TIM LAHAYE
PROPHECY
STUDY BIBLE

KING JAMES VERSION

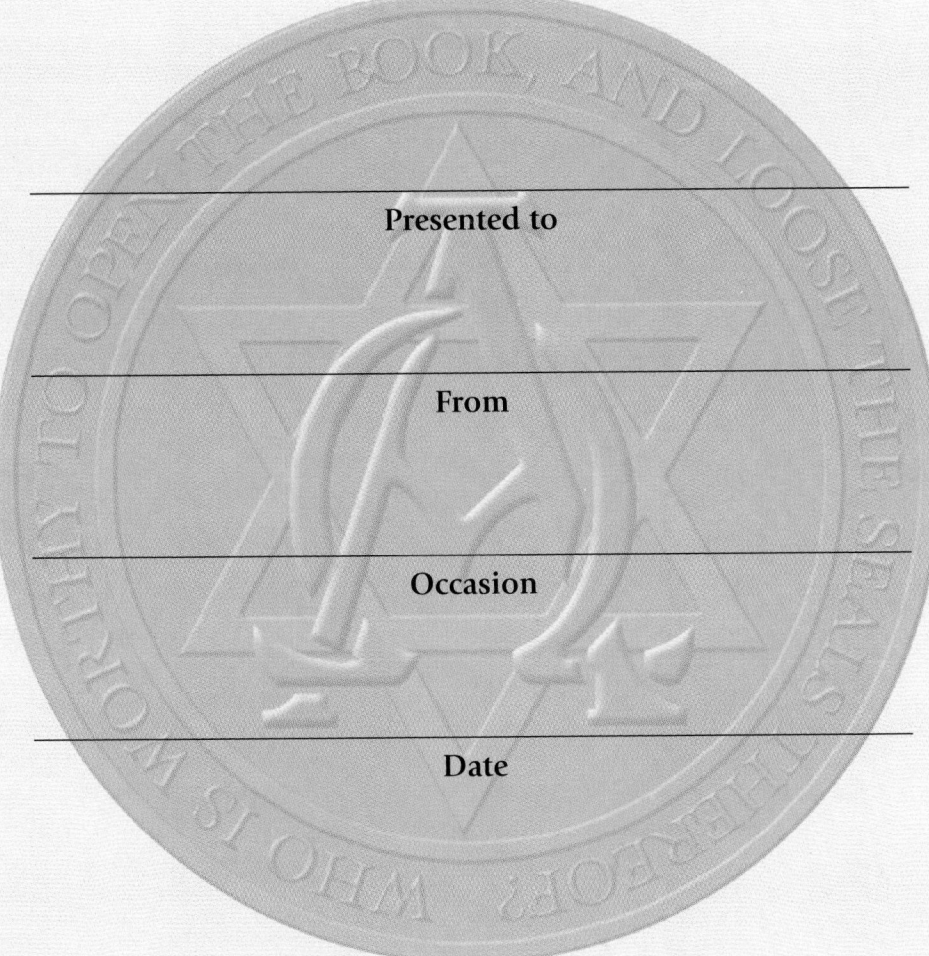

Presented to

From

Occasion

Date

BIBLICAL DISPENSATIONS

Eternity Past — **Eternity Future**

Israel

Dispensations: **Innocence** · **Conscience** · **Human Government** · **Promise** · **Law** · **Church Age** · **Millennial Reign**

Timeline markers:
- Law Fulfilled — Matt. 27:50–51
- Rapture of Saved — 1 Thess. 4:16–17
- Return of Christ in Glory — Rev. 19:11–16
- White Throne
- Lake of Fire

Dispensation	Innocence	Conscience	Human Government	Promise	Law	Church Age	7 Years Tribulation	Millennial Reign
Event	Creation	The Fall	The Flood	Tower of Babel	Exodus	Dispersion of Israel Ezek. 36:16–19 / Regathering of Israel Ezek. 36:20–24	7 Years Tribulation	Armageddon
Responsibility	Obey God Gen. 1:26–28; 2:15–17	Do Good, Blood Sacrifice Gen. 3:5, 7; 22; 4:4	Scatter and Multiply Gen. 8:15—9:7	Dwell in Canaan Gen. 12:1–7	Keep the Whole Law Ex. 19:3–8	Faith in Jesus, Keep Doctrine Pure John 1:12; Rom. 8:1–4; Eph. 2:8–9		Obey and Worship Jesus Isa. 11:3–5; Zech. 14:9, 16
Failure	Disobedience Gen. 3:1–6	Wickedness Gen 6:5–6, 11–12	Did Not Scatter Gen. 11:1–4	Dwelt in Egypt Gen. 12:10; 46:6	Broke Law 2 Kgs. 17:7–20; Matt. 27:1–25	Impure Doctrine John 5:39–40; 2 Tim. 3:1–7		Final Rebellion Rev. 20:7–9
Judgment	Curse and Death Gen. 3:7–19	Flood Gen. 6:7, 13; 7:11–14	Confusion of Languages Gen. 11:5–9	Egyptian Bondage Ex. 1:8–14	Worldwide Dispersion Deut. 28:63–66; Luke 21:20–24	Apostasy, False Doctrine 2 Thess. 2:3; 2 Tim. 4:3		Satan Loosed, Eternal Hell Rev. 20:11–15

The Mountain Peaks of Prophecy

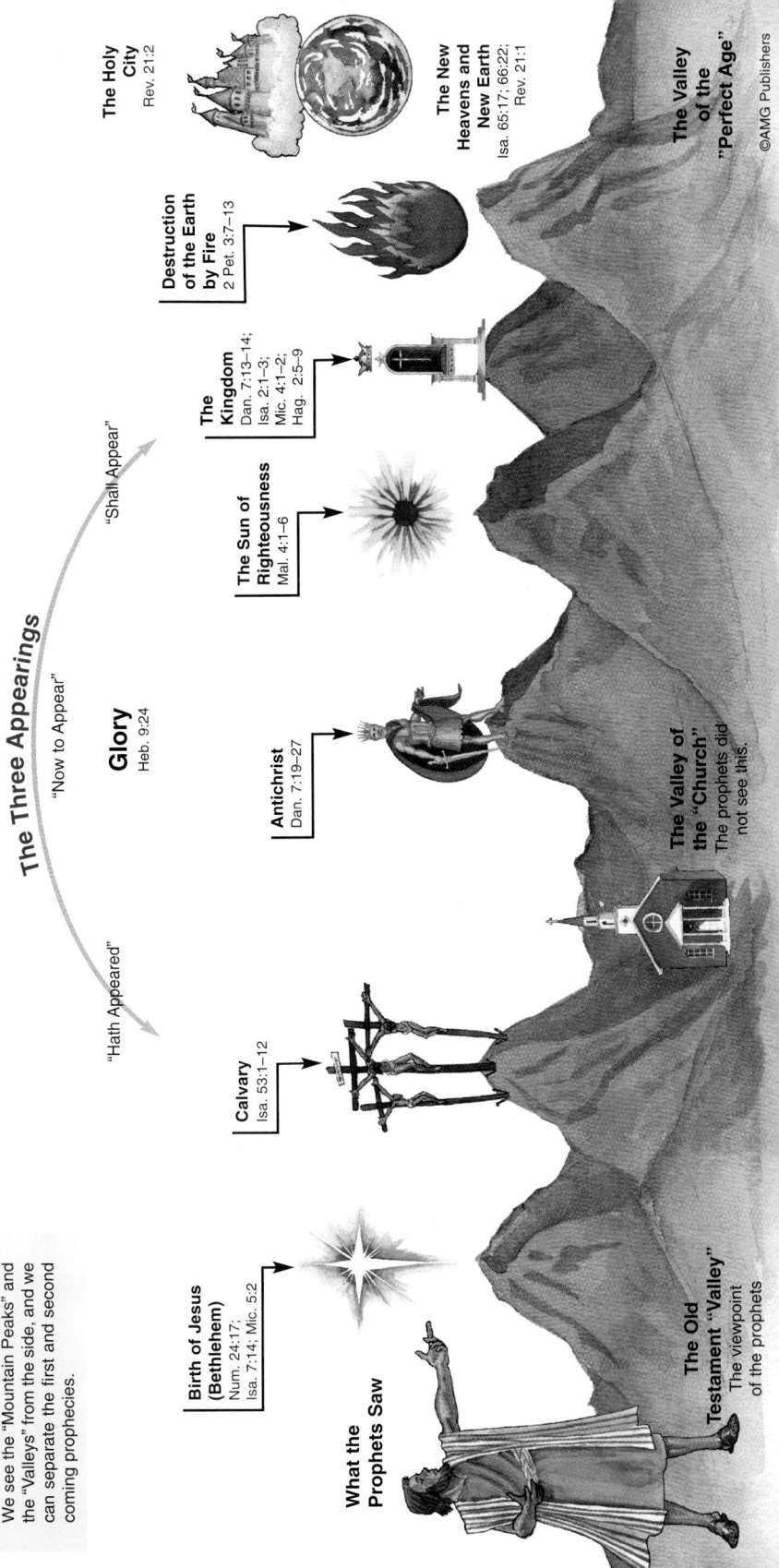

Our Viewpoint

We see the "Mountain Peaks" and the "Valleys" from the side, and we can separate the first and second coming prophecies.

What the Prophets Saw

Priest
Heb. 4:14

The Three Appearings

"Now to Appear"

"Hath Appeared"   "Shall Appear"

Glory
Heb. 9:24

Birth of Jesus (Bethlehem)
Num. 24:17;
Isa. 7:14; Mic. 5:2

Calvary
Isa. 53:1–12

Antichrist
Dan. 7:19–27

The Sun of Righteousness
Mal. 4:1–6

The Kingdom
Dan. 7:13–14;
Isa. 2:1–3;
Mic. 4:1–2;
Hag. 2:5–9

Destruction of the Earth by Fire
2 Pet. 3:7–13

The Holy City
Rev. 21:2

The New Heavens and New Earth
Isa. 65:17; 66:22;
Rev. 21:1

The Old Testament "Valley"
The viewpoint of the prophets

The Valley of the "Church"
The prophets did not see this.

The Valley of the "Perfect Age"

©AMG Publishers

Tabernacle

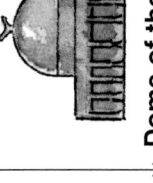

Ark is placed in the Tabernacle

Shechinah Glory fills the Holy of Holies

Conquest & Settlement

The Exodus

Ark is built by Moses & Bezaleel

Tabernacle is constructed

Ark captured and returned

485 Years

1446 BC

First Temple

Ark is transferred to the temple

Shechinah Glory fills the Holy of Holies

Ark is placed beneath Holy of Holies

Monarchy

First temple built (Solomon's)

First temple destroyed

374 Years

1050 BC

960 BC

586 BC

Exile

70 Years

Second Temple

Ark may have been hidden in a secret chamber

Ark is undisturbed by Roman destruction

Roman eagle insignia defiles sanctuary

Gentile Domination

Second temple built (Zerubbabel's)

Second temple enlarged (Herod's)

Second temple destroyed

586 Years

516 BC

19 BC

AD 70

Dome of the Rock

Some believe ark remains hidden during Church Age

Islamic shrine defiles site of the Holy of Holies

Temple site is preserved

Church Age

The search for the ark of the covenant increases as the end of the Church Age nears and the Jews re-establish their sovereignty over the Temple Mount and make preparations to rebuild the temple.

374 Years

Tribulation Temple

Ark may be placed in Third Temple

Seventieth Week
Dan. 9:27

Abomination of Desolation desecrates third temple

Tribulation

Israel enters into a covenant with Antichrist and rebuilds the temple

Temple is desecrated by Antichrist

Midpoint

7 Years

Millennial Temple

Ark may be re-installed by Messiah and Shechinah returns
Ezek. 43:4-7

All of Jerusalem becomes God's Throne (Jer. 3:16–17) and is called "Holy to the Lord" (Zech. 14:20)

Millennial Kingdom

Resumption of animal sacrifices and festival worship schedule

Restoration of national Israel

Reign of Christ on earth

New Heavens and New Earth (Eternal State)

1,000 Years

Their Past (Law)

Entrance into Canaan 2091 BC	Abraham	Shechinah Glory Descends (Ezek. 40:34–38) ←
Exodus from Egypt 1447 BC	Moses, Aaron	
The Wilderness		**God Called to Moses out of the Cloud** Ex. 24:15–18
Jordan	Joshua, Judges	
Canaan		
Divided Kingdom 931 BC	Elijah Called to Heaven	
Crown Removed	Ezek. 21:26–27	God's Presence Departs (Ezek. 11:22–24)

Their Present (Church Age)

606 BC ↑

Babylon — 70 Years Exile (606 BC—536 BC)

Calvary AD 30 — **First Coming (Christ Rejected)**

Jews Scattered (AD 70)

Believing Jews are the Remnant of Israel

The Church

Rapture → **Christ Meets the Church**

• **Antichrist Accepted** John 5:43
• **Judgment of the Jews**
• **Jacob's Trouble** Jer. 30:4–7

Tribulation

Judgment Seat of Christ

Olivet Zech.11:4 Acts 1:8–12

↓

Second Coming (Christ Accepted) ← Revelation

Marriage of the Lamb

Their Future (Righteousness)

Crown Restored
The Throne of David

The Jews Serve as the "Head" of the Nations
Deut. 28:13

Gentile Nations in Blessing
Zech. 8:23

Millennial Kingdom

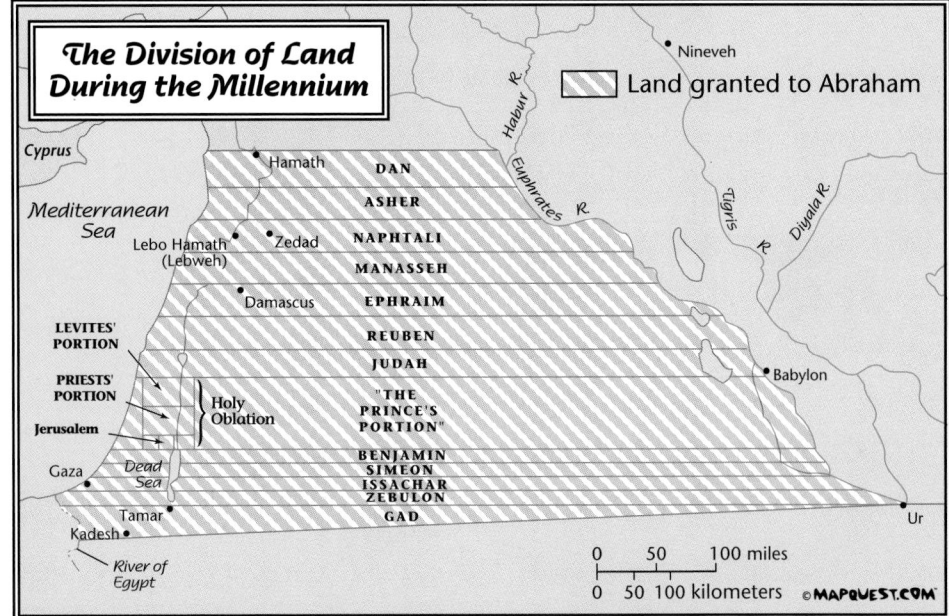

The Division of Land During the Millennium

▨ Land granted to Abraham

Cyprus

Mediterranean Sea

Nineveh

Habur R.

Euphrates R.

Tigris R.

Diyala R.

Hamath — DAN
— ASHER
Lebo Hamath (Lebweh) — Zedad — NAPHTALI
— MANASSEH
Damascus — EPHRAIM
LEVITES' PORTION — REUBEN
PRIESTS' PORTION — JUDAH
Jerusalem — Holy Oblation — "THE PRINCE'S PORTION"
Gaza — Dead Sea — BENJAMIN SIMEON ISSACHAR ZEBULON
Tamar — GAD
Kadesh

Babylon

Ur

River of Egypt

0 — 50 — 100 miles
0 — 50 100 kilometers ©MAPQUEST.COM

DANIEL'S FOREVIEW OF THE ANTICHRIST

606 B.C.

Babylonian Empire

Lion
Dan. 7:1–4

536 B.C.

Medo-Persian Empire

Ram
Dan. 8:1–7

Bear
Dan. 7:5

330 B.C.

Grecian Empire

He-Goat
Dan. 8:5–8

Leopard
Dan. 7:6

323 B.C.

The Four Divisions of Alexander's Kingdom

He-Goat
Dan. 8:8–12

Roman Empire

Fourth Wild Beast
Dan. 7:7–8

Image of the Beast

"The Beast" (Antichrist)
Rev. 13:1–7

"The False Prophet"
(Anti-Spirit)
Rev. 13:11–17

666

John's Foreview of the Antichrist

"The Scarlet Woman"

"The Scarlet Beast"
Rev. 17:3–4

Rev. 11:7   **"Abyss"**   Rev. 17:3–8
Bottomless Pit

"The King of the North"
or "Willful King"
Dan. 11:36–45

Paul's Foreview
of the Antichrist
2 Thess. 2:1–12

NEBUCHADNEZZAR'S DREAM Dan. 2:1–45

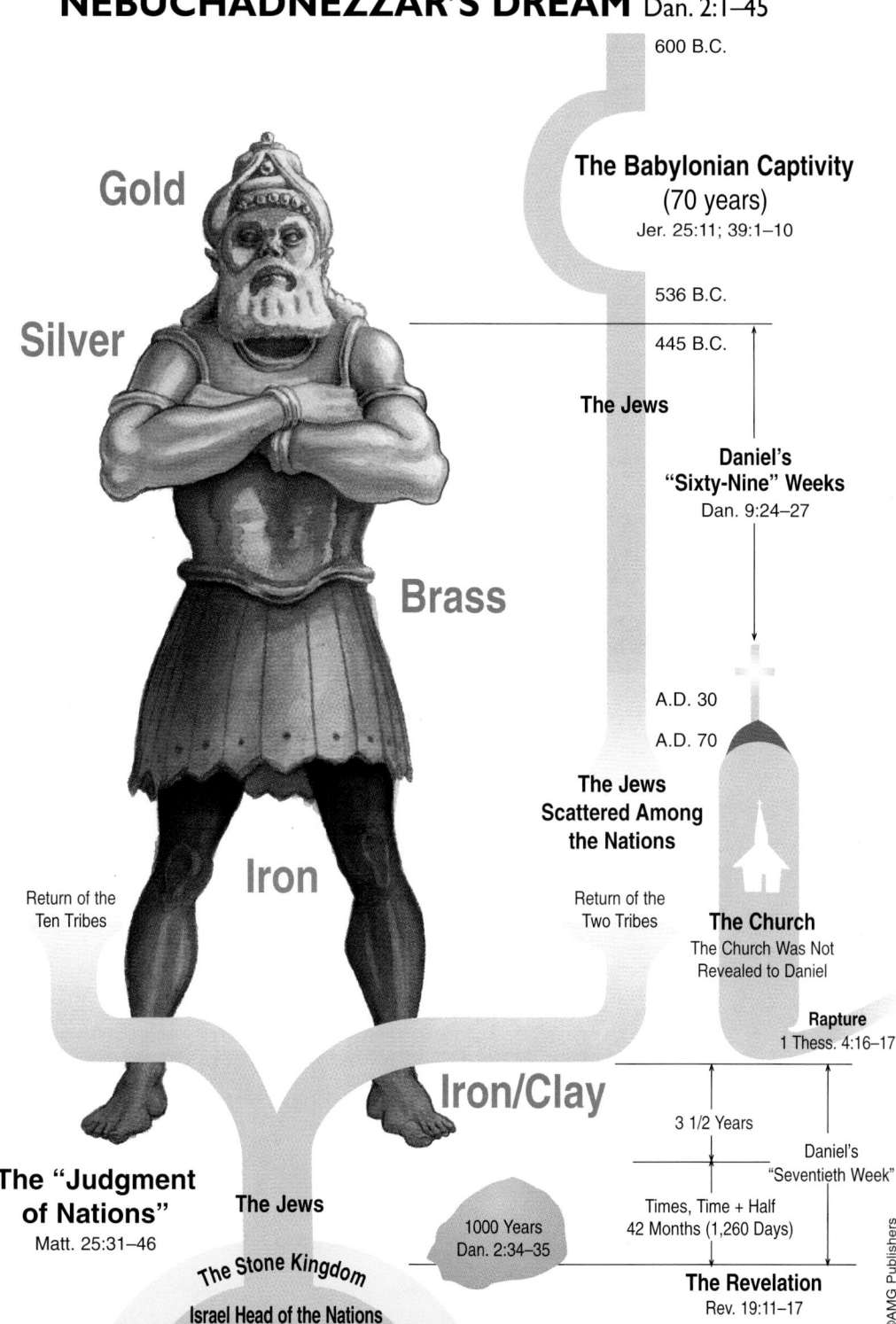

Gold

Silver

Brass

Iron

Iron/Clay

600 B.C.

The Babylonian Captivity
(70 years)
Jer. 25:11; 39:1–10

536 B.C.

445 B.C.

The Jews

Daniel's
"Sixty-Nine" Weeks
Dan. 9:24–27

A.D. 30

A.D. 70

The Jews
Scattered Among
the Nations

Return of the
Ten Tribes

Return of the
Two Tribes

The Church
The Church Was Not
Revealed to Daniel

Rapture
1 Thess. 4:16–17

3 1/2 Years

Daniel's
"Seventieth Week"

The "Judgment
of Nations"
Matt. 25:31–46

The Jews

1000 Years
Dan. 2:34–35

Times, Time + Half
42 Months (1,260 Days)

The Revelation
Rev. 19:11–17

The Stone Kingdom

Israel Head of the Nations
Deut. 28:13

©AMG Publishers

First Temple
Solomon's

Shechinah Present
1 Kings 5—8

First temple built
(Solomon's)

First temple destroyed
(by Babylonians)

Monarchy

374 Years

960 BC
586 BC

---

70 Years

Second Temple
Zerubbabel's & Herod's

Roman eagle present
Ezra 3:7—6:18; Matt. 24:1—2;
Mark 13:1—2; Luke 21:5—6

586 Years

Gentile Domination

Second temple built
(Zerubbabel's)

Second temple enlarged
(Herod's)

516 BC
19 BC

Dome of the Rock
Dome of the Rock

**Dome of the Rock
dominates site**

**Jewish Diaspora
Church Age**

Gentile Inclusion
Rom. 9—11

374 Years

**The Church—
Christ's Spiritual Temple**
Acts 2; Eph. 2

Second temple destroyed
(by Romans)

Third temple built

AD 70

Tribulation Temple
Antichrist Desecrates

**Abomination of
Desolation**
2 Thess. 2:4; Rev. 11:1—2

7 Years

Tribulation

Midpoint

**Temple is
desecrated by
Antichrist**
Dan. 9:26—27;
11:31; 12:11
Matt. 13:14; 24:15

Millennial Temple
Messiah's Memorial Temple

Shechinah present
Ezek. 40:1—43:27;
Isa. 2:2—3; 56:7

1,000 Years

**Millennium—
Messianic Age**

Isa. 2:2—4; 11; 29:6; Ps. 2;
Dan. 7:13—14; Jer. 23:5;
Zech. 14:9—21; Matt. 19:28;
Acts 1:6—7; 3:18—24;
Rom. 8:18—22; Heb. 2:10;
Rev. 11:5; 20

Fourth temple built
(by Messiah)

TIM LaHAYE
PROPHECY
STUDY BIBLE

TIM LAHAYE
PROPHECY
STUDY BIBLE

KING JAMES VERSION

Tim LaHaye, D.Min., Litt.D.
GENERAL EDITOR

Edward Hindson, Th.D., D.Phil.
ASSOCIATE EDITOR

Thomas Ice, Ph.D.
ASSOCIATE EDITOR

James Combs, D.Min., Litt.D.
ASSOCIATE EDITOR

Warren Baker, D.R.E.
MANAGING EDITOR

AMG Publishers

Tim LaHaye Prophecy Study Bible
Copyright © 2000 by AMG Publishers
All rights reserved.

Genuine Black	ISBN 0–89957–932–9
Genuine Burgundy	ISBN 0–89957–934–5
Bonded Black	ISBN 0–89957–926–4
Bonded Burgundy	ISBN 0–89957–928–0
Hardback	ISBN 0–89957–924–8

Also available in thumb-index editions.

Center-Column Reference System. Copyright © 1991, 2000 by AMG Publishers.

Bible Concordance. Copyright © 1991, 2000 by AMG Publishers.

Master Index to Bible Prophecy. Copyright © 1999, 2000 by Thomas Nelson Publishers. Used by permission.

Unless otherwise noted, all maps are the property of Mapquest.com. Used by permission.

The "Left Behind" Series is a registered trademark of Tyndale House Publishers.

AMG Editorial Staff: Warren Baker (Managing Editor), Richard Steele, Jr. (Associate Editor), Vickie Overcash, Evelyn Stoner, Dennis Wisdom.
Chart design by Phillip Rodgers. Illustrations by David Barber.
Page design and layout by LivingStone Corporation.

Printed in the United States of America.
04 03 02 01 00 –R– 9 8 7 6 5 4 3 2 1

*To the millions of readers of the LEFT BEHIND series
of end-time novels, many of whom have for the first time
developed a keen interest in understanding
Bible prophecy, and particularly to the incredible number
of individuals who have received Christ as their Lord and Savior
through the reading of those novels.*

Preface

Prophecy is history written in advance. It is God's way of telling us what will happen in the future. It involves the prediction of specific events before they actually happen. The Bible contains over one thousand predictions of future events. Many of these have already been fulfilled in specific detail. Many more will be fulfilled in the future. These include prophecies of the "End Times," which come under the study of "eschatology," or "last things."

The Tim LaHaye Prophecy Study Bible covers both aspects of prophecy and eschatology. It has been prepared by a team of biblical scholars committed to the belief that the Bible is the inerrant Word of God (a "sure word of prophecy"—2 Pet. 1:19). For nearly ten years, the members of the Pre-Trib Research Center have discussed the need for a comprehensive prophecy study Bible that was faithful to the pretribulational view of Bible prophecy and easy to understand. From the beginning of these discussions, our goal has been to produce the most complete prophecy study Bible ever published. We have endeavored to comment on every predictive passage, making God's faithfulness clear in fulfilling both past and future prophetic predictions.

We have attempted to focus on each prophetic passage of Scripture in a manner that is faithful to the historical-grammatical exegesis of the biblical text, while avoiding undue speculation about prophecies that are yet to be fulfilled. The theological position of the editorial team is both premillennial and pretribulational. In other words, we confidently believe the rapture of the Church will precede the Tribulation period and the Millennial Kingdom of Christ on earth. Beyond this central theological premise, the views of the contributors may vary somewhat from subject to subject.

In addition, the editors and contributors of this Bible have interpreted each passage according to its primary literal sense, unless context indicates some other method of interpretation. While we recognize that the Scriptures contain symbolic language, allegories, and figures of speech, wherever possible, we have interpreted the prophecies of the Scripture in the same way past prophecies were fulfilled—literally.

We believe we are living in the most incredible times the world has ever known. As we continue to come closer to the final fulfillment of Bible predictions concerning the End Times, we sense a growing interest in the study of Bible prophecy. Our sincere hope is that these study notes, charts, and maps will enhance your understanding of Bible prophecy. We pray that God will challenge your mind and encourage your heart by the power of His predictive Word, motivating you to a life of commitment and service to our coming King and Savior—Jesus Christ.

Tim LaHaye, Edward Hindson,
Thomas Ice, James Combs
Editors

About the Editors

Tim LaHaye is a noted author, minister, educator, and nationally recognized speaker on Bible prophecy. He is the President of Tim LaHaye Ministries and founder of the Pre-Trib Research Center.

Dr. LaHaye is one of the nation's most popular authors, having written over forty books on a wide range of subjects including family life, temperaments, Bible prophecy, and secular humanism. His current fiction works are the "Left Behind" series, which he co-authored with Jerry Jenkins. The series is being used of God to lead thousands to Christ and many others to rededicate their lives to Him.

Dr. LaHaye holds a D.Min. degree from Western Theological Seminary and the Litt.D. degree from Liberty University. He and his wife, Beverly, live in California.

Edward Hindson is Professor of Religion, Dean of the Institute of Biblical Studies, and Assistant to the Chancellor at Liberty University in Lynchburg, Virginia. He has authored several books, including *Earth's Final Hour* and *Totally Sufficient,* and also has served as co-editor of the *Knowing Jesus Study Bible*, contributor to *The Complete Bible Commentary*, and as one of the translators for the New King James Version of the Bible. Dr. Hindson is a member of the Executive Committee of the Pre-Trib Research Center and has served as a guest lecturer at both Harvard and Oxford Universities. Dr. Hindson's solid academic scholarship combined with his dynamic and practical teaching style communicates biblical truth in a powerful and positive manner.

Dr. Hindson holds degrees from several institutions, including a Th.D. from Trinity Graduate School, a D.Min. from Westminster Theological Seminary, and a D.Phil. from the University of South Africa. He has also done graduate study at Acadia University in Nova Scotia, Canada. Ed and his wife, Donna, live in Lynchburg, Virginia.

Thomas Ice is Executive Director of the Pre-Trib Research Center in Arlington, Texas, which he co-founded with Dr. Tim LaHaye in 1994 to research, teach, and defend the pretribulational view of the Rapture and related Bible prophecy doctrines. Dr. Ice has co-authored twenty books, including *Ready to Rebuild* and *When the Trumpet Sounds*. He has also written dozens of articles and is a frequent conference speaker. He has served as a pastor for fifteen years.

Dr. Ice has a Th.M. from Dallas Theological Seminary, and a Ph.D. from Tyndale Theological Seminary. Tommy and his wife, Janice, live in Arlington, Texas.

James Combs has been in the ministry for fifty-five years, beginning at the age of sixteen. As an evangelist and speaker on biblical prophecy, he has spoken in nearly one thousand churches. Dr. Combs previously served as Editor of the "Baptist Bible Tribune," official publication of the Baptist Bible Fellowship, and as Editor-in-Chief of "National Liberty Journal." The author of several books, Dr. Combs presently serves as Provost of Louisiana Baptist University and Theological Seminary.

Dr. Combs received his D.Min. degree from Louisiana Baptist and his Litt.D. from Liberty Baptist Theological Seminary in Lynchburg, Virginia. Jim and his wife, Jeri, live in Springfield, Missouri.

Contributors

Jim Anderson, Th.D.
Anderson Evangelistic Enterprises
Belton, MO

John Ankerberg, D.Min.
The Ankerberg Theological Research Institute
Chattanooga, TN

Warren P. Baker, S.T.M., D.R.E.
Managing Editor, AMG Publishers
Chattanooga, TN

Paul Benware, Th.M., Th.D.
Professor of Theology and Bible, Philadelphia College of Bible
Langhorne, PA

David W. Breese, Ph.D.
Christian Destiny, Inc.
Hillsboro, KS

Charles A. Clough, Th.M., M.S.
Meteorologist, U.S. Army
Bel Air, MD

James Combs, D.Min., Litt.D.
Provost of Louisiana Baptist University and Theological Seminary
Shreveport, LA

Mal Couch, Th.M., Th.D., Ph.D.
Founder and president, Tyndale Theological Seminary and Biblical Institute
Fort Worth, TX

Larry V. Crutchfield, M.Phil., Ph.D.
Professor of Early Christian History and Culture, Columbia Evangelical Seminary
Longview, WA

Robert L. Dean, Jr., Th.M., Ph.D. Cand.
Senior Pastor, Preston City Bible Church
Preston City, CT

Timothy J. Demy, Th.D., Ph.D. Cand.
Military Chaplain, Bible Teacher
Newport, RI

Jimmy DeYoung, Ph.D.
Shofar Communications
Chattanooga, TN

Anthony T. Evans, Th.D.
President, The Urban Alternative
Senior Pastor, Oak Cliff Bible Fellowship
Dallas, TX

Gary Frazier, D.D.
President, Discovery Ministries, Inc.
Arlington, TX

Arno Froese
Midnight Call Ministries
Columbia, SC

Arnold Fruchtenbaum, Th.M., Ph.D.
Founder and Director, Ariel Ministries
Tustin, CA

Norman L. Geisler, Ph.D.
Professor of Theology and Apologetics, Southern Evangelical Seminary
Charlotte, NC

Kenneth E. Gillming, Th.M., D.D., Litt.D.
President, Baptist Bible Fellowship International
Senior Pastor, Cherry Street Baptist Church
Springfield, MO

Robert Gromacki, Th.D.
Professor of Bible and Greek, Cedarville College
Cedarville, OH

Edward Hindson, Th.D., D.Phil.
Professor of Religion, Dean of the Institute of Biblical Studies, and
Assistant to the Chancellor, Liberty University
Lynchburg, VA

Mark Hitchcock, J.D., Ph.D. Cand.
Pastor, Faith Bible Church
Edmond, OK

Stanley M. Horton, Th.D.
Distinguished Professor Emeritus, Assemblies of God Theological Seminary
Springfield, MO

Dave Hunt
The Berean Call
Bend, OR

Thomas Ice, Ph.D.
Executive Director of the Pre-Trib Research Center
Arlington, TX

William T. James
Benton, AK

David Jeremiah, Th.M., D.D.
Senior Pastor, Shadow Mountain Community Church
Turning Point Ministries
El Cajon, CA

James M. Kinnebrew, Ph.D.
Academic Dean, Luther Rice Seminary
Atlanta, GA

Adrian Rogers
Pastor, Bellevue Baptist Church
Memphis, TN

James Sewell, Ph.D.
Professor of Bible, Baptist Bible College
Springfield, MO

Renald E. Showers, Th.D.
The Friends of Israel Gospel Ministry
Willow Street, PA

Chuck Smith
Pastor, Calvary Chapel
Costa Mesa, CA

Joseph M. Stowell, III, Th.M., D.D.
President, Moody Bible Institute
Chicago, IL

Paul Lee Tan, Th.D.
Bible Communications, Inc.
Dallas, TX

Robert L. Thomas, Th.M., Th.D.
Professor of New Testament, The Master's Seminary
Sun Valley, CA

Stanley D. Toussaint, Th.D.
Senior Professor Emeritus of Bible Exposition, Dallas Theological Seminary
Dallas, TX

Elmer L. Towns, D.Min., D.D.
Dean of the School of Religion, Liberty University
Lynchburg, VA

Jack Van Impe, Ph.D., Th.D., D.Min., D.D.
Jack Van Impe Ministries International
Rochester Hills, MI

John F. Walvoord, Th.D.
Chancellor, Dallas Theological Seminary
Dallas, TX

John C. Whitcomb, Th.D.
Whitcomb Ministries, Inc.
Orange Park, FL

Harold L. Willmington, D.Min.
Dean, Liberty Bible Institute
Forest, VA

Tim LaHaye, D.Min., Litt.D.
President of Tim LaHaye Ministries and founder of the Pre-Trib Research Center
El Cajon, CA

Zola Levitt, Ph.D., Th.D.
Zola Levitt Ministries, Inc.
Dallas, TX

David Allan Lewis, D.D., Litt.D.
President, Christians United for Israel
Springfield, MO

Erwin Lutzer, Th.M, L.L.D., D.D.
Senior Pastor, The Moody Church
Chicago, IL

Richard L. Mayhue, Th.M., Th.D.
Professor of Theology and Pastoral Ministries, The Master's Seminary
Sun Valley, CA

Thomas S. McCall, Th.M., Th.D.
Senior Theologian, Zola Levitt Ministries, Inc.
Dallas, TX

Josh McDowell, Th.D., D.D.
Josh McDowell Ministry
Dallas, TX

Charles W. Missler, Ph.D.
Koinonia House
Couer d'Alene, ID

David T. Moore
Pastor, Southwest Community Church
Indian Wells, CA

Henry Morris, Ph.D.
President Emeritus, Institute for Creation Research
Santee, CA

Richard Patterson, Th.M., Ph.D.
Distinguished Professor Emeritus, Liberty University
Lynchburg, VA

J. Dwight Pentecost, Th.M., Th.D.
Distinguished Professor of Bible Exposition, Emeritus, Dallas Theological Seminary
Dallas, TX

Randall Price, Th.M., Ph.D.
World of the Bible Ministries
San Marcos, TX

Earl D. Radmacher, Th.D.
President and Professor of Systematic Theology Emeritus, Western Seminary
Portland, OR

David R. Reagan, Ph.D.
Senior Evangelist, Lamb & Lion Ministries
Princeton, TX

How to Study Bible Prophecy

By Tim LaHaye

Prophecy is God's roadmap to show us where history is going. The Bible's predictions claim literal and specific fulfillments that verify that such prophecies are indeed from God. The key to interpreting Bible prophecy is in discerning what is literal and what is symbolic. Therefore, the best way to avoid confusion in the study of prophetic scripture is to follow these simple directions:

1. Interpret prophecy literally wherever possible. God meant what He said and said what He meant when He inspired "holy men of God [who] spake as they were moved by the Holy Ghost" (1 Pet. 1:21) to write the Bible. Consequently we can take the Bible literally most of the time. Where God intends for us to interpret symbolically, He makes it obvious. One of the reasons the book of Revelation is difficult for some people to understand is that they try to spiritualize the symbols used in the book. However, since many Old Testament prophecies have already been literally fulfilled, such as God turning water to blood (Ex. 4:9; 7:17–21), it should not be difficult to imagine that future prophetic events can and will be literally fulfilled at the appropriate time. Only when symbols or figures of speech make absolutely no literal sense, should anything but a literal interpretation be sought.

2. Prophecies concerning Israel and the Church should not be transposed. The promises of God to Israel to be fulfilled "in the latter days," particularly those concerning Israel's punishment during the Tribulation have absolutely nothing to do with the Church. The Bible gives specific promises for the Church that she will be raptured into heaven before the Tribulation (John 14:2–3; 1 Cor. 15:51–52; 1 Thess. 4:13–18).

3. For symbolic passages, compare Scripture with Scripture. The Bible is not contradictory. Even though written by numerous, divinely inspired men over a period of sixteen hundred years, it is supernaturally consistent in its use of terms. For example, the word "beast" is used thirty-four times in Revelation and many other times in Scripture. Daniel explains that the word is symbolic of either a king or kingdom (see Dan. 7—8). By examining the contexts in Revelation and Daniel, you will find that "beast" has the same meaning in both books. Many other symbols used in Revelation are also taken directly from the Old Testament. These include "the tree of life" (Rev. 2:7; 22:2, 14), "the book of life" (Rev. 3:5ff.), and Babylon (Rev. 14:8ff.).

Some symbols in Revelation are drawn from other New Testament passages. These include terms such as "the Word of God" (1:2, 9ff.), "Son of man" (1:13; 14:14), "marriage supper" (19:9), "the Bride" (21:9; 22:17), "first resurrection" (20:5–6), and "second death" (2:11; 20:6, 14; 21:8). Other symbols in Revelation are explained and identified in their context. For example, "alpha and omega" represents Jesus Christ (1:8, 11; 21:6; 22:13); the "seven candlesticks" (1:13, 20) are the seven churches; the "dragon" is Satan (12:3ff.); and the "man child" is Jesus (12:5, 13).

Though some prophetic passages should be interpreted symbolically, it is important to remember that symbols in the Bible depict real people, things, and events. For example, the "seven candlesticks" in Revelation 1 represent real churches that actually existed when the prophecy was given.

Table of Contents

THE OLD TESTAMENT

THE NEW TESTAMENT

STUDY HELPS

See the List of Articles and the List of Tables and Charts for the locations of other featured items.

List of Articles

List of Tables and Charts

Title . . . .**Page**

Title . . . . **.Page**

THE
OLD TESTAMENT

Genesis

The book of Genesis is a fitting introduction to the rest of the Bible. From the grandeur of God's creative acts to the beginnings of marriage, sin, sacrifice for sin, family, work, murder, races, civilization, and God's chosen people (Israel), the book of Genesis lays the foundation of God's revelation of Himself to man. Genesis answers basic questions about the origin of all living things, the origin of evil in the world, and the beginning of God's plan to redeem the human race.

The first eleven chapters of the book summarize early human experience. The remainder of the book focuses on Israel's history and destiny, a theme that propels the redemptive drama throughout the Old Testament. These events and the historical and spiritual lessons surrounding them involve seven major personalities: Adam, Enoch, Noah, Abraham, Isaac, Jacob, and Joseph.

All the prophecies of the Bible are either conditional or unconditional. Conditional prophecies are called such because the fulfillment of these prophecies depends on human responses. God's declaration that death would follow disobedience was a conditional prophecy (Gen. 2:16–17). Unconditional prophecies, which are sometimes referred to as prophetic promises, do not depend on man's response. Three of the most significant unconditional prophecies are found in the book of Genesis: **1)** the triumph of the "seed of the woman" over the serpent (Gen. 3:14–15), fulfilled by Jesus Christ; **2)** God's prophetic covenant with Abraham (Gen. 12:1–7; 17:1–21); and **3)** the prophetic blessing of Jacob on the twelve tribes of Israel (Gen. 49).

Also significant are prophetic types, actions that have meaning in their day, but that also reflect some truth about the future life and work of Jesus Christ. For instance, proper Old Testament sacrifices and offerings are symbolic forecasts of Christ's atonement for sin, even Abraham's offering of Isaac (cf. Gen. 22 with Heb. 11:17–19).

Including conditional prophecies, prophetic types and/or specific predictions, Genesis contains 77 distinct prophecies, involving 212 out of 1,533 verses, or 14 percent of the book.

Author	
Moses	
Date	
15th Century B.C.	
Key Truth	
Beginnings	
Historic Time	
Creation to Patriarchs	
Key Verse	
1:1	
In the beginning God created the heaven and the earth.	

14%
Prophecy

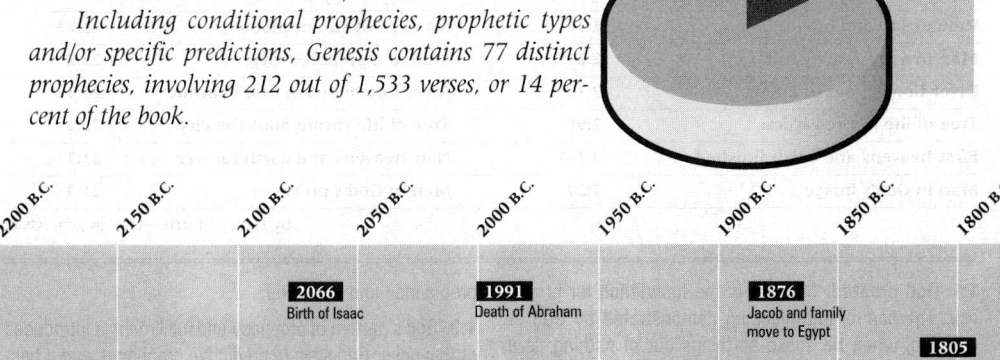

2166 Birth of Abraham

2079 Birth of Ishmael

2066 Birth of Isaac

2006 Birth of Jacob and Esau

1991 Death of Abraham

1929–1909 Jacob lives in Haran with Laban

1898 Joseph sold to the Ishmeelites

1876 Jacob and family move to Egypt

1805 Death of Joseph

2200 B.C.   2150 B.C.   2100 B.C.   2050 B.C.   2000 B.C.   1950 B.C.   1900 B.C.   1850 B.C.   1800 B.C.

CHAPTER 1
Creation

1 In the beginning God created the heaven and the earth.

2 And the earth was without form, and void; and darkness *was* upon the face of the deep. And the Spirit of God moved upon the face of the waters.

3 And God said, Let there be light: and there was light.

4 And God saw the light, that *it was* good: and God divided the light from the darkness.

5 And God called the light Day, and the darkness he called Night. And the evening and the morning were the first day.

6 And God said, Let there be a firmament in the midst of the waters, and let it divide the waters from the waters.

7 And God made the firmament, and divided the waters which *were* under the firmament from the waters which *were* above the firmament: and it was so.

8 And God called the firmament Heaven. And the evening and the morning were the second day.

9 And God said, Let the waters under the heaven be gathered together unto one place, and let the dry *land* appear: and it was so.

10 And God called the dry *land* Earth; and the gathering together of the waters called he Seas: and God saw that *it was* good.

11 And God said, Let the earth bring forth grass, the herb yielding seed, *and* the fruit tree yielding fruit after his kind, whose seed *is* in itself, upon the earth: and it was so.

12 And the earth brought forth grass, *and* herb yielding seed after his kind, and the tree yielding fruit, whose seed *was* in itself, after his kind: and God saw that *it was* good.

13 And the evening and the morning were the third day.

14 And God said, Let there be lights in the firmament of the heaven to divide the day from the night; and let them be for signs, and for seasons, and for days, and years:

15 And let them be for lights in the firmament of the heaven to give light upon the earth: and it was so.

16 And God made two great lights; the greater light to rule the day, and the lesser light to rule the night: *he made* the stars also.

17 And God set them in the firmament of the heaven to give light upon the earth,

18 And to rule over the day and over the night, and to divide the light from the darkness: and God saw that *it was* good.

19 And the evening and the morning were the fourth day.

20 And God said, Let the waters bring forth abundantly the moving creature that hath life, and fowl *that* may fly above the earth in the open firmament of heaven.

21 And God created great whales, and every living creature that moveth, which the

Cross references

1 Ps. 8:3; 33:6; 89:11, 12; 102:25; 136:5; 146:6; Isa. 44:24; Jer. 10:12; 51:15; Zech. 12:1; John 1:1, 2; Acts 14:15; 17:24; Col. 1:16, 17; Heb. 1:10; 11:3; Rev. 4:11; 10:6

2 Ps. 33:6; Isa. 40:13, 14

3 Ps. 33:9; 2Cor. 4:6

5 Ps. 74:16; 104:20

6 Job 37:18; Ps. 136:5; Jer. 10:12; 51:15

7 Ps. 148:4; Prov. 8:28

9 Job 26:10; 38:8; Ps. 33:7; 95:5; 104:9; 136:6; Prov. 8:29; Jer. 5:22; 2Pet. 3:5

11 Luke 6:44; Heb. 6:7

14 Deut. 4:19; Ps. 74:16, 17; 104:19

Comparisons between the Created World and the Eternal World

Probationary World	Genesis	Eternal World	Revelation
Division of light and darkness	1:4	No night	21:25
Division of land and sea	1:10	No more sea	21:1
Rule of sun and moon	1:16	No need of sun or moon	21:23
Man in a prepared garden	2:8–9	Man in a prepared city	21:2
River flowing out of Eden	2:10	River flowing from God's throne	22:1
Tree of life in the garden	2:9	Tree of life throughout the city	22:2
First heavens and earth finished	2:1–3	New heavens and earth forever	21:1
Man in God's image	1:27	Man in God's presence	21:3

By Henry Morris—*Used by permission.*

1:1 God created. Creation is the foundation for prophecy. The control and planning demonstrated by God at creation, when He spoke all things out of nothing, is a necessary prerequisite for predictive prophecy. Hebrews 11:3 ("the worlds—lit. 'ages'—were framed by the word of God") indicates that God creates history, which is preplanned and predicted.

1:3 God's pattern of prophecy and fulfillment is introduced at this point. God says (a predictive prophecy), and it happens (fulfillment of prophecy). This pattern is followed throughout Genesis 1 (see vv. 3, 6, 9, 14, 24, 26).

waters brought forth abundantly, after their kind, and every winged fowl after his kind: and God saw that *it was* good.

22 And God blessed them, saying, Be fruitful, and multiply, and fill the waters in the seas, and let fowl multiply in the earth.

23 And the evening and the morning were the fifth day.

24 And God said, Let the earth bring forth the living creature after his kind, cattle, and creeping thing, and beast of the earth after his kind: and it was so.

25 And God made the beast of the earth after his kind, and cattle after their kind, and every thing that creepeth upon the earth after his kind: and God saw that *it was* good.

26 And God said, Let us make man in our image, after our likeness: and let them have dominion over the fish of the sea, and over the fowl of the air, and over the cattle, and over all the earth, and over every creeping thing that creepeth upon the earth.

27 So God created man in his *own* image, in the image of God created he him; male and female created he them.

28 And God blessed them, and God said unto them, Be fruitful, and multiply, and replenish the earth, and subdue it: and have dominion over the fish of the sea, and over the fowl of the air, and over every living thing that moveth upon the earth.

29 And God said, Behold, I have given you every herb bearing seed, which *is* upon the face of all the earth, and every tree, in the which *is* the fruit of a tree yielding seed; to you it shall be for meat.

30 And to every beast of the earth, and to every fowl of the air, and to every thing that creepeth upon the earth, wherein *there is* life, *I have given* every green herb for meat: and it was so.

31 And God saw every thing that he had made, and, behold, *it was* very good. And the evening and the morning were the sixth day.

CHAPTER 2

1 Thus the heavens and the earth were finished, and all the host of them.

2 And on the seventh day God ended his work which he had made; and he rested on the seventh day from all his work which he had made.

3 And God blessed the seventh day, and sanctified it: because that in it he had rested from all his work which God created and made.

Adam and Eve in the Garden

4 These *are* the generations of the heavens and of the earth when they were created, in the day that the LORD God made the earth and the heavens,

5 And every plant of the field before it was

Cross references (center column):

22 Gen. 8:17

26 Gen. 5:1; 9:2, 6; Ps. 8:6; 100:3; Eccl. 7:29; Acts 17:26, 28, 29; 1Cor. 11:7; Eph. 4:24; Col. 3:10; James 3:9

27 Gen. 5:2; Mal. 2:15; Matt. 19:4; Mark 10:6; 1Cor. 11:7

28 Gen. 9:1, 7; Lev. 26:9; Ps. 127:3; 128:3, 4

29 Gen. 9:3; Job 36:31; Acts 14:17

30 Job 38:41; Ps. 145:15, 16; 147:9

31 Ps. 104:24; 1Tim. 4:4

1 Ps. 33:6

2 Ex. 20:11; 31:17; Deut. 5:14; Heb. 4:4

3 Neh. 9:14; Isa. 58:13

4 Gen. 1:1; Ps. 90:1, 2

1:22 This is the first time the word "blessed" is used in Genesis. One cannot prosper in God's creation without His blessing.

1:26–28 This passage, often called the Cultural Mandate, is a prophecy relating to the call and purpose for mankind. Psalm 8 indicates that the Cultural Mandate is meant to be operational throughout all history (Ps. 8:3–8). This passage provides the basis for human involvement in society, culture, labor, politics, and science.

God has revealed seven dispensations in Scripture: 1) Innocence (Gen. 1:28), 2) Conscience (Gen. 3:7), 3) Human Government (Gen. 8:15), 4) Promise (Gen. 12:1), 5) Law (Ex. 19:1), 6) Church Age (Acts 2:1), and 7) Kingdom (Rev. 20:4). Each dispensation includes a revelation of God's will, a declaration of man's responsibility, and consequences for failing in that responsibility. In each succeeding dispensation some aspects cease while others continue into future dispensations.

The first of these dispensations commences in this passage (see article on Dispensations). The Dispensation of Innocence begins with the creation of Adam and Eve and God's commissioning of them. This dispensation was a time when mankind, through Adam (Rom. 5:12–21;

1 Cor. 15:21–22), was created morally good but able to fall into sin. This apparently short-lived age ceased at the fall into sin as recorded in Genesis 3. God's revelation of His will was "thou shalt not eat of the tree of the knowledge of good and evil" (Gen. 2:17). Man's responsibility was to obey God and not partake. One consequence of disobedience was that "thou shalt surely die" (Gen. 2:17).

2:1–3 God completed in history that which He had planned to do. In this, we see God fulfilling that which He plans and prophesies He will do. So it is for the totality of history.

2:4 After explaining where the heavens and the earth came from, Moses organizes the rest of the book around eleven uses of the words, "the generations." The Hebrew word is *toledoth* and is most commonly translated "generations." In Genesis, it presents the idea of "this is what became of. . . ." In other words, "this is what became of the heavens and the earth. . . ." *Toledoth* is the organizing word that introduces the reader to each of the eleven sections throughout the rest of Genesis (2:4; 5:1; 6:9; 10:1; 11:10; 11:27; 25:12; 25:19; 36:1; 36:9; 37:2).

in the earth, and every herb of the field before it grew: for the LORD God had not caused it to rain upon the earth, and *there was* not a man to till the ground.

6 But there went up a mist from the earth, and watered the whole face of the ground.

7 And the LORD God formed man *of* the dust of the ground, and breathed into his nostrils the breath of life; and man became a living soul.

8 And the LORD God planted a garden eastward in Eden; and there he put the man whom he had formed.

9 And out of the ground made the LORD God to grow every tree that is pleasant to the sight, and good for food; the tree of life also in the midst of the garden, and the tree of knowledge of good and evil.

7 Gen. 3:19, 23; 7:22; Job 33:4; Ps. 103:14; Eccl. 12:7; Isa. 2:22; 64:8; Acts 17:25

8 Gen. 2:15; 3:24; 4:16; 13:10; 2Kgs. 19:12; Isa. 51:3; Ezek. 27:23; 28:13; Joel 2:3

9 Gen. 1:17; 3:22; Prov. 3:18; 11:30; Ezek. 31:8; Rev. 2:7; 22:2, 14

11 Gen. 25:18

14 Dan. 10:4

10 And a river went out of Eden to water the garden; and from thence it was parted, and became into four heads.

11 The name of the first *is* Pison: that *is* it which compasseth the whole land of Havilah, where *there is* gold;

12 And the gold of that land *is* good: there *is* bdellium and the onyx stone.

13 And the name of the second river *is* Gihon: the same *is* it that compasseth the whole land of Ethiopia.

14 And the name of the third river *is* Hiddekel: that *is* it which goeth toward the east of Assyria. And the fourth river *is* Euphrates.

15 And the LORD God took the man, and put him into the garden of Eden to dress it and to keep it.

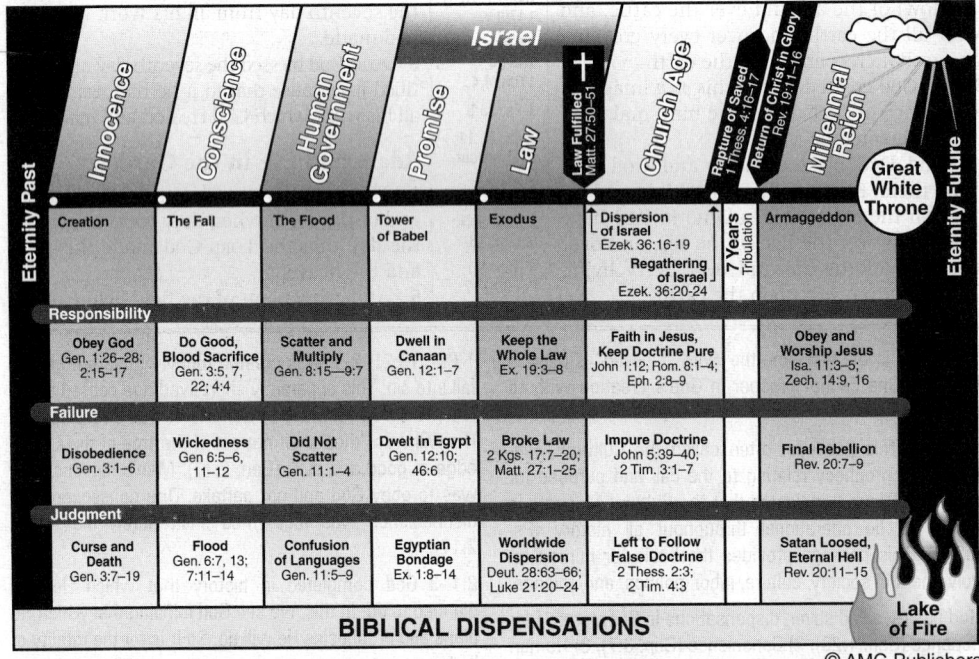

BIBLICAL DISPENSATIONS

© AMG Publishers

2:8 planted a garden. History begins in an undeveloped garden and climaxes in a city—New Jerusalem (Rev. 21:2).

2:9 the tree of life. This tree appears at the beginning of history and at the end for eternity (Rev. 20:2, 14).

2:15–17 The first of the biblical covenants is struck in these verses. The Edenic covenant provides the pre-fall basis that God employs to establish His rule and relationship to mankind. The Edenic covenant, in conjunction with the Cultural Mandate (Gen. 1:26–28), provides the basis for social, political, and economic duties, as well as human responsibility before God. After the fall into sin, other covenants augment this foundational relationship.

The six stated biblical covenants are 1) the Noahic (Gen. 9:16), 2) the Abrahamic (Gen. 12:1–3), 3) the Mosaic (Ex. 19:5), 4) the priestly (Num. 25:10–13), 5) the Davidic (2 Sam. 7:16), and 6) the new covenant (Jer. 31:31–34). Three other covenants are intimated in Scripture: the Edenic (Gen. 2:16), the Adamic (Gen. 3:15), and the Land of Israel (Deut. 30:3).

16 And the Lord God commanded the man, saying, Of every tree of the garden thou mayest freely eat:

17 But of the tree of the knowledge of good and evil, thou shalt not eat of it: for in the day that thou eatest thereof thou shalt surely die.

18 And the Lord God said, *It is* not good that the man should be alone; I will make him an help meet for him.

19 And out of the ground the Lord God formed every beast of the field, and every fowl of the air; and brought *them* unto Adam to see what he would call them: and whatsoever Adam called every living creature, that *was* the name thereof.

20 And Adam gave names to all cattle, and to the fowl of the air, and to every beast of the field; but for Adam there was not found an help meet for him.

21 And the Lord God caused a deep sleep to fall upon Adam, and he slept: and he took one of his ribs, and closed up the flesh instead thereof;

22 And the rib, which the Lord God had taken from man, made he a woman, and brought her unto the man.

23 And Adam said, This *is* now bone of my bones, and flesh of my flesh: she shall be called Woman, because she was taken out of Man.

24 Therefore shall a man leave his father and his mother, and shall cleave unto his wife: and they shall be one flesh.

25 And they were both naked, the man and his wife, and were not ashamed.

CHAPTER 3
Fall of Man

1 Now the serpent was more subtil than any beast of the field which the Lord God had made. And he said unto the woman,

Yea, hath God said, Ye shall not eat of every tree of the garden?

2 And the woman said unto the serpent, We may eat of the fruit of the trees of the garden:

3 But of the fruit of the tree which *is* in the midst of the garden, God hath said, Ye shall not eat of it, neither shall ye touch it, lest ye die.

4 And the serpent said unto the woman, Ye shall not surely die:

5 For God doth know that in the day ye eat thereof, then your eyes shall be opened, and ye shall be as gods, knowing good and evil.

6 And when the woman saw that the tree *was* good for food, and that it *was* pleasant to the eyes, and a tree to be desired to make *one* wise, she took of the fruit thereof, and did eat, and gave also unto her husband with her; and he did eat.

7 And the eyes of them both were opened, and they knew that they *were* naked; and they sewed fig leaves together, and made themselves aprons.

8 And they heard the voice of the Lord God walking in the garden in the cool of the day: and Adam and his wife hid themselves from the presence of the Lord God amongst the trees of the garden.

9 And the Lord God called unto Adam, and said unto him, Where *art* thou?

10 And he said, I heard thy voice in the garden, and I was afraid, because I *was* naked; and I hid myself.

11 And he said, Who told thee that thou *wast* naked? Hast thou eaten of the tree, whereof I commanded thee that thou shouldest not eat?

12 And the man said, The woman whom thou gavest *to be* with me, she gave me of the tree, and I did eat.

Cross-references

17 Gen. 1:9; 3:1, 3, 11, 17, 19; Rom. 6:23; 1Cor. 15:56; James 1:15; 1John 5:16

18 Gen. 3:12; 1Cor. 11:9; 1Tim. 2:13

19 Gen. 1:20, 24; Ps. 8:6, See Gen. 6:20

21 Gen. 15:12; 1Sam. 26:12

22 Prov. 18:22; Heb. 13:4

23 Gen. 29:14; Judg. 9:2; 2Sam. 5:1; 19:13; 1Cor. 11:8; Eph. 5:30

24 Gen. 31:15; Ps. 45:10; Matt. 19:5; Mark 10:7; 1Cor. 6:16; Eph. 5:31

25 Gen. 3:7, 10, 11; Ex. 32:25; Isa. 47:3

1 Matt. 10:16; 2Cor. 11:3; Rev. 12:9; 20:2

3 Gen. 2:17

4 Gen. 3:13; 2Cor. 11:3; 1Tim. 2:14

5 Gen. 3:7; Acts 26:18

6 Gen. 3:12, 17; 1Tim. 2:14

2:17 in the day that thou eatest thereof thou shalt surely die. This is the first prophecy of judgment in the Scriptures. This prophecy began to be fulfilled when Adam and Eve fell into sin (Gen. 3:15–19).

3:1 Yea, hath God said? Satan's temptation began by questioning the truth of God's prophetic word.

3:3 neither shall ye touch it, lest ye die. God warns in Deuteronomy 4:2 that His prophetic word is to be obeyed, not added to or taken away from. Here Eve adds to what God had said.

3:4–5 Ye shall not surely die . . . ye shall be as gods. Satan's dialogue with the woman progresses to the point of outright contradiction and denial of God's prophetic word.

3:7 The Dispensation of Conscience begins with the fall into sin leading to the Flood of Noah. This dispensation demonstrates that man needs more than his conscience to walk upright before God (see article on Dispensations). During this dispensation, God revealed His will through the curse (Gen. 3:14–24). Man's responsibility was to master sin that desired to rule over him (Gen. 4:6–7). The consequences of neglecting his conscience would be the global Flood in the days of Noah (Gen. 6:5–7).

13 And the LORD God said unto the woman, What *is* this *that* thou hast done? And the woman said, The serpent beguiled me, and I did eat.

God Judges

14 And the LORD God said unto the serpent, Because thou hast done this, thou *art* cursed above all cattle, and above every beast of the field; upon thy belly shalt thou go, and dust shalt thou eat all the days of thy life:

15 And I will put enmity between thee and the woman, and between thy seed and her seed; it shall bruise thy head, and thou shalt bruise his heel.

16 Unto the woman he said, I will greatly multiply thy sorrow and thy conception; in sorrow thou shalt bring forth children; and

thy desire *shall be* to thy husband, and he shall rule over thee.

17 And unto Adam he said, Because thou hast hearkened unto the voice of thy wife, and hast eaten of the tree, of which I commanded thee, saying, Thou shalt not eat of it: cursed *is* the ground for thy sake; in sorrow shalt thou eat *of* it all the days of thy life;

18 Thorns also and thistles shall it bring forth to thee; and thou shalt eat the herb of the field;

19 In the sweat of thy face shalt thou eat bread, till thou return unto the ground; for out of it wast thou taken: for dust thou *art*, and unto dust shalt thou return.

20 And Adam called his wife's name Eve; because she was the mother of all living.

21 Unto Adam also and to his wife did the

Cross references (center column):

13 2Cor. 11:3
14 Isa. 65:25
15 Ps. 132:11; Isa. 7:14; Matt. 1:23, 25; 3:7; 13:38; 23:33; Luke 1:31, 34, 35; John 8:44
16 Gen. 4:7; Ps. 48:6; 1Cor. 11:3; Eph. 5:22, 23, 24; 1Pet. 3:1, 5, 6
17 Gen. 2:17; 3:6; Rom. 8:20
19 Eccl. 1:13; 3:20; 12:7

3:14–24 The first major prophetic section in Scripture, these verses contain God's curse of the serpent, Adam, and Eve. In verses 14–19 God prophesies punishment, but in verses 20–24 He predicts provision.

3:14 God curses the serpent through a prophetic word. To curse means to impose a ban or a barrier, a paralysis on movement or other capabilities. The curse of the serpent means that more than any cattle or beast of the field (i.e., all the animals), the snake will be limited by being made to swivel on its belly and grovel in the dust. God's purpose in cursing the serpent is to remind us of the fall every time we see or think of a snake.

3:15–17 The Adamic covenant is initiated between God and mankind because of Adam's sin. This covenant contains the cursed status of man and creation that he must endure throughout history. The curse will be primarily removed during the Millennial reign of Christ (Rom. 8:19–23), and death will finally be eliminated during the eternal state (1 Cor. 15:53–57; Rev. 21:4; 22:3).

3:15 This verse has been labeled the Protevangelium, because it is the first statement containing a reference to the gospel; it will be enlarged upon throughout Scripture. This is also the first messianic prophecy in the Bible.

This verse pronounces a prophetic curse on the power behind the snake (Satan), and a prophecy of the perpetual struggle between satanic forces and mankind. Revelation 12:9 and 20:2 tell us plainly that Satan, the devil, is the one acting through the snake. The struggle will be between Satan and the seed (offspring/descendant) of the woman. This is seen immediately through Cain in Genesis 4, and then through Christ and His followers. The seed of the serpent includes demons and all humanity not following Christ (John 8:44). As a snake strikes at the heel of man while in the field, so Satan will wound mankind;

but Christ shall crush the head of Satan, much like a man in the field grinding a snake under foot.

3:16 thy desire shall be to thy husband. God now prophetically curses the woman in the area of her primary calling. Pain in childbirth and other female hardships were not part of God's original creation, but arrived as a result of this curse. This prophecy also speaks of the battle of the sexes. God intends for the man to lovingly lead his wife and for her to graciously submit.

3:17 cursed is the ground for thy sake. Here the man is prophetically cursed in the area of his calling, to tend the garden. Just as the woman has pain in labor, the man will experience pain in his labor to till the ground.

3:18 Thorns also and thistles shall it bring forth to thee. The obstacles that we experience today are all due to the curse. When the Messiah reigns in His kingdom, the obstacles will be removed (Isa. 55:12–13; 65:23). Till then, as we observe the present cursed earth, it should remind us that the ground that was put under man's feet rebels against man, because man rebels against God.

3:19 In the sweat of thy face . . . till thou return unto the ground. Because of his fall into sin, man will experience hardship until the relief of death returns his body to its place of origin. The wearing of the crown of thorns on Christ's sweat-filled brow during the crucifixion pictured in part His bearing the curse set upon mankind (Matt. 27:29).

3:21 did the LORD God make coats of skins, and clothed them. This gracious provision paints a picture, and thus a prophecy, of salvation through the blood of an innocent substitute. This will become a major theme throughout Scripture.

LORD God make coats of skins, and clothed them.

Adam and Eve Leave Eden

22 And the LORD God said, Behold, the man is become as one of us, to know good and evil: and now, lest he put forth his hand, and take also of the tree of life, and eat, and live for ever:
23 Therefore the LORD God sent him forth from the garden of Eden, to till the ground from whence he was taken.
24 So he drove out the man; and he placed at the east of the garden of Eden Cherubims, and a flaming sword which turned every way, to keep the way of the tree of life.

CHAPTER 4
Cain and Abel

1 And Adam knew Eve his wife; and she conceived, and bare Cain, and said, I have gotten a man from the LORD.
2 And she again bare his brother Abel. And Abel was a keeper of sheep, but Cain was a tiller of the ground.
3 And in process of time it came to pass, that Cain brought of the fruit of the ground an offering unto the LORD.

22 Gen. 2:9; 3:5; Isa. 19:12; 47:12, 13; Jer. 22:23
23 Gen. 4:2; 9:20
24 Gen. 2:8; Ps. 104:4; Heb. 1:7
2 Gen. 3:23; 9:20
3 Num. 18:12
4 Num. 18:17; Prov. 3:9; Heb. 11:4
5 Gen. 31:2
7 Gen. 3:16; Heb. 11:4
8 Matt. 23:35; 1John 3:12; Jude 11
9 Ps. 9:12; John 8:44
10 Heb. 12:24; Rev. 6:10

4 And Abel, he also brought of the firstlings of his flock and of the fat thereof. And the LORD had respect unto Abel and to his offering:
5 But unto Cain and to his offering he had not respect. And Cain was very wroth, and his countenance fell.
6 And the LORD said unto Cain, Why art thou wroth? and why is thy countenance fallen?
7 If thou doest well, shalt thou not be accepted? and if thou doest not well, sin lieth at the door. And unto thee *shall be* his desire, and thou shalt rule over him.
8 And Cain talked with Abel his brother: and it came to pass, when they were in the field, that Cain rose up against Abel his brother, and slew him.
9 And the LORD said unto Cain, Where *is* Abel thy brother? And he said, I know not: *Am* I my brother's keeper?
10 And he said, What hast thou done? the voice of thy brother's blood crieth unto me from the ground.
11 And now *art* thou cursed from the earth, which hath opened her mouth to receive thy brother's blood from thy hand;
12 When thou tillest the ground, it shall not

Comparisons between the Cursed World and the Redeemed World

Cursed World	Genesis	Redeemed World	Revelation
Cursed ground	3:17	No more curse	22:3
Daily sorrow	3:17	No more sorrow	21:4
Returning to the dust	3:19	No more death	21:4
Satan opposing	3:15	Satan banished	20:10
Kept from the tree of life	3:24	Access to tree of life	22:14
Redeemer promised	3:15	Redemption accomplished	5:9–10
Evil continually	6:5	Nothing that defileth	21:27
Cherubim guarding	3:24	Angels inviting	21:9

By Henry Morris—*Used by permission.*

4:1–15 Cain is the fulfillment of the prophecy that Eve would bear a son (Gen. 3:15).

4:1 I have gotten a man from the LORD. Adam and Eve must have been greatly disappointed to realize that their first-born son did not crush the head of the serpent. Instead, Cain's legacy was closer to that of the seed of the serpent.

4:7 sin lieth at the door. The Lord predicts that man's choice to do wrong empowers sin. Cain is commanded to master sin.

4:11 now art thou cursed from the earth. The Lord prophetically curses Cain in much the same way He

cursed the serpent and Cain's parents in Genesis 3. Because Cain brought a sacrifice of his own choosing, the fruit of the ground, God now curses Cain "from the earth," that is, his physical productivity. Within God's economy, the punishment always fits the crime.

4:12 a fugitive and a vagabond shalt thou be in the earth. Because of God's curse of the earth, Cain will no longer successfully till the ground. Instead he will become a wanderer of the earth. The phrase "a fugitive and a vagabond" means "a wandering fugitive."

henceforth yield unto thee her strength; a fugitive and a vagabond shalt thou be in the earth.

13 And Cain said unto the LORD, My punishment *is* greater than I can bear.

14 Behold, thou hast driven me out this day from the face of the earth; and from thy face shall I be hid; and I shall be a fugitive and a vagabond in the earth; and it shall come to pass, *that* every one that findeth me shall slay me.

15 And the LORD said unto him, Therefore whosoever slayeth Cain, vengeance shall be taken on him sevenfold. And the LORD set a mark upon Cain, lest any finding him should kill him.

16 And Cain went out from the presence of the LORD, and dwelt in the land of Nod, on the cast of Eden.

17 And Cain knew his wife; and she conceived, and bare Enoch: and he builded a city, and called the name of the city, after the name of his son, Enoch.

18 And unto Enoch was born Irad: and Irad begat Mehujael: and Mehujael begat Methusael: and Methusael begat Lamech.

19 And Lamech took unto him two wives: the name of the one *was* Adah, and the name of the other Zillah.

20 And Adah bare Jabal: he was the father of such as dwell in tents, and *of such as have* cattle.

21 And his brother's name *was* Jubal: he was the father of all such as handle the harp and organ.

22 And Zillah, she also bare Tubal-cain, an instructer of every artificer in brass and iron: and the sister of Tubal-cain *was* Naamah.

23 And Lamech said unto his wives, Adah and Zillah, Hear my voice; ye wives of Lamech, hearken unto my speech: for I have slain a man to my wounding, and a young man to my hurt.

24 If Cain shall be avenged sevenfold, truly Lamech seventy and sevenfold.

Another Son

25 And Adam knew his wife again; and she bare a son, and called his name Seth: For

God, *said she*, hath appointed me another seed instead of Abel, whom Cain slew.

26 And to Seth, to him also there was born a son; and he called his name Enos: then began men to call upon the name of the LORD.

CHAPTER 5
Adam's Family Record

1 This *is* the book of the generations of Adam. In the day that God created man, in the likeness of God made he him;

2 Male and female created he them; and blessed them, and called their name Adam, in the day when they were created.

3 And Adam lived an hundred and thirty years, and begat *a son* in his own likeness, after his image; and called his name Seth:

4 And the days of Adam after he had begotten Seth were eight hundred years: and he begat sons and daughters:

5 And all the days that Adam lived were nine hundred and thirty years: and he died.

6 And Seth lived an hundred and five years, and begat Enos:

7 And Seth lived after he begat Enos eight hundred and seven years, and begat sons and daughters:

8 And all the days of Seth were nine hundred and twelve years: and he died.

9 And Enos lived ninety years, and begat Cainan:

10 And Enos lived after he begat Cainan eight hundred and fifteen years, and begat sons and daughters:

11 And all the days of Enos were nine hundred and five years: and he died.

12 And Cainan lived seventy years, and begat Mahalaleel:

13 And Cainan lived after he begat Mahalaleel eight hundred and forty years, and begat sons and daughters:

14 And all the days of Cainan were nine hundred and ten years: and he died.

15 And Mahalaleel lived sixty and five years, and begat Jared:

16 And Mahalaleel lived after he begat Jared eight hundred and thirty years, and begat sons and daughters:

Cross references:

14 Gen. 9:6; Num. 35:19, 21, 27; Job 15:20-24; Ps. 51:11

15 Ps. 79:12; Ezek. 9:4, 6

16 2Kgs. 13:23; 24:20; Jer. 23:39; 52:3

17 Ps. 49:11

21 Rom. 4:11, 12

24 Gen. 4:15

25 Gen. 5:3

26 Gen. 5:6; 1Kgs. 18:24; Ps. 116:17; Joel 2:32; Zeph. 3:9; 1Cor. 1:2

1 Gen. 1:26; 1Chr. 1:1; Luke 3:38; Eph. 4:24; Col. 3:10

2 Gen. 1:27

3 Gen. 4:25

4 Gen. 1:28; 1Chr. 1:1

5 Gen. 3:19; Heb. 9:27

6 Gen. 4:26

4:14 it shall come to pass, that every one that findeth me shall slay me. Cain predicts that, since he will be unproductive in an agrarian world, some (apparently his siblings) will want to kill him, perhaps because they see him as a potential thief. Those who know what he did may want to kill him because they fear he will murder someone else.

4:15 vengeance shall be taken on him sevenfold. The Lord prophesies that He will exact great revenge on any that harm Cain. This would hopefully dissuade other family members from taking revenge.

5:1 This is the book of the generations of Adam. This is the second *toledoth* (see note on Gen. 2:4).

17 And all the days of Mahalaleel were eight hundred ninety and five years: and he died.

18 And Jared lived an hundred sixty and two years, and he begat Enoch:

19 And Jared lived after he begat Enoch eight hundred years, and begat sons and daughters:

20 And all the days of Jared were nine hundred sixty and two years: and he died.

21 And Enoch lived sixty and five years, and begat Methuselah:

22 And Enoch walked with God after he begat Methuselah three hundred years, and begat sons and daughters:

23 And all the days of Enoch were three hundred sixty and five years:

Enoch Is a Type of the Rapture

24 And Enoch walked with God: and he *was* not; for God took him.

25 And Methuselah lived an hundred eighty and seven years, and begat Lamech:

26 And Methuselah lived after he begat Lamech seven hundred eighty and two years, and begat sons and daughters:

27 And all the days of Methuselah were nine hundred sixty and nine years: and he died.

28 And Lamech lived an hundred eighty and two years, and begat a son:

29 And he called his name Noah, saying, This *same* shall comfort us concerning our work and toil of our hands, because of the ground which the LORD hath cursed.

30 And Lamech lived after he begat Noah five hundred ninety and five years, and begat sons and daughters:

31 And all the days of Lamech were seven hundred seventy and seven years: and he died.

32 And Noah was five hundred years old: and Noah begat Shem, Ham, and Japheth.

CHAPTER 6
Evil Rules over Mankind

1 And it came to pass, when men began to multiply on the face of the earth, and daughters were born unto them,

2 That the sons of God saw the daughters of men that they *were* fair; and they took them wives of all which they chose.

3 And the LORD said, My spirit shall not always strive with man, for that he also *is* flesh: yet his days shall be an hundred and twenty years.

4 There were giants in the earth in those days; and also after that, when the sons of God came in unto the daughters of men, and they bare *children* to them, the same *became* mighty men which *were* of old, men of renown.

5 And GOD saw that the wickedness of man *was* great in the earth, and *that* every imagination of the thoughts of his heart *was* only evil continually.

6 And it repented the LORD that he had made man on the earth, and it grieved him at his heart.

7 And the LORD said, I will destroy man whom I have created from the face of the earth; both man, and beast, and the creeping thing, and the fowls of the air; for it repenteth me that I have made them.

Cross references (center column):

18 Jude 1:14, 15

22 Gen. 6:9; 17:1; 24:40; 2Kgs. 20:3; Ps. 16:8; 116:9; 128:1; Mic. 6:8; Mal. 2:6

24 2Kgs. 2:11; Heb. 11:5

29 Gen. 3:17; 4:11; Luke 3:36; Heb. 11:7; 1Pet. 3:20

32 Gen. 6:10; 10:21

1 Gen. 1:28

2 Deut. 7:3, 4

3 Ps. 78:39; Gal. 5:16, 17; 1Pet. 3:19, 20

5 Gen. 8:21; Deut. 29:19; Prov. 6:18; Matt. 15:19

6 Num. 23:19; 1Sam. 15:11, 29; 2Sam. 24:16; Isa. 63:10; Mal. 3:6; Eph. 4:30; James 1:17

5:21–24 Enoch is an intriguing figure in Bible prophecy for a number of reasons. Only Noah (Gen. 6:9) and Enoch are singled out by the phrase **walked with God.** It is said of Enoch moreover that **he was not; for God took him.** This does not mean that he ceased to exist or that he died, as did others in the genealogy. Instead it means that he was taken alive into heaven by God (Heb. 11:5), as was Elijah later (2 Kgs. 2:1–12). Thus, Enoch is a type (i.e., a picture or illustration) of the rapture of the Church, in which the Church is to be "taken" to the Lord (John 14:1–3) before the time of wrath (1 Thess. 1:10; 5:9). On the other hand, Noah is a type of Israel which will go through the wrath of the Tribulation yet be preserved (Ezek. 20:33–44; 22:17–22). Jude tells us in the New Testament (Jude 1:14–15) that Enoch prophesied in his day about the Lord's coming for the purpose of judgment, that is, at the Second Coming of Christ. Thus, Enoch was

a prophet during his tenure upon earth.

5:27 Methuselah is the oldest man recorded in the Bible, having lived 969 years. His name is believed to mean, "when he dies, judgment." Methuselah dies in the year of the Flood (Gen. 7:6).

5:29 Lamech utters a prophecy by naming his son. Noah, whose name means "to rest," is associated with the comfort that God gave him. Noah rested safe in the ark, sheltered from God's curse of the Flood.

6:3 yet his days shall be an hundred and twenty years. The Lord predicts that mankind will have a set amount of time before the global Flood occurs.

6:7 I will destroy man. Following the predictive pattern of Genesis 1, the Lord sovereignly declares that He will destroy the humanity He created.

Dispensations

By Robert Dean, Jr.

Dispensationalism is the interpretive key that unlocks the pages of Scripture, opens the door for our understanding of prophecy, and orients our thinking about God's blueprint for human history.

Three complementary principles form the foundation of Dispensational theology. The first principle states that the Bible must be consistently understood in terms of the plain, literal meaning of words, including the use of figures of speech where the context indicates. A second principle lies in the premise that God has a plan for ethnic and national Israel that is distinct from His plan for the New Testament Church. The third principle of Dispensationalism is that human history is the outworking of an eternal plan of God that culminates in bringing maximum glory to Himself.

The Greek word for "dispensation," *oikonómos*, means administration, stewardship. A dispensation therefore is a distinct and identifiable administration in the development of God's design for human history (Eph. 3:2; Col. 1:25–26). God manages the entirety of human history as a household, moving humanity through sequential stages of His administration. Each stage, or dispensation, is determined by the level of revelation the Lord has provided up to that time in history. That revelation specifies man's responsibilities, tests regarding those responsibilities, and God's gracious provision of a solution when failure occurs.

Salvation is by grace through faith in Christ alone.

Though each dispensation has distinct and identifiable characteristics, the truths and principles of God's revelation and plan for redemption are constant. Salvation is by grace through faith in Christ alone. Prior to the cross, faith anticipated fulfillment of the divine promise of salvation through the work of Messiah. Since the crucifixion of Jesus Christ, faith looks back to His finished, substitutionary atonement on the cross. Other characteristics are modified as God's revelation progresses, such as the practice of animal sacrifice.

Dispensationalists sometimes differ as to the exact number of dispensations revealed in Scripture, but they usually list these seven:

1. Innocence: Adam to the Fall
2. Conscience: Fall to Flood
3. Human Government: Flood to Abraham
4. Promise: Abraham to Moses
5. Mosaic Law: Moses to the Cross
6. Church Age: the Day of Pentecost to the Rapture
7. Millennial Kingdom: The literal 1,000 year reign of Jesus Christ following His Second Advent.

Dispensational theology enables us to correctly understand God's prophetic timetable for humanity. The current era focuses on the church as the people of God, not on Israel. Yet for Daniel's prophecy (Dan. 9:27) to be literally fulfilled in the same way the initial sixty-nine weeks were fulfilled (Dan. 9:25–26), the church must be removed from the earth. Only then will God begin to fulfill all He promised to Israel in the Old Testament. The removal of the Church is called the rapture of the church (1 Thess. 4:16–17), and many Dispensationalists believe that the Rapture precedes the last seven years of God's decree for Israel, known as the Tribulation. These seven years, which are technically a completion of the age of the Mosaic Law, begin after the rapture of the church and end with the Second Advent. Thus, the doctrine of the pretribulational rapture of the church is closely identified with Dispensational theology.

8 But Noah found grace in the eyes of the LORD.

Noah

9 These *are* the generations of Noah: Noah was a just man *and* perfect in his generations, *and* Noah walked with God.
10 And Noah begat three sons, Shem, Ham, and Japheth.
11 The earth also was corrupt before God, and the earth was filled with violence.
12 And God looked upon the earth, and, behold, it was corrupt; for all flesh had corrupted his way upon the earth.
13 And God said unto Noah, The end of all flesh is come before me; for the earth is filled with violence through them; and, behold, I will destroy them with the earth.
14 Make thee an ark of gopher wood; rooms shalt thou make in the ark, and shalt pitch it within and without with pitch.
15 And this *is the fashion* which thou shalt make it *of*: The length of the ark *shall be* three hundred cubits, the breadth of it fifty cubits, and the height of it thirty cubits.
16 A window shalt thou make to the ark, and in a cubit shalt thou finish it above; and the door of the ark shalt thou set in the side thereof; *with* lower, second, and third *stories* shalt thou make it.
17 And, behold, I, even I, do bring a flood of waters upon the earth, to destroy all flesh, wherein *is* the breath of life, from under heaven; *and* every thing that *is* in the earth shall die.

The Noahic Covenant as a Type of Prophetic Promise

18 But with thee will I establish my covenant; and thou shalt come into the ark, thou, and thy sons, and thy wife, and thy sons' wives with thee.

19 And of every living thing of all flesh, two of every *sort* shalt thou bring into the ark, to keep *them* alive with thee; they shall be male and female.
20 Of fowls after their kind, and of cattle after their kind, of every creeping thing of the earth after his kind, two of every *sort* shall come unto thee, to keep *them* alive.
21 And take thou unto thee of all food that is eaten, and thou shalt gather *it* to thee; and it shall be for food for thee, and for them.
22 Thus did Noah; according to all that God commanded him, so did he.

CHAPTER 7
The Flood

1 And the LORD said unto Noah, Come thou and all thy house into the ark; for thee have I seen righteous before me in this generation.
2 Of every clean beast thou shalt take to thee by sevens, the male and his female: and of beasts that *are* not clean by two, the male and his female.
3 Of fowls also of the air by sevens, the male and the female; to keep seed alive upon the face of all the earth.
4 For yet seven days, and I will cause it to rain upon the earth forty days and forty nights; and every living substance that I have made will I destroy from off the face of the earth.
5 And Noah did according unto all that the LORD commanded him.
6 And Noah *was* six hundred years old when the flood of waters was upon the earth.
7 And Noah went in, and his sons, and his wife, and his sons' wives with him, into the ark, because of the waters of the flood.
8 Of clean beasts, and of beasts that *are* not clean, and of fowls, and of every thing that creepeth upon the earth,

Cross-references

8 Gen. 19:19; Ex. 33:12, 13, 16, 17; Luke 1:30; Acts 7:46
9 Gen. 5:22; 7:1; Ezek. 14:14, 20; Rom. 1:17; Heb. 11:7; 2Pet. 2:5
10 Gen. 5:32
11 Gen. 7:1; 10:9; 13:13; 2Chr. 34:27; Ezek. 8:17; 28:16; Hab. 2:8, 17; Luke 1:6; Rom. 2:13; 3:19
12 Gen. 18:21; Ps. 14:2; 33:13, 14; 53:2, 3
13 Gen. 6:1; Jer. 51:13; Ezek. 7:2, 3, 6; Amos 8:2; 1Pet. 4:7
17 Gen. 6:13; 7:4, 21-23; 2Pet. 2:5
18 Gen. 7:1, 7, 13; 1Pet. 3:20; 2Pet. 2:5
19 Gen. 7:8, 9, 15, 16
20 Gen. 2:19; 7:9, 15
22 Gen. 7:5, 9, 16; Ex. 40:16; Heb. 11:7
1 Prov. 10:9; Matt. 24:38; Luke 17:26; Heb. 11:7
2 Lev. 10:10; 11:2-4

6:8 But Noah found grace in the eyes of the LORD. God will save Noah, his family, and the animals in the ark, because of His grace. Whether physical or spiritual, salvation is always due to God's favor, totally apart from anything that man has to offer.

6:9 These are the generations of Noah. This is the third *toledoth* (see note on Gen. 2:4).

6:13 the earth is filled with violence through them. God supplies the reason why He will destroy humanity. The violence that He speaks of here is associated with "giants" that were in the earth in those days (Gen. 6:4).

6:17–22 every thing that is in the earth shall die. The Lord once again predicts the global Flood that will de-

stroy all flesh. However, the Lord will preserve a remnant, namely Noah, his wife, their three sons and their wives, and two of every kind of animal. Noah's response to God in doing **all that God commanded him** is a model of the proper response to God's prophetic declaration.

6:18 This is the first use of the word "covenant" in the Bible, even though there were covenants previous to this.

7:1–24 God reveals that in seven days after the ark is finished, the Flood will come. The events God predicted in chapter six are fulfilled in this chapter. Literal prediction followed by literal fulfillment sets a prophetic pattern that is followed throughout the whole Bible.

9 There went in two and two unto Noah into the ark, the male and the female, as God had commanded Noah.

10 And it came to pass after seven days, that the waters of the flood were upon the earth.

11 In the six hundredth year of Noah's life, in the second month, the seventeenth day of the month, the same day were all the fountains of the great deep broken up, and the windows of heaven were opened.

12 And the rain was upon the earth forty days and forty nights.

13 In the selfsame day entered Noah, and Shem, and Ham, and Japheth, the sons of Noah, and Noah's wife, and the three wives of his sons with them, into the ark;

14 They, and every beast after his kind, and all the cattle after their kind, and every creeping thing that creepeth upon the earth after his kind, and every fowl after his kind, every bird of every sort.

15 And they went in unto Noah into the ark, two and two of all flesh, wherein *is* the breath of life.

16 And they that went in, went in male and female of all flesh, as God had commanded him: and the LORD shut him in.

17 And the flood was forty days upon the earth; and the waters increased, and bare up the ark, and it was lift up above the earth.

18 And the waters prevailed, and were increased greatly upon the earth; and the ark went upon the face of the waters.

19 And the waters prevailed exceedingly upon the earth; and all the high hills, that *were* under the whole heaven, were covered.

20 Fifteen cubits upward did the waters prevail; and the mountains were covered.

21 And all flesh died that moved upon the earth, both of fowl, and of cattle, and of beast, and of every creeping thing that creepeth upon the earth, and every man:

22 All in whose nostrils *was* the breath of life, of all that *was* in the dry *land*, died.

23 And every living substance was destroyed which was upon the face of the ground, both man, and cattle, and the creeping things, and the fowl of the heaven; and they were destroyed from the earth: and Noah only remained *alive*, and they that *were* with him in the ark.

24 And the waters prevailed upon the earth an hundred and fifty days.

CHAPTER 8
The Flood Ends

1 And God remembered Noah, and every living thing, and all the cattle that *was* with him in the ark: and God made a wind to pass over the earth, and the waters asswaged;

2 The fountains also of the deep and the windows of heaven were stopped, and the rain from heaven was restrained;

3 And the waters returned from off the earth continually: and after the end of the hundred and fifty days the waters were abated.

4 And the ark rested in the seventh month, on the seventeenth day of the month, upon the mountains of Ararat.

5 And the waters decreased continually until the tenth month: in the tenth *month*, on the first *day* of the month, were the tops of the mountains seen.

6 And it came to pass at the end of forty days, that Noah opened the window of the ark which he had made:

7 And he sent forth a raven, which went forth to and fro, until the waters were dried up from off the earth.

8 Also he sent forth a dove from him, to see if the waters were abated from off the face of the ground;

9 But the dove found no rest for the sole of her foot, and she returned unto him into the ark, for the waters *were* on the face of the whole earth: then he put forth his hand, and took her, and pulled her in unto him into the ark.

10 And he stayed yet other seven days; and again he sent forth the dove out of the ark;

11 And the dove came in to him in the evening; and, lo, in her mouth *was* an olive leaf pluckt off: so Noah knew that the waters were abated from off the earth.

12 And he stayed yet other seven days; and sent forth the dove; which returned not again unto him any more.

13 And it came to pass in the six hundredth and first year, in the first *month*, the first *day* of the month, the waters were dried up from off the earth: and Noah removed the covering of the ark, and looked, and, behold, the face of the ground was dry.

14 And in the second month, on the seven

Cross references:

11 Gen. 1:7; 8:2; Ps. 78:23; Prov. 8:28; Ezek. 26:19
12 Gen. 7:4, 17
13 Gen. 2:1, 7; 6:18; Heb. 11:7; 1Pet. 3:20; 2Pet. 2:5
14 Gen. 7:2, 3, 8, 9
15 Gen. 6:20
16 Gen. 7:2, 3
17 Gen. 7:4, 12
18 Ps. 104:26
19 Ps. 104:6; Jer. 3:23
21 Gen. 6:13, 17; 7:4; Job 22:16; Matt. 24:39; Luke 17:27; 2Pet. 3:6
22 Gen. 2:7
23 1Pet. 3:20; 2Pet. 2:5; 3:6
24 Gen. 8:3, 4; cf. Gen. 7:11
1 Gen. 19:29; Ex. 2:24; 14:21; 1Sam. 1:19
2 Gen. 7:11; Job 38:37
3 Gen. 7:24
6 Gen. 6:16

8:13 The Dispensation of Human Government begins after the Flood when Noah and his family leave the ark (see article on Dispensations). Mankind did not invent civil government. God Himself instituted it after the Flood, as seen in

and twentieth day of the month, was the earth dried.

15 And God spake unto Noah, saying,
16 Go forth of the ark, thou, and thy wife, and thy sons, and thy sons' wives with thee.
17 Bring forth with thee every living thing that *is* with thee, of all flesh, *both* of fowl, and of cattle, and of every creeping thing that creepeth upon the earth; that they may breed abundantly in the earth, and be fruitful, and multiply upon the earth.
18 And Noah went forth, and his sons, and his wife, and his sons' wives with him:
19 Every beast, every creeping thing, and every fowl, *and* whatsoever creepeth upon the earth, after their kinds, went forth out of the ark.
20 And Noah builded an altar unto the Lord; and took of every clean beast, and of every clean fowl, and offered burnt offerings on the altar.
21 And the Lord smelled a sweet savour; and the Lord said in his heart, I will not again curse the ground any more for man's sake; for the imagination of man's heart *is* evil from his youth; neither will I again smite any more every thing living, as I have done.
22 While the earth remaineth, seedtime and harvest, and cold and heat, and summer and winter, and day and night shall not cease.

CHAPTER 9
Noahic Covenant

1 And God blessed Noah and his sons, and said unto them, Be fruitful, and multiply, and replenish the earth.
2 And the fear of you and the dread of you shall be upon every beast of the earth, and upon every fowl of the air, upon all that moveth *upon* the earth, and upon all the fishes of the sea; into your hand are they delivered.
3 Every moving thing that liveth shall be meat for you; even as the green herb have I given you all things.
4 But flesh with the life thereof, *which is* the blood thereof, shall ye not eat.
5 And surely your blood of your lives will I require; at the hand of every beast will I require it, and at the hand of man; at the hand of every man's brother will I require the life of man.
6 Whoso sheddeth man's blood, by man shall his blood be shed: for in the image of God made he man.
7 And you, be ye fruitful, and multiply; bring forth abundantly in the earth, and multiply therein.
8 And God spake unto Noah, and to his sons with him, saying,
9 And I, behold, I establish my covenant with you, and with your seed after you;

Cross references (center column):

20 Lev. 11:1-47
21 Gen. 3:17; 6:5, 17; Lev. 1:9; Jer. 17:9; Ezek. 20:41
1 Gen. 1:28; 9:7, 19; 10:32
2 Gen. 1:28; Hos. 2:18
3 Gen. 1:29; Deut. 12:15; 14:3, 9, 11; Acts 10:12, 13; Rom. 14:14, 20; 1Cor. 10:23, 26; Col. 2:16; 1Tim. 4:3, 4
4 Lev. 17:10, 11, 14; 19:26; Deut. 12:23; Acts 15:20, 29
5 Ex. 21:28
6 Ex. 21:12, 14; Lev. 24:17; Matt. 26:52; Rev. 13:10
7 Gen. 1:28; 8:1, 19
9 Gen. 6:18; Isa. 54:9

---

this passage. God's reveals that evil is to be restrained through civil government. Man's responsibility was to restrain evil through capital punishment of certain offenses (Gen. 9:6; Rom. 13:1-7; 1 Pet. 2:13-17). However, because man did not fully carry out this mandate, God intervened at the tower of Babel (Gen. 11:1-9).

8:21 The Lord was satisfied with Noah's sacrifice. This is a prophetic picture of what is needed to deal with man's sin.

8:22 God promises that there will be ecological stability upon the earth until the end of history. The cycles of seedtime and harvest, cold and heat, summer and winter, and day and night shall not cease throughout history. This element of regularity is the basis for science.

9:1-17 The Noahic Covenant (Gen. 9:1) restates God's authority over man and his duties as found in the Adamic Covenant, and then adds further responsibilities. These new items include the following: 1) animosity between mankind and the animal kingdom (9:2); 2) the allowance of animal flesh for food (9:3); 3) the forbiddance of consumption of blood (9:4); 4) capital punishment for murder (9:5-6); and 5) the command to "be fruitful, and multiply, and replenish the earth" (Gen. 9:1, 7). The Noahic covenant is made between God and man, and affects the en-

tire animal kingdom (9:8-10). In this covenant, God promises never again to destroy the world through a flood (9:11). The sign that God will keep His promise is the rainbow set within a cloud (9:12-17). A rainbow is likely chosen because it is presented elsewhere as an item that surrounds the very throne of God (Ezek. 1:28; Rev. 4:3), representing His blessing. The Noahic covenant is mentioned in Isaiah 54:9-10.

9:6 Capital punishment is here established as part of human government. To not exact such punishment when murder occurs is a sin against God. Capital punishment continues until the Second Coming of Christ (Rom. 13:1-7; 1 Pet. 2:13-17). Since God's standard of justice is substitution, the only thing valuable enough to pay for the life of a human being is the life of another. This principle forms the backbone of the gospel and the need for Christ's substitutionary death on the cross.

9:8-17 God prophesied that He would set a rainbow as a sign of His covenant. This prophecy is fulfilled every time a rainbow appears in the cloud.

9:9 Through this covenant, God promises to keep alive a seed that will eventually curse the seed of the serpent (Gen. 3:15).

10 And with every living creature that *is* with you, of the fowl, of the cattle, and of every beast of the earth with you; from all that go out of the ark, to every beast of the earth.

11 And I will establish my covenant with you; neither shall all flesh be cut off any more by the waters of a flood; neither shall there any more be a flood to destroy the earth.

12 And God said, This *is* the token of the covenant which I make between me and you and every living creature that *is* with you, for perpetual generations:

13 I do set my bow in the cloud, and it shall be for a token of a covenant between me and the earth.

14 And it shall come to pass, when I bring a cloud over the earth, that the bow shall be seen in the cloud:

15 And I will remember my covenant, which *is* between me and you and every living creature of all flesh; and the waters shall no more become a flood to destroy all flesh.

16 And the bow shall be in the cloud; and I will look upon it, that I may remember the everlasting covenant between God and every living creature of all flesh that *is* upon the earth.

17 And God said unto Noah, This *is* the token of the covenant, which I have established between me and all flesh that *is* upon the earth.

Noah's Sons

18 And the sons of Noah, that went forth of the ark, were Shem, and Ham, and Japheth: and Ham *is* the father of Canaan.

19 These *are* the three sons of Noah: and of them was the whole earth overspread.

20 And Noah began *to be* an husbandman, and he planted a vineyard:

21 And he drank of the wine, and was drunken; and he was uncovered within his tent.

22 And Ham, the father of Canaan, saw the nakedness of his father, and told his two brethren without.

23 And Shem and Japheth took a garment, and laid *it* upon both their shoulders, and went backward, and covered the nakedness of their father; and their faces *were* backward, and they saw not their father's nakedness.

24 And Noah awoke from his wine, and knew what his younger son had done unto him.

25 And he said, Cursed *be* Canaan; a servant of servants shall he be unto his brethren.

26 And he said, Blessed *be* the LORD God of Shem; and Canaan shall be his servant.

27 God shall enlarge Japheth, and he shall dwell in the tents of Shem; and Canaan shall be his servant.

28 And Noah lived after the flood three hundred and fifty years.

29 And all the days of Noah were nine hundred and fifty years: and he died.

CHAPTER 10
Noah's Family Record

1 Now these *are* the generations of the sons of Noah, Shem, Ham, and Japheth: and unto them were sons born after the flood.

2 The sons of Japheth; Gomer, and Magog, and Madai, and Javan, and Tubal, and Meshech, and Tiras.

3 And the sons of Gomer; Ashkenaz, and Riphath, and Togarmah.

4 And the sons of Javan; Elishah, and Tarshish, Kittim, and Dodanim.

5 By these were the isles of the Gentiles

Cross references (center column)

10 Ps. 145:9
11 Isa. 54:9
12 Gen. 17:11
13 Rev. 4:3
15 Ex. 28:12; Lev. 26:42, 45; Ezek. 16:60
16 Gen. 17:13, 19
18 Gen. 10:6
19 Gen. 5:32; 10:32; 1Chr. 1:4
20 Gen. 3:19, 23; 4:2; Prov. 12:11
21 Prov. 20:1; 1Cor. 10:12
23 Ex. 20:12; Gal. 6:1
25 Deut. 27:16; Josh. 9:23; 1Kgs. 9:20, 21
26 Ps. 144:15; Heb. 11:16
27 Eph. 2:13, 14; 3:6

1 Gen. 9:1, 7, 19

2 1Chr. 1:5

5 Ps. 72:10; Jer. 2:10; 25:22; Zeph. 2:11

9:16 The rainbow is a reminder to mankind of God's promise.

9:24–27 This passage includes another prophecy, this time concerning the destinies of the Noah's three sons: Shem, Ham (through Canaan), and Japheth. This prophecy provides an outline of post-Flood history. Ham dishonored his father by viewing his nakedness. Shem and Japheth respected their father and refused to look.

9:26 Blessed be the LORD God of Shem. The messianic line that ran through Seth, Enoch, and Noah before the Flood would now run through Shem, Eber, and Abraham and eventually on to Jesus Christ (Gen. 11:10–27; Matt. 1:12–16). God's chosen nation, Israel, would descend through Shem. Thus, through Shem God would meet the spiritual needs of mankind.

9:27 God shall enlarge Japheth. The word "enlarge" is ordinarily coupled with "borders" (cf. Ex. 34:24; Deut. 12:20; 19:8), implying the multiplication of descendants.

10:1 These are the generations of the sons of Noah, Shem, Ham, and Japheth. This is the fourth *toledoth* (see note on Gen. 2:4).

10:1–32 The prophetic significance of the genealogies in this chapter lies in the fact that this is the last time that the generations of Ham and Japheth are traced. Since the promised seed will come through Shem, there are other genealogies of him after this passage.

divided in their lands; every one after his tongue, after their families, in their nations.

6 And the sons of Ham; Cush, and Mizraim, and Phut, and Canaan.

7 And the sons of Cush; Seba, and Havilah, and Sabtah, and Raamah, and Sabtecha: and the sons of Raamah; Sheba, and Dedan.

8 And Cush begat Nimrod: he began to be a mighty one in the earth.

9 He was a mighty hunter before the LORD: wherefore it is said, Even as Nimrod the mighty hunter before the LORD.

10 And the beginning of his kingdom was Babel, and Erech, and Accad, and Calneh, in the land of Shinar.

11 Out of that land went forth Asshur, and builded Nineveh, and the city Rehoboth, and Calah,

12 And Resen between Nineveh and Calah: the same *is* a great city.

13 And Mizraim begat Ludim, and Anamim, and Lehabim, and Naphtuhim,

14 And Pathrusim, and Casluhim, (out of whom came Philistim,) and Caphtorim.

15 And Canaan begat Sidon his firstborn, and Heth,

16 And the Jebusite, and the Amorite, and the Girgasite,

17 And the Hivite, and the Arkite, and the Sinite,

18 And the Arvadite, and the Zemarite, and the Hamathite: and afterward were the families of the Canaanites spread abroad.

19 And the border of the Canaanites was from Sidon, as thou comest to Gerar, unto Gaza; as thou goest, unto Sodom, and Gomorrah, and Admah, and Zeboim, even unto Lasha.

20 These *are* the sons of Ham, after their families, after their tongues, in their countries, *and* in their nations.

21 Unto Shem also the father of all the children of Eber, the brother of Japheth the elder, even to him were *children* born.

22 The children of Shem; Elam, and Asshur, and Arphaxad, and Lud, and Aram.

23 And the children of Aram; Uz, and Hul, and Gether, and Mash.

24 And Arphaxad begat Salah; and Salah begat Eber.

25 And unto Eber were born two sons: the name of one *was* Peleg; for in his days was the earth divided; and his brother's name *was* Joktan.

26 And Joktan begat Almodad, and Sheleph, and Hazarmaveth, and Jerah,

27 And Hadoram, and Uzal, and Diklah,

28 And Obal, and Abimael, and Sheba,

29 And Ophir, and Havilah, and Jobab: all these *were* the sons of Joktan.

30 And their dwelling was from Mesha, as thou goest unto Sephar a mount of the east.

31 These *are* the sons of Shem, after their families, after their tongues, in their lands, after their nations.

32 These *are* the families of the sons of Noah, after their generations, in their nations: and by these were the nations divided in the earth after the flood.

CHAPTER 11
The Tower of Babel

1 And the whole earth was of one language, and of one speech.

2 And it came to pass, as they journeyed from the east, that they found a plain in the land of Shinar; and they dwelt there.

3 And they said one to another, Go to, let us make brick, and burn them throughly. And they had brick for stone, and slime had they for morter.

4 And they said, Go to, let us build us a city and a tower, whose top *may reach* unto heaven; and let us make us a name, lest we be scattered abroad upon the face of the whole earth.

5 And the LORD came down to see the city and the tower, which the children of men builded.

Cross references (center column)

6 1Chr. 1:8
9 Gen. 6:11; Jer. 16:16; Mic. 7:2
10 Mic. 5:6
14 1Chr. 1:12
19 Gen. 13:12, 14, 15, 17; 15:18-21; Num. 34:2-12; Josh. 12:7, 8
22 1Chr. 1:17
24 Gen. 11:12
25 1Chr. 1:19
32 Gen. 9:19; 10:1
2 Gen. 13:11; 2Sam. 6:2; 1Chr. 13:6
4 Deut. 1:28
5 Gen. 18:21

10:8–10 Scripture traces the nativity of Babel to Nimrod, a descendant of Ham. Nimrod is often viewed as a type of the Antichrist, based upon the description of him in this passage. Babel is the birthplace of the kingdom of man that opposes God's kingdom. Babylon plays the most prominent role in the history of man's opposition to God (Gen. 11; Dan. 2, 7). Babylon will be revived during the seven-year Tribulation (Rev. 17—18).

10:32 after their generations. The word *toledoth*, "generations," is used here in continuation of the fourth section of the book (see notes on Gen. 2:4 and

Gen. 10:1).

11:1–9 The Tower of Babel incident is a judgment on the Dispensation of Human Government, because of man's failure to disperse throughout the earth as commanded by God (Gen. 9:1, 7). This passage provides the student of prophecy with the rationale as to why global government is opposed by God. Such a government is opposed to God. This is why the Antichrist will install a global government during the last half of the Tribulation. The government will fail, as those at Babel failed, because God will intervene.

6 And the LORD said, Behold, the people *is* one, and they have all one language; and this they begin to do: and now nothing will be restrained from them, which they have imagined to do.

7 Go to, let us go down, and there confound their language, that they may not understand one another's speech.

8 So the LORD scattered them abroad from thence upon the face of all the earth: and they left off to build the city.

9 Therefore is the name of it called Babel; because the LORD did there confound the language of all the earth: and from thence did the LORD scatter them abroad upon the face of all the earth.

Shem's Family Record

10 These *are* the generations of Shem: Shem *was* an hundred years old, and begat Arphaxad two years after the flood:

11 And Shem lived after he begat Arphaxad five hundred years, and begat sons and daughters.

12 And Arphaxad lived five and thirty years, and begat Salah:

13 And Arphaxad lived after he begat Salah four hundred and three years, and begat sons and daughters.

14 And Salah lived thirty years, and begat Eber:

15 And Salah lived after he begat Eber four hundred and three years, and begat sons and daughters.

16 And Eber lived four and thirty years, and begat Peleg:

17 And Eber lived after he begat Peleg four hundred and thirty years, and begat sons and daughters.

18 And Peleg lived thirty years, and begat Reu:

19 And Peleg lived after he begat Reu two hundred and nine years, and begat sons and daughters.

20 And Reu lived two and thirty years, and begat Serug:

21 And Reu lived after he begat Serug two hundred and seven years, and begat sons and daughters.

22 And Serug lived thirty years, and begat Nahor:

23 And Serug lived after he begat Nahor two hundred years, and begat sons and daughters.

24 And Nahor lived nine and twenty years, and begat Terah:

25 And Nahor lived after he begat Terah an hundred and nineteen years, and begat sons and daughters.

26 And Terah lived seventy years, and begat Abram, Nahor, and Haran.

27 Now these *are* the generations of Terah: Terah begat Abram, Nahor, and Haran; and Haran begat Lot.

28 And Haran died before his father Terah in the land of his nativity, in Ur of the Chaldees.

29 And Abram and Nahor took them wives: the name of Abram's wife *was* Sarai; and the name of Nahor's wife, Milcah, the daughter of Haran, the father of Milcah, and the father of Iscah.

30 But Sarai was barren; she *had* no child.

31 And Terah took Abram his son, and Lot the son of Haran his son's son, and Sarai his daughter-in-law, his son Abram's wife; and they went forth with them from Ur of the Chaldees, to go into the land of Canaan; and they came unto Haran, and dwelt there.

32 And the days of Terah were two hundred and five years: and Terah died in Haran.

CHAPTER 12
God Calls Abram

1 Now the LORD had said unto Abram, Get thee out of thy country, and from thy kindred, and from thy father's house, unto a land that I will shew thee:

Cross references
6 Gen. 9:19; 11:1; Ps. 2:1; Acts 17:26
7 Gen. 1:26; 42:23; Deut. 28:49; Ps. 2:4; Jer. 5:15; Acts 2:4-6; 1Cor. 14:2, 11
8 Gen. 10:25, 32; Luke 1:51
9 1Cor. 14:23
10 Gen. 10:22; 1Chr. 1:17
12 Luke 3:36
16 1Chr. 1:19; Luke 3:35, *Phalec*
20 Luke 3:35, *Saruch*
24 Luke 3:34, *Thara*
26 Josh. 24:2; 1Chr. 1:26
29 Gen. 17:15; 20:12; 22:20
30 Gen. 16:1, 2; 18:11, 12
31 Gen. 10:19; 12:1; Neh. 9:7; Acts 7:4
1 Gen. 15:7; Neh. 9:7; Isa. 41:2; Acts 7:3; Heb. 11:8

11:6–8 God fulfilled what He predicted, confounding men's languages. This is why nations to this day speak various tongues.

11:10 These are the generations of Shem. This is the fifth *toledoth* (see note on Gen. 2:4).

11:27 These are the generations of Terah. This is the sixth *toledoth* (see note on Gen. 2:4).

12:1–3 The Abrahamic covenant is the chief redemptive covenant. Every blessing that redeems believers, within both Israel and the church, flows from this covenant. While the covenant is first introduced in this passage, it is reaffirmed in Genesis 15:1–21 and Genesis 17:1–21, and then renewed with Isaac in Genesis 26:2–5 and Jacob in Genesis 28:10–17. It is a covenant in which God unconditionally promises to bring to pass definite blessings. The three major provisions of the Abrahamic covenant are 1) land for Abram and Israel, 2) descendants (including Christ), and 3) a worldwide blessing. In all, the Abrahamic covenant incorporates over a dozen provisions. Some apply to Abraham, some to Israel, the seed, others to Gentiles.

12:1 unto a land. The land of Israel was divinely given to the Jews. This promise still applies to Israel today.

2 And I will make of thee a great nation, and I will bless thee, and make thy name great; and thou shalt be a blessing:

3 And I will bless them that bless thee, and curse him that curseth thee: and in thee shall all families of the earth be blessed.

4 So Abram departed, as the LORD had spoken unto him; and Lot went with him: and Abram *was* seventy and five years old when he departed out of Haran.

5 And Abram took Sarai his wife, and Lot his brother's son, and all their substance that they had gathered, and the souls that they had gotten in Haran; and they went forth to go into the land of Canaan; and into the land of Canaan they came.

6 And Abram passed through the land unto the place of Sichem, unto the plain of Moreh. And the Canaanite *was* then in the land.

7 And the LORD appeared unto Abram, and said, Unto thy seed will I give this land: and there builded he an altar unto the LORD, who appeared unto him.

8 And he removed from thence unto a mountain on the east of Beth-el, and pitched his tent, *having* Beth-el on the west, and Hai on the east: and there he builded an altar unto the LORD, and called upon the name of the LORD.

9 And Abram journeyed, going on still toward the south.

Abram Goes to Egypt

10 And there was a famine in the land: and Abram went down into Egypt to sojourn there; for the famine *was* grievous in the land.

11 And it came to pass, when he was come near to enter into Egypt, that he said unto Sarai his wife, Behold now, I know that thou *art* a fair woman to look upon:

12 Therefore it shall come to pass, when the Egyptians shall see thee, that they shall say, This *is* his wife: and they will kill me, but they will save thee alive.

13 Say, I pray thee, thou *art* my sister: that it may be well with me for thy sake; and my soul shall live because of thee.

14 And it came to pass, that, when Abram was come into Egypt, the Egyptians beheld the woman that she *was* very fair.

15 The princes also of Pharaoh saw her, and commended her before Pharaoh: and the woman was taken into Pharaoh's house.

16 And he entreated Abram well for her sake: and he had sheep, and oxen, and he asses, and menservants, and maidservants, and she asses, and camels.

17 And the LORD plagued Pharaoh and his house with great plagues because of Sarai Abram's wife.

18 And Pharaoh called Abram, and said, What *is* this *that* thou hast done unto me? why didst thou not tell me that she *was* thy wife?

19 Why saidst thou, She *is* my sister? so I might have taken her to me to wife: now therefore behold thy wife, take *her*, and go thy way.

20 And Pharaoh commanded *his* men concerning him: and they sent him away, and his wife, and all that he had.

CHAPTER 13
Abram and Lot Separate

1 And Abram went up out of Egypt, he, and his wife, and all that he had, and Lot with him, into the south.

2 And Abram *was* very rich in cattle, in silver, and in gold.

3 And he went on his journeys from the south even to Beth-el, unto the place where his tent had been at the beginning, between Beth-el and Hai;

Cross references

2 Gen. 17:6; 18:18; 24:35; 28:4; Deut. 26:5; 1Kgs. 3:8; Gal. 3:14

3 Gen. 18:18; 22:18; 26:4; 27:29; Ex. 23:22; Num. 24:9; Ps. 72:17; Acts 3:25; Gal. 3:8

5 Gen. 11:31; 14:14

6 Gen. 10:18, 19; 13:7; Deut. 11:30; Judg. 7:1; Heb. 11:9

7 Gen. 13:4, 15; 17:1, 8; Ps. 105:9, 11

8 Gen. 13:4

9 Gen. 13:3

10 Gen. 26:1; 43:1; Ps. 105:13

11 Gen. 12:14; 26:7

12 Gen. 20:11; 26:7

13 Gen. 20:5, 13; 26:7

14 Gen. 39:7; Matt. 5:28

15 Gen. 20:2

16 Gen. 20:14

17 Gen. 20:18; 1Chr. 16:21; Ps. 105:14; Heb. 13:4

18 Gen. 20:9; 26:10

20 Prov. 21:1

Israel will permanently be given her land at the Second Coming of Christ and will dwell in it without conflict from that point on.

The Dispensation of Promise (so named by Paul in Gal. 3:15–22; 4:23, 28) begins with the call of Abram and ends with the foundation of Israel as a nation at the giving of the Law at Mount Sinai (Ex. 19). (See article on Dispensations.) During the Dispensation of Promise, God revealed His will through the Abrahamic covenant. Abram's responsibility was to dwell in the land. When Israel disobeyed God, He would chasten His people.

12:2 I will make of thee. Note the hand of God at work in history to accomplish all these promises. Through God's special blessing upon the people of Israel, the entire world has received a blessing. These promises have certainly come to pass in history, even in our own day, and will reach even greater heights during the future Tribulation and Millennial Kingdom.

12:3 History is the outworking of this covenant through the nation of Israel.

12:7 Unto thy seed will I give this land. This is a simple and direct prophecy of God's gift of the land to Abraham's offspring—Israel. There are no conditions attached to this promise; it is the unconditional declaration of a sovereign God. Neither is there a time limit placed upon the duration of Israel's ownership.

4 Unto the place of the altar, which he had made there at the first: and there Abram called on the name of the LORD.

5 And Lot also, which went with Abram, had flocks, and herds, and tents.

6 And the land was not able to bear them, that they might dwell together: for their substance was great, so that they could not dwell together.

7 And there was a strife between the herdmen of Abram's cattle and the herdmen of Lot's cattle: and the Canaanite and the Perizzite dwelled then in the land.

8 And Abram said unto Lot, Let there be no strife, I pray thee, between me and thee, and between my herdmen and thy herdmen; for we *be* brethren.

9 *Is* not the whole land before thee? separate thyself, I pray thee, from me: if *thou wilt take* the left hand, then I will go to the right; or if *thou depart* to the right hand, then I will go to the left.

10 And Lot lifted up his eyes, and beheld all the plain of Jordan, that it *was* well watered every where, before the LORD destroyed Sodom and Gomorrah, *even* as the garden of the LORD, like the land of Egypt, as thou comest unto Zoar.

11 Then Lot chose him all the plain of Jordan; and Lot journeyed east: and they separated themselves the one from the other.

12 Abram dwelled in the land of Canaan, and Lot dwelled in the cities of the plain, and pitched *his* tent toward Sodom.

13 But the men of Sodom *were* wicked and sinners before the LORD exceedingly.

Abram Moves to Hebron

14 And the LORD said unto Abram, after that Lot was separated from him, Lift up now thine eyes, and look from the place where thou art northward, and southward, and eastward, and westward:

15 For all the land which thou seest, to thee will I give it, and to thy seed for ever.

16 And I will make thy seed as the dust of the earth: so that if a man can number the dust of the earth, *then* shall thy seed also be numbered.

17 Arise, walk through the land in the length of it and in the breadth of it; for I will give it unto thee.

18 Then Abram removed *his* tent, and came

and dwelt in the plain of Mamre, which *is* in Hebron, and built there an altar unto the LORD.

CHAPTER 14
Abram Rescues Lot

1 And it came to pass in the days of Amraphel king of Shinar, Arioch king of Ellasar, Chedorlaomer king of Elam, and Tidal king of nations;

2 *That these* made war with Bera king of Sodom, and with Birsha king of Gomorrah, Shinab king of Admah, and Shemeber king of Zeboiim, and the king of Bela, which is Zoar.

3 All these were joined together in the vale of Siddim, which is the salt sea.

4 Twelve years they served Chedorlaomer, and in the thirteenth year they rebelled.

5 And in the fourteenth year came Chedorlaomer, and the kings that *were* with him, and smote the Rephaims in Ashteroth Karnaim, and the Zuzims in Ham, and the Emims in Shaveh Kiriathaim,

6 And the Horites in their mount Seir, unto El-paran, which *is* by the wilderness.

7 And they returned, and came to Enmishpat, which *is* Kadesh, and smote all the country of the Amalekites, and also the Amorites, that dwelt in Hazezon-tamar.

8 And there went out the king of Sodom, and the king of Gomorrah, and the king of Admah, and the king of Zeboiim, and the king of Bela (the same *is* Zoar) and they joined battle with them in the vale of Siddim;

9 With Chedorlaomer the king of Elam, and with Tidal king of nations, and Amraphel king of Shinar, and Arioch king of Ellasar; four kings with five.

10 And the vale of Siddim *was full of* slimepits; and the kings of Sodom and Gomorrah fled, and fell there; and they that remained fled to the mountain.

11 And they took all the goods of Sodom and Gomorrah, and all their victuals, and went their way.

12 And they took Lot, Abram's brother's son, who dwelt in Sodom, and his goods, and departed.

13 And there came one that had escaped, and told Abram the Hebrew; for he dwelt in the plain of Mamre the Amorite, brother of

Cross references

4 Gen. 12:7, 8; Ps. 116:17
6 Gen. 36:7
7 Gen. 12:6; 26:20
8 1Cor. 6:7
9 Gen. 20:15; 34:10; Rom. 12:18; Heb. 12:14; James 3:17
10 Gen. 2:10; 14:2, 8; 19:17, 22, 24, 25; Deut. 34:3; Ps. 107:34; Isa. 51:3
12 Gen. 14:12; 19:1, 29; 2Pet. 2:7, 8
13 Gen. 6:11; 18:20; Ezek. 16:49; 2Pet. 2:7, 8
14 Gen. 13:11; 28:14
15 Num. 34:12; Deut. 34:4; 2Chr. 20:7; Ps. 37:22, 29; 112:2
16 Gen. 15:5; 22:17; 26:4; 28:14; 32:12; Ex. 32:13; Num. 23:10; Deut. 1:10
18 Gen. 14:13; 35:27; 37:14
1 Gen. 10:10; 11:2; Isa. 11:11
2 Gen. 19:22; Deut. 29:23
3 Num. 34:12; Deut. 3:17; Josh. 3:16; Ps. 107:34
4 Gen. 9:26
5 Gen. 15:20; Deut. 2:10, 11, 20; 3:11; Josh. 12:4; 13:12
6 Deut. 2:12, 22
7 2Chr. 20:2

13:14–16 The Lord reiterates and expands upon two of the Abrahamic promises: 1) Abram and his descendants will possess the land forever and 2) Abram's seed will be made as numerous "as the dust of the earth." These promises will be ultimately fulfilled in the Millennial Kingdom.

Eshcol, and brother of Aner: and these *were* confederate with Abram.

14 And when Abram heard that his brother was taken captive, he armed his trained *servants*, born in his own house, three hundred and eighteen, and pursued *them* unto Dan.

15 And he divided himself against them, he and his servants, by night, and smote them, and pursued them unto Hobah, which *is* on the left hand of Damascus.

16 And he brought back all the goods, and also brought again his brother Lot, and his goods, and the women also, and the people.

Melchizedek Blesses Abram

17 And the king of Sodom went out to meet him after his return from the slaughter of Chedorlaomer, and of the kings that *were* with him, at the valley of Shaveh, which *is* the king's dale.

18 And Melchizedek king of Salem brought forth bread and wine: and he *was* the priest of the most high God.

19 And he blessed him, and said, Blessed *be* Abram of the most high God, possessor of heaven and earth:

20 And blessed be the most high God, which hath delivered thine enemies into thy hand. And he gave him tithes of all.

21 And the king of Sodom said unto Abram, Give me the persons, and take the goods to thyself.

22 And Abram said to the king of Sodom, I have lift up mine hand unto the LORD, the most high God, the possessor of heaven and earth,

23 That I will not *take* from a thread even to a shoelatchet, and that I will not take any thing that *is* thine, lest thou shouldest say, I have made Abram rich:

24 Save only that which the young men have eaten, and the portion of the men

which went with me, Aner, Eshcol, and Mamre; let them take their portion.

CHAPTER 15
Abrahamic Covenant

1 After these things the word of the LORD came unto Abram in a vision, saying, Fear not, Abram: I *am* thy shield, *and* thy exceeding great reward.

2 And Abram said, Lord GOD, what wilt thou give me, seeing I go childless, and the steward of my house *is* this Eliezer of Damascus?

3 And Abram said, Behold, to me thou hast given no seed: and, lo, one born in my house is mine heir.

4 And, behold, the word of the LORD *came* unto him, saying, This shall not be thine heir; but he that shall come forth out of thine own bowels shall be thine heir.

5 And he brought him forth abroad, and said, Look now toward heaven, and tell the stars, if thou be able to number them: and he said unto him, So shall thy seed be.

6 And he believed in the LORD; and he counted it to him for righteousness.

7 And he said unto him, I *am* the LORD that brought thee out of Ur of the Chaldees, to give thee this land to inherit it.

8 And he said, Lord GOD, whereby shall I know that I shall inherit it?

9 And he said unto him, Take me an heifer of three years old, and a she goat of three years old, and a ram of three years old, and a turtledove, and a young pigeon.

10 And he took unto him all these, and divided them in the midst, and laid each piece one against another: but the birds divided he not.

11 And when the fowls came down upon the carcases, Abram drove them away.

12 And when the sun was going down, a deep sleep fell upon Abram; and, lo, an horror of great darkness fell upon him.

Cross-references (center column):

14 Gen. 13:8; 15:3; 17:12, 27

15 Isa. 41:2, 3

17 Judg. 11:34; 1 Sam. 18:6; 2 Sam. 18:18; Heb. 7:1

18 Ps. 110:4; Mic. 6:6; Acts 16:17; Heb. 5:6; 7:1

19 Ruth 3:10; 2 Sam. 2:5; Matt. 11:25

20 Gen. 24:27; Heb. 7:4

22 Gen. 14:19; 21:33; Dan. 12:7; Rev. 10:5, 6

23 Esth. 9:15, 16

1 Ps. 16:5; Prov. 11:18

2 Acts 7:5

4 2 Sam. 7:12; 16:11; 2 Chr. 32:21

5 Ex. 32:13; Deut. 1:10; 10:22; 1 Chr. 27:23; Rom. 4:18; Heb. 11:12

6 Ps. 106:31; Rom. 4:3, 9, 22; Gal. 3:6; James 2:23

7 Gen. 11:28, 31; 12:1

8 2 Kgs. 20:8; Luke 1:18

12 Gen. 2:21; Job 4:13

14:18 Melchizedek king of Salem . . . priest of the most high God. The name Melchizedek means "My King is Righteous." Salem is an earlier name for Jerusalem. Abram does not want to share the glory of his victory with those who do not worship God. Therefore, after this victory he partakes of bread and wine with the priest of God. In this way, Melchizedek is a prophetic type of the Messiah's priesthood. (A type is an event, person, teaching, or symbol that foreshadows something to come.) Psalm 110:4 predicts that Messiah will be **a priest for ever after the order of Melchizedek.** Hebrews 5—7 draws parallels between Christ's eternal priesthood and Melchizedek's temporary priesthood.

14:19–20 And he gave him tithes of all. Abram is blessed and the most high God is blessed. Abram gave a tithe (one-tenth) of everything in recognition of the Lord's provision of victory.

15:4–5 This is another reaffirmation of the Abrahamic covenant. This time the emphasis is upon Abraham's descendants. His seed will become as numerous as the stars in heaven.

God's Covenants with Man

By Richard Mayhue

God explicitly made six distinct covenants with promise: **1)** the Noahic (Gen. 6:18; 9:8–17); **2)** the Abrahamic (Gen. 15:1–21; 17:1–22; 26:2–5, 24; 28:13–17); **3)** the Mosaic (Ex. 19–20, 24); **4)** the priestly (Num. 25:10–13); **5)** the Davidic (2 Sam. 7:12–16); and **6)** the new covenant (Jer. 31:31–34). Five are unconditional and everlasting, and one, the Mosaic covenant, is conditional and temporary.

The word "covenant," an agreement that binds two parties together, first appears in the **Noahic Covenant** (Gen. 6:18; 9:9, 11–13, 15–17). God unilaterally covenanted with Noah prior to the flood to preserve the human race and animals from total extinction (Gen. 6:18), and after the flood to provide mankind with a promise that He would not destroy mankind or the whole earth by another flood. This covenant, though it is not mentioned in the New Testament, is unconditional and everlasting; it is signi-fied by the rainbow (Gen. 9:12–17). In the Noahic covenant common grace is mercifully and compassionately extended to the entire human race.

> *A covenant is an agreement that binds two parties together.*

God made the sacred **Abrahamic covenant** (Gen. 15) with Abraham, Isaac, and Jacob. The terms are stated or reaffirmed at least eight times in the Old Testament. The sign of the Abra-hamic Covenant was circumcision. This covenant promised **1)** physical descendants (a great nation); **2)** spiritual descendants; **3)** a Savior (Gen. 15:5; John 8:56); **4)** personal blessing and protection; and **5)** blessings and curses to the nations, dependent upon their treatment of Abraham's descendants (Gen. 12:3).

The **Mosaic covenant** was made at Mt. Sinai (Ex. 19—20) with the newly formed nation of Israel (Ex. 19:8; 24:3–7; 34:27). The ordinances and rituals of this covenant extended only for the covenant's effective life. The hopeless outcome of this strictly legal covenant was Israel's continuous rebellion. Ultimately, however, the righteousness sought in this covenant is fulfilled by the saving work of Jesus Christ in the new covenant, a cov-enant of faith.

The original Levitic/Aaronic priesthood, which was conditionally covenanted by God as part of the Mosaic covenant, would remain in effect only for the life of that covenant. However, the priesthood took on new dimensions in duration and direction as an everlast-ing **priestly covenant** because of Phinehas' brave loyalty to God (Num. 25).

God promised David that one of his descendents would rule over Israel and the world. This **Davidic covenant** is both unconditional and everlasting. Jesus Christ is the specific Davidic seed whom God intends to enthrone for a future, earthly rule over Israel and the nations during the Millennial kingdom (Matt. 1:1, 20; Luke 1:69; Acts 2:30; 13:33–36; Rom. 1:3).

The unconditional **New covenant** fulfills the redemptive conditions envisioned by the conditional old/Mosaic Covenant. Originally promised to Israel (Jer. 32; Ezek. 11, 36), this covenant extended salvation to the Gentiles through Christ, the messenger and mediator of a better covenant purchased with His own blood. In this covenant, through Christ, believ-ers receive **1)** Grace (Heb. 10:29), **2)** Peace (Isa. 54:10; Ezek. 34:25; 37:26), **3)** Spirit of God (Isa. 59:21), **4)** Redemption (Isa. 49:8; Jer. 31:34; Heb. 10:19–20), **5)** Removal of Sin (Jer. 31:34; Rom. 11:27; Heb. 10:17), **6)** New heart (Jer. 31:33; Heb. 8:10; 10:16), and **7)** New relationship with God (Jer. 31:33; Ezek. 16:62; 37:26–27; Heb. 8:10).

13 And he said unto Abram, Know of a surety that thy seed shall be a stranger in a land *that is* not theirs, and shall serve them; and they shall afflict them four hundred years;
14 And also that nation, whom they shall serve, will I judge: and afterward shall they come out with great substance.
15 And thou shalt go to thy fathers in peace; thou shalt be buried in a good old age.
16 But in the fourth generation they shall come hither again: for the iniquity of the Amorites *is* not yet full.
17 And it came to pass, that, when the sun went down, and it was dark, behold a smoking furnace, and a burning lamp that passed between those pieces.
18 In the same day the LORD made a covenant with Abram, saying, Unto thy seed have I given this land, from the river of Egypt unto the great river, the river Euphrates:
19 The Kenites, and the Kenizzites, and the Kadmonites,
20 And the Hittites, and the Perizzites, and the Rephaims,
21 And the Amorites, and the Canaanites, and the Girgashites, and the Jebusites.

CHAPTER 16
Hagar and Ishmael

1 Now Sarai Abram's wife bare him no children: and she had an handmaid, an Egyptian, whose name *was* Hagar.
2 And Sarai said unto Abram, Behold now, the LORD hath restrained me from bearing: I pray thee, go in unto my maid; it may be that I may obtain children by her. And Abram hearkened to the voice of Sarai.
3 And Sarai Abram's wife took Hagar her maid the Egyptian, after Abram had dwelt ten years in the land of Canaan, and gave her to her husband Abram to be his wife.
4 And he went in unto Hagar, and she con-

13 Ex. 1:11; 12:40; Ps. 105:23, 25; Acts 7:6
14 Ex. 6:6; 12:36; Deut. 6:22; Ps. 105:37
15 Gen. 25:8; Job 5:26; Acts 13:36
16 Ex. 12:40; 1Kgs. 21:26; Dan. 8:23; Matt. 23:32; 1Thess. 2:16
17 Jer. 34:18, 19
18 Gen. 12:7; 13:15; 24:7; 26:4; Deut. 1:7; 11:24; 34:4; Josh. 1:4; Isa. 27:12
1 Gen. 15:2, 3; 21:9; Gal. 4:24
2 Gen. 3:17; 20:18; 30:2, 3, 9; 1Sam. 1:5, 6
3 Gen. 12:5
4 2Sam. 6:16; Prov. 30:21, 23
5 Gen. 31:53; 1Sam. 24:12
6 Ex. 2:15; Job 2:6; Ps. 106:41, 42; Prov. 15:1; Jer. 38:5; 1Pet. 3:7
7 Gen. 25:18; Ex. 15:22
9 Titus 2:9
12 Gen. 21:20; 25:18
15 Deut. 10:17; 18:13

ceived: and when she saw that she had conceived, her mistress was despised in her eyes.
5 And Sarai said unto Abram, My wrong *be* upon thee: I have given my maid into thy bosom; and when she saw that she had conceived, I was despised in her eyes: the LORD judge between me and thee.
6 But Abram said unto Sarai, Behold, thy maid *is* in thy hand; do to her as it pleaseth thee. And when Sarai dealt hardly with her, she fled from her face.
7 And the angel of the LORD found her by a fountain of water in the wilderness, by the fountain in the way to Shur.
8 And he said, Hagar, Sarai's maid, whence camest thou? and whither wilt thou go? And she said, I flee from the face of my mistress Sarai.
9 And the angel of the LORD said unto her, Return to thy mistress, and submit thyself under her hands.
10 And the angel of the LORD said unto her, I will multiply thy seed exceedingly, that it shall not be numbered for multitude.
11 And the angel of the LORD said unto her, Behold, thou *art* with child, and shalt bear a son, and shalt call his name Ishmael; because the LORD hath heard thy affliction.
12 And he will be a wild man; his hand *will be* against every man, and every man's hand against him; and he shall dwell in the presence of all his brethren.
13 And she called the name of the LORD that spake unto her, Thou God seest me: for she said, Have I also here looked after him that seeth me?
14 Wherefore the well was called Beerlahai-roi; behold, *it is* between Kadesh and Bered.
15 And Hagar bare Abram a son: and Abram called his son's name, which Hagar bare, Ishmael.
16 And Abram *was* fourscore and six years old, when Hagar bare Ishmael to Abram.

15:13–16 To assure Abram that everything He has promised will come to pass, God predicts seven things about the future of Abram's descendants: 1) They will be strangers in a land they do not own; 2) they will become slaves in the land; 3) this slavery will last for 400 years; 4) the nation that afflicts them will be judged; 5) Abram's descendants will come out of the land with great substance; 6) Abram will die in peace after a long life; and 7) in the fourth generation his descendants will return, after the sin of the Amorites is complete. How did God confirm these promises to Abram? He made an uncondi-

tional covenant with him (Gen. 15:17).

15:18–21 The dimensions of the land that the Lord will ultimately provide for Abram's seed far exceed anything Israel has ever occupied. This specific prophecy will be fulfilled in the future after the return of Christ (Deut. 30:3; Jer. 23:5–8; Ezek. 37:21–25; Acts 15:14–17).

16:10–12 This prophecy relating to Ishmael further narrows down the land promised to the seed of Isaac (17:21). The conflict over the land of Israel began 4,000 years ago with Ishmael and continues to this day.

CHAPTER 17
Circumcision Is the Sign of the Covenant

1 And when Abram was ninety years old and nine, the LORD appeared to Abram, and said unto him, I *am* the Almighty God; walk before me, and be thou perfect.

2 And I will make my covenant between me and thee, and will multiply thee exceedingly.

3 And Abram fell on his face: and God talked with him, saying,

4 As for me, behold, my covenant *is* with thee, and thou shalt be a father of many nations.

5 Neither shall thy name any more be called Abram, but thy name shall be Abraham; for a father of many nations have I made thee.

6 And I will make thee exceeding fruitful, and I will make nations of thee, and kings shall come out of thee.

7 And I will establish my covenant between me and thee and thy seed after thee in their generations for an everlasting covenant, to be a God unto thee, and to thy seed after thee.

8 And I will give unto thee, and to thy seed after thee, the land wherein thou art a stranger, all the land of Canaan, for an everlasting possession; and I will be their God.

9 And God said unto Abraham, Thou shalt keep my covenant therefore, thou, and thy seed after thee in their generations.

10 This *is* my covenant, which ye shall keep, between me and you and thy seed after thee; Every man child among you shall be circumcised.

11 And ye shall circumcise the flesh of your foreskin; and it shall be a token of the covenant betwixt me and you.

12 And he that is eight days old shall be circumcised among you, every man child in your generations, he that is born in the house, or bought with money of any stranger, which *is* not of thy seed.

13 He that is born in thy house, and he that is bought with thy money, must needs be circumcised: and my covenant shall be in your flesh for an everlasting covenant.

Cross references:
2 Gen. 12:2; 13:16; 22:17
4 Rom. 4:11, 12, 16; Gal. 3:29
5 Neh. 9:7; Rom. 4:17
6 Gen. 17:16; 35:11; Matt. 1:6
7 Gen. 26:24; 28:13; Heb. 11:16; Rom. 9:8; Gal. 3:17
8 Gen. 12:7; 13:15; 23:4; 28:4; Ex. 6:7; Lev. 26:12; Deut. 4:37; 14:2; 26:18; 29:13; Ps. 105:9, 11
10 Acts 7:8
11 Acts 7:8; Rom. 4:11
12 Lev. 12:3; Luke 2:21; John 7:22; Phil. 3:5

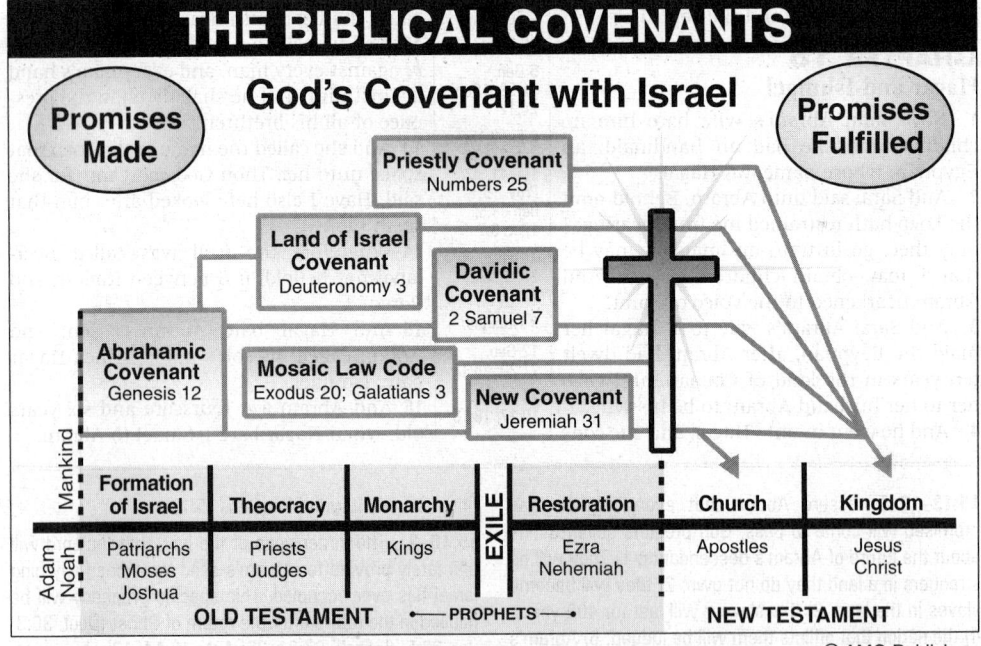

THE BIBLICAL COVENANTS

God's Covenant with Israel

Promises Made

Promises Fulfilled

Priestly Covenant
Numbers 25

Land of Israel Covenant
Deuteronomy 3

Davidic Covenant
2 Samuel 7

Abrahamic Covenant
Genesis 12

Mosaic Law Code
Exodus 20; Galatians 3

New Covenant
Jeremiah 31

Mankind	Formation of Israel	Theocracy	Monarchy	EXILE	Restoration	Church	Kingdom
Adam Noah	Patriarchs Moses Joshua	Priests Judges	Kings		Ezra Nehemiah	Apostles	Jesus Christ

OLD TESTAMENT ←— PROPHETS —→ NEW TESTAMENT

© AMG Publishers

17:1–22 Here circumcision is established as the sign of the covenant. The promises made to Abraham in Genesis 12 and 15 are reiterated. At 99 years of age, Abraham is promised that he will become a father of many nations.

17:11 Circumcision is established as the token or sign of God's eternal covenant with Abraham.

14 And the uncircumcised man child whose flesh of his foreskin is not circumcised, that soul shall be cut off from his people; he hath broken my covenant.

15 And God said unto Abraham, As for Sarai thy wife, thou shalt not call her name Sarai, but Sarah *shall* her name *be*.

16 And I will bless her, and give thee a son also of her: yea, I will bless her, and she shall be *a mother* of nations; kings of people shall be of her.

17 Then Abraham fell upon his face, and laughed, and said in his heart, Shall *a child* be born unto him that is an hundred years old? and shall Sarah, that is ninety years old, bear?

18 And Abraham said unto God, O that Ishmael might live before thee!

19 And God said, Sarah thy wife shall bear thee a son indeed; and thou shalt call his name Isaac: and I will establish my covenant with him for an everlasting covenant, *and* with his seed after him.

20 And as for Ishmael, I have heard thee: Behold, I have blessed him, and will make him fruitful, and will multiply him exceedingly; twelve princes shall he beget, and I will make him a great nation.

21 But my covenant will I establish with Isaac, which Sarah shall bear unto thee at this set time in the next year.

22 And he left off talking with him, and God went up from Abraham.

23 And Abraham took Ishmael his son, and all that were born in his house, and all that were bought with his money, every male among the men of Abraham's house; and circumcised the flesh of their foreskin in the selfsame day, as God had said unto him.

24 And Abraham *was* ninety years old and nine, when he was circumcised in the flesh of his foreskin.

25 And Ishmael his son *was* thirteen years old, when he was circumcised in the flesh of his foreskin.

26 In the selfsame day was Abraham circumcised, and Ishmael his son.

27 And all the men of his house, born in the house, and bought with money of the stranger, were circumcised with him.

CHAPTER 18
The Promise of a Son

1 And the LORD appeared unto him in the plains of Mamre: and he sat in the tent door in the heat of the day;

2 And he lift up his eyes and looked, and, lo, three men stood by him: and when he saw *them*, he ran to meet them from the tent door, and bowed himself toward the ground,

3 And said, My Lord, if now I have found favour in thy sight, pass not away, I pray thee, from thy servant:

4 Let a little water, I pray you, be fetched, and wash your feet, and rest yourselves under the tree:

5 And I will fetch a morsel of bread, and comfort ye your hearts; after that ye shall pass on: for therefore are ye come to your servant. And they said, So do, as thou hast said.

6 And Abraham hastened into the tent unto Sarah, and said, Make ready quickly three measures of fine meal, knead *it*, and make cakes upon the hearth.

7 And Abraham ran unto the herd, and fetcht a calf tender and good, and gave *it* unto a young man; and he hasted to dress it.

8 And he took butter, and milk, and the calf which he had dressed, and set *it* before them; and he stood by them under the tree, and they did eat.

9 And they said unto him, Where *is* Sarah thy wife? And he said, Behold, in the tent.

10 And he said, I will certainly return unto thee according to the time of life; and, lo, Sarah thy wife shall have a son. And Sarah heard *it* in the tent door, which *was* behind him.

Cross-refs: **14** Ex. 4:24 · **16** Gen. 18:10; 35:11; Gal. 4:31; 1Pet. 3:6 · **17** Gen. 18:12; 21:6 · **19** Gen. 18:10; 21:2; Gal. 4:28 · **20** Gen. 16:10; 21:18; 25:12, 16 · **21** Gen. 21:2 · **27** Gen. 18:19 · **1** Gen. 13:18; 14:13 · **2** Gen. 19:1; Heb. 13:2; 1Pet. 4:9 · **4** Gen. 19:2; 43:24 · **5** Gen. 19:8; 33:10; Judg. 6:18; 13:15; 19:5; Ps. 104:15 · **8** Gen. 19:3 · **9** Gen. 24:67 · **10** Gen. 17:19, 21; 19:4; 21:2; 2Kgs. 4:16; Rom. 9:9

17:15–18 Abraham fell upon his face, and laughed. He laughs because he is ninety-nine and his wife Sarai is ninety, both well past childbearing age. To Abraham God's plan appears to be a joke. He responds by asking **that Ishmael might live before** God, that is, that he might be the object of God's promises regarding Abraham's descendants. But God had not chosen Ishmael to fulfill the promises He made to Abraham. This plea to substitute some other way before God is a common response to a prophecy that one does not accept or understand. For this reason many are tempted to interpret the prophetic statements of God's Word in a figurative sense, because the literal interpretation seems too incredible. Yet, as incredible as God's prophetic promise may have seemed to Abraham, God fulfilled it literally.

17:20 Ishmael . . . I will make him a great nation. In addition to Israel, other great nations will spring from Abraham through Ishmael. Today many of these descendants are known as the Arab nations. The genealogy and names of Ishmael's twelve sons are recorded in 1 Chronicles 1:29–31.

11 Now Abraham and Sarah *were* old *and* well stricken in age; *and* it ceased to be with Sarah after the manner of women.

12 Therefore Sarah laughed within herself, saying, After I am waxed old shall I have pleasure, my lord being old also?

13 And the LORD said unto Abraham, Wherefore did Sarah laugh, saying, Shall I of a surety bear a child, which am old?

14 Is any thing too hard for the LORD? At the time appointed I will return unto thee, according to the time of life, and Sarah shall have a son.

15 Then Sarah denied, saying, I laughed not; for she was afraid. And he said, Nay; but thou didst laugh.

Abraham Begs for Sodom

16 And the men rose up from thence, and looked toward Sodom: and Abraham went with them to bring them on the way.

17 And the LORD said, Shall I hide from Abraham that thing which I do;

18 Seeing that Abraham shall surely become a great and mighty nation, and all the nations of the earth shall be blessed in him?

19 For I know him, that he will command his children and his household after him, and they shall keep the way of the LORD, to do justice and judgment; that the LORD may bring upon Abraham that which he hath spoken of him.

20 And the LORD said, Because the cry of Sodom and Gomorrah is great, and because their sin is very grievous;

21 I will go down now, and see whether they have done altogether according to the cry of it, which is come unto me; and if not, I will know.

22 And the men turned their faces from thence, and went toward Sodom: but Abraham stood yet before the LORD.

23 And Abraham drew near, and said, Wilt thou also destroy the righteous with the wicked?

24 Peradventure there be fifty righteous within the city: wilt thou also destroy and not spare the place for the fifty righteous that *are* therein?

25 That be far from thee to do after this manner, to slay the righteous with the wicked: and that the righteous should be as the wicked, that be far from thee: Shall not the Judge of all the earth do right?

26 And the LORD said, If I find in Sodom fifty righteous within the city, then I will spare all the place for their sakes.

27 And Abraham answered and said, Behold now, I have taken upon me to speak unto the Lord, which *am but* dust and ashes:

28 Peradventure there shall lack five of the fifty righteous: wilt thou destroy all the city for *lack of* five? And he said, If I find there forty and five, I will not destroy *it*.

29 And he spake unto him yet again, and said, Peradventure there shall be forty found there. And he said, I will not do *it* for forty's sake.

30 And he said *unto him*, Oh let not the Lord be angry, and I will speak: Peradventure there shall thirty be found there. And he said, I will not do *it*, if I find thirty there.

31 And he said, Behold now, I have taken upon me to speak unto the Lord: Peradventure there shall be twenty found there. And he said, I will not destroy *it* for twenty's sake.

32 And he said, Oh let not the Lord be angry, and I will speak yet but this once: Peradventure ten shall be found there. And he said, I will not destroy *it* for ten's sake.

33 And the LORD went his way, as soon as he had left communing with Abraham: and Abraham returned unto his place.

CHAPTER 19
God Destroys Sodom and Gomorrah

1 And there came two angels to Sodom at even; and Lot sat in the gate of Sodom: and Lot seeing *them* rose up to meet them; and he bowed himself with his face toward the ground;

2 And he said, Behold now, my lords, turn in, I pray you, into your servant's house, and tarry all night, and wash your feet, and ye shall rise up early, and go on your ways. And they said, Nay; but we will abide in the street all night.

3 And he pressed upon them greatly; and they turned in unto him, and entered into his house; and he made them a feast, and did bake unleavened bread, and they did eat.

Cross references

11 Gen. 17:17; 31:35; Rom. 4:19; Heb. 11:11, 12, 19

12 Luke 1:18; 1Pet. 3:6

14 Gen. 17:21; 19:10; 2Kgs. 4:16; Jer. 32:17; Zech. 8:6; Matt. 3:9; 19:26; Luke 1:37

16 Rom. 15:24; 3John 1:6

17 Ps. 25:14; Amos 3:7; John 15:15

18 Gen. 12:3; 22:18; Acts 3:25; Gal. 3:8

19 Deut. 4:9, 10; 6:7; Josh. 24:15; Eph. 6:4

20 Gen. 4:10; 19:13; James 5:4

21 Gen. 11:5; Ex. 3:8; Deut. 8:2; 13:3; Josh. 22:22; Luke 16:15; 2Cor. 11:11

22 Gen. 18:1; 19:1

23 Num. 16:22; 2Sam. 24:17; Heb. 10:22

24 Jer. 5:1

25 Job 8:3, 20; 34:17; Ps. 58:11; 94:2; Isa. 3:10, 11; Rom. 3:6

26 Jer. 5:1; Ezek. 22:30

27 Gen. 3:19; Job 4:19; Eccl. 12:7; Luke 18:1; 1Cor. 15:47, 48; 2Cor. 5:1

32 Gen. 18:1, 22

18:20–22 God's prophecy regarding the destruction of Sodom and Gomorrah would come to pass in the near future. This event would strengthen Abraham's faith and devotion to God.

19:1–29 The destruction of Sodom and Gomorrah, along with the Flood of Noah, typify judgments to come (Isa. 13:19; Jer. 49:18; 50:40; Matt. 11:23–24; Luke 17:29; 2 Pet. 2:6; Jude 1:7).

4 But before they lay down, the men of the city, *even* the men of Sodom, compassed the house round, both old and young, all the people from every quarter:

5 And they called unto Lot, and said unto him, Where *are* the men which came in to thee this night? bring them out unto us, that we may know them.

6 And Lot went out at the door unto them, and shut the door after him,

7 And said, I pray you, brethren, do not so wickedly.

8 Behold now, I have two daughters which have not known man; let me, I pray you, bring them out unto you, and do ye to them as *is* good in your eyes: only unto these men do nothing; for therefore came they under the shadow of my roof.

9 And they said, Stand back. And they said *again*, This one *fellow* came in to sojourn, and he will needs be a judge: now will we deal worse with thee, than with them. And they pressed sore upon the man, *even* Lot, and came near to break the door.

10 But the men put forth their hand, and pulled Lot into the house to them, and shut to the door.

11 And they smote the men that *were* at the door of the house with blindness, both small and great: so that they wearied themselves to find the door.

12 And the men said unto Lot, Hast thou here any besides? son-in-law, and thy sons, and thy daughters, and whatsoever thou hast in the city, bring *them* out of this place:

13 For we will destroy this place, because the cry of them is waxen great before the face of the LORD; and the LORD hath sent us to destroy it.

14 And Lot went out, and spake unto his sons-in-law, which married his daughters, and said, Up, get you out of this place; for the LORD will destroy this city. But he seemed as one that mocked unto his sons-in-law.

15 And when the morning arose, then the angels hastened Lot, saying, Arise, take thy wife, and thy two daughters, which are here; lest thou be consumed in the iniquity of the city.

16 And while he lingered, the men laid hold upon his hand, and upon the hand of his wife, and upon the hand of his two daughters; the LORD being merciful unto him: and they brought him forth, and set him without the city.

17 And it came to pass, when they had brought them forth abroad, that he said, Escape for thy life; look not behind thee, neither stay thou in all the plain; escape to the mountain, lest thou be consumed.

18 And Lot said unto them, Oh, not so, my Lord:

19 Behold now, thy servant hath found grace in thy sight, and thou hast magnified thy mercy, which thou hast shewed unto me in saving my life; and I cannot escape to the mountain, lest some evil take me, and I die:

20 Behold now, this city *is* near to flee unto, and it *is* a little one: Oh, let me escape thither, (*is* it not a little one?) and my soul shall live.

21 And he said unto him, See, I have accepted thee concerning this thing also, that I will not overthrow this city, for the which thou hast spoken.

22 Haste thee, escape thither; for I cannot do any thing till thou be come thither. Therefore the name of the city was called Zoar.

23 The sun was risen upon the earth when Lot entered into Zoar.

24 Then the LORD rained upon Sodom and upon Gomorrah brimstone and fire from the LORD out of heaven;

25 And he overthrew those cities, and all the plain, and all the inhabitants of the cities, and that which grew upon the ground.

26 But his wife looked back from behind him, and she became a pillar of salt.

27 And Abraham gat up early in the morning to the place where he stood before the LORD:

28 And he looked toward Sodom and Gomorrah, and toward all the land of the plain, and beheld, and, lo, the smoke of the country went up as the smoke of a furnace.

29 And it came to pass, when God destroyed the cities of the plain, that God remembered Abraham, and sent Lot out of the midst of the overthrow, when he overthrew the cities in the which Lot dwelt.

Cross-references:

5 Rom. 1:24, 27; Jude 1:7
6 Judg. 19:23
8 Judg. 19:24
9 Ex. 2:14; 2Pet. 2:7, 8
11 2Kgs. 6:18; Acts 13:11
12 2Pet. 2:7, 9
13 1Chr. 21:15
14 Ex. 9:21; Num. 16:21, 45; Matt. 1:18; Luke 17:28; 24:11
15 Num. 16:24, 26; Rev. 18:4
16 Ps. 34:22; Luke 18:13; Rom. 9:15, 16
17 Gen. 19:26; 1Kgs. 19:3; Matt. 24:16, 17, 18; Luke 9:62
18 Acts 10:14
21 Job 42:8, 9; Ps. 145:19
22 Gen. 13:10; 14:2; 19:20; 32:25, 26; Ex. 32:10; Deut. 9:14; Mark 6:5
24 Deut. 29:23; Isa. 13:19; Jer. 20:16; 50:40; Ezek. 16:49, 50; Hos. 11:8; Amos 4:11; Zeph. 2:9; Luke 17:29; 2Pet. 2:6; Jude 1:7
25 Gen. 14:3; Ps. 107:34
26 Luke 17:32
28 Rev. 18:9

19:24 brimstone and fire from the LORD out of heaven. An important lesson concerning the interpretation of Bible prophecy should be learned from the judgment of Sodom and Gomorrah. The brimstone and fire were clearly literal. Revelation tells us that God will send judgments from out of heaven (e.g., the trumpet judgments in Rev. 8—9). The destruction of Sodom and Gomorrah provide a precedent for taking future judgments literally.

Incest

30 And Lot went up out of Zoar, and dwelt in the mountain, and his two daughters with him; for he feared to dwell in Zoar: and he dwelt in a cave, he and his two daughters.

31 And the firstborn said unto the younger, Our father *is* old, and *there is* not a man in the earth to come in unto us after the manner of all the earth:

32 Come, let us make our father drink wine, and we will lie with him, that we may preserve seed of our father.

33 And they made their father drink wine that night: and the firstborn went in, and lay with her father; and he perceived not when she lay down, nor when she arose.

34 And it came to pass on the morrow, that the firstborn said unto the younger, Behold, I lay yesternight with my father: let us make him drink wine this night also; and go thou in, *and* lie with him, that we may preserve seed of our father.

35 And they made their father drink wine that night also: and the younger arose, and lay with him; and he perceived not when she lay down, nor when she arose.

36 Thus were both the daughters of Lot with child by their father.

37 And the firstborn bare a son, and called his name Moab: the same *is* the father of the Moabites unto this day.

38 And the younger, she also bare a son, and called his name Ben-ammi: the same *is* the father of the children of Ammon unto this day.

CHAPTER 20
Abraham and Abimelech

1 And Abraham journeyed from thence toward the south country, and dwelled between Kadesh and Shur, and sojourned in Gerar.

2 And Abraham said of Sarah his wife, She *is* my sister: and Abimelech king of Gerar sent, and took Sarah.

3 But God came to Abimelech in a dream by night, and said to him, Behold, thou *art but* a dead man, for the woman which thou hast taken; for she *is* a man's wife.

4 But Abimelech had not come near her: and he said, Lord, wilt thou slay also a righteous nation?

5 Said he not unto me, She *is* my sister? and she, even she herself said, He *is* my brother: in the integrity of my heart and innocency of my hands have I done this.

6 And God said unto him in a dream, Yea, I know that thou didst this in the integrity of thy heart; for I also withheld thee from sinning against me: therefore suffered I thee not to touch her.

7 Now therefore restore the man *his* wife; for he *is* a prophet, and he shall pray for thee, and thou shalt live: and if thou restore *her* not, know thou that thou shalt surely die, thou, and all that *are* thine.

8 Therefore Abimelech rose early in the morning, and called all his servants, and told all these things in their ears: and the men were sore afraid.

9 Then Abimelech called Abraham, and said unto him, What hast thou done unto us? and what have I offended thee, that thou hast brought on me and on my kingdom a great sin? thou hast done deeds unto me that ought not to be done.

10 And Abimelech said unto Abraham, What sawest thou, that thou hast done this thing?

11 And Abraham said, Because I thought, Surely the fear of God *is* not in this place; and they will slay me for my wife's sake.

12 And yet indeed *she is* my sister; she *is* the daughter of my father, but not the daughter of my mother; and she became my wife.

13 And it came to pass, when God caused me to wander from my father's house, that I said unto her, This *is* thy kindness which thou shalt shew unto me; at every place whither we shall come, say of me, He *is* my brother.

14 And Abimelech took sheep, and oxen, and menservants, and womenservants, and gave *them* unto Abraham, and restored him Sarah his wife.

15 And Abimelech said, Behold, my land *is* before thee: dwell where it pleaseth thee.

16 And unto Sarah he said, Behold, I have given thy brother a thousand *pieces* of silver: behold, he *is* to thee a covering of the eyes, unto all that *are* with thee, and with all *other*: thus she was reproved.

17 So Abraham prayed unto God: and God healed Abimelech, and his wife, and his maidservants; and they bare *children*.

18 For the LORD had fast closed up all the wombs of the house of Abimelech, because of Sarah Abraham's wife.

CHAPTER 21
Isaac Is Born

1 And the LORD visited Sarah as he had said, and the LORD did unto Sarah as he had spoken.

---

30 Gen. 19:17, 19
31 Gen. 16:2, 4; 38:8, 9; Deut. 25:5
32 Mark 12:19
37 Deut. 2:9
38 Deut. 2:19
1 Gen. 16:7, 14; 18:1; 26:6
2 Gen. 12:13, 15; 26:7
3 Gen. 20:7; Job 33:15; Ps. 105:14
4 Gen. 18:23; 20:18
5 2Kgs. 20:3; 2Cor. 1:12
6 Gen. 31:7; 35:5; 39:9; Ex. 34:24; Lev. 6:2; 1Sam. 25:26, 34; Ps. 51:4
7 Gen. 2:17; Num. 16:32, 33; 1Sam. 7:5; 2Kgs. 5:11; Job 42:8; James 5:14, 15; 1John 5:16
9 Gen. 26:10; 34:7; Ex. 32:21; Josh. 7:25
11 Gen. 12:12; 26:7; 42:18; Ps. 36:1; Prov. 16:6
12 Gen. 11:29
13 Gen. 12:1, 9, 11, 13; Heb. 11:8
14 Gen. 12:16
15 Gen. 13:9
16 Gen. 20:5; 24:65; 26:11
17 Job 42:9, 10
18 Gen. 12:17
1 Gen. 17:19; 18:10, 14; 1Sam. 2:21; Gal. 4:23, 28

2 For Sarah conceived, and bare Abraham a son in his old age, at the set time of which God had spoken to him.

3 And Abraham called the name of his son that was born unto him, whom Sarah bare to him, Isaac.

4 And Abraham circumcised his son Isaac being eight days old, as God had commanded him.

5 And Abraham was an hundred years old, when his son Isaac was born unto him.

6 And Sarah said, God hath made me to laugh, *so that* all that hear will laugh with me.

7 And she said, Who would have said unto Abraham, that Sarah should have given children suck? for I have born *him* a son in his old age.

Hagar and Ishmael Are Sent Away

8 And the child grew, and was weaned: and Abraham made a great feast the *same* day that Isaac was weaned.

9 And Sarah saw the son of Hagar the Egyptian, which she had born unto Abraham, mocking.

10 Wherefore she said unto Abraham, Cast out this bondwoman and her son: for the son of this bondwoman shall not be heir with my son, *even* with Isaac.

11 And the thing was very grievous in Abraham's sight because of his son.

12 And God said unto Abraham, Let it not be grievous in thy sight because of the lad, and because of thy bondwoman; in all that Sarah hath said unto thee, hearken unto her voice; for in Isaac shall thy seed be called.

13 And also of the son of the bondwoman will I make a nation, because he *is* thy seed.

14 And Abraham rose up early in the morning, and took bread, and a bottle of water, and gave *it* unto Hagar, putting *it* on her shoulder, and the child, and sent her away: and she departed, and wandered in the wilderness of Beer-sheba.

15 And the water was spent in the bottle, and she cast the child under one of the shrubs.

16 And she went, and sat her down over against *him* a good way off, as it were a bowshot: for she said, Let me not see the death of the child. And she sat over against *him*, and lift up her voice, and wept.

17 And God heard the voice of the lad; and the angel of God called to Hagar out of heaven, and said unto her, What aileth thee, Hagar? fear not; for God hath heard the voice of the lad where he *is*.

18 Arise, lift up the lad, and hold him in thine hand; for I will make him a great nation.

19 And God opened her eyes, and she saw a well of water; and she went, and filled the bottle with water, and gave the lad drink.

20 And God was with the lad; and he grew, and dwelt in the wilderness, and became an archer.

21 And he dwelt in the wilderness of Paran: and his mother took him a wife out of the land of Egypt.

Abraham Makes an Agreement with Abimelech

22 And it came to pass at that time, that Abimelech and Phichol the chief captain of his host spake unto Abraham, saying, God *is* with thee in all that thou doest:

23 Now therefore swear unto me here by God that thou wilt not deal falsely with me, nor with my son, nor with my son's son: *but* according to the kindness that I have done unto thee, thou shalt do unto me, and to the land wherein thou hast sojourned.

24 And Abraham said, I will swear.

25 And Abraham reproved Abimelech because of a well of water, which Abimelech's servants had violently taken away.

26 And Abimelech said, I wot not who hath done this thing: neither didst thou tell me, neither yet heard I *of it*, but today.

27 And Abraham took sheep and oxen, and gave them unto Abimelech; and both of them made a covenant.

28 And Abraham set seven ewe lambs of the flock by themselves.

29 And Abimelech said unto Abraham, What *mean* these seven ewe lambs which thou hast set by themselves?

30 And he said, For *these* seven ewe lambs shalt thou take of my hand, that they may be a witness unto me, that I have digged this well.

31 Wherefore he called that place Beer-sheba; because there they sware both of them.

32 Thus they made a covenant at Beer-sheba:

---

2 Gen. 17:21; Acts 7:8; Gal. 4:22; Heb. 11:11
3 Gen. 17:19
4 Gen. 17:10, 12; Acts 7:8
5 Gen. 17:1, 17
6 Ps. 126:2; Isa. 54:1; Luke 1:58; Gal. 4:27
7 Gen. 18:11, 12
9 Gen. 16:1, 15; Gal. 4:29
10 Gen. 25:6; 36:6, 7; Gal. 4:30
11 Gen. 17:18
12 Rom. 9:7, 8; Heb. 11:18
13 Gen. 16:20; 17:2; 21:18
14 John 8:35
17 Ex. 3:7
18 Gen. 21:13
19 Num. 22:31; 2Kgs. 6:17, 18, 20; Luke 24:16, 31
20 Gen. 16:12; 28:15; 39:2, 3, 21
21 Gen. 24:4
22 Gen. 20:2; 26:26, 28
23 Josh. 2:12; 1Sam. 24:21
25 Gen. 26:15, 18, 20-22
27 Gen. 26:31
29 Gen. 33:8
30 Gen. 31:48, 52
31 Gen. 26:33

21:18 I will make him a great nation. In the midst of Hagar and Ishmael's personal crisis, God reaffirms His prophecy regarding Ishmael and allows him to survive to fulfill His future purpose.

then Abimelech rose up, and Phichol the chief captain of his host, and they returned into the land of the Philistines.

33 And *Abraham* planted a grove in Beersheba, and called there on the name of the LORD, the everlasting God.

34 And Abraham sojourned in the Philistines' land many days.

CHAPTER 22
God Tests Abraham

1 And it came to pass after these things, that God did tempt Abraham, and said unto him, Abraham: and he said, Behold, *here* I *am.*

2 And he said, Take now thy son, thine only *son* Isaac, whom thou lovest, and get thee into the land of Moriah; and offer him there for a burnt offering upon one of the mountains which I will tell thee of.

3 And Abraham rose up early in the morning, and saddled his ass, and took two of his young men with him, and Isaac his son, and clave the wood for the burnt offering, and rose up, and went unto the place of which God had told him.

4 Then on the third day Abraham lifted up his eyes, and saw the place afar off.

5 And Abraham said unto his young men, Abide ye here with the ass; and I and the lad will go yonder and worship, and come again to you.

6 And Abraham took the wood of the burnt offering, and laid *it* upon Isaac his son; and he took the fire in his hand, and a knife; and they went both of them together.

7 And Isaac spake unto Abraham his father, and said, My father: and he said, Here

am I, my son. And he said, Behold the fire and the wood: but where *is* the lamb for a burnt offering?

8 And Abraham said, My son, God will provide himself a lamb for a burnt offering: so they went both of them together.

9 And they came to the place which God had told him of; and Abraham built an altar there, and laid the wood in order, and bound Isaac his son, and laid him on the altar upon the wood.

10 And Abraham stretched forth his hand, and took the knife to slay his son.

11 And the angel of the LORD called unto him out of heaven, and said, Abraham, Abraham: and he said, Here *am* I.

12 And he said, Lay not thine hand upon the lad, neither do thou any thing unto him: for now I know that thou fearest God, seeing thou hast not withheld thy son, thine only *son* from me.

13 And Abraham lifted up his eyes, and looked, and behold behind *him* a ram caught in a thicket by his horns: and Abraham went and took the ram, and offered him up for a burnt offering in the stead of his son.

14 And Abraham called the name of that place Jehovah-jireh: as it is said *to* this day, In the mount of the LORD it shall be seen.

15 And the angel of the LORD called unto Abraham out of heaven the second time,

16 And said, By myself have I sworn, saith the LORD, for because thou hast done this thing, and hast not withheld thy son, thine only *son:*

17 That in blessing I will bless thee, and in multiplying I will multiply thy seed as the

Cross references

33 Gen. 4:26; Deut. 33:27; Isa. 40:28; Rom. 16:26; 1Tim. 1:17

1 1Cor. 10:13; Heb. 11:17; James 1:12; 1Pet. 1:7

2 2Chr. 3:1; John 19:17; Heb. 11:17

9 Heb. 11:17; James 2:21

12 Gen. 26:5; 1Sam. 15:22; Mic. 6:7, 8; James 2:22

16 Ps. 105:9; Luke 1:73; Heb. 6:13, 14

17 Gen. 13:16; 15:5; 24:60; Jer. 33:22; Mic. 1:9

22:2 into the land of Moriah . . . upon one of the mountains. The mountain to which the Lord led Abraham is the Temple Mount in Jerusalem, which became the location for Israel's temple.

22:5–14 The whole sequence of events in this passage is a prophetic prefiguring of the offering of God's own Son, Jesus, on the cross for the sins of the world.

22:6 Abraham took the wood . . . and laid it upon Isaac his son. This pictures Christ's burden of the cross that He carried up Calvary.

22:8 God will provide himself a lamb for a burnt offering. This prophecy, fulfilled first in verse 13, was ultimately fulfilled when God the Father provided Jesus Christ as the perfect sacrifice for sin (John 1:29).

22:9 and bound Isaac his son, and laid him on the altar. In this setting, Isaac is a picture of Christ as the

obedient son who is willing to die in order to satisfy the will of His Father.

22:12 thy son, thine only son. The pattern continues, providing a prophetic picture that the Son of God would follow 2,000 years later. The New Testament tells us that Abraham believed that if he did as God commanded, God would raise Isaac from the dead (Heb. 11:19), an inference from the promise of seed (descendants) through Isaac.

22:13 behold behind him a ram caught in a thicket. Abraham had told Isaac that God would provide the sacrifice (v. 8). Sure enough, God provided the ram while Abraham was being tested.

22:17–18 thy seed shall possess the gate of his enemies. As a climax of this faith-testing event, the Lord reconfirms His prophetic promise to multiply Abraham's

stars of the heaven, and as the sand which *is* upon the sea shore; and thy seed shall possess the gate of his enemies;

18 And in thy seed shall all the nations of the earth be blessed; because thou hast obeyed my voice.

19 So Abraham returned unto his young men, and they rose up and went together to Beer-sheba; and Abraham dwelt at Beer-sheba.

Nahor's Family

20 And it came to pass after these things, that it was told Abraham, saying, Behold, Milcah, she hath also born children unto thy brother Nahor;

21 Huz his firstborn, and Buz his brother, and Kemuel the father of Aram,

22 And Chesed, and Hazo, and Pildash, and Jidlaph, and Bethuel.

23 And Bethuel begat Rebekah: these eight Milcah did bear to Nahor, Abraham's brother.

24 And his concubine, whose name *was* Reumah, she bare also Tebah, and Gaham, and Thahash, and Maachah.

CHAPTER 23
The Death of Sarah

1 And Sarah was an hundred and seven and twenty years old: *these were* the years of the life of Sarah.

2 And Sarah died in Kirjath-arba; the same *is* Hebron in the land of Canaan: and Abraham came to mourn for Sarah, and to weep for her.

3 And Abraham stood up from before his dead, and spake unto the sons of Heth, saying,

4 I *am* a stranger and a sojourner with you: give me a possession of a buryingplace with you, that I may bury my dead out of my sight.

5 And the children of Heth answered Abraham, saying unto him,

6 Hear us, my lord: thou *art* a mighty prince among us: in the choice of our sepulchres bury thy dead; none of us shall withhold from thee his sepulchre, but that thou mayest bury thy dead.

7 And Abraham stood up, and bowed himself to the people of the land, *even* to the children of Heth.

8 And he communed with them, saying, If it be your mind that I should bury my dead out of my sight; hear me, and intreat for me to Ephron the son of Zohar,

9 That he may give me the cave of Machpelah, which he hath, which *is* in the end of his field; for as much money as it is worth he shall give it me for a possession of a buryingplace amongst you.

10 And Ephron dwelt among the children of Heth: and Ephron the Hittite answered Abraham in the audience of the children of Heth, *even* of all that went in at the gate of his city, saying,

11 Nay, my lord, hear me: the field give I thee, and the cave that *is* therein, I give it thee; in the presence of the sons of my people give I it thee: bury thy dead.

12 And Abraham bowed down himself before the people of the land.

13 And he spake unto Ephron in the audience of the people of the land, saying, But if thou *wilt give it*, I pray thee, hear me: I will give thee money for the field; take *it* of me, and I will bury my dead there.

14 And Ephron answered Abraham, saying unto him,

15 My lord, hearken unto me: the land *is worth* four hundred shekels of silver; what *is* that betwixt me and thee? bury therefore thy dead.

16 And Abraham hearkened unto Ephron; and Abraham weighed to Ephron the silver, which he had named in the audience of the sons of Heth, four hundred shekels of silver, current *money* with the merchant.

17 And the field of Ephron, which *was* in Machpelah, which *was* before Mamre, the field, and the cave which *was* therein, and all the trees that *were* in the field, that *were* in all the borders round about, were made sure

18 Unto Abraham for a possession in the presence of the children of Heth, before all that went in at the gate of his city.

19 And after this, Abraham buried Sarah his wife in the cave of the field of Machpelah before Mamre: the same *is* Hebron in the land of Canaan.

20 And the field, and the cave that *is* therein, were made sure unto Abraham for a possession of a buryingplace by the sons of Heth.

Cross references (center column)

18 Gen. 12:3; 18:18; 22:3, 10; 26:4, 5; Acts 3:25; Gal. 3:8, 9, 16, 18

19 Gen. 21:31

20 Gen. 11:29

21 Job 1:1; 32:2

23 Gen. 13:18; 23:19; 24:15; Josh. 14:15; Judg. 1:10; Rom. 9:10, *Rebecca*

4 Gen. 17:8; 1Chr. 29:15; Ps. 105:12; Acts 7:5; Heb. 11:9, 13

6 Gen. 13:2; 14:14; 24:35

10 Gen. 34:20, 24; Ruth 4:4

11 2Sam. 24:21-24

15 Ex. 30:13; Ezek. 45:12

16 Jer. 32:9

17 Gen. 25:9; 49:30-32; 50:13; Acts 7:16

20 Ruth 4:7-10; Jer. 32:10, 11

---

seed, but this time He adds another blessing. Abraham's descendants will be not only numerous, but also dominant. This was locally fulfilled in their conquest of the Promised Land, but it will also be universally realized in their global rule during the Millennial Kingdom.

CHAPTER 24
Isaac Marries Rebekah

1 And Abraham was old, *and* well stricken in age: and the LORD had blessed Abraham in all things.
2 And Abraham said unto his eldest servant of his house, that ruled over all that he had, Put, I pray thee, thy hand under my thigh:
3 And I will make thee swear by the LORD, the God of heaven, and the God of the earth, that thou shalt not take a wife unto my son of the daughters of the Canaanites, among whom I dwell:
4 But thou shalt go unto my country, and to my kindred, and take a wife unto my son Isaac.
5 And the servant said unto him, Peradventure the woman will not be willing to follow me unto this land: must I needs bring thy son again unto the land from whence thou camest?
6 And Abraham said unto him, Beware thou that thou bring not my son thither again.
7 The LORD God of heaven, which took me from my father's house, and from the land of my kindred, and which spake unto me, and that sware unto me, saying, Unto thy seed will I give this land; he shall send his angel before thee, and thou shalt take a wife unto my son from thence.
8 And if the woman will not be willing to follow thee, then thou shalt be clear from this my oath: only bring not my son thither again.
9 And the servant put his hand under the thigh of Abraham his master, and sware to him concerning that matter.
10 And the servant took ten camels of the camels of his master, and departed; for all the goods of his master *were* in his hand: and he arose, and went to Mesopotamia, unto the city of Nahor.
11 And he made his camels to kneel down without the city by a well of water at the time of the evening, *even* the time that women go out to draw *water*.
12 And he said, O LORD God of my master Abraham, I pray thee, send me good speed this day, and shew kindness unto my master Abraham.
13 Behold, I stand *here* by the well of water;

and the daughters of the men of the city come out to draw water:
14 And let it come to pass, that the damsel to whom I shall say, Let down thy pitcher, I pray thee, that I may drink; and she shall say, Drink, and I will give thy camels drink also: *let the same be* she *that* thou hast appointed for thy servant Isaac; and thereby shall I know that thou hast shewed kindness unto my master.
15 And it came to pass, before he had done speaking, that, behold, Rebekah came out, who was born to Bethuel, son of Milcah, the wife of Nahor, Abraham's brother, with her pitcher upon her shoulder.
16 And the damsel *was* very fair to look upon, a virgin, neither had any man known her: and she went down to the well, and filled her pitcher, and came up.
17 And the servant ran to meet her, and said, Let me, I pray thee, drink a little water of thy pitcher.
18 And she said, Drink, my lord: and she hasted, and let down her pitcher upon her hand, and gave him drink.
19 And when she had done giving him drink, she said, I will draw *water* for thy camels also, until they have done drinking.
20 And she hasted, and emptied her pitcher into the trough, and ran again unto the well to draw *water*, and drew for all his camels.
21 And the man wondering at her held his peace, to wit whether the LORD had made his journey prosperous or not.
22 And it came to pass, as the camels had done drinking, that the man took a golden earring of half a shekel weight, and two bracelets for her hands of ten *shekels* weight of gold;
23 And said, Whose daughter *art* thou? tell me, I pray thee: is there room *in* thy father's house for us to lodge in?
24 And she said unto him, I *am* the daughter of Bethuel the son of Milcah, which she bare unto Nahor.
25 She said moreover unto him, We have both straw and provender enough, and room to lodge in.
26 And the man bowed down his head, and worshipped the LORD.
27 And he said, Blessed *be* the LORD God of my master Abraham, who hath not left destitute my master of his mercy and his truth:

24:7 he shall send his angel before thee, and thou shalt take a wife unto my son. This prophecy of Abraham is fulfilled in the immediate context when the servant returns and Isaac and Rebekah marry.

I *being* in the way, the LORD led me to the house of my master's brethren.

28 And the damsel ran, and told *them of* her mother's house these things.

29 And Rebekah had a brother, and his name *was* Laban: and Laban ran out unto the man, unto the well.

30 And it came to pass, when he saw the earring and bracelets upon his sister's hands, and when he heard the words of Rebekah his sister, saying, Thus spake the man unto me; that he came unto the man; and, behold, he stood by the camels at the well.

31 And he said, Come in, thou blessed of the LORD; wherefore standest thou without? for I have prepared the house, and room for the camels.

32 And the man came into the house: and he ungirded his camels, and gave straw and provender for the camels, and water to wash his feet, and the men's feet that *were* with him.

33 And there was set *meat* before him to eat: but he said, I will not eat, until I have told mine errand. And he said, Speak on.

34 And he said, I *am* Abraham's servant.

35 And the LORD hath blessed my master greatly; and he is become great: and he hath given him flocks, and herds, and silver, and gold, and menservants, and maidservants, and camels, and asses.

36 And Sarah my master's wife bare a son to my master when she was old: and unto him hath he given all that he hath.

37 And my master made me swear, saying, Thou shalt not take a wife to my son of the daughters of the Canaanites, in whose land I dwell:

38 But thou shalt go unto my father's house, and to my kindred, and take a wife unto my son.

39 And I said unto my master, Peradventure the woman will not follow me.

40 And he said unto me, The LORD, before whom I walk, will send his angel with thee, and prosper thy way; and thou shalt take a wife for my son of my kindred, and of my father's house:

41 Then shalt thou be clear from *this* my oath, when thou comest to my kindred; and if they give not thee *one*, thou shalt be clear from my oath.

42 And I came this day unto the well, and said, O LORD God of my master Abraham, if now thou do prosper my way which I go:

43 Behold, I stand by the well of water; and it shall come to pass, that when the virgin cometh forth to draw *water*, and I say to her,

Give me, I pray thee, a little water of thy pitcher to drink;

44 And she say to me, Both drink thou, and I will also draw for thy camels: *let* the same *be* the woman whom the LORD hath appointed out for my master's son.

45 And before I had done speaking in mine heart, behold, Rebekah came forth with her pitcher on her shoulder; and she went down unto the well, and drew *water*: and I said unto her, Let me drink, I pray thee.

46 And she made haste, and let down her pitcher from her *shoulder*, and said, Drink, and I will give thy camels drink also: so I drank, and she made the camels drink also.

47 And I asked her, and said, Whose daughter *art* thou? And she said, The daughter of Bethuel, Nahor's son, whom Milcah bare unto him: and I put the earring upon her face, and the bracelets upon her hands.

48 And I bowed down my head, and worshipped the LORD, and blessed the LORD God of my master Abraham, which had led me in the right way to take my master's brother's daughter unto his son.

49 And now if ye will deal kindly and truly with my master, tell me: and if not, tell me; that I may turn to the right hand, or to the left.

50 Then Laban and Bethuel answered and said, The thing proceedeth from the LORD: we cannot speak unto thee bad or good.

51 Behold, Rebekah *is* before thee, take *her*, and go, and let her be thy master's son's wife, as the LORD hath spoken.

52 And it came to pass, that, when Abraham's servant heard their words, he worshipped the LORD, *bowing himself* to the earth.

53 And the servant brought forth jewels of silver, and jewels of gold, and raiment, and gave *them* to Rebekah: he gave also to her brother and to her mother precious things.

54 And they did eat and drink, he and the men that *were* with him, and tarried all night; and they rose up in the morning, and he said, Send me away unto my master.

55 And her brother and her mother said, Let the damsel abide with us *a few* days, at the least ten; after that she shall go.

56 And he said unto them, Hinder me not, seeing the LORD hath prospered my way; send me away that I may go to my master.

57 And they said, We will call the damsel, and inquire at her mouth.

58 And they called Rebekah, and said unto her, Wilt thou go with this man? And she said, I will go.

---

29 Gen. 29:5

31 Gen. 26:29; Judg. 17:2; Ruth 3:10; Ps. 115:15

32 Gen. 43:24; Judg. 19:21

33 Job 23:12; John 4:34; Eph. 6:5-7

35 Gen. 13:2; 24:1

36 Gen. 21:2, 10; 25:5

37 Gen. 24:3

38 Gen. 24:4

39 Gen. 24:5

40 Gen. 17:1; 24:7

41 Gen. 24:8

42 Gen. 24:12

43 Gen. 24:13

45 Gen. 24:15-28; 1Sam. 1:13

47 Ezek. 16:11, 12

48 Gen. 22:23; 24:26

49 Gen. 47:29; Josh. 2:14

50 Gen. 31:24; Ps. 118:23; Matt. 21:42; Mark 12:11

51 Gen. 20:15

52 Gen. 24:26

53 Ex. 3:22; 11:2; 12:35; 2Chr. 21:3; Ezra 1:6

54 Gen. 24:56, 59

55 Judg. 14:8

59 And they sent away Rebekah their sister, and her nurse, and Abraham's servant, and his men.

60 And they blessed Rebekah, and said unto her, Thou *art* our sister, be thou *the mother* of thousands of millions, and let thy seed possess the gate of those which hate them.

61 And Rebekah arose, and her damsels, and they rode upon the camels, and followed the man: and the servant took Rebekah, and went his way.

62 And Isaac came from the way of the well Lahai-roi; for he dwelt in the south country.

63 And Isaac went out to meditate in the field at the eventide: and he lifted up his eyes, and saw, and, behold, the camels *were* coming.

64 And Rebekah lifted up her eyes, and when she saw Isaac, she lighted off the camel.

65 For she *had* said unto the servant, What man *is* this that walketh in the field to meet us? And the servant *had* said, It *is* my master: therefore she took a vail, and covered herself.

66 And the servant told Isaac all things that he had done.

67 And Isaac brought her into his mother Sarah's tent, and took Rebekah, and she became his wife; and he loved her: and Isaac was comforted after his mother's *death*.

CHAPTER 25
Abraham's Other Family

1 Then again Abraham took a wife, and her name *was* Keturah.

2 And she bare him Zimran, and Jokshan, and Medan, and Midian, and Ishbak, and Shuah.

3 And Jokshan begat Sheba, and Dedan. And the sons of Dedan were Asshurim, and Letushim, and Leummim.

4 And the sons of Midian; Ephah, and Epher, and Hanoch, and Abida, and Eldaah. All these *were* the children of Keturah.

5 And Abraham gave all that he had unto Isaac.

6 But unto the sons of the concubines, which Abraham had, Abraham gave gifts, and sent them away from Isaac his son, while he yet lived, eastward, unto the east country.

The Death of Abraham

7 And these *are* the days of the years of Abraham's life which he lived, an hundred threescore and fifteen years.

8 Then Abraham gave up the ghost, and died in a good old age, an old man, and full *of years*; and was gathered to his people.

9 And his sons Isaac and Ishmael buried him in the cave of Machpelah, in the field of Ephron the son of Zohar the Hittite, which *is* before Mamre;

10 The field which Abraham purchased of the sons of Heth: there was Abraham buried, and Sarah his wife.

11 And it came to pass after the death of Abraham, that God blessed his son Isaac; and Isaac dwelt by the well Lahai-roi.

Ishmael's Family

12 Now these *are* the generations of Ishmael, Abraham's son, whom Hagar the Egyptian, Sarah's handmaid, bare unto Abraham:

13 And these *are* the names of the sons of Ishmael, by their names, according to their generations: the firstborn of Ishmael, Nebajoth; and Kedar, and Adbeel, and Mibsam,

14 And Mishma, and Dumah, and Massa,

15 And Hadar, and Tema, Jetur, Naphish, and Kedemah:

16 These *are* the sons of Ishmael, and these *are* their names, by their towns, and by their castles; twelve princes according to their nations.

17 And these *are* the years of the life of Ishmael, an hundred and thirty and seven

Cross references

59 Gen. 35:8
60 Gen. 17:16; 22:17
62 Gen. 16:14; 25:11
63 Josh. 1:8; Ps. 1:2; 77:12; 119:15; 143:5
64 Josh. 15:18
67 Gen. 38:12
2 Gen. 24:36; 1Chr. 1:32
6 Gen. 21:14; Judg. 6:3
8 Gen. 15:15; 35:29; 49:29, 33
9 Gen. 35:29; 50:13
10 Gen. 23:16; 49:31
11 Gen. 16:14; 24:62
12 Gen. 16:15
13 1Chr. 1:29
15 1Chr. 1:30
16 Gen. 17:20
17 Gen. 25:8

24:60 be thou the mother of thousands of millions. Rebekah is included in the blessings of the Abrahamic covenant prior to her marriage to Isaac. (In Hebrew, the word "millions" sounds similar to Rebekah, so this may be a play on words.) The ancient custom of blessing on the occasion of a wedding is reflected here in this prophecy, which is similar to the promise made to Abraham and Sarah (Gen. 17:15–16). The theme of the seed occurs again. This is a prophecy of dominance over enemies in the possession of the land of Canaan (Gen. 13:17; 15:7, 16; 17:8).

25:7–8 This passage declares the fulfillment of the prophecy in Genesis 15:15 that Abraham would live a long life. He lived to be 175 years old. The phrase **was gathered to his people** indicates that they viewed one who had died as departing to be with their ancestors—a tacit indicator of their belief in the existence of the soul after death.

25:12 These are the generations of Ishmael. This is the seventh *toledoth* (see note on Gen. 2:4). In a continuation of this section of the book, the word *toledoth* is repeated in verse 13, where the sons of Ishmael are listed.

years: and he gave up the ghost and died; and was gathered unto his people.

18 And they dwelt from Havilah unto Shur, that is before Egypt, as thou goest toward Assyria: and he died in the presence of all his brethren.

Isaac's Twin Boys

19 And these are the generations of Isaac, Abraham's son: Abraham begat Isaac:

20 And Isaac was forty years old when he took Rebekah to wife, the daughter of Bethuel the Syrian of Padan-aram, the sister to Laban the Syrian.

21 And Isaac intreated the LORD for his wife, because she was barren: and the LORD was intreated of him, and Rebekah his wife conceived.

22 And the children struggled together within her; and she said, If it be so, why am I thus? And she went to inquire of the LORD.

23 And the LORD said unto her, Two nations are in thy womb, and two manner of people shall be separated from thy bowels; and the one people shall be stronger than the other people; and the elder shall serve the younger.

24 And when her days to be delivered were fulfilled, behold, there were twins in her womb.

25 And the first came out red, all over like an hairy garment; and they called his name Esau.

26 And after that came his brother out, and his hand took hold on Esau's heel; and his name was called Jacob: and Isaac was threescore years old when she bare them.

27 And the boys grew: and Esau was a cunning hunter, a man of the field; and Jacob was a plain man, dwelling in tents.

28 And Isaac loved Esau, because he did eat of his venison: but Rebekah loved Jacob.

29 And Jacob sod pottage: and Esau came from the field, and he was faint:

30 And Esau said to Jacob, Feed me, I pray thee, with that same red pottage; for I am faint: therefore was his name called Edom.

31 And Jacob said, Sell me this day thy birthright.

32 And Esau said, Behold, I am at the point to die: and what profit shall this birthright do to me?

33 And Jacob said, Swear to me this day; and he sware unto him: and he sold his birthright unto Jacob.

34 Then Jacob gave Esau bread and pottage of lentiles; and he did eat and drink, and rose up, and went his way: thus Esau despised his birthright.

CHAPTER 26
Isaac Moves to Gerar

1 And there was a famine in the land, beside the first famine that was in the days of Abraham. And Isaac went unto Abimelech king of the Philistines unto Gerar.

2 And the LORD appeared unto him, and said, Go not down into Egypt; dwell in the land which I shall tell thee of:

3 Sojourn in this land, and I will be with thee, and will bless thee; for unto thee, and unto thy seed, I will give all these countries, and I will perform the oath which I sware unto Abraham thy father;

4 And I will make thy seed to multiply as the stars of heaven, and will give unto thy seed all these countries; and in thy seed shall all the nations of the earth be blessed;

5 Because that Abraham obeyed my voice, and kept my charge, my commandments, my statutes, and my laws.

6 And Isaac dwelt in Gerar:

7 And the men of the place asked him of his wife; and he said, She is my sister: for he feared to say, She is my wife; lest, said he, the

---

Cross references column:

18 Gen. 16:12; 1Sam. 15:7; Ps. 78:64

19 Matt. 1:2

20 Gen. 22:23; 24:29

21 1Chr. 5:20; 2Chr. 33:13; Ezra 8:23; Rom. 9:10

22 1Sam. 9:9; 10:22

23 Gen. 17:16; 24:60; 27:29; 2Sam. 8:14; Mal. 1:3; Rom. 9:12

25 Gen. 27:11, 16, 23

26 Gen. 27:36; Hos. 12:3

27 Gen. 27:3, 5; Job 1:1, 8; 2:3; Ps. 37:37; Heb. 11:9

28 Gen. 27:6, 19, 25, 31

33 Heb. 12:16

34 Eccl. 8:15; Isa. 22:13; 1Cor. 15:32

1 Gen. 12:10; 20:2

2 Gen. 12:1

3 Gen. 12:2; 13:15; 15:18; 20:1; 22:16; 28:15; Ps. 39:12; 105:9; Heb. 11:9

4 Gen. 12:3; 15:5; 22:17

7 Gen. 12:13

25:19 These are the generations of Isaac. This is the eighth toledoth (see note on Gen. 2:4).

25:23 the elder shall serve the younger. In the ancient world the birth of twins was considered a special blessing. Ancient tradition also taught that the first-born son had special rights and privileges over subsequent sons. Here God inverts this tradition by favoring the younger of Rebekah's sons over the elder.

25:29–34 In this incident, we see the outworking of the prophecy the Lord gave Rebekah in Genesis 25:23. Esau actually trades his birthright for a bowl of stewed meat.

26:2–6 the LORD appeared unto. Throughout its history,

Israel has tended to rely upon the reputed safety and security of Egypt. So the Lord came to Isaac and renewed the promise of the Abrahamic covenant. The same three promises of land, seed, and extended blessing are repeated to Isaac. Isaac obeys the Lord.

26:2 Egypt is a temptation to the patriarchs to trust human invention and not God's provision in the land He has promised. For believers today, it is a type of the world that tempts us to "go it alone" and not depend on God for His blessing.

26:3 To "sojourn" means to live as a resident alien.

men of the place should kill me for Rebekah; because she *was* fair to look upon.

8 And it came to pass, when he had been there a long time, that Abimelech king of the Philistines looked out at a window, and saw, and, behold, Isaac *was* sporting with Rebekah his wife.

9 And Abimelech called Isaac, and said, Behold, of a surety she *is* thy wife: and how saidst thou, She *is* my sister? And Isaac said unto him, Because I said, Lest I die for her.

10 And Abimelech said, What *is* this thou hast done unto us? one of the people might lightly have lien with thy wife, and thou shouldest have brought guiltiness upon us.

11 And Abimelech charged all *his* people, saying, He that toucheth this man or his wife shall surely be put to death.

12 Then Isaac sowed in that land, and received in the same year an hundredfold: and the LORD blessed him.

13 And the man waxed great, and went forward, and grew until he became very great:

14 For he had possession of flocks, and possession of herds, and great store of servants: and the Philistines envied him.

15 For all the wells which his father's servants had digged in the days of Abraham his father, the Philistines had stopped them, and filled them with earth.

16 And Abimelech said unto Isaac, Go from us; for thou art much mightier than we.

17 And Isaac departed thence, and pitched his tent in the valley of Gerar, and dwelt there.

18 And Isaac digged again the wells of water, which they had digged in the days of Abraham his father; for the Philistines had stopped them after the death of Abraham: and he called their names after the names by which his father had called them.

19 And Isaac's servants digged in the valley, and found there a well of springing water.

20 And the herdmen of Gerar did strive with Isaac's herdmen, saying, The water *is* ours: and he called the name of the well Esek; because they strove with him.

21 And they digged another well, and strove for that also: and he called the name of it Sitnah.

22 And he removed from thence, and digged another well; and for that they strove not: and he called the name of it Rehoboth; and he said, For now the LORD hath made room for us, and we shall be fruitful in the land.

23 And he went up from thence to Beersheba.

24 And the LORD appeared unto him the same night, and said, I *am* the God of Abraham thy father: fear not, for I *am* with thee, and will bless thee, and multiply thy seed for my servant Abraham's sake.

25 And he builded an altar there, and called upon the name of the LORD, and pitched his tent there: and there Isaac's servants digged a well.

Isaac Makes an Agreement with Abimelech

26 Then Abimelech went to him from Gerar, and Ahuzzath one of his friends, and Phichol the chief captain of his army.

27 And Isaac said unto them, Wherefore come ye to me, seeing ye hate me, and have sent me away from you?

28 And they said, We saw certainly that the LORD was with thee: and we said, Let there be now an oath betwixt us, *even* betwixt us and thee, and let us make a covenant with thee;

29 That thou wilt do us no hurt, as we have not touched thee, and as we have done unto thee nothing but good, and have sent thee away in peace: thou *art* now the blessed of the LORD.

30 And he made them a feast, and they did eat and drink.

31 And they rose up betimes in the morning, and sware one to another: and Isaac sent them away, and they departed from him in peace.

32 And it came to pass the same day, that Isaac's servants came, and told him concerning the well which they had digged, and said unto him, We have found water.

Cross References
10 Gen. 20:9
11 Ps. 105:15
12 Gen. 24:1, 35; 25:3; Job 42:12; Matt. 13:8; Mark 4:8
13 Gen. 24:35; Ps. 112:3; Prov. 10:22
14 Gen. 37:11; Eccl. 4:4
15 Gen. 21:30
16 Ex. 1:9
18 Gen. 21:31
20 Gen. 21:25
22 Gen. 17:6; 28:3; 41:52; Ex. 1:7
24 Gen. 15:1; 17:7; 24:12; 26:3, 4; 28:13; Ex. 3:6; Acts 7:32
25 Gen. 12:7; 13:18; Ps. 116:17
26 Gen. 21:22
27 Gen. 26:16; Judg. 11:7
28 Gen. 21:22, 23
29 Gen. 24:31; Ps. 115:15
30 Gen. 19:3
31 Gen. 21:31

26:24 In a time of conflict, the Lord reassures Isaac with His prophetic promise.

26:25 he builded an altar there. Isaac responds to this test in faith, just as his father Abraham had responded in Genesis 12:7–8.

26:28–29 This prophecy of blessing, intended for Esau but given to Jacob, was fulfilled in Israel's possession and enjoyment of the land. Isaac predicts that Jacob's descendants will rule over other people. This will be fulfilled in Christ's reign with His people, Israel, during the Millennial Kingdom. God clearly prophesied Jacob's primacy over Esau (Gen. 25:23), and He would work it out. Rebekah and Jacob's scheme to accomplish God's plan demonstrates a lack of trust. Nevertheless, God's prophecy was fulfilled.

33 And he called it Shebah: therefore the name of the city *is* Beer-sheba unto this day. **34** And Esau was forty years old when he took to wife Judith the daughter of Beeri the Hittite, and Bashemath the daughter of Elon the Hittite: **35** Which were a grief of mind unto Isaac and to Rebekah.

CHAPTER 27
Jacob Steals Isaac's Blessing

1 And it came to pass, that when Isaac was old, and his eyes were dim, so that he could not see, he called Esau his eldest son, and said unto him, My son: and he said unto him, Behold, *here am* I.
2 And he said, Behold now, I am old, I know not the day of my death:
3 Now therefore take, I pray thee, thy weapons, thy quiver and thy bow, and go out to the field, and take me *some* venison;
4 And make me savoury meat, such as I love, and bring *it* to me, that I may eat; that my soul may bless thee before I die.
5 And Rebekah heard when Isaac spake to Esau his son. And Esau went to the field to hunt *for* venison, *and* to bring *it*.
6 And Rebekah spake unto Jacob her son, saying, Behold, I heard thy father speak unto Esau thy brother, saying,
7 Bring me venison, and make me savoury meat, that I may eat, and bless thee before the LORD before my death.
8 Now therefore, my son, obey my voice according to that which I command thee.
9 Go now to the flock, and fetch me from thence two good kids of the goats; and I will make them savoury meat for thy father, such as he loveth:
10 And thou shalt bring *it* to thy father, that he may eat, and that he may bless thee before his death.
11 And Jacob said to Rebekah his mother, Behold, Esau my brother *is* a hairy man, and I *am* a smooth man:
12 My father peradventure will feel me, and I shall seem to him as a deceiver; and I shall bring a curse upon me, and not a blessing.
13 And his mother said unto him, Upon me *be* thy curse, my son: only obey my voice, and go fetch me *them*.
14 And he went, and fetched, and brought *them* to his mother: and his mother made savoury meat, such as his father loved.

15 And Rebekah took goodly raiment of her eldest son Esau, which *were* with her in the house, and put them upon Jacob her younger son:
16 And she put the skins of the kids of the goats upon his hands, and upon the smooth of his neck:
17 And she gave the savoury meat and the bread, which she had prepared, into the hand of her son Jacob.
18 And he came unto his father, and said, My father: and he said, Here *am* I; who *art* thou, my son?
19 And Jacob said unto his father, I *am* Esau thy firstborn; I have done according as thou badest me: arise, I pray thee, sit and eat of my venison, that thy soul may bless me.
20 And Isaac said unto his son, How *is* it that thou hast found *it* so quickly, my son? And he said, Because the LORD thy God brought *it* to me.
21 And Isaac said unto Jacob, Come near, I pray thee, that I may feel thee, my son, whether thou *be* my very son Esau or not.
22 And Jacob went near unto Isaac his father; and he felt him, and said, The voice *is* Jacob's voice, but the hands *are* the hands of Esau.
23 And he discerned him not, because his hands were hairy, as his brother Esau's hands: so he blessed him.
24 And he said, *Art* thou my very son Esau? And he said, I *am*.
25 And he said, Bring *it* near to me, and I will eat of my son's venison, that my soul may bless thee. And he brought *it* near to him, and he did eat: and he brought him wine, and he drank.
26 And his father Isaac said unto him, Come near now, and kiss me, my son.
27 And he came near, and kissed him: and he smelled the smell of his raiment, and blessed him, and said, See, the smell of my son *is* as the smell of a field which the LORD hath blessed:
28 Therefore God give thee of the dew of heaven, and the fatness of the earth, and plenty of corn and wine:
29 Let people serve thee, and nations bow down to thee: be lord over thy brethren, and let thy mother's sons bow down to thee: cursed *be* every one that curseth thee, and blessed *be* he that blesseth thee.

---

33 Gen. 21:31
34 Gen. 36:2
35 Gen. 27:46; 28:1, 8
1 Gen. 48:10; 1Sam. 3:2
2 Prov. 27:1; James 4:14
3 Gen. 25:27, 28
4 Gen. 27:27; 48:9, 15; 49:28; Deut. 33:1
8 Gen. 27:13
9 Gen. 27:4
10 Gen. 27:4
11 Gen. 25:25
12 Gen. 9:25; 27:22; Deut. 27:18
13 Gen. 43:9; 1Sam. 25:24; 2Sam. 14:9; Matt. 27:25
14 Gen. 27:4, 9
15 Gen. 27:27
19 Gen. 27:4
21 Gen. 27:12
23 Gen. 27:16
25 Gen. 27:4
27 Hos. 14:6
28 Gen. 45:18; Deut. 33:13, 28; 2Sam. 1:21; Heb. 11:20
29 Gen. 9:25; 12:3; 25:23; 49:8; Num. 24:9

26:34 Esau acts contrary to the covenant by marrying heathen wives.

30 And it came to pass, as soon as Isaac had made an end of blessing Jacob, and Jacob was yet scarce gone out from the presence of Isaac his father, that Esau his brother came in from his hunting.

31 And he also had made savoury meat, and brought it unto his father, and said unto his father, Let my father arise, and eat of his son's venison, that thy soul may bless me.

32 And Isaac his father said unto him, Who *art* thou? And he said, I *am* thy son, thy firstborn Esau.

33 And Isaac trembled very exceedingly, and said, Who? where *is* he that hath taken venison, and brought *it* me, and I have eaten of all before thou camest, and have blessed him? yea, *and* he shall be blessed.

34 And when Esau heard the words of his father, he cried with a great and exceeding bitter cry, and said unto his father, Bless me, *even* me also, O my father.

35 And he said, Thy brother came with subtilty, and hath taken away thy blessing.

36 And he said, Is not he rightly named Jacob? for he hath supplanted me these two times: he took away my birthright; and, behold, now he hath taken away my blessing. And he said, Hast thou not reserved a blessing for me?

37 And Isaac answered and said unto Esau, Behold, I have made him thy lord, and all his brethren have I given to him for servants; and with corn and wine have I sustained him: and what shall I do now unto thee, my son?

38 And Esau said unto his father, Hast thou but one blessing, my father? bless me, *even* me also, O my father. And Esau lifted up his voice, and wept.

39 And Isaac his father answered and said unto him, Behold, thy dwelling shall be the fatness of the earth, and of the dew of heaven from above;

40 And by thy sword shalt thou live, and shalt serve thy brother; and it shall come to pass when thou shalt have the dominion, that thou shalt break his yoke from off thy neck.

Jacob Runs Away from Esau

41 And Esau hated Jacob because of the blessing wherewith his father blessed him: and Esau said in his heart, The days of mourning for my father are at hand; then will I slay my brother Jacob.

42 And these words of Esau her elder son were told to Rebekah: and she sent and called Jacob her younger son, and said unto him, Behold, thy brother Esau, as touching thee, doth comfort himself, *purposing* to kill thee.

43 Now therefore, my son, obey my voice; and arise, flee thou to Laban my brother to Haran;

44 And tarry with him a few days, until thy brother's fury turn away;

45 Until thy brother's anger turn away from thee, and he forget *that* which thou hast done to him: then I will send, and fetch thee from thence: why should I be deprived also of you both in one day?

46 And Rebekah said to Isaac, I am weary of my life because of the daughters of Heth: if Jacob take a wife of the daughters of Heth, such as these *which are* of the daughters of the land, what good shall my life do me?

CHAPTER 28

1 And Isaac called Jacob, and blessed him, and charged him, and said unto him, Thou shalt not take a wife of the daughters of Canaan.

2 Arise, go to Padan-aram, to the house of Bethuel thy mother's father; and take thee a wife from thence of the daughters of Laban thy mother's brother.

3 And God Almighty bless thee, and make thee fruitful, and multiply thee, that thou mayest be a multitude of people;

4 And give thee the blessing of Abraham, to thee, and to thy seed with thee; that thou mayest inherit the land wherein thou art a

Cross references

31 Gen. 27:4
33 Gen. 28:3, 4; Rom. 11:29
34 Heb. 12:17
36 Gen. 25:26, 33
37 Gen. 27:28, 29; 2Sam. 8:14
38 Heb. 12:17
39 Gen. 27:28; Heb. 11:20
40 Gen. 25:23; 2Sam. 8:14; 2Kgs. 8:20; Obad. 1:18, 19, 20
41 Gen. 37:4, 8; 50:3, 4, 10; Obad. 1:10
42 Ps. 64:5
43 Gen. 11:31
46 Gen. 24:3; 26:35; 28:8
1 Gen. 24:3; 27:33
2 Gen. 22:23; 24:29; 25:20; Hos. 12:12
3 Gen. 17:1, 6
4 Gen. 12:2; 17:8

27:39 thy dwelling shall be the fatness of the earth. Isaac gives Esau the prophetic blessing usually given to a lesser or younger son. Esau and his descendants settle in Edom (Gen. 36:7–8), away from the land of Israel.

27:40 shalt serve thy brother. Israel did come to dominate the descendants of Esau, known as the Edomites, especially under David who conquered Edom (2 Sam. 8:14). The Old Testament chronicles subsequent Edomite history as a series of revolts and reconquests by Israel. Edom ceased to exist as a separate nation by 100 B.C.

27:41 In the anger of the moment, Esau makes a prediction that does not come true.

28:3–4 that thou mayest inherit the land. As Jacob leaves home to flee from Esau and to take a wife, the Lord renews the Abrahamic covenant with Jacob. The themes of land, seed, and an extended blessing continue. Though Esau, like Ishmael, is blessed generally, only Abraham, Isaac, Jacob and his descendants are given the promise of land.

stranger, which God gave unto Abraham.

5 And Isaac sent away Jacob: and he went to Padan-aram unto Laban, son of Bethuel the Syrian, the brother of Rebekah, Jacob's and Esau's mother.

6 When Esau saw that Isaac had blessed Jacob, and sent him away to Padan-aram, to take him a wife from thence; and that as he blessed him he gave him a charge, saying, Thou shalt not take a wife of the daughters of Canaan;

7 And that Jacob obeyed his father and his mother, and was gone to Padan-aram;

8 And Esau seeing that the daughters of Canaan pleased not Isaac his father;

9 Then went Esau unto Ishmael, and took unto the wives which he had Mahalath the daughter of Ishmael Abraham's son, the sister of Nebajoth, to be his wife.

Jacob Has a Dream at Bethel

10 And Jacob went out from Beer-sheba, and went toward Haran.

11 And he lighted upon a certain place, and tarried there all night, because the sun was set; and he took of the stones of that place, and put *them for* his pillows, and lay down in that place to sleep.

12 And he dreamed, and behold a ladder set up on the earth, and the top of it reached to heaven: and behold the angels of God ascending and descending on it.

13 And, behold, the LORD stood above it, and said, I *am* the LORD God of Abraham thy father, and the God of Isaac: the land whereon thou liest, to thee will I give it, and to thy seed;

14 And thy seed shall be as the dust of the earth, and thou shalt spread abroad to the west, and to the east, and to the north, and to the south: and in thee and in thy seed shall all the families of the earth be blessed.

15 And, behold, I *am* with thee, and will keep thee in all *places* whither thou goest, and will bring thee again into this land; for I will not leave thee, until I have done *that* which I have spoken to thee of.

16 And Jacob awaked out of his sleep, and he said, Surely the LORD is in this place; and I knew *it* not.

17 And he was afraid, and said, How dreadful *is* this place! this *is* none other but the house of God, and this *is* the gate of heaven.

18 And Jacob rose up early in the morning, and took the stone that he had put *for* his pillows, and set it up *for* a pillar, and poured oil upon the top of it.

19 And he called the name of that place Beth-el: but the name of that city *was called* Luz at the first.

20 And Jacob vowed a vow, saying, If God will be with me, and will keep me in this way that I go, and will give me bread to eat, and raiment to put on,

21 So that I come again to my father's house in peace; then shall the LORD be my God:

22 And this stone, which I have set *for* a pillar, shall be God's house: and of all that thou shalt give me I will surely give the tenth unto thee.

CHAPTER 29
Jacob Arrives at Laban's House

1 Then Jacob went on his journey, and came into the land of the people of the east.

2 And he looked, and behold a well in the field, and, lo, there *were* three flocks of sheep lying by it; for out of that well they watered the flocks: and a great stone *was* upon the well's mouth.

3 And thither were all the flocks gathered: and they rolled the stone from the well's mouth, and watered the sheep, and put the stone again upon the well's mouth in his place.

4 And Jacob said unto them, My brethren, whence *be* ye? And they said, Of Haran *are* we.

5 And he said unto them, Know ye Laban the son of Nahor? And they said, We know *him*.

6 And he said unto them, *Is* he well? And they said, *He is* well: and, behold, Rachel his daughter cometh with the sheep.

7 And he said, Lo, *it is* yet high day, neither *is it* time that the cattle should be gathered together: water ye the sheep, and go *and* feed *them*.

8 And they said, We cannot, until all the

Cross references (center column)

8 Gen. 24:3; 26:35
9 Gen. 25:13; 36:3, she is called *Bashemath*
10 Hos. 12:12; Acts 7:2, *Charran*
12 Gen. 41:1; Job 33:15; John 1:51; Heb. 1:14
13 Gen. 13:15; 26:24; 35:1, 12; 48:3
14 Gen. 12:3; 13:14, 16; 18:18; 22:18; 26:4; Deut. 12:20
15 Gen. 28:20, 21; 26:24; 31:3; 35:6; 48:16; Num. 23:19; Deut. 31:6, 8; Josh. 1:5; 1Kgs. 8:57; Ps. 121:5, 7, 8; Heb. 13:5
16 Ex. 3:5; Josh. 5:15
18 Gen. 31:13, 45; 35:14; Lev. 8:10-12; Num. 7:1
19 Judg. 1:23, 26; Hos. 4:15
20 Gen. 28:15; 31:13; Judg. 11:30; 2Sam. 15:8; 1Tim. 6:8
21 Deut. 26:17; Judg. 11:31; 2Sam. 15:8; 19:24, 30; 2Kgs. 5:17
22 Gen. 35:7, 14; Lev. 27:30
1 Num. 23:7; Hos. 12:12
6 Gen. 43:27

28:9 Esau continues to act contrary to the covenant, this time by taking wives from the line of Ishmael.

28:13–15 the LORD God of Abraham thy father, and the God of Isaac. The Lord reveals Himself to Jacob as the God of the elect line to which Jacob was now heir. God confirms to Jacob the Abrahamic covenant of land, seed, and blessing. To this He adds the specific promise of His special presence and blessing. This prediction is worked out in the next chapters of Genesis. Twenty years later, Jacob returns to the land with a great family and possessions (Gen. 33:18). At that time, Jacob cites this promise (Gen. 35:3).

flocks be gathered together, and *till* they roll the stone from the well's mouth; then we water the sheep.

9 And while he yet spake with them, Rachel came with her father's sheep: for she kept them.

10 And it came to pass, when Jacob saw Rachel the daughter of Laban his mother's brother, and the sheep of Laban his mother's brother, that Jacob went near, and rolled the stone from the well's mouth, and watered the flock of Laban his mother's brother.

11 And Jacob kissed Rachel, and lifted up his voice, and wept.

12 And Jacob told Rachel that he *was* her father's brother, and that he *was* Rebekah's son: and she ran and told her father.

13 And it came to pass, when Laban heard the tidings of Jacob his sister's son, that he ran to meet him, and embraced him, and kissed him, and brought him to his house. And he told Laban all these things.

14 And Laban said to him, Surely thou *art* my bone and my flesh. And he abode with him the space of a month.

Jacob Tricked into Working for Two Wives

15 And Laban said unto Jacob, Because thou *art* my brother, shouldest thou therefore serve me for nought? tell me, what *shall* thy wages *be*?

16 And Laban had two daughters: the name of the elder *was* Leah, and the name of the younger *was* Rachel.

17 Leah *was* tender eyed; but Rachel was beautiful and well favoured.

18 And Jacob loved Rachel; and said, I will serve thee seven years for Rachel thy younger daughter.

19 And Laban said, *It is* better that I give her to thee, than that I should give her to another man: abide with me.

20 And Jacob served seven years for Rachel; and they seemed unto him *but* a few days, for the love he had to her.

21 And Jacob said unto Laban, Give *me* my wife, for my days are fulfilled, that I may go in unto her.

22 And Laban gathered together all the men of the place, and made a feast.

23 And it came to pass in the evening, that he took Leah his daughter, and brought her to him; and he went in unto her.

24 And Laban gave unto his daughter Leah Zilpah his maid *for* an handmaid.

25 And it came to pass, that in the morning,

behold, it *was* Leah: and he said to Laban, What *is* this thou hast done unto me? did not I serve with thee for Rachel? wherefore then hast thou beguiled me?

26 And Laban said, It must not be so done in our country, to give the younger before the firstborn.

27 Fulfil her week, and we will give thee this also for the service which thou shalt serve with me yet seven other years.

28 And Jacob did so, and fulfilled her week: and he gave him Rachel his daughter to wife also.

29 And Laban gave to Rachel his daughter Bilhah his handmaid to be her maid.

30 And he went in also unto Rachel, and he loved also Rachel more than Leah, and served with him yet seven other years.

Jacob's Family Record

31 And when the LORD saw that Leah *was* hated, he opened her womb: but Rachel *was* barren.

32 And Leah conceived, and bare a son, and she called his name Reuben: for she said, Surely the LORD hath looked upon my affliction; now therefore my husband will love me.

33 And she conceived again, and bare a son; and said, Because the LORD hath heard that I *was* hated, he hath therefore given me this *son* also: and she called his name Simeon.

34 And she conceived again, and bare a son; and said, Now this time will my husband be joined unto me, because I have born him three sons: therefore was his name called Levi.

35 And she conceived again, and bare a son: and she said, Now will I praise the LORD: therefore she called his name Judah; and left bearing.

CHAPTER 30

1 And when Rachel saw that she bare Jacob no children, Rachel envied her sister; and said unto Jacob, Give me children, or else I die.

2 And Jacob's anger was kindled against Rachel: and he said, *Am* I in God's stead, who hath withheld from thee the fruit of the womb?

3 And she said, Behold my maid Bilhah, go in unto her; and she shall bear upon my knees, that I may also have children by her.

4 And she gave him Bilhah her handmaid to wife: and Jacob went in unto her.

5 And Bilhah conceived, and bare Jacob a son.

Cross references

9 Ex. 2:16
10 Ex. 2:17
11 Gen. 33:4; 45:14, 15
12 Gen. 13:8; 14:14, 16; 24:28
13 Gen. 24:29
14 Gen. 2:23; Judg. 9:2; 2Sam. 5:1; 19:12, 13
18 Gen. 31:41; 2Sam. 3:14
20 Gen. 30:26; Hos. 12:12
21 Judg. 15:1
22 Judg. 14:10; John 2:1, 2
27 Judg. 14:12
30 Gen. 29:20; 30:26; 31:41; Deut. 21:15; Hos. 12:12
31 Gen. 30:1; Ps. 127:3
32 Ex. 3:7; 4:31; Deut. 26:7; Ps. 25:18; 106:44
34 Num. 18:2, 4
35 Matt. 1:2

1 Gen. 29:31; 37:11; Job 5:2
2 Gen. 16:2; 1Sam. 1:5
3 Gen. 16:2; 50:23; Job 3:12
4 Gen. 16:3; 35:22

6 And Rachel said, God hath judged me, and hath also heard my voice, and hath given me a son: therefore called she his name Dan.

7 And Bilhah Rachel's maid conceived again, and bare Jacob a second son.

8 And Rachel said, With great wrestlings have I wrestled with my sister, and I have prevailed: and she called his name Naphtali.

9 When Leah saw that she had left bearing, she took Zilpah her maid, and gave her Jacob to wife.

10 And Zilpah Leah's maid bare Jacob a son.

11 And Leah said, A troop cometh: and she called his name Gad.

12 And Zilpah Leah's maid bare Jacob a second son.

13 And Leah said, Happy am I, for the daughters will call me blessed: and she called his name Asher.

14 And Reuben went in the days of wheat harvest, and found mandrakes in the field, and brought them unto his mother Leah. Then Rachel said to Leah, Give me, I pray thee, of thy son's mandrakes.

15 And she said unto her, Is it a small matter that thou hast taken my husband? and wouldest thou take away my son's mandrakes also? And Rachel said, Therefore he shall lie with thee tonight for thy son's mandrakes.

16 And Jacob came out of the field in the evening, and Leah went out to meet him, and said, Thou must come in unto me; for surely I have hired thee with my son's mandrakes. And he lay with her that night.

17 And God hearkened unto Leah, and she conceived, and bare Jacob the fifth son.

18 And Leah said, God hath given me my hire, because I have given my maiden to my husband: and she called his name Issachar.

19 And Leah conceived again, and bare Jacob the sixth son.

20 And Leah said, God hath endued me with a good dowry; now will my husband dwell with me, because I have born him six sons: and she called his name Zebulun.

21 And afterwards she bare a daughter, and called her name Dinah.

22 And God remembered Rachel, and God hearkened to her, and opened her womb.

23 And she conceived, and bare a son; and said, God hath taken away my reproach:

24 And she called his name Joseph; and said, The LORD shall add to me another son.

Jacob's Bargain

25 And it came to pass, when Rachel had born Joseph, that Jacob said unto Laban,

Send me away, that I may go unto mine own place, and to my country.

26 Give me my wives and my children, for whom I have served thee, and let me go: for thou knowest my service which I have done thee.

27 And Laban said unto him, I pray thee, if I have found favour in thine eyes, tarry: for I have learned by experience that the LORD hath blessed me for thy sake.

28 And he said, Appoint me thy wages, and I will give it.

29 And he said unto him, Thou knowest how I have served thee, and how thy cattle was with me.

30 For it was little which thou hadst before I came, and it is now increased unto a multitude; and the LORD hath blessed thee since my coming: and now when shall I provide for mine own house also?

31 And he said, What shall I give thee? And Jacob said, Thou shalt not give me any thing: if thou wilt do this thing for me, I will again feed and keep thy flock:

32 I will pass through all thy flock today, removing from thence all the speckled and spotted cattle, and all the brown cattle among the sheep, and the spotted and speckled among the goats: and of such shall be my hire.

33 So shall my righteousness answer for me in time to come, when it shall come for my hire before thy face: every one that is not speckled and spotted among the goats, and brown among the sheep, that shall be counted stolen with me.

34 And Laban said, Behold, I would it might be according to thy word.

35 And he removed that day the he goats that were ringstraked and spotted, and all the she goats that were speckled and spotted, and every one that had some white in it, and all the brown among the sheep, and gave them into the hand of his sons.

36 And he set three days' journey betwixt himself and Jacob: and Jacob fed the rest of Laban's flocks.

37 And Jacob took him rods of green poplar, and of the hazel and chestnut tree; and pilled white strakes in them, and made the white appear which was in the rods.

38 And he set the rods which he had pilled before the flocks in the gutters in the watering troughs when the flocks came to drink, that they should conceive when they came to drink.

39 And the flocks conceived before the rods,

---

6 Ps. 35:24; 43:1; Lam. 3:59

8 Matt. 4:13, Nephthalim

9 Gen. 30:4

11 Isa. 65:11

13 Prov. 31:28; Luke 1:48

14 Gen. 25:30

15 Num. 16:9, 13

20 Matt. 4:13, Zabulon

22 Gen. 8:1; 29:31; 1Sam. 1:19

23 1Sam. 1:6; Isa. 4:1; Luke 1:25

24 Gen. 35:17

25 Gen. 18:33; 24:54, 56; 31:55

26 Gen. 29:20, 30

27 Gen. 26:24; 39:3, 5

28 Gen. 29:15

29 Gen. 31:6, 38-40; Matt. 24:45; Titus 2:10

30 Gen. 30:43; 1Tim. 5:8

32 Gen. 31:8

33 Ex. 13:14; Ps. 37:6

37 Gen. 31:9-12

and brought forth cattle ringstraked, speckled, and spotted.

40 And Jacob did separate the lambs, and set the faces of the flocks toward the ringstraked, and all the brown in the flock of Laban; and he put his own flocks by themselves, and put them not unto Laban's cattle.

41 And it came to pass, whensoever the stronger cattle did conceive, that Jacob laid the rods before the eyes of the cattle in the gutters, that they might conceive among the rods.

42 But when the cattle were feeble, he put *them* not in: so the feebler were Laban's, and the stronger Jacob's.

43 And the man increased exceedingly, and had much cattle, and maidservants, and menservants, and camels, and asses.

CHAPTER 31
Jacob Runs Away from His Uncle

1 And he heard the words of Laban's sons, saying, Jacob hath taken away all that *was* our father's; and of *that* which *was* our father's hath he gotten all this glory.

2 And Jacob beheld the countenance of Laban, and, behold, it *was* not toward him as before.

3 And the LORD said unto Jacob, Return unto the land of thy fathers, and to thy kindred; and I will be with thee.

4 And Jacob sent and called Rachel and Leah to the field unto his flock,

5 And said unto them, I see your father's countenance, that it *is* not toward me as before; but the God of my father hath been with me.

6 And ye know that with all my power I have served your father.

7 And your father hath deceived me, and changed my wages ten times; but God suffered him not to hurt me.

8 If he said thus, The speckled shall be thy wages; then all the cattle bare speckled: and if he said thus, The ringstraked shall be thy hire; then bare all the cattle ringstraked.

9 Thus God hath taken away the cattle of your father, and given *them* to me.

10 And it came to pass at the time that the cattle conceived, that I lifted up mine eyes, and saw in a dream, and, behold, the rams which leaped upon the cattle *were* ringstraked, speckled, and grisled.

11 And the angel of God spake unto me in a dream, *saying,* Jacob: And I said, Here *am* I.

12 And he said, Lift up now thine eyes, and see, all the rams which leap upon the cattle

are ringstraked, speckled, and grisled: for I have seen all that Laban doeth unto thee.

13 I *am* the God of Beth-el, where thou anointedst the pillar, *and* where thou vowedst a vow unto me: now arise, get thee out from this land, and return unto the land of thy kindred.

14 And Rachel and Leah answered and said unto him, *Is there* yet any portion or inheritance for us in our father's house?

15 Are we not counted of him strangers? for he hath sold us, and hath quite devoured also our money.

16 For all the riches which God hath taken from our father, that *is* ours, and our children's: now then, whatsoever God hath said unto thee, do.

17 Then Jacob rose up, and set his sons and his wives upon camels;

18 And he carried away all his cattle, and all his goods which he had gotten, the cattle of his getting, which he had gotten in Padan-aram, for to go to Isaac his father in the land of Canaan.

19 And Laban went to shear his sheep: and Rachel had stolen the images that *were* her father's.

20 And Jacob stole away unawares to Laban the Syrian, in that he told him not that he fled.

21 So he fled with all that he had; and he rose up, and passed over the river, and set his face *toward* the mount Gilead.

Laban Pursues Jacob

22 And it was told Laban on the third day that Jacob was fled.

23 And he took his brethren with him, and pursued after him seven days' journey; and they overtook him in the mount Gilead.

24 And God came to Laban the Syrian in a dream by night, and said unto him, Take heed that thou speak not to Jacob either good or bad.

25 Then Laban overtook Jacob. Now Jacob had pitched his tent in the mount: and Laban with his brethren pitched in the mount of Gilead.

26 And Laban said to Jacob, What hast thou done, that thou hast stolen away unawares to me, and carried away my daughters, as captives *taken* with the sword?

27 Wherefore didst thou flee away secretly, and steal away from me; and didst not tell me, that I might have sent thee away with mirth, and with songs, with tabret, and with harp?

28 And hast not suffered me to kiss my

Marginal references:

43 Gen. 13:2; 24:35; 26:13, 14; 30:30

1 Ps. 49:16

2 Gen. 4:5; Deut. 28:54; 1Sam. 19:7

3 Gen. 28:15, 20, 21; 32:9

5 Gen. 31:2, 3

6 Gen. 30:29; Gen. 31:38-41

7 Gen. 20:6; 31:41; Num. 14:22; Neh. 4:12; Job 19:3; Ps. 105:14; Zech. 8:23

8 Gen. 30:32

9 Gen. 31:1, 16

11 Gen. 48:16

12 Ex. 3:7

13 Gen. 28:18-20; 31:3; Gen. 32:9

14 Gen. 2:24

15 Gen. 29:15, 27

19 Gen. 35:2; Judg. 17:5; 1Sam. 19:13; Hos. 3:4

21 Gen. 46:28; 2Kgs. 12:17; Luke 9:51, 53

23 Gen. 13:8

24 Gen. 20:3; 24:50; Job 33:15; Matt. 1:20

26 1Sam. 30:2

28 Gen. 31:5; Ruth 1:9, 14; 1Sam. 13:13; 1Kgs. 19:20; 2Chr. 16:9; Acts 20:37

sons and my daughters? thou hast now done foolishly in *so* doing.

29 It is in the power of my hand to do you hurt: but the God of your father spake unto me yesternight, saying, Take thou heed that thou speak not to Jacob either good or bad.

30 And now, *though* thou wouldest needs be gone, because thou sore longedst after thy father's house, *yet* wherefore hast thou stolen my gods?

31 And Jacob answered and said to Laban, Because I was afraid: for I said, Peradventure thou wouldest take by force thy daughters from me.

32 With whomsoever thou findest thy gods, let him not live: before our brethren discern thou what *is* thine with me, and take *it* to thee. For Jacob knew not that Rachel had stolen them.

33 And Laban went into Jacob's tent, and into Leah's tent, and into the two maidservants' tents; but he found *them* not. Then went he out of Leah's tent, and entered into Rachel's tent.

34 Now Rachel had taken the images, and put them in the camel's furniture, and sat upon them. And Laban searched all the tent, but found *them* not.

35 And she said to her father, Let it not displease my lord that I cannot rise up before thee; for the custom of women *is* upon me. And he searched, but found not the images.

36 And Jacob was wroth, and chode with Laban: and Jacob answered and said to Laban, What *is* my trespass? what *is* my sin, that thou hast so hotly pursued after me?

37 Whereas thou hast searched all my stuff, what hast thou found of all thy household stuff? set *it* here before my brethren and thy brethren, that they may judge betwixt us both.

38 This twenty years *have* I *been* with thee; thy ewes and thy she goats have not cast their young, and the rams of thy flock have I not eaten.

39 That which was torn *of beasts* I brought not unto thee; I bare the loss of it; of my hand didst thou require it, *whether* stolen by day, or stolen by night.

40 *Thus* I was; in the day the drought consumed me, and the frost by night; and my sleep departed from mine eyes.

41 Thus have I been twenty years in thy house; I served thee fourteen years for thy two daughters, and six years for thy cattle: and thou hast changed my wages ten times.

42 Except the God of my father, the God of Abraham, and the fear of Isaac, had been with me, surely thou hadst sent me away now empty. God hath seen mine affliction and the labour of my hands, and rebuked *thee* yesternight.

Jacob's New Agreement with Laban

43 And Laban answered and said unto Jacob, *These* daughters *are* my daughters, and *these* children *are* my children, and *these* cattle *are* my cattle, and all that thou seest *is* mine: and what can I do this day unto these my daughters, or unto their children which they have born?

44 Now therefore come thou, let us make a covenant, I and thou; and let it be for a witness between me and thee.

45 And Jacob took a stone, and set it up *for* a pillar.

46 And Jacob said unto his brethren, Gather stones; and they took stones, and made an heap: and they did eat there upon the heap.

47 And Laban called it Jegar-sahadutha: but Jacob called it Galeed.

48 And Laban said, This heap *is* a witness between me and thee this day. Therefore was the name of it called Galeed;

49 And Mizpah; for he said, The LORD watch between me and thee, when we are absent one from another.

50 If thou shalt afflict my daughters, or if thou shalt take *other* wives beside my daughters, no man *is* with us; see, God *is* witness betwixt me and thee.

51 And Laban said to Jacob, Behold this heap, and behold *this* pillar, which I have cast betwixt me and thee;

52 This heap *be* witness, and *this* pillar *be* witness, that I will not pass over this heap to thee, and that thou shalt not pass over this heap and this pillar unto me, for harm.

53 The God of Abraham, and the God of Nahor, the God of their father, judge betwixt us. And Jacob sware by the fear of his father Isaac.

54 Then Jacob offered sacrifice upon the mount, and called his brethren to eat bread: and they did eat bread, and tarried all night in the mount.

55 And early in the morning Laban rose up, and kissed his sons and his daughters, and blessed them: and Laban departed, and returned unto his place.

CHAPTER 32
Jacob Prepares to Meet Esau

1 And Jacob went on his way, and the angels of God met him.

Center column references:

29 Gen. 28:13; 31:24, 53
30 Gen. 31:19; Judg. 18:24
32 Gen. 44:9
35 Ex. 20:12; Lev. 19:32
39 Ex. 22:10-13
41 Gen. 29:27, 28; 31:7
42 Gen. 29:32; 31:53; Ex. 3:7; 1Chr. 12:17; Ps. 124:1, 2; Isa. 8:13; Jude 1:9
44 Gen. 26:28; Josh. 24:27
45 Gen. 28:18
48 Josh. 24:27
49 Judg. 11:29; 1Sam. 7:5
53 Gen. 16:5; 21:23; 31:42
55 Gen. 18:33; 28:1; 30:25
1 Ps. 91:11; Heb. 1:14

2 And when Jacob saw them, he said, This *is* God's host: and he called the name of that place Mahanaim.

3 And Jacob sent messengers before him to Esau his brother unto the land of Seir, the country of Edom.

4 And he commanded them, saying, Thus shall ye speak unto my lord Esau; Thy servant Jacob saith thus, I have sojourned with Laban, and stayed there until now:

5 And I have oxen, and asses, flocks, and menservants, and womenservants: and I have sent to tell my lord, that I may find grace in thy sight.

6 And the messengers returned to Jacob, saying, We came to thy brother Esau, and also he cometh to meet thee, and four hundred men with him.

7 Then Jacob was greatly afraid and distressed: and he divided the people that *was* with him, and the flocks, and herds, and the camels, into two bands;

8 And said, If Esau come to the one company, and smite it, then the other company which is left shall escape.

9 And Jacob said, O God of my father Abraham, and God of my father Isaac, the Lord which saidst unto me, Return unto thy country, and to thy kindred, and I will deal well with thee:

10 I am not worthy of the least of all the mercies, and of all the truth, which thou hast shewed unto thy servant; for with my staff I passed over this Jordan; and now I am become two bands.

11 Deliver me, I pray thee, from the hand of my brother, from the hand of Esau: for I fear him, lest he will come and smite me, *and* the mother with the children.

12 And thou saidst, I will surely do thee good, and make thy seed as the sand of the sea, which cannot be numbered for multitude.

13 And he lodged there that same night; and took of that which came to his hand a present for Esau his brother;

14 Two hundred she goats, and twenty goats, two hundred ewes, and twenty rams,

15 Thirty milch camels with their colts, forty kine, and ten bulls, twenty she asses, and ten foals.

16 And he delivered *them* into the hand of his servants, every drove by themselves; and said unto his servants, Pass over before me, and put a space betwixt drove and drove.

17 And he commanded the foremost, saying, When Esau my brother meeteth thee, and asketh thee, saying, Whose *art* thou? and whither goest thou? and whose *are* these before thee?

18 Then thou shalt say, *They be* thy servant Jacob's; it *is* a present sent unto my lord Esau: and, behold, also he *is* behind us.

19 And so commanded he the second, and the third, and all that followed the droves, saying, On this manner shall ye speak unto Esau, when ye find him.

20 And say ye moreover, Behold, thy servant Jacob *is* behind us. For he said, I will appease him with the present that goeth before me, and afterward I will see his face; peradventure he will accept of me.

21 So went the present over before him: and himself lodged that night in the company.

Jacob Wrestles with God

22 And he rose up that night, and took his two wives, and his two womenservants, and his eleven sons, and passed over the ford Jabbok.

23 And he took them, and sent them over the brook, and sent over that he had.

24 And Jacob was left alone; and there wrestled a man with him until the breaking of the day.

25 And when he saw that he prevailed not against him, he touched the hollow of his thigh; and the hollow of Jacob's thigh was out of joint, as he wrestled with him.

26 And he said, Let me go, for the day breaketh. And he said, I will not let thee go, except thou bless me.

27 And he said unto him, What *is* thy name? And he said, Jacob.

28 And he said, Thy name shall be called no more Jacob, but Israel: for as a prince hast

Cross references (center column)

2 Josh. 5:14; Ps. 103:21; 148:2; Luke 2:13
3 Gen. 33:14, 16; 36:6-8; Deut. 2:5; Josh. 24:4
4 Prov. 15:1
5 Gen. 30:43; Gen. 33:8, 15
6 Gen. 33:1
7 Gen. 35:3
9 Gen. 28:13; 31:3, 13; Ps. 50:15
10 Gen. 24:27; Job 8:7
11 Ps. 59:1, 2; Hos. 10:14
12 Gen. 28:13-15
13 Gen. 43:11; Prov. 18:16
20 Job 42:8, 9; Prov. 21:14
22 Deut. 3:16
24 Hos. 12:3, 4; Eph. 6:12
25 Matt. 26:41; 2Cor. 12:7
26 Hos. 12:4; Luke 24:28
28 Gen. 25:31; 27:33; 35:10; 2Kgs. 17:34; Hos. 12:3, 4

32:9–12 As Jacob returns to the Promised Land, he reminds God of the promises that He made to him in the past (see note on Gen. 28:13–15).

32:24–30 When Jacob departed from the land, he was visited by the Lord as he slept (Gen. 28:13–15). Upon his return, he has this second visitation.

32:24 wrestled a man. This "man" is called an "angel"

in Hosea 12:4. He was likely the "Angel of the Lord," a term that may refer to Christ, whom many believe appeared to men at various times prior to His incarnation.

32:26 except thou bless me. In contrast to Esau, Jacob values the blessing of God and tenaciously wrestles with the angel.

32:28 shall be called no more Jacob, but Israel.

thou power with God and with men, and hast prevailed.

29 And Jacob asked *him*, and said, Tell *me*, I pray thee, thy name. And he said, Wherefore *is* it *that* thou dost ask after my name? And he blessed him there.

30 And Jacob called the name of the place Peniel: for I have seen God face to face, and my life is preserved.

31 And as he passed over Penuel the sun rose upon him, and he halted upon his thigh.

32 Therefore the children of Israel eat not *of* the sinew which shrank, which *is* upon the hollow of the thigh, unto this day: because he touched the hollow of Jacob's thigh in the sinew that shrank.

CHAPTER 33
Jacob Meets Esau

1 And Jacob lifted up his eyes, and looked, and, behold, Esau came, and with him four hundred men. And he divided the children unto Leah, and unto Rachel, and unto the two handmaids.

2 And he put the handmaids and their children foremost, and Leah and her children after, and Rachel and Joseph hindermost.

3 And he passed over before them, and bowed himself to the ground seven times, until he came near to his brother.

4 And Esau ran to meet him, and embraced him, and fell on his neck, and kissed him: and they wept.

5 And he lifted up his eyes, and saw the women and the children; and said, Who *are* those with thee? And he said, The children which God hath graciously given thy servant.

6 Then the handmaidens came near, they and their children, and they bowed themselves.

7 And Leah also with her children came near, and bowed themselves: and after came Joseph near and Rachel, and they bowed themselves.

8 And he said, What *meanest* thou by all this drove which I met? And he said, *These are* to find grace in the sight of my lord.

9 And Esau said, I have enough, my

Cross references (center column):
29 Judg. 13:18
30 Gen. 16:13; Ex. 24:11; 33:20; Deut. 5:24; Judg. 6:22; 13:22; Isa. 6:5
1 Gen. 32:6
3 Gen. 18:2; 42:6; 43:26
4 Gen. 32:28; 45:14, 15
5 Gen. 48:9; Ps. 127:3; Isa. 8:18
8 Gen. 32:5, 16
10 Gen. 43:3; 2Sam. 3:13; 14:24, 28, 32; Matt. 18:10
11 Judg. 1:15; 1Sam. 25:27; 30:26; 2Kgs. 5:15, 23; Phil. 4:18
14 Gen. 32:3
15 Gen. 34:11; 47:25; Ruth 2:13
17 Josh. 13:27; Judg. 8:5; Ps. 60:6
18 Josh. 24:1; Judg. 9:1; John 3:23
19 Josh. 24:32; John 4:5
20 Gen. 35:7
1 Gen. 30:21; Titus 2:5
2 Gen. 6:2; 20:2; Deut. 22:29; Judg. 14:1

brother; keep that thou hast unto thyself.

10 And Jacob said, Nay, I pray thee, if now I have found grace in thy sight, then receive my present at my hand: for therefore I have seen thy face, as though I had seen the face of God, and thou wast pleased with me.

11 Take, I pray thee, my blessing that is brought to thee; because God hath dealt graciously with me, and because I have enough. And he urged him, and he took *it*.

12 And he said, Let us take our journey, and let us go, and I will go before thee.

13 And he said unto him, My lord knoweth that the children *are* tender, and the flocks and herds with young *are* with me: and if men should overdrive them one day, all the flock will die.

14 Let my lord, I pray thee, pass over before his servant: and I will lead on softly, according as the cattle that goeth before me and the children be able to endure, until I come unto my lord unto Seir.

15 And Esau said, Let me now leave with thee *some* of the folk that *are* with me. And he said, What needeth it? let me find grace in the sight of my lord.

16 So Esau returned that day on his way unto Seir.

17 And Jacob journeyed to Succoth, and built him an house, and made booths for his cattle: therefore the name of the place is called Succoth.

18 And Jacob came to Shalem, a city of Shechem, which *is* in the land of Canaan, when he came from Padan-aram; and pitched his tent before the city.

19 And he bought a parcel of a field, where he had spread his tent, at the hand of the children of Hamor, Shechem's father, for an hundred pieces of money.

20 And he erected there an altar, and called it El-elohe-Israel.

CHAPTER 34
Dinah Is Raped

1 And Dinah the daughter of Leah, which she bare unto Jacob, went out to see the daughters of the land.

2 And when Shechem the son of Hamor the Hivite, prince of the country, saw her, he took her, and lay with her, and defiled her.

Jacob means "heel-catcher" or "deceiver," while the new name, Israel, means "prince of God," "God's fighter," or "he struggles with God." Jacob's whole life was a struggle. He struggles with his brother (Gen. 25, 27), his father (Gen. 27), his father-in-law (Gen. 29—31), his wives (Gen. 30), and now with God (Gen. 32:28).

32:29 And he blessed him there. Though the man (angel) did not reveal His name, He did give His blessing to Israel. Many believe that this was Christ (see note on Gen. 32:24).

3 And his soul clave unto Dinah the daughter of Jacob, and he loved the damsel, and spake kindly unto the damsel.

4 And Shechem spake unto his father Hamor, saying, Get me this damsel to wife.

5 And Jacob heard that he had defiled Dinah his daughter: now his sons were with his cattle in the field: and Jacob held his peace until they were come.

6 And Hamor the father of Shechem went out unto Jacob to commune with him.

7 And the sons of Jacob came out of the field when they heard *it*: and the men were grieved, and they were very wroth, because he had wrought folly in Israel in lying with Jacob's daughter; which thing ought not to be done.

8 And Hamor communed with them, saying, The soul of my son Shechem longeth for your daughter: I pray you give her him to wife.

9 And make ye marriages with us, *and* give your daughters unto us, and take our daughters unto you.

10 And ye shall dwell with us: and the land shall be before you; dwell and trade ye therein, and get you possessions therein.

11 And Shechem said unto her father and unto her brethren, Let me find grace in your eyes, and what ye shall say unto me I will give.

12 Ask me never so much dowry and gift, and I will give according as ye shall say unto me: but give me the damsel to wife.

13 And the sons of Jacob answered Shechem and Hamor his father deceitfully, and said, because he had defiled Dinah their sister:

14 And they said unto them, We cannot do this thing, to give our sister to one that is uncircumcised; for that *were* a reproach unto us:

15 But in this will we consent unto you: If ye will be as we *be*, that every male of you be circumcised;

16 Then will we give our daughters unto you, and we will take your daughters to us, and we will dwell with you, and we will become one people.

17 But if ye will not hearken unto us, to be circumcised; then will we take our daughter, and we will be gone.

18 And their words pleased Hamor, and Shechem Hamor's son.

19 And the young man deferred not to do the thing, because he had delight in Jacob's daughter: and he *was* more honourable than all the house of his father.

20 And Hamor and Shechem his son came unto the gate of their city, and communed with the men of their city, saying,

21 These men *are* peaceable with us; therefore let them dwell in the land, and trade therein; for the land, behold, *it is* large enough for them; let us take their daughters to us for wives, and let us give them our daughters.

22 Only herein will the men consent unto us for to dwell with us, to be one people, if every male among us be circumcised, as they *are* circumcised.

23 *Shall* not their cattle and their substance and every beast of theirs *be* ours? only let us consent unto them, and they will dwell with us.

24 And unto Hamor and unto Shechem his son hearkened all that went out of the gate of his city; and every male was circumcised, all that went out of the gate of his city.

25 And it came to pass on the third day, when they were sore, that two of the sons of Jacob, Simeon and Levi, Dinah's brethren, took each man his sword, and came upon the city boldly, and slew all the males.

26 And they slew Hamor and Shechem his son with the edge of the sword, and took Dinah out of Shechem's house, and went out.

27 The sons of Jacob came upon the slain, and spoiled the city, because they had defiled their sister.

28 They took their sheep, and their oxen, and their asses, and that which *was* in the city, and that which *was* in the field,

29 And all their wealth, and all their little ones, and their wives took they captive, and spoiled even all that *was* in the house.

30 And Jacob said to Simeon and Levi, Ye have troubled me to make me to stink among the inhabitants of the land, among the Canaanites and the Perizzites: and I *being* few in number, they shall gather themselves together against me, and slay me; and I shall be destroyed, I and my house.

31 And they said, Should he deal with our sister as with an harlot?

CHAPTER 35
Jacob Returns to Bethel

1 And God said unto Jacob, Arise, go up to Beth-el, and dwell there: and make there an altar unto God, that appeared unto thee when thou fleddest from the face of Esau thy brother.

2 Then Jacob said unto his household, and

Cross references (center column):

3 Isa. 40:2; Hos. 2:14

4 Judg. 14:2

5 1Sam. 10:27; 2Sam. 13:22

7 Gen. 49:7; Deut. 23:17; Josh. 7:15; Judg. 20:6; 2Sam. 13:12, 21

10 Gen. 13:9; 20:15; 42:34; 47:27

12 Ex. 22:16, 17; Deut. 22:29; 1Sam. 18:25

13 2Sam. 13:24-33

14 Josh. 5:9

19 1Chr. 4:9

24 Gen. 23:10

25 Gen. 49:5-7

30 Gen. 49:6; Ex. 5:21; Deut. 4:27; Josh. 7:25; 1Sam. 13:4; Ps. 105:12

1 Gen. 27:43; 28:13, 19

2 Gen. 18:19; 31:19, 34; Ex. 19:10; Josh. 24:2, 15, 23; 1Sam. 7:3

to all that *were* with him, Put away the strange gods that *are* among you, and be clean, and change your garments:

3 And let us arise, and go up to Beth-el; and I will make there an altar unto God, who answered me in the day of my distress, and was with me in the way which I went.

4 And they gave unto Jacob all the strange gods which *were* in their hand, and *all their* earrings which *were* in their ears; and Jacob hid them under the oak which *was* by Shechem.

5 And they journeyed: and the terror of God was upon the cities that *were* round about them, and they did not pursue after the sons of Jacob.

6 So Jacob came to Luz, which *is* in the land of Canaan, that *is*, Beth-el, he and all the people that *were* with him.

7 And he built there an altar, and called the place El-Beth-el: because there God appeared unto him, when he fled from the face of his brother.

8 But Deborah Rebekah's nurse died, and she was buried beneath Beth-el under an oak: and the name of it was called Allon-bachuth.

9 And God appeared unto Jacob again, when he came out of Padan-aram, and blessed him.

10 And God said unto him, Thy name *is* Jacob: thy name shall not be called any more Jacob, but Israel shall be thy name: and he called his name Israel.

11 And God said unto him, I *am* God Almighty: be fruitful and multiply; a nation and a company of nations shall be of thee, and kings shall come out of thy loins;

12 And the land which I gave Abraham and Isaac, to thee I will give it, and to thy seed after thee will I give the land.

13 And God went up from him in the place where he talked with him.

14 And Jacob set up a pillar in the place where he talked with him, *even* a pillar of stone: and he poured a drink offering thereon, and he poured oil thereon.

15 And Jacob called the name of the place where God spake with him, Beth-el.

Rachel Dies

16 And they journeyed from Beth-el; and there was but a little way to come to Ephrath: and Rachel travailed, and she had hard labour.

17 And it came to pass, when she was in hard labour, that the midwife said unto her, Fear not; thou shalt have this son also.

18 And it came to pass, as her soul was in departing, (for she died) that she called his name Ben-oni: but his father called him Benjamin.

19 And Rachel died, and was buried in the way to Ephrath, which *is* Beth-lehem.

20 And Jacob set a pillar upon her grave: that *is* the pillar of Rachel's grave unto this day.

21 And Israel journeyed, and spread his tent beyond the tower of Edar.

Jacob's Sons

22 And it came to pass, when Israel dwelt in that land, that Reuben went and lay with Bilhah his father's concubine: and Israel heard *it*. Now the sons of Jacob were twelve:

23 The sons of Leah; Reuben, Jacob's firstborn, and Simeon, and Levi, and Judah, and Issachar, and Zebulun:

24 The sons of Rachel; Joseph, and Benjamin:

25 And the sons of Bilhah, Rachel's handmaid; Dan, and Naphtali:

26 And the sons of Zilpah, Leah's handmaid; Gad, and Asher: these *are* the sons of Jacob, which were born to him in Padan-aram.

The Death of Isaac

27 And Jacob came unto Isaac his father unto Mamre, unto the city of Arbah, which *is* Hebron, where Abraham and Isaac sojourned.

28 And the days of Isaac were an hundred and fourscore years.

29 And Isaac gave up the ghost, and died, and was gathered unto his people, *being* old and full of days: and his sons Esau and Jacob buried him.

Cross references:

3 Gen. 28:20; 31:3, 42; 32:7, 24; Ps. 107:6
4 Josh. 24:26; Judg. 9:6; Hos. 2:13
5 Ex. 15:16; 23:27; 34:24; Deut. 11:25; Josh. 2:9; 5:1; 1Sam. 14:15; 2Chr. 14:14
6 Gen. 28:19, 22
7 Gen. 28:13; Eccl. 5:4
8 Gen. 24:59
9 Hos. 12:4
10 Gen. 17:5; 32:28
11 Gen. 17:1, 5, 6, 16; 28:3; 48:3, 4; Ex. 6:3
12 Gen. 12:7; 13:15; 26:3, 4; 28:13
13 Gen. 17:22
14 Gen. 28:18
17 Gen. 30:24; 1Sam. 4:20
19 Gen. 48:7; Ruth 1:2; 4:11; Mic. 5:2; Matt. 2:6
20 1Sam. 10:2; 2Sam. 18:18
21 Mic. 4:8
22 Gen. 49:4; 2Sam. 16:22; 20:3; 1Chr. 5:1; 1Cor. 5:1
23 Gen. 46:8; Ex. 1:2
27 Gen. 13:18

35:10 Israel shall be thy name. God reiterates Jacob's new name (cf. Gen. 32:28–29).

35:11–12 kings shall come out of thy loins. The Abrahamic promise of a land, seed, and blessing is reaffirmed to Jacob, who is now called Israel. While other promises had been restated many times to Abraham, Isaac, and Jacob, this is the first time since Genesis 17:6–16 that the prophetic promise of future royalty is repeated.

35:29 gathered unto his people. Isaac dies at 180 years of age, the oldest of the patriarchs (see note on Gen. 25:7–8).

CHAPTER 36
Esau's Family Record

1 Now these *are* the generations of Esau, who *is* Edom.

2 Esau took his wives of the daughters of Canaan; Adah the daughter of Elon the Hittite, and Aholibamah the daughter of Anah the daughter of Zibeon the Hivite;

3 And Bashemath Ishmael's daughter, sister of Nebajoth.

4 And Adah bare to Esau Eliphaz; and Bashemath bare Reuel;

5 And Aholibamah bare Jeush, and Jaalam, and Korah: these *are* the sons of Esau, which were born unto him in the land of Canaan.

6 And Esau took his wives, and his sons, and his daughters, and all the persons of his house, and his cattle, and all his beasts, and all his substance, which he had got in the land of Canaan; and went into the country from the face of his brother Jacob.

7 For their riches were more than that they might dwell together; and the land wherein they were strangers could not bear them because of their cattle.

8 Thus dwelt Esau in mount Seir: Esau *is* Edom.

9 And these *are* the generations of Esau the father of the Edomites in mount Seir:

10 These *are* the names of Esau's sons; Eliphaz the son of Adah the wife of Esau, Reuel the son of Bashemath the wife of Esau.

11 And the sons of Eliphaz were Teman, Omar, Zepho, and Gatam, and Kenaz.

12 And Timna was concubine to Eliphaz Esau's son; and she bare to Eliphaz Amalek: these *were* the sons of Adah Esau's wife.

13 And these *are* the sons of Reuel; Nahath, and Zerah, Shammah, and Mizzah: these were the sons of Bashemath Esau's wife.

14 And these were the sons of Aholibamah, the daughter of Anah the daughter of Zibeon, Esau's wife: and she bare to Esau Jeush, and Jaalam, and Korah.

15 These *were* dukes of the sons of Esau: the sons of Eliphaz the firstborn *son* of Esau; duke Teman, duke Omar, duke Zepho, duke Kenaz,

16 Duke Korah, duke Gatam, *and* duke Amalek: these *are* the dukes *that came* of Eliphaz in the land of Edom; these *were* the sons of Adah.

17 And these *are* the sons of Reuel Esau's son; duke Nahath, duke Zerah, duke Shammah, duke Mizzah: these *are* the dukes *that came* of Reuel in the land of Edom; these *are* the sons of Bashemath Esau's wife.

18 And these *are* the sons of Aholibamah Esau's wife; duke Jeush, duke Jaalam, duke Korah: these *were* the dukes *that came* of Aholibamah the daughter of Anah, Esau's wife.

19 These *are* the sons of Esau, who *is* Edom, and these *are* their dukes.

20 These *are* the sons of Seir the Horite, who inhabited the land; Lotan, and Shobal, and Zibeon, and Anah,

21 And Dishon, and Ezer, and Dishan: these *are* the dukes of the Horites, the children of Seir in the land of Edom.

22 And the children of Lotan were Hori and Hemam; and Lotan's sister *was* Timna.

23 And the children of Shobal *were* these; Alvan, and Manahath, and Ebal, Shepho, and Onam.

24 And these *are* the children of Zibeon; both Ajah, and Anah: this *was that* Anah that found the mules in the wilderness, as he fed the asses of Zibeon his father.

25 And the children of Anah *were* these; Dishon, and Aholibamah the daughter of Anah.

26 And these *are* the children of Dishon; Hemdan, and Esh-ban, and Ithran, and Cheran.

27 The children of Ezer *are* these; Bilhan, and Zaavan, and Akan.

28 The children of Dishan *are* these; Uz, and Aran.

29 These *are* the dukes *that came* of the Horites; duke Lotan, duke Shobal, duke Zibeon, duke Anah,

30 Duke Dishon, duke Ezer, duke Dishan: these *are* the dukes *that came* of Hori, among their dukes in the land of Seir.

31 And these *are* the kings that reigned in the land of Edom, before there reigned any king over the children of Israel.

32 And Bela the son of Beor reigned in Edom: and the name of his city *was* Dinhabah.

33 And Bela died, and Jobab the son of Zerah of Bozrah reigned in his stead.

34 And Jobab died, and Husham of the land of Temani reigned in his stead.

Cross references
1 Gen. 25:30
2 Gen. 26:34; 36:25
3 Gen. 28:9
4 1Chr. 1:35
7 Gen. 13:6, 11; 17:8; 28:4
8 Gen. 32:3; 36:1; Deut. 2:5; Josh. 24:4
10 1Chr. 1:35-37
11 1Chr. 1:36
12 Ex. 17:8, 14; Num. 24:20; 1Sam. 15:2-9
20 Gen. 14:6; Deut. 2:12, 22; 1Chr. 1:38
22 1Chr. 1:39
23 1Chr. 1:40
24 Lev. 19:19
26 1Chr. 1:41
27 1Chr. 1:42
31 1Chr. 1:43

36:1 these are the generations of Esau, who is Edom. This is the ninth *toledoth* (see note on Gen. 2:4).

36:9 these are the generations of Esau the father of the Edomites in mount Seir. This is the tenth *toledoth* (see note on Gen. 2:4).

35 And Husham died, and Hadad the son of Bedad, who smote Midian in the field of Moab, reigned in his stead: and the name of his city *was* Avith.

36 And Hadad died, and Samlah of Masrekah reigned in his stead.

37 And Samlah died, and Saul of Rehoboth *by* the river reigned in his stead.

38 And Saul died, and Baalhanan the son of Achbor reigned in his stead.

39 And Baalhanan the son of Achbor died, and Hadar reigned in his stead: and the name of his city *was* Pau; and his wife's name *was* Mehetabel, the daughter of Matred, the daughter of Mezahab.

40 And these *are* the names of the dukes *that came* of Esau, according to their families, after their places, by their names; duke Timnah, duke Alvah, duke Jetheth,

41 Duke Aholibamah, duke Elah, duke Pinon,

42 Duke Kenaz, duke Teman, duke Mibzar,

43 Duke Magdiel, duke Iram: these *be* the dukes of Edom, according to their habitations in the land of their possession: he *is* Esau the father of the Edomites.

CHAPTER 37
Joseph Has a Dream

1 And Jacob dwelt in the land wherein his father was a stranger, in the land of Canaan.

2 These *are* the generations of Jacob. Joseph, *being* seventeen years old, was feeding the flock with his brethren; and the lad *was* with the sons of Bilhah, and with the sons of Zilpah, his father's wives: and Joseph brought unto his father their evil report.

3 Now Israel loved Joseph more than all his children, because he *was* the son of his old age: and he made him a coat of *many* colours.

4 And when his brethren saw that their father loved him more than all his brethren, they hated him, and could not speak peaceably unto him.

5 And Joseph dreamed a dream, and he told *it* his brethren: and they hated him yet the more.

6 And he said unto them, Hear, I pray you, this dream which I have dreamed:

7 For, behold, we *were* binding sheaves in the field, and, lo, my sheaf arose, and also stood upright; and, behold, your sheaves stood round about, and made obeisance to my sheaf.

8 And his brethren said to him, Shalt thou indeed reign over us? or shalt thou indeed have dominion over us? And they hated him yet the more for his dreams, and for his words.

9 And he dreamed yet another dream, and told it his brethren, and said, Behold, I have dreamed a dream more; and, behold, the sun and the moon and the eleven stars made obeisance to me.

10 And he told *it* to his father, and to his brethren: and his father rebuked him, and said unto him, What *is* this dream that thou hast dreamed? Shall I and thy mother and thy brethren indeed come to bow down ourselves to thee to the earth?

11 And his brethren envied him; but his father observed the saying.

Joseph Sold into Slavery

12 And his brethren went to feed their father's flock in Shechem.

13 And Israel said unto Joseph, Do not thy brethren feed *the flock* in Shechem? come, and I will send thee unto them. And he said to him, Here *am* I.

14 And he said to him, Go, I pray thee, see whether it be well with thy brethren, and well with the flocks; and bring me word again. So he sent him out of the vale of Hebron, and he came to Shechem.

15 And a certain man found him, and, behold, *he was* wandering in the field: and the man asked him, saying, What seekest thou?

16 And he said, I seek my brethren: tell me, I pray thee, where they feed *their flocks*.

Cross-references
39 1Chr. 1:50
40 1Chr. 1:51
1 Gen. 17:8; 23:4; 28:4; 36:7; Heb. 11:9
2 1Sam. 2:22-24
3 Gen. 44:20; Judg. 5:30; 2Sam. 13:18
4 Gen. 27:41; 49:23
7 Gen. 42:6, 9; 43:26; 44:14
9 Gen. 45:9
10 Gen. 27:29
11 Dan. 7:28; Luke 2:19, 51; Acts 7:9
14 Gen. 29:6; 35:27
16 Song 1:7

37:1, 3 Jacob . . . Israel. When Abraham's name was changed in Genesis 17:5, his new name was used from that point forward. However, after Jacob's name was changed, both old and new names were used.

37:2 These are the generations of Jacob. This is the eleventh and last *toledoth* (see note on Gen. 2:4). The rest of Genesis traces the history of Jacob and his sons.

37:3 Israel loved Joseph more than all his children, because he was the son of his old age. The Hebrew word for "coat" denotes a garment with long sleeves. It was clearly a garment representing Jacob's favor, similar to what a crown prince might be given.

37:6–11 this dream which I have dreamed. Joseph's two prophetic dreams included his rise in status (37:7), and the corresponding homage of his family (37:9). These dreams came from God and were fulfilled in history (Gen. 42:6; 43:26, 28; 44:14). Similar imagery to that in Joseph's dreams is found in Revelation 12:1.

17 And the man said, They are departed hence; for I heard them say, Let us go to Dothan. And Joseph went after his brethren, and found them in Dothan.

18 And when they saw him afar off, even before he came near unto them, they conspired against him to slay him.

19 And they said one to another, Behold, this dreamer cometh.

20 Come now therefore, and let us slay him, and cast him into some pit, and we will say, Some evil beast hath devoured him: and we shall see what will become of his dreams.

21 And Reuben heard *it*, and he delivered him out of their hands; and said, Let us not kill him.

22 And Reuben said unto them, Shed no blood, *but* cast him into this pit that *is* in the wilderness, and lay no hand upon him; that he might rid him out of their hands, to deliver him to his father again.

23 And it came to pass, when Joseph was come unto his brethren, that they strip Joseph out of his coat, *his* coat of *many* colours that *was* on him;

24 And they took him, and cast him into a pit: and the pit *was* empty, *there was* no water in it.

25 And they sat down to eat bread: and they lifted up their eyes and looked, and, behold, a company of Ishmeelites came from Gilead with their camels bearing spicery and balm and myrrh, going to carry *it* down to Egypt.

26 And Judah said unto his brethren, What profit *is it* if we slay our brother, and conceal his blood?

27 Come, and let us sell him to the Ishmeelites, and let not our hand be upon him; for he *is* our brother *and* our flesh. And his brethren were content.

28 Then there passed by Midianites merchantmen; and they drew and lifted up Joseph out of the pit, and sold Joseph to the Ishmeelites for twenty *pieces* of silver: and they brought Joseph into Egypt.

29 And Reuben returned unto the pit; and, behold, Joseph *was* not in the pit; and he rent his clothes.

30 And he returned unto his brethren, and said, The child *is* not; and I, whither shall I go?

31 And they took Joseph's coat, and killed a kid of the goats, and dipped the coat in the blood;

32 And they sent the coat of *many* colours, and they brought *it* to their father; and said,

This have we found: know now whether it *be* thy son's coat or no.

33 And he knew it, and said, *It is* my son's coat; an evil beast hath devoured him; Joseph is without doubt rent in pieces.

34 And Jacob rent his clothes, and put sackcloth upon his loins, and mourned for his son many days.

35 And all his sons and all his daughters rose up to comfort him; but he refused to be comforted; and he said, For I will go down into the grave unto my son mourning. Thus his father wept for him.

36 And the Midianites sold him into Egypt unto Potiphar, an officer of Pharaoh's, *and* captain of the guard.

CHAPTER 38
Judah's Indiscretion with Tamar

1 And it came to pass at that time, that Judah went down from his brethren, and turned in to a certain Adullamite, whose name *was* Hirah.

2 And Judah saw there a daughter of a certain Canaanite, whose name *was* Shuah; and he took her, and went in unto her.

3 And she conceived, and bare a son; and he called his name Er.

4 And she conceived again, and bare a son; and she called his name Onan.

5 And she yet again conceived, and bare a son; and called his name Shelah: and he was at Chezib, when she bare him.

6 And Judah took a wife for Er his firstborn, whose name *was* Tamar.

7 And Er, Judah's firstborn, was wicked in the sight of the LORD; and the LORD slew him.

8 And Judah said unto Onan, Go in unto thy brother's wife, and marry her, and raise up seed to thy brother.

9 And Onan knew that the seed should not be his; and it came to pass, when he went in unto his brother's wife, that he spilled *it* on the ground, lest that he should give seed to his brother.

10 And the thing which he did displeased the LORD: wherefore he slew him also.

11 Then said Judah to Tamar his daughter-in-law, Remain a widow at thy father's house, till Shelah my son be grown: for he said, Lest peradventure he die also, as his brethren *did*. And Tamar went and dwelt in her father's house.

12 And in process of time the daughter of Shuah Judah's wife died; and Judah was comforted, and went up unto his sheepshearers to Timnath, he and his friend Hirah the Adullamite.

Cross references (center column):

17 2Kgs. 6:13

18 1Sam. 19:1; Ps. 31:13; 37:12, 32; 94:21; Matt. 27:1; Mark 14:1; John 11:53; Acts 23:12

20 Prov. 1:11, 16; 6:17; 27:4

21 Gen. 42:22

25 Gen. 37:28, 36; Prov. 30:20; Jer. 8:22; Amos 6:6

26 Gen. 4:10; 37:20; Job 16:18

27 Gen. 29:14; 42:21; 1Sam. 18:17

28 Gen. 45:4, 5; Judg. 6:3; Ps. 105:17; Matt. 27:9; Acts 7:9

29 Job 1:20

30 Gen. 42:13, 36; Jer. 31:15

31 Gen. 37:23

33 Gen. 37:20; 44:28

34 Gen. 37:29; 2Sam. 3:31

35 Gen. 42:38; 44:29, 31; 2Sam. 12:17

36 Gen. 39:1; Esth. 1:10

1 Gen. 19:3; 2Kgs. 4:8

2 Gen. 34:2; 1Chr. 2:3

3 Gen. 46:12; Num. 26:19

4 Gen. 46:12; Num. 26:19

5 Gen. 46:12; Num. 26:20

6 Gen. 21:21

7 Gen. 46:12; Num. 26:19; 1Chr. 2:3

9 Deut. 25:6

13 And it was told Tamar, saying, Behold thy father-in-law goeth up to Timnath to shear his sheep.

14 And she put her widow's garments off from her, and covered her with a vail, and wrapped herself, and sat in an open place, which *is* by the way to Timnath; for she saw that Shelah was grown, and she was not given unto him to wife.

15 When Judah saw her, he thought her *to be* an harlot; because she had covered her face.

16 And he turned unto her by the way, and said, Go to, I pray thee, let me come in unto thee; (for he knew not that she *was* his daughter-in-law.) And she said, What wilt thou give me, that thou mayest come in unto me?

17 And he said, I will send *thee* a kid from the flock. And she said, Wilt thou give *me* a pledge, till thou send *it*?

18 And he said, What pledge shall I give thee? And she said, Thy signet, and thy bracelets, and thy staff that *is* in thine hand. And he gave *it* her, and came in unto her, and she conceived by him.

19 And she arose, and went away, and laid by her vail from her, and put on the garments of her widowhood.

20 And Judah sent the kid by the hand of his friend the Adullamite, to receive *his* pledge from the woman's hand: but he found her not.

21 Then he asked the men of that place, saying, Where *is* the harlot, that *was* openly by the way side? And they said, There was no harlot in this *place*.

22 And he returned to Judah, and said, I cannot find her; and also the men of the place said, *that* there was no harlot in this *place*.

23 And Judah said, Let her take *it* to her, lest we be shamed: behold, I sent this kid, and thou hast not found her.

24 And it came to pass about three months after, that it was told Judah, saying, Tamar thy daughter-in-law hath played the harlot; and also, behold, she *is* with child by whoredom. And Judah said, Bring her forth, and let her be burnt.

25 When she *was* brought forth, she sent to her father-in-law, saying, By the man, whose these *are, am* I with child: and she said, Discern, I pray thee, whose *are* these, the signet, and bracelets, and staff.

26 And Judah acknowledged *them*, and said, She hath been more righteous than I; because that I gave her not to Shelah my son. And he knew her again no more.

27 And it came to pass in the time of her travail, that, behold, twins *were* in her womb.

28 And it came to pass, when she travailed, that *the one* put out *his* hand: and the midwife took and bound upon his hand a scarlet thread, saying, This came out first.

29 And it came to pass, as he drew back his hand, that, behold, his brother came out: and she said, How hast thou broken forth? *this* breach *be* upon thee: therefore his name was called Pharez.

30 And afterward came out his brother, that had the scarlet thread upon his hand: and his name was called Zarah.

CHAPTER 39
Joseph and Potiphar's Wife

1 And Joseph was brought down to Egypt; and Potiphar, an officer of Pharaoh, captain of the guard, an Egyptian, bought him of the hands of the Ishmeelites, which had brought him down thither.

2 And the LORD was with Joseph, and he was a prosperous man; and he was in the house of his master the Egyptian.

3 And his master saw that the LORD *was* with him, and that the LORD made all that he did to prosper in his hand.

4 And Joseph found grace in his sight, and he served him: and he made him overseer over his house, and all *that* he had he put into his hand.

5 And it came to pass from the time *that* he had made him overseer in his house, and over all that he had, that the LORD blessed the Egyptian's house for Joseph's sake; and the blessing of the LORD was upon all that he had in the house, and in the field.

6 And he left all that he had in Joseph's hand; and he knew not ought he had, save the bread which he did eat. And Joseph was *a* goodly *person*, and well favoured.

7 And it came to pass after these things, that his master's wife cast her eyes upon Joseph; and she said, Lie with me.

8 But he refused, and said unto his master's wife, Behold, my master wotteth not what *is* with me in the house, and he hath committed all that he hath to my hand;

9 *There is* none greater in this house than I; neither hath he kept back any thing from me but thee, because thou *art* his wife: how then can I do this great wickedness, and sin against God?

10 And it came to pass, as she spake to

Cross References

13 Josh. 15:10, 57; Judg. 14:1

14 Gen. 38:11, 26; Prov. 7:12

17 Gen. 38:20; Ezek. 16:33

18 Gen. 38:25

19 Gen. 38:14

24 Lev. 21:9; Deut. 22:21; Judg. 19:2

25 Gen. 37:32; 38:18

26 Gen. 37:33; 38:14; 1Sam. 24:17; Job 34:31, 32

29 Gen. 46:12; Num. 26:20; 1Chr. 2:4; Matt. 1:3

1 Gen. 37:28, 36; Ps. 105:17

2 Gen. 21:22; 26:24, 28; 28:15; 39:21; 1Sam. 16:18; 18:14, 28; Acts 7:9

3 Ps. 1:3

4 Gen. 18:3; 19:19; 24:2; 39:21

5 Gen. 30:27

6 1Sam. 16:12

7 2Sam. 13:11

9 Gen. 20:6; Lev. 6:2; 2Sam. 12:13; Ps. 51:4; Prov. 6:29, 32

Joseph day by day, that he hearkened not unto her, to lie by her, *or* to be with her.

11 And it came to pass about this time, that *Joseph* went into the house to do his business; and *there was* none of the men of the house there within.

12 And she caught him by his garment, saying, Lie with me: and he left his garment in her hand, and fled, and got him out.

13 And it came to pass, when she saw that he had left his garment in her hand, and was fled forth,

14 That she called unto the men of her house, and spake unto them, saying, See, he hath brought in an Hebrew unto us to mock us; he came in unto me to lie with me, and I cried with a loud voice:

15 And it came to pass, when he heard that I lifted up my voice and cried, that he left his garment with me, and fled, and got him out.

16 And she laid up his garment by her, until his lord came home.

17 And she spake unto him according to these words, saying, The Hebrew servant, which thou hast brought unto us, came in unto me to mock me:

18 And it came to pass, as I lifted up my voice and cried, that he left his garment with me, and fled out.

19 And it came to pass, when his master heard the words of his wife, which she spake unto him, saying, After this manner did thy servant to me; that his wrath was kindled.

20 And Joseph's master took him, and put him into the prison, a place where the king's prisoners *were* bound: and he was there in the prison.

21 But the LORD was with Joseph, and shewed him mercy, and gave him favour in the sight of the keeper of the prison.

22 And the keeper of the prison committed to Joseph's hand all the prisoners that *were* in the prison; and whatsoever they did there, he was the doer *of it*.

23 The keeper of the prison looked not to any thing *that was* under his hand; because the LORD was with him, and *that* which he did, the LORD made *it* to prosper.

Cross references (center column):

12 Prov. 7:13-20

17 Ex. 23:1; Ps. 120:3

19 Prov. 6:34, 35

20 Gen. 40:3, 15; 41:14; Ps. 105:18; 1Pet. 2:19

21 Ex. 3:21; 11:3; 12:36; Ps. 106:46; Prov. 16:7; Dan. 1:9; Acts 7:9, 10

22 Gen. 40:3, 4

23 Gen. 39:2, 3

1 Neh. 1:11

2 Prov. 16:14

3 Gen. 39:20, 23

7 Neh. 2:2

8 Gen. 41:15, 16; Dan. 2:11, 28, 47

12 Gen. 40:18; 41:12, 25, 26; Judg. 7:14; Dan. 2:36; 4:19

13 2Kgs. 25:27; Ps. 3:3; Jer. 52:31

CHAPTER 40
Joseph Interprets the Prisoners' Dreams

1 And it came to pass after these things, *that* the butler of the king of Egypt and *his* baker had offended their lord the king of Egypt.

2 And Pharaoh was wroth against two *of* his officers, against the chief of the butlers, and against the chief of the bakers.

3 And he put them in ward in the house of the captain of the guard, into the prison, the place where Joseph *was* bound.

4 And the captain of the guard charged Joseph with them, and he served them: and they continued a season in ward.

5 And they dreamed a dream both of them, each man his dream in one night, each man according to the interpretation of his dream, the butler and the baker of the king of Egypt, which *were* bound in the prison.

6 And Joseph came in unto them in the morning, and looked upon them, and, behold, they *were* sad.

7 And he asked Pharaoh's officers that *were* with him in the ward of his lord's house, saying, Wherefore look ye *so* sadly today?

8 And they said unto him, We have dreamed a dream, and *there is* no interpreter of it. And Joseph said unto them, *Do* not interpretations *belong* to God? tell me *them*, I pray you.

9 And the chief butler told his dream to Joseph, and said to him, In my dream, behold, a vine *was* before me;

10 And in the vine *were* three branches: and it *was* as though it budded, *and* her blossoms shot forth; and the clusters thereof brought forth ripe grapes:

11 And Pharaoh's cup *was* in my hand: and I took the grapes, and pressed them into Pharaoh's cup, and I gave the cup into Pharaoh's hand.

12 And Joseph said unto him, This *is* the interpretation of it: The three branches *are* three days:

13 Yet within three days shall Pharaoh lift up thine head, and restore thee unto thy

---

40:8 Do not interpretations belong to God? Joseph and Daniel (Dan. 2:26–28; 7:1) were two sons of Israel capable of interpreting prophetic dreams while serving among Gentile powers. Like Daniel (Dan. 2:28), Joseph here declares to a Gentile ruler that only the God of Israel can interpret dreams.

40:9–23 These are prophetic dreams. They are first given (Gen. 40:9–11, 16–17), then correctly interpreted by Joseph, then embedded in prophecy (Gen. 40:12–13, 18–19), and finally fulfilled (Gen. 40:20–23).

place: and thou shalt deliver Pharaoh's cup into his hand, after the former manner when thou wast his butler.

14 But think on me when it shall be well with thee, and shew kindness, I pray thee, unto me, and make mention of me unto Pharaoh, and bring me out of this house:

15 For indeed I was stolen away out of the land of the Hebrews: and here also have I done nothing that they should put me into the dungeon.

16 When the chief baker saw that the interpretation was good, he said unto Joseph, I also *was* in my dream, and, behold, *I had* three white baskets on my head:

17 And in the uppermost basket *there was* of all manner of bakemeats for Pharaoh; and the birds did eat them out of the basket upon my head.

18 And Joseph answered and said, This *is* the interpretation thereof: The three baskets *are* three days:

19 Yet within three days shall Pharaoh lift up thy head from off thee, and shall hang thee on a tree; and the birds shall eat thy flesh from off thee.

20 And it came to pass the third day, *which was* Pharaoh's birthday, that he made a feast unto all his servants: and he lifted up the head of the chief butler and of the chief baker among his servants.

21 And he restored the chief butler unto his butlership again; and he gave the cup into Pharaoh's hand:

22 But he hanged the chief baker: as Joseph had interpreted to them.

23 Yet did not the chief butler remember Joseph, but forgat him.

CHAPTER 41
Joseph Interprets Pharaoh's Dreams

1 And it came to pass at the end of two full years, that Pharaoh dreamed: and, behold, he stood by the river.

2 And, behold, there came up out of the river seven well favoured kine and fatfleshed; and they fed in a meadow.

3 And, behold, seven other kine came up after them out of the river, ill favoured and leanfleshed; and stood by the *other* kine upon the brink of the river.

4 And the ill favoured and leanfleshed kine did eat up the seven well favoured and fat kine. So Pharaoh awoke.

5 And he slept and dreamed the second time: and, behold, seven ears of corn came up upon one stalk, rank and good.

6 And, behold, seven thin ears and blasted with the east wind sprung up after them.

7 And the seven thin ears devoured the seven rank and full ears. And Pharaoh awoke, and, behold, *it was* a dream.

8 And it came to pass in the morning that his spirit was troubled; and he sent and called for all the magicians of Egypt, and all the wise men thereof: and Pharaoh told them his dream; but *there was* none that could interpret them unto Pharaoh.

9 Then spake the chief butler unto Pharaoh, saying, I do remember my faults this day:

10 Pharaoh was wroth with his servants, and put me in ward in the captain of the guard's house, *both* me and the chief baker:

11 And we dreamed a dream in one night, I and he; we dreamed each man according to the interpretation of his dream.

12 And *there was* there with us a young man, an Hebrew, servant to the captain of the guard; and we told him, and he interpreted to us our dreams; to each man according to his dream he did interpret.

13 And it came to pass, as he interpreted to us, so it was; me he restored unto mine office, and him he hanged.

14 Then Pharaoh sent and called Joseph, and they brought him hastily out of the dungeon: and he shaved *himself*, and changed his raiment, and came in unto Pharaoh.

15 And Pharaoh said unto Joseph, I have dreamed a dream, and *there is* none that can interpret it: and I have heard say of thee, *that* thou canst understand a dream to interpret it.

Cross references

14 Josh. 2:12; 1Sam. 20:14, 15; 2Sam. 9:1; 1Kgs. 2:7; Luke 23:42
15 Gen. 39:20
18 Gen. 40:12
19 Gen. 40:13
20 Gen. 40:13, 19; Matt. 14:6; Mark 6:21
21 Gen. 40:13; Neh. 2:1
22 Gen. 40:19
23 Job 19:14; Ps. 31:12; Eccl. 9:15, 16; Amos 6:6
8 Ex. 7:11, 22; Isa. 29:14; Dan. 1:20; 2:1, 2; 4:5, 7, 19; Matt. 2:1
10 Gen. 39:20; 40:2, 3
11 Gen. 40:5
12 Gen. 37:36; 40:12-23
13 Gen. 40:22
14 1Sam. 2:8; Ps. 105:20; 113:7, 8; Dan. 2:25
15 Gen. 41:12; Ps. 25:14; Dan. 5:16

41:1–7 Like the butler and chief baker, Pharaoh receives a dream from God that troubles him. The dream includes an image of kine, which means cows. It is then repeated with an image of corn.

41:1 Pharaoh dreamed. The word Pharaoh means "the great house." Originally it was not so much a title for Egypt's king as it was a reference to his palace. The ancient Egyptians believed that Pharaoh was the living representation of their chief god, Horus. The fact that Pharaoh could not understand his own dream reflected badly, therefore, upon both Horus and Pharaoh, his mediator.

41:8 The fact that no one in Pharaoh's court could interpret the dream demonstrates the shortcomings of the gods the Egyptians worshiped.

16 And Joseph answered Pharaoh, saying, *It is* not in me: God shall give Pharaoh an answer of peace.

17 And Pharaoh said unto Joseph, In my dream, behold, I stood upon the bank of the river:

18 And, behold, there came up out of the river seven kine, fatfleshed and well favoured; and they fed in a meadow:

19 And, behold, seven other kine came up after them, poor and very ill favoured and leanfleshed, such as I never saw in all the land of Egypt for badness:

20 And the lean and the ill favoured kine did eat up the first seven fat kine:

21 And when they had eaten them up, it could not be known that they had eaten them; but they *were* still ill favoured, as at the beginning. So I awoke.

22 And I saw in my dream, and, behold, seven ears came up in one stalk, full and good:

23 And, behold, seven ears, withered, thin, *and* blasted with the east wind, sprung up after them:

24 And the thin ears devoured the seven good ears: and I told *this* unto the magicians; but *there was* none that could declare *it* to me.

25 And Joseph said unto Pharaoh, The dream of Pharaoh *is* one: God hath shewed Pharaoh what he *is* about to do.

26 The seven good kine *are* seven years; and the seven good ears *are* seven years: the dream *is* one.

27 And the seven thin and ill favoured kine that came up after them *are* seven years; and the seven empty ears blasted with the east wind shall be seven years of famine.

28 This *is* the thing which I have spoken unto Pharaoh: What God *is* about to do he sheweth unto Pharaoh.

29 Behold, there come seven years of great plenty throughout all the land of Egypt:

30 And there shall arise after them seven years of famine; and all the plenty shall be forgotten in the land of Egypt; and the famine shall consume the land;

31 And the plenty shall not be known in the land by reason of that famine following; for it *shall be* very grievous.

32 And for that the dream was doubled unto Pharaoh twice; *it is* because the thing *is* established by God, and God will shortly bring it to pass.

33 Now therefore let Pharaoh look out a man discreet and wise, and set him over the land of Egypt.

34 Let Pharaoh do *this*, and let him appoint officers over the land, and take up the fifth part of the land of Egypt in the seven plenteous years.

35 And let them gather all the food of those good years that come, and lay up corn under the hand of Pharaoh, and let them keep food in the cities.

36 And that food shall be for store to the land against the seven years of famine, which shall be in the land of Egypt; that the land perish not through the famine.

Pharaoh Makes Joseph a Ruler

37 And the thing was good in the eyes of Pharaoh, and in the eyes of all his servants.

38 And Pharaoh said unto his servants, Can we find *such a one* as this *is*, a man in whom the Spirit of God *is*?

39 And Pharaoh said unto Joseph, Forasmuch as God hath shewed thee all this, *there is* none so discreet and wise as thou *art*:

40 Thou shalt be over my house, and according unto thy word shall all my people be ruled: only in the throne will I be greater than thou.

Cross references:

16 Gen. 40:8; Dan. 2:22, 28, 30, 47; 4:2; Acts 3:12; 2Cor. 3:5

17 Gen. 41:1

24 Gen. 41:8; Dan. 4:7

25 Dan. 2:28, 29, 45; Rev. 4:1

27 2Kgs. 8:1

28 Gen. 41:25

29 Gen. 41:47

30 Gen. 41:54; 47:13

32 Num. 23:19; Isa. 46:10, 11

34 Prov. 6:6-8

35 Gen. 41:48

36 Gen. 47:15, 19

37 Ps. 105:19; Acts 7:10

38 Num. 27:18; Job 32:8; Prov. 2:6; Dan. 4:8, 18; 5:11, 14; 6:3

40 Ps. 105:21, 22; Acts 7:10

41:16 It is not in me. Joseph's ability to interpret dreams, like Daniel's (Dan. 2:28), is not something that can be learned. It is, rather, a miraculous, direct, verbal revelation from God to a favored servant. Both Joseph and Daniel understood that they were mouthpieces for God.

41:25 God hath shewed Pharaoh. God's prophecies incorporate Gentile nations that rub shoulders with His people Israel. God gave Pharaoh, leader of the most powerful country of his day, a dream because of the Abrahamic covenant and Joseph's presence among the Egyptians (Gen. 45:5–11). Joseph interprets the dream and advises Pharaoh on what he should do about the coming famine. This phrase is repeated in Genesis 41:28 for emphasis.

41:33 discreet and wise. Discreet means discerning.

Thus, Joseph was suggesting that Pharaoh choose an exceedingly wise man to prepare Egypt for the oncoming famine. Joseph informed Pharaoh that the situation needed to be correctly handled. If Pharaoh had not received direct revelation from God through Joseph, he would not have made proper preparations for the seven lean years.

41:34–36 No doubt, Joseph's plan and administration was from the Lord as well.

41:38 a man in whom the spirit of God is? The Holy Spirit is recognized as the means used by God to communicate His prophetic messages to His servants.

41 And Pharaoh said unto Joseph, See, I have set thee over all the land of Egypt.

42 And Pharaoh took off his ring from his hand, and put it upon Joseph's hand, and arrayed him in vestures of fine linen, and put a gold chain about his neck;

43 And he made him to ride in the second chariot which he had; and they cried before him, Bow the knee: and he made him *ruler* over all the land of Egypt.

44 And Pharaoh said unto Joseph, I *am* Pharaoh, and without thee shall no man lift up his hand or foot in all the land of Egypt.

45 And Pharaoh called Joseph's name Zaphnath-paaneah; and he gave him to wife Asenath the daughter of Poti-pherah priest of On. And Joseph went out over *all* the land of Egypt.

46 And Joseph *was* thirty years old when he stood before Pharaoh king of Egypt. And Joseph went out from the presence of Pharaoh, and went throughout all the land of Egypt.

47 And in the seven plenteous years the earth brought forth by handfuls.

48 And he gathered up all the food of the seven years, which were in the land of Egypt, and laid up the food in the cities: the food of the field, which *was* round about every city, laid he up in the same.

49 And Joseph gathered corn as the sand of the sea, very much, until he left numbering; for *it was* without number.

50 And unto Joseph were born two sons before the years of famine came, which Asenath the daughter of Poti-pherah priest of On bare unto him.

51 And Joseph called the name of the firstborn Manasseh: For God, *said he*, hath made me forget all my toil, and all my father's house.

52 And the name of the second called he Ephraim: For God hath caused me to be fruitful in the land of my affliction.

53 And the seven years of plenteousness, that was in the land of Egypt, were ended.

54 And the seven years of dearth began to come, according as Joseph had said: and the dearth was in all lands; but in all the land of Egypt there was bread.

55 And when all the land of Egypt was famished, the people cried to Pharaoh for bread: and Pharaoh said unto all the Egyptians, Go unto Joseph; what he saith to you, do.

56 And the famine was over all the face of

the earth: And Joseph opened all the storehouses, and sold unto the Egyptians; and the famine waxed sore in the land of Egypt.

57 And all countries came into Egypt to Joseph for to buy *corn*; because that the famine was *so* sore in all lands.

CHAPTER 42
Joseph's Brothers Come to Buy Food

1 Now when Jacob saw that there was corn in Egypt, Jacob said unto his sons, Why do ye look one upon another?

2 And he said, Behold, I have heard that there is corn in Egypt: get you down thither, and buy for us from thence; that we may live, and not die.

3 And Joseph's ten brethren went down to buy corn in Egypt.

4 But Benjamin, Joseph's brother, Jacob sent not with his brethren; for he said, Lest peradventure mischief befall him.

5 And the sons of Israel came to buy *corn* among those that came: for the famine was in the land of Canaan.

6 And Joseph *was* the governor over the land, *and* he *it was* that sold to all the people of the land: and Joseph's brethren came, and bowed down themselves before him *with* their faces to the earth.

7 And Joseph saw his brethren, and he knew them, but made himself strange unto them, and spake roughly unto them; and he said unto them, Whence come ye? And they said, From the land of Canaan to buy food.

8 And Joseph knew his brethren, but they knew not him.

9 And Joseph remembered the dreams which he dreamed of them, and said unto them, Ye *are* spies; to see the nakedness of the land ye are come.

10 And they said unto him, Nay, my lord, but to buy food are thy servants come.

11 We *are* all one man's sons; we *are* true *men*, thy servants are no spies.

12 And he said unto them, Nay, but to see the nakedness of the land ye are come.

13 And they said, Thy servants *are* twelve brethren, the sons of one man in the land of Canaan; and, behold, the youngest *is* this day with our father, and one *is* not.

14 And Joseph said unto them, That *is it* that I spake unto you, saying, Ye *are* spies:

15 Hereby ye shall be proved: By the life of Pharaoh ye shall not go forth hence, except your youngest brother come hither.

Cross-references

41 Dan. 6:3

42 Esth. 3:10; 8:2, 8, 15; Dan. 5:7, 29

43 Gen. 42:6; 45:8, 26; Esth. 6:9; Acts 7:10

45 Ex. 2:16; 2Sam. 8:18; 20:26

46 1Sam. 16:21; 1Kgs. 12:6, 8; Dan. 1:19

49 Gen. 22:17; Judg. 7:12; 1Sam. 13:5; Ps. 78:27

50 Gen. 41:45; 46:20; 48:5; 2Sam. 8:18

52 Gen. 49:22

54 Gen. 41:30; Ps. 105:16; Acts 7:11

56 Gen. 42:6; 47:14, 24

57 Deut. 9:28

1 Acts 7:12

2 Gen. 43:8; Ps. 118:17; Isa. 38:1

4 Gen. 42:38

5 Acts 7:11

6 Gen. 37:7; 41:41

9 Gen. 37:5, 9

13 Gen. 37:30; 44:20; Lam. 5:7

15 1Sam. 1:26; 17:55

41:47–54 Pharaoh's dream is literally fulfilled by the seven years of plenty and the seven years of famine.

16 Send one of you, and let him fetch your brother, and ye shall be kept in prison, that your words may be proved, whether *there be any* truth in you: or else by the life of Pharaoh surely ye *are* spies.

17 And he put them all together into ward three days.

18 And Joseph said unto them the third day, This do, and live; *for* I fear God:

19 If ye *be* true *men*, let one of your brethren be bound in the house of your prison: go ye, carry corn for the famine of your houses:

20 But bring your youngest brother unto me; so shall your words be verified, and ye shall not die. And they did so.

21 And they said one to another, We *are* verily guilty concerning our brother, in that we saw the anguish of his soul, when he besought us, and we would not hear; therefore is this distress come upon us.

22 And Reuben answered them, saying, Spake I not unto you, saying, Do not sin against the child; and ye would not hear? therefore, behold, also his blood is required.

23 And they knew not that Joseph understood *them*; for he spake unto them by an interpreter.

24 And he turned himself about from them, and wept; and returned to them again, and communed with them, and took from them Simeon, and bound him before their eyes.

25 Then Joseph commanded to fill their sacks with corn, and to restore every man's money into his sack, and to give them provision for the way: and thus did he unto them.

26 And they laded their asses with the corn, and departed thence.

27 And as one of them opened his sack to give his ass provender in the inn, he espied his money; for, behold, it *was* in his sack's mouth.

28 And he said unto his brethren, My money is restored; and, lo, *it is* even in my sack: and their heart failed *them*, and they were afraid, saying one to another, What *is* this *that* God hath done unto us?

29 And they came unto Jacob their father unto the land of Canaan, and told him all that befell unto them; saying,

30 The man, *who is* the lord of the land, spake roughly to us, and took us for spies of the country.

31 And we said unto him, We *are* true *men*; we are no spies:

32 We *be* twelve brethren, sons of our fa-

ther; one *is* not, and the youngest *is* this day with our father in the land of Canaan.

33 And the man, the lord of the country, said unto us, Hereby shall I know that ye *are* true *men;* leave one of your brethren *here* with me, and take *food for* the famine of your households, and be gone:

34 And bring your youngest brother unto me: then shall I know that ye *are* no spies, but *that* ye *are* true *men: so* will I deliver you your brother, and ye shall traffick in the land.

35 And it came to pass as they emptied their sacks, that, behold, every man's bundle of money *was* in his sack: and when *both* they and their father saw the bundles of money, they were afraid.

36 And Jacob their father said unto them, Me have ye bereaved *of my children:* Joseph *is* not, and Simeon *is* not, and ye will take Benjamin *away:* all these things are against me.

37 And Reuben spake unto his father, saying, Slay my two sons, if I bring him not to thee: deliver him into my hand, and I will bring him to thee again.

38 And he said, My son shall not go down with you; for his brother is dead, and he is left alone: if mischief befall him by the way in the which ye go, then shall ye bring down my grey hairs with sorrow to the grave.

CHAPTER 43
The Brothers' Second Trip to Egypt

1 And the famine *was* sore in the land.

2 And it came to pass, when they had eaten up the corn which they had brought out of Egypt, their father said unto them, Go again, buy us a little food.

3 And Judah spake unto him, saying, The man did solemnly protest unto us, saying, Ye shall not see my face, except your brother *be* with you.

4 If thou wilt send our brother with us, we will go down and buy thee food:

5 But if thou wilt not send *him*, we will not go down: for the man said unto us, Ye shall not see my face, except your brother *be* with you.

6 And Israel said, Wherefore dealt ye *so* ill with me, *as* to tell the man whether ye had yet a brother?

7 And they said, The man asked us straitly of our state, and of our kindred, saying, *Is* your father yet alive? have ye *another* brother? and we told him according to the tenor of these words: could we certainly know that he would say, Bring your brother down?

Center column references

18 Lev. 25:43; Neh. 5:15

20 Gen. 42:34; 43:5; 44:23

21 Job 36:8, 9; Prov. 21:13; Hos. 5:15; Matt. 7:2

22 Gen. 9:5; 37:21; 1Kgs. 2:32; 2Chr. 24:22; Ps. 9:12; Luke 11:50, 51

25 Matt. 5:44; Rom. 12:17, 20, 21

27 Gen. 43:21

30 Gen. 42:7

33 Gen. 42:15, 19, 20

34 Gen. 34:10

35 Gen. 43:21

36 Gen. 43:14

38 Gen. 37:33; 42:4, 13; 44:28, 29

1 Gen. 41:54, 57

3 Gen. 42:20; 44:23

8 And Judah said unto Israel his father, Send the lad with me, and we will arise and go; that we may live, and not die, both we, and thou, *and* also our little ones.

9 I will be surety for him; of my hand shalt thou require him: if I bring him not unto thee, and set him before thee, then let me bear the blame for ever:

10 For except we had lingered, surely now we had returned this second time.

11 And their father Israel said unto them, If *it must be* so now, do this; take of the best fruits in the land in your vessels, and carry down the man a present, a little balm, and a little honey, spices, and myrrh, nuts, and almonds:

12 And take double money in your hand; and the money that was brought again in the mouth of your sacks, carry *it* again in your hand; peradventure it *was* an oversight:

13 Take also your brother, and arise, go again unto the man:

14 And God Almighty give you mercy before the man, that he may send away your other brother, and Benjamin. If I be bereaved *of my children*, I am bereaved.

15 And the men took that present, and they took double money in their hand, and Benjamin; and rose up, and went down to Egypt, and stood before Joseph.

16 And when Joseph saw Benjamin with them, he said to the ruler of his house, Bring *these* men home, and slay, and make ready; for *these* men shall dine with me at noon.

17 And the man did as Joseph bade; and the man brought the men into Joseph's house.

18 And the men were afraid, because they were brought into Joseph's house; and they said, Because of the money that was returned in our sacks at the first time are we brought in; that he may seek occasion against us, and fall upon us, and take us for bondmen, and our asses.

19 And they came near to the steward of Joseph's house, and they communed with him at the door of the house,

20 And said, O sir, we came indeed down at the first time to buy food:

21 And it came to pass, when we came to the inn, that we opened our sacks, and, behold, *every* man's money *was* in the mouth of his sack, our money in full weight: and we have brought it again in our hand.

22 And other money have we brought down in our hands to buy food: we cannot tell who put our money in our sacks.

23 And he said, Peace *be* to you, fear not: your God, and the God of your father, hath given you treasure in your sacks: I had your money. And he brought Simeon out unto them.

24 And the man brought the men into Joseph's house, and gave *them* water, and they washed their feet; and he gave their asses provender.

25 And they made ready the present against Joseph came at noon: for they heard that they should eat bread there.

26 And when Joseph came home, they brought him the present which *was* in their hand into the house, and bowed themselves to him to the earth.

27 And he asked them of *their* welfare, and said, *Is* your father well, the old man of whom ye spake? *Is* he yet alive?

28 And they answered, Thy servant our father *is* in good health, he *is* yet alive. And they bowed down their heads, and made obeisance.

29 And he lifted up his eyes, and saw his brother Benjamin, his mother's son, and said, *Is* this your younger brother, of whom ye spake unto me? And he said, God be gracious unto thee, my son.

30 And Joseph made haste; for his bowels did yearn upon his brother: and he sought *where* to weep; and he entered into *his* chamber, and wept there.

31 And he washed his face, and went out, and refrained himself, and said, Set on bread.

32 And they set on for him by himself, and for them by themselves, and for the Egyptians, which did eat with him, by themselves: because the Egyptians might not eat bread with the Hebrews; for that *is* an abomination unto the Egyptians.

33 And they sat before him, the firstborn according to his birthright, and the youngest according to his youth: and the men marvelled one at another.

34 And he took *and sent* messes unto them from before him: but Benjamin's mess was five times so much as any of theirs. And they drank, and were merry with him.

CHAPTER 44
Joseph's Cup Is Hidden in Benjamin's Sack

1 And he commanded the steward of his house, saying, Fill the men's sacks *with* food, as much as they can carry, and put every man's money in his sack's mouth.

2 And put my cup, the silver cup, in the

9 Gen. 44:32; Phile. 1:18, 19

11 Gen. 32:20; 37:25; Prov. 18:16; Jer. 8:22

12 Gen. 42:25, 35

14 Esth. 4:16

16 Gen. 24:2; 39:4; 44:1; 1Sam. 25:11

18 Job 30:14

20 Gen. 42:3, 10

21 Gen. 42:27, 35

24 Gen. 18:4; 24:32

26 Gen. 37:7, 10

27 Gen. 37:14; 42:11, 13

28 Gen. 37:7, 10

29 Gen. 35:17, 18; 42:13

30 Gen. 42:24; 1Kgs. 3:26

31 Gen. 43:25

32 Gen. 46:34; Ex. 8:26

34 Gen. 45:22; Hag. 1:6; John 2:10

sack's mouth of the youngest, and his corn money. And he did according to the word that Joseph had spoken.

3 As soon as the morning was light, the men were sent away, they and their asses.

4 *And* when they were gone out of the city, *and* not *yet* far off, Joseph said unto his steward, Up, follow after the men; and when thou dost overtake them, say unto them, Wherefore have ye rewarded evil for good?

5 *Is* not this *it* in which my lord drinketh, and whereby indeed he divineth? ye have done evil in so doing.

6 And he overtook them, and he spake unto them these same words.

7 And they said unto him, Wherefore saith my lord these words? God forbid that thy servants should do according to this thing:

8 Behold, the money, which we found in our sacks' mouths, we brought again unto thee out of the land of Canaan: how then should we steal out of thy lord's house silver or gold?

9 With whomsoever of thy servants it be found, both let him die, and we also will be my lord's bondmen.

10 And he said, Now also *let* it *be* according unto your words: he with whom it is found shall be my servant; and ye shall be blameless.

11 Then they speedily took down every man his sack to the ground, and opened every man his sack.

12 And he searched, *and* began at the eldest, and left at the youngest: and the cup was found in Benjamin's sack.

13 Then they rent their clothes, and laded every man his ass, and returned to the city.

14 And Judah and his brethren came to Joseph's house; for he *was* yet there: and they fell before him on the ground.

15 And Joseph said unto them, What deed *is* this that ye have done? wot ye not that such a man as I can certainly divine?

16 And Judah said, What shall we say unto my lord? what shall we speak? or how shall we clear ourselves? God hath found out the iniquity of thy servants: behold, we *are* my lord's servants, both we, and *he* also with whom the cup is found.

17 And he said, God forbid that I should do so: *but* the man in whose hand the cup is found, he shall be my servant; and as for you, get you up in peace unto your father.

18 Then Judah came near unto him, and

said, Oh my lord, let thy servant, I pray thee, speak a word in my lord's ears, and let not thine anger burn against thy servant: for thou *art* even as Pharaoh.

19 My lord asked his servants, saying, Have ye a father, or a brother?

20 And we said unto my lord, We have a father, an old man, and a child of his old age, a little one; and his brother is dead, and he alone is left of his mother, and his father loveth him.

21 And thou saidst unto thy servants, Bring him down unto me, that I may set mine eyes upon him.

22 And we said unto my lord, The lad cannot leave his father: for *if* he should leave his father, *his father* would die.

23 And thou saidst unto thy servants, Except your youngest brother come down with you, ye shall see my face no more.

24 And it came to pass when we came up unto thy servant my father, we told him the words of my lord.

25 And our father said, Go again, *and* buy us a little food.

26 And we said, We cannot go down: if our youngest brother be with us, then will we go down: for we may not see the man's face, except our youngest brother *be* with us.

27 And thy servant my father said unto us, Ye know that my wife bare me two *sons*:

28 And the one went out from me, and I said, Surely he is torn in pieces; and I saw him not since:

29 And if ye take this also from me, and mischief befall him, ye shall bring down my grey hairs with sorrow to the grave.

30 Now therefore when I come to thy servant my father, and the lad *be* not with us; seeing that his life is bound up in the lad's life;

31 It shall come to pass, when he seeth that the lad *is* not *with us*, that he will die: and thy servants shall bring down the grey hairs of thy servant our father with sorrow to the grave.

32 For thy servant became surety for the lad unto my father, saying, If I bring him not unto thee, then I shall bear the blame to my father for ever.

33 Now therefore, I pray thee, let thy servant abide instead of the lad a bondman to my lord; and let the lad go up with his brethren.

34 For how shall I go up to my father, and the lad *be* not with me? lest peradventure I see the evil that shall come on my father.

---

8 Gen. 43:21
9 Gen. 31:32
13 Gen. 37:29, 34; Num. 14:6; 2Sam. 1:11
14 Gen. 37:7
15 Gen. 44:5
16 Gen. 44:9
17 Prov. 17:15
18 Gen. 18:30, 32; Ex. 32:22
20 Gen. 37:3
21 Gen. 42:15, 20
23 Gen. 43:3, 5
25 Gen. 43:2
27 Gen. 46:19
28 Gen. 37:33
29 Gen. 42:36, 38
30 1Sam. 18:1
32 Gen. 43:9
33 Ex. 32:32
34 Ex. 18:8; Job 31:29; Ps. 116:3; 119:143

CHAPTER 45
Joseph Reveals Himself to His Brothers

1 Then Joseph could not refrain himself before all them that stood by him; and he cried, Cause every man to go out from me. And there stood no man with him, while Joseph made himself known unto his brethren.

2 And he wept aloud: and the Egyptians and the house of Pharaoh heard.

3 And Joseph said unto his brethren, I *am* Joseph; doth my father yet live? And his brethren could not answer him; for they were troubled at his presence.

4 And Joseph said unto his brethren, Come near to me, I pray you. And they came near. And he said, I *am* Joseph your brother, whom ye sold into Egypt.

5 Now therefore be not grieved, nor angry with yourselves, that ye sold me hither: for God did send me before you to preserve life.

6 For these two years *hath* the famine *been* in the land: and yet *there are* five years, in the which *there shall* neither *be* earing nor harvest.

7 And God sent me before you to preserve you a posterity in the earth, and to save your lives by a great deliverance.

8 So now *it was* not you *that* sent me hither, but God: and he hath made me a father to Pharaoh, and lord of all his house, and a ruler throughout all the land of Egypt.

9 Haste ye, and go up to my father, and say unto him, Thus saith thy son Joseph, God hath made me lord of all Egypt: come down unto me, tarry not:

10 And thou shalt dwell in the land of Goshen, and thou shalt be near unto me, thou, and thy children, and thy children's children, and thy flocks, and thy herds, and all that thou hast:

11 And there will I nourish thee; for yet *there are* five years of famine; lest thou, and thy household, and all that thou hast, come to poverty.

12 And, behold, your eyes see, and the eyes of my brother Benjamin, that *it is* my mouth that speaketh unto you.

13 And ye shall tell my father of all my glory in Egypt, and of all that ye have seen; and ye shall haste and bring down my father hither.

14 And he fell upon his brother Benjamin's neck, and wept; and Benjamin wept upon his neck.

15 Moreover he kissed all his brethren, and wept upon them: and after that his brethren talked with him.

16 And the fame thereof was heard in Pharaoh's house, saying, Joseph's brethren are come: and it pleased Pharaoh well, and his servants.

17 And Pharaoh said unto Joseph, Say unto thy brethren, This do ye; lade your beasts, and go, get you unto the land of Canaan;

18 And take your father and your households, and come unto me: and I will give you the good of the land of Egypt, and ye shall eat the fat of the land.

19 Now thou art commanded, this do ye; take you wagons out of the land of Egypt for your little ones, and for your wives, and bring your father, and come.

20 Also regard not your stuff; for the good of all the land of Egypt *is* yours.

21 And the children of Israel did so: and Joseph gave them wagons, according to the commandment of Pharaoh, and gave them provision for the way.

22 To all of them he gave each man changes of raiment; but to Benjamin he gave three hundred *pieces* of silver, and five changes of raiment.

23 And to his father he sent after this *manner*; ten asses laden with the good things of Egypt, and ten she asses laden with corn and bread and meat for his father by the way.

24 So he sent his brethren away, and they departed: and he said unto them, See that ye fall not out by the way.

25 And they went up out of Egypt, and came into the land of Canaan unto Jacob their father,

26 And told him, saying, Joseph *is* yet alive, and he *is* governor over all the land of Egypt. And Jacob's heart fainted, for he believed them not.

27 And they told him all the words of Joseph, which he had said unto them: and when he saw the wagons which Joseph had sent to carry him, the spirit of Jacob their father revived:

28 And Israel said, *It is* enough; Joseph my son *is* yet alive: I will go and see him before I die.

---

2 Num. 14:1

3 Job 4:5; 23:15; Matt. 14:26; Mark 6:50; Acts 7:13

4 Gen. 37:28

5 Gen. 50:20; 2 Sam. 16:10, 11; Ps. 105:16, 17; Isa. 40:2; Acts 4:27, 28; 2 Cor. 2:7

8 Gen. 41:43; Judg. 17:10; Job 29:16

10 Gen. 47:1

12 Gen. 42:23

13 Acts 7:14

16 Gen. 41:33

18 Gen. 27:28; Num. 18:12, 29

21 Num. 3:16

22 Gen. 43:34

26 Job 29:24; Ps. 126:1; Luke 24:11, 41

45:5–11 Joseph explains God's purpose in sending him to Egypt to save lives.

45:7 to preserve . . . and to save. Joseph has the family of Israel in mind as well as the Egyptians.

CHAPTER 46

Jacob and His Family Move to Egypt

1 And Israel took his journey with all that he had, and came to Beer-sheba, and offered sacrifices unto the God of his father Isaac.

2 And God spake unto Israel in the visions of the night, and said, Jacob, Jacob. And he said, Here *am* I.

3 And he said, I *am* God, the God of thy father: fear not to go down into Egypt; for I will there make of thee a great nation:

4 I will go down with thee into Egypt; and I will also surely bring thee up *again*: and Joseph shall put his hand upon thine eyes.

5 And Jacob rose up from Beer-sheba: and the sons of Israel carried Jacob their father, and their little ones, and their wives, in the wagons which Pharaoh had sent to carry him.

6 And they took their cattle, and their goods, which they had gotten in the land of Canaan, and came into Egypt, Jacob, and all his seed with him:

7 His sons, and his sons' sons with him, his daughters, and his sons' daughters, and all his seed brought he with him into Egypt.

8 And these *are* the names of the children of Israel, which came into Egypt, Jacob and his sons: Reuben, Jacob's firstborn.

9 And the sons of Reuben; Hanoch, and Phallu, and Hezron, and Carmi.

10 And the sons of Simeon; Jemuel, and Jamin, and Ohad, and Jachin, and Zohar, and Shaul the son of a Canaanitish woman.

11 And the sons of Levi; Gershon, Kohath, and Merari.

12 And the sons of Judah; Er, and Onan, and Shelah, and Pharez, and Zerah: but Er and Onan died in the land of Canaan. And the sons of Pharez were Hezron and Hamul.

13 And the sons of Issachar; Tola, and Phuvah, and Job, and Shimron.

14 And the sons of Zebulun; Sered, and Elon, and Jahleel.

15 These *be* the sons of Leah, which she bare unto Jacob in Padan-aram, with his daughter Dinah: all the souls of his sons and his daughters *were* thirty and three.

16 And the sons of Gad; Ziphion, and Haggi, Shuni, and Ezbon, Eri, and Arodi, and Areli.

17 And the sons of Asher; Jimnah, and Ishuah, and Isui, and Beriah, and Serah their sister: and the sons of Beriah; Heber, and Malchiel.

18 These *are* the sons of Zilpah, whom Laban gave to Leah his daughter, and these she bare unto Jacob, *even* sixteen souls.

19 The sons of Rachel Jacob's wife; Joseph, and Benjamin.

20 And unto Joseph in the land of Egypt were born Manasseh and Ephraim, which Asenath the daughter of Poti-pherah priest of On bare unto him.

21 And the sons of Benjamin *were* Belah, and Becher, and Ashbel, Gera, and Naaman, Ehi, and Rosh, Muppim, and Huppim, and Ard.

22 These *are* the sons of Rachel, which were born to Jacob: all the souls *were* fourteen.

23 And the sons of Dan; Hushim.

24 And the sons of Naphtali; Jahzeel, and Guni, and Jezer, and Shillem.

25 These *are* the sons of Bilhah, which Laban gave unto Rachel his daughter, and she bare these unto Jacob: all the souls *were* seven.

26 All the souls that came with Jacob into Egypt, which came out of his loins, besides Jacob's sons' wives, all the souls *were* threescore and six;

27 And the sons of Joseph, which were born him in Egypt, *were* two souls: all the souls of the house of Jacob, which came into Egypt, *were* threescore and ten.

28 And he sent Judah before him unto Joseph, to direct his face unto Goshen; and they came into the land of Goshen.

29 And Joseph made ready his chariot, and went up to meet Israel his father, to Goshen, and presented himself unto him; and he fell on his neck, and wept on his neck a good while.

30 And Israel said unto Joseph, Now let me die, since I have seen thy face, because thou *art* yet alive.

31 And Joseph said unto his brethren, and unto his father's house, I will go up, and shew Pharaoh, and say unto him, My brethren, and my father's house, which *were* in the land of Canaan, are come unto me;

32 And the men *are* shepherds, for their trade hath been to feed cattle; and they

Cross references

1 Gen. 21:31, 33; 26:24, 25; 28:10, 13; 31:42
2 Gen. 15:1; Job 33:14, 15
3 Gen. 12:2; 28:13; Deut. 26:5
4 Gen. 15:16; 28:15; 48:21; 50:1, 13, 24, 25; Ex. 3:8
5 Gen. 45:19, 21; Acts 7:15
6 Deut. 26:5; Josh. 24:4; Ps. 105:23; Isa. 52:4
8 Ex. 1:1; 6:14; Num. 26:5; 1Chr. 5:1
10 Ex. 6:15; 1Chr. 4:24
11 1Chr. 6:1, 16
12 Gen. 38:3, 7, 10, 29; 1Chr. 2:3, 5; 4:21
13 1Chr. 7:1
16 Num. 26:15, *Zephon*
17 1Chr. 7:30
18 Gen. 29:24; 30:10
19 Gen. 44:27
20 Gen. 41:50
21 1Chr. 7:6; 8:1
23 1Chr. 7:12
24 1Chr. 7:13
25 Gen. 29:29; 30:5, 7
26 Gen. 35:14; Ex. 1:5
27 Deut. 10:22; Acts 7:14

46:2–4 fear not to go down into Egypt. Since Jacob was told to dwell in the land of Canaan and since Abraham and Isaac had bad experiences in Egypt (Gen. 12:10–20; 26:2), Jacob could be afraid of what would happen if he moved to Egypt. Accordingly, the Lord commands Jacob not to fear the move on the basis that even in Egypt God would make a great nation out of him.

46:27 See note on Deuteronomy 32:8.

have brought their flocks, and their herds, and all that they have.

33 And it shall come to pass, when Pharaoh shall call you, and shall say, What *is* your occupation?

34 That ye shall say, Thy servants' trade hath been about cattle from our youth even until now, both we, *and* also our fathers: that ye may dwell in the land of Goshen; for every shepherd *is* an abomination unto the Egyptians.

CHAPTER 47

1 Then Joseph came and told Pharaoh, and said, My father and my brethren, and their flocks, and their herds, and all that they have, are come out of the land of Canaan; and, behold, they *are* in the land of Goshen.

2 And he took some of his brethren, *even* five men, and presented them unto Pharaoh.

3 And Pharaoh said unto his brethren, What *is* your occupation? And they said unto Pharaoh, Thy servants *are* shepherds, both we, *and* also our fathers.

4 They said moreover unto Pharaoh, For to sojourn in the land are we come; for thy servants have no pasture for their flocks; for the famine *is* sore in the land of Canaan: now therefore, we pray thee, let thy servants dwell in the land of Goshen.

5 And Pharaoh spake unto Joseph, saying, Thy father and thy brethren are come unto thee:

6 The land of Egypt *is* before thee; in the best of the land make thy father and brethren to dwell; in the land of Goshen let them dwell: and if thou knowest *any* men of activity among them, then make them rulers over my cattle.

7 And Joseph brought in Jacob his father, and set him before Pharaoh: and Jacob blessed Pharaoh.

8 And Pharaoh said unto Jacob, How old *art* thou?

9 And Jacob said unto Pharaoh, The days of the years of my pilgrimage *are* an hundred and thirty years: few and evil have the days of the years of my life been, and have not attained unto the days of the years of the life of my fathers in the days of their pilgrimage.

10 And Jacob blessed Pharaoh, and went out from before Pharaoh.

11 And Joseph placed his father and his brethren, and gave them a possession in the land of Egypt, in the best of the land, in the

land of Rameses, as Pharaoh had commanded.

12 And Joseph nourished his father, and his brethren, and all his father's household, with bread, according to *their* families.

The Seven Years of Famine

13 And *there was* no bread in all the land; for the famine *was* very sore, so that the land of Egypt and *all* the land of Canaan fainted by reason of the famine.

14 And Joseph gathered up all the money that was found in the land of Egypt, and in the land of Canaan, for the corn which they bought: and Joseph brought the money into Pharaoh's house.

15 And when money failed in the land of Egypt, and in the land of Canaan, all the Egyptians came unto Joseph, and said, Give us bread: for why should we die in thy presence? for the money faileth.

16 And Joseph said, Give your cattle; and I will give you for your cattle, if money fail.

17 And they brought their cattle unto Joseph: and Joseph gave them bread *in exchange* for horses, and for the flocks, and for the cattle of the herds, and for the asses: and he fed them with bread for all their cattle for that year.

18 When that year was ended, they came unto him the second year, and said unto him, We will not hide *it* from my lord, how that our money is spent; my lord also hath our herds of cattle; there is not ought left in the sight of my lord, but our bodies, and our lands:

19 Wherefore shall we die before thine eyes, both we and our land? buy us and our land for bread, and we and our land will be servants unto Pharaoh: and give *us* seed, that we may live, and not die, that the land be not desolate.

20 And Joseph bought all the land of Egypt for Pharaoh; for the Egyptians sold every man his field, because the famine prevailed over them: so the land became Pharaoh's.

21 And as for the people, he removed them to cities from *one* end of the borders of Egypt even to the *other* end thereof.

22 Only the land of the priests bought he not; for the priests had a portion *assigned them* of Pharaoh, and did eat their portion which Pharaoh gave them: wherefore they sold not their lands.

23 Then Joseph said unto the people, Behold, I have bought you this day and your land for Pharaoh: lo, *here is* seed for you, and ye shall sow the land.

---

34 Gen. 30:35; 34:5; 37:12; 43:32; 46:32; Ex. 8:26

1 Gen. 45:10; 46:28, 31

2 Acts 7:13

3 Gen. 46:33, 34

4 Gen. 15:13; 43:1; 46:34; Deut. 26:5; Acts 7:11

6 Gen. 20:15; 47:4

9 Gen. 25:7; 35:28; Job 14:1; Ps. 39:12; Heb. 11:9, 13

10 Gen. 47:7

11 Gen. 47:6; Ex. 1:11; 12:37

12 Gen. 50:21

13 Gen. 41:30; Acts 7:11

14 Gen. 41:56

15 Gen. 47:19

22 Gen. 41:45; 2Sam. 8:18; Ezra 7:24

24 And it shall come to pass in the increase, that ye shall give the fifth *part* unto Pharaoh, and four parts shall be your own, for seed of the field, and for your food, and for them of your households, and for food for your little ones.

25 And they said, Thou hast saved our lives: let us find grace in the sight of my lord, and we will be Pharaoh's servants.

26 And Joseph made it a law over the land of Egypt unto this day, *that* Pharaoh should have the fifth *part*; except the land of the priests only, *which* became not Pharaoh's.

Jacob's Last Wish

27 And Israel dwelt in the land of Egypt, in the country of Goshen; and they had possessions therein, and grew, and multiplied exceedingly.

28 And Jacob lived in the land of Egypt seventeen years: so the whole age of Jacob was an hundred forty and seven years.

29 And the time drew nigh that Israel must die: and he called his son Joseph, and said unto him, If now I have found grace in thy sight, put, I pray thee, thy hand under my thigh, and deal kindly and truly with me; bury me not, I pray thee, in Egypt:

30 But I will lie with my fathers, and thou shalt carry me out of Egypt, and bury me in their buryingplace. And he said, I will do as thou hast said.

31 And he said, Swear unto me. And he sware unto him. And Israel bowed himself upon the bed's head.

CHAPTER 48
Jacob Gives His Blessing to Joseph's Two Sons

1 And it came to pass after these things, that *one* told Joseph, Behold, thy father *is* sick: and he took with him his two sons, Manasseh and Ephraim.

2 And *one* told Jacob, and said, Behold, thy son Joseph cometh unto thee: and Israel strengthened himself, and sat upon the bed.

3 And Jacob said unto Joseph, God Almighty appeared unto me at Luz in the land of Canaan, and blessed me,

4 And said unto me, Behold, I will make

thee fruitful, and multiply thee, and I will make of thee a multitude of people; and will give this land to thy seed after thee *for* an everlasting possession.

5 And now thy two sons, Ephraim and Manasseh, which were born unto thee in the land of Egypt before I came unto thee into Egypt, *are* mine; as Reuben and Simeon, they shall be mine.

6 And thy issue, which thou begettest after them, shall be thine, *and* shall be called after the name of their brethren in their inheritance.

7 And as for me, when I came from Padan, Rachel died by me in the land of Canaan in the way, when yet *there was* but a little way to come unto Ephrath: and I buried her there in the way of Ephrath; the same *is* Beth-lehem.

8 And Israel beheld Joseph's sons, and said, Who *are* these?

9 And Joseph said unto his father, They *are* my sons, whom God hath given me in this *place*. And he said, Bring them, I pray thee, unto me, and I will bless them.

10 Now the eyes of Israel were dim for age, *so that* he could not see. And he brought them near unto him; and he kissed them, and embraced them.

11 And Israel said unto Joseph, I had not thought to see thy face: and, lo, God hath shewed me also thy seed.

12 And Joseph brought them out from between his knees, and he bowed himself with his face to the earth.

13 And Joseph took them both, Ephraim in his right hand toward Israel's left hand, and Manasseh in his left hand toward Israel's right hand, and brought *them* near unto him.

14 And Israel stretched out his right hand, and laid *it* upon Ephraim's head, who *was* the younger, and his left hand upon Manasseh's head, guiding his hands wittingly; for Manasseh *was* the firstborn.

15 And he blessed Joseph, and said, God, before whom my fathers Abraham and Isaac did walk, the God which fed me all my life long unto this day,

16 The Angel which redeemed me from all

Cross references

25 Gen. 33:15

26 Gen. 47:22

27 Gen. 46:3; 47:11

29 Gen. 24:2, 49; 50:25; Deut. 31:14; 1Kgs. 2:1

30 Gen. 49:29; 50:5, 13; 2Sam. 19:37

31 Gen. 48:2; 1Kgs. 1:47; Heb. 11:21

3 Gen. 28:13, 19; 35:6, 9-15

4 Gen. 17:8

5 Gen. 41:50; 46:20; Josh. 13:7; 14:4

7 Gen. 35:9, 16, 19

9 Gen. 27:4; Gen. 33:5

10 Gen. 27:1, 27; Isa. 6:10; 59:1

11 Gen. 45:26

14 Gen. 48:19

15 Gen. 17:1; 24:40; Heb. 11:21

16 Gen. 28:15; 31:11, 13, 24; Num. 26:34, 37; Ps. 34:22; 121:7; Amos 9:12; Acts 15:17

48:3–6 Jacob recounts the Abrahamic promises to Joseph and his two sons, Ephraim and Manasseh.

48:5 thy two sons . . . are mine. Jacob reverses the birth order of Joseph's two sons and says that they are as much his sons as are Reuben and Simeon, Jacob's first two sons (Gen. 29:32–33). Because of their con-

temptible deeds, Reuben (Gen. 35:22) and Simeon (Gen. 34:25) fell from their father's favor.

48:15–16 he blessed Joseph. Jacob blesses Joseph and once again tells him about God's call to redeem him from all evil.

evil, bless the lads; and let my name be named on them, and the name of my fathers Abraham and Isaac; and let them grow into a multitude in the midst of the earth.

17 And when Joseph saw that his father laid his right hand upon the head of Ephraim, it displeased him: and he held up his father's hand, to remove it from Ephraim's head unto Manasseh's head.

18 And Joseph said unto his father, Not so, my father: for this *is* the firstborn; put thy right hand upon his head.

19 And his father refused, and said, I know *it,* my son, I know *it:* he also shall become a people, and he also shall be great: but truly his younger brother shall be greater than he, and his seed shall become a multitude of nations.

20 And he blessed them that day, saying, In thee shall Israel bless, saying, God make thee as Ephraim and as Manasseh: and he set Ephraim before Manasseh.

21 And Israel said unto Joseph, Behold, I die: but God shall be with you, and bring you again unto the land of your fathers.

22 Moreover I have given to thee one portion above thy brethren, which I took out of the hand of the Amorite with my sword and with my bow.

17 Gen. 28:8; 48:14
19 Num. 1:33, 35; 2:19, 21; Deut. 33:17; Rev. 7:6, 8
22 Gen. 15:16 34:28
1 Num. 24:14; Deut. 4:30; 33:1; Isa. 2:2; 39:6; Jer. 23:20; Dan. 2:28, 29; Amos 3:7; Acts 2:17; Heb. 1:2
2 Ps. 34:11
3 Gen. 29:32; Deut. 21:17; Ps. 78:51
4 Gen. 35:22
5 Gen. 29:33, 34; 34:25
6 Gen. 34:26

CHAPTER 49
Jacob Gives a Blessing to All His Sons

1 And Jacob called unto his sons, and said, Gather yourselves together, that I may tell you *that* which shall befall you in the last days.

2 Gather yourselves together, and hear, ye sons of Jacob; and hearken unto Israel your father.

3 Reuben, thou *art* my firstborn, my might, and the beginning of my strength, the excellency of dignity, and the excellency of power:

4 Unstable as water, thou shalt not excel; because thou wentest up to thy father's bed; then defiledst thou *it:* he went up to my couch.

5 Simeon and Levi *are* brethren; instruments of cruelty *are in* their habitations.

6 O my soul, come not thou into their secret; unto their assembly, mine honour, be not thou united: for in their anger they slew a man, and in their selfwill they digged down a wall.

48:16 bless the lads; and let my name be named on them. This is yet another conveyance of the Abrahamic Covenant, specifically to the two sons of Joseph. The tribes of Ephraim and Manasseh were given an inheritance in the Promised Land (Joshua 16—17). Regarding the Angel mentioned here, see the note on Genesis 32:24.

48:19–20 As in the case of Jacob and Esau, God favors the second-born son, Ephraim, over the firstborn, Manasseh.

48:21 but God shall be with you. Over and over we see one of the purposes of prophecy being played out in Genesis—to encourage us that God can be trusted to fulfill His word in the future.

49:1–28 The most densely prophetic portion of Genesis is the overview of the specific destiny of each of Israel's twelve sons. The prophetic utterances are correlated with the characters of each son. It was common in the ancient world for a patriarch to bless his prodigy. Here, however, Jacob both blesses and prophesies concerning each of his twelve sons.

49:1 in the last days. This is the first use in the Bible of this prophetic expression. The context of each occurrence defines what time period is in view. It often refers to the future time of Israel's Tribulation (Deut. 4:30; 31:29; Isa. 2:2; Jer. 23:20; 49:39; Ezek. 38:16; Dan. 2:28;

10:14; Mic. 4:1; Acts 2:17). At other times it refers to the entire church age (Heb. 1:2) or to the conclusion of the church age (1 Tim. 4:1; 2 Tim. 3:1).

49:3–4 Reuben, thou art my firstborn. One custom of the ancient world was that the oldest received a double share of the inheritance. As noted in Genesis 48:4–6 and 1 Chronicles 5:1–2, Joseph replaced Reuben as the favored one, and the birthright was divided between Ephraim and Manasseh.

49:4 Unstable as water. Reuben's instability was exhibited in his incest with Bilhah (Gen. 35:22). As a result, the tribe was isolated in the southern part of Transjordan (Josh. 13:15–23). Reuben's tribe was the first to be carried into captivity by Assyria (Judg. 5:15–16; 1 Chr. 5:26).

49:5–7 Simeon and Levi . . . I will divide them. These two brothers are punished because they acted together in their revenge against Shechem and his people (Gen. 34). Even though Shechem had raped their sister, their response was viewed as cruel. Because of their cruelty, the Lord says He will divide and scatter them. This was fulfilled when it came time to possess the land. Simeon's descendants were the fewest and they were given only a few cities (Joshua 19:1). The tribe of Levi was not given a specific territory, but was scattered to several cities (Joshua 21:1–3).

7 Cursed *be* their anger, for *it was* fierce; and their wrath, for it was cruel: I will divide them in Jacob, and scatter them in Israel.

8 Judah, thou *art he* whom thy brethren shall praise: thy hand *shall be* in the neck of thine enemies; thy father's children shall bow down before thee.

9 Judah *is* a lion's whelp: from the prey, my son, thou art gone up: he stooped down, he couched as a lion, and as an old lion; who shall rouse him up?

10 The sceptre shall not depart from Judah, nor a lawgiver from between his feet, until Shiloh come; and unto him *shall* the gathering of the people *be*.

11 Binding his foal unto the vine, and his ass's colt unto the choice vine; he washed his garments in wine, and his clothes in the blood of grapes:

12 His eyes *shall be* red with wine, and his teeth white with milk.

13 Zebulun shall dwell at the haven of the sea; and he *shall be* for an haven of ships; and his border *shall be* unto Zidon.

14 Issachar *is* a strong ass couching down between two burdens:

15 And he saw that rest *was* good, and the land that *it was* pleasant; and bowed his shoulder to bear, and became a servant unto tribute.

16 Dan shall judge his people, as one of the tribes of Israel.

17 Dan shall be a serpent by the way, an adder in the path, that biteth the horse heels, so that his rider shall fall backward.

18 I have waited for thy salvation, O LORD.

19 Gad, a troop shall overcome him: but he shall overcome at the last.

20 Out of Asher his bread *shall be* fat, and he shall yield royal dainties.

21 Naphtali *is* a hind let loose: he giveth goodly words.

22 Joseph *is* a fruitful bough, *even* a fruitful

Cross references:

7 Josh. 19:1; 21:5-7; 1Chr. 4:24, 39
8 Gen. 27:29; 29:35; Deut. 33:7; 1Chr. 5:2; Ps. 18:40
9 Num. 23:24; 24:9; Hos. 5:14; Rev. 5:5
10 Deut. 28:57; Ps. 60:7; 108:8; Isa. 2:2; 11:1, 10; 55:4, 5; 60:1; Zech. 10:11
13 Deut. 33:18, 19
16 Deut. 33:22
18 Ps. 25:5; 119:166, 174

49:8 whom thy brethren shall praise. This is a play on the meaning of Judah's name, "Let the Lord be praised." Jacob assigns the forfeited leadership to Judah, who interceded on behalf of Benjamin (Gen. 44:18–34). Judah was the most dominant of the twelve tribes (1 Chr. 5:2).

49:9 A lion is an ancient symbol for royalty.

49:10 The sceptre shall not depart . . . until Shiloh come. This verse contains two messianic prophecies. The first prophecy is that the future Messiah will come from the tribe of Judah (Rev. 2:27; 12:5; 19:15). The second prophecy is that the Messiah will come as Shiloh, the "Peaceful one" or "Rest-giver." This verse is a very significant messianic prophecy in which deliverance is clearly promised through a single individual.

49:11–12 Jacob's prophecy includes a testimony to the Millennial blessing of the One who comes through Judah's line. Wine and milk will be commodities during Messiah's rule.

49:13 shall dwell at the haven of the sea. The tribe of Zebulun was situated near the sea and became heavily involved in sea trade.

49:14–15 a strong ass couching down between two burdens. In the ancient world, a strong donkey with a heavy burden pictured forced labor. Issachar's descendants became prosperous through trade. Later, Manasseh came to control part of Issachar's territory (Josh. 17:11).

49:16 Dan shall judge . . . as one of the tribes. Dan struggled to gain recognition among the twelve tribes. Samson was one of the judges that came from the tribe of Dan (Judg. 13:2, 25).

49:17 his rider shall fall backward. Dan means "judge," but this prophecy indicates that he would not live up to this calling. Instead, he would make people fall. A small tribe assigned land close to the Philistines, Dan was warlike and withstood many threats from those around him. Dan is omitted from the list of the twelve tribes comprising the 144,000 "sealed ones" of Israel in the Tribulation (Rev. 7:4–8).

49:18 Jacob pleas for God's deliverance before continuing his prophecy. The negative nature of these prophecies apparently led him to realize that things could be salvaged only by the gracious deliverance of the Lord.

49:19 Gad means "attack." At first, the enemy will overrun Gad, but in the end, Gad will overcome. The tribe of Gad endured many surprise attacks in the land (1 Chr. 5:18–19).

49:20 The tribe of Asher was located in the most fertile part of the land of Israel. They were agriculturally productive. In recognition of this, Deuteronomy 33:24 says that Asher would **dip his foot in** olive **oil.**

49:21 a hind let loose. Deer-like speed and agility enhanced Naphtali's military effort (Judg. 4:6; 5:18). The best known of his descendants was Barak who, through Deborah, won a great military victory over the Canaanites (Judg. 4:6, 15). Naphtali also has a way with words, evidenced by the song Deborah and Barak composed to celebrate the victory (Judg. 5:1–31).

49:22–26 Joseph receives the longest prophetic statement from Jacob, and it concerns Ephraim and Manasseh. His sons will be fruitful and prosperous, though still affected by the hostility and conflict typical of the entire

bough by a well; *whose* branches run over the wall:

23 The archers have sorely grieved him, and shot *at him*, and hated him:

24 But his bow abode in strength, and the arms of his hands were made strong by the hands of the mighty *God* of Jacob; (from thence *is* the shepherd, the stone of Israel:)

25 *Even* by the God of thy father, who shall help thee; and by the Almighty, who shall bless thee with blessings of heaven above, blessings of the deep that lieth under, blessings of the breasts, and of the womb:

26 The blessings of thy father have prevailed above the blessings of my progenitors unto the utmost bound of the everlasting hills: they shall be on the head of Joseph, and on the crown of the head of him that was separate from his brethren.

27 Benjamin shall ravin *as* a wolf: in the morning he shall devour the prey, and at night he shall divide the spoil.

28 All these *are* the twelve tribes of Israel: and this *is it* that their father spake unto them, and blessed them; every one according to his blessing he blessed them.

The Death of Jacob

29 And he charged them, and said unto them, I am to be gathered unto my people: bury me with my fathers in the cave that *is* in the field of Ephron the Hittite,

30 In the cave that *is* in the field of Machpelah, which *is* before Mamre, in the land of Canaan, which Abraham bought with the field of Ephron the Hittite for a possession of a buryingplace.

31 There they buried Abraham and Sarah his wife; there they buried Isaac and Rebekah his wife; and there I buried Leah.

32 The purchase of the field and of the cave that *is* therein *was* from the children of Heth.

33 And when Jacob had made an end of commanding his sons, he gathered up his

feet into the bed, and yielded up the ghost, and was gathered unto his people.

CHAPTER 50
Joseph Comforts His Brothers

1 And Joseph fell upon his father's face, and wept upon him, and kissed him.

2 And Joseph commanded his servants the physicians to embalm his father: and the physicians embalmed Israel.

3 And forty days were fulfilled for him; for so are fulfilled the days of those which are embalmed: and the Egyptians mourned for him threescore and ten days.

4 And when the days of his mourning were past, Joseph spake unto the house of Pharaoh, saying, If now I have found grace in your eyes, speak, I pray you, in the ears of Pharaoh, saying,

5 My father made me swear, saying, Lo, I die: in my grave which I have digged for me in the land of Canaan, there shalt thou bury me. Now therefore let me go up, I pray thee, and bury my father, and I will come again.

6 And Pharaoh said, Go up, and bury thy father, according as he made thee swear.

7 And Joseph went up to bury his father: and with him went up all the servants of Pharaoh, the elders of his house, and all the elders of the land of Egypt,

8 And all the house of Joseph, and his brethren, and his father's house: only their little ones, and their flocks, and their herds, they left in the land of Goshen.

9 And there went up with him both chariots and horsemen: and it was a very great company.

10 And they came to the threshingfloor of Atad, which *is* beyond Jordan, and there they mourned with a great and very sore lamentation: and he made a mourning for his father seven days.

11 And when the inhabitants of the land, the Canaanites, saw the mourning in the floor of Atad, they said, This *is* a grievous mourning to the Egyptians: wherefore the

---

23 Gen. 37:4, 24, 28; 39:20; 42:21; Ps. 118:13

24 Gen. 45:11; 47:12; 50:21; Job 29:20; Ps. 37:15; Ps. 80:1; Ps. 132:2, 5; Isa. 28:16

25 Gen. 17:1; 28:13, 21; 35:3, 11; 43:23; Deut. 33:13

26 Deut. 33:15, 16; Hab. 3:6

27 Num. 23:24; Judg. 20:21, 25; Ezek. 22:25, 27

28 Esth. 8:11; Ezek. 39:10; Zech. 14:1, 7

29 Gen. 15:15; 25:8; Gen. 47:30; Gen. 50:13; 2Sam. 19:37

30 Gen. 23:16

31 Gen. 23:19; 25:9; 35:29

33 Gen. 49:29

1 Gen. 46:4; 2Kgs. 13:14

2 Gen. 50:26; 2Chr. 16:14; Matt. 26:12; Mark 14:8; 16:1; Luke 24:1; John 12:7; 19:39, 40

3 Num. 20:29; Deut. 34:8

4 Esth. 4:2

5 Gen. 47:29

---

family. Greater blessings were predicted for Joseph than for any of the others (vv. 25–26). Samuel descended from Ephraim and Gideon from Manasseh.

49:27 Benjamin is pictured as a ravenous wolf. The warlike tribe of Benjamin was well known for its archers and left-handed slingers (Judg. 20:16; 1 Chr. 8:40; 12:2; 2 Chr. 14:8; 17:17). Israel's second judge was the violent Ehud of Benjamin (Judg. 3:15–23, 26–29). Saul, the first king of Israel (1 Sam. 9:1–2), and Saul, the apostle whose

name was changed to Paul (Phil. 3:5), were both from the tribe of Benjamin.

49:28–29 Jacob's dying words were completely carried out (Gen. 50:12–14).

49:33 gathered unto his people. The same phrase is used of Jacob that was used of Abraham and Isaac before him (Gen. 25:8; 35:29). (See note on Genesis 25:7–8.)

name of it was called Abel-mizraim, which *is* beyond Jordan.

12 And his sons did unto him according as he commanded them:

13 For his sons carried him into the land of Canaan, and buried him in the cave of the field of Machpelah, which Abraham bought with the field for a possession of a burying-place of Ephron the Hittite, before Mamre.

14 And Joseph returned into Egypt, he, and his brethren, and all that went up with him to bury his father, after he had buried his father.

The Death of Joseph

15 And when Joseph's brethren saw that their father was dead, they said, Joseph will peradventure hate us, and will certainly requite us all the evil which we did unto him.

16 And they sent a messenger unto Joseph, saying, Thy father did command before he died, saying,

17 So shall ye say unto Joseph, Forgive, I pray thee now, the trespass of thy brethren, and their sin; for they did unto thee evil: and now, we pray thee, forgive the trespass of the servants of the God of thy father. And Joseph wept when they spake unto him.

18 And his brethren also went and fell down before his face; and they said, Behold, we *be* thy servants.

19 And Joseph said unto them, Fear not: for *am* I in the place of God?

20 But as for you, ye thought evil against me; *but* God meant it unto good, to bring to pass, as *it is* this day, to save much people alive.

21 Now therefore fear ye not: I will nourish you, and your little ones. And he comforted them, and spake kindly unto them.

22 And Joseph dwelt in Egypt, he, and his father's house: and Joseph lived an hundred and ten years.

23 And Joseph saw Ephraim's children of the third *generation*: the children also of Machir the son of Manasseh were brought up upon Joseph's knees.

24 And Joseph said unto his brethren, I die: and God will surely visit you, and bring you out of this land unto the land which he sware to Abraham, to Isaac, and to Jacob.

25 And Joseph took an oath of the children of Israel, saying, God will surely visit you, and ye shall carry up my bones from hence.

26 So Joseph died, *being* an hundred and ten years old: and they embalmed him, and he was put in a coffin in Egypt.

Cross-references

13 Gen. 23:16; 49:29, 30; Acts 7:16

15 Job 15:21, 22

17 Gen. 49:25; Prov. 28:13

18 Gen. 37:7, 10

19 Gen. 45:5; Deut. 32:35; 2Kgs. 5:7; Job 34:29; Rom. 12:19; Heb. 10:30

20 Gen. 45:5, 7; Ps. 56:5; Isa. 10:7; Acts 3:13-15

21 Gen. 34:3; 47:12; Matt. 5:44

23 Gen. 30:3; Num. 32:39; Job 42:16

24 Gen. 15:14, 18; Ex. 3:16, 17; Heb. 11:22

25 Ex. 13:19

50:24 God will surely visit you. Shortly before his death, Joseph prophesies to his descendants that God will return them to the land of promise. The books of Exodus through Joshua detail the fulfillment of this last prophecy in Genesis.

50:25 ye shall carry up my bones. Just as Jacob had insisted on being buried in the Promised Land (Gen. 49:29–30), so too did Joseph. Exodus 13:19 records that Moses took Joseph's bones with him in the Exodus. The bones were later reburied at Shechem in fulfillment of Joseph's wishes (Josh. 24:32).

Exodus

E xodus takes its name from the "exit" of God's chosen people from bondage in Egypt. Seventy people were welcomed into Egypt in Joseph's time and multiplied to well over 1,000,000. Enslaved by Pharaohs who "knew not Joseph" (1:8), the once privileged Israelites are now under the severe bondage of forced labor.

Exodus is the dramatic story of Israel's redemption from slavery by the supernatural power of God and by the blood of the Passover lamb. Divinely chosen to be the great liberator and lawgiver, Moses lived his first forty years as a prince of Egypt, spent forty years in desert exile, then returned to lead and instruct Israel for his final forty years.

The historical section (1—18) details Moses' call at the burning bush, the judgment plagues upon the Egyptians, the miraculous passage through the Red Sea, and the encampment at Sinai. There follows a legislative section (19—24) with the Ten Commandments and the beginning of the Dispensation of Law (19:18) which ended at the cross (Rom. 10:4). A ceremonial section (25—40) concludes the book with descriptions of the Tabernacle, laws for the priesthood, and a wonderful dedication.

Practically everything about the Tabernacle worship has a spiritual or typical application to Christ, who came and "dwelt" or "tabernacled" among us, as the book of Hebrews reveals (Heb. 9:11).

Exodus stands as a monument to the commandments and promises of God. Israel stands as a monument to man's limited obedience and God's limited blessing. Israel's lost opportunities are incalculable. Only when they recognize their promised Messiah and what He did for them on Calvary's cross will they fully receive the fulfillment of all God's promises.

Including these types and other fulfilled prophecies about Israel, Egypt, and the plagues, 487 of the total 1,213 verses are predictive, or 40 percent of the content. Among these there are 69 distinct predictions.

Author
Moses

Date
1440–1400 B.C.

Key Truth
Deliverance

Historic Time
The Exodus from Egypt

Key Verse
3:8
And I am come down to deliver them . . .

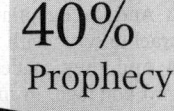

40%
Prophecy

1800 B.C.   1750 B.C.   1700 B.C.   1650 B.C.   1600 B.C.   1550 B.C.   1500 B.C.   1450 B.C.   1400 B.C.

1805
Death of Joseph

1527
Moses in Pharaoh's court

1487
Moses flees to Midian

1447
Exodus from Egypt

1805-1446
Book of Exodus

1407
Entrance into Canaan

1730-1447
Bondage in Egypt begins

Bondage in Egypt ends

1447
The Ten Commandments

CHAPTER 1
A New King in Egypt

1 Now these *are* the names of the children of Israel, which came into Egypt; every man and his household came with Jacob.

2 Reuben, Simeon, Levi, and Judah,

3 Issachar, Zebulun, and Benjamin,

4 Dan, and Naphtali, Gad, and Asher.

5 And all the souls that came out of the loins of Jacob were seventy souls: for Joseph was in Egypt *already*.

6 And Joseph died, and all his brethren, and all that generation.

7 And the children of Israel were fruitful, and increased abundantly, and multiplied, and waxed exceeding mighty; and the land was filled with them.

8 Now there arose up a new king over Egypt, which knew not Joseph.

9 And he said unto his people, Behold, the people of the children of Israel *are* more and mightier than we:

10 Come on, let us deal wisely with them; lest they multiply, and it come to pass, that, when there falleth out any war, they join also unto our enemies, and fight against us, and *so* get them up out of the land.

11 Therefore they did set over them taskmasters to afflict them with their burdens. And they built for Pharaoh treasure cities, Pithom and Raamses.

12 But the more they afflicted them, the more they multiplied and grew. And they were grieved because of the children of Israel.

13 And the Egyptians made the children of Israel to serve with rigour:

14 And they made their lives bitter with hard bondage, in morter, and in brick, and in all manner of service in the field: all their service, wherein they made them serve, *was* with rigour.

15 And the king of Egypt spake to the Hebrew midwives, of which the name of the one *was* Shiphrah, and the name of the other Puah:

16 And he said, When ye do the office of a midwife to the Hebrew women, and see *them* upon the stools; if it *be* a son, then ye shall kill him: but if it *be* a daughter, then she shall live.

17 But the midwives feared God, and did not as the king of Egypt commanded them, but saved the men children alive.

18 And the king of Egypt called for the midwives, and said unto them, Why have ye done this thing, and have saved the men children alive?

19 And the midwives said unto Pharaoh, Because the Hebrew women *are* not as the Egyptian women; for they *are* lively, and are delivered ere the midwives come in unto them.

20 Therefore God dealt well with the midwives: and the people multiplied, and waxed very mighty.

21 And it came to pass, because the midwives feared God, that he made them houses.

22 And Pharaoh charged all his people, saying, Every son that is born ye shall cast into the river, and every daughter ye shall save alive.

CHAPTER 2
Moses Is Born

1 And there went a man of the house of Levi, and took *to wife* a daughter of Levi.

2 And the woman conceived, and bare a son: and when she saw him that he *was a* goodly *child*, she hid him three months.

3 And when she could not longer hide him, she took for him an ark of bulrushes, and daubed it with slime and with pitch, and put the child therein; and she laid *it* in the flags by the river's brink.

4 And his sister stood afar off, to wit what would be done to him.

5 And the daughter of Pharaoh came down to wash *herself* at the river; and her maidens walked along by the river's side; and when she saw the ark among the flags, she sent her maid to fetch it.

6 And when she had opened *it*, she saw the child: and, behold, the babe wept. And she had compassion on him, and said, This *is one* of the Hebrews' children.

7 Then said his sister to Pharaoh's daughter, Shall I go and call to thee a nurse of the Hebrew women, that she may nurse the child for thee?

8 And Pharaoh's daughter said to her, Go. And the maid went and called the child's mother.

9 And Pharaoh's daughter said unto her, Take this child away, and nurse it for me, and I will give *thee* thy wages. And the woman took the child, and nursed it.

10 And the child grew, and she brought him unto Pharaoh's daughter, and he became her son. And she called his name Moses: and she said, Because I drew him out of the water.

Moses Runs Away

11 And it came to pass in those days, when Moses was grown, that he went out unto

---

1 Gen. 46:8; Ex. 6:14

5 Gen. 46:26, 27; Ex. 1:20; Deut. 10:22

6 Gen. 50:26; Acts 7:15

7 Gen. 46:3; Deut. 26:5; Ps. 105:24; Acts 7:17

8 Acts 7:18

9 Ps. 105:24

10 Job 5:13; Ps. 10:2; 83:3, 4; 105:25; Prov. 16:25; 21:30; Acts 7:19

11 Gen. 15:13; 47:11; Ex. 2:11; 3:7; 5:4, 5; Deut. 26:6; Ps. 81:6

14 Ex. 2:23; 6:9; Num. 20:15; Ps. 81:6; Acts 7:19, 34

17 Prov. 16:6; Dan. 3:16, 18; 6:13; Acts 5:29

19 2Sam. 17:19, 20

20 Prov. 11:18; Eccl. 8:12; Isa. 3:10; Heb. 6:10

21 1Sam. 2:35; 2Sam. 7:11, 13, 27, 29; 1Kgs. 2:24; 11:38; Ps. 127:1

22 Ex. 6:20; Num. 26:59; 1Chr. 23:14; Acts 7:19

2 Acts 7:20; Heb. 11:23

4 Ex. 15:20; Num. 26:59

5 Acts 7:21

10 Acts 7:21

11 Ex. 1:11; Acts 7:23, 24; Heb. 11:24-26

his brethren, and looked on their burdens: and he spied an Egyptian smiting an Hebrew, one of his brethren.

12 And he looked this way and that way, and when he saw that *there was* no man, he slew the Egyptian, and hid him in the sand.

13 And when he went out the second day, behold, two men of the Hebrews strove together: and he said to him that did the wrong, Wherefore smitest thou thy fellow?

14 And he said, Who made thee a prince and a judge over us? intendest thou to kill me, as thou killedst the Egyptian? And Moses feared, and said, Surely this thing is known.

15 Now when Pharaoh heard this thing, he sought to slay Moses. But Moses fled from the face of Pharaoh, and dwelt in the land of Midian: and he sat down by a well.

16 Now the priest of Midian had seven daughters: and they came and drew *water*, and filled the troughs to water their father's flock.

17 And the shepherds came and drove them away: but Moses stood up and helped them, and watered their flock.

18 And when they came to Reuel their father, he said, How *is it that* ye are come so soon today?

19 And they said, An Egyptian delivered us out of the hand of the shepherds, and also drew *water* enough for us, and watered the flock.

20 And he said unto his daughters, And where *is* he? why *is it that* ye have left the man? call him, that he may eat bread.

21 And Moses was content to dwell with the man: and he gave Moses Zipporah his daughter.

22 And she bare *him* a son, and he called his name Gershom: for he said, I have been a stranger in a strange land.

23 And it came to pass in process of time, that the king of Egypt died: and the children of Israel sighed by reason of the bondage, and they cried, and their cry came up unto God by reason of the bondage.

24 And God heard their groaning, and God remembered his covenant with Abraham, with Isaac, and with Jacob.

25 And God looked upon the children of Israel, and God had respect unto *them*.

12 Acts 7:24
13 Acts 7:26
15 Heb. 11:27
16 Gen. 24:18; 29:10; Ex. 3:1; 1Sam. 9:11
18 Ex. 3:1; 4:18; 18:1; Num. 10:29
21 Ex. 4:25; 18:2
22 Ex. 18:3; Acts 7:29; Heb. 11:13, 14
23 Ps. 12:5; James 5:4
24 Ex. 6:5; Ps. 105:8, 42
25 Luke 1:25
1 Ex. 2:16; 18:5
2 Deut. 33:16; Isa. 63:9
3 Ps. 111:2; Acts 7:31
4 Deut. 33:16
5 Ex. 19:12; Josh. 5:15; Acts 7:33
6 1Kgs. 19:13; Luke 20:37; Acts 7:32
7 Ex. 1:11; 2:23-25; Ps. 106:44
8 Gen. 50:24; Num. 13:27; Jer. 11:5; 32:22; Ezek. 20:6
9 Ex. 1:11, 13, 14, 22; 2:23
10 Ps. 105:26; Mic. 6:4
11 Ex. 6:12; 1Sam. 18:18; Isa. 6:5, 8; Jer. 1:6
12 Gen. 31:3; Deut. 31:23; Josh. 1:5; Rom. 8:31

CHAPTER 3
God Sends Moses to Egypt

1 Now Moses kept the flock of Jethro his father-in-law, the priest of Midian: and he led the flock to the backside of the desert, and came to the mountain of God, *even to* Horeb.

2 And the angel of the LORD appeared unto him in a flame of fire out of the midst of a bush: and he looked, and, behold, the bush burned with fire, and the bush *was* not consumed.

3 And Moses said, I will now turn aside, and see this great sight, why the bush is not burnt.

4 And when the LORD saw that he turned aside to see, God called unto him out of the midst of the bush, and said, Moses, Moses. And he said, Here *am* I.

5 And he said, Draw not nigh hither: put off thy shoes from off thy feet, for the place whereon thou standest *is* holy ground.

6 Moreover he said, I *am* the God of thy father, the God of Abraham, the God of Isaac, and the God of Jacob. And Moses hid his face; for he was afraid to look upon God.

7 And the LORD said, I have surely seen the affliction of my people which *are* in Egypt, and have heard their cry by reason of their taskmasters; for I know their sorrows;

8 And I am come down to deliver them out of the hand of the Egyptians, and to bring them up out of that land unto a good land and a large, unto a land flowing with milk and honey; unto the place of the Canaanites, and the Hittites, and the Amorites, and the Perizzites, and the Hivites, and the Jebusites.

9 Now therefore, behold, the cry of the children of Israel is come unto me: and I have also seen the oppression wherewith the Egyptians oppress them.

10 Come now therefore, and I will send thee unto Pharaoh, that thou mayest bring forth my people the children of Israel out of Egypt.

11 And Moses said unto God, Who *am* I, that I should go unto Pharaoh, and that I should bring forth the children of Israel out of Egypt?

12 And he said, Certainly I will be with thee; and this *shall be* a token unto thee, that

---

3:8 God promised to bring the children of Israel up out of Egypt into a blessed land then occupied by pagan nations. This was fulfilled after the forty years in the wilderness (caused by their unbelief) under the leadership of Joshua (3:14–17).

I have sent thee: When thou hast brought forth the people out of Egypt, ye shall serve God upon this mountain.

13 And Moses said unto God, Behold, *when* I come unto the children of Israel, and shall say unto them, The God of your fathers hath sent me unto you; and they shall say to me, What *is* his name? what shall I say unto them?

14 And God said unto Moses, I AM THAT I AM: and he said, Thus shalt thou say unto the children of Israel, I AM hath sent me unto you.

15 And God said moreover unto Moses, Thus shalt thou say unto the children of Israel, The LORD God of your fathers, the God of Abraham, the God of Isaac, and the God of Jacob, hath sent me unto you: this *is* my name for ever, and this *is* my memorial unto all generations.

16 Go, and gather the elders of Israel together, and say unto them, The LORD God of your fathers, the God of Abraham, of Isaac, and of Jacob, appeared unto me, saying, I have surely visited you, and *seen* that which is done to you in Egypt:

17 And I have said, I will bring you up out of the affliction of Egypt unto the land of the Canaanites, and the Hittites, and the Amorites, and the Perizzites, and the Hivites, and the Jebusites, unto a land flowing with milk and honey.

18 And they shall hearken to thy voice: and thou shalt come, thou and the elders of Israel, unto the king of Egypt, and ye shall say unto him, The LORD God of the Hebrews hath met with us: and now let us go, we beseech thee, three days' journey into the wilderness, that we may sacrifice to the LORD our God.

19 And I am sure that the king of Egypt will not let you go, no, not by a mighty hand.

20 And I will stretch out my hand, and smite Egypt with all my wonders which I will do in the midst thereof: and after that he will let you go.

21 And I will give this people favour in the sight of the Egyptians: and it shall come to pass, that, when ye go, ye shall not go empty:

22 But every woman shall borrow of her neighbour, and of her that sojourneth in her house, jewels of silver, and jewels of gold, and raiment: and ye shall put *them* upon your sons, and upon your daughters; and ye shall spoil the Egyptians.

CHAPTER 4
God Gives Power to Moses

1 And Moses answered and said, But, behold, they will not believe me, nor hearken unto my voice: for they will say, The LORD hath not appeared unto thee.

2 And the LORD said unto him, What *is* that in thine hand? And he said, A rod.

3 And he said, Cast it on the ground. And he cast it on the ground, and it became a serpent; and Moses fled from before it.

4 And the LORD said unto Moses, Put forth thine hand, and take it by the tail. And he put forth his hand, and caught it, and it became a rod in his hand:

5 That they may believe that the LORD God of their fathers, the God of Abraham, the God of Isaac, and the God of Jacob, hath appeared unto thee.

6 And the LORD said furthermore unto him, Put now thine hand into thy bosom. And he put his hand into his bosom: and when he took it out, behold, his hand *was* leprous as snow.

7 And he said, Put thine hand into thy bosom again. And he put his hand into his bosom again; and plucked it out of his bosom, and, behold, it was turned again as his *other* flesh.

8 And it shall come to pass, if they will not believe thee, neither hearken to the voice of the first sign, that they will believe the voice of the latter sign.

9 And it shall come to pass, if they will not believe also these two signs, neither hearken unto thy voice, that thou shalt take of the water of the river, and pour *it* upon the dry *land*: and the water which thou takest out of the river shall become blood upon the dry *land*.

10 And Moses said unto the LORD, O my Lord, I *am* not eloquent, neither heretofore, nor since thou hast spoken unto thy ser-

Cross-references (center column):

14 Ex. 6:3; John 8:58; 2Cor. 1:20; Heb. 13:8; Rev. 1:4

15 Ps. 135:13; Hos. 12:5

16 Gen. 50:24; Ex. 2:25; 4:29, 31; Luke 1:68

17 Gen. 15:14, 16; Ex. 3:8

18 Ex. 4:31; 5:1, 3; Num. 23:3, 4, 15, 16

19 Ex. 5:2; 7:4

20 Ex. 6:6; 7:1—13:22; Deut. 6:22; Neh. 9:10; Ps. 105:27; 135:9; Jer. 32:20; Acts 7:36

21 Ex. 11:3; 12:36; Ps. 106:46; Prov. 16:7

22 Gen. 15:14; Ex. 11:2; 12:35, 36; Job 27:17; Prov. 13:22; Ezek. 39:10

2 Ex. 4:17, 20

5 Ex. 3:15; 19:9

6 Num. 12:10; 2Kgs. 5:27

7 Num. 12:13, 14; Deut. 32:39; 2Kgs. 5:14; Matt. 8:3

9 Ex. 7:19

10 Ex. 6:12; Jer. 1:6

3:14 I AM. This is one of the three names used by God to define Himself, sometimes translated "Jehovah" (Hebr. *Yahweh*) and found 6,000 times in Scripture. "I AM" literally means "the source" or "the uncaused cause of all things." It is the name Jesus used of Himself that so angered the Jews (John 8:58).

3:15–17 out of the affliction of Egypt . . . unto a land flowing with milk and honey. The God of both the living and the dead predicted the Israelites' deliverance, which was accomplished as He promised at the Exodus.

The Reliability of the Old Testament

By David Moore

The thirty-nine books of the Old Testament were completed around 400 B.C. Since none of the original writings still exist, critics of the Old Testament have often claimed that today's Old Testament is seriously flawed. Is the Old Testament a reliable source of information? After all, it's been translated, retranslated, copied, and recopied multiple-thousands of times by fallible people.

From A.D. 100–500, people called the "Talmudists" produced copies of the Old Testament, a task so sacred that they worked in full Jewish dress and washed their entire body before copying a single word. Every scroll was made of particular materials, and penned in special ink. Not a single word could be written from memory, and, to prevent mistakes, every column had to contain exactly thirty letters. Unfortunately, none of their work remains today.

Following the Talmudists was a time known as the Masoretic Period. Copyists took great care to enumerate, count, and compare, tallying every time a letter of the alphabet occurred in each book. They identified the middle letter and middle word of each book, then the Pentateuch, then the entire Old Testament. If anything didn't match up perfectly, the entire manuscript was destroyed. Until 1947 these were the best copies in existence, but they still left a gap of 1200 to 1500 years between them and the originals. This situation left a lot of room for questions about their accuracy.

> *Bottom line: The text, history, and prophecy are reliable.*

All that changed in 1947 with the discovery of the Dead Sea Scrolls written about 150 B.C. Suddenly, these manuscripts took us at least one thousand years closer to the originals. Critics claimed we would have to make serious revisions to correct scores of errors in our Old Testament, but the Dead Sea Scrolls actually revealed nothing less than the miraculous. On average, experts found only one variation per every 1580 words. Ninety-eight percent of them were simple spelling variations, and none of the variances affected the meaning of the text! Bottom line: The text is reliable.

Archaeology affirms once again that the Old Testament is reliable. For example, critics of the Bible claimed for decades that the Hittites of the Old Testament didn't really exist and that the writers had invented them to establish a literary enemy. All that changed when 1200 years of Hittite history were discovered! Bottom line: This history is reliable.

While both literary discoveries and archaeology support the reliability of the Old Testament, the most amazing affirmation is its fulfilled prophecy. For example, around 700 B.C., the prophet Isaiah predicted that one day a king named Cyrus would issue a decree to rebuild the temple (Isa. 44:28; 45:1), which at that time was still intact. His prediction (160 years before Cyrus or his kingdom existed) seemed ludicrous at the time, since Jerusalem was secure and the temple was intact. About a hundred years later (586 B.C.), a Babylonian king named Nebuchadnezzar destroyed Jerusalem and the temple (2 Kgs. 25:8–10). Then in 539, a king named Cyrus came to power and issued the decree (Ezra 1:1–2). Bottom line: The prophecy is remarkable!

When you read from the Old Testament, you may do so with the absolute assurance that it is the unchanged, uncorrupted, inspired, and authentic word of God.

vant: but I *am* slow of speech, and of a slow tongue.

11 And the LORD said unto him, Who hath made man's mouth? or who maketh the dumb, or deaf, or the seeing, or the blind? have not I the LORD?

12 Now therefore go, and I will be with thy mouth, and teach thee what thou shalt say.

13 And he said, O my Lord, send, I pray thee, by the hand *of him whom* thou wilt send.

14 And the anger of the LORD was kindled against Moses, and he said, *Is* not Aaron the Levite thy brother? I know that he can speak well. And also, behold, he cometh forth to meet thee: and when he seeth thee, he will be glad in his heart.

15 And thou shalt speak unto him, and put words in his mouth: and I will be with thy mouth, and with his mouth, and will teach you what ye shall do.

16 And he shall be thy spokesman unto the people: and he shall be, *even* he shall be to thee instead of a mouth, and thou shalt be to him instead of God.

17 And thou shalt take this rod in thine hand, wherewith thou shalt do signs.

Moses Returns to Egypt

18 And Moses went and returned to Jethro his father-in-law, and said unto him, Let me go, I pray thee, and return unto my brethren which *are* in Egypt, and see whether they be yet alive. And Jethro said to Moses, Go in peace.

19 And the LORD said unto Moses in Midian, Go, return into Egypt: for all the men are dead which sought thy life.

20 And Moses took his wife and his sons, and set them upon an ass, and he returned to the land of Egypt: and Moses took the rod of God in his hand.

21 And the LORD said unto Moses, When thou goest to return into Egypt, see that thou do all those wonders before Pharaoh, which I have put in thine hand: but I will harden his heart, that he shall not let the people go.

22 And thou shalt say unto Pharaoh, Thus saith the LORD, Israel *is* my son, *even* my firstborn:

23 And I say unto thee, Let my son go, that he may serve me: and if thou refuse to let him go, behold, I will slay thy son, *even* thy firstborn.

24 And it came to pass by the way in the inn, that the LORD met him, and sought to kill him.

25 Then Zipporah took a sharp stone, and cut off the foreskin of her son, and cast *it* at his feet, and said, Surely a bloody husband *art* thou to me.

26 So he let him go: then she said, A bloody husband *thou art*, because of the circumcision.

27 And the LORD said to Aaron, Go into the wilderness to meet Moses. And he went, and met him in the mount of God, and kissed him.

28 And Moses told Aaron all the words of the LORD who had sent him, and all the signs which he had commanded him.

29 And Moses and Aaron went and gathered together all the elders of the children of Israel:

30 And Aaron spake all the words which the LORD had spoken unto Moses, and did the signs in the sight of the people.

31 And the people believed: and when they heard that the LORD had visited the children of Israel, and that he had looked upon their affliction, then they bowed their heads and worshipped.

CHAPTER 5
Moses and Aaron Meet Pharaoh

1 And afterward Moses and Aaron went in, and told Pharaoh, Thus saith the LORD God of Israel, Let my people go, that they may hold a feast unto me in the wilderness.

2 And Pharaoh said, Who *is* the LORD, that I should obey his voice to let Israel go? I know not the LORD, neither will I let Israel go.

3 And they said, The God of the Hebrews hath met with us: let us go, we pray thee, three days' journey into the desert, and sacrifice unto the LORD our God; lest he fall upon us with pestilence, or with the sword.

4 And the king of Egypt said unto them, Wherefore do ye, Moses and Aaron, let the people from their works? get you unto your burdens.

5 And Pharaoh said, Behold, the people of the land now *are* many, and ye make them rest from their burdens.

6 And Pharaoh commanded the same day the taskmasters of the people, and their officers, saying,

Cross references (center column)

11 Ps. 94:9

12 Isa. 50:4; Jer. 1:9; Matt. 10:19; Mark 13:11; Luke 12:11, 12; 21:14, 15

13 Jon. 1:3

14 Ex. 4:27; 1Sam. 10:2, 3, 5

15 Ex. 7:1, 2; Num. 22:38; 23:5, 12, 16; Deut. 5:31; 18:18; Isa. 51:16; Jer. 1:9

16 Ex. 7:1; 18:19

17 Ex. 4:2

19 Ex. 2:15, 23; Matt. 2:20

20 Ex. 17:9; Num. 20:8, 9

21 Ex. 3:20; 7:3, 13; 9:12, 35; 10:1; 14:8; Deut. 2:30; Josh. 11:20; Isa. 63:17; John 12:40; Rom. 9:18

22 Jer. 31:9; Hos. 11:1; Rom. 9:4; 2Cor. 6:18; James 1:18

23 Ex. 11:5; 12:29

24 Gen. 17:14; Num. 22:22

25 Josh. 5:2, 3

27 Ex. 3:1; 4:14

28 Ex. 4:8, 9, 15, 16

30 Ex. 4:16

31 Gen. 24:26; Ex. 2:25; 3:7, 16, 18; 4:8, 9; 12:27; 1Chr. 29:20

1 Ex. 10:9

2 Ex. 3:19; 2Kgs. 18:35; Job 21:15

4 Ex. 1:11

5 Ex. 1:7, 9

4:12 go, and I will be with thy mouth. God has given this promise many times to those commissioned to serve Him (see Deut. 31:6; Matt. 28:20; Luke 12:12). This promise was fulfilled throughout the career of Moses.

7 Ye shall no more give the people straw to make brick, as heretofore: let them go and gather straw for themselves.

8 And the tale of the bricks, which they did make heretofore, ye shall lay upon them; ye shall not diminish *ought* thereof: for they *be* idle; therefore they cry, saying, Let us go *and* sacrifice to our God.

9 Let there more work be laid upon the men, that they may labour therein; and let them not regard vain words.

10 And the taskmasters of the people went out, and their officers, and they spake to the people, saying, Thus saith Pharaoh, I will not give you straw.

11 Go ye, get you straw where ye can find it: yet not ought of your work shall be diminished.

12 So the people were scattered abroad throughout all the land of Egypt to gather stubble instead of straw.

13 And the taskmasters hasted *them*, saying, Fulfil your works, *your* daily tasks, as when there was straw.

14 And the officers of the children of Israel, which Pharaoh's taskmasters had set over them, were beaten, *and* demanded, Wherefore have ye not fulfilled your task in making brick both yesterday and today, as heretofore?

15 Then the officers of the children of Israel came and cried unto Pharaoh, saying, Wherefore dealest thou thus with thy servants?

16 There is no straw given unto thy servants, and they say to us, Make brick: and, behold, thy servants *are* beaten; but the fault *is* in thine own people.

17 But he said, Ye *are* idle, *ye are* idle: therefore ye say, Let us go *and* do sacrifice to the LORD.

18 Go therefore now, *and* work; for there shall no straw be given you, yet shall ye deliver the tale of bricks.

19 And the officers of the children of Israel did see *that* they *were* in evil *case*, after it was said, Ye shall not minish *ought* from your bricks of your daily task.

20 And they met Moses and Aaron, who stood in the way, as they came forth from Pharaoh:

21 And they said unto them, The LORD look upon you, and judge; because ye have made

our savour to be abhorred in the eyes of Pharaoh, and in the eyes of his servants, to put a sword in their hand to slay us.

God Promises to Deliver Israel

22 And Moses returned unto the LORD, and said, Lord, wherefore hast thou *so* evil entreated this people? why *is* it *that* thou hast sent me?

23 For since I came to Pharaoh to speak in thy name, he hath done evil to this people; neither hast thou delivered thy people at all.

CHAPTER 6

1 Then the LORD said unto Moses, Now shalt thou see what I will do to Pharaoh: for with a strong hand shall he let them go, and with a strong hand shall he drive them out of his land.

2 And God spake unto Moses, and said unto him, I *am* the LORD:

3 And I appeared unto Abraham, unto Isaac, and unto Jacob, by *the name of* God Almighty, but by my name JEHOVAH was I not known to them.

4 And I have also established my covenant with them, to give them the land of Canaan, the land of their pilgrimage, wherein they were strangers.

5 And I have also heard the groaning of the children of Israel, whom the Egyptians keep in bondage; and I have remembered my covenant.

6 Wherefore say unto the children of Israel, I *am* the LORD, and I will bring you out from under the burdens of the Egyptians, and I will rid you out of their bondage, and I will redeem you with a stretched out arm, and with great judgments:

7 And I will take you to me for a people, and I will be to you a God: and ye shall know that I *am* the LORD your God, which bringeth you out from under the burdens of the Egyptians.

8 And I will bring you in unto the land, concerning the which I did swear to give it to Abraham, to Isaac, and to Jacob; and I will give it you for an heritage: I *am* the LORD.

9 And Moses spake so unto the children of Israel: but they hearkened not unto Moses for anguish of spirit, and for cruel bondage.

10 And the LORD spake unto Moses, saying,

21 Gen. 34:30; Ex. 6:9; 1Sam. 13:4; 27:12; 2Sam. 10:6; 1Chr. 19:6

1 Ex. 3:19, 11:1; 12:31, 33, 39

3 Gen. 17:1; 35:11; 48:3; Ex. 3:14; Ps. 68:4; 83:18; John 8:58; Rev. 1:4

4 Gen. 15:18; 17:4, 7, 8; 28:4

5 Ex. 2:24

6 Ex. 3:17; 6:2, 8, 29; 7:4; 15:13; Deut. 7:8; 26:8; 1Chr. 17:21; Neh. 1:10; Ps. 81:6; 136:11, 12

7 Gen. 17:7, 8; Ex. 5:4, 5; 29:45, 46; Deut. 4:20; 7:6; 14:2; 26:18; 29:13; 2Sam. 7:24; Ps. 81:6; Rev. 21:7

8 Gen. 15:18; 26:3; 28:13; 35:12

9 Ex. 5:21

6:6–8 God promised Israel that they would be brought out of Egypt, delivered from slavery, redeemed as the people of God, brought into the land of promise, and given an inheritance. These promises were all fulfilled in ways that illustrate His faithfulness to those who trust Him.

11 Go in, speak unto Pharaoh king of Egypt, that he let the children of Israel go out of his land.

12 And Moses spake before the LORD, saying, Behold, the children of Israel have not hearkened unto me; how then shall Pharaoh hear me, who *am* of uncircumcised lips?

13 And the LORD spake unto Moses and unto Aaron, and gave them a charge unto the children of Israel, and unto Pharaoh king of Egypt, to bring the children of Israel out of the land of Egypt.

Moses' and Aaron's Family Record

14 These *be* the heads of their fathers' houses: The sons of Reuben the firstborn of Israel; Hanoch, and Pallu, Hezron, and Carmi: these *be* the families of Reuben.

15 And the sons of Simeon; Jemuel, and Jamin, and Ohad, and Jachin, and Zohar, and Shaul the son of a Canaanitish woman: these *are* the families of Simeon.

16 And these *are* the names of the sons of Levi according to their generations; Gershon, and Kohath, and Merari: and the years of the life of Levi *were* an hundred thirty and seven years.

17 The sons of Gershon; Libni, and Shimi, according to their families.

18 And the sons of Kohath; Amram, and Izhar, and Hebron, and Uzziel: and the years of the life of Kohath *were* an hundred thirty and three years.

19 And the sons of Merari; Mahali and Mushi: these *are* the families of Levi according to their generations.

20 And Amram took him Jochebed his father's sister to wife; and she bare him Aaron and Moses: and the years of the life of Amram *were* an hundred and thirty and seven years.

21 And the sons of Izhar; Korah, and Nepheg, and Zichri.

22 And the sons of Uzziel; Mishael, and Elzaphan, and Zithri.

23 And Aaron took him Elisheba, daughter of Amminadab, sister of Naashon, to wife; and she bare him Nadab, and Abihu, Eleazar, and Ithamar.

24 And the sons of Korah; Assir, and Elkanah, and Abiasaph: these *are* the families of the Korhites.

25 And Eleazar Aaron's son took him one of the daughters of Putiel to wife; and she bare him Phinehas: these *are* the heads of the fathers of the Levites according to their families.

26 These *are* that Aaron and Moses, to whom the LORD said, Bring out the children of Israel from the land of Egypt according to their armies.

27 These *are* they which spake to Pharaoh king of Egypt, to bring out the children of Israel from Egypt: these *are* that Moses and Aaron.

Moses and Aaron Return to Pharaoh

28 And it came to pass on the day *when* the LORD spake unto Moses in the land of Egypt,

29 That the LORD spake unto Moses, saying, I *am* the LORD: speak thou unto Pharaoh king of Egypt all that I say unto thee.

30 And Moses said before the LORD, Behold, I *am* of uncircumcised lips, and how shall Pharaoh hearken unto me?

CHAPTER 7

1 And the LORD said unto Moses, See, I have made thee a god to Pharaoh: and Aaron thy brother shall be thy prophet.

2 Thou shalt speak all that I command thee: and Aaron thy brother shall speak unto Pharaoh, that he send the children of Israel out of his land.

3 And I will harden Pharaoh's heart, and multiply my signs and my wonders in the land of Egypt.

4 But Pharaoh shall not hearken unto you, that I may lay my hand upon Egypt, and bring forth mine armies, *and* my people the children of Israel, out of the land of Egypt by great judgments.

5 And the Egyptians shall know that I *am* the LORD, when I stretch forth mine hand upon Egypt, and bring out the children of Israel from among them.

6 And Moses and Aaron did as the LORD commanded them, so did they.

7 And Moses *was* fourscore years old, and Aaron fourscore and three years old, when they spake unto Pharaoh.

8 And the LORD spake unto Moses and unto Aaron, saying,

9 When Pharaoh shall speak unto you, saying, Shew a miracle for you: then thou

Cross references (center column)

12 Ex. 4:10; 6:12, 30; Jer. 1:6
14 Gen. 46:9; 1Chr. 5:3
15 Gen. 46:10; 1Chr. 4:24
16 Gen. 46:11; Num. 3:17; 1Chr. 6:1, 16
17 1Chr. 6:17; 23:7
18 Num. 26:57; 1Chr. 6:2, 18
19 1Chr. 6:19; 23:21
20 Ex. 2:1, 2; Num. 26:59
23 Lev. 10:1; Num. 3:2; 26:60; Ruth 4:19, 20; 1Chr. 2:10; 6:3; 24:1; Matt. 1:4
24 Num. 26:11
25 Num. 25:7, 11; Josh. 24:33
26 Ex. 6:13; 7:4; 12:17, 51; Num. 33:1
27 Ex. 5:1, 3; 6:13; 7:10; 32:7; 33:1; Ps. 77:20
29 Ex. 6:2, 11; 7:2
30 Ex. 4:10; 6:12
1 Ex. 4:16; Jer. 1:10
2 Ex. 4:15
3 Ex. 4:7, 21; 11:9
4 Ex. 6:6; 10:1; 11:9
5 Ex. 3:20; 7:17; 8:22; 14:4, 18; Ps. 9:16
7 Deut. 29:5; 31:2; 34:7; Acts 7:23, 30

7:3 I will harden Pharaoh's heart. No small controversy has arisen from the nine references to Pharaoh hardening his heart while ten times it says that God hardened his heart (4:21–26). Both are true! God's miracles and messages harden or melt the heart of the sinner according to His own will.

shalt say unto Aaron, Take thy rod, and cast *it* before Pharaoh, *and* it shall become a serpent.

10 And Moses and Aaron went in unto Pharaoh, and they did so as the Lord had commanded: and Aaron cast down his rod before Pharaoh, and before his servants, and it became a serpent.

11 Then Pharaoh also called the wise men and the sorcerers: now the magicians of Egypt, they also did in like manner with their enchantments.

12 For they cast down every man his rod, and they became serpents: but Aaron's rod swallowed up their rods.

13 And he hardened Pharaoh's heart, that he hearkened not unto them; as the Lord had said.

The Waters Turned to Blood

14 And the Lord said unto Moses, Pharaoh's heart *is* hardened, he refuseth to let the people go.

15 Get thee unto Pharaoh in the morning; lo, he goeth out unto the water; and thou shalt stand by the river's brink against he come; and the rod which was turned to a serpent shalt thou take in thine hand.

16 And thou shalt say unto him, The Lord God of the Hebrews hath sent me unto thee, saying, Let my people go, that they may serve me in the wilderness: and, behold, hitherto thou wouldest not hear.

17 Thus saith the Lord, In this thou shalt know that I *am* the Lord: behold, I will smite with the rod that *is* in mine hand upon the waters which *are* in the river, and they shall be turned to blood.

18 And the fish that *is* in the river shall die, and the river shall stink; and the Egyptians shall lothe to drink of the water of the river.

19 And the Lord spake unto Moses, Say unto Aaron, Take thy rod, and stretch out thine hand upon the waters of Egypt, upon their streams, upon their rivers, and upon their ponds, and upon all their pools of water, that they may become blood; and *that* there may be blood throughout all the land of Egypt, both in *vessels of* wood, and in *vessels of* stone.

20 And Moses and Aaron did so, as the Lord commanded; and he lifted up the rod, and smote the waters that *were* in the river, in the sight of Pharaoh, and in the sight of his servants; and all the waters that *were* in the river were turned to blood.

21 And the fish that *was* in the river died; and the river stank, and the Egyptians could

not drink of the water of the river; and there was blood throughout all the land of Egypt.

22 And the magicians of Egypt did so with their enchantments: and Pharaoh's heart was hardened, neither did he hearken unto them; as the Lord had said.

23 And Pharaoh turned and went into his house, neither did he set his heart to this also.

24 And all the Egyptians digged round about the river for water to drink; for they could not drink of the water of the river.

25 And seven days were fulfilled, after that the Lord had smitten the river.

CHAPTER 8
The Plague of Frogs

1 And the Lord spake unto Moses, Go unto Pharaoh, and say unto him, Thus saith the Lord, Let my people go, that they may serve me.

2 And if thou refuse to let *them* go, behold, I will smite all thy borders with frogs:

3 And the river shall bring forth frogs abundantly, which shall go up and come into thine house, and into thy bedchamber, and upon thy bed, and into the house of thy servants, and upon thy people, and into thine ovens, and into thy kneadingtroughs:

4 And the frogs shall come up both on thee, and upon thy people, and upon all thy servants.

5 And the Lord spake unto Moses, Say unto Aaron, Stretch forth thine hand with thy rod over the streams, over the rivers, and over the ponds, and cause frogs to come up upon the land of Egypt.

6 And Aaron stretched out his hand over the waters of Egypt; and the frogs came up, and covered the land of Egypt.

7 And the magicians did so with their enchantments, and brought up frogs upon the land of Egypt.

8 Then Pharaoh called for Moses and Aaron, and said, Intreat the Lord, that he may take away the frogs from me, and from my people; and I will let the people go, that they may do sacrifice unto the Lord.

9 And Moses said unto Pharaoh, Glory over me: when shall I intreat for thee, and for thy servants, and for thy people, to destroy the frogs from thee and thy houses, *that* they may remain in the river only?

10 And he said, To morrow. And he said, *Be it* according to thy word: that thou mayest know that *there is* none like unto the Lord our God.

Cross references (center column):

10 Ex. 4:3; Ex. 7:9

11 Gen. 41:8; Ex. 7:22; 8:7, 18; 2Tim. 3:8

13 Ex. 4:21; 7:4

14 Ex. 8:15; 10:1, 20, 27

15 Ex. 4:2, 3; 7:10

16 Ex. 3:12, 18; 5:1, 3

17 Ex. 4:9; 5:2; 7:5; Rev. 16:4, 6

18 Ex. 7:24

19 Ex. 8:5, 6, 16; 9:22; 10:12, 21; 14:21, 26

20 Ex. 17:5; Ps. 78:44; 105:29

21 Ex. 7:18

22 Ex. 7:3, 11

1 Ex. 3:12, 18

2 Ex. 7:14; 9:2; Rev. 16:13

3 Ps. 105:30

5 Ex. 7:19

6 Ps. 78:45; 105:30

7 Ex. 7:11

8 Ex. 9:28; 10:17; Num. 21:7; 1Kgs. 13:6; Acts 8:24

10 Ex. 9:14; Deut. 33:26; 2Sam. 7:22; 1Chr. 17:20; Ps. 86:8; Isa. 46:9; Jer. 10:6, 7

11 And the frogs shall depart from thee and from thy houses, and from thy servants, and from thy people; they shall remain in the river only.

12 And Moses and Aaron went out from Pharaoh: and Moses cried unto the LORD because of the frogs which he had brought against Pharaoh.

13 And the LORD did according to the word of Moses; and the frogs died out of the houses, out of the villages, and out of the fields.

14 And they gathered them together upon heaps: and the land stank.

15 But when Pharaoh saw that there was respite, he hardened his heart, and hearkened not unto them; as the LORD had said.

The Plague of Lice

16 And the LORD said unto Moses, Say unto Aaron, Stretch out thy rod, and smite the dust of the land, that it may become lice throughout all the land of Egypt.

17 And they did so; for Aaron stretched out his hand with his rod, and smote the dust of the earth, and it became lice in man, and in beast; all the dust of the land became lice throughout all the land of Egypt.

18 And the magicians did so with their enchantments to bring forth lice, but they could not: so there were lice upon man, and upon beast.

19 Then the magicians said unto Pharaoh, This *is* the finger of God: and Pharaoh's heart was hardened, and he hearkened not unto them; as the LORD had said.

Swarms of Flies

20 And the LORD said unto Moses, Rise up early in the morning, and stand before Pharaoh; lo, he cometh forth to the water; and say unto him, Thus saith the LORD, Let my people go, that they may serve me.

21 Else, if thou wilt not let my people go, behold, I will send swarms *of flies* upon thee, and upon thy servants, and upon thy people, and into thy houses: and the houses of the Egyptians shall be full of swarms *of flies*, and also the ground whereon they *are*.

22 And I will sever in that day the land of Goshen, in which my people dwell, that no swarms *of flies* shall be there; to the end thou mayest know that I *am* the LORD in the midst of the earth.

23 And I will put a division between my people and thy people: to morrow shall this sign be.

24 And the LORD did so; and there came a grievous swarm *of flies* into the house of Pharaoh, and *into* his servants' houses, and into all the land of Egypt: the land was corrupted by reason of the swarm *of flies*.

25 And Pharaoh called for Moses and for Aaron, and said, Go ye, sacrifice to your God in the land.

26 And Moses said, It is not meet so to do; for we shall sacrifice the abomination of the Egyptians to the LORD our God: lo, shall we sacrifice the abomination of the Egyptians before their eyes, and will they not stone us?

27 We will go three days' journey into the wilderness, and sacrifice to the LORD our God, as he shall command us.

28 And Pharaoh said, I will let you go, that ye may sacrifice to the LORD your God in the wilderness; only ye shall not go very far away: intreat for me.

29 And Moses said, Behold, I go out from thee, and I will intreat the LORD that the swarms *of flies* may depart from Pharaoh, from his servants, and from his people, to morrow: but let not Pharaoh deal deceitfully any more in not letting the people go to sacrifice to the LORD.

30 And Moses went out from Pharaoh, and intreated the LORD.

31 And the LORD did according to the word of Moses; and he removed the swarms *of flies* from Pharaoh, from his servants, and from his people; there remained not one.

32 And Pharaoh hardened his heart at this time also, neither would he let the people go.

CHAPTER 9
The Animals Die

1 Then the LORD said unto Moses, Go in unto Pharaoh, and tell him, Thus saith the LORD God of the Hebrews, Let my people go, that they may serve me.

2 For if thou refuse to let *them* go, and wilt hold them still,

3 Behold, the hand of the LORD is upon thy cattle which *is* in the field, upon the horses, upon the asses, upon the camels, upon the oxen, and upon the sheep: *there shall be* a very grievous murrain.

8:11 The ten plagues of frogs, flies, locusts, water to blood, and so forth, were all literally fulfilled, just as similar plagues of Rev. 6—16 will be literally fulfilled during the Tribulation period.

4 And the LORD shall sever between the cattle of Israel and the cattle of Egypt: and there shall nothing die of all *that is* the children's of Israel.

5 And the LORD appointed a set time, saying, To morrow the LORD shall do this thing in the land.

6 And the LORD did that thing on the morrow, and all the cattle of Egypt died: but of the cattle of the children of Israel died not one.

7 And Pharaoh sent, and, behold, there was not one of the cattle of the Israelites dead. And the heart of Pharaoh was hardened, and he did not let the people go.

The Boils

8 And the LORD said unto Moses and unto Aaron, Take to you handfuls of ashes of the furnace, and let Moses sprinkle it toward the heaven in the sight of Pharaoh.

9 And it shall become small dust in all the land of Egypt, and shall be a boil breaking forth *with* blains upon man, and upon beast, throughout all the land of Egypt.

10 And they took ashes of the furnace, and stood before Pharaoh; and Moses sprinkled it up toward heaven; and it became a boil breaking forth *with* blains upon man, and upon beast.

11 And the magicians could not stand before Moses because of the boils; for the boil was upon the magicians, and upon all the Egyptians.

12 And the LORD hardened the heart of Pharaoh, and he hearkened not unto them; as the LORD had spoken unto Moses.

The Plague of Hail

13 And the LORD said unto Moses, Rise up early in the morning, and stand before Pharaoh, and say unto him, Thus saith the LORD God of the Hebrews, Let my people go, that they may serve me.

14 For I will at this time send all my plagues upon thine heart, and upon thy servants, and upon thy people; that thou mayest know that *there is* none like me in all the earth.

15 For now I will stretch out my hand, that I may smite thee and thy people with pestilence; and thou shalt be cut off from the earth.

16 And in very deed for this *cause* have I raised thee up, for to shew *in* thee my power; and that my name may be declared throughout all the earth.

17 As yet exaltest thou thyself against my people, that thou wilt not let them go?

18 Behold, to morrow about this time I will

4 Ex. 8:22
6 Ps. 78:50
7 Ex. 7:14; 8:32
9 Rev. 16:2
10 Deut. 28:27
11 Ex. 8:18, 19; 2Tim. 3:9
12 Ex. 4:21
13 Ex. 8:20
14 Ex. 8:10
15 Ex. 3:20
16 Ex. 14:17; Prov. 16:4; Rom. 9:17; 1Pet. 2:9

Comparison of Plagues to Vial Judgments

Sixth Egyptian Plague Ex. 9:8–12	First Egyptian Plague Ex. 7:19–21		Ninth Egyptian Plague Ex. 10:21–23			Seventh Egyptian Plague Ex. 9:22–26
Boils	Blood Sea	Blood Rivers	Great Heat	Darkness	Euphrates Dried Up	Great Hail
First Vial Rev. 16:1–2	Second Vial Rev. 16:3	Third Vial Rev. 16:4–7	Fourth Vial Rev. 16:8–9	Fifth Vial Rev. 16:10–11	Sixth Vial Rev. 16:12–16	Seventh Vial Rev. 16:17–21

cause it to rain a very grievous hail, such as hath not been in Egypt since the foundation thereof even until now.

19 Send therefore now, *and* gather thy cattle, and all that thou hast in the field; *for* upon every man and beast which shall be found in the field, and shall not be brought home, the hail shall come down upon them, and they shall die.

20 He that feared the word of the Lord among the servants of Pharaoh made his servants and his cattle flee into the houses:

21 And he that regarded not the word of the Lord left his servants and his cattle in the field.

22 And the Lord said unto Moses, Stretch forth thine hand toward heaven, that there may be hail in all the land of Egypt, upon man, and upon beast, and upon every herb of the field, throughout the land of Egypt.

23 And Moses stretched forth his rod toward heaven: and the Lord sent thunder and hail, and the fire ran along upon the ground; and the Lord rained hail upon the land of Egypt.

24 So there was hail, and fire mingled with the hail, very grievous, such as there was none like it in all the land of Egypt since it became a nation.

25 And the hail smote throughout all the land of Egypt all that *was* in the field, both man and beast; and the hail smote every herb of the field, and brake every tree of the field.

26 Only in the land of Goshen, where the children of Israel *were*, was there no hail.

27 And Pharaoh sent, and called for Moses and Aaron, and said unto them, I have sinned this time: the Lord *is* righteous, and I and my people *are* wicked.

28 Intreat the Lord (for *it is* enough) that there be no *more* mighty thunderings and hail; and I will let you go, and ye shall stay no longer.

29 And Moses said unto him, As soon as I am gone out of the city, I will spread abroad my hands unto the Lord; *and* the thunder shall cease, neither shall there be any more hail; that thou mayest know how that the earth *is* the Lord's.

30 But as for thee and thy servants, I know that ye will not yet fear the Lord God.

31 And the flax and the barley was smitten: for the barley *was* in the ear, and the flax *was* bolled.

32 But the wheat and the rie were not smitten: for they *were* not grown up.

33 And Moses went out of the city from Pharaoh, and spread abroad his hands unto the Lord: and the thunders and hail ceased, and the rain was not poured upon the earth.

34 And when Pharaoh saw that the rain and the hail and the thunders were ceased, he sinned yet more, and hardened his heart, he and his servants.

35 And the heart of Pharaoh was hardened, neither would he let the children of Israel go; as the Lord had spoken by Moses.

CHAPTER 10
Locusts

1 And the Lord said unto Moses, Go in unto Pharaoh: for I have hardened his heart, and the heart of his servants, that I might shew these my signs before him:

2 And that thou mayest tell in the ears of thy son, and of thy son's son, what things I have wrought in Egypt, and my signs which I have done among them; that ye may know how that I *am* the Lord.

3 And Moses and Aaron came in unto Pharaoh, and said unto him, Thus saith the Lord God of the Hebrews, How long wilt thou refuse to humble thyself before me? let my people go, that they may serve me.

4 Else, if thou refuse to let my people go, behold, to morrow will I bring the locusts into thy coast:

5 And they shall cover the face of the earth, that one cannot be able to see the earth: and they shall eat the residue of that which is escaped, which remaineth unto you from the hail, and shall eat every tree which groweth for you out of the field:

6 And they shall fill thy houses, and the houses of all thy servants, and the houses of all the Egyptians; which neither thy fathers, nor thy fathers' fathers have seen, since the day that they were upon the earth unto this day. And he turned himself, and went out from Pharaoh.

7 And Pharaoh's servants said unto him, How long shall this man be a snare unto us? let the men go, that they may serve the Lord their God: knowest thou not yet that Egypt is destroyed?

8 And Moses and Aaron were brought again unto Pharaoh: and he said unto them, Go, serve the Lord your God: *but* who *are* they that shall go?

9 And Moses said, We will go with our young and with our old, with our sons and with our daughters, with our flocks and with our herds will we go; for we *must hold* a feast unto the Lord.

10 And he said unto them, Let the Lord be

21 Ex. 7:23

22 Rev. 16:21

23 Josh. 10:11; Ps. 18:13; 78:47; 105:32; 148:8; Isa. 30:30; Ezek. 38:22; Rev. 8:7

25 Ps. 105:33

26 Ex. 8:22; 9:4, 6; 10:23; 11:7; 12:13; Isa. 32:18, 19

27 Ex. 10:16; 2Chr. 12:6; Ps. 129:4; 145:17; Lam. 1:18; Dan. 9:14

28 Ex. 8:8, 28; 10:17; Ps. 29:3, 4; Acts 8:24

29 1Kgs. 8:22, 38; Ps. 24:1; 143:6; Isa. 1:15; 1Cor. 10:26, 28

30 Isa. 26:10

31 Ruth 1:22; 2:23

33 Ex. 8:12; 9:29

35 Ex. 4:13, 21

1 Ex. 4:21; 7:4, 14

2 Deut. 4:9; Ps. 44:1; 71:18; 78:5; Joel 1:3

3 1Kgs. 21:29; 2Chr. 7:14; 34:27; Job 42:6; Jer. 13:18; James 4:10; 1Pet. 5:6

4 Prov. 30:27; Rev. 9:3

5 Ex. 9:32; 10:15; Joel 1:4; 2:25

6 Ex. 8:3, 21

7 Ex. 23:33; Josh. 23:13; 1Sam. 18:21; Eccl. 7:26; 1Cor. 7:35

9 Ex. 5:1

so with you, as I will let you go, and your little ones: look *to it*; for evil *is* before you.

11 Not so: go now ye *that are* men, and serve the LORD; for that ye did desire. And they were driven out from Pharaoh's presence.

12 And the LORD said unto Moses, Stretch out thine hand over the land of Egypt for the locusts, that they may come up upon the land of Egypt, and eat every herb of the land, *even* all that the hail hath left.

13 And Moses stretched forth his rod over the land of Egypt, and the LORD brought an east wind upon the land all that day, and all *that* night; *and* when it was morning, the east wind brought the locusts.

14 And the locusts went up over all the land of Egypt, and rested in all the coasts of Egypt: very grievous *were they*; before them there were no such locusts as they, neither after them shall be such.

15 For they covered the face of the whole earth, so that the land was darkened; and they did eat every herb of the land, and all the fruit of the trees which the hail had left: and there remained not any green thing in the trees, or in the herbs of the field, through all the land of Egypt.

16 Then Pharaoh called for Moses and Aaron in haste; and he said, I have sinned against the LORD your God, and against you.

17 Now therefore forgive, I pray thee, my sin only this once, and intreat the LORD your God, that he may take away from me this death only.

18 And he went out from Pharaoh, and intreated the LORD.

19 And the LORD turned a mighty strong west wind, which took away the locusts, and cast them into the Red sea; there remained not one locust in all the coasts of Egypt.

20 But the LORD hardened Pharaoh's heart, so that he would not let the children of Israel go.

Three Days of Darkness

21 And the LORD said unto Moses, Stretch out thine hand toward heaven, that there may be darkness over the land of Egypt, even darkness *which* may be felt.

22 And Moses stretched forth his hand toward heaven; and there was a thick darkness in all the land of Egypt three days:

23 They saw not one another, neither rose any from his place for three days: but all the children of Israel had light in their dwellings.

24 And Pharaoh called unto Moses, and

said, Go ye, serve the LORD; only let your flocks and your herds be stayed: let your little ones also go with you.

25 And Moses said, Thou must give us also sacrifices and burnt offerings, that we may sacrifice unto the LORD our God.

26 Our cattle also shall go with us; there shall not an hoof be left behind; for thereof must we take to serve the LORD our God; and we know not with what we must serve the LORD, until we come thither.

27 But the LORD hardened Pharaoh's heart, and he would not let them go.

28 And Pharaoh said unto him, Get thee from me, take heed to thyself, see my face no more; for in *that* day thou seest my face thou shalt die.

29 And Moses said, Thou hast spoken well, I will see thy face again no more.

CHAPTER 11
All Firstborn Must Die

1 And the LORD said unto Moses, Yet will I bring one plague *more* upon Pharaoh, and upon Egypt; afterwards he will let you go hence: when he shall let *you* go, he shall surely thrust you out hence altogether.

2 Speak now in the ears of the people, and let every man borrow of his neighbour, and every woman of her neighbour, jewels of silver, and jewels of gold.

3 And the LORD gave the people favour in the sight of the Egyptians. Moreover the man Moses *was* very great in the land of Egypt, in the sight of Pharaoh's servants, and in the sight of the people.

4 And Moses said, Thus saith the LORD, About midnight will I go out into the midst of Egypt:

5 And all the firstborn in the land of Egypt shall die, from the firstborn of Pharaoh that sitteth upon his throne, even unto the firstborn of the maidservant that *is* behind the mill; and all the firstborn of beasts.

6 And there shall be a great cry throughout all the land of Egypt, such as there was none like it, nor shall be like it any more.

7 But against any of the children of Israel shall not a dog move his tongue, against man or beast: that ye may know how that the LORD doth put a difference between the Egyptians and Israel.

8 And all these thy servants shall come down unto me, and bow down themselves unto me, saying, Get thee out, and all the people that follow thee: and after that I will go out. And he went out from Pharaoh in a great anger.

---

12 Ex. 7:19; 10:5

14 Ps. 78:46; 105:34; Joel 2:2

15 Ex. 10:5; Ps. 105:35

16 Ex. 9:27

17 Ex. 9:28; 1Kgs. 13:6

18 Ex. 8:30

19 Joel 2:20

20 Ex. 4:21; 11:10

21 Ex. 9:22

22 Ps. 105:28

23 Ex. 8:22

24 Ex. 10:8, 10

27 Ex. 4:21; 10:20; 14:4, 8

29 Heb. 11:27

1 Ex. 12:31, 33, 39

2 Ex. 3:22; 12:35

3 Ex. 3:21; 12:36; 2Sam. 7:9; Esth. 9:4; Ps. 106:46

4 Ex. 12:12, 23, 29; Amos 5:17

5 Ex. 12:12, 29; Amos 4:10

6 Ex. 12:30; Amos 5:17

7 Ex. 8:22; Josh. 10:21

8 Ex. 12:33; Judg. 4:10; 8:5; 1Kgs. 20:10; 2Kgs. 3:9

9 And the LORD said unto Moses, Pharaoh shall not hearken unto you; that my wonders may be multiplied in the land of Egypt.
10 And Moses and Aaron did all these wonders before Pharaoh: and the LORD hardened Pharaoh's heart, so that he would not let the children of Israel go out of his land.

CHAPTER 12
The Passover

1 And the LORD spake unto Moses and Aaron in the land of Egypt, saying,
2 This month *shall be* unto you the beginning of months: it *shall be* the first month of the year to you.
3 Speak ye unto all the congregation of Israel, saying, In the tenth *day* of this month they shall take to them every man a lamb, according to the house of *their* fathers, a lamb for an house:
4 And if the household be too little for the lamb, let him and his neighbour next unto his house take *it* according to the number of the souls; every man according to his eating shall make your count for the lamb.
5 Your lamb shall be without blemish, a male of the first year: ye shall take *it* out from the sheep, or from the goats:
6 And ye shall keep it up until the fourteenth day of the same month: and the whole assembly of the congregation of Israel shall kill it in the evening.
7 And they shall take of the blood, and strike *it* on the two side posts and on the upper door post of the houses, wherein they shall eat it.
8 And they shall eat the flesh in that night, roast with fire, and unleavened bread; *and* with bitter *herbs* they shall eat it.
9 Eat not of it raw, nor sodden at all with water, but roast *with* fire; his head with his legs, and with the purtenance thereof.
10 And ye shall let nothing of it remain until the morning; and that which remaineth of it until the morning ye shall burn with fire.
11 And thus shall ye eat it; *with* your loins girded, your shoes on your feet, and your staff in your hand; and ye shall eat it in haste: it *is* the LORD's passover.
12 For I will pass through the land of Egypt this night, and will smite all the firstborn in the land of Egypt, both man and beast; and against all the gods of Egypt I will execute judgment: I *am* the LORD.
13 And the blood shall be to you for a token upon the houses where ye *are*: and when I see the blood, I will pass over you, and the plague shall not be upon you to destroy *you*, when I smite the land of Egypt.
14 And this day shall be unto you for a memorial; and ye shall keep it a feast to the LORD throughout your generations; ye shall keep it a feast by an ordinance for ever.
15 Seven days shall ye eat unleavened bread; even the first day ye shall put away leaven out of your houses: for whosoever eateth leavened bread from the first day until the seventh day, that soul shall be cut off from Israel.
16 And in the first day *there shall be* an holy convocation, and in the seventh day there shall be an holy convocation to you; no manner of work shall be done in them, save *that* which every man must eat, that only may be done of you.
17 And ye shall observe *the feast of* unleavened bread; for in this selfsame day have I brought your armies out of the land of Egypt: therefore shall ye observe this day in your generations by an ordinance for ever.
18 In the first *month*, on the fourteenth day of the month at even, ye shall eat unleavened bread, until the one and twentieth day of the month at even.
19 Seven days shall there be no leaven found in your houses: for whosoever eateth that which is leavened, even that soul shall be cut off from the congregation of Israel, whether he be a stranger, or born in the land.
20 Ye shall eat nothing leavened; in all your habitations shall ye eat unleavened bread.
21 Then Moses called for all the elders of

Cross references:
9 Ex. 3:19; 7:3, 4; 10:1
10 Ex. 10:20, 27; Rom. 2:5; 9:22
2 Ex. 13:4; Deut. 16:1
5 Lev. 22:19-21; 23:12; Mal. 1:8, 14; Heb. 9:14; 1Pet. 1:19
6 Ex. 16:12; Lev. 23:5; Num. 9:3; 28:16; Deut. 16:1, 6
8 Ex. 34:25; Num. 9:11; Deut. 16:3; 1Cor. 5:8
9 Deut. 16:7
10 Ex. 23:18; 34:25
11 Deut. 16:5
12 Ex. 6:2; 11:4, 5; 21:6; 22:28; Num. 33:4; Ps. 82:1, 6; Amos 5:17; John 10:34, 35
14 Ex. 12:24, 43; 13:9, 10; Lev. 23:4, 5; 2Kgs. 23:21
15 Gen. 17:14; Ex. 34:18, 25; Lev. 23:5, 6; Num. 9:13; 28:17; Deut. 16:3, 8; 1Cor. 5:7
16 Lev. 23:7, 8; Num. 28:18, 25
17 Ex. 13:3
18 Lev. 23:5; Num. 28:16
19 Ex. 23:15; 34:18; Num. 9:13; Deut. 16:3; 1Cor. 5:7, 8

12:2 This Passover is the point at which the Jewish calendar began. The time corresponds with our March-April.

12:13–14 The promise of God exempted the families who, in obedience to Him, killed an innocent lamb and placed its blood over the doorpost of their home. By this act of obedience, they would not lose their firstborn; and the sacrificial lamb became a picture of Christ, "the Lamb of God" (John 1:29) who would die for the sins of the world. This Passover was to be a memorial and is to this day celebrated annually by faithful Jews. The fact that they would "keep it a feast by an ordinance for ever" (v. 14) may explain why the Jews during the Millennium will reinstate the sacrificial system. The Passover serves as a perpetual memorial of our eternal deliverance from death by the death of Christ, much as we observe the communion service today as a memorial to His death and Resurrection.

Israel, and said unto them, Draw out and take you a lamb according to your families, and kill the passover.

22 And ye shall take a bunch of hyssop, and dip *it* in the blood that *is* in the bason, and strike the lintel and the two side posts with the blood that *is* in the bason; and none of you shall go out at the door of his house until the morning.

23 For the LORD will pass through to smite the Egyptians; and when he seeth the blood upon the lintel, and on the two side posts, the LORD will pass over the door, and will not suffer the destroyer to come in unto your houses to smite *you*.

24 And ye shall observe this thing for an ordinance to thee and to thy sons for ever.

25 And it shall come to pass, when ye be come to the land which the LORD will give you, according as he hath promised, that ye shall keep this service.

26 And it shall come to pass, when your children shall say unto you, What mean ye by this service?

27 That ye shall say, It *is* the sacrifice of the LORD's passover, who passed over the houses of the children of Israel in Egypt, when he smote the Egyptians, and delivered our houses. And the people bowed the head and worshipped.

28 And the children of Israel went away, and did as the LORD had commanded Moses and Aaron, so did they.

The Death of the Firstborn

29 And it came to pass, that at midnight the LORD smote all the firstborn in the land of Egypt, from the firstborn of Pharaoh that sat on his throne unto the firstborn of the captive that *was* in the dungeon; and all the firstborn of cattle.

30 And Pharaoh rose up in the night, he, and all his servants, and all the Egyptians; and there was a great cry in Egypt; for *there was* not a house where *there was* not one dead.

31 And he called for Moses and Aaron by night, and said, Rise up, *and* get you forth from among my people, both ye and the children of Israel; and go, serve the LORD, as ye have said.

32 Also take your flocks and your herds, as

ye have said, and be gone; and bless me also.

33 And the Egyptians were urgent upon the people, that they might send them out of the land in haste; for they said, We *be* all dead *men*.

34 And the people took their dough before it was leavened, their kneadingtroughs being bound up in their clothes upon their shoulders.

35 And the children of Israel did according to the word of Moses; and they borrowed of the Egyptians jewels of silver, and jewels of gold, and raiment:

36 And the LORD gave the people favour in the sight of the Egyptians, so that they lent unto them *such things as they required.* And they spoiled the Egyptians.

The Long Trip Begins

37 And the children of Israel journeyed from Rameses to Succoth, about six hundred thousand on foot *that were* men, beside children.

38 And a mixed multitude went up also with them; and flocks, and herds, *even* very much cattle.

39 And they baked unleavened cakes of the dough which they brought forth out of Egypt, for it was not leavened; because they were thrust out of Egypt, and could not tarry, neither had they prepared for themselves any victual.

40 Now the sojourning of the children of Israel, who dwelt in Egypt, *was* four hundred and thirty years.

41 And it came to pass at the end of the four hundred and thirty years, even the selfsame day it came to pass, that all the hosts of the LORD went out from the land of Egypt.

42 It *is* a night to be much observed unto the LORD for bringing them out from the land of Egypt: this *is* that night of the LORD to be observed of all the children of Israel in their generations.

43 And the LORD said unto Moses and Aaron, This *is* the ordinance of the passover: There shall no stranger eat thereof:

44 But every man's servant that is bought for money, when thou hast circumcised him, then shall he eat thereof.

45 A foreigner and an hired servant shall not eat thereof.

22 Ex. 12:7; Heb. 11:28
23 Ex. 12:13; 2Sam. 24:16; Ezek. 9:6; 1Cor. 10:10; Heb. 11:28; Rev. 7:3; 9:4
25 Ex. 3:8, 17
26 Ex. 13:8, 14; Deut. 32:7; Josh. 4:6; Ps. 78:6
27 Ex. 4:31; 12:11
28 Heb. 11:28
29 Ex. 4:23; 11:4, 5; Num. 8:17; 33:4; Ps. 78:51; 105:36
30 Ex. 11:6; Prov. 21:13; Amos 5:17; James 2:13
31 Ex. 10:9; 11:1; Ps. 105:38
32 Gen. 27:34; Ex. 10:26
33 Gen. 20:3; Ex. 11:8; Ps. 105:38
36 Gen. 15:14; Ex. 3:21, 22; 11:3; Ps. 105:37
37 Gen. 12:2; 46:3; 47:11; Ex. 38:26; Num. 1:46; 11:21; 33:3, 5
39 Ex. 6:1; 11:1; 12:33
40 Gen. 15:13; Acts 7:6; Gal. 3:17
41 Ex. 7:4; 12:51
42 Deut. 16:6
43 Num. 9:14
44 Gen. 17:12, 13
45 Lev. 22:10

12:41 four hundred thirty years, even the selfsame day. This shows the exact fulfillment of the Abrahamic covenant given 430 years before (Gen. 15:13–16), thirty years under Joseph and his benevolent government and 400 years of bondage.

46 In one house shall it be eaten; thou shalt not carry forth ought of the flesh abroad out of the house; neither shall ye break a bone thereof.

47 All the congregation of Israel shall keep it.

48 And when a stranger shall sojourn with thee, and will keep the passover to the LORD, let all his males be circumcised, and then let him come near and keep it; and he shall be as one that is born in the land: for no uncircumcised person shall eat thereof.

49 One law shall be to him that is homeborn, and unto the stranger that sojourneth among you.

50 Thus did all the children of Israel; as the LORD commanded Moses and Aaron, so did they.

51 And it came to pass the selfsame day, *that* the LORD did bring the children of Israel out of the land of Egypt by their armies.

CHAPTER 13
The Consecration of the Firstborn

1 And the LORD spake unto Moses, saying,

2 Sanctify unto me all the firstborn, whatsoever openeth the womb among the children of Israel, *both* of man and of beast: it *is* mine.

3 And Moses said unto the people, Remember this day, in which ye came out from Egypt, out of the house of bondage; for by strength of hand the LORD brought you out from this *place*: there shall no leavened bread be eaten.

4 This day came ye out in the month Abib.

5 And it shall be when the LORD shall bring thee into the land of the Canaanites, and the Hittites, and the Amorites, and the Hivites, and the Jebusites, which he sware unto thy fathers to give thee, a land flowing with milk and honey, that thou shalt keep this service in this month.

6 Seven days thou shalt eat unleavened bread, and in the seventh day *shall be* a feast to the LORD.

7 Unleavened bread shall be eaten seven days; and there shall no leavened bread be seen with thee, neither shall there be leaven seen with thee in all thy quarters.

8 And thou shalt shew thy son in that day, saying, *This is done* because of that *which* the LORD did unto me when I came forth out of Egypt.

9 And it shall be for a sign unto thee upon thine hand, and for a memorial between thine eyes, that the LORD's law may be in thy mouth: for with a strong hand

hath the LORD brought thee out of Egypt.

10 Thou shalt therefore keep this ordinance in his season from year to year.

11 And it shall be when the LORD shall bring thee into the land of the Canaanites, as he sware unto thee and to thy fathers, and shall give it thee,

12 That thou shalt set apart unto the LORD all that openeth the matrix, and every firstling that cometh of a beast which thou hast; the males *shall be* the LORD's.

13 And every firstling of an ass thou shalt redeem with a lamb; and if thou wilt not redeem it, then thou shalt break his neck: and all the firstborn of man among thy children shalt thou redeem.

14 And it shall be when thy son asketh thee in time to come, saying, What *is* this? that thou shalt say unto him, By strength of hand the LORD brought us out from Egypt, from the house of bondage:

15 And it came to pass, when Pharaoh would hardly let us go, that the LORD slew all the firstborn in the land of Egypt, both the firstborn of man, and the firstborn of beast: therefore I sacrifice to the LORD all that openeth the matrix, being males; but all the firstborn of my children I redeem.

16 And it shall be for a token upon thine hand, and for frontlets between thine eyes: for by strength of hand the LORD brought us forth out of Egypt.

God Leads Them

17 And it came to pass, when Pharaoh had let the people go, that God led them not *through* the way of the land of the Philistines, although that *was* near; for God said, Lest peradventure the people repent when they see war, and they return to Egypt:

18 But God led the people about, *through* the way of the wilderness of the Red sea: and the children of Israel went up harnessed out of the land of Egypt.

19 And Moses took the bones of Joseph with him: for he had straitly sworn the children of Israel, saying, God will surely visit you; and ye shall carry up my bones away hence with you.

20 And they took their journey from Succoth, and encamped in Etham, in the edge of the wilderness.

21 And the LORD went before them by day in a pillar of a cloud, to lead them the way; and by night in a pillar of fire, to give them light; to go by day and night:

22 He took not away the pillar of the cloud

Cross references (center column)

46 Num. 9:12; John 19:33, 36

47 Ex. 12:6; Num. 9:13

48 Num. 9:14

49 Num. 9:14; 15:15, 16; Gal. 3:28

51 Ex. 6:26; 12:41

2 Lev. 27:26; Num. 3:13; 8:16, 17; 18:15; Deut. 15:19; Luke 2:23

3 Ex. 6:1; 12:8, 42; Deut. 16:3

5 Ex. 3:8; 6:8; 12:25, 26

6 Ex. 12:15, 16

8 Ex. 12:26; 13:14

9 Ex. 12:14; 13:16; Num. 15:39; Deut. 6:8; 11:18; Prov. 1:9; Isa. 49:16; Jer. 22:24; Matt. 23:5

12 Ex. 13:2; 22:29; 34:19; Lev. 27:26; Num. 8:17; 18:15; Deut. 15:19; Ezek. 44:30

14 Ex. 12:26; 13:3; Deut. 6:20; Josh. 4:6, 21

15 Ex. 12:29

16 Ex. 13:9

17 Ex. 14:11, 12; Num. 14:1-4; Deut. 17:16

18 Ex. 14:2; Num. 33:6

19 Gen. 50:25; Josh. 24:32; Acts 7:16

21 Ex. 14:19, 24; 40:38; Num. 9:15; 10:34; 14:14; Deut. 1:33; Neh. 9:12, 19; Ps. 78:14; 99:7; 105:39; Isa. 4:5; 1Cor. 10:1

by day, nor the pillar of fire by night, *from* before the people.

CHAPTER 14
God Divides the Waters

1 And the LORD spake unto Moses, saying,

2 Speak unto the children of Israel, that they turn and encamp before Pi-hahiroth, between Migdol and the sea, over against Baal-zephon: before it shall ye encamp by the sea.

3 For Pharaoh will say of the children of Israel, They *are* entangled in the land, the wilderness hath shut them in.

4 And I will harden Pharaoh's heart, that he shall follow after them; and I will be honoured upon Pharaoh, and upon all his host; that the Egyptians may know that I *am* the LORD. And they did so.

5 And it was told the king of Egypt that the people fled: and the heart of Pharaoh and of his servants was turned against the people, and they said, Why have we done this, that we have let Israel go from serving us?

6 And he made ready his chariot, and took his people with him:

7 And he took six hundred chosen chariots, and all the chariots of Egypt, and captains over every one of them.

8 And the LORD hardened the heart of Pharaoh king of Egypt, and he pursued after the children of Israel: and the children of Israel went out with an high hand.

9 But the Egyptians pursued after them, all the horses *and* chariots of Pharaoh, and his horsemen, and his army, and overtook them encamping by the sea, beside Pi-hahiroth, before Baal-zephon.

10 And when Pharaoh drew nigh, the children of Israel lifted up their eyes, and, behold, the Egyptians marched after them; and they were sore afraid: and the children of Israel cried out unto the LORD.

11 And they said unto Moses, Because *there were* no graves in Egypt, hast thou taken us away to die in the wilderness? wherefore hast thou dealt thus with us, to carry us forth out of Egypt?

12 *Is* not this the word that we did tell thee in Egypt, saying, Let us alone, that we may serve the Egyptians? For *it had been* better for us to serve the Egyptians,

than that we should die in the wilderness.

13 And Moses said unto the people, Fear ye not, stand still, and see the salvation of the LORD, which he will shew to you today: for the Egyptians whom ye have seen today, ye shall see them again no more for ever.

14 The LORD shall fight for you, and ye shall hold your peace.

15 And the LORD said unto Moses, Wherefore criest thou unto me? speak unto the children of Israel, that they go forward:

16 But lift thou up thy rod, and stretch out thine hand over the sea, and divide it: and the children of Israel shall go on dry *ground* through the midst of the sea.

17 And I, behold, I will harden the hearts of the Egyptians, and they shall follow them: and I will get me honour upon Pharaoh, and upon all his host, upon his chariots, and upon his horsemen.

18 And the Egyptians shall know that I *am* the LORD, when I have gotten me honour upon Pharaoh, upon his chariots, and upon his horsemen.

19 And the angel of God, which went before the camp of Israel, removed and went behind them; and the pillar of the cloud went from before their face, and stood behind them:

20 And it came between the camp of the Egyptians and the camp of Israel; and it was a cloud and darkness *to them*, but it gave light by night *to these*: so that the one came not near the other all the night.

21 And Moses stretched out his hand over the sea; and the LORD caused the sea to go *back* by a strong east wind all that night, and made the sea dry *land*, and the waters were divided.

22 And the children of Israel went into the midst of the sea upon the dry *ground*: and the waters *were* a wall unto them on their right hand, and on their left.

23 And the Egyptians pursued, and went in after them to the midst of the sea, *even* all Pharaoh's horses, his chariots, and his horsemen.

24 And it came to pass, that in the morning watch the LORD looked unto the host of the Egyptians through the pillar of fire and of the cloud, and troubled the host of the Egyptians,

25 And took off their chariot wheels, that

Cross-references

2 Ex. 13:18; Num. 33:7; Jer. 44:1

3 Ps. 71:11

4 Ex. 4:21; 7:3, 5; 9:16; 14:17, 18; Rom. 9:17, 22, 23

5 Ps. 105:25

7 Ex. 15:4

8 Ex. 6:1; 13:9; 14:4; Num. 33:3

9 Ex. 15:9; Josh. 24:6

10 Josh. 24:7; Neh. 9:9; Ps. 34:17; 107:6

11 Ps. 106:7, 8

12 Ex. 5:21; 6:9

13 2Chr. 20:15, 17; Isa. 41:10, 13, 14

14 Ex. 14:25; Deut. 1:30; 3:22; 20:4; Josh. 10:14, 42; 2Chr. 20:29; Neh. 4:20; Isa. 30:15; 31:4

16 Ex. 7:19; 14:21, 26

17 Ex. 7:3; 14:4, 8

19 Ex. 13:21; 23:20; 32:34; Num. 20:16; Isa. 63:9

20 Isa. 8:14; 2Cor. 4:3

21 Ex. 14:16; 15:8; Josh. 3:16; 4:23; Neh. 9:11; Ps. 66:6; 74:13; 106:9; 114:3; Isa. 63:12

22 Ex. 14:29; 15:19; Num. 33:8; Ps. 66:6; 78:13; Isa. 63:13; Hab. 3:10; 1Cor. 10:1; Heb. 11:29

24 Ps. 77:17

14:4 God was not taken by surprise by Pharaoh's change of heart and warned Moses so he and the Israelites would not be taken unawares.

14:13 This dramatic event was prophesied (revealed in advance) and happened exactly as God predicted.

they drave them heavily: so that the Egyptians said, Let us flee from the face of Israel; for the LORD fighteth for them against the Egyptians.

26 And the LORD said unto Moses, Stretch out thine hand over the sea, that the waters may come again upon the Egyptians, upon their chariots, and upon their horsemen.

27 And Moses stretched forth his hand over the sea, and the sea returned to his strength when the morning appeared; and the Egyptians fled against it; and the LORD overthrew the Egyptians in the midst of the sea.

28 And the waters returned, and covered the chariots, and the horsemen, *and* all the host of Pharaoh that came into the sea after them; there remained not so much as one of them.

29 But the children of Israel walked upon dry *land* in the midst of the sea; and the waters *were* a wall unto them on their right hand, and on their left.

30 Thus the LORD saved Israel that day out of the hand of the Egyptians; and Israel saw the Egyptians dead upon the sea shore.

31 And Israel saw that great work which the LORD did upon the Egyptians: and the people feared the LORD, and believed the LORD, and his servant Moses.

CHAPTER 15
Moses' Song

1 Then sang Moses and the children of Israel this song unto the LORD, and spake, saying, I will sing unto the LORD, for he hath triumphed gloriously: the horse and his rider hath he thrown into the sea.

2 The LORD *is* my strength and song, and he is become my salvation: he *is* my God, and I will prepare him an habitation; my father's God, and I will exalt him.

3 The LORD *is* a man of war: the LORD *is* his name.

4 Pharaoh's chariots and his host hath he cast into the sea: his chosen captains also are drowned in the Red sea.

5 The depths have covered them: they sank into the bottom as a stone.

6 Thy right hand, O LORD, is become glorious in power: thy right hand, O LORD, hath dashed in pieces the enemy.

7 And in the greatness of thine excellency thou hast overthrown them that rose up against thee: thou sentest forth thy wrath, *which* consumed them as stubble.

8 And with the blast of thy nostrils the waters were gathered together, the floods stood upright as an heap, *and* the depths

were congealed in the heart of the sea.

9 The enemy said, I will pursue, I will overtake, I will divide the spoil; my lust shall be satisfied upon them; I will draw my sword, my hand shall destroy them.

10 Thou didst blow with thy wind, the sea covered them: they sank as lead in the mighty waters.

11 Who *is* like unto thee, O LORD, among the gods? who *is* like thee, glorious in holiness, fearful *in* praises, doing wonders?

12 Thou stretchedst out thy right hand, the earth swallowed them.

13 Thou in thy mercy hast led forth the people which thou hast redeemed: thou hast guided *them* in thy strength unto thy holy habitation.

14 The people shall hear, *and* be afraid: sorrow shall take hold on the inhabitants of Palestina.

15 Then the dukes of Edom shall be amazed; the mighty men of Moab, trembling shall take hold upon them; all the inhabitants of Canaan shall melt away.

16 Fear and dread shall fall upon them; by the greatness of thine arm they shall be *as* still as a stone; till thy people pass over, O LORD, till thy people pass over, which thou hast purchased.

17 Thou shalt bring them in, and plant them in the mountain of thine inheritance, *in* the place, O LORD, *which* thou hast made for thee to dwell in, *in* the Sanctuary, O Lord, *which* thy hands have established.

18 The LORD shall reign for ever and ever.

Miriam's Song

19 For the horse of Pharaoh went in with his chariots and with his horsemen into the sea, and the LORD brought again the waters of the sea upon them; but the children of Israel went on dry *land* in the midst of the sea.

20 And Miriam the prophetess, the sister of Aaron, took a timbrel in her hand; and all the women went out after her with timbrels and with dances.

21 And Miriam answered them, Sing ye to the LORD, for he hath triumphed gloriously; the horse and his rider hath he thrown into the sea.

The Bitter Water at Marah

22 So Moses brought Israel from the Red sea, and they went out into the wilderness of Shur; and they went three days in the wilderness, and found no water.

23 And when they came to Marah, they could not drink of the waters of Marah, for

they *were* bitter: therefore the name of it was called Marah.

24 And the people murmured against Moses, saying, What shall we drink?

25 And he cried unto the LORD; and the LORD shewed him a tree, *which* when he had cast into the waters, the waters were made sweet: there he made for them a statute and an ordinance, and there he proved them,

26 And said, If thou wilt diligently hearken to the voice of the LORD thy God, and wilt do that which is right in his sight, and wilt give ear to his commandments, and keep all his statutes, I will put none of these diseases upon thee, which I have brought upon the Egyptians: for I *am* the LORD that healeth thee.

27 And they came to Elim, where *were* twelve wells of water, and threescore and ten palm trees: and they encamped there by the waters.

CHAPTER 16
Manna and Quail

1 And they took their journey from Elim, and all the congregation of the children of Israel came unto the wilderness of Sin, which *is* between Elim and Sinai, on the fifteenth day of the second month after their departing out of the land of Egypt.

2 And the whole congregation of the children of Israel murmured against Moses and Aaron in the wilderness:

3 And the children of Israel said unto them, Would to God we had died by the hand of the LORD in the land of Egypt, when we sat by the flesh pots, *and* when we did eat bread to the full; for ye have brought us forth into this wilderness, to kill this whole assembly with hunger.

4 Then said the LORD unto Moses, Behold, I will rain bread from heaven for you; and the people shall go out and gather a certain rate every day, that I may prove them, whether they will walk in my law, or no.

5 And it shall come to pass, that on the sixth day they shall prepare *that* which they bring in; and it shall be twice as much as they gather daily.

6 And Moses and Aaron said unto all the children of Israel, At even, then ye shall know that the LORD hath brought you out from the land of Egypt:

7 And in the morning, then ye shall see the glory of the LORD; for that he heareth your murmurings against the LORD: and what *are* we, that ye murmur against us?

8 And Moses said, *This shall be,* when the LORD shall give you in the evening flesh to eat, and in the morning bread to the full; for that the LORD heareth your murmurings which ye murmur against him: and what *are* we? your murmurings *are* not against us, but against the LORD.

9 And Moses spake unto Aaron, Say unto all the congregation of the children of Israel, Come near before the LORD: for he hath heard your murmurings.

10 And it came to pass, as Aaron spake unto the whole congregation of the children of Israel, that they looked toward the wilderness, and, behold, the glory of the LORD appeared in the cloud.

11 And the LORD spake unto Moses, saying,

12 I have heard the murmurings of the children of Israel: speak unto them, saying, At even ye shall eat flesh, and in the morning ye shall be filled with bread; and ye shall know that I *am* the LORD your God.

13 And it came to pass, that at even the quails came up, and covered the camp: and in the morning the dew lay round about the host.

14 And when the dew that lay was gone up, behold, upon the face of the wilderness *there lay* a small round thing, *as* small as the hoar frost on the ground.

15 And when the children of Israel saw *it,* they said one to another, It *is* manna: for they wist not what it *was.* And Moses said unto them, This *is* the bread which the LORD hath given you to eat.

16 This *is* the thing which the LORD hath commanded, Gather of it every man according to his eating, an omer for every man, *according to* the number of your persons; take ye every man for *them* which *are* in his tents.

17 And the children of Israel did so, and gathered, some more, some less.

18 And when they did mete *it* with an omer, he that gathered much had nothing over, and he that gathered little had no lack; they gathered every man according to his eating.

19 And Moses said, Let no man leave of it till the morning.

20 Notwithstanding they hearkened not unto Moses; but some of them left of it until the morning, and it bred worms, and stank: and Moses was wroth with them.

21 And they gathered it every morning, every man according to his eating: and when the sun waxed hot, it melted.

22 And it came to pass, *that* on the sixth day they gathered twice as much bread, two omers for one *man*: and all the rulers of the congregation came and told Moses.

Cross references (center column):

24 Ex. 16:2; 17:3

25 Ex. 16:4; Deut. 8:2, 16; Josh. 24:25; Judg. 2:22; 3:1, 4; 2Kgs. 2:21; 4:41; Ps. 66:10; 81:7

26 Ex. 23:25; Deut. 7:12, 15; 28:27, 60; Ps. 41:3, 4; 103:3; 147:3

27 Num. 33:9

1 Num. 33:10, 11; Ezek. 30:15

2 Ex. 15:24; Ps. 106:25; 1Cor. 10:10

3 Num. 11:4, 5; Lam. 4:9

4 Ex. 15:25; Deut. 8:2, 16; Ps. 78:24, 25; 105:40; Prov. 30:8; Matt. 6:11; John 6:31, 32; 1Cor. 10:3

5 Ex. 16:22; Lev. 25:21

6 Ex. 6:7; 16:12, 13; Num. 16:28, 29, 30

7 Ex. 16:10; Num. 16:11; Isa. 35:2; 40:5; John 11:4, 40

8 1Sam. 8:7; Luke 10:16; Rom. 13:2

9 Num. 16:16

10 Ex. 13:21; 16:7; Num. 16:19; 1Kgs. 8:10, 11

13 Num. 11:31; Ps. 78:27, 28; 105:40

15 Num. 11:7; Deut. 8:3; Neh. 9:15; Ps. 78:24; 105:40; John 6:31, 49, 58; 1Cor. 10:3

18 2Cor. 8:15

23 And he said unto them, This *is that* which the LORD hath said, To morrow *is* the rest of the holy sabbath unto the LORD: bake *that* which ye will bake *today,* and seethe that ye will seethe; and that which remaineth over lay up for you to be kept until the morning.

24 And they laid it up till the morning, as Moses bade: and it did not stink, neither was there any worm therein.

25 And Moses said, Eat that today; for today *is* a sabbath unto the LORD: today ye shall not find it in the field.

26 Six days ye shall gather it; but on the seventh day, *which is* the sabbath, in it there shall be none.

27 And it came to pass, *that* there went out *some* of the people on the seventh day for to gather, and they found none.

28 And the LORD said unto Moses, How long refuse ye to keep my commandments and my laws?

29 See, for that the LORD hath given you the sabbath, therefore he giveth you on the sixth day the bread of two days; abide ye every man in his place, let no man go out of his place on the seventh day.

30 So the people rested on the seventh day.

31 And the house of Israel called the name thereof Manna: and it *was* like coriander seed, white; and the taste of it *was* like wafers *made* with honey.

32 And Moses said, This *is* the thing which the LORD commandeth, Fill an omer of it to be kept for your generations; that they may see the bread wherewith I have fed you in the wilderness, when I brought you forth from the land of Egypt.

33 And Moses said unto Aaron, Take a pot, and put an omer full of manna therein, and lay it up before the LORD, to be kept for your generations.

34 As the LORD commanded Moses, so Aaron laid it up before the Testimony, to be kept.

35 And the children of Israel did eat manna forty years, until they came to a land inhabited; they did eat manna, until they came unto the borders of the land of Canaan.

36 Now an omer *is* the tenth *part* of an ephah.

CHAPTER 17
Water Flows from the Rock

1 And all the congregation of the children of Israel journeyed from the wilderness of Sin, after their journeys, according to the commandment of the LORD, and pitched in

23 Gen. 2:3;
Ex. 20:8;
31:15; 35:3;
Lev. 23:3

24 Ex. 16:20

26 Ex. 20:9, 10

28 2Kgs. 17:14; Ps. 78:10, 22; 106:13

31 Num. 11:7, 8

33 Heb. 9:4

35 Ex. 25:16, 21; 40:20; Num. 17:10; 33:38; Deut. 8:2, 3; 10:5; Josh. 5:12; 1Kgs. 8:9; Neh. 9:15, 20, 21; John 6:31, 49

1 Ex. 16:1; Num. 33:12, 14

2 Num. 20:3, 4; Deut. 6:16; Ps. 78:18, 41; Isa. 7:12; Matt. 4:7; 1Cor. 10:9

3 Ex. 16:2

4 Ex. 14:15; 1Sam. 30:6; John 8:59; 10:31

5 Ex. 7:20; Num. 20:8; Ezek. 2:6

6 Num. 20:10, 11; Ps. 78:15, 20; 105:41; 114:8; 1Cor. 10:4

7 Num. 20:13; Ps. 81:7; 95:8; Heb. 3:8

8 Gen. 36:12; Num. 24:20; Deut. 25:17; 1Sam. 15:2

9 Ex. 4:20; Acts 7:45; Heb. 4:8

11 James 5:16

14 Ex. 34:27; Num. 24:20; Deut. 25:19; 1Sam. 5:3, 7; 30:1, 17; 2Sam. 8:12; Ezra 9:14

Rephidim: and *there was* no water for the people to drink.

2 Wherefore the people did chide with Moses, and said, Give us water that we may drink. And Moses said unto them, Why chide ye with me? wherefore do ye tempt the LORD?

3 And the people thirsted there for water; and the people murmured against Moses, and said, Wherefore *is* this *that* thou hast brought us up out of Egypt, to kill us and our children and our cattle with thirst?

4 And Moses cried unto the LORD, saying, What shall I do unto this people? they be almost ready to stone me.

5 And the LORD said unto Moses, Go on before the people, and take with thee of the elders of Israel; and thy rod, wherewith thou smotest the river, take in thine hand, and go.

6 Behold, I will stand before thee there upon the rock in Horeb; and thou shalt smite the rock, and there shall come water out of it, that the people may drink. And Moses did so in the sight of the elders of Israel.

7 And he called the name of the place Massah, and Meribah, because of the chiding of the children of Israel, and because they tempted the LORD, saying, Is the LORD among us, or not?

The First Battle

8 Then came Amalek, and fought with Israel in Rephidim.

9 And Moses said unto Joshua, Choose us out men, and go out, fight with Amalek: to morrow I will stand on the top of the hill with the rod of God in mine hand.

10 So Joshua did as Moses had said to him, and fought with Amalek: and Moses, Aaron, and Hur went up to the top of the hill.

11 And it came to pass, when Moses held up his hand, that Israel prevailed: and when he let down his hand, Amalek prevailed.

12 But Moses' hands *were* heavy; and they took a stone, and put *it* under him, and he sat thereon; and Aaron and Hur stayed up his hands, the one on the one side, and the other on the other side; and his hands were steady until the going down of the sun.

13 And Joshua discomfited Amalek and his people with the edge of the sword.

14 And the LORD said unto Moses, Write this *for* a memorial in a book, and rehearse *it* in the ears of Joshua: for I will utterly put

out the remembrance of Amalek from under heaven.

15 And Moses built an altar, and called the name of it Jehovah-nissi:

16 For he said, Because the LORD hath sworn *that* the LORD *will have* war with Amalek from generation to generation.

CHAPTER 18
The First Judges

1 When Jethro, the priest of Midian, Moses' father-in-law, heard of all that God had done for Moses, and for Israel his people, *and* that the LORD had brought Israel out of Egypt;

2 Then Jethro, Moses' father-in-law, took Zipporah, Moses' wife, after he had sent her back,

3 And her two sons; of which the name of the one *was* Gershom; for he said, I have been an alien in a strange land:

4 And the name of the other *was* Eliezer; for the God of my father, *said he, was* mine help, and delivered me from the sword of Pharaoh:

5 And Jethro, Moses' father-in-law, came with his sons and his wife unto Moses into the wilderness, where he encamped at the mount of God:

6 And he said unto Moses, I thy father-in-law Jethro am come unto thee, and thy wife, and her two sons with her.

7 And Moses went out to meet his father-in-law, and did obeisance, and kissed him; and they asked each other of *their* welfare; and they came into the tent.

8 And Moses told his father-in-law all that the LORD had done unto Pharaoh and to the Egyptians for Israel's sake, *and* all the travail that had come upon them by the way, and how the LORD delivered them.

9 And Jethro rejoiced for all the goodness which the LORD had done to Israel, whom he had delivered out of the hand of the Egyptians.

10 And Jethro said, Blessed *be* the LORD, who hath delivered you out of the hand of the Egyptians, and out of the hand of Pharaoh, who hath delivered the people from under the hand of the Egyptians.

11 Now I know that the LORD *is* greater than all gods: for in the thing wherein they dealt proudly *he was* above them.

12 And Jethro, Moses' father-in-law, took a

burnt offering and sacrifices for God: and Aaron came, and all the elders of Israel, to eat bread with Moses' father-in-law before God.

13 And it came to pass on the morrow, that Moses sat to judge the people: and the people stood by Moses from the morning unto the evening.

14 And when Moses' father-in-law saw all that he did to the people, he said, What *is* this thing that thou doest to the people? why sittest thou thyself alone, and all the people stand by thee from morning unto even?

15 And Moses said unto his father-in-law, Because the people come unto me to inquire of God:

16 When they have a matter, they come unto me; and I judge between one and another, and I do make *them* known the statutes of God, and his laws.

17 And Moses' father-in-law said unto him, The thing that thou doest *is* not good.

18 Thou wilt surely wear away, both thou, and this people that *is* with thee: for this thing *is* too heavy for thee; thou art not able to perform it thyself alone.

19 Hearken now unto my voice, I will give thee counsel, and God shall be with thee: Be thou for the people to Godward, that thou mayest bring the causes unto God:

20 And thou shalt teach them ordinances and laws, and shalt shew them the way wherein they must walk, and the work that they must do.

21 Moreover thou shalt provide out of all the people able men, such as fear God, men of truth, hating covetousness; and place *such* over them, *to be* rulers of thousands, *and* rulers of hundreds, rulers of fifties, and rulers of tens:

22 And let them judge the people at all seasons: and it shall be, *that* every great matter they shall bring unto thee, but every small matter they shall judge: so shall it be easier for thyself, and they shall bear *the burden* with thee.

23 If thou shalt do this thing, and God command thee *so*, then thou shalt be able to endure, and all this people shall also go to their place in peace.

24 So Moses hearkened to the voice of his father-in-law, and did all that he had said.

25 And Moses chose able men out of all Israel, and made them heads over the people,

---

Center reference column:

15 Judg. 6:24

1 Ex. 2:16; 3:1; Ps. 105:5, 43; 106:2, 8

2 Ex. 4:26

3 Ex. 2:22; Acts 7:29

5 Ex. 3:1, 12

7 1Kgs. 2:19; 2Sam. 11:7

8 Gen. 44:34; Num. 20:14; Ps. 78:42; 81:7; 106:10; 107:2

10 Gen. 14:20; 2Sam. 18:28; Luke 1:68

11 Ex. 1:10, 16, 22; 5:2, 7; 14:8, 18; 2Chr. 2:5; Ps. 95:3; 97:9; 135:5

12 1Cor. 10:18, 21, 31

15 Lev. 24:12; Num. 15:34

16 Deut. 17:8; Acts 18:15; 1Cor. 6:1

18 Num. 11:14, 17; Deut. 1:9, 12

19 Ex. 3:12; 4:16; 20:19; Deut. 5:5

20 Deut. 4:1, 5; 5:1; 6:1, 2; 7:11; Ps. 143:8

21 Deut. 1:15, 16, 18; Ezek. 18:8; Acts 6:3

22 Ex. 18:26; Lev. 24:11; Num. 11:17; 15:33; 27:2; 36:1; Deut. 1:17; 17:8

23 Gen. 18:33; 30:25; Ex. 16:29; 18:18; 2Sam. 19:39

25 Deut. 1:15; Acts 6:5

17:14 Just as God predicted, the memory of the Amalekites, who were once a great nation, has been so destroyed, that since the eighth century B.C., no evidence of them has ever been found.

rulers of thousands, rulers of hundreds, rulers of fifties, and rulers of tens.

26 And they judged the people at all seasons: the hard causes they brought unto Moses, but every small matter they judged themselves.

27 And Moses let his father-in-law depart; and he went his way into his own land.

CHAPTER 19
Mount Sinai

1 In the third month, when the children of Israel were gone forth out of the land of Egypt, the same day came they *into* the wilderness of Sinai.

2 For they were departed from Rephidim, and were come *to* the desert of Sinai, and had pitched in the wilderness; and there Israel camped before the mount.

3 And Moses went up unto God, and the LORD called unto him out of the mountain, saying, Thus shalt thou say to the house of Jacob, and tell the children of Israel;

4 Ye have seen what I did unto the Egyptians, and *how* I bare you on eagles' wings, and brought you unto myself.

5 Now therefore, if ye will obey my voice indeed, and keep my covenant, then ye shall be a peculiar treasure unto me above all people: for all the earth *is* mine:

6 And ye shall be unto me a kingdom of priests, and an holy nation. These *are* the words which thou shalt speak unto the children of Israel.

7 And Moses came and called for the elders of the people, and laid before their faces all these words which the LORD commanded him.

8 And all the people answered together, and said, All that the LORD hath spoken we will do. And Moses returned the words of the people unto the LORD.

9 And the LORD said unto Moses, Lo, I come unto thee in a thick cloud, that the people may hear when I speak with thee, and believe thee for ever. And Moses told the words of the people unto the LORD.

10 And the LORD said unto Moses, Go unto

26 Ex. 18:22; Job 29:16
27 Num. 10:29, 30
1 Num. 33:15
3 Ex. 3:4; 20:21; Acts 7:38
4 Deut. 29:2; 32:11; Isa. 63:9; Rev. 12:14
5 Deut. 5:2
6 1Cor. 3:17; 1Thess. 5:27; 1Pet. 2:5, 9; Rev. 1:6; 5:10; 20:6
8 Ex. 24:3, 7; Deut. 5:27; 26:17
9 Ex. 19:16; Deut. 4:11, 12, 36
10 Gen. 35:2; Ex. 19:14; Lev. 11:44, 45; 15:5; Heb. 10:22
11 Ex. 19:16, 18; 34:5; Deut. 33:2
12 Heb. 12:20
15 Ex. 19:11; 1Sam. 21:4, 5; Zech. 7:3; 1Cor. 7:5
16 Ex. 19:19; 40:34; 2Chr. 5:14; Ps. 77:18; Rev. 1:10; 4:1, 5; 8:5; 11:19
18 Ex. 3:2; 24:17; 2Chr. 7:1–3; Heb. 12:26; Rev. 15:8
19 Ex. 19:13; Neh. 9:13; Ps. 81:7; Heb. 12:21
21 Ex. 3:5; 1Sam. 6:19

the people, and sanctify them today and to morrow, and let them wash their clothes,

11 And be ready against the third day: for the third day the LORD will come down in the sight of all the people upon mount Sinai.

12 And thou shalt set bounds unto the people round about, saying, Take heed to yourselves, *that ye go not* up into the mount, or touch the border of it: whosoever toucheth the mount shall be surely put to death:

13 There shall not an hand touch it, but he shall surely be stoned, or shot through; whether *it be* beast or man, it shall not live: when the trumpet soundeth long, they shall come up to the mount.

14 And Moses went down from the mount unto the people, and sanctified the people; and they washed their clothes.

15 And he said unto the people, Be ready against the third day: come not at *your* wives.

16 And it came to pass on the third day in the morning, that there were thunders and lightnings, and a thick cloud upon the mount, and the voice of the trumpet exceeding loud; so that all the people that *was* in the camp trembled.

17 And Moses brought forth the people out of the camp to meet with God; and they stood at the nether part of the mount.

18 And mount Sinai was altogether on a smoke, because the LORD descended upon it in fire: and the smoke thereof ascended as the smoke of a furnace, and the whole mount quaked greatly.

19 And when the voice of the trumpet sounded long, and waxed louder and louder, Moses spake, and God answered him by a voice.

20 And the LORD came down upon mount Sinai, on the top of the mount: and the LORD called Moses *up* to the top of the mount; and Moses went up.

21 And the LORD said unto Moses, Go down, charge the people, lest they break through unto the LORD to gaze, and many of them perish.

22 And let the priests also, which come near

19:1–8 The Mosaic covenant is contemporaneous with the Dispensation of Law. This significant passage introduces one of the longest dispensations in Scripture, almost 1500 years. It runs from the giving of the Ten Commandments to the promised redeemer, Jesus Christ. Keeping the law cannot save anyone, but God promised to bless those who did keep it and curse those who did not. The history of Israel is a perfect example of the fulfillment of that promise; when they obeyed Him, they enjoyed His blessing and bountiful provision. When they disobeyed Him, particularly in the worship of other gods, He cursed them with the worst periods of bondage in their history. The Mosaic covenant did not make the Abrahamic covenant obsolete, but rather supplemented it.

to the LORD, sanctify themselves, lest the LORD break forth upon them.

23 And Moses said unto the LORD, The people cannot come up to mount Sinai: for thou chargedst us, saying, Set bounds about the mount, and sanctify it.

24 And the LORD said unto him, Away, get thee down, and thou shalt come up, thou, and Aaron with thee: but let not the priests and the people break through to come up unto the LORD, lest he break forth upon them.

25 So Moses went down unto the people, and spake unto them.

CHAPTER 20
The Ten Commandments

1 And God spake all these words, saying,

2 I *am* the LORD thy God, which have brought thee out of the land of Egypt, out of the house of bondage.

3 Thou shalt have no other gods before me.

4 Thou shalt not make unto thee any graven image, or any likeness *of any thing* that *is* in heaven above, or that *is* in the earth beneath, or that *is* in the water under the earth:

5 Thou shalt not bow down thyself to them, nor serve them: for I the LORD thy God *am* a jealous God, visiting the iniquity of the fathers upon the children unto the third and fourth *generation* of them that hate me;

6 And shewing mercy unto thousands of them that love me, and keep my commandments.

7 Thou shalt not take the name of the LORD thy God in vain; for the LORD will not hold him guiltless that taketh his name in vain.

8 Remember the sabbath day, to keep it holy.

9 Six days shalt thou labour, and do all thy work:

10 But the seventh day *is* the sabbath of the LORD thy God: *in it* thou shalt not do any work, thou, nor thy son, nor thy daughter, thy manservant, nor thy maidservant, nor thy cattle, nor thy stranger that *is* within thy gates:

11 For *in* six days the LORD made heaven and earth, the sea, and all that in them *is*, and rested the seventh day: wherefore the LORD blessed the sabbath day, and hallowed it.

12 Honour thy father and thy mother: that thy days may be long upon the land which the LORD thy God giveth thee.

13 Thou shalt not kill.

14 Thou shalt not commit adultery.

15 Thou shalt not steal.

16 Thou shalt not bear false witness against thy neighbour.

17 Thou shalt not covet thy neighbour's house, thou shalt not covet thy neighbour's wife, nor his manservant, nor his maidservant, nor his ox, nor his ass, nor any thing that *is* thy neighbour's.

18 And all the people saw the thunderings, and the lightnings, and the noise of the trumpet, and the mountain smoking: and when the people saw *it*, they removed, and stood afar off.

19 And they said unto Moses, Speak thou with us, and we will hear: but let not God speak with us, lest we die.

20 And Moses said unto the people, Fear not: for God is come to prove you, and that his fear may be before your faces, that ye sin not.

21 And the people stood afar off, and Moses drew near unto the thick darkness where God *was*.

Instructions for Building an Altar

22 And the LORD said unto Moses, Thus thou shalt say unto the children of Israel, Ye have seen that I have talked with you from heaven.

23 Ye shall not make with me gods of silver, neither shall ye make unto you gods of gold.

24 An altar of earth thou shalt make unto me, and shalt sacrifice thereon thy burnt offerings, and thy peace offerings, thy sheep, and thine oxen: in all places where I record my name I will come unto thee, and I will bless thee.

25 And if thou wilt make me an altar of stone, thou shalt not build it of hewn stone: for if thou lift up thy tool upon it, thou hast polluted it.

26 Neither shalt thou go up by steps unto mine altar, that thy nakedness be not discovered thereon.

CHAPTER 21
The Treatment of Servants

1 Now these *are* the judgments which thou shalt set before them.

2 If thou buy an Hebrew servant, six years he shall serve: and in the seventh he shall go out free for nothing.

3 If he came in by himself, he shall go out by himself: if he were married, then his wife shall go out with him.

4 If his master have given him a wife, and she have born him sons or daughters; the

---

3 Deut. 5:7; 6:14; 2Kgs. 17:35; Jer. 25:6; 35:15

4 Lev. 26:1; Deut. 4:16; 5:8; 27:15; Ps. 97:7

5 Ex. 34:7, 14; Deut. 4:24; 6:15; Nah. 1:2

7 Ex. 23:1; Lev. 19:12; Deut. 5:11; Ps. 15:4; Mic. 6:11; Matt. 5:33

8 Ex. 31:13, 14; Lev. 19:3, 30; 26:2; Deut. 5:12

11 Gen. 2:2

12 Lev. 19:3; Matt. 15:4; Luke 18:20; Eph. 6:2

13 Deut. 5:17; Matt. 5:21; Rom. 13:9

14 Deut. 5:18; Matt. 5:27

15 Lev. 19:11; 1Thess. 4:6

16 Ex. 23:1; Deut. 5:20; 19:16; Matt. 19:18

17 Mic. 2:2; Hab. 2:9; Luke 12:15; Acts 20:33; Rom. 7:7; 13:9; Heb. 13:5

18 Ex. 19:18; Heb. 12:18; Rev. 1:10, 12

19 Gal. 3:19, 20; Heb. 12:19

22 Deut. 4:36; Neh. 9:13

23 2Cor. 6:14-16

24 Deut. 12:5, 11, 21

1 Ex. 24:3, 4; Deut. 4:14; 6:1

2 Lev. 25:39, 40, 41; Deut. 15:12; Jer. 34:14

wife and her children shall be her master's, and he shall go out by himself.

5 And if the servant shall plainly say, I love my master, my wife, and my children; I will not go out free:

6 Then his master shall bring him unto the judges; he shall also bring him to the door, or unto the door post; and his master shall bore his ear through with an aul; and he shall serve him for ever.

7 And if a man sell his daughter to be a maidservant, she shall not go out as the menservants do.

8 If she please not her master, who hath betrothed her to himself, then shall he let her be redeemed: to sell her unto a strange nation he shall have no power, seeing he hath dealt deceitfully with her.

9 And if he have betrothed her unto his son, he shall deal with her after the manner of daughters.

10 If he take him another *wife*; her food, her raiment, and her duty of marriage, shall he not diminish.

11 And if he do not these three unto her, then shall she go out free without money.

Laws against Violence

12 He that smiteth a man, so that he die, shall be surely put to death.

13 And if a man lie not in wait, but God deliver *him* into his hand; then I will appoint thee a place whither he shall flee.

14 But if a man come presumptuously upon his neighbour, to slay him with guile; thou shalt take him from mine altar, that he may die.

15 And he that smiteth his father, or his mother, shall be surely put to death.

16 And he that stealeth a man, and selleth him, or if he be found in his hand, he shall surely be put to death.

17 And he that curseth his father, or his mother, shall surely be put to death.

18 And if men strive together, and one smite another with a stone, or with *his* fist, and he die not, but keepeth *his* bed:

19 If he rise again, and walk abroad upon his staff, then shall he that smote *him* be quit: only he shall pay *for* the loss of his time, and shall cause *him* to be thoroughly healed.

20 And if a man smite his servant, or his maid, with a rod, and he die under his hand; he shall be surely punished.

21 Notwithstanding, if he continue a day or two, he shall not be punished: for he *is* his money.

22 If men strive, and hurt a woman with child, so that her fruit depart *from her*, and

yet no mischief follow: he shall be surely punished, according as the woman's husband will lay upon him; and he shall pay as the judges *determine*.

23 And if *any* mischief follow, then thou shalt give life for life,

24 Eye for eye, tooth for tooth, hand for hand, foot for foot,

25 Burning for burning, wound for wound, stripe for stripe.

26 And if a man smite the eye of his servant, or the eye of his maid, that it perish; he shall let him go free for his eye's sake.

27 And if he smite out his manservant's tooth, or his maidservant's tooth; he shall let him go free for his tooth's sake.

28 If an ox gore a man or a woman, that they die: then the ox shall be surely stoned, and his flesh shall not be eaten; but the owner of the ox *shall be* quit.

29 But if the ox were wont to push with his horn in time past, and it hath been testified to his owner, and he hath not kept him in, but that he hath killed a man or a woman; the ox shall be stoned, and his owner also shall be put to death.

30 If there be laid on him a sum of money, then he shall give for the ransom of his life whatsoever is laid upon him.

31 Whether he have gored a son, or have gored a daughter, according to this judgment shall it be done unto him.

32 If the ox shall push a manservant or a maidservant; he shall give unto their master thirty shekels of silver, and the ox shall be stoned.

33 And if a man shall open a pit, or if a man shall dig a pit, and not cover it, and an ox or an ass fall therein;

34 The owner of the pit shall make *it* good, *and* give money unto the owner of them; and the dead *beast* shall be his.

35 And if one man's ox hurt another's, that he die; then they shall sell the live ox, and divide the money of it; and the dead *ox* also they shall divide.

36 Or if it be known that the ox hath used to push in time past, and his owner hath not kept him in; he shall surely pay ox for ox; and the dead shall be his own.

CHAPTER 22
Laws about Repayment

1 If a man shall steal an ox, or a sheep, and kill it, or sell it; he shall restore five oxen for an ox, and four sheep for a sheep.

2 If a thief be found breaking up, and be smitten that he die, *there shall* no blood *be* shed for him.

---

5 Deut. 15:16, 17

6 Ex. 12:12; 22:8, 28; Ps. 40:6

7 Ex. 21:2, 3; Neh. 5:5

10 1Cor. 7:5

12 Gen. 9:6; Lev. 24:17; Num. 35:30, 31; Matt. 26:52

13 Num. 35:11, 22; Deut. 19:3, 4, 5; Josh. 20:2; 1Sam. 24:4, 10, 18

14 Num. 15:30; 35:20; Deut. 19:11, 12; 1Kgs. 2:28-34; 2Kgs. 11:15; Heb. 10:26

16 Gen. 37:28; Ex. 22:4; Deut. 24:7

17 Lev. 20:9; Prov. 20:20; Matt. 15:4; Mark 7:10

19 2Sam. 3:29

20 Gen. 4:15, 24; Rom. 13:4

21 Lev. 25:45, 46

22 Ex. 21:30; Deut. 22:18, 19

24 Lev. 24:20; Deut. 19:21; Matt. 5:38

28 Gen. 9:5

30 Ex. 21:22; Num. 35:31

32 Ex. 21:28; Zech. 11:12, 13; Matt. 26:15; Phil. 2:7

1 2Sam. 12:6; Prov. 6:31; Luke 19:8

2 Num. 35:27; Matt. 24:43

3 If the sun be risen upon him, *there shall be* blood *shed* for him; *for* he should make full restitution; if he have nothing, then he shall be sold for his theft.

4 If the theft be certainly found in his hand alive, whether it be ox, or ass, or sheep; he shall restore double.

5 If a man shall cause a field or vineyard to be eaten, and shall put in his beast, and shall feed in another man's field; of the best of his own field, and of the best of his own vineyard, shall he make restitution.

6 If fire break out, and catch in thorns, so that the stacks of corn, or the standing corn, or the field, be consumed *therewith*; he that kindled the fire shall surely make restitution.

7 If a man shall deliver unto his neighbour money or stuff to keep, and it be stolen out of the man's house; if the thief be found, let him pay double.

8 If the thief be not found, then the master of the house shall be brought unto the judges, *to see* whether he have put his hand unto his neighbour's goods.

9 For all manner of trespass, *whether it be* for ox, for ass, for sheep, for raiment, *or* for any manner of lost thing, which *another* challengeth to be his, the cause of both parties shall come before the judges; *and* whom the judges shall condemn, he shall pay double unto his neighbour.

10 If a man deliver unto his neighbour an ass, or an ox, or a sheep, or any beast, to keep; and it die, or be hurt, or driven away, no man seeing *it*:

11 *Then* shall an oath of the LORD be between them both, that he hath not put his hand unto his neighbour's goods; and the owner of it shall accept *thereof*, and he shall not make *it* good.

12 And if it be stolen from him, he shall make restitution unto the owner thereof.

13 If it be torn in pieces, *then* let him bring it *for* witness, *and* he shall not make good that which was torn.

14 And if a man borrow *ought* of his neighbour, and it be hurt, or die, the owner thereof *being* not with it, he shall surely make *it* good.

15 *But* if the owner thereof *be* with it, he shall not make *it* good: if it *be* an hired *thing*, it came for his hire.

Laws of Human Relations

16 And if a man entice a maid that is not betrothed, and lie with her, he shall surely endow her to be his wife.

17 If her father utterly refuse to give her

unto him, he shall pay money according to the dowry of virgins.

18 Thou shalt not suffer a witch to live.

19 Whosoever lieth with a beast shall surely be put to death.

20 He that sacrificeth unto *any* god, save unto the LORD only, he shall be utterly destroyed.

21 Thou shalt neither vex a stranger, nor oppress him: for ye were strangers in the land of Egypt.

22 Ye shall not afflict any widow, or fatherless child.

23 If thou afflict them in any wise, and they cry at all unto me, I will surely hear their cry;

24 And my wrath shall wax hot, and I will kill you with the sword; and your wives shall be widows, and your children fatherless.

25 If thou lend money to *any of* my people *that is* poor by thee, thou shalt not be to him as a usurer, neither shalt thou lay upon him usury.

26 If thou at all take thy neighbour's raiment to pledge, thou shalt deliver it unto him by that the sun goeth down:

27 For that *is* his covering only, it *is* his raiment for his skin: wherein shall he sleep? and it shall come to pass, when he crieth unto me, that I will hear; for I *am* gracious.

28 Thou shalt not revile the gods, nor curse the ruler of thy people.

29 Thou shalt not delay *to offer* the first of thy ripe fruits, and of thy liquors: the firstborn of thy sons shalt thou give unto me.

30 Likewise shalt thou do with thine oxen, *and* with thy sheep: seven days it shall be with his dam; on the eighth day thou shalt give it me.

31 And ye shall be holy men unto me: neither shall ye eat *any* flesh *that is* torn of beasts in the field; ye shall cast it to the dogs.

CHAPTER 23

1 Thou shalt not raise a false report: put not thine hand with the wicked to be an unrighteous witness.

2 Thou shalt not follow a multitude to *do* evil; neither shalt thou speak in a cause to decline after many to wrest *judgment*:

3 Neither shalt thou countenance a poor man in his cause.

4 If thou meet thine enemy's ox or his ass going astray, thou shalt surely bring it back to him again.

5 If thou see the ass of him that hateth

Cross references (center column):

3 Ex. 21:2
4 Ex. 21:16
7 Ex. 22:4
8 Ex. 21:6; 22:28
9 Deut. 25:1; 2Chr. 19:10
11 Heb. 6:16
12 Gen. 31:39
16 Deut. 22:28, 29
17 Gen. 23:16; 34:12; Deut. 22:29; 1Sam. 18:25
18 Lev. 20:27; 1Sam. 28:3, 9
19 Lev. 18:23; 20:15
20 Deut. 17:2, 3, 5
21 Deut. 10:19
22 Isa. 1:17, 23; 10:2; Zech. 7:10; James 1:27
23 Luke 18:7; James 5:4
24 Lam. 5:3
25 Lev. 25:35-37; Ps. 15:5
26 Deut. 24:6, 10, 13, 17; Amos 2:8
27 Ex. 22:23; 34:6; 2Chr. 30:9; Ps. 86:15
28 Ex. 22:8, 9; Eccl. 10:20; Acts 23:5; Jude 8
29 Ex. 13:2, 12; 34:19
30 Lev. 22:27
1 Lev. 19:16; Prov. 10:18; Matt. 26:59-61
2 Lev. 19:15; Prov. 4:14; Mark 15:15
4 Deut. 22:1; Job 31:29; Prov. 24:17; 25:21; Matt. 5:44; Rom. 12:20; 1Thess. 5:15
5 Deut. 22:1

thee lying under his burden, and wouldest forbear to help him, thou shalt surely help with him.

6 Thou shalt not wrest the judgment of thy poor in his cause.

7 Keep thee far from a false matter; and the innocent and righteous slay thou not: for I will not justify the wicked.

8 And thou shalt take no gift: for the gift blindeth the wise, and perverteth the words of the righteous.

9 Also thou shalt not oppress a stranger: for ye know the heart of a stranger, seeing ye were strangers in the land of Egypt.

The Seventh Day

10 And six years thou shalt sow thy land, and shalt gather in the fruits thereof:

11 But the seventh *year* thou shalt let it rest and lie still; that the poor of thy people may eat: and what they leave the beasts of the field shall eat. In like manner thou shalt deal with thy vineyard, *and* with thy olive-yard.

12 Six days thou shalt do thy work, and on the seventh day thou shalt rest: that thine ox and thine ass may rest, and the son of thy handmaid, and the stranger, may be refreshed.

13 And in all *things* that I have said unto you be circumspect: and make no mention of the name of other gods, neither let it be heard out of thy mouth.

Three Festivals Each Year

14 Three times thou shalt keep a feast unto me in the year.

15 Thou shalt keep the feast of unleavened bread: (thou shalt eat unleavened bread seven days, as I commanded thee, in the time appointed of the month Abib; for in it thou camest out from Egypt: and none shall appear before me empty:)

16 And the feast of harvest, the firstfruits of thy labours, which thou hast sown in the field: and the feast of ingathering, *which is* in the end of the year, when thou hast gathered in thy labours out of the field.

17 Three times in the year all thy males shall appear before the Lord GOD.

18 Thou shalt not offer the blood of my sacrifice with leavened bread; neither shall the

6 Amos 5:12; Mal. 3:5

7 Matt. 27:4; Luke 3:14; Rom. 1:18; Eph. 4:25

8 1Sam. 8:3; Amos 5:12

9 Matt. 18:33

10 Lev. 25:3

12 Ex. 20:8, 9; Deut. 5:13; Luke 13:14

13 Deut. 4:9; Josh. 22:5; Ps. 39:1; Hos. 2:17; Eph. 5:15; 1Tim. 4:16

14 Ex. 34:23; Lev. 23:4; Num. 32:38; Deut. 12:3; 16:16; Josh. 23:7; Ps. 16:4; Zech. 13:2

15 Ex. 12:15; 13:6; 34:18, 20; Lev. 23:6; Deut. 16:8, 16

17 Ex. 34:23; Deut. 16:16

18 Ex. 12:8; 34:25; Lev. 2:11; Deut. 16:4

19 Lev. 23:10, 17; Neh. 10:35

20 Ex. 14:19; 32:34; 33:2, 14; Num. 20:16; Josh. 5:13; 6:2; Ps. 91:11; Isa. 63:9

21 John 10:30, 38; Eph. 4:30

25 Deut. 7:13, 15; 28:5, 8

27 Gen. 35:5

fat of my sacrifice remain until the morning.

19 The first of the firstfruits of thy land thou shalt bring into the house of the LORD thy God. Thou shalt not seethe a kid in his mother's milk.

God's Angel

20 Behold, I send an Angel before thee, to keep thee in the way, and to bring thee into the place which I have prepared.

21 Beware of him, and obey his voice, provoke him not; for he will not pardon your transgressions: for my name *is* in him.

22 But if thou shalt indeed obey his voice, and do all that I speak; then I will be an enemy unto thine enemies, and an adversary unto thine adversaries.

23 For mine Angel shall go before thee, and bring thee in unto the Amorites, and the Hittites, and the Perizzites, and the Canaanites, the Hivites, and the Jebusites: and I will cut them off.

24 Thou shalt not bow down to their gods, nor serve them, nor do after their works: but thou shalt utterly overthrow them, and quite break down their images.

25 And ye shall serve the LORD your God, and he shall bless thy bread, and thy water; and I will take sickness away from the midst of thee.

26 There shall nothing cast their young, nor be barren, in thy land: the number of thy days I will fulfil.

27 I will send my fear before thee, and will destroy all the people to whom thou shalt come, and I will make all thine enemies turn their backs unto thee.

28 And I will send hornets before thee, which shall drive out the Hivite, the Canaanite, and the Hittite, from before thee.

29 I will not drive them out from before thee in one year; lest the land become desolate, and the beast of the field multiply against thee.

30 By little and little I will drive them out from before thee, until thou be increased, and inherit the land.

31 And I will set thy bounds from the Red sea even unto the sea of the Philistines, and from the desert unto the river: for I will de-

---

23:25–31 God promised that Israel would be able to drive their enemies out of their land little by little. This was fulfilled primarily in Joshua and the other books of history in direct proportion to the nation's obedience to God. Unfortunately, Israel never claimed their entire inheritance from the Mediterranean Sea to "the river" (the Euphrates).

liver the inhabitants of the land into your hand; and thou shalt drive them out before thee.

32 Thou shalt make no covenant with them, nor with their gods.

33 They shall not dwell in thy land, lest they make thee sin against me: for if thou serve their gods, it will surely be a snare unto thee.

CHAPTER 24
The Agreement Is Signed

1 And he said unto Moses, Come up unto the LORD, thou, and Aaron, Nadab, and Abihu, and seventy of the elders of Israel; and worship ye afar off.

2 And Moses alone shall come near the LORD: but they shall not come nigh; neither shall the people go up with him.

3 And Moses came and told the people all the words of the LORD, and all the judgments: and all the people answered with one voice, and said, All the words which the LORD hath said will we do.

4 And Moses wrote all the words of the LORD, and rose up early in the morning, and builded an altar under the hill, and twelve pillars, according to the twelve tribes of Israel.

5 And he sent young men of the children of Israel, which offered burnt offerings, and sacrificed peace offerings of oxen unto the LORD.

6 And Moses took half of the blood, and put it in basons; and half of the blood he sprinkled on the altar.

7 And he took the book of the covenant, and read in the audience of the people: and they said, All that the LORD hath said will we do, and be obedient.

8 And Moses took the blood, and sprinkled it on the people, and said, Behold the blood of the covenant, which the LORD hath made with you concerning all these words.

9 Then went up Moses, and Aaron, Nadab, and Abihu, and seventy of the elders of Israel:

10 And they saw the God of Israel: and there was under his feet as it were a paved work of a sapphire stone, and as it were the body of heaven in his clearness.

11 And upon the nobles of the children of Israel he laid not his hand: also they saw God, and did eat and drink.

The Tablets of Stone

12 And the LORD said unto Moses, Come up to me into the mount, and be there: and I will give thee tables of stone, and a law, and

commandments which I have written; that thou mayest teach them.

13 And Moses rose up, and his minister Joshua: and Moses went up into the mount of God.

14 And he said unto the elders, Tarry ye here for us, until we come again unto you: and, behold, Aaron and Hur are with you: if any man have any matters to do, let him come unto them.

15 And Moses went up into the mount, and a cloud covered the mount.

16 And the glory of the LORD abode upon mount Sinai, and the cloud covered it six days: and the seventh day he called unto Moses out of the midst of the cloud.

17 And the sight of the glory of the LORD was like devouring fire on the top of the mount in the eyes of the children of Israel.

18 And Moses went into the midst of the cloud, and gat him up into the mount: and Moses was in the mount forty days and forty nights.

CHAPTER 25
Gifts for the Tent

1 And the LORD spake unto Moses, saying,

2 Speak unto the children of Israel, that they bring me an offering: of every man that giveth it willingly with his heart ye shall take my offering.

3 And this is the offering which ye shall take of them; gold, and silver, and brass,

4 And blue, and purple, and scarlet, and fine linen, and goats' hair,

5 And rams' skins dyed red, and badgers' skins, and shittim wood,

6 Oil for the light, spices for anointing oil, and for sweet incense,

7 Onyx stones, and stones to be set in the ephod, and in the breastplate.

8 And let them make me a sanctuary; that I may dwell among them.

9 According to all that I shew thee, after the pattern of the tabernacle, and the pattern of all the instruments thereof, even so shall ye make it.

The Ark of the Covenant

10 And they shall make an ark of shittim wood: two cubits and a half shall be the length thereof, and a cubit and a half the breadth thereof, and a cubit and a half the height thereof.

11 And thou shalt overlay it with pure gold, within and without shalt thou overlay it, and shalt make upon it a crown of gold round about.

---

33 Ex. 34:12; Deut. 7:16; 12:30; Josh. 23:13; Judg. 2:3; 1Sam. 18:21; Ps. 106:36

1 Ex. 1:5; 28:1; Lev. 10:1, 2; Num. 11:16

3 Ex. 19:8; 24:7; Deut. 5:27; Gal. 3:19, 20

4 Gen. 28:18; 31:45; Deut. 31:9

7 Ex. 24:3; Heb. 9:19

8 Heb. 9:20; 13:20; 1Pet. 1:2

10 Judg. 13:22; Isa. 6:1, 5; Ezek. 1:26; 10:1; Matt. 17:2; John 1:18; 1Tim. 6:16; 1John 4:12; Rev. 4:3

11 Gen. 16:13; 31:54; 32:30; Ex. 18:12; 19:21; 24:10; 33:20

12 Ex. 24:2, 15, 18; 31:18; 32:15, 16; Deut. 5:22

15 Ex. 19:9; 16; Matt. 17:5

16 Ex. 16:10; Num. 14:10

17 Ex. 3:2; 19:18; Deut. 4:36; Heb. 12:18, 29

18 Ex. 34:28; Deut. 9:9

2 Ex. 35:5, 21; 1Chr. 29:3, 5, 9, 14; Ezra 2:68; 3:5; 7:16; Neh. 11:2; 2Cor. 8:12; 9:7

8 Ex. 29:45; 36:1, 3, 4; Lev. 4:6; 10:4; 21:12; 1Kgs. 6:13; 2Cor. 6:16; Heb. 3:6; 9:1, 2; Rev. 21:3

10 Ex. 37:1; Deut. 10:3; Heb. 9:4

Inerrancy of the Bible

By Norman Geisler

The inerrant quality of the Word of God is an inference from the nature of God. Jesus taught that His Father is "the only true God" (John 17:3) and that His Word is truth (John 17:17). Equivalently, the apostles taught that God cannot lie (Heb. 6:18) and that "no lie is of the truth" (1 John 2:21).

Inspiration does not extend to just the thoughts or oral pronouncements of prophets but to their very "words." Moses "wrote all the words of the Lord" (Ex. 24:4), and David confessed, "His word was in my tongue" (2 Sam. 23:2). Jeremiah was told to "diminish not a word" (Jer. 26:2). Repeatedly, the prophets prefaced their declarations with the authoritative phrase, "Thus saith the Lord" (as in Judg. 6:8; 2 Sam. 7:5; Isa. 7:7; Hag. 1:5; Zech. 1:3). Jesus defined Old Testament revelation by what "is written" (Matt. 4:4, 7). Paul testified that he spoke words taught by the Spirit (1 Cor. 2:13), and he taught Timothy that "all scripture is given by inspiration of God" (2 Tim. 3:16).

> *Our hope is based on the inerrant fulfillment of prophecy.*

Jesus also affirmed that the whole Old Testament was inspired of God. Everything recorded by Moses and the prophets is from God (Matt. 5:17–18) and therefore must be fulfilled (Luke 24:44, cf. Rom. 15:4). This claim of inspiration, of course, is only for the writings originally given by God, that is, the autographs, not copies subjected to minor scribal errors. The necessary conclusion is that the Scriptures are without error. Whatever God utters is true and without error. With respect to prophecy, the Lord promises to bring to pass the events He predicts (Gen. 41:32; Isa. 46:11).

Second Timothy 3:16 declares, "All scripture is given by inspiration of God," which contextually refers to the "holy scriptures" of the Jewish faith in which young Timothy was taught (v. 15). The New Testament often refers to the authoritative writings of the Jews as "the scriptures." Jesus said, for example, "The scripture cannot be broken" (John 10:35), and concerning prophecy, Jesus claimed to be the fulfillment of the whole of Old Testament Law and prophecy on many occasions (Matt. 5:17; Luke 24:27, 44).

Furthermore, Jesus promised the inspiration of New Testament doctrine, prophecy, and ethics as well. He promised His disciples that He would send them the Holy Spirit who would teach them and help them remember the things they had seen and heard when Jesus was among them (John 14:26).

Later, the apostles wrote that the Son of God was the final revelation of the Father (Heb. 1:3). They testified that their own writings were equal in authority to those of the Old Testament (Luke 1:1–4; 2 Pet. 3:16; Rev. 1:3; 19:10) and were indeed the "word of God" (Acts 4:31; 17:13; 1 Thess. 2:13).

The connection between inerrancy, prophecy, and personal assurance is explained in Hebrews 6:18: "That by two immutable things, in which it was impossible for God to lie, we might have a strong consolation, who have fled for refuge to lay hold upon the hope set before us." Our hope is based on the inerrant fulfillment of prophecy. Jesus Christ fulfilled Old Testament prophecy to the letter, and His return will fulfill both Old and New Testament predictions.

12 And thou shalt cast four rings of gold for it, and put *them* in the four corners thereof; and two rings *shall be* in the one side of it, and two rings in the other side of it.

13 And thou shalt make staves *of* shittim wood, and overlay them with gold.

14 And thou shalt put the staves into the rings by the sides of the ark, that the ark may be borne with them.

15 The staves shall be in the rings of the ark: they shall not be taken from it.

16 And thou shalt put into the ark the testimony which I shall give thee.

17 And thou shalt make a mercy seat *of* pure gold: two cubits and a half *shall be* the length thereof, and a cubit and a half the breadth thereof.

18 And thou shalt make two cherubims *of* gold, *of* beaten work shalt thou make them, in the two ends of the mercy seat.

19 And make one cherub on the one end, and the other cherub on the other end: *even* of the mercy seat shall ye make the cherubims on the two ends thereof.

20 And the cherubims shall stretch forth *their* wings on high, covering the mercy seat with their wings, and their faces *shall look* one to another; toward the mercy seat shall the faces of the cherubims be.

21 And thou shalt put the mercy seat above upon the ark; and in the ark thou shalt put the testimony that I shall give thee.

22 And there I will meet with thee, and I will commune with thee from above the mercy seat, from between the two cherubims which *are* upon the ark of the testimony, of all *things* which I will give thee in commandment unto the children of Israel.

The Table for the Shewbread

23 Thou shalt also make a table *of* shittim wood: two cubits *shall be* the length thereof, and a cubit the breadth thereof, and a cubit and a half the height thereof.

24 And thou shalt overlay it with pure gold, and make thereto a crown of gold round about.

25 And thou shalt make unto it a border of an handbreadth round about, and thou shalt make a golden crown to the border thereof round about.

26 And thou shalt make for it four rings of gold, and put the rings in the four corners that *are* on the four feet thereof.

27 Over against the border shall the rings be for places of the staves to bear the table.

28 And thou shalt make the staves *of* shittim wood, and overlay them with gold, that the table may be borne with them.

29 And thou shalt make the dishes thereof, and spoons thereof, and covers thereof, and

Cross references:
15 1Kgs. 8:8
16 Ex. 16:34; 31:18; Deut. 10:2, 5; 31:26; 1Kgs. 8:9; 2Kgs. 11:12; Heb. 9:4
17 Ex. 37:6; Rom. 3:25; Heb. 9:5
20 1Kgs. 8:7; 1Chr. 28:18; Heb. 9:5
21 Ex. 25:16; Ex. 26:34
22 Ex. 29:42, 43; 30:6, 36; Lev. 16:2; Num. 7:89; 17:4; 1Sam. 4:4; 2Sam. 6:2; 2Kgs. 19:15; Ps. 80:1; 90:1; Isa. 37:16
23 Ex. 37:10; 1Kgs. 7:48; 2Chr. 4:8; Heb. 9:2
29 Ex. 37:16; Num. 4:7

The Tabernacle

Holy of Holies, where the Ark of the Covenant was kept

The Veil

Holy Place, where the table for the shewbread, golden candlestick, and incense altar were kept

Laver of brass

Brasen altar

Entrance

bowls thereof, to cover withal: *of* pure gold shalt thou make them.

30 And thou shalt set upon the table shewbread before me alway.

31 And thou shalt make a candlestick *of* pure gold: *of* beaten work shall the candlestick be made: his shaft, and his branches, his bowls, his knops, and his flowers, shall be of the same.

32 And six branches shall come out of the sides of it; three branches of the candlestick out of the one side, and three branches of the candlestick out of the other side:

33 Three bowls made like unto almonds, *with* a knop and a flower in one branch; and three bowls made like almonds in the other branch, *with* a knop and a flower: so in the six branches that come out of the candlestick.

34 And in the candlestick *shall be* four bowls made like unto almonds, *with* their knops and their flowers.

35 And *there shall be* a knop under two branches of the same, and a knop under two branches of the same, and a knop under two branches of the same, according to the six branches that proceed out of the candlestick.

36 Their knops and their branches shall be of the same: all it *shall be* one beaten work *of* pure gold.

37 And thou shalt make the seven lamps thereof: and they shall light the lamps thereof, that they may give light over against it.

38 And the tongs thereof, and the snuffdishes thereof, *shall be of* pure gold.

39 *Of* a talent of pure gold shall he make it, with all these vessels.

40 And look that thou make *them* after their pattern, which was shewed thee in the mount.

CHAPTER 26
The Tabernacle

1 Moreover thou shalt make the tabernacle *with* ten curtains *of* fine twined linen, and blue, and purple, and scarlet: *with* cherubims of cunning work shalt thou make them.

2 The length of one curtain *shall be* eight and twenty cubits, and the breadth of one curtain four cubits: and every one of the curtains shall have one measure.

3 The five curtains shall be coupled together one to another; and *other* five curtains *shall be* coupled one to another.

4 And thou shalt make loops of blue upon the edge of the one curtain from the

selvedge in the coupling; and likewise shalt thou make in the uttermost edge of *another* curtain, in the coupling of the second.

5 Fifty loops shalt thou make in the one curtain, and fifty loops shalt thou make in the edge of the curtain that *is* in the coupling of the second; that the loops may take hold one of another.

6 And thou shalt make fifty taches of gold, and couple the curtains together with the taches: and it shall be one tabernacle.

7 And thou shalt make curtains *of* goats' hair to be a covering upon the tabernacle: eleven curtains shalt thou make.

8 The length of one curtain *shall be* thirty cubits, and the breadth of one curtain four cubits: and the eleven curtains *shall be all* of one measure.

9 And thou shalt couple five curtains by themselves, and six curtains by themselves, and shalt double the sixth curtain in the forefront of the tabernacle.

10 And thou shalt make fifty loops on the edge of the one curtain *that is* outmost in the coupling, and fifty loops in the edge of the curtain which coupleth the second.

11 And thou shalt make fifty taches of brass, and put the taches into the loops, and couple the tent together, that it may be one.

12 And the remnant that remaineth of the curtains of the tent, the half curtain that remaineth, shall hang over the backside of the tabernacle.

13 And a cubit on the one side, and a cubit on the other side of that which remaineth in the length of the curtains of the tent, it shall hang over the sides of the tabernacle on this side and on that side, to cover it.

14 And thou shalt make a covering for the tent *of* rams' skins dyed red, and a covering above *of* badgers' skins.

15 And thou shalt make boards for the tabernacle *of* shittim wood standing up.

16 Ten cubits *shall be* the length of a board, and a cubit and a half *shall be* the breadth of one board.

17 Two tenons *shall there be* in one board, set in order one against another: thus shalt thou make for all the boards of the tabernacle.

18 And thou shalt make the boards for the tabernacle, twenty boards on the south side southward.

19 And thou shalt make forty sockets of silver under the twenty boards; two sockets under one board for his two tenons, and two sockets under another board for his two tenons.

Cross references

30 Lev. 24:5, 6

31 Ex. 37:17; 1Kgs. 7:49; Zech. 4:2; Heb. 9:2; Rev. 1:12; 4:5

37 Ex. 27:21; 30:8; Lev. 24:3, 4; Num. 8:2; 2Chr. 13:11

40 Ex. 26:30; Num. 8:4; 1Chr. 28:11, 19; Acts 7:44; Heb. 8:5

1 Ex. 36:8

7 Ex. 36:14

14 Ex. 36:19

20 And for the second side of the tabernacle on the north side *there shall be* twenty boards:

21 And their forty sockets *of* silver; two sockets under one board, and two sockets under another board.

22 And for the sides of the tabernacle westward thou shalt make six boards.

23 And two boards shalt thou make for the corners of the tabernacle in the two sides.

24 And they shall be coupled together beneath, and they shall be coupled together above the head of it unto one ring: thus shall it be for them both; they shall be for the two corners.

25 And they shall be eight boards, and their sockets *of* silver, sixteen sockets; two sockets under one board, and two sockets under another board.

26 And thou shalt make bars *of* shittim wood; five for the boards of the one side of the tabernacle,

27 And five bars for the boards of the other side of the tabernacle, and five bars for the boards of the side of the tabernacle, for the two sides westward.

28 And the middle bar in the midst of the boards shall reach from end to end.

29 And thou shalt overlay the boards with gold, and make their rings *of* gold *for* places for the bars: and thou shalt overlay the bars with gold.

30 And thou shalt rear up the tabernacle according to the fashion thereof which was shewed thee in the mount.

31 And thou shalt make a vail *of* blue, and purple, and scarlet, and fine twined linen of cunning work: with cherubims shall it be made:

32 And thou shalt hang it upon four pillars of shittim *wood* overlaid with gold: their hooks *shall be of* gold, upon the four sockets of silver.

33 And thou shalt hang up the vail under the taches, that thou mayest bring in thither within the vail the ark of the testimony: and the vail shall divide unto you between the holy *place* and the most holy.

34 And thou shalt put the mercy seat upon the ark of the testimony in the most holy *place*.

35 And thou shalt set the table without the vail, and the candlestick over against the table on the side of the tabernacle toward the south: and thou shalt put the table on the north side.

36 And thou shalt make an hanging for the door of the tent, *of* blue, and purple, and scarlet, and fine twined linen, wrought with needlework.

37 And thou shalt make for the hanging five pillars *of* shittim *wood*, and overlay them with gold, *and* their hooks *shall be of* gold: and thou shalt cast five sockets of brass for them.

CHAPTER 27
The Altar of Burnt Offering

1 And thou shalt make an altar *of* shittim wood, five cubits long, and five cubits broad; the altar shall be foursquare: and the height thereof *shall be* three cubits.

Cross-references:
30 Ex. 25:9, 40; 27:8; Acts 7:44; Heb. 8:5
31 Ex. 36:35; Lev. 16:2; 2Chr. 3:14; Matt. 27:51; Heb. 9:3
33 Ex. 25:16; 40:21; Lev. 16:2; Heb. 9:2, 3
34 Ex. 25:21; 40:20; Heb. 9:5
35 Ex. 40:22, 24; Heb. 9:2
36 Ex. 36:37
37 Ex. 36:38
1 Ex. 38:1; Ezek. 43:13

The Furnishings of the Tabernacle

FURNISHING	EXODUS	SYMBOL	FORESHADOWS OF CHRIST	REFERENCES
Door	29:4	Salvation	Door to Eternal Life	Ex. 27:16; John 10:7–9
Brazen Altar	38:1–2	Regeneration	Once-for-all Sin Offering	Heb. 10:1–17
Laver	30:18	Purification	Cleansing of All Sin	Eph. 5:25–26; 1 John 1:9
Golden Lampstand	25:31	Illumination	Light of the World	John 1:6–8; 8:12; Rev. 1:13
Table of Shewbread	25:30	Spiritual Nourishment	Bread of Life	John 6:35, 50–51
Altar of Incense	37:25	Intercession	Intercessor	Ps. 66:15; 141:2; Heb. 7:25; Rev. 8:4
Veil	26:31	Access to God	Mediator	Matt. 27:50–51; Heb. 10:19–28
Ark of the Covenant	25:10–16	Representation	Incarnation	John 1:14; 14:6

By James Sewell

2 And thou shalt make the horns of it upon the four corners thereof: his horns shall be of the same: and thou shalt overlay it with brass.

3 And thou shalt make his pans to receive his ashes, and his shovels, and his basons, and his fleshhooks, and his firepans: all the vessels thereof thou shalt make of brass.

4 And thou shalt make for it a grate of network of brass; and upon the net shalt thou make four brasen rings in the four corners thereof.

5 And thou shalt put it under the compass of the altar beneath, that the net may be even to the midst of the altar.

6 And thou shalt make staves for the altar, staves of shittim wood, and overlay them with brass.

7 And the staves shall be put into the rings, and the staves shall be upon the two sides of the altar, to bear it.

8 Hollow with boards shalt thou make it: as it was shewed thee in the mount, so shall they make it.

The Enclosure of the Tabernacle

9 And thou shalt make the court of the tabernacle: for the south side southward there shall be hangings for the court of fine twined linen of an hundred cubits long for one side:

10 And the twenty pillars thereof and their twenty sockets shall be of brass; the hooks of the pillars and their fillets shall be of silver.

11 And likewise for the north side in length there shall be hangings of an hundred cubits long, and his twenty pillars and their twenty sockets of brass; the hooks of the pillars and their fillets of silver.

12 And for the breadth of the court on the west side shall be hangings of fifty cubits: their pillars ten, and their sockets ten.

13 And the breadth of the court on the east side eastward shall be fifty cubits.

14 The hangings of one side of the gate shall be fifteen cubits: their pillars three, and their sockets three.

15 And on the other side shall be hangings fifteen cubits: their pillars three, and their sockets three.

16 And for the gate of the court shall be an hanging of twenty cubits, of blue, and purple, and scarlet, and fine twined linen, wrought with needlework: and their pillars shall be four, and their sockets four.

17 All the pillars round about the court shall be filleted with silver; their hooks shall be of silver, and their sockets of brass.

18 The length of the court shall be an hundred cubits, and the breadth fifty every where, and the height five cubits of fine twined linen, and their sockets of brass.

19 All the vessels of the tabernacle in all the service thereof, and all the pins thereof, and all the pins of the court, shall be of brass.

Taking Care of the Lamp

20 And thou shalt command the children of Israel, that they bring thee pure oil olive beaten for the light, to cause the lamp to burn always.

21 In the tabernacle of the congregation without the vail, which is before the testimony, Aaron and his sons shall order it from evening to morning before the LORD: it shall be a statute for ever unto their generations on the behalf of the children of Israel.

CHAPTER 28
The Priests' Clothes

1 And take thou unto thee Aaron thy brother, and his sons with him, from among the children of Israel, that he may minister unto me in the priest's office, even Aaron, Nadab and Abihu, Eleazar and Ithamar, Aaron's sons.

2 And thou shalt make holy garments for Aaron thy brother for glory and for beauty.

3 And thou shalt speak unto all that are wise hearted, whom I have filled with the spirit of wisdom, that they may make Aaron's garments to consecrate him, that he may minister unto me in the priest's office.

4 And these are the garments which they shall make; a breastplate, and an ephod, and a robe, and an broidered coat, a mitre, and a girdle: and they shall make holy garments for Aaron thy brother, and his sons, that he may minister unto me in the priest's office.

5 And they shall take gold, and blue, and purple, and scarlet, and fine linen.

6 And they shall make the ephod of gold, of blue, and of purple, of scarlet, and fine twined linen, with cunning work.

7 It shall have the two shoulderpieces thereof joined at the two edges thereof; and so it shall be joined together.

8 And the curious girdle of the ephod, which is upon it, shall be of the same, according to the work thereof; even of gold, of blue, and purple, and scarlet, and fine twined linen.

9 And thou shalt take two onyx stones, and grave on them the names of the children of Israel:

---

2 Num. 16:38

8 Ex. 25:40; 26:30

9 Ex. 38:9

20 Lev. 24:2

21 Ex. 26:31, 33; 28:43; 29:9, 28; 30:8; Lev. 3:17; 16:34; 24:9; Num. 18:23; 19:21; 1Sam. 3:3; 30:25; 2Chr. 13:11

1 Num. 18:7; Heb. 5:1, 4

2 Ex. 29:5, 29; 31:10; 39:1, 2; Lev. 8:7, 30; Num. 20:26, 28

3 Ex. 31:3, 6; 35:30, 31; 36:1

4 Ex. 28:6, 15, 31, 39

6 Ex. 39:2

10 Six of their names on one stone, and *the other* six names of the rest on the other stone, according to their birth.

11 With the work of an engraver in stone, *like* the engravings of a signet, shalt thou engrave the two stones with the names of the children of Israel: thou shalt make them to be set in ouches of gold.

12 And thou shalt put the two stones upon the shoulders of the ephod *for* stones of memorial unto the children of Israel: and Aaron shall bear their names before the LORD upon his two shoulders for a memorial.

13 And thou shalt make ouches *of* gold;

14 And two chains *of* pure gold at the ends; *of* wreathen work shalt thou make them, and fasten the wreathen chains to the ouches.

15 And thou shalt make the breastplate of judgment with cunning work; after the work of the ephod thou shalt make it; *of* gold, *of* blue, and *of* purple, and *of* scarlet, and *of* fine twined linen, shalt thou make it.

16 Foursquare it shall be *being* doubled; a span *shall be* the length thereof, and a span *shall be* the breadth thereof.

17 And thou shalt set in it settings of stones, *even* four rows of stones: *the first* row *shall be* a sardius, a topaz, and a carbuncle: *this shall be* the first row.

18 And the second row *shall be* an emerald, a sapphire, and a diamond.

19 And the third row a ligure, an agate, and an amethyst.

20 And the fourth row a beryl, and an onyx, and a jasper: they shall be set in gold in their inclosings.

21 And the stones shall be with the names of the children of Israel, twelve, according to their names, *like* the engravings of a signet; every one with his name shall they be according to the twelve tribes.

22 And thou shalt make upon the breastplate chains at the ends *of* wreathen work *of* pure gold.

23 And thou shalt make upon the breastplate two rings of gold, and shalt put the two rings on the two ends of the breastplate.

24 And thou shalt put the two wreathen *chains* of gold in the two rings *which are* on the ends of the breastplate.

25 And *the other* two ends of the two wreathen *chains* thou shalt fasten in the two ouches, and put *them* on the shoulderpieces of the ephod before it.

26 And thou shalt make two rings of gold,

and thou shalt put them upon the two ends of the breastplate in the border thereof, which *is* in the side of the ephod inward.

27 And two *other* rings of gold thou shalt make, and shalt put them on the two sides of the ephod underneath, toward the forepart thereof, over against the *other* coupling thereof, above the curious girdle of the ephod.

28 And they shall bind the breastplate by the rings thereof unto the rings of the ephod with a lace of blue, that *it* may be above the curious girdle of the ephod, and that the breastplate be not loosed from the ephod.

29 And Aaron shall bear the names of the children of Israel in the breastplate of judgment upon his heart, when he goeth in unto the holy *place*, for a memorial before the LORD continually.

30 And thou shalt put in the breastplate of judgment the Urim and the Thummim; and they shall be upon Aaron's heart, when he goeth in before the LORD: and Aaron shall bear the judgment of the children of Israel upon his heart before the LORD continually.

31 And thou shalt make the robe of the ephod all *of* blue.

32 And there shall be an hole in the top of it, in the midst thereof: it shall have a binding of woven work round about the hole of it, as it were the hole of an habergeon, that it be not rent.

33 And *beneath* upon the hem of it thou shalt make pomegranates *of* blue, and *of* purple, and *of* scarlet, round about the hem thereof; and bells of gold between them round about:

34 A golden bell and a pomegranate, a golden bell and a pomegranate, upon the hem of the robe round about.

35 And it shall be upon Aaron to minister: and his sound shall be heard when he goeth in unto the holy *place* before the LORD, and when he cometh out, that he die not.

36 And thou shalt make a plate of pure gold, and grave upon it, *like* the engravings of a signet, HOLINESS TO THE LORD.

37 And thou shalt put it on a blue lace, that it may be upon the mitre; upon the forefront of the mitre it shall be.

38 And it shall be upon Aaron's forehead, that Aaron may bear the iniquity of the holy things, which the children of Israel shall hallow in all their holy gifts; and it shall be always upon his forehead, that they may be accepted before the LORD.

39 And thou shalt embroider the coat of

12 Ex. 28:29; 39:7; Josh. 4:7; Zech. 6:14

15 Ex. 39:8

17 Ex. 39:10-14

29 Ex. 28:12

30 Lev. 8:8; Num. 27:21; Deut. 33:8; 1Sam. 28:6; Ezra 2:63; Neh. 7:65

31 Ex. 39:22

36 Ex. 39:30; Zech. 14:20

38 Ex. 28:43; Lev. 1:4; 10:17; 22:9, 27; 23:11; Num. 18:1; Isa. 53:11; 56:7; Ezek. 4:4-6; John 1:29; Heb. 9:28; 1Pet. 2:24

fine linen, and thou shalt make the mitre *of fine linen*, and thou shalt make the girdle *of needlework*.

40 And for Aaron's sons thou shalt make coats, and thou shalt make for them girdles, and bonnets shalt thou make for them, for glory and for beauty.

41 And thou shalt put them upon Aaron thy brother, and his sons with him; and shalt anoint them, and consecrate them, and sanctify them, that they may minister unto me in the priest's office.

42 And thou shalt make them linen breeches to cover their nakedness; from the loins even unto the thighs they shall reach:

43 And they shall be upon Aaron, and upon his sons, when they come in unto the tabernacle of the congregation, or when they come near unto the altar to minister in the holy *place*; that they bear not iniquity, and die: *it shall be* a statute for ever unto him and his seed after him.

CHAPTER 29
The Dedication of Aaron and His Sons

1 And this *is* the thing that thou shalt do unto them to hallow them, to minister unto me in the priest's office: Take one young bullock, and two rams without blemish,

2 And unleavened bread, and cakes unleavened tempered with oil, and wafers unleavened anointed with oil: *of* wheaten flour shalt thou make them.

3 And thou shalt put them into one basket, and bring them in the basket, with the bullock and the two rams.

4 And Aaron and his sons thou shalt bring unto the door of the tabernacle of the congregation, and shalt wash them with water.

5 And thou shalt take the garments, and put upon Aaron the coat, and the robe of the ephod, and the ephod, and the breastplate, and gird him with the curious girdle of the ephod:

6 And thou shalt put the mitre upon his head, and put the holy crown upon the mitre.

7 Then shalt thou take the anointing oil, and pour *it* upon his head, and anoint him.

8 And thou shalt bring his sons, and put coats upon them.

9 And thou shalt gird them with girdles, Aaron and his sons, and put the bonnets on them: and the priest's office shall be theirs for a perpetual statute: and thou shalt consecrate Aaron and his sons.

10 And thou shalt cause a bullock to be brought before the tabernacle of the congregation: and Aaron and his sons shall put their hands upon the head of the bullock.

11 And thou shalt kill the bullock before the LORD, *by* the door of the tabernacle of the congregation.

12 And thou shalt take of the blood of the bullock, and put *it* upon the horns of the altar with thy finger, and pour all the blood beside the bottom of the altar.

13 And thou shalt take all the fat that covereth the inwards, and the caul *that is* above the liver, and the two kidneys, and the fat that *is* upon them, and burn *them* upon the altar.

14 But the flesh of the bullock, and his skin, and his dung, shalt thou burn with fire without the camp: it *is* a sin offering.

15 Thou shalt also take one ram; and Aaron and his sons shall put their hands upon the head of the ram.

16 And thou shalt slay the ram, and thou shalt take his blood, and sprinkle *it* round about upon the altar.

17 And thou shalt cut the ram in pieces, and wash the inwards of him, and his legs, and put *them* unto his pieces, and unto his head.

18 And thou shalt burn the whole ram upon the altar: it *is* a burnt offering unto the LORD: it *is* a sweet savour, an offering made by fire unto the LORD.

19 And thou shalt take the other ram; and Aaron and his sons shall put their hands upon the head of the ram.

20 Then shalt thou kill the ram, and take of his blood, and put *it* upon the tip of the right ear of Aaron, and upon the tip of the right ear of his sons, and upon the thumb of their right hand, and upon the great toe of their right foot, and sprinkle the blood upon the altar round about.

21 And thou shalt take of the blood that *is* upon the altar, and of the anointing oil, and sprinkle *it* upon Aaron, and upon his garments, and upon his sons, and upon the garments of his sons with him: and he shall be hallowed, and his garments, and his sons, and his sons' garments with him.

22 Also thou shalt take of the ram the fat and the rump, and the fat that covereth the inwards, and the caul *above* the liver, and the two kidneys, and the fat that *is* upon them, and the right shoulder; for it *is* a ram of consecration:

23 And one loaf of bread, and one cake of oiled bread, and one wafer out of the basket

---

40 Ex. 28:4; 39:27-29, 41; Ezek. 44:17, 18

41 Ex. 29:7, 9-35; 30:30; 40:15; Lev. 8:1-30; 10:7; Heb. 7:28

42 Ex. 39:28; Lev. 6:10; 16:4; Ezek. 44:18

43 Ex. 20:26; 27:21; Lev. 5:1, 17; 17:7; 20:19, 20; 22:9; Num. 9:13; 18:22

1 Lev. 8:2

2 Lev. 2:4; 6:20-22

4 Ex. 40:12; Lev. 8:6; Heb. 10:22

5 Ex. 28:2, 8; Lev. 8:7

6 Lev. 8:9

7 Ex. 28:41; 30:25; Lev. 8:12; 10:7; 21:10; Num. 35:25

8 Lev. 8:13

9 Ex. 28:41; Lev. 8:22; Num. 18:7; Heb. 7:28

10 Lev. 1:4; 8:14

12 Ex. 27:2; 30:2; Lev. 8:15

13 Lev. 3:3

14 Lev. 4:11, 12, 21; Heb. 13:11

15 Lev. 1:4-9; 8:18

18 Gen. 8:21

19 Ex. 29:3; Lev. 8:22

21 Ex. 29:1; 30:25, 31; Lev. 8:30; Heb. 9:22

23 Lev. 8:26

of the unleavened bread that *is* before the LORD:

24 And thou shalt put all in the hands of Aaron, and in the hands of his sons; and shalt wave them *for* a wave offering before the LORD.

25 And thou shalt receive them of their hands, and burn *them* upon the altar for a burnt offering, for a sweet savour before the LORD: it *is* an offering made by fire unto the LORD.

26 And thou shalt take the breast of the ram of Aaron's consecration, and wave it *for* a wave offering before the LORD: and it shall be thy part.

27 And thou shalt sanctify the breast of the wave offering, and the shoulder of the heave offering, which is waved, and which is heaved up, of the ram of the consecration, *even* of *that* which *is* for Aaron, and of *that* which is for his sons:

28 And it shall be Aaron's and his sons' by a statute for ever from the children of Israel: for it *is* an heave offering: and it shall be an heave offering from the children of Israel of the sacrifice of their peace offerings, *even* their heave offering unto the LORD.

29 And the holy garments of Aaron shall be his sons' after him, to be anointed therein, and to be consecrated in them.

30 *And* that son that is priest in his stead shall put them on seven days, when he cometh into the tabernacle of the congregation to minister in the holy *place.*

31 And thou shalt take the ram of the consecration, and seethe his flesh in the holy place.

32 And Aaron and his sons shall eat the flesh of the ram, and the bread that *is* in the basket, *by* the door of the tabernacle of the congregation.

33 And they shall eat those things wherewith the atonement was made, to consecrate *and* to sanctify them: but a stranger shall not eat *thereof,* because they *are* holy.

34 And if ought of the flesh of the consecrations, or of the bread, remain unto the morning, then thou shalt burn the remainder with fire: it shall not be eaten, because it *is* holy.

35 And thus shalt thou do unto Aaron, and to his sons, according to all *things* which I have commanded thee: seven days shalt thou consecrate them.

36 And thou shalt offer every day a bullock *for* a sin offering for atonement: and thou shalt cleanse the altar, when thou hast

made an atonement for it, and thou shalt anoint it, to sanctify it.

37 Seven days thou shalt make an atonement for the altar, and sanctify it; and it shall be an altar most holy: whatsoever toucheth the altar shall be holy.

Two Lambs Every Day

38 Now this *is that* which thou shalt offer upon the altar; two lambs of the first year day by day continually.

39 The one lamb thou shalt offer in the morning; and the other lamb thou shalt offer at even:

40 And with the one lamb a tenth deal of flour mingled with the fourth part of an hin of beaten oil; and the fourth part of an hin of wine *for* a drink offering.

41 And the other lamb thou shalt offer at even, and shalt do thereto according to the meat offering of the morning, and according to the drink offering thereof, for a sweet savour, an offering made by fire unto the LORD.

42 *This shall be* a continual burnt offering throughout your generations *at* the door of the tabernacle of the congregation before the LORD: where I will meet you, to speak there unto thee.

43 And there I will meet with the children of Israel, and *the tabernacle* shall be sanctified by my glory.

44 And I will sanctify the tabernacle of the congregation, and the altar: I will sanctify also both Aaron and his sons, to minister to me in the priest's office.

45 And I will dwell among the children of Israel, and will be their God.

46 And they shall know that I *am* the LORD their God, that brought them forth out of the land of Egypt, that I may dwell among them: I *am* the LORD their God.

CHAPTER 30
The Incense Altar

1 And thou shalt make an altar to burn incense upon: *of* shittim wood shalt thou make it.

2 A cubit *shall be* the length thereof, and a cubit the breadth thereof; foursquare shall it be: and two cubits *shall be* the height thereof: the horns thereof *shall be* of the same.

3 And thou shalt overlay it with pure gold, the top thereof, and the sides thereof round about, and the horns thereof; and thou shalt make unto it a crown of gold round about.

4 And two golden rings shalt thou make to it under the crown of it, by the two corners

---

24 Lev. 7:30

26 Lev. 8:29; Ps. 99:6

27 Lev. 7:31, 34; Num. 18:11, 18; Deut. 18:3

28 Lev. 7:34; Lev. 10:15

29 Num. 18:8; 20:26, 28; 35:25

30 Lev. 8:35; 9:1, 8; Num. 20:28

32 Matt. 12:4

33 Lev. 10:14, 15, 17; 22:10

35 Ex. 40:12; Lev. 8:33-35

36 Ex. 30:26, 28, 29; 40:10; Heb. 10:11

37 Matt. 23:19

38 Num. 28:3; 1Chr. 16:40; 2Chr. 2:4; 13:11; 31:3; Ezra 3:3; Dan. 9:27; 12:11

41 1Kgs. 18:29, 36; 2Kgs. 16:15; Ezra 9:4, 5; Ps. 141:2; Dan. 9:21

42 Ex. 25:22; 29:38; 30:6, 8, 36; Num. 17:4; 28:6; Dan. 8:11-13

43 Ex. 40:34; 1Kgs. 8:11; 2Chr. 5:14; 7:1-3; Ezek. 43:5; Hag. 2:7, 9; Mal. 3:1

44 Lev. 21:15; 22:9, 16

45 Ex. 25:8; Lev. 26:12; Zech. 2:10; John 14:17, 23; 2Cor. 6:16; Rev. 21:3

46 Ex. 20:2

1 Ex. 30:7, 8, 10; 37:25; 40:5; Rev. 4:7, 18; Rev. 8:3

thereof, upon the two sides of it shalt thou make *it*; and they shall be for places for the staves to bear it withal.

5 And thou shalt make the staves *of* shittim wood, and overlay them with gold.

6 And thou shalt put it before the vail that *is* by the ark of the testimony, before the mercy seat that *is* over the testimony, where I will meet with thee.

7 And Aaron shall burn thereon sweet incense every morning: when he dresseth the lamps, he shall burn incense upon it.

8 And when Aaron lighteth the lamps at even, he shall burn incense upon it, a perpetual incense before the Lord throughout your generations.

9 Ye shall offer no strange incense thereon, nor burnt sacrifice, nor meat offering; neither shall ye pour drink offering thereon.

10 And Aaron shall make an atonement upon the horns of it once in a year with the blood of the sin offering of atonements: once in the year shall he make atonement upon it throughout your generations: it *is* most holy unto the Lord.

A Tax for the Tent

11 And the Lord spake unto Moses, saying,

12 When thou takest the sum of the children of Israel after their number, then shall they give every man a ransom for his soul unto the Lord, when thou numberest them; that there be no plague among them, when *thou* numberest them.

13 This they shall give, every one that passeth among them that are numbered, half a shekel after the shekel of the sanctuary: (a shekel *is* twenty gerahs:) an half shekel *shall be* the offering of the Lord.

14 Every one that passeth among them that are numbered, from twenty years old and above, shall give an offering unto the Lord.

15 The rich shall not give more, and the poor shall not give less than half a shekel, when *they* give an offering unto the Lord, to make an atonement for your souls.

16 And thou shalt take the atonement money of the children of Israel, and shalt appoint it for the service of the tabernacle of the congregation; that it may be a memorial unto the children of Israel before the Lord, to make an atonement for your souls.

The Brass Basin

17 And the Lord spake unto Moses, saying,

18 Thou shalt also make a laver *of* brass, and his foot *also of* brass, to wash *withal*: and thou shalt put it between the tabernacle of

the congregation and the altar, and thou shalt put water therein.

19 For Aaron and his sons shall wash their hands and their feet thereat:

20 When they go into the tabernacle of the congregation, they shall wash with water, that they die not; or when they come near to the altar to minister, to burn offering made by fire unto the Lord:

21 So they shall wash their hands and their feet, that they die not: and it shall be a statute for ever to them, *even* to him and to his seed throughout their generations.

How to Make the Oil

22 Moreover the Lord spake unto Moses, saying,

23 Take thou also unto thee principal spices, of pure myrrh five hundred *shekels*, and of sweet cinnamon half so much, *even* two hundred and fifty *shekels*, and of sweet calamus two hundred and fifty *shekels*,

24 And of cassia five hundred *shekels*, after the shekel of the sanctuary, and of oil olive an hin:

25 And thou shalt make it an oil of holy ointment, an ointment compound after the art of the apothecary: it shall be an holy anointing oil.

26 And thou shalt anoint the tabernacle of the congregation therewith, and the ark of the testimony,

27 And the table and all his vessels, and the candlestick and his vessels, and the altar of incense,

28 And the altar of burnt offering with all his vessels, and the laver and his foot.

29 And thou shalt sanctify them, that they may be most holy: whatsoever toucheth them shall be holy.

30 And thou shalt anoint Aaron and his sons, and consecrate them, that *they* may minister unto me in the priest's office.

31 And thou shalt speak unto the children of Israel, saying, This shall be an holy anointing oil unto me throughout your generations.

32 Upon man's flesh shall it not be poured, neither shall ye make *any other* like it, after the composition of it: it *is* holy, *and* it shall be holy unto you.

33 Whosoever compoundeth *any* like it, or whosoever putteth *any* of it upon a stranger, shall even be cut off from his people.

How to Make the Incense

34 And the Lord said unto Moses, Take unto thee sweet spices, stacte, and onycha,

---

Cross references (center column):

6 Ex. 25:21, 22
7 Ex. 27:21; 30:34; 1Sam. 2:28; 1Chr. 23:13; Luke 1:9
8 Ex. 12:6
9 Lev. 10:1
10 Lev. 16:18; 23:27
12 Ex. 38:25; Num. 1:2, 5; 26:2; 31:50; 2Sam. 24:2, 15; Job 33:24; 36:18; Ps. 49:7; Matt. 20:28; Mark 10:45; 1Tim. 2:6; 1Pet. 1:18, 19
13 Ex. 38:26; Lev. 27:25; Num. 3:47; Ezek. 45:12; Matt. 17:24
15 Ex. 30:12; Job 34:19; Prov. 22:2; Eph. 6:9; Col. 3:25
16 Ex. 38:25; Num. 16:40
18 Ex. 38:8; 40:7, 30; 1Kgs. 7:38
19 Ex. 40:31, 32; Ps. 26:6; Isa. 52:11; John 13:10; Heb. 10:22
21 Ex. 28:43
23 Ps. 45:8; Prov. 7:17; Song 4:14; Jer. 6:20; Ezek. 27:22
24 Ex. 29:40; Ps. 45:8
25 Ex. 37:29; Num. 35:25; Ps. 89:20; 133:2
26 Ex. 40:9; Lev. 8:10; Num. 7:1
29 Ex. 29:37
30 Ex. 29:7-14; Lev. 8:12, 30
32 Ex. 30:25, 37
33 Gen. 17:14; Ex. 12:15; 30:38; Lev. 7:20, 21
34 Ex. 25:6; 37:29

and galbanum; *these* sweet spices with pure frankincense: of each shall there be a like *weight*:

35 And thou shalt make it a perfume, a confection after the art of the apothecary, tempered together, pure *and* holy:

36 And thou shalt beat *some* of it very small, and put of it before the testimony in the tabernacle of the congregation, where I will meet with thee: it shall be unto you most holy.

37 And *as for* the perfume which thou shalt make, ye shall not make to yourselves according to the composition thereof: it shall be unto thee holy for the LORD.

38 Whosoever shall make like unto that, to smell thereto, shall even be cut off from his people.

CHAPTER 31
God Appoints the Builders

1 And the LORD spake unto Moses, saying,

2 See, I have called by name Bezaleel the son of Uri, the son of Hur, of the tribe of Judah:

3 And I have filled him with the spirit of God, in wisdom, and in understanding, and in knowledge, and in all manner of workmanship,

4 To devise cunning works, to work in gold, and in silver, and in brass,

5 And in cutting of stones, to set *them*, and in carving of timber, to work in all manner of workmanship.

6 And I, behold, I have given with him Aholiab, the son of Ahisamach, of the tribe of Dan: and in the hearts of all that are wise hearted I have put wisdom, that they may make all that I have commanded thee;

7 The tabernacle of the congregation, and the ark of the testimony, and the mercy seat that *is* thereupon, and all the furniture of the tabernacle,

8 And the table and his furniture, and the pure candlestick with all his furniture, and the altar of incense,

9 And the altar of burnt offering with all his furniture, and the laver and his foot,

10 And the cloths of service, and the holy garments for Aaron the priest, and the garments of his sons, to minister in the priest's office,

11 And the anointing oil, and sweet incense for the holy *place*: according to all that I have commanded thee shall they do.

Rest on the Seventh Day

12 And the LORD spake unto Moses, saying,

13 Speak thou also unto the children of Is-

rael, saying, Verily my sabbaths ye shall keep: for it *is* a sign between me and you throughout your generations; that *ye* may know that I *am* the LORD that doth sanctify you.

14 Ye shall keep the sabbath therefore; for it *is* holy unto you: every one that defileth it shall surely be put to death: for whosoever doeth *any* work therein, that soul shall be cut off from among his people.

15 Six days may work be done; but in the seventh *is* the sabbath of rest, holy to the LORD: whosoever doeth *any* work in the sabbath day, he shall surely be put to death.

16 Wherefore the children of Israel shall keep the sabbath, to observe the sabbath throughout their generations, *for* a perpetual covenant.

17 It *is* a sign between me and the children of Israel for ever: for *in* six days the LORD made heaven and earth, and on the seventh day he rested, and was refreshed.

18 And he gave unto Moses, when he had made an end of communing with him upon mount Sinai, two tables of testimony, tables of stone, written with the finger of God.

CHAPTER 32
The Golden Calf

1 And when the people saw that Moses delayed to come down out of the mount, the people gathered themselves together unto Aaron, and said unto him, Up, make us gods, which shall go before us; for *as for* this Moses, the man that brought us up out of the land of Egypt, we wot not what is become of him.

2 And Aaron said unto them, Break off the golden earrings, which *are* in the ears of your wives, of your sons, and of your daughters, and bring *them* unto me.

3 And all the people brake off the golden earrings which *were* in their ears, and brought *them* unto Aaron.

4 And he received *them* at their hand, and fashioned it with a graving tool, after he had made it a molten calf: and they said, These *be* thy gods, O Israel, which brought thee up out of the land of Egypt.

5 And when Aaron saw *it*, he built an altar before it; and Aaron made proclamation, and said, To morrow *is* a feast to the LORD.

6 And they rose up early on the morrow, and offered burnt offerings, and brought peace offerings; and the people sat down to eat and to drink, and rose up to play.

7 And the LORD said unto Moses, Go, get thee down; for thy people, which thou

Center column cross-references

35 Ex. 30:25; Lev. 2:13

36 Ex. 29:37, 42; 30:32; Lev. 2:3; 16:2

2 Ex. 35:30; 36:1; 1Chr. 2:20

3 Ex. 35:31; 1Kgs. 7:14

6 Ex. 28:3; 35:10, 34, 35; 36:1

7 Ex. 36:8; Ex. 37:1, 6

8 Ex. 37:10, 17

9 Ex. 38:1, 8

10 Ex. 39:1, 41; Num. 4:5-15

11 Ex. 30:25, 31, 34; 37:29

13 Lev. 19:3, 30; 26:2; Ezek. 20:12, 20; 44:24

14 Ex. 20:8; 35:2; Num. 15:35; Deut. 5:12; Ezek. 20:12

15 Gen. 2:2; Ex. 16:23; 20:9, 10

17 Gen. 1:31; 2:2; Ex. 31:13; Ezek. 20:12, 20

18 Ex. 24:12; 32:15, 16; 34:28, 29; Deut. 4:13; 5:22; 9:10, 11; 2Cor. 3:3

1 Ex. 13:21; 24:18; Deut. 9:9; Acts 7:40

2 Judg. 8:24-27

4 Ex. 20:23; Deut. 9:16; Judg. 17:3, 4; 1Kgs. 12:28; Neh. 9:18; Ps. 106:19; Isa. 46:6; Acts 7:41; Rom. 1:23

5 Lev. 23:2, 4, 21, 37; 2Kgs. 10:20; 2Chr. 30:5

6 1Cor. 10:7

broughtest out of the land of Egypt, have corrupted *themselves*:

8 They have turned aside quickly out of the way which I commanded them: they have made them a molten calf, and have worshipped it, and have sacrificed thereunto, and said, These *be* thy gods, O Israel, which have brought thee up out of the land of Egypt.

9 And the LORD said unto Moses, I have seen this people, and, behold, it *is* a stiffnecked people:

10 Now therefore let me alone, that my wrath may wax hot against them, and that I may consume them: and I will make of thee a great nation.

11 And Moses besought the LORD his God, and said, LORD, why doth thy wrath wax hot against thy people, which thou hast brought forth out of the land of Egypt with great power, and with a mighty hand?

12 Wherefore should the Egyptians speak, and say, For mischief did he bring them out, to slay them in the mountains, and to consume them from the face of the earth? Turn from thy fierce wrath, and repent of this evil against thy people.

13 Remember Abraham, Isaac, and Israel, thy servants, to whom thou swarest by thine own self, and saidst unto them, I will multiply your seed as the stars of heaven, and all this land that I have spoken of will I give unto your seed, and they shall inherit *it* for ever.

14 And the LORD repented of the evil which he thought to do unto his people.

15 And Moses turned, and went down from the mount, and the two tables of the testimony *were* in his hand: the tables *were* written on both their sides; on the one side and on the other *were* they written.

16 And the tables *were* the work of God, and the writing *was* the writing of God, graven upon the tables.

17 And when Joshua heard the noise of the people as they shouted, he said unto Moses, *There is* a noise of war in the camp.

18 And he said, *It is* not the voice of *them that* shout for mastery, neither *is it* the voice of *them that* cry for being overcome: *but* the noise of *them that* sing do I hear.

19 And it came to pass, as soon as he came nigh unto the camp, that he saw the calf,

and the dancing: and Moses' anger waxed hot, and he cast the tables out of his hands, and brake them beneath the mount.

20 And he took the calf which they had made, and burnt *it* in the fire, and ground *it* to powder, and strawed *it* upon the water, and made the children of Israel drink *of it*.

21 And Moses said unto Aaron, What did this people unto thee, that thou hast brought so great a sin upon them?

22 And Aaron said, Let not the anger of my lord wax hot: thou knowest the people, that they *are set* on mischief.

23 For they said unto me, Make us gods, which shall go before us: for *as for* this Moses, the man that brought us up out of the land of Egypt, we wot not what is become of him.

24 And I said unto them, Whosoever hath any gold, let them break *it* off. So they gave *it* me: then I cast it into the fire, and there came out this calf.

25 And when Moses saw that the people *were* naked; (for Aaron had made them naked unto *their* shame among their enemies:)

26 Then Moses stood in the gate of the camp, and said, Who *is* on the LORD's side? *let him come* unto me. And all the sons of Levi gathered themselves together unto him.

27 And he said unto them, Thus saith the LORD God of Israel, Put every man his sword by his side, *and* go in and out from gate to gate throughout the camp, and slay every man his brother, and every man his companion, and every man his neighbour.

28 And the children of Levi did according to the word of Moses: and there fell of the people that day about three thousand men.

29 For Moses had said, Consecrate yourselves today to the LORD, even every man upon his son, and upon his brother; that he may bestow upon you a blessing this day.

30 And it came to pass on the morrow, that Moses said unto the people, Ye have sinned a great sin: and now I will go up unto the LORD; peradventure I shall make an atonement for your sin.

31 And Moses returned unto the LORD, and said, Oh, this people have sinned a great sin, and have made them gods of gold.

32 Yet now, if thou wilt forgive their sin;

8 Ex. 20:3, 4, 23; Deut. 9:16; 1Kgs. 12:28

9 Ex. 33:3, 5; 34:9; Deut. 9:6, 13; 31:27; 2Chr. 30:8; Isa. 48:4; Acts 7:51

10 Ex. 22:24; Num. 14:12

11 Deut. 9:18, 26-29; Ps. 74:1, 2; 106:23

12 Ex. 32:14; Num. 14:13; Deut. 9:28; 32:27

13 Gen. 12:7; 13:15; 15:7, 18; 22:16; 26:4; 28:13; 35:11, 12; Heb. 6:13

14 Deut. 32:26; 2Sam. 24:16; 1Chr. 21:15; Ps. 106:45; Jer. 18:8; 26:13, 19; Joel 2:13; Jon. 3:10; 4:2

15 Deut. 9:15

20 Deut. 9:21

21 Gen. 20:9; 26:10

22 Ex. 14:11; 15:24; 16:2; 20, 28; 17:2, 4

25 Ex. 33:4, 5; 2Chr. 28:19

29 Num. 25:11-13; Deut. 13:6-11; 33:9, 10; 1Sam. 15:18, 22; Prov. 21:3; Zech. 13:3; Matt. 10:37

30 Num. 25:13; 1Sam. 12:20, 23; 2Sam. 16:12; Amos 5:15; Luke 15:18

31 Ex. 20:23; Deut. 9:18

32:13 Moses reminds God of His covenant, which is the only reason God spared Israel as He had promised. Unfortunately, because Israel did not obey the Lord fully, they never possessed their complete inheritance—but they will during the Millennial Kingdom.

and if not, blot me, I pray thee, out of thy book which thou hast written.

33 And the LORD said unto Moses, Whosoever hath sinned against me, him will I blot out of my book.

34 Therefore now go, lead the people unto *the place* of which I have spoken unto thee: behold, mine Angel shall go before thee: nevertheless in the day when I visit I will visit their sin upon them.

35 And the LORD plagued the people, because they made the calf, which Aaron made.

CHAPTER 33
God Gives the Orders to March

1 And the LORD said unto Moses, Depart, *and* go up hence, thou and the people which thou hast brought up out of the land of Egypt, unto the land which I sware unto Abraham, to Isaac, and to Jacob, saying, Unto thy seed will I give it:

2 And I will send an angel before thee; and I will drive out the Canaanite, the Amorite, and the Hittite, and the Perizzite, the Hivite, and the Jebusite:

3 Unto a land flowing with milk and honey: for I will not go up in the midst of thee; for thou *art* a stiffnecked people: lest I consume thee in the way.

4 And when the people heard these evil tidings, they mourned: and no man did put on him his ornaments.

5 For the LORD had said unto Moses, Say unto the children of Israel, Ye *are* a stiffnecked people: I will come up into the midst of thee in a moment, and consume thee: therefore now put off thy ornaments from thee, that I may know what to do unto thee.

6 And the children of Israel stripped themselves of their ornaments by the mount Horeb.

7 And Moses took the tabernacle, and pitched it without the camp, afar off from the camp, and called it the Tabernacle of the congregation. And it came to pass, *that* every one which sought the LORD went out unto the tabernacle of the congregation, which *was* without the camp.

8 And it came to pass, when Moses went out unto the tabernacle, *that* all the people rose up, and stood every man *at* his tent door, and looked after Moses, until he was gone into the tabernacle.

9 And it came to pass, as Moses entered into the tabernacle, the cloudy pillar descended, and stood *at* the door of the tabernacle, and *the* LORD talked with Moses.

10 And all the people saw the cloudy pillar stand *at* the tabernacle door: and all the people rose up and worshipped, every man *in* his tent door.

11 And the LORD spake unto Moses face to face, as a man speaketh unto his friend. And he turned again into the camp: but his servant Joshua, the son of Nun, a young man, departed not out of the tabernacle.

12 And Moses said unto the LORD, See, thou sayest unto me, Bring up this people: and thou hast not let me know whom thou wilt send with me. Yet thou hast said, I know thee by name, and thou hast also found grace in my sight.

13 Now therefore, I pray thee, if I have found grace in thy sight, shew me now thy way, that I may know thee, that I may find grace in thy sight: and consider that this nation *is* thy people.

14 And he said, My presence shall go *with thee*, and I will give thee rest.

15 And he said unto him, If thy presence go not *with me*, carry us not up hence.

16 For wherein shall it be known here that I and thy people have found grace in thy sight? *is it* not in that thou goest with us? so shall we be separated, I and thy people, from all the people that *are* upon the face of the earth.

17 And the LORD said unto Moses, I will do this thing also that thou hast spoken: for thou hast found grace in my sight, and I know thee by name.

18 And he said, I beseech thee, shew me thy glory.

19 And he said, I will make all my goodness pass before thee, and I will proclaim the name of the LORD before thee; and will be gracious to whom I will be gracious, and will shew mercy on whom I will shew mercy.

20 And he said, Thou canst not see my face: for there shall no man see me, and live.

21 And the LORD said, Behold, *there is* a place by me, and thou shalt stand upon a rock:

22 And it shall come to pass, while my glory passeth by, that I will put thee in a clift of the rock, and will cover thee with my hand while I pass by:

23 And I will take away mine hand, and thou shalt see my back parts: but my face shall not be seen.

CHAPTER 34
The New Tablets

1 And the LORD said unto Moses, Hew thee two tables of stone like unto the first: and I

---

33 Lev. 23:30; Ezek. 18:4

34 Deut. 32:35; Amos 3:14; Rom. 2:5, 6

35 2Sam. 12:9; Acts 7:41

1 Gen. 12:7; Ex. 32:7, 13

2 Ex. 32:34; 34:11; Deut. 7:22; Josh. 24:11

7 Ex. 29:42, 43; Deut. 4:29; 2Sam. 21:1

8 Num. 16:27

9 Ex. 25:22; 31:18; Ps. 99:7

10 Ex. 4:31

11 Gen. 32:30; Ex. 24:13; Num. 12:8; Deut. 34:10

12 Gen. 18:19; Ps. 1:6; Jer. 1:5; John 10:14, 15; 2Tim. 2:19

13 Deut. 9:26, 29; Joel 2:17

14 Ex. 13:21; Isa. 63:9

15 Ex. 33:3; 34:9

16 Ex. 34:10; Deut. 4:7, 34; 2Sam. 7:23; 1Kgs. 8:53; Ps. 147:20

17 Gen. 19:21; Ex. 33:12; James 5:16

18 Ex. 33:20; 1Tim. 6:16

19 Ex. 34:5-7; Jer. 31:14

20 Gen. 32:30; Ex. 24:10; Deut. 5:24; Judg. 6:22; 13:22; Isa. 6:5; Rev. 1:16, 17

22 Ps. 91:1, 4; Isa. 2:21

23 Ex. 33:20; John 1:18

The Book of Life

By Tim LaHaye

The book of life is alluded to several times in the Old Testament. The psalmist speaks of "the book of the living" (Ps. 69:28), so we perceive that it is a book that contains the names of all the souls of men. It is also referred to as God the Father's book in Exodus 32:32–33, and it records all those whom God the Creator has made. It is, then, the book of the living, much like a modern county records book, only much more important, as Psalm 139:16 implies that more than just our names are written in this book.

There are several ways that an individual might have his or her name blotted out of the book of life. Exodus 32:33 says, "Whosoever hath sinned against me, him will I blot out of my book." It is possible, therefore, to have one's name erased from the book of life because of sin.

Revelation 3:5 promises, "He that overcometh, the same shall be clothed in white raiment; and I will not blot out his name out of the book of life." An "overcomer" here is one who is clothed in the white garments of Christ through His substitutionary atonement, guaranteeing that his name will not be blotted out of the book of life.

> The "book of life" contains the names of all the souls of men.

There is another way in which a person can have his or her name removed from the book of life. Revelation 22:19 explains, "And if any man shall take away from the words of the book of this prophecy, God shall take away his part out of the book of life." This severe warning is to false teachers who would seek to destroy the prophetic truth of the Word of God. Such will have their names removed from the book of life upon their deaths.

When we are born, our names are automatically written in the book of life, and they remain there as long as we live. Upon our deaths if we have sinned (and all have sinned) and have not been redeemed by the Lamb, and/or if we have detracted from the words of His prophecy, our names are blotted out of the book of life.

Revelation 13:8 tells us about a similar book, the "book of life of the Lamb." The Lamb referred to is Jesus Christ, the "Lamb of God, which taketh away the sin of the world" (John 1:29). The Lamb's book of life is the book of Jesus Christ in which are entered the names of those who have received eternal life (see Daniel 12:1). Primarily because a person's name can be blotted out of the book of life, I am convinced that the book of life and the Lamb's book of life are not the same book. Psalm 69:28 says, "Let them be blotted out of the book of the living, and not be written with the righteous." The book of life is a book that contains the names of everyone who has ever lived. If an individual has accepted Christ and His forgiveness of sins, this person's name is indelibly recorded in the Lamb's book of life ("written with the righteous"), and entrance into the Holy City is guaranteed (Rev. 21:27). If an individual never calls upon the Lord Jesus Christ for salvation, this person's name will not be recorded in the Lamb's book and will be blotted out of the book of life (see Rev. 20:15).

will write upon *these* tables the words that were in the first tables, which thou brakest.

2 And be ready in the morning, and come up in the morning unto mount Sinai, and present thyself there to me in the top of the mount.

3 And no man shall come up with thee, neither let any man be seen throughout all the mount; neither let the flocks nor herds feed before that mount.

4 And he hewed two tables of stone like unto the first; and Moses rose up early in the morning, and went up unto mount Sinai, as the LORD had commanded him, and took in his hand the two tables of stone.

5 And the LORD descended in the cloud, and stood with him there, and proclaimed the name of the LORD.

6 And the LORD passed by before him, and proclaimed, The LORD, The LORD God, merciful and gracious, longsuffering, and abundant in goodness and truth,

7 Keeping mercy for thousands, forgiving iniquity and transgression and sin, and that will by no means clear *the guilty*; visiting the iniquity of the fathers upon the children, and upon the children's children, unto the third and to the fourth *generation*.

8 And Moses made haste, and bowed his head toward the earth, and worshipped.

9 And he said, If now I have found grace in thy sight, O Lord, let my Lord, I pray thee, go among us; for it *is* a stiffnecked people; and pardon our iniquity and our sin, and take us for thine inheritance.

God's Agreement

10 And he said, Behold, I make a covenant: before all thy people I will do marvels, such as have not been done in all the earth, nor in any nation: and all the people among which thou *art* shall see the work of the LORD: for it *is* a terrible thing that I will do with thee.

11 Observe thou that which I command thee this day: behold, I drive out before thee the Amorite, and the Canaanite, and the Hittite, and the Perizzite, and the Hivite, and the Jebusite.

12 Take heed to thyself, lest thou make a covenant with the inhabitants of the land

whither thou goest, lest it be for a snare in the midst of thee:

13 But ye shall destroy their altars, break their images, and cut down their groves:

14 For thou shalt worship no other god: for the LORD, whose name *is* Jealous, *is* a jealous God:

15 Lest thou make a covenant with the inhabitants of the land, and they go a whoring after their gods, and do sacrifice unto their gods, and *one* call thee, and thou eat of his sacrifice;

16 And thou take of their daughters unto thy sons, and their daughters go a whoring after their gods, and make thy sons go a whoring after their gods.

17 Thou shalt make thee no molten gods.

18 The feast of unleavened bread shalt thou keep. Seven days thou shalt eat unleavened bread, as I commanded thee, in the time of the month Abib: for in the month Abib thou camest out from Egypt.

19 All that openeth the matrix *is* mine; and every firstling among thy cattle, *whether* ox or sheep, *that is* male.

20 But the firstling of an ass thou shalt redeem with a lamb: and if thou redeem *him* not, then shalt thou break his neck. All the firstborn of thy sons thou shalt redeem. And none shall appear before me empty.

21 Six days thou shalt work, but on the seventh day thou shalt rest: in earing time and in harvest thou shalt rest.

22 And thou shalt observe the feast of weeks, of the firstfruits of wheat harvest, and the feast of ingathering at the year's end.

23 Thrice in the year shall all your men children appear before the Lord GOD, the God of Israel.

24 For I will cast out the nations before thee, and enlarge thy borders: neither shall any man desire thy land, when thou shalt go up to appear before the LORD thy God thrice in the year.

25 Thou shalt not offer the blood of my sacrifice with leaven; neither shall the sacrifice of the feast of the passover be left unto the morning.

26 The first of the firstfruits of thy land thou shalt bring unto the house of the LORD

Center column references

2 Ex. 19:20; 24:12

3 Ex. 19:12, 13, 21

5 Ex. 33:19; Num. 14:17

6 Joel 2:13; Rom. 2:4

7 Ex. 20:6; Deut. 5:10; Job 10:14; Mic. 6:11; Nah. 1:3

8 Ex. 4:31

9 Deut. 32:9; Zech. 2:12

10 2Sam. 7:23; Ps. 77:14; 78:12; 145:6; 147:20; Isa. 64:3

13 Judg. 2:2; 6:25; 2Kgs. 18:4; 23:14; 2Chr. 31:1; 34:3, 4

14 Ex. 20:3, 5; Isa. 9:6; 57:15

15 Num. 25:2; 1Cor. 10:27

17 Ex. 32:8; Lev. 19:4

19 Luke 2:23

20 Ex. 13:13; 23:15; Num. 18:15; Deut. 16:16; 1Sam. 9:7, 8; 2Sam. 24:24

21 Ex. 20:9; 23:12; 35:2; Deut. 5:12, 13; Luke 13:14

23 Ex. 23:14, 17; Deut. 16:16

24 Gen. 35:5; 2Chr. 17:10; Acts 18:10

25 Ex. 12:10; 23:18

26 Ex. 23:19; Deut. 14:21; 26:2, 10

34:10–14 The influence of Egyptian pagan idolatry was still in the Hebrews, even though they were physically out of Egypt. During the very time God was writing the Ten Commandments for Moses, the people sinned. But God forgave them when they repented, and He renewed His promise to bless them IF they would cease from idolatry and worship Him only. They failed to take this action, and their failure is the reason why the nation of Israel has been so persecuted through the ages and even today occupies only a meager portion of the land God gave them.

thy God. Thou shalt not seethe a kid in his mother's milk.

27 And the LORD said unto Moses, Write thou these words: for after the tenor of these words I have made a covenant with thee and with Israel.

28 And he was there with the LORD forty days and forty nights; he did neither eat bread, nor drink water. And he wrote upon the tables the words of the covenant, the ten commandments.

29 And it came to pass, when Moses came down from mount Sinai with the two tables of testimony in Moses' hand, when he came down from the mount, that Moses wist not that the skin of his face shone while he talked with him.

30 And when Aaron and all the children of Israel saw Moses, behold, the skin of his face shone; and they were afraid to come nigh him.

31 And Moses called unto them; and Aaron and all the rulers of the congregation returned unto him: and Moses talked with them.

32 And afterward all the children of Israel came nigh: and he gave them in commandment all that the LORD had spoken with him in mount Sinai.

33 And till Moses had done speaking with them, he put a vail on his face.

34 But when Moses went in before the LORD to speak with him, he took the vail off, until he came out. And he came out, and spake unto the children of Israel that which he was commanded.

35 And the children of Israel saw the face of Moses, that the skin of Moses' face shone: and Moses put the vail upon his face again, until he went in to speak with him.

CHAPTER 35
Regulations for the Sabbath

1 And Moses gathered all the congregation of the children of Israel together, and said unto them, These are the words which the LORD hath commanded, that ye should do them.

2 Six days shall work be done, but on the seventh day there shall be to you an holy day, a sabbath of rest to the LORD: whosoever doeth work therein shall be put to death.

3 Ye shall kindle no fire throughout your habitations upon the sabbath day.

Collecting the Building Materials

4 And Moses spake unto all the congrega-

Cross references

27 Ex. 33:10; Deut. 4:13; 31:9

28 Ex. 24:18; 31:18; 32:16; 33:1; Deut. 4:13; 9:9, 18; 10:2, 4

29 Ex. 32:15; Matt. 17:2; 2Cor. 3:7, 13

32 Ex. 24:3

33 2Cor. 3:13

34 2Cor. 3:16

1 Ex. 34:32

2 Ex. 20:9; 31:14, 15; Lev. 23:3; Num. 15:32; Deut. 5:12; Luke 13:14

3 Ex. 16:23

4 Ex. 25:1, 2

5 Ex. 25:2

8 Ex. 25:6

10 Ex. 31:6

11 Ex. 26:1—27:21

12 Ex. 25:10-22

13 Ex. 25:23, 30; Lev. 24:5, 6

14 Ex. 25:31-40

15 Ex. 30:1, 23, 34

16 Ex. 27:1

17 Ex. 27:9

19 Ex. 31:10; 39:1, 41; Num. 4:5, 6

21 Ex. 25:2; 35:5, 22, 26, 29; 36:2; 1Chr. 28:2, 9; 29:9; Ezra 7:27; 2Cor. 8:12; 9:7

tion of the children of Israel, saying, This is the thing which the LORD commanded, saying,

5 Take ye from among you an offering unto the LORD: whosoever is of a willing heart, let him bring it, an offering of the LORD; gold, and silver, and brass,

6 And blue, and purple, and scarlet, and fine linen, and goats' hair,

7 And rams' skins dyed red, and badgers' skins, and shittim wood,

8 And oil for the light, and spices for anointing oil, and for the sweet incense,

9 And onyx stones, and stones to be set for the ephod, and for the breastplate.

10 And every wise hearted among you shall come, and make all that the LORD hath commanded;

11 The tabernacle, his tent, and his covering, his taches, and his boards, his bars, his pillars, and his sockets,

12 The ark, and the staves thereof, with the mercy seat, and the vail of the covering,

13 The table, and his staves, and all his vessels, and the shewbread,

14 The candlestick also for the light, and his furniture, and his lamps, with the oil for the light,

15 And the incense altar, and his staves, and the anointing oil, and the sweet incense, and the hanging for the door at the entering in of the tabernacle,

16 The altar of burnt offering, with his brasen grate, his staves, and all his vessels, the laver and his foot,

17 The hangings of the court, his pillars, and their sockets, and the hanging for the door of the court,

18 The pins of the tabernacle, and the pins of the court, and their cords,

19 The cloths of service, to do service in the holy place, the holy garments for Aaron the priest, and the garments of his sons, to minister in the priest's office.

20 And all the congregation of the children of Israel departed from the presence of Moses.

21 And they came, every one whose heart stirred him up, and every one whom his spirit made willing, and they brought the LORD's offering to the work of the tabernacle of the congregation, and for all his service, and for the holy garments.

22 And they came, both men and women, as many as were willing hearted, and brought bracelets, and earrings, and rings, and tablets, all jewels of gold: and every man that offered offered an offering of gold unto the LORD.

23 And every man, with whom was found blue, and purple, and scarlet, and fine linen, and goats' *hair*, and red skins of rams, and badgers' skins, brought *them*.

24 Every one that did offer an offering of silver and brass brought the LORD's offering: and every man, with whom was found shittim wood for any work of the service, brought *it*.

25 And all the women that were wise hearted did spin with their hands, and brought that which they had spun, *both* of blue, and of purple, *and* of scarlet, and of fine linen.

26 And all the women whose heart stirred them up in wisdom spun goats' *hair*.

27 And the rulers brought onyx stones, and stones to be set, for the ephod, and for the breastplate;

28 And spice, and oil for the light, and for the anointing oil, and for the sweet incense.

29 The children of Israel brought a willing offering unto the LORD, every man and woman, whose heart made them willing to bring for all manner of work, which the LORD had commanded to be made by the hand of Moses.

30 And Moses said unto the children of Israel, See, the LORD hath called by name Bezaleel the son of Uri, the son of Hur, of the tribe of Judah;

31 And he hath filled him with the spirit of God, in wisdom, in understanding, and in knowledge, and in all manner of workmanship;

32 And to devise curious works, to work in gold, and in silver, and in brass,

33 And in the cutting of stones, to set *them*, and in carving of wood, to make any manner of cunning work.

34 And he hath put in his heart that he may teach, *both* he, and Aholiab, the son of Ahisamach, of the tribe of Dan.

35 Them hath he filled with wisdom of heart, to work all manner of work, of the engraver, and of the cunning workman, and of the embroiderer, in blue, and in purple, in scarlet, and in fine linen, and of the weaver, *even* of them that do any work, and of those that devise cunning work.

CHAPTER 36

1 Then wrought Bezaleel and Aholiab, and every wise hearted man, in whom the LORD put wisdom and understanding to know how to work all manner of work for the service of the sanctuary, according to all that the LORD had commanded.

23 1Chr. 29:8
25 Ex. 28:3; 31:6; 36:1; 2Kgs. 23:7; Prov. 31:19, 22, 24
27 1Chr. 29:6; Ezra 2:68
28 Ex. 30:23
29 Ex. 35:21; 1Chr. 29:9
30 Ex. 31:2-5
34 Ex. 31:6
35 Ex. 31:3, 6; 35:31; 1Kgs. 7:14; 2Chr. 2:14; Isa. 28:26
1 Ex. 25:8; 28:3; 31:6; 35:10, 35
2 Ex. 35:21, 26; 1Chr. 29:5
3 Ex. 35:27
5 2Cor. 8:2, 3

8 Ex. 26:1

12 Ex. 26:5

14 Ex. 26:7

2 And Moses called Bezaleel and Aholiab, and every wise hearted man, in whose heart the LORD had put wisdom, *even* every one whose heart stirred him up to come unto the work to do it:

3 And they received of Moses all the offering, which the children of Israel had brought for the work of the service of the sanctuary, to make it *withal*. And they brought yet unto him free offerings every morning.

4 And all the wise men, that wrought all the work of the sanctuary, came every man from his work which they made;

5 And they spake unto Moses, saying, The people bring much more than enough for the service of the work, which the LORD commanded to make.

6 And Moses gave commandment, and they caused it to be proclaimed throughout the camp, saying, Let neither man nor woman make any more work for the offering of the sanctuary. So the people were restrained from bringing.

7 For the stuff they had was sufficient for all the work to make it, and too much.

The Making of the Tabernacle

8 And every wise hearted man among them that wrought the work of the tabernacle made ten curtains *of* fine twined linen, and blue, and purple, and scarlet: *with* cherubims of cunning work made he them.

9 The length of one curtain *was* twenty and eight cubits, and the breadth of one curtain four cubits: the curtains *were* all of one size.

10 And he coupled the five curtains one unto another: and *the other* five curtains he coupled one unto another.

11 And he made loops of blue on the edge of one curtain from the selvedge in the coupling: likewise he made in the uttermost side of *another* curtain, in the coupling of the second.

12 Fifty loops made he in one curtain, and fifty loops made he in the edge of the curtain which *was* in the coupling of the second: the loops held one *curtain* to another.

13 And he made fifty taches of gold, and coupled the curtains one unto another with the taches: so it became one tabernacle.

14 And he made curtains *of* goats' *hair* for the tent over the tabernacle: eleven curtains he made them.

15 The length of one curtain *was* thirty cubits, and four cubits *was* the breadth of one curtain: the eleven curtains *were* of one size.

16 And he coupled five curtains by themselves, and six curtains by themselves.

17 And he made fifty loops upon the uttermost edge of the curtain in the coupling, and fifty loops made he upon the edge of the curtain which coupleth the second.

18 And he made fifty taches *of* brass to couple the tent together, that it might be one.

19 And he made a covering for the tent *of* rams' skins dyed red, and a covering *of* badgers' skins above *that.*

20 And he made boards for the tabernacle *of* shittim wood, standing up.

21 The length of a board *was* ten cubits, and the breadth of a board one cubit and a half.

22 One board had two tenons, equally distant one from another: thus did he make for all the boards of the tabernacle.

23 And he made boards for the tabernacle; twenty boards for the south side southward:

24 And forty sockets of silver he made under the twenty boards; two sockets under one board for his two tenons, and two sockets under another board for his two tenons.

25 And for the other side of the tabernacle, *which is* toward the north corner, he made twenty boards,

26 And their forty sockets of silver; two sockets under one board, and two sockets under another board.

27 And for the sides of the tabernacle westward he made six boards.

28 And two boards made he for the corners of the tabernacle in the two sides.

29 And they were coupled beneath, and coupled together at the head thereof, to one ring: thus he did to both of them in both the corners.

30 And there were eight boards; and their sockets *were* sixteen sockets of silver, under every board two sockets.

31 And he made bars of shittim wood; five for the boards of the one side of the tabernacle,

32 And five bars for the boards of the other side of the tabernacle, and five bars for the boards of the tabernacle for the sides westward.

33 And he made the middle bar to shoot through the boards from the one end to the other.

34 And he overlaid the boards with gold, and made their rings *of* gold *to be* places for the bars, and overlaid the bars with gold.

35 And he made a vail *of* blue, and purple, and scarlet, and fine twined linen: *with* cherubims made he it of cunning work.

36 And he made thereunto four pillars *of*

19 Ex. 26:14
20 Ex. 26:15
31 Ex. 26:26
35 Ex. 26:31
37 Ex. 26:36

1 Ex. 25:10

6 Ex. 25:17

10 Ex. 25:23

shittim *wood,* and overlaid them with gold: their hooks *were of* gold; and he cast for them four sockets of silver.

37 And he made an hanging for the tabernacle door *of* blue, and purple, and scarlet, and fine twined linen, of needlework;

38 And the five pillars of it with their hooks: and he overlaid their chapiters and their fillets with gold: but their five sockets *were of* brass.

CHAPTER 37
Making the Ark of God

1 And Bezaleel made the ark *of* shittim wood: two cubits and a half *was* the length of it, and a cubit and a half the breadth of it, and a cubit and a half the height of it:

2 And he overlaid it with pure gold within and without, and made a crown of gold to it round about.

3 And he cast for it four rings of gold, *to be set* by the four corners of it; even two rings upon the one side of it, and two rings upon the other side of it.

4 And he made staves *of* shittim wood, and overlaid them with gold.

5 And he put the staves into the rings by the sides of the ark, to bear the ark.

6 And he made the mercy seat *of* pure gold: two cubits and a half *was* the length thereof, and one cubit and a half the breadth thereof.

7 And he made two cherubims *of* gold, beaten out of one piece made he them, on the two ends of the mercy seat;

8 One cherub on the end on this side, and another cherub on the *other* end on that side: out of the mercy seat made he the cherubims on the two ends thereof.

9 And the cherubims spread out *their* wings on high, *and* covered with their wings over the mercy seat, with their faces one to another; *even* to the mercy seatward were the faces of the cherubims.

Making the Table

10 And he made the table *of* shittim wood: two cubits *was* the length thereof, and a cubit the breadth thereof, and a cubit and a half the height thereof:

11 And he overlaid it with pure gold, and made thereunto a crown of gold round about.

12 Also he made thereunto a border of an handbreadth round about; and made a crown of gold for the border thereof round about.

13 And he cast for it four rings of gold, and

put the rings upon the four corners that *were* in the four feet thereof.

14 Over against the border were the rings, the places for the staves to bear the table.

15 And he made the staves *of* shittim wood, and overlaid them with gold, to bear the table.

16 And he made the vessels which *were* upon the table, his dishes, and his spoons, and his bowls, and his covers to cover withal, *of* pure gold.

Making the Lampstand

17 And he made the candlestick *of* pure gold: *of* beaten work made he the candlestick; his shaft, and his branch, his bowls, his knops, and his flowers, were of the same:

18 And six branches going out of the sides thereof; three branches of the candlestick out of the one side thereof, and three branches of the candlestick out of the other side thereof:

19 Three bowls made after the fashion of almonds in one branch, a knop and a flower; and three bowls made like almonds in another branch, a knop and a flower: so throughout the six branches going out of the candlestick.

20 And in the candlestick *were* four bowls made like almonds, his knops, and his flowers:

21 And a knop under two branches of the same, and a knop under two branches of the same, and a knop under two branches of the same, according to the six branches going out of it.

22 Their knops and their branches were of the same: all of it *was* one beaten work *of* pure gold.

23 And he made his seven lamps, and his snuffers, and his snuffdishes, *of* pure gold.

24 *Of* a talent of pure gold made he it, and all the vessels thereof.

Making the Incense Altar

25 And he made the incense altar *of* shittim wood: the length of it *was* a cubit, and the breadth of it a cubit; *it was* foursquare; and two cubits *was* the height of it; the horns thereof were of the same.

26 And he overlaid it with pure gold, *both* the top of it, and the sides thereof round about, and the horns of it: also he made unto it a crown of gold round about.

27 And he made two rings of gold for it under the crown thereof, by the two corners of it, upon the two sides thereof, to be places for the staves to bear it withal.

28 And he made the staves *of* shittim wood, and overlaid them with gold.

29 And he made the holy anointing oil, and the pure incense of sweet spices, according to the work of the apothecary.

CHAPTER 38
Making the Altar and the Basin

1 And he made the altar of burnt offering *of* shittim wood: five cubits *was* the length thereof, and five cubits the breadth thereof; *it was* foursquare; and three cubits the height thereof.

2 And he made the horns thereof on the four corners of it; the horns thereof were of the same: and he overlaid it with brass.

3 And he made all the vessels of the altar, the pots, and the shovels, and the basons, *and* the fleshhooks, and the firepans: all the vessels thereof made he *of* brass.

4 And he made for the altar a brasen grate of network under the compass thereof beneath unto the midst of it.

5 And he cast four rings for the four ends of the grate of brass, *to be* places for the staves.

6 And he made the staves *of* shittim wood, and overlaid them with brass.

7 And he put the staves into the rings on the sides of the altar, to bear it withal; he made the altar hollow with boards.

8 And he made the laver *of* brass, and the foot of it *of* brass, of the lookingglasses of *the women* assembling, which assembled *at* the door of the tabernacle of the congregation.

Making the Enclosure

9 And he made the court: on the south side southward the hangings of the court *were of* fine twined linen, an hundred cubits:

10 Their pillars *were* twenty, and their brasen sockets twenty; the hooks of the pillars and their fillets *were of* silver.

11 And for the north side *the hangings were* an hundred cubits, their pillars *were* twenty, and their sockets of brass twenty; the hooks of the pillars and their fillets *of* silver.

12 And for the west side *were* hangings of fifty cubits, their pillars ten, and their sockets ten; the hooks of the pillars and their fillets *of* silver.

13 And for the east side eastward fifty cubits.

14 The hangings of the one side *of the gate were* fifteen cubits; their pillars three, and their sockets three.

15 And for the other side of the court gate, on this hand and that hand, *were* hangings

16 Ex. 25:29
17 Ex. 25:31
25 Ex. 30:1
29 Ex. 30:23, 34
1 Ex. 27:1

8 Ex. 30:18; 1Sam. 2:22

9 Ex. 27:9

of fifteen cubits; their pillars three, and their sockets three.

16 All the hangings of the court round about *were* of fine twined linen.

17 And the sockets for the pillars *were of* brass; the hooks of the pillars and their fillets *of* silver; and the overlaying of their chapiters *of* silver; and all the pillars of the court *were* filleted with silver.

18 And the hanging for the gate of the court *was* needlework, *of* blue, and purple, and scarlet, and fine twined linen: and twenty cubits *was* the length, and the height in the breadth *was* five cubits, answerable to the hangings of the court.

19 And their pillars *were* four, and their sockets *of* brass four; their hooks *of* silver, and the overlaying of their chapiters and their fillets *of* silver.

20 And all the pins of the tabernacle, and of the court round about, *were of* brass.

"The Sum of the Tabernacle"

21 This is the sum of the tabernacle, *even* of the tabernacle of testimony, as it was counted, according to the commandment of Moses, *for* the service of the Levites, by the hand of Ithamar, son to Aaron the priest.

22 And Bezaleel the son of Uri, the son of Hur, of the tribe of Judah, made all that the LORD commanded Moses.

23 And with him *was* Aholiab, son of Ahisamach, of the tribe of Dan, an engraver, and a cunning workman, and an embroiderer in blue, and in purple, and in scarlet, and fine linen.

24 All the gold that was occupied for the work in all the work of the holy *place*, even the gold of the offering, was twenty and nine talents, and seven hundred and thirty shekels, after the shekel of the sanctuary.

25 And the silver of them that were numbered of the congregation *was* an hundred talents, and a thousand seven hundred and threescore and fifteen shekels, after the shekel of the sanctuary:

26 A bekah for every man, *that is*, half a shekel, after the shekel of the sanctuary, for every one that went to be numbered, from twenty years old and upward, for six hundred thousand and three thousand and five hundred and fifty *men*.

27 And of the hundred talents of silver were cast the sockets of the sanctuary, and the sockets of the vail; an hundred sockets of the hundred talents, a talent for a socket.

28 And of the thousand seven hundred seventy and five shekels he made hooks for the pillars, and overlaid their chapiters, and filleted them.

29 And the brass of the offering *was* seventy talents, and two thousand and four hundred shekels.

30 And therewith he made the sockets to the door of the tabernacle of the congregation, and the brasen altar, and the brasen grate for it, and all the vessels of the altar,

31 And the sockets of the court round about, and the sockets of the court gate, and all the pins of the tabernacle, and all the pins of the court round about.

CHAPTER 39
The Making of the Priests' Clothes

1 And of the blue, and purple, and scarlet, they made cloths of service, to do service in the holy *place*, and made the holy garments for Aaron; as the LORD commanded Moses.

2 And he made the ephod *of* gold, blue, and purple, and scarlet, and fine twined linen.

3 And they did beat the gold into thin plates, and cut *it into* wires, to work *it* in the blue, and in the purple, and in the scarlet, and in the fine linen, *with* cunning work.

4 They made shoulderpieces for it, to couple *it* together: by the two edges was it coupled together.

5 And the curious girdle of his ephod, that *was* upon it, *was* of the same, according to the work thereof; *of* gold, blue, and purple, and scarlet, and fine twined linen; as the LORD commanded Moses.

6 And they wrought onyx stones inclosed in ouches of gold, graven, as signets are graven, with the names of the children of Israel.

7 And he put them on the shoulders of the ephod, *that they should be* stones for a memorial to the children of Israel; as the LORD commanded Moses.

8 And he made the breastplate *of* cunning work, like the work of the ephod; *of* gold, blue, and purple, and scarlet, and fine twined linen.

9 It was foursquare; they made the breastplate double: a span *was* the length thereof, and a span the breadth thereof, *being* doubled.

10 And they set in it four rows of stones: *the first* row *was* a sardius, a topaz, and a carbuncle: this *was* the first row.

11 And the second row, an emerald, a sapphire, and a diamond.

12 And the third row, a ligure, an agate, and an amethyst.

Cross-references (center column):

20 Ex. 27:19
21 Num. 1:50, 53; 4:28, 33; 9:15; 10:11; 17:7, 8; 18:2; 2Chr. 24:6; Acts 7:44
22 Ex. 31:2, 6
24 Ex. 30:13, 24; Lev. 5:15; 27:3, 25; Num. 3:47; 18:16
26 Ex. 30:13, 15; Num. 1:46
27 Ex. 26:19, 21, 25, 32
1 Ex. 28:4; 31:10; 35:19, 23
2 Ex. 28:6
6 Ex. 28:9
7 Ex. 28:12
8 Ex. 28:15
10 Ex. 28:17, 21

13 And the fourth row, a beryl, an onyx, and a jasper: *they were* inclosed in ouches of gold in their inclosings.

14 And the stones *were* according to the names of the children of Israel, twelve, according to their names, *like* the engravings of a signet, every one with his name, according to the twelve tribes.

15 And they made upon the breastplate chains at the ends, *of* wreathen work *of* pure gold.

16 And they made two ouches *of* gold, and two gold rings; and put the two rings in the two ends of the breastplate.

17 And they put the two wreathen chains of gold in the two rings on the ends of the breastplate.

18 And the two ends of the two wreathen chains they fastened in the two ouches, and put them on the shoulderpieces of the ephod, before it.

19 And they made two rings of gold, and put *them* on the two ends of the breastplate, upon the border of it, which *was* on the side of the ephod inward.

20 And they made two *other* golden rings, and put them on the two sides of the ephod underneath, toward the forepart of it, over against the *other* coupling thereof, above the curious girdle of the ephod.

21 And they did bind the breastplate by his rings unto the rings of the ephod with a lace of blue, that it might be above the curious girdle of the ephod, and that the breastplate might not be loosed from the ephod; as the LORD commanded Moses.

22 And he made the robe of the ephod *of* woven work, all *of* blue.

23 And *there was* an hole in the midst of the robe, as the hole of an habergeon, *with* a band round about the hole, that it should not rend.

24 And they made upon the hems of the robe pomegranates *of* blue, and purple, and scarlet, *and* twined *linen*.

25 And they made bells *of* pure gold, and put the bells between the pomegranates upon the hem of the robe, round about between the pomegranates;

26 A bell and a pomegranate, a bell and a pomegranate, round about the hem of the robe to minister *in*; as the LORD commanded Moses.

27 And they made coats *of* fine linen *of* woven work for Aaron, and for his sons,

28 And a mitre *of* fine linen, and goodly bonnets *of* fine linen, and linen breeches *of* fine twined linen,

29 And a girdle *of* fine twined linen, and

blue, and purple, and scarlet, *of* needlework; as the LORD commanded Moses.

30 And they made the plate of the holy crown *of* pure gold, and wrote upon it a writing, *like to* the engravings of a signet, HOLINESS TO THE LORD.

31 And they tied unto it a lace of blue, to fasten *it* on high upon the mitre; as the LORD commanded Moses.

The Tabernacle Is Completed!

32 Thus was all the work of the tabernacle of the tent of the congregation finished: and the children of Israel did according to all that the LORD commanded Moses, so did they.

33 And they brought the tabernacle unto Moses, the tent, and all his furniture, his taches, his boards, his bars, and his pillars, and his sockets,

34 And the covering of rams' skins dyed red, and the covering of badgers' skins, and the vail of the covering,

35 The ark of the testimony, and the staves thereof, and the mercy seat,

36 The table, *and* all the vessels thereof, and the shewbread,

37 The pure candlestick, *with* the lamps thereof, *even with* the lamps to be set in order, and all the vessels thereof, and the oil for light,

38 And the golden altar, and the anointing oil, and the sweet incense, and the hanging for the tabernacle door,

39 The brasen altar, and his grate of brass, his staves, and all his vessels, the laver and his foot,

40 The hangings of the court, his pillars, and his sockets, and the hanging for the court gate, his cords, and his pins, and all the vessels of the service of the tabernacle, for the tent of the congregation,

41 The cloths of service to do service in the holy *place*, and the holy garments for Aaron the priest, and his sons' garments, to minister in the priest's office.

42 According to all that the LORD commanded Moses, so the children of Israel made all the work.

43 And Moses did look upon all the work, and, behold, they had done it as the LORD had commanded, even so had they done it: and Moses blessed them.

CHAPTER 40
Setting Up the Tabernacle

1 And the LORD spake unto Moses, saying,

2 On the first day of the first month shalt

22 Ex. 28:31
25 Ex. 28:33
27 Ex. 28:39, 40
28 Ex. 28:4, 39, 42; Ezek. 44:18
29 Ex. 28:39
30 Ex. 28:36, 37
32 Ex. 25:40; 39:42, 43
42 Ex. 35:10
43 Lev. 9:22, 23; Num. 6:23; Josh. 22:6; 2Sam. 6:18; 1Kgs. 8:14; 2Chr. 30:27
2 Ex. 12:2; 13:4; 26:1, 30; 40:17

thou set up the tabernacle of the tent of the congregation.

3 And thou shalt put therein the ark of the testimony, and cover the ark with the vail.

4 And thou shalt bring in the table, and set in order the things that are to be set in order upon it; and thou shalt bring in the candlestick, and light the lamps thereof.

5 And thou shalt set the altar of gold for the incense before the ark of the testimony, and put the hanging of the door to the tabernacle.

6 And thou shalt set the altar of the burnt offering before the door of the tabernacle of the tent of the congregation.

7 And thou shalt set the laver between the tent of the congregation and the altar, and shalt put water therein.

8 And thou shalt set up the court round about, and hang up the hanging at the court gate.

9 And thou shalt take the anointing oil, and anoint the tabernacle, and all that is therein, and shalt hallow it, and all the vessels thereof: and it shall be holy.

10 And thou shalt anoint the altar of the burnt offering, and all his vessels, and sanctify the altar: and it shall be an altar most holy.

11 And thou shalt anoint the laver and his foot, and sanctify it.

12 And thou shalt bring Aaron and his sons unto the door of the tabernacle of the congregation, and wash them with water.

13 And thou shalt put upon Aaron the holy garments, and anoint him, and sanctify him; that he may minister unto me in the priest's office.

14 And thou shalt bring his sons, and clothe them with coats:

15 And thou shalt anoint them, as thou didst anoint their father, that they may minister unto me in the priest's office: for their anointing shall surely be an everlasting priesthood throughout their generations.

16 Thus did Moses: according to all that the LORD commanded him, so did he.

17 And it came to pass in the first month in the second year, on the first day of the month, that the tabernacle was reared up.

18 And Moses reared up the tabernacle, and fastened his sockets, and set up the boards thereof, and put in the bars thereof, and reared up his pillars.

19 And he spread abroad the tent over the tabernacle, and put the covering of the tent

3 Ex. 26:33; 40:21; Num. 4:5

4 Ex. 25:30; 26:35; 40:22, 23, 24, 25

5 Ex. 40:26

7 Ex. 30:18; 40:30

9 Ex. 30:26

10 Ex. 29:36, 37

12 Lev. 8:1-13

13 Ex. 28:41

15 Num. 25:13

17 Ex. 40:1; Num. 7:1

20 Ex. 25:16

21 Ex. 26:33; 35:12

22 Ex. 26:35

23 Ex. 40:4

24 Ex. 26:35

25 Ex. 25:37; 40:4

26 Ex. 30:6; 40:5

27 Ex. 30:7

28 Ex. 26:36; 40:5

29 Ex. 29:38-42; 40:6

30 Ex. 30:18; 40:7

32 Ex. 30:19, 20

33 Ex. 27:9, 16; 40:8

34 Ex. 29:43; Lev. 16:2; Num. 9:15; 1Kgs. 8:10, 11; 2Chr. 5:13; 7:2; Isa. 6:4; Hag. 2:7, 9; Rev. 15:8

35 Lev. 16:2; 1Kgs. 8:11; 2Chr. 5:14

36 Num. 9:17; 10:11; Neh. 9:19

37 Num. 9:19-22

above upon it; as the LORD commanded Moses.

20 And he took and put the testimony into the ark, and set the staves on the ark, and put the mercy seat above upon the ark:

21 And he brought the ark into the tabernacle, and set up the vail of the covering, and covered the ark of the testimony; as the LORD commanded Moses.

22 And he put the table in the tent of the congregation, upon the side of the tabernacle northward, without the vail.

23 And he set the bread in order upon it before the LORD; as the LORD had commanded Moses.

24 And he put the candlestick in the tent of the congregation, over against the table, on the side of the tabernacle southward.

25 And he lighted the lamps before the LORD; as the LORD commanded Moses.

26 And he put the golden altar in the tent of the congregation before the vail:

27 And he burnt sweet incense thereon; as the LORD commanded Moses.

28 And he set up the hanging at the door of the tabernacle.

29 And he put the altar of burnt offering by the door of the tabernacle of the tent of the congregation, and offered upon it the burnt offering and the meat offering; as the LORD commanded Moses.

30 And he set the laver between the tent of the congregation and the altar, and put water there, to wash withal.

31 And Moses and Aaron and his sons washed their hands and their feet thereat:

32 When they went into the tent of the congregation, and when they came near unto the altar, they washed; as the LORD commanded Moses.

33 And he reared up the court round about the tabernacle and the altar, and set up the hanging of the court gate. So Moses finished the work.

The Glory of the Lord Fills the Tabernacle

34 Then a cloud covered the tent of the congregation, and the glory of the LORD filled the tabernacle.

35 And Moses was not able to enter into the tent of the congregation, because the cloud abode thereon, and the glory of the LORD filled the tabernacle.

36 And when the cloud was taken up from over the tabernacle, the children of Israel went onward in all their journeys:

37 But if the cloud were not taken up, then

they journeyed not till the day that it was taken up.

38 For the cloud of the LORD *was* upon the

38 Ex. 13:21; Num. 9:15

tabernacle by day, and fire was on it by night, in the sight of all the house of Israel, throughout all their journeys.

Leviticus

This third volume of the Torah is called "Leviticus," first so named in the Latin Vulgate (A.D. 400). Also called the book of atonement, it is a manual of sacrifices and a guidebook of worship practices primarily for Hebrew priests. In addition, it teaches the nation Israel, which has just emerged from Egypt, principles of spiritual holiness, physical cleanliness, and dietary health.

The book covers about one month (Ex. 40:17; Num. 1:1), from the construction of the Tabernacle to the numbering of the people for war. In Exodus the Tabernacle was built; in Leviticus the Israelites learn how to worship.

Author
Moses

Date
1440 B.C.

Key Truth
Holiness

Historic Time
Completion of the Tabernacle

Key Verse
19:2
. . . Ye shall be holy: for I the LORD your God am holy.

The terms "holiness," "holy," and "sanctify" appear about 152 times, "atonement" some 45 times, and "priest" 189 times. The New Testament cites Leviticus at least 90 times.

At Sinai the Israelites officially became "a peculiar people" for the Lord (Deut. 14:2), a "theocracy" under His rule, dedicated to God and His worship.

All sacrifices and offerings forecast various aspects of Christ's atoning ministry (Heb. 7—10). Of special significance are the seven feasts of the Lord in chapter 23, which foreshadow **1)** "Christ our Passover," **2)** Unleavened Bread—the Bread of Life, **3)** Firstfruits—Christ's resurrection, **4)** Weeks, fifty days after Firstfruits—Pentecost, **5)** Trumpets—Israel's future regathering, **6)** Day of Atonement—Christ and Israel in the Last Days, **7)** Tabernacles—a celebration of past and future deliverance for Israel. (See the article on the Seven Feasts of Israel.) To gain insight into the typical and larger meanings of the feasts, study Hebrews 4:13—5:10; 6:19—10:31.

Future experiences of the Israelites are also forecast in chapter 26, including drought, distress, and dispersion as chastisements for their waywardness.

Thirty-seven distinct prophecies appear in 506 out of 839 verses or 59 percent of the book, but 91 percent of these prophecies are typological, that is, they are examples or patterns of people or events.

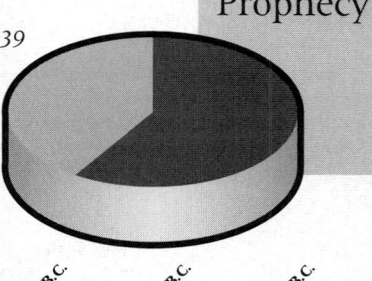

59%
Prophecy

1750 B.C.	1700 B.C.	1650 B.C.	1600 B.C.	1550 B.C.	1500 B.C.	1450 B.C.	1400 B.C.	1350 B.

1527 Moses in Pharaoh's court

1487 Moses flees to Midian

1447 Exodus from Egypt

1407 Entrance into Canaan

1446 Book of Leviticus

1730-1447 Bondage in Egypt begins

Bondage in Egypt ends

1446 The Tabernacle constructed

1375-1050 Israel ruled by Judges

CHAPTER 1
Burnt Offerings

1 And the LORD called unto Moses, and spake unto him out of the tabernacle of the congregation, saying,

2 Speak unto the children of Israel, and say unto them, If any man of you bring an offering unto the LORD, ye shall bring your offering of the cattle, *even* of the herd, and of the flock.

3 If his offering *be* a burnt sacrifice of the herd, let him offer a male without blemish: he shall offer it of his own voluntary will at the door of the tabernacle of the congregation before the LORD.

4 And he shall put his hand upon the head of the burnt offering; and it shall be accepted for him to make atonement for him.

5 And he shall kill the bullock before the LORD: and the priests, Aaron's sons, shall bring the blood, and sprinkle the blood round about upon the altar that *is by the* door of the tabernacle of the congregation.

6 And he shall flay the burnt offering, and cut it into his pieces.

7 And the sons of Aaron the priest shall put fire upon the altar, and lay the wood in order upon the fire:

8 And the priests, Aaron's sons, shall lay the parts, the head, and the fat, in order upon the wood that *is* on the fire which *is* upon the altar:

9 But his inwards and his legs shall he wash in water: and the priest shall burn all on the altar, *to be* a burnt sacrifice, an offering made by fire, of a sweet savour unto the LORD.

10 And if his offering *be* of the flocks, *namely*, of the sheep, or of the goats, for a burnt sacrifice; he shall bring it a male without blemish.

11 And he shall kill it on the side of the altar northward before the LORD: and the priests, Aaron's sons, shall sprinkle his blood round about upon the altar.

12 And he shall cut it into his pieces, with his head and his fat: and the priest shall lay them in order on the wood that *is* on the fire which *is* upon the altar:

13 But he shall wash the inwards and the legs with water: and the priest shall bring *it* all, and burn *it* upon the altar: it *is* a burnt

Cross references

1 Ex. 19:3; 40:34, 35; Num. 12:4, 5
2 Lev. 22:18, 19
3 Ex. 3:1; 12:5; 22:20, 21; Eph. 5:27; Heb. 9:14; 1Pet. 1:19
4 Ex. 29:10, 15, 19; Lev. 3:2, 8, 13; 4:15, 20, 26, 31, 35; 8:14, 22; 9:7; Num. 15:25; Rom. 5:11
5 Lev. 3:8; 2Chr. 35:11; Mic. 6:6; Heb. 10:11; 12:24; 1Pet. 1:2
7 Gen. 22:9
9 Gen. 8:21; 2Cor. 2:15
10 Lev. 1:3
11 Lev. 1:5

1:2 bring an offering. All sacrifices described in this book typically point to Jesus Christ, who gave Himself without spot unto God. They are thus predictive figures, called types. Aaron the high priest also typifies Christ, our high priest (Heb. 4:15; 5:4–6; 9:7–14).

1:3 burnt sacrifice. Several animals could be used in this sacrifice. The bullock or ox suggests Christ's atoning death, wherein He experienced the fires of divine judgment for us. The sheep or lamb remind us of the Passover and the shed blood, which protects and delivers. The goat is usually descriptive of transgressors (Matt. 25:33), but Jesus, who "was numbered with the transgressors" (Isa. 53:12), took our place. The turtle dove or young pigeon was available for the poor who could not afford a stock animal, reminding us that Jesus Himself "became poor" for us (2 Cor. 8:9). This was the offering of Joseph and Mary upon the birth of Jesus, indicating that they were poor (Luke 2:22–24).

1:4 atonement for him. All the blood sacrifices were to "make atonement," or to cover or wipe away sins, anticipating that Jesus would make one sacrifice, fulfilling all types and validating all past offerings which could never permanently take away sins (see Heb. 10:4–12).

1:5 sprinkle the blood round about upon the altar. The slaying of the animal victim set forth symbolically the transfer of sin and guilt from the offerer to the sacrifice itself. The animal bore the penalty for sin, for "the wages of sin is death" (Rom. 6:23). The sacrifices represented the final and efficacious sacrifice of Jesus, shedding His blood to make full and complete atonement for sin (see Ps. 40:6).

1:8 fire which is upon the altar. Fire usually indicates wrath, judgment, and punishment. The fire here suggests the consuming wrath of God that comes upon the animal and not the offerer. That the bullock was totally consumed teaches that Christ's sacrifice completely satisfied the demands of divine justice.

1:9 a sweet savour. The first three of the five major sacrifices in Leviticus 1—7 are presented as sweet savor offerings, meaning literally "an aroma that placates." This indicated God's satisfaction with the offerings and the propitiation for sin that He accepted, thus satisfying and placating the righteous judgment and wrath of God. They pointed typically to the redemptive work of Christ, whose personal sacrifice to the Father was a "sweet aroma" that satisfied the righteous judgment of God upon sin.

1:10 sheep, or of the goats . . . a male without blemish. A sheep or lamb without blemish typified the perfection and submission without objection that our Lord manifested, as He was "brought as a lamb to the slaughter, and . . . openeth not his mouth" (Isa. 53:7).

1:12 The perfection of these Old Testament sacrifices prefigured the sinlessness of Christ, who was "holy, harmless, undefiled, separated from sinners" (Heb. 7:26, cf. 9:24).

sacrifice, an offering made by fire, of a sweet savour unto the LORD.

14 And if the burnt sacrifice for his offering to the LORD *be* of fowls, then he shall bring his offering of turtledoves, or of young pigeons.

15 And the priest shall bring it unto the altar, and wring off his head, and burn *it* on the altar; and the blood thereof shall be wrung out at the side of the altar:

16 And he shall pluck away his crop with his feathers, and cast it beside the altar on the east part, by the place of the ashes:

17 And he shall cleave it with the wings thereof, *but* shall not divide *it* asunder: and the priest shall burn it upon the altar, upon the wood that *is* upon the fire: *it is* a burnt sacrifice, an offering made by fire, of a sweet savour unto the LORD.

CHAPTER 2
Meat Offerings

1 And when any will offer a meat offering unto the LORD, his offering shall be *of* fine flour; and he shall pour oil upon it, and put frankincense thereon:

2 And he shall bring it to Aaron's sons the priests: and he shall take thereout his handful of the flour thereof, and of the oil thereof, with all the frankincense thereof; and the priest shall burn the memorial of it upon the altar, *to be* an offering made by fire, of a sweet savour unto the LORD:

3 And the remnant of the meat offering *shall be* Aaron's and his sons': *it is* a thing most holy of the offerings of the LORD made by fire.

4 And if thou bring an oblation of a meat offering baken in the oven, *it shall be* unleavened cakes of fine flour mingled with oil, or unleavened wafers anointed with oil.

5 And if thy oblation *be* a meat offering *baken* in a pan, it shall be *of* fine flour unleavened, mingled with oil.

6 Thou shalt part it in pieces, and pour oil thereon: it *is* a meat offering.

7 And if thy oblation *be* a meat offering *baken* in the frying pan, it shall be made *of* fine flour with oil.

8 And thou shalt bring the meat offering that is made of these things unto the LORD: and when it is presented unto the priest, he shall bring it unto the altar.

9 And the priest shall take from the meat offering a memorial thereof, and shall burn *it* upon the altar: *it is* an offering made by fire, of a sweet savour unto the LORD.

10 And that which is left of the meat offering *shall be* Aaron's and his sons': *it is* a thing most holy of the offerings of the LORD made by fire.

11 No meat offering, which ye shall bring unto the LORD, shall be made with leaven: for ye shall burn no leaven, nor any honey, in any offering of the LORD made by fire.

12 As for the oblation of the firstfruits, ye shall offer them unto the LORD: but they shall not be burnt on the altar for a sweet savour.

13 And every oblation of thy meat offering shalt thou season with salt; neither shalt thou suffer the salt of the covenant of thy God to be lacking from thy meat offering: with all thine offerings thou shalt offer salt.

14 And if thou offer a meat offering of thy firstfruits unto the LORD, thou shalt offer for the meat offering of thy firstfruits green ears of corn dried by the fire, *even* corn beaten out of full ears.

15 And thou shalt put oil upon it, and lay frankincense thereon: it *is* a meat offering.

16 And the priest shall burn the memorial

Cross references (center column)

14 Lev. 5:7; 12:8; Luke 2:24

16 Lev. 6:10

17 Gen. 15:10; Lev. 1:9, 13

1 Lev. 6:14; 9:17; Num. 15:4

2 Lev. 2:9; 5:12; 6:15; 24:7; Isa. 66:3; Acts 10:4

3 Ex. 29:37; Lev. 7:9; 10:12, 13; Num. 18:9

4 Ex. 29:2

9 Ex. 29:18; Lev. 2:2

10 Lev. 2:3

11 Lev. 6:17; Matt. 16:12; Mark 8:15; Luke 12:1; 1Cor. 5:8; Gal. 5:9

12 Ex. 22:29; Lev. 23:10, 11

13 Num. 18:19; Ezek. 43:24; Mark 9:49; Col. 4:6

14 Lev. 23:10, 14; 2Kgs. 4:42

15 Lev. 2:1

16 Lev. 2:2

2:1 meat offering. As the burnt offering typified Christ in His death, the meal offering typifies Him in life. It speaks of His loving and living obedience through a spotless life, dedicated to God and satisfying the demands of the law (Matt. 3:15). Without leaven, typifying malice, wickedness, and erroneous doctrine (1 Cor. 5:6–9; Matt. 16:12), the bread symbolized the consecration of one's life and substance (Lev. 2:14). Jesus used the unleavened bread during the Passover to symbolize His body, broken for us (1 Cor. 11:23–24), an act which is memorialized by the Lord's Supper in this Church Age. Oil usually signifies the Holy Spirit, given to Him without measure (John 3:34). Frankincense, a sweet resin used in perfumes and burned for its pleasant aroma, speaks of spiritual dedication and communion (see Mal. 1:11; Rev. 5:8; 8:3–4), exemplified in Christ's life and ministry.

2:11 Leaven or yeast was always a symbol of error or sin. Jesus spoke of the "leaven of the Pharisees," which is outward religiosity without inner reality (Luke 12:1), the leaven of the Sadducees, which is erroneous doctrines, such as not believing in the resurrection of the dead (Matt. 16:6–12), and the "leaven of Herod," which is worldly compromise with ungodly civil leaders (Mark 8:15). Paul mentions the "leaven of malice and wickedness" (1 Cor. 5:8). None of these evils were found in Christ, nor should they be found in us.

2:13 with all thine offerings thou shalt offer salt. Jesus alludes to this passage in Mark 9:49–50. Believers are to be "the salt of the earth" (Matt. 5:13).

of it, *part* of the beaten corn thereof, and *part* of the oil thereof, with all the frankincense thereof: *it is* an offering made by fire unto the LORD.

CHAPTER 3
Peace Offerings

1 And if his oblation *be* a sacrifice of peace offering, if he offer *it* of the herd; whether *it be* a male or female, he shall offer it without blemish before the LORD.

2 And he shall lay his hand upon the head of his offering, and kill it *at* the door of the tabernacle of the congregation: and Aaron's sons the priests shall sprinkle the blood upon the altar round about.

3 And he shall offer of the sacrifice of the peace offering an offering made by fire unto the LORD; the fat that covereth the inwards, and all the fat that *is* upon the inwards,

4 And the two kidneys, and the fat that *is* on them, which *is* by the flanks, and the caul above the liver, with the kidneys, it shall he take away.

5 And Aaron's sons shall burn it on the altar upon the burnt sacrifice, which *is* upon the wood that *is* on the fire: *it is* an offering made by fire, of a sweet savour unto the LORD.

6 And if his offering for a sacrifice of peace offering unto the LORD *be* of the flock; male or female, he shall offer it without blemish.

7 If he offer a lamb for his offering, then shall he offer it before the LORD.

8 And he shall lay his hand upon the head of his offering, and kill it before the tabernacle of the congregation: and Aaron's sons shall sprinkle the blood thereof round about upon the altar.

9 And he shall offer of the sacrifice of the peace offering an offering made by fire unto the LORD; the fat thereof, *and* the whole

rump, it shall he take off hard by the backbone; and the fat that covereth the inwards, and all the fat that *is* upon the inwards,

10 And the two kidneys, and the fat that *is* upon them, which *is* by the flanks, and the caul above the liver, with the kidneys, it shall he take away.

11 And the priest shall burn it upon the altar: *it is* the food of the offering made by fire unto the LORD.

12 And if his offering *be* a goat, then he shall offer it before the LORD.

13 And he shall lay his hand upon the head of it, and kill it before the tabernacle of the congregation: and the sons of Aaron shall sprinkle the blood thereof upon the altar round about.

14 And he shall offer thereof his offering, *even* an offering made by fire unto the LORD; the fat that covereth the inwards, and all the fat that *is* upon the inwards,

15 And the two kidneys, and the fat that *is* upon them, which *is* by the flanks, and the caul above the liver, with the kidneys, it shall he take away.

16 And the priest shall burn them upon the altar: *it is* the food of the offering made by fire for a sweet savour: all the fat *is* the LORD's.

17 *It shall be* a perpetual statute for your generations throughout all your dwellings, that ye eat neither fat nor blood.

CHAPTER 4
Sin Offerings

1 And the LORD spake unto Moses, saying,

2 Speak unto the children of Israel, saying, If a soul shall sin through ignorance against any of the commandments of the LORD *concerning things* which ought not to be done, and shall do against any of them:

Cross references (center column):

1 Lev. 1:3; 7:11, 29; 22:21

2 Ex. 29:10; Lev. 1:4, 5

3 Ex. 29:13, 22; Lev. 4:8, 9

5 Ex. 29:13; Lev. 6:12

6 Lev. 3:1

11 Lev. 21:6, 8, 17, 21, 22; 22:25; Ezek. 44:7; Mal. 1:7, 12

12 Lev. 3:1, 7

16 Lev. 7:23, 25; 1Sam. 2:15; 2Chr. 7:7

17 Gen. 9:4; Lev. 3:16; 6:18; 7:23, 26, 36; 17:7, 10, 14; 23:14; Deut. 12:16; cf. Deut. 32:14; 1Sam. 14:33; Neh. 8:10; Ezek. 44:7, 15

2 Lev. 5:15, 17; Num. 15:22-29; 1Sam. 14:27; Ps. 19:12

3:1 peace offering. The slain animal offering differs from the burnt offering. The fat and the kidneys were removed from the bullock or heifer, after the blood. If it was a lamb being offered, the rump was also removed. The inner parts were burned and the remainder provided sustenance for the priests. This typifies Christ as our peace offering on the cross, for He is also our "peace" (Eph. 2:13–17).

3:8 he shall lay his hand upon the head. The offerer of the sacrifice, by touching the head with the hand, indicates identification, symbolically shifting the guilt and penalty for his own sins to the sacrifice. This act finds its typical fulfillment in justification by faith through Christ. This is the third and last of the sweet savor offerings,

which show Christ in His own human perfection, and His willingness to lovingly obey the Father's will.

4:2–3 sin offering. This sacrifice could be offered for a specific sin (5:1–4) with personal confession involved (4:21; 5:5). Christ was made sin for us (2 Cor. 5:21; 1 John 1:9). The sin offering and the trespass offering were not voluntary, as were the three sweet savor offerings. This offering was required by the Law of Moses to be offered by those who unintentionally or inadvertently committed sins out of ignorance, weakness, or sudden response to a situation. God holds people accountable for their sins. Therefore ignorance is not an excuse.

3 If the priest that is anointed do sin according to the sin of the people; then let him bring for his sin, which he hath sinned, a young bullock without blemish unto the LORD for a sin offering.

4 And he shall bring the bullock unto the door of the tabernacle of the congregation before the LORD; and shall lay his hand upon the bullock's head, and kill the bullock before the LORD.

5 And the priest that is anointed shall take of the bullock's blood, and bring it to the tabernacle of the congregation:

6 And the priest shall dip his finger in the blood, and sprinkle of the blood seven times before the LORD, before the vail of the sanctuary.

7 And the priest shall put *some* of the blood upon the horns of the altar of sweet incense before the LORD, which *is* in the tabernacle of the congregation; and shall pour all the blood of the bullock at the bottom of the altar of the burnt offering, which *is at* the door of the tabernacle of the congregation.

8 And he shall take off from it all the fat of the bullock for the sin offering; the fat that covereth the inwards, and all the fat that *is* upon the inwards,

9 And the two kidneys, and the fat that *is* upon them, which *is* by the flanks, and the caul above the liver, with the kidneys, it shall he take away,

10 As it was taken off from the bullock of the sacrifice of peace offerings: and the priest shall burn them upon the altar of the burnt offering.

11 And the skin of the bullock, and all his flesh, with his head, and with his legs, and his inwards, and his dung,

12 Even the whole bullock shall he carry forth without the camp unto a clean place, where the ashes are poured out, and burn him on the wood with fire: where the ashes are poured out shall he be burnt.

13 And if the whole congregation of Israel sin through ignorance, and the thing be hid from the eyes of the assembly, and they have done *somewhat against* any of the commandments of the LORD *concerning things*

14 When the sin, which they have sinned against it, is known, then the congregation shall offer a young bullock for the sin, and bring him before the tabernacle of the congregation.

15 And the elders of the congregation shall lay their hands upon the head of the bullock before the LORD: and the bullock shall be killed before the LORD.

16 And the priest that is anointed shall bring of the bullock's blood to the tabernacle of the congregation:

17 And the priest shall dip his finger *in some* of the blood, and sprinkle *it* seven times before the LORD, *even* before the vail.

18 And he shall put *some* of the blood upon the horns of the altar which *is* before the LORD, that *is* in the tabernacle of the congregation, and shall pour out all the blood at the bottom of the altar of the burnt offering, which *is at* the door of the tabernacle of the congregation.

19 And he shall take all his fat from him, and burn *it* upon the altar.

20 And he shall do with the bullock as he did with the bullock for a sin offering, so shall he do with this: and the priest shall make an atonement for them, and it shall be forgiven them.

21 And he shall carry forth the bullock without the camp, and burn him as he burned the first bullock: it *is* a sin offering for the congregation.

22 When a ruler hath sinned, and done *somewhat* through ignorance *against* any of the commandments of the LORD his God *concerning things* which should not be done, and is guilty;

23 Or if his sin, wherein he hath sinned, come to his knowledge; he shall bring his offering, a kid of the goats, a male without blemish:

24 And he shall lay his hand upon the head of the goat, and kill it in the place where they kill the burnt offering before the LORD: it *is* a sin offering.

25 And the priest shall take of the blood of the sin offering with his finger, and put *it*

Cross references

3 Lev. 8:12; 9:2
4 Lev. 1:3, 4
5 Lev. 16:14; Num. 19:4
7 Lev. 5:9; 8:15; 9:9; 16:18
10 Lev. 3:3-5
11 Ex. 29:14; Num. 19:5
12 Lev. 6:11; Heb. 13:11
13 Lev. 5:2-4, 17; Num. 15:24; Josh. 7:11
15 Lev. 1:4
16 Lev. 4:5; Heb. 9:12, 13, 14
20 Lev. 4:3; Num. 15:25; Dan. 9:24; Rom. 5:11; Heb. 2:17; 10:10-12; 1 John 1:7; 2:2
22 Lev. 4:2, 13
23 Lev. 4:14
24 Lev. 4:4-7
25 Lev. 4:30

4:3 the priest that is anointed. This designated the high priest (8:12). If he as the spiritual leader of the people violated some law of God, his guilt affected the people. This affirms the inability of human priests to remove sin from even their own lives. Only Christ, our high priest, was sinless (2 Cor. 5:21).

4:4–7 The details of the killing of the bullock and the shedding of its blood remind us that "without shedding of blood" there is no forgiveness of sin (Heb. 9:22).

4:12 without the camp. The remainder of the animal was not consumed on the altar but removed outside the camp to be burned in a clean place. That type is fulfilled in Jesus, who "that he might sanctify the people with his own blood, suffered without the gate" (Heb. 13:12).

upon the horns of the altar of burnt offering, and shall pour out his blood at the bottom of the altar of burnt offering.

26 And he shall burn all his fat upon the altar, as the fat of the sacrifice of peace offerings: and the priest shall make an atonement for him as concerning his sin, and it shall be forgiven him.

27 And if any one of the common people sin through ignorance, while he doeth *somewhat against* any of the commandments of the LORD *concerning things* which ought not to be done, and be guilty;

28 Or if his sin, which he hath sinned, come to his knowledge: then he shall bring his offering, a kid of the goats, a female without blemish, for his sin which he hath sinned.

29 And he shall lay his hand upon the head of the sin offering, and slay the sin offering in the place of the burnt offering.

30 And the priest shall take of the blood thereof with his finger, and put *it* upon the horns of the altar of burnt offering, and shall pour out all the blood thereof at the bottom of the altar.

31 And he shall take away all the fat thereof, as the fat is taken away from off the sacrifice of peace offerings; and the priest shall burn *it* upon the altar for a sweet savour unto the LORD; and the priest shall make an atonement for him, and it shall be forgiven him.

32 And if he bring a lamb for a sin offering, he shall bring it a female without blemish.

33 And he shall lay his hand upon the head of the sin offering, and slay it for a sin offering in the place where they kill the burnt offering.

34 And the priest shall take of the blood of the sin offering with his finger, and put *it* upon the horns of the altar of burnt offering, and shall pour out all the blood thereof at the bottom of the altar:

35 And he shall take away all the fat thereof, as the fat of the lamb is taken away from the sacrifice of the peace offerings; and the priest shall burn them upon the altar, according to the offerings made by fire unto the LORD: and the priest shall make an

atonement for his sin that he hath committed, and it shall be forgiven him.

CHAPTER 5
Situations

1 And if a soul sin, and hear the voice of swearing, and *is* a witness, whether he hath seen or known *of it*; if he do not utter *it*, then he shall bear his iniquity.

2 Or if a soul touch any unclean thing, whether *it be* a carcase of an unclean beast, or a carcase of unclean cattle, or the carcase of unclean creeping things, and *if* it be hidden from him; he also shall be unclean, and guilty.

3 Or if he touch the uncleanness of man, whatsoever uncleanness *it be* that a man shall be defiled withal, and it be hid from him; when he knoweth *of it*, then he shall be guilty.

4 Or if a soul swear, pronouncing with *his* lips to do evil, or to do good, whatsoever *it be* that a man shall pronounce with an oath, and it be hid from him; when he knoweth *of it*, then he shall be guilty in one of these.

5 And it shall be, when he shall be guilty in one of these *things*, that he shall confess that he hath sinned in that *thing*:

6 And he shall bring his trespass offering unto the LORD for his sin which he hath sinned, a female from the flock, a lamb or a kid of the goats, for a sin offering; and the priest shall make an atonement for him concerning his sin.

7 And if he be not able to bring a lamb, then he shall bring for his trespass, which he hath committed, two turtledoves, or two young pigeons, unto the LORD; one for a sin offering, and the other for a burnt offering.

8 And he shall bring them unto the priest, who shall offer *that* which *is* for the sin offering first, and wring off his head from his neck, but shall not divide *it* asunder:

9 And he shall sprinkle of the blood of the sin offering upon the side of the altar; and the rest of the blood shall be wrung out at the bottom of the altar: it *is* a sin offering.

10 And he shall offer the second *for* a burnt offering, according to the manner: and the

Cross references (center column)

26 Lev. 3:5; 4:20; Num. 15:28
27 Lev. 4:2; Num. 15:27
28 Lev. 4:23
29 Lev. 4:4, 24
31 Ex. 29:18; Lev. 1:9; 3:3, 14; 4:26
32 Lev. 4:28
35 Lev. 3:5; 4:26, 31
1 Lev. 5:17; 7:18; 17:16; 19:8; 20:17; Num. 9:13; 1Kgs. 8:31; Matt. 26:63
2 Lev. 5:17; 11:24, 28, 31, 39; Num. 19:11, 13, 16
3 Lev. 12:1; 13:59; 15:1-33
4 1Sam. 25:22; Acts 23:12; Mark 6:23
5 Lev. 16:21; 26:40; Num. 5:7; Ezra 10:11, 12
7 Lev. 1:14; 12:8; 14:21
8 Lev. 1:15
9 Lev. 4:7, 18, 30, 34
10 Lev. 1:14; Lev. 4:26

4:27–28 any one of the common people. Ordinary people with fewer resources could bring their sin offerings in the form of an unblemished female goat or a young lamb. An atonement or covering was made for sin in all of these cases. Every sacrifice typified and was fulfilled in the suffering and death of Jesus on the cross.

5:6 trespass offering. This special ceremony concerns sins involving dishonesty, theft, deceit, or lying to cover up other sins. The guilty party, if repentant, can receive forgiveness, but is expected to make restitution. Christ died for our sins of ignorance, our unintentional sins as well as our intentional sins (6:1–7). All sin can be forgiven through His sacrifice, but true and sincere repentance should result in restitution.

Levitical Offerings and Sacrifices

By Arnold Fruchtenbaum

The five special offerings outlined in Leviticus 1–7 are a guidebook, if you will, to a relationship with God. These sacrifices were indicative of the state of one's heart, a representation of obedience to God and faith in the Sacrifice to come. The perfect fulfillment of these offerings is the Lord Jesus Christ who sacrificed Himself to redeem us to God (Heb. 9:26; 10:7–12).

The first of these five offerings is the **burnt offering** (Hebr. *olah,* "to go up"), the name indicating that the whole offering went up in smoke. This is the oldest of the offerings, found as early as the Book of Genesis. This was a voluntary offering in which the worshiper devoted his whole offering—all of it—to God through the fire. The underlying purpose of the burnt offering was to secure atonement for sins, but the immediate purpose was to express total dedication to God. Hence, the burnt offering is symbolic of the sanctification of the whole man in self-surrender to the Lord.

> *The perfect fulfillment of these offerings is the Lord Jesus Christ.*

The second offering is called a **meal offering** (Hebr. *korban minchah,* "to give a present" in the context of giving a gift to gain the favor of a superior). The basic concept is that of a present (Gen. 32:13, 18). The basic content of the meal offering was usually either wheat or barley. Often, the meal offering is mentioned in conjunction with the burnt offering, and the two offerings are very closely connected (Josh. 22:23, 29; Judg. 13:19, 23; 1 Kgs. 8:64; 2 Kgs. 16:13). The meal offering was the only offering that was bloodless; however, it was normally accompanied by a blood offering of some type (Lev. 23:9–14; Num. 15:1–16; Ezra 7:17). It was offered to God in thanksgiving and then given to the priest for the purpose of ministry. The meal offering represents the fruit of that sanctification.

The third offering, called the **peace offering** (Hebr. *zebach shlamim,* "sacrifices of peace [pl.]"), was a voluntary thanksgiving offering. There were three motivations for the peace offering: **1)** a thanksgiving offering (Lev. 7:12–15; 22:29) or an acknowledgement of God's deliverance or blessing bestowed as an answer to prayer (Ps. 56:12–13; 107:22); **2)** a votive offering, which involved making a vow (Lev. 7:16); and **3)** a free will offering to express devotion of thanksgiving to God for some unexpected blessing (Lev. 7:16; 22:17–20). This offering denotes the blossoming of the possession and enjoyment of saving grace.

The fourth offering is the **sin offering** (Hebr. *chattath,* "expiation, missing the mark"). This was a mandatory offering for sins done unwittingly or unintentionally. In other words, this offering was for sins committed through ignorance, error, or oversight, rising out of human infirmity or from the weakness of the flesh. The key result of the sin offering was forgiveness.

The fifth and final offering is called the **trespass offering** (Hebr. *asham,* which carries the concept of guilt and *moal,* "a violation"). Thus, this offering is often referred to as either a trespass offering, a reparation offering, or a guilt offering. The sin offering focused on the sin itself, while the trespass offering focuses our attention on the practice of sin. With this offering the emphasis is on the harmful effects of sin; therefore, it requires confession, compensation, and restitution for the wrong done.

priest shall make an atonement for him for his sin which he hath sinned, and it shall be forgiven him.

11 But if he be not able to bring two turtledoves, or two young pigeons, then he that sinned shall bring for his offering the tenth part of an ephah of fine flour for a sin offering; he shall put no oil upon it, neither shall he put *any* frankincense thereon: for it *is* a sin offering.

12 Then shall he bring it to the priest, and the priest shall take his handful of it, *even* a memorial thereof, and burn *it* on the altar, according to the offerings made by fire unto the LORD: it *is* a sin offering.

13 And the priest shall make an atonement for him as touching his sin that he hath sinned in one of these, and it shall be forgiven him: and *the remnant* shall be the priest's, as a meat offering.

Trepass Offerings

14 And the LORD spake unto Moses, saying,

15 If a soul commit a trespass, and sin through ignorance, in the holy things of the LORD; then he shall bring for his trespass unto the LORD a ram without blemish out of the flocks, with thy estimation by shekels of silver, after the shekel of the sanctuary, for a trespass offering:

16 And he shall make amends for the harm that he hath done in the holy thing, and shall add the fifth part thereto, and give it unto the priest: and the priest shall make an atonement for him with the ram of the trespass offering, and it shall be forgiven him.

17 And if a soul sin, and commit any of these things which are forbidden to be done by the commandments of the LORD; though he wist *it* not, yet is he guilty, and shall bear his iniquity.

18 And he shall bring a ram without blemish out of the flock, with thy estimation, for a trespass offering, unto the priest: and the priest shall make an atonement for him concerning his ignorance wherein he erred and wist *it* not, and it shall be forgiven him.

19 It *is* a trespass offering: he hath certainly trespassed against the LORD.

CHAPTER 6

1 And the LORD spake unto Moses, saying,

2 If a soul sin, and commit a trespass against the LORD, and lie unto his neighbour in that which was delivered him to keep, or in fellowship, or in a thing taken away by violence, or hath deceived his neighbour;

3 Or have found that which was lost, and lieth concerning it, and sweareth falsely; in any of all these that a man doeth, sinning therein:

4 Then it shall be, because he hath sinned, and is guilty, that he shall restore that which he took violently away, or the thing which he hath deceitfully gotten, or that which was delivered him to keep, or the lost thing which he found,

5 Or all that about which he hath sworn falsely; he shall even restore it in the principal, and shall add the fifth part more thereto, *and* give it unto him to whom it appertaineth, in the day of his trespass offering.

6 And he shall bring his trespass offering unto the LORD, a ram without blemish out of the flock, with thy estimation, for a trespass offering, unto the priest:

7 And the priest shall make an atonement for him before the LORD: and it shall be forgiven him for any thing of all that he hath done in trespassing therein.

The Law of the Offerings

8 And the LORD spake unto Moses, saying,

9 Command Aaron and his sons, saying, This *is* the law of the burnt offering: It *is* the burnt offering, because of the burning upon the altar all night unto the morning, and the fire of the altar shall be burning in it.

10 And the priest shall put on his linen garment, and his linen breeches shall he put upon his flesh, and take up the ashes which the fire hath consumed with the burnt offering on the altar, and he shall put them beside the altar.

11 Num. 5:15

12 Lev. 2:2; Lev. 4:35

13 Lev. 2:3; Lev. 4:26

15 Ex. 30:13; Lev. 22:14; 27:25; Ezra 10:19

16 Lev. 4:26; 6:5; 22:14; 27:13, 15, 27, 31; Num. 5:7

17 Lev. 4:2, 13, 22, 27; 5:1, 2, 15; Ps. 19:12; Luke 12:48

18 Lev. 5:15, 16

19 Ezra 10:2

2 Ex. 22:7, 10; Lev. 19:11; Num. 5:6; Prov. 24:28; 26:19; Acts 5:4; Col. 3:9

3 Ex. 22:11; Lev. 19:12; Deut. 22:1, 2, 3; Jer. 7:9; Zech. 5:4

5 Lev. 5:16; Num. 5:7; 2Sam. 12:6; Luke 19:8

6 Lev. 5:15

7 Lev. 4:26

10 Ex. 28:39, 40, 41, 43; Lev. 1:16; 16:4; Ezek. 44:17, 18

5:15–16 When an injustice was done toward another person, or another person's possessions were unintentionally affected by some action or mistake, not only was a financial settlement in favor of the offended party required (besides an animal sacrifice), but twenty percent was to be added to that amount. However, redemption before God is never through money, for "ye were not redeemed with corruptible things. . . . But with the precious blood of Christ" (1 Pet. 1:18–19).

6:1–7 commit a trespass. Several kinds of sins against God and persons are included here in connection with the trespass offering: fraud, violence, deceit, perjury, extortion, theft, embezzlement, and finding and keeping something known to belong to someone else. In all cases, an additional penalty of twenty percent was required as restitution.

11 And he shall put off his garments, and put on other garments, and carry forth the ashes without the camp unto a clean place.
12 And the fire upon the altar shall be burning in it; it shall not be put out: and the priest shall burn wood on it every morning, and lay the burnt offering in order upon it; and he shall burn thereon the fat of the peace offerings.
13 The fire shall ever be burning upon the altar; it shall never go out.

Grain Offerings

14 And this *is* the law of the meat offering: the sons of Aaron shall offer it before the LORD, before the altar.
15 And he shall take of it his handful, of the flour of the meat offering, and of the oil thereof, and all the frankincense which *is* upon the meat offering, and shall burn *it* upon the altar *for* a sweet savour, *even* the memorial of it, unto the LORD.
16 And the remainder thereof shall Aaron and his sons eat: with unleavened bread shall it be eaten in the holy place; in the court of the tabernacle of the congregation they shall eat it.
17 It shall not be baken with leaven. I have given it *unto them for* their portion of my offerings made by fire; it *is* most holy, as *is* the sin offering, and as the trespass offering.
18 All the males among the children of Aaron shall eat of it. *It shall be* a statute for ever in your generations concerning the offerings of the LORD made by fire: every one that toucheth them shall be holy.
19 And the LORD spake unto Moses, saying,
20 This *is* the offering of Aaron and of his sons, which they shall offer unto the LORD in the day when he is anointed; the tenth part of an ephah of fine flour for a meat offering perpetual, half of it in the morning, and half thereof at night.
21 In a pan it shall be made with oil; *and when it is* baken, thou shalt bring it in: *and* the baken pieces of the meat offering shalt thou offer *for* a sweet savour unto the LORD.
22 And the priest of his sons that is anointed in his stead shall offer it: *it is* a statute for ever unto the LORD; it shall be wholly burnt.
23 For every meat offering for the priest shall be wholly burnt: it shall not be eaten.

Sin Offerings

24 And the LORD spake unto Moses, saying,
25 Speak unto Aaron and to his sons, saying, This *is* the law of the sin offering: In the

place where the burnt offering is killed shall the sin offering be killed before the LORD: it *is* most holy.
26 The priest that offereth it for sin shall eat it: in the holy place shall it be eaten, in the court of the tabernacle of the congregation.
27 Whatsoever shall touch the flesh thereof shall be holy: and when there is sprinkled of the blood thereof upon any garment, thou shalt wash that whereon it was sprinkled in the holy place.
28 But the earthen vessel wherein it is sodden shall be broken: and if it be sodden in a brasen pot, it shall be both scoured, and rinsed in water.
29 All the males among the priests shall eat thereof: it *is* most holy.
30 And no sin offering, whereof *any* of the blood is brought into the tabernacle of the congregation to reconcile *withal* in the holy *place*, shall be eaten: it shall be burnt in the fire.

CHAPTER 7
Regulations for Repayment Offerings

1 Likewise this *is* the law of the trespass offering: it *is* most holy.
2 In the place where they kill the burnt offering shall they kill the trespass offering: and the blood thereof shall he sprinkle round about upon the altar.
3 And he shall offer of it all the fat thereof; the rump, and the fat that covereth the inwards,
4 And the two kidneys, and the fat that *is* on them, which *is* by the flanks, and the caul *that is* above the liver, with the kidneys, it shall he take away:
5 And the priest shall burn them upon the altar *for* an offering made by fire unto the LORD: it *is* a trespass offering.
6 Every male among the priests shall eat thereof: it shall be eaten in the holy place: it *is* most holy.
7 As the sin offering *is*, so *is* the trespass offering: *there is* one law for them: the priest that maketh atonement therewith shall have *it*.
8 And the priest that offereth any man's burnt offering, *even* the priest shall have to himself the skin of the burnt offering which he hath offered.
9 And all the meat offering that is baken in the oven, and all that is dressed in the frying pan, and in the pan, shall be the priest's that offereth it.
10 And every meat offering, mingled with

Cross references

11 Lev. 4:12; Ezek. 44:19
12 Lev. 3:3, 9, 14
14 Lev. 2:1; Num. 15:4
15 Lev. 2:2, 9
16 Lev. 2:3; 6:26; 10:12, 13; Num. 18:10; Ezek. 44:29
17 Ex. 29:37; Lev. 2:3, 11; 6:25; 7:1; Num. 18:9, 10
18 Ex. 29:37; Lev. 3:17; 6:29; 22:3-7; Num. 18:10
20 Ex. 16:36; Ex. 29:2
22 Ex. 29:25; Lev. 4:3
25 Lev. 1:3, 5, 11; 4:2, 24, 29, 33; 6:17; 21:22
26 Lev. 6:16; 10:17, 18; Num. 18:9, 10; Ezek. 44:28, 29
27 Ex. 29:37; 30:29
28 Lev. 11:33; 15:12
29 Lev. 6:18, 25; Num. 18:10
30 Lev. 4:7, 11, 12, 18, 21; 10:18; 16:27; Heb. 13:11
1 Lev. 5:1-19; 6:1-7, 17, 25; 21:22
2 Lev. 1:3, 5, 11; 4:24, 29, 33
3 Ex. 29:13; Lev. 3:4, 9, 10, 14-16; 4:8-9
6 Lev. 2:3; 6:16-18; Num. 18:9, 10
7 Lev. 6:25, 26; 14:13
9 Lev. 2:3, 10; Num. 18:9; Ezek. 44:29

oil, and dry, shall all the sons of Aaron have, one *as much* as another.

Peace Offerings

11 And this *is* the law of the sacrifice of peace offerings, which he shall offer unto the LORD.
12 If he offer it for a thanksgiving, then he shall offer with the sacrifice of thanksgiving unleavened cakes mingled with oil, and unleavened wafers anointed with oil, and cakes mingled with oil, of fine flour, fried.
13 Besides the cakes, he shall offer *for* his offering leavened bread with the sacrifice of thanksgiving of his peace offerings.
14 And of it he shall offer one out of the whole oblation *for* an heave offering unto the LORD, *and* it shall be the priest's that sprinkleth the blood of the peace offerings.
15 And the flesh of the sacrifice of his peace offerings for thanksgiving shall be eaten the same day that it is offered; he shall not leave any of it until the morning.
16 But if the sacrifice of his offering *be* a vow, or a voluntary offering, it shall be eaten the same day that he offereth his sacrifice: and on the morrow also the remainder of it shall be eaten:
17 But the remainder of the flesh of the sacrifice on the third day shall be burnt with fire.

11 Lev. 3:1; 22:18, 21
12 Lev. 2:4; Num. 6:15
13 Amos 4:5
14 Num. 18:8, 11, 19
15 Lev. 22:30
16 Lev. 19:6-8
18 Lev. 11:10, 11, 41; 19:7; Num. 18:27
20 Gen. 17:14; Lev. 15:3
21 Lev. 7:20; 11:24, 28; 12:1-3; 13:59; 15:1-33; Ezek. 4:14
23 Lev. 3:17
24 Lev. 17:15; Deut. 14:21; Ezek. 4:14; 44:31

18 And if *any* of the flesh of the sacrifice of his peace offerings be eaten at all on the third day, it shall not be accepted, neither shall it be imputed unto him that offereth it: it shall be an abomination, and the soul that eateth of it shall bear his iniquity.
19 And the flesh that toucheth any unclean *thing* shall not be eaten; it shall be burnt with fire: and as for the flesh, all that be clean shall eat thereof.
20 But the soul that eateth *of* the flesh of the sacrifice of peace offerings, that *pertain* unto the LORD, having his uncleanness upon him, even that soul shall be cut off from his people.
21 Moreover the soul that shall touch any unclean *thing, as* the uncleanness of man, or *any* unclean beast, or any abominable unclean *thing*, and eat of the flesh of the sacrifice of peace offerings, which *pertain* unto the LORD, even that soul shall be cut off from his people.
22 And the LORD spake unto Moses, saying,
23 Speak unto the children of Israel, saying, Ye shall eat no manner of fat, of ox, or of sheep, or of goat.
24 And the fat of the beast that dieth of itself, and the fat of that which is torn with beasts, may be used in any other use: but ye shall in no wise eat of it.
25 For whosoever eateth the fat of the

The Sacrifices of Israel

SACRIFICE	REASON	MEANING	TYPE OF CHRIST	REFERENCES
Burnt Offering	Annual voluntary worship for divine favor	Total dedication to God, Atonement	No spot or blemish, Lamb of God	Lev. 1:3–17; 6:8–13; Num. 28:3—29:39
Meal Grain	General thanksgiving, Securing divine good will, Sin offering for very poor	Dedication of everyday life, A living relationship	Sinlessness, Perfection	Lev. 2:1–16; 6:14–23; Num. 15:1–12
Peace	General thanksgiving, Unexpected blessing, Completion of a vow	Peace and wholeness, God's faithfulness, Communion	Made peace with God for us on the cross. Fellowship with believers	Lev. 3:1–17; 7:11–36; 22:18–30; 23:19; Num. 6:14; 10:10
Sin Offering	Unintentional sin, Purification from sin	Atonement and forgiveness, Cleansing from sins of omission	Substitutionary sacrifice	Lev. 4:1—5:13; 6:24–30 Num. 28:15—29:38
Trespass Offering Guilt Offering	Misappropriation or denial of what belongs to God	Expiation and restitution, Cursing to blessing	Atonement for damages and harm caused by sin	Lev. 5:14—6:7; 7:1–6
Drink Offering	Auxiliary to burnt or peace offerings but never sin or guilt offerings	Symbol of Joy	Christ's blood	Lev. 23; Num. 15:1–10; 28:31

By Arnold Fruchtenbaum

beast, of which men offer an offering made by fire unto the LORD, even the soul that eateth *it* shall be cut off from his people.

26 Moreover ye shall eat no manner of blood, *whether it be* of fowl or of beast, in any of your dwellings.

27 Whatsoever soul *it be* that eateth any manner of blood, even that soul shall be cut off from his people.

28 And the LORD spake unto Moses, saying,

29 Speak unto the children of Israel, saying, He that offereth the sacrifice of his peace offerings unto the LORD shall bring his oblation unto the LORD of the sacrifice of his peace offerings.

30 His own hands shall bring the offerings of the LORD made by fire, the fat with the breast, it shall he bring, that the breast may be waved *for* a wave offering before the LORD.

31 And the priest shall burn the fat upon the altar: but the breast shall be Aaron's and his sons'.

32 And the right shoulder shall ye give unto the priest *for* an heave offering of the sacrifices of your peace offerings.

33 He among the sons of Aaron, that offereth the blood of the peace offerings, and the fat, shall have the right shoulder for *his* part.

34 For the wave breast and the heave shoulder have I taken of the children of Israel from off the sacrifices of their peace offerings, and have given them unto Aaron the priest and unto his sons by a statute for ever from among the children of Israel.

35 This *is the portion* of the anointing of Aaron, and of the anointing of his sons, out of the offerings of the LORD made by fire, in the day *when* he presented them to minister unto the LORD in the priest's office;

36 Which the LORD commanded to be given them of the children of Israel, in the day that he anointed them, *by* a statute for ever throughout their generations.

37 This *is* the law of the burnt offering, of the meat offering, and of the sin offering, and of the trespass offering, and of the consecrations, and of the sacrifice of the peace offerings;

38 Which the LORD commanded Moses in mount Sinai, in the day that he commanded the children of Israel to offer their oblations unto the LORD, in the wilderness of Sinai.

26 Gen. 9:4; Lev. 3:17; 17:10-14
29 Lev. 3:1
30 Ex. 29:24, 27; Lev. 3:3, 4, 9, 14; 8:27; 9:21; Num. 6:20
31 Lev. 3:5, 11, 16; 7:34
32 Lev. 7:34; 9:21; Num. 6:20
34 Ex. 29:28; Lev. 10:14, 15; Num. 18:18, 19; Deut. 18:3
36 Ex. 40:13, 15; Lev. 8:12, 30
37 Ex. 29:1; 6:20; Lev. 6:9, 14, 25; 7:1, 11
38 Lev. 1:2
2 Ex. 28:2, 4; 29:1-3; 30:24, 25
5 Ex. 29:4
6 Ex. 29:4
7 Ex. 28:4; 29:5
8 Ex. 28:30
9 Ex. 28:36-43; 29:6
10 Ex. 30:26-29
12 Ex. 29:7; 30:30; Lev. 21:10, 12; Ps. 133:2
13 Ex. 29:8, 9
14 Ex. 29:10; Lev. 4:4; Ezek. 43:19
15 Ex. 29:12, 36; Lev. 4:7; Ezek. 43:20, 26; Heb. 9:22

CHAPTER 8
Aaron and His Sons Are Ordained

1 And the LORD spake unto Moses, saying,

2 Take Aaron and his sons with him, and the garments, and the anointing oil, and a bullock for the sin offering, and two rams, and a basket of unleavened bread;

3 And gather thou all the congregation together unto the door of the tabernacle of the congregation.

4 And Moses did as the LORD commanded him; and the assembly was gathered together unto the door of the tabernacle of the congregation.

5 And Moses said unto the congregation, This *is* the thing which the LORD commanded to be done.

6 And Moses brought Aaron and his sons, and washed them with water.

7 And he put upon him the coat, and girded him with the girdle, and clothed him with the robe, and put the ephod upon him, and he girded him with the curious girdle of the ephod, and bound *it* unto him therewith.

8 And he put the breastplate upon him: also he put in the breastplate the Urim and the Thummim.

9 And he put the mitre upon his head; also upon the mitre, *even* upon his forefront, did he put the golden plate, the holy crown; as the LORD commanded Moses.

10 And Moses took the anointing oil, and anointed the tabernacle and all that *was* therein, and sanctified them.

11 And he sprinkled thereof upon the altar seven times, and anointed the altar and all his vessels, both the laver and his foot, to sanctify them.

12 And he poured of the anointing oil upon Aaron's head, and anointed him, to sanctify him.

13 And Moses brought Aaron's sons, and put coats upon them, and girded them with girdles, and put bonnets upon them; as the LORD commanded Moses.

14 And he brought the bullock for the sin offering: and Aaron and his sons laid their hands upon the head of the bullock for the sin offering.

15 And he slew *it*; and Moses took the blood, and put *it* upon the horns of the altar round about with his finger, and purified

---

8:6 Presenting their bodies a living sacrifice (Rom. 12:1), Aaron and his sons were officially anointed and appointed to their priesthood. By comparison, Jesus needed no preliminary sacrifices, as He had no sin.

the altar, and poured the blood at the bottom of the altar, and sanctified it, to make reconciliation upon it.

16 And he took all the fat that *was* upon the inwards, and the caul *above* the liver, and the two kidneys, and their fat, and Moses burned *it* upon the altar.

17 But the bullock, and his hide, his flesh, and his dung, he burnt with fire without the camp; as the LORD commanded Moses.

18 And he brought the ram for the burnt offering: and Aaron and his sons laid their hands upon the head of the ram.

19 And he killed *it*; and Moses sprinkled the blood upon the altar round about.

20 And he cut the ram into pieces; and Moses burnt the head, and the pieces, and the fat.

21 And he washed the inwards and the legs in water; and Moses burnt the whole ram upon the altar: it *was* a burnt sacrifice for a sweet savour, *and* an offering made by fire unto the LORD; as the LORD commanded Moses.

22 And he brought the other ram, the ram of consecration: and Aaron and his sons laid their hands upon the head of the ram.

23 And he slew *it*; and Moses took of the blood of it, and put *it* upon the tip of Aaron's right ear, and upon the thumb of his right hand, and upon the great toe of his right foot.

24 And he brought Aaron's sons, and Moses put of the blood upon the tip of their right ear, and upon the thumbs of their right hands, and upon the great toes of their right feet: and Moses sprinkled the blood upon the altar round about.

25 And he took the fat, and the rump, and all the fat that *was* upon the inwards, and the caul *above* the liver, and the two kidneys, and their fat, and the right shoulder:

26 And out of the basket of unleavened bread, that *was* before the LORD, he took one unleavened cake, and a cake of oiled bread, and one wafer, and put *them* on the fat, and upon the right shoulder:

27 And he put all upon Aaron's hands, and upon his sons' hands, and waved them *for* a wave offering before the LORD.

28 And Moses took them from off their hands, and burnt *them* on the altar upon the burnt offering: they *were* consecrations for a sweet savour: it *is* an offering made by fire unto the LORD.

29 And Moses took the breast, and waved it *for* a wave offering before the LORD: *for* of the ram of consecration it was Moses' part; as the LORD commanded Moses.

30 And Moses took of the anointing oil, and of the blood which *was* upon the altar, and sprinkled *it* upon Aaron, *and* upon his garments, and upon his sons, and upon his sons' garments with him; and sanctified Aaron, *and* his garments, and his sons, and his sons' garments with him.

31 And Moses said unto Aaron and to his sons, Boil the flesh *at* the door of the tabernacle of the congregation: and there eat it with the bread that *is* in the basket of consecrations, as I commanded, saying, Aaron and his sons shall eat it.

32 And that which remaineth of the flesh and of the bread shall ye burn with fire.

33 And ye shall not go out of the door of the tabernacle of the congregation *in* seven days, until the days of your consecration be at an end: for seven days shall he consecrate you.

34 As he hath done this day, *so* the LORD hath commanded to do, to make an atonement for you.

35 Therefore shall ye abide *at* the door of the tabernacle of the congregation day and night seven days, and keep the charge of the LORD, that ye die not: for so I am commanded.

36 So Aaron and his sons did all things which the LORD commanded by the hand of Moses.

CHAPTER 9
Aaron Offers Sacrifices

1 And it came to pass on the eighth day, *that* Moses called Aaron and his sons, and the elders of Israel;

2 And he said unto Aaron, Take thee a young calf for a sin offering, and a ram for a burnt offering, without blemish, and offer *them* before the LORD.

3 And unto the children of Israel thou shalt speak, saying, Take ye a kid of the goats for a sin offering; and a calf and a lamb, *both* of the first year, without blemish, for a burnt offering;

4 Also a bullock and a ram for peace offerings, to sacrifice before the LORD; and a meat offering mingled with oil: for today the LORD will appear unto you.

5 And they brought *that* which Moses commanded before the tabernacle of the congregation: and all the congregation drew near and stood before the LORD.

6 And Moses said, This *is* the thing which the LORD commanded that ye should do: and the glory of the LORD shall appear unto you.

Cross references (center column):

16 Ex. 29:13; Lev. 4:8
17 Ex. 29:14; Lev. 4:11, 12
18 Ex. 29:15
21 Ex. 29:18
22 Ex. 29:19, 31
25 Ex. 29:22
26 Ex. 29:23
27 Ex. 29:24, 28
28 Ex. 29:25
29 Ex. 29:26
30 Ex. 29:21; 30:30; Num. 3:3
31 Ex. 29:31, 32
32 Ex. 29:34
33 Ex. 29:30, 35; Ezek. 43:25, 26
34 Heb. 7:16
35 Num. 3:7; 9:19; Deut. 11:1; 1Kgs. 2:3

1 Ezek. 43:27
2 Ex. 29:1; Lev. 4:3; 8:14, 18
3 Lev. 4:23; Ezra 6:17; 10:19
4 Ex. 29:43; Lev. 2:4; 9:6, 23
6 Ex. 24:16; Lev. 9:23

7 And Moses said unto Aaron, Go unto the altar, and offer thy sin offering, and thy burnt offering, and make an atonement for thyself, and for the people: and offer the offering of the people, and make an atonement for them; as the LORD commanded.

8 Aaron therefore went unto the altar, and slew the calf of the sin offering, which *was* for himself.

9 And the sons of Aaron brought the blood unto him: and he dipped his finger in the blood, and put *it* upon the horns of the altar, and poured out the blood at the bottom of the altar:

10 But the fat, and the kidneys, and the caul above the liver of the sin offering, he burnt upon the altar; as the LORD commanded Moses.

11 And the flesh and the hide he burnt with fire without the camp.

12 And he slew the burnt offering; and Aaron's sons presented unto him the blood, which he sprinkled round about upon the altar.

13 And they presented the burnt offering unto him, with the pieces thereof, and the head: and he burnt *them* upon the altar.

14 And he did wash the inwards and the legs, and burnt *them* upon the burnt offering on the altar.

15 And he brought the people's offering, and took the goat, which *was* the sin offering for the people, and slew it, and offered it for sin, as the first.

16 And he brought the burnt offering, and offered it according to the manner.

17 And he brought the meat offering, and took an handful thereof, and burnt *it* upon the altar, beside the burnt sacrifice of the morning.

18 He slew also the bullock and the ram *for* a sacrifice of peace offerings, which *was* for the people: and Aaron's sons presented unto him the blood, which he sprinkled upon the altar round about,

19 And the fat of the bullock and of the ram, the rump, and that which covereth *the inwards*, and the kidneys, and the caul *above* the liver:

20 And they put the fat upon the breasts, and he burnt the fat upon the altar:

21 And the breasts and the right shoulder Aaron waved *for* a wave offering before the LORD; as Moses commanded.

22 And Aaron lifted up his hand toward the people, and blessed them, and came down from offering of the sin offering, and the burnt offering, and peace offerings.

23 And Moses and Aaron went into the tabernacle of the congregation, and came out, and blessed the people: and the glory of the LORD appeared unto all the people.

24 And there came a fire out from before the LORD, and consumed upon the altar the burnt offering and the fat: *which* when all the people saw, they shouted, and fell on their faces.

CHAPTER 10
Nadab and Abihu Sin

1 And Nadab and Abihu, the sons of Aaron, took either of them his censer, and put fire therein, and put incense thereon, and offered strange fire before the LORD, which he commanded them not.

2 And there went out fire from the LORD, and devoured them, and they died before the LORD.

3 Then Moses said unto Aaron, This *is it* that the LORD spake, saying, I will be sanctified in them that come nigh me, and before all the people I will be glorified. And Aaron held his peace.

4 And Moses called Mishael and Elzaphan, the sons of Uzziel the uncle of Aaron, and said unto them, Come near, carry your brethren from before the sanctuary out of the camp.

5 So they went near, and carried them in their coats out of the camp; as Moses had said.

6 And Moses said unto Aaron, and unto Eleazar and unto Ithamar, his sons, Uncover not your heads, neither rend your clothes; lest ye die, and lest wrath come upon all the people: but let your brethren, the whole house of Israel, bewail the burning which the LORD hath kindled.

Cross references (center column):

7 Lev. 4:3, 16, 20
9 Lev. 4:7; 8:15
10 Lev. 4:8; 8:16
11 Lev. 4:11; 8:17
12 Lev. 1:5; 8:19
13 Lev. 8:20
14 Lev. 8:21
16 Lev. 1:3, 10
17 Ex. 29:38; Lev. 2:1, 2; 9:4
18 Lev. 3:1-17
20 Lev. 3:5, 16
21 Ex. 29:24, 26; Lev. 7:30-34
22 Num. 6:23; Deut. 21:5
23 Lev. 9:6; Num. 14:10; 16:19, 42
24 Gen. 4:4; Judg. 6:21; 1Kgs. 18:38, 39; 2Chr. 7:1
1 Ex. 30:9; Lev. 16:1, 12; 22:9; Num. 3:3, 4; 1Chr. 24:2
2 Lev. 9:24; Num. 16:35; 2Sam. 6:7
3 Ex. 19:22; 29:43; Lev. 21:6, 17, 21; John 13:31, 32; 14:13
4 Lev. 6:18, 22; Num. 3:19, 30; Luke 7:12; Acts 5:6, 9, 10; 8:2
6 Ex. 33:5; Lev. 13:45; 21:1, 10; Josh. 7:1; 22:18, 20

9:24 there came a fire out from before the LORD. This fire was probably the beginning of the continual burnt offering (6:12–13), which was always on the altar. Ideally the flame was never to go out, having been ignited by God in His holiness and in His righteous judgment.

10:1 Nadab and Abihu . . . offered strange fire. God's service requires the right approach to God, the right source for God's power, and the right spiritual attitude. Nadab and Abihu failed to seek the mind of God and acted in self-will. The act typifies the use of carnal means to kindle fires of true devotion and praise.

7 And ye shall not go out from the door of the tabernacle of the congregation, lest ye die: for the anointing oil of the LORD *is* upon you. And they did according to the word of Moses.

Rules for Priests

8 And the LORD spake unto Aaron, saying,
9 Do not drink wine nor strong drink, thou, nor thy sons with thee, when ye go into the tabernacle of the congregation, lest ye die: *it shall be* a statute for ever throughout your generations:
10 And that ye may put difference between holy and unholy, and between unclean and clean;
11 And that ye may teach the children of Israel all the statutes which the LORD hath spoken unto them by the hand of Moses.
12 And Moses spake unto Aaron, and unto Eleazar and unto Ithamar, his sons that were left, Take the meat offering that remaineth of the offerings of the LORD made by fire, and eat it without leaven beside the altar: for it *is* most holy:
13 And ye shall eat it in the holy place, because it *is* thy due, and thy sons' due, of the sacrifices of the LORD made by fire: for so I am commanded.
14 And the wave breast and heave shoulder shall ye eat in a clean place; thou, and thy sons, and thy daughters with thee: for *they be* thy due, and thy sons' due, *which* are given out of the sacrifices of peace offerings of the children of Israel.
15 The heave shoulder and the wave breast shall they bring with the offerings made by fire of the fat, to wave *it for* a wave offering before the LORD; and it shall be thine, and thy sons' with thee, by a statute for ever; as the LORD hath commanded.
16 And Moses diligently sought the goat of the sin offering, and, behold, it was burnt: and he was angry with Eleazar and Ithamar, the sons of Aaron *which were* left *alive*, saying,
17 Wherefore have ye not eaten the sin offering in the holy place, seeing it *is* most holy, and *God* hath given it you to bear the iniquity of the congregation, to make atonement for them before the LORD?
18 Behold, the blood of it was not brought in within the holy *place*: ye should indeed have eaten it in the holy *place*, as I commanded.
19 And Aaron said unto Moses, Behold, this day have they offered their sin offering and their burnt offering before the LORD; and such things have befallen me: and *if* I had

eaten the sin offering today, should it have been accepted in the sight of the LORD?
20 And when Moses heard *that*, he was content.

CHAPTER 11
Clean and Unclean Animals

1 And the LORD spake unto Moses and to Aaron, saying unto them,
2 Speak unto the children of Israel, saying, These *are* the beasts which ye shall eat among all the beasts that *are* on the earth.
3 Whatsoever parteth the hoof, and is clovenfooted, *and* cheweth the cud, among the beasts, that shall ye eat.
4 Nevertheless these shall ye not eat of them that chew the cud, or of them that divide the hoof: *as* the camel, because he cheweth the cud, but divideth not the hoof; he *is* unclean unto you.
5 And the coney, because he cheweth the cud, but divideth not the hoof; he *is* unclean unto you.
6 And the hare, because he cheweth the cud, but divideth not the hoof; he *is* unclean unto you.
7 And the swine, though he divide the hoof, and be clovenfooted, yet he cheweth not the cud; he *is* unclean to you.
8 Of their flesh shall ye not eat, and their carcase shall ye not touch; they *are* unclean to you.
9 These shall ye eat of all that *are* in the waters: whatsoever hath fins and scales in the waters, in the seas, and in the rivers, them shall ye eat.
10 And all that have not fins and scales in the seas, and in the rivers, of all that move in the waters, and of any living thing which *is* in the waters, they *shall be* an abomination unto you:
11 They shall be even an abomination unto you; ye shall not eat of their flesh, but ye shall have their carcases in abomination.
12 Whatsoever hath no fins nor scales in the waters, that *shall be* an abomination unto you.
13 And these *are they which* ye shall have in abomination among the fowls; they shall not be eaten, they *are* an abomination: the eagle, and the ossifrage, and the ospray,
14 And the vulture, and the kite after his kind;
15 Every raven after his kind;
16 And the owl, and the night hawk, and the cuckow, and the hawk after his kind,
17 And the little owl, and the cormorant, and the great owl,

Cross References

7 Ex. 28:41; Lev. 8:30; 21:12
9 Ezek. 44:21; Luke 1:15; 1 Tim. 3:3; Titus 1:7
10 Lev. 11:47; 20:25; Jer. 15:19; Ezek. 22:6; 44:23
11 Deut. 24:8; Neh. 8:2, 8, 9, 13; Jer. 18:18; Mal. 2:7
12 Ex. 29:2; Lev. 6:16; 21:22; Num. 18:9, 10
13 Lev. 2:3; 6:16
14 Ex. 29:24, 26, 27; Lev. 7:31, 34; Num. 18:11
15 Lev. 7:29, 30, 34
16 Lev. 9:3, 15
17 Lev. 6:26, 29
18 Lev. 6:26, 30
19 Lev. 9:8, 12; Jer. 6:20; 14:12; Hos. 9:4; Mal. 1:10, 13
2 Deut. 14:4; Acts 10:12, 14
7 Isa. 65:4; 66:3, 17
8 Isa. 52:11; Matt. 15:11, 20; Mark 7:2, 15, 18; Acts 10:14, 15; 15:29; Rom. 14:14, 17; 1 Cor. 8:8; Col. 2:16, 21; Heb. 9:10
9 Deut. 14:9
10 Lev. 7:18; Deut. 14:3
13 Deut. 14:12

18 And the swan, and the pelican, and the gier eagle,

19 And the stork, the heron after her kind, and the lapwing, and the bat.

20 All fowls that creep, going upon *all* four, *shall be* an abomination unto you.

21 Yet these may ye eat of every flying creeping thing that goeth upon *all* four, which have legs above their feet, to leap withal upon the earth;

22 *Even* these of them ye may eat; the locust after his kind, and the bald locust after his kind, and the beetle after his kind, and the grasshopper after his kind.

23 But all *other* flying creeping things, which have four feet, *shall be* an abomination unto you.

24 And for these ye shall be unclean: whosoever toucheth the carcase of them shall be unclean until the even.

25 And whosoever beareth *ought* of the carcase of them shall wash his clothes, and be unclean until the even.

26 *The carcases* of every beast which divideth the hoof, and *is* not clovenfooted, nor cheweth the cud, *are* unclean unto you: every one that toucheth them shall be unclean.

27 And whatsoever goeth upon his paws, among all manner of beasts that go on *all* four, those *are* unclean unto you: whoso toucheth their carcase shall be unclean until the even.

28 And he that beareth the carcase of them shall wash his clothes, and be unclean until the even: they *are* unclean unto you.

29 These also *shall be* unclean unto you among the creeping things that creep upon the earth; the weasel, and the mouse, and the tortoise after his kind,

30 And the ferret, and the chameleon, and the lizard, and the snail, and the mole.

31 These *are* unclean to you among all that creep: whosoever doth touch them, when they be dead, shall be unclean until the even.

32 And upon whatsoever *any* of them, when they are dead, doth fall, it shall be unclean; whether *it be* any vessel of wood, or raiment, or skin, or sack, whatsoever vessel *it be*, wherein *any* work is done, it must be put into water, and it shall be unclean until the even; so it shall be cleansed.

33 And every earthen vessel, whereinto *any* of them falleth, whatsoever *is* in it shall be unclean; and ye shall break it.

34 Of all meat which may be eaten, *that* on which *such* water cometh shall be unclean: and all drink that may be drunk in every *such* vessel shall be unclean.

35 And every *thing* whereupon *any part* of their carcase falleth shall be unclean; *whether it be* oven, or ranges for pots, they shall be broken down: *for* they *are* unclean, and shall be unclean unto you.

36 Nevertheless a fountain or pit, *wherein there is* plenty of water, shall be clean: but that which toucheth their carcase shall be unclean.

37 And if *any part* of their carcase fall upon any sowing seed which is to be sown, it *shall be* clean.

38 But if *any* water be put upon the seed, and *any part* of their carcase fall thereon, it *shall be* unclean unto you.

39 And if any beast, of which ye may eat, die; he that toucheth the carcase thereof shall be unclean until the even.

40 And he that eateth of the carcase of it shall wash his clothes, and be unclean until the even: he also that beareth the carcase of it shall wash his clothes, and be unclean until the even.

41 And every creeping thing that creepeth upon the earth *shall be* an abomination; it shall not be eaten.

42 Whatsoever goeth upon the belly, and whatsoever goeth upon *all* four, or whatsoever hath more feet among all creeping things that creep upon the earth, them ye shall not eat; for they *are* an abomination.

43 Ye shall not make yourselves abominable with any creeping thing that creepeth, neither shall ye make yourselves unclean with them, that ye should be defiled thereby.

44 For I *am* the LORD your God: ye shall therefore sanctify yourselves, and ye shall be holy; for I *am* holy: neither shall ye defile yourselves with any manner of creeping thing that creepeth upon the earth.

45 For I *am* the LORD that bringeth you up out of the land of Egypt, to be your God: ye shall therefore be holy, for I *am* holy.

46 This *is* the law of the beasts, and of the fowl, and of every living creature that moveth in the waters, and of every creature that creepeth upon the earth:

47 To make a difference between the unclean and the clean, and between the beast that may be eaten and the beast that may not be eaten.

CHAPTER 12
The Purification of Women after Childbirth

1 And the LORD spake unto Moses, saying,

2 Speak unto the children of Israel, saying, If a woman have conceived seed, and borne

---

Cross references (center column):

22 Matt. 3:4; Mark 1:6

25 Lev. 14:8; 15:5; Num. 19:10, 22; 31:24

29 Isa. 66:17

32 Lev. 15:12

33 Lev. 6:28; 15:12

40 Lev. 17:15; 22:8; Deut. 14:21; Ezek. 4:14; 44:31

43 Lev. 20:25

44 Ex. 19:6; Lev. 19:2; 20:7, 26; 1Thess. 4:7; 1Pet. 1:15, 16

45 Ex. 6:7; Lev. 11:44

47 Lev. 10:10

2 Lev. 15:19; Luke 2:22

a man child: then she shall be unclean seven days; according to the days of the separation for her infirmity shall she be unclean.

3 And in the eighth day the flesh of his foreskin shall be circumcised.

4 And she shall then continue in the blood of her purifying three and thirty days; she shall touch no hallowed thing, nor come into the sanctuary, until the days of her purifying be fulfilled.

5 But if she bear a maid child, then she shall be unclean two weeks, as in her separation: and she shall continue in the blood of her purifying threescore and six days.

6 And when the days of her purifying are fulfilled, for a son, or for a daughter, she shall bring a lamb of the first year for a burnt offering, and a young pigeon, or a turtledove, for a sin offering, unto the door of the tabernacle of the congregation, unto the priest:

7 Who shall offer it before the Lord, and make an atonement for her; and she shall be cleansed from the issue of her blood. This is the law for her that hath born a male or a female.

8 And if she be not able to bring a lamb, then she shall bring two turtles, or two young pigeons; the one for the burnt offering, and the other for a sin offering: and the priest shall make an atonement for her, and she shall be clean.

CHAPTER 13
Laws Concerning Leprosy

1 And the Lord spake unto Moses and Aaron, saying,

2 When a man shall have in the skin of his flesh a rising, a scab, or bright spot, and it be in the skin of his flesh like the plague of leprosy; then he shall be brought unto Aaron the priest, or unto one of his sons the priests:

3 And the priest shall look on the plague in the skin of the flesh: and when the hair in the plague is turned white, and the plague in sight be deeper than the skin of his flesh, it is a plague of leprosy: and the priest shall look on him, and pronounce him unclean.

4 If the bright spot be white in the skin of his flesh, and in sight be not deeper than the

skin, and the hair thereof be not turned white; then the priest shall shut up him that hath the plague seven days:

5 And the priest shall look on him the seventh day: and, behold, if the plague in his sight be at a stay, and the plague spread not in the skin; then the priest shall shut him up seven days more:

6 And the priest shall look on him again the seventh day: and, behold, if the plague be somewhat dark, and the plague spread not in the skin, the priest shall pronounce him clean: it is but a scab: and he shall wash his clothes, and be clean.

7 But if the scab spread much abroad in the skin, after that he hath been seen of the priest for his cleansing, he shall be seen of the priest again:

8 And if the priest see that, behold, the scab spreadeth in the skin, then the priest shall pronounce him unclean: it is a leprosy.

9 When the plague of leprosy is in a man, then he shall be brought unto the priest;

10 And the priest shall see him: and, behold, if the rising be white in the skin, and it have turned the hair white, and there be quick raw flesh in the rising;

11 It is an old leprosy in the skin of his flesh, and the priest shall pronounce him unclean, and shall not shut him up: for he is unclean.

12 And if a leprosy break out abroad in the skin, and the leprosy cover all the skin of him that hath the plague from his head even to his foot, wheresoever the priest looketh;

13 Then the priest shall consider: and, behold, if the leprosy have covered all his flesh, he shall pronounce him clean that hath the plague: it is all turned white: he is clean.

14 But when raw flesh appeareth in him, he shall be unclean.

15 And the priest shall see the raw flesh, and pronounce him to be unclean: for the raw flesh is unclean: it is a leprosy.

16 Or if the raw flesh turn again, and be changed unto white, he shall come unto the priest;

17 And the priest shall see him: and, behold, if the plague be turned into white; then the priest shall pronounce him clean that hath the plague: he is clean.

Cross references (center column):
3 Gen. 17:12; Luke 1:59; 2:21; John 7:22, 23
6 Luke 2:22
8 Lev. 4:26; 5:7; Luke 2:24
2 Deut. 17:8, 9; 24:8; 28:27; Isa. 3:17; Luke 17:14
6 Lev. 11:25; 14:8
10 Num. 12:10, 12; 2Kgs. 5:27; 2Chr. 26:20

12:3 circumcised. Jesus refers to this passage in responding to those who criticized Him for healing on the Sabbath day, since they claimed it was a labor that should not be done on the Sabbath. Christ pointed out that circumcision was performed on newborn males eight days after birth, which would often fall on the Sabbath day. Why then, Jesus asked, should His healing a paralyzed man on the Sabbath (John 5:1–16) be called into question?

18 The flesh also, in which, *even* in the skin thereof, was a boil, and is healed,

19 And in the place of the boil there be a white rising, or a bright spot, white, and somewhat reddish, and it be shewed to the priest;

20 And if, when the priest seeth it, behold, it *be* in sight lower than the skin, and the hair thereof be turned white; the priest shall pronounce him unclean: it *is* a plague of leprosy broken out of the boil.

21 But if the priest look on it, and, behold, *there be* no white hairs therein, and *if* it *be* not lower than the skin, but *be* somewhat dark; then the priest shall shut him up seven days:

22 And if it spread much abroad in the skin, then the priest shall pronounce him unclean: it *is* a plague.

23 But if the bright spot stay in his place, *and* spread not, it *is* a burning boil; and the priest shall pronounce him clean.

24 Or if there be *any* flesh, in the skin whereof *there is* a hot burning, and the quick *flesh* that burneth have a white bright spot, somewhat reddish, or white;

25 Then the priest shall look upon it: and, behold, *if* the hair in the bright spot be turned white, and it *be in* sight deeper than the skin; it *is* a leprosy broken out of the burning: wherefore the priest shall pronounce him unclean: it *is* the plague of leprosy.

26 But if the priest look on it, and, behold, *there be* no white hair in the bright spot, and it *be* no lower than the *other* skin, but *be* somewhat dark; then the priest shall shut him up seven days:

27 And the priest shall look upon him the seventh day: *and* if it be spread much abroad in the skin, then the priest shall pronounce him unclean: it *is* the plague of leprosy.

28 And if the bright spot stay in his place, *and* spread not in the skin, but it *be* somewhat dark; it *is* a rising of the burning, and the priest shall pronounce him clean: for it *is* an inflammation of the burning.

29 If a man or woman have a plague upon the head or the beard;

30 Then the priest shall see the plague: and, behold, if it *be* in sight deeper than the skin; *and there be* in it a yellow thin hair; then the priest shall pronounce him unclean: it *is* a dry scall, *even* a leprosy upon the head or beard.

31 And if the priest look on the plague of the scall, and, behold, it *be* not in sight deeper than the skin, and *that there is* no black hair in it; then the priest shall shut up

18 Ex. 9:9

45 Lam. 4:15; Ezek. 24:17, 22; Mic. 3:7

46 Num. 5:2; 12:14; 2Kgs. 7:3; 15:5; 2Chr. 26:21; Luke 17:12

him that hath the plague of the scall seven days:

32 And in the seventh day the priest shall look on the plague: and, behold, *if* the scall spread not, and there be in it no yellow hair, and the scall *be* not in sight deeper than the skin;

33 He shall be shaven, but the scall shall he not shave; and the priest shall shut up *him that hath* the scall seven days more:

34 And in the seventh day the priest shall look on the scall: and, behold, *if* the scall be not spread in the skin, nor *be* in sight deeper than the skin; then the priest shall pronounce him clean: and he shall wash his clothes, and be clean.

35 But if the scall spread much in the skin after his cleansing;

36 Then the priest shall look on him: and, behold, if the scall be spread in the skin, the priest shall not seek for yellow hair; he *is* unclean.

37 But if the scall be in his sight at a stay, and *that* there is black hair grown up therein; the scall is healed, he *is* clean: and the priest shall pronounce him clean.

38 If a man also or a woman have in the skin of their flesh bright spots, *even* white bright spots;

39 Then the priest shall look: and, behold, *if* the bright spots in the skin of their flesh *be* darkish white; it *is* a freckled spot *that* groweth in the skin; he *is* clean.

40 And the man whose hair is fallen off his head, he *is* bald; *yet is* he clean.

41 And he that hath his hair fallen off from the part of his head toward his face, he *is* forehead bald: *yet is* he clean.

42 And if there be in the bald head, or bald forehead, a white reddish sore; it *is* a leprosy sprung up in his bald head, or his bald forehead.

43 Then the priest shall look upon it: and, behold, *if* the rising of the sore *be* white reddish in his bald head, or in his bald forehead, as the leprosy appeareth in the skin of the flesh;

44 He is a leprous man, he *is* unclean: the priest shall pronounce him utterly unclean; his plague *is* in his head.

45 And the leper in whom the plague *is*, his clothes shall be rent, and his head bare, and he shall put a covering upon his upper lip, and shall cry, Unclean, unclean.

46 All the days wherein the plague *shall be* in him he shall be defiled; he *is* unclean: he shall dwell alone; without the camp *shall* his habitation *be*.

47 The garment also that the plague of leprosy is in, *whether it be* a woolen garment, or a linen garment;

48 Whether *it be* in the warp, or woof; of linen, or of woolen; whether in a skin, or in any thing made of skin;

49 And if the plague be greenish or reddish in the garment, or in the skin, either in the warp, or in the woof, or in any thing of skin; it *is* a plague of leprosy, and shall be shewed unto the priest:

50 And the priest shall look upon the plague, and shut up *it that hath* the plague seven days:

51 And he shall look on the plague on the seventh day: if the plague be spread in the garment, either in the warp, or in the woof, or in a skin, *or* in any work that is made of skin; the plague *is* a fretting leprosy; it *is* unclean.

52 He shall therefore burn that garment, whether warp or woof, in woolen or in linen, or any thing of skin, wherein the plague is: for it *is* a fretting leprosy; it shall be burnt in the fire.

53 And if the priest shall look, and, behold, the plague be not spread in the garment, either in the warp, or in the woof, or in any thing of skin;

54 Then the priest shall command that they wash *the thing* wherein the plague *is*, and he shall shut it up seven days more:

55 And the priest shall look on the plague, after that it is washed: and, behold, *if* the plague have not changed his colour, and the plague be not spread; it *is* unclean; thou shalt burn it in the fire; it *is* fret inward, *whether* it *be* bare within or without.

56 And if the priest look, and, behold, the plague *be* somewhat dark after the washing of it; then he shall rend it out of the garment, or out of the skin, or out of the warp, or out of the woof:

57 And if it appear still in the garment, either in the warp, or in the woof, or in any thing of skin; it *is* a spreading *plague*: thou shalt burn that wherein the plague *is* with fire.

58 And the garment, either warp, or woof, or whatsoever thing of skin *it be*, which thou shalt wash, if the plague be departed from them, then it shall be washed the second time, and shall be clean.

59 This *is* the law of the plague of leprosy in a garment of woolen or linen, either in the warp, or woof, or any thing of skins, to pronounce it clean, or to pronounce it unclean.

CHAPTER 14
Purification of a Leper

1 And the LORD spake unto Moses, saying,

2 This shall be the law of the leper in the day of his cleansing: He shall be brought unto the priest:

3 And the priest shall go forth out of the camp; and the priest shall look, and, behold, *if* the plague of leprosy be healed in the leper;

4 Then shall the priest command to take for him that is to be cleansed two birds alive *and* clean, and cedar wood, and scarlet, and hyssop:

5 And the priest shall command that one of the birds be killed in an earthen vessel over running water:

6 As for the living bird, he shall take it, and the cedar wood, and the scarlet, and the hyssop, and shall dip them and the living bird in the blood of the bird *that was* killed over the running water:

7 And he shall sprinkle upon him that is to be cleansed from the leprosy seven times, and shall pronounce him clean, and shall let the living bird loose into the open field.

8 And he that is to be cleansed shall wash his clothes, and shave off all his hair, and wash himself in water, that he may be clean: and after that he shall come into the camp, and shall tarry abroad out of his tent seven days.

9 But it shall be on the seventh day, that he shall shave all his hair off his head and his beard and his eyebrows, even all his hair he shall shave off: and he shall wash his clothes, also he shall wash his flesh in water, and he shall be clean.

10 And on the eighth day he shall take two he lambs without blemish, and one ewe lamb of the first year without blemish, and three tenth deals of fine flour *for* a meat offering, mingled with oil, and one log of oil.

11 And the priest that maketh *him* clean shall present the man that is to be made clean, and those things, before the LORD, *at* the door of the tabernacle of the congregation:

51 Lev. 14:44

2 Matt. 8:2, 4; Mark 1:40, 44; Luke 5:12, 14; 17:14

4 Num. 19:6; Ps. 51:7; Heb. 9:19

7 2Kgs. 5:10, 14; Heb. 9:13

8 Lev. 13:6; Num. 12:15

10 Lev. 2:1; Num. 15:4, 15; Matt. 8:4; Mark 1:44; Luke 5:14

14:2 leper . . . brought unto the priest. In Matthew 8:4 and Luke 17:14, Jesus is seen instructing healed lepers to follow God's law and go to the priest for appropriate ceremonies and offerings. In the present dispensation, those healed may go directly to Jesus our High Priest with thanksgiving (Phil. 4:6).

12 And the priest shall take one he lamb, and offer him for a trespass offering, and the log of oil, and wave them *for* a wave offering before the LORD:

13 And he shall slay the lamb in the place where he shall kill the sin offering and the burnt offering, in the holy place: for as the sin offering *is* the priest's, *so is* the trespass offering: it *is* most holy:

14 And the priest shall take *some* of the blood of the trespass offering, and the priest shall put *it* upon the tip of the right ear of him that is to be cleansed, and upon the thumb of his right hand, and upon the great toe of his right foot:

15 And the priest shall take *some* of the log of oil, and pour *it* into the palm of his own left hand:

16 And the priest shall dip his right finger in the oil that *is* in his left hand, and shall sprinkle of the oil with his finger seven times before the LORD:

17 And of the rest of the oil that *is* in his hand shall the priest put upon the tip of the right ear of him that is to be cleansed, and upon the thumb of his right hand, and upon the great toe of his right foot, upon the blood of the trespass offering:

18 And the remnant of the oil that *is* in the priest's hand he shall pour upon the head of him that is to be cleansed: and the priest shall make an atonement for him before the LORD.

19 And the priest shall offer the sin offering, and make an atonement for him that is to be cleansed from his uncleanness; and afterward he shall kill the burnt offering:

20 And the priest shall offer the burnt offering and the meat offering upon the altar: and the priest shall make an atonement for him, and he shall be clean.

21 And if he *be* poor, and cannot get so much; then he shall take one lamb *for* a trespass offering to be waved, to make an atonement for him, and one tenth deal of fine flour mingled with oil for a meat offering, and a log of oil;

22 And two turtledoves, or two young pigeons, such as he is able to get; and the one shall be a sin offering, and the other a burnt offering.

23 And he shall bring them on the eighth day for his cleansing unto the priest, unto the door of the tabernacle of the congregation, before the LORD.

24 And the priest shall take the lamb of the trespass offering, and the log of oil, and the priest shall wave them *for* a wave offering before the LORD:

25 And he shall kill the lamb of the trespass offering, and the priest shall take *some* of the blood of the trespass offering, and put *it* upon the tip of the right ear of him that is to be cleansed, and upon the thumb of his right hand, and upon the great toe of his right foot:

26 And the priest shall pour of the oil into the palm of his own left hand:

27 And the priest shall sprinkle with his right finger *some* of the oil that *is* in his left hand seven times before the LORD:

28 And the priest shall put of the oil that *is* in his hand upon the tip of the right ear of him that is to be cleansed, and upon the thumb of his right hand, and upon the great toe of his right foot, upon the place of the blood of the trespass offering:

29 And the rest of the oil that *is* in the priest's hand he shall put upon the head of him that is to be cleansed, to make an atonement for him before the LORD.

30 And he shall offer the one of the turtledoves, or of the young pigeons, such as he can get;

31 *Even* such as he is able to get, the one *for* a sin offering, and the other *for* a burnt offering, with the meat offering: and the priest shall make an atonement for him that is to be cleansed before the LORD.

32 This *is* the law *of him* in whom *is* the plague of leprosy, whose hand is not able to get *that which pertaineth* to his cleansing.

Cleansing Infected Houses

33 And the LORD spake unto Moses and unto Aaron, saying,

34 When ye be come into the land of Canaan, which I give to you for a possession, and I put the plague of leprosy in a house of the land of your possession;

35 And he that owneth the house shall come and tell the priest, saying, It seemeth to me *there is* as it were a plague in the house:

36 Then the priest shall command that they empty the house, before the priest go *into it* to see the plague, that all that *is* in the house be not made unclean: and afterward the priest shall go in to see the house:

37 And he shall look on the plague, and, behold, *if* the plague *be* in the walls of the house with hollow strakes, greenish or reddish, which in sight *are* lower than the wall;

38 Then the priest shall go out of the house to the door of the house, and shut up the house seven days:

39 And the priest shall come again the sev-

Cross References (center column)

12 Ex. 29:24; Lev. 5:2, 18; 6:6, 7
13 Ex. 29:11; Lev. 1:5, 11; 2:3; 4:4, 24; 7:6, 7; 21:22
14 Ex. 29:20; Lev. 8:23
18 Lev. 4:26
19 Lev. 5:1, 6; 12:7
21 Lev. 5:7; 12:8
22 Lev. 12:8; 15:14, 15
23 Lev. 14:10, 11
24 Lev. 14:12
25 Lev. 14:14
30 Lev. 14:22; 15:15
32 Lev. 14:10
34 Gen. 17:8; Num. 32:22; Deut. 7:1; 32:49
35 Ps. 91:10; Prov. 3:33; Zech. 5:4

enth day, and shall look: and, behold, *if* the plague be spread in the walls of the house;

40 Then the priest shall command that they take away the stones in which the plague *is*, and they shall cast them into an unclean place without the city:

41 And he shall cause the house to be scraped within round about, and they shall pour out the dust that they scrape off without the city into an unclean place:

42 And they shall take other stones, and put *them* in the place of those stones; and he shall take other morter, and shall plaister the house.

43 And if the plague come again, and break out in the house, after that he hath taken away the stones, and after he hath scraped the house, and after it is plaistered;

44 Then the priest shall come and look, and, behold, *if* the plague be spread in the house, it *is* a fretting leprosy in the house: it *is* unclean.

45 And he shall break down the house, the stones of it, and the timber thereof, and all the morter of the house; and he shall carry *them* forth out of the city into an unclean place.

46 Moreover he that goeth into the house all the while that it is shut up shall be unclean until the even.

47 And he that lieth in the house shall wash his clothes; and he that eateth in the house shall wash his clothes.

48 And if the priest shall come in, and look *upon it*, and, behold, the plague hath not spread in the house, after the house was plaistered: then the priest shall pronounce the house clean, because the plague is healed.

49 And he shall take to cleanse the house two birds, and cedar wood, and scarlet, and hyssop:

50 And he shall kill the one of the birds in an earthen vessel over running water:

51 And he shall take the cedar wood, and the hyssop, and the scarlet, and the living bird, and dip them in the blood of the slain bird, and in the running water, and sprinkle the house seven times:

52 And he shall cleanse the house with the blood of the bird, and with the running water, and with the living bird, and with the cedar wood, and with the hyssop, and with the scarlet:

53 But he shall let go the living bird out of the city into the open fields, and make an atonement for the house: and it shall be clean.

54 This *is* the law for all manner of plague of leprosy, and scall,

55 And for the leprosy of a garment, and of a house,

56 And for a rising, and for a scab, and for a bright spot:

57 To teach when *it is* unclean, and when *it is* clean: this *is* the law of leprosy.

CHAPTER 15
Unclean Discharges from the Body

1 And the LORD spake unto Moses and to Aaron, saying,

2 Speak unto the children of Israel, and say unto them, When any man hath a running issue out of his flesh, *because of* his issue he *is* unclean.

3 And this shall be his uncleanness in his issue: whether his flesh run with his issue, or his flesh be stopped from his issue, it *is* his uncleanness.

4 Every bed, whereon he lieth that hath the issue, is unclean: and every thing, whereon he sitteth, shall be unclean.

5 And whosoever toucheth his bed shall wash his clothes, and bathe *himself* in water, and be unclean until the even.

6 And he that sitteth on *any* thing whereon he sat that hath the issue shall wash his clothes, and bathe *himself* in water, and be unclean until the even.

7 And he that toucheth the flesh of him that hath the issue shall wash his clothes, and bathe *himself* in water, and be unclean until the even.

8 And if he that hath the issue spit upon him that is clean; then he shall wash his clothes, and bathe *himself* in water, and be unclean until the even.

9 And what saddle soever he rideth upon that hath the issue shall be unclean.

10 And whosoever toucheth any thing that was under him shall be unclean until the even: and he that beareth *any of* those things shall wash his clothes, and bathe *himself* in water, and be unclean until the even.

11 And whomsoever he toucheth that hath the issue, and hath not rinsed his hands in water, he shall wash his clothes, and bathe *himself* in water, and be unclean until the even.

12 And the vessel of earth, that he toucheth which hath the issue, shall be broken: and every vessel of wood shall be rinsed in water.

13 And when he that hath an issue is cleansed of his issue; then he shall number to himself seven days for his cleansing, and

44 Lev. 13:51; Zech. 5:4

49 Lev. 14:4

53 Lev. 14:20

54 Lev. 13:30

55 Lev. 13:47; 14:34

56 Lev. 13:2

57 Deut. 24:8; Ezek. 44:23

2 Lev. 22:4; Num. 5:2; 2Sam. 3:29; Matt. 9:20; Mark 5:25; Luke 8:43

5 Lev. 11:25; 17:15

12 Lev. 6:28; 11:32, 33

13 Lev. 14:8; 15:28

wash his clothes, and bathe his flesh in running water, and shall be clean.

14 And on the eighth day he shall take to him two turtledoves, or two young pigeons, and come before the LORD unto the door of the tabernacle of the congregation, and give them unto the priest:

15 And the priest shall offer them, the one *for* a sin offering, and the other *for* a burnt offering; and the priest shall make an atonement for him before the LORD for his issue.

16 And if any man's seed of copulation go out from him, then he shall wash all his flesh in water, and be unclean until the even.

17 And every garment, and every skin, whereon is the seed of copulation, shall be washed with water, and be unclean until the even.

18 The woman also with whom man shall lie *with* seed of copulation, they shall *both* bathe *themselves* in water, and be unclean until the even.

19 And if a woman have an issue, *and* her issue in her flesh be blood, she shall be put apart seven days: and whosoever toucheth her shall be unclean until the even.

20 And every thing that she lieth upon in her separation shall be unclean: every thing also that she sitteth upon shall be unclean.

21 And whosoever toucheth her bed shall wash his clothes, and bathe *himself* in water, and be unclean until the even.

22 And whosoever toucheth any thing that she sat upon shall wash his clothes, and bathe *himself* in water, and be unclean until the even.

23 And if it *be* on *her* bed, or on any thing whereon she sitteth, when he toucheth it, he shall be unclean until the even.

24 And if any man lie with her at all, and her flowers be upon him, he shall be unclean seven days; and all the bed whereon he lieth shall be unclean.

25 And if a woman have an issue of her blood many days out of the time of her separation, or if it run beyond the time of her separation; all the days of the issue of her uncleanness shall be as the days of her separation: she *shall be* unclean.

26 Every bed whereon she lieth all the days of her issue shall be unto her as the bed of her separation: and whatsoever she sitteth upon shall be unclean, as the uncleanness of her separation.

27 And whosoever toucheth those things shall be unclean, and shall wash his clothes,

14 Lev. 14:22, 23
15 Lev. 14:19, 30, 31
16 Lev. 22:4; Deut. 23:10
18 1Sam. 21:4
19 Lev. 12:2
24 Lev. 20:18
25 Matt. 9:20; Mark 5:25; Luke 8:43
28 Lev. 15:13
31 Lev. 11:47; Deut. 24:8; Ezek. 44:23
32 Lev. 15:2, 16
33 Lev. 15:19, 24, 25

1 Lev. 10:1, 2

2 Ex. 25:22; 30:10; 40:34; Lev. 23:27; 1Kgs. 8:10-12; Heb. 9:7; 10:19

3 Lev. 4:3; Heb. 9:7, 12, 24, 25

4 Ex. 28:39, 42, 43; 30:20; Lev. 6:10; 8:6, 7; Ezek. 44:17, 18

5 Lev. 14:14; Num. 29:11; 2Chr. 29:21; Ezra 6:17; Ezek. 45:22, 23

6 Lev. 9:7; Heb. 5:2; 7:27, 28; 9:7

and bathe *himself* in water, and be unclean until the even.

28 But if she be cleansed of her issue, then she shall number to herself seven days, and after that she shall be clean.

29 And on the eighth day she shall take unto her two turtles, or two young pigeons, and bring them unto the priest, to the door of the tabernacle of the congregation.

30 And the priest shall offer the one *for* a sin offering, and the other *for* a burnt offering; and the priest shall make an atonement for her before the LORD for the issue of her uncleanness.

31 Thus shall ye separate the children of Israel from their uncleanness; that they die not in their uncleanness, when they defile my tabernacle that *is* among them.

32 This *is* the law of him that hath an issue, and *of him* whose seed goeth from him, and is defiled therewith;

33 And of her that is sick of her flowers, and of him that hath an issue, of the man, and of the woman, and of him that lieth with her that is unclean.

CHAPTER 16
The Day of Atonement

1 And the LORD spake unto Moses after the death of the two sons of Aaron, when they offered before the LORD, and died;

2 And the LORD said unto Moses, Speak unto Aaron thy brother, that he come not at all times into the holy *place* within the vail before the mercy seat, which *is* upon the ark; that he die not: for I will appear in the cloud upon the mercy seat.

3 Thus shall Aaron come into the holy *place*: with a young bullock for a sin offering, and a ram for a burnt offering.

4 He shall put on the holy linen coat, and he shall have the linen breeches upon his flesh, and shall be girded with a linen girdle, and with the linen mitre shall he be attired: these *are* holy garments; therefore shall he wash his flesh in water, and *so* put them on.

5 And he shall take of the congregation of the children of Israel two kids of the goats for a sin offering, and one ram for a burnt offering.

6 And Aaron shall offer his bullock of the sin offering, which *is* for himself, and make an atonement for himself, and for his house.

7 And he shall take the two goats, and present them before the LORD *at* the door of the tabernacle of the congregation.

8 And Aaron shall cast lots upon the two

goats; one lot for the LORD, and the other lot for the scapegoat.

9 And Aaron shall bring the goat upon which the LORD's lot fell, and offer him *for a* sin offering.

10 But the goat, on which the lot fell to be the scapegoat, shall be presented alive before the LORD, to make an atonement with him, *and* to let him go for a scapegoat into the wilderness.

11 And Aaron shall bring the bullock of the sin offering, which *is* for himself, and shall make an atonement for himself, and for his house, and shall kill the bullock of the sin offering which *is* for himself:

12 And he shall take a censer full of burning coals of fire from off the altar before the LORD, and his hands full of sweet incense beaten small, and bring *it* within the vail:

13 And he shall put the incense upon the fire before the LORD, that the cloud of the incense may cover the mercy seat that *is* upon the testimony, that he die not:

14 And he shall take of the blood of the bullock, and sprinkle *it* with his finger upon the mercy seat eastward; and before the mercy seat shall he sprinkle of the blood with his finger seven times.

15 Then shall he kill the goat of the sin offering, that *is* for the people, and bring his blood within the vail, and do with that blood as he did with the blood of the bullock, and sprinkle it upon the mercy seat, and before the mercy seat:

16 And he shall make an atonement for the holy *place*, because of the uncleanness of the children of Israel, and because of their transgressions in all their sins: and so shall he do for the tabernacle of the congregation, that remaineth among them in the midst of their uncleanness.

17 And there shall be no man in the tabernacle of the congregation when he goeth in to make an atonement in the holy *place*, until he come out, and have made an atonement for himself, and for his household, and for all the congregation of Israel.

18 And he shall go out unto the altar that *is* before the LORD, and make an atonement for it; and shall take of the blood of the bullock, and of the blood of the goat, and put *it* upon the horns of the altar round about.

19 And he shall sprinkle of the blood upon it with his finger seven times, and cleanse it, and hallow it from the uncleanness of the children of Israel.

The Scapegoat

20 And when he hath made an end of reconciling the holy *place*, and the tabernacle of the congregation, and the altar, he shall bring the live goat:

21 And Aaron shall lay both his hands upon the head of the live goat, and confess over him all the iniquities of the children of Israel, and all their transgressions in all their sins, putting them upon the head of the goat, and shall send *him* away by the hand of a fit man into the wilderness:

22 And the goat shall bear upon him all their iniquities unto a land not inhabited: and he shall let go the goat in the wilderness.

23 And Aaron shall come into the tabernacle of the congregation, and shall put off the linen garments, which he put on when he went into the holy *place*, and shall leave them there:

24 And he shall wash his flesh with water in the holy place, and put on his garments, and come forth, and offer his burnt offering, and the burnt offering of the people, and make an atonement for himself, and for the people.

25 And the fat of the sin offering shall he burn upon the altar.

26 And he that let go the goat for the scapegoat shall wash his clothes, and bathe his flesh in water, and afterward come into the camp.

27 And the bullock *for* the sin offering, and the goat *for* the sin offering, whose blood was brought in to make atonement in the holy *place*, shall *one* carry forth without the camp; and they shall burn in the fire their skins, and their flesh, and their dung.

28 And he that burneth them shall wash his clothes, and bathe his flesh in water, and afterward he shall come into the camp.

Regulations for the Day of Atonement

29 And *this* shall be a statute for ever unto you: *that* in the seventh month, on the tenth

Cross-references (center column)

10 1John 2:2
12 Ex. 30:34; Lev. 10:1; Num. 16:18, 46; Rev. 8:5
13 Ex. 25:21; 30:1, 7, 8; Num. 16:7, 18, 46; Rev. 8:3, 4
14 Lev. 4:5, 6; Heb. 9:13, 25; 10:4
15 Lev. 16:2; Heb. 2:17; 5:2; 6:19; 9:3, 7, 12, 28
16 Ex. 29:36; Ezek. 45:18; Heb. 9:22, 23
17 Ex. 34:3; Luke 1:10
18 Ex. 30:10; Lev. 4:7, 18; Heb. 9:22, 23
19 Ezek. 43:20
20 Lev. 16:16; Ezek. 45:20
21 Isa. 53:6
22 Isa. 53:11, 12; John 1:29; Heb. 9:28; 1Pet. 2:24
23 Ezek. 42:14; 44:19
24 Lev. 16:3, 5
25 Lev. 4:10
26 Lev. 15:5
27 Lev. 4:12, 21; 6:30; Heb. 13:11
29 Ex. 30:10; Lev. 23:27; Num. 29:7; Isa. 58:3, 5; Dan. 10:3, 12

16:10 make an atonement. The Day of Atonement necessitated two goats, one allowed to live and go free, signifying that Christ took away our sins. The other was slain on the altar, the blood being taken into the Holy of Holies and sprinkled on the mercy seat above the Ark of the Covenant. This signified that Christ shed His blood, then presented Himself in heaven to appear in the presence of God for us.

day of the month, ye shall afflict your souls, and do no work at all, *whether it be* one of your own country, or a stranger that sojourneth among you:

30 For on that day shall *the priest* make an atonement for you, to cleanse you, *that* ye may be clean from all your sins before the LORD.

31 It *shall be* a sabbath of rest unto you, and ye shall afflict your souls, by a statute for ever.

32 And the priest, whom he shall anoint, and whom he shall consecrate to minister in the priest's office in his father's stead, shall make the atonement, and shall put on the linen clothes, *even* the holy garments:

33 And he shall make an atonement for the holy sanctuary, and he shall make an atonement for the tabernacle of the congregation, and for the altar, and he shall make an atonement for the priests, and for all the people of the congregation.

34 And this shall be an everlasting statute unto you, to make an atonement for the children of Israel for all their sins once a year. And he did as the LORD commanded Moses.

CHAPTER 17
Blood Is Sacred

1 And the LORD spake unto Moses, saying,

2 Speak unto Aaron, and unto his sons, and unto all the children of Israel, and say unto them; This *is* the thing which the LORD hath commanded, saying,

3 What man soever *there be* of the house of Israel, that killeth an ox, or lamb, or goat, in the camp, or that killeth *it* out of the camp,

4 And bringeth it not unto the door of the tabernacle of the congregation, to offer an offering unto the LORD before the tabernacle of the LORD; blood shall be imputed unto that man; he hath shed blood; and that man shall be cut off from among his people:

5 To the end that the children of Israel may bring their sacrifices, which they offer in the open field, even that they may bring them unto the LORD, unto the door of the tabernacle of the congregation, unto the priest, and offer them *for* peace offerings unto the LORD.

6 And the priest shall sprinkle the blood upon the altar of the LORD *at* the door of the tabernacle of the congregation, and burn the fat for a sweet savour unto the LORD.

7 And they shall no more offer their sacrifices unto devils, after whom they have gone a whoring. This shall be a statute for ever unto them throughout their generations.

8 And thou shalt say unto them, Whatsoever man *there be* of the house of Israel, or of the strangers which sojourn among you, that offereth a burnt offering or sacrifice,

9 And bringeth it not unto the door of the tabernacle of the congregation, to offer it unto the LORD; even that man shall be cut off from among his people.

10 And whatsoever man *there be* of the house of Israel, or of the strangers that sojourn among you, that eateth any manner of blood; I will even set my face against that soul that eateth blood, and will cut him off from among his people.

11 For the life of the flesh *is* in the blood: and I have given it to you upon the altar to make an atonement for your souls: for it *is* the blood *that* maketh an atonement for the soul.

12 Therefore I said unto the children of Israel, No soul of you shall eat blood, neither shall any stranger that sojourneth among you eat blood.

13 And whatsoever man *there be* of the children of Israel, or of the strangers that sojourn among you, which hunteth and catcheth any beast or fowl that may be eaten; he shall even pour out the blood thereof, and cover it with dust.

14 For *it is* the life of all flesh; the blood of it *is* for the life thereof: therefore I said unto the children of Israel, Ye shall eat the blood of no manner of flesh: for the life of all flesh *is* the blood thereof: whosoever eateth it shall be cut off.

15 And every soul that eateth that which died *of itself*, or that which was torn *with beasts*, *whether it be* one of your own country, or a stranger, he shall both wash his clothes, and bathe *himself* in water, and be unclean until the even: then shall he be clean.

16 But if he wash *them* not, nor bathe his flesh; then he shall bear his iniquity.

CHAPTER 18
Forbidden Sexual Practices

1 And the LORD spake unto Moses, saying,

2 Speak unto the children of Israel, and say unto them, I am the LORD your God.

---

30 Eph. 5:26; Heb. 9:13, 14; 10:1, 2; 1John 1:7, 9
31 Lev. 23:32
32 Ex. 29:29, 30; Lev. 4:3, 5, 16; 16:4
33 Lev. 16:6, 16-18, 24
34 Ex. 30:10; Lev. 23:31; Num. 29:7; Heb. 9:7, 25
3 Deut. 12:5, 15, 21
4 Deut. 12:5, 6, 13, 14; Rom. 5:13
5 Deut. 12:2; Ezek. 20:28; 22:9
6 Ex. 29:18; Lev. 3:2, 5, 11, 16; 4:31; Num. 18:17
7 Ex. 34:15; Lev. 20:5; Deut. 31:16; 32:17; 1Cor. 10:20; Rev. 9:20
8 Lev. 1:2, 3
9 Lev. 17:4
10 Lev. 3:17; 7:26, 27; 19:26; 20:3, 5, 6; 26:17; Deut. 12:16, 23; 15:23; 1Sam. 14:33; Ezek. 14:8; 15:7; 44:7
11 Matt. 26:28; Mark 14:24; Rom. 3:25; 5:9; Eph. 1:7; Heb. 9:22; 13:12
14 Gen. 9:4; Lev. 17:11, 12; Deut. 12:23
15 Ex. 22:31; Lev. 11:25; 15:5; 22:8; Deut. 14:21
16 Lev. 5:1; 7:18; 19:8; Num. 19:20
2 Ex. 6:7; 18:4; Lev. 11:44; 19:4, 10, 34; 20:7

17:11 the life of the flesh is in the blood. When Christ died, He shed His blood to redeem us—He poured out His life (1 Pet. 1:18–20).

3 After the doings of the land of Egypt, wherein ye dwelt, shall ye not do: and after the doings of the land of Canaan, whither I bring you, shall ye not do: neither shall ye walk in their ordinances.

4 Ye shall do my judgments, and keep mine ordinances, to walk therein: I *am* the LORD your God.

5 Ye shall therefore keep my statutes, and my judgments: which if a man do, he shall live in them: I *am* the LORD.

6 None of you shall approach to any that is near of kin to him, to uncover *their* nakedness: I *am* the LORD.

7 The nakedness of thy father, or the nakedness of thy mother, shalt thou not uncover: she *is* thy mother; thou shalt not uncover her nakedness.

8 The nakedness of thy father's wife shalt thou not uncover: it *is* thy father's nakedness.

9 The nakedness of thy sister, the daughter of thy father, or daughter of thy mother, *whether she be* born at home, or born abroad, *even* their nakedness thou shalt not uncover.

10 The nakedness of thy son's daughter, or of thy daughter's daughter, *even* their nakedness thou shalt not uncover: for theirs *is* thine own nakedness.

11 The nakedness of thy father's wife's daughter, begotten of thy father, she *is* thy sister, thou shalt not uncover her nakedness.

12 Thou shalt not uncover the nakedness of thy father's sister: she *is* thy father's near kinswoman.

13 Thou shalt not uncover the nakedness of thy mother's sister: for she *is* thy mother's near kinswoman.

14 Thou shalt not uncover the nakedness of thy father's brother, thou shalt not approach to his wife: she *is* thine aunt.

15 Thou shalt not uncover the nakedness of thy daughter-in-law: she *is* thy son's wife; thou shalt not uncover her nakedness.

16 Thou shalt not uncover the nakedness of thy brother's wife: it *is* thy brother's nakedness.

17 Thou shalt not uncover the nakedness of a woman and her daughter, neither shalt thou take her son's daughter, or her daughter's daughter, to uncover her nakedness; *for*

they *are* her near kinswomen: it *is* wickedness.

18 Neither shalt thou take a wife to her sister, to vex *her*, to uncover her nakedness, beside the other in her life *time*.

19 Also thou shalt not approach unto a woman to uncover her nakedness, as long as she is put apart for her uncleanness.

20 Moreover thou shalt not lie carnally with thy neighbour's wife, to defile thyself with her.

21 And thou shalt not let any of thy seed pass through *the fire* to Molech, neither shalt thou profane the name of thy God: I *am* the LORD.

22 Thou shalt not lie with mankind, as with womankind: it *is* abomination.

23 Neither shalt thou lie with any beast to defile thyself therewith: neither shall any woman stand before a beast to lie down thereto: it *is* confusion.

24 Defile not ye yourselves in any of these things: for in all these the nations are defiled which I cast out before you:

25 And the land is defiled: therefore I do visit the iniquity thereof upon it, and the land itself vomiteth out her inhabitants.

26 Ye shall therefore keep my statutes and my judgments, and shall not commit *any* of these abominations; *neither* any of your own nation, nor any stranger that sojourneth among you:

27 (For all these abominations have the men of the land done, which *were* before you, and the land is defiled;)

28 That the land spue not you out also, when ye defile it, as it spued out the nations that *were* before you.

29 For whosoever shall commit any of these abominations, even the souls that commit *them* shall be cut off from among their people.

30 Therefore shall ye keep mine ordinance, that *ye* commit not *any one* of these abominable customs, which were committed before you, and that ye defile not yourselves therein: I *am* the LORD your God.

CHAPTER 19
Laws of Holiness and Justice

1 And the LORD spake unto Moses, saying,

2 Speak unto all the congregation of the

---

3 Ex. 23:24; Lev. 20:23; Deut. 12:4, 30, 31

4 Deut. 4:1, 2; 6:1; Ezek. 20:19

5 Ex. 6:2, 6, 29; Ezek. 20:11, 13, 21

8 Lev. 20:11; Deut. 22:30; 27:20; Ezek. 22:10; 1Cor. 5:1

15 Gen. 38:18, 26; Ezek. 22:11

16 Deut. 25:5; Mark 12:19

17 Lev. 20:14

18 1Sam. 1:6, 8

19 Lev. 20:18

20 Ex. 20:14; Lev. 20:10; Deut. 5:18; 22:22; Prov. 6:29, 32; Matt. 5:27

21 Lev. 19:12; 20:2, 3; 1Kgs. 11:7, 33; 2Kgs. 16:3; 21:6; 23:10; Jer. 19:5; Ezek. 20:31

22 Lev. 20:13; Rom. 1:27

23 Ex. 22:19; Lev. 20:12, 15, 16

24 Lev. 18:30; 20:23; Deut. 18:12

25 Num. 35:34; Jer. 2:7; 5:9, 29; 9:9; 14:10; 16:18; 23:2

28 Jer. 9:19; Ezek. 36:13, 17

30 Deut. 18:9

2 Lev. 11:44; 20:7, 26; 1Pet. 1:16

19:2 Ye shall be holy. The word "holy" signifies something that is separated, set apart in a particular way or for a particular purpose. Hence, when applied to mankind, we are to separate ourselves from sin and defilement unto obedience to God. The apostle Peter quotes from Leviticus in his instruction to New Testament believers in 1 Peter 1:15–16 (cf. Lev. 11:44–45). A similar command is expressed by Jesus in Matthew 5:48, "Be ye . . . perfect."

children of Israel, and say unto them, Ye shall be holy: for I the LORD your God *am* holy.

3 Ye shall fear every man his mother, and his father, and keep my sabbaths: I *am* the LORD your God.

4 Turn ye not unto idols, nor make to yourselves molten gods: I *am* the LORD your God.

5 And if ye offer a sacrifice of peace offerings unto the LORD, ye shall offer it at your own will.

6 It shall be eaten the same day ye offer it, and on the morrow: and if ought remain until the third day, it shall be burnt in the fire.

7 And if it be eaten at all on the third day, it *is* abominable; it shall not be accepted.

8 Therefore *every one* that eateth it shall bear his iniquity, because he hath profaned the hallowed thing of the LORD: and that soul shall be cut off from among his people.

9 And when ye reap the harvest of your land, thou shalt not wholly reap the corners of thy field, neither shalt thou gather the gleanings of thy harvest.

10 And thou shalt not glean thy vineyard, neither shalt thou gather *every* grape of thy vineyard; thou shalt leave them for the poor and stranger: I *am* the LORD your God.

11 Ye shall not steal, neither deal falsely, neither lie one to another.

12 And ye shall not swear by my name falsely, neither shalt thou profane the name of thy God: I *am* the LORD.

13 Thou shalt not defraud thy neighbour, neither rob *him*: the wages of him that is hired shall not abide with thee all night until the morning.

14 Thou shalt not curse the deaf, nor put a stumblingblock before the blind, but shalt fear thy God: I *am* the LORD.

15 Ye shall do no unrighteousness in judgment: thou shalt not respect the person of the poor, nor honour the person of the mighty: *but* in righteousness shalt thou judge thy neighbour.

16 Thou shalt not go up and down *as* a talebearer among thy people: neither shalt thou stand against the blood of thy neighbour: I *am* the LORD.

17 Thou shalt not hate thy brother in thine heart: thou shalt in any wise rebuke thy neighbour, and not suffer sin upon him.

18 Thou shalt not avenge, nor bear any grudge against the children of thy people, but thou shalt love thy neighbour as thyself: I *am* the LORD.

19 Ye shall keep my statutes. Thou shalt not let thy cattle gender with a diverse kind: thou shalt not sow thy field with mingled seed: neither shall a garment mingled of linen and woolen come upon thee.

20 And whosoever lieth carnally with a woman, that *is* a bondmaid, betrothed to an husband, and not at all redeemed, nor freedom given her; she shall be scourged; they shall not be put to death, because she was not free.

21 And he shall bring his trespass offering unto the LORD, unto the door of the tabernacle of the congregation, *even* a ram for a trespass offering.

22 And the priest shall make an atonement for him with the ram of the trespass offering before the LORD for his sin which he hath done: and the sin which he hath done shall be forgiven him.

23 And when ye shall come into the land, and shall have planted all manner of trees for food, then ye shall count the fruit thereof as uncircumcised: three years shall it be as uncircumcised unto you: it shall not be eaten of.

24 But in the fourth year all the fruit thereof shall be holy to praise the LORD *withal*.

25 And in the fifth year shall ye eat of the fruit thereof, that it may yield unto you the increase thereof: I *am* the LORD your God.

26 Ye shall not eat *any thing* with the blood: neither shall ye use enchantment, nor observe times.

27 Ye shall not round the corners of your heads, neither shalt thou mar the corners of thy beard.

28 Ye shall not make any cuttings in your flesh for the dead, nor print any marks upon you: I *am* the LORD.

29 Do not prostitute thy daughter, to cause her to be a whore; lest the land fall to whoredom, and the land become full of wickedness.

30 Ye shall keep my sabbaths, and reverence my sanctuary: I *am* the LORD.

3 Ex. 20:8, 12; 31:13
4 Ex. 20:4; 34:17; Lev. 26:1; Deut. 27:15
5 Lev. 7:16
9 Lev. 23:22; Deut. 24:19-21; Ruth 2:15, 16
11 Ex. 20:15; 22:1, 7, 10-12; Lev. 6:2; Deut. 5:19
12 Ex. 20:7; Lev. 6:3; 18:21; Deut. 5:11
13 Deut. 24:14, 15
14 Deut. 27:18; Eccl. 5:7
15 Ex. 23:2, 3; Deut. 1:17; 16:19
16 Ex. 23:1, 7; Ps. 15:3; 50:20; Prov. 11:13; 20:19
17 Matt. 18:15; Luke 17:3; Gal. 6:1; 1John 2:9, 11; 3:15
18 Matt. 5:43; 22:39; James 2:8; 5:9; 1Pet. 2:1
19 Deut. 22:9, 10, 11
21 Lev. 5:15; 6:6
24 Deut. 12:17, 18; Prov. 3:9
26 Deut. 12:23; 2Chr. 33:6; Mal. 3:5
27 Lev. 21:5; Isa. 15:2; Jer. 9:26; 48:37
28 Lev. 21:5; Deut. 14:1
29 Deut. 23:17
30 Lev. 19:3; 26:2; Eccl. 5:1

19:11 Ye shall not. Based on the Ten Commandments (Ex. 20), this teaching against stealing and lying is reemphasized by Jesus in Matthew 19:18–19 in speaking to the rich young ruler.

19:18 thou shalt love thy neighbor as thyself. Jesus called this the "second commandment," after first loving God (Matt. 22:37–40; Mark 12:28–31; Luke 10:25–28).

31 Regard not them that have familiar spirits, neither seek after wizards, to be defiled by them: I *am* the LORD your God.

32 Thou shalt rise up before the hoary head, and honour the face of the old man, and fear thy God: I *am* the LORD.

33 And if a stranger sojourn with thee in your land, ye shall not vex him.

34 *But* the stranger that dwelleth with you shall be unto you as one born among you, and thou shalt love him as thyself; for ye were strangers in the land of Egypt: I *am* the LORD your God.

35 Ye shall do no unrighteousness in judgment, in meteyard, in weight, or in measure.

36 Just balances, just weights, a just ephah, and a just hin, shall ye have: I *am* the LORD your God, which brought you out of the land of Egypt.

37 Therefore shall ye observe all my statutes, and all my judgments, and do them: I *am* the LORD.

CHAPTER 20
The Penalties for Sin

1 And the LORD spake unto Moses, saying,

2 Again, thou shalt say to the children of Israel, Whosoever *he be* of the children of Israel, or of the strangers that sojourn in Israel, that giveth *any* of his seed unto Molech; he shall surely be put to death: the people of the land shall stone him with stones.

3 And I will set my face against that man, and will cut him off from among his people; because he hath given of his seed unto Molech, to defile my sanctuary, and to profane my holy name.

4 And if the people of the land do any ways hide their eyes from the man, when he giveth of his seed unto Molech, and kill him not:

5 Then I will set my face against that man, and against his family, and will cut him off, and all that go a whoring after him, to commit whoredom with Molech, from among their people.

6 And the soul that turneth after such as have familiar spirits, and after wizards, to go a whoring after them, I will even set my face against that soul, and will cut him off from among his people.

7 Sanctify yourselves therefore, and be ye holy: for I *am* the LORD your God.

8 And ye shall keep my statutes, and do them: I *am* the LORD which sanctify you.

9 For every one that curseth his father or his mother shall be surely put to death: he hath cursed his father or his mother; his blood *shall be* upon him.

10 And the man that committeth adultery with *another* man's wife, *even he* that committeth adultery with his neighbour's wife, the adulterer and the adulteress shall surely be put to death.

11 And the man that lieth with his father's wife hath uncovered his father's nakedness: both of them shall surely be put to death; their blood *shall be* upon them.

12 And if a man lie with his daughter-in-law, both of them shall surely be put to death: they have wrought confusion; their blood *shall be* upon them.

13 If a man also lie with mankind, as he lieth with a woman, both of them have committed an abomination: they shall surely be put to death; their blood *shall be* upon them.

14 And if a man take a wife and her mother, it *is* wickedness: they shall be burnt with fire, both he and they; that there be no wickedness among you.

15 And if a man lie with a beast, he shall surely be put to death: and ye shall slay the beast.

16 And if a woman approach unto any beast, and lie down thereto, thou shalt kill the woman, and the beast: they shall surely be put to death; their blood *shall be* upon them.

17 And if a man shall take his sister, his father's daughter, or his mother's daughter, and see her nakedness, and she see his nakedness; it *is* a wicked thing; and they shall be cut off in the sight of their people: he hath uncovered his sister's nakedness; he shall bear his iniquity.

18 And if a man shall lie with a woman having her sickness, and shall uncover her nakedness; he hath discovered her fountain, and she hath uncovered the fountain of her blood: and both of them shall be cut off from among their people.

19 And thou shalt not uncover the nakedness of thy mother's sister, nor of thy

---

31 Ex. 22:18; Lev. 20:6, 27; Acts 16:16

32 Lev. 19:14; Prov. 20:29; 1Tim. 5:1

33 Ex. 22:21; 23:9

34 Ex. 12:48, 49; Deut. 10:19

35 Lev. 19:15

36 Deut. 25:13, 15; Prov. 11:1; 16:11; 20:10

37 Lev. 18:4, 5; Deut. 4:5, 6; 5:1; 6:25

2 Deut. 12:31; 2Kgs. 17:17; Jer. 7:31; Ezek. 20:26, 31

3 Lev. 17:10; 18:21; Ezek. 5:11; 23:38, 39

4 Deut. 17:2, 3, 5

5 Ex. 20:5; Lev. 17:7, 10

6 Lev. 19:31

7 Lev. 11:44; 19:2; 1Pet. 1:16

8 Ex. 31:13; Lev. 19:37; 21:8; Ezek. 37:28

9 Ex. 21:17; Lev. 20:11-13, 16, 27; Deut. 27:16

10 Lev. 18:20; Deut. 22:22; John 8:4, 5

11 Lev. 18:8; Deut. 27:23

13 Gen. 19:5

15 Lev. 18:23

17 Gen. 20:12; Deut. 27:22

18 Lev. 15:24; 18:19

20:9 curseth his father or his mother. Quoting this verse and Exodus 20:12, Jesus stresses the spirit as well as the letter of honoring one's parents, by exposing the practice of claiming that what children might provide for elderly parents could instead be donated as a gift to someone else or an institution, such as the temple (see Matt. 15:1–6). This made the Word of God of none effect through human tradition or practices.

father's sister: for he uncovereth his near kin: they shall bear their iniquity.

20 And if a man shall lie with his uncle's wife, he hath uncovered his uncle's nakedness: they shall bear their sin; they shall die childless.

21 And if a man shall take his brother's wife, it *is* an unclean thing: he hath uncovered his brother's nakedness; they shall be childless.

22 Ye shall therefore keep all my statutes, and all my judgments, and do them: that the land, whither I bring you to dwell therein, spue you not out.

23 And ye shall not walk in the manners of the nation, which I cast out before you: for they committed all these things, and therefore I abhorred them.

24 But I have said unto you, Ye shall inherit their land, and I will give it unto you to possess it, a land that floweth with milk and honey: I *am* the LORD your God, which have separated you from *other* people.

25 Ye shall therefore put difference between clean beasts and unclean, and between unclean fowls and clean: and ye shall not make your souls abominable by beast, or by fowl, or by any manner of living thing that creepeth on the ground, which I have separated from you as unclean.

26 And ye shall be holy unto me: for I the LORD *am* holy, and have severed you from *other* people, that ye should be mine.

27 A man also or woman that hath a familiar spirit, or that is a wizard, shall surely be put to death: they shall stone them with stones: their blood *shall be* upon them.

CHAPTER 21
The Holiness of the Priests

1 And the LORD said unto Moses, Speak unto the priests the sons of Aaron, and say unto them, There shall none be defiled for the dead among his people:

2 But for his kin, that is near unto him, *that is,* for his mother, and for his father, and for his son, and for his daughter, and for his brother,

3 And for his sister a virgin, that is nigh unto him, which hath had no husband; for her may he be defiled.

4 *But* he shall not defile himself, *being* a chief man among his people, to profane himself.

5 They shall not make baldness upon their head, neither shall they shave off the corner of their beard, nor make any cuttings in their flesh.

6 They shall be holy unto their God, and not profane the name of their God: for the offerings of the LORD made by fire, *and* the bread of their God, they do offer: therefore they shall be holy.

7 They shall not take a wife *that is* a whore, or profane; neither shall they take a woman put away from her husband: for he *is* holy unto his God.

8 Thou shalt sanctify him therefore; for he offereth the bread of thy God: he shall be holy unto thee: for I the LORD, which sanctify you, *am* holy.

9 And the daughter of any priest, if she profane herself by playing the whore, she profaneth her father: she shall be burnt with fire.

10 And *he that is* the high priest among his brethren, upon whose head the anointing oil was poured, and that is consecrated to put on the garments, shall not uncover his head, nor rend his clothes;

11 Neither shall he go in to any dead body, nor defile himself for his father, or for his mother;

12 Neither shall he go out of the sanctuary, nor profane the sanctuary of his God; for the crown of the anointing oil of his God *is* upon him: I *am* the LORD.

13 And he shall take a wife in her virginity.

14 A widow, or a divorced woman, or profane, *or* an harlot, these shall he not take: but he shall take a virgin of his own people to wife.

15 Neither shall he profane his seed among his people: for I the LORD do sanctify him.

16 And the LORD spake unto Moses, saying,

17 Speak unto Aaron, saying, Whosoever *he be* of thy seed in their generations that hath *any* blemish, let him not approach to offer the bread of his God.

18 For whatsoever man *he be* that hath a blemish, he shall not approach: a blind man, or a lame, or he that hath a flat nose, or any thing superfluous,

19 Or a man that is brokenfooted, or brokenhanded,

20 Or crookbackt, or a dwarf, or that hath a blemish in his eye, or be scurvy, or scabbed, or hath his stones broken;

21 No man that hath a blemish of the seed of Aaron the priest shall come nigh to offer the offerings of the LORD made by fire: he hath a blemish; he shall not come nigh to offer the bread of his God.

22 He shall eat the bread of his God, *both* of the most holy, and of the holy.

23 Only he shall not go in unto the vail, nor

Center reference column

20 Lev. 18:14

21 Lev. 18:16

22 Lev. 18:25, 26, 28; 19:37

23 Lev. 18:3, 24, 27, 30; Deut. 9:5

24 Ex. 3:17; 6:8; 19:5; 33:16; Lev. 20:26; Deut. 7:6; 14:2; 1Kgs. 8:53

25 Lev. 11:43, 47; Deut. 14:4

26 Lev. 19:2; 20:7, 24; Titus 2:14; 1Pet. 1:16

27 Ex. 22:18; Lev. 19:31; 20:9; Deut. 18:10, 11; 1Sam. 28:7, 8

1 Ezek. 44:25

5 Lev. 19:27, 28; Deut. 14:1; Ezek. 44:20

6 Lev. 3:11; 18:21; 19:12

7 Deut. 24:1, 2; Ezek. 44:22

8 Lev. 20:7, 8

9 Gen. 38:24

10 Ex. 28:2; 29:29, 30; Lev. 8:12, 10:6; 16:32; Num. 35:25

11 Lev. 21:1, 2; Num. 19:14

12 Ex. 28:36; Lev. 8:9, 12, 30; 10:7

13 Lev. 21:7; Ezek. 44:22

15 Lev. 21:8

17 Lev. 10:3; Num. 16:5; Ps. 65:4

18 Lev. 22:23

20 Deut. 23:1

21 Lev. 21:6

22 Lev. 2:3, 10; 6:17, 29; 7:1; 22:10, 11, 12; 24:9

come nigh unto the altar, because he hath a blemish; that he profane not my sanctuaries: for I the LORD do sanctify them.

24 And Moses told *it* unto Aaron, and to his sons, and unto all the children of Israel.

CHAPTER 22
The Holiness of the Offerings

1 And the LORD spake unto Moses, saying,

2 Speak unto Aaron and to his sons, that they separate themselves from the holy things of the children of Israel, and that they profane not my holy name *in those things* which they hallow unto me: I *am* the LORD.

3 Say unto them, Whosoever *he be* of all your seed among your generations, that goeth unto the holy things, which the children of Israel hallow unto the LORD, having his uncleanness upon him, that soul shall be cut off from my presence: I *am* the LORD.

4 What man soever of the seed of Aaron *is* a leper, or hath a running issue; he shall not eat of the holy things, until he be clean. And whoso toucheth any thing *that is* unclean *by* the dead, or a man whose seed goeth from him;

5 Or whosoever toucheth any creeping thing, whereby he may be made unclean, or a man of whom he may take uncleanness, whatsoever uncleanness he hath;

6 The soul which hath touched any such shall be unclean until even, and shall not eat of the holy things, unless he wash his flesh with water.

7 And when the sun is down, he shall be clean, and shall afterward eat of the holy things; because it *is* his food.

8 That which dieth of itself, or is torn *with beasts*, he shall not eat to defile himself therewith: I *am* the LORD.

9 They shall therefore keep mine ordinance, lest they bear sin for it, and die therefore, if they profane it: I the LORD do sanctify them.

10 There shall no stranger eat *of* the holy thing: a sojourner of the priest, or an hired servant, shall not eat *of* the holy thing.

11 But if the priest buy *any* soul with his money, he shall eat of it, and he that is born in his house: they shall eat of his meat.

12 If the priest's daughter also be *married* unto a stranger, she may not eat of an offering of the holy things.

13 But if the priest's daughter be a widow, or divorced, and have no child, and is returned unto her father's house, as in her youth, she shall eat of her father's meat: but there shall no stranger eat thereof.

14 And if a man eat *of* the holy thing unwittingly, then he shall put the fifth *part* thereof unto it, and shall give *it* unto the priest with the holy thing.

15 And they shall not profane the holy things of the children of Israel, which they offer unto the LORD;

16 Or suffer them to bear the iniquity of trespass, when they eat their holy things: for I the LORD do sanctify them.

17 And the LORD spake unto Moses, saying,

18 Speak unto Aaron, and to his sons, and unto all the children of Israel, and say unto them, Whatsoever *he be* of the house of Israel, or of the strangers in Israel, that will offer his oblation for all his vows, and for all his freewill offerings, which they will offer unto the LORD for a burnt offering;

19 *Ye shall offer* at your own will a male without blemish, of the beeves, of the sheep, or of the goats.

20 *But* whatsoever hath a blemish, *that* shall ye not offer: for it shall not be acceptable for you.

21 And whosoever offereth a sacrifice of peace offerings unto the LORD to accomplish *his* vow, or a freewill offering in beeves or sheep, it shall be perfect to be accepted; there shall be no blemish therein.

22 Blind, or broken, or maimed, or having a wen, or scurvy, or scabbed, ye shall not offer these unto the LORD, nor make an offering by fire of them upon the altar unto the LORD.

23 Either a bullock or a lamb that hath any thing superfluous or lacking in his parts, that mayest thou offer *for* a freewill offering; but for a vow it shall not be accepted.

24 Ye shall not offer unto the LORD that which is bruised, or crushed, or broken, or cut; neither shall ye make *any offering thereof* in your land.

25 Neither from a stranger's hand shall ye offer the bread of your God of any of these; because their corruption *is* in them, *and* blemishes *be* in them: they shall not be accepted for you.

26 And the LORD spake unto Moses, saying,

27 When a bullock, or a sheep, or a goat, is brought forth, then it shall be seven days under the dam; and from the eighth day and thenceforth it shall be accepted for an offering made by fire unto the LORD.

28 And *whether it be* cow or ewe, ye shall not kill it and her young both in one day.

29 And when ye will offer a sacrifice of thanksgiving unto the LORD, offer *it* at your own will.

Cross references

2 Ex. 28:38; Lev. 18:21; Num. 6:3; 18:32; Deut. 15:19

3 Lev. 7:20

4 Lev. 14:2; 15:2, 13, 16; Num. 19:11, 22

5 Lev. 11:24, 43, 44; 15:7, 19

6 Lev. 15:5; Heb. 10:22

7 Lev. 21:22; Num. 18:11, 13

8 Ex. 22:31; Lev. 17:15; Ezek. 44:31

9 Lev. 28:43; Num. 18:22, 32

10 1Sam. 21:6

11 Num. 18:11, 13

13 Gen. 38:11; Num. 10:14; Num. 18:11, 19

14 Lev. 5:15, 16

15 Num. 18:32

16 Lev. 22:9

18 Lev. 1:2, 3, 10; Num. 15:14

19 Lev. 1:3

20 Deut. 15:21; 17:1; Mal. 1:8, 14; Eph. 5:27; Heb. 9:14; 1Pet. 1:19

21 Lev. 3:1, 6; 7:16; Num. 15:3, 8; Deut. 23:21, 23; Ps. 61:8; 65:1; Eccl. 5:4, 5

22 Lev. 1:9, 13; 3:3, 5; 22:20; Mal. 1:8

23 Lev. 21:18

25 Lev. 21:6, 17; Num. 15:15, 16; Mal. 1:14

27 Ex. 22:30

28 Deut. 22:6

30 On the same day it shall be eaten up; ye shall leave none of it until the morrow: I *am* the LORD.

31 Therefore shall ye keep my commandments, and do them: I *am* the LORD.

32 Neither shall ye profane my holy name; but I will be hallowed among the children of Israel: I *am* the LORD which hallow you,

33 That brought you out of the land of Egypt, to be your God: I *am* the LORD.

CHAPTER 23
The Appointed Festivals

1 And the LORD spake unto Moses, saying,

2 Speak unto the children of Israel, and say unto them, *Concerning* the feasts of the LORD, which ye shall proclaim *to be* holy convocations, *even* these *are* my feasts.

3 Six days shall work be done: but the seventh day *is* the sabbath of rest, an holy convocation; ye shall do no work *therein: it is* the sabbath of the LORD in all your dwellings.

4 These *are* the feasts of the LORD, *even* holy convocations, which ye shall proclaim in their seasons.

5 In the fourteenth *day* of the first month at even *is* the LORD's passover.

6 And on the fifteenth day of the same month *is* the feast of unleavened bread unto the LORD: seven days ye must eat unleavened bread.

7 In the first day ye shall have an holy convocation: ye shall do no servile work therein.

8 But ye shall offer an offering made by fire unto the LORD seven days: in the seventh day *is* an holy convocation: ye shall do no servile work *therein*.

9 And the LORD spake unto Moses, saying,

10 Speak unto the children of Israel, and say unto them, When ye be come into the land which I give unto you, and shall reap the harvest thereof, then ye shall bring a sheaf of the firstfruits of your harvest unto the priest:

11 And he shall wave the sheaf before the LORD, to be accepted for you: on the morrow after the sabbath the priest shall wave it.

12 And ye shall offer that day when ye wave the sheaf an he lamb without blemish of the first year for a burnt offering unto the LORD.

13 And the meat offering thereof *shall be* two tenth deals of fine flour mingled with oil, an offering made by fire unto the LORD *for* a sweet savour: and the drink offering thereof *shall be* of wine, the fourth *part* of an hin.

14 And ye shall eat neither bread, nor parched corn, nor green ears, until the selfsame day that ye have brought an offering unto your God: it shall be a statute for ever throughout your generations in all your dwellings.

15 And ye shall count unto you from the morrow after the sabbath, from the day that ye brought the sheaf of the wave offering; seven sabbaths shall be complete:

16 Even unto the morrow after the seventh sabbath shall ye number fifty days; and ye shall offer a new meat offering unto the LORD.

17 Ye shall bring out of your habitations two wave loaves of two tenth deals: they shall be of fine flour; they shall be baken with leaven; *they are* the firstfruits unto the LORD.

18 And ye shall offer with the bread seven lambs without blemish of the first year, and one young bullock, and two rams: they shall be *for* a burnt offering unto the LORD, with their meat offering, and their drink offerings, *even* an offering made by fire, of sweet savour unto the LORD.

19 Then ye shall sacrifice one kid of the goats for a sin offering, and two lambs of the first year for a sacrifice of peace offerings.

20 And the priest shall wave them with the bread of the firstfruits *for* a wave offering before the LORD, with the two lambs: they shall be holy to the LORD for the priest.

21 And ye shall proclaim on the selfsame day, *that* it may be an holy convocation unto you: ye shall do no servile work *therein: it shall be* a statute for ever in all your dwellings throughout your generations.

---

30 Lev. 7:15
31 Lev. 19:37; Num. 15:40; Deut. 4:40
32 Lev. 10:3; 18:21; 20:8; Matt. 6:9; Luke 11:2
33 Ex. 6:7; Lev. 11:45; 19:36; 25:38; Num. 15:41
2 Ex. 32:5; Lev. 23:4, 37; 2Kgs. 10:20; Ps. 81:3
3 Ex. 20:9; 23:12; 31:15; 34:21; Lev. 19:3; Deut. 5:13; Luke 13:14
4 Ex. 23:14; Lev. 23:2, 37
5 Ex. 12:6, 14, 18; Num. 9:2, 3; 28:16, 17; Deut. 16:1-8
7 Ex. 12:16; Num. 28:18
10 Ex. 23:16, 19; Num. 15:2, 18; Deut. 16:9; Rom. 11:16; 1Cor. 15:20; James 1:18
11 Ex. 29:24
13 Lev. 2:14-16
15 Ex. 34:22; Lev. 25:8; Deut. 16:9
16 Num. 28:26; Acts 2:1
17 Ex. 22:29; Num. 15:17-21; Deut. 26:1
19 Lev. 3:1; Num. 28:30
20 Num. 18:12; Deut. 18:4

22:32 I will be hallowed among the children of Israel. Jesus makes hallowing, or keeping God's name holy and revered, the first request in the Lord's Prayer (Matt. 6:9; Luke 11:2).

23:2 these are my feasts. The Seven Feasts are 1) Passover, typifying Christ's death; 2) Unleavened Bread, showing Christ's body being broken as Jesus revealed (Luke 22:13–20); 3) Firstfruits, symbolizing His resurrection (1 Cor. 15:23); 4) Pentecost (fifty days), anticipating the coming of the Spirit (Acts 2:2; Zech. 12:10); 5) Trumpets, indicating Israel's regathering (Matt. 24:31); 6) Day of Atonement, typifying Christ's atoning death (Heb. 9:12), which the Jews will come to understand (Zech. 12:11–13; 13:1–7), and 7) Tabernacles, which will be observed in the Millennial Kingdom (Zech. 14:16).

The Seven Feasts of Israel

By Zola Levitt

The seven feasts of Israel, as found in Leviticus 23, provide a prophetic preview of the vital future events that relate to Christ, the Church, and the Jews. The seven feasts are important to comprehend so the believer can have a basic understanding of God's calendar.

The first feast on the festival calendar was **Passover**, the feast of redemption (Lev. 23:5). A lamb without spot or blemish was to be sacrificed and his blood shed for deliverance and salvation. It was by divine design from the beginning of time that our Lord Jesus was to be sacrificed on Passover day. Passover represents our salvation in that "the Lamb of God" (John 1:36) takes away the sin of the world.

The **Feast of Unleavened Bread** begins on the night after Passover (Lev. 23:6). God commanded the Jews to eat unleavened bread during the week following Passover, symbolizing a holy walk with the Lord. The unleavened bread of the New Testament is the body of our Lord Jesus Christ. He is called "the bread of life" (John 6:35), and His body was buried during this feast.

> *The seven feasts provide a prophetic preview of vital future events.*

The **Feast of Firstfruits** (Lev. 23:10–11) is held on the Sunday following Unleavened Bread. In it Israel would acknowledge Him as the One who gave them the fertility of the land. They were to bring the firstfruits of the early crops to the priest in the Temple to be waved before the Lord on their behalf. We not only celebrate the resurrection of our Lord on this feast day, but also the resurrection of the Church (see 1 Cor. 15:23).

Pentecost, connoting fifty days, was to occur fifty days after Firstfruits (see Lev. 23:15–17) and involved taking "two wave loaves" baked with leaven and of equal weight. Since they are baked with leaven (which symbolizes sin), they represent sinful men. Thus, God was predicting that the Church would be comprised of two equal parts, Jews and Gentiles. When the Holy Spirit came, there was a harvest of 3,000 souls (Acts 2:41), only a small token of the great harvest to come in the rapture of the Church.

Trumpets were to be blown at the commencement of the **Feast of Trumpets** (Lev. 23:24), which finds its exact parallel and fulfillment in the rapture of the Church (see 1 Cor. 15:51–52 and 1 Thess. 4:16–17) when that great trumpet sounds. The graves will give up those who died in faith and believers that are alive will rise from the earth. All the believers will be mysteriously changed and outfitted for immortality.

On the solemn **Day of Atonement**, the high priest of Israel entered into the Holy of Holies and made a sacrifice on his own behalf and for all the sins of Israel (see Lev. 23:27). Jesus is the final atonement for all sins once and forever (see Heb. 9—10). The Day of Atonement will be fulfilled in a wonderful way when the Lord returns at His Second Coming, at which point Israel will finally accept His atonement.

The **Feast of Tabernacles** celebrates the fact that God wanted to provide shelter for the Israelites in the wilderness (see Lev. 23:39–43). Each year devout Jews build little shelters outside their houses and worship in them. The Lord's great tabernacle will exist in Jerusalem during the Millennial Kingdom. The entire world will come every year to appear before the King and worship Him.

22 And when ye reap the harvest of your land, thou shalt not make clean riddance of the corners of thy field when thou reapest, neither shalt thou gather any gleaning of thy harvest: thou shalt leave them unto the poor, and to the stranger: I *am* the LORD your God.

23 And the LORD spake unto Moses, saying,

24 Speak unto the children of Israel, saying, In the seventh month, in the first *day* of the month, shall ye have a sabbath, a memorial of blowing of trumpets, an holy convocation.

25 Ye shall do no servile work *therein*: but ye shall offer an offering made by fire unto the LORD.

26 And the LORD spake unto Moses, saying,

27 Also on the tenth *day* of this seventh month *there shall be* a day of atonement: it shall be an holy convocation unto you; and ye shall afflict your souls, and offer an offering made by fire unto the LORD.

28 And ye shall do no work in that same day: for it *is* a day of atonement, to make an atonement for you before the LORD your God.

29 For whatsoever soul *it be* that shall not be afflicted in that same day, he shall be cut off from among his people.

30 And whatsoever soul *it be* that doeth any work in that same day, the same soul will I destroy from among his people.

31 Ye shall do no manner of work: *it shall be* a statute for ever throughout your generations in all your dwellings.

32 It *shall be* unto you a sabbath of rest, and

ye shall afflict your souls: in the ninth *day* of the month at even, from even unto even, shall ye celebrate your sabbath.

33 And the LORD spake unto Moses, saying,

34 Speak unto the children of Israel, saying, The fifteenth day of this seventh month *shall be* the feast of tabernacles *for* seven days unto the LORD.

35 On the first day *shall be* an holy convocation: ye shall do no servile work *therein*.

36 Seven days ye shall offer an offering made by fire unto the LORD: on the eighth day shall be an holy convocation unto you; and ye shall offer an offering made by fire unto the LORD: it *is* a solemn assembly; *and* ye shall do no servile work *therein*.

37 These *are* the feasts of the LORD, which ye shall proclaim *to be* holy convocations, to offer an offering made by fire unto the LORD, a burnt offering, and a meat offering, a sacrifice, and drink offerings, every thing upon his day:

38 Beside the sabbaths of the LORD, and beside your gifts, and beside all your vows, and beside all your freewill offerings, which ye give unto the LORD.

39 Also in the fifteenth day of the seventh month, when ye have gathered in the fruit of the land, ye shall keep a feast unto the LORD seven days: on the first day *shall be* a sabbath, and on the eighth day *shall be* a sabbath.

40 And ye shall take you on the first day the boughs of goodly trees, branches of palm trees, and the boughs of thick trees, and

22 Lev. 19:9; Deut. 24:19
24 Lev. 25:9; Num. 29:1
27 Lev. 16:30; Num. 29:7
29 Gen. 17:14
30 Lev. 20:3, 5, 6
34 Ex. 23:16; Num. 29:12; Deut. 16:13; Ezra 3:4; Neh. 8:14; Zech. 14:16; John 7:2
36 Num. 29:35; Deut. 16:8; 2Chr. 7:9; Neh. 8:18; Joel 1:14; 2:15; John 7:37
37 Lev. 23:2, 4
38 Num. 29:39
39 Ex. 23:16; Deut. 16:13
40 Deut. 16:14, 15; Neh. 8:15

The Feasts of Israel

FEAST	OCCASION	MEANING	TYPE OF CHRIST	REFERENCES
Passover	Plague on the firstborn of Egypt	Passed over by God's judgment	Lamb of God	Ex. 12; Lev. 23:5; 1 Cor. 5:7
Unleavened Bread	The Exodus	A peculiar people, holy unto God	Death on the cross	Lev. 23:6; 1 Cor. 5:7; 10:16–17
Firstfruits	Harvest	God gives the harvest	Resurrection	Lev. 23:10–11; 1 Cor. 15:20, 23
Pentecost	End of harvest	God provides	Lord of all	Deut. 16:9; Lev. 23:15–20; Acts 2; Rom. 8:32
Trumpets	Unknown	Celebration	Second Coming	Lev. 23:24; 1 Thess. 4:16
Day of Atonement	Sacrifice for sin	Salvation requires a blood sacrifice	Christ our High Priest	Num. 29:7–11 Lev. 16:1–34; 23:27; Heb. 9:7, 11–12
Tabernacles	Forty years in the wilderness	God is with us	Christ in you	Ex. 23:16; 34:22 Lev. 23:39–43; Eph. 2:22; 3:17

By Warren Baker

willows of the brook; and ye shall rejoice before the LORD your God seven days.

41 And ye shall keep it a feast unto the LORD seven days in the year. *It shall be* a statute for ever in your generations: ye shall celebrate it in the seventh month.

42 Ye shall dwell in booths seven days; all that are Israelites born shall dwell in booths:

43 That your generations may know that I made the children of Israel to dwell in booths, when I brought them out of the land of Egypt: I *am* the LORD your God.

44 And Moses declared unto the children of Israel the feasts of the LORD.

CHAPTER 24
Taking Care of the Lamps

1 And the LORD spake unto Moses, saying,

2 Command the children of Israel, that they bring unto thee pure oil olive beaten for the light, to cause the lamps to burn continually.

3 Without the vail of the testimony, in the tabernacle of the congregation, shall Aaron order it from the evening unto the morning before the LORD continually: *it shall be* a statute for ever in your generations.

4 He shall order the lamps upon the pure candlestick before the LORD continually.

The Shewbread

5 And thou shalt take fine flour, and bake twelve cakes thereof: two tenth deals shall be in one cake.

6 And thou shalt set them in two rows, six on a row, upon the pure table before the LORD.

7 And thou shalt put pure frankincense upon *each* row, that it may be on the bread for a memorial, *even* an offering made by fire unto the LORD.

8 Every sabbath he shall set it in order be-

fore the LORD continually, *being taken* from the children of Israel by an everlasting covenant.

9 And it shall be Aaron's and his sons'; and they shall eat it in the holy place: for it *is* most holy unto him of the offerings of the LORD made by fire by a perpetual statute.

The Punishment for Blasphemy

10 And the son of an Israelitish woman, whose father *was* an Egyptian, went out among the children of Israel: and this son of the Israelitish *woman* and a man of Israel strove together in the camp;

11 And the Israelitish woman's son blasphemed the name *of the* LORD, and cursed. And they brought him unto Moses: (and his mother's name *was* Shelomith, the daughter of Dibri, of the tribe of Dan:)

12 And they put him in ward, that the mind of the LORD might be shewed them.

13 And the LORD spake unto Moses, saying,

14 Bring forth him that hath cursed without the camp; and let all that heard *him* lay their hands upon his head, and let all the congregation stone him.

15 And thou shalt speak unto the children of Israel, saying, Whosoever curseth his God shall bear his sin.

16 And he that blasphemeth the name of the LORD, he shall surely be put to death, *and* all the congregation shall certainly stone him: as well the stranger, as he that is born in the land, when he blasphemeth the name *of the* LORD, shall be put to death.

17 And he that killeth any man shall surely be put to death.

18 And he that killeth a beast shall make it good; beast for beast.

19 And if a man cause a blemish in his neighbour; as he hath done, so shall it be done to him;

20 Breach for breach, eye for eye, tooth for

Cross references (center column)

41 Num. 29:12; Neh. 8:18

42 Neh. 8:14-16

43 Deut. 31:13; Ps. 78:5, 6

44 Lev. 23:2

2 Ex. 27:20, 21

4 Ex. 31:8; 39:37

5 Ex. 25:30

6 1Kgs. 7:48; 2Chr. 4:19; 13:1; Heb. 9:2

8 Num. 4:7; 1Chr. 9:32; 2Chr. 2:4

9 Ex. 20:33; Lev. 8:31; 1Sam. 21:6; Matt. 12:4

11 Ex. 18:22, 26; Lev. 24:6; Isa. 8:21

12 Ex. 18:15, 16; Num. 15:34; 27:5; 36:5, 6

14 Deut. 13:9; 17:7

15 Lev. 5:1; 20:17; Num. 9:13

16 1Kgs. 21:10, 13; Ps. 74:10, 18; Matt. 12:31; Mark 3:28; James 2:7

17 Ex. 21:12

19 Deut. 19:21; Matt. 5:38; 7:2

24:9 they shall eat it in the holy place. Normally only the priests in actual service at the time could eat of the twelve loaves of bread from the table of shewbread in the ancient Tabernacle. Jesus, citing how David and his men, hungry and weary, ate the sacred bread on the Sabbath (Luke 6:1–4), answered His Pharisaical critics. They had questioned His disciples' plucking "ears of corn" on the Sabbath to satisfy their hunger, thus "working." Jesus enunciated a higher law when He announced, "the Son of man is Lord also of the sabbath" (Luke 6:5).

24:20 eye for eye, tooth for tooth. This basically means that the punishment should fit the crime. This idea of retributive justice is a key element in God's plan of redemp-

tion. God's justice for sin demanded our death; this is the punishment that fits the crime (2 Kgs. 14:6; Rom. 6:23). God did not do away with retributive justice to redeem us, but rather sent Christ to His death on the cross to be our substitute (Isa. 53:12; 2 Cor. 5:21). Jesus told His disciples to "resist not evil," but to reach out even to the wicked in patience, love, and forgiveness (Matt. 5:38–42). This does not mean that punishments should no longer fit the crime, or that sin and wickedness do not have consequences for the offender in society. What it means is that it was never right to use this verse in Leviticus to claim a right to personal revenge on one that has injured us.

tooth: as he hath caused a blemish in a man, so shall it be done to him *again*.

21 And he that killeth a beast, he shall restore it: and he that killeth a man, he shall be put to death.

22 Ye shall have one manner of law, as well for the stranger, as for one of your own country: for I *am* the LORD your God.

23 And Moses spake to the children of Israel, that they should bring forth him that had cursed out of the camp, and stone him with stones. And the children of Israel did as the LORD commanded Moses.

CHAPTER 25
Sabbath Years and the Year of Jubilee

1 And the LORD spake unto Moses in mount Sinai, saying,

2 Speak unto the children of Israel, and say unto them, When ye come into the land which I give you, then shall the land keep a sabbath unto the LORD.

3 Six years thou shalt sow thy field, and six years thou shalt prune thy vineyard, and gather in the fruit thereof;

4 But in the seventh year shall be a sabbath of rest unto the land, a sabbath for the LORD: thou shalt neither sow thy field, nor prune thy vineyard.

5 That which groweth of its own accord of thy harvest thou shalt not reap, neither gather the grapes of thy vine undressed: *for* it is a year of rest unto the land.

6 And the sabbath of the land shall be meat for you; for thee, and for thy servant, and for thy maid, and for thy hired servant, and for thy stranger that sojourneth with thee,

7 And for thy cattle, and for the beast that *are* in thy land, shall all the increase thereof be meat.

8 And thou shalt number seven sabbaths of years unto thee, seven times seven years; and the space of the seven sabbaths of years shall be unto thee forty and nine years.

9 Then shalt thou cause the trumpet of the jubile to sound on the tenth *day* of the seventh month, in the day of atonement shall ye make the trumpet sound throughout all your land.

10 And ye shall hallow the fiftieth year, and

proclaim liberty throughout *all* the land unto all the inhabitants thereof: it shall be a jubile unto you; and ye shall return every man unto his possession, and ye shall return every man unto his family.

11 A jubile shall that fiftieth year be unto you: ye shall not sow, neither reap that which groweth of itself in it, nor gather *the grapes* in it of thy vine undressed.

12 For it *is* the jubile; it shall be holy unto you: ye shall eat the increase thereof out of the field.

13 In the year of this jubile ye shall return every man unto his possession.

14 And if thou sell ought unto thy neighbour, or buyest *ought* of thy neighbour's hand, ye shall not oppress one another:

15 According to the number of years after the jubile thou shalt buy of thy neighbour, *and* according unto the number of years of the fruits he shall sell unto thee:

16 According to the multitude of years thou shalt increase the price thereof, and according to the fewness of years thou shalt diminish the price of it: for *according* to the number *of the years* of the fruits doth he sell unto thee.

17 Ye shall not therefore oppress one another; but thou shalt fear thy God: for I *am* the LORD your God.

18 Wherefore ye shall do my statutes, and keep my judgments, and do them; and ye shall dwell in the land in safety.

19 And the land shall yield her fruit, and ye shall eat your fill, and dwell therein in safety.

20 And if ye shall say, What shall we eat the seventh year? behold, we shall not sow, nor gather in our increase:

21 Then I will command my blessing upon you in the sixth year, and it shall bring forth fruit for three years.

22 And ye shall sow the eighth year, and eat *yet* of old fruit until the ninth year; until her fruits come in ye shall eat *of* the old *store*.

23 The land shall not be sold for ever: for the land *is* mine; for ye *are* strangers and sojourners with me.

24 And in all the land of your possession ye shall grant a redemption for the land.

25 If thy brother be waxen poor, and hath sold away *some* of his possession, and if any

Cross references (center column):

21 Ex. 21:33; Lev. 24:17, 18

22 Ex. 12:49; Lev. 19:34; Num. 15:16

23 Lev. 24:14

2 Ex. 23:10; Lev. 26:34, 35; 2Chr. 36:21

5 2Kgs. 19:29

9 Lev. 23:24, 27

10 Lev. 25:13; Num. 36:4; Isa. 61:2; 63:4; Jer. 34:8, 15, 17; Luke 4:19

11 Lev. 25:5

12 Lev. 25:6, 7

13 Lev. 25:10; Num. 36:4

14 Lev. 19:13; 1Cor. 6:8

15 Lev. 27:18, 23

17 Lev. 19:14, 32; 25:14, 45

18 Lev. 19:37; Deut. 12:10; Prov. 1:33

19 Lev. 26:5; Ezek. 34:25, 27, 28

20 Lev. 25:4, 5; Matt. 6:25, 31

21 Ex. 16:29; Deut. 28:8

22 Josh. 5:11, 12; 2Kgs. 19:29

23 Deut. 32:43; 1Chr. 29:15; 2Chr. 7:20; Ps. 39:12; 85:1; 119:19

25 Ruth 2:20; 3:2, 9, 12; 4:4, 6; Jer. 32:7, 8

25:10 it shall be a jubile unto you. Every fiftieth year was to be a Jubilee year, when servants would be freed and properties reverted to original owners, a system for Israel's agrarian economy to preserve tribal inheritance. This freeing of slaves was a type of individual deliverance at Christ's first coming and universal deliverance at His second coming (Rom. 8:18–23).

of his kin come to redeem it, then shall he redeem that which his brother sold.

26 And if the man have none to redeem it, and himself be able to redeem it;

27 Then let him count the years of the sale thereof, and restore the overplus unto the man to whom he sold it; that he may return unto his possession.

28 But if he be not able to restore *it* to him, then that which is sold shall remain in the hand of him that hath bought it until the year of jubile: and in the jubile it shall go out, and he shall return unto his possession.

29 And if a man sell a dwelling house in a walled city, then he may redeem it within a whole year after it is sold; *within* a full year may he redeem it.

30 And if it be not redeemed within the space of a full year, then the house that *is* in the walled city shall be established for ever to him that bought it throughout his generations: it shall not go out in the jubile.

31 But the houses of the villages which have no wall round about them shall be counted as the fields of the country: they may be redeemed, and they shall go out in the jubile.

32 Notwithstanding the cities of the Levites, *and* the houses of the cities of their possession, may the Levites redeem at any time.

33 And if a man purchase of the Levites, then the house that was sold, and the city of his possession, shall go out in *the year of* jubile: for the houses of the cities of the Levites *are* their possession among the children of Israel.

34 But the field of the suburbs of their cities may not be sold; for it *is* their perpetual possession.

35 And if thy brother be waxen poor, and fallen in decay with thee; then thou shalt relieve him: *yea, though he be* a stranger, or a sojourner; that he may live with thee.

36 Take thou no usury of him, or increase: but fear thy God; that thy brother may live with thee.

37 Thou shalt not give him thy money upon usury, nor lend him thy victuals for increase.

38 I *am* the LORD your God, which brought you forth out of the land of Egypt, to give

you the land of Canaan, *and* to be your God.

39 And if thy brother *that dwelleth* by thee be waxen poor, and be sold unto thee; thou shalt not compel him to serve as a bondservant:

40 *But* as an hired servant, *and* as a sojourner, he shall be with thee, *and* shall serve thee unto the year of jubile:

41 And *then* shall he depart from thee, *both* he and his children with him, and shall return unto his own family, and unto the possession of his fathers shall he return.

42 For they *are* my servants, which I brought forth out of the land of Egypt: they shall not be sold as bondmen.

43 Thou shalt not rule over him with rigour; but shalt fear thy God.

44 Both thy bondmen, and thy bondmaids, which thou shalt have, *shall be* of the heathen that are round about you; of them shall ye buy bondmen and bondmaids.

45 Moreover of the children of the strangers that do sojourn among you, of them shall ye buy, and of their families that *are* with you, which they begat in your land: and they shall be your possession.

46 And ye shall take them as an inheritance for your children after you, to inherit *them for* a possession; they shall be your bondmen for ever: but over your brethren the children of Israel, ye shall not rule one over another with rigour.

47 And if a sojourner or stranger wax rich by thee, and thy brother *that dwelleth* by him wax poor, and sell himself unto the stranger *or* sojourner by thee, or to the stock of the stranger's family:

48 After that he is sold he may be redeemed again; one of his brethren may redeem him:

49 Either his uncle, or his uncle's son, may redeem him, or *any* that is nigh of kin unto him of his family may redeem him; or if he be able, he may redeem himself.

50 And he shall reckon with him that bought him from the year that he was sold to him unto the year of jubile: and the price of his sale shall be according unto the number of years, according to the time of an hired servant shall it be with him.

51 If *there be* yet many years *behind*, according unto them he shall give again the price

Cross references

27 Lev. 25:50-52
28 Lev. 25:13
32 Num. 35:2; Josh. 21:2, 3
33 Lev. 25:28
34 Acts 4:36, 37
35 Deut. 15:7, 8; Ps. 37:26; 41:1; 112:5, 9; Prov. 14:31; Luke 6:35; Acts 11:29; Rom. 12:10; 1John 3:17
36 Ex. 22:25; Lev. 25:17; Deut. 23:19; Neh. 5:7, 9; Ps. 15:5; Prov. 28:8; Ezek. 18:8, 13, 17; 22:12
38 Lev. 22:32, 33
39 Ex. 21:2; Deut. 15:12; 1Kgs. 9:22; 2Kgs. 4:1; Neh. 5:5; Jer. 34:14
41 Ex. 21:3; Lev. 25:28
42 Lev. 25:55; Rom. 6:22; 1Cor. 7:23
43 Ex. 1:13, 17, 21; Lev. 23:46; 25:17; Deut. 25:18; Mal. 3:5; Eph. 6:9; Col. 4:1
45 Isa. 56:3, 6
46 Lev. 25:43; Isa. 14:2
47 Lev. 25:25, 35
48 Neh. 5:5
49 Lev. 25:26
50 Job 7:1; Isa. 16:14; 21:16

25:49 nigh of kin unto him of his family may redeem him. The verse refers to Israelites who, in poverty, sold themselves into slavery for survival. A near-kinsman could redeem and grant to the slave again his freedom by paying an appropriate price. This is the basis for the redemption of Ruth by Boaz (Ruth 4:1–12). It is also a type of Christ, our Kinsman-Redeemer who paid the supreme price on the cross to redeem out of the slave market of sin all who will come to Him and receive Him.

of his redemption out of the money that he was bought for.

52 And if there remain but few years unto the year of jubile, then he shall count with him, *and* according unto his years shall he give him again the price of his redemption.

53 *And* as a yearly hired servant shall he be with him: *and the other* shall not rule with rigour over him in thy sight.

54 And if he be not redeemed in these *years*, then he shall go out in the year of jubile, *both* he, and his children with him.

55 For unto me the children of Israel *are* servants; they *are* my servants whom I brought forth out of the land of Egypt: I *am* the LORD your God.

CHAPTER 26
Blessings for Obedience

1 Ye shall make you no idols nor graven image, neither rear you up a standing image, neither shall ye set up *any* image of stone in your land, to bow down unto it: for I *am* the LORD your God.

2 Ye shall keep my sabbaths, and reverence my sanctuary: I *am* the LORD.

3 If ye walk in my statutes, and keep my commandments, and do them;

4 Then I will give you rain in due season, and the land shall yield her increase, and the trees of the field shall yield their fruit.

5 And your threshing shall reach unto the vintage, and the vintage shall reach unto the sowing time: and ye shall eat your bread to the full, and dwell in your land safely.

6 And I will give peace in the land, and ye shall lie down, and none shall make *you* afraid: and I will rid evil beasts out of the land, neither shall the sword go through your land.

7 And ye shall chase your enemies, and they shall fall before you by the sword.

8 And five of you shall chase an hundred, and an hundred of you shall put ten thousand to flight: and your enemies shall fall before you by the sword.

9 For I will have respect unto you, and make you fruitful, and multiply you, and establish my covenant with you.

10 And ye shall eat old store, and bring forth the old because of the new.

11 And I will set my tabernacle among you: and my soul shall not abhor you.

12 And I will walk among you, and will be your God, and ye shall be my people.

13 I *am* the LORD your God, which brought you forth out of the land of Egypt, that ye should not be their bondmen; and I have

broken the bands of your yoke, and made you go upright.

Warnings to Israel

14 But if ye will not hearken unto me, and will not do all these commandments;

15 And if ye shall despise my statutes, or if your soul abhor my judgments, so that ye will not do all my commandments, *but* that ye break my covenant:

16 I also will do this unto you; I will even appoint over you terror, consumption, and the burning ague, that shall consume the eyes, and cause sorrow of heart: and ye shall sow your seed in vain, for your enemies shall eat it.

17 And I will set my face against you, and ye shall be slain before your enemies: they that hate you shall reign over you; and ye shall flee when none pursueth you.

18 And if ye will not yet for all this hearken unto me, then I will punish you seven times more for your sins.

19 And I will break the pride of your power; and I will make your heaven as iron, and your earth as brass:

20 And your strength shall be spent in vain: for your land shall not yield her increase, neither shall the trees of the land yield their fruits.

21 And if ye walk contrary unto me, and will not hearken unto me; I will bring seven times more plagues upon you according to your sins.

22 I will also send wild beasts among you, which shall rob you of your children, and destroy your cattle, and make you few in number; and your *high* ways shall be desolate.

23 And if ye will not be reformed by me by these things, but will walk contrary unto me;

24 Then will I also walk contrary unto you, and will punish you yet seven times for your sins.

25 And I will bring a sword upon you, that shall avenge the quarrel of *my* covenant: and when ye are gathered together within your cities, I will send the pestilence among you; and ye shall be delivered into the hand of the enemy.

26 *And* when I have broken the staff of your bread, ten women shall bake your bread in one oven, and they shall deliver *you* your bread again by weight: and ye shall eat, and not be satisfied.

27 And if ye will not for all this hearken unto me, but walk contrary unto me;

---

1 Ex. 20:4, 5; Deut. 5:8; 16:22; 27:15; Ps. 97:7

2 Lev. 19:30

3 Deut. 11:13; 14:15; 28:1-14

4 Ps. 67:7; 85:12; Isa. 30:23; Zech. 8:12

5 Deut. 11:15; Ezek. 34:25, 27, 28

6 2Kgs. 10:25; Ps. 3:5; 4:8; 147:14; Isa. 35:9; 45:7; Ezek. 5:17

8 Deut. 32:30; Josh. 23:10

9 Gen. 17:6, 7; Ex. 2:25; 2Kgs. 13:23; Neh. 9:23; Ps. 107:38

10 Lev. 25:22

11 Ex. 25:8; Lev. 20:23; Deut. 32:19; Ps. 76:2

12 Jer. 7:23; 11:4; 30:22; Ezek. 11:20

13 Lev. 25:38, 42

14 Deut. 28:15

16 Deut. 28:22, 33; Mic. 6:15

17 Deut. 28:25; Ps. 53:5

18 1Sam. 2:5; Ps. 119:164

19 Deut. 28:23; Ezek. 7:24

20 Deut. 11:17; Isa. 49:4

22 Deut. 32:24; 2Kgs. 17:25

24 2Sam. 22:27; Ps. 18:26

25 Num. 14:12; Jer. 14:12; Ezek. 5:17; 6:3; 14:17

26 Isa. 3:1

28 Then I will walk contrary unto you also in fury; and I, even I, will chastise you seven times for your sins.

29 And ye shall eat the flesh of your sons, and the flesh of your daughters shall ye eat.

30 And I will destroy your high places, and cut down your images, and cast your carcases upon the carcases of your idols, and my soul shall abhor you.

31 And I will make your cities waste, and bring your sanctuaries unto desolation, and I will not smell the savour of your sweet odours.

32 And I will bring the land into desolation: and your enemies which dwell therein shall be astonished at it.

33 And I will scatter you among the heathen, and will draw out a sword after you: and your land shall be desolate, and your cities waste.

34 Then shall the land enjoy her sabbaths, as long as it lieth desolate, and ye *be* in your enemies' land; *even* then shall the land rest, and enjoy her sabbaths.

35 As long as it lieth desolate it shall rest; because it did not rest in your sabbaths, when ye dwelt upon it.

36 And upon them that are left *alive* of you I will send a faintness into their hearts in the lands of their enemies; and the sound of a shaken leaf shall chase them; and they shall flee, as fleeing from a sword; and they shall fall when none pursueth.

37 And they shall fall one upon another, as it were before a sword, when none pursueth: and ye shall have no power to stand before your enemies.

38 And ye shall perish among the heathen, and the land of your enemies shall eat you up.

39 And they that are left of you shall pine away in their iniquity in your enemies' lands; and also in the iniquities of their fathers shall they pine away with them.

40 If they shall confess their iniquity, and the iniquity of their fathers, with their trespass which they trespassed against me, and that also they have walked contrary unto me;

41 And *that* I also have walked contrary unto them, and have brought them into the land of their enemies; if then their uncircumcised hearts be humbled, and they then accept of the punishment of their iniquity:

42 Then will I remember my covenant with Jacob, and also my covenant with Isaac, and also my covenant with Abraham will I remember; and I will remember the land.

43 The land also shall be left of them, and shall enjoy her sabbaths, while she lieth desolate without them: and they shall accept of the punishment of their iniquity: because, even because they despised my judgments, and because their soul abhorred my statutes.

44 And yet for all that, when they be in the land of their enemies, I will not cast them away, neither will I abhor them, to destroy them utterly, and to break my covenant with them: for I *am* the LORD their God.

45 But I will for their sakes remember the covenant of their ancestors, whom I brought forth out of the land of Egypt in the sight of the heathen, that I might be their God: I *am* the LORD.

46 These *are* the statutes and judgments and laws, which the LORD made between him and the children of Israel in mount Sinai by the hand of Moses.

CHAPTER 27
Laws about Dedications

1 And the LORD spake unto Moses, saying,

2 Speak unto the children of Israel, and say unto them, When a man shall make a singular vow, the persons *shall be* for the LORD by thy estimation.

3 And thy estimation shall be of the male from twenty years old even unto sixty years old, even thy estimation shall be fifty shekels of silver, after the shekel of the sanctuary.

4 And if it *be* a female, then thy estimation shall be thirty shekels.

5 And if *it be* from five years old even unto twenty years old, then thy estimation shall be of the male twenty shekels, and for the female ten shekels.

Cross-references:
- **28** Isa. 59:18
- **29** Deut. 28:53; 2Kgs. 6:29; Lam. 4:10
- **30** 2Kgs. 23:20; Jer. 14:19; Ezek. 6:3-6, 13
- **31** Neh. 2:3; Jer. 4:7
- **32** Deut. 28:37; 1Kgs. 9:8; Jer. 9:11; 18:16; 19:8; 25:11, 18; Ezek. 5:15
- **33** Deut. 4:27; 28:64; Jer. 9:16
- **34** 2Chr. 36:21
- **35** Lev. 25:2
- **36** Lev. 26:17
- **37** Judg. 2:14; 7:22; 1Sam. 14:15, 16
- **39** Deut. 4:27; 28:65; Jer. 3:25
- **40** Num. 5:7; Neh. 9:2; Luke 15:18; 1John 1:9
- **41** 2Chr. 12:6, 7, 12; Jer. 6:10; 9:25, 26; Rom. 2:29
- **42** Ps. 106:45; 136:23
- **44** Deut. 4:31; 2Kgs. 13:23; Rom. 11:2
- **45** Ps. 98:2; Rom. 11:28
- **46** Lev. 25:1; 27:34; Deut. 6:1
- **2** Num. 6:2; Judg. 11:30, 31, 39
- **3** Ex. 30:13

26:33 I will scatter you among the heathen [Gentiles]. This entire chapter sets forth the blessings for Israel for obedience and the punishment for disobedience. It is parallel to Deuteronomy 28. Two thousand years of Jewish history are forecast in this passage. The consequences for disobedience include disease, war, famine, destructive animals and other judgments, some of which occurred in Old Testament times, but which culminated in the destruction of Jerusalem in A.D. 70 and the subsequent worldwide dispersion (vv. 38–39). While the end is not yet and the Tribulation will be the "time of Jacob's trouble" (Jer. 30:7), deliverance "shall come" (Zech. 14:5), when the Messiah appears.

6 And if *it be* from a month old even unto five years old, then thy estimation shall be of the male five shekels of silver, and for the female thy estimation *shall be* three shekels of silver.

7 And if *it be* from sixty years old and above; if *it be* a male, then thy estimation shall be fifteen shekels, and for the female ten shekels.

8 But if he be poorer than thy estimation, then he shall present himself before the priest, and the priest shall value him; according to his ability that vowed shall the priest value him.

9 And if *it be* a beast, whereof men bring an offering unto the LORD, all that *any man* giveth of such unto the LORD shall be holy.

10 He shall not alter it, nor change it, a good for a bad, or a bad for a good: and if he shall at all change beast for beast, then it and the exchange thereof shall be holy.

11 And if *it be* any unclean beast, of which they do not offer a sacrifice unto the LORD, then he shall present the beast before the priest:

12 And the priest shall value it, whether it be good or bad: as thou valuest it, *who art* the priest, so shall it be.

13 But if he will at all redeem it, then he shall add a fifth *part* thereof unto thy estimation.

14 And when a man shall sanctify his house *to be* holy unto the LORD, then the priest shall estimate it, whether it be good or bad: as the priest shall estimate it, so shall it stand.

15 And if he that sanctified it will redeem his house, then he shall add the fifth *part* of the money of thy estimation unto it, and it shall be his.

16 And if a man shall sanctify unto the LORD *some part* of a field of his possession, then thy estimation shall be according to the seed thereof: an homer of barley seed *shall be valued* at fifty shekels of silver.

17 If he sanctify his field from the year of jubile, according to thy estimation it shall stand.

18 But if he sanctify his field after the jubile, then the priest shall reckon unto him the money according to the years that remain, even unto the year of the jubile, and it shall be abated from thy estimation.

19 And if he that sanctified the field will in any wise redeem it, then he shall add the fifth *part* of the money of thy estimation unto it, and it shall be assured to him.

20 And if he will not redeem the field, or if he have sold the field to another man, it shall not be redeemed any more.

21 But the field, when it goeth out in the jubile, shall be holy unto the LORD, as a field devoted; the possession thereof shall be the priest's.

22 And if *a man* sanctify unto the LORD a field which he hath bought, which *is* not of the fields of his possession;

23 Then the priest shall reckon unto him the worth of thy estimation, *even* unto the year of the jubile: and he shall give thine estimation in that day, *as* a holy thing unto the LORD.

24 In the year of the jubile the field shall return unto him of whom it was bought, *even* to him to whom the possession of the land *did belong*.

25 And all thy estimations shall be according to the shekel of the sanctuary: twenty gerahs shall be the shekel.

26 Only the firstling of the beasts, which should be the LORD's firstling, no man shall sanctify it; whether *it be* ox, or sheep: it *is* the LORD's.

27 And if *it be* of an unclean beast, then he shall redeem *it* according to thine estimation, and shall add a fifth *part* of it thereto: or if it be not redeemed, then it shall be sold according to thy estimation.

28 Notwithstanding no devoted thing, that a man shall devote unto the LORD of all that he hath, *both* of man and beast, and of the field of his possession, shall be sold or redeemed: every devoted thing *is* most holy unto the LORD.

29 None devoted, which shall be devoted of men, shall be redeemed; *but* shall surely be put to death.

30 And all the tithe of the land, *whether* of the seed of the land, *or* of the fruit of the tree, *is* the LORD's: *it is* holy unto the LORD.

31 And if a man will at all redeem *ought* of his tithes, he shall add thereto the fifth *part* thereof.

32 And concerning the tithe of the herd, or of the flock, *even* of whatsoever passeth under the rod, the tenth shall be holy unto the LORD.

33 He shall not search whether it be good or bad, neither shall he change it: and if he change it at all, then both it and the change thereof shall be holy; it shall not be redeemed.

34 These *are* the commandments, which the LORD commanded Moses for the children of Israel in mount Sinai.

Cross references (center column):

13 Lev. 27:15, 19
15 Lev. 27:13
18 Lev. 25:15, 16
19 Lev. 27:13
21 Lev. 25:10, 28, 31; 27:28; Num. 18:14; Ezek. 44:29
22 Lev. 25:10, 25
23 Lev. 27:18
24 Lev. 25:28
25 Ex. 30:13; Num. 3:47; 18:16
26 Ex. 13:2, 12; 22:30; Num. 18:17; Deut. 15:19
27 Lev. 27:11-13
28 Lev. 27:21; Josh. 6:17-19
29 Num. 21:2, 3
30 Gen. 28:22; Num. 18:21, 24; 2Chr. 31:5, 6, 12; Neh. 13:12; Mal. 3:8, 10
31 Lev. 27:13
32 Jer. 33:13; Ezek. 20:37; Mic. 7:14
33 Lev. 27:10
34 Lev. 26:46

father's sister: for he uncovereth his near kin: they shall bear their iniquity.

20 And if a man shall lie with his uncle's wife, he hath uncovered his uncle's nakedness: they shall bear their sin; they shall die childless.

21 And if a man shall take his brother's wife, it *is* an unclean thing: he hath uncovered his brother's nakedness; they shall be childless.

22 Ye shall therefore keep all my statutes, and all my judgments, and do them: that the land, whither I bring you to dwell therein, spue you not out.

23 And ye shall not walk in the manners of the nation, which I cast out before you: for they committed all these things, and therefore I abhorred them.

24 But I have said unto you, Ye shall inherit their land, and I will give it unto you to possess it, a land that floweth with milk and honey: I *am* the LORD your God, which have separated you from *other* people.

25 Ye shall therefore put difference between clean beasts and unclean, and between unclean fowls and clean: and ye shall not make your souls abominable by beast, or by fowl, or by any manner of living thing that creepeth on the ground, which I have separated from you as unclean.

26 And ye shall be holy unto me: for I the LORD *am* holy, and have severed you from *other* people, that ye should be mine.

27 A man also or woman that hath a familiar spirit, or that is a wizard, shall surely be put to death: they shall stone them with stones: their blood *shall be* upon them.

CHAPTER 21
The Holiness of the Priests

1 And the LORD said unto Moses, Speak unto the priests the sons of Aaron, and say unto them, There shall none be defiled for the dead among his people:

2 But for his kin, that is near unto him, *that is*, for his mother, and for his father, and for his son, and for his daughter, and for his brother,

3 And for his sister a virgin, that is nigh unto him, which hath had no husband; for her may he be defiled.

4 *But* he shall not defile himself, *being* a chief man among his people, to profane himself.

5 They shall not make baldness upon their head, neither shall they shave off the corner of their beard, nor make any cuttings in their flesh.

6 They shall be holy unto their God, and not profane the name of their God: for the offerings of the LORD made by fire, *and* the bread of their God, they do offer: therefore they shall be holy.

7 They shall not take a wife *that is* a whore, or profane; neither shall they take a woman put away from her husband: for he *is* holy unto his God.

8 Thou shalt sanctify him therefore; for he offereth the bread of thy God: he shall be holy unto thee: for I the LORD, which sanctify you, *am* holy.

9 And the daughter of any priest, if she profane herself by playing the whore, she profaneth her father: she shall be burnt with fire.

10 And *he that is* the high priest among his brethren, upon whose head the anointing oil was poured, and that is consecrated to put on the garments, shall not uncover his head, nor rend his clothes;

11 Neither shall he go in to any dead body, nor defile himself for his father, or for his mother;

12 Neither shall he go out of the sanctuary, nor profane the sanctuary of his God; for the crown of the anointing oil of his God *is* upon him: I *am* the LORD.

13 And he shall take a wife in her virginity.

14 A widow, or a divorced woman, or profane, *or* an harlot, these shall he not take: but he shall take a virgin of his own people to wife.

15 Neither shall he profane his seed among his people: for I the LORD do sanctify him.

16 And the LORD spake unto Moses, saying,

17 Speak unto Aaron, saying, Whosoever *he be* of thy seed in their generations that hath *any* blemish, let him not approach to offer the bread of his God.

18 For whatsoever man *he be* that hath a blemish, he shall not approach: a blind man, or a lame, or he that hath a flat nose, or any thing superfluous,

19 Or a man that is brokenfooted, or brokenhanded,

20 Or crookbackt, or a dwarf, or that hath a blemish in his eye, or be scurvy, or scabbed, or hath his stones broken;

21 No man that hath a blemish of the seed of Aaron the priest shall come nigh to offer the offerings of the LORD made by fire: he hath a blemish; he shall not come nigh to offer the bread of his God.

22 He shall eat the bread of his God, *both* of the most holy, and of the holy.

23 Only he shall not go in unto the vail, nor

Cross references

20 Lev. 18:14
21 Lev. 18:16
22 Lev. 18:25, 26, 28; 19:37
23 Lev. 18:3, 24, 27, 30; Deut. 9:5
25 Lev. 11:43, 47; Deut. 14:4
26 Lev. 19:2; 20:7, 24; 1Kgs. 8:53
27 Ex. 22:18; 19:31; 20:9; Deut. 18:10, 11; 1Sam. 28:7, 8
1 Ezek. 44:25
5 Lev. 19:27; Deut. 14:1; Ezek. 44:20
6 Lev. 6:8; 19:5; Deut. 7:6; 14:2; 26:26; 33:16
8 1Pet. 1:16
9 Gen. 38:24
10 Ex. 28:2; 29:29, 30; Lev. 8:12; 16:32; 21:12; Num. 35:25
11 Lev. 21:1, 2; Num. 19:14
12 Ex. 28:36; Lev. 8:9, 12, 30; 10:7
13 Lev. 21:7; Ezek. 44:22
14 Deut. 24:1; Ezek. 44:22
15 Lev. 21:8
17 Lev. 10:3; Num. 16:5; Ps. 65:4
18 Lev. 22:23
20 Deut. 23:1
22 Lev. 2:3, 10; 6:17, 29; 7:1; 22:10, 11, 12; 24:9
23 Lev. 21:6

20:9 curseth his father or his mother. Quoting this verse and Exodus 20:12, Jesus stresses the spirit as well as the letter of honoring one's parents, by exposing the practice of claiming that what children might provide for elderly parents could instead be donated as a gift to someone else or an institution, such as the temple (see Matt. 15:1–6). This made the Word of God of none effect through human tradition or practices.

31 Regard not them that have familiar spirits, neither seek after wizards, to be defiled by them: I *am* the LORD your God.

32 Thou shalt rise up before the hoary head, and honour the face of the old man, and fear thy God: I *am* the LORD.

33 And if a stranger sojourn with thee in your land, ye shall not vex him.

34 *But* the stranger that dwelleth with you shall be unto you as one born among you, and thou shalt love him as thyself; for ye were strangers in the land of Egypt: I *am* the LORD your God.

35 Ye shall do no unrighteousness in judgment, in meteyard, in weight, or in measure.

36 Just balances, just weights, a just ephah, and a just hin, shall ye have: I *am* the LORD your God, which brought you out of the land of Egypt.

37 Therefore shall ye observe all my statutes, and all my judgments, and do them: I *am* the LORD.

CHAPTER 20
The Penalties for Sin

1 And the LORD spake unto Moses, saying,

2 Again, thou shalt say to the children of Israel, Whosoever *he be* of the children of Israel, or of the strangers that sojourn in Israel, that giveth *any* of his seed unto Molech; he shall surely be put to death: the people of the land shall stone him with stones.

3 And I will set my face against that man, and will cut him off from among his people; because he hath given of his seed unto Molech, to defile my sanctuary, and to profane my holy name.

4 And if the people of the land do any ways hide their eyes from the man, when he giveth of his seed unto Molech, and kill him not:

5 Then I will set my face against that man, and against his family, and will cut him off, and all that go a whoring after him, to commit whoredom with Molech, from among their people.

6 And the soul that turneth after such as have familiar spirits, and after wizards, to go a whoring after them, I will even set my face against that soul, and will cut him off from among his people.

7 Sanctify yourselves therefore, and be ye holy: for I *am* the LORD your God.

8 And ye shall keep my statutes, and do them: I *am* the LORD which sanctify you.

9 For every one that curseth his father or his mother shall be surely put to death: he hath cursed his father or his mother; his blood *shall be* upon him.

10 And the man that committeth adultery with *another* man's wife, *even he* that committeth adultery with his neighbour's wife, the adulterer and the adulteress shall surely be put to death.

11 And the man that lieth with his father's wife hath uncovered his father's nakedness: both of them shall surely be put to death; their blood *shall be* upon them.

12 And if a man lie with his daughter-in-law, both of them shall surely be put to death: they have wrought confusion; their blood *shall be* upon them.

13 If a man also lie with mankind, as he lieth with a woman, both of them have committed an abomination: they shall surely be put to death; their blood *shall be* upon them.

14 And if a man take a wife and her mother, it *is* wickedness: they shall be burnt with fire, both he and they; that there be no wickedness among you.

15 And if a man lie with a beast, he shall surely be put to death: and ye shall slay the beast.

16 And if a woman approach unto any beast, and lie down thereto, thou shalt kill the woman, and the beast: they shall surely be put to death; their blood *shall be* upon them.

17 And if a man shall take his sister, his father's daughter, or his mother's daughter, and see her nakedness, and she see his nakedness; it *is* a wicked thing; and they shall be cut off in the sight of their people: he hath uncovered his sister's nakedness; he shall bear his iniquity.

18 And if a man shall lie with a woman having her sickness, and shall uncover her nakedness; he hath discovered her fountain, and she hath uncovered the fountain of her blood: and both of them shall be cut off from among their people.

19 And thou shalt not uncover the naked-ness of thy mother's sister, nor of thy

Cross references:

31 Ex. 22:18; Lev. 20:6, 27; Acts 16:16
32 Lev. 19:14; Prov. 20:29; 1Tim. 5:1
33 Ex. 22:21; 23:9
34 Ex. 12:48, 49; Deut. 10:19
35 Lev. 19:15
36 Deut. 25:13, 15; Prov. 11:1
37 Lev. 18:4, 5; Deut. 4:5; 5:1; 6:25
2 Deut. 12:31; 2Kgs. 17:17; Jer. 7:31; Ezek. 20:26, 31
4 Deut. 17:2, 3, 5
5 Ex. 20:5; Lev. 20:6
6 Lev. 19:31
7 Lev. 11:44; 19:2; 1Pet. 1:16
8 Ex. 31:13; Lev. 19:37; Ezek. 20:12
9 Ex. 21:17; Deut. 27:16
10 Deut. 22:22; John 8:4, 5
11 Deut. 27:23
13 Gen. 19:5
15 Lev. 18:23
17 Gen. 20:12; Deut. 27:22
18 Lev. 15:24; 18:19

Numbers

The title for the book of Numbers describes the two numberings of the Israelites during their forty years in the wilderness. The first census counted the multitude that had come out of Egypt; the second numbered the new generation that was preparing to enter the promised land. Of those over age twenty who came from Egypt, only two men, Joshua and Caleb entered Canaan.

Numbers, much like Genesis, is primarily a book of historical records without the legal language found in the latter half of Exodus, Leviticus, and Deuteronomy. The subject matter in Numbers pertains to the historical record of Israel's numerous shortcomings during the nation's forty years in the desert. Perhaps the words that best summarize the book are the words found in 32:23, "Be sure your sins will find you out."

Numbers is also a book of murmuring, warning, wandering, and training. The people chosen in Genesis, redeemed in Exodus, instructed in Leviticus, and now organized in Numbers, appear to be ready to enter the land of promise. But instead of trusting their Great Benefactor, the people rebel, justifying God's divine complaint: "Forty years long was I grieved with this generation" (Ps. 95:10).

Seven distinct examples of murmuring appear in the text: complaints about the way (11:1–3); the food (11:4–6); the giants (13:31—14:2); the leaders (16:3); the divine judgments (16:41); the desert (20:2–5); and the manna (21:5).

Author
Moses

Date
1440–1405 B.C.

Key Truth
Wanderings

Historic Time
The Wilderness Journey

Key Verse
14:33
And your children shall wander in the wilderness forty years . . .

Nevertheless, God was also training the new generation to obey His laws, worship at the Tabernacle, and to prepare for their future nationhood.

Predictions that none of the adult population, except Caleb and Joshua, would enter Canaan were fulfilled (14:2–34). A vivid type of Christ in the brazen serpent is described in 21:8–9 (cf. John 3:14–15). Of special interest are the prophecies of Balaam (23—24), who was hired to curse Israel by the Moabite king, but blessed them instead.

The book contains 1,288 verses of which 458, or 36 percent, concern 50 predictions, most of which are typical or conditional on obedience.

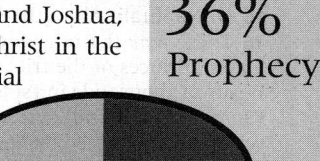

36%
Prophecy

1550 B.C.	1525 B.C.	1500 B.C.	1475 B.C.	1450 B.C.	1425 B.C.	1400 B.C.	1375 B.C.	1350 B.C.

1527 Moses in Pharaoh's court

1487 Moses flees to Midian

1447 Exodus from Egypt

1446 The Tabernacle constructed

1407 Entrance into Canaan

1447 The Ten Commandments

1407 The second census (Num. 26)

1446-1407 Book of Numbers

1375-1050 Israel ruled by Judges

730-1447 ondage in Egypt

1445 The first census (Num. 1–4)

CHAPTER 1

Census of Israel at Sinai

1 And the LORD spake unto Moses in the wilderness of Sinai, in the tabernacle of the congregation, on the first *day* of the second month, in the second year after they were come out of the land of Egypt, saying,

2 Take ye the sum of all the congregation of the children of Israel, after their families, by the house of their fathers, with the number of *their* names, every male by their polls;

3 From twenty years old and upward, all that are able to go forth to war in Israel: thou and Aaron shall number them by their armies.

4 And with you there shall be a man of every tribe; every one head of the house of his fathers.

5 And these *are* the names of the men that shall stand with you: of *the tribe of* Reuben; Elizur the son of Shedeur.

6 Of Simeon; Shelumiel the son of Zurishaddai.

7 Of Judah; Nahshon the son of Amminadab.

8 Of Issachar; Nethaneel the son of Zuar.

9 Of Zebulun; Eliab the son of Helon.

10 Of the children of Joseph: of Ephraim; Elishama the son of Ammihud: of Manasseh; Gamaliel the son of Pedahzur.

11 Of Benjamin; Abidan the son of Gideoni.

12 Of Dan; Ahiezer the son of Ammishaddai.

13 Of Asher; Pagiel the son of Ocran.

14 Of Gad; Eliasaph the son of Deuel.

15 Of Naphtali; Ahira the son of Enan.

16 These *were* the renowned of the congregation, princes of the tribes of their fathers, heads of thousands in Israel.

17 And Moses and Aaron took these men which are expressed by *their* names:

18 And they assembled all the congregation together on the first *day* of the second month, and they declared their pedigrees

after their families, by the house of their fathers, according to the number of the names, from twenty years old and upward, by their polls.

19 As the LORD commanded Moses, so he numbered them in the wilderness of Sinai.

20 And the children of Reuben, Israel's eldest son, by their generations, after their families, by the house of their fathers, according to the number of the names, by their polls, every male from twenty years old and upward, all that were able to go forth to war;

21 Those that were numbered of them, *even* of the tribe of Reuben, *were* forty and six thousand and five hundred.

22 Of the children of Simeon, by their generations, after their families, by the house of their fathers, those that were numbered of them, according to the number of the names, by their polls, every male from twenty years old and upward, all that were able to go forth to war;

23 Those that were numbered of them, *even* of the tribe of Simeon, *were* fifty and nine thousand and three hundred.

24 Of the children of Gad, by their generations, after their families, by the house of their fathers, according to the number of the names, from twenty years old and upward, all that were able to go forth to war;

25 Those that were numbered of them, *even* of the tribe of Gad, *were* forty and five thousand six hundred and fifty.

26 Of the children of Judah, by their generations, after their families, by the house of their fathers, according to the number of the names, from twenty years old and upward, all that were able to go forth to war;

27 Those that were numbered of them, *even* of the tribe of Judah, *were* threescore and fourteen thousand and six hundred.

28 Of the children of Issachar, by their generations, after their families, by the house of

1 Ex. 19:1; 25:22; Num. 10:11, 12

2 Ex. 30:12; 38:26; Num. 26:2, 63, 64; 2Sam. 24:2; 1Chr. 21:2

14 Num. 2:14, he is called *Reuel*

16 Ex. 18:21, 25; Num. 7:2; 1Chr. 27:16

Numbering the Israelites

Tribe	1st Census (Num. 1)	2nd Census (Num. 26)	Tribe	1st Census (Num. 1)	2nd Census (Num. 26)
1. Reuben	46,500	43,730	7. Ephraim	40,500	32,500
2. Simeon	59,300	22,200	8. Manasseh	32,200	52,700
3. Gad	45,650	40,500	9. Benjamin	35,400	45,600
4. Judah	74,600	76,500	10. Dan	62,700	64,400
5. Issachar	54,400	64,300	11. Asher	41,500	53,400
6. Zebulun	57,400	60,500	12. Naphtali	53,400	45,400
			Total	603,550	601,730

their fathers, according to the number of the names, from twenty years old and upward, all that were able to go forth to war;

29 Those that were numbered of them, *even* of the tribe of Issachar, *were* fifty and four thousand and four hundred.

30 Of the children of Zebulun, by their generations, after their families, by the house of their fathers, according to the number of the names, from twenty years old and upward, all that were able to go forth to war;

31 Those that were numbered of them, *even* of the tribe of Zebulun, *were* fifty and seven thousand and four hundred.

32 Of the children of Joseph, *namely*, of the children of Ephraim, by their generations, after their families, by the house of their fathers, according to the number of the names, from twenty years old and upward, all that were able to go forth to war;

33 Those that were numbered of them, *even* of the tribe of Ephraim, *were* forty thousand and five hundred.

34 Of the children of Manasseh, by their generations, after their families, by the house of their fathers, according to the number of the names, from twenty years old and upward, all that were able to go forth to war;

35 Those that were numbered of them, *even* of the tribe of Manasseh, *were* thirty and two thousand and two hundred.

36 Of the children of Benjamin, by their generations, after their families, by the house of their fathers, according to the number of the names, from twenty years old and upward, all that were able to go forth to war;

37 Those that were numbered of them, *even* of the tribe of Benjamin, *were* thirty and five thousand and four hundred.

38 Of the children of Dan, by their generations, after their families, by the house of their fathers, according to the number of the names, from twenty years old and upward, all that were able to go forth to war;

39 Those that were numbered of them, *even* of the tribe of Dan, *were* threescore and two thousand and seven hundred.

40 Of the children of Asher, by their generations, after their families, by the house of

their fathers, according to the number of the names, from twenty years old and upward, all that were able to go forth to war;

41 Those that were numbered of them, *even* of the tribe of Asher, *were* forty and one thousand and five hundred.

42 Of the children of Naphtali, throughout their generations, after their families, by the house of their fathers, according to the number of the names, from twenty years old and upward, all that were able to go forth to war;

43 Those that were numbered of them, *even* of the tribe of Naphtali, *were* fifty and three thousand and four hundred.

44 These *are* those that were numbered, which Moses and Aaron numbered, and the princes of Israel, *being* twelve men: each one was for the house of his fathers.

45 So were all those that were numbered of the children of Israel, by the house of their fathers, from twenty years old and upward, all that were able to go forth to war in Israel;

46 Even all they that were numbered were six hundred thousand and three thousand and five hundred and fifty.

The Levites Are Exempted

47 But the Levites after the tribe of their fathers were not numbered among them.

48 For the LORD had spoken unto Moses, saying,

49 Only thou shalt not number the tribe of Levi, neither take the sum of them among the children of Israel:

50 But thou shalt appoint the Levites over the tabernacle of testimony, and over all the vessels thereof, and over all things that *belong* to it: they shall bear the tabernacle, and all the vessels thereof; and they shall minister unto it, and shall encamp round about the tabernacle.

51 And when the tabernacle setteth forward, the Levites shall take it down: and when the tabernacle is to be pitched, the Levites shall set it up: and the stranger that cometh nigh shall be put to death.

52 And the children of Israel shall pitch their tents, every man by his own camp, and every man by his own standard, throughout their hosts.

44 Num. 26:64

46 Ex. 23:37; 38:26; Num. 2:32; 26:51

47 Num. 2:33; 3:4; 26:57; 1Chr. 21:6

49 Num. 2:33; 26:62

50 Ex. 38:21; Num. 3:7, 8, 23, 29, 35, 38; 4:15, 25-27, 33

51 Num. 3:10, 38; 10:17, 21; 18:22

52 Num. 2:2, 34

1:47 not numbered among them. It has been said that order is heaven's first law. The numbering of every male twenty years of age and older was to declare his allegiance as a willing soldier (v. 28).

The tribe of Levi was not numbered among warriors, because a special work had been appointed for that tribe (vv. 49–50). They were to be the priests for the entire nation of Israel. As a result, they were not given a portion of the land, but rather 48 cities within the other tribes' portions (chap. 35).

53 But the Levites shall pitch round about the tabernacle of testimony, that there be no wrath upon the congregation of the children of Israel: and the Levites shall keep the charge of the tabernacle of testimony.

54 And the children of Israel did according to all that the LORD commanded Moses, so did they.

CHAPTER 2
Tribal Arrangement of the Camp

1 And the LORD spake unto Moses and unto Aaron, saying,

2 Every man of the children of Israel shall pitch by his own standard, with the ensign of their father's house: far off about the tabernacle of the congregation shall they pitch.

3 And on the east side toward the rising of the sun shall they of the standard of the camp of Judah pitch throughout their armies: and Nahshon the son of Amminadab *shall be* captain of the children of Judah.

4 And his host, and those that were numbered of them, *were* threescore and fourteen thousand and six hundred.

5 And those that do pitch next unto him *shall be* the tribe of Issachar: and Nethaneel the son of Zuar *shall be* captain of the children of Issachar.

6 And his host, and those that were numbered thereof, *were* fifty and four thousand and four hundred.

7 *Then* the tribe of Zebulun: and Eliab the son of Helon *shall be* captain of the children of Zebulun.

8 And his host, and those that were numbered thereof, *were* fifty and seven thousand and four hundred.

9 All that were numbered in the camp of Judah *were* an hundred thousand and fourscore thousand and six thousand and four hundred, throughout their armies. These shall first set forth.

10 On the south side *shall be* the standard of the camp of Reuben according to their armies: and the captain of the children of

Reuben *shall be* Elizur the son of Shedeur.

11 And his host, and those that were numbered thereof, *were* forty and six thousand and five hundred.

12 And those which pitch by him *shall be* the tribe of Simeon: and the captain of the children of Simeon *shall be* Shelumiel the son of Zurishaddai.

13 And his host, and those that were numbered of them, *were* fifty and nine thousand and three hundred.

14 Then the tribe of Gad: and the captain of the sons of Gad *shall be* Eliasaph the son of Reuel.

15 And his host, and those that were numbered of them, *were* forty and five thousand and six hundred and fifty.

16 All that were numbered in the camp of Reuben *were* an hundred thousand and fifty and one thousand and four hundred and fifty, throughout their armies. And they shall set forth in the second rank.

17 Then the tabernacle of the congregation shall set forward with the camp of the Levites in the midst of the camp: as they encamp, so shall they set forward, every man in his place by their standards.

18 On the west side *shall be* the standard of the camp of Ephraim according to their armies: and the captain of the sons of Ephraim *shall be* Elishama the son of Ammihud.

19 And his host, and those that were numbered of them, *were* forty thousand and five hundred.

20 And by him *shall be* the tribe of Manasseh: and the captain of the children of Manasseh *shall be* Gamaliel the son of Pedahzur.

21 And his host, and those that were numbered of them, *were* thirty and two thousand and two hundred.

22 Then the tribe of Benjamin: and the captain of the sons of Benjamin *shall be* Abidan the son of Gideoni.

23 And his host, and those that were numbered of them, *were* thirty and five thousand and four hundred.

53 Lev. 10:6; Num. 1:50; 3:7, 8; 8:19, 24-26; 16:46; 18:3-5; 31:30, 47; 1Sam. 6:19; 1Chr. 23:32; 2Chr. 13:11

2 Num. 1:52; Josh. 3:4

3 Num. 10:14; Ruth 4:20; 1Chr. 2:10; Matt. 1:4; Luke 3:32, 33

9 Num. 10:14

14 Num. 1:14; 7:42, 47; 10:20

16 Num. 10:18

17 Num. 10:17, 21

2:2 by his own standard, with the ensign of their father's house. With the Tabernacle in the center, over which floated the pillar of cloud by day and the pillar of fire by night, the twelve tribes in their years of wandering encamped in assigned areas. The Levites were the closest, while Ephraim and Manasseh (descendants of Joseph) were counted as two tribes, making a total of twelve without Levi. Each tribe flew the ensign or banner with the tribe's logo, evidently on a pole. The four ban-

ners that were of special significance were the eagle, representing Dan; the ox, representing Ephraim; the man, representing Reuben; and the lion, representing Judah. Compare the faces of the living creature in Ezekiel 1:10 and Revelation 4:7. The banners of the twelve tribes reflected a heavenly reality. Some suggest they also became symbolic of the four Gospels: Matthew—lion; Mark—ox; Luke—man; John—eagle.

24 All that were numbered of the camp of Ephraim *were* an hundred thousand and eight thousand and an hundred, throughout their armies. And they shall go forward in the third rank.

25 The standard of the camp of Dan *shall be* on the north side by their armies: and the captain of the children of Dan *shall be* Ahiezer the son of Ammishaddai.

26 And his host, and those that were numbered of them, *were* threescore and two thousand and seven hundred.

27 And those that encamp by him *shall be* the tribe of Asher: and the captain of the children of Asher *shall be* Pagiel the son of Ocran.

28 And his host, and those that were numbered of them, *were* forty and one thousand and five hundred.

29 Then the tribe of Naphtali: and the captain of the children of Naphtali *shall be* Ahira the son of Enan.

30 And his host, and those that were numbered of them, *were* fifty and three thousand and four hundred.

31 All they that were numbered in the camp of Dan *were* an hundred thousand and fifty and seven thousand and six hundred. They shall go hindmost with their standards.

32 These *are* those which were numbered of the children of Israel by the house of their fathers: all those that were numbered of the camps throughout their hosts *were* six hundred thousand and three thousand and five hundred and fifty.

33 But the Levites were not numbered among the children of Israel; as the LORD commanded Moses.

34 And the children of Israel did according to all that the LORD commanded Moses: so they pitched by their standards, and so they set forward, every one after their families, according to the house of their fathers.

CHAPTER 3
The Levites Are Set Apart

1 These also *are* the generations of Aaron and Moses in the day *that* the LORD spake with Moses in mount Sinai.

2 And these *are* the names of the sons of Aaron; Nadab the firstborn, and Abihu, Eleazar, and Ithamar.

3 These *are* the names of the sons of Aaron, the priests which were anointed, whom he consecrated to minister in the priest's office.

4 And Nadab and Abihu died before the LORD, when they offered strange fire before the LORD, in the wilderness of Sinai, and they had no children: and Eleazar and Ithamar ministered in the priest's office in the sight of Aaron their father.

5 And the LORD spake unto Moses, saying,

6 Bring the tribe of Levi near, and present them before Aaron the priest, that they may minister unto him.

7 And they shall keep his charge, and the charge of the whole congregation before the tabernacle of the congregation, to do the service of the tabernacle.

8 And they shall keep all the instruments of the tabernacle of the congregation, and the charge of the children of Israel, to do the service of the tabernacle.

9 And thou shalt give the Levites unto Aaron and to his sons: they *are* wholly given unto him out of the children of Israel.

10 And thou shalt appoint Aaron and his sons, and they shall wait on their priest's office: and the stranger that cometh nigh shall be put to death.

The Redemption of the Firstborn

11 And the LORD spake unto Moses, saying,

12 And I, behold, I have taken the Levites from among the children of Israel instead of all the firstborn that openeth the matrix among the children of Israel: therefore the Levites shall be mine;

13 Because all the firstborn *are* mine; *for* on the day that I smote all the firstborn in the land of Egypt I hallowed unto me all the firstborn in Israel, both man and beast: mine shall they be: I *am* the LORD.

14 And the LORD spake unto Moses in the wilderness of Sinai, saying,

15 Number the children of Levi after the house of their fathers, by their families: every male from a month old and upward shalt thou number them.

Cross-references (center column):
24 Num. 10:22
31 Num. 10:25
32 Ex. 38:26; Num. 1:46; 11:21
33 Num. 1:47
34 Num. 24:2, 5, 6
2 Ex. 6:23
3 Ex. 28:41; Lev. 8
4 Lev. 10:1; Num. 26:61; 1Chr. 24:2
6 Num. 8:6; 18:2
7 Num. 1:50; 8:11, 15, 24, 26
9 Num. 8:19; 18:6
10 Num. 1:51; 3:38; 16:40; 18:7
12 Num. 3:41; 8:16; 18:6
13 Ex. 13:2, 12, 15; Lev. 27:26; Num. 8:16, 17; Luke 2:23
15 Num. 3:39; 26:62

3:6 the tribe of Levi. In earlier times, Levi and Simeon, two of Jacob's sons, perpetrated an act of revenge for an injustice against their sister, Dinah (see Gen. 34). For this and other reasons, Jacob in his prophetic blessing upon his children (Gen. 49) pronounced a curse upon them, predicting they would be divided and scattered in Israel (Gen. 49:5–7). Because of the Levites' stand on the Lord's side in the episode of the golden calf (Ex. 32:25–29), God assigned them a holy ministry. They would be scattered in Israel among the tribes, but would serve as priests, thus reversing the patriarchal curse and making them a blessing to the nation as a whole.

16 And Moses numbered them according to the word of the LORD, as he was commanded.

17 And these were the sons of Levi by their names; Gershon, and Kohath, and Merari.

Duties of the Gershonites

18 And these *are* the names of the sons of Gershon by their families; Libni, and Shimei.

19 And the sons of Kohath by their families; Amram, and Izehar, Hebron, and Uzziel.

20 And the sons of Merari by their families; Mahli, and Mushi. These *are* the families of the Levites according to the house of their fathers.

21 Of Gershon *was* the family of the Libnites, and the family of the Shimites: these *are* the families of the Gershonites.

22 Those that were numbered of them, according to the number of all the males, from a month old and upward, *even* those that were numbered of them *were* seven thousand and five hundred.

23 The families of the Gershonites shall pitch behind the tabernacle westward.

24 And the chief of the house of the father of the Gershonites *shall be* Eliasaph the son of Lael.

25 And the charge of the sons of Gershon in the tabernacle of the congregation *shall be* the tabernacle, and the tent, the covering thereof, and the hanging for the door of the tabernacle of the congregation,

26 And the hangings of the court, and the curtain for the door of the court, which *is* by the tabernacle, and by the altar round about, and the cords of it for all the service thereof.

Duties of the Kohathites

27 And of Kohath *was* the family of the Amramites, and the family of the Izeharites, and the family of the Hebronites, and the family of the Uzzielites: these *are* the families of the Kohathites.

28 In the number of all the males, from a month old and upward, *were* eight thousand and six hundred, keeping the charge of the sanctuary.

29 The families of the sons of Kohath shall pitch on the side of the tabernacle southward.

30 And the chief of the house of the father of the families of the Kohathites *shall be* Elizaphan the son of Uzziel.

31 And their charge *shall be* the ark, and the

table, and the candlestick, and the altars, and the vessels of the sanctuary wherewith they minister, and the hanging, and all the service thereof.

32 And Eleazar the son of Aaron the priest *shall be* chief over the chief of the Levites, *and have* the oversight of them that keep the charge of the sanctuary.

Duties of the Sons of Merari

33 Of Merari *was* the family of the Mahlites, and the family of the Mushites: these *are* the families of Merari.

34 And those that were numbered of them, according to the number of all the males, from a month old and upward, *were* six thousand and two hundred.

35 And the chief of the house of the father of the families of Merari *was* Zuriel the son of Abihail: *these* shall pitch on the side of the tabernacle northward.

36 And *under* the custody and charge of the sons of Merari *shall be* the boards of the tabernacle, and the bars thereof, and the pillars thereof, and the sockets thereof, and all the vessels thereof, and all that serveth thereto,

37 And the pillars of the court round about, and their sockets, and their pins, and their cords.

38 But those that encamp before the tabernacle toward the east, *even* before the tabernacle of the congregation eastward, *shall be* Moses, and Aaron and his sons, keeping the charge of the sanctuary for the charge of the children of Israel; and the stranger that cometh nigh shall be put to death.

39 All that were numbered of the Levites, which Moses and Aaron numbered at the commandment of the LORD, throughout their families, all the males from a month old and upward, *were* twenty and two thousand.

40 And the LORD said unto Moses, Number all the firstborn of the males of the children of Israel from a month old and upward, and take the number of their names.

41 And thou shalt take the Levites for me (I *am* the LORD) instead of all the firstborn among the children of Israel; and the cattle of the Levites instead of all the firstlings among the cattle of the children of Israel.

42 And Moses numbered, as the LORD commanded him, all the firstborn among the children of Israel.

43 And all the firstborn males by the number of names, from a month old and upward, of those that were numbered of them, were twenty and two thousand two hundred and threescore and thirteen.

Cross references (center column):

17 Gen. 46:11; Ex. 6:16; Num. 26:57; 1Chr. 6:1, 16; 23:6

18 Ex. 6:17

19 Ex. 6:18

20 Ex. 6:19

23 Num. 1:53

25 Ex. 25:9; 26:1, 7, 14, 36; Num. 4:24-26

26 Ex. 27:9, 16; 35:18

27 1Chr. 26:23

29 Num. 1:53

31 Ex. 25:10, 23, 31; 26:32; 27:1; 30:1; Num. 4:15

35 Num. 1:53

36 Num. 4:31, 32

38 Num. 1:53; 3:7, 8, 10; 18:5

39 Num. 26:62

40 Num. 3:15

41 Num. 3:12, 45

44 And the LORD spake unto Moses, saying,

45 Take the Levites instead of all the firstborn among the children of Israel, and the cattle of the Levites instead of their cattle; and the Levites shall be mine: I *am* the LORD.

46 And for those that are to be redeemed of the two hundred and threescore and thirteen of the firstborn of the children of Israel, which are more than the Levites;

47 Thou shalt even take five shekels apiece by the poll, after the shekel of the sanctuary shalt thou take *them*: (the shekel *is* twenty gerahs:)

48 And thou shalt give the money, wherewith the odd number of them is to be redeemed, unto Aaron and to his sons.

49 And Moses took the redemption money of them that were over and above them that were redeemed by the Levites:

50 Of the firstborn of the children of Israel took he the money; a thousand three hundred and threescore and five *shekels*, after the shekel of the sanctuary:

51 And Moses gave the money of them that were redeemed unto Aaron and to his sons, according to the word of the LORD, as the LORD commanded Moses.

CHAPTER 4
Further Duties of the Levites

1 And the LORD spake unto Moses and unto Aaron, saying,

2 Take the sum of the sons of Kohath from among the sons of Levi, after their families, by the house of their fathers,

3 From thirty years old and upward even until fifty years old, all that enter into the host, to do the work in the tabernacle of the congregation.

4 This *shall be* the service of the sons of Kohath in the tabernacle of the congregation, *about* the most holy things:

5 And when the camp setteth forward, Aaron shall come, and his sons, and they shall take down the covering vail, and cover the ark of testimony with it:

6 And shall put thereon the covering of badgers' skins, and shall spread over *it* a cloth wholly of blue, and shall put in the staves thereof.

7 And upon the table of shewbread they shall spread a cloth of blue, and put thereon

the dishes, and the spoons, and the bowls, and covers to cover withal: and the continual bread shall be thereon:

8 And they shall spread upon them a cloth of scarlet, and cover the same with a covering of badgers' skins, and shall put in the staves thereof.

9 And they shall take a cloth of blue, and cover the candlestick of the light, and his lamps, and his tongs, and his snuffdishes, and all the oil vessels thereof, wherewith they minister unto it:

10 And they shall put it and all the vessels thereof within a covering of badgers' skins, and shall put *it* upon a bar.

11 And upon the golden altar they shall spread a cloth of blue, and cover it with a covering of badgers' skins, and shall put to the staves thereof:

12 And they shall take all the instruments of ministry, wherewith they minister in the sanctuary, and put *them* in a cloth of blue, and cover them with a covering of badgers' skins, and shall put *them* on a bar:

13 And they shall take away the ashes from the altar, and spread a purple cloth thereon:

14 And they shall put upon it all the vessels thereof, wherewith they minister about it, *even* the censers, the fleshhooks, and the shovels, and the basons, all the vessels of the altar; and they shall spread upon it a covering of badgers' skins, and put to the staves of it.

15 And when Aaron and his sons have made an end of covering the sanctuary, and all the vessels of the sanctuary, as the camp is to set forward; after that, the sons of Kohath shall come to bear *it*: but they shall not touch *any* holy thing, lest they die. These *things are* the burden of the sons of Kohath in the tabernacle of the congregation.

16 And to the office of Eleazar the son of Aaron the priest *pertaineth* the oil for the light, and the sweet incense, and the daily meat offering, and the anointing oil, *and* the oversight of all the tabernacle, and of all that therein *is*, in the sanctuary, and in the vessels thereof.

17 And the LORD spake unto Moses and unto Aaron, saying,

18 Cut ye not off the tribe of the families of the Kohathites from among the Levites:

Center column cross-references:

45 Num. 3:12, 41
46 Ex. 13:13; Num. 3:39, 43; 18:15
47 Ex. 30:13; Lev. 27:6, 25; Num. 18:16; Ezek. 45:12
50 Num. 3:46, 47
51 Num. 3:48
3 Num. 8:24; 1Chr. 23:3, 24, 27
4 Num. 4:15, 19
5 Ex. 25:10, 16; 26:31
6 Ex. 25:13
7 Ex. 25:23, 29, 30; Lev. 24:6, 8
9 Ex. 25:31, 37, 38
11 Ex. 30:1, 3
15 Num. 3:31; 7:9; 10:21; Deut. 31:9; 2Sam. 6:6, 7, 13; 1Chr. 13:9, 10; 15:2, 15
16 Ex. 25:6; 29:40; 30:23, 34; Lev. 24:2

4:15 the sons of Kohath. The Kohathites, descendants of Kohath, one of Levi's three sons (Num. 3:17), served as the immediate assistants to the priests in charge of the Tabernacle furniture. Serving the priests was a serious responsibility, as the incident of improperly touching the Ark of the Covenant in David's time reveals (2 Sam. 6:6–7).

Thoughts from the Church Fathers

By Larry Crutchfield

The leaders of the post-apostolic church, including many who lived closest to the time of the apostles, held the Bible prophets of old in the very highest esteem. They diligently studied the prophets' predictions and carefully noted the perfect accuracy with which they were fulfilled. These church leaders proclaimed with boldness and certitude that prophecies related to the future would just as surely come to pass, and that prophetic Scripture was an important aid to faith, and thus, an example for righteous living.

The confidence these leaders had in Bible prophecy was inseparably linked to their belief that the prophets were God's divinely inspired spokesmen, a view clearly stated by trained philosopher Justin Martyr (ca. A.D. 100–165). Justin wrote, "The prophets are inspired by no other than the Divine Word" (*First Apology* 33). "With our own eyes we behold things that have happened and are happening just as they were predicted" (*First Apology* 30).

While Bible prophecies reveal God's future plans for His people, as Irenaeus (ca. A.D. 120–202), bishop of Lyon observed, they were also given "in order that our faith might be firmly established" (*Against Heresies* 4.22.2). The African father Tertullian (A.D. 150–225) expressed it this way: "Well, the truth of a prophecy, I think is the demonstration of its being from above. Hence there is among us an assured faith in regard to coming events as things already proved to us, for they were predicted along with what we have day by day fulfilled" (*Apology* 20).

> *These church leaders proclaimed that prophetic Scripture was an important aid to faith.*

Cyprian (ca. A.D. 200–258), bishop of Carthage, urged Christians not to let "the excessive and headlong faithlessness of many move or disturb" them, but rather to "strengthen [their] faith in the truthfulness which has foretold the matter" (*Treatises* 1.17). While the church fathers believed the study of prophetic Scripture resulted in passive benefits, such as greater faith and hope, they also taught that it required an active response.

At the beginning of the third century, the Roman presbyter and teacher Hippolytus asked, "what man shall have any excuse who hears these things in the Church from prophets and apostles, and from the Lord Himself, and yet will give no heed to the care of his soul, and to the time of the consummation, and to that approaching hour when we shall have to stand at the judgment seat of Christ?" (*Appendix to Works of Hippolytus* 2). Hippolytus also wrote, "Let all of you, then, of necessity, open the eyes of your hearts and the ears of your soul, and receive the word which we are about to speak . . . [concerning] the consummation, and in particular, of the seduction of the whole world by the enemy and devil; and after these things, the second coming of our Lord Jesus Christ" (*Treatise on Christ and Antichrist* 5).

Perhaps Lactantius (ca. A.D. 240–320), Latin rhetorician, Christian apologist, and historian best summarized the response believers should have as they encounter the truth revealed by God's prophetic Word. "Let us therefore apply ourselves to righteousness, which will alone, as an inseparable companion, lead us to God; and 'while a spirit rules these limbs,' let us serve God with unwearied service, let us keep our posts and watches, let us boldly engage with the enemy whom we know, that victorious and triumphant over our conquered adversary, we may obtain from the Lord that reward of valour which He himself has promised" (*Divine Institutes* 7.27).

19 But thus do unto them, that they may live, and not die, when they approach unto the most holy things: Aaron and his sons shall go in, and appoint them every one to his service and to his burden:

20 But they shall not go in to see when the holy things are covered, lest they die.

21 And the LORD spake unto Moses, saying,

22 Take also the sum of the sons of Gershon, throughout the houses of their fathers, by their families;

23 From thirty years old and upward until fifty years old shalt thou number them; all that enter in to perform the service, to do the work in the tabernacle of the congregation.

24 This *is* the service of the families of the Gershonites, to serve, and for burdens:

25 And they shall bear the curtains of the tabernacle, and the tabernacle of the congregation, his covering, and the covering of the badgers' skins that *is* above upon it, and the hanging for the door of the tabernacle of the congregation,

26 And the hangings of the court, and the hanging for the door of the gate of the court, which *is* by the tabernacle and by the altar round about, and their cords, and all the instruments of their service, and all that is made for them: so shall they serve.

27 At the appointment of Aaron and his sons shall be all the service of the sons of the Gershonites, in all their burdens, and in all their service: and ye shall appoint unto them in charge all their burdens.

28 This *is* the service of the families of the sons of Gershon in the tabernacle of the congregation: and their charge *shall be* under the hand of Ithamar the son of Aaron the priest.

29 As for the sons of Merari, thou shalt number them after their families, by the house of their fathers;

30 From thirty years old and upward even unto fifty years old shalt thou number them, every one that entereth into the service, to do the work of the tabernacle of the congregation.

31 And this *is* the charge of their burden, according to all their service in the tabernacle of the congregation; the boards of the tabernacle, and the bars thereof, and the pillars thereof, and sockets thereof,

32 And the pillars of the court round about, and their sockets, and their pins, and their cords, with all their instruments, and with all their service: and by name ye shall reckon the instruments of the charge of their burden.

33 This *is* the service of the families of the sons of Merari, according to all their service, in the tabernacle of the congregation, under the hand of Ithamar the son of Aaron the priest.

The Number of Eligible Levites for Service

34 And Moses and Aaron and the chief of the congregation numbered the sons of the Kohathites after their families, and after the house of their fathers,

35 From thirty years old and upward even unto fifty years old, every one that entereth into the service, for the work in the tabernacle of the congregation:

36 And those that were numbered of them by their families were two thousand seven hundred and fifty.

37 These *were* they that were numbered of the families of the Kohathites, all that might do service in the tabernacle of the congregation, which Moses and Aaron did number according to the commandment of the LORD by the hand of Moses.

38 And those that were numbered of the sons of Gershon, throughout their families, and by the house of their fathers,

39 From thirty years old and upward even unto fifty years old, every one that entereth into the service, for the work in the tabernacle of the congregation,

40 Even those that were numbered of them, throughout their families, by the house of their fathers, were two thousand and six hundred and thirty.

41 These *are* they that were numbered of the families of the sons of Gershon, of all that might do service in the tabernacle of the congregation, whom Moses and Aaron did number according to the commandment of the LORD.

42 And those that were numbered of the families of the sons of Merari, throughout their families, by the house of their fathers,

43 From thirty years old and upward even unto fifty years old, every one that entereth into the service, for the work in the tabernacle of the congregation,

44 Even those that were numbered of them after their families, were three thousand and two hundred.

45 These *be* those that were numbered of the families of the sons of Merari, whom Moses and Aaron numbered according to the word of the LORD by the hand of Moses.

46 All those that were numbered of the Levites, whom Moses and Aaron and the chief

19 Num. 4:4
20 Ex. 19:21; 1Sam. 6:19
23 Num. 4:3
25 Num. 3:25, 26
30 Num. 4:3
31 Ex. 26:15; Num. 3:36, 37
32 Ex. 38:21
34 Num. 4:2

41 Num. 4:22

45 Num. 4:29

of Israel numbered, after their families, and after the house of their fathers,

47 From thirty years old and upward even unto fifty years old, every one that came to do the service of the ministry, and the service of the burden in the tabernacle of the congregation,

48 Even those that were numbered of them, were eight thousand and five hundred and fourscore.

49 According to the commandment of the LORD they were numbered by the hand of Moses, every one according to his service, and according to his burden: thus were they numbered of him, as the LORD commanded Moses.

CHAPTER 5
Unclean People

1 And the LORD spake unto Moses, saying,

2 Command the children of Israel, that they put out of the camp every leper, and every one that hath an issue, and whosoever is defiled by the dead:

3 Both male and female shall ye put out, without the camp shall ye put them; that they defile not their camps, in the midst whereof I dwell.

4 And the children of Israel did so, and put them out without the camp: as the LORD spake unto Moses, so did the children of Israel.

Restitution for Wrongs

5 And the LORD spake unto Moses, saying,

6 Speak unto the children of Israel, When a man or woman shall commit any sin that men commit, to do a trespass against the LORD, and that person be guilty;

7 Then they shall confess their sin which they have done: and he shall recompense his trespass with the principal thereof, and add unto it the fifth *part* thereof, and give *it* unto *him* against whom he hath trespassed.

8 But if the man have no kinsman to recompense the trespass unto, let the trespass be recompensed unto the LORD, *even* to the priest; beside the ram of the atonement, whereby an atonement shall be made for him.

9 And every offering of all the holy things of the children of Israel, which they bring unto the priest, shall be his.

10 And every man's hallowed things shall be his: whatsoever any man giveth the priest, it shall be his.

Wives Suspected of Adultery

11 And the LORD spake unto Moses, saying,

12 Speak unto the children of Israel, and

say unto them, If any man's wife go aside, and commit a trespass against him,

13 And a man lie with her carnally, and it be hid from the eyes of her husband, and be kept close, and she be defiled, and *there be* no witness against her, neither she be taken *with the manner;*

14 And the spirit of jealousy come upon him, and he be jealous of his wife, and she be defiled: or if the spirit of jealousy come upon him, and he be jealous of his wife, and she be not defiled:

15 Then shall the man bring his wife unto the priest, and he shall bring her offering for her, the tenth *part* of an ephah of barley meal; he shall pour no oil upon it, nor put frankincense thereon; for it *is* an offering of jealousy, an offering of memorial, bringing iniquity to remembrance.

16 And the priest shall bring her near, and set her before the LORD:

17 And the priest shall take holy water in an earthen vessel; and of the dust that is in the floor of the tabernacle the priest shall take, and put *it* into the water:

18 And the priest shall set the woman before the LORD, and uncover the woman's head, and put the offering of memorial in her hands, which *is* the jealousy offering: and the priest shall have in his hand the bitter water that causeth the curse:

19 And the priest shall charge her by an oath, and say unto the woman, If no man have lain with thee, and if thou hast not gone aside to uncleanness *with another* instead of thy husband, be thou free from this bitter water that causeth the curse:

20 But if thou hast gone aside *to another* instead of thy husband, and if thou be defiled, and some man have lain with thee beside thine husband:

21 Then the priest shall charge the woman with an oath of cursing, and the priest shall say unto the woman, The LORD make thee a curse and an oath among thy people, when the LORD doth make thy thigh to rot, and thy belly to swell;

22 And this water that causeth the curse shall go into thy bowels, to make *thy* belly to swell, and *thy* thigh to rot: And the woman shall say, Amen, amen.

23 And the priest shall write these curses in a book, and he shall blot *them* out with the bitter water:

24 And he shall cause the woman to drink the bitter water that causeth the curse: and the water that causeth the curse shall enter into her, *and become* bitter.

47 Num. 4:3, 23, 30

49 Num. 4:1, 15, 21, 24, 31

2 Lev. 13:3, 46; 15:2; 21:1; Num. 9:6, 10; 12:14; 19:11, 13; 31:19

3 Lev. 26:11, 12; 2Cor. 6:16

6 Lev. 6:2, 3

7 Lev. 5:5; 6:5; 26:40; Josh. 7:19

8 Lev. 6:6, 7; 7:7

9 Ex. 29:28; Lev. 6:17, 18, 26; 7:6, 7, 9, 10, 14; Num. 18:8, 9, 19; Deut. 18:3, 4; Ezek. 44:29, 30

10 Lev. 10:13

13 Lev. 18:20

15 1Kgs. 17:18; Ezek. 29:16

21 Josh. 6:26; 1Sam. 14:24; Neh. 10:29; Jer. 29:22

22 Deut. 27:15; Ps. 109:18

25 Then the priest shall take the jealousy-offering out of the woman's hand, and shall wave the offering before the LORD, and offer it upon the altar:

26 And the priest shall take an handful of the offering, *even* the memorial thereof, and burn *it* upon the altar, and afterward shall cause the woman to drink the water.

27 And when he hath made her to drink the water, then it shall come to pass, *that*, if she be defiled, and have done trespass against her husband, that the water that causeth the curse shall enter into her, *and become* bitter, and her belly shall swell, and her thigh shall rot: and the woman shall be a curse among her people.

28 And if the woman be not defiled, but be clean; then she shall be free, and shall conceive seed.

29 This *is* the law of jealousies, when a wife goeth aside *to another* instead of her husband, and is defiled;

30 Or when the spirit of jealousy cometh upon him, and he be jealous over his wife, and shall set the woman before the LORD, and the priest shall execute upon her all this law.

31 Then shall the man be guiltless from iniquity, and this woman shall bear her iniquity.

CHAPTER 6
The Nazarite Vow

1 And the LORD spake unto Moses, saying,

2 Speak unto the children of Israel, and say unto them, When either man or woman shall separate *themselves* to vow a vow of a Nazarite, to separate *themselves* unto the LORD:

3 He shall separate *himself* from wine and strong drink, and shall drink no vinegar of wine, or vinegar of strong drink, neither shall he drink any liquor of grapes, nor eat moist grapes, or dried.

4 All the days of his separation shall he eat nothing that is made of the vine tree, from the kernels even to the husk.

5 All the days of the vow of his separation there shall no razor come upon his head: until the days be fulfilled, in the which he separateth *himself* unto the LORD, he shall be holy, *and* shall let the locks of the hair of his head grow.

6 All the days that he separateth *himself* unto the LORD he shall come at no dead body.

7 He shall not make himself unclean for his father, or for his mother, for his brother, or for his sister, when they die: because the consecration of his God *is* upon his head.

8 All the days of his separation he *is* holy unto the LORD.

9 And if any man die very suddenly by him, and he hath defiled the head of his consecration; then he shall shave his head in the day of his cleansing, on the seventh day shall he shave it.

10 And on the eighth day he shall bring two turtles, or two young pigeons, to the priest, to the door of the tabernacle of the congregation:

11 And the priest shall offer the one for a sin offering, and the other for a burnt offering, and make an atonement for him, for that he sinned by the dead, and shall hallow his head that same day.

12 And he shall consecrate unto the LORD the days of his separation, and shall bring a lamb of the first year for a trespass offering: but the days that were before shall be lost, because his separation was defiled.

13 And this *is* the law of the Nazarite, when the days of his separation are fulfilled: he shall be brought unto the door of the tabernacle of the congregation:

14 And he shall offer his offering unto the LORD, one he lamb of the first year without blemish for a burnt offering, and one ewe lamb of the first year without blemish for a sin offering, and one ram without blemish for peace offerings,

15 And a basket of unleavened bread, cakes of fine flour mingled with oil, and wafers of unleavened bread anointed with oil, and their meat offering, and their drink offerings.

16 And the priest shall bring *them* before the LORD, and shall offer his sin offering, and his burnt offering:

17 And he shall offer the ram *for* a sacrifice of peace offerings unto the LORD, with the basket of unleavened bread: the priest shall offer also his meat offering, and his drink offering.

18 And the Nazarite shall shave the head of

Cross references

25 Lev. 8:27
26 Lev. 2:2, 9
27 Deut. 28:37; Ps. 83:9, 11; Jer. 24:9; 29:18, 22; 42:18; Zech. 8:13
29 Num. 5:19
31 Lev. 20:17, 19, 20
2 Lev. 27:2; Judg. 13:5; Acts 21:23; Rom. 1:1
3 Amos 2:12; Luke 1:15
5 Judg. 13:5; 16:17; 1Sam. 1:11
6 Lev. 21:11; Num. 19:11, 16
7 Lev. 21:1, 2, 11; Num. 9:6
9 Acts 18:18; 21:24
10 Lev. 5:7; 14:22; 15:14, 29
12 Lev. 5:6
13 Acts 21:26
14 Lev. 3:6; 4:2, 27, 32
15 Ex. 29:2; Lev. 2:4; Num. 15:5, 7, 10
18 Acts 21:24

6:2 a vow of a Nazarite. A Nazarite was either a man or a woman who was especially dedicated to God. The word is derived from a Hebrew root *nazar*, meaning "separated," and denoted voluntary abstention from alcoholic beverages, contacts with dead bodies, and from cutting the hair or the beard. The vow to be a Nazarite could be lifelong or limited to thirty, sixty, or one hundred days.

his separation *at* the door of the tabernacle of the congregation, and shall take the hair of the head of his separation, and put *it* in the fire which *is* under the sacrifice of the peace offerings.

19 And the priest shall take the sodden shoulder of the ram, and one unleavened cake out of the basket, and one unleavened wafer, and shall put *them* upon the hands of the Nazarite, after *the hair of* his separation is shaven:

20 And the priest shall wave them *for a* wave offering before the LORD: this *is* holy for the priest, with the wave breast and heave shoulder: and after that the Nazarite may drink wine.

21 This *is* the law of the Nazarite who hath vowed, *and of* his offering unto the LORD for his separation, beside *that* that his hand shall get: according to the vow which he vowed, so he must do after the law of his separation.

The Priestly Blessing

22 And the LORD spake unto Moses, saying,
23 Speak unto Aaron and unto his sons, saying, On this wise ye shall bless the children of Israel, saying unto them,
24 The LORD bless thee, and keep thee:
25 The LORD make his face shine upon thee, and be gracious unto thee:
26 The LORD lift up his countenance upon thee, and give thee peace.
27 And they shall put my name upon the children of Israel; and I will bless them.

CHAPTER 7
Offerings at the Tabernacle Dedication

1 And it came to pass on the day that Moses had fully set up the tabernacle, and had anointed it, and sanctified it, and all the instruments thereof, both the altar and all the vessels thereof, and had anointed them, and sanctified them;
2 That the princes of Israel, heads of the house of their fathers, who *were* the princes of the tribes, and were over them that were numbered, offered:
3 And they brought their offering before the LORD, six covered wagons, and twelve oxen; a wagon for two of the princes, and for each one an ox: and they brought them before the tabernacle.
4 And the LORD spake unto Moses, saying,
5 Take *it* of them, that they may be to do the service of the tabernacle of the congregation; and thou shalt give them unto the

Levites, to every man according to his service.
6 And Moses took the wagons and the oxen, and gave them unto the Levites.
7 Two wagons and four oxen he gave unto the sons of Gershon, according to their service:
8 And four wagons and eight oxen he gave unto the sons of Merari, according unto their service, under the hand of Ithamar the son of Aaron the priest.
9 But unto the sons of Kohath he gave none: because the service of the sanctuary belonging unto them *was that* they should bear upon their shoulders.
10 And the princes offered for dedicating of the altar in the day that it was anointed, even the princes offered their offering before the altar.
11 And the LORD said unto Moses, They shall offer their offering, each prince on his day, for the dedicating of the altar.
12 And he that offered his offering the first day was Nahshon the son of Amminadab, of the tribe of Judah:
13 And his offering *was* one silver charger, the weight thereof *was* an hundred and thirty *shekels*, one silver bowl of seventy shekels, after the shekel of the sanctuary; both of them *were* full of fine flour mingled with oil for a meat offering:
14 One spoon of ten *shekels* of gold, full of incense:
15 One young bullock, one ram, one lamb of the first year, for a burnt offering:
16 One kid of the goats for a sin offering:
17 And for a sacrifice of peace offerings, two oxen, five rams, five he goats, five lambs of the first year: this *was* the offering of Nahshon the son of Amminadab.
18 On the second day Nethaneel the son of Zuar, prince of Issachar, did offer:
19 He offered *for* his offering one silver charger, the weight whereof *was* an hundred and thirty *shekels*, one silver bowl of seventy shekels, after the shekel of the sanctuary; both of them full of fine flour mingled with oil for a meat offering:
20 One spoon of gold of ten *shekels*, full of incense:
21 One young bullock, one ram, one lamb of the first year, for a burnt offering:
22 One kid of the goats for a sin offering:
23 And for a sacrifice of peace offerings, two oxen, five rams, five he goats, five lambs of the first year: this *was* the offering of Nethaneel the son of Zuar.
24 On the third day Eliab the son of Helon,

Center column cross-references:

19 Ex. 29:23, 24; 1Sam. 2:15

20 Ex. 29:27, 28

23 Lev. 9:22; 1Chr. 23:13

24 Ps. 121:7; John 17:11

25 Gen. 43:29; Ps. 31:16; 67:1; 80:3, 7, 19; 119:135; Dan. 9:17

26 Ps. 4:6; John 14:27; 2Thess. 3:16

27 Deut. 28:10; 2Chr. 7:14; Ps. 115:12; Isa. 43:7; Dan. 9:18, 19

1 Ex. 40:18; Lev. 8:10, 11

2 Num. 1:4

7 Num. 4:25

8 Num. 4:28, 31, 33

9 Num. 4:6, 8, 10, 12, 14, 15; 2Sam. 6:13

10 Deut. 20:5; 1Kgs. 8:63; 2Chr. 7:5, 9; Ezra 6:16; Neh. 12:27

12 Num. 2:3

13 Ex. 30:13; Lev. 2:1

14 Ex. 30:34

15 Lev. 1:2

16 Lev. 4:23

17 Lev. 3:1

prince of the children of Zebulun, *did offer*:

25 His offering *was* one silver charger, the weight whereof *was* an hundred and thirty *shekels*, one silver bowl of seventy shekels, after the shekel of the sanctuary; both of them full of fine flour mingled with oil for a meat offering:

26 One golden spoon of ten *shekels*, full of incense:

27 One young bullock, one ram, one lamb of the first year, for a burnt offering:

28 One kid of the goats for a sin offering:

29 And for a sacrifice of peace offerings, two oxen, five rams, five he goats, five lambs of the first year: this *was* the offering of Eliab the son of Helon.

30 On the fourth day Elizur the son of Shedeur, prince of the children of Reuben, *did offer*:

31 His offering *was* one silver charger of the weight of an hundred and thirty *shekels*, one silver bowl of seventy shekels, after the shekel of the sanctuary; both of them full of fine flour mingled with oil for a meat offering:

32 One golden spoon of ten *shekels*, full of incense:

33 One young bullock, one ram, one lamb of the first year, for a burnt offering:

34 One kid of the goats for a sin offering:

35 And for a sacrifice of peace offerings, two oxen, five rams, five he goats, five lambs of the first year: this *was* the offering of Elizur the son of Shedeur.

36 On the fifth day Shelumiel the son of Zurishaddai, prince of the children of Simeon, *did offer*:

37 His offering *was* one silver charger, the weight whereof *was* an hundred and thirty *shekels*, one silver bowl of seventy shekels, after the shekel of the sanctuary; both of them full of fine flour mingled with oil for a meat offering:

38 One golden spoon of ten *shekels*, full of incense:

39 One young bullock, one ram, one lamb of the first year, for a burnt offering:

40 One kid of the goats for a sin offering:

41 And for a sacrifice of peace offerings, two oxen, five rams, five he goats, five lambs of the first year: this *was* the offering of Shelumiel the son of Zurishaddai.

42 On the sixth day Eliasaph the son of Deuel, prince of the children of Gad, *offered*:

43 His offering *was* one silver charger of the weight of an hundred and thirty *shekels*, a silver bowl of seventy shekels, after the shekel of the sanctuary; both of them full of

fine flour mingled with oil for a meat offering:

44 One golden spoon of ten *shekels*, full of incense:

45 One young bullock, one ram, one lamb of the first year, for a burnt offering:

46 One kid of the goats for a sin offering:

47 And for a sacrifice of peace offerings, two oxen, five rams, five he goats, five lambs of the first year: this *was* the offering of Eliasaph the son of Deuel.

48 On the seventh day Elishama the son of Ammihud, prince of the children of Ephraim, *offered*:

49 His offering *was* one silver charger, the weight whereof *was* an hundred and thirty *shekels*, one silver bowl of seventy shekels, after the shekel of the sanctuary; both of them full of fine flour mingled with oil for a meat offering:

50 One golden spoon of ten *shekels*, full of incense:

51 One young bullock, one ram, one lamb of the first year, for a burnt offering:

52 One kid of the goats for a sin offering:

53 And for a sacrifice of peace offerings, two oxen, five rams, five he goats, five lambs of the first year: this *was* the offering of Elishama the son of Ammihud.

54 On the eighth day *offered* Gamaliel the son of Pedahzur, prince of the children of Manasseh:

55 His offering *was* one silver charger of the weight of an hundred and thirty *shekels*, one silver bowl of seventy shekels, after the shekel of the sanctuary; both of them full of fine flour mingled with oil for a meat offering:

56 One golden spoon of ten *shekels*, full of incense:

57 One young bullock, one ram, one lamb of the first year, for a burnt offering:

58 One kid of the goats for a sin offering:

59 And for a sacrifice of peace offerings, two oxen, five rams, five he goats, five lambs of the first year: this *was* the offering of Gamaliel the son of Pedahzur.

60 On the ninth day Abidan the son of Gideoni, prince of the children of Benjamin, *offered*:

61 His offering *was* one silver charger, the weight whereof *was* an hundred and thirty *shekels*, one silver bowl of seventy shekels, after the shekel of the sanctuary; both of them full of fine flour mingled with oil for a meat offering:

62 One golden spoon of ten *shekels*, full of incense:

63 One young bullock, one ram, one lamb of the first year, for a burnt offering:

64 One kid of the goats for a sin offering:

65 And for a sacrifice of peace offerings, two oxen, five rams, five he goats, five lambs of the first year: this *was* the offering of Abidan the son of Gideoni.

66 On the tenth day Ahiezer the son of Ammishaddai, prince of the children of Dan, *offered*:

67 His offering *was* one silver charger, the weight whereof *was* an hundred and thirty *shekels*, one silver bowl of seventy shekels, after the shekel of the sanctuary; both of them full of fine flour mingled with oil for a meat offering:

68 One golden spoon of ten *shekels*, full of incense:

69 One young bullock, one ram, one lamb of the first year, for a burnt offering:

70 One kid of the goats for a sin offering:

71 And for a sacrifice of peace offerings, two oxen, five rams, five he goats, five lambs of the first year: this *was* the offering of Ahiezer the son of Ammishaddai.

72 On the eleventh day Pagiel the son of Ocran, prince of the children of Asher, *offered*:

73 His offering *was* one silver charger, the weight whereof *was* an hundred and thirty *shekels*, one silver bowl of seventy shekels, after the shekel of the sanctuary; both of them full of fine flour mingled with oil for a meat offering:

74 One golden spoon of ten *shekels*, full of incense:

75 One young bullock, one ram, one lamb of the first year, for a burnt offering:

76 One kid of the goats for a sin offering:

77 And for a sacrifice of peace offerings, two oxen, five rams, five he goats, five lambs of the first year: this *was* the offering of Pagiel the son of Ocran.

78 On the twelfth day Ahira the son of Enan, prince of the children of Naphtali, *offered*:

79 His offering *was* one silver charger, the weight whereof *was* an hundred and thirty *shekels*, one silver bowl of seventy shekels, after the shekel of the sanctuary; both of them full of fine flour mingled with oil for a meat offering:

80 One golden spoon of ten *shekels*, full of incense:

81 One young bullock, one ram, one lamb of the first year, for a burnt offering:

82 One kid of the goats for a sin offering:

83 And for a sacrifice of peace offerings,

two oxen, five rams, five he goats, five lambs of the first year: this *was* the offering of Ahira the son of Enan.

84 This *was* the dedication of the altar, in the day when it was anointed, by the princes of Israel: twelve chargers of silver, twelve silver bowls, twelve spoons of gold:

85 Each charger of silver *weighing* an hundred and thirty *shekels*, each bowl seventy: all the silver vessels *weighed* two thousand and four hundred *shekels*, after the shekel of the sanctuary:

86 The golden spoons *were* twelve, full of incense, *weighing* ten *shekels* apiece, after the shekel of the sanctuary: all the gold of the spoons *was* an hundred and twenty *shekels*.

87 All the oxen for the burnt offering *were* twelve bullocks, the rams twelve, the lambs of the first year twelve, with their meat offering: and the kids of the goats for sin offering twelve.

88 And all the oxen for the sacrifice of the peace offerings *were* twenty and four bullocks, the rams sixty, the he goats sixty, the lambs of the first year sixty. This *was* the dedication of the altar, after that it was anointed.

89 And when Moses was gone into the tabernacle of the congregation to speak with him, then he heard the voice of one speaking unto him from off the mercy seat that *was* upon the ark of testimony, from between the two cherubims: and he spake unto him.

CHAPTER 8
The Seven Lamps

1 And the LORD spake unto Moses, saying,

2 Speak unto Aaron, and say unto him, When thou lightest the lamps, the seven lamps shall give light over against the candlestick.

3 And Aaron did so; he lighted the lamps thereof over against the candlestick, as the LORD commanded Moses.

4 And this work of the candlestick *was of* beaten gold, unto the shaft thereof, unto the flowers thereof, *was* beaten work: according unto the pattern which the LORD had shewed Moses, so he made the candlestick.

Levites Are Purified

5 And the LORD spake unto Moses, saying,

6 Take the Levites from among the children of Israel, and cleanse them.

7 And thus shalt thou do unto them, to cleanse them: Sprinkle water of purifying upon them, and let them shave all their

---

Cross references (center column):

88 Ex. 25:22; 33:9, 11; Num. 6:1; 12:8

2 Ex. 25:37; 40:25

4 Ex. 25:18, 31, 40

7 Lev. 14:8, 9; Num. 19:9, 17, 18

flesh, and let them wash their clothes, and *so* make themselves clean.

8 Then let them take a young bullock with his meat offering, *even* fine flour mingled with oil, and another young bullock shalt thou take for a sin offering.

9 And thou shalt bring the Levites before the tabernacle of the congregation: and thou shalt gather the whole assembly of the children of Israel together:

10 And thou shalt bring the Levites before the LORD: and the children of Israel shall put their hands upon the Levites:

11 And Aaron shall offer the Levites before the LORD *for* an offering of the children of Israel, that they may execute the service of the LORD.

12 And the Levites shall lay their hands upon the heads of the bullocks: and thou shalt offer the one *for* a sin offering, and the other *for* a burnt offering, unto the LORD, to make an atonement for the Levites.

13 And thou shalt set the Levites before Aaron, and before his sons, and offer them *for* an offering unto the LORD.

14 Thus shalt thou separate the Levites from among the children of Israel: and the Levites shall be mine.

15 And after that shall the Levites go in to do the service of the tabernacle of the congregation: and thou shalt cleanse them, and offer them *for* an offering.

16 For they *are* wholly given unto me from among the children of Israel; instead of such as open every womb, *even instead of* the firstborn of all the children of Israel, have I taken them unto me.

17 For all the firstborn of the children of Israel *are* mine, *both* man and beast: on the day that I smote every firstborn in the land of Egypt I sanctified them for myself.

18 And I have taken the Levites for all the firstborn of the children of Israel.

19 And I have given the Levites *as* a gift to Aaron and to his sons from among the children of Israel, to do the service of the children of Israel in the tabernacle of the congregation, and to make an atonement for the children of Israel: that there be no plague among the children of Israel, when the children of Israel come nigh unto the sanctuary.

20 And Moses, and Aaron, and all the congregation of the children of Israel, did to the Levites according unto all that the LORD commanded Moses concerning the Levites, so did the children of Israel unto them.

21 And the Levites were purified, and they

washed their clothes; and Aaron offered them *as* an offering before the LORD; and Aaron made an atonement for them to cleanse them.

22 And after that went the Levites in to do their service in the tabernacle of the congregation before Aaron, and before his sons: as the LORD had commanded Moses concerning the Levites, so did they unto them.

23 And the LORD spake unto Moses, saying,

24 This *is it* that *belongeth* unto the Levites: from twenty and five years old and upward they shall go in to wait upon the service of the tabernacle of the congregation:

25 And from the age of fifty years they shall cease waiting upon the service *thereof*, and shall serve no more:

26 But shall minister with their brethren in the tabernacle of the congregation, to keep the charge, and shall do no service. Thus shalt thou do unto the Levites touching their charge.

CHAPTER 9
The Passover

1 And the LORD spake unto Moses in the wilderness of Sinai, in the first month of the second year after they were come out of the land of Egypt, saying,

2 Let the children of Israel also keep the passover at his appointed season.

3 In the fourteenth day of this month, at even, ye shall keep it in his appointed season: according to all the rites of it, and according to all the ceremonies thereof, shall ye keep it.

4 And Moses spake unto the children of Israel, that they should keep the passover.

5 And they kept the passover on the fourteenth day of the first month at even in the wilderness of Sinai: according to all that the LORD commanded Moses, so did the children of Israel.

6 And there were certain men, who were defiled by the dead body of a man, that they could not keep the passover on that day: and they came before Moses and before Aaron on that day:

7 And those men said unto him, We *are* defiled by the dead body of a man: wherefore are we kept back, that we may not offer an offering of the LORD in his appointed season among the children of Israel?

8 And Moses said unto them, Stand still, and I will hear what the LORD will command concerning you.

9 And the LORD spake unto Moses, saying,

10 Speak unto the children of Israel, saying,

Cross references (center column):

8 Lev. 2:1
9 Ex. 29:4; 40:12; Lev. 8:3
10 Lev. 1:4
12 Ex. 29:10
14 Num. 3:45; 16:9
15 Num. 8:11, 13
16 Num. 3:12, 45
17 Ex. 3:13; 13:2, 12, 13, 15; Luke 2:23
19 Num. 1:53; 3:9; 16:46; 18:5; 2Chr. 26:16
21 Num. 8:7, 11, 12
22 Num. 8:5-22
24 Num. 4:3; 1Chr. 23:3, 24, 27; 1Tim. 1:18
26 Num. 1:53

2 Ex. 12:1, 14-17; Lev. 23:5; Num. 28:16; Deut. 16:1, 2
3 Ex. 12:6

5 Josh. 5:10

6 Ex. 18:15, 19, 26; Num. 5:2; 19:11, 16; 27:2; John 18:28

8 Num. 27:5

If any man of you or of your posterity shall be unclean by reason of a dead body, or *be* in a journey afar off, yet he shall keep the passover unto the LORD.

11 The fourteenth day of the second month at even they shall keep it, *and* eat it with unleavened bread and bitter *herbs*.

12 They shall leave none of it unto the morning, nor break any bone of it: according to all the ordinances of the passover they shall keep it.

13 But the man that *is* clean, and is not in a journey, and forbeareth to keep the passover, even the same soul shall be cut off from among his people: because he brought not the offering of the LORD in his appointed season, that man shall bear his sin.

14 And if a stranger shall sojourn among you, and will keep the passover unto the LORD; according to the ordinance of the passover, and according to the manner thereof, so shall he do: ye shall have one ordinance, both for the stranger, and for him that was born in the land.

The Cloud over the Tabernacle

15 And on the day that the tabernacle was reared up the cloud covered the tabernacle, *namely*, the tent of the testimony: and at even there was upon the tabernacle as it were the appearance of fire, until the morning.

16 So it was alway: the cloud covered it *by day*, and the appearance of fire by night.

17 And when the cloud was taken up from the tabernacle, then after that the children of Israel journeyed: and in the place where the cloud abode, there the children of Israel pitched their tents.

18 At the commandment of the LORD the children of Israel journeyed, and at the commandment of the LORD they pitched: as long as the cloud abode upon the tabernacle they rested in their tents.

19 And when the cloud tarried long upon the tabernacle many days, then the children of Israel kept the charge of the LORD, and journeyed not.

20 And *so* it was, when the cloud was a few days upon the tabernacle; according to the commandment of the LORD they abode in their tents, and according to the commandment of the LORD they journeyed.

21 And *so* it was, when the cloud abode from even unto the morning, and *that* the cloud was taken up in the morning, then they journeyed: whether *it was* by day or by night that the cloud was taken up, they journeyed.

22 Or *whether it were* two days, or a month, or a year, that the cloud tarried upon the tabernacle, remaining thereon, the children of Israel abode in their tents, and journeyed not: but when it was taken up, they journeyed.

23 At the commandment of the LORD they rested in the tents, and at the commandment of the LORD they journeyed: they kept the charge of the LORD, at the commandment of the LORD by the hand of Moses.

CHAPTER 10
The Silver Trumpets

1 And the LORD spake unto Moses, saying,

2 Make thee two trumpets of silver; of a whole piece shalt thou make them: that thou mayest use them for the calling of the assembly, and for the journeying of the camps.

3 And when they shall blow with them, all the assembly shall assemble themselves to thee at the door of the tabernacle of the congregation.

Cross references (center column):

11 Ex. 12:8; 2Chr. 30:2, 15
12 Ex. 12:10, 43, 46; John 19:36
13 Gen. 17:14; Ex. 12:15; Num. 5:31; 8:13
14 Ex. 12:49
15 Ex. 13:21; 40:34, 38; Neh. 9, 12, 19; Ps. 78:14
17 Ex. 40:36; Num. 10:11, 33, 34; Ps. 80:1
18 1Cor. 10:1
19 Num. 1:53; 3:8
22 Ex. 40:36, 37
23 Num. 9:19
2 Isa. 1:13
3 Jer. 4:5; Joel 2:15

9:16 the cloud covered it by day, and the appearance of fire by night. This was the *Shechinah* cloud, from Hebrew meaning "residence [of God]." The word was used by the Jews to denote physical manifestations of God's glory or light, but does not actually appear in the Bible. Its presence, however, is first recorded in Exodus 13:21–22, when this manifestation of the glory of the Lord protected them from the advancing Egyptian army (Ex. 14:10). Hovering above the encamped Israelites in their journeys, it also was especially evident between the cherubim above the mercy seat on the Ark of the Covenant in the Tabernacle. At the dedication of Solomon's Temple, this same phenomena, called "the glory of the LORD," filled the house (2 Chr. 5:14). Centuries later Ezek-

iel saw it withdrawn progressively from the temple (Ezek. 9:3; 10:18–19; 11:22–23) as judgment and captivity loomed with destruction of the temple only a few years away. The Shechinah will return to the Millennial Temple after the Tribulation and the glorious appearing of Christ (Ezek. 43:1–6).

10:1–2 two trumpets of silver. The first trumpet's sound was to call the people together that they might ready themselves for the journey. The second or last trumpet's sound was to begin the march. Some think that Paul had this analogy in mind when he predicted that the living saints would rise to meet the Lord in the Rapture at the last trumpet (1 Cor. 15:52).

4 And if they blow *but* with one *trumpet,* then the princes, *which are* heads of the thousands of Israel, shall gather themselves unto thee.

5 When ye blow an alarm, then the camps that lie on the east parts shall go forward.

6 When ye blow an alarm the second time, then the camps that lie on the south side shall take their journey: they shall blow an alarm for their journeys.

7 But when the congregation is to be gathered together, ye shall blow, but ye shall not sound an alarm.

8 And the sons of Aaron, the priests, shall blow with the trumpets; and they shall be to you for an ordinance for ever throughout your generations.

9 And if ye go to war in your land against the enemy that oppresseth you, then ye shall blow an alarm with the trumpets; and ye shall be remembered before the LORD your God, and ye shall be saved from your enemies.

10 Also in the day of your gladness, and in your solemn days, and in the beginnings of your months, ye shall blow with the trumpets over your burnt offerings, and over the sacrifices of your peace offerings; that they may be to you for a memorial before your God: I *am* the LORD your God.

The Israelites Leave Sinai

11 And it came to pass on the twentieth *day* of the second month, in the second year, that the cloud was taken up from off the tabernacle of the testimony.

12 And the children of Israel took their journeys out of the wilderness of Sinai; and the cloud rested in the wilderness of Paran.

13 And they first took their journey according to the commandment of the LORD by the hand of Moses.

14 In the first *place* went the standard of the camp of the children of Judah according to their armies: and over his host *was* Nahshon the son of Amminadab.

15 And over the host of the tribe of the children of Issachar *was* Nethaneel the son of Zuar.

16 And over the host of the tribe of the children of Zebulun *was* Eliab the son of Helon.

17 And the tabernacle was taken down; and the sons of Gershon and the sons of Merari set forward, bearing the tabernacle.

18 And the standard of the camp of Reuben set forward according to their armies: and over his host *was* Elizur the son of Shedeur.

19 And over the host of the tribe of the children of Simeon *was* Shelumiel the son of Zurishaddai.

20 And over the host of the tribe of the chil-

Cross references: 4 Ex. 18:21; Num. 1:16; 7:2 · 5 Num. 2:3 · 7 Joel 2:1 · 8 Num. 31:6; Josh. 6:4 · 9 Gen. 8:1; Judg. 2:18; 4:3; 6:9; 10:8, 12; 1Sam. 10:18; 2Chr. 13:14 · 10 Lev. 23:24; Num. 10:9; 29:1; 1Chr. 15:24; 2Chr. 5:12; 7:6; 29:26; Ezra 3:10; Neh. 12:35 · 11 Num. 9:17 · 12 Gen. 21:21; 12:16; 13:3, 26; Ex. 19:1; 40:36; Num. 1:1; 2:9, 16, 24, 31; 9:5; Deut. 1:1 · 14 Num. 1:7; 2:3, 9 · 17 Num. 1:51; 4:24, 31; 7:6-8

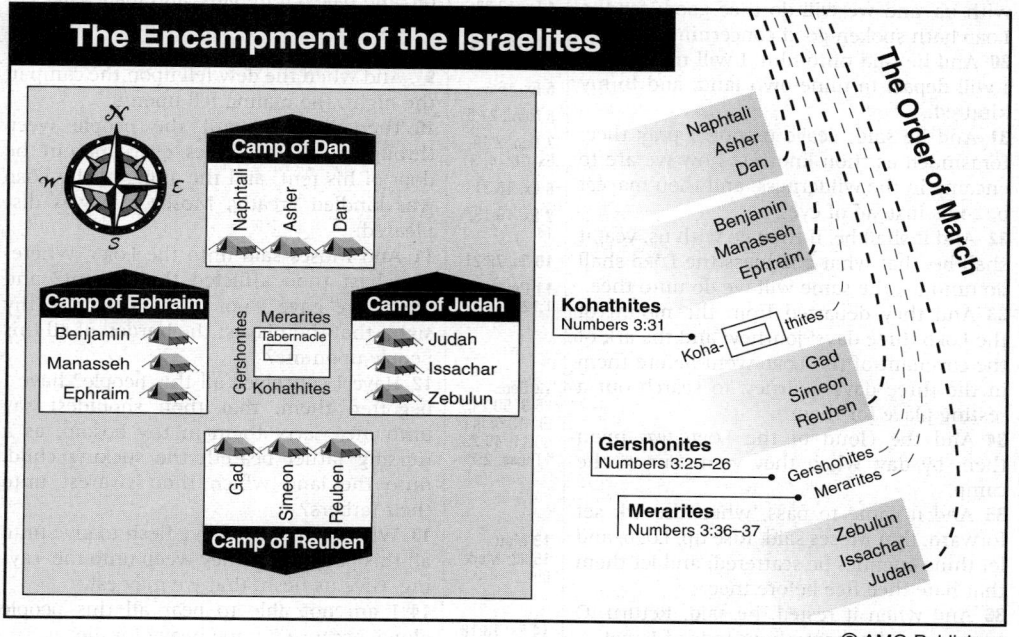

The Encampment of the Israelites

© AMG Publishers

dren of Gad *was* Eliasaph the son of Deuel.
21 And the Kohathites set forward, bearing the sanctuary: and *the other* did set up the tabernacle against they came.
22 And the standard of the camp of the children of Ephraim set forward according to their armies: and over his host *was* Elishama the son of Ammihud.
23 And over the host of the tribe of the children of Manasseh *was* Gamaliel the son of Pedahzur.
24 And over the host of the tribe of the children of Benjamin *was* Abidan the son of Gideoni.
25 And the standard of the camp of the children of Dan set forward, *which was* the rereward of all the camps throughout their hosts: and over his host *was* Ahiezer the son of Ammishaddai.
26 And over the host of the tribe of the children of Asher *was* Pagiel the son of Ocran.
27 And over the host of the tribe of the children of Naphtali *was* Ahira the son of Enan.
28 Thus *were* the journeyings of the children of Israel according to their armies, when they set forward.
29 And Moses said unto Hobab, the son of Raguel the Midianite, Moses' father-in-law, We are journeying unto the place of which the LORD said, I will give it you: come thou with us, and we will do thee good: for the LORD hath spoken good concerning Israel.
30 And he said unto him, I will not go; but I will depart to mine own land, and to my kindred.
31 And he said, Leave us not, I pray thee; forasmuch as thou knowest how we are to encamp in the wilderness, and thou mayest be to us instead of eyes.
32 And it shall be, if thou go with us, yea, it shall be, that what goodness the LORD shall do unto us, the same will we do unto thee.
33 And they departed from the mount of the LORD three days' journey: and the ark of the covenant of the LORD went before them in the three days' journey, to search out a resting place for them.
34 And the cloud of the LORD *was* upon them by day, when they went out of the camp.
35 And it came to pass, when the ark set forward, that Moses said, Rise up, LORD, and let thine enemies be scattered; and let them that hate thee flee before thee.
36 And when it rested, he said, Return, O LORD, unto the many thousands of Israel.

CHAPTER 11
God Sends Fire

1 And *when* the people complained, it displeased the LORD: and the LORD heard *it*; and his anger was kindled; and the fire of the LORD burnt among them, and consumed *them that were* in the uttermost parts of the camp.
2 And the people cried unto Moses; and when Moses prayed unto the LORD, the fire was quenched.
3 And he called the name of the place Taberah: because the fire of the LORD burnt among them.

God Sends Quail

4 And the mixed multitude that *was* among them fell a lusting: and the children of Israel also wept again, and said, Who shall give us flesh to eat?
5 We remember the fish, which we did eat in Egypt freely; the cucumbers, and the melons, and the leeks, and the onions, and the garlick:
6 But now our soul *is* dried away: *there is* nothing at all, beside this manna, *before* our eyes.
7 And the manna *was* as coriander seed, and the colour thereof as the colour of bedellium.
8 *And* the people went about, and gathered *it*, and ground *it* in mills, or beat *it* in a mortar, and baked *it* in pans, and made cakes of it: and the taste of it was as the taste of fresh oil.
9 And when the dew fell upon the camp in the night, the manna fell upon it.
10 Then Moses heard the people weep throughout their families, every man in the door of his tent: and the anger of the LORD was kindled greatly; Moses also was displeased.
11 And Moses said unto the LORD, Wherefore hast thou afflicted thy servant? and wherefore have I not found favour in thy sight, that thou layest the burden of all this people upon me?
12 Have I conceived all this people? have I begotten them, that thou shouldest say unto me, Carry them in thy bosom, as a nursing father beareth the sucking child, unto the land which thou swarest unto their fathers?
13 Whence should I have flesh to give unto all this people? for they weep unto me, saying, Give us flesh, that we may eat.
14 I am not able to bear all this people alone, because *it is* too heavy for me.

15 And if thou deal thus with me, kill me, I pray thee, out of hand, if I have found favour in thy sight; and let me not see my wretchedness.

16 And the LORD said unto Moses, Gather unto me seventy men of the elders of Israel, whom thou knowest to be the elders of the people, and officers over them; and bring them unto the tabernacle of the congregation, that they may stand there with thee.

17 And I will come down and talk with thee there: and I will take of the spirit which *is* upon thee, and will put *it* upon them; and they shall bear the burden of the people with thee, that thou bear *it* not thyself alone.

18 And say thou unto the people, Sanctify yourselves against to morrow, and ye shall eat flesh: for ye have wept in the ears of the LORD, saying, Who shall give us flesh to eat? for *it was* well with us in Egypt: therefore the LORD will give you flesh, and ye shall eat.

19 Ye shall not eat one day, nor two days, nor five days, neither ten days, nor twenty days;

20 *But* even a whole month, until it come out at your nostrils, and it be loathsome unto you: because that ye have despised the LORD which *is* among you, and have wept before him, saying, Why came we forth out of Egypt?

21 And Moses said, The people, among whom I *am, are* six hundred thousand footmen; and thou hast said, I will give them flesh, that they may eat a whole month.

22 Shall the flocks and the herds be slain for them, to suffice them? or shall all the fish of the sea be gathered together for them, to suffice them?

23 And the LORD said unto Moses, Is the LORD's hand waxed short? thou shalt see now whether my word shall come to pass unto thee or not.

24 And Moses went out, and told the people the words of the LORD, and gathered the seventy men of the elders of the people, and set them round about the tabernacle.

25 And the LORD came down in a cloud, and spake unto him, and took of the spirit that *was* upon him, and gave *it* unto the seventy elders: and it came to pass, *that,* when the spirit rested upon them, they prophesied, and did not cease.

26 But there remained two *of the* men in the camp, the name of the one *was* Eldad, and the name of the other Medad: and the spirit rested upon them; and they *were* of them

that were written, but went not out unto the tabernacle: and they prophesied in the camp.

27 And there ran a young man, and told Moses, and said, Eldad and Medad do prophesy in the camp.

28 And Joshua the son of Nun, the servant of Moses, *one* of his young men, answered and said, My lord Moses, forbid them.

29 And Moses said unto him, Enviest thou for my sake? would God that all the LORD's people were prophets, *and* that the LORD would put his spirit upon them!

30 And Moses gat him into the camp, he and the elders of Israel.

31 And there went forth a wind from the LORD, and brought quails from the sea, and let *them* fall by the camp, as it were a day's journey on this side, and as it were a day's journey on the other side, round about the camp, and as it were two cubits *high* upon the face of the earth.

32 And the people stood up all that day, and all *that* night, and all the next day, and they gathered the quails: he that gathered least gathered ten homers: and they spread *them* all abroad for themselves round about the camp.

33 And while the flesh *was* yet between their teeth, ere it was chewed, the wrath of the LORD was kindled against the people, and the LORD smote the people with a very great plague.

34 And he called the name of that place Kibroth-hattaavah: because there they buried the people that lusted.

35 *And* the people journeyed from Kibroth-hattaavah unto Hazeroth; and abode at Hazeroth.

CHAPTER 12
Miriam Is Punished

1 And Miriam and Aaron spake against Moses because of the Ethiopian woman whom he had married: for he had married an Ethiopian woman.

2 And they said, Hath the LORD indeed spoken only by Moses? hath he not spoken also by us? And the LORD heard *it*.

3 (Now the man Moses *was* very meek, above all the men which *were* upon the face of the earth.)

4 And the LORD spake suddenly unto Moses, and unto Aaron, and unto Miriam, Come out ye three unto the tabernacle of the congregation. And they three came out.

5 And the LORD came down in the pillar of the cloud, and stood *in* the door of the

tabernacle, and called Aaron and Miriam: and they both came forth.

6 And he said, Hear now my words: If there be a prophet among you, *I* the LORD will make myself known unto him in a vision, *and* will speak unto him in a dream.

7 My servant Moses *is* not so, who *is* faithful in all mine house.

8 With him will I speak mouth to mouth, even apparently, and not in dark speeches; and the similitude of the LORD shall he behold: wherefore then were ye not afraid to speak against my servant Moses?

9 And the anger of the LORD was kindled against them; and he departed.

10 And the cloud departed from off the tabernacle; and, behold, Miriam *became* leprous, *white* as snow: and Aaron looked upon Miriam, and, behold, *she was* leprous.

11 And Aaron said unto Moses, Alas, my lord, I beseech thee, lay not the sin upon us, wherein we have done foolishly, and wherein we have sinned.

12 Let her not be as one dead, of whom the flesh is half consumed when he cometh out of his mother's womb.

13 And Moses cried unto the LORD, saying, Heal her now, O God, I beseech thee.

14 And the LORD said unto Moses, If her father had but spit in her face, should she not be ashamed seven days? let her be shut out from the camp seven days, and after that let her be received in *again*.

15 And Miriam was shut out from the camp seven days: and the people journeyed not till Miriam was brought in *again*.

16 And afterward the people removed from Hazeroth, and pitched in the wilderness of Paran.

CHAPTER 13
The Spies Explore Canaan

1 And the LORD spake unto Moses, saying,

2 Send thou men, that they may search the land of Canaan, which I give unto the children of Israel: of every tribe of their fathers shall ye send a man, every one a ruler among them.

3 And Moses by the commandment of the LORD sent them from the wilderness of Paran: all those men *were* heads of the children of Israel.

4 And these *were* their names: of the tribe of Reuben, Shammua the son of Zaccur.

5 Of the tribe of Simeon, Shaphat the son of Hori.

6 Of the tribe of Judah, Caleb the son of Jephunneh.

Cross references:

6 Gen. 15:1; 31:10, 11; 46:2; 1Kgs. 3:5; Job 33:15; Ezek. 1:1; Dan. 8:2; 10:8, 16, 17; Matt. 1:20; Luke 1:11, 22; Acts 10:11, 17; 22:17, 18

7 Ps. 105:26; 1Tim. 3:15; Heb. 3:2, 5

8 Ex. 33:11, 19; Deut. 34:10; 1Cor. 13:12; 2Pet. 2:10; Jude 1:8

10 Deut. 24:9; 2Kgs. 5:27; 15:5; 2Chr. 26:19, 20

11 2Sam. 19:19; 24:10; Prov. 30:32

14 Lev. 13:46; Num. 5:2, 3; Heb. 12:9

15 Deut. 24:9; 2Chr. 26:20, 21

2 Num. 32:8; Deut. 1:22

3 Num. 32:8; Deut. 1:19; 9:23

6 Num. 13:30; 14:6, 30; 34:19; Josh. 14:6, 7, 13, 14; Judg. 1:12; 1Chr. 4:15

16 Ex. 17:9; Num. 13:8; 14:6, 30

17 Gen. 14:10; Num. 13:21; Judg. 1:9, 19

20 Deut. 31:6, 7, 23; Neh. 9:25, 35; Ezek. 34:14

21 Josh. 15:1; 19:28

22 Josh. 11:21, 22; 15:13, 14; 21:11; Judg. 1:10; Isa. 19:11; 30:4

23 Num. 32:9; Deut. 1:24, 25; Judg. 16:4

---

7 Of the tribe of Issachar, Igal the son of Joseph.

8 Of the tribe of Ephraim, Oshea the son of Nun.

9 Of the tribe of Benjamin, Palti the son of Raphu.

10 Of the tribe of Zebulun, Gaddiel the son of Sodi.

11 Of the tribe of Joseph, *namely*, of the tribe of Manasseh, Gaddi the son of Susi.

12 Of the tribe of Dan, Ammiel the son of Gemalli.

13 Of the tribe of Asher, Sethur the son of Michael.

14 Of the tribe of Naphtali, Nahbi the son of Vophsi.

15 Of the tribe of Gad, Geuel the son of Machi.

16 These *are* the names of the men which Moses sent to spy out the land. And Moses called Oshea the son of Nun Jehoshua.

17 And Moses sent them to spy out the land of Canaan, and said unto them, Get you up this *way* southward, and go up into the mountain:

18 And see the land, what it *is*; and the people that dwelleth therein, whether they *be* strong or weak, few or many;

19 And what the land *is* that they dwell in, whether it *be* good or bad; and what cities *they be* that they dwell in, whether in tents, or in strong holds;

20 And what the land *is*, whether it *be* fat or lean, whether there be wood therein, or not. And be ye of good courage, and bring of the fruit of the land. Now the time *was* the time of the firstripe grapes.

21 So they went up, and searched the land from the wilderness of Zin unto Rehob, as men come to Hamath.

22 And they ascended by the south, and came unto Hebron; where Ahiman, Sheshai, and Talmai, the children of Anak, *were*. (Now Hebron was built seven years before Zoan in Egypt.)

23 And they came unto the brook of Eshcol, and cut down from thence a branch with one cluster of grapes, and they bare it between two upon a staff; and *they brought* of the pomegranates, and of the figs.

24 The place was called the brook Eshcol, because of the cluster of grapes which the children of Israel cut down from thence.

25 And they returned from searching of the land after forty days.

26 And they went and came to Moses, and to Aaron, and to all the congregation of the children of Israel, unto the wilderness of

Paran, to Kadesh; and brought back word unto them, and unto all the congregation, and shewed them the fruit of the land.

27 And they told him, and said, We came unto the land whither thou sentest us, and surely it floweth with milk and honey; and this *is* the fruit of it.

28 Nevertheless the people *be* strong that dwell in the land, and the cities *are* walled, *and* very great: and moreover we saw the children of Anak there.

29 The Amalekites dwell in the land of the south: and the Hittites, and the Jebusites, and the Amorites, dwell in the mountains: and the Canaanites dwell by the sea, and by the coast of Jordan.

30 And Caleb stilled the people before Moses, and said, Let us go up at once, and possess it; for we are well able to overcome it.

31 But the men that went up with him said, We be not able to go up against the people; for they *are* stronger than we.

32 And they brought up an evil report of the land which they had searched unto the children of Israel, saying, The land, through which we have gone to search it, *is* a land that eateth up the inhabitants thereof; and all the people that we saw in it *are* men of a great stature.

33 And there we saw the giants, the sons of Anak, *which come* of the giants: and we were in our own sight as grasshoppers, and so we were in their sight.

CHAPTER 14
The People Rebel

1 And all the congregation lifted up their voice, and cried; and the people wept that night.

2 And all the children of Israel murmured against Moses and against Aaron: and the whole congregation said unto them, Would God that we had died in the land of Egypt! or would God we had died in this wilderness!

3 And wherefore hath the LORD brought us unto this land, to fall by the sword, that our wives and our children should be a prey? were it not better for us to return into Egypt?

4 And they said one to another, Let us make a captain, and let us return into Egypt.

5 Then Moses and Aaron fell on their faces before all the assembly of the congregation of the children of Israel.

6 And Joshua the son of Nun, and Caleb the son of Jephunneh, *which were* of them that searched the land, rent their clothes:

7 And they spake unto all the company of the children of Israel, saying, The land, which we passed through to search it, *is* an exceeding good land.

8 If the LORD delight in us, then he will bring us into this land, and give it us; a land which floweth with milk and honey.

9 Only rebel not ye against the LORD, neither fear ye the people of the land; for they *are* bread for us: their defence is departed from them, and the LORD *is* with us: fear them not.

10 But all the congregation bade stone them with stones. And the glory of the LORD appeared in the tabernacle of the congregation before all the children of Israel.

11 And the LORD said unto Moses, How long will this people provoke me? and how long will it be ere they believe me, for all the signs which I have shewed among them?

12 I will smite them with the pestilence, and disinherit them, and will make of thee a greater nation and mightier than they.

13 And Moses said unto the LORD, Then the Egyptians shall hear *it*, (for thou broughtest up this people in thy might from among them;)

14 And they will tell *it* to the inhabitants of this land: *for* they have heard that thou LORD *art* among this people, that thou LORD art seen face to face, and *that* thy cloud standeth over them, and *that* thou goest before them, by day time in a pillar of a cloud, and in a pillar of fire by night.

15 Now *if* thou shalt kill *all* this people as one man, then the nations which have heard the fame of thee will speak, saying,

16 Because the LORD was not able to bring this people into the land which he sware unto them therefore he hath slain them in the wilderness.

17 And now, I beseech thee, let the power of my Lord be great, according as thou hast spoken, saying,

18 The LORD *is* longsuffering, and of great mercy, forgiving iniquity and transgression, and by no means clearing *the guilty*, visiting

---

13:32 they brought up an evil report of the land. Less than a year after the Exodus, after the Israelites had beheld the marvelous works of God in delivering them and preserving them, they nevertheless failed at Kadesh-Barnea. For the spiritual typology of this tragic event, see Hebrews 3:7—4:11.

Cross references: 27 Ex. 3:8; 33:3; Deut. 1:25; 28 Num. 13:33; Deut. 1:28; 9:1, 2; 29 Ex. 17:8; Num. 14:43; Judg. 6:3; 1Sam. 14:48; 15:3; 30 Num. 14:6, 24; Josh. 14:7; 31 Num. 32:9; Deut. 1:28; Josh. 14:8; 32 Amos 2:9; 33 Deut. 17:42; Isa. 40:22; 2 Ex. 16:2; 17:3; Num. 16:41; Ps. 106:25; 4 Deut. 17:16; Neh. 9:17; Acts 7:39; 7 Num. 13:27; Deut. 1:25; 8 Deut. 10:15; 2Sam. 15:25, 26; 22:20; 1Kgs. 10:9; Ps. 22:8; 147:10, 11; Isa. 62:4; 10 Ex. 16:10; 17:4; 24:16, 17; 40:34; Lev. 9:23; Num. 16:19, 42; 20:6; 11 Deut. 1:32; John 12:37; Heb. 3:8, 16, 18; 14 Ex. 13:21; 15:14; 40:38; Josh. 2:9, 10; 5:1; Neh. 9:12; Ps. 78:14; 105:39; 16 Deut. 9:28; Josh. 7:9; 18 Ex. 20:5; 34:6, 7; Ps. 103:8; 145:8; Jon. 4:2

the iniquity of the fathers upon the children unto the third and fourth *generation*.

19 Pardon, I beseech thee, the iniquity of this people according unto the greatness of thy mercy, and as thou hast forgiven this people, from Egypt even until now.

God Punishes Israel

20 And the Lord said, I have pardoned according to thy word:

21 But *as* truly *as* I live, all the earth shall be filled with the glory of the Lord.

22 Because all those men which have seen my glory, and my miracles, which I did in Egypt and in the wilderness, and have tempted me now these ten times, and have not hearkened to my voice;

23 Surely they shall not see the land which I sware unto their fathers, neither shall any of them that provoked me see it:

24 But my servant Caleb, because he had another spirit with him, and hath followed me fully, him will I bring into the land whereinto he went; and his seed shall possess it.

25 (Now the Amalekites and the Canaanites dwelt in the valley.) To morrow turn you, and get you into the wilderness by the way of the Red sea.

26 And the Lord spake unto Moses and unto Aaron saying,

27 How long *shall I bear with* this evil congregation, which murmur against me? I have heard the murmurings of the children of Israel, which they murmur against me.

28 Say unto them, *As truly as* I live, saith the Lord, as ye have spoken in mine ears, so will I do to you:

29 Your carcases shall fall in this wilderness; and all that were numbered of you, according to your whole number, from twenty years old and upward, which have murmured against me,

30 Doubtless ye shall not come into the land, *concerning* which I sware to make you dwell therein, save Caleb the son of Jephunneh, and Joshua the son of Nun.

31 But your little ones, which ye said should be a prey, them will I bring in, and they shall know the land which ye have despised.

32 But *as for* you, your carcases, they shall fall in this wilderness.

33 And your children shall wander in the wilderness forty years, and bear your whoredoms, until your carcases be wasted in the wilderness.

34 After the number of the days in which ye searched the land, *even* forty days, each day for a year, shall ye bear your iniquities, *even* forty years, and ye shall know my breach of promise.

35 I the Lord have said, I will surely do it unto all this evil congregation, that are gathered together against me: in this wilderness they shall be consumed, and there they shall die.

36 And the men, which Moses sent to search the land, who returned, and made all the congregation to murmur against him, by bringing up a slander upon the land,

37 Even those men that did bring up the evil report upon the land, died by the plague before the Lord.

38 But Joshua the son of Nun, and Caleb the son of Jephunneh, *which were* of the men that went to search the land, lived *still*.

39 And Moses told these sayings unto all the children of Israel: and the people mourned greatly.

40 And they rose up early in the morning, and gat them up into the top of the mountain, saying, Lo, we *be here*, and will go up unto the place which the Lord hath promised: for we have sinned.

41 And Moses said, Wherefore now do ye transgress the commandment of the Lord? but it shall not prosper.

42 Go not up, for the Lord *is* not among you; that ye be not smitten before your enemies.

43 For the Amalekites and the Canaanites *are* there before you, and ye shall fall by the sword: because ye are turned away from the Lord, therefore the Lord will not be with you.

44 But they presumed to go up unto the hill top: nevertheless the ark of the covenant of the Lord, and Moses, departed not out of the camp.

45 Then the Amalekites came down, and the Canaanites which dwelt in that hill, and smote them, and discomfited them, *even* unto Hormah.

19 Ex. 34:9; Ps. 78:38; 106:45

20 Ps. 106:23; James 5:16; 1John 5:14-16

22 Gen. 31:7; Deut. 1:35; Ps. 95:11; 106:26; Heb. 3:17, 18

23 Num. 32:11; Ezek. 20:15

24 Deut. 1:36; Josh. 14:6, 8, 9, 14

27 Ex. 16:12, 28; Num. 14:11; Matt. 17:17

28 Num. 26:65; 32:11; Deut. 1:35; Heb. 3:17

30 Gen. 14:22; Num. 32:12; Deut. 1:36, 38

31 Ps. 106:24

32 1Cor. 10:5; Heb. 3:17

33 Num. 32:13; Deut. 2:14; Ps. 107:40; Ezek. 23:35

34 1Kgs. 8:56; Ezek. 4:6; Heb. 4:1

35 Num. 23:19; 26:65; 1Cor. 10:5

37 1Cor. 10:10; Heb. 3:17; Jude 1:5

38 Josh. 14:6, 10

40 Deut. 1:41

41 2Chr. 24:20

43 2Chr. 15:2

45 Deut. 1:44; Judg. 1:17

14:20–24 The people of God failed to trust the Lord to lead them into the land of promise. Therefore, none of those over twenty would enter Canaan, because the forty extra years in the wilderness would claim their lives. This prediction was fulfilled (Num. 26:63–65), with only Joshua and Caleb surviving to be the leaders of the conquering armies.

CHAPTER 15
Laws about Offerings

1 And the LORD spake unto Moses, saying,

2 Speak unto the children of Israel, and say unto them, When ye be come into the land of your habitations, which I give unto you,

3 And will make an offering by fire unto the LORD, a burnt offering, or a sacrifice in performing a vow, or in a freewill offering, or in your solemn feasts, to make a sweet savour unto the LORD, of the herd, or of the flock:

4 Then shall he that offereth his offering unto the LORD bring a meat offering of a tenth deal of flour mingled with the fourth *part* of an hin of oil.

5 And the fourth *part* of an hin of wine for a drink offering shalt thou prepare with the burnt offering or sacrifice, for one lamb.

6 Or for a ram, thou shalt prepare *for* a meat offering two tenth deals of flour mingled with the third *part* of an hin of oil.

7 And for a drink offering thou shalt offer the third *part* of an hin of wine, *for* a sweet savour unto the LORD.

8 And when thou preparest a bullock *for* a burnt offering, or *for* a sacrifice in performing a vow, or peace offerings unto the LORD:

9 Then shall he bring with a bullock a meat offering of three tenth deals of flour mingled with half an hin of oil.

10 And thou shalt bring for a drink offering half an hin of wine, *for* an offering made by fire, of a sweet savour unto the LORD.

11 Thus shall it be done for one bullock, or for one ram, or for a lamb, or a kid.

12 According to the number that ye shall prepare, so shall ye do to every one according to their number.

13 All that are born of the country shall do these things after this manner, in offering an offering made by fire, of a sweet savour unto the LORD.

14 And if a stranger sojourn with you, or whosoever *be* among you in your generations, and will offer an offering made by fire, of a sweet savour unto the LORD; as ye do, so he shall do.

15 One ordinance *shall be both* for you of the congregation, and also for the stranger that sojourneth *with you*, an ordinance for ever in your generations: as ye *are*, so shall the stranger be before the LORD.

16 One law and one manner shall be for you, and for the stranger that sojourneth with you.

17 And the LORD spake unto Moses, saying,

18 Speak unto the children of Israel, and say unto them, When ye come into the land whither I bring you,

19 Then it shall be, that, when ye eat of the bread of the land, ye shall offer up an heave offering unto the LORD.

20 Ye shall offer up a cake of the first of your dough *for* an heave offering: as *ye do* the heave offering of the threshingfloor, so shall ye heave it.

21 Of the first of your dough ye shall give unto the LORD an heave offering in your generations.

22 And if ye have erred, and not observed all these commandments, which the LORD hath spoken unto Moses,

23 *Even* all that the LORD hath commanded you by the hand of Moses, from the day that the LORD commanded *Moses*, and henceforward among your generations;

24 Then it shall be, if *ought* be committed by ignorance without the knowledge of the congregation, that all the congregation shall offer one young bullock for a burnt offering, for a sweet savour unto the LORD, with his meat offering, and his drink offering, according to the manner, and one kid of the goats for a sin offering.

25 And the priest shall make an atonement for all the congregation of the children of Israel, and it shall be forgiven them; for it *is* ignorance: and they shall bring their offering, a sacrifice made by fire unto the LORD, and their sin offering before the LORD, for their ignorance:

26 And it shall be forgiven all the congregation of the children of Israel, and the stranger that sojourneth among them; seeing all the people *were* in ignorance.

27 And if any soul sin through ignorance, then he shall bring a she goat of the first year for a sin offering.

28 And the priest shall make an atonement for the soul that sinneth ignorantly, when he sinneth by ignorance before the LORD, to make an atonement for him; and it shall be forgiven him.

29 Ye shall have one law for him that sinneth through ignorance, *both for* him that is born among the children of Israel, and for the stranger that sojourneth among them.

30 But the soul that doeth *ought* presumptuously, *whether he be* born in the land, or a stranger, the same reproacheth the LORD; and that soul shall be cut off from among his people.

31 Because he hath despised the word of

Cross references

2 Lev. 23:10; Num. 15:18; Deut. 7:1

3 Gen. 8:21; Ex. 29:18; Lev. 1:2, 5; 7:16; 22:18, 21; 23:8, 12, 36; Num. 28:19, 27; 29:2, 8, 13; Deut. 16:10

4 Ex. 20:40; Lev. 2:1; 6:14; 14:10; 23:13; Num. 28:5

5 Num. 28:7, 14

6 Num. 28:12, 14

8 Lev. 7:11

9 Num. 28:12, 14

15 Ex. 12:49; Num. 9:14; 15:29

18 Num. 15:2; Deut. 26:1

19 Josh. 5:11, 12

20 Lev. 2:14; 23:10, 16; Deut. 26:2, 10; Prov. 3:9, 10

22 Lev. 4:2

24 Lev. 4:13, 23; Num. 15:8-10; 28:15; Ezra 6:17; 8:35

25 Lev. 4:20

27 Lev. 4:27, 28

28 Lev. 4:35

29 Num. 15:15

30 Deut. 17:12; Ps. 19:13; Heb. 10:26; 2Pet. 2:10

31 Lev. 5:1; 2Sam. 12:9; Prov. 13:13; Ezek. 18:20

the LORD, and hath broken his commandment, that soul shall utterly be cut off; his iniquity *shall be* upon him.

A Sabbath Breaker Is Punished

32 And while the children of Israel were in the wilderness, they found a man that gathered sticks upon the sabbath day.
33 And they that found him gathering sticks brought him unto Moses and Aaron, and unto all the congregation.
34 And they put him in ward, because it was not declared what should be done to him.
35 And the LORD said unto Moses, The man shall be surely put to death: all the congregation shall stone him with stones without the camp.
36 And all the congregation brought him without the camp, and stoned him with stones, and he died; as the LORD commanded Moses.

Fringes of Their Garments

37 And the LORD spake unto Moses, saying,
38 Speak unto the children of Israel, and bid them that they make them fringes in the borders of their garments throughout their generations, and that they put upon the fringe of the borders a ribband of blue:
39 And it shall be unto you for a fringe, that ye may look upon it, and remember all the commandments of the LORD, and do them; and that ye seek not after your own heart and your own eyes, after which ye use to go a whoring:
40 That ye may remember, and do all my commandments, and be holy unto your God.
41 I *am* the LORD your God, which brought you out of the land of Egypt, to be your God: I *am* the LORD your God.

CHAPTER 16
Korah's Rebellion

1 Now Korah, the son of Izhar, the son of Kohath, the son of Levi, and Dathan and Abiram, the sons of Eliab, and On, the son of Peleth, sons of Reuben, took *men*:
2 And they rose up before Moses, with certain of the children of Israel, two hundred and fifty princes of the assembly, famous in the congregation, men of renown:
3 And they gathered themselves together against Moses and against Aaron, and said unto them, *Ye take* too much upon you, seeing all the congregation *are* holy, every one of them, and the LORD *is* among them: wherefore then lift ye up yourselves above the congregation of the LORD?
4 And when Moses heard *it*, he fell upon his face:
5 And he spake unto Korah and unto all his company, saying, Even to morrow the LORD will shew who *are* his, and *who is* holy; and will cause *him* to come near unto him: even *him* whom he hath chosen will he cause to come near unto him.
6 This do; Take you censers, Korah, and all his company;
7 And put fire therein, and put incense in them before the LORD to morrow: and it shall be *that* the man whom the LORD doth choose, he *shall be* holy: *ye take* too much upon you, ye sons of Levi.
8 And Moses said unto Korah, Hear, I pray you, ye sons of Levi:
9 *Seemeth it but* a small thing unto you, that the God of Israel hath separated you from the congregation of Israel, to bring you near to himself to do the service of the tabernacle of the LORD, and to stand before the congregation to minister unto them?
10 And he hath brought thee near *to him*, and all thy brethren the sons of Levi with thee: and seek ye the priesthood also?
11 For which cause *both* thou and all thy company *are* gathered together against the LORD: and what *is* Aaron, that ye murmur against him?
12 And Moses sent to call Dathan and Abiram, the sons of Eliab: which said, We will not come up:
13 *Is it* a small thing that thou hast brought us up out of a land that floweth with milk and honey, to kill us in the wilderness, except thou make thyself altogether a prince over us?
14 Moreover thou hast not brought us into a land that floweth with milk and honey, or

Cross references

32 Ex. 31:14, 15; 35:2, 3
34 Lev. 24:12
35 Ex. 31:14, 15; Lev. 24:14; 1Kgs. 21:13; Acts 7:58
38 Deut. 22:12; Matt. 23:5
39 Deut. 29:19; Job 31:7; Ps. 73:27; 106:39; Jer. 9:14; Ezek. 6:9; James 4:4
40 Lev. 11:44, 45; Rom. 12:1; Col. 1:22; 1Pet. 1:15, 16

1 Ex. 6:21; Num. 26:9; 27:3; Jude 1:11
2 Num. 26:9
3 Ex. 19:6; 29:45; Num. 14:14; 35:34; Ps. 106:16
4 Num. 14:5; 20:6
5 Ex. 28:1; Lev. 10:3; 21:6-8, 12, 15, 17, 18; Num. 3:10; 16:3; 17:5; 1Sam. 2:28; Ps. 105:26; Ezek. 40:46; 44:15, 16
9 Num. 3:41, 45; 8:14; Deut. 10:8; 1Sam. 18:23; Isa. 7:13
11 Ex. 16:8; 1Cor. 3:5
13 Ex. 2:14; Num. 16:9; Acts 7:27, 35
14 Ex. 3:8; Lev. 20:24

16:1 Korah, a descendent of Levi, led an attempted revolt against Moses and Aaron. Korah's rebellion was an arrogant rejection of the divinely appointed leaders, an intrusion into the priestly office, and an ill-fated critical public slander against Moses, whom they had accused of evil motives and failure (vv. 13–14). In response to Moses' prayer, the earth opened and swallowed up Korah and his cohorts Dathan, Abiram (all three Reubenites) and 250 princes of the congregation. The Israelites reacted so rebelliously to this situation that they then accused Moses and Aaron of killing the people of the Lord (v. 41).

given us inheritance of fields and vineyards: wilt thou put out the eyes of these men? we will not come up.

15 And Moses was very wroth, and said unto the LORD, Respect not thou their offering: I have not taken one ass from them, neither have I hurt one of them.

16 And Moses said unto Korah, Be thou and all thy company before the LORD, thou, and they, and Aaron, to morrow:

17 And take every man his censer, and put incense in them, and bring ye before the LORD every man his censer, two hundred and fifty censers; thou also, and Aaron, each *of you* his censer.

18 And they took every man his censer, and put fire in them, and laid incense thereon, and stood in the door of the tabernacle of the congregation with Moses and Aaron.

19 And Korah gathered all the congregation against them unto the door of the tabernacle of the congregation: and the glory of the LORD appeared unto all the congregation.

20 And the LORD spake unto Moses and unto Aaron, saying,

21 Separate yourselves from among this congregation, that I may consume them in a moment.

22 And they fell upon their faces, and said, O God, the God of the spirits of all flesh, shall one man sin, and wilt thou be wroth with all the congregation?

23 And the LORD spake unto Moses, saying,

24 Speak unto the congregation, saying, Get you up from about the tabernacle of Korah, Dathan, and Abiram.

25 And Moses rose up and went unto Dathan and Abiram; and the elders of Israel followed him.

26 And he spake unto the congregation, saying, Depart, I pray you, from the tents of these wicked men, and touch nothing of theirs, lest ye be consumed in all their sins.

27 So they gat up from the tabernacle of Korah, Dathan, and Abiram, on every side: and Dathan and Abiram came out, and stood in the door of their tents, and their wives, and their sons, and their little children.

28 And Moses said, Hereby ye shall know that the LORD hath sent me to do all these works; for *I have* not *done them* of mine own mind.

29 If these men die the common death of all

men, or if they be visited after the visitation of all men; *then* the LORD hath not sent me.

30 But if the LORD make a new thing, and the earth open her mouth, and swallow them up, with all that *appertain* unto them, and they go down quick into the pit; then ye shall understand that these men have provoked the LORD.

31 And it came to pass, as he had made an end of speaking all these words, that the ground clave asunder that *was* under them:

32 And the earth opened her mouth, and swallowed them up, and their houses, and all the men that *appertained* unto Korah, and all *their* goods.

33 They, and all that *appertained* to them, went down alive into the pit, and the earth closed upon them: and they perished from among the congregation.

34 And all Israel that *were* round about them fled at the cry of them: for they said, Lest the earth swallow us up *also*.

35 And there came out a fire from the LORD, and consumed the two hundred and fifty men that offered incense.

36 And the LORD spake unto Moses, saying,

37 Speak unto Eleazar the son of Aaron the priest, that he take up the censers out of the burning, and scatter thou the fire yonder; for they are hallowed.

38 The censers of these sinners against their own souls, let them make them broad plates *for* a covering of the altar: for they offered them before the LORD, therefore they are hallowed: and they shall be a sign unto the children of Israel.

39 And Eleazar the priest took the brasen censers, wherewith they that were burnt had offered; and they were made broad *plates for* a covering of the altar:

40 *To be* a memorial unto the children of Israel, that no stranger, which *is* not of the seed of Aaron, come near to offer incense before the LORD; that he be not as Korah, and as his company: as the LORD said to him by the hand of Moses.

Others Complain and Die

41 But on the morrow all the congregation of the children of Israel murmured against Moses and against Aaron, saying, Ye have killed the people of the LORD.

42 And it came to pass, when the congregation was gathered against Moses and

Cross references

15 Gen. 4:4, 5; 1Sam. 12:3; Acts 20:33; 2Cor. 7:2

16 1Sam. 12:3, 7

19 Ex. 16:7, 10; Lev. 9:6, 23; Num. 14:10; 16:42

21 Gen. 19:17, 22; Ex. 32:10; 33:5; Jer. 51:6; Acts 2:40; Rev. 18:4

22 Num. 14:5; 16:45; 27:16; Job 12:10; Eccl. 12:7; Isa. 57:16; Zech. 12:1; Heb. 12:9

26 Gen. 19:12, 14; Isa. 52:11; 2Cor. 6:17; Rev. 18:4

28 Ex. 3:12; Deut. 18:22; Zech. 2:9, 11; 4:9; John 5:30, 36; 6:38

29 Ex. 20:5; 32:34; Job 35:15; Isa. 10:3; Jer. 5:9

30 Job 31:3; Isa. 28:21

31 Deut. 11:6; Ps. 106:17

32 Num. 16:17; 26:11; 1Chr. 6:22, 37

35 Lev. 10:2; Num. 11:1; 16:17; Ps. 106:18

37 Lev. 27:28

38 ; Prov. 20:2; Ezek. 14:8; Hab. 2:10

40 Num. 3:10; 2Chr. 26:18

42 Ex. 40:34; Num. 16:19; 20:6

16:42 the glory of the LORD appeared. God miraculously intervened and responded to Moses' prayer of intercession for the people, but nevertheless sent a plague into their midst that resulted in 14,700 deaths, besides the original

against Aaron, that they looked toward the tabernacle of the congregation: and, behold, the cloud covered it, and the glory of the LORD appeared.

43 And Moses and Aaron came before the tabernacle of the congregation.

44 And the LORD spake unto Moses, saying,

45 Get you up from among this congregation, that I may consume them as in a moment. And they fell upon their faces.

46 And Moses said unto Aaron, Take a censer, and put fire therein from off the altar, and put on incense, and go quickly unto the congregation, and make an atonement for them: for there is wrath gone out from the LORD; the plague is begun.

47 And Aaron took as Moses commanded, and ran into the midst of the congregation; and, behold, the plague was begun among the people: and he put on incense, and made an atonement for the people.

48 And he stood between the dead and the living; and the plague was stayed.

49 Now they that died in the plague were fourteen thousand and seven hundred, beside them that died about the matter of Korah.

50 And Aaron returned unto Moses unto the door of the tabernacle of the congregation: and the plague was stayed.

CHAPTER 17
Aaron's Rod Yields Almonds

1 And the LORD spake unto Moses, saying,

2 Speak unto the children of Israel, and take of every one of them a rod according to the house of *their* fathers, of all their princes according to the house of their fathers twelve rods: write thou every man's name upon his rod.

3 And thou shalt write Aaron's name upon the rod of Levi: for one rod *shall be* for the head of the house of their fathers.

4 And thou shalt lay them up in the tabernacle of the congregation before the testimony, where I will meet with you.

5 And it shall come to pass, *that* the man's rod, whom I shall choose, shall blossom: and I will make to cease from me the murmurings of the children of Israel, whereby they murmur against you.

6 And Moses spake unto the children of Israel, and every one of their princes gave him a rod apiece, for each prince one, according to their fathers' houses, *even* twelve rods: and the rod of Aaron *was* among their rods.

7 And Moses laid up the rods before the LORD in the tabernacle of witness.

8 And it came to pass, that on the morrow Moses went into the tabernacle of witness; and, behold, the rod of Aaron for the house of Levi was budded, and brought forth buds, and bloomed blossoms, and yielded almonds.

9 And Moses brought out all the rods from before the LORD unto all the children of Israel: and they looked, and took every man his rod.

10 And the LORD said unto Moses, Bring Aaron's rod again before the testimony, to be kept for a token against the rebels; and thou shalt quite take away their murmurings from me, that they die not.

11 And Moses did *so*: as the LORD commanded him, so did he.

12 And the children of Israel spake unto Moses, saying, Behold, we die, we perish, we all perish.

13 Whosoever cometh any thing near unto the tabernacle of the LORD shall die: shall we be consumed with dying?

CHAPTER 18
The Priests' and Levites' Duties

1 And the LORD said unto Aaron, Thou and thy sons and thy father's house with thee shall bear the iniquity of the sanctuary: and thou and thy sons with thee shall bear the iniquity of your priesthood.

2 And thy brethren also of the tribe of Levi, the tribe of thy father, bring thou with thee, that they may be joined unto thee, and minister unto thee: but thou and thy sons with thee *shall minister* before the tabernacle of witness.

3 And they shall keep thy charge, and the charge of all the tabernacle: only they shall not come nigh the vessels of the sanctuary and the altar, that neither they, nor ye also, die.

4 And they shall be joined unto thee, and keep the charge of the tabernacle of the con-

---

45 Num. 16:21, 22, 24; 20:6

46 Lev. 10:6; Num. 1:53; 8:19; 11:33; 18:5; 1Chr. 27:24; Ps. 106:29

4 Ex. 25:22; 29:42, 43; 30:36

5 Num. 16:5, 11

7 Ex. 38:21; Num. 18:2; Acts 7:44

10 Num. 16:38; 17:5; Heb. 9:4

13 Num. 1:51, 53; 18:4, 7

1 Ex. 28:38; Num. 17:13

2 Gen. 29:34; Num. 3:6, 7, 10

3 Num. 3:25, 31, 36; 4:15; 16:40

4 Num. 3:10

---

crowd with Korah. In all ages including the present dispensation, there have been religious leaders who followed in the steps of Korah (Jude 1:11), rejecting true biblical leadership and bringing upon themselves and their followers much suffering and sometimes death.

17:8 the rod of Aaron. The restoration of life and fruitfulness to Aaron's rod not only solidified his leadership over the priesthood, but also suggests the resurrection of Christ, showing He is the LIFE. See the note on Hebrews 9:4.

gregation, for all the service of the tabernacle: and a stranger shall not come nigh unto you.

5 And ye shall keep the charge of the sanctuary, and the charge of the altar: that there be no wrath any more upon the children of Israel.

6 And I, behold, I have taken your brethren the Levites from among the children of Israel: to you *they are* given *as* a gift for the LORD, to do the service of the tabernacle of the congregation.

7 Therefore thou and thy sons with thee shall keep your priest's office for every thing of the altar, and within the vail; and ye shall serve: I have given your priest's office *unto you* as a service of gift: and the stranger that cometh nigh shall be put to death.

The Priests' and Levites' Shares

8 And the LORD spake unto Aaron, Behold, I also have given thee the charge of mine heave offerings of all the hallowed things of the children of Israel; unto thee have I given them by reason of the anointing, and to thy sons, by an ordinance for ever.

9 This shall be thine of the most holy things, *reserved* from the fire: every oblation of theirs, every meat offering of theirs, and every sin offering of theirs, and every trespass offering of theirs, which they shall render unto me, *shall be* most holy for thee and for thy sons.

10 In the most holy *place* shalt thou eat it; every male shall eat it: it shall be holy unto thee.

11 And this *is* thine; the heave offering of their gift, with all the wave offerings of the children of Israel: I have given them unto thee, and to thy sons and to thy daughters with thee, by a statute for ever: every one that is clean in thy house shall eat of it.

12 All the best of the oil, and all the best of the wine, and of the wheat, the firstfruits of them which they shall offer unto the LORD, them have I given thee.

13 *And* whatsoever is first ripe in the land, which they shall bring unto the LORD, shall be thine; every one that is clean in thine house shall eat *of* it.

14 Every thing devoted in Israel shall be thine.

15 Every thing that openeth the matrix in all flesh, which they bring unto the LORD, *whether it be* of men or beasts, shall be thine: nevertheless the firstborn of man shalt thou surely redeem, and the firstling of unclean beasts shalt thou redeem.

16 And those that are to be redeemed from a month old shalt thou redeem, according to thine estimation, for the money of five shekels, after the shekel of the sanctuary, which *is* twenty gerahs.

17 But the firstling of a cow, or the firstling of a sheep, or the firstling of a goat, thou shalt not redeem; they *are* holy: thou shalt sprinkle their blood upon the altar, and shalt burn their fat *for* an offering made by fire, for a sweet savour unto the LORD.

18 And the flesh of them shall be thine, as the wave breast and as the right shoulder are thine.

19 All the heave offerings of the holy things, which the children of Israel offer unto the LORD, have I given thee, and thy sons and thy daughters with thee, by a statute for ever: it *is* a covenant of salt for ever before the LORD unto thee and to thy seed with thee.

20 And the LORD spake unto Aaron, Thou shalt have no inheritance in their land, neither shalt thou have any part among them: I *am* thy part and thine inheritance among the children of Israel.

21 And, behold, I have given the children of Levi all the tenth in Israel for an inheritance, for their service which they serve, *even* the service of the tabernacle of the congregation.

22 Neither must the children of Israel henceforth come nigh the tabernacle of the congregation, lest they bear sin, and die.

23 But the Levites shall do the service of the tabernacle of the congregation, and they shall bear their iniquity: *it shall be* a statute for ever throughout your generations, that among the children of Israel they have no inheritance.

24 But the tithes of the children of Israel, which they offer *as* an heave offering unto the LORD, I have given to the Levites to inherit: therefore I have said unto them, Among the children of Israel they shall have no inheritance.

25 And the LORD spake unto Moses, saying,

26 Thus speak unto the Levites, and say unto them, When ye take of the children of Israel the tithes which I have given you from them for your inheritance, then ye shall offer up an heave offering of it for the LORD, *even* a tenth *part* of the tithe.

27 And *this* your heave offering shall be reckoned unto you, as though *it were* the corn of the threshingfloor, and as the fulness of the winepress.

28 Thus ye also shall offer an heave offering

Cross references

5 Ex. 27:21; 30:7; Lev. 24:3; Num. 8:2; 16:46

7 Num. 3:10; Heb. 9:3, 6

8 Ex. 29:29; 40:13, 15; Lev. 6:16, 18, 26; 7:6, 32; Num. 5:9

9 Lev. 2:2, 3; 4:22, 27; 5:1; 6:25, 26; 7:7; 10:12, 13; 14:13

10 Lev. 6:16, 18, 26, 29; 7:6

11 Ex. 29:27, 28; Lev. 7:30, 34; 10:14; 22:2, 3, 11-13

12 Num. 18:29; Deut. 18:4; Neh. 10:35, 36

13 Ex. 22:29; 23:19; 34:26; Lev. 2:14; Num. 15:19; Deut. 26:2

15 Ex. 13:2, 13; 22:29; 34:20; Lev. 27:26; Num. 3:13

16 Ex. 30:13; Num. 3:47; Ezek. 45:12

17 Lev. 3:2, 5; Deut. 15:19

18 Ex. 29:26, 28; Lev. 7:31, 32, 34

19 Lev. 2:13; 2Chr. 13:5

20 Deut. 10:9; 12:12; 14:27, 29; 18:1, 2; Josh. 13:14, 33; 14:3; 18:7; Ezek. 44:28

21 Lev. 27:30, 32; Num. 3:7, 8; Neh. 10:37; 12:44; Heb. 7:5, 8, 9

22 Lev. 22:9; Num. 1:51

23 Num. 3:7

24 Deut. 10:9; 14:27, 29; 18:1

26 Neh. 10:38

unto the LORD of all your tithes, which ye receive of the children of Israel; and ye shall give thereof the LORD's heave offering to Aaron the priest.

29 Out of all your gifts ye shall offer every heave offering of the LORD, of all the best thereof, *even* the hallowed part thereof out of it.

30 Therefore thou shalt say unto them, When ye have heaved the best thereof from it, then it shall be counted unto the Levites as the increase of the threshingfloor, and as the increase of the winepress.

31 And ye shall eat it in every place, ye and your households: for it *is* your reward for your service in the tabernacle of the congregation.

32 And ye shall bear no sin by reason of it, when ye have heaved from it the best of it: neither shall ye pollute the holy things of the children of Israel, lest ye die.

CHAPTER 19
Purifying an Unclean Person

1 And the LORD spake unto Moses and unto Aaron, saying,

2 This *is* the ordinance of the law which the LORD hath commanded, saying, Speak unto the children of Israel, that they bring thee a red heifer without spot, wherein *is* no blemish, *and* upon which never came yoke:

3 And ye shall give her unto Eleazar the priest, that he may bring her forth without the camp, and *one* shall slay her before his face:

4 And Eleazar the priest shall take of her blood with his finger, and sprinkle of her blood directly before the tabernacle of the congregation seven times:

5 And *one* shall burn the heifer in his sight; her skin, and her flesh, and her blood, with her dung, shall he burn:

6 And the priest shall take cedar wood, and hyssop, and scarlet, and cast *it* into the midst of the burning of the heifer.

7 Then the priest shall wash his clothes, and he shall bathe his flesh in water, and af-

terward he shall come into the camp, and the priest shall be unclean until the even.

8 And he that burneth her shall wash his clothes in water, and bathe his flesh in water, and shall be unclean until the even.

9 And a man *that is* clean shall gather up the ashes of the heifer, and lay *them* up without the camp in a clean place, and it shall be kept for the congregation of the children of Israel for a water of separation: it *is* a purification for sin.

10 And he that gathereth the ashes of the heifer shall wash his clothes, and be unclean until the even: and it shall be unto the children of Israel, and unto the stranger that sojourneth among them, for a statute for ever.

11 He that toucheth the dead body of any man shall be unclean seven days.

12 He shall purify himself with it on the third day, and on the seventh day he shall be clean: but if he purify not himself the third day, then the seventh day he shall not be clean.

13 Whosoever toucheth the dead body of any man that is dead, and purifieth not himself, defileth the tabernacle of the LORD; and that soul shall be cut off from Israel: because the water of separation was not sprinkled upon him, he shall be unclean; his uncleanness *is* yet upon him.

14 This *is* the law, when a man dieth in a tent: all that come into the tent, and all that *is* in the tent, shall be unclean seven days.

15 And every open vessel, which hath no covering bound upon it, *is* unclean.

16 And whosoever toucheth one that is slain with a sword in the open fields, or a dead body, or a bone of a man, or a grave, shall be unclean seven days.

17 And for an unclean *person* they shall take of the ashes of the burnt heifer of purification for sin, and running water shall be put thereto in a vessel:

18 And a clean person shall take hyssop, and dip *it* in the water, and sprinkle *it* upon the tent, and upon all the vessels, and upon

29 Num. 18:12

30 Num. 18:27

31 Matt. 10:10; Luke 10:7; 1Cor. 9:13; 1Tim. 5:18

32 Lev. 19:8; 22:2, 15, 16

2 Deut. 21:3; 1Sam. 6:7

3 Lev. 4:12, 21; 16:27; Heb. 13:11

4 Lev. 4:6; 16:14, 19; Heb. 9:13

5 Ex. 29:14; Lev. 4:11, 12

6 Lev. 14:4, 6, 49

7 Lev. 11:25; 15:5

9 Num. 19:13, 20, 21; 31:23; Heb. 9:13

11 Lev. 21:1; Num. 5:2; 9:6, 10; 19:16; 31:19; Lam. 4:14; Hag. 2:13

12 Num. 31:19

13 Lev. 7:20; 15:31; 22:3; Num. 8:7; 19:9

15 Lev. 11:32; Num. 31:20

16 Num. 19:11

17 Gen. 26:19; Num. 19:9

18 Ps. 51:7

19:2 a red heifer without spot. This special animal was not used for a regular offering at the Tabernacle or temple, but was slain outside the camp. Seven times the priest sprinkled a small portion of the blood toward the Tabernacle. Then the entire cow was burned to ash. Mixed with water, the ashes were used to purify persons who had come in contact with a dead body. Typically, the red heifer depicts the sacrifice of Jesus as the means of cleansing the defilement from the believer who lives in a polluted world. The ceremony of the red heifer has not been observed since the temple was destroyed in A.D. 70. Many orthodox Jews believe that a perfect red heifer without blemish must be found and ceremonially burned to ash. Then the blood must be sprinkled toward the rebuilt temple and the ashes used to cleanse and purify the priesthood, those who would conduct service in the temple. Only by this process can Israel prepare to worship in a properly dedicated temple.

the persons that were there, and upon him that touched a bone, or one slain, or one dead, or a grave:

19 And the clean *person* shall sprinkle upon the unclean on the third day, and on the seventh day: and on the seventh day he shall purify himself, and wash his clothes, and bathe himself in water, and shall be clean at even.

20 But the man that shall be unclean, and shall not purify himself, that soul shall be cut off from among the congregation, because he hath defiled the sanctuary of the LORD: the water of separation hath not been sprinkled upon him; he *is* unclean.

21 And it shall be a perpetual statute unto them, that he that sprinkleth the water of separation shall wash his clothes; and he that toucheth the water of separation shall be unclean until even.

22 And whatsoever the unclean *person* toucheth shall be unclean; and the soul that toucheth *it* shall be unclean until even.

CHAPTER 20
Moses and Aaron Sin

1 Then came the children of Israel, *even* the whole congregation, into the desert of Zin in the first month: and the people abode in Kadesh; and Miriam died there, and was buried there.

2 And there was no water for the congregation: and they gathered themselves together against Moses and against Aaron.

3 And the people chode with Moses, and spake, saying, Would God that we had died when our brethren died before the LORD!

4 And why have ye brought up the congregation of the Lord into this wilderness, that we and our cattle should die there?

5 And wherefore have ye made us to come up out of Egypt, to bring us in unto this evil place? it *is* no place of seed, or of figs, or of vines, or of pomegranates; neither *is* there any water to drink.

6 And Moses and Aaron went from the presence of the assembly unto the door of the tabernacle of the congregation, and they fell upon their faces: and the glory of the LORD appeared unto them.

7 And the LORD spake unto Moses, saying,

8 Take the rod, and gather thou the assembly together, thou, and Aaron thy brother, and speak ye unto the rock before their eyes; and it shall give forth his water, and thou shalt bring forth to them water out of the rock: so thou shalt give the congregation and their beasts drink.

9 And Moses took the rod from before the LORD, as he commanded him.

10 And Moses and Aaron gathered the congregation together before the rock, and he said unto them, Hear now, ye rebels; must we fetch you water out of this rock?

11 And Moses lifted up his hand, and with his rod he smote the rock twice: and the water came out abundantly, and the congregation drank, and their beasts *also*.

12 And the LORD spake unto Moses and Aaron, Because ye believed me not, to sanctify me in the eyes of the children of Israel, therefore ye shall not bring this congregation into the land which I have given them.

13 This *is* the water of Meribah; because the children of Israel strove with the LORD, and he was sanctified in them.

Edom Refuses Passage to Israel

14 And Moses sent messengers from Kadesh unto the king of Edom, Thus saith thy brother Israel, Thou knowest all the travail that hath befallen us:

15 How our fathers went down into Egypt, and we have dwelt in Egypt a long time; and the Egyptians vexed us, and our fathers:

16 And when we cried unto the LORD, he heard our voice, and sent an angel, and hath brought us forth out of Egypt: and, behold, we *are* in Kadesh, a city in the uttermost of thy border:

17 Let us pass, I pray thee, through thy country: we will not pass through the fields, or through the vineyards, neither will we drink *of* the water of the wells: we will go by the king's *high* way, we will not turn to the right hand nor to the left, until we have passed thy borders.

18 And Edom said unto him, Thou shalt not pass by me, lest I come out against thee with the sword.

19 And the children of Israel said unto him, We will go by the high way: and if I and my cattle drink of thy water, then I will pay for it: I will only, without *doing* any thing *else*, go through on my feet.

20 And he said, Thou shalt not go through. And Edom came out against him with much people, and with a strong hand.

21 Thus Edom refused to give Israel passage through his border: wherefore Israel turned away from him.

Aaron's Death

22 And the children of Israel, *even* the whole congregation, journeyed from Kadesh, and came unto mount Hor.

---

19 Lev. 14:9
22 Lev. 15:5; Hag. 2:13
1 Ex. 15:20; Num. 26:59; 33:36
2 Ex. 17:1; Num. 16:19, 42
3 Ex. 17:2; Num. 11:1, 33; 14:2, 37; 16:32, 35, 49
4 Ex. 17:3
6 Num. 14:5, 10; 16:4, 22, 45
8 Ex. 17:5; Neh. 9:15; Ps. 78:15, 16; 105:41; 114:8; Isa. 43:20; 48:21
9 Num. 17:10
10 Ps. 106:33
11 Ex. 17:6; Deut. 8:15; 1 Cor. 10:4
12 Lev. 10:3; Num. 27:14; Deut. 1:37; 3:26; 32:51; Ezek. 20:41; 36:23; 38:16; 1 Pet. 3:15
13 Deut. 33:8; Ps. 95:8; 106:32-43
14 Ex. 18:8; Deut. 2:4-9; 23:7; Judg. 11:16, 17; Obad. 1:10, 12
15 Gen. 46:6; Ex. 1:11; 12:40; Deut. 26:6; Acts 7:15, 19
16 Ex. 2:23; 3:2, 7; 3:2; 14:19; 23:20; 33:2
17 Num. 21:22; Deut. 2:27
19 Deut. 2:6, 28
20 Judg. 11:17
21 Deut. 2:4, 5, 8, 27, 29; Judg. 11:18
22 Num. 21:4; 33:37

23 And the LORD spake unto Moses and Aaron in mount Hor, by the coast of the land of Edom, saying,

24 Aaron shall be gathered unto his people: for he shall not enter into the land which I have given unto the children of Israel, because ye rebelled against my word at the water of Meribah.

25 Take Aaron and Eleazar his son, and bring them up unto mount Hor:

26 And strip Aaron of his garments, and put them upon Eleazar his son: and Aaron shall be gathered *unto his people*, and shall die there.

27 And Moses did as the LORD commanded: and they went up into mount Hor in the sight of all the congregation.

28 And Moses stripped Aaron of his garments, and put them upon Eleazar his son; and Aaron died there in the top of the mount: and Moses and Eleazar came down from the mount.

29 And when all the congregation saw that Aaron was dead, they mourned for Aaron thirty days, *even* all the house of Israel.

CHAPTER 21
Victory over Canaanites

1 And *when* king Arad the Canaanite, which dwelt in the south, heard tell that Israel came by the way of the spies; then he fought against Israel, and took *some* of them prisoners.

2 And Israel vowed a vow unto the LORD, and said, If thou wilt indeed deliver this people into my hand, then I will utterly destroy their cities.

3 And the LORD hearkened to the voice of Israel, and delivered up the Canaanites; and they utterly destroyed them and their cities: and he called the name of the place Hormah.

The Bronze Snake

4 And they journeyed from mount Hor by the way of the Red sea, to compass the land of Edom: and the soul of the people was much discouraged because of the way.

5 And the people spake against God, and against Moses, Wherefore have ye brought us up out of Egypt to die in the wilderness? for *there is* no bread, neither *is there any* water; and our soul loatheth this light bread.

6 And the LORD sent fiery serpents among the people, and they bit the people; and much people of Israel died.

7 Therefore the people came to Moses, and said, We have sinned, for we have spoken against the LORD, and against thee; pray unto the LORD, that he take away the serpents from us. And Moses prayed for the people.

8 And the LORD said unto Moses, Make thee a fiery serpent, and set it upon a pole: and it shall come to pass, that every one that is bitten, when he looketh upon it, shall live.

9 And Moses made a serpent of brass, and put it upon a pole, and it came to pass, that if a serpent had bitten any man, when he beheld the serpent of brass, he lived.

Israel Moves to East of the Jordan

10 And the children of Israel set forward, and pitched in Oboth.

11 And they journeyed from Oboth, and pitched at Ije-abarim, in the wilderness which *is* before Moab, toward the sunrising.

12 From thence they removed, and pitched in the valley of Zared.

13 From thence they removed, and pitched on the other side of Arnon, which *is* in the wilderness that cometh out of the coasts of the Amorites: for Arnon *is* the border of Moab, between Moab and the Amorites.

14 Wherefore it is said in the book of the wars of the LORD, What he did in the Red sea, and in the brooks of Arnon,

15 And at the stream of the brooks that goeth down to the dwelling of Ar, and lieth upon the border of Moab.

16 And from thence *they went* to Beer: that *is* the well whereof the LORD spake unto Moses, Gather the people together, and I will give them water.

17 Then Israel sang this song, Spring up, O well; sing ye unto it:

18 The princes digged the well, the nobles of the people digged it, by *the direction of* the

Cross references:
24 Gen. 25:8; Num. 27:13; 31:2; Deut. 32:50
25 Num. 33:38; Deut. 32:50
28 Ex. 29:29, 30; Num. 33:38; Deut. 10:6; 32:50
29 Deut. 34:8
1 Num. 13:21; 33:40; Judg. 1:16
2 Gen. 28:20; Lev. 27:28; Judg. 11:30
4 Ex. 6:9; Num. 20:22; 33:41; Judg. 11:18
5 Ex. 16:3; 17:3; Num. 11:6; Ps. 78:19
6 Deut. 8:15; 1Cor. 10:9
7 Ex. 8:8, 28; Num. 21:5; 1Sam. 12:19; 1Kgs. 13:6; Ps. 78:34; Acts 8:24
9 2Kgs. 18:4; John 3:14, 15
10 Num. 33:43
11 Num. 33:44
12 Deut. 2:13
13 Num. 22:36; Judg. 11:18
15 Deut. 2:18, 29
16 Judg. 9:21
17 Ex. 15:1; Ps. 105:2; 106:12
18 Isa. 33:22

21:8–9 Make thee a fiery serpent. In a night conversation with Nicodemus (John 3:14–15), Jesus used this historical event of the serpent of brass as a symbol and type of His being lifted up on the cross. Every bitten Israelite who looked, then lived; every sinner ("the wages of sin is death" [Rom. 6:23]) who looks to Christ on the cross in faith believing, receives eternal life from Him and is healed from the venom of sin. The serpent is used in Scripture in connection with evil. Jesus, who knew no sin, became sin for us, thus taking upon Him the evil and iniquity of the human race, all of whom are under the penalty of death.

Biblical Typology

By Thomas Ice

The apostle Paul writes in 1 Corinthians 10:6, "Now these things were our examples." The Greek word *tupos* is translated "examples" and has the idea of "pattern," "illustration," or "type." Paul notes "all these things happened unto them for ensamples [adverb of *tupos*]: and they are written for our admonition" (1 Cor. 10:11). What things? In this case, Paul refers to events related to the Exodus in the Old Testament. Thus, a type is a biblical pattern or illustration, usually from the Old Testament, taking the form of patterns relating to persons or things.

Hebrews 8:5 tells us that the Tabernacle was based upon a heavenly pattern shown to Moses on Mount Sinai. "And look that thou make them after their pattern, which was shewed thee in the mount" (Ex. 25:40). Stephen noted in his sermon, "Our fathers had the tabernacle of witness in the wilderness, as he had appointed, speaking unto Moses, that he should make it according to the fashion that he had seen" (Acts 7:44). The Tabernacle, and later the temple, are types that become patterns revealing key elements in God's plan of salvation.

Many examples of how patterns in individual lives provide a type can be seen from key events in the lives of early Old Testament figures such as Abraham, Isaac, and Joseph. In Genesis 22, the pattern of Abraham offering Isaac shadows many events that mirror the death and resurrection of Jesus. The Lord said to Abraham, "Take now thy son, thine only son Isaac, whom thou lovest, and get thee into the land of Moriah . . . upon one of the mountains" (Gen. 22:2). This verse parallels God the Father's offering of Jesus, His only-begotten Son. The mountain in the land of Moriah is believed to be the very hill in Jerusalem where Israel's temple was built and Israel practiced sacrifice. Jesus' ministry greatly revolved around that location. Isaac is a willing sacrifice (Gen. 22:5–9), as was Jesus. The willingness of Abraham to sacrifice Isaac and the eventual sacrifice of a ram (Gen. 22:9–14) pictures the ultimate sacrifice and provision of Christ for our sin.

> *In prophetic terms, a "type" is a pattern or illustration that reveals key elements in God's plan of salvation.*

Certain events in the life of Joseph are a type and foreshadowing of Israel's relationship with their Messiah. Joseph reveals to his brothers a dream that pictures him ruling over them (Gen. 37:5–9). Joseph is rejected by his brothers (Gen. 37:10–11). His brothers plot to kill him (Gen. 37:18–20), yet they sell him into slavery (Gen. 37:25–27), which pictures the death, burial, and resurrection of Christ. Meanwhile, unknown to Jacob, his father, Joseph rises to a position of great power and influence over the Gentile nations through the events of a famine (Gen. 41). His brothers come to Egypt for food from the Gentiles, and at that time Joseph mercifully reveals himself and restores the broken relationship (Gen. 42—45). This pictures the end-time conversion of Israel to Jesus as her Messiah during the Tribulation, resulting in the millennial blessing for Israel (Gen. 46).

There are many possible types in the Bible. However, a biblical event or concept can be established as a type only after the text has been interpreted historically and the pattern of events determined. Typological connotation should not be used as a primary interpretive approach to any passage. Proper typology can be established only in hindsight, comparing the patterns of historical events to God's plan for history, past and future.

lawgiver, with their staves. And from the wilderness *they went* to Mattanah:

19 And from Mattanah to Nahaliel: and from Nahaliel to Bamoth:

20 And from Bamoth *in* the valley, that *is* in the country of Moab, to the top of Pisgah, which looketh toward Jeshimon.

21 And Israel sent messengers unto Sihon king of the Amorites, saying,

22 Let me pass through thy land: we will not turn into the fields, or into the vineyards; we will not drink *of* the waters of the well: *but* we will go along by the king's *high* way, until we be past thy borders.

23 And Sihon would not suffer Israel to pass through his border: but Sihon gathered all his people together, and went out against Israel into the wilderness: and he came to Jahaz, and fought against Israel.

24 And Israel smote him with the edge of the sword, and possessed his land from Arnon unto Jabbok, even unto the children of Ammon: for the border of the children of Ammon *was* strong.

25 And Israel took all these cities: and Israel dwelt in all the cities of the Amorites, in Heshbon, and in all the villages thereof.

26 For Heshbon *was* the city of Sihon the king of the Amorites, who had fought against the former king of Moab, and taken all his land out of his hand, even unto Arnon.

27 Wherefore they that speak in proverbs say, Come into Heshbon, let the city of Sihon be built and prepared:

28 For there is a fire gone out of Heshbon, a flame from the city of Sihon: it hath consumed Ar of Moab, *and* the lords of the high places of Arnon.

29 Woe to thee, Moab! thou art undone, O people of Chemosh: he hath given his sons that escaped, and his daughters, into captivity unto Sihon king of the Amorites.

30 We have shot at them; Heshbon is perished even unto Dibon, and we have laid them waste even unto Nophah, which *reacheth* unto Medeba.

31 Thus Israel dwelt in the land of the Amorites.

32 And Moses sent to spy out Jaazer, and they took the villages thereof, and drove out the Amorites that *were* there.

33 And they turned and went up by the way of Bashan: and Og the king of Bashan went out against them, he, and all his people, to the battle at Edrei.

34 And the LORD said unto Moses, Fear him not: for I have delivered him into thy hand, and all his people, and his land; and thou shalt do to him as thou didst unto Sihon king of the Amorites, which dwelt at Heshbon.

35 So they smote him, and his sons, and all his people, until there was none left him alive: and they possessed his land.

CHAPTER 22
Balak Sends for Balaam

1 And the children of Israel set forward, and pitched in the plains of Moab on this side Jordan *by* Jericho.

2 And Balak the son of Zippor saw all that Israel had done to the Amorites.

3 And Moab was sore afraid of the people, because they *were* many: and Moab was distressed because of the children of Israel.

4 And Moab said unto the elders of Midian, Now shall this company lick up all *that are* round about us, as the ox licketh up the grass of the field. And Balak the son of Zippor *was* king of the Moabites at that time.

5 He sent messengers therefore unto Balaam the son of Beor to Pethor, which *is* by the river of the land of the children of his people, to call him, saying, Behold, there is a people come out from Egypt: behold, they cover the face of the earth, and they abide over against me:

6 Come now therefore, I pray thee, curse

Cross references (center column):

20 Num. 23:28
21 Deut. 2:26, 27; Judg. 11:19
22 Num. 20:17
23 Judg. 11:20
24 Deut. 2:33; 29:7; Josh. 12:1, 2; 24:8; Neh. 9:22; Ps. 135:10, 11; 136:19; Amos 2:9
28 Deut. 2:9, 18; Isa. 15:1; Jer. 48:45, 46
29 Judg. 11:24; 1Kgs. 11:7, 33; 2Kgs. 23:13; Jer. 48:7, 13
30 Isa. 15:2; Jer. 48:18, 22
32 Num. 32:1; Jer. 48:32
33 Deut. 3:1; 29:7; Josh. 13:12
35 Deut. 3:3, 4
1 Num. 33:48
2 Judg. 11:25
3 Ex. 15:15
4 Num. 31:8; Josh. 13:21
5 Num. 23:7; Deut. 23:4; Josh. 13:22; 24:9; Neh. 13:1, 2; Mic. 6:5; 2Pet. 2:15; Jude 1:11; Rev. 2:14
6 Num. 23:7

22:1—24:25 I pray thee, curse me this people. Balaam, which means "devourer," was originally a pagan spiritualist or magician, called in Joshua 13:22 a "soothsayer." Evidently, Balaam was aware of the God of Israel and included Him as a god he recognized. When Balaam arrived to join Balak and receive his reward, God overruled whatever evil intentions he had and caused him to bless Israel. The prophecies of blessings for Israel that he uttered came true. A man with the potential to be a true servant of God, he mixed truth with error (except in these prophecies) and became known as a false prophet. Later, he advised Balak to send Moabite women into the camp of Israel to seduce the people into immorality, idolatry and sin (Num. 25). Revelation 2:14 records that the "doctrine of Balaam" was being practiced in the compromising worldly church at Pergamos, where Satan's seat existed. This "doctrine of Balaam" was a mingling of the wicked ways of the world with the church, corrupting biblical principles (see 1 John 2:15–16).

me this people; for they *are* too mighty for me: peradventure I shall prevail, *that* we may smite them, and *that* I may drive them out of the land: for I wot that he whom thou blessest *is* blessed, and he whom thou cursest is cursed.

7 And the elders of Moab and the elders of Midian departed with the rewards of divination in their hand; and they came unto Balaam, and spake unto him the words of Balak.

8 And he said unto them, Lodge here this night, and I will bring you word again, as the LORD shall speak unto me: and the princes of Moab abode with Balaam.

9 And God came unto Balaam, and said, What men *are* these with thee?

10 And Balaam said unto God, Balak the son of Zippor, king of Moab, hath sent unto me, *saying,*

11 Behold, *there is* a people come out of Egypt, which covereth the face of the earth: come now, curse me them; peradventure I shall be able to overcome them, and drive them out.

12 And God said unto Balaam, Thou shalt not go with them; thou shalt not curse the people: for they *are* blessed.

13 And Balaam rose up in the morning, and said unto the princes of Balak, Get you into your land: for the LORD refuseth to give me leave to go with you.

14 And the princes of Moab rose up, and they went unto Balak, and said, Balaam refuseth to come with us.

15 And Balak sent yet again princes, more, and more honourable than they.

16 And they came to Balaam, and said to him, Thus saith Balak the son of Zippor, Let nothing, I pray thee, hinder thee from coming unto me:

17 For I will promote thee unto very great honour, and I will do whatsoever thou sayest unto me: come therefore, I pray thee, curse me this people.

18 And Balaam answered and said unto the servants of Balak, If Balak would give me his house full of silver and gold, I cannot go beyond the word of the LORD my God, to do less or more.

19 Now therefore, I pray you, tarry ye also here this night, that I may know what the LORD will say unto me more.

20 And God came unto Balaam at night, and said unto him, If the men come to call thee, rise up, *and* go with them; but yet the word which I shall say unto thee, that shalt thou do.

7 1Sam. 9:7, 8
8 Num. 22:19
9 Gen. 20:3; Num. 22:20
12 Num. 23:20; Rom. 11:29
17 Num. 22:6
18 Num. 24:13; 1Kgs. 22:14; 2Chr. 18:13
19 Num. 22:8
20 Num. 22:9, 35; 23:12, 26; 24:13
22 Ex. 4:24
23 2Kgs. 6:17; Dan. 10:7; Acts 22:9; 2Pet. 2:16; Jude 1:11
28 2Pet. 2:16
29 Prov. 12:10
30 2Pet. 2:16
31 Gen. 21:19; Ex. 34:8; 2Kgs. 6:17; Luke 24:16, 31
32 2Pet. 2:14, 15
34 1Sam. 15:24, 30; 26:21; 2Sam. 12:13; Job 34:31, 32

Balaam Meets the Angel of the Lord

21 And Balaam rose up in the morning, and saddled his ass, and went with the princes of Moab.

22 And God's anger was kindled because he went: and the angel of the LORD stood in the way for an adversary against him. Now he was riding upon his ass, and his two servants *were* with him.

23 And the ass saw the angel of the LORD standing in the way, and his sword drawn in his hand: and the ass turned aside out of the way, and went into the field: and Balaam smote the ass, to turn her into the way.

24 But the angel of the LORD stood in a path of the vineyards, a wall *being* on this side, and a wall on that side.

25 And when the ass saw the angel of the LORD, she thrust herself unto the wall, and crushed Balaam's foot against the wall: and he smote her again.

26 And the angel of the LORD went further, and stood in a narrow place, where *was* no way to turn either to the right hand or to the left.

27 And when the ass saw the angel of the LORD, she fell down under Balaam: and Balaam's anger was kindled, and he smote the ass with a staff.

28 And the LORD opened the mouth of the ass, and she said unto Balaam, What have I done unto thee, that thou hast smitten me these three times?

29 And Balaam said unto the ass, Because thou hast mocked me: I would there were a sword in mine hand, for now would I kill thee.

30 And the ass said unto Balaam, *Am* not I thine ass, upon which thou hast ridden ever since *I was* thine unto this day? was I ever wont to do so unto thee? And he said, Nay.

31 Then the LORD opened the eyes of Balaam, and he saw the angel of the LORD standing in the way, and his sword drawn in his hand: and he bowed down his head, and fell flat on his face.

32 And the angel of the LORD said unto him, Wherefore hast thou smitten thine ass these three times? behold, I went out to withstand thee, because *thy* way is perverse before me:

33 And the ass saw me, and turned from me these three times: unless she had turned from me, surely now also I had slain thee, and saved her alive.

34 And Balaam said unto the angel of the LORD, I have sinned; for I knew not that

thou stoodest in the way against me: now therefore, if it displease thee, I will get me back again.

35 And the angel of the LORD said unto Balaam, Go with the men: but only the word that I shall speak unto thee, that thou shalt speak. So Balaam went with the princes of Balak.

Balaam Arrives and Blesses Israel

36 And when Balak heard that Balaam was come, he went out to meet him unto a city of Moab, which *is* in the border of Arnon, which *is* in the utmost coast.

37 And Balak said unto Balaam, Did I not earnestly send unto thee to call thee? wherefore camest thou not unto me? am I not able indeed to promote thee to honour?

38 And Balaam said unto Balak, Lo, I am come unto thee: have I now any power at all to say any thing? the word that God putteth in my mouth, that shall I speak.

39 And Balaam went with Balak, and they came unto Kirjath-huzoth.

40 And Balak offered oxen and sheep, and sent to Balaam, and to the princes that *were* with him.

41 And it came to pass on the morrow, that Balak took Balaam, and brought him up into the high places of Baal, that thence he might see the utmost *part* of the people.

CHAPTER 23

1 And Balaam said unto Balak, Build me here seven altars, and prepare me here seven oxen and seven rams.

2 And Balak did as Balaam had spoken; and Balak and Balaam offered on *every* altar a bullock and a ram.

3 And Balaam said unto Balak, Stand by thy burnt offering, and I will go: peradventure the LORD will come to meet me: and whatsoever he sheweth me I will tell thee. And he went to an high place.

4 And God met Balaam: and he said unto

him, I have prepared seven altars, and I have offered upon *every* altar a bullock and a ram.

5 And the LORD put a word in Balaam's mouth, and said, Return unto Balak, and thus thou shalt speak.

6 And he returned unto him, and, lo, he stood by his burnt sacrifice, he, and all the princes of Moab.

7 And he took up his parable, and said, Balak the king of Moab hath brought me from Aram, out of the mountains of the east, *saying*, Come, curse me Jacob, and come, defy Israel.

8 How shall I curse, whom God hath not cursed? or how shall I defy, *whom* the LORD hath not defied?

9 For from the top of the rocks I see him, and from the hills I behold him: lo, the people shall dwell alone, and shall not be reckoned among the nations.

10 Who can count the dust of Jacob, and the number of the fourth *part* of Israel? Let me die the death of the righteous, and let my last end be like his!

11 And Balak said unto Balaam, What hast thou done unto me? I took thee to curse mine enemies, and, behold, thou hast blessed *them* altogether.

12 And he answered and said, Must I not take heed to speak that which the LORD hath put in my mouth?

13 And Balak said unto him, Come, I pray thee, with me unto another place, from whence thou mayest see them: thou shalt see but the utmost part of them, and shalt not see them all: and curse me them from thence.

14 And he brought him into the field of Zophim, to the top of Pisgah, and built seven altars, and offered a bullock and a ram on *every* altar.

15 And he said unto Balak, Stand here by thy burnt offering, while I meet *the* LORD yonder.

Cross references (center column):

35 Num. 22:20
36 Gen. 14:17; Num. 21:13
37 Num. 22:17; 24:11
38 Num. 23:26; 24:13; 1Kgs. 22:14; 2Chr. 18:13
41 Deut. 12:2
1 Num. 23:29
2 Num. 23:14, 30
3 Num. 23:15; 24:1
4 Num. 23:16
5 Num. 22:35; 23:16; Deut. 18:18; Jer. 1:9
7 Num. 22:6, 11, 17; 23:18; 24:3, 15, 23; 1Sam. 17:10; Job 27:1; 29:1; Ps. 78:2; Ezek. 17:2; Mic. 2:4; Hab. 2:6
8 Isa. 47:12, 13
9 Ex. 33:16; Deut. 33:28; Ezra 9:2; Eph. 2:14
10 Gen. 13:16; 22:17; Ps. 116:15
11 Num. 22:11, 17; 24:10
12 Num. 22:38
14 Num. 23:14

23:8 How shall I curse, whom God hath not cursed? Balaam had doubtless sought for enchantments (Num. 23:1), but God "put a word in Balaam's mouth" (v. 5) and the prophecies he spoke proclaimed blessings.

23:1–12 The first prophecy and the response: Balaam blesses Israel under the direct control of God (vv. 7–11); Balak objects and the location for the ongoing ceremonies is changed (vv. 13–15). He predicts their uniqueness and marvels at their vast numbers.

23:13–30 The second prophecy and the response:

Balaam announced the divine selection of Israel as His special people, never to be revoked or reversed; they are to be seen as a purified people, ultimately to hear "the shout of a king" (v. 21), a prediction partially fulfilled by David, but evidently to be perfectly applied to the Messiah-King, the Son of David. When He rules, the world will say, "What hath God wrought!" (v. 23). Again the location for sacrificial offerings, part of Balaam's directed ceremonies, is changed.

16 And the LORD met Balaam, and put a word in his mouth, and said, Go again unto Balak, and say thus.
17 And when he came to him, behold, he stood by his burnt offering, and the princes of Moab with him. And Balak said unto him, What hath the LORD spoken?
18 And he took up his parable, and said, Rise up, Balak, and hear; hearken unto me, thou son of Zippor:
19 God is not a man, that he should lie; neither the son of man, that he should repent: hath he said, and shall he not do it? or hath he spoken, and shall he not make it good?
20 Behold, I have received commandment to bless: and he hath blessed; and I cannot reverse it.
21 He hath not beheld iniquity in Jacob, neither hath he seen perverseness in Israel: the LORD his God is with him, and the shout of a king is among them.
22 God brought them out of Egypt; he hath as it were the strength of a unicorn.
23 Surely there is no enchantment against Jacob, neither is there any divination against Israel: according to this time it shall be said of Jacob and of Israel, What hath God wrought!
24 Behold, the people shall rise up as a great lion, and lift up himself as a young lion: he shall not lie down until he eat of the prey, and drink the blood of the slain.
25 And Balak said unto Balaam, Neither curse them at all, nor bless them at all.
26 But Balaam answered and said unto Balak, Told not I thee, saying, All that the LORD speaketh, that I must do?
27 And Balak said unto Balaam, Come, I pray thee, I will bring thee unto another place; peradventure it will please God that thou mayest curse me them from thence.
28 And Balak brought Balaam unto the top of Peor, that looketh toward Jeshimon.
29 And Balaam said unto Balak, Build me here seven altars, and prepare me here seven bullocks and seven rams.
30 And Balak did as Balaam had said, and offered a bullock and a ram on every altar.

CHAPTER 24

1 And when Balaam saw that it pleased the LORD to bless Israel, he went not, as at other times, to seek for enchantments, but he set his face toward the wilderness.

2 And Balaam lifted up his eyes, and he saw Israel abiding in his tents according to their tribes; and the spirit of God came upon him.
3 And he took up his parable, and said, Balaam the son of Beor hath said, and the man whose eyes are open hath said:
4 He hath said, which heard the words of God, which saw the vision of the Almighty, falling into a trance, but having his eyes open:
5 How goodly are thy tents, O Jacob, and thy tabernacles, O Israel!
6 As the valleys are they spread forth, as gardens by the river's side, as the trees of lign aloes which the LORD hath planted, and as cedar trees beside the waters.
7 He shall pour the water out of his buckets, and his seed shall be in many waters, and his king shall be higher than Agag, and his kingdom shall be exalted.
8 God brought him forth out of Egypt; he hath as it were the strength of a unicorn: he shall eat up the nations his enemies, and shall break their bones, and pierce them through with his arrows.
9 He couched, he lay down as a lion, and as a great lion: who shall stir him up? Blessed is he that blesseth thee, and cursed is he that curseth thee.

Balaam's Prophecy

10 And Balak's anger was kindled against Balaam, and he smote his hands together: and Balak said unto Balaam, I called thee to curse mine enemies, and, behold, thou hast altogether blessed them these three times.
11 Therefore now flee thou to thy place: I thought to promote thee unto great honour; but, lo, the LORD hath kept thee back from honour.
12 And Balaam said unto Balak, Spake I not also to thy messengers which thou sentest unto me, saying,
13 If Balak would give me his house full of silver and gold, I cannot go beyond the commandment of the LORD, to do either good or bad of mine own mind; but what the LORD saith, that will I speak?
14 And now, behold, I go unto my people: come therefore, and I will advertise thee what this people shall do to thy people in the latter days.

Cross References (center column)

18 Judg. 3:20
19 1Sam. 15:29; Mal. 3:6; Rom. 11:29; Titus 1:2; James 1:17
20 Gen. 12:2; 22:17
21 Ex. 13:21; 29:45, 46; 33:14; Ps. 89:15; Rom. 4:7, 8
22 Num. 24:8; Deut. 33:17; Job 39:10, 11
23 Ps. 31:19; 44:1
24 Gen. 49:9, 27
26 1Kgs. 22:14
2 Num. 2:2; 11:25; 1Sam. 10:10; 19:20, 23; 2Chr. 15:1
3 Num. 23:7, 18
4 1Sam. 19:24; Ezek. 1:28; Dan. 8:18; 10:15, 16; 2Cor. 12:2, 3, 4; Rev. 1:10, 17
6 Ps. 1:3; 104:16; Jer. 17:8
7 1Sam. 15:9; 2Sam. 5:12; 1Chr. 14:2; Jer. 51:13; Rev. 17:1, 15
8 Num. 14:9; 23:22, 24; Ps. 2:9; 45:5; Isa. 38:13; Jer. 50:9, 17
9 Gen. 12:3; 27:29; 49:9
10 Deut. 23:4, 5; Josh. 24:9, 10; Neh. 13:2; Ezek. 21:14, 17; 22:13
14 Gen. 49:1; Dan. 2:28; 10:14; Mic. 6:5; Rev. 2:14

24:1–14 The third prophecy: Israel is to enjoy their own land with prosperity and military victories assured. The future Messiah-King would be successful "as a great lion" (v. 9, cf. Rev. 5:5).

15 And he took up his parable, and said, Balaam the son of Beor hath said, and the man whose eyes are open hath said:
16 He hath said, which heard the words of God, and knew the knowledge of the most High, *which* saw the vision of the Almighty, falling *into a trance*, but having his eyes open:
17 I shall see him, but not now: I shall behold him, but not nigh: there shall come a Star out of Jacob, and a Sceptre shall rise out of Israel, and shall smite the corners of Moab, and destroy all the children of Sheth.
18 And Edom shall be a possession, Seir also shall be a possession for his enemies; and Israel shall do valiantly.
19 Out of Jacob shall come he that shall have dominion, and shall destroy him that remaineth of the city.
20 And when he looked on Amalek, he took up his parable, and said, Amalek *was* the first of the nations; but his latter end *shall be* that he perish for ever.
21 And he looked on the Kenites, and took up his parable, and said, Strong is thy dwellingplace, and thou puttest thy nest in a rock.
22 Nevertheless the Kenite shall be wasted, until Asshur shall carry thee away captive.
23 And he took up his parable, and said, Alas, who shall live when God doeth this!
24 And ships *shall come* from the coast of Chittim, and shall afflict Asshur, and shall afflict Eber, and he also shall perish for ever.
25 And Balaam rose up, and went and returned to his place: and Balak also went his way.

CHAPTER 25
Moabite Women Seduce Israel

1 And Israel abode in Shittim, and the people began to commit whoredom with the daughters of Moab.

Cross references
17 Gen. 49:10; 2Sam. 8:2; Ps. 110:2; Jer. 48:45; Matt. 2:2; Rev. 1:7; 22:16
18 2Sam. 8:14; Ps. 60:8, 9, 12
19 Gen. 49:10
20 Ex. 17:8, 14; 1Sam. 15:3, 8
22 Gen. 15:19
24 Gen. 10:4, 21, 25; Dan. 11:30
1 Num. 31:16; 33:49; 1Cor. 10:8
2 Ex. 20:5; 34:15, 16; Josh. 22:17; Ps. 106:28; Hos. 9:10; 1Cor. 10:20
4 Deut. 4:3; 13:17; Josh. 22:17
5 Ex. 18:21, 25; 32:27; Deut. 13:6, 9, 13, 15
6 Joel 2:17
7 Ex. 6:25; Ps. 106:30
9 Deut. 4:3; 1Cor. 10:8
11 Ex. 20:5; Deut. 32:16, 21; 1Kgs. 14:22; Ps. 78:58; 106:30; Ezek. 16:38; Zeph. 1:18; 3:8
12 Mal. 2:4, 5; 3:1

2 And they called the people unto the sacrifices of their gods: and the people did eat, and bowed down to their gods.
3 And Israel joined himself unto Baal-peor: and the anger of the LORD was kindled against Israel.
4 And the LORD said unto Moses, Take all the heads of the people, and hang them up before the LORD against the sun, that the fierce anger of the LORD may be turned away from Israel.
5 And Moses said unto the judges of Israel, Slay ye every one his men that were joined unto Baal-peor.
6 And, behold, one of the children of Israel came and brought unto his brethren a Midianitish woman in the sight of Moses, and in the sight of all the congregation of the children of Israel, who *were* weeping *before* the door of the tabernacle of the congregation.
7 And when Phinehas, the son of Eleazar, the son of Aaron the priest, saw *it*, he rose up from among the congregation, and took a javelin in his hand;
8 And he went after the man of Israel into the tent, and thrust both of them through, the man of Israel, and the woman through her belly. So the plague was stayed from the children of Israel.
9 And those that died in the plague were twenty and four thousand.
10 And the LORD spake unto Moses, saying,
11 Phinehas, the son of Eleazar, the son of Aaron the priest, hath turned my wrath away from the children of Israel, while he was zealous for my sake among them, that I consumed not the children of Israel in my jealousy.
12 Wherefore say, Behold, I give unto him my covenant of peace:
13 And he shall have it, and his seed after him, *even* the covenant of an everlasting

---

24:15–24 The fourth prophecy (after which Balaam departs) is that a great personality and leader would someday arise, pointing directly to the Messiah-King, Jesus.

24:17 a Star out of Jacob, and a Sceptre. This remarkable prophecy spoke of the Messiah, the bright and morning star (Rev. 22:16), who will use the scepter of power as King. The Hebrew word for "star" carries the idea of an immense, rolling, shining, blazing reality. Some think this forecasts the star which appeared in the East to guide the Magi to Jesus at Bethlehem (Matt. 2:2). Stars are mentioned both literally and in a figurative sense throughout the Bible, especially in Revelation (fourteen times).

A scepter is an ornate rod or staff, borne as a symbol of authority and used in ancient and modern times. A scepter could be long (like a staff), touching the ground, or short (like a wand) and carried in the hand. Here, the word figuratively speaks of the royal and sovereign authority and power to be exercised by the future king. His domain would include all of the surrounding hostile territories, which may portray Gentile world powers in the future Tribulation and the Millennial Kingdom to follow (vv. 21–24). Some of these areas were temporarily in the empire of David and Solomon, but final fulfillment is still to come.

priesthood; because he was zealous for his God, and made an atonement for the children of Israel.

14 Now the name of the Israelite that was slain *even* that was slain with the Midianitish woman, *was* Zimri, the son of Salu, a prince of a chief house among the Simeonites.

15 And the name of the Midianitish woman that was slain *was* Cozbi, the daughter of Zur; he *was* head over a people, *and* of a chief house in Midian.

16 And the LORD spake unto Moses, saying,

17 Vex the Midianites, and smite them:

18 For they vex you with their wiles, wherewith they have beguiled you in the matter of Peor, and in the matter of Cozbi, the daughter of a prince of Midian, their sister, which was slain in the day of the plague for Peor's sake.

CHAPTER 26
The Second Census

1 And it came to pass after the plague, that the Lord spake unto Moses and unto Eleazar the son of Aaron the priest, saying,

2 Take the sum of all the congregation of the children of Israel, from twenty years old and upward, throughout their fathers' house, all that are able to go to war in Israel.

3 And Moses and Eleazar the priest spake with them in the plains of Moab by Jordan *near* Jericho, saying,

4 *Take the sum of the people*, from twenty years old and upward; as the LORD commanded Moses and the children of Israel, which went forth out of the land of Egypt.

5 Reuben, the eldest son of Israel: the children of Reuben; Hanoch, *of whom cometh* the family of the Hanochites: of Pallu, the family of the Palluites:

6 Of Hezron, the family of the Hezronites: of Carmi, the family of the Carmites.

7 These *are* the families of the Reubenites: and they that were numbered of them were forty and three thousand and seven hundred and thirty.

8 And the sons of Pallu; Eliab.

9 And the sons of Eliab; Nemuel, and Dathan, and Abiram. This *is that* Dathan and

Abiram, *which were* famous in the congregation, who strove against Moses and against Aaron in the company of Korah, when they strove against the LORD:

10 And the earth opened her mouth, and swallowed them up together with Korah, when that company died, what time the fire devoured two hundred and fifty men: and they became a sign.

11 Notwithstanding the children of Korah died not.

12 The sons of Simeon after their families: of Nemuel, the family of the Nemuelites: of Jamin, the family of the Jaminites: of Jachin, the family of the Jachinites:

13 Of Zerah, the family of the Zarhites: of Shaul, the family of the Shaulites.

14 These *are* the families of the Simeonites, twenty and two thousand and two hundred.

15 The children of Gad after their families: of Zephon, the family of the Zephonites: of Haggi, the family of the Haggites: of Shuni, the family of the Shunites:

16 Of Ozni, the family of the Oznites: of Eri, the family of the Erites:

17 Of Arod, the family of the Arodites: of Areli, the family of the Arelites.

18 These *are* the families of the children of Gad according to those that were numbered of them, forty thousand and five hundred.

19 The sons of Judah *were* Er and Onan: and Er and Onan died in the land of Canaan.

20 And the sons of Judah after their families were; of Shelah, the family of the Shelanites: of Pharez, the family of the Pharzites: of Zerah, the family of the Zarhites.

21 And the sons of Pharez were; of Hezron, the family of the Hezronites: of Hamul, the family of the Hamulites.

22 These *are* the families of Judah according to those that were numbered of them, threescore and sixteen thousand and five hundred.

23 *Of* the sons of Issachar after their families: *of* Tola, the family of the Tolaites: of Pua, the family of the Punites:

24 Of Jashub, the family of the Jashubites: of Shimron, the family of the Shimronites.

25 These *are* the families of Issachar accord-

Cross references (center column):

15 Num. 31:8; Josh. 13:21

17 Num. 31:2

18 Num. 31:16; Rev. 2:14

2 Ex. 30:12; 38:25, 26; Num. 1:2, 3

3 Num. 22:1; 26:63; 31:12; 33:48; 35:1

4 Num. 1:1

5 Gen. 46:8; Ex. 6:14; 1Chr. 5:1

9 Num. 16:1, 2

10 Num. 16:32, 35, 38; 1Cor. 10:6; 2Pet. 2:6

11 Ex. 6:24; 1Chr. 6:22

12 Gen. 46:10; Ex. 6:15, *Jemuel*; 1Chr. 4:24, *Jarib*

13 Gen. 46:10, *Zohar*

15 Gen. 46:16, *Ziphion*

16 Gen. 46:16

17 Gen. 46:16, *Arodi*

19 Gen. 38:2-10; 46:12

20 1Chr. 2:3

23 Gen. 46:13; 1Chr. 7:1

26:2–51 the sum of all the congregation. This second numbering or census of the able-bodied warriors over twenty, with scarcely any over sixty other than Caleb and Joshua, revealed that the population was stable. The older generation over the forty years of wandering had died off, and a new generation totaling 601,730 were preparing to enter the land. From Hebrews 4:2, we learn that they who suffered the consequences of their unbelief, rebellion, and rejection of Moses' leadership were a type of those who fail to believe in Jesus as the Messiah and Savior.

ing to those that were numbered of them, threescore and four thousand and three hundred.

26 Of the sons of Zebulun after their families: of Sered, the family of the Sardites: of Elon, the family of the Elonites: of Jahleel, the family of the Jahleelites.

27 These *are* the families of the Zebulunites according to those that were numbered of them, threescore thousand and five hundred.

28 The sons of Joseph after their families *were* Manasseh and Ephraim.

29 Of the sons of Manasseh: of Machir, the family of the Machirites: and Machir begat Gilead: of Gilead *come* the family of the Gileadites.

30 These *are* the sons of Gilead: *of* Jeezer, the family of the Jeezerites: of Helek, the family of the Helekites:

31 And *of* Asriel, the family of the Asrielites: and *of* Shechem, the family of the Shechemites:

32 And *of* Shemida, the family of the Shemidaites: and *of* Hepher, the family of the Hepherites.

33 And Zelophehad the son of Hepher had no sons, but daughters: and the names of the daughters of Zelophehad *were* Mahlah, and Noah, Hoglah, Milcah, and Tirzah.

34 These *are* the families of Manasseh, and those that were numbered of them, fifty and two thousand and seven hundred.

35 These *are* the sons of Ephraim after their families: of Shuthelah, the family of the Shuthalhites: of Becher, the family of the Bachrites: of Tahan, the family of the Tahanites.

36 And these *are* the sons of Shuthelah: of Eran, the family of the Eranites.

37 These *are* the families of the sons of Ephraim according to those that were numbered of them, thirty and two thousand and five hundred. These *are* the sons of Joseph after their families.

38 The sons of Benjamin after their families: of Bela, the family of the Belaites: of Ashbel, the family of the Ashbelites: of Ahiram, the family of the Ahiramites:

39 Of Shupham, the family of the Shuphamites: of Hupham, the family of the Huphamites.

40 And the sons of Bela were Ard and Naaman: *of Ard*, the family of the Ardites: *and of* Naaman, the family of the Naamites.

41 These *are* the sons of Benjamin after their families: and they that were numbered of them *were* forty and five thousand and six hundred.

42 These *are* the sons of Dan after their families: of Shuham, the family of the Shuhamites. These *are* the families of Dan after their families.

43 All the families of the Shuhamites, according to those that were numbered of them, *were* threescore and four thousand and four hundred.

44 Of the children of Asher after their families: of Jimna, the family of the Jimnites: of Jesui, the family of the Jesuites: of Beriah, the family of the Beriites.

45 Of the sons of Beriah: of Heber, the family of the Heberites: of Malchiel, the family of the Malchielites.

46 And the name of the daughter of Asher *was* Sarah.

47 These *are* the families of the sons of Asher according to those that were numbered of them; *who were* fifty and three thousand and four hundred.

48 Of the sons of Naphtali after their families: of Jahzeel, the family of the Jahzeelites: of Guni, the family of the Gunites:

49 Of Jezer, the family of the Jezerites: of Shillem, the family of the Shillemites.

50 These *are* the families of Naphtali according to their families: and they that were numbered of them *were* forty and five thousand and four hundred.

51 These *were* the numbered of the children of Israel, six hundred thousand and a thousand seven hundred and thirty.

52 And the LORD spake unto Moses, saying,

53 Unto these the land shall be divided for an inheritance according to the number of names.

54 To many thou shalt give the more inheritance, and to few thou shalt give the less inheritance: to every one shall his inheritance be given according to those that were numbered of him.

55 Notwithstanding the land shall be divided by lot: according to the names of the tribes of their fathers they shall inherit.

56 According to the lot shall the possession thereof be divided between many and few.

57 And these *are* they that were numbered of the Levites after their families: of Gershon, the family of the Gershonites: of Kohath, the family of the Kohathites: of Merari, the family of the Merarites.

58 These *are* the families of the Levites: the family of the Libnites, the family of the Hebronites, the family of the Mahlites, the family of the Mushites, the family of the Korathites. And Kohath begat Amram.

59 And the name of Amram's wife *was*

Cross references:

26 Gen. 46:14

28 Gen. 46:20

29 Josh. 17:1; 1Chr. 7:14, 15

30 Josh. 17:2; Judg. 6:11, 24, 34, *Abiezer*

33 Num. 27:1; 36:11

35 1Chr. 7:20, *Bered*

38 Gen. 46:21; 1Chr. 7:6; 8:1, *Aharah*

39 Gen. 46:21, *Muppim and Huppim*

40 1Chr. 8:3, *Addar*

42 Gen. 46:23

44 Gen. 46:17; 1Chr. 7:30

48 Gen. 46:24; 1Chr. 7:13

49 1Chr. 7:13, *Shallum*

51 Num. 1:46

53 Josh. 11:23; 14:1

54 Num. 33:54

55 Num. 33:54; 34:13; Josh. 11:23; 14:2

57 Gen. 46:11; Ex. 6:16-19; 1Chr. 6:1, 16

59 Ex. 2:1, 2; 6:20

Jochebed, the daughter of Levi, whom *her mother* bare to Levi in Egypt: and she bare unto Amram Aaron and Moses, and Miriam their sister.

60 And unto Aaron was born Nadab, and Abihu, Eleazar, and Ithamar.

61 And Nadab and Abihu died, when they offered strange fire before the LORD.

62 And those that were numbered of them were twenty and three thousand, all males from a month old and upward: for they were not numbered among the children of Israel, because there was no inheritance given them among the children of Israel.

63 These *are* they that were numbered by Moses and Eleazar the priest, who numbered the children of Israel in the plains of Moab by Jordan *near* Jericho.

64 But among these there was not a man of them whom Moses and Aaron the priest numbered, when they numbered the children of Israel in the wilderness of Sinai.

65 For the LORD had said of them, They shall surely die in the wilderness. And there was not left a man of them, save Caleb the son of Jephunneh, and Joshua the son of Nun.

CHAPTER 27
The Law of Inheritance

1 Then came the daughters of Zelophehad, the son of Hepher, the son of Gilead, the son of Machir, the son of Manasseh, of the families of Manasseh the son of Joseph: and these *are* the names of his daughters; Mahlah, Noah, and Hoglah, and Milcah, and Tirzah.

2 And they stood before Moses, and before Eleazar the priest, and before the princes and all the congregation, *by* the door of the tabernacle of the congregation, saying,

3 Our father died in the wilderness, and he was not in the company of them that gathered themselves together against the LORD in the company of Korah; but died in his own sin, and had no sons.

4 Why should the name of our father be done away from among his family, because he hath no son? Give unto us *therefore* a possession among the brethren of our father.

5 And Moses brought their cause before the LORD.

6 And the LORD spake unto Moses, saying,

7 The daughters of Zelophehad speak right: thou shalt surely give them a possession of an inheritance among their father's brethren; and thou shalt cause the inheritance of their father to pass unto them.

8 And thou shalt speak unto the children of Israel, saying, If a man die, and have no son, then ye shall cause his inheritance to pass unto his daughter.

9 And if he have no daughter, then ye shall give his inheritance unto his brethren.

10 And if he have no brethren, then ye shall give his inheritance unto his father's brethren.

11 And if his father have no brethren, then ye shall give his inheritance unto his kinsman that is next to him of his family, and he shall possess it: and it shall be unto the children of Israel a statute of judgment, as the LORD commanded Moses.

Joshua Named to Succeed Moses

12 And the LORD said unto Moses, Get thee up into this mount Abarim, and see the land which I have given unto the children of Israel.

13 And when thou hast seen it, thou also shalt be gathered unto thy people, as Aaron thy brother was gathered.

14 For ye rebelled against my commandment in the desert of Zin, in the strife of the congregation, to sanctify me at the water before their eyes: that *is* the water of Meribah in Kadesh in the wilderness of Zin.

15 And Moses spake unto the LORD, saying,

16 Let the LORD, the God of the spirits of all flesh, set a man over the congregation,

17 Which may go out before them, and which may go in before them, and which may lead them out, and which may bring them in; that the congregation of the LORD be not as sheep which have no shepherd.

18 And the LORD said unto Moses, Take thee Joshua the son of Nun, a man in whom *is* the spirit, and lay thine hand upon him;

19 And set him before Eleazar the priest, and before all the congregation; and give him a charge in their sight.

20 And thou shalt put *some* of thine honour upon him, that all the congregation of the children of Israel may be obedient.

21 And he shall stand before Eleazar the priest, who shall ask *counsel* for him after the judgment of Urim before the LORD: at his word shall they go out, and at his word they shall come in, *both* he, and all the children of Israel with him, even all the congregation.

22 And Moses did as the LORD commanded him: and he took Joshua, and set him before Eleazar the priest, and before all the congregation:

23 And he laid his hands upon him, and

Cross references

60 Num. 3:2

61 Lev. 10:1, 2; Num. 3:4; 1Chr. 24:2

62 Num. 1:49; 3:39; 18:20, 23, 24; Deut. 10:9; Josh. 13:14, 33; 14:3

63 Num. 26:3

64 Deut. 2:14, 15

65 Num. 14:28, 29, 30; 1Cor. 10:5, 6

1 Num. 26:33; 36:1, 11; Josh. 17:3

3 Num. 14:35; 16:1, 2; 26:64, 65

4 Josh. 17:4

5 Ex. 18:15, 19

12 Num. 33:47; Deut. 3:27; 32:49; 34:1

13 Num. 20:24, 28; 31:2; Deut. 10:6

14 Ex. 17:7; Num. 20:12, 24; Deut. 1:37; 32:51; Ps. 106:32

16 Num. 16:22; Heb. 12:9

17 Deut. 31:2; 1Sam. 8:20; 18:13; 1Kgs. 22:17; 2Chr. 1:10; Zech. 10:2; Matt. 9:36; Mark 6:34

18 Gen. 41:38; Deut. 34:9; Judg. 3:10; 11:29; 1Sam. 16:13, 18

19 Deut. 31:7

20 Num. 11:17, 28; Josh. 1:16, 17; 1Sam. 10:6, 9; 2Kgs. 2:15

21 Ex. 28:30

23 Deut. 3:28; 31:7

gave him a charge, as the LORD commanded by the hand of Moses.

CHAPTER 28
Laws for Offerings

1 And the LORD spake unto Moses, saying,

2 Command the children of Israel, and say unto them, My offering, *and* my bread for my sacrifices made by fire, *for* a sweet savour unto me, shall ye observe to offer unto me in their due season.

3 And thou shalt say unto them, This *is* the offering made by fire which ye shall offer unto the LORD; two lambs of the first year without spot day by day, *for* a continual burnt offering.

4 The one lamb shalt thou offer in the morning, and the other lamb shalt thou offer at even;

5 And a tenth *part* of an ephah of flour for a meat offering, mingled with the fourth *part* of an hin of beaten oil.

6 *It is* a continual burnt offering, which was ordained in mount Sinai for a sweet savour, a sacrifice made by fire unto the LORD.

7 And the drink offering thereof *shall be* the fourth *part* of an hin for the one lamb: in the holy *place* shalt thou cause the strong wine to be poured unto the LORD *for* a drink offering.

8 And the other lamb shalt thou offer at even: as the meat offering of the morning, and as the drink offering thereof, thou shalt offer *it*, a sacrifice made by fire, of a sweet savour unto the LORD.

9 And on the sabbath day two lambs of the first year without spot, and two tenth deals of flour *for* a meat offering, mingled with oil, and the drink offering thereof:

10 *This is* the burnt offering of every sabbath, beside the continual burnt offering, and his drink offering.

11 And in the beginnings of your months ye shall offer a burnt offering unto the LORD; two young bullocks, and one ram, seven lambs of the first year without spot;

12 And three tenth deals of flour *for* a meat offering, mingled with oil, for one bullock; and two tenth deals of flour *for* a meat offering, mingled with oil, for one ram;

13 And a several tenth deal of flour mingled with oil *for* a meat offering unto one lamb; *for* a burnt offering of a sweet savour, a sacrifice made by fire unto the LORD.

14 And their drink offerings shall be half an hin of wine unto a bullock, and the third *part* of an hin unto a ram, and a fourth *part*

of an hin unto a lamb: this *is* the burnt offering of every month throughout the months of the year.

15 And one kid of the goats for a sin offering unto the LORD shall be offered, beside the continual burnt offering, and his drink offering.

Offerings at the Annual Assemblies

16 And in the fourteenth day of the first month *is* the passover of the LORD.

17 And in the fifteenth day of this month *is* the feast: seven days shall unleavened bread be eaten.

18 In the first day *shall be* an holy convocation; ye shall do no manner of servile work *therein*:

19 But ye shall offer a sacrifice made by fire *for* a burnt offering unto the LORD; two young bullocks, and one ram, and seven lambs of the first year: they shall be unto you without blemish:

20 And their meat offering *shall be of* flour mingled with oil: three tenth deals shall ye offer for a bullock, and two tenth deals for a ram;

21 A several tenth deal shalt thou offer for every lamb, throughout the seven lambs:

22 And one goat *for* a sin offering, to make an atonement for you.

23 Ye shall offer these beside the burnt offering in the morning, which *is* for a continual burnt offering.

24 After this manner ye shall offer daily, throughout the seven days, the meat of the sacrifice made by fire, of a sweet savour unto the LORD: it shall be offered beside the continual burnt offering, and his drink offering.

25 And on the seventh day ye shall have an holy convocation; ye shall do no servile work.

26 Also in the day of the firstfruits, when ye bring a new meat offering unto the LORD, after your weeks *be out*, ye shall have an holy convocation; ye shall do no servile work:

27 But ye shall offer the burnt offering for a sweet savour unto the LORD; two young bullocks, one ram, seven lambs of the first year;

28 And their meat offering of flour mingled with oil, three tenth deals unto one bullock, two tenth deals unto one ram,

29 A several tenth deal unto one lamb, throughout the seven lambs;

30 *And* one kid of the goats, to make an atonement for you.

31 Ye shall offer *them* beside the continual burnt offering, and his meat offering, (they

Cross references (center column)

2 Lev. 3:11; 21:6, 8; Mal. 1:7, 12

3 Ex. 29:38

5 Ex. 16:36; 29:40; Lev. 2:1; Num. 15:4

6 Ex. 29:42; Amos 5:25

7 Ex. 29:42

10 Ezek. 46:4

11 Num. 10:10; 1Sam. 20:5; 1Chr. 23:31; 2Chr. 2:4; Ezra 3:5; Neh. 10:33; Isa. 1:13, 14; Ezek. 45:17; 46:6; Hos. 2:11; Col. 2:16

12 Num. 15:4-12

15 Num. 15:24; 28:22

16 Ex. 12:6, 18; Lev. 23:5; Num. 9:3; Deut. 16:1; Ezek. 45:21

17 Lev. 23:6

18 Ex. 12:16; Lev. 23:7

19 Num. 28:31; 29:8; Lev. 22:20; Deut. 15:21

22 Num. 28:15

25 Ex. 12:16; 13:6; Lev. 23:8

26 Ex. 23:16; 34:22; Num. 23:10, 15; Deut. 16:10; Acts 2:1

27 Lev. 23:18, 19

31 Num. 28:19

shall be unto you without blemish) and their drink offerings.

CHAPTER 29

1 And in the seventh month, on the first *day* of the month, ye shall have an holy convocation; ye shall do no servile work: it is a day of blowing the trumpets unto you.
2 And ye shall offer a burnt offering for a sweet savour unto the LORD; one young bullock, one ram, *and* seven lambs of the first year without blemish:
3 And their meat offering *shall be of* flour mingled with oil, three tenth deals *to* a bullock, *and* two tenth deals for a ram,
4 And one tenth deal for one lamb, throughout the seven lambs:
5 And one kid of the goats *for* a sin offering, to make an atonement for you:
6 Beside the burnt offering of the month, and his meat offering, and the daily burnt offering, and his meat offering, and their drink offerings, according unto their manner, for a sweet savour, a sacrifice made by fire unto the LORD.
7 And ye shall have on the tenth *day* of this seventh month an holy convocation; and ye shall afflict your souls: ye shall not do any work *therein*:
8 But ye shall offer a burnt offering unto the LORD *for* a sweet savour; one young bullock, one ram, *and* seven lambs of the first year; they shall be unto you without blemish:
9 And their meat offering *shall be of* flour mingled with oil, three tenth deals to a bullock, *and* two tenth deals to one ram,
10 A several tenth deal for one lamb, throughout the seven lambs:
11 One kid of the goats *for* a sin offering; beside the sin offering of atonement, and the continual burnt offering, and the meat offering of it, and their drink offerings.
12 And on the fifteenth day of the seventh month ye shall have an holy convocation; ye shall do no servile work, and ye shall keep a feast unto the LORD seven days:
13 And ye shall offer a burnt offering, a sacrifice made by fire, of a sweet savour unto the LORD; thirteen young bullocks, two rams, *and* fourteen lambs of the first year; they shall be without blemish:
14 And their meat offering *shall be of* flour mingled with oil, three tenth deals unto every bullock of the thirteen bullocks, two tenth deals to each ram of the two rams,
15 And a several tenth deal to each lamb of the fourteen lambs:

16 And one kid of the goats *for* a sin offering; beside the continual burnt offering, his meat offering, and his drink offering.
17 And on the second day *ye shall offer* twelve young bullocks, two rams, fourteen lambs of the first year without spot:
18 And their meat offering and their drink offerings for the bullocks, for the rams, and for the lambs, *shall be* according to their number, after the manner:
19 And one kid of the goats *for* a sin offering; beside the continual burnt offering, and the meat offering thereof, and their drink offerings.
20 And on the third day eleven bullocks, two rams, fourteen lambs of the first year without blemish;
21 And their meat offering and their drink offerings for the bullocks, for the rams, and for the lambs, *shall be* according to their number, after the manner:
22 And one goat *for* a sin offering; beside the continual burnt offering, and his meat offering, and his drink offering.
23 And on the fourth day ten bullocks, two rams, *and* fourteen lambs of the first year without blemish:
24 Their meat offering and their drink offerings for the bullocks, for the rams, and for the lambs, *shall be* according to their number, after the manner:
25 And one kid of the goats *for* a sin offering; beside the continual burnt offering, his meat offering, and his drink offering.
26 And on the fifth day nine bullocks, two rams, *and* fourteen lambs of the first year without spot:
27 And their meat offering and their drink offerings for the bullocks, for the rams, and for the lambs, *shall be* according to their number, after the manner:
28 And one goat *for* a sin offering; beside the continual burnt offering, and his meat offering, and his drink offering.
29 And on the sixth day eight bullocks, two rams, *and* fourteen lambs of the first year without blemish:
30 And their meat offering and their drink offerings for the bullocks, for the rams, and for the lambs, *shall be* according to their number, after the manner:
31 And one goat *for* a sin offering; beside the continual burnt offering, his meat offering, and his drink offering.
32 And on the seventh day seven bullocks, two rams, *and* fourteen lambs of the first year without blemish:
33 And their meat offering and their drink

1 Lev. 23:24
6 Num. 15:11, 12; 28:3, 11
7 Lev. 16:29; 23:27; Ps. 35:13; Isa. 58:5
8 Num. 28:19
11 Lev. 16:3, 5
12 Lev. 23:34; Deut. 16:13; Ezek. 45:25
13 Ezra 3:4
18 Num. 15:12; 28:7, 14; 29:3, 4, 9, 10
21 Num. 29:18

offerings for the bullocks, for the rams, and for the lambs, *shall be* according to their number, after the manner:

34 And one goat *for* a sin offering; beside the continual burnt offering, his meat offering, and his drink offering.

35 On the eighth day ye shall have a solemn assembly: ye shall do no servile work *therein*:

36 But ye shall offer a burnt offering, a sacrifice made by fire, of a sweet savour unto the LORD: one bullock, one ram, seven lambs of the first year without blemish:

37 Their meat offering and their drink offerings for the bullock, for the ram, and for the lambs, *shall be* according to their number, after the manner:

38 And one goat *for* a sin offering; beside the continual burnt offering, and his meat offering, and his drink offering.

39 These *things* ye shall do unto the LORD in your set feasts, beside your vows, and your freewill offerings, for your burnt offerings, and for your meat offerings, and for your drink offerings, and for your peace offerings.

40 And Moses told the children of Israel according to all that the LORD commanded Moses.

CHAPTER 30
Women's Vows

1 And Moses spake unto the heads of the tribes concerning the children of Israel, saying, This *is* the thing which the LORD hath commanded.

2 If a man vow a vow unto the LORD, or swear an oath to bind his soul with a bond; he shall not break his word, he shall do according to all that proceedeth out of his mouth.

3 If a woman also vow a vow unto the LORD, and bind herself by a bond, *being* in her father's house in her youth;

4 And her father hear her vow, and her bond wherewith she hath bound her soul, and her father shall hold his peace at her: then all her vows shall stand, and every bond wherewith she hath bound her soul shall stand.

5 But if her father disallow her in the day that he heareth; not any of her vows, or of her bonds wherewith she hath bound her soul, shall stand: and the LORD shall forgive her, because her father disallowed her.

6 And if she had at all an husband, when she vowed, or uttered ought out of her lips, wherewith she bound her soul;

7 And her husband heard *it*, and held his

peace at her in the day that he heard *it*: then her vows shall stand, and her bonds wherewith she bound her soul shall stand.

8 But if her husband disallowed her on the day that he heard *it*; then he shall make her vow which she vowed, and that which she uttered with her lips, wherewith she bound her soul, of none effect: and the LORD shall forgive her.

9 But every vow of a widow, and of her that is divorced, wherewith they have bound their souls, shall stand against her.

10 And if she vowed in her husband's house, or bound her soul by a bond with an oath;

11 And her husband heard *it*, and held his peace at her, *and* disallowed her not: then all her vows shall stand, and every bond wherewith she bound her soul shall stand.

12 But if her husband hath utterly made them void on the day he heard *them*; *then* whatsoever proceeded out of her lips concerning her vows, or concerning the bond of her soul, shall not stand: her husband hath made them void; and the LORD shall forgive her.

13 Every vow, and every binding oath to afflict the soul, her husband may establish it, or her husband may make it void.

14 But if her husband altogether hold his peace at her from day to day; then he establisheth all her vows, or all her bonds, which *are* upon her: he confirmeth them, because he held his peace at her in the day that he heard *them*.

15 But if he shall any ways make them void after that he hath heard *them*; then he shall bear her iniquity.

16 These *are* the statutes, which the LORD commanded Moses, between a man and his wife, between the father and his daughter, *being yet* in her youth in her father's house.

CHAPTER 31
War against Midian

1 And the LORD spake unto Moses, saying,

2 Avenge the children of Israel of the Midianites: afterward shalt thou be gathered unto thy people.

3 And Moses spake unto the people, saying, Arm some of yourselves unto the war, and let them go against the Midianites, and avenge the LORD of Midian.

4 Of every tribe a thousand, throughout all the tribes of Israel, shall ye send to the war.

5 So there were delivered out of the thousands of Israel, a thousand of *every* tribe, twelve thousand armed for war.

6 And Moses sent them to the war, a thou-

Cross references

35 Lev. 23:36

39 Lev. 7:11, 16; 22:21, 23; 23:2; 1Chr. 23:31; 2Chr. 31:3; Ezra 3:5; Neh. 10:33; Isa. 1:14

1 Num. 1:4, 16; 7:2

2 Lev. 5:4; 27:2; Deut. 23:21; Judg. 11:30, 35; Job 22:27; Ps. 22:25; 50:14; 55:20; 66:13, 14; 116:14, 18; Eccl. 5:4; Nah. 1:15; Matt. 14:9; Acts 23:14

6 Ps. 56:12

8 Gen. 3:16

2 Num. 25:17; 27:13

6 Num. 10:9

sand of *every* tribe, them and Phinehas the son of Eleazar the priest, to the war, with the holy instruments, and the trumpets to blow in his hand.

7 And they warred against the Midianites, as the LORD commanded Moses; and they slew all the males.

8 And they slew the kings of Midian, beside the rest of them that were slain; *namely,* Evi, and Rekem, and Zur, and Hur, and Reba, five kings of Midian: Balaam also the son of Beor they slew with the sword.

9 And the children of Israel took *all* the women of Midian captives, and their little ones, and took the spoil of all their cattle, and all their flocks, and all their goods.

10 And they burnt all their cities wherein they dwelt, and all their goodly castles, with fire.

11 And they took all the spoil, and all the prey, *both* of men and of beasts.

12 And they brought the captives, and the prey, and the spoil, unto Moses, and Eleazar the priest, and unto the congregation of the children of Israel, unto the camp at the plains of Moab, which *are* by Jordan *near* Jericho.

13 And Moses, and Eleazar the priest, and all the princes of the congregation, went forth to meet them without the camp.

14 And Moses was wroth with the officers of the host, *with* the captains over thousands, and captains over hundreds, which came from the battle.

15 And Moses said unto them, Have ye saved all the women alive?

16 Behold, these caused the children of Israel, through the counsel of Balaam, to commit trespass against the LORD in the matter of Peor, and there was a plague among the congregation of the LORD.

17 Now therefore kill every male among the little ones, and kill every woman that hath known man by lying with him.

18 But all the women children, that have not known a man by lying with him, keep alive for yourselves.

19 And do ye abide without the camp seven days: whosoever hath killed any person, and whosoever hath touched any slain, purify *both* yourselves and your captives on the third day, and on the seventh day.

20 And purify all *your* raiment, and all that is made of skins, and all work of goats' *hair,* and all things made of wood.

Division of the Spoils

21 And Eleazar the priest said unto the men of war which went to the battle, This *is* the

---

7 Deut. 20:13; Judg. 6:1, 2, 33; 21:11; 1Sam. 27:9; 1Kgs. 11:15, 16

8 Josh. 13:21, 22

11 Deut. 20:14

15 Deut. 20:14; 1Sam. 15:3

16 Num. 24:14; 25:2, 9; 2Pet. 2:15; Rev. 2:14

17 Judg. 21:11

19 Num. 5:2; 19:11

23 Num. 19:9, 17

24 Lev. 11:25

27 Josh. 22:8; 1Sam. 30:24

28 Num. 18:26; 31:30, 47

30 Num. 3:7, 8, 25, 31, 36; 18:3, 4; 31:42-47

---

ordinance of the law which the LORD commanded Moses;

22 Only the gold, and the silver, the brass, the iron, the tin, and the lead,

23 Every thing that may abide the fire, ye shall make *it* go through the fire, and it shall be clean: nevertheless it shall be purified with the water of separation: and all that abideth not the fire ye shall make go through the water.

24 And ye shall wash your clothes on the seventh day, and ye shall be clean, and afterward ye shall come into the camp.

25 And the LORD spake unto Moses, saying,

26 Take the sum of the prey that was taken, *both* of man and of beast, thou, and Eleazar the priest, and the chief fathers of the congregation:

27 And divide the prey into two parts; between them that took the war upon them, who went out to battle, and between all the congregation:

28 And levy a tribute unto the LORD of the men of war which went out to battle: one soul of five hundred, *both* of the persons, and of the beeves, and of the asses, and of the sheep:

29 Take *it* of their half, and give it unto Eleazar the priest, *for* an heave offering of the LORD.

30 And of the children of Israel's half, thou shalt take one portion of fifty, of the persons, of the beeves, of the asses, and of the flocks, of all manner of beasts, and give them unto the Levites, which keep the charge of the tabernacle of the LORD.

31 And Moses and Eleazar the priest did as the LORD commanded Moses.

32 And the booty, *being* the rest of the prey which the men of war had caught, was six hundred thousand and seventy thousand and five thousand sheep,

33 And threescore and twelve thousand beeves,

34 And threescore and one thousand asses,

35 And thirty and two thousand persons in all, of women that had not known man by lying with him.

36 And the half, *which was* the portion of them that went out to war, was in number three hundred thousand and seven and thirty thousand and five hundred sheep:

37 And the LORD's tribute of the sheep was six hundred and threescore and fifteen.

38 And the beeves *were* thirty and six thousand; of which the LORD's tribute *was* threescore and twelve.

39 And the asses *were* thirty thousand and

five hundred; of which the LORD's tribute *was* threescore and one.

40 And the persons *were* sixteen thousand; of which the LORD's tribute *was* thirty and two persons.

41 And Moses gave the tribute, *which was* the LORD's heave offering, unto Eleazar the priest, as the LORD commanded Moses.

42 And of the children of Israel's half, which Moses divided from the men that warred,

43 (Now the half *that pertained unto* the congregation was three hundred thousand and thirty thousand *and* seven thousand and five hundred sheep,

44 And thirty and six thousand beeves,

45 And thirty thousand asses and five hundred,

46 And sixteen thousand persons;)

47 Even of the children of Israel's half, Moses took one portion of fifty, *both* of man and of beast, and gave them unto the Levites, which kept the charge of the tabernacle of the LORD; as the LORD commanded Moses.

48 And the officers which *were* over thousands of the host, the captains of thousands, and captains of hundreds, came near unto Moses:

49 And they said unto Moses, Thy servants have taken the sum of the men of war which *are* under our charge, and there lacketh not one man of us.

50 We have therefore brought an oblation for the LORD, what every man hath gotten, of jewels of gold, chains, and bracelets, rings, earrings, and tablets, to make an atonement for our souls before the LORD.

51 And Moses and Eleazar the priest took the gold of them, *even* all wrought jewels.

52 And all the gold of the offering that they offered up to the LORD, of the captains of thousands, and of the captains of hundreds, was sixteen thousand seven hundred and fifty shekels.

53 (*For* the men of war had taken spoil, every man for himself.)

54 And Moses and Eleazar the priest took the gold of the captains of thousands and of hundreds, and brought it into the tabernacle of the congregation, *for* a memorial for the children of Israel before the LORD.

CHAPTER 32
Three Tribes Settle East of the Jordan

1 Now the children of Reuben and the children of Gad had a very great multitude of cattle: and when they saw the land of Jazer, and the land of Gilead, that, behold, the place *was* a place for cattle;

2 The children of Gad and the children of Reuben came and spake unto Moses, and to Eleazar the priest, and unto the princes of the congregation, saying,

3 Ataroth, and Dibon, and Jazer, and Nimrah, and Heshbon, and Elealeh, and Shebam, and Nebo, and Beon,

4 *Even* the country which the LORD smote before the congregation of Israel, *is* a land for cattle, and thy servants have cattle:

5 Wherefore, said they, if we have found grace in thy sight, let this land be given unto thy servants for a possession, *and* bring us not over Jordan.

6 And Moses said unto the children of Gad and to the children of Reuben, Shall your brethren go to war, and shall ye sit here?

7 And wherefore discourage ye the heart of the children of Israel from going over into the land which the LORD hath given them?

8 Thus did your fathers, when I sent them from Kadesh-barnea to see the land.

9 For when they went up unto the valley of Eshcol, and saw the land, they discouraged the heart of the children of Israel, that they should not go into the land which the LORD had given them.

10 And the LORD's anger was kindled the same time, and he sware, saying,

11 Surely none of the men that came up out of Egypt, from twenty years old and upward, shall see the land which I sware unto Abraham, unto Isaac, and unto Jacob; because they have not wholly followed me:

12 Save Caleb the son of Jephunneh the Kenezite, and Joshua the son of Nun: for they have wholly followed the LORD.

13 And the LORD's anger was kindled against Israel, and he made them wander in the wilderness forty years, until all the generation, that had done evil in the sight of the LORD, was consumed.

14 And, behold, ye are risen up in your fathers' stead, an increase of sinful men, to augment yet the fierce anger of the LORD toward Israel.

15 For if ye turn away from after him, he will yet again leave them in the wilderness; and ye shall destroy all this people.

16 And they came near unto him, and said, We will build sheepfolds here for our cattle, and cities for our little ones:

17 But we ourselves will go ready armed before the children of Israel, until we have brought them unto their place: and our lit-

Cross references (center column)

41 Num. 18:8, 19

47 Num. 31:30

50 Ex. 30:12, 16

53 Deut. 20:14

54 Ex. 30:16

1 Num. 21:32; Josh. 13:25; 2Sam. 24:5

3 Num. 32:36, *Beth-nimrah;* 32:38, *Shibmah, Baal-meon*

4 Num. 21:24, 34

8 Num. 13:3, 26; Deut. 1:22

9 Num. 13:24, 31; Deut. 1:24, 28

10 Num. 14:11, 21; Deut. 1:34

11 Num. 14:24, 28, 29, 30; Deut. 1:35

12 Num. 14:24; Deut. 1:36; Josh. 14:8, 9

13 Num. 14:33-35; 26:64, 65

14 Deut. 1:34

15 Deut. 30:17; Josh. 22:16, 18; 2Chr. 7:19; 15:2

17 Josh. 4:12, 13

tle ones shall dwell in the fenced cities because of the inhabitants of the land.

18 We will not return unto our houses, until the children of Israel have inherited every man his inheritance.

19 For we will not inherit with them on yonder side Jordan, or forward; because our inheritance is fallen to us on this side Jordan eastward.

20 And Moses said unto them, If ye will do this thing, if ye will go armed before the LORD to war,

21 And will go all of you armed over Jordan before the LORD, until he hath driven out his enemies from before him,

22 And the land be subdued before the LORD: then afterward ye shall return, and be guiltless before the LORD, and before Israel; and this land shall be your possession before the LORD.

23 But if ye will not do so, behold, ye have sinned against the LORD: and be sure your sin will find you out.

24 Build you cities for your little ones, and folds for your sheep; and do that which hath proceeded out of your mouth.

25 And the children of Gad and the children of Reuben spake unto Moses, saying, Thy servants will do as my lord commandeth.

26 Our little ones, our wives, our flocks, and all our cattle, shall be there in the cities of Gilead:

27 But thy servants will pass over, every man armed for war, before the LORD to battle, as my lord saith.

28 So concerning them Moses commanded Eleazar the priest, and Joshua the son of Nun, and the chief fathers of the tribes of the children of Israel:

29 And Moses said unto them, If the children of Gad and the children of Reuben will pass with you over Jordan, every man armed to battle, before the LORD, and the land shall be subdued before you; then ye shall give them the land of Gilead for a possession:

30 But if they will not pass over with you armed, they shall have possessions among you in the land of Canaan.

31 And the children of Gad and the children of Reuben answered, saying, As the

LORD hath said unto thy servants, so will we do.

32 We will pass over armed before the LORD into the land of Canaan, that the possession of our inheritance on this side Jordan *may be* ours.

33 And Moses gave unto them, *even* to the children of Gad, and to the children of Reuben, and unto half the tribe of Manasseh the son of Joseph, the kingdom of Sihon king of the Amorites, and the kingdom of Og king of Bashan, the land, with the cities thereof in the coasts, *even* the cities of the country round about.

34 And the children of Gad built Dibon, and Ataroth, and Aroer,

35 And Atroth, Shophan, and Jaazer, and Jogbehah,

36 And Beth-nimrah, and Beth-haran, fenced cities: and folds for sheep.

37 And the children of Reuben built Heshbon, and Elealeh, and Kirjathaim,

38 And Nebo, and Baal-meon, (their names being changed), and Shibmah: and gave other names unto the cities which they builded.

39 And the children of Machir the son of Manasseh went to Gilead, and took it, and dispossessed the Amorite which *was* in it.

40 And Moses gave Gilead unto Machir the son of Manasseh; and he dwelt therein.

41 And Jair the son of Manasseh went and took the small towns thereof, and called them Havoth-jair.

42 And Nobah went and took Kenath, and the villages thereof, and called it Nobah, after his own name.

CHAPTER 33
Israel's Wilderness Itinerary

1 These *are* the journeys of the children of Israel, which went forth out of the land of Egypt with their armies under the hand of Moses and Aaron.

2 And Moses wrote their goings out according to their journeys by the commandment of the LORD: and these *are* their journeys according to their goings out.

3 And they departed from Rameses in the first month, on the fifteenth day of the first month; on the morrow after the passover the children of Israel went out with an

Cross-references (center column)

18 Josh. 22:4

19 Num. 32:33; Josh. 12:1; 13:8

20 Deut. 3:18; Josh. 1:14; 4:12, 13

22 Deut. 3: 12, 15, 16, 18, 20; Josh. 1:15; 11:23; 13:8, 32; 18:1; 22:4, 9

23 Gen. 4:7; 44:16; Isa. 59:12

24 Num. 32:16, 34-42

26 Josh. 1:14

27 Josh. 4:12

28 Josh. 1:13

33 Num. 21:24, 33, 35; Deut. 3:12-17; 29:8; Josh. 12:6; 13:8; 22:4

34 Num. 33:45, 46; Deut. 2:36

35 Num. 32:1, 3, *Jazer*

36 Num. 32:3, *Nimrah*

37 Num. 21:27

38 Ex. 23:13; Num. 22:41; 32:3; Josh. 23:7; Isa. 46:1

39 Gen. 50:23

40 Deut. 3:12, 13, 15; Josh. 13:31; 17:1

41 Deut. 3:14; Josh. 13:30; Judg. 10:4; 1Kgs. 4:13; 1Chr. 2:21-23

3 Ex. 12:2, 37; 13:4; 14:8

33:2 according to their journeys. This entire chapter lists forty distinct places where the Israelites encamped after the Exodus from Egypt and prior to their arrival in the plains of Moab. During all of those years God provided their food, and the people were trained in the ways of God and the worship procedures of the Tabernacle. Yet murmurings and periodic challenges marred even this long period of training.

high hand in the sight of all the Egyptians.
4 For the Egyptians buried all *their* first-born, which the LORD had smitten among them: upon their gods also the LORD executed judgments.
5 And the children of Israel removed from Rameses, and pitched in Succoth.
6 And they departed from Succoth, and pitched in Etham, which *is* in the edge of the wilderness.
7 And they removed from Etham, and turned again unto Pi-hahiroth, which *is* before Baal-zephon: and they pitched before Migdol.
8 And they departed from before Pi-hahiroth, and passed through the midst of the sea into the wilderness, and went three days' journey in the wilderness of Etham, and pitched in Marah.
9 And they removed from Marah, and came unto Elim: and in Elim *were* twelve fountains of water, and threescore and ten palm trees; and they pitched there.
10 And they removed from Elim, and encamped by the Red sea.
11 And they removed from the Red sea, and encamped in the wilderness of Sin.
12 And they took their journey out of the wilderness of Sin, and encamped in Dophkah.
13 And they departed from Dophkah, and encamped in Alush.
14 And they removed from Alush, and encamped at Rephidim, where was no water for the people to drink.
15 And they departed from Rephidim, and pitched in the wilderness of Sinai.
16 And they removed from the desert of Sinai, and pitched at Kibroth-hattaavah.
17 And they departed from Kibroth-hattaavah, and encamped at Hazeroth.
18 And they departed from Hazeroth, and pitched in Rithmah.
19 And they departed from Rithmah, and pitched at Rimmon-parez.
20 And they departed from Rimmon-parez, and pitched in Libnah.
21 And they removed from Libnah, and pitched at Rissah.
22 And they journeyed from Rissah, and pitched in Kehelathah.
23 And they went from Kehelathah, and pitched in mount Shapher.
24 And they removed from mount Shapher, and encamped in Haradah.
25 And they removed from Haradah, and pitched in Makheloth.
26 And they removed from Makheloth, and encamped at Tahath.

27 And they departed from Tahath, and pitched at Tarah.
28 And they removed from Tarah, and pitched in Mithcah.
29 And they went from Mithcah, and pitched in Hashmonah.
30 And they departed from Hashmonah, and encamped at Moseroth.
31 And they departed from Moseroth, and pitched in Bene-jaakan.
32 And they removed from Bene-jaakan, and encamped at Horhagidgad.
33 And they went from Horhagidgad, and pitched in Jotbathah.
34 And they removed from Jotbathah, and encamped at Ebronah.
35 And they departed from Ebronah, and encamped at Ezion-gaber.
36 And they removed from Ezion-gaber, and pitched in the wilderness of Zin, which *is* Kadesh.
37 And they removed from Kadesh, and pitched in mount Hor, in the edge of the land of Edom.
38 And Aaron the priest went up into mount Hor at the commandment of the LORD, and died there, in the fortieth year after the children of Israel were come out of the land of Egypt, in the first *day* of the fifth month.
39 And Aaron *was* an hundred and twenty and three years old when he died in mount Hor.
40 And king Arad the Canaanite, which dwelt in the south in the land of Canaan, heard of the coming of the children of Israel.
41 And they departed from mount Hor, and pitched in Zalmonah.
42 And they departed from Zalmonah, and pitched in Punon.
43 And they departed from Punon, and pitched in Oboth.
44 And they departed from Oboth, and pitched in Ije-abarim, in the border of Moab.
45 And they departed from Iim, and pitched in Dibon-gad.
46 And they removed from Dibon-gad, and encamped in Almon-diblathaim.
47 And they removed from Almon-diblathaim, and pitched in the mountains of Abarim, before Nebo.
48 And they departed from the mountains of Abarim, and pitched in the plains of Moab by Jordan *near* Jericho.
49 And they pitched by Jordan, from Beth-jesimoth *even* unto Abel-shittim in the plains of Moab.

Cross references (center column):
4 Ex. 12:12, 29; 18:11; Isa. 19:1; Rev. 12:8
5 Ex. 12:37
6 Ex. 13:20
7 Ex. 14:2, 9
8 Ex. 14:22; 15:22, 23
9 Ex. 15:27
11 Ex. 16:1
14 Ex. 17:1; 19:2
15 Ex. 16:1; 19:1, 2
16 Num. 11:34
17 Num. 11:35
18 Num. 12:16
30 Deut. 10:6
32 Gen. 36:27; Deut. 10:6, 7; 1Chr. 1:42
35 Deut. 2:8; 1Kgs. 9:26; 22:48
36 Num. 20:1; 27:14
37 Num. 20:22, 23; 21:4
38 Num. 20:25, 28; Deut. 10:6; 32:50
40 Num. 21:1-3
41 Num. 21:4
43 Num. 21:10
44 Num. 21:11
45 Num. 32:34
46 Jer. 48:22; Ezek. 6:14
47 Num. 21:20; Deut. 32:49
48 Num. 22:1
49 Num. 25:1; Josh. 2:1

Instructions for Taking Over Canaan

50 And the LORD spake unto Moses in the plains of Moab by Jordan *near* Jericho, saying,

51 Speak unto the children of Israel, and say unto them, When ye are passed over Jordan into the land of Canaan;

52 Then ye shall drive out all the inhabitants of the land from before you, and destroy all their pictures, and destroy all their molten images and quite pluck down all their high places:

53 And ye shall dispossess *the inhabitants* of the land, and dwell therein: for I have given you the land to possess it.

54 And ye shall divide the land by lot for an inheritance among your families: *and* to the more ye shall give the more inheritance, and to the fewer ye shall give the less inheritance: every man's *inheritance* shall be in the place where his lot falleth; according to the tribes of your fathers ye shall inherit.

55 But if ye will not drive out the inhabitants of the land from before you; then it shall come to pass, that those which ye let remain of them *shall be* pricks in your eyes, and thorns in your sides, and shall vex you in the land wherein ye dwell.

56 Moreover it shall come to pass, *that* I shall do unto you, as I thought to do unto them.

CHAPTER 34

1 And the LORD spake unto Moses, saying,

2 Command the children of Israel, and say unto them, When ye come into the land of Canaan; (this *is* the land that shall fall unto you for an inheritance, *even* the land of Canaan with the coasts thereof:)

3 Then your south quarter shall be from the wilderness of Zin along by the coast of Edom, and your south border shall be the outmost coast of the salt sea eastward:

4 And your border shall turn from the south to the ascent of Akrabbim, and pass on to Zin: and the going forth thereof shall be from the south to Kadesh-barnea, and shall go on to Hazar-addar, and pass on to Azmon:

5 And the border shall fetch a compass from Azmon unto the river of Egypt, and the goings out of it shall be at the sea.

6 And *as for* the western border, ye shall even have the great sea for a border: this shall be your west border.

7 And this shall be your north border: from the great sea ye shall point out for you mount Hor:

8 From mount Hor ye shall point out *your border* unto the entrance of Hamath; and the goings forth of the border shall be to Zedad:

9 And the border shall go on to Ziphron, and the goings out of it shall be at Hazar-enan: this shall be your north border.

10 And ye shall point out your east border from Hazar-enan to Shepham:

11 And the coast shall go down from Shepham to Riblah, on the east side of Ain; and the border shall descend, and shall reach unto the side of the sea of Chinnereth eastward:

12 And the border shall go down to Jordan, and the goings out of it shall be at the salt sea: this shall be your land with the coasts thereof round about.

13 And Moses commanded the children of Israel, saying, This *is* the land which ye shall inherit by lot, which the LORD commanded to give unto the nine tribes, and to the half tribe:

14 For the tribe of the children of Reuben according to the house of their fathers, and the tribe of the children of Gad according to the house of their fathers, have received *their inheritance*; and half the tribe of Manasseh have received their inheritance:

15 The two tribes and the half tribe have received their inheritance on this side Jordan *near* Jericho eastward, toward the sunrising.

16 And the LORD spake unto Moses, saying,

17 These *are* the names of the men which shall divide the land unto you: Eleazar the priest, and Joshua the son of Nun.

18 And ye shall take one prince of every tribe, to divide the land by inheritance.

19 And the names of the men *are* these: Of the tribe of Judah, Caleb the son of Jephunneh.

20 And of the tribe of the children of Simeon, Shemuel the son of Ammihud.

21 Of the tribe of Benjamin, Elidad the son of Chislon.

22 And the prince of the tribe of the children of Dan, Bukki the son of Jogli.

Cross references (center column)

51 Deut. 7:1, 2; 9:1; Josh. 3:17

52 Ex. 23:24, 33; 34:13; Deut. 7:2, 5; 12:3; Josh. 11:12; Judg. 2:2

54 Num. 26:53-55

55 Josh. 23:13; Judg. 2:3; Ps. 106:34, 36; Ezek. 28:24

2 Gen. 17:8; Deut. 1:7; Ps. 78:55; 105:11; Ezek. 47:14

3 Gen. 14:3; Josh. 15:1, 2; Ezek. 47:13

4 Num. 13:26; 32:8; Josh. 15:3, 4

5 Gen. 15:18; Josh. 15:4, 47; 1Kgs. 8:65; Isa. 27:12

7 Num. 33:37

8 Num. 13:21; 2Kgs. 14:25; Ezek. 47:15

9 Ezek. 47:17

11 Deut. 3:17; Josh. 11:2; 19:35; 2Kgs. 23:33; Jer. 39:5, 6; Matt. 14:34; Luke 5:1

12 Num. 34:3

13 Num. 34:1; Josh. 14:1, 2

14 Num. 32:33; Josh. 14:2, 3

17 Josh. 14:1; 19:51

18 Num. 1:4, 16

33:51–56 When ye are passed over Jordan into . . . Canaan. God instructed his people to drive out and completely replace all of the wicked inhabitants of the land. Their failure to comply with this divine directive would result in the pagans that remained becoming thorns who would "vex [them] in the land." This prophecy came to pass, resulting in the varied history of Israel through the next thousand years.

23 The prince of the children of Joseph, for the tribe of the children of Manasseh, Hanniel the son of Ephod.

24 And the prince of the tribe of the children of Ephraim, Kemuel the son of Shiphtan.

25 And the prince of the tribe of the children of Zebulun, Elizaphan the son of Parnach.

26 And the prince of the tribe of the children of Issachar, Paltiel the son of Azzan.

27 And the prince of the tribe of the children of Asher, Ahihud the son of Shelomi.

28 And the prince of the tribe of the children of Naphtali, Pedahel the son of Ammihud.

29 These *are they* whom the LORD commanded to divide the inheritance unto the children of Israel in the land of Canaan.

CHAPTER 35
Cities for the Levites

1 And the LORD spake unto Moses in the plains of Moab by Jordan *near* Jericho, saying,

2 Command the children of Israel, that they give unto the Levites of the inheritance of their possession cities to dwell in; and ye shall give *also* unto the Levites suburbs for the cities round about them.

3 And the cities shall they have to dwell in; and the suburbs of them shall be for their cattle, and for their goods, and for all their beasts.

4 And the suburbs of the cities, which ye shall give unto the Levites, *shall reach* from the wall of the city and outward a thousand cubits round about.

5 And ye shall measure from without the city on the east side two thousand cubits, and on the south side two thousand cubits, and on the west side two thousand cubits, and on the north side two thousand cubits; and the city *shall be* in the midst: this shall be to them the suburbs of the cities.

6 And among the cities which ye shall give unto the Levites *there shall be* six cities for refuge, which ye shall appoint for the manslayer, that he may flee thither: and to them ye shall add forty and two cities.

7 *So* all the cities which ye shall give to the Levites *shall be* forty and eight cities: them *shall ye give* with their suburbs.

8 And the cities which ye shall give *shall be*

of the possession of the children of Israel: from *them that have* many ye shall give many; but from *them that have* few ye shall give few: every one shall give of his cities unto the Levites according to his inheritance which he inheriteth.

The Cities of Refuge

9 And the LORD spake unto Moses, saying,

10 Speak unto the children of Israel, and say unto them, When ye be come over Jordan into the land of Canaan;

11 Then ye shall appoint you cities to be cities of refuge for you; that the slayer may flee thither, which killeth any person at unawares.

12 And they shall be unto you cities for refuge from the avenger; that the manslayer die not, until he stand before the congregation in judgment.

13 And of these cities which ye shall give six cities shall ye have for refuge.

14 Ye shall give three cities on this side Jordan, and three cities shall ye give in the land of Canaan, *which* shall be cities of refuge.

15 These six cities shall be a refuge, *both* for the children of Israel, and for the stranger, and for the sojourner among them: that every one that killeth any person unawares may flee thither.

16 And if he smite him with an instrument of iron, so that he die, he *is* a murderer: the murderer shall surely be put to death.

17 And if he smite him with throwing a stone, wherewith he may die, and he die, he *is* a murderer: the murderer shall surely be put to death.

18 Or *if* he smite him with an hand weapon of wood, wherewith he may die, and he die, he *is* a murderer: the murderer shall surely be put to death.

19 The revenger of blood himself shall slay the murderer: when he meeteth him, he shall slay him.

20 But if he thrust him of hatred, or hurl at him by laying of wait, that he die;

21 Or in enmity smite him with his hand, that he die: he that smote *him* shall surely be put to death; *for* he *is* a murderer: the revenger of blood shall slay the murderer, when he meeteth him.

22 But if he thrust him suddenly without

Cross references (center column)

2 Josh. 14:3, 4; 21:2; Ezek. 45:1-5; 48:8-10

6 Num. 35:13; Deut. 4:41; Josh. 20:2, 7, 8; 21:3, 13, 21, 27, 32, 36, 38

7 Josh. 21:41

8 Num. 26:54; Josh. 21:3

10 Deut. 19:2; Josh. 20:2

11 Ex. 21:13

12 Deut. 19:6; Josh. 20:3, 5, 6

13 Num. 35:6

14 Deut. 4:41; Josh. 20:8

15 Num. 15:16

16 Ex. 21:12, 14; Lev. 24:17; Deut. 19:11, 12

19 Num. 35:21, 24, 27; Deut. 19:6, 12; Josh. 20:3, 5

20 Gen. 4:8; Ex. 21:14; Deut. 19:11; 2Sam. 3:27; 20:10; 1Kgs. 2:31, 32

22 Ex. 21:13

35:14 Six of the forty-eight cities of the Levites would be designated as places of safety for any who were guilty of accidental homicide in those difficult times. There, according to the Law, no relative could seek to avenge the unintentional crime by slaying the guilty. These cities of refuge may be considered as a type of Christ, sheltering the sinner from judgment and death (cf. Heb. 6:18).

enmity, or have cast upon him any thing without laying of wait,

23 Or with any stone, wherewith a man may die, seeing *him* not, and cast *it* upon him, that he die, and *was* not his enemy, neither sought his harm:

24 Then the congregation shall judge between the slayer and the revenger of blood according to these judgments:

25 And the congregation shall deliver the slayer out of the hand of the revenger of blood, and the congregation shall restore him to the city of his refuge, whither he was fled: and he shall abide in it unto the death of the high priest, which was anointed with the holy oil.

26 But if the slayer shall at any time come without the border of the city of his refuge, whither he was fled;

27 And the revenger of blood find him without the borders of the city of his refuge, and the revenger of blood kill the slayer; he shall not be guilty of blood:

28 Because he should have remained in the city of his refuge until the death of the high priest: but after the death of the high priest the slayer shall return into the land of his possession.

29 So these *things* shall be for a statute of judgment unto you throughout your generations in all your dwellings.

30 Whoso killeth any person, the murderer shall be put to death by the mouth of witnesses: but one witness shall not testify against any person *to cause him* to die.

31 Moreover ye shall take no satisfaction for the life of a murderer, which *is* guilty of death: but he shall be surely put to death.

32 And ye shall take no satisfaction for him that is fled to the city of his refuge, that he should come again to dwell in the land, until the death of the priest.

33 So ye shall not pollute the land wherein ye *are*: for blood it defileth the land: and the land cannot be cleansed of the blood that is shed therein, but by the blood of him that shed it.

34 Defile not therefore the land which ye shall inhabit, wherein I dwell: for I the LORD dwell among the children of Israel.

CHAPTER 36
Further Instructions on Inheritance

1 And the chief fathers of the families of the children of Gilead, the son of Machir, the son of Manasseh, of the families of the sons of Joseph, came near, and spake before Moses, and before the princes, the chief fathers of the children of Israel:

2 And they said, The LORD commanded my lord to give the land for an inheritance by lot to the children of Israel: and my lord was commanded by the LORD to give the inheritance of Zelophehad our brother unto his daughters.

3 And if they be married to any of the sons of the *other* tribes of the children of Israel, then shall their inheritance be taken from the inheritance of our fathers, and shall be put to the inheritance of the tribe whereunto they are received: so shall it be taken from the lot of our inheritance.

4 And when the jubile of the children of Israel shall be, then shall their inheritance be put unto the inheritance of the tribe whereunto they are received: so shall their inheritance be taken away from the inheritance of the tribe of our fathers.

5 And Moses commanded the children of Israel according to the word of the LORD, saying, The tribe of the sons of Joseph hath said well.

6 This *is* the thing which the LORD doth command concerning the daughters of Zelophehad, saying, Let them marry to whom they think best; only to the family of the tribe of their father shall they marry.

7 So shall not the inheritance of the children of Israel remove from tribe to tribe: for every one of the children of Israel shall keep himself to the inheritance of the tribe of his fathers.

8 And every daughter, that possesseth an inheritance in any tribe of the children of Israel, shall be wife unto one of the family of the tribe of her father, that the children of Israel may enjoy every man the inheritance of his fathers.

9 Neither shall the inheritance remove from *one* tribe to another tribe; but every one of the tribes of the children of Israel shall keep himself to his own inheritance.

10 Even as the LORD commanded Moses, so did the daughters of Zelophehad:

11 For Mahlah, Tirzah, and Hoglah, and Milcah, and Noah, the daughters of Zelophehad, were married unto their father's brothers' sons:

12 *And* they were married into the families of the sons of Manasseh the son of Joseph, and their inheritance remained in the tribe of the family of their father.

13 These *are* the commandments and the judgments, which the LORD commanded by the hand of Moses unto the children of Israel in the plains of Moab by Jordan *near* Jericho.

Cross references (center column):

24 Num. 35:12; Josh. 20:6

25 Ex. 29:7; Lev. 4:3; 21:10; Josh. 20:6

27 Ex. 22:2

29 Num. 27:11

30 Deut. 17:6; 19:15; Matt. 18:16; 2Cor. 13:1; Heb. 10:28

33 Gen. 9:6; Ps. 106:38; Mic. 4:11

34 Ex. 29:45, 46; Lev. 18:25; Deut. 21:23

1 Num. 26:29

2 Num. 26:55; 27:1, 7; 33:54; Josh. 17:3, 4

4 Lev. 25:10

5 Num. 27:7

6 Num. 36:12

7 1Kgs. 21:3

8 1Chr. 23:22

11 Num. 27:1

13 Num. 26:3; 33:50

Deuteronomy

Deuteronomy is not merely a "second law" (the meaning of the Greek word from which the name comes), but an expansion of truth, reviewing the past with an eye to the future. There are three major addresses by Moses: the appointment of Joshua, Moses' song and exhortation, and Moses' parting blessing on the people, as well as a small appendix with his last words. The book teaches that God's laws are outward expressions of His love. In response, love toward God is demonstrated by obedience.

Still strong at the age of 120, Moses instructs the new generation that is preparing to enter the Promised Land. He reminds this generation of the promise of divine grace; he reviews Jehovah's faithfulness and love; he restates the absolute necessity of obedience; he recalls their own failures and rebellion; he reveals future punishments for disobedience; and he renews promises of blessing.

Author
Moses

Date
1405–1400 B.C.

Key Truth
God's Law and God's Love

Historic Time
Shortly before Moses' death

Key Verse
10:12
. . . what doth the LORD thy God require of thee?

Appearing twice is the strong emphasis on love (6:4–5; 10:12; see Mark 12:29–30), where Jesus quotes 6:4, "Hear O Israel; the Lord our God is one Lord," just as Jews recite it today.

This fifth and final book of Moses contains many major predictions. One oft-repeated prophecy is God's promise that Israel would inherit the land of Canaan. Predictive statements about Christ include a description of the future coming of a great prophet like unto Moses (18:15–18, cf. Acts 3:22; 7:37) and a foreshadowing of the Crucifixion (21:22–23, cf. Gal. 3:13). The worldwide dispersion of the children of Israel, which has been literally fulfilled (chap. 28), various chastisements, and Israel's ultimate restoration are all forecast by Moses (29—30; 33).

Deuteronomy's impact on those who penned the books of the New Testament (some 1400 years later) is evident in that quotations from the book appear nearly two hundred times in the New Testament. Christ quotes from Deuteronomy exclusively in His answers to Satan's temptations (Matt. 4:1–11 [cf. Deut. 6:13, 16; 8:3]).

Counting types as well as fulfilled and unfulfilled prophecies, there are 58 distinct predictions in 344 verses out of 959, or 36 percent of the book.

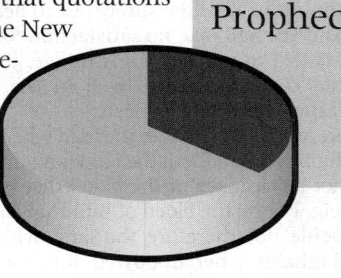

36%
Prophecy

1750 B.C.	1700 B.C.	1650 B.C.	1600 B.C.	1550 B.C.	1500 B.C.	1450 B.C.	1400 B.C.	1350 B.C.

1527
Moses in Pharaoh's court

1487
Moses flees to Midian

1447
Exodus from Egypt

1407
Entrance into Canaan

1447
The Ten Commandments

1407
Book of Deuteronomy

1730-1447
Bondage in Egypt begins

Bondage in Egypt ends

1375-1050
Israel ruled by judges

CHAPTER 1
Israel at Horeb

1 These *be* the words which Moses spake unto all Israel on this side Jordan in the wilderness, in the plain over against the Red *sea*, between Paran, and Tophel, and Laban, and Hazeroth, and Dizahab.

2 (*There are* eleven days *journey* from Horeb by the way of mount Seir unto Kadesh-barnea.)

3 And it came to pass in the fortieth year, in the eleventh month, on the first *day* of the month, *that* Moses spake unto the children of Israel, according unto all that the LORD had given him in commandment unto them;

4 After he had slain Sihon the king of the Amorites, which dwelt in Heshbon, and Og the king of Bashan, which dwelt at Astaroth in Edrei:

5 On this side Jordan, in the land of Moab, began Moses to declare this law, saying,

6 The LORD our God spake unto us in Horeb, saying, Ye have dwelt long enough in this mount:

7 Turn you, and take your journey, and go to the mount of the Amorites, and unto all *the places* nigh thereunto, in the plain, in the hills, and in the vale, and in the south, and by the sea side, to the land of the Canaanites, and unto Lebanon, unto the great river, the river Euphrates.

8 Behold, I have set the land before you: go in and possess the land which the LORD sware unto your fathers, Abraham, Isaac, and Jacob, to give unto them and to their seed after them.

9 And I spake unto you at that time, saying, I am not able to bear you myself alone:

10 The LORD your God hath multiplied you, and, behold, ye *are* this day as the stars of heaven for multitude.

11 (The LORD God of your fathers make you a thousand times so many more as ye *are*, and bless you, as he hath promised you!)

12 How can I myself alone bear your cumbrance, and your burden, and your strife?

13 Take you wise men, and understanding, and known among your tribes, and I will make them rulers over you.

14 And ye answered me, and said, The thing which thou hast spoken *is* good *for us* to do.

15 So I took the chief of your tribes, wise men, and known, and made them heads over you, captains over thousands, and captains over hundreds, and captains over fifties, and captains over tens, and officers among your tribes.

16 And I charged your judges at that time, saying, Hear *the causes* between your brethren, and judge righteously between *every* man and his brother, and the stranger *that is* with him.

17 Ye shall not respect persons in judgment; *but* ye shall hear the small as well as the great; ye shall not be afraid of the face of man; for the judgment *is* God's: and the cause that is too hard for you, bring *it* unto me, and I will hear it.

18 And I commanded you at that time all the things which ye should do.

The Spies and God's Punishment

19 And when we departed from Horeb, we went through all that great and terrible wilderness, which ye saw by the way of the mountain of the Amorites, as the LORD our God commanded us; and we came to Kadesh-barnea.

20 And I said unto you, Ye are come unto the mountain of the Amorites, which the LORD our God doth give unto us.

21 Behold, the LORD thy God hath set the land before thee: go up *and* possess *it*, as the LORD God of thy fathers hath said unto thee; fear not, neither be discouraged.

22 And ye came near unto me every one of you, and said, We will send men before us, and they shall search us out the land, and bring us word again by what way we must go up, and into what cities we shall come.

23 And the saying pleased me well: and I took twelve men of you, one of a tribe:

Cross-references
1 Josh. 9:1, 10; 22:4, 7
2 Num. 13:26; Deut. 9:23
3 Num. 33:38
4 Num. 21:24, 33; Josh. 13:12
6 Ex. 3:1; 19:1; Num. 10:11
8 Gen. 12:7; 15:18; 17:7, 8; 26:4; 28:13
9 Ex. 18:18; Num. 11:14
10 Gen. 15:5; Deut. 10:22; 28:62
11 Gen. 15:5; 22:17; 26:4; Ex. 32:13; 2Sam. 24:3
12 1Kgs. 3:8, 9
13 Ex. 18:21; Num. 11:16, 17
15 Ex. 18:25
16 Lev. 24:22; Deut. 16:18; John 7:24
17 Ex. 18:22, 26; Lev. 19:15; Deut. 16:19; 1Sam. 16:7; 2Chr. 19:6; Prov. 24:23; James 2:1
19 Num. 10:12; 13:26; Deut. 8:15; Jer. 2:6
21 Josh. 1:9
23 Num. 13:3

1:8 the land which the LORD sware unto your fathers. When did the Lord promise this land to Israel? The land of Israel is part of God's covenant pledge to the nation (Gen. 15:18–21; 26:3). That Israel had, and still has, the right to the land is clear from the command to "go in and possess the land." The fact that Israel never brought this area under her total control does not nullify the promise that it will yet happen in the future, during the millennial reign of Christ (Ezek. 47:15–20).

1:20–21 Moses repeats the prophetic promise of the land of Israel from 1:8, but adds, "which the LORD our God doth give unto us." This reiterates the divine prerogative to give the land of Israel to whomever He wants. The Lord further encourages Israel to "fear not, neither be discouraged." Fear and discouragement motivated the ten spies to bring back an evil report about the land, an action which delayed Israel's entry into the land by forty years.

24 And they turned and went up into the mountain, and came unto the valley of Eshcol, and searched it out.

25 And they took of the fruit of the land in their hands, and brought *it* down unto us, and brought us word again, and said, *It is* a good land which the Lord our God doth give us.

26 Notwithstanding ye would not go up, but rebelled against the commandment of the Lord your God:

27 And ye murmured in your tents, and said, Because the Lord hated us, he hath brought us forth out of the land of Egypt, to deliver us into the hand of the Amorites, to destroy us.

28 Whither shall we go up? our brethren have discouraged our heart, saying, The people *is* greater and taller than we; the cities *are* great and walled up to heaven; and moreover we have seen the sons of the Anakims there.

29 Then I said unto you, Dread not, neither be afraid of them.

30 The Lord your God which goeth before you, he shall fight for you, according to all that he did for you in Egypt before your eyes;

31 And in the wilderness, where thou hast seen how that the Lord thy God bare thee, as a man doth bear his son, in all the way that ye went, until ye came into this place.

32 Yet in this thing ye did not believe the Lord your God,

33 Who went in the way before you, to search you out a place to pitch your tents *in*, in fire by night, to shew you by what way ye should go, and in a cloud by day.

34 And the Lord heard the voice of your words, and was wroth, and sware, saying,

35 Surely there shall not one of these men of this evil generation see that good land, which I sware to give unto your fathers,

36 Save Caleb the son of Jephunneh; he shall see it, and to him will I give the land that he hath trodden upon, and to his children, because he hath wholly followed the Lord.

37 Also the Lord was angry with me for your sakes, saying, Thou also shalt not go in thither.

38 *But* Joshua the son of Nun, which standeth before thee, he shall go in thither: encourage him: for he shall cause Israel to inherit it.

39 Moreover your little ones, which ye said should be a prey, and your children, which in that day had no knowledge between good and evil, they shall go in thither, and unto them will I give it, and they shall possess it.

40 But *as for* you, turn you, and take your journey into the wilderness by the way of the Red sea.

41 Then ye answered and said unto me, We have sinned against the Lord, we will go up and fight, according to all that the Lord our God commanded us. And when ye had girded on every man his weapons of war, ye were ready to go up into the hill.

42 And the Lord said unto me, Say unto them, Go not up, neither fight; for I *am* not among you; lest ye be smitten before your enemies.

43 So I spake unto you; and ye would not hear, but rebelled against the commandment of the Lord, and went presumptuously up into the hill.

44 And the Amorites, which dwelt in that mountain, came out against you, and chased you, as bees do, and destroyed you in Seir, *even* unto Hormah.

45 And ye returned and wept before the Lord; but the Lord would not hearken to your voice, nor give ear unto you.

46 So ye abode in Kadesh many days, according unto the days that ye abode *there*.

Cross references:

25 Num. 13:27
26 Num. 14:1-4; Ps. 106:24, 25
27 Deut. 9:28
28 Num. 13:28, 31-33; Deut. 9:1, 2
30 Ex. 14:14, 25; Neh. 4:20
31 Ex. 19:4; Deut. 32:11, 12
32 Ps. 106:24; Jude 1:5
33 Ex. 13:21; Num. 10:33
34 Deut. 2:14, 15
35 Num. 14:22, 23; Ps. 95:11
36 Num. 14:24, 30; Josh. 14:9
37 Num. 3:26; 4:21
38 Ex. 24:13; 33:11; Num. 14:30; 27:18, 19; Deut. 31:7, 23; 1Sam. 16:22
39 Num. 14:3, 31; Rom. 9:11
40 Num. 14:25
41 Num. 14:40
42 Num. 14:42
46 Num. 13:25; 20:1, 22; Judg. 11:17

1:25 It is a good land which the Lord our God doth give us. This prophetic word of the Lord through the twelve spies should have been enough for the earlier generation of Israelites to believe. As a result of Israel's unbelief, the Lord would give the land of Israel to a new generation of His people.

1:35–36 Moses recalls the Lord's statement that "not one of these men of this evil generation" would see the land (Num. 14:29). This prophecy came true as the nation, a generation later, is ready to enter the land of promise. The only exceptions to this promise were Caleb, "because he hath wholly followed the Lord," and Joshua.

1:37 Thou also shalt not go in thither. It was predicted that Moses would not enter the land because he disobeyed the Lord by striking the rock at Meribah (Num. 20:10–13).

1:38–39 he shall cause Israel to inherit it. Joshua, along with Caleb, is allowed into the land because of his trust in God (Num. 13:30—14:28). Moses exhorted and encouraged Joshua to lead the people into the land by transferring his authority to him (Deut. 3:28; 31:1–29; 34:9). The Hebrew name of Joshua is the same name rendered "Jesus" in the New Testament. Joshua is often depicted as a type of Christ. For fulfillment of this prophecy see Joshua 18:4–5.

CHAPTER 2

The Journey in the Wilderness

1 Then we turned, and took our journey into the wilderness by the way of the Red sea, as the LORD spake unto me: and we compassed mount Seir many days.

2 And the LORD spake unto me, saying,

3 Ye have compassed this mountain long enough: turn you northward.

4 And command thou the people, saying, Ye *are* to pass through the coast of your brethren the children of Esau, which dwell in Seir; and they shall be afraid of you: take ye good heed unto yourselves therefore:

5 Meddle not with them; for I will not give you of their land, no, not so much as a foot breadth; because I have given mount Seir unto Esau *for* a possession.

6 Ye shall buy meat of them for money, that ye may eat; and ye shall also buy water of them for money, that ye may drink.

7 For the LORD thy God hath blessed thee in all the works of thy hand: he knoweth thy walking through this great wilderness: these forty years the LORD thy God *hath been* with thee; thou hast lacked nothing.

8 And when we passed by from our brethren the children of Esau, which dwelt in Seir, through the way of the plain from Elath, and from Ezion-gaber, we turned and passed by the way of the wilderness of Moab.

9 And the LORD said unto me, Distress not the Moabites, neither contend with them in battle: for I will not give thee of their land *for* a possession; because I have given Ar unto the children of Lot *for* a possession.

10 The Emims dwelt therein in times past, a people great, and many, and tall, as the Anakims;

11 Which also were accounted giants, as the Anakims; but the Moabites call them Emims.

12 The Horims also dwelt in Seir beforetime; but the children of Esau succeeded them, when they had destroyed them from before them, and dwelt in their stead; as Israel did unto the land of his possession, which the LORD gave unto them.

13 Now rise up, *said I*, and get you over the brook Zered. And we went over the brook Zered.

14 And the space in which we came from Kadesh-barnea, until we were come over the brook Zered, *was* thirty and eight years; until all the generation of the men of war were wasted out from among the host, as the LORD sware unto them.

15 For indeed the hand of the LORD was against them, to destroy them from among the host, until they were consumed.

16 So it came to pass, when all the men of war were consumed and dead from among the people,

17 That the LORD spake unto me, saying,

18 Thou art to pass over through Ar the coast of Moab, this day:

19 And *when* thou comest nigh over against the children of Ammon, distress them not, nor meddle with them: for I will not give thee of the land of the children of Ammon *any* possession; because I have given it unto the children of Lot *for* a possession.

20 (That also was accounted a land of giants: giants dwelt therein in old time; and the Ammonites call them Zamzummims;

21 A people great, and many, and tall, as the Anakims; but the LORD destroyed them before them; and they succeeded them, and dwelt in their stead:

22 As he did to the children of Esau, which dwelt in Seir, when he destroyed the Horims from before them; and they succeeded them, and dwelt in their stead even unto this day:

23 And the Avims which dwelt in Hazerim, *even* unto Azzah, the Caphtorims, which came forth out of Caphtor, destroyed them, and dwelt in their stead.)

24 Rise ye up, take your journey, and pass over the river Arnon: behold, I have given into thine hand Sihon the Amorite, king of Heshbon, and his land: begin to possess *it*, and contend with him in battle.

25 This day will I begin to put the dread of thee and the fear of thee upon the nations *that are* under the whole heaven, who shall hear report of thee, and shall tremble, and be in anguish because of thee.

Israel Defeats Sihon

26 And I sent messengers out of the wilderness of Kedemoth unto Sihon king of Heshbon with words of peace, saying,

27 Let me pass through thy land: I will go along by the highway, I will neither turn unto the right hand nor to the left.

Cross references (center column):

1 Num. 14:25; Deut. 1:40

3 Deut. 2:7, 14

4 Num. 20:14

5 Gen. 36:8; Josh. 24:4

7 Deut. 8:2-4

8 Judg. 11:18; 1Kgs. 9:26

9 Gen. 19:36, 37; Num. 21:28

10 Gen. 14:5; Num. 13:22, 33; Deut. 9:2

12 Gen. 14:6; 36:20; Deut. 2:22

13 Num. 21:12

14 Num. 13:26; 14:25, 33; 26:64; Deut. 1:34, 35; Ezek. 20:15

15 Ps. 78:33; 106:26

19 Gen. 19:38

20 Gen. 14:5

21 Deut. 2:10

22 Gen. 14:6; 36:8, 20-30; Deut. 2:12

23 Gen. 10:14; Josh. 13:3; Jer. 25:20; Amos 9:7

24 Num. 21:13, 14; Judg. 11:18, 21

25 Ex. 15:14, 15; Deut. 11:25; Josh. 2:9, 10

26 Deut. 20:10

27 Num. 21:21, 22; Judg. 11:19

2:24–25 Moses refers to a past prophecy that is recorded here in Scripture for the first time. Though God intends to give them victory over Sihon, king of Heshbon, Israel still must "contend with him in battle." One of the miraculous things that the Lord does for Israel is that He put fear into the nations surrounding the Promised Land.

28 Thou shalt sell me meat for money, that I may eat; and give me water for money, that I may drink: only I will pass through on my feet;

29 (As the children of Esau which dwell in Seir, and the Moabites which dwell in Ar, did unto me;) until I shall pass over Jordan into the land which the LORD our God giveth us.

30 But Sihon king of Heshbon would not let us pass by him: for the LORD thy God hardened his spirit, and made his heart obstinate, that he might deliver him into thy hand, as *appeareth* this day.

31 And the LORD said unto me, Behold, I have begun to give Sihon and his land before thee: begin to possess, that thou mayest inherit his land.

32 Then Sihon came out against us, he and all his people, to fight at Jahaz.

33 And the LORD our God delivered him before us; and we smote him, and his sons, and all his people.

34 And we took all his cities at that time, and utterly destroyed the men, and the women, and the little ones, of every city, we left none to remain:

35 Only the cattle we took for a prey unto ourselves, and the spoil of the cities which we took.

36 From Aroer, which *is* by the brink of the river of Arnon, and *from* the city that *is* by the river, even unto Gilead, there was not one city too strong for us: the LORD our God delivered all unto us.

37 Only unto the land of the children of Ammon thou camest not, *nor* unto any place of the river Jabbok, nor unto the cities in the mountains, nor unto whatsoever the LORD our God forbad us.

CHAPTER 3
Israel Defeats Og

1 Then we turned, and went up the way to Bashan: and Og the king of Bashan came out against us, he and all his people, to battle at Edrei.

2 And the LORD said unto me, Fear him not: for I will deliver him, and all his people, and his land, into thy hand; and thou shalt do unto him as thou didst unto Sihon king of the Amorites, which dwelt at Heshbon.

3 So the LORD our God delivered into our hands Og also, the king of Bashan, and all his people: and we smote him until none was left to him remaining.

4 And we took all his cities at that time, there was not a city which we took not from them, threescore cities, all the region of Argob, the kingdom of Og in Bashan.

5 All these cities *were* fenced with high walls, gates, and bars; beside unwalled towns a great many.

6 And we utterly destroyed them, as we did unto Sihon king of Heshbon, utterly destroying the men, women, and children, of every city.

7 But all the cattle, and the spoil of the cities, we took for a prey to ourselves.

8 And we took at that time out of the hand of the two kings of the Amorites the land that *was* on this side Jordan, from the river of Arnon unto mount Hermon;

9 (*Which* Hermon the Sidonians call Sirion; and the Amorites call it Shenir;)

10 All the cities of the plain, and all Gilead, and all Bashan, unto Salchah and Edrei, cities of the kingdom of Og in Bashan.

11 For only Og king of Bashan remained of the remnant of giants; behold, his bedstead *was* a bedstead of iron; *is* it not in Rabbath of the children of Ammon? nine cubits *was* the length thereof, and four cubits the breadth of it, after the cubit of a man.

The Transjordanic Tribes

12 And this land, *which* we possessed at that time, from Aroer, which *is* by the river Arnon, and half mount Gilead, and the cities thereof, gave I unto the Reubenites and to the Gadites.

13 And the rest of Gilead, and all Bashan, *being* the kingdom of Og, gave I unto the half tribe of Manasseh; all the region of Argob, with all Bashan, which was called the land of giants.

14 Jair the son of Manasseh took all the country of Argob unto the coasts of Geshuri and Maachathi; and called them after his own name, Bashan-havoth-jair, unto this day.

15 And I gave Gilead unto Machir.

16 And unto the Reubenites and unto the Gadites I gave from Gilead even unto the river Arnon half the valley, and the border even unto the river Jabbok, *which is* the border of the children of Ammon;

Cross references (center column)

28 Num. 20:19
29 Num. 20:18; Deut. 23:3, 4; Judg. 11:17, 18
30 Ex. 4:21; Num. 21:23; Josh. 11:20
31 Deut. 1:8
32 Num. 21:23
33 Num. 21:24; Deut. 7:2; 20:7, 16
34 Lev. 27:28; Deut. 7:2, 26
36 Deut. 3:12; 4:48; Josh. 13:9; Ps. 44:3
37 Gen. 32:22; Num. 21:24; Deut. 2:5, 9, 19; 3:16
1 Num. 21:33-35; Deut. 1:4; 29:7
2 Num. 21:34
3 Num. 21:35
4 1Kgs. 4:13
6 Deut. 2:24; Ps. 135:10-12; 136:19-21
9 Deut. 4:48; 1Chr. 5:23; Ps. 29:6
10 Deut. 4:49; Josh. 12:5; 13:11
11 Gen. 14:5; 2Sam. 12:26; Jer. 49:2; Ezek. 21:20; Amos 2:9
12 Num. 32:33; Deut. 2:36; Josh. 12:2, 6; 13:8
13 Josh. 13:29
14 Num. 32:41; Josh. 13:13; 2Sam. 3:3; 10:6; 1Chr. 2:22

2:31 The prophecy from verses 24–25 begins to be fulfilled against King Sihon leading to his defeat before Israel.

3:1–2 The Lord predicts victory over King Og, even though he likely stood around thirteen feet tall (v. 11). The prediction of victory was rapidly fulfilled (vv. 3–12).

17 The plain also, and Jordan, and the coast *thereof*, from Chinnereth even unto the sea of the plain, *even* the salt sea, under Ashdoth-pisgah eastward.

18 And I commanded you at that time, saying, The LORD your God hath given you this land to possess it: ye shall pass over armed before your brethren the children of Israel, all *that are* meet for the war.

19 But your wives, and your little ones, and your cattle, (*for* I know that ye have much cattle,) shall abide in your cities which I have given you;

20 Until the LORD have given rest unto your brethren, as well as unto you, and *until* they also possess the land which the LORD your God hath given them beyond Jordan: and *then* shall ye return every man unto his possession, which I have given you.

21 And I commanded Joshua at that time, saying, Thine eyes have seen all that the LORD your God hath done unto these two kings: so shall the LORD do unto all the kingdoms whither thou passest.

22 Ye shall not fear them: for the LORD your God he shall fight for you.

Moses Is Forbidden to Enter Canaan

23 And I besought the LORD at that time, saying,

24 O Lord GOD, thou hast begun to shew thy servant thy greatness, and thy mighty hand: for what God *is there* in heaven or in earth, that can do according to thy works, and according to thy might?

25 I pray thee, let me go over, and see the good land that *is* beyond Jordan, that goodly mountain, and Lebanon.

26 But the LORD was wroth with me for your sakes, and would not hear me: and the LORD said unto me, Let it suffice thee; speak no more unto me of this matter.

27 Get thee up into the top of Pisgah, and lift up thine eyes westward, and northward, and southward, and eastward, and behold *it* with thine eyes: for thou shalt not go over this Jordan.

28 But charge Joshua, and encourage him,

and strengthen him: for he shall go over before this people, and he shall cause them to inherit the land which thou shalt see.

29 So we abode in the valley over against Beth-peor.

CHAPTER 4
Moses Urges Obedience

1 Now therefore hearken, O Israel, unto the statutes and unto the judgments, which I teach you, for to do *them*, that ye may live, and go in and possess the land which the LORD God of your fathers giveth you.

2 Ye shall not add unto the word which I command you, neither shall ye diminish *ought* from it, that ye may keep the commandments of the LORD your God which I command you.

3 Your eyes have seen what the LORD did because of Baal-peor: for all the men that followed Baal-peor, the LORD thy God hath destroyed them from among you.

4 But ye that did cleave unto the LORD your God *are* alive every one of you this day.

5 Behold, I have taught you statutes and judgments, even as the LORD my God commanded me, that ye should do so in the land whither ye go to possess it.

6 Keep therefore and do *them*; for this *is* your wisdom and your understanding in the sight of the nations, which shall hear all these statutes, and say, Surely this great nation *is* a wise and understanding people.

7 For what nation *is there* so great, who *hath* God so nigh unto them, as the LORD our God *is* in all *things that* we call upon him *for*?

8 And what nation *is there* so great, that hath statutes and judgments *so* righteous as all this law, which I set before you this day?

9 Only take heed to thyself, and keep thy soul diligently, lest thou forget the things which thine eyes have seen, and lest they depart from thy heart all the days of thy life: but teach them thy sons, and thy sons' sons;

10 *Specially* the day that thou stoodest before the LORD thy God in Horeb, when the LORD said unto me, Gather me the people together, and I will make them hear my

Cross references (center column):

17 Gen. 14:3; Num. 34:11, 12; Deut. 4:49; Josh. 12:3

18 Num. 32:20-33

20 Josh. 22:4

21 Num. 27:18

22 Ex. 14:14; Deut. 1:30; 20:4

23 2Cor. 12:8, 9

24 Ex. 15:11; Deut. 11:2

25 Ex. 3:8; Deut. 4:22

26 Num. 20:12; Deut. 31:2

27 Num. 27:12

28 Num. 27:18, 23; Deut. 1:38; 31:3, 7

29 Deut. 4:46; 34:6

1 Lev. 19:37; Deut. 5:1; Rom. 10:5

2 Deut. 12:32; Josh. 1:7; Prov. 30:6; Eccl. 12:13; Rev. 22:18, 19

3 Num. 25:4, 5; Josh. 22:17; Ps. 106:28, 29

6 Job 28:28; Ps. 19:7; 111:10; Prov. 1:7

7 2Sam. 7:23; Ps. 46:1

9 Prov. 3:1, 3; 4:21, 23

10 Ex. 19:9, 16; 20:18; Heb. 12:18, 19

3:21–22 the Lord your God he shall fight for you. The Lord promised that He would give Israel victory over any kingdom that they desired in their new land as He had done to Kings Sihon and Og.

3:28 encourage him, and strengthen him. As in Deuteronomy 1:38, Moses is commanded to prepare Joshua. Joshua is pictured here as a type of Christ because he is the one through whom God works. Clearly

Moses wants the people to learn that it is the Lord who gives them the victory.

4:1 unto the statues and unto the judgments. The condition for continued victory was to hearken unto God. Moses did not obey God, and he must die without entering the land. Now Israel must hearken and obey the Lord's statutes and judgments so that the nation can "go in and possess the land."

words, that they may learn to fear me all the days that they shall live upon the earth, and *that* they may teach their children.

11 And ye came near and stood under the mountain; and the mountain burned with fire unto the midst of heaven, with darkness, clouds, and thick darkness.

12 And the LORD spake unto you out of the midst of the fire: ye heard the voice of the words, but saw no similitude; only *ye heard* a voice.

13 And he declared unto you his covenant, which he commanded you to perform, *even* ten commandments; and he wrote them upon two tables of stone.

14 And the LORD commanded me at that time to teach you statutes and judgments, that ye might do them in the land whither ye go over to possess it.

Idolatry and Its Consequences

15 Take ye therefore good heed unto yourselves; for ye saw no manner of similitude on the day *that* the LORD spake unto you in Horeb out of the midst of the fire:

16 Lest ye corrupt *yourselves*, and make you a graven image, the similitude of any figure, the likeness of male or female,

17 The likeness of any beast that *is* on the earth, the likeness of any winged fowl that flieth in the air,

18 The likeness of any thing that creepeth on the ground, the likeness of any fish that *is* in the waters beneath the earth:

19 And lest thou lift up thine eyes unto heaven, and when thou seest the sun, and the moon, and the stars, *even* all the host of heaven, shouldest be driven to worship them, and serve them, which the LORD thy God hath divided unto all nations under the whole heaven.

20 But the LORD hath taken you, and brought you forth out of the iron furnace, *even* out of Egypt, to be unto him a people of inheritance, as *ye are* this day.

21 Furthermore the LORD was angry with me for your sakes, and sware that I should not go over Jordan, and that I should not go in unto that good land, which the LORD thy God giveth thee *for* an inheritance:

22 But I must die in this land, I must not go over Jordan: but ye shall go over, and possess that good land.

23 Take heed unto yourselves, lest ye forget the covenant of the LORD your God, which he made with you, and make you a graven image, *or* the likeness of any *thing*, which the LORD thy God hath forbidden thee.

24 For the LORD thy God *is* a consuming fire, *even* a jealous God.

25 When thou shalt beget children, and children's children, and ye shall have remained long in the land, and shall corrupt *yourselves*, and make a graven image, *or* the likeness of any *thing*, and shall do evil in the

Cross references

11 Ex. 19:18; Deut. 5:23
12 Ex. 20:22; Deut. 4:33, 36; 5:4, 22; 1Kgs. 19:12
13 Ex. 24:12; 31:18; 34:28; Deut. 9:9, 11
14 Ex. 21:1; 22:1—23:33
15 Ex. 20:4, 5; 32:7; Rom. 1:23
19 Gen. 2:1; Deut. 17:3
20 Ex. 19:5; Deut. 9:29; 32:9; 1Kgs. 8:51; Jer. 11:4
21 Num. 20:12; Deut. 1:37; 3:26
22 Deut. 3:25, 27; 2Pet. 1:13-15
23 Ex. 20:4, 5; Deut. 4:9, 16
24 Ex. 20:5; Isa. 33:14; 42:8; Heb. 12:29
25 Deut. 4:16; 2Kgs. 17:17

Outline of Prophetic Events

DEUTERONOMY 4

1. Israel and her descendants would remain "long in the land" (v. 25).
2. Israel would act corruptly and slip into idolatry (v. 25).
3. Israel would be forced out of the land (v. 26).
4. "The LORD shall scatter [them] among the nations" (v. 27).
5. Israel would be given over to idolatry during their wanderings (v. 28).
6. While dispersed among the nations, Israel will seek and find the LORD when they search for Him with all their hearts (v. 29).
7. There will come a time of tribulation, said to occur "in the latter days," during which time they will turn to the LORD (v. 30).

(For the Lord thy God is a merciful God;) he will not forsake thee, neither destroy thee, nor forget the covenant of thy fathers which he sware unto them. Deuteronomy 4:31

4:13 even ten commandments. Often called "The Sinaitic Covenant," these commandments were to be an expression of Israel's love and devotion to their Lord. There were two copies of this covenant, one for each party to the covenant. In this case, there was one complete copy for God and another for the twelve tribes.

4:22 Moses reiterates the prophecy about his personal destiny because of the Meribah incident (Num. 20:10–13).

4:25–31 This section provides a prophetic road map of Israel from that point in history all the way to eternity future. See the table entitled "Outline of Prophetic Events."

sight of the LORD thy God, to provoke him to anger:

26 I call heaven and earth to witness against you this day, that ye shall soon utterly perish from off the land whereunto ye go over Jordan to possess it; ye shall not prolong *your* days upon it, but shall utterly be destroyed.

27 And the LORD shall scatter you among the nations, and ye shall be left few in number among the heathen, whither the LORD shall lead you.

28 And there ye shall serve gods, the work of men's hands, wood and stone, which neither see, nor hear, nor eat, nor smell.

29 But if from thence thou shalt seek the LORD thy God, thou shalt find *him*, if thou seek him with all thy heart and with all thy soul.

30 When thou art in tribulation, and all these things are come upon thee, *even* in the latter days, if thou turn to the LORD thy God, and shalt be obedient unto his voice;

31 (For the LORD thy God *is* a merciful God;) he will not forsake thee, neither destroy thee, nor forget the covenant of thy fathers which he sware unto them.

Exhortation to Keep God's Law

32 For ask now of the days that are past, which were before thee, since the day that God created man upon the earth, and *ask* from the one side of heaven unto the other, whether there hath been *any such thing* as this great thing *is*, or hath been heard like it?

33 Did *ever* people hear the voice of God speaking out of the midst of the fire, as thou hast heard, and live?

34 Or hath God assayed to go *and* take him a nation from the midst of *another* nation, by temptations, by signs, and by wonders, and by war, and by a mighty hand, and by a stretched out arm, and by great terrors, according to all that the LORD your God did for you in Egypt before your eyes?

35 Unto thee it was shewed, that thou mightest know that the LORD he *is* God; *there is* none else beside him.

36 Out of heaven he made thee to hear his voice, that he might instruct thee: and upon earth he shewed thee his great fire; and thou heardest his words out of the midst of the fire.

37 And because he loved thy fathers, therefore he chose their seed after them, and brought thee out in his sight with his mighty power out of Egypt;

38 To drive out nations from before thee greater and mightier than thou *art*, to bring thee in, to give thee their land *for* an inheritance, as *it is* this day.

39 Know therefore this day, and consider *it* in thine heart, that the LORD he *is* God in heaven above, and upon the earth beneath: *there is* none else.

40 Thou shalt keep therefore his statutes, and his commandments, which I command thee this day, that it may go well with thee, and with thy children after thee, and that thou mayest prolong *thy* days upon the earth, which the LORD thy God giveth thee, for ever.

Eastern Cities of Refuge

41 Then Moses severed three cities on this side Jordan toward the sunrising;

42 That the slayer might flee thither, which should kill his neighbour unawares, and hated him not in times past; and that fleeing unto one of these cities he might live:

43 *Namely*, Bezer in the wilderness, in the plain country, of the Reubenites; and Ramoth in Gilead, of the Gadites; and Golan in Bashan, of the Manassites.

Moses Reiterates the Law

44 And this *is* the law which Moses set before the children of Israel:

45 These *are* the testimonies, and the statutes, and the judgments, which Moses spake unto the children of Israel, after they came forth out of Egypt,

46 On this side Jordan, in the valley over against Beth-peor, in the land of Sihon king of the Amorites, who dwelt at Heshbon, whom Moses and the children of Israel smote, after they were come forth out of Egypt:

47 And they possessed his land, and the land of Og king of Bashan, two kings of the

Cross References

26 Deut. 30:18, 19; Isa. 1:2; Mic. 6:2

27 Lev. 26:33; Deut. 28:62, 64; Neh. 1:8

28 Deut. 28:64; Isa. 44:9; 46:7; Jer. 16:13

29 Lev. 26:39, 40; Isa. 55:6, 7; Jer. 29:12-14

30 Deut. 31:29; Jer. 23:20

31 2Chr. 30:9; Neh. 9:31; Ps. 116:5; Jon. 4:2

32 Job 8:8; Matt. 24:31

33 Ex. 24:11; 33:20; Deut. 5:24, 26

34 Ex. 6:6; 7:3; 13:3; Deut. 7:19; 26:8; 29:3; 34:12

35 Isa. 45:5, 18, 22; Mark 12:29, 32

36 Ex. 19:9, 19; 20:18, 22; 24:16; Heb. 12:18

37 Ex. 13:3, 9, 14; Deut. 10:15

38 Deut. 7:1; 9:1, 4, 5

39 Deut. 4:35; Josh. 2:11

40 Lev. 22:31; Eph. 6:3

43 Josh. 20:8

46 Num. 21:24; Deut. 1:4; 3:29

47 Num. 21:35; Deut. 3:3, 4

4:40 This conditional, prophetic promise is repeated often through Deuteronomy as the condition for blessing within the land. God gave Israel the land, but the promise of Israel staying in the land and enjoying its blessings was contingent upon the people's obedience. However, since God has made sovereign, prophetic declarations about the land which have yet to be fulfilled, He will bring them to pass through the means of the positive choices of Israel in the future (Zech. 12:10).

Amorites, which *were* on this side Jordan toward the sunrising;

48 From Aroer, which *is* by the bank of the river Arnon, even unto mount Sion, which *is* Hermon,

49 And all the plain on this side Jordan eastward, even unto the sea of the plain, under the springs of Pisgah.

CHAPTER 5
The Ten Commandments

1 And Moses called all Israel, and said unto them, Hear, O Israel, the statutes and judgments which I speak in your ears this day, that ye may learn them, and keep, and do them.

2 The LORD our God made a covenant with us in Horeb.

3 The LORD made not this covenant with our fathers, but with us, *even* us, who *are* all of us here alive this day.

4 The LORD talked with you face to face in the mount out of the midst of the fire,

5 (I stood between the LORD and you at that time, to shew you the word of the LORD: for ye were afraid by reason of the fire, and went not up into the mount;) saying,

6 I *am* the LORD thy God, which brought thee out of the land of Egypt, from the house of bondage.

7 Thou shalt have none other gods before me.

8 Thou shalt not make thee *any* graven image, *or* any likeness *of any thing* that *is* in heaven above, or that *is* in the earth beneath, or that *is* in the waters beneath the earth:

9 Thou shalt not bow down thyself unto them, nor serve them: for I the LORD thy God *am* a jealous God, visiting the iniquity of the fathers upon the children unto the third and fourth *generation* of them that hate me,

10 And shewing mercy unto thousands of them that love me and keep my commandments.

11 Thou shalt not take the name of the LORD thy God in vain: for the LORD will not hold *him* guiltless that taketh his name in vain.

12 Keep the sabbath day to sanctify it, as the LORD thy God hath commanded thee.

13 Six days thou shalt labour, and do all thy work:

14 But the seventh day *is* the sabbath of the LORD thy God: *in it* thou shalt not do any work, thou, nor thy son, nor thy daughter, nor thy manservant, nor thy maidservant, nor thine ox, nor thine ass, nor any of thy cattle, nor thy stranger that *is* within thy gates; that thy manservant and thy maidservant may rest as well as thou.

15 And remember that thou wast a servant in the land of Egypt, and *that* the LORD thy God brought thee out thence through a mighty hand and by a stretched out arm: therefore the LORD thy God commanded thee to keep the sabbath day.

16 Honour thy father and thy mother, as the LORD thy God hath commanded thee; that thy days may be prolonged, and that it may go well with thee, in the land which the LORD thy God giveth thee.

17 Thou shalt not kill.

18 Neither shalt thou commit adultery.

19 Neither shalt thou steal.

20 Neither shalt thou bear false witness against thy neighbour.

21 Neither shalt thou desire thy neighbour's wife, neither shalt thou covet thy neighbour's house, his field, or his manservant, or his maidservant, his ox, or his ass, or any *thing* that *is* thy neighbour's.

22 These words the LORD spake unto all your assembly in the mount out of the midst of the fire, of the cloud, and of the thick darkness, with a great voice: and he added no more. And he wrote them in two tables of stone, and delivered them unto me.

23 And it came to pass, when ye heard the voice out of the midst of the darkness, (for the mountain did burn with fire,) that ye came near unto me, *even* all the heads of your tribes, and your elders;

24 And ye said, Behold, the LORD our God hath shewed us his glory and his greatness, and we have heard his voice out of the midst of the fire: we have seen this day that God doth talk with man, and he liveth.

25 Now therefore why should we die? for this great fire will consume us: if we hear the voice of the LORD our God any more, then we shall die.

26 For who *is there of* all flesh, that hath heard the voice of the living God speaking out of the midst of the fire, as we *have*, and lived?

Cross References

48 Deut. 2:36; 3:9; 8:12; Ps. 133:3
49 Deut. 3:17
2 Ex. 19:5; Deut. 4:23
3 Matt. 13:17; Heb. 8:9
4 Ex. 19:9, 19; 20:22
5 Ex. 19:16; 20:18, 21; 24:2; Gal. 3:19
6 Ex. 20:2; Lev. 26:1
7 Ex. 20:3
8 Ex. 20:4
9 Ex. 34:7
10 Jer. 32:18; Dan. 9:4
11 Ex. 20:7; Lev. 19:12; Matt. 5:33
12 Ex. 20:8
13 Ex. 23:12; 35:2; Ezek. 20:12
14 Gen. 2:2; Ex. 16:29, 30; Heb. 4:4
15 Deut. 4:34, 37; 15:15; 16:12; 24:18, 22
16 Ex. 20:12; Lev. 19:3; Eph. 6:2, 3
17 Ex. 20:13; Matt. 5:21
18 Ex. 20:14; Luke 18:20; James 2:11
19 Ex. 20:15; Rom. 13:9
20 Ex. 20:16
21 Ex. 20:17; Luke 12:15
22 Ex. 24:12; 31:18; Deut. 4:13
23 Ex. 20:18, 19
25 Deut. 18:16
26 Deut. 4:33

5:16 Honour thy father and thy mother. In the midst of the giving of the Ten Commandments, the Lord makes a prophetic promise. Long life in the land of Israel was directly dependant upon how well His people would obey this command.

27 Go thou near, and hear all that the LORD our God shall say: and speak thou unto us all that the LORD our God shall speak unto thee; and we will hear *it*, and do *it*.

28 And the LORD heard the voice of your words, when ye spake unto me; and the LORD said unto me, I have heard the voice of the words of this people, which they have spoken unto thee: they have well said all that they have spoken.

29 O that there were such an heart in them, that they would fear me, and keep all my commandments always, that it might be well with them, and with their children for ever!

30 Go say to them, Get you into your tents again.

31 But as for thee, stand thou here by me, and I will speak unto thee all the commandments, and the statutes, and the judgments, which thou shalt teach them, that they may do *them* in the land which I give them to possess it.

32 Ye shall observe to do therefore as the LORD your God hath commanded you: ye shall not turn aside to the right hand or to the left.

33 Ye shall walk in all the ways which the LORD your God hath commanded you, that ye may live, and *that it may be* well with you, and *that* ye may prolong *your* days in the land which ye shall possess.

CHAPTER 6
Remember God Every Day

1 Now these *are* the commandments, the statutes, and the judgments, which the LORD your God commanded to teach you, that ye might do *them* in the land whither ye go to possess it:

2 That thou mightest fear the LORD thy God, to keep all his statutes and his commandments, which I command thee, thou, and thy son, and thy son's son, all the days of thy life; and that thy days may be prolonged.

3 Hear therefore, O Israel, and observe to do *it*; that it may be well with thee, and that ye may increase mightily, as the LORD God of thy fathers hath promised thee, in the land that floweth with milk and honey.

4 Hear, O Israel: The LORD our God *is* one LORD:

5 And thou shalt love the LORD thy God with all thine heart, and with all thy soul, and with all thy might.

6 And these words, which I command thee this day, shall be in thine heart:

7 And thou shalt teach them diligently unto thy children, and shalt talk of them when thou sittest in thine house, and when thou walkest by the way, and when thou liest down, and when thou risest up.

8 And thou shalt bind them for a sign upon thine hand, and they shall be as frontlets between thine eyes.

9 And thou shalt write them upon the posts of thy house, and on thy gates.

10 And it shall be, when the LORD thy God shall have brought thee into the land which he sware unto thy fathers, to Abraham, to Isaac, and to Jacob, to give thee great and goodly cities, which thou buildedst not,

11 And houses full of all good *things*, which thou filledst not, and wells digged, which thou diggedst not, vineyards and olive trees, which thou plantedst not; when thou shalt have eaten and be full;

12 *Then* beware lest thou forget the LORD, which brought thee forth out of the land of Egypt, from the house of bondage.

13 Thou shalt fear the LORD thy God, and serve him, and shalt swear by his name.

14 Ye shall not go after other gods, of the gods of the people which *are* round about you;

15 (For the LORD thy God *is* a jealous God among you) lest the anger of the LORD thy God be kindled against thee, and destroy thee from off the face of the earth.

16 Ye shall not tempt the LORD your God, as ye tempted *him* in Massah.

17 Ye shall diligently keep the commandments of the LORD your God, and his testimonies, and his statutes, which he hath commanded thee.

18 And thou shalt do *that which is* right and good in the sight of the LORD: that it may be well with thee, and that thou mayest go in and possess the good land which the LORD sware unto thy fathers,

19 To cast out all thine enemies from before thee, as the LORD hath spoken.

20 *And* when thy son asketh thee in time to come, saying, What *mean* the testimonies, and the statutes, and the judgments, which the LORD our God hath commanded you?

21 Then thou shalt say unto thy son, We

Cross References

27 Ex. 20:19; Heb. 12:19
28 Deut. 18:17
29 Ps. 81:13; Isa. 48:18; Matt. 23:37
31 Gal. 3:19
32 Deut. 17:20; Josh. 1:7; 23:6; Prov. 4:27
33 Ps. 119:6; Jer. 7:23
1 Deut. 4:1; 5:31; 12:1
2 Ex. 20:20; Ps. 111:10; 128:1
3 Gen. 15:5; 22:17; Ex. 3:8
4 Isa. 42:8; Mark 12:29, 32
5 Deut. 10:12; 2Kgs. 23:25; Matt. 22:37
6 Ps. 37:31; 40:8; 119:11, 98; Prov. 3:3
7 Deut. 4:9; 11:19; Ps. 78:4-6; Eph. 6:4
8 Ex. 13:9, 16; Prov. 3:3
9 Isa. 57:8
10 Josh. 24:13; Ps. 105:44
13 Ps. 63:11; Isa. 45:23; Jer. 4:2; 5:7
14 Jer. 25:6
15 Ex. 20:5
16 Ex. 17:2, 7; Num. 20:3, 4; Matt. 4:7
17 Deut. 11:13, 22; Ps. 119:4
18 Ex. 15:26; Deut. 12:28; 13:18
19 Num. 33:52, 53
20 Ex. 13:14
21 Ex. 3:19; 13:3

6:3 the LORD God of thy fathers. The Lord promised to bless Israel if the people would live obediently to Him in the land.

were Pharaoh's bondmen in Egypt; and the LORD brought us out of Egypt with a mighty hand:

22 And the LORD shewed signs and wonders, great and sore, upon Egypt, upon Pharaoh, and upon all his household, before our eyes:

23 And he brought us out from thence, that he might bring us in, to give us the land which he sware unto our fathers.

24 And the LORD commanded us to do all these statutes, to fear the LORD our God, for our good always, that he might preserve us alive, as *it is* at this day.

25 And it shall be our righteousness, if we observe to do all these commandments before the LORD our God, as he hath commanded us.

CHAPTER 7
Destroy the Nations in the Land

1 When the LORD thy God shall bring thee into the land whither thou goest to possess it, and hath cast out many nations before thee, the Hittites, and the Girgashites, and the Amorites, and the Canaanites, and the Perizzites, and the Hivites, and the Jebusites, seven nations greater and mightier than thou;

2 And when the LORD thy God shall deliver them before thee; thou shalt smite them, *and* utterly destroy them; thou shalt make no covenant with them, nor shew mercy unto them:

3 Neither shalt thou make marriages with them; thy daughter thou shalt not give unto his son, nor his daughter shalt thou take unto thy son.

4 For they will turn away thy son from following me, that they may serve other gods: so will the anger of the LORD be kindled against you, and destroy thee suddenly.

5 But thus shall ye deal with them; ye shall destroy their altars, and break down their images, and cut down their groves, and burn their graven images with fire.

6 For thou *art* an holy people unto the LORD thy God: the LORD thy God hath cho-

sen thee to be a special people unto himself, above all people that *are* upon the face of the earth.

7 The LORD did not set his love upon you, nor choose you, because ye were more in number than any people; for ye *were* the fewest of all people:

8 But because the LORD loved you, and because he would keep the oath which he had sworn unto your fathers, hath the LORD brought you out with a mighty hand, and redeemed you out of the house of bondmen, from the hand of Pharaoh king of Egypt.

9 Know therefore that the LORD thy God, he *is* God, the faithful God, which keepeth covenant and mercy with them that love him and keep his commandments to a thousand generations;

10 And repayeth them that hate him to their face, to destroy them: he will not be slack to him that hateth him, he will repay him to his face.

11 Thou shalt therefore keep the commandments, and the statutes, and the judgments, which I command thee this day, to do them.

12 Wherefore it shall come to pass, if ye hearken to these judgments, and keep, and do them, that the LORD thy God shall keep unto thee the covenant and the mercy which he sware unto thy fathers:

13 And he will love thee, and bless thee, and multiply thee: he will also bless the fruit of thy womb, and the fruit of thy land, thy corn, and thy wine, and thine oil, the increase of thy kine, and the flocks of thy sheep, in the land which he sware unto thy fathers to give thee.

14 Thou shalt be blessed above all people: there shall not be male or female barren among you, or among your cattle.

15 And the LORD will take away from thee all sickness, and will put none of the evil diseases of Egypt, which thou knowest, upon thee; but will lay them upon all *them* that hate thee.

16 And thou shalt consume all the people which the LORD thy God shall deliver thee; thine eye shall have no pity upon them: nei-

Cross references

22 Ex. 7:1—12:51
24 Job 35:7, 8; Jer. 32:39
25 Lev. 18:5; Rom. 10:3, 5
1 Ex. 33:2
2 Ex. 23:32; 34:12, 15, 16; Josh. 2:14; Judg. 1:24; 2:2
3 Ezra 9:2
4 Deut. 6:15
5 Ex. 23:24; 34:13; Ps. 50:5; Jer. 2:3; Amos 3:2
7 Deut. 10:22
8 Ex. 13:3, 14; 32:13; Ps. 105:8, 9, 10
9 Ex. 20:6; Isa. 49:7; Dan. 9:4; 1John 1:9
10 Deut. 32:35; Isa. 59:18; Nah. 1:2
12 Lev. 26:3; Deut. 28:1; Ps. 105:8, 9; Luke 1:55, 72, 73
13 Deut. 28:4; John 14:21
14 Ex. 23:26
15 Ex. 9:14; 15:26; Deut. 28:27, 60
16 Ex. 23:33; Deut. 7:2; 12:30; 13:8; 19:13, 21; 25:12; Judg. 8:27; Ps. 106:36

7:4 and destroy thee suddenly. Moses warns the people that intermarriage with the Canaanites would direct the people to other gods. Moses warns and predicts that such behavior would be one of the things that would cause Israel's destruction.

7:6–9 a special people unto himself. Here, Moses reveals to Israel the reason that God wants His people to be faithful to Him. This special purpose is the reason why

the Lord "set his love upon" Israel. Because of this special relationship between the Lord and His people, Israel can be assured of the Lord's blessing.

7:14–15 shalt be blessed above all people. Moses reiterates the blessings to come if the people of Israel will obey God. The promised blessing will mean that there will be no sickness among them, and the diseases common to Egypt will be put upon those who hate God.

ther shalt thou serve their gods; for that *will be* a snare unto thee.

17 If thou shalt say in thine heart, These nations *are* more than I; how can I dispossess them?

18 Thou shalt not be afraid of them: *but* shalt well remember what the LORD thy God did unto Pharaoh, and unto all Egypt;

19 The great temptations which thine eyes saw, and the signs, and the wonders, and the mighty hand, and the stretched out arm, whereby the LORD thy God brought thee out: so shall the LORD thy God do unto all the people of whom thou art afraid.

20 Moreover the LORD thy God will send the hornet among them, until they that are left, and hide themselves from thee, be destroyed.

21 Thou shalt not be affrighted at them: for the LORD thy God *is* among you, a mighty God and terrible.

22 And the LORD thy God will put out those nations before thee by little and little: thou mayest not consume them at once, lest the beasts of the field increase upon thee.

23 But the LORD thy God shall deliver them unto thee, and shall destroy them with a mighty destruction, until they be destroyed.

24 And he shall deliver their kings into thine hand, and thou shalt destroy their name from under heaven: there shall no man be able to stand before thee, until thou have destroyed them.

25 The graven images of their gods shall ye burn with fire: thou shalt not desire the silver or gold *that is* on them, nor take *it* unto thee, lest thou be snared therein: for it *is* an abomination to the LORD thy God.

26 Neither shalt thou bring an abomination into thine house, lest thou be a cursed thing like it: *but* thou shalt utterly detest it, and thou shalt utterly abhor it; for it *is* a cursed thing.

CHAPTER 8
Israel to Remember God in Canaan

1 All the commandments which I command thee this day shall ye observe to do, that ye may live, and multiply, and go in and possess the land which the LORD sware unto your fathers.

2 And thou shalt remember all the way which the LORD thy God led thee these forty years in the wilderness, to humble thee, *and* to prove thee, to know what *was* in thine heart, whether thou wouldest keep his commandments, or no.

3 And he humbled thee, and suffered thee to hunger, and fed thee with manna, which

---

17 Num. 33:53

18 Deut. 31:6; Ps. 105:5

20 Ex. 23:28; Josh. 24:12

21 Num. 11:20; 14:9, 14, 42; 16:3; Josh. 3:10

22 Ex. 23:29, 30

24 Ex. 17:14; Josh. 1:5; 10:8, 24, 25, 42; 11:8

25 Ex. 32:20; Josh. 7:1, 21; Judg. 8:27

26 Lev. 27:28; Deut. 13:17; Josh. 6:17, 18; 7:1

1 Deut. 4:1; 5:32, 33; 6:1-3

2 Ex. 16:4; 2Chr. 32:31; John 2:25

3 Ex. 16:2, 3, 12, 14, 35; Ps. 104:29; Matt. 4:4; Luke 4:4

4 Deut. 29:5; Neh. 9:21

5 2Sam. 7:14; Ps. 89:32; Prov. 3:12; Heb. 12:5, 6; Rev. 3:19

6 Deut. 5:33

7 Deut. 11:10-12

9 Deut. 33:25

10 Deut. 6:11, 12

12 Prov. 30:9; Hos. 13:6

14 Ps. 106:21; 1Cor. 4:7

15 Num. 20:11; Ps. 78:15; 114:8; Jer. 2:6; Hos. 13:5

16 Ex. 16:15; Deut. 8:3; Jer. 24:5, 6; Heb. 12:11

18 Prov. 10:22; Hos. 2:8

---

thou knewest not, neither did thy fathers know; that he might make thee know that man doth not live by bread only, but by every *word* that proceedeth out of the mouth of the LORD doth man live.

4 Thy raiment waxed not old upon thee, neither did thy foot swell, these forty years.

5 Thou shalt also consider in thine heart, that, as a man chasteneth his son, *so* the LORD thy God chasteneth thee.

6 Therefore thou shalt keep the commandments of the LORD thy God, to walk in his ways, and to fear him.

7 For the LORD thy God bringeth thee into a good land, a land of brooks of water, of fountains and depths that spring out of valleys and hills;

8 A land of wheat, and barley, and vines, and fig trees, and pomegranates; a land of oil olive, and honey;

9 A land wherein thou shalt eat bread without scarceness, thou shalt not lack any *thing* in it; a land whose stones *are* iron, and out of whose hills thou mayest dig brass.

10 When thou hast eaten and art full, then thou shalt bless the LORD thy God for the good land which he hath given thee.

11 Beware that thou forget not the LORD thy God, in not keeping his commandments, and his judgments, and his statutes, which I command thee this day:

12 Lest *when* thou hast eaten and art full, and hast built goodly houses, and dwelt *therein*;

13 And *when* thy herds and thy flocks multiply, and thy silver and thy gold is multiplied, and all that thou hast is multiplied;

14 Then thine heart be lifted up, and thou forget the LORD thy God, which brought thee forth out of the land of Egypt, from the house of bondage;

15 Who led thee through that great and terrible wilderness, *wherein were* fiery serpents, and scorpions, and drought, where *there was* no water; who brought thee forth water out of the rock of flint;

16 Who fed thee in the wilderness with manna, which thy fathers knew not, that he might humble thee, and that he might prove thee, to do thee good at thy latter end;

17 And thou say in thine heart, My power and the might of *mine* hand hath gotten me this wealth.

18 But thou shalt remember the LORD thy God: for *it is* he that giveth thee power to get wealth, that he may establish his covenant which he sware unto thy fathers, as *it is* this day.

19 And it shall be, if thou do at all forget the LORD thy God, and walk after other gods, and serve them, and worship them, I testify against you this day that ye shall surely perish.

20 As the nations which the LORD destroyeth before your face, so shall ye perish; because ye would not be obedient unto the voice of the LORD your God.

CHAPTER 9
God Will Destroy the Canaanites

1 Hear, O Israel: Thou *art* to pass over Jordan this day, to go in to possess nations greater and mightier than thyself, cities great and fenced up to heaven,

2 A people great and tall, the children of the Anakims, whom thou knowest, and *of whom* thou hast heard *say*, Who can stand before the children of Anak!

3 Understand therefore this day, that the LORD thy God *is* he which goeth over before thee; *as* a consuming fire he shall destroy them, and he shall bring them down before thy face: so shalt thou drive them out, and destroy them quickly, as the LORD hath said unto thee.

4 Speak not thou in thine heart, after that the LORD thy God hath cast them out from before thee, saying, For my righteousness the LORD hath brought me in to possess this land: but for the wickedness of these nations the LORD doth drive them out from before thee.

5 Not for thy righteousness, or for the uprightness of thine heart, dost thou go to possess their land: but for the wickedness of these nations the LORD thy God doth drive them out from before thee, and that he may perform the word which the LORD sware unto thy fathers, Abraham, Isaac, and Jacob.

Remember the Rebellions in the Wilderness

6 Understand therefore, that the LORD thy God giveth thee not this good land to possess it for thy righteousness; for thou *art* a stiffnecked people.

7 Remember, *and* forget not, how thou provokedst the LORD thy God to wrath in the wilderness: from the day that thou didst depart out of the land of Egypt, until ye came unto this place, ye have been rebellious against the LORD.

8 Also in Horeb ye provoked the LORD to wrath, so that the LORD was angry with you to have destroyed you.

9 When I was gone up into the mount to receive the tables of stone, *even* the tables of the covenant which the LORD made with you, then I abode in the mount forty days and forty nights, I neither did eat bread nor drink water:

10 And the LORD delivered unto me two tables of stone written with the finger of God; and on them *was written* according to all the words, which the LORD spake with you in the mount out of the midst of the fire in the day of the assembly.

11 And it came to pass at the end of forty days and forty nights, *that* the LORD gave me the two tables of stone, *even* the tables of the covenant.

12 And the LORD said unto me, Arise, get thee down quickly from hence; for thy people which thou hast brought forth out of Egypt have corrupted *themselves*; they are quickly turned aside out of the way which I commanded them; they have made them a molten image.

13 Furthermore the LORD spake unto me, saying, I have seen this people, and, behold, it *is* a stiffnecked people:

14 Let me alone, that I may destroy them, and blot out their name from under heaven: and I will make of thee a nation mightier and greater than they.

15 So I turned and came down from the mount, and the mount burned with fire: and the two tables of the covenant *were* in my two hands.

16 And I looked, and, behold, ye had sinned against the LORD your God, *and* had made you a molten calf: ye had turned aside quickly out of the way which the LORD had commanded you.

17 And I took the two tables, and cast them out of my two hands, and brake them before your eyes.

18 And I fell down before the LORD, as at the first, forty days and forty nights: I did neither eat bread, nor drink water, because of all your sins which ye sinned, in doing wickedly in the sight of the LORD, to provoke him to anger.

19 For I was afraid of the anger and hot displeasure, wherewith the LORD was wroth against you to destroy you. But the LORD hearkened unto me at that time also.

20 And the LORD was very angry with Aaron to have destroyed him: and I prayed for Aaron also the same time.

21 And I took your sin, the calf which ye had made, and burnt it with fire, and stamped it, *and* ground *it* very small, *even*

Cross references (center column)

19 Deut. 4:26; 30:18

20 Dan. 9:11, 12

1 Deut. 1:28; 4:38; 7:1; 11:23, 31; Josh. 3:16; 4:19

2 Num. 13:22, 28, 32, 33

3 Ex. 23:31; Deut. 4:24; 7:23, 24; 31:3; Josh. 3:11; Heb. 12:29

4 Gen. 15:16; Lev. 18:24, 25; Deut. 8:17; 18:12; Rom. 11:6, 20; 1Cor. 4:4, 7

5 Gen. 12:7; 13:15; 15:7; 17:8; 26:4; 28:13; Titus 3:5

6 Ex. 32:9; 33:3; 34:9; Deut. 9:3

7 Ex. 14:11; 16:2; 17:2; Num. 11:4; 20:2; 25:2; Deut. 31:27

8 Ex. 32:4; Ps. 106:19

9 Ex. 24:12, 15, 18; 34:28

10 Ex. 19:17; 20:1; 31:18; Deut. 4:10; 10:4; 18:16

12 Ex. 32:7; Deut. 31:29; Judg. 2:17

13 Ex. 32:9; Deut. 9:10; 10:16; 31:27; 2Kgs. 17:14

14 Ex. 32:10; Num. 14:12; Deut. 29:20; Ps. 9:5; 109:13

15 Ex. 19:18; 32:15; Deut. 4:11; 5:23

16 Ex. 32:19

18 Ex. 34:28; Ps. 106:23

19 Ex. 32:10, 11, 14; 33:17; Deut. 10:10; Ps. 106:23

21 Ex. 32:20; Isa. 31:7

until it was as small as dust: and I cast the dust thereof into the brook that descended out of the mount.

22 And at Taberah, and at Massah, and at Kibroth-hattaavah, ye provoked the LORD to wrath.

23 Likewise when the LORD sent you from Kadesh-barnea, saying, Go up and possess the land which I have given you; then ye rebelled against the commandment of the LORD your God, and ye believed him not, nor hearkened to his voice.

24 Ye have been rebellious against the LORD from the day that I knew you.

25 Thus I fell down before the LORD forty days and forty nights, as I fell down *at the first*; because the LORD had said he would destroy you.

26 I prayed therefore unto the LORD, and said, O Lord GOD, destroy not thy people and thine inheritance, which thou hast redeemed through thy greatness, which thou hast brought forth out of Egypt with a mighty hand.

27 Remember thy servants, Abraham, Isaac, and Jacob; look not unto the stubbornness of this people, nor to their wickedness, nor to their sin:

28 Lest the land whence thou broughtest us out say, Because the LORD was not able to bring them into the land which he promised them, and because he hated them, he hath brought them out to slay them in the wilderness.

29 Yet they *are* thy people and thine inheritance, which thou broughtest out by thy mighty power and by thy stretched out arm.

CHAPTER 10
The Second Set of Stone Tablets

1 At that time the LORD said unto me, Hew thee two tables of stone like unto the first, and come up unto me into the mount, and make thee an ark of wood.

2 And I will write on the tables the words that were in the first tables which thou brakest, and thou shalt put them in the ark.

3 And I made an ark *of* shittim wood, and hewed two tables of stone like unto the first, and went up into the mount, having the two tables in mine hand.

4 And he wrote on the tables, according to the first writing, the ten commandments,

which the LORD spake unto you in the mount out of the midst of the fire in the day of the assembly: and the LORD gave them unto me.

5 And I turned myself and came down from the mount, and put the tables in the ark which I had made; and there they be, as the LORD commanded me.

6 And the children of Israel took their journey from Beeroth of the children of Jaakan to Mosera: there Aaron died, and there he was buried; and Eleazar his son ministered in the priest's office in his stead.

7 From thence they journeyed unto Gudgodah; and from Gudgodah to Jotbath, a land of rivers of waters.

8 At that time the LORD separated the tribe of Levi, to bear the ark of the covenant of the LORD, to stand before the LORD to minister unto him, and to bless in his name, unto this day.

9 Wherefore Levi hath no part nor inheritance with his brethren; the LORD *is* his inheritance, according as the LORD thy God promised him.

10 And I stayed in the mount, according to the first time, forty days and forty nights; and the LORD hearkened unto me at that time also, *and* the LORD would not destroy thee.

11 And the LORD said unto me, Arise, take *thy* journey before the people, that they may go in and possess the land, which I sware unto their fathers to give unto them.

What God Requires

12 And now, Israel, what doth the LORD thy God require of thee, but to fear the LORD thy God, to walk in all his ways, and to love him, and to serve the LORD thy God with all thy heart and with all thy soul,

13 To keep the commandments of the LORD, and his statutes, which I command thee this day for thy good?

14 Behold, the heaven and the heaven of heavens *is* the LORD's thy God, the earth *also*, with all that therein *is*.

15 Only the LORD had a delight in thy fathers to love them, and he chose their seed after them, *even* you above all people, as *it is* this day.

16 Circumcise therefore the foreskin of your heart, and be no more stiffnecked.

Cross references (center column):

22 Ex. 17:7; Num. 11:1, 3, 4, 34; 5

23 Num. 13:3; 14:1; Ps. 106:24, 25

26 Ex. 32:11-13

28 Ex. 32:12; Num. 14:16

29 Ex. 25:10; 1Kgs. 8:51

2 Ex. 25:16, 21

3 Ex. 25:5, 10; 34:4; 37:1

4 Ex. 19:17; 9:10; 18:16; 34:28

5 Ex. 34:29; 40:20; 1Kgs. 8:9

6 Num. 20:28; 33:30, 31, 38

7 Num. 33:32, 33

8 Lev. 9:22; Num. 3:6

9 Num. 18:20, 24; Deut. 18:1, 2; Ezek. 44:28

10 Ex. 32:14, 33, 34; 33:17; 34:28; Deut. 9:10, 18, 25

11 Ex. 32:34; 33:1

12 Deut. 5:33; 6:5, 13; 11:13; 30:16, 20; Mic. 6:8; Matt. 22:37

13 Deut. 6:24

14 Gen. 14:19; Ex. 19:5; 1Kgs. 8:27; Ps. 24:1; 115:16; 148:4

15 Deut. 4:37

16 Lev. 26:41; Deut. 9:6, 13; 30:6; Jer. 4:4; Rom. 2:28, 29; Col. 2:11

10:1–5 The Lord reveals to Israel instructions for the ark of the covenant which would contain the record of the covenantal relationship between Himself and His people. Moses broke the first copy of the covenant when he came down from the mountain and saw Israel in idolatry (Ex. 32).

17 For the LORD your God *is* God of gods, and Lord of lords, a great God, a mighty, and a terrible, which regardeth not persons, nor taketh reward:
18 He doth execute the judgment of the fatherless and widow, and loveth the stranger, in giving him food and raiment.
19 Love ye therefore the stranger: for ye were strangers in the land of Egypt.
20 Thou shalt fear the LORD thy God; him shalt thou serve, and to him shalt thou cleave, and swear by his name.
21 He *is* thy praise, and he *is* thy God, that hath done for thee these great and terrible things, which thine eyes have seen.
22 Thy fathers went down into Egypt with threescore and ten persons; and now the LORD thy God hath made thee as the stars of heaven for multitude.

CHAPTER 11
God's Great Acts

1 Therefore thou shalt love the LORD thy God, and keep his charge, and his statutes, and his judgments, and his commandments, alway.
2 And know ye this day: for *I speak* not with your children which have not known, and which have not seen the chastisement of the LORD your God, his greatness, his mighty hand, and his stretched out arm,
3 And his miracles, and his acts, which he did in the midst of Egypt unto Pharaoh the king of Egypt, and unto all his land;
4 And what he did unto the army of Egypt, unto their horses, and to their chariots; how he made the water of the Red sea to overflow them as they pursued after you, and *how* the LORD hath destroyed them unto this day;
5 And what he did unto you in the wilderness, until ye came into this place;
6 And what he did unto Dathan and Abiram, the sons of Eliab, the son of Reuben: how the earth opened her mouth, and swallowed them up, and their households, and their tents, and all the substance that *was* in their possession, in the midst of all Israel:
7 But your eyes have seen all the great acts of the LORD which he did.

New Life in the New Land

8 Therefore shall ye keep all the commandments which I command you this day, that ye may be strong, and go in and possess the land, whither ye go to possess it;
9 And that ye may prolong *your* days in the land, which the LORD sware unto your fathers to give unto them and to their seed, a land that floweth with milk and honey.
10 For the land, whither thou goest in to possess it, *is* not as the land of Egypt, from whence ye came out, where thou sowedst thy seed, and wateredst *it* with thy foot, as a garden of herbs:
11 But the land, whither ye go to possess it, *is* a land of hills and valleys, *and* drinketh water of the rain of heaven:
12 A land which the LORD thy God careth for the eyes of the LORD thy God *are* always upon it, from the beginning of the year even unto the end of the year.
13 And it shall come to pass, if ye shall hearken diligently unto my commandments

Cross references
17 Josh. 22:22; 2Chr. 19:7; Acts 10:34; Rom. 2:11; Eph. 6:9; Rev. 17:14; 19:16
18 Ps. 68:5; 146:9
19 Lev. 19:33, 34
20 Deut. 6:13; 13:4; Ps. 63:11; Matt. 4:10; Luke 4:8
21 2Sam. 7:23; Ps. 22:3
22 Gen. 15:5; 46:27; Ex. 1:5
1 Deut. 10:12; 30:16, 20; Zech. 3:7
3 Ps. 78:12; 135:9
4 Ex. 14:27, 28; 15:9, 10; Ps. 106:11
6 Num. 16:1, 31; 27:3
7 Deut. 5:3; 7:19
8 Josh. 1:6, 7
9 Ex. 3:8; Deut. 4:40; 5:16; 9:5; Prov. 10:27
10 Zech. 14:18
12 1Kgs. 9:3

The Land Promised to Israel

1. This land was promised to their fathers.	Deut. 1:7–8; 6:10, 23; 9:5; 11:21; 19:8; 24:4; 26:15; 28:11; 30:5, 20; 31:7, 20, 23; 34:4
2. This land is the gift of God to the children of Israel.	Deut. 3:18; 4:21; 5:16; 6:23; 8:10; 9:5–6; 11:17, 31; 12:10; 15:4, 7; 19:1; 25:15, 19; 26:1–2, 9–10; 27:2; 28:8, 11; 32:49, 52
3. This land has a promise of blessing from God.	Deut. 1:25; 4:21–22; 6:3; 8:7–10; 11:11–12, 17; 26:9, 15; 27:3; 30:9; 31:20; 33:13
4. The land He promised has specific borders.	Deut. 2:5, 9, 19, 37
5. The land is to be marked by obedience to God.	Deut. 4:1, 5, 14; 5:16, 31, 33; 6:1; 8:1, 11; 12:1, 17; 16:20; 18:9; 24:4; 25:15; 30:16; 31:13; 32:46–47
6. God will remove them from the land if they are disobedient.	Deut. 4:25–26; 28:18, 21, 24, 33, 52, 63; 29:22, 24, 27–28
7. God predicts their disobedience.	Deut. 30:18; 31:16, 20–21
8. God predicts vengeance on those who conquer the land.	Deut. 32:41–43
9. In the Millennium, the Jews will obey and possess all the land.	Deut. 28:1; 30:4

which I command you this day, to love the LORD your God, and to serve him with all your heart and with all your soul,

14 That I will give *you* the rain of your land in his due season, the first rain and the latter rain, that thou mayest gather in thy corn, and thy wine, and thine oil.

15 And I will send grass in thy fields for thy cattle, that thou mayest eat and be full.

16 Take heed to yourselves, that your heart be not deceived, and ye turn aside, and serve other gods, and worship them;

17 And *then* the LORD's wrath be kindled against you, and he shut up the heaven, that there be no rain, and that the land yield not her fruit; and *lest* ye perish quickly from off the good land which the LORD giveth you.

18 Therefore shall ye lay up these my words in your heart and in your soul, and bind them for a sign upon your hand, that they may be as frontlets between your eyes.

19 And ye shall teach them your children, speaking of them when thou sittest in thine house, and when thou walkest by the way, when thou liest down, and when thou risest up.

20 And thou shalt write them upon the door posts of thine house, and upon thy gates:

21 That your days may be multiplied, and the days of your children, in the land which the LORD sware unto your fathers to give them, as the days of heaven upon the earth.

22 For if ye shall diligently keep all these commandments which I command you, to do them, to love the LORD your God, to walk in all his ways, and to cleave unto him;

23 Then will the LORD drive out all these nations from before you, and ye shall possess greater nations and mightier than yourselves.

24 Every place whereon the soles of your feet shall tread shall be yours: from the wilderness and Lebanon, from the river, the river Euphrates, even unto the uttermost sea shall your coast be.

25 There shall no man be able to stand before you: *for* the LORD your God shall lay the fear of you and the dread of you upon all the land that ye shall tread upon, as he hath said unto you.

26 Behold, I set before you this day a blessing and a curse;

27 A blessing, if ye obey the commandments of the LORD your God, which I command you this day:

28 And a curse, if ye will not obey the commandments of the LORD your God, but turn aside out of the way which I command you this day, to go after other gods, which ye have not known.

29 And it shall come to pass, when the LORD thy God hath brought thee in unto the land whither thou goest to possess it, that thou shalt put the blessing upon mount Gerizim, and the curse upon mount Ebal.

30 *Are* they not on the other side Jordan, by the way where the sun goeth down, in the land of the Canaanites, which dwell in the champaign over against Gilgal, beside the plains of Moreh?

31 For ye shall pass over Jordan to go in to possess the land which the LORD your God giveth you, and ye shall possess it, and dwell therein.

32 And ye shall observe to do all the statutes and judgments which I set before you this day.

CHAPTER 12
Worship Only in the Special Place

1 These *are* the statutes and judgments, which ye shall observe to do in the land, which the LORD God of thy fathers giveth thee to possess it, all the days that ye live upon the earth.

2 Ye shall utterly destroy all the places, wherein the nations which ye shall possess served their gods, upon the high mountains, and upon the hills, and under every green tree:

3 And ye shall overthrow their altars, and break their pillars, and burn their groves with fire; and ye shall hew down the graven images of their gods, and destroy the names of them out of that place.

4 Ye shall not do so unto the LORD your God.

5 But unto the place which the LORD your God shall choose out of all your tribes to put his name there, *even* unto his habitation shall ye seek, and thither thou shalt come:

6 And thither ye shall bring your burnt

Cross references

14 Lev. 26:4; Deut. 28:12; Joel 2:23; James 5:7
15 Deut. 6:11; Ps. 104:14; Joel 2:19
16 Deut. 8:19; 29:18; 30:17; Job 31:27
17 Josh. 23:13, 15, 16
18 Deut. 6:6, 8; 32:46
19 Deut. 4:9, 10; 6:7
20 Deut. 6:9
21 Deut. 4:40; 6:2; Prov. 3:2; 4:10; 9:11
24 Gen. 15:18; Ex. 23:31
25 Ex. 23:27
26 Deut. 30:1, 15, 19
27 Deut. 28:2
28 Deut. 28:15
29 Deut. 27:12, 13; Josh. 8:33
30 Gen. 12:6; Judg. 7:1
31 Josh. 1:11
2 Ex. 34:13; Deut. 7:5; 2Kgs. 16:4; 17:10, 11; Jer. 3:6
3 Num. 33:52; Judg. 2:2
4 Deut. 12:31
5 Deut. 12:11; 26:2; Josh. 9:27; 1Kgs. 8:29; 2Chr. 7:12; Ps. 78:68
6 Lev. 17:3, 4; Deut. 12:17; 14:22, 23; 15:19, 20

11:22–28 This message is mainly a prediction of Israel's dominance if they obey the Lord. Here the Lord lays down the rules that will govern His covenant. This prediction of dominance will ultimately be fulfilled in the Millennium.

12:5 to put his name there. This prophecy is a reference to the temple. It was fulfilled through God's choice of Mount Moriah in what is now Jerusalem (1 Chr. 22:1; 2 Chr. 6:6).

offerings, and your sacrifices, and your tithes, and heave offerings of your hand, and your vows, and your freewill offerings, and the firstlings of your herds and of your flocks:

7 And there ye shall eat before the LORD your God, and ye shall rejoice in all that ye put your hand unto, ye and your households, wherein the LORD thy God hath blessed thee.

8 Ye shall not do after all *the things* that we do here this day, every man whatsoever *is* right in his own eyes.

9 For ye are not as yet come to the rest and to the inheritance, which the LORD your God giveth you.

10 But *when* ye go over Jordan, and dwell in the land which the LORD your God giveth you to inherit, and *when* he giveth you rest from all your enemies round about, so that ye dwell in safety;

11 Then there shall be a place which the LORD your God shall choose to cause his name to dwell there; thither shall ye bring all that I command you; your burnt offerings, and your sacrifices, your tithes, and the heave offering of your hand, and all your choice vows which ye vow unto the LORD:

12 And ye shall rejoice before the LORD your God, ye, and your sons, and your daughters, and your menservants, and your maidservants, and the Levite that *is* within your gates; forasmuch as he hath no part nor inheritance with you.

13 Take heed to thyself that thou offer not thy burnt offerings in every place that thou seest:

14 But in the place which the LORD shall choose in one of thy tribes, there thou shalt offer thy burnt offerings, and there thou shalt do all that I command thee.

15 Notwithstanding thou mayest kill and eat flesh in all thy gates, whatsoever thy soul lusteth after, according to the blessing of the LORD thy God which he hath given thee: the unclean and the clean may eat thereof, as of the roebuck, and as of the hart.

16 Only ye shall not eat the blood; ye shall pour it upon the earth as water.

17 Thou mayest not eat within thy gates the tithe of thy corn, or of thy wine, or of thy oil, or the firstlings of thy herds or of thy flock, nor any of thy vows which thou vowest, nor thy freewill offerings, or heave offering of thine hand:

18 But thou must eat them before the LORD

thy God in the place which the LORD thy God shall choose, thou, and thy son, and thy daughter, and thy manservant, and thy maidservant, and the Levite that *is* within thy gates: and thou shalt rejoice before the LORD thy God in all that thou puttest thine hands unto.

19 Take heed to thyself that thou forsake not the Levite as long as thou livest upon the earth.

20 When the LORD thy God shall enlarge thy border, as he hath promised thee, and thou shalt say, I will eat flesh, because thy soul longeth to eat flesh; thou mayest eat flesh, whatsoever thy soul lusteth after.

21 If the place which the LORD thy God hath chosen to put his name there be too far from thee, then thou shalt kill of thy herd and of thy flock, which the LORD hath given thee as I have commanded thee, and thou shalt eat in thy gates whatsoever thy soul lusteth after.

22 Even as the roebuck and the hart is eaten, so thou shalt eat them: the unclean and the clean shall eat *of* them alike.

23 Only be sure that thou eat not the blood: for the blood *is* the life; and thou mayest not eat the life with the flesh.

24 Thou shalt not eat it; thou shalt pour it upon the earth as water.

25 Thou shalt not eat it; that it may go well with thee, and with thy children after thee, when thou shalt do *that which is* right in the sight of the LORD.

26 Only thy holy things which thou hast, and thy vows, thou shalt take, and go unto the place which the LORD shall choose:

27 And thou shalt offer thy burnt offerings, the flesh and the blood, upon the altar of the LORD thy God: and the blood of thy sacrifices shall be poured out upon the altar of the LORD thy God, and thou shalt eat the flesh.

28 Observe and hear all these words which I command thee, that it may go well with thee, and with thy children after thee for ever, when thou doest *that which is* good and right in the sight of the LORD thy God.

Destroy All Idol Worship

29 When the LORD thy God shall cut off the nations from before thee, whither thou goest to possess them, and thou succeedest them, and dwellest in their land;

30 Take heed to thyself that thou be not snared by following them, after that they be destroyed from before thee; and that thou inquire not after their gods, saying, How did

7 Lev. 23:40; Deut. 12:12, 18; 14:26; 16:11, 14, 15; 26:11; 27:7

8 Judg. 17:6; 21:25

10 Deut. 11:31

11 Deut. 12:5, 14, 18, 21, 26; 14:23; 15:20; 16:2; 17:8; 18:6; 23:16; 26:2; 31:11; Josh. 18:1; 1Kgs. 8:29; Ps. 78:68

12 Deut. 10:9; 12:7; 14:20

13 Lev. 17:4

14 Deut. 12:11

15 Deut. 12:21, 22; 14:5; 15:22

16 Gen. 9:4; Lev. 7:26; 17:10; Deut. 12:23, 24; 15:23

18 Deut. 12:11, 12; 14:23

19 Deut. 14:27

20 Gen. 15:18; 28:14; Ex. 34:24; Deut. 11:24; 19:8

22 Deut. 12:15

23 Gen. 9:4; Lev. 17:11, 14; Deut. 12:16

25 Ex. 13:18; 15:26; Deut. 4:40; 1Kgs. 11:38; Isa. 3:10

26 Num. 5:9, 10; 18:19; 1Sam. 1:21, 22, 24

27 Lev. 1:5, 9, 13; 17:11

28 Deut. 12:25

29 Ex. 23:23; Deut. 19:1; Josh. 23:4

30 Deut. 7:16

these nations serve their gods? even so will I do likewise.

31 Thou shalt not do so unto the LORD thy God: for every abomination to the LORD, which he hateth, have they done unto their gods; for even their sons and their daughters they have burnt in the fire to their gods.

32 What thing soever I command you, observe to do it: thou shalt not add thereto, nor diminish from it.

CHAPTER 13

1 If there arise among you a prophet, or a dreamer of dreams, and giveth thee a sign or a wonder,

2 And the sign or the wonder come to pass, whereof he spake unto thee, saying, Let us go after other gods, which thou hast not known, and let us serve them;

3 Thou shalt not hearken unto the words of that prophet, or that dreamer of dreams: for the LORD your God proveth you, to know whether ye love the LORD your God with all your heart and with all your soul.

4 Ye shall walk after the LORD your God, and fear him, and keep his commandments, and obey his voice, and ye shall serve him, and cleave unto him.

5 And that prophet, or that dreamer of dreams, shall be put to death; because he hath spoken to turn *you* away from the LORD your God, which brought you out of the land of Egypt, and redeemed you out of the house of bondage, to thrust thee out of the way which the LORD thy God commanded thee to walk in. So shalt thou put the evil away from the midst of thee.

6 If thy brother, the son of thy mother, or thy son, or thy daughter, or the wife of thy bosom, or thy friend, which *is* as thine own soul, entice thee secretly, saying, Let us go and serve other gods, which thou hast not known, thou, nor thy fathers;

7 *Namely*, of the gods of the people which *are* round about you, nigh unto thee, or far off from thee, from the *one* end of the earth even unto the *other* end of the earth;

8 Thou shalt not consent unto him, nor hearken unto him; neither shall thine eye pity him, neither shalt thou spare, neither shalt thou conceal him:

9 But thou shalt surely kill him; thine hand shall be first upon him to put him to death, and afterwards the hand of all the people.

10 And thou shalt stone him with stones, that he die; because he hath sought to thrust thee away from the LORD thy God, which brought thee out of the land of Egypt, from the house of bondage.

11 And all Israel shall hear, and fear, and shall do no more any such wickedness as this is among you.

12 If thou shalt hear *say* in one of thy cities, which the LORD thy God hath given thee to dwell there, saying,

13 *Certain* men, the children of Belial, are gone out from among you, and have withdrawn the inhabitants of their city, saying, Let us go and serve other gods, which ye have not known;

14 Then shalt thou inquire, and make search, and ask diligently; and, behold, *if it be* truth, *and* the thing certain, *that* such abomination is wrought among you;

15 Thou shalt surely smite the inhabitants of that city with the edge of the sword, destroying it utterly, and all that *is* therein, and the cattle thereof, with the edge of the sword.

16 And thou shalt gather all the spoil of it into the midst of the street thereof, and shalt burn with fire the city, and all the spoil thereof every whit, for the LORD thy God: and it shall be an heap for ever; it shall not be built again.

17 And there shall cleave nought of the cursed thing to thine hand: that the LORD may turn from the fierceness of his anger, and shew thee mercy, and have compassion upon thee, and multiply thee, as he hath sworn unto thy fathers;

18 When thou shalt hearken to the voice of the LORD thy God, to keep all his commandments which I command thee this day, to do *that which is* right in the eyes of the LORD thy God.

CHAPTER 14

1 Ye *are* the children of the LORD your God: ye shall not cut yourselves, nor make any baldness between your eyes for the dead.

2 For thou *art* an holy people unto the LORD thy God, and the LORD hath chosen thee to be a peculiar people unto himself,

13:1–5 Moses provides the first of two tests the people should apply to examine the message of one declaring himself to be a prophet (cf. Deut. 18:20–22). If a prophet made a prediction that came true, then asked the people to follow other gods, he should not be followed, but should immediately be put to death.

above all the nations that *are* upon the earth.

Clean and Unclean Food

3 Thou shalt not eat any abominable thing.

4 These *are* the beasts which ye shall eat: the ox, the sheep, and the goat,

5 The hart, and the roebuck, and the fallow deer, and the wild goat, and the pygarg, and the wild ox, and the chamois.

6 And every beast that parteth the hoof, and cleaveth the cleft into two claws, *and* cheweth the cud among the beasts, that ye shall eat.

7 Nevertheless these ye shall not eat of them that chew the cud, or of them that divide the cloven hoof; *as* the camel, and the hare, and the coney: for they chew the cud, but divide not the hoof; *therefore* they *are* unclean unto you.

8 And the swine, because it divideth the hoof, yet cheweth not the cud, it *is* unclean unto you: ye shall not eat of their flesh, nor touch their dead carcase.

9 These ye shall eat of all that *are* in the waters: all that have fins and scales shall ye eat:

10 And whatsoever hath not fins and scales ye may not eat; it *is* unclean unto you.

11 Of all clean birds ye shall eat.

12 But these *are they* of which ye shall not eat: the eagle, and the ossifrage, and the ospray,

13 And the glede, and the kite, and the vulture after his kind,

14 And every raven after his kind,

15 And the owl, and the night hawk, and the cuckow, and the hawk after his kind,

16 The little owl, and the great owl, and the swan,

17 And the pelican, and the gier eagle, and the cormorant,

18 And the stork, and the heron after her kind, and the lapwing, and the bat.

19 And every creeping thing that flieth *is* unclean unto you: they shall not be eaten.

20 *But of* all clean fowls ye may eat.

21 Ye shall not eat *of* any thing that dieth of itself: thou shalt give it unto the stranger that *is* in thy gates, that he may eat it; or thou mayest sell it unto an alien: for thou *art* an holy people unto the LORD thy God. Thou shalt not seethe a kid in his mother's milk.

Tithing

22 Thou shalt truly tithe all the increase of thy seed, that the field bringeth forth year by year.

23 And thou shalt eat before the LORD thy God, in the place which he shall choose to place his name there, the tithe of thy corn, of thy wine, and of thine oil, and the firstlings of thy herds and of thy flocks; that thou mayest learn to fear the LORD thy God always.

24 And if the way be too long for thee, so that thou art not able to carry it; *or* if the place be too far from thee, which the LORD thy God shall choose to set his name there, when the LORD thy God hath blessed thee:

25 Then shalt thou turn *it* into money, and bind up the money in thine hand, and shalt go unto the place which the LORD thy God shall choose:

26 And thou shalt bestow that money for whatsoever thy soul lusteth after, for oxen, or for sheep, or for wine, or for strong drink, or for whatsoever thy soul desireth: and thou shalt eat there before the LORD thy God, and thou shalt rejoice, thou, and thine household,

27 And the Levite that *is* within thy gates; thou shalt not forsake him; for he hath no part nor inheritance with thee.

28 At the end of three years thou shalt bring forth all the tithe of thine increase the same year, and shalt lay *it* up within thy gates:

29 And the Levite, (because he hath no part nor inheritance with thee,) and the stranger, and the fatherless, and the widow, which *are* within thy gates, shall come, and shall eat and be satisfied; that the LORD thy God may bless thee in all the work of thine hand which thou doest.

CHAPTER 15
The Seventh Year

1 At the end of *every* seven years thou shalt make a release.

2 And this *is* the manner of the release: Every creditor that lendeth *ought* unto his neighbour shall release *it*; he shall not exact *it* of his neighbour, or of his brother; because it is called the LORD's release.

3 Of a foreigner thou mayest exact *it* *again*: but *that* which is thine with thy brother thine hand shall release;

4 Save when there shall be no poor among you; for the LORD shall greatly bless thee in the land which the LORD thy God giveth thee *for* an inheritance to possess it:

5 Only if thou carefully hearken unto the voice of the LORD thy God, to observe to do all these commandments which I command thee this day.

3 Ezek. 4:14; Acts 10:13, 14
4 Lev. 11:2
8 Lev. 11:26, 27
9 Lev. 11:9
12 Lev. 11:13
19 Lev. 11:20, 21
21 Ex. 23:19; 34:26; Lev. 17:15; 22:8; Deut. 14:2; Ezek. 4:14
22 Lev. 27:30; Deut. 12:6, 17; Neh. 10:37
23 Deut. 12:5-7, 17, 18; 15:19, 20
24 Deut. 12:21
26 Deut. 12:7, 18; 26:11
27 Num. 18:20; Deut. 12:12, 18, 19; 18:1, 2
28 Deut. 26:12; Amos 4:4
29 Deut. 12:12; 14:27; 15:10; 26:12; Prov. 3:9, 10; Mal. 3:10

1 Ex. 21:2; 23:10, 11; Lev. 25:2, 4; Deut. 31:10; Jer. 34:14

3 Deut. 23:20

4 Deut. 28:8

5 Deut. 28:1

6 For the Lord thy God blesseth thee, as he promised thee: and thou shalt lend unto many nations, but thou shalt not borrow; and thou shalt reign over many nations, but they shall not reign over thee.

7 If there be among you a poor man of one of thy brethren within any of thy gates in thy land which the Lord thy God giveth thee, thou shalt not harden thine heart, nor shut thine hand from thy poor brother:

8 But thou shalt open thine hand wide unto him, and shalt surely lend him sufficient for his need, *in that* which he wanteth.

9 Beware that there be not a thought in thy wicked heart, saying, The seventh year, the year of release, is at hand; and thine eye be evil against thy poor brother, and thou givest him nought; and he cry unto the Lord against thee, and it be sin unto thee.

10 Thou shalt surely give him, and thine heart shall not be grieved when thou givest unto him: because that for this thing the Lord thy God shall bless thee in all thy works, and in all that thou puttest thine hand unto.

11 For the poor shall never cease out of the land: therefore I command thee, saying, Thou shalt open thine hand wide unto thy brother, to thy poor, and to thy needy, in thy land.

12 *And* if thy brother, an Hebrew man, or an Hebrew woman, be sold unto thee, and serve thee six years; then in the seventh year thou shalt let him go free from thee.

13 And when thou sendest him out free from thee, thou shalt not let him go away empty:

14 Thou shalt furnish him liberally out of thy flock, and out of thy floor, and out of thy winepress: *of that* wherewith the Lord thy God hath blessed thee thou shalt give unto him.

15 And thou shalt remember that thou wast a bondman in the land of Egypt, and the Lord thy God redeemed thee: therefore I command thee this thing today.

16 And it shall be, if he say unto thee, I will not go away from thee; because he loveth thee and thine house, because he is well with thee;

17 Then thou shalt take an aul, and thrust *it* through his ear unto the door, and he shall be thy servant for ever. And also unto thy maidservant thou shalt do likewise.

18 It shall not seem hard unto thee, when thou sendest him away free from thee; for he hath been worth a double hired servant *to thee*, in serving thee six years: and the

Lord thy God shall bless thee in all that thou doest.

Firstborn Animals

19 All the firstling males that come of thy herd and of thy flock thou shalt sanctify unto the Lord thy God: thou shalt do no work with the firstling of thy bullock, nor shear the firstling of thy sheep.

20 Thou shalt eat *it* before the Lord thy God year by year in the place which the Lord shall choose, thou and thy household.

21 And if there be *any* blemish therein, *as if it be* lame, or blind, *or have* any ill blemish, thou shalt not sacrifice it unto the Lord thy God.

22 Thou shalt eat it within thy gates: the unclean and the clean *person shall eat it* alike, as the roebuck, and as the hart.

23 Only thou shalt not eat the blood thereof; thou shalt pour it upon the ground as water.

CHAPTER 16
Three Festivals Each Year

1 Observe the month of Abib, and keep the passover unto the Lord thy God: for in the month of Abib the Lord thy God brought thee forth out of Egypt by night.

2 Thou shalt therefore sacrifice the passover unto the Lord thy God, of the flock and the herd, in the place which the Lord shall choose to place his name there.

3 Thou shalt eat no leavened bread with it; seven days shalt thou eat unleavened bread therewith, *even* the bread of affliction; for thou camest forth out of the land of Egypt in haste: that thou mayest remember the day when thou camest forth out of the land of Egypt all the days of thy life.

4 And there shall be no leavened bread seen with thee in all thy coast seven days; neither shall there *any thing* of the flesh, which thou sacrificedst the first day at even, remain all night until the morning.

5 Thou mayest not sacrifice the passover within any of thy gates, which the Lord thy God giveth thee:

6 But at the place which the Lord thy God shall choose to place his name in, there thou shalt sacrifice the passover at even, at the going down of the sun, at the season that thou camest forth out of Egypt.

7 And thou shalt roast and eat *it* in the place which the Lord thy God shall choose: and thou shalt turn in the morning, and go unto thy tents.

8 Six days thou shalt eat unleavened

6 Deut. 28:12, 13, 44; Prov. 22:7

7 1John 3:17

8 Lev. 25:35; Matt. 5:42; Luke 6:34, 35

9 Deut. 24:15; 28:54, 56; Prov. 23:6; 28:22; Matt. 20:15; 25:41, 42

10 Deut. 14:29; 24:19; Ps. 41:1; Prov. 22:9; 2Cor. 9:5, 7

11 Matt. 26:11; Mark 14:7; John 12:8

12 Ex. 21:2; Lev. 25:39; Jer. 34:14

14 Prov. 10:22

15 Deut. 5:15; 16:12

18 Isa. 16:14; 21:16

19 Ex. 13:2; 34:19; Lev. 27:26; Num. 3:13

20 Deut. 12:5, 6, 7, 17; 14:23; 16:11, 14

21 Lev. 22:20; Deut. 17:1

22 Deut. 12:15, 22

23 Deut. 12:16, 23

1 Ex. 12:2, 29, 42; 13:4; 34:18

2 Num. 28:19; Deut. 12:5, 26

3 Ex. 12:15, 19, 39; 13:3, 6, 7; 34:18

4 Ex. 12:10; 13:7; 34:25

6 Ex. 12:6

7 Ex. 12:8, 9; 2Kgs. 23:23; Chr. 35:13; John 2:13, 23; 11:55

8 Ex. 12:16; 13:6; Lev. 23:8

bread: and on the seventh day *shall be* a
solemn assembly to the LORD thy God: thou
shalt do no work *therein*.
9 Seven weeks shalt thou number unto
thee: begin to number the seven weeks
from *such time as* thou beginnest *to put* the
sickle to the corn.
10 And thou shalt keep the feast of weeks
unto the LORD thy God with a tribute of a
freewill offering of thine hand, which thou
shalt give *unto the LORD thy God*, according as
the LORD thy God hath blessed thee:
11 And thou shalt rejoice before the LORD
thy God, thou, and thy son, and thy daughter, and thy manservant, and thy maidservant, and the Levite that *is* within thy gates,
and the stranger, and the fatherless, and the
widow, that *are* among you, in the place
which the LORD thy God hath chosen to
place his name there.
12 And thou shalt remember that thou wast
a bondman in Egypt: and thou shalt observe
and do these statutes.
13 Thou shalt observe the feast of tabernacles seven days, after that thou hast gathered in thy corn and thy wine:
14 And thou shalt rejoice in thy feast, thou,
and thy son, and thy daughter, and thy
manservant, and thy maidservant, and the
Levite, the stranger, and the fatherless, and
the widow, that *are* within thy gates.
15 Seven days shalt thou keep a solemn
feast unto the LORD thy God in the place
which the LORD shall choose: because the
LORD thy God shall bless thee in all thine increase, and in all the works of thine hands,
therefore thou shalt surely rejoice.
16 Three times in a year shall all thy males
appear before the LORD thy God in the place
which he shall choose; in the feast of unleavened bread, and in the feast of weeks,
and in the feast of tabernacles: and they
shall not appear before the LORD empty:
17 Every man *shall give* as he is able, according to the blessing of the LORD thy God
which he hath given thee.

The Legal System

18 Judges and officers shalt thou make thee
in all thy gates, which the LORD thy God
giveth thee, throughout thy tribes: and they
shall judge the people with just judgment.
19 Thou shalt not wrest judgment; thou
shalt not respect persons, neither take a gift:
for a gift doth blind the eyes of the wise,
and pervert the words of the righteous.
20 That which is altogether just shalt thou
follow, that thou mayest live, and inherit the
land which the LORD thy God giveth thee.
21 Thou shalt not plant thee a grove of any
trees near unto the altar of the LORD thy
God, which thou shalt make thee.
22 Neither shalt thou set thee up *any* image;
which the LORD thy God hateth.

CHAPTER 17

1 Thou shalt not sacrifice unto the LORD
thy God *any* bullock, or sheep, wherein is
blemish, *or* any evilfavouredness: for that *is*
an abomination unto the LORD thy God.
2 If there be found among you, within any
of thy gates which the LORD thy God giveth
thee, man or woman, that hath wrought
wickedness in the sight of the LORD thy God,
in transgressing his covenant,
3 And hath gone and served other gods,
and worshipped them, either the sun, or
moon, or any of the host of heaven, which I
have not commanded;
4 And it be told thee, and thou hast heard
of it, and inquired diligently, and, behold, *it*
be true, *and* the thing certain, *that* such
abomination is wrought in Israel:
5 Then shalt thou bring forth that man or
that woman, which have committed that
wicked thing, unto thy gates, *even* that man
or that woman, and shalt stone them with
stones, till they die.
6 At the mouth of two witnesses, or three
witnesses, shall he that is worthy of death
be put to death; *but* at the mouth of one witness he shall not be put to death.
7 The hands of the witnesses shall be first
upon him to put him to death, and afterward the hands of all the people. So thou
shalt put the evil away from among you.
8 If there arise a matter too hard for thee
in judgment, between blood and blood, between plea and plea, and between stroke
and stroke, *being* matters of controversy
within thy gates: then shalt thou arise, and
get thee up into the place which the LORD
thy God shall choose;
9 And thou shalt come unto the priests the
Levites, and unto the judge that shall be in
those days, and inquire; and they shall shew
thee the sentence of judgment:
10 And thou shalt do according to the sentence, which they of that place which the
LORD shall choose shall shew thee; and thou
shalt observe to do according to all that they
inform thee:
11 According to the sentence of the law
which they shall teach thee, and according
to the judgment which they shall tell thee,
thou shalt do: thou shalt not decline from

9 Ex. 23:16; 34:22; Lev. 23:15; Num. 28:26
13 Ex. 23:16; Lev. 23:34; Num. 29:12
14 Neh. 8:9
15 Lev. 23:39, 40
16 Ex. 23:14, 15, 17; 34:20, 23
18 Deut. 1:16; 1Chr. 23:4; 26:29; 2Chr. 19:5, 8
19 Ex. 23:2, 6, 8; Lev. 19:15; Prov. 17:23; 24:23
21 Ex. 34:13; 1Kgs. 14:15; 16:33; 2Kgs. 17:16; 21:3; 2Chr. 33:3
22 Lev. 26:1
1 Mal. 1:8, 13, 14
2 Josh. 7:11, 15; 23:16; Judg. 2:20
3 Deut. 4:19; Job 31:26; Jer. 7:22, 23, 31; 19:5; 32:35
4 Deut. 13:12, 14
5 Lev. 24:14, 16; Deut. 13:10; Josh. 7:25
6 Num. 35:30; Deut. 19:15; Matt. 18:16; John 8:17; 2Cor. 13:1; 1Tim. 5:19; Heb. 10:28
7 Deut. 13:5, 9; 17:12; 19:19; Acts 7:58
8 Ex. 21:13, 20, 22, 28; 22:2; Num. 35:11, 16, 19; Deut. 12:5; 19:4, 10, 11, 17; 2Chr. 19:10; Ps. 122:5; Hag. 2:11; Mal. 2:7
9 Deut. 19:17; Jer. 18:18; Ezek. 44:24

the sentence which they shall shew thee, *to* the right hand, nor *to* the left.

12 And the man that will do presumptuously, and will not hearken unto the priest that standeth to minister there before the Lord thy God, or unto the judge, even that man shall die: and thou shalt put away the evil from Israel.

13 And all the people shall hear, and fear, and do no more presumptuously.

A Future King for Israel

14 When thou art come unto the land which the Lord thy God giveth thee, and shalt possess it, and shalt dwell therein, and shalt say, I will set a king over me, like as all the nations that *are* about me;

15 Thou shalt in any wise set *him* king over thee, whom the Lord thy God shall choose: *one* from among thy brethren shalt thou set king over thee: thou mayest not set a stranger over thee, which *is* not thy brother.

16 But he shall not multiply horses to himself, nor cause the people to return to Egypt, to the end that he should multiply horses: forasmuch as the Lord hath said unto you, Ye shall henceforth return no more that way.

17 Neither shall he multiply wives to himself, that his heart turn not away: neither shall he greatly multiply to himself silver and gold.

18 And it shall be, when he sitteth upon the throne of his kingdom, that he shall write him a copy of this law in a book out of *that which is* before the priests the Levites:

19 And it shall be with him, and he shall read therein all the days of his life: that he may learn to fear the Lord his God, to keep all the words of this law and these statutes, to do them:

20 That his heart be not lifted up above his brethren, and that he turn not aside from the commandment, *to* the right hand, or *to* the left: to the end that he may prolong *his* days in his kingdom, he, and his children, in the midst of Israel.

CHAPTER 18
The Priest and Levites' Share

1 The priests the Levites, *and* all the tribe of Levi, shall have no part nor inheritance with Israel: they shall eat the offerings of

the Lord made by fire, and his inheritance.

2 Therefore shall they have no inheritance among their brethren: the Lord *is* their inheritance, as he hath said unto them.

3 And this shall be the priest's due from the people, from them that offer a sacrifice, whether *it be* ox or sheep; and they shall give unto the priest the shoulder, and the two cheeks, and the maw.

4 The firstfruit *also* of thy corn, of thy wine, and of thine oil, and the first of the fleece of thy sheep, shalt thou give him.

5 For the Lord thy God hath chosen him out of all thy tribes, to stand to minister in the name of the Lord, him and his sons for ever.

6 And if a Levite come from any of thy gates out of all Israel, where he sojourned, and come with all the desire of his mind unto the place which the Lord shall choose;

7 Then he shall minister in the name of the Lord his God, as all his brethren the Levites *do*, which stand there before the Lord.

8 They shall have like portions to eat, beside that which cometh of the sale of his patrimony.

Forbidden Practices

9 When thou art come into the land which the Lord thy God giveth thee, thou shalt not learn to do after the abominations of those nations.

10 There shall not be found among you *any one* that maketh his son or his daughter to pass through the fire, *or* that useth divination, *or* an observer of times, or an enchanter, or a witch,

11 Or a charmer, or a consulter with familiar spirits, or a wizard, or a necromancer.

12 For all that do these things *are* an abomination unto the Lord: and because of these abominations the Lord thy God doth drive them out from before thee.

13 Thou shalt be perfect with the Lord thy God.

14 For these nations, which thou shalt possess, hearkened unto observers of times, and unto diviners: but as for thee, the Lord thy God hath not suffered thee so *to do*.

The Prophet like Moses

15 The Lord thy God will raise up unto thee a Prophet from the midst of thee, of thy

Cross references (center column)

12 Num. 15:30; Ezra 10:8; Hos. 4:4

14 1Sam. 8:5, 19, 20

15 1Sam. 9:15; 10:24; 16:12; 1Chr. 22:10; Jer. 30:21

16 Ex. 13:17; Num. 14:3, 4; Deut. 28:68; Isa. 31:1; Jer. 42:15; Ezek. 17:15; Hos. 11:5

17 1Kgs. 11:3, 4

18 Deut. 31:9, 26; 2Kgs. 11:12; 22:8

19 Josh. 1:8; Ps. 119:97, 98

20 Num. 18: 8, 9, 20; 26:62; Deut. 5:32; 10:9; 1Kgs. 15:5; 1Cor. 9:13

3 Lev. 7:30-34

4 Ex. 22:29; Num. 18:12, 24

5 Ex. 28:1; Num. 3:10; Deut. 10:8; 17:12

6 Num. 35:2, 3; Deut. 12:5

7 2Chr. 31:2

8 2Chr. 31:4; Neh. 12:44, 47

9 Lev. 18:26, 27, 30

10 Lev. 18:21; 19:26, 31; 20:27; Deut. 12:31; Isa. 8:19

11 Lev. 20:27; 1Sam. 28:7

15 Deut. 18:18; John 1:45; Acts 3:22; 7:37

17:14 as all the nations that are about me. The Lord predicted that after Israel lived in the land for a while they would want a king. This prophecy was fulfilled when they selected Saul as their first king (1 Sam. 10:24).

18:15–19 a Prophet from the midst of thee, of thy brethren, like unto me. The singular pronoun emphasizes the ultimate Prophet who was to come. Jesus fulfills this prophecy according to Acts 3:20–24; 7:37.

False Prophecy

By Jim Anderson

A s we consider the phenomenon of fulfilled prophecy we must remind ourselves that all prophecy which claims to come from God is not of God. So in order to avoid the confusion that false prophecy brings, we should briefly note the character, causes, and consequences of false prophecy.

Some false prophets are **objectively** false. That is, they deny the true God and very openly and clearly follow a false god such as Baal, Osiris, Zeus, Mithra, Dagon, or some other false deity. Unfortunately, there are many false prophets who are **subjectively** false. That is, they claim to believe in the true God, the Bible, and in Jesus. But they actually do not believe the Bible, nor follow Jesus. Jesus warned of these: "Beware of false prophets, which come to you in sheep's clothing, but inwardly they are ravening wolves" (Matt. 7:15).

The Bible lays down some tests we may give to the message of a professed prophet to see whether his prophecy is truly from God. One of the external tests is to determine whether or not the prophecy comes true. Those prophets who truly come from God will have their prophecies come true (Deut. 18:22). Another test is that among prophets where moral excellence is absent, the prophecy is to be considered false (see Jer. 23:9–32). Still another of the external tests for false prophecy is that of checking out the prophet's "signs" with the character of God (Deut. 13:1–3).

> *The ultimate consequence of false prophecy is death and destruction.*

There were also the internal tests regarding the ethical character of the prophet himself (Jer. 23:21–22) and the uninhibited truthfulness of a credible prophet, which, of course, was lacking in the false prophets of the Bible who were addicted to speaking "lying words" (Jer. 7:4, 8–10).

A very humorous incident is recorded in 1 Kings 22:1–18 and embellished in 2 Chronicles 18:4–27, but the tragedy of it is that there were false prophets in Israel who spoke just to please the king and told lies in the process! Another internal test that would expose the false prophet was the personal bias of the false prophet in favor of Israel. False prophets would always claim that Israel was going to prosper because God's temple was in their midst. Unfortunately these so-called prophets failed to consider that they could not confine the Lord to the temple, which was only a symbol of God's presence (cf. Jer. 7:4–14; 23:9–32; and 1 Sam. 4:21).

There are dire consequences for either producing false prophecies or heeding false prophets. One of those consequences is the failure of the prophecy itself. Since it is false, it is doomed to ultimate failure (cf. Jer. 28:9; Deut. 18:20–22; 2 Chr. 18:12–27). Another consequence is the shame, spiritual depravity, and moral corruption that follow. When people listen to error, follow error, and live in error, the result is always a corrupt, shameful life (Mic. 3:11–12). One very pathetic consequence of false prophecy is that the lives of people other than the false prophet are contaminated. Jesus said of the religious hypocrites of His day, that when they gained a convert they caused that person to become "twofold more the child of hell" (Matt. 23:15). The ultimate consequence of false prophecy is that the false prophet himself receives death and destruction (cf. Jer. 28:16–17).

brethren, like unto me; unto him ye shall hearken;

16 According to all that thou desiredst of the LORD thy God in Horeb in the day of the assembly, saying, Let me not hear again the voice of the LORD my God, neither let me see this great fire any more, that I die not.

17 And the LORD said unto me, They have well *spoken that* which they have spoken.

18 I will raise them up a Prophet from among their brethren, like unto thee, and will put my words in his mouth; and he shall speak unto them all that I shall command him.

19 And it shall come to pass, *that* whosoever will not hearken unto my words which he shall speak in my name, I will require *it* of him.

20 But the prophet, which shall presume to speak a word in my name, which I have not commanded him to speak, or that shall speak in the name of other gods, even that prophet shall die.

21 And if thou say in thine heart, How shall we know the word which the LORD hath not spoken?

22 When a prophet speaketh in the name of the LORD, if the thing follow not, nor come to pass, that *is* the thing which the LORD hath not spoken, *but* the prophet hath spoken it presumptuously: thou shalt not be afraid of him.

CHAPTER 19
The Cities of Refuge

1 When the LORD thy God hath cut off the nations, whose land the LORD thy God giveth thee, and thou succeedest them, and dwellest in their cities, and in their houses;

2 Thou shalt separate three cities for thee in the midst of thy land, which the LORD thy God giveth thee to possess it.

3 Thou shalt prepare thee a way, and divide the coasts of thy land, which the LORD thy God giveth thee to inherit, into three parts, that every slayer may flee thither.

4 And this *is* the case of the slayer, which shall flee thither, that he may live: Whoso killeth his neighbour ignorantly, whom he hated not in time past;

5 As when a man goeth into the wood with his neighbour to hew wood, and his hand fetcheth a stroke with the axe to cut down the tree, and the head slippeth from the helve, and lighteth upon his neighbour, that he die; he shall flee unto one of those cities, and live:

6 Lest the avenger of the blood pursue the slayer, while his heart is hot, and overtake him, because the way is long, and slay him; whereas he *was* not worthy of death, inasmuch as he hated him not in time past.

7 Wherefore I command thee, saying, Thou shalt separate three cities for thee.

8 And if the LORD thy God enlarge thy coast, as he hath sworn unto thy fathers, and give thee all the land which he promised to give unto thy fathers;

9 If thou shalt keep all these commandments to do them, which I command thee this day, to love the LORD thy God, and to walk ever in his ways; then shalt thou add three cities more for thee, beside these three:

10 That innocent blood be not shed in thy land, which the LORD thy God giveth thee *for* an inheritance, and *so* blood be upon thee.

11 But if any man hate his neighbour, and lie in wait for him, and rise up against him, and smite him mortally that he die, and fleeth into one of these cities:

12 Then the elders of his city shall send and fetch him thence, and deliver him into the hand of the avenger of blood, that he may die.

13 Thine eye shall not pity him, but thou shalt put away *the guilt of* innocent blood from Israel, that it may go well with thee.

14 Thou shalt not remove thy neighbour's landmark, which they of old time have set in thine inheritance, which thou shalt inherit in the land that the LORD thy God giveth thee to possess it.

Witnesses

15 One witness shall not rise up against a man for any iniquity, or for any sin, in any sin that he sinneth: at the mouth of two witnesses, or at the mouth of three witnesses, shall the matter be established.

Cross References

16 Ex. 20:19; Deut. 9:10; Heb. 12:19
17 Deut. 5:28
18 Deut. 18:15; Isa. 51:16; John 1:45; 4:25; 8:28; 12:49, 50; 17:8; Acts 3:22; 7:37
19 Acts 3:23
20 Deut. 13:1, 2, 5; Jer. 2:8; 14:14, 15; Zech. 13:3
22 Deut. 13:2; 18:20; Jer. 28:9
1 Deut. 12:29
2 Ex. 21:13; Num. 35:10, 14; Josh. 20:2
4 Num. 35:15; Deut. 4:42
6 Num. 35:12
8 Gen. 15:18; Deut. 12:20
9 Josh. 20:7, 8
11 Ex. 21:12; Num. 35:16, 24; Deut. 27:24; Prov. 28:17
13 Num. 35:33, 34; Deut. 13:8; 21:9; 25:12; 1Kgs. 2:31
14 Deut. 27:17; Job 24:2; Prov. 22:28; Hos. 5:10
15 Num. 35:30; Deut. 17:6; Matt. 18:16; John 8:17; 2Cor. 13:1; 1Tim. 5:19; Heb. 10:28

Jesus, like Moses, would receive and preach God's revelation and lead the people in the way of truth. Here Moses is said to be a prophet, thus, Israel's first prophet.

18:20–22 This is the second of two tests the people should apply to examine the message of one declaring to be a prophet (cf. Deut. 13:1–5). This test consists of determining whether what the prophet predicted actually happened or not. This instruction for discernment is part of the reason why the Jewish leaders properly tested Jesus. The problem arose, however, when He passed all the tests and they still rejected Him.

16 If a false witness rise up against any man to testify against him *that which is* wrong;

17 Then both the men, between whom the controversy *is*, shall stand before the LORD, before the priests and the judges, which shall be in those days;

18 And the judges shall make diligent inquisition: and, behold, *if* the witness *be* a false witness, *and* hath testified falsely against his brother;

19 Then shall ye do unto him, as he had thought to have done unto his brother: so shalt thou put the evil away from among you.

20 And those which remain shall hear, and fear, and shall henceforth commit no more any such evil among you.

21 And thine eye shall not pity; *but* life *shall go* for life, eye for eye, tooth for tooth, hand for hand, foot for foot.

CHAPTER 20
How to Wage War

1 When thou goest out to battle against thine enemies, and seest horses, and chariots, *and* a people more than thou, be not afraid of them: for the LORD thy God *is* with thee, which brought thee up out of the land of Egypt.

2 And it shall be, when ye are come nigh unto the battle, that the priest shall approach and speak unto the people,

3 And shall say unto them, Hear, O Israel, ye approach this day unto battle against your enemies: let not your hearts faint, fear not, and do not tremble, neither be ye terrified because of them;

4 For the LORD your God *is* he that goeth with you, to fight for you against your enemies, to save you.

5 And the officers shall speak unto the people, saying, What man *is there* that hath built a new house, and hath not dedicated it? let him go and return to his house, lest he die in the battle, and another man dedicate it.

6 And what man *is he* that hath planted a vineyard, and hath not *yet* eaten of it? let him *also* go and return unto his house, lest he die in the battle, and another man eat of it.

7 And what man *is there* that hath betrothed a wife, and hath not taken her? let him go and return unto his house, lest he die in the battle, and another man take her.

8 And the officers shall speak further unto the people, and they shall say, What man *is there that is* fearful and fainthearted? let him go and return unto his house, lest his

Cross references

16 Ps. 27:12; 35:11
17 Deut. 17:9; 21:5
19 Deut. 13:5; 17:7; 21:21; 22:21, 24; 24:7; Prov. 19:5, 9; Dan. 6:24
20 Deut. 17:13; 21:21
21 Ex. 21:23, 24; Lev. 24:20; Deut. 19:13; Matt. 5:38
1 Num. 23:21; Deut. 31:6, 8; 2Chr. 13:12; 32:7, 8; Ps. 20:7; Isa. 31:1
4 Deut. 1:30; 3:22; Josh. 23:10
5 Neh. 12:27
6 Lev. 19:23, 24; Deut. 28:30
7 Deut. 24:5
8 Judg. 7:3
10 2Sam. 20:18, 20
13 Num. 31:7
14 Josh. 8:2; 22:8
16 Num. 21:2, 3, 35; 33:52; Deut. 7:1, 2; Josh. 11:14
18 Ex. 23:33; Deut. 7:4; 12:30, 31; 18:9

brethren's heart faint as well as his heart.

9 And it shall be, when the officers have made an end of speaking unto the people, that they shall make captains of the armies to lead the people.

10 When thou comest nigh unto a city to fight against it, then proclaim peace unto it.

11 And it shall be, if it make thee answer of peace, and open unto thee, then it shall be, *that* all the people *that is* found therein shall be tributaries unto thee, and they shall serve thee.

12 And if it will make no peace with thee, but will make war against thee, then thou shalt besiege it:

13 And when the LORD thy God hath delivered it into thine hands, thou shalt smite every male thereof with the edge of the sword:

14 But the women, and the little ones, and the cattle, and all that is in the city, *even* all the spoil thereof, shalt thou take unto thyself; and thou shalt eat the spoil of thine enemies, which the LORD thy God hath given thee.

15 Thus shalt thou do unto all the cities *which are* very far off from thee, which *are* not of the cities of these nations.

16 But of the cities of these people, which the LORD thy God doth give thee *for* an inheritance, thou shalt save alive nothing that breatheth:

17 But thou shalt utterly destroy them; *namely*, the Hittites, and the Amorites, the Canaanites, and the Perizzites, the Hivites, and the Jebusites; as the LORD thy God hath commanded thee:

18 That they teach you not to do after all their abominations, which they have done unto their gods; so should ye sin against the LORD your God.

19 When thou shalt besiege a city a long time, in making war against it to take it, thou shalt not destroy the trees thereof by forcing an axe against them: for thou mayest eat of them, and thou shalt not cut them down (for the tree of the field *is* man's *life*) to employ *them* in the siege:

20 Only the trees which thou knowest that they *be* not trees for meat, thou shalt destroy and cut them down; and thou shalt build bulwarks against the city that maketh war with thee, until it be subdued.

CHAPTER 21
Atonement for Innocent Blood

1 If *one* be found slain in the land which the LORD thy God giveth thee to possess it,

lying in the field, *and* it be not known who hath slain him:

2 Then thy elders and thy judges shall come forth, and they shall measure unto the cities which *are* round about him that is slain:

3 And it shall be, *that* the city *which is* next unto the slain man, even the elders of that city shall take an heifer, which hath not been wrought with, *and* which hath not drawn in the yoke;

4 And the elders of that city shall bring down the heifer unto a rough valley, which is neither eared nor sown, and shall strike off the heifer's neck there in the valley:

5 And the priests the sons of Levi shall come near; for them the LORD thy God hath chosen to minister unto him, and to bless in the name of the LORD; and by their word shall every controversy and every stroke be *tried*:

6 And all the elders of that city, *that are* next unto the slain *man*, shall wash their hands over the heifer that is beheaded in the valley:

7 And they shall answer and say, Our hands have not shed this blood, neither have our eyes seen *it*.

8 Be merciful, O LORD, unto thy people Israel, whom thou hast redeemed, and lay not innocent blood unto thy people of Israel's charge. And the blood shall be forgiven them.

9 So shalt thou put away the *guilt of* innocent blood from among you, when thou shalt do *that which is* right in the sight of the LORD.

Laws Pertaining to the Family

10 When thou goest forth to war against thine enemies, and the LORD thy God hath delivered them into thine hands, and thou hast taken them captive,

11 And seest among the captives a beautiful woman, and hast a desire unto her, that thou wouldest have her to thy wife;

12 Then thou shalt bring her home to thine house; and she shall shave her head, and pare her nails;

13 And she shall put the raiment of her captivity from off her, and shall remain in thine house, and bewail her father and her mother a full month: and after that thou shalt go in unto her, and be her husband, and she shall be thy wife.

14 And it shall be, if thou have no delight in her, then thou shalt let her go whither she will; but thou shalt not sell her at all for

money, thou shalt not make merchandise of her, because thou hast humbled her.

15 If a man have two wives, one beloved, and another hated, and they have born him children, *both* the beloved and the hated; and *if* the firstborn son be hers that was hated:

16 Then it shall be, when he maketh his sons to inherit *that* which he hath, *that* he may not make the son of the beloved firstborn before the son of the hated, *which is indeed* the firstborn:

17 But he shall acknowledge the son of the hated *for* the firstborn, by giving him a double portion of all that he hath: for he *is* the beginning of his strength; the right of the firstborn *is* his.

18 If a man have a stubborn and rebellious son, which will not obey the voice of his father, or the voice of his mother, and *that*, when they have chastened him, will not hearken unto them:

19 Then shall his father and his mother lay hold on him, and bring him out unto the elders of his city, and unto the gate of his place;

20 And they shall say unto the elders of his city, This our son *is* stubborn and rebellious, he will not obey our voice; *he is* a glutton, and a drunkard.

21 And all the men of his city shall stone him with stones, that he die: so shalt thou put evil away from among you; and all Israel shall hear, and fear.

Various Laws

22 And if a man have committed a sin worthy of death, and he be to be put to death, and thou hang him on a tree:

23 His body shall not remain all night upon the tree, but thou shalt in any wise bury him that day; (for he that is hanged *is* accursed of God;) that thy land be not defiled, which the LORD thy God giveth thee *for* an inheritance.

CHAPTER 22

1 Thou shalt not see thy brother's ox or his sheep go astray, and hide thyself from them: thou shalt in any case bring them again unto thy brother.

2 And if thy brother *be* not nigh unto thee, or if thou know him not, then thou shalt bring it unto thine own house, and it shall be with thee until thy brother seek after it, and thou shalt restore it to him again.

3 In like manner shalt thou do with his ass; and so shalt thou do with his raiment;

5 Deut. 10:8; 17:8, 9; 1Chr. 23:13

6 Ps. 19:12; 26:6; Matt. 27:24

8 Jon. 1:14

9 Deut. 19:13

13 Ps. 45:10

14 Gen. 34:2; Deut. 22:29; Judg. 19:24

15 Gen. 29:33

16 Gen. 25:31, 33; 49:3; 1Chr. 5:1, 2; 26:10; 2Chr. 11:19, 22

21 Deut. 13:5, 11; 19:19, 20; 22:21, 24

22 Deut. 19:6; 22:26; Acts 23:29; 25:11, 25; 26:31

23 Lev. 18:25; Num. 35:34; Josh. 8:29; 10:26, 27; John 19:31; Gal. 3:13

1 Ex. 23:4

and with all lost thing of thy brother's, which he hath lost, and thou hast found, shalt thou do likewise: thou mayest not hide thyself.

4 Thou shalt not see thy brother's ass or his ox fall down by the way, and hide thyself from them: thou shalt surely help him to lift *them* up again.

5 The woman shall not wear that which pertaineth unto a man, neither shall a man put on a woman's garment: for all that do so *are* abomination unto the LORD thy God.

6 If a bird's nest chance to be before thee in the way in any tree, or on the ground, *whether they be* young ones, or eggs, and the dam sitting upon the young, or upon the eggs, thou shalt not take the dam with the young:

7 *But* thou shalt in any wise let the dam go, and take the young to thee; that it may be well with thee, and *that* thou mayest prolong *thy* days.

8 When thou buildest a new house, then thou shalt make a battlement for thy roof, that thou bring not blood upon thine house, if any man fall from thence.

9 Thou shalt not sow thy vineyard with divers seeds: lest the fruit of thy seed which thou hast sown, and the fruit of thy vineyard, be defiled.

10 Thou shalt not plow with an ox and an ass together.

11 Thou shalt not wear a garment of divers sorts, *as* of woolen and linen together.

12 Thou shalt make thee fringes upon the four quarters of thy vesture, wherewith thou coverest *thyself*.

Sexual Matters

13 If any man take a wife, and go in unto her, and hate her,

14 And give occasions of speech against her, and bring up an evil name upon her, and say, I took this woman, and when I came to her, I found her not a maid:

15 Then shall the father of the damsel, and her mother, take and bring forth *the tokens of* the damsel's virginity unto the elders of the city in the gate:

16 And the damsel's father shall say unto the elders, I gave my daughter unto this man to wife, and he hateth her;

17 And, lo, he hath given occasions of speech *against her*, saying, I found not thy daughter a maid; and yet these *are the tokens of* my daughter's virginity. And they shall spread the cloth before the elders of the city.

18 And the elders of that city shall take that man and chastise him;

4 Ex. 23:5
6 Lev. 22:28
7 Deut. 4:40
9 Lev. 19:19
10 2Cor. 6:14-16
11 Lev. 19:19
12 Num. 15:38; Matt. 23:5
13 Gen. 29:21; Judg. 15:1
21 Gen. 34:7; Deut. 13:5; Judg. 20:6, 10; 2Sam. 13:12, 13
22 Lev. 20:10; John 8:5
23 Matt. 1:18, 19
24 Deut. 21:14; 22:21, 22

28 Ex. 22:16, 17

29 Deut. 22:21

30 Lev. 18:8; 20:11; 27:20; Ruth 3:9; Ezek. 16:8; 1Cor. 5:1

19 And they shall amerce him in an hundred *shekels* of silver, and give *them* unto the father of the damsel, because he hath brought up an evil name upon a virgin of Israel: and she shall be his wife; he may not put her away all his days.

20 But if this thing be true, *and the tokens of* virginity be not found for the damsel:

21 Then they shall bring out the damsel to the door of her father's house, and the men of her city shall stone her with stones that she die: because she hath wrought folly in Israel, to play the whore in her father's house: so shalt thou put evil away from among you.

22 If a man be found lying with a woman married to an husband, then they shall both of them die, *both* the man that lay with the woman, and the woman: so shalt thou put away evil from Israel.

23 If a damsel *that is* a virgin be betrothed unto an husband, and a man find her in the city, and lie with her;

24 Then ye shall bring them both out unto the gate of that city, and ye shall stone them with stones that they die; the damsel, because she cried not, *being* in the city; and the man, because he hath humbled his neighbour's wife: so thou shalt put away evil from among you.

25 But if a man find a betrothed damsel in the field, and the man force her, and lie with her: then the man only that lay with her shall die:

26 But unto the damsel thou shalt do nothing; *there is* in the damsel no sin *worthy* of death: for as when a man riseth against his neighbour, and slayeth him, even so *is* this matter:

27 For he found her in the field, *and* the betrothed damsel cried, and *there was* none to save her.

28 If a man find a damsel *that is* a virgin, which is not betrothed, and lay hold on her, and lie with her, and they be found;

29 Then the man that lay with her shall give unto the damsel's father fifty *shekels* of silver, and she shall be his wife; because he hath humbled her, he may not put her away all his days.

30 A man shall not take his father's wife, nor discover his father's skirt.

CHAPTER 23
Persons Excluded from the Congregation

1 He that is wounded in the stones, or hath his privy member cut off, shall not

enter into the congregation of the LORD.
2 A bastard shall not enter into the congregation of the LORD; even to his tenth generation shall he not enter into the congregation of the LORD.
3 An Ammonite or Moabite shall not enter into the congregation of the LORD; even to their tenth generation shall they not enter into the congregation of the LORD for ever:
4 Because they met you not with bread and with water in the way, when ye came forth out of Egypt; and because they hired against thee Balaam the son of Beor of Pethor of Mesopotamia, to curse thee.
5 Nevertheless the LORD thy God would not hearken unto Balaam; but the LORD thy God turned the curse into a blessing unto thee, because the LORD thy God loved thee.
6 Thou shalt not seek their peace nor their prosperity all thy days for ever.
7 Thou shalt not abhor an Edomite; for he *is* thy brother: thou shalt not abhor an Egyptian; because thou wast a stranger in his land.
8 The children that are begotten of them shall enter into the congregation of the LORD in their third generation.

Purity during War

9 When the host goeth forth against thine enemies, then keep thee from every wicked thing.
10 If there be among you any man, that is not clean by reason of uncleanness that chanceth him by night, then shall he go abroad out of the camp, he shall not come within the camp:
11 But it shall be, when evening cometh on, he shall wash *himself* with water: and when the sun is down, he shall come into the camp *again*.
12 Thou shalt have a place also without the camp, whither thou shalt go forth abroad:
13 And thou shalt have a paddle upon thy weapon; and it shall be, when thou wilt ease thyself abroad, thou shalt dig therewith, and shalt turn back and cover that which cometh from thee:
14 For the LORD thy God walketh in the midst of thy camp, to deliver thee, and to give up thine enemies before thee; therefore shall thy camp be holy: that he see no unclean thing in thee, and turn away from thee.

Various Laws

15 Thou shalt not deliver unto his master the servant which is escaped from his master unto thee:

16 He shall dwell with thee, *even* among you, in that place which he shall choose in one of thy gates, where it liketh him best: thou shalt not oppress him.
17 There shall be no whore of the daughters of Israel, nor a sodomite of the sons of Israel.
18 Thou shalt not bring the hire of a whore, or the price of a dog, into the house of the LORD thy God for any vow: for even both these *are* abomination unto the LORD thy God.
19 Thou shalt not lend upon usury to thy brother; usury of money, usury of victuals, usury of any thing that is lent upon usury:
20 Unto a stranger thou mayest lend upon usury; but unto thy brother thou shalt not lend upon usury: that the LORD thy God may bless thee in all that thou settest thine hand to in the land whither thou goest to possess it.
21 When thou shalt vow a vow unto the LORD thy God, thou shalt not slack to pay it: for the LORD thy God will surely require it of thee; and it would be sin in thee.
22 But if thou shalt forbear to vow, it shall be no sin in thee.
23 That which is gone out of thy lips thou shalt keep and perform; *even* a freewill offering, according as thou hast vowed unto the LORD thy God, which thou hast promised with thy mouth.
24 When thou comest into thy neighbour's vineyard, then thou mayest eat grapes thy fill at thine own pleasure; but thou shalt not put *any* in thy vessel.
25 When thou comest into the standing corn of thy neighbour, then thou mayest pluck the ears with thine hand; but thou shalt not move a sickle unto thy neighbour's standing corn.

CHAPTER 24

1 When a man hath taken a wife, and married her, and it come to pass that she find no favour in his eyes, because he hath found some uncleanness in her: then let him write her a bill of divorcement, and give *it* in her hand, and send her out of his house.
2 And when she is departed out of his house, she may go and be another man's *wife*.
3 And *if* the latter husband hate her, and write her a bill of divorcement, and giveth *it* in her hand, and sendeth her out of his house; or if the latter husband die, which took her *to be* his wife;

---

3 Neh. 13:1, 2
4 Num. 22:5, 6; Deut. 2:29
6 Ezra 9:12
7 Gen. 25:24-26; Ex. 22:21; 23:9; Lev. 19:34; Deut. 10:19; Obad. 1:10, 12
10 Lev. 15:16
11 Lev. 15:5
14 Lev. 26:12
15 1Sam. 30:15
16 Ex. 22:21
17 Gen. 19:5; Lev. 19:29; 2Kgs. 23:7; Prov. 2:16
19 Ex. 22:25; Lev. 25:36, 37; Neh. 5:2, 7; Ps. 15:5; Luke 6:34, 35
20 Lev. 15:3; 19:34; Deut. 15:10
21 Num. 30:2; Eccl. 5:4, 5
23 Num. 30:2; Ps. 66:13, 14
25 Matt. 12:1; Mark 2:23; Luke 6:1

1 Matt. 5:31; 19:7; Mark 10:4

4 Her former husband, which sent her away, may not take her again to be his wife, after that she is defiled; for that *is* abomination before the LORD: and thou shalt not cause the land to sin, which the LORD thy God giveth thee *for* an inheritance.

5 When a man hath taken a new wife, he shall not go out to war, neither shall he be charged with any business: *but* he shall be free at home one year, and shall cheer up his wife which he hath taken.

6 No man shall take the nether or the upper millstone to pledge: for he taketh *a man's* life to pledge.

7 If a man be found stealing any of his brethren of the children of Israel, and maketh merchandise of him, or selleth him; then that thief shall die; and thou shalt put evil away from among you.

8 Take heed in the plague of leprosy, that thou observe diligently, and do according to all that the priests the Levites shall teach you: as I commanded them, *so* ye shall observe to do.

9 Remember what the LORD thy God did unto Miriam by the way, after that ye were come forth out of Egypt.

10 When thou dost lend thy brother any thing, thou shalt not go into his house to fetch his pledge.

11 Thou shalt stand abroad, and the man to whom thou dost lend shall bring out the pledge abroad unto thee.

12 And if the man *be* poor, thou shalt not sleep with his pledge:

13 In any case thou shalt deliver him the pledge again when the sun goeth down, that he may sleep in his own raiment, and bless thee: and it shall be righteousness unto thee before the LORD thy God.

14 Thou shalt not oppress an hired servant *that is* poor and needy, *whether he be* of thy brethren, or of thy strangers that *are* in thy land within thy gates:

15 At his day thou shalt give *him* his hire, neither shall the sun go down upon it; for he *is* poor, and setteth his heart upon it: lest he cry against thee unto the LORD, and it be sin unto thee.

16 The fathers shall not be put to death for the children, neither shall the children be put to death for the fathers: every man shall be put to death for his own sin.

17 Thou shalt not pervert the judgment of the stranger, *nor* of the fatherless; nor take a widow's raiment to pledge:

18 But thou shalt remember that thou wast a bondman in Egypt, and the LORD thy God

redeemed thee thence: therefore I command thee to do this thing.

19 When thou cuttest down thine harvest in thy field, and hast forgot a sheaf in the field, thou shalt not go again to fetch it: it shall be for the stranger, for the fatherless, and for the widow: that the LORD thy God may bless thee in all the work of thine hands.

20 When thou beatest thine olive tree, thou shalt not go over the boughs again: it shall be for the stranger, for the fatherless, and for the widow.

21 When thou gatherest the grapes of thy vineyard, thou shalt not glean *it* afterward: it shall be for the stranger, for the fatherless, and for the widow.

22 And thou shalt remember that thou wast a bondman in the land of Egypt: therefore I command thee to do this thing.

CHAPTER 25

1 If there be a controversy between men, and they come unto judgment, that *the judges* may judge them; then they shall justify the righteous, and condemn the wicked.

2 And it shall be, if the wicked man *be* worthy to be beaten, that the judge shall cause him to lie down, and to be beaten before his face, according to his fault, by a certain number.

3 Forty stripes he may give him, *and* not exceed: lest, *if* he should exceed, and beat him above these with many stripes, then thy brother should seem vile unto thee.

4 Thou shalt not muzzle the ox when he treadeth out *the corn.*

5 If brethren dwell together, and one of them die, and have no child, the wife of the dead shall not marry without unto a stranger: her husband's brother shall go in unto her, and take her to him to wife, and perform the duty of an husband's brother unto her.

6 And it shall be, *that* the firstborn which she beareth shall succeed in the name of his brother *which is* dead, that his name be not put out of Israel.

7 And if the man like not to take his brother's wife, then let his brother's wife go up to the gate unto the elders, and say, My husband's brother refuseth to raise up unto his brother a name in Israel, he will not perform the duty of my husband's brother.

8 Then the elders of his city shall call him, and speak unto him: and if he stand *to it,* and say, I like not to take her;

9 Then shall his brother's wife come unto

Cross references

5 Deut. 20:7; Prov. 5:18

7 Ex. 21:16; Deut. 19:19

8 Lev. 13:2; 14:2

9 Num. 12:10; Luke 17:32; 1Cor. 10:6

13 Ex. 22:26; Deut. 6:25; Job 29:11, 13; 31:20; Ps. 106:31; 112:9; Dan. 4:27; 2Cor. 9:13; 2Tim. 1:18

14 Mal. 3:5

15 Lev. 19:13; Ps. 25:1; 86:4; Jer. 22:13; James 5:4

16 2Kgs. 14:6; 2Chr. 25:4; Jer. 31:29, 30; Ezek. 18:20

17 Ex. 22:21, 22, 26; Prov. 22:22; Isa. 1:23; Jer. 5:28; 22:3; Ezek. 22:29; Zech. 7:10; Mal. 3:5

18 Deut. 16:12; 24:22

19 Lev. 19:9, 10; 23:22; Deut. 15:10; Ps. 41:1; Prov. 19:17

22 Deut. 24:18

1 Deut. 19:17; Prov. 17:15; Ezek. 44:24

2 Matt. 10:17; Luke 12:48

3 Job 18:3; 2Cor. 11:24

4 Prov. 12:10; 1Cor. 9:9; 1Tim. 5:18

5 Matt. 22:24; Mark 12:19; Luke 20:28

6 Gen. 38:9; Ruth 4:10

7 Ruth 4:1, 2

8 Ruth 4:6

9 Ruth 4:7, 11

him in the presence of the elders, and loose his shoe from off his foot, and spit in his face, and shall answer and say, So shall it be done unto that man that will not build up his brother's house.

10 And his name shall be called in Israel, The house of him that hath his shoe loosed.

11 When men strive together one with another, and the wife of the one draweth near for to deliver her husband out of the hand of him that smiteth him, and putteth forth her hand, and taketh him by the secrets:

12 Then thou shalt cut off her hand, thine eye shall not pity *her.*

13 Thou shalt not have in thy bag divers weights, a great and a small.

14 Thou shalt not have in thine house divers measures, a great and a small.

15 *But* thou shalt have a perfect and just weight, a perfect and just measure shalt thou have: that thy days may be lengthened in the land which the LORD thy God giveth thee.

16 For all that do such things, *and* all that do unrighteously, *are* an abomination unto the LORD thy God.

Destroy Amalek

17 Remember what Amalek did unto thee by the way, when ye were come forth out of Egypt;

18 How he met thee by the way, and smote the hindmost of thee, *even* all *that were* feeble behind thee, when thou *wast* faint and weary; and he feared not God.

19 Therefore it shall be, when the LORD thy God hath given thee rest from all thine enemies round about, in the land which the LORD thy God giveth thee *for* an inheritance to possess it, *that* thou shalt blot out the remembrance of Amalek from under heaven; thou shalt not forget *it.*

CHAPTER 26
Harvest Offerings

1 And it shall be, when thou *art* come in unto the land which the LORD thy God giveth thee *for* an inheritance, and possessest it, and dwellest therein;

2 That thou shalt take of the first of all the fruit of the earth, which thou shalt bring of thy land that the LORD thy God giveth thee, and shalt put *it* in a basket, and shalt go unto the place which the LORD thy God shall choose to place his name there.

3 And thou shalt go unto the priest that shall be in those days, and say unto him, I profess this day unto the LORD thy God, that

12 Deut. 19:13

13 Lev. 19:35, 36; Prov. 11:1; Ezek. 45:10; Mic. 6:11

15 Ex. 20:12

16 Prov. 11:1; 1Thess. 4:6

17 Ex. 17:8

18 Ps. 36:1; Prov. 16:6; Rom. 3:18

19 Ex. 17:14; 1Sam. 15:3

2 Ex. 23:19; 34:26; Num. 18:13; Deut. 12:5; 16:10; Prov. 3:9

5 Gen. 43:1, 2; 45:7, 11; 46:1, 6, 27; Deut. 10:22; Hos. 12:12; Acts 7:15

6 Ex. 1:11, 14

7 Ex. 2:23-25; 3:9; 4:31

8 Ex. 12:37, 51; 13:3, 14, 16; Deut. 4:34; 5:15

9 Ex. 3:8

11 Deut. 12:7, 12, 18; 16:11

12 Lev. 27:30; Num. 18:24; Deut. 14:28, 29

13 Ps. 119:141, 153, 176

14 Lev. 7:20; 21:1, 11; Hos. 9:4

15 Isa. 63:15; Zech. 2:13

I am come unto the country which the LORD sware unto our fathers for to give us.

4 And the priest shall take the basket out of thine hand, and set it down before the altar of the LORD thy God.

5 And thou shalt speak and say before the LORD thy God, A Syrian ready to perish *was* my father, and he went down into Egypt, and sojourned there with a few, and became there a nation, great, mighty, and populous:

6 And the Egyptians evil entreated us, and afflicted us, and laid upon us hard bondage:

7 And when we cried unto the LORD God of our fathers, the LORD heard our voice, and looked on our affliction, and our labour, and our oppression:

8 And the LORD brought us forth out of Egypt with a mighty hand, and with an outstretched arm, and with great terribleness, and with signs, and with wonders:

9 And he hath brought us into this place, and hath given us this land, *even* a land that floweth with milk and honey.

10 And now, behold, I have brought the firstfruits of the land, which thou, O LORD, hast given me. And thou shalt set it before the LORD thy God, and worship before the LORD thy God:

11 And thou shalt rejoice in every good *thing* which the LORD thy God hath given unto thee, and unto thine house, thou, and the Levite, and the stranger that *is* among you.

12 When thou hast made an end of tithing all the tithes of thine increase the third year, *which is* the year of tithing, and hast given *it* unto the Levite, the stranger, the fatherless, and the widow, that they may eat within thy gates, and be filled;

13 Then thou shalt say before the LORD thy God, I have brought away the hallowed things out of *mine* house, and also have given them unto the Levite, and unto the stranger, to the fatherless, and to the widow, according to all thy commandments which thou hast commanded me: I have not transgressed thy commandments, neither have I forgotten *them:*

14 I have not eaten thereof in my mourning, neither have I taken away *ought* thereof for *any* unclean *use,* nor given *ought* thereof for the dead: *but* I have hearkened to the voice of the LORD my God, *and* have done according to all that thou hast commanded me.

15 Look down from thy holy habitation, from heaven, and bless thy people Israel, and the land which thou hast given us, as

thou swarest unto our fathers, a land that floweth with milk and honey.

Concluding Charge

16 This day the LORD thy God hath commanded thee to do these statutes and judgments: thou shalt therefore keep and do them with all thine heart, and with all thy soul.

17 Thou hast avouched the LORD this day to be thy God, and to walk in his ways, and to keep his statutes, and his commandments, and his judgments, and to hearken unto his voice:

18 And the LORD hath avouched thee this day to be his peculiar people, as he hath promised thee, and that *thou* shouldest keep all his commandments;

19 And to make thee high above all nations which he hath made, in praise, and in name, and in honour; and that thou mayest be an holy people unto the LORD thy God, as he hath spoken.

CHAPTER 27
The Law at Mount Ebal

1 And Moses with the elders of Israel commanded the people, saying, Keep all the commandments which I command you this day.

2 And it shall be on the day when ye shall pass over Jordan unto the land which the LORD thy God giveth thee, that thou shalt set thee up great stones, and plaister them with plaister:

3 And thou shalt write upon them all the words of this law, when thou art passed over, that thou mayest go in unto the land which the LORD thy God giveth thee, a land that floweth with milk and honey; as the LORD God of thy fathers hath promised thee.

4 Therefore it shall be when ye be gone over Jordan, *that* ye shall set up these stones, which I command you this day, in mount Ebal, and thou shalt plaister them with plaister.

5 And there shalt thou build an altar unto the LORD thy God, an altar of stones: thou shalt not lift up *any* iron *tool* upon them.

6 Thou shalt build the altar of the LORD thy God of whole stones: and thou shalt offer

burnt offerings thereon unto the LORD thy God:

7 And thou shalt offer peace offerings, and shalt eat there, and rejoice before the LORD thy God.

8 And thou shalt write upon the stones all the words of this law very plainly.

9 And Moses and the priests the Levites spake unto all Israel, saying, Take heed, and hearken, O Israel; this day thou art become the people of the LORD thy God.

10 Thou shalt therefore obey the voice of the LORD thy God, and do his commandments and his statutes, which I command thee this day.

The Curses at Mount Ebal

11 And Moses charged the people the same day, saying,

12 These shall stand upon mount Gerizim to bless the people, when ye are come over Jordan; Simeon, and Levi, and Judah, and Issachar, and Joseph, and Benjamin:

13 And these shall stand upon mount Ebal to curse; Reuben, Gad, and Asher, and Zebulun, Dan, and Naphtali.

14 And the Levites shall speak, and say unto all the men of Israel with a loud voice,

15 Cursed *be* the man that maketh *any* graven or molten image, an abomination unto the LORD, the work of the hands of the craftsman, and putteth *it* in *a* secret *place*. And all the people shall answer and say, Amen.

16 Cursed *be* he that setteth light by his father or his mother. And all the people shall say, Amen.

17 Cursed *be* he that removeth his neighbour's landmark. And all the people shall say, Amen.

18 Cursed *be* he that maketh the blind to wander out of the way. And all the people shall say, Amen.

19 Cursed *be* he that perverteth the judgment of the stranger, fatherless, and widow. And all the people shall say, Amen.

20 Cursed *be* he that lieth with his father's wife; because he uncovereth his father's skirt. And all the people shall say, Amen.

21 Cursed *be* he that lieth with any manner of beast. And all the people shall say, Amen.

17 Ex. 20:19

18 Ex. 6:7; 19:5; Deut. 7:6; 14:2; 28:9

19 Ex. 19:6; Deut. 4:7, 8; 7:6; 28:1, 9; Ps. 148:14; 1Pet. 2:9

2 Josh. 4:1; 8:32

4 Deut. 11:29; Josh. 8:30

5 Ex. 20:25; Josh. 8:31

9 Deut. 26:18

12 Deut. 11:29; Josh. 8:33; Judg. 9:7

13 Deut. 11:29; Josh. 8:33

14 Deut. 33:10; Josh. 8:33; Dan. 9:11

15 Ex. 20:4, 23; 34:17; Lev. 19:4; 26:1; Num. 5:22; Deut. 4:16, 23; 5:8; Isa. 44:9; Jer. 11:5; Hos. 13:2; 1Cor. 14:16

16 Ex. 20:12; 21:17; Lev. 19:3; Deut. 21:18

17 Deut. 19:14; Prov. 22:28

18 Lev. 19:14

19 Ex. 22:21, 22; Deut. 10:18; 24:17; Mal. 3:5

20 Lev. 18:8; 20:11; Deut. 22:30

21 Lev. 18:23; 20:15

26:16–19 This section is likely the nation's ratification of the covenant that Moses is putting forth in Deuteronomy. Here the people acknowledge that the Lord is their God. Thus, they promise wholehearted love, devotion, and obedience to God as expressed in the stipulations of this treaty. In response, the Lord promises the nation that they will be highly praised and holy, set apart, unto God. For fulfillment of this promise, see Isaiah 60 and Zephaniah 3:19–20.

22 Cursed *be* he that lieth with his sister, the daughter of his father, or the daughter of his mother. And all the people shall say, Amen.
23 Cursed *be* he that lieth with his mother-in-law. And all the people shall say, Amen.
24 Cursed *be* he that smiteth his neighbour secretly. And all the people shall say, Amen.
25 Cursed *be* he that taketh reward to slay an innocent person. And all the people shall say, Amen.
26 Cursed *be* he that confirmeth not *all* the words of this law to do them. And all the people shall say, Amen.

CHAPTER 28
The Blessings for Obedience

1 And it shall come to pass, if thou shalt hearken diligently unto the voice of the LORD thy God, to observe *and* to do all his commandments which I command thee this day, that the LORD thy God will set thee on high above all nations of the earth:

22 Lev. 18:9; 20:17
23 Lev. 18:17; 20:14
24 Ex. 20:13; Lev. 24:17; Num. 35:31
25 Ex. 23:7, 8
26 Ps. 119:21
1 Ex. 15:26; Lev. 26:3; Isa. 55:2
2 Zech. 1:6
3 Ps. 128:1, 4
4 Ps. 107:38; 127:3; 128:3; 1Tim. 4:8
6 Ps. 121:8
7 Lev. 26:7, 8; Ps. 89:23, 25

2 And all these blessings shall come on thee, and overtake thee, if thou shalt hearken unto the voice of the LORD thy God.
3 Blessed *shalt* thou *be* in the city, and blessed *shalt* thou *be* in the field.
4 Blessed *shall be* the fruit of thy body, and the fruit of thy ground, and the fruit of thy cattle, the increase of thy kine, and the flocks of thy sheep.
5 Blessed *shall be* thy basket and thy store.
6 Blessed *shalt* thou *be* when thou comest in, and blessed *shalt* thou *be* when thou goest out.
7 The LORD shall cause thine enemies that rise up against thee to be smitten before thy face: they shall come out against thee one way, and flee before thee seven ways.
8 The LORD shall command the blessing upon thee in thy storehouses, and in all that thou settest thine hand unto; and he shall bless thee in the land which the LORD thy God giveth thee.

A Prophetic Overview of Israel's History

Leviticus 26 — *given at Sinai*
vv. 27-33
vv. 34–39
vv. 40–45
Church Age
Rapture
Second Coming of Jesus Christ
Israel Scattered among the Nations
Millennium
Deuteronomy 28 — *given on the plains of Moab*
vv. 36-48
vv. 47-63
vv. 64-68
Babylonian Captivity
Fall of Jerusalem — *A.D. 70*
The Tribulation

© AMG Publishers

28:1–68 This is the blessings and curses section of the covenant. Chapter 28 parallels Leviticus 26. The Lord promises blessings for obedience (Deut. 28:1–14) and curses for disobedience (vv. 15–68). This section also provides the basis for future evaluation of the nation in history. The prophetic judgments that happened much later in Israel's history were the application of these curses upon future Israel. Millennial blessing will be the application of the abundance upon the future people of Israel.

28:1 set thee on high above all nations of the earth. This has not yet happened, but will be fulfilled in Christ's Millennial Kingdom when Israel will live in obedience (Zech. 13:1—14:21; Rom. 11:25–27).

9 The LORD shall establish thee an holy people unto himself, as he hath sworn unto thee, if thou shalt keep the commandments of the LORD thy God, and walk in his ways.

10 And all people of the earth shall see that thou art called by the name of the LORD; and they shall be afraid of thee.

11 And the LORD shall make thee plenteous in goods, in the fruit of thy body, and in the fruit of thy cattle, and in the fruit of thy ground, in the land which the LORD sware unto thy fathers to give thee.

12 The LORD shall open unto thee his good treasure, the heaven to give the rain unto thy land in his season, and to bless all the work of thine hand: and thou shalt lend unto many nations, and thou shalt not borrow.

13 And the LORD shall make thee the head, and not the tail; and thou shalt be above only, and thou shalt not be beneath; if that thou hearken unto the commandments of the LORD thy God, which I command thee this day, to observe and to do *them*:

14 And thou shalt not go aside from any of the words which I command thee this day, *to* the right hand, or *to* the left, to go after other gods to serve them.

The Punishment for Disobedience

15 But it shall come to pass, if thou wilt not hearken unto the voice of the LORD thy God, to observe to do all his commandments and his statutes which I command thee this day; that all these curses shall come upon thee, and overtake thee:

16 Cursed *shalt* thou *be* in the city, and cursed *shalt* thou *be* in the field.

17 Cursed *shall be* thy basket and thy store.

18 Cursed *shall be* the fruit of thy body, and the fruit of thy land, the increase of thy kine, and the flocks of thy sheep.

19 Cursed *shalt* thou *be* when thou comest in, and cursed *shalt* thou *be* when thou goest out.

20 The LORD shall send upon thee cursing, vexation, and rebuke, in all that thou settest thine hand unto for to do, until thou be destroyed, and until thou perish quickly; be-cause of the wickedness of thy doings, whereby thou hast forsaken me.

21 The LORD shall make the pestilence cleave unto thee, until he have consumed thee from off the land, whither thou goest to possess it.

22 The LORD shall smite thee with a consumption, and with a fever, and with an inflammation, and with an extreme burning, and with the sword, and with blasting, and with mildew; and they shall pursue thee until thou perish.

23 And thy heaven that *is* over thy head shall be brass, and the earth that is under thee *shall be* iron.

24 The LORD shall make the rain of thy land powder and dust: from heaven shall it come down upon thee, until thou be destroyed.

25 The LORD shall cause thee to be smitten before thine enemies: thou shalt go out one way against them, and flee seven ways before them: and shalt be removed into all the kingdoms of the earth.

26 And thy carcase shall be meat unto all fowls of the air, and unto the beasts of the earth, and no man shall fray *them* away.

27 The LORD will smite thee with the botch of Egypt, and with the emerods, and with the scab, and with the itch, whereof thou canst not be healed.

28 The LORD shall smite thee with madness, and blindness, and astonishment of heart:

29 And thou shalt grope at noonday, as the blind gropeth in darkness, and thou shalt not prosper in thy ways: and thou shalt be only oppressed and spoiled evermore, and no man shall save *thee*.

30 Thou shalt betroth a wife, and another man shall lie with her: thou shalt build an house, and thou shalt not dwell therein: thou shalt plant a vineyard, and shalt not gather the grapes thereof.

31 Thine ox *shall be* slain before thine eyes, and thou shalt not eat thereof: thine ass *shall be* violently taken away from before thy face, and shall not be restored to thee: thy sheep *shall be* given unto thine enemies, and thou shalt have none to rescue *them*.

Cross references:
9 Ex. 19:5, 6; Deut. 7:6; 26:18, 19; 29:13
10 Num. 6:27; Deut. 11:25; 2Chr. 7:14; Isa. 63:19; Dan. 9:18, 19
11 Deut. 28:4; 30:9; Prov. 10:22
12 Lev. 26:4; Deut. 11:14; 14:29; 15:6
13 Isa. 9:14, 15
14 Deut. 5:32; 11:16
15 Lev. 26:14; Deut. 28:2; Lam. 2:17
16 Deut. 28:3
20 Isa. 30:17; 51:20
21 Lev. 26:25; Jer. 24:10
22 Lev. 26:16; Amos 4:9
23 Lev. 26:19
25 Lev. 26:17, 37; Isa. 30:17; Jer. 15:4; 24:9
26 1Sam. 17:44, 46; Ps. 79:2; Jer. 7:33; 16:4; 34:20
27 Ex. 9:9; 1Sam. 5:6
28 Jer. 4:9
29 Isa. 59:10
30 Deut. 20:6; Job 31:8, 10; Jer. 8:10; 12:13; Amos 5:11; Mic. 6:15; Zeph. 1:13

28:20 until thou be destroyed. This refers to Israel's removal from the land as will be explained in 28:49–68, not total annihilation of the population. Judgment in Scripture is often pictured as sudden and unexpected to those experiencing God's anger (Deut. 4:26; 1 Thess. 5:1–11).

28:23–25 Bad weather, agricultural failure, and military defeat in Israel were not the fault of poor planning and execution, but instead were to be a sign to the nation that she was not obeying the covenant with the Lord.

28:30 These three curses were in contrast to the exemptions from military service granted in 20:5–7. When Israel disobeyed the Lord, then He would no longer fight for them, and the nation was no different at that point than any other nation. Those normally exempted from fighting would be forced to fight and be killed.

32 Thy sons and thy daughters *shall be* given unto another people, and thine eyes shall look, and fail *with longing* for them all the day long: and *there shall be* no might in thine hand.
33 The fruit of thy land, and all thy labours, shall a nation which thou knowest not eat up; and thou shalt be only oppressed and crushed alway:
34 So that thou shalt be mad for the sight of thine eyes which thou shalt see.
35 The LORD shall smite thee in the knees, and in the legs, with a sore botch that cannot be healed, from the sole of thy foot unto the top of thy head.
36 The LORD shall bring thee, and thy king which thou shalt set over thee, unto a nation which neither thou nor thy fathers have known; and there shalt thou serve other gods, wood and stone.
37 And thou shalt become an astonishment, a proverb, and a byword, among all nations whither the LORD shall lead thee.
38 Thou shalt carry much seed out into the field, and shalt gather *but* little in; for the locust shall consume it.
39 Thou shalt plant vineyards, and dress *them*, but shalt neither drink *of* the wine, nor gather *the grapes*; for the worms shall eat them.
40 Thou shalt have olive trees throughout all thy coasts, but thou shalt not anoint *thyself* with the oil; for thine olive shall cast *his* fruit.
41 Thou shalt beget sons and daughters, but thou shalt not enjoy them; for they shall go into captivity.
42 All thy trees and fruit of thy land shall the locust consume.
43 The stranger that *is* within thee shall get up above thee very high; and thou shalt come down very low.
44 He shall lend to thee, and thou shalt not lend to him: he shall be the head, and thou shalt be the tail.
45 Moreover all these curses shall come upon thee, and shall pursue thee, and overtake thee, till thou be destroyed; because thou hearkenedst not unto the voice of the

LORD thy God, to keep his commandments and his statutes which he commanded thee:
46 And they shall be upon thee for a sign and for a wonder, and upon thy seed for ever.
47 Because thou servedst not the LORD thy God with joyfulness, and with gladness of heart, for the abundance of all *things*;
48 Therefore shalt thou serve thine enemies which the LORD shall send against thee, in hunger, and in thirst, and in nakedness, and in want of all *things*: and he shall put a yoke of iron upon thy neck, until he have destroyed thee.
49 The LORD shall bring a nation against thee from far, from the end of the earth, *as swift* as the eagle flieth; a nation whose tongue thou shalt not understand;
50 A nation of fierce countenance, which shall not regard the person of the old, nor shew favour to the young:
51 And he shall eat the fruit of thy cattle, and the fruit of thy land, until thou be destroyed: which *also* shall not leave thee *either* corn, wine, or oil, *or* the increase of thy kine, or flocks of thy sheep, until he have destroyed thee.
52 And he shall besiege thee in all thy gates, until thy high and fenced walls come down, wherein thou trustedst, throughout all thy land: and he shall besiege thee in all thy gates throughout all thy land, which the LORD thy God hath given thee.
53 And thou shalt eat the fruit of thine own body, the flesh of thy sons and of thy daughters, which the LORD thy God hath given thee, in the siege, and in the straitness, wherewith thine enemies shall distress thee:
54 *So that* the man *that is* tender among you, and very delicate, his eye shall be evil toward his brother, and toward the wife of his bosom, and toward the remnant of his children which he shall leave:
55 So that he will not give to any of them of the flesh of his children whom he shall eat: because he hath nothing left him in the siege, and in the straitness, wherewith thine enemies shall distress thee in all thy gates.

Cross references:
32 Ps. 119:82
33 Lev. 26:16; Deut. 28:51; Jer. 5:17
34 Deut. 28:67
35 Deut. 28:27
36 Deut. 4:28; 28:64; 2Kgs. 17:4, 6; 24:12, 14; 25:7, 11; 2Chr. 33:11; 36:6, 20; Jer. 16:13
37 1Kgs. 9:7, 8; Ps. 44:14; Jer. 24:9; 25:9; Zech. 8:13
38 Joel 1:4; Mic. 6:15; Hag. 1:6
41 Lam. 1:5
44 Deut. 28:12, 13; Lam. 1:5
45 Deut. 28:15
46 Isa. 8:18; Ezek. 14:8
47 Deut. 32:15; Neh. 9:35-37
48 Jer. 28:14
49 Jer. 5:15; 6:22, 23; 48:40; 49:22; Lam. 4:19; Ezek. 17:3, 12; Hos. 8:1; Luke 19:43
50 2Chr. 36:17; Prov. 7:13; Eccl. 8:1; Isa. 47:6; Dan. 8:23
51 Deut. 28:33; Isa. 1:7; 62:8
52 2Kgs. 25:1, 2, 4
53 Lev. 26:29; 2Kgs. 6:28, 29

28:37 an astonishment, a proverb, and a byword. These are the opposite of the blessed condition promised for obedience in verse 13 where the Lord would make Israel supreme among the nations.

28:49 The symbol for Babylon in the ancient world was the eagle. The Chaldean, Aramaic language was unknown at this time. This prophecy was given over 800 years before it was fulfilled.

28:49-68 This is a specific prophecy of some of the historical details relating to God's most severe judgment against Israel—deportation. Historical details of two different episodes of deportation are prophesied: the one relating to Babylon in 586 B.C. (vv. 49–63) and the second involving Rome in A.D. 70 (vv. 64–68).

56 The tender and delicate woman among you, which would not adventure to set the sole of her foot upon the ground for delicateness and tenderness, her eye shall be evil toward the husband of her bosom, and toward her son, and toward her daughter,

57 And toward her young one that cometh out from between her feet, and toward her children which she shall bear: for she shall eat them for want of all *things* secretly in the siege and straitness, wherewith thine enemy shall distress thee in thy gates.

58 If thou wilt not observe to do all the words of this law that are written in this book, that thou mayest fear this glorious and fearful name, THE LORD THY GOD;

59 Then the LORD will make thy plagues wonderful, and the plagues of thy seed, *even* great plagues, and of long continuance, and sore sicknesses, and of long continuance.

60 Moreover he will bring upon thee all the diseases of Egypt, which thou wast afraid of; and they shall cleave unto thee.

61 Also every sickness, and every plague, which *is* not written in the book of this law, them will the LORD bring upon thee, until thou be destroyed.

62 And ye shall be left few in number, whereas ye were as the stars of heaven for multitude; because thou wouldest not obey the voice of the LORD thy God.

63 And it shall come to pass, *that* as the LORD rejoiced over you to do you good, and to multiply you; so the LORD will rejoice over you to destroy you, and to bring you to nought; and ye shall be plucked from off the land whither thou goest to possess it.

64 And the LORD shall scatter thee among all people, from the one end of the earth even unto the other; and there thou shalt serve other gods, which neither thou nor thy fathers have known, *even* wood and stone.

65 And among these nations shalt thou find no ease, neither shall the sole of thy foot have rest: but the LORD shall give thee there a trembling heart, and failing of eyes, and sorrow of mind:

66 And thy life shall hang in doubt before thee; and thou shalt fear day and night, and shalt have none assurance of thy life:

67 In the morning thou shalt say, Would God it were even! and at even thou shalt say, Would God it were morning! for the fear of thine heart wherewith thou shalt fear, and for the sight of thine eyes which thou shalt see.

68 And the LORD shall bring thee into Egypt again with ships, by the way whereof I spake unto thee, Thou shalt see it no more again: and there ye shall be sold unto your enemies for bondmen and bondwomen, and no man shall buy *you*.

CHAPTER 29
Covenant Renewal

1 These *are* the words of the covenant, which the LORD commanded Moses to make with the children of Israel in the land of Moab, beside the covenant which he made with them in Horeb.

2 And Moses called unto all Israel, and said unto them, Ye have seen all that the LORD did before your eyes in the land of Egypt unto Pharaoh, and unto all his servants, and unto all his land;

3 The great temptations which thine eyes have seen, the signs, and those great miracles:

4 Yet the LORD hath not given you an heart to perceive, and eyes to see, and ears to hear, unto this day.

28:52–57 besiege thee in all thy gates. This describes the siege of Jerusalem under the Babylonians. The first deportation was primarily to Babylon.

28:64–68 from the one end of the earth even unto the other. This is a prophecy of deportation and dispersion of the Jewish people among all people, after the destruction of Jerusalem by the Roman Empire in A.D. 70. This prediction is still in effect to a large extent since only about one third of the Jews worldwide currently live in Israel.

28:65–67 This passage provides a sad, but apt description of the last two thousand years of Jewish life outside the land of Israel. Israel, "among these nations [has found] no ease . . . [nor] rest." Too often Gentile hostilities have arisen to persecute the Jew. It is estimated that during the two thousand years of this dispersion, over eleven million Jews have been killed while in Gentile lands.

28:68 into Egypt again. This prophecy was written almost fifteen hundred years before it was fulfilled under the Romans. Those Jews who survived the siege and destruction of Jerusalem in A.D. 70 were taken on Roman ships back to Egypt where they glutted the slave market for years because there were so many offered for sale.

29:4 This verse anticipates the need for the coming of the new covenant for Israel during the Millennium (Isa. 59:20–21; Jer. 31:31–34; 32:37–40; Ezek. 16:60–63; 37:21–28).

5 And I have led you forty years in the wilderness: your clothes are not waxen old upon you, and thy shoe is not waxen old upon thy foot.
6 Ye have not eaten bread, neither have ye drunk wine or strong drink: that ye might know that I *am* the LORD your God.
7 And when ye came unto this place, Sihon the king of Heshbon, and Og the king of Bashan, came out against us unto battle, and we smote them:
8 And we took their land, and gave it for an inheritance unto the Reubenites, and to the Gadites, and to the half tribe of Manasseh.
9 Keep therefore the words of this covenant, and do them, that ye may prosper in all that ye do.
10 Ye stand this day all of you before the LORD your God; your captains of your tribes, your elders, and your officers, *with* all the men of Israel,
11 Your little ones, your wives, and thy stranger that *is* in thy camp, from the hewer of thy wood unto the drawer of thy water:
12 That thou shouldest enter into covenant with the LORD thy God, and into his oath, which the LORD thy God maketh with thee this day:
13 That he may establish thee today for a people unto himself, and *that* he may be unto thee a God, as he hath said unto thee, and as he hath sworn unto thy fathers, to Abraham, to Isaac, and to Jacob.
14 Neither with you only do I make this covenant and this oath;
15 But with *him* that standeth here with us this day before the LORD our God, and also with *him* that *is* not here with us this day:
16 (For ye know how we have dwelt in the land of Egypt; and how we came through the nations which ye passed by;
17 And ye have seen their abominations, and their idols, wood and stone, silver and gold, which *were* among them:)
18 Lest there should be among you man, or woman, or family, or tribe, whose heart turneth away this day from the LORD our God, to go *and* serve the gods of these nations; lest there should be among you a root that beareth gall and wormwood;

19 And it come to pass, when he heareth the words of this curse, that he bless himself in his heart, saying, I shall have peace, though I walk in the imagination of mine heart, to add drunkenness to thirst:
20 The LORD will not spare him, but then the anger of the LORD and his jealousy shall smoke against that man, and all the curses that are written in this book shall lie upon him, and the LORD shall blot out his name from under heaven.
21 And the LORD shall separate him unto evil out of all the tribes of Israel, according to all the curses of the covenant that are written in this book of the law:
22 So that the generation to come of your children that shall rise up after you, and the stranger that shall come from a far land, shall say, when they see the plagues of that land, and the sicknesses which the LORD hath laid upon it;
23 *And that* the whole land thereof *is* brimstone, and salt, *and* burning, *that* it is not sown, nor beareth, nor any grass groweth therein, like the overthrow of Sodom, and Gomorrah, Admah, and Zeboim, which the LORD overthrew in his anger, and in his wrath:
24 Even all nations shall say, Wherefore hath the LORD done thus unto this land? what *meaneth* the heat of this great anger?
25 Then men shall say, Because they have forsaken the covenant of the LORD God of their fathers, which he made with them when he brought them forth out of the land of Egypt:
26 For they went and served other gods, and worshipped them, gods whom they knew not, and *whom* he had not given unto them:
27 And the anger of the LORD was kindled against this land, to bring upon it all the curses that are written in this book:
28 And the LORD rooted them out of their land in anger, and in wrath, and in great indignation, and cast them into another land, as *it is* this day.
29 The secret *things belong* unto the LORD our God: but those *things which are* revealed *belong* unto us and to our children for ever, that *we* may do all the words of this law.

29:29 The secret things. These are generally all the unrevealed things of God, but specifically in this context, Israel's unknown future. The only way anyone can know the things of God is if He tells us through revelation. God has revealed many things to Israel. The purpose that God has in revealing things is so that Israel "may do all the words of this law." We cannot know everything about the future, but what God has revealed to us should be acted upon.

CHAPTER 30
God's Promise Remains Constant

1 And it shall come to pass, when all these things are come upon thee, the blessing and the curse, which I have set before thee, and thou shalt call *them* to mind among all the nations, whither the LORD thy God hath driven thee,

2 And shalt return unto the LORD thy God, and shalt obey his voice according to all that I command thee this day, thou and thy children, with all thine heart, and with all thy soul;

3 That then the LORD thy God will turn thy captivity, and have compassion upon thee, and will return and gather thee from all the nations, whither the LORD thy God hath scattered thee.

4 If *any* of thine be driven out unto the outmost *parts* of heaven, from thence will the LORD thy God gather thee, and from thence will he fetch thee:

5 And the LORD thy God will bring thee into the land which thy fathers possessed, and thou shalt possess it; and he will do thee good, and multiply thee above thy fathers.

6 And the LORD thy God will circumcise thine heart, and the heart of thy seed, to love the LORD thy God with all thine heart, and with all thy soul, that thou mayest live.

7 And the LORD thy God will put all these curses upon thine enemies, and on them that hate thee, which persecuted thee.

8 And thou shalt return and obey the voice of the LORD, and do all his commandments which I command thee this day.

9 And the LORD thy God will make thee plenteous in every work of thine hand, in the fruit of thy body, and in the fruit of thy cattle, and in the fruit of thy land, for good:

for the LORD will again rejoice over thee for good, as he rejoiced over thy fathers:

10 If thou shalt hearken unto the voice of the LORD thy God, to keep his commandments and his statutes which are written in this book of the law, *and* if thou turn unto the LORD thy God with all thine heart, and with all thy soul.

11 For this commandment which I command thee this day, it *is* not hidden from thee, neither *is* it far off.

12 It *is* not in heaven, that thou shouldest say, Who shall go up for us to heaven, and bring it unto us, that we may hear it, and do it?

13 Neither *is* it beyond the sea, that thou shouldest say, Who shall go over the sea for us, and bring it unto us, that we may hear it, and do it?

14 But the word *is* very nigh unto thee, in thy mouth, and in thy heart, that thou mayest do it.

Choose Life

15 See, I have set before thee this day life and good, and death and evil;

16 In that I command thee this day to love the LORD thy God, to walk in his ways, and to keep his commandments and his statutes and his judgments, that thou mayest live and multiply: and the LORD thy God shall bless thee in the land whither thou goest to possess it.

17 But if thine heart turn away, so that thou wilt not hear, but shalt be drawn away, and worship other gods, and serve them;

18 I denounce unto you this day, that ye shall surely perish, *and that* ye shall not prolong *your* days upon the land, whither thou passest over Jordan to go to possess it.

19 I call heaven and earth to record this day

Cross references (center column)

2 Neh. 1:9; Isa. 55:7; Lam. 3:40; Joel 2:12, 13

3 Ps. 106:45; 126:1, 4; 147:2; Jer. 29:14; 32:37; Lam. 3:22, 32; Ezek. 34:13; 36:24

4 Deut. 28:64; Neh. 1:9

6 Deut. 10:16; Jer. 32:39; Ezek. 11:19; 36:26

9 Deut. 28:11, 63; Jer. 32:41

11 Isa. 45:19

12 Rom. 10:6

15 Deut. 11:26; 30:1, 19

18 Deut. 4:26; 8:19

19 Deut. 4:26; 30:15; 31:28

30:1–10 After two chapters predicting disobedience and judgment, and deportation from the land, the Lord foretells of ultimate repentance and blessing upon national Israel. The Lord binds Himself to this ultimate destiny for Israel by establishing the land of Israel covenant, in which He promises the land to Israel forever.

30:2 according to all that I command thee this day. The nation of Israel was prophesied to return in unbelief in preparation for the Tribulation which will lead to repentance and fulfillment of this verse shortly before the second coming of Christ (Isa. 11:11–12; Ezek. 20:33–38; 22:17–22; 36:22–38; Zeph. 2:1–2).

30:3 and gather thee from all the nations. Israel's restoration in repentance and belief is often predicted in

the Old Testament in addition to this passage (Deut. 4:29–31; Isa. 27:12–13; 43:5–7; Jer. 16:14–15; 31:7–10; Ezek. 11:14–18; Amos 9:14–15; Zech. 10:8–12; Matt. 24:31).

30:6 the LORD thy God will circumcise thine heart. A prediction of the new covenant which will enable sinful Israel to obey, from the heart, all that the Lord commands her (see also Isa. 59:20–21; Jer. 31:31–34; 32:37–40; Ezek. 16:60–63; 37:21–28).

30:7 the LORD thy God will put all these curses upon thine enemies. This will occur during the Tribulation period leading up to the second coming of Christ (Rev. 6—19), as well as during Christ's Millennial Kingdom (Zech. 14:16–19).

237

against you, *that* I have set before you life and death, blessing and cursing: therefore choose life, that both thou and thy seed may live:

20 That thou mayest love the L ORD thy God, *and* that thou mayest obey his voice, and that thou mayest cleave unto him: for he *is* thy life, and the length of thy days: that thou mayest dwell in the land which the L ORD sware unto thy fathers, to Abraham, to Isaac, and to Jacob, to give them.

CHAPTER 31
Joshua Is Appointed the New Leader

1 And Moses went and spake these words unto all Israel.

2 And he said unto them, I *am* an hundred and twenty years old this day; I can no more go out and come in: also the L ORD hath said unto me, Thou shalt not go over this Jordan.

3 The L ORD thy God, he will go over before thee, *and* he will destroy these nations from before thee, and thou shalt possess them: *and* Joshua, he shall go over before thee, as the L ORD hath said.

4 And the L ORD shall do unto them as he did to Sihon and to Og, kings of the Amorites, and unto the land of them, whom he destroyed.

5 And the L ORD shall give them up before your face, that ye may do unto them according unto all the commandments which I have commanded you.

6 Be strong and of a good courage, fear not, nor be afraid of them: for the L ORD thy God, he *it is* that doth go with thee; he will not fail thee, nor forsake thee.

7 And Moses called unto Joshua, and said unto him in the sight of all Israel, Be strong and of a good courage: for thou must go with this people unto the land which the L ORD hath sworn unto their fathers to give them; and thou shalt cause them to inherit it.

8 And the L ORD, he *it is* that doth go before thee; he will be with thee, he will not fail thee, neither forsake thee: fear not, neither be dismayed.

9 And Moses wrote this law, and delivered it unto the priests the sons of Levi, which bare the ark of the covenant of the L ORD, and unto all the elders of Israel.

10 And Moses commanded them, saying, At the end of *every* seven years, in the solem-

nity of the year of release, in the feast of tabernacles,

11 When all Israel is come to appear before the L ORD thy God in the place which he shall choose, thou shalt read this law before all Israel in their hearing.

12 Gather the people together, men, and women, and children, and thy stranger that *is* within thy gates, that they may hear, and that they may learn, and fear the L ORD your God, and observe to do all the words of this law:

13 And *that* their children, which have not known *any thing*, may hear, and learn to fear the L ORD your God, as long as ye live in the land whither ye go over Jordan to possess it.

14 And the L ORD said unto Moses, Behold, thy days approach that thou must die: call Joshua, and present yourselves in the tabernacle of the congregation, that I may give him a charge. And Moses and Joshua went, and presented themselves in the tabernacle of the congregation.

15 And the L ORD appeared in the tabernacle in a pillar of a cloud: and the pillar of the cloud stood over the door of the tabernacle.

16 And the L ORD said unto Moses, Behold, thou shalt sleep with thy fathers; and this people will rise up, and go a whoring after the gods of the strangers of the land, whither they go *to be* among them, and will forsake me, and break my covenant which I have made with them.

17 Then my anger shall be kindled against them in that day, and I will forsake them, and I will hide my face from them, and they shall be devoured, and many evils and troubles shall befall them; so that they will say in that day, Are not these evils come upon us, because our God *is* not among us?

18 And I will surely hide my face in that day for all the evils which they shall have wrought, in that they are turned unto other gods.

19 Now therefore write ye this song for you, and teach it the children of Israel: put it in their mouths, that this song may be a witness for me against the children of Israel.

20 For when I shall have brought them into the land which I sware unto their fathers, that floweth with milk and honey; and they shall have eaten and filled themselves, and waxen fat; then will they turn unto other gods, and serve them, and provoke me, and break my covenant.

31:16–18 This is a prediction of Israel's apostasy after the death of Moses. After all that the Lord had done for the nation, she would not remain faithful.

21 And it shall come to pass, when many evils and troubles are befallen them, that this song shall testify against them as a witness; for it shall not be forgotten out of the mouths of their seed: for I know their imagination which they go about, even now, before I have brought them into the land which I sware.
22 Moses therefore wrote this song the same day, and taught it the children of Israel.
23 And he gave Joshua the son of Nun a charge, and said, Be strong and of a good courage: for thou shalt bring the children of Israel into the land which I sware unto them: and I will be with thee.

Moses Speaks to the Levites

24 And it came to pass, when Moses had made an end of writing the words of this law in a book, until they were finished,
25 That Moses commanded the Levites, which bare the ark of the covenant of the LORD, saying,
26 Take this book of the law, and put it in the side of the ark of the covenant of the LORD your God, that it may be there for a witness against thee.
27 For I know thy rebellion, and thy stiff neck: behold, while I am yet alive with you this day, ye have been rebellious against the LORD; and how much more after my death?
28 Gather unto me all the elders of your tribes, and your officers, that I may speak these words in their ears, and call heaven and earth to record against them.
29 For I know that after my death ye will utterly corrupt *yourselves*, and turn aside from the way which I have commanded you; and evil will befall you in the latter days; because ye will do evil in the sight of the LORD, to provoke him to anger through the work of your hands.
30 And Moses spake in the ears of all the congregation of Israel the words of this song, until they were ended.

CHAPTER 32
Moses' Song

1 Give ear, O ye heavens, and I will speak; and hear, O earth, the words of my mouth.
2 My doctrine shall drop as the rain, my speech shall distil as the dew, as the small rain upon the tender herb, and as the showers upon the grass:

21 Hos. 5:3; 13:5, 6; Amos 5:25, 26
23 Josh. 1:6
26 2Kgs. 22:8
27 Ex. 32:9; Deut. 9:6, 24; 32:20
29 Gen. 49:1; Deut. 4:30; 28:15; 32:5; Judg. 2:19; Hos. 9:9
1 Ps. 50:4; Isa. 1:2; Jer. 2:12; 6:19
2 Ps. 72:6; Isa. 55:10, 11; Mic. 5:7; 1Cor. 3:6-8
3 1Chr. 29:11
4 2Sam. 22:3, 31; 23:3; Job 34:10; Ps. 18:2, 31, 46; 92:15; Jer. 10:10; Dan. 4:37; Hab. 1:12; Rev. 15:3
5 Matt. 17:17; Luke 9:41; Phil. 2:15
6 Ps. 74:2; 116:12; Isa. 27:11; 44:2; 63:16
7 Ex. 13:14; Ps. 44:1; 78:3, 4
8 Gen. 11:8; Zech. 9:2; Acts 17:26
9 Ex. 15:16; 19:5; 1Sam. 10:1; Ps. 78:71
10 Ps. 17:8; Prov. 7:2
13 Job 29:6; Ps. 81:16; Isa. 58:14; Ezek. 36:2
15 1Sam. 2:29
16 1Kgs. 14:22; 1Cor. 10:22
17 Lev. 17:7; Ps. 106:37; Rev. 9:20

3 Because I will publish the name of the LORD: ascribe ye greatness unto our God.
4 *He is* the Rock, his work *is* perfect: for all his ways *are* judgment: a God of truth and without iniquity, just and right *is* he.
5 They have corrupted themselves, their spot *is* not *the spot* of his children: *they are* a perverse and crooked generation.
6 Do ye thus requite the LORD, O foolish people and unwise? is not he thy father *that* hath bought thee? hath he not made thee, and established thee?
7 Remember the days of old, consider the years of many generations: ask thy father, and he will shew thee; thy elders, and they will tell thee.
8 When the most High divided to the nations their inheritance, when he separated the sons of Adam, he set the bounds of the people according to the number of the children of Israel.
9 For the LORD's portion *is* his people; Jacob *is* the lot of his inheritance.
10 He found him in a desert land, and in the waste howling wilderness; he led him about, he instructed him, he kept him as the apple of his eye.
11 As an eagle stirreth up her nest, fluttereth over her young, spreadeth abroad her wings, taketh them, beareth them on her wings:
12 *So* the LORD alone did lead him, and *there was* no strange god with him.
13 He made him ride on the high places of the earth, that he might eat the increase of the fields; and he made him to suck honey out of the rock, and oil out of the flinty rock;
14 Butter of kine, and milk of sheep, with fat of lambs, and rams of the breed of Bashan, and goats, with the fat of kidneys of wheat; and thou didst drink the pure blood of the grape.
15 But Jeshurun waxed fat, and kicked: thou art waxen fat, thou art grown thick, thou art covered *with fatness*; then he forsook God *which* made him, and lightly esteemed the Rock of his salvation.
16 They provoked him to jealousy with strange *gods*, with abominations provoked they him to anger.
17 They sacrificed unto devils, not to God; to gods whom they knew not, to new *gods that* came newly up, whom your fathers feared not.

31:28–29 call heaven and earth. Moses puts the nation on official notice concerning their responsibility to keep the covenant with the Lord, even though he knew with certainty that they would not.

Fulfilled Prophecy and Israel

By Arnold G. Fruchtenbaum

In Deuteronomy 32:8–9, Moses declared: "When the Most High delivered to the nations their inheritance, when he separated the sons of Adam, he set the bounds of the people according to the number of the children of Israel. For the LORD's portion is his people; Jacob is the lot of his inheritance." God has an overall prophetic program that we often subdivide into three distinct plans: a plan for Israel, a plan for the Church, and a plan for the Gentile nations, all three of which center around the Jewish people.

In connection with Israel, God's sovereign purpose is accomplished through the eternal, conditional covenants God made with the Jewish people (the Abrahamic, land, Davidic, and new covenants). But how does God's program in connection with the Church relate to Israel? Paul teaches that the spiritual blessings the Church enjoys are actually Jewish spiritual blessings which come from the Jewish covenants; therefore, Gentiles are partakers of these spiritual blessings of the Jewish covenants (Eph. 2:11–16; 3:5–6; Rom. 11:17; 15:25–27). The key purpose of the Rapture is to remove the Church from the earth before God pours out His wrath upon Israel and the unrepentant Gentiles.

> *Israel is truly God's timepiece of history and prophecy.*

While the outpouring of God's wrath upon the Gentile world is due to the violation of the Noahic Covenant (Isa. 24:5–6), God's outpouring of judgment upon Israel is to bring its people to national repentance.

How God deals with the Gentile nations has consistently been the outworking of a principle within the Abrahamic covenant: "I will bless them that bless thee, and curse him that curseth thee" (Gen. 12:3). In fact, in the judgment of the Gentiles (the sheep and goats of Matt. 25:31–46), only the sheep, those believing Gentiles whose faith will be evidenced by their positive treatment of the Jews during the Tribulation, will enter the kingdom. The goats, unbelieving Gentiles, will be excluded from the kingdom and go into eternal punishment (see also Joel 3:1–3). How God deals with the future Gentile nations in the kingdom will be based upon their relationship to Israel in the past. His judgments upon them and the fulfillment of His prophecies concerning these nations are often based upon his statement to Israel in Zechariah 2:8, "He that toucheth you toucheth the apple of his eye."

One of the most famous prophecies related to the issue of time, prophecy, and chronology is the "seventy weeks" prophecy in Daniel 9:24–27. God tells Daniel these seventy weeks are decreed "upon thy people" and "upon thy holy city," that is, Israel and Jerusalem. This prophecy does not apply to the Church.

Israel is truly God's timepiece of history and prophecy. God's overall prophetic program, be it for Israel, the Church, or the Gentile nations, works its way out directly or indirectly through the Jewish people. Too often believers have attempted to see where they are in God's prophetic program based upon how world events affect their particular country. But the true determination as to where we are in history is based upon how world events affect Jewish history and the Jewish people. Thus when world-shaking events take place, the criteria for their relation to Bible prophecy is not how they affect the Church, or any particular Gentile nation, no matter how great and powerful, but how they are affecting Jewish history and the people of Israel.

18 Of the Rock *that* begat thee thou art unmindful, and hast forgotten God that formed thee.

19 And when the LORD saw *it*, he abhorred *them*, because of the provoking of his sons, and of his daughters.

20 And he said, I will hide my face from them, I will see what their end *shall be*: for they *are* a very froward generation, children in whom *is* no faith.

21 They have moved me to jealousy with *that which is* not God; they have provoked me to anger with their vanities: and I will move them to jealousy with *those which are* not a people; I will provoke them to anger with a foolish nation.

22 For a fire is kindled in mine anger, and shall burn unto the lowest hell, and shall consume the earth with her increase, and set on fire the foundations of the mountains.

23 I will heap mischiefs upon them; I will spend mine arrows upon them.

24 *They shall be* burnt with hunger, and devoured with burning heat, and with bitter destruction: I will also send the teeth of beasts upon them, with the poison of serpents of the dust.

25 The sword without, and terror within, shall destroy both the young man and the virgin, the suckling *also* with the man of grey hairs.

26 I said, I would scatter them into corners, I would make the remembrance of them to cease from among men:

27 Were it not that I feared the wrath of the enemy, lest their adversaries should behave themselves strangely, *and* lest they should say, Our hand *is* high, and the LORD hath not done all this.

28 For they *are* a nation void of counsel, neither *is there any* understanding in them.

29 O that they were wise, *that* they understood this, *that* they would consider their latter end!

30 How should one chase a thousand, and two put ten thousand to flight, except their Rock had sold them, and the LORD had shut them up?

31 For their rock *is* not as our Rock, even our enemies themselves *being* judges.

32 For their vine *is* of the vine of Sodom, and of the fields of Gomorrah: their grapes *are* grapes of gall, their clusters *are* bitter:

33 Their wine *is* the poison of dragons, and the cruel venom of asps.

34 *Is* not this laid up in store with me *and* sealed up among my treasures?

35 To me *belongeth* vengeance, and recompence; their foot shall slide in *due* time: for the day of their calamity *is* at hand, and the things that shall come upon them make haste.

36 For the LORD shall judge his people, and repent himself for his servants, when he seeth that *their* power is gone, and *there is* none shut up, or left.

37 And he shall say, Where *are* their gods, *their* rock in whom they trusted,

38 Which did eat the fat of their sacrifices, *and* drank the wine of their drink offerings? let them rise up and help you, *and* be your protection.

39 See now that I, *even* I, *am* he, and *there is* no god with me: I kill, and I make alive; I wound, and I heal: neither *is there any* that can deliver out of my hand.

40 For I lift up my hand to heaven, and say, I live for ever.

41 If I whet my glittering sword, and mine

Cross references

18 Jer. 2:32
20 Isa. 30:9; Matt. 17:17
21 Hos. 1:10; Rom. 10:19
22 Jer. 15:14; Lam. 4:11
25 Lam. 1:20
26 Ezek. 20:13, 14, 23
27 Ps. 140:8; Jer. 19:4
28 Jer. 4:22
29 Luke 19:42
30 Lev. 26:8; Isa. 30:17
31 1Sam. 2:2; 4:8; Jer. 40:3
32 Isa. 1:10
34 Job 14:17; Jer. 2:22; Hos. 13:12; Rom. 2:5
35 Ps. 94:1; 2Pet. 2:3
36 Judg. 2:18; Ps. 106:45; Jer. 31:20
37 Judg. 10:14; Jer. 2:28
39 Job 5:18; Ps. 68:20; Hos. 6:1
40 Gen. 14:22
41 Isa. 27:1; 34:5; 66:16

32:21 with a foolish nation. This will have to be some Gentile entity. God's plan for Israel will involve His restoration of them to Him by making them jealous of a "nonpeople" and a foolish nation. Paul speaks of this in Romans 10:19, quoting this passage, to the effect that God would use Gentiles to make His chosen people Israel envious, leading to their repentance and belief. This will be accomplished in the latter half of the Tribulation, after the Antichrist desecrates the temple in Jerusalem (2 Thess. 2:8; Rev. 12).

32:26–27 make the remembrance of them to cease. This is a threat that God does not carry out. The reason He decides against wiping out the nation of Israel is that the Gentiles would misinterpret its significance. Thus, the lesson that should be learned in history would be lost on the Gentiles who would surely twist its meaning.

32:36 repent himself for his servants. The word "repent" in the Hebrew has the idea of "comfort," or "compassion." When the nation comes to the end of herself, then God will repent and show mercy to them, even in the midst of judgment. God shows mercy on some as He sees fit. To the world it may seem that God changes his mind or becomes something He was not, but in reality the "repentance" spoken of here represents a change in the heart of men and was a part of God's plan from all eternity.

32:41–43 vengeance to mine enemies. Lest the Gentile nations think that because God so severely deals with His nation that they are off the hook, the Lord answers with one of the most militant statements of vengeance in the Bible.

hand take hold on judgment; I will render vengeance to mine enemies, and will reward them that hate me.

42 I will make mine arrows drunk with blood, and my sword shall devour flesh; *and that* with the blood of the slain and of the captives, from the beginning of revenges upon the enemy.

43 Rejoice, O ye nations, *with* his people: for he will avenge the blood of his servants, and will render vengeance to his adversaries, and will be merciful unto his land, *and* to his people.

44 And Moses came and spake all the words of this song in the ears of the people, he, and Hoshea the son of Nun.

45 And Moses made an end of speaking all these words to all Israel:

46 And he said unto them, Set your hearts unto all the words which I testify among you this day, which ye shall command your children to observe to do, all the words of this law.

47 For it *is* not a vain thing for you; because it *is* your life: and through this thing ye shall prolong *your* days in the land, whither ye go over Jordan to possess it.

God Prepares Moses for Death

48 And the LORD spake unto Moses that selfsame day, saying,

49 Get thee up into this mountain Abarim, *unto* mount Nebo, which *is* in the land of Moab, that *is* over against Jericho; and behold the land of Canaan, which I give unto the children of Israel for a possession:

50 And die in the mount whither thou goest up, and be gathered unto thy people; as Aaron thy brother died in mount Hor, and was gathered unto his people:

51 Because ye trespassed against me among the children of Israel at the waters of Meribah-Kadesh, in the wilderness of Zin; because ye sanctified me not in the midst of the children of Israel.

52 Yet thou shalt see the land before *thee;*

but thou shalt not go thither unto the land which I give the children of Israel.

CHAPTER 33
Moses Blesses Israel

1 And this *is* the blessing, wherewith Moses the man of God blessed the children of Israel before his death.

2 And he said, The LORD came from Sinai, and rose up from Seir unto them; he shined forth from mount Paran, and he came with ten thousands of saints: from his right hand *went* a fiery law for them.

3 Yea, he loved the people; all his saints *are* in thy hand: and they sat down at thy feet; *every one* shall receive of thy words.

4 Moses commanded us a law, *even* the inheritance of the congregation of Jacob.

5 And he was king in Jeshurun, when the heads of the people *and* the tribes of Israel were gathered together.

6 Let Reuben live, and not die; and let *not* his men be few.

7 And this *is the blessing* of Judah: and he said, Hear, LORD, the voice of Judah, and bring him unto his people: let his hands be sufficient for him; and be thou an help *to him* from his enemies.

8 And of Levi he said, *Let* thy Thummim and thy Urim *be* with thy holy one, whom thou didst prove at Massah, *and with* whom thou didst strive at the waters of Meribah;

9 Who said unto his father and to his mother, I have not seen him; neither did he acknowledge his brethren, nor knew his own children: for they have observed thy word, and kept thy covenant.

10 They shall teach Jacob thy judgments, and Israel thy law: they shall put incense before thee, and whole burnt sacrifice upon thine altar.

11 Bless, LORD, his substance, and accept the work of his hands: smite through the loins of them that rise against him, and of them that hate him, that they rise not again.

Cross references (center column):

42 Jer. 30:14; 46:10; Lam. 2:5

43 Ps. 85:1; Rev. 6:10; 19:2

47 Lev. 18:5

49 Num. 33:47, 48

50 Num. 20:25, 28; 33:38

51 Lev. 10:3; Num. 20:11-13; 27:14;

52 Num. 27:12

2 Ex. 19:18, 20; Ps. 68:17; Rev. 5:11; 9:16

3 Ex. 19:5; Prov. 2:1; Hos. 11:1; Luke 10:39

4 John 1:17; 7:19; Ps. 119:111

5 Judg. 9:2; 17:6

7 Gen. 49:8; Ps. 146:5

8 Ex. 17:7; 28:30; Num. 20:13; Deut. 8:2, 3, 16; Ps. 81:7

9 Gen. 29:32; Ex. 32:26-28; 1Chr. 17:17; Job 37:24; Jer. 18:18

10 Ex. 30:7, 8; Lev. 1:9, 13, 17; 10:11; Num. 16:40

11 2Sam. 24:23; Ps. 20:3; Ezek. 20:40, 41; 43:27

33:1–29 Before his death, Moses gives a prophetic blessing to the tribes of Israel, within the tradition of Abraham, Isaac, Jacob, and Joseph.

33:5 king in Jeshurun. Jeshurun is a pet name for Israel (Deut. 32:15; 33:26; Isa. 44:2) suggesting its ideal uprightness, from the Hebrew root "to be right."

33:6 let not his men be few. Moses predicts that the tribe of Reuben would have a future, but not a glorious one (cf. Gen. 49:3–4). This was fulfilled as Reuben's tribe

declined in population and merged into the nation as a whole, losing its tribal identity (cf. 2 Kings 10:33).

33:8–11 thy Thummim and thy Urim be with thy holy one. Moses desires that Levi will responsibly fulfill their priestly duties, as reference to the Thummim and Urim would indicate. The Thummim and Urim were the precious stones of the breastpiece of the chief priest for the purpose of casting sacred lots to determine God's will for the people.

12 *And* of Benjamin he said, The beloved of the LORD shall dwell in safety by him; *and the* LORD shall cover him all the day long, and he shall dwell between his shoulders.

13 And of Joseph he said, Blessed of the LORD *be* his land, for the precious things of heaven, for the dew, and for the deep that coucheth beneath,

14 And for the precious fruits *brought forth* by the sun, and for the precious things put forth by the moon,

15 And for the chief things of the ancient mountains, and for the precious things of the lasting hills,

16 And for the precious things of the earth and fulness thereof, and *for* the good will of him that dwelt in the bush: let *the blessing* come upon the head of Joseph, and upon the top of the head of him *that was* separated from his brethren.

17 His glory *is like* the firstling of his bullock, and his horns *are like* the horns of unicorns: with them he shall push the people together to the ends of the earth: and they *are* the ten thousands of Ephraim, and they *are* the thousands of Manasseh.

18 And of Zebulun he said, Rejoice, Zebulun, in thy going out; and, Issachar, in thy tents.

19 They shall call the people unto the mountain; there they shall offer sacrifices of righteousness: for they shall suck *of* the abundance of the seas, and *of* treasures hid in the sand.

20 And of Gad he said, Blessed *be* he that enlargeth Gad: he dwelleth as a lion, and teareth the arm with the crown of the head.

21 And he provided the first part for himself, because there, *in* a portion of the lawgiver, *was he* seated; and he came with the heads of the people, he executed the justice of the LORD, and his judgments with Israel.

22 And of Dan he said, Dan *is* a lion's whelp: he shall leap from Bashan.

23 And of Naphtali he said, O Naphtali, satisfied with favour, and full with the blessing of the LORD: possess thou the west and the south.

24 And of Asher he said, *Let* Asher be

blessed with children; let him be acceptable to his brethren, and let him dip his foot in oil.

25 Thy shoes *shall be* iron and brass; and as thy days, *so shall* thy strength *be*.

26 *There is* none like unto the God of Jeshurun, *who* rideth upon the heaven in thy help, and in his excellency on the sky.

27 The eternal God *is thy* refuge, and underneath *are* the everlasting arms: and he shall thrust out the enemy from before thee; and shall say, Destroy *them*.

28 Israel then shall dwell in safety alone: the fountain of Jacob *shall be* upon a land of corn and wine; also his heavens shall drop down dew.

29 Happy *art* thou, O Israel: who *is* like unto thee, O people saved by the LORD, the shield of thy help, and who *is* the sword of thy excellency! and thine enemies shall be found liars unto thee; and thou shalt tread upon their high places.

CHAPTER 34
Moses Sees the Land but Is Not Allowed to Enter

1 And Moses went up from the plains of Moab unto the mountain of Nebo, to the top of Pisgah, that *is* over against Jericho. And the LORD shewed him all the land of Gilead, unto Dan,

2 And all Naphtali, and the land of Ephraim, and Manasseh, and all the land of Judah, unto the utmost sea,

3 And the south, and the plain of the valley of Jericho, the city of palm trees, unto Zoar.

4 And the LORD said unto him, This *is* the land which I sware unto Abraham, unto Isaac, and unto Jacob, saying, I will give it unto thy seed: I have caused thee to see *it* with thine eyes, but thou shalt not go over thither.

Moses' Death

5 So Moses the servant of the LORD died there in the land of Moab, according to the word of the LORD.

6 And he buried him in a valley in the land

Cross references (center column)

13 Gen. 27:28; 49:25
15 Gen. 49:26; Hab. 3:6
16 Gen. 49:26; Ex. 3:2, 4; Acts 7:30, 35
17 Gen. 48:19; Num. 23:22; 1Kgs. 22:11; 1Chr. 5:1; Ps. 44:5; 92:10
18 Gen. 49:13-15
19 Ps. 4:5; Isa. 2:3
20 Josh. 13:10; 1Chr. 12:8
21 Num. 32:16, 17; Josh. 4:12
22 Josh. 19:47; Judg. 18:27
23 Gen. 49:21; Josh. 19:32
24 Gen. 49:20; Job 29:6
25 Deut. 8:9
26 Ex. 15:11; Ps. 68:4, 33, 34
27 Deut. 9:3-5; Ps. 90:1
28 Num. 23:9; Jer. 23:6
29 2Sam. 7:23; 22:45
1 Num. 27:12; 33:47
4 Gen. 12:7; 13:15; 15:18; 26:3; 28:13; Deut. 3:27; 32:52
5 Deut. 32:50; Josh. 1:1, 2
6 Jude 1:9

33:13–17 The prophetic blessing upon Joseph was through his two sons, Ephraim and Manasseh. It consists of a wish for fertility, productivity of their land, and for strength so that they might be instruments of God's judgment of the nations (cf. Gen. 49:22–26).

33:23 satisfied with favour, and full with the blessing of the LORD. This tribe is highly favored of the Lord. This favor is expressed tangibly in Naphtali's advantageous location that touched upon the Sea of Galilee. It is important to note that Jesus, the Messiah, spent most of his life and exercised much of His ministry within this area (cf. Gen. 49:21).

of Moab, over against Beth-peor: but no man knoweth of his sepulchre unto this day.

7 And Moses *was* an hundred and twenty years old when he died: his eye was not dim, nor his natural force abated.

8 And the children of Israel wept for Moses in the plains of Moab thirty days: so the days of weeping *and* mourning for Moses were ended.

9 And Joshua the son of Nun was full of the spirit of wisdom; for Moses had laid his hands upon him: and the children of Israel

hearkened unto him, and did as the LORD commanded Moses.

10 And there arose not a prophet since in Israel like unto Moses, whom the LORD knew face to face,

11 In all the signs and the wonders, which the LORD sent him to do in the land of Egypt to Pharaoh, and to all his servants, and to all his land,

12 And in all that mighty hand, and in all the great terror which Moses shewed in the sight of all Israel.

7 Josh. 14:10, 11

8 Gen. 50:3, 10; Num. 20:29

9 Isa. 11:2; Dan. 6:3

10 Ex. 33:11; Num. 12:6, 8; Deut. 5:4; 18:15, 18

11 Deut. 4:34; 7:19

Joshua

The book of Joshua introduces the twelve historical books. While Joshua was the primary writer and compiler of his book, some portions, including the commentary on Joshua's death, were written by unknown authors.

Joshua's name means "Jehovah saves" or "Jehovah is salvation." The Greek translation of his name is "Jesus" (see Heb. 4:8). Born in slavery, Joshua was over forty when the Exodus began and worked faithfully with Moses since the giving of the Ten Commandments at Mount Sinai. He continued to serve with Moses as he and his godly colleague, Caleb, were the only two spies out of twelve who believed that God would enable them to conquer the land (see Num. 13—14). Consequently, Joshua and Caleb were the only two members of their generation that God permitted to journey across the Jordan River. After aiding Moses for the forty years of wanderings, Joshua led the conquering Israelites when he was in his eighties, and then enjoyed dwelling in the land until his death at the age of 110.

Author
Joshua and Others
Date
Ca. 1405–1380 B.C.
Key Truth
Total Victory
Historic Time
Conquest of Canaan
Key Verse
1:3
. . . that have I given unto you, as I said unto Moses.

Beginning with Joshua's assumption of command and the marshalling of Israel's military forces, the people then crossed the Jordan River, which had miraculously and temporarily dried up. They were now ready to "possess the land" (see Josh. 18:3; 23:5; 24:8).

The book of Joshua is about conquests and compromises, since all the wicked and idolatrous inhabitants were not driven out as God had instructed (3:10; 13:6; 23:5). Strong pockets of idolatrous inhabitants, some in large territories, continued to resist the Israelites. Each generation of Israelites would have to "choose . . . whom [they would] serve" (24:15).

Numerous prophecies about land, conquests, and predictions of victory appear (chaps. 6—7, 10, 21) and were fulfilled in Joshua's lifetime. A future possession of the land will come to pass during the millennial reign of Christ. God did not fail in His promises, but ancient Israel failed to completely obey God and possess their possessions.

Twenty-seven predictions appear in 89 out of 658 verses (12% of the content).

12%
Prophecy

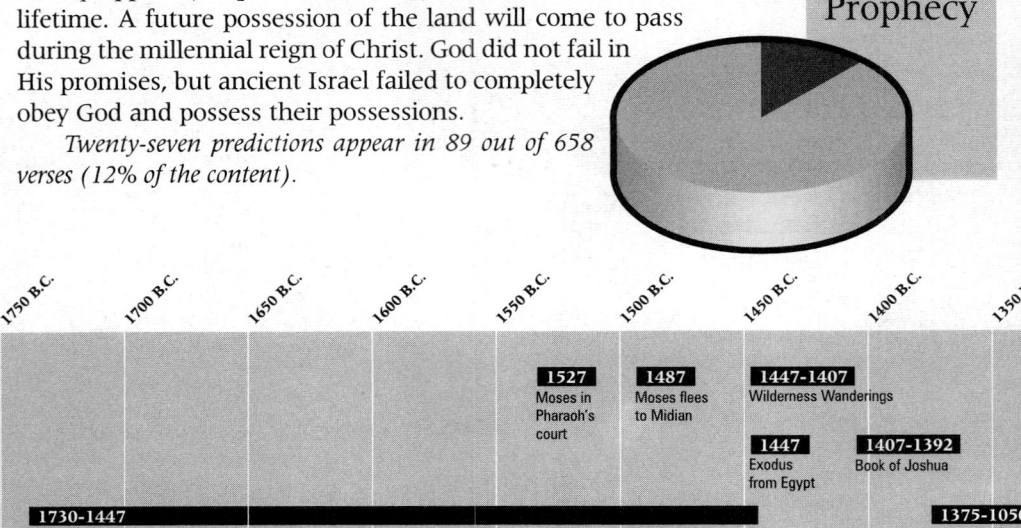

| 1750 B.C. | 1700 B.C. | 1650 B.C. | 1600 B.C. | 1550 B.C. | 1500 B.C. | 1450 B.C. | 1400 B.C. | 1350 |

1527
Moses in Pharaoh's court

1487
Moses flees to Midian

1447-1407
Wilderness Wanderings

1447
Exodus from Egypt

1407-1392
Book of Joshua

1730-1447
Bondage in Egypt begins

Bondage in Egypt ends

1375-1050
Israel ruled by Judges

CHAPTER 1
God's Charge to Joshua

1 Now after the death of Moses the servant of the LORD it came to pass, that the LORD spake unto Joshua the son of Nun, Moses' minister, saying,

2 Moses my servant is dead; now therefore arise, go over this Jordan, thou, and all this people, unto the land which I do give to them, *even* to the children of Israel.

3 Every place that the sole of your foot shall tread upon, that have I given unto you, as I said unto Moses.

4 From the wilderness and this Lebanon even unto the great river, the river Euphrates, all the land of the Hittites, and unto the great sea toward the going down of the sun, shall be your coast.

5 There shall not any man be able to stand before thee all the days of thy life: as I was with Moses, *so* I will be with thee: I will not fail thee, nor forsake thee.

6 Be strong and of a good courage: for unto this people shalt thou divide for an inheritance the land, which I sware unto their fathers to give them.

7 Only be thou strong and very courageous, that thou mayest observe to do according to all the law, which Moses my servant commanded thee: turn not from it *to* the right hand or *to* the left, that thou mayest prosper whithersoever thou goest.

8 This book of the law shall not depart out of thy mouth; but thou shalt meditate therein day and night, that thou mayest observe to do according to all that is written therein: for then thou shalt make thy way prosperous, and then thou shalt have good success.

9 Have not I commanded thee? Be strong and of a good courage; be not afraid, neither be thou dismayed: for the LORD thy God *is* with thee whithersoever thou goest.

10 Then Joshua commanded the officers of the people, saying,

11 Pass through the host, and command the people, saying, Prepare you victuals; for within three days ye shall pass over this Jordan, to go in to possess the land, which the LORD your God giveth you to possess it.

12 And to the Reubenites, and to the Gadites, and to half the tribe of Manasseh, spake Joshua, saying,

13 Remember the word which Moses the servant of the LORD commanded you, saying, The LORD your God hath given you rest, and hath given you this land.

14 Your wives, your little ones, and your cattle, shall remain in the land which Moses gave you on this side Jordan; but ye shall pass before your brethren armed, all the mighty men of valour, and help them;

15 Until the LORD have given your brethren rest, as *he hath given* you, and they also have possessed the land which the LORD your God giveth them: then ye shall return unto the land of your possession, and enjoy it, which Moses the LORD's servant gave you on this side Jordan toward the sunrising.

16 And they answered Joshua, saying, All that thou commandest us we will do, and whithersoever thou sendest us, we will go.

17 According as we hearkened unto Moses in all things, so will we hearken unto thee: only the LORD thy God be with thee, as he was with Moses.

18 Whosoever *he be* that doth rebel against thy commandment, and will not hearken unto thy words in all that thou commandest him, he shall be put to death: only be strong and of a good courage.

CHAPTER 2
Joshua Sends Spies

1 And Joshua the son of Nun sent out of Shittim two men to spy secretly, saying, Go view the land, even Jericho. And they went, and came into an harlot's house, named Rahab, and lodged there.

2 And it was told the king of Jericho, saying, Behold, there came men in hither tonight of the children of Israel to search out the country.

3 And the king of Jericho sent unto Rahab, saying, Bring forth the men that are come to thee, which are entered into thine house:

Cross-references (center column)

1 Ex. 24:13; Deut. 1:38

2 Deut. 34:5

3 Deut. 11:24; Josh. 14:9

4 Gen. 15:18; Ex. 23:31; Num. 34:3-12

5 Ex. 3:12; Deut. 7:24; 31:6, 8, 23; Josh. 1:9, 17; 3:7; 6:27; Isa. 43:2, 5; Heb. 13:5

6 Deut. 31:7, 23

7 Num. 27:23; Deut. 5:32; 28:14; 31:7; Josh. 11:15

8 Deut. 17:18, 19; Ps. 1:2

9 Deut. 31:7, 8, 23; Ps. 27:1; Jer. 1:8

11 Deut. 9:1; 11:31; Josh. 3:2

13 Num. 32:20-28; Josh. 22:2-4

15 Josh. 22:4-6

17 Josh. 1:5; 1Sam. 20:13; 1Kgs. 1:37

1 Num. 25:1; Matt. 1:5; Heb. 11:31; James 2:25

2 Ps. 127:1; Prov. 21:30

1:4–6 This reaffirmation of the land-grant promise to Israel was only partially fulfilled in that day. God gave them all the land Joshua physically walked on, but even he did not fully possess all the land that was promised to him. However, it will be possessed by Israel during the Millennial Kingdom.

1:5–9 I will be with thee. The most practical guarantee in all of Scripture, given to Moses, the children of Israel (Deut. 31:6), Joshua, and others, and confirmed by Jesus to Christians through the ages in the Great Commission (Matt. 28:19–20).

1:8–9 The promise of success is given to those who meditate on the word of God.

for they be come to search out all the country.

4 And the woman took the two men, and hid them, and said thus, There came men unto me, but I wist not whence they *were*:

5 And it came to pass *about the time* of shutting of the gate, when it was dark, that the men went out: whither the men went I wot not: pursue after them quickly; for ye shall overtake them.

6 But she had brought them up to the roof of the house, and hid them with the stalks of flax, which she had laid in order upon the roof.

7 And the men pursued after them the way to Jordan unto the fords: and as soon as they which pursued after them were gone out, they shut the gate.

8 And before they were laid down, she came up unto them upon the roof;

9 And she said unto the men, I know that the LORD hath given you the land, and that your terror is fallen upon us, and that all the inhabitants of the land faint because of you.

10 For we have heard how the LORD dried up the water of the Red sea for you, when ye came out of Egypt; and what ye did unto the two kings of the Amorites, that *were* on the other side Jordan, Sihon and Og, whom ye utterly destroyed:

11 And as soon as we had heard *these things*, our hearts did melt, neither did there remain any more courage in any man because of you: for the LORD your God, he *is* God in heaven above, and in earth beneath.

12 Now therefore, I pray you, swear unto me by the LORD, since I have shewed you kindness, that ye will also shew kindness unto my father's house, and give me a true token:

13 And *that* ye will save alive my father, and my mother, and my brethren, and my sisters, and all that they have, and deliver our lives from death.

14 And the men answered her, Our life for yours, if ye utter not this our business. And it shall be, when the LORD hath given us the land, that we will deal kindly and truly with thee.

15 Then she let them down by a cord through the window: for her house *was* upon the town wall, and she dwelt upon the wall.

16 And she said unto them, Get you to the mountain, lest the pursuers meet you; and hide yourselves there three days, until the pursuers be returned: and afterward may ye go your way.

17 And the men said unto her, We *will be* blameless of this thine oath which thou hast made us swear.

18 Behold, *when* we come into the land,

4 2Sam. 17:19, 20
6 Ex. 1:17; 2Sam. 17:19
9 Gen. 35:5; Ex. 23:27; Deut. 2:25; 11:25
10 Ex. 14:21; Num. 21:24, 34, 35; Josh. 4:23
11 Ex. 15:14, 15; Deut. 4:39; Josh. 5:1; 7:5; Isa. 13:7
12 Josh. 2:18; 1Sam. 20:14, 15, 17; 1Tim. 5:8
14 Judg. 1:24; Matt. 5:7
15 Acts 9:25
17 Ex. 20:7
18 Josh. 2:12; 6:23

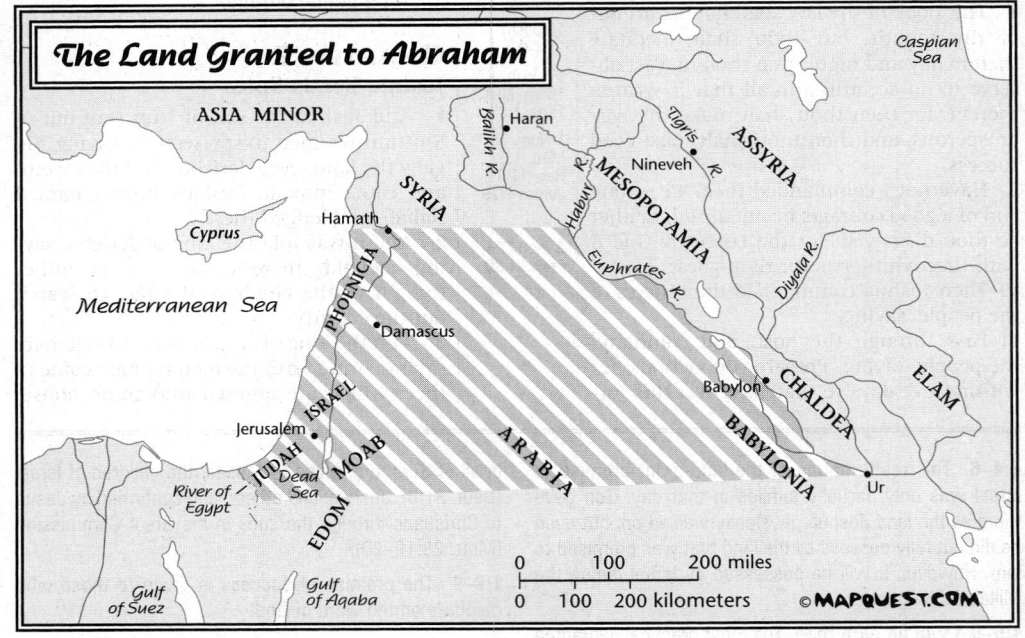

The Land Granted to Abraham

Caspian Sea

ASIA MINOR

Balikh R. Haran

ASSYRIA

SYRIA

Habur R. MESOPOTAMIA Tigris R.

Nineveh

Cyprus Hamath

PHOENICIA Euphrates R. Diyala R.

Mediterranean Sea

Damascus

ELAM

Babylon CHALDEA

Jerusalem ISRAEL

BABYLONIA

JUDAH Dead MOAB

River of / Sea

Egypt EDOM ARABIA

Ur

Gulf of Suez Gulf of Aqaba

0   100   200 miles

0   100   200 kilometers

©MAPQUEST.COM

thou shalt bind this line of scarlet thread in the window which thou didst let us down by: and thou shalt bring thy father, and thy mother, and thy brethren, and all thy father's household, home unto thee.

19 And it shall be, *that* whosoever shall go out of the doors of thy house into the street, his blood *shall be* upon his head, and we *will be* guiltless: and whosoever shall be with thee in the house, his blood *shall be* on our head, if *any* hand be upon him.

20 And if thou utter this our business, then we will be quit of thine oath which thou hast made us to swear.

21 And she said, According unto your words, so *be* it. And she sent them away, and they departed: and she bound the scarlet line in the window.

22 And they went, and came unto the mountain, and abode there three days, until the pursuers were returned: and the pursuers sought *them* throughout all the way, but found *them* not.

23 So the two men returned, and descended from the mountain, and passed over, and came to Joshua the son of Nun, and told him all *things* that befell them:

24 And they said unto Joshua, Truly the LORD hath delivered into our hands all the land; for even all the inhabitants of the country do faint because of us.

CHAPTER 3
Israel Crosses the Jordan

1 And Joshua rose early in the morning; and they removed from Shittim, and came to Jordan, he and all the children of Israel, and lodged there before they passed over.

2 And it came to pass after three days, that the officers went through the host;

3 And they commanded the people, saying, When ye see the ark of the covenant of the LORD your God, and the priests the Levites bearing it, then ye shall remove from your place, and go after it.

4 Yet there shall be a space between you and it, about two thousand cubits by measure: come not near unto it, that ye may know the way by which ye must go: for ye have not passed *this* way heretofore.

5 And Joshua said unto the people, Sanctify yourselves: for to morrow the LORD will do wonders among you.

6 And Joshua spake unto the priests, saying, Take up the ark of the covenant, and pass over before the people. And they took up the ark of the covenant, and went before the people.

7 And the LORD said unto Joshua, This day will I begin to magnify thee in the sight of all Israel, that they may know that, as I was with Moses, *so* I will be with thee.

8 And thou shalt command the priests that bear the ark of the covenant, saying, When ye are come to the brink of the water of Jordan, ye shall stand still in Jordan.

9 And Joshua said unto the children of Israel, Come hither, and hear the words of the LORD your God.

10 And Joshua said, Hereby ye shall know that the living God *is* among you, and *that* he will without fail drive out from before you the Canaanites, and the Hittites, and the Hivites, and the Perizzites, and the Girgashites, and the Amorites, and the Jebusites.

11 Behold, the ark of the covenant of the Lord of all the earth passeth over before you into Jordan.

12 Now therefore take you twelve men out of the tribes of Israel, out of every tribe a man.

13 And it shall come to pass, as soon as the soles of the feet of the priests that bear the ark of the LORD, the Lord of all the earth, shall rest in the waters of Jordan, *that* the waters of Jordan shall be cut off *from* the waters that come down from above; and they shall stand upon an heap.

14 And it came to pass, when the people removed from their tents, to pass over Jordan, and the priests bearing the ark of the covenant before the people;

15 And as they that bare the ark were come unto Jordan, and the feet of the priests that bare the ark were dipped in the brim of the water, (for Jordan overfloweth all his banks all the time of harvest,)

16 That the waters which came down from above stood *and* rose up upon an heap very far from the city Adam, that *is* beside Zaretan: and those that came down toward the sea of the plain, *even* the salt sea, failed, *and* were cut off: and the people passed over right against Jericho.

17 And the priests that bare the ark of the covenant of the LORD stood firm on dry ground in the midst of Jordan, and all the Israelites passed over on dry ground, until all the people were passed clean over Jordan.

CHAPTER 4
Stone Monument Set Up at Gilgal

1 And it came to pass, when all the people were clean passed over Jordan, that the LORD spake unto Joshua, saying,

Cross references (center column)

19 Matt. 27:25

24 Ex. 23:31; Josh. 6:2; 21:44

1 Josh. 2:1

2 Josh. 1:10, 11

3 Num. 10:33; Deut. 31:9, 25

4 Ex. 19:12

5 Ex. 19:10, 14, 15; Lev. 20:7; Num. 11:18; Josh. 7:13; 1Sam. 16:5; Joel 2:16

6 Num. 4:15

7 Josh. 1:5; 4:14; 1Chr. 29:25; 2Chr. 1:1

8 Josh. 3:3, 17

10 Ex. 33:2; Deut. 5:26; 7:1; 1Sam. 17:26; 2Kgs. 19:4; Ps. 44:2; Hos. 1:10; Matt. 16:16; 1Thess. 1:9

11 Josh. 3:13; Mic. 4:13; Zech. 4:14; 6:5

12 Josh. 4:2

13 Josh. 3:11, 15, 16; Ps. 78:13; 114:3

14 Acts 7:45

15 Josh. 3:13; 4:18; 5:10, 12; 1Chr. 12:15; Jer. 12:5; 49:19

16 Gen. 14:3; Num. 34:3; Deut. 3:17; 1Kgs. 4:12; 7:46

17 Ex. 14:29

1 Deut. 27:2; Josh. 3:17

2 Take you twelve men out of the people, out of every tribe a man,

3 And command ye them, saying, Take you hence out of the midst of Jordan, out of the place where the priests' feet stood firm, twelve stones, and ye shall carry them over with you, and leave them in the lodging place, where ye shall lodge this night.

4 Then Joshua called the twelve men, whom he had prepared of the children of Israel, out of every tribe a man:

5 And Joshua said unto them, Pass over before the ark of the LORD your God into the midst of Jordan, and take ye up every man of you a stone upon his shoulder, according unto the number of the tribes of the children of Israel:

6 That this may be a sign among you, *that* when your children ask *their fathers* in time to come, saying, What *mean* ye by these stones?

7 Then ye shall answer them, That the waters of Jordan were cut off before the ark of the covenant of the LORD; when it passed over Jordan, the waters of Jordan were cut off: and these stones shall be for a memorial unto the children of Israel for ever.

8 And the children of Israel did so as Joshua commanded, and took up twelve stones out of the midst of Jordan, as the LORD spake unto Joshua, according to the number of the tribes of the children of Israel, and carried them over with them unto the place where they lodged, and laid them down there.

9 And Joshua set up twelve stones in the midst of Jordan, in the place where the feet of the priests which bare the ark of the covenant stood: and they are there unto this day.

10 For the priests which bare the ark stood in the midst of Jordan, until every thing was finished that the LORD commanded Joshua to speak unto the people, according to all that Moses commanded Joshua: and the people hasted and passed over.

11 And it came to pass, when all the people were clean passed over, that the ark of the LORD passed over, and the priests, in the presence of the people.

12 And the children of Reuben, and the children of Gad, and half the tribe of Manasseh, passed over armed before the children of Israel, as Moses spake unto them:

13 About forty thousand prepared for war passed over before the LORD unto battle, to the plains of Jericho.

14 On that day the LORD magnified Joshua

in the sight of all Israel; and they feared him, as they feared Moses, all the days of his life.

15 And the LORD spake unto Joshua, saying,

16 Command the priests that bear the ark of the testimony, that they come up out of Jordan.

17 Joshua therefore commanded the priests, saying, Come ye up out of Jordan.

18 And it came to pass, when the priests that bare the ark of the covenant of the LORD were come up out of the midst of Jordan, *and* the soles of the priests' feet were lifted up unto the dry land, that the waters of Jordan returned unto their place, and flowed over all his banks, as *they did* before.

19 And the people came up out of Jordan on the tenth *day* of the first month, and encamped in Gilgal, in the east border of Jericho.

20 And those twelve stones, which they took out of Jordan, did Joshua pitch in Gilgal.

21 And he spake unto the children of Israel, saying, When your children shall ask their fathers in time to come, saying, What *mean* these stones?

22 Then ye shall let your children know, saying, Israel came over this Jordan on dry land.

23 For the LORD your God dried up the waters of Jordan from before you, until ye were passed over, as the LORD your God did to the Red sea, which he dried up from before us, until we were gone over:

24 That all the people of the earth might know the hand of the LORD, that it *is* mighty: that ye might fear the LORD your God for ever.

CHAPTER 5
Circumcision and Passover at Gilgal

1 And it came to pass, when all the kings of the Amorites, which *were* on the side of Jordan westward, and all the kings of the Canaanites, which *were* by the sea, heard that the LORD had dried up the waters of Jordan from before the children of Israel, until we were passed over, that their heart melted, neither was there spirit in them any more, because of the children of Israel.

2 At that time the LORD said unto Joshua, Make thee sharp knives, and circumcise again the children of Israel the second time.

3 And Joshua made him sharp knives, and circumcised the children of Israel at the hill of the foreskins.

4 And this *is* the cause why Joshua did cir-

---

2 Josh. 3:12

3 Josh. 3:13; 4:19, 20

6 Ex. 12:26; 13:14; Deut. 6:20; Josh. 4:21; Ps. 44:1; 78:3-6

7 Ex. 12:14; Num. 16:40; Josh. 3:13, 16

12 Num. 32:20, 27, 28

14 Josh. 3:7

16 Ex. 25:16, 22

18 Josh. 3:15

19 Josh. 5:9

20 Josh. 4:3

21 Josh. 4:6

22 Josh. 3:17

23 Ex. 14:21

24 Ex. 14:31; 15:16; Deut. 6:2; 1Kgs. 8:42, 43; 2Kgs. 19:19; 1Chr. 29:12; Ps. 89:7, 13; 106:8; Jer. 10:7

1 Ex. 15:14, 15; Num. 13:29; Josh. 2:9-11; 1Kgs. 10:5; Ps. 48:6; Ezek. 21:7

2 Ex. 4:25

4 Num. 14:29; 26:64, 65; Deut. 2:16

cumcise: All the people that came out of Egypt, *that were* males, *even* all the men of war, died in the wilderness by the way, after they came out of Egypt.

5 Now all the people that came out were circumcised: but all the people *that were* born in the wilderness by the way as they came forth out of Egypt, *them* they had not circumcised.

6 For the children of Israel walked forty years in the wilderness, till all the people *that were* men of war, which came out of Egypt, were consumed, because they obeyed not the voice of the LORD: unto whom the LORD sware that he would not shew them the land, which the LORD sware unto their fathers that he would give us, a land that floweth with milk and honey.

7 And their children, *whom* he raised up in their stead, them Joshua circumcised: for they were uncircumcised, because they had not circumcised them by the way.

8 And it came to pass, when they had done circumcising all the people, that they abode in their places in the camp, till they were whole.

9 And the LORD said unto Joshua, This day have I rolled away the reproach of Egypt from off you. Wherefore the name of the place is called Gilgal unto this day.

10 And the children of Israel encamped in Gilgal, and kept the passover on the fourteenth day of the month at even in the plains of Jericho.

11 And they did eat of the old corn of the land on the morrow after the passover, unleavened cakes, and parched *corn* in the selfsame day.

12 And the manna ceased on the morrow after they had eaten of the old corn of the land; neither had the children of Israel manna any more; but they did eat of the fruit of the land of Canaan that year.

13 And it came to pass, when Joshua was by Jericho, that he lifted up his eyes and looked, and, behold, there stood a man over against him with his sword drawn in his hand: and Joshua went unto him, and said unto him, *Art* thou for us, or for our adversaries?

14 And he said, Nay; but *as* captain of the host of the LORD am I now come. And

Joshua fell on his face to the earth, and did worship, and said unto him, What saith my lord unto his servant?

15 And the captain of the LORD's host said unto Joshua, Loose thy shoe from off thy foot; for the place whereon thou standest *is* holy. And Joshua did so.

CHAPTER 6
Jericho Falls

1 Now Jericho was straitly shut up because of the children of Israel: none went out, and none came in.

2 And the LORD said unto Joshua, See, I have given into thine hand Jericho, and the king thereof, *and* the mighty men of valour.

3 And ye shall compass the city, all *ye* men of war, *and* go round about the city once. Thus shalt thou do six days.

4 And seven priests shall bear before the ark seven trumpets of rams' horns: and the seventh day ye shall compass the city seven times, and the priests shall blow with the trumpets.

5 And it shall come to pass, that when they make a long blast with the ram's horn, *and* when ye hear the sound of the trumpet, all the people shall shout with a great shout; and the wall of the city shall fall down flat, and the people shall ascend up every man straight before him.

6 And Joshua the son of Nun called the priests, and said unto them, Take up the ark of the covenant, and let seven priests bear seven trumpets of rams' horns before the ark of the LORD.

7 And he said unto the people, Pass on, and compass the city, and let him that is armed pass on before the ark of the LORD.

8 And it came to pass, when Joshua had spoken unto the people, that the seven priests bearing the seven trumpets of rams' horns passed on before the LORD, and blew with the trumpets: and the ark of the covenant of the LORD followed them.

9 And the armed men went before the priests that blew with the trumpets, and the rereward came after the ark, *the priests* going on, and blowing with the trumpets.

10 And Joshua had commanded the people, saying, Ye shall not shout, nor make any noise with your voice, neither shall *any*

Cross-references (center column):

6 Ex. 3:8; Num. 14:23, 33; Deut. 1:3; 2:7, 14; Ps. 95:10, 11; Heb. 3:11

7 Num. 14:31; Deut. 1:39

8 Gen. 34:25

9 Gen. 34:14; Lev. 18:3; Josh. 4:19; 24:14; 1Sam. 14:6; Ezek. 20:7; 23:3, 8

10 Ex. 12:6; Num. 9:5

12 Ex. 16:35

13 Gen. 18:2; 32:24; Ex. 23:23; Num. 22:23; Zech. 1:8; Acts 1:10

14 Gen. 17:3; Ex. 23:20; Dan. 10:13, 21; 12:1; Rev. 12:7; 19:11, 14

15 Ex. 3:5; Acts 7:33

2 Deut. 7:24; Josh. 2:9, 24; 8:1

4 Num. 10:8; Judg. 7:16, 22

9 Num. 10:25

6:1–25 I have given into thine hand Jericho. This prophecy of supernatural deliverance of one of the most ancient cities of that day was miraculously fulfilled. Its ruins today show evidence it was destroyed the way God predicted—sparing only the family of Rahab, who believed in and trusted in God. As a testimony of God's grace to all nations, this gentile woman is included in the lineage of David and the Christ.

word proceed out of your mouth, until the day I bid you shout; then shall ye shout.

11 So the ark of the LORD compassed the city, going about *it* once: and they came into the camp, and lodged in the camp.

12 And Joshua rose early in the morning, and the priests took up the ark of the LORD.

13 And seven priests bearing seven trumpets of rams' horns before the ark of the LORD went on continually, and blew with the trumpets: and the armed men went before them; but the rereward came after the ark of the LORD, *the priests* going on, and blowing with the trumpets.

14 And the second day they compassed the city once, and returned into the camp: so they did six days.

15 And it came to pass on the seventh day, that they rose early about the dawning of the day, and compassed the city after the same manner seven times: only on that day they compassed the city seven times.

16 And it came to pass at the seventh time, when the priests blew with the trumpets, Joshua said unto the people, Shout; for the LORD hath given you the city.

17 And the city shall be accursed, *even* it, and all that *are* therein, to the LORD: only Rahab the harlot shall live, she and all that *are* with her in the house, because she hid the messengers that we sent.

18 And ye, in any wise keep *yourselves* from the accursed thing, lest ye make *yourselves* accursed, when ye take of the accursed thing, and make the camp of Israel a curse, and trouble it.

19 But all the silver, and gold, and vessels of brass and iron, *are* consecrated unto the LORD: they shall come into the treasury of the LORD.

20 So the people shouted when *the priests* blew with the trumpets: and it came to pass, when the people heard the sound of the trumpet, and the people shouted with a great shout, that the wall fell down flat, so that the people went up into the city, every man straight before him, and they took the city.

21 And they utterly destroyed all that *was* in the city, both man and woman, young and old, and ox, and sheep, and ass, with the edge of the sword.

22 But Joshua had said unto the two men that had spied out the country, Go into the harlot's house, and bring out thence the

woman, and all that she hath, as ye sware unto her.

23 And the young men that were spies went in, and brought out Rahab, and her father, and her mother, and her brethren, and all that she had; and they brought out all her kindred, and left them without the camp of Israel.

24 And they burnt the city with fire, and all that *was* therein: only the silver, and the gold, and the vessels of brass and of iron, they put into the treasury of the house of the LORD.

25 And Joshua saved Rahab the harlot alive, and her father's household, and all that she had; and she dwelleth in Israel *even* unto this day; because she hid the messengers, which Joshua sent to spy out Jericho.

26 And Joshua adjured *them* at that time, saying, Cursed *be* the man before the LORD, that riseth up and buildeth this city Jericho: he shall lay the foundation thereof in his firstborn, and in his youngest *son* shall he set up the gates of it.

27 So the LORD was with Joshua; and his fame was *noised* throughout all the country.

CHAPTER 7
Achan's Sin

1 But the children of Israel committed a trespass in the accursed thing: for Achan, the son of Carmi, the son of Zabdi, the son of Zerah, of the tribe of Judah, took of the accursed thing: and the anger of the LORD was kindled against the children of Israel.

2 And Joshua sent men from Jericho to Ai, which *is* beside Beth-aven, on the east side of Beth-el, and spake unto them, saying, Go up and view the country. And the men went up and viewed Ai.

3 And they returned to Joshua, and said unto him, Let not all the people go up; but let about two or three thousand men go up and smite Ai; *and* make not all the people to labour thither; for they *are but* few.

4 So there went up thither of the people about three thousand men: and they fled before the men of Ai.

5 And the men of Ai smote of them about thirty and six men: for they chased them *from* before the gate *even* unto Shebarim, and smote them in the going down: wherefore the hearts of the people melted, and became as water.

12 Deut. 31:25

17 Lev. 27:28; Josh. 2:4; Mic. 4:13

18 Deut. 7:26; 13:17; Josh. 7:1, 11, 12, 25; 1Kgs. 18:17, 18; Jon. 1:12

20 Josh. 6:5; Heb. 11:30

21 Deut. 7:2

22 Josh. 2:14; Heb. 11:31

23 Josh. 2:13

24 Josh. 6:19

25 Matt. 1:5

26 1Kgs. 16:34

27 Deut. 1:5; 9:1, 3

1 Josh. 22:20; 1Chr. 2:7

4 Lev. 26:17; Deut. 28:25

5 Lev. 26:36; Josh. 2:9, 11; Ps. 22:14

6:26 Cursed be the man . . . that . . . buildeth this city. Even the warning of the death of his "firstborn, and . . . youngest" was fulfilled in Ahab's time (1 Kgs. 16:34).

6 And Joshua rent his clothes, and fell to the earth upon his face before the ark of the LORD until the eventide, he and the elders of Israel, and put dust upon their heads.
7 And Joshua said, Alas, O Lord GOD, wherefore hast thou at all brought this people over Jordan, to deliver us into the hand of the Amorites, to destroy us? would to God we had been content, and dwelt on the other side Jordan!
8 O Lord, what shall I say, when Israel turneth their backs before their enemies!
9 For the Canaanites and all the inhabitants of the land shall hear *of it*, and shall environ us round, and cut off our name from the earth: and what wilt thou do unto thy great name?
10 And the LORD said unto Joshua, Get thee up; wherefore liest thou thus upon thy face?
11 Israel hath sinned, and they have also transgressed my covenant which I commanded them: for they have even taken of the accursed thing, and have also stolen, and dissembled also, and they have put *it* even among their own stuff.
12 Therefore the children of Israel could not stand before their enemies, *but* turned *their* backs before their enemies, because they were accursed: neither will I be with you any more, except ye destroy the accursed from among you.
13 Up, sanctify the people, and say, Sanctify yourselves against to morrow: for thus saith the Lord God of Israel, *There is* an accursed thing in the midst of thee, O Israel: thou canst not stand before thine enemies, until ye take away the accursed thing from among you.
14 In the morning therefore ye shall be brought according to your tribes: and it shall be, *that* the tribe which the LORD taketh shall come according to the families *thereof*; and the family which the LORD shall take shall come by households; and the household which the LORD shall take shall come man by man.
15 And it shall be, *that* he that is taken with the accursed thing shall be burnt with fire, he and all that he hath: because he hath transgressed the covenant of the LORD, and because he hath wrought folly in Israel.
16 So Joshua rose up early in the morning, and brought Israel by their tribes; and the tribe of Judah was taken:

17 And he brought the family of Judah; and he took the family of the Zarhites: and he brought the family of the Zarhites man by man; and Zabdi was taken:
18 And he brought his household man by man; and Achan, the son of Carmi, the son of Zabdi, the son of Zerah, of the tribe of Judah, was taken.
19 And Joshua said unto Achan, My son, give, I pray thee, glory to the LORD God of Israel, and make confession unto him; and tell me now what thou hast done; hide *it* not from me.
20 And Achan answered Joshua, and said, Indeed I have sinned against the LORD God of Israel, and thus and thus have I done:
21 When I saw among the spoils a goodly Babylonish garment, and two hundred shekels of silver, and a wedge of gold of fifty shekels weight, then I coveted them, and took them; and, behold, they *are* hid in the earth in the midst of my tent, and the silver under it.
22 So Joshua sent messengers, and they ran unto the tent; and, behold, *it was* hid in his tent, and the silver under it.
23 And they took them out of the midst of the tent, and brought them unto Joshua, and unto all the children of Israel, and laid them out before the LORD.
24 And Joshua, and all Israel with him, took Achan the son of Zerah, and the silver, and the garment, and the wedge of gold, and his sons, and his daughters, and his oxen, and his asses, and his sheep, and his tent, and all that he had: and they brought them unto the valley of Achor.
25 And Joshua said, Why hast thou troubled us? the LORD shall trouble thee this day. And all Israel stoned him with stones, and burned them with fire, after they had stoned them with stones.
26 And they raised over him a great heap of stones unto this day. So the LORD turned from the fierceness of his anger. Wherefore the name of that place was called, The valley of Achor, unto this day.

CHAPTER 8
Ai Falls

1 And the LORD said unto Joshua, Fear not, neither be thou dismayed: take all the people of war with thee, and arise, go up to Ai: see, I have given into thy hand the king of

Cross References

6 Gen. 37:29, 34; 1Sam. 4:12; 2Sam. 1:2; 13:19; Neh. 9:1; Job 2:12
7 Ex. 5:22; 2Kgs. 3:10
9 Ex. 32:12; Num. 14:13; Ps. 83:4
11 Josh. 6:17, 18; 7:1; Acts 5:1, 2
12 Num. 14:45; Deut. 7:26; Josh. 6:18; Judg. 2:14
13 Ex. 19:10; Josh. 3:5
14 Prov. 16:33
15 Gen. 34:7; Josh. 7:11; Judg. 20:6; 1Sam. 14:38, 39
18 1Sam. 14:42
19 Num. 5:6, 7; 1Sam. 6:5; 14:43; 2Chr. 30:22; Ps. 51:3; Jer. 13:16; Dan. 9:4; John 9:24
24 Josh. 7:26; 15:7
25 Deut. 17:5; Josh. 6:18; 1Chr. 2:7; Gal. 5:12
26 Deut. 8:29; 13:17; Josh. 7:24; 2Sam. 18:17; 21:14; Isa. 65:10; Lam. 3:53; Hos. 2:15
1 Deut. 1:21; 7:18; 31:8; Josh. 1:9; 6:2

8:1–29 Even after an abortive attempt to take the city of Ai, because of sin in the camp, God promised how He would deliver the city into their hand—and He did, exactly as He promised.

Ai, and his people, and his city, and his land:

2 And thou shalt do to Ai and her king as thou didst unto Jericho and her king: only the spoil thereof, and the cattle thereof, shall ye take for a prey unto yourselves: lay thee an ambush for the city behind it.

3 So Joshua arose, and all the people of war, to go up against Ai: and Joshua chose out thirty thousand mighty men of valour, and sent them away by night.

4 And he commanded them, saying, Behold, ye shall lie in wait against the city, *even* behind the city: go not very far from the city, but be ye all ready:

5 And I, and all the people that *are* with me, will approach unto the city: and it shall come to pass, when they come out against us, as at the first, that we will flee before them,

6 (For they will come out after us) till we have drawn them from the city; for they will say, They flee before us, as at the first: therefore we will flee before them.

7 Then ye shall rise up from the ambush, and seize upon the city: for the Lord your God will deliver it into your hand.

8 And it shall be, when ye have taken the city, *that* ye shall set the city on fire: according to the commandment of the Lord shall ye do. See, I have commanded you.

9 Joshua therefore sent them forth: and they went to lie in ambush, and abode between Beth-el and Ai, on the west side of Ai: but Joshua lodged that night among the people.

10 And Joshua rose up early in the morning, and numbered the people, and went up, he and the elders of Israel, before the people to Ai.

11 And all the people, *even the people* of war that *were* with him, went up, and drew nigh, and came before the city, and pitched on the north side of Ai: now *there was* a valley between them and Ai.

12 And he took about five thousand men, and set them to lie in ambush between Beth-el and Ai, on the west side of the city.

13 And when they had set the people, *even* all the host that *was* on the north of the city, and their liers in wait on the west of the city, Joshua went that night into the midst of the valley.

14 And it came to pass, when the king of Ai saw *it*, that they hasted and rose up early, and the men of the city went out against Israel to battle, he and all his people, at a time appointed, before the plain; but he wist not that *there were* liers in ambush against him behind the city.

15 And Joshua and all Israel made as if they were beaten before them, and fled by the way of the wilderness.

16 And all the people that *were* in Ai were called together to pursue after them: and they pursued after Joshua, and were drawn away from the city.

17 And there was not a man left in Ai or Beth-el, that went not out after Israel: and they left the city open, and pursued after Israel.

18 And the Lord said unto Joshua, Stretch out the spear that *is* in thy hand toward Ai; for I will give it into thine hand. And Joshua stretched out the spear that *he had* in his hand toward the city.

19 And the ambush arose quickly out of their place, and they ran as soon as he had stretched out his hand: and they entered into the city, and took it, and hasted and set the city on fire.

20 And when the men of Ai looked behind them, they saw, and, behold, the smoke of the city ascended up to heaven, and they had no power to flee this way or that way: and the people that fled to the wilderness turned back upon the pursuers.

21 And when Joshua and all Israel saw that the ambush had taken the city, and that the smoke of the city ascended, then they turned again, and slew the men of Ai.

22 And the other issued out of the city against them; so they were in the midst of Israel, some on this side, and some on that side: and they smote them, so that they let none of them remain or escape.

23 And the king of Ai they took alive, and brought him to Joshua.

24 And it came to pass, when Israel had made an end of slaying all the inhabitants of Ai in the field, in the wilderness wherein they chased them, and when they were all fallen on the edge of the sword, until they were consumed, that all the Israelites returned unto Ai, and smote it with the edge of the sword.

25 And *so* it was, *that* all that fell that day, both of men and women, *were* twelve thousand, *even* all the men of Ai.

26 For Joshua drew not his hand back, wherewith he stretched out the spear, until he had utterly destroyed all the inhabitants of Ai.

27 Only the cattle and the spoil of that city Israel took for a prey unto themselves, according unto the word of the Lord which he commanded Joshua.

28 And Joshua burnt Ai, and made it an

Cross references:

2 Deut. 20:14; Josh. 6:21

4 Judg. 20:29

5 Judg. 20:32

8 2Sam. 13:28

11 Josh. 8:5

13 Josh. 8:4

14 Judg. 20:34; Eccl. 9:12

15 Judg. 20:36

22 Deut. 7:2

27 Num. 31:22, 26; Josh. 8:2

28 Deut. 13:16

heap for ever, *even* a desolation unto this day.

29 And the king of Ai he hanged on a tree until eventide: and as soon as the sun was down, Joshua commanded that they should take his carcase down from the tree, and cast it at the entering of the gate of the city, and raise thereon a great heap of stones, *that remaineth* unto this day.

The Ceremony at Mount Ebal

30 Then Joshua built an altar unto the LORD God of Israel in mount Ebal,
31 As Moses the servant of the Lord commanded the children of Israel, as it is written in the book of the law of Moses, an altar of whole stones, over which no man hath lift up *any* iron: and they offered thereon burnt offerings unto the LORD, and sacrificed peace offerings.
32 And he wrote there upon the stones a copy of the law of Moses, which he wrote in the presence of the children of Israel.
33 And all Israel, and their elders, and officers, and their judges, stood on this side the ark and on that side before the priests the Levites, which bare the ark of the covenant of the LORD, as well the stranger, as he that was born among them; half of them over against mount Gerizim, and half of them over against mount Ebal; as Moses the servant of the Lord had commanded before, that they should bless the people of Israel.
34 And afterward he read all the words of the law, the blessings and cursings, according to all that is written in the book of the law.
35 There was not a word of all that Moses commanded, which Joshua read not before all the congregation of Israel, with the women, and the little ones, and the strangers that were conversant among them.

CHAPTER 9
The Gibeonites Deceive Joshua

1 And it came to pass, when all the kings which *were* on this side Jordan, in the hills, and in the valleys, and in all the coasts of the great sea over against Lebanon, the Hittite, and the Amorite, the Canaanite, the Perizzite, the Hivite, and the Jebusite, heard *thereof*;
2 That they gathered themselves together, to fight with Joshua and with Israel, with one accord.
3 And when the inhabitants of Gibeon heard what Joshua had done unto Jericho and to Ai,

4 They did work wilily, and went and made as if they had been ambassadors, and took old sacks upon their asses, and wine bottles, old, and rent, and bound up;
5 And old shoes and clouted upon their feet, and old garments upon them; and all the bread of their provision was dry *and* mouldy.
6 And they went to Joshua unto the camp at Gilgal, and said unto him, and to the men of Israel, We be come from a far country: now therefore make ye a league with us.
7 And the men of Israel said unto the Hivites, Peradventure ye dwell among us; and how shall we make a league with you?
8 And they said unto Joshua, We *are* thy servants. And Joshua said unto them, Who *are* ye? and from whence come ye?
9 And they said unto him, From a very far country thy servants are come because of the name of the LORD thy God: for we have heard the fame of him, and all that he did in Egypt,
10 And all that he did to the two kings of the Amorites, that *were* beyond Jordan, to Sihon king of Heshbon, and to Og king of Bashan, which *was* at Ashtaroth.
11 Wherefore our elders and all the inhabitants of our country spake to us, saying, Take victuals with you for the journey, and go to meet them, and say unto them, We *are* your servants: therefore now make ye a league with us.
12 This our bread we took hot *for* our provision out of our houses on the day we came forth to go unto you; but now, behold, it is dry, and it is mouldy:
13 And these bottles of wine, which we filled, *were* new; and, behold, they be rent: and these our garments and our shoes are become old by reason of the very long journey.
14 And the men took of their victuals, and asked not *counsel* at the mouth of the LORD.
15 And Joshua made peace with them, and made a league with them, to let them live: and the princes of the congregation sware unto them.
16 And it came to pass at the end of three days after they had made a league with them, that they heard that they *were* their neighbours, and *that* they dwelt among them.
17 And the children of Israel journeyed, and came unto their cities on the third day. Now their cities *were* Gibeon, and Chephirah, and Beeroth, and Kirjath-jearim.
18 And the children of Israel smote them

Cross References

29 Deut. 21:23; Josh. 7:26; 10:26, 27; Ps. 107:40; 110:5
30 Deut. 27:4, 5
31 Ex. 20:24, 25; Deut. 27:5, 6
32 Deut. 27:2, 8
33 Deut. 11:29; 27:12; 31:9, 12, 25
34 Deut. 28:2, 15, 45; 29:20, 21; 30:19; 31:11; Neh. 8:3
35 Deut. 31:12; Josh. 8:33
1 Ex. 3:17; 23:23; Num. 34:6
2 Ps. 83:3, 5
3 Josh. 6:27; 10:2; 2Sam. 21:1, 2
6 Josh. 5:10
7 Ex. 23:32; Deut. 7:2; 20:16; Josh. 11:19; Judg. 2:2
8 Deut. 20:11; 2Kgs. 10:5
9 Ex. 15:14; Deut. 20:15; Josh. 2:10
10 Num. 21:24, 33
14 Num. 27:21; Judg. 1:1; 1Sam. 22:10; 23:10, 11; 30:8; 2Sam. 2:1; 5:19; Isa. 30:1, 2
15 Josh. 11:19; 2Sam. 21:2
17 Josh. 18:25, 26, 28; Ezra 2:25
18 Ps. 15:4; Eccl. 5:2

not, because the princes of the congregation had sworn unto them by the LORD God of Israel. And all the congregation murmured against the princes.

19 But all the princes said unto all the congregation, We have sworn unto them by the LORD God of Israel: now therefore we may not touch them.

20 This we will do to them; we will even let them live, lest wrath be upon us, because of the oath which we sware unto them.

21 And the princes said unto them, Let them live; but let them be hewers of wood and drawers of water unto all the congregation; as the princes had promised them.

22 And Joshua called for them, and he spake unto them, saying, Wherefore have ye beguiled us, saying, We *are* very far from you; when ye dwell among us?

23 Now therefore ye *are* cursed, and there shall none of you be freed from being bondmen, and hewers of wood and drawers of water for the house of my God.

24 And they answered Joshua, and said, Because it was certainly told thy servants, how that the LORD thy God commanded his servant Moses to give you all the land, and to destroy all the inhabitants of the land from before you, therefore we were sore afraid of our lives because of you, and have done this thing.

25 And now, behold, we *are* in thine hand: as it seemeth good and right unto thee to do unto us, do.

26 And so did he unto them, and delivered them out of the hand of the children of Israel, that they slew them not.

27 And Joshua made them that day hewers of wood and drawers of water for the congregation, and for the altar of the LORD, even unto this day, in the place which he should choose.

CHAPTER 10
The Amorites Are Defeated

1 Now it came to pass, when Adoni-zedek king of Jerusalem had heard how Joshua had taken Ai, and had utterly destroyed it; as he had done to Jericho and her king, so he had done to Ai and her king; and how the inhabitants of Gibeon had made peace with Israel, and were among them;

2 That they feared greatly, because Gibeon *was* a great city, as one of the royal cities, and because it *was* greater than Ai, and all the men thereof *were* mighty.

3 Wherefore Adoni-zedek king of Jerusalem sent unto Hoham king of Hebron,

and unto Piram king of Jarmuth, and unto Japhia king of Lachish, and unto Debir king of Eglon, saying,

4 Come up unto me, and help me, that we may smite Gibeon: for it hath made peace with Joshua and with the children of Israel.

5 Therefore the five kings of the Amorites, the king of Jerusalem, the king of Hebron, the king of Jarmuth, the king of Lachish, the king of Eglon, gathered themselves together, and went up, they and all their hosts, and encamped before Gibeon, and made war against it.

6 And the men of Gibeon sent unto Joshua to the camp to Gilgal, saying, Slack not thy hand from thy servants; come up to us quickly, and save us, and help us: for all the kings of the Amorites that dwell in the mountains are gathered together against us.

7 So Joshua ascended from Gilgal, he, and all the people of war with him, and all the mighty men of valour.

8 And the LORD said unto Joshua, Fear them not: for I have delivered them into thine hand; there shall not a man of them stand before thee.

9 Joshua therefore came unto them suddenly, *and* went up from Gilgal all night.

10 And the LORD discomfited them before Israel, and slew them with a great slaughter at Gibeon, and chased them along the way that goeth up to Beth-horon, and smote them to Azekah, and unto Makkedah.

11 And it came to pass, as they fled from before Israel, *and* were in the going down to Beth-horon, that the LORD cast down great stones from heaven upon them unto Azekah, and they died: *they were* more which died with hailstones than *they* whom the children of Israel slew with the sword.

12 Then spake Joshua to the LORD in the day when the LORD delivered up the Amorites before the children of Israel, and he said in the sight of Israel, Sun, stand thou still upon Gibeon; and thou, Moon, in the valley of Ajalon.

13 And the sun stood still, and the moon stayed, until the people had avenged themselves upon their enemies. *Is* not this written in the book of Jasher? So the sun stood still in the midst of heaven, and hasted not to go down about a whole day.

14 And there was no day like that before it or after it, that the LORD hearkened unto the voice of a man: for the LORD fought for Israel.

15 And Joshua returned, and all Israel with him, unto the camp to Gilgal.

20 2Sam. 21:1, 2, 6; Ezek. 17:13, 15, 18, 19; Zech. 5:3, 4; Mal. 3:5

21 Deut. 29:11; Josh. 9:15

22 Josh. 9:6, 9, 16

23 Gen. 9:25; Josh. 9:21, 27

24 Ex. 15:14; 23:32; Deut. 7:1, 2

25 Gen. 16:6

27 Deut. 12:5; Josh. 9:21, 23; 1Chr. 9:2; Ezra 8:20

1 Josh. 6:21; 8:22, 26, 28; 9:15

2 Ex. 15:14-16; Deut. 11:25

4 Josh. 9:15; 10:1

5 Josh. 9:2

6 Josh. 5:10; 9:6

7 Josh. 8:1

8 Josh. 1:5; 11:6; Judg. 4:14

10 Josh. 15:35; Josh. 16:3, 5; Judg. 4:15; 1Sam. 7:10, 12; Ps. 18:14; Isa. 28:21

11 Ps. 18:13, 14; 77:17; Isa. 30:30; Rev. 16:21

12 Judg. 12:12; Isa. 28:21; Hab. 3:11

13 2Sam. 1:18

14 Deut. 1:30; Josh. 10:42; 23:3; Isa. 38:8

15 Josh. 10:43

16 But these five kings fled, and hid themselves in a cave at Makkedah.

17 And it was told Joshua, saying, The five kings are found hid in a cave at Makkedah.

18 And Joshua said, Roll great stones upon the mouth of the cave, and set men by it for to keep them:

19 And stay ye not, *but* pursue after your enemies, and smite the hindmost of them; suffer them not to enter into their cities: for the LORD your God hath delivered them into your hand.

20 And it came to pass, when Joshua and the children of Israel had made an end of slaying them with a very great slaughter, till they were consumed, that the rest *which* remained of them entered into fenced cities.

21 And all the people returned to the camp to Joshua at Makkedah in peace: none moved his tongue against any of the children of Israel.

22 Then said Joshua, Open the mouth of the cave, and bring out those five kings unto me out of the cave.

23 And they did so, and brought forth those five kings unto him out of the cave, the king of Jerusalem, the king of Hebron, the king of Jarmuth, the king of Lachish, *and* the king of Eglon.

24 And it came to pass, when they brought out those kings unto Joshua, that Joshua called for all the men of Israel, and said unto the captains of the men of war which went with him, Come near, put your feet upon the necks of these kings. And they came near, and put their feet upon the necks of them.

25 And Joshua said unto them, Fear not, nor be dismayed, be strong and of good courage: for thus shall the LORD do to all your enemies against whom ye fight.

26 And afterward Joshua smote them, and slew them, and hanged them on five trees: and they were hanging upon the trees until the evening.

27 And it came to pass at the time of the going down of the sun, *that* Joshua commanded, and they took them down off the trees, and cast them into the cave wherein they had been hid, and laid great stones in the cave's mouth, *which remain* until this very day.

Joshua Smites the Southern Cities

28 And that day Joshua took Makkedah, and smote it with the edge of the sword, and the king thereof he utterly destroyed them, and all the souls that *were* therein; he

let none remain: and he did to the king of Makkedah as he did unto the king of Jericho.

29 Then Joshua passed from Makkedah, and all Israel with him, unto Libnah, and fought against Libnah:

30 And the LORD delivered it also, and the king thereof, into the hand of Israel; and he smote it with the edge of the sword, and all the souls that *were* therein; he let none remain in it; but did unto the king thereof as he did unto the king of Jericho.

31 And Joshua passed from Libnah, and all Israel with him, unto Lachish, and encamped against it, and fought against it:

32 And the LORD delivered Lachish into the hand of Israel, which took it on the second day, and smote it with the edge of the sword, and all the souls that *were* therein, according to all that he had done to Libnah.

33 Then Horam king of Gezer came up to help Lachish; and Joshua smote him and his people, until he had left him none remaining.

34 And from Lachish Joshua passed unto Eglon, and all Israel with him; and they encamped against it, and fought against it:

35 And they took it on that day, and smote it with the edge of the sword, and all the souls that *were* therein he utterly destroyed that day, according to all that he had done to Lachish.

36 And Joshua went up from Eglon, and all Israel with him, unto Hebron; and they fought against it:

37 And they took it, and smote it with the edge of the sword, and the king thereof, and all the cities thereof, and all the souls that *were* therein; he left none remaining, according to all that he had done to Eglon; but destroyed it utterly, and all the souls that *were* therein.

38 And Joshua returned, and all Israel with him, to Debir; and fought against it:

39 And he took it, and the king thereof, and all the cities thereof; and they smote them with the edge of the sword, and utterly destroyed all the souls that *were* therein; he left none remaining: as he had done to Hebron, so he did to Debir, and to the king thereof; as he had done also to Libnah, and to her king.

40 So Joshua smote all the country of the hills, and of the south, and of the vale, and of the springs, and all their kings: he left none remaining, but utterly destroyed all that breathed, as the LORD God of Israel commanded.

---

21 Ex. 11:7

24 Ps. 107:40; 110:5; 149:8, 9; Isa. 26:5, 6; Mal. 4:3

25 Deut. 3:21; 7:19; 31:6, 8; Josh. 1:9

26 Josh. 8:29

27 Deut. 21:23; Josh. 8:29

28 Josh. 6:21

36 Josh. 14:13; 15:13; Judg. 1:10

38 Josh. 15:15; Judg. 1:11

40 Deut. 20:16, 17

41 And Joshua smote them from Kadesh-barnea even unto Gaza, and all the country of Goshen, even unto Gibeon.

42 And all these kings and their land did Joshua take at one time, because the LORD God of Israel fought for Israel.

43 And Joshua returned, and all Israel with him, unto the camp to Gilgal.

CHAPTER 11
Northern Kings Are Defeated

1 And it came to pass, when Jabin king of Hazor had heard *those things*, that he sent to Jobab king of Madon, and to the king of Shimron, and to the king of Achshaph,

2 And to the kings that *were* on the north of the mountains, and of the plains south of Chinneroth, and in the valley, and in the borders of Dor on the west,

3 *And to* the Canaanite on the east and on the west, and *to* the Amorite, and the Hittite, and the Perizzite, and the Jebusite in the mountains, and *to* the Hivite under Hermon in the land of Mizpeh.

4 And they went out, they and all their hosts with them, much people, even as the sand that *is* upon the sea shore in multitude, with horses and chariots very many.

5 And when all these kings were met together, they came and pitched together at the waters of Merom, to fight against Israel.

6 And the LORD said unto Joshua, Be not afraid because of them: for to morrow about this time will I deliver them up all slain before Israel: thou shalt hough their horses, and burn their chariots with fire.

7 So Joshua came, and all the people of war with him, against them by the waters of Merom suddenly; and they fell upon them.

8 And the LORD delivered them into the hand of Israel, who smote them, and chased them unto great Zidon, and unto Misrephoth-maim, and unto the valley of Mizpeh eastward; and they smote them, until they left them none remaining.

9 And Joshua did unto them as the LORD bade him: he houghed their horses, and burnt their chariots with fire.

10 And Joshua at that time turned back, and took Hazor, and smote the king thereof with the sword: for Hazor beforetime was the head of all those kingdoms.

11 And they smote all the souls that *were* therein with the edge of the sword, utterly

destroying *them*: there was not any left to breathe: and he burnt Hazor with fire.

12 And all the cities of those kings, and all the kings of them, did Joshua take, and smote them with the edge of the sword, *and* he utterly destroyed them, as Moses the servant of the LORD commanded.

13 But *as for* the cities that stood still in their strength, Israel burned none of them, save Hazor only; *that* did Joshua burn.

14 And all the spoil of these cities, and the cattle, the children of Israel took for a prey unto themselves; but every man they smote with the edge of the sword, until they had destroyed them, neither left they any to breathe.

15 As the LORD commanded Moses his servant, so did Moses command Joshua, and so did Joshua; he left nothing undone of all that the LORD commanded Moses.

Summary of Joshua's Victories

16 So Joshua took all that land, the hills, and all the south country, and all the land of Goshen, and the valley, and the plain, and the mountain of Israel, and the valley of the same;

17 *Even* from the mount Halak, that goeth up to Seir, even unto Baal-gad in the valley of Lebanon under mount Hermon: and all their kings he took, and smote them, and slew them.

18 Joshua made war a long time with all those kings.

19 There was not a city that made peace with the children of Israel, save the Hivites the inhabitants of Gibeon: all *other* they took in battle.

20 For it was of the LORD to harden their hearts, that they should come against Israel in battle, that he might destroy them utterly, *and* that they might have no favour, but that he might destroy them, as the LORD commanded Moses.

21 And at that time came Joshua, and cut off the Anakims from the mountains, from Hebron, from Debir, from Anab, and from all the mountains of Judah, and from all the mountains of Israel: Joshua destroyed them utterly with their cities.

22 There was none of the Anakims left in the land of the children of Israel: only in Gaza, in Gath, and in Ashdod, there remained.

23 So Joshua took the whole land, accord-

Cross-references (center column)

41 Gen. 10:19; Josh. 11:16

42 Josh. 10:14

1 Josh. 10:3; 19:15

2 Num. 34:11; Josh. 17:11; Judg. 1:27; 1Kgs. 4:11

3 Gen. 31:49; Josh. 13:11; Judg. 3:3

4 Gen. 22:17; 32:12; Judg. 7:12; 1Sam. 13:5

6 Josh. 10:8; 2Sam. 8:4

8 Josh. 13:6

9 Josh. 11:6

12 Num. 33:52; Deut. 7:2; 20:16, 17

15 Ex. 34:11, 12; Deut. 7:2; Josh. 1:7

16 Josh. 10:41; 12:8

17 Deut. 7:24; Josh. 12:7

19 Josh. 9:3, 7

20 Deut. 2:30; 20:16, 17; Judg. 14:4; 1Sam. 2:25; 1Kgs. 12:15; Rom. 9:18

21 Num. 13:22, 33; Deut. 1:28; Josh. 15:13, 14

22 Josh. 15:46; 1Sam. 17:4

23 Num. 26:53; 34:2; Josh. 11:18; 14; 15; 16; 17; 18; 19; 21:44; 22:4; 23:1

11:11–23 and the land rested from war. Joshua, after approximately fifteen years of war, rehearsed how God had faithfully defeated all their enemies and delivered the land to Israel, as He promised. Joshua and Israel were

ing to all that the LORD said unto Moses; and Joshua gave it for an inheritance unto Israel according to their divisions by their tribes. And the land rested from war.

CHAPTER 12
The Kings Defeated under Moses

1 Now these *are* the kings of the land, which the children of Israel smote, and possessed their land on the other side Jordan toward the rising of the sun, from the river Arnon unto mount Hermon, and all the plain on the east:
2 Sihon king of the Amorites, who dwelt in Heshbon, *and* ruled from Aroer, which *is* upon the bank of the river Arnon, and from the middle of the river, and from half Gilead, even unto the river Jabbok, *which is the* border of the children of Ammon;
3 And from the plain to the sea of Chinneroth on the east, and unto the sea of the plain, *even* the salt sea on the east, the way to Beth-jeshimoth; and from the south, under Ashdoth-pisgah:
4 And the coast of Og king of Bashan, *which was* of the remnant of the giants, that dwelt at Ashtaroth and at Edrei,
5 And reigned in mount Hermon, and in Salcah, and in all Bashan, unto the border of the Geshurites and the Maachathites, and half Gilead, the border of Sihon king of Heshbon.
6 Them did Moses the servant of the LORD and the children of Israel smite: and Moses the servant of the LORD gave it *for* a possession unto the Reubenites, and the Gadites, and the half tribe of Manasseh.

The Kings Defeated under Joshua

7 And these *are* the kings of the country which Joshua and the children of Israel smote on this side Jordan on the west, from Baal-gad in the valley of Lebanon even unto the mount Halak, that goeth up to Seir; which Joshua gave unto the tribes of Israel *for* a possession according to their divisions;
8 In the mountains, and in the valleys, and in the plains, and in the springs, and in the wilderness, and in the south country; the Hittites, the Amorites, and the Canaanites, the Perizzites, the Hivites, and the Jebusites:
9 The king of Jericho, one; the king of Ai, which *is* beside Beth-el, one;

10 The king of Jerusalem, one; the king of Hebron, one;
11 The king of Jarmuth, one; the king of Lachish, one;
12 The king of Eglon, one; the king of Gezer, one;
13 The king of Debir, one; the king of Geder, one;
14 The king of Hormah, one; the king of Arad, one;
15 The king of Libnah, one; the king of Adullam, one;
16 The king of Makkedah, one; the king of Beth-el, one;
17 The king of Tappuah, one; the king of Hepher, one;
18 The king of Aphek, one; the king of Lasharon, one;
19 The king of Madon, one; the king of Hazor, one;
20 The king of Shimron-meron, one; the king of Achshaph, one;
21 The king of Taanach, one; the king of Megiddo, one;
22 The king of Kedesh, one; the king of Jokneam of Carmel, one;
23 The king of Dor in the coast of Dor, one; the king of the nations of Gilgal, one;
24 The king of Tirzah, one: all the kings thirty and one.

CHAPTER 13
The Unconquered Territory

1 Now Joshua was old *and* stricken in years; and the LORD said unto him, Thou art old *and* stricken in years, and there remaineth yet very much land to be possessed.
2 This *is* the land that yet remaineth: all the borders of the Philistines, and all Geshuri,
3 From Sihor, which *is* before Egypt, even unto the borders of Ekron northward, *which* is counted to the Canaanite: five lords of the Philistines; the Gazathites, and the Ashdothites, the Eshkalonites, the Gittites, and the Ekronites; also the Avites:
4 From the south, all the land of the Canaanites, and Mearah that *is* beside the Sidonians, unto Aphek, to the borders of the Amorites:
5 And the land of the Giblites, and all Lebanon, toward the sunrising, from Baal-gad

Cross References (center column)

2 Num. 21:24; Deut. 2:33, 36
3 Deut. 3:17; 4:49
4 Num. 21:35; Deut. 1:4; Josh. 13:12
6 Num. 21:24, 33; 32:29, 33; Deut. 3:11, 12; Josh. 13:8
7 Gen. 14:6; 32:3; Deut. 2:1, 4; Josh. 11:17, 23
8 Ex. 3:8; 23:23; Josh. 9:1; 10:40; 11:16
9 Josh. 6:2; 8:29
10 Josh. 10:23
12 Josh. 10:33
13 Josh. 10:38
15 Josh. 10:29
16 Josh. 8:17; 10:28; Judg. 1:22
17 1Kgs. 4:10
19 Josh. 11:10
20 Josh. 11:1; 19:15
22 Josh. 19:37
23 Gen. 14:1, 2; Josh. 11:2; Isa. 9:1
1 Josh. 14:10; 23:1
2 Judg. 3:1
3 Deut. 2:23; Judg. 3:3; 1Sam. 6:4, 16; Jer. 2:18; Zeph. 2:5
4 Josh. 19:30; Judg. 1:34
5 Josh. 12:7; 1Kgs. 5:18; Ps. 83:7; Ezek. 27:9

---

victorious because they obeyed the Lord, providing more than ample evidence that He would do so in the future. Unfortunately for the children of Israel, they did not obey Him, incurring the wrath of God instead of His blessing, just as He predicted.

under mount Hermon unto the entering into Hamath.

6 All the inhabitants of the hill country from Lebanon unto Misrephoth-maim, *and* all the Sidonians, them will I drive out from before the children of Israel: only divide thou it by lot unto the Israelites for an inheritance, as I have commanded thee.

Division of the Land East of the Jordan

7 Now therefore divide this land for an inheritance unto the nine tribes, and the half tribe of Manasseh,

8 With whom the Reubenites and the Gadites have received their inheritance, which Moses gave them, beyond Jordan eastward, *even* as Moses the servant of the LORD gave them;

9 From Aroer, that *is* upon the bank of the river Arnon, and the city that *is* in the midst of the river, and all the plain of Medeba unto Dibon;

10 And all the cities of Sihon king of the Amorites, which reigned in Heshbon, unto the border of the children of Ammon;

11 And Gilead, and the border of the Geshurites and Maachathites, and all mount Hermon, and all Bashan unto Salcah;

12 All the kingdom of Og in Bashan, which reigned in Ashtaroth and in Edrei, who remained of the remnant of the giants: for these did Moses smite, and cast them out.

13 Nevertheless the children of Israel expelled not the Geshurites, nor the Maachathites: but the Geshurites and Maachathites dwell among the Israelites until this day.

14 Only unto the tribe of Levi he gave none inheritance; the sacrifices of the LORD God of Israel made by fire *are* their inheritance, as he said unto them.

15 And Moses gave unto the tribe of the children of Reuben *inheritance* according to their families.

16 And their coast was from Aroer, that *is* on the bank of the river Arnon, and the city that *is* in the midst of the river, and all the plain by Medeba;

17 Heshbon, and all her cities that *are* in the plain; Dibon, and Bamoth-baal, and Beth-baal-meon,

18 And Jahazah, and Kedemoth, and Mephaath,

19 And Kirjathaim, and Sibmah, and Zareth-shahar in the mount of the valley,

20 And Beth-peor, and Ashdoth-pisgah, and Beth-jeshimoth,

21 And all the cities of the plain, and all the kingdom of Sihon king of the Amorites, which reigned in Heshbon, whom Moses smote with the princes of Midian, Evi, and Rekem, and Zur, and Hur, and Reba, *which were* dukes of Sihon, dwelling in the country.

22 Balaam also the son of Beor, the soothsayer, did the children of Israel slay with the sword among them that were slain by them.

23 And the border of the children of Reuben was Jordan, and the border *thereof.* This *was* the inheritance of the children of Reuben after their families, the cities and the villages thereof.

24 And Moses gave *inheritance* unto the tribe of Gad, *even* unto the children of Gad according to their families.

25 And their coast was Jazer, and all the cities of Gilead, and half the land of the children of Ammon, unto Aroer that *is* before Rabbah;

26 And from Heshbon unto Ramathmizpeh, and Betonim; and from Mahanaim unto the border of Debir;

27 And in the valley, Beth-aram, and Beth-nimrah, and Succoth, and Zaphon, the rest of the kingdom of Sihon king of Heshbon, Jordan and *his* border, *even* unto the edge of the sea of Chinnereth on the other side Jordan eastward.

28 This *is* the inheritance of the children of Gad after their families, the cities, and their villages.

29 And Moses gave *inheritance* unto the half tribe of Manasseh: and *this* was *the possession* of the half tribe of the children of Manasseh by their families.

30 And their coast was from Mahanaim, all Bashan, all the kingdom of Og king of Bashan, and all the towns of Jair, which *are* in Bashan, threescore cities:

31 And half Gilead, and Ashtaroth, and Edrei, cities of the kingdom of Og in Bashan, *were pertaining* unto the children of Machir the son of Manasseh, *even* to the one half of the children of Machir by their families.

32 These *are the countries* which Moses did distribute for inheritance in the plains of Moab, on the other side Jordan, by Jericho, eastward.

33 But unto the tribe of Levi Moses gave not *any* inheritance: the LORD God of Israel *was* their inheritance, as he said unto them.

CHAPTER 14
Division of Canaan

1 And these *are the countries* which the children of Israel inherited in the land of Ca-

Cross References

6 Josh. 11:8; 14:1, 2; 23:13; Judg. 2:21, 23
8 Num. 32:33; Deut. 3:12, 13; Josh. 22:4
9 Num. 21:30; Josh. 13:16
10 Num. 21:24, 25
11 Josh. 12:5
12 Num. 21:24, 35; Deut. 3:11; Josh. 12:4
13 Josh. 13:11
14 Num. 18:20, 23, 24; Josh. 13:33; 14:3, 4
16 Num. 21:28, 30; Josh. 12:2; 13:9
18 Num. 21:23
19 Num. 32:37, 38
20 Deut. 3:17; Josh. 12:3
21 Num. 21:24; 31:8; Deut. 3:10
22 Num. 22:5; 31:8
25 Num. 21:26, 28, 29; 32:35; Deut. 2:19; Judg. 11:13, 15; 2Sam. 11:1; 12:26
27 Gen. 33:17; Num. 32:36; 34:11; 1Kgs. 7:46
30 Num. 32:41; 1Chr. 2:23
31 Num. 32:39, 40; Josh. 12:4
33 Num. 18:20; Deut. 10:9; 18:1, 2; Josh. 13:14; 18:7
1 Num. 34:17, 18

naan, which Eleazar the priest, and Joshua the son of Nun, and the heads of the fathers of the tribes of the children of Israel, distributed for inheritance to them.

2 By lot *was* their inheritance, as the LORD commanded by the hand of Moses, for the nine tribes, and *for* the half tribe.

3 For Moses had given the inheritance of two tribes and an half tribe on the other side Jordan: but unto the Levites he gave none inheritance among them.

4 For the children of Joseph were two tribes, Manasseh and Ephraim: therefore they gave no part unto the Levites in the land, save cities to dwell *in*, with their suburbs for their cattle and for their substance.

5 As the LORD commanded Moses, so the children of Israel did, and they divided the land.

Caleb's Inheritance

6 Then the children of Judah came unto Joshua in Gilgal: and Caleb the son of Jephunneh the Kenezite said unto him, Thou knowest the thing that the LORD said unto Moses the man of God concerning me and thee in Kadesh-barnea.

7 Forty years old *was* I when Moses the servant of the LORD sent me from Kadesh-barnea to espy out the land; and I brought him word again as *it was* in mine heart.

8 Nevertheless my brethren that went up with me made the heart of the people melt: but I wholly followed the LORD my God.

9 And Moses sware on that day, saying, Surely the land whereon thy feet have trodden shall be thine inheritance, and thy children's for ever, because thou hast wholly followed the LORD my God.

10 And now, behold, the LORD hath kept me alive, as he said, these forty and five years, even since the LORD spake this word unto Moses, while *the children of* Israel wandered in the wilderness: and now, lo, I *am* this day fourscore and five years old.

11 As yet I *am as* strong this day as *I was* in the day that Moses sent me: as my strength *was* then, even so *is* my strength now, for war, both to go out, and to come in.

12 Now therefore give me this mountain, whereof the LORD spake in that day; for thou heardest in that day how the Anakims *were* there, and *that* the cities *were* great *and* fenced: if so be the LORD *will be* with me, then I shall be able to drive them out, as the LORD said.

13 And Joshua blessed him, and gave unto

Caleb the son of Jephunneh Hebron for an inheritance.

14 Hebron therefore became the inheritance of Caleb the son of Jephunneh the Kenezite unto this day, because that he wholly followed the LORD God of Israel.

15 And the name of Hebron before *was* Kirjath-arba; *which Arba was* a great man among the Anakims. And the land had rest from war.

CHAPTER 15
Judah's Portion

1 *This* then was the lot of the tribe of the children of Judah by their families; *even* to the border of Edom the wilderness of Zin southward *was* the uttermost part of the south coast.

2 And their south border was from the shore of the salt sea, from the bay that looketh southward:

3 And it went out to the south side to Maaleh-acrabbim, and passed along to Zin, and ascended up on the south side unto Kadesh-barnea, and passed along to Hezron, and went up to Adar, and fetched a compass to Karkaa:

4 *From thence* it passed toward Azmon, and went out unto the river of Egypt; and the goings out of that coast were at the sea: this shall be your south coast.

5 And the east border *was* the salt sea, *even* unto the end of Jordan. And *their* border in the north quarter *was* from the bay of the sea at the uttermost part of Jordan:

6 And the border went up to Beth-hogla, and passed along by the north of Beth-arabah; and the border went up to the stone of Bohan the son of Reuben:

7 And the border went up toward Debir from the valley of Achor, and so northward, looking toward Gilgal, that *is* before the going up to Adummim, which *is* on the south side of the river: and the border passed toward the waters of En-shemesh, and the goings out thereof were at En-rogel:

8 And the border went up by the valley of the son of Hinnom unto the south side of the Jebusite; the same *is* Jerusalem: and the border went up to the top of the mountain that *lieth* before the valley of Hinnom westward, which *is* at the end of the valley of the giants northward:

9 And the border was drawn from the top of the hill unto the fountain of the water of Nephtoah, and went out to the cities of mount Ephron; and the border was drawn to Baalah, which *is* Kirjath-jearim:

Cross references (center column):

2 Num. 26:55; 33:54; 34:13

3 Josh. 13:8, 32, 33

4 Gen. 48:5; 1Chr. 5:1, 2

5 Num. 35:2; Josh. 21:2

6 Num. 13:26; 14:24, 30; 32:12; Deut. 1:36, 38; Josh. 15:17

7 Num. 13:6; 14:6

8 Num. 13:31, 32; 14:24; Deut. 1:28, 36

9 Num. 13:22; 14:23, 24; Deut. 1:36; Josh. 1:3

10 Num. 14:30

11 Deut. 31:2, 7

12 Num. 13:28, 33; Josh. 15:14; Judg. 1:20; Ps. 18:32, 34; 60:12; Rom. 8:31

13 Josh. 10:37; 15:13; 21:11, 12; 22:6; Judg. 1:20; 1Chr. 6:55, 56

14 Josh. 14:8, 9; 21:12

15 Gen. 23:2; Josh. 11:23; 15:13

1 Num. 33:36; 34:3

3 Num. 34:4

4 Num. 34:5

6 Josh. 18:17, 19

7 Josh. 7:26; 2Sam. 17:17; 1Kgs. 1:9

8 Josh. 18:16, 28; Judg. 1:21; 19:10; 2Kgs. 23:10; Jer. 19:2, 6

9 Josh. 18:15; Judg. 18:12; 1Chr. 13:6

10 And the border compassed from Baalah westward unto mount Seir, and passed along unto the side of mount Jearim, which *is* Chesalon, on the north side, and went down to Beth-shemesh, and passed on to Timnah:

11 And the border went out unto the side of Ekron northward: and the border was drawn to Shicron, and passed along to mount Baalah, and went out unto Jabneel; and the goings out of the border were at the sea.

12 And the west border *was* to the great sea, and the coast *thereof*. This *is* the coast of the children of Judah round about according to their families.

13 And unto Caleb the son of Jephunneh he gave a part among the children of Judah, according to the commandment of the LORD to Joshua, *even* the city of Arba the father of Anak, which *city is* Hebron.

14 And Caleb drove thence the three sons of Anak, Sheshai, and Ahiman, and Talmai, the children of Anak.

15 And he went up thence to the inhabitants of Debir: and the name of Debir before *was* Kirjath-sepher.

16 And Caleb said, He that smiteth Kirjath-sepher, and taketh it, to him will I give Achsah my daughter to wife.

17 And Othniel the son of Kenaz, the brother of Caleb, took it: and he gave him Achsah his daughter to wife.

18 And it came to pass, as she came *unto him*, that she moved him to ask of her father a field: and she lighted off *her* ass; and Caleb said unto her, What wouldest thou?

19 Who answered, Give me a blessing; for thou hast given me a south land; give me also springs of water. And he gave her the upper springs, and the nether springs.

20 This *is* the inheritance of the tribe of the children of Judah according to their families.

21 And the uttermost cities of the tribe of the children of Judah toward the coast of Edom southward were Kabzeel, and Eder, and Jagur,

22 And Kinah, and Dimonah, and Adadah,

23 And Kedesh, and Hazor, and Ithnan,

24 Ziph, and Telem, and Bealoth,

25 And Hazor, Hadattah, and Kerioth, *and* Hezron, which *is* Hazor,

26 Amam, and Shema, and Moladah,

27 And Hazar-gaddah, and Heshmon, and Beth-palet,

28 And Hazarshual, and Beer-sheba, and Bizjothjah,

29 Baalah, and Iim, and Azem,

30 And Eltolad, and Chesil, and Hormah,

31 And Ziklag, and Madmannah, and Sansannah,

32 And Lebaoth, and Shilhim, and Ain, and Rimmon: all the cities *are* twenty and nine, with their villages:

33 *And* in the valley, Eshtaol, and Zoreah, and Ashnah,

34 And Zanoah, and En-gannim, Tappuah, and Enam,

35 Jarmuth, and Adullam, Socoh, and Azekah,

36 And Sharaim, and Adithaim, and Gederah, and Gederothaim; fourteen cities with their villages:

37 Zenan, and Hadashah, and Migdal-gad,

38 And Dilean, and Mizpeh, and Joktheel,

39 Lachish, and Bozkath, and Eglon,

40 And Cabbon, and Lahmam, and Kithlish,

41 And Gederoth, Beth-dagon, and Naamah, and Makkedah; sixteen cities with their villages:

42 Libnah, and Ether, and Ashan,

43 And Jiphtah, and Ashnah, and Nezib,

44 And Keilah, and Achzib, and Mareshah; nine cities with their villages:

45 Ekron, with her towns and her villages:

46 From Ekron even unto the sea, all that *lay* near Ashdod, with their villages:

47 Ashdod with her towns and her villages, Gaza with her towns and her villages, unto the river of Egypt, and the great sea, and the border *thereof*:

48 And in the mountains, Shamir, and Jattir, and Socoh,

49 And Dannah, and Kirjath-sannah, which *is* Debir,

50 And Anab, and Eshtemoh, and Anim,

51 And Goshen, and Holon, and Giloh; eleven cities with their villages:

52 Arab, and Dumah, and Eshean,

53 And Janum, and Beth-tappuah, and Aphekah,

54 And Humtah, and Kirjath-arba, which *is* Hebron, and Zior; nine cities with their villages:

55 Maon, Carmel, and Ziph, and Juttah,

56 And Jezreel, and Jokdeam, and Zanoah,

57 Cain, Gibeah, and Timnah; ten cities with their villages:

58 Halhul, Beth-zur, and Gedor,

59 And Maarath, and Beth-anoth, and Eltekon; six cities with their villages:

60 Kirjath-baal, which *is* Kirjath-jearim, and Rabbah; two cities with their villages:

61 In the wilderness, Beth-arabah, Middin, and Secacah,

Cross references (center column):

10 Gen. 38:13; Judg. 14:1
11 Josh. 19:43
12 Num. 34:6, 7; Josh. 15:47
13 Josh. 14:13, 15
14 Num. 13:22; Judg. 1:10, 20
15 Josh. 10:38; Judg. 1:11
16 Judg. 1:12
17 Num. 32:12; Josh. 14:6; Judg. 1:13; 3:9
18 Gen. 24:64; Judg. 1:14; 1Sam. 25:23
19 Gen. 33:11
31 1Sam. 27:6
33 Num. 13:23
38 2Kgs. 14:7
47 Num. 34:6; Josh. 15:4
51 Josh. 10:41; 11:16
54 Josh. 14:15; 15:13
60 Josh. 18:14

62 And Nibshan, and the city of Salt, and En-gedi; six cities with their villages.

63 As for the Jebusites the inhabitants of Jerusalem, the children of Judah could not drive them out: but the Jebusites dwell with the children of Judah at Jerusalem unto this day.

CHAPTER 16

Ephraim and Manasseh's Portions

1 And the lot of the children of Joseph fell from Jordan by Jericho, unto the water of Jericho on the east, to the wilderness that goeth up from Jericho throughout mount Beth-el,

2 And goeth out from Beth-el to Luz, and passeth along unto the borders of Archi to Ataroth,

3 And goeth down westward to the coast of Japhleti, unto the coast of Beth-horon the nether, and to Gezer: and the goings out thereof are at the sea.

4 So the children of Joseph, Manasseh and Ephraim, took their inheritance.

5 And the border of the children of Ephraim according to their families was *thus*: even the border of their inheritance on the east side was Ataroth-addar, unto Beth-horon the upper;

6 And the border went out toward the sea to Michmethah on the north side; and the border went about eastward unto Taanath-shiloh, and passed by it on the east to Janohah;

7 And it went down from Janohah to Ataroth, and to Naarath, and came to Jericho, and went out at Jordan.

8 The border went out from Tappuah westward unto the river Kanah; and the goings out thereof were at the sea. This *is* the inheritance of the tribe of the children of Ephraim by their families.

9 And the separate cities for the children of Ephraim *were* among the inheritance of the children of Manasseh, all the cities with their villages.

10 And they drave not out the Canaanites that dwelt in Gezer: but the Canaanites dwell among the Ephraimites unto this day, and serve under tribute.

CHAPTER 17

1 There was also a lot for the tribe of Manasseh; for he *was* the firstborn of Joseph; *to wit*, for Machir the firstborn of Manasseh, the father of Gilead: because he was a man of war, therefore he had Gilead and Bashan.

2 There was also *a lot* for the rest of the children of Manasseh by their families; for the children of Abiezer, and for the children of Helek, and for the children of Asriel, and for the children of Shechem, and for the children of Hepher, and for the children of Shemida: these *were* the male children of Manasseh the son of Joseph by their families.

3 But Zelophehad, the son of Hepher, the son of Gilead, the son of Machir, the son of Manasseh, had no sons, but daughters: and these *are* the names of his daughters, Mahlah, and Noah, Hoglah, Milcah, and Tirzah.

4 And they came near before Eleazar the priest, and before Joshua the son of Nun, and before the princes, saying, The LORD commanded Moses to give us an inheritance among our brethren. Therefore according to the commandment of the LORD he gave them an inheritance among the brethren of their father.

5 And there fell ten portions to Manasseh, beside the land of Gilead and Bashan, which *were* on the other side Jordan;

6 Because the daughters of Manasseh had an inheritance among his sons: and the rest of Manasseh's sons had the land of Gilead.

7 And the coast of Manasseh was from Asher to Michmethah, that *lieth* before Shechem; and the border went along on the right hand unto the inhabitants of En-tappuah.

8 *Now* Manasseh had the land of Tappuah: but Tappuah on the border of Manasseh *belonged* to the children of Ephraim;

9 And the coast descended unto the river Kanah, southward of the river: these cities of Ephraim *are* among the cities of Manasseh: the coast of Manasseh also *was* on the north side of the river, and the outgoings of it were at the sea:

10 Southward *it was* Ephraim's, and northward *it was* Manasseh's, and the sea is his border; and they met together in Asher on the north, and in Issachar on the east.

11 And Manasseh had in Issachar and in Asher Beth-shean and her towns, and Ibleam and her towns, and the inhabitants of Dor and her towns, and the inhabitants of Endor and her towns, and the inhabitants of Taanach and her towns, and the inhabitants of Megiddo and her towns, *even* three countries.

12 Yet the children of Manasseh could not drive out *the inhabitants of* those cities; but the Canaanites would dwell in that land.

13 Yet it came to pass, when the children of Israel were waxen strong, that they put the

---

63 Judg. 1:8, 21; 2Sam. 5:6

2 Josh. 18:13; Judg. 1:26

3 Josh. 18:13; 1Kgs. 9:15; 1Chr. 7:28; 2Chr. 8:5

4 Josh. 17:14

5 Josh. 18:13; 2Chr. 8:5

6 Josh. 17:7

7 1Chr. 7:28

8 Josh. 17:9

9 Josh. 17:9

10 Judg. 1:29; 1Kgs. 9:16

1 Gen. 41:51; 46:20; 48:18; 50:23; Num. 26:29; 32:39, 40; Deut. 3:15; 1Chr. 7:14

2 Num. 26:29-32; 1Chr. 7:18

3 Num. 26:33; 27:1; 36:2

4 Num. 27:6, 7; Josh. 14:1

7 Josh. 16:6

8 Josh. 16:8

9 Josh. 16:8, 9

11 1Sam. 31:10; 1Kgs. 4:12; 1Chr. 7:29

12 Judg. 1:27, 28

13 Josh. 16:10

Canaanites to tribute; but did not utterly drive them out.

14 And the children of Joseph spake unto Joshua, saying, Why hast thou given me *but* one lot and one portion to inherit, seeing I *am* a great people, forasmuch as the LORD hath blessed me hitherto?

15 And Joshua answered them, If thou *be* a great people, *then* get thee up to the wood *country,* and cut down for thyself there in the land of the Perizzites and of the giants, if mount Ephraim be too narrow for thee.

16 And the children of Joseph said, The hill is not enough for us: and all the Canaanites that dwell in the land of the valley have chariots of iron, *both they* who *are* of Beth-shean and her towns, and *they* who *are* of the valley of Jezreel.

17 And Joshua spake unto the house of Joseph, *even* to Ephraim and to Manasseh, saying, Thou *art* a great people, and hast great power: thou shalt not have one lot only:

18 But the mountain shall be thine; for it *is* a wood, and thou shalt cut it down: and the outgoings of it shall be thine: for thou shalt drive out the Canaanites, though they have iron chariots, *and* though they *be* strong.

CHAPTER 18
The Remaining Land Is Divided

1 And the whole congregation of the children of Israel assembled together at Shiloh, and set up the tabernacle of the congregation there. And the land was subdued before them.

2 And there remained among the children of Israel seven tribes, which had not yet received their inheritance.

3 And Joshua said unto the children of Israel, How long *are* ye slack to go to possess the land, which the LORD God of your fathers hath given you?

4 Give out from among you three men for *each* tribe: and I will send them, and they shall rise, and go through the land, and describe it according to the inheritance of them; and they shall come *again* to me.

5 And they shall divide it into seven parts: Judah shall abide in their coast on the south, and the house of Joseph shall abide in their coasts on the north.

6 Ye shall therefore describe the land *into* seven parts, and bring *the description* hither to me, that I may cast lots for you here before the LORD our God.

7 But the Levites have no part among you; for the priesthood of the LORD *is* their inher-

itance: and Gad, and Reuben, and half the tribe of Manasseh, have received their inheritance beyond Jordan on the east, which Moses the servant of the LORD gave them.

8 And the men arose, and went away: and Joshua charged them that went to describe the land, saying, Go and walk through the land, and describe it, and come again to me, that I may here cast lots for you before the LORD in Shiloh.

9 And the men went and passed through the land, and described it by cities into seven parts in a book, and came *again* to Joshua to the host at Shiloh.

10 And Joshua cast lots for them in Shiloh before the LORD: and there Joshua divided the land unto the children of Israel according to their divisions.

Benjamin's Portion

11 And the lot of the tribe of the children of Benjamin came up according to their families: and the coast of their lot came forth between the children of Judah and the children of Joseph.

12 And their border on the north side was from Jordan; and the border went up to the side of Jericho on the north side, and went up through the mountains westward; and the goings out thereof were at the wilderness of Beth-aven.

13 And the border went over from thence toward Luz, to the side of Luz, which *is* Beth-el, southward; and the border descended to Ataroth-adar, near the hill that *lieth* on the south side of the nether Beth-horon.

14 And the border was drawn *thence,* and compassed the corner of the sea southward, from the hill that *lieth* before Beth-horon southward; and the goings out thereof were at Kirjath-baal, which *is* Kirjath-jearim, a city of the children of Judah: this *was* the west quarter.

15 And the south quarter *was* from the end of Kirjath-jearim, and the border went out on the west, and went out to the well of waters of Nephtoah:

16 And the border came down to the end of the mountain that *lieth* before the valley of the son of Hinnom, *and* which *is* in the valley of the giants on the north, and descended to the valley of Hinnom, to the side of Jebusi on the south, and descended to En-rogel,

17 And was drawn from the north, and went forth to En-shemesh, and went forth toward Geliloth, which *is* over against the

---

Cross-references (center column):

14 Gen. 48:19, 22; Num. 26:34, 37; Josh. 16:4

16 Josh. 19:18; Judg. 1:19; 4:3; 1Kgs. 4:12

18 Deut. 20:1

1 Josh. 19:51; 21:2; 22:9; Judg. 18:31; 1Sam. 1:3, 24; 4:3, 4; Jer. 7:12

3 Judg. 18:9

5 Josh. 15:1; 16:1, 4

6 Josh. 14:2; 18:10

7 Josh. 13:8, 33

12 Josh. 16:1

13 Gen. 28:19; Josh. 16:3; Judg. 1:23

14 Josh. 15:9

15 Josh. 15:9

16 Josh. 15:7, 8

17 Josh. 15:6

going up of Adummim, and descended to the stone of Bohan the son of Reuben,

18 And passed along toward the side over against Arabah northward, and went down unto Arabah:

19 And the border passed along to the side of Beth-hoglah northward: and the outgoings of the border were at the north bay of the salt sea at the south end of Jordan: this *was* the south coast.

20 And Jordan was the border of it on the east side. This *was* the inheritance of the children of Benjamin, by the coasts thereof round about, according to their families.

21 Now the cities of the tribe of the children of Benjamin according to their families were Jericho, and Beth-hoglah, and the valley of Keziz,

22 And Beth-arabah, and Zemaraim, and Beth-el,

23 And Avim, and Parah, and Ophrah,

24 And Chephar-haammonai, and Ophni, and Gaba; twelve cities with their villages:

25 Gibeon, and Ramah, and Beeroth,

26 And Mizpeh, and Chephirah, and Mozah,

27 And Rekem, and Irpeel, and Taralah,

28 And Zelah, Eleph, and Jebusi, which *is* Jerusalem, Gibeath, *and* Kirjath; fourteen cities with their villages. This *is* the inheritance of the children of Benjamin according to their families.

CHAPTER 19
Simeon's Portion

1 And the second lot came forth to Simeon, *even* for the tribe of the children of Simeon according to their families: and their inheritance was within the inheritance of the children of Judah.

2 And they had in their inheritance Beersheba, or Sheba, and Moladah,

3 And Hazarshual, and Balah, and Azem,

4 And Eltolad, and Bethul, and Hormah,

5 And Ziklag, and Beth-marcaboth, and Hazar-susah,

6 And Beth-lebaoth, and Sharuhen; thirteen cities and their villages:

7 Ain, Remmon, and Ether, and Ashan; four cities and their villages:

8 And all the villages that *were* round about these cities to Baalath-beer, Ramath of the south. This *is* the inheritance of the tribe of the children of Simeon according to their families.

9 Out of the portion of the children of Judah *was* the inheritance of the children of Simeon: for the part of the children of

Judah was too much for them: therefore the children of Simeon had their inheritance within the inheritance of them.

Zebulun's Portion

10 And the third lot came up for the children of Zebulun according to their families: and the border of their inheritance was unto Sarid:

11 And their border went up toward the sea, and Maralah, and reached to Dabbasheth, and reached to the river that *is* before Jokneam;

12 And turned from Sarid eastward toward the sunrising unto the border of Chisloth-tabor, and then goeth out to Daberath, and goeth up to Japhia,

13 And from thence passeth on along on the east to Gittah-hepher, to Ittah-kazin, and goeth out to Remmon-methoar to Neah;

14 And the border compasseth it on the north side to Hannathon: and the outgoings thereof are in the valley of Jipthah-el:

15 And Kattath, and Nahallal, and Shimron, and Idalah, and Beth-lehem: twelve cities with their villages.

16 This *is* the inheritance of the children of Zebulun according to their families, these cities with their villages.

Issachar's Portion

17 *And* the fourth lot came out to Issachar, for the children of Issachar according to their families.

18 And their border was toward Jezreel, and Chesulloth, and Shunem,

19 And Hapharaim, and Shion, and Anaharath,

20 And Rabbith, and Kishion, and Abez,

21 And Remeth, and En-gannim, and Enhaddah, and Beth-pazzez;

22 And the coast reacheth to Tabor, and Shahazimah, and Beth-shemesh; and the outgoings of their border were at Jordan: sixteen cities with their villages.

23 This *is* the inheritance of the tribe of the children of Issachar according to their families, the cities and their villages.

Asher's Portion

24 And the fifth lot came out for the tribe of the children of Asher according to their families.

25 And their border was Helkath, and Hali, and Beten, and Achshaph,

26 And Alammelech, and Amad, and

---

18 Josh. 15:6

28 Josh. 15:8

1 Josh. 19:9

2 1Chr. 4:28

9 Josh. 19:1

11 Gen. 49:13; Josh. 12:22

Misheal; and reacheth to Carmel westward, and to Shihor-libnath;

27 And turneth toward the sunrising to Beth-dagon, and reacheth to Zebulun, and to the valley of Jipthah-el toward the north side of Beth-emek, and Neiel, and goeth out to Cabul on the left hand,

28 And Hebron, and Rehob, and Hammon, and Kanah, *even* unto great Zidon;

29 And *then* the coast turneth to Ramah, and to the strong city Tyre; and the coast turneth to Hosah; and the outgoings thereof are at the sea from the coast to Achzib:

30 Ummah also, and Aphek, and Rehob: twenty and two cities with their villages.

31 This *is* the inheritance of the tribe of the children of Asher according to their families, these cities with their villages.

Naphtali's Portion

32 The sixth lot came out to the children of Naphtali, *even* for the children of Naphtali according to their families.

33 And their coast was from Heleph, from Allon to Zaanannim, and Adami, Nekeb, and Jabneel, unto Lakum; and the outgoings thereof were at Jordan:

34 And *then* the coast turneth westward to Aznoth-tabor, and goeth out from thence to Hukkok, and reacheth to Zebulun on the south side, and reacheth to Asher on the west side, and to Judah upon Jordan toward the sunrising.

35 And the fenced cities *are* Ziddim, Zer, and Hammath, Rakkath, and Chinnereth,

36 And Adamah, and Ramah, and Hazor,

37 And Kedesh, and Edrei, and En-hazor,

38 And Iron, and Migdal-el, Horem, and Beth-anath, and Beth-shemesh; nineteen cities with their villages.

39 This *is* the inheritance of the tribe of the children of Naphtali according to their families, the cities and their villages.

Dan's Portion

40 *And* the seventh lot came out for the tribe of the children of Dan according to their families.

41 And the coast of their inheritance was Zorah, and Eshtaol, and Ir-shemesh,

42 And Shaalabbin, and Ajalon, and Jethlah,

43 And Elon, and Thimnathah, and Ekron,

44 And Eltekeh, and Gibbethon, and Baalath,

45 And Jehud, and Bene-berak, and Gath-rimmon,

46 And Me-jarkon, and Rakkon, with the border before Japho.

47 And the coast of the children of Dan went out *too little* for them: therefore the children of Dan went up to fight against Leshem, and took it, and smote it with the edge of the sword, and possessed it, and dwelt therein, and called Leshem, Dan, after the name of Dan their father.

48 This *is* the inheritance of the tribe of the children of Dan according to their families, these cities with their villages.

Joshua's Portion

49 When they had made an end of dividing the land for inheritance by their coasts, the children of Israel gave an inheritance to Joshua the son of Nun among them:

50 According to the word of the LORD they gave him the city which he asked, *even* Timnathserah in mount Ephraim: and he built the city, and dwelt therein.

51 These *are* the inheritances, which Eleazar the priest, and Joshua the son of Nun, and the heads of the fathers of the tribes of the children of Israel, divided for an inheritance by lot in Shiloh before the LORD, at the door of the tabernacle of the congregation. So they made an end of dividing the country.

CHAPTER 20
The Cities of Refuge

1 The LORD also spake unto Joshua, saying,

2 Speak to the children of Israel, saying, Appoint out for you cities of refuge, whereof I spake unto you by the hand of Moses:

3 That the slayer that killeth *any* person unawares *and* unwittingly may flee thither: and they shall be your refuge from the avenger of blood.

4 And when he that doth flee unto one of those cities shall stand at the entering of the gate of the city, and shall declare his cause in the ears of the elders of that city, they shall take him into the city unto them, and give him a place, that he may dwell among them.

5 And if the avenger of blood pursue after him, then they shall not deliver the slayer up into his hand; because he smote his neighbour unwittingly, and hated him not beforetime.

6 And he shall dwell in that city, until he stand before the congregation for judgment, *and* until the death of the high priest that shall be in those days: then shall the slayer return, and come unto his own city, and

---

Center column references:

28 Josh. 11:8; Judg. 1:31

29 Gen. 38:5; Judg. 1:31; Mic. 1:14

34 Deut. 33:23

42 Judg. 1:35

47 Judg. 18:29

50 Josh. 24:30; 1Chr. 7:24

51 Num. 34:17; Josh. 14:1; 18:1, 10

2 Ex. 21:13; Num. 35:6, 11, 14; Deut. 19:2, 9

4 Ruth 4:1, 2

5 Num. 35:12

6 Num. 35:12, 25

unto his own house, unto the city from whence he fled.

7 And they appointed Kedesh in Galilee in mount Naphtali, and Shechem in mount Ephraim, and Kirjath-arba, which *is* Hebron, in the mountain of Judah.

8 And on the other side Jordan by Jericho eastward, they assigned Bezer in the wilderness upon the plain out of the tribe of Reuben, and Ramoth in Gilead out of the tribe of Gad, and Golan in Bashan out of the tribe of Manasseh.

9 These were the cities appointed for all the children of Israel, and for the stranger that sojourneth among them, that whosoever killeth *any* person at unawares might flee thither, and not die by the hand of the avenger of blood, until he stood before the congregation.

CHAPTER 21
The Levites' Cities

1 Then came near the heads of the fathers of the Levites unto Eleazar the priest, and unto Joshua the son of Nun, and unto the heads of the fathers of the tribes of the children of Israel;

2 And they spake unto them at Shiloh in the land of Canaan, saying, The LORD commanded by the hand of Moses to give us cities to dwell in, with the suburbs thereof for our cattle.

3 And the children of Israel gave unto the Levites out of their inheritance, at the commandment of the LORD, these cities and their suburbs.

4 And the lot came out for the families of the Kohathites: and the children of Aaron the priest, *which were* of the Levites, had by lot out of the tribe of Judah, and out of the tribe of Simeon, and out of the tribe of Benjamin, thirteen cities.

5 And the rest of the children of Kohath *had* by lot out of the families of the tribe of Ephraim, and out of the tribe of Dan, and out of the half tribe of Manasseh, ten cities.

6 And the children of Gershon *had* by lot out of the families of the tribe of Issachar, and out of the tribe of Asher, and out of the tribe of Naphtali, and out of the half tribe of Manasseh in Bashan, thirteen cities.

7 The children of Merari by their families *had* out of the tribe of Reuben, and out of the tribe of Gad, and out of the tribe of Zebulun, twelve cities.

8 And the children of Israel gave by lot unto the Levites these cities with their sub-

---

7 Josh. 14:15; 21:11, 13, 21, 32; 1Chr. 6:76; 2Chr. 10:1; Luke 1:39

8 Deut. 4:43; Josh. 21:27, 36, 38; 1Kgs. 22:3; 1Chr. 6:78

9 Num. 35:15; Josh. 20:6

1 Josh. 14:1; 17:1

2 Num. 35:2; Josh. 18:1

4 Josh. 21:8, 19; 24:33

5 Josh. 29:20-26

6 Josh. 21:27-33

7 Josh. 21:34-42

8 Num. 35:2; Josh. 21:3

10 Josh. 21:4

11 Josh. 15:13, 14; 20:7; 1Chr. 6:55; Luke 1:39

12 Josh. 14:14; 1Chr. 6:56

13 Josh. 15:42, 54; 20:7; 1Chr. 6:57

14 Josh. 15:48, 50

15 Josh. 15:49, 51; 1Chr. 10:28

16 Josh. 15:10, 42, 55; 1Chr. 6:59

17 Josh. 18:25

18 1Chr. 6:60

20 Josh. 21:5; 1Chr. 6:66

21 Josh. 20:7

27 Josh. 20:8; 21:6; 1Chr. 6:71

---

urbs, as the LORD commanded by the hand of Moses.

9 And they gave out of the tribe of the children of Judah, and out of the tribe of the children of Simeon, these cities which are *here* mentioned by name,

10 Which the children of Aaron, *being* of the families of the Kohathites, *who were* of the children of Levi, had: for theirs was the first lot.

11 And they gave them the city of Arba the father of Anak, which *city is* Hebron, in the hill *country* of Judah, with the suburbs thereof round about it.

12 But the fields of the city, and the villages thereof, gave they to Caleb the son of Jephunneh for his possession.

13 Thus they gave to the children of Aaron the priest Hebron with her suburbs, *to be* a city of refuge for the slayer; and Libnah with her suburbs,

14 And Jattir with her suburbs, and Eshtemoa with her suburbs,

15 And Holon with her suburbs, and Debir with her suburbs,

16 And Ain with her suburbs, and Juttah with her suburbs, *and* Beth-shemesh with her suburbs; nine cities out of those two tribes.

17 And out of the tribe of Benjamin, Gibeon with her suburbs, Geba with her suburbs,

18 Anathoth with her suburbs, and Almon with her suburbs; four cities.

19 All the cities of the children of Aaron, the priests, *were* thirteen cities with their suburbs.

20 And the families of the children of Kohath, the Levites which remained of the children of Kohath, even they had the cities of their lot out of the tribe of Ephraim.

21 For they gave them Shechem with her suburbs in mount Ephraim, *to be* a city of refuge for the slayer; and Gezer with her suburbs,

22 And Kibzaim with her suburbs, and Beth-horon with her suburbs; four cities.

23 And out of the tribe of Dan, Eltekeh with her suburbs, Gibbethon with her suburbs,

24 Aijalon with her suburbs, Gath-rimmon with her suburbs; four cities.

25 And out of the half tribe of Manasseh, Tanach with her suburbs, and Gath-rimmon with her suburbs; two cities.

26 All the cities *were* ten with their suburbs for the families of the children of Kohath that remained.

27 And unto the children of Gershon, of the families of the Levites, out of the *other* half

tribe of Manasseh *they gave* Golan in Bashan with her suburbs, *to be* a city of refuge for the slayer; and Beesh-terah with her suburbs; two cities.

28 And out of the tribe of Issachar, Kishon with her suburbs, Daberath with her suburbs,

29 Jarmuth with her suburbs, En-gannim with her suburbs; four cities.

30 And out of the tribe of Asher, Mishal with her suburbs, Abdon with her suburbs,

31 Helkath with her suburbs, and Rehob with her suburbs; four cities.

32 And out of the tribe of Naphtali, Kedesh in Galilee with her suburbs, *to be* a city of refuge for the slayer; and Hammoth-dor with her suburbs, and Kartan with her suburbs; three cities.

33 All the cities of the Gershonites according to their families *were* thirteen cities with their suburbs.

34 And unto the families of the children of Merari, the rest of the Levites, out of the tribe of Zebulun, Jokneam with her suburbs, and Kartah with her suburbs,

35 Dimnah with her suburbs, Nahalal with her suburbs; four cities.

36 And out of the tribe of Reuben, Bezer with her suburbs, and Jahazah with her suburbs,

37 Kedemoth with her suburbs, and Mephaath with her suburbs; four cities.

38 And out of the tribe of Gad, Ramoth in Gilead with her suburbs, *to be* a city of refuge for the slayer; and Mahanaim with her suburbs,

39 Heshbon with her suburbs, Jazer with her suburbs; four cities in all.

40 So all the cities for the children of Merari by their families, which were remaining of the families of the Levites, were *by* their lot twelve cities.

41 All the cities of the Levites within the possession of the children of Israel *were* forty and eight cities with their suburbs.

42 These cities were every one with their suburbs round about them: thus *were* all these cities.

Israel Settles the Land

43 And the LORD gave unto Israel all the land which he sware to give unto their fathers; and they possessed it, and dwelt therein.

44 And the LORD gave them rest round about, according to all that he sware unto their fathers: and there stood not a man of all their enemies before them; the LORD

delivered all their enemies into their hand.

45 There failed not ought of any good thing which the LORD had spoken unto the house of Israel; all came to pass.

CHAPTER 22
The Eastern Tribes Are Sent Home

1 Then Joshua called the Reubenites, and the Gadites, and the half tribe of Manasseh,

2 And said unto them, Ye have kept all that Moses the servant of the LORD commanded you, and have obeyed my voice in all that I commanded you:

3 Ye have not left your brethren these many days unto this day, but have kept the charge of the commandment of the LORD your God.

4 And now the LORD your God hath given rest unto your brethren, as he promised them: therefore now return ye, and get you unto your tents, *and* unto the land of your possession, which Moses the servant of the LORD gave you on the other side Jordan.

5 But take diligent heed to do the commandment and the law, which Moses the servant of the LORD charged you, to love the LORD your God, and to walk in all his ways, and to keep his commandments, and to cleave unto him, and to serve him with all your heart and with all your soul.

6 So Joshua blessed them, and sent them away: and they went unto their tents.

7 Now to the *one* half of the tribe of Manasseh Moses had given *possession* in Bashan: but unto the *other* half thereof gave Joshua among their brethren on this side Jordan westward. And when Joshua sent them away also unto their tents, then he blessed them,

8 And he spake unto them, saying, Return with much riches unto your tents, and with very much cattle, with silver, and with gold, and with brass, and with iron, and with very much raiment: divide the spoil of your enemies with your brethren.

9 And the children of Reuben and the children of Gad and the half tribe of Manasseh returned, and departed from the children of Israel out of Shiloh, which *is* in the land of Canaan, to go unto the country of Gilead, to the land of their possession, whereof they were possessed, according to the word of the LORD by the hand of Moses.

10 And when they came unto the borders of Jordan, that *are* in the land of Canaan, the children of Reuben and the children of Gad and the half tribe of Manasseh built there an altar by Jordan, a great altar to see to.

32 Josh. 20:7

34 Josh. 21:7; 1Chr. 6:77

36 Josh. 20:8

38 Josh. 20:8

41 Num. 35:7

43 Gen. 13:15; 15:18; 26:3; 28:4, 13

44 Deut. 7:24; Josh. 11:23; 22:4

45 Josh. 23:14

2 Num. 32:20; Deut. 3:18; Josh. 1:16, 17

4 Num. 32:33; Deut. 29:8; Josh. 13:8

5 Deut. 6:6, 17; 10:12; 11:22

6 Gen. 47:7; Ex. 39:43; Josh. 14:13; 2Sam. 6:18; Luke 24:50

7 Josh. 17:5

8 Num. 31:27; 32:1, 26, 29; 1Sam. 30:24

11 And the children of Israel heard say, Behold, the children of Reuben and the children of Gad and the half tribe of Manasseh have built an altar over against the land of Canaan, in the borders of Jordan, at the passage of the children of Israel.
12 And when the children of Israel heard *of* it, the whole congregation of the children of Israel gathered themselves together at Shiloh, to go up to war against them.
13 And the children of Israel sent unto the children of Reuben, and to the children of Gad, and to the half tribe of Manasseh, into the land of Gilead, Phinehas the son of Eleazar the priest,
14 And with him ten princes, of each chief house a prince throughout all the tribes of Israel; and each one *was* an head of the house of their fathers among the thousands of Israel.
15 And they came unto the children of Reuben, and to the children of Gad, and to the half tribe of Manasseh, unto the land of Gilead, and they spake with them, saying,
16 Thus saith the whole congregation of the LORD, What trespass *is* this that ye have committed against the God of Israel, to turn away this day from following the LORD, in that ye have builded you an altar, that ye might rebel this day against the LORD?
17 *Is* the iniquity of Peor too little for us, from which we are not cleansed until this day, although there was a plague in the congregation of the LORD,
18 But that ye must turn away this day from following the LORD? and it will be, *seeing* ye rebel today against the LORD, that to morrow he will be wroth with the whole congregation of Israel.
19 Notwithstanding, if the land of your possession *be* unclean, *then* pass ye over unto the land of the possession of the LORD, wherein the LORD's tabernacle dwelleth, and take possession among us: but rebel not against the LORD, nor rebel against us, in building you an altar beside the altar of the LORD our God.
20 Did not Achan the son of Zerah commit a trespass in the accursed thing, and wrath fell on all the congregation of Israel? and that man perished not alone in his iniquity.
21 Then the children of Reuben and the children of Gad and the half tribe of Manasseh answered, and said unto the heads of the thousands of Israel,
22 The LORD God of gods, the LORD God of gods, he knoweth, and Israel he shall know;

if *it be* in rebellion, or if in transgression against the LORD, (save us not this day,)
23 That we have built us an altar to turn from following the LORD, or if to offer thereon burnt offering or meat offering, or if to offer peace offerings thereon, let the LORD himself require *it*;
24 And if we have not *rather* done it for fear of *this* thing, saying, In time to come your children might speak unto our children, saying, What have ye to do with the LORD God of Israel?
25 For the LORD hath made Jordan a border between us and you, ye children of Reuben and children of Gad; ye have no part in the LORD: so shall your children make our children cease from fearing the LORD.
26 Therefore we said, Let us now prepare to build us an altar, not for burnt offering, nor for sacrifice:
27 But *that* it *may be* a witness between us, and you, and our generations after us, that we might do the service of the LORD before him with our burnt offerings, and with our sacrifices, and with our peace offerings; that your children may not say to our children in time to come, Ye have no part in the LORD.
28 Therefore said we, that it shall be, when they should *so* say to us or to our generations in time to come, that we may say *again*, Behold the pattern of the altar of the LORD, which our fathers made, not for burnt offerings, nor for sacrifices; but it *is* a witness between us and you.
29 God forbid that we should rebel against the LORD, and turn this day from following the LORD, to build an altar for burnt offerings, for meat offerings, or for sacrifices, beside the altar of the LORD our God that *is* before his tabernacle.
30 And when Phinehas the priest, and the princes of the congregation and heads of the thousands of Israel which *were* with him, heard the words that the children of Reuben and the children of Gad and the children of Manasseh spake, it pleased them.
31 And Phinehas the son of Eleazar the priest said unto the children of Reuben, and to the children of Gad, and to the children of Manasseh, This day we perceive that the LORD *is* among us, because ye have not committed this trespass against the LORD: now ye have delivered the children of Israel out of the hand of the LORD.
32 And Phinehas the son of Eleazar the priest, and the princes, returned from the children of Reuben, and from the children of Gad, out of the land of Gilead, unto the

land of Canaan, to the children of Israel, and brought them word again.

33 And the thing pleased the children of Israel; and the children of Israel blessed God, and did not intend to go up against them in battle, to destroy the land wherein the children of Reuben and Gad dwelt.

34 And the children of Reuben and the children of Gad called the altar *Ed*: for it *shall be* a witness between us that the LORD *is* God.

CHAPTER 23
Joshua's Charge to the People

1 And it came to pass a long time after that the LORD had given rest unto Israel from all their enemies round about, that Joshua waxed old *and* stricken in age.

2 And Joshua called for all Israel, *and* for their elders, and for their heads, and for their judges, and for their officers, and said unto them, I am old *and* stricken in age:

3 And ye have seen all that the LORD your God hath done unto all these nations because of you; for the LORD your God *is* he that hath fought for you.

4 Behold, I have divided unto you by lot these nations that remain, to be an inheritance for your tribes, from Jordan, with all the nations that I have cut off, even unto the great sea westward.

5 And the LORD your God, he shall expel them from before you, and drive them from out of your sight; and ye shall possess their land, as the LORD your God hath promised unto you.

6 Be ye therefore very courageous to keep and to do all that is written in the book of the law of Moses, that ye turn not aside therefrom *to* the right hand or *to* the left;

7 That ye come not among these nations, these that remain among you; neither make mention of the name of their gods, nor cause to swear *by them*, neither serve them, nor bow yourselves unto them:

8 But cleave unto the LORD your God, as ye have done unto this day.

9 For the LORD hath driven out from before you great nations and strong: but *as for* you, no man hath been able to stand before you unto this day.

10 One man of you shall chase a thousand:

for the LORD your God, he *it is* that fighteth for you, as he hath promised you.

11 Take good heed therefore unto yourselves, that ye love the LORD your God.

12 Else if ye do in any wise go back, and cleave unto the remnant of these nations, *even* these that remain among you, and shall make marriages with them, and go in unto them, and they to you:

13 Know for a certainty that the LORD your God will no more drive out *any of* these nations from before you; but they shall be snares and traps unto you, and scourges in your sides, and thorns in your eyes, until ye perish from off this good land which the LORD your God hath given you.

14 And, behold, this day I *am* going the way of all the earth: and ye know in all your hearts and in all your souls, that not one thing hath failed of all the good things which the LORD your God spake concerning you; all are come to pass unto you, *and* not one thing hath failed thereof.

15 Therefore it shall come to pass, *that* as all good things are come upon you, which the LORD your God promised you; so shall the LORD bring upon you all evil things, until he have destroyed you from off this good land which the LORD your God hath given you.

16 When ye have transgressed the covenant of the LORD your God, which he commanded you, and have gone and served other gods, and bowed yourselves to them; then shall the anger of the LORD be kindled against you, and ye shall perish quickly from off the good land which he hath given unto you.

CHAPTER 24
Joshua's Farewell Address at Shechem

1 And Joshua gathered all the tribes of Israel to Shechem, and called for the elders of Israel, and for their heads, and for their judges, and for their officers; and they presented themselves before God.

2 And Joshua said unto all the people, Thus saith the LORD God of Israel, Your fathers dwelt on the other side of the flood in old time, *even* Terah, the father of Abraham, and the father of Nachor: and they served other gods.

Cross-references (center column)

33 1Chr. 29:20; Luke 2:28

1 Josh. 13:1; 21:44; 22:4

2 Deut. 31:28; Josh. 24:1; 1Chr. 28:1

3 Ex. 14:14; Josh. 10:14, 42

4 Josh. 13:2, 6; 18:10

5 Ex. 23:30; Num. 33:53; Deut. 11:23; Josh. 13:6

6 Deut. 5:32; 28:14; Josh. 1:7

7 Ex. 23:13, 33; Num. 32:38; Deut. 7:2, 3

8 Deut. 10:20; 11:22; 13:4; Josh. 22:5

9 Deut. 11:23; Josh. 1:5

10 Deut. 3:22; 32:30

11 Josh. 22:5

12 Deut. 7:3; Heb. 10:38, 39; 2Pet. 2:20, 21

13 Ex. 23:33; Num. 33:55; Deut. 7:16; Judg. 2:3; 1Kgs. 11:4

14 Josh. 21:45; 1Kgs. 2:2; Luke 21:33; Heb. 9:27

15 Lev. 26:16; Deut. 28:15, 16, 63

1 Gen. 35:4; Josh. 23:2; 1Sam. 10:19

2 Gen. 11:26, 31; 31:53

23:13–16 Not one thing hath failed. God was faithful to Israel, giving them all the land they had taken possession of and victory over all the enemies they fought, but they did not claim the lands to the river Euphrates. Instead, they allowed the idolatrous nations to coexist with them, contrary to the will of God, and eventually intermarried with the people of these nations and worshiped their idols—ending in Israel's total captivity and dispersion—just as God predicted.

3 And I took your father Abraham from the other side of the flood, and led him throughout all the land of Canaan, and multiplied his seed, and gave him Isaac.

4 And I gave unto Isaac Jacob and Esau: and I gave unto Esau mount Seir, to possess it; but Jacob and his children went down into Egypt.

5 I sent Moses also and Aaron, and I plagued Egypt, according to that which I did among them: and afterward I brought you out.

6 And I brought your fathers out of Egypt: and ye came unto the sea; and the Egyptians pursued after your fathers with chariots and horsemen unto the Red sea.

7 And when they cried unto the LORD, he put darkness between you and the Egyptians, and brought the sea upon them, and covered them; and your eyes have seen what I have done in Egypt: and ye dwelt in the wilderness a long season.

8 And I brought you into the land of the Amorites, which dwelt on the other side Jordan; and they fought with you: and I gave them into your hand, that ye might possess their land; and I destroyed them from before you.

9 Then Balak the son of Zippor, king of Moab, arose and warred against Israel, and sent and called Balaam the son of Beor to curse you:

10 But I would not hearken unto Balaam; therefore he blessed you still: so I delivered you out of his hand.

11 And ye went over Jordan, and came unto Jericho: and the men of Jericho fought against you, the Amorites, and the Perizzites, and the Canaanites, and the Hittites, and the Girgashites, the Hivites, and the Jebusites; and I delivered them into your hand.

12 And I sent the hornet before you, which drave them out from before you, *even* the two kings of the Amorites; *but* not with thy sword, nor with thy bow.

13 And I have given you a land for which ye did not labour, and cities which ye built not, and ye dwell in them; of the vineyards and oliveyards which ye planted not do ye eat.

14 Now therefore fear the LORD, and serve him in sincerity and in truth: and put away the gods which your fathers served on the other side of the flood, and in Egypt; and serve ye the LORD.

15 And if it seem evil unto you to serve the LORD, choose you this day whom ye will serve; whether the gods which your fathers

served that *were* on the other side of the flood, or the gods of the Amorites, in whose land ye dwell: but as for me and my house, we will serve the LORD.

16 And the people answered and said, God forbid that we should forsake the LORD, to serve other gods;

17 For the LORD our God, he *it is* that brought us up and our fathers out of the land of Egypt, from the house of bondage, and which did those great signs in our sight, and preserved us in all the way wherein we went, and among all the people through whom we passed:

18 And the LORD drave out from before us all the people, even the Amorites which dwelt in the land: *therefore* will we also serve the LORD; for he *is* our God.

19 And Joshua said unto the people, Ye cannot serve the LORD: for he *is* an holy God; he *is* a jealous God; he will not forgive your transgressions nor your sins.

20 If ye forsake the LORD, and serve strange gods, then he will turn and do you hurt, and consume you, after that he hath done you good.

21 And the people said unto Joshua, Nay; but we will serve the LORD.

22 And Joshua said unto the people, Ye *are* witnesses against yourselves that ye have chosen you the LORD, to serve him. And they said, *We are* witnesses.

23 Now therefore put away, *said he*, the strange gods which *are* among you, and incline your heart unto the LORD God of Israel.

24 And the people said unto Joshua, The LORD our God will we serve, and his voice will we obey.

25 So Joshua made a covenant with the people that day, and set them a statute and an ordinance in Shechem.

26 And Joshua wrote these words in the book of the law of God, and took a great stone, and set it up there under an oak, that *was* by the sanctuary of the LORD.

27 And Joshua said unto all the people, Behold, this stone shall be a witness unto us; for it hath heard all the words of the LORD which he spake unto us: it shall be therefore a witness unto you, lest ye deny your God.

28 So Joshua let the people depart, every man unto his inheritance.

The Leaders' Deaths

29 And it came to pass after these things, that Joshua the son of Nun, the servant of the LORD, died, *being* an hundred and ten years old.

---

3 Gen. 12:1; 21:2, 3; Ps. 127:3; Acts 7:2, 3

4 Gen. 25:24-26; 36:8; 46:1, 6; Deut. 2:5; Acts 7:15

5 Ex. 3:10

6 Ex. 12:37, 51; 14:2, 9

7 Ex. 14:10, 20, 27, 28; Deut. 4:34; 29:2; Josh. 5:6

8 Num. 21:21, 33; Deut. 2:32; 3:1

9 Num. 22:5; Deut. 23:4; Judg. 11:25

10 Num. 23:11, 20; 24:10; Deut. 23:5

11 Josh. 3:14, 17; 4:10, 11, 12; 6:1; 10:1; 11:1

12 Ex. 23:28; Deut. 7:20; Ps. 44:3, 6

13 Deut. 6:10, 11; Josh. 11:13

14 Lev. 17:7; Deut. 10:12; 18:13; Ezek. 20:7, 8, 18; 23:3

15 Ex. 23:24, 32, 33; 34:15; Judg. 6:10; 1Kgs. 18:21; Ezek. 20:39

19 Ex. 20:5; 23:21; Lev. 19:2; 1Sam. 6:20; Ps. 99:5, 9; Isa. 5:16; Matt. 6:24

20 2Chr. 15:2; Ezra 8:22

22 Ps. 119:173

23 Judg. 10:16

27 Deut. 31:19, 21, 26; 32:1

28 Judg. 2:6

29 Judg. 2:8

30 And they buried him in the border of his inheritance in Timnathserah, which *is* in mount Ephraim, on the north side of the hill of Gaash.

31 And Israel served the LORD all the days of Joshua, and all the days of the elders that overlived Joshua, and which had known all the works of the LORD, that he had done for Israel.

32 And the bones of Joseph, which the chil-

dren of Israel brought up out of Egypt, buried they in Shechem, in a parcel of ground which Jacob bought of the sons of Hamor the father of Shechem for an hundred pieces of silver: and it became the inheritance of the children of Joseph.

33 And Eleazar the son of Aaron died; and they buried him in a hill *that pertained to* Phinehas his son, which was given him in mount Ephraim.

30 Josh. 19:50; Judg. 2:9

31 Deut. 11:2; 31:13; Judg. 2:7

32 Gen. 33:19; 50:25; Ex. 13:19

33 Ex. 6:25; Judg. 20:28

Judges

The book of Judges takes its name from the history of the fourteen men and one woman (not counting one usurper, Abimelech, son of Gideon) who delivered and ruled Israel without a central government. Only thirteen judges appear in this book, but a total of fifteen judges are mentioned in the Bible as Eli and Samuel are also considered to have ruled as judges. The Hebrew word "to judge" carries the idea of ruling, liberating, or delivering. The judges were supposed to acknowledge God as their supreme ruler in what could be called a theocracy, a period that lasted about 350 years until Samuel, the last judge, anointed Israel's first king, Saul.

In the book of Joshua, Israel disobeyed God by not driving out all the wicked and corrupt peoples from the land. Therefore, they committed apostasy against the true God, and lapsed into idolatry (chaps. 1—16), at which point God allowed one of the surrounding nations to oppress them. Seven times they did this, and seven times the Lord raised up judges to deliver them (2:16–19).

The thirteen judges mentioned in this book are Othniel (3:5–11), Ehud (3:12–30), Shamgar (3:31), Deborah and Barak (4:1—5:31), Gideon (6:1—8:32), Tola (10:1–2), Jair (10:3–5), Jephthah (11:1—12:7), Ibzan (12:8–10), Elon (12:11–12), Abdon (12:13–15), and Samson (13:1—16:31). Some may have ruled over separate areas as contemporaries.

Judges details Israel's incomplete possession of the land, their insufficient victory over evil, and their inconsistent manner of life. Here is the awful example of spiritual decline after great spiritual blessings, and God's grace and faithfulness in pursuing and restoring those who stray. While most Israelites wallowed in wickedness, God delivered His people and preserved a remnant.

Only 41 verses out of 618 (7% of the content) contain predictive statements, all fulfilled in those times. This lack of spiritual utterances sent from God is attested to later, "The word of the Lord was rare in those days" (1 Sam. 3:1).

Author
Possibly Samuel

Date
11th Century B.C.

Key Truth
Cycles of Judgment and Deliverance

Historic Time
Period of the Judges

Key Verse
21:25
. . . every man did that which was right in his own eyes.

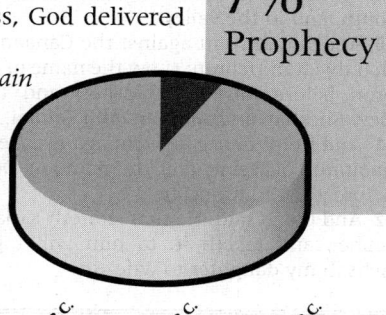

7%
Prophecy

1400 B.C. 1350 B.C. 1300 B.C. 1250 B.C. 1200 B.C. 1150 B.C. 1100 B.C. 1050 B.C. 1000 B.C.

1275-1215
Ehud

1353-1313
Othniel

1195-1155
Deborah and Barak

1148-1108
Gideon

1105-1099
Jephthah

1108-1105
Abimelech

1043-1011
Saul's reign

1105
Birth of Samuel

1069-1049
Samson

Dates may vary as some judges ruled over different areas at the same time.

1375-1050
Book of Judges

CHAPTER 1
Additional Land Is Conquered

1 Now after the death of Joshua it came to pass, that the children of Israel asked the LORD, saying, Who shall go up for us against the Canaanites first, to fight against them?
2 And the LORD said, Judah shall go up: behold, I have delivered the land into his hand.
3 And Judah said unto Simeon his brother, Come up with me into my lot, that we may fight against the Canaanites; and I likewise will go with thee into thy lot. So Simeon went with him.
4 And Judah went up; and the LORD delivered the Canaanites and the Perizzites into their hand: and they slew of them in Bezek ten thousand men.
5 And they found Adoni-bezek in Bezek: and they fought against him, and they slew the Canaanites and the Perizzites.
6 But Adoni-bezek fled; and they pursued after him, and caught him, and cut off his thumbs and his great toes.
7 And Adoni-bezek said, Threescore and ten kings, having their thumbs and their great toes cut off, gathered *their meat* under my table: as I have done, so God hath requited me. And they brought him to Jerusalem, and there he died.
8 Now the children of Judah had fought against Jerusalem, and had taken it, and smitten it with the edge of the sword, and set the city on fire.
9 And afterward the children of Judah went down to fight against the Canaanites, that dwelt in the mountain, and in the south, and in the valley.
10 And Judah went against the Canaanites that dwelt in Hebron: (now the name of Hebron before *was* Kirjath-arba:) and they slew Sheshai, and Ahiman, and Talmai.
11 And from thence he went against the inhabitants of Debir: and the name of Debir before *was* Kirjath-sepher:
12 And Caleb said, He that smiteth Kirjath-sepher, and taketh it, to him will I give Achsah my daughter to wife.

13 And Othniel the son of Kenaz, Caleb's younger brother, took it: and he gave him Achsah his daughter to wife.
14 And it came to pass, when she came *to him,* that she moved him to ask of her father a field: and she lighted from off *her* ass; and Caleb said unto her, What wilt thou?
15 And she said unto him, Give me a blessing: for thou hast given me a south land; give me also springs of water. And Caleb gave her the upper springs and the nether springs.
16 And the children of the Kenite, Moses' father-in-law, went up out of the city of palm trees with the children of Judah into the wilderness of Judah, which *lieth* in the south of Arad; and they went and dwelt among the people.
17 And Judah went with Simeon his brother, and they slew the Canaanites that inhabited Zephath, and utterly destroyed it. And the name of the city was called Hormah.
18 Also Judah took Gaza with the coast thereof, and Askelon with the coast thereof, and Ekron with the coast thereof.
19 And the LORD was with Judah; and he drave out *the inhabitants of* the mountain; but could not drive out the inhabitants of the valley, because they had chariots of iron.
20 And they gave Hebron unto Caleb, as Moses said: and he expelled thence the three sons of Anak.
21 And the children of Benjamin did not drive out the Jebusites that inhabited Jerusalem; but the Jebusites dwell with the children of Benjamin in Jerusalem unto this day.
22 And the house of Joseph, they also went up against Beth-el: and the LORD *was* with them.
23 And the house of Joseph sent to descry Beth-el. (Now the name of the city before *was* Luz.)
24 And the spies saw a man come forth out of the city, and they said unto him, Shew us, we pray thee, the entrance into the city, and we will shew thee mercy.

Cross references

2 Gen. 49:8
3 Judg. 1:17
4 1Sam. 11:8
7 Lev. 24:19; 1Sam. 15:33; James 2:13
8 Josh. 15:63
9 Josh. 10:36; 11:21; 15:13
10 Josh. 14:15; 15:13, 14
11 Josh. 15:15
12 Josh. 15:16, 17
13 Judg. 3:9
14 Josh. 15:18, 19
15 Gen. 33:11
16 Num. 10:32; 21:1; Deut. 34:3; Judg. 4:11, 17; 1Sam. 15:6; 1Chr. 2:55; Jer. 35:2
17 Num. 21:3; Josh. 19:4; Judg. 1:3
18 Josh. 11:22
19 Josh. 17:16, 18; Judg. 1:2; 2Kgs. 18:7
20 Num. 14:24; Deut. 1:36; Josh. 14:9, 13; 15:13, 14
21 Josh. 15:63; 18:28
22 Judg. 1:19
23 Gen. 28:19

1:2 The book of Judges (Hebr. *shophetim*), is the story of the Hebrew heroes who were empowered by the Spirit of God to execute the judgment of God on behalf of the people of Israel and deliver them from their enemies. In partial fulfillment of Jacob's prophecy that Judah would lead the twelve tribes (see Gen. 49:8–10), the Lord tells Judah to go up against the Canaanites. Despite their initial success in capturing Jerusalem (Judg. 1:8) and Hebron (1:10), Judah later failed to keep its position of leadership among the tribes during the period of the judges. It was not until the time of David that Judah again rose to prominence among the tribes of Israel. Ultimately, Jacob's prophecy was fulfilled in the person of Jesus Christ who came from the tribe of Judah through the line of David (see Matt. 1:1–17).

25 And when he shewed them the entrance into the city, they smote the city with the edge of the sword; but they let go the man and all his family.

26 And the man went into the land of the Hittites, and built a city, and called the name thereof Luz: which *is* the name thereof unto this day.

Some Land Is Not Conquered

27 Neither did Manasseh drive out *the inhabitants of* Beth-shean and her towns, nor Taanach and her towns, nor the inhabitants of Dor and her towns, nor the inhabitants of Ibleam and her towns, nor the inhabitants of Megiddo and her towns: but the Canaanites would dwell in that land.

28 And it came to pass, when Israel was strong, that they put the Canaanites to tribute, and did not utterly drive them out.

29 Neither did Ephraim drive out the Canaanites that dwelt in Gezer; but the Canaanites dwelt in Gezer among them.

30 Neither did Zebulun drive out the inhabitants of Kitron, nor the inhabitants of Nahalol; but the Canaanites dwelt among them, and became tributaries.

31 Neither did Asher drive out the inhabitants of Accho, nor the inhabitants of Zidon, nor of Ahlab, nor of Achzib, nor of Helbah, nor of Aphik, nor of Rehob:

32 But the Asherites dwelt among the Canaanites, the inhabitants of the land: for they did not drive them out.

33 Neither did Naphtali drive out the inhabitants of Beth-shemesh, nor the inhabitants of Beth-anath; but he dwelt among the Canaanites, the inhabitants of the land: nevertheless the inhabitants of Beth-shemesh and of Beth-anath became tributaries unto them.

34 And the Amorites forced the children of Dan into the mountain: for they would not suffer them to come down to the valley:

35 But the Amorites would dwell in mount Heres in Aijalon, and in Shaalbim: yet the hand of the house of Joseph prevailed, so that they became tributaries.

36 And the coast of the Amorites *was* from the going up to Akrabbim, from the rock, and upward.

CHAPTER 2
God Sends His Angel

1 And an angel of the LORD came up from Gilgal to Bochim, and said, I made you to go up out of Egypt, and have brought you unto the land which I sware unto your fathers; and I said, I will never break my covenant with you.

2 And ye shall make no league with the inhabitants of this land; ye shall throw down their altars: but ye have not obeyed my voice: why have ye done this?

3 Wherefore I also said, I will not drive them out from before you; but they shall be *as thorns* in your sides, and their gods shall be a snare unto you.

4 And it came to pass, when the angel of the LORD spake these words unto all the children of Israel, that the people lifted up their voice, and wept.

5 And they called the name of that place Bochim: and they sacrificed there unto the LORD.

Joshua's Death

6 And when Joshua had let the people go, the children of Israel went every man unto his inheritance to possess the land.

7 And the people served the LORD all the days of Joshua, and all the days of the elders that outlived Joshua, who had seen all the great works of the LORD, that he did for Israel.

8 And Joshua the son of Nun, the servant of the LORD, died, *being* an hundred and ten years old.

9 And they buried him in the border of his inheritance in Timnath-heres, in the mount of Ephraim, on the north side of the hill Gaash.

10 And also all that generation were gathered unto their fathers: and there arose another generation after them, which knew

27 Josh. 17:11-13
29 Josh. 16:10; 1Kgs. 9:16
30 Josh. 19:15
31 Josh. 19:24-30
32 Ps. 106:34, 35
33 Josh. 19:38; Judg. 1:30, 32
35 Josh. 19:42
36 Num. 34:4; Josh. 15:3
1 Gen. 17:7; Judg. 2:5
2 Deut. 7:2; 12:3; Judg. 2:20; Ps. 106:34
3 Ex. 23:33; 34:12; Deut. 7:16; Josh. 23:13; Judg. 3:6; Ps. 106:36
6 Josh. 22:6; 24:28
7 Josh. 24:29, 31
9 Josh. 19:50; 24:30
10 Ex. 5:2; 1Sam. 2:12; 1Chr. 28:9; Jer. 9:3; 22:16; Gal. 4:8; 2Thess. 1:8; Titus 1:16

2:1 an angel of the LORD. This is actually the Lord himself. When the angel speaks, it is actually the Lord speaking. He is called "LORD," the Hebrew name for Yahweh (or Jehovah) and "God" (cf. Gen. 16:7,13; 48:15–16). Since the Bible clearly states that God the Father is unseen by mortal men (John 1:18), this must be Christ, the second person of the Trinity. These temporary visible appearances of Christ in human form in the Old Testament are called theophanies, or better Christophanies. The ministry of the "angel of the LORD" included divine activity such as revelation, salvation, and judgment. In this passage, He traveled from Gilgal, the place where Joshua set up his battle camp (Josh. 5:10), to Bochim ("weepers") to rebuke the Israelites for violating their covenant with Him.

not the LORD, nor yet the works which he had done for Israel.

Preview of Israel's Sin

11 And the children of Israel did evil in the sight of the LORD, and served Baalim:

12 And they forsook the LORD God of their fathers, which brought them out of the land of Egypt, and followed other gods, of the gods of the people that *were* round about them, and bowed themselves unto them, and provoked the LORD to anger.

13 And they forsook the LORD, and served Baal and Ashtaroth.

14 And the anger of the LORD was hot against Israel, and he delivered them into the hands of spoilers that spoiled them, and he sold them into the hands of their enemies round about, so that they could not any longer stand before their enemies.

15 Whithersoever they went out, the hand of the LORD was against them for evil, as the LORD had said, and as the LORD had sworn unto them: and they were greatly distressed.

16 Nevertheless the LORD raised up judges, which delivered them out of the hand of those that spoiled them.

17 And yet they would not hearken unto their judges, but they went a whoring after other gods, and bowed themselves unto them: they turned quickly out of the way which their fathers walked in, obeying the commandments of the LORD; *but* they did not so.

18 And when the LORD raised them up judges, then the LORD was with the judge, and delivered them out of the hand of their enemies all the days of the judge: for it repented the LORD because of their groanings by reason of them that oppressed them and vexed them.

19 And it came to pass, when the judge was dead, *that* they returned, and corrupted *themselves* more than their fathers, in following other gods to serve them, and to bow down unto them; they ceased not from their own doings, nor from their stubborn way.

20 And the anger of the LORD was hot against Israel; and he said, Because that this people hath transgressed my covenant

which I commanded their fathers, and have not hearkened unto my voice;

21 I also will not henceforth drive out any from before them of the nations which Joshua left when he died:

22 That through them I may prove Israel, whether they will keep the way of the LORD to walk therein, as their fathers did keep *it*, or not.

23 Therefore the LORD left those nations, without driving them out hastily; neither delivered he them into the hand of Joshua.

CHAPTER 3
The Nations Not Conquered

1 Now these *are* the nations which the LORD left, to prove Israel by them, *even* as many *of Israel* as had not known all the wars of Canaan;

2 Only that the generations of the children of Israel might know, to teach them war, at the least such as before knew nothing thereof;

3 *Namely*, five lords of the Philistines, and all the Canaanites, and the Sidonians, and the Hivites that dwelt in mount Lebanon, from mount Baal-hermon unto the entering in of Hamath.

4 And they were to prove Israel by them, to know whether they would hearken unto the commandments of the LORD, which he commanded their fathers by the hand of Moses.

5 And the children of Israel dwelt among the Canaanites, Hittites, and Amorites, and Perizzites, and Hivites, and Jebusites:

6 And they took their daughters to be their wives, and gave their daughters to their sons, and served their gods.

Othniel

7 And the children of Israel did evil in the sight of the LORD, and forgat the LORD their God, and served Baalim and the groves.

8 Therefore the anger of the LORD was hot against Israel, and he sold them into the hand of Chushan-rishathaim king of Mesopotamia: and the children of Israel served Chushan-rishathaim eight years.

9 And when the children of Israel cried unto the LORD, the LORD raised up a deliverer to the children of Israel, who delivered

---

Cross references (center column):

12 Ex. 20:5; Deut. 6:14; 31:16

13 Judg. 3:7; 10:6; Ps. 100:36

14 Lev. 26:37; Josh. 7:12, 13; Judg. 3:8; 4:2; 2Kgs. 17:20; Ps. 44:12; 106:40-42; Isa. 50:1

16 Judg. 3:9, 10, 15; 1Sam. 12:11; Acts 13:20

17 Ex. 34:15, 16; Lev. 17:7

18 Gen. 6:6; Deut. 32:36; Josh. 1:5; Ps. 106:44, 45

19 Judg. 3:12; 4:1; 8:33

20 Josh. 23:16; Judg. 2:14

21 Josh. 23:13

22 Deut. 8:2, 16; 13:3; Judg. 3:1, 4

1 Judg. 2:21, 22

3 Josh. 13:3

4 Judg. 2:22

5 Ps. 106:35

6 Ex. 34:16; Deut. 7:3

7 Ex. 34:13; Deut. 16:21; Judg. 2:11, 13; 6:25

8 Judg. 2:14; Hab. 3:7

9 Judg. 1:13; 2:16; 3:15; 4:3; 6:7; 10:10; 1Sam. 12:10; Neh. 9:27; Ps. 22:5; 106:44; 107:13, 19

2:20–23 Because of Israel's failure to eradicate its enemies, God predicted He would not drive out any more people on its behalf, but would leave those people in the land to prove (or "test") Israel's devotion to Him. Even before the six cycles of judgment-repentance-restoration-relapse that follow in chapters 3—16, Israel had already failed to keep her promises to God and suffered the consequences for several generations to come.

them, *even* Othniel the son of Kenaz, Caleb's younger brother.

10 And the Spirit of the LORD came upon him, and he judged Israel, and went out to war: and the LORD delivered Chushan-rishathaim king of Mesopotamia into his hand; and his hand prevailed against Chushan-rishathaim.

11 And the land had rest forty years. And Othniel the son of Kenaz died.

Ehud

12 And the children of Israel did evil again in the sight of the LORD: and the LORD strengthened Eglon the king of Moab against Israel, because they had done evil in the sight of the LORD.

13 And he gathered unto him the children of Ammon and Amalek, and went and smote Israel, and possessed the city of palm trees.

14 So the children of Israel served Eglon the king of Moab eighteen years.

15 But when the children of Israel cried unto the LORD, the LORD raised them up a deliverer, Ehud the son of Gera, a Benjamite, a man lefthanded: and by him the children of Israel sent a present unto Eglon the king of Moab.

16 But Ehud made him a dagger which had two edges, of a cubit length; and he did gird it under his raiment upon his right thigh.

17 And he brought the present unto Eglon king of Moab: and Eglon *was* a very fat man.

18 And when he had made an end to offer the present, he sent away the people that bare the present.

19 But he himself turned again from the quarries that *were* by Gilgal, and said, I have a secret errand unto thee, O king: who said, Keep silence. And all that stood by him went out from him.

20 And Ehud came unto him; and he was sitting in a summer parlour, which he had for himself alone. And Ehud said, I have a message from God unto thee. And he arose out of *his* seat.

21 And Ehud put forth his left hand, and took the dagger from his right thigh, and thrust it into his belly:

22 And the haft also went in after the blade; and the fat closed upon the blade, so that he could not draw the dagger out of his belly; and the dirt came out.

23 Then Ehud went forth through the porch, and shut the doors of the parlour upon him, and locked them.

24 When he was gone out, his servants came; and when they saw that, behold, the doors of the parlour *were* locked, they said, Surely he covereth his feet in his summer chamber.

25 And they tarried till they were ashamed: and, behold, he opened not the doors of the parlour; therefore they took a key, and opened *them*: and, behold, their lord *was* fallen down dead on the earth.

26 And Ehud escaped while they tarried, and passed beyond the quarries, and escaped unto Seirath.

27 And it came to pass, when he was come, that he blew a trumpet in the mountain of Ephraim, and the children of Israel went down with him from the mount, and he before them.

28 And he said unto them, Follow after me: for the LORD hath delivered your enemies the Moabites into your hand. And they went down after him, and took the fords of Jordan toward Moab, and suffered not a man to pass over.

29 And they slew of Moab at that time about ten thousand men, all lusty, and all men of valour; and there escaped not a man.

30 So Moab was subdued that day under the hand of Israel. And the land had rest fourscore years.

Shamgar

31 And after him was Shamgar the son of Anath, which slew of the Philistines six hundred men with an ox goad: and he also delivered Israel.

CHAPTER 4
Deborah

1 And the children of Israel again did evil in the sight of the LORD, when Ehud was dead.

Cross-references (center column)

10 Num. 27:18; Judg. 6:34; 11:29; 13:25; 14:6, 19; 1Sam. 11:6; 2Chr. 15:1

12 Judg. 2:19; 1Sam. 12:9

13 Judg. 1:16; 5:14

14 Deut. 28:48

15 Judg. 3:9; 20:16; Ps. 78:34

19 Josh. 4:20

20 Amos 3:15

24 1Sam. 24:3

27 Josh. 17:15; Judg. 5:14; 6:34; 7:24; 17:1; 19:1; 1Sam. 13:3

28 Josh. 2:7; Judg. 7:9, 15; 12:5; 1Sam. 17:47

30 Judg. 3:11

31 Judg. 2:16; 4:1, 3–10; 5:6, 8; 10:7, 17; 11:4; 1Sam. 4:1; 13:19, 22; 17:47, 50

1 Judg. 2:19

4:1–11 Deborah, a prophetess. She predicted Israel's victory over the Canaanites at Mount Tabor (4:6–7). Deborah challenged Barak to lead the Israelites against the army of Jabin, King of Hazor, promising that God would defeat Sisera, Jabin's captain at the River Kishon, which flows in the valley below Mount Tabor. When Barak revealed his reluctance, Deborah predicted that a woman would get credit for the victory. Her predictions were fulfilled when Sisera's chariots were bogged down in the flooded riverbed (cf. 4:13–15; 5:21), and the Israelites slaughtered the Canaanite invaders in the valley of Megiddo (5:19).

2 And the LORD sold them into the hand of Jabin king of Canaan, that reigned in Hazor; the captain of whose host *was* Sisera, which dwelt in Harosheth of the Gentiles.

3 And the children of Israel cried unto the LORD: for he had nine hundred chariots of iron; and twenty years he mightily oppressed the children of Israel.

4 And Deborah, a prophetess, the wife of Lapidoth, she judged Israel at that time.

5 And she dwelt under the palm tree of Deborah between Ramah and Beth-el in mount Ephraim: and the children of Israel came up to her for judgment.

6 And she sent and called Barak the son of Abinoam out of Kedesh-naphtali, and said unto him, Hath not the LORD God of Israel commanded, *saying*, Go and draw toward mount Tabor, and take with thee ten thousand men of the children of Naphtali and of the children of Zebulun?

7 And I will draw unto thee to the river Kishon Sisera, the captain of Jabin's army, with his chariots and his multitude; and I will deliver him into thine hand.

8 And Barak said unto her, If thou wilt go with me, then I will go: but if thou wilt not go with me, *then* I will not go.

9 And she said, I will surely go with thee: notwithstanding the journey that thou takest shall not be for thine honour; for the LORD shall sell Sisera into the hand of a woman. And Deborah arose, and went with Barak to Kedesh.

10 And Barak called Zebulun and Naphtali to Kedesh; and he went up with ten thousand men at his feet: and Deborah went up with him.

11 Now Heber the Kenite, *which was* of the children of Hobab the father-in-law of Moses, had severed himself from the Kenites, and pitched his tent unto the plain of Zaanaim, which *is* by Kedesh.

12 And they shewed Sisera that Barak the son of Abinoam was gone up to mount Tabor.

13 And Sisera gathered together all his chariots, *even* nine hundred chariots of iron, and all the people that *were* with him, from Harosheth of the Gentiles unto the river of Kishon.

14 And Deborah said unto Barak, Up; for this *is* the day in which the LORD hath delivered Sisera into thine hand: is not the LORD gone out before thee? So Barak went down from mount Tabor, and ten thousand men after him.

15 And the LORD discomfited Sisera, and all

his chariots, and all *his* host, with the edge of the sword before Barak; so that Sisera lighted down off *his* chariot, and fled away on his feet.

16 But Barak pursued after the chariots, and after the host, unto Harosheth of the Gentiles: and all the host of Sisera fell upon the edge of the sword; *and* there was not a man left.

17 Howbeit Sisera fled away on his feet to the tent of Jael the wife of Heber the Kenite: for *there was* peace between Jabin the king of Hazor and the house of Heber the Kenite.

18 And Jael went out to meet Sisera, and said unto him, Turn in, my lord, turn in to me; fear not. And when he had turned in unto her into the tent, she covered him with a mantle.

19 And he said unto her, Give me, I pray thee, a little water to drink; for I am thirsty. And she opened a bottle of milk, and gave him drink, and covered him.

20 Again he said unto her, Stand in the door of the tent, and it shall be, when any man doth come and inquire of thee, and say, Is there any man here? that thou shalt say, No.

21 Then Jael Heber's wife took a nail of the tent, and took an hammer in her hand, and went softly unto him, and smote the nail into his temples, and fastened it into the ground: for he was fast asleep and weary. So he died.

22 And, behold, as Barak pursued Sisera, Jael came out to meet him, and said unto him, Come, and I will shew thee the man whom thou seekest. And when he came into her *tent*, behold, Sisera lay dead, and the nail *was* in his temples.

23 So God subdued on that day Jabin the king of Canaan before the children of Israel.

24 And the hand of the children of Israel prospered, and prevailed against Jabin the king of Canaan, until they had destroyed Jabin king of Canaan.

CHAPTER 5
Deborah's Song

1 Then sang Deborah and Barak the son of Abinoam on that day, saying,

2 Praise ye the LORD for the avenging of Israel, when the people willingly offered themselves.

3 Hear, O ye kings; give ear, O ye princes; I, *even* I, will sing unto the LORD; I will sing *praise* to the LORD God of Israel.

4 LORD, when thou wentest out of Seir, when thou marchedst out of the field of Edom, the earth trembled, and the heavens

---

Cross references (center column):

2 Josh. 11:1, 10; 19:36; Judg. 2:14; 1Sam. 12:9; Ps. 83:9

3 Judg. 1:19; 5:8; Ps. 106:42

5 Gen. 35:8

6 Josh. 19:37; Heb. 11:32

7 Ex. 14:4; Judg. 5:21; 1Kgs. 18:40; Ps. 83:9, 10

9 Judg. 2:14

10 Ex. 11:8; Judg. 5:18; 1Kgs. 20:10

11 Num. 10:29; Judg. 1:16; 4:6

14 Deut. 9:3; 2Sam. 5:24; Ps. 68:7; Isa. 52:12

15 Josh. 10:10; Ps. 83:9, 10

19 Judg. 5:25

21 Judg. 5:26

23 Ps. 18:47

1 Ex. 15:1

2 2Chr. 17:16; Ps. 18:47

3 Deut. 32:1, 3; Ps. 2:10

4 Deut. 33:2; 2Sam. 22:8; Ps. 68:7, 8; Isa. 64:3; Hab. 3:3, 10

dropped, the clouds also dropped water.
5 The mountains melted from before the LORD, *even* that Sinai from before the LORD God of Israel.
6 In the days of Shamgar the son of Anath, in the days of Jael, the highways were unoccupied, and the travellers walked through byways.
7 *The inhabitants of* the villages ceased, they ceased in Israel, until that I Deborah arose, that I arose a mother in Israel.
8 They chose new gods; then *was* war in the gates: was there a shield or spear seen among forty thousand in Israel?
9 My heart *is* toward the governors of Israel, that offered themselves willingly among the people. Bless ye the LORD.
10 Speak, ye that ride on white asses, ye that sit in judgment, and walk by the way.
11 *They that are delivered* from the noise of archers in the places of drawing water, there shall they rehearse the righteous acts of the LORD, *even* the righteous acts *toward the inhabitants* of his villages in Israel: then shall the people of the LORD go down to the gates.
12 Awake, awake, Deborah: awake, awake, utter a song: arise, Barak, and lead thy captivity captive, thou son of Abinoam.
13 Then he made him that remaineth have dominion over the nobles among the people: the LORD made me have dominion over the mighty.
14 Out of Ephraim *was there* a root of them against Amalek; after thee, Benjamin, among thy people; out of Machir came down governors, and out of Zebulun they that handle the pen of the writer.
15 And the princes of Issachar *were* with Deborah; even Issachar, and also Barak: he was sent on foot into the valley. For the divisions of Reuben *there were* great thoughts of heart.
16 Why abodest thou among the sheepfolds, to hear the bleatings of the flocks? For the divisions of Reuben *there were* great searchings of heart.
17 Gilead abode beyond Jordan: and why did Dan remain in ships? Asher continued on the sea shore, and abode in his breaches.
18 Zebulun and Naphtali *were* a people that jeoparded their lives unto the death in the high places of the field.
19 The kings came *and* fought, then fought the kings of Canaan in Taanach by the waters of Megiddo; they took no gain of money.
20 They fought from heaven; the stars in their courses fought against Sisera.
21 The river of Kishon swept them away,

that ancient river, the river Kishon. O my soul, thou hast trodden down strength.
22 Then were the horsehoofs broken by the means of the pransings, the pransings of their mighty ones.
23 Curse ye Meroz, said the angel of the LORD, curse ye bitterly the inhabitants thereof; because they came not to the help of the LORD, to the help of the LORD against the mighty.
24 Blessed above women shall Jael the wife of Heber the Kenite be, blessed shall she be above women in the tent.
25 He asked water, *and* she gave *him* milk; she brought forth butter in a lordly dish.
26 She put her hand to the nail, and her right hand to the workmen's hammer; and with the hammer she smote Sisera, she smote off his head, when she had pierced and stricken through his temples.
27 At her feet he bowed, he fell, he lay down: at her feet he bowed, he fell: where he bowed, there he fell down dead.
28 The mother of Sisera looked out at a window, and cried through the lattice, Why is his chariot *so* long in coming? why tarry the wheels of his chariots?
29 Her wise ladies answered her, yea, she returned answer to herself,
30 Have they not sped? have they *not* divided the prey; to every man a damsel *or* two; to Sisera a prey of divers colours, a prey of divers colours of needlework, of divers colours of needlework on both sides, *meet* for the necks of *them that take* the spoil?
31 So let all thine enemies perish, O LORD: but *let* them that love him *be* as the sun when he goeth forth in his might. And the land had rest forty years.

CHAPTER 6
Gideon's Call

1 And the children of Israel did evil in the sight of the LORD: and the LORD delivered them into the hand of Midian seven years.
2 And the hand of Midian prevailed against Israel: *and* because of the Midianites the children of Israel made them the dens which *are* in the mountains, and caves, and strong holds.
3 And *so* it was, when Israel had sown, that the Midianites came up, and the Amalekites, and the children of the east, even they came up against them;
4 And they encamped against them, and destroyed the increase of the earth, till thou come unto Gaza, and left no sustenance for Israel, neither sheep, nor ox, nor ass.

Center column references:

5 Ex. 19:18; Deut. 4:11; Ps. 97:5
6 2Chr. 15:5
7 Isa. 49:23
8 Deut. 32:16; Judg. 2:12, 17; 4:3; 1Sam. 13:19, 22
9 Judg. 5:2
10 Judg. 10:4; 12:14; Ps. 105:2; 107:32; 145:5
11 1Sam. 12:7; Ps. 145:7
12 Ps. 57:8; 68:18
13 Num. 32:39, 40; Judg. 3:13, 27; Ps. 49:14
15 Judg. 4:14
16 Num. 32:1
17 Josh. 13:25, 31; 19:29, 31
18 Judg. 4:10
19 Judg. 4:16; 5:30; Ps. 44:12
20 Josh. 10:11; Judg. 4:15; Ps. 77:17, 18
21 Judg. 4:7
23 Judg. 21:9, 10; 1Sam. 17:47; 18:17; 25:28; Neh. 3:5
24 Judg. 4:17; Luke 1:28
25 Judg. 4:19
26 Judg. 4:21
30 Ex. 15:9
31 2Sam. 23:4; Ps. 19:5; 83:9, 10
1 Judg. 2:19; Hab. 3:7
2 1Sam. 13:6
3 Gen. 29:1; Job 1:3
4 Deut. 28:30, 33, 51

5 For they came up with their cattle and their tents, and they came as grasshoppers for multitude; *for* both they and their camels were without number: and they entered into the land to destroy it.

6 And Israel was greatly impoverished because of the Midianites; and the children of Israel cried unto the LORD.

7 And it came to pass, when the children of Israel cried unto the LORD because of the Midianites,

8 That the LORD sent a prophet unto the children of Israel, which said unto them, Thus saith the LORD God of Israel, I brought you up from Egypt, and brought you forth out of the house of bondage;

9 And I delivered you out of the hand of the Egyptians, and out of the hand of all that oppressed you, and drave them out from before you, and gave them their land;

10 And I said unto you, I *am* the LORD your God; fear not the gods of the Amorites, in whose land ye dwell: but ye have not obeyed my voice.

11 And there came an angel of the LORD, and sat under an oak which *was* in Ophrah, that *pertained* unto Joash the Abi-ezrite: and his son Gideon threshed wheat by the winepress, to hide *it* from the Midianites.

12 And the angel of the LORD appeared unto him, and said unto him, The LORD *is* with thee, thou mighty man of valour.

13 And Gideon said unto him, Oh my Lord, if the LORD be with us, why then is all this befallen us? and where *be* all his miracles which our fathers told us of, saying, Did not the LORD bring us up from Egypt? but now the LORD hath forsaken us, and delivered us into the hands of the Midianites.

14 And the LORD looked upon him, and said, Go in this thy might, and thou shalt save Israel from the hand of the Midianites: have not I sent thee?

15 And he said unto him, Oh my Lord, wherewith shall I save Israel? behold, my family *is* poor in Manasseh, and I *am* the least in my father's house.

16 And the LORD said unto him, Surely I will be with thee, and thou shalt smite the Midianites as one man.

17 And he said unto him, If now I have

found grace in thy sight, then shew me a sign that thou talkest with me.

18 Depart not hence, I pray thee, until I come unto thee, and bring forth my present, and set *it* before thee. And he said, I will tarry until thou come again.

19 And Gideon went in, and made ready a kid, and unleavened cakes of an ephah of flour: the flesh he put in a basket, and he put the broth in a pot, and brought *it* out unto him under the oak, and presented *it*.

20 And the angel of God said unto him, Take the flesh and the unleavened cakes, and lay *them* upon this rock, and pour out the broth. And he did so.

21 Then the angel of the LORD put forth the end of the staff that *was* in his hand, and touched the flesh and the unleavened cakes; and there rose up fire out of the rock, and consumed the flesh and the unleavened cakes. Then the angel of the LORD departed out of his sight.

22 And when Gideon perceived that he *was* an angel of the LORD, Gideon said, Alas, O Lord GOD! for because I have seen an angel of the LORD face to face.

23 And the LORD said unto him, Peace *be* unto thee; fear not: thou shalt not die.

24 Then Gideon built an altar there unto the LORD, and called it Jehovah-shalom: unto this day it *is* yet in Ophrah of the Abi-ezrites.

Gideon Destroys Altar of Baal

25 And it came to pass the same night, that the LORD said unto him, Take thy father's young bullock, even the second bullock of seven years old, and throw down the altar of Baal that thy father hath, and cut down the grove that *is* by it:

26 And build an altar unto the LORD thy God upon the top of this rock, in the ordered place, and take the second bullock, and offer a burnt sacrifice with the wood of the grove which thou shalt cut down.

27 Then Gideon took ten men of his servants, and did as the LORD had said unto him: and *so* it was, because he feared his father's household, and the men of the city, that he could not do *it* by day, that he did *it* by night.

28 And when the men of the city arose early

Cross references (center column)

5 Judg. 7:12
6 Judg. 3:15; Hos. 5:15
9 Ps. 44:2, 3
10 2Kgs. 17:35, 37, 38; Jer. 10:2
11 Josh. 17:2; Heb. 11:32
12 Josh. 1:5; Judg. 13:3; Luke 1:11, 28
13 2Chr. 15:2; Ps. 44:1; 89:49; Isa. 59:1; 63:15
14 Josh. 1:9; Judg. 4:6; 1Sam. 12:11; Heb. 11:32, 34
15 Ex. 18:21, 25; 1Sam. 9:21; Mic. 5:2
16 Ex. 3:12; Josh. 1:5
17 Ex. 4:1-8; Judg. 6:36, 37; 2Kgs. 20:8; Ps. 86:17; Isa. 7:11
18 Gen. 18:3, 5; Judg. 13:15
19 Gen. 18:6-8
20 Judg. 13:19; 1Kgs. 18:33, 34
21 Lev. 9:24; 1Kgs. 18:38; 2Chr. 7:1
22 Gen. 16:13; 32:30; Ex. 33:20; Judg. 13:21, 22
23 Dan. 10:19
24 Gen. 22:14; Ex. 17:15; Judg. 8:32; Jer. 33:16; Ezek. 48:35
25 Ex. 34:13; Deut. 7:5

6:11–24 The "angel of the LORD" appeared to Gideon, a fearful Israelite of the tribe of Manasseh, and predicted that He would use him to defeat the alliance of Midianite and Amalekite bandits that were oppressing Israel at that time (Judg. 6:14). Despite Gideon's initial hesitation, God convinced him to use three hundred men to frighten the invaders into fleeing for their lives (see 7:1–25).

Angels

By David Jeremiah

Plain and simple, angels are created spirit beings from outside this world who exist in an innumerable company (Heb. 13:22). Within that loose meaning are two broad categories of angels: good and bad. The good ones we call God's angels. The bad ones are fallen angels—Satan and his demons. Some interpreters believe that all angels were created on the second day of creation (see Ps. 104), but regardless of when they were created, some time in that early period, for purposes beyond our understanding, Satan instigated an angelic rebellion (see the article on Fallen Angels). For the remainder of this article, the angels discussed are referring to "good" angels.

God's angels—that is, the "good" angels—definitely call God's heaven their home. These holy angels belong only to the God of the Bible, and therefore to heaven. They do not belong to earth or to any earthly religion or philosophy. Through their actions on earth and in heaven, as revealed in the Scriptures, we observe that God uses angels in connection with the human race, sometimes to bring protection and blessing and at other times as messengers of judgment, as in the book of Revelation. They are specifically called "ministering spirits, sent forth to minister (serve) for them who shall be heirs of salvation," or "who will inherit salvation" (Heb. 1:14).

> *We must never let angels replace God in our lives.*

There are three principles, key warnings actually, that will guide us to a biblical perspective about angels and our relationship to them. The first is that *we must not create or reshape angels according to our own fancy.* This is being done in our present society, where the creations of mankind's imagination are sold in the form of figurines and paintings that are called "angels." The angels mentioned in the Bible are created spirit beings, not humans in afterlife. Unlike humans, angels are not permanently housed in physical bodies. They do not have to "earn their wings," nor do they act on their own reasoning and volition. Though only two angels are ever mentioned by name, Gabriel (Dan. 8:16; 9:21; Luke 1:19, 26) and Michael the Archangel (Dan. 10:13, 21; 12:1; Jude 1:9; Rev. 12:7), wherever gender is mentioned, the angels in the Bible are described as male beings.

The second warning is that *we must never let angels replace God in our lives.* Angels may be "other-worldly" and powerful; however, they do not act but by the power of Almighty God. In this age where many are consumed with "spiritual" things apart from the God of the Bible, fascination with angels is one more vain attempt to overcome the spiritual void that only a relationship with Christ can fill. Before we desire to be led by angels, we must remember that the children of Israel were filled with mourning at the thought that they would be led by an angel rather than the God of heaven (Ex. 33:1–4).

The third warning is that *angels must never receive our worship* (Col. 2:18). In heaven all worship is directed only to God (Rev. 19:10; 22:9).

Nearly every book in the Bible alludes to angels. Angels are present not only to give new revelations but to provide watchcare and protection for God's people. They are worshipers and warriors (the Lord's Host); they have different ranks (thrones, powers, rulers, authorities—Col. 1:16; Eph. 1:20–21; 3:10); and they are immortal.

in the morning, behold, the altar of Baal was cast down, and the grove was cut down that *was* by it, and the second bullock was offered upon the altar *that was* built.

29 And they said one to another, Who hath done this thing? And when they inquired and asked, they said, Gideon the son of Joash hath done this thing.

30 Then the men of the city said unto Joash, Bring out thy son, that he may die: because he hath cast down the altar of Baal, and because he hath cut down the grove that *was* by it.

31 And Joash said unto all that stood against him, Will ye plead for Baal? will ye save him? he that will plead for him, let him be put to death whilst *it is yet* morning: if he *be* a god, let him plead for himself, because *one* hath cast down his altar.

32 Therefore on that day he called him Jerubbaal, saying, Let Baal plead against him, because he hath thrown down his altar.

Gideon Prepares for Battle

33 Then all the Midianites and the Amalekites and the children of the east were gathered together, and went over, and pitched in the valley of Jezreel.

34 But the Spirit of the LORD came upon Gideon, and he blew a trumpet; and Abiezer was gathered after him.

35 And he sent messengers throughout all Manasseh; who also was gathered after him: and he sent messengers unto Asher, and unto Zebulun, and unto Naphtali; and they came up to meet them.

36 And Gideon said unto God, If thou wilt save Israel by mine hand, as thou hast said,

37 Behold, I will put a fleece of wool in the floor; *and* if the dew be on the fleece only, and *it be* dry upon all the earth *beside*, then shall I know that thou wilt save Israel by mine hand, as thou hast said.

38 And it was so: for he rose up early on the morrow, and thrust the fleece together, and wringed the dew out of the fleece, a bowl full of water.

39 And Gideon said unto God, Let not thine anger be hot against me and I will speak but this once: let me prove, I pray thee, but this once with the fleece; let it now be dry only upon the fleece, and upon all the ground let there be dew.

40 And God did so that night: for it was dry upon the fleece only, and there was dew on all the ground.

32 1Sam. 12:11; 2Sam. 11:21

33 Josh. 17:16; Judg. 6:3

34 Num. 10:3; 3:27; Judg. 3:10; 1Chr. 12:18; 2Chr. 24:20

37 Ex. 4:3, 4, 6, 7

39 Gen. 18:32

1 Judg. 6:32

2 Deut. 8:17; Isa. 10:13; 1Cor. 1:29; 2Cor. 4:7

3 Deut. 20:8

7 1Sam. 14:6

9 Gen. 46:2, 3

11 Gen. 24:14; Ex. 13:18; Judg. 7:13-15; 1Sam. 14:9, 10

CHAPTER 7

1 Then Jerubbaal, who *is* Gideon, and all the people that *were* with him, rose up early, and pitched beside the well of Harod: so that the host of the Midianites were on the north side of them, by the hill of Moreh, in the valley.

2 And the LORD said unto Gideon, The people that *are* with thee *are* too many for me to give the Midianites into their hands, lest Israel vaunt themselves against me, saying, Mine own hand hath saved me.

3 Now therefore go to, proclaim in the ears of the people, saying, Whosoever *is* fearful and afraid, let him return and depart early from mount Gilead. And there returned of the people twenty and two thousand; and there remained ten thousand.

4 And the LORD said unto Gideon, The people *are* yet *too* many; bring them down unto the water, and I will try them for thee there: and it shall be, *that* of whom I say unto thee, This shall go with thee, the same shall go with thee; and of whomsoever I say unto thee, This shall not go with thee, the same shall not go.

5 So he brought down the people unto the water: and the LORD said unto Gideon, Every one that lappeth of the water with his tongue, as a dog lappeth, him shalt thou set by himself; likewise every one that boweth down upon his knees to drink.

6 And the number of them that lapped, *putting* their hand to their mouth, were three hundred men: but all the rest of the people bowed down upon their knees to drink water.

7 And the LORD said unto Gideon, By the three hundred men that lapped will I save you, and deliver the Midianites into thine hand: and let all the *other* people go every man unto his place.

8 So the people took victuals in their hand, and their trumpets: and he sent all *the rest of* Israel every man unto his tent, and retained those three hundred men: and the host of Midian was beneath him in the valley.

The Battle

9 And it came to pass the same night, that the LORD said unto him, Arise, get thee down unto the host; for I have delivered it into thine hand.

10 But if thou fear to go down, go thou with Phurah thy servant down to the host:

11 And thou shalt hear what they say; and afterward shall thine hands be strengthened

to go down unto the host. Then went he down with Phurah his servant unto the outside of the armed men that *were* in the host.

12 And the Midianites and the Amalekites and all the children of the east lay along in the valley like grasshoppers for multitude; and their camels *were* without number, as the sand by the sea side for multitude.

13 And when Gideon was come, behold, *there was* a man that told a dream unto his fellow, and said, Behold, I dreamed a dream, and, lo, a cake of barley bread tumbled into the host of Midian, and came unto a tent, and smote it that it fell, and overturned it, that the tent lay along.

14 And his fellow answered and said, This *is* nothing else save the sword of Gideon the son of Joash, a man of Israel: *for* into his hand hath God delivered Midian, and all the host.

15 And it was *so*, when Gideon heard the telling of the dream, and the interpretation thereof, that he worshipped, and returned into the host of Israel, and said, Arise; for the LORD hath delivered into your hand the host of Midian.

16 And he divided the three hundred men *into* three companies, and he put a trumpet in every man's hand, with empty pitchers, and lamps within the pitchers.

17 And he said unto them, Look on me, and do likewise: and, behold, when I come to the outside of the camp, it shall be *that*, as I do, so shall ye do.

18 When I blow with a trumpet, I and all that *are* with me, then blow ye the trumpets also on every side of all the camp, and say, *The sword* of the LORD, and of Gideon.

19 So Gideon, and the hundred men that *were* with him, came unto the outside of the camp in the beginning of the middle watch; and they had but newly set the watch: and they blew the trumpets, and brake the pitchers that *were* in their hands.

20 And the three companies blew the trumpets, and brake the pitchers, and held the lamps in their left hands, and the trumpets in their right hands to blow *withal*: and they cried, The sword of the LORD, and of Gideon.

21 And they stood every man in his place round about the camp: and all the host ran, and cried, and fled.

22 And the three hundred blew the trumpets, and the LORD set every man's sword against his fellow, even throughout all the host: and the host fled to Beth-shittah in Zererath, *and* to the border of Abel-meholah, unto Tabbath.

23 And the men of Israel gathered themselves together out of Naphtali, and out of Asher, and out of all Manasseh, and pursued after the Midianites.

24 And Gideon sent messengers throughout all mount Ephraim, saying, Come down against the Midianites, and take before them the waters unto Beth-barah and Jordan. Then all the men of Ephraim gathered themselves together, and took the waters unto Beth-barah and Jordan.

25 And they took two princes of the Midianites, Oreb and Zeeb; and they slew Oreb upon the rock Oreb, and Zeeb they slew at the winepress of Zeeb, and pursued Midian, and brought the heads of Oreb and Zeeb to Gideon on the other side Jordan.

CHAPTER 8
Gideon Pursues the Escaping Kings

1 And the men of Ephraim said unto him, Why hast thou served us thus, that thou calledst us not, when thou wentest to fight with the Midianites? And they did chide with him sharply.

2 And he said unto them, What have I done now in comparison of you? *Is* not the gleaning of the grapes of Ephraim better than the vintage of Abi-ezer?

3 God hath delivered into your hands the princes of Midian, Oreb and Zeeb: and what was I able to do in comparison of you? Then their anger was abated toward him, when he had said that.

4 And Gideon came to Jordan, *and* passed over, he, and the three hundred men that *were* with him, faint, yet pursuing *them*.

5 And he said unto the men of Succoth, Give, I pray you, loaves of bread unto the people that follow me; for they *be* faint, and I am pursuing after Zebah and Zalmunna, kings of Midian.

6 And the princes of Succoth said, *Are* the hands of Zebah and Zalmunna now in thine hand, that we should give bread unto thine army?

7 And Gideon said, Therefore when the LORD hath delivered Zebah and Zalmunna into mine hand, then I will tear your flesh with the thorns of the wilderness and with briers.

8 And he went up thence to Penuel, and spake unto them likewise: and the men of Penuel answered him as the men of Succoth had answered *him*.

9 And he spake also unto the men of Penuel, saying, When I come again in peace, I will break down this tower.

Center column cross-references

12 Judg. 6:5, 33; 8:10

21 Ex. 14:13, 14; 2Kgs. 7:7; 2Chr. 20:17

22 Josh. 6:4, 16, 20; 1Sam. 14:20; 2Chr. 20:23; Ps. 83:9; Isa. 9:4; 2Cor. 4:7

24 Judg. 3:27, 28; John 1:28

25 Judg. 8:3, 4; Ps. 83:11; Isa. 10:26

1 Judg. 12:1; 2Sam. 19:41

3 Judg. 7:24, 25; Prov. 15:1; Phil. 2:3

5 Gen. 33:17; Ps. 60:6

6 1Sam. 25:11; 1Kgs. 20:11

7 Judg. 8:16

8 Gen. 32:30; 1Kgs. 12:25

9 Judg. 8:17; 1Kgs. 22:27

10 Now Zebah and Zalmunna *were* in Karkor, and their hosts with them, about fifteen thousand *men*, all that were left of all the hosts of the children of the east: for there fell an hundred and twenty thousand men that drew sword.

11 And Gideon went up by the way of them that dwelt in tents on the east of Nobah and Jogbehah, and smote the host: for the host was secure.

12 And when Zebah and Zalmunna fled, he pursued after them, and took the two kings of Midian, Zebah and Zalmunna, and discomfited all the host.

13 And Gideon the son of Joash returned from battle before the sun *was up*,

14 And caught a young man of the men of Succoth, and inquired of him: and he described unto him the princes of Succoth, and the elders thereof, *even* threescore and seventeen men.

15 And he came unto the men of Succoth, and said, Behold Zebah and Zalmunna, with whom ye did upbraid me, saying, *Are* the hands of Zebah and Zalmunna now in thine hand, that we should give bread unto thy men *that are* weary?

16 And he took the elders of the city, and thorns of the wilderness and briers, and with them he taught the men of Succoth.

17 And he beat down the tower of Penuel, and slew the men of the city.

18 Then said he unto Zebah and Zalmunna, What manner of men *were they* whom ye slew at Tabor? And they answered, As thou *art*, so *were* they; each one resembled the children of a king.

19 And he said, They *were* my brethren, *even* the sons of my mother: *as* the LORD liveth, if ye had saved them alive, I would not slay you.

20 And he said unto Jether his firstborn, Up, *and* slay them. But the youth drew not his sword: for he feared, because he *was* yet a youth.

21 Then Zebah and Zalmunna said, Rise thou, and fall upon us: for as the man *is, so is* his strength. And Gideon arose, and slew Zebah and Zalmunna, and took away the ornaments that *were* on their camels' necks.

Gideon's Later Years

22 Then the men of Israel said unto Gideon, Rule thou over us, both thou, and thy son, and thy son's son also: for thou hast delivered us from the hand of Midian.

23 And Gideon said unto them, I will not

rule over you, neither shall my son rule over you: the LORD shall rule over you.

24 And Gideon said unto them, I would desire a request of you, that ye would give me every man the earrings of his prey. (For they had golden earrings, because they *were* Ishmeelites.)

25 And they answered, We will willingly give *them*. And they spread a garment, and did cast therein every man the earrings of his prey.

26 And the weight of the golden earrings that he requested was a thousand and seven hundred *shekels* of gold; beside ornaments, and collars, and purple raiment that *was* on the kings of Midian, and beside the chains that *were* about their camels' necks.

27 And Gideon made an ephod thereof, and put it in his city, *even* in Ophrah: and all Israel went thither a whoring after it: which thing became a snare unto Gideon, and to his house.

28 Thus was Midian subdued before the children of Israel, so that they lifted up their heads no more. And the country was in quietness forty years in the days of Gideon.

29 And Jerubbaal the son of Joash went and dwelt in his own house.

30 And Gideon had threescore and ten sons of his body begotten: for he had many wives.

31 And his concubine that *was* in Shechem, she also bare him a son, whose name he called Abimelech.

32 And Gideon the son of Joash died in a good old age, and was buried in the sepulchre of Joash his father, in Ophrah of the Abi-ezrites.

33 And it came to pass, as soon as Gideon was dead, that the children of Israel turned again, and went a whoring after Baalim, and made Baal-berith their god.

34 And the children of Israel remembered not the LORD their God, who had delivered them out of the hands of all their enemies on every side:

35 Neither shewed they kindness to the house of Jerubbaal, *namely*, Gideon, according to all the goodness which he had shewed unto Israel.

CHAPTER 9
Abimelech

1 And Abimelech the son of Jerubbaal went to Shechem unto his mother's brethren, and communed with them, and with all the family of the house of his mother's father, saying,

---

10 Judg. 7:12; 20:2, 15, 17, 25; 2Kgs. 3:26

11 Num. 32:35, 42; Judg. 18:27; 1Thess. 5:3

12 Ps. 83:11

15 Judg. 8:6

16 Judg. 8:7

17 Judg. 8:9; 1Kgs. 12:25

18 Judg. 4:6; Ps. 89:12

21 Ps. 83:11

23 1Sam. 8:7; 10:19; 12:12

24 Gen. 25:13; 37:25, 28

27 Deut. 7:16; Judg. 6:24; 17:5; Ps. 106:39

28 Judg. 5:31

30 Judg. 9:2, 5

31 Judg. 9:1

32 Gen. 25:8; Judg. 6:24; 8:27; Job 5:26

33 Judg. 2:17, 19; 9:4, 46

34 Ps. 73:11, 42; 106:13, 21

35 Judg. 9:16-18; Eccl. 9:14, 15

1 Judg. 8:31

2 Speak, I pray you, in the ears of all the men of Shechem, Whether *is* better for you, either that all the sons of Jerubbaal, *which are* threescore and ten persons, reign over you, or that one reign over you? remember also that I *am* your bone and your flesh.

3 And his mother's brethren spake of him in the ears of all the men of Shechem all these words: and their hearts inclined to follow Abimelech; for they said, He *is* our brother.

4 And they gave him threescore and ten *pieces* of silver out of the house of Baal-berith, wherewith Abimelech hired vain and light persons, which followed him.

5 And he went unto his father's house at Ophrah, and slew his brethren the sons of Jerubbaal, *being* threescore and ten persons, upon one stone: notwithstanding yet Jotham the youngest son of Jerubbaal was left; for he hid himself.

6 And all the men of Shechem gathered together, and all the house of Millo, and went, and made Abimelech king, by the plain of the pillar that *was* in Shechem.

7 And when they told *it* to Jotham, he went and stood in the top of mount Gerizim, and lifted up his voice, and cried, and said unto them, Hearken unto me, ye men of Shechem, that God may hearken unto you.

8 The trees went forth *on a time* to anoint a king over them; and they said unto the olive tree, Reign thou over us.

9 But the olive tree said unto them, Should I leave my fatness, wherewith by me they honour God and man, and go to be promoted over the trees?

10 And the trees said to the fig tree, Come thou, *and* reign over us.

11 But the fig tree said unto them, Should I forsake my sweetness, and my good fruit, and go to be promoted over the trees?

12 Then said the trees unto the vine, Come thou, *and* reign over us.

13 And the vine said unto them, Should I leave my wine, which cheereth God and man, and go to be promoted over the trees?

14 Then said all the trees unto the bramble, Come thou, *and* reign over us.

15 And the bramble said unto the trees, If in truth ye anoint me king over you, *then* come *and* put your trust in my shadow: and if not, let fire come out of the bramble, and devour the cedars of Lebanon.

16 Now therefore, if ye have done truly and sincerely, in that ye have made Abimelech king, and if ye have dealt well with Jerub-

baal and his house, and have done unto him according to the deserving of his hands;

17 (For my father fought for you, and adventured his life far, and delivered you out of the hand of Midian:

18 And ye are risen up against my father's house this day, and have slain his sons, threescore and ten persons, upon one stone, and have made Abimelech, the son of his maidservant, king over the men of Shechem, because he *is* your brother;)

19 If ye then have dealt truly and sincerely with Jerubbaal and with his house this day, *then* rejoice ye in Abimelech, and let him also rejoice in you:

20 But if not, let fire come out from Abimelech, and devour the men of Shechem, and the house of Millo; and let fire come out from the men of Shechem, and from the house of Millo, and devour Abimelech.

21 And Jotham ran away, and fled, and went to Beer, and dwelt there, for fear of Abimelech his brother.

22 When Abimelech had reigned three years over Israel,

23 Then God sent an evil spirit between Abimelech and the men of Shechem; and the men of Shechem dealt treacherously with Abimelech:

24 That the cruelty *done* to the threescore and ten sons of Jerubbaal might come, and their blood be laid upon Abimelech their brother, which slew them; and upon the men of Shechem, which aided him in the killing of his brethren.

25 And the men of Shechem set liers in wait for him in the top of the mountains, and they robbed all that came along that way by them: and it was told Abimelech.

26 And Gaal the son of Ebed came with his brethren, and went over to Shechem: and the men of Shechem put their confidence in him.

27 And they went out into the fields, and gathered their vineyards, and trode *the grapes*, and made merry, and went into the house of their god, and did eat and drink, and cursed Abimelech.

28 And Gaal the son of Ebed said, Who *is* Abimelech, and who *is* Shechem, that we should serve him? *is* not *he* the son of Jerubbaal? and Zebul his officer? serve the men of Hamor the father of Shechem: for why should we serve him?

29 And would to God this people were under my hand! then would I remove Abimelech. And he said to Abimelech, Increase thine army, and come out.

2 Gen. 29:14; Judg. 8:30
3 Gen. 29:15
4 Judg. 8:33; 11:3; 2Chr. 13:7; Prov. 12:11; Acts 17:5
5 Judg. 6:24; 2Kgs. 11:1, 2
6 Josh. 24:26
7 Deut. 11:29; 27:12; Josh. 8:33; John 4:20
8 Judg. 8:22, 23; 2Kgs. 14:9
9 Ps. 104:15
13 Ps. 104:15
15 Num. 21:28; Judg. 9:20; 2Kgs. 14:9; Ps. 104:16; Isa. 2:13; 30:2; 37:24; Ezek. 19:14; 31:3; Dan. 4:12; Hos. 14:7
16 Judg. 8:35
18 Judg. 9:5, 6
19 Judg. 9:15, 56, 57; Isa. 8:6; Phil. 3:3
21 2Sam. 20:14
23 1Sam. 16:14; 18:9, 10; 1Kgs. 12:15; 22:22; 2Chr. 10:15; 18:19-34; Isa. 19:2, 14; 33:1
24 1Kgs. 2:32; Esth. 9:25; Ps. 7:16; Matt. 23:35, 36
27 Judg. 9:4; Isa. 16:9, 10; Jer. 25:30
28 Gen. 34:2, 6; 1Sam. 25:10; 1Kgs. 12:16
29 2Sam. 15:4

30 And when Zebul the ruler of the city heard the words of Gaal the son of Ebed, his anger was kindled.

31 And he sent messengers unto Abimelech privily, saying, Behold, Gaal the son of Ebed and his brethren be come to Shechem; and, behold, they fortify the city against thee.

32 Now therefore up by night, thou and the people that *is* with thee, and lie in wait in the field:

33 And it shall be, *that* in the morning, as soon as the sun is up, thou shalt rise early, and set upon the city: and, behold, *when* he and the people that *is* with him come out against thee, then mayest thou do to them as thou shalt find occasion.

34 And Abimelech rose up, and all the people that *were* with him, by night, and they laid wait against Shechem in four companies.

35 And Gaal the son of Ebed went out, and stood in the entering of the gate of the city: and Abimelech rose up, and the people that *were* with him, from lying in wait.

36 And when Gaal saw the people, he said to Zebul, Behold, there come people down from the top of the mountains. And Zebul said unto him, Thou seest the shadow of the mountains as *if they were* men.

37 And Gaal spake again and said, See there come people down by the middle of the land, and another company come along by the plain of Meonenim.

38 Then said Zebul unto him, Where *is* now thy mouth, wherewith thou saidst, Who *is* Abimelech, that we should serve him? *is* not this the people that thou hast despised? go out, I pray now, and fight with them.

39 And Gaal went out before the men of Shechem, and fought with Abimelech.

40 And Abimelech chased him, and he fled before him, and many were overthrown *and* wounded, *even* unto the entering of the gate.

41 And Abimelech dwelt at Arumah: and Zebul thrust out Gaal and his brethren, that they should not dwell in Shechem.

42 And it came to pass on the morrow, that the people went out into the field; and they told Abimelech.

43 And he took the people, and divided them into three companies, and laid wait in the field, and looked, and, behold, the people *were* come forth out of the city; and he rose up against them, and smote them.

44 And Abimelech, and the company that *was* with him, rushed forward, and stood in the entering of the gate of the city: and the two *other* companies ran upon all *the people* that *were* in the fields, and slew them.

45 And Abimelech fought against the city all that day; and he took the city, and slew the people that *was* therein, and beat down the city, and sowed it with salt.

46 And when all the men of the tower of Shechem heard *that*, they entered into an hold of the house of the god Berith.

47 And it was told Abimelech, that all the men of the tower of Shechem were gathered together.

48 And Abimelech gat him up to mount Zalmon, he and all the people that *were* with him; and Abimelech took an axe in his hand, and cut down a bough from the trees, and took it, and laid *it* on his shoulder, and said unto the people that *were* with him, What ye have seen me do, make haste, *and* do as I *have done.*

49 And all the people likewise cut down every man his bough, and followed Abimelech, and put *them* to the hold, and set the hold on fire upon them; so that all the men of the tower of Shechem died also, about a thousand men and women.

50 Then went Abimelech to Thebez, and encamped against Thebez, and took it.

51 But there was a strong tower within the city, and thither fled all the men and women, and all they of the city, and shut *it* to them, and gat them up to the top of the tower.

52 And Abimelech came unto the tower, and fought against it, and went hard unto the door of the tower to burn it with fire.

53 And a certain woman cast a piece of a millstone upon Abimelech's head, and all to brake his skull.

54 Then he called hastily unto the young man his armourbearer, and said unto him, Draw thy sword, and slay me, that men say not of me, A woman slew him. And his young man thrust him through, and he died.

55 And when the men of Israel saw that Abimelech was dead, they departed every man unto his place.

56 Thus God rendered the wickedness of Abimelech, which he did unto his father, in slaying his seventy brethren:

57 And all the evil of the men of Shechem did God render upon their heads: and upon them came the curse of Jotham the son of Jerubbaal.

CHAPTER 10
Tola

1 And after Abimelech there arose to defend Israel Tola the son of Puah, the son of

---

33 1Sam. 10:7; 25:8; Eccl. 9:10

37 Deut. 18:14

38 Judg. 9:28, 29

45 Deut. 29:23; Judg. 9:20; 1Kgs. 12:25; 2Kgs. 3:25

46 Judg. 8:33

48 Ps. 68:14

53 2Sam. 11:21

54 1Sam. 31:4

56 Judg. 9:24; Job 31:3; Ps. 94:23; Prov. 5:22

57 Judg. 9:20

1 Judg. 2:16

Dodo, a man of Issachar; and he dwelt in Shamir in mount Ephraim.

2 And he judged Israel twenty and three years, and died, and was buried in Shamir.

Jair

3 And after him arose Jair, a Gileadite, and judged Israel twenty and two years.

4 And he had thirty sons that rode on thirty ass colts, and they had thirty cities, which are called Havoth-jair unto this day, which are in the land of Gilead.

5 And Jair died, and was buried in Camon.

6 And the children of Israel did evil again in the sight of the LORD, and served Baalim, and Ashtaroth, and the gods of Syria, and the gods of Zidon, and the gods of Moab, and the gods of the children of Ammon, and the gods of the Philistines, and forsook the LORD, and served not him.

7 And the anger of the LORD was hot against Israel, and he sold them into the hands of the Philistines, and into the hands of the children of Ammon.

8 And that year they vexed and oppressed the children of Israel: eighteen years, all the children of Israel that were on the other side Jordan in the land of the Amorites, which is in Gilead.

9 Moreover the children of Ammon passed over Jordan to fight also against Judah, and against Benjamin, and against the house of Ephraim; so that Israel was sore distressed.

10 And the children of Israel cried unto the LORD, saying, We have sinned against thee, both because we have forsaken our God, and also served Baalim.

11 And the LORD said unto the children of Israel, Did not I deliver you from the Egyptians, and from the Amorites, from the children of Ammon, and from the Philistines?

12 The Zidonians also, and the Amalekites, and the Maonites, did oppress you; and ye cried to me, and I delivered you out of their hand.

13 Yet ye have forsaken me, and served other gods: wherefore I will deliver you no more.

14 Go and cry unto the gods which ye have chosen; let them deliver you in the time of your tribulation.

15 And the children of Israel said unto the LORD, We have sinned: do thou unto us whatsoever seemeth good unto thee; deliver us only, we pray thee, this day.

16 And they put away the strange gods from among them, and served the LORD: and his soul was grieved for the misery of Israel.

4 Num. 32:41; Deut. 3:14; Judg. 5:10; 12:14

6 Judg. 2:11, 12, 13; 3:7; 4:1; 6:1; 13:1; 1Kgs. 11:33; Ps. 106:36

7 Judg. 2:14; 1Sam. 12:9

10 1Sam. 12:10

11 Ex. 14:30; Num. 21:21; 24, 25; Ps. 3:12, 13, 31

12 Judg. 5:19; 6:3; Ps. 106:42, 43

13 Deut. 32:15; Jer. 2:13

14 Deut. 32:37, 38; 2Kgs. 3:13; Jer. 2:28

15 1Sam. 3:18; 2Sam. 15:26

16 2Chr. 7:14; 15:8; Ps. 106:44, 45; Isa. 63:9; Jer. 18:7, 8

17 Gen. 31:49; Judg. 11:11, 29

18 Judg. 11:8, 11

1 Judg. 6:12; 2Kgs. 5:1; Heb. 11:32

3 Judg. 9:4; 1Sam. 22:2

7 Gen. 26:27

8 Judg. 10:18; Luke 17:4

10 Jer. 42:5

11 Judg. 10:17; 11:8; 20:1; 1Sam. 10:17; 11:15

17 Then the children of Ammon were gathered together, and encamped in Gilead. And the children of Israel assembled themselves together, and encamped in Mizpeh.

18 And the people and princes of Gilead said one to another, What man is he that will begin to fight against the children of Ammon? he shall be head over all the inhabitants of Gilead.

CHAPTER 11
Jephthah Is Asked to Lead Gilead's Army

1 Now Jephthah the Gileadite was a mighty man of valour, and he was the son of an harlot: and Gilead begat Jephthah.

2 And Gilead's wife bare him sons; and his wife's sons grew up, and they thrust out Jephthah, and said unto him, Thou shalt not inherit in our father's house; for thou art the son of a strange woman.

3 Then Jephthah fled from his brethren, and dwelt in the land of Tob: and there were gathered vain men to Jephthah, and went out with him.

4 And it came to pass in process of time, that the children of Ammon made war against Israel.

5 And it was so, that when the children of Ammon made war against Israel, the elders of Gilead went to fetch Jephthah out of the land of Tob:

6 And they said unto Jephthah, Come, and be our captain, that we may fight with the children of Ammon.

7 And Jephthah said unto the elders of Gilead, Did not ye hate me, and expel me out of my father's house? and why are ye come unto me now when ye are in distress?

8 And the elders of Gilead said unto Jephthah, Therefore we turn again to thee now, that thou mayest go with us, and fight against the children of Ammon, and be our head over all the inhabitants of Gilead.

9 And Jephthah said unto the elders of Gilead, If ye bring me home again to fight against the children of Ammon, and the LORD deliver them before me, shall I be your head?

10 And the elders of Gilead said unto Jephthah, The LORD be witness between us, if we do not so according to thy words.

11 Then Jephthah went with the elders of Gilead, and the people made him head and captain over them: and Jephthah uttered all his words before the LORD in Mizpeh.

12 And Jephthah sent messengers unto the king of the children of Ammon, saying,

What hast thou to do with me, that thou art come against me to fight in my land?

13 And the king of the children of Ammon answered unto the messengers of Jephthah, Because Israel took away my land, when they came up out of Egypt, from Arnon even unto Jabbok, and unto Jordan: now therefore restore those *lands* again peaceably.

14 And Jephthah sent messengers again unto the king of the children of Ammon:

15 And said unto him, Thus saith Jephthah, Israel took not away the land of Moab, nor the land of the children of Ammon:

16 But when Israel came up from Egypt, and walked through the wilderness unto the Red sea, and came to Kadesh;

17 Then Israel sent messengers unto the king of Edom, saying, Let me, I pray thee, pass through thy land: but the king of Edom would not hearken *thereto*. And in like manner they sent unto the king of Moab: but he would not *consent*: and Israel abode in Kadesh.

18 Then they went along through the wilderness, and compassed the land of Edom, and the land of Moab, and came by the east side of the land of Moab, and pitched on the other side of Arnon, but came not within the border of Moab: for Arnon *was* the border of Moab.

19 And Israel sent messengers unto Sihon king of the Amorites, the king of Heshbon; and Israel said unto him, Let us pass, we pray thee, through thy land into my place.

20 But Sihon trusted not Israel to pass through his coast: but Sihon gathered all his people together, and pitched in Jahaz, and fought against Israel.

21 And the LORD God of Israel delivered Sihon and all his people into the hand of Israel, and they smote them: so Israel possessed all the land of the Amorites, the inhabitants of that country.

22 And they possessed all the coasts of the Amorites, from Arnon even unto Jabbok, and from the wilderness even unto Jordan.

23 So now the LORD God of Israel hath dispossessed the Amorites from before his people Israel, and shouldest thou possess it?

24 Wilt not thou possess that which Chemosh thy god giveth thee to possess? So whomsoever the LORD our God shall drive out from before us, them will we possess.

25 And now *art* thou any thing better than Balak the son of Zippor, king of Moab? did he ever strive against Israel, or did he ever fight against them,

26 While Israel dwelt in Heshbon and her

towns, and in Aroer and her towns, and in all the cities that *be* along by the coasts of Arnon, three hundred years? why therefore did ye not recover *them* within that time?

27 Wherefore I have not sinned against thee, but thou doest me wrong to war against me: the LORD the Judge be judge this day between the children of Israel and the children of Ammon.

28 Howbeit the king of the children of Ammon hearkened not unto the words of Jephthah which he sent him.

Jephthah's Vow

29 Then the Spirit of the LORD came upon Jephthah, and he passed over Gilead, and Manasseh, and passed over Mizpeh of Gilead, and from Mizpeh of Gilead he passed over *unto* the children of Ammon.

30 And Jephthah vowed a vow unto the LORD, and said, If thou shalt without fail deliver the children of Ammon into mine hands,

31 Then it shall be, that whatsoever cometh forth of the doors of my house to meet me, when I return in peace from the children of Ammon, shall surely be the LORD's, and I will offer it up for a burnt offering.

32 So Jephthah passed over unto the children of Ammon to fight against them; and the LORD delivered them into his hands.

33 And he smote them from Aroer, even till thou come to Minnith, *even* twenty cities, and unto the plain of the vineyards, with a very great slaughter. Thus the children of Ammon were subdued before the children of Israel.

34 And Jephthah came to Mizpeh unto his house, and, behold, his daughter came out to meet him with timbrels and with dances: and she *was his* only child; beside her he had neither son nor daughter.

35 And it came to pass, when he saw her, that he rent his clothes, and said, Alas, my daughter! thou hast brought me very low, and thou art one of them that trouble me: for I have opened my mouth unto the LORD, and I cannot go back.

36 And she said unto him, My father, *if* thou hast opened thy mouth unto the LORD, do to me according to that which hath proceeded out of thy mouth; forasmuch as the LORD hath taken vengeance for thee of thine enemies, *even* of the children of Ammon.

37 And she said unto her father, Let this thing be done for me: let me alone two months, that I may go up and down upon

---

13 Gen. 32:22; Num. 21:24-26

15 Deut. 2:9, 19

16 Num. 13:26; 14:25; 20:1; Deut. 1:40, 46; Josh. 5:6

17 Num. 20:1, 14, 18, 21;

18 Num. 21:4, 11, 13, 14; 22:36; Deut. 2:1-8

19 Num. 21:21, 22; Deut. 2:26, 27

20 Num. 21:23; Deut. 2:32

21 Num. 21:24, 25; Deut. 2:33, 34

22 Deut. 2:36

24 Num. 21:29; Deut. 9:4, 5; 18:12; Josh. 3:10

25 Num. 22:2; Josh. 24:9

26 Num. 21:25; Deut. 2:36

27 Gen. 16:5; 18:25; 31:53; 1Sam. 24:12, 15

29 Judg. 3:10

30 Gen. 28:20; 1Sam. 1:11

31 Lev. 27:2, 3, 11, 12; 1Sam. 1:11, 28; 2:18; Ps. 66:13

33 Ezek. 27:17

34 Ex. 15:20; Judg. 10:17; 11:11; 1Sam. 18:6; Ps. 68:25; Jer. 31:4

35 Gen. 37:29; 34; Num. 30:2; Ps. 15:4; Eccl. 5:2, 4, 5

36 Num. 30:2; 2Sam. 18:19, 31

the mountains, and bewail my virginity, I and my fellows.

38 And he said, Go. And he sent her away *for* two months: and she went with her companions, and bewailed her virginity upon the mountains.

39 And it came to pass at the end of two months, that she returned unto her father, who did with her *according* to his vow which he had vowed: and she knew no man. And it was a custom in Israel,

40 *That* the daughters of Israel went yearly to lament the daughter of Jephthah the Gileadite four days in a year.

CHAPTER 12
Jephthah Defeats Ephraim

1 And the men of Ephraim gathered themselves together, and went northward, and said unto Jephthah, Wherefore passedst thou over to fight against the children of Ammon, and didst not call us to go with thee? we will burn thine house upon thee with fire.

2 And Jephthah said unto them, I and my people were at great strife with the children of Ammon; and when I called you, ye delivered me not out of their hands.

3 And when I saw that ye delivered *me* not, I put my life in my hands, and passed over against the children of Ammon, and the LORD delivered them into my hand: wherefore then are ye come up unto me this day, to fight against me?

4 Then Jephthah gathered together all the men of Gilead, and fought with Ephraim: and the men of Gilead smote Ephraim, because they said, Ye Gileadites *are* fugitives of Ephraim among the Ephraimites, *and* among the Manassites.

5 And the Gileadites took the passages of Jordan before the Ephraimites: and it was *so*, that when those Ephraimites which were escaped said, Let me go over; that the men of Gilead said unto him, *Art* thou an Ephraimite? If he said, Nay;

6 Then said they unto him, Say now Shibboleth: and he said Sibboleth: for he could not frame to pronounce *it* right. Then they took him, and slew him at the passages of Jordan: and there fell at that time of the Ephraimites forty and two thousand.

7 And Jephthah judged Israel six years. Then died Jephthah the Gileadite, and was buried in *one of* the cities of Gilead.

Ibzan

8 And after him Ibzan of Beth-lehem judged Israel.

9 And he had thirty sons, and thirty daughters, *whom* he sent abroad, and took in thirty daughters from abroad for his sons. And he judged Israel seven years.

10 Then died Ibzan, and was buried at Beth-lehem.

Elon

11 And after him Elon, a Zebulonite, judged Israel; and he judged Israel ten years.

12 And Elon the Zebulonite died, and was buried in Aijalon in the country of Zebulun.

Abdon

13 And after him Abdon the son of Hillel, a Pirathonite, judged Israel.

14 And he had forty sons and thirty nephews, that rode on threescore and ten ass colts: and he judged Israel eight years.

15 And Abdon the son of Hillel the Pirathonite died, and was buried in Pirathon in the land of Ephraim, in the mount of the Amalekites.

CHAPTER 13
Samson's Birth

1 And the children of Israel did evil again in the sight of the LORD; and the LORD delivered them into the hand of the Philistines forty years.

2 And there was a certain man of Zorah, of the family of the Danites, whose name *was*

39 Judg. 11:31; 1Sam. 1:22, 24; 2:18
40 Judg. 5:11
1 Judg. 8:1
3 1Sam. 19:5; 28:21; Job 13:14; Ps. 119:109
4 1Sam. 25:10; Ps. 78:9
5 Josh. 22:11; Judg. 3:28; 7:24
6 Ps. 69:2, 15; Isa. 27:12
14 Judg. 5:10; 10:4
15 Judg. 3:13, 27; 5:14
1 Judg. 2:11; 3:7; 4:1; 6:1; 10:6; 1Sam. 12:9
2 Josh. 19:41

13:2–5 Again, the "angel of the LORD," a theophany of Christ, appeared to the wife of Manoah of the tribe of the Danites, who had already vacated their inherited territory because of pressure from the Philistines and fled north to the city of Laish (18:1–20). Manoah's family remained behind in what appears to be a displaced person's camp (13:25) on the border of the Philistines. The irony of this story is that God predicts that He will raise up a man from Israel's weakest tribe to defeat her greatest enemy. He promised the woman she would give birth to a son who would be a Nazarite ("separated" or "consecrated") unto God, and that he would "begin to deliver" Israel from the Philistines. This prediction was fulfilled in the birth of Samson (13:24), who held the Philistines at bay for twenty years but failed to finish the job because of the wiles of Delilah and his own lustful desires (16:4–31). The task begun by Samson would later be completed by David's conquest of the Philistines (cf. 2 Sam. 5:17–25; 8:1).

Manoah; and his wife *was* barren, and bare not.

3 And the angel of the Lord appeared unto the woman, and said unto her, Behold now, thou *art* barren, and bearest not: but thou shalt conceive, and bear a son.

4 Now therefore beware, I pray thee, and drink not wine nor strong drink, and eat not any unclean *thing*:

5 For, lo, thou shalt conceive, and bear a son; and no razor shall come on his head: for the child shall be a Nazarite unto God from the womb: and he shall begin to deliver Israel out of the hand of the Philistines.

6 Then the woman came and told her husband, saying, A man of God came unto me, and his countenance *was* like the countenance of an angel of God, very terrible: but I asked him not whence he *was*, neither told he me his name:

7 But he said unto me, Behold, thou shalt conceive, and bear a son; and now drink no wine nor strong drink, neither eat any unclean *thing*: for the child shall be a Nazarite to God from the womb to the day of his death.

8 Then Manoah intreated the Lord, and said, O my Lord, let the man of God which thou didst send come again unto us, and teach us what we shall do unto the child that shall be born.

9 And God hearkened to the voice of Manoah; and the angel of God came again unto the woman as she sat in the field: but Manoah her husband *was* not with her.

10 And the woman made haste, and ran, and shewed her husband, and said unto him, Behold, the man hath appeared unto me, that came unto me the *other* day.

11 And Manoah arose, and went after his wife, and came to the man, and said unto him, *Art* thou the man that spakest unto the woman? And he said, I *am*.

12 And Manoah said, Now let thy words come to pass. How shall we order the child, and *how* shall we do unto him?

13 And the angel of the Lord said unto Manoah, Of all that I said unto the woman let her beware.

14 She may not eat of any *thing* that cometh of the vine, neither let her drink wine or strong drink, nor eat any unclean *thing*: all that I commanded her let her observe.

15 And Manoah said unto the angel of the Lord, I pray thee, let us detain thee, until we shall have made ready a kid for thee.

16 And the angel of the Lord said unto Ma-

3 Judg. 6:12; Luke 1:11, 13, 28, 31

4 Num. 6:2, 3; Judg. 13:4; Luke 1:15

5 Num. 6:2, 5; 1Sam. 1:11; 7:13; 2Sam. 8:1; 1Chr. 18:1

6 Deut. 33:1; Judg. 13:17, 18; 1Sam. 2:27; 9:6; 1Kgs. 17:24; Matt. 28:3; Luke 9:29; Acts 6:15

14 Judg. 13:4

15 Gen. 18:5; Judg. 6:18

18 Gen. 32:29; Isa. 9:6

19 Judg. 6:19, 20

20 Lev. 9:24; 1Chr. 21:16; Ezek. 1:28; Matt. 17:6

21 Judg. 6:22

22 Gen. 32:30; Ex. 33:20; Deut. 5:26; Judg. 6:22

24 1Sam. 3:19; Luke 1:80; 2:52; Heb. 11:32

25 Josh. 15:33; Judg. 3:10; 18:11, 12; 1Sam. 11:6; Matt. 4:1

1 Gen. 34:2; 38:13; Josh. 15:10

2 Gen. 21:21; 34:4

3 Gen. 24:3, 4; 34:14; Ex. 34:16; Deut. 7:3

4 Deut. 28:48; Josh. 11:20; Judg. 13:1; 1Kgs. 12:15; 2Kgs. 6:33; 2Chr. 10:15; 22:7; 25:20

noah, Though thou detain me, I will not eat of thy bread: and if thou wilt offer a burnt offering, thou must offer it unto the Lord. For Manoah knew not that he *was* an angel of the Lord.

17 And Manoah said unto the angel of the Lord, What *is* thy name, that when thy sayings come to pass we may do thee honour?

18 And the angel of the Lord said unto him, Why askest thou thus after my name, seeing it *is* secret?

19 So Manoah took a kid with a meat offering, and offered *it* upon a rock unto the Lord: and *the angel* did wondrously; and Manoah and his wife looked on.

20 For it came to pass, when the flame went up toward heaven from off the altar, that the angel of the Lord ascended in the flame of the altar. And Manoah and his wife looked on *it*, and fell on their faces to the ground.

21 But the angel of the Lord did no more appear to Manoah and to his wife. Then Manoah knew that he *was* an angel of the Lord.

22 And Manoah said unto his wife, We shall surely die, because we have seen God.

23 But his wife said unto him, If the Lord were pleased to kill us, he would not have received a burnt offering and a meat offering at our hands, neither would he have shewed us all these *things*, nor would as at this time have told us *such things* as these.

24 And the woman bare a son, and called his name Samson: and the child grew, and the Lord blessed him.

25 And the Spirit of the Lord began to move him at times in the camp of Dan between Zorah and Eshtaol.

CHAPTER 14
Samson's First Wife

1 And Samson went down to Timnath, and saw a woman in Timnath of the daughters of the Philistines.

2 And he came up, and told his father and his mother, and said, I have seen a woman in Timnath of the daughters of the Philistines: now therefore get her for me to wife.

3 Then his father and his mother said unto him, *Is there* never a woman among the daughters of thy brethren, or among all my people, that thou goest to take a wife of the uncircumcised Philistines? And Samson said unto his father, Get her for me; for she pleaseth me well.

4 But his father and his mother knew not

that it *was* of the L ORD , that he sought an occasion against the Philistines: for at that time
the Philistines had dominion over Israel.

5 Then went Samson down, and his father
and his mother, to Timnath, and came to
the vineyards of Timnath: and, behold, a
young lion roared against him.

6 And the Spirit of the L ORD came mightily
upon him, and he rent him as he would
have rent a kid, and *he had* nothing in his
hand: but he told not his father or his
mother what he had done.

7 And he went down, and talked with the
woman; and she pleased Samson well.

8 And after a time he returned to take her,
and he turned aside to see the carcase of the
lion: and, behold, *there was* a swarm of bees
and honey in the carcase of the lion.

9 And he took thereof in his hands, and
went on eating, and came to his father and
mother, and he gave them, and they did eat:
but he told not them that he had taken the
honey out of the carcase of the lion.

10 So his father went down unto the
woman: and Samson made there a feast; for
so used the young men to do.

11 And it came to pass, when they saw him,
that they brought thirty companions to be
with him.

12 And Samson said unto them, I will now
put forth a riddle unto you: if ye can certainly declare it me within the seven days of
the feast, and find *it* out, then I will give you
thirty sheets and thirty change of garments:

13 But if ye cannot declare *it* me, then shall
ye give me thirty sheets and thirty change of
garments. And they said unto him, Put
forth thy riddle, that we may hear it.

14 And he said unto them, Out of the eater
came forth meat, and out of the strong
came forth sweetness. And they could not
in three days expound the riddle.

15 And it came to pass on the seventh day,
that they said unto Samson's wife, Entice
thy husband, that he may declare unto us
the riddle, lest we burn thee and thy father's house with fire: have ye called us to
take that we have? *is it* not *so?*

16 And Samson's wife wept before him,
and said, Thou dost but hate me, and lovest
me not: thou hast put forth a riddle unto
the children of my people, and hast not told
it me. And he said unto her, Behold, I have
not told *it* my father nor my mother, and
shall I tell *it* thee?

17 And she wept before him the seven days,
while their feast lasted: and it came to pass
on the seventh day, that he told her, because

she lay sore upon him: and she told the riddle to the children of her people.

18 And the men of the city said unto him
on the seventh day before the sun went
down, What *is* sweeter than honey? and
what *is* stronger than a lion? And he said
unto them, If ye had not plowed with my
heifer, ye had not found out my riddle.

19 And the Spirit of the L ORD came upon
him, and he went down to Ashkelon, and
slew thirty men of them, and took their
spoil, and gave change of garments unto
them which expounded the riddle. And his
anger was kindled, and he went up to his
father's house.

20 But Samson's wife was *given* to his companion, whom he had used as his friend.

CHAPTER 15

1 But it came to pass within a while after,
in the time of wheat harvest, that Samson
visited his wife with a kid; and he said, I
will go in to my wife into the chamber. But
her father would not suffer him to go in.

2 And her father said, I verily thought that
thou hadst utterly hated her; therefore I
gave her to thy companion: *is* not her
younger sister fairer than she? take her,
I pray thee, instead of her.

3 And Samson said concerning them, Now
shall I be more blameless than the Philistines, though I do them a displeasure.

4 And Samson went and caught three
hundred foxes, and took firebrands, and
turned tail to tail, and put a firebrand in the
midst between two tails.

5 And when he had set the brands on fire,
he let *them* go into the standing corn of the
Philistines, and burnt up both the shocks,
and also the standing corn, with the vineyards *and* olives.

6 Then the Philistines said, Who hath
done this? And they answered, Samson, the
son-in-law of the Timnite, because he had
taken his wife, and given her to his companion. And the Philistines came up, and
burnt her and her father with fire.

7 And Samson said unto them, Though ye
have done this, yet will I be avenged of you,
and after that I will cease.

8 And he smote them hip and thigh with a
great slaughter: and he went down and
dwelt in the top of the rock Etam.

Samson Kills a Thousand Philistines

9 Then the Philistines went up, and pitched
in Judah, and spread themselves in Lehi.

---

6 Judg. 3:10;
13:25; 1Sam.
11:6

12 Gen.
29:27; 45:22;
1Kgs. 10:1;
2Kgs. 5:22;
Ezek. 17:2;
Luke 14:7

15 Judg.
15:6; 16:5

16 Judg.
16:15

19 Judg.
3:10; 13:25

20 Judg.
15:2; John
3:29

2 Judg.
14:20

9 Judg.
15:19

10 And the men of Judah said, Why are ye come up against us? And they answered, To bind Samson are we come up, to do to him as he hath done to us.

11 Then three thousand men of Judah went to the top of the rock Etam, and said to Samson, Knowest thou not that the Philistines *are* rulers over us? what *is* this *that* thou hast done unto us? And he said unto them, As they did unto me, so have I done unto them.

12 And they said unto him, We are come down to bind thee, that we may deliver thee into the hand of the Philistines. And Samson said unto them, Swear unto me, that ye will not fall upon me yourselves.

13 And they spake unto him, saying, No; but we will bind thee fast, and deliver thee into their hand: but surely we will not kill thee. And they bound him with two new cords, and brought him up from the rock.

14 *And* when he came unto Lehi, the Philistines shouted against him: and the Spirit of the LORD came mightily upon him, and the cords that *were* upon his arms became as flax that was burnt with fire, and his bands loosed from off his hands.

15 And he found a new jawbone of an ass, and put forth his hand, and took it, and slew a thousand men therewith.

16 And Samson said, With the jawbone of an ass, heaps upon heaps, with the jaw of an ass have I slain a thousand men.

17 And it came to pass, when he had made an end of speaking, that he cast away the jawbone out of his hand, and called that place Ramath-lehi.

18 And he was sore athirst, and called on the LORD, and said, Thou hast given this great deliverance into the hand of thy servant: and now shall I die for thirst, and fall into the hand of the uncircumcised?

19 But God clave an hollow place that *was* in the jaw, and there came water thereout; and when he had drunk, his spirit came again, and he revived: wherefore he called the name thereof En-hakkore, which *is* in Lehi unto this day.

20 And he judged Israel in the days of the Philistines twenty years.

CHAPTER 16

Samson Removes Gaza's City Gates

1 Then went Samson to Gaza, and saw there an harlot, and went in unto her.

2 *And it was told* the Gazites, saying, Samson is come hither. And they compassed *him* in, and laid wait for him all night in the gate

Cross references (center column):

11 Judg. 14:4

14 Judg. 3:10; 14:6

15 Lev. 26:8; Josh. 23:10; Judg. 3:31

18 Ps. 3:7

19 Gen. 45:27; Isa. 40:29

20 Judg. 13:1

2 1Sam. 23:26; Ps. 118:10-12; Acts 9:24

5 Judg. 14:15; Prov. 2:16-19; 5:3-11; 6:24-26; 7:21-23

of the city, and were quiet all the night, saying, In the morning, when it is day, we shall kill him.

3 And Samson lay till midnight, and arose at midnight, and took the doors of the gate of the city, and the two posts, and went away with them, bar and all, and put *them* upon his shoulders, and carried them up to the top of an hill that *is* before Hebron.

Samson and Delilah

4 And it came to pass afterward, that he loved a woman in the valley of Sorek, whose name *was* Delilah.

5 And the lords of the Philistines came up unto her, and said unto her, Entice him, and see wherein his great strength *lieth*, and by what *means* we may prevail against him, that we may bind him to afflict him: and we will give thee every one of us eleven hundred *pieces* of silver.

6 And Delilah said to Samson, Tell me, I pray thee, wherein thy great strength *lieth*, and wherewith thou mightest be bound to afflict thee.

7 And Samson said unto her, If they bind me with seven green withs that were never dried, then shall I be weak, and be as another man.

8 Then the lords of the Philistines brought up to her seven green withs which had not been dried, and she bound him with them.

9 Now *there were* men lying in wait, abiding with her in the chamber. And she said unto him, The Philistines *be* upon thee, Samson. And he brake the withs, as a thread of tow is broken when it toucheth the fire. So his strength was not known.

10 And Delilah said unto Samson, Behold, thou hast mocked me, and told me lies: now tell me, I pray thee, wherewith thou mightest be bound.

11 And he said unto her, If they bind me fast with new ropes that never were occupied, then shall I be weak, and be as another man.

12 Delilah therefore took new ropes, and bound him therewith, and said unto him, The Philistines *be* upon thee, Samson. And *there were* liers in wait abiding in the chamber. And he brake them from off his arms like a thread.

13 And Delilah said unto Samson, Hitherto thou hast mocked me, and told me lies: tell me wherewith thou mightest be bound. And he said unto her, If thou weavest the seven locks of my head with the web.

14 And she fastened *it* with the pin, and

said unto him, The Philistines *be* upon thee, Samson. And he awaked out of his sleep, and went away with the pin of the beam, and with the web.

15 And she said unto him, How canst thou say, I love thee, when thine heart *is* not with me? thou hast mocked me these three times, and hast not told me wherein thy great strength *lieth*.

16 And it came to pass, when she pressed him daily with her words, and urged him, *so* that his soul was vexed unto death;

17 That he told her all his heart, and said unto her, There hath not come a razor upon mine head; for I *have been* a Nazarite unto God from my mother's womb: if I be shaven, then my strength will go from me, and I shall become weak, and be like any *other* man.

18 And when Delilah saw that he had told her all his heart, she sent and called for the lords of the Philistines, saying, Come up this once, for he hath shewed me all his heart. Then the lords of the Philistines came up unto her, and brought money in their hand.

19 And she made him sleep upon her knees; and she called for a man, and she caused him to shave off the seven locks of his head; and she began to afflict him, and his strength went from him.

20 And she said, The Philistines *be* upon thee, Samson. And he awoke out of his sleep, and said, I will go out as at other times before, and shake myself. And he wist not that the LORD was departed from him.

21 But the Philistines took him, and put out his eyes, and brought him down to Gaza, and bound him with fetters of brass; and he did grind in the prison house.

22 Howbeit the hair of his head began to grow again after he was shaven.

Samson's Death

23 Then the lords of the Philistines gathered them together for to offer a great sacrifice unto Dagon their god, and to rejoice: for they said, Our god hath delivered Samson our enemy into our hand.

24 And when the people saw him, they praised their god: for they said, Our god hath delivered into our hands our enemy, and the destroyer of our country, which slew many of us.

25 And it came to pass, when their hearts were merry, that they said, Call for Samson, that he may make us sport. And they called for Samson out of the prison house; and he

made them sport: and they set him between the pillars.

26 And Samson said unto the lad that held him by the hand, Suffer me that I may feel the pillars whereupon the house standeth, that I may lean upon them.

27 Now the house was full of men and women; and all the lords of the Philistines *were* there; and *there were* upon the roof about three thousand men and women, that beheld while Samson made sport.

28 And Samson called unto the LORD, and said, O Lord GOD, remember me, I pray thee, and strengthen me, I pray thee, only this once, O God, that I may be at once avenged of the Philistines for my two eyes.

29 And Samson took hold of the two middle pillars upon which the house stood, and on which it was borne up, of the one with his right hand, and of the other with his left.

30 And Samson said, Let me die with the Philistines. And he bowed himself with *all his* might; and the house fell upon the lords, and upon all the people that *were* therein. So the dead which he slew at his death were more than *they* which he slew in his life.

31 Then his brethren and all the house of his father came down, and took him, and brought *him* up, and buried him between Zorah and Eshtaol in the burying place of Manoah his father. And he judged Israel twenty years.

CHAPTER 17
Micah's Idols

1 And there was a man of mount Ephraim, whose name *was* Micah.

2 And he said unto his mother, The eleven hundred *shekels* of silver that were taken from thee, about which thou cursedst, and spakest of also in mine ears, behold, the silver *is* with me; I took it. And his mother said, Blessed *be thou* of the LORD, my son.

3 And when he had restored the eleven hundred *shekels* of silver to his mother, his mother said, I had wholly dedicated the silver unto the LORD from my hand for my son, to make a graven image and a molten image: now therefore I will restore it unto thee.

4 Yet he restored the money unto his mother; and his mother took two hundred *shekels* of silver, and gave them to the founder, who made thereof a graven image and a molten image: and they were in the house of Micah.

5 And the man Micah had an house of

Cross references (center column)

15 Judg. 14:16.

17 Num. 6:5; Judg. 13:5; Mic. 7:5

19 Prov. 7:26, 27

20 Num. 14:9, 42, 43; Josh. 7:12; 1Sam. 16:14; 18:12; 28:15, 16; 2Chr. 15:2

24 Dan. 5:4

25 Judg. 9:27

27 Deut. 22:8

28 Jer. 15:15

31 Judg. 13:25

2 Gen. 14:19; Ruth 3:10

3 Ex. 20:4, 23; Lev. 19:4

4 Isa. 46:6

5 Gen. 31:19, 30; Ex. 29:9; Judg. 8:27; 1Kgs. 13:33; Hos. 3:4

gods, and made an ephod, and teraphim, and consecrated one of his sons, who became his priest.

6 In those days *there was* no king in Israel, *but* every man did *that which was* right in his own eyes.

Micah's Priest

7 And there was a young man out of Bethlehem-judah of the family of Judah, who *was* a Levite, and he sojourned there.

8 And the man departed out of the city from Beth-lehem-judah to sojourn where he could find *a place*: and he came to mount Ephraim to the house of Micah, as he journeyed.

9 And Micah said unto him, Whence comest thou? And he said unto him, I *am* a Levite of Beth-lehem-judah, and I go to sojourn where I may find *a place*.

10 And Micah said unto him, Dwell with me, and be unto me a father and a priest, and I will give thee ten *shekels* of silver by the year, and a suit of apparel, and thy victuals. So the Levite went in.

11 And the Levite was content to dwell with the man; and the young man was unto him as one of his sons.

12 And Micah consecrated the Levite; and the young man became his priest, and was in the house of Micah.

13 Then said Micah, Now know I that the LORD will do me good, seeing I have a Levite to *my* priest.

CHAPTER 18
Micah and the Tribe of Dan

1 In those days *there was* no king in Israel: and in those days the tribe of the Danites sought them an inheritance to dwell in; for unto that day *all their* inheritance had not fallen unto them among the tribes of Israel.

2 And the children of Dan sent of their family five men from their coasts, men of valour, from Zorah, and from Eshtaol, to spy out the land, and to search it; and they said unto them, Go, search the land: who when they came to mount Ephraim, to the house of Micah, they lodged there.

3 When they *were* by the house of Micah, they knew the voice of the young man the Levite: and they turned in thither, and said unto him, Who brought thee hither? and what makest thou in this *place*? and what hast thou here?

4 And he said unto them, Thus and thus dealeth Micah with me, and hath hired me, and I am his priest.

5 And they said unto him, Ask counsel, we pray thee, of God, that we may know whether our way which we go shall be prosperous.

6 And the priest said unto them, Go in peace: before the LORD *is* your way wherein ye go.

7 Then the five men departed, and came to Laish, and saw the people that *were* therein, how they dwelt careless, after the manner of the Zidonians, quiet and secure; and *there was* no magistrate in the land, that might put *them* to shame in *any* thing; and they *were* far from the Zidonians, and had no business with *any* man.

8 And they came unto their brethren to Zorah and Eshtaol: and their brethren said unto them, What *say* ye?

9 And they said, Arise, that we may go up against them: for we have seen the land, and, behold, it *is* very good: and *are* ye still? be not slothful to go, *and* to enter to possess the land.

10 When ye go, ye shall come unto a people secure, and to a large land: for God hath given it into your hands; a place where *there is* no want of any thing that *is* in the earth.

11 And there went from thence of the family of the Danites, out of Zorah and out of Eshtaol, six hundred men appointed with weapons of war.

12 And they went up, and pitched in Kirjath-jearim, in Judah: wherefore they called that place Mahaneh-dan unto this day: behold, *it is* behind Kirjath-jearim.

13 And they passed thence unto mount Ephraim, and came unto the house of Micah.

14 Then answered the five men that went to spy out the country of Laish, and said unto their brethren, Do ye know that there is in these houses an ephod, and teraphim, and a graven image, and a molten image? now therefore consider what ye have to do.

15 And they turned thitherward, and came to the house of the young man the Levite, *even* unto the house of Micah, and saluted him.

16 And the six hundred men appointed with their weapons of war, which *were* of the children of Dan, stood by the entering of the gate.

17 And the five men that went to spy out the land went up, *and* came in thither, *and* took the graven image, and the ephod, and the teraphim, and the molten image: and the priest stood in the entering of the gate with the six hundred men *that were* appointed with weapons of war.

Cross references (center column):

6 Deut. 12:8; 33:5; Judg. 18:1; 19:1; 21:25

7 Josh. 19:15; Judg. 19:1; Ruth 1:1, 2; Mic. 5:2; Matt. 2:1, 5, 6

10 Gen. 45:8; Judg. 18:19; Job 29:16

12 Judg. 17:5; 18:30

1 Josh. 19:47; Judg. 17:6; 21:25

2 Num. 13:17; Josh. 2:1; Judg. 13:25; 17:1

4 Judg. 17:10

5 Judg. 17:5; 18:14; 1Kgs. 22:5; Isa. 30:1; Hos. 4:12

6 1Kgs. 22:6

7 Josh. 19:47; Judg. 18:27, 28

8 Judg. 18:2

9 Num. 13:30; Josh. 2:23, 24; 1Kgs. 22:3

10 Deut. 8:9; Judg. 18:7, 27

12 Josh. 15:60; Judg. 13:25

13 Judg. 18:2

14 Judg. 17:5; 1Sam. 14:28;

16 Judg. 18:11

17 Judg. 17:4, 5; 18:2, 14

18 And these went into Micah's house, and fetched the carved image, the ephod, and the teraphim, and the molten image. Then said the priest unto them, What do ye?

19 And they said unto him, Hold thy peace, lay thine hand upon thy mouth, and go with us, and be to us a father and a priest: *is it* better for thee to be a priest unto the house of one man, or that thou be a priest unto a tribe and a family in Israel?

20 And the priest's heart was glad, and he took the ephod, and the teraphim, and the graven image, and went in the midst of the people.

21 So they turned and departed, and put the little ones and the cattle and the carriage before them.

22 *And* when they were a good way from the house of Micah, the men that *were* in the houses near to Micah's house were gathered together, and overtook the children of Dan.

23 And they cried unto the children of Dan. And they turned their faces, and said unto Micah, What aileth thee, that thou comest with such a company?

24 And he said, Ye have taken away my gods which I made, and the priest, and ye are gone away: and what have I more? and what *is* this *that* ye say unto me, What aileth thee?

25 And the children of Dan said unto him, Let not thy voice be heard among us, lest angry fellows run upon thee, and thou lose thy life, with the lives of thy household.

26 And the children of Dan went their way: and when Micah saw that they *were* too strong for him, he turned and went back unto his house.

27 And they took *the things* which Micah had made, and the priest which he had, and came unto Laish, unto a people *that were* at quiet and secure: and they smote them with the edge of the sword, and burnt the city with fire.

28 And *there was* no deliverer, because it *was* far from Zidon, and they had no business with *any* man; and it was in the valley that *lieth* by Beth-rehob. And they built a city, and dwelt therein.

29 And they called the name of the city Dan, after the name of Dan their father, who was born unto Israel: howbeit the name of the city *was* Laish at the first.

30 And the children of Dan set up the graven image: and Jonathan, the son of Gershom, the son of Manasseh, he and his sons were priests to the tribe of Dan until the day of the captivity of the land.

31 And they set them up Micah's graven image, which he made, all the time that the house of God was in Shiloh.

CHAPTER 19
The Levite and His Concubine

1 And it came to pass in those days, when *there was* no king in Israel, that there was a certain Levite sojourning on the side of mount Ephraim, who took to him a concubine out of Beth-lehem-judah.

2 And his concubine played the whore against him, and went away from him unto her father's house to Beth-lehem-judah, and was there four whole months.

3 And her husband arose, and went after her, to speak friendly unto her, *and* to bring her again, having his servant with him, and a couple of asses: and she brought him into her father's house: and when the father of the damsel saw him, he rejoiced to meet him.

4 And his father-in-law, the damsel's father, retained him; and he abode with him three days: so they did eat and drink, and lodged there.

5 And it came to pass on the fourth day, when they arose early in the morning, that he rose up to depart: and the damsel's father said unto his son-in-law, Comfort thine heart with a morsel of bread, and afterward go your way.

6 And they sat down, and did eat and drink both of them together: for the damsel's father had said unto the man, Be content, I pray thee, and tarry all night, and let thine heart be merry.

7 And when the man rose up to depart, his father-in-law urged him: therefore he lodged there again.

8 And he arose early in the morning on the fifth day to depart: and the damsel's father said, Comfort thine heart, I pray thee. And they tarried until afternoon, and they did eat both of them.

9 And when the man rose up to depart, he, and his concubine, and his servant, his father-in-law, the damsel's father, said unto him, Behold, now the day draweth toward evening, I pray you tarry all night: behold, the day groweth to an end, lodge here, that thine heart may be merry; and to morrow get you early on your way, that thou mayest go home.

10 But the man would not tarry that night, but he rose up and departed, and came over against Jebus, which *is* Jerusalem; and *there were* with him two asses saddled, his concubine also *was* with him.

---

19 Judg. 17:10; Job 21:5; 29:9; 40:4; Prov. 30:32; Mic. 7:16;

25 2Sam. 17:8

27 Deut. 33:22; Josh. 19:47; Judg. 18:7, 10

28 Num. 13:21; Judg. 18:7; 2Sam. 10:6

29 Gen. 14:14; Josh. 19:47; Judg. 20:1; 1Kgs. 12:29, 30; 15:20

30 Judg. 13:1; 1Sam. 4:2, 3, 10, 11; Ps. 78:60, 61

31 Josh. 18:1; Judg. 19:18; 21:12

1 Judg. 17:6, 7; 18:1; 21:25

3 Gen. 34:3

5 Gen. 18:5

10 Josh. 18:28

11 *And* when they *were* by Jebus, the day was far spent; and the servant said unto his master, Come, I pray thee, and let us turn in into this city of the Jebusites, and lodge in it.
12 And his master said unto him, We will not turn aside hither into the city of a stranger, that *is* not of the children of Israel; we will pass over to Gibeah.
13 And he said unto his servant, Come, and let us draw near to one of these places to lodge all night, in Gibeah, or in Ramah.
14 And they passed on and went their way; and the sun went down upon them *when they were* by Gibeah, which *belongeth* to Benjamin.
15 And they turned aside thither, to go in *and* to lodge in Gibeah: and when he went in, he sat him down in a street of the city: for *there was* no man that took them into his house to lodging.
16 And, behold, there came an old man from his work out of the field at even, which *was* also of mount Ephraim; and he sojourned in Gibeah: but the men of the place *were* Benjamites.
17 And when he had lifted up his eyes, he saw a wayfaring man in the street of the city: and the old man said, Whither goest thou? and whence comest thou?
18 And he said unto him, We *are* passing from Beth-lehem-judah toward the side of mount Ephraim; from thence *am* I: and I went to Beth-lehem-judah, but I *am now* going to the house of the LORD; and there *is* no man that receiveth me to house.
19 Yet there is both straw and provender for our asses; and there is bread and wine also for me, and for thy handmaid, and for the young man *which is* with thy servants: *there is* no want of any thing.
20 And the old man said, Peace *be* with thee; howsoever *let* all thy wants *lie* upon me; only lodge not in the street.
21 So he brought him into his house, and gave provender unto the asses: and they washed their feet, and did eat and drink.
22 *Now* as they were making their hearts merry, behold, the men of the city, certain sons of Belial, beset the house round about, *and* beat at the door, and spake to the master of the house, the old man, saying, Bring forth the man that came into thine house, that we may know him.
23 And the man, the master of the house, went out unto them, and said unto them, Nay, my brethren, *nay*, I pray you, do not *so* wickedly; seeing that this man is come into mine house, do not this folly.

24 Behold, *here is* my daughter a maiden, and his concubine; them I will bring out now, and humble ye them, and do with them what seemeth good unto you: but unto this man do not so vile a thing.
25 But the men would not hearken to him: so the man took his concubine, and brought her forth unto them; and they knew her, and abused her all the night until the morning: and when the day began to spring, they let her go.
26 Then came the woman in the dawning of the day, and fell down at the door of the man's house where her lord *was*, till it was light.
27 And her lord rose up in the morning, and opened the doors of the house, and went out to go his way: and, behold, the woman his concubine was fallen down *at* the door of the house, and her hands *were* upon the threshold.
28 And he said unto her, Up, and let us be going. But none answered. Then the man took her *up* upon an ass, and the man rose up, and gat him unto his place.
29 And when he was come into his house, he took a knife, and laid hold on his concubine, and divided her, *together* with her bones, into twelve pieces, and sent her into all the coasts of Israel.
30 And it was so, that all that saw it said, There was no such deed done nor seen from the day that the children of Israel came up out of the land of Egypt unto this day: consider of it, take advice, and speak *your minds*.

CHAPTER 20
Israel Punishes Benjamin for Its Sin

1 Then all the children of Israel went out, and the congregation was gathered together as one man, from Dan even to Beer-sheba, with the land of Gilead, unto the LORD in Mizpeh.
2 And the chief of all the people, *even* of all the tribes of Israel, presented themselves in the assembly of the people of God, four hundred thousand footmen that drew sword.
3 (Now the children of Benjamin heard that the children of Israel were gone up to Mizpeh.) Then said the children of Israel, Tell *us*, how was this wickedness?
4 And the Levite, the husband of the woman that was slain, answered and said, I came into Gibeah that *belongeth* to Benjamin, I and my concubine, to lodge.
5 And the men of Gibeah rose against me, and beset the house round about upon me

11 Josh. 15:8, 63; Judg. 1:21; 2Sam. 5:6
12 Josh. 18:28
13 Josh. 18:25
15 Matt. 25:43; Heb. 13:2
16 Ps. 104:23
18 Josh. 18:1, 31; Judg. 20:18; 1Sam. 1:3, 7
20 Gen. 19:2; 43:23; Judg. 6:23
21 Gen. 18:4; 24:32; 43:24; John 13:5
22 Gen. 19:4, 5; Deut. 13:13; Judg. 20:5; Hos. 9:9; 10:9; Rom. 1:26, 27
23 Gen. 19:6, 7; 2Sam. 13:12
24 Gen. 19:8; 34:2; Deut. 21:14
25 Gen. 4:1
28 Judg. 20:5
29 Judg. 20:6; 1Sam. 11:7
30 Judg. 20:7; Prov. 13:10
1 Deut. 13:12; Josh. 22:12; Judg. 10:17; 11:11; 18:29; 21:5; 1Sam. 3:20; 7:5; 10:17; 11:7; 2Sam. 3:10; 24:2;
2 Judg. 8:10
4 Judg. 19:15
5 Judg. 19:22, 25, 26

by night, *and* thought to have slain me: and my concubine have they forced, that she is dead.

6 And I took my concubine, and cut her in pieces, and sent her throughout all the country of the inheritance of Israel: for they have committed lewdness and folly in Israel.

7 Behold, ye *are* all children of Israel; give here your advice and counsel.

8 And all the people arose as one man, saying, We will not any *of us* go to his tent, neither will we any *of us* turn into his house.

9 But now this *shall be* the thing which we will do to Gibeah; *we will go up* by lot against it;

10 And we will take ten men of an hundred throughout all the tribes of Israel, and an hundred of a thousand, and a thousand out of ten thousand, to fetch victual for the people, that they may do, when they come to Gibeah of Benjamin, according to all the folly that they have wrought in Israel.

11 So all the men of Israel were gathered against the city, knit together as one man.

12 And the tribes of Israel sent men through all the tribe of Benjamin, saying, What wickedness *is* this that is done among you?

13 Now therefore deliver *us* the men, the children of Belial, which *are* in Gibeah, that we may put them to death, and put away evil from Israel. But the children of Benjamin would not hearken to the voice of their brethren the children of Israel:

14 But the children of Benjamin gathered themselves together out of the cities unto Gibeah, to go out to battle against the children of Israel.

15 And the children of Benjamin were numbered at that time out of the cities twenty and six thousand men that drew sword, beside the inhabitants of Gibeah, which were numbered seven hundred chosen men.

16 Among all this people *there were* seven hundred chosen men lefthanded; every one could sling stones at an hair *breadth*, and not miss.

17 And the men of Israel, beside Benjamin, were numbered four hundred thousand men that drew sword: all these *were* men of war.

18 And the children of Israel arose, and went up to the house of God, and asked

counsel of God, and said, Which of us shall go up first to the battle against the children of Benjamin? And the LORD said, Judah *shall go up* first.

19 And the children of Israel rose up in the morning, and encamped against Gibeah.

20 And the men of Israel went out to battle against Benjamin; and the men of Israel put themselves in array to fight against them at Gibeah.

21 And the children of Benjamin came forth out of Gibeah, and destroyed down to the ground of the Israelites that day twenty and two thousand men.

22 And the people the men of Israel encouraged themselves, and set their battle again in array in the place where they put themselves in array the first day.

23 (And the children of Israel went up and wept before the LORD until even, and asked counsel of the LORD, saying, Shall I go up again to battle against the children of Benjamin my brother? And the LORD said, Go up against him.)

24 And the children of Israel came near against the children of Benjamin the second day.

25 And Benjamin went forth against them out of Gibeah the second day, and destroyed down to the ground of the children of Israel again eighteen thousand men; all these drew the sword.

26 Then all the children of Israel, and all the people, went up, and came unto the house of God, and wept, and sat there before the LORD, and fasted that day until even, and offered burnt offerings and peace offerings before the LORD.

27 And the children of Israel inquired of the LORD, (for the ark of the covenant of God *was* there in those days,

28 And Phinehas, the son of Eleazar, the son of Aaron, stood before it in those days,) saying, Shall I yet again go out to battle against the children of Benjamin my brother, or shall I cease? And the LORD said, Go up; for to morrow I will deliver them into thine hand.

29 And Israel set liers in wait round about Gibeah.

30 And the children of Israel went up against the children of Benjamin on the third day, and put themselves in array against Gibeah, as at other times.

Cross references (center column):

6 Josh. 7:15; Judg. 19:29
7 Judg. 19:30
12 Deut. 13:14; Josh. 22:13, 16
13 Deut. 13:13; 17:12; Judg. 19:22
16 Judg. 3:15; 1Chr. 12:2
18 Num. 27:21; Judg. 1:1; 20:23, 26
21 Gen. 49:27
23 Judg. 20:26, 27
25 Judg. 20:21
26 Judg. 20:18
27 Josh. 18:1; 1Sam. 4:3, 4
28 Deut. 10:8; 18:5; Josh. 24:33
29 Josh. 8:4

20:8 the people arose as one man. God predicted the victory of the tribes of Israel over the tribe of Benjamin to end the terrible civil war between them.

31 And the children of Benjamin went out against the people, *and* were drawn away from the city; and they began to smite of the people, *and* kill, as at other times, in the highways, of which one goeth up to the house of God, and the other to Gibeah in the field, about thirty men of Israel.

32 And the children of Benjamin said, They *are* smitten down before us, as at the first. But the children of Israel said, Let us flee, and draw them from the city unto the highways.

33 And all the men of Israel rose up out of their place, and put themselves in array at Baal-tamar: and the liers in wait of Israel came forth out of their places, *even* out of the meadows of Gibeah.

34 And there came against Gibeah ten thousand chosen men out of all Israel, and the battle was sore: but they knew not that evil *was* near them.

35 And the LORD smote Benjamin before Israel: and the children of Israel destroyed of the Benjamites that day twenty and five thousand and an hundred men: all these drew the sword.

36 So the children of Benjamin saw that they were smitten: for the men of Israel gave place to the Benjamites, because they trusted unto the liers in wait which they had set beside Gibeah.

37 And the liers in wait hasted, and rushed upon Gibeah; and the liers in wait drew *themselves* along, and smote all the city with the edge of the sword.

38 Now there was an appointed sign between the men of Israel and the liers in wait, that they should make a great flame with smoke rise up out of the city.

39 And when the men of Israel retired in the battle, Benjamin began to smite *and* kill of the men of Israel about thirty persons: for they said, Surely they are smitten down before us, as *in* the first battle.

40 But when the flame began to arise up out of the city with a pillar of smoke, the Benjamites looked behind them, and, behold, the flame of the city ascended up to heaven.

41 And when the men of Israel turned again, the men of Benjamin were amazed: for they saw that evil was come upon them.

42 Therefore they turned *their backs* before the men of Israel unto the way of the wilderness; but the battle overtook them; and them which *came* out of the cities they destroyed in the midst of them.

43 *Thus* they inclosed the Benjamites round about, *and* chased them, *and* trode them down with ease over against Gibeah toward the sunrising.

44 And there fell of Benjamin eighteen thousand men; all these *were* men of valour.

45 And they turned and fled toward the wilderness unto the rock of Rimmon: and they gleaned of them in the highways five thousand men; and pursued hard after them unto Gidom, and slew two thousand men of them.

46 So that all which fell that day of Benjamin were twenty and five thousand men that drew the sword; all these *were* men of valour.

47 But six hundred men turned and fled to the wilderness unto the rock Rimmon, and abode in the rock Rimmon four months.

48 And the men of Israel turned again upon the children of Benjamin, and smote them with the edge of the sword, as well the men of *every* city, as the beast, and all that came to hand: also they set on fire all the cities that they came to.

CHAPTER 21
Wives for the Tribe of Benjamin

1 Now the men of Israel had sworn in Mizpeh, saying, There shall not any of us give his daughter unto Benjamin to wife.

2 And the people came to the house of God, and abode there till even before God, and lifted up their voices, and wept sore;

3 And said, O LORD God of Israel, why is this come to pass in Israel, that there should be today one tribe lacking in Israel?

4 And it came to pass on the morrow, that the people rose early, and built there an altar, and offered burnt offerings and peace offerings.

5 And the children of Israel said, Who *is there* among all the tribes of Israel that came not up with the congregation unto the LORD? For they had made a great oath concerning him that came not up to the LORD to Mizpeh, saying, He shall surely be put to death.

6 And the children of Israel repented them for Benjamin their brother, and said, There is one tribe cut off from Israel this day.

7 How shall we do for wives for them that remain, seeing we have sworn by the LORD that we will not give them of our daughters to wives?

8 And they said, What one *is there* of the tribes of Israel that came not up to Mizpeh to the LORD? And, behold, there came none to the camp from Jabesh-gilead to the assembly.

Cross references:

34 Josh. 8:14; Isa. 47:11
36 Josh. 8:15
37 Josh. 6:5; 8:19
40 Josh. 8:20
45 Josh. 15:32
47 Judg. 21:13
1 Judg. 20:1
2 Judg. 20:18, 26
4 2Sam. 24:25
5 Judg. 5:23
8 1Sam. 11:1; 31:11

9 For the people were numbered, and, behold, *there were* none of the inhabitants of Jabesh-gilead there.

10 And the congregation sent hither twelve thousand men of the valiantest, and commanded them, saying, Go and smite the inhabitants of Jabesh-gilead with the edge of the sword, with the women and the children.

11 And this *is* the thing that ye shall do, Ye shall utterly destroy every male, and every woman that hath lain by man.

12 And they found among the inhabitants of Jabesh-gilead four hundred young virgins, that had known no man by lying with any male: and they brought them unto the camp to Shiloh, which *is* in the land of Canaan.

13 And the whole congregation sent *some* to speak to the children of Benjamin that *were* in the rock Rimmon, and to call peaceably unto them.

14 And Benjamin came again at that time; and they gave them wives which they had saved alive of the women of Jabesh-gilead: and yet so they sufficed them not.

15 And the people repented them for Benjamin, because that the LORD had made a breach in the tribes of Israel.

16 Then the elders of the congregation said, How shall we do for wives for them that remain, seeing the women are destroyed out of Benjamin?

17 And they said, *There must be* an inheritance for them that be escaped of Benjamin, that a tribe be not destroyed out of Israel.

18 Howbeit we may not give them wives of our daughters: for the children of Israel have sworn, saying, Cursed *be* he that giveth a wife to Benjamin.

19 Then they said, Behold, *there is* a feast of the LORD in Shiloh yearly *in a place* which *is* on the north side of Beth-el, on the east side of the highway that goeth up from Beth-el to Shechem, and on the south of Lebonah.

20 Therefore they commanded the children of Benjamin, saying, Go and lie in wait in the vineyards;

21 And see, and, behold, if the daughters of Shiloh come out to dance in dances, then come ye out of the vineyards, and catch you every man his wife of the daughters of Shiloh, and go to the land of Benjamin.

22 And it shall be, when their fathers or their brethren come unto us to complain, that we will say unto them, Be favourable unto them for our sakes: because we reserved not to each man his wife in the war: for ye did not give unto them at this time, *that* ye should be guilty.

23 And the children of Benjamin did so, and took *them* wives, according to their number, of them that danced, whom they caught: and they went and returned unto their inheritance, and repaired the cities, and dwelt in them.

24 And the children of Israel departed thence at that time, every man to his tribe and to his family, and they went out from thence every man to his inheritance.

25 In those days *there was* no king in Israel: every man did *that which was* right in his own eyes.

Cross references:

10 Judg. 5:23; 21:5; 1Sam. 11:7

11 Num. 31:17

12 Josh. 18:1

13 Deut. 20:10; Judg. 20:47

15 Judg. 21:6

18 Judg. 11:35; 21:1

21 Judg. 11:34; 1Sam. 18:6; Jer. 31:13

23 Judg. 20:48

25 Deut. 12:8; Judg. 17:6; 18:1; 19:1

Ruth

The book of Ruth, sometimes called "the romance of redemption," is a charming, idyllic story of faith, devotion, and love. The unfolding romance in Ruth should be viewed in light of ancient Hebrew custom. When judged this way, there is nothing immodest or indecorous in this beautiful story of true love purely requited.

Ruth may have originally been part of the book of Judges. However, by New Testament times, it was included on a scroll with four other books that were read publicly at the feasts of Israel. These books were known as the Five Megilloth (scrolls) and arranged to be read on Jewish holy days in this order: *Song of Solomon, Ruth, Lamentations, Ecclesiastes,* and *Esther.* Ruth was read publicly at the Feast of the Harvest (Pentecost) because much of the story is set in the harvest fields.

According to Mosaic Law (Deut. 25:5), a near kinsman had first option to buy land in the estate of a deceased Israelite, but he was expected to marry the widow of the deceased. The nearest kinsmen to Ruth's deceased husband declined to marry Ruth, since it would complicate his own inheritance, so the next closest kinsman, Boaz, could then "redeem" the land and claim the widow as his wife.

This Gentile (Moabitess) is one of four women included in the genealogy of Jesus (Matt. 1:5). However, she was a descendent of Terah, who was also Abraham's father (Gen. 11:31). The genealogy in the last chapter documents the "seed of Abraham" passing to David, the human ancestor of both Joseph and Mary (Matt. 1; Luke 3; Gen. 22:18).

No predictive revelations appear in Ruth. However, many Bible scholars have compared the relationship of Boaz, the bridegroom, and Ruth, the bride, with Christ's relationship with His Church.

Of the 85 total verses in the book of Ruth, 15 (18%) are typologically predictive of Christ and the Church. Like Boaz, Jesus comes from Bethlehem seeking a Gentile Bride, fulfilling the messianic prophecies of the Davidic line of kings.

Author
Unknown

Date
11th Century B.C.

Key Truth
Romance of Redemption

Historic Time
The Period of the Judges

Key Verse
4:4
. . . for there is none to redeem it beside thee. . . .

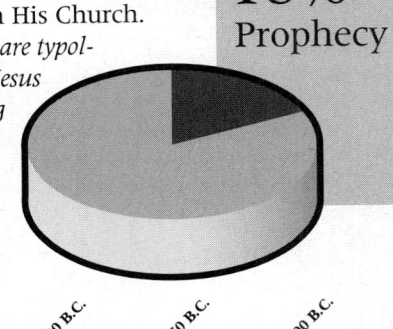

18%
Prophecy

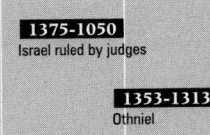

1450 B.C. 1400 B.C. 1350 B.C. 1300 B.C. 1250 B.C. 1200 B.C. 1150 B.C. 1100 B.C. 1050

1375-1050
Israel ruled by judges

1275-1215
Ehud

1195-1155
Deborah and Barak

1148-1108
Gideon

1105-1099
Jephthah

1353-1313
Othniel

1108-1105
Abimelech

1150-1120
Book of Ruth

1105
Birth of Samuel

Samson

Dates may vary as some judges ruled over different areas at the same time.

thou shalt mark the place where he shall lie, and thou shalt go in, and uncover his feet, and lay thee down; and he will tell thee what thou shalt do.

5 And she said unto her, All that thou sayest unto me I will do.

6 And she went down unto the floor, and did according to all that her mother-in-law bade her.

7 And when Boaz had eaten and drunk, and his heart was merry, he went to lie down at the end of the heap of corn: and she came softly, and uncovered his feet, and laid her down.

8 And it came to pass at midnight, that the man was afraid, and turned himself: and, behold, a woman lay at his feet.

9 And he said, Who *art* thou? And she answered, I *am* Ruth thine handmaid: spread therefore thy skirt over thine handmaid; for thou *art* a near kinsman.

10 And he said, Blessed *be* thou of the LORD, my daughter: *for* thou hast shewed more kindness in the latter end than at the beginning, inasmuch as thou followedst not young men, whether poor or rich.

11 And now, my daughter, fear not; I will do to thee all that thou requirest: for all the city of my people doth know that thou *art* a virtuous woman.

12 And now it is true that I *am thy* near kinsman: howbeit there is a kinsman nearer than I.

13 Tarry this night, and it shall be in the morning, *that* if he will perform unto thee the part of a kinsman, well; let him do the kinsman's part: but if he will not do the part of a kinsman to thee, then will I do the part of a kinsman to thee, *as* the LORD liveth: lie down until the morning.

14 And she lay at his feet until the morning: and she rose up before one could know another. And he said, Let it not be known that a woman came into the floor.

15 Also he said, Bring the vail that *thou hast* upon thee, and hold it. And when she held it, he measured six *measures* of barley, and laid *it* on her: and she went into the city.

16 And when she came to her mother-in-law,

7 Judg. 19:6, 9, 22; 2Sam. 13:28; Esth. 1:10

9 Ruth 2:20; 3:12; Ezek. 16:8

10 Ruth 1:8; Ruth 2:20

11 Prov. 12:4

12 Ruth 3:9; 4:1

13 Deut. 25:5; Judg. 8:19; Ruth 4:5; Jer. 4:2; Matt. 22:24

14 Rom. 12:17; 14:16; 1Cor. 10:32; 2Cor. 8:21; 1Thess. 5:22

18 Ps. 37:3, 5

1 Ruth 3:12

2 1Kgs. 21:8; Prov. 31:23

4 Gen. 23:18; Lev. 25:25; Jer. 32:7, 8

5 Gen. 38:8; Deut. 25:5, 6; Ruth 3:3; Matt. 22:24

6 Ruth 3:12, 13

7 Deut. 25:7, 9

she said, Who *art* thou, my daughter? And she told her all that the man had done to her.

17 And she said, These six *measures* of barley gave he me; for he said to me, Go not empty unto thy mother-in-law.

18 Then said she, Sit still, my daughter, until thou know how the matter will fall: for the man will not be in rest, until he have finished the thing this day.

CHAPTER 4
Boaz Marries Ruth

1 Then went Boaz up to the gate, and sat him down there: and, behold, the kinsman of whom Boaz spake came by; unto whom he said, Ho, such a one! turn aside, sit down here. And he turned aside, and sat down.

2 And he took ten men of the elders of the city, and said, Sit ye down here. And they sat down.

3 And he said unto the kinsman, Naomi, that is come again out of the country of Moab, selleth a parcel of land, which *was* our brother Elimelech's:

4 And I thought to advertise thee, saying, Buy *it* before the inhabitants, and before the elders of my people. If thou wilt redeem *it*, redeem *it*: but if thou wilt not redeem *it*, *then* tell me, that I may know: for *there is* none to redeem *it* beside thee; and I *am* after thee. And he said, I will redeem *it*.

5 Then said Boaz, What day thou buyest the field of the hand of Naomi, thou must buy *it* also of Ruth the Moabitess, the wife of the dead, to raise up the name of the dead upon his inheritance.

6 And the kinsman said, I cannot redeem *it* for myself, lest I mar mine own inheritance: redeem thou my right to thyself; for I cannot redeem *it*.

7 Now this *was the manner* in former time in Israel concerning redeeming and concerning changing, for to confirm all things; a man plucked off his shoe, and gave *it* to his neighbour: and this *was* a testimony in Israel.

8 Therefore the kinsman said unto Boaz, Buy *it* for thee. So he drew off his shoe.

9 And Boaz said unto the elders, and *unto*

4:1–11 the kinsman of whom Boaz spake. A kinsman is a relative of Ruth's deceased husband who is authorized by Old Testament law to redeem her from widowhood by marrying her (cf. Deut. 25:5; Matt. 22:23–28). The biblical concept of redemption is illustrated beautifully in the relationship between Boaz and Ruth. She was a Gentile widow and he was a Hebrew from Bethlehem who offers to be her redeemer (Hebr. *goel*). Together, they form a prophetic type of Christ and His Bride, the Church. In the New Testament, redemption illustrates the work of Christ on our behalf (Luke 1:68; Acts 20:28; 1 Cor. 6:20; 7:23; Gal. 3:13; Heb. 9:12; 1 Pet. 1:19; Rev. 5:9).

all the people, Ye *are* witnesses this day, that I have bought all that *was* Elimelech's, and all that *was* Chilion's and Mahlon's, of the hand of Naomi.

10 Moreover Ruth the Moabitess, the wife of Mahlon, have I purchased to be my wife, to raise up the name of the dead upon his inheritance, that the name of the dead be not cut off from among his brethren, and from the gate of his place: ye *are* witnesses this day.

11 And all the people that *were* in the gate, and the elders, said, *We are* witnesses. The LORD make the woman that is come into thine house like Rachel and like Leah, which two did build the house of Israel: and do thou worthily in Ephratah, and be famous in Beth-lehem:

12 And let thy house be like the house of Pharez, whom Tamar bare unto Judah, of the seed which the LORD shall give thee of this young woman.

The Genealogy of Boaz

13 So Boaz took Ruth, and she was his wife: and when he went in unto her, the LORD

gave her conception, and she bare a son.

14 And the women said unto Naomi, Blessed *be* the LORD, which hath not left thee this day without a kinsman, that his name may be famous in Israel.

15 And he shall be unto thee a restorer of *thy* life, and a nourisher of thine old age: for thy daughter-in-law, which loveth thee, which is better to thee than seven sons, hath born him.

16 And Naomi took the child, and laid it in her bosom, and became nurse unto it.

17 And the women her neighbours gave it a name, saying, There is a son born to Naomi; and they called his name Obed: he *is* the father of Jesse, the father of David.

18 Now these *are* the generations of Pharez: Pharez begat Hezron,

19 And Hezron begat Ram, and Ram begat Amminadab,

20 And Amminadab begat Nahshon, and Nahshon begat Salmon,

21 And Salmon begat Boaz, and Boaz begat Obed,

22 And Obed begat Jesse, and Jesse begat David.

Cross references

10	Deut. 25:6
11	Gen. 35:16, 19; Deut. 25:9; Ps. 127:3; 128:3
12	Gen. 38:29; 1Sam. 2:20; 1Chr. 2:4; Matt. 1:3
13	Gen. 29:31; 33:5; Ruth 3:11
14	Luke 1:58; Rom. 12:15
15	Gen. 45:11; 1Sam. 1:8; Ps. 55:22
17	Luke 1:58, 59
18	1Chr. 2:4; Matt. 1:3
20	Num. 1:7; Matt. 1:4
22	1Chr. 2:15; Matt. 1:6

The Redemptive Line of Messiah

ANCESTRY	DESCRIPTION	OT REFERENCE
From Adam and Eve	The woman's Seed	Genesis 3:15
From Abraham	All the earth shall be blessed through his Seed	Genesis 22:18
From Jacob	The younger son	Genesis 25:23
From Judah	Shiloh, Sceptre, Star	Genesis 49:10 Numbers 24:17
From Obed	Son of Boaz and Ruth, father of Jesse	Ruth 4:11–22
From Jesse	Rod out of the Stem	Isaiah 11:1

See Matthew 1:1–17 and Luke 3:23–38 for the genealogy of Jesus from Adam, Abraham, and David

4:14 famous in Israel. The blessing of the women of Bethlehem predicts that the name of the kinsman will be famous. Their blessing came true in the redemption provided by Boaz that propagated the line of the Messiah and was fulfilled in the births of David and Jesus at Bethlehem (see Matt. 1:1–17).

1 Samuel

T his book of transition is named after the last judge and first great prophet of Israel. Samuel was one of the greatest of the Hebrew leaders God raised up at special times, along with Abraham, the great patriarch, and Moses, the warrior and lawgiver. Samuel's influence lay not in military exploits, diplomatic skill, or political shrewdness, but in personal integrity and unceasing loyalty to God.

Though not of the Levitical priestly tribe, Samuel was specially called to be a priest. He established the schools of the prophets (1 Sam. 19:20; 1 Kgs. 2:3–5; 4:38), and, after anointing both Saul and David to be kings, gradually relinquished his political position to the monarchy. Recording the transition from theocracy (government by God) to monarchy, 1 Samuel covers a period of nearly 100 years from the birth of Samuel to the death of Saul.

Author
Samuel and Others

Date
10th Century B.C.

Key Truth
The Lord's Anointed

Historic Time
Birth of Samuel to Death of Saul

Key Verse
13:14
. . . the LORD hath sought him a man after his own heart. . . .

The book also contrasts the characters of Israel's first two kings. Saul was a "man after the flesh," who never reached his spiritual potential but was selfish, jealous, depressive, and self-willed. David was heroic, courageous, spiritual, and dedicated to God. Here we see David as a shepherd lad, musician, armour-bearer, soldier, king's son-in-law, king designate, psalm writer and fugitive.

The books of 1 and 2 Samuel were originally one book. Although its division into two parts first appeared in the Greek Septuagint version of the Old Testament, it remained undivided in the Hebrew text until the publishing of the Hebrew Bible in A.D. 1517. Most of the prophecies in 1 Samuel were fulfilled in ancient times, but predictions of a strong monarchy may foreshadow the reign of Jesus, who was born of the lineage of David and is even called the "Son of David."

Thirty-one predictions are distributed throughout the book, relating to various historical persons and events. These predictions are found in 124 verses out of 810 or 15 percent of the book.

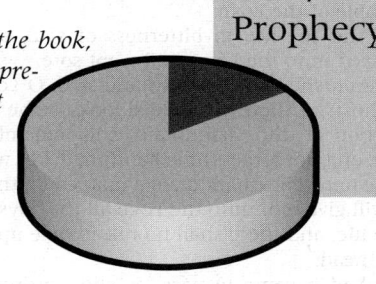

15%
Prophecy

| 1300 B.C. | 1250 B.C. | 1200 B.C. | 1150 B.C. | 1100 B.C. | 1050 B.C. | 1000 B.C. | 950 B.C. | 900 B.C. |

Israel ruled by judges

1043-1011
Saul's reign

990
Birth of Solomon

1105-1011
Book of 1 Samuel

971-931
Solomon's reign

1080
Birth of Saul

1026
David anointed

1011-971
David's reign

1105
Birth of Samuel

1040
Birth of David

CHAPTER 1
Samuel's Birth

1 Now there was a certain man of Ramathaim-zophim, of mount Ephraim, and his name *was* Elkanah, the son of Jeroham, the son of Elihu, the son of Tohu, the son of Zuph, an Ephrathite.

2 And he had two wives; the name of the one *was* Hannah, and the name of the other Peninnah: and Peninnah had children, but Hannah had no children.

3 And this man went up out of his city yearly to worship and to sacrifice unto the Lᴏʀᴅ of hosts in Shiloh. And the two sons of Eli, Hophni and Phinehas, the priests of the Lᴏʀᴅ, *were* there.

4 And when the time was that Elkanah offered, he gave to Peninnah his wife, and to all her sons and her daughters, portions:

5 But unto Hannah he gave a worthy portion; for he loved Hannah: but the Lᴏʀᴅ had shut up her womb.

6 And her adversary also provoked her sore, for to make her fret, because the Lᴏʀᴅ had shut up her womb.

7 And *as* he did so year by year, when she went up to the house of the Lᴏʀᴅ, so she provoked her; therefore she wept, and did not eat.

8 Then said Elkanah her husband to her, Hannah, why weepest thou? and why eatest thou not? and why is thy heart grieved? *am* not I better to thee than ten sons?

9 So Hannah rose up after they had eaten in Shiloh, and after they had drunk. Now Eli the priest sat upon a seat by a post of the temple of the Lᴏʀᴅ.

10 And she *was* in bitterness of soul, and prayed unto the Lᴏʀᴅ, and wept sore.

11 And she vowed a vow, and said, O Lᴏʀᴅ of hosts, if thou wilt indeed look on the affliction of thine handmaid, and remember me, and not forget thine handmaid, but wilt give unto thine handmaid a man child, then I will give him unto the Lᴏʀᴅ all the days of his life, and there shall no razor come upon his head.

12 And it came to pass, as she continued

praying before the Lᴏʀᴅ, that Eli marked her mouth.

13 Now Hannah, she spake in her heart; only her lips moved, but her voice was not heard: therefore Eli thought she had been drunken.

14 And Eli said unto her, How long wilt thou be drunken? put away thy wine from thee.

15 And Hannah answered and said, No, my lord, I *am* a woman of a sorrowful spirit: I have drunk neither wine nor strong drink, but have poured out my soul before the Lᴏʀᴅ.

16 Count not thine handmaid for a daughter of Belial: for out of the abundance of my complaint and grief have I spoken hitherto.

17 Then Eli answered and said, Go in peace: and the God of Israel grant *thee* thy petition that thou hast asked of him.

18 And she said, Let thine handmaid find grace in thy sight. So the woman went her way, and did eat, and her countenance was no more *sad*.

19 And they rose up in the morning early, and worshipped before the Lᴏʀᴅ, and returned, and came to their house to Ramah: and Elkanah knew Hannah his wife; and the Lᴏʀᴅ remembered her.

20 Wherefore it came to pass, when the time was come about after Hannah had conceived, that she bare a son, and called his name Samuel, *saying*, Because I have asked him of the Lᴏʀᴅ.

21 And the man Elkanah, and all his house, went up to offer unto the Lᴏʀᴅ the yearly sacrifice, and his vow.

22 But Hannah went not up; for she said unto her husband, *I will not go up* until the child be weaned, and *then* I will bring him, that he may appear before the Lᴏʀᴅ, and there abide for ever.

23 And Elkanah her husband said unto her, Do what seemeth thee good; tarry until thou have weaned him; only the Lᴏʀᴅ establish his word. So the woman abode, and gave her son suck until she weaned him.

24 And when she had weaned him, she

Cross-references
1 Ruth 1:2; 1Chr. 6:27, 34
3 Ex. 23:14; Deut. 12:5-7; 16:16; Josh. 18:1; Luke 2:41
4 Deut. 12:17, 18; 16:11
5 Gen. 30:2
6 Job 24:21
8 Ruth 4:15
9 1Sam. 3:3
10 Job 7:11; 10:1
11 Gen. 8:1; 28:20; 29:32; 30:22; Ex. 4:31; Num. 6:5; 30:3; Judg. 11:30; 13:5; 2Sam. 16:12; Ps. 25:18
15 Ps. 62:8; 142:2
16 Deut. 13:13
17 Judg. 18:6; Ps. 20:4, 5; Mark 5:34; Luke 7:50; 8:48
18 Gen. 33:15; Ruth 2:13; Eccl. 9:7
19 Gen. 4:1; 30:22
21 1Sam. 1:3
22 Ex. 21:6; 1Sam. 1:11, 28; 2:11, 18; 3:1 Luke 2:22
23 Num. 30:7; 2Sam. 7:25
24 Deut. 12:5, 6, 11; Josh. 18:1

1:3 The Lᴏʀᴅ of hosts. This major majestic title (Hebr. *Jehovah Sabaoth*), first used here and then in 1:11 by Hannah in her prayer for a son, does not appear in the Pentateuch. After this, it occurs over 280 times in the Old Testament, especially in the prophets (Isaiah, Jeremiah, Zechariah, Malachi). The term "hosts" is used in the Bible for heavenly bodies (Gen 2:1; Neh. 9:6; Isa. 40:26), for angels (Luke 2:13), armies (1 Kgs. 11:15), and sinners (Judg. 4:2). God is able to marshal His heavenly armies of angels, as well as earthly armies, to carry out His divine program for this world. The title teaches us that all things are under His divine and providential control. The divine title may be used for Christ. Compare Isaiah 6:1–3 with John 12:41 and Isaiah 8:13–14 with 1 Peter 2:5–8.

took him up with her, with three bullocks, and one ephah of flour, and a bottle of wine, and brought him unto the house of the LORD in Shiloh: and the child *was* young.

25 And they slew a bullock, and brought the child to Eli.

26 And she said, Oh my lord, *as* thy soul liveth, my lord, I *am* the woman that stood by thee here, praying unto the LORD.

27 For this child I prayed; and the LORD hath given me my petition which I asked of him:

28 Therefore also I have lent him to the LORD; as long as he liveth he shall be lent to the LORD. And he worshipped the LORD there.

CHAPTER 2
Hannah's Prayer

1 And Hannah prayed, and said, My heart rejoiceth in the LORD, mine horn is exalted in the LORD: my mouth is enlarged over mine enemies; because I rejoice in thy salvation.

2 *There is* none holy as the LORD: for *there is* none beside thee: neither *is there* any rock like our God.

3 Talk no more so exceeding proudly; let *not* arrogancy come out of your mouth: for the LORD *is* a God of knowledge, and by him actions are weighed.

4 The bows of the mighty men *are* broken, and they that stumbled are girded with strength.

5 *They that were* full have hired out themselves for bread; and *they that were* hungry ceased: so that the barren hath born seven; and she that hath many children is waxed feeble.

6 The LORD killeth, and maketh alive: he bringeth down to the grave, and bringeth up.

7 The LORD maketh poor, and maketh rich: he bringeth low, and lifteth up.

8 He raiseth up the poor out of the dust, *and* lifteth up the beggar from the dunghill, to set *them* among princes, and to make them inherit the throne of glory: for the pillars of the earth *are* the LORD's, and he hath set the world upon them.

9 He will keep the feet of his saints, and the wicked shall be silent in darkness; for by strength shall no man prevail.

10 The adversaries of the LORD shall be broken to pieces; out of heaven shall he thunder upon them: the LORD shall judge the ends of the earth; and he shall give strength unto his king, and exalt the horn of his anointed.

11 And Elkanah went to Ramah to his house. And the child did minister unto the LORD before Eli the priest.

Eli's Corrupt Sons

12 Now the sons of Eli *were* sons of Belial; they knew not the LORD.

13 And the priests' custom with the people *was, that,* when any man offered sacrifice, the priest's servant came, while the flesh was in seething, with a fleshhook of three teeth in his hand;

14 And he struck *it* into the pan, or kettle, or caldron, or pot; all that the fleshhook brought up the priest took for himself. So they did in Shiloh unto all the Israelites that came thither.

15 Also before they burnt the fat, the priest's servant came, and said to the man that sacrificed, Give flesh to roast for the priest; for he will not have sodden flesh of thee, but raw.

16 And *if* any man said unto him, Let them not fail to burn the fat presently, and *then* take *as much* as thy soul desireth; then he would answer him, Nay; but thou shalt give *it me* now: and if not, I will take *it* by force.

17 Wherefore the sin of the young men was

Cross-references

25 Luke 2:22
26 Gen. 42:15; 2Kgs. 2:2, 4, 6
27 Matt. 7:7
28 Gen. 24:26, 52; 1Sam. 1:11, 22
1 Ps. 9:14; 13:5; 20:5; 35:9; 92:10; 112:9; Luke 1:46; Phil. 4:6
2 Ex. 15:11; Deut. 3:24; 2Sam. 22:32; Ps. 86:8
3 Ps. 94:4; Mal. 3:13; Jude 1:15
4 Ps. 37:15, 17; 76:3
5 Ps. 34:10; 113:9; Isa. 54:1; Jer. 15:9; Luke 1:53
6 Deut. 32:39; Job 5:18; Hos. 6:1
7 Job 1:21; Ps. 75:7
8 Job 36:7; Ps. 24:2; 102:25; Luke 1:52; Heb. 1:3
9 Ps. 91:11; 121:3
10 1Sam. 7:10; Ps. 2:9; 18:13; 89:24
11 1Sam. 2:18; 3:1
12 Deut. 13:13
15 Lev. 3:3-5, 16

2:1 And Hannah prayed. Before he was born, Hannah dedicated Samuel to God to be a Nazarite. When he was very young, she brought him to the Tabernacle and to the high priest Eli. This noble woman in her song of thanksgiving (vv. 1–10) demonstrated such wisdom and insight that she could be ranked as a prophetess.

2:10 anointed. Hannah's song concludes with the prophecy that the adversaries of the Lord would be defeated; that thunderous judgment out of heaven would come upon the earth; that God would give His king great strength; and finally, that He would exalt "the horn" (Hebr. for "horn" means "strength"), or his anointed. This is the first mention in Scripture of Jehovah's Messiah ("the anointed one") and it is sung by a woman. Eleven centuries later, Mary sang her famous "magnificat," magnifying the Lord and anticipating the ministry of her son, the Messiah, the Anointed One. Compare Psalm 2:1–9, where the anointed is said to be the Son of the LORD.

2:10 the LORD shall judge the ends of the earth. This is an inspired early prediction of the glorious reign of Jesus in the millennial age, a concept Hannah herself could not have originated. Another Hannah (Anna), a prophetess, rejoiced over the predictions of Simeon covering the Messiah's future triumphs, given in the temple, when Jesus was only eight days old (Luke 2:21–38).

very great before the LORD: for men abhorred the offering of the LORD.

18 But Samuel ministered before the LORD, *being* a child, girded with a linen ephod.

19 Moreover his mother made him a little coat, and brought *it* to him from year to year, when she came up with her husband to offer the yearly sacrifice.

20 And Eli blessed Elkanah and his wife, and said, The LORD give thee seed of this woman for the loan which is lent to the LORD. And they went unto their own home.

21 And the LORD visited Hannah, so that she conceived, and bare three sons and two daughters. And the child Samuel grew before the LORD.

22 Now Eli was very old, and heard all that his sons did unto all Israel; and how they lay with the women that assembled *at* the door of the tabernacle of the congregation.

23 And he said unto them, Why do ye such things? for I hear of your evil dealings by all this people.

24 Nay, my sons; for *it is* no good report that I hear: ye make the LORD's people to transgress.

25 If one man sin against another, the judge shall judge him: but if a man sin against the LORD, who shall intreat for him? Notwithstanding they hearkened not unto the voice of their father, because the LORD would slay them.

26 And the child Samuel grew on, and was in favour both with the LORD, and also with men.

27 And there came a man of God unto Eli, and said unto him, Thus saith the LORD, Did I plainly appear unto the house of thy father, when they were in Egypt in Pharaoh's house?

28 And did I choose him out of all the tribes of Israel *to be* my priest, to offer upon mine altar, to burn incense, to wear an ephod before me? and did I give unto the house of thy father all the offerings made by fire of the children of Israel?

29 Wherefore kick ye at my sacrifice and at mine offering, which I have commanded *in* my habitation; and honourest thy sons above me, to make yourselves fat with the

chiefest of all the offerings of Israel my people?

30 Wherefore the LORD God of Israel saith, I said indeed *that* thy house, and the house of thy father, should walk before me for ever: but now the LORD saith, Be it far from me; for them that honour me I will honour, and they that despise me shall be lightly esteemed.

31 Behold, the days come, that I will cut off thine arm, and the arm of thy father's house, that there shall not be an old man in thine house.

32 And thou shalt see an enemy *in my* habitation, in all *the wealth* which God shall give Israel: and there shall not be an old man in thine house for ever.

33 And the man of thine, *whom* I shall not cut off from mine altar, *shall be* to consume thine eyes, and to grieve thine heart: and all the increase of thine house shall die in the flower of their age.

34 And this *shall be* a sign unto thee, that shall come upon thy two sons, on Hophni and Phinehas; in one day they shall die both of them.

35 And I will raise me up a faithful priest, *that* shall do according to *that* which *is* in mine heart and in my mind: and I will build him a sure house; and he shall walk before mine anointed for ever.

36 And it shall come to pass, *that* every one that is left in thine house shall come *and* crouch to him for a piece of silver and a morsel of bread, and shall say, Put me, I pray thee, into one of the priests' offices, that I may eat a piece of bread.

CHAPTER 3
Samuel's Call

1 And the child Samuel ministered unto the LORD before Eli. And the word of the LORD was precious in those days; *there was* no open vision.

2 And it came to pass at that time, when Eli *was* laid down in his place, and his eyes began to wax dim, *that* he could not see;

3 And ere the lamp of God went out in the temple of the LORD, where the ark of God *was*, and Samuel was laid down *to sleep*;

Cross references

18 Ex. 28:4;
1Sam. 2:11;
2Sam. 6:14

19 1Sam.
1:3

20 Gen.
14:19; 1Sam.
1:28

21 Gen.
21:1; Judg.
13:24; 1Sam.
2:26; 3:19;
Luke 1:80;
2:40

22 Ex. 38:8

25 Num.
15:30; Josh.
11:20; Prov.
15:10

26 1Sam.
2:21; Prov.
3:4; Luke
2:52; Acts
2:47; Rom.
14:18

27 Ex. 4:14,
27; 1Kgs.
13:1

28 Ex. 28:1,
4; Lev. 2:3,
10; 6:16; 7:7,
8, 34, 35;
Num. 5:9,
10; 16:5

29 Deut.
12:5, 6;
32:15

30 Ex. 29:9;
Ps. 18:20;
91:14; Jer.
18:9, 10;
Mal. 2:9

31 1Sam.
4:11; 14:3;
1Kgs. 2:27;
Ezek. 44:10

32 Zech. 8:4

34 1Sam.
4:11; 1Kgs.
13:3

35 2Sam.
7:11, 27;
1Kgs. 2:35;
11:38; 1Chr.
29:22

36 1Kgs.
2:27

1 Amos 8:11

3 Ex. 27:21;
Lev. 24:3

2:26 the child Samuel. While Samuel, whose very name means "name of God," is not specifically cited in the New Testament as a type of Christ, there are several similarities that tend to forecast the Savior's ministry. Samuel was a prophet, priest, and ruler, as Jesus is. He grew in stature and in favor both with the Lord and men (cf. Luke 2:52). He was a great intercessor, saying of the rebellious nation, "God forbid that I should sin against the LORD in ceasing to pray for you" (12:23). Jesus, who cannot sin, "ever liveth to make intercession for [us]" (Heb. 7:25).

4 That the LORD called Samuel: and he answered, Here *am* I.

5 And he ran unto Eli, and said, Here *am* I; for thou calledst me. And he said, I called not; lie down again. And he went and lay down.

6 And the LORD called yet again, Samuel. And Samuel arose and went to Eli, and said, Here *am* I; for thou didst call me. And he answered, I called not, my son; lie down again.

7 Now Samuel did not yet know the LORD, neither was the word of the LORD yet revealed unto him.

8 And the LORD called Samuel again the third time. And he arose and went to Eli, and said, Here *am* I; for thou didst call me. And Eli perceived that the LORD had called the child.

9 Therefore Eli said unto Samuel, Go, lie down: and it shall be, if he call thee, that thou shalt say, Speak, LORD; for thy servant heareth. So Samuel went and lay down in his place.

10 And the LORD came, and stood, and called as at other times, Samuel, Samuel. Then Samuel answered, Speak; for thy servant heareth.

11 And the LORD said to Samuel, Behold, I will do a thing in Israel, at which both the ears of every one that heareth it shall tingle.

12 In that day I will perform against Eli all *things* which I have spoken concerning his house: when I begin, I will also make an end.

13 For I have told him that I will judge his house for ever for the iniquity which he knoweth; because his sons made themselves vile, and he restrained them not.

14 And therefore I have sworn unto the house of Eli, that the iniquity of Eli's house shall not be purged with sacrifice nor offering for ever.

15 And Samuel lay until the morning, and opened the doors of the house of the LORD. And Samuel feared to shew Eli the vision.

16 Then Eli called Samuel, and said, Samuel, my son. And he answered, Here *am* I.

17 And he said, What *is* the thing that the LORD hath said unto thee? I pray thee hide *it*

not from me: God do so to thee, and more also, if thou hide *any* thing from me of all the things that he said unto thee.

18 And Samuel told him every whit, and hid nothing from him. And he said, It *is* the LORD: let him do what seemeth him good.

19 And Samuel grew, and the LORD was with him, and did let none of his words fall to the ground.

20 And all Israel from Dan even to Beersheba knew that Samuel *was* established *to be* a prophet of the LORD.

21 And the LORD appeared again in Shiloh: for the LORD revealed himself to Samuel in Shiloh by the word of the LORD.

CHAPTER 4
The Philistines Capture the Ark of God

1 And the word of Samuel came to all Israel. Now Israel went out against the Philistines to battle, and pitched beside Ebenezer: and the Philistines pitched in Aphek.

2 And the Philistines put themselves in array against Israel: and when they joined battle, Israel was smitten before the Philistines: and they slew of the army in the field about four thousand men.

3 And when the people were come into the camp, the elders of Israel said, Wherefore hath the LORD smitten us today before the Philistines? Let us fetch the ark of the covenant of the LORD out of Shiloh unto us, that, when it cometh among us, it may save us out of the hand of our enemies.

4 So the people sent to Shiloh, that they might bring from thence the ark of the covenant of the LORD of hosts, which dwelleth *between* the cherubims: and the two sons of Eli, Hophni and Phinehas, *were* there with the ark of the covenant of God.

5 And when the ark of the covenant of the LORD came into the camp, all Israel shouted with a great shout, so that the earth rang again.

6 And when the Philistines heard the noise of the shout, they said, What *meaneth* the noise of this great shout in the camp of the Hebrews? And they understood that the ark of the LORD was come into the camp.

Cross references

7 Acts 19:2

11 2Kgs. 21:12; Jer. 19:3

12 1Sam. 2:30-36

13 1Sam. 2: 12, 17, 22, 23, 25, 29-31; Ezek. 7:3; 18:30

14 Num. 15:30, 31; Isa. 22:14

17 Ruth 1:17

18 Job 1:21; 2:10; Ps. 39:9; Isa. 39:8

19 Gen. 39:2, 21, 23; 1Sam. 2:21; 9:6

20 Judg. 20:1

21 1Sam. 3:1, 4

1 1Sam. 5:1; 7:12

4 Ex. 25:18, 22; Num. 7:89; 2Sam. 6:2; Ps. 80:1; 99:1

3:4 the LORD called Samuel. While still a lad, probably no more than ten years old, Samuel received a special divine revelation. Not only did God speak to him in the night in a voice that he heard, but to him was revealed the coming tragedy and downfall of the house of Eli. Reluctantly, he shared the message with the aging high priest. As Samuel continued to mature, his spiritual influence increased and the entire nation knew that he was "established to be a prophet of the LORD" (v. 20). Young people in the Bible with a divine call and destiny include Joseph, David (1 Sam. 16:11–13), Jeremiah (Jer. 5:1–10), John the Baptist, and Jesus (Luke 1—3).

7 And the Philistines were afraid, for they said, God is come into the camp. And they said, Woe unto us! for there hath not been such a thing heretofore.

8 Woe unto us! who shall deliver us out of the hand of these mighty Gods? these *are* the Gods that smote the Egyptians with all the plagues in the wilderness.

9 Be strong, and quit yourselves like men, O ye Philistines, that ye be not servants unto the Hebrews, as they have been to you: quit yourselves like men, and fight.

10 And the Philistines fought, and Israel was smitten, and they fled every man into his tent: and there was a very great slaughter; for there fell of Israel thirty thousand footmen.

11 And the ark of God was taken; and the two sons of Eli, Hophni and Phinehas, were slain.

Eli's Death

12 And there ran a man of Benjamin out of the army, and came to Shiloh the same day with his clothes rent, and with earth upon his head.

13 And when he came, lo, Eli sat upon a seat by the wayside watching: for his heart trembled for the ark of God. And when the man came into the city, and told *it*, all the city cried out.

14 And when Eli heard the noise of the crying, he said, What *meaneth* the noise of this tumult? And the man came in hastily, and told Eli.

15 Now Eli was ninety and eight years old; and his eyes were dim, that he could not see.

16 And the man said unto Eli, I *am* he that came out of the army, and I fled today out of the army. And he said, What is there done, my son?

17 And the messenger answered and said, Israel is fled before the Philistines, and there hath been also a great slaughter among the people, and thy two sons also, Hophni and Phinehas, are dead, and the ark of God is taken.

18 And it came to pass, when he made mention of the ark of God, that he fell from off the seat backward by the side of the gate, and his neck brake, and he died: for he was an old man, and heavy. And he had judged Israel forty years.

19 And his daughter-in-law, Phinehas' wife, was with child, *near* to be delivered: and when she heard the tidings that the ark of God was taken, and that her father-in-law

and her husband were dead, she bowed herself and travailed; for her pains came upon her.

20 And about the time of her death the women that stood by her said unto her, Fear not; for thou hast born a son. But she answered not, neither did she regard *it*.

21 And she named the child Ichabod, saying, The glory is departed from Israel: because the ark of God was taken, and because of her father-in-law and her husband.

22 And she said, The glory is departed from Israel: for the ark of God is taken.

CHAPTER 5
God Judges the Philistines

1 And the Philistines took the ark of God, and brought it from Ebenezer unto Ashdod.

2 When the Philistines took the ark of God, they brought it into the house of Dagon, and set it by Dagon.

3 And when they of Ashdod arose early on the morrow, behold, Dagon *was* fallen upon his face to the earth before the ark of the LORD. And they took Dagon, and set him in his place again.

4 And when they arose early on the morrow morning, behold, Dagon *was* fallen upon his face to the ground before the ark of the LORD; and the head of Dagon and both the palms of his hands *were* cut off upon the threshold; only *the stump of* Dagon was left to him.

5 Therefore neither the priests of Dagon, nor any that come into Dagon's house, tread on the threshold of Dagon in Ashdod unto this day.

6 But the hand of the LORD was heavy upon them of Ashdod, and he destroyed them, and smote them with emerods, *even* Ashdod and the coasts thereof.

7 And when the men of Ashdod saw that *it was* so, they said, The ark of the God of Israel shall not abide with us: for his hand is sore upon us, and upon Dagon our god.

8 They sent therefore and gathered all the lords of the Philistines unto them, and said, What shall we do with the ark of the God of Israel? And they answered, Let the ark of the God of Israel be carried about unto Gath. And they carried the ark of the God of Israel about *thither*.

9 And it was *so*, that, after they had carried it about, the hand of the LORD was against the city with a very great destruction: and he smote the men of the city, both small and great, and they had emerods in their secret parts.

10 Therefore they sent the ark of God to Ekron. And it came to pass, as the ark of God came to Ekron, that the Ekronites cried out, saying, They have brought about the ark of the God of Israel to us, to slay us and our people.

11 So they sent and gathered together all the lords of the Philistines, and said, Send away the ark of the God of Israel, and let it go again to his own place, that it slay us not, and our people: for there was a deadly destruction throughout all the city; the hand of God was very heavy there.

12 And the men that died not were smitten with the emerods: and the cry of the city went up to heaven.

CHAPTER 6
The Philistines Return the Ark to Israel

1 And the ark of the LORD was in the country of the Philistines seven months.

2 And the Philistines called for the priests and the diviners, saying, What shall we do to the ark of the LORD? tell us wherewith we shall send it to his place.

3 And they said, If ye send away the ark of the God of Israel, send it not empty; but in any wise return him a trespass offering: then ye shall be healed, and it shall be known to you why his hand is not removed from you.

4 Then said they, What *shall be* the trespass offering which we shall return to him? They answered, Five golden emerods, and five golden mice, *according to* the number of the lords of the Philistines: for one plague *was* on you all, and on your lords.

5 Wherefore ye shall make images of your emerods, and images of your mice that mar the land; and ye shall give glory unto the God of Israel: peradventure he will lighten his hand from off you, and from off your gods, and from off your land.

6 Wherefore then do ye harden your hearts, as the Egyptians and Pharaoh hardened their hearts? when he had wrought wonderfully among them, did they not let the people go, and they departed?

7 Now therefore make a new cart, and take two milch kine, on which there hath come no yoke, and tie the kine to the cart, and bring their calves home from them:

8 And take the ark of the LORD, and lay it upon the cart; and put the jewels of gold, which ye return him *for* a trespass offering, in a coffer by the side thereof; and send it away, that it may go.

9 And see, if it goeth up by the way of his own coast to Beth-shemesh, *then* he hath done us this great evil: but if not, then we shall know that *it is* not his hand *that* smote us: it *was* a chance *that* happened to us.

10 And the men did so; and took two milch kine, and tied them to the cart, and shut up their calves at home:

11 And they laid the ark of the LORD upon the cart, and the coffer with the mice of gold and the images of their emerods.

12 And the kine took the straight way to the way of Beth-shemesh, *and* went along the highway, lowing as they went, and turned not aside *to* the right hand or *to* the left; and the lords of the Philistines went after them unto the border of Beth-she-mesh.

13 And *they of* Beth-shemesh *were* reaping their wheat harvest in the valley: and they lifted up their eyes, and saw the ark, and rejoiced to see *it.*

14 And the cart came into the field of Joshua, a Beth-shemite, and stood there, where *there was* a great stone: and they clave the wood of the cart, and offered the kine a burnt offering unto the LORD.

15 And the Levites took down the ark of the LORD, and the coffer that *was* with it, wherein the jewels of gold *were,* and put *them* on the great stone: and the men of Beth-shemesh offered burnt offerings and sacrificed sacrifices the same day unto the LORD.

16 And when the five lords of the Philistines had seen *it,* they returned to Ekron the same day.

17 And these *are* the golden emerods which the Philistines returned *for* a trespass offering unto the LORD; for Ashdod one, for Gaza one, for Askelon one, for Gath one, for Ekron one;

18 And the golden mice, *according to* the number of all the cities of the Philistines *belonging* to the five lords, *both* of fenced cities, and of country villages, even unto the great *stone of* Abel, whereon they set down the ark of the LORD: *which stone remaineth* unto this day in the field of Joshua, the Beth-shemite.

19 And he smote the men of Beth-shemesh, because they had looked into the ark of the LORD, even he smote of the people fifty thousand and threescore and ten men: and the people lamented, because the LORD had smitten *many* of the people with a great slaughter.

20 And the men of Beth-shemesh said, Who is able to stand before this holy LORD

Cross-references (center column):

11 1Sam. 5:6, 9

2 Gen. 41:8; Ex. 7:11; Dan. 2:2; 5:7; Matt. 2:4

3 Ex. 23:15; Lev. 5:15, 16; Deut. 16:16; 1Sam. 6:9

4 Josh. 13:3; Judg. 3:3; 1Sam. 6:17, 18

5 Josh. 7:19; 1Sam. 5: 3, 4, 7, 6, 11; Ps. 39:10; Isa. 42:12; Mal. 2:2; John 9:24

6 Ex. 7:13; 8:15; 12:31; 14:17

7 Num. 19:2; 2Sam. 6:3

8 1Sam. 6:4, 5

9 Josh. 15:10; 1Sam. 6:3

16 Josh. 13:3

17 1Sam. 6:4

19 Ex. 19:21; Num. 4:5, 15, 20; 2Sam. 6:7

20 2Sam. 6:9; Mal. 3:2

God? and to whom shall he go up from us?
21 And they sent messengers to the inhabitants of Kirjath-jearim, saying, The Philistines have brought again the ark of the LORD; come ye down, *and* fetch it up to you.

CHAPTER 7

1 And the men of Kirjath-jearim came, and fetched up the ark of the LORD, and brought it into the house of Abinadab in the hill, and sanctified Eleazar his son to keep the ark of the LORD.
2 And it came to pass, while the ark abode in Kirjath-jearim, that the time was long; for it was twenty years: and all the house of Israel lamented after the LORD.

Samuel Leads Israel

3 And Samuel spake unto all the house of Israel, saying, If ye do return unto the LORD with all your hearts, *then* put away the strange gods and Ashtaroth from among you, and prepare your hearts unto the LORD, and serve him only: and he will deliver you out of the hand of the Philistines.
4 Then the children of Israel did put away Baalim and Ashtaroth, and served the LORD only.
5 And Samuel said, Gather all Israel to Mizpeh, and I will pray for you unto the LORD.
6 And they gathered together to Mizpeh, and drew water, and poured *it* out before the LORD, and fasted on that day, and said there, We have sinned against the LORD. And Samuel judged the children of Israel in Mizpeh.
7 And when the Philistines heard that the children of Israel were gathered together to Mizpeh, the lords of the Philistines went up against Israel. And when the children of Israel heard *it*, they were afraid of the Philistines.
8 And the children of Israel said to Samuel, Cease not to cry unto the LORD our God for us, that he will save us out of the hand of the Philistines.
9 And Samuel took a sucking lamb, and offered *it for* a burnt offering wholly unto

the LORD: and Samuel cried unto the LORD for Israel; and the LORD heard him.
10 And as Samuel was offering up the burnt offering, the Philistines drew near to battle against Israel: but the LORD thundered with a great thunder on that day upon the Philistines, and discomfited them; and they were smitten before Israel.
11 And the men of Israel went out of Mizpeh, and pursued the Philistines, and smote them, until *they came* under Beth-car.
12 Then Samuel took a stone, and set *it* between Mizpeh and Shen, and called the name of it Ebenezer, saying, Hitherto hath the LORD helped us.
13 So the Philistines were subdued, and they came no more into the coast of Israel: and the hand of the LORD was against the Philistines all the days of Samuel.
14 And the cities which the Philistines had taken from Israel were restored to Israel, from Ekron even unto Gath; and the coasts thereof did Israel deliver out of the hands of the Philistines. And there was peace between Israel and the Amorites.
15 And Samuel judged Israel all the days of his life.
16 And he went from year to year in circuit to Beth-el, and Gilgal, and Mizpeh, and judged Israel in all those places.
17 And his return *was* to Ramah; for there *was* his house; and there he judged Israel; and there he built an altar unto the LORD.

CHAPTER 8

Israel Asks for a King

1 And it came to pass, when Samuel was old, that he made his sons judges over Israel.
2 Now the name of his firstborn was Joel; and the name of his second, Abiah: *they were* judges in Beer-sheba.
3 And his sons walked not in his ways, but turned aside after lucre, and took bribes, and perverted judgment.
4 Then all the elders of Israel gathered themselves together, and came to Samuel unto Ramah,

Cross references (center column):
21 Josh. 18:14; Judg. 18:12; Chr. 13:5, 6
1 1Sam. 6:21; 2Sam. 6:4; Ps. 132:6
3 Gen. 35:2; Deut. 6:13; 10:20; 13:4; 30:2-10; Josh. 24:14, 23; Judg. 2:13; 1Kgs. 8:48; 2Chr. 30:19; Job 11:13, 14; Isa. 55:7; Hos. 6:1; Joel 2:12; Matt. 4:10; Luke 4:8
4 Judg. 2:11
5 Judg. 20:1; 2Kgs. 25:23
6 Judg. 10:10; 2Sam. 14:14; 1Kgs. 8:47; Neh. 9:1, 2; Ps. 106:6; Dan. 9:3-5; Joel 2:12
8 Isa. 37:4
9 Ps. 99:6; Jer. 15:1
10 Josh. 10:10; Judg. 4:15; 5:20; 1Sam. 2:10; 2Sam. 22:14, 15
12 Gen. 28:18; 31:45; 35:14; Josh. 4:9; 24:26
13 Judg. 13:1; 1Sam. 13:5
15 Judg. 2:16; 1Sam. 7:6; 12:11
17 Judg. 21:4; 1Sam. 8:4
1 Deut. 16:18; Judg. 10:4; 12:14

7:15 Samuel judged Israel all the days of his life. Samuel, the last and greatest of the judges and the first of the prophets (Acts 3:24) was the most important leader since Moses (see Jer. 15:1), who also was a great intercessor for his people (see Ex. 32:30–35). Although a descendant of Ephraim and not of the priestly tribe of Levi, Samuel was divinely chosen to serve as judge and priest. From his boyhood he was recognized by the people as the coming spiritual leader in their midst. He succeeded Eli, the high priest in the Aaronic line, upon his death, following the defeat of Israel and the capture of the Ark of the Covenant by the Philistines. Samuel has the unique distinction of anointing the first two kings of Israel (1 Sam. 10:1; 16:13).

5 And said unto him, Behold, thou art old, and thy sons walk not in thy ways: now make us a king to judge us like all the nations.

6 But the thing displeased Samuel, when they said, Give us a king to judge us. And Samuel prayed unto the LORD.

7 And the LORD said unto Samuel, Hearken unto the voice of the people in all that they say unto thee: for they have not rejected thee, but they have rejected me, that I should not reign over them.

8 According to all the works which they have done since the day that I brought them up out of Egypt even unto this day, wherewith they have forsaken me, and served other gods, so do they also unto thee.

9 Now therefore hearken unto their voice: howbeit yet protest solemnly unto them, and shew them the manner of the king that shall reign over them.

10 And Samuel told all the words of the LORD unto the people that asked of him a king.

11 And he said, This will be the manner of the king that shall reign over you: He will take your sons, and appoint them for himself, for his chariots, and to be his horsemen; and some shall run before his chariots.

12 And he will appoint him captains over thousands, and captains over fifties; and will set them to ear his ground, and to reap his harvest, and to make his instruments of war, and instruments of his chariots.

13 And he will take your daughters to be confectionaries, and to be cooks, and to be bakers.

14 And he will take your fields, and your vineyards, and your oliveyards, even the best of them, and give them to his servants.

15 And he will take the tenth of your seed, and of your vineyards, and give to his officers, and to his servants.

16 And he will take your menservants, and your maidservants, and your goodliest young men, and your asses, and put them to his work.

17 He will take the tenth of your sheep: and ye shall be his servants.

18 And ye shall cry out in that day because of your king which ye shall have chosen you; and the LORD will not hear you in that day.

19 Nevertheless the people refused to obey the voice of Samuel; and they said, Nay; but we will have a king over us;

20 That we also may be like all the nations; and that our king may judge us, and go out before us, and fight our battles.

21 And Samuel heard all the words of the people, and he rehearsed them in the ears of the LORD.

22 And the LORD said to Samuel, Hearken unto their voice, and make them a king. And Samuel said unto the men of Israel, Go ye every man unto his city.

CHAPTER 9
Samuel Anoints Saul King

1 Now there was a man of Benjamin, whose name was Kish, the son of Abiel, the son of Zeror, the son of Bechorath, the son of Aphiah, a Benjamite, a mighty man of power.

2 And he had a son, whose name was Saul, a choice young man, and a goodly: and there was not among the children of Israel a goodlier person than he: from his shoulders and upward he was higher than any of the people.

3 And the asses of Kish Saul's father were lost. And Kish said to Saul his son, Take now one of the servants with thee, and arise, go seek the asses.

4 And he passed through mount Ephraim, and passed through the land of Shalisha, but they found them not: then they passed through the land of Shalim, and there they

8:6 Give us a king. Desiring both to avoid having Samuel's irresponsible sons in leadership and to be more like surrounding nations, the elders of Israel launched a monarchist movement. Samuel prophesies to the people what they should expect from a monarchy form of government. Nevertheless, the people were determined to have a king. Although they had rejected the theocracy with Samuel as leader, it was still earlier prophesied by Moses that a king would indeed reign (Deut. 17:14–20; 28:36). Hannah, evidently a prophetess, also speaks of a king and an "anointed one" or Messiah (1 Sam. 2:10) It was, however, the providential plan of God to establish the Davidic dynasty, which would culminate in the coming of Jesus, "the king of the Jews," who was crucified (Matt. 27:37). At His return, Jesus will assume His rightful role as "the root of David," and the Israelites and all the peoples of the world will come to Jerusalem to worship the King (Zech. 14:9, 16–17 [cf. Jer. 30:9; Ezek. 37:24–25]).

9:2 Saul, a choice young man. At first reluctant to serve, Saul was anointed king by Samuel (1 Sam. 10:1), as God had instructed him (1 Sam. 8:22).

The Office of the Prophet

By Edward Hindson

The Hebrew prophets were spokesmen for God. They wrote both the books of history and the books of prophecy in the Old Testament. The prophetic books of history are followed in the Hebrew Bible by the prophetic books of prediction. The two categories of prophetic books form a unit in the middle of the Hebrew Scriptures, under the common term "prophets" (Hebr. *nebiyim*).

The term *nabiy* itself designates the prophet as a spokesman for God. While the prophet preached to his own generation, he also predicted events in the future. The twofold aspect of the prophet's ministry included declaring God's message and foretelling God's actions. Thus, the prophet was also called a "seer" (Hebr. *roeh*), because he could see future events before they happened.

The prophet is depicted in the Bible as one who was admitted into the divine council chambers where God "reveals" His "secrets" (Amos 3:7) by "uncovering the ear" of the prophet (1 Sam. 9:15). By the process of divine inspiration, God revealed what was hidden (2 Sam. 7:27), so that the prophet perceives what the Lord had said (Jer. 23:18). This communion with God was essential for God's truth to be revealed by the process of prophetic inspiration. The word of the Lord was communicated to the prophet and mediated to the people by the Holy Spirit—with powerful conviction and precise accuracy.

> *The prophet's ministry included declaring God's message and foretelling God's actions.*

The Old Testament prophets foresaw the coming of a divine Messiah with God-like characteristics. The purpose of messianic prophecy was to clearly identify the Messiah after He had fulfilled the specific events predicted about Him by God's prophets. Such predictions were so deliberate and specific that there could be no mistaking their intended designation. The best guideline for determining which prophecies refer to the predicted Messiah is the New Testament, which clearly applies these predictions to Jesus of Nazareth.

The New Testament recognizes the value of predictive prophecy and its fulfillment as evidence to prove the supernatural credibility of Christianity. The prophets clearly predicted the coming of a divine being into the human race, who would be born of a virgin (Isa. 7:14) at Bethlehem (Mic. 5:2) from the line of Abraham (Gen. 15:1–4) and David (2 Sam. 7:16). That person is none other than Jesus Christ. He alone clearly fulfills over one hundred specific biblical prophecies about the coming Messiah. Jesus Himself said, "All things must be fulfilled, which were written in the law of Moses, and in the prophets, and in the psalms, concerning me" (Luke 24:44). Jesus willingly submitted Himself to the course that these prophecies had prescribed for Him and considered the details of His life and death as something that must take place, because it was written in the Word of God. At the same time, Jesus saw Himself as the culminating point to which the whole of prophecy was directed.

The New Testament also provides the best guideline for determining whether or not a certain event is fulfilled. It tells us where the prophets spoke of Christ. The New Testament clearly indicates that the Old Testament messianic references point to one person—Jesus of Nazareth. "To him give all the prophets witness, that through his name whosoever believeth in him shall receive remission of sins" (Acts 10:43).

were not: and he passed through the land of the Benjamites, but they found *them* not.

5 *And* when they were come to the land of Zuph, Saul said to his servant that *was* with him, Come, and let us return; lest my father leave *caring* for the asses, and take thought for us.

6 And he said unto him, Behold now, *there is* in this city a man of God, and *he is* an honourable man; all that he saith cometh surely to pass: now let us go thither; peradventure he can shew us our way that we should go.

7 Then said Saul to his servant, But, behold, *if* we go, what shall we bring the man? for the bread is spent in our vessels, and *there is* not a present to bring to the man of God: what have we?

8 And the servant answered Saul again, and said, Behold, I have here at hand the fourth part of a shekel of silver: *that* will I give to the man of God, to tell us our way.

9 (Beforetime in Israel, when a man went to inquire of God, thus he spake, Come, and let us go to the seer: for *he that is* now *called* a Prophet was beforetime called a Seer.)

10 Then said Saul to his servant, Well said; come, let us go. So they went unto the city where the man of God *was*.

11 *And* as they went up the hill to the city, they found young maidens going out to draw water, and said unto them, Is the seer here?

12 And they answered them, and said, He is; behold, *he is* before you: make haste now, for he came today to the city; for *there is* a sacrifice of the people today in the high place:

13 As soon as ye be come into the city, ye shall straightway find him, before he go up to the high place to eat: for the people will not eat until he come, because he doth bless the sacrifice; *and* afterwards they eat that be bidden. Now therefore get you up; for about this time ye shall find him.

14 And they went up into the city: *and* when they were come into the city, behold, Samuel came out against them, for to go up to the high place.

15 Now the LORD had told Samuel in his ear a day before Saul came, saying,

16 To morrow about this time I will send thee a man out of the land of Benjamin, and thou shalt anoint him *to be* captain over my people Israel, that he may save my people out of the hand of the Philistines: for I have looked upon my people, because their cry is come unto me.

17 And when Samuel saw Saul, the LORD said unto him, Behold the man whom I spake to thee of! this same shall reign over my people.

18 Then Saul drew near to Samuel in the gate, and said, Tell me, I pray thee, where the seer's house *is*.

19 And Samuel answered Saul, and said, I *am* the seer: go up before me unto the high place; for ye shall eat with me today, and to morrow I will let thee go, and will tell thee all that *is* in thine heart.

20 And as for thine asses that were lost three days ago, set not thy mind on them; for they are found. And on whom *is* all the desire of Israel? *Is it* not on thee, and on all thy father's house?

21 And Saul answered and said, *Am* not I a Benjamite, of the smallest of the tribes of Israel? and my family the least of all the families of the tribe of Benjamin? wherefore then speakest thou so to me?

22 And Samuel took Saul and his servant, and brought them into the parlour, and made them sit in the chiefest place among them that were bidden, which *were* about thirty persons.

23 And Samuel said unto the cook, Bring the portion which I gave thee, of which I said unto thee, Set it by thee.

24 And the cook took up the shoulder, and *that* which *was* upon it, and set *it* before Saul. And *Samuel* said, Behold that which is left! set *it* before thee, *and* eat: for unto this time hath it been kept for thee since I said, I have invited the people. So Saul did eat with Samuel that day.

25 And when they were come down from the high place into the city, *Samuel* communed with Saul upon the top of the house.

26 And they arose early: and it came to pass about the spring of the day, that Samuel called Saul to the top of the house, saying, Up, that I may send thee away. And Saul arose, and they went out both of them, he and Samuel, abroad.

27 *And* as they were going down to the end of the city, Samuel said to Saul, Bid the servant pass on before us, (and he passed on,) but stand thou still a while, that I may shew thee the word of God.

CHAPTER 10

1 Then Samuel took a vial of oil, and poured *it* upon his head, and kissed him, and said, *Is it* not because the LORD hath anointed thee *to be* captain over his inheritance?

Cross references

6 Deut. 33:1; 1Sam. 3:19; 1Kgs. 13:1

7 Judg. 6:18; 13:17; 1Kgs. 14:3; 2Kgs. 4:42; 8:8

9 Gen. 25:22; 2Sam. 24:11; 2Kgs. 17:13; 1Chr. 26:28; 29:29; 2Chr. 16:7, 10; Isa. 30:10; Amos 7:12

11 Gen. 24:11

12 Gen. 31:54; 1Sam. 16:2; 1Kgs. 3:2

15 1Sam. 15:1; 20:2; Acts 13:21

16 Ex. 2:25; 3:7, 9; 1Sam. 10:1

17 1Sam. 16:12; Hos. 13:11

20 1Sam. 8:5, 19; 9:3; 12:13

21 Judg. 6:15; 20:46-48; 1Sam. 15:17; Ps. 68:27

24 Lev. 7:32, 33; Ezek. 24:4

25 Deut. 22:8; 2Sam. 11:2; Acts 10:9

1 Deut. 32:9; 1Sam. 9:16; 16:13; 2Kgs. 9:3, 6; Ps. 2:12; 78:71; Acts 13:21

2 When thou art departed from me today, then thou shalt find two men by Rachel's sepulchre in the border of Benjamin at Zelzah; and they will say unto thee, The asses which thou wentest to seek are found: and, lo, thy father hath left the care of the asses, and sorroweth for you, saying, What shall I do for my son?

3 Then shalt thou go on forward from thence, and thou shalt come to the plain of Tabor, and there shall meet thee three men going up to God to Beth-el, one carrying three kids, and another carrying three loaves of bread, and another carrying a bottle of wine:

4 And they will salute thee, and give thee two *loaves* of bread; which thou shalt receive of their hands.

5 After that thou shalt come to the hill of God, where *is* the garrison of the Philistines: and it shall come to pass, when thou art come thither to the city, that thou shalt meet a company of prophets coming down from the high place with a psaltery, and a tabret, and a pipe, and a harp, before them; and they shall prophesy:

6 And the Spirit of the LORD will come upon thee, and thou shalt prophesy with them, and shalt be turned into another man.

7 And let it be, when these signs are come unto thee, *that* thou do as occasion serve thee; for God *is* with thee.

8 And thou shalt go down before me to Gilgal; and, behold, I will come down unto thee, to offer burnt offerings, *and* to sacrifice sacrifices of peace offerings: seven days shalt thou tarry, till I come to thee, and shew thee what thou shalt do.

Saul Prophesies

9 And it was *so*, that when he had turned his back to go from Samuel, God gave him another heart: and all those signs came to pass that day.

10 And when they came thither to the hill, behold, a company of prophets met him; and the Spirit of God came upon him, and he prophesied among them.

11 And it came to pass, when all that knew him beforetime saw that, behold, he prophesied among the prophets, then the people said one to another, What *is* this *that* is come unto the son of Kish? *Is* Saul also among the prophets?

12 And one of the same place answered and said, But who *is* their father? Therefore it became a proverb, *Is* Saul also among the prophets?

13 And when he had made an end of prophesying, he came to the high place.

14 And Saul's uncle said unto him and to his servant, Whither went ye? And he said, To seek the asses: and when we saw that *they were* no where, we came to Samuel.

15 And Saul's uncle said, Tell me, I pray thee, what Samuel said unto you.

16 And Saul said unto his uncle, He told us plainly that the asses were found. But of the matter of the kingdom, whereof Samuel spake, he told him not.

Saul Becomes King

17 And Samuel called the people together unto the LORD to Mizpeh;

18 And said unto the children of Israel, Thus saith the LORD God of Israel, I brought up Israel out of Egypt, and delivered you out of the hand of the Egyptians, and out of the hand of all kingdoms, *and* of them that oppressed you:

19 And ye have this day rejected your God, who himself saved you out of all your adversities and your tribulations; and ye have said unto him, *Nay*, but set a king over us. Now therefore present yourselves before the LORD by your tribes, and by your thousands.

20 And when Samuel had caused all the tribes of Israel to come near, the tribe of Benjamin was taken.

Cross references:

2 Gen. 35:19, 20; Josh. 18:28

3 Gen. 28:22; 35:1, 3, 7

4 Judg. 18:15

5 Ex. 15:20, 21; 1Sam. 9:12; 10:10; 13:3; 2Kgs. 3:15; 1Cor. 14:1

6 Num. 11:25; 1Sam. 10:10; 16:13; 19:23, 24

7 Ex. 4:8; Judg. 6:12; 9:33; Luke 2:12

8 1Sam. 11:14, 15; 13:4, 8

10 1Sam. 10:5, 6; 19:20

11 1Sam. 19:24; Matt. 13:54, 55; John 7:15; Acts 4:13

12 Isa. 54:13; John 6:45; 7:16

17 Judg. 11:11; 20:1; 1Sam. 7:5, 6; 11:15

18 Judg. 6:8, 9

19 1Sam. 8:7, 19; 12:12

20 Josh. 7:14, 16, 17; Acts 1:24, 26

10:11 Is Saul also among the prophets? Following his official anointing, as Saul met a company of prophets, the Spirit of the Lord came upon him and he prophesied. No record of his words or behavior is given, but evidently God gave him a great opportunity to serve. The aging prophet proclaimed him as king, launching Saul's forty-year reign. As for the proverb about Saul being a prophet, it was repeated on a later occasion (1 Sam. 19:23–24), when he was restrained for a time from attacking David, whom he then considered a possible rival for the throne. That Saul was "a man after the flesh" (Rom. 8:5—9:13) there can be no doubt. He was unable to overcome his own jealousy, ill temper, and depression. Yet the Spirit of God had been with him and there were victories. God's Spirit would come and go upon Israel's leaders to empower them to fulfill their kingly office. God would often withhold His Spirit when a leader was disobedient or rebellious. The story of Saul is the story of a king who might have been truly great. It is the account of a monarch who squandered his opportunities. His tragic example is a warning to all spiritual leaders.

21 When he had caused the tribe of Benjamin to come near by their families, the family of Matri was taken, and Saul the son of Kish was taken: and when they sought him, he could not be found.

22 Therefore they inquired of the LORD further, if the man should yet come thither. And the LORD answered, Behold, he hath hid himself among the stuff.

23 And they ran and fetched him thence: and when he stood among the people, he was higher than any of the people from his shoulders and upward.

24 And Samuel said to all the people, See ye him whom the LORD hath chosen, that *there is* none like him among all the people? And all the people shouted, and said, God save the king.

25 Then Samuel told the people the manner of the kingdom, and wrote *it* in a book, and laid *it* up before the LORD. And Samuel sent all the people away, every man to his house.

26 And Saul also went home to Gibeah; and there went with him a band of men, whose hearts God had touched.

27 But the children of Belial said, How shall this man save us? And they despised him, and brought him no presents. But he held his peace.

CHAPTER 11
Saul Rescues Jabesh-gilead

1 Then Nahash the Ammonite came up, and encamped against Jabesh-gilead: and all the men of Jabesh said unto Nahash, Make a covenant with us, and we will serve thee.

2 And Nahash the Ammonite answered them, On this *condition* will I make *a covenant* with you, that I may thrust out all your right eyes, and lay it *for* a reproach upon all Israel.

3 And the elders of Jabesh said unto him, Give us seven days' respite, that we may send messengers unto all the coasts of Israel: and then, if *there be* no man to save us, we will come out to thee.

4 Then came the messengers to Gibeah of Saul, and told the tidings in the ears of the people: and all the people lifted up their voices, and wept.

5 And, behold, Saul came after the herd out of the field; and Saul said, What *aileth* the people that they weep? And they

told him the tidings of the men of Jabesh.

6 And the Spirit of God came upon Saul when he heard those tidings, and his anger was kindled greatly.

7 And he took a yoke of oxen, and hewed them in pieces, and sent *them* throughout all the coasts of Israel by the hands of messengers, saying, Whosoever cometh not forth after Saul and after Samuel, so shall it be done unto his oxen. And the fear of the LORD fell on the people, and they came out with one consent.

8 And when he numbered them in Bezek, the children of Israel were three hundred thousand, and the men of Judah thirty thousand.

9 And they said unto the messengers that came, Thus shall ye say unto the men of Jabesh-gilead, To morrow, by *that time* the sun be hot, ye shall have help. And the messengers came and shewed *it* to the men of Jabesh; and they were glad.

10 Therefore the men of Jabesh said, To morrow we will come out unto you, and ye shall do with us all that seemeth good unto you.

11 And it was *so* on the morrow, that Saul put the people in three companies; and they came into the midst of the host in the morning watch, and slew the Ammonites until the heat of the day: and it came to pass, that they which remained were scattered, so that two of them were not left together.

12 And the people said unto Samuel, Who *is* he that said, Shall Saul reign over us? bring the men, that we may put them to death.

13 And Saul said, There shall not a man be put to death this day: for today the LORD hath wrought salvation in Israel.

14 Then said Samuel to the people, Come, and let us go to Gilgal, and renew the kingdom there.

15 And all the people went to Gilgal; and there they made Saul king before the LORD in Gilgal; and there they sacrificed sacrifices of peace offerings before the LORD; and there Saul and all the men of Israel rejoiced greatly.

CHAPTER 12
Samuel Addresses Israel

1 And Samuel said unto all Israel, Behold, I have hearkened unto your voice in all that

Cross-references

22 1Sam. 23:2, 4, 10, 11
23 1Sam. 9:2
24 2Sam. 21:6; 1Kgs. 1:25, 39; 2Kgs. 11:12
25 Deut. 17:14; 1Sam. 8:11
26 Judg. 20:14; 1Sam. 11:4
27 Deut. 13:13; 1Sam. 11:12; 2Sam. 8:2; 1Kgs. 4:21; 10:25; 2Chr. 17:5; Ps. 72:10; Matt. 2:11
1 Gen. 26:28; Ex. 23:32; Judg. 21:8; 1Sam. 12:12; 1Kgs. 20:34; Job 41:4; Ezek. 17:13
2 Gen. 34:14; 1Sam. 17:26
4 Judg. 2:4; 21:2; 1Sam. 10:26; 15:34; 2Sam. 21:6
6 Judg. 3:10; 6:34; 11:29; 13:25; 14:6; 1Sam. 10:10; 16:13
7 Judg. 19:29; 20:1; 21:5, 8, 10
8 Judg. 1:5; 2Sam. 24:9
10 1Sam. 11:3
11 Judg. 7:16; 1Sam. 31:11
12 1Sam. 10:27; Luke 19:27
13 Ex. 14:13, 30; 1Sam. 19:5; 2Sam. 19:22
14 1Sam. 10:8
15 1Sam. 10:8, 17

12:1–25 Samuel said. Samuel brings a prophetic address to a large assembly of Israelites and their leaders at Gilgal. He reminds the people of his own selfless dedication. Samuel then reviews several cases of divine deliverance under judges, raised up by God, "when the LORD your God was your king" (v. 12), inferring that responsibility for wanting a

ye said unto me, and have made a king over you.

2 And now, behold, the king walketh before you: and I am old and greyheaded; and, behold, my sons *are* with you: and I have walked before you from my childhood unto this day.

3 Behold, here I *am*: witness against me before the Lord, and before his anointed: whose ox have I taken? or whose ass have I taken? or whom have I defrauded? whom have I oppressed? or of whose hand have I received *any* bribe to blind mine eyes therewith? and I will restore it you.

4 And they said, Thou hast not defrauded us, nor oppressed us, neither hast thou taken ought of any man's hand.

5 And he said unto them, The Lord *is* witness against you, and his anointed *is* witness this day, that ye have not found ought in my hand. And they answered, *He is* witness.

6 And Samuel said unto the people, *It is* the Lord that advanced Moses and Aaron, and that brought your fathers up out of the land of Egypt.

7 Now therefore stand still, that I may reason with you before the Lord of all the righteous acts of the Lord, which he did to you and to your fathers.

8 When Jacob was come into Egypt, and your fathers cried unto the Lord, then the Lord sent Moses and Aaron, which brought forth your fathers out of Egypt, and made them dwell in this place.

9 And when they forgat the Lord their God, he sold them into the hand of Sisera, captain of the host of Hazor, and into the hand of the Philistines, and into the hand of the king of Moab, and they fought against them.

10 And they cried unto the Lord, and said, We have sinned, because we have forsaken the Lord, and have served Baalim and Ashtaroth: but now deliver us out of the hand of our enemies, and we will serve thee.

11 And the Lord sent Jerubbaal, and Bedan, and Jephthah, and Samuel, and delivered you out of the hand of your enemies on every side, and ye dwelled safe.

12 And when ye saw that Nahash the king of the children of Ammon came against you, ye said unto me, Nay; but a king shall

reign over us: when the Lord your God *was* your king.

13 Now therefore behold the king whom ye have chosen, *and* whom ye have desired! and, behold, the Lord hath set a king over you.

14 If ye will fear the Lord, and serve him, and obey his voice, and not rebel against the commandment of the Lord, then shall both ye and also the king that reigneth over you continue following the Lord your God:

15 But if ye will not obey the voice of the Lord, but rebel against the commandment of the Lord, then shall the hand of the Lord be against you, as *it was* against your fathers.

16 Now therefore stand and see this great thing, which the Lord will do before your eyes.

17 *Is it* not wheat harvest today? I will call unto the Lord, and he shall send thunder and rain; that ye may perceive and see that your wickedness *is* great, which ye have done in the sight of the Lord, in asking you a king.

18 So Samuel called unto the Lord; and the Lord sent thunder and rain that day: and all the people greatly feared the Lord and Samuel.

19 And all the people said unto Samuel, Pray for thy servants unto the Lord thy God, that we die not: for we have added unto all our sins *this* evil, to ask us a king.

20 And Samuel said unto the people, Fear not: ye have done all this wickedness: yet turn not aside from following the Lord, but serve the Lord with all your heart;

21 And turn ye not aside: for *then should ye go* after vain *things*, which cannot profit nor deliver; for they *are* vain.

22 For the Lord will not forsake his people for his great name's sake: because it hath pleased the Lord to make you his people.

23 Moreover as for me, God forbid that I should sin against the Lord in ceasing to pray for you: but I will teach you the good and the right way:

24 Only fear the Lord, and serve him in truth with all your heart: for consider how great *things* he hath done for you.

25 But if ye shall still do wickedly, ye shall be consumed, both ye and your king.

Cross references (center column):

2 Num. 27:17; 1Sam. 8:1, 5, 20

3 Num. 16:15; Deut. 16:19

5 Ex. 22:4; John 18:38; Acts 23:9; 24:16, 20

6 Mic. 6:4

7 Judg. 5:11; Isa. 1:18; 5:3, 4; Mic. 6:2, 3

8 Gen. 46:5, 6; Ex. 2:23; 3:10; 4:16

9 Judg. 3:7, 12; 4:2; 10:7; 13:1

10 Judg. 2:13; Judg. 10:10, 15, 16

11 Judg. 6:14, 32; 11:1; 1Sam. 7:13

12 Judg. 8:23; 1Sam. 8:5, 7, 19; 10:19; 11:1

13 1Sam. 8:5; 9:20; 10:24; Hos. 13:11

14 Josh. 24:14; Ps. 81:13, 14

15 Lev. 26:14, 15; Deut. 28:15

16 Ex. 14:13, 31

17 Josh. 10:12; Prov. 26:1

18 Ex. 14:31; Ezra 10:9

21 1Cor. 8:4

22 Deut. 7:7, 8; 14:2

23 Ps. 34:11; Prov. 4:11; Rom. 1:9; Col. 1:9; 2Tim. 1:3

24 Eccl. 12:13; Isa. 5:12

25 Deut. 28:36; Josh. 24:20

---

king rested with the people. Even though King Saul was now fully installed as the sovereign, God sent thunder and rain that day, which struck fear in the hearts of the people. They realized that they had sinned by asking for a king, basically from wrong motives.

CHAPTER 13
Saul's First Sin at Gilgal

1 Saul reigned one year; and when he had reigned two years over Israel,

2 Saul chose him three thousand *men* of Israel; *whereof* two thousand were with Saul in Michmash and in mount Beth-el, and a thousand were with Jonathan in Gibeah of Benjamin: and the rest of the people he sent every man to his tent.

3 And Jonathan smote the garrison of the Philistines that *was* in Geba, and the Philistines heard *of it.* And Saul blew the trumpet throughout all the land, saying, Let the Hebrews hear.

4 And all Israel heard say *that* Saul had smitten a garrison of the Philistines, and *that* Israel also was had in abomination with the Philistines. And the people were called together after Saul to Gilgal.

5 And the Philistines gathered themselves together to fight with Israel, thirty thousand chariots, and six thousand horsemen, and people as the sand which *is* on the sea shore in multitude: and they came up, and pitched in Michmash, eastward from Beth-aven.

6 When the men of Israel saw that they were in a strait, (for the people were distressed,) then the people did hide themselves in caves, and in thickets, and in rocks, and in high places, and in pits.

7 And *some of* the Hebrews went over Jordan to the land of Gad and Gilead. As for Saul, he *was* yet in Gilgal, and all the people followed him trembling.

8 And he tarried seven days, according to the set time that Samuel *had appointed*: but Samuel came not to Gilgal; and the people were scattered from him.

9 And Saul said, Bring hither a burnt offering to me, and peace offerings. And he offered the burnt offering.

10 And it came to pass, that as soon as he had made an end of offering the burnt offering, behold, Samuel came; and Saul went out to meet him, that he might salute him.

11 And Samuel said, What hast thou done? And Saul said, Because I saw that the people were scattered from me, and *that* thou camest not within the days appointed, and *that* the Philistines gathered themselves together at Michmash;

12 Therefore said I, The Philistines will come down now upon me to Gilgal, and I have not made supplication unto the LORD: I forced myself therefore, and offered a burnt offering.

13 And Samuel said to Saul, Thou hast done foolishly: thou hast not kept the commandment of the LORD thy God, which he commanded thee: for now would the LORD have established thy kingdom upon Israel for ever.

14 But now thy kingdom shall not continue: the LORD hath sought him a man after his own heart, and the LORD hath commanded him *to be* captain over his people, because thou hast not kept *that* which the LORD commanded thee.

15 And Samuel arose, and gat him up from Gilgal unto Gibeah of Benjamin. And Saul numbered the people *that were* present with him, about six hundred men.

16 And Saul, and Jonathan his son, and the people *that were* present with them, abode in Gibeah of Benjamin: but the Philistines encamped in Michmash.

17 And the spoilers came out of the camp of the Philistines in three companies: one company turned unto the way *that leadeth to* Ophrah, unto the land of Shual:

18 And another company turned the way *to* Beth-horon: and another company turned *to* the way of the border that looketh to the valley of Zeboim toward the wilderness.

Israel's Lack of Weapons

19 Now there was no smith found throughout all the land of Israel: for the Philistines said, Lest the Hebrews make *them* swords or spears:

20 But all the Israelites went down to the Philistines, to sharpen every man his share, and his coulter, and his axe, and his mattock.

21 Yet they had a file for the mattocks, and for the coulters, and for the forks, and for the axes, and to sharpen the goads.

22 So it came to pass in the day of battle,

Cross references (center column):

2 1Sam. 10:26
3 1Sam. 10:5
4 Gen. 34:30; Ex. 5:21
6 Judg. 6:2
8 1Sam. 10:8
13 1Sam. 15:11; 2Chr. 16:9
14 1Sam. 15:28; Ps. 89:20; Acts 13:22
15 1Sam. 14:2
17 Josh. 18:23
18 Josh. 16:3; 18:13, 14; Neh. 11:34
19 2Kgs. 24:14; Jer. 24:1
22 Judg. 5:8

13:14 thy kingdom shall not continue. Because of Saul's intrusion into the priest's role (vv. 8–14), Samuel predicts that his dynasty will not continue. This early failure, after only two years in power, was a portent of what was to come. Samuel's prophecy that Saul's kingdom would not be permanent was prompted by Saul's disobedience, self-will, and arrogance. This forecast was later acknowledged by Jonathan, Saul's son and heir (1 Sam. 23:17), and by Saul himself (1 Sam. 24:20).

that there was neither sword nor spear found in the hand of any of the people that *were* with Saul and Jonathan: but with Saul and with Jonathan his son was there found.

23 And the garrison of the Philistines went out to the passage of Michmash.

CHAPTER 14
Jonathan's Daring Attack

1 Now it came to pass upon a day, that Jonathan the son of Saul said unto the young man that bare his armour, Come, and let us go over to the Philistines' garrison, that *is* on the other side. But he told not his father.

2 And Saul tarried in the uttermost part of Gibeah under a pomegranate tree which *is* in Migron: and the people that *were* with him *were* about six hundred men;

3 And Ahiah, the son of Ahitub, Ichabod's brother, the son of Phinehas, the son of Eli, the LORD's priest in Shiloh, wearing an ephod. And the people knew not that Jonathan was gone.

4 And between the passages, by which Jonathan sought to go over unto the Philistines' garrison, *there was* a sharp rock on the one side, and a sharp rock on the other side: and the name of the one *was* Bozez, and the name of the other Seneh.

5 The forefront of the one *was* situated northward over against Michmash, and the other southward over against Gibeah.

6 And Jonathan said to the young man that bare his armour, Come, and let us go over unto the garrison of these uncircumcised: it may be that the LORD will work for us: for *there is* no restraint to the LORD to save by many or by few.

7 And his armourbearer said unto him, Do all that *is* in thine heart: turn thee; behold, I *am* with thee according to thy heart.

8 Then said Jonathan, Behold, we will pass over unto *these* men, and we will discover ourselves unto them.

9 If they say thus unto us, Tarry until we come to you; then we will stand still in our place, and will not go up unto them.

10 But if they say thus, Come up unto us; then we will go up: for the LORD hath delivered them into our hand: and this *shall be* a sign unto us.

11 And both of them discovered themselves unto the garrison of the Philistines: and the Philistines said, Behold, the Hebrews come forth out of the holes where they had hid themselves.

12 And the men of the garrison answered Jonathan and his armourbearer, and said, Come up to us, and we will shew you a thing. And Jonathan said unto his armourbearer, Come up after me: for the LORD hath delivered them into the hand of Israel.

13 And Jonathan climbed up upon his hands and upon his feet, and his armourbearer after him: and they fell before Jonathan; and his armourbearer slew after him.

14 And that first slaughter, which Jonathan and his armourbearer made, was about twenty men, within as it were an half acre of land, *which* a yoke *of oxen might plow.*

15 And there was trembling in the host, in the field, and among all the people: the garrison, and the spoilers, they also trembled, and the earth quaked: so it was a very great trembling.

Israel Defeats the Philistines

16 And the watchmen of Saul in Gibeah of Benjamin looked; and, behold, the multitude melted away, and they went on beating down *one another.*

17 Then said Saul unto the people that *were* with him, Number now, and see who is gone from us. And when they had numbered, behold, Jonathan and his armourbearer *were* not *there.*

18 And Saul said unto Ahiah, Bring hither the ark of God. For the ark of God was at that time with the children of Israel.

19 And it came to pass, while Saul talked unto the priest, that the noise that *was* in the host of the Philistines went on and increased: and Saul said unto the priest, Withdraw thine hand.

20 And Saul and all the people that *were* with him assembled themselves, and they came to the battle: and, behold, every man's sword was against his fellow, *and there was* a very great discomfiture.

21 Moreover the Hebrews *that* were with the Philistines before that time, which went up with them into the camp *from the country* round about, even they also *turned* to be with the Israelites that *were* with Saul and Jonathan.

22 Likewise all the men of Israel which had hid themselves in mount Ephraim, *when* they heard that the Philistines fled, even they also followed hard after them in the battle.

23 So the LORD saved Israel that day: and the battle passed over unto Beth-aven.

Cross references (center column):

23 1Sam. 14:1, 4

2 1Sam. 13:15

3 1Sam. 2:28; 4:21; 22:9, 11, 20

4 1Sam. 13:23

6 Judg. 7:4, 7; 2Chr. 14:11

10 Gen. 24:14; Judg. 7:11

13 Judg. 7:21

15 Gen. 35:5; 1Sam. 13:17; 2Kgs. 7:7; Job 18:11

16 1Sam. 13:20

19 Num. 27:21

20 Judg. 7:22; 2Chr. 20:23

22 1Sam. 13:6

23 Ex. 14:30; 1Sam. 13:5; Ps. 44:6, 7; Hos. 1:7

Jonathan and Saul's Oath

24 And the men of Israel were distressed that day: for Saul had adjured the people, saying, Cursed *be* the man that eateth *any* food until evening, that I may be avenged on mine enemies. So none of the people tasted *any* food.

25 And all *they of* the land came to a wood; and there was honey upon the ground.

26 And when the people were come into the wood, behold, the honey dropped; but no man put his hand to his mouth: for the people feared the oath.

27 But Jonathan heard not when his father charged the people with the oath: wherefore he put forth the end of the rod that *was* in his hand, and dipped it in an honeycomb, and put his hand to his mouth; and his eyes were enlightened.

28 Then answered one of the people, and said, Thy father straitly charged the people with an oath, saying, Cursed *be* the man that eateth *any* food this day. And the people were faint.

29 Then said Jonathan, My father hath troubled the land: see, I pray you, how mine eyes have been enlightened, because I tasted a little of this honey.

30 How much more, if haply the people had eaten freely today of the spoil of their enemies which they found? for had there not been now a much greater slaughter among the Philistines?

31 And they smote the Philistines that day from Michmash to Aijalon: and the people were very faint.

32 And the people flew upon the spoil, and took sheep, and oxen, and calves, and slew *them* on the ground: and the people did eat *them* with the blood.

33 Then they told Saul, saying, Behold, the people sin against the LORD, in that they eat with the blood. And he said, Ye have transgressed: roll a great stone unto me this day.

34 And Saul said, Disperse yourselves among the people, and say unto them, Bring me hither every man his ox, and every man his sheep, and slay *them* here, and eat; and sin not against the LORD in eating with the blood. And all the people brought every man his ox with him that night, and slew *them* there.

35 And Saul built an altar unto the LORD: the same was the first altar that he built unto the LORD.

36 And Saul said, Let us go down after the Philistines by night, and spoil them until the morning light, and let us not leave a man of them. And they said, Do whatsoever seemeth good unto thee. Then said the priest, Let us draw near hither unto God.

37 And Saul asked counsel of God, Shall I go down after the Philistines? wilt thou deliver them into the hand of Israel? But he answered him not that day.

38 And Saul said, Draw ye near hither, all the chief of the people: and know and see wherein this sin hath been this day.

39 For, *as* the LORD liveth, which saveth Israel, though it be in Jonathan my son, he shall surely die. But *there was* not a man among all the people *that* answered him.

40 Then said he unto all Israel, Be ye on one side, and I and Jonathan my son will be on the other side. And the people said unto Saul, Do what seemeth good unto thee.

41 Therefore Saul said unto the LORD God of Israel, Give a perfect *lot*. And Saul and Jonathan were taken: but the people escaped.

42 And Saul said, Cast *lots* between me and Jonathan my son. And Jonathan was taken.

43 Then Saul said to Jonathan, Tell me what thou hast done. And Jonathan told him, and said, I did but taste a little honey with the end of the rod that *was* in mine hand, *and*, lo, I must die.

44 And Saul answered, God do so and more also: for thou shalt surely die, Jonathan.

45 And the people said unto Saul, Shall Jonathan die, who hath wrought this great salvation in Israel? God forbid: *as* the LORD liveth, there shall not one hair of his head fall to the ground; for he hath wrought with God this day. So the people rescued Jonathan, that he died not.

46 Then Saul went up from following the Philistines: and the Philistines went to their own place.

Summary of Saul's Military Leadership

47 So Saul took the kingdom over Israel, and fought against all his enemies on every

---

24 Josh. 6:26

25 Ex. 3:8; Num. 13:27; Deut. 9:28; Matt. 3:4, 5

32 Lev. 3:17; 7:26; 17:10; 19:26; Deut. 12:16, 23, 24

35 1Sam. 7:17

37 1Sam. 28:6

38 Josh. 7:14; 1Sam. 10:19

39 2Sam. 12:5

41 Josh. 7:16; 1Sam. 10:20, 21; Prov. 16:33; Acts 1:24

43 Josh. 7:19; 1Sam. 14:27

44 Ruth 1:17; 1Sam. 14:39

45 2Sam. 14:11; 1Kgs. 1:52; Luke 21:18

47 1Sam. 11:11; 2Sam. 10:6

14:47 Saul took the kingdom. Fighting enemies on every side, including the neighboring tribal nations of Moab, Edom, Ammon, Zobah, and the Philistines, Saul demonstrated his leadership abilities, winning many victories and establishing the royal realm as a strong political state. Rather than erecting a major palace headquarters, he and his court moved about the nation, encamping in strategic places and solidifying his support. Nevertheless, his tendency to substitute his own judgment for the direction of the LORD continued.

side, against Moab, and against the children of Ammon, and against Edom, and against the kings of Zobah, and against the Philistines: and whithersoever he turned himself, he vexed *them*.

48 And he gathered an host, and smote the Amalekites, and delivered Israel out of the hands of them that spoiled them.

49 Now the sons of Saul were Jonathan, and Ishui, and Melchi-shua: and the names of his two daughters *were these*; the name of the firstborn Merab, and the name of the younger Michal:

50 And the name of Saul's wife *was* Ahinoam, the daughter of Ahimaaz: and the name of the captain of his host *was* Abner, the son of Ner, Saul's uncle.

51 And Kish *was* the father of Saul; and Ner the father of Abner *was* the son of Abiel.

52 And there was sore war against the Philistines all the days of Saul: and when Saul saw any strong man, or any valiant man, he took him unto him.

CHAPTER 15
Saul's Second Sin at Gilgal

1 Samuel also said unto Saul, The LORD sent me to anoint thee *to be* king over his people, over Israel: now therefore hearken thou unto the voice of the words of the LORD.

2 Thus saith the LORD of hosts, I remember *that* which Amalek did to Israel, how he laid *wait* for him in the way, when he came up from Egypt.

3 Now go and smite Amalek, and utterly destroy all that they have, and spare them not; but slay both man and woman, infant and suckling, ox and sheep, camel and ass.

4 And Saul gathered the people together, and numbered them in Telaim, two hundred thousand footmen, and ten thousand men of Judah.

5 And Saul came to a city of Amalek, and laid wait in the valley.

6 And Saul said unto the Kenites, Go, depart, get you down from among the Amalekites, lest I destroy you with them: for ye shewed kindness to all the children of Israel, when they came up out of Egypt. So the Kenites departed from among the Amalekites.

7 And Saul smote the Amalekites from

48 1Sam. 15:3, 7
49 1Sam. 31:2; 1Chr. 8:33
51 1Sam. 9:1
52 1Sam. 8:11
1 1Sam. 9:16
2 Ex. 17:8, 14; Num. 24:20; Deut. 25:17-19
3 Lev. 27:28, 29; Josh. 6:17, 21
6 Gen. 18:25; 19:12, 14; Ex. 18:10, 19; Num. 10:29, 32; 24:21; Judg. 1:16; 4:11; Rev. 18:4
7 Gen. 2:11; 16:7; 25:18; 1Sam. 14:48
8 1Sam. 30:1; 1Kgs. 20:34, 35
9 1Sam. 15:3, 15
11 Gen. 6:6, 7; Josh. 22:16; 1Sam. 13:13; 15: 3, 9, 35; 16:1; 2Sam. 24:16; 1Kgs. 9:6
12 Josh. 15:55
13 Gen. 14:19; Judg. 17:2; Ruth 3:10
15 Gen. 3:12; 1Sam. 15:9, 21; Prov. 28:13
17 1Sam. 9:21
20 1Sam. 15:13

Havilah *until* thou comest to Shur, that *is* over against Egypt.

8 And he took Agag the king of the Amalekites alive, and utterly destroyed all the people with the edge of the sword.

9 But Saul and the people spared Agag, and the best of the sheep, and of the oxen, and of the fatlings, and the lambs, and all *that was* good, and would not utterly destroy them: but every thing *that was* vile and refuse, that they destroyed utterly.

10 Then came the word of the LORD unto Samuel, saying,

11 It repenteth me that I have set up Saul *to be* king: for he is turned back from following me, and hath not performed my commandments. And it grieved Samuel; and he cried unto the LORD all night.

12 And when Samuel rose early to meet Saul in the morning, it was told Samuel, saying, Saul came to Carmel, and, behold, he set him up a place, and is gone about, and passed on, and gone down to Gilgal.

13 And Samuel came to Saul: and Saul said unto him, Blessed *be* thou of the LORD: I have performed the commandment of the LORD.

14 And Samuel said, What *meaneth* then this bleating of the sheep in mine ears, and the lowing of the oxen which I hear?

15 And Saul said, They have brought them from the Amalekites: for the people spared the best of the sheep and of the oxen, to sacrifice unto the LORD thy God; and the rest we have utterly destroyed.

16 Then Samuel said unto Saul, Stay, and I will tell thee what the LORD hath said to me this night. And he said unto him, Say on.

17 And Samuel said, When thou *wast* little in thine own sight, *wast* thou not *made* the head of the tribes of Israel, and the LORD anointed thee king over Israel?

18 And the LORD sent thee on a journey, and said, Go and utterly destroy the sinners the Amalekites, and fight against them until they be consumed.

19 Wherefore then didst thou not obey the voice of the LORD, but didst fly upon the spoil, and didst evil in the sight of the LORD?

20 And Saul said unto Samuel, Yea, I have obeyed the voice of the LORD, and have gone the way which the LORD sent me, and have brought Agag the king of Amalek, and have utterly destroyed the Amalekites.

15:20–35 rejected thee from being king. After Saul's disobedience, Samuel predicts that the kingdom will be taken from him. Samuel states three great principles of timeless value: 1) to obey (God) is better than sacrifice; 2) rebellion is as the sin of witchcraft; and 3) stubbornness is as iniquity and idolatry. Saul's insincere attempt

21 But the people took of the spoil, sheep and oxen, the chief of the things which should have been utterly destroyed, to sacrifice unto the LORD thy God in Gilgal.

22 And Samuel said, Hath the LORD *as great* delight in burnt offerings and sacrifices, as in obeying the voice of the LORD? Behold, to obey *is* better than sacrifice, *and* to hearken than the fat of rams.

23 For rebellion *is as* the sin of witchcraft, and stubbornness *is as* iniquity and idolatry. Because thou hast rejected the word of the LORD, he hath also rejected thee from *being* king.

24 And Saul said unto Samuel, I have sinned: for I have transgressed the commandment of the LORD, and thy words: because I feared the people, and obeyed their voice.

25 Now therefore, I pray thee, pardon my sin, and turn again with me, that I may worship the LORD.

26 And Samuel said unto Saul, I will not return with thee: for thou hast rejected the word of the LORD, and the LORD hath rejected thee from being king over Israel.

27 And as Samuel turned about to go away, he laid hold upon the skirt of his mantle, and it rent.

28 And Samuel said unto him, The LORD hath rent the kingdom of Israel from thee this day, and hath given it to a neighbour of thine, *that is* better than thou.

29 And also the Strength of Israel will not lie nor repent: for he *is* not a man, that he should repent.

30 Then he said, I have sinned: *yet* honour me now, I pray thee, before the elders of my people, and before Israel, and turn again with me, that I may worship the LORD thy God.

31 So Samuel turned again after Saul; and Saul worshipped the LORD.

32 Then said Samuel, Bring ye hither to me Agag the king of the Amalekites. And Agag came unto him delicately. And Agag said, Surely the bitterness of death is past.

33 And Samuel said, As thy sword hath made women childless, so shall thy mother be childless among women. And Samuel hewed Agag in pieces before the LORD in Gilgal.

34 Then Samuel went to Ramah; and Saul went up to his house to Gibeah of Saul.

35 And Samuel came no more to see Saul until the day of his death: nevertheless Samuel mourned for Saul: and the LORD repented that he had made Saul king over Israel.

CHAPTER 16
Samuel Anoints David King

1 And the LORD said unto Samuel, How long wilt thou mourn for Saul, seeing I have rejected him from reigning over Israel? fill thine horn with oil, and go, I will send thee to Jesse the Beth-lehemite: for I have provided me a king among his sons.

2 And Samuel said, How can I go? if Saul hear *it*, he will kill me. And the LORD said, Take an heifer with thee, and say, I am come to sacrifice to the LORD.

3 And call Jesse to the sacrifice, and I will shew thee what thou shalt do: and thou shalt anoint unto me *him* whom I name unto thee.

4 And Samuel did that which the LORD spake, and came to Beth-lehem. And the elders of the town trembled at his coming, and said, Comest thou peaceably?

5 And he said, Peaceably: I am come to sacrifice unto the LORD: sanctify yourselves, and come with me to the sacrifice. And he sanctified Jesse and his sons, and called them to the sacrifice.

6 And it came to pass, when they were come, that he looked on Eliab, and said, Surely the LORD's anointed *is* before him.

7 But the LORD said unto Samuel, Look not on his countenance, or on the height of his stature; because I have refused him: for *the LORD seeth* not as man seeth; for man looketh on the outward appearance, but the LORD looketh on the heart.

8 Then Jesse called Abinadab, and made him pass before Samuel. And he said, Neither hath the LORD chosen this.

9 Then Jesse made Shammah to pass by. And he said, Neither hath the LORD chosen this.

10 Again, Jesse made seven of his sons to pass before Samuel. And Samuel said unto Jesse, The LORD hath not chosen these.

11 And Samuel said unto Jesse, Are here all *thy* children? And he said, There remaineth yet the youngest, and, behold, he keepeth

Cross References

21 1Sam. 15:15
22 Ps. 50:8, 9; Prov. 21:3; Jer. 7:22, 23; Hos. 6:6; Matt. 5:24; Mark 12:33
23 1Sam. 13:14
24 Ex. 23:2; 2Sam. 12:13; Prov. 29:25; Isa. 51:12, 13
26 1Sam. 2:30
27 1Kgs. 11:30
28 1Sam. 28:17, 18; 1Kgs. 11:31
29 Num. 23:19; Ezek. 24:14; 2Tim. 2:13; Titus 1:2
30 John 5:44; 12:43
33 Ex. 17:11; Num. 14:45; Judg. 1:7
34 1Sam. 11:4
35 1Sam. 15:11; 16:1; 19:24;
1 2Kgs. 9:1; Ps. 78:70; 89:19, 20
2 1Sam. 9:12; 20:29
3 Ex. 4:15; 1Sam. 9:16
4 1Sam. 21:1; 1Kgs. 2:13; 2Kgs. 9:22
5 Ex. 19:10, 14
6 1Sam. 17:13; 1Kgs. 12:26; 1Chr. 27:18, *Elihu*
7 1Kgs. 8:39; Ps. 7:9; Jer. 11:20; Acts 1:24; 2Cor. 10:7
11 1Sam. 17:12; 2Sam. 7:8; Ps. 78:70

at repentance (vv. 24–25) was followed by a profound pronouncement from Samuel, another timeless principle: "Thou hast rejected the word of the LORD, and the LORD hath rejected thee from being king over Israel" (v. 26). Saul never saw Samuel again until the strange scene in 1 Samuel 28:7–20.

the sheep. And Samuel said unto Jesse, Send and fetch him: for we will not sit down till he come hither.

12 And he sent, and brought him in. Now he *was* ruddy, *and* withal of a beautiful countenance, and goodly to look to. And the LORD said, Arise, anoint him: for this *is* he.

13 Then Samuel took the horn of oil, and anointed him in the midst of his brethren: and the Spirit of the LORD came upon David from that day forward. So Samuel rose up, and went to Ramah.

David Becomes Saul's Musician

14 But the Spirit of the LORD departed from Saul, and an evil spirit from the LORD troubled him.

15 And Saul's servants said unto him, Behold now, an evil spirit from God troubleth thee.

16 Let our lord now command thy servants, *which are* before thee, to seek out a man, *who is* a cunning player on an harp: and it shall come to pass, when the evil spirit from God is upon thee, that he shall play with his hand, and thou shalt be well.

17 And Saul said unto his servants, Provide me now a man that can play well, and bring *him* to me.

18 Then answered one of the servants, and said, Behold, I have seen a son of Jesse the Beth-lehemite, *that is* cunning in playing, and a mighty valiant man, and a man of war, and prudent in matters, and a comely person, and the LORD *is* with him.

19 Wherefore Saul sent messengers unto Jesse, and said, Send me David thy son, which *is* with the sheep.

20 And Jesse took an ass *laden* with bread, and a bottle of wine, and a kid, and sent *them* by David his son unto Saul.

21 And David came to Saul, and stood before him: and he loved him greatly; and he became his armourbearer.

22 And Saul sent to Jesse, saying, Let David, I pray thee, stand before me; for he hath found favour in my sight.

23 And it came to pass, when the *evil* spirit from God was upon Saul, that David took an harp, and played with his hand: so Saul

was refreshed, and was well, and the evil spirit departed from him.

CHAPTER 17
David and Goliath

1 Now the Philistines gathered together their armies to battle, and were gathered together at Shochoh, which *belongeth* to Judah, and pitched between Shochoh and Azekah, in Ephes-dammim.

2 And Saul and the men of Israel were gathered together, and pitched by the valley of Elah, and set the battle in array against the Philistines.

3 And the Philistines stood on a mountain on the one side, and Israel stood on a mountain on the other side: and *there was* a valley between them.

4 And there went out a champion out of the camp of the Philistines, named Goliath, of Gath, whose height *was* six cubits and a span.

5 And *he had* an helmet of brass upon his head, and he *was* armed with a coat of mail; and the weight of the coat *was* five thousand shekels of brass.

6 And *he had* greaves of brass upon his legs, and a target of brass between his shoulders.

7 And the staff of his spear *was* like a weaver's beam; and his spear's head *weighed* six hundred shekels of iron: and one bearing a shield went before him.

8 And he stood and cried unto the armies of Israel, and said unto them, Why are ye come out to set *your* battle in array? *am* not I a Philistine, and ye servants to Saul? choose you a man for you, and let him come down to me.

9 If he be able to fight with me, and to kill me, then will we be your servants: but if I prevail against him, and kill him, then shall ye be our servants, and serve us.

10 And the Philistine said, I defy the armies of Israel this day; give me a man, that we may fight together.

11 When Saul and all Israel heard those words of the Philistine, they were dismayed, and greatly afraid.

12 Now David *was* the son of that

Cross references (center column)

12 1Sam. 17:42; Song 5:10
13 Num. 27:18; Judg. 11:29; 13:25; 14:6; 1Sam. 10:1, 6, 10; Ps. 89:20
14 Judg. 9:23; 16:20; 1Sam. 11:6; 18:10, 12; 19:9; 28:15; Ps. 51:11
16 Gen. 41:46; 1Sam. 16:21, 22, 23; 1Kgs. 10:8; 2Kgs. 3:15
18 1Sam. 3:19; 17:32, 34-36; 18:12, 14
19 1Sam. 16:11; 17:15, 34
20 Gen. 43:11; 1Sam. 10:27; 17:18; Prov. 18:16
21 Gen. 41:46; 1Kgs. 10:8; Prov. 22:29
23 1Sam. 16:14, 16
1 Josh. 15:35; 1Sam. 13:5; 1Chr. 11:13; 2Chr. 28:18
4 Josh. 11:22; 2Sam. 21:19
7 2Sam. 21:19
8 1Sam. 8:17
9 1Sam. 11:1
10 1Sam. 16:26; 2Sam. 21:21
12 Gen. 35:19; Ruth 4:22; 1Sam. 16:1, 18, 10, 11; 17:58; 1Chr. 2:13-15

16:12 Arise, anoint him: for this is he. Sent by the Lord to the family of Jesse, Samuel anoints the eighth and youngest son to be the future king. David, chosen by the Lord in his youth, was from the tribe of Judah (Gen. 49:10) and becomes the second king of Israel. He is an ancestor, humanly speaking, a forerunner and foreshadower of the greater David (Jesus Christ), who is the rightful King of Israel that shall reign as King of kings in the Millennium. That historic day of his anointing by Samuel set in motion a sequence of events which has no end (see Rev. 3:7; 5:5; 22:16).

Fallen Angels

By Chuck Missler

Fallen angels are first introduced in Genesis 6:1–4. In the Old Testament, the term "sons of God" is exclusively used of angels (Job 1:6; 2:1; 38:7). Jesus implies the same in Luke 20:36. The unnatural offspring resulting from their consorting with human wives ("daughters of Adam") are called Nephilim, or "fallen ones" (from the Hebrew *nephal*, to fall). So it was understood by many ancient Jewish scholars, the translators of the Septuagint (an early Greek translation of the Old Testament), and the early Church. (The translation "giants" comes from the Septuagint Greek translation (*gigantes*), which actually means "earth-born.")

This unnatural offspring was apparently a satanic plot to corrupt the human genealogy in an attempt to preclude a redemptive Kinsman-Redeemer, the Messiah, who descended from the line of Seth. This was one reason behind the Flood. Noah was still distinctive in having an unblemished genealogy (Gen. 6:9).

> *The Holy Spirit is restraining the forces of Satan far more than we can understand.*

Similar events apparently may have occurred after the Flood (Gen. 6:4), giving rise to the Nephilim (also called Rephaims, Emims, Horims, and Zamsummims) encountered by Israel in the land of Canaan throughout the Old Testament (Num. 13:33 [cf. Gen. 14:5; 15:20; Deut. 2:10–12, 22; 3:11, 13; Josh. 12:4; 13:12]).

An alternative view emerged in the fifth century, suggesting that Genesis 6 alludes to a failure to keep the "faithful" line of Seth separate from the worldly line of Cain. This widely held view is built on the assumptions that the line of Seth was faithful and the line of Cain was not, and that they were to remain separate (a concept introduced many chapters later). This argument certainly does not explain the unnatural hybrid offspring. (If the line of Seth was faithful, why did they perish in the Flood?)

Nevertheless, many Bible scholars have held to the "line of Seth" and "line of Cain" interpretation of the intermarriages, citing Matthew 22:30 to counter the other interpretations. Certain fallen angels, perhaps those discussed here, are in special confinement (see 1 Pet. 3:19–20; 2 Pet. 2:4–5; Jude 1:6–7).

Satan now leads a vast throng of fallen angels, who evidently joined him in his rebellion (Isa. 14:12–15; Ezek. 28:11–19; Matt. 25:41; Eph. 6:12; Rev. 12:4–9). Fallen angels are not to be confused with the demons of the New Testament. Angels apparently have no problem appearing in our world: they spoke as men, ate meals (Gen. 18:1–8; 19:3), took people by the hand (Gen. 19:10, 16), and were capable of direct combat (2 Kgs. 19:35; Isa. 37:36). Demons, on the other hand, appear to be desperate for embodiment (Matt. 8:28–34; Mark 5:1–20; Luke 8:26–39). Some suggest that the demons may be the disembodied spirits of the Nephilim that perished (cf. Isa. 26:14).

Our Lord's allusion to the "days of [Noah]" in regards to Christ's second coming (Matt. 24:37; Luke 17:26) cause some to anticipate a possible recurrence of the events of Genesis 6. Supernatural deceptions are to be a characteristic of the days prior to our Lord's return (Matt. 24:4, 23–25; 2 Thess. 2:8–12).

The ultimate fallen angel may be behind the Antichrist, who comes out of the *aboussos*, or bottomless pit (Rev. 9:11; 11:7; 17:8) and is the seed of the serpent (Gen. 3:15). The "one who now letteth" (2 Thess. 2:7), the Holy Spirit who restrains the works of evil among men, is presently restraining the forces of Satan far more than we can understand.

Ephrathite of Beth-lehem-judah, whose name *was* Jesse; and he had eight sons: and the man went among men *for* an old man in the days of Saul.

13 And the three eldest sons of Jesse went *and* followed Saul to the battle: and the names of his three sons that went to the battle *were* Eliab the firstborn, and next unto him Abinadab, and the third Shammah.

14 And David *was* the youngest: and the three eldest followed Saul.

15 But David went and returned from Saul to feed his father's sheep at Beth-lehem.

16 And the Philistine drew near morning and evening, and presented himself forty days.

17 And Jesse said unto David his son, Take now for thy brethren an ephah of this parched *corn*, and these ten loaves, and run to the camp to thy brethren;

18 And carry these ten cheeses unto the captain of *their* thousand, and look how thy brethren fare, and take their pledge.

19 Now Saul, and they, and all the men of Israel, *were* in the valley of Elah, fighting with the Philistines.

20 And David rose up early in the morning, and left the sheep with a keeper, and took, and went, as Jesse had commanded him; and he came to the trench, as the host was going forth to the fight, and shouted for the battle.

21 For Israel and the Philistines had put the battle in array, army against army.

22 And David left his carriage in the hand of the keeper of the carriage, and ran into the army, and came and saluted his brethren.

23 And as he talked with them, behold, there came up the champion, the Philistine of Gath, Goliath by name, out of the armies of the Philistines, and spake according to the same words: and David heard *them*.

24 And all the men of Israel, when they saw the man, fled from him, and were sore afraid.

25 And the men of Israel said, Have ye seen this man that is come up? surely to defy Israel is he come up: and it shall be, *that* the man who killeth him, the king will enrich him with great riches, and will give him his daughter, and make his father's house free in Israel.

26 And David spake to the men that stood by him, saying, What shall be done to the man that killeth this Philistine, and taketh away the reproach from Israel? for who *is*

this uncircumcised Philistine, that he should defy the armies of the living God?

27 And the people answered him after this manner, saying, So shall it be done to the man that killeth him.

28 And Eliab his eldest brother heard when he spake unto the men; and Eliab's anger was kindled against David, and he said, Why camest thou down hither? and with whom hast thou left those few sheep in the wilderness? I know thy pride, and the naughtiness of thine heart; for thou art come down that thou mightest see the battle.

29 And David said, What have I now done? *Is there* not a cause?

30 And he turned from him toward another, and spake after the same manner: and the people answered him again after the former manner.

31 And when the words were heard which David spake, they rehearsed *them* before Saul: and he sent for him.

32 And David said to Saul, Let no man's heart fail because of him; thy servant will go and fight with this Philistine.

33 And Saul said to David, Thou art not able to go against this Philistine to fight with him: for thou *art but* a youth, and he a man of war from his youth.

34 And David said unto Saul, Thy servant kept his father's sheep, and there came a lion, and a bear, and took a lamb out of the flock:

35 And I went out after him, and smote him, and delivered *it* out of his mouth: and when he arose against me, I caught *him* by his beard, and smote him, and slew him.

36 Thy servant slew both the lion and the bear: and this uncircumcised Philistine shall be as one of them, seeing he hath defied the armies of the living God.

37 David said moreover, The Lord that delivered me out of the paw of the lion, and out of the paw of the bear, he will deliver me out of the hand of this Philistine. And Saul said unto David, Go, and the Lord be with thee.

38 And Saul armed David with his armour, and he put an helmet of brass upon his head; also he armed him with a coat of mail.

39 And David girded his sword upon his armour, and he assayed to go; for he had not proved *it*. And David said unto Saul, I cannot go with these; for I have not proved *them*. And David put them off him.

40 And he took his staff in his hand, and chose him five smooth stones out of the

---

13 1Sam. 16:6, 8, 9; 1Chr. 2:13

15 1Sam. 16:19

18 Gen. 37:14

20 1Sam. 26:5

23 1Sam. 17:8

25 Josh. 15:16

26 Deut. 5:26; 1Sam. 11:2; 14:6; 17:10

27 1Sam. 17:25

28 Gen. 37:4, 8, 11; Matt. 10:36

29 1Sam. 17:17

30 1Sam. 17:26, 27

32 Deut. 20:1, 3; 1Sam. 16:18

33 Num. 13:31; Deut. 9:2

37 1Sam. 20:13; 1Chr. 22:11, 16; Ps. 18:16, 17; 63:7; 77:11; 2Cor. 1:10; 2Tim. 4:17, 18

brook, and put them in a shepherd's bag which he had, even in a scrip; and his sling *was* in his hand: and he drew near to the Philistine.

41 And the Philistine came on and drew near unto David; and the man that bare the shield *went* before him.

42 And when the Philistine looked about, and saw David, he disdained him: for he was *but* a youth, and ruddy, and of a fair countenance.

43 And the Philistine said unto David, *Am I* a dog, that thou comest to me with staves? And the Philistine cursed David by his gods.

44 And the Philistine said to David, Come to me, and I will give thy flesh unto the fowls of the air, and to the beasts of the field.

45 Then said David to the Philistine, Thou comest to me with a sword, and with a spear, and with a shield: but I come to thee in the name of the LORD of hosts, the God of the armies of Israel, whom thou hast defied.

46 This day will the LORD deliver thee into mine hand; and I will smite thee, and take thine head from thee; and I will give the carcases of the host of the Philistines this day unto the fowls of the air, and to the wild beasts of the earth; that all the earth may know that there is a God in Israel.

47 And all this assembly shall know that the LORD saveth not with sword and spear: for the battle *is* the LORD's, and he will give you into our hands.

48 And it came to pass, when the Philistine arose, and came and drew nigh to meet David, that David hasted, and ran toward the army to meet the Philistine.

49 And David put his hand in his bag, and took thence a stone, and slang *it*, and smote the Philistine in his forehead, that the stone sunk into his forehead; and he fell upon his face to the earth.

50 So David prevailed over the Philistine with a sling and with a stone, and smote the Philistine, and slew him; but *there was* no sword in the hand of David.

51 Therefore David ran, and stood upon the Philistine, and took his sword, and drew it out of the sheath thereof, and slew him, and cut off his head therewith. And when the Philistines saw their champion was dead, they fled.

52 And the men of Israel and of Judah arose, and shouted, and pursued the Philistines, until thou come to the valley, and to the gates of Ekron. And the wounded of the Philistines fell down by the way to Shaaraim, even unto Gath, and unto Ekron.

53 And the children of Israel returned from chasing after the Philistines, and they spoiled their tents.

54 And David took the head of the Philistine, and brought it to Jerusalem; but he put his armour in his tent.

55 And when Saul saw David go forth against the Philistine, he said unto Abner, the captain of the host, Abner, whose son *is* this youth? And Abner said, *As* thy soul liveth, O king, I cannot tell.

56 And the king said, Inquire thou whose son the stripling *is*.

57 And as David returned from the slaughter of the Philistine, Abner took him, and brought him before Saul with the head of the Philistine in his hand.

58 And Saul said to him, Whose son *art* thou, *thou* young man? And David answered, I *am* the son of thy servant Jesse the Beth-lehemite.

CHAPTER 18
David and Jonathan Become Friends

1 And it came to pass, when he had made an end of speaking unto Saul, that the soul of Jonathan was knit with the soul of David, and Jonathan loved him as his own soul.

2 And Saul took him that day, and would let him go no more home to his father's house.

3 Then Jonathan and David made a covenant, because he loved him as his own soul.

4 And Jonathan stripped himself of the robe that *was* upon him, and gave it to David, and his garments, even to his sword, and to his bow, and to his girdle.

5 And David went out whithersoever Saul sent him, *and* behaved himself wisely: and Saul set him over the men of war, and he was accepted in the sight of all the people, and also in the sight of Saul's servants.

---

42 1Sam. 16:12; Ps. 123:3, 4; 1Cor. 1:27, 28

43 1Sam. 24:14; 2Sam. 3:8; 9:8; 16:9; 2Kgs. 8:13

44 1Kgs. 20:10, 11

45 1Sam. 17:10; 2Sam. 22:33, 35; Ps. 124:8; 125:1; 2Cor. 10:4; Heb. 11:33, 34

46 Deut. 28:26; Josh. 4:24; 1Kgs. 8:43; 18:36; 2Kgs. 19:19; Isa. 52:10

47 2Chr. 20:15; Ps. 44:6, 7; Hos. 1:7; Zech. 4:6

50 Judg. 3:31; 15:15; 1Sam. 21:9; 2Sam. 23:21

51 Heb. 11:34

52 Josh. 15:36

55 1Sam. 16:21, 22

57 1Sam. 17:54

58 1Sam. 17:12

1 Gen. 44:30; Deut. 13:6; 1Sam. 19:2; 20:17; 2Sam. 1:26

2 1Sam. 17:15

5 1Sam. 18:14, 15, 30

17:45 I come to thee in the name of the LORD. David, the brave youth, with great faith and courage, challenges the Philistine champion. As was the custom in some ancient societies, a warrior from each opposing side would be selected to wage hand-to-hand combat against his foe, a fight unto death. David's victory against the well-armed and armored giant resulted in the Israelites routing their enemies and confirmed the prophecy that David was to be king.

Saul Becomes Jealous of David

6 And it came to pass as they came, when David was returned from the slaughter of the Philistine, that the women came out of all cities of Israel, singing and dancing, to meet king Saul, with tabrets, with joy, and with instruments of musick.

7 And the women answered *one another* as they played, and said, Saul hath slain his thousands, and David his ten thousands.

8 And Saul was very wroth, and the saying displeased him; and he said, They have ascribed unto David ten thousands, and to me they have ascribed *but* thousands: and *what* can he have more but the kingdom?

9 And Saul eyed David from that day and forward.

10 And it came to pass on the morrow, that the evil spirit from God came upon Saul, and he prophesied in the midst of the house: and David played with his hand, as at other times: and *there was* a javelin in Saul's hand.

11 And Saul cast the javelin; for he said, I will smite David even to the wall *with it.* And David avoided out of his presence twice.

12 And Saul was afraid of David, because the LORD was with him, and was departed from Saul.

13 Therefore Saul removed him from him, and made him his captain over a thousand; and he went out and came in before the people.

14 And David behaved himself wisely in all his ways; and the LORD *was* with him.

15 Wherefore when Saul saw that he behaved himself very wisely, he was afraid of him.

16 But all Israel and Judah loved David, because he went out and came in before them.

David Marries Saul's Daughter

17 And Saul said to David, Behold my elder daughter Merab, her will I give thee to wife: only be thou valiant for me, and fight the LORD's battles. For Saul said, Let not mine hand be upon him, but let the hand of the Philistines be upon him.

18 And David said unto Saul, Who *am* I? and what *is* my life, *or* my father's family in Israel, that I should be son-in-law to the king?

19 But it came to pass at the time when Merab Saul's daughter should have been given to David, that she was given unto Adriel the Meholathite to wife.

20 And Michal Saul's daughter loved David: and they told Saul, and the thing pleased him.

21 And Saul said, I will give him her, that she may be a snare to him, and that the hand of the Philistines may be against him. Wherefore Saul said to David, Thou shalt this day be my son-in-law in the one of the twain.

22 And Saul commanded his servants, *saying,* Commune with David secretly, and say, Behold, the king hath delight in thee, and all his servants love thee: now therefore be the king's son-in-law.

23 And Saul's servants spake those words in the ears of David. And David said, Seemeth it to you *a* light *thing* to be a king's son-in-law, seeing that I *am* a poor man, and lightly esteemed?

24 And the servants of Saul told him, saying, On this manner spake David.

25 And Saul said, Thus shall ye say to David, The king desireth not any dowry, but an hundred foreskins of the Philistines, to be avenged of the king's enemies. But Saul thought to make David fall by the hand of the Philistines.

26 And when his servants told David these words, it pleased David well to be the king's son-in-law: and the days were not expired.

27 Wherefore David arose and went, he and his men, and slew of the Philistines two hundred men; and David brought their foreskins, and they gave them in full tale to the king, that he might be the king's son-in-law. And Saul gave him Michal his daughter to wife.

28 And Saul saw and knew that the LORD *was* with David, and *that* Michal Saul's daughter loved him.

29 And Saul was yet the more afraid of David; and Saul became David's enemy continually.

30 Then the princes of the Philistines went forth: and it came to pass, after they went forth, *that* David behaved himself more

Cross references

6 Ex. 15:20; Judg. 11:34
7 Ex. 15:21; 1Sam. 21:11; 29:5
8 1Sam. 15:28; Eccl. 4:4
10 1Sam. 16:14; 19:9, 24; 1Kgs. 18:29; Acts 16:16
11 1Sam. 19:10; 20:33; Prov. 27:4
12 1Sam. 16:13, 14, 18; 18:15, 29; 28:15
13 Num. 27:17; 1Sam. 18:16; 2Sam. 5:2
14 Gen. 39:2, 3, 23; Josh. 6:27; 1Sam. 18:5
16 1Sam. 18:5
17 Num. 32:20, 27, 29; 1Sam. 17:25; 18:21, 25; 25:28; 2Sam. 12:9
18 1Sam. 9:21; 18:23; 2Sam. 7:18
19 Judg. 7:22; 2Sam. 21:8
20 1Sam. 18:28
21 Ex. 10:7; 1Sam. 18:17, 26
25 Gen. 34:12; Ex. 22:17; 1Sam. 14:24; 18:17
26 1Sam. 18:21
27 1Sam. 18:13; 2Sam. 3:14
30 1Sam. 18:5; 2Sam. 11:1

18:9 And Saul eyed David from that day and forward. Saul, the man after the flesh, and David, the man after God's own heart, were antagonists in a strange conflict that spanned nearly fifteen years. First hired as a court musician (16:17–23), David for a time became Saul's armor bearer, then returned home. Not long after David defeated Goliath, jealousy began to consume Saul because of David's popularity.

wisely than all the servants of Saul; so that his name was much set by.

CHAPTER 19
Saul Tries to Kill David

1 And Saul spake to Jonathan his son, and to all his servants, that they should kill David.
2 But Jonathan Saul's son delighted much in David: and Jonathan told David, saying, Saul my father seeketh to kill thee: now therefore, I pray thee, take heed to thyself until the morning, and abide in a secret *place*, and hide thyself:
3 And I will go out and stand beside my father in the field where thou *art*, and I will commune with my father of thee; and what I see, that I will tell thee.
4 And Jonathan spake good of David unto Saul his father, and said unto him, Let not the king sin against his servant, against David; because he hath not sinned against thee, and because his works *have been* to thee-ward very good:
5 For he did put his life in his hand, and slew the Philistine, and the LORD wrought a great salvation for all Israel: thou sawest *it*, and didst rejoice: wherefore then wilt thou sin against innocent blood, to slay David without a cause?
6 And Saul hearkened unto the voice of Jonathan: and Saul sware, *As* the LORD liveth, he shall not be slain.
7 And Jonathan called David, and Jonathan shewed him all those things. And Jonathan brought David to Saul, and he was in his presence, as in times past.
8 And there was war again: and David went out, and fought with the Philistines, and slew them with a great slaughter; and they fled from him.
9 And the evil spirit from the LORD was upon Saul, as he sat in his house with his javelin in his hand: and David played with *his* hand.
10 And Saul sought to smite David even to the wall with the javelin; but he slipped away out of Saul's presence, and he smote the javelin into the wall: and David fled, and escaped that night.
11 Saul also sent messengers unto David's house, to watch him, and to slay him in the morning: and Michal David's wife told him, saying, If thou save not thy life tonight, to morrow thou shalt be slain.
12 So Michal let David down through a window: and he went, and fled, and escaped.

13 And Michal took an image, and laid *it* in the bed, and put a pillow of goats' *hair* for his bolster, and covered *it* with a cloth.
14 And when Saul sent messengers to take David, she said, He *is* sick.
15 And Saul sent the messengers *again* to see David, saying, Bring him up to me in the bed, that I may slay him.
16 And when the messengers were come in, behold, *there was* an image in the bed, with a pillow of goats' *hair* for his bolster.
17 And Saul said unto Michal, Why hast thou deceived me so, and sent away mine enemy, that he is escaped? And Michal answered Saul, He said unto me, Let me go; why should I kill thee?
18 So David fled, and escaped, and came to Samuel to Ramah, and told him all that Saul had done to him. And he and Samuel went and dwelt in Naioth.
19 And it was told Saul, saying, Behold, David *is* at Naioth in Ramah.
20 And Saul sent messengers to take David: and when they saw the company of the prophets prophesying, and Samuel standing *as* appointed over them, the Spirit of God was upon the messengers of Saul, and they also prophesied.
21 And when it was told Saul, he sent other messengers, and they prophesied likewise. And Saul sent messengers again the third time, and they prophesied also.
22 Then went he also to Ramah, and came to a great well that *is* in Sechu: and he asked and said, Where *are* Samuel and David? And *one* said, Behold, *they be* at Naioth in Ramah.
23 And he went thither to Naioth in Ramah: and the Spirit of God was upon him also, and he went on, and prophesied, until he came to Naioth in Ramah.
24 And he stripped off his clothes also, and prophesied before Samuel in like manner, and lay down naked all that day and all that night. Wherefore they say, *Is* Saul also among the prophets?

CHAPTER 20
Jonathan Helps David Escape

1 And David fled from Naioth in Ramah, and came and said before Jonathan, What have I done? what *is* mine iniquity? and what *is* my sin before thy father, that he seeketh my life?
2 And he said unto him, God forbid; thou shalt not die: behold, my father will do nothing either great or small, but that he will shew it me: and why should my father hide this thing from me? it *is* not *so*.

Cross references (center column):

2 1Sam. 18:1
4 Gen. 42:22; Ps. 35:12; 109:5; Prov. 17:13; 31:8, 9; Jer. 18:20
5 Judg. 9:17; 12:3; 1Sam. 11:13; 17:49, 50; 20:32; 28:21; 1Chr. 11:14; Ps. 119:109; Matt. 27:4
7 1Sam. 16:21; 18:2, 13
9 1Sam. 16:14; 18:10, 11
12 Josh. 2:15; Acts 9:24, 25
17 2Sam. 2:22
20 Num. 11:25; 1Sam. 10:5, 6; Joel 2:28; John 7:32, 45; 1Cor. 14:3, 24, 25
23 1Sam. 10:10
24 1Sam. 10:11; 2Sam. 6:14, 20; Isa. 20:2; Mic. 1:8
2 1Sam. 9:15; 20:12

3 And David sware moreover, and said, Thy father certainly knoweth that I have found grace in thine eyes; and he saith, Let not Jonathan know this, lest he be grieved: but truly *as* the LORD liveth, and *as* thy soul liveth, *there is* but a step between me and death.

4 Then said Jonathan unto David, Whatsoever thy soul desireth, I will even do *it* for thee.

5 And David said unto Jonathan, Behold, to morrow *is* the new moon, and I should not fail to sit with the king at meat: but let me go, that I may hide myself in the field unto the third *day* at even.

6 If thy father at all miss me, then say, David earnestly asked *leave* of me that he might run to Beth-lehem his city: for *there is* a yearly sacrifice there for all the family.

7 If he say thus, *It is* well; thy servant shall have peace: but if he be very wroth, *then* be sure that evil is determined by him.

8 Therefore thou shalt deal kindly with thy servant; for thou hast brought thy servant into a covenant of the LORD with thee: notwithstanding, if there be in me iniquity, slay me thyself; for why shouldest thou bring me to thy father?

9 And Jonathan said, Far be it from thee: for if I knew certainly that evil were determined by my father to come upon thee, then would not I tell it thee?

10 Then said David to Jonathan, Who shall tell me? or what *if* thy father answer thee roughly?

11 And Jonathan said unto David, Come, and let us go out into the field. And they went out both of them into the field.

12 And Jonathan said unto David, O LORD God of Israel, when I have sounded my father about to morrow any time, *or* the third *day*, and, behold, *if there be* good toward David, and I then send not unto thee, and shew it thee;

13 The LORD do so and much more to Jonathan: but if it please my father *to do* thee evil, then I will shew it thee, and send thee away, that thou mayest go in peace: and the LORD be with thee, as he hath been with my father.

14 And thou shalt not only while yet I live shew me the kindness of the LORD, that I die not:

15 But *also* thou shalt not cut off thy kindness from my house for ever: no, not when the LORD hath cut off the enemies of David every one from the face of the earth.

16 So Jonathan made *a covenant* with the

5 Num. 10:10; 28:11; 1Sam. 19:2
6 1Sam. 9:12; 16:4
7 Deut. 1:23; 1Sam. 25:17; 2Sam. 17:4; Esth. 7:7
8 Josh. 2:14; 1Sam. 18:3; 20:16; 23:18; 2Sam. 14:32
12 1Sam. 20:2
13 Josh. 1:5; Ruth 1:17; 1Sam. 17:37; 1Chr. 22:11, 16
15 2Sam. 9:1, 3, 7; 21:7
16 1Sam. 25:22; 31:2; 2Sam. 4:7; 21:8
17 1Sam. 18:1
18 1Sam. 20:5
19 1Sam. 19:2
21 Jer. 4:2
23 1Sam. 20:14, 15, 42
26 Lev. 7:21; 15:5
28 1Sam. 20:6

house of David, *saying*, Let the LORD even require *it* at the hand of David's enemies.

17 And Jonathan caused David to swear again, because he loved him: for he loved him as he loved his own soul.

18 Then Jonathan said to David, To morrow *is* the new moon: and thou shalt be missed, because thy seat will be empty.

19 And *when* thou hast stayed three days, *then* thou shalt go down quickly, and come to the place where thou didst hide thyself when the business was *in hand*, and shalt remain by the stone Ezel.

20 And I will shoot three arrows on the side *thereof*, as though I shot at a mark.

21 And, behold, I will send a lad, *saying*, Go, find out the arrows. If I expressly say unto the lad, Behold, the arrows *are* on this side of thee, take them; then come thou: for *there is* peace to thee, and no hurt; *as* the LORD liveth.

22 But if I say thus unto the young man, Behold, the arrows *are* beyond thee; go thy way: for the LORD hath sent thee away.

23 And *as touching* the matter which thou and I have spoken of, behold, the LORD *be* between thee and me for ever.

24 So David hid himself in the field: and when the new moon was come, the king sat him down to eat meat.

25 And the king sat upon his seat, as at other times, *even* upon a seat by the wall: and Jonathan arose, and Abner sat by Saul's side, and David's place was empty.

26 Nevertheless Saul spake not any thing that day: for he thought, Something hath befallen him, he *is* not clean; surely he *is* not clean.

27 And it came to pass on the morrow, *which was* the second *day* of the month, that David's place was empty: and Saul said unto Jonathan his son, Wherefore cometh not the son of Jesse to meat, neither yesterday, nor today?

28 And Jonathan answered Saul, David earnestly asked *leave* of me *to go* to Bethlehem:

29 And he said, Let me go, I pray thee; for our family hath a sacrifice in the city; and my brother, he hath commanded me *to be there*: and now, if I have found favour in thine eyes, let me get away, I pray thee, and see my brethren. Therefore he cometh not unto the king's table.

30 Then Saul's anger was kindled against Jonathan, and he said unto him, Thou son of the perverse rebellious *woman*, do not I know that thou hast chosen the son of Jesse

to thine own confusion, and unto the confusion of thy mother's nakedness?

31 For as long as the son of Jesse liveth upon the ground, thou shalt not be established, nor thy kingdom. Wherefore now send and fetch him unto me, for he shall surely die.

32 And Jonathan answered Saul his father, and said unto him, Wherefore shall he be slain? what hath he done?

33 And Saul cast a javelin at him to smite him: whereby Jonathan knew that it was determined of his father to slay David.

34 So Jonathan arose from the table in fierce anger, and did eat no meat the second day of the month: for he was grieved for David, because his father had done him shame.

35 And it came to pass in the morning, that Jonathan went out into the field at the time appointed with David, and a little lad with him.

36 And he said unto his lad, Run, find out now the arrows which I shoot. *And* as the lad ran, he shot an arrow beyond him.

37 And when the lad was come to the place of the arrow which Jonathan had shot, Jonathan cried after the lad, and said, *Is* not the arrow beyond thee?

38 And Jonathan cried after the lad, Make speed, haste, stay not. And Jonathan's lad gathered up the arrows, and came to his master.

39 But the lad knew not any thing: only Jonathan and David knew the matter.

40 And Jonathan gave his artillery unto his lad, and said unto him, Go, carry *them* to the city.

41 *And* as soon as the lad was gone, David arose out of *a place* toward the south, and fell on his face to the ground, and bowed himself three times: and they kissed one another, and wept one with another, until David exceeded.

42 And Jonathan said to David, Go in peace, forasmuch as we have sworn both of us in the name of the Lord, saying, The Lord be between me and thee, and between my seed and thy seed for ever. And he arose and departed: and Jonathan went into the city.

CHAPTER 21
David Gets Help from Ahimelech

1 Then came David to Nob to Ahimelech the priest: and Ahimelech was afraid at the meeting of David, and said unto him, Why *art* thou alone, and no man with thee?

2 And David said unto Ahimelech the priest, The king hath commanded me a business, and hath said unto me, Let no man know any thing of the business whereabout I send thee, and what I have commanded thee: and I have appointed *my* servants to such and such a place.

3 Now therefore what is under thine hand? give *me* five *loaves of* bread in mine hand, or what there is present.

4 And the priest answered David, and said, *There is* no common bread under mine hand, but there is hallowed bread; if the young men have kept themselves at least from women.

5 And David answered the priest, and said unto him, Of a truth women *have been* kept from us about these three days, since I came out, and the vessels of the young men are holy, and *the bread is* in a manner common, yea, though it were sanctified this day in the vessel.

6 So the priest gave him hallowed *bread*: for there was no bread there but the shewbread, that was taken from before the Lord, to put hot bread in the day when it was taken away.

7 Now a certain man of the servants of Saul *was* there that day, detained before the Lord; and his name *was* Doeg, an Edomite, the chiefest of the herdmen that *belonged* to Saul.

8 And David said unto Ahimelech, And is there not here under thine hand spear or sword? for I have neither brought my sword nor my weapons with me, because the king's business required haste.

9 And the priest said, The sword of Goliath the Philistine, whom thou slewest in the valley of Elah, behold, it *is here* wrapped in a cloth behind the ephod: if thou wilt take that, take *it*: for *there is* no other save that here. And David said, *There is* none like that; give it me.

David Acts Insane

10 And David arose, and fled that day for fear of Saul, and went to Achish the king of Gath.

11 And the servants of Achish said unto him, *Is* not this David the king of the land? did they not sing one to another of him in dances, saying, Saul hath slain his thousands, and David his ten thousands?

12 And David laid up these words in his heart, and was sore afraid of Achish the king of Gath.

13 And he changed his behaviour before them, and feigned himself mad in their

---

32 1Sam. 19:5; Matt. 27:23; Luke 23:22

33 1Sam. 18:11; 20:7

42 1Sam. 1:17; 20:23

1 1 Sam. 14:3, also called *Ahiah* or *Abiathar*; 16:4; Mark 2:26; 16:4

4 Ex. 19:15; 25:30; Lev. 24:5; Zech. 7:3; Matt. 12:4

5 Lev. 8:26; 1Thess. 4:4

6 Lev. 24:8, 9; Matt. 12:3, 4; Mark 2:25, 26; Luke 6:3, 4

7 1Sam. 22:9

9 1Sam. 17:2, 50; 31:10

11 1Sam. 18:7; 29:5

12 Luke 2:19

hands, and scrabbled on the doors of the gate, and let his spittle fall down upon his beard.

14 Then said Achish unto his servants, Lo, ye see the man is mad: wherefore *then* have ye brought him to me?

15 Have I need of mad men, that ye have brought this *fellow* to play the mad man in my presence? shall this *fellow* come into my house?

CHAPTER 22
David Raises a Small Army

1 David therefore departed thence, and escaped to the cave Adullam: and when his brethren and all his father's house heard *it*, they went down thither to him.

2 And every one *that was* in distress, and every one that *was* in debt, and every one *that was* discontented, gathered themselves unto him; and he became a captain over them: and there were with him about four hundred men.

3 And David went thence to Mizpeh of Moab: and he said unto the king of Moab, Let my father and my mother, I pray thee, come forth, *and be* with you, till I know what God will do for me.

4 And he brought them before the king of Moab: and they dwelt with him all the while that David was in the hold.

5 And the prophet Gad said unto David, Abide not in the hold; depart, and get thee into the land of Judah. Then David departed, and came into the forest of Hareth.

Saul Kills the Priests Who Helped David

6 When Saul heard that David was discovered, and the men that *were* with him, (now Saul abode in Gibeah under a tree in Ramah, having his spear in his hand, and all his servants *were* standing about him;)

7 Then Saul said unto his servants that stood about him, Hear now, ye Benjamites; will the son of Jesse give every one of you fields and vineyards, *and* make you all captains of thousands, and captains of hundreds;

8 That all of you have conspired against me, and *there is* none that sheweth me that my son hath made a league with the son of Jesse, and *there is* none of you that is sorry for me, or sheweth unto me that my son hath stirred up my servant against me, to lie in wait, as at this day?

9 Then answered Doeg the Edomite, which was set over the servants of Saul, and

said, I saw the son of Jesse coming to Nob, to Ahimelech the son of Ahitub.

10 And he inquired of the LORD for him, and gave him victuals, and gave him the sword of Goliath the Philistine.

11 Then the king sent to call Ahimelech the priest, the son of Ahitub, and all his father's house, the priests that *were* in Nob: and they came all of them to the king.

12 And Saul said, Hear now, thou son of Ahitub. And he answered, Here I *am*, my lord.

13 And Saul said unto him, Why have ye conspired against me, thou and the son of Jesse, in that thou hast given him bread, and a sword, and hast inquired of God for him, that he should rise against me, to lie in wait, as at this day?

14 Then Ahimelech answered the king, and said, And who *is so* faithful among all thy servants as David, which is the king's son-in-law, and goeth at thy bidding, and is honourable in thine house?

15 Did I then begin to inquire of God for him? be it far from me: let not the king impute *any* thing unto his servant, *nor* to all the house of my father: for thy servant knew nothing of all this, less or more.

16 And the king said, Thou shalt surely die, Ahimelech, thou, and all thy father's house.

17 And the king said unto the footmen that stood about him, Turn, and slay the priests of the LORD; because their hand also *is* with David, and because they knew when he fled, and did not shew it to me. But the servants of the king would not put forth their hand to fall upon the priests of the LORD.

18 And the king said to Doeg, Turn thou, and fall upon the priests. And Doeg the Edomite turned, and he fell upon the priests, and slew on that day fourscore and five persons that did wear a linen ephod.

19 And Nob, the city of the priests, smote he with the edge of the sword, both men and women, children and sucklings, and oxen, and asses, and sheep, with the edge of the sword.

20 And one of the sons of Ahimelech the son of Ahitub, named Abiathar, escaped, and fled after David.

21 And Abiathar shewed David that Saul had slain the LORD's priests.

22 And David said unto Abiathar, I knew *it* that day, when Doeg the Edomite *was* there, that he would surely tell Saul: I have occasioned *the death* of all the persons of thy father's house.

23 Abide thou with me, fear not: for he that

Cross references (center column):

1 2Sam. 23:13

2 Judg. 11:3

5 2Sam. 24:11; 1Chr. 21:9; 2Chr. 29:25

7 1Sam. 8:14

8 1Sam. 18:3; 20:2, 30

9 1Sam. 14:3; 21:1, 7; 22:1-3

10 Num. 27:21; 1Sam. 21:6, 9

17 Ex. 1:17

18 1Sam. 2:31

19 1Sam. 12:9, 11

20 1Sam. 2:33; 23:6

23 1Kgs. 2:26

seeketh my life seeketh thy life: but with me thou *shalt be* in safeguard.

CHAPTER 23
David Rescues Keilah

1 Then they told David, saying, Behold, the Philistines fight against Keilah, and they rob the threshingfloors.

2 Therefore David inquired of the LORD, saying, Shall I go and smite these Philistines? And the LORD said unto David, Go, and smite the Philistines, and save Keilah.

3 And David's men said unto him, Behold, we be afraid here in Judah: how much more then if we come to Keilah against the armies of the Philistines?

4 Then David inquired of the LORD yet again. And the LORD answered him and said, Arise, go down to Keilah; for I will deliver the Philistines into thine hand.

5 So David and his men went to Keilah, and fought with the Philistines, and brought away their cattle, and smote them with a great slaughter. So David saved the inhabitants of Keilah.

Saul Pursues David

6 And it came to pass, when Abiathar the son of Ahimelech fled to David to Keilah, *that* he came down *with* an ephod in his hand.

7 And it was told Saul that David was come to Keilah. And Saul said, God hath delivered him into mine hand; for he is shut in, by entering into a town that hath gates and bars.

8 And Saul called all the people together to war, to go down to Keilah, to besiege David and his men.

9 And David knew that Saul secretly practised mischief against him; and he said to Abiathar the priest, Bring hither the ephod.

10 Then said David, O LORD God of Israel, thy servant hath certainly heard that Saul seeketh to come to Keilah, to destroy the city for my sake.

11 Will the men of Keilah deliver me up into his hand? will Saul come down, as thy servant hath heard? O LORD God of Israel, I beseech thee, tell thy servant. And the LORD said, He will come down.

12 Then said David, Will the men of Keilah deliver me and my men into the hand of Saul? And the LORD said, They will deliver *thee* up.

13 Then David and his men, *which were* about six hundred, arose and departed out of Keilah, and went whithersoever they could go. And it was told Saul that David was escaped from Keilah; and he forbare to go forth.

14 And David abode in the wilderness in strong holds, and remained in a mountain in the wilderness of Ziph. And Saul sought him every day, but God delivered him not into his hand.

15 And David saw that Saul was come out to seek his life: and David *was* in the wilderness of Ziph in a wood.

16 And Jonathan Saul's son arose, and went to David into the wood, and strengthened his hand in God.

17 And he said unto him, Fear not: for the hand of Saul my father shall not find thee; and thou shalt be king over Israel, and I shall be next unto thee; and that also Saul my father knoweth.

18 And they two made a covenant before the LORD: and David abode in the wood, and Jonathan went to his house.

19 Then came up the Ziphites to Saul to Gibeah, saying, Doth not David hide himself with us in strong holds in the wood, in the hill of Hachilah, which *is* on the south of Jeshimon?

20 Now therefore, O king, come down according to all the desire of thy soul to come down; and our part *shall be* to deliver him into the king's hand.

21 And Saul said, Blessed *be* ye of the LORD; for ye have compassion on me.

22 Go, I pray you, prepare yet, and know and see his place where his haunt is, *and* who hath seen him there: for it is told me *that* he dealeth very subtilly.

23 See therefore, and take knowledge of all the lurking places where he hideth himself, and come ye again to me with the certainty, and I will go with you: and it shall come to pass, if he be in the land, that I will search him out throughout all the thousands of Judah.

24 And they arose, and went to Ziph before Saul: but David and his men *were* in the wilderness of Maon, in the plain on the south of Jeshimon.

25 Saul also and his men went to seek *him*. And they told David: wherefore he came down into a rock, and abode in the wilderness of Maon. And when Saul heard *that*, he pursued after David in the wilderness of Maon.

26 And Saul went on this side of the mountain, and David and his men on that side of the mountain: and David made haste to get

---

Cross references (center column):

1 Josh. 15:44
2 1Sam. 12:4, 6, 9; 30:8; 2Sam. 5:19, 23
6 1Sam. 22:20
9 Num. 27:21; 1Sam. 30:7
10 1Sam. 22:19
13 1Sam. 22:2; 25:13
14 Josh. 15:55; Ps. 11:1; 54:3, 4
17 1Sam. 24:20
18 1Sam. 18:3; 20:16, 42; 2Sam. 21:7
19 1Sam. 26:1
20 Ps. 54:3
24 Josh. 15:55; 1Sam. 25:2
26 Ps. 17:9; 31:22

away for fear of Saul; for Saul and his men compassed David and his men round about to take them.

27 But there came a messenger unto Saul, saying, Haste thee, and come; for the Philistines have invaded the land.

28 Wherefore Saul returned from pursuing after David, and went against the Philistines: therefore they called that place Sela-hammahlekoth.

29 And David went up from thence, and dwelt in strong holds at En-gedi.

CHAPTER 24
David Spares Saul in a Cave

1 And it came to pass, when Saul was returned from following the Philistines, that it was told him, saying, Behold, David is in the wilderness of En-gedi.

2 Then Saul took three thousand chosen men out of all Israel, and went to seek David and his men upon the rocks of the wild goats.

3 And he came to the sheepcotes by the way, where was a cave; and Saul went in to cover his feet: and David and his men remained in the sides of the cave.

4 And the men of David said unto him, Behold the day of which the LORD said unto thee, Behold, I will deliver thine enemy into thine hand, that thou mayest do to him as it shall seem good unto thee. Then David arose, and cut off the skirt of Saul's robe privily.

5 And it came to pass afterward, that David's heart smote him, because he had cut off Saul's skirt.

6 And he said unto his men, The LORD forbid that I should do this thing unto my master, the LORD's anointed, to stretch forth mine hand against him, seeing he is the anointed of the LORD.

7 So David stayed his servants with these words, and suffered them not to rise against Saul. But Saul rose up out of the cave, and went on his way.

8 David also arose afterward, and went out of the cave, and cried after Saul, saying, My lord the king. And when Saul looked behind him, David stooped with his face to the earth, and bowed himself.

9 And David said to Saul, Wherefore hearest thou men's words, saying, Behold, David seeketh thy hurt?

10 Behold, this day thine eyes have seen how that the LORD had delivered thee today into mine hand in the cave: and some bade me kill thee: but mine eye spared thee; and I said, I will not put forth mine hand against

my lord; for he is the LORD's anointed.

11 Moreover, my father, see, yea, see the skirt of thy robe in my hand: for in that I cut off the skirt of thy robe, and killed thee not, know thou and see that there is neither evil nor transgression in mine hand, and I have not sinned against thee; yet thou huntest my soul to take it.

12 The LORD judge between me and thee, and the LORD avenge me of thee: but mine hand shall not be upon thee.

13 As saith the proverb of the ancients, Wickedness proceedeth from the wicked: but mine hand shall not be upon thee.

14 After whom is the king of Israel come out? after whom dost thou pursue? after a dead dog, after a flea.

15 The LORD therefore be judge, and judge between me and thee, and see, and plead my cause, and deliver me out of thine hand.

16 And it came to pass, when David had made an end of speaking these words unto Saul, that Saul said, Is this thy voice, my son David? And Saul lifted up his voice, and wept.

17 And he said to David, Thou art more righteous than I: for thou hast rewarded me good, whereas I have rewarded thee evil.

18 And thou hast shewed this day how that thou hast dealt well with me: forasmuch as when the LORD had delivered me into thine hand, thou killedst me not.

19 For if a man find his enemy, will he let him go well away? wherefore the LORD reward thee good for that thou hast done unto me this day.

20 And now, behold, I know well that thou shalt surely be king, and that the kingdom of Israel shall be established in thine hand.

21 Swear now therefore unto me by the LORD, that thou wilt not cut off my seed after me, and that thou wilt not destroy my name out of my father's house.

22 And David sware unto Saul. And Saul went home; but David and his men gat them up unto the hold.

CHAPTER 25
Samuel's Death

1 And Samuel died; and all the Israelites were gathered together, and lamented him, and buried him in his house at Ramah.

David and Abigail

And David arose, and went down to the wilderness of Paran.

2 And there was a man in Maon, whose possessions were in Carmel; and the man

---

27 2Kgs. 19:9

29 2Chr. 20:2

1 1Sam. 23:28

2 Ps. 38:12

3 Judg. 3:24; Ps. 141:6

4 1Sam. 26:8

5 2Sam. 24:10

6 1Sam. 26:11

7 Ps. 7:4; Matt. 5:44; Rom. 12:17, 19

9 Ps. 141:6; Prov. 16:28; 17:9

11 1Sam. 26:20; Ps. 7:3; 35:7

12 Gen. 16:5; Judg. 11:27; 1Sam. 26:10; Job 5:8

14 1Sam. 17:43; 26:20; 2Sam. 9:8

15 1Sam. 24:12; 2Chr. 24:22; Ps. 35:1; 43:1; 119:154; Mic. 7:9

16 1Sam. 26:17

17 Gen. 38:26; 1Sam. 26:21; Matt. 5:44

18 1Sam. 23:12; 26:8, 23

20 1Sam. 23:17

21 Gen. 21:23; 2Sam. 21:6, 8

22 1Sam. 23:29

1 Gen. 21:21; Num. 20:29; Deut. 34:8; 1Sam. 28:3; Ps. 120:5

2 Josh. 15:55; 1Sam. 23:24

was very great, and he had three thousand sheep, and a thousand goats: and he was shearing his sheep in Carmel.

3 Now the name of the man *was* Nabal; and the name of his wife Abigail: and *she was* a woman of good understanding, and of a beautiful countenance: but the man *was* churlish and evil in his doings; and he *was* of the house of Caleb.

4 And David heard in the wilderness that Nabal did shear his sheep.

5 And David sent out ten young men, and David said unto the young men, Get you up to Carmel, and go to Nabal, and greet him in my name:

6 And thus shall ye say to him that liveth *in prosperity*, Peace *be* both to thee, and peace *be* to thine house, and peace *be* unto all that thou hast.

7 And now I have heard that thou hast shearers: now thy shepherds which were with us, we hurt them not, neither was there ought missing unto them, all the while they were in Carmel.

8 Ask thy young men, and they will shew thee. Wherefore let the young men find favour in thine eyes: for we come in a good day: give, I pray thee, whatsoever cometh to thine hand unto thy servants, and to thy son David.

9 And when David's young men came, they spake to Nabal according to all those words in the name of David, and ceased.

10 And Nabal answered David's servants, and said, Who *is* David? and who *is* the son of Jesse? there be many servants now a days that break away every man from his master.

11 Shall I then take my bread, and my water, and my flesh that I have killed for my shearers, and give *it* unto men, whom I know not whence they *be*?

12 So David's young men turned their way, and went again, and came and told him all those sayings.

13 And David said unto his men, Gird ye on every man his sword. And they girded on every man his sword; and David also girded on his sword: and there went up after David about four hundred men; and two hundred abode by the stuff.

14 But one of the young men told Abigail, Nabal's wife, saying, Behold, David sent messengers out of the wilderness to salute our master; and he railed on them.

15 But the men *were* very good unto us, and we were not hurt, neither missed we any thing, as long as we were conversant with them, when we were in the fields:

16 They were a wall unto us both by night and day, all the while we were with them keeping the sheep.

17 Now therefore know and consider what thou wilt do; for evil is determined against our master, and against all his household: for he *is such* a son of Belial, that *a man* cannot speak to him.

18 Then Abigail made haste, and took two hundred loaves, and two bottles of wine, and five sheep ready dressed, and five measures of parched *corn*, and an hundred clusters of raisins, and two hundred cakes of figs, and laid *them* on asses.

19 And she said unto her servants, Go on before me; behold, I come after you. But she told not her husband Nabal.

20 And it was *so, as* she rode on the ass, that she came down by the covert of the hill, and, behold, David and his men came down against her; and she met them.

21 Now David had said, Surely in vain have I kept all that this *fellow* hath in the wilderness, so that nothing was missed of all that *pertained* unto him: and he hath requited me evil for good.

22 So and more also do God unto the enemies of David, if I leave of all that *pertain* to him by the morning light any that pisseth against the wall.

23 And when Abigail saw David, she hasted, and lighted off the ass, and fell before David on her face, and bowed herself to the ground,

24 And fell at his feet, and said, Upon me, my lord, *upon* me *let this* iniquity *be*: and let thine handmaid, I pray thee, speak in thine audience, and hear the words of thine handmaid.

25 Let not my lord, I pray thee, regard this man of Belial, *even* Nabal: for as his name *is*, so *is* he; Nabal *is* his name, and folly *is* with him: but I thine handmaid saw not the young men of my lord, whom thou didst send.

26 Now therefore, my lord, *as* the Lord liveth, and *as* thy soul liveth, seeing the Lord hath withholden thee from coming to *shed* blood, and from avenging thyself with thine own hand, now let thine enemies, and they that seek evil to my lord, be as Nabal.

27 And now this blessing which thine handmaid hath brought unto my lord, let it even be given unto the young men that follow my lord.

28 I pray thee, forgive the trespass of thine handmaid: for the Lord will certainly make my lord a sure house; because my lord

---

Center cross-reference column:

4 Gen. 38:13; 2Sam. 13:23

6 1Chr. 12:18; Ps. 122:7; Luke 10:5

7 1Sam. 25:15, 21

8 Neh. 8:10; Esth. 9:19

10 Judg. 9:28; Ps. 73:7, 8; 123:3, 4

11 Judg. 8:6

13 1Sam. 30:24

15 1Sam. 25:7

16 Ex. 14:22; Job 1:10

17 Deut. 13:13; Judg. 19:22; 1Sam. 20:7

18 Gen. 32:13; Prov. 18:16; 21:14

19 Gen. 32:16, 20

21 Ps. 109:5; Prov. 17:13

22 Ruth 1:17; 1Sam. 3:17; 20:13, 16; 25:34; 1Kgs. 14:10; 21:21; 2Kgs. 9:8

23 Josh. 15:18; Judg. 1:14

26 Gen. 20:6; 1Sam. 25:33; 2Sam. 18:32; 2Kgs. 2:2; Rom. 12:19

27 Gen. 33:11; 1Sam. 30:26; 2Kgs. 5:15

28 1Sam. 18:17; 24:11; 2Sam. 7:11, 27; 1Kgs. 9:5; 1Chr. 17:10, 25

fighteth the battles of the LORD, and evil hath not been found in thee *all* thy days.

29 Yet a man is risen to pursue thee, and to seek thy soul: but the soul of my lord shall be bound in the bundle of life with the LORD thy God; and the souls of thine enemies, them shall he sling out, *as out* of the middle of a sling.

30 And it shall come to pass, when the LORD shall have done to my lord according to all the good that he hath spoken concerning thee, and shall have appointed thee ruler over Israel;

31 That this shall be no grief unto thee, nor offence of heart unto my lord, either that thou hast shed blood causeless, or that my lord hath avenged himself: but when the LORD shall have dealt well with my lord, then remember thine handmaid.

32 And David said to Abigail, Blessed *be* the LORD God of Israel, which sent thee this day to meet me:

33 And blessed *be* thy advice, and blessed *be* thou, which hast kept me this day from coming to *shed* blood, and from avenging myself with mine own hand.

34 For in very deed, *as* the LORD God of Israel liveth, which hath kept me back from hurting thee, except thou hadst hasted and come to meet me, surely there had not been left unto Nabal by the morning light any that pisseth against the wall.

35 So David received of her hand *that* which she had brought him, and said unto her, Go up in peace to thine house; see, I have hearkened to thy voice, and have accepted thy person.

36 And Abigail came to Nabal; and, behold, he held a feast in his house, like the feast of a king; and Nabal's heart *was* merry within him, for he *was* very drunken: wherefore she told him nothing, less or more, until the morning light.

37 But it came to pass in the morning, when the wine was gone out of Nabal, and his wife had told him these things, that his heart died within him, and he became *as* a stone.

38 And it came to pass about ten days *after*, that the LORD smote Nabal, that he died.

39 And when David heard that Nabal was dead, he said, Blessed *be* the LORD, that hath pleaded the cause of my reproach from the hand of Nabal, and hath kept his servant from evil: for the LORD hath returned the wickedness of Nabal upon his own head. And David sent and communed with Abigail, to take her to him to wife.

40 And when the servants of David were come to Abigail to Carmel, they spake unto her, saying, David sent us unto thee, to take thee to him to wife.

41 And she arose, and bowed herself on *her* face to the earth, and said, Behold, *let* thine handmaid *be* a servant to wash the feet of the servants of my lord.

42 And Abigail hasted, and arose, and rode upon an ass, with five damsels of hers that went after her; and she went after the messengers of David, and became his wife.

43 David also took Ahinoam of Jezreel; and they were also both of them his wives.

44 But Saul had given Michal his daughter, David's wife, to Phalti the son of Laish, which *was* of Gallim.

CHAPTER 26
David Spares Saul Again

1 And the Ziphites came unto Saul to Gibeah, saying, Doth not David hide himself in the hill of Hachilah, *which is* before Jeshimon?

2 Then Saul arose, and went down to the wilderness of Ziph, having three thousand chosen men of Israel with him, to seek David in the wilderness of Ziph.

3 And Saul pitched in the hill of Hachilah, which *is* before Jeshimon, by the way. But David abode in the wilderness, and he saw that Saul came after him into the wilderness.

4 David therefore sent out spies, and understood that Saul was come in very deed.

5 And David arose, and came to the place where Saul had pitched: and David beheld the place where Saul lay, and Abner the son of Ner, the captain of his host: and Saul lay in the trench, and the people pitched round about him.

6 Then answered David and said to Ahimelech the Hittite, and to Abishai the son of Zeruiah, brother to Joab, saying, Who will go down with me to Saul to the camp? And Abishai said, I will go down with thee.

7 So David and Abishai came to the people by night: and, behold, Saul lay sleeping within the trench, and his spear stuck in the ground at his bolster: but Abner and the people lay round about him.

8 Then said Abishai to David, God hath delivered thine enemy into thine hand this day: now therefore let me smite him, I pray thee, with the spear even to the earth at once, and I will not *smite* him the second time.

9 And David said to Abishai, Destroy him

Center column references:

29 Jer. 10:18

32 Gen. 24:27; Ex. 18:10; Ps. 41:13; 72:18; Luke 1:68

33 1Sam. 25:26

34 1Sam. 25:22, 26

35 Gen. 19:21; 1Sam. 20:42; 2Sam. 15:9; 2Kgs. 5:19; Luke 7:50; 8:48

36 2Sam. 13:23

39 1Sam. 25:26, 32; 34; 1Kgs. 2:44; Ps. 7:16; Prov. 22:23

41 Ruth 2:10, 13; Prov. 15:33

43 Josh. 15:56; 1Sam. 27:3; 30:5

44 2Sam. 3:14, 15; Isa. 10:30

1 1Sam. 23:19

5 1Sam. 14:50; 17:20, 55

6 Judg. 7:10, 11; 1Chr. 2:16

8 1Sam. 24:18

9 1Sam. 24:6, 7; 2Sam. 1:16

not: for who can stretch forth his hand against the LORD's anointed, and be guiltless?

10 David said furthermore, As the LORD liveth, the LORD shall smite him; or his day shall come to die; or he shall descend into battle, and perish.

11 The LORD forbid that I should stretch forth mine hand against the LORD's anointed: but, I pray thee, take thou now the spear that is at his bolster, and the cruse of water, and let us go.

12 So David took the spear and the cruse of water from Saul's bolster; and they gat them away, and no man saw it, nor knew it, neither awaked: for they were all asleep; because a deep sleep from the LORD was fallen upon them.

13 Then David went over to the other side, and stood on the top of an hill afar off; a great space being between them:

14 And David cried to the people, and to Abner the son of Ner, saying, Answerest thou not, Abner? Then Abner answered and said, Who art thou that criest to the king?

15 And David said to Abner, Art not thou a valiant man? and who is like to thee in Israel? wherefore then hast thou not kept thy lord the king? for there came one of the people in to destroy the king thy lord.

16 This thing is not good that thou hast done. As the LORD liveth, ye are worthy to die, because ye have not kept your master, the LORD's anointed. And now see where the king's spear is, and the cruse of water that was at his bolster.

17 And Saul knew David's voice, and said, Is this thy voice, my son David? And David said, It is my voice, my lord, O king.

18 And he said, Wherefore doth my lord thus pursue after his servant? for what have I done? or what evil is in mine hand?

19 Now therefore, I pray thee, let my lord the king hear the words of his servant. If the LORD have stirred thee up against me, let him accept an offering: but if they be the children of men, cursed be they before the LORD; for they have driven me out this day from abiding in the inheritance of the LORD, saying, Go, serve other gods.

20 Now therefore, let not my blood fall to the earth before the face of the LORD: for the

king of Israel is come out to seek a flea, as when one doth hunt a partridge in the mountains.

21 Then said Saul, I have sinned: return, my son David: for I will no more do thee harm, because my soul was precious in thine eyes this day: behold, I have played the fool, and have erred exceedingly.

22 And David answered and said, Behold the king's spear! and let one of the young men come over and fetch it.

23 The LORD render to every man his righteousness and his faithfulness: for the LORD delivered thee into my hand today, but I would not stretch forth mine hand against the LORD's anointed.

24 And, behold, as thy life was much set by this day in mine eyes, so let my life be much set by in the eyes of the LORD, and let him deliver me out of all tribulation.

25 Then Saul said to David, Blessed be thou, my son David: thou shalt both do great things, and also shalt still prevail. So David went on his way, and Saul returned to his place.

CHAPTER 27
David Returns to Gath

1 And David said in his heart, I shall now perish one day by the hand of Saul: there is nothing better for me than that I should speedily escape into the land of the Philistines; and Saul shall despair of me, to seek me any more in any coast of Israel: so shall I escape out of his hand.

2 And David arose, and he passed over with the six hundred men that were with him unto Achish, the son of Maoch, king of Gath.

3 And David dwelt with Achish at Gath, he and his men, every man with his household, even David with his two wives, Ahinoam the Jezreelitess, and Abigail the Carmelitess, Nabal's wife.

4 And it was told Saul that David was fled to Gath: and he sought no more again for him.

5 And David said unto Achish, If I have now found grace in thine eyes, let them give me a place in some town in the country, that I may dwell there: for why should thy servant dwell in the royal city with thee?

26:25 Saul said to David, Blessed be thou. For the second time, David had found Saul asleep at night while in pursuit of the young fugitive. This time, David took the king's spear. After David had awakened him by calling from a distant hill, Saul confessed his folly in chasing David, uttering a blessing and a prophecy, "Thou shalt both do great things, and also shalt still prevail."

6 Then Achish gave him Ziklag that day: wherefore Ziklag pertaineth unto the kings of Judah unto this day.

7 And the time that David dwelt in the country of the Philistines was a full year and four months.

8 And David and his men went up, and invaded the Geshurites, and the Gezrites, and the Amalekites: for those *nations were* of old the inhabitants of the land, as thou goest to Shur, even unto the land of Egypt.

9 And David smote the land, and left neither man nor woman alive, and took away the sheep, and the oxen, and the asses, and the camels, and the apparel, and returned, and came to Achish.

10 And Achish said, Whither have ye made a road today? And David said, Against the south of Judah, and against the south of the Jerahmeelites, and against the south of the Kenites.

11 And David saved neither man nor woman alive, to bring *tidings* to Gath, saying, Lest they should tell on us, saying, So did David, and so *will be* his manner all the while he dwelleth in the country of the Philistines.

12 And Achish believed David, saying, He hath made his people Israel utterly to abhor him; therefore he shall be my servant for ever.

CHAPTER 28

1 And it came to pass in those days, that the Philistines gathered their armies together for warfare, to fight with Israel. And Achish said unto David, Know thou assuredly, that thou shalt go out with me to battle, thou and thy men.

2 And David said to Achish, Surely thou shalt know what thy servant can do. And Achish said to David, Therefore will I make thee keeper of mine head for ever.

Saul and the Medium at Endor

3 Now Samuel was dead, and all Israel had lamented him, and buried him in Ramah, even in his own city. And Saul had put away those that had familiar spirits, and the wizards, out of the land.

4 And the Philistines gathered themselves together, and came and pitched in Shunem: and Saul gathered all Israel together, and they pitched in Gilboa.

5 And when Saul saw the host of the Philistines, he was afraid, and his heart greatly trembled.

6 And when Saul inquired of the LORD, the LORD answered him not, neither by dreams, nor by Urim, nor by prophets.

7 Then said Saul unto his servants, Seek me a woman that hath a familiar spirit, that I may go to her, and inquire of her. And his servants said to him, Behold, *there is* a woman that hath a familiar spirit at Endor.

8 And Saul disguised himself, and put on other raiment, and he went, and two men with him, and they came to the woman by night: and he said, I pray thee, divine unto me by the familiar spirit, and bring me *him* up, whom I shall name unto thee.

9 And the woman said unto him, Behold, thou knowest what Saul hath done, how he hath cut off those that have familiar spirits, and the wizards, out of the land: wherefore then layest thou a snare for my life, to cause me to die?

10 And Saul sware to her by the LORD, saying, *As* the LORD liveth, there shall no punishment happen to thee for this thing.

11 Then said the woman, Whom shall I bring up unto thee? And he said, Bring me up Samuel.

12 And when the woman saw Samuel, she cried with a loud voice: and the woman spake to Saul, saying, Why hast thou deceived me? for thou *art* Saul.

13 And the king said unto her, Be not afraid: for what sawest thou? And the woman said unto Saul, I saw gods ascending out of the earth.

14 And he said unto her, What form *is* he of? And she said, An old man cometh up; and he *is* covered with a mantle. And Saul perceived that it *was* Samuel, and he stooped with *his* face to the ground, and bowed himself.

15 And Samuel said to Saul, Why hast thou

Cross references

6 Josh. 15:31; 19:5

7 1Sam. 29:3

8 Gen. 25:18; Ex. 17:16; Josh. 13:2; 16:10; Judg. 1:29; 1Sam. 15:7, 8

10 Judg. 1:16; 1Chr. 2:9, 25

1 1Sam. 29:1

3 Ex. 22:18; Lev. 19:31; 20:27; Deut. 18:10, 11; 1Sam. 25:1; 28:9

4 Josh. 19:18; 1Sam. 31:1; 2Kgs. 4:8

5 Job 18:11

6 Ex. 28:30; Num. 12:6; 27:21; Deut. 33:8; 1Sam. 14:37; Prov. 1:28; Lam. 2:9

8 Deut. 18:11; 1Chr. 10:13; Isa. 8:19

9 1Sam. 28:3

13 Ex. 22:28

14 1Sam. 15:27; 2Kgs. 2:8, 13

15 1Sam. 18:12; 28:6; Prov. 5:11-13; 14:14

28:7 Prohibited by the Law of Moses (Lev. 19:31), necromancy had been largely suppressed in Israel by Saul. Since Samuel had died several years earlier, and God had rejected Saul as king and removed His Spirit from Saul as a means of divine guidance, the desperate seventy-year-old monarch seeks counsel through a spiritist, a medium, who was still practicing as a presumed channeler through whom the dead might communicate. His appearance has been explained as 1) an elaborate hoax, 2) a demonic impersonation, or 3) the actual appearance of Samuel. This strange apparition in no wise endorses any form of spiritism, but the predictions of defeat and death for Saul were accurate (1 Sam. 31:6). True believers are never to be involved in spiritism, sorcery, or demonic, magical arts (see Isa. 47:9, 12; 57:3).

disquieted me, to bring me up? And Saul answered, I am sore distressed; for the Philistines make war against me, and God is departed from me, and answereth me no more, neither by prophets, nor by dreams: therefore I have called thee, that thou mayest make known unto me what I shall do.

16 Then said Samuel, Wherefore then dost thou ask of me, seeing the Lord is departed from thee, and is become thine enemy?

17 And the Lord hath done to him, as he spake by me: for the Lord hath rent the kingdom out of thine hand, and given it to thy neighbour, *even* to David:

18 Because thou obeyedst not the voice of the Lord, nor executedst his fierce wrath upon Amalek, therefore hath the Lord done this thing unto thee this day.

19 Moreover the Lord will also deliver Israel with thee into the hand of the Philistines: and to morrow *shalt* thou and thy sons *be* with me: the Lord also shall deliver the host of Israel into the hand of the Philistines.

20 Then Saul fell straightway all along on the earth, and was sore afraid, because of the words of Samuel: and there was no strength in him; for he had eaten no bread all the day, nor all the night.

21 And the woman came unto Saul, and saw that he was sore troubled, and said unto him, Behold, thine handmaid hath obeyed thy voice, and I have put my life in my hand, and have hearkened unto thy words which thou spakest unto me.

22 Now therefore, I pray thee, hearken thou also unto the voice of thine handmaid, and let me set a morsel of bread before thee; and eat, that thou mayest have strength, when thou goest on thy way.

23 But he refused, and said, I will not eat. But his servants, together with the woman, compelled him; and he hearkened unto their voice. So he arose from the earth, and sat upon the bed.

24 And the woman had a fat calf in the house; and she hasted, and killed it, and took flour, and kneaded *it*, and did bake unleavened bread thereof:

25 And she brought *it* before Saul, and before his servants; and they did eat. Then they rose up, and went away that night.

Chapter 29

The Philistines Question David's Loyalty

1 Now the Philistines gathered together all their armies to Aphek: and the Israelites pitched by a fountain which *is* in Jezreel.

2 And the lords of the Philistines passed on by hundreds, and by thousands: but David and his men passed on in the rereward with Achish.

3 Then said the princes of the Philistines, What *do* these Hebrews *here?* And Achish said unto the princes of the Philistines, *Is* not this David, the servant of Saul the king of Israel, which hath been with me these days, or these years, and I have found no fault in him since he fell *unto me* unto this day?

4 And the princes of the Philistines were wroth with him; and the princes of the Philistines said unto him, Make this fellow return, that he may go again to his place which thou hast appointed him, and let him not go down with us to battle, lest in the battle he be an adversary to us: for wherewith should he reconcile himself unto his master? *should it* not *be* with the heads of these men?

5 *Is* not this David, of whom they sang one to another in dances, saying, Saul slew his thousands, and David his ten thousands?

6 Then Achish called David, and said unto him, Surely, *as* the Lord liveth, thou hast been upright, and thy going out and thy coming in with me in the host *is* good in my sight: for I have not found evil in thee since the day of thy coming unto me unto this day: nevertheless the lords favour thee not.

7 Wherefore now return, and go in peace, that thou displease not the lords of the Philistines.

8 And David said unto Achish, But what have I done? and what hast thou found in thy servant so long as I have been with thee unto this day, that I may not go fight against the enemies of my lord the king?

9 And Achish answered and said to David, I know that thou *art* good in my sight, as an angel of God: notwithstanding the princes of the Philistines have said, He shall not go up with us to the battle.

10 Wherefore now rise up early in the morning with thy master's servants that are come with thee: and as soon as ye be up early in the morning, and have light, depart.

11 So David and his men rose up early to depart in the morning, to return into the land of the Philistines. And the Philistines went up to Jezreel.

Chapter 30

David Defeats the Amalekites

1 And it came to pass, when David and his men were come to Ziklag on the third day,

---

Cross-references (center column):

17 1Sam. 15:28.

18 1Sam. 15:9; 1Kgs. 20:42; 1Chr. 10:13; Jer. 48:10.

21 Judg. 12:3; 1Sam. 19:5; Job 13:14.

1 1Sam. 4:1; 28:1.

2 1Sam. 28:1, 2.

3 1Sam. 27:7; Dan. 6:5.

4 1Sam. 14:21; 1Chr. 12:19.

5 1Sam. 18:7; 21:11.

6 1Sam. 29:2; 2Sam. 3:25; 2Kgs. 19:27.

9 1Sam. 29:4; 2Sam. 14:17, 20; 19:27.

11 2Sam. 4:4.

1 1Sam. 15:7; 27:8.

that the Amalekites had invaded the south, and Ziklag, and smitten Ziklag, and burned it with fire;

2 And had taken the women captives, that *were* therein: they slew not any, either great or small, but carried *them* away, and went on their way.

3 So David and his men came to the city, and, behold, *it was* burned with fire; and their wives, and their sons, and their daughters, were taken captives.

4 Then David and the people that *were* with him lifted up their voice and wept, until they had no more power to weep.

5 And David's two wives were taken captives, Ahinoam the Jezreelitess, and Abigail the wife of Nabal the Carmelite.

6 And David was greatly distressed; for the people spake of stoning him, because the soul of all the people was grieved, every man for his sons and for his daughters: but David encouraged himself in the LORD his God.

7 And David said to Abiathar the priest, Ahimelech's son, I pray thee, bring me hither the ephod. And Abiathar brought thither the ephod to David.

8 And David inquired at the LORD, saying, Shall I pursue after this troop? shall I overtake them? And he answered him, Pursue: for thou shalt surely overtake *them*, and without fail recover *all*.

9 So David went, he and the six hundred men that *were* with him, and came to the brook Besor, where those that were left behind stayed.

10 But David pursued, he and four hundred men: for two hundred abode behind, which were so faint that they could not go over the brook Besor.

11 And they found an Egyptian in the field, and brought him to David, and gave him bread, and he did eat; and they made him drink water;

12 And they gave him a piece of a cake of figs, and two clusters of raisins: and when he had eaten, his spirit came again to him: for he had eaten no bread, nor drunk *any* water, three days and three nights.

13 And David said unto him, To whom *belongest* thou? and whence *art* thou? And he said, I *am* a young man of Egypt, servant to an Amalekite; and my master left me, because three days agone I fell sick.

14 We made an invasion *upon* the south of the Cherethites, and upon *the coast* which *belongeth* to Judah, and upon the south of Caleb; and we burned Ziklag with fire.

15 And David said to him, Canst thou bring me down to this company? And he said, Swear unto me by God, that thou wilt neither kill me, nor deliver me into the hands of my master, and I will bring thee down to this company.

16 And when he had brought him down, behold, *they were* spread abroad upon all the earth, eating and drinking, and dancing, because of all the great spoil that they had taken out of the land of the Philistines, and out of the land of Judah.

17 And David smote them from the twilight even unto the evening of the next day: and there escaped not a man of them, save four hundred young men, which rode upon camels, and fled.

18 And David recovered all that the Amalekites had carried away: and David rescued his two wives.

19 And there was nothing lacking to them, neither small nor great, neither sons nor daughters, neither spoil, nor any *thing* that they had taken to them: David recovered all.

20 And David took all the flocks and the herds, *which* they drave before those *other* cattle, and said, This *is* David's spoil.

21 And David came to the two hundred men, which were so faint that they could not follow David, whom they had made also to abide at the brook Besor: and they went forth to meet David, and to meet the people that *were* with him: and when David came near to the people, he saluted them.

22 Then answered all the wicked men and *men* of Belial, of those that went with David, and said, Because they went not with us, we will not give them *ought* of the spoil that we have recovered, save to every man his wife and his children, that they may lead *them* away, and depart.

23 Then said David, Ye shall not do so, my brethren, with that which the LORD hath given us, who hath preserved us, and delivered the company that came against us into our hand.

---

5 1Sam. 25:42, 43; 2Sam. 2:2

6 Ex. 17:4; Ps. 42:5; 56:3, 4, 11; Hab. 3:17, 18

7 1Sam. 23:6, 9

8 1Sam. 23:2, 4

10 1Sam. 30:21

12 Judg. 15:19; 1Sam. 14:27

14 Josh. 14:13; 15:13; 1Sam. 30:16; 2Sam. 8:18; 1Kgs. 1:38, 44; Ezek. 25:16; Zeph. 2:5

16 1Thess. 5:3

19 1Sam. 30:8

21 1Sam. 30:10

22 Deut. 13:13; Judg. 19:22

30:1–20 David and his men were come to Ziklag. In a closing incident in 1 Samuel, David and his men had been living in exile from Saul in Ziklag, a Philistine city. The city was attacked and burned again by the Amalekites on a rampage. Abiathar the priest prophesies to David that his army would conquer the Amalekites. David then chased the attackers, recovered all they had taken and slew the Amalekite raiders, thus fulfilling Abiathar's prophecy.

24 For who will hearken unto you in this matter? but as his part *is* that goeth down to the battle, so *shall* his part *be* that tarrieth by the stuff: they shall part alike.

25 And it was *so* from that day forward, that he made it a statute and an ordinance for Israel unto this day.

26 And when David came to Ziklag, he sent of the spoil unto the elders of Judah, *even* to his friends, saying, Behold a present for you of the spoil of the enemies of the LORD;

27 To *them* which *were* in Beth-el, and to *them* which *were* in south Ramoth, and to *them* which *were* in Jattir,

28 And to *them* which *were* in Aroer, and to *them* which *were* in Siphmoth, and to *them* which *were* in Eshtemoa,

29 And to *them* which *were* in Rachal, and to *them* which *were* in the cities of the Jerahmeelites, and to *them* which *were* in the cities of the Kenites,

30 And to *them* which *were* in Hormah, and to *them* which *were* in Chor-ashan, and to *them* which *were* in Athach,

31 And to *them* which *were* in Hebron, and to all the places where David himself and his men were wont to haunt.

CHAPTER 31
Saul's Death

1 Now the Philistines fought against Israel: and the men of Israel fled from before the Philistines, and fell down slain in mount Gilboa.

2 And the Philistines followed hard upon Saul and upon his sons; and the Philistines slew Jonathan, and Abinadab, and Malchishua, Saul's sons.

3 And the battle went sore against Saul, and the archers hit him; and he was sore wounded of the archers.

4 Then said Saul unto his armourbearer, Draw thy sword, and thrust me through therewith; lest these uncircumcised come and thrust me through, and abuse me. But his armourbearer would not; for he was sore afraid. Therefore Saul took a sword, and fell upon it.

5 And when his armourbearer saw that Saul was dead, he fell likewise upon his sword, and died with him.

6 So Saul died, and his three sons, and his armourbearer, and all his men, that same day together.

7 And when the men of Israel that *were* on the other side of the valley, and *they* that *were* on the other side Jordan, saw that the men of Israel fled, and that Saul and his sons were dead, they forsook the cities, and fled; and the Philistines came and dwelt in them.

8 And it came to pass on the morrow, when the Philistines came to strip the slain, that they found Saul and his three sons fallen in mount Gilboa.

9 And they cut off his head, and stripped off his armour, and sent into the land of the Philistines round about, to publish *it in* the house of their idols, and among the people.

10 And they put his armour in the house of Ashtaroth: and they fastened his body to the wall of Beth-shan.

11 And when the inhabitants of Jabesh-gilead heard of that which the Philistines had done to Saul;

12 All the valiant men arose, and went all night, and took the body of Saul and the bodies of his sons from the wall of Beth-shan, and came to Jabesh, and burnt them there.

13 And they took their bones, and buried *them* under a tree at Jabesh, and fasted seven days.

Cross references:

24 Num. 31:27; Josh. 22:8
27 Josh. 15:48; 19:8
28 Josh. 13:16; Josh. 15:50
29 Judg. 1:16; 1Sam. 27:10
30 Judg. 1:17
31 Josh. 14:13; 2Sam. 2:1
1 1Sam. 28:4; 1Chr. 10:1-12
2 1Sam. 14:49; 1Chr. 8:33
3 2Sam. 1:6
4 Judg. 9:54; 1Sam. 14:6; 17:26; 2Sam. 1:10, 14
8 2Sam. 1:20
10 Josh. 17:11; Judg. 1:27; Judg. 2:13; 1Sam. 21:9; 2Sam. 21:12
11 1Sam. 11:3, 9, 11
12 1Sam. 11:1-11; 2Sam. 2:4-7; 2Chr. 16:14; Jer. 34:5; Amos 6:10
13 Gen. 50:10; 2Sam. 2:4, 5; 21:12-14

31:6 So Saul died and his three sons . . . that same day together. Wounded and fleeing from the victorious Philistines, Saul chose to end his own life by falling on his sword rather than be taken captive and then slain. Thus ended the forty-year reign of a flawed monarch, who failed to follow the Lord with all his heart. His tragic end demonstrates in a practical manner Paul's words in Romans 8:13: "For if ye live after the flesh, ye shall die."

2 Samuel

Second Samuel presents the history of the founding of Israel's kingdom. The books of 1 and 2 Samuel were originally one book. Although its division into two parts first appeared in the Greek Septuagint version of the Old Testament, it remained undivided in the Hebrew text until the publishing of the Hebrew Bible in A.D. 1517. David, first anointed by Samuel as a lad (1 Sam. 16:1–13), was anointed king of Judah after King Saul's death (2 Sam. 2:1–4). Seven years later, he became king of all Israel (5:1–5) and reigned a total of forty years from 1011 B.C. to 971 B.C.

The monarchy reached its highest development during David's reign, a level continued by David's successor, Solomon. David unified the nation, subdued Israel's enemies, and extended the empire from the Mediterranean to the Euphrates and from the border of Egypt to Damascus in Syria. Prosperity, poetry, music, and public worship became part of the popular culture during the reign of David.

Though David's failures brought rebellions, family trouble and confusion, he remained "a man after [God's] own heart" (1 Sam. 13:14), learning how to repent and worship God in prayer, psalms, and praise.

Several prophecies by God, His prophets, and David were fulfilled soon after being expressed (see chaps. 3, 5—6, 12, 24).

Of prime importance are the prophecies in the Davidic covenant (chap. 7), the seventh of the eight covenants of the Bible. Irrevocable and eternal, this divine agreement and promise to David guaranteed: **1)** an eternal dynasty or "house" (7:16), **2)** an everlasting kingdom (see Luke 1:30–33), and **3)** a perpetual throne (Acts 2:29–30, Rev. 22:16). Only one condition is indicated, that any disobedient descendant of David would be chastised. But the dynasty would last forever. Jesus Christ, "Son of David" (Matt. 1:1) is the final and eternal fulfillment of the Davidic covenant.

Twenty-two definite prophecies appear in the book in 68 of the 695 verses, which amounts to 10 percent of the content.

Author
Unknown
Date
10th Century B.C.
Key Truth
Unity and Blessing
Historic Time
David's Reign
Key Verse
5:12
And David perceived that the LORD had established him king over Israel. . . .

10%
Prophecy

1300 B.C.	1250 B.C.	1200 B.C.	1150 B.C.	1100 B.C.	1050 B.C.		1000 B.C.	950 B.C.	900 B.C.

1375-1050
Israel ruled by judges

1043-1011
Saul's reign

990
Birth of Solomon

1011-971
Book of 2 Samuel

971-931
Solomon's reign

1080
Birth of Saul

1026
David anointed

1011-971
David's reign

1105
Birth of Samuel

1040
Birth of David

CHAPTER 1
David Learns of Saul's Death

1 Now it came to pass after the death of Saul, when David was returned from the slaughter of the Amalekites, and David had abode two days in Ziklag;

2 It came even to pass on the third day, that, behold, a man came out of the camp from Saul with his clothes rent, and earth upon his head: and *so* it was, when he came to David, that he fell to the earth, and did obeisance.

3 And David said unto him, From whence comest thou? And he said unto him, Out of the camp of Israel am I escaped.

4 And David said unto him, How went the matter? I pray thee, tell me. And he answered, That the people are fled from the battle, and many of the people also are fallen and dead; and Saul and Jonathan his son are dead also.

5 And David said unto the young man that told him, How knowest thou that Saul and Jonathan his son be dead?

6 And the young man that told him said, As I happened by chance upon mount Gilboa, behold, Saul leaned upon his spear; and, lo, the chariots and horsemen followed hard after him.

7 And when he looked behind him, he saw me, and called unto me. And I answered, Here *am* I.

8 And he said unto me, Who *art* thou? And I answered him, I *am* an Amalekite.

9 He said unto me again, Stand, I pray thee, upon me, and slay me: for anguish is come upon me, because my life *is* yet whole in me.

10 So I stood upon him, and slew him, because I was sure that he could not live after that he was fallen: and I took the crown that *was* upon his head, and the bracelet that *was* on his arm, and have brought them hither unto my lord.

11 Then David took hold on his clothes, and rent them; and likewise all the men that *were* with him:

12 And they mourned, and wept, and fasted until even, for Saul, and for Jonathan his son, and for the people of the LORD, and for the house of Israel; because they were fallen by the sword.

13 And David said unto the young man that told him, Whence *art* thou? And he answered, I *am* the son of a stranger, an Amalekite.

14 And David said unto him, How wast thou not afraid to stretch forth thine hand to destroy the LORD's anointed?

15 And David called one of the young men, and said, Go near, *and* fall upon him. And he smote him that he died.

16 And David said unto him, Thy blood *be* upon thy head; for thy mouth hath testified against thee, saying, I have slain the LORD's anointed.

David's Lament

17 And David lamented with this lamentation over Saul and over Jonathan his son:

18 (Also he bade them teach the children of Judah *the use of* the bow: behold, *it is* written in the book of Jasher.)

19 The beauty of Israel is slain upon thy high places: how are the mighty fallen!

20 Tell *it* not in Gath, publish *it* not in the streets of Askelon; lest the daughters of the Philistines rejoice, lest the daughters of the uncircumcised triumph.

21 Ye mountains of Gilboa, *let there be* no dew, neither *let there be* rain, upon you, nor fields of offerings: for there the shield of the mighty is vilely cast away, the shield of Saul, *as though he had* not *been* anointed with oil.

22 From the blood of the slain, from the fat of the mighty, the bow of Jonathan turned not back, and the sword of Saul returned not empty.

Cross References

1 1Sam. 30:17, 26

2 1Sam. 4:12; 2Sam. 4:10

6 1Sam. 31:1, 2-4

10 Judg. 9:54

11 2Sam. 3:31; 13:31

14 Num. 12:8; 1Sam. 24:6; 26:9; 31:4; Ps. 105:15

15 2Sam. 4:10, 12

16 1Sam. 26:9; 2Sam. 1:10; 1Kgs. 2:32, 33, 37; Luke 19:22

18 Josh. 10:13; 1Sam. 31:3

19 2Sam. 1:27

20 Ex. 15:20; Judg. 11:34; 1Sam. 18:6; 31:4, 9; Mic. 1:10

21 Judg. 5:23; 1Sam. 10:1; 31:1; Job 3:3, 4; Jer. 20:14

22 1Sam. 18:4

1:6 the young man. This Amalekite, probably a survivor of the battle described in 1 Samuel 30, comes to David shortly after Saul's death, claiming to have found Saul still alive after his attempted suicide. According to his story, he responded to Saul's last request, slaying the monarch, then bringing the king's crown to David. Evidently this was an attempt to curry favor with David, supposing he would be rewarded for killing Saul. Instead, he is summarily executed for slaying "the LORD's anointed" (v. 16). David always respected the office of the king and was grieved by Saul's tragic death. David had no reason at this time to doubt the story, and the event demonstrates how dishonesty can bring swift judgment.

1:17 lamentation over Saul. Out of his sincere grief, David composes and sings a heartfelt lamentation over Israel's defeat and the death of many of his countrymen, three times using the refrain, "How are the mighty fallen!" (v. 19). David's love for Saul and Jonathan, in spite of the former king's animosity towards him was immortalized in this short psalm, still being read after three thousand years.

23 Saul and Jonathan *were* lovely and pleasant in their lives, and in their death they were not divided: they were swifter than eagles, they were stronger than lions.
24 Ye daughters of Israel, weep over Saul, who clothed you in scarlet, with *other* delights, who put on ornaments of gold upon your apparel.
25 How are the mighty fallen in the midst of the battle! O Jonathan, *thou wast* slain in thine high places.
26 I am distressed for thee, my brother Jonathan: very pleasant hast thou been unto me: thy love to me was wonderful, passing the love of women.
27 How are the mighty fallen, and the weapons of war perished!

CHAPTER 2
David Becomes Judah's King

1 And it came to pass after this, that David inquired of the LORD, saying, Shall I go up into any of the cities of Judah? And the LORD said unto him, Go up. And David said, Whither shall I go up? And he said, Unto Hebron.
2 So David went up thither, and his two wives also, Ahinoam the Jezreelitess, and Abigail Nabal's wife the Carmelite.
3 And his men that *were* with him did David bring up, every man with his household: and they dwelt in the cities of Hebron.
4 And the men of Judah came, and there they anointed David king over the house of Judah. And they told David, saying, *That* the men of Jabesh-gilead *were they* that buried Saul.
5 And David sent messengers unto the men of Jabesh-gilead, and said unto them, Blessed *be* ye of the LORD, that ye have shewed this kindness unto your lord, *even* unto Saul, and have buried him.
6 And now the LORD shew kindness and truth unto you: and I also will requite you this kindness, because ye have done this thing.
7 Therefore now let your hands be strengthened, and be ye valiant: for your master Saul is dead, and also the house of Judah have anointed me king over them.

Ish-bosheth Succeeds Saul

8 But Abner the son of Ner, captain of Saul's host, took Ish-bosheth the son of Saul, and brought him over to Mahanaim;
9 And made him king over Gilead, and over the Ashurites, and over Jezreel, and over Ephraim, and over Benjamin, and over all Israel.
10 Ish-bosheth Saul's son *was* forty years old when he began to reign over Israel, and reigned two years. But the house of Judah followed David.
11 And the time that David was king in Hebron over the house of Judah was seven years and six months.

War between Israel and Judah

12 And Abner the son of Ner, and the servants of Ish-bosheth the son of Saul, went out from Mahanaim to Gibeon.
13 And Joab the son of Zeruiah, and the servants of David, went out, and met together by the pool of Gibeon: and they sat down, the one on the one side of the pool, and the other on the other side of the pool.
14 And Abner said to Joab, Let the young men now arise, and play before us. And Joab said, Let them arise.
15 Then there arose and went over by number twelve of Benjamin, which *pertained* to Ish-bosheth the son of Saul, and twelve of the servants of David.
16 And they caught every one his fellow by the head, and *thrust* his sword in his fellow's side; so they fell down together: wherefore that place was called Helkath-hazzurim, which *is* in Gibeon.
17 And there was a very sore battle that day; and Abner was beaten, and the men of Israel, before the servants of David.
18 And there were three sons of Zeruiah there, Joab, and Abishai, and Asahel: and Asahel *was as* light of foot as a wild roe.
19 And Asahel pursued after Abner; and in going he turned not to the right hand nor to the left from following Abner.
20 Then Abner looked behind him, and said, *Art* thou Asahel? And he answered, I *am*.
21 And Abner said to him, Turn thee aside to thy right hand or to thy left, and lay thee hold on one of the young men, and take thee his armour. But Asahel would not turn aside from following of him.
22 And Abner said again to Asahel, Turn thee aside from following me: wherefore should I smite thee to the ground? how

---

Cross-references (center column):

23 Judg. 14:18
26 1Sam. 18:1, 3; 19:2; 20:17, 41; 23:16
27 2Sam. 1:19
1 Judg. 1:1; 1Sam. 23:2, 4, 9; 30:7, 8, 31; 2Sam. 2:11; 5:1, 3; 1Kgs. 2:11
2 1Sam. 30:5
3 1Sam. 27:2, 3; 30:1; 1Chr. 12:1
4 1Sam. 31:11, 13; 2Sam. 2:11; 5:5
5 Ruth 2:20; 3:10; Ps. 115:15
6 2Tim. 1:16, 18
8 1Sam. 14:50; 1Chr. 8:33; 9:39
11 2Sam. 5:5; 1Kgs. 2:11
12 Josh. 18:25
13 Jer. 41:12
18 1Chr. 2:16; 12:8; Ps. 18:33; Song 2:17; 8:14
21 Judg. 14:19

2:4 the men of Judah . . . anointed David. This second anointing of David to be king (cf. 1 Sam. 16:11–13) was performed in Hebron by the men of Judah, who were doubtless the political leaders. Hebron became the capital and David reigned there for over seven years.

then should I hold up my face to Joab thy brother?

23 Howbeit he refused to turn aside: wherefore Abner with the hinder end of the spear smote him under the fifth *rib*, that the spear came out behind him; and he fell down there, and died in the same place: and it came to pass, *that* as many as came to the place where Asahel fell down and died stood still.

24 Joab also and Abishai pursued after Abner: and the sun went down when they were come to the hill of Ammah, that *lieth* before Giah by the way of the wilderness of Gibeon.

25 And the children of Benjamin gathered themselves together after Abner, and became one troop, and stood on the top of an hill.

26 Then Abner called to Joab, and said, Shall the sword devour for ever? knowest thou not that it will be bitterness in the latter end? how long shall it be then, ere thou bid the people return from following their brethren?

27 And Joab said, *As* God liveth, unless thou hadst spoken, surely then in the morning the people had gone up every one from following his brother.

28 So Joab blew a trumpet, and all the people stood still, and pursued after Israel no more, neither fought they any more.

29 And Abner and his men walked all that night through the plain, and passed over Jordan, and went through all Bithron, and they came to Mahanaim.

30 And Joab returned from following Abner: and when he had gathered all the people together, there lacked of David's servants nineteen men and Asahel.

31 But the servants of David had smitten of Benjamin, and of Abner's men, *so that* three hundred and threescore men died.

32 And they took up Asahel, and buried him in the sepulchre of his father, which *was in* Beth-lehem. And Joab and his men went all night, and they came to Hebron at break of day.

CHAPTER 3

1 Now there was long war between the house of Saul and the house of David: but David waxed stronger and stronger, and the house of Saul waxed weaker and weaker.

David's Sons Born at Hebron

2 And unto David were sons born in Hebron: and his firstborn was Amnon, of Ahinoam the Jezreelitess;

3 And his second, Chileab, of Abigail the wife of Nabal the Carmelite; and the third, Absalom the son of Maacah the daughter of Talmai king of Geshur;

4 And the fourth, Adonijah the son of Haggith; and the fifth, Shephatiah the son of Abital;

5 And the sixth, Ithream, by Eglah David's wife. These were born to David in Hebron.

Abner Decides to Join David

6 And it came to pass, while there was war between the house of Saul and the house of David, that Abner made himself strong for the house of Saul.

7 And Saul had a concubine, whose name *was* Rizpah, the daughter of Aiah: and Ishbosheth said to Abner, Wherefore hast thou gone in unto my father's concubine?

8 Then was Abner very wroth for the words of Ish-bosheth, and said, *Am* I a dog's head, which against Judah do shew kindness this day unto the house of Saul thy father, to his brethren, and to his friends, and have not delivered thee into the hand of David, that thou chargest me today with a fault concerning this woman?

9 So do God to Abner, and more also, except, as the Lord hath sworn to David, even so I do to him;

10 To translate the kingdom from the house of Saul, and to set up the throne of David over Israel and over Judah, from Dan even to Beer-sheba.

11 And he could not answer Abner a word again, because he feared him.

12 And Abner sent messengers to David on his behalf, saying, Whose *is* the land? saying *also*, Make thy league with me, and, behold, my hand *shall be* with thee, to bring about all Israel unto thee.

13 And he said, Well; I will make a league with thee: but one thing I require of thee, that is, Thou shalt not see my face, except thou first bring Michal Saul's daughter, when thou comest to see my face.

14 And David sent messengers to Ish-bosheth Saul's son, saying, Deliver *me* my wife Michal, which I espoused to me for an hundred foreskins of the Philistines.

15 And Ish-bosheth sent, and took her from *her* husband, *even* from Phaltiel the son of Laish.

16 And her husband went with her along weeping behind her to Bahurim. Then said Abner unto him, Go, return. And he returned.

17 And Abner had communication with the

Cross references (center column)

23 2Sam. 3:27; 4:6; 20:10

27 2Sam. 2:14; Prov. 17:14

2 1Sam. 25:43; 1Chr. 3:1-4

3 1Sam. 27:8; 2Sam. 13:27; 1Chr. 3:1

4 1Kgs. 1:5

7 2Sam. 16:21; 21:8, 10

8 Deut. 23:18; 1Sam. 24:14; 2Sam. 9:8; 16:9

9 Ruth 1:17; 1Sam. 15:28; 16:1, 12; 28:17; 1Kgs. 19:2; 1Chr. 12:23

10 Judg. 20:1; 2Sam. 17:11; 1Kgs. 4:25

13 Gen. 43:3; 1Sam. 18:20

14 1Sam. 18:25, 27

15 1Sam. 25:44

16 2Sam. 19:16

elders of Israel, saying, Ye sought for David in times past *to be* king over you:

18 Now then do *it*: for the LORD hath spoken of David, saying, By the hand of my servant David I will save my people Israel out of the hand of the Philistines, and out of the hand of all their enemies.

19 And Abner also spake in the ears of Benjamin: and Abner went also to speak in the ears of David in Hebron all that seemed good to Israel, and that seemed good to the whole house of Benjamin.

20 So Abner came to David to Hebron, and twenty men with him. And David made Abner and the men that *were* with him a feast.

21 And Abner said unto David, I will arise and go, and will gather all Israel unto my lord the king, that they may make a league with thee, and that thou mayest reign over all that thine heart desireth. And David sent Abner away; and he went in peace.

Joab Kills Abner

22 And, behold, the servants of David and Joab came from *pursuing* a troop, and brought in a great spoil with them: but Abner *was* not with David in Hebron; for he had sent him away, and he was gone in peace.

23 When Joab and all the host that *was* with him were come, they told Joab, saying, Abner the son of Ner came to the king, and he hath sent him away, and he is gone in peace.

24 Then Joab came to the king, and said, What hast thou done? behold, Abner came unto thee; why *is* it *that* thou hast sent him away, and he is quite gone?

25 Thou knowest Abner the son of Ner, that he came to deceive thee, and to know thy going out and thy coming in, and to know all that thou doest.

26 And when Joab was come out from David, he sent messengers after Abner, which brought him again from the well of Sirah: but David knew *it* not.

27 And when Abner was returned to Hebron, Joab took him aside in the gate to speak with him quietly, and smote him there under the fifth *rib*, that he died, for the blood of Asahel his brother.

28 And afterward when David heard *it*, he said, I and my kingdom *are* guiltless before the LORD for ever from the blood of Abner the son of Ner:

29 Let it rest on the head of Joab, and on all his father's house; and let there not fail

from the house of Joab one that hath an issue, or that is a leper, or that leaneth on a staff, or that falleth on the sword, or that lacketh bread.

30 So Joab and Abishai his brother slew Abner, because he had slain their brother Asahel at Gibeon in the battle.

31 And David said to Joab, and to all the people that *were* with him, Rend your clothes, and gird you with sackcloth, and mourn before Abner. And king David *himself* followed the bier.

32 And they buried Abner in Hebron: and the king lifted up his voice, and wept at the grave of Abner; and all the people wept.

33 And the king lamented over Abner, and said, Died Abner as a fool dieth?

34 Thy hands *were* not bound, nor thy feet put into fetters: as a man falleth before wicked men, *so* fellest thou. And all the people wept again over him.

35 And when all the people came to cause David to eat meat while it was yet day, David sware, saying, So do God to me, and more also, if I taste bread, or ought else, till the sun be down.

36 And all the people took notice *of it*, and it pleased them: as whatsoever the king did pleased all the people.

37 For all the people and all Israel understood that day that it was not of the king to slay Abner the son of Ner.

38 And the king said unto his servants, Know ye not that there is a prince and a great man fallen this day in Israel?

39 And I *am* this day weak, though anointed king; and these men the sons of Zeruiah *be* too hard for me: the LORD shall reward the doer of evil according to his wickedness.

CHAPTER 4
Ish-bosheth Is Assassinated

1 And when Saul's son heard that Abner was dead in Hebron, his hands were feeble, and all the Israelites were troubled.

2 And Saul's son had two men *that were* captains of bands: the name of the one *was* Baanah, and the name of the other Rechab, the sons of Rimmon a Beerothite, of the children of Benjamin: (for Beeroth also was reckoned to Benjamin:

3 And the Beerothites fled to Gittaim, and were sojourners there until this day.)

4 And Jonathan, Saul's son, had a son *that was* lame of *his* feet. He was five years old when the tidings came of Saul and Jonathan out of Jezreel, and his nurse took him

Center cross-reference column

18 2Sam. 3:9

19 1Chr. 12:29

21 2Sam. 3:10, 12; 1Kgs. 11:37

25 1Sam. 29:6; Isa. 37:28

27 2Sam. 2:23; 4:6; 20:9, 10; 1Kgs. 2:5

29 Lev. 15:2; 1Kgs. 2:32, 33

30 2Sam. 2:23

31 Gen. 37:34; Josh. 7:6; 2Sam. 1:2, 11

33 2Sam. 13:12, 13

35 Ruth 1:17; 2Sam. 1:12; 12:17; Jer. 16:7

39 2Sam. 19:7, 13; 1Kgs. 2:5, 6, 33, 34; Ps. 28:4; 62:12; 2Tim. 4:14

1 Ezra 4:4; Isa. 13:7; Matt. 2:3

2 Josh. 18:25

3 Neh. 11:33

4 1Sam. 29:1, 11; 2Sam. 9:3; 1Chr. 8:34; 9:40

up, and fled: and it came to pass, as she made haste to flee, that he fell, and became lame. And his name *was* Mephibosheth.

5 And the sons of Rimmon the Beerothite, Rechab and Baanah, went, and came about the heat of the day to the house of Ish-bosheth, who lay on a bed at noon.

6 And they came thither into the midst of the house, *as though* they would have fetched wheat; and they smote him under the fifth *rib*: and Rechab and Baanah his brother escaped.

7 For when they came into the house, he lay on his bed in his bedchamber, and they smote him, and slew him, and beheaded him, and took his head, and gat them away through the plain all night.

8 And they brought the head of Ish-bosheth unto David to Hebron, and said to the king, Behold the head of Ish-bosheth the son of Saul thine enemy, which sought thy life; and the LORD hath avenged my lord the king this day of Saul, and of his seed.

9 And David answered Rechab and Baanah his brother, the sons of Rimmon the Beerothite, and said unto them, *As* the LORD liveth, who hath redeemed my soul out of all adversity,

10 When one told me, saying, Behold, Saul is dead, thinking to have brought good tidings, I took hold of him, and slew him in Ziklag, who *thought* that I would have given him a reward for his tidings:

11 How much more, when wicked men have slain a righteous person in his own house upon his bed? shall I not therefore now require his blood of your hand, and take you away from the earth?

12 And David commanded his young men, and they slew them, and cut off their hands and their feet, and hanged *them* up over the pool in Hebron. But they took the head of Ish-bosheth, and buried *it* in the sepulchre of Abner in Hebron.

CHAPTER 5
David Also Becomes Israel's King

1 Then came all the tribes of Israel to David unto Hebron, and spake, saying, Behold, we *are* thy bone and thy flesh.

2 Also in time past, when Saul was king over us, thou wast he that leddest out and broughtest in Israel: and the LORD said to thee Thou shalt feed my people Israel, and thou shalt be a captain over Israel.

3 So all the elders of Israel came to the king to Hebron; and king David made a league with them in Hebron before the LORD: and they anointed David king over Israel.

4 David *was* thirty years old when he began to reign, *and* he reigned forty years.

5 In Hebron he reigned over Judah seven years and six months: and in Jerusalem he reigned thirty and three years over all Israel and Judah.

David Captures Zion

6 And the king and his men went to Jerusalem unto the Jebusites, the inhabitants of the land: which spake unto David, saying, Except thou take away the blind and the lame, thou shalt not come in hither: thinking, David cannot come in hither.

7 Nevertheless David took the strong hold of Zion: the same *is* the city of David.

Cross references:

6 2Sam. 2:23

8 1Sam. 19:2, 10, 11; 23:15; 25:29

9 Gen. 48:16; 1Kgs. 1:29; Ps. 31:7

10 2Sam. 1:2, 4, 15

11 Gen. 9:5, 6

12 2Sam. 1:15; 3:32

1 Gen. 29:14; 1Chr. 11:1; 12:23

2 1Sam. 16:1, 12; 18:13; 2Sam. 7:7; Ps. 78:71

3 Judg. 11:11; 1Sam. 23:18; 2Kgs. 11:17; 1Chr. 11:3

4 1Chr. 26:31; 29:27

5 2Sam. 2:11; 1Chr. 3:4

6 Josh. 15:63; Judg. 1:8, 21; 19:11, 12

7 2Sam. 5:9; 1Kgs. 2, 10; 8:1

5:3 anointed David king over Israel. Nearly two decades had elapsed since David's first anointing (1 Sam. 16) and seven and one-half years since he had become king of Judah in Hebron. Now at the age of thirty-seven, he becomes the undisputed king of all Israel at his third anointing (cf. 1 Chr. 12:23–40). This climactic event was the fulfillment of David's prophecy, evidently widely circulated, that he would indeed be "captain over Israel" (v. 2). The celebration over his coronation is a foretaste of that joyous occasion, when the long-rejected Messiah-King, Jesus, returns to Israel in glorious power to establish and consolidate His rightful rule over Israel and the entire world (Isa. 25:6–9; Zech. 4—9).

5:5 in Jerusalem he reigned. After conquering Jerusalem, David reestablished the city as a center for true worship of God. Not since the days of Melchizedek and Abraham nearly one thousand years earlier had a true servant of God ruled the city. One of the most significant Old Testament types of Christ, Melchizedek brought forth bread and wine (foreshadows of the body and blood of Christ, 1 Cor. 11:23–26), blessed Abraham and received tithes from the patriarch (see Heb. 7:1–22). David, as it were, sits upon the throne of Melchizedek as king of Salem (Jerusalem).

5:7 David took the strong hold of Zion. The first occurrence of the word "Zion" was originally used to describe a fortress on the edge of the small community of Jerusalem. Later it was applied to the enlarged growing city of Jerusalem, the capital of Israel. However, the word is frequently found in Scripture applied to the temple mount area and sometimes is equated with the temple itself, the center of religious worship. Found one hundred fifty-four times in the Old Testament, and seven times in the New Testament, the word "Zion" has significance apart from

8 And David said on that day, Whosoever getteth up to the gutter, and smiteth the Jebusites, and the lame and the blind, *that are* hated of David's soul, *he shall be chief and captain.* Wherefore they said, The blind and the lame shall not come into the house.

9 So David dwelt in the fort, and called it the city of David. And David built round about from Millo and inward.

10 And David went on, and grew great, and the LORD God of hosts *was* with him.

David Prospers

11 And Hiram king of Tyre sent messengers to David, and cedar trees, and carpenters, and masons: and they built David an house.

12 And David perceived that the LORD had established him king over Israel, and that he had exalted his kingdom for his people Israel's sake.

13 And David took *him* more concubines and wives out of Jerusalem, after he was come from Hebron: and there were yet sons and daughters born to David.

14 And these *be* the names of those that were born unto him in Jerusalem; Shammua, and Shobab, and Nathan, and Solomon,

15 Ibhar also, and Elishua, and Nepheg, and Japhia,

16 And Elishama, and Eliada, and Eliphalet.

David Defeats the Philistines

17 But when the Philistines heard that they had anointed David king over Israel, all the Philistines came up to seek David; and David heard *of it,* and went down to the hold.

18 The Philistines also came and spread themselves in the valley of Rephaim.

19 And David inquired of the LORD, saying, Shall I go up to the Philistines? wilt thou deliver them into mine hand? And the LORD said unto David, Go up: for I will doubtless deliver the Philistines into thine hand.

20 And David came to Baal-perazim, and David smote them there, and said, The LORD hath broken forth upon mine enemies before me, as the breach of waters. Therefore

he called the name of that place Baal-perazim.

21 And there they left their images, and David and his men burned them.

22 And the Philistines came up yet again, and spread themselves in the valley of Rephaim.

23 And when David inquired of the LORD, he said, Thou shalt not go up; *but* fetch a compass behind them, and come upon them over against the mulberry trees.

24 And let it be, when thou hearest the sound of a going in the tops of the mulberry trees, that then thou shalt bestir thyself: for then shall the LORD go out before thee, to smite the host of the Philistines.

25 And David did so, as the LORD had commanded him; and smote the Philistines from Geba until thou come to Gazer.

CHAPTER 6
David Brings the Ark to Jerusalem

1 Again, David gathered together all *the* chosen *men* of Israel, thirty thousand.

2 And David arose, and went with all the people that *were* with him from Baale of Judah, to bring up from thence the ark of God, whose name is called by the name of the LORD of hosts that dwelleth *between* the cherubims.

3 And they set the ark of God upon a new cart, and brought it out of the house of Abinadab that *was* in Gibeah: and Uzzah and Ahio, the sons of Abinadab, drave the new cart.

4 And they brought it out of the house of Abinadab which *was* at Gibeah, accompanying the ark of God: and Ahio went before the ark.

5 And David and all the house of Israel played before the LORD on all manner of *instruments made of* fir wood, even on harps, and on psalteries, and on timbrels, and on cornets, and on cymbals.

6 And when they came to Nachon's threshingfloor, Uzzah put forth *his hand* to the ark of God, and took hold of it; for the oxen shook *it.*

7 And the anger of the LORD was kindled against Uzzah; and God smote him there for

Cross references (center column)

8 1Chr. 11:6-9
9 2Sam. 5:7
11 1Kgs. 5:2; 1Chr. 14:1
13 Deut. 17:17; 1Chr. 3:9; 14:3
14 1Chr. 3:5; 14:4
15 1Chr. 3:6
16 1Chr. 14:7
17 2Sam. 23:14; 1Chr. 11:16; 14:8
18 Josh. 15:8; Isa. 17:5
19 1Sam. 23:2, 4; 30:8; 2Sam. 2:1
20 Isa. 28:21
21 Deut. 7:5, 25; 1Chr. 14:12
22 1Chr. 14:13
23 2Sam. 5:19
24 Judg. 4:14; 2Kgs. 7:6;
25 Josh. 16:10; 1Chr. 14:16, *Gibeon*
2 Josh. 15:9, 60; 1Sam. 4:4; 1Chr. 13:5, 6; Ps. 80:1
3 Num. 7:9; 1Sam. 6:7
4 1Sam. 7:1
6 Num. 4:15; 1Chr. 13:9, *Chidon*
7 1Sam. 6:19

---

its original use as a geographical location. Historically, it is the City of David (1 Chr. 11:5; Ps. 2:6), the religious, political, and military capital of the united kingdom of Israel and later Judah until 586 B.C., when the city and the temple were destroyed. Prophetically, Zion has reference to Jerusalem as the future capital city of the nation of Israel in the Millennium (Isa. 1:27; 2:3; 4:1–6; Zech. 1:16–17; 8:3–8; Rom. 11:26). Spiritually, but still a literal reality, Zion in Hebrews 12:22 is equated with the heavenly Jerusalem, eternal home of the redeemed (see also Rev. 14:1).

his error; and there he died by the ark of God.

8 And David was displeased, because the LORD had made a breach upon Uzzah: and he called the name of the place Perez-uzzah to this day.

9 And David was afraid of the LORD that day, and said, How shall the ark of the LORD come to me?

10 So David would not remove the ark of the LORD unto him into the city of David: but David carried it aside into the house of Obed-edom the Gittite.

11 And the ark of the LORD continued in the house of Obed-edom the Gittite three months: and the LORD blessed Obed-edom, and all his household.

12 And it was told king David, saying, The LORD hath blessed the house of Obed-edom, and all that *pertaineth* unto him, because of the ark of God. So David went and brought up the ark of God from the house of Obed-edom into the city of David with gladness.

13 And it was *so*, that when they that bare the ark of the LORD had gone six paces, he sacrificed oxen and fatlings.

14 And David danced before the LORD with all *his* might; and David *was* girded with a linen ephod.

15 So David and all the house of Israel brought up the ark of the LORD with shouting, and with the sound of the trumpet.

16 And as the ark of the LORD came into the city of David, Michal Saul's daughter looked through a window, and saw king David leaping and dancing before the LORD; and she despised him in her heart.

17 And they brought in the ark of the LORD, and set it in his place, in the midst of the tabernacle that David had pitched for it: and David offered burnt offerings and peace offerings before the LORD.

18 And as soon as David had made an end of offering burnt offerings and peace offerings, he blessed the people in the name of the LORD of hosts.

19 And he dealt among all the people, *even* among the whole multitude of Israel, as

well to the women as men, to every one a cake of bread, and a good piece *of flesh*, and a flagon *of wine*. So all the people departed every one to his house.

20 Then David returned to bless his household. And Michal the daughter of Saul came out to meet David, and said, How glorious was the king of Israel today, who uncovered himself today in the eyes of the handmaids of his servants, as one of the vain fellows shamelessly uncovereth himself!

21 And David said unto Michal, It was before the LORD, which chose me before thy father, and before all his house, to appoint me ruler over the people of the LORD, over Israel: therefore will I play before the LORD.

22 And I will yet be more vile than thus, and will be base in mine own sight: and of the maidservants which thou hast spoken of, of them shall I be had in honour.

23 Therefore Michal the daughter of Saul had no child unto the day of her death.

CHAPTER 7
God's Promise to David

1 And it came to pass, when the king sat in his house, and the LORD had given him rest round about from all his enemies;

2 That the king said unto Nathan the prophet, See now, I dwell in an house of cedar, but the ark of God dwelleth within curtains.

3 And Nathan said to the king, Go, do all that *is* in thine heart; for the LORD *is* with thee.

4 And it came to pass that night, that the word of the LORD came unto Nathan, saying,

5 Go and tell my servant David, Thus saith the LORD, Shalt thou build me an house for me to dwell in?

6 Whereas I have not dwelt in *any* house since the time that I brought up the children of Israel out of Egypt, even to this day, but have walked in a tent and in a tabernacle.

7 In all *the places* wherein I have walked with all the children of Israel spake I a word with any of the tribes of Israel, whom I

Cross references (center column)

9 Ps. 119:120; Luke 5:8, 9
10 1Chr. 13:13
11 1Chr. 13:14
12 1Chr. 15:25
13 Num. 4:15; 1Kgs. 8:5; 1Chr. 15:2, 15, 26
14 1Sam. 2:18; 1Chr. 15:27; Ps. 30:11
15 1Chr. 15:28
16 1Chr. 15:29
17 1Kgs. 8:5, 62, 63; 1Chr. 15:1; 16:1; Ps. 132:8
18 1Kgs. 8:55; 1Chr. 16:2
19 1Chr. 16:3
20 1Sam. 19:24; 2Sam. 6:14, 16
21 1Sam. 13:14; 15:28
23 1Sam. 15:35
1 1Chr. 17:1-15
2 Ex. 26:1; 40:21; 2Sam. 5:11; Acts 7:46
3 1Kgs. 8:17, 18; 1Chr. 22:7; 28:2
5 1Kgs. 5:3; 8:19; 1Chr. 22:8; 28:3
6 Ex. 40:18, 19, 34; 1Kgs. 8:16
7 Lev. 26:11, 12; Deut. 17:6; Ps. 78:71, 72

6:15 So David and all the house of Israel brought up the ark. The sacred ark of the covenant was now brought according to the Levitical law to the city of Jerusalem (cf. 1 Chr. 15:1–28).

6:17 And they brought in the ark of the LORD, and set it in his place. The ark was the center of Israelite worship, for there was the place where the Shechinah glory of God was manifested between the cherubim on the Day of Atonement each year. The ark was made after the Exodus (Ex. 25:10–22), placed in the inner Holy of Holies, past the Holy Place in the Tabernacle. Centuries later David moved the ark to Jerusalem, then called the City of David, with a spirit of national worship and enthusiasm. The ark was placed in a special tabernacle prepared by David. Later it would be moved into Solomon's Temple, where it remained until the fall of Jerusalem in 586 B.C.

commanded to feed my people Israel, saying, Why build ye not me an house of cedar?

8 Now therefore so shalt thou say unto my servant David, Thus saith the LORD of hosts, I took thee from the sheepcote, from following the sheep, to be ruler over my people, over Israel:

9 And I was with thee whithersoever thou wentest, and have cut off all thine enemies out of thy sight, and have made thee a great name, like unto the name of the great *men* that *are* in the earth.

10 Moreover I will appoint a place for my people Israel, and will plant them, that they may dwell in a place of their own, and move no more; neither shall the children of wickedness afflict them any more, as beforetime,

11 And as since the time that I commanded judges *to be* over my people Israel, and have caused thee to rest from all thine enemies.

Also the LORD telleth thee that he will make thee an house.

12 And when thy days be fulfilled, and thou shalt sleep with thy fathers, I will set up thy seed after thee, which shall proceed out of thy bowels, and I will establish his kingdom.

13 He shall build an house for my name, and I will stablish the throne of his kingdom for ever.

14 I will be his father, and he shall be my son. If he commit iniquity, I will chasten him with the rod of men, and with the stripes of the children of men:

15 But my mercy shall not depart away from him, as I took *it* from Saul, whom I put away before thee.

16 And thine house and thy kingdom shall be established for ever before thee: thy throne shall be established for ever.

17 According to all these words, and according to all this vision, so did Nathan speak unto David.

8 1Sam. 16:11, 12
9 1Sam. 18:14; Ps. 89:23
10 Ps. 44:2; Jer. 24:6; Amos 9:15
11 Judg. 2:14-16; 1Sam. 12:9, 11
12 Deut. 31:16; 1Kgs. 1:21; 2:1; Acts 13:36
13 1Kgs. 5:5; 1Chr. 22:10; Ps. 89:4, 29, 36, 37
14 Ps. 89:26, 27, 30-33
15 1Kgs. 11:13, 34
16 John 12:34

The Promise of a Davidic King

PROPHECY	OT REFERENCE	NT FULFILLMENT
David's royal line to be perpetual	2 Samuel 7:16 cf. Psalm 78:67-70	Luke 1:33; 2:11; John 7:42; Romans 1:3
Sceptre not to depart from Judah	Genesis 49:9-10	Hebrews 7:14; Revelation 5:5
Stem out of Jesse (David's father) to rule	Isaiah 11:1-5	Luke 3:23; 4:18 Romans 11:26
Divine oath to David confirms promise	Psalm 89:2-4; 132:11	Luke 1:32
Government from Davidic throne assured	Isaiah 9:6-7 Jeremiah 23:5	Luke 1:33
Bethlehem designated as Messiah's birthplace	Micah 5:2-4	Matthew 2:1-6
The "Branch" from the root of Jesse and David to reign	Isaiah 11:1 cf. Zechariah 12:8	Revelation 22:16

7:8 so shalt thou say unto my servant David. It had been David's desire to inaugurate a construction program to build a permanent temple in Jerusalem as a center for national worship. But the word of the Lord came to the prophet Nathan, with instructions that David was not to build a temple, for his son was to erect the sacred structure. God then spelled out several promises and one condition in a statement often called the Davidic covenant. David is promised that his "house," his family, and his posterity would be established in perpetuity (v. 13), that a place would be permanently reserved for His people (v. 10), and that a kingdom, a throne, and royal authority would continue forever (v. 13). The angel Gabriel spoke of this everlasting royal authority to the divinely chosen

mother, Mary, saying, "He [Christ] shall reign over the house of Jacob for ever; and of his kingdom there shall be no end" (Luke 1:33).

7:16 thy throne shall be established for ever. Over a period of 500 years, the promise that the Davidic line would continue forever was repeated many times: to David himself, to Solomon, in the Psalms, and by the prophets Isaiah, Jeremiah, Amos, Micah and Zechariah. While individual kings were chastised for disobedience, the covenant was never abrogated. From David a direct line of descent continued for over one thousand years, until Jesus, the Son of Abraham, the Son of David, was born (Matt. 1:1–16). See the note on Acts 1:6–7.

David's Prayer of Appreciation

18 Then went king David in, and sat before the Lord, and he said, Who *am* I, O Lord God? and what *is* my house, that thou hast brought me hitherto?

19 And this was yet a small thing in thy sight, O Lord God; but thou hast spoken also of thy servant's house for a great while to come. And *is* this the manner of man, O Lord God?

20 And what can David say more unto thee? for thou, Lord God, knowest thy servant.

21 For thy word's sake, and according to thine own heart, hast thou done all these great things, to make thy servant know *them*.

22 Wherefore thou art great, O Lord God: for *there is* none like thee, neither *is there any* God beside thee, according to all that we have heard with our ears.

23 And what one nation in the earth *is* like thy people, *even* like Israel, whom God went to redeem for a people to himself, and to make him a name, and to do for you great things and terrible, for thy land, before thy people, which thou redeemedst to thee from Egypt, *from* the nations and their gods?

24 For thou hast confirmed to thyself thy people Israel *to be* a people unto thee for ever: and thou, Lord, art become their God.

25 And now, O Lord God, the word that thou hast spoken concerning thy servant, and concerning his house, establish *it*, for ever, and do as thou hast said.

26 And let thy name be magnified for ever, saying, The Lord of hosts *is* the God over Israel: and let the house of thy servant David be established before thee.

27 For thou, O Lord of hosts, God of Israel, hast revealed to thy servant, saying, I will build thee an house: therefore hath thy servant found in his heart to pray this prayer unto thee.

28 And now, O Lord God, thou *art* that God, and thy words be true, and thou hast promised this goodness unto thy servant:

29 Therefore now let it please thee to bless the house of thy servant, that it may continue for ever before thee: for thou, O Lord God, hast spoken *it*: and with thy blessing let the house of thy servant be blessed for ever.

Cross references (center column)

18 Gen. 32:10
19 2Sam. 7:12, 13; Isa. 55:8
20 Gen. 18:19; Ps. 139:1
22 Deut. 3:24; 4:35; 32:39; 1Sam. 2:2; 1Chr. 16:25; 2Chr. 2:5; Ps. 48:1; 86:8, 10; 89:6, 8; 96:4; 135:5; 145:3; Isa. 45:5, 18, 22; Jer. 10:6
23 Deut. 4:7, 32, 34; 9:26; 33:29; Neh. 1:10; Ps. 147:20
24 Deut. 26:18; Ps. 48:14
28 John 17:17
29 2Sam. 22:51
1 1Chr. 18:1
2 Num. 24:17; 1Sam. 10:27; 2Sam. 8:6; Ps. 72:10
3 Gen. 15:18; 2Sam. 10:6; 1Chr. 18:3
4 Josh. 11:6, 9
5 1Kgs. 11:23-25
6 2Sam. 7:9; 8:2, 14
7 1Kgs. 10:16
8 1Chr. 18:8
9 1Chr. 18:9
10 1Chr. 18:10, *Hadoram*
11 1Kgs. 7:51; 1Chr. 18:11; 26:26
13 2Kgs. 14:7; 1Chr. 18:12

CHAPTER 8

David's Military Success

1 And after this it came to pass, that David smote the Philistines, and subdued them: and David took Metheg-ammah out of the hand of the Philistines.

2 And he smote Moab, and measured them with a line, casting them down to the ground; even with two lines measured he to put to death, and with one full line to keep alive. And *so* the Moabites became David's servants, *and* brought gifts.

3 David smote also Hadadezer, the son of Rehob, king of Zobah, as he went to recover his border at the river Euphrates.

4 And David took from him a thousand *chariots*, and seven hundred horsemen, and twenty thousand footmen: and David houghed all the chariot *horses*, but reserved of them *for* an hundred chariots.

5 And when the Syrians of Damascus came to succour Hadadezer king of Zobah, David slew of the Syrians two and twenty thousand men.

6 Then David put garrisons in Syria of Damascus: and the Syrians became servants to David, *and* brought gifts. And the Lord preserved David whithersoever he went.

7 And David took the shields of gold that were on the servants of Hadadezer, and brought them to Jerusalem.

8 And from Betah, and from Berothai, cities of Hadadezer, king David took exceeding much brass.

9 When Toi king of Hamath heard that David had smitten all the host of Hadadezer,

10 Then Toi sent Joram his son unto king David, to salute him, and to bless him, because he had fought against Hadadezer, and smitten him: for Hadadezer had wars with Toi. And *Joram* brought with him vessels of silver, and vessels of gold, and vessels of brass:

11 Which also king David did dedicate unto the Lord, with the silver and gold that he had dedicated of all nations which he subdued;

12 Of Syria, and of Moab, and of the children of Ammon, and of the Philistines, and of Amalek, and of the spoil of Hadadezer, son of Rehob, king of Zobah.

13 And David gat *him* a name when he returned from smiting of the Syrians in the

---

7:29 the house of thy servant. David wanted to build a "house" for the Lord (a temple), but God makes a "house" for David, the royal family and posterity culminating in Jesus.

valley of salt, *being* eighteen thousand *men.*
14 And he put garrisons in Edom; throughout all Edom put he garrisons, and all they of Edom became David's servants. And the LORD preserved David whithersoever he went.

David's Officials

15 And David reigned over all Israel; and David executed judgment and justice unto all his people.
16 And Joab the son of Zeruiah *was* over the host; and Jehoshaphat the son of Ahilud *was* recorder;
17 And Zadok the son of Ahitub, and Ahimelech the son of Abiathar, *were* the priests; and Seraiah *was* the scribe;
18 And Benaiah the son of Jehoiada *was over* both the Cherethites and the Pelethites; and David's sons were chief rulers.

CHAPTER 9
David's Kindness to Mephibosheth

1 And David said, Is there yet any that is left of the house of Saul, that I may shew him kindness for Jonathan's sake?
2 And *there was* of the house of Saul a servant whose name *was* Ziba. And when they had called him unto David, the king said unto him, *Art* thou Ziba? And he said, Thy servant *is* he.
3 And the king said, *Is* there not yet any of the house of Saul, that I may shew the kindness of God unto him? And Ziba said unto the king, Jonathan hath yet a son, *which is* lame on *his* feet.
4 And the king said unto him, Where *is* he? And Ziba said unto the king, Behold, he *is* in the house of Machir, the son of Ammiel, in Lo-debar.
5 Then king David sent, and fetched him out of the house of Machir, the son of Ammiel, from Lo-debar.
6 Now when Mephibosheth, the son of Jonathan, the son of Saul, was come unto David, he fell on his face, and did reverence. And David said, Mephibosheth. And he answered, Behold thy servant!
7 And David said unto him, Fear not: for I will surely shew thee kindness for Jonathan thy father's sake, and will restore thee all the land of Saul thy father; and thou shalt eat bread at my table continually.
8 And he bowed himself, and said, What *is* thy servant, that thou shouldest look upon such a dead dog as I *am*?
9 Then the king called to Ziba, Saul's servant, and said unto him, I have given unto

thy master's son all that pertained to Saul and to all his house.
10 Thou therefore, and thy sons, and thy servants, shall till the land for him, and thou shalt bring in *the fruits*, that thy master's son may have food to eat: but Mephibosheth thy master's son shall eat bread alway at my table. Now Ziba had fifteen sons and twenty servants.
11 Then said Ziba unto the king, According to all that my lord the king hath commanded his servant, so shall thy servant do. As for Mephibosheth, *said the king*, he shall eat at my table, as one of the king's sons.
12 And Mephibosheth had a young son, whose name *was* Micha. And all that dwelt in the house of Ziba *were* servants unto Mephibosheth.
13 So Mephibosheth dwelt in Jerusalem: for he did eat continually at the king's table; and was lame on both his feet.

CHAPTER 10
Israel Defeats the Ammonites and Syrians

1 And it came to pass after this, that the king of the children of Ammon died, and Hanun his son reigned in his stead.
2 Then said David, I will shew kindness unto Hanun the son of Nahash, as his father shewed kindness unto me. And David sent to comfort him by the hand of his servants for his father. And David's servants came into the land of the children of Ammon.
3 And the princes of the children of Ammon said unto Hanun their lord, Thinkest thou that David doth honour thy father, that he hath sent comforters unto thee? hath not David *rather* sent his servants unto thee, to search the city, and to spy it out, and to overthrow it?
4 Wherefore Hanun took David's servants, and shaved off the one half of their beards, and cut off their garments in the middle, *even* to their buttocks, and sent them away.
5 When they told *it* unto David, he sent to meet them, because the men were greatly ashamed: and the king said, Tarry at Jericho until your beards be grown, and *then* return.
6 And when the children of Ammon saw that they stank before David, the children of Ammon sent and hired the Syrians of Bethrehob, and the Syrians of Zoba, twenty thousand footmen, and of king Maacah a thousand men, and of Ish-tob twelve thousand men.
7 And when David heard of *it*, he sent Joab, and all the host of the mighty men.

14 Gen. 27:29, 37, 40; Num. 24:18; 2Sam. 8:6

16 2Sam. 19:13; 20:23; 1Kgs. 4:3; 1Chr. 11:6; 18:15

17 1Chr. 24:3

18 1Sam. 30:14; 2Sam. 20:26; 1Chr. 18:17

1 1Sam. 18:3; 20:14-17, 42; Prov. 27:10

2 2Sam. 16:1; 19:17, 29

3 1Sam. 20:14; 2Sam. 4:4

4 2Sam. 17:27

6 1Chr. 8:34

7 2Sam. 9:1, 3

8 1Sam. 24:14; 2Sam. 16:9

9 2Sam. 16:4; 19:29

10 2Sam. 9:7, 11, 13; 19:17, 28

12 1Chr. 8:34

13 2Sam. 9:3, 7, 10

1 1Chr. 19:3

4 Isa. 20:4; 47:2

6 Gen. 34:30; Ex. 5:21; Judg. 11:3, 5; 1Sam. 13:4; 2Sam. 8:3, 5

7 2Sam. 23:8

8 And the children of Ammon came out, and put the battle in array at the entering in of the gate: and the Syrians of Zoba, and of Rehob, and Ish-tob, and Maacah, *were* by themselves in the field.

9 When Joab saw that the front of the battle was against him before and behind, he chose of all the choice *men* of Israel, and put *them* in array against the Syrians:

10 And the rest of the people he delivered into the hand of Abishai his brother, that he might put *them* in array against the children of Ammon.

11 And he said, If the Syrians be too strong for me, then thou shalt help me: but if the children of Ammon be too strong for thee, then I will come and help thee.

12 Be of good courage, and let us play the men for our people, and for the cities of our God: and the LORD do that which seemeth him good.

13 And Joab drew nigh, and the people that *were* with him, unto the battle against the Syrians: and they fled before him.

14 And when the children of Ammon saw that the Syrians were fled, then fled they also before Abishai, and entered into the city. So Joab returned from the children of Ammon, and came to Jerusalem.

15 And when the Syrians saw that they were smitten before Israel, they gathered themselves together.

16 And Hadarezer sent, and brought out the Syrians that *were* beyond the river: and they came to Helam; and Shobach the captain of the host of Hadarezer *went* before them.

17 And when it was told David, he gathered all Israel together, and passed over Jordan, and came to Helam. And the Syrians set themselves in array against David, and fought with him.

18 And the Syrians fled before Israel; and David slew *the men of* seven hundred chariots of the Syrians, and forty thousand horsemen, and smote Shobach the captain of their host, who died there.

19 And when all the kings *that were* servants

to Hadarezer saw that they were smitten before Israel, they made peace with Israel, and served them. So the Syrians feared to help the children of Ammon any more.

CHAPTER 11
David and Bath-sheba

1 And it came to pass, after the year was expired, at the time when kings go forth *to battle*, that David sent Joab, and his servants with him, and all Israel; and they destroyed the children of Ammon, and besieged Rabbah. But David tarried still at Jerusalem.

2 And it came to pass in an eveningtide, that David arose from off his bed, and walked upon the roof of the king's house: and from the roof he saw a woman washing herself; and the woman *was* very beautiful to look upon.

3 And David sent and inquired after the woman. And *one* said, Is not this Bathsheba, the daughter of Eliam, the wife of Uriah the Hittite?

4 And David sent messengers, and took her; and she came in unto him, and he lay with her; for she was purified from her uncleanness: and she returned unto her house.

5 And the woman conceived, and sent and told David, and said, I *am* with child.

6 And David sent to Joab, *saying*, Send me Uriah the Hittite. And Joab sent Uriah to David.

7 And when Uriah was come unto him, David demanded *of him* how Joab did, and how the people did, and how the war prospered.

8 And David said to Uriah, Go down to thy house, and wash thy feet. And Uriah departed out of the king's house, and there followed him a mess *of meat* from the king.

9 But Uriah slept at the door of the king's house with all the servants of his lord, and went not down to his house.

10 And when they had told David, saying, Uriah went not down unto his house, David said unto Uriah, Camest thou not from *thy*

Cross references (center column)

8 2Sam. 10:6

12 Deut. 31:6; 1Sam. 3:18; 4:9; 1Cor. 16:13

16 1Chr. 19:16

18 1Chr. 19:18, *footmen*

19 2Sam. 8:6

1 1Chr. 20:1

2 Gen. 34:2; Deut. 22:8; Job 31:1; Matt. 5:28

3 2Sam. 23:39; 1Chr. 3:5

4 Lev. 15:18; James 1:14

8 Gen. 18:4; 19:2

11:4 he lay with her. As great and privileged as David was, he yielded to the lusts of the flesh (Gal. 5:16–21) and suffered tragic consequences. Guilty of adultery and essentially guilty of murder, he sought to cover up his sins and rationalize his conduct. God forgave David, but "the sword" never departed from his house in his lifetime (2 Sam. 12:10). Though David truly repented of his sin, God did not eliminate the consequences of that sin. David's family was henceforth marked by death, sinful practices, and much travail: the death of this first son with Bathsheba (chap. 12), the incestuous rape of Tamar by David's son Amnon, the death of Amnon at the hands of Absalom (chap. 13), the rebellion and attempted coup of Absalom against David, which led to Absalom's death (chaps. 14—18), the insurrection led by Sheba and civil war (chap. 20), and the short-lived plot by Adonijah to supplant Solomon as David's successor (1 Kgs. 1).

journey? why *then* didst thou not go down unto thine house?

11 And Uriah said unto David, The ark, and Israel, and Judah, abide in tents; and my lord Joab, and the servants of my lord, are encamped in the open fields; shall I then go into mine house, to eat and to drink, and to lie with my wife? *as* thou livest, and *as* thy soul liveth, I will not do this thing.

12 And David said to Uriah, Tarry here today also, and to morrow I will let thee depart. So Uriah abode in Jerusalem that day, and the morrow.

13 And when David had called him, he did eat and drink before him; and he made him drunk: and at even he went out to lie on his bed with the servants of his lord, but went not down to his house.

14 And it came to pass in the morning, that David wrote a letter to Joab, and sent *it* by the hand of Uriah.

15 And he wrote in the letter, saying, Set ye Uriah in the forefront of the hottest battle, and retire ye from him, that he may be smitten, and die.

16 And it came to pass, when Joab observed the city, that he assigned Uriah unto a place where he knew that valiant men *were*.

17 And the men of the city went out, and fought with Joab: and there fell *some* of the people of the servants of David; and Uriah the Hittite died also.

18 Then Joab sent and told David all the things concerning the war;

19 And charged the messenger, saying, When thou hast made an end of telling the matters of the war unto the king,

20 And if so be that the king's wrath arise, and he say unto thee, Wherefore approached ye so nigh unto the city when ye did fight? knew ye not that they would shoot from the wall?

21 Who smote Abimelech the son of Jerubbesheth? did not a woman cast a piece of a millstone upon him from the wall, that he died in Thebez? why went ye nigh the wall? then say thou, Thy servant Uriah the Hittite is dead also.

22 So the messenger went, and came and shewed David all that Joab had sent him for.

23 And the messenger said unto David, Surely the men prevailed against us, and came out unto us into the field, and we were upon them even unto the entering of the gate.

24 And the shooters shot from off the wall upon thy servants; and *some* of the king's

---

servants be dead, and thy servant Uriah the Hittite is dead also.

25 Then David said unto the messenger, Thus shalt thou say unto Joab, Let not this thing displease thee, for the sword devoureth one as well as another: make thy battle more strong against the city, and overthrow it: and encourage thou him.

26 And when the wife of Uriah heard that Uriah her husband was dead, she mourned for her husband.

27 And when the mourning was past, David sent and fetched her to his house, and she became his wife, and bare him a son. But the thing that David had done displeased the LORD.

CHAPTER 12
Nathan Confronts David

1 And the LORD sent Nathan unto David. And he came unto him, and said unto him, There were two men in one city; the one rich, and the other poor.

2 The rich *man* had exceeding many flocks and herds:

3 But the poor *man* had nothing, save one little ewe lamb, which he had bought and nourished up: and it grew up together with him, and with his children; it did eat of his own meat, and drank of his own cup, and lay in his bosom, and was unto him as a daughter.

4 And there came a traveller unto the rich man, and he spared to take of his own flock and of his own herd, to dress for the wayfaring man that was come unto him; but took the poor man's lamb, and dressed it for the man that was come to him.

5 And David's anger was greatly kindled against the man; and he said to Nathan, As the LORD liveth, the man that hath done this *thing* shall surely die:

6 And he shall restore the lamb fourfold, because he did this thing, and because he had no pity.

7 And Nathan said to David, Thou *art* the man. Thus saith the LORD God of Israel, I anointed thee king over Israel, and I delivered thee out of the hand of Saul;

8 And I gave thee thy master's house, and thy master's wives into thy bosom, and gave thee the house of Israel and of Judah; and if *that had been* too little, I would moreover have given unto thee such and such things.

9 Wherefore hast thou despised the commandment of the LORD, to do evil in his sight? thou hast killed Uriah the Hittite with the sword, and hast taken his wife *to be*

Center column references:

11 2Sam. 7:2, 6; 20:6

13 Gen. 19:33, 35; 2Sam. 11:9

14 1Kgs. 21:8, 9

15 2Sam. 12:9

21 Judg. 6:32, *Jerub-baal*; 9:53; Jer. 11:13; Hos. 9:10

27 2Sam. 12:9

1 2Sam. 14:5; 1Kgs. 20:35-41; Isa. 5:3

5 1Sam. 26:16

6 Ex. 22:1; Luke 19:8

7 1Sam. 16:13

9 Num. 15:31; 1Sam. 15:19; 2Sam. 11:15-17, 27

thy wife, and hast slain him with the sword of the children of Ammon.

10 Now therefore the sword shall never depart from thine house; because thou hast despised me, and hast taken the wife of Uriah the Hittite to be thy wife.

11 Thus saith the LORD, Behold, I will raise up evil against thee out of thine own house, and I will take thy wives before thine eyes, and give *them* unto thy neighbour, and he shall lie with thy wives in the sight of this sun.

12 For thou didst *it* secretly: but I will do this thing before all Israel, and before the sun.

13 And David said unto Nathan, I have sinned against the LORD. And Nathan said unto David, The LORD also hath put away thy sin; thou shalt not die.

14 Howbeit, because by this deed thou hast given great occasion to the enemies of the LORD to blaspheme, the child also *that is* born unto thee shall surely die.

The Child Dies

15 And Nathan departed unto his house. And the LORD struck the child that Uriah's wife bare unto David, and it was very sick.

16 David therefore besought God for the child; and David fasted, and went in, and lay all night upon the earth.

17 And the elders of his house arose, *and went* to him, to raise him up from the earth: but he would not, neither did he eat bread with them.

18 And it came to pass on the seventh day, that the child died. And the servants of David feared to tell him that the child was dead: for they said, Behold, while the child was yet alive, we spake unto him, and he would not hearken unto our voice: how will he then vex himself, if we tell him that the child is dead?

19 But when David saw that his servants whispered, David perceived that the child was dead: therefore David said unto his servants, Is the child dead? And they said, He is dead.

20 Then David arose from the earth, and washed, and anointed *himself*, and changed his apparel, and came into the house of the LORD, and worshipped: then he came to his own house; and when he required, they set bread before him, and he did eat.

21 Then said his servants unto him, What thing *is* this that thou hast done? thou didst fast and weep for the child, *while it was* alive; but when the child was dead, thou didst rise and eat bread.

22 And he said, While the child was yet alive, I fasted and wept: for I said, Who can tell *whether* GOD will be gracious to me, that the child may live?

23 But now he is dead, wherefore should I fast? can I bring him back again? I shall go to him, but he shall not return to me.

Solomon Is Born

24 And David comforted Bath-sheba his wife, and went in unto her, and lay with her: and she bare a son, and he called his name Solomon: and the LORD loved him.

25 And he sent by the hand of Nathan the prophet; and he called his name Jedidiah, because of the LORD.

Another Victory over the Ammonites

26 And Joab fought against Rabbah of the children of Ammon, and took the royal city.

27 And Joab sent messengers to David, and said, I have fought against Rabbah, and have taken the city of waters.

28 Now therefore gather the rest of the people together, and encamp against the city, and take it: lest I take the city, and it be called after my name.

29 And David gathered all the people together, and went to Rabbah, and fought against it, and took it.

30 And he took their king's crown from off his head, the weight whereof *was* a talent of gold with the precious stones: and it was *set* on David's head. And he brought forth the spoil of the city in great abundance.

31 And he brought forth the people that *were* therein, and put *them* under saws, and under harrows of iron, and under axes of iron, and made them pass through the brickkiln: and thus did he unto all the cities of the children of Ammon. So David and all the people returned unto Jerusalem.

CHAPTER 13
Amnon Rapes Tamar

1 And it came to pass after this, that Absalom the son of David had a fair sister, whose name *was* Tamar; and Amnon the son of David loved her.

2 And Amnon was so vexed, that he fell sick for his sister Tamar; for she *was* a virgin; and Amnon thought it hard for him to do any thing to her.

3 But Amnon had a friend, whose name *was* Jonadab, the son of Shimeah David's brother: and Jonadab *was* a very subtil man.

4 And he said unto him, Why *art* thou,

being the king's son, lean from day to day? wilt thou not tell me? And Amnon said unto him, I love Tamar, my brother Absalom's sister.

5 And Jonadab said unto him, Lay thee down on thy bed, and make thyself sick: and when thy father cometh to see thee, say unto him, I pray thee, let my sister Tamar come, and give me meat, and dress the meat in my sight, that I may see *it*, and eat *it* at her hand.

6 So Amnon lay down, and made himself sick: and when the king was come to see him, Amnon said unto the king, I pray thee, let Tamar my sister come, and make me a couple of cakes in my sight, that I may eat at her hand.

7 Then David sent home to Tamar, saying, Go now to thy brother Amnon's house, and dress him meat.

8 So Tamar went to her brother Amnon's house; and he was laid down. And she took flour, and kneaded *it*, and made cakes in his sight, and did bake the cakes.

9 And she took a pan, and poured *them* out before him; but he refused to eat. And Amnon said, Have out all men from me. And they went out every man from him.

10 And Amnon said unto Tamar, Bring the meat into the chamber, that I may eat of thine hand. And Tamar took the cakes which she had made, and brought *them* into the chamber to Amnon her brother.

11 And when she had brought *them* unto him to eat, he took hold of her, and said unto her, Come lie with me, my sister.

12 And she answered him, Nay, my brother, do not force me; for no such thing ought to be done in Israel: do not thou this folly.

13 And I, whither shall I cause my shame to go? and as for thee, thou shalt be as one of the fools in Israel. Now therefore, I pray thee, speak unto the king; for he will not withhold me from thee.

14 Howbeit he would not hearken unto her voice: but, being stronger than she, forced her, and lay with her.

15 Then Amnon hated her exceedingly; so that the hatred wherewith he hated her *was* greater than the love wherewith he had loved her. And Amnon said unto her, Arise, be gone.

16 And she said unto him, *There is* no cause: this evil in sending me away *is* greater than the other that thou didst unto me. But he would not hearken unto her.

17 Then he called his servant that ministered unto him, and said, Put now this *woman* out from me, and bolt the door after her.

18 And *she had* a garment of divers colours upon her: for with such robes were the king's daughters *that were* virgins apparelled. Then his servant brought her out, and bolted the door after her.

19 And Tamar put ashes on her head, and rent her garment of divers colours that *was* on her, and laid her hand on her head, and went on crying.

Absalom Avenges Tamar

20 And Absalom her brother said unto her, Hath Amnon thy brother been with thee? but hold now thy peace, my sister: he *is* thy brother; regard not this thing. So Tamar remained desolate in her brother Absalom's house.

21 But when king David heard of all these things, he was very wroth.

22 And Absalom spake unto his brother Amnon neither good nor bad: for Absalom hated Amnon, because he had forced his sister Tamar.

23 And it came to pass after two full years, that Absalom had sheepshearers in Baal-hazor, which *is* beside Ephraim: and Absalom invited all the king's sons.

24 And Absalom came to the king, and said, Behold now, thy servant hath sheepshearers; let the king, I beseech thee, and his servants go with thy servant.

25 And the king said to Absalom, Nay, my son, let us not all now go, lest we be chargeable unto thee. And he pressed him: howbeit he would not go, but blessed him.

26 Then said Absalom, If not, I pray thee, let my brother Amnon go with us. And the king said unto him, Why should he go with thee?

27 But Absalom pressed him, that he let Amnon and all the king's sons go with him.

28 Now Absalom had commanded his servants, saying, Mark ye now when Amnon's heart is merry with wine, and when I say unto you, Smite Amnon; then kill him, fear not: have not I commanded you? be courageous, and be valiant.

29 And the servants of Absalom did unto Amnon as Absalom had commanded. Then all the king's sons arose, and every man gat him up upon his mule, and fled.

30 And it came to pass, while they were in the way, that tidings came to David, saying, Absalom hath slain all the king's sons, and there is not one of them left.

31 Then the king arose, and tare his gar-

---

6 Gen. 18:6

9 Gen. 45:1

11 Gen. 39:12

12 Gen. 34:7; Lev. 18:9, 11; 20:17; Judg. 19:23; 20:6

13 Lev. 18:9, 11

14 Deut. 22:25; 2Sam. 12:11

18 Gen. 37:3; Judg. 5:30; Ps. 45:14

19 Josh. 7:6; 2Sam. 1:2; Job 2:12; Jer. 2:37

22 Gen. 24:50; 31:24; Lev. 19:17, 18

23 Gen. 38:12, 13; 1Sam. 25:4, 36

28 Judg. 19:6, 9, 22; Ruth 3:7; 1Sam. 25:36; Esth. 1:10; Ps. 104:15

31 2Sam. 1:11; 12:16

ments, and lay on the earth; and all his servants stood by with their clothes rent.

32 And Jonadab, the son of Shimeah David's brother, answered and said, Let not my lord suppose *that* they have slain all the young men the king's sons; for Amnon only is dead: for by the appointment of Absalom this hath been determined from the day that he forced his sister Tamar.

33 Now therefore let not my lord the king take the thing to his heart, to think that all the king's sons are dead: for Amnon only is dead.

Absalom Escapes

34 But Absalom fled. And the young man that kept the watch lifted up his eyes, and looked, and, behold, there came much people by the way of the hill side behind him.

35 And Jonadab said unto the king, Behold, the king's sons come: as thy servant said, so it is.

36 And it came to pass, as soon as he had made an end of speaking, that, behold, the king's sons came, and lifted up their voice and wept: and the king also and all his servants wept very sore.

37 But Absalom fled, and went to Talmai, the son of Ammihud, king of Geshur. And *David* mourned for his son every day.

38 So Absalom fled, and went to Geshur, and was there three years.

39 And *the soul of* king David longed to go forth unto Absalom: for he was comforted concerning Amnon, seeing he was dead.

CHAPTER 14
Joab Plots Absalom's Return

1 Now Joab the son of Zeruiah perceived that the king's heart *was* toward Absalom.

2 And Joab sent to Tekoah, and fetched thence a wise woman, and said unto her, I pray thee, feign thyself to be a mourner, and put on now mourning apparel, and anoint not thyself with oil, but be as a woman that had a long time mourned for the dead:

3 And come to the king, and speak on this manner unto him. So Joab put the words in her mouth.

4 And when the woman of Tekoah spake to the king, she fell on her face to the ground, and did obeisance, and said, Help, O king.

5 And the king said unto her, What aileth thee? And she answered, I *am* indeed a widow woman, and mine husband is dead.

6 And thy handmaid had two sons, and they two strove together in the field, and

there was none to part them, but the one smote the other, and slew him.

7 And, behold, the whole family is risen against thine handmaid, and they said, Deliver him that smote his brother, that we may kill him, for the life of his brother whom he slew; and we will destroy the heir also: and so they shall quench my coal which is left, and shall not leave to my husband *neither* name nor remainder upon the earth.

8 And the king said unto the woman, Go to thine house, and I will give charge concerning thee.

9 And the woman of Tekoah said unto the king, My lord, O king, the iniquity *be* on me, and on my father's house: and the king and his throne *be* guiltless.

10 And the king said, Whosoever saith *ought* unto thee, bring him to me, and he shall not touch thee any more.

11 Then said she, I pray thee, let the king remember the LORD thy God, that thou wouldest not suffer the revengers of blood to destroy any more, lest they destroy my son. And he said, *As* the LORD liveth, there shall not one hair of thy son fall to the earth.

12 Then the woman said, Let thine handmaid, I pray thee, speak *one* word unto my lord the king. And he said, Say on.

13 And the woman said, Wherefore then hast thou thought such a thing against the people of God? for the king doth speak this thing as one which is faulty, in that the king doth not fetch home again his banished.

14 For we must needs die, and *are* as water spilt on the ground, which cannot be gathered up again; neither doth God respect *any* person: yet doth he devise means, that his banished be not expelled from him.

15 Now therefore that I am come to speak of this thing unto my lord the king, *it is* because the people have made me afraid: and thy handmaid said, I will now speak unto the king; it may be that the king will perform the request of his handmaid.

16 For the king will hear, to deliver his handmaid out of the hand of the man *that would* destroy me and my son together out of the inheritance of God.

17 Then thine handmaid said, The word of my lord the king shall now be comfortable: for as an angel of God, so *is* my lord the king to discern good and bad: therefore the LORD thy God will be with thee.

18 Then the king answered and said unto the woman, Hide not from me, I pray thee,

32 2Sam. 13:3

33 2Sam. 19:19

34 2Sam. 13:38

37 2Sam. 3:3

38 2Sam. 14:23, 32; 15:8

39 Gen. 38:12; Ps. 84:2

1 2Sam. 13:30

2 Ruth 3:3; 2Chr. 11:6

3 Ex. 4:14; 2Sam. 14:19

4 1Sam. 20:41; 2Sam. 1:2; 2Kgs. 6:26, 28

5 2Sam. 12:1

7 Num. 35:19; Deut. 19:12

9 Gen. 27:13; 1Sam. 25:24; 2Sam. 3:28, 29; 1Kgs. 2:33; Matt. 27:25

11 Num. 35:19; 1Sam. 14:45; Acts 27:34

13 Judg. 20:2; 2Sam. 13:37, 38

14 Num. 35:15, 25, 28; Job 34:15; Heb. 9:27

17 2Sam. 14:20; 19:27

the thing that I shall ask thee. And the woman said, Let my lord the king now speak.

19 And the king said, *Is not* the hand of Joab with thee in all this? And the woman answered and said, *As* thy soul liveth, my lord the king, none can turn to the right hand or to the left from ought that my lord the king hath spoken: for thy servant Joab, he bade me, and he put all these words in the mouth of thine handmaid:

20 To fetch about this form of speech hath thy servant Joab done this thing: and my lord *is* wise, according to the wisdom of an angel of God, to know all *things* that *are* in the earth.

21 And the king said unto Joab, Behold now, I have done this thing: go therefore, bring the young man Absalom again.

22 And Joab fell to the ground on his face, and bowed himself, and thanked the king: and Joab said, Today thy servant knoweth that I have found grace in thy sight, my lord, O king, in that the king hath fulfilled the request of his servant.

23 So Joab arose and went to Geshur, and brought Absalom to Jerusalem.

24 And the king said, Let him turn to his own house, and let him not see my face. So Absalom returned to his own house, and saw not the king's face.

Absalom Returns to Jerusalem

25 But in all Israel there was none to be so much praised as Absalom for his beauty: from the sole of his foot even to the crown of his head there was no blemish in him.

26 And when he polled his head, (for it was at every year's end that he polled *it*: because *the hair* was heavy on him, therefore he polled it:) he weighed the hair of his head at two hundred shekels after the king's weight.

27 And unto Absalom there were born three sons, and one daughter, whose name *was* Tamar: she was a woman of a fair countenance.

28 So Absalom dwelt two full years in Jerusalem, and saw not the king's face.

29 Therefore Absalom sent for Joab, to have sent him to the king; but he would not come to him: and when he sent again the second time, he would not come.

30 Therefore he said unto his servants, See, Joab's field is near mine, and he hath barley there; go and set it on fire. And Absalom's servants set the field on fire.

31 Then Joab arose, and came to Absalom

unto *his* house, and said unto him, Wherefore have thy servants set my field on fire?

32 And Absalom answered Joab, Behold, I sent unto thee, saying, Come hither, that I may send thee to the king, to say, Wherefore am I come from Geshur? *it had been* good for me *to have been* there still: now therefore let me see the king's face; and if there be *any* iniquity in me, let him kill me.

33 So Joab came to the king, and told him: and when he had called for Absalom, he came to the king, and bowed himself on his face to the ground before the king: and the king kissed Absalom.

CHAPTER 15
Absalom Prepares for a Revolt

1 And it came to pass after this, that Absalom prepared him chariots and horses, and fifty men to run before him.

2 And Absalom rose up early, and stood beside the way of the gate: and it was *so*, that when any man that had a controversy came to the king for judgment, then Absalom called unto him, and said, Of what city *art* thou? And he said, Thy servant *is* of one of the tribes of Israel.

3 And Absalom said unto him, See, thy matters *are* good and right; but *there is* no man *deputed* of the king to hear thee.

4 Absalom said moreover, Oh that I were made judge in the land, that every man which hath any suit or cause might come unto me, and I would do him justice!

5 And it was *so*, that when any man came nigh *to him* to do him obeisance, he put forth his hand, and took him, and kissed him.

6 And on this manner did Absalom to all Israel that came to the king for judgment: so Absalom stole the hearts of the men of Israel.

7 And it came to pass after forty years, that Absalom said unto the king, I pray thee, let me go and pay my vow, which I have vowed unto the LORD, in Hebron.

8 For thy servant vowed a vow while I abode at Geshur in Syria, saying, If the LORD shall bring me again indeed to Jerusalem, then I will serve the LORD.

9 And the king said unto him, Go in peace. So he arose, and went to Hebron.

10 But Absalom sent spies throughout all the tribes of Israel, saying, As soon as ye hear the sound of the trumpet, then ye shall say, Absalom reigneth in Hebron.

11 And with Absalom went two hundred men out of Jerusalem, *that were* called; and

Cross references (center column)

19 2Sam. 14:3

20 2Sam. 14:17; 19:27

23 2Sam. 13:37

24 Gen. 43:3; 2Sam. 3:13

25 Isa. 1:6

27 2Sam. 18:18

28 2Sam. 14:24

33 Gen. 33:4; 45:14; Luke 15:20

1 2Sam. 12:11; 1Kgs. 1:5

4 Judg. 9:29

6 Rom. 16:18

7 1Sam. 16:1

8 Gen. 28:20, 21; 1Sam. 16:2; 2Sam. 13:38

11 Gen. 20:5; 1Sam. 9:13; 16:3, 5

they went in their simplicity, and they knew not any thing.

12 And Absalom sent for Ahithophel the Gilonite, David's counseller, from his city, *even* from Giloh, while he offered sacrifices. And the conspiracy was strong; for the people increased continually with Absalom.

David Escapes

13 And there came a messenger to David, saying, The hearts of the men of Israel are after Absalom.

14 And David said unto all his servants that *were* with him at Jerusalem, Arise, and let us flee; for we shall not *else* escape from Absalom: make speed to depart, lest he overtake us suddenly, and bring evil upon us, and smite the city with the edge of the sword.

15 And the king's servants said unto the king, Behold, thy servants *are ready to do* whatsoever my lord the king shall appoint.

16 And the king went forth, and all his household after him. And the king left ten women, *which were* concubines, to keep the house.

17 And the king went forth, and all the people after him, and tarried in a place that was far off.

18 And all his servants passed on beside him; and all the Cherethites, and all the Pelethites, and all the Gittites, six hundred men which came after him from Gath, passed on before the king.

19 Then said the king to Ittai the Gittite, Wherefore goest thou also with us? return to thy place, and abide with the king: for thou *art* a stranger, and also an exile.

20 Whereas thou camest *but* yesterday, should I this day make thee go up and down with us? seeing I go whither I may, return thou, and take back thy brethren: mercy and truth *be* with thee.

21 And Ittai answered the king, and said, *As* the LORD liveth, and *as* my lord the king liveth, surely in what place my lord the king shall be, whether in death or life, even there also will thy servant be.

22 And David said to Ittai, Go and pass over. And Ittai the Gittite passed over, and all his men, and all the little ones that *were* with him.

23 And all the country wept with a loud voice, and all the people passed over: the king also himself passed over the brook Kidron, and all the people passed over, toward the way of the wilderness.

24 And lo Zadok also, and all the Levites *were* with him, bearing the ark of the cov-

enant of God: and they set down the ark of God; and Abiathar went up, until all the people had done passing out of the city.

25 And the king said unto Zadok, Carry back the ark of God into the city: if I shall find favour in the eyes of the LORD, he will bring me again, and shew me *both* it, and his habitation:

26 But if he thus say, I have no delight in thee; behold, *here am* I, let him do to me as seemeth good unto him.

27 The king said also unto Zadok the priest, *Art not* thou a seer? return into the city in peace, and your two sons with you, Ahimaaz thy son, and Jonathan the son of Abiathar.

28 See, I will tarry in the plain of the wilderness, until there come word from you to certify me.

29 Zadok therefore and Abiathar carried the ark of God again to Jerusalem: and they tarried there.

30 And David went up by the ascent of *mount* Olivet, and wept as he went up, and had his head covered, and he went barefoot: and all the people that *was* with him covered every man his head, and they went up, weeping as they went up.

31 And *one* told David, saying, Ahithophel *is* among the conspirators with Absalom. And David said, O LORD, I pray thee, turn the counsel of Ahithophel into foolishness.

32 And it came to pass, that *when* David was come to the top *of the mount*, where he worshipped God, behold, Hushai the Archite came to meet him with his coat rent, and earth upon his head:

33 Unto whom David said, If thou passest on with me, then thou shalt be a burden unto me:

34 But if thou return to the city, and say unto Absalom, I will be thy servant, O king; *as* I *have been* thy father's servant hitherto, so *will* I now also *be* thy servant: then mayest thou for me defeat the counsel of Ahithophel.

35 And *hast thou* not there with thee Zadok and Abiathar the priests? therefore it shall be, *that* what thing soever thou shalt hear out of the king's house, thou shalt tell *it* to Zadok and Abiathar the priests.

36 Behold, *they have* there with them their two sons, Ahimaaz Zadok's *son*, and Jonathan Abiathar's *son*; and by them ye shall send unto me every thing that ye can hear.

37 So Hushai David's friend came into the city, and Absalom came into Jerusalem.

---

12 Josh. 15:51; Ps. 3:1; 41:9; 55:12, 13, 14

13 Judg. 9:3; 2Sam. 15:6

14 2Sam. 19:9

16 2Sam. 16:21, 22

18 2Sam. 8:18

19 2Sam. 18:2

20 1Sam. 23:13

21 Ruth 1:16, 17; Prov. 17:17; 18:24

23 2Sam. 16:2; John 18:1, *Cedron*

24 Num. 4:15

25 Ps. 43:3

26 Num. 14:8; 1Sam. 3:18; 2Sam. 22:20; 1Kgs. 10:9; 2Chr. 9:8; Isa. 62:4

27 1Sam. 9:9; 2Sam. 17:17

28 2Sam. 17:16

30 2Sam. 19:4; Esth. 6:12; Ps. 126:6; Isa. 20:2, 4; Jer. 14:3, 4

31 2Sam. 16:23; 17:14, 23; Ps. 3:1, 2; 55:12

32 Josh. 16:2; 2Sam. 1:2

33 2Sam. 19:35

34 2Sam. 16:19

35 2Sam. 17:15, 16

36 2Sam. 15:27

37 2Sam. 16:15, 16; 1Chr. 27:33

CHAPTER 16

1 And when David was a little past the top *of the hill*, behold, Ziba the servant of Mephibosheth met him, with a couple of asses saddled, and upon them two hundred *loaves* of bread, and an hundred bunches of raisins, and an hundred of summer fruits, and a bottle of wine.

2 And the king said unto Ziba, What meanest thou by these? And Ziba said, The asses *be* for the king's household to ride on; and the bread and summer fruit for the young men to eat; and the wine, that such as be faint in the wilderness may drink.

3 And the king said, And where *is* thy master's son? And Ziba said unto the king, Behold, he abideth at Jerusalem: for he said, Today shall the house of Israel restore me the kingdom of my father.

4 Then said the king to Ziba, Behold, thine *are* all that *pertained* unto Mephibosheth. And Ziba said, I humbly beseech thee *that* I may find grace in thy sight, my lord, O king.

5 And when king David came to Bahurim, behold, thence came out a man of the family of the house of Saul, whose name *was* Shimei, the son of Gera: he came forth, and cursed still as he came.

6 And he cast stones at David, and at all the servants of king David: and all the people and all the mighty men *were* on his right hand and on his left.

7 And thus said Shimei when he cursed, Come out, come out, thou bloody man, and thou man of Belial:

8 The LORD hath returned upon thee all the blood of the house of Saul, in whose stead thou hast reigned; and the LORD hath delivered the kingdom into the hand of Absalom thy son: and, behold, thou *art taken* in thy mischief, because thou *art* a bloody man.

9 Then said Abishai the son of Zeruiah unto the king, Why should this dead dog curse my lord the king? let me go over, I pray thee, and take off his head.

10 And the king said, What have I to do with you, ye sons of Zeruiah? so let him curse, because the LORD hath said unto him, Curse David. Who shall then say, Wherefore hast thou done so?

11 And David said to Abishai, and to all his servants, Behold, my son, which came forth of my bowels, seeketh my life: how much more now *may this* Benjamite *do it*? let him alone, and let him curse; for the LORD hath bidden him.

12 It may be that the LORD will look on mine affliction, and that the LORD will requite me good for his cursing this day.

13 And as David and his men went by the way, Shimei went along on the hill's side over against him, and cursed as he went, and threw stones at him, and cast dust.

14 And the king, and all the people that *were* with him, came weary, and refreshed themselves there.

Absalom Returns to Jerusalem

15 And Absalom, and all the people the men of Israel, came to Jerusalem, and Ahithophel with him.

16 And it came to pass, when Hushai the Archite, David's friend, was come unto Absalom, that Hushai said unto Absalom, God save the king, God save the king.

17 And Absalom said to Hushai, *Is* this thy kindness to thy friend? why wentest thou not with thy friend?

18 And Hushai said unto Absalom, Nay; but whom the LORD, and this people, and all the men of Israel, choose, his will I be, and with him will I abide.

19 And again, whom should I serve? *should* I not *serve* in the presence of his son? as I have served in thy father's presence, so will I be in thy presence.

20 Then said Absalom to Ahithophel, Give counsel among you what we shall do.

21 And Ahithophel said unto Absalom, Go in unto thy father's concubines, which he hath left to keep the house; and all Israel shall hear that thou art abhorred of thy father: then shall the hands of all that *are* with thee be strong.

22 So they spread Absalom a tent upon the top of the house; and Absalom went in unto his father's concubines in the sight of all Israel.

23 And the counsel of Ahithophel, which he counselled in those days, *was* as if a man had inquired at the oracle of God: so *was* all the counsel of Ahithophel both with David and with Absalom.

CHAPTER 17
Absalom Receives Counsel

1 Moreover Ahithophel said unto Absalom, Let me now choose out twelve thousand men, and I will arise and pursue after David this night:

2 And I will come upon him while he *is* weary and weak handed, and will make him afraid: and all the people that *are* with him shall flee: and I will smite the king only:

3 And I will bring back all the people unto

Cross references

1 2Sam. 9:2; 15:30, 32
2 2Sam. 15:23; 17:29
3 2Sam. 19:27
4 Prov. 18:13
5 2Sam. 19:16; 1Kgs. 2:8, 44
7 Deut. 13:13
8 Judg. 9:24, 56, 57; 2Sam. 1:16; 3:28, 29; 4:11, 12; 1Kgs. 2:32, 33
9 Ex. 22:28; 1Sam. 24:14; 2Sam. 9:8
10 2Sam. 19:22; 2Kgs. 18:25; Lam. 3:38; Rom. 9:20; 1Pet. 2:23
11 Gen. 15:4; 2Sam. 12:11
12 Rom. 8:28
15 2Sam. 15:37
16 2Sam. 15:37
17 2Sam. 19:25; Prov. 17:17
19 2Sam. 15:34
21 Gen. 34:30; 1Sam. 13:4; 2Sam. 2:7; 15:16; 20:3; Zech. 8:13
22 2Sam. 12:11, 12
23 2Sam. 15:12

2 Deut. 25:18; 2Sam. 16:14; Zech. 13:7

thee: the man whom thou seekest *is* as if all returned: *so* all the people shall be in peace.

4 And the saying pleased Absalom well, and all the elders of Israel.

5 Then said Absalom, Call now Hushai the Archite also, and let us hear likewise what he saith.

6 And when Hushai was come to Absalom, Absalom spake unto him, saying, Ahithophel hath spoken after this manner: shall we do *after* his saying? if not; speak thou.

7 And Hushai said unto Absalom, The counsel that Ahithophel hath given *is* not good at this time.

8 For, said Hushai, thou knowest thy father and his men, that they *be* mighty men, and they *be* chafed in their minds, as a bear robbed of her whelps in the field: and thy father *is* a man of war, and will not lodge with the people.

9 Behold, he is hid now in some pit, or in some *other* place: and it will come to pass, when some of them be overthrown at the first, that whosoever heareth it will say, There is a slaughter among the people that follow Absalom.

10 And he also *that is* valiant, whose heart *is* as the heart of a lion, shall utterly melt: for all Israel knoweth that thy father *is* a mighty man, and *they* which *be* with him *are* valiant men.

11 Therefore I counsel that all Israel be generally gathered unto thee, from Dan even to Beer-sheba, as the sand that *is* by the sea for multitude; and that thou go to battle in thine own person.

12 So shall we come upon him in some place where he shall be found, and we will light upon him as the dew falleth on the ground: and of him and of all the men that *are* with him there shall not be left so much as one.

13 Moreover, if he be gotten into a city, then shall all Israel bring ropes to that city, and we will draw it into the river, until there be not one small stone found there.

14 And Absalom and all the men of Israel said, The counsel of Hushai the Archite *is* better than the counsel of Ahithophel. For the LORD had appointed to defeat the good counsel of Ahithophel, to the intent that the LORD might bring evil upon Absalom.

David Is Warned to Retreat

15 Then said Hushai unto Zadok and to Abiathar the priests, Thus and thus did Ahithophel counsel Absalom and the elders of Israel; and thus and thus have I counselled.

16 Now therefore send quickly, and tell David, saying, Lodge not this night in the plains of the wilderness, but speedily pass over; lest the king be swallowed up, and all the people that *are* with him.

17 Now Jonathan and Ahimaaz stayed by En-rogel; for they might not be seen to come into the city: and a wench went and told them; and they went and told king David.

18 Nevertheless a lad saw them, and told Absalom: but they went both of them away quickly, and came to a man's house in Bahurim, which had a well in his court; whither they went down.

19 And the woman took and spread a covering over the well's mouth, and spread ground corn thereon; and the thing was not known.

20 And when Absalom's servants came to the woman to the house, they said, Where *is* Ahimaaz and Jonathan? And the woman said unto them, They be gone over the brook of water. And when they had sought and could not find *them*, they returned to Jerusalem.

21 And it came to pass, after they were departed, that they came up out of the well, and went and told king David, and said unto David, Arise, and pass quickly over the water: for thus hath Ahithophel counselled against you.

22 Then David arose, and all the people that *were* with him, and they passed over Jordan: by the morning light there lacked not one of them that was not gone over Jordan.

23 And when Ahithophel saw that his counsel was not followed, he saddled *his* ass, and arose, and gat him home to his house, to his city, and put his household in order, and hanged himself, and died, and was buried in the sepulchre of his father.

Absalom Advances on David

24 Then David came to Mahanaim. And Absalom passed over Jordan, he and all the men of Israel with him.

25 And Absalom made Amasa captain of the host instead of Joab: which Amasa *was* a man's son, whose name *was* Ithra an Israelite, that went in to Abigail the daughter of Nahash, sister to Zeruiah Joab's mother.

26 So Israel and Absalom pitched in the land of Gilead.

27 And it came to pass, when David was come to Mahanaim, that Shobi the son of Nahash of Rabbah of the children of Ammon, and Machir the son of Ammiel

---

8 Hos. 13:8

10 Josh. 2:11

11 Gen. 22:17; Judg. 20:1

14 2Sam. 15:31, 34

15 2Sam. 15:35

16 2Sam. 15:28

17 Josh. 2:4; 15:7; 18:16; 2Sam. 15:27, 36

18 2Sam. 16:5

19 Josh. 2:6

20 Ex. 1:19; Josh. 2:4, 5

21 2Sam. 17:15, 16

23 2Sam. 15:12; Matt. 27:5

24 Gen. 32:2; Josh. 13:26; 2Sam. 2:8

25 1Chr. 2:13, 16, 17

27 2Sam. 9:4; 10:1; 12:29; 19:31, 32; 1Kgs. 2:7

of Lo-debar, and Barzillai the Gileadite of Rogelim,

28 Brought beds, and basons, and earthen vessels, and wheat, and barley, and flour, and parched *corn*, and beans, and lentiles, and parched *pulse*,

29 And honey, and butter, and sheep, and cheese of kine, for David, and for the people that *were* with him, to eat: for they said, The people *is* hungry, and weary, and thirsty, in the wilderness.

CHAPTER 18
Absalom's Death

1 And David numbered the people that *were* with him, and set captains of thousands and captains of hundreds over them.

2 And David sent forth a third part of the people under the hand of Joab, and a third part under the hand of Abishai the son of Zeruiah, Joab's brother, and a third part under the hand of Ittai the Gittite. And the king said unto the people, I will surely go forth with you myself also.

3 But the people answered, Thou shalt not go forth: for if we flee away, they will not care for us; neither if half of us die, will they care for us: but now *thou art* worth ten thousand of us: therefore now *it is* better that thou succour us out of the city.

4 And the king said unto them, What seemeth you best I will do. And the king stood by the gate side, and all the people came out by hundreds and by thousands.

5 And the king commanded Joab and Abishai and Ittai, saying, *Deal* gently for my sake with the young man, *even* with Absalom. And all the people heard when the king gave all the captains charge concerning Absalom.

6 So the people went out into the field against Israel: and the battle was in the wood of Ephraim;

7 Where the people of Israel were slain before the servants of David, and there was there a great slaughter that day of twenty thousand *men*.

8 For the battle was there scattered over the face of all the country: and the wood devoured more people that day than the sword devoured.

9 And Absalom met the servants of David. And Absalom rode upon a mule, and the mule went under the thick boughs of a great oak, and his head caught hold of the oak, and he was taken up between the heaven and the earth; and the mule that *was* under him went away.

10 And a certain man saw *it*, and told Joab, and said, Behold, I saw Absalom hanged in an oak.

11 And Joab said unto the man that told him, And, behold, thou sawest *him*, and why didst thou not smite him there to the ground? and I would have given thee ten *shekels* of silver, and a girdle.

12 And the man said unto Joab, Though I should receive a thousand *shekels* of silver in mine hand, *yet* would I not put forth mine hand against the king's son: for in our hearing the king charged thee and Abishai and Ittai, saying, Beware that none *touch* the young man Absalom.

13 Otherwise I should have wrought falsehood against mine own life: for there is no matter hid from the king, and thou thyself wouldest have set thyself against *me*.

14 Then said Joab, I may not tarry thus with thee. And he took three darts in his hand, and thrust them through the heart of Absalom, while he *was* yet alive in the midst of the oak.

15 And ten young men that bare Joab's armour compassed about and smote Absalom, and slew him.

16 And Joab blew the trumpet, and the people returned from pursuing after Israel: for Joab held back the people.

17 And they took Absalom, and cast him into a great pit in the wood, and laid a very great heap of stones upon him: and all Israel fled every one to his tent.

18 Now Absalom in his lifetime had taken and reared up for himself a pillar, which *is* in the king's dale: for he said, I have no son to keep my name in remembrance: and he called the pillar after his own name: and it is called unto this day, Absalom's place.

19 Then said Ahimaaz the son of Zadok, Let me now run, and bear the king tidings, how that the LORD hath avenged him of his enemies.

20 And Joab said unto him, Thou shalt not bear tidings this day, but thou shalt bear tidings another day: but this day thou shalt bear no tidings, because the king's son is dead.

21 Then said Joab to Cushi, Go tell the king what thou hast seen. And Cushi bowed himself unto Joab, and ran.

22 Then said Ahimaaz the son of Zadok yet again to Joab, But howsoever, let me, I pray thee, also run after Cushi. And Joab said, Wherefore wilt thou run, my son, seeing that thou hast no tidings ready?

23 But howsoever, *said he*, let me run. And

Center column references:

29 2Sam. 16:2

2 2Sam. 15:19

3 2Sam. 21:17

5 2Sam. 18:12

6 Josh. 17:15, 18

12 2Sam. 18:5

17 Josh. 7:26

18 Gen. 14:17; 2Sam. 14:27

he said unto him, Run. Then Ahimaaz ran by the way of the plain, and overran Cushi.

24 And David sat between the two gates: and the watchman went up to the roof over the gate unto the wall, and lifted up his eyes, and looked, and behold a man running alone.

25 And the watchman cried, and told the king. And the king said, If he *be* alone, *there is* tidings in his mouth. And he came apace, and drew near.

26 And the watchman saw another man running: and the watchman called unto the porter, and said, Behold *another* man running alone. And the king said, He also bringeth tidings.

27 And the watchman said, Me thinketh the running of the foremost is like the running of Ahimaaz the son of Zadok. And the king said, He *is* a good man, and cometh with good tidings.

28 And Ahimaaz called, and said unto the king, All is well. And he fell down to the earth upon his face before the king, and said, Blessed *be* the LORD thy God, which hath delivered up the men that lifted up their hand against my lord the king.

29 And the king said, Is the young man Absalom safe? And Ahimaaz answered, When Joab sent the king's servant, and *me* thy servant, I saw a great tumult, but I knew not what *it was*.

30 And the king said *unto him,* Turn aside, *and* stand here. And he turned aside, and stood still.

David Mourns Absalom

31 And, behold, Cushi came; and Cushi said, Tidings, my lord the king: for the LORD hath avenged thee this day of all them that rose up against thee.

32 And the king said unto Cushi, Is the young man Absalom safe? And Cushi answered, The enemies of my lord the king, and all that rise against thee to do *thee* hurt, be as *that* young man *is*.

33 And the king was much moved, and went up to the chamber over the gate, and wept: and as he went, thus he said, O my son Absalom, my son, my son Absalom! would God I had died for thee, O Absalom, my son, my son!

CHAPTER 19

1 And it was told Joab, Behold, the king weepeth and mourneth for Absalom.

2 And the victory that day was *turned* into mourning unto all the people: for the people

heard say that day how the king was grieved for his son.

3 And the people gat them by stealth that day into the city, as people being ashamed steal away when they flee in battle.

4 But the king covered his face, and the king cried with a loud voice, O my son Absalom, O Absalom, my son, my son!

5 And Joab came into the house to the king, and said, Thou hast shamed this day the faces of all thy servants, which this day have saved thy life, and the lives of thy sons and of thy daughters, and the lives of thy wives, and the lives of thy concubines;

6 In that thou lovest thine enemies, and hatest thy friends. For thou hast declared this day, that thou regardest neither princes nor servants: for this day I perceive, that if Absalom had lived, and all we had died this day, then it had pleased thee well.

7 Now therefore arise, go forth, and speak comfortably unto thy servants: for I swear by the LORD, if thou go not forth, there will not tarry one with thee this night: and that will be worse unto thee than all the evil that befell thee from thy youth until now.

8 Then the king arose, and sat in the gate. And they told unto all the people, saying, Behold, the king doth sit in the gate. And all the people came before the king: for Israel had fled every man to his tent.

David's Kingdom Is Restored

9 And all the people were at strife throughout all the tribes of Israel, saying, The king saved us out of the hand of our enemies, and he delivered us out of the hand of the Philistines; and now he is fled out of the land for Absalom.

10 And Absalom, whom we anointed over us, is dead in battle. Now therefore why speak ye not a word of bringing the king back?

11 And king David sent to Zadok and to Abiathar the priests, saying, Speak unto the elders of Judah, saying, Why are ye the last to bring the king back to his house? seeing the speech of all Israel is come to the king, *even* to his house.

12 Ye *are* my brethren, ye *are* my bones and my flesh: wherefore then are ye the last to bring back the king?

13 And say ye to Amasa, *Art* thou not of my bone, and of my flesh? God do so to me, and more also, if thou be not captain of the host before me continually in the room of Joab.

14 And he bowed the heart of all the men of Judah, even as *the heart of* one man; so that

---

Cross-references (center column):

24 2Kgs. 9:17

33 2Sam. 19:4

3 2Sam. 19:32

4 2Sam. 15:30; 18:33

9 2Sam. 15:14

12 2Sam. 5:1

13 Ruth 1:17; 2Sam. 17:25

14 Judg. 20:1

they sent *this word* unto the king, Return thou, and all thy servants.

15 So the king returned, and came to Jordan. And Judah came to Gilgal, to go to meet the king, to conduct the king over Jordan.

16 And Shimei the son of Gera, a Benjamite, which *was* of Bahurim, hasted and came down with the men of Judah to meet king David.

17 And *there were* a thousand men of Benjamin with him, and Ziba the servant of the house of Saul, and his fifteen sons and his twenty servants with him; and they went over Jordan before the king.

18 And there went over a ferry boat to carry over the king's household, and to do what he thought good. And Shimei the son of Gera fell down before the king, as he was come over Jordan;

19 And said unto the king, Let not my lord impute iniquity unto me, neither do thou remember that which thy servant did perversely the day that my lord the king went out of Jerusalem, that the king should take it to his heart.

20 For thy servant doth know that I have sinned: therefore, behold, I am come the first this day of all the house of Joseph to go down to meet my lord the king.

21 But Abishai the son of Zeruiah answered and said, Shall not Shimei be put to death for this, because he cursed the LORD's anointed?

22 And David said, What have I to do with you, ye sons of Zeruiah, that ye should this day be adversaries unto me? shall there any man be put to death this day in Israel? for do not I know that I *am* this day king over Israel?

23 Therefore the king said unto Shimei, Thou shalt not die. And the king sware unto him.

24 And Mephibosheth the son of Saul came down to meet the king, and had neither dressed his feet, nor trimmed his beard, nor washed his clothes, from the day the king departed until the day he came *again* in peace.

25 And it came to pass, when he was come to Jerusalem to meet the king, that the king said unto him, Wherefore wentest not thou with me, Mephibosheth?

26 And he answered, My lord, O king, my servant deceived me: for thy servant said, I will saddle me an ass, that I may ride thereon, and go to the king; because thy servant *is* lame.

27 And he hath slandered thy servant unto my lord the king; but my lord the king *is* as an angel of God: do therefore *what is* good in thine eyes.

28 For all *of* my father's house were but dead men before my lord the king: yet didst thou set thy servant among them that did eat at thine own table. What right therefore have I yet to cry any more unto the king?

29 And the king said unto him, Why speakest thou any more of thy matters? I have said, Thou and Ziba divide the land.

30 And Mephibosheth said unto the king, Yea, let him take all, forasmuch as my lord the king is come again in peace unto his own house.

31 And Barzillai the Gileadite came down from Rogelim, and went over Jordan with the king, to conduct him over Jordan.

32 Now Barzillai was a very aged man, *even* fourscore years old: and he had provided the king of sustenance while he lay at Mahanaim; for he *was* a very great man.

33 And the king said unto Barzillai, Come thou over with me, and I will feed thee with me in Jerusalem.

34 And Barzillai said unto the king, How long have I to live, that I should go up with the king unto Jerusalem?

35 I *am* this day fourscore years old: *and* can I discern between good and evil? can thy servant taste what I eat or what I drink? can I hear any more the voice of singing men and singing women? wherefore then should thy servant be yet a burden unto my lord the king?

36 Thy servant will go a little way over Jordan with the king: and why should the king recompense it me with such a reward?

37 Let thy servant, I pray thee, turn back again, that I may die in mine own city, *and be buried* by the grave of my father and of my mother. But behold thy servant Chimham; let him go over with my lord the king; and do to him what shall seem good unto thee.

38 And the king answered, Chimham shall go over with me, and I will do to him that which shall seem good unto thee: and whatsoever thou shalt require of me, *that* will I do for thee.

39 And all the people went over Jordan. And when the king was come over, the king kissed Barzillai, and blessed him; and he returned unto his own place.

40 Then the king went on to Gilgal, and Chimham went on with him: and all the people of Judah conducted the king, and also half the people of Israel.

15 Josh. 5:9
16 2Sam. 16:5; 1Kgs. 2:8
17 2Sam. 9:2, 10; 16:1, 2
19 1Sam. 22:15; 2Sam. 13:33; 16:5, 6
20 2Sam. 16:5
21 Ex. 22:28
22 1Sam. 11:13; 2Sam. 16:10
23 1Kgs. 2:8, 9, 37, 46
24 2Sam. 9:6
25 2Sam. 16:17
27 2Sam. 14:17, 20; 16:3
28 2Sam. 9:7, 10, 13
31 1Kgs. 2:7
32 2Sam. 17:27
35 Ps. 90:10
37 1Kgs. 2:7; Jer. 41:17
39 Gen. 31:55

41 And, behold, all the men of Israel came to the king, and said unto the king, Why have our brethren the men of Judah stolen thee away, and have brought the king, and his household, and all David's men with him, over Jordan?

42 And all the men of Judah answered the men of Israel, Because the king *is* near of kin to us: wherefore then be ye angry for this matter? have we eaten at all of the king's *cost?* or hath he given us any gift?

43 And the men of Israel answered the men of Judah, and said, We have ten parts in the king, and we have also more *right* in David than ye: why then did ye despise us, that our advice should not be first had in bringing back our king? And the words of the men of Judah were fiercer than the words of the men of Israel.

CHAPTER 20
Sheba's Revolt

1 And there happened to be there a man of Belial, whose name *was* Sheba, the son of Bichri, a Benjamite: and he blew a trumpet, and said, We have no part in David, neither have we inheritance in the son of Jesse: every man to his tents, O Israel.

2 So every man of Israel went up from after David, *and* followed Sheba the son of Bichri: but the men of Judah clave unto their king, from Jordan even to Jerusalem.

3 And David came to his house at Jerusalem; and the king took the ten women *his* concubines, whom he had left to keep the house, and put them in ward, and fed them, but went not in unto them. So they were shut up unto the day of their death, living in widowhood.

4 Then said the king to Amasa, Assemble me the men of Judah within three days, and be thou here present.

5 So Amasa went to assemble *the men of* Judah: but he tarried longer than the set time which he had appointed him.

6 And David said to Abishai, Now shall Sheba the son of Bichri do us more harm than *did* Absalom: take thou thy lord's servants, and pursue after him, lest he get him fenced cities, and escape us.

7 And there went out after him Joab's men, and the Cherethites, and the Pelethites, and all the mighty men: and they went out of Jerusalem, to pursue after Sheba the son of Bichri.

8 When they *were* at the great stone which *is* in Gibeon, Amasa went before them. And Joab's garment that he had put on was

girded unto him, and upon it a girdle *with* a sword fastened upon his loins in the sheath thereof; and as he went forth it fell out.

9 And Joab said to Amasa, *Art* thou in health, my brother? And Joab took Amasa by the beard with the right hand to kiss him.

10 But Amasa took no heed to the sword that *was* in Joab's hand: so he smote him therewith in the fifth *rib*, and shed out his bowels to the ground, and struck him not again; and he died. So Joab and Abishai his brother pursued after Sheba the son of Bichri.

11 And one of Joab's men stood by him, and said, He that favoureth Joab, and he that *is* for David, *let him go* after Joab.

12 And Amasa wallowed in blood in the midst of the highway. And when the man saw that all the people stood still, he removed Amasa out of the highway into the field, and cast a cloth upon him, when he saw that every one that came by him stood still.

13 When he was removed out of the highway, all the people went on after Joab, to pursue after Sheba the son of Bichri.

14 And he went through all the tribes of Israel unto Abel, and to Beth-maachah, and all the Berites: and they were gathered together, and went also after him.

15 And they came and besieged him in Abel of Beth-maachah, and they cast up a bank against the city, and it stood in the trench: and all the people that *were* with Joab battered the wall, to throw it down.

16 Then cried a wise woman out of the city, Hear, hear; say, I pray you, unto Joab, Come near hither, that I may speak with thee.

17 And when he was come near unto her, the woman said, *Art* thou Joab? And he answered, I *am* he. Then she said unto him Hear the words of thine handmaid. And he answered, I do hear.

18 Then she spake, saying, They were wont to speak in old time, saying, They shall surely ask *counsel* at Abel: and so they ended *the matter.*

19 I *am one of them that are* peaceable *and* faithful in Israel: thou seekest to destroy a city and a mother in Israel: why wilt thou swallow up the inheritance of the LORD?

20 And Joab answered and said, Far be it, far be it from me, that I should swallow up or destroy.

21 The matter *is* not so: but a man of mount Ephraim, Sheba the son of Bichri by name, hath lifted up his hand against the king,

41 2Sam.
19:15
42 2Sam.
19:12
43 Judg. 8:1;
12:1
1 2Sam.
19:43; 1Kgs.
12:16; 2Chr.
10:16
3 2Sam.
15:16; 16:21,
22
4 2Sam.
19:13
6 2Sam.
11:11; 1Kgs.
1:33
7 2Sam.
8:18; 1Kgs.
1:38
9 Matt.
26:49; Luke
22:47
10 2Sam.
2:23; 1Kgs.
2:5

14 2Kgs.
15:29; 2Chr.
16:4

15 2Kgs.
19:32

18 Deut.
20:11

19 1Sam.
26:19; 2Sam.
21:3

even against David: deliver him only, and I will depart from the city. And the woman said unto Joab, Behold, his head shall be thrown to thee over the wall.

22 Then the woman went unto all the people in her wisdom. And they cut off the head of Sheba the son of Bichri, and cast *it* out to Joab. And he blew a trumpet, and they retired from the city, every man to his tent. And Joab returned to Jerusalem unto the king.

David's Officials

23 Now Joab *was* over all the host of Israel: and Benaiah the son of Jehoiada *was* over the Cherethites and over the Pelethites:
24 And Adoram *was* over the tribute: and Jehoshaphat the son of Ahilud *was* recorder:
25 And Sheva *was* scribe: and Zadok and Abiathar *were* the priests:
26 And Ira also the Jairite was a chief ruler about David.

CHAPTER 21
Gibeonites Are Avenged

1 Then there was a famine in the days of David three years, year after year; and David inquired of the LORD. And the LORD answered, It is for Saul, and for *his* bloody house, because he slew the Gibeonites.
2 And the king called the Gibeonites, and said unto them; (now the Gibeonites *were* not of the children of Israel, but of the remnant of the Amorites; and the children of Israel had sworn unto them: and Saul sought to slay them in his zeal to the children of Israel and Judah.)
3 Wherefore David said unto the Gibeonites, What shall I do for you? and wherewith shall I make the atonement, that ye may bless the inheritance of the LORD?
4 And the Gibeonites said unto him, We will have no silver nor gold of Saul, nor of his house; neither for us shalt thou kill any man in Israel. And he said, What ye shall say, *that* will I do for you.
5 And they answered the king, The man that consumed us, and that devised against us *that* we should be destroyed from remaining in any of the coasts of Israel,
6 Let seven men of his sons be delivered unto us, and we will hang them up unto the LORD in Gibeah of Saul, *whom* the LORD did choose. And the king said, I will give *them*.
7 But the king spared Mephibosheth, the son of Jonathan the son of Saul, because of the LORD's oath that *was* between them, between David and Jonathan the son of Saul.

8 But the king took the two sons of Rizpah the daughter of Aiah, whom she bare unto Saul, Armoni and Mephibosheth; and the five sons of Michal the daughter of Saul, whom she brought up for Adriel the son of Barzillai the Meholathite:
9 And he delivered them into the hands of the Gibeonites, and they hanged them in the hill before the LORD: and they fell *all* seven together, and were put to death in the days of harvest, in the first *days*, in the beginning of barley harvest.
10 And Rizpah the daughter of Aiah took sackcloth, and spread it for her upon the rock, from the beginning of harvest until water dropped upon them out of heaven, and suffered neither the birds of the air to rest on them by day, nor the beasts of the field by night.
11 And it was told David what Rizpah the daughter of Aiah, the concubine of Saul, had done.
12 And David went and took the bones of Saul and the bones of Jonathan his son from the men of Jabesh-gilead, which had stolen them from the street of Beth-shan, where the Philistines had hanged them, when the Philistines had slain Saul in Gilboa:
13 And he brought up from thence the bones of Saul and the bones of Jonathan his son; and they gathered the bones of them that were hanged.
14 And the bones of Saul and Jonathan his son buried they in the country of Benjamin in Zelah, in the sepulchre of Kish his father: and they performed all that the king commanded. And after that God was intreated for the land.

Philistine Giants Die in Battle

15 Moreover the Philistines had yet war again with Israel; and David went down, and his servants with him, and fought against the Philistines: and David waxed faint.
16 And Ishbibenob, which *was* of the sons of the giant, the weight of whose spear *weighed* three hundred *shekels* of brass in weight, he being girded with a new *sword*, thought to have slain David.
17 But Abishai the son of Zeruiah succoured him, and smote the Philistine, and killed him. Then the men of David sware unto him, saying, Thou shalt go no more out with us to battle, that thou quench not the light of Israel.
18 And it came to pass after this, that there was again a battle with the Philistines at

22 Eccl. 9:14, 15
23 2Sam. 8:16, 18
24 2Sam. 8:16; 1Kgs. 4:3, 6
25 2Sam. 8:17; 1Kgs. 4:4
26 Gen. 41:45; Ex. 2:16; 2Sam. 8:18; 23:38
1 Num. 27:21
2 Josh. 9:3, 15-17
3 2Sam. 20:19
6 1Sam. 10:24, 26; 11:4
7 1Sam. 18:3; 20:8, 15, 42; 23:18
8 2Sam. 3:7
9 2Sam. 6:17
10 Deut. 21:23; 2Sam. 3:7; 21:8
12 1Sam. 31:10, 11-13
14 Josh. 7:26; 18:28; 2Sam. 24:25
17 2Sam. 18:3; 1Kgs. 11:36; 15:4; Ps. 132:17
18 1Chr. 11:29; 20:4

Gob: then Sibbechai the Hushathite slew Saph, which *was* of the sons of the giant.

19 And there was again a battle in Gob with the Philistines, where Elhanan the son of Jaare-oregim, a Beth-lehemite, slew *the brother of* Goliath the Gittite, the staff of whose spear *was* like a weaver's beam.

20 And there was yet a battle in Gath, where was a man of *great* stature, that had on every hand six fingers, and on every foot six toes, four and twenty in number; and he also was born to the giant.

21 And when he defied Israel, Jonathan the son of Shimea the brother of David slew him.

22 These four were born to the giant in Gath, and fell by the hand of David, and by the hand of his servants.

CHAPTER 22
David's Song

1 And David spake unto the LORD the words of this song in the day *that* the LORD had delivered him out of the hand of all his enemies, and out of the hand of Saul:

2 And he said, The LORD *is* my rock, and my fortress, and my deliverer;

3 The God of my rock; in him will I trust: *he is* my shield, and the horn of my salvation, my high tower, and my refuge, my saviour; thou savest me from violence.

4 I will call on the LORD, *who is* worthy to be praised: so shall I be saved from mine enemies.

5 When the waves of death compassed me, the floods of ungodly men made me afraid;

6 The sorrows of hell compassed me about; the snares of death prevented me;

7 In my distress I called upon the LORD, and cried to my God: and he did hear my voice out of his temple, and my cry *did enter* into his ears.

8 Then the earth shook and trembled; the foundations of heaven moved and shook, because he was wroth.

9 There went up a smoke out of his nostrils, and fire out of his mouth devoured: coals were kindled by it.

10 He bowed the heavens also, and came down; and darkness *was* under his feet.

11 And he rode upon a cherub, and did fly: and he was seen upon the wings of the wind.

12 And he made darkness pavilions round about him, dark waters, *and* thick clouds of the skies.

13 Through the brightness before him were coals of fire kindled.

14 The LORD thundered from heaven, and the most High uttered his voice.

15 And he sent out arrows, and scattered them; lightning, and discomfited them.

16 And the channels of the sea appeared, the foundations of the world were discovered, at the rebuking of the LORD, at the blast of the breath of his nostrils.

17 He sent from above, he took me; he drew me out of many waters;

18 He delivered me from my strong enemy, *and* from them that hated me: for they were too strong for me.

19 They prevented me in the day of my calamity: but the LORD was my stay.

20 He brought me forth also into a large place: he delivered me, because he delighted in me.

21 The LORD rewarded me according to my righteousness: according to the cleanness of my hands hath he recompensed me.

22 For I have kept the ways of the LORD, and have not wickedly departed from my God.

23 For all his judgments *were* before me: and *as for* his statutes, I did not depart from them.

24 I was also upright before him and have kept myself from mine iniquity.

25 Therefore the LORD hath recompensed me according to my righteousness; according to my cleanness in his eye sight.

26 With the merciful thou wilt shew thyself merciful, *and* with the upright man thou wilt shew thyself upright.

27 With the pure thou wilt shew thyself pure; and with the froward thou wilt shew thyself unsavoury.

28 And the afflicted people thou wilt save: but thine eyes *are* upon the haughty, *that* thou mayest bring *them* down.

29 For thou *art* my lamp, O LORD: and the LORD will lighten my darkness.

30 For by thee I have run through a troop: by my God have I leaped over a wall.

Cross-references (center column)

19 1Chr. 20:5
21 1Sam. 16:9, *Shammah;* 17:10, 25, 26
22 1Chr. 20:8
1 Ex. 15:1; Judg. 5:1; Ps. 34:19
2 Ps. 18:2
3 Ps. 9:9; 14:6; Prov. 18:10; Luke 1:69
6 Ps. 116:3
7 Ex. 3:7; Ps. 34:6, 15, 17; 116:4; 120:1; Jon. 2:2
8 Judg. 5:4; Ps. 77:18; 97:4; Job 26:11
9 Ps. 97:3; Hab. 3:5; Heb. 12:29
10 Ex. 20:21; 1Kgs. 8:12; Ps. 97:2; 144:5; Isa. 64:1
11 Ps. 104:3
12 2Sam. 22:10; Ps. 97:2
13 2Sam. 22:9
14 1Sam. 2:10; 7:10; Ps. 29:3
15 Deut. 32:23; Ps. 7:13; 77:17
16 Ps. 74:1; 106:9
17 Ps. 144:7
18 2Sam. 22:1
20 Ps. 22:8
26 Matt. 5:7
27 Ps. 18:26
28 Ps. 72:12, 13; Isa. 2:11, 12, 17; 5:15
29 Job 29:3; Ps. 27:1

22:2 The Lord is my rock. David wrote this great song of deliverance when he finally experienced victory over all of his enemies. So important is this prophetic ode, that it is included in the book of Psalms as well (Ps. 18). The dramatic and poetic description of victory and deliverance after rejection and suffering (vv. 7–20) suggests Christ's triumphant resurrection and ascension. God's blessings and approval (vv. 21–28) seem to go beyond the earthly David and apply appropriately to the great "Son of David."

31 *As for* God, his way *is* perfect; the word of the LORD *is* tried: he *is* a buckler to all them that trust in him.

32 For who *is* God, save the LORD? and who *is* a rock, save our God?

33 God *is* my strength *and* power: and he maketh my way perfect.

34 He maketh my feet like hinds' *feet*: and setteth me upon my high places.

35 He teacheth my hands to war; so that a bow of steel is broken by mine arms.

36 Thou hast also given me the shield of thy salvation: and thy gentleness hath made me great.

37 Thou hast enlarged my steps under me; so that my feet did not slip.

38 I have pursued mine enemies, and destroyed them; and turned not again until I had consumed them.

39 And I have consumed them, and wounded them, that they could not arise: yea, they are fallen under my feet.

40 For thou hast girded me with strength to battle: them that rose up against me hast thou subdued under me.

41 Thou hast also given me the necks of mine enemies, that I might destroy them that hate me.

42 They looked, but *there was* none to save; *even* unto the LORD, but he answered them not.

43 Then did I beat them as small as the dust of the earth, I did stamp them as the mire of the street, *and* did spread them abroad.

44 Thou also hast delivered me from the strivings of my people, thou hast kept me *to be* head of the heathen: a people *which* I knew not shall serve me.

45 Strangers shall submit themselves unto me: as soon as they hear, they shall be obedient unto me.

46 Strangers shall fade away, and they shall be afraid out of their close places.

47 The LORD liveth; and blessed *be* my rock; and exalted be the God of the rock of my salvation.

48 It *is* God that avengeth me, and that bringeth down the people under me,

49 And that bringeth me forth from mine enemies: thou also hast lifted me up on high above them that rose up against me: thou hast delivered me from the violent man.

50 Therefore I will give thanks unto thee, O LORD, among the heathen, and I will sing praises unto thy name.

51 *He is* the tower of salvation for his king: and sheweth mercy to his anointed, unto David, and to his seed for evermore.

CHAPTER 23
David's Last Words

1 Now these *be* the last words of David. David the son of Jesse said, and the man *who was* raised up on high, the anointed of the God of Jacob, and the sweet psalmist of Israel, said,

2 The Spirit of the LORD spake by me, and his word *was* in my tongue.

3 The God of Israel said, the Rock of Israel spake to me, He that ruleth over men *must be* just, ruling in the fear of God.

4 And *he shall be* as the light of the morning, *when* the sun riseth, *even* a morning without clouds; *as* the tender grass *springing* out of the earth by clear shining after rain.

5 Although my house *be* not so with God; yet he hath made with me an everlasting covenant, ordered in all *things*, and sure: for *this is* all my salvation, and all *my* desire, although he make *it* not to grow.

6 But *the sons* of Belial *shall be* all of them as thorns thrust away, because they cannot be taken with hands:

7 But the man *that* shall touch them must be fenced with iron and the staff of a spear; and they shall be utterly burned with fire in the *same* place.

David's Mighty Men

8 These *be* the names of the mighty men whom David had: The Tachmonite that sat in the seat, chief among the captains; the same *was* Adino the Eznite: *he lift up his spear* against eight hundred, whom he slew at one time.

9 And after him *was* Eleazar the son of Dodo the Ahohite, *one* of the three mighty men with David, when they defied the Philistines *that* were there gathered together to battle, and the men of Israel were gone away:

10 He arose, and smote the Philistines until his hand was weary, and his hand clave unto the sword: and the LORD wrought a

---

Cross references:

31 Deut. 32:4; Ps. 12:6; 119:140; Prov. 30:5; Dan. 4:37; Rev. 15:3

32 1Sam. 2:2; Isa. 45:5, 6

33 Job 22:3; Ps. 27:1; 28:7, 8

34 2Sam. 2:18; Isa. 33:16

35 Ps. 144:1

37 Prov. 4:12

39 Mal. 4:3

40 Ps. 18:32, 39; Ps. 44:5

41 Gen. 49:8; Ex. 23:27; Josh. 10:24

42 Job 27:9; Prov. 1:28

43 2Kgs. 13:7; Ps. 35:5

44 Deut. 28:13; Ps. 2:8; Isa. 55:5

46 Mic. 7:17

47 Ps. 89:26

48 Ps. 144:2

49 Ps. 140:1

51 Ps. 89:20, 29

2 2Pet. 1:21

3 Ex. 18:21; Deut. 32:4, 31; 2Sam. 22:2, 32; 2Chr. 19:7, 9; Ps. 110:2

4 Judg. 5:31; Ps. 89:36; Prov. 4:18; Hos. 6:5

5 2Sam. 7:15, 16; Ps. 89:29; Isa. 55:3

8 1Chr. 11:11; 27:2

9 1Chr. 11:12; 27:4

23:5 everlasting covenant. This last, short psalm by David speaks of the unconditional promise of a perpetual dynasty. Verses 3–4 speak of a righteous reign by a just ruler, who fears God, shining forth like the sun, a forward glimpse of the coming Millennial Kingdom.

great victory that day; and the people returned after him only to spoil.

11 And after him *was* Shammah the son of Agee the Hararite. And the Philistines were gathered together into a troop, where was a piece of ground full of lentiles: and the people fled from the Philistines.

12 But he stood in the midst of the ground, and defended it, and slew the Philistines: and the LORD wrought a great victory.

13 And three of the thirty chief went down, and came to David in the harvest time unto the cave of Adullam: and the troop of the Philistines pitched in the valley of Rephaim.

14 And David *was* then in an hold, and the garrison of the Philistines *was* then in Bethlehem.

15 And David longed, and said, Oh that one would give me drink of the water of the well of Beth-lehem, which *is* by the gate!

16 And the three mighty men brake through the host of the Philistines, and drew water out of the well of Beth-lehem, that *was* by the gate, and took *it*, and brought *it* to David: nevertheless he would not drink thereof, but poured it out unto the LORD.

17 And he said, Be it far from me, O LORD, that I should do this: *is not this* the blood of the men that went in jeopardy of their lives? therefore he would not drink it. These things did these three mighty men.

18 And Abishai, the brother of Joab, the son of Zeruiah, was chief among three. And he lifted up his spear against three hundred, *and* slew *them*, and had the name among three.

19 Was he not most honourable of three? therefore he was their captain: howbeit he attained not unto the *first* three.

20 And Benaiah the son of Jehoiada, the son of a valiant man, of Kabzeel, who had done many acts, he slew two lionlike men of Moab: he went down also and slew a lion in the midst of a pit in time of snow:

21 And he slew an Egyptian, a goodly man: and the Egyptian had a spear in his hand; but he went down to him with a staff, and plucked the spear out of the Egyptian's hand, and slew him with his own spear.

22 These *things* did Benaiah the son of Jehoiada, and had the name among three mighty men.

23 He was more honourable than the thirty, but he attained not to the *first* three. And David set him over his guard.

24 Asahel the brother of Joab *was* one of the thirty; Elhanan the son of Dodo of Bethlehem,

25 Shammah the Harodite, Elika the Harodite,

26 Helez the Paltite, Ira the son of Ikkesh the Tekoite,

27 Abiezer the Anethothite, Mebunnai the Hushathite,

28 Zalmon the Ahohite, Maharai the Netophathite,

29 Heleb the son of Baanah, a Netophathite, Ittai the son of Ribai out of Gibeah of the children of Benjamin,

30 Benaiah the Pirathonite, Hiddai of the brooks of Gaash,

31 Abi-albon the Arbathite, Azmaveth the Barhumite,

32 Eliahba the Shaalbonite, of the sons of Jashen, Jonathan,

33 Shammah the Hararite, Ahiam the son of Sharar the Hararite,

34 Eliphelet the son of Ahasbai, the son of the Maachathite, Eliam the son of Ahithophel the Gilonite,

35 Hezrai the Carmelite, Paarai the Arbite,

36 Igal the son of Nathan of Zobah, Bani the Gadite,

37 Zelek the Ammonite, Naharai the Beerothite, armourbearer to Joab the son of Zeruiah,

38 Ira an Ithrite, Gareb an Ithrite,

39 Uriah the Hittite: thirty and seven in all.

CHAPTER 24
David Takes a Census

1 And again the anger of the LORD was kindled against Israel, and he moved David against them to say, Go, number Israel and Judah.

2 For the king said to Joab the captain of the host, which *was* with him, Go now through all the tribes of Israel, from Dan even to Beer-sheba, and number ye the people, that I may know the number of the people.

3 And Joab said unto the king, Now the LORD thy God add unto the people, how many soever they be an hundredfold, and that the eyes of my lord the king may see *it*: but why doth my lord the king delight in this thing?

4 Notwithstanding the king's word prevailed against Joab, and against the captains of the host. And Joab and the captains of the host went out from the presence of the king, to number the people of Israel.

5 And they passed over Jordan, and pitched in Aroer, on the right side of the city that *lieth* in the midst of the river of Gad, and toward Jazer:

Center column cross-references:

11 1Chr. 11:13, 14, 27
13 1Sam. 22:1; 2Sam. 5:18; 1Chr. 11:15
14 1Sam. 22:4, 5
17 Lev. 17:10
18 1Chr. 11:20
20 Ex. 15:15; Josh. 15:21; 1Chr. 11:22
21 1Chr. 11:23, *a man of great stature*
23 1Sam. 22:14; 2Sam. 8:18; 20:23
24 2Sam. 2:18
25 1Chr. 11:27
30 Deut. 1:24; Judg. 2:9
38 2Sam. 20:26
39 2Sam. 11:3, 6

1 2Sam. 21:2; 1Chr. 21:1; 27:23, 24; James 1:13, 14
2 Judg. 20:1; Jer. 17:5

5 Num. 32:1, 3; Deut. 2:36; Josh. 13:9, 16

6 Then they came to Gilead, and to the land of Tahtim-hodshi; and they came to Dan-jaan, and about to Zidon,

7 And came to the strong hold of Tyre, and to all the cities of the Hivites, and of the Canaanites: and they went out *to* the south of Judah, *even* to Beer-sheba.

8 So when they had gone through all the land, they came to Jerusalem at the end of nine months and twenty days.

9 And Joab gave up the sum of the number of the people unto the king: and there were in Israel eight hundred thousand valiant men that drew the sword; and the men of Judah *were* five hundred thousand men.

David's Punishment

10 And David's heart smote him after that he had numbered the people. And David said unto the LORD, I have sinned greatly in that I have done: and now, I beseech thee, O LORD, take away the iniquity of thy servant; for I have done very foolishly.

11 For when David was up in the morning, the word of the LORD came unto the prophet Gad, David's seer, saying,

12 Go and say unto David, Thus saith the LORD, I offer thee three *things*; choose thee one of them, that I may *do it* unto thee.

13 So Gad came to David, and told him, and said unto him, Shall seven years of famine come unto thee in thy land? or wilt thou flee three months before thine enemies, while they pursue thee? or that there be three days' pestilence in thy land? now advise, and see what answer I shall return to him that sent me.

14 And David said unto Gad, I am in a great strait: let us fall now into the hand of the LORD; for his mercies *are* great: and let me not fall into the hand of man.

15 So the LORD sent a pestilence upon Israel from the morning even to the time appointed: and there died of the people from Dan even to Beer-sheba seventy thousand men.

16 And when the angel stretched out his hand upon Jerusalem to destroy it, the LORD repented him of the evil, and said to the angel that destroyed the people, It is enough: stay now thine hand. And the angel of the LORD was by the threshingplace of Araunah the Jebusite.

17 And David spake unto the LORD when he saw the angel that smote the people, and said, Lo, I have sinned, and I have done wickedly: but these sheep, what have they done? let thine hand, I pray thee, be against me, and against my father's house.

David Offers Sacrifice

18 And Gad came that day to David, and said unto him, Go up, rear an altar unto the LORD in the threshingfloor of Araunah the Jebusite.

19 And David, according to the saying of Gad, went up as the LORD commanded.

20 And Araunah looked, and saw the king and his servants coming on toward him: and Araunah went out, and bowed himself before the king on his face upon the ground.

21 And Araunah said, Wherefore is my lord the king come to his servant? And David said, To buy the threshingfloor of thee, to build an altar unto the LORD, that the plague may be stayed from the people.

22 And Araunah said unto David, Let my lord the king take and offer up what *seemeth* good unto him: behold, *here be* oxen for burnt sacrifice, and threshing instruments and *other* instruments of the oxen for wood.

23 All these *things* did Araunah, *as* a king, give unto the king. And Araunah said unto the king, The LORD thy God accept thee.

24 And the king said unto Araunah, Nay; but I will surely buy *it* of thee at a price: neither will I offer burnt offerings unto the LORD my God of that which doth cost me nothing. So David bought the thresh-

Cross references

6 Josh. 19:28, 47; Judg. 18:28, 29

9 1Chr. 21:5

10 1Sam. 13:13; 24:5; 2Sam. 12:13

11 1Sam. 9:9; 22:5; 1Chr. 29:29

13 1Chr. 21:12

14 Ps. 103:8, 13, 14; 119:156; Isa. 47:6; Zech. 1:15

15 1Chr. 21:14; 27:24

16 Gen. 6:6; Ex. 12:23; 1Sam. 15:11; 2Sam. 24:18; 1Chr. 21:15; 2Chr. 3:1, Ornan; Joel 2:13, 14

17 1Chr. 21:17

18 1Chr. 21:18

21 Gen. 23:8-16; Num. 16:48, 50

22 1Kgs. 19:21

23 Ezek. 20:40, 41

24 1Chr. 21:24, 25

24:16 And the angel of the LORD was by the threshingplace of Araunah the Jebusite. The chastisement for David's unwise sin in proudly conducting a census of all those able to serve in his army in Israel, would take one of three forms. David was given the choice of a seven-year famine, a three-month exile from invading armies, or a three-day pestilence that would afflict the nation. David opted to be in the hands of the Lord, and the pestilence came. Administered by an angel of the Lord, the pestilence stopped at the threshing floor of Araunah. At the direction of the prophet Gad, David erected an altar at that place, buying the property surrounding it for fifty shekels of silver. The site was on Mount Moriah, where Abraham offered Isaac (Gen. 22) and where Solomon would one day build the temple (2 Chr. 3:1).

ingfloor and the oxen for fifty shekels of silver.

25 And David built there an altar unto the

25 2Sam.
21:14; 24:2

LORD, and offered burnt offerings and peace offerings. So the LORD was intreated for the land, and the plague was stayed from Israel.

24:25 David. Though flawed and intensely human, David never was involved in idolatry, necromancy, or rebellion against the true God of Israel. David recognized God as his source of strength and wisdom, seeking to worship and serve Him. Though he sinned with Bathsheba and erred in proudly numbering his people, he nevertheless was Israel's greatest king. In God's divine plan to redeem mankind and to establish righteousness on earth, devised before the foundation of the world, David fulfilled a key role with everlasting results.

1 Kings

Like the books of Samuel, 1 and 2 Kings were originally one book, written to record the history of God's chosen people under its greatest kings, and also the failures of most of the kings who followed.

First Kings opens with the death of David and the accession of Solomon (979 B.C.), under whose reign the Israelite empire dazzled the people with material magnificence and profound wisdom. After being anointed king (chap. 1), his wisdom and reign are described, culminating with the building of the Jerusalem temple. Tragically, Solomon fell into the entrapment of idolatry, and after his death the empire split into two kingdoms, Israel in the North and Judah in the South. The Davidic dynasty continued in Judah under twenty hereditary kings from 931 B.C. until 586 B.C., when Jerusalem was overrun by the Babylonians. Israel had nineteen kings in four dynasties. With the exception of periodic revivals in Judah, the long decline in both kingdoms followed a pattern of disobedience, disruption, disintegration, and disaster.

The appearance of Elijah (17:1) heralds an era when often only a remnant of Israel and Judah were faithful to God. Elijah's eight recorded miracles, his courageous opposition to idolatry, and his dramatic ascension to heaven (2 Kgs. 2) highlight his ministry. For prophecies concerning his return, see Malachi 3:1; 4:5–6; Matthew 17:3, 10–12; 27:47; Luke 1:13–17.

Author
Unknown

Date
6th Century B.C.

Key Truth
Israel's Greatness and Decline

Historic Time
United and Divided Kingdom

Key Verse
6:1
[Solomon] began to build the house of the LORD.

A key prophetic theme of 1 Kings is probably best described in 2:3: "Keep the charge of the LORD thy God, to walk in his ways, to keep his statutes, and his commandments . . . that thou mayest prosper in all that thou doest." Unfortunately, God's chosen people failed miserably at heeding this advice and suffered tragic consequences.

Predictive material, including applications of temple worship that foreshadow Christ's ministry, involve 189 of the 816 verses, or 23 percent. Most of the 44 prophecies were quickly fulfilled. Continuation of the Davidic dynasty was reconfirmed to Solomon (9:1–9), but judgment would later fall on Israel for its disobedience.

23%
Prophecy

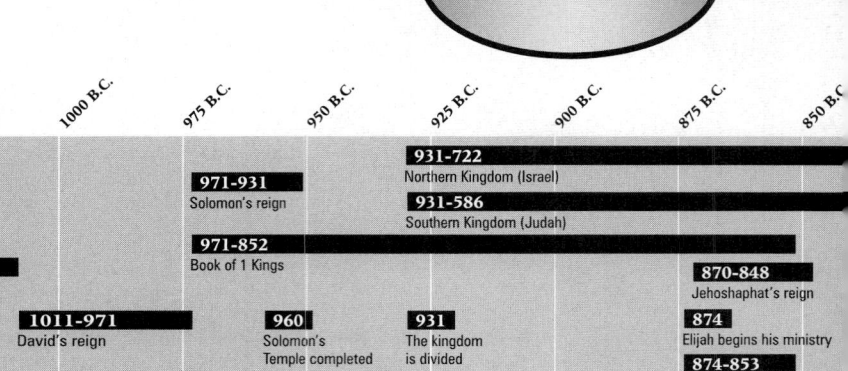

1050 B.C.	1025 B.C.	1000 B.C.	975 B.C.	950 B.C.	925 B.C.	900 B.C.	875 B.C.	850 B.C.

1040 Birth of David

1026 David anointed

1043-1011 Saul's reign

1011-971 David's reign

971-931 Solomon's reign

971-852 Book of 1 Kings

960 Solomon's Temple completed

931-722 Northern Kingdom (Israel)

931-586 Southern Kingdom (Judah)

931 The kingdom is divided

870-848 Jehoshaphat's reign

874 Elijah begins his ministry

874-853 Ahab's reign

CHAPTER 1
David Approaches Death

1 Now king David was old *and* stricken in years; and they covered him with clothes, but he gat no heat.

2 Wherefore his servants said unto the king, Let there be sought for my lord the king a young virgin: and let her stand before the king, and let her cherish him, and let her lie in thy bosom, that my lord the king may get heat.

3 So they sought for a fair damsel throughout all the coasts of Israel, and found Abishag a Shunammite, and brought her to the king.

4 And the damsel *was* very fair, and cherished the king, and ministered to him: but the king knew her not.

Adonijah Usurps David's Throne

5 Then Adonijah the son of Haggith exalted himself, saying, I will be king: and he prepared him chariots and horsemen, and fifty men to run before him.

6 And his father had not displeased him at any time in saying, Why hast thou done so? and he also *was a* very goodly *man;* and *his mother* bare him after Absalom.

7 And he conferred with Joab the son of Zeruiah, and with Abiathar the priest: and they following Adonijah helped *him.*

8 But Zadok the priest, and Benaiah the son of Jehoiada, and Nathan the prophet, and Shimei, and Rei, and the mighty men which *belonged* to David, were not with Adonijah.

9 And Adonijah slew sheep and oxen and fat cattle by the stone of Zoheleth, which *is* by En-rogel, and called all his brethren the king's sons, and all the men of Judah the king's servants:

10 But Nathan the prophet, and Benaiah, and the mighty men, and Solomon his brother, he called not.

11 Wherefore Nathan spake unto Bath-sheba the mother of Solomon, saying, Hast thou not heard that Adonijah the son of Haggith doth reign, and David our lord knoweth *it* not?

12 Now therefore come, let me, I pray thee, give thee counsel, that thou mayest save thine own life, and the life of thy son Solomon.

13 Go and get thee in unto king David, and say unto him, Didst not thou, my lord, O king, swear unto thine handmaid, saying, Assuredly Solomon thy son shall reign after me, and he shall sit upon my throne? why then doth Adonijah reign?

14 Behold, while thou yet talkest there with the king, I also will come in after thee, and confirm thy words.

15 And Bath-sheba went in unto the king into the chamber: and the king was very old; and Abishag the Shunammite ministered unto the king.

16 And Bath-sheba bowed, and did obeisance unto the king. And the king said, What wouldest thou?

17 And she said unto him, My lord, thou swarest by the LORD thy God unto thine handmaid, *saying,* Assuredly Solomon thy son shall reign after me, and he shall sit upon my throne.

18 And now, behold, Adonijah reigneth; and now, my lord the king, thou knowest *it* not:

19 And he hath slain oxen and fat cattle and sheep in abundance, and hath called all the sons of the king, and Abiathar the priest, and Joab the captain of the host: but Solomon thy servant hath he not called.

20 And thou, my lord, O king, the eyes of all Israel *are* upon thee, that thou shouldest tell them who shall sit on the throne of my lord the king after him.

21 Otherwise it shall come to pass, when my lord the king shall sleep with his fathers, that I and my son Solomon shall be counted offenders.

22 And, lo, while she yet talked with the king, Nathan the prophet also came in.

23 And they told the king, saying, Behold Nathan the prophet. And when he was come in before the king, he bowed himself before the king with his face to the ground.

24 And Nathan said, My lord, O king, hast thou said, Adonijah shall reign after me, and he shall sit upon my throne?

25 For he is gone down this day, and hath slain oxen and fat cattle and sheep in abundance, and hath called all the king's sons, and the captains of the host, and Abiathar the priest; and, behold, they eat and drink before him, and say, God save king Adonijah.

Cross References

3 Josh. 19:18

5 2Sam. 3:4; 15:1

6 2Sam. 3:3, 4; 1Chr. 3:2

7 2Sam. 20:25; 1Kgs. 2:22, 28

8 2Sam. 23:8; 1Kgs. 4:18

9 2Sam. 17:17

11 2Sam. 3:4

13 1Chr. 22:9

17 1Kgs. 1:13, 30

19 1Kgs. 1:7-9, 25

21 Deut. 31:16; 1Kgs. 2:10

25 1Sam. 10:24; 1Kgs. 1:19

1:8 Zadok the priest. Zadok was one of the high priests serving during the reign of King David (2 Sam. 8:17). The ancestors of Zadok will provide the priestly stock that will oversee the Millennial Temple during Christ's one thousand-year reign on earth (Ezek. 44:15) because of his faithfulness during a time of apostasy as noted in 1 Kings 2:27, 35.

26 But me, *even* me thy servant, and Zadok the priest, and Benaiah the son of Jehoiada, and thy servant Solomon, hath he not called.

27 Is this thing done by my lord the king, and thou hast not shewed *it* unto thy servant, who should sit on the throne of my lord the king after him?

David Has Solomon Anointed King

28 Then king David answered and said, Call me Bath-sheba. And she came into the king's presence, and stood before the king.

29 And the king sware, and said, *As* the LORD liveth, that hath redeemed my soul out of all distress,

30 Even as I sware unto thee by the LORD God of Israel, saying, Assuredly Solomon thy son shall reign after me, and he shall sit upon my throne in my stead; even so will I certainly do this day.

31 Then Bath-sheba bowed with *her* face to the earth, and did reverence to the king, and said, Let my lord king David live for ever.

32 And king David said, Call me Zadok the priest, and Nathan the prophet, and Benaiah the son of Jehoiada. And they came before the king.

33 The king also said unto them, Take with you the servants of your lord, and cause Solomon my son to ride upon mine own mule, and bring him down to Gihon:

34 And let Zadok the priest and Nathan the prophet anoint him there king over Israel: and blow ye with the trumpet, and say, God save king Solomon.

35 Then ye shall come up after him, that he may come and sit upon my throne; for he shall be king in my stead: and I have appointed him to be ruler over Israel and over Judah.

36 And Benaiah the son of Jehoiada answered the king, and said, Amen: the LORD God of my lord the king say so *too*.

37 As the LORD hath been with my lord the king, even so be he with Solomon, and make his throne greater than the throne of my lord king David.

38 So Zadok the priest, and Nathan the prophet, and Benaiah the son of Jehoiada, and the Cherethites, and the Pelethites, went down, and caused Solomon to ride upon king David's mule, and brought him to Gihon.

39 And Zadok the priest took an horn of oil out of the tabernacle, and anointed Solomon. And they blew the trumpet; and all the people said, God save king Solomon.

40 And all the people came up after him, and the people piped with pipes, and rejoiced with great joy, so that the earth rent with the sound of them.

41 And Adonijah and all the guests that *were* with him heard *it* as they had made an end of eating. And when Joab heard the sound of the trumpet, he said, Wherefore *is this* noise of the city being in an uproar?

42 And while he yet spake, behold, Jonathan the son of Abiathar the priest came: and Adonijah said unto him, Come in; for thou *art* a valiant man, and bringest good tidings.

43 And Jonathan answered and said to Adonijah, Verily our lord king David hath made Solomon king.

44 And the king hath sent with him Zadok the priest, and Nathan the prophet, and Benaiah the son of Jehoiada, and the Cherethites, and the Pelethites, and they have caused him to ride upon the king's mule:

45 And Zadok the priest and Nathan the prophet have anointed him king in Gihon: and they are come up from thence rejoicing, so that the city rang again. This *is* the noise that ye have heard.

46 And also Solomon sitteth on the throne of the kingdom.

47 And moreover the king's servants came to bless our lord king David, saying, God make the name of Solomon better than thy name, and make his throne greater than thy throne. And the king bowed himself upon the bed.

48 And also thus said the king, Blessed *be* the LORD God of Israel, which hath given *one* to sit on my throne this day, mine eyes even seeing *it*.

49 And all the guests that *were* with Adonijah were afraid, and rose up, and went every man his way.

50 And Adonijah feared because of Solomon, and arose, and went, and caught hold on the horns of the altar.

51 And it was told Solomon, saying, Behold, Adonijah feareth king Solomon: for, lo, he hath caught hold on the horns of the altar, saying, Let king Solomon swear unto me today that he will not slay his servant with the sword.

52 And Solomon said, If he will shew himself a worthy man, there shall not an hair of him fall to the earth: but if wickedness shall be found in him, he shall die.

53 So king Solomon sent, and they brought him down from the altar. And he came and

---

Cross references:

29 2Sam. 4:9
30 1Kgs. 1:17
31 Neh. 2:3; Dan. 2:4
33 2Sam. 20:6; 2Chr. 32:30; Esth. 6:8
34 1Sam. 10:1; 16:3, 12; 2Sam. 2:4; 5:3; 15:10; 1Kgs. 19:16; 2Kgs. 9:3, 13; 11:12, 14
37 Josh. 1:5, 17; 1Sam. 20:13; 1Kgs. 1:47
38 2Sam. 8:18; 23:20-23
39 Ex. 30:23, 25, 32; 1Sam. 10:24; 1Chr. 29:22; Ps. 89:20
42 2Sam. 18:27
46 1Chr. 29:23
47 Gen. 47:31; 1Kgs. 1:37
48 1Kgs. 3:6; Ps. 132:11, 12
50 1Kgs. 2:28
52 1Sam. 14:45; 2Sam. 14:11; Acts 27:34

bowed himself to king Solomon: and Solomon said unto him, Go to thine house.

CHAPTER 2
David Gives Instructions to Solomon

1 Now the days of David drew nigh that he should die; and he charged Solomon his son, saying,

2 I go the way of all the earth: be thou strong therefore, and shew thyself a man;

3 And keep the charge of the LORD thy God, to walk in his ways, to keep his statutes, and his commandments, and his judgments, and his testimonies, as it is written in the law of Moses, that thou mayest prosper in all that thou doest, and whithersoever thou turnest thyself:

4 That the LORD may continue his word which he spake concerning me, saying, If thy children take heed to their way, to walk before me in truth with all their heart and with all their soul, there shall not fail thee (said he) a man on the throne of Israel.

5 Moreover thou knowest also what Joab the son of Zeruiah did to me, *and* what he did to the two captains of the hosts of Israel, unto Abner the son of Ner, and unto Amasa the son of Jether, whom he slew, and shed the blood of war in peace, and put the blood of war upon his girdle that *was* about his loins, and in his shoes that *were* on his feet.

6 Do therefore according to thy wisdom, and let not his hoar head go down to the grave in peace.

7 But shew kindness unto the sons of Barzillai the Gileadite, and let them be of those that eat at thy table: for so they came to me when I fled because of Absalom thy brother.

8 And, behold, *thou hast* with thee Shimei the son of Gera, a Benjamite of Bahurim, which cursed me with a grievous curse in the day when I went to Mahanaim: but he came down to meet me at Jordan, and I sware to him by the LORD, saying, I will not put thee to death with the sword.

9 Now therefore hold him not guiltless: for thou *art* a wise man, and knowest what thou oughtest to do unto him; but his hoar head bring thou down to the grave with blood.

David's Death

10 So David slept with his fathers, and was buried in the city of David.

11 And the days that David reigned over Israel *were* forty years: seven years reigned he in Hebron, and thirty and three years reigned he in Jerusalem.

12 Then sat Solomon upon the throne of David his father; and his kingdom was established greatly.

Solomon Consolidates His Rule

13 And Adonijah the son of Haggith came to Bath-sheba the mother of Solomon. And she said, Comest thou peaceably? And he said, Peaceably.

14 He said moreover, I have somewhat to say unto thee. And she said, Say on.

15 And he said, Thou knowest that the kingdom was mine, and *that* all Israel set their faces on me, that I should reign: howbeit the kingdom is turned about, and is become my brother's: for it was his from the LORD.

16 And now I ask one petition of thee, deny me not. And she said unto him, Say on.

17 And he said, Speak, I pray thee, unto Solomon the king, (for he will not say thee nay,) that he give me Abishag the Shunammite to wife.

18 And Bath-sheba said, Well; I will speak for thee unto the king.

19 Bath-sheba therefore went unto king Solomon, to speak unto him for Adonijah. And the king rose up to meet her, and bowed himself unto her, and sat down on his throne, and caused a seat to be set for the king's mother; and she sat on his right hand.

20 Then she said, I desire one small petition of thee; *I pray thee,* say me not nay. And the king said unto her, Ask on, my mother: for I will not say thee nay.

21 And she said, Let Abishag the Shunammite be given to Adonijah thy brother to wife.

Cross references

1 Gen. 47:29; Deut. 31:14

2 Deut. 17:19, 20; Josh. 23:14

3 Deut. 29:9; Josh. 1:7; 1Sam. 18:5, 14, 30; 1Chr. 22:12, 13

4 2Sam. 7:12, 13, 25; 1Kgs. 8:25; 2Kgs. 20:3; Ps. 132:12

5 2Sam. 3:27, 39; 18:5, 12, 14; 19:5-7; 20:10

6 1Kgs. 2:9; Prov. 20:26

7 2Sam. 9:7, 10; 17:27; 19:28, 31, 38

8 2Sam. 16:5; 19:18, 23

9 Gen. 42:38; 44:31; Ex. 20:7; Job 9:28

10 2Sam. 5:7; 1Kgs. 1:21; Acts 2:29; 13:36

11 2Sam. 5:4; 1Chr. 29:26, 27

12 1Chr. 29:23; 2Chr. 1:1

13 1Sam. 16:4, 5

15 1Kgs. 1:5; 1Chr. 22:9, 10; 28:5-7; Prov. 21:30; Dan. 2:21

16 Ps. 132:10

17 1Kgs. 1:3, 4

19 Ex. 20:12; Ps. 45:9

2:4 If thy children take heed. As the death of David draws near, the Lord confirms His plan through another key individual. Earlier the Lord promised in the Davidic covenant (2 Sam. 7:4–17) that a descendant of David would always rule over Israel. First Kings demonstrates that none of the immediate Davidic descendants are worthy to fulfill the promise. Increasingly the history of Israel is pointing to the need for an individual who is able to fulfill for the nation the things necessary to obtain her promises and blessings. Only Jesus the Messiah, son of David, is worthy to fulfill the promise.

22 And king Solomon answered and said unto his mother, And why dost thou ask Abishag the Shunammite for Adonijah? ask for him the kingdom also; for he *is* mine elder brother; even for him, and for Abiathar the priest, and for Joab the son of Zeruiah.

23 Then king Solomon sware by the LORD, saying, God do so to me, and more also, if Adonijah have not spoken this word against his own life.

24 Now therefore, *as* the LORD liveth, which hath established me, and set me on the throne of David my father, and who hath made me an house, as he promised, Adonijah shall be put to death this day.

25 And king Solomon sent by the hand of Benaiah the son of Jehoiada; and he fell upon him that he died.

26 And unto Abiathar the priest said the king, Get thee to Anathoth, unto thine own fields; for thou *art* worthy of death: but I will not at this time put thee to death, because thou barest the ark of the Lord GOD before David my father, and because thou hast been afflicted in all wherein my father was afflicted.

27 So Solomon thrust out Abiathar from being priest unto the LORD; that he might fulfil the word of the LORD, which he spake concerning the house of Eli in Shiloh.

28 Then tidings came to Joab: for Joab had turned after Adonijah, though he turned not after Absalom. And Joab fled unto the tabernacle of the LORD, and caught hold on the horns of the altar.

29 And it was told king Solomon that Joab was fled unto the tabernacle of the LORD; and, behold, *he is* by the altar. Then Solomon sent Benaiah the son of Jehoiada, saying, Go, fall upon him.

30 And Benaiah came to the tabernacle of the LORD, and said unto him, Thus saith the king, Come forth. And he said, Nay; but I will die here. And Benaiah brought the king word again, saying, Thus said Joab, and thus he answered me.

31 And the king said unto him, Do as he hath said, and fall upon him, and bury him; that thou mayest take away the innocent blood, which Joab shed, from me, and from the house of my father.

32 And the LORD shall return his blood upon his own head, who fell upon two men more righteous and better than he, and slew them with the sword, my father David not knowing *thereof, to wit,* Abner the son of Ner, captain of the host of Israel, and

Amasa the son of Jether, captain of the host of Judah.

33 Their blood shall therefore return upon the head of Joab, and upon the head of his seed for ever: but upon David, and upon his seed, and upon his house, and upon his throne, shall there be peace for ever from the LORD.

34 So Benaiah the son of Jehoiada went up, and fell upon him, and slew him: and he was buried in his own house in the wilderness.

35 And the king put Benaiah the son of Jehoiada in his room over the host: and Zadok the priest did the king put in the room of Abiathar.

36 And the king sent and called for Shimei, and said unto him, Build thee an house in Jerusalem, and dwell there, and go not forth thence any whither.

37 For it shall be, *that* on the day thou goest out, and passest over the brook Kidron, thou shalt know for certain that thou shalt surely die: thy blood shall be upon thine own head.

38 And Shimei said unto the king, The saying *is* good: as my lord the king hath said, so will thy servant do. And Shimei dwelt in Jerusalem many days.

39 And it came to pass at the end of three years, that two of the servants of Shimei ran away unto Achish son of Maachah king of Gath. And they told Shimei, saying, Behold, thy servants *be* in Gath.

40 And Shimei arose, and saddled his ass, and went to Gath to Achish to seek his servants: and Shimei went, and brought his servants from Gath.

41 And it was told Solomon that Shimei had gone from Jerusalem to Gath, and was come again.

42 And the king sent and called for Shimei, and said unto him, Did I not make thee to swear by the LORD, and protested unto thee, saying, Know for a certain, on the day thou goest out, and walkest abroad any whither, that thou shalt surely die? and thou saidst unto me, The word *that* I have heard *is* good.

43 Why then hast thou not kept the oath of the LORD, and the commandment that I have charged thee with?

44 The king said moreover to Shimei, Thou knowest all the wickedness which thine heart is privy to, that thou didst to David my father: therefore the LORD shall return thy wickedness upon thine own head;

45 And king Solomon *shall be* blessed, and

Center reference column:

22 1Kgs. 1:7

23 Ruth 1:17

24 2Sam. 7:11, 13; 1Chr. 22:10

26 Josh. 21:18; 1Sam. 22:20, 23; 23:6; 2Sam. 15:24, 29

27 1Sam. 2:31-35

28 1Kgs. 1:7, 50

31 Ex. 21:14; Num. 35:33; Deut. 19:13; 21:8, 9

32 Judg. 9:24, 57; 2Sam. 3:27; 20:10; 2Chr. 21:13; Ps. 7:16

33 2Sam. 3:29; Prov. 25:5

35 Num. 25:11-13; 1Sam. 2:35; 1Kgs. 2:27; 1Chr. 6:53; 24:3

36 2Sam. 16:5; 1Kgs. 2:8

37 Lev. 20:9; Josh. 2:19; 2Sam. 1:16; 15:23

39 1Sam. 27:2

44 2Sam. 16:5; Ps. 7:16; Ezek. 17:19

45 Prov. 25:5

the throne of David shall be established before the LORD for ever.

46 So the king commanded Benaiah the son of Jehoiada; which went out, and fell upon him, that he died. And the kingdom was established in the hand of Solomon.

CHAPTER 3
Solomon Marries Pharaoh's Daughter

1 And Solomon made affinity with Pharaoh king of Egypt, and took Pharaoh's daughter, and brought her into the city of David, until he had made an end of building his own house, and the house of the LORD, and the wall of Jerusalem round about.

2 Only the people sacrificed in high places, because there was no house built unto the name of the LORD, until those days.

Solomon Asks for Wisdom

3 And Solomon loved the LORD, walking in the statutes of David his father: only he sacrificed and burnt incense in high places.

4 And the king went to Gibeon to sacrifice there; for that *was* the great high place: a thousand burnt offerings did Solomon offer upon that altar.

5 In Gibeon the LORD appeared to Solomon in a dream by night: and God said, Ask what I shall give thee.

6 And Solomon said, Thou hast shewed unto thy servant David my father great mercy, according as he walked before thee in truth, and in righteousness, and in uprightness of heart with thee; and thou hast kept for him this great kindness, that thou hast given him a son to sit on his throne, as *it is* this day.

7 And now, O LORD my God, thou hast made thy servant king instead of David my father: and I *am but* a little child: I know not *how* to go out or come in.

8 And thy servant *is* in the midst of thy people which thou hast chosen, a great people, that cannot be numbered nor counted for multitude.

9 Give therefore thy servant an understanding heart to judge thy people, that I may discern between good and bad: for who is able to judge this thy so great a people?

10 And the speech pleased the Lord, that Solomon had asked this thing.

11 And God said unto him, Because thou hast asked this thing, and hast not asked for thyself long life; neither hast asked riches for thyself, nor hast asked the life of thine enemies; but hast asked for thyself understanding to discern judgment;

12 Behold, I have done according to thy words: lo, I have given thee a wise and an understanding heart; so that there was none like thee before thee, neither after thee shall any arise like unto thee.

13 And I have also given thee that which thou hast not asked, both riches, and honour: so that there shall not be any among the kings like unto thee all thy days.

14 And if thou wilt walk in my ways, to keep my statutes and my commandments, as thy father David did walk, then I will lengthen thy days.

15 And Solomon awoke; and, behold, *it was* a dream. And he came to Jerusalem, and stood before the ark of the covenant of the LORD, and offered up burnt offerings, and offered peace offerings, and made a feast to all his servants.

An Example of Solomon's Wisdom

16 Then came there two women, *that were* harlots, unto the king, and stood before him.

17 And the one woman said, O my lord, I and this woman dwell in one house; and I was delivered of a child with her in the house.

---

46 1Kgs. 2:12; 2Chr. 1:1

1 2Sam. 5:7; 1Kgs. 7:1, 8; 9:15, 19, 24

2 Lev. 17:3, 4, 5; Deut. 12:2, 4, 5; 1Kgs. 22:43

3 Deut. 6:5; 30:16, 20; 1Kgs. 3:6, 14; Ps. 31:23; Rom. 8:28; 1Cor. 8:3

4 1Chr. 16:39; 2Chr. 1:3

5 1Kgs. 9:2; 2Chr. 1:7; Matt. 1:20; 2:13, 19

6 1Kgs. 1:48; 2:4; 9:4; 2Kgs. 20:3; 2Chr. 1:8-10; Ps. 15:2

7 Num. 27:17; 1Chr. 29:1

8 Gen. 13:16; 15:5; Deut. 7:6; 2Chr. 1:10; Ps. 72:1, 2;

Prov. 2:3-9; Heb. 5:14; James 1:5

11 James 4:3

12 1Kgs. 4:29, 30, 31; Eccl. 1:16

13 1Kgs. 4:21, 24; Prov. 3:16; Matt. 6:33

14 1Kgs. 15:5; Ps. 91:16; Prov. 3:2

2:45 king Solomon shall be blessed. As is true of other historical books, blessings demonstrate the outworking in history of God's faithfulness and the fact that He keeps His word. In this instance, the Lord furthers the outworking in history of His Davidic promise that "the throne of David shall be established before the LORD for ever."

3:5–15 In these verses, the biblical pattern of the Lord revealing Himself to the covenant seed, in this case Solomon, at the passing of their predecessor, in this case David, is maintained. Here the Lord demonstrates His ability to prophesy by asking Solomon to name his own blessing (v. 5). This is the passage where Solomon demonstrates wisdom by asking God for wisdom (v. 9).

3:7 I am but a little child: I know not how to go out or come in. An expression that reveals Solomon's realization that he needs the oversight and counsel of the Lord to properly lead the nation of Israel.

3:11–14 none like thee. The Lord not only answered Solomon's request for wisdom, but also provided "riches and honor." The extent of that wisdom is seen in 1 Kings 4:32 where three thousand proverbs were given to him plus the 1,005 "songs," some of which can be found in the books of Proverbs, Song of Solomon, and Ecclesiastes.

18 And it came to pass the third day after that I was delivered, that this woman was delivered also: and we *were* together; *there was* no stranger with us in the house, save we two in the house.

19 And this woman's child died in the night; because she overlaid it.

20 And she arose at midnight, and took my son from beside me, while thine handmaid slept, and laid it in her bosom, and laid her dead child in my bosom.

21 And when I rose in the morning to give my child suck, behold, it was dead: but when I had considered it in the morning, behold, it was not my son, which I did bear.

22 And the other woman said, Nay; but the living *is* my son, and the dead *is* thy son. And this said, No; but the dead *is* thy son, and the living *is* my son. Thus they spake before the king.

23 Then said the king, The one saith, This *is* my son that liveth, and thy son *is* the dead: and the other saith, Nay; but thy son *is* the dead, and my son *is* the living.

24 And the king said, Bring me a sword. And they brought a sword before the king.

25 And the king said, Divide the living child in two, and give half to the one, and half to the other.

26 Then spake the woman whose the living child *was* unto the king, for her bowels yearned upon her son, and she said, O my lord, give her the living child, and in no wise slay it. But the other said, Let it be neither mine nor thine, *but* divide *it*.

27 Then the king answered and said, Give her the living child, and in no wise slay it: she *is* the mother thereof.

28 And all Israel heard of the judgment which the king had judged; and they feared the king: for they saw that the wisdom of God *was* in him, to do judgment.

CHAPTER 4
Solomon's Officials

1 So king Solomon was king over all Israel.

2 And these *were* the princes which he had; Azariah the son of Zadok the priest,

3 Elihoreph and Ahiah, the sons of Shisha, scribes; Jehoshaphat the son of Ahilud, the recorder.

4 And Benaiah the son of Jehoiada *was* over the host: and Zadok and Abiathar *were* the priests:

5 And Azariah the son of Nathan *was* over the officers: and Zabud the son of Nathan *was* principal officer, *and* the king's friend:

6 And Ahishar *was* over the household:

and Adoniram the son of Abda *was* over the tribute.

7 And Solomon had twelve officers over all Israel, which provided victuals for the king and his household: each man his month in a year made provision.

8 And these *are* their names: The son of Hur, in mount Ephraim:

9 The son of Dekar, in Makaz, and in Shaalbim, and Beth-shemesh, and Elon-beth-hanan:

10 The son of Hesed, in Aruboth; to him *pertained* Sochoh, and all the land of Hepher:

11 The son of Abinadab, in all the region of Dor; which had Taphath the daughter of Solomon to wife:

12 Baana the son of Ahilud; *to him pertained* Taanach and Megiddo, and all Beth-shean, which *is* by Zartanah beneath Jezreel, from Beth-shean to Abel-meholah, *even* unto *the place that is* beyond Jokneam:

13 The son of Geber, in Ramoth-gilead; to him *pertained* the towns of Jair the son of Manasseh, which *are* in Gilead; to him *also pertained* the region of Argob, which *is* in Bashan, threescore great cities with walls and brasen bars:

14 Ahinadab the son of Iddo *had* Mahanaim:

15 Ahimaaz *was* in Naphtali; he also took Basmath the daughter of Solomon to wife:

16 Baanah the son of Hushai *was* in Asher and in Aloth:

17 Jehoshaphat the son of Paruah, in Issachar:

18 Shimei the son of Elah, in Benjamin:

19 Geber the son of Uri *was* in the country of Gilead, *in* the country of Sihon king of the Amorites, and of Og king of Bashan; and *he was* the only officer which *was* in the land.

Solomon Prospers

20 Judah and Israel *were* many, as the sand which *is* by the sea in multitude, eating and drinking, and making merry.

21 And Solomon reigned over all kingdoms from the river unto the land of the Philistines, and unto the border of Egypt: they brought presents, and served Solomon all the days of his life.

22 And Solomon's provision for one day was thirty measures of fine flour, and threescore measures of meal,

23 Ten fat oxen, and twenty oxen out of the pastures, and an hundred sheep, beside harts, and roebucks, and fallowdeer, and fatted fowl.

Cross References
26 Gen. 43:30; Isa. 49:15; Jer. 31:20; Hos. 11:8

28 1Kgs. 3:9, 11, 12

3 2Sam. 8:16; 20:24

4 1Kgs. 2:27, 35

5 2Sam. 8:18; 15:37; 16:16; 20:26; 1Kgs. 4:7; 1Chr. 27:33

6 1Kgs. 5:14

13 Num. 32:41; Deut. 3:4

19 Deut. 3:8

20 Gen. 22:17; 1Kgs. 3:8; Ps. 72:3, 7; Prov. 14:28; Mic. 4:4

21 Gen. 15:18; Josh. 1:4; 2Chr. 9:26; Ps. 68:29; 72:8, 10, 11

24 For he had dominion over all *the region* on this side the river, from Tiphsah even to Azzah, over all the kings on this side the river: and he had peace on all sides round about him.

25 And Judah and Israel dwelt safely, every man under his vine and under his fig tree, from Dan even to Beer-sheba, all the days of Solomon.

26 And Solomon had forty thousand stalls of horses for his chariots, and twelve thousand horsemen.

27 And those officers provided victual for king Solomon, and for all that came unto king Solomon's table, every man in his month: they lacked nothing.

28 Barley also and straw for the horses and dromedaries brought they unto the place where *the officers* were, every man according to his charge.

29 And God gave Solomon wisdom and understanding exceeding much, and largeness of heart, even as the sand that *is* on the sea shore.

30 And Solomon's wisdom excelled the wisdom of all the children of the east country, and all the wisdom of Egypt.

31 For he was wiser than all men; than Ethan the Ezrahite, and Heman, and Chalcol, and Darda, the sons of Mahol: and his fame was in all nations round about.

32 And he spake three thousand proverbs: and his songs were a thousand and five.

33 And he spake of trees, from the cedar tree that *is* in Lebanon even unto the hyssop that springeth out of the wall: he spake also of beasts, and of fowl, and of creeping things, and of fishes.

34 And there came of all people to hear the wisdom of Solomon, from all kings of the earth, which had heard of his wisdom.

CHAPTER 5
Solomon Prepares to Build the Temple

1 And Hiram king of Tyre sent his servants unto Solomon; for he had heard that they had anointed him king in the room of his father: for Hiram was ever a lover of David.

2 And Solomon sent to Hiram, saying,

3 Thou knowest how that David my father could not build an house unto the name of

the LORD his God for the wars which were about him on every side, until the LORD put them under the soles of his feet.

4 But now the LORD my God hath given me rest on every side, *so that there is* neither adversary nor evil occurrent.

5 And, behold, I purpose to build an house unto the name of the LORD my God, as the LORD spake unto David my father, saying, Thy son, whom I will set upon thy throne in thy room, he shall build an house unto my name.

6 Now therefore command thou that they hew me cedar trees out of Lebanon; and my servants shall be with thy servants: and unto thee will I give hire for thy servants according to all that thou shalt appoint: for thou knowest that *there is* not among us any that can skill to hew timber like unto the Sidonians.

7 And it came to pass, when Hiram heard the words of Solomon, that he rejoiced greatly, and said, Blessed *be* the LORD this day, which hath given unto David a wise son over this great people.

8 And Hiram sent to Solomon, saying, I have considered the things which thou sentest to me for: *and* I will do all thy desire concerning timber of cedar, and concerning timber of fir.

9 My servants shall bring *them* down from Lebanon unto the sea: and I will convey them by sea in floats unto the place that thou shalt appoint me, and will cause them to be discharged there, and thou shalt receive *them*: and thou shalt accomplish my desire, in giving food for my household.

10 So Hiram gave Solomon cedar trees and fir trees *according to* all his desire.

11 And Solomon gave Hiram twenty thousand measures of wheat *for* food to his household, and twenty measures of pure oil: thus gave Solomon to Hiram year by year.

12 And the LORD gave Solomon wisdom, as he promised him: and there was peace between Hiram and Solomon; and they two made a league together.

13 And king Solomon raised a levy out of all Israel; and the levy was thirty thousand men.

14 And he sent them to Lebanon, ten thou-

5:5 to build an house unto the name of the LORD my God. Solomon's desire was inspired by the Spirit of God fulfilling His prophecy to David (2 Sam. 7:12–13) that David's "seed" would build the temple of God. Solomon's Temple, as it was called, became so ingrained in Jewish history until its destruction by Nebuchadnezzar that it stands as proof that God keeps His word and fulfills His prophecies.

sand a month by courses: a month they were in Lebanon, *and* two months at home: and Adoniram *was* over the levy.

15 And Solomon had threescore and ten thousand that bare burdens, and fourscore thousand hewers in the mountains;

16 Beside the chief of Solomon's officers which *were* over the work, three thousand and three hundred, which ruled over the people that wrought in the work.

17 And the king commanded, and they brought great stones, costly stones, *and* hewed stones, to lay the foundation of the house.

18 And Solomon's builders and Hiram's builders did hew *them*, and the stonesquarers: so they prepared timber and stones to build the house.

CHAPTER 6
Solomon Builds the Temple

1 And it came to pass in the four hundred and eightieth year after the children of Israel were come out of the land of Egypt, in the fourth year of Solomon's reign over Israel, in the month Zif, which *is* the second month, that he began to build the house of the LORD.

2 And the house which king Solomon built for the LORD, the length thereof *was* threescore cubits, and the breadth thereof twenty *cubits*, and the height thereof thirty cubits.

3 And the porch before the temple of the house, twenty cubits *was* the length thereof, according to the breadth of the house; *and* ten cubits *was* the breadth thereof before the house.

4 And for the house he made windows of narrow lights.

5 And against the wall of the house he built chambers round about, *against* the walls of the house round about, *both* of the temple and of the oracle: and he made chambers round about:

6 The nethermost chamber *was* five cubits broad, and the middle *was* six cubits broad, and the third *was* seven cubits broad: for without in the wall of the house he made narrowed rests round about, that *the beams* should not be fastened in the walls of the house.

7 And the house, when it was in building, was built of stone made ready before it was brought thither: so that there was neither hammer nor axe *nor* any tool of iron heard in the house, while it was in building.

8 The door for the middle chamber *was* in the right side of the house: and they went up with winding stairs into the middle

Cross references
- **15** 1Kgs. 9:21; 2Chr. 2:17, 18
- **17** 1Chr. 22:2
- **1** 2Chr. 3:1, 2; Acts 7:47
- **2** Ezek. 41:1-5
- **4** Ezek. 40:16; 41:16
- **5** 1Kgs. 6:16; 19-21, 31; Ezek. 41:6
- **7** Deut. 5:18; 27:5, 6

The Temple of Israel

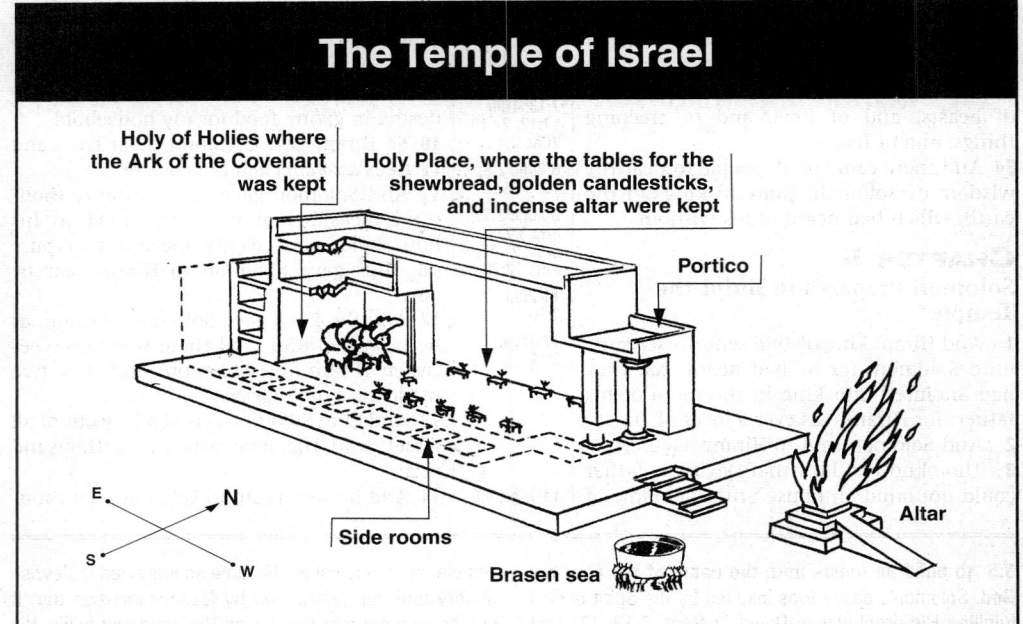

Holy of Holies where the Ark of the Covenant was kept

Holy Place, where the tables for the shewbread, golden candlesticks, and incense altar were kept

Portico

Side rooms

Brasen sea

Altar

E N S W

The Future Temples

By Randall Price

As in the past, the temple will exist in the future to enable Israel to fulfill her national and spiritual existence. The prophecies of the rebuilding of a temple in Jerusalem in the latter days are therefore an inseparable part of the restoration prophecies made to national Israel. Scripture indicates that three temples will appear in the future: a temple in the Tribulation period, a millennial temple, and an eternal temple.

During the Tribulation, unbelieving Jews will rebuild the temple (Isa. 66:1–6), apparently as the result of a covenant made between the Jewish leadership and the Antichrist (Dan. 9:27a). This covenant will be broken by the Antichrist with the "abomination of desolation" (see Dan. 9:27b) when he invades Jerusalem (Dan. 11:45; Rev. 11:2), signaling the midpoint of the seven-year Tribulation period (Matt. 24:15; Mark 13:14 [cf. Rev. 11:1–2]). An unparalleled period of Jewish persecution will then begin, leading up to the rescue of the redeemed remnant at the second advent of Messiah (Zech. 12:8–14; Rev. 19:11–16). The temple in the Tribulation period may be destroyed at the return of Christ when the Mount of Olives splits in half (Zech. 14:4), but it will certainly be removed as part of the extensive topographical changes that will prepare for the millennial Jerusalem and its temple (Zech. 14:10, cf. Isa. 2:2).

> *Scripture indicates that three temples will appear in the future.*

The Millennial Temple will be built by Christ (Zech. 6:12–13), redeemed Jews (Ezek. 43:10–11), and representatives from the Gentile nations (Zech. 6:15; Hag. 2:7 [cf. Isa. 60:10]) at the beginning of the messianic kingdom (Ezek. 37:26–28). Redeemed Gentiles will also be included in worship at this temple (Isa. 60:6; Zeph. 3:10; Zech. 2:11) as predicted by Jesus (Matt. 21:13, cf. Isa. 56:7). The dimensions and architectural design of the Millennial Temple, as well as its priestly personnel and ritual regulations are detailed in Ezekiel 40—48. The ceremonial system in Ezekiel's temple includes blood sacrifices (cf. Isa. 56:6–7; 60:7), the function of which may be memorial in nature, just as the Lord's Supper is today (1 Cor. 11:24–26). The fact that the blood sacrifices are said to be for "atonement" indicates the need for a ritual purification for those saints living in mortal bodies throughout the Millennium and seeking to approach the temple, since God's holy presence will be resident there (Jer. 3:17; Zech. 14:20–21). The Millennial Temple will apparently be besieged by Satan and his army at the end of the Millennial Kingdom (Rev. 20:7–9) and removed at the time of the creation of the new earth (Isa. 65:17; Rev. 21:1).

The final temple revealed in prophecy is the one occupying the New Jerusalem throughout the eternal kingdom (Rev. 21:2, 10). Since all of the saints are now in resurrected bodies without the possibility of sin, there will be no need for a physical structure to prevent direct contact with God (Rev. 21:3; 22:4). John declares that there is no temple in the New Jerusalem, because "the Lord God Almighty and the Lamb are the temple of it" (Rev. 21:22). This holy temple, comprised of God Himself, will fulfill the divine ideal that was begun, but never realized, in the Garden of Eden, where God and man were to experience intimate relationship (Gen. 3:8). As a result, the saints will serve God forever (Rev. 7:15; 21:3) in the New Jerusalem, which itself is an infinitely magnified Holy of Holies (Rev. 21:16, cf. 1 Kgs. 6:20).

chamber, and out of the middle into the third.

9 So he built the house, and finished it; and covered the house with beams and boards of cedar.

10 And *then* he built chambers against all the house, five cubits high: and they rested on the house *with* timber of cedar.

11 And the word of the LORD came to Solomon, saying,

12 *Concerning* this house which thou art in building, if thou wilt walk in my statutes, and execute my judgments, and keep all my commandments to walk in them; then will I perform my word with thee, which I spake unto David thy father:

13 And I will dwell among the children of Israel, and will not forsake my people Israel.

14 So Solomon built the house, and finished it.

15 And he built the walls of the house within with boards of cedar, both the floor of the house, and the walls of the cieling: *and* he covered *them* on the inside with wood, and covered the floor of the house with planks of fir.

16 And he built twenty cubits on the sides of the house, both the floor and the walls with boards of cedar: he even built *them* for it within, *even* for the oracle, *even* for the most holy *place.*

17 And the house, that *is,* the temple before it, was forty cubits *long.*

18 And the cedar of the house within *was* carved with knops and open flowers: all *was* cedar; there was no stone seen.

19 And the oracle he prepared in the house within, to set there the ark of the covenant of the LORD.

20 And the oracle in the forepart *was* twenty cubits in length, and twenty cubits in breadth, and twenty cubits in the height thereof: and he overlaid it with pure gold; and *so* covered the altar *which was* of cedar.

21 So Solomon overlaid the house within with pure gold: and he made a partition by the chains of gold before the oracle; and he overlaid it with gold.

22 And the whole house he overlaid with gold, until he had finished all the house: also the whole altar that *was* by the oracle he overlaid with gold.

23 And within the oracle he made two cherubims *of* olive tree, *each* ten cubits high.

24 And five cubits *was* the one wing of the cherub, and five cubits the other wing of the cherub: from the uttermost part of the one wing unto the uttermost part of the other *were* ten cubits.

25 And the other cherub *was* ten cubits: both the cherubims *were* of one measure and one size.

26 The height of the one cherub *was* ten cubits, and so *was it* of the other cherub.

27 And he set the cherubims within the inner house: and they stretched forth the wings of the cherubims, so that the wing of the one touched the *one* wall, and the wing of the other cherub touched the other wall; and their wings touched one another in the midst of the house.

28 And he overlaid the cherubims with gold.

29 And he carved all the walls of the house round about with carved figures of cherubims and palm trees and open flowers, within and without.

30 And the floor of the house he overlaid with gold, within and without.

31 And for the entering of the oracle he made doors *of* olive tree: the lintel *and* side posts *were* a fifth part *of the wall.*

32 The two doors also *were of* olive tree; and he carved upon them carvings of cherubims and palm trees and open flowers, and overlaid *them* with gold, and spread gold upon the cherubims, and upon the palm trees.

33 So also made he for the door of the temple posts *of* olive tree, a fourth part *of the wall.*

34 And the two doors *were of* fir tree: the two leaves of the one door *were* folding, and the two leaves of the other door *were* folding.

35 And he carved *thereon* cherubims and palm trees and open flowers: and covered *them* with gold fitted upon the carved work.

36 And he built the inner court with three rows of hewed stone, and a row of cedar beams.

37 In the fourth year was the foundation of the house of the LORD laid, in the month Zif:

38 And in the eleventh year, in the month Bul, which *is* the eighth month, was the house finished throughout all the parts thereof, and according to all the fashion of it. So was he seven years in building it.

Cross references (center column):

9 1Kgs. 6:14, 38
12 2Sam. 7:13; 1Kgs. 2:4; 9:4; 1Chr. 22:10
13 Ex. 25:8; Lev. 26:11; Deut. 31:6; 2Cor. 6:16; Rev. 21:3
14 1Kgs. 6:38
16 Ex. 26:33; Lev. 16:2; 1Kgs. 8:6; 2Chr. 3:8; Ezek. 45:3; Heb. 9:3
22 Ex. 30:1, 3, 6
23 Ex. 37:7-9; 2Chr. 3:10-12
27 Ex. 25:20; 37:9; 2Chr. 5:8
34 Ezek. 41:23-25
37 1Kgs. 6:1
38 1Kgs. 6:1

6:11–13 if thou wilt. This is an example of a conditional promise. The tragic history of Israel and the Jewish people is a constant reminder that God keeps His word and blesses those who obey Him, but curses those who disobey Him. Only eternity will reveal what Israel could have accomplished had they obeyed God.

CHAPTER 7

Solomon Completes Other Building Projects

1 But Solomon was building his own house thirteen years, and he finished all his house.

2 He built also the house of the forest of Lebanon; the length thereof *was* an hundred cubits, and the breadth thereof fifty cubits, and the height thereof thirty cubits, upon four rows of cedar pillars, with cedar beams upon the pillars.

3 And *it was* covered with cedar above upon the beams, that *lay* on forty five pillars, fifteen *in* a row.

4 And *there were* windows *in* three rows, and light *was* against light *in* three ranks.

5 And all the doors and posts *were* square, with the windows: and light *was* against light *in* three ranks.

6 And he made a porch of pillars; the length thereof *was* fifty cubits, and the breadth thereof thirty cubits: and the porch *was* before them: and the *other* pillars and the thick beam *were* before them.

7 Then he made a porch for the throne where he might judge, *even* the porch of judgment: and *it was* covered with cedar from one side of the floor to the other.

8 And his house where he dwelt *had* another court within the porch, *which* was of the like work. Solomon made also an house for Pharaoh's daughter, whom he had taken *to wife*, like unto this porch.

9 All these *were of* costly stones, according to the measures of hewed stones, sawed with saws, within and without, even from the foundation unto the coping, and *so on* the outside toward the great court.

10 And the foundation *was of* costly stones, even great stones, stones of ten cubits, and stones of eight cubits.

11 And above *were* costly stones, after the measures of hewed stones, and cedars.

12 And the great court round about *was* with three rows of hewed stones, and a row of cedar beams, both for the inner court of the house of the LORD, and for the porch of the house.

13 And king Solomon sent and fetched Hiram out of Tyre.

14 He *was* a widow's son of the tribe of Naphtali, and his father *was* a man of Tyre, a worker in brass: and he was filled with wisdom, and understanding, and cunning to work all works in brass. And he came to king Solomon, and wrought all his work.

Cross references

1 1Kgs. 9:10; 2Chr. 8:1

8 1Kgs. 3:1; 2Chr. 8:11

12 John 10:23; Acts 3:11

13 2Chr. 4:11, *Huram*; 1Kgs. 7:40

14 Ex. 31:3; 36:1; 2Chr. 2:14; 4:16

15 2Kgs. 25:17; 2Chr. 3:15; 4:12; Jer. 52:21

20 2Chr. 3:16; 4:13; Jer. 52:23

21 1Kgs. 6:3; 2Chr. 3:17

23 2Kgs. 25:13; 2Chr. 4:2; Jer. 52:17

24 2Chr. 4:3

25 2Chr. 4:4, 5; Jer. 52:20

26 2Chr. 4:5

38 2Chr. 4:6

The Two Large Pillars

15 For he cast two pillars of brass, of eighteen cubits high apiece: and a line of twelve cubits did compass either of them about.

16 And he made two chapiters *of* molten brass, to set upon the tops of the pillars: the height of the one chapiter *was* five cubits, and the height of the other chapiter *was* five cubits:

17 *And* nets of checker work, and wreaths of chain work, for the chapiters which *were* upon the top of the pillars; seven for the one chapiter, and seven for the other chapiter.

18 And he made the pillars, and two rows round about upon the one network, to cover the chapiters that *were* upon the top, with pomegranates: and so did he for the other chapiter.

19 And the chapiters that *were* upon the top of the pillars *were* of lily work in the porch, four cubits.

20 And the chapiters upon the two pillars *had pomegranates* also above, over against the belly which *was* by the network: and the pomegranates *were* two hundred in rows round about upon the other chapiter.

21 And he set up the pillars in the porch of the temple: and he set up the right pillar, and called the name thereof Jachin: and he set up the left pillar, and called the name thereof Boaz.

22 And upon the top of the pillars *was* lily work: so was the work of the pillars finished.

Furnishings for the Temple

23 And he made a molten sea, ten cubits from the one brim to the other: *it was* round all about, and his height *was* five cubits: and a line of thirty cubits did compass it round about.

24 And under the brim of it round about *there were* knops compassing it, ten in a cubit, compassing the sea round about: the knops *were* cast in two rows, when it was cast.

25 It stood upon twelve oxen, three looking toward the north, and three looking toward the west, and three looking toward the south, and three looking toward the east: and the sea *was set* above upon them, and all their hinder parts *were* inward.

26 And *it was* an handbreadth thick, and the brim thereof was wrought like the brim of a cup, with flowers of lilies: it contained two thousand baths.

27 And he made ten bases of brass; four

cubits *was* the length of one base, and four cubits the breadth thereof, and three cubits the height of it.

28 And the work of the bases *was* on this *manner*: they had borders, and the borders *were* between the ledges:

29 And on the borders that *were* between the ledges *were* lions, oxen, and cherubims: and upon the ledges *there was* a base above: and beneath the lions and oxen *were* certain additions made of thin work.

30 And every base had four brasen wheels, and plates of brass: and the four corners thereof had undersetters: under the laver *were* undersetters molten, at the side of every addition.

31 And the mouth of it within the chapiter and above *was* a cubit: but the mouth thereof *was* round *after* the work of the base, a cubit and an half: and also upon the mouth of it *were* gravings with their borders, foursquare, not round.

32 And under the borders *were* four wheels; and the axletrees of the wheels *were joined* to the base: and the height of a wheel *was* a cubit and half a cubit.

33 And the work of the wheels *was* like the work of a chariot wheel: their axletrees, and their naves, and their felloes, and their spokes, *were* all molten.

34 And *there were* four undersetters to the four corners of one base: *and* the undersetters *were* of the very base itself.

35 And in the top of the base *was there* a round compass of half a cubit high: and on the top of the base the ledges thereof and the borders thereof *were* of the same.

36 For on the plates of the ledges thereof, and on the borders thereof, he graved cherubims, lions, and palm trees, according to the proportion of every one, and additions round about.

37 After this *manner* he made the ten bases: all of them had one casting, one measure, *and* one size.

38 Then made he ten lavers of brass: one laver contained forty baths: *and* every laver was four cubits: *and* upon every one of the ten bases one laver.

39 And he put five bases on the right side of the house, and five on the left side of the house: and he set the sea on the right side of the house eastward over against the south.

40 And Hiram made the lavers, and the shovels, and the basons. So Hiram made an end of doing all the work that he made king Solomon for the house of the LORD:

41 The two pillars, and the *two* bowls of the chapiters that *were* on the top of the two pillars; and the two networks, to cover the two bowls of the chapiters which *were* upon the top of the pillars;

42 And four hundred pomegranates for the two networks, *even* two rows of pomegranates for one network, to cover the two bowls of the chapiters that *were* upon the pillars;

43 And the ten bases, and ten lavers on the bases;

44 And one sea, and twelve oxen under the sea;

45 And the pots, and the shovels, and the basons: and all these vessels, which Hiram made to king Solomon for the house of the LORD, *were of* bright brass.

46 In the plain of Jordan did the king cast them, in the clay ground between Succoth and Zarthan.

47 And Solomon left all the vessels *unweighed*, because they were exceeding many: neither was the weight of the brass found out.

48 And Solomon made all the vessels that *pertained* unto the house of the LORD: the altar of gold, and the table of gold, whereupon the shewbread *was*,

49 And the candlesticks of pure gold, five on the right *side*, and five on the left, before the oracle, with the flowers, and the lamps, and the tongs *of* gold,

50 And the bowls, and the snuffers, and the basons, and the spoons, and the censers *of* pure gold; and the hinges *of* gold, *both* for the doors of the inner house, the most holy *place, and* for the doors of the house, to wit, of the temple.

51 So was ended all the work that king Solomon made for the house of the LORD. And Solomon brought in the things which David his father had dedicated; *even* the silver, and the gold, and the vessels, did he put among the treasures of the house of the LORD.

CHAPTER 8
Solomon Brings the Ark of God into the Temple

1 Then Solomon assembled the elders of Israel, and all the heads of the tribes, the chief of the fathers of the children of Israel, unto king Solomon in Jerusalem, that they might bring up the ark of the covenant of the LORD out of the city of David, which *is* Zion.

2 And all the men of Israel assembled themselves unto king Solomon at the feast

41 1Kgs. 7:17, 18

45 Ex. 27:3; 2Chr. 4:16

46 Gen. 33:17; Josh. 3:16; 2Chr. 4:17

48 Ex. 25:30; 37:10-16, 25-28; Lev. 24:5-8

51 2Sam. 8:11; 2Chr. 5:1

1 2Sam. 5:7, 9; 6:12, 16, 17; 2Chr. 5:2-5

2 Lev. 23:34; 2Chr. 7:8

in the month Ethanim, which *is* the seventh month.

3 And all the elders of Israel came, and the priests took up the ark.

4 And they brought up the ark of the LORD, and the tabernacle of the congregation, and all the holy vessels that *were* in the tabernacle, even those did the priests and the Levites bring up.

5 And king Solomon, and all the congregation of Israel, that were assembled unto him, *were* with him before the ark, sacrificing sheep and oxen, that could not be told nor numbered for multitude.

6 And the priests brought in the ark of the covenant of the LORD unto his place, into the oracle of the house, to the most holy *place, even* under the wings of the cherubims.

7 For the cherubims spread forth *their* two wings over the place of the ark, and the cherubims covered the ark and the staves thereof above.

8 And they drew out the staves, that the ends of the staves were seen out in the holy *place* before the oracle, and they were not seen without: and there they are unto this day.

9 *There was* nothing in the ark save the two tables of stone, which Moses put there at Horeb, when the LORD made *a covenant* with the children of Israel, when they came out of the land of Egypt.

10 And it came to pass, when the priests were come out of the holy *place*, that the cloud filled the house of the LORD,

11 So that the priests could not stand to minister because of the cloud: for the glory of the LORD had filled the house of the LORD.

Solomon Addresses the People

12 Then spake Solomon, The LORD said that he would dwell in the thick darkness.

13 I have surely built thee an house to dwell in, a settled place for thee to abide in for ever.

14 And the king turned his face about, and blessed all the congregation of Israel: (and all the congregation of Israel stood;)

15 And he said, Blessed *be* the LORD God of Israel, which spake with his mouth unto David my father, and hath with his hand fulfilled *it*, saying,

16 Since the day that I brought forth my people Israel out of Egypt, I chose no city out of all the tribes of Israel to build an house, that my name might be therein; but I chose David to be over my people Israel.

17 And it was in the heart of David my fa-

ther to build an house for the name of the LORD God of Israel.

18 And the LORD said unto David my father, Whereas it was in thine heart to build an house unto my name, thou didst well that it was in thine heart.

19 Nevertheless thou shalt not build the house; but thy son that shall come forth out of thy loins, he shall build the house unto my name.

20 And the LORD hath performed his word that he spake, and I am risen up in the room of David my father, and sit on the throne of Israel, as the LORD promised, and have built an house for the name of the LORD God of Israel.

21 And I have set there a place for the ark, wherein *is* the covenant of the LORD, which he made with our fathers, when he brought them out of the land of Egypt.

Solomon's Temple Prayer

22 And Solomon stood before the altar of the LORD in the presence of all the congregation of Israel, and spread forth his hands toward heaven:

23 And he said, LORD God of Israel, *there is* no God like thee, in heaven above, or on earth beneath, who keepest covenant and mercy with thy servants that walk before thee with all their heart:

24 Who hast kept with thy servant David my father that thou promisedst him: thou spakest also with thy mouth, and hast fulfilled *it* with thine hand, as *it is* this day.

25 Therefore now, LORD God of Israel, keep with thy servant David my father that thou promisedst him, saying, There shall not fail thee a man in my sight to sit on the throne of Israel; so that thy children take heed to their way, that they walk before me as thou hast walked before me.

26 And now, O God of Israel, let thy word, I pray thee, be verified, which thou spakest unto thy servant David my father.

27 But will God indeed dwell on the earth? behold, the heaven and heaven of heavens cannot contain thee; how much less this house that I have builded?

28 Yet have thou respect unto the prayer of thy servant, and to his supplication, O LORD my God, to hearken unto the cry and to the prayer, which thy servant prayeth before thee today:

29 That thine eyes may be open toward this house night and day, *even* toward the place of which thou hast said, My name shall be there: that thou mayest hearken unto the

Cross References

3 Num. 4:15; Deut. 31:9; Josh. 3:3, 6; 1Chr. 15:14, 15

5 2Sam. 6:13

6 Ex. 26:33, 34; 2Sam. 6:17; 1Kgs. 6:19, 27

8 Ex. 25:14; 2Chr. 5:9

9 Ex. 25:21; 34:27, 28; 40:20; Deut. 4:13; 10:2, 5

10 Ex. 40:34, 35; 2Chr. 5:13; 7:2

12 2Chr. 6:1-6; Ps. 18:11; 97:2

13 2Sam. 7:13; Ps. 132:14

14 2Sam. 6:18

15 2Sam. 7:5, 25; Luke 1:68

16 Deut. 12:11; 1Sam. 16:1; 2Sam. 7:6, 8; 1Kgs. 8:29; 1Chr. 28:4; 2Chr. 6:5-7

17 2Sam. 7:2; 1Chr. 17:1

18 2Chr. 6:8, 9

19 2Sam. 7:5, 12, 13; 1Kgs. 5:3, 5

20 1Chr. 28:5, 6

21 Deut. 31:26; 1Kgs. 8:9

22 Ex. 9:33; 2Chr. 6:12-21; Ezra 9:5; Isa. 1:15

23 Gen. 17:1; Deut. 7:9

25 2Sam. 7:12, 16; 1Kgs. 2:4

26 2Sam. 7:25

27 2Chr. 2:6; Isa. 66:1; Jer. 23:24

29 Deut. 12:11; Dan. 6:10

prayer which thy servant shall make toward this place.

30 And hearken thou to the supplication of thy servant, and of thy people Israel, when they shall pray toward this place: and hear thou in heaven thy dwelling place: and when thou hearest, forgive.

31 If any man trespass against his neighbour, and an oath be laid upon him to cause him to swear, and the oath come before thine altar in this house:

32 Then hear thou in heaven, and do, and judge thy servants, condemning the wicked, to bring his way upon his head; and justifying the righteous, to give him according to his righteousness.

33 When thy people Israel be smitten down before the enemy, because they have sinned against thee, and shall turn again to thee, and confess thy name, and pray, and make supplication unto thee in this house:

34 Then hear thou in heaven, and forgive the sin of thy people Israel, and bring them again unto the land which thou gavest unto their fathers.

35 When heaven is shut up, and there is no rain, because they have sinned against thee; if they pray toward this place, and confess thy name, and turn from their sin, when thou afflictest them:

36 Then hear thou in heaven, and forgive the sin of thy servants, and of thy people Israel, that thou teach them the good way wherein they should walk, and give rain upon thy land, which thou hast given to thy people for an inheritance.

37 If there be in the land famine, if there be pestilence, blasting, mildew, locust, *or* if there be caterpiller; if their enemy besiege them in the land of their cities; whatsoever plague, whatsoever sickness *there be*;

38 What prayer and supplication soever be *made* by any man, *or* by all thy people Israel, which shall know every man the plague of his own heart, and spread forth his hands toward this house:

39 Then hear thou in heaven thy dwelling place, and forgive, and do, and give to every man according to his ways, whose heart thou knowest; (for thou, *even* thou only, knowest the hearts of all the children of men;)

40 That they may fear thee all the days that they live in the land which thou gavest unto our fathers.

41 Moreover concerning a stranger, that *is* not of thy people Israel, but cometh out of a far country for thy name's sake;

42 (For they shall hear of thy great name, and of thy strong hand, and of thy stretched out arm;) when he shall come and pray toward this house;

43 Hear thou in heaven thy dwelling place, and do according to all that the stranger calleth to thee for: that all people of the earth may know thy name, to fear thee, as *do* thy people Israel; and that they may know that this house, which I have builded, is called by thy name.

44 If thy people go out to battle against their enemy, whithersoever thou shalt send them, and shall pray unto the LORD toward the city which thou hast chosen, and *toward* the house that I have built for thy name:

45 Then hear thou in heaven their prayer and their supplication, and maintain their cause.

46 If they sin against thee, (for *there is* no man that sinneth not,) and thou be angry with them, and deliver them to the enemy, so that they carry them away captives unto the land of the enemy, far or near;

47 *Yet* if they shall bethink themselves in the land whither they were carried captives, and repent, and make supplication unto thee in the land of them that carried them captives, saying, We have sinned, and have done perversely, we have committed wickedness;

48 And *so* return unto thee with all their heart, and with all their soul, in the land of their enemies, which led them away captive, and pray unto thee toward their land, which thou gavest unto their fathers, the city which thou hast chosen, and the house which I have built for thy name:

49 Then hear thou their prayer and their supplication in heaven thy dwelling place, and maintain their cause,

50 And forgive thy people that have sinned against thee, and all their transgressions wherein they have transgressed against thee, and give them compassion before them who carried them captive, that they may have compassion on them:

51 For they *be* thy people, and thine inheritance, which thou broughtest forth out of Egypt, from the midst of the furnace of iron:

52 That thine eyes may be open unto the supplication of thy servant, and unto the supplication of thy people Israel, to hearken unto them in all that they call for unto thee.

53 For thou didst separate them from among all the people of the earth, *to be* thine inheritance, as thou spakest by the hand of

---

30 2Chr. 20:9; Neh. 1:6

31 Ex. 22:11; Lev. 5:1

32 Deut. 25:1

33 Lev. 26:17, 39, 40; Deut. 28:25; Neh. 1:9

35 Lev. 26:19; Deut. 28:23

36 1Sam. 12:23; Ps. 25:4; 27:11; 94:12; 143:8

37 Lev. 26:16, 25, 26; Deut. 28:21, 22, 27, 38, 42, 52; 2Chr. 20:9

39 1Sam. 16:7; 1Chr. 28:9; Ps. 11:4; Jer. 17:10; Acts 1:24

40 Ps. 130:4

42 Deut. 3:24

43 1Sam. 17:46; 2Kgs. 19:19; Ps. 67:2; 102:15

46 Lev. 26:34, 44; Deut. 28:36, 64; 2Chr. 6:36; Prov. 20:9; Eccl. 7:20; James 3:2; 1John 1:8, 10

47 Lev. 26:40; Neh. 1:6; Ps. 106:6; Dan. 9:5

48 Jer. 29:12-14; Dan. 6:10

50 Ezra 7:6; Ps. 106:46

51 Deut. 4:20; 9:29; Neh. 1:10; Jer. 11:4

53 Ex. 19:5; Deut. 9:26, 29; 14:2

Moses thy servant, when thou broughtest our fathers out of Egypt, O Lord GOD.

Solomon Admonishes the People

54 And it was *so*, that when Solomon had made an end of praying all this prayer and supplication unto the LORD, he arose from before the altar of the LORD, from kneeling on his knees with his hands spread up to heaven.

55 And he stood, and blessed all the congregation of Israel with a loud voice, saying,

56 Blessed *be* the LORD, that hath given rest unto his people Israel, according to all that he promised: there hath not failed one word of all his good promise, which he promised by the hand of Moses his servant.

57 The LORD our God be with us, as he was with our fathers: let him not leave us, nor forsake us:

58 That he may incline our hearts unto him, to walk in all his ways, and to keep his commandments, and his statutes, and his judgments, which he commanded our fathers.

59 And let these my words, wherewith I have made supplication before the LORD, be nigh unto the LORD our God day and night, that he maintain the cause of his servant, and the cause of his people Israel at all times, as the matter shall require:

60 That all the people of the earth may know that the LORD *is* God, *and that there is* none else.

61 Let your heart therefore be perfect with the LORD our God, to walk in his statutes, and to keep his commandments, as at this day.

Sacrifice and Celebration

62 And the king, and all Israel with him, offered sacrifice before the LORD.

63 And Solomon offered a sacrifice of peace offerings, which he offered unto the LORD, two and twenty thousand oxen, and an hundred and twenty thousand sheep. So the king and all the children of Israel dedicated the house of the LORD.

64 The same day did the king hallow the middle of the court that *was* before the house of the LORD: for there he offered burnt offerings, and meat offerings, and the fat of the peace offerings: because the brasen altar that *was* before the LORD *was* too little to re-

ceive the burnt offerings, and meat offerings, and the fat of the peace offerings.

65 And at that time Solomon held a feast, and all Israel with him, a great congregation, from the entering in of Hamath unto the river of Egypt, before the LORD our God, seven days and seven days, *even* fourteen days.

66 On the eighth day he sent the people away: and they blessed the king, and went unto their tents joyful and glad of heart for all the goodness that the LORD had done for David his servant, and for Israel his people.

CHAPTER 9
God Appears to Solomon

1 And it came to pass, when Solomon had finished the building of the house of the LORD, and the king's house, and all Solomon's desire which he was pleased to do,

2 That the LORD appeared to Solomon the second time, as he had appeared unto him at Gibeon.

3 And the LORD said unto him, I have heard thy prayer and thy supplication, that thou hast made before me: I have hallowed this house, which thou hast built, to put my name there for ever; and mine eyes and mine heart shall be there perpetually.

4 And if thou wilt walk before me, as David thy father walked, in integrity of heart, and in uprightness, to do according to all that I have commanded thee, *and* wilt keep my statutes and my judgments:

5 Then I will establish the throne of thy kingdom upon Israel for ever, as I promised to David thy father, saying, There shall not fail thee a man upon the throne of Israel.

6 *But* if ye shall at all turn from following me, ye or your children, and will not keep my commandments *and* my statutes which I have set before you, but go and serve other gods, and worship them:

7 Then will I cut off Israel out of the land which I have given them; and this house, which I have hallowed for my name, will I cast out of my sight; and Israel shall be a proverb and a byword among all people:

8 And at this house, *which* is high, every one that passeth by it shall be astonished, and shall hiss; and they shall say, Why hath the LORD done thus unto this land, and to this house?

Cross References

55 2Sam. 6:18
56 Deut. 12:10; Josh. 21:45; 23:14
57 Deut. 31:6; Josh. 1:5
58 Ps. 119:36
60 Deut. 4:35, 39; Josh. 4:24; 1Sam. 17:46; 2Kgs. 19:19
61 1Kgs. 11:4; 15:3, 14; 2Kgs. 20:3
62 2Chr. 7:4, 5
64 2Chr. 4:1; 7:7
65 Gen. 15:18; Lev. 23:34; Num. 34:5, 8; Josh. 13:5; Judg. 3:3; 2Kgs. 14:25; 2Chr. 7:8
66 2Chr. 7:9, 10
1 1Kgs. 7:1; 2Chr. 7:11; 8:6
2 1Kgs. 3:5
3 Deut. 11:12; 1Kgs. 8:29; 2Kgs. 20:5; Ps. 10:17
4 Gen. 17:1; 1Kgs. 11:4, 6, 38; 14:8; 15:5
5 2Sam. 7:12, 16; 1Kgs. 2:4; 6:12; 1Chr. 22:10; Ps. 132:12
6 2Sam. 7:14; 2Chr. 7:19, 20; Ps. 89:30-32
7 Deut. 4:26; 28:37; 2Kgs. 17:23; 25:21; Ps. 44:14; Jer. 7:14
8 Deut. 29:24-26; 2Chr. 7:21; Jer. 22:8, 9

9:1–5 if thou wilt walk before me. This promise of God to maintain His name perpetually was conditioned on the obedience of the Jewish people. Sadly, their obedience was rarely given. But this promise does guarantee there will be a future Temple during the Millennial Kingdom.

9 And they shall answer, Because they forsook the LORD their God, who brought forth their fathers out of the land of Egypt, and have taken hold upon other gods, and have worshipped them, and served them: therefore hath the LORD brought upon them all this evil.

Solomon's Other Projects

10 And it came to pass at the end of twenty years, when Solomon had built the two houses, the house of the LORD, and the king's house,

11 (*Now* Hiram the king of Tyre had furnished Solomon with cedar trees and fir trees, and with gold, according to all his desire,) that then king Solomon gave Hiram twenty cities in the land of Galilee.

12 And Hiram came out from Tyre to see the cities which Solomon had given him; and they pleased him not.

13 And he said, What cities *are* these which thou hast given me, my brother? And he called them the land of Cabul unto this day.

14 And Hiram sent to the king sixscore talents of gold.

15 And this *is* the reason of the levy which king Solomon raised; for to build the house of the LORD, and his own house, and Millo, and the wall of Jerusalem, and Hazor, and Megiddo, and Gezer.

16 *For* Pharaoh king of Egypt had gone up, and taken Gezer, and burnt it with fire, and slain the Canaanites that dwelt in the city, and given it *for* a present unto his daughter, Solomon's wife.

17 And Solomon built Gezer, and Bethhoron the nether,

18 And Baalath, and Tadmor in the wilderness, in the land,

19 And all the cities of store that Solomon had, and cities for his chariots, and cities for his horsemen, and that which Solomon desired to build in Jerusalem, and in Lebanon, and in all the land of his dominion.

20 *And* all the people *that were* left of the Amorites, Hittites, Perizzites, Hivites, and Jebusites, which *were* not of the children of Israel,

21 Their children that were left after them in the land, whom the children of Israel also were not able utterly to destroy, upon those did Solomon levy a tribute of bondservice unto this day.

22 But of the children of Israel did Solomon make no bondmen: but they *were* men of war, and his servants, and his princes, and his captains, and rulers of his chariots, and his horsemen.

23 These *were* the chief of the officers that *were* over Solomon's work, five hundred and fifty, which bare rule over the people that wrought in the work.

24 But Pharaoh's daughter came up out of the city of David unto her house which *Solomon* had built for her: then did he build Millo.

25 And three times in a year did Solomon offer burnt offerings and peace offerings upon the altar which he built unto the LORD, and he burnt incense upon the altar that *was* before the LORD. So he finished the house.

26 And king Solomon made a navy of ships in Ezion-geber, which *is* beside Eloth, on the shore of the Red sea, in the land of Edom.

27 And Hiram sent in the navy his servants, shipmen that had knowledge of the sea, with the servants of Solomon.

28 And they came to Ophir, and fetched from thence gold, four hundred and twenty talents, and brought *it* to king Solomon.

CHAPTER 10
The Queen of Sheba Visits Solomon

1 And when the queen of Sheba heard of the fame of Solomon concerning the name of the LORD, she came to prove him with hard questions.

2 And she came to Jerusalem with a very great train, with camels that bare spices, and very much gold, and precious stones: and when she was come to Solomon, she communed with him of all that was in her heart.

3 And Solomon told her all her questions: there was not *any* thing hid from the king, which he told her not.

4 And when the queen of Sheba had seen all Solomon's wisdom, and the house that he had built,

5 And the meat of his table, and the sitting of his servants, and the attendance of his ministers, and their apparel, and his cupbearers, and his ascent by which he went up unto the house of the LORD; there was no more spirit in her.

6 And she said to the king, It was a true report that I heard in mine own land of thy acts and of thy wisdom.

7 Howbeit I believed not the words, until I came, and mine eyes had seen *it*: and, behold, the half was not told me: thy wisdom and prosperity exceedeth the fame which I heard.

---

10 1Kgs. 6:37, 38; 7:1; 2Chr. 8:1

11 2Chr. 8:2

13 Josh. 19:27

15 Josh. 16:10; 17:11; 19:36; Judg. 1:29; 2Sam. 5:9; 1Kgs. 5:13; 9:24

16 Josh. 16:10

17 Josh. 16:3; 21:22; 2Chr. 8:5

18 Josh. 19:44; 2Chr. 8:4-6

19 1Kgs. 4:26; 9:1

20 2Chr. 8:7-9

21 Gen. 9:25, 26; Josh. 15:63; 17:12; Judg. 1:21, 27, 28, 29; 3:1; Ezra 2:55, 58; Neh. 7:57; 11:3

22 Lev. 25:39

23 2Chr. 8:10

24 2Sam. 5:9; 11:27; 1Kgs. 3:1; 7:8; 2Chr. 8:11; 32:5

25 2Chr. 8:12, 13, 16

26 Num. 33:35; Deut. 2:8; 2Chr. 8:17, 18

27 1Kgs. 10:11

28 Job 22:24

1 Judg. 14:12; 2Chr. 9:1-9; Prov. 1:6; Matt. 12:42; Luke 11:31

5 1Chr. 26:16

8 Happy *are* thy men, happy *are* these thy servants, which stand continually before thee, *and* that hear thy wisdom.
9 Blessed be the LORD thy God, which delighted in thee, to set thee on the throne of Israel: because the LORD loved Israel for ever, therefore made he thee king, to do judgment and justice.
10 And she gave the king an hundred and twenty talents of gold, and of spices very great store, and precious stones: there came no more such abundance of spices as these which the queen of Sheba gave to king Solomon.
11 And the navy also of Hiram, that brought gold from Ophir, brought in from Ophir great plenty of almug trees, and precious stones.
12 And the king made of the almug trees pillars for the house of the LORD, and for the king's house, harps also and psalteries for singers: there came no such almug trees, nor were seen unto this day.
13 And king Solomon gave unto the queen of Sheba all her desire, whatsoever she asked, beside *that* which Solomon gave her of his royal bounty. So she turned and went to her own country, she and her servants.

Solomon's Wealth and Fame

14 Now the weight of gold that came to Solomon in one year was six hundred threescore and six talents of gold,
15 Beside *that he had* of the merchantmen, and of the traffick of the spice merchants, and of all the kings of Arabia, and of the governors of the country.
16 And king Solomon made two hundred targets *of* beaten gold: six hundred *shekels* of gold went to one target.
17 And *he made* three hundred shields *of* beaten gold; three pound of gold went to one shield: and the king put them in the house of the forest of Lebanon.
18 Moreover the king made a great throne of ivory, and overlaid it with the best gold.
19 The throne had six steps, and the top of the throne *was* round behind: and *there were* stays on either side on the place of the seat, and two lions stood beside the stays.
20 And twelve lions stood there on the one side and on the other upon the six steps: there was not the like made in any kingdom.

21 And all king Solomon's drinking vessels *were of* gold, and all the vessels of the house of the forest of Lebanon *were of* pure gold; none *were of* silver: it was nothing accounted of in the days of Solomon.
22 For the king had at sea a navy of Tharshish with the navy of Hiram: once in three years came the navy of Tharshish, bringing gold, and silver, ivory, and apes, and peacocks.
23 So king Solomon exceeded all the kings of the earth for riches and for wisdom.
24 And all the earth sought to Solomon, to hear his wisdom, which God had put in his heart.
25 And they brought every man his present, vessels of silver, and vessels of gold, and garments, and armour, and spices, horses, and mules, a rate year by year.
26 And Solomon gathered together chariots and horsemen: and he had a thousand and four hundred chariots, and twelve thousand horsemen, whom he bestowed in the cities for chariots, and with the king at Jerusalem.
27 And the king made silver *to be* in Jerusalem as stones, and cedars made he *to be* as the sycomore trees that *are* in the vale, for abundance.
28 And Solomon had horses brought out of Egypt, and linen yarn: the king's merchants received the linen yarn at a price.
29 And a chariot came up and went out of Egypt for six hundred *shekels* of silver, and an horse for an hundred and fifty: and so for all the kings of the Hittites, and for the kings of Syria, did they bring *them* out by their means.

CHAPTER 11
Solomon Turns from God

1 But king Solomon loved many strange women, together with the daughter of Pharaoh, women of the Moabites, Ammonites, Edomites, Zidonians, *and* Hittites;
2 Of the nations *concerning* which the LORD said unto the children of Israel, Ye shall not go in to them, neither shall they come in unto you: *for* surely they will turn away your heart after their gods: Solomon clave unto these in love.
3 And he had seven hundred wives, princesses, and three hundred concubines: and his wives turned away his heart.
4 For it came to pass, when Solomon was

Cross references (center column)

8 Prov. 8:34
9 2Sam. 8:15; 1Kgs. 5:7; Ps. 72:2; Prov. 8:15
10 Ps. 72:10, 15
11 1Kgs. 9:27; 2Chr. 2:8; 9:10, 11
12 2Chr. 9:10, 11
15 2Chr. 9:24; Ps. 72:10
17 1Kgs. 7:2; 14:26
18 2Chr. 9:17-19
21 2Chr. 9:20-22
22 Gen. 10:4; 2Chr. 20:36
23 1Kgs. 3:12, 13; 4:30
26 Deut. 17:16; 1Kgs. 4:26; 2Chr. 1:14; 9:25
27 2Chr. 1:15-17
28 Deut. 17:16; 2Chr. 1:16; 9:28; Ezek. 27:7
29 Josh. 1:4; 2Kgs. 7:6

1 Deut. 17:17; Neh. 13:26

2 Ex. 34:16; Deut. 7:3, 4

4 Deut. 17:17; 1Kgs. 8:61; 9:4; Neh. 13:26

11:4–13 his wives turned away his heart after other gods. Due to his disobedience in the last years of his life, Solomon's seed would not reign over all of Israel. In time, the ten northern tribes withdrew and kept the name Israel.

old, *that* his wives turned away his heart after other gods: and his heart was not perfect with the LORD his God, as *was* the heart of David his father.

5 For Solomon went after Ashtoreth the goddess of the Zidonians, and after Milcom the abomination of the Ammonites.

6 And Solomon did evil in the sight of the LORD, and went not fully after the LORD, as *did* David his father.

7 Then did Solomon build an high place for Chemosh, the abomination of Moab, in the hill that *is* before Jerusalem, and for Molech, the abomination of the children of Ammon.

8 And likewise did he for all his strange wives, which burnt incense and sacrificed unto their gods.

The Consequences of Solomon's Sins

9 And the LORD was angry with Solomon, because his heart was turned from the LORD God of Israel, which had appeared unto him twice,

10 And had commanded him concerning this thing, that he should not go after other gods: but he kept not that which the LORD commanded.

11 Wherefore the LORD said unto Solomon, Forasmuch as this is done of thee, and thou hast not kept my covenant and my statutes, which I have commanded thee, I will surely rend the kingdom from thee, and will give it to thy servant.

12 Notwithstanding in thy days I will not do it for David thy father's sake: *but* I will rend it out of the hand of thy son.

13 Howbeit I will not rend away all the kingdom; *but* will give one tribe to thy son for David my servant's sake, and for Jerusalem's sake which I have chosen.

14 And the LORD stirred up an adversary unto Solomon, Hadad the Edomite: he *was* of the king's seed in Edom.

15 For it came to pass, when David was in Edom, and Joab the captain of the host was gone up to bury the slain, after he had smitten every male in Edom;

16 (For six months did Joab remain there with all Israel, until he had cut off every male in Edom:)

17 That Hadad fled, he and certain Edomites of his father's servants with him, to go into Egypt; Hadad *being* yet a little child.

18 And they arose out of Midian, and came to Paran: and they took men with them out of Paran, and they came to Egypt, unto Pharaoh king of Egypt; which gave him an house, and appointed him victuals, and gave him land.

19 And Hadad found great favour in the sight of Pharaoh, so that he gave him to wife the sister of his own wife, the sister of Tahpenes the queen.

20 And the sister of Tahpenes bare him Genubath his son, whom Tahpenes weaned in Pharaoh's house: and Genubath was in Pharaoh's household among the sons of Pharaoh.

21 And when Hadad heard in Egypt that David slept with his fathers, and that Joab the captain of the host was dead, Hadad said to Pharaoh, Let me depart, that I may go to mine own country.

22 Then Pharaoh said unto him, But what hast thou lacked with me, that, behold, thou seekest to go to thine own country? And he answered, Nothing: howbeit let me go in any wise.

23 And God stirred him up *another* adversary, Rezon the son of Eliadah, which fled from his lord Hadadezer king of Zobah:

24 And he gathered men unto him, and became captain over a band, when David slew them *of Zobah*: and they went to Damascus, and dwelt therein, and reigned in Damascus.

25 And he was an adversary to Israel all the days of Solomon, beside the mischief that Hadad *did*: and he abhorred Israel, and reigned over Syria.

Jeroboam Is Chosen to Rule Ten Tribes

26 And Jeroboam the son of Nebat, an Ephrathite of Zereda, Solomon's servant, whose mother's name *was* Zeruah, a widow woman, even he lifted up *his* hand against the king.

27 And this *was* the cause that he lifted up *his* hand against the king: Solomon built Millo, *and* repaired the breaches of the city of David his father.

28 And the man Jeroboam *was* a mighty man of valour: and Solomon seeing the young man that he was industrious, he made him ruler over all the charge of the house of Joseph.

Cross references:

5 Judg. 2:13; 1Kgs. 11:33; 2Kgs. 23:13

6 Num. 14:24

7 Num. 21:29; 33:52; Judg. 11:24; 2Kgs. 23:13

9 1Kgs. 3:5; 9:2; 11:2, 3

10 1Kgs. 6:12; 9:6

11 1Kgs. 11:31; 12:15, 16

13 Deut. 12:11; 2Sam. 7:15; 1Kgs. 12:20; Ps. 89:33

14 1Chr. 5:26

15 Num. 24:19; Deut. 20:13; 2Sam. 8:14; 1Chr. 18:12, 13

21 1Kgs. 2:10, 34

23 2Sam. 8:3

24 2Sam. 8:3; 10:8, 18

26 2Sam. 20:21; 1Kgs. 12:2; 2Chr. 13:6

27 1Kgs. 9:24

The Southern Kingdom, in and around Jerusalem and including Benjamin, was known as Judah. After the captivity of the Northern Kingdom, Solomon's seed ruled in the land of Judah for over one hundred years.

29 And it came to pass at that time when Jeroboam went out of Jerusalem, that the prophet Ahijah the Shilonite found him in the way; and he had clad himself with a new garment; and they two *were* alone in the field:

30 And Ahijah caught the new garment that *was* on him, and rent it *in* twelve pieces:

31 And he said to Jeroboam, Take thee ten pieces: for thus saith the Lord, the God of Israel, Behold, I will rend the kingdom out of the hand of Solomon, and will give ten tribes to thee:

32 (But he shall have one tribe for my servant David's sake, and for Jerusalem's sake, the city which I have chosen out of all the tribes of Israel:)

33 Because that they have forsaken me, and have worshipped Ashtoreth the goddess of the Zidonians, Chemosh the god of the Moabites, and Milcom the god of the children of Ammon, and have not walked in my ways, to do *that which is* right in mine eyes, and *to keep* my statutes and my judgments, as *did* David his father.

34 Howbeit I will not take the whole kingdom out of his hand: but I will make him prince all the days of his life for David my servant's sake, whom I chose, because he kept my commandments and my statutes:

35 But I will take the kingdom out of his son's hand, and will give it unto thee, *even* ten tribes.

36 And unto his son will I give one tribe, that David my servant may have a light alway before me in Jerusalem, the city which I have chosen me to put my name there.

37 And I will take thee, and thou shalt reign according to all that thy soul desireth, and shalt be king over Israel.

38 And it shall be, if thou wilt hearken unto all that I command thee, and wilt walk in my ways, and do *that is* right in my sight, to keep my statutes and my commandments, as David my servant did; that I will be with thee, and build thee a sure house, as I built for David, and will give Israel unto thee.

39 And I will for this afflict the seed of David, but not for ever.

40 Solomon sought therefore to kill Jeroboam. And Jeroboam arose, and fled into Egypt, unto Shishak king of Egypt, and was in Egypt until the death of Solomon.

Cross-references:
29 1Kgs. 14:2
30 1Sam. 15:27; 24:5
31 1Kgs. 11:11, 13
33 1Kgs. 11:5-7
35 1Kgs. 12:16, 17
36 1Kgs. 15:4; 2Kgs. 8:19; Ps. 132:17
38 Josh. 1:5; 2Sam. 7:11, 27
41 2Chr. 9:29
42 2Chr. 9:30
43 2Chr. 9:31; Matt. 1:7, called *Roboam*
1 2Chr. 10:1-11
2 1Kgs. 11:26, 40
4 1Sam. 8:11-18; 1Kgs. 4:7
7 2Chr. 10:7; Prov. 15:1

Solomon's Death

41 And the rest of the acts of Solomon, and all that he did, and his wisdom, *are* they not written in the book of the acts of Solomon?

42 And the time that Solomon reigned in Jerusalem over all Israel *was* forty years.

43 And Solomon slept with his fathers, and was buried in the city of David his father: and Rehoboam his son reigned in his stead.

CHAPTER 12
The Northern Tribes Revolt

1 And Rehoboam went to Shechem: for all Israel were come to Shechem to make him king.

2 And it came to pass, when Jeroboam the son of Nebat, who was yet in Egypt, heard *of it*, (for he was fled from the presence of king Solomon, and Jeroboam dwelt in Egypt;)

3 That they sent and called him. And Jeroboam and all the congregation of Israel came, and spake unto Rehoboam, saying,

4 Thy father made our yoke grievous: now therefore make thou the grievous service of thy father, and his heavy yoke which he put upon us, lighter, and we will serve thee.

5 And he said unto them, Depart yet *for* three days, then come again to me. And the people departed.

6 And king Rehoboam consulted with the old men, that stood before Solomon his father while he yet lived, and said, How do ye advise that I may answer this people?

7 And they spake unto him, saying, If thou wilt be a servant unto this people this day, and wilt serve them, and answer them, and speak good words to them, then they will be thy servants for ever.

8 But he forsook the counsel of the old men, which they had given him, and consulted with the young men that were grown up with him, *and* which stood before him:

9 And he said unto them, What counsel give ye that we may answer this people, who have spoken to me, saying, Make the yoke which thy father did put upon us lighter?

10 And the young men that were grown up with him spake unto him, saying, Thus shalt thou speak unto this people that spake unto thee, saying, Thy father made our yoke heavy, but make thou *it* lighter unto us; thus shalt thou say unto them, My little *finger* shall be thicker than my father's loins.

11:29–36 Ahijah the prophet tore the garment of Jeroboam into twelve pieces and, by giving him ten, reaffirmed the prophecy that the house of Israel would be divided into two nations.

11 And now whereas my father did lade you with a heavy yoke, I will add to your yoke: my father hath chastised you with whips, but I will chastise you with scorpions.

12 So Jeroboam and all the people came to Rehoboam the third day, as the king had appointed, saying, Come to me again the third day.

13 And the king answered the people roughly, and forsook the old men's counsel that they gave him;

14 And spake to them after the counsel of the young men, saying, My father made your yoke heavy, and I will add to your yoke: my father *also* chastised you with whips, but I will chastise you with scorpions.

15 Wherefore the king hearkened not unto the people; for the cause was from the LORD, that he might perform his saying, which the LORD spake by Ahijah the Shilonite unto Jeroboam the son of Nebat.

16 So when all Israel saw that the king hearkened not unto them, the people answered the king, saying, What portion have we in David? neither *have we* inheritance in the son of Jesse: to your tents, O Israel: now see to thine own house, David. So Israel departed unto their tents.

17 But *as for* the children of Israel which dwelt in the cities of Judah, Rehoboam reigned over them.

18 Then king Rehoboam sent Adoram, who *was* over the tribute; and all Israel stoned him with stones, that he died. Therefore king Rehoboam made speed to get him up to his chariot, to flee to Jerusalem.

19 So Israel rebelled against the house of David unto this day.

20 And it came to pass, when all Israel heard that Jeroboam was come again, that they sent and called him unto the congregation, and made him king over all Israel: there was none that followed the house of David, but the tribe of Judah only.

Civil War Is Averted

21 And when Rehoboam was come to Jerusalem, he assembled all the house of Judah, with the tribe of Benjamin, an hundred and fourscore thousand chosen men, which were warriors, to fight against the house of Israel, to bring the kingdom again to Rehoboam the son of Solomon.

22 But the word of God came unto Shemaiah the man of God, saying,

23 Speak unto Rehoboam, the son of Solomon, king of Judah, and unto all the house of Judah and Benjamin, and to the remnant of the people, saying,

24 Thus saith the LORD, Ye shall not go up, nor fight against your brethren the children of Israel: return every man to his house; for this thing is from me. They hearkened therefore to the word of the LORD, and returned to depart, according to the word of the LORD.

Jeroboam's Apostasy

25 Then Jeroboam built Shechem in mount Ephraim, and dwelt therein; and went out from thence, and built Penuel.

26 And Jeroboam said in his heart, Now shall the kingdom return to the house of David:

27 If this people go up to do sacrifice in the house of the LORD at Jerusalem, then shall the heart of this people turn again unto their lord, *even* unto Rehoboam king of Judah, and they shall kill me, and go again to Rehoboam king of Judah.

28 Whereupon the king took counsel, and made two calves *of* gold, and said unto them, It is too much for you to go up to Jerusalem: behold thy gods, O Israel, which brought thee up out of the land of Egypt.

29 And he set the one in Beth-el, and the other put he in Dan.

30 And this thing became a sin: for the people went *to worship* before the one, *even* unto Dan.

31 And he made an house of high places, and made priests of the lowest of the people, which were not of the sons of Levi.

32 And Jeroboam ordained a feast in the eighth month, on the fifteenth day of the month, like unto the feast that *is* in Judah, and he offered upon the altar. So did he in Beth-el, sacrificing unto the calves that he had made: and he placed in Beth-el the priests of the high places which he had made.

33 So he offered upon the altar which he had made in Beth-el the fifteenth day of the eighth month, *even* in the month which he had devised of his own heart; and ordained a feast unto the children of Israel: and he offered upon the altar, and burnt incense.

CHAPTER 13
A Judean Prophet Warns Jeroboam

1 And, behold, there came a man of God out of Judah by the word of the LORD unto Beth-el: and Jeroboam stood by the altar to burn incense.

15 Judg. 14:4; 1Kgs. 11:11, 31; 12:24; 2Chr. 10:15; 22:7; 25:20
16 2Sam. 20:1
17 1Kgs. 11:13, 36
18 1Kgs. 4:6; 5:14
19 2Kgs. 17:21
20 1Kgs. 11:13, 32
21 2Chr. 11:1
22 2Chr. 11:2
24 1Kgs. 12:15
25 Judg. 8:17; 9:45
27 Deut. 12:5, 6
28 Ex. 32:4, 8; 2Kgs. 10:29; 17:16
29 Gen. 28:19; Judg. 18:29; Hos. 4:15
30 1Kgs. 13:34; 2Kgs. 17:21
31 Num. 3:10; 1Kgs. 13:32, 33; 2Kgs. 17:32; 2Chr. 11:14, 15; Ezek. 44:7, 8
32 Lev. 23:33, 34; Num. 29:12; 1Kgs. 8:2, 5; Amos 7:13
33 Num. 15:39; 1Kgs. 13:1
1 1Kgs. 12:32, 33; 2Kgs. 23:17

2 And he cried against the altar in the word of the LORD, and said, O altar, altar, thus saith the LORD; Behold, a child shall be born unto the house of David, Josiah by name; and upon thee shall he offer the priests of the high places that burn incense upon thee, and men's bones shall be burnt upon thee.

3 And he gave a sign the same day, saying, This *is* the sign which the LORD hath spoken; Behold, the altar shall be rent, and the ashes that *are* upon it shall be poured out.

4 And it came to pass, when king Jeroboam heard the saying of the man of God, which had cried against the altar in Beth-el, that he put forth his hand from the altar, saying, Lay hold on him. And his hand, which he put forth against him, dried up, so that he could not pull it in again to him.

5 The altar also was rent, and the ashes poured out from the altar, according to the sign which the man of God had given by the word of the LORD.

6 And the king answered and said unto the man of God, Intreat now the face of the LORD thy God, and pray for me, that my hand may be restored me again. And the man of God besought the LORD, and the king's hand was restored him again, and became as *it was* before.

7 And the king said unto the man of God, Come home with me, and refresh thyself, and I will give thee a reward.

8 And the man of God said unto the king, If thou wilt give me half thine house, I will not go in with thee, neither will I eat bread nor drink water in this place:

9 For so was it charged me by the word of the LORD, saying, Eat no bread, nor drink water, nor turn again by the same way that thou camest.

10 So he went another way, and returned not by the way that he came to Beth-el.

The Prophet Dies

11 Now there dwelt an old prophet in Beth-el; and his sons came and told him all the works that the man of God had done that day in Beth-el: the words which he had spoken unto the king, them they told also to their father.

12 And their father said unto them, What way went he? For his sons had seen what way the man of God went, which came from Judah.

13 And he said unto his sons, Saddle me the ass. So they saddled him the ass: and he rode thereon,

14 And went after the man of God, and found him sitting under an oak: and he said unto him, Art thou the man of God that camest from Judah? And he said, I *am.*

15 Then he said unto him, Come home with me, and eat bread.

16 And he said, I may not return with thee, nor go in with thee: neither will I eat bread nor drink water with thee in this place:

17 For it was said to me by the word of the LORD, Thou shalt eat no bread nor drink water there, nor turn again to go by the way that thou camest.

18 He said unto him, I *am* a prophet also as thou *art*; and an angel spake unto me by the word of the LORD, saying, Bring him back with thee into thine house, that he may eat bread and drink water. *But* he lied unto him.

19 So he went back with him, and did eat bread in his house, and drank water.

20 And it came to pass, as they sat at the table, that the word of the LORD came unto the prophet that brought him back:

21 And he cried unto the man of God that came from Judah, saying, Thus saith the LORD, Forasmuch as thou hast disobeyed the mouth of the LORD, and hast not kept the commandment which the LORD thy God commanded thee,

22 But camest back, and hast eaten bread and drunk water in the place, of the which *the* LORD did say to thee, Eat no bread, and drink no water; thy carcase shall not come unto the sepulchre of thy fathers.

23 And it came to pass, after he had eaten bread, and after he had drunk, that he saddled for him the ass, *to wit,* for the prophet whom he had brought back.

24 And when he was gone, a lion met him by the way, and slew him: and his carcase

Cross references (center column)

2 2Kgs. 23:15, 16
3 Isa. 7:14; John 2:18; 1Cor. 1:22
6 Ex. 8:8; 9:28; 10:17; Num. 21:7; Acts 8:24; James 5:16
7 1Sam. 9:7; 2Kgs. 5:15
8 Num. 22:18; 24:13
9 1Cor. 5:11
16 1Kgs. 13:8, 9
17 1Kgs. 20:35; 1Thess. 4:15
22 1Kgs. 13:9
24 1Kgs. 20:36

13:1–10 a child shall be born unto the house of David. An unnamed prophet met Jeroboam at the altar of God at Bethel and gave a most amazing prophecy. A reformer by the name of Josiah would become king of Judah and would destroy on that altar the false prophets who were leading the people in the worship of idols. Josiah would not be born for another three hundred years! Yet he fulfilled this amazing prediction, testifying to the faithfulness of God and prophecy (2 Chr. 34:33).

13:11–32 While we admire this "man of God" for refusing the flattery of King Jeroboam, he listened to the lying prophet (v. 18) and disobeyed God, for which he was slain. These events are a tragic reminder that God holds his servants accountable to obey His word.

was cast in the way, and the ass stood by it, the lion also stood by the carcase.

25 And, behold, men passed by, and saw the carcase cast in the way, and the lion standing by the carcase: and they came and told *it* in the city where the old prophet dwelt.

26 And when the prophet that brought him back from the way heard *thereof*, he said, It *is* the man of God, who was disobedient unto the word of the LORD: therefore the LORD hath delivered him unto the lion, which hath torn him, and slain him, according to the word of the LORD, which he spake unto him.

27 And he spake to his sons, saying, Saddle me the ass. And they saddled *him*.

28 And he went and found his carcase cast in the way, and the ass and the lion standing by the carcase: the lion had not eaten the carcase, nor torn the ass.

29 And the prophet took up the carcase of the man of God, and laid it upon the ass, and brought it back: and the old prophet came to the city, to mourn and to bury him.

30 And he laid his carcase in his own grave; and they mourned over him, *saying*, Alas, my brother!

31 And it came to pass, after he had buried him, that he spake to his sons, saying, When I am dead, then bury me in the sepulchre wherein the man of God *is* buried; lay my bones beside his bones:

32 For the saying which he cried by the word of the LORD against the altar in Bethel, and against all the houses of the high places which *are* in the cities of Samaria, shall surely come to pass.

33 After this thing Jeroboam returned not from his evil way, but made again of the lowest of the people priests of the high places: whosoever would, he consecrated him, and he became *one* of the priests of the high places.

34 And this thing became sin unto the house of Jeroboam, even to cut *it* off, and to destroy *it* from off the face of the earth.

CHAPTER 14

Ahijah Prophesies against Jeroboam

1 At that time Abijah the son of Jeroboam fell sick.

2 And Jeroboam said to his wife, Arise, I pray thee, and disguise thyself, that thou be not known to be the wife of Jeroboam; and get thee to Shiloh: behold, there *is* Ahijah the prophet, which told me that *I should be* king over this people.

3 And take with thee ten loaves, and cracknels, and a cruse of honey, and go to him: he shall tell thee what shall become of the child.

4 And Jeroboam's wife did so, and arose, and went to Shiloh, and came to the house of Ahijah. But Ahijah could not see; for his eyes were set by reason of his age.

5 And the LORD said unto Ahijah, Behold, the wife of Jeroboam cometh to ask a thing of thee for her son; for he *is* sick: thus and thus shalt thou say unto her: for it shall be, when she cometh in, that she shall feign herself *to be* another woman.

6 And it was *so*, when Ahijah heard the sound of her feet, as she came in at the door, that he said, Come in, thou wife of Jeroboam; why feignest thou thyself *to be* another? for I *am* sent to thee with heavy *tidings*.

7 Go, tell Jeroboam, Thus saith the LORD God of Israel, Forasmuch as I exalted thee from among the people, and made thee prince over my people Israel,

8 And rent the kingdom away from the house of David, and gave it thee: and *yet* thou hast not been as my servant David, who kept my commandments, and who followed me with all his heart, to do *that* only *which was* right in mine eyes;

9 But hast done evil above all that were before thee: for thou hast gone and made thee other gods, and molten images, to provoke me to anger, and hast cast me behind thy back:

10 Therefore behold, I will bring evil upon the house of Jeroboam, and will cut off from Jeroboam him that pisseth against the wall, *and* him that is shut up and left in Israel, and will take away the remnant of the house of Jeroboam, as a man taketh away dung, till it be all gone.

11 Him that dieth of Jeroboam in the city shall the dogs eat; and him that dieth in the field shall the fowls of the air eat: for the LORD hath spoken *it*.

12 Arise thou therefore, get thee to thine own house: *and* when thy feet enter into the city, the child shall die.

13 And all Israel shall mourn for him, and

30 Jer. 22:18
31 2Kgs. 23:17, 18
32 1Kgs. 13:2; 16:24; 2Kgs. 23:16, 19
33 1Kgs. 12:31, 32; 2Chr. 11:15; 13:9
34 1Kgs. 12:30; 14:10
2 1Kgs. 11:31
3 1Sam. 9:7, 8
4 1Kgs. 11:29
7 2Sam. 12:7, 8; 1Kgs. 16:2
8 1Kgs. 11:31, 33, 38; 15:5
9 1Kgs. 12:28; 2Chr. 11:15; Neh. 9:26; Ps. 50:17; Ezek. 23:35
10 Deut. 32:36; 1Kgs. 15:29; 21:21; 2Kgs. 9:8; 14:26
11 1Kgs. 16:4; 21:24
12 1Kgs. 14:17
13 2Chr. 12:12; 19:3

14:9–16 done evil above all that were before thee. Jeroboam had introduced idolatry and disobedience to God, making "Israel to sin" (v. 16). God determined to slay Jeroboam and his entire seed so that none of his children would reign over Israel. All that God predicted literally came to pass.

bury him: for he only of Jeroboam shall come to the grave, because in him there is found *some* good thing toward the Lord God of Israel in the house of Jeroboam.

14 Moreover the Lord shall raise him up a king over Israel, who shall cut off the house of Jeroboam that day: but what? even now.

15 For the Lord shall smite Israel, as a reed is shaken in the water, and he shall root up Israel out of this good land, which he gave to their fathers, and shall scatter them beyond the river, because they have made their groves, provoking the Lord to anger.

16 And he shall give Israel up because of the sins of Jeroboam, who did sin, and who made Israel to sin.

17 And Jeroboam's wife arose, and departed, and came to Tirzah: *and* when she came to the threshold of the door, the child died;

18 And they buried him; and all Israel mourned for him, according to the word of the Lord, which he spake by the hand of his servant Ahijah the prophet.

Jeroboam's Death

19 And the rest of the acts of Jeroboam, how he warred, and how he reigned, behold, they *are* written in the book of the chronicles of the kings of Israel.

20 And the days which Jeroboam reigned *were* two and twenty years: and he slept with his fathers, and Nadab his son reigned in his stead.

Rehoboam Rules Judah

21 And Rehoboam the son of Solomon reigned in Judah. Rehoboam *was* forty and one years old when he began to reign, and he reigned seventeen years in Jerusalem, the city which the Lord did choose out of all the tribes of Israel, to put his name there. And his mother's name *was* Naamah an Ammonitess.

22 And Judah did evil in the sight of the Lord, and they provoked him to jealousy with their sins which they had committed, above all that their fathers had done.

23 For they also built them high places, and images, and groves, on every high hill, and under every green tree.

24 And there were also sodomites in the land: *and* they did according to all the abominations of the nations which the Lord cast out before the children of Israel.

25 And it came to pass in the fifth year of king Rehoboam, *that* Shishak king of Egypt came up against Jerusalem:

26 And he took away the treasures of the

14 1Kgs. 15:27-29

15 Ex. 34:13; Deut. 12:3, 4; Josh. 23:15, 16; 2Kgs. 15:29; 17:6; Ps. 52:5

16 1Kgs. 12:30; 13:34

17 1Kgs. 14:12; 16:6, 8, 15, 23; Song 6:4

18 1Kgs. 14:13

19 2Chr. 13:2, 3

21 1Kgs. 11:31; 14:31; 2Chr. 12:13

22 Deut. 32:21; 2Chr. 12:1; Ps. 78:58; 1Cor. 10:22

23 Deut. 12:2; 2Kgs. 17:9, 10; Isa. 16:24, 25

24 Deut. 23:17; 1Kgs. 15:12; 22:46; 2Kgs. 23:7

25 1Kgs. 11:40; 2Chr. 12:2

26 2Chr. 12:9, 10, 11; 10:17

29 2Chr. 12:15

30 1Kgs. 12:24; 15:6; 2Chr. 12:15

31 1Kgs. 14:21; 2Chr. 12:16, *Abijah*; Matt. 1:7, *Abia*

1 2Chr. 13:1, 2

2 2Chr. 11:20-22, *Absalom*; 13:2, *Michaiah the daughter of Uriel*

3 1Kgs. 11:4; Ps. 119:80

4 1Kgs. 11:32, 36; 2Chr. 21:7

5 2Sam. 11:4, 15

7 2Chr. 13:2, 3, 22

house of the Lord, and the treasures of the king's house; he even took away all: and he took away all the shields of gold which Solomon had made.

27 And king Rehoboam made in their stead brasen shields, and committed *them* unto the hands of the chief of the guard, which kept the door of the king's house.

28 And it was *so*, when the king went into the house of the Lord, that the guard bare them, and brought them back into the guard chamber.

29 Now the rest of the acts of Rehoboam, and all that he did, *are* they not written in the book of the chronicles of the kings of Judah?

30 And there was war between Rehoboam and Jeroboam all *their* days.

31 And Rehoboam slept with his fathers, and was buried with his fathers in the city of David. And his mother's name *was* Naamah an Ammonitess. And Abijam his son reigned in his stead.

Chapter 15
Abijam Rules Judah

1 Now in the eighteenth year of king Jeroboam the son of Nebat reigned Abijam over Judah.

2 Three years reigned he in Jerusalem. And his mother's name *was* Maachah, the daughter of Abishalom.

3 And he walked in all the sins of his father, which he had done before him: and his heart was not perfect with the Lord his God, as the heart of David his father.

4 Nevertheless for David's sake did the Lord his God give him a lamp in Jerusalem, to set up his son after him, and to establish Jerusalem:

5 Because David did *that which was* right in the eyes of the Lord, and turned not aside from any *thing* that he commanded him all the days of his life, save only in the matter of Uriah the Hittite.

6 And there was war between Rehoboam and Jeroboam all the days of his life.

7 Now the rest of the acts of Abijam, and all that he did, *are* they not written in the book of the chronicles of the kings of Judah? And there was war between Abijam and Jeroboam.

8 And Abijam slept with his fathers; and they buried him in the city of David: and Asa his son reigned in his stead.

Asa Rules Judah

9 And in the twentieth year of Jeroboam king of Israel reigned Asa over Judah.

10 And forty and one years reigned he in Jerusalem. And his mother's name *was* Maachah, the daughter of Abishalom.

11 And Asa did *that which was* right in the eyes of the LORD, as *did* David his father.

12 And he took away the sodomites out of the land, and removed all the idols that his fathers had made.

13 And also Maachah his mother, even her he removed from *being* queen, because she had made an idol in a grove; and Asa destroyed her idol, and burnt *it* by the brook Kidron.

14 But the high places were not removed: nevertheless Asa's heart was perfect with the LORD all his days.

15 And he brought in the things which his father had dedicated, and the things which himself had dedicated, into the house of the LORD, silver, and gold, and vessels.

16 And there was war between Asa and Baasha king of Israel all their days.

17 And Baasha king of Israel went up against Judah, and built Ramah, that he might not suffer any to go out or come in to Asa king of Judah.

18 Then Asa took all the silver and the gold *that were* left in the treasures of the house of the LORD, and the treasures of the king's house, and delivered them into the hand of his servants: and king Asa sent them to Ben-hadad, the son of Tabrimon, the son of Hezion, king of Syria, that dwelt at Damascus, saying,

19 *There is* a league between me and thee, *and* between my father and thy father: behold, I have sent unto thee a present of silver and gold; come and break thy league with Baasha king of Israel, that he may depart from me.

20 So Ben-hadad hearkened unto king Asa, and sent the captains of the hosts which he had against the cities of Israel, and smote Ijon, and Dan, and Abel-beth-maachah, and all Cinneroth, with all the land of Naphtali.

21 And it came to pass, when Baasha heard *thereof*, that he left off building of Ramah, and dwelt in Tirzah.

22 Then king Asa made a proclamation throughout all Judah; none *was* exempted: and they took away the stones of Ramah, and the timber thereof, wherewith Baasha had builded; and king Asa built with them Geba of Benjamin, and Mizpah.

23 The rest of all the acts of Asa, and all his

10 1Kgs. 15:2
11 2Chr. 14:2
12 1Kgs. 14:24; 22:46
13 Ex. 32:20; 2Chr. 15:16
14 1Kgs. 15:3; 22:43; 2Chr. 15:17, 18
17 Josh. 18:25; 1Kgs. 12:27; 2Chr. 16:1-6
18 1Kgs. 11:23, 24; 2Chr. 16:2
20 Judg. 18:29; 2Sam. 20:14; 2Kgs. 15:29
22 Josh. 18:26; 21:17; 2Chr. 16:6
23 2Chr. 16:12
24 2Chr. 17:1; Matt. 1:8, called *Josaphat*
25 1Kgs. 12:30; 14:16
27 Josh. 19:44; 21:23; 1Kgs. 14:14; 16:15
29 1Kgs. 14:10, 14
30 1Kgs. 14:9, 16
32 1Kgs. 15:16
34 1Kgs. 12:28, 29; 13:33; 14:16
1 1Kgs. 16:7; 2Chr. 19:2; 20:34

might, and all that he did, and the cities which he built, *are* they not written in the book of the chronicles of the kings of Judah? Nevertheless in the time of his old age he was diseased in his feet.

24 And Asa slept with his fathers, and was buried with his fathers in the city of David his father: and Jehoshaphat his son reigned in his stead.

Nadab Rules Israel

25 And Nadab the son of Jeroboam began to reign over Israel in the second year of Asa king of Judah, and reigned over Israel two years.

26 And he did evil in the sight of the LORD, and walked in the way of his father, and in his sin wherewith he made Israel to sin.

27 And Baasha the son of Ahijah, of the house of Issachar, conspired against him; and Baasha smote him at Gibbethon, which *belonged* to the Philistines; for Nadab and all Israel laid siege to Gibbethon.

28 Even in the third year of Asa king of Judah did Baasha slay him, and reigned in his stead.

29 And it came to pass, when he reigned, *that* he smote all the house of Jeroboam; he left not to Jeroboam any that breathed, until he had destroyed him, according unto the saying of the LORD, which he spake by his servant Ahijah the Shilonite:

30 Because of the sins of Jeroboam which he sinned, and which he made Israel sin, by his provocation wherewith he provoked the LORD God of Israel to anger.

31 Now the rest of the acts of Nadab, and all that he did, *are* they not written in the book of the chronicles of the kings of Israel?

32 And there was war between Asa and Baasha king of Israel all their days.

Baasha Rules Israel

33 In the third year of Asa king of Judah began Baasha the son of Ahijah to reign over all Israel in Tirzah, twenty and four years.

34 And he did evil in the sight of the LORD, and walked in the way of Jeroboam, and in his sin wherewith he made Israel to sin.

CHAPTER 16

1 Then the word of the LORD came to Jehu the son of Hanani against Baasha, saying,

---

16:1–4 It was predicted of Baasha, the evil king of Israel, that his posterity would be taken away. This was literally fulfilled in verses 11–13.

2 Forasmuch as I exalted thee out of the dust, and made thee prince over my people Israel; and thou hast walked in the way of Jeroboam, and hast made my people Israel to sin, to provoke me to anger with their sins;

3 Behold, I will take away the posterity of Baasha, and the posterity of his house; and will make thy house like the house of Jeroboam the son of Nebat.

4 Him that dieth of Baasha in the city shall the dogs eat; and him that dieth of his in the fields shall the fowls of the air eat.

5 Now the rest of the acts of Baasha, and what he did, and his might, *are* they not written in the book of the chronicles of the kings of Israel?

6 So Baasha slept with his fathers, and was buried in Tirzah: and Elah his son reigned in his stead.

7 And also by the hand of the prophet Jehu the son of Hanani came the word of the LORD against Baasha, and against his house, even for all the evil that he did in the sight of the LORD, in provoking him to anger with the work of his hands, in being like the house of Jeroboam; and because he killed him.

Elah Rules Israel

8 In the twenty and sixth year of Asa king of Judah began Elah the son of Baasha to reign over Israel in Tirzah, two years.

9 And his servant Zimri, captain of half *his* chariots, conspired against him, as he was in Tirzah, drinking himself drunk in the house of Arza steward of *his* house in Tirzah.

10 And Zimri went in and smote him, and killed him, in the twenty and seventh year of Asa king of Judah, and reigned in his stead.

11 And it came to pass, when he began to reign, as soon as he sat on his throne, *that* he slew all the house of Baasha: he left him not one that pisseth against a wall, neither of his kinsfolks, nor of his friends.

12 Thus did Zimri destroy all the house of Baasha, according to the word of the LORD, which he spake against Baasha by Jehu the prophet,

13 For all the sins of Baasha, and the sins of Elah his son, by which they sinned, and by which they made Israel to sin, in provoking the LORD God of Israel to anger with their vanities.

14 Now the rest of the acts of Elah, and all that he did, *are* they not written in the book of the chronicles of the kings of Israel?

Zimri Rules Israel

15 In the twenty and seventh year of Asa king of Judah did Zimri reign seven days in Tirzah. And the people *were* encamped against Gibbethon, which *belonged* to the Philistines.

16 And the people *that were* encamped heard say, Zimri hath conspired, and hath also slain the king: wherefore all Israel made Omri, the captain of the host, king over Israel that day in the camp.

17 And Omri went up from Gibbethon, and all Israel with him, and they besieged Tirzah.

18 And it came to pass, when Zimri saw that the city was taken, that he went into the palace of the king's house, and burnt the king's house over him with fire, and died,

19 For his sins which he sinned in doing evil in the sight of the LORD, in walking in the way of Jeroboam, and in his sin which he did, to make Israel to sin.

20 Now the rest of the acts of Zimri, and his treason that he wrought, *are* they not written in the book of the chronicles of the kings of Israel?

Omri Rules Israel

21 Then were the people of Israel divided into two parts: half of the people followed Tibni the son of Ginath, to make him king; and half followed Omri.

22 But the people that followed Omri prevailed against the people that followed Tibni the son of Ginath: so Tibni died, and Omri reigned.

23 In the thirty and first year of Asa king of Judah began Omri to reign over Israel, twelve years: six years reigned he in Tirzah.

24 And he bought the hill Samaria of Shemer for two talents of silver, and built on the hill, and called the name of the city which he built, after the name of Shemer, owner of the hill, Samaria.

25 But Omri wrought evil in the eyes of the LORD, and did worse than all that *were* before him.

26 For he walked in all the way of Jeroboam the son of Nebat, and in his sin wherewith he made Israel to sin, to provoke the LORD God of Israel to anger with their vanities.

27 Now the rest of the acts of Omri which he did, and his might that he shewed, *are* they not written in the book of the chronicles of the kings of Israel?

28 So Omri slept with his fathers, and was

Cross References

2 1Kgs. 14:7; 15:34
3 1Kgs. 14:10; 15:29; 16:11
4 1Kgs. 14:11
5 2Chr. 16:1
6 1Kgs. 14:7; 15:21
7 1Kgs. 15:27, 29; 16:1; Hos. 1:4
9 2Kgs. 9:31
11 1Sam. 25:22
12 1Kgs. 16:1, 3
13 Deut. 32:21; 1Sam. 12:21; Isa. 41:29; Jon. 2:8; 1Cor. 8:4; 10:19
15 1Kgs. 15:27
19 1Kgs. 12:28; 15:26, 34
24 1Kgs. 13:32; 2Kgs. 17:24; John 4:4
25 Mic. 6:16

buried in Samaria: and Ahab his son reigned in his stead.

Ahab Rules Israel

29 And in the thirty and eighth year of Asa king of Judah began Ahab the son of Omri to reign over Israel: and Ahab the son of Omri reigned over Israel in Samaria twenty and two years.

30 And Ahab the son of Omri did evil in the sight of the LORD above all that *were* before him.

31 And it came to pass, as if it had been a light thing for him to walk in the sins of Jeroboam the son of Nebat, that he took to wife Jezebel the daughter of Ethbaal king of the Zidonians, and went and served Baal, and worshipped him.

32 And he reared up an altar for Baal in the house of Baal, which he had built in Samaria.

33 And Ahab made a grove; and Ahab did more to provoke the LORD God of Israel to anger than all the kings of Israel that were before him.

34 In his days did Hiel the Bethelite build Jericho: he laid the foundation thereof in Abiram his firstborn, and set up the gates thereof in his youngest *son* Segub, according to the word of the LORD, which he spake by Joshua the son of Nun.

CHAPTER 17
Elijah Warns Ahab of a Drought

1 And Elijah the Tishbite, *who was* of the inhabitants of Gilead, said unto Ahab, *As* the LORD God of Israel liveth, before whom I stand, there shall not be dew nor rain these years, but according to my word.

2 And the word of the LORD came unto him, saying,

3 Get thee hence, and turn thee eastward, and hide thyself by the brook Cherith, that *is* before Jordan.

4 And it shall be, *that* thou shalt drink of the brook; and I have commanded the ravens to feed thee there.

5 So he went and did according unto the word of the LORD: for he went and dwelt by the brook Cherith, that *is* before Jordan.

6 And the ravens brought him bread and flesh in the morning, and bread and flesh in the evening; and he drank of the brook.

7 And it came to pass after a while, that the brook dried up, because there had been no rain in the land.

Elijah Raises the Widow's Son

8 And the word of the LORD came unto him, saying,

9 Arise, get thee to Zarephath, which *belongeth* to Zidon, and dwell there: behold, I have commanded a widow woman there to sustain thee.

10 So he arose and went to Zarephath. And when he came to the gate of the city, behold, the widow woman *was* there gathering of sticks: and he called to her, and said, Fetch me, I pray thee, a little water in a vessel, that I may drink.

11 And as she was going to fetch *it*, he called to her, and said, Bring me, I pray thee, a morsel of bread in thine hand.

12 And she said, *As* the LORD thy God liveth, I have not a cake, but an handful of meal in a barrel, and a little oil in a cruse: and, behold, I *am* gathering two sticks, that I may go in and dress it for me and my son, that we may eat it, and die.

13 And Elijah said unto her, Fear not; go *and* do as thou hast said: but make me thereof a little cake first, and bring *it* unto me, and after make for thee and for thy son.

14 For thus saith the LORD God of Israel, The barrel of meal shall not waste, neither shall the cruse of oil fail, until the day *that* the LORD sendeth rain upon the earth.

15 And she went and did according to the saying of Elijah: and she, and he, and her house, did eat *many* days.

16 *And* the barrel of meal wasted not, neither did the cruse of oil fail, according to the word of the LORD, which he spake by Elijah.

17 And it came to pass after these things, *that* the son of the woman, the mistress of the house, fell sick; and his sickness was so sore, that there was no breath left in him.

18 And she said unto Elijah, What have I to do with thee, O thou man of God? art thou

---

Center column cross-references:

31 Deut. 7:3; Judg. 18:7; 1Kgs. 21:25, 26; 2Kgs. 10:18; 17:16

32 2Kgs. 10:21, 26, 27

33 1Kgs. 16:30; 21:25; 2Kgs. 13:6; 17:10; 21:3; Jer. 17:2

34 Josh. 6:26

1 Deut. 10:8; 2Kgs. 3:14; Luke 1:17; 4:25, he is called *Elias;* James 5:17

9 Obad. 20; Luke 4:26, called *Sarepta*

18 Luke 5:8

17:1–2 Elijah ("Jehovah is God") is one of the greatest of the Hebrew prophets. He started the "school of the prophets" and set the standard in Israel of what a prophet should be. Here, "the word of the LORD came unto him," regarding a three-year drought in Israel (see 18:1).

17:8–16 Under the inspiration of the Spirit, the prophet of God told the widow of Zarephath that she would not run out of meal and oil if she took a step of faith and made him a cake of the last of the supply. She did, and the prophecy was fulfilled. Jesus used her as an example to prove that God's love and offer of redemption included the Gentiles (Luke 4:25).

come unto me to call my sin to remembrance, and to slay my son?

19 And he said unto her, Give me thy son. And he took him out of her bosom, and carried him up into a loft, where he abode, and laid him upon his own bed.

20 And he cried unto the LORD, and said, O LORD my God, hast thou also brought evil upon the widow with whom I sojourn, by slaying her son?

21 And he stretched himself upon the child three times, and cried unto the LORD, and said, O LORD my God, I pray thee, let this child's soul come into him again.

22 And the LORD heard the voice of Elijah; and the soul of the child came into him again, and he revived.

23 And Elijah took the child, and brought him down out of the chamber into the house, and delivered him unto his mother: and Elijah said, See, thy son liveth.

24 And the woman said to Elijah, Now by this I know that thou *art* a man of God, *and* that the word of the LORD in thy mouth *is* truth.

CHAPTER 18
Elijah Confronts Ahab Again

1 And it came to pass *after* many days, that the word of the LORD came to Elijah in the third year, saying, Go, shew thyself unto Ahab; and I will send rain upon the earth.

2 And Elijah went to shew himself unto Ahab. And *there was* a sore famine in Samaria.

3 And Ahab called Obadiah, which *was* the governor of *his* house. (Now Obadiah feared the LORD greatly:

4 For it was *so*, when Jezebel cut off the prophets of the LORD, that Obadiah took an hundred prophets, and hid them by fifty in a cave, and fed them with bread and water.)

5 And Ahab said unto Obadiah, Go into the land, unto all fountains of water, and unto all brooks: peradventure we may find grass to save the horses and mules alive, that we lose not all the beasts.

6 So they divided the land between them to pass throughout it: Ahab went one way by himself, and Obadiah went another way by himself.

7 And as Obadiah was in the way, behold,

Elijah met him: and he knew him, and fell on his face, and said, *Art* thou that my lord Elijah?

8 And he answered him, I *am*: go, tell thy lord, Behold, Elijah *is here*.

9 And he said, What have I sinned, that thou wouldest deliver thy servant into the hand of Ahab, to slay me?

10 *As* the LORD thy God liveth, there is no nation or kingdom, whither my lord hath not sent to seek thee: and when they said, *He is* not *there*; he took an oath of the kingdom and nation, that they found thee not.

11 And now thou sayest, Go, tell thy lord, Behold, Elijah *is here*.

12 And it shall come to pass, *as soon as* I am gone from thee, that the Spirit of the LORD shall carry thee whither I know not; and *so* when I come and tell Ahab, and he cannot find thee, he shall slay me: but I thy servant fear the LORD from my youth.

13 Was it not told my lord what I did when Jezebel slew the prophets of the LORD, how I hid an hundred men of the LORD's prophets by fifty in a cave, and fed them with bread and water?

14 And now thou sayest, Go, tell thy lord, Behold, Elijah *is here*: and he shall slay me.

15 And Elijah said, *As* the LORD of hosts liveth, before whom I stand, I will surely shew myself unto him today.

16 So Obadiah went to meet Ahab, and told him: and Ahab went to meet Elijah.

17 And it came to pass, when Ahab saw Elijah, that Ahab said unto him, *Art* thou he that troubleth Israel?

18 And he answered, I have not troubled Israel; but thou, and thy father's house, in that ye have forsaken the commandments of the LORD, and thou hast followed Baalim.

19 Now therefore send, *and* gather to me all Israel unto mount Carmel, and the prophets of Baal four hundred and fifty, and the prophets of the groves four hundred, which eat at Jezebel's table.

Elijah at Mount Carmel

20 So Ahab sent unto all the children of Israel, and gathered the prophets together unto mount Carmel.

21 And Elijah came unto all the people, and said, How long halt ye between two

---

Cross references (center column):

21 2Kgs. 4:34, 35

22 Heb. 11:35

24 John 3:2; 16:30

1 Deut. 28:12; Luke 4:25; James 5:17

12 2Kgs. 2:16; Ezek. 3:12, 14; Matt. 4:1; Acts 8:39

17 Josh. 7:25; 1Kgs. 21:20; Acts 16:20

18 2Chr. 15:2

19 Josh. 19:26; 1Kgs. 16:33

20 1Kgs. 22:6

21 Josh. 24:15; 2Kgs. 17:41; Matt. 6:24

18:17–46 The exciting story of Elijah challenging the four hundred and fifty prophets of Baal and the four hundred false "prophets of the groves" proved that the God of Israel and Judah is the only true God. God's answer by fire is one of the most colorful responses in the Bible. It also shows that nothing is worse than leading people to worship idols. In verse 41, Elijah showed his faith in God's promises that the drought was to end (v. 45).

opinions? if the LORD be God, follow him: but if Baal, *then* follow him. And the people answered him not a word.

22 Then said Elijah unto the people, I, *even* I only, remain a prophet of the LORD; but Baal's prophets *are* four hundred and fifty men.

23 Let them therefore give us two bullocks; and let them choose one bullock for themselves, and cut it in pieces, and lay *it* on wood, and put no fire *under*: and I will dress the other bullock, and lay *it* on wood, and put no fire *under*:

24 And call ye on the name of your gods, and I will call on the name of the LORD: and the God that answereth by fire, let him be God. And all the people answered and said, It is well spoken.

25 And Elijah said unto the prophets of Baal, Choose you one bullock for yourselves, and dress *it* first; for ye *are* many; and call on the name of your gods, but put no fire *under*.

26 And they took the bullock which was given them, and they dressed *it*, and called on the name of Baal from morning even until noon, saying, O Baal, hear us. But *there was* no voice, nor any that answered. And they leaped upon the altar which was made.

27 And it came to pass at noon, that Elijah mocked them, and said, Cry aloud: for he *is* a god; either he is talking, or he is pursuing, or he is in a journey, *or* peradventure he sleepeth, and must be awaked.

28 And they cried aloud, and cut themselves after their manner with knives and lancets, till the blood gushed out upon them.

29 And it came to pass, when midday was past, and they prophesied until the *time* of the offering of the *evening* sacrifice, that *there was* neither voice, nor any to answer, nor any that regarded.

30 And Elijah said unto all the people, Come near unto me. And all the people came near unto him. And he repaired the altar of the LORD *that was* broken down.

31 And Elijah took twelve stones, according to the number of the tribes of the sons of Jacob, unto whom the word of the LORD came, saying, Israel shall be thy name:

32 And with the stones he built an altar in the name of the LORD: and he made a trench about the altar, as great as would contain two measures of seed.

33 And he put the wood in order, and cut the bullock in pieces, and laid *him* on the wood, and said, Fill four barrels with water, and pour *it* on the burnt sacrifice, and on the wood.

34 And he said, Do *it* the second time. And they did *it* the second time. And he said, Do *it* the third time. And they did *it* the third time.

35 And the water ran round about the altar; and he filled the trench also with water.

36 And it came to pass at *the time of* the offering of the *evening* sacrifice, that Elijah the prophet came near, and said, LORD God of Abraham, Isaac, and of Israel, let it be known this day that thou *art* God in Israel, and *that* I *am* thy servant, and *that* I have done all these things at thy word.

37 Hear me, O LORD, hear me, that this people may know that thou *art* the LORD God, and *that* thou hast turned their heart back again.

38 Then the fire of the LORD fell, and consumed the burnt sacrifice, and the wood, and the stones, and the dust, and licked up the water that *was* in the trench.

39 And when all the people saw *it*, they fell on their faces: and they said, The LORD, he *is* the God; the LORD, he *is* the God.

40 And Elijah said unto them, Take the prophets of Baal; let not one of them escape. And they took them: and Elijah brought them down to the brook Kishon, and slew them there.

The Drought Ends

41 And Elijah said unto Ahab, Get thee up, eat and drink; for *there is* a sound of abundance of rain.

42 So Ahab went up to eat and to drink. And Elijah went up to the top of Carmel; and he cast himself down upon the earth, and put his face between his knees,

43 And said to his servant, Go up now, look toward the sea. And he went up, and looked, and said, *There is* nothing. And he said, Go again seven times.

44 And it came to pass at the seventh time, that he said, Behold, there ariseth a little cloud out of the sea, like a man's hand. And he said, Go up, say unto Ahab, Prepare *thy chariot*, and get thee down, that the rain stop thee not.

45 And it came to pass in the meanwhile, that the heaven was black with clouds and wind, and there was a great rain. And Ahab rode, and went to Jezreel.

46 And the hand of the LORD was on Elijah; and he girded up his loins, and ran before Ahab to the entrance of Jezreel.

Cross references (center column):

22 1Kgs. 18:19; 19:10, 14
24 1Kgs. 18:38; 1Chr. 21:26
26 Ps. 115:5; Jer. 10:5; 1Cor. 8:4; 12:2
28 Lev. 19:28; Deut. 14:1
29 1Kgs. 18:26; 1Cor. 14:4, 5
30 1Kgs. 19:10
31 Gen. 32:28; 35:10; 2Kgs. 17:34
32 Col. 3:17
33 Lev. 1:6–8; Judg. 6:20
35 1Kgs. 13:32, 38
36 Ex. 3:6; Num. 16:28; 1Kgs. 8:43; 2Kgs. 19:19; Ps. 83:18
38 Lev. 9:24; Judg. 6:21; 1Chr. 21:26; 2Chr. 7:1
39 1Kgs. 18:24
40 Deut. 13:5; 18:20; 2Kgs. 10:25
42 James 5:17, 18
46 2Kgs. 4:29; 9:1

CHAPTER 19
Elijah Flees to Mount Horeb

1 And Ahab told Jezebel all that Elijah had done, and withal how he had slain all the prophets with the sword.

2 Then Jezebel sent a messenger unto Elijah, saying, So let the gods do *to me*, and more also, if I make not thy life as the life of one of them by to morrow about this time.

3 And when he saw *that*, he arose, and went for his life, and came to Beer-sheba, which *belongeth* to Judah, and left his servant there.

4 But he himself went a day's journey into the wilderness, and came and sat down under a juniper tree: and he requested for himself that he might die; and said, It is enough; now, O LORD, take away my life; for I *am* not better than my fathers.

5 And as he lay and slept under a juniper tree, behold, then an angel touched him, and said unto him, Arise *and* eat.

6 And he looked, and, behold, *there was* a cake baken on the coals, and a cruse of water at his head. And he did eat and drink, and laid him down again.

7 And the angel of the LORD came again the second time, and touched him, and said, Arise *and* eat; because the journey *is* too great for thee.

8 And he arose, and did eat and drink, and went in the strength of that meat forty days and forty nights unto Horeb the mount of God.

God Commissions Elijah

9 And he came thither unto a cave, and lodged there; and, behold, the word of the LORD *came* to him, and he said unto him, What doest thou here, Elijah?

10 And he said, I have been very jealous for the LORD God of hosts: for the children of Israel have forsaken thy covenant, thrown down thine altars, and slain thy prophets with the sword; and I, *even* I only, am left; and they seek my life, to take it away.

11 And he said, Go forth, and stand upon the mount before the LORD. And, behold, the LORD passed by, and a great and strong wind rent the mountains, and brake in pieces the rocks before the LORD; *but* the LORD *was* not in the wind: and after the wind an earthquake; *but* the LORD *was* not in the earthquake:

12 And after the earthquake a fire; *but* the LORD *was* not in the fire: and after the fire a still small voice.

13 And it was *so*, when Elijah heard *it*, that he wrapped his face in his mantle, and went out, and stood in the entering in of the cave. And, behold, *there came* a voice unto him, and said, What doest thou here, Elijah?

14 And he said, I have been very jealous for the LORD God of hosts: because the children of Israel have forsaken thy covenant, thrown down thine altars, and slain thy prophets with the sword; and I, *even* I only, am left; and they seek my life, to take it away.

15 And the LORD said unto him, Go, return on thy way to the wilderness of Damascus: and when thou comest, anoint Hazael *to be* king over Syria:

16 And Jehu the son of Nimshi shalt thou anoint *to be* king over Israel: and Elisha the son of Shaphat of Abel-meholah shalt thou anoint *to be* prophet in thy room.

17 And it shall come to pass, *that* him that escapeth the sword of Hazael shall Jehu slay: and him that escapeth from the sword of Jehu shall Elisha slay.

18 Yet I have left *me* seven thousand in Israel, all the knees which have not bowed unto Baal, and every mouth which hath not kissed him.

Elijah Calls Elisha

19 So he departed thence, and found Elisha the son of Shaphat, who *was* plowing *with* twelve yoke *of oxen* before him, and he with the twelfth: and Elijah passed by him, and cast his mantle upon him.

20 And he left the oxen, and ran after Elijah, and said, Let me, I pray thee, kiss my father and my mother, and *then* I will follow thee. And he said unto him, Go back again: for what have I done to thee?

21 And he returned back from him, and took a yoke of oxen, and slew them, and boiled their flesh with the instruments of the oxen, and gave unto the people, and they did eat. Then he arose, and went after Elijah, and ministered unto him.

CHAPTER 20
The Syrian Army Surrounds Samaria

1 And Ben-hadad the king of Syria gathered all his host together: and *there were* thirty and two kings with him, and horses, and chariots: and he went up and besieged Samaria, and warred against it.

2 And he sent messengers to Ahab king of Israel into the city, and said unto him, Thus saith Ben-hadad,

3 Thy silver and thy gold *is* mine; thy wives

---

1 1Kgs. 18:40

2 Ruth 1:17; 1Kgs. 20:10; 2Kgs. 6:31

4 Num. 11:15; Jon. 4:3, 8

8 Ex. 3:1; 34:28; Deut. 9:9, 18; Matt. 4:2

10 Num. 25:11, 13; 1Kgs. 18:4, 22; Ps. 69:9; Rom. 11:3

11 Ex. 24:12; Ezek. 1:4; 37:7

13 Ex. 3:6; 1Kgs. 19:9; Isa. 6:2

14 1Kgs. 19:10

15 2Kgs. 8:12, 13

16 2Kgs. 9:1–3; Luke 4:27, called *Eliseus*

17 2Kgs. 8:12; 9:14; 10:6; 13:3; Hos. 6:5

18 Hos. 13:2; Rom. 11:4

20 Matt. 8:21, 22; Luke 9:61, 62

21 2Sam. 24:22

also and thy children, *even* the goodliest, *are* mine.

4 And the king of Israel answered and said, My lord, O king, according to thy saying, I *am* thine, and all that I have.

5 And the messengers came again, and said, Thus speaketh Ben-hadad, saying, Although I have sent unto thee, saying, Thou shalt deliver me thy silver, and thy gold, and thy wives, and thy children;

6 Yet I will send my servants unto thee to morrow about this time, and they shall search thine house, and the houses of thy servants; and it shall be, *that* whatsoever is pleasant in thine eyes, they shall put *it* in their hand, and take *it* away.

7 Then the king of Israel called all the elders of the land, and said, Mark, I pray you, and see how this *man* seeketh mischief: for he sent unto me for my wives, and for my children, and for my silver, and for my gold; and I denied him not.

8 And all the elders and all the people said unto him, Hearken not *unto him*, nor consent.

9 Wherefore he said unto the messengers of Ben-hadad, Tell my lord the king, All that thou didst send for to thy servant at the first I will do: but this thing I may not do. And the messengers departed, and brought him word again.

10 And Ben-hadad sent unto him, and said, The gods do so unto me, and more also, if the dust of Samaria shall suffice for handfuls for all the people that follow me.

11 And the king of Israel answered and said, Tell *him*, Let not him that girdeth on *his harness* boast himself as he that putteth it off.

12 And it came to pass, when *Ben-hadad* heard this message, as he *was* drinking, he and the kings in the pavilions, that he said unto his servants, Set *yourselves in array.* And they set *themselves in array* against the city.

A Prophet Predicts Ahab's Victory

13 And, behold, there came a prophet unto Ahab king of Israel, saying, Thus saith the LORD, Hast thou seen all this great multitude? behold, I will deliver it into thine hand this day; and thou shalt know that I *am* the LORD.

14 And Ahab said, By whom? And he said, Thus saith the LORD, *Even* by the young men of the princes of the provinces. Then he said, Who shall order the battle? And he answered, Thou.

15 Then he numbered the young men of the

princes of the provinces, and they were two hundred and thirty two: and after them he numbered all the people, *even* all the children of Israel, *being* seven thousand.

16 And they went out at noon. But Benhadad *was* drinking himself drunk in the pavilions, he and the kings, the thirty and two kings that helped him.

17 And the young men of the princes of the provinces went out first; and Ben-hadad sent out, and they told him, saying, There are men come out of Samaria.

18 And he said, Whether they be come out for peace, take them alive; or whether they be come out for war, take them alive.

19 So these young men of the princes of the provinces came out of the city, and the army which followed them.

20 And they slew every one his man: and the Syrians fled; and Israel pursued them: and Ben-hadad the king of Syria escaped on an horse with the horsemen.

21 And the king of Israel went out, and smote the horses and chariots, and slew the Syrians with a great slaughter.

22 And the prophet came to the king of Israel, and said unto him, Go, strengthen thyself, and mark, and see what thou doest: for at the return of the year the king of Syria will come up against thee.

Ahab Defeats Syria Again

23 And the servants of the king of Syria said unto him, Their gods *are* gods of the hills; therefore they were stronger than we; but let us fight against them in the plain, and surely, we shall be stronger than they.

24 And do this thing, Take the kings away, every man out of his place, and put captains in their rooms:

25 And number thee an army, like the army that thou hast lost, horse for horse, and chariot for chariot: and we will fight against them in the plain, *and* surely we shall be stronger than they. And he hearkened unto their voice, and did so.

26 And it came to pass at the return of the year, that Ben-hadad numbered the Syrians, and went up to Aphek, to fight against Israel.

27 And the children of Israel were numbered, and were all present, and went against them: and the children of Israel pitched before them like two little flocks of kids; but the Syrians filled the country.

28 And there came a man of God, and spake unto the king of Israel, and said, Thus saith the LORD, Because the Syrians have said,

10 Ex. 11:8;
Judg. 4:10;
1Kgs. 19:2

12 1Kgs.
20:16

13 1Kgs.
20:28

16 1Kgs.
16:9; 20:12

22 2Sam.
11:1

26 Josh.
13:4

28 1Kgs.
20:13

The LORD *is* God of the hills, but he *is* not God of the valleys, therefore will I deliver all this great multitude into thine hand, and ye shall know that I *am* the LORD.

29 And they pitched one over against the other seven days. And *so* it was, that in the seventh day the battle was joined: and the children of Israel slew of the Syrians an hundred thousand footmen in one day.

30 But the rest fled to Aphek, into the city; and *there* a wall fell upon twenty and seven thousand of the men *that were* left. And Benhadad fled, and came into the city, into an inner chamber.

31 And his servants said unto him, Behold now, we have heard that the kings of the house of Israel *are* merciful kings: let us, I pray thee, put sackcloth on our loins, and ropes upon our heads, and go out to the king of Israel: peradventure he will save thy life.

32 So they girded sackcloth on their loins, and *put* ropes on their heads, and came to the king of Israel, and said, Thy servant Ben-hadad saith, I pray thee, let me live. And he said, *Is* he yet alive? he *is* my brother.

33 Now the men did diligently observe whether *any thing would come* from him, and did hastily catch *it*: and they said, Thy brother Ben-hadad. Then he said, Go ye, bring him. Then Ben-hadad came forth to him; and he caused him to come up into the chariot.

34 And *Ben-hadad* said unto him, The cities, which my father took from thy father, I will restore; and thou shalt make streets for thee in Damascus, as my father made in Samaria. Then *said Ahab*, I will send thee away with this covenant. So he made a covenant with him, and sent him away.

A Prophet Condemns Ahab

35 And a certain man of the sons of the prophets said unto his neighbour in the word of the LORD, Smite me, I pray thee. And the man refused to smite him.

36 Then said he unto him, Because thou hast not obeyed the voice of the LORD, behold, as soon as thou art departed from me, a lion shall slay thee. And as soon as he was departed from him, a lion found him, and slew him.

37 Then he found another man, and said,

Smite me, I pray thee. And the man smote him, so that in smiting he wounded *him*.

38 So the prophet departed, and waited for the king by the way, and disguised himself with ashes upon his face.

39 And as the king passed by, he cried unto the king: and he said, Thy servant went out into the midst of the battle; and, behold, a man turned aside, and brought a man unto me, and said, Keep this man: if by any means he be missing, then shall thy life be for his life, or else thou shalt pay a talent of silver.

40 And as thy servant was busy here and there, he was gone. And the king of Israel said unto him, So *shall* thy judgment *be*; thyself hast decided *it*.

41 And he hasted, and took the ashes away from his face; and the king of Israel discerned him that he *was* of the prophets.

42 And he said unto him, Thus saith the LORD, Because thou hast let go out of *thy* hand a man whom I appointed to utter destruction, therefore thy life shall go for his life, and thy people for his people.

43 And the king of Israel went to his house heavy and displeased, and came to Samaria.

CHAPTER 21
Naboth's Vineyard

1 And it came to pass after these things, *that* Naboth the Jezreelite had a vineyard, which *was* in Jezreel, hard by the palace of Ahab king of Samaria.

2 And Ahab spake unto Naboth, saying, Give me thy vineyard, that I may have it for a garden of herbs, because it *is* near unto my house: and I will give thee for it a better vineyard than it; *or*, if it seem good to thee, I will give thee the worth of it in money.

3 And Naboth said to Ahab, The LORD forbid it me, that I should give the inheritance of my fathers unto thee.

4 And Ahab came into his house heavy and displeased because of the word which Naboth the Jezreelite had spoken to him: for he had said, I will not give thee the inheritance of my fathers. And he laid him down upon his bed, and turned away his face, and would eat no bread.

5 But Jezebel his wife came to him, and said unto him, Why is thy spirit so sad, that thou eatest no bread?

6 And he said unto her, Because I spake

Cross references (center column)

30 1Kgs. 22:25

31 Gen. 37:34

34 1Kgs. 15:20

35 1Kgs. 13:17, 18; 2Kgs. 2:3, 5, 7, 15

36 1Kgs. 13:24

39 2Kgs. 10:24

42 1Kgs. 22:31-37

43 1Kgs. 21:4

2 1Sam. 8:14

3 Lev. 25:23; Num. 36:7; Ezek. 46:18

20:28–29 God's Spirit will not always strive with man, and He will not let men blaspheme His name forever. The Syrians blasphemed His name and lost one hundred thousand footmen in a single day.

unto Naboth the Jezreelite, and said unto him, Give me thy vineyard for money; or else, if it please thee, I will give thee *another* vineyard for it: and he answered, I will not give thee my vineyard.

7 And Jezebel his wife said unto him, Dost thou now govern the kingdom of Israel? arise, *and* eat bread, and let thine heart be merry: I will give thee the vineyard of Naboth the Jezreelite.

8 So she wrote letters in Ahab's name, and sealed *them* with his seal, and sent the letters unto the elders and to the nobles that *were* in his city, dwelling with Naboth.

9 And she wrote in the letters, saying, Proclaim a fast, and set Naboth on high among the people:

10 And set two men, sons of Belial, before him, to bear witness against him, saying, Thou didst blaspheme God and the king. And *then* carry him out, and stone him, that he may die.

11 And the men of his city, *even* the elders and the nobles who were the inhabitants in his city, did as Jezebel had sent unto them, *and* as it *was* written in the letters which she had sent unto them.

12 They proclaimed a fast, and set Naboth on high among the people.

13 And there came in two men, children of Belial, and sat before him: and the men of Belial witnessed against him, *even* against Naboth, in the presence of the people, saying, Naboth did blaspheme God and the king. Then they carried him forth out of the city, and stoned him with stones, that he died.

14 Then they sent to Jezebel, saying, Naboth is stoned, and is dead.

15 And it came to pass, when Jezebel heard that Naboth was stoned, and was dead, that Jezebel said to Ahab, Arise, take possession of the vineyard of Naboth the Jezreelite, which he refused to give thee for money: for Naboth is not alive, but dead.

16 And it came to pass, when Ahab heard that Naboth was dead, that Ahab rose up to go down to the vineyard of Naboth the Jezreelite, to take possession of it.

17 And the word of the LORD came to Elijah the Tishbite, saying,

18 Arise, go down to meet Ahab king of Israel, which *is* in Samaria: behold, *he is* in the vineyard of Naboth, whither he is gone down to possess it.

19 And thou shalt speak unto him, saying, Thus saith the LORD, Hast thou killed, and also taken possession? And thou shalt speak unto him, saying, Thus saith the LORD, In the place where dogs licked the blood of Naboth shall dogs lick thy blood, even thine.

20 And Ahab said to Elijah, Hast thou found me, O mine enemy? And he answered, I have found *thee*: because thou hast sold thyself to work evil in the sight of the LORD.

21 Behold, I will bring evil upon thee, and will take away thy posterity, and will cut off from Ahab him that pisseth against the wall, and him that is shut up and left in Israel,

22 And will make thine house like the house of Jeroboam the son of Nebat, and like the house of Baasha the son of Ahijah, for the provocation wherewith thou hast provoked *me* to anger, and made Israel to sin.

23 And of Jezebel also spake the LORD, saying, The dogs shall eat Jezebel by the wall of Jezreel.

24 Him that dieth of Ahab in the city the dogs shall eat; and him that dieth in the field shall the fowls of the air eat.

25 But there was none like unto Ahab, which did sell himself to work wickedness in the sight of the LORD, whom Jezebel his wife stirred up.

26 And he did very abominably in following idols, according to all *things* as did the Amorites, whom the LORD cast out before the children of Israel.

27 And it came to pass, when Ahab heard those words, that he rent his clothes, and put sackcloth upon his flesh, and fasted, and lay in sackcloth, and went softly.

28 And the word of the LORD came to Elijah the Tishbite, saying,

29 Seest thou how Ahab humbleth himself before me? because he humbleth himself before me, I will not bring the evil in his days: *but* in his son's days will I bring the evil upon his house.

---

10 Ex. 22:28; Lev. 24:14, 15, 16; Acts 6:11
12 Isa. 58:4
13 2Kgs. 9:26
17 Ps. 9:12
18 1Kgs. 13:32; 2Chr. 22:9
19 1Kgs. 22:38
20 1Kgs. 18:17; 2Kgs. 17:17; Rom. 7:14
21 1Sam. 25:22; 1Kgs. 14:10; 2Kgs. 9:8
22 1Kgs. 15:29; 16:3, 11
23 2Kgs. 9:36
24 1Kgs. 14:11; 16:4
25 1Kgs. 16:30, 31
26 Gen. 15:16; 2Kgs. 21:11
27 Gen. 37:34
29 2Kgs. 9:25

21:17–29 Ahab was one of the most evil kings of Israel (vv. 25–26), and Elijah predicted that his posterity would be cut off and that none of his seed would rule in Israel. God gave Ahab many opportunities to repent, but he continued to rebel against the Lord and was killed in battle.

21:23 The Lord's prophecy of the gruesome death of Jezebel, Ahab's evil wife, was literally fulfilled in 2 Kings 9:30–37.

CHAPTER 22
Micaiah Predicts Ahab's Defeat

1 And they continued three years without war between Syria and Israel.

2 And it came to pass in the third year, that Jehoshaphat the king of Judah came down to the king of Israel.

3 And the king of Israel said unto his servants, Know ye that Ramoth in Gilead *is* ours, and we *be* still, *and* take it not out of the hand of the king of Syria?

4 And he said unto Jehoshaphat, Wilt thou go with me to battle to Ramoth-gilead? And Jehoshaphat said to the king of Israel, I *am* as thou *art*, my people as thy people, my horses as thy horses.

5 And Jehoshaphat said unto the king of Israel, Inquire, I pray thee, at the word of the LORD today.

6 Then the king of Israel gathered the prophets together, about four hundred men, and said unto them, Shall I go against Ramoth-gilead to battle, or shall I forbear? And they said, Go up; for the Lord shall deliver *it* into the hand of the king.

7 And Jehoshaphat said, *Is there* not here a prophet of the LORD besides, that we might inquire of him?

8 And the king of Israel said unto Jehoshaphat, *There is* yet one man, Micaiah the son of Imlah, by whom we may inquire of the LORD: but I hate him; for he doth not prophesy good concerning me, but evil. And Jehoshaphat said, Let not the king say so.

9 Then the king of Israel called an officer, and said, Hasten *hither* Micaiah the son of Imlah.

10 And the king of Israel and Jehoshaphat the king of Judah sat each on his throne, having put on their robes, in a void place in the entrance of the gate of Samaria; and all the prophets prophesied before them.

11 And Zedekiah the son of Chenaanah made him horns of iron: and he said, Thus saith the LORD, With these shalt thou push the Syrians, until thou have consumed them.

12 And all the prophets prophesied so, saying, Go up to Ramoth-gilead, and prosper: for the LORD shall deliver *it* into the king's hand.

13 And the messenger that was gone to call Micaiah spake unto him, saying, Behold now, the words of the prophets *declare* good unto the king with one mouth: let thy word, I pray thee, be like the word of one of them, and speak *that which* is good.

14 And Micaiah said, *As* the LORD liveth, what the LORD saith unto me, that will I speak.

15 So he came to the king. And the king said unto him, Micaiah, shall we go against Ramoth-gilead to battle, or shall we forbear? And he answered him, Go, and prosper: for the LORD shall deliver *it* into the hand of the king.

16 And the king said unto him, How many times shall I adjure thee that thou tell me nothing but *that which is* true in the name of the LORD?

17 And he said, I saw all Israel scattered upon the hills, as sheep that have not a shepherd: and the LORD said, These have no master: let them return every man to his house in peace.

18 And the king of Israel said unto Jehoshaphat, Did I not tell thee that he would prophesy no good concerning me, but evil?

19 And he said, Hear thou therefore the word of the LORD: I saw the LORD sitting on his throne, and all the host of heaven standing by him on his right hand and on his left.

20 And the LORD said, Who shall persuade Ahab, that he may go up and fall at Ramoth-gilead? And one said on this manner, and another said on that manner.

21 And there came forth a spirit, and stood before the LORD, and said, I will persuade him.

22 And the LORD said unto him, Wherewith? And he said, I will go forth, and I will be a lying spirit in the mouth of all his prophets. And he said, Thou shalt persuade *him*, and prevail also: go forth, and do so.

23 Now therefore, behold, the LORD hath put a lying spirit in the mouth of all these thy prophets, and the LORD hath spoken evil concerning thee.

24 But Zedekiah the son of Chenaanah went near, and smote Micaiah on the cheek, and said, Which way went the Spirit of the LORD from me to speak unto thee?

Cross References
- **2** 2Chr. 18:2, 3
- **3** Deut. 4:43
- **4** 2Kgs. 3:7
- **6** 1Kgs. 18:19
- **7** 2Kgs. 3:11
- **14** Num. 22:38
- **17** Matt. 9:36
- **19** Job 1:6; 2:1; Ps. 103:20, 21; Isa. 6:1; Dan. 7:9, 10; Zech. 1:10; Matt. 18:10; Heb. 1:7, 14
- **22** Judg. 9:23; Job 12:16; Ezek. 14:9; 2Thess. 2:11
- **23** Ezek. 14:9
- **24** 2Chr. 18:23

22:17–28 as sheep that have not a shepherd. Micaiah, the prophet of God, stood against all the lying prophets of Israel when he warned that the children of Israel should not go against the king of Syria. Then he said to Ahab, "If thou return at all in peace, the LORD has not spoken by me." Ahab's death is described in verse 34; thus the prophecy was literally fulfilled.

25 And Micaiah said, Behold, thou shalt see in that day, when thou shalt go into an inner chamber to hide thyself.

26 And the king of Israel said, Take Micaiah, and carry him back unto Amon the governor of the city, and to Joash the king's son;

27 And say, Thus saith the king, Put this *fellow* in the prison, and feed him with bread of affliction and with water of affliction, until I come in peace.

28 And Micaiah said, If thou return at all in peace, the LORD hath not spoken by me. And he said, Hearken, O people, every one of you.

Ahab Dies in Battle

29 So the king of Israel and Jehoshaphat the king of Judah went up to Ramoth-gilead.

30 And the king of Israel said unto Jehoshaphat, I will disguise myself, and enter into the battle; but put thou on thy robes. And the king of Israel disguised himself, and went into the battle.

31 But the king of Syria commanded his thirty and two captains that had rule over his chariots, saying, Fight neither with small nor great, save only with the king of Israel.

32 And it came to pass, when the captains of the chariots saw Jehoshaphat, that they said, Surely it *is* the king of Israel. And they turned aside to fight against him: and Jehoshaphat cried out.

33 And it came to pass, when the captains of the chariots perceived that it *was* not the king of Israel, that they turned back from pursuing him.

34 And a *certain* man drew a bow at a venture, and smote the king of Israel between the joints of the harness: wherefore he said unto the driver of his chariot, Turn thine hand, and carry me out of the host; for I am wounded.

35 And the battle increased that day: and the king was stayed up in his chariot against the Syrians, and died at even: and the blood ran out of the wound into the midst of the chariot.

36 And there went a proclamation throughout the host about the going down of the sun, saying, Every man to his city, and every man to his own country.

37 So the king died, and was brought to Samaria; and they buried the king in Samaria.

38 And *one* washed the chariot in the pool of Samaria; and the dogs licked up his

blood; and they washed his armour; according unto the word of the LORD which he spake.

39 Now the rest of the acts of Ahab, and all that he did, and the ivory house which he made, and all the cities that he built, *are* they not written in the book of the chronicles of the kings of Israel?

40 So Ahab slept with his fathers; and Ahaziah his son reigned in his stead.

Jehoshaphat Rules Judah

41 And Jehoshaphat the son of Asa began to reign over Judah in the fourth year of Ahab king of Israel.

42 Jehoshaphat *was* thirty and five years old when he began to reign; and he reigned twenty and five years in Jerusalem. And his mother's name *was* Azubah the daughter of Shilhi.

43 And he walked in all the ways of Asa his father; he turned not aside from it, doing *that which was* right in the eyes of the LORD: nevertheless the high places were not taken away; *for* the people offered and burnt incense yet in the high places.

44 And Jehoshaphat made peace with the king of Israel.

45 Now the rest of the acts of Jehoshaphat, and his might that he shewed, and how he warred, *are* they not written in the book of the chronicles of the kings of Judah?

46 And the remnant of the sodomites, which remained in the days of his father Asa, he took out of the land.

47 *There was* then no king in Edom: a deputy *was* king.

48 Jehoshaphat made ships of Tharshish to go to Ophir for gold: but they went not; for the ships were broken at Ezion-geber.

49 Then said Ahaziah the son of Ahab unto Jehoshaphat, Let my servants go with thy servants in the ships. But Jehoshaphat would not.

50 And Jehoshaphat slept with his fathers, and was buried with his fathers in the city of David his father: and Jehoram his son reigned in his stead.

Ahaziah Rules Israel

51 Ahaziah the son of Ahab began to reign over Israel in Samaria the seventeenth year of Jehoshaphat king of Judah, and reigned two years over Israel.

52 And he did evil in the sight of the LORD, and walked in the way of his father, and in the way of his mother, and in the way of

Cross references

25 1Kgs. 20:30
28 Num. 16:29; Deut. 18:20-22
30 2Chr. 35:22
32 2Chr. 18:31; Prov. 13:20
34 2Sam. 15:11
38 1Kgs. 21:19
39 Amos 3:15
41 2Chr. 20:31
43 1Kgs. 14:23; 15:14; 2Kgs. 12:3; 2Chr. 17:3
44 2Chr. 19:2; 2Cor. 6:14
46 1Kgs. 14:24; 15:12
47 Gen. 25:23; 2Sam. 8:14; 2Kgs. 3:9; 8:20
48 1Kgs. 9:26; 10:22; 2Chr. 20:35, 36, 37
50 2Chr. 21:1
51 1Kgs. 22:40
52 1Kgs. 15:26

Jeroboam the son of Nebat, who made Israel to sin:

53 For he served Baal, and worshipped him,

53 Judg. 2:11; 16:31

and provoked to anger the LORD God of Israel, according to all that his father had done.

2 Kings

This book completes the historical record of the two divided kingdoms that were once the united nation of Israel. This history of God's chosen people opens in 1 Kings with the temple built and ends in 2 Kings with the temple burned to the ground; begins with David's first successor, Solomon, and ends with David's last successor, Jehoiachin, being released after being deposed and imprisoned for thirty-seven years. Second Kings traces the history of the divided kingdoms from the death of King Ahab of Israel (Northern Kingdom) to the conquests of both Israel (722 B.C.) and Judah (586 B.C.) by the Assyrians and the Babylonians respectively, culminating with the destruction of Jerusalem in 586 B.C.

Key expressions like "man of God" (thirty-seven times), "did evil in the sight of the Lord" (twenty-one times) and "did right in the sight of the Lord" (seven times), give the message of Kings. God's standards for morals and worship had been violated. God raised up prophets, "men of God," to warn the people to repent. Their message was often introduced by the authoritative phrase, "Thus saith the Lord."

Of Israel's nineteen kings, none was a true worshiper of Jehovah; of the twenty kings of Judah that succeed Solomon, only seven were godly. Although the kingdom of Judah experienced periodic revivals under such godly kings as Hezekiah and Josiah, eventually the people always returned to their wicked ways. However, the sins of both Hebrew nations did not go unpunished.

Much of the first half of the book focuses on Elijah's anointed successor, Elisha, and his ministry and miracles. Sixteen miracles are recorded, double the number of Elijah's (see 2:9).

Containing some 50 separate prophecies in 144 of its 719 verses, predictions amount to 20 percent of its material, practically all of which were fulfilled in their times. Sacrificial offerings and occasions like Passover are included, but are typical foreshadowing, not specific predictions.

Author
Various

Date
6th Century B.C.

Key Truth
The Fall of Israel and Judah

Historic Time
Divided Kingdom

Key Verse
17:22
For the children of Israel walked in all the sins of Jeroboam. . . .

20% Prophecy

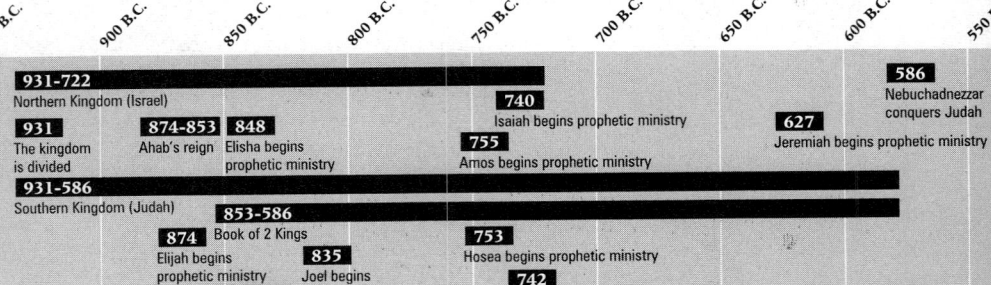

| 950 B.C. | 900 B.C. | 850 B.C. | 800 B.C. | 750 B.C. | 700 B.C. | 650 B.C. | 600 B.C. | 550 |

931–722 Northern Kingdom (Israel)

586 Nebuchadnezzar conquers Judah

931 The kingdom is divided

874–853 Ahab's reign

848 Elisha begins prophetic ministry

740 Isaiah begins prophetic ministry

755 Amos begins prophetic ministry

627 Jeremiah begins prophetic ministry

931–586 Southern Kingdom (Judah)

853–586 Book of 2 Kings

874 Elijah begins prophetic ministry

835 Joel begins prophetic ministry

870–848 Jehoshaphat's reign

753 Hosea begins prophetic ministry

742 Micah begins prophetic ministry

CHAPTER 1
Elijah Predicts Ahaziah's Death

1 Then Moab rebelled against Israel after the death of Ahab.

2 And Ahaziah fell down through a lattice in his upper chamber that *was* in Samaria, and was sick: and he sent messengers, and said unto them, Go, inquire of Baal-zebub the god of Ekron whether I shall recover of this disease.

3 But the angel of the LORD said to Elijah the Tishbite, Arise, go up to meet the messengers of the king of Samaria, and say unto them, *Is it* not because *there is* not a God in Israel, *that* ye go to inquire of Baal-zebub the god of Ekron?

4 Now therefore thus saith the LORD, Thou shalt not come down from that bed on which thou art gone up, but shalt surely die. And Elijah departed.

5 And when the messengers turned back unto him, he said unto them, Why are ye now turned back?

6 And they said unto him, There came a man up to meet us, and said unto us, Go, turn again unto the king that sent you, and say unto him, Thus saith the LORD, *Is it* not because *there is* not a God in Israel, *that* thou sendest to inquire of Baal-zebub the god of Ekron? therefore thou shalt not come down from that bed on which thou art gone up, but shalt surely die.

7 And he said unto them, What manner of man *was he* which came up to meet you, and told you these words?

8 And they answered him, *He was* an hairy man, and girt with a girdle of leather about his loins. And he said, It *is* Elijah the Tishbite.

9 Then the king sent unto him a captain of fifty with his fifty. And he went up to him: and, behold, he sat on the top of an hill. And he spake unto him, Thou man of God, the king hath said, Come down.

10 And Elijah answered and said to the captain of fifty, If I *be* a man of God, then let fire come down from heaven, and consume thee and thy fifty. And there came down fire from heaven, and consumed him and his fifty.

11 Again also he sent unto him another captain of fifty with his fifty. And he answered and said unto him, O man of God, thus hath the king said, Come down quickly.

12 And Elijah answered and said unto them, If I *be* a man of God, let fire come down from heaven, and consume thee and thy fifty. And the fire of God came down from heaven, and consumed him and his fifty.

13 And he sent again a captain of the third fifty with his fifty. And the third captain of fifty went up, and came and fell on his knees before Elijah, and besought him, and said unto him, O man of God, I pray thee, let my life, and the life of these fifty thy servants, be precious in thy sight.

14 Behold, there came fire down from heaven, and burnt up the two captains of the former fifties with their fifties: therefore let my life now be precious in thy sight.

15 And the angel of the LORD said unto Elijah, Go down with him: be not afraid of him. And he arose, and went down with him unto the king.

16 And he said unto him, Thus saith the LORD, Forasmuch as thou hast sent messengers to inquire of Baal-zebub the god of Ekron, *is it* not because *there is* no God in Israel to inquire of his word? therefore thou shalt not come down off that bed on which thou art gone up, but shalt surely die.

17 So he died according to the word of the LORD which Elijah had spoken. And Jehoram reigned in his stead in the second year of Jehoram the son of Jehoshaphat King of Judah: because he had no son.

18 Now the rest of the acts of Ahaziah which he did *are* they not written in the book of the chronicles of the kings of Israel?

CHAPTER 2
Elijah Is Taken Up to Heaven

1 And it came to pass, when the LORD would take up Elijah into heaven by a whirlwind, that Elijah went with Elisha from Gilgal.

2 And Elijah said unto Elisha, Tarry here, I pray thee; for the LORD hath sent me to Beth-el. And Elisha said *unto him,* As the LORD liveth, and *as* thy soul liveth, I will not leave thee. So they went down to Beth-el.

3 And the sons of the prophets that *were* at Beth-el came forth to Elisha, and said unto him, Knowest thou that the LORD will take away thy master from thy head today? And he said, Yea, I know *it;* hold ye your peace.

4 And Elijah said unto him, Elisha, tarry

Cross references (center column):

1 2Sam. 8:2; 2Kgs. 3:5
2 1Sam. 5:10
8 Zech. 13:4; Matt. 3:4
10 Luke 9:54
13 1Sam. 26:21; Ps. 72:14

17 2Kgs. 3:1

1 Gen. 5:24; 1Kgs. 19:21

2 Ruth 1:15, 16; 1Sam. 1:26; 2Kgs. 2:4, 6; 4:30

3 1Kgs. 20:35; 2Kgs. 2:5, 7, 15; 4:1, 38; 9:1

1:4 Elijah's prophecy of the impending death of Ahaziah after his fall was literally fulfilled in verses 16–17, fulfilling the prophecy of Elijah that Ahab's posterity would be "cut off" (1 Kgs. 21:21).

here, I pray thee; for the Lord hath sent me to Jericho. And he said, *As* the Lord liveth, and *as* thy soul liveth, I will not leave thee. So they came to Jericho.

5 And the sons of the prophets that *were* at Jericho came to Elisha, and said unto him, Knowest thou that the Lord will take away thy master from thy head today? And he answered, Yea, I know *it*; hold ye your peace.

6 And Elijah said unto him, Tarry, I pray thee, here; for the Lord hath sent me to Jordan. And he said, *As* the Lord liveth, and *as* thy soul liveth, I will not leave thee. And they two went on.

7 And fifty men of the sons of the prophets went, and stood to view afar off: and they two stood by Jordan.

8 And Elijah took his mantle, and wrapped *it* together, and smote the waters, and they were divided hither and thither, so that they two went over on dry ground.

9 And it came to pass, when they were gone over, that Elijah said unto Elisha, Ask what I shall do for thee, before I be taken away from thee. And Elisha said, I pray thee, let a double portion of thy spirit be upon me.

10 And he said, Thou hast asked a hard thing: *nevertheless,* if thou see me *when I am* taken from thee, it shall be so unto thee; but if not, it shall not be *so.*

11 And it came to pass, as they still went on, and talked, that, behold, *there appeared* a chariot of fire, and horses of fire, and parted them both asunder; and Elijah went up by a whirlwind into heaven.

12 And Elisha saw *it,* and he cried, My father, my father, the chariot of Israel, and the horsemen thereof. And he saw him no more: and he took hold of his own clothes, and rent them in two pieces.

Elisha Returns without Elijah

13 He took up also the mantle of Elijah that fell from him, and went back, and stood by the bank of Jordan;

14 And he took the mantle of Elijah that fell from him, and smote the waters, and said, Where *is* the Lord God of Elijah? and when he also had smitten the waters, they parted hither and thither: and Elisha went over.

15 And when the sons of the prophets which *were* to view at Jericho saw him, they said, The spirit of Elijah doth rest on Elisha. And they came to meet him, and bowed themselves to the ground before him.

16 And they said unto him, Behold now, there be with thy servants fifty strong men; let them go, we pray thee, and seek thy master: lest peradventure the Spirit of the Lord hath taken him up, and cast him upon some mountain, or into some valley. And he said, Ye shall not send.

17 And when they urged him till he was ashamed, he said, Send. They sent therefore fifty men; and they sought three days, but found him not.

18 And when they came again to him, (for he tarried at Jericho,) he said unto them, Did I not say unto you, Go not?

Elisha Purifies a Spring

19 And the men of the city said unto Elisha, Behold, I pray thee, the situation of this city *is* pleasant, as my lord seeth: but the water *is* naught, and the ground barren.

20 And he said, Bring me a new cruse, and put salt therein. And they brought *it* to him.

21 And he went forth unto the spring of the waters, and cast the salt in there, and said, Thus saith the Lord, I have healed these waters; there shall not be from thence any more death or barren *land.*

22 So the waters were healed unto this day, according to the saying of Elisha which he spake.

The Children Curse Elisha

23 And he went up from thence unto Bethel: and as he was going up by the way, there came forth little children out of the city, and mocked him, and said unto him, Go up, thou bald head; go up, thou bald head.

24 And he turned back, and looked on them, and cursed them in the name of the Lord. And there came forth two she bears out of the wood, and tare forty and two children of them.

25 And he went from thence to mount Carmel, and from thence he returned to Samaria.

CHAPTER 3
Elisha Helps Jehoram Defeat Moab

1 Now Jehoram the son of Ahab began to reign over Israel in Samaria the eighteenth year of Jehoshaphat king of Judah, and reigned twelve years.

2 And he wrought evil in the sight of the Lord; but not like his father, and like his mother: for he put away the image of Baal that his father had made.

3 Nevertheless he cleaved unto the sins of Jeroboam the son of Nebat, which made Israel to sin; he departed not therefrom.

8 Ex. 14:21; Josh. 3:16; 2Kgs. 2:14

11 2Kgs. 6:17

12 2Kgs. 13:14

14 2Kgs. 2:8

15 2Kgs. 2:7

16 1Kgs. 18:12; Ezek. 8:3; Acts 8:39

21 Ex. 15:25; 2Kgs. 4:41; 6:6; John 9:6

1 2Kgs. 1:17

2 1Kgs. 16:31, 32

3 1Kgs. 12:28, 31, 32

4 And Mesha king of Moab was a sheepmaster, and rendered unto the king of Israel an hundred thousand lambs, and an hundred thousand rams, with the wool.

5 But it came to pass, when Ahab was dead, that the king of Moab rebelled against the king of Israel.

6 And king Jehoram went out of Samaria the same time, and numbered all Israel.

7 And he went and sent to Jehoshaphat the king of Judah, saying, The king of Moab hath rebelled against me: wilt thou go with me against Moab to battle? And he said, I will go up: I *am* as thou *art*, my people as thy people, *and* my horses as thy horses.

8 And he said, Which way shall we go up? And he answered, The way through the wilderness of Edom.

9 So the king of Israel went, and the king of Judah, and the king of Edom: and they fetched a compass of seven days' journey: and there was no water for the host, and for the cattle that followed them.

10 And the king of Israel said, Alas! that the LORD hath called these three kings together, to deliver them into the hand of Moab!

11 But Jehoshaphat said, *Is there* not here a prophet of the LORD, that we may inquire of the LORD by him? And one of the king of Israel's servants answered and said, Here *is* Elisha the son of Shaphat, which poured water on the hands of Elijah.

12 And Jehoshaphat said, The word of the LORD is with him. So the king of Israel and Jehoshaphat and the king of Edom went down to him.

13 And Elisha said unto the king of Israel, What have I to do with thee? get thee to the prophets of thy father, and to the prophets of thy mother. And the king of Israel said unto him, Nay: for the LORD hath called these three kings together, to deliver them into the hand of Moab.

14 And Elisha said, *As* the LORD of hosts liveth, before whom I stand, surely, were it not that I regard the presence of Jehoshaphat the king of Judah, I would not look toward thee, nor see thee.

15 But now bring me a minstrel. And it came to pass, when the minstrel played, that the hand of the LORD came upon him.

16 And he said, Thus saith the LORD, Make this valley full of ditches.

17 For thus saith the LORD, Ye shall not see wind, neither shall ye see rain; yet that val-

ley shall be filled with water, that ye may drink, both ye, and your cattle, and your beasts.

18 And this is *but* a light thing in the sight of the LORD: he will deliver the Moabites also into your hand.

19 And ye shall smite every fenced city, and every choice city, and shall fell every good tree, and stop all wells of water, and mar every good piece of land with stones.

20 And it came to pass in the morning, when the meat offering was offered, that, behold, there came water by the way of Edom, and the country was filled with water.

21 And when all the Moabites heard that the kings were come up to fight against them, they gathered all that were able to put on armour, and upward, and stood in the border.

22 And they rose up early in the morning, and the sun shone upon the water, and the Moabites saw the water on the other side *as* red as blood:

23 And they said, This *is* blood: the kings are surely slain, and they have smitten one another: now therefore, Moab, to the spoil.

24 And when they came to the camp of Israel, the Israelites rose up and smote the Moabites, so that they fled before them: but they went forward smiting the Moabites, even in *their* country.

25 And they beat down the cities, and on every good piece of land cast every man his stone, and filled it; and they stopped all the wells of water, and felled all the good trees: only in Kir-haraseth left they the stones thereof; howbeit the slingers went about *it*, and smote it.

26 And when the king of Moab saw that the battle was too sore for him, he took with him seven hundred men that drew swords, to break through *even* unto the king of Edom: but they could not.

27 Then he took his eldest son that should have reigned in his stead, and offered him *for* a burnt offering upon the wall. And there was great indignation against Israel: and they departed from him, and returned to *their own* land.

CHAPTER 4
Elisha Helps a Prophet's Widow

1 Now there cried a certain woman of the wives of the sons of the prophets unto

Cross references (center column):
4 Isa. 16:1
5 2Kgs. 1:1
7 1Kgs. 22:4
9 Ex. 11:8
11 1Kgs. 22:7
12 2Kgs. 2:25
13 Judg. 10:14; Ruth 1:15; 1Kgs. 18:19; Ezek. 14:3
14 1Kgs. 17:1; 2Kgs. 5:16
15 1Sam. 10:5; Ezek. 3:14, 22; 8:1
16 2Kgs. 4:3
20 Ex. 29:39, 40
25 Isa. 16:7, 11
7 2Kgs. 8:20; Amos 2:1
1 Lev. 25:39; 1Kgs. 20:35; Matt. 18:25

3:18 The Lord predicted victory for Israel and Judah over the Moabites, which was literally fulfilled in verses 24–26.

Elisha, saying, Thy servant my husband is dead; and thou knowest that thy servant did fear the LORD: and the creditor is come to take unto him my two sons to be bondmen.
2 And Elisha said unto her, What shall I do for thee? tell me, what hast thou in the house? And she said, Thine handmaid hath not any thing in the house, save a pot of oil.
3 Then he said, Go, borrow thee vessels abroad of all thy neighbours, *even* empty vessels; borrow not a few.
4 And when thou art come in, thou shalt shut the door upon thee and upon thy sons, and shalt pour out into all those vessels, and thou shalt set aside that which is full.
5 So she went from him, and shut the door upon her and upon her sons, who brought *the vessels* to her; and she poured out.
6 And it came to pass, when the vessels were full, that she said unto her son, Bring me yet a vessel. And he said unto her, *There is* not a vessel more. And the oil stayed.
7 Then she came and told the man of God. And he said, Go, sell the oil, and pay thy debt, and live thou and thy children of the rest.

Elisha and the Woman from Shunem

8 And it fell on a day, that Elisha passed to Shunem, where *was* a great woman; and she constrained him to eat bread. And *so* it was, *that* as oft as he passed by, he turned in thither to eat bread.
9 And she said unto her husband, Behold now, I perceive that this *is* an holy man of God, which passeth by us continually.
10 Let us make a little chamber, I pray thee, on the wall; and let us set for him there a bed, and a table, and a stool, and a candlestick: and it shall be, when he cometh to us, that he shall turn in thither.
11 And it fell on a day, that he came thither, and he turned into the chamber, and lay there.
12 And he said to Gehazi his servant, Call this Shunammite. And when he had called her, she stood before him.
13 And he said unto him, Say now unto her, Behold, thou hast been careful for us with all this care; what *is* to be done for thee? wouldest thou be spoken for to the king, or to the captain of the host? And she answered, I dwell among mine own people.
14 And he said, What then *is* to be done for her? And Gehazi answered, Verily she hath no child, and her husband is old.
15 And he said, Call her. And when he had called her, she stood in the door.

16 And he said, About this season, according to the time of life, thou shalt embrace a son. And she said, Nay, my lord, *thou* man of God, do not lie unto thine handmaid.
17 And the woman conceived, and bare a son at that season that Elisha had said unto her, according to the time of life.

Elisha Raises the Woman's Son

18 And when the child was grown, it fell on a day, that he went out to his father to the reapers.
19 And he said unto his father, My head, my head. And he said to a lad, Carry him to his mother.
20 And when he had taken him, and brought him to his mother, he sat on her knees till noon, and *then* died.
21 And she went up, and laid him on the bed of the man of God, and shut *the door* upon him, and went out.
22 And she called unto her husband, and said, Send me, I pray thee, one of the young men, and one of the asses, that I may run to the man of God, and come again.
23 And he said, Wherefore wilt thou go to him today? *it is* neither new moon, nor sabbath. And she said, *It shall be* well.
24 Then she saddled an ass, and said to her servant, Drive, and go forward; slack not *thy* riding for me, except I bid thee.
25 So she went and came unto the man of God to mount Carmel. And it came to pass, when the man of God saw her afar off, that he said to Gehazi his servant, Behold, *yonder is* that Shunammite:
26 Run now, I pray thee, to meet her, and say unto her, *Is it* well with thee? *is it* well with thy husband? *is it* well with the child? And she answered, *It is* well.
27 And when she came to the man of God to the hill, she caught him by the feet: but Gehazi came near to thrust her away. And the man of God said, Let her alone; for her soul *is* vexed within her: and the LORD hath hid *it* from me, and hath not told me.
28 Then she said, Did I desire a son of my lord? did I not say, Do not deceive me?
29 Then he said to Gehazi, Gird up thy loins, and take my staff in thine hand, and go thy way: if thou meet any man, salute him not; and if any salute thee, answer him not again: and lay my staff upon the face of the child.
30 And the mother of the child said, *As the* LORD liveth, and *as* thy soul liveth, I will not leave thee. And he arose, and followed her.
31 And Gehazi passed on before them, and

---

3 2Kgs. 3:16
8 Josh. 19:18
16 Gen. 18:10, 14; 2Kgs. 4:28

25 2Kgs. 2:25

28 2Kgs. 4:16

29 Ex. 7:19; 14:16; 1Kgs. 18:46; 2Kgs. 2:8, 14; 9:1; Luke 10:4; Acts 19:12

30 2Kgs. 2:2

31 John 11:11

laid the staff upon the face of the child; but *there was* neither voice, nor hearing. Wherefore he went again to meet him, and told him, saying, The child is not awaked.

32 And when Elisha was come into the house, behold, the child was dead, *and* laid upon his bed.

33 He went in therefore, and shut the door upon them twain, and prayed unto the LORD.

34 And he went up, and lay upon the child, and put his mouth upon his mouth, and his eyes upon his eyes, and his hands upon his hands: and he stretched himself upon the child; and the flesh of the child waxed warm.

35 Then he returned, and walked in the house to and fro; and went up, and stretched himself upon him: and the child sneezed seven times, and the child opened his eyes.

36 And he called Gehazi, and said, Call this Shunammite. So he called her. And when she was come in unto him, he said, Take up thy son.

37 Then she went in, and fell at his feet, and bowed herself to the ground, and took up her son, and went out.

The Poison Food Is Made Edible

38 And Elisha came again to Gilgal: and *there was* a dearth in the land; and the sons of the prophets *were* sitting before him: and he said unto his servant, Set on the great pot, and seethe pottage for the sons of the prophets.

39 And one went out into the field to gather herbs, and found a wild vine, and gathered thereof wild gourds his lap full, and came and shred *them* into the pot of pottage: for they knew *them* not.

40 So they poured out for the men to eat. And it came to pass, as they were eating of the pottage, that they cried out, and said, O *thou* man of God, *there is* death in the pot. And they could not eat *thereof*.

41 But he said, Then bring meal. And he cast *it* into the pot; and he said, Pour out for the people, that they may eat. And there was no harm in the pot.

42 And there came a man from Baal-shalisha, and brought the man of God bread of the firstfruits, twenty loaves of barley, and full ears of corn in the husk thereof. And he said, Give unto the people, that they may eat.

43 And his servitor said, What, should I set this before an hundred men? He said again, Give the people, that they may eat: for thus saith the LORD, They shall eat, and shall leave *thereof*.

44 So he set *it* before them, and they did eat, and left *thereof*, according to the word of the LORD.

CHAPTER 5
Naaman Is Cured of Leprosy

1 Now Naaman, captain of the host of the king of Syria, was a great man with his master, and honourable, because by him the LORD had given deliverance unto Syria: he was also a mighty man in valour, *but he was* a leper.

2 And the Syrians had gone out by companies, and had brought away captive out of the land of Israel a little maid; and she waited on Naaman's wife.

3 And she said unto her mistress, Would God my lord *were* with the prophet that *is* in Samaria! for he would recover him of his leprosy.

4 And *one* went in, and told his lord, saying, Thus and thus said the maid that *is* of the land of Israel.

5 And the king of Syria said, Go to, go, and I will send a letter unto the king of Israel. And he departed, and took with him ten talents of silver, and six thousand *pieces* of gold, and ten changes of raiment.

6 And he brought the letter to the king of Israel, saying, Now when this letter is come unto thee, behold, I have *therewith* sent Naaman my servant to thee, that thou mayest recover him of his leprosy.

7 And it came to pass, when the king of Israel had read the letter, that he rent his clothes, and said, *Am* I God, to kill and to make alive, that this man doth send unto me to recover a man of his leprosy? wherefore consider, I pray you, and see how he seeketh a quarrel against me.

8 And it was *so*, when Elisha the man of God had heard that the king of Israel had rent his clothes, that he sent to the king, saying, Wherefore hast thou rent thy clothes? let him come now to me, and he shall know that there is a prophet in Israel.

9 So Naaman came with his horses and with his chariot, and stood at the door of the house of Elisha.

10 And Elisha sent a messenger unto him,

Cross references:
33 1Kgs. 17:20; 2Kgs. 4:4; Matt. 6:6
34 1Kgs. 17:21; Acts 20:10
35 1Kgs. 17:21; 2Kgs. 8:1, 5
37 1Kgs. 17:23; Heb. 11:35
38 2Kgs. 2:1, 3; 8:1; Luke 10:39; Acts 22:3
40 Ex. 10:17
41 Ex. 15:25; 2Kgs. 2:21; 5:10; John 9:6
42 1Sam. 9:4, 7; 1Cor. 9:11; Gal. 6:6
43 Luke 9:13, 17; John 6:9, 11
44 Matt. 14:20; 15:37; John 6:13
1 Ex. 11:3; Luke 4:27
5 1Sam. 9:8; 2Kgs. 8:8, 9
7 Gen. 30:2; Deut. 32:39; 1Sam. 2:6
10 2Kgs. 4:41; John 9:7

5:10 Elisha told Naaman to wash seven times in the river Jordan and he would be healed of his leprosy. This prediction was literally and miraculously fulfilled in verse 14.

saying, Go and wash in Jordan seven times, and thy flesh shall come again to thee, and thou shalt be clean.

11 But Naaman was wroth, and went away, and said, Behold, I thought, He will surely come out to me, and stand, and call on the name of the LORD his God, and strike his hand over the place, and recover the leper.

12 *Are* not Abana and Pharpar, rivers of Damascus, better than all the waters of Israel? may I not wash in them, and be clean? So he turned and went away in a rage.

13 And his servants came near, and spake unto him, and said, My father, *if* the prophet had bid thee *do some* great thing, wouldest thou not have done *it*? how much rather then, when he saith to thee, Wash, and be clean?

14 Then went he down, and dipped himself seven times in Jordan, according to the saying of the man of God: and his flesh came again like unto the flesh of a little child, and he was clean.

15 And he returned to the man of God, he and all his company, and came, and stood before him: and he said, Behold, now I know that *there is* no God in all the earth, but in Israel: now therefore, I pray thee, take a blessing of thy servant.

16 But he said, *As* the LORD liveth, before whom I stand, I will receive none. And he urged him to take *it*; but he refused.

17 And Naaman said, Shall there not then, I pray thee, be given to thy servant two mules' burden of earth? for thy servant will henceforth offer neither burnt offering nor sacrifice unto other gods, but unto the LORD.

18 In this thing the LORD pardon thy servant, *that* when my master goeth into the house of Rimmon to worship there, and he leaneth on my hand, and I bow myself in the house of Rimmon: when I bow down myself in the house of Rimmon, the LORD pardon thy servant in this thing.

19 And he said unto him, Go in peace. So he departed from him a little way.

Gehazi Gets Naaman's Leprosy

20 But Gehazi, the servant of Elisha the man of God, said, Behold, my master hath spared Naaman this Syrian, in not receiving at his hands that which he brought: but, *as* the LORD liveth, I will run after him, and take somewhat of him.

21 So Gehazi followed after Naaman. And when Naaman saw *him* running after him, he lighted down from the chariot to meet him, and said, *Is* all well?

22 And he said, All *is* well. My master hath sent me, saying, Behold, even now there be come to me from mount Ephraim two young men of the sons of the prophets: give them, I pray thee, a talent of silver, and two changes of garments.

23 And Naaman said, Be content, take two talents. And he urged him, and bound two talents of silver in two bags, with two changes of garments, and laid *them* upon two of his servants; and they bare *them* before him.

24 And when he came to the tower, he took *them* from their hand, and bestowed *them* in the house: and he let the men go, and they departed.

25 But he went in, and stood before his master. And Elisha said unto him, Whence *comest thou*, Gehazi? And he said, Thy servant went no whither.

26 And he said unto him, Went not mine heart *with thee*, when the man turned again from his chariot to meet thee? *Is it* a time to receive money, and to receive garments, and oliveyards, and vineyards, and sheep, and oxen, and menservants, and maidservants?

27 The leprosy therefore of Naaman shall cleave unto thee, and unto thy seed for ever. And he went out from his presence a leper *as white* as snow.

CHAPTER 6
Elisha Makes an Axe Head Float

1 And the sons of the prophets said unto Elisha, Behold now, the place where we dwell with thee is too strait for us.

2 Let us go, we pray thee, unto Jordan, and take thence every man a beam, and let us make us a place there, where we may dwell. And he answered, Go ye.

3 And one said, Be content, I pray thee, and go with thy servants. And he answered, I will go.

4 So he went with them. And when they came to Jordan, they cut down wood.

5 But as one was felling a beam, the axe head fell into the water: and he cried, and said, Alas, master! for it was borrowed.

6 And the man of God said, Where fell it? And he shewed him the place. And he cut

Cross references
14 Job 33:25; Luke 4:27
15 Gen. 33:11; Dan. 2:47; 3:29; 6:26, 27
16 Gen. 14:23; 2Kgs. 3:14; Matt. 10:8; Acts 8:18, 20
18 2Kgs. 7:2, 17
27 Ex. 4:6; Num. 12:10; 2Kgs. 15:5; 1Tim. 6:10
1 2Kgs. 4:38
6 2Kgs. 2:21

5:19–27 Because of his deceitfulness, Gehazi, the servant of Elisha, was cursed with leprosy just as the prophet predicted.

down a stick, and cast *it* in thither; and the iron did swim.

7 Therefore said he, Take *it* up to thee. And he put out his hand, and took it.

Elisha and the Syrian Troops

8 Then the king of Syria warred against Israel, and took counsel with his servants, saying, In such and such a place *shall be* my camp.

9 And the man of God sent unto the king of Israel, saying, Beware that thou pass not such a place; for thither the Syrians are come down.

10 And the king of Israel sent to the place which the man of God told him and warned him of, and saved himself there, not once nor twice.

11 Therefore the heart of the king of Syria was sore troubled for this thing; and he called his servants, and said unto them, Will ye not shew me which of us *is* for the king of Israel?

12 And one of his servants said, None, my lord, O king: but Elisha, the prophet that *is* in Israel, telleth the king of Israel the words that thou speakest in thy bedchamber.

13 And he said, Go and spy where he *is*, that I may send and fetch him. And it was told him, saying, Behold, *he is* in Dothan.

14 Therefore sent he thither horses, and chariots, and a great host: and they came by night, and compassed the city about.

15 And when the servant of the man of God was risen early, and gone forth, behold, an host compassed the city both with horses and chariots. And his servant said unto him, Alas, my master! how shall we do?

16 And he answered, Fear not: for they that *be* with us *are* more than they that *be* with them.

17 And Elisha prayed, and said, LORD, I pray thee, open his eyes, that he may see. And the LORD opened the eyes of the young man; and he saw: and, behold, the mountain *was* full of horses and chariots of fire round about Elisha.

18 And when they came down to him, Elisha prayed unto the LORD, and said, Smite this people, I pray thee, with blindness. And he smote them with blindness according to the word of Elisha.

19 And Elisha said unto them, This *is* not the way, neither *is* this the city: follow me, and I will bring you to the man whom ye seek. But he led them to Samaria.

20 And it came to pass, when they were come into Samaria, that Elisha said, LORD,

open the eyes of these *men*, that they may see. And the LORD opened their eyes, and they saw; and, behold, *they were* in the midst of Samaria.

21 And the king of Israel said unto Elisha, when he saw them, My father, shall I smite *them*? shall I smite *them*?

22 And he answered, Thou shalt not smite *them*: wouldest thou smite those whom thou hast taken captive with thy sword and with thy bow? set bread and water before them, that they may eat and drink, and go to their master.

23 And he prepared great provision for them: and when they had eaten and drunk, he sent them away, and they went to their master. So the bands of Syria came no more into the land of Israel.

The Syrian Army Surrounds Samaria

24 And it came to pass after this, that Benhadad king of Syria gathered all his host, and went up, and besieged Samaria.

25 And there was a great famine in Samaria: and, behold, they besieged it, until an ass's head was *sold* for fourscore *pieces* of silver, and the fourth part of a cab of dove's dung for five *pieces* of silver.

26 And as the king of Israel was passing by upon the wall, there cried a woman unto him, saying, Help, my lord, O king.

27 And he said, If the LORD do not help thee, whence shall I help thee? out of the barnfloor, or out of the winepress?

28 And the king said unto her, What aileth thee? And she answered, This woman said unto me, Give thy son, that we may eat him today, and we will eat my son to morrow.

29 So we boiled my son, and did eat him: and I said unto her on the next day, Give thy son, that we may eat him: and she hath hid her son.

30 And it came to pass, when the king heard the words of the woman, that he rent his clothes; and he passed by upon the wall, and the people looked, and, behold, *he had* sackcloth within upon his flesh.

31 Then he said, God do so and more also to me, if the head of Elisha the son of Shaphat shall stand on him this day.

32 But Elisha sat in his house, and the elders sat with him; and *the king* sent a man from before him: but ere the messenger came to him, he said to the elders, See ye how this son of a murderer hath sent to take away mine head? look, when the messenger cometh, shut the door, and hold him fast at

---

13 Gen. 37:17

16 2Chr. 32:7; Ps. 55:18; Rom. 8:31

17 2Kgs. 2:11; Ps. 34:7; 68:17; Zech. 1:8; 6:1-7

18 Gen. 19:11

22 Rom. 12:20

23 2Kgs. 5:2; 6:8, 9

29 Lev. 26:29; Deut. 28:53, 57

30 1Kgs. 21:27

31 Ruth 1:17; 1Kgs. 19:2

32 1Kgs. 18:4; Ezek. 8:1; 20:1; Luke 13:32

the door: *is* not the sound of his master's feet behind him?

33 And while he yet talked with them, behold, the messenger came down unto him: and he said, Behold, this evil *is* of the LORD; what should I wait for the LORD any longer?

CHAPTER 7

1 Then Elisha said, Hear ye the word of the LORD; Thus saith the LORD, To morrow about this time *shall* a measure of fine flour *be sold* for a shekel, and two measures of barley for a shekel, in the gate of Samaria.

2 Then a lord on whose hand the king leaned answered the man of God, and said, Behold, *if* the LORD would make windows in heaven, might this thing be? And he said, Behold, thou shalt see *it* with thine eyes, but shalt not eat thereof.

The Syrians Retreat

3 And there were four leprous men at the entering in of the gate: and they said one to another, Why sit we here until we die?

4 If we say, We will enter into the city, then the famine *is* in the city, and we shall die there: and if we sit still here, we die also. Now therefore come, and let us fall unto the host of the Syrians: if they save us alive, we shall live; and if they kill us, we shall but die.

5 And they rose up in the twilight, to go unto the camp of the Syrians: and when they were come to the uttermost part of the camp of Syria, behold, *there was* no man there.

6 For the Lord had made the host of the Syrians to hear a noise of chariots, and a noise of horses, *even* the noise of a great host: and they said one to another, Lo, the king of Israel hath hired against us the kings of the Hittites, and the kings of the Egyptians, to come upon us.

7 Wherefore they arose and fled in the twilight, and left their tents, and their horses, and their asses, even the camp as it *was*, and fled for their life.

8 And when these lepers came to the uttermost part of the camp, they went into one tent, and did eat and drink, and carried thence silver, and gold, and raiment, and went and hid *it*; and came again, and entered into another tent, and carried thence *also*, and went and hid *it*.

9 Then they said one to another, We do not well: this day *is* a day of good tidings, and we hold our peace: if we tarry till the morning light, some mischief will come upon us: now therefore come, that we may go and tell the king's household.

10 So they came and called unto the porter of the city: and they told them, saying, We came to the camp of the Syrians, and, behold, *there was* no man there, neither voice of man, but horses tied, and asses tied, and the tents as they *were*.

11 And he called the porters; and they told *it* to the king's house within.

12 And the king arose in the night, and said unto his servants, I will now shew you what the Syrians have done to us. They know that we *be* hungry; therefore are they gone out of the camp to hide themselves in the field, saying, When they come out of the city, we shall catch them alive, and get into the city.

13 And one of his servants answered and said, Let *some* take, I pray thee, five of the horses that remain, which are left in the city, (behold, they *are* as all the multitude of Israel that are left in it: behold, *I say*, they *are* even as all the multitude of the Israelites that are consumed:) and let us send and see.

14 They took therefore two chariot horses; and the king sent after the host of the Syrians, saying, Go and see.

15 And they went after them unto Jordan: and, lo, all the way *was* full of garments and vessels, which the Syrians had cast away in their haste. And the messengers returned, and told the king.

16 And the people went out, and spoiled the tents of the Syrians. So a measure of fine flour was *sold* for a shekel, and two measures of barley for a shekel, according to the word of the LORD.

17 And the king appointed the lord on whose hand he leaned to have the charge of the gate: and the people trode upon him in the gate, and he died, as the man of God had said, who spake when the king came down to him.

18 And it came to pass as the man of God had spoken to the king, saying, Two measures of barley for a shekel, and a measure of fine flour for a shekel, shall be to morrow about this time in the gate of Samaria:

19 And that lord answered the man of God,

---

33 Job 2:9
1 2Kgs. 7:18, 19
2 2Kgs. 7:17, 19, 20; Mal. 3:10
3 Lev. 13:46
6 2Sam. 5:24; 1Kgs. 10:29; 2Kgs. 19:7; Job 15:21
7 Ps. 48:4-6; Prov. 28:1

16 2Kgs. 7:1

17 2Kgs. 6:32; 7:2

18 2Kgs. 7:1

7:1–2 During a famine in Israel, Elisha prophesied that there would be an abundance of food supplied and that the doubting officer would see it but not eat of it. The prophecy was fulfilled in verse 17.

and said, Now, behold, *if* the L ORD should make windows in heaven, might such a thing be? And he said, Behold, thou shalt see it with thine eyes, but shalt not eat thereof.
20 And so it fell out unto him: for the people trode upon him in the gate, and he died.

CHAPTER 8
The Woman Returns to Shunem

1 Then spake Elisha unto the woman, whose son he had restored to life, saying, Arise, and go thou and thine household, and sojourn wheresoever thou canst sojourn: for the L ORD hath called for a famine; and it shall also come upon the land seven years.

2 And the woman arose, and did after the saying of the man of God: and she went with her household, and sojourned in the land of the Philistines seven years.

3 And it came to pass at the seven years' end, that the woman returned out of the land of the Philistines: and she went forth to cry unto the king for her house and for her land.

4 And the king talked with Gehazi the servant of the man of God, saying, Tell me, I pray thee, all the great things that Elisha hath done.

5 And it came to pass, as he was telling the king how he had restored a dead body to life, that, behold, the woman, whose son he had restored to life, cried to the king for her house and for her land. And Gehazi said, My lord, O king, this *is* the woman, and this *is* her son, whom Elisha restored to life.

6 And when the king asked the woman, she told him. So the king appointed unto her a certain officer, saying, Restore all that *was* hers, and all the fruits of the field since the day that she left the land, even until now.

Elisha Predicts Hazael's Rise to Power

7 And Elisha came to Damascus; and Benhadad the king of Syria was sick; and it was told him, saying, The man of God is come hither.

8 And the king said unto Hazael, Take a present in thine hand, and go, meet the man of God, and inquire of the L ORD by him, saying, Shall I recover of this disease?

9 So Hazael went to meet him, and took a present with him, even of every good thing of Damascus, forty camels' burden, and came and stood before him, and said, Thy son Ben-hadad king of Syria hath sent me to thee, saying, Shall I recover of this disease?

10 And Elisha said unto him, Go, say unto him, Thou mayest certainly recover: howbeit the L ORD hath shewed me that he shall surely die.

11 And he settled his countenance stedfastly, until he was ashamed: and the man of God wept.

12 And Hazael said, Why weepeth my lord? And he answered, Because I know the evil that thou wilt do unto the children of Israel: their strong holds wilt thou set on fire, and their young men wilt thou slay with the sword, and wilt dash their children, and rip up their women with child.

13 And Hazael said, But what, *is* thy servant a dog, that he should do this great thing? And Elisha answered, The L ORD hath shewed me that thou *shalt be* king over Syria.

14 So he departed from Elisha, and came to his master; who said to him, What said Elisha to thee? And he answered, He told me *that* thou shouldest surely recover.

15 And it came to pass on the morrow, that he took a thick cloth, and dipped *it* in water, and spread *it* on his face, so that he died: and Hazael reigned in his stead.

Jehoram Rules Judah

16 And in the fifth year of Joram the son of Ahab king of Israel, Jehoshaphat *being* then king of Judah, Jehoram the son of Jehoshaphat king of Judah began to reign.

17 Thirty and two years old was he when he began to reign; and he reigned eight years in Jerusalem.

18 And he walked in the way of the kings of Israel, as did the house of Ahab: for the daughter of Ahab was his wife: and he did evil in the sight of the L ORD.

19 Yet the L ORD would not destroy Judah for David his servant's sake, as he promised him to give him alway a light, *and* to his children.

20 In his days Edom revolted from under the hand of Judah, and made a king over themselves.

Cross references

1 2Kgs. 4:35; Ps. 105:16; Hag. 1:11
4 2Kgs. 5:27
5 2Kgs. 4:35
8 1Sam. 9:7; 1Kgs. 14:3; 19:15; 2Kgs. 1:2; 5:5
10 2Kgs. 8:15
11 Luke 19:41
12 2Kgs. 10:32; 12:17; 13:3, 7; 15:16; Hos. 13:16; Amos 1:3, 13
13 1Sam. 17:43; 1Kgs. 19:15
16 2Chr. 21:3, 4
17 2Chr. 21:5
18 2Kgs. 8:26
19 2Sam. 7:13; 1Kgs. 11:36; 15:4; 2Chr. 21:7
20 Gen. 27:40; 1Kgs. 22:47; 2Kgs. 3:27; 2Chr. 21:8, 9, 10

8:1–15 Elisha predicted that a seven-year famine would come on Israel and that the king of Aram would recover from his illness, yet later die—all of which was fulfilled.

8:13–15 The prophet's prediction that Hazael would become king and kill many Israelites (v. 12) was fulfilled (see 10:32; 12:17–18; 2 Chr. 22:5–6).

21 So Joram went over to Zair, and all the chariots with him: and he rose by night, and smote the Edomites which compassed him about, and the captains of the chariots: and the people fled into their tents.

22 Yet Edom revolted from under the hand of Judah unto this day. Then Libnah revolted at the same time.

23 And the rest of the acts of Joram, and all that he did, *are* they not written in the book of the chronicles of the kings of Judah?

24 And Joram slept with his fathers, and was buried with his fathers in the city of David: and Ahaziah his son reigned in his stead.

Ahaziah Rules Judah

25 In the twelfth year of Joram the son of Ahab king of Israel did Ahaziah the son of Jehoram king of Judah begin to reign.

26 Two and twenty years old *was* Ahaziah when he began to reign; and he reigned one year in Jerusalem. And his mother's name *was* Athaliah, the daughter of Omri king of Israel.

27 And he walked in the way of the house of Ahab, and did evil in the sight of the LORD, as *did* the house of Ahab: for he *was* the son-in-law of the house of Ahab.

28 And he went with Joram the son of Ahab to the war against Hazael king of Syria in Ramoth-gilead; and the Syrians wounded Joram.

29 And king Joram went back to be healed in Jezreel of the wounds which the Syrians had given him at Ramah, when he fought against Hazael king of Syria. And Ahaziah the son of Jehoram king of Judah went down to see Joram the son of Ahab in Jezreel, because he was sick.

CHAPTER 9
Jehu Is Anointed King

1 And Elisha the prophet called one of the children of the prophets, and said unto him, Gird up thy loins, and take this box of oil in thine hand, and go to Ramoth-gilead:

2 And when thou comest thither, look out there Jehu the son of Jehoshaphat the son of Nimshi, and go in, and make him arise up from among his brethren, and carry him to an inner chamber;

3 Then take the box of oil, and pour *it* on his head, and say, Thus saith the LORD, I have anointed thee king over Israel. Then open the door, and flee, and tarry not.

4 So the young man, *even* the young man the prophet, went to Ramoth-gilead.

5 And when he came, behold, the captains of the host *were* sitting; and he said, I have an errand to thee, O captain. And Jehu said, Unto which of all us? And he said, To thee, O captain.

6 And he arose, and went into the house; and he poured the oil on his head, and said unto him, Thus saith the LORD God of Israel, I have anointed thee king over the people of the LORD, *even* over Israel.

7 And thou shalt smite the house of Ahab thy master, that I may avenge the blood of my servants the prophets, and the blood of all the servants of the LORD, at the hand of Jezebel.

8 For the whole house of Ahab shall perish: and I will cut off from Ahab him that pisseth against the wall, and him that is shut up and left in Israel:

9 And I will make the house of Ahab like the house of Jeroboam the son of Nebat, and like the house of Baasha the son of Ahijah:

10 And the dogs shall eat Jezebel in the portion of Jezreel, and *there shall be* none to bury her. And he opened the door, and fled.

11 Then Jehu came forth to the servants of his lord: and *one* said unto him, Is all well? wherefore came this mad *fellow* to thee? And he said unto them, Ye know the man, and his communication.

12 And they said, *It is* false; tell us now. And he said, Thus and thus spake he to me, saying, Thus saith the LORD, I have anointed thee king over Israel.

13 Then they hasted, and took every man his garment, and put *it* under him on the top of the stairs, and blew with trumpets, saying, Jehu is king.

Jehu Assassinates Joram

14 So Jehu the son of Jehoshaphat the son of Nimshi conspired against Joram. (Now Joram had kept Ramoth-gilead, he and all Israel, because of Hazael king of Syria.

15 But king Joram was returned to be healed in Jezreel of the wounds which the Syrians had given him, when he fought with Hazael king of Syria.) And Jehu said, If it be your minds, *then* let none go forth *nor* escape out of the city to go to tell *it* in Jezreel.

16 So Jehu rode in a chariot, and went to Jezreel; for Joram lay there. And Ahaziah king of Judah was come down to see Joram.

17 And there stood a watchman on the tower in Jezreel, and he spied the company of Jehu as he came, and said, I see a com-

Cross references (center column)

22 Gen. 27:40; 2Chr. 21:10
24 2Chr. 21:17; 22:1, 6, *Azariah*; 25:23, *Jehoahaz*
26 2Kgs. 8:18; 2Chr. 22:2
27 2Chr. 22:3, 4
28 2Chr. 22:5
29 2Kgs. 8:28; 9:15, 16; 2Chr. 22:6, 7
1 1Kgs. 20:35; 2Kgs. 4:29; 8:28, 29; Jer. 1:17
2 2Kgs. 9:5, 11
3 1Kgs. 19:16
6 1Kgs. 19:16; 2Chr. 22:7
7 1Kgs. 18:4; 21:15
8 Deut. 32:36; 1Sam. 25:22; 1Kgs. 14:10; 21:21
9 1Kgs. 14:10; 15:29; 16:3, 11; 21:22
10 1Kgs. 21:23; 2Kgs. 9:35, 36
11 Jer. 29:26; John 10:20; Acts 26:24; 1Cor. 4:10
13 Matt. 21:7
15 2Kgs. 8:20
16 2Kgs. 8:29

pany. And Joram said, Take an horseman, and send to meet them, and let him say, *Is it* peace?

18 So there went one on horseback to meet him, and said, Thus saith the king, *Is it* peace? And Jehu said, What hast thou to do with peace? turn thee behind me. And the watchman told, saying, The messenger came to them, but he cometh not again.

19 Then he sent out a second on horseback, which came to them, and said, Thus saith the king, *Is it* peace? And Jehu answered, What hast thou to do with peace? turn thee behind me.

20 And the watchman told, saying, He came even unto them, and cometh not again: and the driving *is* like the driving of Jehu the son of Nimshi; for he driveth furiously.

21 And Joram said, Make ready. And his chariot was made ready. And Joram king of Israel and Ahaziah king of Judah went out, each in his chariot, and they went out against Jehu, and met him in the portion of Naboth the Jezreelite.

22 And it came to pass, when Joram saw Jehu, that he said, *Is it* peace, Jehu? And he answered, What peace, so long as the whoredoms of thy mother Jezebel and her witchcrafts *are so* many?

23 And Joram turned his hands, and fled, and said to Ahaziah, *There is* treachery, O Ahaziah.

24 And Jehu drew a bow with his full strength, and smote Jehoram between his arms, and the arrow went out at his heart, and he sunk down in his chariot.

25 Then said *Jehu* to Bidkar his captain, Take up, *and* cast him in the portion of the field of Naboth the Jezreelite: for remember how that, when I and thou rode together after Ahab his father, the LORD laid this burden upon him;

26 Surely I have seen yesterday the blood of Naboth, and the blood of his sons, saith the LORD; and I will requite thee in this plat, saith the LORD. Now therefore take *and* cast him into the plat *of ground,* according to the word of the LORD.

Jehu Assassinates Ahaziah

27 But when Ahaziah the king of Judah saw *this,* he fled by the way of the garden house. And Jehu followed after him, and said, Smite him also in the chariot. *And they did so* at the going up to Gur, which *is* by Ibleam. And he fled to Megiddo, and died there.

28 And his servants carried him in a chariot to Jerusalem, and buried him in his sepulchre with his fathers in the city of David.

29 And in the eleventh year of Joram the son of Ahab began Ahaziah to reign over Judah.

Jehu Assassinates Jezebel

30 And when Jehu was come to Jezreel, Jezebel heard *of it;* and she painted her face, and tired her head, and looked out at a window.

31 And as Jehu entered in at the gate, she said, *Had* Zimri peace, who slew his master?

32 And he lifted up his face to the window, and said, Who *is* on my side? who? And there looked out to him two *or* three eunuchs.

33 And he said, Throw her down. So they threw her down: and *some* of her blood was sprinkled on the wall, and on the horses: and he trode her under foot.

34 And when he was come in, he did eat and drink, and said, Go, see now this cursed *woman,* and bury her: for she *is* a king's daughter.

35 And they went to bury her: but they found no more of her than the skull, and the feet, and the palms of *her* hands.

36 Wherefore they came again, and told him. And he said, This *is* the word of the LORD, which he spake by his servant Elijah the Tishbite, saying, In the portion of Jezreel shall dogs eat the flesh of Jezebel:

37 And the carcase of Jezebel shall be as dung upon the face of the field in the portion of Jezreel; *so* that they shall not say, This *is* Jezebel.

CHAPTER 10
Ahab and Ahaziah's Family Members Are Assassinated

1 And Ahab had seventy sons in Samaria. And Jehu wrote letters, and sent to Samaria, unto the rulers of Jezreel, to the elders, and to them that brought up Ahab's *children,* saying,

2 Now as soon as this letter cometh to you,

---

21 2Chr. 22:7
25 1Kgs. 21:29
26 1Kgs. 21:19
27 2Chr. 22:9
30 Ezek. 23:40
31 1Kgs. 16:9-20
34 1Kgs. 16:31
36 1Kgs. 21:23
37 Ps. 83:10

9:30–37 This passage describes the gruesome death of Jezebel according to the prophecy of 1 Kings 21:23.

10:1–11, 17 These verses describe the fulfillment of the prediction that Elijah gave in 1 Kings 21:20–22 that the seed of Ahab would be "cut off."

seeing your master's sons *are* with you, and *there are* with you chariots and horses, a fenced city also, and armour;

3 Look even out the best and meetest of your master's sons, and set *him* on his father's throne, and fight for your master's house.

4 But they were exceedingly afraid, and said, Behold, two kings stood not before him: how then shall we stand?

5 And he that *was* over the house, and he that *was* over the city, the elders also, and the bringers up *of the children*, sent to Jehu, saying, We *are* thy servants, and will do all that thou shalt bid us; we will not make any king: do thou *that which is* good in thine eyes.

6 Then he wrote a letter the second time to them, saying, If ye *be* mine, and *if* ye will hearken unto my voice, take ye the heads of the men your master's sons, and come to me to Jezreel by to morrow this time. Now the king's sons, *being* seventy persons, *were* with the great men of the city, which brought them up.

7 And it came to pass, when the letter came to them, that they took the king's sons, and slew seventy persons, and put their heads in baskets, and sent him *them* to Jezreel.

8 And there came a messenger, and told him, saying, They have brought the heads of the king's sons. And he said, Lay ye them in two heaps at the entering in of the gate until the morning.

9 And it came to pass in the morning, that he went out, and stood, and said to all the people, Ye *be* righteous: behold, I conspired against my master, and slew him: but who slew all these?

10 Know now that there shall fall unto the earth nothing of the word of the LORD, which the LORD spake concerning the house of Ahab: for the LORD hath done *that* which he spake by his servant Elijah.

11 So Jehu slew all that remained of the house of Ahab in Jezreel, and all his great men, and his kinsfolks, and his priests, until he left him none remaining.

12 And he arose and departed, and came to Samaria. *And* as he *was* at the shearing house in the way,

13 Jehu met with the brethren of Ahaziah king of Judah, and said, Who *are* ye? And they answered, We *are* the brethren of Ahaziah; and we go down to salute the children of the king and the children of the queen.

14 And he said, Take them alive. And they

took them alive, and slew them at the pit of the shearing house, *even* two and forty men; neither left he any of them.

15 And when he was departed thence, he lighted on Jehonadab the son of Rechab *coming* to meet him: and he saluted him, and said to him, Is thine heart right, as my heart *is* with thy heart? And Jehonadab answered, It is. If it be, give *me* thine hand. And he gave *him* his hand; and he took him up to him into the chariot.

16 And he said, Come with me, and see my zeal for the LORD. So they made him ride in his chariot.

17 And when he came to Samaria, he slew all that remained unto Ahab in Samaria, till he had destroyed him, according to the saying of the LORD, which he spake to Elijah.

Jehu Kills Baal Worshipers

18 And Jehu gathered all the people together, and said unto them, Ahab served Baal a little; *but* Jehu shall serve him much.

19 Now therefore call unto me all the prophets of Baal, all his servants, and all his priests; let none be wanting: for I have a great sacrifice *to do* to Baal; whosoever shall be wanting, he shall not live. But Jehu did *it* in subtilty, to the intent that he might destroy the worshippers of Baal.

20 And Jehu said, Proclaim a solemn assembly for Baal. And they proclaimed *it*.

21 And Jehu sent through all Israel: and all the worshippers of Baal came, so that there was not a man left that came not. And they came into the house of Baal; and the house of Baal was full from one end to another.

22 And he said unto him that *was* over the vestry, Bring forth vestments for all the worshippers of Baal. And he brought them forth vestments.

23 And Jehu went, and Jehonadab the son of Rechab, into the house of Baal, and said unto the worshippers of Baal, Search, and look that there be here with you none of the servants of the LORD, but the worshippers of Baal only.

24 And when they went in to offer sacrifices and burnt offerings, Jehu appointed fourscore men without, and said, *If* any of the men whom I have brought into your hands escape, *he that letteth him go*, his life *shall be* for the life of him.

25 And it came to pass, as soon as he had made an end of offering the burnt offering, that Jehu said to the guard and to the captains, Go in, *and* slay them; let none come forth. And they smote them with the edge

7 1Kgs. 21:21

9 2Kgs. 9:14, 24

10 1Sam. 3:19; 1Kgs. 21:19, 21, 29

13 2Kgs. 8:29; 2Chr. 22:8

15 1Chr. 2:55; Ezra 10:19; Jer. 35:6

16 1Kgs. 19:10

17 1Kgs. 21:21; 2Kgs. 9:8; 2Chr. 22:8

18 1Kgs. 16:31, 32

19 1Kgs. 22:6

21 1Kgs. 16:32

24 1Kgs. 20:39

of the sword; and the guard and the captains cast *them* out, and went to the city of the house of Baal.

26 And they brought forth the images out of the house of Baal, and burned them.

27 And they brake down the image of Baal, and brake down the house of Baal, and made it a draught house unto this day.

28 Thus Jehu destroyed Baal out of Israel.

29 Howbeit *from* the sins of Jeroboam the son of Nebat, who made Israel to sin, Jehu departed not from after them, *to wit*, the golden calves that *were* in Beth-el, and that *were* in Dan.

30 And the LORD said unto Jehu, Because thou hast done well in executing *that which is* right in mine eyes, *and* hast done unto the house of Ahab according to all that *was* in mine heart, thy children of the fourth *generation* shall sit on the throne of Israel.

31 But Jehu took no heed to walk in the law of the LORD God of Israel with all his heart: for he departed not from the sins of Jeroboam, which made Israel to sin.

Jehu's Death

32 In those days the LORD began to cut Israel short: and Hazael smote them in all the coasts of Israel;

33 From Jordan eastward, all the land of Gilead, the Gadites, and the Reubenites, and the Manassites, from Aroer, which *is* by the river Arnon, even Gilead and Bashan.

34 Now the rest of the acts of Jehu, and all that he did, and all his might, *are* they not written in the book of the chronicles of the kings of Israel?

35 And Jehu slept with his fathers: and they buried him in Samaria. And Jehoahaz his son reigned in his stead.

36 And the time that Jehu reigned over Israel in Samaria *was* twenty and eight years.

CHAPTER 11
Athaliah Rules Judah

1 And when Athaliah the mother of Ahaziah saw that her son was dead, she arose and destroyed all the seed royal.

2 But Jehosheba, the daughter of king Joram, sister of Ahaziah, took Joash the son of Ahaziah, and stole him from among the king's sons *which were* slain; and they hid him, *even* him and his nurse, in the bed-

chamber from Athaliah, so that he was not slain.

3 And he was with her hid in the house of the LORD six years. And Athaliah did reign over the land.

4 And the seventh year Jehoiada sent and fetched the rulers over hundreds, with the captains and the guard, and brought them to him into the house of the LORD, and made a covenant with them, and took an oath of them in the house of the LORD, and shewed them the king's son.

5 And he commanded them, saying, This *is* the thing that ye shall do; A third part of you that enter in on the sabbath shall even be keepers of the watch of the king's house;

6 And a third part *shall be* at the gate of Sur; and a third part at the gate behind the guard: so shall ye keep the watch of the house, that it be not broken down.

7 And two parts of all you that go forth on the sabbath, even they shall keep the watch of the house of the LORD about the king.

8 And ye shall compass the king round about, every man with his weapons in his hand: and he that cometh within the ranges, let him be slain: and be ye with the king as he goeth out and as he cometh in.

9 And the captains over the hundreds did according to all *things* that Jehoiada the priest commanded: and they took every man his men that were to come in on the sabbath, with them that should go out on the sabbath, and came to Jehoiada the priest.

10 And to the captains over hundreds did the priest give king David's spears and shields, that *were* in the temple of the LORD.

11 And the guard stood, every man with his weapons in his hand, round about the king, from the right corner of the temple to the left corner of the temple, *along* by the altar and the temple.

12 And he brought forth the king's son, and put the crown upon him, and *gave him* the testimony; and they made him king, and anointed him; and they clapped their hands, and said, God save the king.

13 And when Athaliah heard the noise of the guard *and* of the people, she came to the people into the temple of the LORD.

14 And when she looked, behold, the king stood by a pillar, as the manner *was*, and the princes and the trumpeters by the king, and

---

26 1Kgs. 14:23

27 Ezra 6:11; Dan. 2:5; 3:29

29 1Kgs. 12:28, 29

30 2Kgs. 10:35; 13:1, 10; 14:23; 15:8, 12

31 1Kgs. 14:16

32 2Kgs. 8:12

33 Amos 1:3

1 2Kgs. 8:26; 2Chr. 22:10

2 2Chr. 22:11, Jehoshabeath

4 2Chr. 23:1

5 1Chr. 9:25

9 2Chr. 23:8

12 1Sam. 10:24

13 2Chr. 23:12

14 2Kgs. 23:3; 2Chr. 34:31

10:30 Because Jehu followed the Lord, the Lord declares that Jehu's heirs would follow him to the throne for four generations. Second Kings 15:12 records the literal fulfillment of this prophecy.

all the people of the land rejoiced, and blew with trumpets: and Athaliah rent her clothes, and cried, Treason, Treason.

15 But Jehoiada the priest commanded the captains of the hundreds, the officers of the host, and said unto them, Have her forth without the ranges: and him that followeth her kill with the sword. For the priest had said, Let her not be slain in the house of the LORD.

16 And they laid hands on her; and she went by the way by the which the horses came into the king's house: and there was she slain.

Jehoiada's Reforms

17 And Jehoiada made a covenant between the LORD and the king and the people, that they should be the LORD's people; between the king also and the people.

18 And all the people of the land went into the house of Baal, and brake it down; his altars and his images brake they in pieces thoroughly, and slew Mattan the priest of Baal before the altars. And the priest appointed officers over the house of the LORD.

19 And he took the rulers over hundreds, and the captains, and the guard, and all the people of the land; and they brought down the king from the house of the LORD, and came by the way of the gate of the guard to the king's house. And he sat on the throne of the kings.

20 And all the people of the land rejoiced, and the city was in quiet: and they slew Athaliah with the sword *beside* the king's house.

21 Seven years old *was* Jehoash when he began to reign.

CHAPTER 12
Jehoash Rules Judah

1 In the seventh year of Jehu Jehoash began to reign; and forty years reigned he in Jerusalem. And his mother's name *was* Zibiah of Beer-sheba.

2 And Jehoash did *that which was* right in the sight of the LORD all his days wherein Jehoiada the priest instructed him.

3 But the high places were not taken away: the people still sacrificed and burnt incense in the high places.

4 And Jehoash said to the priests, All the money of the dedicated things that is brought into the house of the LORD, *even* the money of every one that passeth *the account*, the money that every man is set at, *and* all the money that cometh into any man's

heart to bring into the house of the LORD,

5 Let the priests take *it* to them, every man of his acquaintance: and let them repair the breaches of the house, wheresoever any breach shall be found.

6 But it was *so, that* in the three and twentieth year of king Jehoash the priests had not repaired the breaches of the house.

7 Then king Jehoash called for Jehoiada the priest, and the *other* priests, and said unto them, Why repair ye not the breaches of the house? now therefore receive no *more* money of your acquaintance, but deliver it for the breaches of the house.

8 And the priests consented to receive no *more* money of the people, neither to repair the breaches of the house.

9 But Jehoiada the priest took a chest, and bored a hole in the lid of it, and set it beside the altar, on the right side as one cometh into the house of the LORD: and the priests that kept the door put therein all the money *that was* brought into the house of the LORD.

10 And it was *so*, when they saw that *there was* much money in the chest, that the king's scribe and the high priest came up, and they put up in bags, and told the money that was found in the house of the LORD.

11 And they gave the money, being told, into the hands of them that did the work, that had the oversight of the house of the LORD: and they laid it out to the carpenters and builders, that wrought upon the house of the LORD,

12 And to masons, and hewers of stone, and to buy timber and hewed stone to repair the breaches of the house of the LORD, and for all that was laid out for the house to repair *it*.

13 Howbeit there were not made for the house of the LORD bowls of silver, snuffers, basons, trumpets, any vessels of gold, or vessels of silver, of the money *that was* brought into the house of the LORD:

14 But they gave that to the workmen, and repaired therewith the house of the LORD.

15 Moreover they reckoned not with the men, into whose hand they delivered the money to be bestowed on workmen: for they dealt faithfully.

16 The trespass money and sin money was not brought into the house of the LORD: it was the priests.

17 Then Hazael king of Syria went up, and fought against Gath, and took it: and Hazael set his face to go up to Jerusalem.

18 And Jehoash king of Judah took all the hallowed things that Jehoshaphat, and Je-

---

Cross references:

17 2Sam. 5:3; 2Chr. 23:16

18 Deut. 12:3; 2Kgs. 10:26; 2Chr. 23:17, 18

21 2Chr. 24:1

1 2Chr. 24:1

3 1Kgs. 15:14; 22:43; 2Kgs. 14:4

4 Ex. 30:13; 35:5; 2Kgs. 22:4; 1Chr. 29:9

6 2Chr. 24:5

7 2Chr. 24:6

9 2Chr. 24:8

13 2Chr. 24:14

15 2Kgs. 22:7

16 Lev. 5:15, 18; 7:7; Num. 18:9

17 2Kgs. 8:12; 2Chr. 24:23

18 1Kgs. 15:18; 2Kgs. 18:15, 16

horam, and Ahaziah, his fathers, kings of Judah, had dedicated, and his own hallowed things, and all the gold *that was* found in the treasures of the house of the Lord, and in the king's house, and sent *it* to Hazael king of Syria: and he went away from Jerusalem.

19 And the rest of the acts of Joash, and all that he did, *are* they not written in the book of the chronicles of the kings of Judah?

20 And his servants arose, and made a conspiracy, and slew Joash in the house of Millo, which goeth down to Silla.

21 For Jozachar the son of Shimeath, and Jehozabad the son of Shomer, his servants, smote him, and he died; and they buried him with his fathers in the city of David: and Amaziah his son reigned in his stead.

CHAPTER 13
Jehoahaz Rules Israel

1 In the three and twentieth year of Joash the son of Ahaziah king of Judah Jehoahaz the son of Jehu began to reign over Israel in Samaria, *and reigned* seventeen years.

2 And he did *that which was* evil in the sight of the Lord, and followed the sins of Jeroboam the son of Nebat, which made Israel to sin; he departed not therefrom.

3 And the anger of the Lord was kindled against Israel, and he delivered them into the hand of Hazael king of Syria, and into the hand of Ben-hadad the son of Hazael, all *their* days.

4 And Jehoahaz besought the Lord, and the Lord hearkened unto him: for he saw the oppression of Israel, because the king of Syria oppressed them.

5 (And the Lord gave Israel a saviour, so that they went out from under the hand of the Syrians: and the children of Israel dwelt in their tents, as beforetime.

6 Nevertheless they departed not from the sins of the house of Jeroboam, who made Israel sin, *but* walked therein: and there remained the grove also in Samaria.)

7 Neither did he leave of the people to Jehoahaz but fifty horsemen, and ten chariots, and ten thousand footmen; for the king of Syria had destroyed them, and had made them like the dust by threshing.

8 Now the rest of the acts of Jehoahaz, and all that he did, and his might, *are* they not written in the book of the chronicles of the kings of Israel?

9 And Jehoahaz slept with his fathers; and they buried him in Samaria: and Joash his son reigned in his stead.

Jehoash Rules Israel

10 In the thirty and seventh year of Joash king of Judah began Jehoash the son of Jehoahaz to reign over Israel in Samaria, *and reigned* sixteen years.

11 And he did *that which was* evil in the sight of the Lord; he departed not from all the sins of Jeroboam the son of Nebat, who made Israel sin: *but* he walked therein.

12 And the rest of the acts of Joash, and all that he did, and his might wherewith he fought against Amaziah king of Judah, *are* they not written in the book of the chronicles of the kings of Israel?

13 And Joash slept with his fathers; and Jeroboam sat upon his throne: and Joash was buried in Samaria with the kings of Israel.

Elisha's Death

14 Now Elisha was fallen sick of his sickness whereof he died. And Joash the king of Israel came down unto him, and wept over his face, and said, O my father, my father, the chariot of Israel, and the horsemen thereof.

15 And Elisha said unto him, Take bow and arrows. And he took unto him bow and arrows.

16 And he said to the king of Israel, Put thine hand upon the bow. And he put his hand *upon it*: and Elisha put his hands upon the king's hands.

17 And he said, Open the window eastward. And he opened *it*. Then Elisha said, Shoot. And he shot. And he said, The arrow of the Lord's deliverance, and the arrow of deliverance from Syria: for thou shalt smite the Syrians in Aphek, till thou have consumed *them*.

18 And he said, Take the arrows. And he took *them*. And he said unto the king of Israel, Smite upon the ground. And he smote thrice, and stayed.

19 And the man of God was wroth with him, and said, Thou shouldest have smitten five or six times; then hadst thou smitten Syria till thou hadst consumed *it*: whereas now thou shalt smite Syria *but* thrice.

20 And Elisha died, and they buried him.

---

20 2Kgs. 14:5; 2Chr. 24:25
21 2Chr. 24:26, 27, Zabad
3 Judg. 2:14; 2Kgs. 8:12
4 Ex. 3:7; 2Kgs. 14:26; Ps. 78:34
5 2Kgs. 13:25; 14:25, 27
6 1Kgs. 16:33
7 Amos 1:3
9 2Kgs. 13:10, *Jehoash*
10 2Kgs. 14:1
12 2Kgs. 13:14, 25; 14:9, 15; 2Chr. 25:17
14 2Kgs. 2:12
17 1Kgs. 20:26
19 2Kgs. 13:25

13:18 Elisha's dying prediction that Israel would defeat the Syrians "three times" was literally fulfilled (v. 25).

And the bands of the Moabites invaded the land at the coming in of the year.
21 And it came to pass, as they were burying a man, that, behold, they spied a band *of men*; and they cast the man into the sepulchre of Elisha: and when the man was let down, and touched the bones of Elisha, he revived, and stood up on his feet.

Wars with Syria

22 But Hazael king of Syria oppressed Israel all the days of Jehoahaz.
23 And the LORD was gracious unto them, and had compassion on them, and had respect unto them, because of his covenant with Abraham, Isaac, and Jacob, and would not destroy them, neither cast he them from his presence as yet.
24 So Hazael king of Syria died; and Benhadad his son reigned in his stead.
25 And Jehoash the son of Jehoahaz took again out of the hand of Ben-hadad the son of Hazael the cities, which he had taken out of the hand of Jehoahaz his father by war. Three times did Joash beat him, and recovered the cities of Israel.

CHAPTER 14
Amaziah Rules Judah

1 In the second year of Joash son of Jehoahaz king of Israel reigned Amaziah the son of Joash king of Judah.
2 He was twenty and five years old when he began to reign, and reigned twenty and nine years in Jerusalem. And his mother's name *was* Jehoaddan of Jerusalem.
3 And he did *that which was* right in the sight of the LORD, yet not like David his father: he did according to all things as Joash his father did.
4 Howbeit the high places were not taken away: as yet the people did sacrifice and burnt incense on the high places.
5 And it came to pass, as soon as the kingdom was confirmed in his hand, that he slew his servants which had slain the king his father.
6 But the children of the murderers he slew not: according unto that which is written in the book of the law of Moses, wherein the LORD commanded, saying, The fathers shall not be put to death for the children, nor the children be put to death for the fathers; but every man shall be put to death for his own sin.
7 He slew of Edom in the valley of salt ten thousand, and took Selah by war, and called the name of it Joktheel unto this day.

8 Then Amaziah sent messengers to Jehoash, the son of Jehoahaz son of Jehu, king of Israel, saying, Come, let us look one another in the face.
9 And Jehoash the king of Israel sent to Amaziah king of Judah, saying, The thistle that *was* in Lebanon sent to the cedar that *was* in Lebanon, saying, Give thy daughter to my son to wife: and there passed by a wild beast that *was* in Lebanon, and trode down the thistle.
10 Thou hast indeed smitten Edom, and thine heart hath lifted thee up: glory *of this*, and tarry at home: for why shouldest thou meddle to *thy* hurt, that thou shouldest fall, *even* thou, and Judah with thee?
11 But Amaziah would not hear. Therefore Jehoash king of Israel went up; and he and Amaziah king of Judah looked one another in the face at Beth-shemesh, which *belongeth* to Judah.
12 And Judah was put to the worse before Israel; and they fled every man to their tents.
13 And Jehoash king of Israel took Amaziah king of Judah, the son of Jehoash the son of Ahaziah, at Beth-shemesh, and came to Jerusalem, and brake down the wall of Jerusalem from the gate of Ephraim unto the corner gate, four hundred cubits.
14 And he took all the gold and silver, and all the vessels that were found in the house of the LORD, and in the treasures of the king's house, and hostages, and returned to Samaria.

Jehoash's Death

15 Now the rest of the acts of Jehoash which he did, and his might, and how he fought with Amaziah king of Judah, *are* they not written in the book of the chronicles of the kings of Israel?
16 And Jehoash slept with his fathers, and was buried in Samaria with the kings of Israel; and Jeroboam his son reigned in his stead.

Amaziah's Death

17 And Amaziah the son of Joash king of Judah lived after the death of Jehoash son of Jehoahaz king of Israel fifteen years.
18 And the rest of the acts of Amaziah, *are* they not written in the book of the chronicles of the kings of Judah?
19 Now they made a conspiracy against him in Jerusalem: and he fled to Lachish; but they sent after him to Lachish, and slew him there.

22 2Kgs. 8:12
23 Ex. 2:24, 25; 32:13; 2Kgs. 14:27
25 2Kgs. 13:18, 19
1 2Kgs. 13:10; 2Chr. 25:1
4 2Kgs. 12:3
5 2Kgs. 12:20
6 Deut. 24:16; Ezek. 18:4, 20
7 Josh. 15:38; 2Sam. 8:13; 2Chr. 25:11
8 2Chr. 25:17, 18
9 Judg. 9:8; 1Kgs. 4:33
10 Deut. 8:14; 2Chr. 32:25; Ezek. 28:2, 5, 17; Hab. 2:4
11 Josh. 19:38; 21:16
13 Neh. 8:16; 12:39; Jer. 31:38; Zech. 14:10
14 1Kgs. 7:51
15 2Kgs. 13:12
17 2Chr. 25:25
19 Josh. 10:31; 2Chr. 25:27

20 And they brought him on horses: and he was buried at Jerusalem with his fathers in the city of David.

21 And all the people of Judah took Azariah, which *was* sixteen years old, and made him king instead of his father Amaziah.

22 He built Elath, and restored it to Judah, after that the king slept with his fathers.

Jeroboam II Rules Israel

23 In the fifteenth year of Amaziah the son of Joash king of Judah Jeroboam the son of Joash king of Israel began to reign in Samaria, *and reigned* forty and one years.

24 And he did *that which was* evil in the sight of the LORD: he departed not from all the sins of Jeroboam the son of Nebat, who made Israel to sin.

25 He restored the coast of Israel from the entering of Hamath unto the sea of the plain, according to the word of the LORD God of Israel, which he spake by the hand of his servant Jonah, the son of Amittai, the prophet, which *was* of Gath-hepher.

26 For the LORD saw the affliction of Israel, *that it was* very bitter: for *there was* not any shut up, nor any left, nor any helper for Israel.

27 And the LORD said not that he would blot out the name of Israel from under heaven: but he saved them by the hand of Jeroboam the son of Joash.

28 Now the rest of the acts of Jeroboam, and all that he did, and his might, how he warred, and how he recovered Damascus, and Hamath, *which belonged* to Judah, for Israel, are they not written in the book of the chronicles of the kings of Israel?

29 And Jeroboam slept with his fathers, *even* with the kings of Israel; and Zachariah his son reigned in his stead.

CHAPTER 15
Azariah Rules Judah

1 In the twenty and seventh year of Jeroboam king of Israel began Azariah son of Amaziah king of Judah to reign.

2 Sixteen years old was he when he began to reign, and he reigned two and fifty years in Jerusalem. And his mother's name *was* Jecholiah of Jerusalem.

3 And he did *that which was* right in the sight of the LORD, according to all that his father Amaziah had done;

4 Save that the high places were not removed: the people sacrificed and burnt incense still on the high places.

5 And the LORD smote the king, so that he

was a leper unto the day of his death, and dwelt in a several house. And Jotham the king's son *was* over the house, judging the people of the land.

6 And the rest of the acts of Azariah, and all that he did, *are* they not written in the book of the chronicles of the kings of Judah?

7 So Azariah slept with his fathers; and they buried him with his fathers in the city of David: and Jotham his son reigned in his stead.

Zachariah Rules Israel

8 In the thirty and eighth year of Azariah king of Judah did Zachariah the son of Jeroboam reign over Israel in Samaria six months.

9 And he did *that which was* evil in the sight of the LORD, as his fathers had done: he departed not from the sins of Jeroboam the son of Nebat, who made Israel to sin.

10 And Shallum the son of Jabesh conspired against him, and smote him before the people, and slew him, and reigned in his stead.

11 And the rest of the acts of Zachariah, behold, they *are* written in the book of the chronicles of the kings of Israel.

12 This *was* the word of the LORD which he spake unto Jehu, saying, Thy sons shall sit on the throne of Israel unto the fourth *generation*. And so it came to pass.

Shallum Rules Israel

13 Shallum the son of Jabesh began to reign in the nine and thirtieth year of Uzziah king of Judah; and he reigned a full month in Samaria.

14 For Menahem the son of Gadi went up from Tirzah, and came to Samaria, and smote Shallum the son of Jabesh in Samaria, and slew him, and reigned in his stead.

15 And the rest of the acts of Shallum, and his conspiracy which he made, behold, they *are* written in the book of the chronicles of the kings of Israel.

16 Then Menahem smote Tiphsah, and all that *were* therein, and the coasts thereof from Tirzah: because they opened not *to him*, therefore he smote *it; and* all the women therein that were with child he ripped up.

Menahem Rules Israel

17 In the nine and thirtieth year of Azariah king of Judah began Menahem the son of

Gadi to reign over Israel, *and reigned* ten years in Samaria.

18 And he did *that which was* evil in the sight of the LORD: he departed not all his days from the sins of Jeroboam the son of Nebat, who made Israel to sin.

19 *And* Pul the king of Assyria came against the land: and Menahem gave Pul a thousand talents of silver, that his hand might be with him to confirm the kingdom in his hand.

20 And Menahem exacted the money of Israel, *even* of all the mighty men of wealth, of each man fifty shekels of silver, to give to the king of Assyria. So the king of Assyria turned back, and stayed not there in the land.

21 And the rest of the acts of Menahem, and all that he did, *are* they not written in the book of the chronicles of the kings of Israel?

22 And Menahem slept with his fathers; and Pekahiah his son reigned in his stead.

Pekahiah Rules Israel

23 In the fiftieth year of Azariah king of Judah Pekahiah the son of Menahem began to reign over Israel in Samaria, *and reigned* two years.

24 And he did *that which was* evil in the sight of the LORD: he departed not from the sins of Jeroboam the son of Nebat, who made Israel to sin.

25 But Pekah the son of Remaliah, a captain of his, conspired against him, and smote him in Samaria, in the palace of the king's house, with Argob and Arieh, and with him fifty men of the Gileadites: and he killed him, and reigned in his room.

26 And the rest of the acts of Pekahiah, and all that he did, behold, they *are* written in the book of the chronicles of the kings of Israel.

Pekah Rules Israel

27 In the two and fiftieth year of Azariah king of Judah Pekah the son of Remaliah began to reign over Israel in Samaria, *and reigned* twenty years.

28 And he did *that which was* evil in the sight of the LORD: he departed not from the sins of Jeroboam the son of Nebat, who made Israel to sin.

29 In the days of Pekah king of Israel came Tiglathpileser king of Assyria, and took Ijon, and Abel-beth-maachah, and Janoah, and Kedesh, and Hazor, and Gilead, and Galilee, all the land of Naphtali, and carried them captive to Assyria.

30 And Hoshea the son of Elah made a conspiracy against Pekah the son of Remaliah, and smote him, and slew him, and reigned in his stead, in the twentieth year of Jotham the son of Uzziah.

31 And the rest of the acts of Pekah, and all that he did, behold, they *are* written in the book of the chronicles of the kings of Israel.

Jotham Rules Judah

32 In the second year of Pekah the son of Remaliah king of Israel began Jotham the son of Uzziah king of Judah to reign.

33 Five and twenty years old was he when he began to reign, and he reigned sixteen years in Jerusalem. And his mother's name *was* Jerusha, the daughter of Zadok.

34 And he did *that which was* right in the sight of the LORD: he did according to all that his father Uzziah had done.

35 Howbeit the high places were not removed: the people sacrificed and burned incense still in the high places. He built the higher gate of the house of the LORD.

36 Now the rest of the acts of Jotham, and all that he did, *are* they not written in the book of the chronicles of the kings of Judah?

37 In those days the LORD began to send against Judah Rezin the king of Syria, and Pekah the son of Remaliah.

38 And Jotham slept with his fathers, and was buried with his fathers in the city of David his father: and Ahaz his son reigned in his stead.

CHAPTER 16
Ahaz Rules Judah

1 In the seventeenth year of Pekah the son of Remaliah Ahaz the son of Jotham king of Judah began to reign.

2 Twenty years old *was* Ahaz when he began to reign, and reigned sixteen years in Jerusalem, and did not *that which was* right in the sight of the LORD his God, like David his father.

3 But he walked in the way of the kings of Israel, yea, and made his son to pass through the fire, according to the abominations of the heathen, whom the LORD cast out from before the children of Israel.

4 And he sacrificed and burnt incense in the high places, and on the hills, and under every green tree.

5 Then Rezin king of Syria and Pekah son of Remaliah king of Israel came up to Jerusalem to war: and they besieged Ahaz, but could not overcome *him*.

---

19 2Kgs. 14:5; 1Chr. 5:26; Isa. 9:1; Hos. 8:9

27 Isa. 7:1

29 1Kgs. 15:20; 1Chr. 5:26; Isa. 9:1

30 2Kgs. 17:1; Hos. 10:3, 7, 15

32 2Chr. 27:1

34 2Kgs. 15:3

35 2Kgs. 15:4; 2Chr. 27:3

37 2Kgs. 16:5; 15:27; Isa. 7:1

1 2Chr. 28:1

3 Lev. 18:21; Deut. 12:31; 2Chr. 28:3; Ps. 106:37, 38

4 Deut. 12:2; 1Kgs. 14:23

5 Isa. 7:1, 4

6 At that time Rezin king of Syria recovered Elath to Syria, and drave the Jews from Elath: and the Syrians came to Elath, and dwelt there unto this day.
7 So Ahaz sent messengers to Tiglathpileser king of Assyria, saying, I *am* thy servant and thy son: come up, and save me out of the hand of the king of Syria, and out of the hand of the king of Israel, which rise up against me.
8 And Ahaz took the silver and gold that was found in the house of the LORD, and in the treasures of the king's house, and sent *it for* a present to the king of Assyria.
9 And the king of Assyria hearkened unto him: for the king of Assyria went up against Damascus, and took it, and carried *the people of* it captive to Kir, and slew Rezin.
10 And king Ahaz went to Damascus to meet Tiglathpileser king of Assyria, and saw an altar that *was* at Damascus: and king Ahaz sent to Urijah the priest the fashion of the altar, and the pattern of it, according to all the workmanship thereof.
11 And Urijah the priest built an altar according to all that king Ahaz had sent from Damascus: so Urijah the priest made *it* against king Ahaz came from Damascus.
12 And when the king was come from Damascus, the king saw the altar: and the king approached to the altar, and offered thereon.
13 And he burnt his burnt offering and his meat offering, and poured his drink offering, and sprinkled the blood of his peace offerings, upon the altar.
14 And he brought also the brasen altar, which *was* before the LORD, from the forefront of the house, from between the altar and the house of the LORD, and put it on the north side of the altar.
15 And king Ahaz commanded Urijah the priest, saying, Upon the great altar burn the morning burnt offering, and the evening meat offering, and the king's burnt sacrifice, and his meat offering, with the burnt offering of all the people of the land, and their meat offering, and their drink offerings; and sprinkle upon it all the blood of the burnt offering, and all the blood of the sacrifice: and the brasen altar shall be for me to inquire *by*.
16 Thus did Urijah the priest, according to all that king Ahaz commanded.
17 And king Ahaz cut off the borders of the bases, and removed the laver from off them; and took down the sea from off the brasen oxen that *were* under it, and put it upon a pavement of stones.

18 And the covert for the sabbath that they had built in the house, and the king's entry without, turned he from the house of the LORD for the king of Assyria.
19 Now the rest of the acts of Ahaz which he did, *are* they not written in the book of the chronicles of the kings of Judah?
20 And Ahaz slept with his fathers, and was buried with his fathers in the city of David: and Hezekiah his son reigned in his stead.

CHAPTER 17
Hoshea Rules Israel

1 In the twelfth year of Ahaz king of Judah began Hoshea the son of Elah to reign in Samaria over Israel nine years.
2 And he did *that which was* evil in the sight of the LORD, but not as the kings of Israel that were before him.
3 Against him came up Shalmaneser king of Assyria; and Hoshea became his servant, and gave him presents.
4 And the king of Assyria found conspiracy in Hoshea: for he had sent messengers to So king of Egypt, and brought no present to the king of Assyria, as *he had done* year by year: therefore the king of Assyria shut him up, and bound him in prison.
5 Then the king of Assyria came up throughout all the land, and went up to Samaria, and besieged it three years.
6 In the ninth year of Hoshea the king of Assyria took Samaria, and carried Israel away into Assyria, and placed them in Halah and in Habor *by* the river of Gozan, and in the cities of the Medes.

The Reasons for Samaria's Fall and Exile

7 For *so* it was, that the children of Israel had sinned against the LORD their God, which had brought them up out of the land of Egypt, from under the hand of Pharaoh king of Egypt, and had feared other gods,
8 And walked in the statutes of the heathen, whom the LORD cast out from before the children of Israel, and of the kings of Israel, which they had made.
9 And the children of Israel did secretly *those* things that *were* not right against the LORD their God, and they built them high places in all their cities, from the tower of the watchmen to the fenced city.
10 And they set them up images and groves in every high hill, and under every green tree:
11 And there they burnt incense in all the high places, as *did* the heathen whom the

---

6 2Kgs. 14:22
7 2Kgs. 15:29
8 2Kgs. 12:18; 2Chr. 28:21
9 Amos 1:5
12 2Chr. 26:16, 19
14 2Chr. 4:1
15 Ex. 29:39-41
17 1Kgs. 7:23, 25, 27, 28; 2Chr. 28:24
20 2Chr. 28:27
1 2Kgs. 15:30
3 2Kgs. 18:9

5 2Kgs. 18:9
6 Lev. 26:32, 33; Deut. 28:36, 64; 29:27, 28; 2Kgs. 18:10, 11; 1Chr. 5:26; Hos. 13:16

8 Lev. 18:3; Deut. 18:9; 2Kgs. 16:3
9 2Kgs. 18:8
10 Ex. 34:13; Deut. 12:2; 16:21; 1Kgs. 14:23; 2Kgs. 16:4; Isa. 57:5; Mic. 5:14

LORD carried away before them; and wrought wicked things to provoke the LORD to anger:

12 For they served idols, whereof the LORD had said unto them, Ye shall not do this thing.

13 Yet the LORD testified against Israel, and against Judah, by all the prophets, *and by* all the seers, saying, Turn ye from your evil ways, and keep my commandments *and* my statutes, according to all the law which I commanded your fathers, and which I sent to you by my servants the prophets.

14 Notwithstanding they would not hear, but hardened their necks, like to the neck of their fathers, that did not believe in the LORD their God.

15 And they rejected his statutes, and his covenant that he made with their fathers, and his testimonies which he testified against them; and they followed vanity, and became vain, and went after the heathen that *were* round about them, *concerning* whom the LORD had charged them, that they should not do like them.

16 And they left all the commandments of the LORD their God, and made them molten images, *even* two calves, and made a grove, and worshipped all the host of heaven, and served Baal.

17 And they caused their sons and their daughters to pass through the fire, and used divination and enchantments, and sold themselves to do evil in the sight of the LORD, to provoke him to anger.

18 Therefore the LORD was very angry with Israel, and removed them out of his sight: there was none left but the tribe of Judah only.

19 Also Judah kept not the commandments of the LORD their God, but walked in the statutes of Israel which they made.

20 And the LORD rejected all the seed of Israel, and afflicted them, and delivered them into the hand of spoilers, until he had cast them out of his sight.

21 For he rent Israel from the house of David; and they made Jeroboam the son of Nebat king: and Jeroboam drave Israel from following the LORD, and made them sin a great sin.

22 For the children of Israel walked in all the sins of Jeroboam which he did; they departed not from them;

23 Until the LORD removed Israel out of his sight, as he had said by all his servants the prophets. So was Israel carried away out of their own land to Assyria unto this day.

Assyria Settles Foreigners in Israel

24 And the king of Assyria brought *men* from Babylon, and from Cuthah, and from Ava, and from Hamath, and from Sepharvaim, and placed *them* in the cities of Samaria instead of the children of Israel: and they possessed Samaria, and dwelt in the cities thereof.

25 And *so* it was at the beginning of their dwelling there, *that* they feared not the LORD: therefore the LORD sent lions among them, which slew *some* of them.

26 Wherefore they spake to the king of Assyria, saying, The nations which thou hast removed, and placed in the cities of Samaria, know not the manner of the God of the land: therefore he hath sent lions among them, and, behold, they slay them, because they know not the manner of the God of the land.

27 Then the king of Assyria commanded, saying, Carry thither one of the priests whom ye brought from thence; and let them go and dwell there, and let him teach them the manner of the God of the land.

28 Then one of the priests whom they had carried away from Samaria came and dwelt in Beth-el, and taught them how they should fear the LORD.

29 Howbeit every nation made gods of their own, and put *them* in the houses of the high places which the Samaritans had made, every nation in their cities wherein they dwelt.

30 And the men of Babylon made Succoth-benoth, and the men of Cuth made Nergal, and the men of Hamath made Ashima,

31 And the Avites made Nibhaz and Tartak, and the Sepharvites burnt their children in fire to Adrammelech and Anammelech, the gods of Sepharvaim.

32 So they feared the LORD, and made unto themselves of the lowest of them priests of the high places, which sacrificed for them in the houses of the high places.

33 They feared the LORD, and served their own gods, after the manner of the nations whom they carried away from thence.

34 Unto this day they do after the former manners: they fear not the LORD, neither do they after their statutes, or after their ordinances, or after the law and commandment which the LORD commanded the children of Jacob, whom he named Israel;

35 With whom the LORD had made a covenant, and charged them, saying, Ye shall not fear other gods, nor bow yourselves to

---

12 Ex. 20:3, 4; Lev. 26:1; Deut. 4:19; 5:7, 8

13 1 Sam. 9:9; Jer. 18:11; 25:5; 35:15

14 Deut. 31:27; Prov. 29:1

15 Deut. 12:30, 31; 29:25; 32:21; 1 Kgs. 16:13; Ps. 115:8; Rom. 1:21; 1 Cor. 8:4

16 Ex. 32:8; 1 Kgs. 12:28; 14:15, 23; 15:13; 16:31, 33; 22:53; 2 Kgs. 11:18

17 Lev. 18:21; Deut. 18:10; 1 Kgs. 21:20; 2 Kgs. 16:3; Ezek. 23:37

18 1 Kgs. 11:13, 32

19 Jer. 3:8

20 2 Kgs. 13:3; 15:29

21 1 Kgs. 11:11, 31; 12:20, 28

23 1 Kgs. 14:16; 2 Kgs. 17:6

24 2 Kgs. 17:30; 18:34, *Ivah*; Ezra 4:2, 10

30 2 Kgs. 17:24

31 Lev. 18:21; Deut. 12:31; Ezra 4:9

32 1 Kgs. 12:31

33 Zeph. 1:5

34 Gen. 32:28; 35:10; 1 Kgs. 11:31

35 Ex. 20:5; Judg. 6:10

them, nor serve them, nor sacrifice to them:

36 But the LORD, who brought you up out of the land of Egypt with great power and a stretched out arm, him shall ye fear, and him shall ye worship, and to him shall ye do sacrifice.

37 And the statutes, and the ordinances, and the law, and the commandment, which he wrote for you, ye shall observe to do for evermore; and ye shall not fear other gods.

38 And the covenant that I have made with you ye shall not forget; neither shall ye fear other gods.

39 But the LORD your God ye shall fear; and he shall deliver you out of the hand of all your enemies.

40 Howbeit they did not hearken, but they did after their former manner.

41 So these nations feared the LORD, and served their graven images, both their children, and their children's children: as did their fathers, so do they unto this day.

CHAPTER 18
Hezekiah Rules Judah

1 Now it came to pass in the third year of Hoshea son of Elah king of Israel, *that* Hezekiah the son of Ahaz king of Judah began to reign.

2 Twenty and five years old was he when he began to reign; and he reigned twenty and nine years in Jerusalem. His mother's name also *was* Abi, the daughter of Zachariah.

3 And he did *that which was* right in the sight of the LORD, according to all that David his father did.

4 He removed the high places, and brake the images, and cut down the groves, and brake in pieces the brasen serpent that Moses had made: for unto those days the children of Israel did burn incense to it: and he called it Nehushtan.

5 He trusted in the LORD God of Israel; so that after him was none like him among all the kings of Judah, nor *any* that were before him.

6 For he clave to the LORD, *and* departed not from following him, but kept his commandments, which the LORD commanded Moses.

7 And the LORD was with him; *and* he prospered whithersoever he went forth: and he rebelled against the king of Assyria, and served him not.

8 He smote the Philistines, *even* unto Gaza, and the borders thereof, from the tower of the watchmen to the fenced city.

9 And it came to pass in the fourth year of king Hezekiah, which *was* the seventh year of Hoshea son of Elah king of Israel, *that* Shalmaneser king of Assyria came up against Samaria, and besieged it.

10 And at the end of three years they took it: *even* in the sixth year of Hezekiah, that *is* the ninth year of Hoshea king of Israel, Samaria was taken.

11 And the king of Assyria did carry away Israel unto Assyria, and put them in Halah and in Habor *by* the river of Gozan, and in the cities of the Medes:

12 Because they obeyed not the voice of the LORD their God, but transgressed his covenant, *and* all that Moses the servant of the LORD commanded, and would not hear *them*, nor do *them*.

Sennacherib Threatens Jerusalem

13 Now in the fourteenth year of king Hezekiah did Sennacherib king of Assyria come up against all the fenced cities of Judah, and took them.

14 And Hezekiah king of Judah sent to the king of Assyria to Lachish, saying, I have offended; return from me: that which thou puttest on me will I bear. And the king of Assyria appointed unto Hezekiah king of Judah three hundred talents of silver and thirty talents of gold.

15 And Hezekiah gave *him* all the silver that was found in the house of the LORD, and in the treasures of the king's house.

16 At that time did Hezekiah cut off *the gold from* the doors of the temple of the LORD, and *from* the pillars which Hezekiah king of Judah had overlaid, and gave it to the king of Assyria.

17 And the king of Assyria sent Tartan and Rabsaris and Rab-shakeh from Lachish to king Hezekiah with a great host against Jerusalem. And they went up and came to Jerusalem. And when they were come up, they came and stood by the conduit of the upper pool, which *is* in the highway of the fuller's field.

18 And when they had called to the king, there came out to them Eliakim the son of Hilkiah, which *was* over the household, and Shebna the scribe, and Joah the son of Asaph the recorder.

19 And Rab-shakeh said unto them, Speak ye now to Hezekiah, Thus saith the great king, the king of Assyria, What confidence *is* this wherein thou trustest?

20 Thou sayest, (but *they are but* vain words,) *I have* counsel and strength for the

36 Ex. 6:6; Deut. 10:20
37 Deut. 5:32
38 Deut. 4:23
41 2Kgs. 17:32, 33
1 2Chr. 28:27; 29:1
2 2Chr. 29:1, *Abijah*
4 Num. 21:9; 2Chr. 31:1
5 2Kgs. 19:10; 23:25; Job 13:15; Ps. 13:5
6 Deut. 10:20; Josh. 23:8
7 1Sam. 18:5, 14; 2Kgs. 16:7; 2Chr. 15:2; Ps. 60:12
8 2Kgs. 17:9; 1Chr. 4:41; Isa. 14:29
9 2Kgs. 17:3
10 2Kgs. 17:6
11 2Kgs. 17:6; 1Chr. 5:26
12 2Kgs. 17:7; Dan. 9:6, 10
13 2Chr. 32:1; Isa. 36:1
15 2Kgs. 16:8
17 Isa. 7:3
19 2Chr. 32:10

war. Now on whom dost thou trust, that thou rebellest against me?

21 Now, behold, thou trustest upon the staff of this bruised reed, *even* upon Egypt, on which if a man lean, it will go into his hand, and pierce it: so *is* Pharaoh king of Egypt unto all that trust on him.

22 But if ye say unto me, We trust in the LORD our God: *is* not that he, whose high places and whose altars Hezekiah hath taken away, and hath said to Judah and Jerusalem, Ye shall worship before this altar in Jerusalem?

23 Now therefore, I pray thee, give pledges to my lord the king of Assyria, and I will deliver thee two thousand horses, if thou be able on thy part to set riders upon them.

24 How then wilt thou turn away the face of one captain of the least of my master's servants, and put thy trust on Egypt for chariots and for horsemen?

25 Am I now come up without the LORD against this place to destroy it? The LORD said to me, Go up against this land, and destroy it.

26 Then said Eliakim the son of Hilkiah, and Shebna, and Joah, unto Rab-shakeh, Speak, I pray thee, to thy servants in the Syrian language; for we understand *it*: and talk not with us in the Jews' language in the ears of the people that *are* on the wall.

27 But Rab-shakeh said unto them, Hath my master sent me to thy master, and to thee, to speak these words? *hath he* not *sent me* to the men which sit on the wall, that they may eat their own dung, and drink their own piss with you?

28 Then Rab-shakeh stood and cried with a loud voice in the Jews' language, and spake, saying, Hear the word of the great king, the king of Assyria:

29 Thus saith the king, Let not Hezekiah deceive you: for he shall not be able to deliver you out of his hand:

30 Neither let Hezekiah make you trust in the LORD, saying, The LORD will surely deliver us, and this city shall not be delivered into the hand of the king of Assyria.

31 Hearken not to Hezekiah: for thus saith the king of Assyria, Make *an agreement* with me by a present, and come out to me, and *then* eat ye every man of his own vine, and

every one of his fig tree, and drink ye every one the waters of his cistern:

32 Until I come and take you away to a land like your own land, a land of corn and wine, a land of bread and vineyards, a land of oil olive and of honey, that ye may live, and not die: and hearken not unto Hezekiah, when he persuadeth you, saying, The LORD will deliver us.

33 Hath any of the gods of the nations delivered at all his land out of the hand of the king of Assyria?

34 Where *are* the gods of Hamath, and of Arpad? where *are* the gods of Sepharvaim, Hena, and Ivah? have they delivered Samaria out of mine hand?

35 Who *are* they among all the gods of the countries, that have delivered their country out of mine hand, that the LORD should deliver Jerusalem out of mine hand?

36 But the people held their peace, and answered him not a word: for the king's commandment was, saying, Answer him not.

37 Then came Eliakim the son of Hilkiah, which *was* over the household, and Shebna the scribe, and Joah the son of Asaph the recorder, to Hezekiah with *their* clothes rent, and told him the words of Rab-shakeh.

CHAPTER 19
Isaiah Reassures Hezekiah

1 And it came to pass, when king Hezekiah heard *it*, that he rent his clothes, and covered himself with sackcloth, and went into the house of the LORD.

2 And he sent Eliakim, which *was* over the household, and Shebna the scribe, and the elders of the priests, covered with sackcloth, to Isaiah the prophet the son of Amoz.

3 And they said unto him, Thus saith Hezekiah, This day *is* a day of trouble, and of rebuke, and blasphemy: for the children are come to the birth, and *there is* not strength to bring forth.

4 It may be the LORD thy God will hear all the words of Rab-shakeh, whom the king of Assyria his master hath sent to reproach the living God; and will reprove the words which the LORD thy God hath heard: wherefore lift up *thy* prayer for the remnant that are left.

5 So the servants of king Hezekiah came to Isaiah.

Cross references
21 Ezek. 29:6, 7
22 2Kgs. 18:4; 2Chr. 31:1; 32:12
29 2Chr. 32:15
32 Deut. 8:7, 8
33 2Kgs. 19:12; 2Chr. 32:14; Isa. 10:10, 11
34 2Kgs. 17:24, Ava; 19:13
35 Dan. 3:15
37 Isa. 33:7
1 Isa. 37:1
2 Luke 3:4, Ezaias
4 2Sam. 16:12; 2Kgs. 18:35; Ps. 50:21

19:5–7, 20–36 Isaiah, the prophet of God, told Hezekiah, the godly king of Judah, that he would be spared from the hand of the mighty army of the Assyrians and that Sennacherib, king of Assyria, would return to his own land and be killed. The events happened just as the prophet said (vv. 36–37).

6 And Isaiah said unto them, Thus shall ye say to your master, Thus saith the LORD, Be not afraid of the words which thou hast heard, with which the servants of the king of Assyria have blasphemed me.
7 Behold, I will send a blast upon him, and he shall hear a rumour, and shall return to his own land; and I will cause him to fall by the sword in his own land.

Sennacherib Threatens Again

8 So Rab-shakeh returned, and found the king of Assyria warring against Libnah: for he had heard that he was departed from Lachish.
9 And when he heard say of Tirhakah king of Ethiopia, Behold, he is come out to fight against thee: he sent messengers again unto Hezekiah, saying,
10 Thus shall ye speak to Hezekiah king of Judah, saying, Let not thy God in whom thou trustest deceive thee, saying, Jerusalem shall not be delivered into the hand of the king of Assyria.
11 Behold, thou hast heard what the kings of Assyria have done to all lands, by destroying them utterly: and shalt thou be delivered?
12 Have the gods of the nations delivered them which my fathers have destroyed; as Gozan, and Haran, and Rezeph, and the children of Eden which were in Thelasar?
13 Where is the king of Hamath, and the king of Arpad, and the king of the city of Sepharvaim, of Hena, and Ivah?
14 And Hezekiah received the letter of the hand of the messengers, and read it: and Hezekiah went up into the house of the LORD, and spread it before the LORD.
15 And Hezekiah prayed before the LORD, and said, O LORD God of Israel, which dwellest between the cherubims, thou art the God, even thou alone, of all the kingdoms of the earth; thou hast made heaven and earth.
16 LORD, bow down thine ear, and hear: open, LORD, thine eyes, and see: and hear the words of Sennacherib, which hath sent him to reproach the living God.
17 Of a truth, LORD, the kings of Assyria have destroyed the nations and their lands,
18 And have cast their gods into the fire: for they were no gods, but the work of men's hands, wood and stone: therefore they have destroyed them.
19 Now therefore, O LORD our God, I beseech thee, save thou us out of his hand, that all the kingdoms of the earth may

know that thou art the LORD God, even thou only.

Isaiah's Prophecy against Assyria

20 Then Isaiah the son of Amoz sent to Hezekiah, saying, Thus saith the LORD God of Israel, That which thou hast prayed to me against Sennacherib king of Assyria I have heard.
21 This is the word that the LORD hath spoken concerning him; The virgin the daughter of Zion hath despised thee, and laughed thee to scorn; the daughter of Jerusalem hath shaken her head at thee.
22 Whom hast thou reproached and blasphemed? and against whom hast thou exalted thy voice, and lifted up thine eyes on high? even against the Holy One of Israel.
23 By thy messengers thou hast reproached the Lord, and hast said, With the multitude of my chariots I am come up to the height of the mountains, to the sides of Lebanon, and will cut down the tall cedar trees thereof, and the choice fir trees thereof: and I will enter into the lodgings of his borders, and into the forest of his Carmel.
24 I have digged and drunk strange waters, and with the sole of my feet have I dried up all the rivers of besieged places.
25 Hast thou not heard long ago how I have done it, and of ancient times that I have formed it? now have I brought it to pass, that thou shouldest be to lay waste fenced cities into ruinous heaps.
26 Therefore their inhabitants were of small power, they were dismayed and confounded; they were as the grass of the field, and as the green herb, as the grass on the housetops, and as corn blasted before it be grown up.
27 But I know thy abode, and thy going out, and thy coming in, and thy rage against me.
28 Because thy rage against me and thy tumult is come up into mine ears, therefore I will put my hook in thy nose, and my bridle in thy lips, and I will turn thee back by the way by which thou camest.
29 And this shall be a sign unto thee, Ye shall eat this year such things as grow of themselves, and in the second year that which springeth of the same; and in the third year sow ye, and reap, and plant vineyards, and eat the fruits thereof.
30 And the remnant that is escaped of the house of Judah shall yet again take root downward, and bear fruit upward.
31 For out of Jerusalem shall go forth a remnant, and they that escape out of mount

6 2Kgs. 18:17; Isa. 37:6

7 2Kgs. 19:35-37; Jer. 51:1

8 2Kgs. 18:14

9 1Sam. 23:27

10 2Kgs. 18:5

12 2Kgs. 18:33; Ezek. 27:23

13 2Kgs. 18:34

14 Isa. 37:14

15 1Sam. 4:4; 1Kgs. 18:39; Ps. 80:1; Isa. 44:6; Jer. 10:10-12

16 2Kgs. 19:16; 2Chr. 6:40; Ps. 31:2

18 Ps. 115:4; Jer. 10:3

19 Ps. 83:18

20 Isa. 37:21; Ps. 65:2

21 Job 16:4; Ps. 22:7, 8; Lam. 2:13, 15

22 Ps. 71:22; Isa. 5:24; Jer. 51:5

23 2Kgs. 18:17; Ps. 20:7; Isa. 10:18

25 Isa. 10:5; 45:7

26 Ps. 129:6

27 Ps. 139:1

28 2Kgs. 19:33, 36, 37; Job 41:2; Ezek. 29:4; 38:4; Amos 4:2

29 1Sam. 2:34; 2Kgs. 20:8, 9; Isa. 7:11, 14; Luke 2:12

30 2Chr. 32:22, 23

31 Isa. 9:7

Zion: the zeal of the LORD *of hosts* shall do this.

32 Therefore thus saith the LORD concerning the king of Assyria, He shall not come into this city, nor shoot an arrow there, nor come before it with shield, nor cast a bank against it.

33 By the way that he came, by the same shall he return, and shall not come into this city, saith the LORD.

34 For I will defend this city, to save it, for mine own sake, and for my servant David's sake.

35 And it came to pass that night, that the angel of the LORD went out, and smote in the camp of the Assyrians an hundred fourscore and five thousand: and when they arose early in the morning, behold, they *were* all dead corpses.

36 So Sennacherib king of Assyria departed, and went and returned, and dwelt at Nineveh.

37 And it came to pass, as he was worshipping in the house of Nisroch his god, that Adrammelech and Sharezer his sons smote him with the sword: and they escaped into the land of Armenia. And Esarhaddon his son reigned in his stead.

CHAPTER 20
Hezekiah Gets Sick

1 In those days was Hezekiah sick unto death. And the prophet Isaiah the son of Amoz came to him, and said unto him, Thus saith the LORD, Set thine house in order; for thou shalt die, and not live.

2 Then he turned his face to the wall, and prayed unto the LORD, saying,

3 I beseech thee, O LORD, remember now how I have walked before thee in truth and with a perfect heart, and have done *that which is* good in thy sight. And Hezekiah wept sore.

4 And it came to pass, afore Isaiah was gone out into the middle court, that the word of the LORD came to him, saying,

5 Turn again, and tell Hezekiah the captain of my people, Thus saith the LORD, the God of David thy father, I have heard thy prayer, I have seen thy tears: behold, I will heal thee: on the third day thou shalt go up unto the house of the LORD.

6 And I will add unto thy days fifteen years; and I will deliver thee and this city out of the hand of the king of Assyria; and I will defend this city for mine own sake, and for my servant David's sake.

7 And Isaiah said, Take a lump of figs. And they took and laid *it* on the boil, and he recovered.

8 And Hezekiah said unto Isaiah, What *shall be* the sign that the LORD will heal me, and that I shall go up into the house of the LORD the third day?

9 And Isaiah said, This sign shalt thou have of the LORD, that the LORD will do the thing that he hath spoken: shall the shadow go forward ten degrees, or go back ten degrees?

10 And Hezekiah answered, It is a light thing for the shadow to go down ten degrees: nay, but let the shadow return backward ten degrees.

11 And Isaiah the prophet cried unto the LORD: and he brought the shadow ten degrees backward, by which it had gone down in the dial of Ahaz.

Hezekiah Boasts of His Wealth

12 At that time Berodach-baladan, the son of Baladan, king of Babylon, sent letters and a present unto Hezekiah: for he had heard that Hezekiah had been sick.

13 And Hezekiah hearkened unto them, and shewed them all the house of his precious things, the silver, and the gold, and the spices, and the precious ointment, and *all* the house of his armour, and all that was found in his treasures: there was nothing in his house, nor in all his dominion, that Hezekiah shewed them not.

14 Then came Isaiah the prophet unto king Hezekiah, and said unto him, What said these men? and from whence came they unto thee? And Hezekiah said, They are come from a far country, *even* from Babylon.

15 And he said, What have they seen in thine house? And Hezekiah answered, All *the things* that *are* in mine house have they seen: there is nothing among my treasures that I have not shewed them.

Cross references: **34** 1Kgs. 11:12, 13; 2Kgs. 20:6 · **35** 2Chr. 32:21; Isa. 37:36 · **36** Gen. 10:11 · **37** 2Kgs. 19:7; 2Chr. 32:21; Ezra 4:2 · **1** 2Chr. 32:24; Isa. 38:1-3 · **3** Gen. 17:1; 1Kgs. 3:6; Neh. 13:22 · **5** 1Sam. 9:16; 10:1; 2Kgs. 19:20; Ps. 39:12; 56:8; 65:2 · **6** 2Kgs. 19:34 · **7** Isa. 38:21 · **8** Judg. 6:17, 37, 39; Isa. 7:11, 14; 38:22 · **9** Isa. 38:7, 8 · **11** Josh. 10:12, 14; Isa. 38:8 · **12** Isa. 39:1 · **13** 2Chr. 32:27, 31 · **15** 2Kgs. 20:15

20:1–19 During a severe illness, God sent Isaiah to promise the king fifteen additional years of life (v. 6). During Hezekiah's extra years, he opened the treasures of the kingdom to men from Babylon. God warned him that the day would come when the people would "be carried into Babylon" (v. 17) including some of his sons that would one day be eunuchs in the palace of the king of Babylon. This tragic prophecy was literally fulfilled many years later (see Dan. 1:1–6).

16 And Isaiah said unto Hezekiah, Hear the word of the LORD.

17 Behold, the days come, that all that *is* in thine house, and that which thy fathers have laid up in store unto this day, shall be carried into Babylon: nothing shall be left, saith the LORD.

18 And of thy sons that shall issue from thee, which thou shalt beget, shall they take away; and they shall be eunuchs in the palace of the king of Babylon.

19 Then said Hezekiah unto Isaiah, Good *is* the word of the LORD which thou hast spoken. And he said, *Is it* not *good*, if peace and truth be in my days?

Hezekiah's Death

20 And the rest of the acts of Hezekiah, and all his might, and how he made a pool, and a conduit, and brought water into the city, *are* they not written in the book of the chronicles of the kings of Judah?

21 And Hezekiah slept with his fathers: and Manasseh his son reigned in his stead.

CHAPTER 21
Manasseh Rules Judah

1 Manasseh *was* twelve years old when he began to reign, and reigned fifty and five years in Jerusalem. And his mother's name *was* Hephzibah.

2 And he did *that which was* evil in the sight of the LORD, after the abominations of the heathen, whom the LORD cast out before the children of Israel.

3 For he built up again the high places which Hezekiah his father had destroyed; and he reared up altars for Baal, and made a grove, as did Ahab king of Israel; and worshipped all the host of heaven, and served them.

4 And he built altars in the house of the LORD, of which the LORD said, In Jerusalem will I put my name.

5 And he built altars for all the host of heaven in the two courts of the house of the LORD.

6 And he made his son pass through the fire, and observed times, and used enchantments, and dealt with familiar spirits and wizards: he wrought much wickedness in the sight of the LORD, to provoke *him* to anger.

7 And he set a graven image of the grove that he had made in the house, of which the LORD said to David, and to Solomon his son, In this house, and in Jerusalem, which I have chosen out of all tribes of Israel, will I put my name for ever:

8 Neither will I make the feet of Israel move any more out of the land which I gave their fathers; only if they will observe to do according to all that I have commanded them, and according to all the law that my servant Moses commanded them.

9 But they hearkened not: and Manasseh seduced them to do more evil than did the nations whom the LORD destroyed before the children of Israel.

10 And the LORD spake by his servants the prophets, saying,

11 Because Manasseh king of Judah hath done these abominations, *and* hath done wickedly above all that the Amorites did, which *were* before him, and hath made Judah also to sin with his idols:

12 Therefore thus saith the LORD God of Israel, Behold, I *am* bringing *such* evil upon Jerusalem and Judah, that whosoever heareth of it, both his ears shall tingle.

13 And I will stretch over Jerusalem the line of Samaria, and the plummet of the house of Ahab: and I will wipe Jerusalem as *a* man wipeth a dish, wiping *it*, and turning *it* upside down.

14 And I will forsake the remnant of mine inheritance, and deliver them into the hand of their enemies; and they shall become a prey and a spoil to all their enemies;

15 Because they have done *that which was* evil in my sight, and have provoked me to anger, since the day their fathers came forth out of Egypt, even unto this day.

16 Moreover Manasseh shed innocent blood very much, till he had filled Jerusalem from one end to another; beside his sin wherewith he made Judah to sin, in doing *that which was* evil in the sight of the LORD.

17 Now the rest of the acts of Manasseh, and all that he did, and his sin that he sinned, *are* they not written in the book of the chronicles of the kings of Judah?

18 And Manasseh slept with his fathers, and was buried in the garden of his own house, in the garden of Uzza: and Amon his son reigned in his stead.

Cross references (center column):

17 2Kgs. 24:13; 25:13; Jer. 27:21, 22; 52:17
18 2Kgs. 24:12; 2Chr. 33:11
19 1Sam. 3:18; Job 1:21; Ps. 39:9
20 2Chr. 32:30, 32; Neh. 3:16
21 2Chr. 32:33
1 2Chr. 33:1
2 2Kgs. 16:3
3 Deut. 4:19; 17:3; 1Kgs. 16:32, 33; 2Kgs. 17:16; 18:4
4 2Sam. 7:13; 1Kgs. 8:29; 9:3; Jer. 32:34
6 Lev. 18:21; 20:2; 19:26, 31; Deut. 18:10, 11; 2Kgs. 16:3; 17:17
7 2Sam. 7:13; 1Kgs. 8:29; 9:3; 2Kgs. 23:27; Ps. 132:13, 14; Jer. 32:34
8 2Sam. 7:10
9 Prov. 29:12
11 1Kgs. 21:26; 2Kgs. 21:9; 23:26, 27; 24:3, 4; Jer. 15:4
12 1Sam. 3:11; Jer. 19:3
13 Isa. 34:11; Lam. 2:8; Amos 7:7, 8
16 2Kgs. 24:4
17 2Chr. 33:11-19
18 2Chr. 33:20

21:10–16 Through His prophets, the Lord warned of the downfall of Manasseh for all his wickedness, because he led the children of Judah into sins that were worse than the sins of the Amorites. This prophecy was literally fulfilled in 2 Chronicles 33:10–11.

Amon Rules Judah

19 Amon *was* twenty and two years old when he began to reign, and he reigned two years in Jerusalem. And his mother's name *was* Meshullemeth, the daughter of Haruz of Jotbah.

20 And he did *that which was* evil in the sight of the LORD, as his father Manasseh did.

21 And he walked in all the way that his father walked in, and served the idols that his father served, and worshipped them:

22 And he forsook the LORD God of his fathers, and walked not in the way of the LORD.

23 And the servants of Amon conspired against him, and slew the king in his own house.

24 And the people of the land slew all them that had conspired against king Amon; and the people of the land made Josiah his son king in his stead.

25 Now the rest of the acts of Amon which he did, *are* they not written in the book of the chronicles of the kings of Judah?

26 And he was buried in his sepulchre in the garden of Uzza: and Josiah his son reigned in his stead.

CHAPTER 22
Josiah Rules Judah

1 Josiah *was* eight years old when he began to reign, and he reigned thirty and one years in Jerusalem. And his mother's name *was* Jedidah, the daughter of Adaiah of Boscath.

2 And he did *that which was* right in the sight of the LORD, and walked in all the way of David his father, and turned not aside to the right hand or to the left.

A Copy of the Law Is Found

3 And it came to pass in the eighteenth year of king Josiah, *that* the king sent Shaphan the son of Azaliah, the son of Meshullam, the scribe, to the house of the LORD, saying,

4 Go up to Hilkiah the high priest, that he may sum the silver which is brought into the house of the LORD, which the keepers of the door have gathered of the people:

5 And let them deliver it into the hand of the doers of the work, that have the oversight of the house of the LORD: and let them give it to the doers of the work which *is* in the house of the LORD, to repair the breaches of the house,

6 Unto carpenters, and builders, and masons, and to buy timber and hewn stone to repair the house.

7 Howbeit there was no reckoning made with them of the money that was delivered into their hand, because they dealt faithfully.

8 And Hilkiah the high priest said unto Shaphan the scribe, I have found the book of the law in the house of the LORD. And Hilkiah gave the book to Shaphan, and he read it.

9 And Shaphan the scribe came to the king, and brought the king word again, and said, Thy servants have gathered the money that was found in the house, and have delivered it into the hand of them that do the work, that have the oversight of the house of the LORD.

10 And Shaphan the scribe shewed the king, saying, Hilkiah the priest hath delivered me a book. And Shaphan read it before the king.

11 And it came to pass, when the king had heard the words of the book of the law, that he rent his clothes.

12 And the king commanded Hilkiah the priest, and Ahikam the son of Shaphan, and Achbor the son of Michaiah, and Shaphan the scribe, and Asahiah a servant of the king's, saying,

13 Go ye, inquire of the LORD for me, and for the people, and for all Judah, concerning the words of this book that is found: for great *is* the wrath of the LORD that is kindled against us, because our fathers have not hearkened unto the words of this book, to do according unto all that which is written concerning us.

14 So Hilkiah the priest, and Ahikam, and Achbor, and Shaphan, and Asahiah, went unto Huldah the prophetess, the wife of Shallum the son of Tikvah, the son of Harhas, keeper of the wardrobe; (now she dwelt in Jerusalem in the college;) and they communed with her.

15 And she said unto them, Thus saith the LORD God of Israel, Tell the man that sent you to me,

16 Thus saith the LORD, Behold, I will bring evil upon this place, and upon the inhabitants thereof, *even* all the words of the book which the king of Judah hath read:

17 Because they have forsaken me, and have burned incense unto other gods, that they might provoke me to anger with all the works of their hands; therefore my wrath shall be kindled against this place, and shall not be quenched.

---

19 2Chr. 33:21-23

20 2Kgs. 21:2-9

22 1Kgs. 11:33

23 2Chr. 33:24, 25

26 Matt. 1:10, called *Josias*

1 Josh. 15:39; 2Chr. 34:1

2 Deut. 5:32

3 2Chr. 34:8

4 2Kgs. 12:4, 9; Ps. 84:10

5 2Kgs. 12:11, 12, 14

7 2Kgs. 12:15

8 Deut. 31:24; 2Chr. 34:14

12 2Chr. 34:20, *Abdon*

13 Deut. 29:27

14 2Chr. 34:22, *Tikvath*

16 Deut. 29:27; Dan. 9:11-14

17 Deut. 29:25-27

18 But to the king of Judah which sent you to inquire of the LORD, thus shall ye say to him, Thus saith the LORD God of Israel, *As touching* the words which thou hast heard; **19** Because thine heart was tender, and thou hast humbled thyself before the LORD, when thou heardest what I spake against this place, and against the inhabitants thereof, that they should become a desolation and a curse, and hast rent thy clothes, and wept before me; I also have heard *thee*, saith the LORD. **20** Behold therefore, I will gather thee unto thy fathers, and thou shalt be gathered into thy grave in peace; and thine eyes shall not see all the evil which I will bring upon this place. And they brought the king word again.

CHAPTER 23
Josiah's Reforms

1 And the king sent, and they gathered unto him all the elders of Judah and of Jerusalem.
2 And the king went up into the house of the LORD, and all the men of Judah and all the inhabitants of Jerusalem with him, and the priests, and the prophets, and all the people, both small and great: and he read in their ears all the words of the book of the covenant which was found in the house of the LORD.
3 And the king stood by a pillar, and made a covenant before the LORD, to walk after the LORD, and to keep his commandments and his testimonies and his statutes with all *their* heart and all *their* soul, to perform the words of this covenant that were written in this book. And all the people stood to the covenant.
4 And the king commanded Hilkiah the high priest, and the priests of the second order, and the keepers of the door, to bring forth out of the temple of the LORD all the vessels that were made for Baal, and for the grove, and for all the host of heaven: and he burned them without Jerusalem in the fields of Kidron, and carried the ashes of them unto Beth-el.
5 And he put down the idolatrous priests, whom the kings of Judah had ordained to burn incense in the high places in the cities

of Judah, and in the places round about Jerusalem; them also that burned incense unto Baal, to the sun, and to the moon, and to the planets, and to all the host of heaven.
6 And he brought out the grove from the house of the LORD, without Jerusalem, unto the brook Kidron, and burned it at the brook Kidron, and stamped *it* small to powder, and cast the powder thereof upon the graves of the children of the people.
7 And he brake down the houses of the sodomites, that *were* by the house of the LORD, where the women wove hangings for the grove.
8 And he brought all the priests out of the cities of Judah, and defiled the high places where the priests had burned incense, from Geba to Beer-sheba, and brake down the high places of the gates that *were* in the entering in of the gate of Joshua the governor of the city, which *were* on a man's left hand at the gate of the city.
9 Nevertheless the priests of the high places came not up to the altar of the LORD in Jerusalem, but they did eat of the unleavened bread among their brethren.
10 And he defiled Topheth, which *is* in the valley of the children of Hinnom, that no man might make his son or his daughter to pass through the fire to Molech.
11 And he took away the horses that the kings of Judah had given to the sun, at the entering in of the house of the LORD, by the chamber of Nathan-melech the chamberlain, which *was* in the suburbs, and burned the chariots of the sun with fire.
12 And the altars that *were* on the top of the upper chamber of Ahaz, which the kings of Judah had made, and the altars which Manasseh had made in the two courts of the house of the LORD, did the king beat down, and brake *them* down from thence, and cast the dust of them into the brook Kidron.
13 And the high places that *were* before Jerusalem, which *were* on the right hand of the mount of corruption, which Solomon the king of Israel had builded for Ashtoreth the abomination of the Zidonians, and for Chemosh the abomination of the Moabites, and for Milcom the abomination of the children of Ammon, did the king defile.
14 And he brake in pieces the images, and

Cross-references (center column):

18 2Chr. 34:26
19 Lev. 26:31, 32; 1Kgs. 21:29; Ps. 51:17; Isa. 57:15; Jer. 26:6; 44:22
20 Ps. 37:37; Isa. 57:1, 2
1 2Chr. 34:29, 30
2 2Kgs. 22:8
3 2Kgs. 11:14, 17
4 2Kgs. 21:3, 7
5 2Kgs. 21:3
6 2Kgs. 21:7; 2Chr. 34:4
7 1Kgs. 14:24; 15:12; Ezek. 16:16
8 1Kgs. 15:22
9 1Sam. 2:36; Ezek. 44:10-14
10 Lev. 18:21; Deut. 18:10; Josh. 15:8; Isa. 30:33; Jer. 7:31; 19:6, 11-13; Ezek. 23:37, 39
12 2Kgs. 21:5; Jer. 19:13; Zeph. 1:5
13 1Kgs. 11:7
14 Ex. 23:24; Deut. 7:5, 25

22:20 Josiah, a godly king, tried to lead the people to repent and obey the Lord through his "reading of the law." Therefore, God prophesied that the destruction of Jerusalem would not take place on Josiah's watch. Second Kings 23:29–30 describes the death of Josiah while the rest of the book describes the long-predicted captivity of Judah and destruction of Jerusalem.

How We Got Our Bible

By James M. Kinnebrew

The Bible relates many instances where God revealed His Word and His will to man in an instant. As glorious and efficient as these revelations were in their situations, the Bible you hold in your hands came about through a slow, purposeful, and complex work of God Almighty.

As finite creatures in a perplexing world, we have an inherent need for a word from heaven. As a loving Father with infinite wisdom, God has met that need. He has done this, in part, through "general revelation." We can know all the broad truths of God's existence, power, benevolence, and wisdom when we take note of the universe around us (Ps. 19:1–6; Rom. 1:18–32). Likewise, we can discern His presence, holiness, and justice, as well as our own sinfulness, by our own conscience (Eccl. 3:11; Prov. 20:27; Rom. 2:14–16).

Unfortunately, our reasoning powers are not always suffi-
cient to interpret what we see in the world (Ps. 14:1; Isa. 55:8–9), and our consciences can be either too scrupulous (1 Cor. 8:7; Rom. 14:14–23) or too numb (Titus 1:15). In addition, neither creation nor conscience conveys the truth that we need for our eternal salvation. That revelation is found in the inspired Scripture text of the Bible.

> *The protecting hand of God has preserved His Word through the ages.*

The early Christians recognized the sixty-six books of the Bible as inspired Scripture. They recognized these books as Scripture; however, they did not make them such. The Bible is the only collection of writings universally discerned to bear the marks of God's Word. We call the entire collection of books the "canon" (Gr. *kanon*, "measuring rod"). They alone are the rule, the measure of correct belief and action.

Jesus gave unreserved sanction to the divine authority of the Scriptures of His day (Matt. 4:4; 5:17–18; Luke 24:25–27, 44; John 10:35). Those Scriptures included only the thirty-nine books of our Old Testament (see the article entitled "The Apocryphal Literature" by Mal Couch).

The New Testament canon likewise rests on the authority of Christ Himself. In John 14:25–26; 16:12–13, Jesus appointed the apostles as His duly authenticated messengers and promised that the Holy Spirit would remind them of His teachings (the Gospels), lead them into all truth (Acts and the Epistles), and teach them things to come (Revelation). They, in a unique sense, were Christ's ambassadors (2 Cor. 5:20). Of them He said, "he that hears you hears me" (Luke 10:16). Only those books that are authentically apostolic (not forgeries as referred to in 2 Thess. 2:2) or have apostolic sanction (like Mark and Luke) can stand up under scrutiny as the very Word of God. So these sixty-six books (39 in the Old Testament and 27 in the New Testament) comprise the written Word of God.

When we think of how we got our Bible, we recognize the protecting hand of God in preserving His Word through the ages. The Bible has endured the opposition of pagan emperors, godless critics, and even misguided religionists. It has been banned, burned, slandered, and ridiculed—all to no avail. Its survival through unparalleled persecution has been the source of universal amazement. The copy you hold in your hands right now is a testimony to what God will do to get His Word to mankind, to draw them into a saving, eternal relationship with Himself.

cut down the groves, and filled their places with the bones of men.

15 Moreover the altar that *was* at Beth-el, *and* the high place which Jeroboam the son of Nebat, who made Israel to sin, had made, both that altar and the high place he brake down, and burned the high place, *and* stamped *it* small to powder, and burned the grove.

16 And as Josiah turned himself, he spied the sepulchres that *were* there in the mount, and sent, and took the bones out of the sepulchres, and burned *them* upon the altar, and polluted it, according to the word of the LORD which the man of God proclaimed, who proclaimed these words.

17 Then he said, What title *is* that that I see? And the men of the city told him, *It is* the sepulchre of the man of God, which came from Judah, and proclaimed these things that thou hast done against the altar of Beth-el.

18 And he said, Let him alone; let no man move his bones. So they let his bones alone, with the bones of the prophet that came out of Samaria.

19 And all the houses also of the high places that *were* in the cities of Samaria, which the kings of Israel had made to provoke *the* LORD to anger, Josiah took away, and did to them according to all the acts that he had done in Beth-el.

20 And he slew all the priests of the high places that *were* there upon the altars, and burned men's bones upon them, and returned to Jerusalem.

21 And the king commanded all the people, saying, Keep the passover unto the LORD your God, as *it is* written in the book of this covenant.

22 Surely there was not holden such a passover from the days of the judges that judged Israel, nor in all the days of the kings of Israel, nor of the kings of Judah;

23 But in the eighteenth year of king Josiah, *wherein* this passover was holden to the LORD in Jerusalem.

24 Moreover the *workers with* familiar spirits, and the wizards, and the images, and the idols, and all the abominations that were spied in the land of Judah and in Jerusalem, did Josiah put away, that he might perform the words of the law which were written in the book that Hilkiah the priest found in the house of the LORD.

25 And like unto him was there no king before him, that turned to the LORD with all his heart, and with all his soul, and with all

his might, according to all the law of Moses; neither after him arose there *any* like him.

26 Notwithstanding the LORD turned not from the fierceness of his great wrath, wherewith his anger was kindled against Judah, because of all the provocations that Manasseh had provoked him withal.

27 And the LORD said, I will remove Judah also out of my sight, as I have removed Israel, and will cast off this city Jerusalem which I have chosen, and the house of which I said, My name shall be there.

Josiah's Death

28 Now the rest of the acts of Josiah, and all that he did, *are* they not written in the book of the chronicles of the kings of Judah?

29 In his days Pharaoh-nechoh king of Egypt went up against the king of Assyria to the river Euphrates: and king Josiah went against him; and he slew him at Megiddo, when he had seen him.

30 And his servants carried him in a chariot dead from Megiddo, and brought him to Jerusalem, and buried him in his own sepulchre. And the people of the land took Jehoahaz the son of Josiah, and anointed him, and made him king in his father's stead.

Jehoahaz Rules Judah

31 Jehoahaz *was* twenty and three years old when he began to reign; and he reigned three months in Jerusalem. And his mother's name *was* Hamutal, the daughter of Jeremiah of Libnah.

32 And he did *that which was* evil in the sight of the LORD, according to all that his fathers had done.

33 And Pharaoh-nechoh put him in bands at Riblah in the land of Hamath, that he might not reign in Jerusalem; and put the land to a tribute of an hundred talents of silver, and a talent of gold.

34 And Pharaoh-nechoh made Eliakim the son of Josiah king in the room of Josiah his father, and turned his name to Jehoiakim, and took Jehoahaz away: and he came to Egypt, and died there.

Jehoiakim Rules Judah

35 And Jehoiakim gave the silver and the gold to Pharaoh; but he taxed the land to give the money according to the commandment of Pharaoh: he exacted the silver and the gold of the people of the land, of every one according to his taxation, to give *it* unto Pharaoh-nechoh.

Cross references (center column):

15 1Kgs. 12:28, 33
16 1Kgs. 13:2
17 1Kgs. 13:1, 30
18 1Kgs. 13:31
19 2Chr. 34:6, 7
20 Ex. 22:20; 1Kgs. 13:2; 18:40; 2Kgs. 11:18; 2Chr. 34:5
21 Ex. 12:3; Lev. 23:5; Num. 9:2; Deut. 16:2; 2Chr. 35:1
22 2Chr. 35:18, 19
24 Gen. 31:19; Lev. 19:31; Deut. 18:11; 2Kgs. 21:6
25 2Kgs. 18:5
26 2Kgs. 21:11, 12; 24:3, 4; Jer. 15:4
27 1Kgs. 8:29; 9:3; 2Kgs. 17:18, 20; 18:11; 21:4, 7, 13
29 2Kgs. 14:8; 2Chr. 35:20; Zech. 12:11
30 2Chr. 35:24; 36:1
31 2Kgs. 24:18; 1Chr. 3:15; Jer. 22:11
33 2Kgs. 25:6; Jer. 52:27
34 2Kgs. 24:17; 2Chr. 36:4; Jer. 22:11, 12; Ezek. 19:3, 4; Dan. 1:7; Matt. 1:11, called *Jakim*
35 2Kgs. 23:33

36 Jehoiakim *was* twenty and five years old when he began to reign; and he reigned eleven years in Jerusalem. And his mother's name *was* Zebudah, the daughter of Pedaiah of Rumah.

37 And he did *that which was* evil in the sight of the LORD, according to all that his fathers had done.

CHAPTER 24

1 In his days Nebuchadnezzar king of Babylon came up, and Jehoiakim became his servant three years: then he turned and rebelled against him.

2 And the LORD sent against him bands of the Chaldees, and bands of the Syrians, and bands of the Moabites, and bands of the children of Ammon, and sent them against Judah to destroy it, according to the word of the LORD, which he spake by his servants the prophets.

3 Surely at the commandment of the LORD came *this* upon Judah, to remove *them* out of his sight, for the sins of Manasseh, according to all that he did;

4 And also for the innocent blood that he shed: for he filled Jerusalem with innocent blood; which the LORD would not pardon.

5 Now the rest of the acts of Jehoiakim, and all that he did, *are* they not written in the book of the chronicles of the kings of Judah?

6 So Jehoiakim slept with his fathers: and Jehoiachin his son reigned in his stead.

7 And the king of Egypt came not again any more out of his land: for the king of Babylon had taken from the river of Egypt unto the river Euphrates all that pertained to the king of Egypt.

Jehoiachin Rules Judah

8 Jehoiachin *was* eighteen years old when he began to reign, and he reigned in Jerusalem three months. And his mother's name *was* Nehushta, the daughter of Elnathan of Jerusalem.

9 And he did *that which was* evil in the sight of the LORD, according to all that his father had done.

10 At that time the servants of Nebuchadnezzar king of Babylon came up against Jerusalem, and the city was besieged.

11 And Nebuchadnezzar king of Babylon came against the city, and his servants did besiege it.

12 And Jehoiachin the king of Judah went out to the king of Babylon, he, and his mother, and his servants, and his princes,

and his officers: and the king of Babylon took him in the eighth year of his reign.

13 And he carried out thence all the treasures of the house of the LORD, and the treasures of the king's house, and cut in pieces all the vessels of gold which Solomon king of Israel had made in the temple of the LORD, as the LORD had said.

14 And he carried away all Jerusalem, and all the princes, and all the mighty men of valour, *even* ten thousand captives, and all the craftsmen and smiths: none remained, save the poorest sort of the people of the land.

15 And he carried away Jehoiachin to Babylon, and the king's mother, and the king's wives, and his officers, and the mighty of the land, *those* carried he into captivity from Jerusalem to Babylon.

16 And all the men of might, *even* seven thousand, and craftsmen and smiths a thousand, all *that were* strong *and* apt for war, even them the king of Babylon brought captive to Babylon.

17 And the king of Babylon made Mattaniah his father's brother king in his stead, and changed his name to Zedekiah.

Zedekiah Rules Judah

18 Zedekiah *was* twenty and one years old when he began to reign, and he reigned eleven years in Jerusalem. And his mother's name *was* Hamutal, the daughter of Jeremiah of Libnah.

19 And he did *that which was* evil in the sight of the LORD, according to all that Jehoiakim had done.

20 For through the anger of the LORD it came to pass in Jerusalem and Judah, until he had cast them out from his presence, that Zedekiah rebelled against the king of Babylon.

CHAPTER 25

Jerusalem Falls

1 And it came to pass in the ninth year of his reign, in the tenth month, in the tenth *day* of the month, *that* Nebuchadnezzar king of Babylon came, he, and all his host, against Jerusalem, and pitched against it; and they built forts against it round about.

2 And the city was besieged unto the eleventh year of king Zedekiah.

3 And on the ninth *day* of the *fourth* month the famine prevailed in the city, and there was no bread for the people of the land.

4 And the city was broken up, and all the men of war *fled* by night by the way of the

Cross references

36 2Chr. 36:5

1 2Chr. 36:6; Jer. 25:1, 9; Dan. 1:1

2 2Kgs. 20:17; 21:12-14; 23:27; Jer. 25:9; 32:28; Ezek. 19:8

3 2Kgs. 21:2, 11; 23:26

4 2Kgs. 21:16

6 2Chr. 36:6, 8; Jer. 22:18, 19; 36:30

7 Jer. 37:5, 7; 46:2

8 2Chr. 36:9; Jer. 22:24, 28; 24:1

10 Dan. 1:1

12 Jer. 24:1; 25:1; 29:1, 2; 52:28; Ezek. 17:12; 2Kgs. 25:27

13 2Kgs. 20:17; Isa. 39:6; Jer. 20:5; Dan. 5:2, 3

14 1Sam. 13:19, 22; 2Kgs. 25:12; Jer. 24:1; 40:7; 52:28

15 2Chr. 36:10; Esth. 2:6; Jer. 22:24

16 Jer. 52:28

17 2Kgs. 23:34; 1Chr. 3:15; 2Chr. 36:4, 10; Jer. 37:1

18 2Kgs. 23:31; 2Chr. 36:11; Jer. 37:1; 52:1

19 2Chr. 36:12

20 2Chr. 36:13; Ezek. 17:15

1 2Chr. 36:17; Jer. 34:2; 39:1; 52:4, 5; Ezek. 24:1

3 Jer. 39:2; 52:6

4 Jer. 39:2, 4-7; 52:7; Ezek. 12:12

gate between two walls, which *is* by the king's garden: (now the Chaldees *were* against the city round about:) and *the king* went the way toward the plain.

5 And the army of the Chaldees pursued after the king, and overtook him in the plains of Jericho: and all his army were scattered from him.

6 So they took the king, and brought him up to the king of Babylon to Riblah; and they gave judgment upon him.

7 And they slew the sons of Zedekiah before his eyes, and put out the eyes of Zedekiah, and bound him with fetters of brass, and carried him to Babylon.

8 And in the fifth month, on the seventh *day* of the month, which *is* the nineteenth year of king Nebuchadnezzar king of Babylon, came Nebuzaradan, captain of the guard, a servant of the king of Babylon, unto Jerusalem:

9 And he burnt the house of the Lord, and the king's house, and all the houses of Jerusalem, and every great *man's* house burnt he with fire.

10 And all the army of the Chaldees, that *were with* the captain of the guard, brake down the walls of Jerusalem round about.

11 Now the rest of the people *that were* left in the city, and the fugitives that fell away to the king of Babylon, with the remnant of the multitude, did Nebuzaradan the captain of the guard carry away.

12 But the captain of the guard left of the poor of the land *to be* vinedressers and husbandmen.

13 And the pillars of brass that *were* in the house of the Lord, and the bases, and the brasen sea that *was* in the house of the Lord, did the Chaldees break in pieces, and carried the brass of them to Babylon.

14 And the pots, and the shovels, and the snuffers, and the spoons, and all the vessels of brass wherewith they ministered, took they away.

15 And the firepans, and the bowls, *and* such things as *were* of gold, *in* gold, and of silver, *in* silver, the captain of the guard took away.

16 The two pillars, one sea, and the bases which Solomon had made for the house of the Lord; the brass of all these vessels was without weight.

17 The height of the one pillar *was* eighteen cubits, and the chapiter upon it *was* brass: and the height of the chapiter three cubits; and the wreathen work, and pomegranates upon the chapiter round about, all of brass:

and like unto these had the second pillar with wreathen work.

18 And the captain of the guard took Seraiah the chief priest, and Zephaniah the second priest, and the three keepers of the door:

19 And out of the city he took an officer that was set over the men of war, and five men of them that were in the king's presence, which were found in the city, and the principal scribe of the host, which mustered the people of the land, and threescore men of the people of the land *that were* found in the city:

20 And Nebuzaradan captain of the guard took these, and brought them to the king of Babylon to Riblah:

21 And the king of Babylon smote them, and slew them at Riblah in the land of Hamath. So Judah was carried away out of their land.

Gedaliah Becomes Governor of Judah

22 And *as for* the people that remained in the land of Judah, whom Nebuchadnezzar king of Babylon had left, even over them he made Gedaliah the son of Ahikam, the son of Shaphan, ruler.

23 And when all the captains of the armies, they and their men, heard that the king of Babylon had made Gedaliah governor, there came to Gedaliah to Mizpah, even Ishmael the son of Nethaniah, and Johanan the son of Careah, and Seraiah the son of Tanhumeth the Netophathite, and Jaazaniah the son of a Maachathite, they and their men.

24 And Gedaliah sware to them, and to their men, and said unto them, Fear not to be the servants of the Chaldees: dwell in the land, and serve the king of Babylon; and it shall be well with you.

25 But it came to pass in the seventh month, that Ishmael the son of Nethaniah, the son of Elishama, of the seed royal, came, and ten men with him, and smote Gedaliah, that he died, and the Jews and the Chaldees that were with him at Mizpah.

26 And all the people, both small and great, and the captains of the armies, arose, and came to Egypt: for they were afraid of the Chaldees.

Jehoiachin Is Restored to Honor

27 And it came to pass in the seven and thirtieth year of the captivity of Jehoiachin king of Judah, in the twelfth month, on the seven and twentieth *day* of the month, *that*

Cross references

6 2Kgs. 23:33; Jer. 52:9

7 Jer. 39:7; Ezek. 12:13

8 2Kgs. 24:12; 25:27; Jer. 39:9; 52:12-14

9 2Chr. 36:19; Ps. 79:1; Jer. 39:8; Amos 2:5

10 Neh. 1:3; Jer. 52:14

11 Jer. 39:9; 52:15

12 2Kgs. 24:14; Jer. 39:10; 40:7; 52:16

13 1Kgs. 7:15, 23, 27; 2Kgs. 20:17; Jer. 27:19, 22; 52:17-23

14 Ex. 27:3; 1Kgs. 7:45, 50

16 1Kgs. 7:47

17 1Kgs. 7:15; Jer. 52:21

18 1Chr. 6:14; Ezra 7:1; 21:1; 29:25; 52:24

19 Jer. 52:25

21 Lev. 26:33; Deut. 28:36, 64; 2Kgs. 23:27

22 Jer. 40:5

23 Jer. 40:7-9

25 Jer. 41:1, 2

26 Jer. 43:4, 7

27 Gen. 40:13, 20; Jer. 52:31

Evilmerodach king of Babylon in the year that he began to reign did lift up the head of Jehoiachin king of Judah out of prison;

28 And he spake kindly to him, and set his throne above the throne of the kings that *were* with him in Babylon;

29 2Sam. 9:7

29 And changed his prison garments: and he did eat bread continually before him all the days of his life.

30 And his allowance *was* a continual allowance given him of the king, a daily rate for every day, all the days of his life.

1 Chronicles

O riginally 1 and 2 Chronicles were one book, appearing in the closing section of the Hebrew Bible known as "the Writings." Following the genealogies, most of 1 Chronicles is a detailed description of King David's reign.

According to tradition, the books of 1 and 2 Chronicles were written by Ezra the scribe near the end of the Exile period. This is supported by the fact that Ezra's purpose in coming to Jerusalem was to teach the people about God's laws (Ezra 7:10, 25), and by the emphasis of this book on the history of Jewish worship. Furthermore, the style of the book of Ezra is quite similar.

Author
Possibly Ezra

Date
5th Century B.C.

Key Truth
History of God's People

Historic Time
United Kingdom

Key Verse
9:1
So all Israel were reckoned by genealogies. . . .

The Chronicles are more than a supplement to Samuel and Kings, since they view the same events differently. First and Second Chronicles reflect more of a providential standpoint; while 1 and 2 Samuel and 1 and 2 Kings present more of a historical perspective. In Kings, the throne, the palace, and political history are prominent. In Chronicles, the altar, the temple, and spiritual history are emphasized, while the sins of David and Solomon are not mentioned. From the beginning, the writer is concerned with magnifying God and giving Him His rightful place as sovereign Lord over all.

First Chronicles contains the most extensive genealogical lists in the Bible. After the genealogies is a brief account of the death of Saul. Then David's forty-year administration is detailed followed by Solomon's ascension to the throne. The Kingdom of Israel receives scant attention. The main focus is on Judah, the rise and fall of David's monarchy, the temple of Solomon and its worship, and the priests and Levites who served the temple.

No future prophecies appear in the book, although there are twenty-four instances of fulfilled events or conditional prophecies and predictive types. That Israel would endure forever (17:11–15) culminates in the reign of Jesus, King of Kings and "Son of David."

One hundred thirty-two verses have typical or predictive elements, which amounts to 14 percent of the total 942 verses.

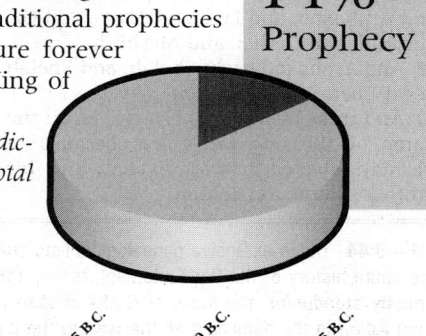

14%
Prophecy

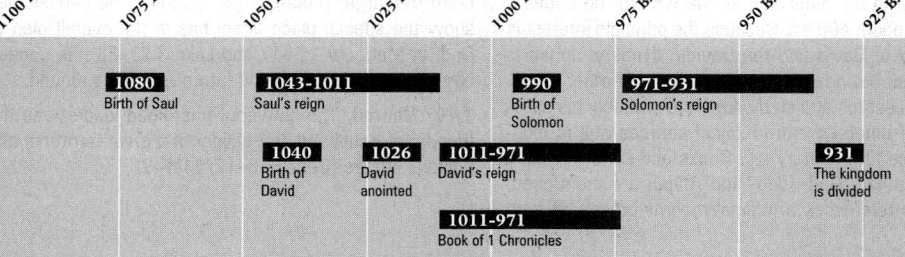

1100 B.C.	1075 B.C.	1050 B.C.	1025 B.C.	1000 B.C.	975 B.C.	950 B.C.	925 B.C.	900 B.C.

1080 Birth of Saul

1043-1011 Saul's reign

990 Birth of Solomon

971-931 Solomon's reign

1040 Birth of David

1026 David anointed

1011-971 David's reign

931 The kingdom is divided

1011-971 Book of 1 Chronicles

CHAPTER 1
Family Records from Adam to Abraham

1 Adam, Sheth, Enosh,
2 Kenan, Mahalaleel, Jered,
3 Henoch, Methuselah, Lamech,
4 Noah, Shem, Ham, and Japheth.
5 The sons of Japheth; Gomer, and Magog, and Madai, and Javan, and Tubal, and Meshech, and Tiras.
6 And the sons of Gomer; Ashchenaz, and Riphath, and Togarmah.
7 And the sons of Javan; Elishah, and Tarshish, Kittim, and Dodanim.
8 The sons of Ham; Cush, and Mizraim, Put, and Canaan.
9 And the sons of Cush; Seba, and Havilah, and Sabta, and Raamah, and Sabtecha. And the sons of Raamah; Sheba, and Dedan.
10 And Cush begat Nimrod: he began to be mighty upon the earth.
11 And Mizraim begat Ludim, and Anamim, and Lehabim, and Naphtuhim,
12 And Pathrusim, and Casluhim, (of whom came the Philistines,) and Caphthorim.
13 And Canaan begat Zidon his firstborn, and Heth,
14 The Jebusite also, and the Amorite, and the Girgashite,
15 And the Hivite, and the Arkite, and the Sinite,
16 And the Arvadite, and the Zemarite, and the Hamathite.
17 The sons of Shem; Elam, and Asshur, and Arphaxad, and Lud, and Aram, and Uz, and Hul, and Gether, and Meshech.
18 And Arphaxad begat Shelah, and Shelah begat Eber.
19 And unto Eber were born two sons: the name of the one *was* Peleg; because in his days the earth was divided: and his brother's name *was* Joktan.
20 And Joktan begat Almodad, and Sheleph, and Hazarmaveth, and Jerah,
21 Hadoram also, and Uzal, and Diklah,
22 And Ebal, and Abimael, and Sheba,
23 And Ophir, and Havilah, and Jobab. All these *were* the sons of Joktan.
24 Shem, Arphaxad, Shelah,
25 Eber, Peleg, Reu,
26 Serug, Nahor, Terah,
27 Abram; the same *is* Abraham.

Ishmael's and Keturah's Family Records

28 The sons of Abraham; Isaac, and Ishmael.
29 These *are* their generations: The firstborn of Ishmael, Nebaioth; then Kedar, and Adbeel, and Mibsam,
30 Mishma, and Dumah, Massa, Hadad, and Tema,
31 Jetur, Naphish, and Kedemah. These are the sons of Ishmael.
32 Now the sons of Keturah, Abraham's concubine: she bare Zimran, and Jokshan, and Medan, and Midian, and Ishbak, and Shuah. And the sons of Jokshan; Sheba, and Dedan.
33 And the sons of Midian; Ephah, and Epher, and Henoch, and Abida, and Eldaah. All these *are* the sons of Keturah.

Esau's Family Record

34 And Abraham begat Isaac. The sons of Isaac; Esau and Israel.
35 The sons of Esau; Eliphaz, Reuel, and Jeush, and Jaalam, and Korah.
36 The sons of Eliphaz; Teman, and Omar, Zephi, and Gatam, Kenaz, and Timna, and Amalek.
37 The sons of Reuel; Nahath, Zerah, Shammah, and Mizzah.
38 And the sons of Seir; Lotan, and Shobal, and Zibeon, and Anah, and Dishon, and Ezer, and Dishan.

Cross references:
1 Gen. 4:25, 26; 5:3, 9
5 Gen. 10:2
8 Gen. 10:6
10 Gen. 10:8, 13
12 Deut. 2:23
13 Gen. 10:15
17 Gen. 10:22, 23; 11:10
19 Gen. 10:25
20 Gen. 10:26
24 Gen. 11:10; Luke 3:34
25 Gen. 11:15
27 Gen. 17:5
28 Gen. 16:11, 15; 21:2, 3
29 Gen. 25:13-16
30 Gen. 25:15
32 Gen. 25:1, 2
34 Gen. 21:2, 3; 25:25, 26
35 Gen. 36:9, 10, 11
38 Gen. 36:20

1:1—9:44 These extensive genealogical lists chronicle the entire history of the Old Testament, telling, from the priestly standpoint, the story of God's chosen people from Adam in the beginning all the way to the author's own time, about 400 B.C. Because the principle interest is the history of David and the Davidic dynasty, Judah is emphasized, but not to the exclusion of the other tribes. Involving research and study, Ezra and probably his associates cite nineteen extra-biblical sources still in existence in the fifth century B.C. Books and annals of such men as Nathan, Gad, Iddo, and Ahijah are mentioned, along with references to official records preserved from the days of Israel's and Judah's kings. However, the inspired Old Testament writings from Genesis to the last Old Testament prophets constituted the main source. From the larger prophetic perspective, the genealogies show the special place Israel has in the overall plan of God. In Matthew 1:1–17 and Luke 3:23–38, the genealogy of Israel's Messiah and future King is continued.

1:10 Nimrod. This powerful post-flood leader was the founder of Babel and first builder of a great territorial and political empire (Gen. 10:8–12; 11:1–9).

39 And the sons of Lotan; Hori, and Homam: and Timna *was* Lotan's sister.
40 The sons of Shobal; Alian, and Manahath, and Ebal, Shephi, and Onam. And the sons of Zibeon; Aiah, and Anah.
41 The sons of Anah; Dishon. And the sons of Dishon; Amram, and Esh-ban, and Ithran, and Cheran.
42 The sons of Ezer; Bilhan, and Zavan, *and* Jakan. The sons of Dishan; Uz, and Aran.
43 Now these *are* the kings that reigned in the land of Edom before *any* king reigned over the children of Israel; Bela the son of Beor: and the name of his city *was* Dinhabah.
44 And when Bela was dead, Jobab the son of Zerah of Bozrah reigned in his stead.
45 And when Jobab was dead, Husham of the land of the Temanites reigned in his stead.
46 And when Husham was dead, Hadad the son of Bedad, which smote Midian in the field of Moab, reigned in his stead: and the name of his city *was* Avith.
47 And when Hadad was dead, Samlah of Masrekah reigned in his stead.
48 And when Samlah was dead, Shaul of Rehoboth by the river reigned in his stead.
49 And when Shaul was dead, Baal-hanan the son of Achbor reigned in his stead.
50 And when Baal-hanan was dead, Hadad reigned in his stead: and the name of his city *was* Pai; and his wife's name *was* Mehetabel, the daughter of Matred, the daughter of Mezahab.
51 Hadad died also. And the dukes of Edom were; duke Timnah, duke Aliah, duke Jetheth,
52 Duke Aholibamah, duke Elah, duke Pinon,
53 Duke Kenaz, duke Teman, duke Mibzar,
54 Duke Magdiel, duke Iram. These *are* the dukes of Edom.

CHAPTER 2
Israel's Sons

1 These *are* the sons of Israel; Reuben, Simeon, Levi, and Judah, Issachar, and Zebulun,
2 Dan, Joseph, and Benjamin, Naphtali, Gad, and Asher.

Judah's Family Record

3 The sons of Judah; Er, and Onan, and Shelah: *which* three were born unto him of the daughter of Shua the Canaanitess. And Er, the firstborn of Judah, was evil in the sight of the LORD; and he slew him.
4 And Tamar his daughter in law bare him Pharez and Zerah. All the sons of Judah *were* five.
5 The sons of Pharez; Hezron, and Hamul.
6 And the sons of Zerah; Zimri, and Ethan, and Heman, and Calcol, and Dara: five of them in all.
7 And the sons of Carmi; Achar, the troubler of Israel, who transgressed in the thing accursed.
8 And the sons of Ethan; Azariah.
9 The sons also of Hezron, that were born unto him; Jerahmeel, and Ram, and Chelubai.
10 And Ram begat Amminadab; and Amminadab begat Nahshon, prince of the children of Judah;
11 And Nahshon begat Salma, and Salma begat Boaz,
12 And Boaz begat Obed, and Obed begat Jesse,
13 And Jesse begat his firstborn Eliab, and Abinadab the second, and Shimma the third,
14 Nethaneel the fourth, Raddai the fifth,
15 Ozem the sixth, David the seventh:
16 Whose sisters *were* Zeruiah, and Abigail. And the sons of Zeruiah; Abishai, and Joab, and Asahel, three.
17 And Abigail bare Amasa: and the father of Amasa *was* Jether the Ishmeelite.
18 And Caleb the son of Hezron begat *children* of Azubah *his* wife, and of Jerioth: her sons *are* these; Jesher, and Shobab, and Ardon.
19 And when Azubah was dead, Caleb took unto him Ephrath, which bare him Hur.
20 And Hur begat Uri, and Uri begat Bezaleel.
21 And afterward Hezron went in to the daughter of Machir the father of Gilead, whom he married when he *was* threescore years old; and she bare him Segub.
22 And Segub begat Jair, who had three and twenty cities in the land of Gilead.

39 Gen. 36:22
40 Gen. 36:23
41 Gen. 36:25, 26
42 Gen. 36:27
43 Gen. 36:31
48 Gen. 36:37
50 Gen. 36:39
51 Gen. 29:32; 30:5; 35:18, 22; 36:40; 46:8
3 Gen. 38:2, 3, 7; 46:12; Num. 26:19
4 Gen. 38:29, 30; Matt. 1:3
5 Gen. 46:12; Ruth 4:18
6 Josh. 7:1; 1Kgs. 4:31
7 Josh. 6:18; 7:1; 2Chr. 4:1
9 1Chr. 2:38, 42; Matt. 1:3, 4
10 Num. 1:7; 2:3; Ruth 4:19, 20; Matt. 1:4
11 Ruth 4:21; Matt. 1:4
13 1Sam. 16:6, 9
16 2Sam. 2:18
17 2Sam. 17:25
19 1Chr. 2:50
20 Ex. 31:2
21 Num. 27:1

2:15 David the seventh. Actually, David was the eighth son of Jesse (1 Sam. 16:10; 17:12). Apparently one son died without descendants, and so was omitted from the genealogy.

2:3–15 Judah . . . David. The divinely planned lineage of the messianic line is recorded from Israel's time to David's era, a period of over eight centuries.

23 And he took Geshur, and Aram, with the towns of Jair, from them, with Kenath, and the towns thereof, *even* threescore cities. All these *belonged to* the sons of Machir the father of Gilead.

24 And after that Hezron was dead in Caleb-ephratah, then Abiah Hezron's wife bare him Ashur the father of Tekoa.

25 And the sons of Jerahmeel the firstborn of Hezron were, Ram the firstborn, and Bunah, and Oren, and Ozem, *and* Ahijah.

26 Jerahmeel had also another wife, whose name *was* Atarah; she *was* the mother of Onam.

27 And the sons of Ram the firstborn of Jerahmeel were, Maaz, and Jamin, and Eker.

28 And the sons of Onam were, Shammai, and Jada. And the sons of Shammai; Nadab, and Abishur.

29 And the name of the wife of Abishur *was* Abihail, and she bare him Ahban, and Molid.

30 And the sons of Nadab; Seled, and Appaim: but Seled died without children.

31 And the sons of Appaim; Ishi. And the sons of Ishi; Sheshan. And the children of Sheshan; Ahlai.

32 And the sons of Jada the brother of Shammai; Jether, and Jonathan: and Jether died without children.

33 And the sons of Jonathan; Peleth, and Zaza. These were the sons of Jerahmeel.

34 Now Sheshan had no sons, but daughters. And Sheshan had a servant, an Egyptian, whose name *was* Jarha.

35 And Sheshan gave his daughter to Jarha his servant to wife; and she bare him Attai.

36 And Attai begat Nathan, and Nathan begat Zabad,

37 And Zabad begat Ephlal, and Ephlal begat Obed,

38 And Obed begat Jehu, and Jehu begat Azariah,

39 And Azariah begat Helez, and Helez begat Eleasah,

40 And Eleasah begat Sisamai, and Sisamai begat Shallum,

41 And Shallum begat Jekamiah, and Jekamiah begat Elishama.

42 Now the sons of Caleb the brother of Jerahmeel *were*, Mesha his firstborn, which was the father of Ziph; and the sons of Mareshah the father of Hebron.

43 And the sons of Hebron; Korah, and Tappuah, and Rekem, and Shema.

44 And Shema begat Raham, the father of Jorkoam: and Rekem begat Shammai.

45 And the son of Shammai *was* Maon: and Maon *was* the father of Beth-zur.

46 And Ephah, Caleb's concubine, bare Haran, and Moza, and Gazez: and Haran begat Gazez.

47 And the sons of Jahdai; Regem, and Jotham, and Geshan, and Pelet, and Ephah, and Shaaph.

48 Maachah, Caleb's concubine, bare Sheber, and Tirhanah.

49 She bare also Shaaph the father of Madmannah, Sheva the father of Machbenah, and the father of Gibea: and the daughter of Caleb *was* Achsah.

50 These were the sons of Caleb the son of Hur, the firstborn of Ephratah; Shobal the father of Kirjath-jearim,

51 Salma the father of Beth-lehem, Hareph the father of Beth-gader.

52 And Shobal the father of Kirjath-jearim had sons; Haroeh, *and* half of the Manahethites.

53 And the families of Kirjath-jearim; the Ithrites, and the Puhites, and the Shumathites, and the Mishraites; of them came the Zareathites, and the Eshtaulites.

54 The sons of Salma; Beth-lehem, and the Netophathites, Ataroth the house of Joab, and half of the Manahethites, the Zorites.

55 And the families of the scribes which dwelt at Jabez; the Tirathites, the Shimeathites, *and* Suchathites. These *are* the Kenites that came of Hemath, the father of the house of Rechab.

CHAPTER 3
David's Sons

1 Now these were the sons of David, which were born unto him in Hebron; the firstborn Amnon, of Ahinoam the Jezreelitess; the second Daniel, of Abigail the Carmelitess:

2 The third, Absalom the son of Maachah the daughter of Talmai king of Geshur: the fourth, Adonijah the son of Haggith:

3 The fifth, Shephatiah of Abital: the sixth, Ithream by Eglah his wife.

4 *These* six were born unto him in Hebron; and there he reigned seven years and six

Cross references (center column):

23 Num. 32:41; Deut. 3:14; Josh. 13:30
24 1Chr. 4:5
31 1Chr. 2:34, 35
36 1Chr. 11:41
49 Josh. 15:17
50 1Chr. 2:19
52 1Chr. 4:2
55 Judg. 1:16; Jer. 35:2
1 Josh. 15:56; 2Sam. 3:2, 3
3 2Sam. 3:5
4 2Sam. 2:11; 5:5

3:1–24 The royal genealogy continues from David through all the kings of Judah, beyond the seventy-year captivity (606–536 B.C.) to Zerubbabel, the head of the house of David at the time (Ezra 2:1–2), and through five more generations to about 425 B.C.

months: and in Jerusalem he reigned thirty and three years.

5 And these were born unto him in Jerusalem; Shimea, and Shobab, and Nathan, and Solomon, four, of Bath-shua the daughter of Ammiel:

6 Ibhar also, and Elishama, and Eliphelet,

7 And Nogah, and Nepheg, and Japhia,

8 And Elishama, and Eliada, and Eliphelet, nine.

9 *These were* all the sons of David, beside the sons of the concubines, and Tamar their sister.

Solomon's Family Record

10 And Solomon's son *was* Rehoboam, Abia his son, Asa his son, Jehoshaphat his son,

11 Joram his son, Ahaziah his son, Joash his son,

12 Amaziah his son, Azariah his son, Jotham his son,

13 Ahaz his son, Hezekiah his son, Manasseh his son,

14 Amon his son, Josiah his son.

15 And the sons of Josiah *were*, the firstborn Johanan, the second Jehoiakim, the third Zedekiah, the fourth Shallum.

16 And the sons of Jehoiakim: Jeconiah his son, Zedekiah his son.

17 And the sons of Jeconiah; Assir, Salathiel his son,

18 Malchiram also, and Pedaiah, and Shenazar, Jecamiah, Hoshama, and Nedabiah.

19 And the sons of Pedaiah *were*, Zerubbabel, and Shimei: and the sons of Zerubbabel; Meshullam, and Hananiah, and Shelomith their sister:

20 And Hashubah, and Ohel, and Berechiah, and Hasadiah, Jushab-hesed, five.

21 And the sons of Hananiah; Pelatiah, and Jesaiah: the sons of Rephaiah, the sons of Arnan, the sons of Obadiah, the sons of Shechaniah.

22 And the sons of Shechaniah; Shemaiah: and the sons of Shemaiah; Hattush, and Igeal, and Bariah, and Neariah, and Shaphat, six.

23 And the sons of Neariah; Elioenai, and Hezekiah, and Azrikam, three.

24 And the sons of Elioenai *were*, Hodaiah,

and Eliashib, and Pelaiah, and Akkub, and Johanan, and Dalaiah, and Anani, seven.

CHAPTER 4
Judah's Family Record

1 The sons of Judah; Pharez, Hezron, and Carmi, and Hur, and Shobal.

2 And Reaiah the son of Shobal begat Jahath; and Jahath begat Ahumai, and Lahad. These *are* the families of the Zorathites.

3 And these *were of* the father of Etam; Jezreel, and Ishma, and Idbash: and the name of their sister *was* Hazelelponi:

4 And Penuel the father of Gedor, and Ezer the father of Hushah. These *are* the sons of Hur, the firstborn of Ephratah, the father of Beth-lehem.

5 And Ashur the father of Tekoa had two wives, Helah and Naarah.

6 And Naarah bare him Ahuzam, and Hepher, and Temeni, and Haahashtari. These *were* the sons of Naarah.

7 And the sons of Helah *were*, Zereth, and Jezoar, and Ethnan.

8 And Coz begat Anub, and Zobebah, and the families of Aharhel the son of Harum.

9 And Jabez was more honourable than his brethren: and his mother called his name Jabez, saying, Because I bare him with sorrow.

10 And Jabez called on the God of Israel, saying, Oh that thou wouldest bless me indeed, and enlarge my coast, and that thine hand might be with me, and that thou wouldest keep *me* from evil, that it may not grieve me! And God granted him that which he requested.

11 And Chelub the brother of Shuah begat Mehir, which *was* the father of Eshton.

12 And Eshton begat Beth-rapha, and Paseah, and Tehinnah the father of *Ir-nahash*. These *are* the men of Rechah.

13 And the sons of Kenaz; Othniel, and Seraiah: and the sons of Othniel; Hathath.

14 And Meonothai begat Ophrah: and Seraiah begat Joab, the father of the valley of Charashim; for they were craftsmen.

15 And the sons of Caleb the son of Jephunneh; Iru, Elah, and Naam: and the sons of Elah, even Kenaz.

Cross references (center column)

5 2Sam. 5:14; 11:3; 12:24; 1Chr. 14:4
6 2Sam. 5:15
8 2Sam. 5:14-16; 1Chr. 14:7
9 2Sam. 13:1
10 1Kgs. 11:43; 15:1, 6
11 2Chr. 21:17, *Jehoahaz*; 22:6, *Azariah*
12 2Kgs. 15:30
15 2Kgs. 23:30, 34; 24:17
16 2Kgs. 24:17; Matt. 1:11
17 Matt. 1:12
22 Ezra 8:2
1 Gen. 38:29; 46:12; 1Chr. 2:9, *Chelubar*; 2:18, Caleb
2 1Chr. 2:52
4 1Chr. 2:50
5 1Chr. 2:24
9 Gen. 34:19
13 Josh. 15:17
14 Neh. 11:35

3:16 Jeconiah. No royal descendants of this wicked king, also known as Coniah and Jehoiachin, would prosper on the throne, according to Jeremiah (Jer. 22:30). Although a descendant of Jeconiah and the direct heir to the Davidic throne, Joseph, the legal father of Jesus and husband of Mary, was not the Savior's biological father, as Jesus was born of the virgin Mary. Mary, however, was a descendant of David through his son Nathan (Luke 3:31). Thus Jesus was free from the curse on Jeconiah, but still "was made of the seed of David according to the flesh" (Rom. 1:3).

16 And the sons of Jehaleleel; Ziph, and Ziphah, Tiria, and Asareel.

17 And the sons of Ezra *were*, Jether, and Mered, and Epher, and Jalon: and she bare Miriam, and Shammai, and Ishbah the father of Eshtemoa.

18 And his wife Jehudijah bare Jered the father of Gedor, and Heber the father of Socho, and Jekuthiel the father of Zanoah. And these *are* the sons of Bithiah the daughter of Pharaoh, which Mered took.

19 And the sons of *his* wife Hodiah the sister of Naham, the father of Keilah the Garmite, and Eshtemoa the Maachathite.

20 And the sons of Shimon *were*, Amnon, and Rinnah, Ben-hanan, and Tilon. And the sons of Ishi *were*, Zoheth, and Ben-zoheth.

21 The sons of Shelah the son of Judah *were*, Er the father of Lecah, and Laadah the father of Mareshah, and the families of the house of them that wrought fine linen, of the house of Ashbea,

22 And Jokim, and the men of Chozeba, and Joash, and Saraph, who had the dominion in Moab, and Jashubi-lehem. And *these are* ancient things.

23 These *were* the potters, and those that dwelt among plants and hedges: there they dwelt with the king for his work.

Simeon's Family Record

24 The sons of Simeon *were*, Nemuel, and Jamin, Jarib, Zerah, *and* Shaul:

25 Shallum his son, Mibsam his son, Mishma his son.

26 And the sons of Mishma; Hamuel his son, Zacchur his son, Shimei his son.

27 And Shimei had sixteen sons and six daughters; but his brethren had not many children, neither did all their family multiply, like to the children of Judah.

28 And they dwelt at Beer-sheba, and Moladah, and Hazar-shual,

29 And at Bilhah, and at Ezem, and at Tolad,

30 And at Bethuel, and at Hormah, and at Ziklag,

31 And at Beth-marcaboth, and Hazar-susim, and at Beth-birei, and at Shaaraim. These *were* their cities unto the reign of David.

32 And their villages *were*, Etam, and Ain, Rimmon, and Tochen, and Ashan, five cities:

33 And all their villages that *were* round about the same cities, unto Baal. These *were* their habitations, and their genealogy.

34 And Meshobab, and Jamlech, and Joshah the son of Amaziah,

35 And Joel, and Jehu the son of Josibiah, the son of Seraiah, the son of Asiel,

36 And Elioenai, and Jaakobah, and Jeshohaiah, and Asaiah, and Adiel, and Jesimiel, and Benaiah,

37 And Ziza the son of Shiphi, the son of Allon, the son of Jedaiah, the son of Shimri, the son of Shemaiah;

38 These mentioned by *their* names *were* princes in their families: and the house of their fathers increased greatly.

39 And they went to the entrance of Gedor, *even* unto the east side of the valley, to seek pasture for their flocks.

40 And they found fat pasture and good, and the land *was* wide, and quiet, and peaceable; for *they* of Ham had dwelt there of old.

41 And these written by name came in the days of Hezekiah king of Judah, and smote their tents, and the habitations that were found there, and destroyed them utterly unto this day, and dwelt in their rooms: because *there was* pasture there for their flocks.

42 And *some* of them, *even* of the sons of Simeon, five hundred men, went to mount Seir, having for their captains Pelatiah, and Neariah, and Rephaiah, and Uzziel, the sons of Ishi.

43 And they smote the rest of the Amalekites that were escaped, and dwelt there unto this day.

Chapter 5
Reuben's Family Record

1 Now the sons of Reuben the firstborn of Israel, (for he *was* the firstborn; but, forasmuch as he defiled his father's bed, his birthright was given unto the sons of Joseph the son of Israel: and the genealogy is not to be reckoned after the birthright.

2 For Judah prevailed above his brethren,

Center column cross-references:

21 Gen. 38:1, 5; 46:12

24 Gen. 46:10; Ex. 6:15; Num. 26:12

28 Josh. 19:2

29 Josh. 19:3, 4

31 Josh. 19:5

32 Josh. 19:7

33 Josh. 19:8

41 2Kgs. 18:8

43 1Sam. 15:8; 30:17; 2Sam. 8:12

1 Gen. 29:32; 35:22; 48:15, 22; 49:3, 4

2 Gen. 49:8, 10; Ps. 60:7; 108:8; Mic. 5:2; Matt. 2:6

4:9–10 Jabez. This descendant of Judah is mentioned only here. The name Jabez means "he makes sorrowful," reflecting on the intense and unusual pain and sorrow preceding and attending his birth. So notable was his spiritual character and so fervent was his prayer requesting material blessings and spiritual protection, that here it is recorded: "God granted him that which he requested."

and of him *came* the chief ruler; but the birthright *was* Joseph's:)

3 The sons, *I say*, of Reuben the firstborn of Israel *were*, Hanoch, and Pallu, Hezron, and Carmi.

4 The sons of Joel; Shemaiah his son, Gog his son, Shimei his son,

5 Micah his son, Reaia his son, Baal his son,

6 Beerah his son, whom Tilgath-pilneser king of Assyria carried away *captive*: he *was* prince of the Reubenites.

7 And his brethren by their families, when the genealogy of their generations was reckoned, *were* the chief, Jeiel, and Zechariah,

8 And Bela the son of Azaz, the son of Shema, the son of Joel, who dwelt in Aroer, even unto Nebo and Baal-meon:

9 And eastward he inhabited unto the entering in of the wilderness from the river Euphrates: because their cattle were multiplied in the land of Gilead.

10 And in the days of Saul they made war with the Hagarites, who fell by their hand: and they dwelt in their tents throughout all the east *land* of Gilead.

Gad's Family Record

11 And the children of Gad dwelt over against them, in the land of Bashan unto Salchah:

12 Joel the chief, and Shapham the next, and Jaanai, and Shaphat in Bashan.

13 And their brethren of the house of their fathers *were*, Michael, and Meshullam, and Sheba, and Jorai, and Jachan, and Zia, and Heber, seven.

14 These *are* the children of Abihail the son of Huri, the son of Jaroah, the son of Gilead, the son of Michael, the son of Jeshishai, the son of Jahdo, the son of Buz;

15 Ahi the son of Abdiel, the son of Guni, chief of the house of their fathers.

16 And they dwelt in Gilead in Bashan, and in her towns, and in all the suburbs of Sharon, upon their borders.

17 All these were reckoned by genealogies in the days of Jotham king of Judah, and in the days of Jeroboam king of Israel.

The Eastern Tribes' Army

18 The sons of Reuben, and the Gadites, and half the tribe of Manasseh, of valiant men, men able to bear buckler and sword, and to shoot with bow, and skilful in war, *were* four and forty thousand seven hundred and threescore, that went out to the war.

19 And they made war with the Hagarites, with Jetur, and Nephish, and Nodab.

20 And they were helped against them, and the Hagarites were delivered into their hand, and all that *were* with them: for they cried to God in the battle, and he was intreated of them; because they put their trust in him.

21 And they took away their cattle; of their camels fifty thousand, and of sheep two hundred and fifty thousand, and of asses two thousand, and of men an hundred thousand.

22 For there fell down many slain, because the war *was* of God. And they dwelt in their steads until the captivity.

Sketch of Eastern Manasseh's History

23 And the children of the half tribe of Manasseh dwelt in the land: they increased from Bashan unto Baalath-hermon and Senir, and unto mount Hermon.

24 And these *were* the heads of the house of their fathers, even Epher, and Ishi, and Eliel, and Azriel, and Jeremiah, and Hodaviah, and Jahdiel, mighty men of valour, famous men, *and* heads of the house of their fathers.

25 And they transgressed against the God of their fathers, and went a whoring after the gods of the people of the land, whom God destroyed before them.

26 And the God of Israel stirred up the spirit of Pul king of Assyria, and the spirit of Tilgath-pilneser king of Assyria, and he carried them away, even the Reubenites, and the Gadites, and the half tribe of Manasseh, and brought them unto Halah, and Habor, and Hara, and to the river Gozan, unto this day.

3 Gen. 46:9; Ex. 6:14; Num. 26:5

6 2Kgs. 15:29; 16:7

7 1Chr. 5:17

8 Josh. 13:15, 16; 1Chr. 5:4

9 Josh. 22:9

10 Gen. 25:12

11 Josh. 13:11, 24

16 1Chr. 27:29

17 2Kgs. 14:16, 28; 15:5, 32

19 Gen. 25:15; 1Chr. 1:31

20 1Chr. 5:22; Ps. 22:4, 5

22 2Kgs. 15:29; 17:6

25 2Kgs. 17:7

26 2Kgs. 15:19, 29; 17:6; 18:11

5:25–26 he carried them away. Because of idolatry and immorality, God sent Tiglath Pileser III (745–727 B.C.), also known as Pul, the king of Assyria and later Babylon, to carry the Israelites east of the Jordan River away into captivity. These included Reuben, Gad, and the half-tribe of Manasseh (also known as Machir and Gilead, the son and grandson of Jacob's son Manasseh). This was the first removal of Israelites by northern conquerors (ca. 758 B.C.). Later, in 722 B.C., the entire Northern Kingdom fell to Shalmaneser and his successor Sargon of Assyria (2 Kgs. 17:3–6).

CHAPTER 6
Levi's Family Record

1 The sons of Levi; Gershon, Kohath, and Merari.

2 And the sons of Kohath; Amram, Izhar, and Hebron, and Uzziel.

3 And the children of Amram; Aaron, and Moses, and Miriam. The sons also of Aaron; Nadab, and Abihu, Eleazar, and Ithamar.

4 Eleazar begat Phinehas, Phinehas begat Abishua,

5 And Abishua begat Bukki, and Bukki begat Uzzi,

6 And Uzzi begat Zerahiah, and Zerahiah begat Meraioth,

7 Meraioth begat Amariah, and Amariah begat Ahitub,

8 And Ahitub begat Zadok, and Zadok begat Ahimaaz,

9 And Ahimaaz begat Azariah, and Azariah begat Johanan,

10 And Johanan begat Azariah, (he *it is* that executed the priest's office in the temple that Solomon built in Jerusalem:)

11 And Azariah begat Amariah, and Amariah begat Ahitub,

12 And Ahitub begat Zadok, and Zadok begat Shallum,

13 And Shallum begat Hilkiah, and Hilkiah begat Azariah,

14 And Azariah begat Seraiah, and Seraiah begat Jehozadak,

15 And Jehozadak went *into captivity*, when the LORD carried away Judah and Jerusalem by the hand of Nebuchadnezzar.

16 The sons of Levi; Gershom, Kohath, and Merari.

17 And these *be* the names of the sons of Gershom; Libni, and Shimei.

18 And the sons of Kohath *were*, Amram, and Izhar, and Hebron, and Uzziel.

19 The sons of Merari; Mahli, and Mushi. And these *are* the families of the Levites according to their fathers.

20 Of Gershom; Libni his son, Jahath his son, Zimmah his son,

21 Joah his son, Iddo his son, Zerah his son, Jeaterai his son.

22 The sons of Kohath; Amminadab his son, Korah his son, Assir his son,

23 Elkanah his son, and Ebiasaph his son, and Assir his son,

24 Tahath his son, Uriel his son, Uzziah his son, and Shaul his son.

25 And the sons of Elkanah; Amasai, and Ahimoth.

26 *As for* Elkanah: the sons of Elkanah; Zophai his son, and Nahath his son,

27 Eliab his son, Jeroham his son, Elkanah his son.

28 And the sons of Samuel; the firstborn Vashni, and Abiah.

29 The sons of Merari; Mahli, Libni his son, Shimei his son, Uzza his son,

30 Shimea his son, Haggiah his son, Asaiah his son.

The Temple Musicians

31 And these *are they* whom David set over the service of song in the house of the LORD, after that the ark had rest.

32 And they ministered before the dwelling place of the tabernacle of the congregation with singing, until Solomon had built the house of the LORD in Jerusalem: and *then* they waited on their office according to their order.

33 And these *are* they that waited with their children. Of the sons of the Kohathites: Heman a singer, the son of Joel, the son of Shemuel,

34 The son of Elkanah, the son of Jeroham, the son of Eliel, the son of Toah,

35 The son of Zuph, the son of Elkanah, the son of Mahath, the son of Amasai,

36 The son of Elkanah, the son of Joel, the son of Azariah, the son of Zephaniah,

37 The son of Tahath, the son of Assir, the son of Ebiasaph, the son of Korah,

38 The son of Izhar, the son of Kohath, the son of Levi, the son of Israel.

39 And his brother Asaph, who stood on his right hand, *even* Asaph the son of Berachiah, the son of Shimea,

40 The son of Michael, the son of Baaseiah, the son of Malchiah,

41 The son of Ethni, the son of Zerah, the son of Adaiah,

42 The son of Ethan, the son of Zimmah, the son of Shimei,

43 The son of Jahath, the son of Gershom, the son of Levi.

44 And their brethren the sons of Merari *stood* on the left hand: Ethan the son of Kishi, the son of Abdi, the son of Malluch,

45 The son of Hashabiah, the son of Amaziah, the son of Hilkiah,

Cross References (center column)

1 Gen. 46:11; Ex. 6:16; Num. 26:57; 1Chr. 23:6

2 1Chr. 6:22

3 Lev. 10:1

8 2Sam. 8:17; 15:27

10 1Kgs. 6; 2Chr. 3; 26:17, 18

11 Ezra 7:3

12 1Chr. 9:11

14 Neh. 11:11

15 2Kgs. 25:18

16 Ex. 6:16

20 1Chr. 6:42

21 1Chr. 6:4, 42

22 1Chr. 6:2, 18, *Izhar*

24 1Chr. 6:36; *Zephaniah, Azariah, Joel*

25 1Chr. 6:35, 36

26 1Sam. 1:1; 1Chr. 6:34, *Toah*

27 1Chr. 6:34, *Eliel*

28 1Sam. 8:2; 1Chr. 6:33

31 1Chr. 16:1

34 1Chr. 6:26, *Nahath*

36 1Chr. 6:24, *Shaul, Uzziah, Uriel*

37 Ex. 6:24

41 1Chr. 6:21

44 1Chr. 9:16; 15:17; 25:1, 3, 6

6:1 sons of Levi. Second only to Judah in prophetic significance was the priestly tribe of Levi. Both Moses and Aaron were descendants of Levi with the latter's descendants to furnish the divinely authorized high priest of Israel.

46 The son of Amzi, the son of Bani, the son of Shamer,

47 The son of Mahli, the son of Mushi, the son of Merari, the son of Levi.

48 Their brethren also the Levites *were* appointed unto all manner of service of the tabernacle of the house of God.

Aaron's Family Record

49 But Aaron and his sons offered upon the altar of the burnt offering, and on the altar of incense, *and were appointed* for all the work of the *place* most holy, and to make an atonement for Israel, according to all that Moses the servant of God had commanded.

50 And these *are* the sons of Aaron; Eleazar his son, Phinehas his son, Abishua his son,

51 Bukki his son, Uzzi his son, Zerahiah his son,

52 Meraioth his son, Amariah his son, Ahitub his son,

53 Zadok his son, Ahimaaz his son.

The Levites' Cities

54 Now these *are* their dwelling places throughout their castles in their coasts, of the sons of Aaron, of the families of the Kohathites: for theirs was the lot.

55 And they gave them Hebron in the land of Judah, and the suburbs thereof round about it.

56 But the fields of the city, and the villages thereof, they gave to Caleb the son of Jephunneh.

57 And to the sons of Aaron they gave the cities of Judah, *namely*, Hebron, *the city* of refuge, and Libnah with her suburbs, and Jattir, and Eshtemoa, with their suburbs,

58 And Hilen with her suburbs, Debir with her suburbs,

59 And Ashan with her suburbs, and Beth-shemesh with her suburbs:

60 And out of the tribe of Benjamin; Geba with her suburbs, and Alemeth with her suburbs, and Anathoth with her suburbs. All their cities throughout their families *were* thirteen cities.

61 And unto the sons of Kohath, *which were* left of the family of that tribe, *were cities given* out of the half tribe, *namely, out of* the half *tribe* of Manasseh, by lot, ten cities.

62 And to the sons of Gershom throughout their families out of the tribe of Issachar, and out of the tribe of Asher, and out of the tribe of Naphtali, and out of the tribe of Manasseh in Bashan, thirteen cities.

63 Unto the sons of Merari *were given* by lot, throughout their families, out of the tribe of Reuben, and out of the tribe of Gad, and out of the tribe of Zebulun, twelve cities.

64 And the children of Israel gave to the Levites *these* cities with their suburbs.

65 And they gave by lot out of the tribe of the children of Judah, and out of the tribe of the children of Simeon, and out of the tribe of the children of Benjamin, these cities, which are called by *their* names.

66 And *the residue* of the families of the sons of Kohath had cities of their coasts out of the tribe of Ephraim.

67 And they gave unto them, *of* the cities of refuge, Shechem in mount Ephraim with her suburbs; *they gave* also Gezer with her suburbs,

68 And Jokmeam with her suburbs, and Beth-horon with her suburbs,

69 And Aijalon with her suburbs, and Gath-rimmon with her suburbs:

70 And out of the half tribe of Manasseh; Aner with her suburbs, and Bileam with her suburbs, for the family of the remnant of the sons of Kohath.

71 Unto the sons of Gershom *were given* out of the family of the half tribe of Manasseh, Golan in Bashan with her suburbs, and Ashtaroth with her suburbs:

72 And out of the tribe of Issachar; Kedesh with her suburbs, Daberath with her suburbs,

73 And Ramoth with her suburbs, and Anem with her suburbs:

74 And out of the tribe of Asher; Mashal with her suburbs, and Abdon with her suburbs,

75 And Hukok with her suburbs, and Rehob with her suburbs:

76 And out of the tribe of Naphtali; Kadesh in Galilee with her suburbs, and Hammon with her suburbs, and Kirjathaim with her suburbs.

77 Unto the rest of the children of Merari *were given* out of the tribe of Zebulun, Rimmon with her suburbs, Tabor with her suburbs:

---

49 Ex. 30:7; Lev. 1:9
54 Josh. 21:7, 10
55 Josh. 21:11, 12
56 Josh. 14:13; 15:13
57 Josh. 21:13
58 Josh. 21:15
59 Josh. 21:16
60 Josh. 21:18
61 Josh. 21:5; 1Chr. 6:66
63 Josh. 21:7, 34
66 1Chr. 6:61
67 Josh. 21:21
68 Josh. 21:22-35, many of these cities have other names

6:53 Zadok. The eleventh in descent from Aaron, Zadok was loyal to King David in a time of rebellion (2 Sam. 19:9–11), and he anointed Solomon to be David's successor (1 Kgs. 2:26–27, 35). His descendants, known in advance by God, will occupy ranking priestly positions in the future Millennial Temple in restored Israel (Ezek. 40:46; 43:19; 44:15; 48:11).

78 And on the other side Jordan by Jericho, on the east side of Jordan, *were given them* out of the tribe of Reuben, Bezer in the wilderness with her suburbs, and Jahzah with her suburbs,

79 Kedemoth also with her suburbs, and Mephaath with her suburbs:

80 And out of the tribe of Gad; Ramoth in Gilead with her suburbs, and Mahanaim with her suburbs,

81 And Heshbon with her suburbs, and Jazer with her suburbs.

CHAPTER 7
Issachar's Family Record

1 Now the sons of Issachar *were*, Tola, and Puah, Jashub, and Shimron, four.

2 And the sons of Tola; Uzzi, and Rephaiah, and Jeriel, and Jahmai, and Jibsam, and Shemuel, heads of their father's house, *to wit*, of Tola: *they were* valiant men of might in their generations; whose number *was* in the days of David two and twenty thousand and six hundred.

3 And the sons of Uzzi; Izrahiah: and the sons of Izrahiah; Michael, and Obadiah, and Joel, Ishiah, five: all of them chief men.

4 And with them, by their generations, after the house of their fathers, *were* bands of soldiers for war, six and thirty thousand *men*: for they had many wives and sons.

5 And their brethren among all the families of Issachar *were* valiant men of might, reckoned in all by their genealogies fourscore and seven thousand.

Benjamin's Family Record

6 *The sons* of Benjamin; Bela, and Becher, and Jediael, three.

7 And the sons of Bela; Ezbon, and Uzzi, and Uzziel, and Jerimoth, and Iri, five; heads of the house of *their* fathers, mighty men of valour; and were reckoned by their genealogies twenty and two thousand and thirty and four.

8 And the sons of Becher; Zemira, and Joash, and Eliezer, and Elioenai, and Omri, and Jerimoth, and Abiah, and Anathoth,

and Alameth. All these *are* the sons of Becher.

9 And the number of them, after their genealogy by their generations, heads of the house of their fathers, mighty men of valour, *was* twenty thousand and two hundred.

10 The sons also of Jediael; Bilhan: and the sons of Bilhan; Jeush, and Benjamin, and Ehud, and Chenaanah, and Zethan, and Tharshish, and Ahishahar.

11 All these the sons of Jediael, by the heads of their fathers, mighty men of valour, *were* seventeen thousand and two hundred *soldiers*, fit to go out for war *and* battle.

12 Shuppim also, and Huppim, the children of Ir, *and* Hushim, the sons of Aher.

Naphtali's Sons

13 The sons of Naphtali; Jahziel, and Guni, and Jezer, and Shallum, the sons of Bilhah.

Manasseh's Family Record

14 The sons of Manasseh; Ashriel, whom she bare: (*but* his concubine the Aramitess bare Machir the father of Gilead:

15 And Machir took to wife *the sister* of Huppim and Shuppim, whose sister's name *was* Maachah;) and the name of the second *was* Zelophehad: and Zelophehad had daughters.

16 And Maachah the wife of Machir bare a son, and she called his name Peresh; and the name of his brother *was* Sheresh; and his sons *were* Ulam and Rakem.

17 And the sons of Ulam; Bedan. These *were* the sons of Gilead, the son of Machir, the son of Manasseh.

18 And his sister Hammoleketh bare Ishod, and Abiezer, and Mahalah.

19 And the sons of Shemida were, Ahian, and Shechem, and Likhi, and Aniam.

Ephraim's Family Record

20 And the sons of Ephraim; Shuthelah, and Bered his son, and Tahath his son, and Eladah his son, and Tahath his son,

21 And Zabad his son, and Shuthelah his son, and Ezer, and Elead, whom the men of

---

Marginal references (center column):

1 Gen. 46:13; Num. 26:23

2 2Sam. 24:1, 2; 1Chr. 27:1

6 Gen. 46:21; Num. 26:38; 1Chr. 8:1

12 Num. 26:38; 26:39, *Shupham, and Hupham;* 1Chr. 7:7

13 Gen. 46:24, *Shillem*

17 1Sam. 12:11

18 Num. 26:30, *Jeezer*

20 Num. 26:35

7:1–40 sons of Issachar. The descendants of Issachar, Benjamin, Naphtali, Manasseh, Ephraim, and Asher are discussed, with each group forming tribal states which lasted for hundreds of years. These six, plus Dan and Zebulon, were part of the Northern Kingdom (Israel) after Solomon's death. Simeon (4:24–43) seems to have been absorbed later into Judah and Benjamin, which constituted the Southern Kingdom (Judah). In the future Tribulation, twelve thousand from each tribe (excluding Dan), whose ancestry is known only by the Lord, will form the 144,000 special sealed witnesses who will preach the gospel of the Kingdom (Rev. 7:2–8; 12:17 [cf. Matt. 24:14]). Territorial borders are described for all twelve tribes, including Dan, who will occupy restored millennial Israel (Ezek. 48:1–8, 23–28).

Gath *that were* born in *that* land slew, because they came down to take away their cattle.

22 And Ephraim their father mourned many days, and his brethren came to comfort him.

23 And when he went in to his wife, she conceived, and bare a son, and he called his name Beriah, because it went evil with his house.

24 (And his daughter *was* Sherah, who built Beth-horon the nether, and the upper, and Uzzen-sherah.)

25 And Rephah *was* his son, also Resheph, and Telah his son, and Tahan his son,

26 Laadan his son, Ammihud his son, Elishama his son,

27 Nun his son, Jehoshua his son.

28 And their possessions and habitations *were*, Beth-el and the towns thereof, and eastward Naaran, and westward Gezer, with the towns thereof; Shechem also and the towns thereof, unto Gaza and the towns thereof:

29 And by the borders of the children of Manasseh, Beth-shean and her towns, Taanach and her towns, Megiddo and her towns, Dor and her towns. In these dwelt the children of Joseph the son of Israel.

Asher's Family Record

30 The sons of Asher; Imnah, and Isuah, and Ishuai, and Beriah, and Serah their sister.

31 And the sons of Beriah; Heber, and Malchiel, who *is* the father of Birzavith.

32 And Heber begat Japhlet, and Shomer, and Hotham, and Shua their sister.

33 And the sons of Japhlet; Pasach, and Bimhal, and Ashvath. These *are* the children of Japhlet.

34 And the sons of Shamer; Ahi, and Rohgah, Jehubbah, and Aram.

35 And the sons of his brother Helem; Zophah, and Imna, and Shelesh, and Amal.

36 The sons of Zophah; Suah, and Harnepher, and Shual, and Beri, and Imrah,

37 Bezer, and Hod, and Shamma, and Shilshah, and Ithran, and Beera.

38 And the sons of Jether; Jephunneh, and Pispah, and Ara.

39 And the sons of Ulla; Arah, and Haniel, and Rezia.

40 All these *were* the children of Asher,

heads of *their* father's house, choice *and* mighty men of valour, chief of the princes. And the number throughout the genealogy of them that were apt to the war *and* to battle *was* twenty and six thousand men.

CHAPTER 8
Benjamin's Family Record

1 Now Benjamin begat Bela his firstborn, Ashbel the second, and Aharah the third,

2 Nohah the fourth, and Rapha the fifth.

3 And the sons of Bela were, Addar, and Gera, and Abihud,

4 And Abishua, and Naaman, and Ahoah,

5 And Gera, and Shephuphan, and Huram.

6 And these *are* the sons of Ehud: these are the heads of the fathers of the inhabitants of Geba, and they removed them to Manahath:

7 And Naaman, and Ahiah, and Gera, he removed them, and begat Uzza, and Ahihud.

8 And Shaharaim begat *children* in the country of Moab, after he had sent them away; Hushim and Baara *were* his wives.

9 And he begat of Hodesh his wife, Jobab, and Zibia, and Mesha, and Malcham,

10 And Jeuz, and Shachia, and Mirma. These *were* his sons, heads of the fathers.

11 And of Hushim he begat Abitub, and Elpaal.

12 The sons of Elpaal; Eber, and Misham, and Shamed, who built Ono, and Lod, with the towns thereof:

13 Beriah also, and Shema, who *were* heads of the fathers of the inhabitants of Aijalon, who drove away the inhabitants of Gath:

14 And Ahio, Shashak, and Jeremoth,

15 And Zebadiah, and Arad, and Ader,

16 And Michael, and Ispah, and Joha, the sons of Beriah;

17 And Zebadiah, and Meshullam, and Hezeki, and Heber,

18 Ishmerai also, and Jezliah, and Jobab, the sons of Elpaal;

19 And Jakim, and Zichri, and Zabdi,

20 And Elienai, and Zilthai, and Eliel,

21 And Adaiah, and Beraiah, and Shimrath, the sons of Shimhi;

22 And Ishpan, and Heber, and Eliel,

23 And Abdon, and Zichri, and Hanan,

24 And Hananiah, and Elam, and Antothijah,

Cross references (center column)

27 Num. 13:8, 16
28 Josh. 16:7, *Naarath*
29 Josh. 17:7, 11
30 Gen. 46:17; Num. 26:44
32 1Chr. 7:34, *Shamer*
34 1Chr. 7:32, *Shomer*
1 Gen. 46:21; Num. 26:38; 1Chr. 7:6
3 Gen. 46:21
5 Num. 26:39; 1Chr. 7:12
6 1Chr. 2:52
13 1Chr. 13:21, *Shimhi*
21 1Chr. 21:13

8:1 Benjamin. Additional genealogical information is given in 1 Chronicles 7:6–11 concerning this tribe from which Saul, Israel's first king, emerged. The apostle Paul in New Testament times was a Benjamite (Phil. 3:4–7).

25 And Iphedeiah, and Penuel, the sons of Shashak;

26 And Shamsherai, and Shehariah, and Athaliah,

27 And Jaresiah, and Eliah, and Zichri, the sons of Jeroham.

28 These *were* heads of the fathers, by their generations, chief *men*. These dwelt in Jerusalem.

29 And at Gibeon dwelt the father of Gibeon; whose wife's name *was* Maachah:

30 And his firstborn son Abdon, and Zur, and Kish, and Baal, and Nadab,

31 And Gedor, and Ahio, and Zacher.

32 And Mikloth begat Shimeah. And these also dwelt with their brethren in Jerusalem, over against them.

33 And Ner begat Kish, and Kish begat Saul, and Saul begat Jonathan, and Malchishua, and Abinadab, and Esh-baal.

34 And the son of Jonathan *was* Merib-baal; and Merib-baal begat Micah.

35 And the sons of Micah *were*, Pithon, and Melech, and Tarea, and Ahaz.

36 And Ahaz begat Jehoadah; and Jehoadah begat Alemeth, and Azmaveth, and Zimri; and Zimri begat Moza,

37 And Moza begat Binea: Rapha *was* his son, Eleasah his son, Azel his son:

38 And Azel had six sons, whose names *are* these, Azrikam, Bocheru, and Ishmael, and Sheariah, and Obadiah, and Hanan. All these *were* the sons of Azel.

39 And the sons of Eshek his brother *were*, Ulam his firstborn, Jehush the second, and Eliphelet the third.

40 And the sons of Ulam were mighty men of valour, archers, and had many sons, and sons' sons, an hundred and fifty. All these *are* of the sons of Benjamin.

CHAPTER 9
Jerusalem's Inhabitants after the Exile

1 So all Israel were reckoned by genealogies; and, behold, they *were* written in the book of the kings of Israel and Judah, *who* were carried away to Babylon for their transgression.

2 Now the first inhabitants that *dwelt* in their possessions in their cities *were*, the Israelites, the priests, Levites, and the Nethinims.

3 And in Jerusalem dwelt of the children of Judah, and of the children of Benjamin, and of the children of Ephraim, and Manasseh;

4 Uthai the son of Ammihud, the son of Omri, the son of Imri, the son of Bani, of the children of Pharez the son of Judah.

5 And of the Shilonites; Asaiah the firstborn, and his sons.

6 And of the sons of Zerah; Jeuel, and their brethren, six hundred and ninety.

7 And of the sons of Benjamin; Sallu the son of Meshullam, the son of Hodaviah, the son of Hasenuah,

8 And Ibneiah the son of Jeroham, and Elah the son of Uzzi, the son of Michri, and Meshullam the son of Shephathiah, the son of Reuel, the son of Ibnijah;

9 And their brethren, according to their generations, nine hundred and fifty and six. All these men *were* chief of the fathers in the house of their fathers.

10 And of the priests; Jedaiah, and Jehoiarib, and Jachin,

11 And Azariah the son of Hilkiah, the son of Meshullam, the son of Zadok, the son of Meraioth, the son of Ahitub, the ruler of the house of God;

12 And Adaiah the son of Jeroham, the son of Pashur, the son of Malchijah, and Maasiai the son of Adiel, the son of Jahzerah, the son of Meshullam, the son of Meshillemith, the son of Immer;

13 And their brethren, heads of the house of their fathers, a thousand and seven hundred and threescore; very able men for the work of the service of the house of God.

14 And of the Levites; Shemaiah the son of Hasshub, the son of Azrikam, the son of Hashabiah, of the sons of Merari;

15 And Bakbakkar, Heresh, and Galal, and Mattaniah the son of Micah, the son of Zichri, the son of Asaph;

16 And Obadiah the son of Shemaiah, the son of Galal, the son of Jeduthun, and Berechiah the son of Asa, the son of Elkanah, that dwelt in the villages of the Netophathites.

17 And the porters *were*, Shallum, and Akkub, and Talmon, and Ahiman, and their brethren: Shallum *was* the chief;

18 Who hitherto *waited* in the king's gate eastward: they *were* porters in the companies of the children of Levi.

19 And Shallum the son of Kore, the son of Ebiasaph, the son of Korah, and his brethren, of the house of his father, the Ko-

29 1Chr. 9:35

31 1Chr. 9:37

32 1Chr. 9:38

33 1Sam. 14:49, *Ishui*; 14:51; 2Sam. 2:8

34 2Sam. 4:4; 9:6, 10, 12

36 1Chr. 9:42, *Jarah*

37 1Chr. 9:43, *Rephaiah*

1 Ezra 2:59

2 Josh. 9:27; Ezra 2:43, 70; 8:20; Neh. 7:73

3 Neh. 11:1

10 Neh. 11:10; 11:11, *Seraiah*

9:2–34 first inhabitants. These were the inhabitants of Jerusalem after the exile, which ended in 536 B.C.

rahites, *were* over the work of the service, keepers of the gates of the tabernacle: and their fathers, *being* over the host of the LORD, *were* keepers of the entry.

20 And Phinehas the son of Eleazar was the ruler over them in time past, *and* the LORD *was* with him.

21 *And* Zechariah the son of Meshelemiah *was* porter of the door of the tabernacle of the congregation.

22 All these *which were* chosen to be porters in the gates *were* two hundred and twelve. These were reckoned by their genealogy in their villages, whom David and Samuel the seer did ordain in their set office.

23 So they and their children *had* the oversight of the gates of the house of the LORD, *namely*, the house of the tabernacle, by wards.

24 In four quarters were the porters, toward the east, west, north, and south.

25 And their brethren, *which were* in their villages, *were* to come after seven days from time to time with them.

26 For these Levites, the four chief porters, were in *their* set office, and were over the chambers and treasuries of the house of God.

27 And they lodged round about the house of God, because the charge *was* upon them, and the opening thereof every morning *pertained* to them.

28 And *certain* of them had the charge of the ministering vessels, that they should bring them in and out by tale.

29 *Some* of them also *were* appointed to oversee the vessels, and all the instruments of the sanctuary, and the fine flour, and the wine, and the oil, and the frankincense, and the spices.

30 And *some* of the sons of the priests made the ointment of the spices.

31 And Mattithiah, *one* of the Levites, who *was* the firstborn of Shallum the Korahite, had the set office over the things that were made in the pans.

32 And *other* of their brethren, of the sons of the Kohathites, *were* over the shewbread, to prepare *it* every sabbath.

33 And these *are* the singers, chief of the fathers of the Levites, *who remaining* in the chambers *were* free: for they were employed in *that* work day and night.

34 These chief fathers of the Levites *were*

chief throughout their generations; these dwelt at Jerusalem.

Saul's Family Record

35 And in Gibeon dwelt the father of Gibeon, Jehiel, whose wife's name *was* Maachah:

36 And his firstborn son Abdon, then Zur, and Kish, and Baal, and Ner, and Nadab,

37 And Gedor, and Ahio, and Zechariah, and Mikloth.

38 And Mikloth begat Shimeam. And they also dwelt with their brethren at Jerusalem, over against their brethren.

39 And Ner begat Kish; and Kish begat Saul; and Saul begat Jonathan, and Malchishua, and Abinadab, and Esh-baal.

40 And the son of Jonathan *was* Merib-baal: and Merib-baal begat Micah.

41 And the sons of Micah *were*, Pithon, and Melech, and Tahrea, *and Ahaz*.

42 And Ahaz begat Jarah; and Jarah begat Alemeth, and Azmaveth, and Zimri; and Zimri begat Moza;

43 And Moza begat Binea; and Rephaiah his son, Eleasah his son, Azel his son.

44 And Azel had six sons, whose names *are* these, Azrikam, Bocheru, and Ishmael, and Shear iah, and Obadiah, and Hanan: these *were* the sons of Azel.

CHAPTER 10
Saul's Death

1 Now the Philistines fought against Israel; and the men of Israel fled from before the Philistines, and fell down slain in mount Gilboa.

2 And the Philistines followed hard after Saul, and after his sons; and the Philistines slew Jonathan, and Abinadab, and Malchishua, the sons of Saul.

3 And the battle went sore against Saul, and the archers hit him, and he was wounded of the archers.

4 Then said Saul to his armourbearer, Draw thy sword, and thrust me through therewith; lest these uncircumcised come and abuse me. But his armourbearer would not; for he was sore afraid. So Saul took a sword, and fell upon it.

5 And when his armourbearer saw that Saul was dead, he fell likewise on the sword, and died.

20 Num. 31:6
22 1Sam. 9:9; 1Chr. 26:1, 2
25 2Kgs. 11:5
30 Ex. 30:23
31 Lev. 2:5; 6:21
32 Lev. 24:8
33 1Chr. 6:31; 25:1
35 1Chr. 8:29
39 1Chr. 8:33
41 1Chr. 8:35

1 1Sam. 31:1, 2

2 1Sam. 14:49

9:35 Gibeon. The ancestry of King Saul and a listing of descendants appear, prior to beginning the narrative record of Saul's death in battle and the succession of David to the throne.

6 So Saul died, and his three sons, and all his house died together.

7 And when all the men of Israel that *were* in the valley saw that they fled, and that Saul and his sons were dead, then they forsook their cities, and fled: and the Philistines came and dwelt in them.

8 And it came to pass on the morrow, when the Philistines came to strip the slain, that they found Saul and his sons fallen in mount Gilboa.

9 And when they had stripped him, they took his head, and his armour, and sent into the land of the Philistines round about, to carry tidings unto their idols, and to the people.

10 And they put his armour in the house of their gods, and fastened his head in the temple of Dagon.

11 And when all Jabesh-gilead heard all that the Philistines had done to Saul,

12 They arose, all the valiant men, and took away the body of Saul, and the bodies of his sons, and brought them to Jabesh, and buried their bones under the oak in Jabesh, and fasted seven days.

13 So Saul died for his transgression which he committed against the LORD, *even* against the word of the LORD, which he kept not, and also for asking *counsel* of *one that had* a familiar spirit, to inquire *of it*;

14 And inquired not of the LORD: therefore he slew him, and turned the kingdom unto David the son of Jesse.

CHAPTER 11
David Becomes King over All Israel

1 Then all Israel gathered themselves to David unto Hebron, saying, Behold, we *are* thy bone and thy flesh.

2 And moreover in time past, even when Saul was king, thou *wast* he that leddest out and broughtest in Israel: and the LORD thy God said unto thee, Thou shalt feed my people Israel, and thou shalt be ruler over my people Israel.

3 Therefore came all the elders of Israel to the king to Hebron; and David made a covenant with them in Hebron before the LORD;

and they anointed David king over Israel, according to the word of the LORD by Samuel.

David Captures Zion

4 And David and all Israel went to Jerusalem, which *is* Jebus; where the Jebusites *were*, the inhabitants of the land.

5 And the inhabitants of Jebus said to David, Thou shalt not come hither. Nevertheless David took the castle of Zion, which *is* the city of David.

6 And David said, Whosoever smiteth the Jebusites first shall be chief and captain. So Joab the son of Zeruiah went first up, and was chief.

7 And David dwelt in the castle; therefore they called it the city of David.

8 And he built the city round about, even from Millo round about: and Joab repaired the rest of the city.

9 So David waxed greater and greater: for the LORD of hosts *was* with him.

David's Mighty Men

10 These also *are* the chief of the mighty men whom David had, who strengthened themselves with him in his kingdom, *and* with all Israel, to make him king, according to the word of the LORD concerning Israel.

11 And this *is* the number of the mighty men whom David had; Jashobeam, an hachmonite, the chief of the captains: he lifted up his spear against three hundred slain *by him* at one time.

12 And after him *was* Eleazar the son of Dodo, the Ahohite, who *was one* of the three mighties.

13 He was with David at Pas-dammim, and there the Philistines were gathered together to battle, where was a parcel of ground full of barley; and the people fled from before the Philistines.

14 And they set themselves in the midst of *that* parcel, and delivered it, and slew the Philistines; and the LORD saved *them* by a great deliverance.

15 Now three of the thirty captains went down to the rock to David, into the cave of

---

Center column references:

10 1Sam. 31:10

13 1Sam. 13:13; 15:23; 28:7

14 1Sam. 15:28; 2Sam. 3:9, 10; 5:3

1 2Sam. 5:1

2 Ps. 78:71

3 1Sam. 16:1, 12, 13; 2Sam. 5:3

4 Judg. 1:21; 19:10; 2Sam. 5:6

7 2Sam. 5:7

10 1Sam. 16:1, 12; 2Sam. 23:8

13 1Sam. 17:1

15 2Sam. 23:13; 1Chr. 14:9

10:13 Saul died. The writer explains why Saul came to a tragic end. First, he disobeyed the Lord's command given through the prophet Samuel (1 Sam. 15:3–9), and second, he sought the advice of a medium, a necromancer (one who claims to communicate with the dead), which Mosaic law forbade (1 Sam. 28:6–19; cf. Deut. 18:9–14).

11:1 David ruled over Judah in Hebron for seven and a half years, from approximately 1010 B.C. to 1003 B.C. (2 Sam. 2—4). David's rule over Israel began at this point (see 2 Sam. 5:1–10). His reign totaled over forty years (1 Kgs. 2:11).

Adullam; and the host of the Philistines encamped in the valley of Rephaim.

16 And David *was* then in the hold, and the Philistines' garrison *was* then at Beth-lehem.

17 And David longed, and said, Oh that one would give me drink of the water of the well of Beth-lehem, that *is* at the gate!

18 And the three brake through the host of the Philistines, and drew water out of the well of Beth-lehem, that *was* by the gate, and took *it*, and brought *it* to David: but David would not drink *of* it, but poured it out to the LORD,

19 And said, My God forbid it me, that I should do this thing: shall I drink the blood of these men that have put their lives in jeopardy? for with *the jeopardy of* their lives they brought it. Therefore he would not drink it. These things did these three mightiest.

20 And Abishai the brother of Joab, he was chief of the three: for lifting up his spear against three hundred, he slew *them*, and had a name among the three.

21 Of the three, he was more honourable than the two; for he was their captain: howbeit he attained not to the *first* three.

22 Benaiah the son of Jehoiada, the son of a valiant man of Kabzeel, who had done many acts; he slew two lionlike men of Moab: also he went down and slew a lion in a pit in a snowy day.

23 And he slew an Egyptian, a man of *great* stature, five cubits high; and in the Egyptian's hand *was* a spear like a weaver's beam; and he went down to him with a staff, and plucked the spear out of the Egyptian's hand, and slew him with his own spear.

24 These *things* did Benaiah the son of Jehoiada, and had the name among the three mighties.

25 Behold, he was honourable among the thirty, but attained not to the *first* three: and David set him over his guard.

26 Also the valiant men of the armies *were*, Asahel the brother of Joab, Elhanan the son of Dodo of Beth-lehem,

27 Shammoth the Harorite, Helez the Pelonite,

28 Ira the son of Ikkesh the Tekoite, Abiezer the Antothite,

29 Sibbecai the Hushathite, Ilai the Ahohite,

30 Maharai the Netophathite, Heled the son of Baanah the Netophathite,

31 Ithai the son of Ribai of Gibeah, *that pertained* to the children of Benjamin, Benaiah the Pirathonite,

32 Hurai of the brooks of Gaash, Abiel the Arbathite,

33 Azmaveth the Baharumite, Eliahba the Shaalbonite,

34 The sons of Hashem the Gizonite, Jonathan the son of Shage the Hararite,

35 Ahiam the son of Sacar the Hararite, Eliphal the son of Ur,

36 Hepher the Mecherathite, Ahijah the Pelonite,

37 Hezro the Carmelite, Naarai the son of Ezbai,

38 Joel the brother of Nathan, Mibhar the son of Haggeri,

39 Zelek the Ammonite, Naharai the Berothite, the armourbearer of Joab the son of Zeruiah,

40 Ira the Ithrite, Gareb the Ithrite,

41 Uriah the Hittite, Zabad the son of Ahlai,

42 Adina the son of Shiza the Reubenite, a captain of the Reubenites, and thirty with him,

43 Hanan the son of Maachah, and Joshaphat the Mithnite,

44 Uzzia the Ashterathite, Shama and Jehiel the sons of Hothan the Aroerite,

45 Jediael the son of Shimri, and Joha his brother, the Tizite,

46 Eliel the Mahavite, and Jeribai, and Joshaviah, the sons of Elnaam, and Ithmah the Moabite,

47 Eliel, and Obed, and Jasiel the Mesobaite.

CHAPTER 12
David's Personal Army

1 Now these *are* they that came to David to Ziklag, while he yet kept himself close because of Saul the son of Kish: and they *were* among the mighty men, helpers of the war.

2 *They were* armed with bows, and could use both the right hand and the left in *hurling* stones and *shooting* arrows out of a bow, *even* of Saul's brethren of Benjamin.

3 The chief *was* Ahiezer, then Joash, the sons of Shemaah the Gibeathite; and Jeziel, and Pelet, the sons of Azmaveth; and Berachah, and Jehu the Antothite,

4 And Ismaiah the Gibeonite, a mighty man among the thirty, and over the thirty; and Jeremiah, and Jahaziel, and Johanan, and Josabad the Gederathite,

5 Eluzai, and Jerimoth, and Bealiah, and Shemariah, and Shephatiah the Haruphite,

6 Elkanah, and Jesiah, and Azareel, and Joezer, and Jashobeam, the Korhites,

Cross references (center column)

20 2Sam. 23:18

21 2Sam. 23:19

22 2Sam. 23:20

26 2Sam. 23:24

27 2Sam. 23:25, 26

34 2Sam. 23:32, 33

1 1Sam. 27:2, 6

2 Judg. 20:16

7 And Joelah, and Zebadiah, the sons of Jeroham of Gedor.

8 And of the Gadites there separated themselves unto David into the hold to the wilderness men of might, *and* men of war *fit* for the battle, that could handle shield and buckler, whose faces *were like* the faces of lions, and *were* as swift as the roes upon the mountains;

9 Ezer the first, Obadiah the second, Eliab the third,

10 Mishmannah the fourth, Jeremiah the fifth,

11 Attai the sixth, Eliel the seventh,

12 Johanan the eighth, Elzabad the ninth,

13 Jeremiah the tenth, Machbanai the eleventh.

14 These *were* of the sons of Gad, captains of the host: one of the least *was* over an hundred, and the greatest over a thousand.

15 These *are* they that went over Jordan in the first month, when it had overflown all his banks; and they put to flight all *them* of the valleys, *both* toward the east, and toward the west.

16 And there came of the children of Benjamin and Judah to the hold unto David.

17 And David went out to meet them, and answered and said unto them, If ye be come peaceably unto me to help me, mine heart shall be knit unto you: but if *ye be come* to betray me to mine enemies, seeing *there is* no wrong in mine hands, the God of our fathers look *thereon*, and rebuke *it*.

18 Then the spirit came upon Amasai, *who was* chief of the captains, *and he said*, Thine *are* we, David, and on thy side, thou son of Jesse: peace, peace *be* unto thee, and peace *be* to thine helpers; for thy God helpeth thee. Then David received them, and made them captains of the band.

19 And there fell *some* of Manasseh to David, when he came with the Philistines against Saul to battle: but they helped them not: for the lords of the Philistines upon advisement sent him away, saying, He will fall to his master Saul to *the jeopardy of* our heads.

20 As he went to Ziklag, there fell to him of Manasseh, Adnah, and Jozabad, and Jediael, and Michael, and Jozabad, and Elihu, and Zilthai, captains of the thousands that *were* of Manasseh.

21 And they helped David against the band *of the rovers*: for they *were* all mighty men of valour, and were captains in the host.

22 For at *that* time day by day there came to David to help him, until *it was* a great host, like the host of God.

23 And these *are* the numbers of the bands *that were* ready armed to the war, *and* came to David to Hebron, to turn the kingdom of Saul to him, according to the word of the LORD.

24 The children of Judah that bare shield and spear *were* six thousand and eight hundred, ready armed to the war.

25 Of the children of Simeon, mighty men of valour for the war, seven thousand and one hundred.

26 Of the children of Levi four thousand and six hundred.

27 And Jehoiada *was* the leader of the Aaronites, and with him *were* three thousand and seven hundred;

28 And Zadok, a young man mighty of valour, and of his father's house twenty and two captains.

29 And of the children of Benjamin, the kindred of Saul, three thousand: for hitherto the greatest part of them had kept the ward of the house of Saul.

30 And of the children of Ephraim twenty thousand and eight hundred, mighty men of valour, famous throughout the house of their fathers.

31 And of the half tribe of Manasseh eighteen thousand, which were expressed by name, to come and make David king.

32 And of the children of Issachar, *which were men* that had understanding of the times, to know what Israel ought to do; the heads of them *were* two hundred; and all their brethren *were* at their commandment.

33 Of Zebulun, such as went forth to battle, expert in war, with all instruments of war, fifty thousand, which could keep rank: *they were* not of double heart.

34 And of Naphtali a thousand captains, and with them with shield and spear thirty and seven thousand.

35 And of the Danites expert in war twenty and eight thousand and six hundred.

36 And of Asher, such as went forth to battle, expert in war, forty thousand.

37 And on the other side of Jordan, of the Reubenites, and the Gadites, and of the half tribe of Manasseh, with all manner of instruments of war for the battle, an hundred and twenty thousand.

Cross references (center column):

8 2Sam. 2:18

15 Josh. 3:15

18 Judg. 6:34; 2Sam. 17:25

19 1Sam. 29:2, 4

21 1Sam. 30:1, 9, 10

23 1Sam. 16:1, 3; 2Sam. 2:3, 4; 5:1; 1Chr. 10:14; 11:1

28 2Sam. 8:17

29 Gen. 31:23; 2Sam. 2:8, 9

32 Esth. 1:13

33 Ps. 12:2

12:23–37 This section records the period of David's rule over Judah until he was crowned king of all Israel in Hebron.

38 All these men of war, that could keep rank, came with a perfect heart to Hebron, to make David king over all Israel: and all the rest also of Israel *were* of one heart to make David king.

39 And there they were with David three days, eating and drinking: for their brethren had prepared for them.

40 Moreover they that were nigh them, *even* unto Issachar and Zebulun and Naphtali, brought bread on asses, and on camels, and on mules, and on oxen, *and* meat, meal, cakes of figs, and bunches of raisins, and wine, and oil, and oxen, and sheep abundantly: for *there was* joy in Israel.

CHAPTER 13
David Moves the Ark of God

1 And David consulted with the captains of thousands and hundreds, *and* with every leader.

2 And David said unto all the congregation of Israel, If *it seem* good unto you, and *that it be* of the LORD our God, let us send abroad unto our brethren every where, *that are* left in all the land of Israel, and with them *also* to the priests and Levites *which are* in their cities *and* suburbs, that they may gather themselves unto us:

3 And let us bring again the ark of our God to us: for we inquired not at it in the days of Saul.

4 And all the congregation said that they would do so: for the thing was right in the eyes of all the people.

5 So David gathered all Israel together, from Shihor of Egypt even unto the entering of Hemath, to bring the ark of God from Kirjath-jearim.

6 And David went up, and all Israel, to Baalah, *that is*, to Kirjath-jearim, which *belonged* to Judah, to bring up thence the ark of God the LORD, that dwelleth *between* the cherubims, whose name is called *on it*.

7 And they carried the ark of God in a new cart out of the house of Abinadab: and Uzza and Ahio drave the cart.

8 And David and all Israel played before God with all *their* might, and with singing, and with harps, and with psalteries, and with timbrels, and with cymbals, and with trumpets.

9 And when they came unto the threshingfloor of Chidon, Uzza put forth his hand to hold the ark; for the oxen stumbled.

10 And the anger of the LORD was kindled against Uzza, and he smote him, because he put his hand to the ark: and there he died before God.

11 And David was displeased, because the LORD had made a breach upon Uzza: wherefore that place is called Perez-uzza to this day.

12 And David was afraid of God that day, saying, How shall I bring the ark of God *home* to me?

13 So David brought not the ark *home* to himself to the city of David, but carried it aside into the house of Obed-edom the Gittite.

14 And the ark of God remained with the family of Obed-edom in his house three months. And the LORD blessed the house of Obed-edom, and all that he had.

CHAPTER 14
David Prospers

1 Now Hiram king of Tyre sent messengers to David, and timber of cedars, with masons and carpenters, to build him an house.

2 And David perceived that the LORD had confirmed him king over Israel, for his kingdom was lifted up on high, because of his people Israel.

3 And David took more wives at Jerusalem: and David begat more sons and daughters.

4 Now these *are* the names of *his* children which he had in Jerusalem; Shammua, and Shobab, Nathan, and Solomon,

---

Cross references (center column):

2 1Sam. 31:1; Isa. 37:4
3 1Sam. 7:1, 2
5 Josh. 13:3; 1Sam. 6:21; 7:1; 2Sam. 6:1
6 Josh. 15:9, 60; 1Sam. 4:4; 2Sam. 6:2
7 Num. 4:15; 1Sam. 7:1; 1Chr. 15:2, 13
8 2Sam. 6:5
9 2Sam. 6:6
10 Lev. 10:2; Num. 4:15; 1Chr. 15:13, 15
14 Gen. 30:27; 2Sam. 6:11; 1Chr. 26:5
1 2Sam. 5:11
4 1Chr. 3:5

12:39–40 This joyous coronation feast is described with the same enthusiasm as in verse 23, where David's earlier followers and soldiers are compared to a great army, like an army of God (see 2 Sam. 5).

13:9–10 Responsible for covering the ark and other furniture for travel (Num. 4:5–14), the priests were not to touch the ark while it was in transit. In charge of conveying the ark using the rings and poles provided (Ex. 25:14), the family of Kohathites were promised death if they touched it (Num. 4:15). It was not to be carried on wagons, but on human shoulders (Num. 7:9). The priests and others alike somehow ignored the law and instead did that which was "right in the eyes of all the people" (vv. 3–4). Trying to do the right thing in the wrong way brought divine judgment. Uzza's death was consistent with the warning given to the Kohathites. The event stood out as an example which effectively checked further disobedience from spreading among the people (1 Chr. 15:2–13, cf. 2 Sam. 6:1–11).

5 And Ibhar, and Elishua, and Elpalet,
6 And Nogah, and Nepheg, and Japhia,
7 And Elishama, and Beeliada, and Eliphalet.

David Defeats the Philistines

8 And when the Philistines heard that David was anointed king over all Israel, all the Philistines went up to seek David. And David heard *of it*, and went out against them.
9 And the Philistines came and spread themselves in the valley of Rephaim.
10 And David inquired of God, saying, Shall I go up against the Philistines? and wilt thou deliver them into mine hand? And the LORD said unto him, Go up; for I will deliver them into thine hand.
11 So they came up to Baal-perazim; and David smote them there. Then David said, God hath broken in upon mine enemies by mine hand like the breaking forth of waters: therefore they called the name of that place Baal-perazim.
12 And when they had left their gods there, David gave a commandment, and they were burned with fire.
13 And the Philistines yet again spread themselves abroad in the valley.
14 Therefore David inquired again of God; and God said unto him Go not up after them; turn away from them, and come upon them over against the mulberry trees.
15 And it shall be, when thou shalt hear a sound of going in the tops of the mulberry trees, *that* then thou shalt go out to battle: for God is gone forth before thee to smite the host of the Philistines.
16 David therefore did as God commanded him: and they smote the host of the Philistines from Gibeon even to Gazer.
17 And the fame of David went out into all lands; and the LORD brought the fear of him upon all nations.

CHAPTER 15
David Brings the Ark of God to Jerusalem

1 And *David* made him houses in the city of David, and prepared a place for the ark of God, and pitched for it a tent.

2 Then David said, None ought to carry the ark of God but the Levites: for them hath the LORD chosen to carry the ark of God, and to minister unto him for ever.
3 And David gathered all Israel together to Jerusalem, to bring up the ark of the LORD unto his place, which he had prepared for it.
4 And David assembled the children of Aaron, and the Levites:
5 Of the sons of Kohath; Uriel the chief, and his brethren an hundred and twenty:
6 Of the sons of Merari; Asaiah the chief, and his brethren two hundred and twenty:
7 Of the sons of Gershom; Joel the chief, and his brethren an hundred and thirty:
8 Of the sons of Elizaphan; Shemaiah the chief, and his brethren two hundred:
9 Of the sons of Hebron; Eliel the chief, and his brethren fourscore:
10 Of the sons of Uzziel; Amminadab the chief, and his brethren an hundred and twelve.
11 And David called for Zadok and Abiathar the priests, and for the Levites, for Uriel, Asaiah, and Joel, Shemaiah, and Eliel, and Amminadab,
12 And said unto them, Ye *are* the chief of the fathers of the Levites: sanctify yourselves, *both* ye and your brethren, that ye may bring up the ark of the LORD God of Israel unto *the place that* I have prepared for it.
13 For because ye *did it* not at the first, the LORD our God made a breach upon us, for that we sought him not after the due order.
14 So the priests and the Levites sanctified themselves to bring up the ark of the LORD God of Israel.
15 And the children of the Levites bare the ark of God upon their shoulders with the staves thereon, as Moses commanded according to the word of the LORD.
16 And David spake to the chief of the Levites to appoint their brethren *to be* the singers with instruments of musick, psalteries and harps and cymbals, sounding, by lifting up the voice with joy.
17 So the Levites appointed Heman the son of Joel; and of his brethren, Asaph the son of Berechiah; and of the sons of Merari their brethren, Ethan the son of Kushaiah;

Cross-references (center column)

7 2Sam. 5:16
8 2Sam. 5:17
9 1Chr. 11:15
13 2Sam. 5:22
14 2Sam. 5:23
16 2Sam. 5:25, *Geba*
17 Deut. 2:25; 11:25; Josh. 6:27; 2Chr. 26:8
1 1Chr. 16:1
2 Num. 4:2, 15; Deut. 10:8; 31:9
3 1Kgs. 8:1; 1Chr. 13:5
8 Ex. 6:22
9 Ex. 6:18
13 2Sam. 6:3; 1Chr. 13:7, 10, 11
15 Ex. 25:14; Num. 4:15; 7:9
17 1Chr. 6:33, 39, 44

14:12 Burning idols was required by the Law of Moses (Deut. 7:5, 25).

15:1–29 After the three months that the ark was kept in the home of Obed-edom, David then carefully followed the directions of the Law to move the ark (Num. 4:1–39; Deut. 10:8; 18:5). He also prepared a temporary tabernacle in Jerusalem, which would be the center for worship until the temple was constructed (Deut. 12:5–7).

18 And with them their brethren of the second *degree*, Zechariah, Ben, and Jaaziel, and Shemiramoth, and Jehiel, and Unni, Eliab, and Benaiah, and Maaseiah, and Mattithiah, and Elipheleh, and Mikneiah, and Obed-edom, and Jeiel, the porters.
19 So the singers, Heman, Asaph, and Ethan, *were appointed* to sound with cymbals of brass;
20 And Zechariah, and Aziel, and Shemiramoth, and Jehiel, and Unni, and Eliab, and Maaseiah, and Benaiah, with psalteries on Alamoth;
21 And Mattithiah, and Elipheleh, and Mikneiah, and Obed-edom, and Jeiel, and Azaziah, with harps on the Sheminith to excel.
22 And Chenaniah, chief of the Levites, *was* for song: he instructed about the song, because he *was* skilful.
23 And Berechiah and Elkanah *were* doorkeepers for the ark.
24 And Shebaniah, and Jehoshaphat, and Nethaneel, and Amasai, and Zechariah, and Benaiah, and Eliezer, the priests, did blow with the trumpets before the ark of God: and Obed-edom and Jehiah *were* doorkeepers for the ark.
25 So David, and the elders of Israel, and the captains over thousands, went to bring up the ark of the covenant of the LORD out of the house of Obed-edom with joy.
26 And it came to pass, when God helped the Levites that bare the ark of the covenant of the LORD, that they offered seven bullocks and seven rams.
27 And David *was* clothed with a robe of fine linen, and all the Levites that bare the ark, and the singers, and Chenaniah the master of the song with the singers: David also *had* upon him an ephod of linen.
28 Thus all Israel brought up the ark of the covenant of the LORD with shouting, and with sound of the cornet, and with trumpets, and with cymbals, making a noise with psalteries and harps.
29 And it came to pass, *as* the ark of the covenant of the LORD came to the city of David, that Michal the daughter of Saul looking out at a window saw king David dancing and playing: and she despised him in her heart.

CHAPTER 16

1 So they brought the ark of God, and set it in the midst of the tent that David had pitched for it: and they offered burnt sacrifices and peace offerings before God.
2 And when David had made an end of offering the burnt offerings and the peace offerings, he blessed the people in the name of the LORD.
3 And he dealt to every one of Israel, both man and woman, to every one a loaf of bread, and a good piece of flesh, and a flagon *of wine*.
4 And he appointed *certain* of the Levites to minister before the ark of the LORD, and to record, and to thank and praise the LORD God of Israel:
5 Asaph the chief, and next to him Zechariah, Jeiel, and Shemiramoth, and Jehiel, and Mattithiah, and Eliab, and Benaiah, and Obed-edom: and Jeiel with psalteries and with harps; but Asaph made a sound with cymbals;
6 Benaiah also and Jahaziel the priests with trumpets continually before the ark of the covenant of God.

David's Psalm of Thanksgiving

7 Then on that day David delivered first *this psalm* to thank the LORD into the hand of Asaph and his brethren.
8 Give thanks unto the LORD, call upon his name, make known his deeds among the people.
9 Sing unto him, sing psalms unto him, talk ye of all his wondrous works.
10 Glory ye in his holy name: let the heart of them rejoice that seek the LORD.
11 Seek the LORD and his strength, seek his face continually.
12 Remember his marvellous works that he hath done, his wonders, and the judgments of his mouth;
13 O ye seed of Israel his servant, ye children of Jacob, his chosen ones.
14 He *is* the LORD our God; his judgments *are* in all the earth.
15 Be ye mindful always of his covenant; the word *which* he commanded to a thousand generations;
16 *Even of the covenant* which he made with Abraham, and of his oath unto Isaac;

20 1Chr. 15:18, *Jaaziel*
24 Num. 10:8; Ps. 81:3
25 2Sam. 6:12, 13; 1Kgs. 8:1
28 1Chr. 13:8
29 2Sam. 6:16
1 2Sam. 6:17-19
7 2Sam. 23:1
8 Ps. 105:1-15
16 Gen. 17:2; 26:3; 28:13; 35:11

16:7–36 This was evidently the first public concert of praise, introducing a thanksgiving psalm by David, sung by Asaph's choir with instrumental accompaniment. The hymn is composed of phrases also used in other psalms: 1) verses 8–22 (cf. Ps. 105:1–15); 2) verses 22–33 (cf. Ps. 96:1–13); 3) verses 34–36 (cf. Ps. 106:1, 47–48).

17 And hath confirmed the same to Jacob for a law, *and* to Israel *for* an everlasting covenant,

18 Saying, Unto thee will I give the land of Canaan, the lot of your inheritance;

19 When ye were but few, even a few, and strangers in it.

20 And *when* they went from nation to nation, and from *one* kingdom to another people;

21 He suffered no man to do them wrong: yea, he reproved kings for their sakes,

22 *Saying,* Touch not mine anointed, and do my prophets no harm.

23 Sing unto the LORD, all the earth; shew forth from day to day his salvation.

24 Declare his glory among the heathen; his marvellous works among all nations.

25 For great *is* the LORD, and greatly to be praised: he also *is* to be feared above all gods.

26 For all the gods of the people *are* idols: but the LORD made the heavens.

27 Glory and honour *are* in his presence; strength and gladness *are* in his place.

28 Give unto the LORD, ye kindreds of the people, give unto the LORD glory and strength.

29 Give unto the LORD the glory *due* unto his name: bring an offering, and come before him: worship the LORD in the beauty of holiness.

30 Fear before him, all the earth: the world also shall be stable, that it be not moved.

31 Let the heavens be glad, and let the earth rejoice: and let *men* say among the nations, The LORD reigneth.

32 Let the sea roar, and the fulness thereof: let the fields rejoice, and all that *is* therein.

33 Then shall the trees of the wood sing out at the presence of the LORD, because he cometh to judge the earth.

34 O give thanks unto the LORD; for *he is* good; for his mercy *endureth* for ever.

35 And say ye, Save us, O God of our salvation, and gather us together, and deliver us from the heathen, that we may give thanks to thy holy name, *and* glory in thy praise.

36 Blessed *be* the LORD God of Israel for ever and ever. And all the people said, Amen, and praised the LORD.

Those That Served in the Tabernacle

37 So he left there before the ark of the covenant of the LORD Asaph and his brethren, to minister before the ark continually, as every day's work required:

38 And Obed-edom with their brethren, threescore and eight; Obed-edom also the son of Jeduthun and Hosah *to be* porters:

39 And Zadok the priest, and his brethren the priests, before the tabernacle of the LORD in the high place that *was* at Gibeon,

40 To offer burnt offerings unto the LORD upon the altar of the burnt offering continually morning and evening, and *to do* according to all that is written in the law of the LORD, which he commanded Israel;

41 And with them Heman and Jeduthun, and the rest that were chosen, who were expressed by name, to give thanks to the LORD, because his mercy *endureth* for ever;

42 And with them Heman and Jeduthun with trumpets and cymbals for those that should make a sound, and with musical instruments of God. And the sons of Jeduthun *were* porters.

43 And all the people departed every man to his house: and David returned to bless his house.

CHAPTER 17
God's Promise to David

1 Now it came to pass, as David sat in his house, that David said to Nathan the prophet, Lo, I dwell in an house of cedars, but the ark of the covenant of the LORD *remaineth* under curtains.

2 Then Nathan said unto David, Do all that *is* in thine heart; for God *is* with thee.

3 And it came to pass the same night, that the word of God came to Nathan, saying,

4 Go and tell David my servant, Thus saith the LORD, Thou shalt not build me an house to dwell in:

5 For I have not dwelt in an house since the day that I brought up Israel unto this day; but have gone from tent to tent, and from *one* tabernacle *to another.*

6 Wheresoever I have walked with all Israel, spake I a word to any of the judges of Israel, whom I commanded to feed my peo-

Cross references (center column):
19 Gen. 34:30
21 Gen. 12:17; 20:3; Ex. 7:15-18
22 Ps. 105:15
23 Ps. 96:1
26 Lev. 19:4
34 Ps. 106:1; 107:1; 118:1; 136:1
35 Ps. 106:47, 48
36 Deut. 27:15; 1Kgs. 8:15
39 1Kgs. 3:4; 1Chr. 21:29; 2Chr. 1:3
40 Ex. 29:38; Num. 28:3
41 1Chr. 16:34; 2Chr. 5:13; 7:3; Ezra 3:11; Jer. 33:11
43 2Sam. 6:19, 20
1 2Sam. 7:1

17:4 Because David was a man of warfare, God did not allow David to build the temple (1 Chr. 22:8; 28:3), but he was allowed to accumulate a large part of the materials needed for construction (1 Chr. 22:2–4, 14–16) in antici-pation of his son Solomon being able to accomplish the task. Solomon was approved by God because he would be a "man of rest" (1 Chr. 22:9).

ple, saying, Why have ye not built me an house of cedars?

7 Now therefore thus shalt thou say unto my servant David, Thus saith the LORD of hosts, I took thee from the sheepcote, *even* from following the sheep, that thou shouldest be ruler over my people Israel:

8 And I have been with thee whithersoever thou hast walked, and have cut off all thine enemies from before thee, and have made thee a name like the name of the great men that *are* in the earth.

9 Also I will ordain a place for my people Israel, and will plant them, and they shall dwell in their place, and shall be moved no more; neither shall the children of wickedness waste them any more, as at the beginning,

10 And since the time that I commanded judges *to be* over my people Israel. Moreover I will subdue all thine enemies. Furthermore I tell thee that the LORD will build thee an house.

11 And it shall come to pass, when thy days be expired that thou must go *to be* with thy fathers, that I will raise up thy seed after thee, which shall be of thy sons; and I will establish his kingdom.

12 He shall build me an house, and I will stablish his throne for ever.

13 I will be his father, and he shall be my son: and I will not take my mercy away from him, as I took *it* from *him* that was before thee:

14 But I will settle him in mine house and in my kingdom for ever: and his throne shall be established for evermore.

15 According to all these words, and according to all this vision, so did Nathan speak unto David.

David's Prayer of Appreciation

16 And David the king came and sat before the LORD, and said, Who *am* I, O LORD God, and what *is* mine house, that thou hast brought me hitherto?

17 And *yet* this was a small thing in thine eyes, O God; for thou hast *also* spoken of thy servant's house for a great while to come, and hast regarded me according to the estate of a man of high degree, O LORD God.

18 What can David *speak* more to thee for the honour of thy servant? for thou knowest thy servant.

19 O LORD, for thy servant's sake, and according to thine own heart, hast thou done all this greatness, in making known all *these* great things.

20 O LORD, *there is* none like thee, neither *is there any* God beside thee, according to all that we have heard with our ears.

21 And what one nation in the earth *is* like thy people Israel, whom God went to redeem *to be* his own people, to make thee a name of greatness and terribleness, by driving out nations from before thy people, whom thou hast redeemed out of Egypt?

22 For thy people Israel didst thou make thine own people for ever; and thou, LORD, becamest their God.

23 Therefore now, LORD, let the thing that thou hast spoken concerning thy servant and concerning his house be established for ever, and do as thou hast said.

24 Let it even be established, that thy name may be magnified for ever, saying, The LORD of hosts *is* the God of Israel, *even* a God to Israel: and *let* the house of David thy servant be established before thee.

25 For thou, O my God, hast told thy servant that thou wilt build him an house: therefore thy servant hath found *in his heart* to pray before thee.

26 And now, LORD, thou art God, and hast promised this goodness unto thy servant:

27 Now therefore let it please thee to bless the house of thy servant, that it may be before thee for ever: for thou blessest, O LORD, and *it shall be* blessed for ever.

CHAPTER 18
David's Military Success

1 Now after this it came to pass, that David smote the Philistines, and subdued them, and took Gath and her towns out of the hand of the Philistines.

---

13 2Sam. 7:14, 15
14 Luke 1:33
16 2Sam. 7:18

1 2Sam. 8:1

17:7–15 The great Davidic covenant is also found in 2 Samuel 7:8–29. Principle prophetic promises include a guarantee that Israel's territory would be a permanent dwelling place (v. 9), that David's house (not a building but his posterity) would continue (v. 10), that the seed or descendants of David would be established in the monarchy (v. 11), and that his son would build the temple (v. 12). The continuity of the temple as the center of worship includes Solomon's Temple, the second temple after the captivity, the third temple in the future Tribulation (Rev. 11:1–2), and the Millennial Temple (Ezek. 40—48). The Davidic dynasty through Solomon and his successors would continue forever (v. 14). All the promises to David merge in Jesus Christ, who in the messianic kingdom will sit on the throne of David (Luke 1:32–33). This is not a heavenly throne, but will be on earth.

2 And he smote Moab; and the Moabites became David's servants, *and* brought gifts.

3 And David smote Hadarezer king of Zobah unto Hamath, as he went to stablish his dominion by the river Euphrates.

4 And David took from him a thousand chariots, and seven thousand horsemen, and twenty thousand footmen: David also houghed all the chariot *horses*, but reserved of them an hundred chariots.

5 And when the Syrians of Damascus came to help Hadarezer king of Zobah, David slew of the Syrians two and twenty thousand men.

6 Then David put *garrisons* in Syria-damascus; and the Syrians became David's servants, *and* brought gifts. Thus the LORD preserved David whithersoever he went.

7 And David took the shields of gold that were on the servants of Hadarezer, and brought them to Jerusalem.

8 Likewise from Tibhath, and from Chun, cities of Hadarezer, brought David very much brass, wherewith Solomon made the brasen sea, and the pillars, and the vessels of brass.

9 Now when Tou king of Hamath heard how David had smitten all the host of Hadarezer king of Zobah;

10 He sent Hadoram his son to king David, to inquire of his welfare, and to congratulate him, because he had fought against Hadarezer, and smitten him; (for Hadarezer had war with Tou;) and *with him* all manner of vessels of gold and silver and brass.

11 Them also king David dedicated unto the LORD, with the silver and the gold that he brought from all *these* nations; from Edom, and from Moab, and from the children of Ammon, and from the Philistines, and from Amalek.

12 Moreover Abishai the son of Zeruiah slew of the Edomites in the valley of salt eighteen thousand.

13 And he put garrisons in Edom; and all the Edomites became David's servants. Thus the LORD preserved David whithersoever he went.

David's Officials

14 So David reigned over all Israel, and executed judgment and justice among all his people.

15 And Joab the son of Zeruiah *was* over the host; and Jehoshaphat the son of Ahilud, recorder.

16 And Zadok the son of Ahitub, and Abimelech the son of Abiathar, *were* the priests; and Shavsha was scribe;

17 And Benaiah the son of Jehoiada *was* over the Cherethites and the Pelethites; and the sons of David *were* chief about the king.

CHAPTER 19

Israel Defeats the Ammonites and Syrians

1 Now it came to pass after this, that Nahash the king of the children of Ammon died, and his son reigned in his stead.

2 And David said, I will shew kindness unto Hanun the son of Nahash, because his father shewed kindness to me. And David sent messengers to comfort him concerning his father. So the servants of David came into the land of the children of Ammon to Hanun, to comfort him.

3 But the princes of the children of Ammon said to Hanun, Thinkest thou that David doth honour thy father, that he hath sent comforters unto thee? are not his servants come unto thee for to search, and to overthrow, and to spy out the land?

4 Wherefore Hanun took David's servants, and shaved them, and cut off their garments in the midst hard by their buttocks, and sent them away.

5 Then there went *certain*, and told David how the men were served. And he sent to meet them: for the men were greatly ashamed. And the king said, Tarry at Jericho until your beards be grown, and *then* return.

6 And when the children of Ammon saw that they had made themselves odious to David, Hanun and the children of Ammon sent a thousand talents of silver to hire them chariots and horsemen out of Mesopotamia, and out of Syria-maachah, and out of Zobah.

7 So they hired thirty and two thousand chariots, and the king of Maachah and his people; who came and pitched before Medeba. And the children of Ammon gathered themselves together from their cities, and came to battle.

Cross-references (center column):

3 2Sam. 8:3

4 2Sam. 8:4, *seven hundred*

8 1Kgs. 7:15, 23; 2Chr. 4:12, 15, 16

9 2Sam. 8:9

10 2Sam. 8:10

12 2Sam. 8:13

13 2Sam. 8:14

16 2Sam. 8:17, *Seraiah*; 1Kgs. 4:3, *Shisha*

17 2Sam. 8:18

1 2Sam. 10:1

6 1Chr. 18:5, 9

18:8 much brass. This brass, or bronze, was collected for the temple. The materials David had accumulated for Solomon's Temple are described in 1 Chronicles 22:2–5, 14–16.

19:1–2 Nahash. There is some question as to whether this is the same Nahash of Ammon whom Saul fought some fifty-five years before (1 Sam. 11:1–15). It may have been a son who had the same name.

8 And when David heard *of it*, he sent Joab, and all the host of the mighty men.

9 And the children of Ammon came out, and put the battle in array before the gate of the city: and the kings that were come *were* by themselves in the field.

10 Now when Joab saw that the battle was set against him before and behind, he chose out of all the choice of Israel, and put *them* in array against the Syrians.

11 And the rest of the people he delivered unto the hand of Abishai his brother, and they set *themselves* in array against the children of Ammon.

12 And he said, If the Syrians be too strong for me, then thou shalt help me: but if the children of Ammon be too strong for thee, then I will help thee.

13 Be of good courage, and let us behave ourselves valiantly for our people, and for the cities of our God: and let the LORD do *that which is* good in his sight.

14 So Joab and the people that *were* with him drew nigh before the Syrians unto the battle; and they fled before him.

15 And when the children of Ammon saw that the Syrians were fled, they likewise fled before Abishai his brother, and entered into the city. Then Joab came to Jerusalem.

16 And when the Syrians saw that they were put to the worse before Israel, they sent messengers, and drew forth the Syrians that *were* beyond the river: and Shophach the captain of the host of Hadarezer *went* before them.

17 And it was told David; and he gathered all Israel, and passed over Jordan, and came upon them, and set *the battle* in array against them. So when David had put the battle in array against the Syrians, they fought with him.

18 But the Syrians fled before Israel; and David slew of the Syrians seven thousand *men which fought in* chariots, and forty thousand footmen, and killed Shophach the captain of the host.

19 And when the servants of Hadarezer saw that they were put to the worse before Israel, they made peace with David, and became his servants: neither would the Syrians help the children of Ammon any more.

CHAPTER 20
Another Victory over the Ammonites

1 And it came to pass, that after the year was expired, at the time that kings go out *to battle*, Joab led forth the power of the army, and wasted the country of the children of Ammon, and came and besieged Rabbah. But David tarried at Jerusalem. And Joab smote Rabbah, and destroyed it.

2 And David took the crown of their king from off his head, and found it to weigh a talent of gold, and *there were* precious stones in it; and it was set upon David's head: and he brought also exceeding much spoil out of the city.

3 And he brought out the people that *were* in it, and cut *them* with saws, and with harrows of iron, and with axes. Even so dealt David with all the cities of the children of Ammon. And David and all the people returned to Jerusalem.

Philistine Giants Die in Battle

4 And it came to pass after this, that there arose war at Gezer with the Philistines; at which time Sibbechai the Hushathite slew Sippai, *that was* of the children of the giant: and they were subdued.

5 And there was war again with the Philistines; and Elhanan the son of Jair slew Lahmi the brother of Goliath the Gittite, whose spear staff *was* like a weaver's beam.

6 And yet again there was war at Gath, where was a man of *great* stature, whose fingers and toes *were* four and twenty, six *on each hand*, and six *on each foot*: and he also was the son of the giant.

7 But when he defied Israel, Jonathan the son of Shimea David's brother slew him.

8 These were born unto the giant in Gath; and they fell by the hand of David, and by the hand of his servants.

CHAPTER 21
David Takes a Census

1 And Satan stood up against Israel, and provoked David to number Israel.

---

16 2Sam. 10:16

1 2Sam. 11:1; 12:26

2 2Sam. 12:30, 31

4 2Sam. 21:18; 1Chr. 11:29

5 2Sam. 21:19

6 2Sam. 21:20

7 1Sam. 16:9

1 2Sam. 24:1

20:3 cut them with saws. The proper understanding of the wording of this verse is that David did not mutilate the Ammonites, but forced them to labor in the fields and in building projects (see 2 Sam. 12:31). The tools mentioned here were those which were to be used on buildings and in fields.

21:1 Satan. There are no other instances in the historical books of the Old Testament where Satan ("adversary," a name which emphasizes what he does) is referred to by this title. The only other places in the Old Testament are Job (used fourteen times in chapters 1 and 2), Psalm 109:6 and in Zechariah 3:1–2.

2 And David said to Joab and to the rulers of the people, Go, number Israel from Beersheba even to Dan; and bring the number of them to me, that I may know *it*.

3 And Joab answered, The LORD make his people an hundred times so many more as they *be*: but, my lord the king, *are* they not all my lord's servants? why then doth my lord require this thing? why will he be a cause of trespass to Israel?

4 Nevertheless the king's word prevailed against Joab. Wherefore Joab departed, and went throughout all Israel, and came to Jerusalem.

5 And Joab gave the sum of the number of the people unto David. And all *they of* Israel were a thousand thousand and an hundred thousand men that drew sword: and Judah *was* four hundred threescore and ten thousand men that drew sword.

6 But Levi and Benjamin counted he not among them: for the king's word was abominable to Joab.

David's Punishment

7 And God was displeased with this thing; therefore he smote Israel.

8 And David said unto God, I have sinned greatly, because I have done this thing: but now, I beseech thee, do away the iniquity of thy servant; for I have done very foolishly.

9 And the LORD spake unto Gad, David's seer, saying,

10 Go and tell David, saying, Thus saith the LORD, I offer thee three *things*: choose thee one of them, that I may do *it* unto thee.

11 So Gad came to David, and said unto him, Thus saith the LORD, Choose thee

12 Either three years' famine; or three months to be destroyed before thy foes, while that the sword of thine enemies overtaketh *thee*; or else three days the sword of the LORD, even the pestilence, in the land, and the angel of the LORD destroying throughout all the coasts of Israel. Now therefore advise thyself what word I shall bring again to him that sent me.

13 And David said unto Gad, I am in a great strait: let me fall now into the hand of the LORD; for very great *are* his mercies: but let me not fall into the hand of man.

14 So the LORD sent pestilence upon Israel: and there fell of Israel seventy thousand men.

15 And God sent an angel unto Jerusalem to destroy it: and as he was destroying, the LORD beheld, and he repented him of the evil, and said to the angel that destroyed, It

is enough, stay now thine hand. And the angel of the LORD stood by the threshingfloor of Ornan the Jebusite.

16 And David lifted up his eyes, and saw the angel of the LORD stand between the earth and the heaven, having a drawn sword in his hand stretched out over Jerusalem. Then David and the elders *of Israel, who were* clothed in sackcloth, fell upon their faces.

17 And David said unto God, Is it not I *that* commanded the people to be numbered? even I it is that have sinned and done evil indeed; but *as for* these sheep, what have they done? let thine hand, I pray thee, O LORD my God, be on me, and on my father's house; but not on thy people, that they should be plagued.

David Offers a Sacrifice

18 Then the angel of the LORD commanded Gad to say to David, that David should go up, and set up an altar unto the LORD in the threshingfloor of Ornan the Jebusite.

19 And David went up at the saying of Gad, which he spake in the name of the LORD.

20 And Ornan turned back, and saw the angel; and his four sons with him hid themselves. Now Ornan was threshing wheat.

21 And as David came to Ornan, Ornan looked and saw David, and went out of the threshingfloor, and bowed himself to David with *his* face to the ground.

22 Then David said to Ornan, Grant me the place of *this* threshingfloor, that I may build an altar therein unto the LORD: thou shalt grant it me for the full price: that the plague may be stayed from the people.

23 And Ornan said unto David, Take *it* to thee, and let my lord the king do *that which is* good in his eyes: lo, I give *thee* the oxen *also* for burnt offerings, and the threshing instruments for wood, and the wheat for the meat offering; I give it all.

24 And king David said to Ornan, Nay; but I will verily buy it for the full price: for I will not take *that* which *is* thine for the LORD, nor offer burnt offerings without cost.

25 So David gave to Ornan for the place six hundred shekels of gold by weight.

26 And David built there an altar unto the LORD, and offered burnt offerings and peace offerings, and called upon the LORD; and he answered him from heaven by fire upon the altar of burnt offering.

27 And the LORD commanded the angel; and he put up his sword again into the sheath thereof.

Cross references
2 1Chr. 27:23
6 1Chr. 27:24
8 2Sam. 12:13; 24:10
9 1Sam. 9:9
12 2Sam. 24:13
15 Gen. 6:6; 2Sam. 24:16
16 2Chr. 3:1
18 2Chr. 3:1
25 2Sam. 24:24
26 Lev. 9:24; 2Chr. 3:1; 7:1

28 At that time when David saw that the LORD had answered him in the threshingfloor of Ornan the Jebusite, then he sacrificed there.

29 For the tabernacle of the LORD, which Moses made in the wilderness, and the altar of the burnt offering, *were* at that season in the high place at Gibeon.

30 But David could not go before it to inquire of God: for he was afraid because of the sword of the angel of the LORD.

CHAPTER 22

1 Then David said, This *is* the house of the LORD God, and this *is* the altar of the burnt offering for Israel.

David's Preparation for the Temple

2 And David commanded to gather together the strangers that *were* in the land of Israel; and he set masons to hew wrought stones to build the house of God.

3 And David prepared iron in abundance for the nails for the doors of the gates, and for the joinings; and brass in abundance without weight;

4 Also cedar trees in abundance: for the Zidonians and they of Tyre brought much cedar wood to David.

5 And David said, Solomon my son *is* young and tender, and the house *that is* to be builded for the LORD *must be* exceeding magnifical, of fame and of glory throughout all countries: I will *therefore* now make preparation for it. So David prepared abundantly before his death.

6 Then he called for Solomon his son, and charged him to build an house for the LORD God of Israel.

7 And David said to Solomon, My son, as for me, it was in my mind to build an house unto the name of the LORD my God:

8 But the word of the LORD came to me, saying, Thou hast shed blood abundantly, and hast made great wars: thou shalt not build an house unto my name, because thou hast shed much blood upon the earth in my sight.

9 Behold, a son shall be born to thee, who shall be a man of rest; and I will give him

rest from all his enemies round about: for his name shall be Solomon, and I will give peace and quietness unto Israel in his days.

10 He shall build an house for my name; and he shall be my son, and I *will be* his father; and I will establish the throne of his kingdom over Israel for ever.

11 Now, my son, the LORD be with thee; and prosper thou, and build the house of the LORD thy God, as he hath said of thee.

12 Only the LORD give thee wisdom and understanding, and give thee charge concerning Israel, that thou mayest keep the law of the LORD thy God.

13 Then shalt thou prosper, if thou takest heed to fulfil the statutes and judgments which the LORD charged Moses with concerning Israel: be strong, and of good courage; dread not, nor be dismayed.

14 Now, behold, in my trouble I have prepared for the house of the LORD an hundred thousand talents of gold, and a thousand thousand talents of silver; and of brass and iron without weight; for it is in abundance: timber also and stone have I prepared; and thou mayest add thereto.

15 Moreover *there are* workmen with thee in abundance, hewers and workers of stone and timber, and all manner of cunning men for every manner of work.

16 Of the gold, the silver, and the brass, and the iron, *there is* no number. Arise *therefore*, and be doing, and the LORD be with thee.

17 David also commanded all the princes of Israel to help Solomon his son, *saying*,

18 *Is* not the LORD your God with you? and hath he *not* given you rest on every side? for he hath given the inhabitants of the land into mine hand; and the land is subdued before the LORD, and before his people.

19 Now set your heart and your soul to seek the LORD your God; arise therefore, and build ye the sanctuary of the LORD God, to bring the ark of the covenant of the LORD, and the holy vessels of God, into the house that is to be built to the name of the LORD.

CHAPTER 23

1 So when David was old and full of days, he made Solomon his son king over Israel.

Cross references (center column)

29 1Kgs. 3:4; 1Chr. 16:39; 2Chr. 1:3

1 Deut. 12:5; 2Sam. 24:18; 1Chr. 21:18, 19, 26, 28; 2Chr. 3:1

2 1Kgs. 9:21

3 1Kgs. 7:47; 1Chr. 22:14

4 1Kgs. 5:6

5 1Chr. 19:1

7 Deut. 12:5, 11; 2Sam. 7:2; 1Kgs. 8:17; 1Chr. 17:1; 28:2

8 1Kgs. 5:3; 1Chr. 28:3

9 1Kgs. 4:25; 5:4; 1Chr. 28:5

10 2Sam. 7:13; 1Kgs. 5:5; 1Chr. 17:12, 13; 28:6; Heb. 1:5

11 1Chr. 22:16

12 1Kgs. 3:9, 12; Ps. 72:1

13 Deut. 31:7, 8; Josh. 1:6, 7, 8, 9; 1Chr. 28:7, 20

14 1Chr. 22:3

16 1Chr. 22:11

18 Deut. 12:10; Josh. 22:4; 2Sam. 7:1; 1Chr. 23:25

19 1Kgs. 5:3; 8:6, 21; 1Chr. 22:7; 2Chr. 5:7; 6:11; 20:3

1 1Kgs. 1:33-39; 1Chr. 28:5

22:8–9 Solomon. To emphasize the tranquil era to follow David's tumultuous reign, God instructed him to bestow the name "Solomon" upon his heir. The word Solomon means "peaceful." Under Solomon, the kingdom reached its peak of prosperity and military strength.

23:1 Solomon his son king over Israel. For a description of the events leading up to the ascension of Solomon to the throne, see the notes for 1 Kings 1—2.

The Levites and Their Duties

2 And he gathered together all the princes of Israel, with the priests and the Levites.
3 Now the Levites were numbered from the age of thirty years and upward: and their number by their polls, man by man, was thirty and eight thousand.
4 Of which, twenty and four thousand *were* to set forward the work of the house of the LORD; and six thousand *were* officers and judges:
5 Moreover four thousand *were* porters; and four thousand praised the LORD with the instruments which I made, *said David*, to praise *therewith*.
6 And David divided them into courses among the sons of Levi, *namely*, Gershon, Kohath, and Merari.
7 Of the Gershonites *were*, Laadan, and Shimei.
8 The sons of Laadan; the chief *was* Jehiel, and Zetham, and Joel, three.
9 The sons of Shimei; Shelomith, and Haziel, and Haran, three. These *were* the chief of the fathers of Laadan.
10 And the sons of Shimei *were*, Jahath, Zina, and Jeush, and Beriah. These four *were* the sons of Shimei.
11 And Jahath was the chief, and Zizah the second: but Jeush and Beriah had not many sons; therefore they were in one reckoning, according to *their* father's house.
12 The sons of Kohath; Amram, Izhar, Hebron, and Uzziel, four.
13 The sons of Amram; Aaron and Moses: and Aaron was separated, that he should sanctify the most holy things, he and his sons for ever, to burn incense before the LORD, to minister unto him, and to bless in his name for ever.
14 Now *concerning* Moses the man of God, his sons were named of the tribe of Levi.
15 The sons of Moses *were*, Gershom, and Eliezer.
16 Of the sons of Gershom, Shebuel *was* the chief.
17 And the sons of Eliezer *were*, Rehabiah the chief. And Eliezer had none other sons; but the sons of Rehabiah were very many.
18 Of the sons of Izhar; Shelomith the chief.
19 Of the sons of Hebron; Jeriah the first, Amariah the second, Jahaziel the third, and Jekameam the fourth.
20 Of the sons of Uzziel; Michah the first, and Jesiah the second.
21 The sons of Merari; Mahli, and Mushi. The sons of Mahli; Eleazar, and Kish.

22 And Eleazar died, and had no sons, but daughters: and their brethren the sons of Kish took them.
23 The sons of Mushi; Mahli, and Eder, and Jeremoth, three.
24 These *were* the sons of Levi after the house of their fathers; *even* the chief of the fathers, as they were counted by number of names by their polls, that did the work for the service of the house of the LORD, from the age of twenty years and upward.
25 For David said, The LORD God of Israel hath given rest unto his people, that they may dwell in Jerusalem for ever:
26 And also unto the Levites; they shall no more carry the tabernacle, nor any vessels of it for the service thereof.
27 For by the last words of David the Levites *were* numbered from twenty years old and above:
28 Because their office *was* to wait on the sons of Aaron for the service of the house of the LORD, in the courts, and in the chambers, and in the purifying of all holy things, and the work of the service of the house of God;
29 Both for the shewbread, and for the fine flour for meat offering, and for the unleavened cakes, and for *that which is baked in* the pan, and for that which is fried, and for all manner of measure and size;
30 And to stand every morning to thank and praise the LORD, and likewise at even;
31 And to offer all burnt sacrifices unto the LORD in the sabbaths, in the new moons, and on the set feasts, by number, according to the order commanded unto them, continually before the LORD:
32 And that they should keep the charge of the tabernacle of the congregation, and the charge of the holy *place*, and the charge of the sons of Aaron their brethren, in the service of the house of the LORD.

CHAPTER 24
The Organization of the Priests

1 Now *these are* the divisions of the sons of Aaron. The sons of Aaron; Nadab, and Abihu, Eleazar, and Ithamar.
2 But Nadab and Abihu died before their father, and had no children: therefore Eleazar and Ithamar executed the priest's office.
3 And David distributed them, both Zadok of the sons of Eleazar, and Ahimelech of the sons of Ithamar, according to their offices in their service.
4 And there were more chief men found of the sons of Eleazar than of the sons of Ithamar; and *thus* were they divided. Among the

3 Num. 4:3, 47
4 Deut. 16:18; 1Chr. 26:29; 2Chr. 19:8
5 2Chr. 29:25, 26; Amos 6:5
6 Ex. 6:16; Num. 26:57; 1Chr. 6:1; 2Chr. 8:14; 29:25
7 1Chr. 6:17; 26:21
10 1Chr. 23:11
12 Ex. 6:18
13 Ex. 6:20; 28:1; 30:7; Num. 6:23; 16:40; Deut. 21:5; 1Sam. 2:28; Heb. 5:4
15 Ex. 2:22; 18:3, 4
16 1Chr. 26:24
17 1Chr. 26:25
19 1Chr. 24:23
21 1Chr. 24:26, 29
22 Num. 36:6, 8; 1Chr. 24:28
23 1Chr. 24:30
24 Num. 1:3; 4:3; 8:24; 10:17, 21; 1Chr. 23:27; Ezra 3:8
25 1Chr. 22:18
26 Num. 4:5
28 Neh. 11:24
29 Ex. 25:30; Lev. 2:4, 5, 7; 6:20; 19:35; 1Chr. 9:29
31 Lev. 23:4; Num. 10:10; Ps. 81:3
32 Num. 1:53; 3:6-9
1 Lev. 10:1, 6; Num. 26:60
2 Num. 3:4; 26:61

sons of Eleazar *there were* sixteen chief men of the house of *their* fathers, and eight among the sons of Ithamar according to the house of their fathers.

5 Thus were they divided by lot, one sort with another; for the governors of the sanctuary, and governors *of the house* of God, were of the sons of Eleazar, and of the sons of Ithamar.

6 And Shemaiah the son of Nethaneel the scribe, *one* of the Levites, wrote them before the king, and the princes, and Zadok the priest, and Ahimelech the son of Abiathar, and *before* the chief of the fathers of the priests and Levites: one principal household being taken for Eleazar, and *one* taken for Ithamar.

7 Now the first lot came forth to Jehoiarib, the second to Jedaiah,

8 The third to Harim, the fourth to Seorim,

9 The fifth to Malchijah, the sixth to Mijamin,

10 The seventh to Hakkoz, the eighth to Abijah,

11 The ninth to Jeshua, the tenth to Shecaniah,

12 The eleventh to Eliashib, the twelfth to Jakim,

13 The thirteenth to Huppah, the fourteenth to Jeshebeab,

14 The fifteenth to Bilgah, the sixteenth to Immer,

15 The seventeenth to Hezir, the eighteenth to Aphses,

16 The nineteenth to Pethahiah, the twentieth to Jehezekel,

17 The one and twentieth to Jachin, the two and twentieth to Gamul,

18 The three and twentieth to Delaiah, the four and twentieth to Maaziah.

19 These *were* the orderings of them in their service to come into the house of the LORD, according to their manner, under Aaron their father, as the LORD God of Israel had commanded him.

The Levites Again

20 And the rest of the sons of Levi *were these*: Of the sons of Amram; Shubael: of the sons of Shubael; Jehdeiah.

21 Concerning Rehabiah: of the sons of Rehabiah, the first *was* Isshiah.

22 Of the Izharites; Shelomoth: of the sons of Shelomoth; Jahath.

23 And the sons *of Hebron*; Jeriah *the first*, Amariah the second, Jahaziel the third, Jekameam the fourth.

24 *Of* the sons of Uzziel; Michah: of the sons of Michah; Shamir.

25 The brother of Michah *was* Isshiah: of the sons of Isshiah; Zechariah.

26 The sons of Merari *were* Mahli and Mushi: the sons of Jaaziah; Beno.

27 The sons of Merari by Jaaziah; Beno, and Shoham, and Zaccur, and Ibri.

28 Of Mahli *came* Eleazar, who had no sons.

29 Concerning Kish: the son of Kish *was* Jerahmeel.

30 The sons also of Mushi; Mahli, and Eder, and Jerimoth. These *were* the sons of the Levites after the house of their fathers.

31 These likewise cast lots over against their brethren the sons of Aaron in the presence of David the king, and Zadok, and Ahimelech, and the chief of the fathers of the priests and Levites, even the principal fathers over against their younger brethren.

CHAPTER 25
The Temple Musicians and Their Duties

1 Moreover David and the captains of the host separated to the service of the sons of Asaph, and of Heman, and of Jeduthun, who should prophesy with harps, with psalteries, and with cymbals: and the number of the workmen according to their service was:

2 Of the sons of Asaph; Zaccur, and Joseph, and Nethaniah, and Asarelah, the

10 Neh. 12:4, 17; Luke 1:5

19 1Chr. 9:25

20 1Chr. 23:16, *Shebuel*

21 1Chr. 23:17

22 1Chr. 23:18, *Shelomith*

23 1Chr. 23:19; 26:31

26 Ex. 6:19; 1Chr. 23:21

28 1Chr. 23:22

30 1Chr. 23:23

1 1Chr. 6:33, 39, 44

24:4–19 These twenty-four classes or courses continued in New Testament times as the basis for rotating the priestly duties. As some of these classes died out or had to be consolidated with others, new ones were formed to take their places. In the return from exile in 538 B.C., four registered classes were represented: David's second, third and sixteenth, and a new class, Pashur (Ezra 2:36–39). By 522 B.C., twenty-two courses had been reinstated (Neh. 12:1–7 [cf. Neh. 10:2–9; 12:12–21]). A New Testament reference to this system appears in the account of Zacharias, father of John the Baptist, who saw an angel during his term of duty in the temple (see Luke 1:8–23).

25:1 prophesy. These musicians did not necessarily prophesy in the same sense as Nathan or Gad (contemporary prophets with David), but they did inspire worship and service through the lyrics of the psalms. Prophesying can mean proclaiming God's truth to His people (1 Cor. 14:3). David and his fellow musicians led the people in spiritual worship through music, as is done today in Christian assemblies.

sons of Asaph under the hands of Asaph, which prophesied according to the order of the king.

3 Of Jeduthun: the sons of Jeduthun; Gedaliah, and Zeri, and Jeshaiah, Hashabiah, and Mattithiah, six, under the hands of their father Jeduthun, who prophesied with a harp, to give thanks and to praise the LORD.

4 Of Heman: the sons of Heman; Bukkiah, Mattaniah, Uzziel, Shebuel, and Jerimoth, Hananiah, Hanani, Eliathah, Giddalti, and Romamti-ezer, Joshbekashah, Mallothi, Hothir, *and* Mahazioth:

5 All these *were* the sons of Heman the king's seer in the words of God, to lift up the horn. And God gave to Heman fourteen sons and three daughters.

6 All these *were* under the hands of their father for song *in* the house of the LORD, with cymbals, psalteries, and harps, for the service of the house of God, according to the king's order to Asaph, Jeduthun, and Heman.

7 So the number of them, with their brethren that were instructed in the songs of the LORD, *even* all that were cunning, was two hundred fourscore and eight.

8 And they cast lots, ward against *ward*, as well the small as the great, the teacher as the scholar.

9 Now the first lot came forth for Asaph to Joseph: the second to Gedaliah, who with his brethren and sons *were* twelve:

10 The third to Zaccur, *he*, his sons, and his brethren, *were* twelve:

11 The fourth to Izri, *he*, his sons, and his brethren, *were* twelve:

12 The fifth to Nethaniah, *he*, his sons, and his brethren, *were* twelve:

13 The sixth to Bukkiah, *he*, his sons, and his brethren, *were* twelve:

14 The seventh to Jesharelah, *he*, his sons, and his brethren, *were* twelve:

15 The eighth to Jeshaiah, *he*, his sons, and his brethren, *were* twelve:

16 The ninth to Mattaniah, *he*, his sons, and his brethren, *were* twelve:

17 The tenth to Shimei, *he*, his sons, and his brethren, *were* twelve:

18 The eleventh to Azareel, *he*, his sons, and his brethren, *were* twelve:

19 The twelfth to Hashabiah, *he*, his sons, and his brethren, *were* twelve:

20 The thirteenth to Shubael, *he*, his sons, and his brethren, *were* twelve:

21 The fourteenth to Mattithiah, *he*, his sons, and his brethren, *were* twelve:

22 The fifteenth to Jeremoth, *he*, his sons, and his brethren, *were* twelve:

23 The sixteenth to Hananiah, *he*, his sons, and his brethren, *were* twelve:

24 The seventeenth to Joshbekashah, *he*, his sons, and his brethren, *were* twelve:

25 The eighteenth to Hanani, *he*, his sons, and his brethren, *were* twelve:

26 The nineteenth to Mallothi, *he*, his sons, and his brethren, *were* twelve:

27 The twentieth to Eliathah, *he*, his sons, and his brethren, *were* twelve:

28 The one and twentieth to Hothir, *he*, his sons, and his brethren, *were* twelve:

29 The two and twentieth to Giddalti, *he*, his sons, and his brethren, *were* twelve:

30 The three and twentieth to Mahazioth, *he*, his sons, and his brethren, *were* twelve:

31 The four and twentieth to Romamti-ezer, *he*, his sons, and his brethren, *were* twelve.

CHAPTER 26
Other Temple Workers

1 Concerning the divisions of the porters: Of the Korhites *was* Meshelemiah the son of Kore, of the sons of Asaph.

2 And the sons of Meshelemiah *were*, Zechariah the firstborn, Jediael the second, Zebadiah the third, Jathniel the fourth,

3 Elam the fifth, Jehohanan the sixth, Elioenai the seventh.

4 Moreover the sons of Obed-edom *were*, Shemaiah the firstborn, Jehozabad the second, Joah the third, and Sacar the fourth, and Nethaneel the fifth,

5 Ammiel the sixth, Issachar the seventh, Peulthai the eighth: for God blessed him.

6 Also unto Shemaiah his son were sons born, that ruled throughout the house of their father: for they *were* mighty men of valour.

7 The sons of Shemaiah; Othni, and Rephael, and Obed, Elzabad, whose brethren *were* strong men, Elihu, and Semachiah.

8 All these of the sons of Obed-edom: they and their sons and their brethren, able men

Cross-references: 4 1Chr. 25:18, 20 · 6 1Chr. 25:2 · 8 2Chr. 23:13 · 8 1Chr. 6:37; 9:19; 26:14 · 5 1Chr. 13:14

26:1–32 David's administration involved extensive organization and the delegation of leadership and responsibility. Some Christians have supposed that efficient and effective organization is not necessary to carry on God's work. But both in the Old Testament and the New Testament, the principles of organization, planning, and dedicated service are very clear.

for strength for the service, *were* threescore and two of Obed-edom.

9 And Meshelemiah had sons and brethren, strong men, eighteen.

10 Also Hosah, of the children of Merari, had sons; Simri the chief, (for *though* he was not the firstborn, yet his father made him the chief;)

11 Hilkiah the second, Tebaliah the third, Zechariah the fourth: all the sons and brethren of Hosah *were* thirteen.

12 Among these *were* the divisions of the porters, *even* among the chief men, *having* wards one against another, to minister in the house of the LORD.

13 And they cast lots, as well the small as the great, according to the house of their fathers, for every gate.

14 And the lot eastward fell to Shelemiah. Then for Zechariah his son, a wise counseller, they cast lots; and his lot came out northward.

15 To Obed-edom southward; and to his sons the house of Asuppim.

16 To Shuppim and Hosah *the lot came forth* westward, with the gate Shallecheth, by the causeway of the going up, ward against ward.

17 Eastward *were* six Levites, northward four a day, southward four a day, and toward Asuppim two *and* two.

18 At Parbar westward, four at the causeway, *and* two at Parbar.

19 These *are* the divisions of the porters among the sons of Kore, and among the sons of Merari.

20 And of the Levites, Ahijah *was* over the treasures of the house of God, and over the treasures of the dedicated things.

21 *As concerning* the sons of Laadan; the sons of the Gershonite Laadan, chief fathers, *even* of Laadan the Gershonite, *were* Jehieli.

22 The sons of Jehieli; Zetham, and Joel his brother, *which were* over the treasures of the house of the LORD.

23 Of the Amramites, *and* the Izharites, the Hebronites, *and* the Uzzielites:

24 And Shebuel the son of Gershom, the son of Moses, *was* ruler of the treasures.

25 And his brethren by Eliezer; Rehabiah his son, and Jeshaiah his son, and Joram his son, and Zichri his son, and Shelomith his son.

26 Which Shelomith and his brethren *were* over all the treasures of the dedicated things, which David the king, and the chief fathers, the captains over thousands and hundreds, and the captains of the host, had dedicated.

27 Out of the spoils won in battles did they dedicate to maintain the house of the LORD.

28 And all that Samuel the seer, and Saul the son of Kish, and Abner the son of Ner, and Joab the son of Zeruiah, had dedicated; *and* whosoever had dedicated *any thing, it was* under the hand of Shelomith, and of his brethren.

Other Public Servants

29 Of the Izharites, Chenaniah and his sons *were* for the outward business over Israel, for officers and judges.

30 *And* of the Hebronites, Hashabiah and his brethren, men of valour, a thousand and seven hundred, *were* officers among them of Israel on this side Jordan westward in all the business of the LORD, and in the service of the king.

31 Among the Hebronites *was* Jerijah the chief, *even* among the Hebronites, according to the generations of his fathers. In the fortieth year of the reign of David they were sought for, and there were found among them mighty men of valour at Jazer of Gilead.

32 And his brethren, men of valour, *were* two thousand and seven hundred chief fathers, whom king David made rulers over the Reubenites, the Gadites, and the half tribe of Manasseh, for every matter pertaining to God, and affairs of the king.

CHAPTER 27
Monthly Organization of Public Service

1 Now the children of Israel after their number, *to wit,* the chief fathers and captains of thousands and hundreds, and their officers that served the king in any matter of the courses, which came in and went out month by month throughout all the months of the year, of every course *were* twenty and four thousand.

2 Over the first course for the first month *was* Jashobeam the son of Zabdiel: and in his course *were* twenty and four thousand.

3 Of the children of Perez *was* the chief of all the captains of the host for the first month.

4 And over the course of the second month *was* Dodai an Ahohite, and of his course *was* Mikloth also the ruler: in his course likewise *were* twenty and four thousand.

5 The third captain of the host for the third month *was* Benaiah the son of Jehoiada, a chief priest: and in his course *were* twenty and four thousand.

Cross references

10 1Chr. 16:38
14 1Chr. 26:1
16 1Kgs. 10:5; 2Chr. 9:4
20 1Chr. 28:12; Mal. 3:10
21 1Chr. 6:17; 23:8; 29:8
24 1Chr. 23:16
25 1Chr. 23:18
28 1Sam. 9:9
29 1Chr. 23:4
31 Josh. 21:39; 1Chr. 23:19
32 2Chr. 19:11
2 2Sam. 23:8; 1Chr. 11:11
4 2Sam. 23:9
5 1Kgs. 4:5

6 This *is that* Benaiah, *who was* mighty among the thirty, and above the thirty: and in his course *was* Ammizabad his son.

7 The fourth *captain* for the fourth month *was* Asahel the brother of Joab, and Zebadiah his son after him: and in his course *were* twenty and four thousand.

8 The fifth captain for the fifth month *was* Shamhuth the Izrahite: and in his course *were* twenty and four thousand.

9 The sixth *captain* for the sixth month *was* Ira the son of Ikkesh the Tekoite: and in his course *were* twenty and four thousand.

10 The seventh *captain* for the seventh month *was* Helez the Pelonite, of the children of Ephraim: and in his course *were* twenty and four thousand.

11 The eighth *captain* for the eighth month *was* Sibbecai the Hushathite, of the Zarhites: and in his course *were* twenty and four thousand.

12 The ninth *captain* for the ninth month *was* Abiezer the Anetothite, of the Benjamites: and in his course *were* twenty and four thousand.

13 The tenth *captain* for the tenth month *was* Maharai the Netophathite, of the Zarhites: and in his course *were* twenty and four thousand.

14 The eleventh *captain* for the eleventh month *was* Benaiah the Pirathonite, of the children of Ephraim: and in his course *were* twenty and four thousand.

15 The twelfth *captain* for the twelfth month *was* Heldai the Netophathite, of Othniel: and in his course *were* twenty and four thousand.

Tribal Leaders

16 Furthermore over the tribes of Israel: the ruler of the Reubenites *was* Eliezer the son of Zichri: of the Simeonites, Shephatiah the son of Maachah:

17 Of the Levites, Hashabiah the son of Kemuel: of the Aaronites, Zadok:

18 Of Judah, Elihu, *one* of the brethren of David: of Issachar, Omri the son of Michael:

19 Of Zebulun, Ishmaiah the son of Obadiah: of Naphtali, Jerimoth the son of Azriel:

20 Of the children of Ephraim, Hoshea the son of Azaziah: of the half tribe of Manasseh, Joel the son of Pedaiah:

21 Of the half *tribe* of Manasseh in Gilead, Iddo the son of Zechariah: of Benjamin, Jaasiel the son of Abner:

22 Of Dan, Azareel the son of Jeroham. These *were* the princes of the tribes of Israel.

23 But David took not the number of them from twenty years old and under: because the LORD had said he would increase Israel like to the stars of the heavens.

24 Joab the son of Zeruiah began to number, but he finished not, because there fell wrath for it against Israel; neither was the number put in the account of the chronicles of king David.

Administrators of David's Property

25 And over the king's treasures *was* Azmaveth the son of Adiel: and over the storehouses in the fields, in the cities, and in the villages, and in the castles, *was* Jehonathan the son of Uzziah:

26 And over them that did the work of the field for tillage of the ground *was* Ezri the son of Chelub:

27 And over the vineyards *was* Shimei the Ramathite: over the increase of the vineyards for the wine cellars *was* Zabdi the Shiphmite:

28 And over the olive trees and the sycomore trees that *were* in the low plains *was* Baal-hanan the Gederite: and over the cellars of oil *was* Joash:

29 And over the herds that fed in Sharon *was* Shitrai the Sharonite: and over the herds *that were* in the valleys *was* Shaphat the son of Adlai:

30 Over the camels also *was* Obil the Ishmeelite: and over the asses *was* Jehdeiah the Meronothite:

31 And over the flocks *was* Jaziz the Hagerite. All these *were* the rulers of the substance which *was* king David's.

Those Close to David

32 Also Jonathan David's uncle was a counseller, a wise man, and a scribe: and Jehiel the son of Hachmoni *was* with the king's sons:

33 And Ahithophel *was* the king's counseller: and Hushai the Archite *was* the king's companion:

34 And after Ahithophel *was* Jehoiada the

Cross-references (center column):

6 2Sam. 23:20, 22, 23; 1Chr. 11:22
7 2Sam. 23:24; 1Chr. 11:26
9 1Chr. 11:28
10 1Chr. 11:27
11 2Sam. 21:18; 1Chr. 11:29
12 1Chr. 11:28
13 2Sam. 23:28; 1Chr. 11:30
14 1Chr. 11:31
15 1Chr. 11:30
17 1Chr. 26:30
18 1Sam. 16:6, *Eliab*
23 Gen. 15:5
24 2Sam. 24:15; 1Chr. 21:7
33 2Sam. 15:12, 37; 16:16
34 1Kgs. 1:7; 1Chr. 11:6

27:27–34 Ahithophel had deserted David in order to follow Absalom, who attempted to usurp the throne (2 Sam. 15:12, 31; 16:20–23). When frustrated by Hushai, who was actually loyal to David (2 Sam. 15:32, 37; 17:1–16), he committed suicide (2 Sam. 17:23).

son of Benaiah, and Abiathar: and the general of the king's army *was* Joab.

CHAPTER 28
God Has Chosen Solomon to Build the Temple

1 And David assembled all the princes of Israel, the princes of the tribes, and the captains of the companies that ministered to the king by course, and the captains over the thousands, and captains over the hundreds, and the stewards over all the substance and possession of the king, and of his sons, with the officers, and with the mighty men, and with all the valiant men, unto Jerusalem.

2 Then David the king stood up upon his feet, and said, Hear me, my brethren, and my people: *As for me,* I *had* in mine heart to build an house of rest for the ark of the covenant of the LORD, and for the footstool of our God, and had made ready for the building:

3 But God said unto me, Thou shalt not build an house for my name, because thou *hast been* a man of war, and hast shed blood.

4 Howbeit the LORD God of Israel chose me before all the house of my father to be king over Israel for ever: for he hath chosen Judah *to be* the ruler; and of the house of Judah, the house of my father; and among the sons of my father he liked me to make *me* king over all Israel:

5 And of all my sons, (for the LORD hath given me many sons,) he hath chosen Solomon my son to sit upon the throne of the kingdom of the LORD over Israel.

6 And he said unto me, Solomon thy son, he shall build my house and my courts: for I have chosen him *to be* my son, and I will be his father.

7 Moreover I will establish his kingdom for ever, if he be constant to do my commandments and my judgments, as at this day.

8 Now therefore in the sight of all Israel the congregation of the LORD, and in the audience of our God, keep and seek for all the commandments of the LORD your God: that ye may possess this good land, and leave *it* for an inheritance for your children after you for ever.

9 And thou, Solomon my son, know thou the God of thy father, and serve him with a

perfect heart and with a willing mind: for the LORD searcheth all hearts, and understandeth all the imaginations of the thoughts: if thou seek him, he will be found of thee; but if thou forsake him, he will cast thee off for ever.

10 Take heed now; for the LORD hath chosen thee to build an house for the sanctuary: be strong, and do *it.*

11 Then David gave to Solomon his son the pattern of the porch, and of the houses thereof, and of the treasuries thereof, and of the upper chambers thereof, and of the inner parlours thereof, and of the place of the mercy seat,

12 And the pattern of all that he had by the spirit, of the courts of the house of the LORD, and of all the chambers round about, of the treasuries of the house of God, and of the treasuries of the dedicated things:

13 Also for the courses of the priests and the Levites, and for all the work of the service of the house of the LORD, and for all the vessels of service in the house of the LORD.

14 *He gave* of gold by weight for *things* of gold, for all instruments of all manner of service; *silver also* for all instruments of silver by weight, for all instruments of every kind of service:

15 Even the weight for the candlesticks of gold, and for their lamps of gold, by weight for every candlestick, and for the lamps thereof: and for the candlesticks of silver by weight, *both* for the candlestick, and *also* for the lamps thereof, according to the use of every candlestick.

16 And by weight *he gave* gold for the tables of shewbread, for every table; and *likewise* silver for the tables of silver:

17 Also pure gold for the fleshhooks, and the bowls, and the cups: and for the golden basons *he gave gold* by weight for every bason; and *likewise silver* by weight for every bason of silver:

18 And for the altar of incense refined gold by weight; and gold for the pattern of the chariot of the cherubims, that spread out *their wings,* and covered the ark of the covenant of the LORD.

19 All *this, said David,* the LORD made me understand in writing by *his* hand upon me, *even* all the works of this pattern.

20 And David said to Solomon his son, Be strong and of good courage, and do *it:* fear

1	1Chr. 11:10; 27:1, 2, 16, 25
2	2Sam. 7:2; Ps. 99:5; 132:3-5, 7
3	2Sam. 7:5, 13; 1Kgs. 5:3; 1Chr. 17:4; 22:8
4	Gen. 49:8; 1Sam. 16:1, 7-13; 1Chr. 5:2; Ps. 60:7; 78:68
5	1Chr. 3:1; 22:9; 23:1
6	2Sam. 7:13, 14; 1Chr. 22:9, 10; 2Chr. 1:9
7	1Chr. 22:13
9	1Sam. 16:7; 1Kgs. 8:39; 2Kgs. 20:3; 1Chr. 29:17; 2Chr. 15:2; Ps. 7:9; 101:2; 139:2; Prov. 17:3; Jer. 9:24; 11:20; 17:10; 20:12; Hos. 4:1; John 2:23; Rev. 2:23
10	1Chr. 28:6
11	Ex. 25:40; 1Chr. 28:19
12	1Chr. 26:20
18	Ex. 25:18-22; 1Sam. 4:4; 1Kgs. 6:23
19	Ex. 25:40; 1Chr. 28:11, 12
20	Deut. 31:7, 8; Josh. 1:5, 6, 7, 9; 1Chr. 22:13

28:20 be strong and of good courage. David musters the strength to bring a powerful challenge to his leaders and to Solomon shortly before his death.

not, nor be dismayed: for the Lord God, *even my God, will be* with thee; he will not fail thee, nor forsake thee, until thou hast finished all the work for the service of the house of the Lord.

21 And, behold, the courses of the priests and the Levites, *even they shall be with thee* for all the service of the house of God: and *there shall be* with thee for all manner of workmanship every willing skilful man, for any manner of service: also the princes and all the people *will be* wholly at thy commandment.

CHAPTER 29
An Offering for the Temple

1 Furthermore David the king said unto all the congregation, Solomon my son, whom alone God hath chosen, *is yet* young and tender, and the work *is* great: for the palace *is* not for man, but for the Lord God.

2 Now I have prepared with all my might for the house of my God the gold for *things to be made* of gold, and the silver for *things* of silver, and the brass for *things* of brass, the iron for *things* of iron, and wood for *things* of wood; onyx stones, and *stones* to be set, glistering stones, and of divers colours, and all manner of precious stones, and marble stones in abundance.

3 Moreover, because I have set my affection to the house of my God, I have of mine own proper good, of gold and silver, *which* I have given to the house of my God, over and above all that I have prepared for the holy house,

4 *Even* three thousand talents of gold, of the gold of Ophir, and seven thousand talents of refined silver, to overlay the walls of the houses *withal*:

5 The gold for *things* of gold, and the silver for *things* of silver, and for all manner of work *to be made* by the hands of artificers. And who *then* is willing to consecrate his service this day unto the Lord?

6 Then the chief of the fathers and princes of the tribes of Israel, and the captains of thousands and of hundreds, with the rulers of the king's work, offered willingly,

7 And gave for the service of the house of God of gold five thousand talents and ten thousand drams, and of silver ten thousand

Cross References
21 Ex. 35:25, 26; 36:1, 2
1 1Kgs. 3:7; 1Chr. 22:5; Prov. 4:3
2 Isa. 54:11, 12; Rev. 21:18
4 1Kgs. 9:28
6 1Chr. 27:1
8 1Chr. 26:21
9 2Cor. 9:7
11 Matt. 6:13; 1Tim. 1:17; Rev. 5:13
12 Rom. 11:36
15 Job 14:2; Ps. 30:12; 90:9; 102:11; 144:4; Heb. 11:13; 1Pet. 2:11
17 1Sam. 16:7; 1Chr. 28:9; Prov. 11:20
18 Ps. 10:17
19 1Chr. 22:14; 29:2; Ps. 72:1

talents, and of brass eighteen thousand talents, and one hundred thousand talents of iron.

8 And they with whom *precious* stones were found gave *them* to the treasure of the house of the Lord, by the hand of Jehiel the Gershonite.

9 Then the people rejoiced, for that they offered willingly, because with perfect heart they offered willingly to the Lord: and David the king also rejoiced with great joy.

David Prays

10 Wherefore David blessed the Lord before all the congregation: and David said, Blessed *be* thou, Lord God of Israel our father, for ever and ever.

11 Thine, O Lord, *is* the greatness, and the power, and the glory, and the victory, and the majesty: for all *that is* in the heaven and in the earth *is thine*; thine *is* the kingdom, O Lord, and thou art exalted as head above all.

12 Both riches and honour *come* of thee, and thou reignest over all; and in thine hand *is* power and might; and in thine hand *it is* to make great, and to give strength unto all.

13 Now therefore, our God, we thank thee, and praise thy glorious name.

14 But who *am* I, and what *is* my people, that we should be able to offer so willingly after this sort? for all things *come* of thee, and of thine own have we given thee.

15 For we *are* strangers before thee, and sojourners, as *were* all our fathers: our days on the earth *are* as a shadow, and *there is* none abiding.

16 O Lord our God, all this store that we have prepared to build thee an house for thine holy name *cometh* of thine hand, and *is* all thine own.

17 I know also, my God, that thou triest the heart, and hast pleasure in uprightness. As for me, in the uprightness of mine heart I have willingly offered all these things: and now have I seen with joy thy people, which are present here, to offer willingly unto thee.

18 O Lord God of Abraham, Isaac, and of Israel, our fathers, keep this for ever in the imagination of the thoughts of the heart of thy people, and prepare their heart unto thee:

19 And give unto Solomon my son a perfect

29:1–19 David the king said unto all. Concluding his final farewell address as the sovereign, David publicly describes the vast amount of accumulated materials and treasures to be used for the construction of the temple under Solomon's reign. With thanksgiving and prayer, a great official celebration is held in honor of the full coronation of Solomon into the kingly office.

heart, to keep thy commandments, thy testimonies, and thy statutes, and to do all *these things*, and to build the palace, *for the* which I have made provision.

20 And David said to all the congregation, Now bless the LORD your God. And all the congregation blessed the LORD God of their fathers, and bowed down their heads, and worshipped the LORD, and the king.

Solomon Begins His Reign

21 And they sacrificed sacrifices unto the LORD, and offered burnt offerings unto the LORD, on the morrow after that day, *even a* thousand bullocks, a thousand rams, *and* a thousand lambs, with their drink offerings, and sacrifices in abundance for all Israel:

22 And did eat and drink before the LORD on that day with great gladness. And they made Solomon the son of David king the second time, and anointed *him* unto the LORD *to be* the chief governor, and Zadok *to be* priest.

23 Then Solomon sat on the throne of the LORD as king instead of David his father, and prospered; and all Israel obeyed him.

24 And all the princes, and the mighty men, and all the sons likewise of king David, submitted themselves unto Solomon the king.

25 And the LORD magnified Solomon exceedingly in the sight of all Israel, and bestowed upon him *such* royal majesty as had not been on any king before him in Israel.

David's Death

26 Thus David the son of Jesse reigned over all Israel.

27 And the time that he reigned over Israel *was* forty years; seven years reigned he in Hebron, and thirty and three *years* reigned he in Jerusalem.

28 And he died in a good old age, full of days, riches, and honour: and Solomon his son reigned in his stead.

29 Now the acts of David the king, first and last, behold, they *are* written in the book of Samuel the seer, and in the book of Nathan the prophet, and in the book of Gad the seer,

30 With all his reign and his might, and the times that went over him, and over Israel, and over all the kingdoms of the countries.

Cross references

22 1Kgs. 1:35, 39
24 Eccl. 8:2
25 1Kgs. 3:13; 2Chr. 1:12; Eccl. 2:9
27 2Sam. 5:4, 5; 1Kgs. 2:11
28 Gen. 25:8; 1Chr. 23:1
30 Dan. 2:21

29:22 made Solomon . . . king the second time. This refers to the grand public ceremony subsequent to the private installation of Solomon (1 Kgs. 1:35–39), held to counteract the attempt of Adonijah to take over the throne. With this ceremony, probably performed by Zadok the high priest, David transfers all authority to Solomon, who then sits upon the throne. The descendants of Zadok will perform the priestly duties in the Millennial Temple (Ezek. 40—48).

29:29 Nathan . . . Gad. Most likely, these were ancient prophets' writings perhaps similar to Jasher's works (Josh. 10:13; 2 Sam. 1:18), which were available to Ezra, but have since been long lost. It is assumed that many nameless but true prophets of God have written books of which parts have been incorporated into Scripture.

2 Chronicles

T he book of 2 Chronicles was originally included with 1 Chronicles. Ezra, the generally accepted author for the book (see introduction to 1 Chr.), restates the history of Israel and Judah as it related to the people's spiritual condition. Covering a period from 971 to 586 B.C. or about 385 years, this book opens with Solomon enthroned in splendor and closes with the beginning of Judah's seventy years of captivity and the decree of King Cyrus to allow the Jews to return to Jerusalem (536 B.C.). After describing the accession of Solomon, a detailed account is given of the building and dedication of the temple in Jerusalem (1—9).

Author
Ezra

Date
6th Century B.C.

Key Truth
Judah's Greatness and Fall

Historic Time
Divided Kingdom

Key Verse
30:18–19
. . . The good LORD pardon every one that prepareth his heart to seek God. . . .

In this record of the royal house and history of Judah, the fall from the greatness of David and Solomon's reigns is clear. Revivals had occurred under five of the eight best kings—Asa (chap. 15), Jehoshaphat (20), Joash (23—24), Hezekiah (29—31), and Josiah (35)—yet formalism, apostasy, and spiritual neglect increased throughout Judah. The revivals that took place never lasted long because those kings who were right with God raised children who became evil idolaters (e.g., Hezekiah and Manasseh).

After King Josiah's death in about 610 B.C., the four evil kings (Jehoahaz, Jehoiakim, Jehoiachin, and Zedekiah) sealed the nation's fate with their disobedience. The Babylonians, in three invasions which began the seventy years of captivity (36:20–21 and Jer. 25), carried away large numbers of Israelites and destroyed Jerusalem (606 B.C., 597 B.C., and 586 B.C.).

The book closes with practically the same words that open Ezra, ending the seventy years of captivity in 536 B.C.

Only chapters 7 and 8, recording Solomon's prayer and the Lord's appearance to the king after the temple's dedication, contain conditional prophecies about Israel's future disobedience and fall. Yet there is a suggestion of the perpetual preciousness of the temple area (7:15–16).

The 37 separate predictions are mostly already fulfilled or concerned with typology. Of 882 verses, 268, or 31 percent, are predictive in nature.

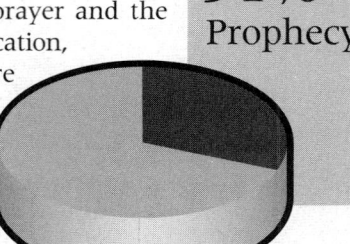

31%
Prophecy

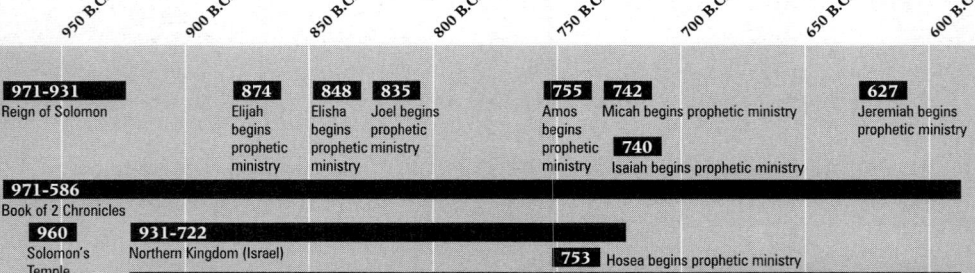

950 B.C.	900 B.C.	850 B.C.	800 B.C.	750 B.C.	700 B.C.	650 B.C.	600 B.C.	550 B.C.

971-931
Reign of Solomon

874 Elijah begins prophetic ministry

848 Elisha begins prophetic ministry **835** Joel begins prophetic ministry

755 Amos begins prophetic ministry **742** Micah begins prophetic ministry

740 Isaiah begins prophetic ministry

627 Jeremiah begins prophetic ministry

971-586
Book of 2 Chronicles

960
Solomon's Temple completed

931-722
Northern Kingdom (Israel)

753 Hosea begins prophetic ministry

931-586
Southern Kingdom (Judah)

CHAPTER 1

Solomon Asks for Wisdom

1 And Solomon the son of David was strengthened in his kingdom, and the LORD his God *was* with him, and magnified him exceedingly.

2 Then Solomon spake unto all Israel, to the captains of thousands and of hundreds, and to the judges, and to every governor in all Israel, the chief of the fathers.

3 So Solomon, and all the congregation with him, went to the high place that *was* at Gibeon; for there was the tabernacle of the congregation of God, which Moses the servant of the LORD had made in the wilderness.

4 But the ark of God had David brought up from Kirjath-jearim to *the place which* David had prepared for it: for he had pitched a tent for it at Jerusalem.

5 Moreover the brasen altar, that Bezaleel the son of Uri, the son of Hur, had made, he put before the tabernacle of the LORD: and Solomon and the congregation sought unto it.

6 And Solomon went up thither to the brasen altar before the LORD, which *was* at the tabernacle of the congregation, and offered a thousand burnt offerings upon it.

7 In that night did God appear unto Solomon, and said unto him, Ask what I shall give thee.

8 And Solomon said unto God, Thou hast shewed great mercy unto David my father, and hast made me to reign in his stead.

9 Now, O LORD God, let thy promise unto David my father be established: for thou hast made me king over a people like the dust of the earth in multitude.

10 Give me now wisdom and knowledge, that I may go out and come in before this people: for who can judge this thy people, *that is so* great?

11 And God said to Solomon, Because this was in thine heart, and thou hast not asked riches, wealth, or honour, nor the life of thine enemies, neither yet hast asked long life; but hast asked wisdom and knowledge for thyself, that thou mayest judge my people, over whom I have made thee king:

12 Wisdom and knowledge *is* granted unto thee; and I will give thee riches, and wealth, and honour, such as none of the kings have had that *have been* before thee, neither shall there any after thee have the like.

13 Then Solomon came *from his journey* to the high place that *was* at Gibeon to Jerusalem, from before the tabernacle of the congregation, and reigned over Israel.

Solomon's Horses and Chariots

14 And Solomon gathered chariots and horsemen: and he had a thousand and four hundred chariots, and twelve thousand horsemen, which he placed in the chariot cities, and with the king at Jerusalem.

15 And the king made silver and gold at Jerusalem *as plenteous* as stones, and cedar trees made he as the sycomore trees that *are* in the vale for abundance.

16 And Solomon had horses brought out of Egypt, and linen yarn: the king's merchants received the linen yarn at a price.

17 And they fetched up, and brought forth out of Egypt a chariot for six hundred *shekels* of silver, and an horse for an hundred and fifty: and so brought they out *horses* for all the kings of the Hittites, and for the kings of Syria, by their means.

CHAPTER 2

Solomon Prepares to Build the Temple

1 And Solomon determined to build an house for the name of the LORD, and an house for his kingdom.

2 And Solomon told out threescore and ten thousand men to bear burdens, and fourscore thousand to hew in the mountain, and three thousand and six hundred to oversee them.

3 And Solomon sent to Huram the king of Tyre, saying, As thou didst deal with David my father, and didst send him cedars to

---

Cross references (center column):

1 Gen. 39:2; 1Kgs. 2:46; 1Chr. 29:25

2 1Chr. 27:1

3 1Kgs. 3:4; 1Chr. 16:39; 21:29

4 2Sam. 6:2, 17; 1Chr. 15:1

5 Ex. 27:1, 2; 31:2; 38:1, 2

6 1Kgs. 3:4

7 1Kgs. 3:5, 6

8 1Chr. 28:5

9 1Kgs. 3:7, 8

10 Num. 27:17; Deut. 31:2; 1Kgs. 3:9

11 1Kgs. 3:11-13

12 1Chr. 29:25; 2Chr. 9:22; Eccl. 2:9

14 1Kgs. 4:26; 10:26; 2Chr. 9:25

15 1Kgs. 10:27; 2Chr. 9:27; Job 22:24

16 1Kgs. 10:28, 29

1 1Kgs. 5:5

2 1Kgs. 5:15; 2Chr. 2:18

3 1Kgs. 5:1; 1Chr. 14:1

1:3 Gibeon. Although David had erected a tent to house the ark itself in the capital (1 Chr. 15:1–2), the ancient Tabernacle with its brazen (bronze) altar was still six miles away at Gibeon, where worship was still being conducted.

1:10 Give me now wisdom. Solomon's request for wisdom (1 Kgs. 3:12), granted by God (see James 1:5–7), resulted in the production of both Proverbs and Ecclesiastes.

1:14 Solomon gathered chariots and horsemen. Notwithstanding the Mosaic regulations on multiplying horses and wives (Deut. 17:16), Solomon proceeded to acquire both, with his wives eventually influencing him into spiritual decline and idolatry (1 Kgs. 11:1–13). Even the wisest of men can err in departing from God's will and Word, leaving a tragic example of failure later in life.

build him an house to dwell therein, *even so deal with me.*

4 Behold, I build an house to the name of the LORD my God, to dedicate *it* to him, *and* to burn before him sweet incense, and for the continual shewbread, and for the burnt offerings morning and evening, on the sabbaths, and on the new moons, and on the solemn feasts of the LORD our God. This *is an ordinance* for ever to Israel.

5 And the house which I build *is* great: for great *is* our God above all gods.

6 But who is able to build him an house, seeing the heaven and heaven of heavens cannot contain him? who *am* I then, that I should build him an house, save only to burn sacrifice before him?

7 Send me now therefore a man cunning to work in gold, and in silver, and in brass, and in iron, and in purple, and crimson, and blue, and that can skill to grave with the cunning men that *are* with me in Judah and in Jerusalem, whom David my father did provide.

8 Send me also cedar trees, fir trees, and algum trees, out of Lebanon: for I know that thy servants can skill to cut timber in Lebanon; and, behold, my servants *shall be* with thy servants,

9 Even to prepare me timber in abundance: for the house which I am about to build *shall be* wonderful great.

10 And, behold, I will give to thy servants, the hewers that cut timber, twenty thousand measures of beaten wheat, and twenty thousand measures of barley, and twenty thousand baths of wine, and twenty thousand baths of oil.

11 Then Huram the king of Tyre answered in writing, which he sent to Solomon, Because the LORD hath loved his people, he hath made thee king over them.

12 Huram said moreover, Blessed *be* the LORD God of Israel, that made heaven and earth, who hath given to David the king a wise son, endued with prudence and understanding, that might build an house for the LORD, and an house for his kingdom.

13 And now I have sent a cunning man, endued with understanding, of Huram my father's,

14 The son of a woman of the daughters of Dan, and his father *was* a man of Tyre, skilful to work in gold, and in silver, in brass, in iron, in stone, and in timber, in purple, in blue, and in fine linen, and in crimson; also to grave any manner of graving, and to find out every device which shall be put to him, with thy cunning men, and with the cunning men of my lord David thy father.

15 Now therefore the wheat, and the barley, the oil, and the wine, which my lord hath spoken of, let him send unto his servants:

16 And we will cut wood out of Lebanon, as much as thou shalt need: and we will bring it to thee in floats by sea to Joppa; and thou shalt carry it up to Jerusalem.

17 And Solomon numbered all the strangers that *were* in the land of Israel, after the numbering wherewith David his father had numbered them; and they were found an hundred and fifty thousand and three thousand and six hundred.

18 And he set threescore and ten thousand of them *to be* bearers of burdens, and fourscore thousand *to be* hewers in the mountain, and three thousand and six hundred overseers to set the people a work.

CHAPTER 3
Solomon Builds the Temple

1 Then Solomon began to build the house of the LORD at Jerusalem in mount Moriah, where *the* LORD appeared unto David his father, in the place that David had prepared in the threshingfloor of Ornan the Jebusite.

2 And he began to build in the second *day* of the second month, in the fourth year of his reign.

3 Now these *are the things wherein* Solomon was instructed for the building of the house of God. The length by cubits after the first

Cross References

4 Ex. 25:30; 30:7; Num. 28:3, 9, 11; Lev. 24:8; 2Chr. 2:1

5 Ps. 135:5

6 1Kgs. 8:27; 2Chr. 6:18; Isa. 66:1

7 1Chr. 22:15

8 1Kgs. 5:6; 10:11

10 1Kgs. 5:11

11 1Kgs. 10:9; 2Chr. 9:8

12 Gen. 1, 2; 1Kgs. 5:7; Ps. 33:6; 102:25; 124:8; 136:5, 6; Acts 4:24; 14:15; Rev. 10:6

14 1Kgs. 7:13, 14

15 2Chr. 2:10

16 Josh. 19:46; 1Kgs. 5:8, 9; Acts 9:36

17 1Chr. 22:2; 2Chr. 2:2; 8:7, 8; 1Kgs. 5:13, 15, 16; 9:20, 21

18 2Chr. 2:2

1 Gen. 22:2, 14; 2Sam. 24:18; 1Kgs. 6:1; 1Chr. 21:18; 22:1

3 1Kgs. 6:2

2:13–14 Huram, the king of Tyre, is called Hiram in 1 Kings 5:11, cf. 2 Sam. 5:11. He is to be distinguished from Huram, the master craftsman (1 Kgs. 7:13), who is also called Hiram in 1 Kings.

3:1 Mount Moriah . . . threshingfloor. A threshingfloor is a level and hard-beaten plot of ground on which sheaves of grain were threshed to beat out the grain from the husks. The top of a rock was a favorite spot for this process. It is believed that Abraham offered Isaac on the rock still situated in the center of what is now called the Dome of the Rock, an Islamic place of worship in Jerusalem. This place, purchased by David (2 Sam. 24:18–25) as the site for the temple, became the focus for the construction of the first truly holy building in the history of the world. For three thousand years it has been considered a sacred place. The next temple, during the Tribulation, will be built on this site, and the Millennial Temple will one day incorporate the sacred site.

measure *was* threescore cubits, and the breadth twenty cubits.

4 And the porch that *was* in the front *of the house*, the length *of it was* according to the breadth of the house, twenty cubits, and the height *was* an hundred and twenty: and he overlaid it within with pure gold.

5 And the greater house he cieled with fir tree, which he overlaid with fine gold, and set thereon palm trees and chains.

6 And he garnished the house with precious stones for beauty: and the gold *was* gold of Parvaim.

7 He overlaid also the house, the beams, the posts, and the walls thereof, and the doors thereof, with gold; and graved cherubims on the walls.

8 And he made the most holy house, the length whereof *was* according to the breadth of the house, twenty cubits, and the breadth thereof twenty cubits: and he overlaid it with fine gold, *amounting* to six hundred talents.

9 And the weight of the nails *was* fifty shekels of gold. And he overlaid the upper chambers with gold.

10 And in the most holy house he made two cherubims of image work, and overlaid them with gold.

11 And the wings of the cherubims *were* twenty cubits long: one wing *of the one cherub was* five cubits, reaching to the wall of the house: and the other wing *was likewise* five cubits, reaching to the wing of the other cherub.

12 And *one* wing of the other cherub *was* five cubits, reaching to the wall of the house: and the other wing *was* five cubits *also*, joining to the wing of the other cherub.

13 The wings of these cherubims spread themselves forth twenty cubits: and they stood on their feet, and their faces *were* inward.

14 And he made the vail *of* blue, and purple, and crimson, and fine linen, and wrought cherubims thereon.

15 Also he made before the house two pillars of thirty and five cubits high, and the chapiter that *was* on the top of each of them *was* five cubits.

16 And he made chains, *as* in the oracle, and put *them* on the heads of the pillars; and

made an hundred pomegranates, and put *them* on the chains.

17 And he reared up the pillars before the temple, one on the right hand, and the other on the left; and called the name of that on the right hand Jachin, and the name of that on the left Boaz.

CHAPTER 4
Furnishings for the Temple

1 Moreover he made an altar of brass, twenty cubits the length thereof, and twenty cubits the breadth thereof, and ten cubits the height thereof.

2 Also he made a molten sea of ten cubits from brim to brim, round in compass, and five cubits the height thereof; and a line of thirty cubits did compass it round about.

3 And under it *was* the similitude of oxen, which did compass it round about: ten in a cubit, compassing the sea round about. Two rows of oxen *were* cast, when it was cast.

4 It stood upon twelve oxen, three looking toward the north, and three looking toward the west, and three looking toward the south, and three looking toward the east: and the sea *was set* above upon them, and all their hinder parts *were* inward.

5 And the thickness of it *was* an handbreadth, and the brim of it like the work of the brim of a cup, with flowers of lilies; *and* it received and held three thousand baths.

6 He made also ten lavers, and put five on the right hand, and five on the left, to wash in them: such things as they offered for the burnt offering they washed in them; but the sea *was* for the priests to wash in.

7 And he made ten candlesticks of gold according to their form, and set *them* in the temple, five on the right hand, and five on the left.

8 He made also ten tables, and placed *them* in the temple, five on the right side, and five on the left. And he made an hundred basons of gold.

9 Furthermore he made the court of the priests, and the great court, and doors for the court, and overlaid the doors of them with brass.

10 And he set the sea on the right side of the east end, over against the south.

11 And Huram made the pots, and the

Cross references (center column):

4 1Kgs. 6:3
5 1Kgs. 6:17
10 1Kgs. 6:23
14 Ex. 26:31; Matt. 27:51; Heb. 9:3
15 1Kgs. 7:15-21; Jer. 52:21
16 1Kgs. 7:20
17 1Kgs. 7:21
1 Ex. 27:1, 2; 2Kgs. 16:14; Ezek. 43:13, 16
2 1Kgs. 7:23
3 1Kgs. 7:24-26
5 1Kgs. 7:26
6 1Kgs. 7:38
7 Ex. 25:31, 40; 1Kgs. 7:49; 1Chr. 28:12, 19
8 1Kgs. 7:48
9 1Kgs. 6:36
10 1Kgs. 7:39
11 1Kgs. 7:40

4:1–22 Continuing from chapter 3, more temple furnishings are described (cf. 1 Kgs. 7:23–51), including the bronze altar and the huge molten sea which replaced the brazen laver of the Tabernacle. The temple, its furnishings, and all of the sacrifices in 2 Chronicles have a broadly typical significance and may be considered prophetic, pointing to Jesus (cf. John 2:18–21).

shovels, and the basons. And Huram finished the work that he was to make for king Solomon for the house of God;

12 *To wit*, the two pillars, and the pommels, and the chapiters *which were* on the top of the two pillars, and the two wreaths to cover the two pommels of the chapiters which *were* on the top of the pillars;

13 And four hundred pomegranates on the two wreaths; two rows of pomegranates on each wreath, to cover the two pommels of the chapiters which *were* upon the pillars.

14 He made also bases, and lavers made he upon the bases;

15 One sea, and twelve oxen under it.

16 The pots also, and the shovels, and the fleshhooks, and all their instruments, did Huram his father make to king Solomon for the house of the LORD of bright brass.

17 In the plain of Jordan did the king cast them, in the clay ground between Succoth and Zeredathah.

18 Thus Solomon made all these vessels in great abundance: for the weight of the brass could not be found out.

19 And Solomon made all the vessels that *were for* the house of God, the golden altar also, and the tables whereon the shewbread *was set;*

20 Moreover the candlesticks with their lamps, that they should burn after the manner before the oracle, of pure gold;

21 And the flowers, and the lamps, and the tongs, *made he of* gold, *and* that perfect gold;

22 And the snuffers, and the basons, and the spoons, and the censers, *of* pure gold: and the entry of the house, the inner doors thereof for the most holy *place*, and the doors of the house of the temple, *were of* gold.

CHAPTER 5

1 Thus all the work that Solomon made for the house of the LORD was finished: and Solomon brought in *all* the things that David his father had dedicated; and the silver, and the gold, and all the instruments, put he among the treasures of the house of God.

Solomon Brings the Ark of God into the Temple

2 Then Solomon assembled the elders of Israel, and all the heads of the tribes, the chief of the fathers of the children of Israel, unto Jerusalem, to bring up the ark of the covenant of the LORD out of the city of David, which *is* Zion.

3 Wherefore all the men of Israel assembled themselves unto the king in the feast which *was* in the seventh month.

4 And all the elders of Israel came; and the Levites took up the ark.

5 And they brought up the ark, and the tabernacle of the congregation, and all the holy vessels that *were* in the tabernacle, these did the priests *and* the Levites bring up.

6 Also king Solomon, and all the congregation of Israel that were assembled unto him before the ark, sacrificed sheep and oxen, which could not be told nor numbered for multitude.

7 And the priests brought in the ark of the covenant of the LORD unto his place, to the oracle of the house, into the most holy *place, even* under the wings of the cherubims:

8 For the cherubims spread forth *their* wings over the place of the ark, and the cherubims covered the ark and the staves thereof above.

9 And they drew out the staves *of the ark*, that the ends of the staves were seen from the ark before the oracle; but they were not seen without. And there it is unto this day.

10 *There was* nothing in the ark save the two tables which Moses put *therein* at Horeb, when the LORD made *a covenant* with the children of Israel, when they came out of Egypt.

11 And it came to pass, when the priests were come out of the holy *place*: (for all the priests *that were* present were sanctified, *and* did not *then* wait by course:

12 Also the Levites *which were* the singers, all of them of Asaph, of Heman, of Jeduthun, with their sons and their brethren, *being* arrayed in white linen, having cymbals and psalteries and harps, stood at the east

12 1Kgs. 7:41
13 1Kgs. 7:20
14 1Kgs. 7:27, 43
16 1Kgs. 7:14, 45
17 1Kgs. 7:46
18 1Kgs. 7:47
19 Ex. 25:30; 1Kgs. 7:48-50
20 Ex. 27:20, 21
21 Ex. 25:31
1 1Kgs. 7:51
2 2Sam. 6:12; 1Kgs. 8:1
3 1Kgs. 8:2; 2Chr. 7:8-10
9 1Kgs. 8:8
10 Deut. 10:2, 5; 2Chr. 6:11
12 1Chr. 15:24; 25:1

5:1 the house of the Lord was finished. The seven-year building program produced the most magnificent temple in human history, exceeding the idolatrous structures that had been erected throughout the world.

5:10 nothing in the ark save the two tables. In Moses' time, five hundred years earlier, the ark, a cabinet of acacia wood overlaid with gold, contained the two tablets of stone on which were inscribed the Ten Commandments. The ark also contained a pot of manna (Ex. 16:33) and Aaron's rod that budded (Num. 17:1–13, Heb 9:4). Apparently both the pot and the rod were lost when the ark was held by the Philistines (1 Kgs. 8:9).

end of the altar, and with them an hundred and twenty priests sounding with trumpets:)

13 It came even to pass, as the trumpeters and singers *were* as one, to make one sound to be heard in praising and thanking the LORD; and when they lifted up *their* voice with the trumpets and cymbals and instruments of musick, and praised the LORD, *saying*, For *he is* good; for his mercy *endureth* for ever: that *then* the house was filled with a cloud, *even* the house of the LORD;

14 So that the priests could not stand to minister by reason of the cloud: for the glory of the LORD had filled the house of God.

CHAPTER 6
Solomon Addresses the People

1 Then said Solomon, The LORD hath said that he would dwell in the thick darkness.

2 But I have built an house of habitation for thee, and a place for thy dwelling for ever.

3 And the king turned his face, and blessed the whole congregation of Israel: and all the congregation of Israel stood.

4 And he said, Blessed *be* the LORD God of Israel, who hath with his hands fulfilled *that* which he spake with his mouth to my father David, saying,

5 Since the day that I brought forth my people out of the land of Egypt I chose no city among all the tribes of Israel to build an house in, that my name might be there; neither chose I any man to be a ruler over my people Israel:

6 But I have chosen Jerusalem, that my name might be there; and have chosen David to be over my people Israel.

7 Now it was in the heart of David my father to build an house for the name of the LORD God of Israel.

8 But the LORD said to David my father, Forasmuch as it was in thine heart to build an house for my name, thou didst well in that it was in thine heart:

9 Notwithstanding thou shalt not build the house; but thy son which shall come forth out of thy loins, he shall build the house for my name.

10 The LORD therefore hath performed his word that he hath spoken: for I am risen up

in the room of David my father, and am set on the throne of Israel, as the LORD promised, and have built the house for the name of the LORD God of Israel.

11 And in it have I put the ark, wherein *is* the covenant of the LORD, that he made with the children of Israel.

Solomon's Temple Prayer

12 And he stood before the altar of the LORD in the presence of all the congregation of Israel, and spread forth his hands:

13 For Solomon had made a brasen scaffold, of five cubits long, and five cubits broad, and three cubits high, and had set it in the midst of the court: and upon it he stood, and kneeled down upon his knees before all the congregation of Israel, and spread forth his hands toward heaven,

14 And said, O LORD God of Israel, *there is* no God like thee in the heaven, nor in the earth; which keepest covenant, and *shewest* mercy unto thy servants, that walk before thee with all their hearts:

15 Thou which hast kept with thy servant David my father that which thou hast promised him; and spakest with thy mouth, and hast fulfilled *it* with thine hand, as *it is* this day.

16 Now therefore, O LORD God of Israel, keep with thy servant David my father that which thou hast promised him, saying, There shall not fail thee a man in my sight to sit upon the throne of Israel; yet so that thy children take heed to their way to walk in my law, as thou hast walked before me.

17 Now then, O LORD God of Israel, let thy word be verified, which thou hast spoken unto thy servant David.

18 But will God in very deed dwell with men on the earth? behold, heaven and the heaven of heavens cannot contain thee; how much less this house which I have built!

19 Have respect therefore to the prayer of thy servant, and to his supplication, O LORD my God, to hearken unto the cry and the prayer which thy servant prayeth before thee:

20 That thine eyes may be open upon this house day and night, upon the place whereof thou hast said that thou wouldest

Cross references (center column)

13 1Chr. 16:34, 41; Ps. 136
14 Ex. 40:35; 2Chr. 7:2
1 Lev. 16:2; 1Kgs. 8:12
6 1Chr. 28:4; 2Chr. 12:13
7 2Sam. 7:2; 1Chr. 17:1; 28:2
11 2Chr. 5:10
12 1Kgs. 8:22
14 Ex. 15:11; Deut. 4:39; 7:9
15 1Chr. 22:9
16 2Sam. 7:12, 16; 1Kgs. 2:4; 6:12; 2Chr. 7:18; Ps. 132:12
18 2Chr. 2:6; Isa. 66:1; Acts 7:49

6:14–42 This prayer is one of the most beautiful in all of Scripture. It reveals Solomon's great familiarity with and reverence for the warnings of God, which were given to all Israel through Moses (Lev. 26—27).

6:16 Solomon seemed to be conscious of God's conditions in the promise that He gave to David (see 1 Kgs. 2:4; 6:12 [cf. Ex. 32:13; Num. 14:18; Neh. 1:8–9; Dan. 9:13]).

put thy name there; to hearken unto the prayer which thy servant prayeth toward this place.

21 Hearken therefore unto the supplications of thy servant, and of thy people Israel, which they shall make toward this place: hear thou from thy dwelling place, *even* from heaven; and when thou hearest, forgive.

22 If a man sin against his neighbour, and an oath be laid upon him to make him swear, and the oath come before thine altar in this house;

23 Then hear thou from heaven, and do, and judge thy servants, by requiting the wicked, by recompensing his way upon his own head; and by justifying the righteous, by giving him according to his righteousness.

24 And if thy people Israel be put to the worse before the enemy, because they have sinned against thee; and shall return and confess thy name, and pray and make supplication before thee in this house;

25 Then hear thou from the heavens, and forgive the sin of thy people Israel, and bring them again unto the land which thou gavest to them and to their fathers.

26 When the heaven is shut up, and there is no rain, because they have sinned against thee; *yet* if they pray toward this place, and confess thy name, and turn from their sin, when thou dost afflict them;

27 Then hear thou from heaven, and forgive the sin of thy servants, and of thy people Israel, when thou hast taught them the good way, wherein they should walk; and send rain upon thy land, which thou hast given unto thy people for an inheritance.

28 If there be dearth in the land, if there be pestilence, if there be blasting, or mildew, locusts, or caterpillers; if their enemies besiege them in the cities of their land; whatsoever sore or whatsoever sickness *there be*:

29 *Then* what prayer *or* what supplication soever shall be made of any man, or of all thy people Israel, when every one shall know his own sore and his own grief, and shall spread forth his hands in this house:

30 Then hear thou from heaven thy dwelling place, and forgive, and render unto every man according unto all his ways, whose heart thou knowest; (for thou only knowest the hearts of the children of men:)

31 That they may fear thee, to walk in thy ways, so long as they live in the land which thou gavest unto our fathers.

32 Moreover concerning the stranger, which is not of thy people Israel, but is come from a far country for thy great name's sake, and thy mighty hand, and thy stretched out arm; if they come and pray in this house;

33 Then hear thou from the heavens, *even* from thy dwelling place, and do according to all that the stranger calleth to thee for; that all people of the earth may know thy name, and fear thee, as *doth* thy people Israel, and may know that this house which I have built is called by thy name.

34 If thy people go out to war against their enemies by the way that thou shalt send them, and they pray unto thee toward this city which thou hast chosen, and the house which I have built for thy name;

35 Then hear thou from the heavens their prayer and their supplication, and maintain their cause.

36 If they sin against thee, (for *there is* no man which sinneth not,) and thou be angry with them, and deliver them over before *their* enemies, and they carry them away captives unto a land far off or near;

37 Yet *if* they bethink themselves in the land whither they are carried captive, and turn and pray unto thee in the land of their captivity, saying, We have sinned, we have done amiss, and have dealt wickedly;

38 If they return to thee with all their heart and with all their soul in the land of their captivity, whither they have carried them captives, and pray toward their land, which thou gavest unto their fathers, and *toward* the city which thou hast chosen, and toward the house which I have built for thy name:

39 Then hear thou from the heavens, *even* from thy dwelling place, their prayer and their supplications, and maintain their cause, and forgive thy people which have sinned against thee.

40 Now, my God, let, I beseech thee, thine eyes be open, and *let* thine ears *be* attent unto the prayer *that is made* in this place.

41 Now therefore arise, O LORD God, into thy resting place, thou, and the ark of thy strength: let thy priests, O LORD God, be clothed with salvation, and let thy saints rejoice in goodness.

42 O LORD God, turn not away the face of

---

26 1Kgs. 17:1

28 2Chr. 20:9

30 1Chr. 28:9

32 John 12:20; Acts 8:27

36 Prov. 20:9; Eccl. 7:20; James 3:2; 1John 1:8

41 1Chr. 28:2; Neh. 9:25; Ps. 132:8-10, 16

42 Ps. 132:1; Isa. 55:3

6:37–39 Daniel later acted according to the elements in Solomon's prayer (Dan. 9:5 [see also Ps. 106:6]).

thine anointed: remember the mercies of David thy servant.

CHAPTER 7
God's Glory Fills the Temple

1 Now when Solomon had made an end of praying, the fire came down from heaven, and consumed the burnt offering and the sacrifices; and the glory of the LORD filled the house.

2 And the priests could not enter into the house of the LORD, because the glory of the LORD had filled the LORD's house.

3 And when all the children of Israel saw how the fire came down, and the glory of the LORD upon the house, they bowed themselves with their faces to the ground upon the pavement, and worshipped, and praised the LORD, *saying*, For *he is* good; for his mercy *endureth* for ever.

Sacrifice and Celebrations

4 Then the king and all the people offered sacrifices before the LORD.

5 And king Solomon offered a sacrifice of twenty and two thousand oxen, and an hundred and twenty thousand sheep: so the king and all the people dedicated the house of God.

6 And the priests waited on their offices: the Levites also with instruments of musick of the LORD, which David the king had made to praise the LORD, because his mercy *endureth* for ever, when David praised by their ministry; and the priests sounded trumpets before them, and all Israel stood.

7 Moreover Solomon hallowed the middle of the court that *was* before the house of the LORD: for there he offered burnt offerings, and the fat of the peace offerings, because the brasen altar which Solomon had made was not able to receive the burnt offerings, and the meat offerings, and the fat.

8 Also at the same time Solomon kept the feast seven days, and all Israel with him, a very great congregation, from the entering in of Hamath unto the river of Egypt.

9 And in the eighth day they made a solemn assembly: for they kept the dedica-tion of the altar seven days, and the feast seven days.

10 And on the three and twentieth day of the seventh month he sent the people away into their tents, glad and merry in heart for the goodness that the LORD had shewed unto David, and to Solomon, and to Israel his people.

God Appears to Solomon

11 Thus Solomon finished the house of the LORD, and the king's house: and all that came into Solomon's heart to make in the house of the LORD, and in his own house, he prosperously effected.

12 And the LORD appeared to Solomon by night, and said unto him, I have heard thy prayer, and have chosen this place to myself for an house of sacrifice.

13 If I shut up heaven that there be no rain, or if I command the locusts to devour the land, or if I send pestilence among my people;

14 If my people, which are called by my name, shall humble themselves, and pray, and seek my face, and turn from their wicked ways; then will I hear from heaven, and will forgive their sin, and will heal their land.

15 Now mine eyes shall be open, and mine ears attent unto the prayer *that is made* in this place.

16 For now have I chosen and sanctified this house, that my name may be there for ever: and mine eyes and mine heart shall be there perpetually.

17 And as for thee, if thou wilt walk before me, as David thy father walked, and do according to all that I have commanded thee, and shalt observe my statutes and my judgments;

18 Then will I stablish the throne of thy kingdom, according as I have covenanted with David thy father, saying, There shall not fail thee a man *to be* ruler in Israel.

19 But if ye turn away, and forsake my statutes and my commandments, which I have set before you, and shall go and serve other gods, and worship them;

---

1 Lev. 9:24; Judg. 6:21; 1Kgs. 8:10, 11, 54; 18:38; 1Chr. 21:26; 2Chr. 5:13, 14; Ezek. 10:3, 4

2 2Chr. 5:14

3 1Chr. 16:41; 2Chr. 5:13; 20:21; Ps. 136:1

4 1Kgs. 8:62, 63

6 1Chr. 15:16; 2Chr. 5:12

7 1Kgs. 8:64

8 Josh. 13:3; 1Kgs. 8:65

10 1Kgs. 8:66

11 1Kgs. 9:1

12 Deut. 12:5

13 2Chr. 6:26, 28

14 2Chr. 6:27, 30; James 4:10

15 2Chr. 6:40

16 1Kgs. 9:3; 2Chr. 6:6

17 1Kgs. 9:4

18 2Chr. 6:16

19 Lev. 26:14, 33; Deut. 28:15, 36, 37

7:2 The occurrence of God's glory filling the temple is very similar to what happened at the dedication of the Tabernacle (Ex. 40:34–35). The progressive removal of the glory of God, His Shechinah presence, is recorded in Ezekiel 9:3, 10:18 and 11:23. This divine phenomenon will not be seen again until the Millennial Temple stands in Israel in all of its splendor (Ezek. 43:2–5).

7:12–14 Sacrifice was a central element in Old Testament worship (Lev. 17:11; Heb. 9:22). This key Old Testament passage presents the conditions of true repentance: humbling oneself, praying, seeking God's face, and turning from evil. This formula for revival, which relates to the people called by His name, is based on Deuteronomy 28 and Leviticus 26 (see 2 Chr. 6:24).

20 Then will I pluck them up by the roots out of my land which I have given them; and this house, which I have sanctified for my name, will I cast out of my sight, and will make it *to be* a proverb and a byword among all nations.

21 And this house, which is high, shall be an astonishment to every one that passeth by it; so that he shall say, Why hath the LORD done thus unto this land, and unto this house?

22 And it shall be answered, Because they forsook the LORD God of their fathers, which brought them forth out of the land of Egypt, and laid hold on other gods, and worshipped them, and served them: therefore hath he brought all this evil upon them.

CHAPTER 8
Solomon's Other Projects

1 And it came to pass at the end of twenty years, wherein Solomon had built the house of the LORD, and his own house,

2 That the cities which Huram had restored to Solomon, Solomon built them, and caused the children of Israel to dwell there.

3 And Solomon went to Hamath-zobah, and prevailed against it.

4 And he built Tadmor in the wilderness, and all the store cities, which he built in Hamath.

5 Also he built Beth-horon the upper, and Beth-horon the nether, fenced cities, with walls, gates, and bars;

6 And Baalath, and all the store cities that Solomon had, and all the chariot cities, and the cities of the horsemen, and all that Solomon desired to build in Jerusalem, and in Lebanon, and throughout all the land of his dominion.

7 *As for* all the people *that were* left of the Hittites, and the Amorites, and the Perizzites, and the Hivites, and the Jebusites, which *were* not of Israel,

8 *But* of their children, who were left after them in the land, whom the children of Israel consumed not, them did Solomon make to pay tribute until this day.

9 But of the children of Israel did Solomon make no servants for his work; but they *were* men of war, and chief of his captains, and captains of his chariots and horsemen.

10 And these *were* the chief of king Solomon's officers, *even* two hundred and fifty, that bare rule over the people.

11 And Solomon brought up the daughter of Pharaoh out of the city of David unto the house that he had built for her: for he said, My wife shall not dwell in the house of David king of Israel, because *the places are* holy, whereunto the ark of the LORD hath come.

12 Then Solomon offered burnt offerings unto the LORD on the altar of the LORD, which he had built before the porch,

13 Even after a certain rate every day, offering according to the commandment of Moses, on the sabbaths, and on the new moons, and on the solemn feasts, three times in the year, *even* in the feast of unleavened bread, and in the feast of weeks, and in the feast of tabernacles.

14 And he appointed, according to the order of David his father, the courses of the priests to their service, and the Levites to their charges, to praise and minister before the priests, as the duty of every day required: the porters also by their courses at every gate: for so had David the man of God commanded.

15 And they departed not from the commandment of the king unto the priests and Levites concerning any matter, or concerning the treasures.

16 Now all the work of Solomon was prepared unto the day of the foundation of the house of the LORD, and until it was finished. *So* the house of the LORD was perfected.

17 Then went Solomon to Ezion-geber, and to Eloth, at the sea side in the land of Edom.

18 And Huram sent him by the hands of his servants ships, and servants that had knowledge of the sea; and they went with the servants of Solomon to Ophir, and took thence four hundred and fifty talents of gold, and brought *them* to king Solomon.

CHAPTER 9
The Queen of Sheba Visits Solomon

1 And when the queen of Sheba heard of the fame of Solomon, she came to prove

Center column cross-references

21 Deut. 29:24; Jer. 22:8, 9
1 1Kgs. 9:10
4 1Kgs. 9:17
7 1Kgs. 9:20
10 1Kgs. 9:23
11 1Kgs. 3:1; 7:8; 9:24
13 Ex. 23:14; 29:38; Num. 20:1; 28:3, 9, 11, 26; Deut. 16:16
14 1Chr. 9:17; 24:1; 25:1; 26:1
17 Deut. 2:8; 1Kgs. 9:26; 2Kgs. 14:22
18 1Kgs. 9:27; 2Chr. 9:10, 13
1 1Kgs. 10:1; Matt. 12:42; Luke 11:31

8:1 twenty years. Seven years were spent in building the temple (1 Kgs. 6:37–38), while thirteen years were needed for Solomon's palace (1 Kgs. 7:1).

9:1 Sheba. This land was located in southwestern Arabia, some twelve hundred miles from Jerusalem.

The Queen of Sheba's visit to Israel is also described in 1 Kings 10:1–13. While impressed with Solomon's wisdom and wealth, there is no indication in the text that she forsook idolatry and became a believer in the true God alone.

Solomon with hard questions at Jerusalem, with a very great company, and camels that bare spices, and gold in abundance, and precious stones: and when she was come to Solomon, she communed with him of all that was in her heart.

2 And Solomon told her all her questions: and there was nothing hid from Solomon which he told her not.

3 And when the queen of Sheba had seen the wisdom of Solomon, and the house that he had built,

4 And the meat of his table, and the sitting of his servants, and the attendance of his ministers, and their apparel; his cupbearers also, and their apparel; and his ascent by which he went up into the house of the LORD; there was no more spirit in her.

5 And she said to the king, *It was* a true report which I heard in mine own land of thine acts, and of thy wisdom:

6 Howbeit I believed not their words, until I came, and mine eyes had seen *it*: and, behold, the one half of the greatness of thy wisdom was not told me: *for* thou exceedest the fame that I heard.

7 Happy *are* thy men, and happy *are* these thy servants, which stand continually before thee, and hear thy wisdom.

8 Blessed be the LORD thy God, which delighted in thee to set thee on his throne, *to be* king for the LORD thy God: because thy God loved Israel, to establish them for ever, therefore made he thee king over them, to do judgment and justice.

9 And she gave the king an hundred and twenty talents of gold, and of spices great abundance, and precious stones: neither was there any such spice as the queen of Sheba gave king Solomon.

10 And the servants also of Huram, and the servants of Solomon, which brought gold from Ophir, brought algum trees and precious stones.

11 And the king made *of* the algum trees terraces to the house of the LORD, and to the king's palace, and harps and psalteries for singers: and there were none such seen before in the land of Judah.

12 And king Solomon gave to the queen of Sheba all her desire, whatsoever she asked, beside *that* which she had brought unto the king. So she turned, and went away to her own land, she and her servants.

Solomon's Wealth and Fame

13 Now the weight of gold that came to Solomon in one year was six hundred

and threescore and six talents of gold;

14 Beside *that which* chapmen and merchants brought. And all the kings of Arabia and governors of the country brought gold and silver to Solomon.

15 And king Solomon made two hundred targets *of* beaten gold: six hundred *shekels* of beaten gold went to one target.

16 And three hundred shields *made he of* beaten gold: three hundred *shekels* of gold went to one shield. And the king put them in the house of the forest of Lebanon.

17 Moreover the king made a great throne of ivory, and overlaid it with pure gold.

18 And *there were* six steps to the throne, with a footstool of gold, *which were* fastened to the throne, and stays on each side of the sitting place, and two lions standing by the stays:

19 And twelve lions stood there on the one side and on the other upon the six steps. There was not the like made in any kingdom.

20 And all the drinking vessels of king Solomon *were of* gold, and all the vessels of the house of the forest of Lebanon *were of* pure gold: none *were of* silver; it was *not* any thing accounted of in the days of Solomon.

21 For the king's ships went to Tarshish with the servants of Huram: every three years once came the ships of Tarshish bringing gold, and silver, ivory, and apes, and peacocks.

22 And king Solomon passed all the kings of the earth in riches and wisdom.

23 And all the kings of the earth sought the presence of Solomon, to hear his wisdom, that God had put in his heart.

24 And they brought every man his present, vessels of silver, and vessels of gold, and raiment, harness, and spices, horses, and mules, a rate year by year.

25 And Solomon had four thousand stalls for horses and chariots, and twelve thousand horsemen; whom he bestowed in the chariot cities, and with the king at Jerusalem.

26 And he reigned over all the kings from the river even unto the land of the Philistines, and to the border of Egypt.

27 And the king made silver in Jerusalem as stones, and cedar trees made he as the sycomore trees that *are* in the low plains in abundance.

28 And they brought unto Solomon horses out of Egypt, and out of all lands.

10 1Kgs. 10:11, *almug trees;* 2Chr. 8:18

25 1Kgs. 4:26; 10:26; 2Chr. 1:14

26 Gen. 15:18; 1Kgs. 4:21; Ps. 72:8

27 1Kgs. 10:27; 2Chr. 1:15

28 1Kgs. 10:28; 2Chr. 1:16

Solomon's Death

29 Now the rest of the acts of Solomon, first and last, *are* they not written in the book of Nathan the prophet, and in the prophecy of Ahijah the Shilonite, and in the visions of Iddo the seer against Jeroboam the son of Nebat? **30** And Solomon reigned in Jerusalem over all Israel forty years. **31** And Solomon slept with his fathers, and he was buried in the city of David his father: and Rehoboam his son reigned in his stead.

CHAPTER 10
The Northern Tribes Revolt

1 And Rehoboam went to Shechem: for to Shechem were all Israel come to make him king. **2** And it came to pass, when Jeroboam the son of Nebat, who *was* in Egypt, whither he had fled from the presence of Solomon the king, heard *it*, that Jeroboam returned out of Egypt. **3** And they sent and called him. So Jeroboam and all Israel came and spake to Rehoboam, saying, **4** Thy father made our yoke grievous: now therefore ease thou somewhat the grievous servitude of thy father, and his heavy yoke that he put upon us, and we will serve thee. **5** And he said unto them, Come again unto me after three days. And the people departed. **6** And king Rehoboam took counsel with the old men that had stood before Solomon his father while he yet lived, saying, What counsel give ye *me* to return answer to this people? **7** And they spake unto him, saying, If thou be kind to this people, and please them, and speak good words to them, they will be thy servants for ever.

29 1Kgs. 11:29, 41; 2Chr. 12:15; 13:22

30 1Kgs. 11:42, 43

1 1Kgs. 12:1

2 1Kgs. 11:40

15 1Sam. 2:25; 1Kgs. 11:29; 12:15, 24

8 But he forsook the counsel which the old men gave him, and took counsel with the young men that were brought up with him, that stood before him. **9** And he said unto them, What advice give ye that we may return answer to this people, which have spoken to me, saying, Ease somewhat the yoke that thy father did put upon us? **10** And the young men that were brought up with him spake unto him, saying, Thus shalt thou answer the people that spake unto thee, saying, Thy father made our yoke heavy, but make thou *it* somewhat lighter for us; thus shalt thou say unto them, My little *finger* shall be thicker than my father's loins. **11** For whereas my father put a heavy yoke upon you, I will put more to your yoke: my father chastised you with whips, but I *will chastise you* with scorpions. **12** So Jeroboam and all the people came to Rehoboam on the third day, as the king bade, saying, Come again to me on the third day. **13** And the king answered them roughly; and king Rehoboam forsook the counsel of the old men, **14** And answered them after the advice of the young men, saying, My father made your yoke heavy, but I will add thereto: my father chastised you with whips, but I *will chastise you* with scorpions. **15** So the king hearkened not unto the people: for the cause was of God, that the LORD might perform his word, which he spake by the hand of Ahijah the Shilonite to Jeroboam the son of Nebat. **16** And when all Israel *saw* that the king would not hearken unto them, the people answered the king, saying, What portion have we in David? and *we have* none inheritance in the son of Jesse: every man to your

---

9:29 acts of Solomon. Among the sources Ezra used to compile and complete this chronicle of Solomon's reign, in addition to 1 Kings 1—11, were the books of Nathan the prophet, Ahijah the Shilonite (an inhabitant of Shiloh), and the visions of Iddo. These materials were never included in the canon of the Scripture and are long lost. Another book, the Acts of Solomon, is mentioned in 1 Kings 11:41. Official recorders in the royal courts of the kings also kept historical records. The books of 1 and 2 Samuel and 1 and 2 Kings detail God's interpretation of how the nation was doing in keeping the Mosaic covenant. The chronicler here is focusing on encouraging the returning Jews from Babylon with God's promises of a glorious future in the Davidic covenant.

9:31 Solomon slept with his fathers. This expression in Hebrew is a euphemistic way of saying that Solomon has died. Never again would Israel rise to so high a peak of influence and wealth. At this particular time in history both the Egyptian empire and the Assyrian-Babylonian realm were at a low ebb in strength.

10:16 What portion have we in David? This slogan was used previously by Sheba in his rebellion against David (2 Sam. 20:1). The people here used it against Rehoboam to emphasize that they did not have to follow someone of David's lineage.

tents, O Israel: *and* now, David, see to thine own house. So all Israel went to their tents.
17 But *as for* the children of Israel that dwelt in the cities of Judah, Rehoboam reigned over them.
18 Then king Rehoboam sent Hadoram that *was* over the tribute; and the children of Israel stoned him with stones, that he died. But king Rehoboam made speed to get him up to *his* chariot, to flee to Jerusalem.
19 And Israel rebelled against the house of David unto this day.

CHAPTER 11
Civil War Is Averted

1 And when Rehoboam was come to Jerusalem, he gathered of the house of Judah and Benjamin an hundred and fourscore thousand chosen *men*, which were warriors, to fight against Israel, that he might bring the kingdom again to Rehoboam.
2 But the word of the LORD came to Shemaiah the man of God, saying,
3 Speak unto Rehoboam the son of Solomon, king of Judah, and to all Israel in Judah and Benjamin, saying,
4 Thus saith the LORD, Ye shall not go up, nor fight against your brethren: return every man to his house: for this thing is done of me. And they obeyed the words of the LORD, and returned from going against Jeroboam.

Rehoboam Prospers

5 And Rehoboam dwelt in Jerusalem, and built cities for defence in Judah.
6 He built even Beth-lehem, and Etam, and Tekoa,
7 And Beth-zur, and Shoco, and Adullam,
8 And Gath, and Mareshah, and Ziph,
9 And Adoraim, and Lachish, and Azekah,
10 And Zorah, and Aijalon, and Hebron, which *are* in Judah and in Benjamin fenced cities.
11 And he fortified the strong holds, and put captains in them, and store of victual, and of oil and wine.
12 And in every several city *he put* shields and spears, and made them exceeding strong, having Judah and Benjamin on his side.

13 And the priests and the Levites that *were* in all Israel resorted to him out of all their coasts.
14 For the Levites left their suburbs and their possession, and came to Judah and Jerusalem: for Jeroboam and his sons had cast them off from executing the priest's office unto the LORD:
15 And he ordained him priests for the high places, and for the devils, and for the calves which he had made.
16 And after them out of all the tribes of Israel such as set their hearts to seek the LORD God of Israel came to Jerusalem, to sacrifice unto the LORD God of their fathers.
17 So they strengthened the kingdom of Judah, and made Rehoboam the son of Solomon strong, three years: for three years they walked in the way of David and Solomon.
18 And Rehoboam took him Mahalath the daughter of Jerimoth the son of David to wife, *and* Abihail the daughter of Eliab the son of Jesse;
19 Which bare him children; Jeush, and Shamariah, and Zaham.
20 And after her he took Maachah the daughter of Absalom; which bare him Abijah, and Attai, and Ziza, and Shelomith.
21 And Rehoboam loved Maachah the daughter of Absalom above all his wives and his concubines: (for he took eighteen wives, and threescore concubines; and begat twenty and eight sons, and threescore daughters.)
22 And Rehoboam made Abijah the son of Maachah the chief, *to be* ruler among his brethren: for *he thought* to make him king.
23 And he dealt wisely, and dispersed of all his children throughout all the countries of Judah and Benjamin, unto every fenced city: and he gave them victual in abundance. And he desired many wives.

CHAPTER 12
Rehoboam Sins and Is Punished

1 And it came to pass, when Rehoboam had established the kingdom, and had strengthened himself, he forsook the law of the LORD, and all Israel with him.

Cross references: 19 1Kgs. 12:19; 1 1Kgs. 12:21; 2 2Chr. 12:15; 14 Num. 35:2; 2Chr. 13:9; 15 Lev. 17:7; 1Kgs. 12:28, 31; 13:33; 14:9; Hos. 13:2; 1Cor. 10:20; 16 2Chr. 15:9; 30:11, 18; 17 2Chr. 12:1; 20 1Kgs. 15:2. She is also called *Michaiah the daughter of Uriel*, 2Chr. 13:2; 22 Deut. 21:15-17; 1 1Kgs. 14:22-24; 2Chr. 11:17

11:4 Ye shall not go up. Shemaiah the man of God forbade Rehoboam to fight to regain the ten tribes, now ruled by Jeroboam the son of Nebat. God had promised the kingdom to Jeroboam after Solomon's slide into idolatry had begun (1 Kgs. 11:26–40).

12:1 forsook the law of the LORD. Decline and apostasy in Israel, led by Solomon's son, resulted in divine chastisement and an invasion from Egypt. Repentance avoided total destruction (vv. 5–12), but Rehoboam became a temporary vassal of the Egyptian king.

2 And it came to pass, *that* in the fifth year of king Rehoboam Shishak king of Egypt came up against Jerusalem, because they had transgressed against the LORD,
3 With twelve hundred chariots, and threescore thousand horsemen: and the people *were* without number that came with him out of Egypt; the Lubims, the Sukkiims, and the Ethiopians.
4 And he took the fenced cities which *pertained* to Judah, and came to Jerusalem.
5 Then came Shemaiah the prophet to Rehoboam, and *to* the princes of Judah, that were gathered together to Jerusalem because of Shishak, and said unto them, Thus saith the LORD, Ye have forsaken me, and therefore have I also left you in the hand of Shishak.
6 Whereupon the princes of Israel and the king humbled themselves; and they said, The LORD *is* righteous.
7 And when the LORD saw that they humbled themselves, the word of the LORD came to Shemaiah, saying, They have humbled themselves; *therefore* I will not destroy them, but I will grant them some deliverance; and my wrath shall not be poured out upon Jerusalem by the hand of Shishak.
8 Nevertheless they shall be his servants; that they may know my service, and the service of the kingdoms of the countries.
9 So Shishak king of Egypt came up against Jerusalem, and took away the treasures of the house of the LORD, and the treasures of the king's house; he took all: he carried away also the shields of gold which Solomon had made.
10 Instead of which king Rehoboam made shields of brass, and committed *them* to the hands of the chief of the guard, that kept the entrance of the king's house.
11 And when the king entered into the house of the LORD, the guard came and fetched them, and brought them again into the guard chamber.
12 And when he humbled himself, the wrath of the LORD turned from him, that he would not destroy *him* altogether: and also in Judah things went well.

Rehoboam's Death

13 So king Rehoboam strengthened himself in Jerusalem, and reigned: for Rehoboam *was* one and forty years old when he began to reign, and he reigned seventeen years in Jerusalem, the city which the LORD had chosen out of all the tribes of Israel, to put his name there. And his mother's name *was* Naamah an Ammonitess.
14 And he did evil, because he prepared not his heart to seek the LORD.
15 Now the acts of Rehoboam, first and last, *are* they not written in the book of Shemaiah the prophet, and of Iddo the seer concerning genealogies? And *there were* wars between Rehoboam and Jeroboam continually.
16 And Rehoboam slept with his fathers, and was buried in the city of David: and Abijah his son reigned in his stead.

CHAPTER 13
Abijah Rules Judah

1 Now in the eighteenth year of king Jeroboam began Abijah to reign over Judah.
2 He reigned three years in Jerusalem. His mother's name also *was* Michaiah the daughter of Uriel of Gibeah. And there was war between Abijah and Jeroboam.
3 And Abijah set the battle in array with an army of valiant men of war, *even* four hundred thousand chosen men: Jeroboam also set the battle in array against him with eight hundred thousand chosen men, *being* mighty men of valour.
4 And Abijah stood up upon mount Zemaraim, which *is* in mount Ephraim, and said, Hear me, thou Jeroboam, and all Israel;
5 Ought ye not to know that the LORD God of Israel gave the kingdom over Israel to David for ever, *even* to him and to his sons by a covenant of salt?
6 Yet Jeroboam the son of Nebat, the servant of Solomon the son of David, is risen up, and hath rebelled against his lord.
7 And there are gathered unto him vain men, the children of Belial, and have strengthened themselves against Rehoboam the son of Solomon, when Rehoboam was

Cross references (center column):

2 1Kgs. 14:24, 25
3 2Chr. 16:8
5 2Chr. 11:2; 15:2
6 Ex. 9:27; James 4:10
7 1Kgs. 21:28, 29
8 Deut. 28:47, 48; Isa. 26:13
9 1Kgs. 10:16, 17; 14:25, 26; 2Chr. 9:15, 16
10 2Sam. 8:18
12 Gen. 18:24; 1Kgs. 14:13; 2Chr. 19:3
13 1Kgs. 14:21; 2Chr. 6:6
15 1Kgs. 14:30; 2Chr. 9:29; 13:22
16 1Kgs. 14:31, *Abijam*
1 1Kgs. 15:1
2 2Chr. 11:20
4 Josh. 18:22
5 Num. 18:19; 2Sam. 7:12, 13, 16
6 1Kgs. 11:26; 12:20
7 Judg. 9:4

13:2 Michaiah is called Maachah in 1 Kings 15:2 and 2 Chronicles 11:20. She is called the daughter of Absalom, though she was actually his granddaughter. It was a common practice among the Hebrews to call someone a son or daughter even if they were a distant ancestor (cf. Jesus in Matt. 1 for a similar customary practice).

13:5 covenant of salt. Salt was used in the perpetual sacrifices of the Old Testament; therefore, it seems that this was a covenant sealed by the parties involved through an animal sacrifice. A covenant of salt could not be changed (see Num. 18:19, cf. Mark 9:49).

young and tenderhearted, and could not withstand them.

8 And now ye think to withstand the kingdom of the LORD in the hand of the sons of David; and ye *be* a great multitude, and *there are* with you golden calves, which Jeroboam made you for gods.

9 Have ye not cast out the priests of the LORD, the sons of Aaron, and the Levites, and have made you priests after the manner of the nations of *other* lands? so that whosoever cometh to consecrate himself with a young bullock and seven rams, *the same* may be a priest of *them that are* no gods.

10 But as for us, the LORD *is* our God, and we have not forsaken him; and the priests, which minister unto the LORD, *are* the sons of Aaron, and the Levites *wait* upon *their* business:

11 And they burn unto the LORD every morning and every evening burnt sacrifices and sweet incense: the shewbread also *set they in order* upon the pure table; and the candlestick of gold with the lamps thereof, to burn every evening: for we keep the charge of the LORD our God; but ye have forsaken him.

12 And, behold, God himself *is* with us for *our* captain, and his priests with sounding trumpets to cry alarm against you. O children of Israel, fight ye not against the LORD God of your fathers; for ye shall not prosper.

13 But Jeroboam caused an ambushment to come about behind them: so they were before Judah, and the ambushment *was* behind them.

14 And when Judah looked back, behold, the battle *was* before and behind: and they cried unto the LORD, and the priests sounded with the trumpets.

15 Then the men of Judah gave a shout: and as the men of Judah shouted, it came to pass, that God smote Jeroboam and all Israel before Abijah and Judah.

16 And the children of Israel fled before Judah: and God delivered them into their hand.

17 And Abijah and his people slew them with a great slaughter: so there fell down slain of Israel five hundred thousand chosen men.

18 Thus the children of Israel were brought under at that time, and the children of Judah prevailed, because they relied upon the LORD God of their fathers.

19 And Abijah pursued after Jeroboam, and

took cities from him, Beth-el with the towns thereof, and Jeshanah with the towns thereof, and Ephrain with the towns thereof.

20 Neither did Jeroboam recover strength again in the days of Abijah: and the LORD struck him, and he died.

21 But Abijah waxed mighty, and married fourteen wives, and begat twenty and two sons, and sixteen daughters.

22 And the rest of the acts of Abijah, and his ways, and his sayings, *are* written in the story of the prophet Iddo.

CHAPTER 14
Asa Rules Judah

1 So Abijah slept with his fathers, and they buried him in the city of David: and Asa his son reigned in his stead. In his days the land was quiet ten years.

2 And Asa did *that which was* good and right in the eyes of the LORD his God:

3 For he took away the altars of the strange *gods*, and the high places, and brake down the images, and cut down the groves:

4 And commanded Judah to seek the LORD God of their fathers, and to do the law and the commandment.

5 Also he took away out of all the cities of Judah the high places and the images: and the kingdom was quiet before him.

6 And he built fenced cities in Judah: for the land had rest, and he had no war in those years; because the LORD had given him rest.

7 Therefore he said unto Judah, Let us build these cities, and make about *them* walls, and towers, gates, and bars, *while* the land *is* yet before us; because we have sought the LORD our God, we have sought *him*, and he hath given us rest on every side. So they built and prospered.

8 And Asa had an army *of men* that bare targets and spears, out of Judah three hundred thousand; and out of Benjamin, that bare shields and drew bows, two hundred and fourscore thousand: all these *were* mighty men of valour.

9 And there came out against them Zerah the Ethiopian with an host of a thousand thousand, and three hundred chariots; and came unto Mareshah.

10 Then Asa went out against him, and they set the battle in array in the valley of Zephathah at Mareshah.

11 And Asa cried unto the LORD his God,

Cross references (center column)

8 1Kgs. 12:28; 14:9; Hos. 8:6

9 Ex. 29:1, 35; Lev. 8:2; 2Chr. 11:14, 15

11 Ex. 27:20, 21; Lev. 24:2, 3, 6; 2Chr. 2:4

12 Num. 10:8; Acts 5:39

15 2Chr. 14:12

18 1Chr. 5:20; Ps. 22:5

19 Josh. 15:9

20 1Sam. 25:38; 1Kgs. 14:20

22 2Chr. 12:15

1 1Kgs. 15:8

3 Ex. 34:13; 1Kgs. 11:7; 15:14; 2Chr. 15:17

9 Josh. 15:44; 2Chr. 16:8

11 Ex. 14:10; 1Sam. 14:6; 17:45; 2Chr. 13:14; Ps. 22:5; Prov. 18:10

14:11 Asa cried unto the LORD. Asa was one of the better kings whose faith and prayer led to triumph over the invading Ethiopians.

and said, LORD, *it is* nothing with thee to help, whether with many, or with them that have no power: help us, O LORD our God; for we rest on thee, and in thy name we go against this multitude. O LORD, thou *art* our God; let not man prevail against thee.

12 So the LORD smote the Ethiopians before Asa, and before Judah; and the Ethiopians fled.

13 And Asa and the people that *were* with him pursued them unto Gerar: and the Ethiopians were overthrown, that they could not recover themselves; for they were destroyed before the LORD, and before his host; and they carried away very much spoil.

14 And they smote all the cities round about Gerar; for the fear of the LORD came upon them: and they spoiled all the cities; for there was exceeding much spoil in them.

15 They smote also the tents of cattle, and carried away sheep and camels in abundance, and returned to Jerusalem.

CHAPTER 15
Asa's Reforms

1 And the Spirit of God came upon Azariah the son of Oded:

2 And he went out to meet Asa, and said unto him, Hear ye me, Asa, and all Judah and Benjamin; The LORD *is* with you, while ye be with him; and if ye seek him, he will be found of you; but if ye forsake him, he will forsake you.

3 Now for a long season Israel *hath been* without the true God, and without a teaching priest, and without law.

4 But when they in their trouble did turn unto the LORD God of Israel, and sought him, he was found of them.

5 And in those times *there was* no peace to him that went out, nor to him that came in, but great vexations *were* upon all the inhabitants of the countries.

6 And nation was destroyed of nation, and city of city: for God did vex them with all adversity.

7 Be ye strong therefore, and let not your

hands be weak: for your work shall be rewarded.

8 And when Asa heard these words, and the prophecy of Oded the prophet, he took courage, and put away the abominable idols out of all the land of Judah and Benjamin, and out of the cities which he had taken from mount Ephraim, and renewed the altar of the LORD, that *was* before the porch of the LORD.

9 And he gathered all Judah and Benjamin, and the strangers with them out of Ephraim and Manasseh, and out of Simeon: for they fell to him out of Israel in abundance, when they saw that the LORD his God *was* with him.

10 So they gathered themselves together at Jerusalem in the third month, in the fifteenth year of the reign of Asa.

11 And they offered unto the LORD the same time, of the spoil *which* they had brought, seven hundred oxen and seven thousand sheep.

12 And they entered into a covenant to seek the LORD God of their fathers with all their heart and with all their soul;

13 That whosoever would not seek the LORD God of Israel should be put to death, whether small or great, whether man or woman.

14 And they sware unto the LORD with a loud voice, and with shouting, and with trumpets, and with cornets.

15 And all Judah rejoiced at the oath: for they had sworn with all their heart, and sought him with their whole desire; and he was found of them: and the LORD gave them rest round about.

16 And also *concerning* Maachah the mother of Asa the king, he removed her from *being* queen, because she had made an idol in a grove: and Asa cut down her idol, and stamped *it*, and burnt *it* at the brook Kidron.

17 But the high places were not taken away out of Israel: nevertheless the heart of Asa was perfect all his days.

18 And he brought into the house of God the things that his father had dedicated,

Cross references

12 2Chr. 13:15
13 Gen. 10:19; 20:1
14 Gen. 35:5; 2Chr. 17:10
1 Num. 24:2; Judg. 3:10; 2Chr. 20:14; 24:20
2 1Chr. 28:9; 2Chr. 15:4, 15; 33:12, 13; 24:20; Jer. 29:13; Matt. 7:7; James 4:8
3 Lev. 10:11; Hos. 3:4
4 Deut. 4:29
5 Judg. 5:6
6 Matt. 24:7
8 2Chr. 13:19
9 2Chr. 11:16
11 2Chr. 14:13, 15
12 2Kgs. 23:3; 2Chr. 34:31; Neh. 10:29
13 Ex. 22:20; Deut. 13:5, 9, 15
15 2Chr. 15:2
16 1Kgs. 15:2, 10, 13
17 1Kgs. 15:14; 2Chr. 14:3, 5

15:9 all Judah and Benjamin. Under the revival and reforms Asa initiated, many citizens of the Northern Kingdom, then steeped in idolatry, migrated into the Southern Kingdom, including people from the tribes of Ephraim and Manasseh. Simeon's descendants were already partially assimilated into Judah.

15:12 entered into a covenant to seek the LORD. This

was the strongest reaffirmation of spiritual dedications since Solomon's decline.

15:16 Maachah was Absalom's granddaughter, as well as King Rehoboam's favorite wife (see 1 Kgs. 15:10; 2 Chr. 13:2). Although Asa was her grandson, he removed her from being queen mother because of her promotion of idolatry.

and that he himself had dedicated, silver, and gold, and vessels.

19 And there was no *more* war unto the five and thirtieth year of the reign of Asa.

CHAPTER 16
Asa Seeks Syria's Help

1 In the six and thirtieth year of the reign of Asa Baasha king of Israel came up against Judah, and built Ramah, to the intent that he might let none go out or come in to Asa king of Judah.

2 Then Asa brought out silver and gold out of the treasures of the house of the LORD and of the king's house, and sent to Ben-hadad king of Syria, that dwelt at Damascus, saying,

3 *There is* a league between me and thee, as *there was* between my father and thy father: behold, I have sent thee silver and gold; go, break thy league with Baasha king of Israel, that he may depart from me.

4 And Ben-hadad hearkened unto king Asa, and sent the captains of his armies against the cities of Israel; and they smote Ijon, and Dan, and Abel-maim, and all the store cities of Naphtali.

5 And it came to pass, when Baasha heard *it*, that he left off building of Ramah, and let his work cease.

6 Then Asa the king took all Judah; and they carried away the stones of Ramah, and the timber thereof, wherewith Baasha was building; and he built therewith Geba and Mizpah.

7 And at that time Hanani the seer came to Asa king of Judah, and said unto him, Because thou hast relied on the king of Syria, and not relied on the LORD thy God, therefore is the host of the king of Syria escaped out of thine hand.

8 Were not the Ethiopians and the Lubims a huge host, with very many chariots and horsemen? yet, because thou didst rely on the LORD, he delivered them into thine hand.

9 For the eyes of the LORD run to and fro throughout the whole earth, to shew himself strong in the behalf of *them* whose heart

is perfect toward him. Herein thou hast done foolishly: therefore from henceforth thou shalt have wars.

10 Then Asa was wroth with the seer, and put him in a prison house; for *he was* in a rage with him because of this *thing*. And Asa oppressed *some* of the people the same time.

Asa's Death

11 And, behold, the acts of Asa, first and last, lo, they *are* written in the book of the kings of Judah and Israel.

12 And Asa in the thirty and ninth year of his reign was diseased in his feet, until his disease *was* exceeding *great*: yet in his disease he sought not to the LORD, but to the physicians.

13 And Asa slept with his fathers, and died in the one and fortieth year of his reign.

14 And they buried him in his own sepulchres, which he had made for himself in the city of David, and laid him in the bed which was filled with sweet odours and divers kinds of *spices* prepared by the apothecaries' art: and they made a very great burning for him.

CHAPTER 17
Jehoshaphat Rules Judah

1 And Jehoshaphat his son reigned in his stead, and strengthened himself against Israel.

2 And he placed forces in all the fenced cities of Judah, and set garrisons in the land of Judah, and in the cities of Ephraim, which Asa his father had taken.

3 And the LORD was with Jehoshaphat, because he walked in the first ways of his father David, and sought not unto Baalim;

4 But sought to the LORD God of his father, and walked in his commandments, and not after the doings of Israel.

5 Therefore the LORD stablished the kingdom in his hand; and all Judah brought to Jehoshaphat presents; and he had riches and honour in abundance.

6 And his heart was lifted up in the ways of the LORD: moreover he took away the high places and groves out of Judah.

Cross references (center column):

1 1Kgs. 15:17; 2Chr. 15:9

7 1Kgs. 16:1; 2Chr. 19:2; Isa. 31:1; Jer. 17:5

8 2Chr. 12:3; 14:9

9 1Sam. 13:13; 1Kgs. 15:32; Job 34:21; Prov. 5:21; 15:3; Jer. 16:17; 32:19; Zech. 4:10

10 2Chr. 18:26; Jer. 20:2; Matt. 14:3

11 1Kgs. 15:23

12 1Kgs. 15:24; Jer. 17:5

14 Gen. 50:2; 2Chr. 21:19; Jer. 34:5; Mark 16:1; John 19:39, 40

1 1Kgs. 15:24

2 2Chr. 15:8

4 1Kgs. 12:28

5 1Sam. 10:27; 1Kgs. 10:25, 27; 2Chr. 18:1

6 1Kgs. 22:43; 2Chr. 15:17; 19:3; 20:33

16:9 thou hast done foolishly. Because in his later years Asa relied on the king of Syria rather than God to protect him from the forces of King Baasha of Israel, God's prophet Hanani rebuked him. Instead of repenting, Asa became angry and imprisoned Hanani. Nevertheless, Hanani's prophecy that Asa would have continuing wars was fulfilled. Persecuting a faithful servant of God for delivering an unpopular message always leads to serious consequences.

17:1 Jehosaphat. Asa's son resumed the reforms. Jehoshaphat sought the Lord and was blessed with riches, honor and abundance.

7 Also in the third year of his reign he sent to his princes, *even* to Ben-hail, and to Obadiah, and to Zechariah, and to Nethaneel, and to Michaiah, to teach in the cities of Judah.

8 And with them *he sent* Levites, *even* Shemaiah, and Nethaniah, and Zebadiah, and Asahel, and Shemiramoth, and Jehonathan, and Adonijah, and Tobijah, and Tob-adonijah, Levites; and with them Elishama and Jehoram, priests.

9 And they taught in Judah, and *had* the book of the law of the LORD with them, and went about throughout all the cities of Judah, and taught the people.

10 And the fear of the LORD fell upon all the kingdoms of the lands that *were* round about Judah, so that they made no war against Jehoshaphat.

11 Also *some* of the Philistines brought Jehoshaphat presents, and tribute silver; and the Arabians brought him flocks, seven thousand and seven hundred rams, and seven thousand and seven hundred he goats.

12 And Jehoshaphat waxed great exceedingly; and he built in Judah castles, and cities of store.

13 And he had much business in the cities of Judah: and the men of war, mighty men of valour, *were* in Jerusalem.

14 And these *are* the numbers of them according to the house of their fathers: Of Judah, the captains of thousands; Adnah the chief, and with him mighty men of valour three hundred thousand.

15 And next to him *was* Jehohanan the captain, and with him two hundred and fourscore thousand.

16 And next him *was* Amasiah the son of Zichri, who willingly offered himself unto the LORD; and with him two hundred thousand mighty men of valour.

17 And of Benjamin; Eliada a mighty man of valour, and with him armed men with bow and shield two hundred thousand.

18 And next him *was* Jehozabad, and with him an hundred and fourscore thousand ready prepared for the war.

19 These waited on the king, beside *those* whom the king put in the fenced cities throughout all Judah.

Cross references

7 2Chr. 15:3
9 2Chr. 35:3; Neh. 8:7
10 Gen. 35:5
11 2Sam. 8:2
16 Judg. 5:2, 9
19 2Chr. 17:2
1 2Kgs. 8:18; 2Chr. 17:5
2 1Kgs. 22:2
4 1Sam. 23:2, 4, 9; 2Sam. 2:1

CHAPTER 18
Micaiah Predicts Ahab and Jehoshaphat's Defeat

1 Now Jehoshaphat had riches and honour in abundance, and joined affinity with Ahab.

2 And after *certain* years he went down to Ahab to Samaria. And Ahab killed sheep and oxen for him in abundance, and for the people that *he had* with him, and persuaded him to go up *with him* to Ramoth-gilead.

3 And Ahab king of Israel said unto Jehoshaphat king of Judah, Wilt thou go with me to Ramoth-gilead? And he answered him, I *am* as thou *art*, and my people as thy people; and *we will be* with thee in the war.

4 And Jehoshaphat said unto the king of Israel, Inquire, I pray thee, at the word of the LORD today.

5 Therefore the king of Israel gathered together of prophets four hundred men, and said unto them, Shall we go to Ramoth-gilead to battle, or shall I forbear? And they said, Go up; for God will deliver *it* into the king's hand.

6 But Jehoshaphat said, *Is there* not here a prophet of the LORD besides, that we might inquire of him?

7 And the king of Israel said unto Jehoshaphat, *There is* yet one man, by whom we may inquire of the LORD: but I hate him; for he never prophesied good unto me, but always evil: the same *is* Micaiah the son of Imla. And Jehoshaphat said, Let not the king say so.

8 And the king of Israel called for one *of his* officers, and said, Fetch quickly Micaiah the son of Imla.

9 And the king of Israel and Jehoshaphat king of Judah sat either of them on his throne, clothed in *their* robes, and they sat in a void place at the entering in of the gate of Samaria; and all the prophets prophesied before them.

10 And Zedekiah the son of Chenaanah had made him horns of iron, and said, Thus saith the LORD, With these thou shalt push Syria until they be consumed.

11 And all the prophets prophesied so, saying, Go up to Ramoth-gilead, and prosper:

18:1 Jehoshaphat's son, Jehoram, was given in marriage to Athaliah, the daughter of Ahab and Jezebel (2 Chr. 21:6). This alliance was condemned by God (2 Chr. 19:2; see also Amos 3:3; 1 Cor. 7:39; 2 Cor. 6:14).

18:5–6 These prophets were probably those involved in the calf worship established by King Jeroboam in Dan and Bethel. Although the religion of these prophets may have been presented as an alternate way to worship Jehovah, there can be no doubt it was idolatry (1 Kgs. 12:28).

for the LORD shall deliver *it* into the hand of the king.

12 And the messenger that went to call Micaiah spake to him, saying, Behold, the words of the prophets *declare* good to the king with one assent; let thy word therefore, I pray thee, be like one of theirs, and speak thou good.

13 And Micaiah said, *As* the LORD liveth, even what my God saith, that will I speak.

14 And when he was come to the king, the king said unto him, Micaiah, shall we go to Ramoth-gilead to battle, or shall I forbear? And he said, Go ye up, and prosper, and they shall be delivered into your hand.

15 And the king said to him, How many times shall I adjure thee that thou say nothing but the truth to me in the name of the LORD?

16 Then he said, I did see all Israel scattered upon the mountains, as sheep that have no shepherd: and the LORD said, These have no master; let them return *therefore* every man to his house in peace.

17 And the king of Israel said to Jehoshaphat, Did I not tell thee *that* he would not prophesy good unto me, but evil?

18 Again he said, Therefore hear the word of the LORD; I saw the LORD sitting upon his throne, and all the host of heaven standing on his right hand and *on* his left.

19 And the LORD said, Who shall entice Ahab king of Israel, that he may go up and fall at Ramoth-gilead? And one spake saying after this manner, and another saying after that manner.

20 Then there came out a spirit, and stood before the LORD, and said, I will entice him. And the LORD said unto him, Wherewith?

21 And he said, I will go out, and be a lying spirit in the mouth of all his prophets. And *the LORD* said, Thou shalt entice *him*, and thou shalt also prevail: go out, and do *even* so.

22 Now therefore, behold, the LORD hath put a lying spirit in the mouth of these thy prophets, and the LORD hath spoken evil against thee.

23 Then Zedekiah the son of Chenaanah came near, and smote Micaiah upon the cheek, and said, Which way went the Spirit of the LORD from me to speak unto thee?

24 And Micaiah said, Behold, thou shalt see on that day when thou shalt go into an inner chamber to hide thyself.

25 Then the king of Israel said, Take ye Micaiah, and carry him back to Amon the governor of the city, and to Joash the king's son;

26 And say, Thus saith the king, Put this *fellow* in the prison, and feed him with bread of affliction and with water of affliction, until I return in peace.

27 And Micaiah said, If thou certainly return in peace, *then* hath not the LORD spoken by me. And he said, Hearken, all ye people.

Ahab Dies in Battle

28 So the king of Israel and Jehoshaphat the king of Judah went up to Ramoth-gilead.

29 And the king of Israel said unto Jehoshaphat, I will disguise myself, and will go to the battle; but put thou on thy robes. So the king of Israel disguised himself; and they went to the battle.

30 Now the king of Syria had commanded the captains of the chariots that *were* with him, saying, Fight ye not with small or great, save only with the king of Israel.

31 And it came to pass, when the captains of the chariots saw Jehoshaphat, that they said, It *is* the king of Israel. Therefore they compassed about him to fight: but Jehoshaphat cried out, and the LORD helped him; and God moved them *to depart* from him.

32 For it came to pass, that, when the captains of the chariots perceived that it was not the king of Israel, they turned back again from pursuing him.

33 And a *certain* man drew a bow at a venture, and smote the king of Israel between the joints of the harness: therefore he said to his chariot man, Turn thine hand, that thou mayest carry me out of the host; for I am wounded.

34 And the battle increased that day: howbeit the king of Israel stayed *himself* up in *his* chariot against the Syrians until the even: and about the time of the sun going down he died.

CHAPTER 19
Jehu Confronts Jehoshaphat

1 And Jehoshaphat the king of Judah returned to his house in peace to Jerusalem.

Cross references (center column):

13 Num. 22:18, 20, 35; 23:12, 26; 24:13; 1Kgs. 22:14

20 Job 1:6

22 Job 12:16; Isa. 19:14; Ezek. 14:9

23 Jer. 20:2; Mark 14:65; Acts 23:2

26 2Chr. 16:10

18:13 Micaiah. Though this faithful prophet was unpopular for his prediction of Ahab's defeat, and though he was wrongfully imprisoned for his prophetic message, this man of God was vindicated by history. Ahab did not return in peace and victory, but died on the battlefield.

2 And Jehu the son of Hanani the seer went out to meet him, and said to king Jehoshaphat, Shouldest thou help the ungodly, and love them that hate the LORD? therefore *is* wrath upon thee from before the LORD.

3 Nevertheless there are good things found in thee, in that thou hast taken away the groves out of the land, and hast prepared thine heart to seek God.

Jehoshaphat Appoints Judges

4 And Jehoshaphat dwelt at Jerusalem: and he went out again through the people from Beer-sheba to mount Ephraim, and brought them back unto the LORD God of their fathers.

5 And he set judges in the land throughout all the fenced cities of Judah, city by city,

6 And said to the judges, Take heed what ye do: for ye judge not for man, but for the LORD, who *is* with you in the judgment.

7 Wherefore now let the fear of the LORD be upon you; take heed and do *it*: for *there is* no iniquity with the LORD our God, nor respect of persons, nor taking of gifts.

8 Moreover in Jerusalem did Jehoshaphat set of the Levites, and *of* the priests, and of the chief of the fathers of Israel, for the judgment of the LORD, and for controversies, when they returned to Jerusalem.

9 And he charged them, saying, Thus shall ye do in the fear of the LORD, faithfully, and with a perfect heart.

10 And what cause soever shall come to you of your brethren that dwell in their cities, between blood and blood, between law and commandment, statutes and judgments, ye shall even warn them that they trespass not against the LORD, and *so* wrath come upon you, and upon your brethren: this do, and ye shall not trespass.

11 And, behold, Amariah the chief priest *is* over you in all matters of the LORD; and Zebadiah the son of Ishmael, the ruler of the house of Judah, for all the king's matters: also the Levites *shall be* officers before you.

2 1Sam. 9:9;
2Chr. 32:25;
Ps. 139:21

3 2Chr.
12:12; 17:4,
6; 30:19;
Ezra 7:10

6 Deut. 1:17;
Ps. 82:1;
Eccl. 5:8

7 Deut.
10:17; 32:4;
Job 34:19;
Acts 10:34;
Rom. 2:11;
9:14; Gal.
2:6; Eph. 6:9;
Col. 3:25;
1Pet. 1:17

8 Deut.
16:18; 2Chr.
17:8

9 2Sam.
23:3

10 Num.
16:46; Deut.
17:8; Ezek.
3:18

11 1Chr.
26:30; 2Chr.
15:2

2 Gen. 14:7;
Josh. 15:62

3 2Chr. 19:3;
Ezra 8:21;
Jer. 36:9;
Jon. 3:5

6 Deut. 4:39;
Josh. 2:11;
1Kgs. 8:23;
1Chr. 29:12;
Ps. 47:2, 8;
62:11; Dan.
4:17, 25, 32;
Matt. 6:9, 13

7 Gen. 17:7;
Ex. 6:7; Ps.
44:2; Isa.
41:8; James
2:23

9 1Kgs. 8:33,
37; 2Chr.
6:20, 28-30

10 Num.
20:21; Deut.
2:4, 9, 19

11 Ps. 83:12

Deal courageously, and the LORD shall be with the good.

CHAPTER 20
Moab and Ammon Are Defeated

1 It came to pass after this also, *that* the children of Moab, and the children of Ammon, and with them *other* beside the Ammonites, came against Jehoshaphat to battle.

2 Then there came some that told Jehoshaphat, saying, There cometh a great multitude against thee from beyond the sea on this side Syria; and, behold, they *be* in Hazazon-tamar, which *is* En-gedi.

3 And Jehoshaphat feared, and set himself to seek the LORD, and proclaimed a fast throughout all Judah.

4 And Judah gathered themselves together, to ask *help* of the LORD: even out of all the cities of Judah they came to seek the LORD.

5 And Jehoshaphat stood in the congregation of Judah and Jerusalem, in the house of the LORD, before the new court,

6 And said, O LORD God of our fathers, *art* not thou God in heaven? and rulest *not* thou over all the kingdoms of the heathen? and in thine hand *is there not* power and might, so that none is able to withstand thee?

7 *Art* not thou our God, *who* didst drive out the inhabitants of this land before thy people Israel, and gavest it to the seed of Abraham thy friend for ever?

8 And they dwelt therein, and have built thee a sanctuary therein for thy name, saying,

9 If, *when* evil cometh upon us, *as* the sword, judgment, or pestilence, or famine, we stand before this house, and in thy presence, (for thy name *is* in this house,) and cry unto thee in our affliction, then thou wilt hear and help.

10 And now, behold, the children of Ammon and Moab and mount Seir, whom thou wouldest not let Israel invade, when they came out of the land of Egypt, but they turned from them, and destroyed them not;

11 Behold, *I say, how* they reward us, to

19:2 Jehu the son of Hanani the seer. Hanani had rebuked Asa the king for seeking help from the king of Syria against King Baasha of Israel. Baasha had built military fortifications to prevent transit to and from Judah (1 Chr. 16:1–9). Jehu, Hanani's son, first denounced Baasha (1 Kgs. 16:1, 7) and then after a period of thirty years, reappears here to reprove Jehoshaphat for his alliance with Ahab. He later wrote a record of Jehoshaphat's reign (2 Chr. 20:34).

20:2 beyond the sea. The sea mentioned here is the Dead Sea. The countries of Ammon and Moab were east of that "sea of salt."

come to cast us out of thy possession, which thou hast given us to inherit.

12 O our God, wilt thou not judge them? for we have no might against this great company that cometh against us; neither know we what to do: but our eyes *are* upon thee.

13 And all Judah stood before the LORD, with their little ones, their wives, and their children.

14 Then upon Jahaziel the son of Zechariah, the son of Benaiah, the son of Jeiel, the son of Mattaniah, a Levite of the sons of Asaph, came the Spirit of the LORD in the midst of the congregation;

15 And he said, Hearken ye, all Judah, and ye inhabitants of Jerusalem, and thou king Jehoshaphat, Thus saith the LORD unto you, Be not afraid nor dismayed by reason of this great multitude; for the battle *is* not yours, but God's.

16 To morrow go ye down against them: behold, they come up by the cliff of Ziz; and ye shall find them at the end of the brook, before the wilderness of Jeruel.

17 Ye shall not *need* to fight in this *battle*: set yourselves, stand ye *still*, and see the salvation of the LORD with you, O Judah and Jerusalem: fear not, nor be dismayed; to morrow go out against them: for the LORD *will be* with you.

18 And Jehoshaphat bowed his head with *his* face to the ground: and all Judah and the inhabitants of Jerusalem fell before the LORD, worshipping the LORD.

19 And the Levites, of the children of the Kohathites, and of the children of the Korhites, stood up to praise the LORD God of Israel with a loud voice on high.

20 And they rose early in the morning, and went forth into the wilderness of Tekoa: and as they went forth, Jehoshaphat stood and said, Hear me, O Judah, and ye inhabitants of Jerusalem; Believe in the LORD your God, so shall ye be established; believe his prophets, so shall ye prosper.

21 And when he had consulted with the people, he appointed singers unto the LORD, and that should praise the beauty of holiness, as they went out before the army, and to say, Praise the LORD; for his mercy *endureth* for ever.

22 And when they began to sing and to praise, the LORD set ambushments against the children of Ammon, Moab, and mount Seir, which were come against Judah; and they were smitten.

23 For the children of Ammon and Moab stood up against the inhabitants of mount Seir, utterly to slay and destroy *them*: and when they had made an end of the inhabitants of Seir, every one helped to destroy another.

24 And when Judah came toward the watch tower in the wilderness, they looked unto the multitude, and, behold, they *were* dead bodies fallen to the earth, and none escaped.

25 And when Jehoshaphat and his people came to take away the spoil of them, they found among them in abundance both riches with the dead bodies, and precious jewels, which they stripped off for themselves, more than they could carry away: and they were three days in gathering of the spoil, it was so much.

26 And on the fourth day they assembled themselves in the valley of Berachah; for there they blessed the LORD: therefore the name of the same place was called, The valley of Berachah, unto this day.

27 Then they returned, every man of Judah and Jerusalem, and Jehoshaphat in the forefront of them, to go again to Jerusalem with joy; for the LORD had made them to rejoice over their enemies.

28 And they came to Jerusalem with psalteries and harps and trumpets unto the house of the LORD.

29 And the fear of God was on all the kingdoms of *those* countries, when they had heard that the LORD fought against the enemies of Israel.

30 So the realm of Jehoshaphat was quiet: for his God gave him rest round about.

Summary of Jehoshaphat's Reign

31 And Jehoshaphat reigned over Judah: *he was* thirty and five years old when he began to reign, and he reigned twenty and five years in Jerusalem. And his mother's name *was* Azubah the daughter of Shilhi.

32 And he walked in the way of Asa his

Cross references (center column):

12 1Sam. 3:13; Ps. 25:15; 121:1, 2; 123:1, 2; 141:8

14 Num. 11:25, 26; 24:2; 2Chr. 15:1; 24:20

15 Ex. 14:13, 14; Deut. 1:29, 30; 31:6, 8; 2Chr. 32:7

17 Ex. 14:13, 14; Num. 14:9; 2Chr. 15:2; 32:8

18 Ex. 4:31

20 Isa. 7:9

21 1Chr. 16:29, 34, 41; 2Chr. 5:13; 7:3, 6; Ps. 136:1

22 Judg. 7:22; 1Sam. 14:20

27 Neh. 12:43

29 2Chr. 17:10

30 2Chr. 15:15; Job 34:29

31 1Kgs. 22:41

20:15 the battle is not yours, but God's. This expression is similar to what Moses said at the Exodus (Ex. 14:13–14) and David said when he faced Goliath (1 Sam. 17:47). Deliverance came in each case through divine intervention.

20:22–23 the Lord set ambushments. As the armies of Ammon and Moab became involved with the Edomites in Seir, confusion ensued, and the armies destroyed each other. This was similar to God's internvention in Gideon's day (Judg. 7:15–23).

father, and departed not from it, doing *that which was* right in the sight of the LORD.

33 Howbeit the high places were not taken away: for as yet the people had not prepared their hearts unto the God of their fathers.

34 Now the rest of the acts of Jehoshaphat, first and last, behold, they *are* written in the book of Jehu the son of Hanani, who *is* mentioned in the book of the kings of Israel.

35 And after this did Jehoshaphat king of Judah join himself with Ahaziah king of Israel, who did very wickedly:

36 And he joined himself with him to make ships to go to Tarshish: and they made the ships in Ezion-geber.

37 Then Eliezer the son of Dodavah of Mareshah prophesied against Jehoshaphat, saying, Because thou hast joined thyself with Ahaziah, the LORD hath broken thy works. And the ships were broken, that they were not able to go to Tarshish.

CHAPTER 21

1 Now Jehoshaphat slept with his fathers, and was buried with his fathers in the city of David. And Jehoram his son reigned in his stead.

Jehoram Rules Judah

2 And he had brethren the sons of Jehoshaphat, Azariah, and Jehiel, and Zechariah, and Azariah, and Michael, and Shephatiah: all these *were* the sons of Jehoshaphat king of Israel.

3 And their father gave them great gifts of silver, and of gold, and of precious things, with fenced cities in Judah: but the kingdom gave he to Jehoram; because he *was* the firstborn.

4 Now when Jehoram was risen up to the kingdom of his father, he strengthened himself, and slew all his brethren with the sword, and *divers* also of the princes of Israel.

5 Jehoram *was* thirty and two years old when he began to reign, and he reigned eight years in Jerusalem.

6 And he walked in the way of the kings of Israel, like as did the house of Ahab: for he had the daughter of Ahab to wife: and he wrought *that which was* evil in the eyes of the LORD.

7 Howbeit the LORD would not destroy the house of David, because of the covenant that he had made with David, and as he promised to give a light to him and to his sons for ever.

8 In his days the Edomites revolted from under the dominion of Judah, and made themselves a king.

9 Then Jehoram went forth with his princes, and all his chariots with him: and he rose up by night, and smote the Edomites which compassed him in, and the captains of the chariots.

10 So the Edomites revolted from under the hand of Judah unto this day. The same time *also* did Libnah revolt from under his hand; because he had forsaken the LORD God of his fathers.

11 Moreover he made high places in the mountains of Judah, and caused the inhabitants of Jerusalem to commit fornication, and compelled Judah *thereto*.

12 And there came a writing to him from Elijah the prophet, saying, Thus saith the LORD God of David thy father, Because thou hast not walked in the ways of Jehoshaphat thy father, nor in the ways of Asa king of Judah,

13 But hast walked in the way of the kings of Israel, and hast made Judah and the inhabitants of Jerusalem to go a whoring, like to the whoredoms of the house of Ahab, and also hast slain thy brethren of thy father's house, *which were* better than thyself:

14 Behold, with a great plague will the LORD smite thy people, and thy children, and thy wives, and all thy goods:

15 And thou *shalt have* great sickness by disease of thy bowels, until thy bowels fall out by reason of the sickness day by day.

16 Moreover the LORD stirred up against Jehoram the spirit of the Philistines, and of the Arabians, that *were* near the Ethiopians:

17 And they came up into Judah, and brake into it, and carried away all the substance that was found in the king's house, and his

Cross-references

33 2Chr. 12:14; 17:6; 19:3
34 1Kgs. 16:1, 7
35 1Kgs. 22:48, 49
36 1Kgs. 22:49
37 1Kgs. 22:48; 2Chr. 9:21
1 1Kgs. 22:50
3 2Kgs. 8:16
5 2Kgs. 8:17
6 2Chr. 22:2
7 2Sam. 7:12, 13; 1Kgs. 11:36; 2Kgs. 8:19; Ps. 132:11
8 2Kgs. 8:20
11 Lev. 17:7; 20:5; 2Chr. 21:13
12 2Kgs. 2:1
13 Ex. 34:15; Deut. 31:16; 1Kgs. 16:31-33; 2Kgs. 9:22; 2Chr. 21:4, 11
15 2Chr. 21:18, 19
16 1Kgs. 11:14, 23
17 2Chr. 22:1; 24:7

21:1 Jehoram. This wicked king, eldest son of Jehoshaphat, came to power, and reigned eight years. His reign is marked by his slaughter of all the princes in the realm and his endeavor to reverse every righteous trend started by his father. Jehoram promoted immorality and idolatry (v. 11). His wife was Athaliah, the daughter of Ahab and Jezebel.

21:12 a writing to him from Elijah the prophet. Shortly before his translation (2 Kgs. 2:1–11), Elijah had written a letter concerning Jehoram's evil reign and painful death. This may have been composed while Jehoram was co-regent with his father Jehoshaphat—in prophetic anticipation of what was yet to come.

sons also, and his wives; so that there was never a son left him, save Jehoahaz, the youngest of his sons.

18 And after all this the LORD smote him in his bowels with an incurable disease.

19 And it came to pass, that in process of time, after the end of two years, his bowels fell out by reason of his sickness: so he died of sore diseases. And his people made no burning for him, like the burning of his fathers.

20 Thirty and two years old was he when he began to reign, and he reigned in Jerusalem eight years, and departed without being desired. Howbeit they buried him in the city of David, but not in the sepulchres of the kings.

CHAPTER 22
Ahaziah Rules Judah

1 And the inhabitants of Jerusalem made Ahaziah his youngest son king in his stead: for the band of men that came with the Arabians to the camp had slain all the eldest. So Ahaziah the son of Jehoram king of Judah reigned.

2 Forty and two years old was Ahaziah when he began to reign, and he reigned one year in Jerusalem. His mother's name also was Athaliah the daughter of Omri.

3 He also walked in the ways of the house of Ahab: for his mother was his counseller to do wickedly.

4 Wherefore he did evil in the sight of the LORD like the house of Ahab: for they were his counsellers after the death of his father to his destruction.

5 He walked also after their counsel, and went with Jehoram the son of Ahab king of Israel to war against Hazael king of Syria at Ramoth-gilead: and the Syrians smote Joram.

6 And he returned to be healed in Jezreel because of the wounds which were given him at Ramah, when he fought with Hazael king of Syria. And Azariah the son of Jeho-

ram king of Judah went down to see Jehoram the son of Ahab at Jezreel, because he was sick.

Jehu Assassinates Ahaziah

7 And the destruction of Ahaziah was of God by coming to Joram: for when he was come, he went out with Jehoram against Jehu the son of Nimshi, whom the LORD had anointed to cut off the house of Ahab.

8 And it came to pass, that, when Jehu was executing judgment upon the house of Ahab, and found the princes of Judah, and the sons of the brethren of Ahaziah, that ministered to Ahaziah, he slew them.

9 And he sought Ahaziah: and they caught him, (for he was hid in Samaria,) and brought him to Jehu: and when they had slain him, they buried him: Because, said they, he is the son of Jehoshaphat, who sought the LORD with all his heart. So the house of Ahaziah had no power to keep still the kingdom.

Athaliah Rules Judah

10 But when Athaliah the mother of Ahaziah saw that her son was dead, she arose and destroyed all the seed royal of the house of Judah.

11 But Jehoshabeath, the daughter of the king, took Joash the son of Ahaziah, and stole him from among the king's sons that were slain, and put him and his nurse in a bedchamber. So Jehoshabeath, the daughter of king Jehoram, the wife of Jehoiada the priest, (for she was the sister of Ahaziah,) hid him from Athaliah, so that she slew him not.

12 And he was with them hid in the house of God six years: and Athaliah reigned over the land.

CHAPTER 23

1 And in the seventh year Jehoiada strengthened himself, and took the captains

Cross-references (center column)

18 2Kgs. 9:29; 2Chr. 21:15

19 2Chr. 16:14

20 Jer. 22:18

1 2Kgs. 8:24; 2Chr. 21:17; 22:6

2 2Kgs. 8:26; 2Chr. 21:6

5 2Kgs. 8:28

6 2Kgs. 9:15

7 Judg. 14:4; 1Kgs. 12:15; 2Kgs. 9:6, 7, 21; 2Chr. 10:15

8 2Kgs. 10:10, 11, 13, 14

9 2Kgs. 9:27, at *Megiddo* in the kingdom of *Samaria;* 2Chr. 17:4

10 2Kgs. 11:1

11 2Kgs. 11:2, *Jehosheba*

1 2Kgs. 11:4

22:2 Athaliah the daughter of Omri. This wicked woman, who would usurp the throne of Judah, was the daughter of Ahab and Jezebel and granddaughter of Omri, an earlier king of Israel. The word "daughter" is being used to mean "female descendant," just as the word "son" is often used in Hebrew to designate a male descendant.

22:5 Jehoram, or the shorter spelling, Joram, is the name of two separate individuals, one who ruled over Israel and the other over Judah. Even more confusing,

these two men were in power during the same time period. While the name Joram is almost always applied to the King of Israel (2 Kgs. 8:21, 23–24, 28; 9:14–17, 21–23; 2 Chr. 22:7), he is referred to as Jehoram in 2 Kings 3:1; 9:24 and in 2 Chronicles 22:7, both spellings being used. The king of Judah is normally referred to as Jehoram (1 Kgs. 22:50; 2 Kgs. 12:18; 2 Chr. 21:1, 3–5, 16; 22:1, 11) though on two occasions he is called Joram (2 Kgs. 11:2; 1 Chr. 3:11). Both kings are called Jehoram in 2 Chronicles 22:6.

of hundreds, Azariah the son of Jeroham, and Ishmael the son of Jehohanan, and Azariah the son of Obed, and Maaseiah the son of Adaiah, and Elishaphat the son of Zichri, into covenant with him.

2 And they went about in Judah, and gathered the Levites out of all the cities of Judah, and the chief of the fathers of Israel, and they came to Jerusalem.

3 And all the congregation made a covenant with the king in the house of God. And he said unto them, Behold, the king's son shall reign, as the LORD hath said of the sons of David.

4 This *is* the thing that ye shall do; A third part of you entering on the sabbath, of the priests and of the Levites, *shall be* porters of the doors;

5 And a third part *shall be* at the king's house; and a third part at the gate of the foundation: and all the people *shall be* in the courts of the house of the LORD.

6 But let none come into the house of the LORD, save the priests, and they that minister of the Levites; they shall go in, for they *are* holy: but all the people shall keep the watch of the LORD.

7 And the Levites shall compass the king round about, every man with his weapons in his hand; and whosoever *else* cometh into the house, he shall be put to death: but be ye with the king when he cometh in, and when he goeth out.

8 So the Levites and all Judah did according to all things that Jehoiada the priest had commanded, and took every man his men that were to come in on the sabbath, with them that were to go *out* on the sabbath: for Jehoiada the priest dismissed not the courses.

9 Moreover Jehoiada the priest delivered to the captains of hundreds spears, and bucklers, and shields, that *had been* king David's, which *were* in the house of God.

10 And he set all the people, every man having his weapon in his hand, from the right side of the temple to the left side of the temple, along by the altar and the temple, by the king round about.

11 Then they brought out the king's son, and put upon him the crown, and *gave him* the testimony, and made him king. And Jehoiada and his sons anointed him, and said, God save the king.

12 Now when Athaliah heard the noise of the people running and praising the king, she came to the people into the house of the LORD:

13 And she looked, and, behold, the king stood at his pillar at the entering in, and the princes and the trumpets by the king: and all the people of the land rejoiced, and sounded with trumpets, also the singers with instruments of musick, and such as taught to sing praise. Then Athaliah rent her clothes, and said, Treason, Treason.

14 Then Jehoiada the priest brought out the captains of hundreds that were set over the host, and said unto them, Have her forth of the ranges: and whoso followeth her, let him be slain with the sword. For the priest said, Slay her not in the house of the LORD.

15 So they laid hands on her; and when she was come to the entering of the horse gate by the king's house, they slew her there.

Jehoiada's Reform

16 And Jehoiada made a covenant between him, and between all the people, and between the king, that they should be the LORD's people.

17 Then all the people went to the house of Baal, and brake it down, and brake his altars and his images in pieces, and slew Mattan the priest of Baal before the altars.

18 Also Jehoiada appointed the offices of the house of the LORD by the hand of the priests the Levites, whom David had distributed in the house of the LORD, to offer the burnt offerings of the LORD, as *it is* written in the law of Moses, with rejoicing and with singing, *as it was ordained* by David.

19 And he set the porters at the gates of the house of the LORD, that none *which was* unclean in any thing should enter in.

20 And he took the captains of hundreds, and the nobles, and the governors of the people, and all the people of the land, and brought down the king from the house of the LORD: and they came through the high gate into the king's house, and set the king upon the throne of the kingdom.

21 And all the people of the land rejoiced: and the city was quiet, after that they had slain Athaliah with the sword.

Cross references: 3 2Sam. 7:12; 1Kgs. 2:4; 9:5; 2Chr. 6:16; 7:18; 21:7 | 4 1Chr. 9:25 | 6 1Chr. 23:28, 29 | 11 Deut. 17:18 | 13 1Chr. 25:8 | 15 Neh. 3:28 | 17 Deut. 13:9 | 18 Num. 28:2; 1Chr. 23:6, 30, 31; 24:1; 25:2, 6 | 19 1Chr. 26:1 | 20 2Kgs. 11:19

23:11 the testimony. This refers to the Law of Moses (Ex. 25:21), which was meant to be the king's constant guide (Deut. 17:19–20). He was supposed to write his own copy (Deut. 17:18). There is no record that any king ever did.

CHAPTER 24
Joash Rules Judah

1 Joash *was* seven years old when he began to reign, and he reigned forty years in Jerusalem. His mother's name also *was* Zibiah of Beer-sheba.

2 And Joash did *that which was* right in the sight of the LORD all the days of Jehoiada the priest.

3 And Jehoiada took for him two wives; and he begat sons and daughters.

4 And it came to pass after this, *that* Joash was minded to repair the house of the LORD.

5 And he gathered together the priests and the Levites, and said to them, Go out unto the cities of Judah, and gather of all Israel money to repair the house of your God from year to year, and see that ye hasten the matter. Howbeit the Levites hastened *it* not.

6 And the king called for Jehoiada the chief, and said unto him, Why hast thou not required of the Levites to bring in out of Judah and out of Jerusalem the collection, *according to the commandment* of Moses the servant of the LORD, and of the congregation of Israel, for the tabernacle of witness?

7 For the sons of Athaliah, that wicked woman, had broken up the house of God; and also all the dedicated things of the house of the LORD did they bestow upon Baalim.

8 And at the king's commandment they made a chest, and set it without at the gate of the house of the LORD.

9 And they made a proclamation through Judah and Jerusalem, to bring in to the LORD the collection *that* Moses the servant of God *laid* upon Israel in the wilderness.

10 And all the princes and all the people rejoiced, and brought in, and cast into the chest, until they had made an end.

11 Now it came to pass, that at what time the chest was brought unto the king's office

by the hand of the Levites, and when they saw that *there was* much money, the king's scribe and the high priest's officer came and emptied the chest, and took it, and carried it to his place again. Thus they did day by day, and gathered money in abundance.

12 And the king and Jehoiada gave it to such as did the work of the service of the house of the LORD, and hired masons and carpenters to repair the house of the LORD, and also such as wrought iron and brass to mend the house of the LORD.

13 So the workmen wrought, and the work was perfected by them, and they set the house of God in his state, and strengthened it.

14 And when they had finished *it,* they brought the rest of the money before the king and Jehoiada, whereof were made vessels for the house of the LORD, *even* vessels to minister, and to offer *withal,* and spoons, and vessels of gold and silver. And they offered burnt offerings in the house of the LORD continually all the days of Jehoiada.

15 But Jehoiada waxed old, and was full of days when he died; an hundred and thirty years old *was* he when he died.

16 And they buried him in the city of David among the kings, because he had done good in Israel, both toward God, and toward his house.

17 Now after the death of Jehoiada came the princes of Judah, and made obeisance to the king. Then the king hearkened unto them.

18 And they left the house of the LORD God of their fathers, and served groves and idols: and wrath came upon Judah and Jerusalem for this their trespass.

19 Yet he sent prophets to them, to bring them again unto the LORD; and they testified against them: but they would not give ear.

20 And the Spirit of God came upon Zecha-

Cross references

1 2Kgs. 11:21; 12:1
2 2Chr. 26:5
5 2Kgs. 12:4
6 Ex. 30:12-14, 16; Num. 1:50; 2Kgs. 12:7; Acts 7:44
7 2Kgs. 12:4; 2Chr. 21:17
8 2Kgs. 12:9
9 2Chr. 22:6
11 2Kgs. 12:10
14 2Kgs. 12:13
18 Judg. 5:8; 1Kgs. 14:23; 2Chr. 19:2; 28:13; 29:8; 32:25
19 2Chr. 36:15; Jer. 7:25, 26; 25:4
20 Num. 14:41; Judg. 6:34; 2Chr. 15:1, 2; 20:14

24:6 the tabernacle of witness. The Tabernacle was called "the tent of the testimony" (Num. 9:15), because it housed the tables of the law of testimony (Ex. 25:16). "Temple" was also used as a name for the Tabernacle (1 Sam. 1:9; 3:3; 2 Sam. 22:7).

24:17 after the death of Jehoiada. This godly high priest led the fight against idols, encouraged the revolt against wicked Queen Athaliah, the usurper, and secured the throne for the sole surviving son of Ahaziah, son of Jehoram and grandson of Jehoshaphat. Thus King Joash, as a seven-year-old boy, became king of Judah with Jehoiada as co-regent. After Jehoiada's death at the age of 130, the king's courtiers persuaded Joash to return to

idolatry. Later he was assassinated (v. 25).

24:20 Zechariah the son of Jehoiada. This is not the same Zechariah, son of Berechiah (Zech. 1:1) who lived over three hundred years later (ca. 525–475 B.C.). This murdered prophet, whose father was called both Jehoida and Berechiah, was the one mentioned by Jesus in Matthew 23:35 in His denunciation of the hypocritical scribes and pharisees of His time. Jesus was suggesting that from the first murder of a righteous man (Abel) to the last murder of a prophet in the Old Testament "may come all the righteous blood shed upon the earth. . . . Shall come upon this generation" (Matt. 23:35, 36). This prediction related to the fall of Jerusalem.

riah the son of Jehoiada the priest, which stood above the people, and said unto them, Thus saith God, Why transgress ye the commandments of the LORD, that ye cannot prosper? because ye have forsaken the LORD, he hath also forsaken you.

21 And they conspired against him, and stoned him with stones at the commandment of the king in the court of the house of the LORD.

22 Thus Joash the king remembered not the kindness which Jehoiada his father had done to him, but slew his son. And when he died, he said, The LORD look upon *it,* and require *it.*

23 And it came to pass at the end of the year, *that* the host of Syria came up against him: and they came to Judah and Jerusalem, and destroyed all the princes of the people from among the people, and sent all the spoil of them unto the king of Damascus.

24 For the army of the Syrians came with a small company of men, and the LORD delivered a very great host into their hand, because they had forsaken the LORD God of their fathers. So they executed judgment against Joash.

25 And when they were departed from him, (for they left him in great diseases,) his own servants conspired against him for the blood of the sons of Jehoiada the priest, and slew him on his bed, and he died: and they buried him in the city of David, but they buried him not in the sepulchres of the kings.

26 And these are they that conspired against him; Zabad the son of Shimeath an Ammonitess, and Jehozabad the son of Shimrith a Moabitess.

27 Now *concerning* his sons, and the greatness of the burdens *laid* upon him, and the repairing of the house of God, behold, they *are* written in the story of the book of the kings. And Amaziah his son reigned in his stead.

CHAPTER 25
Amaziah Rules Judah

1 Amaziah *was* twenty and five years old *when* he began to reign, and he reigned twenty and nine years in Jerusalem. And his mother's name *was* Jehoaddan of Jerusalem.

2 And he did *that which was* right in the sight of the LORD, but not with a perfect heart.

3 Now it came to pass, when the kingdom was established to him, that he slew his servants that had killed the king his father.

4 But he slew not their children, but *did* as *it is* written in the law in the book of Moses, where the LORD commanded, saying, The fathers shall not die for the children, neither shall the children die for the fathers, but every man shall die for his own sin.

5 Moreover Amaziah gathered Judah together, and made them captains over thousands, and captains over hundreds, according to the houses of *their* fathers, throughout all Judah and Benjamin: and he numbered them from twenty years old and above, and found them three hundred thousand choice *men, able* to go forth to war, that could handle spear and shield.

6 He hired also an hundred thousand mighty men of valour out of Israel for an hundred talents of silver.

7 But there came a man of God to him, saying, O king, let not the army of Israel go with thee; for the LORD *is* not with Israel, *to wit, with* all the children of Ephraim.

8 But if thou wilt go, do *it,* be strong for the battle: God shall make thee fall before the enemy: for God hath power to help, and to cast down.

9 And Amaziah said to the man of God, But what shall we do for the hundred talents which I have given to the army of Israel? And the man of God answered, The LORD is able to give thee much more than this.

10 Then Amaziah separated them, *to wit,* the army that was come to him out of Ephraim, to go home again: wherefore their anger was greatly kindled against Judah, and they returned home in great anger.

11 And Amaziah strengthened himself, and led forth his people, and went to the valley of salt, and smote of the children of Seir ten thousand.

12 And *other* ten thousand *left* alive did the children of Judah carry away captive, and brought them unto the top of the rock, and cast them down from the top of the rock, that they all were broken in pieces.

13 But the soldiers of the army which Amaziah sent back, that they should not go

Cross references (center column)

21 Matt. 23:35; Acts 7:58, 59
23 2Kgs. 12:17
24 Lev. 26:8, 25; Deut. 28:25; 32:30; 2Chr. 22:8; Isa. 10:5; 30:17
25 2Kgs. 12:20; 24:21
26 2Kgs. 12:21
27 2Kgs. 12:18, 21
1 2Kgs. 14:1
2 2Kgs. 14:4; 2Chr. 25:14
3 2Kgs. 14:5
4 Deut. 24:16; 2Kgs. 14:6; Jer. 31:30; Ezek. 18:20
5 Num. 1:3
8 2Chr. 20:6
9 Prov. 10:22
11 2Kgs. 14:7

25:9 The LORD is able to give thee much more than this. This phrase asserts what is promised in Matthew 6:33, Ephesians 3:20, and Philippians 4:19.

with him to battle, fell upon the cities of Judah, from Samaria even unto Beth-horon, and smote three thousand of them, and took much spoil.

14 Now it came to pass, after that Amaziah was come from the slaughter of the Edomites, that he brought the gods of the children of Seir, and set them up *to be* his gods, and bowed down himself before them, and burned incense unto them.

15 Wherefore the anger of the LORD was kindled against Amaziah, and he sent unto him a prophet, which said unto him, Why hast thou sought after the gods of the people, which could not deliver their own people out of thine hand?

16 And it came to pass, as he talked with him, that *the king* said unto him, Art thou made of the king's counsel? forbear; why shouldest thou be smitten? Then the prophet forbare, and said, I know that God hath determined to destroy thee, because thou hast done this, and hast not hearkened unto my counsel.

17 Then Amaziah king of Judah took advice, and sent to Joash, the son of Jehoahaz, the son of Jehu, king of Israel, saying, Come, let us see one another in the face.

18 And Joash king of Israel sent to Amaziah king of Judah, saying, The thistle that *was* in Lebanon sent to the cedar that *was* in Lebanon, saying, Give thy daughter to my son to wife: and there passed by a wild beast that *was* in Lebanon, and trode down the thistle.

19 Thou sayest, Lo, thou hast smitten the Edomites; and thine heart lifteth thee up to boast: abide now at home; why shouldest thou meddle to *thine* hurt, that thou shouldest fall, *even* thou, and Judah with thee?

20 But Amaziah would not hear; for it *came* of God, that he might deliver them into the hand *of their enemies*, because they sought after the gods of Edom.

21 So Joash the king of Israel went up; and they saw one another in the face, *both* he and Amaziah king of Judah, at Beth-shemesh, which *belongeth* to Judah.

22 And Judah was put to the worse before Israel, and they fled every man to his tent.

23 And Joash the king of Israel took Amaziah king of Judah, the son of Joash, the son of Jehoahaz, at Beth-shemesh, and brought him to Jerusalem, and brake down the wall of Jerusalem from the gate of Ephraim to the corner gate, four hundred cubits.

24 And *he took* all the gold and the silver, and all the vessels that were found in the house of God with Obed-edom, and the treasures of the king's house, the hostages also, and returned to Samaria.

25 And Amaziah the son of Joash king of Judah lived after the death of Joash son of Jehoahaz king of Israel fifteen years.

26 Now the rest of the acts of Amaziah, first and last, behold, *are* they not written in the book of the kings of Judah and Israel?

27 Now after the time that Amaziah did turn away from following the LORD they made a conspiracy against him in Jerusalem; and he fled to Lachish: but they sent to Lachish after him, and slew him there.

28 And they brought him upon horses, and buried him with his fathers in the city of Judah.

CHAPTER 26
Uzziah Rules Judah

1 Then all the people of Judah took Uzziah, who *was* sixteen years old, and made him king in the room of his father Amaziah.

2 He built Eloth, and restored it to Judah, after that the king slept with his fathers.

3 Sixteen years old *was* Uzziah when he began to reign, and he reigned fifty and two years in Jerusalem. His mother's name also *was* Jecoliah of Jerusalem.

4 And he did *that which was* right in the sight of the LORD, according to all that his father Amaziah did.

5 And he sought God in the days of Zechariah, who had understanding in the visions of God: and as long as he sought the LORD, God made him to prosper.

6 And he went forth and warred against the Philistines, and brake down the wall of Gath, and the wall of Jabneh, and the wall of Ashdod, and built cities about Ashdod, and among the Philistines.

7 And God helped him against the Philistines, and against the Arabians that dwelt in Gur-baal, and the Mehunims.

8 And the Ammonites gave gifts to Uzziah: and his name spread abroad *even* to the entering in of Egypt; for he strengthened *himself* exceedingly.

9 Moreover Uzziah built towers in Jeru-

Marginal references: **14** Ex. 20:3, 5; 2Chr. 28:23 · **15** 2Chr. 25:11; Ps. 96:5 · **16** 1Sam. 2:25 · **17** 2Kgs. 14:8, 9 · **20** 1Kgs. 12:15; 2Chr. 22:7; 25:14 · **23** 2Chr. 21:17; 22:1, 6 · **25** 2Kgs. 14:17 · **28** 2Kgs. 14:20 · **1** 2Kgs. 14:21, 22; 15:1 · **5** Gen. 41:15; 2Chr. 24:2; Dan. 1:17; 2:19; 10:1 · **6** Isa. 14:29 · **7** 2Chr. 21:16 · **8** 2Sam. 8:2; 2Chr. 17:11 · **9** 2Kgs. 14:13; Neh. 3:13, 19, 32; Zech. 14:10

26:1 Uzziah. His reign was long and prosperous (51 years). Like the better kings of Judah, he also erred, intruding into the priest's office. He was struck with leprosy and died in quarantine (v. 21).

salem at the corner gate, and at the valley gate, and at the turning *of the wall*, and fortified them.

10 Also he built towers in the desert, and digged many wells: for he had much cattle, both in the low country, and in the plains: husbandmen *also*, and vine dressers in the mountains, and in Carmel: for he loved husbandry.

11 Moreover Uzziah had an host of fighting men, that went out to war by bands, according to the number of their account by the hand of Jeiel the scribe and Maaseiah the ruler, under the hand of Hananiah, *one* of the king's captains.

12 The whole number of the chief of the fathers of the mighty men of valour *were* two thousand and six hundred.

13 And under their hand *was* an army, three hundred thousand and seven thousand and five hundred, that made war with mighty power, to help the king against the enemy.

14 And Uzziah prepared for them throughout all the host shields, and spears, and helmets, and habergeons, and bows, and slings *to cast* stones.

15 And he made in Jerusalem engines, invented by cunning men, to be on the towers and upon the bulwarks, to shoot arrows and great stones withal. And his name spread far abroad; for he was marvellously helped, till he was strong.

16 But when he was strong, his heart was lifted up to *his* destruction: for he transgressed against the Lord his God, and went into the temple of the Lord to burn incense upon the altar of incense.

17 And Azariah the priest went in after him, and with him fourscore priests of the Lord, *that were* valiant men:

18 And they withstood Uzziah the king, and said unto him, It *appertaineth* not unto thee, Uzziah, to burn incense unto the Lord, but to the priests the sons of Aaron, that are consecrated to burn incense: go out of the sanctuary; for thou hast trespassed; neither *shall it be* for thine honour from the Lord God.

19 Then Uzziah was wroth, and *had* a censer in his hand to burn incense: and while he was wroth with the priests, the leprosy even rose up in his forehead before the priests in the house of the Lord, from beside the incense altar.

20 And Azariah the chief priest, and all the priests, looked upon him, and, behold, he *was* leprous in his forehead, and they thrust him out from thence; yea, himself hasted also to go out, because the Lord had smitten him.

21 And Uzziah the king was a leper unto the day of his death, and dwelt in a several house, *being* a leper; for he was cut off from the house of the Lord: and Jotham his son *was* over the king's house, judging the people of the land.

22 Now the rest of the acts of Uzziah, first and last, did Isaiah the prophet, the son of Amoz, write.

23 So Uzziah slept with his fathers, and they buried him with his fathers in the field of the burial which *belonged* to the kings; for they said, He *is* a leper: and Jotham his son reigned in his stead.

CHAPTER 27
Jotham Rules Judah

1 Jotham *was* twenty and five years old when he began to reign, and he reigned sixteen years in Jerusalem. His mother's name also *was* Jerushah, the daughter of Zadok.

2 And he did *that which was* right in the sight of the Lord, according to all that his father Uzziah did: howbeit he entered not into the temple of the Lord. And the people did yet corruptly.

3 He built the high gate of the house of the Lord, and on the wall of Ophel he built much.

4 Moreover he built cities in the mountains of Judah, and in the forests he built castles and towers.

5 He fought also with the king of the Ammonites, and prevailed against them. And the children of Ammon gave him the same year an hundred talents of silver, and ten thousand measures of wheat, and ten thousand of barley. So much did the children of Ammon pay unto him, both the second year, and the third.

6 So Jotham became mighty, because he prepared his ways before the Lord his God.

7 Now the rest of the acts of Jotham, and all his wars, and his ways, lo, they *are* written in the book of the kings of Israel and Judah.

8 He was five and twenty years old when he began to reign, and reigned sixteen years in Jerusalem.

16 Deut. 8:14; 32:15; 2Kgs. 16:12, 13; 2Chr. 25:19

17 1Chr. 6:10

18 Ex. 30:7, 8; Num. 16:40; 18:7

19 Num. 12:10; 2Kgs. 5:27

20 Esth. 6:12

21 Lev. 13:46; Num. 5:2; 2Kgs. 15:5

22 Isa. 1:1

23 2Kgs. 15:7; Isa. 6:1

1 2Kgs. 15:32

2 2Kgs. 15:35

3 2Chr. 33:14; Neh. 3:26

27:1-2 Jothan. This son of Uzziah was a good and prosperous king, with building projects to his credit; but the people continued to live "corruptly." His only apparent flaw is that his leadership did not impact the population spiritually.

9 And Jotham slept with his fathers, and they buried him in the city of David: and Ahaz his son reigned in his stead.

CHAPTER 28
Ahaz Rules Judah

1 Ahaz *was* twenty years old when he began to reign, and he reigned sixteen years in Jerusalem: but he did not *that which was* right in the sight of the LORD, like David his father:

2 For he walked in the ways of the kings of Israel, and made also molten images for Baalim.

3 Moreover he burnt incense in the valley of the son of Hinnom, and burnt his children in the fire, after the abominations of the heathen whom the LORD had cast out before the children of Israel.

4 He sacrificed also and burnt incense in the high places, and on the hills, and under every green tree.

5 Wherefore the LORD his God delivered him into the hand of the king of Syria; and they smote him, and carried away a great multitude of them captives, and brought *them* to Damascus. And he was also delivered into the hand of the king of Israel, who smote him with a great slaughter.

6 For Pekah the son of Remaliah slew in Judah an hundred and twenty thousand in one day, *which were* all valiant men; because they had forsaken the LORD God of their fathers.

7 And Zichri, a mighty man of Ephraim, slew Maaseiah the king's son, and Azrikam the governor of the house, and Elkanah *that was* next to the king.

8 And the children of Israel carried away captive of their brethren two hundred thousand, women, sons, and daughters, and took also away much spoil from them, and brought the spoil to Samaria.

9 But a prophet of the LORD was there, whose name *was* Oded: and he went out before the host that came to Samaria, and said unto them, Behold, because the LORD God of your fathers was wroth with Judah, he hath delivered them into your hand, and ye have slain them in a rage *that* reacheth up to heaven.

10 And now ye purpose to keep under the children of Judah and Jerusalem for bondmen and bondwomen unto you: *but are there not* with you, even with you, sins against the LORD your God?

11 Now hear me therefore, and deliver the captives again, which ye have taken captive of your brethren: for the fierce wrath of the LORD *is* upon you.

12 Then certain of the heads of the children of Ephraim, Azariah the son of Johanan, Berechiah the son of Meshillemoth, and Jehizkiah the son of Shallum, and Amasa the son of Hadlai, stood up against them that came from the war,

13 And said unto them, Ye shall not bring in the captives hither: for whereas we have offended against the LORD *already*, ye intend to add *more* to our sins and to our trespass: for our trespass is great, and *there is* fierce wrath against Israel.

14 So the armed men left the captives and the spoil before the princes and all the congregation.

15 And the men which were expressed by name rose up, and took the captives, and with the spoil clothed all that were naked among them, and arrayed them, and shod them, and gave them to eat and to drink, and anointed them, and carried all the feeble of them upon asses, and brought them to Jericho, the city of palm trees, to their brethren: then they returned to Samaria.

16 At that time did king Ahaz send unto the kings of Assyria to help him.

17 For again the Edomites had come and smitten Judah, and carried away captives.

18 The Philistines also had invaded the cities of the low country, and of the south of Judah, and had taken Beth-shemesh, and Ajalon, and Gederoth, and Shocho with the villages thereof, and Timnah with the villages thereof, Gimzo also and the villages thereof: and they dwelt there.

19 For the LORD brought Judah low because of Ahaz king of Israel; for he made Judah naked, and transgressed sore against the LORD.

20 And Tilgath-pilneser king of Assyria came unto him, and distressed him, but strengthened him not.

21 For Ahaz took away a portion *out* of the house of the LORD, and *out* of the house of

---

Cross References

9 2Kgs. 15:38

1 2Kgs. 16:2

2 Ex. 34:17; Lev. 19:4; Judg. 2:11

3 Lev. 18:21; 2Kgs. 16:3; 23:10; 2Chr. 33:6

5 2Kgs. 16:5, 6; Isa. 7:1

6 2Kgs. 15:27

8 2Chr. 11:4

9 Ezra 9:6; Ps. 69:26; Isa. 10:5; 47:6; Ezek. 25:12, 15; 26:2; Obad. 1:10; Zech. 1:15; Rev. 18:5

10 Lev. 25:39, 42, 43, 46

11 James 2:13

15 Deut. 34:3; Judg. 1:16; 2Kgs. 6:22; 2Chr. 28:12; Prov. 25:21, 22; Luke 6:27; Rom. 12:20

16 2Kgs. 16:7

18 Ezek. 16:27, 57

19 Ex. 32:25; 2Chr. 21:2

20 2Kgs. 15:29; 16:7-9

28:1 Ahaz. Another wicked king, Ahaz sank to even lower levels of immoral, idolatrous evil and rejection of the true God than any of his predecessors. The nation, threatened by neighboring powers, became weak and unstable. Yet Ahaz continued on his evil course, and even went so far as to shut the doors of the house of the Lord (v. 24). All of his evil practice provoked the Lord to anger (v. 25).

the king, and of the princes, and gave *it* unto the king of Assyria: but he helped him not.

22 And in the time of his distress did he trespass yet more against the LORD: this *is that* king Ahaz.

23 For he sacrificed unto the gods of Damascus, which smote him: and he said, Because the gods of the kings of Syria help them, *therefore* will I sacrifice to them, that they may help me. But they were the ruin of him, and of all Israel.

24 And Ahaz gathered together the vessels of the house of God, and cut in pieces the vessels of the house of God, and shut up the doors of the house of the LORD, and he made him altars in every corner of Jerusalem.

25 And in every several city of Judah he made high places to burn incense unto other gods, and provoked to anger the LORD God of his fathers.

26 Now the rest of his acts and of all his ways, first and last, behold, they *are* written in the book of the kings of Judah and Israel.

27 And Ahaz slept with his fathers, and they buried him in the city, *even* in Jerusalem: but they brought him not into the sepulchres of the kings of Israel: and Hezekiah his son reigned in his stead.

CHAPTER 29
Hezekiah Rules Judah

1 Hezekiah began to reign *when he was* five and twenty years old, and he reigned nine and twenty years in Jerusalem. And his mother's name *was* Abijah, the daughter of Zechariah.

2 And he did *that which was* right in the sight of the LORD, according to all that David his father had done.

Hezekiah's Temple Reforms

3 He in the first year of his reign, in the first month, opened the doors of the house of the LORD, and repaired them.

4 And he brought in the priests and the Levites, and gathered them together into the east street,

5 And said unto them, Hear me, ye Levites, sanctify now yourselves, and sanctify the house of the LORD God of your fathers, and carry forth the filthiness out of the holy *place*.

6 For our fathers have trespassed, and done *that which was* evil in the eyes of the LORD our God, and have forsaken him, and have turned away their faces from the habitation of the LORD, and turned *their* backs.

7 Also they have shut up the doors of the porch, and put out the lamps, and have not burned incense nor offered burnt offerings in the holy *place* unto the God of Israel.

8 Wherefore the wrath of the LORD was upon Judah and Jerusalem, and he hath delivered them to trouble, to astonishment, and to hissing, as ye see with your eyes.

9 For, lo, our fathers have fallen by the sword, and our sons and our daughters and our wives *are* in captivity for this.

10 Now *it is* in mine heart to make a covenant with the LORD God of Israel, that his fierce wrath may turn away from us.

11 My sons, be not now negligent: for the LORD hath chosen you to stand before him, to serve him, and that ye should minister unto him, and burn incense.

12 Then the Levites arose, Mahath the son of Amasai, and Joel the son of Azariah, of the sons of the Kohathites: and of the sons of Merari, Kish the son of Abdi, and Azariah the son of Jehalelel: and of the Gershonites; Joah the son of Zimmah, and Eden the son of Joah:

Cross references
23 2Chr. 25:14; Jer. 44:17, 18
24 2Chr. 29:3, 7
26 2Kgs. 16:19, 20
1 2Kgs. 18:1; 2Chr. 26:5
3 2Chr. 28:24; 29:7
5 1Chr. 15:12; 2Chr. 35:6
6 Jer. 2:27; Ezek. 8:16
7 2Chr. 28:24
8 Deut. 28:25; 1Kgs. 9:8; 2Chr. 24:18; Jer. 18:16; 19:8; 25:9, 18; 29:18
9 2Chr. 28:5, 6, 8, 17
10 2Chr. 15:12
11 Num. 3:6; 8:14; 18:2, 6

29:1 Hezekiah. Of the twenty kings of Judah, only eight "did that which was right in the sight of the LORD," and none of them were untarnished by compromise or failure. Hezekiah was the greatest and best of the monarchs of Judah, yet even he erred by revealing his treasures unreservedly to a delegation from Babylon. A century later, the armies of Babylon would pillage and destroy Jerusalem and carry the Jews into captivity (2 Kgs. 20:12–19; 2 Chr. 32:31; 36:15–21). Hezekiah's godly reign and the spiritual revival he initiated are so significant, that his story is presented in three Old Testament books: 2 Kings 18—20, 2 Chronicles 29—32, and Isaiah 36—39. The prophets Isaiah, (Isa. 1:1), Hosea (Hos. 1:1)

and Micah (Mic. 1:1) were Hezekiah's contemporaries. His trust in the Lord, and consequent success and prosperity, was unequaled by any of his predecessors or successors (2 Kgs. 18:5–7). Two miraculous deliverances occurred in his life: the national deliverance from the invading Assyrians when the angel of the Lord slew 185,000 soldiers (2 Kgs. 19:35–36; 2 Chr. 32:21), and the healing of Hezekiah, whose life was extended fifteen years (2 Kgs. 20:1–6; Isa. 38).

29:3 doors of the house of the LORD. At the outset of His reign, Hezekiah reopened the doors of the temple that Ahaz, his idolatrous father, had shut (2 Chr. 28:24).

13 And of the sons of Elizaphan; Shimri, and Jeiel: and of the sons of Asaph; Zechariah, and Mattaniah:

14 And of the sons of Heman; Jehiel, and Shimei: and of the sons of Jeduthun; Shemaiah, and Uzziel.

15 And they gathered their brethren, and sanctified themselves, and came, according to the commandment of the king, by the words of the LORD, to cleanse the house of the LORD.

16 And the priests went into the inner part of the house of the LORD, to cleanse it, and brought out all the uncleanness that they found in the temple of the LORD into the court of the house of the LORD. And the Levites took it, to carry it out abroad into the brook Kidron.

17 Now they began on the first day of the first month to sanctify, and on the eighth day of the month came they to the porch of the LORD: so they sanctified the house of the LORD in eight days; and in the sixteenth day of the first month they made an end.

18 Then they went in to Hezekiah the king, and said, We have cleansed all the house of the LORD, and the altar of burnt offering, with all the vessels thereof, and the shewbread table, with all the vessels thereof.

19 Moreover all the vessels, which king Ahaz in his reign did cast away in his transgression, have we prepared and sanctified, and, behold, they are before the altar of the LORD.

20 Then Hezekiah the king rose early, and gathered the rulers of the city, and went up to the house of the LORD.

21 And they brought seven bullocks, and seven rams, and seven lambs, and seven he goats, for a sin offering for the kingdom, and for the sanctuary, and for Judah. And he commanded the priests the sons of Aaron to offer them on the altar of the LORD.

22 So they killed the bullocks, and the priests received the blood, and sprinkled it on the altar: likewise, when they had killed the rams, they sprinkled the blood upon the altar: they killed also the lambs, and they sprinkled the blood upon the altar.

23 And they brought forth the he goats for the sin offering before the king and the congregation; and they laid their hands upon them:

24 And the priests killed them, and they made reconciliation with their blood upon the altar, to make an atonement for all Israel: for the king commanded that the burnt offering and the sin offering should be made for all Israel.

25 And he set the Levites in the house of the LORD with cymbals, with psalteries, and with harps, according to the commandment of David, and of Gad the king's seer, and Nathan the prophet: for so was the commandment of the LORD by his prophets.

26 And the Levites stood with the instruments of David, and the priests with the trumpets.

27 And Hezekiah commanded to offer the burnt offering upon the altar. And when the burnt offering began, the song of the LORD began also with the trumpets, and with the instruments ordained by David king of Israel.

28 And all the congregation worshipped, and the singers sang, and the trumpeters sounded: and all this continued until the burnt offering was finished.

29 And when they had made an end of offering, the king and all that were present with him bowed themselves, and worshipped.

30 Moreover Hezekiah the king and the princes commanded the Levites to sing praise unto the LORD with the words of David, and of Asaph the seer. And they sang praises with gladness, and they bowed their heads and worshipped.

31 Then Hezekiah answered and said, Now ye have consecrated yourselves unto the LORD, come near and bring sacrifices and thank offerings into the house of the LORD. And the congregation brought in sacrifices and thank offerings; and as many as were of a free heart burnt offerings.

32 And the number of the burnt offerings, which the congregation brought, was threescore and ten bullocks, an hundred rams, and two hundred lambs: all these were for a burnt offering to the LORD.

33 And the consecrated things were six hundred oxen and three thousand sheep.

34 But the priests were too few, so that they could not flay all the burnt offerings: wherefore their brethren the Levites did help them, till the work was ended, and until the other priests had sanctified themselves: for the Levites were more upright in heart to sanctify themselves than the priests.

Cross references:

15 1Chr. 23:28; 2Chr. 29:5; 30:12

19 2Chr. 28:24

21 Lev. 4:3, 14

22 Lev. 8:14, 15, 19, 24; Heb. 9:21

23 Lev. 4:15, 24

24 Lev. 14:20

25 2Sam. 24:11; 1Chr. 16:4; 23:5; 25:1, 6; 2Chr. 8:14; 30:12

26 Num. 10:8, 10; 1Chr. 15:24; 16:6; 23:5; Amos 6:5

27 2Chr. 23:18

29 2Chr. 20:18

31 Lev. 7:12; 2Chr. 13:9

34 2Chr. 30:3; 35:11; Ps. 7:10

29:20–36 Temple forms of worship, as practiced in Solomon's reign, and the long-neglected songs of David and Asaph, together with appropriate Mosaic sacrifices, were reinstituted quickly with great joy in a cleansed temple.

35 And also the burnt offerings *were* in abundance, with the fat of the peace offerings, and the drink offerings for *every* burnt offering. So the service of the house of the LORD was set in order.

36 And Hezekiah rejoiced, and all the people, that God had prepared the people: for the thing was *done* suddenly.

CHAPTER 30
Hezekiah Celebrates the Passover

1 And Hezekiah sent to all Israel and Judah, and wrote letters also to Ephraim and Manasseh, that they should come to the house of the LORD at Jerusalem, to keep the passover unto the LORD God of Israel.

2 For the king had taken counsel, and his princes, and all the congregation in Jerusalem, to keep the passover in the second month.

3 For they could not keep it at that time, because the priests had not sanctified themselves sufficiently, neither had the people gathered themselves together to Jerusalem.

4 And the thing pleased the king and all the congregation.

5 So they established a decree to make proclamation throughout all Israel, from Beer-sheba even to Dan, that they should come to keep the passover unto the LORD God of Israel at Jerusalem: for they had not done *it* of a long *time in such sort* as it was written.

6 So the posts went with the letters from the king and his princes throughout all Israel and Judah, and according to the commandment of the king, saying, Ye children of Israel, turn again unto the LORD God of Abraham, Isaac, and Israel, and he will return to the remnant of you, that are escaped out of the hand of the kings of Assyria.

7 And be not ye like your fathers, and like your brethren, which trespassed against the LORD God of their fathers, *who* therefore gave them up to desolation, as ye see.

8 Now be ye not stiffnecked, as your fa-thers *were,* *but* yield yourselves unto the LORD, and enter into his sanctuary, which he hath sanctified for ever: and serve the LORD your God, that the fierceness of his wrath may turn away from you.

9 For if ye turn again unto the LORD, your brethren and your children *shall find* compassion before them that lead them captive, so that they shall come again into this land: for the LORD your God *is* gracious and merciful, and will not turn away *his* face from you, if ye return unto him.

10 So the posts passed from city to city through the country of Ephraim and Manasseh even unto Zebulun: but they laughed them to scorn, and mocked them.

11 Nevertheless divers of Asher and Manasseh and of Zebulun humbled themselves, and came to Jerusalem.

12 Also in Judah the hand of God was to give them one heart to do the commandment of the king and of the princes, by the word of the LORD.

13 And there assembled at Jerusalem much people to keep the feast of unleavened bread in the second month, a very great congregation.

14 And they arose and took away the altars that *were* in Jerusalem, and all the altars for incense took they away, and cast *them* into the brook Kidron.

15 Then they killed the passover on the fourteenth *day* of the second month: and the priests and the Levites were ashamed, and sanctified themselves, and brought in the burnt offerings into the house of the LORD.

16 And they stood in their place after their manner, according to the law of Moses the man of God: the priests sprinkled the blood, *which they received* of the hand of the Levites.

17 For *there were* many in the congregation that were not sanctified: therefore the Levites had the charge of the killing of the passovers for every one *that was* not clean, to sanctify *them* unto the LORD.

Cross references

35 Lev. 3:16; Num. 15:5, 7, 10
2 Num. 9:10, 11
3 Ex. 12:6, 18; 2Chr. 29:34
6 2Kgs. 15:19, 29; Jer. 4:1; Joel 2:13
7 2Chr. 29:8; Ezek. 20:18
8 Deut. 10:16; 1Chr. 29:24; 2Chr. 29:10; Ezra 10:19
9 Ex. 34:6; Ps. 106:46; Isa. 55:7
10 2Chr. 36:16
11 2Chr. 11:16; 30:18, 21
12 2Chr. 29:25; Phil. 2:13
14 2Chr. 28:24
15 2Chr. 29:34
17 2Chr. 29:34

30:1–27 passover. The annual memorial of Israel's deliverance from Egypt over seven hundred years earlier was celebrated. Not since the reign of Solomon had that solemn, but joyful, season been so widely and universally observed. Over seven hundred years later, Jesus celebrated the Passover in Jerusalem and fulfilled its typology as the Lamb of God, becoming "Christ our Passover sacrificed for us" (Matt. 26:17–19; 1 Cor. 5:7). In the Millennium, the Passover will be annually observed to commemorate ceremonially all that deliverance by the blood of the Lamb has meant (Ezek. 45:21). Even in the New Jerusalem, Christ will be known eternally as the Lamb (Rev. 21:14, 22–23; 22:1, 3). This title is used of Christ twenty-seven times in Revelation in relation to Israel, the Church, the world, and eternity.

30:13 second month. Under appropriate conditions the Passover could be properly observed on the fourteenth day of the second month rather than the first (Num. 9:10–11).

18 For a multitude of the people, *even* many of Ephraim, and Manasseh, Issachar, and Zebulun, had not cleansed themselves, yet did they eat the passover otherwise than it was written. But Hezekiah prayed for them, saying, The good LORD pardon every one

19 *That* prepareth his heart to seek God, the LORD God of his fathers, though *he be* not *cleansed* according to the purification of the sanctuary.

20 And the LORD hearkened to Hezekiah, and healed the people.

21 And the children of Israel that were present at Jerusalem kept the feast of unleavened bread seven days with great gladness: and the Levites and the priests praised the LORD day by day, *singing* with loud instruments unto the LORD.

22 And Hezekiah spake comfortably unto all the Levites that taught the good knowledge of the LORD: and they did eat throughout the feast seven days, offering peace offerings, and making confession to the LORD God of their fathers.

23 And the whole assembly took counsel to keep other seven days: and they kept *other* seven days with gladness.

24 For Hezekiah king of Judah did give to the congregation a thousand bullocks and seven thousand sheep; and the princes gave to the congregation a thousand bullocks and ten thousand sheep: and a great number of priests sanctified themselves.

25 And all the congregation of Judah, with the priests and the Levites, and all the congregation that came out of Israel, and the strangers that came out of the land of Israel, and that dwelt in Judah, rejoiced.

26 So there was great joy in Jerusalem: for since the time of Solomon the son of David king of Israel *there was* not the like in Jerusalem.

27 Then the priests the Levites arose and blessed the people: and their voice was heard, and their prayer came *up* to his holy dwelling place, *even* unto heaven.

CHAPTER 31
Religious Reforms Continue

1 Now when all this was finished, all Israel that were present went out to the cities of Judah, and brake the images in pieces, and cut down the groves, and threw down

the high places and the altars out of all Judah and Benjamin, in Ephraim also and Manasseh, until they had utterly destroyed them all. Then all the children of Israel returned, every man to his possession, into their own cities.

Hezekiah Provides for the Priests and Levites

2 And Hezekiah appointed the courses of the priests and the Levites after their courses, every man according to his service, the priests and Levites for burnt offerings and for peace offerings, to minister, and to give thanks, and to praise in the gates of the tents of the LORD.

3 *He appointed* also the king's portion of his substance for the burnt offerings, *to wit,* for the morning and evening burnt offerings, and the burnt offerings for the sabbaths, and for the new moons, and for the set feasts, as *it is* written in the law of the LORD.

4 Moreover he commanded the people that dwelt in Jerusalem to give the portion of the priests and the Levites, that they might be encouraged in the law of the LORD.

5 And as soon as the commandment came abroad, the children of Israel brought in abundance the firstfruits of corn, wine, and oil, and honey, and of all the increase of the field; and the tithe of all *things* brought they in abundantly.

6 And *concerning* the children of Israel and Judah, that dwelt in the cities of Judah, they also brought in the tithe of oxen and sheep, and the tithe of holy things which were consecrated unto the LORD their God, and laid *them* by heaps.

7 In the third month they began to lay the foundation of the heaps, and finished *them* in the seventh month.

8 And when Hezekiah and the princes came and saw the heaps, they blessed the LORD, and his people Israel.

9 Then Hezekiah questioned with the priests and the Levites concerning the heaps.

10 And Azariah the chief priest of the house of Zadok answered him, and said, Since *the people* began to bring the offerings into the house of the LORD, we have had enough to eat, and have left plenty: for the LORD hath

---

18	Ex. 12:43; 2Chr. 30:11
19	2Chr. 19:3
21	Ex. 12:15; 13:6
22	Deut. 33:10; 2Chr. 17:9; 35:3; Ezra 10:11
23	1Kgs. 8:65
24	2Chr. 29:34; 35:7, 8
25	2Chr. 30:11, 18
27	Num. 6:23; Ps. 68:5
1	2Kgs. 13:4; 2Chr. 30:14
2	1Chr. 23:6, 30, 31; 24:1
3	Num. 28, 29
4	Num. 18:8; Neh. 13:10; Mal. 2:7
5	Ex. 22:29; Neh. 13:12
6	Lev. 27:30; Deut. 14:28
10	Mal. 3:10

31:4 The priests and the Levites depended on the gifts of the people for their livelihood (Num. 18:12, 21, 24). Therefore, in times of backsliding, the priests and Levites were tempted to use other means to make a living (Judg. 17:10; 1 Sam. 2:36). It was essential to restore proper tithing for a consecrated priesthood.

blessed his people; and that which is left *is* this great store.

11 Then Hezekiah commanded to prepare chambers in the house of the LORD; and they prepared *them*,

12 And brought in the offerings and the tithes and the dedicated *things* faithfully: over which Cononiah the Levite *was* ruler, and Shimei his brother *was* the next.

13 And Jehiel, and Azaziah, and Nahath, and Asahel, and Jerimoth, and Jozabad, and Eliel, and Ismachiah, and Mahath, and Benaiah, *were* overseers under the hand of Cononiah and Shimei his brother, at the commandment of Hezekiah the king, and Azariah the ruler of the house of God.

14 And Kore the son of Imnah the Levite, the porter toward the east, *was* over the freewill offerings of God, to distribute the oblations of the LORD, and the most holy things.

15 And next him *were* Eden, and Miniamin, and Jeshua, and Shemaiah, Amariah, and Shecaniah, in the cities of the priests, in *their* set office, to give to their brethren by courses, as well to the great as to the small:

16 Beside their genealogy of males, from three years old and upward, *even* unto every one that entereth into the house of the LORD, his daily portion for their service in their charges according to their courses;

17 Both to the genealogy of the priests by the house of their fathers, and the Levites from twenty years old and upward, in their charges by their courses;

18 And to the genealogy of all their little ones, their wives, and their sons, and their daughters, through all the congregation: for in their set office they sanctified themselves in holiness:

19 Also of the sons of Aaron the priests, *which were* in the fields of the suburbs of their cities, in every several city, the men that were expressed by name, to give portions to all the males among the priests, and to all that were reckoned by genealogies among the Levites.

20 And thus did Hezekiah throughout all Judah, and wrought *that which was* good and right and truth before the LORD his God.

21 And in every work that he began in the service of the house of God, and in the law, and in the commandments, to seek his God, he did *it* with all his heart, and prospered.

CHAPTER 32
Sennacherib Threatens Jerusalem

1 After these things, and the establishment thereof, Sennacherib king of Assyria came, and entered into Judah, and encamped against the fenced cities, and thought to win them for himself.

2 And when Hezekiah saw that Sennacherib was come, and that he was purposed to fight against Jerusalem,

3 He took counsel with his princes and his mighty men to stop the waters of the fountains which *were* without the city: and they did help him.

4 So there was gathered much people together, who stopped all the fountains, and the brook that ran through the midst of the land, saying, Why should the kings of Assyria come, and find much water?

5 Also he strengthened himself, and built up all the wall that was broken, and raised *it* up to the towers, and another wall without, and repaired Millo *in* the city of David, and made darts and shields in abundance.

6 And he set captains of war over the people, and gathered them together to him in the street of the gate of the city, and spake comfortably to them, saying,

7 Be strong and courageous, be not afraid nor dismayed for the king of Assyria, nor for all the multitude that *is* with him: for *there be* more with us than with him:

8 With him *is* an arm of flesh; but with us *is* the LORD our God to help us, and to fight our battles. And the people rested themselves upon the words of Hezekiah king of Judah.

9 After this did Sennacherib king of Assyria send his servants to Jerusalem, (but he *himself laid siege* against Lachish, and all his power with him,) unto Hezekiah king of Judah, and unto all Judah that *were* at Jerusalem, saying,

10 Thus saith Sennacherib king of Assyria, Whereon do ye trust, that ye abide in the siege in Jerusalem?

11 Doth not Hezekiah persuade you to give over yourselves to die by famine and by thirst, saying, The LORD our God shall deliver us out of the hand of the king of Assyria?

12 Hath not the same Hezekiah taken away his high places and his altars, and commanded Judah and Jerusalem, saying, Ye shall worship before one altar, and burn incense upon it?

13 Know ye not what I and my fathers have done unto all the people of *other* lands? were the gods of the nations of those lands any ways able to deliver their lands out of mine hand?

14 Who *was there* among all the gods of

Cross references (center column):

12 Neh. 13:13

15 Josh. 21:9; 1Chr. 9:22

17 1Chr. 23:24, 27

19 Lev. 25:34; Num. 35:2; 2Chr. 31:12-15

20 2Kgs. 20:3

1 2Kgs. 18:13; Isa. 36:1

5 2Sam. 5:9; 1Kgs. 9:24; 2Chr. 25:23; Isa. 22:9, 10

6 2Chr. 30:22; Isa. 40:2

7 Deut. 31:6; 2Kgs. 6:16; 2Chr. 20:15

8 2Chr. 13:12; Jer. 17:5; Rom. 8:31; 1John 4:4

9 2Kgs. 18:17

10 2Kgs. 18:19

11 2Kgs. 18:30

12 2Kgs. 18:22

13 2Kgs. 18:33-35

those nations that my fathers utterly destroyed, that could deliver his people out of mine hand, that your God should be able to deliver you out of mine hand?

15 Now therefore let not Hezekiah deceive you, nor persuade you on this manner, neither yet believe him: for no god of any nation or kingdom was able to deliver his people out of mine hand, and out of the hand of my fathers: how much less shall your God deliver you out of mine hand?

16 And his servants spake yet *more* against the LORD God, and against his servant Hezekiah.

17 He wrote also letters to rail on the LORD God of Israel, and to speak against him, saying, As the gods of the nations of *other* lands have not delivered their people out of mine hand, so shall not the God of Hezekiah deliver his people out of mine hand.

18 Then they cried with a loud voice in the Jews' speech unto the people of Jerusalem that *were* on the wall, to affright them, and to trouble them; that they might take the city.

19 And they spake against the God of Jerusalem, as against the gods of the people of the earth, *which were* the work of the hands of man.

God Rescues Jerusalem

20 And for this *cause* Hezekiah the king, and the prophet Isaiah the son of Amoz, prayed and cried to heaven.

21 And the LORD sent an angel, which cut off all the mighty men of valour, and the leaders and captains in the camp of the king of Assyria. So he returned with shame of face to his own land. And when he was come into the house of his god, they that came forth of his own bowels slew him there with the sword.

22 Thus the LORD saved Hezekiah and the inhabitants of Jerusalem from the hand of Sennacherib the king of Assyria, and from the hand of all *other*, and guided them on every side.

23 And many brought gifts unto the LORD to Jerusalem, and presents to Hezekiah king of Judah: so that he was magnified in the sight of all nations from thenceforth.

Hezekiah Gets Sick

24 In those days Hezekiah was sick to the death, and prayed unto the LORD: and he spake unto him, and he gave him a sign.

25 But Hezekiah rendered not again according to the benefit *done* unto him; for his heart was lifted up: therefore there was wrath upon him, and upon Judah and Jerusalem.

26 Notwithstanding Hezekiah humbled himself for the pride of his heart, *both* he and the inhabitants of Jerusalem, so that the wrath of the LORD came not upon them in the days of Hezekiah.

Hezekiah Prospers

27 And Hezekiah had exceeding much riches and honour: and he made himself treasuries for silver, and for gold, and for precious stones, and for spices, and for shields, and for all manner of pleasant jewels;

28 Storehouses also for the increase of corn, and wine, and oil; and stalls for all manner of beasts, and cotes for flocks.

29 Moreover he provided him cities, and possessions of flocks and herds in abundance: for God had given him substance very much.

30 This same Hezekiah also stopped the upper watercourse of Gihon, and brought it straight down to the west side of the city of David. And Hezekiah prospered in all his works.

31 Howbeit in *the business of* the ambassadors of the princes of Babylon, who sent unto him to inquire of the wonder that was *done* in the land, God left him, to try him, that he might know all *that was* in his heart.

Hezekiah's Death

32 Now the rest of the acts of Hezekiah, and his goodness, behold, they *are* written in the vision of Isaiah the prophet, the son of Amoz, *and* in the book of the kings of Judah and Israel.

33 And Hezekiah slept with his fathers, and they buried him in the chiefest of the sepulchres of the sons of David: and all Judah and the inhabitants of Jerusalem did him

---

Cross references (center column):

15 2Kgs. 18:29
17 2Kgs. 19:9, 12
18 2Kgs. 18:26-28
19 2Kgs. 19:18
20 2Kgs. 19:2, 4, 15
21 2Kgs. 19:35
23 2Chr. 1:1; 17:5
24 2Kgs. 20:1; Isa. 38:1
25 2Chr. 24:18; 26:16; Ps. 116:12; Hab. 2:4
26 2Kgs. 20:19; Jer. 26:18, 19
29 1Chr. 29:12
30 Isa. 22:9, 11
31 Deut. 8:2; 2Kgs. 20:12; Isa. 39:1
32 2Kgs. 18:19, 20
33 2Kgs. 20:21; Prov. 10:7

32:20 Hezekiah . . . and . . . Isaiah . . . prayed. Some years after the fall of the Northern Kingdom (Israel) to the Assyrians under Shalmaneser (2 Kgs. 17:1-6) in about 722 B.C., Sennacherib invaded Judah intent on conquering Hezekiah and carrying the people away into captivity, as previous monarchs had done to the Northern Kingdom (2 Kgs. 17:1-41). A mighty victory wrought by prayer brought deliverance through direct, divine intervention (v. 21). Not only did 185,000 Assyrians die overnight, but not long afterwards Sennacherib was assassinated (2 Kgs. 19:35-37).

honour at his death. And Manasseh his son reigned in his stead.

CHAPTER 33
Manasseh Rules Judah

1 Manasseh *was* twelve years old when he began to reign, and he reigned fifty and five years in Jerusalem:

2 But did *that which was* evil in the sight of the LORD, like unto the abominations of the heathen, whom the LORD had cast out before the children of Israel.

3 For he built again the high places which Hezekiah his father had broken down, and he reared up altars for Baalim, and made groves, and worshipped all the host of heaven, and served them.

4 Also he built altars in the house of the LORD, whereof the LORD had said, In Jerusalem shall my name be for ever.

5 And he built altars for all the host of heaven in the two courts of the house of the LORD.

6 And he caused his children to pass through the fire in the valley of the son of Hinnom: also he observed times, and used enchantments, and used witchcraft, and dealt with a familiar spirit, and with wizards: he wrought much evil in the sight of the LORD, to provoke him to anger.

7 And he set a carved image, the idol which he had made, in the house of God, of which God had said to David and to Solomon his son, In this house, and in Jerusalem, which I have chosen before all the tribes of Israel, will I put my name for ever:

8 Neither will I any more remove the foot of Israel from out of the land which I have appointed for your fathers; so that they will take heed to do all that I have commanded them, according to the whole law and the statutes and the ordinances by the hand of Moses.

9 So Manasseh made Judah and the inhabitants of Jerusalem to err, *and* to do worse than the heathen, whom the LORD had destroyed before the children of Israel.

10 And the LORD spake to Manasseh, and to his people: but they would not hearken.

11 Wherefore the LORD brought upon them the captains of the host of the king of Assyria, which took Manasseh among the thorns, and bound him with fetters, and carried him to Babylon.

12 And when he was in affliction, he besought the LORD his God, and humbled himself greatly before the God of his fathers,

13 And prayed unto him: and he was intreated of him, and heard his supplication, and brought him again to Jerusalem into his kingdom. Then Manasseh knew that the LORD he *was* God.

14 Now after this he built a wall without the city of David, on the west side of Gihon, in the valley, even to the entering in at the fish gate and compassed about Ophel, and raised it up a very great height, and put captains of war in all the fenced cities of Judah.

15 And he took away the strange gods, and the idol out of the house of the LORD, and all the altars that he had built in the mount of the house of the LORD, and in Jerusalem, and cast *them* out of the city.

16 And he repaired the altar of the LORD, and sacrificed thereon peace offerings and thank offerings, and commanded Judah to serve the LORD God of Israel.

17 Nevertheless the people did sacrifice still in the high places, *yet* unto the LORD their God only.

18 Now the rest of the acts of Manasseh, and his prayer unto his God, and the words of the seers that spake to him in the name of the LORD God of Israel, behold, they *are* written in the book of the kings of Israel.

19 His prayer also, and *how God* was intreated of him, and all his sin, and his trespass, and the places wherein he built high places, and set up groves and graven images, before he was humbled: behold, they *are* written among the sayings of the seers.

20 So Manasseh slept with his fathers, and they buried him in his own house: and Amon his son reigned in his stead.

Amon Rules Judah

21 Amon *was* two and twenty years old when he began to reign, and reigned two years in Jerusalem.

Cross references (center column):

1 2Kgs. 21:1

2 Deut. 18:9; 2Chr. 28:3

3 Deut. 16:21; 17:3; 2Kgs. 18:4; 2Chr. 30:14; 31:1; 32:12

4 Deut. 12:11; 1Kgs. 8:29; 9:3; 2Chr. 6:6; 7:16

5 2Chr. 4:9

6 Lev. 18:21; Deut. 18:10, 11; 2Kgs. 21:6; 23:10; 2Chr. 28:3; Ezek. 23:37, 39

7 2Kgs. 21:7; Ps. 132:14

8 2Sam. 7:10

11 Deut. 28:36; Job 36:8; Ps. 107:10, 11

12 1Pet. 5:6

13 1Chr. 5:20; Ezra 8:23; Ps. 9:16; Dan. 4:25

14 1Kgs. 1:33; 2Chr. 27:3

15 2Chr. 33:3, 5, 7

16 Lev. 7:12

17 2Chr. 32:12

18 1Sam. 9:9

20 2Kgs. 21:18

21 2Kgs. 21:19

33:1–6 Manasseh. Following the best king of Judah's twenty monarchs came the worst king, who reinaugurated Baal worship, built altars to worship the "host of heaven" (the sun, moon, stars, and mythical gods connected with constellations), and worst of all, practiced human sacrifice and even infanticide.

33:12 in affliction, he besought the LORD. Conquered and imprisoned by the king of Assyria, Manasseh finally turned to the true God and was restored to his kingdom. There he removed the idols from Jerusalem and restored temple worship, commanding "Judah to serve the LORD God of Israel" (v. 16).

33:21 Amon. This son of Manasseh returned to idolatry but was assassinated after a two-year reign.

22 But he did *that which was* evil in the sight of the LORD, as did Manasseh his father: for Amon sacrificed unto all the carved images which Manasseh his father had made, and served them;

23 And humbled not himself before the LORD, as Manasseh his father had humbled himself; but Amon trespassed more and more.

24 And his servants conspired against him, and slew him in his own house.

25 But the people of the land slew all them that had conspired against king Amon; and the people of the land made Josiah his son king in his stead.

CHAPTER 34
Josiah Rules Judah

1 Josiah *was* eight years old when he began to reign, and he reigned in Jerusalem one and thirty years.

2 And he did *that which was* right in the sight of the LORD, and walked in the ways of David his father, and declined *neither* to the right hand, nor to the left.

Josiah Brings about Reforms

3 For in the eighth year of his reign, while he was yet young, he began to seek after the God of David his father: and in the twelfth year he began to purge Judah and Jerusalem from the high places, and the groves, and the carved images, and the molten images.

4 And they brake down the altars of Baalim in his presence; and the images, that *were* on high above them, he cut down; and the groves, and the carved images, and the molten images, he brake in pieces, and made dust *of them*, and strowed *it* upon the graves of them that had sacrificed unto them.

5 And he burnt the bones of the priests upon their altars, and cleansed Judah and Jerusalem.

6 And *so did he* in the cities of Manasseh,

and Ephraim, and Simeon, even unto Naphtali, with their mattocks round about.

7 And when he had broken down the altars and the groves, and had beaten the graven images into powder, and cut down all the idols throughout all the land of Israel, he returned to Jerusalem.

A Copy of the Law Is Found

8 Now in the eighteenth year of his reign, when he had purged the land, and the house, he sent Shaphan the son of Azaliah, and Maaseiah the governor of the city, and Joah the son of Joahaz the recorder, to repair the house of the LORD his God.

9 And when they came to Hilkiah the high priest, they delivered the money that was brought into the house of God, which the Levites that kept the doors had gathered of the hand of Manasseh and Ephraim, and of all the remnant of Israel, and of all Judah and Benjamin; and they returned to Jerusalem.

10 And they put *it* in the hand of the workmen that had the oversight of the house of the LORD, and they gave it to the workmen that wrought in the house of the LORD, to repair and amend the house:

11 Even to the artificers and builders gave they *it*, to buy hewn stone, and timber for couplings, and to floor the houses which the kings of Judah had destroyed.

12 And the men did the work faithfully: and the overseers of them *were* Jahath and Obadiah, the Levites, of the sons of Merari; and Zechariah and Meshullam, of the sons of the Kohathites, to set *it* forward; and *other of* the Levites, all that could skill of instruments of musick.

13 Also *they were* over the bearers of burdens, and *were* overseers of all that wrought the work in any manner of service: and of the Levites *there were* scribes, and officers, and porters.

14 And when they brought out the money that was brought into the house of the LORD,

Cross references

23 2Chr. 33:12
24 2Kgs. 21:23, 24
1 2Kgs. 22:1
3 1Kgs. 13:2; 2Chr. 15:2; 33:17, 22
4 Lev. 26:30; 2Kgs. 23:4, 6
5 1Kgs. 13:2
7 Deut. 9:21
8 2Kgs. 22:3
9 2Kgs. 12:4
13 1Chr. 23:4, 5
14 2Kgs. 22:8

34:1 Josiah. Coming to the throne at an early age, Josiah, in the eighth year of his reign at age sixteen, "began to seek after the God of David" (v. 3). By age twenty (v. 20), he began purging Judah of idolatrous worship, extending his influence and activities for God among the Israelites in the former Northern Kingdom who had not been taken captive to other lands. This area included cities in Manasseh, Ephraim, and as far north as Naphtali, near Syria.

34:14 found a book of the law. During the restoration of the long-neglected temple, Hilkiah the priest found a copy of the Law of Moses, which had been out of circulation during Manasseh's long and evil reign. Some suggest that this copy was merely a transcript of Deuteronomy, but it was more likely the entire Pentateuch. Such blessings and curses as recorded in Leviticus 26 and Deuteronomy 28—30 were instrumental in beginning Josiah's revival.

Hilkiah the priest found a book of the law of the LORD *given* by Moses.

15 And Hilkiah answered and said to Shaphan the scribe, I have found the book of the law in the house of the LORD. And Hilkiah delivered the book to Shaphan.

16 And Shaphan carried the book to the king, and brought the king word back again, saying, All that was committed to thy servants, they do *it*.

17 And they have gathered together the money that was found in the house of the LORD, and have delivered it into the hand of the overseers, and to the hand of the workmen.

18 Then Shaphan the scribe told the king, saying, Hilkiah the priest hath given me a book. And Shaphan read it before the king.

19 And it came to pass, when the king had heard the words of the law, that he rent his clothes.

20 And the king commanded Hilkiah, and Ahikam the son of Shaphan, and Abdon the son of Micah, and Shaphan the scribe, and Asaiah a servant of the king's, saying,

21 Go, inquire of the LORD for me, and for them that are left in Israel and in Judah, concerning the words of the book that is found: for great *is* the wrath of the LORD that is poured out upon us, because our fathers have not kept the word of the LORD, to do after all that is written in this book.

22 And Hilkiah, and *they* that the king *had appointed*, went to Huldah the prophetess, the wife of Shallum the son of Tikvath, the son of Hasrah, keeper of the wardrobe; (now she dwelt in Jerusalem in the college:) and they spake to her to that *effect*.

23 And she answered them, Thus saith the LORD God of Israel, Tell ye the man that sent you to me,

24 Thus saith the LORD, Behold, I will bring evil upon this place, and upon the inhabitants thereof, *even* all the curses that are written in the book which they have read before the king of Judah:

25 Because they have forsaken me, and have burned incense unto other gods, that they might provoke me to anger with all the works of their hands; therefore my wrath shall be poured out upon this place, and shall not be quenched.

26 And as for the king of Judah, who sent you to inquire of the LORD, so shall ye say unto him, Thus saith the LORD God of Israel *concerning* the words which thou hast heard;

27 Because thine heart was tender, and thou didst humble thyself before God, when thou heardest his words against this place, and against the inhabitants thereof, and humbledst thyself before me, and didst rend thy clothes, and weep before me; I have even heard *thee* also, saith the LORD.

28 Behold, I will gather thee to thy fathers, and thou shalt be gathered to thy grave in peace, neither shall thine eyes see all the evil that I will bring upon this place, and upon the inhabitants of the same. So they brought the king word again.

29 Then the king sent and gathered together all the elders of Judah and Jerusalem.

30 And the king went up into the house of the LORD, and all the men of Judah, and the inhabitants of Jerusalem, and the priests, and the Levites, and all the people, great and small: and he read in their ears all the words of the book of the covenant that was found in the house of the LORD.

31 And the king stood in his place, and made a covenant before the LORD, to walk after the LORD, and to keep his commandments, and his testimonies, and his statutes, with all his heart, and with all his soul, to perform the words of the covenant which are written in this book.

32 And he caused all that were present in Jerusalem and Benjamin to stand *to it*. And the inhabitants of Jerusalem did according to the covenant of God, the God of their fathers.

33 And Josiah took away all the abominations out of all the countries that *pertained* to the children of Israel, and made all that were present in Israel to serve, *even* to serve the LORD their God. *And* all his days they departed not from following the LORD, the God of their fathers.

CHAPTER 35
Josiah Celebrates the Passover

1 Moreover Josiah kept a passover unto the LORD in Jerusalem: and they killed the

Cross references
- **20** 2Kgs. 22:12
- **22** 2Kgs. 22:14
- **29** 2Kgs. 23:1
- **31** 2Kgs. 11:14; 23:3; 2Chr. 6:13
- **33** 1Kgs. 11:5; Jer. 3:10
- **1** Ex. 12:6; 2Kgs. 23:21, 22; Ezra 6:19

34:31 the king . . . made a covenant before the LORD. This last good king of Judah made a public commitment to observe and renew the past covenants God had made with Israel, as set forth in the Pentateuch. Until Josiah died, the people and the land were free of public, idolatrous abominations. But the seeds of evil remained in the hearts of many, re-emerging under the rule of the last three monarchs of Judah and resulting in divine judgment and the Babylonian Captivity.

passover on the fourteenth *day* of the first month.

2 And he set the priests in their charges, and encouraged them to the service of the house of the LORD,

3 And said unto the Levites that taught all Israel, which were holy unto the LORD, Put the holy ark in the house which Solomon the son of David king of Israel did build; *it shall* not *be* a burden upon *your* shoulders: serve now the LORD your God, and his people Israel,

4 And prepare *yourselves* by the houses of your fathers, after your courses, according to the writing of David king of Israel, and according to the writing of Solomon his son.

5 And stand in the holy *place* according to the divisions of the families of the fathers of your brethren the people, and *after* the division of the families of the Levites.

6 So kill the passover, and sanctify yourselves, and prepare your brethren, that *they* may do according to the word of the LORD by the hand of Moses.

7 And Josiah gave to the people, of the flock, lambs and kids, all for the passover offerings, for all that were present, to the number of thirty thousand, and three thousand bullocks: these *were* of the king's substance.

8 And his princes gave willingly unto the people, to the priests, and to the Levites: Hilkiah and Zechariah and Jehiel, rulers of the house of God, gave unto the priests for the passover offerings two thousand and six hundred *small cattle*, and three hundred oxen.

9 Conaniah also, and Shemaiah and Nethaneel, his brethren, and Hashabiah and Jeiel and Jozabad, chief of the Levites, gave unto the Levites for passover offerings five thousand *small cattle*, and five hundred oxen.

10 So the service was prepared, and the priests stood in their place, and the Levites

in their courses, according to the king's commandment.

11 And they killed the passover, and the priests sprinkled *the blood* from their hands, and the Levites flayed *them*.

12 And they removed the burnt offerings, that they might give according to the divisions of the families of the people, to offer unto the LORD, as *it is* written in the book of Moses. And so *did they* with the oxen.

13 And they roasted the passover with fire according to the ordinance: but the *other* holy *offerings* sod they in pots, and in caldrons, and in pans, and divided *them* speedily among all the people.

14 And afterward they made ready for themselves, and for the priests: because the priests the sons of Aaron *were busied* in offering of burnt offerings and the fat until night; therefore the Levites prepared for themselves, and for the priests the sons of Aaron.

15 And the singers the sons of Asaph *were* in their place, according to the commandment of David, and Asaph, and Heman, and Jeduthun the king's seer; and the porters *waited* at every gate; they might not depart from their service; for their brethren the Levites prepared for them.

16 So all the service of the LORD was prepared the same day, to keep the passover, and to offer burnt offerings upon the altar of the LORD, according to the commandment of king Josiah.

17 And the children of Israel that were present kept the passover at that time, and the feast of unleavened bread seven days.

18 And there was no passover like to that kept in Israel from the days of Samuel the prophet; neither did all the kings of Israel keep such a passover as Josiah kept, and the priests, and the Levites, and all Judah and Israel that were present, and the inhabitants of Jerusalem.

19 In the eighteenth year of the reign of Josiah was this passover kept.

Cross references:

2 2Chr. 23:18; 29:5, 11; Ezra 6:18
3 Deut. 33:10; 1Chr. 23:26; 2Chr. 5:7; 30:22; 34:14; Mal. 2:7
4 1Chr. 9:10; 2Chr. 8:14
5 Ps. 134:1
6 2Chr. 29:5, 15; 30:3, 15; Ezra 6:20
7 2Chr. 30:24
10 Ezra 6:18
11 2Chr. 29:22, 34
12 Lev. 3:3
13 Ex. 12:8, 9; Deut. 16:7; 1Sam. 2:13-15
15 1Chr. 9:17, 18; 25:1; 26:14
17 Ex. 12:15; 13:6; 2Chr. 30:21
18 2Kgs. 23:22, 23

35:3 the holy ark. No mention is made of the ark of the covenant after this order from Josiah that it be restored to the temple. Several theories have been advanced in ancient and modern times as to its possible location, if it still exists. Some think it was consumed in the fiery destruction of the temple in 586 B.C. Others think it may have been carried away to Babylon by King Nebuchadnezzar prior to Jerusalem's final fall. Jewish lore has it that Jeremiah hid it in a cave, while some believe Jeremiah or the priests buried it deep beneath the Temple Mount. There is also a Jewish tradition that suggests that the priests

did indeed hide the ark before Nebuchadnezzar plundered the temple. Though it is not required in the scheme of biblical prophecy, many Jewish traditions teach that the ark will be found when its hiding place is revealed by the Messiah at His coming. His knowledge of its whereabouts will, the Jews declare, be proof of His claims.

35:18 passover. This last great Passover celebration was more in accordance with the Law of Moses and was attended and observed by a larger crowd than was ever witnessed during the reign of Hezekiah (2 Chr. 30).

Josiah's Death

20 After all this, when Josiah had prepared the temple, Necho king of Egypt came up to fight against Carchemish by Euphrates: and Josiah went out against him.

21 But he sent ambassadors to him, saying, What have I to do with thee, thou king of Judah? *I come* not against thee this day, but against the house wherewith I have war: for God commanded me to make haste: forbear thee from *meddling with* God, who *is* with me, that he destroy thee not.

22 Nevertheless Josiah would not turn his face from him, but disguised himself, that he might fight with him, and hearkened not unto the words of Necho from the mouth of God, and came to fight in the valley of Megiddo.

23 And the archers shot at king Josiah; and the king said to his servants, Have me away; for I am sore wounded.

24 His servants therefore took him out of that chariot, and put him in the second chariot that he had; and they brought him to Jerusalem, and he died, and was buried in *one of* the sepulchres of his fathers. And all Judah and Jerusalem mourned for Josiah.

25 And Jeremiah lamented for Josiah: and all the singing men and the singing women spake of Josiah in their lamentations to this day, and made them an ordinance in Israel: and, behold, they *are* written in the lamentations.

26 Now the rest of the acts of Josiah, and his goodness, according to *that which was* written in the law of the LORD,

27 And his deeds, first and last, behold, they *are* written in the book of the kings of Israel and Judah.

CHAPTER 36

Jehoahaz Rules Judah

1 Then the people of the land took Jehoahaz the son of Josiah, and made him king in his father's stead in Jerusalem.

2 Jehoahaz *was* twenty and three years old when he began to reign, and he reigned three months in Jerusalem.

3 And the king of Egypt put him down at Jerusalem, and condemned the land in an hundred talents of silver and a talent of gold.

4 And the king of Egypt made Eliakim his brother king over Judah and Jerusalem, and turned his name to Jehoiakim. And Necho took Jehoahaz his brother, and carried him to Egypt.

Jehoiakim Rules Judah

5 Jehoiakim *was* twenty and five years old when he began to reign, and he reigned eleven years in Jerusalem: and he did *that which was* evil in the sight of the LORD his God.

6 Against him came up Nebuchadnezzar king of Babylon, and bound him in fetters, to carry him to Babylon.

7 Nebuchadnezzar also carried of the vessels of the house of the LORD to Babylon, and put them in his temple at Babylon.

8 Now the rest of the acts of Jehoiakim, and his abominations which he did, and that which was found in him, behold, they

Cross references (center column):
- 20 2Kgs. 23:29; Jer. 46:2
- 22 1Kgs. 22:30
- 23 1Kgs. 22:34
- 24 2Kgs. 23:30; Zech. 12:11
- 25 Jer. 22:20; Lam. 4:20; Matt. 9:23
- 1 2Kgs. 23:30
- 5 2Kgs. 23:36, 37
- 6 2Kgs. 24:1, 6; Jer. 22:18, 19; 36:30; Hab. 1:6
- 7 2Kgs. 24:13; Dan. 1:1, 2; 5:2
- 8 1Chr. 3:16, Jeconiah; Jer. 22:24, Coniah

35:22 Megiddo. In spite of his dedication, Josiah apparently erred in becoming involved in fighting the king of Egypt, who was moving through Judah's area with a vast army to attack Assyria. Mortally wounded in a battle in the valley of Megiddo, he was brought back to Jerusalem and died. Many battles in history have been fought in this valley in central Israel, which will be the scene of the final "battle of that great day of God Almighty" (Rev. 16:13–16). There the rulers of the earth and the whole world will gather against Israel (Zech. 14:2–3). Returning as King of Kings, Jesus, the Messiah of Israel, will be the great victor there (Rev. 19:16–21, cf. Zech. 12:10).

35:25 Jeremiah lamented. The specific lamentations for Josiah are not recorded in Scripture, but Jeremiah, then a young prophet, was already prominent in the realm. Other contemporary prophets were Habbakuk and Zephaniah (Zeph. 1:1).

36:6 Nebuchadnezzar. In about 606 B.C., the king of Babylon defeated the Egyptian Pharaoh Necho at Carchemish, capital of Assyria at the time and north of Judah, and he subsequently conquered all of Syria and the area which had been Israel. The retreating king of Egypt deposed Josiah's son, Jehoahaz, after a three-month reign, installing Eliakim, also known as Jehoiakim, on the throne. Although Jehoiakim was "bound in fetters," he was evidently not taken to Babylon. Some suggest that when Nebuchadnezzar's father, Nabopolasser, died suddenly, Nebuchadnezzar, co-regent with his father, hurried back to Babylon to confirm his sole kingship, allowing Jehoiakim to remain king of Judah. A few years later, Jehoiakim rebelled against Nebuchadnezzar. Before the Babylonian king could respond, God sent groups of the Chaldeans, Syrians, Moabites and Ammonites to fight against Judah and Jehoiakim died in battle (2 Kgs. 24:1, 5; Jer. 36:30–31).

The Literal Babylon

By Arno Froese

Genesis 10:10 names Nimrod, the son of Cush, as the founder of Babel, "in the land of Shinar," which later became known as the city of Babylon, in what is now modern-day Iraq. Nimrod's name means "rebellious," "revolt," "indignation," even "disgraceful," displaying the rebellious heart of man without God.

In Genesis 11, the people of Babylon, who had the concept of self-redemption, built a city and a tower to accomplish unity, fame, and prosperity. They cried out, "Let us build us a city and a tower, whose top may reach unto heaven" (Gen. 11:4). Neither Nimrod nor any other strong personality is mentioned in Genesis 11. The people were in charge, as is evident from the repeated use of the word "us" in verse 4.

Uniformity apparently was the key to the city's initial success. Even the building material, "brick for stone" and "slime . . . for mortar," expresses the unifying of Babel. Stones come in different sizes and forms; therefore, they must have been difficult to work with. The "slime" they used may have been similar to our asphalt. Such "mortar" made separation almost impossible.

The ruins of ancient Babylon are located in modern-day Iraq.

The Lord's reaction to the tower-builders is found in Genesis 11:6–7. "So the Lord scattered them" (v. 8). From that point on, nothing is recorded in the Bible about Babylon until the end of the ten-tribe kingdom of Israel, when Babylon assumes prominence with the ascension of King Nebuchadnezzar. This king's rulership marks the beginning of Gentile world dominion and the golden age of Babylonia.

The prophet Daniel summarizes the significance of Babylon and her role in the Gentile world dominion. A classic example of this in Daniel is Nebuchadnezzar's image. World history, the present, and the future, are revealed in this image in Daniel 2:32–33. The Scripture explains, "Thou, O king, art a king of kings. . . . Thou art this head of gold" (vv. 37–38). The golden head signifies Nebuchadnezzar's superiority over any other Gentile empire.

The end of the city is predicted in Jeremiah 51:37. "Babylon shall become heaps, a dwellingplace for dragons, an astonishment, and an hissing, without an inhabitant." Isaiah also predicted the complete demise of the once beautiful Babylon. "Babylon, the glory of kingdoms, the beauty of the Chaldees' excellency . . . shall never be inhabited . . . her time is near to come, and her days shall not be prolonged" (Isa. 13:19–22).

The city of Babylon had no promise of perpetual existence. Cyrus the Persian crossed the Tigris River in 547 B.C. and conquered the kingdom of Lydia. He then turned his armies southward, conquering the outlying cities of Babylonia on his way to the capital. The city of Babylon fell in one night to Cyrus in 539 B.C., and ceased to be a world power from that time. Persian governors ruled the city for the next sixty years, including Xerxes (the Ahasuerus of Esther 1:1), who represented his father, Darius the Great, in the city. When Xerxes himself became ruler of Persia, the inhabitants of Babylon rebelled against the Persian government. Xerxes responded in 482 B.C. by destroying the fortifications of the city. Over time, the city of Babylon became an uninhabited mound of ruins, just as the prophets had predicted. Hence, the literal city of Babylon, which no longer exists, is not to be confused with "Mystery Babylon" in Revelation 17 (see the article entitled "The Figurative Babylon" by Arno Froese). However, some expositors believe Babylon will be rebuilt under the Antichrist and then finally destroyed at the end of the Tribulation.

are written in the book of the kings of Israel and Judah: and Jehoiachin his son reigned in his stead.

Jehoiachin Is Taken to Babylon

9 Jehoiachin *was* eight years old when he began to reign, and he reigned three months and ten days in Jerusalem: and he did *that which was* evil in the sight of the LORD.

10 And when the year was expired, king Nebuchadnezzar sent, and brought him to Babylon, with the goodly vessels of the house of the LORD, and made Zedekiah his brother king over Judah and Jerusalem.

Zedekiah Rules Judah

11 Zedekiah *was* one and twenty years old when he began to reign, and reigned eleven years in Jerusalem.

12 And he did *that which was* evil in the sight of the LORD his God, *and* humbled not himself before Jeremiah the prophet *speaking* from the mouth of the LORD.

13 And he also rebelled against king Nebuchadnezzar, who had made him swear by God: but he stiffened his neck, and hardened his heart from turning unto the LORD God of Israel.

14 Moreover all the chief of the priests, and the people, transgressed very much after all the abominations of the heathen; and polluted the house of the LORD which he had hallowed in Jerusalem.

15 And the LORD God of their fathers sent to them by his messengers, rising up betimes,

and sending; because he had compassion on his people, and on his dwelling place:

16 But they mocked the messengers of God, and despised his words, and misused his prophets, until the wrath of the LORD arose against his people, till *there was* no remedy.

Judah Goes into Exile

17 Therefore he brought upon them the king of the Chaldees, who slew their young men with the sword in the house of their sanctuary, and had no compassion upon young man or maiden, old man, or him that stooped for age: he gave *them* all into his hand.

18 And all the vessels of the house of God, great and small, and the treasures of the house of the LORD, and the treasures of the king, and of his princes; all *these* he brought to Babylon.

19 And they burnt the house of God, and brake down the wall of Jerusalem, and burnt all the palaces thereof with fire, and destroyed all the goodly vessels thereof.

20 And them that had escaped from the sword carried he away to Babylon; where they were servants to him and his sons until the reign of the kingdom of Persia:

21 To fulfil the word of the LORD by the mouth of Jeremiah, until the land had enjoyed her sabbaths: *for* as long as she lay desolate she kept sabbath, to fulfil threescore and ten years.

Cyrus Frees the Exiles

22 Now in the first year of Cyrus king of Persia, that the word of the LORD *spoken* by

Cross References

9 2Kgs. 24:8
10 2Kgs. 24:10-17; Jer. 37:1; Dan. 1:1, 2; 5:2
11 2Kgs. 24:18; Jer. 52:1
13 2Kgs. 17:14; Jer. 52:3; Ezek. 17:15, 18
15 Jer. 25:3, 4; 35:15; 44:4
16 Jer. 5:12, 13; 32:3; 38:6; Ps. 74:1; 79:5; Prov. 1:25, 30; Matt. 23:34
18 2Kgs. 25:13
19 2Kgs. 25:9; Ps. 74:6, 7; 79:1, 7
20 2Kgs. 25:11; Jer. 27:7
21 Lev. 25:4, 5; 26:34, 35, 43; Jer. 25:9, 11, 12; 26:6, 7; 29:10; Dan. 9:2
22 Ezra 1:1; Isa. 44:28; Jer. 25:12, 13; 29:10; 33:10, 11, 14

36:9–10 Jehoiachin. This young man reigned only one hundred days, when Jerusalem was again invaded by the Babylonians and a second deportation of people from Judah took place (597 B.C.). Zedekiah was given the throne by the Babylonians.

36:10 Zedekiah. The last of the Davidic line to rule, Zedekiah was actually Jehoiachin's uncle. "Brother" was a common term Hebrews used for near relatives, including uncles and cousins. Jesus, Son of David, Son of Abraham (Matt. 1:1) will be the last and everlasting King of Israel in the Davidic dynasty in the glorious future Millennium.

36:19 they burnt the house of God. Following an eleven-year rule, Zedekiah revolted in spite of the prophet Jeremiah's appeals. This time when the armies of Nebuchadnezzar arrived, Jerusalem was devastated and the temple consumed by fire. The third and final deportation of the people from Judah then took place in about 586 B.C. According to Jewish history the first temple (Solo-

mon's Temple) was destroyed on the ninth of Av (a summer date) that year and the second temple (Herod's Temple) was burned by the Romans on the ninth of Av in A.D. 70. Jewish tradition, not Scripture, teaches that the next temple will be dedicated on the ninth of Av.

36:21 the word of the LORD by . . . Jeremiah. The prophet stated that the reason for the Babylonian Captivity was the people's stubborn refusal to obey the word of the Lord (Jer. 25:1–11). The length of the period of punishment was chosen by God to highlight Israel's disobedience in not keeping the sabbatical years (Lev. 25:1–7), which had not been honored for 490 years, dating back to the days of Eli (1 Sam. 1—4; see also Lev. 26:27–46). This was only one of the many sins of the people, but the penalty was a tangible lesson from the Lord that was important for them to learn.

36:22–23 In the Hebrew Bible the Old Testament ends with this book and these words, concluding a section of

the mouth of Jeremiah might be accomplished, the LORD stirred up the spirit of Cyrus king of Persia, that he made a proclamation throughout all his kingdom, and *put it* also in writing, saying,

23 Thus saith Cyrus king of Persia, All the

23 Ezra 1:2, 3

kingdoms of the earth hath the LORD God of heaven given me; and he hath charged me to build him an house in Jerusalem, which *is* in Judah. Who *is there* among you of all his people? The LORD his God *be* with him, and let him go up.

Scripture called "the Writings." These included the poetic books (Job, Psalms, Proverbs, Ecclesiastes, and Song of Solomon), as well as Ruth, Esther, Daniel, Ezra, Nehemiah, and 1–2 Chronicles.

Ezra

The books of Ezra and Nehemiah were originally one volume. The Vulgate (a Latin translation of the Scripture) was the first edition of the Bible to separate them, but at that time they were designated as 1 and 2 Ezra. Like the book of Daniel, portions of Ezra were written in Aramaic, the language of Babylon.

Ezra is the first of the six post-exilic books, which also include Nehemiah, Esther, Haggai, Zechariah, and Malachi. The book of Ezra records how mainly through Ezra, priest and scribe, the Word of God, for the first time, gained its rightful position in Israel. A descendent of Hilkiah (who in 2 Chr. 34:14 had found a copy of the law during the reign of Josiah), Ezra played a major role in re-establishing the true worship of God in Israel, and records the rebuilding of the temple under Zerubbabel sixty years earlier.

Author	Ezra
Date	5th Century B.C.
Key Truth	Return and Rebuilding
Historic Time	The Persian Empire
Key Verse	9:9 . . . our God hath not forsaken us in our bondage.

Ezra was a great revivalist and reformer. That revival began with prayer, confession, and repentance, with the Jews reestablishing their identity and separating from non-Jewish mates. Ezra organized the synagogue movement and was a prime founder of the order of the scribes, whose ministry was to copy the Old Testament books and to explain their teachings.

Under the leadership of Jeshua, the high priest, and Zerubbabel, proper worship and the ceremonies of the temple were restored to Jerusalem. The temple's construction was begun about 536 B.C. but not completed until about 516 B.C., after the motivating ministries of Haggai and Zechariah. About 50,000 Israelites (all but 11,000 from Judah) returned as a result of Cyrus' decree, issued about 538 B.C. The great majority of exiled Jews, however, stayed in Babylon or migrated elsewhere, leading to the Diaspora (see Acts 2:1ff).

All the prophetic material in Ezra is typical, with the institutions of Israel (i.e., the temple, offerings, feasts, priests' garments, etc.) foreshadowing the work of Christ. There are 10 of these types occupying 63 out of the 280 verses, or 23 percent.

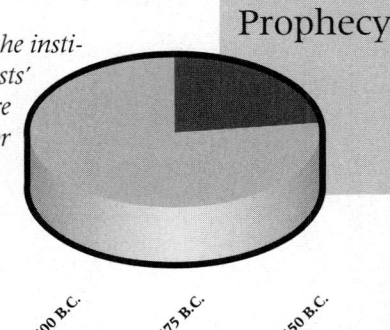

23%
Prophecy

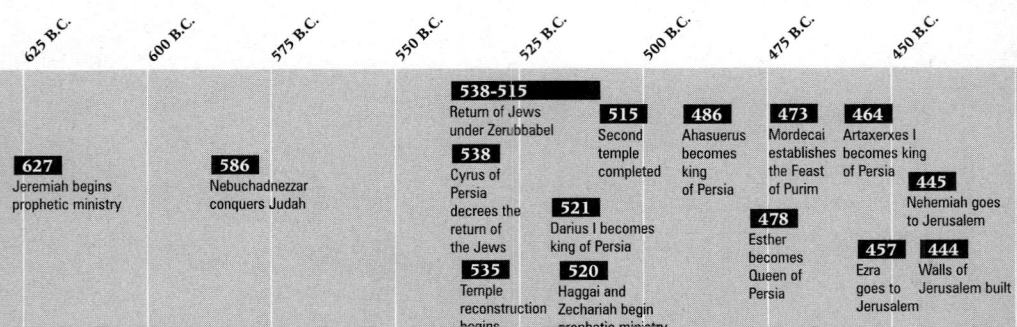

625 B.C.	600 B.C.	575 B.C.	550 B.C.	525 B.C.	500 B.C.	475 B.C.	450 B.C.	425 B.

538-515
Return of Jews under Zerubbabel

515
Second temple completed

486
Ahasuerus becomes king of Persia

473
Mordecai establishes the Feast of Purim

464
Artaxerxes I becomes king of Persia

627
Jeremiah begins prophetic ministry

586
Nebuchadnezzar conquers Judah

538
Cyrus of Persia decrees the return of the Jews

521
Darius I becomes king of Persia

478
Esther becomes Queen of Persia

445
Nehemiah goes to Jerusalem

535
Temple reconstruction begins

520
Haggai and Zechariah begin prophetic ministry

457
Ezra goes to Jerusalem

444
Walls of Jerusalem built

CHAPTER 1
The Edict of Cyrus

1 Now in the first year of Cyrus king of Persia, that the word of the LORD by the mouth of Jeremiah might be fulfilled, the LORD stirred up the spirit of Cyrus king of Persia, that he made a proclamation throughout all his kingdom, and *put it* also in writing, saying,

2 Thus saith Cyrus king of Persia, The LORD God of heaven hath given me all the kingdoms of the earth; and he hath charged me to build him an house at Jerusalem, which *is* in Judah.

3 Who *is there* among you of all his people? his God be with him, and let him go up to Jerusalem, which *is* in Judah, and build the house of the LORD God of Israel, (he *is* the God,) which *is* in Jerusalem.

4 And whosoever remaineth in any place where he sojourneth, let the men of his place help him with silver, and with gold, and with goods, and with beasts, beside the freewill offering for the house of God that *is* in Jerusalem.

The Jewish Exiles Return to Jerusalem

5 Then rose up the chief of the fathers of Judah and Benjamin, and the priests, and the Levites, with all *them* whose spirit God had raised, to go up to build the house of the LORD which *is* in Jerusalem.

6 And all they that *were* about them strengthened their hands with vessels of silver, with gold, with goods, and with beasts, and with precious things, beside all *that* was willingly offered.

7 Also Cyrus the king brought forth the vessels of the house of the LORD, which Nebuchadnezzar had brought forth out of Jerusalem, and had put them in the house of his gods;

8 Even those did Cyrus king of Persia bring forth by the hand of Mithredath the treasurer, and numbered them unto Sheshbazzar, the prince of Judah.

9 And this *is* the number of them: thirty chargers of gold, a thousand chargers of silver, nine and twenty knives,

10 Thirty basons of gold, silver basons of a second *sort* four hundred and ten, *and* other vessels a thousand.

11 All the vessels of gold and of silver *were* five thousand and four hundred. All *these* did Sheshbazzar bring up with *them of* the captivity that were brought up from Babylon unto Jerusalem.

CHAPTER 2
The Record of Those Who Returned

1 Now these *are* the children of the province that went up out of the captivity, of those which had been carried away, whom Nebuchadnezzar the king of Babylon had carried away unto Babylon, and came again unto Jerusalem and Judah, every one unto his city;

2 Which came with Zerubbabel: Jeshua, Nehemiah, Seraiah, Reelaiah, Mordecai, Bilshan, Mispar, Bigvai, Rehum, Baanah. The number of the men of the people of Israel:

3 The children of Parosh, two thousand an hundred seventy and two.

4 The children of Shephatiah, three hundred seventy and two.

5 The children of Arah, seven hundred seventy and five.

6 The children of Pahath-moab, of the children of Jeshua *and* Joab, two thousand eight hundred and twelve.

7 The children of Elam, a thousand two hundred fifty and four.

8 The children of Zattu, nine hundred forty and five.

Cross references (center column):

1 2Chr. 36:22, 23; Ezra 5:13, 14; Jer. 25:12; 29:10
2 Isa. 44:28; 45:1, 13
3 Dan. 6:26
5 Phil. 2:13
7 2Kgs. 24:13; 2Chr. 36:7; Ezra 5:14; 6:5
8 Ezra 5:14

1 2Kgs. 24:14-16; 25:11; 2Chr. 36:20; Neh. 7:6

2 Neh. 7:7

5 Neh. 7:10

6 Neh. 7:11

1:1 in the first year of Cyrus king of Persia, that the word of the LORD by the mouth of Jeremiah might be fulfilled. Prior to the first invasion by Babylonian King Nebuchadnezzar in 606 B.C., Jeremiah, the weeping prophet, had warned Jerusalem and Judah that a time of captivity was imminent (Jer. 25:1–14). The whole land would be in desolation, and the people would serve the king of Babylon seventy years. That began with the first conquest and deportation of multiplied thousands to Babylon. In 536 B.C. (the first year of Cyrus' reign) the Babylonian Empire had been conquered and absorbed by Persia. Prince Zerubbabel, great-grandson of Judah's last godly king, Josiah, led fifty thousand Jews back to Jerusalem and their national homeland (Jer. 29:10; Dan. 9:2).

2:1 that went up out of the captivity. The stages in the restoration are threefold: First the return in 536 B.C. under Zerubbabel and Joshua, the high priest, with Haggai and Zechariah as contemporary prophets (Ezra 1—6); second, the group led by Ezra the priest, a direct descendant of Aaron, in 457 B.C. (Ezra 7—10); third, the group who came with Nehemiah in 445 B.C. who spearheaded the reconstruction of the walls.

9 The children of Zaccai, seven hundred and threescore.
10 The children of Bani, six hundred forty and two.
11 The children of Bebai, six hundred twenty and three.
12 The children of Azgad, a thousand two hundred twenty and two.
13 The children of Adonikam, six hundred sixty and six.
14 The children of Bigvai, two thousand fifty and six.
15 The children of Adin, four hundred fifty and four.
16 The children of Ater of Hezekiah, ninety and eight.
17 The children of Bezai, three hundred twenty and three.
18 The children of Jorah, an hundred and twelve.
19 The children of Hashum, two hundred twenty and three.
20 The children of Gibbar, ninety and five.
21 The children of Beth-lehem, an hundred twenty and three.
22 The men of Netophah, fifty and six.
23 The men of Anathoth, an hundred twenty and eight.
24 The children of Azmaveth, forty and two.
25 The children of Kirjath-arim, Chephirah, and Beeroth, seven hundred and forty and three.
26 The children of Ramah and Gaba, six hundred twenty and one.
27 The men of Michmas, an hundred twenty and two.
28 The men of Beth-el and Ai, two hundred twenty and three.
29 The children of Nebo, fifty and two.
30 The children of Magbish, an hundred fifty and six.
31 The children of the other Elam, a thousand two hundred fifty and four.
32 The children of Harim, three hundred and twenty.
33 The children of Lod, Hadid, and Ono, seven hundred twenty and five.
34 The children of Jericho, three hundred forty and five.
35 The children of Senaah, three thousand and six hundred and thirty.
36 The priests: the children of Jedaiah, of the house of Jeshua, nine hundred seventy and three.
37 The children of Immer, a thousand fifty and two.
38 The children of Pashur, a thousand two hundred forty and seven.

39 The children of Harim, a thousand and seventeen.
40 The Levites: the children of Jeshua and Kadmiel, of the children of Hodaviah, seventy and four.
41 The singers: the children of Asaph, an hundred twenty and eight.
42 The children of the porters: the children of Shallum, the children of Ater, the children of Talmon, the children of Akkub, the children of Hatita, the children of Shobai, *in* all an hundred thirty and nine.
43 The Nethinims: the children of Ziha, the children of Hasupha, the children of Tabbaoth,
44 The children of Keros, the children of Siaha, the children of Padon,
45 The children of Lebanah, the children of Hagabah, the children of Akkub,
46 The children of Hagab, the children of Shalmai, the children of Hanan,
47 The children of Giddel, the children of Gahar, the children of Reaiah,
48 The children of Rezin, the children of Nekoda, the children of Gazzam,
49 The children of Uzza, the children of Paseah, the children of Besai,
50 The children of Asnah, the children of Mehunim, the children of Nephusim,
51 The children of Bakbuk, the children of Hakupha, the children of Harhur,
52 The children of Bazluth, the children of Mehida, the children of Harsha,
53 The children of Barkos, the children of Sisera, the children of Thamah,
54 The children of Neziah, the children of Hatipha.
55 The children of Solomon's servants: the children of Sotai, the children of Sophereth, the children of Peruda,
56 The children of Jaalah, the children of Darkon, the children of Giddel,
57 The children of Shephatiah, the children of Hattil, the children of Pochereth of Zebaim, the children of Ami.
58 All the Nethinims, and the children of Solomon's servants, *were* three hundred ninety and two.
59 And these *were* they which went up from Tel-melah, Tel-harsa, Cherub, Addan, *and* Immer: but they could not shew their father's house, and their seed, whether they *were* of Israel:
60 The children of Delaiah, the children of Tobiah, the children of Nekoda, six hundred fifty and two.
61 And of the children of the priests: the children of Habaiah, the children of Koz, the

Center column cross-references:
10 Neh. 7:15
18 Neh. 7:24
20 Neh. 7:25
24 Neh. 7:28
31 Ezra 2:7
36 1Chr. 24:7
37 1Chr. 24:14
38 1Chr. 9:12
39 1Chr. 24:8
40 Neh. 7:43, *Hodevah*
43 1Chr. 9:2
52 Neh. 7:54
55 1Kgs. 9:21; Neh. 7:57
57 Neh. 7:59
58 Josh. 9:21, 27; 1Kgs. 9:21; 1Chr. 9:2
59 Neh. 7:61
61 2Sam. 17:27

children of Barzillai; which took a wife of the daughters of Barzillai the Gileadite, and was called after their name:

62 These sought their register *among* those that were reckoned by genealogy, but they were not found: therefore were they, as polluted, put from the priesthood.

63 And the Tirshatha said unto them, that they should not eat of the most holy things, till there stood up a priest with Urim and with Thummim.

64 The whole congregation together *was* forty and two thousand three hundred *and* threescore,

65 Beside their servants and their maids, of whom *there were* seven thousand three hundred thirty and seven: and *there were* among them two hundred singing men and singing women.

66 Their horses *were* seven hundred thirty and six; their mules, two hundred forty and five;

67 Their camels, four hundred thirty and five; *their* asses, six thousand seven hundred and twenty.

68 And *some* of the chief of the fathers, when they came to the house of the LORD which *is* at Jerusalem, offered freely for the house of God to set it up in his place:

69 They gave after their ability unto the treasure of the work threescore and one thousand drams of gold, and five thousand pound of silver, and one hundred priests' garments.

70 So the priests, and the Levites, and *some* of the people, and the singers, and the porters, and the Nethinims, dwelt in their cities, and all Israel in their cities.

CHAPTER 3
Worship Is Restored

1 And when the seventh month was come, and the children of Israel *were* in the cities, the people gathered themselves together as one man to Jerusalem.

2 Then stood up Jeshua the son of Jozadak, and his brethren the priests, and Zerubbabel the son of Shealtiel, and his brethren, and builded the altar of the God of Israel, to offer burnt offerings thereon, as *it is* written in the law of Moses the man of God.

3 And they set the altar upon his bases; for fear *was* upon them because of the people of those countries: and they offered burnt offerings thereon unto the LORD, *even* burnt offerings morning and evening.

4 They kept also the feast of tabernacles, as *it is* written, and *offered* the daily burnt offerings by number, according to the custom, as the duty of every day required;

5 And afterward *offered* the continual burnt offering, both of the new moons, and of all the set feasts of the LORD that were consecrated, and of every one that willingly offered a freewill offering unto the LORD.

6 From the first day of the seventh month began they to offer burnt offerings unto the LORD. But the foundation of the temple of the LORD was not *yet* laid.

7 They gave money also unto the masons, and to the carpenters; and meat, and drink, and oil, unto them of Zidon, and to them of Tyre, to bring cedar trees from Lebanon to the sea of Joppa, according to the grant that they had of Cyrus king of Persia.

Rebuilding the Temple

8 Now in the second year of their coming unto the house of God at Jerusalem, in the second month, began Zerubbabel the son of Shealtiel, and Jeshua the son of Jozadak, and the remnant of their brethren the priests and the Levites, and all they that were come out of the captivity unto Jerusalem; and appointed the Levites, from twenty years old and upward, to set forward the work of the house of the LORD.

9 Then stood Jeshua *with* his sons and his brethren, Kadmiel and his sons, the sons of Judah, together, to set forward the workmen in the house of God: the sons of Henadad, *with* their sons and their brethren the Levites.

10 And when the builders laid the foundation of the temple of the LORD, they set the priests in their apparel with trumpets, and the Levites the sons of Asaph with cymbals, to praise the LORD, after the ordinance of David king of Israel.

11 And they sang together by course in praising and giving thanks unto the LORD;

Cross references (center column)

62 Num. 3:10
63 Ex. 28:30; Lev. 22:2, 10, 15, 16; Num. 27:21; Neh. 8:9
64 Neh. 7:66
68 Or, Neh. 7:70
69 1Chr. 26:20
70 Ezra 6:16, 17; Neh. 7:73
2 Deut. 12:5; Hag. 1:1; 2:2; Zech. 3:1; Matt. 1:12; Luke 3:27
3 Num. 28:3, 4
4 Ex. 23:16; Num. 29:12; Neh. 8:14, 17; 14:16, 17
5 Ex. 29:38; Num. 28:3, 11, 19, 26; 29:2, 8, 13
7 1Kgs. 5:6, 9; 2Chr. 2:10, 16; Ezra 6:3; Acts 9:36; 12:20
8 1Chr. 23:24, 27
9 Ezra 2:40
10 1Chr. 6:31; 16:4, 5, 6, 42; 25:1
11 Ex. 15:21; 1Chr. 16:34, 41; 2Chr. 7:3; Neh. 12:24; Ps. 136:1; Jer. 33:11

3:1 the children of Israel. Those who returned seem to represent all of the Israelites, but were relatively few in number. The vast majority of Jewish people remained in Babylon and Persia, gradually spreading throughout many nations.

3:11 his mercy endureth for ever toward Israel. These words are performed by a vast choir, accompanied by an orchestra, at the laying of the foundation of Zerubbabel's Temple. This is the only prophetic affirmation in the book, stating that God's mercy continues and will continue toward Israel.

because *he is* good, for his mercy *endureth* for ever toward Israel. And all the people shouted with a great shout, when they praised the LORD, because the foundation of the house of the LORD was laid.

12 But many of the priests and Levites and chief of the fathers, *who were* ancient men, that had seen the first house, when the foundation of this house was laid before their eyes, wept with a loud voice; and many shouted aloud for joy:

13 So that the people could not discern the noise of the shout of joy from the noise of the weeping of the people: for the people shouted with a loud shout, and the noise was heard afar off.

CHAPTER 4
Enemies Oppose the Work

1 Now when the adversaries of Judah and Benjamin heard that the children of the captivity builded the temple unto the LORD God of Israel;

2 Then they came to Zerubbabel, and to the chief of the fathers, and said unto them, Let us build with you: for we seek your God, as ye *do*; and we do sacrifice unto him since the days of Esar-haddon king of Assur, which brought us up hither.

3 But Zerubbabel, and Jeshua, and the rest of the chief of the fathers of Israel, said unto them, Ye have nothing to do with us to build an house unto our God; but we ourselves together will build unto the LORD God of Israel, as king Cyrus the king of Persia hath commanded us.

4 Then the people of the land weakened the hands of the people of Judah, and troubled them in building,

5 And hired counsellers against them, to frustrate their purpose, all the days of Cyrus king of Persia, even until the reign of Darius king of Persia.

6 And in the reign of Ahasuerus, in the beginning of his reign, wrote they *unto him* an accusation against the inhabitants of Judah and Jerusalem.

7 And in the days of Artaxerxes wrote Bishlam, Mithredath, Tabeel, and the rest of their companions, unto Artaxerxes king of Persia; and the writing of the letter *was* written in the Syrian tongue, and interpreted in the Syrian tongue.

8 Rehum the chancellor and Shimshai the scribe wrote a letter against Jerusalem to Artaxerxes the king in this sort:

9 Then *wrote* Rehum the chancellor, and Shimshai the scribe, and the rest of their companions; the Dinaites, the Apharsathchites, the Tarpelites, the Apharsites, the Archevites, the Babylonians, the Susanchites, the Dehavites, *and* the Elamites,

10 And the rest of the nations whom the great and noble Asnappar brought over, and set in the cities of Samaria, and the rest *that are* on this side the river, and at such a time.

11 This *is* the copy of the letter that they sent unto him, *even* unto Artaxerxes the king; Thy servants the men on this side the river, and at such a time.

12 Be it known unto the king, that the Jews which came up from thee to us are come unto Jerusalem, building the rebellious and the bad city, and have set up the walls *thereof*, and joined the foundations.

13 Be it known now unto the king, that, if this city be builded, and the walls set up *again, then* will they not pay toll, tribute, and custom, and *so* thou shalt endamage the revenue of the kings.

14 Now because we have maintenance from *the king's* palace, and it was not meet for us to see the king's dishonour, therefore have we sent and certified the king;

15 That search may be made in the book of the records of thy fathers: so shalt thou find in the book of the records, and know that this city *is* a rebellious city, and hurtful unto kings and provinces, and that they have moved sedition within the same of old time: for which cause was this city destroyed.

16 We certify the king that, if this city be builded *again*, and the walls thereof set up, by this means thou shalt have no portion on this side the river.

17 *Then* sent the king an answer unto Rehum the chancellor, and *to* Shimshai the scribe, and *to* the rest of their companions that dwell in Samaria, and *unto* the rest beyond the river, Peace, and at such a time.

18 The letter which ye sent unto us hath been plainly read before me.

19 And I commanded, and search hath been made, and it is found that this city of old time hath made insurrection against kings, and *that* rebellion and sedition have been made therein.

20 There have been mighty kings also over Jerusalem, which have ruled over all *countries* beyond the river; and toll, tribute, and custom, was paid unto them.

21 Give ye now commandment to cause these men to cease, and that this city be not builded, until *another* commandment shall be given from me.

22 Take heed now that ye fail not to do this:

Cross references (center column):

12 Hag. 2:3
1 Ezra 4:7-9
2 2Kgs. 17:24, 32, 33; 19:37; Ezra 4:10
3 Ezra 1:1-3; Neh. 2:20
4 Ezra 3:3
9 2Kgs. 17:30, 31
10 Ezra 4:10, 11, 17; 7:12
13 Ezra 7:24

20 Gen. 15:18; Josh. 1:4; 1Kgs. 4:21; Ps. 72:8

why should damage grow to the hurt of the kings?

23 Now when the copy of king Artaxerxes' letter *was* read before Rehum, and Shimshai the scribe, and their companions, they went up in haste to Jerusalem unto the Jews, and made them to cease by force and power.

24 Then ceased the work of the house of God which *is* at Jerusalem. So it ceased unto the second year of the reign of Darius king of Persia.

CHAPTER 5
The Temple Is Rebuilt

1 Then the prophets, Haggai the prophet, and Zechariah the son of Iddo, prophesied unto the Jews that *were* in Judah and Jerusalem in the name of the God of Israel, *even* unto them.

2 Then rose up Zerubbabel the son of Shealtiel, and Jeshua the son of Jozadak, and began to build the house of God which *is* at Jerusalem: and with them *were* the prophets of God helping them.

3 At the same time came to them Tatnai, governor on this side the river, and Shethar-boznai, and their companions, and said thus unto them, Who hath commanded you to build this house, and to make up this wall?

4 Then said we unto them after this manner, What are the names of the men that make this building?

5 But the eye of their God was upon the elders of the Jews, that they could not cause them to cease, till the matter came to Darius: and then they returned answer by letter concerning this *matter*.

6 The copy of the letter that Tatnai, governor on this side the river, and Shethar-boznai, and his companions the Apharsachites, which *were* on this side the river, sent unto Darius the king:

7 They sent a letter unto him, wherein was written thus; Unto Darius the king, all peace.

8 Be it known unto the king, that we went into the province of Judea, to the house of the great God, which is builded with great stones, and timber is laid in the walls, and this work goeth fast on, and prospereth in their hands.

9 Then asked we those elders, *and* said unto them thus, Who commanded you to build this house, and to make up these walls?

10 We asked their names also, to certify thee, that we might write the names of the men that *were* the chief of them.

11 And thus they returned us answer, saying, We are the servants of the God of heaven and earth, and build the house that was builded these many years ago, which a great king of Israel builded and set up.

12 But after that our fathers had provoked the God of heaven unto wrath, he gave them into the hand of Nebuchadnezzar the king of Babylon, the Chaldean, who destroyed this house, and carried the people away into Babylon.

13 But in the first year of Cyrus the king of Babylon *the same* king Cyrus made a decree to build this house of God.

14 And the vessels also of gold and silver of the house of God, which Nebuchadnezzar took out of the temple that *was* in Jerusalem, and brought them into the temple of Babylon, those did Cyrus the king take out of the temple of Babylon, and they were delivered unto *one*, whose name *was* Sheshbazzar, whom he had made governor;

15 And said unto him, Take these vessels, go, carry them into the temple that *is* in Jerusalem, and let the house of God be builded in his place.

16 Then came the same Sheshbazzar, *and* laid the foundation of the house of God which *is* in Jerusalem: and since that time even until now hath it been in building, and *yet* it is not finished.

17 Now therefore, if *it seem* good to the king, let there be search made in the king's treasure house, which *is* there at Babylon, whether it be *so*, that a decree was made of Cyrus the king to build this house of God at Jerusalem, and let the king send his pleasure to us concerning this matter.

1 Hag. 1:1; Zech. 1:1
2 Ezra 3:2
3 Ezra 5:6, 9; 6:6
4 Ezra 5:10
5 Ezra 6:6; 7:6, 28; Ps. 33:18
6 Ezra 4:9
9 Ezra 5:3, 4
11 1Kgs. 6:1
12 2Kgs. 24:2; 25:8, 9, 11; 2Chr. 36:16, 17
13 Ezra 1:1
14 Ezra 1:7, 8; 6:5; Hag. 1:14; 2:2, 21
16 Ezra 3:8, 10; 6:15
17 Ezra 6:1, 2

4:24 Then ceased the work of the house of God. Both the peoples who had been transferred from other lands to Canaan and their neighbors strenuously objected to the return of the Jews. Through their opposition and intrigue, the slow work of rebuilding the temple and restoring the walls was stopped by the Persian government about 520 B.C.

5:1 the prophets, Haggai . . . and Zechariah. These prophets inspired Prince Zerubbabel and Jeshua the high priest to restart the building program. Opposition again arose, but a new king, Darius, was in power. Upon an examination of the records of Cyrus, Darius ordered the work to begin again at once (v. 13).

CHAPTER 6
Cyrus' Edict Is Rediscovered

1 Then Darius the king made a decree, and search was made in the house of the rolls, where the treasures were laid up in Babylon.
2 And there was found at Achmetha, in the palace that *is* in the province of the Medes, a roll, and therein *was* a record thus written:
3 In the first year of Cyrus the king *the same* Cyrus the king made a decree *concerning* the house of God at Jerusalem, Let the house be builded, the place where they offered sacrifices, and let the foundations thereof be strongly laid; the height thereof threescore cubits, *and* the breadth thereof threescore cubits;
4 *With* three rows of great stones, and a row of new timber: and let the expences be given out of the king's house:
5 And also let the golden and silver vessels of the house of God, which Nebuchadnezzar took forth out of the temple which *is* at Jerusalem, and brought unto Babylon, be restored, and brought again unto the temple which *is* at Jerusalem, *every one* to his place, and place *them* in the house of God.
6 Now *therefore*, Tatnai, governor beyond the river, Shethar-boznai, and your companions the Apharsachites, which *are* beyond the river, be ye far from thence:
7 Let the work of this house of God alone; let the governor of the Jews and the elders of the Jews build this house of God in his place.
8 Moreover I make a decree what ye shall do to the elders of these Jews for the building of this house of God: that of the king's goods, *even* of the tribute beyond the river, forthwith expences be given unto these men, that they be not hindered.
9 And that which they have need of, both young bullocks, and rams, and lambs, for the burnt offerings of the God of heaven, wheat, salt, wine, and oil, according to the appointment of the priests which *are* at Jerusalem, let it be given them day by day without fail:
10 That they may offer sacrifices of sweet savours unto the God of heaven, and pray for the life of the king, and of his sons.
11 Also I have made a decree, that whosoever shall alter this word, let timber be pulled down from his house, and being set up, let him be hanged thereon; and let his house be made a dunghill for this.
12 And the God that hath caused his name to dwell there destroy all kings and people, that shall put to their hand to alter *and* to destroy this house of God which *is* at Jerusalem. I Darius have made a decree; let it be done with speed.

The Temple Is Dedicated

13 Then Tatnai, governor on this side the river, Shethar-boznai, and their companions, according to that which Darius the king had sent, so they did speedily.
14 And the elders of the Jews builded, and they prospered through the prophesying of Haggai the prophet and Zechariah the son of Iddo. And they builded, and finished *it*, according to the commandment of the God of Israel, and according to the commandment of Cyrus, and Darius, and Artaxerxes king of Persia.
15 And this house was finished on the third day of the month Adar, which was in the sixth year of the reign of Darius the king.
16 And the children of Israel, the priests, and the Levites, and the rest of the children of the captivity, kept the dedication of this house of God with joy,
17 And offered at the dedication of this house of God an hundred bullocks, two hundred rams, four hundred lambs; and for a sin offering for all Israel, twelve he goats, according to the number of the tribes of Israel.
18 And they set the priests in their divisions, and the Levites in their courses, for the service of God, which *is* at Jerusalem; as it is written in the book of Moses.
19 And the children of the captivity kept the passover upon the fourteenth *day* of the first month.
20 For the priests and the Levites were purified together, all of them *were* pure, and killed the passover for all the children of the

Cross references
1 Ezra 5:17
4 1Kgs. 6:36
5 Ezra 1:7, 8; 5:14
6 Ezra 5:3
10 Ezra 7:23; Jer. 29:7; 1Tim. 2:1, 2
11 Dan. 2:5; 3:29
12 1Kgs. 9:3
14 Ezra 1:1; 4:24; 5:1, 2, 13; 6:3; 7:1
16 1Kgs. 8:63; 2Chr. 7:5
17 Ezra 8:35
18 Num. 3:6; 8:9; 1Chr. 23:6; 24:1
19 Ex. 12:6
20 2Chr. 30:15; 35:11

6:14 **they builded, and finished it.** The temple was completed about 516 B.C. (compare the books of Hag. and Zech. 1—6 for relevant prophecies). According to the Jewish Talmud, this second temple lacked five things that were in Solomon's Temple: the ark, the sacred fire, the Shechinah cloud, the Holy Spirit, and the Urim and Thummim. Generally called the "second temple," the structure was gradually improved. A vast expansion commenced about 18 B.C. and had continued for forty-six years when Jesus began His ministry (John 2:20). The entire religious complex was finished about A.D. 64 and destroyed by the Romans in A.D. 70.

captivity, and for their brethren the priests, and for themselves.

21 And the children of Israel, which were come again out of captivity, and all such as had separated themselves unto them from the filthiness of the heathen of the land, to seek the LORD God of Israel, did eat,

22 And kept the feast of unleavened bread seven days with joy: for the LORD had made them joyful, and turned the heart of the king of Assyria unto them, to strengthen their hands in the work of the house of God, the God of Israel.

CHAPTER 7
Ezra Arrives

1 Now after these things, in the reign of Artaxerxes king of Persia, Ezra the son of Seraiah, the son of Azariah, the son of Hilkiah,

2 The son of Shallum, the son of Zadok, the son of Ahitub,

3 The son of Amariah, the son of Azariah, the son of Meraioth,

4 The son of Zerahiah, the son of Uzzi, the son of Bukki,

5 The son of Abishua, the son of Phinehas, the son of Eleazar, the son of Aaron the chief priest:

6 This Ezra went up from Babylon; and he *was* a ready scribe in the law of Moses, which the LORD God of Israel had given: and the king granted him all his request, according to the hand of the LORD his God upon him.

7 And there went up *some* of the children of Israel, and of the priests, and the Levites, and the singers, and the porters, and the Nethinims, unto Jerusalem, in the seventh year of Artaxerxes the king.

8 And he came to Jerusalem in the fifth month, which *was* in the seventh year of the king.

9 For upon the first *day* of the first month began he to go up from Babylon, and on the first *day* of the fifth month came he to Jerusalem, according to the good hand of his God upon him.

10 For Ezra had prepared his heart to seek the law of the LORD, and to do *it*, and to teach in Israel statutes and judgments.

11 Now this *is* the copy of the letter that the king Artaxerxes gave unto Ezra the priest, the scribe, *even* a scribe of the words of the commandments of the LORD, and of his statutes to Israel.

12 Artaxerxes, king of kings, unto Ezra the priest, a scribe of the law of the God of heaven, perfect *peace*, and at such a time.

13 I make a decree, that all they of the people of Israel, and *of* his priests and Levites, in my realm, which are minded of their own freewill to go up to Jerusalem, go with thee.

14 Forasmuch as thou art sent of the king, and of his seven counsellers, to inquire concerning Judah and Jerusalem, according to the law of thy God which *is* in thine hand;

15 And to carry the silver and gold, which the king and his counsellers have freely offered unto the God of Israel, whose habitation *is* in Jerusalem,

16 And all the silver and gold that thou canst find in all the province of Babylon, with the freewill offering of the people, and of the priests, offering willingly for the house of their God which *is* in Jerusalem:

17 That thou mayest buy speedily with this money bullocks, rams, lambs, with their meat offerings and their drink offerings, and offer them upon the altar of the house of your God which *is* in Jerusalem.

18 And whatsoever shall seem good to thee, and to thy brethren, to do with the rest of the silver and the gold, that do after the will of your God.

19 The vessels also that are given thee for

Cross references

21 Ezra 9:11
22 Ex. 12:15; 13:6; 2Kgs. 23:29; 2Chr. 30:21; 33:11; 35:17; Ezra 1:1; 6:6; Prov. 21:1
1 1Chr. 6:14; Neh. 2:1
6 Ezra 7:9, 11, 12, 21; 8:22, 31
7 Ezra 2:43; 8:1, 15, 20
9 Ezra 7:6; Neh. 2:8, 18
10 Deut. 33:10; Ezra 6:25; Neh. 8:1-8; Ps. 119:45; Mal. 2:7
12 Ezra 4:10; Ezek. 26:7; Dan. 2:37
14 Esth. 1:14
15 2Chr. 6:2; Ps. 135:21
16 1Chr. 29:6, 9; Ezra 8:25
17 Num. 15:4-13; Deut. 12:5, 11

7:1 Ezra the son of Seraiah. In 457 B.C., some eighty years after that first return under Zerubbabel, Ezra the scribe, who had prepared his heart to seek the Lord, led another large number of exiles back to Jerusalem. Ezra was authorized by King Artaxerxes I of Persia and furnished with an immense amount of money, contributed both by the king and through freewill offerings from exiled Jews who did not return. He set about to enhance worship at the temple, organize civil and religious authorities throughout the land, and enforce the laws of God. Ezra acted under the authorization of the third imperial decree, issued by Artaxerxes in this case (earlier decrees date from Cyrus in 536 B.C. and Darius in 520 B.C.). The 457 B.C. date is used by those prophetic researchers who insist on using a 365 and one-fourth day solar year, when computing the seventy weeks of years in Daniel which total 490 years (see Dan. 9:2, 20–25). The 483 years (seven weeks of years plus sixty-two weeks of years), starting at 457 B.C., ends about 26 A.D., the year of Christ's baptism. Other scholars more accurately use the 360-day prophetic year beginning with the second decree of Artaxerxes (445 B.C.), authorizing Nehemiah to be Tirshatha or governor of Judah and to rebuild the walls. With the slightly shorter year the terminus is about 30 A.D., when Jesus was crucified. See notes on Daniel 9.

the service of the house of thy God, *those* deliver thou before the God of Jerusalem.

20 And whatsoever more shall be needful for the house of thy God, which thou shalt have occasion to bestow, bestow *it* out of the king's treasure house.

21 And I, *even* I Artaxerxes the king, do make a decree to all the treasurers which *are* beyond the river, that whatsoever Ezra the priest, the scribe of the law of the God of heaven, shall require of you, it be done speedily,

22 Unto an hundred talents of silver, and to an hundred measures of wheat, and to an hundred baths of wine, and to an hundred baths of oil, and salt without prescribing *how much*.

23 Whatsoever is commanded by the God of heaven, let it be diligently done for the house of the God of heaven: for why should there be wrath against the realm of the king and his sons?

24 Also we certify you, that touching any of the priests and Levites, singers, porters, Nethinims, or ministers of this house of God, it shall not be lawful to impose toll, tribute, or custom, upon them.

25 And thou, Ezra, after the wisdom of thy God, that *is* in thine hand, set magistrates and judges, which may judge all the people that *are* beyond the river, all such as know the laws of thy God; and teach ye them that know *them* not.

26 And whosoever will not do the law of thy God, and the law of the king, let judgment be executed speedily upon him, whether *it be* unto death, or to banishment, or to confiscation of goods, or to imprisonment.

27 Blessed *be* the LORD God of our fathers, which hath put *such a thing* as this in the king's heart, to beautify the house of the LORD which *is* in Jerusalem:

28 And hath extended mercy unto me before the king, and his counsellers, and before all the king's mighty princes. And I was strengthened as the hand of the LORD my God *was* upon me, and I gathered together out of Israel chief men to go up with me.

CHAPTER 8
Those Who Returned with Ezra

1 These *are* now the chief of their fathers, and *this is* the genealogy of them that went up with me from Babylon, in the reign of Artaxerxes the king.

2 Of the sons of Phinehas; Gershom: of the sons of Ithamar; Daniel: of the sons of David; Hattush.

3 Of the sons of Shechaniah, of the sons of Pharosh; Zechariah: and with him were reckoned by genealogy of the males an hundred and fifty.

4 Of the sons of Pahath-moab; Elihoenai the son of Zerahiah, and with him two hundred males.

5 Of the sons of Shechaniah; the son of Jahaziel, and with him three hundred males.

6 Of the sons also of Adin; Ebed the son of Jonathan, and with him fifty males.

7 And of the sons of Elam; Jeshaiah the son of Athaliah, and with him seventy males.

8 And of the sons of Shephatiah; Zebadiah the son of Michael, and with him fourscore males.

9 Of the sons of Joab; Obadiah the son of Jehiel, and with him two hundred and eighteen males.

10 And of the sons of Shelomith; the son of Josiphiah, and with him an hundred and threescore males.

11 And of the sons of Bebai; Zechariah the son of Bebai, and with him twenty and eight males.

12 And of the sons of Azgad; Johanan the son of Hakkatan, and with him an hundred and ten males.

13 And of the last sons of Adonikam, whose names *are* these, Eliphelet, Jeiel, and Shemaiah, and with them threescore males.

14 Of the sons also of Bigvai; Uthai, and Zabbud, and with them seventy males.

15 And I gathered them together to the river that runneth to Ahava; and there abode we in tents three days: and I viewed the people, and the priests, and found there none of the sons of Levi.

16 Then sent I for Eliezer, for Ariel, for Shemaiah, and for Elnathan, and for Jarib, and for Elnathan, and for Nathan, and for Zechariah, and for Meshullam, chief men; also for Joiarib, and for Elnathan, men of understanding.

17 And I sent them with commandment unto Iddo the chief at the place Casiphia, and I told them what they should say unto

25 Ex. 18:21, 22; Deut. 16:18; 2Chr. 17:7; Ezra 7:10; Mal. 2:7; Matt. 23:2, 3

27 1Chr. 29:10; Ezra 6:22

28 Ezra 5:5; 7:6, 9; 8:18; 9:9

2 1Chr. 3:22

3 Ezra 2:3

15 Ezra 7:7

17 2Sam. 14:3, 19

7:27 in the king's heart. Some researchers believe that Artaxerxes, the son of Xerxes (called Ahasuerus in Esther and other places), was the son or stepson of Queen Esther.

7:28 I was strengthened. Here Ezra moves to autobiographical reporting, continuing through chapter nine.

Iddo, *and* to his brethren the Nethinims, at the place Casiphia, that they should bring unto us ministers for the house of our God.
18 And by the good hand of our God upon us they brought us a man of understanding, of the sons of Mahli, the son of Levi, the son of Israel; and Sherebiah, with his sons and his brethren, eighteen;
19 And Hashabiah, and with him Jeshaiah of the sons of Merari, his brethren and their sons, twenty;
20 Also of the Nethinims, whom David and the princes had appointed for the service of the Levites, two hundred and twenty Nethinims: all of them were expressed by name.

Ezra Leads the People
21 Then I proclaimed a fast there, at the river of Ahava, that we might afflict ourselves before our God, to seek of him a right way for us, and for our little ones, and for all our substance.
22 For I was ashamed to require of the king a band of soldiers and horsemen to help us against the enemy in the way: because we had spoken unto the king, saying, The hand of our God *is* upon all them for good that seek him; but his power and his wrath *is* against all them that forsake him.
23 So we fasted and besought our God for this: and he was intreated of us.
24 Then I separated twelve of the chief of the priests, Sherebiah, Hashabiah, and ten of their brethren with them,
25 And weighed unto them the silver, and the gold, and the vessels, *even* the offering of the house of our God, which the king, and his counsellers, and his lords, and all Israel *there* present, had offered:
26 I even weighed unto their hand six hundred and fifty talents of silver, and silver vessels an hundred talents, *and* of gold an hundred talents;
27 Also twenty basons of gold, of a thousand drams; and two vessels of fine copper, precious as gold.
28 And I said unto them, Ye *are* holy unto the LORD; the vessels *are* holy also; and the silver and the gold *are* a freewill offering unto the LORD God of your fathers.
29 Watch ye, and keep *them*, until ye weigh *them* before the chief of the priests and the Levites, and chief of the fathers of Israel, at Jerusalem, in the chambers of the house of the LORD.
30 So took the priests and the Levites the weight of the silver, and the gold, and the

vessels, to bring *them* to Jerusalem unto the house of our God.
31 Then we departed from the river of Ahava on the twelfth *day* of the first month, to go unto Jerusalem: and the hand of our God was upon us, and he delivered us from the hand of the enemy, and of such as lay in wait by the way.
32 And we came to Jerusalem, and abode there three days.
33 Now on the fourth day was the silver and the gold and the vessels weighed in the house of our God by the hand of Meremoth the son of Uriah the priest; and with him *was* Eleazar the son of Phinehas; and with them *was* Jozabad the son of Jeshua, and Noadiah the son of Binnui, Levites;
34 By number *and* by weight of every one: and all the weight was written at that time.
35 *Also* the children of those that had been carried away, which were come out of the captivity, offered burnt offerings unto the God of Israel, twelve bullocks for all Israel, ninety and six rams, seventy and seven lambs, twelve he goats *for* a sin offering: all *this was* a burnt offering unto the LORD.
36 And they delivered the king's commissions unto the king's lieutenants, and to the governors on this side the river: and they furthered the people, and the house of God.

CHAPTER 9
Intermarriage with Pagans
1 Now when these things were done, the princes came to me, saying, The people of Israel, and the priests, and the Levites, have not separated themselves from the people of the lands, *doing* according to their abominations, *even* of the Canaanites, the Hittites, the Perizzites, the Jebusites, the Ammonites, the Moabites, the Egyptians, and the Amorites.
2 For they have taken of their daughters for themselves, and for their sons: so that the holy seed have mingled themselves with the people of *those* lands: yea, the hand of the princes and rulers hath been chief in this trespass.
3 And when I heard this thing, I rent my garment and my mantle, and plucked off the hair of my head and of my beard, and sat down astonied.
4 Then were assembled unto me every one that trembled at the words of the God of Israel, because of the transgression of those that had been carried away; and I sat astonied until the evening sacrifice.

---

18 Neh. 8:7; 9:4, 5
20 Ezra 2:43
21 Lev. 16:29; 23:29; 2Chr. 20:3; Ps. 5:8; Isa. 58:3, 5
22 2Chr. 15:2; Ezra 7:6, 9, 28; Ps. 33:18, 19; 34:15, 16, 22; Rom. 8:28; 1Cor. 9:15
23 1Chr. 5:20; 2Chr. 33:13; Isa. 19:22
25 Ezra 7:15, 16
28 Lev. 21:6-8; 22:2, 3; Deut. 33:8; Num. 4:4, 15, 19, 20
31 Ezra 7:6, 9, 28
32 Neh. 2:11
33 Ezra 8:26, 30
35 Ezra 6:17
36 Ezra 7:21

1 Deut. 12:30, 31; Ezra 6:21; Neh. 9:2

2 Ex. 19:6; 22:31; 34:16; Deut. 7:3, 6; 14:2; Neh. 13:23; 2Cor. 6:14

3 Job 1:20; Ps. 143:4

4 Ex. 29:39; Ezra 10:3; Isa. 66:2

5 And at the evening sacrifice I arose up from my heaviness; and having rent my garment and my mantle, I fell upon my knees, and spread out my hands unto the LORD my God,

6 And said, O my God, I am ashamed and blush to lift up my face to thee, my God: for our iniquities are increased over *our* head, and our trespass is grown up unto the heavens.

7 Since the days of our fathers *have* we *been* in a great trespass unto this day; and for our iniquities have we, our kings, *and* our priests, been delivered into the hand of the kings of the lands, to the sword, to captivity, and to a spoil, and to confusion of face, as *it is* this day.

8 And now for a little space grace hath been *shewed* from the LORD our God, to leave us a remnant to escape, and to give us a nail in his holy place, that our God may lighten our eyes, and give us a little reviving in our bondage.

9 For we *were* bondmen; yet our God hath not forsaken us in our bondage, but hath extended mercy unto us in the sight of the kings of Persia, to give us a reviving, to set up the house of our God, and to repair the desolations thereof, and to give us a wall in Judah and in Jerusalem.

10 And now, O our God, what shall we say after this? for we have forsaken thy commandments,

11 Which thou hast commanded by thy servants the prophets, saying, The land, unto which ye go to possess it, is an unclean land with the filthiness of the people of the lands, with their abominations, which have filled it from one end to another with their uncleanness.

12 Now therefore give not your daughters unto their sons, neither take their daughters unto your sons, nor seek their peace or their wealth for ever: that ye may be strong, and eat the good of the land, and leave *it* for an inheritance to your children for ever.

13 And after all that is come upon us for our evil deeds, and for our great trespass, seeing that thou our God hast punished us less than our iniquities *deserve*, and hast given us *such* deliverance as this;

14 Should we again break thy commandments, and join in affinity with the people of these abominations? wouldest not thou be angry with us till thou hadst consumed *us*, so that *there should be* no remnant nor escaping?

15 O LORD God of Israel, thou *art* righteous: for we remain yet escaped, as *it is* this day: behold, we *are* before thee in our trespasses: for we cannot stand before thee because of this.

CHAPTER 10
Putting Away Foreign Wives and Children

1 Now when Ezra had prayed, and when he had confessed, weeping and casting himself down before the house of God, there assembled unto him out of Israel a very great congregation of men and women and children: for the people wept very sore.

2 And Shechaniah the son of Jehiel, *one* of the sons of Elam, answered and said unto Ezra, We have trespassed against our God, and have taken strange wives of the people of the land: yet now there is hope in Israel concerning this thing.

3 Now therefore let us make a covenant with our God to put away all the wives, and such as are born of them, according to the counsel of my lord, and of those that tremble at the commandment of our God; and let it be done according to the law.

4 Arise; for *this* matter *belongeth* unto thee: we also *will be* with thee: be of good courage, and do *it*.

5 Then arose Ezra, and made the chief priests, the Levites, and all Israel, to swear that they should do according to this word. And they sware.

6 Then Ezra rose up from before the house of God, and went into the chamber of Johanan the son of Eliashib: and *when* he came thither, he did eat no bread, nor drink water: for he mourned because of the transgression of them that had been carried away.

7 And they made proclamation throughout Judah and Jerusalem unto all the children of the captivity, that they should gather themselves together unto Jerusalem;

Cross references (center column):

5 Ex. 9:29, 33
6 2Chr. 28:9; Ps. 38:4; Dan. 9:7, 8; Rev. 18:5
7 Deut. 28:36, 64; Neh. 9:30; Ps. 106:6; Dan. 9:5, 6, 7, 8
8 Ps. 13:3; 34:5; Isa. 22:23
9 Ezra 7:28; Neh. 9:36; Ps. 136:23; Isa. 5:2
11 2Kgs. 21:16; Ezra 6:21
12 Ex. 23:32; 34:16; Deut. 7:3; 23:6; Prov. 13:22; 20:7
13 Ps. 103:10
14 Deut. 9:8; Ezra 9:2; Neh. 13:23, 27; John 5:14; 2Pet. 2:20, 21
15 Neh. 9:33; Ps. 130:3; Dan. 9:14; Rom. 3:19; 1Cor. 15:17
1 2Chr. 20:9; Dan. 9:20
2 Neh. 13:27
3 Deut. 7:2, 3; 2Chr. 34:31; Ezra 9:4
4 1Chr. 28:10
5 Neh. 5:12
6 Deut. 9:18

9:5 I fell upon my knees. Ezra's prayer of national repentance resulted from the deterioration of the purity of God's earthly chosen people through intermarriage with their heathen neighbors (v. 1). Revival and drastic action were necessary or the chosen race would have become diffused and diluted through the centuries, eventually disappearing altogether. Therefore, severe measures were enforced to rescue the people from encroaching idolatry and racial absorption.

8 And that whosoever would not come within three days, according to the counsel of the princes and the elders, all his substance should be forfeited, and himself separated from the congregation of those that had been carried away.

9 Then all the men of Judah and Benjamin gathered themselves together unto Jerusalem within three days. It *was* the ninth month, on the twentieth *day* of the month; and all the people sat in the street of the house of God, trembling because of *this* matter, and for the great rain.

10 And Ezra the priest stood up, and said unto them, Ye have transgressed, and have taken strange wives, to increase the trespass of Israel.

11 Now therefore make confession unto the LORD God of your fathers, and do his pleasure: and separate yourselves from the people of the land, and from the strange wives.

12 Then all the congregation answered and said with a loud voice, As thou hast said, so must we do.

13 But the people *are* many, and *it is* a time of much rain, and we are not able to stand without, neither *is this* a work of one day or two: for we are many that have transgressed in this thing.

14 Let now our rulers of all the congregation stand, and let all them which have taken strange wives in our cities come at appointed times, and with them the elders of every city, and the judges thereof, until the fierce wrath of our God for this matter be turned from us.

15 Only Jonathan the son of Asahel and Jahaziah the son of Tikvah were employed about this *matter*: and Meshullam and Shabbethai the Levite helped them.

16 And the children of the captivity did so. And Ezra the priest, *with* certain chief of the fathers, after the house of their fathers, and all of them by *their* names, were separated, and sat down in the first day of the tenth month to examine the matter.

17 And they made an end with all the men that had taken strange wives by the first day of the first month.

The List of Men with Foreign Wives

18 And among the sons of the priests there were found that had taken strange wives: *namely*, of the sons of Jeshua the son of Jozadak, and his brethren; Maaseiah, and Eliezer, and Jarib, and Gedaliah.

19 And they gave their hands that they would put away their wives; and *being* guilty, *they offered* a ram of the flock for their trespass.

20 And of the sons of Immer; Hanani, and Zebadiah.

21 And of the sons of Harim; Maaseiah, and Elijah, and Shemaiah, and Jehiel, and Uzziah.

22 And of the sons of Pashur; Elioenai, Maaseiah, Ishmael, Nethaneel, Jozabad, and Elasah.

23 Also of the Levites; Jozabad, and Shimei, and Kelaiah, (the same *is* Kelita,) Pethahiah, Judah, and Eliezer.

24 Of the singers also; Eliashib: and of the porters; Shallum, and Telem, and Uri.

25 Moreover of Israel: of the sons of Parosh; Ramiah, and Jeziah, and Malchiah, and Miamin, and Eleazar, and Malchijah, and Benaiah.

26 And of the sons of Elam; Mattaniah, Zechariah, and Jehiel, and Abdi, and Jeremoth, and Eliah.

27 And of the sons of Zattu; Elioenai, Eliashib, Mattaniah, and Jeremoth, and Zabad, and Aziza.

28 Of the sons also of Bebai; Jehohanan, Hananiah, Zabbai, *and* Athlai.

29 And of the sons of Bani; Meshullam, Malluch, and Adaiah, Jashub, and Sheal, and Ramoth.

30 And of the sons of Pahath-moab; Adna, and Chelal, Benaiah, Maaseiah, Mattaniah, Bezaleel, and Binnui, and Manasseh.

31 And *of* the sons of Harim; Eliezer, Ishijah, Malchiah, Shemaiah, Shimeon,

32 Benjamin, Malluch, *and* Shemariah.

33 Of the sons of Hashum; Mattenai, Mattathah, Zabad, Eliphelet, Jeremai, Manasseh, *and* Shimei.

34 Of the sons of Bani; Maadai, Amram, and Uel,

35 Benaiah, Bedeiah, Chelluh,

36 Vaniah, Meremoth, Eliashib,

37 Mattaniah, Mattenai, and Jaasau,

38 And Bani, and Binnui, Shimei,

39 And Shelemiah, and Nathan, and Adaiah,

40 Machnadebai, Shashai, Sharai,

41 Azareel, and Shelemiah, Shemariah,

42 Shallum, Amariah, *and* Joseph.

43 Of the sons of Nebo; Jeiel, Mattithiah, Zabad, Zebina, Jadau, and Joel, Benaiah.

44 All these had taken strange wives: and *some* of them had wives by whom they had children.

Cross references

9 1Sam. 12:18.

11 Josh. 7:19; Ezra 10:3; Prov. 28:13.

14 2Chr. 30:8.

19 Lev. 6:4, 6; 2Kgs. 10:15; 1Chr. 29:24; 2Chr. 30:8.

Nehemiah

The books of Ezra and Nehemiah were originally one volume, but Jerome (ca. A.D. 342–420) split them into 1 and 2 Ezra in the Vulgate, a Latin translation of the Bible. Not long afterward, the second portion was named "Nehemiah" after its principal character. The name "Nehemiah" means "Jehovah comforts."

Nehemiah, a descendent of those Jews who went into the Babylonian Captivity (606–536 B.C.) rose to the high office of cupbearer to the Persian king. His responsibility of testing whatever the king ate, in case it was poisoned, made him a close companion and advisor to the ruler.

Author	Nehemiah and Ezra
Date	445–430 B.C.
Key Truth	Rebuilding Jerusalem
Historic Time	Persian Empire
Key Verse	Nehemiah 13:31 . . . Remember me, O my God, for good.

In the twentieth year of the reign of Artaxerxes I, Nehemiah received royal permission to return to Jerusalem to rebuild the city's ruined walls. He held the office of governor or "Tirshatha." Within fifty-two days and in the face of opposition from other cities and peoples and discouragement from within, the walls were reconstructed and the twelve gates completed.

Ezra, the priest and scribe, worked closely with Nehemiah, the governor and political ruler. Social, economic, and religious abuses were corrected. After twelve years, during which civil and religious order were restored in Jerusalem, Nehemiah returned to Babylon. However, during Nehemiah's absence, flagrant moral and religious abuses arose again in Jerusalem. Nehemiah hastened back to the city and acted swiftly and sternly to remedy the distressing situation.

Nehemiah faced ridicule, anger, conspiracy, discouragement, usury, intimidation, and neglect of spiritual responsibilities by the leadership and the people. But through prayer and perseverance, preparedness and strong leadership, he prevailed.

One specific prophecy (2:20) indicates that God would give success to the wall reconstruction project (6:15–16). The twelve gates of Jerusalem (chap. 3) may foreshadow the twelve gates of the New Jerusalem (Rev. 21).

Fourteen predictions, including announcements and foreshadowing sacrifices and types, involve 45 of 406 verses, or 11 percent of the book. Like Ezra, institutional modes of worship at the temple, including sacrifices, offerings, and feasts, foreshadow the redemptive work of Christ.

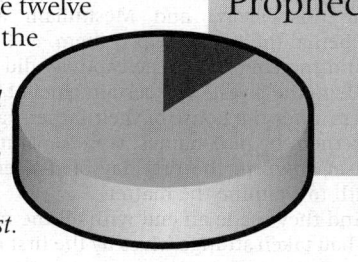

11%
Prophecy

625 B.C.	600 B.C.	575 B.C.	550 B.C.	525 B.C.	500 B.C.	475 B.C.	450 B.C.	425 B.C.

627 Jeremiah begins prophetic ministry

586 Nebuchadnezzar conquers Judah

538-515 Return of Jews under Zerubbabel

538 Cyrus of Persia decrees the return of the Jews

535 Temple reconstruction begins

515 Second temple completed

521 Darius I becomes king of Persia

520 Haggai and Zechariah begin prophetic ministry

486 Ahasuerus becomes king of Persia

473 Mordecai establishes the Feast of Purim

478 Esther becomes queen of Persia

464 Artaxerxes I becomes king of Persia

457 Ezra goes to Jerusalem

444 Walls of Jerusalem built

445 Nehemiah goes to Jerusalem

445-424 Book of Nehemiah

CHAPTER 1
Nehemiah Prays for Jerusalem

1 The words of Nehemiah the son of Hachaliah. And it came to pass in the month Chisleu, in the twentieth year, as I was in Shushan the palace,

2 That Hanani, one of my brethren, came, he and *certain* men of Judah; and I asked them concerning the Jews that had escaped, which were left of the captivity, and concerning Jerusalem.

3 And they said unto me, The remnant that are left of the captivity there in the province *are* in great affliction and reproach: the wall of Jerusalem also *is* broken down, and the gates thereof are burned with fire.

4 And it came to pass, when I heard these words, that I sat down and wept, and mourned *certain* days, and fasted, and prayed before the God of heaven,

5 And said, I beseech thee, O LORD God of heaven, the great and terrible God, that keepeth covenant and mercy for them that love him and observe his commandments:

6 Let thine ear now be attentive, and thine eyes open, that thou mayest hear the prayer of thy servant, which I pray before thee now, day and night, for the children of Israel thy servants, and confess the sins of the children of Israel, which we have sinned against thee: both I and my father's house have sinned.

7 We have dealt very corruptly against thee, and have not kept the commandments, nor the statutes, nor the judgments, which thou commandedst thy servant Moses.

8 Remember, I beseech thee, the word that thou commandedst thy servant Moses, saying, *If* ye transgress, I will scatter you abroad among the nations:

9 But *if* ye turn unto me, and keep my commandments, and do them; though there were of you cast out unto the uttermost part of the heaven, *yet* will I gather them from thence, and will bring them unto the place that I have chosen to set my name there.

10 Now these *are* thy servants and thy people, whom thou hast redeemed by thy great power, and by thy strong hand.

11 O Lord, I beseech thee, let now thine ear be attentive to the prayer of thy servant, and to the prayer of thy servants, who desire to fear thy name: and prosper, I pray thee, thy servant this day, and grant him mercy in the sight of this man. For I was the king's cupbearer.

CHAPTER 2
Nehemiah Goes to Jerusalem

1 And it came to pass in the month Nisan, in the twentieth year of Artaxerxes the king, *that* wine *was* before him: and I took up the wine, and gave *it* unto the king. Now I had not been *beforetime* sad in his presence.

2 Wherefore the king said unto me, Why *is* thy countenance sad, seeing thou *art* not sick? this *is* nothing *else* but sorrow of heart. Then I was very sore afraid,

3 And said unto the king, Let the king live for ever: why should not my countenance be sad, when the city, the place of my fathers' sepulchres, *lieth* waste, and the gates thereof are consumed with fire?

4 Then the king said unto me, For what dost thou make request? So I prayed to the God of heaven.

5 And I said unto the king, If it please the king, and if thy servant have found favour in thy sight, that thou wouldest send me unto Judah, unto the city of my fathers' sepulchres, that I may build it.

Cross References

1 Neh. 10:1

3 2Kgs. 25:10; Neh. 2:17

5 Ex. 20:6; Dan. 9:4

6 1Kgs. 8:28, 29; 2Chr. 6:40; Dan. 9:17, 18, 20

7 Deut. 28:15; Ps. 106:6; Dan. 9:5

8 Lev. 26:33; Deut. 4:25-27; 28:64

9 Lev. 26:39-45; Deut. 4:29-31; 30:2, 4

10 Deut. 9:29; Dan. 9:15

11 Neh. 1:6; 2:1; Isa. 26:8; Heb. 13:18

1 Ezra 7:1; Neh. 1:11

2 Prov. 15:13

3 1Kgs. 1:31; Neh. 1:3; Dan. 2:4; 5:10; 6:6, 21

1:3 the wall of Jerusalem also is broken down. An unwalled city in those days was very vulnerable to marauders, thieves, and military attack. Since 586 B.C., a period of 140 years, the walls had been in disrepair. Although the temple had been built eighty years earlier, attempts to repair the walls had been futile.

1:4 I sat down and wept . . . and prayed. Nehemiah was a man of prayer, courage, perseverance and deep dedication to God. Prayer was his first response to a need (see 2:4; 4:4, 9; 6:9, 14). His example and encouragement led to the great prayer of the Levite spiritual leaders of the nation (chap. 9).

1:11 I was the king's cupbearer. Hearing of the conditions in Jerusalem, realizing he was an official in the Persian government, and seeking the will of God, Nehemiah knows God can answer his prayer, and that He can use him as part of the answer.

2:1 I took up the wine, and gave it unto the king. Usually pleasant and positive in the king's presence (that was expected), Nehemiah was obviously saddened by the conditions in Jerusalem. Four months had passed since his brother Hanani had informed him (Neh. 1:2). Boldly, Nehemiah asked for a special commission, with full authority and necessary resources, to rebuild much of Jerusalem. Artaxerxes immediately approved the request and provided a large military escort (v. 9).

6 And the king said unto me, (the queen also sitting by him,) For how long shall thy journey be? and when wilt thou return? So it pleased the king to send me; and I set him a time.
7 Moreover I said unto the king, If it please the king, let letters be given to me to the governors beyond the river, that they may convey me over till I come into Judah;
8 And a letter unto Asaph the keeper of the king's forest, that he may give me timber to make beams for the gates of the palace which *appertained* to the house, and for the wall of the city, and for the house that I shall enter into. And the king granted me, according to the good hand of my God upon me.
9 Then I came to the governors beyond the river, and gave them the king's letters. Now the king had sent captains of the army and horsemen with me.
10 When Sanballat the Horonite, and Tobiah the servant, the Ammonite, heard *of it,* it grieved them exceedingly that there was come a man to seek the welfare of the children of Israel.
11 So I came to Jerusalem, and was there three days.
12 And I arose in the night, I and some few men with me; neither told I *any* man what my God had put in my heart to do at Jerusalem: neither *was there any* beast with me, save the beast that I rode upon.
13 And I went out by night by the gate of the valley, even before the dragon well, and to the dung port, and viewed the walls of Jerusalem, which were broken down, and the gates thereof were consumed with fire.
14 Then I went on to the gate of the fountain, and to the king's pool: but *there was* no

place for the beast *that was* under me to pass.
15 Then went I up in the night by the brook, and viewed the wall, and turned back, and entered by the gate of the valley, and *so* returned.
16 And the rulers knew not whither I went, or what I did; neither had I as yet told *it* to the Jews, nor to the priests, nor to the nobles, nor to the rulers, nor to the rest that did the work.
17 Then said I unto them, Ye see the distress that we *are* in, how Jerusalem *lieth* waste, and the gates thereof are burned with fire: come, and let us build up the wall of Jerusalem, that we be no more a reproach.
18 Then I told them of the hand of my God which was good upon me; as also the king's words that he had spoken unto me. And they said, Let us rise up and build. So they strengthened their hands for *this* good *work.*
19 But when Sanballat the Horonite, and Tobiah the servant, the Ammonite, and Geshem the Arabian, heard *it,* they laughed us to scorn, and despised us, and said, What *is* this thing that ye do? will ye rebel against the king?
20 Then answered I them, and said unto them, The God of heaven, he will prosper us; therefore we his servants will arise and build: but ye have no portion, nor right, nor memorial, in Jerusalem.

CHAPTER 3
Rebuilding the Wall

1 Then Eliashib the high priest rose up with his brethren the priests, and they builded the sheep gate; they sanctified it, and set up the doors of it; even unto the

Cross references (center column):
6 Neh. 5:14; 13:6
8 Ezra 5:5; 7:6, 9, 28; Neh. 2:18; 3:7
11 Ezra 8:32
13 2Chr. 26:9; Neh. 1:3; 2:17; 3:13
14 Neh. 3:15
15 2Sam. 15:23; Jer. 31:40
17 Neh. 1:3; Ps. 44:13; 79:4; Ezek. 24:9; Ezek. 5:14, 15; 22:4
18 2Sam. 2:7; Neh. 2:8
19 Neh. 6:6; Ps. 44:13; 79:4; 80:6
20 Ezra 4:3
1 Neh. 12:10, 39; Jer. 31:38; Zech. 14:10; John 5:2

2:6 the queen. Some commentators think this may have been Queen Esther.

2:11 I came to Jerusalem. During his first three days in Jerusalem, Nehemiah personally and privately surveyed the situation without confiding in the local priests, nobles, or rulers. Then he gathered the leaders and announced his plan, inspiring them to rise up and build. As with any divinely endorsed enterprise, opposition was encountered. The critics used sarcastic laughter, public scorn, and despicable allegations, accusing Nehemiah of planning to foment rebellion.

2:20 he will prosper us. This prediction, directed toward those who ridiculed Nehemiah's program to rebuild the walls of Jerusalem, was literally fulfilled (Neh. 6:15–16). The wall was finished in the record time of fifty-two days

of organized, guarded labor by dedicated Jews.

3:1 sheep gate. Twelve gates were completed with doors during the 52-day construction program. The names are recorded by Nehemiah and provide an interesting study. They were 1) the sheep gate, 2) the fish gate, 3) the old gate, 4) the valley gate, 5) the dung gate, 6) the fountain gate, 7) the water gate, 8) the horse gate, 9) the east gate, 10) the Miphkad ("appointment") gate. Two more, the prison gate and the gate of Ephraim, are mentioned in 12:39. In the Bible, twelve is sometimes used as the number of divine government, i.e., twelve tribes, twelve apostles, twelve gates, and so forth. Compare the twelve gates of the millennial city of Jerusalem in Ezekiel 48:30–35 and the twelve gates of the New Jerusalem in Rev. 21:10–13.

tower of Meah they sanctified it, unto the tower of Hananeel.

2 And next unto him builded the men of Jericho. And next to them builded Zaccur the son of Imri.

3 But the fish gate did the sons of Hassenaah build, who *also* laid the beams thereof, and set up the doors thereof, the locks thereof, and the bars thereof.

4 And next unto them repaired Meremoth the son of Urijah, the son of Koz. And next unto them repaired Meshullam the son of Berechiah, the son of Meshezabeel. And next unto them repaired Zadok the son of Baana.

5 And next unto them the Tekoites repaired; but their nobles put not their necks to the work of their Lord.

6 Moreover the old gate repaired Jehoiada the son of Paseah, and Meshullam the son of Besodeiah; they laid the beams thereof, and set up the doors thereof, and the locks thereof, and the bars thereof.

7 And next unto them repaired Melatiah the Gibeonite, and Jadon the Meronothite, the men of Gibeon, and of Mizpah, unto the throne of the governor on this side the river.

8 Next unto him repaired Uzziel the son of Harhaiah, of the goldsmiths. Next unto him also repaired Hananiah the son of *one of* the apothecaries, and they fortified Jerusalem unto the broad wall.

9 And next unto them repaired Rephaiah the son of Hur, the ruler of the half part of Jerusalem.

10 And next unto them repaired Jedaiah the son of Harumaph, even over against his house. And next unto him repaired Hattush the son of Hashabniah.

11 Malchijah the son of Harim, and Hashub the son of Pahath-moab, repaired the other piece, and the tower of the furnaces.

12 And next unto him repaired Shallum the son of Halohesh, the ruler of the half part of Jerusalem, he and his daughters.

13 The valley gate repaired Hanun, and the inhabitants of Zanoah; they built it, and set up the doors thereof, the locks thereof, and the bars thereof, and a thousand cubits on the wall unto the dung gate.

14 But the dung gate repaired Malchiah the son of Rechab, the ruler of part of Beth-haccerem; he built it, and set up the doors thereof, the locks thereof, and the bars thereof.

15 But the gate of the fountain repaired Shallun the son of Col-hozeh, the ruler of part of Mizpah; he built it, and covered it,

and set up the doors thereof, the locks thereof, and the bars thereof, and the wall of the pool of Siloah by the king's garden, and unto the stairs that go down from the city of David.

16 After him repaired Nehemiah the son of Azbuk, the ruler of the half part of Beth-zur, unto *the place* over against the sepulchres of David, and to the pool that was made, and unto the house of the mighty.

17 After him repaired the Levites, Rehum the son of Bani. Next unto him repaired Hashabiah, the ruler of the half part of Keilah, in his part.

18 After him repaired their brethren, Bavai the son of Henadad, the ruler of the half part of Keilah.

19 And next to him repaired Ezer the son of Jeshua, the ruler of Mizpah, another piece over against the going up to the armoury at the turning *of the wall*.

20 After him Baruch the son of Zabbai earnestly repaired the other piece, from the turning *of the wall* unto the door of the house of Eliashib the high priest.

21 After him repaired Meremoth the son of Urijah the son of Koz another piece, from the door of the house of Eliashib even to the end of the house of Eliashib.

22 And after him repaired the priests, the men of the plain.

23 After him repaired Benjamin and Hashub over against their house. After him repaired Azariah the son of Maaseiah the son of Ananiah by his house.

24 After him repaired Binnui the son of Henadad another piece, from the house of Azariah unto the turning *of the wall*, even unto the corner.

25 Palal the son of Uzai, over against the turning *of the wall*, and the tower which lieth out from the king's high house, that *was* by the court of the prison. After him Pedaiah the son of Parosh.

26 Moreover the Nethinims dwelt in Ophel, unto *the place* over against the water gate toward the east, and the tower that lieth out.

27 After them the Tekoites repaired another piece, over against the great tower that lieth out, even unto the wall of Ophel.

28 From above the horse gate repaired the priests, every one over against his house.

29 After them repaired Zadok the son of Immer over against his house. After him repaired also Shemaiah the son of Shechaniah, the keeper of the east gate.

30 After him repaired Hananiah the son of Shelemiah, and Hanun the sixth son of

Center column cross-references:

2 Ezra 2:34

3 2Chr. 33:14; Neh. 6:1; 7:1; 12:39; Zeph. 1:10

5 Judg. 5:23

6 Neh. 12:39

7 Neh. 2:8

8 Neh. 12:38

11 Neh. 12:38

13 Neh. 2:13

15 Neh. 2:14; John 9:7

16 2Kgs. 20:20; Isa. 22:11

19 2Chr. 26:9

24 Neh. 3:19

25 Jer. 32:2; 33:1; 37:21

26 2Chr. 27:3; Ezra 2:43; Neh. 8:1, 3; 11:21; 12:37

28 2Kgs. 11:16; 2Chr. 23:15; Jer. 31:40

Zalaph, another piece. After him repaired Meshullam the son of Berechiah over against his chamber.

31 After him repaired Malchiah the goldsmith's son unto the place of the Nethinims, and of the merchants, over against the gate Miphkad, and to the going up of the corner.

32 And between the going up of the corner unto the sheep gate repaired the goldsmiths and the merchants.

CHAPTER 4
The Workers Guard the Wall

1 But it came to pass, that when Sanballat heard that we builded the wall, he was wroth, and took great indignation, and mocked the Jews.

2 And he spake before his brethren and the army of Samaria, and said, What do these feeble Jews? will they fortify themselves? will they sacrifice? will they make an end in a day? will they revive the stones out of the heaps of the rubbish which are burned?

3 Now Tobiah the Ammonite *was* by him, and he said, Even that which they build, if a fox go up, he shall even break down their stone wall.

4 Hear, O our God; for we are despised: and turn their reproach upon their own head, and give them for a prey in the land of captivity:

5 And cover not their iniquity, and let not their sin be blotted out from before thee: for they have provoked *thee* to anger before the builders.

6 So built we the wall; and all the wall was joined together unto the half thereof: for the people had a mind to work.

7 But it came to pass, *that* when Sanballat, and Tobiah, and the Arabians, and the Ammonites, and the Ashdodites, heard that the walls of Jerusalem were made up, *and* that the breaches began to be stopped, then they were very wroth,

8 And conspired all of them together to come *and* to fight against Jerusalem, and to hinder it.

9 Nevertheless we made our prayer unto our God, and set a watch against them day and night, because of them.

10 And Judah said, The strength of the bearers of burdens is decayed, and *there is* much rubbish; so that we are not able to build the wall.

11 And our adversaries said, They shall not know, neither see, till we come in the midst among them, and slay them, and cause the work to cease.

12 And it came to pass, that when the Jews which dwelt by them came, they said unto us ten times, From all places whence ye

1 Neh. 2:10, 19
3 Neh. 2:10, 19
4 Ps. 79:12; 123:3, 4; Prov. 3:34
5 Ps. 69:27, 28; 109:14, 15; Jer. 18:23
7 Neh. 4:1
8 Ps. 83:3-5
9 Ps. 50:15

4:1 Sanballat. One of the three principle leaders of the opposition to Nehemiah's goals, Sanballat was an appointed official of the Persian government who held some military or civil command in Samaria. His two companions in this hostile opposition were Tobiah the Ammonite and Geshem (Gashmu) the Arabian (2:19; 4:7; 6:1, 6).

4:2 Samaria. Once the capital of the Northern Kingdom, the name evolved to designate the mixed peoples, whom the king of Assyria transported from various conquered lands to settle, intermarry, and mingle with the Israelites that were not deported (see 2 Kgs. 17:1–6; 24–41). By 445 B.C., nearly 300 years later, the Samaritans had developed into a cultural and ethnic group themselves. Through the centuries they drifted from idolatry to worshiping the Lord with their own brand of religion, an adaptation of Judaism. In Christ's time "the Jews [had] no dealings with the Samaritans" (John 4:9), but Jesus reached out to them and included them in His global commission (John 4:1–42; Acts 1:8).

4:2–3 What do these feeble Jews? Opposition by ridicule was a psychological ploy, calculated to bolster the attitude among the Samaritans that the project was

doomed to failure, as well as to mock the Jews, dissuading them from the ambitious undertaking. Fervent prayer and dedicated work overcame this verbal attack (vv. 4–6).

4:6 the people had a mind to work. Undeterred by the ridicule, the people maintained a positive mental and spiritual attitude about their project and rebuilt half the wall.

4:7–8 Attempts to forcibly stop the work by anger, plots, and conspiracies did not succeed. The long-time enemies of Israel who had settled in the land—the Arabians, Ammonites, Ashdodites (Philistines) and Moabites (13:1, 23)—allied with the Samaritan leader Sanballat, who bitterly opposed the Jews' every effort toward national re-establishment.

4:10–23 Opposition resulted in discouragement among the wall builders and their families. The enemies' strategies were partially successful. Nehemiah and his faithful coworkers and the military detachment organized the people to resist a secret planned attack (v. 11). Nehemiah challenged the people saying, "The LORD which is great and terrible . . . and fight" (v. 14). Seeing that the Jews were prepared to fight, the attack was canceled.

shall return unto us *they will be upon you.*
13 Therefore set I in the lower places behind the wall, *and* on the higher places, I even set the people after their families with their swords, their spears, and their bows.
14 And I looked, and rose up, and said unto the nobles, and to the rulers, and to the rest of the people, Be not ye afraid of them: remember the Lord, *which is* great and terrible, and fight for your brethren, your sons, and your daughters, your wives, and your houses.
15 And it came to pass, when our enemies heard that it was known unto us, and God had brought their counsel to nought, that we returned all of us to the wall, every one unto his work.
16 And it came to pass from that time forth, *that* the half of my servants wrought in the work, and the other half of them held both the spears, the shields, and the bows, and the habergeons; and the rulers *were* behind all the house of Judah.
17 They which builded on the wall, and they that bare burdens, with those that laded, *every one* with one of his hands wrought in the work, and with the other *hand* held a weapon.
18 For the builders, every one had his sword girded by his side, and *so* builded. And he that sounded the trumpet *was* by me.
19 And I said unto the nobles, and to the rulers, and to the rest of the people, The work *is* great and large, and we are separated upon the wall, one far from another.
20 In what place *therefore* ye hear the sound of the trumpet, resort ye thither unto us: our God shall fight for us.
21 So we laboured in the work: and half of them held the spears from the rising of the morning till the stars appeared.
22 Likewise at the same time said I unto the people, Let every one with his servant lodge within Jerusalem, that in the night they may be a guard to us, and labour on the day.
23 So neither I, nor my brethren, nor my servants, nor the men of the guard which followed me, none of us put off our clothes, *saving that* every one put them off for washing.

14 Num. 14:9; Deut. 1:29; 10:17; 2Sam. 10:12

15 Job 5:12

20 Ex. 14:14, 25; Deut. 1:30; 3:22; 20:4; Josh. 23:10

23 Judg. 5:11

1 Lev. 25:35-37; Deut. 15:7; Isa. 5:7

5 Ex. 21:7; Lev. 25:39; Isa. 58:7

7 Ex. 22:25; Lev. 25:36; Ezek. 22:12

8 Lev. 25:48

9 Lev. 25:36; 2Sam. 12:14; Rom. 2:24; 1Pet. 2:12

CHAPTER 5
Abolishing Interest Payments

1 And there was a great cry of the people and of their wives against their brethren the Jews.
2 For there were that said, We, our sons, and our daughters, *are* many: therefore we take up corn *for them,* that we may eat, and live.
3 *Some* also there were that said, We have mortgaged our lands, vineyards, and houses, that we might buy corn, because of the dearth.
4 There were also that said, We have borrowed money for the king's tribute, *and that upon* our lands and vineyards.
5 Yet now our flesh *is* as the flesh of our brethren, our children as their children: and, lo, we bring into bondage our sons and our daughters to be servants, and *some* of our daughters are brought unto bondage *already:* neither *is it* in our power *to redeem them;* for other men have our lands and vineyards.
6 And I was very angry when I heard their cry and these words.
7 Then I consulted with myself, and I rebuked the nobles, and the rulers, and said unto them, Ye exact usury, every one of his brother. And I set a great assembly against them.
8 And I said unto them, We after our ability have redeemed our brethren the Jews, which were sold unto the heathen; and will ye even sell your brethren? or shall they be sold unto us? Then held they their peace, and found nothing *to answer.*
9 Also I said, It *is* not good that ye do: ought ye not to walk in the fear of our God because of the reproach of the heathen our enemies?
10 I likewise, *and* my brethren, and my servants, might exact of them money and corn: I pray you, let us leave off this usury.
11 Restore, I pray you, to them, even this day, their lands, their vineyards, their oliveyards, and their houses, also the hundredth *part* of the money, and of the corn, the wine, and the oil, that ye exact of them.

5:1 a great cry. Opposition by selfish greed came not from other peoples, but among the Jews themselves, who were divided between the rich and poor. The wealthy were practically enslaving the farmers and merchants by charging high interest and exacting other fees. Nehemiah's remedy was full restitution, demonstrated by his personal example of unselfish service, never taking any salary or allowances from the people for himself or his entourage during his entire term as Tirshatha (Pers. from *Tarsta,* "his excellency"), a term used for the governor's office.

12 Then said they, We will restore *them*, and will require nothing of them; so will we do as thou sayest. Then I called the priests, and took an oath of them, that they should do according to this promise.

13 Also I shook my lap, and said, So God shake out every man from his house, and from his labour, that performeth not this promise, even thus be he shaken out, and emptied. And all the congregation said, Amen, and praised the LORD. And the people did according to this promise.

14 Moreover from the time that I was appointed to be their governor in the land of Judah, from the twentieth year even unto the two and thirtieth year of Artaxerxes the king, *that is*, twelve years, I and my brethren have not eaten the bread of the governor.

15 But the former governors that *had been* before me were chargeable unto the people, and had taken of them bread and wine, beside forty shekels of silver; yea, even their servants bare rule over the people: but so did not I, because of the fear of God.

16 Yea, also I continued in the work of this wall, neither bought we any land: and all my servants *were* gathered thither unto the work.

17 Moreover *there were* at my table an hundred and fifty of the Jews and rulers, beside those that came unto us from among the heathen that *are* about us.

18 Now *that* which was prepared *for me* daily *was* one ox *and* six choice sheep; also fowls were prepared for me, and once in ten days store of all sorts of wine: yet for all this required not I the bread of the governor, because the bondage was heavy upon this people.

19 Think upon me, my God, for good, *according* to all that I have done for this people.

CHAPTER 6
Plots against Nehemiah

1 Now it came to pass, when Sanballat, and Tobiah, and Geshem the Arabian, and the rest of our enemies, heard that I had builded the wall, and *that* there was no breach left therein; (though at that time I had not set up the doors upon the gates;)

2 That Sanballat and Geshem sent unto me, saying, Come, let us meet together in *some one of* the villages in the plain of Ono. But they thought to do me mischief.

3 And I sent messengers unto them, saying, I *am* doing a great work, so that I cannot come down: why should the work cease, whilst I leave it, and come down to you?

4 Yet they sent unto me four times after this sort; and I answered them after the same manner.

5 Then sent Sanballat his servant unto me in like manner the fifth time with an open letter in his hand;

6 Wherein *was* written, It is reported among the heathen, and Gashmu saith *it, that* thou and the Jews think to rebel: for which cause thou buildest the wall, that thou mayest be their king, according to these words.

7 And thou hast also appointed prophets to preach of thee at Jerusalem, saying, There is a king in Judah: and now shall it be reported to the king according to these words. Come now therefore, and let us take counsel together.

8 Then I sent unto him, saying, There are no such things done as thou sayest, but thou feignest them out of thine own heart.

9 For they all made us afraid, saying, Their hands shall be weakened from the work, that it be not done. Now therefore, *O God*, strengthen my hands.

10 Afterward I came unto the house of Shemaiah the son of Delaiah the son of Mehetabeel, who *was* shut up; and he said, Let us meet together in the house of God, within the temple, and let us shut the doors of the temple: for they will come to slay thee; yea, in the night will they come to slay thee.

11 And I said, Should such a man as I flee? and who *is there*, that, *being* as I *am*, would go into the temple to save his life? I will not go in.

12 And, lo, I perceived that God had not sent him; but that he pronounced this

Cross references

12 Ezra 10:5; Jer. 34:8, 9
13 2Kgs. 23:3; Matt. 10:14; Acts 13:51; 18:6
14 Neh. 13:6; 1Cor. 9:4, 15
15 Neh. 5:9; 2Cor. 11:9; 12:13
17 2Sam. 9:7; 1Kgs. 18:19
18 1Kgs. 4:22; Neh. 5:14, 15
19 Neh. 13:22
1 Neh. 2:10, 19; 3:1, 3; 4:1, 7; 6:6
2 1Chr. 8:12; Neh. 11:35; Ps. 37:12, 32; Prov. 26:24, 25
6 Neh. 2:19; 6:1
12 Ezek. 13:22

6:1–2 Opposition by compromise, craftiness, and slander was the last major effort by Sanballat, Tobiah, and Geshem and their cohorts to thwart the completion of the wall project. Repeatedly, they called for a meeting to discuss the matter, then accused Nehemiah of planning to rebel against Persia and become king. Finally, conspirators arranged for a man named Shemaiah to advise Nehemiah to hide himself in the temple, alleging that assassins would come to slay him. Nehemiah rebuffed this presumed prophet, who, it was learned, had been hired by Sanballat and Tobiah in an attempt to frighten the governor. Prayer, faith, courage, and work sustained the great leader in every crisis.

prophecy against me: for Tobiah and Sanballat had hired him.

13 Therefore *was* he hired, that I should be afraid, and do so, and sin, and *that* they might have *matter* for an evil report, that they might reproach me.

14 My God, think thou upon Tobiah and Sanballat according to these their works, and on the prophetess Noadiah, and the rest of the prophets, that would have put me in fear.

15 So the wall was finished in the twenty and fifth *day* of *the month* Elul, in fifty and two days.

16 And it came to pass, that when all our enemies heard *thereof*, and all the heathen that *were* about us saw *these things*, they were much cast down in their own eyes: for they perceived that this work was wrought of our God.

17 Moreover in those days the nobles of Judah sent many letters unto Tobiah, and *the letters* of Tobiah came unto them.

18 For *there were* many in Judah sworn unto him, because he *was* the son in law of Shechaniah the son of Arah; and his son Johanan had taken the daughter of Meshullam the son of Berechiah.

19 Also they reported his good deeds before me, and uttered my words to him. *And* Tobiah sent letters to put me in fear.

CHAPTER 7
Nehemiah Appoints Rulers

1 Now it came to pass, when the wall was built, and I had set up the doors, and the porters and the singers and the Levites were appointed,

2 That I gave my brother Hanani, and Hananiah the ruler of the palace, charge over Jerusalem: for he *was* a faithful man, and feared God above many.

3 And I said unto them, Let not the gates of Jerusalem be opened until the sun be hot; and while they stand by, let them shut the doors, and bar *them*: and appoint watches of the inhabitants of Jerusalem, every one in his watch, and every one *to be* over against his house.

4 Now the city *was* large and great: but the

people *were* few therein, and the houses *were* not builded.

The List of Returning Exiles

5 And my God put into mine heart to gather together the nobles, and the rulers, and the people, that they might be reckoned by genealogy. And I found a register of the genealogy of them which came up at the first, and found written therein,

6 These *are* the children of the province, that went up out of the captivity, of those that had been carried away, whom Nebuchadnezzar the king of Babylon had carried away, and came again to Jerusalem and to Judah, every one unto his city;

7 Who came with Zerubbabel, Jeshua, Nehemiah, Azariah, Raamiah, Nahamani, Mordecai, Bilshan, Mispereth, Bigvai, Nehum, Baanah. The number, *I say*, of the men of the people of Israel *was this*;

8 The children of Parosh, two thousand an hundred seventy and two.

9 The children of Shephatiah, three hundred seventy and two.

10 The children of Arah, six hundred fifty and two.

11 The children of Pahath-moab, of the children of Jeshua and Joab, two thousand and eight hundred *and* eighteen.

12 The children of Elam, a thousand two hundred fifty and four.

13 The children of Zattu, eight hundred forty and five.

14 The children of Zaccai, seven hundred and threescore.

15 The children of Binnui, six hundred forty and eight.

16 The children of Bebai, six hundred twenty and eight.

17 The children of Azgad, two thousand three hundred twenty and two.

18 The children of Adonikam, six hundred threescore and seven.

19 The children of Bigvai, two thousand threescore and seven.

20 The children of Adin, six hundred fifty and five.

21 The children of Ater of Hezekiah, ninety and eight.

14 Neh. 13:29; Ezek. 13:17

16 Neh. 2:10; 4:1, 7; 6:1; Ps. 126:2

1 Neh. 6:1

2 Ex. 18:21; Neh. 2:8

6 Ezra 2:1

7 Ezra 2:2

6:15–16 the wall was finished. For the first time in over 140 years, the city was a secure enclosure, surrounded by substantial new walls with twelve gates. To complete the project in just fifty-two days was an amazing achievement, which indeed had been wrought of our God.

6:17 letters. Tobiah launched a letter-writing campaign to gain favor with the Jews, even after all the opposition he had mounted. Since he had married into a Jewish family, some actually defended him to Nehemiah. He also sought to intimidate Nehemiah, intending to frighten him or reduce his influence (see 13:7–9).

22 The children of Hashum, three hundred twenty and eight.
23 The children of Bezai, three hundred twenty and four.
24 The children of Hariph, an hundred and twelve.
25 The children of Gibeon, ninety and five.
26 The men of Beth-lehem and Netophah, an hundred fourscore and eight.
27 The men of Anathoth, an hundred twenty and eight.
28 The men of Beth-azmaveth, forty and two.
29 The men of Kirjath-jearim, Chephirah, and Beeroth, seven hundred forty and three.
30 The men of Ramah and Geba, six hundred twenty and one.
31 The men of Michmas, an hundred and twenty and two.
32 The men of Beth-el and Ai, an hundred twenty and three.
33 The men of the other Nebo, fifty and two.
34 The children of the other Elam, a thousand two hundred fifty and four.
35 The children of Harim, three hundred and twenty.
36 The children of Jericho, three hundred forty and five.
37 The children of Lod, Hadid, and Ono, seven hundred twenty and one.
38 The children of Senaah, three thousand nine hundred and thirty.
39 The priests: the children of Jedaiah, of the house of Jeshua, nine hundred seventy and three.
40 The children of Immer, a thousand fifty and two.
41 The children of Pashur, a thousand two hundred forty and seven.
42 The children of Harim, a thousand and seventeen.
43 The Levites: the children of Jeshua, of Kadmiel, *and* of the children of Hodevah, seventy and four.
44 The singers: the children of Asaph, an hundred forty and eight.
45 The porters: the children of Shallum, the children of Ater, the children of Talmon, the children of Akkub, the children of Hatita, the children of Shobai, an hundred thirty and eight.
46 The Nethinims: the children of Ziha, the children of Hashupha, the children of Tabbaoth,
47 The children of Keros, the children of Sia, the children of Padon,

48 The children of Lebana, the children of Hagaba, the children of Shalmai,
49 The children of Hanan, the children of Giddel, the children of Gahar,
50 The children of Reaiah, the children of Rezin, the children of Nekoda,
51 The children of Gazzam, the children of Uzza, the children of Phaseah,
52 The children of Besai, the children of Meunim, the children of Nephishesim,
53 The children of Bakbuk, the children of Hakupha, the children of Harhur,
54 The children of Bazlith, the children of Mehida, the children of Harsha,
55 The children of Barkos, the children of Sisera, the children of Tamah,
56 The children of Neziah, the children of Hatipha.
57 The children of Solomon's servants: the children of Sotai, the children of Sophereth, the children of Perida,
58 The children of Jaala, the children of Darkon, the children of Giddel,
59 The children of Shephatiah, the children of Hattil, the children of Pochereth of Zebaim, the children of Amon.
60 All the Nethinims, and the children of Solomon's servants, *were* three hundred ninety and two.
61 And these *were* they which went up *also* from Tel-melah, Tel-haresha, Cherub, Addon, and Immer: but they could not shew their father's house, nor their seed, whether they *were* of Israel.
62 The children of Delaiah, the children of Tobiah, the children of Nekoda, six hundred forty and two.
63 And of the priests: the children of Habaiah, the children of Koz, the children of Barzillai, which took *one* of the daughters of Barzillai the Gileadite to wife, and was called after their name.
64 These sought their register *among* those that were reckoned by genealogy, but it was not found: therefore were they, as polluted, put from the priesthood.
65 And the Tirshatha said unto them, that they should not eat of the most holy things, till there stood *up* a priest with Urim and Thummim.
66 The whole congregation together *was* forty and two thousand three hundred and threescore,
67 Beside their manservants and their maidservants, of whom *there were* seven thousand three hundred thirty and seven: and they had two hundred forty and five singing men and singing women.

34 Neh. 7:12
39 1Chr. 24:7
40 1Chr. 24:14
41 1Chr. 9:12; 24:9
42 1Chr. 24:8
43 Ezra 2:40, *Hodaviah;* 3:9; *Judah*
61 Ezra 2:59

65 Neh. 8:9

68 Their horses, seven hundred thirty and six: their mules, two hundred forty and five:
69 *Their* camels, four hundred thirty and five: six thousand seven hundred and twenty asses.
70 And some of the chief of the fathers gave unto the work. The Tirshatha gave to the treasure a thousand drams of gold, fifty basons, five hundred and thirty priests' garments.
71 And *some* of the chief of the fathers gave to the treasure of the work twenty thousand drams of gold, and two thousand and two hundred pound of silver.
72 And *that* which the rest of the people gave *was* twenty thousand drams of gold, and two thousand pound of silver, and threescore and seven priests' garments.
73 So the priests, and the Levites, and the porters, and the singers, and *some* of the people, and the Nethinims, and all Israel, dwelt in their cities; and when the seventh month came, the children of Israel *were* in their cities.

CHAPTER 8
Ezra Reads the Law to the People

1 And all the people gathered themselves together as one man into the street that *was* before the water gate; and they spake unto Ezra the scribe to bring the book of the law of Moses, which the LORD had commanded to Israel.
2 And Ezra the priest brought the law before the congregation both of men and women, and all that could hear with understanding, upon the first day of the seventh month.
3 And he read therein before the street that *was* before the water gate from the morning until midday, before the men and the women, and those that could understand; and the ears of all the people *were attentive* unto the book of the law.

4 And Ezra the scribe stood upon a pulpit of wood, which they had made for the purpose; and beside him stood Mattithiah, and Shema, and Anaiah, and Urijah, and Hilkiah, and Maaseiah, on his right hand; and on his left hand, Pedaiah, and Mishael, and Malchiah, and Hashum, and Hashbadana, Zechariah, *and* Meshullam.
5 And Ezra opened the book in the sight of all the people; (for he was above all the people;) and when he opened it, all the people stood up:
6 And Ezra blessed the LORD, the great God. And all the people answered, Amen, Amen, with lifting up their hands: and they bowed their heads, and worshipped the LORD with *their* faces to the ground.
7 Also Jeshua, and Bani, and Sherebiah, Jamin, Akkub, Shabbethai, Hodijah, Maaseiah, Kelita, Azariah, Jozabad, Hanan, Pelaiah, and the Levites, caused the people to understand the law: and the people *stood* in their place.
8 So they read in the book in the law of God distinctly, and gave the sense, and caused *them* to understand the reading.
9 And Nehemiah, which *is* the Tirshatha, and Ezra the priest the scribe, and the Levites that taught the people, said unto all the people, This day *is* holy unto the LORD your God; mourn not, nor weep. For all the people wept, when they heard the words of the law.
10 Then he said unto them, Go your way, eat the fat, and drink the sweet, and send portions unto them for whom nothing is prepared: for *this* day *is* holy unto our Lord: neither be ye sorry; for the joy of the LORD is your strength.
11 So the Levites stilled all the people, saying, Hold your peace, for the day *is* holy; neither be ye grieved.
12 And all the people went their way to eat, and to drink, and to send portions, and to

Cross references
70 Neh. 8:9
71 Ezra 2:69
73 Ezra 3:1
1 Ezra 3:1; 7:6; Neh. 3:26
2 Lev. 23:24; Deut. 31:11, 12
5 Judg. 3:20
6 Ex. 4:31; 12:27; 2Chr. 20:18; Lam. 3:41; 1Cor. 14:16; 1Tim. 2:8
7 Lev. 10:11; Deut. 33:10; 2Chr. 17:7-9; Mal. 2:7
9 Lev. 23:24; Num. 29:1; Deut. 16:14, 15; 2Chr. 35:3; Ezra 2:63; Neh. 7:65; 8:8; 10:1; Eccl. 3:4
10 Esth. 9:19, 22; Rev. 11:10
12 Neh. 8:7, 8, 10

8:2 Ezra the priest. Since Ezra's previous activities (Ezra 7—10) occupied only about 8 months in 457 B.C., and he is not mentioned again until 445 B.C., it is thought by some that he returned to Babylon for some years. Suddenly, he is again prominent and participating with Nehemiah in reacquainting the Jews with the tenets, teachings, and ceremonies of the Law.

8:3 he read. Ezra convened a huge open-air assembly, stood upon a high platform to be seen and heard, along with other spiritual leaders, and read from the Law. With the nation now reestablished, they needed to learn the Law.

8:8 Here is a divinely inspired formula for teaching the Word of God: 1) Read distinctly, 2) Give the sense, explaining in simple, understandable terms what the Scriptures mean, and 3) Cause people to understand through illustrations, explanations and applications.

8:10 the joy of the LORD is your strength. Nehemiah declared the day when the Word of God was so powerfully presented to the people to be a special holy occasion, emphasizing that it was a time for rejoicing and mirth.

make great mirth, because they had understood the words that were declared unto them.

The Feast of Tabernacles

13 And on the second day were gathered together the chief of the fathers of all the people, the priests, and the Levites, unto Ezra the scribe, even to understand the words of the law.

14 And they found written in the law which the LORD had commanded by Moses, that the children of Israel should dwell in booths in the feast of the seventh month:

15 And that they should publish and proclaim in all their cities, and in Jerusalem, saying, Go forth unto the mount, and fetch olive branches, and pine branches, and myrtle branches, and palm branches, and branches of thick trees, to make booths, as *it is* written.

16 So the people went forth, and brought *them*, and made themselves booths, every one upon the roof of his house, and in their courts, and in the courts of the house of God, and in the street of the water gate, and in the street of the gate of Ephraim.

17 And all the congregation of them that were come again out of the captivity made booths, and sat under the booths: for since the days of Jeshua the son of Nun unto that day had not the children of Israel done so. And there was very great gladness.

18 Also day by day, from the first day unto the last day, he read in the book of the law of God. And they kept the feast seven days; and on the eighth day *was* a solemn assembly, according unto the manner.

CHAPTER 9
The People Confess Their Sins

1 Now in the twenty and fourth day of this month the children of Israel were assembled with fasting, and with sackclothes, and earth upon them.

2 And the seed of Israel separated themselves from all strangers, and stood and

confessed their sins, and the iniquities of their fathers.

3 And they stood up in their place, and read in the book of the law of the LORD their God one fourth part of the day; and *another* fourth part they confessed, and worshipped the LORD their God.

4 Then stood up upon the stairs, of the Levites, Jeshua, and Bani, Kadmiel, Shebaniah, Bunni, Sherebiah, Bani, *and* Chenani, and cried with a loud voice unto the LORD their God.

5 Then the Levites, Jeshua, and Kadmiel, Bani, Hashabniah, Sherebiah, Hodijah, Shebaniah, *and* Pethahiah, said, Stand up *and* bless the LORD your God for ever and ever: and blessed be thy glorious name, which is exalted above all blessing and praise.

6 Thou, *even* thou, *art* LORD alone; thou hast made heaven, the heaven of heavens, with all their host, the earth, and all *things* that *are* therein, the seas, and all that *is* therein, and thou preservest them all; and the host of heaven worshippeth thee.

7 Thou *art* the LORD the God, who didst choose Abram, and broughtest him forth out of Ur of the Chaldees, and gavest him the name of Abraham;

8 And foundest his heart faithful before thee, and madest a covenant with him to give the land of the Canaanites, the Hittites, the Amorites, and the Perizzites, and the Jebusites, and the Girgashites, to give *it*, *I say*, to his seed, and hast performed thy words; for thou *art* righteous:

9 And didst see the affliction of our fathers in Egypt, and heardest their cry by the Red sea;

10 And shewedst signs and wonders upon Pharaoh, and on all his servants, and on all the people of his land: for thou knewest that they dealt proudly against them. So didst thou get thee a name, as *it is* this day.

11 And thou didst divide the sea before them, so that they went through the midst of the sea on the dry land; and their persecutors thou threwest into the deeps, as a stone into the mighty waters.

Cross-references (center column)

14 Lev. 23:34, 42; Deut. 16:13

15 Lev. 23:4, 40; Deut. 16:16

16 Deut. 22:8; 2Kgs. 14:13; Neh. 12:37, 39

17 2Chr. 30:21

18 Lev. 23:36; Num. 29:35; Deut. 31:10-13

1 Josh. 7:6; 1Sam. 4:12; 2Sam. 1:2; Neh. 8:2; Job 2:12

2 Ezra 10:11; Neh. 13:3, 30

3 Neh. 8:7, 8

5 1Chr. 29:13

6 Gen. 1:1; 2:1; Ex. 20:11; Deut. 10:14; 1Kgs. 8:27; 2Kgs. 19:15, 19; Ps. 36:6; 86:10; Isa. 37:16, 20; Rev. 14:7

7 Gen. 11:31; 12:1; 17:5

8 Gen. 12:7; 15:6, 18; 17:7, 8; Josh. 23:14

9 Ex. 2:25; 3:7; 14:10

10 Ex. 9:16; 18:11; Isa. 63:12, 14; Jer. 32:20; Dan. 9:15

11 Ex. 14:21, 22, 27, 28; 15:5, 10; Ps. 78:13

8:14-18 dwell in booths. While the Feast of Tabernacles had been observed periodically for centuries, the occasion was reinstituted here as an annual event (see Ex. 23:16; 34:22; Lev. 23:33–44; Deut. 16:13). Historically, it was a memorial of experiences, when the Israelites came out of Egypt. Prophetically, it points to the kingdom age, when Israel is finally freed forever from persecution, bondage, and oppression (Zech. 14:16–21).

9:1-38 This great prayer, beginning in verse six, is one of the longest in the Bible and recounts the past experiences of Israel. It then includes honest and humble confession of the past national and personal sins. In a spirit of revival, the leaders and people "make a sure covenant, . . . write it . . . and seal it" (v. 30), rededicating themselves to God.

12 Moreover thou leddest them in the day by a cloudy pillar; and in the night by a pillar of fire, to give them light in the way wherein they should go.

13 Thou camest down also upon mount Sinai, and spakest with them from heaven, and gavest them right judgments, and true laws, good statutes and commandments:

14 And madest known unto them thy holy sabbath, and commandedst them precepts, statutes, and laws, by the hand of Moses thy servant:

15 And gavest them bread from heaven for their hunger, and broughtest forth water for them out of the rock for their thirst, and promisedst them that they should go in to possess the land which thou hadst sworn to give them.

16 But they and our fathers dealt proudly, and hardened their necks, and hearkened not to thy commandments,

17 And refused to obey, neither were mindful of thy wonders that thou didst among them; but hardened their necks, and in their rebellion appointed a captain to return to their bondage: but thou *art* a God ready to pardon, gracious and merciful, slow to anger, and of great kindness, and forsookest them not.

18 Yea, when they had made them a molten calf, and said, This *is* thy God that brought thee up out of Egypt, and had wrought great provocations;

19 Yet thou in thy manifold mercies forsookest them not in the wilderness: the pillar of the cloud departed not from them by day, to lead them in the way; neither the pillar of fire by night, to shew them light, and the way wherein they should go.

20 Thou gavest also thy good spirit to instruct them, and withheldest not thy manna from their mouth, and gavest them water for their thirst.

21 Yea, forty years didst thou sustain them in the wilderness, *so that* they lacked nothing; their clothes waxed not old, and their feet swelled not.

22 Moreover thou gavest them kingdoms and nations, and didst divide them into corners: so they possessed the land of Sihon, and the land of the king of Heshbon, and the land of Og king of Bashan.

23 Their children also multipliedst thou as the stars of heaven, and broughtest them into the land, concerning which thou hadst promised to their fathers, that they should go in to possess *it*.

24 So the children went in and possessed

the land, and thou subduedst before them the inhabitants of the land, the Canaanites, and gavest them into their hands, with their kings, and the people of the land, that they might do with them as they would.

25 And they took strong cities, and a fat land, and possessed houses full of all goods, wells digged, vineyards, and oliveyards, and fruit trees in abundance: so they did eat, and were filled, and became fat, and delighted themselves in thy great goodness.

26 Nevertheless they were disobedient, and rebelled against thee, and cast thy law behind their backs, and slew thy prophets which testified against them to turn them to thee, and they wrought great provocations.

27 Therefore thou deliveredst them into the hand of their enemies, who vexed them: and in the time of their trouble, when they cried unto thee, thou heardest *them* from heaven; and according to thy manifold mercies thou gavest them saviours, who saved them out of the hand of their enemies.

28 But after they had rest, they did evil again before thee: therefore leftest thou them in the hand of their enemies, so that they had the dominion over them: yet when they returned, and cried unto thee, thou heardest *them* from heaven; and many times didst thou deliver them according to thy mercies;

29 And testifiedst against them, that thou mightest bring them again unto thy law: yet they dealt proudly, and hearkened not unto thy commandments, but sinned against thy judgments, (which if a man do, he shall live in them;) and withdrew the shoulder, and hardened their neck, and would not hear.

30 Yet many years didst thou forbear them, and testifiedst against them by thy spirit in thy prophets: yet would they not give ear: therefore gavest thou them into the hand of the people of the lands.

31 Nevertheless for thy great mercies' sake thou didst not utterly consume them, nor forsake them; for thou *art* a gracious and merciful God.

32 Now therefore, our God, the great, the mighty, and the terrible God, who keepest covenant and mercy, let not all the trouble seem little before thee, that hath come upon us, on our kings, on our princes, and on our priests, and on our prophets, and on our fathers, and on all thy people, since the time of the kings of Assyria unto this day.

33 Howbeit thou *art* just in all that is

---

12 Ex. 13:21
13 Ex. 19:20; 20:1
14 Gen. 2:3; Ex. 20:8, 11
15 Ex. 16:14, 15; 17:6; Num. 20:9-13; Deut. 1:8
16 Deut. 31:27; 2Kgs. 17:14
17 Ex. 34:6; Num. 14:4, 18
18 Ex. 32:4
19 Ex. 13:21, 22; Ps. 106:45
20 Ex. 16:15; 17:6; Num. 11:17; Josh. 5:12; Isa. 63:11
21 Deut. 2:7; 8:4; 29:5
22 Num. 21:21-26
23 Gen. 22:17
24 Josh. 1:2-6; Ps. 44:2, 3
25 Num. 13:27; Deut. 6:11; 8:7, 8; 32:15; Neh. 9:35; Ezek. 20:6; Hos. 3:5
26 Judg. 2:11, 12; 1Kgs. 14:9; 18:4; 19:10; 2Chr. 24:20, 21; Ps. 50:17; Ezek. 20:21; Matt. 23:37; Acts 7:52
27 Judg. 2:14, 18; 3:8-11; Ps. 106:41, 42, 44
28 Judg. 3:11, 12, 30; 4:1; 5:31
29 Lev. 18:5; Gal. 3:12
30 2Kgs. 17:13; 2Chr. 36:15; Jer. 7:25
31 Jer. 4:27
32 Ex. 1:5; 34:6, 7
33 Ps. 106:6; 119:137; Dan. 9:5, 6, 8, 14

brought upon us; for thou hast done right, but we have done wickedly:

34 Neither have our kings, our princes, our priests, nor our fathers, kept thy law, nor hearkened unto thy commandments and thy testimonies, wherewith thou didst testify against them.

35 For they have not served thee in their kingdom, and in thy great goodness that thou gavest them, and in the large and fat land which thou gavest before them, neither turned they from their wicked works.

36 Behold, we *are* servants this day, and *for* the land that thou gavest unto our fathers to eat the fruit thereof and the good thereof, behold, we *are* servants in it:

37 And it yieldeth much increase unto the kings whom thou hast set over us because of our sins: also they have dominion over our bodies, and over our cattle, at their pleasure, and we *are* in great distress.

The People Make a Pledge

38 And because of all this we make a sure *covenant*, and write *it*; and our princes, Levites, *and* priests, seal *unto it*.

CHAPTER 10

1 Now those that sealed *were*, Nehemiah, the Tirshatha, the son of Hachaliah, and Zidkijah,

2 Seraiah, Azariah, Jeremiah,

3 Pashur, Amariah, Malchijah,

4 Hattush, Shebaniah, Malluch,

5 Harim, Meremoth, Obadiah,

6 Daniel, Ginnethon, Baruch,

7 Meshullam, Abijah, Mijamin,

8 Maaziah, Bilgai, Shemaiah: these *were* the priests.

9 And the Levites: both Jeshua the son of Azaniah, Binnui of the sons of Henadad, Kadmiel;

10 And their brethren, Shebaniah, Hodijah, Kelita, Pelaiah, Hanan,

11 Micha, Rehob, Hashabiah,

12 Zaccur, Sherebiah, Shebaniah,

13 Hodijah, Bani, Beninu.

14 The chief of the people; Parosh, Pahathmoab, Elam, Zatthu, Bani,

15 Bunni, Azgad, Bebai,

16 Adonijah, Bigvai, Adin,

17 Ater, Hizkijah, Azzur,

18 Hodijah, Hashum, Bezai,

19 Hariph, Anathoth, Nebai,

20 Magpiash, Meshullam, Hezir,

21 Meshezabeel, Zadok, Jaddua,

22 Pelatiah, Hanan, Anaiah,

23 Hoshea, Hananiah, Hashub,

24 Hallohesh, Pileha, Shobek,

25 Rehum, Hashabnah, Maaseiah,

26 And Ahijah, Hanan, Anan,

27 Malluch, Harim, Baanah.

28 And the rest of the people, the priests, the Levites, the porters, the singers, the Nethinims, and all they that had separated themselves from the people of the lands unto the law of God, their wives, their sons, and their daughters, every one having knowledge, and having understanding;

29 They clave to their brethren, their nobles, and entered into a curse, and into an oath, to walk in God's law, which was given by Moses the servant of God, and to observe and do all the commandments of the LORD our Lord, and his judgments and his statutes;

30 And that we would not give our daughters unto the people of the land, nor take their daughters for our sons:

31 And *if* the people of the land bring ware or any victuals on the sabbath day to sell, *that* we would not buy it of them on the sabbath, or on the holy day: and *that* we would leave the seventh year, and the exaction of every debt.

32 Also we made ordinances for us, to charge ourselves yearly with the third part of a shekel for the service of the house of our God;

33 For the shewbread, and for the continual meat offering, and for the continual burnt offering, of the sabbaths, of the new moons, for the set feasts, and for the holy *things*, and for the sin offerings to make an atonement for Israel, and *for* all the work of the house of our God.

34 And we cast the lots among the priests, the Levites, and the people, for the wood offering, to bring *it* into the house of our God, after the houses of our fathers, at times appointed year by year, to burn upon the altar of the LORD our God, as *it is* written in the law:

35 And to bring the firstfruits of our ground, and the firstfruits of all fruit of all trees, year by year, unto the house of the LORD:

36 Also the firstborn of our sons, and of our

Cross references (center column)

35 Deut. 28:47; Neh. 9:25

36 Deut. 28:48; Ezra 9:9

37 Deut. 28:33, 48, 51

38 2Kgs. 23:3; 2Chr. 29:10; 34:31; Ezra 10:3; Neh. 10:1, 29

1 Neh. 1:1; 8:9

2 Neh. 12:1-21

14 Ezra 2:3-58; Neh. 7:8-63

28 Ezra 2:36-43; 9:1; 10:11, 12, 19; Neh. 13:3

29 Deut. 29:12, 14; 2Kgs. 23:3; 2Chr. 34:31; Neh. 5:12, 13; Ps. 119:106

30 Ex. 34:16; Deut. 7:3; Ezra 9:12, 14

31 Ex. 20:10; 23:10, 11; Lev. 23:3; 25:4; Deut. 5:12; 15:1, 2; Neh. 5:12; 13:15-18

33 Lev. 24:5-9; 2Chr. 2:4

34 Lev. 6:12; Neh. 13:31; Isa. 40:16

35 Ex. 23:19; 34:26; Lev. 19:23; Num. 18:12; Deut. 26:2

36 Ex. 13:2, 12, 13; Lev. 27:26, 27; Num. 18:15, 16

10:1 those that sealed. Led by governor Nehemiah, many leaders signed and sealed the covenant, while the people promised not to forsake the house of God (see 10:39).

cattle, as *it is* written in the law, and the firstlings of our herds and of our flocks, to bring to the house of our God, unto the priests that minister in the house of our God:

37 And *that* we should bring the firstfruits of our dough, and our offerings, and the fruit of all manner of trees, of wine and of oil, unto the priests, to the chambers of the house of our God; and the tithes of our ground unto the Levites, that the same Levites might have the tithes in all the cities of our tillage.

38 And the priest the son of Aaron shall be with the Levites, when the Levites take tithes: and the Levites shall bring up the tithe of the tithes unto the house of our God, to the chambers, into the treasure house.

39 For the children of Israel and the children of Levi shall bring the offering of the corn, of the new wine, and the oil, unto the chambers, where *are* the vessels of the sanctuary, and the priests that minister, and the porters, and the singers: and we will not forsake the house of our God.

CHAPTER 11
Those in Jerusalem

1 And the rulers of the people dwelt at Jerusalem: the rest of the people also cast lots, to bring one of ten to dwell in Jerusalem the holy city, and nine parts *to dwell* in *other* cities.

2 And the people blessed all the men, that willingly offered themselves to dwell at Jerusalem.

3 Now these *are* the chief of the province that dwelt in Jerusalem: but in the cities of Judah dwelt every one in his possession in their cities, *to wit*, Israel, the priests, and the Levites, and the Nethinims, and the children of Solomon's servants.

4 And at Jerusalem dwelt *certain* of the children of Judah, and of the children of Benjamin. Of the children of Judah; Athaiah the son of Uzziah, the son of Zechariah, the son of Amariah, the son of Shephatiah, the son of Mahalaleel, of the children of Perez;

5 And Maaseiah the son of Baruch, the son of Col-hozeh, the son of Hazaiah, the son of Adaiah, the son of Joiarib, the son of Zechariah, the son of Shiloni.

6 All the sons of Perez that dwelt at Jerusalem *were* four hundred threescore and eight valiant men.

7 And these *are* the sons of Benjamin; Sallu the son of Meshullam, the son of Joed,

the son of Pedaiah, the son of Kolaiah, the son of Maaseiah, the son of Ithiel, the son of Jesaiah.

8 And after him Gabbai, Sallai, nine hundred twenty and eight.

9 And Joel the son of Zichri *was* their overseer: and Judah the son of Senuah *was* second over the city.

10 Of the priests: Jedaiah the son of Joiarib, Jachin.

11 Seraiah the son of Hilkiah, the son of Meshullam, the son of Zadok, the son of Meraioth, the son of Ahitub, *was* the ruler of the house of God.

12 And their brethren that did the work of the house *were* eight hundred twenty and two: and Adaiah the son of Jeroham, the son of Pelaliah, the son of Amzi, the son of Zechariah, the son of Pashur, the son of Malchiah,

13 And his brethren, chief of the fathers, two hundred forty and two: and Amashai the son of Azareel, the son of Ahasai, the son of Meshillemoth, the son of Immer,

14 And their brethren, mighty men of valour, an hundred twenty and eight: and their overseer *was* Zabdiel, the son of *one of* the great men.

15 Also of the Levites: Shemaiah the son of Hashub, the son of Azrikam, the son of Hashabiah, the son of Bunni;

16 And Shabbethai and Jozabad, of the chief of the Levites, *had* the oversight of the outward business of the house of God.

17 And Mattaniah the son of Micha, the son of Zabdi, the son of Asaph, *was* the principal to begin the thanksgiving in prayer: and Bakbukiah the second among his brethren, and Abda the son of Shammua, the son of Galal, the son of Jeduthun.

18 All the Levites in the holy city *were* two hundred fourscore and four.

19 Moreover the porters, Akkub, Talmon, and their brethren that kept the gates, *were* an hundred seventy and two.

20 And the residue of Israel, of the priests, *and* the Levites, *were* in all the cities of Judah, every one in his inheritance.

21 But the Nethinims dwelt in Ophel: and Ziha and Gispa *were* over the Nethinims.

22 The overseer also of the Levites at Jerusalem *was* Uzzi the son of Bani, the son of Hashabiah, the son of Mattaniah, the son of Micha. Of the sons of Asaph, the singers *were* over the business of the house of God.

23 For *it was* the king's commandment concerning them, that a certain portion should be for the singers, due for every day.

Cross references (center column):

37 Lev. 23:17; 27:30; Num. 15:19; 18:12-19, 21-24; Deut. 18:4; 26:2

38 Num. 18:26; 1Chr. 9:26; 2Chr. 31:11

39 Deut. 12:6, 11; 2Chr. 31:12; Neh. 13:10, 11, 12

1 Neh. 11:18; Matt. 4:5; 27:53

2 Judg. 5:9

3 1Chr. 9:2, 3; Ezra 2:43, 55

4 Gen. 38:29, *Pharez;* 1Chr. 9:3-9

10 1Chr. 9:10-13

16 1Chr. 26:29

18 Neh. 11:1

21 Neh. 3:26

23 Ezra 6:8, 9; 7:20-23

24 And Pethahiah the son of Meshezabeel, of the children of Zerah the son of Judah, *was* at the king's hand in all matters concerning the people.

Surrounding Towns and Villages
25 And for the villages, with their fields, *some* of the children of Judah dwelt at Kirjath-arba, and *in* the villages thereof, and at Dibon, and *in* the villages thereof, and at Jekabzeel, and *in* the villages thereof,
26 And at Jeshua, and at Moladah, and at Beth-phelet,
27 And at Hazar-shual, and at Beer-sheba, and *in* the villages thereof,
28 And at Ziklag, and at Mekonah, and in the villages thereof,
29 And at En-rimmon, and at Zareah, and at Jarmuth,
30 Zanoah, Adullam, and *in* their villages, at Lachish, and the fields thereof, at Azekah, and *in* the villages thereof. And they dwelt from Beer-sheba unto the valley of Hinnom.
31 The children also of Benjamin from Geba *dwelt* at Michmash, and Aija, and Beth-el, and *in* their villages,
32 *And* at Anathoth, Nob, Ananiah,
33 Hazor, Ramah, Gittaim,
34 Hadid, Zeboim, Neballat,
35 Lod, and Ono, the valley of craftsmen.
36 And of the Levites *were* divisions *in* Judah, *and* in Benjamin.

CHAPTER 12
The List of Priests and Levites
1 Now these *are* the priests and the Levites that went up with Zerubbabel the son of Shealtiel, and Jeshua: Seraiah, Jeremiah, Ezra,
2 Amariah, Malluch, Hattush,
3 Shechaniah, Rehum, Meremoth,
4 Iddo, Ginnetho, Abijah,
5 Miamin, Maadiah, Bilgah,
6 Shemaiah, and Joiarib, Jedaiah,
7 Sallu, Amok, Hilkiah, Jedaiah. These *were* the chief of the priests and of their brethren in the days of Jeshua.
8 Moreover the Levites: Jeshua, Binnui, Kadmiel, Sherebiah, Judah, *and* Mattaniah, *which was* over the thanksgiving, he and his brethren.
9 Also Bakbukiah and Unni, their

brethren, *were* over against them in the watches.
10 And Jeshua begat Joiakim, Joiakim also begat Eliashib, and Eliashib begat Joiada,
11 And Joiada begat Jonathan, and Jonathan begat Jaddua.
12 And in the days of Joiakim were priests, the chief of the fathers: of Seraiah, Meraiah; of Jeremiah, Hananiah;
13 Of Ezra, Meshullam; of Amariah, Jehohanan;
14 Of Melicu, Jonathan; of Shebaniah, Joseph;
15 Of Harim, Adna; of Meraioth, Helkai;
16 Of Iddo, Zechariah; of Ginnethon, Meshullam;
17 Of Abijah, Zichri; of Miniamin, of Moadiah, Piltai;
18 Of Bilgah, Shammua; of Shemaiah, Jehonathan;
19 And of Joiarib, Mattenai; of Jedaiah, Uzzi;
20 Of Sallai, Kallai; of Amok, Eber;
21 Of Hilkiah, Hashabiah; of Jedaiah, Nethaneel.
22 The Levites in the days of Eliashib, Joiada, and Johanan, and Jaddua, *were* recorded chief of the fathers: also the priests, to the reign of Darius the Persian.
23 The sons of Levi, the chief of the fathers, *were* written in the book of the chronicles, even until the days of Johanan the son of Eliashib.
24 And the chief of the Levites: Hashabiah, Sherebiah, and Jeshua the son of Kadmiel, with their brethren over against them, to praise *and* to give thanks, according to the commandment of David the man of God, ward over against ward.
25 Mattaniah, and Bakbukiah, Obadiah, Meshullam, Talmon, Akkub, *were* porters keeping the ward at the thresholds of the gates.
26 These *were* in the days of Joiakim the son of Jeshua, the son of Jozadak, and in the days of Nehemiah the governor, and of Ezra the priest, the scribe.

Nehemiah Dedicates the Wall
27 And at the dedication of the wall of Jerusalem they sought the Levites out of all their places, to bring them to Jerusalem, to keep the dedication with gladness, both

Cross references (center column):
24 Gen. 38:30, *Zarah*; 1Chr. 18:17; 23:28
25 Josh. 14:15
35 1Chr. 4:14
1 Ezra 2:1, 2; Neh. 10:2-8
2 Neh. 12:14
3 Neh. 12:14, 15
4 Neh. 12:16; Luke 1:5
5 Neh. 12:17
7 Ezra 3:2; Neh. 12:20; Hag. 1:1; Zech. 3:1
8 Neh. 11:17
23 1Chr. 9:14-34
24 1Chr. 23; 25; 26; Ezra 3:11
26 Ezra 7:6, 11; Neh. 8:9
27 Deut. 20:5; 1Chr. 25:6; 2Chr. 5:13; 7:6

12:27 dedication. A great celebration followed the rebuilding of the walls. The rededication of the people and the new spirit of revival culminated in temple-centered worship and praise. It was a fitting program for the dedication of the walls.

with thanksgivings, and with singing, *with* cymbals, psalteries, and with harps.

28 And the sons of the singers gathered themselves together, both out of the plain country round about Jerusalem, and from the villages of Netophathi;

29 Also from the house of Gilgal, and out of the fields of Geba and Azmaveth: for the singers had builded them villages round about Jerusalem.

30 And the priests and the Levites purified themselves, and purified the people, and the gates, and the wall.

31 Then I brought up the princes of Judah upon the wall, and appointed two great *companies of them that gave* thanks, whereof one went on the right hand upon the wall toward the dung gate:

32 And after them went Hoshaiah, and half of the princes of Judah,

33 And Azariah, Ezra, and Meshullam,

34 Judah, and Benjamin, and Shemaiah, and Jeremiah,

35 And *certain* of the priests' sons with trumpets; *namely,* Zechariah the son of Jonathan, the son of Shemaiah, the son of Mattaniah, the son of Michaiah, the son of Zaccur, the son of Asaph:

36 And his brethren, Shemaiah, and Azarael, Milalai, Gilalai, Maai, Nethaneel, and Judah, Hanani, with the musical instruments of David the man of God, and Ezra the scribe before them.

37 And at the fountain gate, which was over against them, they went up by the stairs of the city of David, at the going up of the wall, above the house of David, even unto the water gate eastward.

38 And the other *company of them that gave* thanks went over against *them,* and I after them, and the half of the people upon the wall, from beyond the tower of the furnaces even unto the broad wall;

39 And from above the gate of Ephraim, and above the old gate, and above the fish gate, and the tower of Hananeel, and the tower of Meah, even unto the sheep gate: and they stood still in the prison gate.

40 So stood the two *companies of them that gave* thanks in the house of God, and I, and the half of the rulers with me:

41 And the priests; Eliakim, Maaseiah, Miniamin, Michaiah, Elioenai, Zechariah, *and* Hananiah, with trumpets;

42 And Maaseiah, and Shemaiah, and Eleazar, and Uzzi, and Jehohanan, and Malchijah, and Elam, and Ezer. And the singers sang loud, with Jezrahiah *their* overseer.

43 Also that day they offered great sacrifices, and rejoiced: for God had made them rejoice with great joy: the wives also and the children rejoiced: so that the joy of Jerusalem was heard even afar off.

Providing for Worship

44 And at that time were some appointed over the chambers for the treasures, for the offerings, for the firstfruits, and for the tithes, to gather into them out of the fields of the cities the portions of the law for the priests and Levites: for Judah rejoiced for the priests and for the Levites that waited.

45 And both the singers and the porters kept the ward of their God, and the ward of the purification, according to the commandment of David, *and* of Solomon his son.

46 For in the days of David and Asaph of old *there were* chief of the singers, and songs of praise and thanksgiving unto God.

47 And all Israel in the days of Zerubbabel, and in the days of Nehemiah, gave the portions of the singers and the porters, every day his portion: and they sanctified *holy things* unto the Levites; and the Levites sanctified *them* unto the children of Aaron.

CHAPTER 13
The Reforms of Nehemiah

1 On that day they read in the book of Moses in the audience of the people; and therein was found written, that the Ammonite and the Moabite should not come into the congregation of God for ever;

2 Because they met not the children of Israel with bread and with water, but hired Balaam against them, that he should curse them: howbeit our God turned the curse into a blessing.

3 Now it came to pass, when they had heard the law, that they separated from Israel all the mixed multitude.

4 And before this, Eliashib the priest, having the oversight of the chamber of the house of our God, *was* allied unto Tobiah:

5 And he had prepared for him a great chamber, where aforetime they laid the meat offerings, the frankincense, and the vessels, and the tithes of the corn, the new wine, and the oil, which was commanded *to be given* to the Levites, and the singers, and the porters; and the offerings of the priests.

6 But in all this *time* was not I at Jerusalem: for in the two and thirtieth year of Artaxerxes king of Babylon came I unto the

Cross references

31 Neh. 2:13; 3:13; 12:38

35 Num. 10:2, 8

36 1Chr. 23:5

37 Neh. 2:14; 3:15, 26; 8:1, 3, 16

38 Neh. 3:8, 11; 12:31

39 2Kgs. 14:13; Neh. 3:1, 3, 6, 32; 8:16; Jer. 32:2

44 Neh. 13:5, 12, 13

45 1Chr. 25; 26

46 1Chr. 25:1-7; 2Chr. 29:30

47 Num. 18:21, 24, 26

1 Deut. 23:3, 4, 31:11, 12; 2Kgs. 23:2; Neh. 8:3, 8; 9:3; Isa. 34:16

2 Num. 22:5; 23:11; 24:10; Deut. 23:5; Josh. 24:9, 10

3 Neh. 9:2; 10:28

5 Num. 18:21, 24; Neh. 12:44

6 Neh. 5:14

king, and after certain days obtained I leave of the king:

7 And I came to Jerusalem, and understood of the evil that Eliashib did for Tobiah, in preparing him a chamber in the courts of the house of God.

8 And it grieved me sore: therefore I cast forth all the household stuff of Tobiah out of the chamber.

9 Then I commanded, and they cleansed the chambers: and thither brought I again the vessels of the house of God, with the meat offering and the frankincense.

10 And I perceived that the portions of the Levites had not been given *them*: for the Levites and the singers, that did the work, were fled every one to his field.

11 Then contended I with the rulers, and said, Why is the house of God forsaken? And I gathered them together, and set them in their place.

12 Then brought all Judah the tithe of the corn and the new wine and the oil unto the treasuries.

13 And I made treasurers over the treasuries, Shelemiah the priest, and Zadok the scribe, and of the Levites, Pedaiah: and next to them *was* Hanan the son of Zaccur, the son of Mattaniah: for they were counted faithful, and their office *was* to distribute unto their brethren.

14 Remember me, O my God, concerning this, and wipe not out my good deeds that I have done for the house of my God, and for the offices thereof.

15 In those days saw I in Judah *some* treading wine presses on the sabbath, and bringing in sheaves, and lading asses; as also wine, grapes, and figs, and all *manner of* burdens, which they brought into Jerusalem on the sabbath day: and I testified *against them* in the day wherein they sold victuals.

16 There dwelt men of Tyre also therein, which brought fish, and all manner of ware, and sold on the sabbath unto the children of Judah, and in Jerusalem.

17 Then I contended with the nobles of Judah, and said unto them, What evil thing *is* this that ye do, and profane the sabbath day?

18 Did not your fathers thus, and did not

our God bring all this evil upon us, and upon this city? yet ye bring more wrath upon Israel by profaning the sabbath.

19 And it came to pass, that when the gates of Jerusalem began to be dark before the sabbath, I commanded that the gates should be shut, and charged that they should not be opened till after the sabbath: and *some* of my servants set I at the gates, *that* there should no burden be brought in on the sabbath day.

20 So the merchants and sellers of all kind of ware lodged without Jerusalem once or twice.

21 Then I testified against them, and said unto them, Why lodge ye about the wall? if ye do *so* again, I will lay hands on you. From that time forth came they no *more* on the sabbath.

22 And I commanded the Levites that they should cleanse themselves, and *that* they should come *and* keep the gates, to sanctify the sabbath day. Remember me, O my God, *concerning* this also, and spare me according to the greatness of thy mercy.

23 In those days also saw I Jews *that* had married wives of Ashdod, of Ammon, *and* of Moab:

24 And their children spake half in the speech of Ashdod, and could not speak in the Jews' language, but according to the language of each people.

25 And I contended with them, and cursed them, and smote certain of them, and plucked off their hair, and made them swear by God, *saying*, Ye shall not give your daughters unto their sons, nor take their daughters unto your sons, or for yourselves.

26 Did not Solomon king of Israel sin by these things? yet among many nations was there no king like him, who was beloved of his God, and God made him king over all Israel: nevertheless even him did outlandish women cause to sin.

27 Shall we then hearken unto you to do all this great evil, to transgress against our God in marrying strange wives?

28 And *one* of the sons of Joiada, the son of Eliashib the high priest, *was* son in law to Sanballat the Horonite: therefore I chased him from me.

7 Neh. 13:1, 5
9 2Chr. 29:5, 15, 16, 18
10 Num. 35:2; Mal. 3:8
11 Neh. 10:39; 13:17, 25; Prov. 28:4
12 Neh. 10:38, 39; 12:44
13 2Chr. 31:12; Neh. 7:2; 12:44; 1Cor. 4:2
14 Neh. 5:19; 13:22, 31
15 Ex. 20:10; Neh. 10:31; Jer. 17:21, 22
17 Neh. 13:11
18 Jer. 17:21-23
19 Lev. 23:32; Jer. 17:21, 22
22 Neh. 12:30; 13:14, 31
23 Ezra 9:2
25 Ezra 10:5; Neh. 10:29, 30; 13:11; Prov. 28:4
26 2Sam. 12:24; 1Kgs. 3:13; 11:1-3, 4-8; 2Chr. 1:12
27 Ezra 10:2
28 Neh. 12:10, 22

13:7 I came to Jerusalem. After twelve years, Nehemiah, in about 434 B.C., returned to Persia, but he eventually came back to Jerusalem to find that new abuses had arisen. Tobiah was actually using a special suite of rooms in the temple itself, evidently because Eliashib, the high priest, was related by marriage to Sanballat (cf. 13:28). Nehemiah expelled Tobiah the Ammonite from the temple chamber and initiated better arrangements for the support of the temple (vv. 10–14) and for Sabbath observance (vv. 15–22).

29 Remember them, O my God, because they have defiled the priesthood, and the covenant of the priesthood, and of the Levites.
30 Thus cleansed I them from all strangers,

30 Neh. 10:30; 12:1-26

31 Neh. 10:34; 13:14, 22

and appointed the wards of the priests and the Levites, every one in his business;
31 And for the wood offering, at times appointed, and for the firstfruits. Remember me, O my God, for good.

13:31 Remember me, O my God, for good. The book closes with Nehemiah's prayer, a spiritual sentiment that all who humbly serve God might echo from their hearts.

Esther

The book of Esther was the last of five books in a collection known as the Five Megilloth (scrolls). Each of these five books was designated to be read publicly at one of the five major feasts of the Jews. For the sake of convenience, all the books were placed on one scroll. The other four books were the Song of Solomon, Ruth, Lamentations, and Ecclesiastes. Esther was read at the Feast of Purim, the commemoration of the great deliverance of the Jews that God brought about through Esther.

Esther, the "romance of providence," is the only Bible book besides Ruth named after a woman. The book records the beginnings of the festival of Purim and preserves the memory of the great deliverance of the Jews under Xerxes, events which happened between the return of Zerubbabel from Babylon to Jerusalem (536 B.C.) and the arrival of Ezra (457 B.C.). Though the name of God is not openly mentioned, His providential protection, guidance and care are evident.

This story of intrigue and ruthlessness is set in an Oriental palace. The five main characters are King Ahasuerus (also known as Xerxes); Vashti, the deposed queen; Mordecai, uncle of Esther and a court official; Esther, who initially kept her Jewish origins a secret; and Haman the Agagite, probably a descendent of Amalek and Agag (see Num. 24:7; 1 Sam. 15:1).

The king, after suffering numerous defeats, has sought solace in his palace activities. At a banquet, Queen Vashti refuses to display herself before the officials and is therefore deposed. Esther is chosen as queen after a nationwide search. By divine providence, Esther is positioned to intervene against an evil plot by Haman to destroy the Jews, and thereby delivers her people.

The book of Esther is an important link in a chain of events leading to the coming of the Messiah.

Only Esther 6:13 is predictive, when Haman's wife anticipates his fall, which is one verse out of 167, or 1 percent of the total.

Author
Unknown, Possibly Mordecai

Date
483–473 B.C.

Key Truth
Deliverance

Historic Time
Persian Empire

Key Verse
4:14
. . . who knoweth whether thou art come to the kingdom for such a time as this?

1% Prophecy

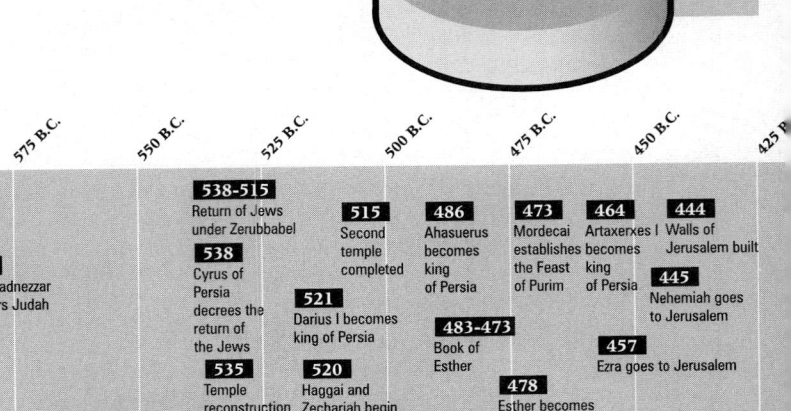

625 B.C.	600 B.C.	575 B.C.	550 B.C.	525 B.C.	500 B.C.	475 B.C.	450 B.C.	425 B.

722 Assyria conquers Israel

627 Jeremiah begins prophetic ministry

586 Nebuchadnezzar conquers Judah

538-515 Return of Jews under Zerubbabel

538 Cyrus of Persia decrees the return of the Jews

535 Temple reconstruction begins

521 Darius I becomes king of Persia

520 Haggai and Zechariah begin prophetic ministry

515 Second temple completed

486 Ahasuerus becomes king of Persia

483-473 Book of Esther

478 Esther becomes queen of Persia

473 Mordecai establishes the Feast of Purim

464 Artaxerxes I becomes king of Persia

457 Ezra goes to Jerusalem

444 Walls of Jerusalem built

445 Nehemiah goes to Jerusalem

CHAPTER 1

Queen Vashti Defies King Ahasuerus

1 Now it came to pass in the days of Ahasuerus, (this *is* Ahasuerus which reigned, from India even unto Ethiopia, *over* an hundred and seven and twenty provinces:)
2 *That* in those days, when the king Ahasuerus sat on the throne of his kingdom, which *was* in Shushan the palace,
3 In the third year of his reign, he made a feast unto all his princes and his servants; the power of Persia and Media, the nobles and princes of the provinces, *being* before him:
4 When he shewed the riches of his glorious kingdom and the honour of his excellent majesty many days, *even* an hundred and fourscore days.
5 And when these days were expired, the king made a feast unto all the people that were present in Shushan the palace, both unto great and small, seven days, in the court of the garden of the king's palace;
6 *Where were* white, green, and blue, *hangings*, fastened with cords of fine linen and purple to silver rings and pillars of marble: the beds *were of* gold and silver, upon a pavement of red, and blue, and white, and black marble.
7 And they gave *them* drink in vessels of gold, (the vessels being diverse one from another,) and royal wine in abundance, according to the state of the king.
8 And the drinking *was* according to the law; none did compel: for so the king had appointed to all the officers of his house, that they should do according to every man's pleasure.
9 Also Vashti the queen made a feast for the women *in* the royal house which *belonged* to king Ahasuerus.
10 On the seventh day, when the heart of the king was merry with wine, he commanded Mehuman, Biztha, Harbona, Bigtha, and Abagtha, Zethar, and Carcas, the seven chamberlains that served in the presence of Ahasuerus the king,
11 To bring Vashti the queen before the king with the crown royal, to shew the people and the princes her beauty: for she *was* fair to look on.
12 But the queen Vashti refused to come at the king's commandment by *his* chamberlains: therefore was the king very wroth, and his anger burned in him.
13 Then the king said to the wise men, which knew the times, (for so *was* the king's manner toward all that knew law and judgment:
14 And the next unto him *was* Carshena, Shethar, Admatha, Tarshish, Meres, Marsena, *and* Memucan, the seven princes of Persia and Media, which saw the king's face, *and* which sat the first in the kingdom;)
15 What shall we do unto the queen Vashti according to law, because she hath not performed the commandment of the king Ahasuerus by the chamberlains?
16 And Memucan answered before the king and the princes, Vashti the queen hath not done wrong to the king only, but also to all the princes, and to all the people that *are* in all the provinces of the king Ahasuerus.
17 For *this* deed of the queen shall come abroad unto all women, so that they shall despise their husbands in their eyes, when it shall be reported, The king Ahasuerus commanded Vashti the queen to be brought in before him, but she came not.
18 *Likewise* shall the ladies of Persia and Media say this day unto all the king's princes, which have heard of the deed of the queen. Thus *shall there arise* too much contempt and wrath.
19 If it please the king, let there go a royal commandment from him, and let it be

Cross references

1 Ezra 4:6; Esth. 8:9; Dan. 6:1; 9:1
2 1Kgs. 1:46; Neh. 1:1
3 Gen. 40:20; Esth. 2:18; Mark 6:21
6 Esth. 7:8; Ezek. 23:41; Amos 2:8; 6:4
10 2Sam. 13:28; Esth. 7:9
13 1Chr. 12:32; Jer. 10:7; Dan. 2:12; Matt. 2:1
14 2Kgs. 25:19; Ezra 7:14
17 Eph. 5:33
19 Esth. 8:8; Dan. 6:8, 12, 15

1:1 Ahasuerus. The name is the Hebrew translation of the Persian name, Khshayarsha. He is better known by his Greek name, Xerxes.

1:2 Shushan the palace. The Hebrew word means "lily," and the Greek form is Susa. It is believed that lilies blossomed in the area. The palace was the winter residence and capitol of the great Persian kings. The famous Code of Hammurabi was found there in A.D. 1901. Daniel lived in this palace on occasion (Dan. 8:1–2). Research has shown the palace to be a splendid and vast structure, beautifully designed, adorned, and furnished.

1:11–12 Vashti refused. While Vashti deserves sympathy for her refusal to appear publicly to show the people and the princes her beauty in some risqué manner, it must be remembered that the king's command was considered irrevocable law. Ahasuerus' response was not execution, as might have been the case under more ruthless Babylonian kings, but divorce. He also issued a decree requiring wives to give their husbands "honor" (v. 20).

written among the laws of the Persians and the Medes, that it be not altered, That Vashti come no more before king Ahasuerus; and let the king give her royal estate unto another that is better than she.

20 And when the king's decree which he shall make shall be published throughout all his empire, (for it is great,) all the wives shall give to their husbands honour, both to great and small.

21 And the saying pleased the king and the princes; and the king did according to the word of Memucan:

22 For he sent letters into all the king's provinces, into every province according to the writing thereof, and to every people after their language, that every man should bear rule in his own house, and that *it* should be published according to the language of every people.

CHAPTER 2
Esther Is Made Queen

1 After these things, when the wrath of king Ahasuerus was appeased, he remembered Vashti, and what she had done, and what was decreed against her.

2 Then said the king's servants that ministered unto him, Let there be fair young virgins sought for the king:

3 And let the king appoint officers in all the provinces of his kingdom, that they may gather together all the fair young virgins unto Shushan the palace, to the house of the women, unto the custody of Hege the king's chamberlain, keeper of the women; and let their things for purification be given *them*:

4 And let the maiden which pleaseth the king be queen instead of Vashti. And the thing pleased the king; and he did so.

5 *Now* in Shushan the palace there was a certain Jew, whose name *was* Mordecai, the son of Jair, the son of Shimei, the son of Kish, a Benjamite;

6 Who had been carried away from Jerusalem with the captivity which had been carried away with Jeconiah king of Judah, whom Nebuchadnezzar the king of Babylon had carried away.

7 And he brought up Hadassah, that *is*, Es-

ther, his uncle's daughter: for she had neither father nor mother, and the maid *was* fair and beautiful; whom Mordecai, when her father and mother were dead, took for his own daughter.

8 So it came to pass, when the king's commandment and his decree was heard, and when many maidens were gathered together unto Shushan the palace, to the custody of Hegai, that Esther was brought also unto the king's house, to the custody of Hegai, keeper of the women.

9 And the maiden pleased him, and she obtained kindness of him; and he speedily gave her her things for purification, with such things as belonged to her, and seven maidens, *which were* meet to be given her, out of the king's house: and he preferred her and her maids unto the best *place* of the house of the women.

10 Esther had not shewed her people nor her kindred: for Mordecai had charged her that she should not shew *it*.

11 And Mordecai walked every day before the court of the women's house, to know how Esther did, and what should become of her.

12 Now when every maid's turn was come to go in to king Ahasuerus, after that she had been twelve months, according to the manner of the women, (for so were the days of their purifications accomplished, *to wit*, six months with oil of myrrh, and six months with sweet odours, and with *other* things for the purifying of the women;)

13 Then thus came *every* maiden unto the king; whatsoever she desired was given her to go with her out of the house of the women unto the king's house.

14 In the evening she went, and on the morrow she returned into the second house of the women, to the custody of Shaashgaz, the king's chamberlain, which kept the concubines: she came in unto the king no more, except the king delighted in her, and that she were called by name.

15 Now when the turn of Esther, the daughter of Abihail the uncle of Mordecai, who had taken her for his daughter, was come to go in unto the king, she required nothing but what Hegai the king's cham-

Cross references
20 Eph. 5:33; Col. 3:18; 1Pet. 3:1
22 Esth. 8:9; Eph. 5:22-24; 1Tim. 2:12
1 Esth. 1:19, 20
3 Esth. 2:8
6 2Kgs. 24:6, 14, 15; 2Chr. 36:10, 20; Jer. 24:1
7 Esth. 2:15; Eph. 6:4
8 Esth. 2:3
9 Esth. 2:3, 12
10 Esth. 2:20
15 Esth. 2:7

2:2 fair young virgins. An empire-wide contest is conducted to select the most beautiful in the king's eyes.

2:7 Esther's uncle Mordecai, a prominent official, brought Esther to the palace to participate in the program. Esther's Hebrew name was Hadassah, which means "myrtle." The word "Esther" probably comes from the Persian word *stara*, from which the word star is derived. Evidently she had been orphaned and subsequently adopted by Mordecai.

berlain, the keeper of the women, appointed. And Esther obtained favour in the sight of all them that looked upon her.

16 So Esther was taken unto king Ahasuerus into his house royal in the tenth month, which *is* the month Tebeth, in the seventh year of his reign.

17 And the king loved Esther above all the women, and she obtained grace and favour in his sight more than all the virgins; so that he set the royal crown upon her head, and made her queen instead of Vashti.

18 Then the king made a great feast unto all his princes and his servants, *even* Esther's feast; and he made a release to the provinces, and gave gifts, according to the state of the king.

Mordecai Saves the King's Life

19 And when the virgins were gathered together the second time, then Mordecai sat in the king's gate.

20 Esther had not *yet* shewed her kindred nor her people; as Mordecai had charged her: for Esther did the commandment of Mordecai, like as when she was brought up with him.

21 In those days, while Mordecai sat in the king's gate, two of the king's chamberlains, Bigthan and Teresh, of those which kept the door, were wroth, and sought to lay hand on the king Ahasuerus.

22 And the thing was known to Mordecai, who told *it* unto Esther the queen; and Esther certified the king *thereof* in Mordecai's name.

23 And when inquisition was made of the matter, it was found out; therefore they were both hanged on a tree: and it was written in the book of the chronicles before the king.

Chapter 3
Haman's Plot

1 After these things did king Ahasuerus promote Haman the son of Hammedatha the Agagite, and advanced him, and set his seat above all the princes that *were* with him.

2 And all the king's servants, that *were* in the king's gate, bowed, and reverenced Haman: for the king had so commanded concerning him. But Mordecai bowed not, nor did *him* reverence.

3 Then the king's servants, which *were* in the king's gate, said unto Mordecai, Why transgressest thou the king's commandment?

4 Now it came to pass, when they spake daily unto him, and he hearkened not unto them, that they told Haman, to see whether Mordecai's matters would stand: for he had told them that he *was* a Jew.

5 And when Haman saw that Mordecai bowed not, nor did him reverence, then was Haman full of wrath.

6 And he thought scorn to lay hands on Mordecai alone; for they had shewed him the people of Mordecai: wherefore Haman sought to destroy all the Jews that *were* throughout the whole kingdom of Ahasuerus, *even* the people of Mordecai.

7 In the first month, that *is*, the month Nisan, in the twelfth year of king Ahasuerus, they cast Pur, that *is*, the lot, before Haman from day to day, and from month to month, *to* the twelfth *month*, that *is*, the month Adar.

8 And Haman said unto king Ahasuerus, There is a certain people scattered abroad and dispersed among the people in all the provinces of thy kingdom; and their laws *are*

Cross References:
18 Esth. 1:3
19 Esth. 2:21; 3:2
20 Esth. 2:10
21 Esth. 6:2
22 Esth. 6:2
23 Esth. 6:1
1 Num. 24:7; 1Sam. 15:8
2 Esth. 2:19; 3:5; Ps. 15:4
3 Esth. 3:2
5 Esth. 3:2; 5:9; Dan. 3:19
6 Ps. 83:4
7 Esth. 9:24
8 Ezra 4:13; Acts 16:20

2:17 the king loved Esther. By divine providence, this fair, beautiful woman, who told no one she was a Jew (v. 10), was crowned queen, replacing Vashti. This was about 478 B.C., two years after the defeat of Ahasuerus' forces by the Greeks at the Island of Salamis, where half the Persian fleet was sunk. This was the last major imperialist expansion to the West by the Persians. The king found solace in his beautiful palace, his wife, Queen Esther (and as Oriental kings did, with his harem), his vast empire and great riches.

3:5 then was Haman full of wrath. Appointed "grand vizier" of the Persian Empire, the wicked Haman, an Agagite (possibly a descendent of Agag, king of the Amalekites during the time of Samuel and Saul [1 Sam. 15:5–33]), deeply resented and despised Mordecai the Jew for not showing him reverential respect and bowing in submission. His hatred of Mordecai led to this major persecution of the Jews in a foreign land.

3:7 Pur is not a Hebrew word, but comes from the Assyrian *puru*, which means a pebble or small stone, rather like dice, something used for casting lots. Here the lot was cast systematically by days and months in order to determine which date in particular would be best to destroy the Jews. In verse 13 it is seen that specifically the thirteenth day of the twelfth month was chosen. The Feast of Purim, the Jewish feast celebrating the events in Esther, takes its name from this practice.

diverse from all people; neither keep they the king's laws: therefore it *is* not for the king's profit to suffer them.

9 If it please the king, let it be written that they may be destroyed: and I will pay ten thousand talents of silver to the hands of those that have the charge of the business, to bring *it* into the king's treasuries.

10 And the king took his ring from his hand, and gave it unto Haman the son of Hammedatha the Agagite, the Jews' enemy.

11 And the king said unto Haman, The silver *is* given to thee, the people also, to do with them as it seemeth good to thee.

12 Then were the king's scribes called on the thirteenth day of the first month, and there was written according to all that Haman had commanded unto the king's lieutenants, and to the governors that *were* over every province, and to the rulers of every people of every province according to the writing thereof, and *to* every people after their language; in the name of king Ahasuerus was it written, and sealed with the king's ring.

13 And the letters were sent by posts into all the king's provinces, to destroy, to kill, and to cause to perish, all Jews, both young and old, little children and women, in one day, *even* upon the thirteenth *day* of the twelfth month, which is the month Adar, and *to take* the spoil of them for a prey.

14 The copy of the writing for a commandment to be given in every province was published unto all people, that they should be ready against that day.

15 The posts went out, being hastened by the king's commandment, and the decree was given in Shushan the palace. And the king and Haman sat down to drink; but the city Shushan was perplexed.

CHAPTER 4
Mordecai Asks for Esther's Help

1 When Mordecai perceived all that was done, Mordecai rent his clothes, and put on sackcloth with ashes, and went out into the midst of the city, and cried with a loud and a bitter cry;

2 And came even before the king's gate: for none *might* enter into the king's gate clothed with sackcloth.

3 And in every province, whithersoever the king's commandment and his decree came, *there was* great mourning among the Jews, and fasting, and weeping, and wailing; and many lay in sackcloth and ashes.

4 So Esther's maids and her chamberlains came and told *it* her. Then was the queen exceedingly grieved; and she sent raiment to clothe Mordecai, and to take away his sackcloth from him: but he received *it* not.

5 Then called Esther for Hatach, *one* of the king's chamberlains, whom he had appointed to attend upon her, and gave him a commandment to Mordecai, to know what it *was*, and why it *was*.

6 So Hatach went forth to Mordecai unto the street of the city, which *was* before the king's gate.

7 And Mordecai told him of all that had happened unto him, and of the sum of the money that Haman had promised to pay to the king's treasuries for the Jews, to destroy them.

8 Also he gave him the copy of the writing of the decree that was given at Shushan to destroy them, to shew *it* unto Esther, and to declare *it* unto her, and to charge her that she should go in unto the king, to make supplication unto him, and to make request before him for her people.

9 And Hatach came and told Esther the words of Mordecai.

10 Again Esther spake unto Hatach, and gave him commandment unto Mordecai;

11 All the king's servants, and the people of the king's provinces, do know, that whosoever, whether man or woman, shall come unto the king into the inner court, who is not called, *there is* one law of his to put *him* to death, except such to whom the king shall hold out the golden sceptre, that he may live: but I have not been called to come in unto the king these thirty days.

12 And they told to Mordecai Esther's words.

13 Then Mordecai commanded to answer Esther, Think not with thyself that thou shalt escape in the king's house, more than all the Jews.

14 For if thou altogether holdest thy peace at this time, *then* shall there enlargement and deliverance arise to the Jews from an-

Cross references (center column)

10 Gen. 41:42; Esth. 7:6; 8:2, 8

12 1Kgs. 21:8; Esth. 1:22; 8:8, 9, 10

13 Esth. 8:10, 11, 12-17

14 Esth. 8:13, 14

15 Esth. 8:15; Prov. 29:2

1 Gen. 27:34; Josh. 7:6; 2Sam. 1:11; Ezek. 27:30

3 Isa. 58:5; Dan. 9:3

7 Esth. 3:9

8 Esth. 3:14, 15

11 Esth. 5:1, 2; 8:4; Dan. 2:9

14 Job 9:18

3:9 they may be destroyed. Wicked Haman convinces the king that Jews, different from other people with their customs and practices (v. 8), deserved eradication.

4:14 thou art come to the kingdom. Mordecai urges Esther to intercede with the king to rescue the Jews. While asserting that God could raise up deliverance from another source, he expresses the principle, "thou art come to the kingdom for such a time as this."

other place; but thou and thy father's house shall be destroyed: and who knoweth whether thou art come to the kingdom for *such* a time as this?

15 Then Esther bade *them* return Mordecai *this answer,*

16 Go, gather together all the Jews that are present in Shushan, and fast ye for me, and neither eat nor drink three days, night or day: I also and my maidens will fast likewise; and so will I go in unto the king, which *is* not according to the law: and if I perish, I perish.

17 So Mordecai went his way, and did according to all that Esther had commanded him.

CHAPTER 5
The Banquet

1 Now it came to pass on the third day, that Esther put on *her* royal *apparel*, and stood in the inner court of the king's house, over against the king's house: and the king sat upon his royal throne in the royal house, over against the gate of the house.

2 And it was so, when the king saw Esther the queen standing in the court, *that* she obtained favour in his sight: and the king held out to Esther the golden sceptre that *was* in his hand. So Esther drew near, and touched the top of the sceptre.

3 Then said the king unto her, What wilt thou, queen Esther? and what *is* thy request? it shall be even given thee to the half of the kingdom.

4 And Esther answered, If *it seem* good unto the king, let the king and Haman come this day unto the banquet that I have prepared for him.

5 Then the king said, Cause Haman to make haste, that he may do as Esther hath said. So the king and Haman came to the banquet that Esther had prepared.

6 And the king said unto Esther at the banquet of wine, What *is* thy petition? and

it shall be granted thee: and what *is* thy request? even to the half of the kingdom it shall be performed.

7 Then answered Esther, and said, My petition and my request *is*;

8 If I have found favour in the sight of the king, and if it please the king to grant my petition, and to perform my request, let the king and Haman come to the banquet that I shall prepare for them, and I will do to morrow as the king hath said.

9 Then went Haman forth that day joyful and with a glad heart: but when Haman saw Mordecai in the king's gate, that he stood not up, nor moved for him, he was full of indignation against Mordecai.

10 Nevertheless Haman refrained himself: and when he came home, he sent and called for his friends, and Zeresh his wife.

11 And Haman told them of the glory of his riches, and the multitude of his children, and all *the things* wherein the king had promoted him, and how he had advanced him above the princes and servants of the king.

12 Haman said moreover, Yea, Esther the queen did let no man come in with the king unto the banquet that she had prepared but myself; and to morrow am I invited unto her also with the king.

13 Yet all this availeth me nothing, so long as I see Mordecai the Jew sitting at the king's gate.

14 Then said Zeresh his wife and all his friends unto him, Let a gallows be made of fifty cubits high, and to morrow speak thou unto the king that Mordecai may be hanged thereon: then go thou in merrily with the king unto the banquet. And the thing pleased Haman; and he caused the gallows to be made.

CHAPTER 6
The King Honors Mordecai

1 On that night could not the king sleep, and he commanded to bring the book of

---

Cross references (center column):

16 Gen. 43:14; Esth. 5:1

1 Esth. 4:11, 16; 6:4

2 Esth. 4:11; 8:4; Prov. 21:1

3 Mark 6:23

6 Esth. 7:2; 9:12

9 Esth. 3:5

10 2Sam. 13:22

11 Esth. 3:1; 9:7-10

14 Esth. 6:4; 7:9, 10

1 Esth. 2:23

4:16 According to Persian protocol, no one could come into the king's presence uninvited. Anyone who dared to appear before the throne without a proper invitation was subject to immediate execution. The protocol was to protect the king from assassins. Not even the queen had unrestricted access to the king. For Esther to enter the king's presence unannounced might result in the king's displeasure and her untimely death. Realizing this, after three days of fasting, she sends word to Mordecai that she will go into the king regardless of the consequences.

5:2 the golden sceptre. Entering the king's presence,

Esther is received with favor. Indicating his welcoming sentiment, he extends toward her his beautiful, long, golden sceptre. In accordance with customary protocols, she touches the top of the scepter. Some commentators have looked upon this act as an illustration of salvation. Esther is then able to set in a motion a plan for the Jews' deliverance.

6:1–14 In one of the amazing, and perhaps most amusing, incidents in the Scriptures, the king orders Haman (who was there to get permission to hang Mordecai) to honor Mordecai publicly in a parade through the streets of Susa as an example of how the king would honor a hero.

records of the chronicles; and they were read before the king.

2 And it was found written, that Mordecai had told of Bigthana and Teresh, two of the king's chamberlains, the keepers of the door, who sought to lay hand on the king Ahasuerus.

3 And the king said, What honour and dignity hath been done to Mordecai for this? Then said the king's servants that ministered unto him, There is nothing done for him.

4 And the king said, Who is in the court? Now Haman was come into the outward court of the king's house, to speak unto the king to hang Mordecai on the gallows that he had prepared for him.

5 And the king's servants said unto him, Behold, Haman standeth in the court. And the king said, Let him come in.

6 So Haman came in. And the king said unto him, What shall be done unto the man whom the king delighteth to honour? Now Haman thought in his heart, To whom would the king delight to do honour more than to myself?

7 And Haman answered the king, For the man whom the king delighteth to honour,

8 Let the royal apparel be brought which the king useth to wear, and the horse that the king rideth upon, and the crown royal which is set upon his head:

9 And let this apparel and horse be delivered to the hand of one of the king's most noble princes, that they may array the man withal whom the king delighteth to honour, and bring him on horseback through the street of the city, and proclaim before him, Thus shall it be done to the man whom the king delighteth to honour.

10 Then the king said to Haman, Make haste, and take the apparel and the horse, as thou hast said, and do even so to Mordecai the Jew, that sitteth at the king's gate: let nothing fail of all that thou hast spoken.

11 Then took Haman the apparel and the horse, and arrayed Mordecai, and brought him on horseback through the street of the city, and proclaimed before him, Thus shall it be done unto the man whom the king delighteth to honour.

12 And Mordecai came again to the king's gate. But Haman hasted to his house mourning, and having his head covered.

13 And Haman told Zeresh his wife and all his friends every thing that had befallen him. Then said his wise men and Zeresh his wife unto him, If Mordecai be of the seed of

the Jews, before whom thou hast begun to fall, thou shalt not prevail against him, but shalt surely fall before him.

14 And while they were yet talking with him, came the king's chamberlains, and hasted to bring Haman unto the banquet that Esther had prepared.

CHAPTER 7
Haman Is Hanged

1 So the king and Haman came to banquet with Esther the queen.

2 And the king said again unto Esther on the second day at the banquet of wine, What is thy petition, queen Esther? and it shall be granted thee: and what is thy request? and it shall be performed, even to the half of the kingdom.

3 Then Esther the queen answered and said, If I have found favour in thy sight, O king, and if it please the king, let my life be given me at my petition, and my people at my request:

4 For we are sold, I and my people, to be destroyed, to be slain, and to perish. But if we had been sold for bondmen and bondwomen, I had held my tongue, although the enemy could not countervail the king's damage.

5 Then the king Ahasuerus answered and said unto Esther the queen, Who is he, and where is he, that durst presume in his heart to do so?

6 And Esther said, The adversary and enemy is this wicked Haman. Then Haman was afraid before the king and the queen.

7 And the king arising from the banquet of wine in his wrath went into the palace garden: and Haman stood up to make request for his life to Esther the queen; for he saw that there was evil determined against him by the king.

8 Then the king returned out of the palace garden into the place of the banquet of wine; and Haman was fallen upon the bed whereon Esther was. Then said the king, Will he force the queen also before me in the house? As the word went out of the king's mouth, they covered Haman's face.

9 And Harbonah, one of the chamberlains, said before the king, Behold also, the gallows fifty cubits high, which Haman had made for Mordecai, who had spoken good for the king, standeth in the house of Haman. Then the king said, Hang him thereon.

10 So they hanged Haman on the gallows that he had prepared for Mordecai. Then was the king's wrath pacified.

---

2 Esth. 2:21
4 Esth. 5:1, 5:14
8 1Kgs. 1:33
9 Gen. 41:43
12 2Sam. 15:30; 2Chr. 26:20; Jer. 14:3, 4
14 Esth. 5:8
2 Esth. 5:6

4 Esth. 3:9; 4:7

8 Esth. 1:6; Job 9:24

9 Esth. 1:10; 5:14; Ps. 7:16; Prov. 11:5, 6

10 Ps. 37:35, 36; Dan. 6:24

CHAPTER 8
The Jews Are Authorized to Defend Themselves

1 On that day did the king Ahasuerus give the house of Haman the Jews' enemy unto Esther the queen. And Mordecai came before the king; for Esther had told what he *was* unto her.

2 And the king took off his ring, which he had taken from Haman, and gave it unto Mordecai. And Esther set Mordecai over the house of Haman.

3 And Esther spake yet again before the king, and fell down at his feet, and besought him with tears to put away the mischief of Haman the Agagite, and his device that he had devised against the Jews.

4 Then the king held out the golden sceptre toward Esther. So Esther arose, and stood before the king,

5 And said, If it please the king, and if I have found favour in his sight, and the thing *seem* right before the king, and I *be* pleasing in his eyes, let it be written to reverse the letters devised by Haman the son of Hammedatha the Agagite, which he wrote to destroy the Jews which *are* in all the king's provinces:

6 For how can I endure to see the evil that shall come unto my people? or how can I endure to see the destruction of my kindred?

7 Then the king Ahasuerus said unto Esther the queen and to Mordecai the Jew, Behold, I have given Esther the house of Haman, and him they have hanged upon the gallows, because he laid his hand upon the Jews.

8 Write ye also for the Jews, as it liketh you, in the king's name, and seal *it* with the king's ring: for the writing which is written in the king's name, and sealed with the king's ring, may no man reverse.

9 Then were the king's scribes called at that time in the third month, that *is*, the month Sivan, on the three and twentieth *day* thereof; and it was written according to all that Mordecai commanded unto the Jews, and to the lieutenants, and the deputies and rulers of the provinces which *are* from India unto Ethiopia, an hundred twenty and seven provinces, unto every province according to the writing thereof,

and unto every people after their language, and to the Jews according to their writing, and according to their language.

10 And he wrote in the king Ahasuerus' name, and sealed *it* with the king's ring, and sent letters by posts on horseback, *and* riders on mules, camels, *and* young dromedaries:

11 Wherein the king granted the Jews which *were* in every city to gather themselves together, and to stand for their life, to destroy, to slay, and to cause to perish, all the power of the people and province that would assault them, *both* little ones and women, and *to take* the spoil of them for a prey,

12 Upon one day in all the provinces of king Ahasuerus, *namely*, upon the thirteenth *day* of the twelfth month, which *is* the month Adar.

13 The copy of the writing for a commandment to be given in every province *was* published unto all people, and that the Jews should be ready against that day to avenge themselves on their enemies.

14 *So* the posts that rode upon mules *and* camels went out, being hastened and pressed on by the king's commandment. And the decree was given at Shushan the palace.

15 And Mordecai went out from the presence of the king in royal apparel of blue and white, and with a great crown of gold, and with a garment of fine linen and purple: and the city of Shushan rejoiced and was glad.

16 The Jews had light, and gladness, and joy, and honour.

17 And in every province, and in every city, whithersoever the king's commandment and his decree came, the Jews had joy and gladness, a feast and a good day. And many of the people of the land became Jews; for the fear of the Jews fell upon them.

CHAPTER 9
The Jews Destroy Their Enemies

1 Now in the twelfth month, that *is*, the month Adar, on the thirteenth day of the same, when the king's commandment and his decree drew near to be put in execution, in the day that the enemies of the Jews hoped to have power over them, (though it

Cross references
1 Esth. 2:7
2 Esth. 3:10
4 Esth. 4:11; 5:2
6 Neh. 2:3; Esth. 7:4
7 Esth. 8:1; Prov. 13:22
8 Esth. 1:19; Dan. 6:8, 12, 15
9 Esth. 1:1, 22; 3:12
10 1Kgs. 21:8; Esth. 3:12, 13
11 Esth. 9:10, 15, 16
12 Esth. 3:13-15; 9:1
13 Esth. 3:14, 15
15 Esth. 3:15; Prov. 29:2
16 Ps. 97:11
17 Gen. 35:5; Ex. 15:16; Deut. 2:25; 11:25; 1Sam. 25:8; Esth. 9:2, 19, 22; Ps. 18:43
1 2Sam. 22:41; Esth. 3:13; 8:12

8:1–17 While the king under the law of the Medes and Persians could not revoke his decree that would allow the Jews to be slain, he could and did issue a new decree, authorizing them to defend themselves and slay their attackers, seventy-five thousand of whom died.

was turned to the contrary, that the Jews had rule over them that hated them;)

2 The Jews gathered themselves together in their cities throughout all the provinces of the king Ahasuerus, to lay hand on such as sought their hurt: and no man could withstand them; for the fear of them fell upon all people.

3 And all the rulers of the provinces, and the lieutenants, and the deputies, and officers of the king, helped the Jews; because the fear of Mordecai fell upon them.

4 For Mordecai *was* great in the king's house, and his fame went out throughout all the provinces: for this man Mordecai waxed greater and greater.

5 Thus the Jews smote all their enemies with the stroke of the sword, and slaughter, and destruction, and did what they would unto those that hated them.

6 And in Shushan the palace the Jews slew and destroyed five hundred men.

7 And Parshandatha, and Dalphon, and Aspatha,

8 And Poratha, and Adalia, and Aridatha,

9 And Parmashta, and Arisai, and Aridai, and Vajezatha,

10 The ten sons of Haman the son of Hammedatha, the enemy of the Jews, slew they; but on the spoil laid they not their hand.

11 On that day the number of those that were slain in Shushan the palace was brought before the king.

12 And the king said unto Esther the queen, The Jews have slain and destroyed five hundred men in Shushan the palace, and the ten sons of Haman; what have they done in the rest of the king's provinces? now what *is* thy petition? and it shall be granted thee: or what *is* thy request further? and it shall be done.

13 Then said Esther, If it please the king, let it be granted to the Jews which *are* in Shushan to do to morrow also according unto this day's decree, and let Haman's ten sons be hanged upon the gallows.

14 And the king commanded it so to be done: and the decree was given at Shushan; and they hanged Haman's ten sons.

15 For the Jews that *were* in Shushan gathered themselves together on the fourteenth day also of the month Adar, and slew three

hundred men at Shushan; but on the prey they laid not their hand.

The Feast of Purim

16 But the other Jews that *were* in the king's provinces gathered themselves together, and stood for their lives, and had rest from their enemies, and slew of their foes seventy and five thousand, but they laid not their hands on the prey,

17 On the thirteenth day of the month Adar; and on the fourteenth day of the same rested they, and made it a day of feasting and gladness.

18 But the Jews that *were* at Shushan assembled together on the thirteenth *day* thereof, and on the fourteenth thereof; and on the fifteenth *day* of the same they rested, and made it a day of feasting and gladness.

19 Therefore the Jews of the villages, that dwelt in the unwalled towns, made the fourteenth day of the month Adar *a day of* gladness and feasting, and a good day, and of sending portions one to another.

20 And Mordecai wrote these things, and sent letters unto all the Jews that *were* in all the provinces of the king Ahasuerus, *both* nigh and far,

21 To stablish *this* among them, that they should keep the fourteenth day of the month Adar, and the fifteenth day of the same, yearly,

22 As the days wherein the Jews rested from their enemies, and the month which was turned unto them from sorrow to joy, and from mourning into a good day: that they should make them days of feasting and joy, and of sending portions one to another, and gifts to the poor.

23 And the Jews undertook to do as they had begun, and as Mordecai had written unto them;

24 Because Haman the son of Hammedatha, the Agagite, the enemy of all the Jews, had devised against the Jews to destroy them, and had cast Pur, that *is*, the lot, to consume them, and to destroy them;

25 But when *Esther* came before the king, he commanded by letters that his wicked device, which he devised against the Jews, should return upon his own head, and that he and his sons should be hanged on the gallows.

26 Wherefore they called these days Purim

Cross references (center column):

2 Esth. 8:11, 17; 9:16; Ps. 71:13, 24

4 2Sam. 3:1; 1Chr. 11:9; Prov. 4:18

10 Esth. 5:11; 8:11; Job 18:19; 27:13-15; Ps. 21:10

12 Esth. 5:6; 7:2

13 2Sam. 21:6, 9; Esth. 8:11

15 Esth. 9:2, 10; 8:11

16 Esth. 9:2; 8:11

18 Esth. 9:11, 15

19 Deut. 16:11, 14; Neh. 8:10, 12; Esth. 8:17; 9:22

22 Neh. 8:10; Esth. 9:19; Ps. 30:11

24 Esth. 3:6, 7

25 Esth. 7:5-10; 8:3-8; 9:13, 14; Ps. 7:16

26 Esth. 9:20

9:26 they called these days Purim. After the Jews' deliverance, they commemorated the event with a special festival that became known as the Feast of Purim. It is still annually observed from the thirteenth through the fifteenth days of the Hebrew month Adar (midautumn).

after the name of Pur. Therefore for all the words of this letter, and *of that* which they had seen concerning this matter, and which had come unto them,

27 The Jews ordained, and took upon them, and upon their seed, and upon all such as joined themselves unto them, so as it should not fail, that they would keep these two days according to their writing, and according to their *appointed* time every year;

28 And *that* these days *should be* remembered and kept throughout every generation, every family, every province, and every city; and *that* these days of Purim should not fail from among the Jews, nor the memorial of them perish from their seed.

29 Then Esther the queen, the daughter of Abihail, and Mordecai the Jew, wrote with all authority, to confirm this second letter of Purim.

30 And he sent the letters unto all the Jews, to the hundred twenty and seven provinces of the kingdom of Ahasuerus, *with* words of peace and truth,

31 To confirm these days of Purim in their times *appointed*, according as Mordecai the Jew and Esther the queen had enjoined them, and as they had decreed for themselves and for their seed, the matters of the fastings and their cry.

32 And the decree of Esther confirmed these matters of Purim; and it was written in the book.

CHAPTER 10
Mordecai's Greatness

1 And the king Ahasuerus laid a tribute upon the land, and *upon* the isles of the sea.

2 And all the acts of his power and of his might, and the declaration of the greatness of Mordecai, whereunto the king advanced him, *are* they not written in the book of the chronicles of the kings of Media and Persia?

3 For Mordecai the Jew *was* next unto king Ahasuerus, and great among the Jews, and accepted of the multitude of his brethren, seeking the wealth of his people, and speaking peace to all his seed.

---

27 Esth. 8:17; Isa. 56:3, 6; Zech. 2:11
29 Esth. 2:15; 8:10; 9:20
30 Esth. 1:1
31 Esth. 4:3, 16
1 Gen. 10:5; Ps. 72:10; Isa. 24:15
2 Esth. 8:15; 9:4
3 Gen. 41:40; 2Chr. 28:7; Neh. 2:10; Ps. 122:8, 9

9:31 To confirm these days of Purim. While not specifically predictive, the annual observance of this feast reminds the Jews of God's deliverance from the first widespread anti-Semitic program in world history. Tragically, governmental, religious, and personal persecution of the Jews has occurred periodically throughout the centuries that followed. Prophetically, a final time of Jacob's trouble (Jer. 30:7), perpetrated by the future Antichrist in the Tribulation, will occur. The return of the Messiah to establish His kingdom will elevate Israel to the most blessed nation of all time.

Job

The first of the five poetical books, Job (meaning "one who is persecuted") is titled after the principle character. Most scholars agree that the book of Job may have been the first book ever written. However, the book's authorship is a subject of wide debate as Elihu, Moses, Solomon, Isaiah, Hezekiah, Jeremiah, Baruch, and even Job himself have been considered to be possible authors. Though no solid evidence supports any one of these potential authors, it is commonly believed that Job lived during the patriarchal period (i.e., the time of Abraham, Isaac, and Jacob).

The introduction (1—2) is prose; the main body is poetry, usually couplets with comparative or contrasting ideas in each clause. Seven personalities appear in this dramatic account of Job's sufferings, questions, and deliverance: the LORD, Satan, Job, Eliphaz, Bildad, Zophar, and Elihu. Perhaps the Bible's oldest book, Job does not refer to the Law, the temple, or anything related to the ancient history of Israel, yet the Scriptures quote or refer to it fifty-seven times, and James 5:10 specifically mentions Job. Ezekiel compares Job's godliness with Noah and Daniel.

After Job presents his initial complaint (chap. 4), three debates pit Eliphaz, Bildad, and Zophar, all insisting that Job's sufferings are punishments, against Job defending himself. After the debates, young Elihu urges Job not to blame God for his misfortunes. Finally the response of the Lord in divine revelation brings Job to his knees. Job finds peace in trusting the infinite and omnipotent God. The last chapter shows the ultimate aim of God to bless his people. "Ye have heard of the patience of Job," writes James (5:11), that He is "very pitiful and tender in mercy."

The strongest prophecy in the entire book is Job's affirmation of his faith that he would see, in his resurrected flesh, his living Redeemer standing upon the earth (19:25–27).

Out of 1,070 verses, only 22 are predictive (2%). Most are general prophecies of blessings for obedience (11:14–20), the transience of life (14:12–15) or the certainty of deliverance (23:10–11).

Author
Unknown

Date
1500 B.C.

Key Truth
Why Do the Righteous Suffer?

Historic Time
The Time of the Patriarchs

Key Verse
1:21
. . . the LORD gave, and . . . hath taken away; blessed be the name of the LORD.

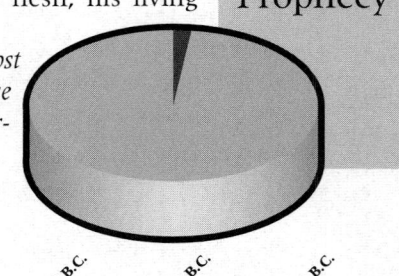

2% Prophecy

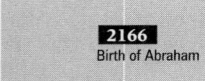
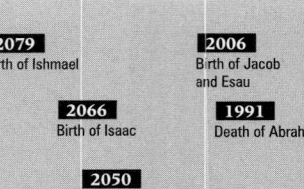
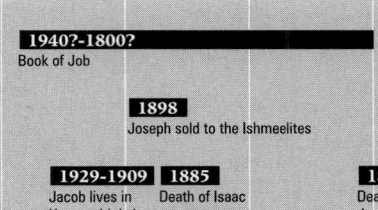

2200 B.C.	2150 B.C.	2100 B.C.	2050 B.C.	2000 B.C.	1950 B.C.	1900 B.C.	1850 B.C.	1800

2166 Birth of Abraham

2079 Birth of Ishmael

2006 Birth of Jacob and Esau

1940?-1800? Book of Job

2066 Birth of Isaac

1991 Death of Abraham

1898 Joseph sold to the Ishmeelites

2050 Sodom and Gomorah destroyed

1929-1909 Jacob lives in Haran with Leban

1885 Death of Isaac

180? Death o Joseph

1876 Jacob and his family move to Egypt

CHAPTER 1
The Testing of Job

1 There was a man in the land of Uz, whose name *was* Job; and that man was perfect and upright, and one that feared God, and eschewed evil.

2 And there were born unto him seven sons and three daughters.

3 His substance also was seven thousand sheep, and three thousand camels, and five hundred yoke of oxen, and five hundred she asses, and a very great household; so that this man was the greatest of all the men of the east.

4 And his sons went and feasted *in their* houses, every one his day; and sent and called for their three sisters to eat and to drink with them.

5 And it was so, when the days of *their* feasting were gone about, that Job sent and sanctified them, and rose up early in the morning, and offered burnt offerings *according* to the number of them all: for Job said, It may be that my sons have sinned, and cursed God in their hearts. Thus did Job continually.

6 Now there was a day when the sons of God came to present themselves before the LORD, and Satan came also among them.

7 And the LORD said unto Satan, Whence comest thou? Then Satan answered the LORD, and said, From going to and fro in the earth, and from walking up and down in it.

8 And the LORD said unto Satan, Hast thou considered my servant Job, that *there is* none like him in the earth, a perfect and an upright man, one that feareth God, and escheweth evil?

9 Then Satan answered the LORD, and said, Doth Job fear God for nought?

10 Hast not thou made an hedge about him, and about his house, and about all that he hath on every side? thou hast blessed the work of his hands, and his substance is increased in the land.

11 But put forth thine hand now, and touch all that he hath, and he will curse thee to thy face.

12 And the LORD said unto Satan, Behold,

all that he hath *is* in thy power; only upon himself put not forth thine hand. So Satan went forth from the presence of the LORD.

13 And there was a day when his sons and his daughters *were* eating and drinking wine in their eldest brother's house:

14 And there came a messenger unto Job, and said, The oxen were plowing, and the asses feeding beside them:

15 And the Sabeans fell *upon them*, and took them away; yea, they have slain the servants with the edge of the sword; and I only am escaped alone to tell thee.

16 While he *was* yet speaking, there came also another, and said, The fire of God is fallen from heaven, and hath burned up the sheep, and the servants, and consumed them; and I only am escaped alone to tell thee.

17 While he *was* yet speaking, there came also another, and said, The Chaldeans made out three bands, and fell upon the camels, and have carried them away, yea, and slain the servants with the edge of the sword; and I only am escaped alone to tell thee.

18 While he *was* yet speaking, there came also another, and said, Thy sons and thy daughters *were* eating and drinking wine in their eldest brother's house:

19 And, behold, there came a great wind from the wilderness, and smote the four corners of the house, and it fell upon the young men, and they are dead; and I only am escaped alone to tell thee.

20 Then Job arose, and rent his mantle, and shaved his head, and fell down upon the ground, and worshipped,

21 And said, Naked came I out of my mother's womb, and naked shall I return thither: the LORD gave, and the LORD hath taken away; blessed be the name of the LORD.

22 In all this Job sinned not, nor charged God foolishly.

CHAPTER 2
Job Is Tested Again

1 Again there was a day when the sons of God came to present themselves before the

1 Gen. 6:9; 17:1; 22:20, 21; Job 2:3; Prov. 8:13; 16:6; Ezek. 14:14; James 5:11

5 Gen. 8:20; 1Kgs. 21:10, 13; Job 42:8

6 1Kgs. 22:19; 1Chr. 21:1; Job 2:1; Rev. 12:9, 10

7 Job 2:2; Matt. 12:43; 1Pet. 5:8

8 Job 1:1; 2:3

10 Ps. 34:7; 128:1, 2; Prov. 10:22; Isa. 5:2

11 Job 2:5; 19:21; Isa. 8:21; Mal. 3:13, 14

12 Gen. 16:6

13 Eccl. 9:12

18 Job 1:4, 13

20 Gen. 37:29; Ezra 9:3; 1Pet. 5:6

21 Ps. 49:17; Eccl. 5:15, 19; Matt. 20:15; Eph. 5:20; 1Thess. 5:18; 1Tim. 6:7; James 1:17

22 Job 2:10

1 Job 1:6

1:1—2:7 Although Satan and his demons have been able to tempt believers in all ages, there is no evidence that God has ever again lowered His hedge of protection to the level that He did with Job. First Corinthians 10:13 assures us that we can never be tempted beyond our endurance and that God always provides "a way to escape," if we desire to take it.

1:6 The word "Satan" is used here for the first time as the name for the devil. Literally it means "accuser" or "adversary"; and according to Revelation 12:10 he is seen as the accuser of the brethren. Satan, when he has access to God, loves to accuse the brethren of unfaithfulness.

Satan

By Stanley M. Horton

The Bible does not give a great deal of attention to Satan. It is more concerned with the revelation of God and His plan of redemption, His grace, and His holy love and concern for humankind. Rather than emphasizing Satan, the Bible emphasizes God's power to save and restore. Nevertheless, Satan, whose name literally means "the adversary," opposes God and people from Genesis to Revelation.

In the form of a serpent, Satan tempted Eve in Genesis 3—identified in Revelation 12:9 as "that old serpent, called the Devil, and Satan." In the prologue to the book of Job, Satan questions Job's loyalty to God, and God permits him to afflict Job—but God sets the limits on what Satan can do. In the New Testament, Satan tried to get Jesus to break His identity with humankind that He declared in His baptism by John the Baptist (John 1). Jesus won a decisive victory using only what is available to us all—the Word of God. James 4:7 advises us that we too can win victories over Satan by submitting to God and resisting the devil (literally, "the slanderer").

Though the Bible does not tell us all there is to know about Satan, it does mention his fall from heaven (Luke 10:18; Jude 1:6; Rev. 12:7–9). It warns us that he blinds the minds of the ungodly (2 Cor. 4:4). He can come sometimes as a roaring lion (1 Peter 5:8), and sometimes masked as an angel of light (2 Cor. 11:14). By prayer, the Word, and the power of the Holy Spirit, we can defeat him.

> *Satan's doom is inevitable.*

Satan's doom is inevitable. After the Church is raptured, he will concentrate his rebellion in the person of the Antichrist as his agent. The Antichrist, "after the working of Satan" will come "with all power and signs and lying wonders" (2 Thess. 2:9). Satan, the Dragon of Revelation 12:9, is prepared for the Antichrist, giving him his satanic power, authority, and throne (Rev. 13:2). God will then permit Satan to give the Antichrist the appearance of duplicating the resurrection of Christ (Rev. 13:3), and the people will worship Satan and the Antichrist (Rev. 13:4). But after the Antichrist and His armies are defeated by the returning Jesus and His army (Rev. 19:19–21), an angel from heaven will bind Satan with a great chain and lock him in the bottomless pit (Greek, *abussos*, "abyss") for a thousand years (Rev. 20:1–2).

After the Millennium, Satan will be released. The Scripture does not elaborate on why this must be done. Perhaps it is a final vindication of God's justice. For even after a thousand years of Christ's glorious reign, a multitude ("as the sands of the sea") will follow Satan. This multitude will enjoy the blessings of Christ's reign and still rebel against God. Therefore, God will condemn them to be separated from Him and His blessings forever. Then Satan will find that he will be cast into the lake of fire and brimstone forever (Rev. 20:7–10). In the new heavens and the new earth, neither sin nor Satan will ever mar the joy and blessed fellowship we shall share with the Lord.

LORD, and Satan came also among them to
present himself before the LORD.
2 And the LORD said unto Satan, From
whence comest thou? And Satan answered the
LORD, and said, From going to and fro in the
earth, and from walking up and down in it.
3 And the LORD said unto Satan, Hast thou
considered my servant Job, that *there is* none
like him in the earth, a perfect and an upright man, one that feareth God, and escheweth evil? and still he holdeth fast his
integrity, although thou movedst me against
him, to destroy him without cause.
4 And Satan answered the LORD, and said,
Skin for skin, yea, all that a man hath will
he give for his life.
5 But put forth thine hand now, and touch
his bone and his flesh, and he will curse
thee to thy face.
6 And the LORD said unto Satan, Behold,
he *is* in thine hand; but save his life.
7 So went Satan forth from the presence
of the LORD, and smote Job with sore boils
from the sole of his foot unto his crown.
8 And he took him a potsherd to scrape
himself withal; and he sat down among the
ashes.
9 Then said his wife unto him, Dost thou
still retain thine integrity? curse God, and
die.
10 But he said unto her, Thou speakest as
one of the foolish women speaketh. What?
shall we receive good at the hand of God,
and shall we not receive evil? In all this did
not Job sin with his lips.

Job's Three Friends

11 Now when Job's three friends heard of
all this evil that was come upon him, they
came every one from his own place; Eliphaz
the Temanite, and Bildad the Shuhite, and
Zophar the Naamathite: for they had made
an appointment together to come to mourn
with him and to comfort him.
12 And when they lifted up their eyes afar
off, and knew him not, they lifted up their
voice, and wept; and they rent every one
his mantle, and sprinkled dust upon their
heads toward heaven.
13 So they sat down with him upon the
ground seven days and seven nights, and
none spake a word unto him: for they saw
that *his* grief was very great.

CHAPTER 3

Job Complains to God

1 After this opened Job his mouth, and
cursed his day.

2 Job 1:7
3 Job 1:1, 8; 9:17; 27:5, 6
5 Job 1:11; 19:20
6 Job 1:12
7 Isa. 1:6
8 2Sam. 13:19; Job 42:6; Ezek. 27:30; Matt. 11:21
9 Job 2:3; 21:15
10 Job 1:21, 22; Ps. 39:1; Rom. 12:12; James 5:10, 11
11 Gen. 25:2; 36:11; Job 42:11; Prov. 17:17; Jer. 49:7; Rom. 12:15
12 Neh. 9:1; Lam. 2:10; Ezek. 27:30
13 Gen. 50:10
3 Job 10:18, 19; Jer. 15:10; 20:14
5 Job 10:21, 22; 16:16; 28:3; Ps. 23:4; 44:19; 107:10, 14; Jer. 13:16; Amos 5:8; 8:10
8 Jer. 9:17, 18
9 Job 41:18
11 Job 10:18
12 Gen. 30:3; Isa. 66:12
14 Job 15:28
16 Ps. 58:8
18 Job 39:7
20 1Sam. 1:10; 2Kgs. 4:27; Prov. 31:6; Jer. 20:18
21 Prov. 2:4; Rev. 9:6
23 Job 19:8; Lam. 3:7

2 And Job spake, and said,
3 Let the day perish wherein I was born,
and the night *in which* it was said, There is a
man child conceived.
4 Let that day be darkness; let not God regard it from above, neither let the light
shine upon it.
5 Let darkness and the shadow of death
stain it; let a cloud dwell upon it; let the
blackness of the day terrify it.
6 As *for* that night, let darkness seize upon
it; let it not be joined unto the days of the
year, let it not come into the number of the
months.
7 Lo, let that night be solitary, let no joyful
voice come therein.
8 Let them curse it that curse the day, who
are ready to raise up their mourning.
9 Let the stars of the twilight thereof be
dark; let it look for light, but *have* none; neither let it see the dawning of the day:
10 Because it shut not up the doors of my
mother's womb, nor hid sorrow from mine
eyes.
11 Why died I not from the womb? *why* did
I *not* give up the ghost when I came out of
the belly?
12 Why did the knees prevent me? or why
the breasts that I should suck?
13 For now should I have lain still and been
quiet, I should have slept: then had I been
at rest,
14 With kings and counsellers of the earth,
which built desolate places for themselves;
15 Or with princes that had gold, who filled
their houses with silver:
16 Or as an hidden untimely birth I had not
been; as infants *which* never saw light.
17 There the wicked cease *from* troubling;
and there the weary be at rest.
18 *There* the prisoners rest together; they
hear not the voice of the oppressor.
19 The small and great are there; and the
servant *is* free from his master.
20 Wherefore is light given to him that is in
misery, and life unto the bitter *in* soul;
21 Which long for death, but it *cometh* not;
and dig for it more than for hid treasures;
22 Which rejoice exceedingly, *and* are glad,
when they can find the grave?
23 *Why is light given* to a man whose way is
hid, and whom God hath hedged in?
24 For my sighing cometh before I eat,
and my roarings are poured out like the
waters.
25 For the thing which I greatly feared is
come upon me, and that which I was afraid
of is come unto me.

26 I was not in safety, neither had I rest, neither was I quiet; yet trouble came.

CHAPTER 4
Eliphaz Rebukes Job

1 Then Eliphaz the Temanite answered and said,

2 *If* we assay to commune with thee, wilt thou be grieved? but who can withhold himself from speaking?

3 Behold, thou hast instructed many, and thou hast strengthened the weak hands.

4 Thy words have upholden him that was falling, and thou hast strengthened the feeble knees.

5 But now it is come upon thee, and thou faintest; it toucheth thee, and thou art troubled.

6 *Is* not *this* thy fear, thy confidence, thy hope, and the uprightness of thy ways?

7 Remember, I pray thee, who *ever* perished, being innocent? or where were the righteous cut off?

8 Even as I have seen, they that plow iniquity, and sow wickedness, reap the same.

9 By the blast of God they perish, and by the breath of his nostrils are they consumed.

10 The roaring of the lion, and the voice of the fierce lion, and the teeth of the young lions, are broken.

11 The old lion perisheth for lack of prey, and the stout lion's whelps are scattered abroad.

12 Now a thing was secretly brought to me, and mine ear received a little thereof.

13 In thoughts from the visions of the night, when deep sleep falleth on men,

14 Fear came upon me, and trembling, which made all my bones to shake.

15 Then a spirit passed before my face; the hair of my flesh stood up:

16 It stood still, but I could not discern the form thereof: an image *was* before mine eyes, *there was* silence, and I heard a voice, *saying,*

17 Shall mortal man be more just than God? shall a man be more pure than his maker?

18 Behold, he put no trust in his servants; and his angels he charged with folly:

19 How much less *in* them that dwell in houses of clay, whose foundation *is* in the dust, *which* are crushed before the moth?

20 They are destroyed from morning to evening: they perish for ever without any regarding *it.*

21 Doth not their excellency *which is* in

Cross references (center column):
- 3 Isa. 35:3
- 4 Isa. 35:3; Heb. 12:12
- 6 Job 1:1; Prov. 3:26
- 7 Ps. 37:25
- 8 Ps. 7:14; Prov. 22:8; Hos. 10:13; Gal. 6:7, 8
- 9 Ex. 15:8; Isa. 11:4; 30:33
- 10 Ps. 58:6
- 11 Ps. 34:10
- 13 Job 33:15
- 17 Job 9:2
- 18 Job 15:15; 25:5; 2Pet. 2:4
- 19 Job 15:16; 2Cor. 4:7; 5:1
- 20 Ps. 90:5, 6
- 3 Ps. 37:35, 36; Jer. 12:2, 3
- 4 Ps. 109:12; 119:155; 127:5
- 5 Job 18:9
- 7 Gen. 3:17-19; 1Cor. 10:13
- 9 Job 9:10; Ps. 40:5; 145:3
- 10 Job 28:26; Ps. 65:9, 10; 147:8
- 11 1Sam. 2:7; Ps. 113:7
- 12 Ps. 33:10
- 13 Ps. 9:15; 1Cor. 3:19
- 15 Ps. 35:10
- 16 Ps. 107:42
- 17 Ps. 94:12; Prov. 3:11, 12
- 19 Ps. 34:19; 91:3, 10; Prov. 24:16; 1Cor. 10:13
- 20 Ps. 33:19; 37:19
- 21 Ps. 31:20
- 22 Isa. 11:9; 35:9; 65:25; Ezek. 34:25

them go away? they die, even without wisdom.

CHAPTER 5

1 Call now, if there be any that will answer thee; and to which of the saints wilt thou turn?

2 For wrath killeth the foolish man, and envy slayeth the silly one.

3 I have seen the foolish taking root: but suddenly I cursed his habitation.

4 His children are far from safety, and they are crushed in the gate, neither *is there* any to deliver *them.*

5 Whose harvest the hungry eateth up, and taketh it even out of the thorns, and the robber swalloweth up their substance.

6 Although affliction cometh not forth of the dust, neither doth trouble spring out of the ground;

7 Yet man is born unto trouble, as the sparks fly upward.

8 I would seek unto God, and unto God would I commit my cause:

9 Which doeth great things and unsearchable; marvellous things without number:

10 Who giveth rain upon the earth, and sendeth waters upon the fields:

11 To set up on high those that be low; that those which mourn may be exalted to safety.

12 He disappointeth the devices of the crafty, so that their hands cannot perform *their* enterprise.

13 He taketh the wise in their own craftiness: and the counsel of the froward is carried headlong.

14 They meet with darkness in the daytime, and grope in the noonday as in the night.

15 But he saveth the poor from the sword, from their mouth, and from the hand of the mighty.

16 So the poor hath hope, and iniquity stoppeth her mouth.

17 Behold, happy *is* the man whom God correcteth: therefore despise not thou the chastening of the Almighty:

18 For he maketh sore, and bindeth up: he woundeth, and his hands make whole.

19 He shall deliver thee in six troubles: yea, in seven there shall no evil touch thee.

20 In famine he shall redeem thee from death: and in war from the power of the sword.

21 Thou shalt be hid from the scourge of the tongue: neither shalt thou be afraid of destruction when it cometh.

22 At destruction and famine thou shalt

laugh: neither shalt thou be afraid of the beasts of the earth.

23 For thou shalt be in league with the stones of the field: and the beasts of the field shall be at peace with thee.

24 And thou shalt know that thy tabernacle *shall be* in peace; and thou shalt visit thy habitation, and shalt not sin.

25 Thou shalt know also that thy seed *shall be* great, and thine offspring as the grass of the earth.

26 Thou shalt come to *thy* grave in a full age, like as a shock of corn cometh in in his season.

27 Lo this, we have searched it, so it *is*; hear it, and know thou *it* for thy good.

CHAPTER 6
Job Answers

1 But Job answered and said,

2 Oh that my grief were throughly weighed, and my calamity laid in the balances together!

3 For now it would be heavier than the sand of the sea: therefore my words are swallowed up.

4 For the arrows of the Almighty *are* within me, the poison whereof drinketh up my spirit: the terrors of God do set themselves in array against me.

5 Doth the wild ass bray when he hath grass? or loweth the ox over his fodder?

6 Can that which is unsavoury be eaten without salt? or is there *any* taste in the white of an egg?

7 The things *that* my soul refused to touch *are* as my sorrowful meat.

8 Oh that I might have my request; and that God would grant *me* the thing that I long for!

9 Even that it would please God to destroy me; that he would let loose his hand, and cut me off!

10 Then should I yet have comfort; yea, I would harden myself in sorrow: let him not spare; for I have not concealed the words of the Holy One.

11 What *is* my strength, that I should hope? and what *is* mine end, that I should prolong my life?

12 *Is* my strength the strength of stones? or *is* my flesh of brass?

13 *Is* not my help in me? and is wisdom driven quite from me?

14 To him that is afflicted pity *should be shewed* from his friend; but he forsaketh the fear of the Almighty.

15 My brethren have dealt deceitfully as a brook, *and* as the stream of brooks they pass away;

16 Which are blackish by reason of the ice, *and* wherein the snow is hid:

17 What time they wax warm, they vanish: when it is hot, they are consumed out of their place.

18 The paths of their way are turned aside; they go to nothing, and perish.

19 The troops of Tema looked, the companies of Sheba waited for them.

20 They were confounded because they had hoped; they came thither, and were ashamed.

21 For now ye are nothing; ye see *my* casting down, and are afraid.

22 Did I say, Bring unto me? or, Give a reward for me of your substance?

23 Or, Deliver me from the enemy's hand? or, Redeem me from the hand of the mighty?

24 Teach me, and I will hold my tongue: and cause me to understand wherein I have erred.

25 How forcible are right words! but what doth your arguing reprove?

26 Do ye imagine to reprove words, and the speeches of one that is desperate, *which are* as wind?

27 Yea, ye overwhelm the fatherless, and ye dig *a pit* for your friend.

28 Now therefore be content, look upon me; for *it is* evident unto you if I lie.

29 Return, I pray you, let it not be iniquity; yea, return again, my righteousness *is* in it.

30 Is there iniquity in my tongue? cannot my taste discern perverse things?

CHAPTER 7

1 *Is there* not an appointed time to man upon earth? *are not* his days also like the days of an hireling?

2 As a servant earnestly desireth the shadow, and as an hireling looketh for *the reward of* his work:

3 So am I made to possess months of

Cross references (center column):

23 Ps. 91:12; Hos. 2:18
25 Ps. 72:16; 112:2
26 Prov. 9:11; 10:27
27 Ps. 111:2
3 Ps. 77:4; Prov. 27:3
4 Ps. 38:2; 88:15, 16
9 1Kgs. 19:4
10 Lev. 19:2; Isa. 57:15; Hos. 11:9; Acts 20:20
14 Prov. 17:17
15 Ps. 38:11; 41:9; Jer. 15:18
19 Gen. 25:15; 1Kgs. 10:1; Ps. 72:10; Ezek. 27:22, 23
20 Jer. 14:3
21 Job 13:4; Ps. 38:11
27 Ps. 57:6
29 Job 17:10
1 Job 14:5, 13, 14; Ps. 39:4
3 Job 29:2

7:1 Is there not an appointed time to man upon earth? This suggests that our days are indeed numbered; however, several Scriptures indicate we can lengthen or shorten the number of our days by obeying or disobeying the commands of God.

vanity, and wearisome nights are appointed to me.

4 When I lie down, I say, When shall I arise, and the night be gone? and I am full of tossings to and fro unto the dawning of the day.

5 My flesh is clothed with worms and clods of dust; my skin is broken, and become loathsome.

6 My days are swifter than a weaver's shuttle, and are spent without hope.

7 O remember that my life *is* wind: mine eye shall no more see good.

8 The eye of him that hath seen me shall see me no *more*: thine eyes *are* upon me, and I *am* not.

9 *As* the cloud is consumed and vanisheth away: so he that goeth down to the grave shall come up no *more*.

10 He shall return no more to his house, neither shall his place know him any more.

11 Therefore I will not refrain my mouth; I will speak in the anguish of my spirit; I will complain in the bitterness of my soul.

12 *Am* I a sea, or a whale, that thou settest a watch over me?

13 When I say, My bed shall comfort me, my couch shall ease my complaint;

14 Then thou scarest me with dreams, and terrifiest me through visions:

15 So that my soul chooseth strangling, *and* death rather than my life.

16 I loathe *it*; I would not live alway: let me alone; for my days *are* vanity.

17 What *is* man, that thou shouldest magnify him? and that thou shouldest set thine heart upon him?

18 And *that* thou shouldest visit him every morning, *and* try him every moment?

19 How long wilt thou not depart from me, nor let me alone till I swallow down my spittle?

20 I have sinned; what shall I do unto thee, O thou preserver of men? why hast thou set me as a mark against thee, so that I am a burden to myself?

21 And why dost thou not pardon my transgression, and take away mine iniquity? for now shall I sleep in the dust; and thou shalt seek me in the morning, but I *shall* not *be*.

CHAPTER 8
Bildad Answers Job

1 Then answered Bildad the Shuhite, and said,

2 How long wilt thou speak these *things*? and *how long shall* the words of thy mouth *be* like a strong wind?

---

3 Doth God pervert judgment? or doth the Almighty pervert justice?

4 If thy children have sinned against him, and he have cast them away for their transgression;

5 If thou wouldest seek unto God betimes, and make thy supplication to the Almighty;

6 If thou *wert* pure and upright; surely now he would awake for thee, and make the habitation of thy righteousness prosperous.

7 Though thy beginning was small, yet thy latter end should greatly increase.

8 For inquire, I pray thee, of the former age, and prepare thyself to the search of their fathers:

9 (For we *are but of* yesterday, and know nothing, because our days upon earth *are* a shadow:)

10 Shall not they teach thee, *and* tell thee, and utter words out of their heart?

11 Can the rush grow up without mire? can the flag grow without water?

12 Whilst it *is* yet in his greenness, *and* not cut down, it withereth before any *other* herb.

13 So *are* the paths of all that forget God; and the hypocrite's hope shall perish:

14 Whose hope shall be cut off, and whose trust *shall be* a spider's web.

15 He shall lean upon his house, but it shall not stand: he shall hold it fast, but it shall not endure.

16 He *is* green before the sun, and his branch shooteth forth in his garden.

17 His roots are wrapped about the heap, *and* seeth the place of stones.

18 If he destroy him from his place, then *it* shall deny him, *saying*, I have not seen thee.

19 Behold, this *is* the joy of his way, and out of the earth shall others grow.

20 Behold, God will not cast away a perfect *man*, neither will he help the evil doers:

21 Till he fill thy mouth with laughing, and thy lips with rejoicing.

22 They that hate thee shall be clothed with shame; and the dwelling place of the wicked shall come to nought.

CHAPTER 9
Job Replies

1 Then Job answered and said,

2 I know *it is* so of a truth: but how should man be just with God?

3 If he will contend with him, he cannot answer him one of a thousand.

4 *He is* wise in heart, and mighty in strength: who hath hardened *himself* against him, and hath prospered?

5 Which removeth the mountains, and

Center column cross-references:

4 Deut. 28:67; Job 17:12

5 Isa. 14:11

6 Job 9:25; 16:22; 17:11; Ps. 90:6; 102:11; 103:15; 144:4; Isa. 38:12; 40:6; James 4:14

7 Ps. 78:39; 89:47

8 Job 20:9

9 2Sam. 12:23

11 Ps. 39:1, 9; 40:9

13 Job 9:27

16 Job 10:1, 20; 14:6; Ps. 39:13; 62:9

17 Ps. 8:4; 144:3; Heb. 2:6

20 Job 16:12; Ps. 21:12; 36:6; Lam. 3:12

3 Gen. 18:25; Deut. 32:4; 2Chr. 19:7; Job 34:12, 17

4 Job 1:5, 18

5 Job 5:8; 11:13; 22:23-30

8 Deut. 4:32; 32:7; Job 15:18

9 Gen. 47:9; 1Chr. 29:15; Job 7:6; Ps. 39:5; 102:11; 144:4

12 Ps. 129:6; Jer. 17:6

13 Job 11:20; 18:14; 27:8; Ps. 112:10; Prov. 10:28

14 Isa. 59:5, 6

15 Job 27:18

18 Job 7:10; 20:9; Ps. 37:36

19 Ps. 113:7

22 Ps. 35:26; 109:29

2 Ps. 143:2; Rom. 3:20

4 Job 36:5

they know not: which overturneth them in his anger.

6 Which shaketh the earth out of her place, and the pillars thereof tremble.

7 Which commandeth the sun, and it riseth not; and sealeth up the stars.

8 Which alone spreadeth out the heavens, and treadeth upon the waves of the sea.

9 Which maketh Arcturus, Orion, and Pleiades, and the chambers of the south.

10 Which doeth great things past finding out; yea, and wonders without number.

11 Lo, he goeth by me, and I see *him* not: he passeth on also, but I perceive him not.

12 Behold, he taketh away, who can hinder him? who will say unto him, What doest thou?

13 *If* God will not withdraw his anger, the proud helpers do stoop under him.

14 How much less shall I answer him, *and* choose out my words *to reason* with him?

15 Whom, though I were righteous, *yet* would I not answer, *but* I would make supplication to my judge.

16 If I had called, and he had answered me; *yet* would I not believe that he had hearkened unto my voice.

17 For he breaketh me with a tempest, and multiplieth my wounds without cause.

18 He will not suffer me to take my breath, but filleth me with bitterness.

19 If *I speak* of strength, lo, *he is* strong: and if of judgment, who shall set me a time *to plead?*

20 If I justify myself, mine own mouth shall condemn me: *if I say,* I *am* perfect, it shall also prove me perverse.

21 *Though* I *were* perfect, *yet* would I not know my soul: I would despise my life.

22 This *is* one *thing,* therefore I said *it,* He destroyeth the perfect and the wicked.

23 If the scourge slay suddenly, he will laugh at the trial of the innocent.

24 The earth is given into the hand of the wicked: he covereth the faces of the judges thereof; if not, where, *and* who *is* he?

25 Now my days are swifter than a post: they flee away, they see no good.

26 They are passed away as the swift ships: as the eagle *that* hasteth to the prey.

27 If I say, I will forget my complaint, I will leave off my heaviness, and comfort *myself:*

28 I am afraid of all my sorrows, I know that thou wilt not hold me innocent.

29 *If* I be wicked, why then labour I in vain?

30 If I wash myself with snow water, and make my hands never so clean;

31 Yet shalt thou plunge me in the ditch, and mine own clothes shall abhor me.

6 Job 26:11; Isa. 2:19, 21; Hag. 2:6, 21; Heb. 12:26

8 Gen. 1:6; Ps. 104:2, 3

9 Gen. 1:16; Job 38:31, 32; Amos 5:8

10 Job 5:9; Ps. 71:15

11 Job 23:8, 9; 35:14

12 Job 11:10; Isa. 45:9; Jer. 18:6; Rom. 9:20

13 Job 26:12; Isa. 30:7

15 Job 10:15

17 Job 2:3; 34:6

22 Eccl. 9:2, 3; Ezek. 21:3

24 2Sam. 15:30; 19:4; Jer. 14:4

25 Job 7:6, 7

26 Hab. 1:8

27 Job 7:13

28 Ex. 20:7; Ps. 119:120

30 Jer. 2:22

33 1Sam. 2:25; Job 9:19

34 Job 13:20-22; 33:7; Ps. 39:10

1 1Kgs. 19:4; Job 7:11, 16; Jon. 4:3, 8

3 Ps. 138:8; Isa. 64:8

4 1Sam. 16:7

7 Ps. 139:12

8 Ps. 119:73

9 Gen. 2:7; 3:19; Isa. 64:8

10 Ps. 139:14-16

14 Ps. 139:1

15 Job 9:12, 15, 20, 21; Ps. 25:18

16 Isa. 38:13; Lam. 3:10

17 Ruth 1:21

18 Job 3:11

32 For *he is* not a man, as I *am, that* I should answer him, *and* we should come together in judgment.

33 Neither is there any daysman betwixt us, *that* might lay his hand upon us both.

34 Let him take his rod away from me, and let not his fear terrify me:

35 *Then* would I speak, and not fear him; but *it is* not so with me.

CHAPTER 10

1 My soul is weary of my life; I will leave my complaint upon myself; I will speak in the bitterness of my soul.

2 I will say unto God, Do not condemn me; shew me wherefore thou contendest with me.

3 *Is it* good unto thee that thou shouldest oppress, that thou shouldest despise the work of thine hands, and shine upon the counsel of the wicked?

4 Hast thou eyes of flesh? or seest thou as man seeth?

5 *Are* thy days as the days of man? *are* thy years as man's days,

6 That thou inquirest after mine iniquity, and searchest after my sin?

7 Thou knowest that I am not wicked; and *there is* none that can deliver out of thine hand.

8 Thine hands have made me and fashioned me together round about; yet thou dost destroy me.

9 Remember, I beseech thee, that thou hast made me as the clay; and wilt thou bring me into dust again?

10 Hast thou not poured me out as milk, and curdled me like cheese?

11 Thou hast clothed me with skin and flesh, and hast fenced me with bones and sinews.

12 Thou hast granted me life and favour, and thy visitation hath preserved my spirit.

13 And these *things* hast thou hid in thine heart: I know that this *is* with thee.

14 If I sin, then thou markest me, and thou wilt not acquit me from mine iniquity.

15 If I be wicked, woe unto me; and *if* I be righteous, *yet* will I not lift up my head. I *am* full of confusion; therefore see thou mine affliction;

16 For it increaseth. Thou huntest me as a fierce lion: and again thou shewest thyself marvellous upon me.

17 Thou renewest thy witnesses against me, and increasest thine indignation upon me; changes and war *are* against me.

18 Wherefore then hast thou brought me

forth out of the womb? Oh that I had given up the ghost, and no eye had seen me!

19 I should have been as though I had not been; I should have been carried from the womb to the grave.

20 Are not my days few? cease then, and let me alone, that I may take comfort a little,

21 Before I go whence I shall not return, even to the land of darkness and the shadow of death;

22 A land of darkness, as darkness itself; and of the shadow of death, without any order, and where the light is as darkness.

CHAPTER 11
Zophar Accuses Job of Sin

1 Then answered Zophar the Naamathite, and said,

2 Should not the multitude of words be answered? and should a man full of talk be justified?

3 Should thy lies make men hold their peace? and when thou mockest, shall no man make thee ashamed?

4 For thou hast said, My doctrine is pure, and I am clean in thine eyes.

5 But oh that God would speak, and open his lips against thee;

6 And that he would shew thee the secrets of wisdom, that they are double to that which is! Know therefore that God exacteth of thee less than thine iniquity deserveth.

7 Canst thou by searching find out God? canst thou find out the Almighty unto perfection?

8 It is as high as heaven; what canst thou do? deeper than hell; what canst thou know?

9 The measure thereof is longer than the earth, and broader than the sea.

10 If he cut off, and shut up, or gather together, then who can hinder him?

11 For he knoweth vain men: he seeth wickedness also; will he not then consider it?

12 For vain man would be wise, though man be born like a wild ass's colt.

13 If thou prepare thine heart, and stretch out thine hands toward him;

14 If iniquity be in thine hand, put it far away, and let not wickedness dwell in thy tabernacles.

15 For then shalt thou lift up thy face without spot; yea, thou shalt be stedfast, and shalt not fear:

16 Because thou shalt forget thy misery, and remember it as waters that pass away:

17 And thine age shall be clearer than the

20 Job 7:6, 16, 19; 8:9; Ps. 39:5, 13

21 Ps. 23:4; 88:12

4 Job 6:10; 10:7

6 Ezra 9:13

7 Eccl. 3:11; Rom. 11:33

10 Job 9:12; 12:14; Rev. 3:7

11 Ps. 10:11, 14; 35:22; 94:11

12 Ps. 73:22; 92:6; Eccl. 3:18

13 1Sam. 7:3; Job 5:8; 22:21; Ps. 78:8; 88:9; 143:6

14 Ps. 101:3

15 Job 22:26; Ps. 119:6

16 Isa. 65:16

17 Ps. 37:6; 112:4; Isa. 58:8, 10

18 Lev. 26:5, 6; Ps. 3:5; 4:8; Prov. 3:24

20 Lev. 26:16; Deut. 28:65; Job 8:14; 18:14; Prov. 11:7

3 Job 13:2

4 Job 16:10; 17:2, 6; 21:3; 30:1; Ps. 91:15

5 Prov. 14:2

6 Job 21:7; Ps. 37:1, 35; 73:11, 12; 92:7; Jer. 12:1; Mal. 3:15

10 Num. 16:22; Dan. 5:23; Acts 17:28

11 Job 6:30; 34:3

12 Job 32:7

13 Job 9:4; 36:5

14 Isa. 22:22; Rev. 3:7

15 Gen. 7:11

17 1Cor. 1:19

noonday; thou shalt shine forth, thou shalt be as the morning.

18 And thou shalt be secure, because there is hope; yea, thou shalt dig about thee, and thou shalt take thy rest in safety.

19 Also thou shalt lie down, and none shall make thee afraid; yea, many shall make suit unto thee.

20 But the eyes of the wicked shall fail, and they shall not escape, and their hope shall be as the giving up of the ghost.

CHAPTER 12
Job Responds

1 And Job answered and said,

2 No doubt but ye are the people, and wisdom shall die with you.

3 But I have understanding as well as you; I am not inferior to you: yea, who knoweth not such things as these?

4 I am as one mocked of his neighbour, who calleth upon God, and he answereth him: the just upright man is laughed to scorn.

5 He that is ready to slip with his feet is as a lamp despised in the thought of him that is at ease.

6 The tabernacles of robbers prosper, and they that provoke God are secure; into whose hand God bringeth abundantly.

7 But ask now the beasts, and they shall teach thee; and the fowls of the air, and they shall tell thee:

8 Or speak to the earth, and it shall teach thee: and the fishes of the sea shall declare unto thee.

9 Who knoweth not in all these that the hand of the LORD hath wrought this?

10 In whose hand is the soul of every living thing, and the breath of all mankind.

11 Doth not the ear try words? and the mouth taste his meat?

12 With the ancient is wisdom; and in length of days understanding.

13 With him is wisdom and strength, he hath counsel and understanding.

14 Behold, he breaketh down, and it cannot be built again: he shutteth up a man, and there can be no opening.

15 Behold, he withholdeth the waters, and they dry up: also he sendeth them out, and they overturn the earth.

16 With him is strength and wisdom: the deceived and the deceiver are his.

17 He leadeth counsellers away spoiled, and maketh the judges fools.

18 He looseth the bond of kings, and girdeth their loins with a girdle.

19 He leadeth princes away spoiled, and overthroweth the mighty.

20 He removeth away the speech of the trusty, and taketh away the understanding of the aged.

21 He poureth contempt upon princes, and weakeneth the strength of the mighty.

22 He discovereth deep things out of darkness, and bringeth out to light the shadow of death.

23 He increaseth the nations, and destroyeth them: he enlargeth the nations, and straiteneth them *again*.

24 He taketh away the heart of the chief of the people of the earth, and causeth them to wander in a wilderness *where there is* no way.

25 They grope in the dark without light, and he maketh them to stagger like *a* drunken *man*.

CHAPTER 13

1 Lo, mine eye hath seen all *this*, mine ear hath heard and understood it.

2 What ye know, *the same* do I know also: I *am* not inferior unto you.

3 Surely I would speak to the Almighty, and I desire to reason with God.

4 But ye *are* forgers of lies, ye *are* all physicians of no value.

5 O that ye would altogether hold your peace! and it should be your wisdom.

6 Hear now my reasoning, and hearken to the pleadings of my lips.

7 Will ye speak wickedly for God? and talk deceitfully for him?

8 Will ye accept his person? will ye contend for God?

9 Is it good that he should search you out? or as one man mocketh another, do ye *so* mock him?

10 He will surely reprove you, if ye do secretly accept persons.

11 Shall not his excellency make you afraid? and his dread fall upon you?

12 Your remembrances *are* like unto ashes, your bodies to bodies of clay.

13 Hold your peace, let me alone, that I may speak, and let come on me what *will*.

14 Wherefore do I take my flesh in my teeth, and put my life in mine hand?

15 Though he slay me, yet will I trust in him: but I will maintain mine own ways before him.

16 He also *shall be* my salvation: for an hypocrite shall not come before him.

17 Hear diligently my speech, and my declaration with your ears.

18 Behold now, I have ordered *my* cause; I know that I shall be justified.

19 Who *is* he *that* will plead with me? for now, if I hold my tongue, I shall give up the ghost.

20 Only do not two *things* unto me: then will I not hide myself from thee.

21 Withdraw thine hand far from me: and let not thy dread make me afraid.

22 Then call thou, and I will answer: or let me speak, and answer thou me.

23 How many *are* mine iniquities and sins? make me to know my transgression and my sin.

24 Wherefore hidest thou thy face, and holdest me for thine enemy?

25 Wilt thou break a leaf driven to and fro? and wilt thou pursue the dry stubble?

26 For thou writest bitter things against me, and makest me to possess the iniquities of my youth.

27 Thou puttest my feet also in the stocks, and lookest narrowly unto all my paths; thou settest a print upon the heels of my feet.

28 And he, as a rotten thing, consumeth, as a garment that is moth eaten.

CHAPTER 14

1 Man *that is* born of a woman *is* of few days, and full of trouble.

2 He cometh forth like a flower, and is cut down: he fleeth also as a shadow, and continueth not.

3 And dost thou open thine eyes upon such an one, and bringest me into judgment with thee?

4 Who can bring a clean *thing* out of an unclean? not one.

5 Seeing his days *are* determined, the number of his months *are* with thee, thou hast appointed his bounds that he cannot pass;

6 Turn from him, that he may rest, till he shall accomplish, as an hireling, his day.

7 For there is hope of a tree, if it be cut down, that it will sprout again, and that the tender branch thereof will not cease.

8 Though the root thereof wax old in the earth, and the stock thereof die in the ground;

9 *Yet* through the scent of water it will bud, and bring forth boughs like a plant.

10 But man dieth, and wasteth away: yea, man giveth up the ghost, and where *is* he?

11 *As* the waters fail from the sea, and the flood decayeth and drieth up:

Cross-references (center column):

20 Job 32:9; Isa. 3:1-3
21 Ps. 107:40; Dan. 2:21
22 Dan. 2:22; Matt. 10:26; 1Cor. 4:5
23 Ps. 107:38; Isa. 9:3; 26:15
24 Ps. 107:4, 40
25 Deut. 28:29; Job 5:14; Ps. 107:27
2 Job 12:3
3 Job 23:3; 31:35
4 Job 6:21; 16:2
5 Prov. 17:28
7 Job 17:5; 32:21; 36:4
14 1Sam. 28:21; Job 18:4; Ps. 119:109
15 Job 27:5; Ps. 23:4; Prov. 14:32
19 Job 33:6; Isa. 50:8
20 Job 9:34; 33:7
21 Ps. 39:10
24 Deut. 32:20; 32:42; Ruth 1:21; Job 16:9; 19:11; 33:10; Ps. 13:1; 44:24; 88:14; Isa. 8:17; Lam. 2:5
25 Isa. 42:3
26 Job 20:11; Ps. 25:7
27 Job 33:11
1 Job 5:7; Eccl. 2:23
2 Job 8:9; Ps. 90:5, 6, 9; 102:11; 103:15; 144:4; Isa. 40:6; 1Pet. 1:24
3 Ps. 143:2; 144:3
4 Ps. 51:5; Rom. 5:12
5 Job 7:1

12 So man lieth down, and riseth not: till the heavens *be* no more, they shall not awake, nor be raised out of their sleep.

13 O that thou wouldest hide me in the grave, that thou wouldest keep me secret, until thy wrath be past, that thou wouldest appoint me a set time, and remember me!

14 If a man die, shall he live *again*? all the days of my appointed time will I wait, till my change come.

15 Thou shalt call, and I will answer thee: thou wilt have a desire to the work of thine hands.

16 For now thou numberest my steps: dost thou not watch over my sin?

17 My transgression *is* sealed up in a bag, and thou sewest up mine iniquity.

18 And surely the mountain falling cometh to nought, and the rock is removed out of his place.

19 The waters wear the stones: thou washest away the things which grow *out* of the dust of the earth; and thou destroyest the hope of man.

20 Thou prevailest for ever against him, and he passeth: thou changest his countenance, and sendest him away.

21 His sons come to honour, and he knoweth *it* not; and they are brought low, but he perceiveth *it* not of them.

22 But his flesh upon him shall have pain, and his soul within him shall mourn.

CHAPTER 15
Eliphaz Reprimands Job

1 Then answered Eliphaz the Temanite, and said,

2 Should a wise man utter vain knowledge, and fill his belly with the east wind?

3 Should he reason with unprofitable talk? or with speeches wherewith he can do no good?

4 Yea, thou castest off fear, and restrainest prayer before God.

5 For thy mouth uttereth thine iniquity, and thou choosest the tongue of the crafty.

6 Thine own mouth condemneth thee, and not I: yea, thine own lips testify against thee.

7 *Art* thou the first man *that* was born? or wast thou made before the hills?

8 Hast thou heard the secret of God? and dost thou restrain wisdom to thyself?

9 What knowest thou, that we know not? *what* understandest thou, which *is* not in us?

10 With us *are* both the greyheaded and very aged men, much elder than thy father.

11 *Are* the consolations of God small with thee? is there any secret thing with thee?

12 Why doth thine heart carry thee away? and what do thy eyes wink at,

13 That thou turnest thy spirit against God, and lettest *such* words go out of thy mouth?

14 What *is* man, that he should be clean? and *he which is* born of a woman, that he should be righteous?

15 Behold, he putteth no trust in his saints; yea, the heavens are not clean in his sight.

16 How much more abominable and filthy *is* man, which drinketh iniquity like water?

17 I will shew thee, hear me; and that *which* I have seen I will declare;

18 Which wise men have told from their fathers, and have not hid *it*:

19 Unto whom alone the earth was given, and no stranger passed among them.

20 The wicked man travaileth with pain all *his* days, and the number of years is hidden to the oppressor.

21 A dreadful sound *is* in his ears: in prosperity the destroyer shall come upon him.

22 He believeth not that he shall return out of darkness, and he is waited for of the sword.

23 He wandereth abroad for bread, *saying*, Where *is it*? he knoweth that the day of darkness is ready at his hand.

24 Trouble and anguish shall make him afraid; they shall prevail against him, as a king ready to the battle.

25 For he stretcheth out his hand against God, and strengtheneth himself against the Almighty.

26 He runneth upon him, *even on his* neck, upon the thick bosses of his bucklers:

27 Because he covereth his face with his fatness, and maketh collops of fat on *his* flanks.

Cross references

12 Ps. 102:26; Isa. 51:6; 65:17; 66:22; Acts 3:21; Rom. 8:20; 2Pet. 3:7, 10, 11; Rev. 20:11; 21:1

14 Job 13:15; 14:7

15 Job 13:22

16 Job 10:6, 14; 13:27; 31:4; 34:21; Ps. 56:8; 139:1-3; Prov. 5:21; Jer. 32:19

17 Deut. 32:34; Hos. 13:12

21 Eccl. 9:5; Isa. 63:16

6 Luke 19:22

7 Ps. 90:2; Prov. 8:25

8 Rom. 11:34; 1Cor. 2:11

9 Job 13:2

10 Job 32:6, 7

14 1Kgs. 8:46; 2Chr. 6:36; Job 14:4; Ps. 14:3; Prov. 20:9; Eccl. 7:20; 1John 1:8, 10

15 Job 4:18; 25:5

16 Job 4:19; 34:7; Ps. 14:3; 53:3; Prov. 19:28

18 Job 8:8

19 Joel 3:17

20 Ps. 90:12

21 1Thess. 5:3

23 Job 18:12; Ps. 59:15; 109:10

27 Ps. 17:10

14:12–13 Job is so certain of a resurrection he just assumes it and ties it in with the time that "the heavens be no more," which accords with Jesus' words, "Heaven and earth shall pass away: but my words shall not pass away" (Matt. 24:35).

14:14–15 One of the great philosophical questions of life is asked by Job, "If a man die, shall he live again?" A driving force in all religion is life in the hereafter. The Jews had a strong belief in a future resurrection, yet it is the Christian message, based on the resurrection of Jesus, that is the most definitive and satisfying. The real answer to Job's classic question is found in his great prophecy in 19:25–27.

28 And he dwelleth in desolate cities, *and in* houses which no man inhabiteth, which are ready to become heaps.

29 He shall not be rich, neither shall his substance continue, neither shall he prolong the perfection thereof upon the earth.

30 He shall not depart out of darkness; the flame shall dry up his branches, and by the breath of his mouth shall he go away.

31 Let not him that is deceived trust in vanity: for vanity shall be his recompence.

32 It shall be accomplished before his time, and his branch shall not be green.

33 He shall shake off his unripe grape as the vine, and shall cast off his flower as the olive.

34 For the congregation of hypocrites *shall be* desolate, and fire shall consume the tabernacles of bribery.

35 They conceive mischief, and bring forth vanity, and their belly prepareth deceit.

CHAPTER 16
Job Complains Again

1 Then Job answered and said,

2 I have heard many such things: miserable comforters *are* ye all.

3 Shall vain words have an end? or what emboldeneth thee that thou answerest?

4 I also could speak as ye *do*: if your soul were in my soul's stead, I could heap up words against you, and shake mine head at you.

5 *But* I would strengthen you with my mouth, and the moving of my lips should assuage *your grief.*

6 Though I speak, my grief is not asswaged: and *though* I forbear, what am I eased?

7 But now he hath made me weary: thou hast made desolate all my company.

8 And thou hast filled me with wrinkles, *which* is a witness *against me*: and my leanness rising up in me beareth witness to my face.

9 He teareth *me* in his wrath, who hateth me: he gnasheth upon me with his teeth; mine enemy sharpeneth his eyes upon me.

10 They have gaped upon me with their mouth; they have smitten me upon the cheek reproachfully; they have gathered themselves together against me.

11 God hath delivered me to the ungodly, and turned me over into the hands of the wicked.

12 I was at ease, but he hath broken me asunder: he hath also taken *me* by my neck, and shaken me to pieces, and set me up for his mark.

13 His archers compass me round about, he cleaveth my reins asunder, and doth not spare; he poureth out my gall upon the ground.

14 He breaketh me with breach upon breach, he runneth upon me like a giant.

15 I have sewed sackcloth upon my skin, and defiled my horn in the dust.

16 My face is foul with weeping, and on my eyelids *is* the shadow of death;

17 Not for *any* injustice in mine hands: also my prayer *is* pure.

18 O earth, cover not thou my blood, and let my cry have no place.

19 Also now, behold, my witness *is* in heaven, and my record *is* on high.

20 My friends scorn me: *but* mine eye poureth out *tears* unto God.

21 O that one might plead for a man with God, as a man *pleadeth* for his neighbour!

22 When a few years are come, then I shall go the way *whence* I shall not return.

CHAPTER 17

1 My breath is corrupt, my days are extinct, the graves *are ready* for me.

2 *Are there* not mockers with me? and doth not mine eye continue in their provocation?

3 Lay down now, put me in a surety with thee; who *is* he *that* will strike hands with me?

4 For thou hast hid their heart from understanding: therefore shalt thou not exalt *them.*

5 He that speaketh flattery to *his* friends, even the eyes of his children shall fail.

6 He hath made me also a byword of the people; and aforetime I was as a tabret.

7 Mine eye also is dim by reason of sorrow, and all my members *are* as a shadow.

8 Upright *men* shall be astonied at this, and the innocent shall stir up himself against the hypocrite.

9 The righteous also shall hold on his way, and he that hath clean hands shall be stronger and stronger.

10 But as for you all, do ye return, and come now: for I cannot find *one* wise *man* among you.

11 My days are past, my purposes are broken off, *even* the thoughts of my heart.

12 They change the night into day: the light *is* short because of darkness.

13 If I wait, the grave *is* mine house: I have made my bed in the darkness.

14 I have said to corruption, Thou *art* my father: to the worm, *Thou art* my mother, and my sister.

Center cross-references:

30 Job 4:9
31 Isa. 59:4
32 Job 22:16; Ps. 55:23
35 Ps. 7:14; Isa. 59:4; Hos. 10:13
2 Job 13:4
4 Ps. 22:7; 109:25; Lam. 2:15
9 Job 10:16, 17; 13:24
10 Ps. 22:13; 35:15; Lam. 3:30; Mic. 5:1
11 Job 1:15, 17
12 Job 7:20
15 Job 30:19; Ps. 7:5
18 Job 27:9; Ps. 66:18, 19
19 Rom. 1:9
21 Job 31:35; Eccl. 6:10; Isa. 45:9; Rom. 9:20
22 Eccl. 12:5
1 Ps. 88:3, 4
2 1Sam. 1:6, 7
3 Prov. 6:1; 17:18; 22:26
6 Job 30:9
7 Ps. 6:7; 31:9
9 Ps. 24:4
10 Job 6:29
11 Job 7:6; 9:25

15 And where *is* now my hope? as for my hope, who shall see it?
16 They shall go down to the bars of the pit, when *our* rest together *is* in the dust.

CHAPTER 18
Bildad's Sermon

1 Then answered Bildad the Shuhite, and said,
2 How long *will it be ere* ye make an end of words? mark, and afterwards we will speak.
3 Wherefore are we counted as beasts, *and* reputed vile in your sight?
4 He teareth himself in his anger: shall the earth be forsaken for thee? and shall the rock be removed out of his place?
5 Yea, the light of the wicked shall be put out, and the spark of his fire shall not shine.
6 The light shall be dark in his tabernacle, and his candle shall be put out with him.
7 The steps of his strength shall be straitened, and his own counsel shall cast him down.
8 For he is cast into a net by his own feet, and he walketh upon a snare.
9 The gin shall take *him* by the heel, *and* the robber shall prevail against him.
10 The snare *is* laid for him in the ground, and a trap for him in the way.
11 Terrors shall make him afraid on every side, and shall drive him to his feet.
12 His strength shall be hungerbitten, and destruction *shall be* ready at his side.
13 It shall devour the strength of his skin: *even* the firstborn of death shall devour his strength.
14 His confidence shall be rooted out of his tabernacle, and it shall bring him to the king of terrors.
15 It shall dwell in his tabernacle, because *it is* none of his: brimstone shall be scattered upon his habitation.
16 His roots shall be dried up beneath, and above shall his branch be cut off.
17 His remembrance shall perish from the earth, and he shall have no name in the street.
18 He shall be driven from light into darkness, and chased out of the world.
19 He shall neither have son nor nephew among his people, nor any remaining in his dwellings.
20 They that come after *him* shall be astonied at his day, as they that went before were affrighted.
21 Surely such *are* the dwellings of the wicked, and this *is* the place *of him that* knoweth not God.

CHAPTER 19
Job Is Confident

1 Then Job answered and said,
2 How long will ye vex my soul, and break me in pieces with words?
3 These ten times have ye reproached me: ye are not ashamed *that* ye make yourselves strange to me.
4 And be it indeed *that* I have erred, mine error remaineth with myself.
5 If indeed ye will magnify *yourselves* against me, and plead against me my reproach:
6 Know now that God hath overthrown me, and hath compassed me with his net.
7 Behold, I cry out of wrong, but I am not heard: I cry aloud, but *there is* no judgment.
8 He hath fenced up my way that I cannot pass, and he hath set darkness in my paths.
9 He hath stripped me of my glory, and taken the crown *from* my head.
10 He hath destroyed me on every side, and I am gone: and mine hope hath he removed like a tree.
11 He hath also kindled his wrath against me, and he counteth me unto him as *one of* his enemies.
12 His troops come together, and raise up their way against me, and encamp round about my tabernacle.
13 He hath put my brethren far from me, and mine acquaintance are verily estranged from me.
14 My kinsfolk have failed, and my familiar friends have forgotten me.
15 They that dwell in mine house, and my maids, count me for a stranger: I am an alien in their sight.
16 I called my servant, and he gave *me* no answer; I intreated him with my mouth.
17 My breath is strange to my wife, though I intreated for the children's *sake* of mine own body.
18 Yea, young children despised me; I arose, and they spake against me.
19 All my inward friends abhorred me: and they whom I loved are turned against me.
20 My bone cleaveth to my skin and to my flesh, and I am escaped with the skin of my teeth.
21 Have pity upon me, have pity upon me, O ye my friends; for the hand of God hath touched me.
22 Why do ye persecute me as God, and are not satisfied with my flesh?
23 Oh that my words were now written! oh that they were printed in a book!

Cross References

16 Job 3:17–19; 18:13
3 Ps. 73:22
4 Job 13:14
5 Prov. 13:9; 20:20; 24:20
6 Job 21:17; Ps. 18:28
7 Job 5:13
8 Job 22:10; Ps. 9:15; 35:8
9 Job 5:5
11 Job 15:21; 20:25; Jer. 6:25; 20:3; Mal. 4:1
12 Job 15:23
14 Job 8:14; 11:20; Ps. 112:10; Prov. 10:28
16 Job 29:19; Isa. 5:24; Amos 2:9; Mal. 4:1
17 Ps. 34:16; 109:13; Prov. 2:22; 10:7
19 Isa. 14:22; Jer. 22:30
20 Ps. 37:13
21 Jer. 9:3; 10:25; 1Thess. 4:5; 2Thess. 1:8; Titus 1:16
3 Gen. 31:7; Lev. 26:26
5 Ps. 38:16
8 Job 3:23; Ps. 88:8
9 Ps. 89:44
11 Job 13:24; Lam. 2:5
12 Job 30:12
13 Ps. 31:11; 38:11; 69:8; 88:8, 18
18 2Kgs. 2:23
19 Ps. 41:9; 55:13, 14, 20
20 Job 30:30; Ps. 102:5; Lam. 4:8
21 Job 1:11; Ps. 38:2
22 Ps. 60:26

How to Keep a Spiritual Journal

By Tim LaHaye

The best tool I use to get the greatest blessing out of devotional reading is in habitually keeping a daily spiritual journal. A fancy journal or notebook is not necessary; an ordinary sheet of paper or a small spiral notebook will suffice. Allowing one page per day, write the day of the week, the month, and the date at the top of your journal entry, with space for the text to be read.

There are five things you should include in your daily journal:

1. God's Message to You Today

The first thing to look for is that special message from God for the day. Naturally, this will be influenced largely by the passage under study for that day and your own particular need at the time.

2. A Promise from God

The Bible is filled with promises from God to His children. You will not find one in every passage, but promises are so common that you will locate them very frequently. In many passages you will find several, and for that reason you should select the best one from the three or four chapters you read that day. There are two things to consider in claiming promises: 1) make sure they are universal promises, and 2) make sure they apply to you. Some are for Israel; some are for the people in the Millennium; and some are promised judgments on the wicked. Always examine the Bible in the light of the people to whom it is directly written and in light of the context.

Daily journals offer practical applications to your life.

Another thing to keep in mind when looking for promises is whether there are any conditions to the promise. You should always write down the conditions that precede a promise so you will know whether or not it is legitimate for you to claim.

3. A Command to Keep

The Bible is filled with commands for God's people to obey. These commands are for our good, since the keeping of them enriches our lives. As you come upon these commands in your reading, select the most important of them for your life at that moment and enter it into your journal.

4. A Timeless Principle

One reason why the Bible is the greatest manual ever written on human behavior is that it contains thousands of timeless principles for daily living. These divine insights guide us as believers and help program our minds in advance so that we do not have to go through agonizing thought processes when decisions need to be made. Obeying timeless principles produces happiness and fulfillment in the lives of God's people.

5. Your Application

As a principal tool in implementing the above "finds" in your daily reading, pick out one that is in the area of your greatest need, and list how you intend to implement it in your daily life. Ask God to help you apply the biblical principles you study to areas in your life where you feel you need the most improvement.

Daily journals offer simple but practical applications to your life concerning the daily challenges you find in God's Word. These applications will transform your life into the growing, consistent Christian walk that every child of God needs.

24 That they were graven with an iron pen and lead in the rock for ever!

25 For I know *that* my redeemer liveth, and *that* he shall stand at the latter *day* upon the earth:

26 And *though* after my skin *worms* destroy this *body*, yet in my flesh shall I see God:

27 Whom I shall see for myself, and mine eyes shall behold, and not another; *though* my reins be consumed within me.

28 But ye should say, Why persecute we him, seeing the root of the matter is found in me?

29 Be ye afraid of the sword: for wrath *bringeth* the punishments of the sword, that ye may know *there is* a judgment.

Chapter 20
Zophar's Sermon

1 Then answered Zophar the Naamathite, and said,

2 Therefore do my thoughts cause me to answer, and for *this* I make haste.

3 I have heard the check of my reproach, and the spirit of my understanding causeth me to answer,

4 Knowest thou *not* this of old, since man was placed upon earth,

5 That the triumphing of the wicked *is* short, and the joy of the hypocrite *but* for a moment?

6 Though his excellency mount up to the heavens, and his head reach unto the clouds;

7 *Yet* he shall perish for ever like his own dung: they which have seen him shall say, Where *is* he?

8 He shall fly away as a dream, and shall not be found: yea, he shall be chased away as a vision of the night.

9 The eye also *which* saw him shall *see him* no more; neither shall his place any more behold him.

10 His children shall seek to please the poor, and his hands shall restore their goods.

11 His bones are full *of the sin* of his youth, which shall lie down with him in the dust.

12 Though wickedness be sweet in his mouth, *though* he hide it under his tongue;

13 *Though* he spare it, and forsake it not; but keep it still within his mouth:

14 *Yet* his meat in his bowels is turned, *it is* the gall of asps within him.

15 He hath swallowed down riches, and he shall vomit them up again: God shall cast them out of his belly.

16 He shall suck the poison of asps: the viper's tongue shall slay him.

17 He shall not see the rivers, the floods, the brooks of honey and butter.

18 That which he laboured for shall he restore, and shall not swallow *it* down: according to *his* substance *shall* the restitution *be*, and he shall not rejoice *therein*.

19 Because he hath oppressed *and* hath forsaken the poor; *because* he hath violently taken away an house which he builded not;

20 Surely he shall not feel quietness in his belly, he shall not save of that which he desired.

21 There shall none of his meat be left; therefore shall no man look for his goods.

22 In the fulness of his sufficiency he shall be in straits: every hand of the wicked shall come upon him.

23 *When* he is about to fill his belly, *God* shall cast the fury of his wrath upon him, and shall rain *it* upon him while he is eating.

24 He shall flee from the iron weapon, *and* the bow of steel shall strike him through.

25 It is drawn, and cometh out of the body; yea, the glittering sword cometh out of his gall: terrors *are* upon him.

26 All darkness *shall be* hid in his secret places: a fire not blown shall consume him; it shall go ill with him that is left in his tabernacle.

27 The heaven shall reveal his iniquity; and the earth shall rise up against him.

28 The increase of his house shall depart, *and his goods* shall flow away in the day of his wrath.

29 This *is* the portion of a wicked man from God, and the heritage appointed unto him by God.

Chapter 21
Job Describes the Wicked

1 But Job answered and said,

2 Hear diligently my speech, and let this be your consolations.

Cross references
26 Ps. 17:15; 1Cor. 13:12; 1John 3:2
28 Job 19:22
29 Ps. 58:10, 11
5 Ps. 37:35, 36
6 Isa. 14:13, 14; Obad. 1:3, 4
7 Ps. 83:10
8 Ps. 73:20; 90:5
9 Job 7:8, 10; 8:18; Ps. 37:36; 103:16
10 Job 20:18
11 Job 13:26; 21:26; Ps. 25:7
17 Ps. 36:9; Jer. 17:6
18 Job 20:10, 15
20 Eccl. 5:13, 14
23 Num. 11:33; Ps. 78:30, 31
24 Isa. 24:18; Jer. 48:43; Amos 5:19
25 Job 16:13; 18:11
26 Ps. 21:9
29 Job 27:13; 31:2, 3

19:25–27 This memorable statement of Job's faith is more than a classic declaration of faith, particularly in view of the lack of a Bible to guide him; it is truly one of the great prophecies of Scripture. Because God is a living "redeemer," our bodies will not remain "dead" even after they decay, but their elements will be used to make new bodies of our flesh which "shall see God" with our "own eyes." That means there will not only be life in the hereafter for believers, but life will also be even better than this one, for we cannot "see God" now, but then we will (see 1 Cor. 13:12)! It is likely that not only our sight will be better in the resurrection, but also everything else will be.

3 Suffer me that I may speak; and after that I have spoken, mock on.

4 As for me, *is* my complaint to man? and if *it were so*, why should not my spirit be troubled?

5 Mark me, and be astonished, and lay *your* hand upon *your* mouth.

6 Even when I remember I am afraid, and trembling taketh hold on my flesh.

7 Wherefore do the wicked live, become old, yea, are mighty in power?

8 Their seed is established in their sight with them, and their offspring before their eyes.

9 Their houses *are* safe from fear, neither *is* the rod of God upon them.

10 Their bull gendereth, and faileth not; their cow calveth, and casteth not her calf.

11 They send forth their little ones like a flock, and their children dance.

12 They take the timbrel and harp, and rejoice at the sound of the organ.

13 They spend their days in wealth, and in a moment go down to the grave.

14 Therefore they say unto God, Depart from us; for we desire not the knowledge of thy ways.

15 What *is* the Almighty, that we should serve him? and what profit should we have, if we pray unto him?

16 Lo, their good *is* not in their hand: the counsel of the wicked is far from me.

17 How oft is the candle of the wicked put out! and *how oft* cometh their destruction upon them! *God* distributeth sorrows in his anger.

18 They are as stubble before the wind, and as chaff that the storm carrieth away.

19 God layeth up his iniquity for his children: he rewardeth him, and he shall know it.

20 His eyes shall see his destruction, and he shall drink of the wrath of the Almighty.

21 For what pleasure *hath* he in his house after him, when the number of his months is cut off in the midst?

22 Shall *any* teach God knowledge? seeing he judgeth those that are high.

23 One dieth in his full strength, being wholly at ease and quiet.

24 His breasts are full of milk, and his bones are moistened with marrow.

25 And another dieth in the bitterness of his soul, and never eateth with pleasure.

26 They shall lie down alike in the dust, and the worms shall cover them.

27 Behold, I know your thoughts, and the devices *which* ye wrongfully imagine against me.

---

28 For ye say, Where *is* the house of the prince? and where *are* the dwelling places of the wicked?

29 Have ye not asked them that go by the way? and do ye not know their tokens,

30 That the wicked is reserved to the day of destruction? they shall be brought forth to the day of wrath.

31 Who shall declare his way to his face? and who shall repay him *what* he hath done?

32 Yet shall he be brought to the grave, and shall remain in the tomb.

33 The clods of the valley shall be sweet unto him, and every man shall draw after him, as *there are* innumerable before him.

34 How then comfort ye me in vain, seeing in your answers there remaineth falsehood?

CHAPTER 22
Eliphaz Accuses Job

1 Then Eliphaz the Temanite answered and said,

2 Can a man be profitable unto God, as he that is wise may be profitable unto himself?

3 *Is it* any pleasure to the Almighty, that thou art righteous? or *is it* gain *to him*, that thou makest thy ways perfect?

4 Will he reprove thee for fear of thee? will he enter with thee into judgment?

5 *Is* not thy wickedness great? and thine iniquities infinite?

6 For thou hast taken a pledge from thy brother for nought, and stripped the naked of their clothing.

7 Thou hast not given water to the weary to drink, and thou hast withholden bread from the hungry.

8 But *as for* the mighty man, he had the earth; and the honourable man dwelt in it.

9 Thou hast sent widows away empty, and the arms of the fatherless have been broken.

10 Therefore snares *are* round about thee, and sudden fear troubleth thee;

11 Or darkness, *that* thou canst not see; and abundance of waters cover thee.

12 *Is* not God in the height of heaven? and behold the height of the stars, how high they are!

13 And thou sayest, How doth God know? can he judge through the dark cloud?

14 Thick clouds *are* a covering to him, that he seeth not; and he walketh in the circuit of heaven.

15 Hast thou marked the old way which wicked men have trodden?

16 Which were cut down out of time, whose foundation was overflown with a flood:

---

3 Job 16:10; 17:2

5 Judg. 18:19; Job 29:9; 40:4; Ps. 39:9

7 Job 12:6; Ps. 17:10, 14; 73:3, 12; Jer. 12:1; Hab. 1:16

9 Ps. 73:5

10 Ex. 23:26

13 Job 36:11

14 Job 22:17

15 Ex. 5:2; Job 34:9; 35:3; Mal. 3:14

16 Job 22:18; Ps. 1:1; Prov. 1:10

17 Job 18:6; Luke 12:46

18 Ps. 1:4; 35:5; Isa. 17:13; 29:5; Hos. 13:3

19 Ex. 20:5

20 Ps. 75:8; Isa. 51:17; Jer. 25:15; Rev. 14:10; 19:15

22 Isa. 40:13; 45:9; Rom. 11:34; 1Cor. 2:16

26 Job 20:11; Eccl. 9:2

28 Job 20:7

30 Prov. 16:4; 2Pet. 2:9

31 Gal. 2:11

33 Heb. 9:27

2 Job 35:7; Ps. 16:2; Luke 17:10

6 Ex. 22:26, 27; Deut. 24:10-13; Job 24:3, 9; Ezek. 18:12

7 Deut. 15:7-11; Job 31:17; Isa. 58:7; Ezek. 18:7, 16; Matt. 25:42

9 Job 31:21; Isa. 10:2; Ezek. 22:7

10 Job 18:8-10; 19:6

11 Ps. 69:1

17 Which said unto God, Depart from us: and what can the Almighty do for them?

18 Yet he filled their houses with good *things*: but the counsel of the wicked is far from me.

19 The righteous see *it*, and are glad: and the innocent laugh them to scorn.

20 Whereas our substance is not cut down, but the remnant of them the fire consumeth.

21 Acquaint now thyself with him, and be at peace: thereby good shall come unto thee.

22 Receive, I pray thee, the law from his mouth, and lay up his words in thine heart.

23 If thou return to the Almighty, thou shalt be built up, thou shalt put away iniquity far from thy tabernacles.

24 Then shalt thou lay up gold as dust, and the *gold* of Ophir as the stones of the brooks.

25 Yea, the Almighty shall be thy defence, and thou shalt have plenty of silver.

26 For then shalt thou have thy delight in the Almighty, and shalt lift up thy face unto God.

27 Thou shalt make thy prayer unto him, and he shall hear thee, and thou shalt pay thy vows.

28 Thou shalt also decree a thing, and it shall be established unto thee: and the light shall shine upon thy ways.

29 When *men* are cast down, then thou shalt say, *There is* lifting up; and he shall save the humble person.

30 He shall deliver the island of the innocent: and it is delivered by the pureness of thine hands.

CHAPTER 23
Job Wants Access to God

1 Then Job answered and said,

2 Even today *is* my complaint bitter: my stroke is heavier than my groaning.

3 Oh that I knew where I might find him! *that* I might come *even* to his seat!

4 I would order *my* cause before him, and fill my mouth with arguments.

5 I would know the words *which* he would answer me, and understand what he would say unto me.

6 Will he plead against me with *his* great power? No; but he would put *strength* in me.

7 There the righteous might dispute with him; so should I be delivered for ever from my judge.

8 Behold, I go forward, but he *is not there*; and backward, but I cannot perceive him:

9 On the left hand, where he doth work, but I cannot behold *him*: he hideth himself on the right hand, that I cannot see *him*:

10 But he knoweth the way that I take: *when* he hath tried me, I shall come forth as gold.

11 My foot hath held his steps, his way have I kept, and not declined.

12 Neither have I gone back from the commandment of his lips; I have esteemed the words of his mouth more than my necessary *food*.

13 But he *is* in one *mind*, and who can turn him? and *what* his soul desireth, even *that* he doeth.

14 For he performeth *the thing that is* appointed for me: and many such *things are* with him.

15 Therefore am I troubled at his presence: when I consider, I am afraid of him.

16 For God maketh my heart soft, and the Almighty troubleth me:

17 Because I was not cut off before the darkness, *neither* hath he covered the darkness from my face.

CHAPTER 24

1 Why, seeing times are not hidden from the Almighty, do they that know him not see his days?

2 *Some* remove the landmarks; they violently take away flocks, and feed *thereof*.

3 They drive away the ass of the fatherless, they take the widow's ox for a pledge.

4 They turn the needy out of the way: the poor of the earth hide themselves together.

5 Behold, *as* wild asses in the desert, go they forth to their work; rising betimes for a prey: the wilderness *yieldeth* food for them *and* for *their* children.

6 They reap *every one* his corn in the field: and they gather the vintage of the wicked.

7 They cause the naked to lodge without clothing, that *they have* no covering in the cold.

8 They are wet with the showers of the

Cross references (center column)

17 Job 21:14; Ps. 4:6
18 Job 21:16
19 Ps. 58:10; 107:42
21 Isa. 27:5
22 Ps. 119:11
23 Job 8:5, 6; 11:13, 14
24 2Chr. 1:15
26 Job 11:15; 27:10; Isa. 58:14
27 Ps. 50:14, 15; Isa. 58:9
29 Prov. 29:23; James 4:6; 1Pet. 5:5
30 Gen. 18:26-33
3 Job 13:3; 16:21
6 Isa. 27:4, 8; 57:16
8 Job 9:11
10 Ps. 17:3; 66:10; 139:1-3; James 1:12
11 Ps. 44:18
12 John 4:32, 34
13 Job 12:12-14; Ps. 115:3; Rom. 9:19
14 1Thess. 3:3
16 Ps. 22:14
1 Acts 1:7
2 Deut. 19:14; 27:17; Prov. 22:28; 23:10; Hos. 5:10
3 Deut. 24:6, 10, 12, 17; Job 22:6
4 Prov. 28:28
7 Ex. 22:26, 27; Deut. 24:12, 13; Job 22:6
8 Lam. 4:5

23:10 God's ability to know all things is not limited to just what Job was going to do in his moment of trial, for He knows "the end from the beginning" (Isa. 46:10). Even before Satan proposed to test Job, God knew that His servant would prove himself faithful. Nothing man does in life takes God by surprise. It is this characteristic of omniscience that allows Him to know the past, present, and future for individuals, nations, and worlds. This is why we can rely on Bible prophecy; it is given by the God who knows all things.

mountains, and embrace the rock for want of a shelter.

9 They pluck the fatherless from the breast, and take a pledge of the poor.

10 They cause *him* to go naked without clothing, and they take away the sheaf *from* the hungry;

11 *Which* make oil within their walls, *and* tread *their* winepresses, and suffer thirst.

12 Men groan from out of the city, and the soul of the wounded crieth out: yet God layeth not folly *to them.*

13 They are of those that rebel against the light; they know not the ways thereof, nor abide in the paths thereof.

14 The murderer rising with the light killeth the poor and needy, and in the night is as a thief.

15 The eye also of the adulterer waiteth for the twilight, saying, No eye shall see me: and disguiseth *his* face.

16 In the dark they dig through houses, *which* they had marked for themselves in the daytime: they know not the light.

17 For the morning *is* to them even as the shadow of death: if *one* know *them,* they are *in* the terrors of the shadow of death.

18 He *is* swift as the waters; their portion is cursed in the earth: he beholdeth not the way of the vineyards.

19 Drought and heat consume the snow waters: *so doth* the grave *those which* have sinned.

20 The womb shall forget him; the worm shall feed sweetly on him; he shall be no more remembered; and wickedness shall be broken as a tree.

21 He evil entreateth the barren *that* beareth not: and doeth not good to the widow.

22 He draweth also the mighty with his power: he riseth up, and no *man* is sure of life.

23 *Though* it be given him *to be* in safety, whereon he resteth; yet his eyes *are* upon their ways.

24 They are exalted for a little while, but are gone and brought low; they are taken out of the way as all *other,* and cut off as the tops of the ears of corn.

25 And if *it be* not *so* now, who will make me a liar, and make my speech nothing worth?

CHAPTER 25
Bildad Protests

1 Then answered Bildad the Shuhite, and said,

2 Dominion and fear *are* with him, he maketh peace in his high places.

3 Is there any number of his armies? and upon whom doth not his light arise?

4 How then can man be justified with God? or how can he be clean *that is* born of a woman?

5 Behold even to the moon, and it shineth not; yea, the stars are not pure in his sight.

6 How much less man, *that is* a worm? and the son of man, *which is* a worm?

CHAPTER 26
Job's Rebuttal

1 But Job answered and said,

2 How hast thou helped *him that is* without power? *how* savest thou the arm *that hath* no strength?

3 How hast thou counselled *him that hath* no wisdom? and *how* hast thou plentifully declared the thing as it is?

4 To whom hast thou uttered words? and whose spirit came from thee?

5 Dead *things* are formed from under the waters, and the inhabitants thereof.

6 Hell *is* naked before him, and destruction hath no covering.

7 He stretcheth out the north over the empty place, *and* hangeth the earth upon nothing.

8 He bindeth up the waters in his thick clouds; and the cloud is not rent under them.

9 He holdeth back the face of his throne, *and* spreadeth his cloud upon it.

10 He hath compassed the waters with bounds, until the day and night come to an end.

11 The pillars of heaven tremble and are astonished at his reproof.

12 He divideth the sea with his power, and by his understanding he smiteth through the proud.

13 By his spirit he hath garnished the heavens; his hand hath formed the crooked serpent.

14 Lo, these *are* parts of his ways: but how little a portion is heard of him? but the thunder of his power who can understand?

CHAPTER 27
Job Describes the Fate of the Wicked

1 Moreover Job continued his parable, and said,

2 *As* God liveth, *who* hath taken away my judgment; and the Almighty, *who* hath vexed my soul;

3 All the while my breath *is* in me, and the spirit of God *is* in my nostrils;

Cross-references: 14 Ps. 10:8; 15 Ps. 10:11; Prov. 7:9; 16 John 3:20; 20 Prov. 10:7; 23 Ps. 11:4; Prov. 15:3; 3 James 1:17; 4 Job 4:17-21; 15:14-16; 6 Ps. 139:8, 11; Prov. 15:11; Heb. 4:13; 7 Job 9:8; Ps. 24:2; 104:2-5; 8 Prov. 30:4; 10 Job 38:8; Ps. 33:7; 104:9; Prov. 8:29; Jer. 5:22; 12 Ex. 14:21; Ps. 74:13; Isa. 51:15; Jer. 31:35; 13 Ps. 33:6; Isa. 27:1; 2 Ruth 1:20; 2Kgs. 4:27; Job 34:5; 3 Gen. 2:7

4 My lips shall not speak wickedness, nor my tongue utter deceit.

5 God forbid that I should justify you: till I die I will not remove mine integrity from me.

6 My righteousness I hold fast, and will not let it go: my heart shall not reproach *me* so long as I live.

7 Let mine enemy be as the wicked, and he that riseth up against me as the unrighteous.

8 For what *is* the hope of the hypocrite, though he hath gained, when God taketh away his soul?

9 Will God hear his cry when trouble cometh upon him?

10 Will he delight himself in the Almighty? will he always call upon God?

11 I will teach you by the hand of God: *that* which *is* with the Almighty will I not conceal.

12 Behold, all ye yourselves have seen *it*; why then are ye thus altogether vain?

13 This *is* the portion of a wicked man with God, and the heritage of oppressors, *which* they shall receive of the Almighty.

14 If his children be multiplied, *it is* for the sword: and his offspring shall not be satisfied with bread.

15 Those that remain of him shall be buried in death: and his widows shall not weep.

16 Though he heap up silver as the dust, and prepare raiment as the clay;

17 He may prepare *it*, but the just shall put *it* on, and the innocent shall divide the silver.

18 He buildeth his house as a moth, and as a booth *that* the keeper maketh.

19 The rich man shall lie down, but he shall not be gathered: he openeth his eyes, and he *is* not.

20 Terrors take hold on him as waters, a tempest stealeth him away in the night.

21 The east wind carrieth him away, and he departeth: and as a storm hurleth him out of his place.

22 For *God* shall cast upon him, and not spare: he would fain flee out of his hand.

23 *Men* shall clap their hands at him, and shall hiss him out of his place.

CHAPTER 28
In Praise of Wisdom

1 Surely there is a vein for the silver, and a place for gold *where* they fine *it*.

2 Iron is taken out of the earth, and brass *is* molten *out of* the stone.

3 He setteth an end to darkness, and

searcheth out all perfection: the stones of darkness, and the shadow of death.

4 The flood breaketh out from the inhabitant; *even the waters* forgotten of the foot: they are dried up, they are gone away from men.

5 *As for* the earth, out of it cometh bread: and under it is turned up as it were fire.

6 The stones of it *are* the place of sapphires: and it hath dust of gold.

7 *There is* a path which no fowl knoweth, and which the vulture's eye hath not seen:

8 The lion's whelps have not trodden it, nor the fierce lion passed by it.

9 He putteth forth his hand upon the rock; he overturneth the mountains by the roots.

10 He cutteth out rivers among the rocks; and his eye seeth every precious thing.

11 He bindeth the floods from overflowing; and *the thing that is* hid bringeth he forth to light.

12 But where shall wisdom be found? and where *is* the place of understanding?

13 Man knoweth not the price thereof; neither is it found in the land of the living.

14 The depth saith, It *is* not in me: and the sea saith, *It is* not with me.

15 It cannot be gotten for gold, neither shall silver be weighed *for* the price thereof.

16 It cannot be valued with the gold of Ophir, with the precious onyx, or the sapphire.

17 The gold and the crystal cannot equal it: and the exchange of it *shall not be for* jewels of fine gold.

18 No mention shall be made of coral, or of pearls: for the price of wisdom *is* above rubies.

19 The topaz of Ethiopia shall not equal it, neither shall it be valued with pure gold.

20 Whence then cometh wisdom? and where *is* the place of understanding?

21 Seeing it is hid from the eyes of all living, and kept close from the fowls of the air.

22 Destruction and death say, We have heard the fame thereof with our ears.

23 God understandeth the way thereof, and he knoweth the place thereof.

24 For he looketh to the ends of the earth, *and* seeth under the whole heaven;

25 To make the weight for the winds; and he weigheth the waters by measure.

26 When he made a decree for the rain, and a way for the lightning of the thunder:

27 Then did he see it, and declare it; he prepared it, yea, and searched it out.

28 And unto man he said, Behold, the fear

Center column cross-references

5 Job 2:9; 13:15
6 Job 2:3; Acts 24:16
8 Matt. 16:26; Luke 12:20
9 Job 35:12; Ps. 18:41; 109:7; Prov. 1:28; 28:9; Isa. 1:15; Jer. 14:12; Ezek. 8:18; Mic. 3:4; John 9:31; James 4:3
10 Job 22:26, 27
13 Job 20:29
14 Deut. 28:41; Esth. 9:10; Hos. 9:13
15 Ps. 78:64
17 Prov. 28:8; Eccl. 2:26
18 Isa. 1:8; Lam. 2:6
20 Job 18:11
12 Job 28:20; Eccl. 7:24
13 Prov. 3:15
14 Job 28:22; Rom. 11:33, 34
15 Prov. 3:13-15; 8:10, 11, 19; 16:16
20 Job 28:12
22 Job 28:14
24 Prov. 15:3
25 Ps. 135:7
26 Job 38:25
28 Deut. 4:6; Ps. 111:10; Prov. 1:7; 9:10; Eccl. 12:13

of the Lord, that *is* wisdom; and to depart from evil *is* understanding.

CHAPTER 29
Job Remembers

1 Moreover Job continued his parable, and said,

2 Oh that I were as *in* months past, as *in* the days *when* God preserved me;

3 When his candle shined upon my head, *and when* by his light I walked *through* darkness;

4 As I was in the days of my youth, when the secret of God *was* upon my tabernacle;

5 When the Almighty *was* yet with me, *when* my children *were* about me;

6 When I washed my steps with butter, and the rock poured me out rivers of oil;

7 When I went out to the gate through the city, *when* I prepared my seat in the street!

8 The young men saw me, and hid themselves: and the aged arose, *and* stood up.

9 The princes refrained talking, and laid *their* hand on their mouth.

10 The nobles held their peace, and their tongue cleaved to the roof of their mouth.

11 When the ear heard *me*, then it blessed me; and when the eye saw *me*, it gave witness to me:

12 Because I delivered the poor that cried, and the fatherless, and *him that had* none to help him.

13 The blessing of him that was ready to perish came upon me: and I caused the widow's heart to sing for joy.

14 I put on righteousness, and it clothed me: my judgment *was* as a robe and a diadem.

15 I was eyes to the blind, and feet *was* I to the lame.

16 I *was* a father to the poor: and the cause *which* I knew not I searched out.

17 And I brake the jaws of the wicked, and plucked the spoil out of his teeth.

18 Then I said, I shall die in my nest, and I shall multiply *my* days as the sand.

19 My root *was* spread out by the waters, and the dew lay all night upon my branch.

20 My glory *was* fresh in me, and my bow was renewed in my hand.

21 Unto me *men* gave ear, and waited, and kept silence at my counsel.

22 After my words they spake not again and my speech dropped upon them.

23 And they waited for me as for the rain; and they opened their mouth wide *as* for the latter rain.

24 *If* I laughed on them, they believed *it*

not; and the light of my countenance they cast not down.

25 I chose out their way, and sat chief, and dwelt as a king in the army, as one *that* comforteth the mourners.

CHAPTER 30

1 But now *they that are* younger than I have me in derision, whose fathers I would have disdained to have set with the dogs of my flock.

2 Yea, whereto *might* the strength of their hands *profit* me, in whom old age was perished?

3 For want and famine *they were* solitary; fleeing into the wilderness in former time desolate and waste.

4 Who cut up mallows by the bushes, and juniper roots *for* their meat.

5 They were driven forth from among *men*, (they cried after them as *after* a thief;)

6 To dwell in the clifts of the valleys, *in* caves of the earth, and *in* the rocks.

7 Among the bushes they brayed; under the nettles they were gathered together.

8 *They were* children of fools, yea, children of base men: they were viler than the earth.

9 And now am I their song, yea, I am their byword.

10 They abhor me, they flee far from me, and spare not to spit in my face.

11 Because he hath loosed my cord, and afflicted me, they have also let loose the bridle before me.

12 Upon *my* right *hand* rise the youth; they push away my feet, and they raise up against me the ways of their destruction.

13 They mar my path, they set forward my calamity, they have no helper.

14 They came *upon me* as a wide breaking in *of waters*: in the desolation they rolled themselves *upon me*.

15 Terrors are turned upon me: they pursue my soul as the wind: and my welfare passeth away as a cloud.

16 And now my soul is poured out upon me; the days of affliction have taken hold upon me.

17 My bones are pierced in me in the night season: and my sinews take no rest.

18 By the great force *of my disease* is my garment changed: it bindeth me about as the collar of my coat.

19 He hath cast me into the mire, and I am become like dust and ashes.

20 I cry unto thee, and thou dost not hear me: I stand up, and thou regardest me *not*.

21 Thou art become cruel to me: with thy

Cross references (center column):

2 Job 7:3

3 Job 18:6; Ps. 18:28

4 Ps. 25:14

6 Gen. 49:11; Deut. 32:13; 33:24; Job 20:17; Ps. 81:16

9 Job 21:5

10 Ps. 137:6

12 Ps. 72:12; Prov. 21:13; 24:11

14 Deut. 24:13; Ps. 132:9; Isa. 59:17; 61:10; Eph. 6:14; 1 Thess. 5:8

15 Num. 10:31

16 Prov. 29:7

17 Ps. 58:6; Prov. 30:14

18 Ps. 30:6

19 Job 18:16; Ps. 1:3; Jer. 17:8

20 Gen. 49:24

23 Zech. 10:1

9 Job 17:6; Ps. 35:15; 69:12; Lam. 3:14, 63

10 Num. 12:14; Deut. 25:9; Isa. 50:6; Matt. 26:67; 27:30

11 Job 12:18

12 Job 19:12

16 Ps. 42:4

strong hand thou opposest thyself against me.

22 Thou liftest me up to the wind; thou causest me to ride *upon it*, and dissolvest my substance.

23 For I know *that* thou wilt bring me *to* death, and *to* the house appointed for all living.

24 Howbeit he will not stretch out *his* hand to the grave, though they cry in his destruction.

25 Did not I weep for him that was in trouble? was *not* my soul grieved for the poor?

26 When I looked for good, then evil came *unto me*: and when I waited for light, there came darkness.

27 My bowels boiled, and rested not: the days of affliction prevented me.

28 I went mourning without the sun: I stood up, *and* I cried in the congregation.

29 I am a brother to dragons, and a companion to owls.

30 My skin is black upon me, and my bones are burned with heat.

31 My harp also is *turned* to mourning, and my organ into the voice of them that weep.

CHAPTER 31

1 I made a covenant with mine eyes; why then should I think upon a maid?

2 For what portion of God *is there* from above? and *what* inheritance of the Almighty from on high?

3 *Is* not destruction to the wicked? and a strange *punishment* to the workers of iniquity?

4 Doth not he see my ways, and count all my steps?

5 If I have walked with vanity, or if my foot hath hasted to deceit;

6 Let me be weighed in an even balance, that God may know mine integrity.

7 If my step hath turned out of the way, and mine heart walked after mine eyes, and if any blot hath cleaved to mine hands;

8 *Then* let me sow, and let another eat; yea, let my offspring be rooted out.

9 If mine heart have been deceived by a woman, or *if* I have laid wait at my neighbour's door;

10 *Then* let my wife grind unto another, and let others bow down upon her.

11 For this *is* an heinous crime; yea, it *is* an iniquity *to be punished by* the judges.

12 For it *is* a fire *that* consumeth to destruction, and would root out all mine increase.

13 If I did despise the cause of my manser-

---

23 Heb. 9:27
25 Ps. 35:13, 14; Rom. 12:15
26 Jer. 8:15
28 Ps. 38:6; 42:9; 43:2
29 Ps. 102:6; Mic. 1:8
30 Ps. 102:3; 119:83; Lam. 4:8; 5:10
2 Job 20:29; 27:13
4 Job 34:21; Prov. 5:21
7 Num. 15:39; Eccl. 11:9; Ezek. 6:9; Matt. 5:29
8 Lev. 26:16; Deut. 28:30, 38-48
10 2Sam. 12:11; Jer. 8:10
11 Gen. 38:24; Lev. 20:10; Deut. 22:22; Job 31:28
14 Ps. 44:21
15 Job 34:19; Prov. 14:31; 22:2; Mal. 2:10
20 Deut. 24:13
21 Job 22:9
23 Isa. 13:6; Joel 1:15
24 Mark 10:24; 1Tim. 6:17
25 Ps. 62:10; Prov. 11:28
26 Deut. 4:19; 11:16; 17:3; Ezek. 8:16
28 Job 31:11
29 Prov. 17:5
30 Matt. 5:44; Rom. 12:14
32 Gen. 19:2, 3; Judg. 19:20, 21; Rom. 12:13; Heb. 13:2; 1Pet. 4:9
33 Gen. 3:8, 12
35 Job 13:22; 33:6

---

vant or of my maidservant, when they contended with me;

14 What then shall I do when God riseth up? and when he visiteth, what shall I answer him?

15 Did not he that made me in the womb make him? and did not one fashion us in the womb?

16 If I have withheld the poor from *their* desire, or have caused the eyes of the widow to fail;

17 Or have eaten my morsel myself alone, and the fatherless hath not eaten thereof;

18 (For from my youth he was brought up with me, as *with* a father, and I have guided her from my mother's womb;)

19 If I have seen any perish for want of clothing, or any poor without covering;

20 If his loins have not blessed me, and *if* he were *not* warmed with the fleece of my sheep;

21 If I have lifted up my hand against the fatherless, when I saw my help in the gate:

22 *Then* let mine arm fall from my shoulder blade, and mine arm be broken from the bone.

23 For destruction *from* God *was* a terror to me, and by reason of his highness I could not endure.

24 If I have made gold my hope, or have said to the fine gold, *Thou art* my confidence;

25 If I rejoiced because my wealth *was* great, and because mine hand had gotten much;

26 If I beheld the sun when it shined, or the moon walking *in* brightness;

27 And my heart hath been secretly enticed, or my mouth hath kissed my hand:

28 This also *were* an iniquity *to be punished by* the judge: for I should have denied the God *that is* above.

29 If I rejoiced at the destruction of him that hated me, or lifted up myself when evil found him:

30 Neither have I suffered my mouth to sin by wishing a curse to his soul.

31 If the men of my tabernacle said not, Oh that we had of his flesh! we cannot be satisfied.

32 The stranger did not lodge in the street: *but* I opened my doors to the traveller.

33 If I covered my transgressions as Adam, by hiding mine iniquity in my bosom:

34 Did I fear a great multitude, or did the contempt of families terrify me, that I kept silence, *and* went not out of the door?

35 Oh that one would hear me! behold, my

desire *is, that* the Almighty would answer me, and *that* mine adversary had written a book.

36 Surely I would take it upon my shoulder, *and* bind it *as* a crown to me.

37 I would declare unto him the number of my steps; as a prince would I go near unto him.

38 If my land cry against me, or that the furrows likewise thereof complain;

39 If I have eaten the fruits thereof without money, or have caused the owners thereof to lose their life:

40 Let thistles grow instead of wheat, and cockle instead of barley. The words of Job are ended.

CHAPTER 32
Elihu Speaks

1 So these three men ceased to answer Job, because he *was* righteous in his own eyes.

2 Then was kindled the wrath of Elihu the son of Barachel the Buzite, of the kindred of Ram: against Job was his wrath kindled, because he justified himself rather than God.

3 Also against his three friends was his wrath kindled, because they had found no answer, and *yet* had condemned Job.

4 Now Elihu had waited till Job had spoken, because they *were* elder than he.

5 When Elihu saw that *there was* no answer in the mouth of *these* three men, then his wrath was kindled.

6 And Elihu the son of Barachel the Buzite answered and said, I *am* young, and ye *are* very old; wherefore I was afraid, and durst not shew you mine opinion.

7 I said, Days should speak, and multitude of years should teach wisdom.

8 But *there is* a spirit in man: and the inspiration of the Almighty giveth them understanding.

9 Great men are not *always* wise: neither do the aged understand judgment.

10 Therefore I said, Hearken to me; I also will shew mine opinion.

11 Behold, I waited for your words; I gave ear to your reasons, whilst ye searched out what to say.

12 Yea, I attended unto you, and, behold, *there was* none of you that convinced Job, *or* that answered his words:

13 Lest ye should say, We have found out wisdom: God thrusteth him down, not man.

14 Now he hath not directed *his* words against me: neither will I answer him with your speeches.

15 They were amazed, they answered no more: they left off speaking.

16 When I had waited, (for they spake not, but stood still, *and* answered no more;)

17 *I said,* I will answer also my part, I also will shew mine opinion.

18 For I am full of matter, the spirit within me constraineth me.

19 Behold, my belly *is* as wine *which* hath no vent; it is ready to burst like new bottles.

20 I will speak, that I may be refreshed: I will open my lips and answer.

21 Let me not, I pray you, accept any man's person, neither let me give flattering titles unto man.

22 For I know not to give flattering titles; *in so doing* my maker would soon take me away.

CHAPTER 33

1 Wherefore, Job, I pray thee, hear my speeches, and hearken to all my words.

2 Behold, now I have opened my mouth, my tongue hath spoken in my mouth.

3 My words *shall be of* the uprightness of my heart: and my lips shall utter knowledge clearly.

4 The Spirit of God hath made me, and the breath of the Almighty hath given me life.

5 If thou canst answer me, set *thy words* in order before me, stand up.

6 Behold, I *am* according to thy wish in God's stead: I also am formed out of the clay.

7 Behold, my terror shall not make thee afraid, neither shall my hand be heavy upon thee.

8 Surely thou hast spoken in mine hearing, and I have heard the voice of *thy* words, *saying,*

9 I am clean without transgression, I *am* innocent; neither *is there* iniquity in me.

10 Behold, he findeth occasions against me, he counteth me for his enemy,

11 He putteth my feet in the stocks, he marketh all my paths.

12 Behold, *in* this thou art not just: I will answer thee, that God is greater than man.

13 Why dost thou strive against him? for he giveth not account of any of his matters.

14 For God speaketh once, yea twice, *yet* man perceiveth it not.

15 In a dream, in a vision of the night, when deep sleep falleth upon men, in slumberings upon the bed;

16 Then he openeth the ears of men, and sealeth their instruction,

17 That he may withdraw man *from his* purpose, and hide pride from man.

Cross references

39 1Kgs. 21:19; James 5:4
40 Gen. 3:18
1 Job 33:9
2 Gen. 22:21
6 Job 15:10
8 1Kgs. 3:12; 4:29; Job 35:11; 38:36; Prov. 2:6; Eccl. 2:26; Dan. 1:17; 2:21; Matt. 11:25; James 1:5
9 1Cor. 1:26
13 Jer. 9:23; 1Cor. 1:29
21 Lev. 19:15; Deut. 1:17; 16:19; Prov. 24:23; Matt. 22:16
4 Gen. 2:7
6 Job 9:34, 35; 13:20, 21; 31:35
7 Job 9:34; 13:21
9 Job 9:17; 10:7; 11:4; 16:17; 23:10, 11; 27:5; 29:14; 31:1
10 Job 13:24; 16:9; 19:11
11 Job 13:27; 14:16; 31:4
13 Isa. 45:9
14 Job 40:5; Ps. 62:11
15 Num. 12:6; Job 4:13
16 Job 36:10, 15

18 He keepeth back his soul from the pit, and his life from perishing by the sword.

19 He is chastened also with pain upon his bed, and the multitude of his bones with strong *pain*:

20 So that his life abhorreth bread, and his soul dainty meat.

21 His flesh is consumed away, that it cannot be seen; and his bones *that* were not seen stick out.

22 Yea, his soul draweth near unto the grave, and his life to the destroyers.

23 If there be a messenger with him, an interpreter, one among a thousand, to shew unto man his uprightness:

24 Then he is gracious unto him, and saith, Deliver him from going down to the pit: I have found a ransom.

25 His flesh shall be fresher than a child's: he shall return to the days of his youth:

26 He shall pray unto God, and he will be favourable unto him: and he shall see his face with joy: for he will render unto man his righteousness.

27 He looketh upon men, and *if any* say, I have sinned, and perverted *that which was* right, and it profited me not;

28 He will deliver his soul from going into the pit, and his life shall see the light.

29 Lo, all these *things* worketh God oftentimes with man,

30 To bring back his soul from the pit, to be enlightened with the light of the living.

31 Mark well, O Job, hearken unto me: hold thy peace, and I will speak.

32 If thou hast any thing to say, answer me: speak, for I desire to justify thee.

33 If not, hearken unto me: hold thy peace, and I shall teach thee wisdom.

CHAPTER 34

1 Furthermore Elihu answered and said,

2 Hear my words, O ye wise *men*; and give ear unto me, ye that have knowledge.

3 For the ear trieth words, as the mouth tasteth meat.

4 Let us choose to us judgment: let us know among ourselves what *is* good.

5 For Job hath said, I am righteous: and God hath taken away my judgment.

6 Should I lie against my right? my wound *is* incurable without transgression.

7 What man *is* like Job, *who* drinketh up scorning like water?

8 Which goeth in company with the workers of iniquity, and walketh with wicked men.

9 For he hath said, It profiteth a man

---

20 Ps. 107:18

27 2Sam. 12:13; Prov. 28:13; Luke 15:21; Rom. 6:21; 1John 1:9

28 Isa. 38:17

30 Job 33:28; Ps. 56:13

33 Ps. 34:11

3 Job 6:30; 12:11

5 Job 27:2; 33:9

6 Job 6:4; 9:17; 16:13

7 Job 15:16

9 Job 9:22, 23, 30; 35:3; Mal. 3:14

10 Gen. 18:25; Deut. 32:4; 2Chr. 19:7; Job 8:3; 36:23; Ps. 92:15; Rom. 9:14

11 Ps. 62:12; Prov. 24:12; Jer. 32:19; Ezek. 33:20; Matt. 16:27; Rom. 2:6; 2Cor. 5:10; 1Pet. 1:17; Rev. 22:12

12 Job 8:3

14 Ps. 104:29

15 Gen. 3:19; Eccl. 12:7

17 Gen. 18:25; 2Sam. 23:3

18 Ex. 22:28

19 Deut. 10:17; 2Chr. 19:7; Job 31:15; Col. 3:25; 1Pet. 1:17

20 Ex. 12:29, 30

21 2Chr. 16:9; Job 31:4; Ps. 34:15; Prov. 5:21; 15:3; Jer. 16:17; 32:19

22 Ps. 139:12; Amos 9:2, 3

24 Dan. 2:21

28 Ex. 22:23

---

nothing that he should delight himself with God.

10 Therefore hearken unto me, ye men of understanding: far be it from God, *that he should do* wickedness; and *from* the Almighty, *that he should commit* iniquity.

11 For the work of a man shall he render unto him, and cause every man to find according to *his* ways.

12 Yea, surely God will not do wickedly, neither will the Almighty pervert judgment.

13 Who hath given him a charge over the earth? or who hath disposed the whole world?

14 If he set his heart upon man, *if* he gather unto himself his spirit and his breath;

15 All flesh shall perish together, and man shall turn again unto dust.

16 If now *thou hast* understanding, hear this: hearken to the voice of my words.

17 Shall even he that hateth right govern? and wilt thou condemn him that is most just?

18 *Is it fit* to say to a king, *Thou art* wicked? *and* to princes, *Ye are* ungodly?

19 *How much less to him* that accepteth not the persons of princes, nor regardeth the rich more than the poor? for they all *are* the work of his hands.

20 In a moment shall they die, and the people shall be troubled at midnight, and pass away: and the mighty shall be taken away without hand.

21 For his eyes *are* upon the ways of man, and he seeth all his goings.

22 *There is* no darkness, nor shadow of death, where the workers of iniquity may hide themselves.

23 For he will not lay upon man more *than right*; that he should enter into judgment with God.

24 He shall break in pieces mighty men without number, and set others in their stead.

25 Therefore he knoweth their works, and he overturneth *them* in the night, so that they are destroyed.

26 He striketh them as wicked men in the open sight of others;

27 Because they turned back from him, and would not consider any of his ways:

28 So that they cause the cry of the poor to come unto him, and he heareth the cry of the afflicted.

29 When he giveth quietness, who then can make trouble? and when he hideth *his* face, who then can behold him? whether *it be done* against a nation, or against a man only:

30 That the hypocrite reign not, lest the people be ensnared.

31 Surely it is meet to be said unto God, I have borne *chastisement*, I will not offend *any more*:

32 *That which* I see not teach thou me: if I have done iniquity, I will do no more.

33 *Should it be* according to thy mind? he will recompense it, whether thou refuse, or whether thou choose; and not I: therefore speak what thou knowest.

34 Let men of understanding tell me, and let a wise man hearken unto me.

35 Job hath spoken without knowledge, and his words *were* without wisdom.

36 My desire *is that* Job may be tried unto the end because of *his* answers for wicked men.

37 For he addeth rebellion unto his sin, he clappeth *his hands* among us, and multiplieth his words against God.

CHAPTER 35

1 Elihu spake moreover, and said,

2 Thinkest thou this to be right, *that* thou saidst, My righteousness *is* more than God's?

3 For thou saidst, What advantage will it be unto thee? *and*, What profit shall I have, *if I be cleansed* from my sin?

4 I will answer thee, and thy companions with thee.

5 Look unto the heavens, and see; and behold the clouds *which* are higher than thou.

6 If thou sinnest, what doest thou against him? or *if* thy transgressions be multiplied, what doest thou unto him?

7 If thou be righteous, what givest thou him? or what receiveth he of thine hand?

8 Thy wickedness *may hurt* a man as thou *art*; and thy righteousness *may profit* the son of man.

9 By reason of the multitude of oppressions they make *the oppressed* to cry: they cry out by reason of the arm of the mighty.

10 But none saith, Where *is* God my maker, who giveth songs in the night;

11 Who teacheth us more than the beasts of the earth, and maketh us wiser than the fowls of heaven?

12 There they cry, but none giveth answer, because of the pride of evil men.

13 Surely God will not hear vanity, neither will the Almighty regard it.

14 Although thou sayest thou shalt not see him, *yet* judgment *is* before him; therefore trust thou in him.

15 But now, because *it is* not *so*, he hath vis-

Cross references

30 1Kgs. 12:28, 30; 2Kgs. 21:9
31 Dan. 9:7-14
35 Job 35:16
3 Job 21:15; 34:9
4 Job 34:8
5 Job 22:12
6 Prov. 8:36; Jer. 7:19
7 Job 22:2, 3; Ps. 16:2; Prov. 9:12; Rom. 11:35
9 Ex. 2:23; Job 34:28
10 Ps. 42:8; 77:6; 149:5; Isa. 51:13; Acts 16:25
11 Ps. 94:12
12 Prov. 1:28
13 Job 27:9; Prov. 15:29; Isa. 1:15; Jer. 11:11
14 Job 9:11; Ps. 37:5, 6
15 Ps. 89:32
16 Job 34:35, 37; 38:2
5 Job 9:4; 12:13, 16; 37:23; Ps. 99:4
7 Ps. 33:18; 34:15; 113:8
8 Ps. 107:10
10 Job 33:16, 23
11 Job 21:13; Isa. 1:19, 20
13 Rom. 2:5
14 Deut. 23:17; Job 15:32; 22:16; Ps. 55:23;
16 Ps. 18:19; 23:5; 31:8; 36:8; 118:5
18 Ps. 49:7
19 Prov. 11:4
21 Ps. 66:18; Heb. 11:25

ited in his anger; yet he knoweth *it* not in great extremity:

16 Therefore doth Job open his mouth in vain; he multiplieth words without knowledge.

CHAPTER 36

1 Elihu also proceeded, and said,

2 Suffer me a little, and I will shew thee that *I have* yet to speak on God's behalf.

3 I will fetch my knowledge from afar, and will ascribe righteousness to my Maker.

4 For truly my words *shall* not *be* false: he that is perfect in knowledge *is* with thee.

5 Behold, God *is* mighty, and despiseth not *any*: he *is* mighty in strength *and* wisdom.

6 He preserveth not the life of the wicked: but giveth right to the poor.

7 He withdraweth not his eyes from the righteous: but with kings *are they* on the throne; yea, he doth establish them for ever, and they are exalted.

8 And if *they be* bound in fetters, *and* be holden in cords of affliction;

9 Then he sheweth them their work, and their transgressions that they have exceeded.

10 He openeth also their ear to discipline, and commandeth that they return from iniquity.

11 If they obey and serve *him*, they shall spend their days in prosperity, and their years in pleasures.

12 But if they obey not, they shall perish by the sword, and they shall die without knowledge.

13 But the hypocrites in heart heap up wrath: they cry not when he bindeth them.

14 They die in youth, and their life *is* among the unclean.

15 He delivereth the poor in his affliction, and openeth their ears in oppression.

16 Even so would he have removed thee out of the strait *into* a broad place, where *there is* no straitness; and that which should be set on thy table *should be* full of fatness.

17 But thou hast fulfilled the judgment of the wicked: judgment and justice take hold *on thee*.

18 Because *there is* wrath, *beware* lest he take thee away with *his* stroke: then a great ransom cannot deliver thee.

19 Will he esteem thy riches? *no*, not gold, nor all the forces of strength.

20 Desire not the night, when people are cut off in their place.

21 Take heed, regard not iniquity: for this hast thou chosen rather than affliction.

22 Behold, God exalteth by his power: who teacheth like him?

23 Who hath enjoined him his way? or who can say, Thou hast wrought iniquity?

24 Remember that thou magnify his work, which men behold.

25 Every man may see it; man may behold *it* afar off.

26 Behold, God *is* great, and we know *him* not neither can the number of his years be searched out.

27 For he maketh small the drops of water: they pour down rain according to the vapour thereof:

28 Which the clouds do drop *and* distil upon man abundantly.

29 Also can *any* understand the spreadings of the clouds, *or* the noise of his tabernacle?

30 Behold, he spreadeth his light upon it, and covereth the bottom of the sea.

31 For by them judgeth he the people; he giveth meat in abundance.

32 With clouds he covereth the light; and commandeth it *not to shine* by *the cloud* that cometh betwixt.

33 The noise thereof sheweth concerning it, the cattle also concerning the vapour.

CHAPTER 37

1 At this also my heart trembleth, and is moved out of his place.

2 Hear attentively the noise of his voice, and the sound *that* goeth out of his mouth.

3 He directeth it under the whole heaven, and his lightning unto the ends of the earth.

4 After it a voice roareth: he thundereth with the voice of his excellency; and he will not stay them when his voice is heard.

5 God thundereth marvellously with his voice; great things doeth he, which we cannot comprehend.

6 For he saith to the snow, Be thou *on* the earth; likewise to the small rain, and to the great rain of his strength.

7 He sealeth up the hand of every man; that all men may know his work.

8 Then the beasts go into dens, and remain in their places.

9 Out of the south cometh the whirlwind: and cold out of the north.

10 By the breath of God frost is given: and the breadth of the waters is straitened.

11 Also by watering he wearieth the thick cloud: he scattereth his bright cloud:

12 And it is turned round about by his counsels: that they may do whatsoever he commandeth them upon the face of the world in the earth.

Cross-references (center column):

22 Isa. 40:13, 14; Rom. 11:34; 1Cor. 2:16
23 Job 34:10, 13
24 Ps. 92:5; Rev. 15:3
26 Ps. 90:2; 102:24, 27; 1Cor. 13:12; Heb. 1:12
27 Ps. 147:8
28 Prov. 3:20
30 Job 37:3
31 Job 37:13; 38:23; Ps. 136:25; Acts 14:17
32 Ps. 147:8
33 1Kgs. 18:41, 45
4 Ps. 29:3; 68:33
5 Job 5:9; 9:10; 36:26; Rev. 15:3
6 Ps. 147:16, 17
7 Ps. 109:27
8 Ps. 104:22
10 Job 38:29, 30; Ps. 147:17, 18
12 Ps. 148:8
13 2Sam. 21:10; 1Kgs. 18:45
14 Ps. 111:2
16 Job 36:4, 29
18 Gen. 1:6; Isa. 44:24
23 Job 36:5; 1Tim. 6:16
24 Matt. 10:28; 11:25; 1Cor. 1:26
1 Ex. 19:16, 18; 1Kgs. 19:11; Ezek. 1:4; Nah. 1:3
2 Job 34:35; 42:3; 1Tim. 1:7
3 Job 40:7
4 Ps. 104:5; Prov. 8:29; 30:4
7 Job 1:6
8 Gen. 1:9; Ps. 33:7; 104:9; Prov. 8:29

---

13 He causeth it to come, whether for correction, or for his land, or for mercy.

14 Hearken unto this, O Job: stand still, and consider the wondrous works of God.

15 Dost thou know when God disposed them, and caused the light of his cloud to shine?

16 Dost thou know the balancings of the clouds, the wondrous works of him which is perfect in knowledge?

17 How thy garments *are* warm, when he quieteth the earth by the south *wind*?

18 Hast thou with him spread out the sky, *which is* strong, *and* as a molten looking glass?

19 Teach us what we shall say unto him; *for* we cannot order *our speech* by reason of darkness.

20 Shall it be told him that I speak? if a man speak, surely he shall be swallowed up.

21 And now *men* see not the bright light which *is* in the clouds: but the wind passeth, and cleanseth them.

22 Fair weather cometh out of the north: with God *is* terrible majesty.

23 *Touching* the Almighty, we cannot find him out: *he is* excellent in power, and in judgment, and in plenty of justice: he will not afflict.

24 Men do therefore fear him: he respecteth not any *that are* wise of heart.

CHAPTER 38
God Speaks

1 Then the LORD answered Job out of the whirlwind, and said,

2 Who *is* this that darkeneth counsel by words without knowledge?

3 Gird up now thy loins like a man; for I will demand of thee, and answer thou me.

4 Where wast thou when I laid the foundations of the earth? declare, if thou hast understanding.

5 Who hath laid the measures thereof, if thou knowest? or who hath stretched the line upon it?

6 Whereupon are the foundations thereof fastened? or who laid the corner stone thereof;

7 When the morning stars sang together, and all the sons of God shouted for joy?

8 Or *who* shut up the sea with doors, when it brake forth, *as if* it had issued out of the womb?

9 When I made the cloud the garment thereof, and thick darkness a swaddling band for it,

10 And brake up for it my decreed *place*, and set bars and doors,

11 And said, Hitherto shalt thou come, but no further: and here shall thy proud waves be stayed?

12 Hast thou commanded the morning since thy days; *and* caused the dayspring to know his place;

13 That it might take hold of the ends of the earth, that the wicked might be shaken out of it?

14 It is turned as clay *to* the seal; and they stand as a garment.

15 And from the wicked their light is withholden, and the high arm shall be broken.

16 Hast thou entered into the springs of the sea? or hast thou walked in the search of the depth?

17 Have the gates of death been opened unto thee? or hast thou seen the doors of the shadow of death?

18 Hast thou perceived the breadth of the earth? declare if thou knowest it all.

19 Where *is* the way *where* light dwelleth? and *as for* darkness, where *is* the place thereof,

20 That thou shouldest take it to the bound thereof, and that thou shouldest know the paths *to* the house thereof?

21 Knowest thou *it*, because thou wast then born? or *because* the number of thy days *is* great?

22 Hast thou entered into the treasures of the snow? or hast thou seen the treasures of the hail,

23 Which I have reserved against the time of trouble, against the day of battle and war?

24 By what way is the light parted, *which* scattereth the east wind upon the earth?

25 Who hath divided a watercourse for the overflowing of waters, or a way for the lightning of thunder;

26 To cause it to rain on the earth, *where* no man *is; on* the wilderness, wherein *there is* no man;

27 To satisfy the desolate and waste *ground*; and to cause the bud of the tender herb to spring forth?

28 Hath the rain a father? or who hath begotten the drops of dew?

29 Out of whose womb came the ice? and the hoary frost of heaven, who hath gendered it?

30 The waters are hid as *with* a stone, and the face of the deep is frozen.

31 Canst thou bind the sweet influences of Pleiades, or loose the bands of Orion?

32 Canst thou bring forth Mazzaroth in his season? or canst thou guide Arcturus with his sons?

33 Knowest thou the ordinances of heaven? canst thou set the dominion thereof in the earth?

34 Canst thou lift up thy voice to the clouds, that abundance of waters may cover thee?

35 Canst thou send lightnings, that they may go, and say unto thee, Here we *are*?

36 Who hath put wisdom in the inward parts? or who hath given understanding to the heart?

37 Who can number the clouds in wisdom? or who can stay the bottles of heaven,

38 When the dust groweth into hardness, and the clods cleave fast together?

39 Wilt thou hunt the prey for the lion? or fill the appetite of the young lions,

40 When they couch in *their* dens, *and* abide in the covert to lie in wait?

41 Who provideth for the raven his food? when his young ones cry unto God, they wander for lack of meat.

CHAPTER 39

1 Knowest thou the time when the wild goats of the rock bring forth? *or* canst thou mark when the hinds do calve?

2 Canst thou number the months *that* they fulfil? or knowest thou the time when they bring forth?

3 They bow themselves, they bring forth their young ones, they cast out their sorrows.

4 Their young ones are in good liking, they grow up with corn; they go forth, and return not unto them.

5 Who hath sent out the wild ass free? or who hath loosed the bands of the wild ass?

6 Whose house I have made the wilderness, and the barren land his dwellings.

7 He scorneth the multitude of the city, neither regardeth he the crying of the driver.

8 The range of the mountains *is* his pasture, and he searcheth after every green thing.

9 Will the unicorn be willing to serve thee, or abide by thy crib?

Cross references (center column)

10 Job 26:10
11 Ps. 89:9; 93:4
12 Ps. 74:16; 148:5
13 Ps. 104:35
15 Job 18:5; Ps. 10:15
16 Ps. 77:19
17 Ps. 9:13
22 Ps. 135:7
23 Ex. 9:18; Josh. 10:11; Isa. 30:30; Ezek. 13:11, 13; Rev. 16:21
25 Job 28:26
27 Ps. 107:35
28 Ps. 147:8; Jer. 14:22
29 Ps. 147:16
30 Job 37:10
31 Job 9:9; Amos 5:8
33 Jer. 31:35
36 Job 32:8; Ps. 51:6; Eccl. 2:26
39 Ps. 104:21; 145:15
41 Ps. 147:9; Matt. 6:26
1 Ps. 29:9
6 Job 24:5; Jer. 2:24; Hos. 8:9
7 Job 3:18
9 Num. 23:22; Deut. 33:17

38:13 This verse is an allusion to the day of judgment for mankind, nations, kings, and those in authority. In that day "the wicked," those without faith in the living God will be "shaken out." From other passages we see that the wicked will indeed be judged and face a Christless eternity.

10 Canst thou bind the unicorn with his band in the furrow? or will he harrow the valleys after thee?

11 Wilt thou trust him, because his strength *is* great? or wilt thou leave thy labour to him?

12 Wilt thou believe him, that he will bring home thy seed, and gather *it into* thy barn?

13 *Gavest thou* the goodly wings unto the peacocks? or wings and feathers unto the ostrich?

14 Which leaveth her eggs in the earth, and warmeth them in dust,

15 And forgetteth that the foot may crush them, or that the wild beast may break them.

16 She is hardened against her young ones, as though *they were* not hers: her labour is in vain without fear;

17 Because God hath deprived her of wisdom, neither hath he imparted to her understanding.

18 What time she lifteth up herself on high, she scorneth the horse and his rider.

19 Hast thou given the horse strength? hast thou clothed his neck with thunder?

20 Canst thou make him afraid as a grasshopper? the glory of his nostrils *is* terrible.

21 He paweth in the valley, and rejoiceth in *his* strength: he goeth on to meet the armed men.

22 He mocketh at fear, and is not affrighted; neither turneth he back from the sword.

23 The quiver rattleth against him, the glittering spear and the shield.

24 He swalloweth the ground with fierceness and rage: neither believeth he that *it is* the sound of the trumpet.

25 He saith among the trumpets, Ha, ha; and he smelleth the battle afar off, the thunder of the captains, and the shouting.

26 Doth the hawk fly by thy wisdom, *and* stretch her wings toward the south?

27 Doth the eagle mount up at thy command, and make her nest on high?

28 She dwelleth and abideth on the rock, upon the crag of the rock, and the strong place.

29 From thence she seeketh the prey, *and* her eyes behold afar off.

30 Her young ones also suck up blood: and where the slain *are*, there *is* she.

CHAPTER 40

1 Moreover the LORD answered Job, and said,

2 Shall he that contendeth with the

Almighty instruct *him*? he that reproveth God, let him answer it.

3 Then Job answered the LORD, and said,

4 Behold, I am vile; what shall I answer thee? I will lay mine hand upon my mouth.

5 Once have I spoken; but I will not answer: yea, twice; but I will proceed no further.

6 Then answered the LORD unto Job out of the whirlwind, and said,

7 Gird up thy loins now like a man: I will demand of thee, and declare thou unto me.

8 Wilt thou also disannul my judgment? wilt thou condemn me, that thou mayest be righteous?

9 Hast thou an arm like God? or canst thou thunder with a voice like him?

10 Deck thyself now *with* majesty and excellency; and array thyself with glory and beauty.

11 Cast abroad the rage of thy wrath: and behold every one *that is* proud, and abase him.

12 Look on every one *that is* proud, *and* bring him low; and tread down the wicked in their place.

13 Hide them in the dust together; *and* bind their faces in secret.

14 Then will I also confess unto thee that thine own right hand can save thee.

15 Behold now behemoth, which I made with thee; he eateth grass as an ox.

16 Lo now, his strength *is* in his loins, and his force *is* in the navel of his belly.

17 He moveth his tail like a cedar: the sinews of his stones are wrapped together.

18 His bones *are as* strong pieces of brass; his bones *are* like bars of iron.

19 He *is* the chief of the ways of God: he that made him can make his sword to approach *unto him*.

20 Surely the mountains bring him forth food, where all the beasts of the field play.

21 He lieth under the shady trees, in the covert of the reed, and fens.

22 The shady trees cover him *with* their shadow; the willows of the brook compass him about.

23 Behold, he drinketh up a river, *and* hasteth not: he trusteth that he can draw up Jordan into his mouth.

24 He taketh it with his eyes: *his* nose pierceth through snares.

CHAPTER 41

1 Canst thou draw out leviathan with an hook? or his tongue with a cord *which* thou lettest down?

16 Lam. 4:3

17 Job 35:11

21 Jer. 8:6

27 Jer. 49:16; Obad. 1:4

30 Matt. 24:28; Luke 17:37

2 Job 33:13

4 Ezra 9:6; Job 29:9; 42:6; Ps. 39:9; 51:4

6 Job 38:1

7 Job 38:3; 42:4

8 Ps. 51:4; Rom. 3:4

9 Job 37:4; Ps. 29:3, 4

10 Ps. 93:1; 104:1

12 Isa. 2:12; Dan. 4:37

20 Ps. 104:14

24 Job 41:1, 2

1 Ps. 104:26; Isa. 27:1

2 Canst thou put an hook into his nose? or bore his jaw through with a thorn?
3 Will he make many supplications unto thee? will he speak soft *words* unto thee?
4 Will he make a covenant with thee? wilt thou take him for a servant for ever?
5 Wilt thou play with him as *with* a bird? or wilt thou bind him for thy maidens?
6 Shall the companions make a banquet of him? shall they part him among the merchants?
7 Canst thou fill his skin with barbed irons? or his head with fish spears?
8 Lay thine hand upon him, remember the battle, do no more.
9 Behold, the hope of him is in vain: shall not *one* be cast down even at the sight of him?
10 None *is so* fierce that dare stir him up: who then is able to stand before me?
11 Who hath prevented me, that I should repay *him? whatsoever is* under the whole heaven is mine.
12 I will not conceal his parts, nor his power, nor his comely proportion.
13 Who can discover the face of his garment? *or* who can come *to him* with his double bridle?
14 Who can open the doors of his face? his teeth *are* terrible round about.
15 *His* scales *are his* pride, shut up together *as with* a close seal.
16 One is so near to another, that no air can come between them.
17 They are joined one to another, they stick together, that they cannot be sundered.
18 By his neesings a light doth shine, and his eyes *are* like the eyelids of the morning.
19 Out of his mouth go burning lamps, *and* sparks of fire leap out.
20 Out of his nostrils goeth smoke, as *out of* a seething pot or caldron.
21 His breath kindleth coals, and a flame goeth out of his mouth.
22 In his neck remaineth strength, and sorrow is turned into joy before him.
23 The flakes of his flesh are joined together: they are firm in themselves; they cannot be moved.
24 His heart is as firm as a stone; yea, as hard as a piece of the nether *millstone.*
25 When he raiseth up himself, the mighty are afraid: by reason of breakings they purify themselves.
26 The sword of him that layeth at him cannot hold: the spear, the dart, nor the habergeon.

27 He esteemeth iron as straw, *and* brass as rotten wood.
28 The arrow cannot make him flee: slingstones are turned with him into stubble.
29 Darts are counted as stubble: he laugheth at the shaking of a spear.
30 Sharp stones *are* under him: he spreadeth sharp pointed things upon the mire.
31 He maketh the deep to boil like a pot: he maketh the sea like a pot of ointment.
32 He maketh a path to shine after him; *one* would think the deep *to be* hoary.
33 Upon earth there is not his like, who is made without fear.
34 He beholdeth all high *things*: he *is* a king over all the children of pride.

CHAPTER 42
Job's Humility

1 Then Job answered the LORD, and said,
2 I know that thou canst do every *thing*, and *that* no thought can be withholden from thee.
3 Who *is* he that hideth counsel without knowledge? therefore have I uttered that I understood not; things too wonderful for me, which I knew not.
4 Hear, I beseech thee, and I will speak: I will demand of thee, and declare thou unto me.
5 I have heard of thee by the hearing of the ear: but now mine eye seeth thee.
6 Wherefore I abhor *myself*, and repent in dust and ashes.
7 And it was *so*, that after the LORD had spoken these words unto Job, the LORD said to Eliphaz the Temanite, My wrath is kindled against thee, and against thy two friends: for ye have not spoken of me the *thing that is* right, as my servant Job *hath*.
8 Therefore take unto you now seven bullocks and seven rams, and go to my servant Job, and offer up for yourselves a burnt offering; and my servant Job shall pray for you: for him will I accept: lest I deal with you *after your* folly, in that ye have not spoken of me *the thing which is* right, like my servant Job.
9 So Eliphaz the Temanite and Bildad the Shuhite *and* Zophar the Naamathite went, and did according as the LORD commanded them: the LORD also accepted Job.

The Restoration of Job's Prosperity

10 And the LORD turned the captivity of Job, when he prayed for his friends: also the LORD gave Job twice as much as he had before.

Cross references:

2 Isa. 37:29
11 Ex. 19:5; Deut. 10:14; Ps. 24:1; 50:12; Rom. 11:35; 1Cor. 10:26, 28
2 Gen. 18:14; Matt. 19:26; Mark 10:27; 14:37; Luke 18:27
3 Job 38:2; Ps. 40:5; 131:1; 139:6
4 Job 38:3; 40:7
6 Ezra 9:6; Job 40:4
8 Gen. 20:17; Num. 23:1; 1Sam. 25:35; Mal. 1:8; Matt. 5:24; James 5:15, 16; 1John 5:16
10 Ps. 14:7; 126:1; Isa. 40:2

11 Then came there unto him all his brethren, and all his sisters, and all they that had been of his acquaintance before, and did eat bread with him in his house: and they bemoaned him, and comforted him over all the evil that the LORD had brought upon him: every man also gave him a piece of money, and every one an earring of gold.

12 So the LORD blessed the latter end of Job more than his beginning: for he had fourteen thousand sheep, and six thousand camels, and a thousand yoke of oxen, and a thousand she asses.

13 He had also seven sons and three daughters.

14 And he called the name of the first, Jemima; and the name of the second, Kezia; and the name of the third, Kerenhappuch.

15 And in all the land were no women found so fair as the daughters of Job: and their father gave them inheritance among their brethren.

16 After this lived Job an hundred and forty years, and saw his sons, and his sons' sons, even four generations.

17 So Job died, being old and full of days.

11 Job 19:13
12 Job 1:3; 8:7; James 5:11
13 Job 1:2

16 Job 5:26; Prov. 3:16

17 Gen. 25:8

Psalms

T he book of Psalms was the hymnal of the Hebrews, containing songs of praise (what the Hebrew name actually means) which could be chanted or recited responsively, but could also be arranged in simple melodies. Orchestral or instrumental accompaniment was common, with stringed instruments like the harp or lyre, wind instruments like the horn, flute, or trumpet, and percussion instruments like the cymbals or early tambourine. Psalm 150 lists several instruments of that time.

About half the psalms were written by David, twelve by Asaph, eleven by the Children of Korah, two by Solomon, one by Moses, one by Heman, and one by Ethan. Forty-nine are by anonymous authors.

The psalms contain elements of worship, praise, history, prayer, doctrine, thanksgiving, lamentations, and prayers for deliverance—all written with a wide range of human and spiritual emotions. Individual psalms are often classified according to their content: Didactic Psalms are those which give instruction (e.g., Ps. 119); the Messianic Psalms contain prophecy relating to the Messiah; the Imprecatory Psalms involve pleas to God for the punishment of the wicked; Penitential Psalms express not only the feelings of a repentant heart but also appeal for divine cleansing (see Ps. 6, 32, 38, 51, 102, 130, 143).

Of special interest are the Messianic Psalms and the psalms that allude to Christ's Millennial Kingdom. Major Messianic Psalms predicting the first or second advents of Christ include: 2, 8, 16, 22, 24, 40, 45, 69, 72, 89, 102, 109, 110, 118, 132. In addition, Psalms 96—99 are millennial, referring to the enthronement of the King. Other psalms such as 9, 21, and 50 seem to be messianic. Quoted in the New Testament more than any other Old Testament writing, Psalms was specifically mentioned by Jesus as containing prophecies to be fulfilled in His ministry (Luke 24:44–53).

The book of Psalms contains 59 specific predictions in 242 (approximately 10%) of the 2,526 total verses.

Author
David and Others

Date
collected by 400 B.C.

Key Truth
Praise, Worship, and Trust

Historic Time
Moses to Babylonian Captivity

Key Verse
29:2
. . . worship the LORD in the beauty of holiness.

10%
Prophecy

1300 B.C.	1200 B.C.	1100 B.C.	1000 B.C.	900 B.C.	800 B.C.	700 B.C.	600 B.C.	500 B.C.

105??
lm 90, Moses

75-1050
el ruled by judges

971-931
Solomon's reign

1011-971
David's reign

931-722
Northern Kingdom (Israel)

990
Birth of Solomon

931-586
Southern Kingdom (Judah)

1025-930
Most of the psalms

605-536
Babylonian Captivity

515
Psalms 126; 137 after captivity

516
Rebuilding of the temple complete

BOOK I

PSALM 1
The Righteous Are Blessed

1 Blessed *is* the man that walketh not in the counsel of the ungodly, nor standeth in the way of sinners, nor sitteth in the seat of the scornful.

2 But his delight *is* in the law of the LORD; and in his law doth he meditate day and night.

3 And he shall be like a tree planted by the rivers of water, that bringeth forth his fruit in his season; his leaf also shall not wither; and whatsoever he doeth shall prosper.

4 The ungodly *are* not so: but *are* like the chaff which the wind driveth away.

5 Therefore the ungodly shall not stand in the judgment, nor sinners in the congregation of the righteous.

6 For the LORD knoweth the way of the righteous: but the way of the ungodly shall perish.

PSALM 2
The Anointed One

1 Why do the heathen rage, and the people imagine a vain thing?

2 The kings of the earth set themselves, and the rulers take counsel together, against the LORD, and against his anointed, *saying*,

3 Let us break their bands asunder, and cast away their cords from us.

4 He that sitteth in the heavens shall laugh: the Lord shall have them in derision.

5 Then shall he speak unto them in his wrath, and vex them in his sore displeasure.

6 Yet have I set my king upon my holy hill of Zion.

7 I will declare the decree: the LORD hath said unto me, Thou *art* my Son; this day have I begotten thee.

8 Ask of me, and I shall give *thee* the heathen *for* thine inheritance, and the uttermost parts of the earth *for* thy possession.

9 Thou shalt break them with a rod of iron; thou shalt dash them in pieces like a potter's vessel.

10 Be wise now therefore, O ye kings: be instructed, ye judges of the earth.

11 Serve the LORD with fear, and rejoice with trembling.

12 Kiss the Son, lest he be angry, and ye perish *from* the way, when his wrath is kindled but a little. Blessed *are* all they that put their trust in him.

PSALM 3
A Morning Prayer

A Psalm of David, when he fled from Absalom his son.

1 LORD, how are they increased that trouble me! many *are* they that rise up against me.

2 Many *there be* which say of my soul, *There is* no help for him in God. Selah.

3 But thou, O LORD, *art* a shield for me; my glory, and the lifter up of mine head.

4 I cried unto the LORD with my voice, and he heard me out of his holy hill. Selah.

5 I laid me down and slept; I awaked; for the LORD sustained me.

6 I will not be afraid of ten thousands of people, that have set *themselves* against me round about.

7 Arise, O LORD; save me, O my God: for

Cross-references

1 Ps. 26:4; Prov. 4:14, 15; Jer. 15:17

2 Josh. 1:8; Ps. 119:1, 35, 47, 92, 97

3 Gen. 39:3, 23; Ezek. 47:12

4 Job 21:18; Ps. 35:5; Isa. 17:13; 29:5

6 Ps. 37:18; 2Tim. 2:19

1 Ps. 46:6

2 Ps. 45:7; John 1:41

3 Jer. 5:5; Luke 19:14

4 Ps. 11:4; Prov. 1:26

6 2Sam. 5:7

7 Acts 13:33

8 Ps. 22:27; John 17:4, 5; 19:15

9 Ps. 89:23; Rev. 2:27; 12:5

11 Phil. 2:12

12 Prov. 16:20; John 5:23

3 Ps. 27:6

5 Lev. 26:6; Ps. 4:8; Prov. 3:24

6 Ps. 27:3

7 Job 16:10; 29:17; Ps. 58:6; Lam. 3:30

1:1–6 Psalm 1 is a preface to the entire collection of psalms. It begins with a beatitude, or blessing. Like Jesus' beatitudes in the Sermon on the Mount (Matt. 5:3–12), the psalmist announces "happy" and "approved" is the righteous man, in contrast to the ungodly man whose destiny is the judgment of God (v. 4). Only those who seek God with a sincere heart will be truly blessed.

2:6–7 my king . . . my Son. This is the first of the Messianic Psalms. These are psalms that predict various aspects of the life and ministry of the coming Messiah. In some cases they describe the experiences of Israel's kings, but in every case they point ahead to the King of kings. Psalm 2 is attributed to David in Acts 4:25 and quoted frequently in the New Testament as referring to Jesus Christ (cf. Acts 13:33; Heb. 1:5; Rev. 19:15). Almost one-third of the New Testament quotations taken from the Hebrew Bible (112 of 360) are taken from the book of Psalms.

2:12 Kiss the Son. Here we are invited to make peace with God by submitting to His Son as our Lord and Savior. Compare John 5:23, "He that honoureth not the Son honoureth not the Father which hath sent him."

3:1–8 Some of the psalms are songs of war. They interweave expressions of praise with appeals for judgment and justice. These Imprecatory Psalms represent the appeal of the psalmist for God to intervene with justice in a fallen, sinful world. These are not just the emotional cries of distraught humans but war cries of the Prince of Peace. Jesus quoted some of these psalms Himself (Ps. 35:19; 69:4; John 15:25). God's promised Messiah will come with justice to judge and make war when He returns at the Battle of Armageddon (Rev. 19:11–16).

thou hast smitten all mine enemies *upon* the cheek bone; thou hast broken the teeth of the ungodly.

8 Salvation *belongeth* unto the LORD: thy blessing *is* upon thy people. Selah.

PSALM 4
An Evening Prayer
To the chief Musician on Neginoth, A Psalm of David.

1 Hear me when I call, O God of my righteousness: thou hast enlarged me *when I was* in distress; have mercy upon me, and hear my prayer.

2 O ye sons of men, how long *will ye turn* my glory into shame? *how long* will ye love vanity, *and* seek after leasing? Selah.

3 But know that the LORD hath set apart him that is godly for himself: the LORD will hear when I call unto him.

4 Stand in awe, and sin not: commune with your own heart upon your bed, and be still. Selah.

5 Offer the sacrifices of righteousness, and put your trust in the LORD.

6 *There be* many that say, Who will shew us *any* good? LORD, lift thou up the light of thy countenance upon us.

7 Thou hast put gladness in my heart, more than in the time *that* their corn and their wine increased.

8 I will both lay me down in peace, and sleep: for thou, LORD, only makest me dwell in safety.

PSALM 5
A Prayer for Protection
To the chief Musician upon Nehiloth, A Psalm of David.

1 Give ear to my words, O LORD, consider my meditation.

2 Hearken unto the voice of my cry, my King, and my God: for unto thee will I pray.

3 My voice shalt thou hear in the morning, O LORD; in the morning will I direct *my prayer* unto thee, and will look up.

4 For thou *art* not a God that hath pleasure in wickedness: neither shall evil dwell with thee.

5 The foolish shall not stand in thy sight: thou hatest all workers of iniquity.

6 Thou shalt destroy them that speak leasing: the LORD will abhor the bloody and deceitful man.

7 But as for me, I will come *into* thy house in the multitude of thy mercy: *and* in thy fear will I worship toward thy holy temple.

8 Lead me, O LORD, in thy righteousness

---

8 Prov. 21:31; Isa. 43:11; Jer. 3:23; Hos. 13:4; Jon. 2:9; Rev. 7:10; 19:1

3 2Tim. 2:19; 2Pet. 2:9

4 Eph. 4:26; Ps. 77:6; 2Cor. 13:5

5 Deut. 33:19; 2Sam. 15:12; Ps. 37:3; 50:14

6 Num. 6:26; Ps. 80:3, 7, 19; 119:135

7 Isa. 9:3

8 Lev. 25:18, 19; 26:5; Deut. 12:10; Job 11:18, 19; Ps. 3:5

2 Ps. 3:4; 65:2

3 Ps. 30:5; 88:13; 130:6

5 Hab. 1:13

6 Ps. 55:23; Rev. 21:8

7 1Kgs. 8:29, 30, 35, 38; Ps. 28:2; 132:7; 138:2

8 Ps. 25:4, 5; 27:11

9 Ps. 62:4; Rom. 3:13

10 2Sam. 15:31; 17:14, 23

11 Isa. 65:13

12 Ps. 115:13

1 Ps. 38:1; Jer. 10:24; 46:28

2 Ps. 41:4; Hos. 6:1

3 Ps. 90:13

5 Ps. 30:9; 88:11; 115:17; 118:17; Isa. 38:18

7 Job 17:7; Ps. 31:9; 38:10; 88:9; Lam. 5:17

8 Ps. 3:4; 119:115; Matt. 7:23; 25:41; Luke 13:27

2 Ps. 50:22; Isa. 38:13

---

because of mine enemies; make thy way straight before my face.

9 For *there is* no faithfulness in their mouth; their inward part *is* very wickedness; their throat *is* an open sepulchre; they flatter with their tongue.

10 Destroy thou them, O God; let them fall by their own counsels; cast them out in the multitude of their transgressions; for they have rebelled against thee.

11 But let all those that put their trust in thee rejoice: let them ever shout for joy, because thou defendest them: let them also that love thy name be joyful in thee.

12 For thou, LORD, wilt bless the righteous; with favour wilt thou compass him as *with* a shield.

PSALM 6
A Prayer for Mercy in Time of Trouble
To the chief Musician on Neginoth upon Sheminith, A Psalm of David.

1 O LORD, rebuke me not in thine anger, neither chasten me in thy hot displeasure.

2 Have mercy upon me, O LORD; for I *am* weak: O LORD, heal me; for my bones are vexed.

3 My soul is also sore vexed: but thou, O LORD, how long?

4 Return, O LORD, deliver my soul: oh save me for thy mercies' sake.

5 For in death *there is* no remembrance of thee: in the grave who shall give thee thanks?

6 I am weary with my groaning; all the night make I my bed to swim; I water my couch with my tears.

7 Mine eye is consumed because of grief; it waxeth old because of all mine enemies.

8 Depart from me, all ye workers of iniquity; for the LORD hath heard the voice of my weeping.

9 The LORD hath heard my supplication; the LORD will receive my prayer.

10 Let all mine enemies be ashamed and sore vexed: let them return *and* be ashamed suddenly.

PSALM 7
A Prayer for Justice
Shiggaion of David, which he sang unto the LORD, concerning the words of Cush the Benjamite.

1 O LORD my God, in thee do I put my trust: save me from all them that persecute me, and deliver me:

2 Lest he tear my soul like a lion, rending *it* in pieces, while *there is* none to deliver.

3 O LORD my God, if I have done this; if there be iniquity in my hands;

4 If I have rewarded evil unto him that was at peace with me; (yea, I have delivered him that without cause is mine enemy:)

5 Let the enemy persecute my soul, and take *it*; yea, let him tread down my life upon the earth, and lay mine honour in the dust. Selah.

6 Arise, O LORD, in thine anger, lift up thyself because of the rage of mine enemies: and awake for me *to* the judgment *that* thou hast commanded.

7 So shall the congregation of the people compass thee about: for their sakes therefore return thou on high.

8 The LORD shall judge the people: judge me, O LORD, according to my righteousness, and according to mine integrity *that is* in me.

9 Oh let the wickedness of the wicked come to an end; but establish the just: for the righteous God trieth the hearts and reins.

10 My defence *is* of God, which saveth the upright in heart.

11 God judgeth the righteous, and God is angry *with the wicked* every day.

12 If he turn not, he will whet his sword; he hath bent his bow, and made it ready.

13 He hath also prepared for him the instruments of death; he ordaineth his arrows against the persecutors.

14 Behold, he travaileth with iniquity, and hath conceived mischief, and brought forth falsehood.

15 He made a pit, and digged it, and is fallen into the ditch *which* he made.

16 His mischief shall return upon his own head, and his violent dealing shall come down upon his own pate.

17 I will praise the LORD according to his righteousness: and will sing praise to the name of the LORD most high.

PSALM 8
God's Glory and Man's Honor
To the chief Musician upon Gittith, A Psalm of David.

1 O LORD our Lord, how excellent *is* thy name in all the earth! who hast set thy glory above the heavens.

2 Out of the mouth of babes and sucklings hast thou ordained strength because of thine enemies, that thou mightest still the enemy and the avenger.

3 When I consider thy heavens, the work of thy fingers, the moon and the stars, which thou hast ordained;

4 What is man, that thou art mindful of him? and the son of man, that thou visitest him?

5 For thou hast made him a little lower than the angels, and hast crowned him with glory and honour.

6 Thou madest him to have dominion over the works of thy hands; thou hast put all *things* under his feet:

7 All sheep and oxen, yea, and the beasts of the field;

8 The fowl of the air, and the fish of the sea, *and whatsoever* passeth through the paths of the seas.

9 O LORD our Lord, how excellent *is* thy name in all the earth!

PSALM 9
Thanksgiving for God's Justice
To the chief Musician upon Muth-labben, A Psalm of David.

1 I will praise *thee*, O LORD, with my whole heart; I will shew forth all thy marvellous works.

2 I will be glad and rejoice in thee: I will sing praise to thy name, O thou most High.

3 When mine enemies are turned back, they shall fall and perish at thy presence.

4 For thou hast maintained my right and my cause; thou satest in the throne judging right.

5 Thou hast rebuked the heathen, thou hast destroyed the wicked, thou hast put out their name for ever and ever.

6 O thou enemy, destructions are come to a perpetual end: and thou hast destroyed cities; their memorial is perished with them.

7 But the LORD shall endure for ever: he hath prepared his throne for judgment.

8 And he shall judge the world in right-

Cross references (center column):

3 1Sam. 24:11; 2Sam. 16:7, 8
4 1Sam. 24:7; 26:9
6 Ps. 44:23; 94:2
8 Ps. 18:20; 35:24
9 Ps. 139:1; Jer. 11:20; 17:10; 20:12; Rev. 2:23
10 Ps. 125:4
12 Deut. 32:41
13 Deut. 32:23, 42; Ps. 64:7
14 Job 15:35; Isa. 33:11; 59:4; James 1:15
15 Ps. 9:15; 10:2; 35:8; 94:23; 141:10; Prov. 5:22; 26:27
16 1Kgs. 2:32; Esth. 9:25
1 Ps. 113:4; 148:13
2 Ps. 44:16; Matt. 11:25; 21:16; 1Cor. 1:27
3 Ps. 111:2
4 Job 7:17; Ps. 144:3; Heb. 2:6
6 Gen. 1:26, 28; 1Cor. 15:27; Heb. 2:8
9 Ps. 8:1
2 Ps. 5:11; 56:2; 83:18
5 Deut. 9:14; Prov. 10:7
7 Ps. 102:12, 26; Heb. 1:11
8 Ps. 96:13; 98:9

8:4–5 a little lower than the angels. In quoting this text, Hebrews 2:6–9, which follows the Septuagint text, points out that though humans are presently "lower" than the angels, they will ultimately be crowned with "glory and honor" through the work of Christ on their behalf. In this way, the author of Hebrews answers the question: If Christ became man and experienced death, how could He be superior to the angels? Part of the answer is that He will judge angels, and so shall we (1 Cor. 6:3) because we will be elevated by Christ to a position higher than the angels.

9:1–20 This psalm anticipates the coming rule of Christ on earth during the Millennium (vv. 7–9) as well as God's ultimate judgment of unbelievers at the Great White Throne Judgment (vv. 16–17, 19; cf. Rev. 20:11–15).

eousness, he shall minister judgment to the people in uprightness.

9 The LORD also will be a refuge for the oppressed, a refuge in times of trouble.

10 And they that know thy name will put their trust in thee: for thou, LORD, hast not forsaken them that seek thee.

11 Sing praises to the LORD, which dwelleth in Zion: declare among the people his doings.

12 When he maketh inquisition for blood, he remembereth them: he forgetteth not the cry of the humble.

13 Have mercy upon me, O LORD; consider my trouble *which I suffer* of them that hate me, thou that liftest me up from the gates of death:

14 That I may shew forth all thy praise in the gates of the daughter of Zion: I will rejoice in thy salvation.

15 The heathen are sunk down in the pit *that* they made: in the net which they hid is their own foot taken.

16 The LORD is known *by* the judgment *which* he executeth: the wicked is snared in the work of his own hands. Higgaion. Selah.

17 The wicked shall be turned into hell, *and* all the nations that forget God.

18 For the needy shall not alway be forgotten: the expectation of the poor shall *not* perish for ever.

19 Arise, O LORD; let not man prevail: let the heathen be judged in thy sight.

20 Put them in fear, O LORD: *that* the nations may know themselves *to be but* men. Selah.

PSALM 10
A Prayer for Justice

1 Why standest thou afar off, O LORD? *why* hidest thou *thyself* in times of trouble?

2 The wicked in *his* pride doth persecute the poor: let them be taken in the devices that they have imagined.

3 For the wicked boasteth of his heart's desire, and blesseth the covetous, *whom* the LORD abhorreth.

4 The wicked, through the pride of his countenance, will not seek *after God*: God *is* not in all his thoughts.

5 His ways are always grievous; thy judgments *are* far above out of his sight: *as for* all his enemies, he puffeth at them.

6 He hath said in his heart, I shall not be moved: for *I shall* never *be* in adversity.

7 His mouth is full of cursing and deceit and fraud: under his tongue *is* mischief and vanity.

8 He sitteth in the lurking places of the villages: in the secret places doth he murder the innocent: his eyes are privily set against the poor.

9 He lieth in wait secretly as a lion in his den: he lieth in wait to catch the poor: he doth catch the poor, when he draweth him into his net.

10 He croucheth, *and* humbleth himself, that the poor may fall by his strong ones.

11 He hath said in his heart, God hath forgotten: he hideth his face; he will never see *it*.

12 Arise, O LORD; O God, lift up thine hand: forget not the humble.

13 Wherefore doth the wicked contemn God? he hath said in his heart, Thou wilt not require *it*.

14 Thou hast seen *it*; for thou beholdest mischief and spite, to requite *it* with thy hand: the poor committeth himself unto thee; thou art the helper of the fatherless.

15 Break thou the arm of the wicked and the evil *man*: seek out his wickedness *till* thou find none.

16 The LORD *is* King for ever and ever: the heathen are perished out of his land.

17 LORD, thou hast heard the desire of the humble: thou wilt prepare their heart, thou wilt cause thine ear to hear:

18 To judge the fatherless and the oppressed, that the man of the earth may no more oppress.

PSALM 11
Trusting God

To the chief Musician, A Psalm of David.

1 In the LORD put I my trust: how say ye to my soul, Flee *as* a bird to your mountain?

2 For, lo, the wicked bend *their* bow, they make ready their arrow upon the string, that they may privily shoot at the upright in heart.

3 If the foundations be destroyed, what can the righteous do?

4 The LORD *is* in his holy temple, the LORD's throne *is* in heaven: his eyes behold, his eyelids try, the children of men.

5 The LORD trieth the righteous: but the wicked and him that loveth violence his soul hateth.

---

9 Ps. 32:7; 37:39; 46:1; 91:2
10 Ps. 91:14
12 Gen. 9:5
14 Ps. 13:5
15 Prov. 5:22; 22:8
16 Ex. 7:5; 14:4, 10, 31; Ps. 19:14
17 Job 8:13; Ps. 50:22
18 Ps. 9:12; 12:5; Prov. 23:18; 24:14
2 Ps. 7:16; 9:15, 16; Prov. 5:22
3 Ps. 94:4; Prov. 28:4
4 Ps. 14:1, 2; 53:1
5 Ps. 12:5; Prov. 24:7; Isa. 26:11
6 Eccl. 8:11; Isa. 56:12; Rev. 18:7
7 Job 20:12; Ps. 12:2; Rom. 3:14
8 Ps. 17:11; Hab. 3:14
9 Ps. 17:12; Mic. 7:2
11 Job 22:13; Ps. 73:11; 94:7; Ezek. 8:12; 9:9
12 Mic. 5:9
14 Hos. 14:3; 2Tim. 1:12
15 Ps. 37:17
16 Ps. 29:10; Jer. 10:10; Lam. 5:19; Dan. 4:34; 6:26
18 Ps. 82:3; Isa. 11:4
1 Ps. 56:11
3 Ps. 82:5
4 Isa. 66:1; Hab. 2:20; Matt. 5:34; 23:22; Rev. 4:2
5 Gen. 22:1; James 1:12

10:16–18 This psalm foresees the rule of Christ on earth during His millennial reign. Psalms 10—14 emphasize that we cannot plan the future without submitting our lives to the One who controls the future.

6 Upon the wicked he shall rain snares, fire and brimstone, and an horrible tempest: *this shall be* the portion of their cup.

7 For the righteous LORD loveth righteousness; his countenance doth behold the upright.

PSALM 12
A Plea for Help

To the chief Musician upon Sheminith, A Psalm of David.

1 Help, LORD; for the godly man ceaseth; for the faithful fail from among the children of men.

2 They speak vanity every one with his neighbour: *with* flattering lips *and* with a double heart do they speak.

3 The LORD shall cut off all flattering lips, *and* the tongue that speaketh proud things:

4 Who have said, With our tongue will we prevail; our lips *are* our own: who *is* lord over us?

5 For the oppression of the poor, for the sighing of the needy, now will I arise, saith the LORD; I will set *him* in safety *from him that* puffeth at him.

6 The words of the LORD *are* pure words: *as* silver tried in a furnace of earth, purified seven times.

7 Thou shalt keep them, O LORD, thou shalt preserve them from this generation for ever.

8 The wicked walk on every side, when the vilest men are exalted.

PSALM 13
A Prayer for Help

To the chief Musician, A Psalm of David.

1 How long wilt thou forget me, O LORD? for ever? how long wilt thou hide thy face from me?

2 How long shall I take counsel in my soul, *having* sorrow in my heart daily? how long shall mine enemy be exalted over me?

3 Consider *and* hear me, O LORD my God: lighten mine eyes, lest I sleep the *sleep of* death;

4 Lest mine enemy say, I have prevailed against him; *and* those that trouble me rejoice when I am moved.

5 But I have trusted in thy mercy; my heart shall rejoice in thy salvation.

6 I will sing unto the LORD, because he hath dealt bountifully with me.

PSALM 14
The Sinfulness of Men

To the chief Musician, A Psalm of David.

1 The fool hath said in his heart, *There is* no God. They are corrupt, they have done abominable works, *there is* none that doeth good.

2 The LORD looked down from heaven upon the children of men, to see if there were any that did understand, *and* seek God.

3 They are all gone aside, they are *all* together become filthy: *there is* none that doeth good, no, not one.

4 Have all the workers of iniquity no knowledge? who eat up my people *as* they eat bread, and call not upon the LORD.

5 There were they in great fear: for God *is* in the generation of the righteous.

6 Ye have shamed the counsel of the poor, because the LORD *is* his refuge.

7 Oh that the salvation of Israel *were come* out of Zion! when the LORD bringeth back the captivity of his people, Jacob shall rejoice, *and* Israel shall be glad.

PSALM 15
True Worshipers

A Psalm of David.

1 LORD, who shall abide in thy tabernacle? who shall dwell in thy holy hill?

2 He that walketh uprightly, and worketh righteousness, and speaketh the truth in his heart.

3 *He that* backbiteth not with his tongue, nor doeth evil to his neighbour, nor taketh up a reproach against his neighbour.

4 In whose eyes a vile person is contemned; but he honoureth them that fear the LORD. *He that* sweareth to *his own* hurt, and changeth not.

5 *He that* putteth not out his money to usury, nor taketh reward against the innocent. He that doeth these *things* shall never be moved.

PSALM 16
A Prayer of Confidence

Michtam of David.

1 Preserve me, O God: for in thee do I put my trust.

Cross references

6 Gen. 10:24; 43:34; 1Sam. 1:4; 9:23; Ps. 75:8; Ezek. 38:22

7 Job 36:7; Ps. 33:18; 34:15; 45:7; 146:8; 1Pet. 3:12

1 Isa. 57:1; Mic. 7:2

2 Ps. 10:7; 28:3

3 1Sam. 2:3; Ps. 17:10; Dan. 7:8, 25

5 Ex. 3:7, 8; Ps. 10:5; Isa. 33:10

6 2Sam. 22:31; Ps. 18:30; 19:8; Prov. 30:5

1 Job 13:24; Ps. 44:24

3 Ezra 9:8; Jer. 51:39

4 Ps. 25:2; 35:19; 38:16

5 Ps. 33:21

6 Ps. 116:7; 119:17

1 Gen. 6:11, 12; Ps. 10:4; 53:1; Rom. 3:10

2 Ps. 33:13; 102:19

3 Rom. 3:10-12

4 Ps. 79:6; Isa. 64:7; Jer. 10:25; Amos 8:4; Mic. 3:3

5 Ps. 53:5

6 Ps. 9:9; 142:5

7 Job 42:10; Ps. 53:6; 126:1; Rom. 11:26

3 Ps. 34:13

4 Judg. 11:35; Esth. 3:2

5 Ex. 22:25; Ezek. 18:8

14:7 the LORD bringeth back the captivity of his people (v. 7). This verse has reference to the future restoration of Israel by the Messiah. While God is currently regathering the Jews in the land of Israel, this prophecy will not be ultimately fulfilled until the Millennial Kingdom, when Christ rules from Jerusalem over all the earth.

2 *O my soul*, thou hast said unto the Lord, Thou *art* my Lord: my goodness *extendeth* not to thee;

3 *But* to the saints that *are* in the earth, and *to* the excellent, in whom *is* all my delight.

4 Their sorrows shall be multiplied *that* hasten *after* another *god*: their drink offerings of blood will I not offer, nor take up their names into my lips.

5 The Lord *is* the portion of mine inheritance and of my cup: thou maintainest my lot.

6 The lines are fallen unto me in pleasant *places*; yea, I have a goodly heritage.

7 I will bless the Lord, who hath given me counsel: my reins also instruct me in the night seasons.

8 I have set the Lord always before me: because *he is* at my right hand, I shall not be moved.

9 Therefore my heart is glad, and my glory rejoiceth: my flesh also shall rest in hope.

10 For thou wilt not leave my soul in hell; neither wilt thou suffer thine Holy One to see corruption.

11 Thou wilt shew me the path of life: in thy presence *is* fulness of joy; at thy right hand *there are* pleasures for evermore.

PSALM 17
An Innocent Man's Prayer
A Prayer of David.

1 Hear the right, O Lord attend unto my cry, give ear unto my prayer, *that goeth* not out of feigned lips.

2 Let my sentence come forth from thy presence; let thine eyes behold the things that are equal.

3 Thou hast proved mine heart; thou hast visited *me* in the night; thou hast tried me, *and* shalt find nothing; I am purposed *that* my mouth shall not transgress.

4 Concerning the works of men, by the word of thy lips I have kept *me from* the paths of the destroyer.

5 Hold up my goings in thy paths, *that* my footsteps slip not.

6 I have called upon thee, for thou wilt hear me, O God: incline thine ear unto me, and hear my speech.

7 Shew thy marvellous lovingkindness, O thou that savest by thy right hand them which put their trust *in thee* from those that rise up *against them*.

8 Keep me as the apple of the eye, hide me under the shadow of thy wings,

9 From the wicked that oppress me, *from* my deadly enemies, *who* compass me about.

10 They are inclosed in their own fat: with their mouth they speak proudly.

11 They have now compassed us in our steps: they have set their eyes bowing down to the earth;

12 Like as a lion *that* is greedy of his prey, and as it were a young lion lurking in secret places.

13 Arise, O Lord, disappoint him, cast him down: deliver my soul from the wicked, *which is* thy sword:

14 From men *which are* thy hand, O Lord, from men of the world, *which have* their portion in *this* life, and whose belly thou fillest with thy hid *treasure*: they are full of children, and leave the rest of their *substance* to their babes.

15 As for me, I will behold thy face in righteousness: I shall be satisfied, when I awake, with thy likeness.

PSALM 18
A Song of Victory
To the chief Musician, A Psalm of David, the servant of the Lord, who spake unto the Lord the words of this song in the day that the Lord delivered him from the hand of all his enemies, and from the hand of Saul: And he said,

1 I will love thee, O Lord, my strength.

2 The Lord *is* my rock, and my fortress, and my deliverer; my God, my strength, in whom I will trust; my buckler, and the horn of my salvation, *and* my high tower.

3 I will call upon the Lord, *who is worthy* to be praised: so shall I be saved from mine enemies.

4 The sorrows of death compassed me, and the floods of ungodly men made me afraid.

5 The sorrows of hell compassed me about: the snares of death prevented me.

6 In my distress I called upon the Lord, and cried unto my God: he heard my voice

Center reference column
2 Job 22:2, 3; 35:7, 8; Ps. 50:9; Rom. 11:35

4 Ex. 23:13; Josh. 23:7; Hos. 2:16, 17

5 Deut. 32:9; Ps. 11:6; 73:26; 119:57; 142:5; Jer. 10:16; Lam. 3:24

7 Ps. 17:3

8 Ps. 15:5; 73:23; 110:5; 121:5; Acts 2:25

9 Ps. 30:12; 57:8

10 Lev. 19:28; Num. 6:6; Ps. 49:15; Acts 2:27, 31; 13:35

11 Ps. 17:15; 21:6; 36:8; Matt. 5:8; 7:14; 1Cor. 13:12; 1John 3:2

3 Job 23:10; Ps. 16:7; 26:2; 66:10; 139:2; Zech. 13:9; Mal. 3:2, 3; 1Pet. 1:7

5 Ps. 119:133

6 Ps. 116:2

7 Ps. 31:21

8 Deut. 32:10; Ps. 91:1, 4; Zech. 2:8

11 1Sam. 23:26; Ps. 10:8, 9, 10

13 Isa. 10:5

14 Ps. 73:12; Luke 16:25; James 5:5

15 Ps. 4:6, 7; 1John 3:2

2 Heb. 2:13

4 Ps. 116:3

16:9–10 This is one of the Messianic Psalms. Initially, David expresses his faith in eternal life. He is convinced that his dead body will not be left in the grave. But he looks beyond his own experience to predict that God's Holy One will not "see corruption" (lit. "experience decay"). This phrase cannot be limited to David since his dead body has obviously decayed. It foresees the resurrection of Christ after He was in the grave only three days and is so quoted by Peter (Acts 2:25–28) and by Paul (Acts 13:35). Jesus died for our sins and then came back to life again to guarantee our eternal life as well.

out of his temple, and my cry came before him, *even* into his ears.

7 Then the earth shook and trembled; the foundations also of the hills moved and were shaken, because he was wroth.

8 There went up a smoke out of his nostrils, and fire out of his mouth devoured: coals were kindled by it.

9 He bowed the heavens also, and came down: and darkness *was* under his feet.

10 And he rode upon a cherub, and did fly: yea, he did fly upon the wings of the wind.

11 He made darkness his secret place; his pavilion round about him *were* dark waters *and* thick clouds of the skies.

12 At the brightness *that was* before him his thick clouds passed, hail *stones* and coals of fire.

13 The LORD also thundered in the heavens, and the Highest gave his voice; hail *stones* and coals of fire.

14 Yea, he sent out his arrows, and scattered them; and he shot out lightnings, and discomfited them.

15 Then the channels of waters were seen, and the foundations of the world were discovered at thy rebuke, O LORD, at the blast of the breath of thy nostrils.

16 He sent from above, he took me, he drew me out of many waters.

17 He delivered me from my strong enemy, and from them which hated me: for they were too strong for me.

18 They prevented me in the day of my calamity: but the LORD was my stay.

19 He brought me forth also into a large place; he delivered me, because he delighted in me.

20 The LORD rewarded me according to my righteousness; according to the cleanness of my hands hath he recompensed me.

21 For I have kept the ways of the LORD, and have not wickedly departed from my God.

22 For all his judgments *were* before me, and I did not put away his statutes from me.

23 I was also upright before him, and I kept myself from mine iniquity.

24 Therefore hath the LORD recompensed me according to my righteousness, according to the cleanness of my hands in his eyesight.

25 With the merciful thou wilt shew thyself merciful; with an upright man thou wilt shew thyself upright;

26 With the pure thou wilt shew thyself pure; and with the froward thou wilt shew thyself froward.

27 For thou wilt save the afflicted people; but wilt bring down high looks.

28 For thou wilt light my candle: the LORD my God will enlighten my darkness.

29 For by thee I have run through a troop; and by my God have I leaped over a wall.

30 *As for* God, his way *is* perfect: the word of the LORD is tried: he *is* a buckler to all those that trust in him.

31 For who *is* God save the LORD? or who *is* a rock save our God?

32 *It is* God that girdeth me with strength, and maketh my way perfect.

33 He maketh my feet like hinds' *feet*, and setteth me upon my high places.

34 He teacheth my hands to war, so that a bow of steel is broken by mine arms.

35 Thou hast also given me the shield of thy salvation: and thy right hand hath holden me up, and thy gentleness hath made me great.

36 Thou hast enlarged my steps under me, that my feet did not slip.

37 I have pursued mine enemies, and overtaken them: neither did I turn again till they were consumed.

38 I have wounded them that they were not able to rise: they are fallen under my feet.

39 For thou hast girded me with strength unto the battle: thou hast subdued under me those that rose up against me.

40 Thou hast also given me the necks of mine enemies; that I might destroy them that hate me.

41 They cried, but *there was* none to save *them: even* unto the LORD, but he answered them not.

42 Then did I beat them small as the dust before the wind: I did cast them out as the dirt in the streets.

43 Thou hast delivered me from the strivings of the people; *and* thou hast made me the head of the heathen: a people *whom* I have not known shall serve me.

44 As soon as they hear of me, they shall obey me: the strangers shall submit themselves unto me.

45 The strangers shall fade away, and be afraid out of their close places.

46 The LORD liveth; and blessed *be* my rock; and let the God of my salvation be exalted.

47 *It is* God that avengeth me, and subdueth the people under me.

48 He delivereth me from mine enemies: yea, thou liftest me up above those that rise up against me: thou hast delivered me from the violent man.

49 Therefore will I give thanks unto thee, O

---

7 Acts 4:31
9 Ps. 144:5
10 Ps. 99:1; 104:3
11 Ps. 97:2
12 Ps. 97:3
13 Ps. 29:3
14 Josh. 10:10; Ps. 144:6; Isa. 30:30
15 Ex. 15:8; Ps. 106:9
16 Ps. 144:7
19 Ps. 31:8; 118:5
20 1Sam. 24:19
24 1Sam. 26:23
25 1Kgs. 8:32
26 Lev. 26:23, 24, 27, 28; Prov. 3:34
27 Ps. 101:5; Prov. 6:17
28 Job 18:6; 29:3
30 Deut. 32:4; Ps. 119:140; Prov. 30:5
31 Deut. 32:31, 39; 1Sam. 2:2; Ps. 86:8; Isa. 45:5
32 Ps. 91:2
33 Deut. 32:13; 33:29; 2Sam. 2:18; Hab. 3:19
34 Ps. 144:4
36 Prov. 4:12
41 Isa. 1:15; Jer. 11:11; 14:12; Ezek. 8:18; Mic. 3:4; Zech. 7:13
42 Zech. 10:5
43 2Sam. 2:9, 10; 3:1; 8; Isa. 52:15; 55:5
44 Deut. 33:29; Ps. 66:3; 81:15
45 Mic. 7:17
48 Ps. 59:1
49 Rom. 15:9

LORD, among the heathen, and sing praises unto thy name.

50 Great deliverance giveth he to his king; and sheweth mercy to his anointed, to David, and to his seed for evermore.

PSALM 19
God's Creation

To the chief Musician, A Psalm of David.

1 The heavens declare the glory of God; and the firmament sheweth his handywork.
2 Day unto day uttereth speech, and night unto night sheweth knowledge.
3 *There is* no speech nor language, *where* their voice is not heard.
4 Their line is gone out through all the earth, and their words to the end of the world. In them hath he set a tabernacle for the sun,
5 Which *is* as a bridegroom coming out of his chamber, *and* rejoiceth as a strong man to run a race.
6 His going forth *is* from the end of the heaven, and his circuit unto the ends of it: and there is nothing hid from the heat thereof.

God's Law

7 The law of the LORD *is* perfect, converting the soul: the testimony of the LORD *is* sure, making wise the simple.
8 The statutes of the LORD *are* right, rejoicing the heart: the commandment of the LORD *is* pure, enlightening the eyes.
9 The fear of the LORD *is* clean, enduring for ever: the judgments of the LORD *are* true *and* righteous altogether.
10 More to be desired *are they* than gold, yea, than much fine gold: sweeter also than honey and the honeycomb.
11 Moreover by them is thy servant warned: *and* in keeping of them *there is* great reward.
12 Who can understand *his* errors? cleanse thou me from secret *faults.*
13 Keep back thy servant also from presumptuous *sins*; let them not have dominion

over me: then shall I be upright, and I shall be innocent from the great transgression.
14 Let the words of my mouth, and the meditation of my heart, be acceptable in thy sight, O LORD, my strength, and my redeemer.

PSALM 20
A Prayer for Victory

To the chief Musician, A Psalm of David.

1 The LORD hear thee in the day of trouble; the name of the God of Jacob defend thee;
2 Send thee help from the sanctuary, and strengthen thee out of Zion;
3 Remember all thy offerings, and accept thy burnt sacrifice; Selah.
4 Grant thee according to thine own heart, and fulfil all thy counsel.
5 We will rejoice in thy salvation, and in the name of our God we will set up *our* banners: the LORD fulfil all thy petitions.
6 Now know I that the LORD saveth his anointed; he will hear him from his holy heaven with the saving strength of his right hand.
7 Some *trust* in chariots, and some in horses: but we will remember the name of the LORD our God.
8 They are brought down and fallen: but we are risen, and stand upright.
9 Save, LORD: let the king hear us when we call.

PSALM 21
Praise for Victory

To the chief Musician, A Psalm of David.

1 The king shall joy in thy strength, O LORD; and in thy salvation how greatly shall he rejoice!
2 Thou hast given him his heart's desire, and hast not withholden the request of his lips. Selah.
3 For thou preventest him with the blessings of goodness: thou settest a crown of pure gold on his head.
4 He asked life of thee, *and* thou gavest *it* him, *even* length of days for ever and ever.

Cross references (center column):

50 2Sam. 7:13; Ps. 144:10

1 Gen. 1:6; Isa. 40:22; Rom. 1:19, 20

4 Rom. 10:18

5 Eccl. 1:5

7 Ps. 111:7

8 Ps. 12:6; 13:3

10 Ps. 119:72, 103, 127; Prov. 8:10, 11, 19

11 Prov. 29:18

12 Lev. 4:2; Ps. 40:12; 90:8

13 Gen. 20:6; 1Sam. 25:32, 33, 34, 39; Ps. 119:133; Rom. 6:12, 14

14 Ps. 18:1; 51:15; Isa. 43:14; 44:6; 47:4; 1Thess. 1:10

1 Prov. 18:10

2 1Kgs. 6:16; 2Chr. 20:8; Ps. 73:17

4 Ps. 21:2

5 Ex. 17:15; Ps. 9:14; 60:4

7 2Chr. 32:8; Ps. 33:16, 17; Prov. 21:31; Isa. 31:1

1 Ps. 20:5, 6

2 Ps. 20:4, 5

3 2Sam. 12:30; 1Chr. 20:2

4 Ps. 61:5, 6; 91:16

20:1—21:13 The Royal Psalms (see Psalms 2, 20, 21, 45, 61, 72, 89, 110) are Messianic Psalms that celebrate the line of Davidic kings and ultimately point to the Messiah himself, the ultimate King of Israel. Psalms 20 and 21 go together. Psalm 20 is a psalm of prayer for the king before battle, and Psalm 21 is a psalm of thanksgiving for his victory.

20:6 the LORD saveth his anointed. This is a reference

to the Messiah and God's promise to protect Him (cf. Ps. 2:2).

21:3 a crown of pure gold. This reference to victory finds its ultimate fulfillment in the crown of Christ (see Rev. 14:14). David and the kings who followed him in his family line foreshadowed the coming of Jesus Christ, the only one who could fulfill these prophecies and secure David's throne forever (see Luke 1:33).

5 His glory *is* great in thy salvation: honour and majesty hast thou laid upon him.

6 For thou hast made him most blessed for ever: thou hast made him exceeding glad with thy countenance.

7 For the king trusteth in the LORD, and through the mercy of the most High he shall not be moved.

8 Thine hand shall find out all thine enemies: thy right hand shall find out those that hate thee.

9 Thou shalt make them as a fiery oven in the time of thine anger: the LORD shall swallow them up in his wrath, and the fire shall devour them.

10 Their fruit shalt thou destroy from the earth, and their seed from among the children of men.

11 For they intended evil against thee: they imagined a mischievous device, *which* they are not able *to perform.*

12 Therefore shalt thou make them turn their back, *when* thou shalt make ready *thine arrows* upon thy strings against the face of them.

13 Be thou exalted, LORD, in thine own strength: *so* will we sing and praise thy power.

PSALM 22
Anguish and Praise

To the chief Musician upon Aijeleth Shahar, A Psalm of David.

1 My God, my God, why hast thou forsaken me? *why art thou so* far from helping me, *and from* the words of my roaring?

2 O my God, I cry in the daytime, but thou hearest not; and in the night season, and am not silent.

3 But thou *art* holy, *O thou* that inhabitest the praises of Israel.

4 Our fathers trusted in thee: they trusted, and thou didst deliver them.

5 They cried unto thee, and were delivered: they trusted in thee, and were not confounded.

6 But I *am* a worm, and no man; a re-

7 Ps. 16:8
8 1Sam. 31:3
9 Isa. 26:11; Mal. 4:1
10 Ps. 37:28; 109:13; Isa. 14:20
1 Matt. 27:46; Mark 15:34
5 Ps. 25:2, 3; Rom. 9:33
6 Job 25:6; Isa. 53:3
7 Matt. 27:39; Mark 15:29; Luke 23:35
8 Ps. 91:14; Matt. 27:43
12 Deut. 32:14; Ps. 68:30; Ezek. 39:18; Amos 4:1
13 Job 16:10; Ps. 35:21; Lam. 2:16; 3:46
14 Josh. 7:5; Job 23:16
15 Job 29:10; John 19:28
16 Matt. 27:35; Mark 15:24; Luke 23:33; John 19:23, 37; 20:25
17 Luke 23:27, 35
18 Luke 23:34; John 19:23, 24
19 Ps. 10:1
20 Ps. 22:16
21 Acts 4:27; 2Tim. 4:17
22 Ps. 40:9; Rom. 8:29
24 Heb. 5:7

proach of men, and despised of the people.

7 All they that see me laugh me to scorn: they shoot out the lip, they shake the head, *saying,*

8 He trusted on the LORD *that* he would deliver him: let him deliver him, seeing he delighted in him.

9 But thou *art* he that took me out of the womb: thou didst make me hope *when I was* upon my mother's breasts.

10 I was cast upon thee from the womb: thou *art* my God from my mother's belly.

11 Be not far from me; for trouble *is* near; for *there is* none to help.

12 Many bulls have compassed me: strong *bulls* of Bashan have beset me round.

13 They gaped upon me *with* their mouths, *as* a ravening and a roaring lion.

14 I am poured out like water, and all my bones are out of joint: my heart is like wax; it is melted in the midst of my bowels.

15 My strength is dried up like a potsherd; and my tongue cleaveth to my jaws; and thou hast brought me into the dust of death.

16 For dogs have compassed me: the assembly of the wicked have inclosed me: they pierced my hands and my feet.

17 I may tell all my bones: they look *and* stare upon me.

18 They part my garments among them, and cast lots upon my vesture.

19 But be not thou far from me, O LORD: O my strength, haste thee to help me.

20 Deliver my soul from the sword; my darling from the power of the dog.

21 Save me from the lion's mouth: for thou hast heard me from the horns of the unicorns.

22 I will declare thy name unto my brethren: in the midst of the congregation will I praise thee.

23 Ye that fear the LORD, praise him; all ye the seed of Jacob, glorify him; and fear him, all ye the seed of Israel.

24 For he hath not despised nor abhorred the affliction of the afflicted; neither hath

---

22:1–31 This psalm has often been called the "Song of the Cross." It is impossible to read this psalm without noticing that it points beyond David's own experience to the suffering and death of Christ, God's promised Messiah. The psalm even predicts Jesus' exact words from the cross: "My God, my God, why hast thou forsaken me?" (cf. Matt. 27:46; Mark 15:34). David vividly described the excruciating pain of the crucifixion of Christ down to the minute details—hundreds of years before crucifixion was used as a means of capital punishment. His cry to God (v. 1), the piercing of His hands and feet (v. 16), the taunting crowd (vv. 7–13), His suffering (v. 14), His thirst (v. 15), and even the soldiers gambling for His robe (v. 18) are all examples of detailed messianic prophecy in this psalm. David's prophecy foresees the rejection of the Messiah by His own people when Jesus took our sins upon Himself and died in our place on the cross (see Matt. 27:39–43).

The Messianic Psalms

By Warren Baker

The term "messianic psalms" is used to describe those psalms that contain prophecies regarding the Messiah. These psalms are classified into two categories: the Suffering Messiah Psalms and the Royal Psalms. The Suffering Messiah Psalms relate Christ's suffering on behalf of sinners (especially Ps. 16; 22; 40; see also Ps. 35; 41; 55; 69; 109), while the Royal Psalms describe Christ as King, particularly with respect to His reign during the Millennial Kingdom and throughout eternity (especially Ps. 2; 45; 72; 110; see also Ps. 18; 20; 21; 61; 89; 118; 132). Other psalms speak of God's rule or of Christ in an indirect way; however, though these psalms may be prophetic (most are not), they are not messianic (see Ps. 8; 9; 10; 14; 23; 24; 27; 31:5; 34; 38).

How can we determine whether a particular psalm is messianic? The first proof is based upon tradition. In other words, we should ask, "Did the Jews of antiquity view the passage as a prophecy of the coming Messiah?" or "Did the early Christian Church believe that Christ uniquely fulfilled what was written?" The wording of the question the High Priest asked of Christ in Matthew 26:63 proves that Jewish tradition held that Psalm 2, on which his question is based, was truly messianic (cf. John 1:49). The second proof is based upon the content of the psalm itself. Regarding content, we need to ask, "Does the psalm describe an event that could not possibly apply to anyone but the Messiah of God, Jesus Christ?" In Psalm 45:7-8 and 110:5 the name *Adonai* ("Lord"), a name reserved for God alone, is applied to the King; this can refer to none other than Jesus Christ.

> *The term "messianic psalms" is used to describe those psalms that contain prophecies regarding the Messiah.*

Within any of the psalms there are general principles and truths that can apply to Christ, to the psalmist himself, and to followers of God in general. To be truly messianic, however, a psalm must reveal some specific truth about Christ and must not contain anything in the immediate context that would disallow a messianic interpretation. The third proof comes from parallel Old Testament usage. For example, the messianic content of Psalm 72:8 is reinforced by the parallel use in Zechariah 9:10. The fourth and final proof and ultimate confirmation that a particular psalm is indeed messianic is the testimony of Christ and the New Testament to that effect. In Matthew 22:41-46, Jesus, using the text of Psalm 110:1 questioned the Pharisees regarding the Messiah. Jesus thus affirmed the messianic content of Psalm 110, and the Jews, who did not question His interpretation of the psalm as messianic, affirmed Jewish tradition regarding the psalm.

Hebrew poetry adds to the content of the Messianic Psalms by serving as an instrument of expression for what might otherwise be so overwhelming as to stifle the heart and vision of the psalmist. Whether the Hebrew pattern of rhyming ideas (instead of words) is used to describe Christ's suffering or His coming glory, these poetic frameworks help to draw out the emotion of the moment. It not only allows for, but also prescribes by its very format, that the psalmist give a detailed description of the event. The emotional descriptions and personal assessment of future events that these psalms give us help reinforce the literalness of their fulfillment. It is one thing to read a prophecy that Messiah will suffer, it is quite another to read detailed descriptions of His agony.

he hid his face from him; but when he cried unto him, he heard.

25 My praise *shall be* of thee in the great congregation: I will pay my vows before them that fear him.

26 The meek shall eat and be satisfied: they shall praise the LORD that seek him: your heart shall live for ever.

27 All the ends of the world shall remember and turn unto the LORD: and all the kindreds of the nations shall worship before thee.

28 For the kingdom *is* the LORD's: and he *is* the governor among the nations.

29 All *they that be* fat upon earth shall eat and worship: all they that go down to the dust shall bow before him: and none can keep alive his own soul.

30 A seed shall serve him; it shall be accounted to the Lord for a generation.

31 They shall come, and shall declare his righteousness unto a people that shall be born, that he hath done *this*.

PSALM 23
"The Lord Is My Shepherd"
A Psalm of David.

1 The LORD *is* my shepherd; I shall not want.

2 He maketh me to lie down in green pastures: he leadeth me beside the still waters.

3 He restoreth my soul: he leadeth me in the paths of righteousness for his name's sake.

4 Yea, though I walk through the valley of the shadow of death, I will fear no evil: for thou *art* with me; thy rod and thy staff they comfort me.

5 Thou preparest a table before me in the presence of mine enemies: thou anointest my head with oil; my cup runneth over.

6 Surely goodness and mercy shall follow me all the days of my life: and I will dwell in the house of the LORD for ever.

Cross references:
25 Ps. 35:18; 40:9, 10
26 Lev. 7:11, 12, 15, 16
27 Ps. 96:7; 98:3; Isa. 49:6
28 Obad. 21; Matt. 6:13
29 Phil. 2:10
31 Ps. 78:6; Isa. 60:3
1 Jer. 23:4; John 10:11; Phil. 4:19
3 Prov. 8:20
4 Job 3:5; 10:21, 22; Isa. 43:2
1 Job 41:11
2 Gen. 1:9; Job 38:6; Ps. 104:5; 136:6; 2Pet. 3:5
3 Ps. 15:1
4 Job 17:9; Ps. 15:4; Isa. 33:15, 16; Matt. 5:8; 1Tim. 2:8
6 Ps. 27:8; 105:4
7 Ps. 97:6; Isa. 26:2; Hag. 2:7; Mal. 3:1; 1Cor. 2:8
1 Ps. 86:4; 143:8; Lam. 3:41
2 Ps. 13:4; 22:5; 31:1; 34:8; Isa. 28:16; 49:23; Rom. 10:11
4 Ex. 33:13; Ps. 5:8; 27:11; 86:11; 119; 143:8, 10

PSALM 24
The "King of Glory"
A Psalm of David.

1 The earth *is* the LORD's, and the fulness thereof; the world, and they that dwell therein.

2 For he hath founded it upon the seas, and established it upon the floods.

3 Who shall ascend into the hill of the LORD? or who shall stand in his holy place?

4 He that hath clean hands, and a pure heart; who hath not lifted up his soul unto vanity, nor sworn deceitfully.

5 He shall receive the blessing from the LORD, and righteousness from the God of his salvation.

6 This *is* the generation of them that seek him, that seek thy face, O Jacob. Selah.

7 Lift up your heads, O ye gates; and be ye lift up, ye everlasting doors; and the King of glory shall come in.

8 Who *is* this King of glory? The LORD strong and mighty, the LORD mighty in battle.

9 Lift up your heads, O ye gates; even lift *them* up, ye everlasting doors; and the King of glory shall come in.

10 Who is this King of glory? The LORD of hosts, he *is* the King of glory. Selah.

PSALM 25
A Prayer for Guidance and Protection
A Psalm of David.

1 Unto thee, O LORD, do I lift up my soul.

2 O my God, I trust in thee: let me not be ashamed, let not mine enemies triumph over me.

3 Yea, let none that wait on thee be ashamed: let them be ashamed which transgress without cause.

4 Shew me thy ways, O LORD; teach me thy paths.

22:27–31 This psalm ends with the promise that the nations will turn to the Lord and worship Him in the Millennial Kingdom.

23:1–6 The twenty-third psalm describes Jesus as our Shepherd-King and anticipates His role as our Good Shepherd (see John 10). The imagery of this psalm is one of the most intimate word pictures in all the psalms. The "shepherd" is pictured living with his sheep—loving, guiding, and protecting them. The relationship between the shepherd and the sheep is a beautiful picture of God's love for His people. Jesus used this same imagery to illustrate His love for us, promising even to lay down His life for us (John 10:15).

24:7–10 Psalm 24 looks ahead to the time when Jesus Christ will return in a triumphal procession to Jerusalem, at His Second Coming. As the eternal Son of God, He is the "King of glory." The Bible predicts that when Christ returns to earth, He will come into Jerusalem, the royal city of the kingdom of God, as the victorious conqueror, the "King over all the earth" (cf. Zech. 14:1–9; Ezek. 43:1–5; Acts 1:11–12).

5 Lead me in thy truth, and teach me: for thou *art* the God of my salvation; on thee do I wait all the day.
6 Remember, O LORD, thy tender mercies and thy lovingkindnesses; for they *have been* ever of old.
7 Remember not the sins of my youth, nor my transgressions: according to thy mercy remember thou me for thy goodness' sake, O LORD.
8 Good and upright *is* the LORD: therefore will he teach sinners in the way.
9 The meek will he guide in judgment: and the meek will he teach his way.
10 All the paths of the LORD *are* mercy and truth unto such as keep his covenant and his testimonies.
11 For thy name's sake, O LORD, pardon mine iniquity; for it *is* great.
12 What man *is* he that feareth the LORD? him shall he teach in the way *that* he shall choose.
13 His soul shall dwell at ease; and his seed shall inherit the earth.
14 The secret of the LORD *is* with them that fear him; and he will shew them his covenant.
15 Mine eyes *are* ever toward the LORD; for he shall pluck my feet out of the net.
16 Turn thee unto me, and have mercy upon me; for I *am* desolate and afflicted.
17 The troubles of my heart are enlarged: *O* bring thou me out of my distresses.
18 Look upon mine affliction and my pain; and forgive all my sins.
19 Consider mine enemies; for they are many; and they hate me with cruel hatred.
20 O keep my soul, and deliver me: let me not be ashamed; for I put my trust in thee.
21 Let integrity and uprightness preserve me; for I wait on thee.
22 Redeem Israel, O God, out of all his troubles.

PSALM 26
A Prayer for Protection
A Psalm of David.

1 Judge me, O LORD; for I have walked in mine integrity: I have trusted also in the LORD; *therefore* I shall not slide.
2 Examine me, O LORD, and prove me; try my reins and my heart.
3 For thy lovingkindness *is* before mine eyes: and I have walked in thy truth.
4 I have not sat with vain persons, neither will I go in with dissemblers.
5 I have hated the congregation of evil doers; and will not sit with the wicked.

6 I will wash mine hands in innocency: so will I compass thine altar, O LORD:
7 That I may publish with the voice of thanksgiving, and tell of all thy wondrous works.
8 LORD, I have loved the habitation of thy house, and the place where thine honour dwelleth.
9 Gather not my soul with sinners, nor my life with bloody men:
10 In whose hands *is* mischief, and their right hand is full of bribes.
11 But as for me, I will walk in mine integrity: redeem me, and be merciful unto me.
12 My foot standeth in an even place: in the congregations will I bless the LORD.

PSALM 27
A Prayer of Praise
A Psalm of David.

1 The LORD *is* my light and my salvation; whom shall I fear? the LORD *is* the strength of my life; of whom shall I be afraid?
2 When the wicked, *even* mine enemies and my foes, came upon me to eat up my flesh, they stumbled and fell.
3 Though an host should encamp against me, my heart shall not fear: though war should rise against me, in this *will* I *be* confident.
4 One *thing* have I desired of the LORD, that will I seek after; that I may dwell in the house of the LORD all the days of my life, to behold the beauty of the LORD, and to inquire in his temple.
5 For in the time of trouble he shall hide me in his pavilion: in the secret of his tabernacle shall he hide me; he shall set me up upon a rock.
6 And now shall mine head be lifted up above mine enemies round about me: therefore will I offer in his tabernacle sacrifices of joy; I will sing, yea, I will sing praises unto the LORD.
7 Hear, O LORD, *when* I cry with my voice: have mercy also upon me, and answer me.
8 *When thou saidst*, Seek ye my face; my heart said unto thee, Thy face, LORD, will I seek.
9 Hide not thy face *far* from me; put not thy servant away in anger: thou hast been my help; leave me not, neither forsake me, O God of my salvation.
10 When my father and my mother forsake me, then the LORD will take me up.
11 Teach me thy way, O LORD, and lead me in a plain path, because of mine enemies.
12 Deliver me not over unto the will of mine

Cross references

6 Ps. 103:17; 106:1; 107:1; Isa. 63:15; Jer. 33:11
7 Job 13:26; 20:11; Ps. 51:1; Jer. 3:25
11 Ps. 31:3; 79:9; 109:21; 143:11; Rom. 5:20
12 Ps. 37:23
13 Ps. 37:11, 22, 29; Prov. 19:23
14 Prov. 3:32; John 7:17; 15:15
15 Ps. 141:8
16 Ps. 69:16; 86:16
18 2Sam. 16:12
20 Ps. 25:2
22 Ps. 130:8
1 Ps. 7:8
2 Ps. 7:9; 17:3; 66:10; 139:23; Zech. 13:9
3 2Kgs. 20:3
4 Ps. 1:1; Jer. 15:17
5 Ps. 1:1; 31:6; 139:21, 22
8 Ps. 27:4
9 1Sam. 25:29; Ps. 28:3
10 Ex. 23:8; Deut. 16:19
11 Ps. 26:1
12 Ps. 22:22; 27:11; 40:2; 107:32; 111:1
1 Ex. 15:2; Isa. 12:2; Mic. 7:8
2 Ps. 14:4
3 Ps. 3:6
4 Ps. 65:4; Luke 2:37
5 Ps. 40:2; 83:3
9 Ps. 69:17; 143:7
11 Ps. 5:8; 25:4; 26:12
12 1Sam. 22:9; 2Sam. 16:7, 8; Ps. 35:11, 25; Acts 9:1

enemies: for false witnesses are risen up against me, and such as breathe out cruelty.

13 *I had fainted*, unless I had believed to see the goodness of the LORD in the land of the living.

14 Wait on the LORD: be of good courage, and he shall strengthen thine heart: wait, I say, on the LORD.

PSALM 28
A Prayer for Help
A Psalm of David.

1 Unto thee will I cry, O LORD my rock; be not silent to me: lest, *if* thou be silent to me, I become like them that go down into the pit.

2 Hear the voice of my supplications, when I cry unto thee, when I lift up my hands toward thy holy oracle.

3 Draw me not away with the wicked, and with the workers of iniquity, which speak peace to their neighbours, but mischief *is* in their hearts.

4 Give them according to their deeds, and according to the wickedness of their endeavours: give them after the work of their hands; render to them their desert.

5 Because they regard not the works of the LORD, nor the operation of his hands, he shall destroy them, and not build them up.

6 Blessed *be* the LORD, because he hath heard the voice of my supplications.

7 The LORD *is* my strength and my shield; my heart trusted in him, and I am helped: therefore my heart greatly rejoiceth; and with my song will I praise him.

8 The LORD *is* their strength, and he *is* the saving strength of his anointed.

9 Save thy people, and bless thine inheritance: feed them also, and lift them up for ever.

PSALM 29
"The Voice of the Lord"
A Psalm of David.

1 Give unto the LORD, O ye mighty, give unto the LORD glory and strength.

2 Give unto the LORD the glory due unto his name; worship the LORD in the beauty of holiness.

3 The voice of the LORD *is* upon the waters: the God of glory thundereth: the LORD *is* upon many waters.

4 The voice of the LORD *is* powerful; the voice of the LORD *is* full of majesty.

5 The voice of the LORD breaketh the cedars; yea, the LORD breaketh the cedars of Lebanon.

---

13 Ps. 56:13; 116:9; 142:5; Jer. 11:19; Ezek. 26:20

14 Ps. 31:24; 62:1, 5; 130:5; Isa. 25:9; Hab. 2:3

1 Ps. 83:1; 88:4; 143:7

2 1Kgs. 6:22, 23; 8:28, 29; Ps. 5:7; 138:2

3 Ps. 12:2; 26:9; 55:21; 62:4; Jer. 9:8

4 2Tim. 4:14; Rev. 18:6

5 Job 34:27

7 Ps. 13:5; 18:2; 22:4

8 Ps. 20:6

9 Deut. 9:29; 1Kgs. 8:51, 53; Ps. 78:71

1 1Chr. 16:28, 29; Ps. 96:7, 8, 9

2 2Chr. 20:21

3 Job 37:4, 5

6 Deut. 3:9; Ps. 114:4

8 Num. 13:26

10 Gen. 6:17; Job 38:8, 25; Ps. 10:16

11 Ps. 28:8

1 Ps. 25:2; 28:9; 35:19, 24

2 Ps. 6:2; 103:3

3 Ps. 28:1; 86:13

4 1Chr. 16:4; Ps. 97:12

5 Ps. 63:3; 103:9; 126:5; Isa. 26:20; 54:7, 8; 2Cor. 4:17

6 Job 29:18

7 Ps. 104:29

9 Ps. 6:5; 88:11; 115:17; 118:17; Isa. 38:18

1 Ps. 22:5; 25:2; 71:1; 143:1; Isa. 49:23

---

6 He maketh them also to skip like a calf; Lebanon and Sirion like a young unicorn.

7 The voice of the LORD divideth the flames of fire.

8 The voice of the LORD shaketh the wilderness; the LORD shaketh the wilderness of Kadesh.

9 The voice of the LORD maketh the hinds to calve, and discovereth the forests: and in his temple doth every one speak of *his* glory.

10 The LORD sitteth upon the flood; yea, the LORD sitteth King for ever.

11 The LORD will give strength unto his people; the LORD will bless his people with peace.

PSALM 30
A Prayer of Thanksgiving
A Psalm and Song at the dedication of the house of David.

1 I will extol thee, O LORD; for thou hast lifted me up, and hast not made my foes to rejoice over me.

2 O LORD my God, I cried unto thee, and thou hast healed me.

3 O LORD, thou hast brought up my soul from the grave: thou hast kept me alive, that I should not go down to the pit.

4 Sing unto the LORD, O ye saints of his, and give thanks at the remembrance of his holiness.

5 For his anger *endureth but* a moment; in his favour *is* life: weeping may endure for a night, but joy *cometh* in the morning.

6 And in my prosperity I said, I shall never be moved.

7 LORD, by thy favour thou hast made my mountain to stand strong: thou didst hide thy face, *and* I was troubled.

8 I cried to thee, O LORD; and unto the LORD I made supplication.

9 What profit *is there* in my blood, when I go down to the pit? Shall the dust praise thee? shall it declare thy truth?

10 Hear, O LORD, and have mercy upon me: LORD, be thou my helper.

11 Thou hast turned for me my mourning into dancing: thou hast put off my sackcloth, and girded me with gladness;

12 To the end that *my* glory may sing praise to thee, and not be silent. O LORD my God, I will give thanks unto thee for ever.

PSALM 31
Commitment to God
To the chief Musician, A Psalm of David.

1 In thee, O LORD, do I put my trust; let me never be ashamed: deliver me in thy righteousness.

2 Bow down thine ear to me; deliver me speedily: be thou my strong rock, for an house of defence to save me.

3 For thou *art* my rock and my fortress; therefore for thy name's sake lead me, and guide me.

4 Pull me out of the net that they have laid privily for me: for thou *art* my strength.

5 Into thine hand I commit my spirit: thou hast redeemed me, O LORD God of truth.

6 I have hated them that regard lying vanities: but I trust in the LORD.

7 I will be glad and rejoice in thy mercy: for thou hast considered my trouble; thou hast known my soul in adversities;

8 And hast not shut me up into the hand of the enemy: thou hast set my feet in a large room.

9 Have mercy upon me, O LORD, for I am in trouble: mine eye is consumed with grief, *yea,* my soul and my belly.

10 For my life is spent with grief, and my years with sighing: my strength faileth because of mine iniquity, and my bones are consumed.

11 I was a reproach among all mine enemies, but especially among my neighbours, and a fear to mine acquaintance: they that did see me without fled from me.

12 I am forgotten as a dead man out of mind: I am like a broken vessel.

13 For I have heard the slander of many: fear *was* on every side: while they took counsel together against me, they devised to take away my life.

14 But I trusted in thee, O LORD: I said, Thou *art* my God.

15 My times *are* in thy hand: deliver me from the hand of mine enemies, and from them that persecute me.

16 Make thy face to shine upon thy servant: save me for thy mercies' sake.

17 Let me not be ashamed, O LORD; for I have called upon thee: let the wicked be ashamed, *and* let them be silent in the grave.

18 Let the lying lips be put to silence; which speak grievous things proudly and contemptuously against the righteous.

19 *Oh* how great *is* thy goodness, which thou hast laid up for them that fear thee;

3 Ps. 18:2; 23:3; 25:11
5 Luke 23:46
6 Jon. 2:8
8 1Sam. 17:46; 24:18
9 Ps. 6:7
10 Ps. 32:3; 102:3
11 Job 19:13; Ps. 38:11; 41:8
12 Ps. 88:4, 5
13 Jer. 6:25; 20:3, 10; Lam. 2:22; Matt. 27:1
16 Num. 6:25, 26; Ps. 4:6; 67:1
17 1Sam. 2:9; Ps. 25:2; 115:17
18 1Sam. 2:3; Ps. 12:3; 94:4; Jude 1:15
19 Isa. 64:4; 1Cor. 2:9
20 Job 5:21; Ps. 27:5; 32:7
21 1Sam. 23:7; Ps. 17:7
22 1Sam. 23:26; Lam. 3:54; Jon. 2:4
23 Ps. 34:9
24 Ps. 27:14
1 Ps. 85:2; Rom. 4:6, 7, 8
2 John 1:47; 2Cor. 5:19
5 Prov. 28:13; 1John 1:9
6 Isa. 55:6; John 7:34
7 Ex. 15:1; 2Sam. 22:1; Ps. 9:9; 27:5
9 Job 35:11; Prov. 26:3; James 3:3

which thou hast wrought for them that trust in thee before the sons of men!

20 Thou shalt hide them in the secret of thy presence from the pride of man: thou shalt keep them secretly in a pavilion from the strife of tongues.

21 Blessed *be* the LORD: for he hath shewed me his marvellous kindness in a strong city.

22 For I said in my haste, I am cut off from before thine eyes: nevertheless thou heardest the voice of my supplications when I cried unto thee.

23 O love the LORD, all ye his saints: *for the* LORD preserveth the faithful, and plentifully rewardeth the proud doer.

24 Be of good courage, and he shall strengthen your heart, all ye that hope in the LORD.

PSALM 32
Confession and Forgiveness

A Psalm of David, Maschil.

1 Blessed *is he whose* transgression *is* forgiven, *whose* sin *is* covered.

2 Blessed *is* the man unto whom the LORD imputeth not iniquity, and in whose spirit *there is* no guile.

3 When I kept silence, my bones waxed old through my roaring all the day long.

4 For day and night thy hand was heavy upon me: my moisture is turned into the drought of summer. Selah.

5 I acknowledged my sin unto thee, and mine iniquity have I not hid. I said, I will confess my transgressions unto the LORD; and thou forgavest the iniquity of my sin. Selah.

6 For this shall every one that is godly pray unto thee in a time when thou mayest be found: surely in the floods of great waters they shall not come nigh unto him.

7 Thou *art* my hiding place; thou shalt preserve me from trouble; thou shalt compass me about with songs of deliverance. Selah.

8 I will instruct thee and teach thee in the way which thou shalt go: I will guide thee with mine eye.

9 Be ye not as the horse, *or* as the mule, *which* have no understanding: whose mouth must be held in with bit and bridle, lest they come near unto thee.

31:5 I commit my spirit. These were Jesus' final words from the cross (Luke 24:46). The phrase means to surrender your life and eternal destiny to God. This is the ultimate expression of our acceptance of God's will for our lives. When Jesus died, He died as a human being, enduring every kind of suffering a human being can endure (cf. Heb. 2:18; 4:15). In His dying moments, He could do nothing more than commit His life and destiny to the Father. He died in our place, atoning for our sins and surrendered Himself to the Father.

10 Many sorrows *shall be* to the wicked: but he that trusteth in the LORD, mercy shall compass him about.

11 Be glad in the LORD, and rejoice, ye righteous: and shout for joy, all *ye that are* upright in heart.

PSALM 33
Praising God

1 Rejoice in the LORD, O ye righteous: *for* praise is comely for the upright.

2 Praise the LORD with harp: sing unto him with the psaltery *and* an instrument of ten strings.

3 Sing unto him a new song; play skilfully with a loud noise.

4 For the word of the LORD *is* right; and all his works *are done* in truth.

5 He loveth righteousness and judgment: the earth is full of the goodness of the LORD.

6 By the word of the LORD were the heavens made; and all the host of them by the breath of his mouth.

7 He gathereth the waters of the sea together as an heap: he layeth up the depth in storehouses.

8 Let all the earth fear the LORD: let all the inhabitants of the world stand in awe of him.

9 For he spake, and it was *done*; he commanded, and it stood fast.

10 The LORD bringeth the counsel of the heathen to nought: he maketh the devices of the people of none effect.

11 The counsel of the LORD standeth for ever, the thoughts of his heart to all generations.

12 Blessed *is* the nation whose God *is* the LORD; *and* the people *whom* he hath chosen for his own inheritance.

13 The LORD looketh from heaven; he beholdeth all the sons of men.

14 From the place of his habitation he looketh upon all the inhabitants of the earth.

15 He fashioneth their hearts alike; he considereth all their works.

16 There is no king saved by the multitude of an host: a mighty man is not delivered by much strength.

17 An horse *is* a vain thing for safety: neither shall he deliver *any* by his great strength.

18 Behold, the eye of the LORD *is* upon them that fear him, upon them that hope in his mercy;

19 To deliver their soul from death, and to keep them alive in famine.

20 Our soul waiteth for the LORD: he *is* our help and our shield.

21 For our heart shall rejoice in him, because we have trusted in his holy name.

22 Let thy mercy, O LORD, be upon us, according as we hope in thee.

PSALM 34
Praising God for Deliverance

A Psalm of David, when he changed his behaviour before Abimelech; who drove him away, and he departed.

1 I will bless the LORD at all times: his praise *shall* continually *be* in my mouth.

2 My soul shall make her boast in the LORD: the humble shall hear *thereof*, and be glad.

3 O magnify the LORD with me, and let us exalt his name together.

4 I sought the LORD, and he heard me, and delivered me from all my fears.

5 They looked unto him, and were lightened: and their faces were not ashamed.

6 This poor man cried, and the LORD heard *him*, and saved him out of all his troubles.

7 The angel of the LORD encampeth round about them that fear him, and delivereth them.

8 O taste and see that the LORD *is* good: blessed *is* the man *that* trusteth in him.

9 O fear the LORD, ye his saints: for *there is* no want to them that fear him.

10 The young lions do lack, and suffer hunger: but they that seek the LORD shall not want any good *thing*.

11 Come, ye children, hearken unto me: I will teach you the fear of the LORD.

12 What man *is he that* desireth life, *and* loveth *many* days, that he may see good?

13 Keep thy tongue from evil, and thy lips from speaking guile.

14 Depart from evil, and do good; seek peace, and pursue it.

15 The eyes of the LORD *are* upon the righteous, and his ears *are open* unto their cry.

16 The face of the LORD *is* against them that do evil, to cut off the remembrance of them from the earth.

17 *The righteous* cry, and the LORD heareth, and delivereth them out of all their troubles.

18 The LORD *is* nigh unto them that are of a broken heart; and saveth such as be of a contrite spirit.

19 Many *are* the afflictions of the righteous: but the LORD delivereth him out of them all.

Cross references (center column)

10 Ps. 34:8; Prov. 13:21
1 Ps. 97:12
3 Ps. 96:1; 98:1; Rev. 5:9
5 Ps. 11:7
6 Gen. 1:6, 7; 2:1
7 Gen. 1:9
9 Gen. 1:3
10 Isa. 8:10; 19:3
11 Job 23:13; Prov. 19:21
12 Ex. 19:5; Deut. 7:6; Ps. 65:4; 144:15
13 2Chr. 16:9; Prov. 15:3
17 Ps. 20:7; 147:10; Prov. 21:31
18 Job 36:7; 1Pet. 3:12
19 Job 5:20; Ps. 37:19
20 Ps. 62:1, 5; 115:9, 10, 11; 130:6
21 Ps. 13:5; Zech. 10:7; John 16:22
1 Eph. 5:20; 1Thess. 5:18; 2Thess. 1:3; 2:13
2 Ps. 119:74
6 2Sam. 22:1; Ps. 3:4
7 Gen. 32:1, 2; 2Kgs. 6:17
8 Ps. 2:12; 1Pet. 2:3
11 Ps. 32:8
12 1Pet. 3:10, 11
13 1Pet. 2:22
14 Heb. 12:14
15 Job 36:7
16 Lev. 17:10; Prov. 10:7; Jer. 44:11; Amos 9:4
18 Ps. 51:17; 145:18; Isa. 57:15; 61:1; 66:2
19 Prov. 24:16; 2Tim. 3:11, 12

20 He keepeth all his bones: not one of them is broken.
21 Evil shall slay the wicked: and they that hate the righteous shall be desolate.
22 The LORD redeemeth the soul of his servants: and none of them that trust in him shall be desolate.

PSALM 35
A Prayer for Rescue
A Psalm of David.

1 Plead *my* cause, O LORD, with them that strive with me: fight against them that fight against me.
2 Take hold of shield and buckler, and stand up for mine help.
3 Draw out also the spear, and stop *the way* against them that persecute me: say unto my soul, I *am* thy salvation.
4 Let them be confounded and put to shame that seek after my soul: let them be turned back and brought to confusion that devise my hurt.
5 Let them be as chaff before the wind: and let the angel of the LORD chase *them*.
6 Let their way be dark and slippery: and let the angel of the LORD persecute them.
7 For without cause have they hid for me their net *in* a pit, *which* without cause they have digged for my soul.
8 Let destruction come upon him at unawares; and let his net that he hath hid catch himself: into that very destruction let him fall.
9 And my soul shall be joyful in the LORD: it shall rejoice in his salvation.
10 All my bones shall say, LORD, who *is* like unto thee, which deliverest the poor from him that is too strong for him, yea, the poor and the needy from him that spoileth him?
11 False witnesses did rise up; they laid to my charge *things* that I knew not.
12 They rewarded me evil for good *to* the spoiling of my soul.
13 But as for me, when they were sick, my clothing *was* sackcloth: I humbled my soul with fasting; and my prayer returned into mine own bosom.

14 I behaved myself as though *he had been* my friend *or* brother: I bowed down heavily, as one that mourneth *for his* mother.
15 But in mine adversity they rejoiced, and gathered themselves together: yea, the abjects gathered themselves together against me, and I knew *it* not; they did tear *me*, and ceased not:
16 With hypocritical mockers in feasts, they gnashed upon me with their teeth.
17 Lord, how long wilt thou look on? rescue my soul from their destructions, my darling from the lions.
18 I will give thee thanks in the great congregation: I will praise thee among much people.
19 Let not them that are mine enemies wrongfully rejoice over me: *neither* let them wink with the eye that hate me without a cause.
20 For they speak not peace: but they devise deceitful matters against *them that are* quiet in the land.
21 Yea, they opened their mouth wide against me, *and* said, Aha, aha, our eye hath seen *it*.
22 *This* thou hast seen, O LORD: keep not silence: O Lord, be not far from me.
23 Stir up thyself, and awake to my judgment, *even* unto my cause, my God and my Lord.
24 Judge me, O LORD my God, according to thy righteousness; and let them not rejoice over me.
25 Let them not say in their hearts, Ah, so would we have it: let them not say, We have swallowed him up.
26 Let them be ashamed and brought to confusion together that rejoice at mine hurt: let them be clothed with shame and dishonour that magnify *themselves* against me.
27 Let them shout for joy, and be glad, that favour my righteous cause: yea, let them say continually, Let the LORD be magnified, which hath pleasure in the prosperity of his servant.
28 And my tongue shall speak of thy righteousness *and* of thy praise all the day long.

Cross references
20 John 19:36
21 Ps. 94:23
22 2Sam. 4:9; 1Kgs. 1:29; Ps. 71:23; 103:4; Lam. 3:58
1 Ex. 14:25; Ps. 43:1; 119:154; Lam. 3:58
2 Isa. 42:13
5 Job 21:18; Ps. 1:4; 83:13; Isa. 29:5; Hos. 13:3
6 Ps. 73:18; Jer. 23:12
8 Ps. 7:15, 16; Prov. 5:22; 1Thess. 5:3
12 John 10:32
13 Job 30:25; Matt. 10:13; Luke 10:6
15 Job 16:9; 30:1, 8, 12; Ps. 38:17
16 Job 16:9; Ps. 37:12; Lam. 2:16
17 Ps. 22:20; Hab. 1:13
18 Ps. 22:25, 31; 40:9, 10; 111:1
19 Ps. 119:161; Prov. 6:13; John 15:25
21 Ps. 22:13; 40:15; 54:7; 70:3
22 Ex. 3:7; Ps. 10:1; 28:1; 38:21
24 Ps. 26:1
25 Lam. 2:16
26 Ps. 38:16; 40:14
28 Ps. 50:15; 51:14; 71:24

34:20 not one of them is broken. These words prefigured, a thousand years before the event, that when Jesus would be crucified none of His bones would be broken—in contrast to the treatment of the two thieves (John 19:36). Breaking the legs of crucified victims was a common practice, but Jesus was already dead, making this procedure unnecessary. Instead, the soldiers pierced His side (John 19:34, cf. Rev. 1:7).

35:7 Christ would be hated without a cause (cf. Ps. 69:4; John 15:24–25).

35:11 False witnesses. Such were those who would testify against Christ, but no legitimate accusation would stand against Him (Matt. 26:59–63).

PSALM 36
The Wickedness of Man

To the chief Musician, A Psalm of David the servant of the LORD.

1 The transgression of the wicked saith within my heart, *that there is* no fear of God before his eyes.

2 For he flattereth himself in his own eyes, until his iniquity be found to be hateful.

3 The words of his mouth *are* iniquity and deceit: he hath left off to be wise, *and* to do good.

4 He deviseth mischief upon his bed; he setteth himself in a way *that is* not good; he abhorreth not evil.

The Goodness of God

5 Thy mercy, O LORD, *is* in the heavens; *and* thy faithfulness *reacheth* unto the clouds.

6 Thy righteousness *is* like the great mountains; thy judgments *are* a great deep: O LORD, thou preservest man and beast.

7 How excellent *is* thy lovingkindness, O God! therefore the children of men put their trust under the shadow of thy wings.

8 They shall be abundantly satisfied with the fatness of thy house; and thou shalt make them drink of the river of thy pleasures.

9 For with thee *is* the fountain of life: in thy light shall we see light.

10 O continue thy lovingkindness unto them that know thee; and thy righteousness to the upright in heart.

11 Let not the foot of pride come against me, and let not the hand of the wicked remove me.

12 There are the workers of iniquity fallen: they are cast down, and shall not be able to rise.

PSALM 37
God Takes Care of His Own

A Psalm of David.

1 Fret not thyself because of evildoers, neither be thou envious against the workers of iniquity.

2 For they shall soon be cut down like the grass, and wither as the green herb.

3 Trust in the LORD, and do good; *so* shalt thou dwell in the land, and verily thou shalt be fed.

4 Delight thyself also in the LORD; and he shall give thee the desires of thine heart.

5 Commit thy way unto the LORD; trust also in him; and he shall bring *it* to pass.

6 And he shall bring forth thy righteousness as the light, and thy judgment as the noonday.

7 Rest in the LORD, and wait patiently for him: fret not thyself because of him who prospereth in his way, because of the man who bringeth wicked devices to pass.

8 Cease from anger, and forsake wrath: fret not thyself in any wise to do evil.

9 For evildoers shall be cut off: but those that wait upon the LORD, they shall inherit the earth.

10 For yet a little while, and the wicked *shall* not *be*: yea, thou shalt diligently consider his place, and it *shall* not *be*.

11 But the meek shall inherit the earth; and shall delight themselves in the abundance of peace.

12 The wicked plotteth against the just, and gnasheth upon him with his teeth.

13 The Lord shall laugh at him: for he seeth that his day is coming.

14 The wicked have drawn out the sword, and have bent their bow, to cast down the poor and needy, *and* to slay such as be of upright conversation.

15 Their sword shall enter into their own heart, and their bows shall be broken.

16 A little that a righteous man hath *is* better than the riches of many wicked.

17 For the arms of the wicked shall be broken: but the LORD upholdeth the righteous.

18 The LORD knoweth the days of the upright: and their inheritance shall be for ever.

19 They shall not be ashamed in the evil time: and in the days of famine they shall be satisfied.

20 But the wicked shall perish, and the enemies of the LORD *shall be* as the fat of lambs: they shall consume; into smoke shall they consume away.

21 The wicked borroweth, and payeth not again: but the righteous sheweth mercy, and giveth.

22 For *such as be* blessed of him shall inherit the earth; and *they that be* cursed of him shall be cut off.

23 The steps of a *good* man are ordered by the LORD: and he delighteth in his way.

Cross references

1 Rom. 3:18
4 Mic. 2:1
5 Ps. 57:10; 108:4
6 Job 7:20; 11:8; Rom. 11:33
7 Ruth 2:12
8 Job 20:17; Rev. 22:1
9 Jer. 2:13; John 4:10, 14; 1Pet. 2:9
10 Ps. 7:10; 94:15; 97:11; Jer. 22:16
12 Ps. 1:5

1 Ps. 37:7; 73:3; Prov. 23:17; 24:1, 19
2 Ps. 90:5, 6
4 Isa. 58:14
5 Ps. 55:22; Prov. 16:3; Matt. 6:25; Luke 12:22; 1Pet. 5:7
6 Job 11:17; Mic. 7:9
7 Ps. 37:1, 8; 62:1; Isa. 30:15; Jer. 12:1; Lam. 3:26
8 Ps. 73:3; Eph. 4:26
9 Job 27:13, 14; Ps. 37:11, 22, 29; Isa. 57:13
10 Job 7:10; 20:9; Heb. 10:36, 37
11 Matt. 5:5
16 Prov. 15:16; 16:8
17 Job 38:15; Ezek. 30:21
18 Isa. 60:21
20 Ps. 102:3
21 Ps. 112:5, 9
22 Ps. 37:9; Prov. 3:33
23 1Sam. 2:9; Prov. 16:9

37:11 the meek shall inherit the earth. The reference is a messianic promise to God's people that they will possess the earth during Christ's millennial reign. Jesus quoted this passage in Matthew 5:5. Verses 22, 29, and 34 in this psalm also emphasize this truth.

24 Though he fall, he shall not be utterly cast down: for the Lord upholdeth *him with* his hand.
25 I have been young, and *now* am old; yet have I not seen the righteous forsaken, nor his seed begging bread.
26 *He is* ever merciful, and lendeth; and his seed *is* blessed.
27 Depart from evil, and do good; and dwell for evermore.
28 For the Lord loveth judgment, and forsaketh not his saints; they are preserved for ever: but the seed of the wicked shall be cut off.
29 The righteous shall inherit the land, and dwell therein for ever.
30 The mouth of the righteous speaketh wisdom, and his tongue talketh of judgment.
31 The law of his God *is* in his heart; none of his steps shall slide.
32 The wicked watcheth the righteous, and seeketh to slay him.
33 The Lord will not leave him in his hand, nor condemn him when he is judged.
34 Wait on the Lord, and keep his way, and he shall exalt thee to inherit the land: when the wicked are cut off, thou shalt see *it.*
35 I have seen the wicked in great power, and spreading himself like a green bay tree.
36 Yet he passed away, and, lo, he *was* not: yea, I sought him, but he could not be found.
37 Mark the perfect *man*, and behold the upright: for the end of *that* man *is* peace.
38 But the transgressors shall be destroyed together: the end of the wicked shall be cut off.
39 But the salvation of the righteous *is* of the Lord: *he is* their strength in the time of trouble.
40 And the Lord shall help them, and deliver them: he shall deliver them from the wicked, and save them, because they trust in him.

Psalm 38
A Prayer of Penitence

A Psalm of David, to bring to remembrance.

1 O Lord, rebuke me not in thy wrath: neither chasten me in thy hot displeasure.
2 For thine arrows stick fast in me, and thy hand presseth me sore.
3 *There is* no soundness in my flesh because of thine anger; neither *is there any* rest in my bones because of my sin.
4 For mine iniquities are gone over mine head: as an heavy burden they are too heavy for me.

5 My wounds stink *and* are corrupt because of my foolishness.
6 I am troubled; I am bowed down greatly; I go mourning all the day long.
7 For my loins are filled with a loathsome *disease*: and *there is* no soundness in my flesh.
8 I am feeble and sore broken: I have roared by reason of the disquietness of my heart.
9 Lord, all my desire *is* before thee; and my groaning is not hid from thee.
10 My heart panteth, my strength faileth me: as for the light of mine eyes, it also is gone from me.
11 My lovers and my friends stand aloof from my sore; and my kinsmen stand afar off.
12 They also that seek after my life lay snares *for me*: and they that seek my hurt speak mischievous things, and imagine deceits all the day long.
13 But I, as a deaf *man*, heard not; and *I was* as a dumb man *that* openeth not his mouth.
14 Thus I was as a man that heareth not, and in whose mouth *are* no reproofs.
15 For in thee, O Lord, do I hope: thou wilt hear, O Lord my God.
16 For I said, *Hear me*, lest *otherwise* they should rejoice over me: when my foot slippeth, they magnify *themselves* against me.
17 For I *am* ready to halt, and my sorrow *is* continually before me.
18 For I will declare mine iniquity; I will be sorry for my sin.
19 But mine enemies *are* lively, *and* they are strong: and they that hate me wrongfully are multiplied.
20 They also that render evil for good are mine adversaries; because I follow *the thing that* good *is.*
21 Forsake me not, O Lord: O my God, be not far from me.
22 Make haste to help me, O Lord my salvation.

Psalm 39
Vanity of Life

To the chief Musician, even to Jeduthun, A Psalm of David.

1 I said, I will take heed to my ways, that I sin not with my tongue: I will keep my mouth with a bridle, while the wicked is before me.
2 I was dumb with silence, I held my peace, *even* from good; and my sorrow was stirred.
3 My heart was hot within me, while I was musing the fire burned: *then* spake I with my tongue,

24 Ps. 20; 40:2
25 Job 15:23
28 Prov. 2:22
29 Prov. 2:21
30 Matt. 12:35
31 Deut. 6:6; Isa. 51:7
33 Ps. 109:31
34 Ps. 27:14; 37:9; 52:5, 6; 91:8; Prov. 20:22
35 Job 5:3
37 Isa. 32:17; 57:2
38 Ps. 1:4; 52:5
39 Ps. 3:8; 9:9
40 1Chr. 5:20; Isa. 31:5; Dan. 3:17, 28; 6:23
1 Ps. 6:1
2 Job 6:4; Ps. 32:4
3 Ps. 6:2
4 Ezra 9:6; Ps. 40:12; Matt. 11:28
6 Job 30:28; Ps. 35:14; 42:9; 43:2
7 Job 7:5; Ps. 38:3
8 Job 3:24; Ps. 22:1; Isa. 59:11
10 Ps. 6:7; 88:9
11 Ps. 31:11; Luke 10:31, 32; 23:49
12 2Sam. 16:7, 8
13 2Sam. 16:10
16 Ps. 13:4; 35:26
18 Ps. 32:5
20 1Pet. 3:13; 1John 3:12
22 Ps.62:2, 6; Isa. 12:2
1 1Kgs. 2:4; 2Kgs. 10:31; Ps. 141:3; Col. 4:5; James 3:2
3 Jer. 20:9

4 LORD, make me to know mine end, and the measure of my days, what it *is; that* I may know how frail I *am.*

5 Behold, thou hast made my days *as* an handbreadth; and mine age *is* as nothing before thee: verily every man at his best state *is* altogether vanity. Selah.

6 Surely every man walketh in a vain shew: surely they are disquieted in vain: he heapeth up *riches,* and knoweth not who shall gather them.

7 And now, Lord, what wait I for? my hope *is* in thee.

8 Deliver me from all my transgressions: make me not the reproach of the foolish.

9 I was dumb, I opened not my mouth; because thou didst *it.*

10 Remove thy stroke away from me: I am consumed by the blow of thine hand.

11 When thou with rebukes dost correct man for iniquity, thou makest his beauty to consume away like a moth: surely every man *is* vanity. Selah.

12 Hear my prayer, O LORD, and give ear unto my cry; hold not thy peace at my tears: for I *am* a stranger with thee, *and* a sojourner, as all my fathers *were.*

13 O spare me, that I may recover strength, before I go hence, and be no more.

PSALM 40
A Song of Deliverance
To the chief Musician, A Psalm of David.

1 I waited patiently for the LORD; and he inclined unto me, and heard my cry.

2 He brought me up also out of an horrible pit, out of the miry clay, and set my feet upon a rock, *and* established my goings.

3 And he hath put a new song in my mouth, *even* praise unto our God: many shall see *it,* and fear, and shall trust in the LORD.

4 Blessed *is* that man that maketh the LORD his trust, and respecteth not the proud, nor such as turn aside to lies.

5 Many, O LORD my God, *are* thy wonderful works *which* thou hast done, and thy thoughts *which are* to usward: they cannot be reckoned up in order unto thee: *if* I would declare and speak *of them,* they are more than can be numbered.

6 Sacrifice and offering thou didst not de-

sire; mine ears hast thou opened: burnt offering and sin offering hast thou not required.

7 Then said I, Lo, I come: in the volume of the book *it is* written of me,

8 I delight to do thy will, O my God: yea, thy law *is* within my heart.

9 I have preached righteousness in the great congregation: lo, I have not refrained my lips, O LORD, thou knowest.

10 I have not hid thy righteousness within my heart; I have declared thy faithfulness and thy salvation: I have not concealed thy lovingkindness and thy truth from the great congregation.

11 Withhold not thou thy tender mercies from me, O LORD: let thy lovingkindness and thy truth continually preserve me.

A Prayer for Help

12 For innumerable evils have compassed me about: mine iniquities have taken hold upon me, so that I am not able to look up; they are more than the hairs of mine head: therefore my heart faileth me.

13 Be pleased, O LORD, to deliver me: O LORD, make haste to help me.

14 Let them be ashamed and confounded together that seek after my soul to destroy it; let them be driven backward and put to shame that wish me evil.

15 Let them be desolate for a reward of their shame that say unto me, Aha, aha.

16 Let all those that seek thee rejoice and be glad in thee: let such as love thy salvation say continually, The LORD be magnified.

17 But I *am* poor and needy; *yet* the Lord thinketh upon me: thou *art* my help and my deliverer; make no tarrying, O my God.

PSALM 41
David's Prayer in Sickness
To the chief Musician, A Psalm of David.

1 Blessed *is* he that considereth the poor: the LORD will deliver him in time of trouble.

2 The LORD will preserve him, and keep him alive; *and* he shall be blessed upon the earth: and thou wilt not deliver him unto the will of his enemies.

3 The LORD will strengthen him upon the bed of languishing: thou wilt make all his bed in his sickness.

Center column cross-references:

4 Ps. 90:12; 119:84
5 Ps. 39:11; 62:9; 90:4; 144:4
6 Eccl. 2:18, 21, 26; 5:14; James 4:14
7 Ps. 38:15
8 Ps. 44:13; 79:4
9 2Sam. 16:10
10 Job 9:34; 13:21
11 Job 4:19; 13:28
12 Gen. 47:9; Lev. 25:23
13 Job 10:20, 21; 14:5, 6, 10-12
1 Ps. 27:14; 37:7
2 Ps. 27:5; 37:23; 69:2, 14
3 Ps. 33:3; 52:6
4 Ps. 34:8; 101:3, 7; 125:5; Jer. 17:7
5 Job 5:9; 9:10; Ps. 139:6, 17
6 1Sam. 15:22; Isa. 1:11; 66:3; Matt. 9:13; 12:7; Heb. 10:5
7 Luke 24:44
8 Jer. 31:33; Rom. 7:22
10 Acts 20:20, 27
11 Ps. 43:3; 57:3; 61:7
15 Ps. 70:3; 73:19
16 Ps. 35:27; 70:4
17 Ps. 70:5; 1Pet. 5:7
1 Prov. 14:21
2 Ps. 27:12

40:6–10 Hebrews 10:5–7 quotes these verses as being fulfilled in the birth of Jesus Christ. The words of the psalm anticipate Christ's perfect sacrifice as superior to the sacrifices of the Mosaic Law. The argument in Hebrews 10 is that Jesus' perfect sacrifice accomplished what the Law could not do with its temporary sacrifices.

4 I said, LORD, be merciful unto me: heal my soul; for I have sinned against thee.

5 Mine enemies speak evil of me, When shall he die, and his name perish?

6 And if he come to see *me*, he speaketh vanity: his heart gathereth iniquity to itself; *when* he goeth abroad, he telleth *it*.

7 All that hate me whisper together against me: against me do they devise my hurt.

8 An evil disease, *say they*, cleaveth fast unto him: and *now* that he lieth he shall rise up no more.

9 Yea, mine own familiar friend, in whom I trusted, which did eat of my bread, hath lifted up *his* heel against me.

10 But thou, O LORD, be merciful unto me, and raise me up, that I may requite them.

11 By this I know that thou favourest me, because mine enemy doth not triumph over me.

12 And as for me, thou upholdest me in mine integrity, and settest me before thy face for ever.

13 Blessed *be* the LORD God of Israel from everlasting, and to everlasting. Amen, and Amen.

BOOK II

PSALM 42
Thirsting for God
To the chief Musician, Maschil, for the sons of Korah.

1 As the hart panteth after the water brooks, so panteth my soul after thee, O God.

2 My soul thirsteth for God, for the living God: when shall I come and appear before God?

3 My tears have been my meat day and night, while they continually say unto me, Where *is* thy God?

4 When I remember these *things*, I pour out my soul in me: for I had gone with the multitude, I went with them to the house of God, with the voice of joy and praise, with a multitude that kept holyday.

5 Why art thou cast down, O my soul? and *why* art thou disquieted in me? hope thou in God: for I shall yet praise him *for* the help of his countenance.

6 O my God, my soul is cast down within me: therefore will I remember thee from the land of Jordan, and of the Hermonites, from the hill Mizar.

7 Deep calleth unto deep at the noise of thy waterspouts: all thy waves and thy billows are gone over me.

8 *Yet* the LORD will command his lovingkindness in the daytime, and in the night his song *shall be* with me, *and* my prayer unto the God of my life.

9 I will say unto God my rock, Why hast thou forgotten me? why go I mourning because of the oppression of the enemy?

10 *As* with a sword in my bones, mine enemies reproach me; while they say daily unto me, Where *is* thy God?

11 Why art thou cast down, O my soul? and why art thou disquieted within me? hope thou in God: for I shall yet praise him, *who is* the health of my countenance, and my God.

PSALM 43
A Man in Exile

1 Judge me, O God, and plead my cause against an ungodly nation: O deliver me from the deceitful and unjust man.

2 For thou *art* the God of my strength: why dost thou cast me off? why go I mourning because of the oppression of the enemy?

3 O send out thy light and thy truth: let them lead me; let them bring me unto thy holy hill, and to thy tabernacles.

4 Then will I go unto the altar of God, unto God my exceeding joy: yea, upon the harp will I praise thee, O God my God.

5 Why art thou cast down, O my soul? and why art thou disquieted within me? hope in God: for I shall yet praise him, *who is* the health of my countenance, and my God.

PSALM 44
A Prayer for Protection
To the chief Musician for the sons of Korah, Maschil.

1 We have heard with our ears, O God, our fathers have told us, *what* work thou didst in their days, in the times of old.

2 *How* thou didst drive out the heathen with thy hand, and plantedst them; *how* thou didst afflict the people, and cast them out.

3 For they got not the land in possession by their own sword, neither did their own arm save them: but thy right hand, and thine arm, and the light of thy countenance, because thou hadst a favour unto them.

Cross-references (center column)

4 2Chr. 30:20; Ps. 6:2; 147:3

6 Ps. 12:2; Prov. 26:24-26

9 2Sam. 15:12; Job 19:19; Ps. 55:12, 13, 20; Jer. 20:10; Obad. 1:7; John 13:18

12 Job 36:7; Ps. 34:15

2 Ps. 63:1; 84:2; John 7:37; 1Thess. 1:9

3 Ps. 42:10; 79:10; 80:5; 102:9; 115:2

4 Job 30:16; Ps. 62:8; Isa. 30:29

5 Ps. 42:11; 43:5; Lam. 3:24

7 Ps. 88:7; Jer. 4:20; Ezek. 7:26; Jon. 2:3

8 Lev. 25:21; Deut. 28:8; Job 35:10; Ps. 32:7; 63:6; 133:3; 149:5

9 Ps. 38:6; 43:2

10 Ps. 42:3; Joel 2:17; Mic. 7:10

11 Ps. 42:5; 43:5

1 Ps. 26:1; 35:1, 24

2 Ps. 28:7; 42:9

3 Ps. 3:4; 40:11; 57:3

5 Ps. 42:5, 11

1 Ex. 12:26, 27; Ps. 78:3

2 Ex. 15:17; Deut. 7:1; Ps. 78:55; 80:8

3 Deut. 4:37; 7:7, 8; 8:17; Josh. 24:12

41:9 mine own familiar friend. David's betrayal by his friend Ahithophel prefigures Judas Iscariot's betrayal of Jesus (see Matt. 26:14–16; Mark 14:17–21; Luke 22:21–23; John 13:18–19). The connection of the "familiar friend" and the eating of bread was understood by the disciples as referring to Judas' betrayal of Christ after the Last Supper.

4 Thou art my King, O God: command deliverances for Jacob.

5 Through thee will we push down our enemies: through thy name will we tread them under that rise up against us.

6 For I will not trust in my bow, neither shall my sword save me.

7 But thou hast saved us from our enemies, and hast put them to shame that hated us.

8 In God we boast all the day long, and praise thy name for ever. Selah.

9 But thou hast cast off, and put us to shame; and goest not forth with our armies.

10 Thou makest us to turn back from the enemy: and they which hate us spoil for themselves.

11 Thou hast given us like sheep *appointed* for meat; and hast scattered us among the heathen.

12 Thou sellest thy people for nought, and dost not increase *thy wealth* by their price.

13 Thou makest us a reproach to our neighbours, a scorn and a derision to them that are round about us.

14 Thou makest us a byword among the heathen, a shaking of the head among the people.

15 My confusion *is* continually before me, and the shame of my face hath covered me,

16 For the voice of him that reproacheth and blasphemeth; by reason of the enemy and avenger.

17 All this is come upon us; yet have we not forgotten thee, neither have we dealt falsely in thy covenant.

18 Our heart is not turned back, neither have our steps declined from thy way;

19 Though thou hast sore broken us in the place of dragons, and covered us with the shadow of death.

20 If we have forgotten the name of our God, or stretched out our hands to a strange god;

21 Shall not God search this out? for he knoweth the secrets of the heart.

22 Yea, for thy sake are we killed all the day long; we are counted as sheep for the slaughter.

23 Awake, why sleepest thou, O Lord? arise, cast *us* not off for ever.

24 Wherefore hidest thou thy face, *and* forgettest our affliction and our oppression?

25 For our soul is bowed down to the dust: our belly cleaveth unto the earth.

26 Arise for our help, and redeem us for thy mercies' sake.

PSALM 45
A Royal Wedding Song
To the chief Musician upon Shoshannim, for the sons of Korah, Maschil, A Song of loves.

1 My heart is inditing a good matter: I speak of the things which I have made touching the king: my tongue *is* the pen of a ready writer.

2 Thou art fairer than the children of men: grace is poured into thy lips: therefore God hath blessed thee for ever.

3 Gird thy sword upon *thy* thigh, O *most* mighty, with thy glory and thy majesty.

4 And in thy majesty ride prosperously because of truth and meekness *and* righteousness; and thy right hand shall teach thee terrible things.

5 Thine arrows *are* sharp in the heart of the king's enemies; *whereby* the people fall under thee.

6 Thy throne, O God, *is* for ever and ever: the sceptre of thy kingdom *is* a right sceptre.

7 Thou lovest righteousness, and hatest wickedness: therefore God, thy God, hath anointed thee with the oil of gladness above thy fellows.

8 All thy garments *smell* of myrrh, and aloes, *and* cassia, out of the ivory palaces, whereby they have made thee glad.

9 Kings' daughters *were* among thy honourable women: upon thy right hand did stand the queen in gold of Ophir.

10 Hearken, O daughter, and consider, and incline thine ear; forget also thine own people, and thy father's house;

11 So shall the king greatly desire thy beauty: for he *is* thy Lord; and worship thou him.

12 And the daughter of Tyre *shall be there* with a gift; *even* the rich among the people shall intreat thy favour.

13 The king's daughter *is* all glorious within: her clothing *is* of wrought gold.

14 She shall be brought unto the king in raiment of needlework: the virgins her companions that follow her shall be brought unto thee.

Cross references: 6 Ps. 33:16; Hos. 1:7. 10 Lev. 26:17; Deut. 28:25. 11 Deut. 4:27; 28:64; Rom. 8:36. 12 Isa. 52:3,4; Jer. 15:13. 13 Deut. 28:37; Ps. 79:4; 80:6. 14 2Kgs. 19:21; Jer. 24:9. 16 Ps. 8:2. 17 Dan. 9:13. 18 Job 23:11; Ps. 119:51,157. 19 Ps. 23:4; Isa. 34:13; 35:7. 20 Job 11:13; Ps. 68:31. 21 Job 31:14; Ps. 139:1; Jer. 17:10. 22 Rom. 8:36. 23 Ps. 7:6; 35:23; 44:9; 59:4,5; 78:65. 24 Job 13:24; Ps. 13:1; 88:14. 25 Ps. 119:25. 2 Luke 4:22. 4 Rev. 6:2. 6 Ps. 93:2; Heb. 1:8. 7 1Kgs. 1:39,40. 9 1Kgs. 2:19; Song 6:8. 11 Ps. 95:6; Isa. 54:5. 12 Ps. 22:29; 72:10; Isa. 49:23; 60:3. 13 Rev. 19:7,8. 14 Song 1:4.

45:6–7 This Messianic Psalm pictures the eternal throne of David on which Christ will rule (cf. Luke 1:31). Hebrews 1:8–9 quotes this passage as being fulfilled in the everlasting reign of Christ as King. The psalm also depicts the King on his wedding day pointing prophetically to the Marriage Supper of the Lamb (see Rev. 19:7–9).

15 With gladness and rejoicing shall they be brought: they shall enter into the king's palace.

16 Instead of thy fathers shall be thy children, whom thou mayest make princes in all the earth.

17 I will make thy name to be remembered in all generations: therefore shall the people praise thee for ever and ever.

PSALM 46
"God Is Our Refuge and Strength"
To the chief Musician for the sons of Korah, A Song upon Alamoth.

1 God *is* our refuge and strength, a very present help in trouble.

2 Therefore will not we fear, though the earth be removed, and though the mountains be carried into the midst of the sea;

3 *Though* the waters thereof roar *and* be troubled, *though* the mountains shake with the swelling thereof. Selah.

4 *There is* a river, the streams whereof shall make glad the city of God, the holy *place* of the tabernacles of the most High.

5 God *is* in the midst of her; she shall not be moved: God shall help her, *and that* right early.

6 The heathen raged, the kingdoms were moved: he uttered his voice, the earth melted.

7 The LORD of hosts *is* with us; the God of Jacob *is* our refuge. Selah.

8 Come, behold the works of the LORD, what desolations he hath made in the earth.

9 He maketh wars to cease unto the end of the earth; he breaketh the bow, and cutteth the spear in sunder; he burneth the chariot in the fire.

10 Be still, and know that I *am* God: I will be exalted among the heathen, I will be exalted in the earth.

11 The LORD of hosts *is* with us; the God of Jacob *is* our refuge. Selah.

PSALM 47
God Is King
To the chief Musician, A Psalm for the sons of Korah.

1 O clap your hands, all ye people; shout unto God with the voice of triumph.

16 1Pet. 2:9; Rev. 1:6; 5:10; 20:6
17 Mal. 1:11
1 Ps. 62:7, 8
3 Ps. 93:3, 4; Jer. 5:22; Matt. 7:25
4 Isa. 8:7; 60:14
5 Ex. 14:24, 27; Deut. 23:14; Isa. 12:6; Hos. 11:9; Zeph. 3:15
6 Josh. 2:9, 24; Ps. 2:1
8 Ps. 66:5
9 Isa. 2:4; Ezek. 39:9
10 Isa. 2:11, 17

2 Deut. 7:21
3 Ps. 18:47
4 1Pet. 1:4
5 Ps. 68:24, 25
7 Zech. 14:9; 1Cor. 14:15, 16
8 1Chr. 16:31; Rev. 19:6

1 Isa. 2:2, 3; Mic. 4:1; Zech. 8:3
2 Ps. 50:2; Jer. 3:19; Ezek. 20:6; Dan. 8:9; 11:16
4 2Sam. 10:6, 14, 16, 18, 19
6 Ex. 15:15; Hos. 13:13
7 Jer. 18:17; Ezek. 27:26
8 Isa. 2:2; Mic. 4:1
9 Ps. 26:3; 40:10
10 Deut. 28:58; Josh. 7:9; Ps. 113:3; Mal. 1:11, 14

2 For the LORD most high *is* terrible; *he is* a great King over all the earth.

3 He shall subdue the people under us, and the nations under our feet.

4 He shall choose our inheritance for us, the excellency of Jacob whom he loved. Selah.

5 God is gone up with a shout, the LORD with the sound of a trumpet.

6 Sing praises to God, sing praises: sing praises unto our King, sing praises.

7 For God *is* the King of all the earth: sing ye praises with understanding.

8 God reigneth over the heathen: God sitteth upon the throne of his holiness.

9 The princes of the people are gathered together, *even* the people of the God of Abraham: for the shields of the earth *belong* unto God: he is greatly exalted.

PSALM 48
The Glory of Zion
A Song and Psalm for the sons of Korah.

1 Great *is* the LORD, and greatly to be praised in the city of our God, *in* the mountain of his holiness.

2 Beautiful for situation, the joy of the whole earth, *is* mount Zion, *on* the sides of the north, the city of the great King.

3 God is known in her palaces for a refuge.

4 For, lo, the kings were assembled, they passed by together.

5 They saw *it, and* so they marvelled; they were troubled, *and* hasted away.

6 Fear took hold upon them there, *and* pain, as of a woman in travail.

7 Thou breakest the ships of Tarshish with an east wind.

8 As we have heard, so have we seen in the city of the LORD of hosts, in the city of our God: God will establish it for ever. Selah.

9 We have thought of thy lovingkindness, O God, in the midst of thy temple.

10 According to thy name, O God, so *is* thy praise unto the ends of the earth: thy right hand is full of righteousness.

11 Let mount Zion rejoice, let the daughters of Judah be glad, because of thy judgments.

12 Walk about Zion, and go round about her: tell the towers thereof.

46:1–11 The psalmist foresees the joyful and peaceful prosperity of the Millennial Kingdom of Christ's rule on earth. Only then will Israel experience such glory. Wars will cease, and peace will prevail.

47:8–9 God sitteth upon the throne of his holiness.

The psalmist predicts the glorious victory of the Messiah over the enemies of Israel and foreshadows the millennial reign of Christ when these dreams shall become reality for God's people.

13 Mark ye well her bulwarks, consider her palaces; that ye may tell *it* to the generation following.

14 For this God *is* our God for ever and ever: he will be our guide *even* unto death.

PSALM 49
Trusting Riches Is Foolish
To the chief Musician, A Psalm for the sons of Korah.

1 Hear this, all *ye* people; give ear, all *ye* inhabitants of the world:

2 Both low and high, rich and poor, together.

3 My mouth shall speak of wisdom; and the meditation of my heart *shall be* of understanding.

4 I will incline mine ear to a parable: I will open my dark saying upon the harp.

5 Wherefore should I fear in the days of evil, *when* the iniquity of my heels shall compass me about?

6 They that trust in their wealth, and boast themselves in the multitude of their riches;

7 None *of them* can by any means redeem his brother, nor give to God a ransom for him:

8 (For the redemption of their soul *is* precious, and it ceaseth for ever:)

9 That he should still live for ever, *and* not see corruption.

10 For he seeth *that* wise men die, likewise the fool and the brutish person perish, and leave their wealth to others.

11 Their inward thought *is, that* their houses *shall continue* for ever, *and* their dwelling places to all generations; they call *their* lands after their own names.

12 Nevertheless man *being* in honour abideth not: he is like the beasts *that* perish.

13 This their way *is* their folly: yet their posterity approve their sayings. Selah.

14 Like sheep they are laid in the grave; death shall feed on them; and the upright shall have dominion over them in the morning; and their beauty shall consume in the grave from their dwelling.

15 But God will redeem my soul from the power of the grave: for he shall receive me. Selah.

16 Be not thou afraid when one is made rich, when the glory of his house is increased;

17 For when he dieth he shall carry nothing away: his glory shall not descend after him.

18 Though while he lived he blessed his soul: and *men* will praise thee, when thou doest well to thyself.

19 He shall go to the generation of his fathers; they shall never see light.

20 Man *that is* in honour, and understandeth not, is like the beasts *that* perish.

PSALM 50
God Is the Judge
A Psalm of Asaph.

1 The mighty God, *even* the LORD, hath spoken, and called the earth from the rising of the sun unto the going down thereof.

2 Out of Zion, the perfection of beauty, God hath shined.

3 Our God shall come, and shall not keep silence: a fire shall devour before him, and it shall be very tempestuous round about him.

4 He shall call to the heavens from above, and to the earth, that he may judge his people.

5 Gather my saints together unto me; those that have made a covenant with me by sacrifice.

6 And the heavens shall declare his righteousness: for God *is* judge himself. Selah.

7 Hear, O my people, and I will speak; O Israel, and I will testify against thee: I *am* God, *even* thy God.

8 I will not reprove thee for thy sacrifices or thy burnt offerings, *to have been* continually before me.

9 I will take no bullock out of thy house, *nor* he goats out of thy folds.

10 For every beast of the forest *is* mine, *and* the cattle upon a thousand hills.

11 I know all the fowls of the mountains: and the wild beasts of the field *are* mine.

12 If I were hungry, I would not tell thee: for the world *is* mine, and the fulness thereof.

13 Will I eat the flesh of bulls, or drink the blood of goats?

14 Offer unto God thanksgiving; and pay thy vows unto the most High:

15 And call upon me in the day of trouble: I will deliver thee, and thou shalt glorify me.

16 But unto the wicked God saith, What hast thou to do to declare my statutes, or *that* thou shouldest take my covenant in thy mouth?

17 Seeing thou hatest instruction, and castest my words behind thee.

18 When thou sawest a thief, then thou consentedst with him, and hast been partaker with adulterers.

19 Thou givest thy mouth to evil, and thy tongue frameth deceit.

20 Thou sittest *and* speakest against thy

Center column cross-references:

4 Ps. 78:2; Matt. 13:35
6 Mark 10:24
7 Matt. 16:26
10 Prov. 11:4; Eccl. 2:16, 18, 21
13 Luke 12:20
14 Mal. 4:3; Luke 22:30; Rev. 2:26; 20:4
17 Job 27:19
18 Deut. 29:19; Luke 12:19
20 Ps. 49:12; Eccl. 3:19
1 Neh. 9:32; Isa. 9:6; Jer. 32:18
2 Deut. 33:2; Ps. 48:2; 80:1
3 Lev. 10:2; Num. 16:35; Ps. 97:3; Dan. 7:10
4 Deut. 4:26; 31:28; 32:1; Isa. 1:2; Mic. 6:1, 2
5 Ex. 24:7; Deut. 33:3; Isa. 13:3
6 Ps. 75:7; 97:6
7 Ex. 20:2; Ps. 81:8
8 Isa. 1:11; Jer. 7:22; Hos. 6:6
9 Mic. 6:6; Acts 17:25
12 Ex. 19:5; Deut. 10:14; Job 41:11
14 Deut. 23:21; Job 22:27; Ps. 76:11; Eccl. 5:4, 5; Hos. 14:2; Heb. 13:15
15 Job 22:27; Ps. 22:23; 50:23; 91:15; 107:6, 13, 19, 28; Zech. 13:9
17 Neh. 9:26; Rom. 2:21, 22
18 Rom. 1:32; 1 Tim. 5:22

brother; thou slanderest thine own mother's son.

21 These *things* hast thou done, and I kept silence; thou thoughtest that I was altogether *such a one* as thyself: *but* I will reprove thee, and set *them* in order before thine eyes.

22 Now consider this, ye that forget God, lest I tear *you* in pieces, and *there be* none to deliver.

23 Whoso offereth praise glorifieth me: and to him that ordereth *his* conversation *aright* will I shew the salvation of God.

PSALM 51
A Prayer for Spiritual Cleansing
To the chief Musician, A Psalm of David, when Nathan the prophet came unto him, after he had gone in to Bathsheba.

1 Have mercy upon me, O God, according to thy lovingkindness: according unto the multitude of thy tender mercies blot out my transgressions.

2 Wash me throughly from mine iniquity, and cleanse me from my sin.

3 For I acknowledge my transgressions: and my sin *is* ever before me.

4 Against thee, thee only, have I sinned, and done *this* evil in thy sight: that thou mightest be justified when thou speakest, *and* be clear when thou judgest.

5 Behold, I was shapen in iniquity; and in sin did my mother conceive me.

6 Behold, thou desirest truth in the inward parts: and in the hidden *part* thou shalt make me to know wisdom.

7 Purge me with hyssop, and I shall be clean: wash me, and I shall be whiter than snow.

8 Make me to hear joy and gladness; *that* the bones *which* thou hast broken may rejoice.

9 Hide thy face from my sins, and blot out all mine iniquities.

10 Create in me a clean heart, O God; and renew a right spirit within me.

11 Cast me not away from thy presence; and take not thy holy spirit from me.

12 Restore unto me the joy of thy salvation; and uphold me *with thy* free spirit.

13 *Then* will I teach transgressors thy ways; and sinners shall be converted unto thee.

14 Deliver me from bloodguiltiness, O God, thou God of my salvation: *and* my tongue shall sing aloud of thy righteousness.

15 O Lord, open thou my lips; and my mouth shall shew forth thy praise.

16 For thou desirest not sacrifice; else

21 Isa. 26:10; 57:11; Rom. 2:4
22 Isa. 51:13
23 Ps. 27:6; Rom. 12:1; Gal. 6:16
1 Ps. 51:9; Isa. 43:25; 44:22; Col. 2:14
2 Heb. 9:14; 1John 1:7, 9; Rev. 1:5
4 2Sam. 12:13; Luke 15:21
5 Job 14:4; Ps. 58:3; John 3:6; Rom. 5:12; Eph. 2:3
6 Job 38:36
7 Lev. 14:4, 6, 49; Num. 19:18; Isa. 1:18; Heb. 9:19
8 Matt. 5:4
9 Ps. 51:1; Jer. 16:17
10 Acts 15:9; Eph. 2:10
11 Gen. 4:14; 2Kgs. 13:23; Rom. 8:9; Eph. 4:30
12 2Cor. 3:17
14 Ps. 35:28; 2Sam. 11:17; 12:9
16 Num. 15:27, 30; Ps. 40:6; 50:8; Isa. 1:11; Jer. 7:22; Hos. 6:6
17 Ps. 34:18; Isa. 57:15; 66:2
19 1Sam. 22:9; Ps. 4:5; Ezek. 22:9; Mal. 3:3
1 1Sam. 21:7
5 Prov. 2:22
6 Job 22:19; Mal. 1:5
1 Rom. 3:10
2 2Chr. 15:2; 19:3; Ps. 33:13

would I give *it*: thou delightest not in burnt offering.

17 The sacrifices of God *are* a broken spirit: a broken and a contrite heart, O God, thou wilt not despise.

18 Do good in thy good pleasure unto Zion: build thou the walls of Jerusalem.

19 Then shalt thou be pleased with the sacrifices of righteousness, with burnt offering and whole burnt offering: then shall they offer bullocks upon thine altar.

PSALM 52
God's Judgment and Grace
To the chief Musician, Maschil, A Psalm of David, when Doeg the Edomite came and told Saul, and said unto him, David is come to the house of Ahimelech.

1 Why boastest thou thyself in mischief, O mighty man? the goodness of God *endureth* continually.

2 Thy tongue deviseth mischiefs; like a sharp razor, working deceitfully.

3 Thou lovest evil more than good; *and* lying rather than to speak righteousness. Selah.

4 Thou lovest all devouring words, O *thou* deceitful tongue.

5 God shall likewise destroy thee for ever, he shall take thee away, and pluck thee out of *thy* dwelling place, and root thee out of the land of the living. Selah.

6 The righteous also shall see, and fear, and shall laugh at him:

7 Lo, *this is* the man *that* made not God his strength; but trusted in the abundance of his riches, *and* strengthened himself in his wickedness.

8 But I *am* like a green olive tree in the house of God: I trust in the mercy of God for ever and ever.

9 I will praise thee for ever, because thou hast done *it*: and I will wait on thy name; for *it is* good before thy saints.

PSALM 53
Mankind's Wickedness
To the chief Musician upon Mahalath, Maschil, A Psalm of David.

1 The fool hath said in his heart, *There is* no God. Corrupt are they, and have done abominable iniquity: *there is* none that doeth good.

2 God looked down from heaven upon the children of men, to see if there were *any* that did understand, that did seek God.

3 Every one of them is gone back: they are altogether become filthy; *there is* none that doeth good, no, not one.

4 Have the workers of iniquity no knowledge? who eat up my people *as* they eat bread: they have not called upon God.

5 There were they in great fear, *where* no fear was: for God hath scattered the bones of him that encampeth *against* thee: thou hast put *them* to shame, because God hath despised them.

6 Oh that the salvation of Israel *were come* out of Zion! When God bringeth back the captivity of his people, Jacob shall rejoice, *and* Israel shall be glad.

PSALM 54
A Prayer for Relief

To the chief Musician on Neginoth, Maschil, A Psalm of David, when the Ziphims came and said to Saul, Doth not David hide himself with us?

1 Save me, O God, by thy name, and judge me by thy strength.

2 Hear my prayer, O God; give ear to the words of my mouth.

3 For strangers are risen up against me, and oppressors seek after my soul: they have not set God before them. Selah.

4 Behold, God *is* mine helper: the Lord *is* with them that uphold my soul.

5 He shall reward evil unto mine enemies: cut them off in thy truth.

6 I will freely sacrifice unto thee: I will praise thy name, O Lord; for *it is* good.

7 For he hath delivered me out of all trouble: and mine eye hath seen *his desire* upon mine enemies.

PSALM 55
Betrayed

To the chief Musician on Neginoth, Maschil, A Psalm of David.

1 Give ear to my prayer, O God; and hide not thyself from my supplication.

2 Attend unto me, and hear me: I mourn in my complaint, and make a noise;

3 Because of the voice of the enemy, because of the oppression of the wicked: for they cast iniquity upon me, and in wrath they hate me.

4 My heart is sore pained within me: and the terrors of death are fallen upon me.

5 Fearfulness and trembling are come upon me, and horror hath overwhelmed me.

6 And I said, Oh that I had wings like a dove! *for then* would I fly away, and be at rest.

7 Lo, *then* would I wander far off, *and* remain in the wilderness. Selah.

8 I would hasten my escape from the windy storm *and* tempest.

Cross references (center column):

4 Jer. 4:22
5 Lev. 26:17, 36; Prov. 28:1; Ezek. 6:5
6 Ps. 14:7
3 Ps. 86:14
4 Ps. 118:7
5 Ps. 89:49
6 Ps. 52:9
7 Ps. 59:10; 92:11
2 Isa. 38:14
3 2Sam. 16:7, 8; 19:19
4 Ps. 116:3
9 Jer. 6:7
12 Ps. 35:26; 38:16; 41:9
13 2Sam. 15:12; 16:23; Ps. 41:9; Jer. 9:4
14 Ps. 42:4
15 Num. 16:30
17 Dan. 6:10; Luke 18:1; Acts 3:1; 10:3, 9, 30; 1Thess. 5:17
18 2Chr. 32:7, 8
19 Deut. 33:27
20 Ps. 7:4; Acts 12:1
21 Ps. 28:3; 57:4; 62:4; 64:3; Prov. 5:3, 4; 12:18
22 Ps. 37:5, 24; Matt. 6:25; Luke 12:22; 1Pet. 5:7
23 Job 15:32; Ps. 5:6; Prov. 10:27; Eccl. 7:17

1 Ps. 57:1

2 Ps. 54:5; 57:3

---

9 Destroy, O Lord, *and* divide their tongues: for I have seen violence and strife in the city.

10 Day and night they go about it upon the walls thereof: mischief also and sorrow *are* in the midst of it.

11 Wickedness *is* in the midst thereof: deceit and guile depart not from her streets.

12 For *it was* not an enemy *that* reproached me; then I could have borne *it*: neither *was it* he that hated me *that* did magnify *himself* against me; then I would have hid myself from him:

13 But *it was* thou, a man mine equal, my guide, and mine acquaintance.

14 We took sweet counsel together, *and* walked unto the house of God in company.

15 Let death seize upon them, *and* let them go down quick into hell: for wickedness *is* in their dwellings, *and* among them.

16 As for me, I will call upon God; and the Lord shall save me.

17 Evening, and morning, and at noon, will I pray, and cry aloud: and he shall hear my voice.

18 He hath delivered my soul in peace from the battle *that was* against me: for there were many with me.

19 God shall hear, and afflict them, even he that abideth of old. Selah. Because they have no changes, therefore they fear not God.

20 He hath put forth his hands against such as be at peace with him: he hath broken his covenant.

21 *The words* of his mouth were smoother than butter, but war *was* in his heart: his words were softer than oil, yet *were* they drawn swords.

22 Cast thy burden upon the Lord, and he shall sustain thee: he shall never suffer the righteous to be moved.

23 But thou, O God, shalt bring them down into the pit of destruction: bloody and deceitful men shall not live out half their days; but I will trust in thee.

PSALM 56
A Prayer of Trust

To the chief Musician upon Jonath-elem-rechokim, Michtam of David, when the Philistines took him in Gath.

1 Be merciful unto me, O God: for man would swallow me up; he fighting daily oppresseth me.

2 Mine enemies would daily swallow *me* up: for *they be* many that fight against me, O thou most High.

3 What time I am afraid, I will trust in thee.

4 In God I will praise his word, in God I
have put my trust; I will not fear what flesh
can do unto me.
5 Every day they wrest my words: all their
thoughts *are* against me for evil.
6 They gather themselves together, they
hide themselves, they mark my steps, when
they wait for my soul.
7 Shall they escape by iniquity? in *thine*
anger cast down the people, O God.
8 Thou tellest my wanderings: put thou
my tears into thy bottle: *are they* not in thy
book?
9 When I cry *unto thee,* then shall mine enemies turn back: this I know; for God *is* for
me.
10 In God will I praise *his* word: in the LORD
will I praise *his* word.
11 In God have I put my trust: I will not be
afraid what man can do unto me.
12 Thy vows *are* upon me, O God: I will render praises unto thee.
13 For thou hast delivered my soul from
death: *wilt* not *thou deliver* my feet from falling, that I may walk before God in the light
of the living.

Psalm 57

Pleading for God's Help

To the chief Musician, Al-taschith, Michtam of David,
when he fled from Saul in the cave.

1 Be merciful unto me, O God, be merciful
unto me: for my soul trusteth in thee: yea,
in the shadow of thy wings will I make my
refuge, until *these* calamities be overpast.
2 I will cry unto God most high; unto God
that performeth *all things* for me.
3 He shall send from heaven, and save me
from the reproach of him that would swallow me up. Selah. God shall send forth his
mercy and his truth.
4 My soul *is* among lions: *and* I lie *even*
among them that are set on fire, *even* the
sons of men, whose teeth *are* spears and arrows, and their tongue a sharp sword.
5 Be thou exalted, O God, above the heavens; *let* thy glory *be* above all the earth.
6 They have prepared a net for my steps;
my soul is bowed down: they have digged a
pit before me, into the midst whereof they
are fallen *themselves*. Selah.
7 My heart is fixed, O God, my heart is
fixed: I will sing and give praise.
8 Awake up, my glory; awake, psaltery and
harp: I *myself* will awake early.
9 I will praise thee, O Lord, among the
people: I will sing unto thee among the nations.

4 Ps. 56:10, 11; 118:6; Isa. 31:3; Heb. 13:6
6 Ps. 59:3; 71:10; 140:2
8 Mal. 3:16
9 Rom. 8:31
10 Ps. 56:4
13 Job 33:30; Ps. 116:8
1 Ps. 17:8; 56:1; 63:7; Isa. 26:20
2 Ps. 138:8
3 Ps. 40:11; 43:3; 56:1; 61:7; 144:5, 7
4 Ps. 55:21; 64:3; Prov. 30:14
5 Ps. 57:11; 108:5
6 Ps. 7:15, 16; 9:15
7 Ps. 108:1-5
8 Ps. 16:9; 30:12; 108:1, 2
9 Ps. 108:3
10 Ps. 36:5; 71:19; 103:11; 108:4
11 Ps. 57:5
2 Ps. 94:20; Isa. 10:1
3 Ps. 51:5; Isa. 48:8
4 Ps. 140:3; Eccl. 10:11; Jer. 8:17
6 Job 4:10; Ps. 3:7
7 Josh. 7:5; Ps. 112:10
8 Job 3:16; Eccl. 6:3
9 Prov. 10:25
10 Ps. 52:6; 64:10; 68:23; 107:42
11 Ps. 67:4; 92:15; 96:13; 98:9; Isa. 3:10
1 Ps. 18:48
3 1Sam. 24:11; Ps. 56:6
4 Ps. 35:23; 44:23

10 For thy mercy *is* great unto the heavens,
and thy truth unto the clouds.
11 Be thou exalted, O God, above the heavens: *let* thy glory *be* above all the earth.

Psalm 58

A Prayer for the Punishment of the Wicked

To the chief Musician, Al-taschith, Michtam of David.

1 Do ye indeed speak righteousness, O
congregation? do ye judge uprightly, O ye
sons of men?
2 Yea, in heart ye work wickedness; ye
weigh the violence of your hands in the
earth.
3 The wicked are estranged from the
womb: they go astray as soon as they be
born, speaking lies.
4 Their poison *is* like the poison of a serpent: *they are* like the deaf adder *that* stoppeth her ear;
5 Which will not hearken to the voice of
charmers, charming never so wisely.
6 Break their teeth, O God, in their mouth:
break out the great teeth of the young lions,
O LORD.
7 Let them melt away as waters *which* run
continually: *when* he bendeth *his bow to shoot*
his arrows, let them be as cut in pieces.
8 As a snail *which* melteth, let *every one of*
them pass away: *like* the untimely birth of a
woman, *that* they may not see the sun.
9 Before your pots can feel the thorns, he
shall take them away as with a whirlwind,
both living, and in *his* wrath.
10 The righteous shall rejoice when he
seeth the vengeance: he shall wash his feet
in the blood of the wicked.
11 So that a man shall say, Verily *there is* a
reward for the righteous: verily he is a God
that judgeth in the earth.

Psalm 59

A Prayer for Deliverance

To the chief Musician, Al-taschith, Michtam of David;
when Saul sent, and they watched the house to kill
him.

1 Deliver me from mine enemies, O my
God: defend me from them that rise up
against me.
2 Deliver me from the workers of iniquity,
and save me from bloody men.
3 For, lo, they lie in wait for my soul: the
mighty are gathered against me; not *for* my
transgression, nor *for* my sin, O LORD.
4 They run and prepare themselves without *my* fault: awake to help me, and behold.
5 Thou therefore, O LORD God of hosts, the

God of Israel, awake to visit all the heathen: be not merciful to any wicked transgressors. Selah.

6 They return at evening: they make a noise like a dog, and go round about the city.

7 Behold, they belch out with their mouth: swords *are* in their lips: for who, *say they,* doth hear?

8 But thou, O LORD, shalt laugh at them; thou shalt have all the heathen in derision.

9 *Because of* his strength will I wait upon thee: for God *is* my defence.

10 The God of my mercy shall prevent me: God shall let me see *my desire* upon mine enemies.

11 Slay them not, lest my people forget: scatter them by thy power; and bring them down, O Lord our shield.

12 *For* the sin of their mouth *and* the words of their lips let them even be taken in their pride: and for cursing and lying *which* they speak.

13 Consume *them* in wrath, consume *them,* that they *may* not *be:* and let them know that God ruleth in Jacob unto the ends of the earth. Selah.

14 And at evening let them return; *and* let them make a noise like a dog, and go round about the city.

15 Let them wander up and down for meat, and grudge if they be not satisfied.

16 But I will sing of thy power; yea, I will sing aloud of thy mercy in the morning: for thou hast been my defence and refuge in the day of my trouble.

17 Unto thee, O my strength, will I sing: for God *is* my defence, *and* the God of my mercy.

PSALM 60
A Prayer after Defeat

To the chief Musician upon Shushan-eduth, Michtam of David, to teach; when he strove with Aram-naharaim and with Aram-zobah, when Joab returned, and smote of Edom in the valley of salt twelve thousand.

1 O God, thou hast cast us off, thou hast scattered us, thou hast been displeased; O turn thyself to us again.

2 Thou hast made the earth to tremble; thou hast broken it: heal the breaches thereof; for it shaketh.

3 Thou hast shewed thy people hard things: thou hast made us to drink the wine of astonishment.

4 Thou hast given a banner to them that fear thee, that it may be displayed because of the truth. Selah.

5 That thy beloved may be delivered; save *with* thy right hand, and hear me.

6 God hath spoken in his holiness; I will rejoice, I will divide Shechem, and mete out the valley of Succoth.

7 Gilead *is* mine, and Manasseh *is* mine; Ephraim also *is* the strength of mine head; Judah *is* my lawgiver;

8 Moab *is* my washpot; over Edom will I cast out my shoe: Philistia, triumph thou because of me.

9 Who will bring me *into* the strong city? who will lead me into Edom?

10 *Wilt* not thou, O God, *which* hadst cast us off? and *thou,* O God, *which* didst not go out with our armies?

11 Give us help from trouble: for vain *is* the help of man.

12 Through God we shall do valiantly: for he *it is that* shall tread down our enemies.

PSALM 61
Confidence in God's Protection

To the chief Musician upon Neginah, A Psalm of David.

1 Hear my cry, O God; attend unto my prayer.

2 From the end of the earth will I cry unto thee, when my heart is overwhelmed: lead me to the rock *that* is higher than I.

3 For thou hast been a shelter for me, *and* a strong tower from the enemy.

4 I will abide in thy tabernacle for ever: I will trust in the covert of thy wings. Selah.

5 For thou, O God, hast heard my vows: thou hast given *me* the heritage of those that fear thy name.

6 Thou wilt prolong the king's life: *and* his years as many generations.

7 He shall abide before God for ever: O prepare mercy and truth, *which* may preserve him.

8 So will I sing praise unto thy name for ever, that I may daily perform my vows.

PSALM 62
Depending on God

To the chief Musician, to Jeduthun, A Psalm of David.

1 Truly my soul waiteth upon God: from him *cometh* my salvation.

2 He only *is* my rock and my salvation; *he is* my defence; I shall not be greatly moved.

3 How long will ye imagine mischief against a man? ye shall be slain all of you: as a bowing wall *shall ye be, and as* a tottering fence.

4 They only consult to cast *him* down from

Center reference column

6 Ps. 59:14

7 Ps. 10:11, 13; 57:4; 64:5; 73:11; 94:7; Prov. 12:18

8 1Sam. 19:16; Ps. 2:4

9 Ps. 59:17; 62:2

10 Ps. 21:3; 54:7; 56:2; 92:11; 112:8

11 Gen. 4:12, 15

12 Prov. 12:13; 18:7

13 Ps. 7:9; 83:18

14 Ps. 59:6

15 Job 15:23; Ps. 109:10

17 Ps. 18:1; 59:9, 10

1 Ps. 44:9

2 2Chr. 7:14

3 Ps. 71:20; Isa. 51:17, 22; Jer. 25:15

4 Ps. 20:5

5 Ps. 108:6

6 Gen. 12:6; Josh. 1:6; 13:27; Ps. 89:35

7 Gen. 49:10; Deut. 33:17

8 2Sam. 8:1, 2, 14; Ps. 108:9

9 2Sam. 11:1; 12:26

10 Josh. 7:12; Ps. 44:9; 61:1; 108:11

11 Ps. 118:8; 146:3

12 Num. 24:18; 1Chr. 19:13; Isa. 63:3

3 Prov. 18:10

4 Ps. 17:8; 27:4; 57:1; 91:4

6 Ps. 21:4

7 Ps. 40:11; Prov. 20:28

1 Ps. 33:20; 65:1

2 Ps. 37:24

his excellency: they delight in lies: they bless with their mouth, but they curse inwardly. Selah.

5 My soul, wait thou only upon God; for my expectation *is* from him.

6 He only *is* my rock and my salvation: *he is* my defence; I shall not be moved.

7 In God *is* my salvation and my glory: the rock of my strength, *and* my refuge, *is* in God.

8 Trust in him at all times; *ye* people, pour out your heart before him: God *is* a refuge for us. Selah.

9 Surely men of low degree *are* vanity, *and* men of high degree *are* a lie: to be laid in the balance, they *are* altogether *lighter* than vanity.

10 Trust not in oppression, and become not vain in robbery: if riches increase, set not your heart *upon them*.

11 God hath spoken once; twice have I heard this; that power *belongeth* unto God.

12 Also unto thee, O Lord, *belongeth* mercy: for thou renderest to every man according to his work.

PSALM 63
Yearning for God
A Psalm of David, when he was in the wilderness of Judah.

1 O God, thou *art* my God; early will I seek thee: my soul thirsteth for thee, my flesh longeth for thee in a dry and thirsty land, where no water is;

2 To see thy power and thy glory, so *as* I have seen thee in the sanctuary.

3 Because thy lovingkindness *is* better than life, my lips shall praise thee.

4 Thus will I bless thee while I live: I will lift up my hands in thy name.

5 My soul shall be satisfied as *with* marrow and fatness; and my mouth shall praise *thee* with joyful lips:

6 When I remember thee upon my bed, *and* meditate on thee in the *night* watches.

7 Because thou hast been my help, therefore in the shadow of thy wings will I rejoice.

8 My soul followeth hard after thee: thy right hand upholdeth me.

9 But those *that* seek my soul, to destroy *it*, shall go into the lower parts of the earth.

10 They shall fall by the sword: they shall be a portion for foxes.

11 But the king shall rejoice in God; every one that sweareth by him shall glory: but the mouth of them that speak lies shall be stopped.

---

5 Ps. 62:1, 2

7 Jer. 3:23

8 1Sam. 1:15; Ps. 18:2; 42:4; Lam. 2:19

9 Ps. 39:5, 11; Isa. 40:15, 17; Rom. 3:4

10 Job 31:25; Ps. 52:7; Luke 12:15; 1Tim. 6:17

11 Job 33:14; Rev. 19:1

12 Ezek. 7:27; Matt. 16:27; 1Cor. 3:8; 2Cor. 5:10; Eph. 6:8; 1Pet. 1:17; Rev. 22:12

2 1Sam. 4:21; 1Chr. 16:11; Ps. 27:4; 78:61

3 Ps. 30:5

4 Ps. 104:33; 146:2

5 Ps. 36:8

6 Ps. 42:8; 119:55; 149:5

7 Ps. 61:4

10 Ezek. 35:5

11 Deut. 6:13; Isa. 45:23; 65:16; Zeph. 1:5

3 Ps. 11:2; 57:4; 58:7; Jer. 9:3

5 Ps. 10:11; 59:7; Prov. 1:11

7 Ps. 7:12, 13

8 Ps. 31:11; 52:6; Prov. 12:13; 18:7

9 Ps. 40:3; Jer. 50:28; 51:10

2 Isa. 66:23

3 Isa. 6:7; Heb. 9:14; 1John 1:7, 9

5 Ps. 22:27

6 Ps. 93:1

7 Ps. 76:10; 89:9; 107:29; Isa. 17:12, 13; Matt. 8:26

PSALM 64
A Prayer for Deliverance
To the chief Musician, A Psalm of David.

1 Hear my voice, O God, in my prayer: preserve my life from fear of the enemy.

2 Hide me from the secret counsel of the wicked; from the insurrection of the workers of iniquity:

3 Who whet their tongue like a sword, *and* bend *their bows to shoot* their arrows, *even* bitter words:

4 That they may shoot in secret at the perfect: suddenly do they shoot at him, and fear not.

5 They encourage themselves *in* an evil matter: they commune of laying snares privily; they say, Who shall see them?

6 They search out iniquities; they accomplish a diligent search: both the inward *thought* of every one *of them*, and the heart, *is* deep.

7 But God shall shoot at them *with* an arrow; suddenly shall they be wounded.

8 So they shall make their own tongue to fall upon themselves: all that see them shall flee away.

9 And all men shall fear, and shall declare the work of God; for they shall wisely consider of his doing.

10 The righteous shall be glad in the LORD, and shall trust in him; and all the upright in heart shall glory.

PSALM 65
Thanking God for Nature
To the chief Musician, A Psalm and Song of David.

1 Praise waiteth for thee, O God, in Sion: and unto thee shall the vow be performed.

2 O thou that hearest prayer, unto thee shall all flesh come.

3 Iniquities prevail against me: *as for* our transgressions, thou shalt purge them away.

4 Blessed *is the man whom* thou choosest, and causest to approach *unto thee, that* he may dwell in thy courts: we shall be satisfied with the goodness of thy house, *even* of thy holy temple.

5 *By* terrible things in righteousness wilt thou answer us, O God of our salvation; *who art* the confidence of all the ends of the earth, and of them that are afar off *upon* the sea:

6 Which by his strength setteth fast the mountains; *being* girded with power:

7 Which stilleth the noise of the seas, the noise of their waves, and the tumult of the people.

8 They also that dwell in the uttermost parts are afraid at thy tokens: thou makest the outgoings of the morning and evening to rejoice.

9 Thou visitest the earth, and waterest it: thou greatly enrichest it with the river of God, *which* is full of water: thou preparest them corn, when thou hast so provided for it.

10 Thou waterest the ridges thereof abundantly: thou settlest the furrows thereof: thou makest it soft with showers: thou blessest the springing thereof.

11 Thou crownest the year with thy goodness; and thy paths drop fatness.

12 They drop *upon* the pastures of the wilderness: and the little hills rejoice on every side.

13 The pastures are clothed with flocks; the valleys also are covered over with corn; they shout for joy, they also sing.

PSALM 66
Praise and Thanksgiving
To the chief Musician, A Song or Psalm.

1 Make a joyful noise unto God, all ye lands:

2 Sing forth the honour of his name: make his praise glorious.

3 Say unto God, How terrible *art thou in* thy works! through the greatness of thy power shall thine enemies submit themselves unto thee.

4 All the earth shall worship thee, and shall sing unto thee; they shall sing *to* thy name. Selah.

5 Come and see the works of God: *he is* terrible *in his* doing toward the children of men.

6 He turned the sea into dry *land*: they went through the flood on foot: there did we rejoice in him.

7 He ruleth by his power for ever; his eyes behold the nations: let not the rebellious exalt themselves. Selah.

8 O bless our God, ye people, and make the voice of his praise to be heard:

9 Which holdeth our soul in life, and suffereth not our feet to be moved.

10 For thou, O God, hast proved us: thou hast tried us, as silver is tried.

11 Thou broughtest us into the net; thou laidst affliction upon our loins.

12 Thou hast caused men to ride over our heads; we went through fire and through water: but thou broughtest us out into a wealthy *place*.

13 I will go into thy house with burnt offerings: I will pay thee my vows,

14 Which my lips have uttered, and my mouth hath spoken, when I was in trouble.

15 I will offer unto thee burnt sacrifices of fatlings, with the incense of rams; I will offer bullocks with goats. Selah.

16 Come *and* hear, all ye that fear God, and I will declare what he hath done for my soul.

17 I cried unto him with my mouth, and he was extolled with my tongue.

18 If I regard iniquity in my heart, the Lord will not hear *me*:

19 *But* verily God hath heard *me*; he hath attended to the voice of my prayer.

20 Blessed *be* God, which hath not turned away my prayer, nor his mercy from me.

PSALM 67
Let All Nations Praise God!
To the chief Musician on Neginoth, A Psalm or Song.

1 God be merciful unto us, and bless us; *and* cause his face to shine upon us; Selah.

2 That thy way may be known upon earth, thy saving health among all nations.

3 Let the people praise thee, O God; let all the people praise thee.

4 O let the nations be glad and sing for joy: for thou shalt judge the people righteously, and govern the nations upon earth. Selah.

5 Let the people praise thee, O God; let all the people praise thee.

6 *Then* shall the earth yield her increase; *and* God, *even* our own God, shall bless us.

7 God shall bless us; and all the ends of the earth shall fear him.

PSALM 68
The True God
To the chief Musician, A Psalm or Song of David.

1 Let God arise, let his enemies be scattered: let them also that hate him flee before him.

2 As smoke is driven away, *so* drive *them* away: as wax melteth before the fire, *so* let the wicked perish at the presence of God.

3 But let the righteous be glad; let them

Cross references

9 Deut. 11:12; Ps. 46:4; 68:9, 10; 104:13; Jer. 5:24
13 Isa. 55:12
1 Ps. 100:1
3 Ps. 18:44; 65:5; 81:15
4 Ps. 22:27; 67:3; 96:1, 2; 117:1
5 Ps. 46:8
6 Ex. 14:21; Josh. 3:14, 16
7 Ps. 11:4
9 Ps. 121:3
10 Ps. 17:3; Isa. 48:10; Zech. 13:9; 1Pet. 1:6, 7
11 Lam. 1:13
12 Isa. 43:2; 51:23
13 Ps. 100:4; 116:14, 17, 18, 19; Eccl. 5:4
16 Ps. 34:11
18 Job 27:9; Prov. 15:29; 28:9; Isa. 1:15; John 9:31; James 4:3
19 Ps. 116:1, 2
1 Num. 6:25; Ps. 4:6; 31:16; 80:3, 7, 19; 119:135
2 Luke 2:30, 31; Acts 18:25; Titus 2:11
3 Ps. 66:4
4 Ps. 96:10, 13; 98:9
6 Lev. 26:4; Ps. 85:12; Ezek. 34:27
7 Ps. 22:27
1 Num. 10:35; Isa. 33:3
2 Ps. 97:5; Isa. 9:18; Hos. 13:3

66:4 The psalmist foresees a day when all the earth will worship the Lord and sing unto Him. This will be fulfilled only during the Millennial Kingdom, when Christ rules on earth.

67:4 This psalm also predicts a time when God will judge people righteously and "govern the nations" of the earth through the millennial reign of Christ.

rejoice before God: yea, let them exceedingly rejoice.

4 Sing unto God, sing praises to his name: extol him that rideth upon the heavens by his name JAH, and rejoice before him.

5 A father of the fatherless, and a judge of the widows, *is* God in his holy habitation.

6 God setteth the solitary in families: he bringeth out those which are bound with chains: but the rebellious dwell in a dry *land*.

7 O God, when thou wentest forth before thy people, when thou didst march through the wilderness; Selah:

8 The earth shook, the heavens also dropped at the presence of God: *even* Sinai itself *was moved* at the presence of God, the God of Israel.

9 Thou, O God, didst send a plentiful rain, whereby thou didst confirm thine inheritance, when it was weary.

10 Thy congregation hath dwelt therein: thou, O God, hast prepared of thy goodness for the poor.

11 The Lord gave the word: great *was* the company of those that published *it*.

12 Kings of armies did flee apace: and she that tarried at home divided the spoil.

13 Though ye have lien among the pots, *yet shall ye be as* the wings of a dove covered with silver, and her feathers with yellow gold.

14 When the Almighty scattered kings in it, it was *white* as snow in Salmon.

15 The hill of God *is as* the hill of Bashan; an high hill *as* the hill of Bashan.

16 Why leap ye, ye high hills? *this is* the hill *which* God desireth to dwell in; yea, the Lord will dwell *in it* for ever.

17 The chariots of God *are* twenty thousand, *even* thousands of angels: the Lord *is* among them, *as in* Sinai, in the holy *place*.

18 Thou hast ascended on high, thou hast led captivity captive: thou hast received gifts for men; yea, *for* the rebellious also, that the Lord God might dwell *among them*.

19 Blessed *be* the Lord, *who* daily loadeth us *with benefits, even* the God of our salvation. Selah.

20 *He that is* our God *is* the God of salvation; and unto God the Lord *belong* the issues from death.

21 But God shall wound the head of his enemies, *and* the hairy scalp of such an one as goeth on still in his trespasses.

22 The Lord said, I will bring again from Bashan, I will bring *my people* again from the depths of the sea:

23 That thy foot may be dipped in the blood of *thine* enemies, *and* the tongue of thy dogs in the same.

24 They have seen thy goings, O God; *even* the goings of my God, my King, in the sanctuary.

25 The singers went before, the players on instruments *followed* after; among *them were* the damsels playing with timbrels.

26 Bless ye God in the congregations, *even* the Lord, from the fountain of Israel.

27 There *is* little Benjamin *with* their ruler, the princes of Judah *and* their council, the princes of Zebulun, *and* the princes of Naphtali.

28 Thy God hath commanded thy strength: strengthen, O God, that which thou hast wrought for us.

29 Because of thy temple at Jerusalem shall kings bring presents unto thee.

30 Rebuke the company of spearmen, the multitude of the bulls, with the calves of the people, *till every one* submit himself with pieces of silver: scatter thou the people *that* delight in war.

31 Princes shall come out of Egypt; Ethiopia shall soon stretch out her hands unto God.

32 Sing unto God, ye kingdoms of the earth; O sing praises unto the Lord; Selah:

33 To him that rideth upon the heavens of heavens, *which were* of old; lo, he doth send out his voice, *and that* a mighty voice.

34 Ascribe ye strength unto God: his excellency *is* over Israel, and his strength *is* in the clouds.

35 O God, *thou art* terrible out of thy holy places: the God of Israel *is* he that giveth strength and power unto *his* people. Blessed *be* God.

Psalm 69
A Cry of Distress
To the chief Musician upon Shoshannim,
A Psalm of David.

1 Save me, O God; for the waters are come in unto *my* soul.

2 I sink in deep mire, where *there is* no standing: I am come into deep waters, where the floods overflow me.

3 I am weary of my crying: my throat is dried: mine eyes fail while I wait for my God.

Cross references
4 Ex. 6:3; Deut. 33:26; Ps. 66:4
5 Ps. 10:14, 18; 146:9
7 Ex. 13:21
8 Ex. 19:16, 18; Isa. 64:1, 3
9 Deut. 11:11, 12; Ezek. 34:26
10 Deut. 26:5, 9
12 Num. 31:8, 9, 54; Josh. 10:16; 12:8
14 Num. 21:3; Josh. 10:10; 12:1
16 Deut. 12:5, 11; 1Kgs. 9:3
17 2Kgs. 6:16, 17; Heb. 12:22; Rev. 9:16
18 Acts 1:9; 2:4, 33; Eph. 4:8; 1Tim. 1:13
20 Rev. 1:18; 20:1
21 Hab. 3:13
22 Ex. 14:22; Num. 21:33
23 1Kgs. 21:19
25 1Chr. 13:8; 15:16
27 1Sam. 9:21
29 1Kgs. 10:10, 24, 25; 2Chr. 32:23
30 2Sam. 8:2, 6
31 Isa. 19:19, 21; 45:14; Zeph. 3:10
1 Ps. 69:2, 14, 15; Jon. 2:5
2 Ps. 40:2
3 Ps. 6:6; 119:82, 123; Isa. 38:14

68:18 Ephesians 4:8 quotes this verse as being fulfilled when Jesus ascended victoriously into heaven, leading the souls of the Old Testament saints into glory.

4 They that hate me without a cause are more than the hairs of mine head: they that would destroy me, *being* mine enemies wrongfully, are mighty: then I restored *that* which I took not away.

5 O God, thou knowest my foolishness; and my sins are not hid from thee.

6 Let not them that wait on thee, O Lord GOD of hosts, be ashamed for my sake: let not those that seek thee be confounded for my sake, O God of Israel.

7 Because for thy sake I have borne reproach; shame hath covered my face.

8 I am become a stranger unto my brethren, and an alien unto my mother's children.

9 For the zeal of thine house hath eaten me up; and the reproaches of them that reproached thee are fallen upon me.

10 When I wept, *and chastened* my soul with fasting, that was to my reproach.

11 I made sackcloth also my garment; and I became a proverb to them.

12 They that sit in the gate speak against me; and I *was* the song of the drunkards.

13 But as for me, my prayer *is* unto thee, O LORD, *in* an acceptable time: O God, in the multitude of thy mercy hear me, in the truth of thy salvation.

14 Deliver me out of the mire, and let me not sink: let me be delivered from them that hate me, and out of the deep waters.

15 Let not the waterflood overflow me, neither let the deep swallow me up, and let not the pit shut her mouth upon me.

16 Hear me, O LORD; for thy lovingkindness *is* good: turn unto me according to the multitude of thy tender mercies.

17 And hide not thy face from thy servant; for I am in trouble: hear me speedily.

18 Draw nigh unto my soul, *and* redeem it: deliver me because of mine enemies.

19 Thou hast known my reproach, and my shame, and my dishonour: mine adversaries *are* all before thee.

20 Reproach hath broken my heart; and I am full of heaviness: and I looked *for some* to take pity, but *there was* none; and for comforters, but I found none.

21 They gave me also gall for my meat; and in my thirst they gave me vinegar to drink.

Cross references:
4 John 15:25
8 Isa. 53:3; John 1:11; 7:5
9 John 2:17
11 Jer. 24:9
12 Job 30:9; Ps. 35:15, 16
13 Isa. 49:8; 55:6; 2Cor. 6:2
15 Num. 16:33
16 Ps. 25:16; 63:3; 86:16
17 Ps. 27:9; 102:2
19 Ps. 22:6, 7; Isa. 53:3; Heb. 12:2
20 Job 16:2; Ps. 142:4; Isa. 63:5
21 Matt. 27:34, 48; Mark 15:23; John 19:29
22 Rom. 11:9, 10
23 Isa. 6:9, 10; John 12:39, 40; Rom. 11:10; 2Cor. 3:14
24 1Thess. 2:16
25 Matt. 23:38; Acts 1:20
26 2Chr. 28:9; Isa. 53:4; Zech. 1:15
27 Isa. 26:10; Rom. 1:28; 9:31
28 Ezek. 13:9; Luke 10:20; Rev. 3:5; 13:8
31 Ps. 50:13, 14, 23
32 Ps. 22:26; 34:2
33 Eph. 3:1
35 Isa. 44:26
36 Ps. 102:28

22 Let their table become a snare before them: and *that which should have been* for *their* welfare, *let it become* a trap.

23 Let their eyes be darkened, that they see not; and make their loins continually to shake.

24 Pour out thine indignation upon them, and let thy wrathful anger take hold of them.

25 Let their habitation be desolate; *and let* none dwell in their tents.

26 For they persecute *him* whom thou hast smitten; and they talk to the grief of those whom thou hast wounded.

27 Add iniquity unto their iniquity: and let them not come into thy righteousness.

28 Let them be blotted out of the book of the living, and not be written with the righteous.

29 But I *am* poor and sorrowful: let thy salvation, O God, set me up on high.

30 I will praise the name of God with a song, and will magnify him with thanksgiving.

31 *This* also shall please the LORD better than an ox *or* bullock that hath horns and hoofs.

32 The humble shall see *this, and* be glad: and your heart shall live that seek God.

33 For the LORD heareth the poor, and despiseth not his prisoners.

34 Let the heaven and earth praise him, the seas, and every thing that moveth therein.

35 For God will save Zion, and will build the cities of Judah: that they may dwell there, and have it in possession.

36 The seed also of his servants shall inherit it: and they that love his name shall dwell therein.

PSALM 70
A Prayer for Deliverance

To the chief Musician, A Psalm of David, to bring to remembrance.

1 *Make haste,* O God, to deliver me; make haste to help me, O LORD.

2 Let them be ashamed and confounded that seek after my soul: let them be turned backward, and put to confusion, that desire my hurt.

3 Let them be turned back for a reward of their shame that say, Aha, aha.

69:9 the zeal of thine house. This verse was quoted in John 2:17 to explain Jesus' passion for God's Temple.

69:21 The reference to "gall" (v. 21) is typical of the vinegar offered to Christ on the cross (cf. Matt. 27:48; Mark 15:36; Luke 23:36).

69:25 David's cries for help in this psalm prefigure the sufferings of Christ. Peter applied the reference to being "desolate" to refer to Judas' removal from his place among the twelve disciples (Acts 1:20).

4 Let all those that seek thee rejoice and be glad in thee: and let such as love thy salvation say continually, Let God be magnified.

5 But I *am* poor and needy: make haste unto me, O God: thou *art* my help and my deliverer; O LORD, make no tarrying.

PSALM 71
The Prayer of an Aged Man

1 In thee, O LORD, do I put my trust: let me never be put to confusion.

2 Deliver me in thy righteousness, and cause me to escape: incline thine ear unto me, and save me.

3 Be thou my strong habitation, whereunto I may continually resort: thou hast given commandment to save me; for thou *art* my rock and my fortress.

4 Deliver me, O my God, out of the hand of the wicked, out of the hand of the unrighteous and cruel man.

5 For thou *art* my hope, O Lord GOD: *thou art* my trust from my youth.

6 By thee have I been holden up from the womb: thou art he that took me out of my mother's bowels: my praise *shall be* continually of thee.

7 I am as a wonder unto many; but thou *art* my strong refuge.

8 Let my mouth be filled *with* thy praise *and with* thy honour all the day.

9 Cast me not off in the time of old age; forsake me not when my strength faileth.

10 For mine enemies speak against me; and they that lay wait for my soul take counsel together,

11 Saying, God hath forsaken him: persecute and take him; for *there is* none to deliver *him.*

12 O God, be not far from me: O my God, make haste for my help.

13 Let them be confounded *and* consumed that are adversaries to my soul; let them be covered *with* reproach and dishonour that seek my hurt.

14 But I will hope continually, and will yet praise thee more and more.

15 My mouth shall shew forth thy righteousness *and* thy salvation all the day; for I know not the numbers *thereof.*

16 I will go in the strength of the Lord GOD:

I will make mention of thy righteousness, *even* of thine only.

17 O God, thou hast taught me from my youth: and hitherto have I declared thy wondrous works.

18 Now also when I am old and greyheaded, O God, forsake me not; until I have shewed thy strength unto *this* generation, *and* thy power to every one *that* is to come.

19 Thy righteousness also, O God, *is* very high, who hast done great things: O God, who *is* like unto thee!

20 *Thou,* which hast shewed me great and sore troubles, shalt quicken me again, and shalt bring me up again from the depths of the earth.

21 Thou shalt increase my greatness, and comfort me on every side.

22 I will also praise thee with the psaltery, *even* thy truth, O my God: unto thee will I sing with the harp, O thou Holy One of Israel.

23 My lips shall greatly rejoice when I sing unto thee; and my soul, which thou hast redeemed.

24 My tongue also shall talk of thy righteousness all the day long: for they are confounded, for they are brought unto shame, that seek my hurt.

PSALM 72
A Prayer for the King
A Psalm for Solomon.

1 Give the king thy judgments, O God, and thy righteousness unto the king's son.

2 He shall judge thy people with righteousness, and thy poor with judgment.

3 The mountains shall bring peace to the people, and the little hills, by righteousness.

4 He shall judge the poor of the people, he shall save the children of the needy, and shall break in pieces the oppressor.

5 They shall fear thee as long as the sun and moon endure, throughout all generations.

6 He shall come down like rain upon the mown grass: as showers *that* water the earth.

7 In his days shall the righteous flourish; and abundance of peace so long as the moon endureth.

8 He shall have dominion also from sea to

Center reference column

5 Ps. 40:17; 141:1
1 Ps. 25:2, 3; 31:1
2 Ps. 17:6; 31:1
3 Ps. 31:2, 3; 44:4
4 Ps. 140:1, 4
5 Jer. 17:7, 17
6 Ps. 22:9, 10; Isa. 46:3
7 Isa. 8:18; Zech. 3:8; 1Cor. 4:9
8 Ps. 35:28
9 Ps. 71:18
10 2Sam. 17:1; Matt. 27:1
12 Ps. 22:11, 19; 35:22; 38:21, 22; 70:1
13 Ps. 35:4, 26; 40:14; 70:2; 71:24
15 Ps. 35:28; 40:5; 71:8, 24; 139:17, 18
19 Ps. 35:10; 57:10; 86:8; 89:6, 8
20 Ps. 60:3; Hos. 6:1, 2
22 2Kgs. 19:22; Ps. 92:1, 2, 3; 150:3; Isa. 60:9
23 Ps. 103:4
24 Ps. 71:8, 13, 15
2 Isa. 11:2-4; 32:1
3 Ps. 85:10; Isa. 32:17; 52:7
4 Isa. 11:4
5 Ps. 72:7, 17; 89:36, 37
7 Isa. 2:4; Dan. 2:44; Luke 1:33
8 Zech. 9:10

72:1–20 The inscription refers to this as "A Psalm for Solomon," and the psalm may have been written to celebrate his coronation and predict the success of his reign. As the psalm unfolds, it goes far beyond anything Solomon himself could fulfill and points to the millennial reign of Christ. This psalm has long been considered by both Jews and Christians to be a description of God's promised Messiah—God's Royal Son.

sea, and from the river unto the ends of the earth.

9 They that dwell in the wilderness shall bow before him; and his enemies shall lick the dust.

10 The kings of Tarshish and of the isles shall bring presents: the kings of Sheba and Seba shall offer gifts.

11 Yea, all kings shall fall down before him: all nations shall serve him.

12 For he shall deliver the needy when he crieth; the poor also, and *him* that hath no helper.

13 He shall spare the poor and needy, and shall save the souls of the needy.

14 He shall redeem their soul from deceit and violence: and precious shall their blood be in his sight.

15 And he shall live, and to him shall be given of the gold of Sheba: prayer also shall be made for him continually; *and* daily shall he be praised.

16 There shall be an handful of corn in the earth upon the top of the mountains; the fruit thereof shall shake like Lebanon: and *they* of the city shall flourish like grass of the earth.

17 His name shall endure for ever: his name shall be continued as long as the sun: and *men* shall be blessed in him: all nations shall call him blessed.

18 Blessed *be* the LORD God, the God of Israel, who only doeth wondrous things.

19 And blessed *be* his glorious name for ever: and let the whole earth be filled *with* his glory; Amen, and Amen.

20 The prayers of David the son of Jesse are ended.

BOOK III

PSALM 73
The Fate of the Wicked

A Psalm of Asaph.

1 Truly God *is* good to Israel, *even* to such as are of a clean heart.

2 But as for me, my feet were almost gone; my steps had well nigh slipped.

3 For I was envious at the foolish, *when* I saw the prosperity of the wicked.

4 For *there are* no bands in their death: but their strength *is* firm.

5 They *are* not in trouble *as other* men; neither are they plagued like *other* men.

6 Therefore pride compasseth them about as a chain; violence covereth them *as* a garment.

7 Their eyes stand out with fatness: they have more than heart could wish.

---

9 Ps. 74:14; Isa. 49:23; Mic. 7:17

10 2Chr. 9:21; Ps. 45:12; 68:29; Isa. 49:7; 60:6, 9

11 Isa. 49:22, 23

12 Job 29:12

14 Ps. 116:15

16 1Kgs. 4:20

17 Gen. 12:3; 22:18; Ps. 89:36; Jer. 4:2; Luke 1:48

18 Ex. 15:11; 1Chr. 29:10; Ps. 41:13; 77:14; 106:48; 136:4

19 Num. 14:21; Neh. 9:5; Zech. 14:9

3 Job 21:7; Ps. 37:1; Jer. 12:1

5 Job 21:9

6 Ps. 109:18

7 Job 15:27; Ps. 17:10; 119:70; Jer. 5:28

8 Ps. 53:1; Hos. 7:16; 2Pet. 2:18; Jude 1:16

9 Rev. 13:6

10 Ps. 75:8

11 Job 22:13; Ps. 10:11; 94:7

12 Ps. 73:3

13 Job 21:15; 34:9; 35:3; Ps. 26:6; Mal. 3:14

16 Eccl. 8:17

17 Ps. 37:38; 77:13

20 Job 20:8; Ps. 78:65; 90:5; Isa. 29:7, 8

21 Ps. 73:3

22 Ps. 92:6; Prov. 30:2

24 Ps. 32:8; Isa. 58:8

27 Ex. 34:15; Num. 15:39

---

8 They are corrupt, and speak wickedly *concerning* oppression: they speak loftily.

9 They set their mouth against the heavens, and their tongue walketh through the earth.

10 Therefore his people return hither: and waters of a full *cup* are wrung out to them.

11 And they say, How doth God know? and is there knowledge in the most High?

12 Behold, these *are* the ungodly, who prosper in the world; they increase *in* riches.

13 Verily I have cleansed my heart *in* vain, and washed my hands in innocency.

14 For all the day long have I been plagued, and chastened every morning.

15 If I say, I will speak thus; behold, I should offend *against* the generation of thy children.

16 When I thought to know this, it *was* too painful for me;

17 Until I went into the sanctuary of God; *then* understood I their end.

18 Surely thou didst set them in slippery places: thou castedst them down into destruction.

19 How are they *brought* into desolation, as in a moment! they are utterly consumed with terrors.

20 As a dream when *one* awaketh; *so*, O Lord, when thou awakest, thou shalt despise their image.

21 Thus my heart was grieved, and I was pricked in my reins.

22 So foolish *was* I, and ignorant: I was *as* a beast before thee.

23 Nevertheless I *am* continually with thee: thou hast holden *me* by my right hand.

24 Thou shalt guide me with thy counsel, and afterward receive me *to* glory.

25 Whom have I in heaven *but thee*? and *there is* none upon earth *that* I desire beside thee.

26 My flesh and my heart faileth: *but* God *is* the strength of my heart, and my portion for ever.

27 For, lo, they that are far from thee shall perish: thou hast destroyed all them that go a whoring from thee.

28 But it *is* good for me to draw near to God: I have put my trust in the Lord GOD, that I may declare all thy works.

PSALM 74
An Appeal to God

Maschil of Asaph.

1 O God, why hast thou cast *us* off for ever? *why* doth thine anger smoke against the sheep of thy pasture?

2 Remember thy congregation, *which* thou hast purchased of old; the rod of thine inheritance, *which* thou hast redeemed; this mount Zion, wherein thou hast dwelt.

3 Lift up thy feet unto the perpetual desolations; *even* all *that* the enemy hath done wickedly in the sanctuary.

4 Thine enemies roar in the midst of thy congregations; they set up their ensigns *for* signs.

5 *A man* was famous according as he had lifted up axes upon the thick trees.

6 But now they break down the carved work thereof at once with axes and hammers.

7 They have cast fire into thy sanctuary, they have defiled *by casting down* the dwelling place of thy name to the ground.

8 They said in their hearts, Let us destroy them together: they have burned up all the synagogues of God in the land.

9 We see not our signs: *there is* no more any prophet: neither *is there* among us any that knoweth how long.

10 O God, how long shall the adversary reproach? shall the enemy blaspheme thy name for ever?

11 Why withdrawest thou thy hand, even thy right hand? pluck *it* out of thy bosom.

12 For God *is* my King of old, working salvation in the midst of the earth.

13 Thou didst divide the sea by thy strength: thou brakest the heads of the dragons in the waters.

14 Thou brakest the heads of leviathan in pieces, *and* gavest him *to be* meat to the people inhabiting the wilderness.

15 Thou didst cleave the fountain and the flood: thou driedst up mighty rivers.

16 The day *is* thine, the night also *is* thine: thou hast prepared the light and the sun.

17 Thou hast set all the borders of the earth: thou hast made summer and winter.

18 Remember this, *that* the enemy hath reproached, O LORD, and *that* the foolish people have blasphemed thy name.

19 O deliver not the soul of thy turtledove unto the multitude *of the wicked*: forget not the congregation of thy poor for ever.

20 Have respect unto the covenant: for the dark places of the earth are full of the habitations of cruelty.

21 O let not the oppressed return ashamed: let the poor and needy praise thy name.

22 Arise, O God, plead thine own cause: remember how the foolish man reproacheth thee daily.

23 Forget not the voice of thine enemies:

the tumult of those that rise up against thee increaseth continually.

PSALM 75
God Will Judge Fairly

To the chief Musician, Al-taschith, A Psalm or Song of Asaph.

1 Unto thee, O God, do we give thanks, *unto thee* do we give thanks: for *that* thy name is near thy wondrous works declare.

2 When I shall receive the congregation I will judge uprightly.

3 The earth and all the inhabitants thereof are dissolved: I bear up the pillars of it. Selah.

4 I said unto the fools, Deal not foolishly: and to the wicked, Lift not up the horn:

5 Lift not up your horn on high: speak *not* with a stiff neck.

6 For promotion *cometh* neither from the east, nor from the west, nor from the south.

7 But God *is* the judge: he putteth down one, and setteth up another.

8 For in the hand of the LORD *there is* a cup, and the wine is red; it is full of mixture; and he poureth out of the same: but the dregs thereof, all the wicked of the earth shall wring *them* out, *and* drink *them*.

9 But I will declare for ever; I will sing praises to the God of Jacob.

10 All the horns of the wicked also will I cut off; *but* the horns of the righteous shall be exalted.

PSALM 76
The God of Victory and Judgment

To the chief Musician on Neginoth, A Psalm or Song of Asaph.

1 In Judah *is* God known: his name *is* great in Israel.

2 In Salem also is his tabernacle, and his dwelling place in Zion.

3 There brake he the arrows of the bow, the shield, and the sword, and the battle. Selah.

4 Thou *art* more glorious *and* excellent than the mountains of prey.

5 The stouthearted are spoiled, they have slept their sleep: and none of the men of might have found their hands.

6 At thy rebuke, O God of Jacob, both the chariot and horse are cast into a dead sleep.

7 Thou, *even* thou, *art* to be feared: and who may stand in thy sight when once thou art angry?

8 Thou didst cause judgment to be heard from heaven; the earth feared, and was still,

Cross references

2 Ex. 15:16; Deut. 9:29; 32:9; Jer. 10:16
4 Lam. 2:7; Dan. 6:27
6 1Kgs. 6:18, 29, 32, 35
7 2Kgs. 25:9; Ps. 89:39
8 Ps. 83:4
9 1Sam. 3:1; Amos 8:11
12 Ps. 44:4
13 Ex. 14:21; Isa. 51:9, 10; Ezek. 29:3; 32:2
14 Num. 14:9; Ps. 72:9
15 Ex. 17:5, 6; Num. 20:11; Josh. 3:13; Ps. 105:41; Isa. 48:21
16 Gen. 1:14
17 Gen. 8:22; Acts 17:26
18 Ps. 39:8; 74:22; Rev. 16:19
19 Ps. 68:10; Song 2:14
20 Gen. 17:7, 8; Lev. 26:44, 45; Ps. 106:45; Jer. 33:21
22 Ps. 74:18; 89:51
23 Jon. 1:2
7 1Sam. 2:7; Ps. 50:6; 58:11; Dan. 2:21
8 Jer. 25:15; Rev. 14:10; 16:19
10 Ps. 89:17; 101:8; 148:14; Jer. 48:25
1 Ps. 48:1
3 Ps. 46:9; Ezek. 39:9
4 Ezek. 38:12, 13; 39:4
6 Ex. 15:1, 21; Ezek. 39:20; Nah. 2:13; Zech. 12:4
8 Ezek. 38:20

9 When God arose to judgment, to save all the meek of the earth. Selah.

10 Surely the wrath of man shall praise thee: the remainder of wrath shalt thou restrain.

11 Vow, and pay unto the LORD your God: let all that be round about him bring presents unto him that ought to be feared.

12 He shall cut off the spirit of princes: *he is* terrible to the kings of the earth.

PSALM 77
Comforting Comes from God
To the chief Musician, to Jeduthun, A Psalm of Asaph.

1 I cried unto God with my voice, *even* unto God with my voice; and he gave ear unto me.

2 In the day of my trouble I sought the Lord: my sore ran in the night, and ceased not: my soul refused to be comforted.

3 I remembered God, and was troubled: I complained, and my spirit was overwhelmed. Selah.

4 Thou holdest mine eyes waking: I am so troubled that I cannot speak.

5 I have considered the days of old, the years of ancient times.

6 I call to remembrance my song in the night: I commune with mine own heart: and my spirit made diligent search.

7 Will the Lord cast off for ever? and will he be favourable no more?

8 Is his mercy clean gone for ever? doth *his* promise fail for evermore?

9 Hath God forgotten to be gracious? hath he in anger shut up his tender mercies? Selah.

10 And I said, This *is* my infirmity: *but I will remember* the years of the right hand of the most High.

11 I will remember the works of the LORD: surely I will remember thy wonders of old.

12 I will meditate also of all thy work, and talk of thy doings.

13 Thy way, O God, *is* in the sanctuary: who *is* so great a God as *our* God?

14 Thou *art* the God that doest wonders: thou hast declared thy strength among the people.

15 Thou hast with *thine* arm redeemed thy people, the sons of Jacob and Joseph. Selah.

16 The waters saw thee, O God, the waters saw thee; they were afraid: the depths also were troubled.

Cross references (center column)
9 Ps. 9:7-9; 72:4
10 Ex. 9:16; 18:11; Ps. 65:7
11 2Chr. 32:22, 23; Ps. 68:29; 89:7; Eccl. 5:4-6
12 Ps. 68:35
1 Ps. 3:4
2 Ps. 50:15; Isa. 26:9, 16
3 Ps. 142:3; 143:4
5 Deut. 32:7; Ps. 143:5; Isa. 51:9
6 Ps. 4:4; 42:8
8 Rom. 9:6
9 Isa. 49:15
10 Ps. 31:22
11 Ps. 143:5
13 Ex. 15:11; Ps. 73:17
15 Ex. 6:6; Deut. 9:29
16 Ex. 14:21; Josh. 3:15, 16
17 2Sam. 22:15; Hab. 3:11
18 2Sam. 22:8; Ps. 97:4
19 Ex. 14:28; Hab. 3:15
20 Ex. 13:21; 14:19
1 Isa. 51:4
2 Ps. 49:4; Matt. 13:35
3 Ps. 44:1
4 Ex. 12:26, 27; 13:8, 14; Josh. 4:6, 7
5 Deut. 4:9; 6:7; 11:19
6 Ps. 102:18
8 Ex. 32:9; 2Kgs. 17:14; Ezek. 20:18
10 2Kgs. 17:15
12 Ex. 7—12
13 Ex. 14:21; 15:8

17 The clouds poured out water: the skies sent out a sound: thine arrows also went abroad.

18 The voice of thy thunder *was* in the heaven: the lightnings lightened the world: the earth trembled and shook.

19 Thy way *is* in the sea, and thy path in the great waters, and thy footsteps are not known.

20 Thou leddest thy people like a flock by the hand of Moses and Aaron.

PSALM 78
God Loves His People
Maschil of Asaph.

1 Give ear, O my people, *to* my law: incline your ears to the words of my mouth.

2 I will open my mouth in a parable: I will utter dark sayings of old:

3 Which we have heard and known, and our fathers have told us.

4 We will not hide *them* from their children, shewing to the generation to come the praises of the LORD, and his strength, and his wonderful works that he hath done.

5 For he established a testimony in Jacob, and appointed a law in Israel, which he commanded our fathers, that they should make them known to their children:

6 That the generation to come might know *them, even* the children *which* should be born; *who* should arise and declare *them* to their children:

7 That they might set their hope in God, and not forget the works of God, but keep his commandments:

8 And might not be as their fathers, a stubborn and rebellious generation; a generation *that* set not their heart aright, and whose spirit was not stedfast with God.

9 The children of Ephraim, *being* armed, *and* carrying bows, turned back in the day of battle.

10 They kept not the covenant of God, and refused to walk in his law;

11 And forgat his works, and his wonders that he had shewed them.

12 Marvellous things did he in the sight of their fathers, in the land of Egypt, *in* the field of Zoan.

13 He divided the sea, and caused them to pass through; and he made the waters to stand as an heap.

14 In the daytime also he led them with a

78:2 God tells the people of Israel that He will speak to them "in a parable." The New Testament quotes this as being fulfilled in Jesus' teaching by use of parables (Matt. 13:35).

cloud, and all the night with a light of fire.
15 He clave the rocks in the wilderness, and gave *them* drink as *out of* the great depths.
16 He brought streams also out of the rock, and caused waters to run down like rivers.
17 And they sinned yet more against him by provoking the most High in the wilderness.
18 And they tempted God in their heart by asking meat for their lust.
19 Yea, they spake against God; they said, Can God furnish a table in the wilderness?
20 Behold, he smote the rock, that the waters gushed out, and the streams overflowed; can he give bread also? can he provide flesh for his people?
21 Therefore the LORD heard *this*, and was wroth: so a fire was kindled against Jacob, and anger also came up against Israel;
22 Because they believed not in God, and trusted not in his salvation:
23 Though he had commanded the clouds from above, and opened the doors of heaven,
24 And had rained down manna upon them to eat, and had given them of the corn of heaven.
25 Man did eat angels' food: he sent them meat to the full.
26 He caused an east wind to blow in the heaven: and by his power he brought in the south wind.
27 He rained flesh also upon them as dust, and feathered fowls like as the sand of the sea:
28 And he let *it* fall in the midst of their camp, round about their habitations.
29 So they did eat, and were well filled: for he gave them their own desire;
30 They were not estranged from their lust. But while their meat *was* yet in their mouths,
31 The wrath of God came upon them, and slew the fattest of them, and smote down the chosen *men* of Israel.
32 For all this they sinned still, and believed not for his wondrous works.
33 Therefore their days did he consume in vanity, and their years in trouble.
34 When he slew them, then they sought him: and they returned and inquired early after God.
35 And they remembered that God *was* their rock, and the high God their redeemer.
36 Nevertheless they did flatter him with their mouth, and they lied unto him with their tongues.
37 For their heart was not right with him,

neither were they stedfast in his covenant.
38 But he, *being* full of compassion, forgave *their* iniquity, and destroyed *them* not: yea, many a time turned he his anger away, and did not stir up all his wrath.
39 For he remembered that they *were but* flesh; a wind that passeth away, and cometh not again.
40 How oft did they provoke him in the wilderness, *and* grieve him in the desert!
41 Yea, they turned back and tempted God, and limited the Holy One of Israel.
42 They remembered not his hand, *nor* the day when he delivered them from the enemy.
43 How he had wrought his signs in Egypt, and his wonders in the field of Zoan:
44 And had turned their rivers into blood; and their floods, that they could not drink.
45 He sent divers sorts of flies among them, which devoured them; and frogs, which destroyed them.
46 He gave also their increase unto the caterpiller, and their labour unto the locust.
47 He destroyed their vines with hail, and their sycomore trees with frost.
48 He gave up their cattle also to the hail, and their flocks to hot thunderbolts.
49 He cast upon them the fierceness of his anger, wrath, and indignation, and trouble, by sending evil angels *among them.*
50 He made a way to his anger; he spared not their soul from death, but gave their life over to the pestilence;
51 And smote all the firstborn in Egypt; the chief of *their* strength in the tabernacles of Ham:
52 But made his own people to go forth like sheep, and guided them in the wilderness like a flock.
53 And he led them on safely, so that they feared not: but the sea overwhelmed their enemies.
54 And he brought them to the border of his sanctuary, *even to* this mountain, *which* his right hand had purchased.
55 He cast out the heathen also before them, and divided them an inheritance by line, and made the tribes of Israel to dwell in their tents.
56 Yet they tempted and provoked the most high God, and kept not his testimonies:
57 But turned back, and dealt unfaithfully like their fathers: they were turned aside like a deceitful bow.
58 For they provoked him to anger with their high places, and moved him to jealousy with their graven images.

Cross references (center column):

15 Ex. 17:6; Num. 20:11; 1Cor. 10:4
16 Deut. 9:21; Ps. 105:41
17 Deut. 9:22
18 Ex. 16:2
19 Num. 11:4
20 Ex. 17:6
21 Num. 11:1, 10
24 Ex. 16:4, 14; John 6:31
29 Num. 11:20
34 Hos. 5:15
35 Ex. 15:13; Deut. 7:8; 32:4, 15, 31; Isa. 41:14; 44:6; 63:9
36 Ezek. 33:31
37 Ps. 78:8
38 Num. 14:18, 20; 1Kgs. 21:29; Isa. 48:9
39 Gen. 6:3; Job 7:7, 16; Ps. 103:14, 16; John 3:6; James 4:14
40 Ps. 78:17; 95:9, 10; Isa. 7:13; 63:10; Eph. 4:30; Heb. 3:16, 17
44 Ex. 7:20
45 Ex. 8:6, 24
46 Ex. 10:13, 15
47 Ex. 9:23, 25
50 Ex. 9:3, 6
51 Ex. 12:29
53 Ex. 14:19, 20, 27, 28; 15:10
54 Ex. 15:17
55 Josh. 13:7; 19:51
56 Judg. 2:11, 12
57 Ezek. 20:27, 28; Hos. 7:16
58 1Kgs. 11:7; 12:31; Ezek. 20:28

59 When God heard *this*, he was wroth, and greatly abhorred Israel:

60 So that he forsook the tabernacle of Shiloh, the tent *which* he placed among men;

61 And delivered his strength into captivity, and his glory into the enemy's hand.

62 He gave his people over also unto the sword; and was wroth with his inheritance.

63 The fire consumed their young men; and their maidens were not given to marriage.

64 Their priests fell by the sword; and their widows made no lamentation.

65 Then the Lord awaked as one out of sleep, *and* like a mighty man that shouteth by reason of wine.

66 And he smote his enemies in the hinder parts: he put them to a perpetual reproach.

67 Moreover he refused the tabernacle of Joseph, and chose not the tribe of Ephraim:

68 But chose the tribe of Judah, the mount Zion which he loved.

69 And he built his sanctuary like high *palaces*, like the earth which he hath established for ever.

70 He chose David also his servant, and took him from the sheepfolds:

71 From following the ewes great with young he brought him to feed Jacob his people, and Israel his inheritance.

72 So he fed them according to the integrity of his heart; and guided them by the skilfulness of his hands.

PSALM 79
Sorrow over Jerusalem
A Psalm of Asaph.

1 O God, the heathen are come into thine inheritance; thy holy temple have they defiled; they have laid Jerusalem on heaps.

2 The dead bodies of thy servants have they given *to be* meat unto the fowls of the heaven, the flesh of thy saints unto the beasts of the earth.

3 Their blood have they shed like water round about Jerusalem; and *there was* none to bury *them*.

4 We are become a reproach to our neighbours, a scorn and derision to them that are round about us.

5 How long, LORD? wilt thou be angry for ever? shall thy jealousy burn like fire?

6 Pour out thy wrath upon the heathen that have not known thee, and upon the kingdoms that have not called upon thy name.

7 For they have devoured Jacob, and laid waste his dwelling place.

8 O remember not against us former iniquities: let thy tender mercies speedily prevent us: for we are brought very low.

9 Help us, O God of our salvation, for the glory of thy name: and deliver us, and purge away our sins, for thy name's sake.

10 Wherefore should the heathen say, Where *is* their God? let him be known among the heathen in our sight *by* the revenging of the blood of thy servants *which is* shed.

11 Let the sighing of the prisoner come before thee; according to the greatness of thy power preserve thou those that are appointed to die;

12 And render unto our neighbours sevenfold into their bosom their reproach, wherewith they have reproached thee, O Lord.

13 So we thy people and sheep of thy pasture will give thee thanks for ever: we will shew forth thy praise to all generations.

PSALM 80
A Prayer for Restoration
To the chief Musician upon Shoshannim-eduth, A Psalm of Asaph.

1 Give ear, O Shepherd of Israel, thou that leadest Joseph like a flock; thou that dwellest *between* the cherubims, shine forth.

2 Before Ephraim and Benjamin and Manasseh stir up thy strength, and come *and* save us.

3 Turn us again, O God, and cause thy face to shine; and we shall be saved.

4 O LORD God of hosts, how long wilt thou be angry against the prayer of thy people?

5 Thou feedest them with the bread of tears; and givest them tears to drink in great measure.

6 Thou makest us a strife unto our neighbours: and our enemies laugh among themselves.

7 Turn us again, O God of hosts, and cause thy face to shine; and we shall be saved.

8 Thou hast brought a vine out of Egypt: thou hast cast out the heathen, and planted it.

9 Thou preparedst *room* before it, and didst cause it to take deep root, and it filled the land.

10 The hills were covered with the shadow of it, and the boughs thereof *were like* the goodly cedars.

Cross references (center column):

60 Jer. 7:12, 14
62 1Sam. 4:10
63 Jer. 7:34; 16:9; 25:10
64 1Sam. 4:11; 22:18
65 Ps. 44:23; Isa. 42:13
66 1Sam. 5:6, 12; 6:4
69 1Kgs. 6:1
70 1Sam. 16:11, 12; 2Sam. 7:8
71 2Sam. 5:2; 1Chr. 11:2
1 2Kgs. 25:9, 10; 2Chr. 36:19
2 Jer. 7:33
3 Ps. 141:7; Jer. 14:16; 16:4; Rev. 11:9
5 Zeph. 1:18; 3:8
6 Ps. 53:4; Isa. 45:4, 5; Jer. 10:25; 2Thess. 1:8; Rev. 16:1
8 Deut. 28:43; Ps. 142:6; Isa. 64:9
9 2Chr. 14:11; Jer. 14:7, 21
10 Ps. 42:10; 115:2
11 Ps. 102:20
12 Isa. 65:6, 7; Jer. 32:18; Luke 6:38
13 Ps. 100:3; Isa. 43:21
1 Ex. 25:20, 22; Deut. 33:2
3 Lam. 5:21
5 Isa. 30:20
8 Isa. 5:1, 7; Jer. 2:21; Ezek. 15:6; 17:6; 19:10
9 Ex. 23:28; Josh. 24:12

79:1–4 Asaph foresees the destruction of Jerusalem and the defiling of the temple, perhaps by both the Babylonians in 586 B.C. and the Romans in A.D. 70.

11 She sent out her boughs unto the sea, and her branches unto the river.
12 Why hast thou *then* broken down her hedges, so that all they which pass by the way do pluck her?
13 The boar out of the wood doth waste it, and the wild beast of the field doth devour it.
14 Return, we beseech thee, O God of hosts: look down from heaven, and behold, and visit this vine;
15 And the vineyard which thy right hand hath planted, and the branch *that* thou madest strong for thyself.
16 *It is* burned with fire, *it is* cut down: they perish at the rebuke of thy countenance.
17 Let thy hand be upon the man of thy right hand, upon the son of man *whom* thou madest strong for thyself.
18 So will not we go back from thee: quicken us, and we will call upon thy name.
19 Turn us again, O LORD God of hosts, cause thy face to shine; and we shall be saved.

PSALM 81
A Song for a Feast
To the chief Musician upon Gittith, A Psalm of Asaph.

1 Sing aloud unto God our strength: make a joyful noise unto the God of Jacob.
2 Take a psalm, and bring hither the timbrel, the pleasant harp with the psaltery.
3 Blow up the trumpet in the new moon, in the time appointed, on our solemn feast day.
4 For this *was* a statute for Israel, *and* a law of the God of Jacob.
5 This he ordained in Joseph *for* a testimony, when he went out through the land of Egypt: *where* I heard a language *that* I understood not.
6 I removed his shoulder from the burden: his hands were delivered from the pots.
7 Thou calledst in trouble, and I delivered thee; I answered thee in the secret place of thunder: I proved thee at the waters of Meribah. Selah.
8 Hear, O my people, and I will testify unto thee: O Israel, if thou wilt hearken unto me;
9 There shall no strange god be in thee; neither shalt thou worship any strange god.
10 I *am* the LORD thy God, which brought thee out of the land of Egypt: open thy mouth wide, and I will fill it.
11 But my people would not hearken to my voice; and Israel would none of me.
12 So I gave them up unto their own hearts' lust: *and* they walked in their own counsels.

13 Oh that my people had hearkened unto me, *and* Israel had walked in my ways!
14 I should soon have subdued their enemies, and turned my hand against their adversaries.
15 The haters of the LORD should have submitted themselves unto him: but their time should have endured for ever.
16 He should have fed them also with the finest of the wheat: and with honey out of the rock should I have satisfied thee.

PSALM 82
God Is in Control
A Psalm of Asaph.

1 God standeth in the congregation of the mighty; he judgeth among the gods.
2 How long will ye judge unjustly, and accept the persons of the wicked? Selah.
3 Defend the poor and fatherless: do justice to the afflicted and needy.
4 Deliver the poor and needy: rid *them* out of the hand of the wicked.
5 They know not, neither will they understand; they walk on in darkness: all the foundations of the earth are out of course.
6 I have said, Ye *are* gods; and all of you *are* children of the most High.
7 But ye shall die like men, and fall like one of the princes.
8 Arise, O God, judge the earth: for thou shalt inherit all nations.

PSALM 83
A Prayer for Enemies to Be Defeated
A Song or Psalm of Asaph.

1 Keep not thou silence, O God: hold not thy peace, and be not still, O God.
2 For, lo, thine enemies make a tumult: and they that hate thee have lifted up the head.
3 They have taken crafty counsel against thy people, and consulted against thy hidden ones.
4 They have said, Come, and let us cut them off from *being* a nation; that the name of Israel may be no more in remembrance.
5 For they have consulted together with one consent: they are confederate against thee:
6 The tabernacles of Edom, and the Ishmeelites; of Moab, and the Hagarenes;
7 Gebal, and Ammon, and Amalek; the Philistines with the inhabitants of Tyre;
8 Assur also is joined with them: they have holpen the children of Lot. Selah.
9 Do unto them as *unto* the Midianites; as *to* Sisera, as *to* Jabin, at the brook of Kison:

Cross-references (center column)

12 Isa. 5:5; Nah. 2:2
14 Isa. 63:15
15 Isa. 49:5
17 Ps. 89:21
4 Lev. 23:24; Num. 10:10
6 Ex. 1:14
7 Ex. 2:23; 14:10; 17:6, 7; 19:19; Num. 20:13
10 Ex. 20:2
11 Ex. 32:1; Deut. 32:15, 18
12 Acts 7:42; 14:16; Rom. 1:24, 26
13 Deut. 5:29; 10:12, 13; 32:29; Isa. 48:18
15 Ps. 18; 45; 66:3; Rom. 1:3
16 Deut. 32:13, 14; Job 29:6; Ps. 147:14
1 Ex. 21:6; 22:28; 2Chr. 19:6; Eccl. 5:8
2 Deut. 1:17; 2Chr. 19:7; Prov. 18:5
3 Jer. 22:3
4 Job 29:12; Prov. 24:11
5 Ps. 11:3; 75:3; Mic. 3:1
6 Ex. 22:9, 28; Ps. 82:1; John 10:34
7 Job 21:32; Ps. 49:12; Ezek. 31:14
8 Mic. 7:2, 7
1 Ps. 28:1; 35:22; 109:1
2 Ps. 2:1; 81:15; Acts 4:25
3 Ps. 27:5
4 Esth. 3:6, 9; Jer. 11:19; 31:36
6 2Chr. 20:1, 10, 11
9 Num. 31:7; Judg. 4:15, 24; 5:21; 7:22

10 *Which* perished at Endor: they became *as* dung for the earth.

11 Make their nobles like Oreb, and like Zeeb: yea, all their princes as Zebah, and as Zalmunna:

12 Who said, Let us take to ourselves the houses of God in possession.

13 O my God, make them like a wheel; as the stubble before the wind.

14 As the fire burneth a wood, and as the flame setteth the mountains on fire;

15 So persecute them with thy tempest, and make them afraid with thy storm.

16 Fill their faces with shame; that they may seek thy name, O LORD.

17 Let them be confounded and troubled for ever; yea, let them be put to shame, and perish:

18 That *men* may know that thou, whose name alone *is* JEHOVAH, *art* the most high over all the earth.

PSALM 84
Yearning for God's House

To the chief Musician upon Gittith, A Psalm for the sons of Korah.

1 How amiable *are* thy tabernacles, O LORD of hosts!

2 My soul longeth, yea even fainteth for the courts of the LORD: my heart and my flesh crieth out for the living God.

3 Yea, the sparrow hath found an house, and the swallow a nest for herself, where she may lay her young, *even* thine altars, O LORD of hosts, my King, and my God.

4 Blessed *are* they that dwell in thy house: they will be still praising thee. Selah.

5 Blessed *is* the man whose strength *is* in thee; in whose heart *are* the ways *of them*.

6 *Who* passing through the valley of Baca make it a well; the rain also filleth the pools.

7 They go from strength to strength, *every one of them* in Zion appeareth before God.

8 O LORD God of hosts, hear my prayer: give ear, O God of Jacob. Selah.

9 Behold, O God our shield, and look upon the face of thine anointed.

10 For a day in thy courts *is* better than a thousand. I had rather be a doorkeeper in the house of my God, than to dwell in the tents of wickedness.

11 For the LORD God *is* a sun and shield: the LORD will give grace and glory: no good *thing*

Cross references (center column)

10 2Kgs. 9:37; Zeph. 1:17
11 Judg. 7:25; 8:12, 21
13 Ps. 35:5; Isa. 17:13, 14
14 Deut. 32:22
15 Job 9:17
16 Ps. 35:4, 26
18 Ex. 6:3; Ps. 59:13; 92:8
1 Ps. 27:4
2 Ps. 42:1, 2; 63:1; 73:26; 119:20
4 Ps. 65:4
6 2Sam. 5:22, 23
7 Deut. 16:16; Prov. 4:18; Zech. 14:16; 2Cor. 3:18
9 Gen. 15:1; Ps. 84:11
11 Prov. 2:7; Isa. 60:19
12 Ps. 2:12
1 Ezra 1:11; 2:1; Ps. 14:7; 77:7; Jer. 30:18; 31:23; Ezek. 39:25; Joel 3:1
2 Ps. 32:1
3 Deut. 13:17
4 Ps. 80:7
5 Ps. 74:1; 79:5; 80:4
6 Hab. 3:2
8 Hab. 2:1; Zech. 9:10; 2Pet. 2:20, 21
9 Isa. 46:13; Zech. 2:5; John 1:14
10 Isa. 32:17; Luke 2:14
11 Isa. 45:8
3 Ps. 56:1; 57:1

---

will he withhold from them that walk uprightly.

12 O LORD of hosts, blessed *is* the man that trusteth in thee.

PSALM 85
Invoking God's Mercy

To the chief Musician, A Psalm for the sons of Korah.

1 LORD, thou hast been favourable unto thy land: thou hast brought back the captivity of Jacob.

2 Thou hast forgiven the iniquity of thy people, thou hast covered all their sin. Selah.

3 Thou hast taken away all thy wrath: thou hast turned *thyself* from the fierceness of thine anger.

4 Turn us, O God of our salvation, and cause thine anger toward us to cease.

5 Wilt thou be angry with us for ever? wilt thou draw out thine anger to all generations?

6 Wilt thou not revive us again: that thy people may rejoice in thee?

7 Shew us thy mercy, O LORD, and grant us thy salvation.

8 I will hear what God the LORD will speak: for he will speak peace unto his people, and to his saints: but let them not turn again to folly.

9 Surely his salvation *is* nigh them that fear him; that glory may dwell in our land.

10 Mercy and truth are met together; righteousness and peace have kissed *each other*.

11 Truth shall spring out of the earth; and righteousness shall look down from heaven.

12 Yea, the LORD shall give *that which is* good; and our land shall yield her increase.

13 Righteousness shall go before him; and shall set *us* in the way of his steps.

PSALM 86
A Cry for Help

A Prayer of David.

1 Bow down thine ear, O LORD hear me: for I *am* poor and needy.

2 Preserve my soul; for I *am* holy: O thou my God, save thy servant that trusteth in thee.

3 Be merciful unto me, O Lord: for I cry unto thee daily.

85:1–13 This psalm pictures a time when the Jewish people will return from captivity (v. 1) and experience a spiritual revival (v. 6). Only during the Millennial Kingdom will such conditions prevail when the land will overflow with righteousness (v. 13).

4 Rejoice the soul of thy servant: for unto thee, O Lord, do I lift up my soul.

5 For thou, Lord, *art* good, and ready to forgive; and plenteous in mercy unto all them that call upon thee.

6 Give ear, O LORD, unto my prayer; and attend to the voice of my supplications.

7 In the day of my trouble I will call upon thee: for thou wilt answer me.

8 Among the gods *there is* none like unto thee, O Lord; neither *are there any works* like unto thy works.

9 All nations whom thou hast made shall come and worship before thee, O Lord; and shall glorify thy name.

10 For thou *art* great, and doest wondrous things: thou *art* God alone.

11 Teach me thy way, O LORD; I will walk in thy truth: unite my heart to fear thy name.

12 I will praise thee, O Lord my God, with all my heart: and I will glorify thy name for evermore.

13 For great *is* thy mercy toward me: and thou hast delivered my soul from the lowest hell.

14 O God, the proud are risen against me, and the assemblies of violent *men* have sought after my soul; and have not set thee before them.

15 But thou, O Lord, *art* a God full of compassion, and gracious, longsuffering, and plenteous in mercy and truth.

16 O turn unto me, and have mercy upon me; give thy strength unto thy servant, and save the son of thine handmaid.

17 Shew me a token for good; that they which hate me may see *it*, and be ashamed: because thou, LORD, hast holpen me, and comforted me.

PSALM 87
Zion

A Psalm or Song for the sons of Korah.

1 His foundation *is* in the holy mountains.

2 The LORD loveth the gates of Zion more than all the dwellings of Jacob.

3 Glorious things are spoken of thee, O city of God. Selah.

4 I will make mention of Rahab and Babylon to them that know me: behold Philistia, and Tyre, with Ethiopia; this *man* was born there.

5 And of Zion it shall be said, This and that man was born in her: and the highest himself shall establish her.

6 The LORD shall count, when he writeth

up the people, *that* this *man* was born there. Selah.

7 As well the singers as the players on instruments *shall be there*: all my springs *are* in thee.

PSALM 88
A Prayer for Deliverance from Death

A Song or Psalm for the sons of Korah, to the chief Musician upon Mahalath Leannoth, Maschil of Heman the Ezrahite.

1 O LORD God of my salvation, I have cried day *and* night before thee:

2 Let my prayer come before thee: incline thine ear unto my cry;

3 For my soul is full of troubles: and my life draweth nigh unto the grave.

4 I am counted with them that go down into the pit: I am as a man *that hath* no strength:

5 Free among the dead, like the slain that lie in the grave, whom thou rememberest no more: and they are cut off from thy hand.

6 Thou hast laid me in the lowest pit, in darkness, in the deeps.

7 Thy wrath lieth hard upon me, and thou hast afflicted *me* with all thy waves. Selah.

8 Thou hast put away mine acquaintance far from me; thou hast made me an abomination unto them: *I am* shut up, and I cannot come forth.

9 Mine eye mourneth by reason of affliction: LORD, I have called daily upon thee, I have stretched out my hands unto thee.

10 Wilt thou shew wonders to the dead? shall the dead arise *and* praise thee? Selah.

11 Shall thy lovingkindness be declared in the grave? *or* thy faithfulness in destruction?

12 Shall thy wonders be known in the dark? and thy righteousness in the land of forgetfulness?

13 But unto thee have I cried, O LORD; and in the morning shall my prayer prevent thee.

14 LORD, why castest thou off my soul? *why* hidest thou thy face from me?

15 I *am* afflicted and ready to die from *my* youth up: *while* I suffer thy terrors I am distracted.

16 Thy fierce wrath goeth over me; thy terrors have cut me off.

17 They came round about me daily like water; they compassed me about together.

18 Lover and friend hast thou put far from me, *and* mine acquaintance into darkness.

Cross references (center column):

4 Ps. 25:1; 143:8

5 Ps. 86:15; 130:7; 145:9; Joel 2:13

7 Ps. 50:15

8 Ex. 15:11; Deut. 3:24; Ps. 89:6

9 Ps. 22:31; 102:18; Isa. 43:7; Rev. 15:4

10 Ex. 15:11; Deut. 6:4; 32:39; Ps. 72:18; 77:14; Isa. 37:16; 44:6; Mark 12:29; 1Cor. 8:4; Eph. 4:6

11 Ps. 25:4; 27:11; 119:33; 143:8

13 Ps. 56:13; 116:8

14 Ps. 54:3

15 Ex. 34:6; Num. 14:18; Neh. 9:17; Ps. 86:5; 103:8; 111:4; 130:4, 7; 145:8; Joel 2:13

16 Ps. 25:16; 69:16; 116:16

1 Ps. 48:1

2 Ps. 78:67, 68

4 Ps. 89:10; Isa. 51:9

6 Ps. 22:30; Ezek. 13:9

1 Ps. 27:9; 51:14; Luke 18:7

5 Isa. 53:8

7 Ps. 42:7

8 Job 19:13, 19; Ps. 31:11; 142:4; Lam. 3:7

9 Job 11:13; Ps. 38:10; 86:3; 143:6

10 Ps. 6:5; 30:9; 115:17; 118:17; Isa. 38:18

14 Job 13:24

15 Job 6:4

17 Ps. 22:16

18 Job 19:13; Ps. 31:11; 38:11

PSALM 89
God's Agreement with David

Maschil of Ethan the Ezrahite.

1 I will sing of the mercies of the LORD for ever: with my mouth will I make known thy faithfulness to all generations.

2 For I have said, Mercy shall be built up for ever: thy faithfulness shalt thou establish in the very heavens.

3 I have made a covenant with my chosen, I have sworn unto David my servant,

4 Thy seed will I establish for ever, and build up thy throne to all generations. Selah.

5 And the heavens shall praise thy wonders, O LORD: thy faithfulness also in the congregation of the saints.

6 For who in the heaven can be compared unto the LORD? *who* among the sons of the mighty can be likened unto the LORD?

7 God is greatly to be feared in the assembly of the saints, and to be had in reverence of all *them that are* about him.

8 O LORD God of hosts, who *is* a strong LORD like unto thee? or to thy faithfulness round about thee?

9 Thou rulest the raging of the sea: when the waves thereof arise, thou stillest them.

10 Thou hast broken Rahab in pieces, as one that is slain; thou hast scattered thine enemies with thy strong arm.

11 The heavens *are* thine, the earth also *is* thine: *as for* the world and the fulness thereof, thou hast founded them.

12 The north and the south thou hast created them: Tabor and Hermon shall rejoice in thy name.

13 Thou hast a mighty arm: strong is thy hand, *and* high is thy right hand.

14 Justice and judgment *are* the habitation of thy throne: mercy and truth shall go before thy face.

15 Blessed *is* the people that know the joyful sound: they shall walk, O LORD, in the light of thy countenance.

16 In thy name shall they rejoice all the day: and in thy righteousness shall they be exalted.

17 For thou *art* the glory of their strength:

and in thy favour our horn shall be exalted.

18 For the LORD *is* our defence; and the Holy One of Israel *is* our king.

19 Then thou spakest in vision to thy holy one, and saidst, I have laid help upon *one that is* mighty; I have exalted *one* chosen out of the people.

20 I have found David my servant; with my holy oil have I anointed him:

21 With whom my hand shall be established: mine arm also shall strengthen him.

22 The enemy shall not exact upon him; nor the son of wickedness afflict him.

23 And I will beat down his foes before his face, and plague them that hate him.

24 But my faithfulness and my mercy *shall be* with him: and in my name shall his horn be exalted.

25 I will set his hand also in the sea, and his right hand in the rivers.

26 He shall cry unto me, Thou *art* my father, my God, and the rock of my salvation.

27 Also I will make him *my* firstborn, higher than the kings of the earth.

28 My mercy will I keep for him for evermore, and my covenant shall stand fast with him.

29 His seed also will I make *to endure* for ever, and his throne as the days of heaven.

30 If his children forsake my law, and walk not in my judgments;

31 If they break my statutes, and keep not my commandments;

32 Then will I visit their transgression with the rod, and their iniquity with stripes.

33 Nevertheless my lovingkindness will I not utterly take from him, nor suffer my faithfulness to fail.

34 My covenant will I not break, nor alter the thing that is gone out of my lips.

35 Once have I sworn by my holiness that I will not lie unto David.

36 His seed shall endure for ever, and his throne as the sun before me.

37 It shall be established for ever as the moon, and *as* a faithful witness in heaven. Selah.

38 But thou hast cast off and abhorred, thou hast been wroth with thine anointed.

Cross-references

1 Ps. 89:4; 101:1; 119:90
2 Ps. 119:89
3 2Sam. 7:11
4 Luke 1:32, 33
5 Rev. 7:10, 11, 12
8 1Sam. 2:2
9 Ps. 65:7; 93:3, 4; 107:29
10 Ex. 14:26, 27, 28; Ps. 87:4; Isa. 30:7; 51:9
11 Gen. 1:1; 1Chr. 29:11; Ps. 24:1, 2; 50:12
12 Josh. 12:1; 19:22; Job 26:7
14 Ps. 85:13; 97:2
15 Num. 10:10; 23:21; Ps. 4:6; 44:3; 98:6
17 Ps. 75:10; 89:24; 92:10; 132:17
18 Ps. 47:9
19 1Kgs. 11:34; Ps. 89:3
20 1Sam. 16:1, 12
21 Ps. 80:17
22 2Sam. 7:13
26 2Sam. 7:14; 22:47
28 Isa. 55:3
29 Jer. 33:17
32 2Sam. 7:14; 1Kgs. 11:31
33 2Sam. 7:13
36 2Sam. 7:16; Jer. 33:20; Luke 1:33; John 12:34

89:1 This important messianic psalm underlines the importance of the Davidic covenant. God promised David that his seed would occupy his throne forever (vv. 3–4). Many believe this psalm was written shortly after the nation of Judah was defeated and the last king of David's line was exiled to Babylon (2 Kgs. 24:8–17). Despite these desperate circumstances, God promises that David's line will go on forever (v. 4) and that He will keep His promises to His people (v. 34). The apostle Peter referred to these promises in Acts 2:30, when he reminded his listeners that God promised King David that He would "raise up Christ to sit on his throne."

39 Thou hast made void the covenant of thy servant: thou hast profaned his crown *by casting it* to the ground.
40 Thou hast broken down all his hedges; thou hast brought his strong holds to ruin.
41 All that pass by the way spoil him: he is a reproach to his neighbours.
42 Thou hast set up the right hand of his adversaries; thou hast made all his enemies to rejoice.
43 Thou hast also turned the edge of his sword, and hast not made him to stand in the battle.
44 Thou hast made his glory to cease, and cast his throne down to the ground.
45 The days of his youth hast thou shortened: thou hast covered him with shame. Selah.
46 How long, Lord? wilt thou hide thyself for ever? shall thy wrath burn like fire?
47 Remember how short my time is: wherefore hast thou made all men in vain?
48 What man *is he that* liveth, and shall not see death? shall he deliver his soul from the hand of the grave? Selah.
49 Lord, where *are* thy former lovingkindnesses, *which* thou swarest unto David in thy truth?
50 Remember, Lord, the reproach of thy servants; *how* I do bear in my bosom *the reproach of* all the mighty people;
51 Wherewith thine enemies have reproached, O Lord; wherewith they have reproached the footsteps of thine anointed.
52 Blessed *be* the Lord for evermore. Amen, and Amen.

BOOK IV

PSALM 90
God Is Eternal

A Prayer of Moses the man of God.

1 Lord, thou hast been our dwelling place in all generations.
2 Before the mountains were brought forth, or ever thou hadst formed the earth and the world, even from everlasting to everlasting, thou *art* God.
3 Thou turnest man to destruction; and sayest, Return, ye children of men.
4 For a thousand years in thy sight *are but* as yesterday when it is past, and *as* a watch in the night.
5 Thou carriest them away as with a flood; they are *as* a sleep: in the morning *they are* like grass *which* groweth up.
6 In the morning it flourisheth, and

groweth up; in the evening it is cut down, and withereth.
7 For we are consumed by thine anger, and by thy wrath are we troubled.
8 Thou hast set our iniquities before thee, our secret *sins* in the light of thy countenance.
9 For all our days are passed away in thy wrath: we spend our years as a tale *that is told.*
10 The days of our years *are* threescore years and ten; and if by reason of strength *they be* fourscore years, yet *is* their strength labour and sorrow; for it is soon cut off, and we fly away.
11 Who knoweth the power of thine anger? even according to thy fear, *so is* thy wrath.
12 So teach *us* to number our days, that we may apply *our* hearts unto wisdom.
13 Return, O Lord, how long? and let it repent thee concerning thy servants.
14 O satisfy us early with thy mercy; that we may rejoice and be glad all our days.
15 Make us glad according to the days *wherein* thou hast afflicted us, *and* the years *wherein* we have seen evil.
16 Let thy work appear unto thy servants, and thy glory unto their children.
17 And let the beauty of the Lord our God be upon us: and establish thou the work of our hands upon us; yea, the work of our hands establish thou it.

PSALM 91
In God's Care

1 He that dwelleth in the secret place of the most High shall abide under the shadow of the Almighty.
2 I will say of the Lord, *He is* my refuge and my fortress: my God; in him will I trust.
3 Surely he shall deliver thee from the snare of the fowler, *and* from the noisome pestilence.
4 He shall cover thee with his feathers, and under his wings shalt thou trust: his truth *shall be thy* shield and buckler.
5 Thou shalt not be afraid for the terror by night; *nor* for the arrow *that* flieth by day;
6 *Nor* for the pestilence *that* walketh in darkness; *nor* for the destruction *that* wasteth at noonday.
7 A thousand shall fall at thy side, and ten thousand at thy right hand; *but* it shall not come nigh thee.
8 Only with thine eyes shalt thou behold and see the reward of the wicked.
9 Because thou hast made the Lord, *which is* my refuge, *even* the most High, thy habitation;

Cross references

39 Ps. 74:7; Lam. 5:16
40 Ps. 80:12
41 Ps. 44:13; 79:4
44 Ps. 89:39
46 Ps. 79:5; 78:63
47 Job 7:7; 10:9; 14:1; Ps. 39:5; 119:84
48 Ps. 49:9; Heb. 11:5
49 2Sam. 7:15; Ps. 54:5; Isa. 55:3
50 Ps. 69:9, 19
51 Ps. 74:22
52 Ps. 41:13
1 Deut. 33:27; Ez. 11:16
2 Prov. 8:25, 26
3 Gen. 3:19; Eccl. 12:7
4 2Pet. 3:8
5 Ps. 73:20; 103:15; Isa. 40:6
6 Job 14:2; Ps. 92:7
8 Ps. 19:12; 50:21; Jer. 16:17
12 Ps. 39:4
13 Deut. 32:36; Ps. 135:14
14 Ps. 85:6; 149:2
16 Hab. 3:2
17 Ps. 27:4; Isa. 26:12
1 Ps. 17:8; 27:5; 31:20; 32:7
2 Ps. 142:5
3 Ps. 124:7
4 Ps. 91:8; 57:1; 61:4
5 Job 5:19; Ps. 112:7; 121:6; Prov. 3:23, 24; Isa. 43:2
8 Ps. 37:34; Mal. 1:5
9 Ps. 71:3; 90:1; 91:2

10 There shall no evil befall thee, neither shall any plague come nigh thy dwelling.
11 For he shall give his angels charge over thee, to keep thee in all thy ways.
12 They shall bear thee up in *their* hands, lest thou dash thy foot against a stone.
13 Thou shalt tread upon the lion and adder: the young lion and the dragon shalt thou trample under feet
14 Because he hath set his love upon me, therefore will I deliver him: I will set him on high, because he hath known my name.
15 He shall call upon me, and I will answer him: I *will be* with him in trouble; I will deliver him, and honour him.
16 With long life will I satisfy him, and shew him my salvation.

PSALM 92
God's Goodness
A Psalm or Song for the sabbath day.

1 *It is a* good *thing* to give thanks unto the LORD, and to sing praises unto thy name, O most High:
2 To shew forth thy lovingkindness in the morning, and thy faithfulness every night,
3 Upon an instrument of ten strings, and upon the psaltery; upon the harp with a solemn sound.
4 For thou, LORD, hast made me glad through thy work: I will triumph in the works of thy hands.
5 O LORD, how great are thy works! *and* thy thoughts are very deep.
6 A brutish man knoweth not; neither doth a fool understand this.
7 When the wicked spring as the grass, and when all the workers of iniquity do flourish; *it is* that they shall be destroyed for ever:
8 But thou, LORD, *art most* high for evermore.
9 For, lo, thine enemies, O LORD, for, lo, thine enemies shall perish; all the workers of iniquity shall be scattered.
10 But my horn shalt thou exalt like *the horn of* a unicorn: I shall be anointed with fresh oil.
11 Mine eye also shall see *my desire* on mine enemies, *and* mine ears shall hear *my desire* of the wicked that rise up against me.
12 The righteous shall flourish like the palm tree: he shall grow like a cedar in Lebanon.
13 Those that be planted in the house of the LORD shall flourish in the courts of our God.
14 They shall still bring forth fruit in old age; they shall be fat and flourishing;
15 To shew that the LORD *is* upright: *he is* my rock, and *there is* no unrighteousness in him.

PSALM 93
God's Majesty

1 The LORD reigneth, he is clothed with majesty; the LORD is clothed with strength, *wherewith* he hath girded himself: the world also is stablished, that it cannot be moved.
2 Thy throne *is* established of old: thou *art* from everlasting.
3 The floods have lifted up, O LORD, the floods have lifted up their voice; the floods lift up their waves.
4 The LORD on high *is* mightier than the noise of many waters, *yea, than* the mighty waves of the sea.
5 Thy testimonies are very sure: holiness becometh thine house, O LORD, for ever.

PSALM 94
God Is the Judge

1 O LORD God, to whom vengeance belongeth; O God, to whom vengeance belongeth, shew thyself.
2 Lift up thyself, thou judge of the earth: render a reward to the proud.
3 LORD, how long shall the wicked, how long shall the wicked triumph?
4 *How long* shall they utter *and* speak hard things? *and* all the workers of iniquity boast themselves?
5 They break in pieces thy people, O LORD, and afflict thine heritage.
6 They slay the widow and the stranger, and murder the fatherless.
7 Yet they say, The LORD shall not see, neither shall the God of Jacob regard *it.*
8 Understand, ye brutish among the people: and *ye* fools, when will ye be wise?
9 He that planted the ear, shall he not hear? he that formed the eye, shall he not see?
10 He that chastiseth the heathen, shall not he correct? he that teacheth man knowledge, *shall not he know?*
11 The LORD knoweth the thoughts of man, that they *are* vanity.
12 Blessed *is* the man whom thou chastenest, O LORD, and teachest him out of thy law;

Cross references:
10 Prov. 12:21
11 Matt. 4:6; Luke 4:10, 11; Heb. 1:14
16 Prov. 3:2
1 Ps. 147:1
2 Ps. 89:1
3 1Chr. 23:5; Ps. 9:16; 33:2
5 Ps. 40:5; 139:17; Isa. 28:29; Rom. 11:33, 34
6 Ps. 73:22; 94:8
7 Job 12:6; 21:7; Ps. 37:1, 2, 35, 38; Jer. 12:1, 2; Mal. 3:15
8 Ps. 56:2; 83:18
9 Ps. 68:1; 89:10
10 Ps. 23:5; 89:17, 24
11 Ps. 54:7; 59:10; 112:8
12 Ps. 52:8; Isa. 65:22; Hos. 14:5, 6
13 Ps. 100:4; 135:2
15 Deut. 32:4; Rom. 9:14
1 Ps. 65:6; 96:10; 97:1; 99:1; 104:1; Isa. 52:7; Rev. 19:6
2 Ps. 45:6; Prov. 8:22
4 Ps. 65:7; 89:9
1 Deut. 32:35; Ps. 80:1; Nah. 1:2
2 Gen. 18:25; Ps. 7:6
9 Ex. 4:11
10 Job 35:11; Isa. 28:26
11 1Cor. 3:20
12 Prov. 3:11

94:1 God promises the people of Israel that He will not cast them off nor forsake them (v. 14). God's promises to Old Testament Israel must have a future fulfillment or they cannot be viewed as having any certainty at all.

13 That thou mayest give him rest from the days of adversity, until the pit be digged for the wicked.

14 For the LORD will not cast off his people, neither will he forsake his inheritance.

15 But judgment shall return unto righteousness: and all the upright in heart shall follow it.

16 Who will rise up for me against the evildoers? *or* who will stand up for me against the workers of iniquity?

17 Unless the LORD *had been* my help, my soul had almost dwelt in silence.

18 When I said, My foot slippeth; thy mercy, O LORD, held me up.

19 In the multitude of my thoughts within me thy comforts delight my soul.

20 Shall the throne of iniquity have fellowship with thee, which frameth mischief by a law?

21 They gather themselves together against the soul of the righteous, and condemn the innocent blood.

22 But the LORD is my defence; and my God *is* the rock of my refuge.

23 And he shall bring upon them their own iniquity, and shall cut them off in their own wickedness; *yea,* the LORD our God shall cut them off.

PSALM 95
Praise and Worship

1 O come, let us sing unto the LORD: let us make a joyful noise to the rock of our salvation.

2 Let us come before his presence with thanksgiving, and make a joyful noise unto him with psalms.

3 For the LORD *is* a great God, and a great King above all gods.

4 In his hand *are* the deep places of the earth: the strength of the hills *is* his also.

5 The sea *is* his, and he made it: and his hands formed the dry *land.*

6 O come, let us worship and bow down: let us kneel before the LORD our maker.

7 For he *is* our God; and we *are* the people of his pasture, and the sheep of his hand. Today if ye will hear his voice,

8 Harden not your heart, as in the provocation, *and* as *in* the day of temptation in the wilderness:

Cross references (center column):

14 1Sam. 12:22; Rom. 11:1, 2

20 Ps. 58:2; Isa. 10:1; Amos 6:3

21 Prov. 17:15; Matt. 27:1

22 Ps. 59:9; 62:2, 6

23 Ps. 7:16; Prov. 2:22; 5:22

1 Deut. 32:15; 2Sam. 22:47; Ps. 100:1

3 Ps. 96:4; 97:9; 135:5

5 Gen. 1:9, 10

6 1Cor. 6:20

7 Ps. 79:13; 80:1; 100:3; Heb. 3:7, 15; 4:7

8 Ex. 17:2, 7; Num. 14:22; 20:13; Deut. 6:16

9 Num. 14:22; Ps. 78:18, 40, 56; 1Cor. 10:9

10 Heb. 3:10, 17

11 Num. 14:23, 28, 30; Heb. 3:11, 18; 4:3, 5

1 1Chr. 16:23-33; Ps. 33:3

4 Ps. 18:3; 95:3; 145:3

5 Ps. 115:15; Isa. 42:5; Jer. 10:11, 12

6 Ps. 29:2

9 Ps. 29:2; 110:3

10 Rev. 11:15; 19:6

13 Rev. 19:11

1 Isa. 60:9

---

9 When your fathers tempted me, proved me, and saw my work.

10 Forty years long was I grieved with *this* generation, and said, It *is* a people that do err in their heart, and they have not known my ways:

11 Unto whom I sware in my wrath that they should not enter into my rest.

PSALM 96
God Is the True King

1 O sing unto the LORD a new song: sing unto the LORD, all the earth.

2 Sing unto the LORD, bless his name; shew forth his salvation from day to day.

3 Declare his glory among the heathen, his wonders among all people.

4 For the LORD *is* great, and greatly to be praised: he *is* to be feared above all gods.

5 For all the gods of the nations *are* idols: but the LORD made the heavens.

6 Honour and majesty *are* before him: strength and beauty *are* in his sanctuary.

7 Give unto the LORD, O ye kindreds of the people, give unto the LORD glory and strength.

8 Give unto the LORD the glory *due unto* his name: bring an offering, and come into his courts.

9 O worship the LORD in the beauty of holiness: fear before him, all the earth.

10 Say among the heathen *that* the LORD reigneth: the world also shall be established that it shall not be moved: he shall judge the people righteously.

11 Let the heavens rejoice, and let the earth be glad; let the sea roar, and the fulness thereof.

12 Let the field be joyful, and all that *is* therein: then shall all the trees of the wood rejoice

13 Before the LORD: for he cometh, for he cometh to judge the earth: he shall judge the world with righteousness, and the people with his truth.

PSALM 97
The Power of God

1 The LORD reigneth; let the earth rejoice; let the multitude of isles be glad *thereof.*

2 Clouds and darkness *are* round about

97:1–12 This psalm paints a dramatic picture of the Messiah's victorious conquest of the enemies of God, ushering in His Millennial Kingdom. The book of Revelation uses similar images to depict the return of Christ to judge the world and bring in His kingdom on earth (Rev. 16:16–20). Jesus told His disciples that the "sign of the Son of Man" would appear "in the clouds" with "power and great glory" (Matt. 24:30) in language similar to Psalm 97:2–6.

him: righteousness and judgment *are* the habitation of his throne.

3 A fire goeth before him, and burneth up his enemies round about.

4 His lightnings enlightened the world: the earth saw, and trembled.

5 The hills melted like wax at the presence of the LORD, at the presence of the Lord of the whole earth.

6 The heavens declare his righteousness, and all the people see his glory.

7 Confounded be all they that serve graven images, that boast themselves of idols: worship him, all *ye* gods.

8 Zion heard, and was glad; and the daughters of Judah rejoiced because of thy judgments, O LORD.

9 For thou, LORD, *art* high above all the earth: thou art exalted far above all gods.

10 Ye that love the LORD, hate evil: he preserveth the souls of his saints; he delivereth them out of the hand of the wicked.

11 Light is sown for the righteous, and gladness for the upright in heart.

12 Rejoice in the LORD, ye righteous; and give thanks at the remembrance of his holiness.

PSALM 98
God Rules the World

A Psalm.

1 O sing unto the LORD a new song; for he hath done marvellous things: his right hand, and his holy arm, hath gotten him the victory.

2 The LORD hath made known his salvation: his righteousness hath he openly shewed in the sight of the heathen.

3 He hath remembered his mercy and his truth toward the house of Israel: all the ends of the earth have seen the salvation of our God.

4 Make a joyful noise unto the LORD, all the earth: make a loud noise, and rejoice, and sing praise.

5 Sing unto the LORD with the harp; with the harp, and the voice of a psalm.

6 With trumpets and sound of cornet make a joyful noise before the LORD, the King.

7 Let the sea roar, and the fulness thereof; the world, and they that dwell therein.

8 Let the floods clap *their* hands: let the hills be joyful together

9 Before the LORD; for he cometh to judge the earth: with righteousness shall he judge the world, and the people with equity.

PSALM 99
God Is Faithful

1 The LORD reigneth; let the people tremble: he sitteth *between* the cherubims; let the earth be moved.

2 The LORD *is* great in Zion; and he *is* high above all the people.

3 Let them praise thy great and terrible name; *for* it *is* holy.

4 The king's strength also loveth judgment; thou dost establish equity, thou executest judgment and righteousness in Jacob.

5 Exalt ye the LORD our God, and worship at his footstool; *for* he *is* holy.

6 Moses and Aaron among his priests, and Samuel among them that call upon his name; they called upon the LORD, and he answered them.

7 He spake unto them in the cloudy pillar: they kept his testimonies, and the ordinance *that* he gave them.

8 Thou answeredst them, O LORD our God: thou wast a God that forgavest them, though thou tookest vengeance of their inventions.

9 Exalt the LORD our God, and worship at his holy hill; for the LORD our God *is* holy.

PSALM 100
A Hymn of Praise

A Psalm of praise.

1 Make a joyful noise unto the LORD, all ye lands.

2 Serve the LORD with gladness: come before his presence with singing.

3 Know ye that the LORD he *is* God: *it is* he *that* hath made us, and not we ourselves; *we are* his people, and the sheep of his pasture.

4 Enter into his gates with thanksgiving, *and* into his courts with praise: be thankful unto him, *and* bless his name.

5 For the LORD *is* good; his mercy *is* everlasting; and his truth *endureth* to all generations.

Cross references

3 Ps. 18:8; 50:3; Dan. 7:10; Hab. 3:5

4 Ex. 19:18; Ps. 77:18; 104:32

5 Judg. 5:5; Mic. 1:4; Nah. 1:5

6 Ps. 19:1; 50:6

7 Ex. 20:4; Lev. 26:1; Deut. 5:8; 27:15; Heb. 1:6

9 Ex. 18:11; Ps. 83:18; 95:3; 96:4

10 Prov. 2:8; Amos 5:15

11 Job 22:28; Ps. 112:4; Prov. 4:18

1 Ex. 15:6, 11; Ps. 33:3; Isa. 42:10; 59:16; 63:5

2 Isa. 52:10; 62:2; Luke 2:30, 31; Rom. 3:25, 26

3 Isa. 49:6; 52:10; Luke 1:54, 55, 72; 2:30, 31; 3:6; Acts 13:47; 28:28

4 Ps. 95:1; 100:1

6 Num. 10:10; 1Chr. 15:28; 2Chr. 29:27

7 Ps. 96:11

8 Isa. 55:12

1 Ps. 18:10

3 Rev. 15:4

6 Ex. 14:15; 15:25

7 Ex. 33:9

8 Ex. 32:2; Num. 14:20; 20:12, 24

4 Ps. 66:13; 116:17-19

5 Ps. 89:1; 136:1

98:1 a new song. This psalm echoes the worship and praise of humanity and the song they sing to welcome the millennial reign of Christ. Revelation 5:9 records this "new song" as a song of praise sung to Christ, the Lamb of God, for His redemption.

99:1–9 Similarly to Psalm 98, this psalm alludes to the millennial reign of Christ. He is pictured as the King in Zion with Moses, Aaron, and Samuel attending to Him.

PSALM 101
David's Promise
A Psalm of David.

1 I will sing of mercy and judgment: unto thee, O LORD, will I sing.
2 I will behave myself wisely in a perfect way. O when wilt thou come unto me? I will walk within my house with a perfect heart.
3 I will set no wicked thing before mine eyes: I hate the work of them that turn aside; *it* shall not cleave to me.
4 A froward heart shall depart from me: I will not know a wicked *person*.
5 Whoso privily slandereth his neighbour, him will I cut off: him that hath an high look and a proud heart will not I suffer.
6 Mine eyes *shall be* upon the faithful of the land, that they may dwell with me: he that walketh in a perfect way, he shall serve me.
7 He that worketh deceit shall not dwell within my house: he that telleth lies shall not tarry in my sight.
8 I will early destroy all the wicked of the land; that I may cut off all wicked doers from the city of the LORD.

PSALM 102
An Afflicted Man's Prayer for Help
A Prayer of the afflicted, when he is overwhelmed, and poureth out his complaint before the LORD.

1 Hear my prayer, O LORD, and let my cry come unto thee.
2 Hide not thy face from me in the day *when* I am in trouble; incline thine ear unto me: in the day *when* I call answer me speedily.
3 For my days are consumed like smoke, and my bones are burned as an hearth.
4 My heart is smitten, and withered like grass; so that I forget to eat my bread.
5 By reason of the voice of my groaning my bones cleave to my skin.
6 I am like a pelican of the wilderness: I am like an owl of the desert.
7 I watch, and am as a sparrow alone upon the house top.
8 Mine enemies reproach me all the day; *and* they that are mad against me are sworn against me.

9 For I have eaten ashes like bread, and mingled my drink with weeping,
10 Because of thine indignation and thy wrath: for thou hast lifted me up, and cast me down.
11 My days *are* like a shadow that declineth; and I am withered like grass.
12 But thou, O LORD, shalt endure for ever; and thy remembrance unto all generations.
13 Thou shalt arise, *and* have mercy upon Zion: for the time to favour her, yea, the set time, is come.
14 For thy servants take pleasure in her stones, and favour the dust thereof.
15 So the heathen shall fear the name of the LORD, and all the kings of the earth thy glory.
16 When the LORD shall build up Zion, he shall appear in his glory.
17 He will regard the prayer of the destitute, and not despise their prayer.
18 This shall be written for the generation to come: and the people which shall be created shall praise the LORD.
19 For he hath looked down from the height of his sanctuary; from heaven did the LORD behold the earth;
20 To hear the groaning of the prisoner; to loose those that are appointed to death;
21 To declare the name of the LORD in Zion, and his praise in Jerusalem;
22 When the people are gathered together, and the kingdoms, to serve the LORD.
23 He weakened my strength in the way; he shortened my days.
24 I said, O my God, take me not away in the midst of my days: thy years *are* throughout all generations.
25 Of old hast thou laid the foundation of the earth: and the heavens *are* the work of thy hands.
26 They shall perish, but thou shalt endure: yea, all of them shall wax old like a garment; as a vesture shalt thou change them, and they shall be changed:
27 But thou *art* the same, and thy years shall have no end.
28 The children of thy servants shall continue, and their seed shall be established before thee.

Cross references
2 1Sam. 18:14; 1Kgs. 9:4; 11:4
3 Josh. 23:6
5 Prov. 6:17
8 Jer. 21:12
5 Job 19:20
7 Ps. 38:11; 77:4
8 Acts 23:12; 26:11
9 Ps. 42:3; 80:5
10 Ps. 30:7
11 Job 14:2; Ps. 102:4; 109:23; 144:4; Eccl. 6:12; Isa. 40:6-8; James 1:10
12 Ps. 9:7; 102:26; 135:13; Lam. 5:19
13 Isa. 40:2; 60:10; Zech. 1:12
14 Ps. 79:1
15 1Kgs. 8:43
16 Isa. 60:1, 2
17 Neh. 1:6, 11; 2:8
18 Isa. 43:21; Rom. 15:4; 1Cor. 10:11
23 Job 21:21
24 Ps. 90:2; Isa. 38:10; Hab. 1:12
25 Gen. 1:1; 2:1; Heb. 1:10
26 Ps. 102:12; Isa. 34:4; 51:6; 65:17; 66:22; Rom. 8:20; 2Pet. 3:7, 10-12
27 Mal. 3:6; Heb. 13:8; James 1:17
28 Ps. 69:36

102:16 The psalmist looks forward to the set time (v. 13) when God will once again "build up Zion." This promise ultimately looks ahead to the great restoration of Zion in the Millennial Kingdom when Jesus Christ will reign on the throne of David in fulfillment of God's promises to Israel.

102:25–26 In these verses, which are quoted in Hebrews 1:10–12, the psalmist foresees the destruction of the present earth (cf. 2 Pet. 3:7–10) and anticipates the fact that the heavens and the earth shall be changed (Rev. 21:1).

PSALM 103
God's Love

A Psalm of David.

1 Bless the LORD, O my soul: and all that is within me, *bless* his holy name.
2 Bless the LORD, O my soul, and forget not all his benefits:
3 Who forgiveth all thine iniquities; who healeth all thy diseases;
4 Who redeemeth thy life from destruction; who crowneth thee with lovingkindness and tender mercies;
5 Who satisfieth thy mouth with good *things; so that* thy youth is renewed like the eagle's.
6 The LORD executeth righteousness and judgment for all that are oppressed.
7 He made known his ways unto Moses, his acts unto the children of Israel.
8 The LORD *is* merciful and gracious, slow to anger, and plenteous in mercy.
9 He will not always chide: neither will he keep *his anger* for ever.
10 He hath not dealt with us after our sins; nor rewarded us according to our iniquities.
11 For as the heaven is high above the earth, *so* great is his mercy toward them that fear him.
12 As far as the east is from the west, *so* far hath he removed our transgressions from us.
13 Like as a father pitieth *his* children, *so* the LORD pitieth them that fear him.
14 For he knoweth our frame; he remembereth that we *are* dust.
15 *As for* man, his days *are* as grass: as a flower of the field, so he flourisheth.
16 For the wind passeth over it, and it is gone; and the place thereof shall know it no more.
17 But the mercy of the LORD *is* from everlasting to everlasting upon them that fear him, and his righteousness unto children's children;
18 To such as keep his covenant, and to those that remember his commandments to do them.
19 The LORD hath prepared his throne in the heavens; and his kingdom ruleth over all.
20 Bless the LORD, ye his angels, that excel in strength, that do his commandments, hearkening unto the voice of his word.
21 Bless ye the LORD, all *ye* his hosts; *ye* ministers of his, that do his pleasure.
22 Bless the LORD, all his works in all places of his dominion: bless the LORD, O my soul.

3 Matt. 9:2, 6; Mark 2:5, 10, 11; Luke 7:47
5 Isa. 40:31
8 Ex. 34:6, 7; Num. 14:18
9 Isa. 57:16; Jer. 3:5
10 Ezra 9:13
11 Eph. 3:18
13 Mal. 3:17
14 Gen. 3:19; Eccl. 12:7
16 Job 7:10; 20:9
17 Ex. 20:6
18 Deut. 7:9
19 Ps. 11:4; 47:2; Dan. 4:25, 34, 35
20 Ps. 78:25; 148:2; Matt. 6:10; Heb. 1:14
21 Gen. 32:2; Josh. 5:14; Ps. 68:17; Dan. 7:9, 10; Heb. 1:14
22 Ps. 103:1; 145:10

1 Ps. 93:1; 103:1; 104:35
2 Isa. 40:22; 45:12; Dan. 7:9
3 Ps. 18:10; Isa. 19:1
4 Heb. 1:7
6 Gen. 7:19
7 Gen. 8:1
13 Jer. 10:13; 14:22
14 Gen. 1:29, 30; 3:18; 9:3
15 Judg. 9:13; Ps. 23:5; Prov. 31:6, 7
16 Num. 24:6
18 Prov. 30:26
19 Gen. 1:14; Job 38:12
20 Isa. 45:7
21 Job 38:39; Joel 1:20

PSALM 104
God Is the Creator

1 Bless the LORD, O my soul. O LORD my God, thou art very great; thou art clothed with honour and majesty.
2 Who coverest *thyself* with light as *with* a garment: who stretchest out the heavens like a curtain:
3 Who layeth the beams of his chambers in the waters: who maketh the clouds his chariot: who walketh upon the wings of the wind:
4 Who maketh his angels spirits; his ministers a flaming fire:
5 *Who* laid the foundations of the earth, *that* it should not be removed for ever.
6 Thou coveredst it with the deep as *with* a garment: the waters stood above the mountains.
7 At thy rebuke they fled; at the voice of thy thunder they hasted away.
8 They go up by the mountains; they go down by the valleys unto the place which thou hast founded for them.
9 Thou hast set a bound that they may not pass over; that they turn not again to cover the earth.
10 He sendeth the springs into the valleys, *which* run among the hills.
11 They give drink to every beast of the field: the wild asses quench their thirst.
12 By them shall the fowls of the heaven have their habitation, *which* sing among the branches.
13 He watereth the hills from his chambers: the earth is satisfied with the fruit of thy works.
14 He causeth the grass to grow for the cattle, and herb for the service of man: that he may bring forth food out of the earth;
15 And wine *that* maketh glad the heart of man, *and* oil to make *his* face to shine, and bread *which* strengtheneth man's heart.
16 The trees of the LORD are full *of sap*; the cedars of Lebanon, which he hath planted;
17 Where the birds make their nests: *as for* the stork, the fir trees *are* her house.
18 The high hills *are* a refuge for the wild goats; *and* the rocks for the conies.
19 He appointed the moon for seasons: the sun knoweth his going down.
20 Thou makest darkness, and it is night: wherein all the beasts of the forest do creep *forth*.
21 The young lions roar after their prey, and seek their meat from God.
22 The sun ariseth, they gather themselves

together, and lay them down in their dens.
23 Man goeth forth unto his work and to his labour until the evening.
24 O LORD, how manifold are thy works! in wisdom hast thou made them all: the earth is full of thy riches.
25 *So is* this great and wide sea, wherein *are* things creeping innumerable, both small and great beasts.
26 There go the ships: *there is* that leviathan, *whom* thou hast made to play therein.
27 These wait all upon thee; that thou mayest give *them* their meat in due season.
28 *That* thou givest them they gather: thou openest thine hand, they are filled with good.
29 Thou hidest thy face, they are troubled: thou takest away their breath, they die, and return to their dust.
30 Thou sendest forth thy spirit, they are created: and thou renewest the face of the earth.
31 The glory of the LORD shall endure for ever: the LORD shall rejoice in his works.
32 He looketh on the earth, and it trembleth: he toucheth the hills, and they smoke.
33 I will sing unto the LORD as long as I live: I will sing praise to my God while I have my being.
34 My meditation of him shall be sweet: I will be glad in the LORD.
35 Let the sinners be consumed out of the earth, and let the wicked be no more. Bless thou the LORD, O my soul. Praise ye the LORD.

PSALM 105
God Takes Care of His People

1 O give thanks unto the LORD; call upon his name: make known his deeds among the people.
2 Sing unto him, sing psalms unto him: talk ye of all his wondrous works.
3 Glory ye in his holy name: let the heart of them rejoice that seek the LORD.
4 Seek the LORD, and his strength: seek his face evermore.
5 Remember his marvellous works that he hath done; his wonders, and the judgments of his mouth;
6 O ye seed of Abraham his servant, ye children of Jacob his chosen.

7 He *is* the LORD our God: his judgments *are* in all the earth.
8 He hath remembered his covenant for ever, the word *which* he commanded to a thousand generations.
9 Which *covenant* he made with Abraham, and his oath unto Isaac;
10 And confirmed the same unto Jacob for a law, *and* to Israel *for* an everlasting covenant:
11 Saying, Unto thee will I give the land of Canaan, the lot of your inheritance:
12 When they were *but* a few men in number; yea, very few, and strangers in it.
13 When they went from one nation to another, from *one* kingdom to another people;
14 He suffered no man to do them wrong: yea, he reproved kings for their sakes;
15 *Saying*, Touch not mine anointed, and do my prophets no harm.
16 Moreover he called for a famine upon the land: he brake the whole staff of bread.
17 He sent a man before them, *even* Joseph, who was sold for a servant:
18 Whose feet they hurt with fetters: he was laid in iron:
19 Until the time that his word came: the word of the LORD tried him.
20 The king sent and loosed him; *even* the ruler of the people, and let him go free.
21 He made him lord of his house, and ruler of all his substance:
22 To bind his princes at his pleasure; and teach his senators wisdom.
23 Israel also came into Egypt; and Jacob sojourned in the land of Ham.
24 And he increased his people greatly; and made them stronger than their enemies.
25 He turned their heart to hate his people, to deal subtilly with his servants.
26 He sent Moses his servant; *and* Aaron whom he had chosen.
27 They shewed his signs among them, and wonders in the land of Ham.
28 He sent darkness, and made it dark; and they rebelled not against his word.
29 He turned their waters into blood, and slew their fish.
30 Their land brought forth frogs in abundance, in the chambers of their kings.
31 He spake, and there came divers sorts of flies, *and* lice in all their coasts.

Cross references

23 Gen. 3:10
24 Prov. 3:19
26 Job 41:1
29 Job 34:14, 15; Eccl. 12:7
30 Isa. 32:15; Ezek. 37:9
35 Prov. 2:22
1 1Chr. 16:8-22
7 Isa. 26:9
8 Luke 1:72
9 Gen. 17:2; 22:16; 26:3; 28:13; 35:11; Luke 1:73; Heb. 6:17
11 Gen. 13:15; 15:18
12 Gen. 34:30; Deut. 7:7; 26:5; Heb. 11:9
14 Gen. 12:17; 20:3, 7; 35:5
16 Gen. 41:54; Lev. 26:26; Isa. 3:1; Ezek. 4:16
17 Gen. 37:28, 36; 45:5; 50:20
18 Gen. 39:20; 40:15
19 Gen. 41:25
20 Gen. 41:14
21 Gen. 41:40
23 Gen. 46:6
24 Ex. 1:7
25 Ex. 1:8
26 Ex. 3:10; 4:12, 14
27 Ps. 78:43; 106:22
28 Ex. 10:22; Ps. 99:7
29 Ex. 7:20; Ps. 78:44
30 Ex. 8:6
31 Ex. 8:17, 24; Ps. 78:45

105:8–11 These verses emphasize the longevity and permanence of God's covenant with Abraham, Isaac, and Jacob. This covenant will endure for a "thousand generations"—a metaphor meaning forever. This everlasting covenant grants the land of Canaan to the Jewish people as an eternal inheritance to them from God Himself (cf. Gen. 13:15; 15:18).

32 He gave them hail for rain, *and* flaming fire in their land.

33 He smote their vines also and their fig trees; and brake the trees of their coasts.

34 He spake, and the locusts came, and caterpillers, and that without number,

35 And did eat up all the herbs in their land, and devoured the fruit of their ground.

36 He smote also all the firstborn in their land, the chief of all their strength.

37 He brought them forth also with silver and gold: and *there was* not one feeble *person* among their tribes.

38 Egypt was glad when they departed: for the fear of them fell upon them.

39 He spread a cloud for a covering; and fire to give light in the night.

40 *The people* asked, and he brought quails, and satisfied them with the bread of heaven.

41 He opened the rock, and the waters gushed out; they ran in the dry places *like* a river.

42 For he remembered his holy promise, *and* Abraham his servant.

43 And he brought forth his people with joy, *and* his chosen with gladness:

44 And gave them the lands of the heathen: and they inherited the labour of the people;

45 That they might observe his statutes, and keep his laws. Praise ye the Lord.

PSALM 106
Israel Prone to Rebellion

1 Praise ye the Lord. O give thanks unto the Lord; for *he is* good: for his mercy *endureth* for ever.

2 Who can utter the mighty acts of the Lord? *who* can shew forth all his praise?

3 Blessed *are* they that keep judgment, *and* he that doeth righteousness at all times.

4 Remember me, O Lord, with the favour *that thou bearest unto* thy people: O visit me with thy salvation;

5 That I may see the good of thy chosen, that I may rejoice in the gladness of thy nation, that I may glory with thine inheritance.

6 We have sinned with our fathers, we have committed iniquity, we have done wickedly.

7 Our fathers understood not thy wonders in Egypt; they remembered not the multitude of thy mercies; but provoked *him* at the sea, *even* at the Red sea.

8 Nevertheless he saved them for his name's sake, that he might make his mighty power to be known.

---

32 Ex. 9:23, 25
33 Ps. 78:47
34 Ex. 10:4, 13, 14
36 Ex. 12:29
37 Ex. 12:35
38 Ex. 12:33
39 Ex. 13:21
40 Ex. 16:12
41 Ex. 17:6
42 Gen. 15:14
44 Josh. 13:7; Ps. 78:55
6 Lev. 26:40; 1Kgs. 8:47
7 Ex. 14:11, 12
8 Ex. 9:16; Ezek. 20:14
9 Ex. 14:21; Ps. 18:15; Isa. 63:11-14; Nah. 1:4
10 Ex. 14:30
11 Ex. 14:27, 28; 15:5
12 Ex. 14:31; 15:1
13 Ex. 15:24; 16:2; 17:2
14 Num. 11:4, 33; 1Cor. 10:6
15 Num. 11:31
16 Num. 16:1
17 Num. 16:31, 32
19 Ex. 32:4
23 Ex. 32:10, 11, 32
24 Deut. 8:7
26 Ex. 6:8; Deut. 32:40
28 Num. 25:2, 3
30 Num. 25:7, 8
32 Num. 20:3, 12, 13; Deut. 1:37; 3:26; Ps. 81:7
33 Num. 20:10
34 Deut. 7:2, 16; Judg. 1:21, 27-29; 2:2

---

9 He rebuked the Red sea also, and it was dried up: so he led them through the depths, as through the wilderness.

10 And he saved them from the hand of him that hated *them*, and redeemed them from the hand of the enemy.

11 And the waters covered their enemies: there was not one of them left.

12 Then believed they his words; they sang his praise.

13 They soon forgat his works; they waited not for his counsel:

14 But lusted exceedingly in the wilderness, and tempted God in the desert.

15 And he gave them their request; but sent leanness into their soul.

16 They envied Moses also in the camp, *and* Aaron the saint of the Lord.

17 The earth opened and swallowed up Dathan, and covered the company of Abiram.

18 And a fire was kindled in their company; the flame burned up the wicked.

19 They made a calf in Horeb, and worshipped the molten image.

20 Thus they changed their glory into the similitude of an ox that eateth grass.

21 They forgat God their saviour, which had done great things in Egypt;

22 Wondrous works in the land of Ham, *and* terrible things by the Red sea.

23 Therefore he said that he would destroy them, had not Moses his chosen stood before him in the breach, to turn away his wrath, lest he should destroy *them*.

24 Yea, they despised the pleasant land, they believed not his word:

25 But murmured in their tents, *and* hearkened not unto the voice of the Lord.

26 Therefore he lifted up his hand against them, to overthrow them in the wilderness:

27 To overthrow their seed also among the nations, and to scatter them in the lands.

28 They joined themselves also unto Baalpeor, and ate the sacrifices of the dead.

29 Thus they provoked *him* to anger with their inventions: and the plague brake in upon them.

30 Then stood up Phinehas, and executed judgment: and *so* the plague was stayed.

31 And that was counted unto him for righteousness unto all generations for evermore.

32 They angered *him* also at the waters of strife, so that it went ill with Moses for their sakes:

33 Because they provoked his spirit, so that he spake unadvisedly with his lips.

34 They did not destroy the nations, con-

cerning whom the LORD commanded them:
35 But were mingled among the heathen, and learned their works.
36 And they served their idols: which were a snare unto them.
37 Yea, they sacrificed their sons and their daughters unto devils,
38 And shed innocent blood, *even* the blood of their sons and of their daughters, whom they sacrificed unto the idols of Canaan: and the land was polluted with blood.
39 Thus were they defiled with their own works, and went a whoring with their own inventions.
40 Therefore was the wrath of the LORD kindled against his people, insomuch that he abhorred his own inheritance.
41 And he gave them into the hand of the heathen; and they that hated them ruled over them.
42 Their enemies also oppressed them, and they were brought into subjection under their hand.
43 Many times did he deliver them; but they provoked *him* with their counsel, and were brought low for their iniquity.
44 Nevertheless he regarded their affliction, when he heard their cry:
45 And he remembered for them his covenant, and repented according to the multitude of his mercies.
46 He made them also to be pitied of all those that carried them captives.
47 Save us, O LORD our God, and gather us from among the heathen, to give thanks unto thy holy name, *and* to triumph in thy praise.
48 Blessed *be* the LORD God of Israel from everlasting to everlasting: and let all the people say, Amen. Praise ye the LORD.

BOOK V

PSALM 107
God Rescues Us

1 O give thanks unto the LORD, for *he is* good: for his mercy *endureth* for ever.
2 Let the redeemed of the LORD say *so*, whom he hath redeemed from the hand of the enemy;
3 And gathered them out of the lands, from the east, and from the west, from the north, and from the south.
4 They wandered in the wilderness in a solitary way; they found no city to dwell in.
5 Hungry and thirsty, their soul fainted in them.
6 Then they cried unto the LORD in their

---

35 Judg. 2:2; 3:5, 6; Isa. 2:6
36 Deut. 7:16; Judg. 2:3, 12–19
37 Deut. 32:17; 2Kgs. 16:3; Ezek. 16:20
40 Deut. 9:29; Judg. 2:14
41 Judg. 2:14; Neh. 9:27
43 Judg. 2:16; Neh. 9:27
44 Judg. 3:9
45 Lev. 26:41, 42
46 Ezra 9:9; Jer. 42:12
47 1Chr. 16:35, 36
48 Ps. 41:13
1 Ps. 106:1; 118:1; 119:68; 136:1; Matt. 19:17
2 Ps. 106:10
3 Ps. 106:47; Isa. 43:5, 6; Jer. 29:14; 31:8, 10; Ezek. 39:27, 28
4 Deut. 32:10; Ps. 107:40
6 Ps. 50:15; 107:13, 19, 28; Hos. 5:15
7 Ezra 8:21
9 Luke 1:53
10 Job 36:8; Luke 1:79
12 Isa. 63:5
16 Isa. 45:2
17 Lam. 3:39
20 2Kgs. 20:4, 5; Matt. 8:8
21 Ps. 107:8, 15, 31
22 Lev. 7:12; Ps. 9:11; 50:14; 73:28; 116:17; 118:17; Heb. 13:15
25 Jon. 1:4
26 Ps. 22:14; 119:28; Nah. 2:10

---

trouble, *and* he delivered them out of their distresses.
7 And he led them forth by the right way, that they might go to a city of habitation.
8 Oh that *men* would praise the LORD *for* his goodness, and *for* his wonderful works to the children of men!
9 For he satisfieth the longing soul, and filleth the hungry soul with goodness.
10 Such as sit in darkness and in the shadow of death, *being* bound in affliction and iron;
11 Because they rebelled against the words of God, and contemned the counsel of the most High:
12 Therefore he brought down their heart with labour; they fell down, and *there was* none to help.
13 Then they cried unto the LORD in their trouble, *and* he saved them out of their distresses.
14 He brought them out of darkness and the shadow of death, and brake their bands in sunder.
15 Oh that *men* would praise the LORD *for* his goodness, and *for* his wonderful works to the children of men!
16 For he hath broken the gates of brass, and cut the bars of iron in sunder.
17 Fools because of their transgression, and because of their iniquities, are afflicted.
18 Their soul abhorreth all manner of meat; and they draw near unto the gates of death.
19 Then they cry unto the LORD in their trouble, *and* he saveth them out of their distresses.
20 He sent his word, and healed them, and delivered *them* from their destructions.
21 Oh that *men* would praise the LORD *for* his goodness, and *for* his wonderful works to the children of men!
22 And let them sacrifice the sacrifices of thanksgiving, and declare his works with rejoicing.
23 They that go down to the sea in ships, that do business in great waters;
24 These see the works of the LORD, and his wonders in the deep.
25 For he commandeth, and raiseth the stormy wind, which lifteth up the waves thereof.
26 They mount up to the heaven, they go down again to the depths: their soul is melted because of trouble.
27 They reel to and fro, and stagger like a drunken man, and are at their wits' end.
28 Then they cry unto the LORD in their

trouble, and he bringeth them out of their distresses.

29 He maketh the storm a calm, so that the waves thereof are still.

30 Then are they glad because they be quiet; so he bringeth them unto their desired haven.

31 Oh that *men* would praise the LORD *for* his goodness, and *for* his wonderful works to the children of men!

32 Let them exalt him also in the congregation of the people, and praise him in the assembly of the elders.

33 He turneth rivers into a wilderness, and the watersprings into dry ground;

34 A fruitful land into barrenness, for the wickedness of them that dwell therein.

35 He turneth the wilderness into a standing water, and dry ground into watersprings.

36 And there he maketh the hungry to dwell, that they may prepare a city for habitation;

37 And sow the fields, and plant vineyards, which may yield fruits of increase.

38 He blesseth them also, so that they are multiplied greatly; and suffereth not their cattle to decrease.

39 Again, they are minished and brought low through oppression, affliction, and sorrow.

40 He poureth contempt upon princes, and causeth them to wander in the wilderness, *where there is* no way.

41 Yet setteth he the poor on high from affliction, and maketh *him* families like a flock.

42 The righteous shall see *it*, and rejoice: and all iniquity shall stop her mouth.

43 Whoso *is* wise, and will observe these *things*, even they shall understand the lovingkindness of the LORD.

PSALM 108
A Cry for Help
A Song or Psalm of David.

1 O God, my heart is fixed; I will sing and give praise, even with my glory.

2 Awake, psaltery and harp: I *myself* will awake early.

3 I will praise thee, O LORD, among the people: and I will sing praises unto thee among the nations.

4 For thy mercy *is* great above the heavens: and thy truth *reacheth* unto the clouds.

5 Be thou exalted, O God, above the heavens: and thy glory above all the earth;

6 That thy beloved may be delivered: save *with* thy right hand, and answer me.

7 God hath spoken in his holiness; I will rejoice, I will divide Shechem, and mete out the valley of Succoth.

8 Gilead *is* mine; Manasseh *is* mine; Ephraim also *is* the strength of mine head; Judah *is* my lawgiver;

9 Moab *is* my washpot; over Edom will I cast out my shoe; over Philistia will I triumph.

10 Who will bring me into the strong city? who will lead me into Edom?

11 *Wilt* not *thou*, O God, *who* hast cast us off? and wilt not thou, O God, go forth with our hosts?

12 Give us help from trouble: for vain *is* the help of man.

13 Through God we shall do valiantly: for he *it is that* shall tread down our enemies.

PSALM 109
A Cry for Retribution
To the chief Musician, A Psalm of David.

1 Hold not thy peace, O God of my praise;

2 For the mouth of the wicked and the mouth of the deceitful are opened against me: they have spoken against me with a lying tongue.

3 They compassed me about also with words of hatred; and fought against me without a cause.

4 For my love they are my adversaries: but I *give myself unto* prayer.

5 And they have rewarded me evil for good, and hatred for my love.

6 Set thou a wicked man over him: and let Satan stand at his right hand.

7 When he shall be judged, let him be condemned: and let his prayer become sin.

8 Let his days be few; *and* let another take his office.

9 Let his children be fatherless, and his wife a widow.

10 Let his children be continually vagabonds, and beg: let them seek *their bread* also out of their desolate places.

11 Let the extortioner catch all that he hath; and let the strangers spoil his labour.

12 Let there be none to extend mercy unto

Cross-references (center column)

29 Ps. 89:9; Matt. 8:26
31 Ps. 107:8, 15, 21
32 Ps. 22:22, 25; 111:1
33 1Kgs. 17:1, 7
34 Gen. 13:10; 14:3; 19:25
35 Ps. 114:8; Isa. 41:18
38 Gen. 12:2; 17:16, 20; Ex. 1:7
39 2Kgs. 10:32
40 Job 12:21, 24
41 1Sam. 2:8; Ps. 78:52; 113:7, 8
42 Job 5:16; 22:19; Ps. 52:6; 58:10; 63:11; Prov. 10:11; Rom. 3:19
43 Ps. 64:9; Jer. 9:12; Hos. 14:9
1 Ps. 57:7
2 Ps. 57:8-11
5 Ps. 57:5, 11
6 Ps. 60:5
8 Gen. 49:10
10 Ps. 60:9
13 Ps. 60:12
1 Ps. 83:1
3 Ps. 35:7; 69:4; John 15:25
5 Ps. 35:7, 12; 38:20
6 Zech. 3:1
7 Prov. 28:9
8 Acts 1:20
9 Ex. 22:24
11 Job 5:5; 18:9

109:8 let another take his office. The apostle Peter refers to this verse, combining it with Psalm 69:25 to refer to Judas Iscariot's suicide, which removed him from his place among the twelve disciples and led to his being replaced by Matthias (Acts 1:12–26).

him: neither let there be any to favour his fatherless children.

13 Let his posterity be cut off; *and* in the generation following let their name be blotted out.

14 Let the iniquity of his fathers be remembered with the LORD; and let not the sin of his mother be blotted out.

15 Let them be before the LORD continually, that he may cut off the memory of them from the earth.

16 Because that he remembered not to shew mercy, but persecuted the poor and needy man, that he might even slay the broken in heart.

17 As he loved cursing, so let it come unto him: as he delighted not in blessing, so let it be far from him.

18 As he clothed himself with cursing like as with his garment, so let it come into his bowels like water, and like oil into his bones.

19 Let it be unto him as the garment *which* covereth him, and for a girdle wherewith he is girded continually.

20 *Let* this *be* the reward of mine adversaries from the LORD, and of them that speak evil against my soul.

21 But do thou for me, O GOD the Lord, for thy name's sake: because thy mercy *is* good, deliver thou me.

22 For I *am* poor and needy, and my heart is wounded within me.

23 I am gone like the shadow when it declineth: I am tossed up and down as the locust.

24 My knees are weak through fasting; and my flesh faileth of fatness.

25 I became also a reproach unto them: *when* they looked upon me they shaked their heads.

26 Help me, O LORD my God: O save me according to thy mercy:

27 That they may know that this *is* thy hand; *that* thou, LORD, hast done it.

28 Let them curse, but bless thou: when they arise, let them be ashamed; but let thy servant rejoice.

29 Let mine adversaries be clothed with shame, and let them cover themselves with their own confusion, as with a mantle.

30 I will greatly praise the LORD with my mouth; yea, I will praise him among the multitude.

31 For he shall stand at the right hand of the poor, to save *him* from those that condemn his soul.

PSALM 110
The Chosen King of the Lord
A Psalm of David.

1 The LORD said unto my Lord, Sit thou at my right hand, until I make thine enemies thy footstool.

2 The LORD shall send the rod of thy strength out of Zion: rule thou in the midst of thine enemies.

3 Thy people *shall be* willing in the day of thy power, in the beauties of holiness from the womb of the morning: thou hast the dew of thy youth.

4 The LORD hath sworn, and will not repent, Thou *art* a priest for ever after the order of Melchizedek.

5 The Lord at thy right hand shall strike through kings in the day of his wrath.

6 He shall judge among the heathen, he shall fill *the places* with the dead bodies; he shall wound the heads over many countries.

7 He shall drink of the brook in the way: therefore shall he lift up the head.

PSALM 111
Praising God

1 Praise ye the LORD. I will praise the LORD with *my* whole heart, in the assembly of the upright, and *in* the congregation.

13 Job 18:19; Ps. 37:28; Prov. 10:7
14 Ex. 20:5; Neh. 4:5; Jer. 18:23
15 Job 18:17; Ps. 34:16
16 Ps. 34:18
17 Prov. 14:14; Ezek. 35:6
23 Ps. 102:11; 144:4
24 Heb. 12:12
25 Ps. 22:6, 7; Matt. 27:39
28 2Sam. 16:11, 12; Isa. 65:14
29 Ps. 35:26; 132:18
31 Ps. 16:8; 73:23; 110:5; 121:5
1 Ps. 45:6, 7; Matt. 22:44; Mark 12:36; Luke 20:42; Acts 2:34; 1Cor. 15:25; Heb. 1:13; 1Pet. 3:22
3 Judg. 5:2; Ps. 96:9
4 Num. 23:19; Zech. 6:13; Heb. 5:6; 6:20; 7:17, 21
5 Rev. 11:18
7 Judg. 7:5
1 Ps. 35:18; 89:5; 107:32; 109:30; 149:1

110:1 This psalm is quoted more often in the New Testament than any other. Jesus Himself quoted from it to prove His identity with God the Father (see Matt. 22:41–46). He asked the Pharisees whose son the Messiah was, and they answered, "The Son of David." Then, quoting Psalm 110:1, Jesus pointed out that David called him "Lord" when he said: "The LORD *(Jehovah)* said unto my Lord *(adonai)*, Sit thou at my right hand." In this amazing verse, God the Father speaks to God the Son and invites Him to share His throne. Jesus used this passage to point out that the Christ (Hebr., *Messiah*) was both the son of David and the Lord of David because He was the Son of God who had been born into the human race through the line of David.

110:1–7 In these verses, David pictures the Messiah as both King and Priest. He will rule out of Zion as King and will also function as an eternal Priest according to the "order of Melchizedek." Hebrews 5:6 quotes verse 4 to verify the legitimacy of Jesus' priesthood. He is not a priest after the order of Levi or Aaron, since the Messiah is from the tribe of Judah, but He is an eternal priest of God like Melchizedek (see Gen. 14:18–20). The psalm also looks ahead to the triumphant millennial reign of Christ when He will rule the heathen.

2 The works of the LORD *are* great, sought out of all them that have pleasure therein.
3 His work *is* honourable and glorious: and his righteousness endureth for ever.
4 He hath made his wonderful works to be remembered: the LORD *is* gracious and full of compassion.
5 He hath given meat unto them that fear him: he will ever be mindful of his covenant.
6 He hath shewed his people the power of his works, that he may give them the heritage of the heathen.
7 The works of his hands *are* verity and judgment; all his commandments *are* sure.
8 They stand fast for ever and ever, *and are* done in truth and uprightness.
9 He sent redemption unto his people: he hath commanded his covenant for ever: holy and reverend *is* his name.
10 The fear of the LORD *is* the beginning of wisdom: a good understanding have all they that do *his commandments*: his praise endureth for ever.

PSALM 112
A Godly Person Is Prosperous

1 Praise ye the LORD. Blessed *is* the man *that* feareth the LORD, *that* delighteth greatly in his commandments.
2 His seed shall be mighty upon earth: the generation of the upright shall be blessed.
3 Wealth and riches *shall be* in his house: and his righteousness endureth for ever.
4 Unto the upright there ariseth light in the darkness: *he is* gracious, and full of compassion, and righteous.
5 A good man sheweth favour, and lendeth: he will guide his affairs with discretion.
6 Surely he shall not be moved for ever: the righteous shall be in everlasting remembrance.
7 He shall not be afraid of evil tidings: his heart is fixed, trusting in the LORD.
8 His heart *is* established, he shall not be afraid, until he see *his desire* upon his enemies.
9 He hath dispersed, he hath given to the poor; his righteousness endureth for ever; his horn shall be exalted with honour.
10 The wicked shall see *it*, and be grieved; he shall gnash with his teeth, and melt away: the desire of the wicked shall perish.

PSALM 113
God Raises Up the Humble

1 Praise ye the LORD. Praise, O ye servants of the LORD, praise the name of the LORD.

2 Job 38; 39; 40; 41
5 Matt. 6:26, 33
8 Matt. 5:18; Rev. 15:3
9 Matt. 1:21; Luke 1:49, 68
10 Prov. 1:7; 3:4; 9:10
3 Matt. 6:33
4 Job 11:17; Ps. 97:11
5 Ps. 37:26; Luke 6:35; Eph. 5:15; Col. 4:5
6 Ps. 15:5; Prov. 10:7
7 Ps. 57:7; 64:10; Prov. 1:33
8 Ps. 59:10; 118:7; Prov. 1:33
9 Deut. 24:13; Ps. 75:10; 2Cor. 9:9
10 Ps. 37:12; 58:7, 8; Prov. 10:28; 11:7; Luke 13:28
1 Ps. 135:1
2 Dan. 2:20
3 Isa. 59:19; Mal. 1:11
4 Ps. 8:1; 97:9; 99:2
5 Ps. 89:6
6 Ps. 11:4; 138:6; Isa. 57:15
7 1Sam. 2:8; Ps. 107:41
9 1Sam. 2:5
1 Ex. 13:3
3 Ex. 14:21; Josh. 3:13
5 Hab. 3:8
8 Ex. 17:6; Num. 20:11; Ps. 107:35
1 Isa. 48:11; Ezek. 36:32
2 Ps. 42:3, 10; 79:10; Joel 2:17
3 1Chr. 16:26; Ps. 135:6; Dan. 4:35
4 Deut. 4:28; Ps. 135:15-17; Jer. 10:3

2 Blessed be the name of the LORD from this time forth and for evermore.
3 From the rising of the sun unto the going down of the same the LORD's name *is* to be praised.
4 The LORD *is* high above all nations, *and* his glory above the heavens.
5 Who *is* like unto the LORD our God, who dwelleth on high,
6 Who humbleth *himself* to behold *the things that are* in heaven, and in the earth!
7 He raiseth up the poor out of the dust, *and* lifteth the needy out of the dunghill;
8 That he may set *him* with princes, *even* with the princes of his people.
9 He maketh the barren woman to keep house, *and to be* a joyful mother of children. Praise ye the LORD.

PSALM 114
A Song for the Passover Feast

1 When Israel went out of Egypt, the house of Jacob from a people of strange language;
2 Judah was his sanctuary, *and* Israel his dominion.
3 The sea saw *it*, and fled: Jordan was driven back.
4 The mountains skipped like rams, *and* the little hills like lambs.
5 What *ailed* thee, O thou sea, that thou fleddest? thou Jordan, *that* thou wast driven back?
6 Ye mountains, *that* ye skipped like rams; *and* ye little hills, like lambs?
7 Tremble, thou earth, at the presence of the Lord, at the presence of the God of Jacob;
8 Which turned the rock *into* a standing water, the flint into a fountain of waters.

PSALM 115
The One True God

1 Not unto us, O LORD, not unto us, but unto thy name give glory, for thy mercy, *and* for thy truth's sake.
2 Wherefore should the heathen say, Where *is* now their God?
3 But our God *is* in the heavens: he hath done whatsoever he hath pleased.
4 Their idols *are* silver and gold, the work of men's hands.
5 They have mouths, but they speak not: eyes have they, but they see not:
6 They have ears, but they hear not: noses have they, but they smell not:
7 They have hands, but they handle not:

feet have they, but they walk not: neither speak they through their throat.

8 They that make them are like unto them; *so is* every one that trusteth in them.

9 O Israel, trust thou in the LORD: he *is* their help and their shield.

10 O house of Aaron, trust in the LORD: he *is* their help and their shield.

11 Ye that fear the LORD, trust in the LORD: he *is* their help and their shield.

12 The LORD hath been mindful of us: he will bless *us*; he will bless the house of Israel; he will bless the house of Aaron.

13 He will bless them that fear the LORD, *both* small and great.

14 The LORD shall increase you more and more, you and your children.

15 Ye *are* blessed of the LORD which made heaven and earth.

16 The heaven, *even* the heavens, *are* the LORD's: but the earth hath he given to the children of men.

17 The dead praise not the LORD, neither any that go down into silence.

18 But we will bless the LORD from this time forth and for evermore. Praise the LORD.

PSALM 116
Rescued from Death

1 I love the LORD, because he hath heard my voice *and* my supplications.

2 Because he hath inclined his ear unto me, therefore will I call upon *him* as long as I live.

3 The sorrows of death compassed me, and the pains of hell gat hold upon me: I found trouble and sorrow.

4 Then called I upon the name of the LORD; O LORD, I beseech thee, deliver my soul.

5 Gracious *is* the LORD, and righteous; yea, our God *is* merciful.

6 The LORD preserveth the simple: I was brought low, and he helped me.

7 Return unto thy rest, O my soul; for the LORD hath dealt bountifully with thee.

8 For thou hast delivered my soul from death, mine eyes from tears, *and* my feet from falling.

9 I will walk before the LORD in the land of the living.

10 I believed, therefore have I spoken: I was greatly afflicted:

11 I said in my haste, All men *are* liars.

12 What shall I render unto the LORD *for* all his benefits toward me?

13 I will take the cup of salvation, and call upon the name of the LORD.

8 Ps. 135:18; Isa. 44:9, 10, 11; Jon. 2:8; Hab. 2:18, 19

9 Ps. 33:20; 118:2-4; 135:19, 20; Prov. 30:5

13 Ps. 128:1, 4

15 Gen. 1:1; 14:19; Ps. 96:5

17 Ps. 6:5; 88:10, 11, 12; Isa. 38:18

18 Ps. 113:2; Dan. 2:20

1 Ps. 18:1

3 Ps. 18:4-6

5 Ezra 9:15; Neh. 9:8; Ps. 103:8; 119:137; 145:17

7 Ps. 13:6; 119:17; Jer. 6:16; Matt. 11:29

8 Ps. 56:13

9 Ps. 27:13

10 2Cor. 4:13

11 Ps. 31:22; Rom. 3:4

14 Ps. 22:25; 116:18; Jon. 2:9

16 Ps. 86:16; 119:125; 143:12

17 Lev. 7:12; Ps. 50:14; 107:22

19 Ps. 96:8; 100:4; 135:2

1 Rom. 15:11

2 Ps. 100:5

1 1Chr. 16:8, 34; Ps. 106:1; 107:1; 136:1

5 Ps. 18:19; 120:1

6 Ps. 27:1; 56:4, 11; 146:5; Isa. 51:12; Heb. 13:6

12 Deut. 1:44; Eccl. 7:6; Nah. 1:10

14 Ex. 15:2; Isa. 12:2

14 I will pay my vows unto the LORD now in the presence of all his people.

15 Precious in the sight of the LORD *is* the death of his saints.

16 O LORD, truly I *am* thy servant; I *am* thy servant, *and* the son of thine handmaid: thou hast loosed my bonds.

17 I will offer to thee the sacrifice of thanksgiving, and will call upon the name of the LORD.

18 I will pay my vows unto the LORD now in the presence of all his people,

19 In the courts of the LORD's house, in the midst of thee, O Jerusalem. Praise ye the LORD.

PSALM 117
Praise the Lord

1 O praise the LORD, all ye nations: praise him, all ye people.

2 For his merciful kindness is great toward us: and the truth of the LORD *endureth* for ever. Praise ye the LORD.

PSALM 118
Thanksgiving

1 O give thanks unto the LORD; for *he is* good: because his mercy *endureth* for ever.

2 Let Israel now say, that his mercy *endureth* for ever.

3 Let the house of Aaron now say, that his mercy *endureth* for ever.

4 Let them now that fear the LORD say, that his mercy *endureth* for ever.

5 I called upon the LORD in distress: the LORD answered me, *and set me* in a large place.

6 The LORD *is* on my side; I will not fear: what can man do unto me?

7 The LORD taketh my part with them that help me: therefore shall I see *my desire* upon them that hate me.

8 *It is* better to trust in the LORD than to put confidence in man.

9 *It is* better to trust in the LORD than to put confidence in princes.

10 All nations compassed me about: but in the name of the LORD will I destroy them.

11 They compassed me about; yea, they compassed me about: but in the name of the LORD I will destroy them.

12 They compassed me about like bees; they are quenched as the fire of thorns: for in the name of the LORD I will destroy them.

13 Thou hast thrust sore at me that I might fall: but the LORD helped me.

14 The LORD *is* my strength and song, and is become my salvation.

15 The voice of rejoicing and salvation *is* in the tabernacles of the righteous: the right hand of the Lord doeth valiantly.
16 The right hand of the Lord is exalted: the right hand of the Lord doeth valiantly.
17 I shall not die, but live, and declare the works of the Lord.
18 The Lord hath chastened me sore: but he hath not given me over unto death.
19 Open to me the gates of righteousness: I will go into them, *and* I will praise the Lord:
20 This gate of the Lord, into which the righteous shall enter.
21 I will praise thee: for thou hast heard me, and art become my salvation.
22 The stone *which* the builders refused is become the head *stone* of the corner.
23 This is the Lord's doing; it *is* marvellous in our eyes.
24 This *is* the day *which* the Lord hath made; we will rejoice and be glad in it.
25 Save now, I beseech thee, O Lord: O Lord, I beseech thee, send now prosperity.
26 Blessed *be* he that cometh in the name of the Lord: we have blessed you out of the house of the Lord.
27 God *is* the Lord, which hath shewed us light: bind the sacrifice with cords, *even* unto the horns of the altar.
28 Thou *art* my God, and I will praise thee: *thou art* my God, I will exalt thee.
29 O give thanks unto the Lord; for *he is* good: for his mercy *endureth* for ever.

PSALM 119
The Law of the Lord
א ALEPH
1 Blessed *are* the undefiled in the way, who walk in the law of the Lord.
2 Blessed *are* they that keep his testimonies, *and that* seek him with the whole heart.
3 They also do no iniquity: they walk in his ways.
4 Thou hast commanded *us* to keep thy precepts diligently.
5 O that my ways were directed to keep thy statutes!
6 Then shall I not be ashamed, when I have respect unto all thy commandments.
7 I will praise thee with uprightness of

Cross references (center column)
16 Ex. 15:6
17 Ps. 6:5; 73:28; Hab. 1:12
18 2Cor. 6:9
19 Isa. 26:2
20 Ps. 24:7; Isa. 35:8; Rev. 21:27; 22:14, 15
21 Ps. 116:1; 118:14
22 Matt. 21:42; Mark 12:10; Luke 20:17; Acts 4:11; Eph. 2:20; 1Pet. 2:4, 7
26 Zech. 4:7; Matt. 21:9; 23:39; Mark 11:9; Luke 19:38
27 Esth. 8:16; 1Pet. 2:9
28 Ex. 15:2; Isa. 25:1
29 Ps. 118:1
1 Ps. 128:1
3 1John 3:9; 5:18
6 Job 22:26; 1John 2:28
7 Ps. 119:171
10 2Chr. 15:15; Ps. 119:21, 118
11 Ps. 37:31; Luke 2:19, 51
12 Ps. 25:4; 119:26, 33, 64, 68, 108, 124
13 Ps. 34:11
15 Ps. 1:2; 119:23, 48, 78
16 Ps. 1:2; 119:35, 47, 70, 77
17 Ps. 116:7
19 Gen. 47:9; 1Chr. 29:15; Ps. 39:12

heart, when I shall have learned thy righteous judgments.
8 I will keep thy statutes: O forsake me not utterly.

ב BETH
9 Wherewithal shall a young man cleanse his way? by taking heed *thereto* according to thy word.
10 With my whole heart have I sought thee: O let me not wander from thy commandments.
11 Thy word have I hid in mine heart, that I might not sin against thee.
12 Blessed *art* thou, O Lord: teach me thy statutes.
13 With my lips have I declared all the judgments of thy mouth.
14 I have rejoiced in the way of thy testimonies, as *much as* in all riches.
15 I will meditate in thy precepts, and have respect unto thy ways.
16 I will delight myself in thy statutes: I will not forget thy word.

ג GIMEL
17 Deal bountifully with thy servant, *that* I may live, and keep thy word.
18 Open thou mine eyes, that I may behold wondrous things out of thy law.
19 I *am* a stranger in the earth: hide not thy commandments from me.
20 My soul breaketh for the longing *that it hath* unto thy judgments at all times.
21 Thou hast rebuked the proud *that are* cursed, which do err from thy commandments.
22 Remove from me reproach and contempt; for I have kept thy testimonies.
23 Princes also did sit *and* speak against me: *but* thy servant did meditate in thy statutes.
24 Thy testimonies also *are* my delight *and* my counsellors.

ד DALETH
25 My soul cleaveth unto the dust: quicken thou me according to thy word.
26 I have declared my ways, and thou heardest me: teach me thy statutes.
27 Make me to understand the way of thy precepts: so shall I talk of thy wondrous works.

118:22 The stone which the builders refused. This verse contains one of the most important messianic predictions—that of the rejection and restoration of Christ (cf. Matt. 21:42; Mark 12:10; Luke 20:17; Acts 4:11). Rejected by the "builders" of Israel's religious system, Jesus Christ will still become the "headstone of the corner." Since Jesus truly is the Messiah, He will become the cornerstone of the Christian faith (Eph. 2:20; cf. Isa. 28:16 with 1 Pet. 2:6).

How to Study the Bible

By Tim LaHaye

The foundation of Bible learning must come through Bible reading. It has been my observation that unless a person has a regular habit of reading the Bible, he will not benefit greatly from his studies. I have never met a person who enjoyed studying God's Word who had not first developed the habit of regularly reading it.

When reading the Bible, do not get so bogged down in the complexities of verse or word analysis that you lose the overall purpose and meaning of the writer. To gain the most value from your reading, carefully consider the following techniques:

1. Read Daily

Job 23:12 says, "I have esteemed the words of his mouth more than my necessary food." From that statement we can deduce that daily Bible reading is to your spiritual life what daily eating is to your physical life. We are all familiar with the necessity of regular mealtimes; however, it is also important to set and keep a designated time for Bible reading.

2. Read Devotionally

Prayerfully ask God to send some message each day before you read His Word. Many times He will give you a thought that answers the hunger of your heart. Sometimes He will give you a blessing that you will need later in the day. In either case it will be helpful to write the message down. Devotional reading that emphasizes the truths revealed in Scripture provides the spiritual instruction for daily living that every Christian needs.

> *The Bible is a literal treasure chest of the "wisdom of God" for everyday living.*

3. Do a Subject Analysis

Nothing will complete your understanding of biblical truth like your own personal subject analysis. Doing such an analysis is easy. Just follow these simple steps:

a. Look for more information on the subject you are studying by consulting a good Bible concordance.

b. Look up all cross-references to that subject, particularly those in the New Testament and in Psalms and Proverbs. Start with the New Testament references, for God has revealed to us many things necessary to the Christian life in the New Testament. Psalms and Proverbs are included because God gave them through the wisest man who has ever lived, Solomon, and the man who taught him most of his wisdom, King David.

c. Begin keeping a spiritual journal by jotting down the concepts or basic principles that God is teaching on the subject you are studying. Journal entries should be no more than a full page per each day's Bible reading (see the article entitled "How to Keep a Spiritual Journal" by Tim LaHaye).

d. Search a good Bible dictionary, and examine the definition of the subject being studied. If your analysis is seriously different from that of the dictionary, then you should go back over your analysis to see if you missed something in your study.

The Bible is a literal treasure chest of the "wisdom of God" for everyday living, but most Christians do not know the book sufficiently to provide that wisdom when they need it. Daily reading combined with the subject analysis method is the best way to learn the truths found in the Word of God. Intensive Bible study, along with repetition and Scripture memorization, will give you a thorough grasp of the Bible in a relatively short period of time. Most importantly, it will make you "strong in the Lord, and in the power of his might" (Eph. 6:10).

28 My soul melteth for heaviness: strengthen thou me according unto thy word.

29 Remove from me the way of lying: and grant me thy law graciously.

30 I have chosen the way of truth: thy judgments have I laid *before me.*

31 I have stuck unto thy testimonies: O LORD, put me not to shame.

32 I will run the way of thy commandments, when thou shalt enlarge my heart.

ה HE

33 Teach me, O LORD, the way of thy statutes; and I shall keep it *unto* the end.

34 Give me understanding, and I shall keep thy law; yea, I shall observe it with *my* whole heart.

35 Make me to go in the path of thy commandments; for therein do I delight.

36 Incline my heart unto thy testimonies, and not to covetousness.

37 Turn away mine eyes from beholding vanity; *and* quicken thou me in thy way.

38 Stablish thy word unto thy servant, who *is devoted* to thy fear.

39 Turn away my reproach which I fear: for thy judgments *are* good.

40 Behold, I have longed after thy precepts: quicken me in thy righteousness.

ו VAW

41 Let thy mercies come also unto me, O LORD, *even* thy salvation, according to thy word.

42 So shall I have wherewith to answer him that reproacheth me: for I trust in thy word.

43 And take not the word of truth utterly out of my mouth; for I have hoped in thy judgments.

44 So shall I keep thy law continually for ever and ever.

45 And I will walk at liberty: for I seek thy precepts.

46 I will speak of thy testimonies also before kings, and will not be ashamed.

47 And I will delight myself in thy commandments, which I have loved.

48 My hands also will I lift up unto thy commandments, which I have loved; and I will meditate in thy statutes.

ז ZAYIN

49 Remember the word unto thy servant, upon which thou hast caused me to hope.

50 This *is* my comfort in my affliction: for thy word hath quickened me.

51 The proud have had me greatly in deri-

---

33 Matt. 10:22
34 Prov. 2:6
37 Ps. 119:40; Prov. 23:5; Isa. 33:15
38 2Sam. 7:25
40 Ps. 119:20, 25, 37, 88, 107, 149, 156, 159
41 Ps. 106:4; 119:77
46 Ps. 138:1; Matt. 10:18, 19; Acts 26:1, 2
47 Ps. 119:16
48 Ps. 119:15
49 Ps. 119:74, 81, 147
50 Rom. 15:4
51 Job 23:11; Ps. 44:18; 119:157; Jer. 20:7
53 Ezra 9:3
55 Ps. 63:6
57 Ps. 16:5; Jer. 10:16; Lam. 3:24
58 Ps. 119:41
59 Luke 15:17, 18
62 Acts 16:25
64 Ps. 33:5; 119:12, 26
68 Ps. 106:1
69 Job 13:4
70 Ps. 17:10; 119:35; Isa. 6:10; Acts 28:27
71 Ps. 119:67; Heb. 12:10, 11
72 Ps. 19:10; 119:127; Prov. 8:10, 11, 19
73 Job 10:8; Ps. 100:3; 119:34, 144; 138:8; 139:14
74 Ps. 34:2; 119:49, 147

---

sion: *yet* have I not declined from thy law.

52 I remembered thy judgments of old, O LORD; and have comforted myself.

53 Horror hath taken hold upon me because of the wicked that forsake thy law.

54 Thy statutes have been my songs in the house of my pilgrimage.

55 I have remembered thy name, O LORD, in the night, and have kept thy law.

56 This I had, because I kept thy precepts.

ח HETH

57 *Thou art* my portion, O LORD: I have said that I would keep thy words.

58 I intreated thy favour with *my* whole heart: be merciful unto me according to thy word.

59 I thought on my ways, and turned my feet unto thy testimonies.

60 I made haste, and delayed not to keep thy commandments.

61 The bands of the wicked have robbed me: *but* I have not forgotten thy law.

62 At midnight I will rise to give thanks unto thee because of thy righteous judgments.

63 I *am* a companion of all *them* that fear thee, and of them that keep thy precepts.

64 The earth, O LORD, is full of thy mercy: teach me thy statutes.

ט TETH

65 Thou hast dealt well with thy servant, O LORD, according unto thy word.

66 Teach me good judgment and knowledge: for I have believed thy commandments.

67 Before I was afflicted I went astray: but now have I kept thy word.

68 Thou *art* good, and doest good; teach me thy statutes.

69 The proud have forged a lie against me: *but* I will keep thy precepts with *my* whole heart.

70 Their heart is as fat as grease; *but* I delight in thy law.

71 *It is* good for me that I have been afflicted; that I might learn thy statutes.

72 The law of thy mouth *is* better unto me than thousands of gold and silver.

י YOD

73 Thy hands have made me and fashioned me: give me understanding, that I may learn thy commandments.

74 They that fear thee will be glad when they see me; because I have hoped in thy word.

75 I know, O LORD, that thy judgments *are* right, and *that* thou in faithfulness hast afflicted me.
76 Let, I pray thee, thy merciful kindness be for my comfort, according to thy word unto thy servant.
77 Let thy tender mercies come unto me, that I may live: for thy law *is* my delight.
78 Let the proud be ashamed; for they dealt perversely with me without a cause: *but* I will meditate in thy precepts.
79 Let those that fear thee turn unto me, and those that have known thy testimonies.
80 Let my heart be sound in thy statutes; that I be not ashamed.

כ KAPH
81 My soul fainteth for thy salvation: *but* I hope in thy word.
82 Mine eyes fail for thy word, saying, When wilt thou comfort me?
83 For I am become like a bottle in the smoke; *yet* do I not forget thy statutes.
84 How many *are* the days of thy servant? when wilt thou execute judgment on them that persecute me?
85 The proud have digged pits for me, which *are* not after thy law.
86 All thy commandments *are* faithful: they persecute me wrongfully; help thou me.
87 They had almost consumed me upon earth; but I forsook not thy precepts.
88 Quicken me after thy lovingkindness; so shall I keep the testimony of thy mouth.

ל LAMEDH
89 For ever, O LORD, thy word is settled in heaven.
90 Thy faithfulness *is* unto all generations: thou hast established the earth, and it abideth.
91 They continue this day according to thine ordinances: for all *are* thy servants.
92 Unless thy law *had been* my delights, I should then have perished in mine affliction.
93 I will never forget thy precepts: for with them thou hast quickened me.
94 I *am* thine, save me; for I have sought thy precepts.
95 The wicked have waited for me to destroy me: *but* I will consider thy testimonies.
96 I have seen an end of all perfection: *but* thy commandment *is* exceeding broad.

מ MEM
97 O how love I thy law! it *is* my meditation all the day.

98 Thou through thy commandments hast made me wiser than mine enemies: for they *are* ever with me.
99 I have more understanding than all my teachers: for thy testimonies *are* my meditation.
100 I understand more than the ancients, because I keep thy precepts.
101 I have refrained my feet from every evil way, that I might keep thy word.
102 I have not departed from thy judgments: for thou hast taught me.
103 How sweet are thy words unto my taste! *yea, sweeter* than honey to my mouth!
104 Through thy precepts I get understanding: therefore I hate every false way.

נ NUN
105 Thy word *is* a lamp unto my feet, and a light unto my path.
106 I have sworn, and I will perform *it*, that I will keep thy righteous judgments.
107 I am afflicted very much: quicken me, O LORD, according unto thy word.
108 Accept, I beseech thee, the freewill offerings of my mouth, O LORD, and teach me thy judgments.
109 My soul *is* continually in my hand: yet do I not forget thy law.
110 The wicked have laid a snare for me: yet I erred not from thy precepts.
111 Thy testimonies have I taken as an heritage for ever: for they *are* the rejoicing of my heart.
112 I have inclined mine heart to perform thy statutes alway, *even unto* the end.

ס SAMEKH
113 I hate *vain* thoughts: but thy law do I love.
114 Thou *art* my hiding place and my shield: I hope in thy word.
115 Depart from me, ye evildoers: for I will keep the commandments of my God.
116 Uphold me according unto thy word, that I may live: and let me not be ashamed of my hope.
117 Hold thou me up, and I shall be safe: and I will have respect unto thy statutes continually.
118 Thou hast trodden down all them that err from thy statutes: for their deceit *is* falsehood.
119 Thou puttest away all the wicked of the earth *like* dross: therefore I love thy testimonies.
120 My flesh trembleth for fear of thee; and I am afraid of thy judgments.

---

75 Heb. 12:10
77 Ps. 119:24, 41, 47, 174
78 Ps. 25:3; 119:23, 86
81 Ps. 73:26; 84:2; 119:74, 114
82 Ps. 69:3; 119:123
83 Job 30:30
84 Ps. 39:4; Rev. 6:10
85 Ps. 35:7; Prov. 16:27
86 Ps. 35:19; 38:19; 119:78
88 Ps. 119:40
89 Ps. 89:2; Matt. 24:34, 35; 1Pet. 1:25
90 Ps. 89:1
91 Jer. 33:25
92 Ps. 119:24
96 Matt. 5:18; 24:35
97 Ps. 1:2
98 Deut. 4:6, 8
99 2Tim. 3:15
100 Job 32:7-9
101 Prov. 1:15
103 Ps. 19:10; Prov. 8:11
104 Ps. 119:128
105 Prov. 6:23
106 Neh. 10:29
107 Ps. 119:88
108 Ps. 119:12, 26; Hos. 14:2; Heb. 13:15
110 Ps. 119:10, 21; 140:5; 141:9
116 Rom. 5:5; 9:33; 10:11
119 Ezek. 22:18

ע AYIN

121 I have done judgment and justice: leave me not to mine oppressors.

122 Be surety for thy servant for good: let not the proud oppress me.

123 Mine eyes fail for thy salvation, and for the word of thy righteousness.

124 Deal with thy servant according unto thy mercy, and teach me thy statutes.

125 I *am* thy servant; give me understanding, that I may know thy testimonies.

126 *It is* time for *thee*, LORD, to work: *for* they have made void thy law.

127 Therefore I love thy commandments above gold; yea, above fine gold.

128 Therefore I esteem all *thy* precepts *concerning* all *things to be* right; *and* I hate every false way.

פ PE

129 Thy testimonies *are* wonderful: therefore doth my soul keep them.

130 The entrance of thy words giveth light; it giveth understanding unto the simple.

131 I opened my mouth, and panted: for I longed for thy commandments.

132 Look thou upon me, and be merciful unto me, as thou usest to do unto those that love thy name.

133 Order my steps in thy word: and let not any iniquity have dominion over me.

134 Deliver me from the oppression of man: so will I keep thy precepts.

135 Make thy face to shine upon thy servant; and teach me thy statutes.

136 Rivers of waters run down mine eyes, because they keep not thy law.

צ TSADDE

137 Righteous *art* thou, O LORD, and upright *are* thy judgments.

138 Thy testimonies *that* thou hast commanded *are* righteous and very faithful.

139 My zeal hath consumed me, because mine enemies have forgotten thy words.

140 Thy word *is* very pure: therefore thy servant loveth it.

141 I *am* small and despised: *yet* do not I forget thy precepts.

142 Thy righteousness *is* an everlasting righteousness, and thy law *is* the truth.

143 Trouble and anguish have taken hold on me: *yet* thy commandments *are* my delights.

144 The righteousness of thy testimonies *is* everlasting: give me understanding, and I shall live.

Center references

122 Heb. 7:22
125 Ps. 116:16
128 Ps. 119:104
131 Ps. 119:20
132 Ps. 106:4; 2Thess. 1:6, 7
133 Ps. 17:5; 19:13; Rom. 6:12
134 Luke 1:74
135 Ps. 4:6; 119:12, 26
136 Jer. 9:1; 14:17; Ezek. 9:4
137 Ezra 9:15; Neh. 9:33; Jer. 12:1; Dan. 9:7
138 Ps. 19:7-9
139 Ps. 69:9; John 2:17
140 Ps. 12:6; 18:30; 119:8; Prov. 30:5
142 Ps. 19:9; 119:151; John 17:17
143 Ps. 119:77
144 Ps. 119:34, 73, 169
147 Ps. 5:3; 88:13; 119:74; 130:6
148 Ps. 63:1, 6
149 Ps. 119:40, 154
151 Ps. 119:142; 145:18
152 Luke 21:33
153 Lam. 5:1
154 1Sam. 24:15
158 Ezek. 9:4
161 1Sam. 24:11, 14; 26:18; Ps. 119:23
165 Prov. 3:2; Isa. 32:17

ק QOPH

145 I cried with *my* whole heart; hear me, O LORD: I will keep thy statutes.

146 I cried unto thee; save me, and I shall keep thy testimonies.

147 I prevented the dawning of the morning, and cried: I hoped in thy word.

148 Mine eyes prevent the *night* watches, that I might meditate in thy word.

149 Hear my voice according unto thy lovingkindness: O LORD, quicken me according to thy judgment.

150 They draw nigh that follow after mischief: they are far from thy law.

151 Thou *art* near, O LORD; and all thy commandments *are* truth.

152 Concerning thy testimonies, I have known of old that thou hast founded them for ever.

ר RESH

153 Consider mine affliction, and deliver me: for I do not forget thy law.

154 Plead my cause, and deliver me: quicken me according to thy word.

155 Salvation *is* far from the wicked: for they seek not thy statutes.

156 Great *are* thy tender mercies, O LORD: quicken me according to thy judgments.

157 Many *are* my persecutors and mine enemies; *yet* do I not decline from thy testimonies.

158 I beheld the transgressors, and was grieved; because they kept not thy word.

159 Consider how I love thy precepts: quicken me, O LORD, according to thy lovingkindness.

160 Thy word *is* true *from* the beginning: and every one of thy righteous judgments *endureth* for ever.

ש SHIN

161 Princes have persecuted me without a cause: but my heart standeth in awe of thy word.

162 I rejoice at thy word, as one that findeth great spoil.

163 I hate and abhor lying: *but* thy law do I love.

164 Seven times a day do I praise thee because of thy righteous judgments.

165 Great peace have they which love thy law: and nothing shall offend them.

166 LORD, I have hoped for thy salvation, and done thy commandments.

167 My soul hath kept thy testimonies; and I love them exceedingly.

168 I have kept thy precepts and thy testimonies: for all my ways *are* before thee.

ת TAU

169 Let my cry come near before thee, O LORD: give me understanding according to thy word.

170 Let my supplication come before thee: deliver me according to thy word.

171 My lips shall utter praise, when thou hast taught me thy statutes.

172 My tongue shall speak of thy word: for all thy commandments *are* righteousness.

173 Let thine hand help me; for I have chosen thy precepts.

174 I have longed for thy salvation, O LORD; and thy law *is* my delight.

175 Let my soul live, and it shall praise thee; and let thy judgments help me.

176 I have gone astray like a lost sheep; seek thy servant; for I do not forget thy commandments.

PSALM 120
A Prayer for Deliverance

A Song of degrees.

1 In my distress I cried unto the LORD, and he heard me.

2 Deliver my soul, O LORD, from lying lips, *and* from a deceitful tongue.

3 What shall be given unto thee? or what shall be done unto thee, thou false tongue?

4 Sharp arrows of the mighty, with coals of juniper.

5 Woe is me, that I sojourn in Mesech, *that* I dwell in the tents of Kedar!

6 My soul hath long dwelt with him that hateth peace.

7 I *am for* peace: but when I speak, they *are* for war.

PSALM 121
Help Comes from the Lord

A Song of degrees.

1 I will lift up mine eyes unto the hills, from whence cometh my help.

2 My help *cometh* from the LORD, which made heaven and earth.

3 He will not suffer thy foot to be moved: he that keepeth thee will not slumber.

4 Behold, he that keepeth Israel shall neither slumber nor sleep.

5 The LORD *is* thy keeper: the LORD *is* thy shade upon thy right hand.

6 The sun shall not smite thee by day, nor the moon by night.

7 The LORD shall preserve thee from all evil: he shall preserve thy soul.

8 The LORD shall preserve thy going out and thy coming in from this time forth, and even for evermore.

PSALM 122
Jerusalem

A Song of degrees of David.

1 I was glad when they said unto me, Let us go into the house of the LORD.

2 Our feet shall stand within thy gates, O Jerusalem.

3 Jerusalem is builded as a city that is compact together:

4 Whither the tribes go up, the tribes of the LORD, unto the testimony of Israel, to give thanks unto the name of the LORD.

5 For there are set thrones of judgment, the thrones of the house of David.

6 Pray for the peace of Jerusalem: they shall prosper that love thee.

7 Peace be within thy walls, *and* prosperity within thy palaces.

8 For my brethren and companions' sakes, I will now say, Peace *be* within thee.

9 Because of the house of the LORD our God I will seek thy good.

PSALM 123
A Prayer for Mercy

A Song of degrees.

1 Unto thee lift I up mine eyes, O thou that dwellest in the heavens.

2 Behold, as the eyes of servants *look* unto the hand of their masters, *and* as the eyes of a maiden unto the hand of her mistress; so our eyes *wait* upon the LORD our God, until that he have mercy upon us.

3 Have mercy upon us, O LORD, have mercy upon us: for we are exceedingly filled with contempt.

4 Our soul is exceedingly filled with the scorning of those that are at ease, *and* with the contempt of the proud.

PSALM 124
God Protects His People

A Song of degrees of David.

1 If *it had not been* the LORD who was on our side, now may Israel say;

2 If *it had not been* the LORD who was on our side, when men rose up against us:

3 Then they had swallowed us up quick, when their wrath was kindled against us:

4 Then the waters had overwhelmed us, the stream had gone over our soul:

5 Then the proud waters had gone over our soul.

---

168 Prov. 5:21

169 Ps. 119:144

171 Ps. 119:17

173 Josh. 24:22; Prov. 1:29; Luke 10:42

174 Ps. 119:16, 24, 47, 77, 111, 166

176 Isa. 53:6; Luke 15:4; 1Pet. 2:25

1 Ps. 118:5; Jon. 2:2

5 Gen. 10:2; 25:13; 1Sam. 25:1; Jer. 49:28, 29; Ezek. 27:13

1 Jer. 3:23

2 Ps. 124:8

3 1Sam. 2:9; Ps. 127:1; Prov. 3:23, 26; Isa. 27:3

5 Ps. 16:8; 109:31; Isa. 25:4

6 Ps. 91:5; Isa. 49:10; Rev. 7:16

7 Ps. 41:2; 97:10; 145:20

8 Deut. 28:6; Prov. 2:8; 3:6

1 Isa. 2:3; Zech. 8:21

3 2Sam. 5:9

4 Ex. 16:34; 23:17; Deut. 16:16

5 Deut. 17:8; 2Chr. 19:8

6 Ps. 51:18

9 Neh. 2:10

1 Ps. 2:4; 11:4; 115:3; 121:1; 141:8

1 Ps. 129:1

3 Ps. 56:1, 2; 57:3; Prov. 1:12

6 Blessed *be* the LORD, who hath not given us *as* a prey to their teeth.

7 Our soul is escaped as a bird out of the snare of the fowlers: the snare is broken, and we are escaped.

8 Our help *is* in the name of the LORD, who made heaven and earth.

PSALM 125
God Surrounds His People
A Song of degrees.

1 They that trust in the LORD *shall be* as mount Zion, *which* cannot be removed, *but* abideth for ever.

2 As the mountains *are* round about Jerusalem, so the LORD *is* round about his people from henceforth even for ever.

3 For the rod of the wicked shall not rest upon the lot of the righteous; lest the righteous put forth their hands unto iniquity.

4 Do good, O LORD, unto *those that be* good, and *to them that are* upright in their hearts.

5 As for such as turn aside unto their crooked ways, the LORD shall lead them forth with the workers of iniquity: *but* peace *shall be* upon Israel.

PSALM 126
Thanksgiving for Restoration
A Song of degrees.

1 When the LORD turned again the captivity of Zion, we were like them that dream.

2 Then was our mouth filled with laughter, and our tongue with singing: then said they among the heathen, The LORD hath done great things for them.

3 The LORD hath done great things for us; *whereof* we are glad.

4 Turn again our captivity, O LORD, as the streams in the south.

5 They that sow in tears shall reap in joy.

6 He that goeth forth and weepeth, bearing precious seed, shall doubtless come again with rejoicing, bringing his sheaves *with him.*

PSALM 127
Prosperity Is from the Lord
A Song of degrees for Solomon.

1 Except the LORD build the house, they labour in vain that build it: except the LORD keep the city, the watchman waketh *but* in vain.

2 *It is* vain for you to rise up early, to sit up late, to eat the bread of sorrows: *for* so he giveth his beloved sleep.

3 Lo, children *are* an heritage of the LORD: *and* the fruit of the womb *is his* reward.

4 As arrows *are* in the hand of a mighty man; so *are* children of the youth.

5 Happy *is* the man that hath his quiver full of them: they shall not be ashamed, but they shall speak with the enemies in the gate.

PSALM 128
One Who Reveres God
A Song of degrees.

1 Blessed *is* every one that feareth the LORD; that walketh in his ways.

2 For thou shalt eat the labour of thine hands: happy *shalt* thou *be*, and *it shall be* well with thee.

3 Thy wife *shall be* as a fruitful vine by the sides of thine house: thy children like olive plants round about thy table.

4 Behold, that thus shall the man be blessed that feareth the LORD.

5 The LORD shall bless thee out of Zion: and thou shalt see the good of Jerusalem all the days of thy life.

6 Yea, thou shalt see thy children's children, *and* peace upon Israel.

PSALM 129
A Prayer against the Enemies of Israel
A Song of degrees.

1 Many a time have they afflicted me from my youth, may Israel now say:

2 Many a time have they afflicted me from my youth: yet they have not prevailed against me.

3 The plowers plowed upon my back: they made long their furrows.

4 The LORD *is* righteous: he hath cut asunder the cords of the wicked.

5 Let them all be confounded and turned back that hate Zion.

6 Let them be as the grass *upon* the housetops, which withereth afore it groweth up:

7 Wherewith the mower filleth not his hand; nor he that bindeth sheaves his bosom.

8 Neither do they which go by say, The blessing of the LORD *be* upon you: we bless you in the name of the LORD.

PSALM 130
Hoping for Redemption
A Song of degrees.

1 Out of the depths have I cried unto thee, O LORD.

2 Lord, hear my voice: let thine ears be attentive to the voice of my supplications.

Cross references

7 Ps. 91:3; Prov. 6:5
8 Gen. 1:1; Ps. 121:2; 134:3
3 Prov. 22:8; Isa. 14:5
5 Ps. 128:6; Prov. 2:15; Gal. 6:16
1 Ps. 53:6; 85:1; Hos. 6:11; Joel 3:1; Acts 12:9
2 Job 8:21
4 Jer. 31:9
1 Ps. 121:3, 4, 5
2 Gen. 3:17, 19
3 Gen. 33:5; 48:4; Deut. 28:4; Josh. 24:3, 4
5 Job 5:4; Ps. 18:47, *destroy;* Prov. 27:11
1 Ps. 112:1; 115:13; 119:1
2 Isa. 3:10
3 Ps. 52:8; 144:12; Ezek. 19:10
5 Ps. 134:3
6 Gen. 50:23; Job 42:16; Ps. 125:5
1 Ps. 124:1; Ezek. 23:3; Hos. 2:15; 11:1
6 Ps. 37:2
8 Ruth 2:4; Ps. 118:26
1 Lam. 3:55; Jon. 2:2

3 If thou, LORD, shouldest mark iniquities, O Lord, who shall stand?

4 But *there is* forgiveness with thee, that thou mayest be feared.

5 I wait for the LORD, my soul doth wait, and in his word do I hope.

6 My soul *waiteth* for the Lord more than they that watch for the morning: *I say, more than* they that watch for the morning.

7 Let Israel hope in the LORD: for with the LORD *there is* mercy, and with him *is* plenteous redemption.

8 And he shall redeem Israel from all his iniquities.

PSALM 131
Childlike Trust
A Song of degrees of David.

1 LORD, my heart is not haughty, nor mine eyes lofty: neither do I exercise myself in great matters, or in things too high for me.

2 Surely I have behaved and quieted myself, as a child that is weaned of his mother: my soul *is* even as a weaned child.

3 Let Israel hope in the LORD from henceforth and for ever.

PSALM 132
God's Temple
A Song of degrees.

1 LORD, remember David, *and* all his afflictions:

2 How he sware unto the LORD, *and* vowed unto the mighty *God* of Jacob;

3 Surely I will not come into the tabernacle of my house, nor go up into my bed;

4 I will not give sleep to mine eyes, *or* slumber to mine eyelids,

5 Until I find out a place for the LORD, an habitation for the mighty *God* of Jacob.

6 Lo, we heard of it at Ephratah: we found it in the fields of the wood.

7 We will go into his tabernacles: we will worship at his footstool.

8 Arise, O LORD, into thy rest; thou, and the ark of thy strength.

9 Let thy priests be clothed with righteousness; and let thy saints shout for joy.

10 For thy servant David's sake turn not away the face of thine anointed.

11 The LORD hath sworn *in* truth unto David; he will not turn from it; Of the fruit of thy body will I set upon thy throne.

12 If thy children will keep my covenant and my testimony that I shall teach them, their children shall also sit upon thy throne for evermore.

13 For the LORD hath chosen Zion; he hath desired *it* for his habitation.

14 This *is* my rest for ever: here will I dwell; for I have desired it.

15 I will abundantly bless her provision: I will satisfy her poor with bread.

16 I will also clothe her priests with salvation: and her saints shall shout aloud for joy.

17 There will I make the horn of David to bud: I have ordained a lamp for mine anointed.

18 His enemies will I clothe with shame: but upon himself shall his crown flourish.

PSALM 133
Brotherhood
A Song of degrees of David.

1 Behold, how good and how pleasant *it is* for brethren to dwell together in unity!

2 *It is* like the precious ointment upon the head, that ran down upon the beard, *even* Aaron's beard: that went down to the skirts of his garments;

3 As the dew of Hermon, *and as the dew* that descended upon the mountains of Zion: for there the LORD commanded the blessing, *even* life for evermore.

PSALM 134
Night-Watchers
A Song of degrees.

1 Behold, bless ye the LORD, all *ye* servants of the LORD, which by night stand in the house of the LORD.

2 Lift up your hands *in* the sanctuary, and bless the LORD.

3 The LORD that made heaven and earth bless thee out of Zion.

PSALM 135
The True God and Idols

1 Praise ye the LORD. Praise ye the name of the LORD; praise *him*, O ye servants of the LORD.

2 Ye that stand in the house of the Lord, in the courts of the house of our God,

---

Cross references:

3 Ps. 143:2; Rom. 3:20, 23, 24
4 Ex. 34:7; 1Kgs. 8:40; Ps. 2:11; Jer. 33:8, 9
5 Isa. 8:17; 26:8; 30:18
8 Matt. 1:21
1 Rom. 12:16
2 Matt. 18:3; 1Cor. 14:20
4 Prov. 6:4
5 Acts 7:46
6 1Sam. 7:1; 17:12; 1Chr. 13:5
7 Ps. 5:7; 99:5
8 Num. 10:35; 2Chr. 6:41, 42; Ps. 78:61
9 Job 29:14; Ps. 132:16; Isa. 61:10
11 2Sam. 7:12; 1Kgs. 8:25; 2Chr. 6:16; Ps. 89:3, 4, 33; 110:4; Luke 1:69; Acts 2:30
13 Ps. 48:1, 2
14 Ps. 68:16
15 Ps. 147:14
16 2Chr. 6:41; Ps. 132:9; 149:4; Hos. 11:12
17 1Kgs. 11:36; 15:4; 2Chr. 21:7
1 Heb. 13:1
2 Ex. 30:25, 30
3 Lev. 25:21; Deut. 4:48
1 1Chr. 9:33; Ps. 135:1, 2
2 Luke 2:37

132:11–13 God makes a solemn oath to David to set upon his throne a literal physical descendant of his line (v. 11). This psalm confirms God's covenant oath to David to establish his seed upon the throne at Zion (Jerusalem) forever. The ultimate fulfillment of this promise will be realized when Jesus Christ, the Son of God and the descendant of David, rules from Jerusalem on David's throne in the Millennial Kingdom.

3 Praise the LORD; for the LORD *is* good: sing praises unto his name; for *it is* pleasant.
4 For the LORD hath chosen Jacob unto himself, *and* Israel for his peculiar treasure.
5 For I know that the LORD *is* great, and *that* our Lord *is* above all gods.
6 Whatsoever the LORD pleased, *that* did he in heaven, and in earth, in the seas, and all deep places.
7 He causeth the vapours to ascend from the ends of the earth; he maketh lightnings for the rain; he bringeth the wind out of his treasuries.
8 Who smote the firstborn of Egypt, both of man and beast.
9 *Who* sent tokens and wonders into the midst of thee, O Egypt, upon Pharaoh, and upon all his servants.
10 Who smote great nations, and slew mighty kings;
11 Sihon king of the Amorites, and Og king of Bashan, and all the kingdoms of Canaan:
12 And gave their land *for* an heritage, an heritage unto Israel his people.
13 Thy name, O LORD, *endureth* for ever; *and* thy memorial, O LORD, throughout all generations.
14 For the LORD will judge his people, and he will repent himself concerning his servants.
15 The idols of the heathen *are* silver and gold, the work of men's hands.
16 They have mouths, but they speak not; eyes have they, but they see not;
17 They have ears, but they hear not; neither is there *any* breath in their mouths.
18 They that make them are like unto them: *so is* every one that trusteth in them.
19 Bless the LORD, O house of Israel: bless the LORD, O house of Aaron:
20 Bless the LORD, O house of Levi: ye that fear the LORD, bless the LORD.
21 Blessed be the LORD out of Zion, which dwelleth at Jerusalem. Praise ye the LORD.

PSALM 136
His Mercy Endureth Forever

1 O give thanks unto the LORD; for *he is* good: for his mercy *endureth* for ever.
2 O give thanks unto the God of gods: for his mercy *endureth* for ever.
3 O give thanks to the Lord of lords: for his mercy *endureth* for ever.
4 To him who alone doeth great wonders: for his mercy *endureth* for ever.
5 To him that by wisdom made the heavens: for his mercy *endureth* for ever.
6 To him that stretched out the earth

Cross references (center column):

3 Ps. 119:68; 147:1
4 Ex. 19:5; Deut. 7:6, 7; 10:15
5 Ps. 95:3; 97:9
6 Ps. 115:3
7 Job 28:25, 26; 38:22, 24; Jer. 10:13; 51:16; Zech. 10:1
8 Ex. 12:12, 29; Ps. 78:51; 136:10
9 Ps. 136:15
10 Num. 21:24-26, 34, 35; Ps. 136:17
11 Josh. 12:7
12 Ps. 78:55; 136:21, 22
13 Ex. 3:15; Ps. 102:12
14 Deut. 32:36
1 1Chr. 16:34, 41; 2Chr. 20:21; Ps. 106:1; 107:1; 118:1
2 Deut. 10:17
4 Ps. 72:18
5 Gen. 1:1; Prov. 3:19; Jer. 51:15
6 Gen. 1:9; Ps. 24:2; Jer. 10:12
7 Gen. 1:14
8 Gen. 1:16
10 Ex. 12:29
11 Ex. 12:51; 13:3, 17
12 Ex. 6:6
13 Ex. 14:21, 22; Ps. 78:13
15 Ex. 14:27
16 Ex. 13:18; 15:22; Deut. 8:15
19 Num. 21:21
20 Num. 21:33
21 Josh. 12:1
23 Gen. 8:1; Deut. 32:36
3 Ps. 79:1

above the waters: for his mercy *endureth* for ever.
7 To him that made great lights: for his mercy *endureth* for ever:
8 The sun to rule by day: for his mercy *endureth* for ever:
9 The moon and stars to rule by night: for his mercy *endureth* for ever.
10 To him that smote Egypt in their firstborn: for his mercy *endureth* for ever:
11 And brought out Israel from among them: for his mercy *endureth* for ever:
12 With a strong hand, and with a stretched out arm: for his mercy *endureth* for ever.
13 To him which divided the Red sea into parts: for his mercy *endureth* for ever:
14 And made Israel to pass through the midst of it: for his mercy *endureth* for ever:
15 But overthrew Pharaoh and his host in the Red sea: for his mercy *endureth* for ever.
16 To him which led his people through the wilderness: for his mercy *endureth* for ever.
17 To him which smote great kings: for his mercy *endureth* for ever:
18 And slew famous kings: for his mercy *endureth* for ever:
19 Sihon king of the Amorites: for his mercy *endureth* for ever:
20 And Og the king of Bashan: for his mercy *endureth* for ever:
21 And gave their land for an heritage: for his mercy *endureth* for ever:
22 *Even* an heritage unto Israel his servant: for his mercy *endureth* for ever.
23 Who remembered us in our low estate: for his mercy *endureth* for ever:
24 And hath redeemed us from our enemies: for his mercy *endureth* for ever.
25 Who giveth food to all flesh: for his mercy *endureth* for ever.
26 O give thanks unto the God of heaven: for his mercy *endureth* for ever.

PSALM 137
The Mourning of the Exiles in Babylon

1 By the rivers of Babylon, there we sat down, yea, we wept, when we remembered Zion.
2 We hanged our harps upon the willows in the midst thereof.
3 For there they that carried us away captive required of us a song; and they that wasted us *required of us* mirth, *saying*, Sing us *one* of the songs of Zion.
4 How shall we sing the LORD's song in a strange land?

5 If I forget thee, O Jerusalem, let my right hand forget *her cunning.*

6 If I do not remember thee, let my tongue cleave to the roof of my mouth; if I prefer not Jerusalem above my chief joy.

7 Remember, O LORD, the children of Edom in the day of Jerusalem; who said, Raze *it,* raze *it, even* to the foundation thereof.

8 O daughter of Babylon, who art to be destroyed; happy *shall he be,* that rewardeth thee as thou hast served us.

9 Happy *shall he be,* that taketh and dasheth thy little ones against the stones.

PSALM 138
A Prayer of Thanksgiving
A Psalm of David.

1 I will praise thee with my whole heart: before the gods will I sing praise unto thee.

2 I will worship toward thy holy temple, and praise thy name for thy lovingkindness and for thy truth: for thou hast magnified thy word above all thy name.

3 In the day when I cried thou answeredst me, *and* strengthenedst me *with* strength in my soul.

4 All the kings of the earth shall praise thee, O LORD, when they hear the words of thy mouth.

5 Yea, they shall sing in the ways of the LORD: for great *is* the glory of the LORD.

6 Though the LORD *be* high, yet hath he respect unto the lowly: but the proud he knoweth afar off.

7 Though I walk in the midst of trouble, thou wilt revive me: thou shalt stretch forth thine hand against the wrath of mine enemies, and thy right hand shall save me.

8 The LORD will perfect *that which* concerneth me: thy mercy, O LORD, *endureth* for ever: forsake not the works of thine own hands.

PSALM 139
God Is Omnipresent and Omniscient
To the chief Musician, A Psalm of David.

1 O LORD, thou hast searched me, and known *me.*

2 Thou knowest my downsitting and mine uprising, thou understandest my thought afar off.

3 Thou compassest my path and my lying down, and art acquainted *with* all my ways.

4 For *there is* not a word in my tongue, *but,* lo, O LORD, thou knowest it altogether.

6 Ezek. 3:26

7 Jer. 49:7; Lam. 4:22; Ezek. 25:12; Obad. 1:10

8 Isa. 13:1, 6; 47:1; Jer. 25:12; 50:2, 15, 29; Rev. 18:6

9 Isa. 13:16

1 Ps. 119:46

2 1Kgs. 8:29, 30; Ps. 5:7; 28:2; Isa. 42:21

4 Ps. 102:15, 22

6 Ps. 113:5, 6; Prov. 3:34; Isa. 57:15; James 4:6; 1Pet. 5:5

7 Ps. 23:3, 4

8 Job 10:3, 8; 14:15; Ps. 57:2; Phil. 1:6

1 Ps. 17:3; Jer. 12:3

2 2Kgs. 19:27; Matt. 9:4; John 2:24, 25

3 Job 31:4

4 Heb. 4:13

6 Job 42:3; Ps. 40:5; 131:1

7 Jer. 23:24; Jon. 1:3

8 Job 26:6; Prov. 15:11; Amos 9:2-4

12 Job 26:6; 34:22; Dan. 2:22; Heb. 4:13

15 Job 10:8, 9; Eccl. 11:5

17 Ps. 40:5

19 Ps. 119:115; Isa. 11:4

20 Jude 1:15

21 2Chr. 19:2; Ps. 119:158

23 Job 31:6; Ps. 26:2

24 Ps. 5:8; 143:10

1 Ps. 140:4

2 Ps. 56:6

5 Thou hast beset me behind and before, and laid thine hand upon me.

6 *Such* knowledge *is* too wonderful for me; it is high, I cannot *attain* unto it.

7 Whither shall I go from thy spirit? or whither shall I flee from thy presence?

8 If I ascend up into heaven, thou *art* there: if I make my bed in hell, behold, thou *art there.*

9 *If* I take the wings of the morning, *and* dwell in the uttermost parts of the sea;

10 Even there shall thy hand lead me, and thy right hand shall hold me.

11 If I say, Surely the darkness shall cover me; even the night shall be light about me.

12 Yea, the darkness hideth not from thee; but the night shineth as the day: the darkness and the light *are* both alike *to thee.*

13 For thou hast possessed my reins: thou hast covered me in my mother's womb.

14 I will praise thee; for I am fearfully *and* wonderfully made: marvellous *are* thy works; and *that* my soul knoweth right well.

15 My substance was not hid from thee, when I was made in secret, *and* curiously wrought in the lowest parts of the earth.

16 Thine eyes did see my substance, yet being unperfect; and in thy book all *my members* were written, *which* in continuance were fashioned, when *as yet there was* none of them.

17 How precious also are thy thoughts unto me, O God! how great is the sum of them!

18 *If* I should count them, they are more in number than the sand: when I awake, I am still with thee.

19 Surely thou wilt slay the wicked, O God: depart from me therefore, ye bloody men.

20 For they speak against thee wickedly, *and* thine enemies take *thy name* in vain.

21 Do not I hate them, O LORD, that hate thee? and am not I grieved with those that rise up against thee?

22 I hate them with perfect hatred: I count them mine enemies.

23 Search me, O God, and know my heart: try me, and know my thoughts:

24 And see if *there be any* wicked way in me, and lead me in the way everlasting.

PSALM 140
Relief from Religious Persecution
To the chief Musician, A Psalm of David.

1 Deliver me, O LORD, from the evil man: preserve me from the violent man;

2 Which imagine mischiefs in *their* heart; continually are they gathered together *for* war.

3 They have sharpened their tongues like a serpent; adders' poison *is* under their lips. Selah.

4 Keep me, O LORD, from the hands of the wicked; preserve me from the violent man; who have purposed to overthrow my goings.

5 The proud have hid a snare for me, and cords; they have spread a net by the way-side; they have set gins for me. Selah.

6 I said unto the LORD, Thou *art* my God: hear the voice of my supplications, O LORD.

7 O GOD the Lord, the strength of my sal-vation, thou hast covered my head in the day of battle.

8 Grant not, O LORD, the desires of the wicked: further not his wicked device; *lest* they exalt themselves. Selah.

9 *As for* the head of those that compass me about, let the mischief of their own lips cover them.

10 Let burning coals fall upon them: let them be cast into the fire; into deep pits, that they rise not up again.

11 Let not an evil speaker be established in the earth: evil shall hunt the violent man to overthrow *him*.

12 I know that the LORD will maintain the cause of the afflicted, *and* the right of the poor.

13 Surely the righteous shall give thanks unto thy name: the upright shall dwell in thy presence.

PSALM 141
A Prayer for Preservation from Evil
A Psalm of David.

1 LORD, I cry unto thee: make haste unto me; give ear unto my voice, when I cry unto thee.

2 Let my prayer be set forth before thee *as* incense; *and* the lifting up of my hands *as* the evening sacrifice.

3 Set a watch, O LORD, before my mouth; keep the door of my lips.

4 Incline not my heart to *any* evil thing, to practise wicked works with men that work iniquity: and let me not eat of their dainties.

5 Let the righteous smite me; *it shall be* a kindness: and let him reprove me; *it shall be* an excellent oil, *which* shall not break my head: for yet my prayer also *shall be* in their calamities.

6 When their judges are overthrown in stony places, they shall hear my words; for they are sweet.

7 Our bones are scattered at the grave's mouth, as when one cutteth and cleaveth *wood* upon the earth.

8 But mine eyes *are* unto thee, O GOD the Lord: in thee is my trust; leave not my soul destitute.

9 Keep me from the snares *which* they have laid for me, and the gins of the work-ers of iniquity.

10 Let the wicked fall into their own nets, whilst that I withal escape.

PSALM 142
In Time of Trouble
Maschil of David; A Prayer when he was in the cave.

1 I cried unto the LORD with my voice; with my voice unto the LORD did I make my sup-plication.

2 I poured out my complaint before him; I shewed before him my trouble.

3 When my spirit was overwhelmed within me, then thou knewest my path. In the way wherein I walked have they privily laid a snare for me.

4 I looked on *my* right hand, and beheld, but *there was* no man that would know me: refuge failed me; no man cared for my soul.

5 I cried unto thee, O LORD: I said, Thou *art* my refuge *and* my portion in the land of the living.

6 Attend unto my cry; for I am brought very low: deliver me from my persecutors; for they are stronger than I.

7 Bring my soul out of prison, that I may praise thy name: the righteous shall com-pass me about; for thou shalt deal bounti-fully with me.

PSALM 143
Hear My Prayer!
A Psalm of David.

1 Hear my prayer, O LORD, give ear to my supplications: in thy faithfulness answer me, *and* in thy righteousness.

2 And enter not into judgment with thy servant: for in thy sight shall no man living be justified.

3 For the enemy hath persecuted my soul; he hath smitten my life down to the ground; he hath made me to dwell in dark-ness, as those that have been long dead.

4 Therefore is my spirit overwhelmed within me; my heart within me is desolate.

5 I remember the days of old; I meditate on all thy works; I muse on the work of thy hands.

6 I stretch forth my hands unto thee: my soul *thirsteth* after thee, as a thirsty land. Selah.

7 Hear me speedily, O LORD: my spirit faileth: hide not thy face from me, lest I be

Center reference column
3 Ps. 58:4; Rom. 3:13

4 Ps. 71:4; 140:1

5 Ps. 35:7; 57:6; 119:110; 141:9; Jer. 18:22

8 Deut. 32:27

9 Ps. 7:16; 94:23; Prov. 12:13; 18:7

10 Ps. 11:6

12 1Kgs. 8:45; Ps. 9:4

1 Ps. 70:5

2 Ex. 29:39; Ps. 134:2; 1Tim. 2:8; Rev. 5:8; 8:3, 4

4 Prov. 23:6

5 Prov. 9:8; 19:25; 25:12

7 2Cor. 1:9

8 2Chr. 20:12; Ps. 25:15; 123:1, 2

9 Ps. 119:110; 140:5; 142:3

10 Ps. 35:8

2 Isa. 26:16

3 Ps. 140:5; 143:4

4 Ps. 31:11; 69:20; 88:8, 18

5 Ps. 16:5; 27:13; 46:1; 73:26; 91:2; 119:57; Lam. 3:24

6 Ps. 116:6

7 Ps. 13:6; 34:2; 119:17

1 Ps. 31:1

2 Ex. 34:7; Job 4:17; 9:2; 14:3; 15:14; 25:4; Ps. 130:3; Eccl. 7:20; Rom. 3:20; Gal. 2:16

4 Ps. 77:3; 142:3

5 Ps. 77:5, 10, 11

6 Ps. 63:1; 88:9

7 Ps. 28:1; 88:4

like unto them that go down into the pit.

8 Cause me to hear thy lovingkindness in the morning; for in thee do I trust: cause me to know the way wherein I should walk; for I lift up my soul unto thee.

9 Deliver me, O Lord, from mine enemies: I flee unto thee to hide me.

10 Teach me to do thy will; for thou *art* my God: thy spirit *is* good; lead me into the land of uprightness.

11 Quicken me, O Lord, for thy name's sake: for thy righteousness' sake bring my soul out of trouble.

12 And of thy mercy cut off mine enemies, and destroy all them that afflict my soul: for I *am* thy servant.

PSALM 144
David Thanks God

A Psalm of David.

1 Blessed *be* the Lord my strength, which teacheth my hands to war, *and* my fingers to fight:

2 My goodness, and my fortress; my high tower, and my deliverer; my shield, and *he* in whom I trust; who subdueth my people under me.

3 Lord, what *is* man, that thou takest knowledge of him! *or* the son of man, that thou makest account of him!

4 Man is like to vanity: his days *are* as a shadow that passeth away.

5 Bow thy heavens, O Lord, and come down: touch the mountains, and they shall smoke.

6 Cast forth lightning, and scatter them: shoot out thine arrows, and destroy them.

7 Send thine hand from above; rid me, and deliver me out of great waters, from the hand of strange children;

8 Whose mouth speaketh vanity, and their right hand *is* a right hand of falsehood.

9 I will sing a new song unto thee, O God: upon a psaltery *and* an instrument of ten strings will I sing praises unto thee.

10 *It is he* that giveth salvation unto kings: who delivereth David his servant from the hurtful sword.

11 Rid me, and deliver me from the hand of strange children, whose mouth speaketh vanity, and their right hand *is* a right hand of falsehood:

8 Ps. 5:8; 25:1; 46:5

10 Neh. 9:20; Ps. 25:4, 5; 139:24; Isa. 26:10

11 Ps. 119:25, 37, 40

12 Ps. 54:5; 116:16

1 2Sam. 22:35; Ps. 18:2, 31, 34

2 2Sam. 22:2, 3, 40, 48

3 Job 7:17; Ps. 8:4; Heb. 2:6

4 Job 4:19; 14:2; Ps. 39:5; 62:9; 102:11

5 Ps. 18:9; Isa. 64:1

6 Ps. 18:13, 14

7 Ps. 18:16; 54:3; 144:11; Mal. 2:11

8 Ps. 12:2

9 Ps. 33:2, 3; 40:3

10 Ps. 18:50

11 Ps. 144:7, 8

12 Ps. 128:3

15 Deut. 33:29; Ps. 33:12; 65:4; 146:5

3 Job 5:9; 9:10; Ps. 96:4; 147:5; Rom. 11:33

4 Isa. 33:19

8 Ex. 34:6, 7; Num. 14:18; Ps. 86:5, 15; 103:8

9 Ps. 100:5; Nah. 1:7

10 Ps. 19:1

13 Ps. 146:10; 1Tim. 1:17

12 That our sons *may be* as plants grown up in their youth; *that* our daughters *may be* as corner stones, polished *after* the similitude of a palace:

13 *That* our garners *may be* full, affording all manner of store: *that* our sheep may bring forth thousands and ten thousands in our streets:

14 *That* our oxen *may be* strong to labour; *that there be* no breaking in, nor going out; that *there be* no complaining in our streets.

15 Happy *is that* people, that is in such a case: *yea*, happy *is that* people, whose God *is* the Lord.

PSALM 145
David Praises God

David's Psalm of praise.

1 I will extol thee, my God, O king; and I will bless thy name for ever and ever.

2 Every day will I bless thee; and I will praise thy name for ever and ever.

3 Great *is* the Lord, and greatly to be praised; and his greatness *is* unsearchable.

4 One generation shall praise thy works to another, and shall declare thy mighty acts.

5 I will speak of the glorious honour of thy majesty, and of thy wondrous works.

6 And *men* shall speak of the might of thy terrible acts: and I will declare thy greatness.

7 They shall abundantly utter the memory of thy great goodness, and shall sing of thy righteousness.

8 The Lord *is* gracious, and full of compassion; slow to anger, and of great mercy.

9 The Lord *is* good to all: and his tender mercies *are* over all his works.

10 All thy works shall praise thee, O Lord; and thy saints shall bless thee.

11 They shall speak of the glory of thy kingdom, and talk of thy power;

12 To make known to the sons of men his mighty acts, and the glorious majesty of his kingdom.

13 Thy kingdom *is* an everlasting kingdom, and thy dominion *endureth* throughout all generations.

14 The Lord upholdeth all that fall, and raiseth up all *those that be* bowed down.

15 The eyes of all wait upon thee; and thou givest them their meat in due season.

145:1 Thy kingdom is an everlasting kingdom. Unlike early kingdoms that fade away, or even David's kingdom that was taken into captivity, the eternal kingdom of God will be perpetuated by the Messiah, Jesus Christ. He will reign on David's throne during the Millennium and then, having "delivered up the Kingdom to God [the Father]," He will reign forever (cf. Isa. 9:6–7; 1 Cor. 15:24).

16 Thou openest thine hand, and satisfiest the desire of every living thing.

17 The LORD *is* righteous in all his ways, and holy in all his works.

18 The LORD *is* nigh unto all them that call upon him, to all that call upon him in truth.

19 He will fulfil the desire of them that fear him: he also will hear their cry, and will save them.

20 The LORD preserveth all them that love him: but all the wicked will he destroy.

21 My mouth shall speak the praise of the LORD: and let all flesh bless his holy name for ever and ever.

PSALM 146
God Is an Abundant Help

1 Praise ye the LORD. Praise the LORD, O my soul.

2 While I live will I praise the LORD: I will sing praises unto my God while I have any being.

3 Put not your trust in princes, *nor* in the son of man, in whom *there is* no help.

4 His breath goeth forth, he returneth to his earth; in that very day his thoughts perish.

5 Happy *is he* that *hath* the God of Jacob for his help, whose hope *is* in the LORD his God:

6 Which made heaven, and earth, the sea, and all that therein *is*: which keepeth truth for ever:

7 Which executeth judgment for the oppressed: which giveth food to the hungry. The LORD looseth the prisoners:

8 The LORD openeth *the eyes of* the blind: the LORD raiseth them that are bowed down: the LORD loveth the righteous:

9 The LORD preserveth the strangers; he relieveth the fatherless and widow: but the way of the wicked he turneth upside down.

10 The LORD shall reign for ever, *even* thy God, O Zion, unto all generations. Praise ye the LORD.

PSALM 147
Praising the Almighty

1 Praise ye the LORD: for *it is* good to sing praises unto our God; for *it is* pleasant; *and* praise is comely.

2 The LORD doth build up Jerusalem: he gathereth together the outcasts of Israel.

3 He healeth the broken in heart, and bindeth up their wounds.

4 He telleth the number of the stars; he calleth them all by *their* names.

5 Great *is* our Lord, and of great power: his understanding *is* infinite.

---

18 Deut. 4:7; John 4:24

3 Isa. 2:22

4 Eccl. 12:7

5 Ps. 144:15; Jer. 17:7

6 Gen. 1:1; Rev. 14:7

8 Matt. 9:30; John 9:7-32; Luke 13:13

9 Deut. 10:18

10 Ex. 15:18; Ps. 10:16; 145:13; Rev. 11:15

1 Ps. 33:1; 92:1; 135:3

2 Deut. 30:3; Ps. 102:16

3 Ps. 51:17; Isa. 57:15; 61:1; Luke 4:18

4 Gen. 15:5; Isa. 40:26

5 1 Chr. 16:25; Ps. 48:1; 96:4; 145:3; Isa. 40:28; Nah. 1:3

6 Ps. 146:8, 9

8 Job 38:26, 27; Ps. 104:13, 14

9 Job 38:41; Ps. 104:27, 28; 136:25; 145:15; Matt. 6:26

10 Ps. 33:16, 17, 18; Hos. 1:7

14 Deut. 32:14; Ps. 81:16; 132:15; Isa. 60:17, 18

15 Job 37:12

16 Job 37:6

19 Deut. 33:2-4

20 Deut. 4:32-34; Rom. 3:1, 2

4 Gen. 1:7

5 Gen. 1:1, 6, 7

7 Isa. 43:20

8 Ps. 147:15-18

9 Isa. 44:23; 49:13; 55:12

---

6 The LORD lifteth up the meek: he casteth the wicked down to the ground.

7 Sing unto the LORD with thanksgiving; sing praise upon the harp unto our God:

8 Who covereth the heaven with clouds, who prepareth rain for the earth, who maketh grass to grow upon the mountains.

9 He giveth to the beast his food, *and* to the young ravens which cry.

10 He delighteth not in the strength of the horse: he taketh not pleasure in the legs of a man.

11 The LORD taketh pleasure in them that fear him, in those that hope in his mercy.

12 Praise the LORD, O Jerusalem; praise thy God, O Zion.

13 For he hath strengthened the bars of thy gates; he hath blessed thy children within thee.

14 He maketh peace *in* thy borders, *and* filleth thee with the finest of the wheat.

15 He sendeth forth his commandment *upon* earth: his word runneth very swiftly.

16 He giveth snow like wool: he scattereth the hoarfrost like ashes.

17 He casteth forth his ice like morsels: who can stand before his cold?

18 He sendeth out his word, and melteth them: he causeth his wind to blow, *and* the waters flow.

19 He sheweth his word unto Jacob, his statutes and his judgments unto Israel.

20 He hath not dealt so with any nation: and *as for his* judgments, they have not known them. Praise ye the LORD.

PSALM 148
Praise the Lord!

1 Praise ye the LORD. Praise ye the LORD from the heavens: praise him in the heights.

2 Praise ye him, all his angels: praise ye him, all his hosts.

3 Praise ye him, sun and moon: praise him, all ye stars of light.

4 Praise him, ye heavens of heavens, and ye waters that *be* above the heavens.

5 Let them praise the name of the LORD: for he commanded, and they were created.

6 He hath also stablished them for ever and ever: he hath made a decree which shall not pass.

7 Praise the LORD from the earth, ye dragons, and all deeps:

8 Fire, and hail; snow, and vapour; stormy wind fulfilling his word:

9 Mountains, and all hills; fruitful trees, and all cedars:

10 Beasts, and all cattle; creeping things, and flying fowl:

11 Kings of the earth, and all people; princes, and all judges of the earth:

12 Both young men, and maidens; old men, and children:

13 Let them praise the name of the LORD: for his name alone is excellent; his glory *is* above the earth and heaven.

14 He also exalteth the horn of his people, the praise of all his saints; *even* of the children of Israel, a people near unto him. Praise ye the LORD.

PSALM 149
A Hymn of Praise

1 Praise ye the LORD. Sing unto the LORD a new song, *and* his praise in the congregation of saints.

2 Let Israel rejoice in him that made him: let the children of Zion be joyful in their King.

3 Let them praise his name in the dance: let them sing praises unto him with the timbrel and harp.

4 For the LORD taketh pleasure in his people: he will beautify the meek with salvation.

14 Ps. 75:10; 149:9; Eph. 2:17

1 Ps. 33:3; Isa. 42:10

2 Job 35:10; Ps. 100:3; Isa. 54:5; Zech. 9:9; Matt. 21:5

3 Ps. 81:2; 150:4

4 Ps. 35:27; 132:16

5 Job 35:10

6 Heb. 4:12; Rev. 1:16

9 Deut. 7:1, 2; Ps. 148:14

2 Deut. 3:24; Ps. 145:5, 6

3 Ps. 81:2; 98:6; 149:3

4 Ex. 15:20; Ps. 33:2; 92:3; 144:9; 149:3; Isa. 38:20

5 1Chr. 15:16, 19, 28; 16:5; 25:1, 6

5 Let the saints be joyful in glory: let them sing aloud upon their beds.

6 *Let* the high *praises* of God *be* in their mouth, and a two-edged sword in their hand;

7 To execute vengeance upon the heathen, *and* punishments upon the people;

8 To bind their kings with chains, and their nobles with fetters of iron;

9 To execute upon them the judgment written: this honour have all his saints. Praise ye the LORD.

PSALM 150
"Praise God"

1 Praise ye the LORD. Praise God in his sanctuary: praise him in the firmament of his power.

2 Praise him for his mighty acts: praise him according to his excellent greatness.

3 Praise him with the sound of the trumpet: praise him with the psaltery and harp.

4 Praise him with the timbrel and dance: praise him with stringed instruments and organs.

5 Praise him upon the loud cymbals: praise him upon the high sounding cymbals.

6 Let every thing that hath breath praise the LORD. Praise ye the LORD.

Proverbs

The first of the three wisdom books of Solomon, Proverbs contains a wealth of practical wisdom for everyday living, showing the vast difference between those who are "wise," that is, those who choose to follow God's wisdom, or the way of the "fool," who does his own thing and thus chooses the wrong way that leads to destruction. Proverbs is a collection of poetic observations on life—each observation is like a jewel on a single strand. Together, these strands of observations are intended to teach wisdom, morality, success, and practical truths for everyday application. While Solomon initiated the collection (see 1 Kgs. 4:32), it is possible that other wise sayings were incorporated by him or his successors.

A proverb is a short sentence conveying moral truth in a concise and pointed form, usually containing a poetic comparison or contrast of ideas. In Hebrew poetry, words do not rhyme, but ideas do. This connection of ideas is called parallelism. The three primary types of parallelism are as follows: **1) synonymous** parallelism, in which the second clause restates and amplifies the first clause (19:29); **2) antithetic** parallelism, in which a truth is stated in the first clause and its opposite appears in the second; **3)** and **synthetic** or **progressive** parallelism, where the second clause develops and adds a higher level to the thought of the first. In addition, look for similes, metaphors, personification, and other figures of speech throughout the book.

Author
Solomon and Others
Date
1000 B.C. and Later
Key Truth
Fearing and Reverencing God
Historic Time
King Solomon to King Hezekiah
Key Verses
1:7; 9:10
The fear of the LORD is the beginning of wisdom. . . .

Chapter 7 is a stern warning against immoral (strange) women and their physical enticements, while chapter 8 sets forth wisdom personified as a woman appealing for moral and spiritual values. Chapter 30 contains "the words of Agur" with unusual sets of four aspects of wisdom. In chapter 31, "the words of King Lemuel" (Solomon?) describe the ideal or "virtuous woman."

Only 7 out of 915 verses (less than 1%) can be considered prophetic, and they refer only to sacrifices typical of Jesus.

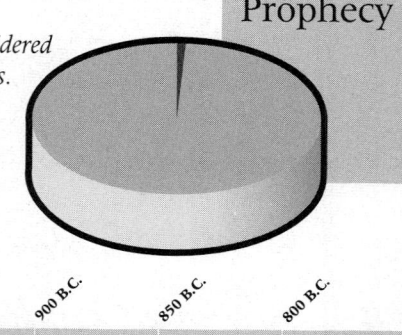

1%
Prophecy

971-931
Solomon's reign

1011-971
David's reign

931-722
Northern Kingdom (Israel)

1375-1050
Israel ruled by judges

990
Birth of Solomon

967-960
Construction of Solomon's Temple

931-586
Southern Kingdom (Judah)

1025-930
Most of Proverbs was written or adapted by Solomon

CHAPTER 1
The Value of Proverbs

1 The proverbs of Solomon the son of David, king of Israel;
2 To know wisdom and instruction; to perceive the words of understanding;
3 To receive the instruction of wisdom, justice, and judgment, and equity;
4 To give subtilty to the simple, to the young man knowledge and discretion.
5 A wise *man* will hear, and will increase learning; and a man of understanding shall attain unto wise counsels:
6 To understand a proverb, and the interpretation; the words of the wise, and their dark sayings.

Advice to Young Men

7 The fear of the LORD *is* the beginning of knowledge: *but* fools despise wisdom and instruction.
8 My son, hear the instruction of thy father, and forsake not the law of thy mother:
9 For they *shall be* an ornament of grace unto thy head, and chains about thy neck.
10 My son, if sinners entice thee, consent thou not.
11 If they say, Come with us, let us lay wait for blood, let us lurk privily for the innocent without cause:
12 Let us swallow them up alive as the grave; and whole, as those that go down into the pit:
13 We shall find all precious substance, we shall fill our houses with spoil:
14 Cast in thy lot among us; let us all have one purse:
15 My son, walk not thou in the way with them; refrain thy foot from their path:
16 For their feet run to evil, and make haste to shed blood.

17 Surely in vain the net is spread in the sight of any bird.
18 And they lay wait for their *own* blood; they lurk privily for their *own* lives.
19 So *are* the ways of every one that is greedy of gain; *which* taketh away the life of the owners thereof.
20 Wisdom crieth without; she uttereth her voice in the streets:
21 She crieth in the chief place of concourse, in the openings of the gates: in the city she uttereth her words, *saying,*
22 How long, ye simple ones, will ye love simplicity? and the scorners delight in their scorning, and fools hate knowledge?
23 Turn you at my reproof: behold, I will pour out my spirit unto you, I will make known my words unto you.
24 Because I have called, and ye refused; I have stretched out my hand, and no man regarded;
25 But ye have set at nought all my counsel, and would none of my reproof:
26 I also will laugh at your calamity; I will mock when your fear cometh;
27 When your fear cometh as desolation, and your destruction cometh as a whirlwind; when distress and anguish cometh upon you.
28 Then shall they call upon me, but I will not answer; they shall seek me early, but they shall not find me:
29 For that they hated knowledge, and did not choose the fear of the LORD:
30 They would none of my counsel: they despised all my reproof.
31 Therefore shall they eat of the fruit of their own way, and be filled with their own devices.
32 For the turning away of the simple shall slay them, and the prosperity of fools shall destroy them.

Cross references: 1 1Kgs. 4:32; Prov. 10:1; 25:1; Eccl. 12:9 · 3 Prov. 2:1, 9 · 4 Prov. 9:4 · 7 Job 28:28; Ps. 111:10 · 8 Prov. 4:1; 6:20 · 9 Prov. 3:22 · 10 Gen. 39:7-12; Ps. 1:1; Eph. 5:11 · 11 Jer. 5:26 · 12 Ps. 28:1; 143:7 · 15 Ps. 1:1; 119:101; Prov. 4:14 · 16 Isa. 59:7; Rom. 3:15 · 19 Prov. 15:27; 1Tim. 6:10 · 23 Joel 2:28 · 24 Isa. 65:12; 66:4; Jer. 7:13; Zech. 7:11 · 25 Ps. 107:11; Prov. 1:30; Luke 7:30 · 26 Ps. 2:4 · 28 Job 27:9; 35:12; Isa. 1:15; Jer. 11:11; 14:12 · 29 Job 21:14; Ps. 119:173 · 31 Job 4:8; Prov. 14:14; 22:8; Isa. 3:11; Jer. 6:19

1:6 To understand a proverb. The book of Proverbs is a special kind of literature with a focus upon providing wisdom (i.e., skill in living) in the details of everyday life. Because of its purpose to provide insight into this present life, it contains virtually no predictive prophecy. A proverb is a literary style that is brief, concrete, and provides a general truth that may have diverse applications. A proverb is not a law, a promise, or a prophecy; it is words of wisdom. Specifically, a proverb is a body of wisdom drawn from meditation upon the Law the Lord gave to Israel. Law often provides sanctions against those found disobeying it. Wisdom, on the other hand, since it merely states what a wise person should do and where such behavior will in and of itself naturally lead (i.e., the end of a matter), is sanctionless.

1:23 pour out my spirit unto you. Using the literary device of personification, wisdom calls to the simple ones to pay attention to her reproof. Correction is hard to take, but if the naive will heed the reprimand of wisdom then she will pour out her spirit. To pour out one's spirit is an idiom that means maximum revelation. In this context, wisdom will tell the submissive son all she knows. This is vindicated by the similarity of the line that follows: "I will make known my words unto you." The expression, "pour out my spirit," is used in other passages of events when God prophetically reveals Himself to His people (cf. Isa. 32:15; Joel 2:28; Acts 2:17; Rom. 5:5).

33 But whoso hearkeneth unto me shall dwell safely, and shall be quiet from fear of evil.

CHAPTER 2
The Rewards of Wisdom

1 My son, if thou wilt receive my words, and hide my commandments with thee;
2 So that thou incline thine ear unto wisdom, *and* apply thine heart to understanding;
3 Yea, if thou criest after knowledge, *and* liftest up thy voice for understanding;
4 If thou seekest her as silver, and searchest for her as *for* hid treasures;
5 Then shalt thou understand the fear of the LORD, and find the knowledge of God.
6 For the LORD giveth wisdom: out of his mouth *cometh* knowledge and understanding.
7 He layeth up sound wisdom for the righteous: *he is* a buckler to them that walk uprightly.
8 He keepeth the paths of judgment, and preserveth the way of his saints.
9 Then shalt thou understand righteousness, and judgment, and equity; *yea,* every good path.
10 When wisdom entereth into thine heart, and knowledge is pleasant unto thy soul;
11 Discretion shall preserve thee, understanding shall keep thee:
12 To deliver thee from the way of the evil *man,* from the man that speaketh froward things;
13 Who leave the paths of uprightness, to walk in the ways of darkness;
14 Who rejoice to do evil, *and* delight in the frowardness of the wicked;
15 Whose ways *are* crooked, and *they* froward in their paths:
16 To deliver thee from the strange woman, *even* from the stranger *which* flattereth with her words;
17 Which forsaketh the guide of her youth, and forgetteth the covenant of her God.
18 For her house inclineth unto death, and her paths unto the dead.
19 None that go unto her return again, neither take they hold of the paths of life.
20 That thou mayest walk in the way of good *men,* and keep the paths of the righteous.

21 For the upright shall dwell in the land, and the perfect shall remain in it.
22 But the wicked shall be cut off from the earth, and the transgressors shall be rooted out of it.

CHAPTER 3
More Advice

1 My son, forget not my law; but let thine heart keep my commandments:
2 For length of days, and long life, and peace, shall they add to thee.
3 Let not mercy and truth forsake thee: bind them about thy neck; write them upon the table of thine heart:
4 So shalt thou find favour and good understanding in the sight of God and man.
5 Trust in the LORD with all thine heart; and lean not unto thine own understanding.
6 In all thy ways acknowledge him, and he shall direct thy paths.
7 Be not wise in thine own eyes: fear the LORD, and depart from evil.
8 It shall be health to thy navel, and marrow to thy bones.
9 Honour the LORD with thy substance, and with the firstfruits of all thine increase:
10 So shall thy barns be filled with plenty, and thy presses shall burst out with new wine.
11 My son, despise not the chastening of the LORD; neither be weary of his correction:
12 For whom the LORD loveth he correcteth; even as a father the son *in whom* he delighteth.
13 Happy *is* the man *that* findeth wisdom, and the man *that* getteth understanding.
14 For the merchandise of it *is* better than the merchandise of silver, and the gain thereof than fine gold.
15 She *is* more precious than rubies: and all the things thou canst desire are not to be compared unto her.
16 Length of days *is* in her right hand; *and* in her left hand riches and honour.
17 Her ways *are* ways of pleasantness, and all her paths *are* peace.
18 She *is* a tree of life to them that lay hold upon her: and happy *is every one* that retaineth her.
19 The LORD by wisdom hath founded the

Cross-references (center column)

33 Ps. 25:12, 13; 112:7
1 Prov. 4:21; 7:1
4 Prov. 3:14; Matt. 13:44
8 1Sam. 2:9
11 Prov. 6:22
14 Rom. 1:32
16 Prov. 5:3, 20; 6:24; 7:5
17 Mal. 2:14, 15
18 Prov. 7:27
21 Ps. 37:29
22 Job 18:17; Ps. 37:28; 104:35
1 Deut. 8:1; 30:16, 20
2 Ps. 119:165
4 1Sam. 2:26; Ps. 111:10; Luke 2:52; Acts 2:47; Rom. 14:18
5 Ps. 37:3, 5; Jer. 9:23
6 1Chr. 28:9; Jer. 10:23
7 Job 1:1; Prov. 16:6; Rom. 12:16
8 Job 21:24
9 Ex. 22:29; 23:19; 34:26; Deut. 26:2; Mal. 3:10; Luke 14:13
10 Deut. 28:8
11 Ps. 94:12; Heb. 12:5, 6
14 Prov. 2:4; 8:11, 19; 16:16
16 Prov. 8:18; 1Tim. 4:8
18 Gen. 2:9; 3:22
19 Ps. 104:24; 136:5; Prov. 8:27; Jer. 10:12; 51:15

2:21–22 Those made "righteous" by the blood of Christ (which is what "perfect" refers to here) will, like the meek which Jesus mentioned, "inherit the earth" (Matt. 5:5) during the Millennial Kingdom (Rev. 20). However, "the wicked shall be cut off from the earth" when the Lord comes to banish the unsaved to outer darkness and establish His kingdom (cf. Matt. 25:31–46).

earth; by understanding hath he established the heavens.

20 By his knowledge the depths are broken up, and the clouds drop down the dew.

21 My son, let not them depart from thine eyes: keep sound wisdom and discretion:

22 So shall they be life unto thy soul, and grace to thy neck.

23 Then shalt thou walk in thy way safely, and thy foot shall not stumble.

24 When thou liest down, thou shalt not be afraid: yea, thou shalt lie down, and thy sleep shall be sweet.

25 Be not afraid of sudden fear, neither of the desolation of the wicked, when it cometh.

26 For the LORD shall be thy confidence, and shall keep thy foot from being taken.

27 Withhold not good from them to whom it is due, when it is in the power of thine hand to do it.

28 Say not unto thy neighbour, Go, and come again, and to morrow I will give; when thou hast it by thee.

29 Devise not evil against thy neighbour, seeing he dwelleth securely by thee.

30 Strive not with a man without cause, if he have done thee no harm.

31 Envy thou not the oppressor, and choose none of his ways.

32 For the froward is abomination to the LORD: but his secret is with the righteous.

33 The curse of the LORD is in the house of the wicked: but he blesseth the habitation of the just.

34 Surely he scorneth the scorners: but he giveth grace unto the lowly.

35 The wise shall inherit glory: but shame shall be the promotion of fools.

CHAPTER 4
The Benefits of Wisdom

1 Hear, ye children, the instruction of a father, and attend to know understanding.

2 For I give you good doctrine, forsake ye not my law.

3 For I was my father's son, tender and only beloved in the sight of my mother.

4 He taught me also, and said unto me, Let thine heart retain my words: keep my commandments, and live.

5 Get wisdom, get understanding: forget it not; neither decline from the words of my mouth.

6 Forsake her not, and she shall preserve thee: love her, and she shall keep thee.

7 Wisdom is the principal thing; therefore get wisdom: and with all thy getting get understanding.

8 Exalt her, and she shall promote thee: she shall bring thee to honour, when thou dost embrace her.

9 She shall give to thine head an ornament of grace: a crown of glory shall she deliver to thee.

10 Hear, O my son, and receive my sayings; and the years of thy life shall be many.

11 I have taught thee in the way of wisdom; I have led thee in right paths.

12 When thou goest, thy steps shall not be straitened; and when thou runnest, thou shalt not stumble.

13 Take fast hold of instruction; let her not go: keep her; for she is thy life.

14 Enter not into the path of the wicked, and go not in the way of evil men.

15 Avoid it, pass not by it, turn from it, and pass away.

16 For they sleep not, except they have done mischief; and their sleep is taken away, unless they cause some to fall.

17 For they eat the bread of wickedness, and drink the wine of violence.

18 But the path of the just is as the shining light, that shineth more and more unto the perfect day.

19 The way of the wicked is as darkness: they know not at what they stumble.

20 My son, attend to my words; incline thine ear unto my sayings.

21 Let them not depart from thine eyes; keep them in the midst of thine heart.

22 For they are life unto those that find them, and health to all their flesh.

23 Keep thy heart with all diligence; for out of it are the issues of life.

24 Put away from thee a froward mouth, and perverse lips put far from thee.

25 Let thine eyes look right on, and let thine eyelids look straight before thee.

26 Ponder the path of thy feet, and let all thy ways be established.

27 Turn not to the right hand nor to the left: remove thy foot from evil.

CHAPTER 5
Warning against Sexual Sin

1 My son, attend unto my wisdom, and bow thine ear to my understanding:

2 That thou mayest regard discretion, and that thy lips may keep knowledge.

3 For the lips of a strange woman drop as an honeycomb, and her mouth is smoother than oil:

4 But her end is bitter as wormwood, sharp as a two-edged sword.

---

20 Gen. 1:9; Deut. 33:28

24 Lev. 26:6; Ps. 3:5; 4:8

25 Ps. 91:5; 112:7

27 Rom. 13:7; Gal. 6:10

28 Lev. 19:13; Deut. 24:15

30 Rom. 12:18

32 Ps. 25:14

33 Lev. 26:14-17; Ps. 1:3; 37:22; Zech. 5:4; Mal. 2:2

34 James 4:6; 1Pet. 5:5

1 Ps. 34:11; Prov. 1:8

3 1Chr. 29:1

4 1Chr. 28:9; Prov. 7:2; Eph. 6:4

6 2Thess. 2:10

7 Matt. 13:44; Luke 10:42

8 1Sam. 2:30

9 Prov. 1:9; 3:22

10 Prov. 3:2

12 Ps. 18:36; 91:11, 12

14 Ps. 1:1; Prov. 1:10, 15

16 Ps. 36:4; Isa. 57:20

18 2Sam. 2:9; Matt. 5:14, 45; Phil. 2:15

19 1Sam. 2:9; Job 18:5, 6; Isa. 59:9, 10; Jer. 23:12; John 12:35

21 Prov. 2:1; 3:3, 21

22 Prov. 3:8; 12:18

27 Deut. 5:32; 28:14

2 Mal. 2:7

4 Eccl. 7:26; Heb. 4:12

5 Her feet go down to death; her steps take hold on hell.

6 Lest thou shouldest ponder the path of life, her ways are moveable, *that* thou canst not know *them*.

7 Hear me now therefore, O ye children, and depart not from the words of my mouth.

8 Remove thy way far from her, and come not nigh the door of her house:

9 Lest thou give thine honour unto others, and thy years unto the cruel:

10 Lest strangers be filled with thy wealth; and thy labours *be* in the house of a stranger;

11 And thou mourn at the last, when thy flesh and thy body are consumed,

12 And say, How have I hated instruction, and my heart despised reproof;

13 And have not obeyed the voice of my teachers, nor inclined mine ear to them that instructed me!

14 I was almost in all evil in the midst of the congregation and assembly.

15 Drink waters out of thine own cistern, and running waters out of thine own well.

16 Let thy fountains be dispersed abroad, *and* rivers of waters in the streets.

17 Let them be only thine own, and not strangers' with thee.

18 Let thy fountain be blessed: and rejoice with the wife of thy youth.

19 *Let her be as* the loving hind and pleasant roe; let her breasts satisfy thee at all times; and be thou ravished always with her love.

20 And why wilt thou, my son, be ravished with a strange woman, and embrace the bosom of a stranger?

21 For the ways of man *are* before the eyes of the LORD, and he pondereth all his goings.

22 His own iniquities shall take the wicked himself, and he shall be holden with the cords of his sins.

23 He shall die without instruction; and in the greatness of his folly he shall go astray.

CHAPTER 6
Warnings against Idleness and Deceit

1 My son, if thou be surety for thy friend, *if* thou hast stricken thy hand with a stranger,

2 Thou art snared with the words of thy mouth, thou art taken with the words of thy mouth.

3 Do this now, my son, and deliver thyself, when thou art come into the hand of thy friend; go, humble thyself, and make sure thy friend.

4 Give not sleep to thine eyes, nor slumber to thine eyelids.

5 Deliver thyself as a roe from the hand *of the hunter*, and as a bird from the hand of the fowler.

6 Go to the ant, thou sluggard; consider her ways, and be wise:

7 Which having no guide, overseer, or ruler,

8 Provideth her meat in the summer, *and* gathereth her food in the harvest.

9 How long wilt thou sleep, O sluggard? when wilt thou arise out of thy sleep?

10 *Yet* a little sleep, a little slumber, a little folding of the hands to sleep:

11 So shall thy poverty come as one that travelleth, and thy want as an armed man.

12 A naughty person, a wicked man, walketh with a froward mouth.

13 He winketh with his eyes, he speaketh with his feet, he teacheth with his fingers;

14 Frowardness *is* in his heart, he deviseth mischief continually; he soweth discord.

15 Therefore shall his calamity come suddenly; suddenly shall he be broken without remedy.

16 These six *things* doth the LORD hate: yea, seven *are* an abomination unto him:

17 A proud look, a lying tongue, and hands that shed innocent blood,

18 An heart that deviseth wicked imaginations, feet that be swift in running to mischief,

19 A false witness *that* speaketh lies, and he that soweth discord among brethren.

Warning against Adultery

20 My son, keep thy father's commandment, and forsake not the law of thy mother:

21 Bind them continually upon thine heart, *and* tie them about thy neck.

22 When thou goest, it shall lead thee; when thou sleepest, it shall keep thee; and *when* thou awakest, it shall talk with thee.

23 For the commandment *is* a lamp; and the law *is* light; and reproofs of instruction *are* the way of life:

24 To keep thee from the evil woman, from the flattery of the tongue of a strange woman.

25 Lust not after her beauty in thine heart; neither let her take thee with her eyelids.

26 For by means of a whorish woman *a man is brought* to a piece of bread: and the adulteress will hunt for the precious life.

Cross references (center column)

5 Prov. 7:27
12 Prov. 1:25, 29; 12:1
18 Mal. 2:14
19 Song 2:9; 4:5; 7:3
20 Prov. 2:16; 7:5
21 2Chr. 16:9; Job 31:4; 34:21; Prov. 15:3; Jer. 16:17; 32:19; Hos. 7:2; Heb. 4:13
22 Ps. 9:15
23 Job 4:21; 36:12
1 Prov. 11:15; 17:18; 20:16; 22:26; 27:13
4 Ps. 132:4
6 Job 12:7
9 Prov. 24:33, 34
11 Prov. 10:4; 13:4; 20:4
13 Job 15:12; Ps. 35:19; Prov. 10:10
14 Prov. 6:19; Mic. 2:1
15 2Chr. 36:16; Jer. 19:11
17 Ps. 18:27; 101:5; 120:2, 3; Isa. 1:15
18 Gen. 6:5; Isa. 59:7; Rom. 3:15
19 Ps. 27:12; Prov. 6:14; 19:5, 9
20 Prov. 1:8; Eph. 6:1
21 Prov. 3:3; 7:3
22 Prov. 2:11; 3:23, 24
23 Ps. 19:8; 119:105
24 Prov. 2:16; 5:3; 7:5
25 Matt. 5:28
26 Gen. 39:14; Prov. 29:3; Ezek. 13:18

27 Can a man take fire in his bosom, and his clothes not be burned?

28 Can one go upon hot coals, and his feet not be burned?

29 So he that goeth in to his neighbour's wife; whosoever toucheth her shall not be innocent.

30 *Men* do not despise a thief, if he steal to satisfy his soul when he is hungry;

31 But *if* he be found, he shall restore sevenfold; he shall give all the substance of his house.

32 *But* whoso committeth adultery with a woman lacketh understanding: he *that* doeth it destroyeth his own soul.

33 A wound and dishonour shall he get; and his reproach shall not be wiped away.

34 For jealousy *is* the rage of a man: therefore he will not spare in the day of vengeance.

35 He will not regard any ransom; neither will he rest content, though thou givest many gifts.

CHAPTER 7
A Prostitute's Trap

1 My son, keep my words, and lay up my commandments with thee.

2 Keep my commandments, and live; and my law as the apple of thine eye.

3 Bind them upon thy fingers, write them upon the table of thine heart.

4 Say unto wisdom, Thou *art* my sister; and call understanding *thy* kinswoman:

5 That they may keep thee from the strange woman, from the stranger *which* flattereth with her words.

6 For at the window of my house I looked through my casement,

7 And beheld among the simple ones, I discerned among the youths, a young man void of understanding,

8 Passing through the street near her corner; and he went the way to her house,

9 In the twilight, in the evening, in the black and dark night:

10 And, behold, there met him a woman *with* the attire of an harlot, and subtil of heart.

11 (She *is* loud and stubborn; her feet abide not in her house:

12 Now *is she* without, now in the streets, and lieth in wait at every corner.)

13 So she caught him, and kissed him, *and* with an impudent face said unto him,

14 *I have* peace offerings with me; this day have I paid my vows.

15 Therefore came I forth to meet thee, diligently to seek thy face, and I have found thee.

16 I have decked my bed with coverings of tapestry, with carved *works*, with fine linen of Egypt.

17 I have perfumed my bed with myrrh, aloes, and cinnamon.

18 Come, let us take our fill of love until the morning: let us solace ourselves with loves.

19 For the goodman *is* not at home, he is gone a long journey:

20 He hath taken a bag of money with him, *and* will come home at the day appointed.

21 With her much fair speech she caused him to yield, with the flattering of her lips she forced him.

22 He goeth after her straightway, as an ox goeth to the slaughter, or as a fool to the correction of the stocks;

23 Till a dart strike through his liver; as a bird hasteth to the snare, and knoweth not that it *is* for his life.

24 Hearken unto me now therefore, O ye children, and attend to the words of my mouth.

25 Let not thine heart decline to her ways, go not astray in her paths.

26 For she hath cast down many wounded: yea, many strong *men* have been slain by her.

27 Her house *is* the way to hell, going down to the chambers of death.

CHAPTER 8
Wisdom

1 Doth not wisdom cry? and understanding put forth her voice?

2 She standeth in the top of high places, by the way in the places of the paths.

3 She crieth at the gates, at the entry of the city, at the coming in at the doors.

Cross references (center column)

31 Ex. 22:1, 4
32 Prov. 7:7
1 Prov. 2:1
2 Lev. 18:5; Deut. 32:10; Prov. 4:4; Isa. 55:3
3 Deut. 6:8; 11:18; Prov. 3:3; 6:21
5 Prov. 2:16; 5:3; 6:24
7 Prov. 6:32; 9:4, 16
9 Job 24:15
11 Prov. 9:13; 1Tim. 5:13; Titus 2:5
16 Isa. 19:9
21 Ps. 12:2; Prov. 5:3
23 Eccl. 9:12
26 Neh. 13:26
27 Prov. 2:18; 5:5; 9:18
1 Prov. 1:20; 9:3
6 Prov. 22:20

8:1–36 Solomon brings his opening argument to a climax (chaps. 1—9) as to why a son should choose wisdom over folly. He does this by presenting wisdom in the form of female personification. This section is not prophetic of Jesus Christ even though He, as God, is all wise. Proverbs admonishes the son to choose wisdom as his helper, his wife, his companion for life, and she will help him navigate the pitfalls of everyday life. Solomon extols the virtues of wisdom as a woman who should be taken as his bride because she will be good for him. Hence, this "lady wisdom" is set in contrast to the strange woman or harlot of Proverbs 7. Such a relationship with wisdom will protect and guide the son throughout his life (Prov. 7:4–5).

4 Unto you, O men, I call; and my voice *is* to the sons of man.

5 O ye simple, understand wisdom: and, ye fools, be ye of an understanding heart.

6 Hear; for I will speak of excellent things; and the opening of my lips *shall be* right things.

7 For my mouth shall speak truth; and wickedness *is* an abomination to my lips.

8 All the words of my mouth *are* in righteousness; *there is* nothing froward or perverse in them.

9 They *are* all plain to him that understandeth, and right to them that find knowledge.

10 Receive my instruction, and not silver; and knowledge rather than choice gold.

11 For wisdom *is* better than rubies; and all the things that may be desired are not to be compared to it.

12 I wisdom dwell with prudence, and find out knowledge of witty inventions.

13 The fear of the LORD *is* to hate evil: pride, and arrogancy, and the evil way, and the froward mouth, do I hate.

14 Counsel *is* mine, and sound wisdom: I *am* understanding; I have strength.

15 By me kings reign, and princes decree justice.

16 By me princes rule, and nobles, *even* all the judges of the earth.

17 I love them that love me; and those that seek me early shall find me.

18 Riches and honour *are* with me; *yea,* durable riches and righteousness.

19 My fruit *is* better than gold, yea, than fine gold; and my revenue than choice silver.

20 I lead in the way of righteousness, in the midst of the paths of judgment:

21 That I may cause those that love me to inherit substance; and I will fill their treasures.

22 The LORD possessed me in the beginning of his way, before his works of old.

23 I was set up from everlasting, from the beginning, or ever the earth was.

24 When *there were* no depths, I was brought forth; when *there were* no fountains abounding with water.

25 Before the mountains were settled, before the hills was I brought forth:

26 While as yet he had not made the earth, nor the fields, nor the highest part of the dust of the world.

27 When he prepared the heavens, I *was* there: when he set a compass upon the face of the depth:

28 When he established the clouds above:

when he strengthened the fountains of the deep:

29 When he gave to the sea his decree, that the waters should not pass his commandment: when he appointed the foundations of the earth:

30 Then I was by him, *as* one brought up *with him*: and I was daily *his* delight, rejoicing always before him;

31 Rejoicing in the habitable part of his earth; and my delights *were* with the sons of men.

32 Now therefore hearken unto me, O ye children: for blessed *are they that* keep my ways.

33 Hear instruction, and be wise, and refuse it not.

34 Blessed *is* the man that heareth me, watching daily at my gates, waiting at the posts of my doors.

35 For whoso findeth me findeth life, and shall obtain favour of the LORD.

36 But he that sinneth against me wrongeth his own soul: all they that hate me love death.

CHAPTER 9
Wisdom and the Foolish Woman

1 Wisdom hath builded her house, she hath hewn out her seven pillars:

2 She hath killed her beasts; she hath mingled her wine; she hath also furnished her table.

3 She hath sent forth her maidens: she crieth upon the highest places of the city,

4 Whoso *is* simple, let him turn in hither: *as for* him that wanteth understanding, she saith to him,

5 Come, eat of my bread, and drink of the wine *which* I have mingled.

6 Forsake the foolish, and live; and go in the way of understanding.

7 He that reproveth a scorner getteth to himself shame: and he that rebuketh a wicked *man getteth* himself a blot.

8 Reprove not a scorner, lest he hate thee: rebuke a wise man, and he will love thee.

9 Give *instruction* to a wise *man,* and he will be yet wiser: teach a just *man,* and he will increase in learning.

10 The fear of the LORD *is* the beginning of wisdom: and the knowledge of the holy *is* understanding.

11 For by me thy days shall be multiplied, and the years of thy life shall be increased.

12 If thou be wise, thou shalt be wise for thyself: but *if* thou scornest, thou alone shalt bear *it.*

---

11 Job 28:15-19; Ps. 19:10; 119:127; Prov. 3:14, 15; 4:5, 7; 16:16

13 Prov. 4:24; 6:17; 16:6

14 Eccl. 7:19

15 Dan. 2:21; Rom. 13:1

17 1Sam. 2:30; Ps. 91:14; John 14:21

18 Prov. 3:16; Matt. 6:33

22 Prov. 3:19; John 1:1

23 Ps. 2:6

25 Job 15:7, 8

29 Gen. 1:9, 10; Job 38:4, 10, 11; Ps. 33:7; 104:9; Jer. 5:22

30 Matt. 3:17; John 1:1, 2, 18; Col. 1:13

31 Ps. 16:3

32 Ps. 119:1, 2; 128:1, 2; Luke 11:28

34 Prov. 3:13, 18

35 Prov. 12:2

36 Prov. 20:2

1 Matt. 16:18; Eph. 2:20, 21, 22; 1Pet. 2:5

2 Prov. 9:5; 23:30; Matt. 22:3, 4

3 Prov. 8:1, 2; 9:14; Rom. 10:15

4 Prov. 6:32; 9:16; Matt. 11:25

5 Prov. 9:2; Song 5:1; Isa. 55:1; John 6:27

8 Ps. 141:5; Matt. 7:6

9 Matt. 13:12

10 Job 28:28; Ps. 111:10; Prov. 1:7

13 A foolish woman *is* clamorous: *she is* simple, and knoweth nothing.

14 For she sitteth at the door of her house, on a seat in the high places of the city,

15 To call passengers who go right on their ways:

16 Whoso *is* simple, let him turn in hither: and *as for* him that wanteth understanding, she saith to him,

17 Stolen waters are sweet, and bread *eaten* in secret is pleasant.

18 But he knoweth not that the dead *are* there; *and that* her guests *are* in the depths of hell.

CHAPTER 10
Some Proverbs of Solomon

1 The proverbs of Solomon. A wise son maketh a glad father: but a foolish son *is* the heaviness of his mother.

2 Treasures of wickedness profit nothing: but righteousness delivereth from death.

3 The LORD will not suffer the soul of the righteous to famish: but he casteth away the substance of the wicked.

4 He becometh poor that dealeth *with* a slack hand: but the hand of the diligent maketh rich.

5 He that gathereth in summer *is* a wise son: *but* he that sleepeth in harvest *is* a son that causeth shame.

6 Blessings *are* upon the head of the just: but violence covereth the mouth of the wicked.

7 The memory of the just *is* blessed: but the name of the wicked shall rot.

8 The wise in heart will receive commandments: but a prating fool shall fall.

9 He that walketh uprightly walketh surely: but he that perverteth his ways shall be known.

10 He that winketh with the eye causeth sorrow: but a prating fool shall fall.

11 The mouth of a righteous *man is* a well of life: but violence covereth the mouth of the wicked.

12 Hatred stirreth up strifes: but love covereth all sins.

13 In the lips of him that hath understanding wisdom is found: but a rod *is* for the back of him that is void of understanding.

14 Wise *men* lay up knowledge: but the mouth of the foolish *is* near destruction.

15 The rich man's wealth *is* his strong city: the destruction of the poor *is* their poverty.

16 The labour of the righteous *tendeth* to life: the fruit of the wicked to sin.

17 He *is in* the way of life that keepeth instruction: but he that refuseth reproof erreth.

18 He that hideth hatred *with* lying lips, and he that uttereth a slander, *is* a fool.

19 In the multitude of words there wanteth not sin: but he that refraineth his lips *is* wise.

20 The tongue of the just *is as* choice silver: the heart of the wicked *is* little worth.

21 The lips of the righteous feed many: but fools die for want of wisdom.

22 The blessing of the LORD, it maketh rich, and he addeth no sorrow with it.

23 *It is* as sport to a fool to do mischief: but a man of understanding hath wisdom.

24 The fear of the wicked, it shall come upon him: but the desire of the righteous shall be granted.

25 As the whirlwind passeth, so *is* the wicked no *more*: but the righteous *is* an everlasting foundation.

26 As vinegar to the teeth, and as smoke to the eyes, so *is* the sluggard to them that send him.

27 The fear of the LORD prolongeth days: but the years of the wicked shall be shortened.

28 The hope of the righteous *shall be* gladness: but the expectation of the wicked shall perish.

29 The way of the LORD *is* strength to the upright: but destruction *shall be* to the workers of iniquity.

30 The righteous shall never be removed: but the wicked shall not inhabit the earth.

31 The mouth of the just bringeth forth wisdom: but the froward tongue shall be cut out.

32 The lips of the righteous know what is acceptable: but the mouth of the wicked *speaketh* frowardness.

Cross references

17 Prov. 20:17
18 Prov. 2:18; 7:27
2 Ps. 49:6-9; Prov. 11:4; Dan. 4:27; Luke 12:19, 20
3 Ps. 10:14; 34:9, 10; 37:25
5 Prov. 12:4; 17:2; 19:26
6 Esth. 7:8; Prov. 10:11
7 Eccl. 8:10
8 Prov. 10:10
9 Ps. 23:4; Prov. 28:18; Isa. 33:15, 16
10 Prov. 6:13; 10:8
11 Ps. 37:30; 107:42; Prov. 10:6; 13:14; 18:4
12 Prov. 17:9; 1Cor. 13:4; 1Pet. 4:8
13 Prov. 26:3
15 Job 31:24; Ps. 52:7; Prov. 18:11; 1Tim. 6:17
19 Eccl. 5:3; James 3:2
23 Prov. 14:9; 15:21
24 1John 5:14, 15
25 Matt. 7:24, 25; 16:18
27 Job 15:32, 33; Eccl. 7:17
29 Ps. 1:6; 37:20
30 Ps. 37:22, 29; 125:1; Prov. 10:25
31 Ps. 37:30

10:30 The great benefit to living this life to the glory of God is that "the righteous shall never be removed." Once we are raptured to be with Jesus, we shall "ever be with the Lord" (1 Thess. 4:17), first in the earthly kingdom for one thousand years and then in heaven forever. By contrast, "the wicked shall not inhabit the earth." God's original plan for man was that he would enjoy the blessings of an Eden-like earth forever (Gen. 1—3). The wicked that reject God's means of blood sacrifice made by His Son will never enjoy this earth where God Himself and His son will dwell forever. This is the tragedy of the ages and the consequence of man's rejection of Jesus and the gift of eternal life through Him alone.

CHAPTER 11

1 A false balance *is* abomination to the LORD: but a just weight *is* his delight.

2 *When* pride cometh, then cometh shame: but with the lowly *is* wisdom.

3 The integrity of the upright shall guide them: but the perverseness of transgressors shall destroy them.

4 Riches profit not in the day of wrath: but righteousness delivereth from death.

5 The righteousness of the perfect shall direct his way: but the wicked shall fall by his own wickedness.

6 The righteousness of the upright shall deliver them: but transgressors shall be taken in *their own* naughtiness.

7 When a wicked man dieth, *his* expectation shall perish: and the hope of unjust *men* perisheth.

8 The righteous is delivered out of trouble, and the wicked cometh in his stead.

9 An hypocrite with *his* mouth destroyeth his neighbour: but through knowledge shall the just be delivered.

10 When it goeth well with the righteous, the city rejoiceth: and when the wicked perish, *there is* shouting.

11 By the blessing of the upright the city is exalted: but it is overthrown by the mouth of the wicked.

12 He that is void of wisdom despiseth his neighbour: but a man of understanding holdeth his peace.

13 A talebearer revealeth secrets: but he that is of a faithful spirit concealeth the matter.

14 Where no counsel *is*, the people fall: but in the multitude of counsellers *there is* safety.

15 He that is surety for a stranger shall smart *for it*: and he that hateth suretiship is sure.

16 A gracious woman retaineth honour: and strong *men* retain riches.

17 The merciful man doeth good to his own soul: but *he that is* cruel troubleth his own flesh.

18 The wicked worketh a deceitful work: but to him that soweth righteousness *shall be* a sure reward.

19 As righteousness *tendeth* to life: so he that pursueth evil *pursueth it* to his own death.

20 They that are of a froward heart *are* abomination to the LORD: but *such as are* upright in *their* way *are* his delight.

21 *Though* hand *join* in hand, the wicked shall not be unpunished: but the seed of the righteous shall be delivered.

22 *As* a jewel of gold in a swine's snout, *so is* a fair woman which is without discretion.

23 The desire of the righteous *is* only good: *but* the expectation of the wicked *is* wrath.

24 There is that scattereth, and yet increaseth; and *there is* that withholdeth more than is meet, but *it tendeth* to poverty.

25 The liberal soul shall be made fat: and he that watereth shall be watered also himself.

26 He that withholdeth corn, the people shall curse him: but blessing *shall be* upon the head of him that selleth *it*.

27 He that diligently seeketh good procureth favour: but he that seeketh mischief, it shall come unto him.

28 He that trusteth in his riches shall fall: but the righteous shall flourish as a branch.

29 He that troubleth his own house shall inherit the wind: and the fool *shall be* servant to the wise of heart.

30 The fruit of the righteous *is* a tree of life; and he that winneth souls *is* wise.

31 Behold, the righteous shall be recompensed in the earth: much more the wicked and the sinner.

CHAPTER 12

1 Whoso loveth instruction loveth knowledge: but he that hateth reproof *is* brutish.

2 A good *man* obtaineth favour of the LORD: but a man of wicked devices will he condemn.

3 A man shall not be established by wickedness: but the root of the righteous shall not be moved.

4 A virtuous woman *is* a crown to her husband: but she that maketh ashamed *is* as rottenness in his bones.

5 The thoughts of the righteous *are* right: *but* the counsels of the wicked *are* deceit.

6 The words of the wicked *are* to lie in wait for blood: but the mouth of the upright shall deliver them.

7 The wicked are overthrown, and *are* not: but the house of the righteous shall stand.

8 A man shall be commended according to his wisdom: but he that is of a perverse heart shall be despised.

9 *He that is* despised, and hath a servant, *is* better than he that honoureth himself, and lacketh bread.

10 A righteous *man* regardeth the life of his beast: but the tender mercies of the wicked *are* cruel.

11 He that tilleth his land shall be satisfied with bread: but he that followeth vain *persons is* void of understanding.

12 The wicked desireth the net of evil *men*:

Cross references

1 Lev. 19:35; 36
2 Prov. 15:33; 16:18
4 Gen. 7:1; Prov. 10:2; Ezek. 7:19; Zeph. 1:18
6 Prov. 5:22; Eccl. 10:8
9 Job 8:13
10 Esth. 8:15; Prov. 28:12, 28
11 Prov. 29:8
13 Lev. 19:16; Prov. 20:19
16 Prov. 31:30
17 Matt. 5:7; 25:34-46
18 Hos. 10:12; Gal. 6:8, 9; James 3:18
21 Ps. 112:2; Prov. 16:5
23 Rom. 2:8, 9
24 Ps. 112:9
25 Matt. 5:7; 2 Cor. 9:6-10
26 Job 29:13; Amos 8:5, 6
27 Esth. 7:10; Ps. 7:15, 16; 9:15, 16; 10:2; 57:6
28 Job 31:24; Ps. 1:3; 52:7, 8; 92:12-15; Jer. 17:8; Mark 10:24; Luke 12:21; 1 Tim. 6:17
29 Eccl. 5:16
30 Dan. 12:3; 1 Cor. 9:19-22; James 5:20
31 Jer. 25:29; 1 Pet. 4:17, 18
1 1 Cor. 11:7
7 Matt. 7:24-27
8 1 Sam. 25:17
9 Prov. 13:7
10 Deut. 25:4
11 Gen. 3:19

but the root of the righteous yieldeth *fruit*.

13 The wicked is snared by the transgression of *his* lips: but the just shall come out of trouble.

14 A man shall be satisfied with good by the fruit of *his* mouth: and the recompence of a man's hands shall be rendered unto him.

15 The way of a fool *is* right in his own eyes: but he that hearkeneth unto counsel *is* wise.

16 A fool's wrath is presently known: but a prudent *man* covereth shame.

17 *He that* speaketh truth sheweth forth righteousness: but a false witness deceit.

18 There is that speaketh like the piercings of a sword: but the tongue of the wise *is* health.

19 The lip of truth shall be established for ever: but a lying tongue *is* but for a moment.

20 Deceit *is* in the heart of them that imagine evil: but to the counsellers of peace *is* joy.

21 There shall no evil happen to the just: but the wicked shall be filled with mischief.

22 Lying lips *are* abomination to the LORD: but they that deal truly *are* his delight.

23 A prudent man concealeth knowledge: but the heart of fools proclaimeth foolishness.

24 The hand of the diligent shall bear rule: but the slothful shall be under tribute.

25 Heaviness in the heart of man maketh it stoop: but a good word maketh it glad.

26 The righteous *is* more excellent than his neighbour: but the way of the wicked seduceth them.

27 The slothful *man* roasteth not that which he took in hunting: but the substance of a diligent man *is* precious.

28 In the way of righteousness *is* life; and *in* the pathway *thereof there is* no death.

CHAPTER 13

1 A wise son *heareth* his father's instruction: but a scorner heareth not rebuke.

2 A man shall eat good by the fruit of *his* mouth: but the soul of the transgressors *shall eat* violence.

3 He that keepeth his mouth keepeth his life: *but* he that openeth wide his lips shall have destruction.

4 The soul of the sluggard desireth, and *hath* nothing: but the soul of the diligent shall be made fat.

5 A righteous *man* hateth lying: but a wicked *man* is loathsome, and cometh to shame.

6 Righteousness keepeth *him that is* up-

right in the way: but wickedness overthroweth the sinner.

7 There is that maketh himself rich, yet *hath* nothing: *there is* that maketh himself poor, yet *hath* great riches.

8 The ransom of a man's life *are* his riches: but the poor heareth not rebuke.

9 The light of the righteous rejoiceth: but the lamp of the wicked shall be put out.

10 Only by pride cometh contention: but with the well advised *is* wisdom.

11 Wealth *gotten* by vanity shall be diminished: but he that gathereth by labour shall increase.

12 Hope deferred maketh the heart sick: but *when* the desire cometh, *it is* a tree of life.

13 Whoso despiseth the word shall be destroyed: but he that feareth the commandment shall be rewarded.

14 The law of the wise *is* a fountain of life, to depart from the snares of death.

15 Good understanding giveth favour: but the way of transgressors *is* hard.

16 Every prudent *man* dealeth with knowledge: but a fool layeth open *his* folly.

17 A wicked messenger falleth into mischief: but a faithful ambassador *is* health.

18 Poverty and shame *shall be to* him that refuseth instruction: but he that regardeth reproof shall be honoured.

19 The desire accomplished is sweet to the soul: but *it is* abomination to fools to depart from evil.

20 He that walketh with wise *men* shall be wise: but a companion of fools shall be destroyed.

21 Evil pursueth sinners: but to the righteous good shall be repayed.

22 A good *man* leaveth an inheritance to his children's children: and the wealth of the sinner *is* laid up for the just.

23 Much food *is in* the tillage of the poor: but there is *that is* destroyed for want of judgment.

24 He that spareth his rod hateth his son: but he that loveth him chasteneth him betimes.

25 The righteous eateth to the satisfying of his soul: but the belly of the wicked shall want.

CHAPTER 14

1 Every wise woman buildeth her house: but the foolish plucketh it down with her hands.

2 He that walketh in his uprightness feareth the LORD: but *he that is* perverse in his ways despiseth him.

Center column cross-references:

13 Prov. 18:7; 2Pet. 2:9
14 Prov. 13:2; 18:20; Isa. 3:10, 11
15 Prov. 3:7; Luke 18:11
16 Prov. 29:11
17 Prov. 14:5
18 Ps. 57:4; 59:7; 64:3
19 Ps. 52:5; Prov. 19:9
22 Prov. 6:17; 11:20; Rev. 22:15
23 Prov. 13:16; 15:2
24 Prov. 10:4
25 Prov. 15:13; Isa. 50:4
3 Ps. 39:1; Prov. 21:23; James 3:2
6 Prov. 11:3, 5, 6
7 Prov. 12:9
9 Job 18:5, 6; 21:17; Prov. 24:20
11 Prov. 10:2; 20:21
12 Prov. 13:19
13 2Chr. 36:16
14 2Sam. 22:6; Prov. 10:11; 14:27; 16:22
16 Prov. 12:23; 15:2
17 Prov. 25:13
18 Prov. 15:5, 31
19 Prov. 13:12
21 Ps. 32:10
22 Job 27:16, 17; Prov. 28:8; Eccl. 2:26
23 Prov. 12:11
24 Prov. 19:18; 22:15
25 Ps. 34:10; 37:3
1 Ruth 4:11; Prov. 24:3
2 Job 12:4

3 In the mouth of the foolish *is* a rod of pride: but the lips of the wise shall preserve them.

4 Where no oxen *are*, the crib *is* clean: but much increase *is* by the strength of the ox.

5 A faithful witness will not lie: but a false witness will utter lies.

6 A scorner seeketh wisdom, and *findeth it* not: but knowledge *is* easy unto him that understandeth.

7 Go from the presence of a foolish man, when thou perceivest not *in him* the lips of knowledge.

8 The wisdom of the prudent *is* to understand his way: but the folly of fools *is* deceit.

9 Fools make a mock at sin: but among the righteous *there is* favour.

10 The heart knoweth his own bitterness; and a stranger doth not intermeddle with his joy.

11 The house of the wicked shall be overthrown: but the tabernacle of the upright shall flourish.

12 There is a way which seemeth right unto a man, but the end thereof *are* the ways of death.

13 Even in laughter the heart is sorrowful; and the end of that mirth *is* heaviness.

14 The backslider in heart shall be filled with his own ways: and a good man *shall be satisfied* from himself.

15 The simple believeth every word: but the prudent *man* looketh well to his going.

16 A wise *man* feareth, and departeth from evil: but the fool rageth, and is confident.

17 *He that is* soon angry dealeth foolishly: and a man of wicked devices is hated.

18 The simple inherit folly: but the prudent are crowned with knowledge.

19 The evil bow before the good; and the wicked at the gates of the righteous.

20 The poor is hated even of his own neighbour: but the rich *hath* many friends.

21 He that despiseth his neighbour sinneth: but he that hath mercy on the poor, happy *is* he.

22 Do they not err that devise evil? but mercy and truth *shall be* to them that devise good.

23 In all labour there is profit: but the talk of the lips *tendeth* only to penury.

24 The crown of the wise *is* their riches: *but* the foolishness of fools *is* folly.

25 A true witness delivereth souls: but a deceitful *witness* speaketh lies.

26 In the fear of the LORD *is* strong confidence: and his children shall have a place of refuge.

27 The fear of the LORD *is* a fountain of life, to depart from the snares of death.

28 In the multitude of people *is* the king's honour: but in the want of people *is* the destruction of the prince.

29 *He that is* slow to wrath *is* of great understanding: but *he that is* hasty of spirit exalteth folly.

30 A sound heart *is* the life of the flesh: but envy the rottenness of the bones.

31 He that oppresseth the poor reproacheth his Maker: but he that honoureth him hath mercy on the poor.

32 The wicked is driven away in his wickedness: but the righteous hath hope in his death.

33 Wisdom resteth in the heart of him that hath understanding: but *that which is* in the midst of fools is made known.

34 Righteousness exalteth a nation: but sin *is* a reproach to any people.

35 The king's favour *is* toward a wise servant: but his wrath is *against* him that causeth shame.

CHAPTER 15

1 A soft answer turneth away wrath: but grievous words stir up anger.

2 The tongue of the wise useth knowledge aright: but the mouth of fools poureth out foolishness.

3 The eyes of the LORD *are* in every place, beholding the evil and the good.

4 A wholesome tongue *is* a tree of life: but perverseness therein *is* a breach in the spirit.

5 A fool despiseth his father's instruction: but he that regardeth reproof is prudent.

6 In the house of the righteous *is* much treasure: but in the revenues of the wicked is trouble.

7 The lips of the wise disperse knowledge: but the heart of the foolish *doeth* not so.

8 The sacrifice of the wicked *is* an abomination to the LORD: but the prayer of the upright *is* his delight.

9 The way of the wicked *is* an abomination unto the LORD: but he loveth him that followeth after righteousness.

10 Correction *is* grievous unto him that forsaketh the way: *and* he that hateth reproof shall die.

11 Hell and destruction *are* before the LORD: how much more then the hearts of the children of men?

12 A scorner loveth not one that reproveth him: neither will he go unto the wise.

13 A merry heart maketh a cheerful counte-

Cross references (center column)

3 Prov. 12:6

5 Ex. 20:16; 23:1; Prov. 6:19; 12:17; 14:25

6 Prov. 8:9; 17:24

9 Prov. 10:23

11 Job 8:15

12 Prov. 16:25; Rom. 6:21

13 Prov. 5:4; Eccl. 2:2

14 Prov. 1:31; 12:14

16 Prov. 22:3

20 Prov. 19:7

21 Ps. 41:1; 112:9

25 Prov. 14:5

29 James 1:19

30 Ps. 112:10; Prov. 12:4

31 Job 31:15, 16

32 Job 13:15; 19:26; Ps. 23:4; 37:37; 2Cor. 1:9; 5:8; 2Tim. 4:18

33 Prov. 12:16; 29:11

35 Matt. 24:45, 47

1 Judg. 8:1-3; 25:15; 1Sam. 25:10; 1Kgs. 12:13, 14, 16

2 Prov. 12:28; 13:16; 15:28

3 Job 5:21; 34:21; Jer. 16:17; 32:19; Heb. 4:13

5 Prov. 10:1; 13:8; 15:31, 32

8 Prov. 21:27; 28:9; Isa. 1:11; 61:8; 66:3; Jer. 6:20; 7:22; Amos 5:22

9 1Tim. 6:11

11 Job 26:6; John 2:24, 25; 21:17; Acts 1:24

12 Amos 5:10; 2Tim. 4:3

nance: but by sorrow of the heart the spirit is broken.

14 The heart of him that hath understanding seeketh knowledge: but the mouth of fools feedeth on foolishness.

15 All the days of the afflicted *are* evil: but he that is of a merry heart *hath* a continual feast.

16 Better *is* little with the fear of the LORD than great treasure and trouble therewith.

17 Better *is* a dinner of herbs where love is, than a stalled ox and hatred therewith.

18 A wrathful man stirreth up strife: but *he that is* slow to anger appeaseth strife.

19 The way of the slothful *man is* as an hedge of thorns: but the way of the righteous *is* made plain.

20 A wise son maketh a glad father: but a foolish man despiseth his mother.

21 Folly *is* joy to *him that is* destitute of wisdom: but a man of understanding walketh uprightly.

22 Without counsel purposes are disappointed: but in the multitude of counsellers they are established.

23 A man hath joy by the answer of his mouth: and a word *spoken* in due season, how good *is it*!

24 The way of life *is* above to the wise, that he may depart from hell beneath.

25 The LORD will destroy the house of the proud: but he will establish the border of the widow.

26 The thoughts of the wicked *are* an abomination to the LORD: but *the words* of the pure *are* pleasant words.

27 He that is greedy of gain troubleth his own house; but he that hateth gifts shall live.

28 The heart of the righteous studieth to answer: but the mouth of the wicked poureth out evil things.

29 The LORD *is* far from the wicked: but he heareth the prayer of the righteous.

30 The light of the eyes rejoiceth the heart: *and* a good report maketh the bones fat.

31 The ear that heareth the reproof of life abideth among the wise.

32 He that refuseth instruction despiseth his own soul: but he that heareth reproof getteth understanding.

33 The fear of the LORD *is* the instruction of wisdom; and before honour *is* humility.

CHAPTER 16

1 The preparations of the heart in man, and the answer of the tongue, *is* from the LORD.

2 All the ways of a man *are* clean in his own eyes; but the LORD weigheth the spirits.

3 Commit thy works unto the LORD, and thy thoughts shall be established.

4 The LORD hath made all *things* for himself: yea, even the wicked for the day of evil.

5 Every one *that is* proud in heart *is* an abomination to the LORD: *though* hand *join* in hand, he shall not be unpunished.

6 By mercy and truth iniquity is purged: and by the fear of the LORD *men* depart from evil.

7 When a man's ways please the LORD, he maketh even his enemies to be at peace with him.

8 Better *is* a little with righteousness than great revenues without right.

9 A man's heart deviseth his way: but the LORD directeth his steps.

10 A divine sentence *is* in the lips of the king: his mouth transgresseth not in judgment.

11 A just weight and balance *are* the LORD's: all the weights of the bag *are* his work.

12 *It is* an abomination to kings to commit wickedness: for the throne is established by righteousness.

13 Righteous lips *are* the delight of kings; and they love him that speaketh right.

14 The wrath of a king *is as* messengers of death: but a wise man will pacify it.

15 In the light of the king's countenance *is* life; and his favour *is* as a cloud of the latter rain.

16 How much better *is it* to get wisdom than gold! and to get understanding rather to be chosen than silver!

17 The highway of the upright *is* to depart from evil: he that keepeth his way preserveth his soul.

18 Pride *goeth* before destruction, and an haughty spirit before a fall.

19 Better *it is to be* of an humble spirit with the lowly, than to divide the spoil with the proud.

20 He that handleth a matter wisely shall find good: and whoso trusteth in the LORD, happy *is* he.

Cross references (center column)

15 Prov. 17:22
16 Ps. 37:16; Prov. 16:8; 1Tim. 6:6
17 Prov. 17:1
18 Prov. 26:21; 29:22
19 Prov. 22:5
20 Prov. 10:1; 29:3
21 Prov. 10:23; Eph. 5:15
22 Prov. 11:14; 20:18
24 Phil. 3:20; Col. 3:1, 2
25 Ps. 68:5, 6; 146:9; Prov. 12:7; 14:11
26 Prov. 6:16, 18; 37:30
27 Prov. 11:19; Isa. 5:8; Jer. 17:11
28 1Pet. 3:15
29 Ps. 10:1; 34:16; 145:18, 19
33 Prov. 1:7; 18:12
1 Jer. 10:23; Matt. 10:19, 20
2 2Sam. 16:7; Prov. 21:2
3 Phil. 4:6; 1Pet. 5:7
4 Job 21:30; Isa. 43:7; Rom. 9:22; 11:36
6 Luke 11:41
9 Ps. 37:23
14 Prov. 19:12; 20:2
15 Zech. 10:1
18 Prov. 11:2; 17:19; 18:12
20 Ps. 2:12; 34:8; 125:1; Isa. 30:18; Jer. 17:7

16:6 By mercy and truth iniquity is purged. While this text speaks of the personal virtues of mercy and truth that should be displayed in the life of an individual, they were perfected and fulfilled through the person of Jesus Christ (John 1:17). Christ also purged our sins through His death and resurrection on the cross (Mark 10:45; Rom. 3:25).

21 The wise in heart shall be called prudent: and the sweetness of the lips increaseth learning.

22 Understanding *is* a wellspring of life unto him that hath it: but the instruction of fools *is* folly.

23 The heart of the wise teacheth his mouth, and addeth learning to his lips.

24 Pleasant words *are as* an honeycomb, sweet to the soul, and health to the bones.

25 There is a way that seemeth right unto a man, but the end thereof *are* the ways of death.

26 He that laboureth laboureth for himself; for his mouth craveth it of him.

27 An ungodly man diggeth up evil: and in his lips *there is* as a burning fire.

28 A froward man soweth strife: and a whisperer separateth chief friends.

29 A violent man enticeth his neighbour, and leadeth him into the way *that is* not good.

30 He shutteth his eyes to devise froward things: moving his lips he bringeth evil to pass.

31 The hoary head *is* a crown of glory, *if* it be found in the way of righteousness.

32 *He that is* slow to anger *is* better than the mighty; and he that ruleth his spirit than he that taketh a city.

33 The lot is cast into the lap; but the whole disposing thereof *is* of the LORD.

CHAPTER 17

1 Better *is* a dry morsel, and quietness therewith, than an house full of sacrifices *with* strife.

2 A wise servant shall have rule over a son that causeth shame, and shall have part of the inheritance among the brethren.

3 The fining pot *is* for silver, and the furnace for gold: but the LORD trieth the hearts.

4 A wicked doer giveth heed to false lips; *and* a liar giveth ear to a naughty tongue.

5 Whoso mocketh the poor reproacheth his Maker: *and* he that is glad at calamities shall not be unpunished.

6 Children's children *are* the crown of old men; and the glory of children *are* their fathers.

7 Excellent speech becometh not a fool: much less do lying lips a prince.

8 A gift *is as* a precious stone in the eyes of him that hath it: whithersoever it turneth, it prospereth.

9 He that covereth a transgression seeketh love; but he that repeateth a matter separateth *very* friends.

22 Prov. 13:14; 14:27
23 Ps. 37:30; Matt. 12:34
25 Prov. 14:12
26 Prov. 9:12; Eccl. 6:7
28 Prov. 6:14, 19; 15:18; 17:9; 26:21; 29:22
29 Prov. 1:10
31 Prov. 20:29
32 Prov. 19:11
1 Prov. 15:17
2 Prov. 10:5; 19:26
3 Ps. 26:2; Prov. 27:21; Jer. 17:10; Mal. 3:3
5 Job 31:29; Prov. 14:31
6 Ps. 127:3; 128:3
8 Prov. 18:16; 19:6
9 Prov. 10:12; 16:28
12 Hos. 13:8
13 Ps. 109:4, 5; Jer. 18:20; Rom. 12:17; 1Thess. 5:15; 1Pet. 3:9
14 1Thess. 4:11
15 Ex. 23:7; Prov. 24:24; Isa. 5:23
16 Prov. 21:25, 26
17 Ruth 1:16; Prov. 18:24
20 James 3:8
21 Prov. 10:1; 17:25; 19:13
22 Ps. 22:15; Prov. 12:25; 15:13, 15
23 Ex. 23:8
24 Eccl. 2:14; 8:1
27 James 1:19
28 Job 13:5
1 Jude 1:19

10 A reproof entereth more into a wise man than an hundred stripes into a fool.

11 An evil *man* seeketh only rebellion: therefore a cruel messenger shall be sent against him.

12 Let a bear robbed of her whelps meet a man, rather than a fool in his folly.

13 Whoso rewardeth evil for good, evil shall not depart from his house.

14 The beginning of strife *is as* when one letteth out water: therefore leave off contention, before it be meddled with.

15 He that justifieth the wicked, and he that condemneth the just, even they both *are* abomination to the LORD.

16 Wherefore *is there* a price in the hand of a fool to get wisdom, seeing *he hath* no heart *to it?*

17 A friend loveth at all times, and a brother is born for adversity.

18 A man void of understanding striketh hands, *and* becometh surety in the presence of his friend.

19 He loveth transgression that loveth strife: *and* he that exalteth his gate seeketh destruction.

20 He that hath a froward heart findeth no good: and he that hath a perverse tongue falleth into mischief.

21 He that begetteth a fool *doeth it* to his sorrow: and the father of a fool hath no joy.

22 A merry heart doeth good *like* a medicine: but a broken spirit drieth the bones.

23 A wicked *man* taketh a gift out of the bosom to pervert the ways of judgment.

24 Wisdom *is* before him that hath understanding; but the eyes of a fool *are* in the ends of the earth.

25 A foolish son *is* a grief to his father, and bitterness to her that bare him.

26 Also to punish the just *is* not good, *nor* to strike princes for equity.

27 He that hath knowledge spareth his words: *and* a man of understanding is of an excellent spirit.

28 Even a fool, when he holdeth his peace, is counted wise: *and* he that shutteth his lips *is esteemed* a man of understanding.

CHAPTER 18

1 Through desire a man, having separated himself, seeketh *and* intermeddleth with all wisdom.

2 A fool hath no delight in understanding, but that his heart may discover itself.

3 When the wicked cometh, *then* cometh also contempt, and with ignominy reproach.

4 The words of a man's mouth *are as* deep waters, *and* the wellspring of wisdom *as a* flowing brook.

5 *It is* not good to accept the person of the wicked, to overthrow the righteous in judgment.

6 A fool's lips enter into contention, and his mouth calleth for strokes.

7 A fool's mouth *is* his destruction, and his lips *are* the snare of his soul.

8 The words of a talebearer *are* as wounds, and they go down into the innermost parts of the belly.

9 He also that is slothful in his work is brother to him that is a great waster.

10 The name of the LORD *is* a strong tower: the righteous runneth into it, and is safe.

11 The rich man's wealth *is* his strong city, and as an high wall in his own conceit.

12 Before destruction the heart of man is haughty, and before honour *is* humility.

13 He that answereth a matter before he heareth *it*, it *is* folly and shame unto him.

14 The spirit of a man will sustain his infirmity; but a wounded spirit who can bear?

15 The heart of the prudent getteth knowledge; and the ear of the wise seeketh knowledge.

16 A man's gift maketh room for him, and bringeth him before great men.

17 *He that is* first in his own cause *seemeth* just; but his neighbour cometh and searcheth him.

18 The lot causeth contentions to cease, and parteth between the mighty.

19 A brother offended *is harder to be won* than a strong city: and *their* contentions *are* like the bars of a castle.

20 A man's belly shall be satisfied with the fruit of his mouth; *and* with the increase of his lips shall he be filled.

21 Death and life *are* in the power of the tongue: and they that love it shall eat the fruit thereof.

22 *Whoso* findeth a wife findeth a good *thing*, and obtaineth favour of the LORD.

23 The poor useth intreaties; but the rich answereth roughly.

24 A man *that hath* friends must shew himself friendly: and there is a friend *that* sticketh closer than a brother.

CHAPTER 19

1 Better *is* the poor that walketh in his integrity, than *he that is* perverse in his lips, and is a fool.

2 Also, *that* the soul *be* without knowledge,

Center references

4 Ps. 78:2
5 Lev. 19:15; Deut. 1:17
7 Prov. 10:14; 12:13; 13:3; Eccl. 10:12
10 2Sam. 22:3, 51; Ps. 18:2; 27:1
13 John 7:51
16 Gen. 32:20; 1Sam. 25:27
20 Prov. 12:14; 13:2
21 Matt. 12:37
22 Prov. 19:14; 31:10
23 James 2:3
24 Prov. 17:17
1 Prov. 28:6
3 Ps. 37:7
4 Prov. 14:20
5 Ex. 23:1; Deut. 19:16, 19; Prov. 6:19; 19:9; 21:28
6 Prov. 17:8; 18:16; 20:26; 21:14
7 Ps. 38:11; Prov. 14:20
8 Prov. 16:20
9 Prov. 19:5
10 Prov. 30:22; Eccl. 10:6, 7
11 Prov. 14:29; 16:32
12 Prov. 16:14, 15; 20:2; 28:15; Hos. 14:5
14 2Cor. 12:14
16 Luke 10:28; 11:28
17 Matt. 10:42; 25:40
18 Prov. 13:24; 23:13
20 Ps. 37:37
21 Job 23:13; Ps. 33:10, 11
23 1Tim. 4:8
24 Prov. 15:19; 26:13, 15

it is not good; and he that hasteth with *his* feet sinneth.

3 The foolishness of man perverteth his way: and his heart fretteth against the LORD.

4 Wealth maketh many friends; but the poor is separated from his neighbour.

5 A false witness shall not be unpunished, and *he that* speaketh lies shall not escape.

6 Many will intreat the favour of the prince: and every man *is* a friend to him that giveth gifts.

7 All the brethren of the poor do hate him: how much more do his friends go far from him? he pursueth *them with* words, *yet* they *are* wanting *to him*.

8 He that getteth wisdom loveth his own soul: he that keepeth understanding shall find good.

9 A false witness shall not be unpunished, and *he that* speaketh lies shall perish.

10 Delight is not seemly for a fool; much less for a servant to have rule over princes.

11 The discretion of a man deferreth his anger; and *it is* his glory to pass over a transgression.

12 The king's wrath *is* as the roaring of a lion; but his favour *is* as dew upon the grass.

13 A foolish son *is* the calamity of his father: and the contentions of a wife *are* a continual dropping.

14 House and riches *are* the inheritance of fathers: and a prudent wife *is* from the LORD.

15 Slothfulness casteth into a deep sleep; and an idle soul shall suffer hunger.

16 He that keepeth the commandment keepeth his own soul; *but* he that despiseth his ways shall die.

17 He that hath pity upon the poor lendeth unto the LORD; and that which he hath given will he pay him again.

18 Chasten thy son while there is hope, and let not thy soul spare for his crying.

19 A man of great wrath shall suffer punishment: for if thou deliver *him*, yet thou must do it again.

20 Hear counsel, and receive instruction, that thou mayest be wise in thy latter end.

21 *There are* many devices in a man's heart; nevertheless the counsel of the LORD, that shall stand.

22 The desire of a man *is* his kindness: and a poor man *is* better than a liar.

23 The fear of the LORD *tendeth* to life: and he *that hath it* shall abide satisfied; he shall not be visited with evil.

24 A slothful *man* hideth his hand in *his* bosom, and will not so much as bring it to his mouth again.

25 Smite a scorner, and the simple will beware: and reprove one that hath understanding, *and* he will understand knowledge.

26 He that wasteth *his* father, *and* chaseth away *his* mother, *is* a son that causeth shame, and bringeth reproach.

27 Cease, my son, to hear the instruction *that causeth* to err from the words of knowledge.

28 An ungodly witness scorneth judgment: and the mouth of the wicked devoureth iniquity.

29 Judgments are prepared for scorners, and stripes for the back of fools.

CHAPTER 20

1 Wine *is* a mocker, strong drink *is* raging: and whosoever is deceived thereby is not wise.

2 The fear of a king *is* as the roaring of a lion: *whoso* provoketh him to anger sinneth *against* his own soul.

3 *It is* an honour for a man to cease from strife: but every fool will be meddling.

4 The sluggard will not plow by reason of the cold; *therefore* shall he beg in harvest, and *have* nothing.

5 Counsel in the heart of man *is like* deep water; but a man of understanding will draw it out.

6 Most men will proclaim every one his own goodness: but a faithful man who can find?

7 The just *man* walketh in his integrity: his children *are* blessed after him.

8 A king that sitteth in the throne of judgment scattereth away all evil with his eyes.

9 Who can say, I have made my heart clean, I am pure from my sin?

10 Divers weights, *and* divers measures, both of them *are* alike abomination to the LORD.

11 Even a child is known by his doings, whether his work *be* pure, and whether *it be* right.

12 The hearing ear, and the seeing eye, the LORD hath made even both of them.

13 Love not sleep, lest thou come to poverty; open thine eyes, *and* thou shalt be satisfied with bread.

14 *It is* naught, *it is* naught, saith the buyer: but when he is gone his way, then he boasteth.

15 There is gold, and a multitude of rubies: but the lips of knowledge *are* a precious jewel.

16 Take his garment that is surety *for a*

Cross-references
25 Deut. 13:11
26 Prov. 17:2
28 Job 15:16; 20:12, 13; 34:7
1 Gen. 9:21; Prov. 23:29, 30
4 Prov. 10:4; 19:15, 24
6 Ps. 12:1; Prov. 25:14
7 Ps. 37:26; 112:2; 2Cor. 1:12
9 1Kgs. 8:46; 2Chr. 6:36; Job 14:4; Ps. 51:5; Eccl. 7:20; 1Cor. 4:4; 1John 1:8
10 Deut. 25:13
11 Matt. 7:16
12 Ex. 4:11; Ps. 94:9
13 Prov. 6:9; 12:11; 19:15; Rom. 12:11
15 Job 28:12, 16-19; Prov. 3:15; 8:11
16 Prov. 22:26, 27; 27:13
17 Prov. 9:17
18 Prov. 15:22; 24:6; Luke 14:31
19 Prov. 11:13; Rom. 16:18
20 Ex. 21:17; Lev. 20:9; Job 18:5, 6; Prov. 24:20; Matt. 15:4
21 Hab. 2:6
22 Rom. 12:17, 19
24 Jer. 10:23
25 Eccl. 5:4, 5
26 Ps. 101:5
2 Prov. 16:2; 24:12; Luke 16:15
3 1Sam. 15:22; Mic. 6:7, 8
6 Prov. 10:2; 13:11; 20:21; 2Pet. 2:3

stranger: and take a pledge of him for a strange woman.

17 Bread of deceit *is* sweet to a man; but afterwards his mouth shall be filled with gravel.

18 *Every* purpose is established by counsel: and with good advice make war.

19 He that goeth about *as* a talebearer revealeth secrets: therefore meddle not with him that flattereth with his lips.

20 Whoso curseth his father or his mother, his lamp shall be put out in obscure darkness.

21 An inheritance *may be* gotten hastily at the beginning; but the end thereof shall not be blessed.

22 Say not thou, I will recompense evil; *but* wait on the LORD, and he shall save thee.

23 Divers weights *are* an abomination unto the LORD; and a false balance *is* not good.

24 Man's goings *are* of the LORD; how can a man then understand his own way?

25 *It is* a snare to the man *who* devoureth *that which* is holy, and after vows to make inquiry.

26 A wise king scattereth the wicked, and bringeth the wheel over them.

27 The spirit of man *is* the candle of the LORD, searching all the inward parts of the belly.

28 Mercy and truth preserve the king: and his throne is upholden by mercy.

29 The glory of young men *is* their strength: and the beauty of old men *is* the grey head.

30 The blueness of a wound cleanseth away evil: so *do* stripes the inward parts of the belly.

CHAPTER 21

1 The king's heart *is* in the hand of the LORD, *as* the rivers of water: he turneth it whithersoever he will.

2 Every way of a man *is* right in his own eyes: but the LORD pondereth the hearts.

3 To do justice and judgment *is* more acceptable to the LORD than sacrifice.

4 An high look, and a proud heart, *and* the plowing of the wicked, *is* sin.

5 The thoughts of the diligent *tend* only to plenteousness; but of every one *that is* hasty only to want.

6 The getting of treasures by a lying tongue *is* a vanity tossed to and fro of them that seek death.

7 The robbery of the wicked shall destroy them; because they refuse to do judgment.

8 The way of man *is* froward and strange: but *as for* the pure, his work *is* right.

9 *It is* better to dwell in a corner of the housetop, than with a brawling woman in a wide house.

10 The soul of the wicked desireth evil: his neighbour findeth no favour in his eyes.

11 When the scorner is punished, the simple is made wise: and when the wise is instructed, he receiveth knowledge.

12 The righteous *man* wisely considereth the house of the wicked: *but God* overthroweth the wicked for *their* wickedness.

13 Whoso stoppeth his ears at the cry of the poor, he also shall cry himself, but shall not be heard.

14 A gift in secret pacifieth anger: and a reward in the bosom strong wrath.

15 *It is* joy to the just to do judgment: but destruction *shall be* to the workers of iniquity.

16 The man that wandereth out of the way of understanding shall remain in the congregation of the dead.

17 He that loveth pleasure *shall be* a poor man: he that loveth wine and oil shall not be rich.

18 The wicked *shall be* a ransom for the righteous, and the transgressor for the upright.

19 *It is* better to dwell in the wilderness, than with a contentious and an angry woman.

20 *There is* treasure to be desired and oil in the dwelling of the wise; but a foolish man spendeth it up.

21 He that followeth after righteousness and mercy findeth life, righteousness, and honour.

22 A wise *man* scaleth the city of the mighty, and casteth down the strength of the confidence thereof.

23 Whoso keepeth his mouth and his tongue keepeth his soul from troubles.

24 Proud *and* haughty scorner *is* his name, who dealeth in proud wrath.

25 The desire of the slothful killeth him; for his hands refuse to labour.

26 He coveteth greedily all the day long: but the righteous giveth and spareth not.

27 The sacrifice of the wicked *is* abomination: how much more, *when* he bringeth it with a wicked mind?

28 A false witness shall perish: but the man that heareth speaketh constantly.

29 A wicked man hardeneth his face: but *as for* the upright, he directeth his way.

30 *There is* no wisdom nor understanding nor counsel against the LORD.

31 The horse *is* prepared against the day of battle: but safety *is* of the LORD.

CHAPTER 22

1 A *good* name *is* rather to be chosen than great riches, *and* loving favour rather than silver and gold.

2 The rich and poor meet together: the LORD *is* the maker of them all.

3 A prudent *man* foreseeth the evil, and hideth himself: but the simple pass on, and are punished.

4 By humility *and* the fear of the LORD *are* riches, and honour, and life.

5 Thorns *and* snares *are* in the way of the froward: he that doth keep his soul shall be far from them.

6 Train up a child in the way he should go: and when he is old, he will not depart from it.

7 The rich ruleth over the poor, and the borrower *is* servant to the lender.

8 He that soweth iniquity shall reap vanity: and the rod of his anger shall fail.

9 He that hath a bountiful eye shall be blessed; for he giveth of his bread to the poor.

10 Cast out the scorner, and contention shall go out; yea, strife and reproach shall cease.

11 He that loveth pureness of heart, *for* the grace of his lips the king *shall be* his friend.

12 The eyes of the LORD preserve knowledge, and he overthroweth the words of the transgressor.

13 The slothful *man* saith, *There is* a lion without, I shall be slain in the streets.

14 The mouth of strange women *is* a deep pit: he that is abhorred of the LORD shall fall therein.

15 Foolishness *is* bound in the heart of a child; *but* the rod of correction shall drive it far from him.

16 He that oppresseth the poor to increase his *riches, and* he that giveth to the rich, *shall* surely *come* to want.

17 Bow down thine ear, and hear the words of the wise, and apply thine heart unto my knowledge.

---

9 Prov. 19:13; 21:19
10 James 4:5
13 Matt. 7:2; 18:30; James 2:13
18 Prov. 11:8; Isa. 43:3, 4
19 Prov. 21:9
20 Ps. 112:3; Matt. 25:3, 4
21 Prov. 15:9; Matt. 5:6
22 Eccl. 9:14
23 Prov. 12:13; 13:3; 18:21; James 3:2
25 Prov. 13:4
26 Ps. 37:26; 112:9
27 Prov. 15:8
28 Prov. 19:5, 9
30 Isa. 8:9, 10; Jer. 9:23; Acts 5:39
31 Ps. 3:8; 20:7; 33:17; Isa. 31:1
1 Eccl. 7:1
2 Job 31:15; Prov. 14:31; 29:13; 1Cor. 12:21
3 Prov. 14:16; 27:12
4 Ps. 112:3; Matt. 6:33
5 Prov. 15:19; 1John 5:18
6 Eph. 6:4; 2Tim. 3:15
7 James 2:6
8 Job 4:8; Hos. 10:13
9 2Cor. 9:6
14 Prov. 2:16; 5:3; 7:5; 23:27; Eccl. 7:26
15 Prov. 13:24; 19:18; 23:13, 14; 29:15, 17

22:6 when he is old, he will not depart from it. "Old" here means mature (a young adult, lit. "when he grows a beard"), not elderly. One who submits to the way of wisdom in his or her childhood will certainly continue on that path as an adult. This is not a prophetic promise that will be fulfilled in history. Instead, it is a statement of wisdom teaching that in proper child training will produce wise adults.

18 For *it is* a pleasant thing if thou keep them within thee; they shall withal be fitted in thy lips.
19 That thy trust may be in the LORD, I have made known to thee this day, even to thee.
20 Have not I written to thee excellent things in counsels and knowledge,
21 That I might make thee know the certainty of the words of truth; that thou mightest answer the words of truth to them that send unto thee?
22 Rob not the poor, because he *is* poor: neither oppress the afflicted in the gate:
23 For the LORD will plead their cause, and spoil the soul of those that spoiled them.
24 Make no friendship with an angry man; and with a furious man thou shalt not go:
25 Lest thou learn his ways, and get a snare to thy soul.
26 Be not thou *one* of them that strike hands, *or* of them that are sureties for debts.
27 If thou hast nothing to pay, why should he take away thy bed from under thee?
28 Remove not the ancient landmark, which thy fathers have set.
29 Seest thou a man diligent in his business? he shall stand before kings; he shall not stand before mean *men*.

CHAPTER 23

1 When thou sittest to eat with a ruler, consider diligently what *is* before thee:
2 And put a knife to thy throat, if thou *be* a man given to appetite.
3 Be not desirous of his dainties: for they *are* deceitful meat.
4 Labour not to be rich: cease from thine own wisdom.
5 Wilt thou set thine eyes upon that which is not? for *riches* certainly make themselves wings; they fly away as an eagle toward heaven.
6 Eat thou not the bread of *him that hath* an evil eye, neither desire thou his dainty meats:
7 For as he thinketh in his heart, so *is* he: Eat and drink, saith he to thee; but his heart *is* not with thee.
8 The morsel *which* thou hast eaten shalt thou vomit up, and lose thy sweet words.

---

21 Luke 1:3, 4; 1Pet. 3:15
22 Ex. 23:6
23 1Sam. 24:12; 25:39; Ps. 12:5
28 Deut. 19:14; 27:17; Prov. 23:10
4 Prov. 3:5; 28:20; Rom. 12:16; 1Tim. 6:9, 10
6 Deut. 15:9; Ps. 141:4
7 Ps. 12:2
9 Prov. 9:8; Matt. 7:6
10 Deut. 19:14; 27:17; Prov. 22:28
11 Job 31:21; Prov. 22:23
13 Prov. 13:24; 19:18; 22:15; 29:15, 17
14 1Cor. 5:5
15 Prov. 23:24, 25; 29:3
17 Ps. 37:1; 73:3; Prov. 3:31; 24:1; 28:14
18 Ps. 37:37; Prov. 24:14; Luke 16:25
19 Prov. 4:23
20 Isa. 5:22; Matt. 24:49; Luke 21:34; Rom. 13:13; Eph. 5:18
21 Prov. 19:15
22 Prov. 1:8
23 Matt. 13:44
28 Eccl. 7:26
29 Gen. 49:12; Isa. 5:11, 22
30 Ps. 75:8; Prov. 9:2; 20:1; Eph. 5:18

---

9 Speak not in the ears of a fool: for he will despise the wisdom of thy words.
10 Remove not the old landmark; and enter not into the fields of the fatherless:
11 For their redeemer *is* mighty; he shall plead their cause with thee.
12 Apply thine heart unto instruction, and thine ears to the words of knowledge.
13 Withhold not correction from the child: for *if* thou beatest him with the rod, he shall not die.
14 Thou shalt beat him with the rod, and shalt deliver his soul from hell.
15 My son, if thine heart be wise, my heart shall rejoice, even mine.
16 Yea, my reins shall rejoice, when thy lips speak right things.
17 Let not thine heart envy sinners: but *be thou* in the fear of the LORD all the day long.
18 For surely there is an end; and thine expectation shall not be cut off.
19 Hear thou, my son, and be wise, and guide thine heart in the way.
20 Be not among winebibbers; among riotous eaters of flesh:
21 For the drunkard and the glutton shall come to poverty: and drowsiness shall clothe *a man* with rags.
22 Hearken unto thy father that begat thee, and despise not thy mother when she is old.
23 Buy the truth, and sell *it* not; *also* wisdom, and instruction, and understanding.
24 The father of the righteous shall greatly rejoice: and he that begetteth a wise *child* shall have joy of him.
25 Thy father and thy mother shall be glad, and she that bare thee shall rejoice.
26 My son, give me thine heart, and let thine eyes observe my ways.
27 For a whore *is* a deep ditch; and a strange woman *is* a narrow pit.
28 She also lieth in wait as *for* a prey, and increaseth the transgressors among men.
29 Who hath woe? who hath sorrow? who hath contentions? who hath babbling? who hath wounds without cause? who hath redness of eyes?
30 They that tarry long at the wine; they that go to seek mixed wine.
31 Look not thou upon the wine when it is

22:22–23 Proverbs is wisdom set within the framework of the Mosaic Law. The Lord told Israel how they should treat the poor (Deut. 22:1–18) under governance of the Law. Their were no penalties that were to be implemented by human agents because the Lord would impose directly the sanctions for mistreatment of the poor (Deut. 15:4–8). Thus, a wise Israelite would not want to rob or afflict the poor. This proverb does not apply to Gentiles since they have never been under the jurisdiction of the Mosaic Law (Ps. 147:19–20).

red, when it giveth his colour in the cup, *when* it moveth itself aright.

32 At the last it biteth like a serpent, and stingeth like an adder.

33 Thine eyes shall behold strange women, and thine heart shall utter perverse things.

34 Yea, thou shalt be as he that lieth down in the midst of the sea, or as he that lieth upon the top of a mast.

35 They have stricken me, *shalt thou say, and* I was not sick; they have beaten me, *and* I felt *it* not: when shall I awake? I will seek it yet again.

CHAPTER 24

1 Be not thou envious against evil men, neither desire to be with them.

2 For their heart studieth destruction, and their lips talk of mischief.

3 Through wisdom is an house builded; and by understanding it is established:

4 And by knowledge shall the chambers be filled with all precious and pleasant riches.

5 A wise man *is* strong; yea, a man of knowledge increaseth strength.

6 For by wise counsel thou shalt make thy war: and in multitude of counsellers *there is* safety.

7 Wisdom *is* too high for a fool: he openeth not his mouth in the gate.

8 He that deviseth to do evil shall be called a mischievous person.

9 The thought of foolishness *is* sin: and the scorner *is* an abomination to men.

10 *If* thou faint in the day of adversity, thy strength *is* small.

11 If thou forbear to deliver *them that are* drawn unto death, and *those that are* ready to be slain;

12 If thou sayest, Behold, we knew it not; doth not he that pondereth the heart consider *it*? and he that keepeth thy soul, doth *not* he know *it*? and shall *not* he render to *every* man according to his works?

13 My son, eat thou honey, because *it is* good; and the honeycomb, *which is* sweet to thy taste:

14 So *shall* the knowledge of wisdom *be* unto thy soul: when thou hast found *it*, then there shall be a reward, and thy expectation shall not be cut off.

15 Lay not wait, O wicked *man*, against the dwelling of the righteous; spoil not his resting place:

16 For a just *man* falleth seven times, and riseth up again: but the wicked shall fall into mischief.

17 Rejoice not when thine enemy falleth,

and let not thine heart be glad when he stumbleth:

18 Lest the LORD see *it*, and it displease him, and he turn away his wrath from him.

19 Fret not thyself because of evil *men*, neither be thou envious at the wicked;

20 For there shall be no reward to the evil *man*; the candle of the wicked shall be put out.

21 My son, fear thou the LORD and the king: *and* meddle not with them that are given to change:

22 For their calamity shall rise suddenly; and who knoweth the ruin of them both?

23 These *things* also *belong* to the wise. *It is* not good to have respect of persons in judgment.

24 He that saith unto the wicked, Thou *art* righteous; him shall the people curse, nations shall abhor him:

25 But to them that rebuke *him* shall be delight, and a good blessing shall come upon them.

26 *Every man* shall kiss *his* lips that giveth a right answer.

27 Prepare thy work without, and make it fit for thyself in the field; and afterwards build thine house.

28 Be not a witness against thy neighbour without cause; and deceive *not* with thy lips.

29 Say not, I will do so to him as he hath done to me: I will render to the man according to his work.

30 I went by the field of the slothful, and by the vineyard of the man void of understanding;

31 And, lo, it was all grown over with thorns, *and* nettles had covered the face thereof, and the stone wall thereof was broken down.

32 Then I saw, *and* considered *it* well: I looked upon *it, and* received instruction.

33 *Yet* a little sleep, a little slumber, a little folding of the hands to sleep:

34 So shall thy poverty come *as* one that travelleth; and thy want as an armed man.

CHAPTER 25
More Proverbs from Solomon

1 These *are* also proverbs of Solomon, which the men of Hezekiah king of Judah copied out.

2 *It is* the glory of God to conceal a thing: but the honour of kings *is* to search out a matter.

3 The heaven for height, and the earth for depth, and the heart of kings *is* unsearchable.

Cross references (center column)

35 Deut. 29:19; Prov. 27:22; Isa. 56:12; Jer. 5:3; Eph. 4:19

1 Ps. 37:1; 73:3; Prov. 1:15; 3:31; 23:17; 24:19

2 Ps. 10:7

5 Prov. 21:22; Eccl. 9:16

6 Luke 14:31

7 Ps. 10:5; Prov. 14:6

8 Rom. 1:30

11 Ps. 82:4; Isa. 58:6, 7; 1 John 3:16

12 Job 34:11; Ps. 62:12; Prov. 21:2; Jer. 32:19; Rom. 2:6; Rev. 2:23; 22:12

13 Song 5:1

14 Ps. 19:10; 119:103; Prov. 23:18

15 Ps. 10:9, 10

16 Esth. 7:10; Job 5:19

17 Job 31:29; Ps. 35:15, 19

19 Ps. 37:1; 73:3

20 Job 18:5, 6; 21:17; Ps. 11:6

21 Rom. 13:7; 1 Pet. 2:17

23 Lev. 19:15; Deut. 1:17; 16:19

24 Isa. 5:23

27 Luke 14:28

28 Eph. 4:25

29 Matt. 5:39, 44; Rom. 12:17, 19

31 Gen. 3:18

33 Prov. 6:9

1 1 Kgs. 4:32

2 Deut. 29:29; Job 29:16; Rom. 11:33

4 Take away the dross from the silver, and there shall come forth a vessel for the finer.
5 Take away the wicked *from* before the king, and his throne shall be established in righteousness.
6 Put not forth thyself in the presence of the king, and stand not in the place of great *men*:
7 For better *it is* that it be said unto thee, Come up hither; than that thou shouldest be put lower in the presence of the prince whom thine eyes have seen.
8 Go not forth hastily to strive, lest *thou know not* what to do in the end thereof, when thy neighbour hath put thee to shame.
9 Debate thy cause with thy neighbour *himself*; and discover not a secret to another:
10 Lest he that heareth *it* put thee to shame, and thine infamy turn not away.
11 A word fitly spoken *is like* apples of gold in pictures of silver.
12 *As* an earring of gold, and an ornament of fine gold, *so is* a wise reprover upon an obedient ear.
13 As the cold of snow in the time of harvest, *so is* a faithful messenger to them that send him: for he refresheth the soul of his masters.
14 Whoso boasteth himself of a false gift *is like* clouds and wind without rain.
15 By long forbearing is a prince persuaded, and a soft tongue breaketh the bone.
16 Hast thou found honey? eat so much as is sufficient for thee, lest thou be filled therewith, and vomit it.
17 Withdraw thy foot from thy neighbour's house; lest he be weary of thee, and *so* hate thee.
18 A man that beareth false witness against his neighbour *is* a maul, and a sword, and a sharp arrow.
19 Confidence in an unfaithful man in time of trouble *is like* a broken tooth, and a foot out of joint.
20 *As* he that taketh away a garment in cold weather, *and as* vinegar upon nitre, so *is* he that singeth songs to an heavy heart.
21 If thine enemy be hungry, give him bread to eat; and if he be thirsty, give him water to drink:
22 For thou shalt heap coals of fire upon his head, and the LORD shall reward thee.
23 The north wind driveth away rain: so *doth* an angry countenance a backbiting tongue.
24 *It is* better to dwell in the corner of the housetop, than with a brawling woman and in a wide house.

25 *As* cold waters to a thirsty soul, so *is* good news from a far country.
26 A righteous man falling down before the wicked *is as* a troubled fountain, and a corrupt spring.
27 *It is* not good to eat much honey: so *for men* to search their own glory *is not* glory.
28 He that *hath* no rule over his own spirit *is like* a city *that is* broken down, *and* without walls.

CHAPTER 26

1 As snow in summer, and as rain in harvest, so honour is not seemly for a fool.
2 As the bird by wandering, as the swallow by flying, so the curse causeless shall not come.
3 A whip for the horse, a bridle for the ass, and a rod for the fool's back.
4 Answer not a fool according to his folly, lest thou also be like unto him.
5 Answer a fool according to his folly, lest he be wise in his own conceit.
6 He that sendeth a message by the hand of a fool cutteth off the feet, *and* drinketh damage.
7 The legs of the lame are not equal: so *is* a parable in the mouth of fools.
8 As he that bindeth a stone in a sling, so *is* he that giveth honour to a fool.
9 *As* a thorn goeth up into the hand of a drunkard, so *is* a parable in the mouth of fools.
10 The great *God* that formed all *things* both rewardeth the fool, and rewardeth transgressors.
11 As a dog returneth to his vomit, *so* a fool returneth to his folly.
12 Seest thou a man wise in his own conceit? *there is* more hope of a fool than of him.
13 The slothful *man* saith, *There is* a lion in the way; a lion *is* in the streets.
14 *As* the door turneth upon his hinges, so *doth* the slothful upon his bed.
15 The slothful hideth his hand in *his* bosom; it grieveth him to bring it again to his mouth.
16 The sluggard *is* wiser in his own conceit than seven men that can render a reason.
17 He that passeth by, *and* meddleth with strife *belonging* not to him, *is like* one that taketh a dog by the ears.
18 As a mad *man* who casteth firebrands, arrows, and death,
19 So *is* the man *that* deceiveth his neighbour, and saith, Am not I in sport?
20 Where no wood is, *there* the fire goeth

4 2Tim. 2:21
5 Prov. 16:12; 20:8; 29:14
7 Luke 14:8-10
8 Prov. 17:14; Matt. 5:25
9 Matt. 5:25; 18:15
11 Prov. 15:23; Isa. 50:4
13 Prov. 13:17
14 Prov. 20:6; Jude 1:12
15 Gen. 32:4; 1Sam. 25:24; Prov. 15:1; 16:14
16 Prov. 25:27
18 Ps. 57:4; 120:3, 4; Prov. 12:18
20 Dan. 6:18; Rom. 12:15
21 Ex. 23:4, 5; Matt. 5:44; Rom. 12:20
22 2Sam. 16:12
23 Job 37:22; Ps. 101:5
24 Prov. 19:13; 21:9, 19
27 Prov. 25:16; 27:2
28 Prov. 16:32
1 1Sam. 12:17
2 Num. 23:8; Deut. 23:5
3 Ps. 32:9; Prov. 10:13
5 Matt. 16:1-4; 21:24-27
11 Ex. 8:15; 2Pet. 2:22
12 Prov. 29:20; Luke 18:11; Rom. 12:16; Rev. 3:17
13 Prov. 22:13
15 Prov. 19:24

out: so where *there is* no talebearer, the strife ceaseth.

21 As coals *are* to burning coals, and wood to fire; so *is* a contentious man to kindle strife.

22 The words of a talebearer *are* as wounds, and they go down into the innermost parts of the belly.

23 Burning lips and a wicked heart *are like* a potsherd covered with silver dross.

24 He that hateth dissembleth with his lips, and layeth up deceit within him;

25 When he speaketh fair, believe him not: for *there are* seven abominations in his heart.

26 *Whose* hatred is covered by deceit, his wickedness shall be shewed before the *whole* congregation.

27 Whoso diggeth a pit shall fall therein: and he that rolleth a stone, it will return upon him.

28 A lying tongue hateth *those that are* afflicted by it; and a flattering mouth worketh ruin.

CHAPTER 27

1 Boast not thyself of to morrow; for thou knowest not what a day may bring forth.

2 Let another man praise thee, and not thine own mouth; a stranger, and not thine own lips.

3 A stone *is* heavy, and the sand weighty; but a fool's wrath *is* heavier than them both.

4 Wrath *is* cruel, and anger *is* outrageous; but who *is* able to stand before envy?

5 Open rebuke *is* better than secret love.

6 Faithful *are* the wounds of a friend; but the kisses of an enemy *are* deceitful.

7 The full soul loatheth an honeycomb; but to the hungry soul every bitter thing is sweet.

8 As a bird that wandereth from her nest, so *is* a man that wandereth from his place.

9 Ointment and perfume rejoice the heart: so *doth* the sweetness of a man's friend by hearty counsel.

10 Thine own friend, and thy father's friend, forsake not; neither go into thy brother's house in the day of thy calamity: *for* better *is* a neighbour *that is* near than a brother far off.

11 My son, be wise, and make my heart

glad, that I may answer him that reproacheth me.

12 A prudent *man* foreseeth the evil, *and* hideth himself; *but* the simple pass on, *and* are punished.

13 Take his garment that is surety for a stranger, and take a pledge of him for a strange woman.

14 He that blesseth his friend with a loud voice, rising early in the morning, it shall be counted a curse to him.

15 A continual dropping in a very rainy day and a contentious woman are alike.

16 Whosoever hideth her hideth the wind, and the ointment of his right hand, *which* bewrayeth *itself*.

17 Iron sharpeneth iron; so a man sharpeneth the countenance of his friend.

18 Whoso keepeth the fig tree shall eat the fruit thereof: so he that waiteth on his master shall be honoured.

19 As in water face *answereth* to face, so the heart of man to man.

20 Hell and destruction are never full; so the eyes of man are never satisfied.

21 *As* the fining pot for silver, and the furnace for gold; so *is* a man to his praise.

22 Though thou shouldest bray a fool in a mortar among wheat with a pestle, *yet* will not his foolishness depart from him.

23 Be thou diligent to know the state of thy flocks, *and* look well to thy herds.

24 For riches *are* not for ever: and doth the crown *endure* to every generation?

25 The hay appeareth, and the tender grass sheweth itself, and herbs of the mountains are gathered.

26 The lambs *are* for thy clothing, and the goats *are* the price of the field.

27 And *thou shalt have* goats' milk enough for thy food, for the food of thy household, and *for* the maintenance for thy maidens.

CHAPTER 28

1 The wicked flee when no man pursueth: but the righteous are bold as a lion.

2 For the transgression of a land many *are* the princes thereof: but by a man of understanding *and* knowledge the state *thereof* shall be prolonged.

3 A poor man that oppresseth the poor *is like* a sweeping rain which leaveth no food.

Cross references (center column)

21 Prov. 15:18; 29:22
22 Prov. 18:8
25 Ps. 28:3; Jer. 9:8
27 Ps. 7:15, 16; 10:2; 57:6; Prov. 28:10; Eccl. 10:8
1 Luke 12:19, 20; James 4:13, 14
2 Prov. 25:27
4 Prov. 6:34; 1John 3:12
5 Prov. 28:23; Gal. 2:14
6 Ps. 141:5
7 Job 6:7
10 Prov. 17:17; 18:24; 19:7
11 Ps. 127:5; Prov. 10:1; 23:15, 24
12 Prov. 22:3
13 Ex. 22:26; Prov. 20:16
15 Prov. 19:13
18 1Cor. 9:7, 13
20 Prov. 30:16; Eccl. 1:8; 6:7; Hab. 2:5
21 Prov. 17:3
22 Prov. 23:35; Isa. 1:5; Jer. 5:3
25 Ps. 104:14
1 Lev. 26:17, 36; Ps. 53:5
3 Matt. 18:28

27:1 thou knowest not what a day may bring forth. Proverbs is a book of wisdom, whose focus is upon the skill of living out the details of this life. Thus, in the daily affairs of life, such as in the business realm, one does not know for sure whether one's activity will bring profit or loss (cf. James 4:13–17). God's prophetic plan for history is certain and should be contemplated when planning one's daily affairs, but the plans of men are not certain.

4 They that forsake the law praise the wicked: but such as keep the law contend with them.

5 Evil men understand not judgment: but they that seek the LORD understand all *things*.

6 Better *is* the poor that walketh in his uprightness, than *he that is* perverse *in his* ways, though he *be* rich.

7 Whoso keepeth the law *is* a wise son: but he that is a companion of riotous *men* shameth his father.

8 He that by usury and unjust gain increaseth his substance, he shall gather it for him that will pity the poor.

9 He that turneth away his ear from hearing the law, even his prayer *shall be* abomination.

10 Whoso causeth the righteous to go astray in an evil way, he shall fall himself into his own pit: but the upright shall have good *things* in possession.

11 The rich man *is* wise in his own conceit; but the poor that hath understanding searcheth him out.

12 When righteous *men* do rejoice, *there is* great glory: but when the wicked rise, a man is hidden.

13 He that covereth his sins shall not prosper: but whoso confesseth and forsaketh *them* shall have mercy.

14 Happy *is* the man that feareth alway: but he that hardeneth his heart shall fall into mischief.

15 *As* a roaring lion, and a ranging bear; *so is* a wicked ruler over the poor people.

16 The prince that wanteth understanding *is* also a great oppressor: *but* he that hateth covetousness shall prolong *his* days.

17 A man that doeth violence to the blood of *any* person shall flee to the pit; let no man stay him.

18 Whoso walketh uprightly shall be saved: but *he that is* perverse *in his* ways shall fall at once.

19 He that tilleth his land shall have plenty of bread: but he that followeth after vain *persons* shall have poverty enough.

20 A faithful man shall abound with blessings: but he that maketh haste to be rich shall not be innocent.

21 To have respect of persons *is* not good: for for a piece of bread *that* man will transgress.

22 He that hasteth to be rich *hath* an evil eye, and considereth not that poverty shall come upon him.

23 He that rebuketh a man afterwards shall find more favour than he that flattereth with the tongue.

24 Whoso robbeth his father or his mother, and saith, *It is* no transgression; the same *is* the companion of a destroyer.

25 He that is of a proud heart stirreth up strife: but he that putteth his trust in the LORD shall be made fat.

26 He that trusteth in his own heart is a fool: but whoso walketh wisely, he shall be delivered.

27 He that giveth unto the poor shall not lack: but he that hideth his eyes shall have many a curse.

28 When the wicked rise, men hide themselves: but when they perish, the righteous increase.

CHAPTER 29

1 He, that being often reproved hardeneth *his* neck, shall suddenly be destroyed, and that without remedy.

2 When the righteous are in authority, the people rejoice: but when the wicked beareth rule, the people mourn.

3 Whoso loveth wisdom rejoiceth his father: but he that keepeth company with harlots spendeth *his* substance.

4 The king by judgment establisheth the land: but he that receiveth gifts overthroweth it.

5 A man that flattereth his neighbour spreadeth a net for his feet.

6 In the transgression of an evil man *there is* a snare: but the righteous doth sing and rejoice.

7 The righteous considereth the cause of the poor: *but* the wicked regardeth not to know *it*.

8 Scornful men bring a city into a snare: but wise *men* turn away wrath.

9 *If* a wise man contendeth with a foolish man, whether he rage or laugh, *there is* no rest.

10 The bloodthirsty hate the upright: but the just seek his soul.

11 A fool uttereth all his mind: but a wise *man* keepeth it in till afterwards.

12 If a ruler hearken to lies, all his servants *are* wicked.

13 The poor and the deceitful man meet together: the LORD lighteneth both their eyes.

14 The king that faithfully judgeth the poor, his throne shall be established for ever.

15 The rod and reproof give wisdom: but a child left *to himself* bringeth his mother to shame.

16 When the wicked are multiplied, trans-

Cross references:

4 1Kgs. 18:18, 21; Matt. 3:7; 14:4

5 John 7:17; 1Cor. 2:15

8 Prov. 13:22; Eccl. 2:26

9 Ps. 66:18; 109:7; Zech. 7:11

10 Prov. 26:27; Matt. 6:33

13 Ps. 32:3, 5; 1John 1:8-10

14 Ps. 16:8; Prov. 23:17; Rom. 2:5; 11:20

15 Ex. 1:14, 16, 22; Matt. 2:16; 1Pet. 5:8

17 Gen. 9:6; Ex. 21:14

18 Prov. 10:9, 25; Prov. 28:6

20 Prov. 13:11; 20:21; 23:4; 28:22; 1Tim. 6:9

21 Prov. 18:5; 24:23; Ezek. 13:19

22 Prov. 28:20

25 Prov. 13:10; 1Tim. 6:6

27 Deut. 15:7; Prov. 19:17; 22:9

28 Job 24:4; Prov. 28:12; 29:2

1 1Sam. 2:25; 2Chr. 36:16

2 Esth. 3:15; 8:15

3 Luke 15:13, 30

7 Job 29:16; 31:13; Ps. 41:1

10 1John 3:12

13 Matt. 5:45

14 Ps. 72:2, 4, 13, 14

16 Ps. 37:36; 58:10; 91:8; 92:11

gression increaseth: but the righteous shall see their fall.

17 Correct thy son, and he shall give thee rest; yea, he shall give delight unto thy soul.

18 Where *there is* no vision, the people perish: but he that keepeth the law, happy *is* he.

19 A servant will not be corrected by words: for though he understand he will not answer.

20 Seest thou a man *that is* hasty in his words? *there is* more hope of a fool than of him.

21 He that delicately bringeth up his servant from a child shall have him become *his* son at the length.

22 An angry man stirreth up strife, and a furious man aboundeth in transgression.

23 A man's pride shall bring him low: but honour shall uphold the humble in spirit.

24 Whoso is partner with a thief hateth his own soul: he heareth cursing, and bewrayeth *it* not.

25 The fear of man bringeth a snare: but whoso putteth his trust in the LORD shall be safe.

26 Many seek the ruler's favour; but *every* man's judgment *cometh* from the LORD.

27 An unjust man *is* an abomination to the just: and *he that is* upright in the way *is* abomination to the wicked.

CHAPTER 30
The Observations of Agur

1 The words of Agur the son of Jakeh, *even* the prophecy: the man spake unto Ithiel, even unto Ithiel and Ucal,

2 Surely I *am* more brutish than *any* man, and have not the understanding of a man.

3 I neither learned wisdom, nor have the knowledge of the holy.

4 Who hath ascended up into heaven, or descended? who hath gathered the wind in his fists? who hath bound the waters in a garment? who hath established all the ends of the earth? what *is* his name, and what *is* his son's name, if thou canst tell?

5 Every word of God *is* pure: he *is* a shield unto them that put their trust in him.

6 Add thou not unto his words, lest he reprove thee, and thou be found a liar.

7 Two *things* have I required of thee; deny me *them* not before I die:

8 Remove far from me vanity and lies: give me neither poverty nor riches; feed me with food convenient for me:

9 Lest I be full, and deny *thee*, and say, Who *is* the LORD? or lest I be poor, and steal, and take the name of my God *in vain*.

10 Accuse not a servant unto his master, lest he curse thee, and thou be found guilty.

11 *There is* a generation *that* curseth their father, and doth not bless their mother.

12 *There is* a generation *that are* pure in their own eyes, and *yet* is not washed from their filthiness.

13 *There is* a generation, O how lofty are their eyes! and their eyelids are lifted up.

14 *There is* a generation, whose teeth *are as* swords, and their jaw teeth *as* knives, to devour the poor from off the earth, and the needy from *among* men.

15 The horseleach hath two daughters, *crying*, Give, give. There are three *things that* are never satisfied, *yea*, four *things* say not, *It is* enough:

16 The grave; and the barren womb; the earth *that* is not filled with water; and the fire *that* saith not, *It is* enough.

17 The eye *that* mocketh at *his* father, and despiseth to obey *his* mother, the ravens of the valley shall pick it out, and the young eagles shall eat it.

18 There be three *things which* are too wonderful for me, yea, four which I know not:

19 The way of an eagle in the air; the way of a serpent upon a rock; the way of a ship in the midst of the sea; and the way of a man with a maid.

20 Such *is* the way of an adulterous woman; she eateth, and wipeth her mouth, and saith, I have done no wickedness.

21 For three *things* the earth is disquieted, and for four *which* it cannot bear:

22 For a servant when he reigneth; and a fool when he is filled with meat;

23 For an odious *woman* when she is married; and an handmaid that is heir to her mistress.

24 There be four *things which are* little upon the earth, but they *are* exceeding wise:

25 The ants *are* a people not strong, yet they prepare their meat in the summer;

26 The conies *are but* a feeble folk, yet make they their houses in the rocks;

27 The locusts have no king, yet go they forth all of them by bands;

28 The spider taketh hold with her hands, and is in kings' palaces.

29 There be three *things* which go well, yea, four are comely in going:

30 A lion *which is* strongest among beasts, and turneth not away for any;

31 A greyhound; an he goat also; and a king, against whom *there is* no rising up.

32 If thou hast done foolishly in lifting up

17 Prov. 13:24; 19:18; 22:15; 23:13-15

18 1Sam. 3:1; Amos 8:11, 12; John 13:17; James 1:25

20 Prov. 26:12

22 Prov. 15:18; 26:21

23 Job 22:29; Matt. 23:12; Luke 14:11; 18:14; Acts 12:23; James 4:6, 10; 1Pet. 5:5

24 Lev. 5:1

25 Gen. 12:12; 20:2, 11

1 Prov. 31:1

2 Ps. 73:22

4 Job 38:4; Ps. 104:3; Isa. 40:12; John 3:13

5 Ps. 12:6; 18:30; 19:8; 84:11; 115:9-11; 119:140

6 Deut. 4:2; 12:32; Rev. 22:18, 19

8 Matt. 6:11

9 Deut. 8:12; 14:17; 31:20; 32:15; Neh. 9:25, 26; Job 31:24, 25, 28; Hos. 13:6

12 Luke 18:11

13 Ps. 131:1; Prov. 6:17

14 Job 29:17; Ps. 14:4; 52:2; 57:4; Prov. 12:18; Amos 8:4

16 Prov. 27:20; Hab. 2:5

17 Gen. 9:22; Lev. 20:9; Prov. 20:20; 23:22

22 Prov. 19:10; Eccl. 10:7

25 Prov. 6:6

26 Ps. 104:18

thyself, or if thou hast thought evil, *lay* thine hand upon thy mouth.

33 Surely the churning of milk bringeth forth butter, and the wringing of the nose bringeth forth blood: so the forcing of wrath bringeth forth strife.

CHAPTER 31
Advice to a King

1 The words of king Lemuel, the prophecy that his mother taught him.

2 What, my son? and what, the son of my womb? and what, the son of my vows?

3 Give not thy strength unto women, nor thy ways to that which destroyeth kings.

4 *It is* not for kings, O Lemuel, *it is* not for kings to drink wine; nor for princes strong drink:

5 Lest they drink, and forget the law, and pervert the judgment of any of the afflicted.

6 Give strong drink unto him that is ready to perish, and wine unto those that be of heavy hearts.

7 Let him drink, and forget his poverty, and remember his misery no more.

8 Open thy mouth for the dumb in the cause of all such as are appointed to destruction.

9 Open thy mouth, judge righteously, and plead the cause of the poor and needy.

A Good Woman

10 Who can find a virtuous woman? for her price *is* far above rubies.

11 The heart of her husband doth safely trust in her, so that he shall have no need of spoil.

12 She will do him good and not evil all the days of her life.

13 She seeketh wool, and flax, and worketh willingly with her hands.

14 She is like the merchants' ships; she bringeth her food from afar.

15 She riseth also while it is yet night, and giveth meat to her household, and a portion to her maidens.

16 She considereth a field, and buyeth it: with the fruit of her hands she planteth a vineyard.

17 She girdeth her loins with strength, and strengtheneth her arms.

18 She perceiveth that her merchandise *is* good: her candle goeth not out by night.

19 She layeth her hands to the spindle, and her hands hold the distaff.

20 She stretcheth out her hand to the poor; yea, she reacheth forth her hands to the needy.

21 She is not afraid of the snow for her household: for all her household *are* clothed with scarlet.

22 She maketh herself coverings of tapestry; her clothing *is* silk and purple.

23 Her husband is known in the gates, when he sitteth among the elders of the land.

24 She maketh fine linen, and selleth *it*; and delivereth girdles unto the merchant.

25 Strength and honour *are* her clothing; and she shall rejoice in time to come.

26 She openeth her mouth with wisdom; and in her tongue *is* the law of kindness.

27 She looketh well to the ways of her household, and eateth not the bread of idleness.

28 Her children arise up, and call her blessed; her husband *also*, and he praiseth her.

29 Many daughters have done virtuously, but thou excellest them all.

30 Favour *is* deceitful, and beauty *is* vain: *but* a woman *that* feareth the LORD, she shall be praised.

31 Give her of the fruit of her hands; and let her own works praise her in the gates.

---

1 Prov. 30:1
2 Isa. 49:15
3 Deut. 17:17; Neh. 13:26; Prov. 5:9; 7:26; Hos. 4:11
4 Eccl. 10:17
5 Hos. 4:11
6 1Sam. 1:10; Ps. 104:15
8 1Sam. 19:4; Esth. 4:16; Job 29:15, 16
9 Lev. 19:15; Deut. 1:16; Job 29:12; Isa. 1:17; Jer. 22:16
10 Prov. 12:4; 18:22; 19:14
15 Luke 12:42; Rom. 12:11
20 Eph. 4:28; Heb. 13:16
23 Prov. 12:4

Ecclesiastes

Ecclesiastes was written in the twilight of Solomon's career, when he seemed to have returned to the Lord after being influenced by the pagan gods and false religions of his many wives. Most of the book is about the futility of a life that is not centered on God and His will. Solomon also stresses that blessing in life comes from obedience to God and the principles laid out in His Word.

The Hebrew name of Ecclesiastes is "the Preacher" (*Qōheleth*), meaning the speaker at an assembly. The title in our Bible comes from the Greek translation of the Hebrew word for "the Preacher." In ancient times, Middle-Easterners enjoyed attending meetings designated for philosophical discussion. Probably written late in Solomon's life, Ecclesiastes declares the emptiness (vanity) of life apart from God. Key phrases include "under the sun" (thirty-one times), "vanity" or "vanities" (thirty-seven times), and "vexation of the spirit" (ten times).

Author	Solomon
Date	935 B.C.
Key Truth	Is Life Worth Living?
Historic Time	Solomon's Reign
Key Verse	1:2 Vanity of vanities, saith the Preacher, vanity of vanities; all is vanity.

The book opens with the immensely wealthy and powerful Solomon trying to find meaning and happiness apart from God. Beginning with the question, "What profit hath a man of all his labor . . . under the sun," that is, on the earth. He then reviews his search for true happiness and satisfaction. Initially, he seeks satisfaction in nature and science. Next, he searches for satisfaction in wisdom and education, to no avail. Then he tries pleasure followed by building projects, vast estates, servants, possessions, art, music, fame and greatness. Looking then at all he had gained and accomplished, he declares it has "no profit under the sun."

Solomon then explores subjects pertaining to philosophy, fatalism, deism, stoicism, good conduct, wealth, reputation, and morality. Finally, he concludes that the only true satisfaction comes from fearing God and keeping His commandments (12:13). Although Solomon investigated many approaches to life, he emphasized that God will bring every work into scrutiny. This will be fulfilled during the final judgment (Rev. 20:11–15).

Only 7 verses, mostly on God's judgments, out of 222 (3 percent) are predictive in nature.

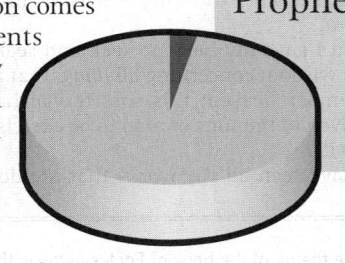

3%
Prophecy

1150 B.C.	1100 B.C.	1050 B.C.	1000 B.C.	950 B.C.	900 B.C.	850 B.C.	800 B.C.	750 B.C.

1043-1011
Saul's reign

971-931
Solomon's reign

1011-971
David's reign

935
Book of Ecclesiastes

1375-1050
rael ruled by judges

967-960
Construction of Solomon's Temple

931-722
Northern Kingdom (Israel)

990
Birth of Solomon

931-586
Southern Kingdom (Judah)

CHAPTER 1
All Is Vanity

1 The words of the Preacher, the son of David, king in Jerusalem.

2 Vanity of vanities, saith the Preacher, vanity of vanities; all *is* vanity.

3 What profit hath a man of all his labour which he taketh under the sun?

4 *One* generation passeth away, and *another* generation cometh: but the earth abideth for ever.

5 The sun also ariseth, and the sun goeth down, and hasteth to his place where he arose.

6 The wind goeth toward the south, and turneth about unto the north; it whirleth about continually, and the wind returneth again according to his circuits.

7 All the rivers run into the sea; yet the sea *is* not full; unto the place from whence the rivers come, thither they return again.

8 All things *are* full of labour; man cannot utter *it*: the eye is not satisfied with seeing, nor the ear filled with hearing.

9 The thing that hath been, it *is that* which shall be; and that which is done *is* that which shall be done: and *there is* no new *thing* under the sun.

10 Is there *any* thing whereof it may be said, See, this *is* new? it hath been already of old time, which was before us.

11 *There is* no remembrance of former *things*; neither shall there be *any* remembrance of *things* that are to come with *those* that shall come after.

Solomon's Own Experience

12 I the Preacher was king over Israel in Jerusalem.

13 And I gave my heart to seek and search out by wisdom concerning all *things* that are done under heaven: this sore travail hath God given to the sons of man to be exercised therewith.

14 I have seen all the works that are done

under the sun; and, behold, all *is* vanity and vexation of spirit.

15 *That which is* crooked cannot be made straight: and that which is wanting cannot be numbered.

16 I communed with mine own heart, saying, Lo, I am come to great estate, and have gotten more wisdom than all *they* that have been before me in Jerusalem: yea, my heart had great experience of wisdom and knowledge.

17 And I gave my heart to know wisdom, and to know madness and folly: I perceived that this also *is* vexation of spirit.

18 For in much wisdom *is* much grief: and he that increaseth knowledge increaseth sorrow.

CHAPTER 2

1 I said in mine heart, Go to now, I will prove thee with mirth, therefore enjoy pleasure: and, behold, this also *is* vanity.

2 I said of laughter, *It is* mad: and of mirth, What doeth it?

3 I sought in mine heart to give myself unto wine, yet acquainting mine heart with wisdom; and to lay hold on folly, till I might see what *was* that good for the sons of men, which they should do under the heaven all the days of their life.

4 I made me great works; I builded me houses; I planted me vineyards:

5 I made me gardens and orchards, and I planted trees in them of all *kind of* fruits:

6 I made me pools of water, to water therewith the wood that bringeth forth trees:

7 I got *me* servants and maidens, and had servants born in my house; also I had great possessions of great and small cattle above all that were in Jerusalem before me:

8 I gathered me also silver and gold, and the peculiar treasure of kings and of the provinces: I gat me men singers and women singers, and the delights of the sons of men, *as* musical instruments, and that of all sorts.

Cross references (center column)

1 Eccl. 1:12; 7:27; 12:8-10

2 Ps. 39:5, 6; 62:9; 144:4; Eccl. 12:8; Rom. 8:20

3 Eccl. 2:22; 3:9

4 Ps. 104:5; 119:90

5 Ps. 19:5, 6

6 John 3:8

7 Job 38:10; Ps. 104:8, 9

8 Prov. 27:20

9 Eccl. 3:15

12 Eccl. 1:1

13 Gen. 3:10, 19

15 Eccl. 7:13

16 1Kgs. 3:12, 13; 4:30; 10:7, 23

17 Eccl. 2:3, 12; 7:23, 25; 1Thess. 5:21

18 Eccl. 12:12

1 Isa. 50:11; Luke 12:19

2 Prov. 14:13; Eccl. 7:6

3 Eccl. 1:17

8 1Kgs. 9:28; 10:10, 14, 21

1:2 The theme of the book of Ecclesiastes is that "under the sun [i.e., 'without God in the picture'], all is vanity." The key word of the book, "vanity," occurs thirty-seven times. It is used to describe outward and tangible things (Eccl. 2:15, 19; 8:10, 14) as well as inward thoughts (Eccl. 1:14; 2:11). The word "vanity" (Hebr. *hevel*) emphasizes that which is empty and passing. The phrase "vanity of vanities" denotes the Hebrew way of expressing a superlative (it could be translated "most futile"). This method is also seen in the phrase "most holy place,"

which in the Hebrew is "holy of Holies" (Ex. 26:34).

1:4 As important as one life or generation is to those living in it, at best, life is temporary but eternity is forever; therefore, we should all live with eternity and its values in view. It is important to note that "the earth abideth for ever." All of God's revealed plans for the future involve a permanent earth—recreated, renewed, and reformed, but eternal (cf. Rev. 21:2–5). This earth in its present form will "pass away" but will be made new and abide forever.

9 So I was great, and increased more than all that were before me in Jerusalem: also my wisdom remained with me.

10 And whatsoever mine eyes desired I kept not from them, I withheld not my heart from any joy; for my heart rejoiced in all my labour: and this was my portion of all my labour.

11 Then I looked on all the works that my hands had wrought, and on the labour that I had laboured to do: and, behold, all *was* vanity and vexation of spirit, and *there was* no profit under the sun.

12 And I turned myself to behold wisdom, and madness, and folly: for what *can* the man *do* that cometh after the king? *even* that which hath been already done.

13 Then I saw that wisdom excelleth folly, as far as light excelleth darkness.

14 The wise man's eyes *are* in his head; but the fool walketh in darkness: and I myself perceived also that one event happeneth to them all.

15 Then said I in my heart, As it happeneth to the fool, *so* it happeneth even to me; and why was I then more wise? Then I said in my heart, that this also *is* vanity.

16 For *there is* no remembrance of the wise more than of the fool for ever; seeing that which now *is* in the days to come shall all be forgotten. And how dieth the wise *man*? as the fool.

17 Therefore I hated life; because the work that is wrought under the sun *is* grievous unto me: for all *is* vanity and vexation of spirit.

18 Yea, I hated all my labour which I had taken under the sun: because I should leave it unto the man that shall be after me.

19 And who knoweth whether he shall be a wise *man* or a fool? yet shall he have rule over all my labour wherein I have laboured, and wherein I have shewed myself wise under the sun. This *is* also vanity.

20 Therefore I went about to cause my heart to despair of all the labour which I took under the sun.

21 For there is a man whose labour *is* in wisdom, and in knowledge, and in equity; yet to a man that hath not laboured therein shall he leave it *for* his portion. This also *is* vanity and a great evil.

22 For what hath man of all his labour, and of the vexation of his heart, wherein he hath laboured under the sun?

23 For all his days *are* sorrows, and his travail grief; yea, his heart taketh not rest in the night. This is also vanity.

24 *There is* nothing better for a man, *than* that he should eat and drink, and *that* he should make his soul enjoy good in his labour. This also I saw, that it *was* from the hand of God.

25 For who can eat, or who else can hasten *hereunto*, more than I?

26 For *God* giveth to a man that *is* good in his sight wisdom, and knowledge, and joy: but to the sinner he giveth travail, to gather and to heap up, that he may give to *him that is* good before God. This also *is* vanity and vexation of spirit.

CHAPTER 3
A Time for Everything

1 To every *thing there is* a season, and a time to every purpose under the heaven:

2 A time to be born, and a time to die; a time to plant, and a time to pluck up *that which is* planted;

3 A time to kill, and a time to heal; a time to break down, and a time to build up;

4 A time to weep, and a time to laugh; a time to mourn, and a time to dance;

5 A time to cast away stones, and a time to gather stones together; a time to embrace, and a time to refrain from embracing;

6 A time to get, and a time to lose; a time to keep, and a time to cast away;

7 A time to rend, and a time to sew; a time to keep silence, and a time to speak;

8 A time to love, and a time to hate; a time of war, and a time of peace.

9 What profit hath he that worketh in that wherein he laboureth?

10 I have seen the travail, which God hath given to the sons of men to be exercised in it.

Cross references
9 Eccl. 1:16
10 Eccl. 3:22; 5:18; 9:9
11 Eccl. 1:3, 14
12 Eccl. 1:17; 7:25
14 Ps. 49:10; Prov. 17:24; Eccl. 8:1; 9:2, 3, 11
18 Ps. 49:10
22 Eccl. 1:3; 3:9
23 Job 5:7; 14:1
24 Eccl. 3:12, 13, 22; 5:18; 8:15
26 Gen. 7:1; Job 27:16, 17; Prov. 28:8; Luke 1:6
1 Eccl. 3:17; 8:6
2 Heb. 9:27
5 Joel 2:16; 1Cor. 7:5
7 Amos 5:13
8 Luke 14:26
9 Eccl. 1:3
10 Eccl. 1:13

2:11 no profit under the sun. This verse is Solomon's reflection on all that he had accomplished. The result of all his accomplishments was emptiness and had become unprofitable. The words that best describe Solomon's feelings at this point are "vanity and vexation of spirit." In all of the supposed pleasures of life, he found no satisfaction (Heb. 11:25). The cause of all this emptiness and sorrow was that Solomon had not learned how to restrain his desires. There are many believers (including preachers and church leaders) who have also not learned this lesson. In the end, however, they will see that the fulfillment of fleshly desires is always unprofitable. Our accomplishments for God are intended to be a testimony of Christ to the world, but the times when our flesh is not restrained will result in a reproach on the cause of Christ.

11 He hath made every *thing* beautiful in his time: also he hath set the world in their heart, so that no man can find out the work that God maketh from the beginning to the end.

12 I know that *there is* no good in them, but for *a* man to rejoice, and to do good in his life.

13 And also that every man should eat and drink, and enjoy the good of all his labour, it *is* the gift of God.

14 I know that, whatsoever God doeth, it shall be for ever: nothing can be put to it, nor any thing taken from it: and God doeth it, that *men* should fear before him.

15 That which hath been is now; and that which is to be hath already been; and God requireth that which is past.

Injustice

16 And moreover I saw under the sun the place of judgment, *that* wickedness *was* there; and the place of righteousness, *that* iniquity *was* there.

17 I said in mine heart, God shall judge the righteous and the wicked: for *there is* a time there for every purpose and for every work.

18 I said in mine heart concerning the estate of the sons of men, that God might manifest them, and that they might see that they themselves are beasts.

19 For that which befalleth the sons of men befalleth beasts; even one thing befalleth them: as the one dieth, so dieth the other; yea, they have all one breath; so that a man hath no preeminence above a beast: for all *is* vanity.

20 All go unto one place; all are of the dust, and all turn to dust again.

21 Who knoweth the spirit of man that goeth upward, and the spirit of the beast that goeth downward to the earth?

22 Wherefore I perceive that *there is* nothing better, than that a man should rejoice in his own works; for that *is* his portion: for who

shall bring him to see what shall be after him?

CHAPTER 4

1 So I returned, and considered all the oppressions that are done under the sun: and behold the tears of *such as were* oppressed, and they had no comforter; and on the side of their oppressors *there was* power; but they had no comforter.

2 Wherefore I praised the dead which are already dead more than the living which are yet alive.

3 Yea, better *is he* than both they, which hath not yet been, who hath not seen the evil work that is done under the sun.

4 Again, I considered all travail, and every right work, that for this a man is envied of his neighbour. This *is* also vanity and vexation of spirit.

5 The fool foldeth his hands together, and eateth his own flesh.

6 Better *is* an handful *with* quietness, than both the hands full *with* travail and vexation of spirit.

7 Then I returned, and I saw vanity under the sun.

8 There is one *alone*, and *there is* not a second; yea, he hath neither child nor brother: yet *is there* no end of all his labour; neither is his eye satisfied with riches; neither *saith he*, For whom do I labour, and bereave my soul of good? This *is* also vanity, yea, it *is* a sore travail.

9 Two *are* better than one; because they have a good reward for their labour.

10 For if they fall, the one will lift up his fellow: but woe to him *that is* alone when he falleth; for *he hath* not another to help him up.

11 Again, if two lie together, then they have heat: but how can one be warm *alone*?

12 And if one prevail against him, two shall withstand him; and a threefold cord is not quickly broken.

13 Better *is* a poor and a wise child than an

Cross-references

| 11 Eccl. 8:17; Rom. 11:33 |
| 12 Eccl. 3:22 |
| 13 Eccl. 2:24 |
| 14 James 1:17 |
| 15 Eccl. 1:9 |
| 16 Eccl. 5:8 |
| 17 Eccl. 3:1; Rom. 2:6, 7, 8; 2Cor. 5:10; 2Thess. 1:6, 7 |
| 19 Ps. 49:12, 20; 73:22; Eccl. 2:16 |
| 20 Gen. 3:19 |
| 21 Eccl. 12:7 |
| 22 Eccl. 2:10, 24; 3:12; 5:18; 6:12; 8:7; 10:14; 11:9 |
| 1 Eccl. 3:16; 5:8 |
| 2 Job 3:17 |
| 3 Job 3:11, 16, 21; Eccl. 6:3 |
| 5 Prov. 6:10; 24:33 |
| 6 Prov. 15:16, 17; 16:8 |
| 8 Ps. 39:6; Prov. 27:20; 1John 2:16 |

3:11 he hath set the world in their heart. A better rendering of the text is, "God has set eternity in their heart." Because he was created to be eternal by an eternal God, man intuitively knows there is life after death—somewhere. This whole existence called "life" is designed for us to either accept God and His will for our lives or do our own thing. The prophetic word does not tell us everything God has in store for our future, but has revealed many wonderful and exciting details that make the study of prophecy so rewarding.

3:17–18 Written on the table of every man's heart is the intuitive knowledge that God will judge him in the next life. "The wicked," those who reject Christ, will be judged for their works at the Great White Throne Judgment (Rev. 20:11–15). The redeemed, who by faith in Christ had their wicked deeds forgiven and are cleansed "as white as snow" (Isa. 1:18), will face Him at the judgment seat of Christ, which is a judgment of reward, not of salvation (1 Cor. 3:11–15).

old and foolish king, who will no more be admonished.

14 For out of prison he cometh to reign; whereas also *he that is* born in his kingdom becometh poor.

15 I considered all the living which walk under the sun, with the second child that shall stand up in his stead.

16 *There is* no end of all the people, *even* of all that have been before them: they also that come after shall not rejoice in him. Surely this also *is* vanity and vexation of spirit.

CHAPTER 5
Rash Promises

1 Keep thy foot when thou goest to the house of God, and be more ready to hear, than to give the sacrifice of fools: for they consider not that they do evil.

2 Be not rash with thy mouth, and let not thine heart be hasty to utter *any* thing before God: for God *is* in heaven, and thou upon earth: therefore let thy words be few.

3 For a dream cometh through the multitude of business; and a fool's voice *is known* by multitude of words.

4 When thou vowest a vow unto God, defer not to pay it; for *he hath* no pleasure in fools: pay that which thou hast vowed.

5 Better *is it* that thou shouldest not vow, than that thou shouldest vow and not pay.

6 Suffer not thy mouth to cause thy flesh to sin; neither say thou before the angel, that it *was* an error: wherefore should God be angry at thy voice, and destroy the work of thine hands?

7 For in the multitude of dreams and many words *there are* also *divers* vanities: but fear thou God.

The Vanity of Life

8 If thou seest the oppression of the poor, and violent perverting of judgment and justice in a province, marvel not at the matter: for *he that is* higher than the highest regardeth; and *there be* higher than they.

9 Moreover the profit of the earth is for all: the king *himself* is served by the field.

10 He that loveth silver shall not be satisfied with silver; nor he that loveth abundance with increase: this *is* also vanity.

11 When goods increase, they are increased that eat them: and what good *is there* to the owners thereof, saving the beholding *of them* with their eyes?

12 The sleep of a labouring man *is* sweet, whether he eat little or much: but the abun-

dance of the rich will not suffer him to sleep.

13 There is a sore evil *which* I have seen under the sun, *namely*, riches kept for the owners thereof to their hurt.

14 But those riches perish by evil travail: and he begetteth a son, and *there is* nothing in his hand.

15 As he came forth of his mother's womb, naked shall he return to go as he came, and shall take nothing of his labour, which he may carry way in his hand.

16 And this also *is* a sore evil, *that* in all points as he came, so shall he go: and what profit hath he that hath laboured for the wind?

17 All his days also he eateth in darkness, and *he hath* much sorrow and wrath with his sickness.

18 Behold *that* which I have seen: *it is* good and comely *for one* to eat and to drink, and to enjoy the good of all his labour that he taketh under the sun all the days of his life, which God giveth him: for it *is* his portion.

19 Every man also to whom God hath given riches and wealth, and hath given him power to eat thereof, and to take his portion, and to rejoice in his labour; this *is* the gift of God.

20 For he shall not much remember the days of his life; because God answereth *him* in the joy of his heart.

CHAPTER 6

1 There is an evil which I have seen under the sun, and it *is* common among men:

2 A man to whom God hath given riches, wealth, and honour, so that he wanteth nothing for his soul of all that he desireth, yet God giveth him not power to eat thereof, but a stranger eateth it: this *is* vanity, and it *is* an evil disease.

3 If a man beget an hundred *children*, and live many years, so that the days of his years be many, and his soul be not filled with good, and also *that* he have no burial; I say, *that* an untimely birth *is* better than he.

4 For he cometh in with vanity, and departeth in darkness, and his name shall be covered with darkness.

5 Moreover he hath not seen the sun, nor known *any thing*: this hath more rest than the other.

6 Yea, though he live a thousand years twice *told*, yet hath he seen no good: do not all go to one place?

7 All the labour of man *is* for his mouth, and yet the appetite is not filled.

---

1 Ex. 3:5;
1Sam. 15:22;
Ps. 50:8;
Prov. 15:8;
21:27; Isa.
1:12; Hos.
6:6

2 Prov.
10:19; Matt.
6:7

3 Prov. 10:19

4 Num. 30:2;
Deut. 23:21,
22, 23; Ps.
50:14; 66:13,
14; 76:11

5 Prov.
20:25; Acts
5:4

6 1Cor. 11:10

7 Eccl. 12:13

8 Ps. 12:5;
58:11; 82:1;
Eccl. 3:16

13 Eccl. 6:1

15 Job 1:21;
Ps. 49:17;
1Tim. 6:7

16 Prov.
11:29; Eccl.
1:3

17 Ps. 127:2

18 Eccl.
2:10, 24;
3:12, 13, 22;
9:7; 11:9;
1Tim. 6:17

19 Eccl.
2:24; 3:13;
6:2

1 Eccl. 5:13

2 Job 21:10;
Ps. 17:14;
73:7; Luke
12:20

3 2Kgs. 9:35;
Job 3:16; Ps.
58:8; Eccl.
4:3; Isa.
14:19, 20;
Jer. 22:19

7 Prov. 16:26

8 For what hath the wise more than the fool? what hath the poor, that knoweth to walk before the living?

9 Better *is* the sight of the eyes than the wandering of the desire: this *is* also vanity and vexation of spirit.

10 That which hath been is named already, and it is known that it *is* man: neither may he contend with him that is mightier than he.

11 Seeing there be many things that increase vanity, what *is* man the better?

12 For who knoweth what *is* good for man in *this* life, all the days of his vain life which he spendeth as a shadow? for who can tell a man what shall be after him under the sun?

CHAPTER 7
Comparing Wisdom and Folly

1 A good name *is* better than precious ointment; and the day of death than the day of one's birth.

2 *It is* better to go to the house of mourning, than to go to the house of feasting: for that *is* the end of all men; and the living will lay *it* to his heart.

3 Sorrow *is* better than laughter: for by the sadness of the countenance the heart is made better.

4 The heart of the wise *is* in the house of mourning; but the heart of fools *is* in the house of mirth.

5 *It is* better to hear the rebuke of the wise, than for a man to hear the song of fools.

6 For as the crackling of thorns under a pot, so *is* the laughter of the fool: this also *is* vanity.

7 Surely oppression maketh a wise man mad; and a gift destroyeth the heart.

8 Better *is* the end of a thing than the beginning thereof: *and* the patient in spirit *is* better than the proud in spirit.

9 Be not hasty in thy spirit to be angry: for anger resteth in the bosom of fools.

10 Say not thou, What is *the cause* that the former days were better than these? for thou dost not inquire wisely concerning this.

11 Wisdom *is* good with an inheritance: and *by it there is* profit to them that see the sun.

12 For wisdom *is* a defence, *and* money *is* a defence: but the excellency of knowledge *is*, *that* wisdom giveth life to them that have it.

13 Consider the work of God: for who can make *that* straight, which he hath made crooked?

14 In the day of prosperity be joyful, but in the day of adversity consider: God also hath

---

10 Job 9:32; Isa. 45:9; Jer. 49:19

12 Ps. 39:6; 102:11; 109:23; 144:4; Eccl. 8:7; James 4:14

1 Prov. 15:30; 22:1

3 2Cor. 7:10

5 Ps. 141:5; Prov. 13:18; 15:31, 32

6 Ps. 118:12; Eccl. 2:2

7 Ex. 23:8; Deut. 16:19

8 Prov. 14:29

9 Prov. 14:17; 16:32; James 1:19

11 Eccl. 11:7

13 Job 12:14; Eccl. 1:15; Isa. 14:27

14 Deut. 28:47; Eccl. 3:4

15 Eccl. 8:14

16 Prov. 25:16; Rom. 12:3

17 Job 15:32; Ps. 55:23; Prov. 10:27

19 Prov. 21:22; 24:5; Eccl. 9:16, 18

20 1Kgs. 8:46; 2Chr. 6:36; Prov. 20:9; Rom. 3:23; 1John 1:8

23 Rom. 1:22

24 Job 28:12, 20; Rom. 11:33; 1Tim. 6:16

25 Eccl. 1:17; 2:12

26 Prov. 5:3, 4; 22:14

27 Eccl. 1:1, 2

28 Job 33:23; Ps. 12:1

29 Gen. 1:27; 3:6, 7

1 Prov. 4:8, 9; 17:24

---

set the one over against the other, to the end that man should find nothing after him.

15 All *things* have I seen in the days of my vanity: there is a just *man* that perisheth in his righteousness, and there is a wicked *man* that prolongeth *his life* in his wickedness.

16 Be not righteous over much; neither make thyself over wise: why shouldest thou destroy thyself?

17 Be not over much wicked, neither be thou foolish: why shouldest thou die before thy time?

18 *It is* good that thou shouldest take hold of this; yea, also from this withdraw not thine hand: for he that feareth God shall come forth of them all.

19 Wisdom strengtheneth the wise more than ten mighty *men* which are in the city.

20 For *there is* not a just man upon earth, that doeth good, and sinneth not.

21 Also take no heed unto all words that are spoken; lest thou hear thy servant curse thee:

22 For oftentimes also thine own heart knoweth that thou thyself likewise hast cursed others.

23 All this have I proved by wisdom: I said, I will be wise; but it *was* far from me.

24 That which is far off, and exceeding deep, who can find it out?

25 I applied mine heart to know, and to search, and to seek out wisdom, and the reason *of things*, and to know the wickedness of folly, even of foolishness *and* madness:

26 And I find more bitter than death the woman, whose heart *is* snares and nets, *and* her hands *as* bands: whoso pleaseth God shall escape from her; but the sinner shall be taken by her.

27 Behold, this have I found, saith the preacher, *counting* one by one, to find out the account:

28 Which yet my soul seeketh, but I find not: one man among a thousand have I found; but a woman among all those have I not found.

29 Lo, this only have I found, that God hath made man upright; but they have sought out many inventions.

CHAPTER 8

1 Who *is* as the wise *man*? and who knoweth the interpretation of a thing? a man's wisdom maketh his face to shine, and the boldness of his face shall be changed.

Obey the King

2 I *counsel thee* to keep the king's commandment, and *that* in regard of the oath of God.

3 Be not hasty to go out of his sight: stand not in an evil thing; for he doeth whatsoever pleaseth him.

4 Where the word of a king *is, there is* power: and who may say unto him, What doest thou?

5 Whoso keepeth the commandment shall feel no evil thing: and a wise man's heart discerneth both time and judgment.

6 Because to every purpose there is time and judgment, therefore the misery of man *is* great upon him.

7 For he knoweth not that which shall be: for who can tell him when it shall be?

8 *There is* no man that hath power over the spirit to retain the spirit; neither *hath he* power in the day of death: and *there is* no discharge in *that* war; neither shall wickedness deliver those that are given to it.

Life Seems Unfair

9 All this have I seen, and applied my heart unto every work that is done under the sun: *there is* a time wherein one man ruleth over another to his own hurt.

10 And so I saw the wicked buried, who had come and gone from the place of the holy, and they were forgotten in the city where they had so done: this *is* also vanity.

11 Because sentence against an evil work is not executed speedily, therefore the heart of the sons of men is fully set in them to do evil.

12 Though a sinner do evil an hundred times, and his *days* be prolonged, yet surely I know that it shall be well with them that fear God, which fear before him:

13 But it shall not be well with the wicked, neither shall he prolong *his* days, *which are* as a shadow; because he feareth not before God.

14 There is a vanity which is done upon the earth; that there be just *men*, unto whom it happeneth according to the work of the wicked; again, there be wicked *men*, to whom it happeneth according to the work of the righteous: I said that this also *is* vanity.

15 Then I commended mirth, because a man hath no better thing under the sun, than to eat, and to drink, and to be merry: for that shall abide with him of his labour the days of his life, which God giveth him under the sun.

16 When I applied mine heart to know wisdom, and to see the business that is done upon the earth: (for also *there is that* neither day nor night seeth sleep with his eyes:)

17 Then I beheld all the work of God, that a man cannot find out the work that is done under the sun: because though a man labour to seek *it* out, yet he shall not find *it*; yea further; though a wise *man* think to know *it*, yet shall he not be able to find *it*.

CHAPTER 9

1 For all this I considered in my heart even to declare all this, that the righteous, and the wise, and their works, *are* in the hand of God: no man knoweth either love or hatred *by* all *that is* before them.

2 All *things come* alike to all: *there is* one event to the righteous, and to the wicked; to the good and to the clean, and to the unclean; to him that sacrificeth, and to him that sacrificeth not: as *is* the good, so *is* the sinner; *and* he that sweareth, as *he* that feareth an oath.

3 This *is* an evil among all *things* that are done under the sun, that *there is* one event unto all: yea, also the heart of the sons of men is full of evil, and madness *is* in their heart while they live, and after that *they go* to the dead.

4 For to him that is joined to all the living there is hope: for a living dog is better than a dead lion.

5 For the living know that they shall die: but the dead know not any thing, neither have they any more a reward; for the memory of them is forgotten.

6 Also their love, and their hatred, and their envy, is now perished; neither have they any more a portion for ever in any *thing* that is done under the sun.

7 Go thy way, eat thy bread with joy, and drink thy wine with a merry heart; for God now accepteth thy works.

8 Let thy garments be always white; and let thy head lack no ointment.

9 Live joyfully with the wife whom thou lovest all the days of the life of thy vanity, which he hath given thee under the sun, all the days of thy vanity: for that *is* thy portion in *this* life, and in thy labour which thou takest under the sun.

10 Whatsoever thy hand findeth to do, do *it* with thy might; for *there is* no work, nor device, nor knowledge, nor wisdom, in the grave, whither thou goest.

11 I returned, and saw under the sun, that the race *is* not to the swift, nor the battle to

Center column references

2 1Chr. 29:24; Ezek. 17:18; Rom. 13:5

3 Eccl. 10:4

4 Job 34:18

6 Eccl. 3:1

7 Prov. 24:22; Eccl. 6:12; 9:12; 10:14

8 Job 14:5; Ps. 49:6, 7

11 Ps. 10:6; 50:21; Isa. 26:10

12 Ps. 37:11, 18, 19; Prov. 1:32, 33; Isa. 3:10, 11; 65:20; Matt. 25:34, 41; Rom. 2:5

14 Ps. 73:14; Eccl. 2:14; 7:15; 9:1-3

15 Eccl. 2:24; 3:12, 22; 5:18; 9:7

17 Job 5:9; Ps. 73:16; Eccl. 3:11; Rom. 11:33

1 Eccl. 8:14

2 Job 21:7; Ps. 73:3, 12, 13; Mal. 3:15

5 Job 7:8-10; 14:21; Isa. 26:14; 63:16

7 Eccl. 8:15

9 Eccl. 2:10, 24; 3:13, 22; 5:18

11 Jer. 9:23; Amos 2:14, 15

the strong, neither yet bread to the wise, nor yet riches to men of understanding, nor yet favour to men of skill; but time and chance happeneth to them all.

12 For man also knoweth not his time: as the fishes that are taken in an evil net, and as the birds that are caught in the snare; so *are* the sons of men snared in an evil time, when it falleth suddenly upon them.

Wisdom and Foolishness

13 This wisdom have I seen also under the sun, and it *seemed* great unto me:

14 *There was* a little city, and few men within it; and there came a great king against it, and besieged it, and built great bulwarks against it:

15 Now there was found in it a poor wise man, and he by his wisdom delivered the city; yet no man remembered that same poor man.

16 Then said I, Wisdom *is* better than strength: nevertheless the poor man's wisdom *is* despised, and his words are not heard.

17 The words of wise *men are* heard in quiet more than the cry of him that ruleth among fools.

18 Wisdom *is* better than weapons of war: but one sinner destroyeth much good.

CHAPTER 10

1 Dead flies cause the ointment of the apothecary to send forth a stinking savour: *so doth* a little folly him that is in reputation for wisdom *and* honour.

2 A wise man's heart *is* at his right hand; but a fool's heart at his left.

3 Yea also, when he that is a fool walketh by the way, his wisdom faileth *him*, and he saith to every one *that* he *is* a fool.

4 If the spirit of the ruler rise up against thee, leave not thy place; for yielding pacifieth great offences.

5 There is an evil *which* I have seen under the sun, as an error *which* proceedeth from the ruler:

6 Folly is set in great dignity, and the rich sit in low place.

7 I have seen servants upon horses, and princes walking as servants upon the earth.

8 He that diggeth a pit shall fall into it; and whoso breaketh an hedge, a serpent shall bite him.

9 Whoso removeth stones shall be hurt therewith; *and* he that cleaveth wood shall be endangered thereby.

10 If the iron be blunt, and he do not whet

the edge, then must he put to more strength: but wisdom *is* profitable to direct.

11 Surely the serpent will bite without enchantment; and a babbler is no better.

12 The words of a wise man's mouth *are* gracious; but the lips of a fool will swallow up himself.

13 The beginning of the words of his mouth *is* foolishness: and the end of his talk *is* mischievous madness.

14 A fool also is full of words: a man cannot tell what shall be; and what shall be after him, who can tell him?

15 The labour of the foolish wearieth every one of them, because he knoweth not how to go to the city.

16 Woe to thee, O land, when thy king *is* a child, and thy princes eat in the morning!

17 Blessed *art* thou, O land, when thy king *is* the son of nobles, and thy princes eat in due season, for strength, and not for drunkenness!

18 By much slothfulness the building decayeth; and through idleness of the hands the house droppeth through.

19 A feast is made for laughter, and wine maketh merry: but money answereth all *things*.

20 Curse not the king, no not in thy thought; and curse not the rich in thy bedchamber: for a bird of the air shall carry the voice, and that which hath wings shall tell the matter.

CHAPTER 11
A Wise Man

1 Cast thy bread upon the waters: for thou shalt find it after many days.

2 Give a portion to seven, and also to eight; for thou knowest not what evil shall be upon the earth.

3 If the clouds be full of rain, they empty *themselves* upon the earth: and if the tree fall toward the south, or toward the north, in the place where the tree falleth, there it shall be.

4 He that observeth the wind shall not sow; and he that regardeth the clouds shall not reap.

5 As thou knowest not what *is* the way of the spirit, *nor* how the bones *do grow* in the womb of her that is with child: even so thou knowest not the works of God who maketh all.

6 In the morning sow thy seed, and in the evening withhold not thine hand: for thou knowest not whether shall prosper, either

12 Prov. 29:6; Eccl. 8:7; Luke 12:20, 39; 17:26; 1Thess. 5:3

14 2Sam. 20:16-22

16 Prov. 21:22; 24:5; Eccl. 7:19; 9:18; Mark 6:2, 3

18 Josh. 7:1, 11, 12; Eccl. 9:16

3 Prov. 13:16; 18:2

4 1Sam. 25:24-35; Prov. 25:15; Eccl. 8:3

6 Esth. 3:1

7 Prov. 19:10; 30:22

8 Ps. 7:15; Prov. 26:27

11 Ps. 58:4, 5; Jer. 8:17

12 Prov. 10:14, 32; 12:13; 18:7

14 Prov. 15:2; Eccl. 3:22; 6:12; 8:7

16 Isa. 3:4, 5, 12; 5:11

17 Prov. 31:4

19 Ps. 104:15

20 Ex. 22:28; Luke 19:40; Acts 23:5

1 Deut. 15:10; Prov. 19:17; Isa. 32:20; Matt. 10:42; 2Cor. 9:8; Gal. 6:9, 10; Heb. 6:10

2 Ps. 112:9; Mic. 5:5; Luke 6:30; Eph. 5:16; 1Tim. 6:18, 19

5 Ps. 139:14, 15; John 3:8

this or that, or whether they both *shall be* alike good.

7 Truly the light *is* sweet, and a pleasant *thing it is* for the eyes to behold the sun:

8 But if a man live many years, *and* rejoice in them all; yet let him remember the days of darkness; for they shall be many. All that cometh *is* vanity.

Advice to Young People

9 Rejoice, O young man, in thy youth; and let thy heart cheer thee in the days of thy youth, and walk in the ways of thine heart, and in the sight of thine eyes: but know thou, that for all these *things* God will bring thee into judgment.

10 Therefore remove sorrow from thy heart, and put away evil from thy flesh: for childhood and youth *are* vanity.

CHAPTER 12

1 Remember now thy Creator in the days of thy youth, while the evil days come not, nor the years draw nigh, when thou shalt say, I have no pleasure in them;

2 While the sun, or the light, or the moon, or the stars, be not darkened, nor the clouds return after the rain:

3 In the day when the keepers of the house shall tremble, and the strong men shall bow themselves, and the grinders cease because they are few, and those that look out of the windows be darkened,

4 And the doors shall be shut in the streets, when the sound of the grinding is low, and he shall rise up at the voice of the bird, and all the daughters of musick shall be brought low;

5 Also *when* they shall be afraid of *that which is* high, and fears *shall be* in the way, and the almond tree shall flourish, and the grasshopper shall be a burden, and desire shall fail: because man goeth to his long home, and the mourners go about the streets:

6 Or ever the silver cord be loosed, or the golden bowl be broken, or the pitcher be broken at the fountain, or the wheel broken at the cistern.

7 Then shall the dust return to the earth as it was: and the spirit shall return unto God who gave it.

8 Vanity of vanities, saith the preacher; all *is* vanity.

The Conclusion

9 And moreover, because the preacher was wise, he still taught the people knowledge; yea, he gave good heed, and sought out, *and* set in order many proverbs.

10 The preacher sought to find out acceptable words: and *that which was* written *was* upright, *even* words of truth.

11 The words of the wise *are* as goads, and as nails fastened *by* the masters of assemblies, *which* are given from one shepherd.

12 And further, by these, my son, be admonished: of making many books *there is* no end; and much study *is* a weariness of the flesh.

13 Let us hear the conclusion of the whole matter: Fear God, and keep his commandments: for this *is* the whole *duty* of man.

14 For God shall bring every work into judgment, with every secret thing, whether *it be* good, or whether *it be* evil.

Cross references (center column):

7 Eccl. 7:11
9 Num. 15:39; Eccl. 12:14; Rom. 2:6-11
10 2Sam. 19:35; Ps. 39:5; Prov. 22:6; Lam. 3:27; 2Cor. 7:1; 2Tim. 2:22
4 2Sam. 19:35
5 Job 17:13; Jer. 9:17
7 Gen. 3:19; Num. 16:22; 27:16; Job 34:14, 15; Ps. 90:3; Eccl. 3:21; Isa. 57:16; Zech. 12:1
8 Ps. 62:9; Eccl. 1:2
9 1Kgs. 4:32
12 Eccl. 1:18
13 Deut. 6:2; 10:12
14 Eccl. 11:9; Matt. 12:36; Acts 17:30, 31; Rom. 2:16; 1Cor. 4:5; 2Cor. 5:10

11:9 for all these things God will bring thee into judgment. It is evident that men and women do not like to dwell on eternal judgment, but God wants them to (which is why He mentions it so often in Scripture). This judgment day is inevitable (see Heb. 9:27). The happiest and best way to live is to make every decision in light of eternity's values and keep our future judgment in view.

12:14 every work into judgment, with every secret thing. This truth reaffirms that 1) we are on this earth to serve God, 2) we are held accountable by God for the way we live our lives, and 3) we will be judged by Him on even the "secret thing[s]" whether "good or evil." (See 1 Cor. 3:11–15 regarding the "judgment" of Christians and Rev. 20:11–15 regarding the judgment of the unsaved.) There is no such thing as a universal judgment. However, God has a judgment planned for believers to determine their rewards in the afterlife and a judgment planned for unbelievers to determine their punishment in damnation.

Song of Solomon

One of more than a thousand songs written by Solomon (1 Kgs. 4:32), this poem's Hebrew title is simply translated "Song of Songs," but it is sometimes called "Canticles" from the Latin translation of *canticum canticorum*. Because the name of God does not appear, and the book is not quoted or alluded to in the New Testament, and because the poem contains "sensuous imagery of human passion," some early Christian scholars questioned its canonicity (acceptance as Holy Scripture). But from ancient times the Jews have included it in Scripture. In fact it is the first of the five scrolls (Five Megilloth) read at five Jewish feasts.

Author
Solomon

Date
950 B.C.

Key Truth
Marital Love

Historic Time
Solomon's Reign

Key Verse
6:3
I am my beloved's, and my beloved is mine: he feedeth among the lilies.

Many Jews and Christians consider Song of Solomon to be an Oriental love lyric, a poem of physical passion between two lovers (Solomon and the Shulamite maiden), showing the sacredness of pure marital relationships. However, some rabbis have interpreted it as an allegory, with Solomon representing the Lord and the maiden representing Israel. Regardless of whether or not Song of Solomon can be interpreted allegorically, it must first be read as a colorful, poetic, and divinely inspired presentation of intimate human love.

This book of the Bible is a collection of reflective poems or "canticles," not necessarily in chronological order. Some expositors have constructed this scenario: Solomon, disguised as a shepherd, goes to inspect his vineyards. While there, he falls in love with the beautiful Shulamite maiden and courts her. He leaves, promising to return. She has no idea that he is the powerful sovereign. Thus when he returns in majestic splendor (3:6–11), she is surprised and overjoyed, and the two are married. The analogy some see here is that Christ came first as the lowly Shepherd, but will come some day for His Bride with power and glory.

Of the 117 total verses in Song of Solomon, none (0%) are considered to be predictive in nature. However, if one considers the entire love poem to be prophetically typological of Christ and the Church, then the entire book would be predictive.

0%
Prophecy

971-931	931
Solomon's reign	The kingdom is divided

1375-1050
Israel ruled by judges

1011-971	965?	931-722
David's reign	Song of Solomon	Northern Kingdom (Israel)

990	967-960	931-586
Birth of Solomon	Construction of Solomon's Temple	Southern Kingdom (Judah)

CHAPTER 1

1 The song of songs, which *is* Solomon's.

The First Song

2 Let him kiss me with the kisses of his mouth: for thy love *is* better than wine.
3 Because of the savour of thy good ointments thy name *is as* ointment poured forth, therefore do the virgins love thee.
4 Draw me, we will run after thee: the king hath brought me into his chambers: we will be glad and rejoice in thee, we will remember thy love more than wine: the upright love thee.
5 I *am* black, but comely, O ye daughters of Jerusalem, as the tents of Kedar, as the curtains of Solomon.
6 Look not upon me, because I *am* black, because the sun hath looked upon me: my mother's children were angry with me; they made me the keeper of the vineyards; *but* mine own vineyard have I not kept.
7 Tell me, O thou whom my soul loveth, where thou feedest, where thou makest *thy flock* to rest at noon: for why should I be as one that turneth aside by the flocks of thy companions?
8 If thou know not, O thou fairest among women, go thy way forth by the footsteps of the flock, and feed thy kids beside the shepherds' tents.
9 I have compared thee, O my love, to a company of horses in Pharaoh's chariots.
10 Thy cheeks are comely with rows *of jewels*, thy neck with chains *of gold*.
11 We will make thee borders of gold with studs of silver.
12 While the king *sitteth* at his table, my spikenard sendeth forth the smell thereof.
13 A bundle of myrrh *is* my wellbeloved unto me; he shall lie all night betwixt my breasts.
14 My beloved *is* unto me *as* a cluster of camphire in the vineyards of En-gedi.
15 Behold, thou *art* fair, my love; behold, thou *art* fair; thou *hast* doves' eyes.
16 Behold, thou *art* fair, my beloved, yea, pleasant: also our bed *is* green.
17 The beams of our house *are* cedar, *and* our rafters of fir.

Cross references

1 1Kgs. 4:32
2 Song 4:10
4 Ps. 45:14, 15; Hos. 11:4; John 6:44; 12:32; 14:2; Eph. 2:6; Phil. 3:12-14
8 Song 5:9; 6:1
9 2Chr. 1:16, 17; Song 2:2, 10, 13; 4:1, 7; 5:2; 6:4; John 15:14, 15
10 Ezek. 16:11-13
14 Song 4:13
15 Song 4:1; 5:12
3 Rev. 22:1, 2
6 Song 8:3
7 Song 3:5; 8:4
9 Song 2:17
10 Song 2:13
13 Song 2:10
14 Song 8:13
15 Ps. 80:13; Ezek. 13:4; Luke 13:32
16 Song 6:3; 7:10
17 Song 2:9; 4:6; 8:14

CHAPTER 2

1 I *am* the rose of Sharon, *and* the lily of the valleys.
2 As the lily among thorns, so *is* my love among the daughters.
3 As the apple tree among the trees of the wood, so *is* my beloved among the sons. I sat down under his shadow with great delight, and his fruit *was* sweet to my taste.
4 He brought me to the banqueting house, and his banner over me *was* love.
5 Stay me with flagons, comfort me with apples: for I *am* sick of love.
6 His left hand *is* under my head, and his right hand doth embrace me.
7 I charge you, O ye daughters of Jerusalem, by the roes, and by the hinds of the field, that ye stir not up, nor awake *my* love, till he please.

The Second Song

8 The voice of my beloved! behold, he cometh leaping upon the mountains, skipping upon the hills.
9 My beloved is like a roe or a young hart: behold, he standeth behind our wall, he looketh forth at the windows, shewing himself through the lattice.
10 My beloved spake, and said unto me, Rise up, my love, my fair one, and come away.
11 For, lo, the winter is past, the rain is over *and* gone;
12 The flowers appear on the earth; the time of the singing *of birds* is come, and the voice of the turtle is heard in our land;
13 The fig tree putteth forth her green figs, and the vines *with* the tender grape give a *good* smell. Arise, my love, my fair one, and come away.
14 O my dove, *that art* in the clefts of the rock, in the secret *places* of the stairs, let me see thy countenance, let me hear thy voice; for sweet *is* thy voice, and thy countenance *is* comely.
15 Take us the foxes, the little foxes, that spoil the vines: for our vines *have* tender grapes.
16 My beloved *is* mine, and I *am* his: he feedeth among the lilies.
17 Until the day break, and the shadows

1:1—8:14 Many interpret this book as a prophetic picture of Christ and His Bride, the Church (see Eph. 5:22–23; Rev. 21:2; 22:17). However, there is no such use of the book by any of the New Testament writers, nor are we instructed that it is to be used allegorically. The main purpose of the book is to give divine approval to the husband and wife prerogative of enjoying each other physically.

flee away, turn, my beloved, and be thou like a roe or a young hart upon the mountains of Bether.

CHAPTER 3

1 By night on my bed I sought him whom my soul loveth: I sought him, but I found him not.

2 I will rise now, and go about the city in the streets, and in the broad ways I will seek him whom my soul loveth: I sought him, but I found him not.

3 The watchmen that go about the city found me: *to whom I said*, Saw ye him whom my soul loveth?

4 *It was* but a little that I passed from them, but I found him whom my soul loveth: I held him, and would not let him go, until I had brought him into my mother's house, and into the chamber of her that conceived me.

5 I charge you, O ye daughters of Jerusalem, by the roes, and by the hinds of the field, that ye stir not up, nor awake *my* love, till he please.

The Third Song

6 Who *is* this that cometh out of the wilderness like pillars of smoke, perfumed with myrrh and frankincense, with all powders of the merchant?

7 Behold his bed, which *is* Solomon's; threescore valiant men *are* about it, of the valiant of Israel.

8 They all hold swords, *being* expert in war: every man *hath* his sword upon his thigh because of fear in the night.

9 King Solomon made himself a chariot of the wood of Lebanon.

10 He made the pillars thereof *of* silver, the bottom thereof *of* gold, the covering of it *of* purple, the midst thereof being paved *with* love, for the daughters of Jerusalem.

11 Go forth, O ye daughters of Zion, and behold king Solomon with the crown wherewith his mother crowned him in the day of his espousals, and in the day of the gladness of his heart.

CHAPTER 4

1 Behold, thou *art* fair, my love; behold, thou *art* fair; thou *hast* doves' eyes within thy locks: thy hair *is* as a flock of goats, that appear from mount Gilead.

2 Thy teeth *are* like a flock *of sheep that are even* shorn, which came up from the washing; whereof every one bear twins, and none *is* barren among them.

3 Thy lips *are* like a thread of scarlet, and thy speech *is* comely: thy temples *are* like a piece of a pomegranate within thy locks.

4 Thy neck *is* like the tower of David builded for an armoury, whereon there hang a thousand bucklers, all shields of mighty men.

5 Thy two breasts *are* like two young roes that are twins, which feed among the lilies.

6 Until the day break, and the shadows flee away, I will get me to the mountain of myrrh, and to the hill of frankincense.

7 Thou *art* all fair, my love; *there is* no spot in thee.

8 Come with me from Lebanon, *my* spouse, with me from Lebanon: look from the top of Amana, from the top of Shenir and Hermon, from the lions' dens, from the mountains of the leopards.

9 Thou hast ravished my heart, my sister, *my* spouse; thou hast ravished my heart with one of thine eyes, with one chain of thy neck.

10 How fair is thy love, my sister, *my* spouse! how much better is thy love than wine! and the smell of thine ointments than all spices!

11 Thy lips, O *my* spouse, drop *as* the honeycomb: honey and milk *are* under thy tongue; and the smell of thy garments *is* like the smell of Lebanon.

12 A garden inclosed *is* my sister, *my* spouse; a spring shut up, a fountain sealed.

13 Thy plants *are* an orchard of pomegranates, with pleasant fruits; camphire, with spikenard,

14 Spikenard and saffron; calamus and cinnamon, with all trees of frankincense; myrrh and aloes, with all the chief spices:

15 A fountain of gardens, a well of living waters, and streams from Lebanon.

16 Awake, O north wind; and come, thou south; blow upon my garden, *that* the spices thereof may flow out. Let my beloved come into his garden, and eat his pleasant fruits.

CHAPTER 5

1 I am come into my garden, my sister, *my* spouse: I have gathered my myrrh with my spice; I have eaten my honeycomb with my honey; I have drunk my wine with my milk: eat, O friends; drink, yea, drink abundantly, O beloved.

The Fourth Song

2 I sleep, but my heart waketh: *it is* the voice of my beloved that knocketh, *saying*,

---

1 Isa. 26:9

3 Song 5:7

5 Song 2:7; 8:4

6 Song 8:5

1 Song 1:15; 5:12; 6:5

2 Song 6:6

3 Song 6:7

4 Neh. 3:19; Song 7:4

5 Prov. 5:19; Song 7:3

6 Song 2:17

7 Eph. 5:27

8 Deut. 3:9

10 Song 1:2

11 Gen. 27:27; Prov. 24:13, 14; Song 5:1; Hos. 14:6, 7

13 Song 1:14

15 John 4:10; 7:38

16 Song 5:1

1 Song 4:11, 16; Luke 15:7, 10; John 3:29; 15:14

2 Rev. 3:20

Open to me, my sister, my love, my dove, my undefiled: for my head is filled with dew, *and* my locks with the drops of the night.

3 I have put off my coat; how shall I put it on? I have washed my feet; how shall I defile them?

4 My beloved put in his hand by the hole *of the door*, and my bowels were moved for him.

5 I rose up to open to my beloved; and my hands dropped *with* myrrh, and my fingers *with* sweet smelling myrrh, upon the handles of the lock.

6 I opened to my beloved; but my beloved had withdrawn himself, *and* was gone: my soul failed when he spake: I sought him, but I could not find him; I called him, but he gave me no answer.

7 The watchmen that went about the city found me, they smote me, they wounded me; the keepers of the walls took away my veil from me.

8 I charge you, O daughters of Jerusalem, if ye find my beloved, that ye tell him, that I *am* sick of love.

9 What *is* thy beloved more than *another* beloved, O thou fairest among women? what *is* thy beloved more than *another* beloved, that thou dost so charge us?

10 My beloved *is* white and ruddy, the chiefest among ten thousand.

11 His head *is as* the most fine gold, his locks *are* bushy, *and* black as a raven.

12 His eyes *are as the eyes* of doves by the rivers of waters, washed with milk, *and* fitly set.

13 His cheeks *are* as a bed of spices, *as* sweet flowers: his lips *like* lilies, dropping sweet smelling myrrh.

14 His hands *are as* gold rings set with the beryl: his belly *is as* bright ivory overlaid *with* sapphires.

15 His legs *are as* pillars of marble, set upon sockets of fine gold: his countenance *is as* Lebanon, excellent as the cedars.

16 His mouth *is* most sweet: yea, he *is* altogether lovely. This *is* my beloved, and this *is* my friend, O daughters of Jerusalem.

Chapter 6

1 Whither is thy beloved gone, O thou fairest among women? whither is thy beloved turned aside? that we may seek him with thee.

2 My beloved is gone down into his garden, to the beds of spices, to feed in the gardens, and to gather lilies.

3 I *am* my beloved's, and my beloved *is* mine: he feedeth among the lilies.

The Fifth Song

4 Thou *art* beautiful, O my love, as Tirzah, comely as Jerusalem, terrible as *an army* with banners.

5 Turn away thine eyes from me, for they have overcome me: thy hair *is* as a flock of goats that appear from Gilead.

6 Thy teeth *are* as a flock of sheep which go up from the washing, whereof every one beareth twins, and *there is* not one barren among them.

7 As a piece of a pomegranate *are* thy temples within thy locks.

8 There are threescore queens, and fourscore concubines, and virgins without number.

9 My dove, my undefiled is *but* one; she *is* the *only* one of her mother, she *is* the choice one of her that bare her. The daughters saw her, and blessed her; *yea*, the queens and the concubines, and they praised her.

10 Who *is* she *that* looketh forth as the morning, fair as the moon, clear as the sun, *and* terrible as *an army* with banners?

11 I went down into the garden of nuts to see the fruits of the valley, *and* to see whether the vine flourished, *and* the pomegranates budded.

12 Or ever I was aware, my soul made me *like* the chariots of Ammi-nadib.

13 Return, return, O Shulamite; return, return, that we may look upon thee. What will ye see in the Shulamite? As it were the company of two armies.

Chapter 7

1 How beautiful are thy feet with shoes, O prince's daughter! the joints of thy thighs *are* like jewels, the work of the hands of a cunning workman.

2 Thy navel *is like* a round goblet, *which* wanteth not liquor: thy belly *is like* an heap of wheat set about with lilies.

3 Thy two breasts *are* like two young roes *that are* twins.

4 Thy neck *is* as a tower of ivory; thine eyes *like* the fishpools in Heshbon, by the gate of Bathrabbim: thy nose *is* as the tower of Lebanon which looketh toward Damascus.

5 Thine head upon thee *is* like Carmel, and the hair of thine head like purple; the king *is* held in the galleries.

6 How fair and how pleasant art thou, O love, for delights!

Cross references (center column)

6 Song 3:1
7 Song 3:3
9 Song 1:8
12 Song 1:15; 4:1
1 Song 1:8
3 Song 2:16; 7:10
4 Song 6:10
5 Song 4:1
6 Song 4:2
7 Song 4:3
10 Song 6:4
11 Song 7:12
13 Gen. 32:2
1 Ps. 45:13
3 Song 4:5
4 Song 4:4

7 This thy stature is like to a palm tree, and thy breasts to clusters *of grapes*.

8 I said, I will go up to the palm tree, I will take hold of the boughs thereof: now also thy breasts shall be as clusters of the vine, and the smell of thy nose like apples;

9 And the roof of thy mouth like the best wine for my beloved, that goeth *down* sweetly, causing the lips of those that are asleep to speak.

10 I *am* my beloved's, and his desire *is* toward me.

11 Come, my beloved, let us go forth into the field; let us lodge in the villages.

12 Let us get up early to the vineyards; let us see if the vine flourish, *whether* the tender grape appear, *and* the pomegranates bud forth: there will I give thee my loves.

13 The mandrakes give a smell, and at our gates *are* all manner of pleasant *fruits*, new and old, *which* I have laid up for thee, O my beloved.

CHAPTER 8

1 O that thou *wert* as my brother, that sucked the breasts of my mother! *when* I should find thee without, I would kiss thee; yea, I should not be despised.

2 I would lead thee, *and* bring thee into my mother's house, *who* would instruct me: I would cause thee to drink of spiced wine of the juice of my pomegranate.

3 His left hand *should be* under my head, and his right hand should embrace me.

4 I charge you, O daughters of Jerusalem, that ye stir not up, nor awake *my* love, until he please.

The Sixth Song

5 Who *is* this that cometh up from the wilderness, leaning upon her beloved? I raised thee up under the apple tree: there thy mother brought thee forth: there she brought thee forth *that* bare thee.

6 Set me as a seal upon thine heart, as a seal upon thine arm: for love *is* strong as death; jealousy *is* cruel as the grave: the coals thereof *are* coals of fire, *which hath a* most vehement flame.

7 Many waters cannot quench love, neither can the floods drown it: if *a* man would give all the substance of his house for love, it would utterly be contemned.

8 We have a little sister, and she hath no breasts: what shall we do for our sister in the day when she shall be spoken for?

9 If she *be* a wall, we will build upon her a palace of silver: and if she *be* a door, we will inclose her with boards of cedar.

10 I *am* a wall, and my breasts like towers: then was I in his eyes as one that found favour.

11 Solomon had a vineyard at Baal-hamon; he let out the vineyard unto keepers; every one for the fruit thereof was to bring a thousand *pieces* of silver.

12 My vineyard, which *is* mine, *is* before me: thou, O Solomon, *must have* a thousand, and those that keep the fruit thereof two hundred.

13 Thou that dwellest in the gardens, the companions hearken to thy voice: cause me to hear *it*.

14 Make haste, my beloved, and be thou like to a roe or to a young hart upon the mountains of spices.

---

10 Ps. 45:11; Song 2:16; 6:3

12 Song 6:11

13 Gen. 30:14; Matt. 13:52

2 Prov. 9:2

3 Song 2:6

4 Song 2:7; 3:5

5 Song 3:6

6 Isa. 49:16; Jer. 22:24; Hag. 2:23

7 Prov. 6:35

8 Ezek. 23:33

11 Matt. 21:33

13 Song 2:14

14 Song 2:17; Rev. 22:17, 20

Isaiah

I saiah's name literally means "salvation of the Lord," the underlying theme of the entire book. In fact, the plan of salvation is so comprehensively revealed in Isaiah's work that Augustine called it "the fifth Gospel," and others have referred to it as "the Bible in miniature."

Isaiah is thought to have been the son of a prince of Judah. He certainly did not feel uncomfortable in the presence of kings (Isa. 7:3–12; 37:21), and the richness of his vocabulary suggests that he was a man of culture and education. Isaiah received a dramatic call to the prophetic ministry sometime during the year of King Uzziah's death (748 B.C.) and ministered for more than forty years thereafter during the reigns of four kings: Uzziah, Jotham in Judah, Ahaz, and Hezekiah. Traditional accounts say that Isaiah was martyred by the wicked king Manasseh by being sawed in half (see Heb. 11:37) after 697 B.C.

While some scholars speculate that chapters 40—66 were written by other authors sometime after the Assyrian captivity (606–536 B.C.), the famous scroll of Isaiah from Qumran (dated 150 B.C.) makes no such distinction at any point in the text. Among the Jewish writers and scholars of ancient times, no other person of any kind is acknowledged as the author. The entire book is a unified narrative with a distinct and broad vocabulary, though the last portion addresses different subjects. In the New Testament, quotations borrowed from the last twenty-seven chapters of the book are credited to Isaiah.

Author
Isaiah

Date
8th Century B.C.

Key Truth
Salvation through the Messiah

Historic Time
King Uzziah to King Manasseh

Key Verse
12:2
. . . God is my salvation; I will trust, and not be afraid. . . .

Some prophecies involve types, but most are either already fulfilled or yet future-specific prophecies. Isaiah presents more messianic predictions than any other Old Testament book. Descriptions of the future kingdom of Israel and the worldwide Millennial Kingdom of Christ are striking. Both the first and second comings of the Messiah are clearly set forth, revealing the "sufferings of Christ" and the "glory that should follow" (see 1 Pet. 1:10–11).

No less than 754 verses out of 1,292 in Isaiah, or 59 percent of the book, are prophetic with 111 separate predictions.

59%
Prophecy

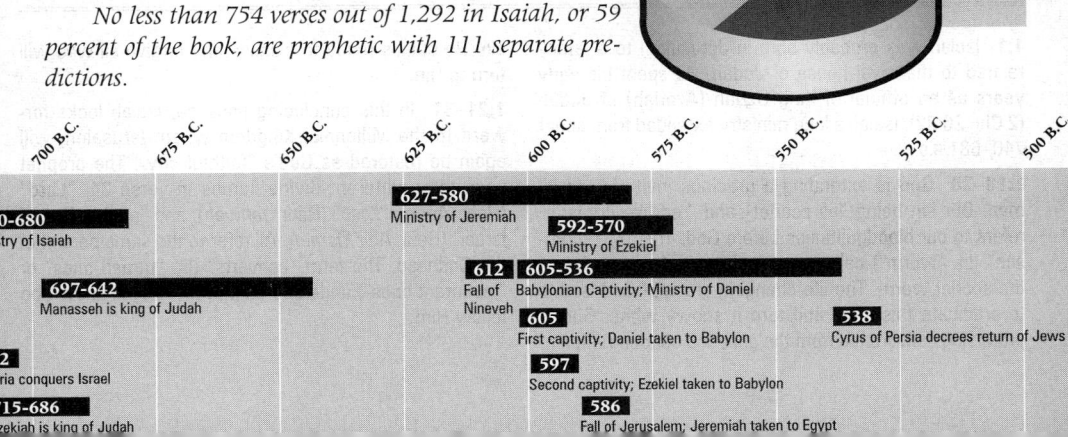

700 B.C.	675 B.C.	650 B.C.	625 B.C.	600 B.C.	575 B.C.	550 B.C.	525 B.C.	500 B.C.

40-680
istry of Isaiah

627-580
Ministry of Jeremiah

592-570
Ministry of Ezekiel

697-642
Manasseh is king of Judah

612
Fall of Nineveh

605-536
Babylonian Captivity; Ministry of Daniel

605
First captivity; Daniel taken to Babylon

538
Cyrus of Persia decrees return of Jews

22
syria conquers Israel

597
Second captivity; Ezekiel taken to Babylon

715-686
ezekiah is king of Judah

586
Fall of Jerusalem; Jeremiah taken to Egypt

CHAPTER 1

1 The vision of Isaiah the son of Amoz, which he saw concerning Judah and Jerusalem in the days of Uzziah, Jotham, Ahaz, *and* Hezekiah, kings of Judah.

A Sinful Nation

2 Hear, O heavens, and give ear, O earth: for the LORD hath spoken, I have nourished and brought up children, and they have rebelled against me.

3 The ox knoweth his owner, and the ass his master's crib: *but* Israel doth not know, my people doth not consider.

4 Ah sinful nation, a people laden with iniquity, a seed of evildoers, children that are corrupters: they have forsaken the LORD, they have provoked the Holy One of Israel unto anger, they are gone away backward.

5 Why should ye be stricken any more? ye will revolt more and more: the whole head is sick, and the whole heart faint.

6 From the sole of the foot even unto the head *there is* no soundness in it; *but* wounds, and bruises, and putrifying sores: they have not been closed, neither bound up, neither mollified with ointment.

7 Your country *is* desolate, your cities *are* burned with fire: your land, strangers devour it in your presence, and *it is* desolate, as overthrown by strangers.

8 And the daughter of Zion is left as a cottage in a vineyard, as a lodge in a garden of cucumbers, as a besieged city.

9 Except the LORD of hosts had left unto us a very small remnant, we should have been as Sodom, *and* we should have been like unto Gomorrah.

10 Hear the word of the LORD, ye rulers of Sodom; give ear unto the law of our God, ye people of Gomorrah.

11 To what purpose *is* the multitude of your sacrifices unto me? saith the LORD: I am full of the burnt offerings of rams, and the fat of fed beasts; and I delight not in the blood of bullocks, or of lambs, or of he goats.

12 When ye come to appear before me, who hath required this at your hand, to tread my courts?

13 Bring no more vain oblations; incense is an abomination unto me; the new moons and sabbaths, the calling of assemblies, I cannot away with; *it is* iniquity, even the solemn meeting.

14 Your new moons and your appointed feasts my soul hateth: they are a trouble unto me; I am weary to bear *them*.

15 And when ye spread forth your hands, I will hide mine eyes from you: yea, when ye make many prayers, I will not hear: your hands are full of blood.

16 Wash you, make you clean; put away the evil of your doings from before mine eyes; cease to do evil;

17 Learn to do well; seek judgment, relieve the oppressed, judge the fatherless, plead for the widow.

18 Come now, and let us reason together, saith the LORD: though your sins be as scarlet, they shall be as white as snow; though they be red like crimson, they shall be as wool.

19 If ye be willing and obedient, ye shall eat the good of the land:

20 But if ye refuse and rebel, ye shall be devoured with the sword: for the mouth of the LORD hath spoken *it*.

Zion, the Sinful City

21 How is the faithful city become an harlot! it was full of judgment; righteousness lodged in it; but now murderers.

22 Thy silver is become dross, thy wine mixed with water:

23 Thy princes *are* rebellious, and companions of thieves: every one loveth gifts, and

Cross references

2 Deut. 32:1; Jer. 2:12
4 Isa. 57:3
5 Jer. 2:30; 5:3
6 Jer. 8:22
7 Deut. 28:51, 52
9 Gen. 19:24; Lam. 3:22; Rom. 9:29
10 Deut. 32:32; Ezek. 16:46
11 1Sam. 15:22; Ps. 50:8, 9; 51:16; Prov. 15:8; 21:27; Isa. 66:3; Jer. 6:20; 7:21; Amos 5:21, 22; Mic. 6:7
12 Ex. 23:17; 34:23
13 Joel 1:14; 2:15; Matt. 15:9
14 Lev. 23:2; Num. 28:11; Isa. 43:24; Lam. 2:6
15 Isa. 59:2, 3; Jer. 14:12
16 Ps. 34:14
17 Mic. 6:8
18 Ps. 51:7; Rev. 7:14
20 Num. 23:19; Titus 1:2
21 Jer. 2:20, 21
22 Jer. 6:28, 30; Ezek. 22:18, 19

1:1 Isaiah was probably born in Jerusalem to a family related to the royal house of Judah. He spent his early years as an official of King Uzziah (Azariah) of Judah (2 Chr. 26:22). Isaiah's long ministry extended from about 740–681 B.C.

1:18–20 God is extending a gracious invitation to all men. Our sin being "as scarlet" and "red like crimson" refers to our bloodguiltiness before God. The term "crimson" (lit. "worm") calls to mind the colorfast red dye of the scarlet worm. The life-changing grace of God is able to eradicate this stain and turn it snowy white. God is promising deliverance from the guilt and condemnation of sin; He stands ready to cleanse and forgive all who will turn to Him.

1:21–31 In this concluding passage, Isaiah looks forward to the Millennial Kingdom when Jerusalem will again be restored as God's "faithful city." The prophet uses three different divine names in verse 24: "Lord" (Hebr. *Adon*); "LORD" (Hebr. *Yahweh*), and "mighty One of Israel" (Hebr. *Abir Yisrael*). All refer to the same person of the Godhead. The term "converts" (lit. "turned ones" or "repentant ones") underscores that those who know God follow Him.

followeth after rewards: they judge not the fatherless, neither doth the cause of the widow come unto them.

24 Therefore saith the Lord, the LORD of hosts, the mighty One of Israel, Ah, I will ease me of mine adversaries, and avenge me of mine enemies:

25 And I will turn my hand upon thee, and purely purge away thy dross, and take away all thy tin:

26 And I will restore thy judges as at the first, and thy counsellers as at the beginning: afterward thou shalt be called, The city of righteousness, the faithful city.

27 Zion shall be redeemed with judgment, and her converts with righteousness.

28 And the destruction of the transgressors and of the sinners *shall be* together, and they that forsake the LORD shall be consumed.

29 For they shall be ashamed of the oaks which ye have desired, and ye shall be confounded for the gardens that ye have chosen.

30 For ye shall be as an oak whose leaf fadeth, and as a garden that hath no water.

31 And the strong shall be as tow, and the maker of it as a spark, and they shall both burn together, and none shall quench *them*.

CHAPTER 2
True Peace

1 The word that Isaiah the son of Amoz saw concerning Judah and Jerusalem.

2 And it shall come to pass in the last days, *that* the mountain of the LORD's house shall be established in the top of the mountains, and shall be exalted above the hills; and all nations shall flow unto it.

3 And many people shall go and say, Come ye, and let us go up to the mountain of the LORD, to the house of the God of Jacob; and he will teach us of his ways, and we will walk in his paths: for out of Zion shall go

forth the law, and the word of the LORD from Jerusalem.

4 And he shall judge among the nations, and shall rebuke many people: and they shall beat their swords into plowshares, and their spears into pruninghooks: nation shall not lift up sword against nation, neither shall they learn war any more.

The Proud Will Be Destroyed

5 O house of Jacob, come ye, and let us walk in the light of the LORD.

6 Therefore thou hast forsaken thy people the house of Jacob, because they be replenished from the east, and *are* soothsayers like the Philistines, and they please themselves in the children of strangers.

7 Their land also is full of silver and gold, neither *is there any* end of their treasures; their land is also full of horses, neither *is there any* end of their chariots:

8 Their land also is full of idols; they worship the work of their own hands, that which their own fingers have made:

9 And the mean man boweth down, and the great man humbleth himself: therefore forgive them not.

10 Enter into the rock, and hide thee in the dust, for fear of the LORD, and for the glory of his majesty.

11 The lofty looks of man shall be humbled, and the haughtiness of men shall be bowed down, and the LORD alone shall be exalted in that day.

12 For the day of the LORD of hosts *shall be* upon every *one that is* proud and lofty, and upon every *one that is* lifted up; and he shall be brought low:

13 And upon all the cedars of Lebanon, *that are* high and lifted up, and upon all the oaks of Bashan,

14 And upon all the high mountains, and upon all the hills *that are* lifted up,

Cross references

24	Deut. 28:63; Ezek. 5:13
25	Jer. 6:29; 9:7; Mal. 3:3
26	Jer. 33:7; Zech. 8:3
28	Job 31:3; Ps. 1:6; 5:6; 73:27; 92:9; 104:35
29	Isa. 57:5; 65:3; 66:17
31	Isa. 43:17; Ezek. 32:21
2	Gen. 49:1; Ps. 68:15, 16; 72:8; Isa. 27:13; Jer. 23:20; Mic. 4:1
3	Jer. 31:6; 50:5; Zech. 8:21, 23; Luke 24:47
4	Ps. 46:9; 72:3, 7; Hos. 2:18; Zech. 9:10
5	Eph. 5:8
6	Num. 23:7; Deut. 18:14; Ps. 106:35; Jer. 10:2
7	Deut. 17:16; 17
8	Jer. 2:28
10	Isa. 2:19, 21; Rev. 6:15
11	Isa. 4:1; 5:15, 16; 52:6; Jer. 30:7, 8; Ezek. 38:14, 19
13	Isa. 14:8; 37:24; Ezek. 31:3; Zech. 11:1, 2
14	Isa. 30:25

2:1–5 The word that Isaiah . . . saw. This phrase from verse 1 indicates that the prophecy of this chapter is separate from that of the previous chapter. The use of the prophetic perfect verb form shows that the prophet sees the future as though it had already happened (see also Mic. 4:1–4). Isaiah envisions the Kingdom Age, when the nations of the world will come to the Holy City (Jerusalem) to learn the ways of God. Christ Himself is the Judge who will direct the affairs of nations, and peace shall prevail. Then the instruments of war and bloodshed will be refashioned into instruments of peace and prosperity.

2:6–9 replenished from the east. This refers to foreign influences from the East, namely, Assyria and Babylon. The literal meaning of the term "soothsayers" (Hebr. *Anan*, "to cloud" or "cover") depicts the actions of these eastern nations as of clouds obstructing the light of God's glory and revelation. Both the "mean man" (lower class) and the "great man" (upper class) were bowing to idols and placing themselves in danger of God's judgment.

2:10–12 hide thee in the dust. The judgment of the "day of the LORD" is at hand. This will be a universal judgment upon all human government (cf. Joel and 2 Thess. 1:7—2:12). In the face of such calamity, Isaiah's challenge is to trust in God.

The Prophecies of Isaiah

By Edward Hindson

Isaiah stands at the peak of the Old Testament as the literary genius of the prophets of Israel. His book is the longest of the prophets and looks further into the future than any of his contemporaries. This amazing book of prophecy includes Isaiah's unique prophecies regarding the coming of Immanuel and the Suffering Servant. It's impressive grandeur, dignity of expression, and dramatic style make it one of the finest examples of Hebrew literature.

Isaiah, the son of Amoz, was one of the most prominent citizens of Jerusalem, having access to both the royal and priestly leadership of Judah. Isaiah stood against the rising threat of Assyria and the emerging spirit of universalism that encouraged the formation of political alliances with other Near Eastern nations. When King Hezekiah ascended to the throne, a new day dawned for Judah. Pursuing a policy of spiritual reform, the new king repaired and cleansed the temple, reinstituted Mosaic Law in determining national policy, and made Isaiah his chief advisor.

Isaiah has been called the "Prince of the Prophets." The grandeur and dignity of his style parallels a liveliness of energy and profusion of imagery that make a lasting impression on his readers. Isaiah's prophecies are generally divided into two major sections: prophetic condemnation (chaps. 1—35) and prophetic consolation (chaps. 40—66), with a historic interlude in chapters 36—39.

> *Isaiah's book looks further into the future than those of his contemporaries.*

The prophet opens with a series of warnings aimed at Judah and Jerusalem (chaps. 1—5). These serve as an overview of his concern for the moral decay of the Jewish nation. In chapter 6, Isaiah includes the story of his call to the prophetic ministry. Next, he brings a series of predictions regarding the coming of the virgin-born Messiah, symbolically identified as Immanuel ("God with us") in chapters 7—12. Then, Isaiah proceeds to a series of prophecies against the nations, including Babylon, Moab, Syria, Ethiopia, Egypt, Babylon, Edom, Arabia, and Phoenicia (chaps. 13—23). In chapter 24, the prophet foresees the tragedies of the Tribulation period, and in chapters 25—27, he foresees the triumphs of the Millennial Kingdom. He repeats a similar parallel in chapters 34—35. In between, are a series of "woes" pronounced upon Israel and Judah (chaps. 28—33).

In the middle of the book are four chapters (36—39) that serve as an interlude between the major sections of the book. These chapters include the story of Assyria's failed attempt to conquer Jerusalem and the rising threat of the Babylonian Empire on the prophetic horizon. The closing section of Isaiah (chaps. 40–66) includes predictions of a future peaceful consolation that will be brought to reality by the servant of the Lord. These prophecies of deliverance foresee the messianic reign of Christ in peace and prosperity that will occur in the Millennium (cf. Rev. 20).

The theme of Isaiah's prophecies points to the coming of Jesus Christ, the virgin's son, Immanuel, the Branch of the Lord, the mighty God, the Prince of Peace, the coming Messiah, the Suffering Servant, the glorious King! He is the one who will judge the nations, atone for our sins, and rule the world in peace and righteousness.

15 And upon every high tower, and upon every fenced wall,

16 And upon all the ships of Tarshish, and upon all pleasant pictures.

17 And the loftiness of man shall be bowed down, and the haughtiness of men shall be made low: and the LORD alone shall be exalted in that day.

18 And the idols he shall utterly abolish.

19 And they shall go into the holes of the rocks, and into the caves of the earth, for fear of the LORD, and for the glory of his majesty, when he ariseth to shake terribly the earth.

20 In that day a man shall cast his idols of silver, and his idols of gold, which they made *each one* for himself to worship, to the moles and to the bats;

21 To go into the clefts of the rocks, and into the tops of the ragged rocks, for fear of the LORD, and for the glory of his majesty, when he ariseth to shake terribly the earth.

22 Cease ye from man, whose breath *is* in his nostrils: for wherein is he to be accounted of?

CHAPTER 3
God Judges Judah and Jerusalem

1 For, behold, the Lord, the LORD of hosts, doth take away from Jerusalem and from Judah the stay and the staff, the whole stay of bread, and the whole stay of water,

2 The mighty man, and the man of war, the judge, and the prophet, and the prudent, and the ancient,

3 The captain of fifty, and the honourable man, and the counseller, and the cunning artificer, and the eloquent orator.

4 And I will give children *to be* their princes, and babes shall rule over them.

5 And the people shall be oppressed, every one by another, and every one by his neighbour: the child shall behave himself proudly against the ancient, and the base against the honourable.

6 When a man shall take hold of his brother of the house of his father, *saying,* Thou hast clothing, be thou our ruler, and *let* this ruin *be* under thy hand:

7 In that day shall he swear, saying, I will not be an healer; for in my house *is* neither bread nor clothing: make me not a ruler of the people.

8 For Jerusalem is ruined, and Judah is fallen: because their tongue and their do-

ings *are* against the LORD, to provoke the eyes of his glory.

9 The shew of their countenance doth witness against them; and they declare their sin as Sodom, they hide *it* not. Woe unto their soul! for they have rewarded evil unto themselves.

10 Say ye to the righteous, that *it shall be* well *with him*: for they shall eat the fruit of their doings.

11 Woe unto the wicked! *it shall be* ill *with him*: for the reward of his hands shall be given him.

12 *As for* my people, children *are* their oppressors, and women rule over them. O my people, they which lead thee cause *thee* to err, and destroy the way of thy paths.

13 The LORD standeth up to plead, and standeth to judge the people.

14 The LORD will enter into judgment with the ancients of his people, and the princes thereof: for ye have eaten up the vineyard; the spoil of the poor *is* in your houses.

15 What mean ye *that* ye beat my people to pieces, and grind the faces of the poor? saith the Lord GOD of hosts.

The Women of Jerusalem

16 Moreover the LORD saith, Because the daughters of Zion are haughty, and walk with stretched forth necks and wanton eyes, walking and mincing *as* they go, and making a tinkling with their feet:

17 Therefore the Lord will smite with a scab the crown of the head of the daughters of Zion, and the LORD will discover their secret parts.

18 In that day the Lord will take away the bravery of *their* tinkling ornaments *about their feet*, and *their* cauls, and *their* round tires like the moon,

19 The chains, and the bracelets, and the mufflers,

20 The bonnets, and the ornaments of the legs, and the headbands, and the tablets, and the earrings,

21 The rings, and nose jewels,

22 The changeable suits of apparel, and the mantles, and the wimples, and the crisping pins,

23 The glasses, and the fine linen, and the hoods, and the vails.

24 And it shall come to pass, *that* instead of sweet smell there shall be stink; and instead of a girdle a rent; and instead of well set

Cross references:
16 1Kgs. 10:22
17 Isa. 2:1, 11
19 Isa. 2:10; 30:32; Hos. 10:8; Hag. 2:6, 21; Luke 23:30; 2Thess. 1:9; Heb. 12:26; Rev. 6:16; 9:6
20 Isa. 30:22; 31:7
21 Isa. 2:10, 19
22 Job 27:3; Ps. 146:3; Jer. 17:5
1 Lev. 26:26; Jer. 37:21; 38:9
2 2Kgs. 24:14
4 Eccl. 10:16
7 Gen. 14:22
8 Mic. 3:12
9 Gen. 13:13; 18:20, 21; 19:5
10 Ps. 128:2; Eccl. 8:12
11 Ps. 11:6; Eccl. 8:13
12 Isa. 3:4; 9:16
13 Mic. 6:2
14 Isa. 5:7; Matt. 21:33
15 Isa. 58:4; Mic. 3:2, 3
17 Deut. 28:27; Isa. 47:2, 3; Jer. 13:22; Nah. 3:5
18 Judg. 8:21
24 Isa. 22:12; Mic. 1:16

2:19–21 he ariseth to shake terribly the earth. These references to shaking the earth are similar to Revelation 6:14.

hair baldness; and instead of a stomacher a girding of sackcloth; *and* burning instead of beauty.

25 Thy men shall fall by the sword, and thy mighty in the war.

26 And her gates shall lament and mourn; and she *being* desolate shall sit upon the ground.

CHAPTER 4

1 And in that day seven women shall take hold of one man, saying, We will eat our own bread, and wear our own apparel: only let us be called by thy name, to take away our reproach.

The Future of Jerusalem

2 In that day shall the branch of the LORD be beautiful and glorious, and the fruit of the earth *shall be* excellent and comely for them that are escaped of Israel.

3 And it shall come to pass, *that he that is* left in Zion, and *he that* remaineth in Jerusalem, shall be called holy, *even* every one that is written among the living in Jerusalem:

4 When the Lord shall have washed away the filth of the daughters of Zion, and shall have purged the blood of Jerusalem from the midst thereof by the spirit of judgment, and by the spirit of burning.

5 And the LORD will create upon every dwelling place of mount Zion, and upon her assemblies, a cloud and smoke by day, and the shining of a flaming fire by night: for upon all the glory *shall be* a defence.

6 And there shall be a tabernacle for a shadow in the daytime from the heat, and for a place of refuge, and for a covert from storm and from rain.

CHAPTER 5
The Parable of the Vineyard

1 Now will I sing to my wellbeloved a song of my beloved touching his vineyard. My

wellbeloved hath a vineyard in a very fruitful hill:

2 And he fenced it, and gathered out the stones thereof, and planted it with the choicest vine, and built a tower in the midst of it, and also made a winepress therein: and he looked that it should bring forth grapes, and it brought forth wild grapes.

3 And now, O inhabitants of Jerusalem, and men of Judah, judge, I pray you, betwixt me and my vineyard.

4 What could have been done more to my vineyard, that I have not done in it? wherefore, when I looked that it should bring forth grapes, brought it forth wild grapes?

5 And now go to; I will tell you what I will do to my vineyard: I will take away the hedge thereof, and it shall be eaten up; *and* break down the wall thereof, and it shall be trodden down:

6 And I will lay it waste: it shall not be pruned, nor digged; but there shall come up briers and thorns: I will also command the clouds that they rain no rain upon it.

7 For the vineyard of the LORD of hosts *is* the house of Israel, and the men of Judah his pleasant plant: and he looked for judgment, but behold oppression; for righteousness, but behold a cry.

The Fate of the Wicked

8 Woe unto them that join house to house, *that* lay field to field, till *there be* no place, that they may be placed alone in the midst of the earth!

9 In mine ears *said* the LORD of hosts, Of a truth many houses shall be desolate, *even* great and fair, without inhabitant.

10 Yea, ten acres of vineyard shall yield one bath, and the seed of an homer shall yield an ephah.

11 Woe unto them that rise up early in the morning, *that* they may follow strong drink; that continue until night, *till* wine inflame them!

---

26 Jer. 14:2; Lam. 1:4; 2:10
1 Isa. 2:11, 17; Luke 1:25; 2Thess. 3:12
2 Jer. 23:5; Zech. 3:8; 6:12
3 Isa. 60:21; Phil. 4:3; Rev. 3:5
4 Mal. 3:2, 3
5 Ex. 13:21; Isa. 8:14; Zech. 2:5
6 Isa. 25:4
1 Ps. 80:8; Song 8:12; Isa. 27:2; Jer. 2:21; Matt. 21:33; Mark 12:1; Luke 20:9
2 Deut. 32:6; Isa. 1:2, 3
3 Rom. 3:4
5 Ps. 80:12
8 Mic. 2:2
9 Isa. 22:14
10 Ezek. 45:11
11 Prov. 23:29, 30; Eccl. 10:16; Isa. 5:22

4:2–6 the branch of the LORD. This title, which refers to the Messiah, is also used in Jeremiah 23:5; 33:15 and Zechariah 3:8; 6:12. In the midst of his warning of judgment, Isaiah unveils a promise of hope in the coming of Messiah. He sees ahead to the Millennial Kingdom when once again the cloud of glory shall go before them by day and the pillar of fire by night.

5:1–7 This is a parable of the vineyard, which symbolized Israel (cf. also Jer. 12:10; Ps. 80:8–19; Matt. 21:33–45). Reminiscent of the Song of Solomon, the poem is called the "song of my beloved," but here it

becomes a song of lament. The beloved is the Lord, and Israel is the vineyard that has brought forth wild grapes. There is a play on sounds and letters in the Hebrew of "he looked for judgment [*mishpat*], but behold oppression [*mispach*]; for righteousness [*tsedaqah*], but behold a cry [*tseaqah*]." What God finds when He comes is the opposite of what He seeks.

5:8 join house to house. This refers to the practice of greedy landowners who, by foreclosing mortgages, acquired adjoining land to form huge estates.

12 And the harp, and the viol, the tabret, and pipe, and wine, are in their feasts: but they regard not the work of the LORD, neither consider the operation of his hands.

13 Therefore my people are gone into captivity, because *they have* no knowledge: and their honourable men *are* famished, and their multitude dried up with thirst.

14 Therefore hell hath enlarged herself, and opened her mouth without measure: and their glory, and their multitude, and their pomp, and he that rejoiceth, shall descend into it.

15 And the mean man shall be brought down, and the mighty man shall be humbled, and the eyes of the lofty shall be humbled:

16 But the LORD of hosts shall be exalted in judgment, and God that is holy shall be sanctified in righteousness.

17 Then shall the lambs feed after their manner, and the waste places of the fat ones shall strangers eat.

18 Woe unto them that draw iniquity with cords of vanity, and sin as it were with a cart rope:

19 That say, Let him make speed, *and* hasten his work, that we may see *it*: and let the counsel of the Holy One of Israel draw nigh and come, that we may know *it*!

20 Woe unto them that call evil good, and good evil; that put darkness for light, and light for darkness; that put bitter for sweet, and sweet for bitter!

21 Woe unto *them that are* wise in their own eyes, and prudent in their own sight!

22 Woe unto *them that are* mighty to drink wine, and men of strength to mingle strong drink:

23 Which justify the wicked for reward, and take away the righteousness of the righteous from him!

24 Therefore as the fire devoureth the stubble, and the flame consumeth the chaff, *so*

their root shall be as rottenness, and their blossom shall go up as dust: because they have cast away the law of the LORD of hosts, and despised the word of the Holy One of Israel.

25 Therefore is the anger of the LORD kindled against his people, and he hath stretched forth his hand against them, and hath smitten them: and the hills did tremble, and their carcases *were* torn in the midst of the streets. For all this his anger is not turned away, but his hand *is* stretched out still.

26 And he will lift up an ensign to the nations from far, and will hiss unto them from the end of the earth: and, behold, they shall come with speed swiftly:

27 None shall be weary nor stumble among them; none shall slumber nor sleep; neither shall the girdle of their loins be loosed, nor the latchet of their shoes be broken:

28 Whose arrows *are* sharp, and all their bows bent, their horses' hoofs shall be counted like flint, and their wheels like a whirlwind:

29 Their roaring *shall be* like a lion, they shall roar like young lions: yea, they shall roar, and lay hold of the prey, and shall carry *it* away safe, and none shall deliver *it*.

30 And in that day they shall roar against them like the roaring of the sea: and if *one* look unto the land, behold darkness *and* sorrow, and the light is darkened in the heavens thereof.

CHAPTER 6
God Calls Isaiah

1 In the year that king Uzziah died I saw also the Lord sitting upon a throne, high and lifted up, and his train filled the temple.

2 Above it stood the seraphims: each one had six wings with twain he covered his face, and with twain he covered his feet, and with twain he did fly.

3 And one cried unto another, and said,

Cross references

12 Job 34:27; Ps. 28:5; Amos 6:5, 6

13 Isa. 1:3; Hos. 4:6; Luke 19:44

15 Isa. 2:9, 11, 17

17 Isa. 10:16

19 Isa. 66:5; Jer. 17:15; Amos 5:18; 2Pet. 3:3, 4

21 Prov. 3:7; Rom. 1:22; 12:16

22 Isa. 5:11

23 Prov. 17:15; 24:24

24 Ex. 15:7; Job 18:16; Hos. 9:16; Amos 2:9

25 Lev. 26:14; 2Kgs. 22:13, 17; Isa. 9:12, 17, 21; 10:4; Jer. 4:24

26 Deut. 28:49; Ps. 72:8; Isa. 7:18; 11:12; Joel 2:7; Mal. 1:11

27 Dan. 5:6

28 Jer. 5:16

30 Isa. 8:22; Jer. 4:23; Lam. 3:2

1 1Kgs. 22:19; 2Kgs. 15:7; John 12:41; Rev. 4:2

2 Ezek. 1:11

3 Ps. 72:19; Rev. 4:8

5:18 draw iniquity with cords. This phrase pictures pulling a load of sin with a rope on a cart. The people of Judah are condemned for parading their sin before God.

5:26–30 he will lift up an ensign [banner] **to the nations.** Isaiah makes it clear that when God stretches forth His hand to undertake judgment, He will not cease until He is finished. The banner that God will raise at the nations serves as a declaration of war; at God's request the invading nations come to destroy Judah.

6:1 In the year that king Uzziah died. Isaiah here tells of his original call to the prophetic ministry in 740 B.C. The

death of godly Uzziah signaled the end of Judah's golden age. Uzziah's leprosy parallels the spiritual decadence that prevailed in Jewish society at the time. At this crucial hour, the prophet's only recourse is to turn to God Himself, the true Sovereign in the affairs of men.

6:3, 8 Holy, holy, holy. The Seraphim (lit. "burning ones") are six-winged angelic creatures that are heard declaring God's holiness. "Holy, holy, holy" may be taken as a suggestion of the Trinity. Note also, when God speaks, He uses the plural pronoun "us" (v. 8).

Holy, holy, holy, *is* the Lord of hosts: the whole earth *is* full of his glory.

4 And the posts of the door moved at the voice of him that cried, and the house was filled with smoke.

5 Then said I, Woe *is* me! for I am undone; because I *am* a man of unclean lips, and I dwell in the midst of a people of unclean lips: for mine eyes have seen the King, the Lord of hosts.

6 Then flew one of the seraphims unto me, having a live coal in his hand, *which* he had taken with the tongs from off the altar:

7 And he laid *it* upon my mouth, and said, Lo, this hath touched thy lips; and thine iniquity is taken away, and thy sin purged.

8 Also I heard the voice of the Lord, saying, Whom shall I send, and who will go for us? Then said I, Here *am* I; send me.

9 And he said, Go, and tell this people, Hear ye indeed, but understand not; and see ye indeed, but perceive not.

10 Make the heart of this people fat, and make their ears heavy, and shut their eyes; lest they see with their eyes, and hear with their ears, and understand with their heart, and convert, and be healed.

11 Then said I, Lord, how long? And he answered, Until the cities be wasted without inhabitant, and the houses without man, and the land be utterly desolate,

12 And the Lord have removed men far away, and *there be* a great forsaking in the midst of the land.

13 But yet in it *shall be* a tenth, and *it* shall return, and shall be eaten: as a teil tree, and as an oak, whose substance *is* in them, when they cast *their leaves: so* the holy seed *shall be* the substance thereof.

CHAPTER 7
A Message for King Ahaz

1 And it came to pass in the days of Ahaz the son of Jotham, the son of Uzziah, king of Judah, *that* Rezin the king of Syria, and Pekah the son of Remaliah, king of Israel, went up toward Jerusalem to war against it, but could not prevail against it.

2 And it was told the house of David, saying, Syria is confederate with Ephraim. And his heart was moved, and the heart of his people, as the trees of the wood are moved with the wind.

3 Then said the Lord unto Isaiah, Go forth now to meet Ahaz, thou, and Shear-jashub thy son, at the end of the conduit of the upper pool in the highway of the fuller's field;

4 And say unto him, Take heed, and be quiet; fear not, neither be fainthearted for the two tails of these smoking firebrands, for the fierce anger of Rezin with Syria, and of the son of Remaliah.

5 Because Syria, Ephraim, and the son of Remaliah, have taken evil counsel against thee, saying,

6 Let us go up against Judah, and vex it, and let us make a breach therein for us, and set a king in the midst of it, *even* the son of Tabeal:

7 Thus saith the Lord God, It shall not stand, neither shall it come to pass.

8 For the head of Syria *is* Damascus, and the head of Damascus *is* Rezin; and within threescore and five years shall Ephraim be broken, that it be not a people.

9 And the head of Ephraim *is* Samaria, and the head of Samaria *is* Remaliah's son. If ye will not believe, surely ye shall not be established.

A Virgin

10 Moreover the Lord spake again unto Ahaz, saying,

11 Ask thee a sign of the Lord thy God; ask it either in the depth, or in the height above.

12 But Ahaz said, I will not ask, neither will I tempt the Lord.

Cross-references: 4 Ex. 40:34; 1Kgs. 8:10 · 5 Ex. 4:10; 6:30; Judg. 6:22; 13:22; Jer. 1:6 · 6 Rev. 8:3 · 7 Jer. 1:9; Dan. 10:16 · 8 Gen. 1:26; 3:22; 11:7 · 9 Isa. 43:8; Matt. 13:14; Mark 4:12; Luke 8:10; John 12:40; Acts 28:26; Rom. 11:8 · 10 Ps. 119:70; Isa. 63:17; Jer. 5:21 · 11 Mic. 3:12 · 12 2Kgs. 25:21 · 13 Ezra 9:2; Mal. 2:15; Rom. 11:5 · 1 2Kgs. 16:5; 2Chr. 28:5, 6 · 3 2Kgs. 18:17; Isa. 6:13; 10:21; 36:2 · 7 Prov. 21:30; Isa. 8:10 · 8 2Sam. 8:6 · 9 2Chr. 20:20 · 11 Judg. 6:36; Matt. 12:38

6:9–13 Isaiah's preaching will, for the most part, fall upon deaf ears. The phrase "hear ye indeed" means "keep on hearing." Judah will continue hearing but not heed the prophet's warning. The more Isaiah preaches, the more the people will harden themselves to his message. Eventually, they will be taken captive to Babylon, after which only a tenth of them will return to the Holy Land.

7:3–9 The Lord sends Isaiah to the House of David to discuss the military threat facing Judah. God further instructs the prophet to bring his son Shear-jashub ("A Remnant Shall Return") as a token of God's promise of hope. The word of the Lord, spoken by Isaiah, told Ahaz not to fear these invading kings, and the description of these kings as stubs of "smoking firebrands" (lit., "smoldering sticks") prophesies the imminent doom that awaits the nations these kings represent. The threatened invasion of Judah will not succeed, and within sixty-five years the Northern Kingdom will cease to exist.

7:10–13 As the spokesman of the Lord (*Yahweh*), Isaiah urges Ahaz to ask for a sign (Hebr. *ot*, "miracle"). The king's response sounds pious, but it actually betrays his

13 And he said, Hear ye now, O house of David; *Is it* a small thing for you to weary men, but will ye weary my God also?

14 Therefore the Lord himself shall give you a sign; Behold, a virgin shall conceive, and bear a son, and shall call his name Immanuel.

15 Butter and honey shall he eat, that he may know to refuse the evil, and choose the good.

16 For before the child shall know to refuse the evil, and choose the good, the land that thou abhorrest shall be forsaken of both her kings.

17 The LORD shall bring upon thee, and upon thy people, and upon thy father's house, days that have not come, from the day that Ephraim departed from Judah; *even* the king of Assyria.

18 And it shall come to pass in that day, *that* the LORD shall hiss for the fly that *is* in the uttermost part of the rivers of Egypt, and for the bee that *is* in the land of Assyria.

19 And they shall come, and shall rest all of them in the desolate valleys, and in the holes of the rocks, and upon all thorns, and upon all bushes.

20 In the same day shall the Lord shave with a razor that is hired, *namely*, by them beyond the river, by the king of Assyria, the head, and the hair of the feet: and it shall also consume the beard.

21 And it shall come to pass in that day, *that* a man shall nourish a young cow, and two sheep;

22 And it shall come to pass, for the abundance of milk *that* they shall give he shall eat butter: for butter and honey shall every one eat that is left in the land.

23 And it shall come to pass in that day, *that* every place shall be, where there were a thousand vines at a thousand silverlings, it shall *even* be for briers and thorns.

24 With arrows and with bows shall *men* come thither; because all the land shall become briers and thorns.

25 And *on* all hills that shall be digged with the mattock, there shall not come thither the fear of briers and thorns: but it shall be for the sending forth of oxen, and for the treading of lesser cattle.

CHAPTER 8
The Sign of Isaiah's Son

1 Moreover the LORD said unto me, Take thee a great roll, and write in it with a man's pen concerning Maher-shalal-hash-baz.

2 And I took unto me faithful witnesses to record, Uriah the priest, and Zechariah the son of Jeberechiah.

3 And I went unto the prophetess; and she conceived, and bare a son. Then said the LORD to me, Call his name Maher-shalal-hash-baz.

4 For before the child shall have knowledge to cry, My father, and my mother, the riches of Damascus and the spoil of Samaria shall be taken away before the king of Assyria.

Cross-references

14 Gen. 4:1, 25; 16:11; 29:32; 30:6, 8; 1Sam. 4:21; Isa. 8:8; 9:6; Matt. 1:23; Luke 1:31, 34

16 2Kgs. 15:30; 16:9; Isa. 8:4

17 1Kgs. 12:16; 2Chr. 28:19

18 Isa. 5:26

19 Isa. 2:19; Jer. 16:16

20 2Kgs. 16:7, 8; 2Chr. 28:20, 21; Ezek. 5:1

23 Isa. 5:6

1 Isa. 30:8; Hab. 2:2

2 2Kgs. 16:10

4 2Kgs. 15:29; 16:9; Isa. 7:16; 17:3

---

unbelief. Isaiah announces that God Himself had chosen a miraculous sign addressed to the house of David. The prophecy would have profound and far-reaching implications for the future of the Davidic kingdom and the messianic ruler who is to be established upon its throne.

7:14 The unusual birth will indeed be a sign (see also Gen. 16:11; Judg. 13:5). The Hebrew is better read "the virgin," rather than "a virgin," the Hebrew word for "virgin" being the unique Hebrew term *almah*. Comparing the six other instances of the word in the Old Testament (Gen. 24:43; Ex. 2:8; Ps. 68:25; Prov. 30:19; Song 1:3; 6:8) it is evident that *almah* is the most precise term Isaiah could have used to indicate that the young woman in view would indeed be a virgin. The more common Hebrew term for virgin, *bethulah*, is not as precise as *almah*. On at least two occasions, *bethulah* is used of a young married woman or a young widow (Deut. 22:19; Joel 1:8). The prophet envisions the miraculous sign of a pregnant virgin who is about to bear a Son. That this prophecy must refer to the virgin birth of Christ is made clear in Matthew 1:23, where the Greek word *parthenos* ("virgin") is used to quote this verse and to declare its fulfillment in the conception of Jesus. See the note on Matthew 1:23.

7:15–16 Isaiah carries the present tense of the prediction into the immediate situation, and his prophecy has both direct significance to Ahaz and ultimately to the line of David in predicting the virgin birth of the Messiah. Though Immanuel would not be born for many years, His infancy symbolized the fact that Judah's present isolation and soon-coming desolation will be short-lived because her enemies will soon be rendered powerless.

7:17–25 Syria fell to Assyria in 732 B.C., and within another ten years, Ephraim (the Northern Kingdom) was also taken captive.

8:1–4 The symbolic name of Isaiah's son Maher-shalal-hash-baz (meaning "Speed the Spoil, Hasten the Prey") symbolizes the speedy and victorious Assyrian conquest of Damascus (Syria) and Samaria (Israel).

The Assyrians Are Coming!

5 The Lord spake also unto me again, saying,

6 Forasmuch as this people refuseth the waters of Shiloah that go softly, and rejoice in Rezin and Remaliah's son;

7 Now therefore, behold, the Lord bringeth up upon them the waters of the river, strong and many, *even* the king of Assyria, and all his glory: and he shall come up over all his channels, and go over all his banks:

8 And he shall pass through Judah; he shall overflow and go over, he shall reach *even* to the neck; and the stretching out of his wings shall fill the breadth of thy land, O Immanuel.

9 Associate yourselves, O ye people, and ye shall be broken in pieces; and give ear, all ye of far countries: gird yourselves, and ye shall be broken in pieces; gird yourselves, and ye shall be broken in pieces.

10 Take counsel together and it shall come to nought; speak the word, and it shall not stand: for God *is* with us.

11 For the Lord spake thus to me with a strong hand, and instructed me that I should not walk in the way of this people, saying,

12 Say ye not, A confederacy, to all *them to* whom this people shall say, A confederacy; neither fear ye their fear, nor be afraid.

13 Sanctify the Lord of hosts himself; and *let* him *be* your fear, and *let* him *be* your dread.

14 And he shall be for a sanctuary; but for a stone of stumbling and for a rock of offence to both the houses of Israel, for a gin and for a snare to the inhabitants of Jerusalem.

15 And many among them shall stumble, and fall, and be broken, and be snared, and be taken.

A Warning

16 Bind up the testimony, seal the law among my disciples.

17 And I will wait upon the Lord, that hideth his face from the house of Jacob, and I will look for him.

18 Behold, I and the children whom the Lord hath given me *are* for signs and for wonders in Israel from the Lord of hosts, which dwelleth in mount Zion.

19 And when they shall say unto you, Seek unto them that have familiar spirits, and unto wizards that peep, and that mutter: should not a people seek unto their God? for the living to the dead?

20 To the law and to the testimony: if they speak not according to this word, *it is* because *there is* no light in them.

21 And they shall pass through it, hardly bestead and hungry: and it shall come to pass, that when they shall be hungry, they shall fret themselves, and curse their king and their God, and look upward.

22 And they shall look unto the earth; and behold trouble and darkness, dimness of anguish; and *they shall be* driven to darkness.

CHAPTER 9
The Prince of Peace

1 Nevertheless the dimness *shall* not *be* such as *was* in her vexation, when at the first he lightly afflicted the land of Zebulun and the land of Naphtali, and afterward did more grievously afflict *her* by the way of the sea, beyond Jordan, in Galilee of the nations.

2 The people that walked in darkness have

Cross references (center column)

6 Neh. 3:15; Isa. 7:1, 2, 6; John 9:7

8 Isa. 7:14; 30:28

9 Joel 3:9, 11

10 Job 5:12; Isa. 7:7, 14; Acts 5:38, 39; Rom. 8:31

13 Num. 20:12; Ps. 76:7; Luke 12:5

14 Isa. 28:16; Ezek. 11:16; Luke 2:34; Rom. 9:33; 1 Pet. 2:8

15 Matt. 21:44; Luke 20:18; Rom. 9:32; 11:25

17 Isa. 54:8; Hab. 2:3; Luke 2:25, 38

18 Ps. 71:7; Zech. 3:8; Heb. 2:13

19 1 Sam. 28:8; Ps. 106:28; Isa. 19:3; 29:4

20 Mic. 3:6; Luke 16:29

21 Rev. 16:11

1 Lev. 26:24; 2 Kgs. 15:29; 17:5, 6

2 Matt. 4:16; Eph. 5:8, 14

8:5–10 the waters of Shiloah. The waters of the pool of Siloam were known for their healing powers (cf. John 9:7). Since the people of Israel have refused the Lord in a time of peace, God will bring upon them the "waters of the river," which are contrasted to those of the gentle pool. Isaiah names in advance the nation that will destroy Israel as a flood. That this invasion will also "pass through Judah," and will overflow "even to the neck," indicates that the Assyrian invasion will not only wipe out the Northern Kingdom, but it will nearly drown the Southern Kingdom as well (cf. Isa. 36—37). Immanuel (v. 8), this one whose name signifies "God with us," is no ordinary person nor is he a contemporary of Isaiah. The language here clearly intends to link the prophecy of the virgin birth of Immanuel (7:14) to the prediction of his coronation as King (9:6–7).

8:14–18 a stone of stumbling and . . . rock of offence. This is a messianic prophecy fulfilled in Christ (cf. Rom. 9:33; 1 Pet. 2:8). Instead of running to the Lord for refuge, the children of Israel will stumble over Him in disbelief. The prophet closes this section by clearly stating that he and his children are intended to be signs to the nation of Judah. Their symbolic names serve as a final warning to the people of Zion.

9:2 upon them hath the light shined. To those who "walk in darkness," the prophet sees "a great light," as though it were already shining. This is quoted as being fulfilled in Jesus' ministry in Galilee (Matt. 4:15–16).

seen a great light: they that dwell in the land of the shadow of death, upon them hath the light shined.

3 Thou hast multiplied the nation, *and* not increased the joy: they joy before thee according to the joy in harvest, *and* as men rejoice when they divide the spoil.

4 For thou hast broken the yoke of his burden, and the staff of his shoulder, the rod of his oppressor, as in the day of Midian.

5 For every battle of the warrior *is* with confused noise, and garments rolled in blood; but *this* shall be with burning *and* fuel of fire.

6 For unto us a child is born, unto us a son is given: and the government shall be upon his shoulder: and his name shall be called Wonderful, Counsellor, The mighty God, The everlasting Father, The Prince of Peace.

7 Of the increase of *his* government and peace *there shall be* no end, upon the throne of David, and upon his kingdom, to order it, and to establish it with judgment and with justice from henceforth even for ever. The zeal of the Lord of hosts will perform this.

God's Anger

8 The Lord sent a word into Jacob, and it hath lighted upon Israel.

9 And all the people shall know, *even* Ephraim and the inhabitant of Samaria, that say in the pride and stoutness of heart,

10 The bricks are fallen down, but we will build with hewn stones: the sycomores are cut down, but we will change *them into* cedars.

11 Therefore the Lord shall set up the adversaries of Rezin against him, and join his enemies together;

12 The Syrians before, and the Philistines behind; and they shall devour Israel with open mouth. For all this his anger is not turned away, but his hand *is* stretched out still.

13 For the people turneth not unto him that smiteth them, neither do they seek the Lord of hosts.

14 Therefore the Lord will cut off from Is-

rael head and tail, branch and rush, in one day.

15 The ancient and honourable, he *is* the head; and the prophet that teacheth lies, he *is* the tail.

16 For the leaders of this people cause *them* to err; and *they that are* led of them *are* destroyed.

17 Therefore the Lord shall have no joy in their young men, neither shall have mercy on their fatherless and widows: for every one *is* an hypocrite and an evildoer, and every mouth speaketh folly. For all this his anger is not turned away, but his hand *is* stretched out still.

18 For wickedness burneth as the fire: it shall devour the briers and thorns, and shall kindle in the thickets of the forest, and they shall mount up *like* the lifting up of smoke.

19 Through the wrath of the Lord of hosts is the land darkened, and the people shall be as the fuel of the fire: no man shall spare his brother.

20 And he shall snatch on the right hand, and be hungry; and he shall eat on the left hand, and they shall not be satisfied: they shall eat every man the flesh of his own arm:

21 Manasseh, Ephraim; and Ephraim, Manasseh: *and* they together *shall be* against Judah. For all this his anger is not turned away, but his hand *is* stretched out still.

CHAPTER 10

1 Woe unto them that decree unrighteous decrees, and that write grievousness *which* they have prescribed;

2 To turn aside the needy from judgment, and to take away the right from the poor of my people, that widows may be their prey, and *that* they may rob the fatherless!

3 And what will ye do in the day of visitation, and in the desolation *which* shall come from far? to whom will ye flee for help? and where will ye leave your glory?

4 Without me they shall bow down under the prisoners, and they shall fall under the slain. For all this his anger is not turned away, but his hand *is* stretched out still.

Cross references (center column)

3 Judg. 5:30

4 Judg. 7:22; Ps. 83:9; Isa. 10:5, 26; 14:5

5 Isa. 66:15, 16

6 Judg. 13:18; Isa. 7:14; Matt. 28:18; Luke 2:11; John 3:16; 1Cor. 15:25; Eph. 2:14; Titus 2:13

7 2Kgs. 19:31; Isa. 37:32; Dan. 2:44; Luke 1:32, 33

12 Isa. 5:25; 10:4; Jer. 4:8

13 Jer. 5:3; Hos. 7:10

14 Isa. 10:17; Rev. 18:8

16 Isa. 3:12

17 Ps. 147:10, 11; Isa. 5:25; 9:12, 21; 10:4; Mic. 7:2

18 Isa. 10:17; Mal. 4:1

19 Isa. 8:22; Mic. 7:2, 6

20 Lev. 26:26; Isa. 49:26; Jer. 19:9

21 Isa. 5:25; 9:12, 17; 10:4

1 Ps. 58:2; 94:20

3 Job 31:14; Hos. 9:7; Luke 19:44

4 Isa. 5:25; 9:12, 17, 21

9:6–7 Again, using the prophetic perfect, the prophet sees the gift-child as though He were already born. This divine child is Immanuel. The word "Wonderful" indicates a miraculous nature, while "Counsellor," often used in parallel with "king" (cf. Mic. 4:9), suggests that the counsel given by this God-like king will be "miraculous." The strongest of the divine titles, "The mighty God," is used to describe one who is indeed God Himself. As a child He is born, but as a Son He comes from eternity and is thus said to be "given." He is the "Prince of Peace," a benevolent ruler who, with His Millennial Kingdom, will bring eternal peace on earth. Thus the obscure figure of Immanuel (7:14) is now revealed as none other than Jesus Christ Himself, God-incarnate!

Assyria, the Instrument of God

5 O Assyrian, the rod of mine anger, and the staff in their hand is mine indignation.

6 I will send him against an hypocritical nation, and against the people of my wrath will I give him a charge, to take the spoil, and to take the prey, and to tread them down like the mire of the streets.

7 Howbeit he meaneth not so, neither doth his heart think so; but *it is* in his heart to destroy and cut off nations not a few.

8 For he saith, *Are* not my princes altogether kings?

9 *Is* not Calno as Carchemish? *is* not Hamath as Arpad? *is* not Samaria as Damascus?

10 As my hand hath found the kingdoms of the idols, and whose graven images did excel them of Jerusalem and of Samaria;

11 Shall I not, as I have done unto Samaria and her idols, so do to Jerusalem and her idols?

12 Wherefore it shall come to pass, *that* when the Lord hath performed his whole work upon mount Zion and on Jerusalem, I will punish the fruit of the stout heart of the king of Assyria, and the glory of his high looks.

13 For he saith, By the strength of my hand I have done *it*, and by my wisdom; for I am prudent: and I have removed the bounds of the people, and have robbed their treasures, and I have put down the inhabitants like a valiant *man*:

14 And my hand hath found as a nest the riches of the people: and as one gathereth eggs *that are* left, have I gathered all the earth; and there was none that moved the wing, or opened the mouth, or peeped.

15 Shall the axe boast itself against him that heweth therewith? *or* shall the saw magnify itself against him that shaketh it? as if the rod should shake *itself* against them that lift it up, *or* as if the staff should lift up *itself, as if it were* no wood.

16 Therefore shall the Lord, the Lord of hosts, send among his fat ones leanness;

and under his glory he shall kindle a burning like the burning of a fire.

17 And the light of Israel shall be for a fire, and his Holy One for a flame: and it shall burn and devour his thorns and his briers in one day;

18 And shall consume the glory of his forest, and of his fruitful field, both soul and body: and they shall be as when a standard-bearer fainteth.

19 And the rest of the trees of his forest shall be few, that a child may write them.

A Remnant Will Return

20 And it shall come to pass in that day, *that* the remnant of Israel, and such as are escaped of the house of Jacob, shall no more again stay upon him that smote them; but shall stay upon the LORD, the Holy One of Israel, in truth.

21 The remnant shall return, *even* the remnant of Jacob, unto the mighty God.

22 For though thy people Israel be as the sand of the sea, *yet* a remnant of them shall return: the consumption decreed shall overflow with righteousness.

23 For the Lord GOD of hosts shall make a consumption, even determined, in the midst of all the land.

24 Therefore thus saith the Lord GOD of hosts, O my people that dwellest in Zion, be not afraid of the Assyrian: he shall smite thee with a rod, and shall lift up his staff against thee, after the manner of Egypt.

25 For yet a very little while, and the indignation shall cease, and mine anger in their destruction.

26 And the LORD of hosts shall stir up a scourge for him according to the slaughter of Midian at the rock of Oreb: and *as* his rod *was* upon the sea, so shall he lift it up after the manner of Egypt.

27 And it shall come to pass in that day, *that* his burden shall be taken away from off thy shoulder, and his yoke from off thy neck, and the yoke shall be destroyed because of the anointing.

Cross references

5 Jer. 51:20
6 Isa. 9:17; Jer. 34:22
7 Gen. 50:20; Mic. 4:12
8 2Kgs. 18:24, 33; 19:10
9 2Kgs. 16:9; 2Chr. 35:20; Amos 6:2
12 2Kgs. 19:31; Jer. 50:18
13 Isa. 37:24; Ezek. 28:4; Dan. 4:30
14 Job 31:25
15 Jer. 51:20
16 Isa. 5:17
17 Isa. 9:18; 27:4
18 2Kgs. 19:23
20 2Kgs. 16:7; 2Chr. 28:20
21 Isa. 7:3
22 Isa. 6:13; 28:22; Rom. 9:27
23 Isa. 28:22; Dan. 9:27; Rom. 9:28
24 Ex. 14; Isa. 37:6
25 Isa. 54:7; Dan. 11:36
26 Ex. 14:26, 27; Judg. 7:25; 2Kgs. 19:35; Isa. 9:4
27 Ps. 105:15; Isa. 14:25; Dan. 9:24; 1John 2:20

10:5 the rod of mine anger. Again as though it were already accomplished, Isaiah declares that Assyria was a rod in the hand of God to discipline Israel, even though the prideful Assyrians did not intend to cooperate with God. The prophet's intention is to make it clear that Assyria will not conquer Israel by her own power but by God's permission.

10:9 The cities listed in this verse are on a direct line from Nineveh (capital of Assyria) to Jerusalem (capital of Judah). Note that Samaria is listed as already fallen.

10:21 The remnant shall return. This is the promise suggested by the name of the prophet's son, Shear-jashub. See the note on 7:3–9.

10:26 the slaughter of Midian at the rock of Oreb. This occurred centuries earlier in the days of Gideon (Judg. 7:15). Here it serves as a reminder of the overwhelming power of divine intervention in human affairs.

The Attack

28 He is come to Aiath, he is passed to Migron; at Michmash he hath laid up his carriages:

29 They are gone over the passage: they have taken up their lodging at Geba; Ramah is afraid; Gibeah of Saul is fled.

30 Lift up thy voice, O daughter of Gallim: cause it to be heard unto Laish, O poor Anathoth.

31 Madmenah is removed; the inhabitants of Gebim gather themselves to flee.

32 As yet shall he remain at Nob that day: he shall shake his hand *against* the mount of the daughter of Zion, the hill of Jerusalem.

33 Behold, the Lord, the LORD of hosts, shall lop the bough with terror: and the high ones of stature *shall be* hewn down, and the haughty shall be humbled.

34 And he shall cut down the thickets of the forest with iron, and Lebanon shall fall by a mighty one.

CHAPTER 11
A Kingdom of Peace

1 And there shall come forth a rod out of the stem of Jesse, and a Branch shall grow out of his roots:

2 And the spirit of the LORD shall rest upon him, the spirit of wisdom and understanding, the spirit of counsel and might, the spirit of knowledge and of the fear of the LORD;

3 And shall make him of quick understanding in the fear of the LORD: and he shall not judge after the sight of his eyes, neither reprove after the hearing of his ears:

4 But with righteousness shall he judge the poor, and reprove with equity for the meek of the earth: and he shall smite the earth with the rod of his mouth, and with the breath of his lips shall he slay the wicked.

5 And righteousness shall be the girdle of his loins, and faithfulness the girdle of his reins.

6 The wolf also shall dwell with the lamb, and the leopard shall lie down with the kid; and the calf and the young lion and the fatling together; and a little child shall lead them.

7 And the cow and the bear shall feed; their young ones shall lie down together: and the lion shall eat straw like the ox.

8 And the sucking child shall play on the hole of the asp, and the weaned child shall put his hand on the cockatrice's den.

9 They shall not hurt nor destroy in all my holy mountain: for the earth shall be full of the knowledge of the LORD, as the waters cover the sea.

Coming Home

10 And in that day there shall be a root of Jesse, which shall stand for an ensign of the people; to it shall the Gentiles seek: and his rest shall be glorious.

11 And it shall come to pass in that day, *that* the Lord shall set his hand again the second time to recover the remnant of his people, which shall be left, from Assyria, and from Egypt, and from Pathros, and from Cush, and from Elam, and from Shinar, and from Hamath, and from the islands of the sea.

12 And he shall set up an ensign for the nations, and shall assemble the outcasts of

Cross-references (center column)

29 1Sam. 11:4; 13:23
30 Josh. 21:18; Judg. 18:7; 1Sam. 25:44
31 Josh. 15:31
32 1Sam. 21:1; 22:19; Neh. 11:32; Isa. 13:2; 37:22
33 Amos 2:9
1 Isa. 4:2; 11:2; 53:2; Jer. 23:5; Zech. 6:12; Acts 13:23; Rev. 5:5
2 Matt. 3:16; John 1:32, 33; 3:34
4 Job 4:9; Ps. 72:2, 4; Mal. 4:6; 2Thess. 2:8; Rev. 1:16; 2:16; 19:11, 15
5 Eph. 6:14
6 Ezek. 34:25; Hos. 2:18
9 Job 5:23; Hab. 2:14
10 Isa. 2:11; 11:1; Rom. 15:10, 12; Heb. 4:1
11 Isa. 2:11; Zech. 10:10
12 John 7:35; James 1:1

11:1—12:6 The millennial reign of Christ is described in this passage. The prophet indicates that Messiah's coming is yet in the distant future. For those who despair that the Davidic line might be lost, Isaiah shows that although the "tree" of the line of David will be cut down, a "rod" (Hebr. *choter*, "shoot" or "sprout") will come forth from the "stem" (Hebr. *geza*, "root" or "stump") of Jesse (David's father and the forefather of the Davidic line). The terms "branch" and "root" are used in parallel with rod.

11:2–5 The spirit of the LORD. The "Branch" is personalized in verse 2 as the Messiah Himself. The description of the Spirit in relation to seven attributes anticipates the sevenfold Spirit of God (cf. Rev. 4:5). The words for "counsel" and "might" are the same as used in 9:6 to describe the divine Child. Because the Spirit of God is upon Him, the Messiah will have true spiritual vision. By the power of His spoken word, Christ will rule the earth with the "rod [Hebr. *shebet*, scepter] of his mouth." He will "slay the wicked" with His breath at His second coming (cf. Rev. 19:15).

11:6–9 the earth shall be full of the knowledge of the LORD. Recalling the idyllic conditions of Eden, the messianic kingdom will be characterized by peace and harmony because the curse of Genesis 3 will be repealed. Ravenous predatory animals—wolf, leopard, lion, and bear—are set in deliberate contrast to the more defenseless lamb, kid, calf, cow, and ox. Even the asp and the cockatrice (snakes) will be harmless to a small child. The prophet sees beyond the restoration of Judah to a time of universal messianic rule.

11:10 to it shall the Gentiles seek. Isaiah is predicting a time when salvation will come to the Gentiles as well as to the Jews. The Messiah is again referred to as a "root of Jesse" as in verse 1.

Israel, and gather together the dispersed of Judah from the four corners of the earth.

13 The envy also of Ephraim shall depart, and the adversaries of Judah shall be cut off: Ephraim shall not envy Judah, and Judah shall not vex Ephraim.

14 But they shall fly upon the shoulders of the Philistines toward the west; they shall spoil them of the east together: they shall lay their hand upon Edom and Moab; and the children of Ammon shall obey them.

15 And the LORD shall utterly destroy the tongue of the Egyptian sea; and with his mighty wind shall he shake his hand over the river, and shall smite it in the seven streams, and make *men* go over dryshod.

16 And there shall be an highway for the remnant of his people, which shall be left, from Assyria; like as it was to Israel in the day that he came up out of the land of Egypt.

CHAPTER 12
A Hymn of Thanksgiving

1 And in that day thou shalt say, O LORD, I will praise thee: though thou wast angry with me, thine anger is turned away, and thou comfortedst me.

2 Behold, God *is* my salvation; I will trust, and not be afraid: for the LORD JEHOVAH *is* my strength and *my* song; he also is become my salvation.

3 Therefore with joy shall ye draw water out of the wells of salvation.

4 And in that day shall ye say, Praise the LORD, call upon his name, declare his doings among the people, make mention that his name is exalted.

5 Sing unto the LORD; for he hath done excellent things: this *is* known in all the earth.

6 Cry out and shout, thou inhabitant of Zion: for great *is* the Holy One of Israel in the midst of thee.

Cross references (center column)

13 Jer. 3:18; Ezek. 37:16, 17, 22; Hos. 1:11
14 Dan. 11:41
15 Zech. 10:11; Rev. 16:12
16 Ex. 14:29; Isa. 63:12, 13
2 Ps. 83:18
3 John 4:10, 14; 7:37, 38
4 1Chr. 16:8; Ps. 34:3; 105:1; 145:4-6
5 Ex. 15:1, 21; Ps. 68:32; 98:1
6 Ps. 71:22; 89:18; Isa. 41:14, 16; 54:1; Zeph. 3:14
1 Jer. 50; 51
2 Isa. 5:26; 10:32; 18:3; Jer. 50:2; 51:25
3 Ps. 149:2, 5, 6; Joel 3:11
6 Job 31:23; Joel 1:15; Zeph. 1:7; Rev. 6:17
8 Ps. 48:6; Isa. 21:3
9 Ps. 104:35; Prov. 2:22; Mal. 4:1
10 Isa. 24:21, 23; Ezek. 32:7; Joel 2:31; 3:15; Matt. 24:29; Mark 13:24; Luke 21:25

CHAPTER 13
Babylon

1 The burden of Babylon, which Isaiah the son of Amoz did see.

2 Lift ye up a banner upon the high mountain, exalt the voice unto them, shake the hand, that they may go into the gates of the nobles.

3 I have commanded my sanctified ones, I have also called my mighty ones for mine anger, *even* them that rejoice in my highness.

4 The noise of a multitude in the mountains, like as of a great people; a tumultuous noise of the kingdoms of nations gathered together: the LORD of hosts mustereth the host of the battle.

5 They come from a far country, from the end of heaven, *even* the LORD, and the weapons of his indignation, to destroy the whole land.

6 Howl ye; for the day of the LORD *is* at hand; it shall come as a destruction from the Almighty.

7 Therefore shall all hands be faint, and every man's heart shall melt:

8 And they shall be afraid: pangs and sorrows shall take hold of them; they shall be in pain as a woman that travaileth: they shall be amazed one at another; their faces *shall be as* flames.

9 Behold, the day of the LORD cometh, cruel both with wrath and fierce anger, to lay the land desolate: and he shall destroy the sinners thereof out of it.

10 For the stars of heaven and the constellations thereof shall not give their light: the sun shall be darkened in his going forth, and the moon shall not cause her light to shine.

11 And I will punish the world for *their* evil, and the wicked for their iniquity; and I will cause the arrogancy of the proud to cease,

---

12:1–6 Behold, God is my salvation. With characteristic imagery, Isaiah draws the Immanuel prophecy (7:1—12:6) to a dramatic climax with a triumphal doxology of praise. The description of God as our strength, song, and salvation is similar to the song of deliverance sung at the crossing of the Red Sea (Ex. 15:2). The "water out of the wells of salvation" seems to anticipate Jesus' word to the woman at the well in John 4:14.

13:1 From this point Isaiah turns his prophetic attention to God's judgment against Israel's neighbors. The prophet's message of judgment is called a "burden" (Hebr. *masa*, "oracle"). The prophet's first message was deliv-

ered against Babylon, the very nation that would eventually carry Judah into captivity. The "sanctified ones" and "mighty ones" (v. 3) are the armies of Medo-Persia, which God will raise up against Babylon to fulfill His purpose.

13:6 the day of the LORD. Isaiah's reference has both immediate and end-time significance. The destruction that is on the immediate horizon is the fall of Babylon in 539 B.C. But Isaiah also foretells the ultimate fall of "Babylon," used here to depict an evil empire that will arise in the Last Days (cf. Rev. 14:8).

The Figurative Babylon

By Arno Froese

The word, "Babylon," may mean "confusion" or "the gate of God." During the building of the tower at Babel, God confused the language; thus, the definition of "confusion" is fitting. The other meaning of Babylon, "gate of God," suggests self-redemption. Even after Babylon no longer existed, the Bible speaks about Babylon in Revelation 17 as an entity that propels the Antichrist to power. Will ancient Babylon be rebuilt and become the center of the world's economy, finances and religion? The Bible mentions, "Mystery, Babylon the great, the mother of harlots and abominations of the Earth" (Rev. 17:5). This verse does not refer to "Babylon" literally, but rather figuratively. This Babylon is a different identity than the one mentioned in Jeremiah 27:6.

While a literal Babylon no longer exists, the spirit of Babylon, characterized by rebellion and confusion, continues. Babylon is a symbol of rebellion against God, whose position in that regard passed to Media-Persia, then to Greece, and finally to Rome. The spirit of Babylonian rebellion and licentiousness continues today and will climax in the great confrontation between light and darkness at the appearing of the Lord Jesus Christ!

> *The spirit of Babylon, characterized by rebellion and confusion, continues.*

Therefore, many assume that ancient Babylon will play no significant role in the development of end-time events. It is not the "Mystery Babylon" of Revelation 17.

The Babylon of Revelation 17 is pictured as a woman "drunken with the blood of Saints, the blood of the martyrs of Jesus" (v. 6). The literal ancient city of Babylon would not be responsible for the death of the Christian martyrs mentioned in Revelation 17:6.

Another reason the literal city of Babylon is not the Babylon mentioned in Revelation 17, is that the "seven heads" of the beast in Revelation are described as "seven mountains" (v. 9), most likely describing the terrain of this region. The literal city of Babylon was established on the "plain of Shinar," a virtual desert, with no mountains nearby.

Who, then, is this "drunken woman," "Mystery Babylon," pictured in Revelation 17, which drank the blood of the martyrs of Jesus and continues to commit spiritual fornication with the political power structure of the world? Rome is the only city in the world that appears to meet the criteria the Bible uses in describing "Mystery Babylon." The Roman Empire was the originator of democracy and a symbol of economic prosperity. I believe that no other city on earth is recognized simultaneously as a religious and political entity. However, some Bible scholars believe that a rebuilt Babylon under Antichrist may be suggested in Revelation 18.

We need not belabor the point regarding the world's current global financial system, where economics ignores sovereign borders. Nor do we need much imagination to see that a one-world religion is already in the formative stages. Under the Babylonian King Nebuchadnezzar, the empire was commanded to worship a false god or suffer the consequences (Dan. 3). This persecution of those unwilling to bow before a false deity is viewed by many to be typical of the final persecution of Israel and Christian converts led by Antichrist during the Tribulation.

Only "Mystery Babylon" will finalize the work of the Tower of Babel builders and King Nebuchadnezzar, a global system under the philosophy of political democracy, free enterprise, unified financial systems, and ultimately a one-world religious faith. You may ask, "Why?" Because the father of lies (Satan) must imitate that which is promised to take place when Jesus comes (Phil. 2:10–11).

and will lay low the haughtiness of the terrible.

12 I will make a man more precious than fine gold; even a man than the golden wedge of Ophir.

13 Therefore I will shake the heavens, and the earth shall remove out of her place, in the wrath of the LORD of hosts, and in the day of his fierce anger.

14 And it shall be as the chased roe, and as a sheep that no man taketh up: they shall every man turn to his own people, and flee every one into his own land.

15 Every one that is found shall be thrust through; and every one that is joined *unto them* shall fall by the sword.

16 Their children also shall be dashed to pieces before their eyes; their houses shall be spoiled, and their wives ravished.

17 Behold, I will stir up the Medes against them, which shall not regard silver; and *as for* gold, they shall not delight in it.

18 *Their* bows also shall dash the young men to pieces; and they shall have no pity on the fruit of the womb; their eye shall not spare children.

19 And Babylon, the glory of kingdoms, the beauty of the Chaldees' excellency, shall be as when God overthrew Sodom and Gomorrah.

20 It shall never be inhabited, neither shall it be dwelt in from generation to generation: neither shall the Arabian pitch tent there; neither shall the shepherds make their fold there.

21 But wild beasts of the desert shall lie there; and their houses shall be full of doleful creatures; and owls shall dwell there, and satyrs shall dance there.

22 And the wild beasts of the islands shall cry in their desolate houses, and dragons in *their* pleasant palaces: and her time *is* near to come, and her days shall not be prolonged.

13 Ps. 110:5; Lam. 1:12; Hag. 2:6
14 Jer. 50:16; 51:9
16 Ps. 137:9; Nah. 3:10; Zech. 14:2
17 Isa. 21:2; Jer. 51:11, 28; Dan. 5:28, 31
19 Gen. 19:24, 25; Deut. 29:23; Isa. 14:4, 22; Jer. 49:18; 50:40
20 Jer. 50:3, 39; 51:29, 62
21 Isa. 34:11-15; Rev. 18:2
22 Jer. 51:33
1 Ps. 102:13; Isa. 60:4, 5, 10; Zech. 1:17; 2:12; Eph. 2:12, 13
2 Isa. 49:22; 60:9, 14; 66:20
4 Isa. 13:19; Hab. 2:6; Rev. 18:16
5 Ps. 125:3
8 Isa. 55:12; Ezek. 31:16
9 Ezek. 32:21

CHAPTER 14
The King of Babylon

1 For the LORD will have mercy on Jacob, and will yet choose Israel, and set them in their own land: and the strangers shall be joined with them, and they shall cleave to the house of Jacob.

2 And the people shall take them, and bring them to their place: and the house of Israel shall possess them in the land of the LORD for servants and handmaids: and they shall take them captives, whose captives they were; and they shall rule over their oppressors.

3 And it shall come to pass in the day that the LORD shall give thee rest from thy sorrow, and from thy fear, and from the hard bondage wherein thou wast made to serve,

4 That thou shalt take up this proverb against the king of Babylon, and say, How hath the oppressor ceased! the golden city ceased!

5 The LORD hath broken the staff of the wicked, *and* the sceptre of the rulers.

6 He who smote the people in wrath with a continual stroke, he that ruled the nations in anger, is persecuted, *and* none hindereth.

7 The whole earth is at rest, *and* is quiet: they break forth into singing.

8 Yea, the fir trees rejoice at thee, *and* the cedars of Lebanon, *saying*, Since thou art laid down, no feller is come up against us.

9 Hell from beneath is moved for thee to meet *thee* at thy coming: it stirreth up the dead for thee, *even* all the chief ones of the earth; it hath raised up from their thrones all the kings of the nations.

10 All they shall speak and say unto thee, Art thou also become weak as we? art thou become like unto us?

11 Thy pomp is brought down to the grave, *and* the noise of thy viols: the worm is spread under thee, and the worms cover thee.

13:19 Isaiah concludes that Babylon will be destroyed and never rebuilt. Indeed, it will never again be inhabited. Refer to Revelation 17–18, which describes the final and everlasting destruction of idolatrous "Babylon."

13:21–22 The reference to "wild beasts" should be taken literally and not interpreted as demons. Likewise, what are made out to be mythic creatures—owls, satyrs, and dragons—are better rendered ostriches, wild goats, and jackals.

14:1–3 the LORD will have mercy on Jacob. In spite of

God's displeasure with Israel, there is coming a time when He will have mercy upon them. This refers to Israel's future restoration in her own land during the millennial reign of Christ.

14:4–11 this proverb against the king of Babylon. Hell (Hebr. *sheol*) is the abode of the dead, a place of fiery judgment for the unrighteous. In this proverb the king of Babylon is being welcomed into hell by the "kings of the nations" (Gentiles). In perverse celebration, they will declare that he has become as weak as they are.

12 How art thou fallen from heaven, O Lucifer, son of the morning! *how* art thou cut down to the ground, which didst weaken the nations!

13 For thou hast said in thine heart, I will ascend into heaven, I will exalt my throne above the stars of God: I will sit also upon the mount of the congregation, in the sides of the north:

14 I will ascend above the heights of the clouds; I will be like the most High.

15 Yet thou shalt be brought down to hell, to the sides of the pit.

16 They that see thee shall narrowly look upon thee, *and* consider thee, *saying, Is* this the man that made the earth to tremble, that did shake kingdoms;

17 *That* made the world as a wilderness, and destroyed the cities thereof; *that* opened not the house of his prisoners?

18 All the kings of the nations, *even* all of them, lie in glory, every one in his own house.

19 But thou art cast out of thy grave like an abominable branch, *and as* the raiment of those that are slain, thrust through with a sword, that go down to the stones of the pit; as a carcase trodden under feet.

20 Thou shalt not be joined with them in burial, because thou hast destroyed thy land, *and* slain thy people: the seed of evildoers shall never be renowned.

21 Prepare slaughter for his children for the iniquity of their fathers; that they do not rise, nor possess the land, nor fill the face of the world with cities.

22 For I will rise up against them, saith the LORD of hosts, and cut off from Babylon the name, and remnant, and son, and nephew, saith the LORD.

23 I will also make it a possession for the bittern, and pools of water: and I will sweep it with the besom of destruction, saith the LORD of hosts.

The Assyrians

24 The LORD of hosts hath sworn, saying, Surely as I have thought, so shall it come to

Cross references:
12 Isa. 34:4
13 Ps. 48:2; Dan. 8:10; Matt. 11:23
14 Isa. 47:8; 2Thess. 2:4
15 Matt. 11:23
20 Job 18:19; Ps. 21:10; 37:28; 109:13
21 Ex. 20:5; Matt. 23:35
22 Isa. 14:10; Job 18:19; Prov. 10:7; Jer. 51:62
23 Isa. 34:11; Zeph. 2:14

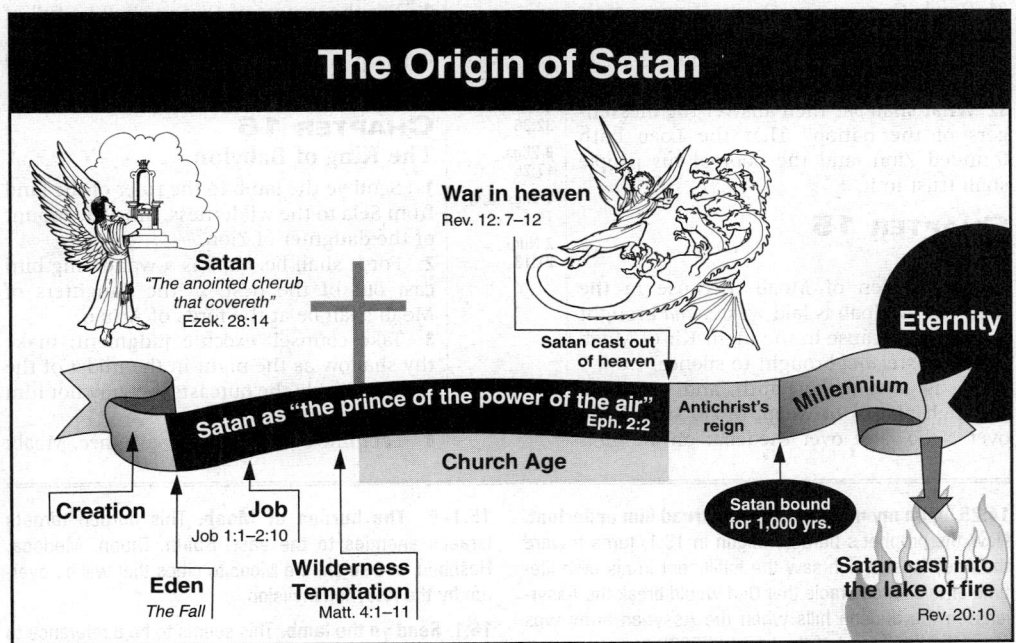

The Origin of Satan

Satan — "The anointed cherub that covereth" Ezek. 28:14

War in heaven — Rev. 12: 7–12

Satan cast out of heaven

Eternity

Satan as "the prince of the power of the air" Eph. 2:2

Antichrist's reign

Millennium

Church Age

Creation

Job — Job 1:1–2:10

Eden — The Fall

Wilderness Temptation — Matt. 4:1–11

Satan bound for 1,000 yrs.

Satan cast into the lake of fire — Rev. 20:10

© AMG Publishers

14:12–23 Lucifer. This is a reference to Satan, the real power behind the evil Gentile monarchs. Isaiah uses the fall of Satan to illustrate the fall of the Babylonian king. The name "Lucifer" is Latin for "the morning star," and a translation of the Hebrew (*helel,* "bright one"). As the morning star speedily disappears before the rising sun, so Satan, "the angel of light," will be banished to outer darkness by the coming of the Son of God (cf. Mal. 4).

pass; and as I have purposed, *so* shall it stand:

25 That I will break the Assyrian in my land, and upon my mountains tread him under foot: then shall his yoke depart from off them, and his burden depart from off their shoulders.

26 This *is* the purpose that is purposed upon the whole earth: and this *is* the hand that is stretched out upon all the nations.

27 For the LORD of hosts hath purposed, and who shall disannul *it*? and his hand *is* stretched out, and who shall turn it back?

The Philistines

28 In the year that king Ahaz died was this burden.

29 Rejoice not thou, whole Palestina, because the rod of him that smote thee is broken: for out of the serpent's root shall come forth a cockatrice, and his fruit *shall be* a fiery flying serpent.

30 And the firstborn of the poor shall feed, and the needy shall lie down in safety: and I will kill thy root with famine, and he shall slay thy remnant.

31 Howl, O gate; cry, O city; thou, whole Palestina, *art* dissolved: for there shall come from the north a smoke, and none *shall be* alone in his appointed times.

32 What shall *one* then answer the messengers of the nation? That the LORD hath founded Zion, and the poor of his people shall trust in it.

CHAPTER 15
Moab

1 The burden of Moab. Because in the night Ar of Moab is laid waste, *and* brought to silence; because in the night Kir of Moab is laid waste, *and* brought to silence;

2 He is gone up to Bajith, and to Dibon, the high places, to weep: Moab shall howl over Nebo, and over Medeba: on all their

Cross references (center column)

25 Isa. 10:27
27 2Chr. 20:6; Job 9:12; 23:13; Ps. 33:11; Prov. 19:21; 21:30; Isa. 43:13; Dan. 4:31, 35
28 2Kgs. 16:20
29 2Kgs. 18:8; 2Chr. 26:6
32 Ps. 87:1, 5; 102:16; Zeph. 3:12; Zech. 11:11
1 Num. 21:28; Jer. 48:1; Ezek; 25:8-11; Amos 2:1
2 Lev. 21:5; Isa. 3:24; 16:12; 22:12; Jer. 47:5; 48:1, 37, 38; Ezek. 7:18
3 Jer. 48:38
4 Isa. 16:9
5 Isa. 16:11, 14; Jer. 48:5, 31, 34
6 Num. 32:36
9 2Kgs. 17:25
1 2Kgs. 3:4; 14:7
2 Num. 21:13

heads *shall be* baldness, *and* every beard cut off.

3 In their streets they shall gird themselves with sackcloth: on the tops of their houses, and in their streets, every one shall howl, weeping abundantly.

4 And Heshbon shall cry, and Elealeh: their voice shall be heard *even* unto Jahaz: therefore the armed soldiers of Moab shall cry out; his life shall be grievous unto him.

5 My heart shall cry out for Moab; his fugitives *shall flee* unto Zoar, an heifer of three years old: for by the mounting up of Luhith with weeping shall they go it up; for in the way of Horonaim they shall raise up a cry of destruction.

6 For the waters of Nimrim shall be desolate: for the hay is withered away, the grass faileth, there is no green thing.

7 Therefore the abundance they have gotten, and that which they have laid up, shall they carry away to the brook of the willows.

8 For the cry is gone round about the borders of Moab; the howling thereof unto Eglaim, and the howling thereof unto Beerelim.

9 For the waters of Dimon shall be full of blood: for I will bring more upon Dimon, lions upon him that escapeth of Moab, and upon the remnant of the land.

CHAPTER 16
The King of Babylon

1 Send ye the lamb to the ruler of the land from Sela to the wilderness, unto the mount of the daughter of Zion.

2 For it shall be, *that*, as a wandering bird cast out of the nest, *so* the daughters of Moab shall be at the fords of Arnon.

3 Take counsel, execute judgment; make thy shadow as the night in the midst of the noonday; hide the outcasts; bewray not him that wandereth.

4 Let mine outcasts dwell with thee, Moab;

14:25 upon my mountains [I will] tread him underfoot. Now the prophet's burden, begun in 13:1, turns toward the Assyrians. Isaiah saw the fulfillment in his own lifetime of this fierce oracle that God would break the Assyrians on the Judean hills when the Assyrian army was struck by the "angel of the LORD" (37:36).

14:28 Ahaz died in 727 B.C.

14:29–32 Here the prophet warns Israel's perennial enemies, including Palestina (Philistia), not to rejoice in Israel's plight because they too shall be invaded "from the north" (i.e., Babylon).

15:1–9 The burden of Moab. This burden targets Israel's enemies to the east. Bajith, Dibon, Medeba, Heshbon, and so on, are Moabite cities that will be overrun by the Assyrian invasion.

16:1 Send ye the lamb. This seems to be a reference to the payment of tribute from Sela (Petra, capital of Edom) to Jerusalem (cf. 2Sam. 8:2; 2Kings 3:4). Moab's only hope to escape the Assyrian invasion was to make peace with Judah.

16:4–5 Let mine outcasts dwell with thee. This seems to anticipate Israel's flight to Petra during the Last Days

be thou a covert to them from the face of the spoiler: for the extortioner is at an end, the spoiler ceaseth, the oppressors are consumed out of the land.

5 And in mercy shall the throne be established: and he shall sit upon it in truth in the tabernacle of David, judging, and seeking judgment, and hasting righteousness.

6 We have heard of the pride of Moab; *he is* very proud: *even* of his haughtiness, and his pride, and his wrath: *but* his lies *shall* not *be* so.

7 Therefore shall Moab howl for Moab, every one shall howl: for the foundations of Kir-hareseth shall ye mourn; surely *they are* stricken.

8 For the fields of Heshbon languish, *and* the vine of Sibmah: the lords of the heathen have broken down the principal plants thereof, they are come *even* unto Jazer, they wandered *through* the wilderness: her branches are stretched out, they are gone over the sea.

9 Therefore I will bewail with the weeping of Jazer the vine of Sibmah: I will water thee with my tears, O Heshbon, and Elealeh: for the shouting for thy summer fruits and for thy harvest is fallen.

10 And gladness is taken away, and joy out of the plentiful field; and in the vineyards there shall be no singing, neither shall there be shouting: the treaders shall tread out no wine in *their* presses; I have made *their vintage* shouting to cease.

11 Wherefore my bowels shall sound like an harp for Moab, and mine inward parts for Kir-haresh.

12 And it shall come to pass, when it is seen that Moab is weary on the high place, that he shall come to his sanctuary to pray; but he shall not prevail.

13 This *is* the word that the LORD hath spoken concerning Moab since that time.

14 But now the LORD hath spoken, saying, Within three years, as the years of an hireling, and the glory of Moab shall be contemned, with all that great multitude; and the remnant *shall be* very small *and* feeble.

CHAPTER 17
Damascus

1 The burden of Damascus. Behold, Damascus is taken away from *being* a city, and it shall be a ruinous heap.

2 The cities of Aroer *are* forsaken: they shall be for flocks, which shall lie down, and none shall make *them* afraid.

3 The fortress also shall cease from Ephraim, and the kingdom from Damascus, and the remnant of Syria: they shall be as the glory of the children of Israel, saith the LORD of hosts.

4 And in that day it shall come to pass, *that* the glory of Jacob shall be made thin, and the fatness of his flesh shall wax lean.

5 And it shall be as when the harvest man gathereth the corn, and reapeth the ears with his arm; and it shall be as he that gathereth ears in the valley of Rephaim.

6 Yet gleaning grapes shall be left in it, as the shaking of an olive tree, two *or* three berries in the top of the uppermost bough, four *or* five in the outmost fruitful branches thereof, saith the LORD God of Israel.

7 At that day shall a man look to his Maker, and his eyes shall have respect to the Holy One of Israel.

8 And he shall not look to the altars, the work of his hands, neither shall respect *that* which his fingers have made, either the groves, or the images.

9 In that day shall his strong cities be as a forsaken bough, and an uppermost branch, which they left because of the children of Israel: and there shall be desolation.

10 Because thou hast forgotten the God of thy salvation, and hast not been mindful of the rock of thy strength, therefore shalt thou plant pleasant plants, and shalt set it with strange slips:

11 In the day shalt thou make thy plant to grow, and in the morning shalt thou make thy seed to flourish: *but* the harvest *shall be* a heap in the day of grief and of desperate sorrow.

12 Woe to the multitude of many people, *which* make a noise like the noise of the seas; and to the rushing of nations, *that*

Cross references: 5 Ps. 72:2; 96:13; 98:9; Dan. 7:14, 27; Mic. 4:7; Luke 1:33. 6 Isa. 28:15; Jer. 48:29; Zeph. 2:10. 7 2Kgs. 3:25; Jer. 48:20. 8 Isa. 16:9; 24:7. 9 Isa. 15:4; Jer. 48:32. 10 Isa. 24:8; Jer. 48:33. 11 Isa. 15:5; 63:15; Jer. 48:36. 12 Isa. 15:2. 14 Isa. 21:16. 1 2Kgs. 16:9; Jer. 49:23; Amos 1:3; Zech. 9:1. 2 Jer. 7:33. 3 Isa. 7:16; 8:4. 4 Isa. 10:16. 5 Jer. 51:33. 6 Isa. 24:13. 7 Mic. 7:7. 10 Ps. 68:19. 12 Jer. 6:23.

to escape the invasion from the North predicted in Ezekiel 38—39.

17:1–14 The burden of Damascus. Here the prophet turns his attention to the capital of Syria. This chapter elaborates on the prophecy given in chapter 7 and predicts the downfall of the coalition between Syria and Ephraim. God used Tiglath-pileser of Syria to destroy Damascus in 732 B.C.

17:4 Jacob shall be made thin. This is a prediction of the devastating famine that followed the Assyrian conquest and deportation of the northern tribes in 722 B.C.

make a rushing like the rushing of mighty waters!

13 The nations shall rush like the rushing of many waters: but *God* shall rebuke them, and they shall flee far off, and shall be chased as the chaff of the mountains before the wind, and like a rolling thing before the whirlwind.

14 And behold at eveningtide trouble; *and* before the morning he *is* not. This *is* the portion of them that spoil us, and the lot of them that rob us.

CHAPTER 18
Ethiopia

1 Woe to the land shadowing with wings, which *is* beyond the rivers of Ethiopia:

2 That sendeth ambassadors by the sea, even in vessels of bulrushes upon the waters, *saying*, Go, ye swift messengers, to a nation scattered and peeled, to a people terrible from their beginning hitherto; a nation meted out and trodden down, whose land the rivers have spoiled!

3 All ye inhabitants of the world, and dwellers on the earth, see ye, when he lifteth up an ensign on the mountains; and when he bloweth a trumpet, hear ye.

4 For so the LORD said unto me, I will take my rest, and I will consider in my dwelling place like a clear heat upon herbs, *and* like a cloud of dew in the heat of harvest.

5 For afore the harvest, when the bud is perfect, and the sour grape is ripening in the flower, he shall both cut off the sprigs with pruning hooks, and take away *and* cut down the branches.

6 They shall be left together unto the fowls of the mountains, and to the beasts of the earth: and the fowls shall summer upon them, and all the beasts of the earth shall winter upon them.

7 In that time shall the present be brought unto the LORD of hosts of a people scattered and peeled, and from a people terrible from their beginning hitherto; a nation meted out and trodden under foot, whose land the rivers have spoiled, to the place of the name of the LORD of hosts, the mount Zion.

CHAPTER 19
Egypt

1 The burden of Egypt. Behold, the LORD rideth upon a swift cloud, and shall come into Egypt: and the idols of Egypt shall be moved at his presence, and the heart of Egypt shall melt in the midst of it.

2 And I will set the Egyptians against the Egyptians: and they shall fight every one against his brother, and every one against his neighbour; city against city, *and* kingdom against kingdom.

3 And the spirit of Egypt shall fail in the midst thereof; and I will destroy the counsel thereof: and they shall seek to the idols, and to the charmers, and to them that have familiar spirits, and to the wizards.

4 And the Egyptians will I give over into the hand of a cruel lord; and a fierce king shall rule over them, saith the Lord, the LORD of hosts.

5 And the waters shall fail from the sea, and the river shall be wasted and dried up.

6 And they shall turn the rivers far away; *and* the brooks of defence shall be emptied and dried up: the reeds and flags shall wither.

7 The paper reeds by the brooks, by the mouth of the brooks, and every thing sown by the brooks, shall wither, be driven away, and be no *more*.

8 The fishers also shall mourn, and all they that cast angle into the brooks shall lament, and they that spread nets upon the waters shall languish.

9 Moreover they that work in fine flax, and they that weave networks, shall be confounded.

10 And they shall be broken in the purposes thereof, all that make sluices *and* ponds for fish.

11 Surely the princes of Zoan *are* fools, the counsel of the wise counsellers of Pharaoh is become brutish: how say ye unto Pharaoh, I *am* the son of the wise, the son of ancient kings?

12 Where *are* they? where *are* thy wise *men*? and let them tell thee now, and let them know what the LORD of hosts hath purposed upon Egypt.

Cross references (center column):

13 Ps. 9:5; 83:13; Hos. 13:3

1 Isa. 20:4, 5; Ezek. 30:4, 5, 9; Zeph. 2:12; 3:10

2 Isa. 13:7

3 Isa. 5:26

7 Ps. 68:31; 72:10; Isa. 13:2; 16:1; Zeph. 3:10; Mal. 1:11

1 Ex. 12:12; Ps. 18:10; 104:3; Jer. 43:12; 46:13; Ezek. 29; 30

2 Judg. 7:22; 1Sam. 14:16, 20; 2Chr. 20:23

3 Isa. 8:19; 47:12

4 Isa. 20:4; Jer. 46:26; Ezek. 29:19

5 Jer. 51:36; Ezek. 30:12

6 2Kgs. 19:24

9 1Kgs. 10:28; Prov. 7:16

11 Num. 13:22

12 1Cor. 1:20

18:1–7 The pen of the burdened prophet now targets the land of Ethiopia (Cush) with its words of woe. This nation once rose to such power that it overran all of Egypt (715 B.C.). Sennacherib of Assyria finally crushed the Ethiopian-Egyptian forces in 701 B.C.

19:1–10 The burden of Egypt. This is a message of both judgment and hope for Egypt. Isaiah writes in advance of the coming Egyptian civil war of the seventh century B.C. Egypt eventually fell to Esar-haddon of Assyria in 671 B.C. The "cruel lord" and "fierce king" prefigure the Assyrian overlords who were to subjugate Egypt for nearly twenty years.

13 The princes of Zoan are become fools, the princes of Noph are deceived; they have also seduced Egypt, *even they that are* the stay of the tribes thereof.
14 The Lord hath mingled a perverse spirit in the midst thereof: and they have caused Egypt to err in every work thereof, as a drunken *man* staggereth in his vomit.
15 Neither shall there be *any* work for Egypt, which the head or tail, branch or rush, may do.
16 In that day shall Egypt be like unto women: and it shall be afraid and fear because of the shaking of the hand of the Lord of hosts, which he shaketh over it.
17 And the land of Judah shall be a terror unto Egypt, every one that maketh mention thereof shall be afraid in himself, because of the counsel of the Lord of hosts, which he hath determined against it.
18 In that day shall five cities in the land of Egypt speak the language of Canaan, and swear to the Lord of hosts; one shall be called, The city of destruction.
19 In that day shall there be an altar to the Lord in the midst of the land of Egypt, and a pillar at the border thereof to the Lord.
20 And it shall be for a sign and for a witness unto the Lord of hosts in the land of Egypt: for they shall cry unto the Lord because of the oppressors, and he shall send them a saviour, and a great one, and he shall deliver them.
21 And the Lord shall be known to Egypt, and the Egyptians shall know the Lord in that day, and shall do sacrifice and oblation; yea, they shall vow a vow unto the Lord, and perform *it.*
22 And the Lord shall smite Egypt: he shall smite and heal *it:* and they shall return *even* to the Lord, and he shall be intreated of them, and shall heal them.
23 In that day shall there be a highway out

of Egypt to Assyria, and the Assyrian shall come into Egypt, and the Egyptian into Assyria, and the Egyptians shall serve with the Assyrians.
24 In that day shall Israel be the third with Egypt and with Assyria, *even* a blessing in the midst of the land:
25 Whom the Lord of hosts shall bless, saying, Blessed *be* Egypt my people, and Assyria the work of my hands, and Israel mine inheritance.

CHAPTER 20
The Captivity of Egypt and Ethiopia

1 In the year that Tartan came unto Ashdod, (when Sargon the king of Assyria sent him,) and fought against Ashdod, and took it;
2 At the same time spake the Lord by Isaiah the son of Amoz, saying, Go and loose the sackcloth from off thy loins, and put off thy shoe from thy foot. And he did so, walking naked and barefoot.
3 And the Lord said, Like as my servant Isaiah hath walked naked and barefoot three years *for* a sign and wonder upon Egypt and upon Ethiopia;
4 So shall the king of Assyria lead away the Egyptians prisoners, and the Ethiopians captives, young and old, naked and barefoot, even with *their* buttocks uncovered, to the shame of Egypt.
5 And they shall be afraid and ashamed of Ethiopia their expectation, and of Egypt their glory.
6 And the inhabitant of this isle shall say in that day, Behold, such *is* our expectation, whither we flee for help to be delivered from the king of Assyria: and how shall we escape?

CHAPTER 21
The Fall of Babylon

1 The burden of the desert of the sea. As whirlwinds in the south pass through; *so* it

13 Jer. 2:16
14 1Kgs. 22:22; Isa. 29:10
15 Isa. 9:14
16 Isa. 11:15; Jer. 51:30; Nah. 3:13
18 Zeph. 3:9
19 Gen. 28:18; Ex. 24:4; Josh. 22:10, 26, 27
20 Josh. 4:20; 22:27
21 Mal. 1:11
23 Isa. 11:16
25 Ps. 100:3; Isa. 29:23; Hos. 2:23; Eph. 2:10
1 2Kgs. 18:17
2 1Sam. 19:24; Mic. 1:8, 11; Zech. 13:4
3 Isa. 8:18
4 2Sam. 10:4; Isa. 3:17; Jer. 13:22, 26; Mic. 1:11
5 2Kgs. 18:21; Isa. 30:3, 5, 7; 36:6
6 Jer. 47:4
1 Zech. 9:14

19:18–25 The city of destruction. This is a deliberate alteration of the name Heliopolis, "City of the Sun." But the prophet sees a day when Egypt will be converted to the knowledge of the Lord. The prediction of an "altar to the Lord" in Egypt was technically fulfilled during the reign of Ptolemy VI by a priest named Onias. However, the "great one" who brings universal blessing must be a reference to the coming Messiah who will embrace Egypt in His Millennial Kingdom. The highway running from Egypt to Assyria through Israel anticipates a time of international peace when Egypt and Assyria will become people of God.

20:1–6 walking naked and barefoot. The date of this

prophecy is 711 B.C., the year of the Assyrian invasion into the Philistine coast. The Assyrian king, Sargon had sent troops to subdue the Philistine city of Ashdod. In a very unusual command, God instructs Isaiah to become a living illustration of their future slavery. Assyria was known not only for humiliating its captives by stripping them naked, but also in some cases for torturing them by peeling their skin off while they were still alive!

21:1 the desert of the sea. The precise location referred to is unclear. However, it seems to refer to Media and Persia, which lay beyond the desert and the Persian Gulf. If so, then Isaiah is foreseeing the invasion of Babylon by Media-Persia.

cometh from the desert, from a terrible land.

2 A grievous vision is declared unto me; the treacherous dealer dealeth treacherously, and the spoiler spoileth. Go up, O Elam: besiege, O Media; all the sighing thereof have I made to cease.

3 Therefore are my loins filled with pain: pangs have taken hold upon me, as the pangs of a woman that travaileth: I was bowed down at the hearing *of it*; I was dismayed at the seeing *of it*.

4 My heart panted, fearfulness affrighted me: the night of my pleasure hath he turned into fear unto me.

5 Prepare the table, watch in the watchtower, eat, drink: arise, ye princes, *and* anoint the shield.

6 For thus hath the Lord said unto me, Go, set a watchman, let him declare what he seeth.

7 And he saw a chariot *with* a couple of horsemen, a chariot of asses, *and* a chariot of camels; and he hearkened diligently with much heed:

8 And he cried, A lion: My lord, I stand continually upon the watchtower in the daytime, and I am set in my ward whole nights:

9 And, behold, here cometh a chariot of men, *with* a couple of horsemen. And he answered and said, Babylon is fallen, is fallen; and all the graven images of her gods he hath broken unto the ground.

10 O my threshing, and the corn of my floor: that which I have heard of the LORD of hosts, the God of Israel, have I declared unto you.

Edom

11 The burden of Dumah. He calleth to me out of Seir, Watchman, what of the night? Watchman, what of the night?

12 The watchman said, The morning

cometh, and also the night: if ye will inquire, inquire ye: return, come.

Arabia

13 The burden upon Arabia. In the forest in Arabia shall ye lodge, O ye travelling companies of Dedanim.

14 The inhabitants of the land of Tema brought water to him that was thirsty, they prevented with their bread him that fled.

15 For they fled from the swords, from the drawn sword, and from the bent bow, and from the grievousness of war.

16 For thus hath the Lord said unto me, Within a year, according to the years of an hireling, and all the glory of Kedar shall fail:

17 And the residue of the number of archers, the mighty men of the children of Kedar, shall be diminished: for the LORD God of Israel hath spoken *it*.

CHAPTER 22
Jerusalem

1 The burden of the valley of vision. What aileth thee now, that thou art wholly gone up to the housetops?

2 Thou that art full of stirs, a tumultuous city, a joyous city: thy slain *men are* not slain with the sword, nor dead in battle.

3 All thy rulers are fled together, they are bound by the archers: all that are found in thee are bound together, *which* have fled from far.

4 Therefore said I, Look away from me; I will weep bitterly, labour not to comfort me, because of the spoiling of the daughter of my people.

5 For *it is* a day of trouble, and of treading down, and of perplexity by the Lord GOD of hosts in the valley of vision, breaking down the walls, and of crying to the mountains.

6 And Elam bare the quiver with chariots of men *and* horsemen, and Kir uncovered the shield.

Cross references (center column):

2 Isa. 13:17; 33:1; Jer. 49:34
3 Isa. 13:8; 15:5; 16:11
4 Deut. 28:67
5 Dan. 5:5
7 Isa. 21:9
8 Hab. 2:1
9 Isa. 46:1; Jer. 50:2; 51:8, 44; Rev. 14:8; 18:2
10 Jer. 51:33
11 1Chr. 1:30; Ezra 35:2; Jer. 49:7, 8; Obad. 1:1
13 1Chr. 1:9, 32; Jer. 49:28
16 Ps. 120:5; Isa. 16:14; 60:7
2 Isa. 32:13
4 Jer. 4:19; 9:1
5 Isa. 37:3; Lam. 1:5; 2:2
6 Isa. 15:1; Jer. 49:35

21:4 the night of my pleasure. This anticipates Belshazzar's banquet in Daniel 5, for on that night, Babylon fell (539 B.C.).

21:9 Babylon is fallen, is fallen. This same exclamation is used in Revelation 14:8.

21:11–12 Edom (Dumah) is hiding out in Seir, where the descendants of Esau settled. Isaiah warns them of impending judgment unless they "return" (Hebr. *shub*, repent).

21:14 the land of Tema. Tema was an oasis beyond Edom in Northern Arabia. While his son Belshazzar ruled

over Babylon, Nabonidus spent much of his time in Tema in seclusion. The prophet predicts that the Arabian tribes of the desert beyond Edom will be unable to stand before the coming Assyrian invasion.

22:1–14 The burden of the valley of vision. The gathering storm of judgment will dump its greatest torrents on Jerusalem herself. The people will go up on the housetops to observe the siege of Babylonian forces against the city. The prophet calls for repentance. Instead the people have developed the attitude of "eat and drink; for to morrow we shall die" (v. 13).

7 And it shall come to pass, *that* thy choicest valleys shall be full of chariots, and the horsemen shall set themselves in array at the gate.

8 And he discovered the covering of Judah, and thou didst look in that day to the armour of the house of the forest.

9 Ye have seen also the breaches of the city of David, that they are many: and ye gathered together the waters of the lower pool.

10 And ye have numbered the houses of Jerusalem, and the houses have ye broken down to fortify the wall.

11 Ye made also a ditch between the two walls for the water of the old pool: but ye have not looked unto the maker thereof, neither had respect unto him that fashioned it long ago.

12 And in that day did the Lord GOD of hosts call to weeping, and to mourning, and to baldness, and to girding with sackcloth:

13 And behold joy and gladness, slaying oxen, and killing sheep, eating flesh, and drinking wine: let us eat and drink; for to morrow we shall die.

14 And it was revealed in mine ears by the LORD of hosts, Surely this iniquity shall not be purged from you till ye die, saith the Lord GOD of hosts.

Shebna

15 Thus saith the Lord GOD of hosts, Go, get thee unto this treasurer, *even* unto Shebna, which *is* over the house, *and say,*

16 What hast thou here? and whom hast thou here, that thou hast hewed thee out a sepulchre here, *as* he that heweth him out a sepulchre on high, *and* that graveth an habitation for himself in a rock?

17 Behold, the LORD will carry thee away with a mighty captivity, and will surely cover thee.

18 He will surely violently turn and toss thee *like* a ball into a large country: there shalt thou die, and there the chariots of thy glory *shall be* the shame of thy lord's house.

19 And I will drive thee from thy station, and from thy state shall he pull thee down.

20 And it shall come to pass in that day, that I will call my servant Eliakim the son of Hilkiah:

21 And I will clothe him with thy robe, and strengthen him with thy girdle, and I will commit thy government into his hand: and he shall be a father to the inhabitants of Jerusalem, and to the house of Judah.

22 And the key of the house of David will I lay upon his shoulder; so he shall open, and none shall shut; and he shall shut, and none shall open.

23 And I will fasten him *as* a nail in a sure place; and he shall be for a glorious throne to his father's house.

24 And they shall hang upon him all the glory of his father's house, the offspring and the issue, all vessels of small quantity, from the vessels of cups, even to all the vessels of flagons.

25 In that day, saith the LORD of hosts, shall the nail that is fastened in the sure place be removed, and be cut down, and fall; and the burden that *was* upon it shall be cut off: for the LORD hath spoken *it.*

CHAPTER 23
Phoenicia

1 The burden of Tyre. Howl, ye ships of Tarshish; for it is laid waste, so that there is no house, no entering in: from the land of Chittim it is revealed to them.

2 Be still, ye inhabitants of the isle; thou

Cross references (center column)

8 1Kgs. 7:2; 10:17
9 2Kgs. 20:20; 2Chr. 32:4, 5, 30
11 Neh. 3:16; Isa. 37:26
12 Ezra 9:3; Isa. 15:2; Joel 1:13; Mic. 1:16
13 Isa. 56:12; 1Cor. 15:32
14 1Sam. 3:14; Isa. 5:9; Ezek. 24:13
15 1Kgs. 4:6; 2Kgs. 18:37; Isa. 36:3
16 2Sam. 18:18; Matt. 27:60
17 Esth. 7:8
20 2Kgs. 18:18
22 Job 12:14; Rev. 3:7
23 Ezra 9:8

1 Isa. 23:12; Jer. 25:22; 47:4; Ezek. 26–28; Amos 1:9; Zech. 9:2, 4

22:15–25 the key of the house of David. This phrase in verse 22 is a reference to the authority attached to the occupant of David's throne (cf. Matt. 16:19). Shebna, the treasurer, apparently was the leader of a pro-Egyptian faction in Jerusalem. Arrogantly assuming his position as treasurer was secure, he had already ordered a large tomb to be constructed in his memory. Isaiah predicts that Shebna will soon be demoted and will die a pauper in a foreign country. Shebna was in fact replaced by Eliakim during the reign of Hezekiah, as indicated in 2 Kings 18:18.

23:1–18 The next burden (oracle) is against Tyre, the major coastal city of the Phoenicians to the north of Judah. The Greeks called them "purple people" because of their famous purple dye. The Phoenicians were the shipping merchants of the ancient Near East. The prophet is declaring that trade with distant regions will cease because of Tyre's destruction. Both Isaiah and Ezekiel (chaps. 27—28) predicted the fall of Tyre. Ezekiel prophesied that the entire city would be thrown into the sea (Ezek. 26). The prophet predicts that Tyre will be laid waste for seventy years, yet will survive, being forced to "sing as an harlot" (v. 15), meaning she would no longer enjoy her independence but would have to pander to the desires of her conquerors. The reference to Tyre's merchandise becoming "holiness to the LORD" (v. 18) may have been fulfilled when the city furnished construction materials to Israel after their period of captivity had ended (Ezra 3:7).

whom the merchants of Zidon, that pass over the sea, have replenished.

3 And by great waters the seed of Sihor, the harvest of the river, *is* her revenue; and she is a mart of nations.

4 Be thou ashamed, O Zidon: for the sea hath spoken, *even* the strength of the sea, saying, I travail not, nor bring forth children, neither do I nourish up young men, *nor* bring up virgins.

5 As at the report concerning Egypt, *so* shall they be sorely pained at the report of Tyre.

6 Pass ye over to Tarshish; howl, ye inhabitants of the isle.

7 *Is* this your joyous *city*, whose antiquity *is* of ancient days? her own feet shall carry her afar off to sojourn.

8 Who hath taken this counsel against Tyre, the crowning *city*, whose merchants *are* princes, whose traffickers *are* the honourable of the earth?

9 The LORD of hosts hath purposed it, to stain the pride of all glory, *and* to bring into contempt all the honourable of the earth.

10 Pass through thy land as a river, O daughter of Tarshish: *there is* no more strength.

11 He stretched out his hand over the sea, he shook the kingdoms: the LORD hath given a commandment against the merchant *city*, to destroy the strong holds thereof.

12 And he said, Thou shalt no more rejoice, O thou oppressed virgin, daughter of Zidon: arise, pass over to Chittim; there also shalt thou have no rest.

13 Behold the land of the Chaldeans; this people was not, *till* the Assyrian founded it for them that dwell in the wilderness: they set up the towers thereof, they raised up the palaces thereof; *and* he brought it to ruin.

14 Howl, ye ships of Tarshish: for your strength is laid waste.

15 And it shall come to pass in that day, that Tyre shall be forgotten seventy years,

according to the days of one king: after the end of seventy years shall Tyre sing as an harlot.

16 Take an harp, go about the city, thou harlot that hast been forgotten; make sweet melody, sing many songs, that thou mayest be remembered.

17 And it shall come to pass after the end of seventy years, that the LORD will visit Tyre, and she shall turn to her hire, and shall commit fornication with all the kingdoms of the world upon the face of the earth.

18 And her merchandise and her hire shall be holiness to the LORD: it shall not be treasured nor laid up; for her merchandise shall be for them that dwell before the LORD, to eat sufficiently, and for durable clothing.

CHAPTER 24
God's Judgment on the Whole Earth

1 Behold, the LORD maketh the earth empty, and maketh it waste, and turneth it upside down, and scattereth abroad the inhabitants thereof.

2 And it shall be, as with the people, so with the priest; as with the servant, so with his master; as with the maid, so with her mistress; as with the buyer, so with the seller; as with the lender, so with the borrower; as with the taker of usury, so with the giver of usury to him.

3 The land shall be utterly emptied, and utterly spoiled: for the LORD hath spoken this word.

4 The earth mourneth *and* fadeth away, the world languisheth *and* fadeth away, the haughty people of the earth do languish.

5 The earth also is defiled under the inhabitants thereof; because they have transgressed the laws, changed the ordinance, broken the everlasting covenant.

6 Therefore hath the curse devoured the earth, and they that dwell therein are desolate: therefore the inhabitants of the earth are burned, and few men left.

Cross references (center column)

3 Ezek. 27:3
5 Isa. 19:16
7 Isa. 22:2
8 Ezek. 28:2, 12
12 Isa. 23:1; Rev. 18:22
13 Ps. 72:9
14 Isa. 23:11; Ezek. 27:25, 30
17 Rev. 17:2
18 Zech. 14:20, 21

2 Ezek. 7:12, 13; Hos. 4:9

5 Gen. 3:17; Num. 35:33

6 Mal. 4:6

23:13 The Chaldeans were the founders of the Neo-Babylonian Empire. Isaiah predicted that they would besiege and destroy Tyre. The Assyrians also would be conquered by the Chaldeans in 612 B.C.

24:1 turneth it upside down. This is better read "distorts." Thus, through war, God will empty the earth and leave it a devastated and distorted wasteland. The cities of the earth are described as desolate and burned as a result of this universal destruction (v. 6).

24:1–12 Chapters 24 through 27 are often called the

"Little Apocalypse." The chapters look beyond the immediate judgment of Israel's Gentile neighbors to the final judgments of the nations during the Tribulation period, which ushers in the messianic kingdom. These chapters present universal judgments followed by universal blessings. The Lord moves in cataclysmic judgment upon the earth, not simply on the "land" of Israel. The severity of the Tribulation period is indicated by the statement, "the Lord maketh the earth empty, and . . . waste."

7 The new wine mourneth, the vine languisheth, all the merryhearted do sigh.
8 The mirth of tabrets ceaseth, the noise of them that rejoice endeth, the joy of the harp ceaseth.
9 They shall not drink wine with a song; strong drink shall be bitter to them that drink it.
10 The city of confusion is broken down: every house is shut up, that no man may come in.
11 *There is* a crying for wine in the streets; all joy is darkened, the mirth of the land is gone.
12 In the city is left desolation, and the gate is smitten with destruction.
13 When thus it shall be in the midst of the land among the people, *there shall be* as the shaking of an olive tree, *and* as the gleaning grapes when the vintage is done.
14 They shall lift up their voice, they shall sing for the majesty of the LORD, they shall cry aloud from the sea.
15 Wherefore glorify ye the LORD in the fires, *even* the name of the LORD God of Israel in the isles of the sea.
16 From the uttermost part of the earth have we heard songs, *even* glory to the righteous. But I said, My leanness, my leanness, woe unto me! the treacherous dealers have dealt treacherously; yea, the treacherous dealers have dealt very treacherously.
17 Fear, and the pit, and the snare, *are* upon thee, O inhabitant of the earth.
18 And it shall come to pass, *that* he who fleeth from the noise of the fear shall fall into the pit; and he that cometh up out of the midst of the pit shall be taken in the snare: for the windows from on high are open, and the foundations of the earth do shake.
19 The earth is utterly broken down, the earth is clean dissolved, the earth is moved exceedingly.
20 The earth shall reel to and fro like a drunkard, and shall be removed like a cottage; and the transgression thereof shall be heavy upon it; and it shall fall, and not rise again.
21 And it shall come to pass in that day, *that* the LORD shall punish the host of the high ones *that are* on high, and the kings of the earth upon the earth.
22 And they shall be gathered together, *as* prisoners are gathered in the pit, and shall be shut up in the prison, and after many days shall they be visited.
23 Then the moon shall be confounded, and the sun ashamed, when the LORD of hosts shall reign in mount Zion, and in Jerusalem, and before his ancients gloriously.

CHAPTER 25
Praise God!

1 O LORD, thou *art* my God; I will exalt thee, I will praise thy name; for thou hast done wonderful *things; thy* counsels of old *are* faithfulness *and* truth.
2 For thou hast made of a city an heap; *of* a defenced city a ruin: a palace of strangers to be no city; it shall never be built.
3 Therefore shall the strong people glorify thee, the city of the terrible nations shall fear thee.
4 For thou hast been a strength to the poor, a strength to the needy in his distress, a refuge from the storm, a shadow from the heat, when the blast of the terrible ones *is* as a storm *against* the wall.
5 Thou shalt bring down the noise of strangers, as the heat in a dry place; *even* the heat with the shadow of a cloud: the branch of the terrible ones shall be brought low.
6 And in this mountain shall the LORD of hosts make unto all people a feast of fat things, a feast of wines on the lees, of fat things full of marrow, of wines on the lees well refined.
7 And he will destroy in this mountain the face of the covering cast over all people, and the vail that is spread over all nations.
8 He will swallow up death in victory; and

24:13 as the shaking of an olive tree. This end-time judgment leaves the people of the earth empty and retaining only negligible remains.

24:18–20 The earth shall reel to and fro. This devastation will be so great that the earth will literally shake from the aftershock. God's judgment will rock the very stability of the planet, reminding its inhabitants that they have rebelled against God Almighty.

24:21–23 the host of the high ones [satanic powers] . . . **and the kings of the earth** [earthly powers]. After a period of time in prison, the host and the kings will be visited (lit. "punished"). Notice the obvious parallel to Revelation 20:1–3 where Satan is bound in the bottomless pit for a thousand years and then loosed for a "little season," only to be finally cast into the lake of fire.

25:7 The "vail" does not refer to the veil of the temple but to the covering of death that hangs over all nations during the Tribulation.

the Lord GOD will wipe away tears from off all faces; and the rebuke of his people shall he take away from off all the earth: for the LORD hath spoken *it*.

9 And it shall be said in that day, Lo, this *is* our God; we have waited for him, and he will save us: this *is* the LORD; we have waited for him, we will be glad and rejoice in his salvation.

10 For in this mountain shall the hand of the LORD rest, and Moab shall be trodden down under him, even as straw is trodden down for the dunghill.

11 And he shall spread forth his hands in the midst of them, as he that swimmeth spreadeth forth *his hands* to swim: and he shall bring down their pride together with the spoils of their hands.

12 And the fortress of the high fort of thy walls shall he bring down, lay low, *and* bring to the ground, *even* to the dust.

CHAPTER 26
God's People Will Be Victorious

1 In that day shall this song be sung in the land of Judah; We have a strong city; salvation will *God* appoint *for* walls and bulwarks.

2 Open ye the gates, that the righteous nation which keepeth the truth may enter in.

3 Thou wilt keep *him* in perfect peace, *whose* mind *is* stayed *on thee*: because he trusteth in thee.

4 Trust ye in the LORD for ever: for in the LORD JEHOVAH *is* everlasting strength:

5 For he bringeth down them that dwell on high; the lofty city, he layeth it low; he layeth it low, *even* to the ground; he bringeth it *even* to the dust.

6 The foot shall tread it down, *even* the feet of the poor, *and* the steps of the needy.

7 The way of the just *is* uprightness: thou, most upright, dost weigh the path of the just.

8 Yea, in the way of thy judgments, O LORD, have we waited for thee; the desire of *our* soul *is* to thy name, and to the remembrance of thee.

9 With my soul have I desired thee in the

Cross references

9 Gen. 49:18; Ps. 20:5; Titus 2:13
12 Isa. 26:5
1 Isa. 2:11; 60:18
2 Ps. 118:19, 20
3 Isa. 57:19
4 Deut. 32:4; Isa. 45:17
5 Isa. 25:12; 32:19
7 Ps. 37:23
8 Isa. 64:5
9 Ps. 63:6; Song 3:1
10 Ps. 143:10; Eccl. 8:12; Rom. 2:4
11 Job 34:27; Ps. 28:5; Isa. 5:12
13 2Chr. 12:8
16 Hos. 5:15
17 Isa. 13:8; John 16:21
18 Ps. 17:14
19 Ezek. 37:1; Dan. 12:2
20 Ex. 12:22, 23; Ps. 30:5; Isa. 54:7, 8; 2Cor. 4:17
21 Mic. 1:3; Jude 1:14

night; yea, with my spirit within me will I seek thee early: for when thy judgments *are* in the earth, the inhabitants of the world will learn righteousness.

10 Let favour be shewed to the wicked, *yet* will he not learn righteousness: in the land of uprightness will he deal unjustly, and will not behold the majesty of the LORD.

11 LORD, *when* thy hand is lifted up, they will not see: *but* they shall see, and be ashamed for *their* envy at the people; yea, the fire of thine enemies shall devour them.

12 LORD, thou wilt ordain peace for us: for thou also hast wrought all our works in us.

13 O LORD our God, *other* lords beside thee have had dominion over us: *but* by thee only will we make mention of thy name.

14 *They are* dead, they shall not live; *they are* deceased, they shall not rise: therefore hast thou visited and destroyed them, and made all their memory to perish.

15 Thou hast increased the nation, O LORD, thou hast increased the nation: thou art glorified: thou hadst removed *it* far *unto* all the ends of the earth.

16 LORD, in trouble have they visited thee, they poured out a prayer *when* thy chastening *was* upon them.

17 Like as a woman with child, *that* draweth near the time of her delivery, is in pain, *and* crieth out in her pangs; so have we been in thy sight, O LORD.

18 We have been with child, we have been in pain, we have as it were brought forth wind; we have not wrought any deliverance in the earth; neither have the inhabitants of the world fallen.

19 Thy dead *men* shall live, *together with* my dead body shall they arise. Awake and sing, ye that dwell in dust: for thy dew *is as* the dew of herbs, and the earth shall cast out the dead.

20 Come, my people, enter thou into thy chambers, and shut thy doors about thee: hide thyself as it were for a little moment, until the indignation be overpast.

21 For, behold, the LORD cometh out of his place to punish the inhabitants of the earth

---

26:3 Israel is promised "perfect peace" (lit., "peace, peace"). This emphatic expression indicates a peace that goes beyond human comprehension (cf. Phil. 4:7) and anticipates the final victory yet to be realized in Christ.

26:19 Thy dead men shall live. This verse is one of the strongest promises in the Old Testament of a physical resurrection. Those believers who have previously died

are called upon to wake from the dead and sing.

26:20–21 The prophet utters a wonderful promise of safety for God's people during the time of worldwide terror in the Tribulation. He urges them, as He urged the children of Israel during the first Passover (Ex. 12), to shut themselves up in their homes "until the indignation be overpast."

for their iniquity: the earth also shall disclose her blood, and shall no more cover her slain.

CHAPTER 27
The Deliverance of Israel

1 In that day the LORD with his sore and great and strong sword shall punish leviathan the piercing serpent, even leviathan that crooked serpent; and he shall slay the dragon that *is* in the sea.

2 In that day sing ye unto her, A vineyard of red wine.

3 I the LORD do keep it; I will water it every moment: lest *any* hurt it, I will keep it night and day.

4 Fury *is* not in me: who would set the briers *and* thorns against me in battle? I would go through them, I would burn them together.

5 Or let him take hold of my strength, *that* he may make peace with me; *and* he shall make peace with me.

6 He shall cause them that come of Jacob to take root: Israel shall blossom and bud, and fill the face of the world with fruit.

7 Hath he smitten him, as he smote those that smote him? *or* is he slain according to the slaughter of them that are slain by him?

8 In measure, when it shooteth forth, thou wilt debate with it: he stayeth his rough wind in the day of the east wind.

9 By this therefore shall the iniquity of Jacob be purged; and this *is* all the fruit to take away his sin; when he maketh all the stones of the altar as chalkstones that are beaten in sunder, the groves and images shall not stand up.

10 Yet the defenced city *shall be* desolate, *and* the habitation forsaken, and left like a wilderness: there shall the calf feed, and there shall he lie down, and consume the branches thereof.

11 When the boughs thereof are withered, they shall be broken off: the women come, *and* set them on fire: for it *is* a people of no understanding: therefore he that made them will not have mercy on them, and he that formed them will shew them no favour.

12 And it shall come to pass in that day, *that* the LORD shall beat off from the channel of the river unto the stream of Egypt, and ye shall be gathered one by one, O ye children of Israel.

13 And it shall come to pass in that day, *that* the great trumpet shall be blown, and they shall come which were ready to perish in the land of Assyria, and the outcasts in the land of Egypt, and shall worship the LORD in the holy mount at Jerusalem.

CHAPTER 28
The Judgment of Ephraim

1 Woe to the crown of pride, to the drunkards of Ephraim, whose glorious beauty *is* a fading flower, which *are* on the head of the fat valleys of them that are overcome with wine!

2 Behold, the Lord hath a mighty and strong one, *which* as a tempest of hail *and* a destroying storm, as a flood of mighty waters overflowing, shall cast down to the earth with the hand.

3 The crown of pride, the drunkards of Ephraim, shall be trodden under feet:

4 And the glorious beauty, which *is* on the head of the fat valley, shall be a fading flower, *and* as the hasty fruit before the summer; which *when* he that looketh upon it seeth, while it is yet in his hand he eateth it up.

5 In that day shall the LORD of hosts be for a crown of glory, and for a diadem of beauty, unto the residue of his people,

6 And for a spirit of judgment to him that sitteth in judgment, and for strength to them that turn the battle to the gate.

A Warning to Jerusalem

7 But they also have erred through wine, and through strong drink are out of the way; the priest and the prophet have erred through strong drink, they are swallowed up of wine, they are out of the way through strong drink; they err in vision, they stumble *in* judgment.

8 For all tables are full of vomit *and* filthiness, *so that there is* no place *clean*.

Cross references

1 Ps. 74:13, 14; Isa. 51:9; Ezek. 29:3; 32:2

2 Ps. 80:8; Isa. 5:1; Jer. 2:21

3 Ps. 121:4, 5

4 2Sam. 23:6; Isa. 9:18

5 Job 22:21; Isa. 25:4

6 Isa. 37:31; Hos. 14:5, 6

8 Job 23:6; Ps. 6:1; 78:38; Jer. 10:24; 30:11; 46:28; 1Cor. 10:13

10 Isa. 17:2; 32:14

11 Deut. 32:18, 28; Isa. 1:3; 43:1, 7; 44:2, 21, 24; Jer. 8:7

13 Isa. 2:11; Matt. 24:31; Rev. 11:15

1 Isa. 28:3, 4

2 Isa. 30:30; Ezek. 13:11

3 Isa. 28:1

4 Isa. 28:1

7 Prov. 20:1; Isa. 56:10, 12; Hos. 4:11

27:1 leviathan. This animal (see Job 41:1; Ps. 74:13–14; 104:26) is used symbolically of "that crooked serpent . . . the dragon," or Satan. Isaiah has in view the final victory of God over Satan (cf. Rev. 20:2).

27:2–13 I will keep it night and day. Isaiah breaks into a joyful song of the "vineyard" (Israel) of the Lord (cf. Isa.

5:1–7). The vineyard will succeed because the Lord, Himself, will keep (lit. "till") it. The wandering Israelites will finally be able to flourish and prosper. This will take place in the Millennial Kingdom when all nations will come up to Jerusalem to worship the true and living God.

9 Whom shall he teach knowledge? and whom shall he make to understand doctrine? *them that are* weaned from the milk, *and* drawn from the breasts.

10 For precept *must be* upon precept, precept upon precept; line upon line, line upon line; here a little, *and* there a little:

11 For with stammering lips and another tongue will he speak to this people.

12 To whom he said, This *is* the rest where-with ye may cause the weary to rest; and this *is* the refreshing: yet they would not hear.

13 But the word of the LORD was unto them precept upon precept, precept upon precept; line upon line, line upon line; here a little, *and* there a little; that they might go, and fall backward, and be broken, and snared, and taken.

The Cornerstone

14 Wherefore hear the word of the LORD, ye scornful men, that rule this people which *is* in Jerusalem.

15 Because ye have said, We have made a covenant with death, and with hell are we at agreement; when the overflowing scourge shall pass through, it shall not come unto us: for we have made lies our refuge, and under falsehood have we hid ourselves:

16 Therefore thus saith the Lord GOD, Behold, I lay in Zion for a foundation a stone, a tried stone, a precious corner *stone*, a sure foundation: he that believeth shall not make haste.

17 Judgment also will I lay to the line, and righteousness to the plummet: and the hail shall sweep away the refuge of lies, and the waters shall overflow the hiding place.

18 And your covenant with death shall be disannulled, and your agreement with hell shall not stand; when the overflowing scourge shall pass through, then ye shall be trodden down by it.

19 From the time that it goeth forth it shall take you: for morning by morning shall it pass over, by day and by night: and it shall be a vexation only *to* understand the report.

20 For the bed is shorter than that a man can stretch himself *on it:* and the covering

narrower than that he can wrap himself *in it.*

21 For the LORD shall rise up as *in* mount Perazim, he shall be wroth as *in* the valley of Gibeon, that he may do his work, his strange work; and bring to pass his act, his strange act.

22 Now therefore be ye not mockers, lest your bands be made strong: for I have heard from the Lord GOD of hosts a consumption, even determined upon the whole earth.

23 Give ye ear, and hear my voice; hearken, and hear my speech.

24 Doth the plowman plow all day to sow? doth he open and break the clods of his ground?

25 When he hath made plain the face thereof, doth he not cast abroad the fitches, and scatter the cummin, and cast in the principal wheat and the appointed barley and the rie in their place?

26 For his God doth instruct him to discretion, *and* doth teach him.

27 For the fitches are not threshed with a threshing instrument, neither is a cart wheel turned about upon the cummin; but the fitches are beaten out with a staff, and the cummin with a rod.

28 Bread *corn* is bruised; because he will not ever be threshing it, nor break *it with* the wheel of his cart, nor bruise *it with* his horsemen.

29 This also cometh forth from the LORD of hosts, *which* is wonderful in counsel, *and* excellent in working.

CHAPTER 29
The Fate of Jerusalem

1 Woe to Ariel, to Ariel, the city *where* David dwelt! add ye year to year; let them kill sacrifices.

2 Yet I will distress Ariel, and there shall be heaviness and sorrow: and it shall be unto me as Ariel.

3 And I will camp against thee round about, and will lay siege against thee with a mount, and I will raise forts against thee.

4 And thou shalt be brought down, *and* shalt speak out of the ground, and thy speech shall be low out of the dust, and thy

Cross references

9 Jer. 6:10
11 1Cor. 14:21
15 Amos 2:4
16 Gen. 49:24; Ps. 118:22; Matt. 21:42; Acts 4:11; Rom. 9:33; 10:11; Eph. 2:20; 1Pet. 2:6-8
17 Isa. 28:15
21 Josh. 10:10, 12; 2Sam. 5:20, 25; 1Chr. 14:11, 16; Lam. 3:33
22 Isa. 10:22, 23; Dan. 9:27

29 Ps. 92:5; Jer. 32:19

1 2Sam. 5:9; Ezek. 43:15, 16

4 Isa. 8:19

28:14–19 a covenant with death. The prophet now turns his attention to the rulers of Jerusalem. Many residents of Judah at that time foolishly thought that a pro-Assyrian alliance would protect them if Samaria fell. The prophecy in these verses is similar to the "sign" to Ahaz in chapter 7. Despite the faithlessness of the people, God promises to lay a "corner stone" in Zion (v. 16). That cornerstone is none other than Jesus Christ (cf. Rom 9:33; 1 Pet. 2:6). Those who believe in Jesus will find Him to be "a sure foundation." To those who reject Him, He becomes a stone of stumbling.

voice shall be, as of one that hath a familiar spirit, out of the ground, and thy speech shall whisper out of the dust.

5 Moreover the multitude of thy strangers shall be like small dust, and the multitude of the terrible ones *shall be* as chaff that passeth away: yea, it shall be at an instant suddenly.

6 Thou shalt be visited of the Lord of hosts with thunder, and with earthquake, and great noise, with storm and tempest, and the flame of devouring fire.

7 And the multitude of all the nations that fight against Ariel, even all that fight against her and her munition, and that distress her, shall be as a dream of a night vision.

8 It shall even be as when an hungry *man* dreameth, and, behold, he eateth; but he awaketh, and his soul is empty: or as when a thirsty man dreameth, and, behold, he drinketh; but he awaketh, and, behold, *he is* faint, and his soul hath appetite: so shall the multitude of all the nations be, that fight against mount Zion.

The Blindness and Hypocrisy of Israel

9 Stay yourselves, and wonder; cry ye out, and cry: they are drunken, but not with wine; they stagger, but not with strong drink.

10 For the Lord hath poured out upon you the spirit of deep sleep, and hath closed your eyes: the prophets and your rulers, the seers hath he covered.

11 And the vision of all is become unto you as the words of a book that is sealed, which *men* deliver to one that is learned, saying, Read this, I pray thee: and he saith, I cannot; for it *is* sealed:

12 And the book is delivered to him that is not learned, saying, Read this, I pray thee: and he saith, I am not learned.

13 Wherefore the Lord said, Forasmuch as this people draw near *me* with their mouth, and with their lips do honour me, but have removed their heart far from me, and their fear toward me is taught by the precept of men:

14 Therefore, behold, I will proceed to do a marvellous work among this people, *even* a marvellous work and a wonder: for the wisdom of their wise *men* shall perish, and the understanding of their prudent *men* shall be hid.

Hope

15 Woe unto them that seek deep to hide their counsel from the Lord, and their works are in the dark, and they say, Who seeth us? and who knoweth us?

16 Surely your turning of things upside down shall be esteemed as the potter's clay: for shall the work say of him that made it, He made me not? or shall the thing framed say of him that framed it, He had no understanding?

17 *Is* it not yet a very little while, and Lebanon shall be turned into a fruitful field, and the fruitful field shall be esteemed as a forest?

18 And in that day shall the deaf hear the words of the book, and the eyes of the blind shall see out of obscurity, and out of darkness.

19 The meek also shall increase *their* joy in the Lord, and the poor among men shall rejoice in the Holy One of Israel.

20 For the terrible one is brought to nought, and the scorner is consumed, and all that watch for iniquity are cut off:

21 That make a man an offender for a word, and lay a snare for him that reproveth in the gate, and turn aside the just for a thing of nought.

22 Therefore thus saith the Lord, who redeemed Abraham, concerning the house of Jacob, Jacob shall not now be ashamed, neither shall his face now wax pale.

23 But when he seeth his children, the work of mine hands, in the midst of him, they shall sanctify my name, and sanctify the Holy One of Jacob, and shall fear the God of Israel.

24 They also that erred in spirit shall come to understanding, and they that murmured shall learn doctrine.

Cross references

5 Job 21:18; Isa. 17:13; 25:5; 30:13
6 Isa. 28:2; 30:30
7 Job 20:8; Isa. 37:36
8 Ps. 73:20
9 Isa. 28:7, 8; 51:21
10 1Sam. 9:9; Ps. 69:23; Isa. 6:10; Rom. 11:8
11 Isa. 8:16; Dan. 12:4, 9; Rev. 5:1-5, 9; 6:1
13 Ezek. 33:31; Matt. 15:8, 9; Mark 7:6, 7
14 Jer. 49:7; Obad. 1:8; Hab. 1:5; 1Cor. 1:19
15 Ps. 94:7; Isa. 30:1
16 Isa. 45:9; Rom. 9:20
17 Isa. 32:15
18 Isa. 35:5
19 Isa. 61:1; James 2:5
20 Isa. 28:14, 22; Mic. 2:1
21 Prov. 28:21; Amos 5:10, 12
22 Josh. 24:3
23 Isa. 19:25; 45:11; 60:21; Eph. 2:10
24 Isa. 28:7

29:13–24 The prophet condemns his own people for honoring God with their mouth and lips but not their heart. Jesus, in Mark 7:6–7, quotes verse 13 as the epitome of Pharisaism. Isaiah further notes that the fear (or reverence) of his contemporaries was merely an intellectual accommodation "taught by the precept of men." Proper worship must begin with a true reverence for God and His Word. Isaiah then declares that since the intellectual leaders of Israel will not follow the Lord, the deaf, blind, meek, and poor (i.e., the Gentiles) shall rejoice in Him (vv. 18–19). This again looks far ahead to the One who would say, "Go out into the highways and hedges and compel them to come in" (Luke 14:23).

CHAPTER 30
Reliance upon Egypt Is Vain

1 Woe to the rebellious children, saith the LORD, that take counsel, but not of me; and that cover with a covering, but not of my spirit, that they may add sin to sin:
2 That walk to go down into Egypt, and have not asked at my mouth; to strengthen themselves in the strength of Pharaoh, and to trust in the shadow of Egypt!
3 Therefore shall the strength of Pharaoh be your shame, and the trust in the shadow of Egypt your confusion.
4 For his princes were at Zoan, and his ambassadors came to Hanes.
5 They were all ashamed of a people that could not profit them, nor be an help nor profit, but a shame, and also a reproach.
6 The burden of the beasts of the south: into the land of trouble and anguish, from whence come the young and old lion, the viper and fiery flying serpent, they will carry their riches upon the shoulders of young asses, and their treasures upon the bunches of camels, to a people that shall not profit them.
7 For the Egyptians shall help in vain, and to no purpose: therefore have I cried concerning this, Their strength is to sit still.
8 Now go, write it before them in a table, and note it in a book, that it may be for the time to come for ever and ever:
9 That this is a rebellious people, lying children, children that will not hear the law of the LORD:
10 Which say to the seers, See not; and to the prophets, Prophesy not unto us right things, speak unto us smooth things, prophesy deceits:
11 Get you out of the way, turn aside out of the path, cause the Holy One of Israel to cease from before us.
12 Wherefore thus saith the Holy One of Israel, Because ye despise this word, and trust in oppression and perverseness, and stay thereon:
13 Therefore this iniquity shall be to you as a breach ready to fall, swelling out in a high wall, whose breaking cometh suddenly at an instant.
14 And he shall break it as the breaking of the potter's vessel that is broken in pieces; he shall not spare: so that there shall not be found in the bursting of it a sherd to take fire from the hearth, or to take water withal out of the pit.
15 For thus saith the Lord GOD, the Holy One of Israel; In returning and rest shall ye be saved; in quietness and in confidence shall be your strength: and ye would not.
16 But ye said, No; for we will flee upon horses; therefore shall ye flee: and, We will ride upon the swift; therefore shall they that pursue you be swift.
17 One thousand shall flee at the rebuke of one; at the rebuke of five shall ye flee: till ye be left as a beacon upon the top of a mountain, and as an ensign on an hill.
18 And therefore will the LORD wait, that he may be gracious unto you, and therefore will he be exalted, that he may have mercy upon you: for the LORD is a God of judgment: blessed are all they that wait for him.

God Will Bless His People

19 For the people shall dwell in Zion at Jerusalem: thou shalt weep no more: he will be very gracious unto thee at the voice of thy cry; when he shall hear it, he will answer thee.
20 And though the Lord give you the bread of adversity, and the water of affliction, yet shall not thy teachers be removed into a corner any more, but thine eyes shall see thy teachers:
21 And thine ears shall hear a word behind thee, saying, This is the way, walk ye in it, when ye turn to the right hand, and when ye turn to the left.
22 Ye shall defile also the covering of thy graven images of silver, and the ornament of thy molten images of gold: thou shalt cast them away as a menstruous cloth; thou shalt say unto it, Get thee hence.
23 Then shall he give the rain of thy seed, that thou shalt sow the ground withal; and bread of the increase of the earth, and it shall be fat and plenteous: in that day shall thy cattle feed in large pastures.
24 The oxen likewise and the young asses that ear the ground shall eat clean provender, which hath been winnowed with the shovel and with the fan.
25 And there shall be upon every high mountain, and upon every high hill, rivers and streams of waters in the day of the great slaughter, when the towers fall.
26 Moreover the light of the moon shall be as the light of the sun, and the light of the sun shall be sevenfold, as the light of seven days, in the day that the LORD bindeth up the breach of his people, and healeth the stroke of their wound.

Assyria's Punishment

27 Behold, the name of the LORD cometh from far, burning with his anger, and the

burden *thereof is* heavy: his lips are full of indignation, and his tongue as a devouring fire:

28 And his breath, as an overflowing stream, shall reach to the midst of the neck, to sift the nations with the sieve of vanity: and *there shall be* a bridle in the jaws of the people, causing *them* to err.

29 Ye shall have a song, as in the night *when* a holy solemnity is kept; and gladness of heart, as when one goeth with a pipe to come into the mountain of the LORD, to the mighty One of Israel.

30 And the LORD shall cause his glorious voice to be heard, and shall shew the lighting down of his arm, with the indignation of *his* anger, and *with* the flame of a devouring fire, *with* scattering, and tempest, and hailstones.

31 For through the voice of the LORD shall the Assyrian be beaten down, *which* smote with a rod.

32 And *in* every place where the grounded staff shall pass, which the LORD shall lay upon him, *it* shall be with tabrets and harps: and in battles of shaking will he fight with it.

33 For Tophet *is* ordained of old; yea, for the king it is prepared; he hath made *it* deep *and* large: the pile thereof *is* fire and much wood; the breath of the LORD, like a stream of brimstone, doth kindle it.

CHAPTER 31
Egypt Is Frail

1 Woe to them that go down to Egypt for help; and stay on horses, and trust in chariots, because *they are* many; and in horsemen, because they are very strong; but they look not unto the Holy One of Israel, neither seek the LORD!

2 Yet he also *is* wise, and will bring evil, and will not call back his words: but will arise against the house of the evildoers, and against the help of them that work iniquity.

3 Now the Egyptians *are* men, and not God; and their horses flesh, and not spirit. When the LORD shall stretch out his hand, both he that helpeth shall fall, and he that is holpen shall fall down, and they all shall fail together.

4 For thus hath the LORD spoken unto me,

Like as the lion and the young lion roaring on his prey, when a multitude of shepherds is called forth against him, *he* will not be afraid of their voice, nor abase himself for the noise of them: so shall the LORD of hosts come down to fight for mount Zion, and for the hill thereof.

5 As birds flying, so will the LORD of hosts defend Jerusalem; defending also he will deliver *it; and* passing over he will preserve it.

6 Turn ye unto *him from* whom the children of Israel have deeply revolted.

7 For in that day every man shall cast away his idols of silver, and his idols of gold, which your own hands have made unto you *for* a sin.

8 Then shall the Assyrian fall with the sword, not of a mighty man; and the sword, not of a mean man, shall devour him: but he shall flee from the sword, and his young men shall be discomfited.

9 And he shall pass over to his strong hold for fear, and his princes shall be afraid of the ensign, saith the LORD, whose fire *is* in Zion, and his furnace in Jerusalem.

CHAPTER 32
The Righteous King

1 Behold, a king shall reign in righteousness, and princes shall rule in judgment.

2 And a man shall be as an hiding place from the wind, and a covert from the tempest; as rivers of water in a dry place, as the shadow of a great rock in a weary land.

3 And the eyes of them that see shall not be dim, and the ears of them that hear shall hearken.

4 The heart also of the rash shall understand knowledge, and the tongue of the stammerers shall be ready to speak plainly.

5 The vile person shall be no more called liberal, nor the churl said *to be* bountiful.

6 For the vile person will speak villany, and his heart will work iniquity, to practise hypocrisy, and to utter error against the LORD, to make empty the soul of the hungry, and he will cause the drink of the thirsty to fail.

7 The instruments also of the churl *are* evil: he deviseth wicked devices to destroy the poor with lying words, even when the needy speaketh right.

Cross references: 28 Isa. 8:8; 11:4; 37:20; 2Thess. 2:8. 29 Deut. 32:4; Ps. 42:4; Isa. 2:3. 30 Isa. 28:2; 29:6; 32:19. 31 Isa. 10:5, 24; 37:36. 32 Isa. 11:15; 19:16. 33 Jer. 7:31; 19:6. 1 Ps. 20:7; Isa. 30:2; 36:6, 9; Ezek. 17:15; Dan. 9:13; Hos. 7:7. 2 Num. 23:19. 3 Ps. 146:3, 5. 4 Isa. 42:13; Hos. 11:10; Amos 3:8. 5 Deut. 32:11; Ps. 37:40; 91:4. 6 Hos. 9:9. 7 1Kgs. 12:30; Isa. 2:20; 30:22. 8 2Kgs. 19:35, 36; Isa. 37:36. 9 Isa. 37:37. 1 Ps. 45:1; Jer. 23:5; Hos. 3:5; Zech. 9:9. 2 Isa. 4:6; 25:4. 3 Isa. 29:18; 35:5, 6.

32:1–8 a king shall reign in righteousness. This King is Christ Himself. His government (promised in 9:6) is totally characterized by righteousness and judgment. Isaiah sees a great day coming when the godly character of those in Judah will be "as the shadow of a great rock in a weary land" (v. 2). In that time, even the ignorant will "understand knowledge" [Hebr. *daat,* "moral discernment"].

8 But the liberal deviseth liberal things; and by liberal things shall he stand.

Judgment and Restoration

9 Rise up, ye women that are at ease; hear my voice, ye careless daughters; give ear unto my speech.
10 Many days and years shall ye be troubled, ye careless women: for the vintage shall fail, the gathering shall not come.
11 Tremble, ye women that are at ease; be troubled, ye careless ones: strip you, and make you bare, and gird *sackcloth* upon *your* loins.
12 They shall lament for the teats, for the pleasant fields, for the fruitful vine.
13 Upon the land of my people shall come up thorns *and* briers; yea, upon all the houses of joy *in* the joyous city:
14 Because the palaces shall be forsaken; the multitude of the city shall be left; the forts and towers shall be for dens for ever, a joy of wild asses, a pasture of flocks;
15 Until the spirit be poured upon us from on high, and the wilderness be a fruitful field, and the fruitful field be counted for a forest.
16 Then judgment shall dwell in the wilderness, and righteousness remain in the fruitful field.
17 And the work of righteousness shall be peace; and the effect of righteousness quietness and assurance for ever.
18 And my people shall dwell in a peaceable habitation, and in sure dwellings, and in quiet resting places;
19 When it shall hail, coming down on the forest; and the city shall be low in a low place.
20 Blessed *are* ye that sow beside all waters, that send forth *thither* the feet of the ox and the ass.

CHAPTER 33
Salvation

1 Woe to thee that spoilest, and thou *wast* not spoiled; and dealest treacherously, and they dealt not treacherously with thee! when thou shalt cease to spoil, thou shalt be spoiled; *and* when thou shalt make an end to deal treacherously, they shall deal treacherously with thee.

2 O LORD, be gracious unto us; we have waited for thee: be thou their arm every morning, our salvation also in the time of trouble.
3 At the noise of the tumult the people fled; at the lifting up of thyself the nations were scattered.
4 And your spoil shall be gathered *like* the gathering of the caterpiller: as the running to and fro of locusts shall he run upon them.
5 The LORD is exalted; for he dwelleth on high: he hath filled Zion with judgment and righteousness.
6 And wisdom and knowledge shall be the stability of thy times, *and* strength of salvation: the fear of the LORD *is* his treasure.
7 Behold, their valiant ones shall cry without: the ambassadors of peace shall weep bitterly.
8 The highways lie waste, the wayfaring man ceaseth: he hath broken the covenant, he hath despised the cities, he regardeth no man.
9 The earth mourneth *and* languisheth: Lebanon is ashamed *and* hewn down: Sharon is like a wilderness; and Bashan and Carmel shake off *their fruits.*
10 Now will I rise, saith the LORD; now will I be exalted; now will I lift up myself.
11 Ye shall conceive chaff, ye shall bring forth stubble: your breath, *as* fire, shall devour you.
12 And the people shall be *as* the burnings of lime: *as* thorns cut up shall they be burned in the fire.
13 Hear, ye *that are* far off, what I have done; and, ye *that are* near, acknowledge my might.
14 The sinners in Zion are afraid; fearfulness hath surprised the hypocrites. Who among us shall dwell with the devouring fire? who among us shall dwell with everlasting burnings?
15 He that walketh righteously, and speaketh uprightly; he that despiseth the gain of oppressions, that shaketh his hands from holding of bribes, that stoppeth his ears from hearing of blood, and shutteth his eyes from seeing evil;

Cross References:
9 Amos 6:1
13 Isa. 22:2; 34:13; Hos. 9:6
14 Isa. 27:10
15 Ps. 104:30; Isa. 29:17; 35:2; Joel 2:28
17 James 3:18
19 Isa. 30:30; Zech. 11:2
20 Isa. 30:24
1 Isa. 21:2; Hab. 2:8; Rev. 13:10
2 Isa. 25:9
5 Ps. 97:9
7 2Kgs. 18:18, 37
8 Judg. 5:6; 2Kgs. 18:14-17
9 Isa. 24:4
10 Ps. 12:5
11 Ps. 7:14; Isa. 59:4
12 Isa. 9:18
13 Isa. 49:1
15 Ps. 15:2; 24:4; 119:37

33:1–12 Isaiah's final woe on Israel and Judah looks beyond to the ultimate devastation that will come in the Last Days. The one that spoils and is not spoiled is a reference to the coming Antichrist and his kingdom. "The time of trouble" (v. 2) is a reference to the Tribulation (cf. Matt. 24). The invading army is likened to a horde of locusts that shall cover the land of Israel (v. 4). In verse 8, Isaiah uses the phrase "he hath broken the covenant," anticipating events in Daniel 9:27 that describe the Antichrist. Both prophets foresaw a time when this evil one who promises sanctuary for Israel will violate the holy places and turn against her during the Tribulation.

16 He shall dwell on high: his place of defence *shall be* the munitions of rocks: bread shall be given him; his waters *shall be* sure.

The Glorious Future

17 Thine eyes shall see the king in his beauty: they shall behold the land that is very far off.

18 Thine heart shall meditate terror. Where *is* the scribe? where *is* the receiver? where *is* he that counted the towers?

19 Thou shalt not see a fierce people, a people of a deeper speech than thou canst perceive; of a stammering tongue, *that thou canst* not understand.

20 Look upon Zion, the city of our solemnities: thine eyes shall see Jerusalem a quiet habitation, a tabernacle *that* shall not be taken down; not one of the stakes thereof shall ever be removed, neither shall any of the cords thereof be broken.

21 But there the glorious LORD *will be* unto us a place of broad rivers *and* streams; wherein shall go no galley with oars, neither shall gallant ship pass thereby.

22 For the LORD *is* our judge, the LORD *is* our lawgiver, the LORD *is* our king; he will save us.

23 Thy tacklings are loosed; they could not well strengthen their mast, they could not spread the sail: then is the prey of a great spoil divided; the lame take the prey.

24 And the inhabitant shall not say, I am sick: the people that dwell therein *shall be* forgiven *their* iniquity.

CHAPTER 34
God's Vengeance

1 Come near, ye nations, to hear; and hearken, ye people: let the earth hear, and all that is therein; the world, and all things that come forth of it.

2 For the indignation of the LORD *is* upon all nations, and *his* fury upon all their armies: he hath utterly destroyed them, he hath delivered them to the slaughter.

3 Their slain also shall be cast out, and their stink shall come up out of their carcases, and the mountains shall be melted with their blood.

4 And all the host of heaven shall be dissolved, and the heavens shall be rolled together as a scroll: and all their host shall fall down, as the leaf falleth off from the vine, and as a falling *fig* from the fig tree.

5 For my sword shall be bathed in heaven: behold, it shall come down upon Idumea, and upon the people of my curse, to judgment.

6 The sword of the LORD is filled with blood, it is made fat with fatness, *and* with the blood of lambs and goats, with the fat of the kidneys of rams: for the LORD hath a sacrifice in Bozrah, and a great slaughter in the land of Idumea.

7 And the unicorns shall come down with them, and the bullocks with the bulls; and their land shall be soaked with blood, and their dust made fat with fatness.

8 For *it is* the day of the LORD's vengeance, *and* the year of recompences for the controversy of Zion.

9 And the streams thereof shall be turned into pitch, and the dust thereof into brimstone, and the land thereof shall become burning pitch.

10 It shall not be quenched night nor day; the smoke thereof shall go up for ever: from generation to generation it shall lie waste; none shall pass through it for ever and ever.

11 But the cormorant and the bittern shall

Center reference column

18 1Cor. 1:20

19 Deut. 28:49, 50; 2Kgs. 19:32; Jer. 5:15

20 Ps. 46:5; 48:12; 125:1, 2; Isa. 37:33; 54:2

22 Ps. 89:18; James 4:12

24 Jer. 50:20

1 Deut. 32:1; Ps. 49:1

3 Joel 2:20

4 Ps. 102:26; Isa. 14:12; Ezek. 32:7, 8; Joel 12:31; 3:15; Matt. 24:29; 2Pet. 3:10; Rev. 6:13, 14

5 Jer. 46:10; 49:7; Mal. 1:4

6 Isa. 63:1; Jer. 49:13; Zeph. 1:7

8 Isa. 63:4

9 Deut. 29:23

10 Mal. 1:4; Rev. 14:11; 18:18; 19:3

11 2Kgs. 21:13; Isa. 14:23; Lam. 2:8; Zeph. 2:14; Rev. 18:2

33:17–22 the king in his beauty. This is Christ Himself, and Isaiah's description of the magnitude of His kingdom looks ahead to the Millennial Kingdom where Christ will rule the world in peace. He will satisfy all of Israel's needs. He will be the Judge, Lawgiver, and King. Thus, in this threefold capacity, "he will save us" (v. 22).

34:1–35:10 Here the reader is confronted with another significant apocalyptic prophecy that actually continues throughout Isaiah. The object of God's wrath during the time of the Tribulation will be the nations, the earth, and the world. Isaiah foresees the Battle of Armageddon when God's indignation and fury are poured out on all Gentile nations. Isaiah also sees a time when even the "mountains shall be melted" and the "host of heaven shall be dissolved" [lit. "melt" or "vanish"]. This judgment will be so cataclysmic that it will affect the earth and its atmosphere and will usher in "new heavens and a new earth" (see Isa. 65:17).

34:8 the day of the LORD's vengeance. This refers to the entire time of God's judgment and justice. This coincides with the final devastation of the world (cf. "day of the LORD": Joel 2:2; Zeph. 1:15; Zech. 14:1; Mal. 4:5; "time of trouble": Dan. 12:1; "time of Jacob's trouble": Jer. 30:7; "the wrath to come": 1 Thess. 1:10; "wrath of the Lamb": Rev. 6:16–17).

34:11–17 God's judgment on the entire Gentile world is pictured in the desolation and depopulation of Idumea (Edom).

possess it; the owl also and the raven shall dwell in it: and he shall stretch out upon it the line of confusion, and the stones of emptiness.

12 They shall call the nobles thereof to the kingdom, but none *shall be* there, and all her princes shall be nothing.

13 And thorns shall come up in her palaces, nettles and brambles in the fortresses thereof: and it shall be an habitation of dragons, *and* a court for owls.

14 The wild beasts of the desert shall also meet with the wild beasts of the island, and the satyr shall cry to his fellow; the screech owl also shall rest there, and find for herself a place of rest.

15 There shall the great owl make her nest, and lay, and hatch, and gather under her shadow: there shall the vultures also be gathered, every one with her mate.

16 Seek ye out of the book of the LORD, and read: no one of these shall fail, none shall want her mate: for my mouth it hath commanded, and his spirit it hath gathered them.

17 And he hath cast the lot for them, and his hand hath divided it unto them by line: they shall possess it for ever, from generation to generation shall they dwell therein.

CHAPTER 35
The Path of Holiness

1 The wilderness and the solitary place shall be glad for them; and the desert shall rejoice, and blossom as the rose.

2 It shall blossom abundantly, and rejoice even with joy and singing: the glory of Lebanon shall be given unto it, the excellency of Carmel and Sharon, they shall see the glory of the LORD, *and* the excellency of our God.

3 Strengthen ye the weak hands, and confirm the feeble knees.

4 Say to them *that are* of a fearful heart, Be strong, fear not: behold, your God will come

with vengeance, *even* God *with* a recompence; he will come and save you.

5 Then the eyes of the blind shall be opened, and the ears of the deaf shall be unstopped.

6 Then shall the lame *man* leap as an hart, and the tongue of the dumb sing: for in the wilderness shall waters break out, and streams in the desert.

7 And the parched ground shall become a pool, and the thirsty land springs of water: in the habitation of dragons, where each lay, *shall be* grass with reeds and rushes.

8 And an highway shall be there, and a way, and it shall be called The way of holiness; the unclean shall not pass over it; but it *shall be* for those: the wayfaring men, though fools, shall not err *therein*.

9 No lion shall be there, nor *any* ravenous beast shall go up thereon, it shall not be found there; but the redeemed shall walk *there*:

10 And the ransomed of the LORD shall return, and come to Zion with songs and everlasting joy upon their heads: they shall obtain joy and gladness, and sorrow and sighing shall flee away.

CHAPTER 36
The Invasion of Sennacherib

1 Now it came to pass in the fourteenth year of king Hezekiah, *that* Sennacherib king of Assyria came up against all the defenced cities of Judah, and took them.

2 And the king of Assyria sent Rab-shakeh from Lachish to Jerusalem unto king Hezekiah with a great army. And he stood by the conduit of the upper pool in the highway of the fuller's field.

3 Then came forth unto him Eliakim, Hilkiah's son, which was over the house, and Shebna the scribe, and Joah, Asaph's son, the recorder.

4 And Rab-shakeh said unto them, Say ye

13 Isa. 13:21; 32:13; Hos. 9:6

16 Mal. 3:16

1 Isa. 55:12

2 Isa. 32:15

3 Job 4:3, 4; Heb. 12:12

5 Isa. 29:18; 32:3, 4; 42:7; Matt. 9:27; 11:5; 12:22; 20:30; 21:14; Mark 7:32; John 9:6, 7

6 Isa. 32:4; 41:18; 43:19; Matt. 9:32, 33; 11:5; 12:22; 15:30; 21:14; John 5:8, 9; 7:38, 39; Acts 3:2; 8:7; 14:8

7 Isa. 34:13

8 Isa. 52:1; Joel 3:17; Rev. 21:27

9 Lev. 26:6; Isa. 11:9; Ezek. 34:25

10 Isa. 25:8; 51:11; 65:19; Rev. 7:17; 21:4

1 2Kgs. 18:13, 17; 2Chr. 32:1

4 2Kgs. 18:19

34:16 the book of the LORD. This is the "book" of God's inspired prophecies concerning the coming day of judgment, probably a reference to Isaiah's own writings.

35:1–10 the desert shall rejoice, and blossom as the rose. The prophet Isaiah now offers a message of hope. After the terrible destruction of the Tribulation will come the blessings of the Millennial Kingdom. All spiritual evil and physical catastrophe will be reversed; the curse is lifted, and the land of promise is restored to pristine conditions.

35:8 an highway shall be there. This highway is contrasted to the desolate desert and its endless maze of shifting sands. It will be the "way of holiness" and will be a freeway to carry the ransomed and redeemed who have survived the Tribulation period on their journey to Zion (Jerusalem), the capital city of the Millennial Kingdom.

36:1—39:8 These three chapters bring the reader back to the historical setting of Isaiah's day. They also record the fulfillment of the prophecies already given concerning Assyria and Babylon. This section shifts from poetry to prose and parallels 2 Kings 18—20 and 2 Chronicles 32.

now to Hezekiah, Thus saith the great king, the king of Assyria, What confidence *is* this wherein thou trustest?

5 I say, *sayest thou*, (but *they are but* vain words) *I have* counsel and strength for war: now on whom dost thou trust, that thou rebellest against me?

6 Lo, thou trustest in the staff of this broken reed, on Egypt; whereon if a man lean, it will go into his hand, and pierce it: so *is* Pharaoh king of Egypt to all that trust in him.

7 But if thou say to me, We trust in the LORD our God: *is it* not he, whose high places and whose altars Hezekiah hath taken away, and said to Judah and to Jerusalem, Ye shall worship before this altar?

8 Now therefore give pledges, I pray thee, to my master the king of Assyria, and I will give thee two thousand horses, if thou be able on thy part to set riders upon them.

9 How then wilt thou turn away the face of one captain of the least of my master's servants, and put thy trust on Egypt for chariots and for horsemen?

10 And am I now come up without the LORD against this land to destroy it? the LORD said unto me, Go up against this land, and destroy it.

11 Then said Eliakim and Shebna and Joah unto Rab-shakeh, Speak, I pray thee, unto thy servants in the Syrian language; for we understand *it*: and speak not to us in the Jews' language, in the ears of the people that *are* on the wall.

12 But Rab-shakeh said, Hath my master sent me to thy master and to thee to speak these words? *hath he* not *sent me* to the men that sit upon the wall, that they may eat their own dung, and drink their own piss with you?

13 Then Rab-shakeh stood, and cried with a loud voice in the Jews' language, and said, Hear ye the words of the great king, the king of Assyria.

14 Thus saith the king, Let not Hezekiah deceive you: for he shall not be able to deliver you.

15 Neither let Hezekiah make you trust in the LORD, saying, The LORD will surely deliver us: this city shall not be delivered into the hand of the king of Assyria.

16 Hearken not to Hezekiah: for thus saith the king of Assyria, Make *an agreement* with me *by* a present, and come out to me: and eat ye every one of his vine, and every one of his fig tree, and drink ye every one the waters of his own cistern;

17 Until I come and take you away to a land like your own land, a land of corn and wine, a land of bread and vineyards.

18 *Beware* lest Hezekiah persuade you, saying, The LORD will deliver us. Hath any of the gods of the nations delivered his land out of the hand of the king of Assyria?

19 Where *are* the gods of Hamath and Arphad? where *are* the gods of Sepharvaim? and have they delivered Samaria out of my hand?

20 Who *are they* among all the gods of these lands, that have delivered their land out of my hand, that the LORD should deliver Jerusalem out of my hand?

21 But they held their peace, and answered him not a word: for the king's commandment was, saying, Answer him not.

22 Then came Eliakim, the son of Hilkiah, that *was* over the household, and Shebna the scribe, and Joah, the son of Asaph, the recorder, to Hezekiah with *their* clothes rent, and told him the words of Rab-shakeh.

CHAPTER 37
Hezekiah's Fear and Isaiah's Encouragement

1 And it came to pass, when king Hezekiah heard *it*, that he rent his clothes, and covered himself with sackcloth, and went into the house of the LORD.

2 And he sent Eliakim, who *was* over the household, and Shebna the scribe, and the elders of the priests covered with sackcloth, unto Isaiah the prophet the son of Amoz.

3 And they said unto him, Thus saith Hezekiah, This day *is* a day of trouble, and of rebuke, and of blasphemy: for the children are come to the birth, and *there is* not strength to bring forth.

4 It may be the LORD thy God will hear the words of Rab-shakeh, whom the king of Assyria his master hath sent to reproach the living God, and will reprove the words which the LORD thy God hath heard: wherefore lift up *thy* prayer for the remnant that is left.

5 So the servants of king Hezekiah came to Isaiah.

6 And Isaiah said unto them, Thus shall ye say unto your master, Thus saith the LORD, Be not afraid of the words that thou hast heard, wherewith the servants of the king of Assyria have blasphemed me.

7 Behold, I will send a blast upon him, and he shall hear a rumour, and return to his own land; and I will cause him to fall by the sword in his own land.

6 Ezek. 29:6, 7
16 Zech. 3:10

1 2 Kgs. 10:1

4 13 Jer. 49:23

8 So Rab-shakeh returned, and found the king of Assyria warring against Libnah: for he had heard that he was departed from Lachish.

9 And he heard say concerning Tirhakah king of Ethiopia, He is come forth to make war with thee. And when he heard *it,* he sent messengers to Hezekiah, saying,

10 Thus shall ye speak to Hezekiah king of Judah, saying, Let not thy God, in whom thou trustest, deceive thee, saying, Jerusalem shall not be given into the hand of the king of Assyria.

11 Behold, thou hast heard what the kings of Assyria have done to all lands by destroying them utterly; and shalt thou be delivered?

12 Have the gods of the nations delivered them which my fathers have destroyed, *as* Gozan, and Haran, and Rezeph, and the children of Eden which *were* in Telassar?

13 Where *is* the king of Hamath, and the king of Arphad, and the king of the city of Sepharvaim, Hena, and Ivah?

14 And Hezekiah received the letter from the hand of the messengers, and read it: and Hezekiah went up unto the house of the Lord, and spread it before the Lord.

15 And Hezekiah prayed unto the Lord, saying,

16 O Lord of hosts, God of Israel, that dwellest *between* the cherubims, thou *art* the God, *even* thou alone, of all the kingdoms of the earth: thou hast made heaven and earth.

17 Incline thine ear, O Lord, and hear; open thine eyes, O Lord, and see: and hear all the words of Sennacherib, which hath sent to reproach the living God.

18 Of a truth, Lord, the kings of Assyria have laid waste all the nations, and their countries,

19 And have cast their gods into the fire: for they *were* no gods, but the work of men's hands, wood and stone: therefore they have destroyed them.

20 Now therefore, O Lord our God, save us from his hand, that all the kingdoms of the earth may know that thou *art* the Lord, *even* thou only.

Isaiah's Message to the King

21 Then Isaiah the son of Amoz sent unto Hezekiah, saying, Thus saith the Lord God

of Israel, Whereas thou hast prayed to me against Sennacherib king of Assyria:

22 This *is* the word which the Lord hath spoken concerning him; The virgin, the daughter of Zion, hath despised thee, *and* laughed thee to scorn; the daughter of Jerusalem hath shaken her head at thee.

23 Whom hast thou reproached and blasphemed? and against whom hast thou exalted *thy* voice, and lifted up thine eyes on high? *even* against the Holy One of Israel.

24 By thy servants hast thou reproached the Lord, and hast said, By the multitude of my chariots am I come up to the height of the mountains, to the sides of Lebanon; and I will cut down the tall cedars thereof, *and* the choice fir trees thereof: and I will enter into the height of his border, *and* the forest of his Carmel.

25 I have digged, and drunk water; and with the sole of my feet have I dried up all the rivers of the besieged places.

26 Hast thou not heard long ago, *how* I have done it; *and* of ancient times, that I have formed it? now have I brought it to pass, that thou shouldest be to lay waste defenced cities *into* ruinous heaps.

27 Therefore their inhabitants *were* of small power, they were dismayed and confounded: they were *as* the grass of the field, and *as* the green herb, *as* the grass on the housetops, and *as corn* blasted before it be grown up.

28 But I know thy abode, and thy going out, and thy coming in, and thy rage against me.

29 Because thy rage against me, and thy tumult, is come up into mine ears, therefore will I put my hook in thy nose, and my bridle in thy lips, and I will turn thee back by the way by which thou camest.

30 And this *shall be* a sign unto thee, Ye shall eat *this* year such as groweth of itself; and the second year that which springeth of the same: and in the third year sow ye, and reap, and plant vineyards, and eat the fruit thereof.

31 And the remnant that is escaped of the house of Judah shall again take root downward, and bear fruit upward:

32 For out of Jerusalem shall go forth a remnant, and they that escape out of mount Zion: the zeal of the Lord of hosts shall do this.

33 Therefore thus saith the Lord concerning

---

17 Dan. 9:18

26 2Kgs. 19:25

29 Isa. 30:28; Ezek. 38:4

32 2Kgs. 19:31; Isa. 9:7

37:33–38 Hezekiah is promised that the king of Assyria will not enter Jerusalem because God will defend it "for my servant David's sake" (i.e., to protect the Davidic line). Just as He had delivered Israel from the Pharaoh of Egypt (Ex.

the king of Assyria, He shall not come into
this city, nor shoot an arrow there, nor come
before it with shields, nor cast a bank
against it.
34 By the way that he came, by the same
shall he return, and shall not come into this
city, saith the LORD.
35 For I will defend this city to save it for
mine own sake, and for my servant David's
sake.
36 Then the angel of the LORD went forth,
and smote in the camp of the Assyrians a
hundred and fourscore and five thousand:
and when they arose early in the morning,
behold, they *were* all dead corpses.
37 So Sennacherib king of Assyria departed,
and went and returned, and dwelt at Nineveh.
38 And it came to pass, as he was worshipping in the house of Nisroch his god, that
Adrammelech and Sharezer his sons smote
him with the sword; and they escaped into
the land of Armenia: and Esar-haddon his
son reigned in his stead.

CHAPTER 38

The Sickness of Hezekiah

1 In those days was Hezekiah sick unto
death. And Isaiah the prophet the son of
Amoz came unto him, and said unto him,
Thus saith the LORD, Set thine house in
order: for thou shalt die, and not live.
2 Then Hezekiah turned his face toward
the wall, and prayed unto the LORD,
3 And said, Remember now, O LORD, I beseech thee, how I have walked before thee
in truth and with a perfect heart, and have
done *that which is* good in thy sight. And
Hezekiah wept sore.
4 Then came the word of the LORD to Isaiah, saying,
5 Go, and say to Hezekiah, Thus saith the
LORD, the God of David thy father, I have
heard thy prayer, I have seen thy tears: behold, I will add unto thy days fifteen years.
6 And I will deliver thee and this city out
of the hand of the king of Assyria: and I will
defend this city.
7 And this *shall be* a sign unto thee from
the LORD, that the LORD will do this thing
that he hath spoken;
8 Behold, I will bring again the shadow of
the degrees, which is gone down in the sun
dial of Ahaz, ten degrees backward. So the
sun returned ten degrees, by which degrees
it was gone down.
9 The writing of Hezekiah king of Judah,
when he had been sick, and was recovered
of his sickness:
10 I said in the cutting off of my days, I
shall go to the gates of the grave: I am deprived of the residue of my years.
11 I said, I shall not see the LORD, *even* the
LORD, in the land of the living: I shall behold
man no more with the inhabitants of the
world.
12 Mine age is departed, and is removed
from me as a shepherd's tent: I have cut off
like a weaver my life: he will cut me off with
pining sickness: from day *even* to night wilt
thou make an end of me.
13 I reckoned till morning, *that,* as a lion, so
will he break all my bones: from day *even* to
night wilt thou make an end of me.
14 Like a crane *or* a swallow, so did I chat-
ter: I did mourn as a dove: mine eyes fail
with looking upward: O LORD, I am oppressed; undertake for me.
15 What shall I say? he hath both spoken
unto me, and himself hath done *it*: I shall go
softly all my years in the bitterness of my
soul.
16 O Lord, by these *things men* live, and in
all these *things is* the life of my spirit: so wilt
thou recover me, and make me to live.
17 Behold, for peace I had great bitterness:
but thou hast in love to my soul *delivered it*

35 2Kgs. 20:6; Isa. 38:6
36 2Kgs. 19:35
1 2Sam. 17:23; 2Kgs. 20:1; 2Chr. 32:24
3 Neh. 13:14
6 Isa. 37:35
7 2Kgs. 20:8; Isa. 7:11
11 Ps. 27:13; 116:9
12 Job 7:6
14 Isa. 59:11
15 Job 7:11; 10:1

12:29), God now delivers Judah from the Assyrians by smiting them in their own camp. Second Kings 19:35 adds the words, "And it came to pass that night" (i.e., the night after Hezekiah had prayed).

37:36 the angel of the LORD. This is probably Christ Himself, who had often appeared in the Old Testament in the form of a Christophany (see Gen. 18:1–33; Josh. 5:13—6:5; Judg. 6:11–23). These temporary, visible appearances of the pre-incarnate Christ were always done on Israel's behalf.

38:1—39:8 The events covered in chapters 38 and 39 do not follow chapters 36 and 37 chronologically. Chapters 37 and 38 form a conclusion to the Assyrian period of Isaiah's ministry, while chapters 38 and 39 form an introduction to the coming Babylonian captivity, which is the central concern in chapters 40 through 66.

38:7 a sign unto thee from the LORD. Deeply broken by Isaiah's prophetic warning that he would die, Hezekiah prayed to the Lord and was given another fifteen years to live. By a supernatural miracle, the falling shadow on the steps (or degree markers) of the sundial was reversed.

from the pit of corruption: for thou hast cast all my sins behind thy back.

18 For the grave cannot praise thee, death can *not* celebrate thee: they that go down into the pit cannot hope for thy truth.

19 The living, the living, he shall praise thee, as I *do* this day: the father to the children shall make known thy truth.

20 The LORD *was ready* to save me: therefore we will sing my songs to the stringed instruments all the days of our life in the house of the LORD.

21 For Isaiah had said, Let them take a lump of figs, and lay *it* for a plaister upon the boil, and he shall recover.

22 Hezekiah also had said, What *is* the sign that I shall go up to the house of the LORD?

CHAPTER 39
Ambassadors from Babylon

1 At that time Merodach-baladan, the son of Baladan, king of Babylon, sent letters and a present to Hezekiah: for he had heard that he had been sick, and was recovered.

2 And Hezekiah was glad of them, and shewed them the house of his precious things, the silver, and the gold, and the spices, and the precious ointment, and all the house of his armour, and all that was found in his treasures: there was nothing in his house, nor in all his dominion, that Hezekiah shewed them not.

3 Then came Isaiah the prophet unto king Hezekiah, and said unto him, What said these men? and from whence came they

unto thee? And Hezekiah said, They are come from a far country unto me, *even* from Babylon.

4 Then said he, What have they seen in thine house? And Hezekiah answered, All that *is* in mine house have they seen: there is nothing among my treasures that I have not shewed them.

5 Then said Isaiah to Hezekiah, Hear the word of the LORD of hosts:

6 Behold, the days come, that all that *is* in thine house, and *that* which thy fathers have laid up in store until this day, shall be carried to Babylon: nothing shall be left, saith the LORD.

7 And of thy sons that shall issue from thee, which thou shalt beget, shall they take away; and they shall be eunuchs in the palace of the king of Babylon.

8 Then said Hezekiah to Isaiah, Good *is* the word of the LORD which thou hast spoken. He said moreover, For there shall be peace and truth in my days.

CHAPTER 40
Words of Comfort

1 Comfort ye, comfort ye my people, saith your God.

2 Speak ye comfortably to Jerusalem, and cry unto her, that her warfare is accomplished, that her iniquity is pardoned: for she hath received of the LORD's hand double for all her sins.

3 The voice of him that crieth in the wilderness, Prepare ye the way of the LORD,

Cross references (center column):
18 Ps. 6:5; 30:9; 88:11; 115:17; Eccl. 9:10
19 Deut. 4:9; 6:7; Ps. 78:3, 4
21 2Kgs. 20:7
22 2Kgs. 20:8
1 2Kgs. 20:12
2 2Chr. 32:31
6 Jer. 20:5
7 Dan. 1:2, 3, 7
8 1Sam. 3:18
2 Job 42:10; Isa. 61:7
3 Ps. 68:4; Isa. 49:11; Mal. 3:1; Matt. 3:3; Mark 1:3; Luke 3:4; John 1:23

39:1–8 Merodach-baladan . . . king of Babylon. Known in the Akkadian texts as Marduk-apal-iddina, he conquered Babylon in 721 B.C. with the help of the Elamites and ruled there eleven years before being driven out by Sargon II of Assyria in 710 B.C. After the death of Sargon, he reentered Babylon briefly in 703 B.C. in an attempt to regain power against the new Assyrian ruler, Sennacherib. Merodach-baladan was attempting to convince regional powers to support him against the Assyrian king. Impressed by the flatteries of this man who would be king, Hezekiah foolishly showed his emissaries the treasures of Jerusalem and of the temple. This was evidently done in vanity and pride, which the people of Israel would later regret. This incident is used by Isaiah to introduce the coming Babylonian captivity. Isaiah predicts that all the royal treasures will be taken to Babylon in the future. News of these great treasures would spread throughout Babylon, provoking the Babylonians to come and take them away.

40:1—48:22 This section of Isaiah's prophecy is often

called the "Book of Consolation" because of its message of salvation and hope.

40:1 comfort ye my people. The Hebrew word for "comfort" (*nachamu*) means both "repent" and "console." True repentance must precede divine consolation. The phrase "my people" recalls the promise to Abraham, Isaac, and Jacob, and refers to the people of God who are in a covenant relationship with Him. This designation appears twelve times in chapters 1—39 and fifteen times in chapters 40—66. As the prophetic word of God regarding the first coming of Christ was offered to encourage and console the people of Israel, so the promises of the Second Coming are an encouragement to the believer (cf. 1 Thess. 4:18).

40:3 The voice of him that crieth in the wilderness. This would be fulfilled by John the Baptist (see Matt. 3:3; Mark 1:3; Luke 3:4; John 1:23). John would call the people of Judah to repentance, to make preparations for the coming of the Messiah.

make straight in the desert a highway for our God.

4 Every valley shall be exalted, and every mountain and hill shall be made low: and the crooked shall be made straight, and the rough places plain:

5 And the glory of the Lord shall be revealed, and all flesh shall see *it* together: for the mouth of the Lord hath spoken *it*.

6 The voice said, Cry. And he said, What shall I cry? All flesh *is* grass, and all the goodliness thereof *is* as the flower of the field:

7 The grass withereth, the flower fadeth: because the spirit of the Lord bloweth upon it: surely the people *is* grass.

8 The grass withereth, the flower fadeth: but the word of our God shall stand for ever.

9 O Zion, that bringest good tidings, get thee up into the high mountain; O Jerusalem, that bringest good tidings, lift up thy voice with strength; lift *it* up, be not afraid; say unto the cities of Judah, Behold your God!

10 Behold, the Lord God will come with strong *hand*, and his arm shall rule for him: behold, his reward *is* with him, and his work before him.

11 He shall feed his flock like a shepherd: he shall gather the lambs with his arm, and carry *them* in his bosom, *and* shall gently lead those that are with young.

Israel's Incomparable God

12 Who hath measured the waters in the hollow of his hand, and meted out heaven with the span, and comprehended the dust of the earth in a measure, and weighed the mountains in scales, and the hills in a balance?

13 Who hath directed the Spirit of the Lord, or *being* his counseller hath taught him?

14 With whom took he counsel, and *who* instructed him, and taught him in the path of judgment, and taught him knowledge, and shewed to him the way of understanding?

15 Behold, the nations *are* as a drop of a bucket, and are counted as the small dust of the balance: behold, he taketh up the isles as a very little thing.

16 And Lebanon *is* not sufficient to burn, nor the beasts thereof sufficient for a burnt offering.

17 All nations before him *are* as nothing; and they are counted to him less than nothing, and vanity.

18 To whom then will ye liken God? or what likeness will ye compare unto him?

19 The workman melteth a graven image, and the goldsmith spreadeth it over with gold, and casteth silver chains.

20 He that *is* so impoverished that he hath no oblation chooseth a tree *that* will not rot; he seeketh unto him a cunning workman to prepare a graven image, *that* shall not be moved.

21 Have ye not known? have ye not heard? hath it not been told you from the beginning? have ye not understood from the foundations of the earth?

22 *It is* he that sitteth upon the circle of the earth, and the inhabitants thereof *are* as grasshoppers; that stretcheth out the heavens as a curtain, and spreadeth them out as a tent to dwell in:

23 That bringeth the princes to nothing; he maketh the judges of the earth as vanity.

24 Yea, they shall not be planted; yea, they shall not be sown: yea, their stock shall not take root in the earth: and he shall also blow upon them, and they shall wither, and the whirlwind shall take them away as stubble.

25 To whom then will ye liken me, or shall I be equal? saith the Holy One.

26 Lift up your eyes on high, and behold who hath created these *things*, that bringeth out their host by number: he calleth them all by names by the greatness of his might, for that *he is* strong in power; not one faileth.

27 Why sayest thou, O Jacob, and speakest, O Israel, My way is hid from the Lord, and my judgment is passed over from my God?

28 Hast thou not known? hast thou not heard, *that* the everlasting God, the Lord, the Creator of the ends of the earth, fainteth not, neither is weary? *there is* no searching of his understanding.

29 He giveth power to the faint; and to *them that have* no might he increaseth strength.

30 Even the youths shall faint and be weary, and the young men shall utterly fall:

31 But they that wait upon the Lord shall renew *their* strength; they shall mount up with wings as eagles; they shall run, and

---

4 Isa. 45:2

6 Job 14:2; Ps. 90:5; 102:11; 103:15; James 1:10; 1Pet. 1:24

7 Ps. 103:16

8 John 12:34; 1Pet. 1:25

9 Isa. 41:27; 52:7

10 Isa. 49:4; 59:16; 62:11; Rev. 22:12

11 Isa. 49:10; Ezek. 34:23; 37:24; John 10:11; Heb. 13:20; 1Pet. 2:25; 5:4; Rev. 7:17

12 Prov. 30:4

13 Job 21:22; 36:22, 23; Rom. 11:34; 1Cor. 2:16

17 Ps. 62:9; Dan. 4:35

18 Isa. 40:25; 46:5; Acts 17:29

19 Isa. 41:6, 7; 44:12; Jer. 10:3

20 Isa. 41:7; Jer. 10:4

21 Ps. 19:1; Acts 14:17; Rom. 1:19, 20

22 Job 9:8; Ps. 104:2; Isa. 42:5; 44:24; 51:13; Jer. 10:12

23 Job 12:21; Ps. 107:40

25 Deut. 4:15; Isa. 40:18

26 Ps. 147:4

28 Ps. 147:5; Rom. 11:33

31 Ps. 103:5

40:9–17 The phrase "Behold your God!" refers to the coming of God incarnate in the person of Jesus Christ, like a shepherd gathering his sheep (see John 10). The questions that follow in verses 12–17 are reminiscent of those in Job 38—41, and each implies the answer: "None but God!"

not be weary; *and* they shall walk, and not faint.

CHAPTER 41
God's Assurance to Israel

1 Keep silence before me, O islands; and let the people renew *their* strength: let them come near; then let them speak: let us come near together to judgment.

2 Who raised up the righteous *man* from the east, called him to his foot, gave the nations before him, and made *him* rule over kings? he gave *them* as the dust to his sword, *and* as driven stubble to his bow.

3 He pursued them, *and* passed safely; *even* by the way *that* he had not gone with his feet.

4 Who hath wrought and done *it*, calling the generations from the beginning? I the LORD, the first, and with the last; I *am* he.

5 The isles saw *it*, and feared; the ends of the earth were afraid, drew near, and came.

6 They helped every one his neighbour; and *every one* said to his brother, Be of good courage.

7 So the carpenter encouraged the goldsmith, *and* he that smootheth *with* the hammer him that smote the anvil, saying, It *is* ready for the sodering: and he fastened it with nails, *that* it should not be moved.

8 But thou, Israel, *art* my servant, Jacob whom I have chosen, the seed of Abraham my friend.

9 *Thou* whom I have taken from the ends of the earth, and called thee from the chief men thereof, and said unto thee, Thou *art* my servant; I have chosen thee, and not cast thee away.

10 Fear thou not; for I *am* with thee: be not dismayed; for I *am* thy God: I will strengthen thee; yea, I will help thee; yea, I will uphold thee with the right hand of my righteousness.

11 Behold, all they that were incensed against thee shall be ashamed and confounded: they shall be as nothing; and they that strive with thee shall perish.

12 Thou shalt seek them, and shalt not find them, *even* them that contended with thee:

they that war against thee shall be as nothing, and as a thing of nought.

13 For I the LORD thy God will hold thy right hand, saying unto thee, Fear not; I will help thee.

14 Fear not, thou worm Jacob, *and* ye men of Israel; I will help thee, saith the LORD, and thy redeemer, the Holy One of Israel.

15 Behold, I will make thee a new sharp threshing instrument having teeth: thou shalt thresh the mountains, and beat *them* small, and shalt make the hills as chaff.

16 Thou shalt fan them, and the wind shall carry them away, and the whirlwind shall scatter them: and thou shalt rejoice in the LORD, *and* shalt glory in the Holy One of Israel.

17 *When* the poor and needy seek water, and *there is* none, *and* their tongue faileth for thirst, I the LORD will hear them, I the God of Israel will not forsake them.

18 I will open rivers in high places, and fountains in the midst of the valleys: I will make the wilderness a pool of water, and the dry land springs of water.

19 I will plant in the wilderness the cedar, the shittah tree, and the myrtle, and the oil tree; I will set in the desert the fir tree, *and* the pine, and the box tree together:

20 That they may see, and know, and consider, and understand together, that the hand of the LORD hath done this, and the Holy One of Israel hath created it.

A Challenge

21 Produce your cause, saith the LORD; bring forth your strong *reasons*, saith the King of Jacob.

22 Let them bring *them* forth, and shew us what shall happen: let them shew the former things, what they *be*, that we may consider them, and know the latter end of them; or declare us things for to come.

23 Shew the things that are to come hereafter, that we may know that ye *are* gods: yea, do good, or do evil, that we may be dismayed, and behold *it* together.

24 Behold, ye *are* of nothing, and your work

Cross references (center column):

1 Zech. 2:13
2 Gen. 14:14; Isa. 41:25; 45:1; 46:11
4 Isa. 41:26; 43:10; 44:6, 7; 46:10; 48:12; Rev. 1:17; 22:13
6 Isa. 40:19; 44:12
7 Isa. 40:19, 20
8 Deut. 7:6; 10:15; 14:2; 2Chr. 20:7; Ps. 135:4; Isa. 43:1; 44:1; James 2:23
10 Deut. 31:6, 8; Isa. 41:13, 14; 43:5
11 Ex. 23:22; Isa. 45:24; 60:12; Zech. 12:3
13 Isa. 41:10
15 Mic. 4:13; 2Cor. 10:4, 5
16 Isa. 45:25; Jer. 51:2
18 Ps. 107:35; Isa. 35:6, 7; 43:19; 44:3
20 Job 12:9
22 Isa. 45:21
23 Isa. 42:9; 44:7, 8; 45:3; Jer. 10:5; John 13:19
24 Ps. 115:8; Isa. 44:9; 1Cor. 8:4

41:1–7 the righteous man from the east. This refers to Cyrus the Great of Persia (558–529 B.C.), who is prophesied by name in 44:28. He is introduced as the one who will be raised up from the East to fulfill the will of God. Both the Hebrew text and the Septuagint (a Greek translation) have "righteousness," a noun rather than an adjective. It is God who raised up righteousness toward His people by the deliverance He provides through Cyrus the Great.

41:19 These seven trees, all common to Syria and Israel, would have been especially well known to an author who lived in that region. They are symbolic of the perfection of God's work on behalf of His people.

of nought: an abomination *is he that* chooseth you.

25 I have raised up *one* from the north, and he shall come: from the rising of the sun shall he call upon my name: and he shall come upon princes as *upon* morter, and as the potter treadeth clay.

26 Who hath declared from the beginning, that we may know? and beforetime, that we may say, *He is* righteous? yea, *there is* none that sheweth, yea, *there is* none that declareth, yea, *there is* none that heareth your words.

27 The first *shall say* to Zion, Behold, behold them: and I will give to Jerusalem one that bringeth good tidings.

28 For I beheld, and *there was* no man; even among them, and *there was* no counsellor, that, when I asked of them, could answer a word.

29 Behold, they *are* all vanity; their works *are* nothing: their molten images *are* wind and confusion.

CHAPTER 42
God's Special Servant

1 Behold my servant, whom I uphold; mine elect, *in whom* my soul delighteth; I have put my spirit upon him: he shall bring forth judgment to the Gentiles.

2 He shall not cry, nor lift up, nor cause his voice to be heard in the street.

3 A bruised reed shall he not break, and the smoking flax shall he not quench: he shall bring forth judgment unto truth.

4 He shall not fail nor be discouraged, till he have set judgment in the earth: and the isles shall wait for his law.

5 Thus saith God the LORD, he that created the heavens, and stretched them out; he that spread forth the earth, and that which cometh out of it; he that giveth breath unto the people upon it, and spirit to them that walk therein:

6 I the LORD have called thee in righteousness, and will hold thine hand, and will keep thee, and give thee for a covenant of the people, for a light of the Gentiles;

7 To open the blind eyes, to bring out the

Cross-references:
25 Ezra 1:2; Isa. 41:2
26 Isa. 43:9
27 Isa. 40:9; 41:4
28 Isa. 63:5
29 Isa. 41:24
1 Isa. 11:2; 43:10; 49:3, 6; 52:13; 53:11; Matt. 3:17; 12:18-20; 17:5; John 3:34; Eph. 1:6; Phil. 2:7
4 Gen. 49:10
5 Ps. 136:6; Isa. 44:24; Zech. 12:1; Acts 17:25
6 Isa. 43:1; 49:6, 8; Luke 2:32; Acts 13:47
7 Isa. 9:2; 35:5; 61:1; Luke 4:18; 2Tim. 2:26; Heb. 2:14, 15
8 Isa. 48:11
10 Ps. 33:3; 40:3; 98:1; 107:23
13 Isa. 31:4
17 Ps. 1:29; 44:11; 45:16; 97:7
19 Isa. 43:8; Ezek. 12:2; John 9:39, 41

---

prisoners from the prison, *and* them that sit in darkness out of the prison house.

8 I *am* the LORD: that *is* my name: and my glory will I not give to another, neither my praise to graven images.

9 Behold, the former things are come to pass, and new things do I declare: before they spring forth I tell you of them.

A Song of Praise

10 Sing unto the LORD a new song, *and* his praise from the end of the earth, ye that go down to the sea, and all that is therein; the isles, and the inhabitants thereof.

11 Let the wilderness and the cities thereof lift up *their voice*, the villages *that* Kedar doth inhabit: let the inhabitants of the rock sing, let them shout from the top of the mountains.

12 Let them give glory unto the LORD, and declare his praise in the islands.

13 The LORD shall go forth as a mighty man, he shall stir up jealousy like a man of war: he shall cry, yea, roar; he shall prevail against his enemies.

14 I have long time holden my peace; I have been still, *and* refrained myself: *now* will I cry like a travailing woman; I will destroy and devour at once.

15 I will make waste mountains and hills, and dry up all their herbs; and I will make the rivers islands, and I will dry up the pools.

16 And I will bring the blind by a way *that* they knew not; I will lead them in paths *that* they have not known: I will make darkness light before them, and crooked things straight. These things will I do unto them, and not forsake them.

17 They shall be turned back, they shall be greatly ashamed, that trust in graven images, that say to the molten images, Ye *are* our gods.

Israel Is Stubborn

18 Hear, ye deaf; and look, ye blind, that ye may see.

19 Who *is* blind, but my servant? or deaf, as my messenger *that* I sent? who *is* blind as *he*

42:1–4 my servant. The servant is more than a personification of the nation of Israel. He is none other than the Messiah, Jesus Christ Himself. He is also called "mine elect" (Hebr. *bechiri*, "set apart for a definite purpose") and the One in whom God put His spirit. The New Testament quotes this prophecy as being fulfilled in the Lord Jesus Christ (Matt. 12:18–21). The ministry of the Servant of the Lord will be to bring forth "judgment to the Gentiles" and "in the earth." Of all the Old Testament prophets, Isaiah presents this fact the most clearly. Messiah's kingdom will know no barriers of nationality or race.

that is perfect, and blind as the LORD's servant?

20 Seeing many things, but thou observest not; opening the ears, but he heareth not.

21 The LORD is well pleased for his righteousness' sake; he will magnify the law, and make *it* honourable.

22 But this *is* a people robbed and spoiled; *they are* all of them snared in holes, and they are hid in prison houses: they are for a prey, and none delivereth; for a spoil, and none saith, Restore.

23 Who among you will give ear to this? *who* will hearken and hear for the time to come?

24 Who gave Jacob for a spoil, and Israel to the robbers? did not the LORD, he against whom we have sinned? for they would not walk in his ways, neither were they obedient unto his law.

25 Therefore he hath poured upon him the fury of his anger, and the strength of battle: and it hath set him on fire round about, yet he knew not; and it burned him, yet he laid *it* not to heart.

CHAPTER 43

1 But now thus saith the LORD that created thee, O Jacob, and he that formed thee, O Israel, Fear not: for I have redeemed thee, I have called *thee* by thy name; thou *art* mine.

2 When thou passest through the waters, I *will be* with thee; and through the rivers, they shall not overflow thee: when thou walkest through the fire, thou shalt not be burned; neither shall the flame kindle upon thee.

3 For I *am* the LORD thy God, the Holy One of Israel, thy Saviour: I gave Egypt *for* thy ransom, Ethiopia and Seba for thee.

4 Since thou wast precious in my sight, thou hast been honourable, and I have loved thee: therefore will I give men for thee, and people for thy life.

5 Fear not: for I *am* with thee: I will bring thy seed from the east, and gather thee from the west;

20 Rom. 2:21

25 2Kgs. 25:9; Hos. 7:9

1 Isa. 42:6; 43:7, 21; 44:2, 6, 21, 24; 45:4

2 Deut. 31:6, 8; Ps. 66:12; 91:3; Dan. 3:25, 27

3 Prov. 11:8; 21:18

5 Isa. 41:10, 14; 44:2; Jer. 30:10, 11

7 Ps. 100:3; Isa. 29:23; 43:1; 63:19; John 3:3, 5; 2Cor. 5:17; Eph. 2:10; James 2:7

8 Isa. 6:9; 42:19; Ezek. 12:2

9 Isa. 41:21, 22, 26

10 Isa. 41:4; 42:1; 44:6, 8; 55:4

11 Isa. 45:21; Hos. 13:4

12 Deut. 32:16; Ps. 81:9; Isa. 43:10; 44:8

13 Job 9:12; Ps. 90:2; Isa. 14:27; John 8:58

16 Ex. 14:16, 22; Josh. 3:13, 16; Ps. 77:19; Isa. 51:10

17 Ex. 14:4-9, 25

18 Jer. 16:14; 23:7

19 Isa. 35:6; 41:18; 2Cor. 5:17; Rev. 21:5

6 I will say to the north, Give up; and to the south, Keep not back: bring my sons from far, and my daughters from the ends of the earth;

7 *Even* every one that is called by my name: for I have created him for my glory, I have formed him; yea, I have made him.

8 Bring forth the blind people that have eyes, and the deaf that have ears.

9 Let all the nations be gathered together, and let the people be assembled: who among them can declare this, and shew us former things? let them bring forth their witnesses, that they may be justified: or let them hear, and say, It *is* truth.

10 Ye *are* my witnesses, saith the LORD, and my servant whom I have chosen: that ye may know and believe me, and understand that I *am* he: before me there was no God formed, neither shall there be after me.

11 I, *even* I, *am* the LORD; and beside me *there is* no saviour.

12 I have declared, and have saved, and I have shewed, when *there was* no strange *god* among you: therefore ye *are* my witnesses, saith the LORD, that I *am* God.

13 Yea, before the day *was* I *am* he; and *there is* none that can deliver out of my hand: I will work, and who shall let it?

14 Thus saith the LORD, your redeemer, the Holy One of Israel; For your sake I have sent to Babylon, and have brought down all their nobles, and the Chaldeans, whose cry *is* in the ships.

15 I *am* the LORD, your Holy One, the creator of Israel, your King.

16 Thus saith the LORD, which maketh a way in the sea, and a path in the mighty waters;

17 Which bringeth forth the chariot and horse, the army and the power; they shall lie down together, they shall not rise: they are extinct, they are quenched as tow.

18 Remember ye not the former things, neither consider the things of old.

19 Behold, I will do a new thing; now it shall spring forth; shall ye not know it?

43:1–13 Fear not: for I have redeemed thee. In spite of Israel's deliberate rejection of the Lord as her rightful king, God reassures the people of that nation that He is their salvation. Twenty-two times in the "Servant" passages of the book of Isaiah the theme of redemption is repeated. It speaks of a redemption from physical and spiritual bondage as well as the end-time redemption yet to come (cf. 43:5–7; 44:22; 49:6–7). But this redemptive word of God is further declared to be extended to "all the nations" (the Gentiles [v. 9]) for salvation.

43:14–28 Isaiah here predicts that God will judge Babylon after using them to judge Israel. The curse of the captivity and the subsequent deliverance of the remnant from Babylon, yet future at the time of Isaiah's writing, are clearly depicted.

43:20 For dragons and owls, see the note on Isaiah 13:21–22.

I will even make a way in the wilderness, *and* rivers in the desert.

20 The beast of the field shall honour me, the dragons and the owls: because I give waters in the wilderness, *and* rivers in the desert, to give drink to my people, my chosen.

21 This people have I formed for myself; they shall shew forth my praise.

22 But thou hast not called upon me, O Jacob; but thou hast been weary of me, O Israel.

23 Thou hast not brought me the small cattle of thy burnt offerings; neither hast thou honoured me with thy sacrifices. I have not caused thee to serve with an offering, nor wearied thee with incense.

24 Thou hast bought me no sweet cane with money, neither hast thou filled me with the fat of thy sacrifices: but thou hast made me to serve with thy sins, thou hast wearied me with thine iniquities.

25 I, *even* I, *am* he that blotteth out thy transgressions for mine own sake, and will not remember thy sins.

26 Put me in remembrance: let us plead together: declare thou, that thou mayest be justified.

27 Thy first father hath sinned, and thy teachers have transgressed against me.

28 Therefore I have profaned the princes of the sanctuary, and have given Jacob to the curse, and Israel to reproaches.

CHAPTER 44
The Lord Is the Only God

1 Yet now hear, O Jacob my servant; and Israel, whom I have chosen:

2 Thus saith the LORD that made thee, and formed thee from the womb, *which* will help thee; Fear not, O Jacob, my servant; and thou, Jesurun, whom I have chosen.

3 For I will pour water upon him that is thirsty, and floods upon the dry ground: I will pour my spirit upon thy seed, and my blessing upon thine offspring:

4 And they shall spring up *as* among the grass, as willows by the water courses.

5 One shall say, I *am* the LORD's; and another shall call *himself* by the name of Jacob; and another shall subscribe *with* his hand unto the LORD, and surname *himself* by the name of Israel.

20 Isa. 48:21
21 Ps. 102:18; Isa. 43:1, 7; Luke 1:74, 75; Eph. 1:5, 6
22 Mal. 1:13
23 Amos 5:25
24 Isa. 1:14; Mal. 2:17
25 Isa. 1:18; 44:22; 48:9; Jer. 31:34; 50:20; Ezek. 36:22; Acts 3:19
27 Mal. 2:7, 8
28 Ps. 79:4; Isa. 47:6; Jer. 24:9; Lam. 2:2, 6, 7; Dan. 9:11; Zech. 8:13
1 Isa. 41:8; 43:1; 44:21; Jer. 30:10; 46:27, 28
2 Deut. 32:15; Isa. 43:1, 7
3 Isa. 35:7; Joel 2:28; John 7:38; Acts 2:18
6 Isa. 41:4; 43:1, 14; 44:24; 48:12; Rev. 1:8, 17; 22:13
7 Isa. 41:4, 22; 45:21
8 Deut. 4:35, 39; 32:4, 39; 1Sam. 2:2; 2Sam. 22:32; Isa. 41:22; 43:10, 12; 45:5
9 Ps. 115:4; Isa. 41:24, 29
10 Jer. 10:5; Hab. 2:18
11 Ps. 97:7; Isa. 1:29; 42:17; 45:16
12 Isa. 40:19; 41:6; Jer. 10:3

6 Thus saith the LORD the King of Israel, and his redeemer the LORD of hosts; I *am* the first, and I *am* the last; and beside me *there is* no God.

7 And who, as I, shall call, and shall declare it, and set it in order for me, since I appointed the ancient people? and the things that are coming, and shall come, let them shew unto them.

8 Fear ye not, neither be afraid: have not I told thee from that time, and have declared *it*? ye *are* even my witnesses. Is there a God beside me? yea, *there is* no God; I know not *any*.

9 They that make a graven image *are* all of them vanity; and their delectable things shall not profit; and they *are* their own witnesses; they see not, nor know; that they may be ashamed.

10 Who hath formed a god, or molten a graven image *that* is profitable for nothing?

11 Behold, all his fellows shall be ashamed: and the workmen, they *are* of men: let them all be gathered together, let them stand up; *yet* they shall fear, *and* they shall be ashamed together.

12 The smith with the tongs both worketh in the coals, and fashioneth it with hammers, and worketh it with the strength of his arms: yea, he is hungry, and his strength faileth: he drinketh no water, and is faint.

13 The carpenter stretcheth out *his* rule; he marketh it out with a line; he fitteth it with planes, and he marketh it out with the compass, and maketh it after the figure of a man, according to the beauty of a man; that it may remain in the house.

14 He heweth him down cedars, and taketh the cypress and the oak, which he strengtheneth for himself among the trees of the forest: he planteth an ash, and the rain doth nourish *it*.

15 Then shall it be for a man to burn: for he will take thereof, and warm himself; yea, he kindleth *it*, and baketh bread; yea, he maketh a god, and worshippeth *it*; he maketh it a graven image, and falleth down thereto.

16 He burneth part thereof in the fire; with part thereof he eateth flesh; he roasteth roast, and is satisfied: yea, he warmeth *himself*, and saith, Aha, I am warm, I have seen the fire:

44:6 beside me there is no God. The prophet here emphasizes the uniqueness of God. Yet, at the same time, the prophet recognizes a distinction between "the LORD the King of Israel" and "his redeemer the LORD of hosts."

By applying the personal name "Yahweh" to both the word "King" and the word "Redeemer," Isaiah penetrates the mystery that the Godhead includes God the Father and God the Son.

17 And the residue thereof he maketh a god, *even* his graven image: he falleth down unto it, and worshippeth *it*, and prayeth unto it, and saith, Deliver me; for thou *art* my god.

18 They have not known nor understood: for he hath shut their eyes, that they cannot see; *and* their hearts, that they cannot understand.

19 And none considereth in his heart, neither *is there* knowledge nor understanding to say, I have burned part of it in the fire; yea, also I have baked bread upon the coals thereof; I have roasted flesh, and eaten *it*: and shall I make the residue thereof an abomination? shall I fall down to the stock of a tree?

20 He feedeth on ashes: a deceived heart hath turned him aside, that he cannot deliver his soul, nor say, *Is there* not a lie in my right hand?

21 Remember these, O Jacob and Israel; for thou *art* my servant: I have formed thee; thou *art* my servant: O Israel, thou shalt not be forgotten of me.

22 I have blotted out, as a thick cloud, thy transgressions, and, as a cloud, thy sins: return unto me; for I have redeemed thee.

23 Sing, O ye heavens; for the LORD hath done *it*: shout, ye lower parts of the earth: break forth into singing, ye mountains, O forest, and every tree therein: for the LORD hath redeemed Jacob, and glorified himself in Israel.

24 Thus saith the LORD, thy redeemer, and he that formed thee from the womb, I *am* the LORD that maketh all *things*; that stretcheth forth the heavens alone; that spreadeth abroad the earth by myself;

25 That frustrateth the tokens of the liars, and maketh diviners mad; that turneth wise *men* backward, and maketh their knowledge foolish;

26 That confirmeth the word of his servant, and performeth the counsel of his messengers; that saith to Jerusalem, Thou shalt be inhabited; and to the cities of Judah, Ye shall be built, and I will raise up the decayed places thereof:

27 That saith to the deep, Be dry, and I will dry up thy rivers:

28 That saith of Cyrus, *He is* my shepherd, and shall perform all my pleasure: even saying to Jerusalem, Thou shalt be built; and to the temple, Thy foundation shall be laid.

CHAPTER 45
God Commissions Cyrus

1 Thus saith the LORD to his anointed, to Cyrus, whose right hand I have holden, to subdue nations before him; and I will loose the loins of kings, to open before him the two leaved gates; and the gates shall not be shut;

2 I will go before thee, and make the crooked places straight: I will break in pieces the gates of brass, and cut in sunder the bars of iron:

3 And I will give thee the treasures of darkness, and hidden riches of secret places, that thou mayest know that I, the LORD, which call *thee* by thy name, *am* the God of Israel.

4 For Jacob my servant's sake, and Israel mine elect, I have even called thee by thy name: I have surnamed thee, though thou hast not known me.

5 I *am* the LORD, and *there is* none else, *there is* no God beside me: I girded thee, though thou hast not known me:

Cross references
19 Isa. 46:8
20 Hos. 4:12; Rom. 1:21; 2Thess. 2:11
21 Isa. 44:1, 2
22 1Cor. 6:20; 1Pet. 1:18, 19
23 Ps. 69:34; 96:11, 12; Isa. 42:10; 49:13; Jer. 51:48; Rev. 18:20
24 Job 9:8; Ps. 104:2; Isa. 40:22; 42:5; 43:1, 14; 44:6; 45:12; 51:13
25 Isa. 47:13; Jer. 50:36; 1Cor. 1:20
26 Zech. 1:6
27 Jer. 50:38; 51:32, 36
28 2Chr. 36:22, 23; Ezra 1:1; Isa. 45:13
1 Isa. 41:2, 13; Dan. 5:30
2 Ps. 107:16; Isa. 40:4
3 Ex. 33:12, 17; Isa. 41:23; 43:1; 49:1
4 Isa. 44:1; 1Thess. 4:5
5 Deut. 4:35, 39; 32:39

44:21–28 This is one of the most amazing prophecies in all of Scripture. In verse 28, Cyrus, the king of Persia, is named as the coming deliverer of the Jews more than 140 years in advance. The structure of the poem in verses 24–28 is arranged deliberately to end with a definite climax, which introduces Cyrus as the deliverer who will allow Jews to return to their homeland. Thus it is announced that Jerusalem will again be inhabited and the surrounding cities will be rebuilt. This is Cyrus II (554–529 B.C.), known as Cyrus the Great in Persian history. The name "Cyrus" was probably an early dynastic throne name used by Persian kings (similar to the Roman's use of "Caesar.") In 539 B.C., Cyrus conquered Babylon and authorized the return of the exiled Jews to rebuild their homeland, including Jerusalem and the foundation of the temple (cf. Ezra 1:2). In A.D. 1879, the discovery of the Cyrus Cylinder (536 B.C.), further affirmed the biblical account. This cylindrical stone is engraved with a declaration by Cyrus in which he states that because the people in Babylon received his rule without violence, he set about to remove the yoke of bondage and restore the buildings of those in Babylon.

45:1–4 Yahweh Himself has declared Cyrus to be "anointed" (Hebr. *meshiach*, messiah). This term originated with the Israelite custom of anointing kings and leaders. Cyrus is given this honorific title only in the sense that he will deliver the Jews from Babylonian bondage; no other Gentile is ever referred to by this title in Scripture. In this passage, Cyrus is deliberately named in advance to reassure the Jews that the God of Israel indeed is still in control of human events.

6 That they may know from the rising of the sun, and from the west, that *there is* none beside me. I *am* the Lord, and *there is* none else.

7 I form the light, and create darkness: I make peace, and create evil: I the Lord do all these *things*.

8 Drop down, ye heavens, from above, and let the skies pour down righteousness: let the earth open, and let them bring forth salvation, and let righteousness spring up together; I the Lord have created it.

The Lord of Creation and History

9 Woe unto him that striveth with his Maker! *Let* the potsherd *strive* with the potsherds of the earth. Shall the clay say to him that fashioneth it, What makest thou? or thy work, He hath no hands?

10 Woe unto him that saith unto *his* father, What begettest thou? or to the woman, What hast thou brought forth?

11 Thus saith the Lord, the Holy One of Israel, and his Maker, Ask me of things to come concerning my sons, and concerning the work of my hands command ye me.

12 I have made the earth, and created man upon it: I, *even* my hands, have stretched out the heavens, and all their host have I commanded.

13 I have raised him up in righteousness, and I will direct all his ways: he shall build my city, and he shall let go my captives, not for price nor reward, saith the Lord of hosts.

14 Thus saith the Lord, The labour of Egypt, and merchandise of Ethiopia and of the Sabeans, men of stature, shall come over unto thee, and they shall be thine: they shall come after thee; in chains they shall come over, and they shall fall down unto thee, they shall make supplication unto thee, *saying*, Surely God *is* in thee; and *there is* none else, *there is* no God.

15 Verily thou *art* a God that hidest thyself, O God of Israel, the Saviour.

16 They shall be ashamed, and also confounded, all of them: they shall go to confusion together *that are* makers of idols.

17 *But* Israel shall be saved in the Lord with an everlasting salvation: ye shall not be ashamed nor confounded world without end.

18 For thus saith the Lord that created the heavens; God himself that formed the earth and made it; he hath established it, he created it not in vain, he formed it to be inhabited: I *am* the Lord; and *there is* none else.

19 I have not spoken in secret, in a dark place of the earth: I said not unto the seed of Jacob, Seek ye me in vain: I the Lord speak righteousness, I declare things that are right.

The False Gods of Babylon

20 Assemble yourselves and come; draw near together, ye *that are* escaped of the nations: they have no knowledge that set up the wood of their graven image, and pray unto a god *that* cannot save.

21 Tell ye, and bring *them* near; yea, let them take counsel together: who hath declared this from ancient time? *who* hath told it from that time? *have* not I the Lord? and *there is* no God else beside me; a just God and a Saviour; *there is* none beside me.

22 Look unto me, and be ye saved, all the ends of the earth: for I *am* God, and *there is* none else.

23 I have sworn by myself, the word is gone out of my mouth *in* righteousness, and shall not return, That unto me every knee shall bow, every tongue shall swear.

24 Surely, shall *one* say, in the Lord have I righteousness and strength: *even* to him shall *men* come; and all that are incensed against him shall be ashamed.

25 In the Lord shall all the seed of Israel be justified, and shall glory.

CHAPTER 46

1 Bel boweth down, Nebo stoopeth, their idols were upon the beasts, and upon the cattle: your carriages *were* heavy loaden; *they are* a burden to the weary *beast*.

2 They stoop, they bow down together; they could not deliver the burden, but themselves are gone into captivity.

3 Hearken unto me, O house of Jacob, and all the remnant of the house of Israel, which are borne *by me* from the belly, which are carried from the womb:

4 And *even* to *your* old age I am he; and *even* to hoar hairs will I carry *you*: I have made, and I will bear; even I will carry, and will deliver *you*.

5 To whom will ye liken me, and make *me*

Cross references

6 Ps. 102:15; Isa. 37:20; Mal. 1:11

7 Amos 3:6

8 Ps. 72:3; 85:11

9 Isa. 29:16; 64:8; Jer. 18:6; Rom. 9:20

11 Isa. 29:23; Jer. 31:9

12 Gen. 1:26, 27; 2:1; Isa. 42:5; Jer. 27:5

13 2Chr. 36:22, 23; Ezra 1:1; Isa. 41:2; 44:28; 52:3; Rom. 3:24

14 Ps. 68:31; 72:10, 11; 149:8; Isa. 45:5; 49:23; 60:9, 10, 14, 16; Zech. 8:22, 23; 1Cor. 14:25

15 Ps. 44:24; Isa. 8:17; 57:17

16 Isa. 44:11

17 Isa. 26:4; 45:25; Rom. 11:26

18 Isa. 42:5; 45:5

19 Deut. 30:11; Ps. 19:8; 119:137, 138; Isa. 48:16

20 Isa. 44:17-19; 46:7; 48:7; Rom. 1:22, 23

21 Isa. 41:22; 43:9; 44:7; 8; 45:5, 14, 18; 46:9, 10; 48:3, 14

22 Ps. 22:27; 65:5

23 Phil. 2:10; Heb. 6:13

1 Jer. 10:5

2 Jer. 48:7

4 Ps. 48:14

45:13–19 raised him up in righteousness. This does not necessarily imply that Cyrus himself was a true believer. Rather, God providentially raised him up as an act of His righteousness to Israel. Cyrus even subsidized the reconstruction.

equal, and compare me, that we may be like?

6 They lavish gold out of the bag, and weigh silver in the balance, *and* hire a goldsmith; and he maketh it a god: they fall down, yea, they worship.

7 They bear him upon the shoulder, they carry him, and set him in his place, and he standeth; from his place shall he not remove: yea, *one* shall cry unto him, yet can he not answer, nor save him out of his trouble.

8 Remember this, and shew yourselves men: bring *it* again to mind, O ye transgressors.

9 Remember the former things of old: for I *am* God, and *there is* none else; *I am* God, and *there is* none like me,

10 Declaring the end from the beginning, and from ancient times *the things* that are not *yet* done, saying, My counsel shall stand, and I will do all my pleasure:

11 Calling a ravenous bird from the east, the man that executeth my counsel from a far country: yea, I have spoken *it*, I will also bring it to pass; I have purposed *it*, I will also do it.

12 Hearken unto me, ye stouthearted, that *are* far from righteousness:

13 I bring near my righteousness; it shall not be far off, and my salvation shall not tarry: and I will place salvation in Zion for Israel my glory.

CHAPTER 47
Judgment on Babylon

1 Come down, and sit in the dust, O virgin daughter of Babylon, sit on the ground: *there is* no throne, O daughter of the Chaldeans: for thou shalt no more be called tender and delicate.

2 Take the millstones, and grind meal: uncover thy locks, make bare the leg, uncover the thigh, pass over the rivers.

3 Thy nakedness shall be uncovered, yea, thy shame shall be seen: I will take vengeance, and I will not meet *thee as* a man.

4 *As for* our redeemer, the LORD of hosts *is* his name, the Holy One of Israel.

5 Sit thou silent, and get thee into darkness, O daughter of the Chaldeans: for thou

shalt no more be called, The lady of kingdoms.

6 I was wroth with my people, I have polluted mine inheritance, and given them into thine hand: thou didst shew them no mercy; upon the ancient hast thou very heavily laid thy yoke.

7 And thou saidst, I shall be a lady for ever: *so* that thou didst not lay these *things* to thy heart, neither didst remember the latter end of it.

8 Therefore hear now this, *thou that art* given to pleasures, that dwellest carelessly, that sayest in thine heart, I *am*, and none else beside me; I shall not sit *as* a widow, neither shall I know the loss of children:

9 But these two *things* shall come to thee in a moment in one day, the loss of children, and widowhood: they shall come upon thee in their perfection for the multitude of thy sorceries, *and* for the great abundance of thine enchantments.

10 For thou hast trusted in thy wickedness: thou hast said, None seeth me. Thy wisdom and thy knowledge, it hath perverted thee; and thou hast said in thine heart, I *am*, and none else beside me.

11 Therefore shall evil come upon thee; thou shalt not know from whence it riseth: and mischief shall fall upon thee; thou shalt not be able to put it off: and desolation shall come upon thee suddenly, *which* thou shalt not know.

12 Stand now with thine enchantments, and with the multitude of thy sorceries, wherein thou hast laboured from thy youth; if so be thou shalt be able to profit, if so be thou mayest prevail.

13 Thou art wearied in the multitude of thy counsels. Let now the astrologers, the stargazers, the monthly prognosticators, stand up, and save thee from *these things* that shall come upon thee.

14 Behold, they shall be as stubble; the fire shall burn them; they shall not deliver themselves from the power of the flame: *there shall* not *be* a coal to warm at, *nor* fire to sit before it.

15 Thus shall they be unto thee with whom thou hast laboured, *even* thy merchants, from thy youth: they shall wander every one to his quarter; none shall save thee.

---

6 Isa. 40:19; 41:6; 44:12, 19; Jer. 10:3

7 Isa. 45:20; Jer. 10:5

8 Isa. 44:19; 47:7

9 Deut. 32:7; Isa. 45:5, 21

10 Ps. 33:11

11 Num. 23:19

12 Ps. 76:5; Rom. 10:3

13 Isa. 51:5; 62:11; Hab. 2:3; Rom. 1:17; 3:21

1 Isa. 3:26; Jer. 48:18

2 Ex. 11:5; Judg. 16:21; Matt. 24:41

3 Isa. 3:17; 20:4; Jer. 13:22, 26; Nah. 3:5; Rom. 12:19

4 Isa. 43:3, 14; Jer. 50:34

5 1Sam. 2:9; Isa. 13:19; 47:7; Dan. 2:37

6 Deut. 28:50; 2Sam. 24:14; 2Chr. 28:9; Isa. 43:28; Zech. 1:15

7 Deut. 32:29; Isa. 46:8; 47:5; Rev. 18:7

8 Isa. 47:10; Zeph. 2:15; Rev. 18:7

9 Isa. 51:19; Nah. 3:4; 1Thess. 5:3

10 Ps. 52:7; Isa. 29:15; 47:8; Ezek. 8:12; 9:9

11 1Thess. 5:3

13 Dan. 2:2

15 Rev. 18:11

47:1–5 In spite of its splendor, ancient Babylon was built upon the dust of the desert of Shinar. Babylon is subsequently pictured as a deposed queen, a naked slave girl reduced to sitting in the dust. She is no longer "the lady [mistress] of kingdoms" (v. 5). This same imagery is found in Revelation, where Babylon is called the "great whore" (17:1; 19:2; cf. 18:3).

CHAPTER 48
God Holds the Future

1 Hear ye this, O house of Jacob, which are called by the name of Israel, and are come forth out of the waters of Judah, which swear by the name of the LORD, and make mention of the God of Israel, *but* not in truth, nor in righteousness.

2 For they call themselves of the holy city, and stay themselves upon the God of Israel; The LORD of hosts *is* his name.

3 I have declared the former things from the beginning; and they went forth out of my mouth, and I shewed them; I did *them* suddenly, and they came to pass.

4 Because I knew that thou *art* obstinate, and thy neck *is* an iron sinew, and thy brow brass;

5 I have even from the beginning declared *it* to thee; before it came to pass I shewed *it* thee: lest thou shouldest say, Mine idol hath done them, and my graven image, and my molten image, hath commanded them.

6 Thou hast heard, see all this; and will not ye declare *it*? I have shewed thee new things from this time, even hidden things, and thou didst not know them.

7 They are created now, and not from the beginning; even before the day when thou heardest them not; lest thou shouldest say, Behold, I knew them.

8 Yea, thou heardest not; yea, thou knewest not; yea, from that time *that* thine ear was not opened: for I knew that thou wouldest deal very treacherously, and wast called a transgressor from the womb.

9 For my name's sake will I defer mine anger, and for my praise will I refrain for thee, that I cut thee not off.

10 Behold, I have refined thee, but not with silver; I have chosen thee in the furnace of affliction.

11 For mine own sake, *even* for mine own sake, will I do *it*: for how should *my name* be polluted? and I will not give my glory unto another.

12 Hearken unto me, O Jacob and Israel, my called; I *am* he; I *am* the first, I also *am* the last.

13 Mine hand also hath laid the foundation of the earth, and my right hand hath spanned the heavens: *when* I call unto them, they stand up together.

14 All ye, assemble yourselves, and hear; which among them hath declared these *things*? The LORD hath loved him: he will do his pleasure on Babylon, and his arm *shall be* on the Chaldeans.

15 I, *even* I, have spoken; yea, I have called him: I have brought him, and he shall make his way prosperous.

16 Come ye near unto me, hear ye this; I have not spoken in secret from the beginning; from the time that it was, there *am* I: and now the Lord GOD, and his Spirit, hath sent me.

17 Thus saith the LORD, thy Redeemer, the Holy One of Israel; I *am* the LORD thy God which teacheth thee to profit, which leadeth thee by the way *that* thou shouldest go.

18 O that thou hadst hearkened to my commandments! then had thy peace been as a river, and thy righteousness as the waves of the sea:

19 Thy seed also had been as the sand, and the offspring of thy bowels like the gravel thereof; his name should not have been cut off nor destroyed from before me.

20 Go ye forth of Babylon, flee ye from the Chaldeans, with a voice of singing declare ye, tell this, utter it *even* to the end of the earth; say ye, The LORD hath redeemed his servant Jacob.

21 And they thirsted not *when* he led them through the deserts: he caused the waters to flow out of the rock for them: he clave the rock also, and the waters gushed out.

22 *There is* no peace, saith the LORD, unto the wicked.

CHAPTER 49
Israel, God's Servant

1 Listen, O isles, unto me; and hearken, ye people, from far; The LORD hath called me from the womb; from the bowels of my mother hath he made mention of my name.

2 And he hath made my mouth like a sharp sword; in the shadow of his hand hath he hid me, and made me a polished shaft; in his quiver hath he hid me;

3 And said unto me, Thou *art* my servant, O Israel, in whom I will be glorified.

4 Then I said, I have laboured in vain, I

Cross References
1 Zeph. 1:5
2 Isa. 52:1; Mic. 3:11; Rom. 2:17
3 Josh. 21:45; Isa. 41:22; 42:9; 43:9; 44:7, 8; 45:21; 46:9, 10
4 Ex. 32:9; Deut. 31:27
8 Ps. 58:3
9 Ps. 78:38; 79:9; 106:8; Isa. 43:25; 48:11; Ezek. 20:9, 14, 22, 44
10 Ps. 66:10; Ezek. 22:20-22
12 Deut. 32:39; Isa. 41:4; 44:6; Rev. 1:17; 22:13
13 Ps. 102:25; Isa. 40:26
14 Isa. 41:22; 43:9; 44:7, 28; 45:1, 20, 21
15 Isa. 45:1, 2
16 Isa. 45:19; 61:1; Zech. 2:8, 9, 11
17 Ps. 32:8; Isa. 43:14; 44:6, 24; 48:20
18 Deut. 32:29; Ps. 81:13; 119:165
19 Gen. 22:17; Hos. 1:10
20 Ex. 19:4-6; Isa. 44:22, 23; 52:11; Jer. 50:8; 51:6, 45
21 Ex. 17:6
1 Jer. 1:5
2 Heb. 4:12; Rev. 1:16

49:1–12 The Servant is distinguished from the servant-nation Israel as one who will come forth from it. The Servant is the Messiah, who was formed from the womb to be the Father's Servant and to bring Jacob to Him in repentance. He is further commissioned to be a "light to the Gentiles," quoted in Acts 13:47 as being fulfilled in Jesus Christ.

Israel in the Millennium

By Timothy J. Demy

The unique role of Israel in biblical prophecy and the covenant relationship between Israel and God culminates during the Millennium. God has a blessed future for Israel. In the one thousand years following the second coming of Jesus Christ, Israel and Jerusalem will truly be a holy land and a holy city which will be the focal point of all earthly activity (Isa. 65:18–23). Especially prominent will be the worship of Jesus Christ in the Millennial Temple (Jer. 33:15–22; Ezek. 40—48; Zech. 14:16–21). During the Millennium, Israel will have a very special role, for at this time Israel's final physical and spiritual restoration, as promised throughout the Bible, will occur (Ezek. 37:21–22).

There are four major facets of Israel's final restoration. Each of these is tied to a specific biblical covenant and is expanded upon by subsequent prophecies.

1. The regeneration of Israel occurs during the Tribulation just prior to the second coming of Jesus Christ. The basis of the regeneration is the new covenant (Jer. 31:31–34). The regeneration will be comprised of the confession of Israel's national sin (Jer. 3:11–18, Hos. 5:15) and a pleading for the return of the Messiah (Zech. 12:10; Matt. 23:37–39). The words of Israel's confession are found in Isaiah 53:1–9. As a result of this confession, Israel as a nation will be saved, fulfilling the prophecy of Romans 11:25–27. Israel's pleading for the Messiah's return is prophesied in Isaiah 64:1–12; Joel 2:28–32; and Zechariah 12:10—13:9. The present unbelief of the nation of Israel is not permanent, and Israel's future acceptance of Jesus Christ as the Messiah will be fully realized in the Millennium.

> *God has a blessed future for Israel.*

2. The national regathering of Israel from all over the world occurs after the regeneration. The basis of the regathering is the land covenant of Deuteronomy 29:1—30:20, especially chapter 30, and is prophesied in other passages (Isa. 11:11—12:6; Jer. 16:14–15; Ezek. 11:14–18; 36:24; Amos 9:14–15; Zeph. 3:18–20; Zech. 10:8–12). The regathering will be total and permanent. Never again will God's chosen people be persecuted or dispersed. The wrongs of history will be righted.

3. The permanent possession of the entire land promised to Abraham as well as the realization of the land's complete productivity also occurs during the Millennium. The promise of this possession and productivity is found in the Abrahamic covenant of Genesis 12:1–3; 13:14–17. After Israel's regeneration, all of the promises of this covenant will be fulfilled (cf. Isa. 27:12–13; Jer. 3:1–6; Ezek. 20:42–44; Joel 2:18–27; Matt. 24:31). For the first time in Israel's long history there will be permanent peace, security, and productivity throughout the land.

4. Jesus Christ the Son of David and King of kings will once again fill David's throne. The promise for this event is found in the Davidic covenant of 2 Samuel 7:11–16 and 1 Chronicles 17:10–14. This covenant with David promised an eternal kingdom, an eternal throne, and an eternal ruler. All of these will be realized in the Millennium with Jesus Christ ruling over a redeemed people in their land (Isa. 9:6–7; Jer. 23:5–6; 33:17–26; Amos 9:11–12; Luke 1:32–33). The reign of Christ from the Davidic throne will extend to the Gentile nations as well as Israel, and all people will know that Jesus Christ is Lord.

have spent my strength for nought, and in vain: *yet* surely my judgment *is* with the Lord, and my work with my God.

5 And now, saith the Lord that formed me from the womb *to be* his servant, to bring Jacob again to him, Though Israel be not gathered, yet shall I be glorious in the eyes of the Lord, and my God shall be my strength.

6 And he said, It is a light thing that thou shouldest be my servant to raise up the tribes of Jacob, and to restore the preserved of Israel: I will also give thee for a light to the Gentiles, that thou mayest be my salvation unto the end of the earth.

7 Thus saith the Lord, the Redeemer of Israel, *and* his Holy One, to him whom man despiseth, to him whom the nation abhorreth, to a servant of rulers, Kings shall see and arise, princes also shall worship, because of the Lord that is faithful, *and* the Holy One of Israel, and he shall choose thee.

Zion Will Be Restored

8 Thus saith the Lord, In an acceptable time have I heard thee, and in a day of salvation have I helped thee: and I will preserve thee, and give thee for a covenant of the people, to establish the earth, to cause to inherit the desolate heritages;

9 That thou mayest say to the prisoners, Go forth; to them that *are* in darkness, Shew yourselves. They shall feed in the ways, and their pastures *shall be* in all high places.

10 They shall not hunger nor thirst; neither shall the heat nor sun smite them: for he that hath mercy on them shall lead them, even by the springs of water shall he guide them.

11 And I will make all my mountains a way, and my highways shall be exalted.

12 Behold, these shall come from far: and, lo, these from the north and from the west; and these from the land of Sinim.

13 Sing, O heavens; and be joyful, O earth; and break forth into singing, O mountains: for the Lord hath comforted his people, and will have mercy upon his afflicted.

14 But Zion said, The Lord hath forsaken me, and my Lord hath forgotten me.

15 Can a woman forget her sucking child, that she should not have compassion on the son of her womb? yea, they may forget, yet will I not forget thee.

16 Behold, I have graven thee upon the palms of *my* hands; thy walls *are* continually before me.

17 Thy children shall make haste; thy destroyers and they that made thee waste shall go forth of thee.

18 Lift up thine eyes round about, and behold: all these gather themselves together, *and* come to thee. As I live, saith the Lord, thou shalt surely clothe thee with them all, as with an ornament, and bind them *on thee*, as a bride *doeth*.

19 For thy waste and thy desolate places, and the land of thy destruction, shall even now be too narrow by reason of the inhabitants, and they that swallowed thee up shall be far away.

20 The children which thou shalt have, after thou hast lost the other, shall say again in thine ears, The place *is* too strait for me: give place to me that I may dwell.

21 Then shalt thou say in thine heart, Who hath begotten me these, seeing I have lost my children, and am desolate, a captive, and removing to and fro? and who hath brought up these? Behold, I was left alone; these, where *had* they *been*?

22 Thus saith the Lord God, Behold, I will lift up mine hand to the Gentiles, and set up my standard to the people: and they shall bring thy sons in *their* arms, and thy daughters shall be carried upon *their* shoulders.

23 And kings shall be thy nursing fathers, and their queens thy nursing mothers: they shall bow down to thee with *their* face toward the earth, and lick up the dust of thy feet; and thou shalt know that I *am* the Lord: for they shall not be ashamed that wait for me.

24 Shall the prey be taken from the mighty, or the lawful captive delivered?

25 But thus saith the Lord, Even the captives of the mighty shall be taken away, and the prey of the terrible shall be delivered: for I will contend with him that contendeth with thee, and I will save thy children.

---

5 Isa. 49:1; Matt. 23:37
6 Isa. 42:6; 60:3; Luke 2:32; Acts 13:47; 26:18
7 Ps. 72:10, 11; Isa. 49:23; 53:3; Matt. 26:67
8 Ps. 69:13; Isa. 42:6; 2Cor. 6:2
9 Isa. 42:7; Zech. 9:12
10 Ps. 23:2; 121:6; Rev. 7:16
11 Isa. 40:4
12 Isa. 43:5, 6
13 Isa. 44:23
14 Isa. 40:27
15 Ps. 103:13; Mal. 3:17; Matt. 7:11; Rom. 11:29
16 Ex. 13:9; Song 8:6
17 Isa. 49:19
18 Prov. 17:6; Isa. 60:4
19 Isa. 54:1, 2; Zech. 2:4; 10:10
20 Isa. 60:4; Matt. 3:9; Rom. 11:11, 12
22 Isa. 60:4; 66:20
23 Ps. 34:22; 72:9, 11; Isa. 49:7; 52:15; 60:16; Mic. 7:17; Rom. 5:5; 9:33; 10:11
24 Matt. 12:29; Luke 11:21, 22

49:8 covenant of the people. This is a reference to the new covenant (testament) by which Christ will gather believers from far (cf. 42:6).

49:16 I have graven [Hebr. *shaqaq*, "to carve, cut, engrave"] **thee upon the palms of my hands.** This statement hints at the eternal security of the salvation of God's people. They are inseparably united to Him. God promises Israel that His new covenant with the Gentiles does not negate His old covenant with Israel (vv. 13–26). Ultimately, however, God will, through the nail-scarred hands of His Son, Jesus Christ, bring both the Gentiles and His people together into one people of God.

26 And I will feed them that oppress thee with their own flesh; and they shall be drunken with their own blood, as with sweet wine: and all flesh shall know that I the LORD *am* thy Saviour and thy Redeemer, the mighty One of Jacob.

CHAPTER 50
God Helps Those Who Trust Him

1 Thus saith the LORD, Where *is* the bill of your mother's divorcement, whom I have put away? or which of my creditors *is it* to whom I have sold you? Behold, for your iniquities have ye sold yourselves, and for your transgressions is your mother put away.
2 Wherefore, when I came, *was there* no man? when I called, *was there* none to answer? Is my hand shortened at all, that it cannot redeem? or have I no power to deliver? behold, at my rebuke I dry up the sea, I make the rivers a wilderness: their fish stinketh, because *there is* no water, and dieth for thirst.
3 I clothe the heavens with blackness, and I make sackcloth their covering.
4 The Lord GOD hath given me the tongue of the learned, that I should know how to speak a word in season to *him that is* weary: he wakeneth morning by morning, he wakeneth mine ear to hear as the learned.
5 The Lord GOD hath opened mine ear, and I was not rebellious, neither turned away back.
6 I gave my back to the smiters, and my cheeks to them that plucked off the hair: I hid not my face from shame and spitting.
7 For the Lord GOD will help me; therefore shall I not be confounded: therefore have I set my face like a flint, and I know that I shall not be ashamed.
8 *He is* near that justifieth me; who will contend with me? let us stand together: who *is* mine adversary? let him come near to me.

9 Behold, the Lord GOD will help me; who *is* he *that* shall condemn me? lo, they all shall wax old as a garment; the moth shall eat them up.
10 Who *is* among you that feareth the LORD, that obeyeth the voice of his servant, that walketh *in* darkness, and hath no light? let him trust in the name of the LORD, and stay upon his God.
11 Behold, all ye that kindle a fire, that compass *yourselves* about with sparks: walk in the light of your fire, and in the sparks *that* ye have kindled. This shall ye have of mine hand; ye shall lie down in sorrow.

CHAPTER 51
Comforting Words for Jerusalem

1 Hearken to me, ye that follow after righteousness, ye that seek the LORD: look unto the rock *whence* ye are hewn, and to the hole of the pit *whence* ye are digged.
2 Look unto Abraham your father, and unto Sarah *that* bare you: for I called him alone, and blessed him, and increased him.
3 For the LORD shall comfort Zion: he will comfort all her waste places; and he will make her wilderness like Eden, and her desert like the garden of the LORD; joy and gladness shall be found therein, thanksgiving, and the voice of melody.
4 Hearken unto me, my people; and give ear unto me, O my nation: for a law shall proceed from me, and I will make my judgment to rest for a light of the people.
5 My righteousness *is* near; my salvation is gone forth, and mine arms shall judge the people; the isles shall wait upon me, and on mine arm shall they trust.
6 Lift up your eyes to the heavens, and look upon the earth beneath: for the heavens shall vanish away like smoke, and the earth shall wax old like a garment, and they that dwell therein shall die in like manner: but my salvation shall be for ever, and my righteousness shall not be abolished.

Cross references:
26 Isa. 60:16; Rev. 14:20; 16:6
1 Deut. 24:1; Jer. 3:8; Matt. 18:25
2 Ex. 7:18, 21; 14:21; Josh. 3:16; Nah. 1:4
3 Ex. 10:21; Rev. 6:12
4 Ex. 4:11; Matt. 11:28
5 Ps. 40:6-8; Matt. 26:39; John 14:31; Phil. 2:8; Heb. 10:5
6 Lam. 3:30; Matt. 26:67; 27:26; John 18:22
7 Ezek. 3:8, 9
8 Rom. 8:32-34
9 Job 13:28; Ps. 102:26; Isa. 51:6, 8
10 2Chr. 20:20; Ps. 20:7; 23:4
11 Ps. 16:4; John 9:39
1 Isa. 51:7; Rom. 9:30-32
2 Gen. 12:1, 2; 24:1, 35; Rom. 4:1, 16; Heb. 11:11, 12
3 Ps. 102:13; Joel 2:3
5 Ps. 67:4; Rom. 1:16, 17
6 Matt. 24:35; 2Pet. 3:10, 12

50:1 Where is the bill of your mother's divorcement? This is a rhetorical question, and the implied answer is that there is none. Contrast Jeremiah 3:8, where the Lord states that He divorced Israel and threatens Judah with the same treatment. In spite of their sins, God never severed Himself from the Davidic line.

50:6 I gave my back to the smiters. The fulfillment of this statement is found in Matthew 27:26 in relation to the scourging that Christ received. The plucking of His hair refers to the plucking out of His beard. And the reference to spitting is verified in Matthew 27:30; Mark 14:65; 15:19. The Servant is again seen as an individual suffering for the sins of the people.

51:6 the heavens . . . shall vanish away . . . and the earth. Isaiah looks to the end of the corridor of human history to when the heavens (atmosphere) and the earth will cease. He likens the earth to an old garment, meaning the earth will one day simply wear out, and only the ransomed and redeemed shall return with singing unto Jerusalem and experience everlasting joy.

7 Hearken unto me, ye that know righteousness, the people in whose heart *is* my law; fear ye not the reproach of men, neither be ye afraid of their revilings.

8 For the moth shall eat them up like a garment, and the worm shall eat them like wool: but my righteousness shall be for ever, and my salvation from generation to generation.

9 Awake, awake, put on strength, O arm of the LORD; awake, as in the ancient days, in the generations of old. *Art* thou not it that hath cut Rahab, *and* wounded the dragon?

10 *Art* thou not it which hath dried the sea, the waters of the great deep; that hath made the depths of the sea a way for the ransomed to pass over?

11 Therefore the redeemed of the LORD shall return, and come with singing unto Zion; and everlasting joy *shall be* upon their head: they shall obtain gladness and joy; *and* sorrow and mourning shall flee away.

12 I, *even* I, *am* he that comforteth you: who *art* thou, that thou shouldest be afraid of a man *that* shall die, and of the son of man *which* shall be made *as* grass;

13 And forgettest the LORD thy maker, that hath stretched forth the heavens, and laid the foundations of the earth; and hast feared continually every day because of the fury of the oppressor, as if he were ready to destroy? and where *is* the fury of the oppressor?

14 The captive exile hasteneth that he may be loosed, and that he should not die in the pit, nor that his bread should fail.

15 But I *am* the LORD thy God, that divided the sea, whose waves roared: The LORD of hosts *is* his name.

16 And I have put my words in thy mouth, and I have covered thee in the shadow of mine hand, that I may plant the heavens, and lay the foundations of the earth, and say unto Zion, Thou *art* my people.

17 Awake, awake, stand up, O Jerusalem, which hast drunk at the hand of the LORD the cup of his fury; thou hast drunken the dregs of the cup of trembling, *and* wrung *them* out.

18 *There is* none to guide her among all the sons *whom* she hath brought forth; neither

is there any that taketh her by the hand of all the sons *that* she hath brought up.

19 These two *things* are come unto thee; who shall be sorry for thee? desolation, and destruction, and the famine, and the sword: by whom shall I comfort thee?

20 Thy sons have fainted, they lie at the head of all the streets, as a wild bull in a net: they are full of the fury of the LORD, the rebuke of thy God.

21 Therefore hear now this, thou afflicted, and drunken, but not with wine:

22 Thus saith thy Lord the LORD, and thy God *that* pleadeth the cause of his people, Behold, I have taken out of thine hand the cup of trembling, *even* the dregs of the cup of my fury; thou shalt no more drink it again:

23 But I will put it into the hand of them that afflict thee; which have said to thy soul, Bow down, that we may go over: and thou hast laid thy body as the ground, and as the street, to them that went over.

CHAPTER 52
Zion Will Escape

1 Awake, awake; put on thy strength, O Zion; put on thy beautiful garments, O Jerusalem, the holy city: for henceforth there shall no more come into thee the uncircumcised and the unclean.

2 Shake thyself from the dust; arise, *and* sit down, O Jerusalem: loose thyself from the bands of thy neck, O captive daughter of Zion.

3 For thus saith the LORD, Ye have sold yourselves for nought; and ye shall be redeemed without money.

4 For thus saith the Lord GOD, My people went down aforetime into Egypt to sojourn there; and the Assyrian oppressed them without cause.

5 Now therefore, what have I here, saith the LORD, that my people is taken away for nought? they that rule over them make them to howl, saith the LORD; and my name continually every day *is* blasphemed.

6 Therefore my people shall know my name: therefore *they shall know* in that day that I *am* he that doth speak: behold, *it is* I.

Cross references (center column):

7 Matt. 10:28

9 Ps. 44:1, 23; 74:13, 14; Rev. 11:17

10 Ex. 14:21; Isa. 43:16

11 Isa. 35:10

12 Ps. 118:6; Isa. 40:6; 51:3; 2Cor. 1:3; 1Pet. 1:24

13 Job 9:8; 20:7; Ps. 104:2; Isa. 40:22; 42:5; 44:24

14 Zech. 9:11

15 Job 26:12; Ps. 74:13; Jer. 31:35

16 Deut. 18:18; Isa. 49:2; 59:21; 65:17; 66:22; John 3:34

17 Deut. 28:28, 34; Job 21:20; Ps. 60:3; 75:8; Isa. 52:1; Jer. 25:15, 16; Ezek. 23:32-34; Zech. 12:2; Rev. 14:10

19 Isa. 47:9; Amos 7:2

20 Lam. 2:11, 12

21 Isa. 51:17; Lam. 3:15

22 Jer. 50:34

23 Ps. 66:11, 12; Jer. 25:17, 26, 28; Zech. 12:2

1 Matt. 4:5; Rev. 21:2, 27

3 Jer. 15:13

4 Gen. 46:6; Acts 7:14

5 Ezek. 36:20, 23

52:1–12 This passage on the Servant of the Lord who will suffer for the sins of His people now carries the theme of God's deliverance for His people to new heights. The prophet foresees the Millennium, when Jerusalem will be "the holy city." At that time the "uncircumcised and the unclean" (the unrighteous) will no longer enter her gates.

7 How beautiful upon the mountains are the feet of him that bringeth good tidings, that publisheth peace; that bringeth good tidings of good, that publisheth salvation; that saith unto Zion, Thy God reigneth!

8 Thy watchmen shall lift up the voice; with the voice together shall they sing: for they shall see eye to eye, when the LORD shall bring again Zion.

9 Break forth into joy, sing together, ye waste places of Jerusalem: for the LORD hath comforted his people, he hath redeemed Jerusalem.

10 The LORD hath made bare his holy arm in the eyes of all the nations; and all the ends of the earth shall see the salvation of our God.

11 Depart ye, depart ye, go ye out from thence, touch no unclean *thing*; go ye out of the midst of her; be ye clean, that bear the vessels of the LORD.

12 For ye shall not go out with haste, nor go by flight: for the LORD will go before you; and the God of Israel *will be* your rereward.

The Suffering Servant

13 Behold, my servant shall deal prudently, he shall be exalted and extolled, and be very high.

14 As many were astonied at thee; his visage was so marred more than any man,

and his form more than the sons of men:

15 So shall he sprinkle many nations; the kings shall shut their mouths at him: for *that* which had not been told them shall they see; and *that* which they had not heard shall they consider.

CHAPTER 53

1 Who hath believed our report? and to whom is the arm of the LORD revealed?

2 For he shall grow up before him as a tender plant, and as a root out of a dry ground: he hath no form nor comeliness; and when we shall see him, *there is* no beauty that we should desire him.

3 He is despised and rejected of men; a man of sorrows, and acquainted with grief: and we hid as it were *our* faces from him; he was despised, and we esteemed him not.

4 Surely he hath borne our griefs, and carried our sorrows: yet we did esteem him stricken, smitten of God, and afflicted.

5 But he *was* wounded for our transgressions, *he was* bruised for our iniquities: the chastisement of our peace *was* upon him; and with his stripes we are healed.

6 All we like sheep have gone astray; we have turned every one to his own way; and the LORD hath laid on him the iniquity of us all.

7 He was oppressed, and he was afflicted,

Cross references (center column):

7 Nah. 1:15; Rom. 10:15

10 Ps. 98:2, 3; Luke 3:6

11 Lev. 22:2; Zech. 2:6, 7; Rev. 18:4

13 Phil. 2:9

14 Ps. 22:6, 7; Isa. 53:2, 3

15 Isa. 49:7, 23; 55:5; Ezek. 36:25; Acts 2:33; Rom. 15:21; 16:25, 26; Eph. 3:5, 9; Heb. 9:13, 14

2 Isa. 11:1; 52:14; Mark 9:12

3 Ps. 22:6; John 1:10, 11

4 Matt. 8:17

5 Rom. 4:25; 1 Pet. 2:24

6 Ps. 119:176; 1 Pet. 2:25

7 Matt. 26:63; 27:12, 14; Mark 14:61; 15:5

52:7 the feet of him that bringeth good tidings. This phrase is used in Nahum 1:15 and is repeated in the New Testament (Rom. 10:15; Eph. 6:15). To bring "good tidings" (Hebr. *mebaser*) means to "preach" or "carry good news." It certainly anticipates the gospel (good news) of the New Testament and results in peace and salvation.

52:13–15 These verses actually introduce the prophecy of the Suffering Servant in chapter 53. The Servant of the Lord is individualized as the Messiah who suffers for sin. This Servant is the fulfillment of all of Isaiah's messianic prophecies. He is the miraculously-born Son of the Virgin—Immanuel, "God with Us" (7:14; cf. Matt. 1:23), the Branch (11:1) who springs up out of the stump of the Davidic line, and the New David (9:7) who deserves to rule the world because He is the One who suffers redemptively for all humanity. Thus He will not always remain in the state of humiliation, but will be given glory, honor, and a name that is above every name (cf. Phil. 2:9–11). Both the common man and the exalted ruler will stand speechless in awe of Him. His visage (appearance, or face) will become so marred (disfigured) by beatings and scourgings that He will be barely recognizable. The Hebrew word translated "sprinkle" is a technical term found in the Mosaic Law for the sprinkling of blood for

cleansing from sin. The Servant of the Lord is viewed as our High Priest who sprinkles His own blood on the mercy seat for our sins.

53:1–12 The prophet brings us on a personal level to the Messiah, the Son of God, who alone can atone for sin. His message is rejected; His person is refused; and His mission is misunderstood. Nevertheless, His vicarious suffering provides atonement for our sins; and though He suffers death and burial, He will ultimately be exalted. No other Scripture better describes the humble appearance of Jesus as a common rabbi from the city of Nazareth.

53:3–5 Note the parallels to the suffering of Christ in the New Testament: the agony in the garden, His battered face, the severe scourging, and the torture of the crucifixion itself. The New Testament teaches the substitutionary atonement of Christ in similar language: "He hath borne our griefs (Hebr. "spiritual sickness") corresponds to the statement that He "bare our sins in his own body on the tree" (1 Pet. 2:24). The phrase "with his stripes [wounds] we are healed [Hebr. *rapa,* to mend or cure]" refers to our spiritual condition being made whole. In Isaiah the term is always used of spiritual healing and forgiveness (see 19:22; 57:18).

yet he opened not his mouth: he is brought as a lamb to the slaughter, and as a sheep before her shearers is dumb, so he openeth not his mouth.

8 He was taken from prison and from judgment: and who shall declare his generation? for he was cut off out of the land of the living: for the transgression of my people was he stricken.

9 And he made his grave with the wicked, and with the rich in his death; because he had done no violence, neither *was any* deceit in his mouth.

10 Yet it pleased the LORD to bruise him; he hath put *him* to grief: when thou shalt make his soul an offering for sin, he shall see *his* seed, he shall prolong *his* days, and the pleasure of the LORD shall prosper in his hand.

11 He shall see of the travail of his soul, *and* shall be satisfied: by his knowledge shall my righteous servant justify many; for he shall bear their iniquities.

12 Therefore will I divide him *a portion* with the great, and he shall divide the spoil with the strong; because he hath poured out his soul unto death: and he was numbered with the transgressors; and he bare the sin of many, and made intercession for the transgressors.

CHAPTER 54
God Loves Israel

1 Sing, O barren, thou *that* didst not bear; break forth into singing, and cry aloud, thou *that* didst not travail with child: for more *are* the children of the desolate than the children of the married wife, saith the LORD.

2 Enlarge the place of thy tent, and let them stretch forth the curtains of thine habitations: spare not, lengthen thy cords, and strengthen thy stakes;

3 For thou shalt break forth on the right hand and on the left; and thy seed shall inherit the Gentiles, and make the desolate cities to be inhabited.

4 Fear not; for thou shalt not be ashamed:

8 Dan. 9:26
9 Matt. 27:57, 58, 60; 1Pet. 2:22; 1John 3:5
10 Rom. 6:9; 2Cor. 5:21; Eph. 1:5, 9; 2Thess. 1:11; 1Pet. 2:24
11 Isa. 42:1; 49:3; 53:4, 5; John 17:3; Rom. 5:18, 19; 2Pet. 1:3; 1John 2:1
12 Ps. 2:8; Mark 15:28; Luke 22:37; 23:34; Rom. 8:34; Phil. 2:9; Col. 2:15; Heb. 7:25; 9:24; 1John 2:1

1 1Sam. 2:5; Zeph. 3:14; Gal. 4:27
2 Isa. 49:19, 20
3 Isa. 55:5; 61:9
5 Jer. 3:14; Zech. 14:9; Luke 1:32; Rom. 3:29
6 Isa. 62:4
7 Ps. 30:5; Isa. 26:20; 60:10; 2Cor. 4:17
8 Isa. 55:3; Jer. 31:3
9 Gen. 8:21; 9:11; Isa. 55:11; Jer. 31:35, 36
10 Ps. 46:2; 89:33, 34; Isa. 51:6; Matt. 5:18
11 1Chr. 29:2; Rev. 21:18
13 John 6:45

neither be thou confounded; for thou shalt not be put to shame: for thou shalt forget the shame of thy youth, and shalt not remember the reproach of thy widowhood any more.

5 For thy Maker *is* thine husband; the LORD of hosts *is* his name; and thy Redeemer the Holy One of Israel; The God of the whole earth shall he be called.

6 For the LORD hath called thee as a woman forsaken and grieved in spirit, and a wife of youth, when thou wast refused, saith thy God.

7 For a small moment have I forsaken thee; but with great mercies will I gather thee.

8 In a little wrath I hid my face from thee for a moment; but with everlasting kindness will I have mercy on thee, saith the LORD thy Redeemer.

9 For this *is as* the waters of Noah unto me: for *as* I have sworn that the waters of Noah should no more go over the earth; so have I sworn that I would not be wroth with thee, nor rebuke thee.

10 For the mountains shall depart, and the hills be removed; but my kindness shall not depart from thee, neither shall the covenant of my peace be removed, saith the LORD that hath mercy on thee.

Jerusalem in the Future

11 O thou afflicted, tossed with tempest, *and* not comforted, behold, I will lay thy stones with fair colours, and lay thy foundations with sapphires.

12 And I will make thy windows of agates, and thy gates of carbuncles, and all thy borders of pleasant stones.

13 And all thy children *shall be* taught of the LORD; and great *shall be* the peace of thy children.

14 In righteousness shalt thou be established: thou shalt be far from oppression; for thou shalt not fear: and from terror; for it shall not come near thee.

15 Behold, they shall surely gather together,

53:8–9 He was taken from prison and from judgment. This refers to the illegitimate trials to which Jesus was subjected. The reference to the Servant making "his grave with the wicked" anticipates Christ's crucifixion between two thieves (see Matt. 27:38). Also the additional phrase "and with the rich in his death" predicts Jesus' burial in the tomb of the wealthy Joseph of Arimathaea (Matt. 27:57).

53:10 it pleased the Lord to bruise [Hebr. *daka*, "to

utterly crush"] **him.** This refers to the same condition in verse 5. That He was "an offering for sin" (Hebr. *asham*, "guilt offering") involves the trespass offering described in Numbers 5:5–10. The phrase "he shall prolong his days" suggests that the Servant's ministry will not end with His violent death. The life of the Suffering Servant will, like Hezekiah's in chapter 38, be supernaturally extended. This we now know refers to Christ's resurrection.

but not by me: whosoever shall gather together against thee shall fall for thy sake.

16 Behold, I have created the smith that bloweth the coals in the fire, and that bringeth forth an instrument for his work; and I have created the waster to destroy.

17 No weapon that is formed against thee shall prosper; and every tongue *that* shall rise against thee in judgment thou shalt condemn. This *is* the heritage of the servants of the LORD, and their righteousness *is* of me, saith the LORD.

CHAPTER 55
God Offers Mercy

1 Ho, every one that thirsteth, come ye to the waters, and he that hath no money; come ye, buy, and eat; yea, come, buy wine and milk without money and without price.

2 Wherefore do ye spend money for *that which is* not bread? and your labour for *that which* satisfieth not? hearken diligently unto me, and eat ye *that which is* good, and let your soul delight itself in fatness.

3 Incline your ear, and come unto me: hear, and your soul shall live; and I will make an everlasting covenant with you, *even* the sure mercies of David.

4 Behold, I have given him *for* a witness to the people, a leader and commander to the people.

5 Behold, thou shalt call a nation *that* thou knowest not, and nations *that* knew not thee shall run unto thee because of the LORD thy God, and for the Holy One of Israel; for he hath glorified thee.

6 Seek ye the LORD while he may be found, call ye upon him while he is near:

7 Let the wicked forsake his way, and the unrighteous man his thoughts: and let him return unto the LORD, and he will have mercy upon him; and to our God, for he will abundantly pardon.

8 For my thoughts *are* not your thoughts, neither *are* your ways my ways, saith the LORD.

9 For *as* the heavens are higher than the earth, so are my ways higher than your ways, and my thoughts than your thoughts.

10 For as the rain cometh down, and the snow from heaven, and returneth not thither, but watereth the earth, and maketh it bring forth and bud, that it may give seed to the sower, and bread to the eater:

11 So shall my word be that goeth forth out of my mouth: it shall not return unto me void, but it shall accomplish that which I please, and it shall prosper *in the thing* whereto I sent it.

12 For ye shall go out with joy, and be led forth with peace: the mountains and the hills shall break forth before you into singing, and all the trees of the field shall clap *their* hands.

13 Instead of the thorn shall come up the fir tree, and instead of the brier shall come up the myrtle tree: and it shall be to the LORD for a name, for an everlasting sign *that* shall not be cut off.

CHAPTER 56
Sabbath-Keeping

1 Thus saith the LORD, Keep ye judgment, and do justice: for my salvation *is* near to come, and my righteousness to be revealed.

2 Blessed *is* the man *that* doeth this, and the son of man *that* layeth hold on it; that keepeth the sabbath from polluting it, and keepeth his hand from doing any evil.

3 Neither let the son of the stranger, that hath joined himself to the LORD, speak, saying, The LORD hath utterly separated me from his people: neither let the eunuch say, Behold, I *am* a dry tree.

4 For thus saith the LORD unto the eunuchs that keep my sabbaths, and choose *the things* that please me, and take hold of my covenant;

5 Even unto them will I give in mine house and within my walls a place and a name better than of sons and of daughters: I will give them an everlasting name, that shall not be cut off.

6 Also the sons of the stranger, that join themselves to the LORD, to serve him, and to love the name of the LORD, to be his servants, every one that keepeth the sabbath from polluting it, and taketh hold of my covenant;

7 Even them will I bring to my holy mountain, and make them joyful in my house of prayer: their burnt offerings and their sacrifices *shall be* accepted upon mine altar; for mine house shall be called an house of prayer for all people.

1 Matt. 13:44, 46; John 4:14; 7:37; Rev. 3:18; 21:6; 22:17

3 2Sam. 7:8; Ps. 89:28; Jer. 32:40; Matt. 11:28; Acts 13:34

4 Jer. 30:9; Ezek. 34:23; Dan. 9:25; Hos. 3:5; John 18:37; Rev. 1:5

5 Isa. 52:15; 60:5, 9; Acts 3:13; Eph. 2:11, 12

6 Ps. 32:6; Matt. 5:25; 25:11; John 7:34; 8:21; 2Cor. 6:1, 2; Heb. 3:13

7 Ps. 130:7; Isa. 1:16; Jer. 3:12; Zech. 8:17

8 2Sam. 7:19

9 Ps. 103:11

10 Deut. 32:2

11 Isa. 54:9

12 1Chr. 16:33; Ps. 96:12; 98:8; Isa. 14:8; 35:1, 2, 10; 42:11; 65:13, 14

13 Isa. 41:10; Jer. 13:11; Mic. 7:4

1 Isa. 46:13; Matt. 3:2; 4:17; Rom. 13:11, 12

2 Isa. 58:13

3 Deut. 23:1-3; Acts 8:27; 10:1, 2, 34; 17:4; 18:7; 1Pet. 1:1

5 John 1:12; 1Tim. 3:15

7 Matt. 21:13; Mark 11:17; Luke 19:46

56:1–6 Now Isaiah turns his attention to God's message of condemnation to those who refuse His offer of salvation. The blessed man is the one who turns away from "doing any evil." The "sons of the stranger" refer to Gentiles who are willing to love and serve the Lord and thereby partake of His covenant.

8 The Lord GOD which gathereth the outcasts of Israel saith, Yet will I gather *others* to him, beside those that are gathered unto him.

Israel's Leaders Are Condemned

9 All ye beasts of the field, come to devour, *yea*, all ye beasts in the forest.

10 His watchmen *are* blind: they are all ignorant, they *are* all dumb dogs, they cannot bark; sleeping, lying down, loving to slumber.

11 Yea, *they are* greedy dogs *which* can never have enough, and they *are* shepherds *that* cannot understand: they all look to their own way, every one for his gain, from his quarter.

12 Come ye, *say they*, I will fetch wine, and we will fill ourselves with strong drink; and to morrow shall be as this day, *and* much more abundant.

CHAPTER 57
Condemnation of Israel's Idolatry

1 The righteous perisheth, and no man layeth *it* to heart: and merciful men *are* taken away, none considering that the righteous is taken away from the evil *to come*.

2 He shall enter into peace: they shall rest in their beds, *each one* walking *in* his uprightness.

3 But draw near hither, ye sons of the sorceress, the seed of the adulterer and the whore.

4 Against whom do ye sport yourselves? against whom make ye a wide mouth, *and* draw out the tongue? *are* ye not children of transgression, a seed of falsehood,

5 Enflaming yourselves with idols under every green tree, slaying the children in the valleys under the clifts of the rocks?

6 Among the smooth *stones* of the stream *is* thy portion; they, they *are* thy lot: even to them hast thou poured a drink offering, thou hast offered a meat offering. Should I receive comfort in these?

7 Upon a lofty and high mountain hast thou set thy bed: even thither wentest thou up to offer sacrifice.

8 Behind the doors also and the posts hast thou set up thy remembrance: for thou hast discovered *thyself to another* than me, and art gone up; thou hast enlarged thy bed, and made thee *a covenant* with them; thou lovedst their bed where thou sawest *it*.

9 And thou wentest to the king with oint-

ment, and didst increase thy perfumes, and didst send thy messengers far off, and didst debase *thyself even* unto hell.

10 Thou art wearied in the greatness of thy way; *yet* saidst thou not, There is no hope: thou hast found the life of thine hand; therefore thou wast not grieved.

11 And of whom hast thou been afraid or feared, that thou hast lied, and hast not remembered me, nor laid *it* to thy heart? have not I held my peace even of old, and thou fearest me not?

12 I will declare thy righteousness, and thy works; for they shall not profit thee.

13 When thou criest, let thy companies deliver thee; but the wind shall carry them all away; vanity shall take *them*: but he that putteth his trust in me shall possess the land, and shall inherit my holy mountain;

Return to God!

14 And shall say, Cast ye up, cast ye up, prepare the way, take up the stumblingblock out of the way of my people.

15 For thus saith the high and lofty One that inhabiteth eternity, whose name *is* Holy; I dwell in the high and holy *place*, with him also *that is* of a contrite and humble spirit, to revive the spirit of the humble, and to revive the heart of the contrite ones.

16 For I will not contend for ever, neither will I be always wroth: for the spirit should fail before me, and the souls *which* I have made.

17 For the iniquity of his covetousness was I wroth, and smote him: I hid me, and was wroth, and he went on frowardly in the way of his heart.

18 I have seen his ways, and will heal him: I will lead him also, and restore comforts unto him and to his mourners.

19 I create the fruit of the lips; Peace, peace to *him that is* far off, and to *him that is* near, saith the LORD; and I will heal him.

20 But the wicked *are* like the troubled sea, when it cannot rest, whose waters cast up mire and dirt.

21 *There is* no peace, saith my God, to the wicked.

CHAPTER 58
Genuine Fasting

1 Cry aloud, spare not, lift up thy voice like a trumpet, and shew my people their trans-

Cross References

8 Ps. 147:2; John 10:16; Eph. 1:10; 2:14-16
9 Jer. 12:9
10 Matt. 15:14; 23:16; Phil. 3:2
11 Ezek. 34:2, 3; Mic. 3:11
12 Prov. 23:35; Luke 12:19
1 1Kgs. 14:13; 2Kgs. 22:20; Ps. 12:1; Mic. 7:2
2 2Chr. 16:14; Luke 2:29
3 Matt. 16:4
5 Lev. 18:21; 20:2; 2Kgs. 16:3, 4; 17:10; 23:10; Isa. 1:29; Jer. 2:20; 7:31; Ezek. 16:20; 20:26
7 Ezek. 16:16, 25; 23:41
8 Ezek. 16:26, 28; 23:2-20
9 Isa. 30:6; Ezek. 16:33; 23:16; Hos. 7:11; 12:1
10 Jer. 2:25
11 Ps. 50:21; Isa. 51:12, 13
14 Isa. 40:3; 62:10
15 Job 6:10; Ps. 34:18; 51:17; 68:4; 138:6; 147:3; Isa. 61:1; 66:2; Zech. 2:13; Luke 1:49
16 Num. 16:22; Job 34:14; Ps. 85:5; 103:9; Mic. 7:18; Heb. 12:9
17 Isa. 8:17; 9:13; 45:15; Jer. 6:13
19 Eph. 2:17

58:1–2 In the closing chapters of Isaiah (chaps. 58—66) the reader is carried beyond the first coming of Messiah to the future coming when He will bring peace to the world. In His second coming, Christ comes as Lord, Judge, and King

gression, and the house of Jacob their sins.
2 Yet they seek me daily, and delight to know my ways, as a nation that did righteousness, and forsook not the ordinance of their God: they ask of me the ordinances of justice; they take delight in approaching to God.
3 Wherefore have we fasted, *say they*, and thou seest not? *wherefore* have we afflicted our soul, and thou takest no knowledge? Behold, in the day of your fast ye find pleasure, and exact all your labours.
4 Behold, ye fast for strife and debate, and to smite with the fist of wickedness: ye shall not fast as *ye do this* day, to make your voice to be heard on high.
5 Is it such a fast that I have chosen? a day for a man to afflict his soul? *is it* to bow down his head as a bulrush, and to spread sackcloth and ashes *under him*? wilt thou call this a fast, and an acceptable day to the LORD?
6 *Is* not this the fast that I have chosen? to loose the bands of wickedness, to undo the heavy burdens, and to let the oppressed go free, and that ye break every yoke?
7 *Is it* not to deal thy bread to the hungry, and that thou bring the poor that are cast out to thy house? when thou seest the naked, that thou cover him; and that thou hide not thyself from thine own flesh?
8 Then shall thy light break forth as the morning, and thine health shall spring forth speedily: and thy righteousness shall go before thee; the glory of the LORD shall be thy rereward.
9 Then shalt thou call, and the LORD shall answer; thou shalt cry, and he shall say, Here I *am*. If thou take away from the midst of thee the yoke, the putting forth of the finger, and speaking vanity;
10 And *if* thou draw out thy soul to the hungry, and satisfy the afflicted soul; then shall thy light rise in obscurity, and thy darkness *be* as the noonday:
11 And the LORD shall guide thee continually, and satisfy thy soul in drought, and make fat thy bones: and thou shalt be like a watered garden, and like a spring of water, whose waters fail not.
12 And *they that shall be* of thee shall build the old waste places: thou shalt raise up the foundations of many generations; and thou shalt be called, The repairer of the breach, The restorer of paths to dwell in.

Keeping the Sabbath

13 If thou turn away thy foot from the sabbath, *from* doing thy pleasure on my holy day; and call the sabbath a delight, the holy of the LORD, honourable; and shalt honour him, not doing thine own ways, nor finding thine own pleasure, nor speaking *thine own* words:
14 Then shalt thou delight thyself in the LORD; and I will cause thee to ride upon the high places of the earth, and feed thee with the heritage of Jacob thy father: for the mouth of the LORD hath spoken *it*.

CHAPTER 59
Isaiah Reproves Israel

1 Behold, the LORD's hand is not shortened, that it cannot save; neither his ear heavy, that it cannot hear:
2 But your iniquities have separated between you and your God, and your sins have hid *his* face from you, that he will not hear.
3 For your hands are defiled with blood, and your fingers with iniquity; your lips have spoken lies, your tongue hath muttered perverseness.
4 None calleth for justice, nor *any* pleadeth for truth: they trust in vanity, and speak lies; they conceive mischief, and bring forth iniquity.
5 They hatch cockatrice' eggs, and weave the spider's web: he that eateth of their eggs dieth, and that which is crushed breaketh out into a viper.
6 Their webs shall not become garments, neither shall they cover themselves with their works: their works *are* works of iniquity, and the act of violence *is* in their hands.
7 Their feet run to evil, and they make haste to shed innocent blood: their thoughts *are* thoughts of iniquity; wasting and destruction *are* in their paths.
8 The way of peace they know not; and *there is* no judgment in their goings: they have made them crooked paths: whosoever goeth therein shall not know peace.
9 Therefore is judgment far from us, neither doth justice overtake us: we wait for light, but behold obscurity; for brightness, *but* we walk in darkness.
10 We grope for the wall like the blind, and we grope as if *we had* no eyes: we stumble at

Cross references: 3 Lev. 16:29, 31; 23:27; Mal. 3:14 · 4 1Kgs. 21:9, 12, 13 · 5 Lev. 16:29; Esth. 4:3; Job 2:8; Dan. 9:3; Jon. 3:6; Zech. 7:5 · 6 Neh. 5:10-12; Jer. 34:9 · 7 Gen. 29:14; Neh. 5:5; Job 31:19; Ezek. 18:7, 16; Matt. 25:35 · 8 Ex. 14:19; Job 11:17; Isa. 52:12 · 9 Ps. 12:2 · 12 Isa. 61:4 · 13 Isa. 56:2 · 14 Deut. 32:13; 33:29; Job 22:26; Isa. 1:20; 40:5; Mic. 4:4 · 1 Num. 11:23; Isa. 50:2 · 3 Isa. 1:15 · 4 Job 15:35; Ps. 7:14 · 6 Job 8:14, 15 · 7 Prov. 1:16; Rom. 3:15 · 8 Ps. 125:5; Prov. 2:15 · 9 Jer. 8:15 · 10 Deut. 28:29; Job 5:14; Amos 8:9

noonday as in the night; *we are* in desolate places as dead *men*.

11 We roar all like bears, and mourn sore like doves: we look for judgment, but *there is* none; for salvation, *but* it is far off from us.

12 For our transgressions are multiplied before thee, and our sins testify against us: for our transgressions *are* with us; and *as for* our iniquities, we know them;

13 In transgressing and lying against the LORD, and departing away from our God, speaking oppression and revolt, conceiving and uttering from the heart words of falsehood.

14 And judgment is turned away backward, and justice standeth afar off: for truth is fallen in the street, and equity cannot enter.

15 Yea, truth faileth; and he *that* departeth from evil maketh himself a prey: and the LORD saw *it*, and it displeased him that *there was* no judgment.

16 And he saw that *there was* no man, and wondered that *there was* no intercessor: therefore his arm brought salvation unto him; and his righteousness, it sustained him.

17 For he put on righteousness as a breastplate, and an helmet of salvation upon his head; and he put on the garments of vengeance *for* clothing, and was clad with zeal as a cloke.

18 According to *their* deeds, accordingly he will repay, fury to his adversaries, recompence to his enemies; to the islands he will repay recompence.

19 So shall they fear the name of the LORD from the west, and his glory from the rising of the sun. When the enemy shall come in like a flood, the Spirit of the LORD shall lift up a standard against him.

20 And the Redeemer shall come to Zion, and unto them that turn from transgression in Jacob, saith the LORD.

21 As for me, this *is* my covenant with them, saith the LORD; My spirit that *is* upon thee, and my words which I have put in thy mouth, shall not depart out of thy mouth, nor out of the mouth of thy seed, nor out of the mouth of thy seed's seed, saith the LORD, from henceforth and for ever.

CHAPTER 60
The Future Glory of Zion

1 Arise, shine; for thy light is come, and the glory of the LORD is risen upon thee.

2 For, behold, the darkness shall cover the earth, and gross darkness the people: but the LORD shall arise upon thee, and his glory shall be seen upon thee.

3 And the Gentiles shall come to thy light, and kings to the brightness of thy rising.

4 Lift up thine eyes round about, and see: all they gather themselves together, they come to thee: thy sons shall come from far, and thy daughters shall be nursed at *thy* side.

5 Then thou shalt see, and flow together, and thine heart shall fear, and be enlarged; because the abundance of the sea shall be converted unto thee, the forces of the Gentiles shall come unto thee.

6 The multitude of camels shall cover thee, the dromedaries of Midian and Ephah; all they from Sheba shall come: they shall bring gold and incense; and they shall shew forth the praises of the LORD.

7 All the flocks of Kedar shall be gathered together unto thee, the rams of Nebaioth shall minister unto thee: they shall come up with acceptance on mine altar, and I will glorify the house of my glory.

8 Who *are* these *that* fly as a cloud, and as the doves to their windows?

9 Surely the isles shall wait for me, and the ships of Tarshish first, to bring thy sons from far, their silver and their gold with them, unto the name of the LORD thy God, and to the Holy One of Israel, because he hath glorified thee.

10 And the sons of strangers shall build up thy walls, and their kings shall minister unto thee: for in my wrath I smote thee, but in my favour have I had mercy on thee.

11 Therefore thy gates shall be open continually; they shall not be shut day nor night; that *men* may bring unto thee the forces of the Gentiles, and *that* their kings *may be* brought.

12 For the nation and kingdom that will not serve thee shall perish; yea, *those* nations shall be utterly wasted.

13 The glory of Lebanon shall come unto thee, the fir tree, the pine tree, and the box together, to beautify the place of my sanctuary; and I will make the place of my feet glorious.

14 The sons also of them that afflicted thee shall come bending unto thee; and all they that despised thee shall bow themselves

---

11 Isa. 38:14; Ezek. 7:16

13 Matt. 12:34

15 Ps. 98:1; Isa. 63:5; Ezek. 22:30; Mark 6:6

17 Eph. 6:14, 17; 1Thess. 5:8

18 Isa. 63:6

19 Ps. 113:3; Mal. 1:11; Rev. 12:15

20 Rom. 11:26

21 Heb. 8:10; 10:16

1 Mal. 4:2; Eph. 5:14

3 Isa. 49:6, 23; Rev. 21:24

4 Isa. 49:18, 20-22; 66:12

5 Isa. 60:11; 61:6; Rom. 11:25

6 Gen. 25:4; Ps. 72:10; Isa. 61:6; Matt. 2:11

7 Gen. 25:13; Hag. 2:7, 9

9 Ps. 68:30; 72:10; Isa. 42:4; 51:5; 55:5; Jer. 3:17; Zech. 14:14; Gal. 4:26

10 Isa. 49:23; 54:7, 8; 57:17; Zech. 6:15; Rev. 21:24

11 Isa. 60:5; Rev. 21:25

12 Zech. 14:17, 19; Matt. 21:44

13 1Chr. 28:2; Ps. 132:7; Isa. 35:2; 41:19

14 Isa. 49:23; Heb. 12:22; Rev. 3:9; 14:1

60:1–22 Isaiah foresees a time when Israel will arise out of her darkness and shine with God's glory. Then the "Gentiles shall come" to her light. These verses describe in detail the worship of the nations at Jerusalem when they will bow down at Jerusalem. See the similar description in Revelation 21:23; 22:5.

down at the soles of thy feet; and they shall call thee, The city of the LORD, The Zion of the Holy One of Israel.

15 Whereas thou hast been forsaken and hated, so that no man went through *thee,* I will make thee an eternal excellency, a joy of many generations.

16 Thou shalt also suck the milk of the Gentiles, and shalt suck the breast of kings: and thou shalt know that I the LORD *am* thy Saviour and thy Redeemer, the mighty One of Jacob.

17 For brass I will bring gold, and for iron I will bring silver, and for wood brass, and for stones iron: I will also make thy officers peace, and thine exactors righteousness.

18 Violence shall no more be heard in thy land, wasting nor destruction within thy borders; but thou shalt call thy walls Salvation, and thy gates Praise.

19 The sun shall be no more thy light by day; neither for brightness shall the moon

give light unto thee: but the LORD shall be unto thee an everlasting light, and thy God thy glory.

20 Thy sun shall no more go down; neither shall thy moon withdraw itself: for the LORD shall be thine everlasting light, and the days of thy mourning shall be ended.

21 Thy people also *shall be* all righteous: they shall inherit the land for ever, the branch of my planting, the work of my hands, that I may be glorified.

22 A little one shall become a thousand, and a small one a strong nation: I the LORD will hasten it in his time.

CHAPTER 61
Those Who Endure Affliction Will Be Exalted

1 The Spirit of the Lord GOD *is* upon me; because the LORD hath anointed me to preach good tidings unto the meek; he hath

Marginal references:
16 Isa. 43:3; 49:23; 61:6; 66:11, 12
18 Isa. 26:1
19 Zech. 2:5; Rev. 21:23; 22:5
20 Amos 8:9
21 Ps. 37:11, 22; Isa. 29:23; 45:11; 52:1; 61:3; Matt. 5:5; 15:13; John 15:2; Eph. 2:10; Rev. 21:27
22 Matt. 13:31, 32
1 Ps. 45:7; 147:3; Isa. 11:2; 42:7; 57:15; Jer. 34:8; Luke 4:18; John 1:32; 3:34

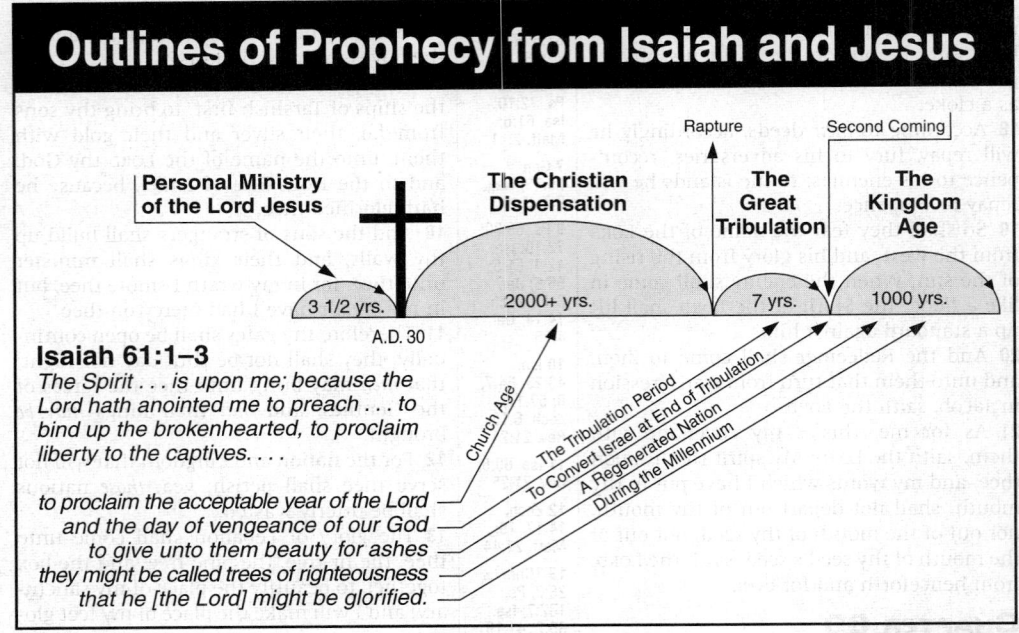

Outlines of Prophecy from Isaiah and Jesus

Rapture   Second Coming

Personal Ministry of the Lord Jesus | The Christian Dispensation | The Great Tribulation | The Kingdom Age

3 1/2 yrs. | 2000+ yrs. | 7 yrs. | 1000 yrs.

A.D. 30

Isaiah 61:1–3
The Spirit . . . is upon me; because the Lord hath anointed me to preach . . . to bind up the brokenhearted, to proclaim liberty to the captives. . . .

Church Age

The Tribulation Period
To Convert Israel at End of Tribulation
A Regenerated Nation During the Millennium

to proclaim the acceptable year of the Lord
and the day of vengeance of our God
to give unto them beauty for ashes
they might be called trees of righteousness
that he [the Lord] might be glorified.

© AMG Publishers

61:1–3 Now Isaiah introduces the King who is to rule in the glorious kingdom he has just described. Jesus read from this passage in the synagogue (Luke 4:17–21), after which He said, "This day is this scripture fulfilled in your ears." The person on whom the Spirit rests is Christ, the One whom God anointed "to preach good tidings" and to "proclaim liberty." When Jesus quoted this passage, He stopped at this point, indicating that the "day of vengeance," the final judgment, had not yet come. The distance separating the first coming of Christ, at His advent, and the Second Coming was thus signified.

The Millennial Kingdom

By Chuck Smith

The Bible teaches that Jesus is coming again to this earth. In Acts 1:11 as the disciples were watching Jesus ascend into heaven, the two men standing by them in white apparel said to them, "Ye men of Galilee, why stand ye here gazing up into heaven? this same Jesus, which is taken up from you into heaven, shall so come in like manner as ye have seen him go into heaven." Matthew 24:30 tells us, that "they shall see the Son of man coming in the clouds of heaven with power and great glory." Revelation 1:7 tells us, "Behold, he cometh with clouds; and every eye shall see him, and they also which pierced him." Zechariah, speaking for the Lord, said, "And they shall look upon me whom they have pierced" (Zech.12:10).

The purpose of the second coming of Christ is to establish the kingdom of God on the earth. In His model prayer, Jesus told His disciples to pray, "Thy kingdom come. Thy will be done in earth, as it is in heaven" (Matt. 6:10). During the Millennium, the damage of the Tribulation will be reversed, and Christ will reign on the throne of David (Isa. 9:6–7; Zech. 12:10). In Revelation 5:10, John said, "And hast made us unto our God kings and priests: and we shall reign on the earth." Hence, when Jesus comes to reign, the Church will reign with Him. Revelation 20:4 tells us that the length of our reign on the earth will be one thousand years. In Latin a thousand years is *mille annum,* from which we get our English word "millennium."

> **When Jesus comes to reign, the Church will reign with Him.**

Revelation 5:9–10 speaks of the new song the Church will be singing in heaven of the worthiness of the Lamb to take the book and loose the seals: "for thou wast slain, and hast redeemed us to God by thy blood out of every kindred, and tongue, and people, and nation; and hast made us unto our God kings and priests: and we shall reign on the earth."

His kingdom will not be meat or drink, "but righteousness, and peace, and joy in the Holy Ghost" (Rom. 14:17). It is at this time that "the wolf . . . shall dwell with the lamb, and the leopard shall lie down with the kid; and the calf and the young lion and the fatling together; and a little child shall lead them" (Isa. 11:6). "The wolf and the lamb shall feed together, and the lion shall eat straw like the bullock" (Isa. 65:25). This is the time when "they shall beat their swords into plowshares, and their spears into pruninghooks: nation shall not lift up a sword against nation, neither shall they learn war any more" (Mic. 4:3). God's promises to Israel included both earthly and spiritual blessings. Christ's disciples, who understood the earthly aspect of the blessings on Israel, asked Christ just prior to His ascension when he would fulfill the earthly blessings and establish His kingdom (Acts 1:6). They were then ignorant of the fact that this phase of Christ's kingdom would not take place until the End Times.

Until Christ returns, our purpose and commission is to be at work declaring His gospel to the world (Matt. 24:14). "Even so, come [quickly], Lord Jesus" (Rev. 22:20).

sent me to bind up the brokenhearted, to proclaim liberty to the captives, and the opening of the prison to *them that are* bound;

2 To proclaim the acceptable year of the LORD, and the day of vengeance of our God; to comfort all that mourn;

3 To appoint unto them that mourn in Zion, to give unto them beauty for ashes, the oil of joy for mourning, the garment of praise for the spirit of heaviness; that they might be called trees of righteousness, the planting of the LORD, that he might be glorified.

4 And they shall build the old wastes, they shall raise up the former desolations, and they shall repair the waste cities, the desolations of many generations.

5 And strangers shall stand and feed your flocks, and the sons of the alien *shall be* your plowmen and your vinedressers.

6 But ye shall be named the Priests of the LORD: *men* shall call you the Ministers of our God: ye shall eat the riches of the Gentiles, and in their glory shall ye boast yourselves.

7 For your shame *ye shall have* double; and *for* confusion they shall rejoice in their portion: therefore in their land they shall possess the double: everlasting joy shall be unto them.

8 For I the LORD love judgment, I hate robbery for burnt offering; and I will direct their work in truth, and I will make an everlasting covenant with them.

9 And their seed shall be known among the Gentiles, and their offspring among the people: all that see them shall acknowledge them, that they *are* the seed *which* the LORD hath blessed.

10 I will greatly rejoice in the LORD, my soul shall be joyful in my God; for he hath clothed me with the garments of salvation, he hath covered me with the robe of righteousness, as a bridegroom decketh *himself* with ornaments, and as a bride adorneth *herself* with her jewels.

11 For as the earth bringeth forth her bud, and as the garden causeth the things that are sown in it to spring forth; so the Lord GOD will cause righteousness and praise to spring forth before all the nations.

Cross references (center column)

2 Lev. 25:9; Isa. 34:8; 57:18; 63:4; 66:14; Mal. 4:1, 3; Matt. 5:4; 2Thess. 1:7-9

3 Ps. 30:11; Isa. 60:21; John 15:8

4 Isa. 49:8; 58:12; Ezek. 36:33-36

5 Eph. 2:12

6 Ex. 19:6; Isa. 60:5, 11, 16, 17; 66:21; 1Pet. 2:5, 9; Rev. 1:6; 5:10

7 Isa. 40:2; Zech. 9:12

8 Ps. 11:7; Isa. 1:11, 13; 55:3

9 Isa. 65:23

10 Ps. 132:9, 16; Isa. 49:18; Hab. 3:18; Rev. 21:2

11 Ps. 72:3; 85:11; Isa. 60:18; 62:7

2 Isa. 60:3; 62:4, 12; 65:15

3 Zech. 9:16

4 Isa. 49:14; 54:1, 6, 7; Hos. 1:10; 1Pet. 2:10

5 Isa. 65:19

6 Ezek. 3:17; 33:7

7 Isa. 61:11; Zeph. 3:20

8 Deut. 28:31; Jer. 5:17

9 Deut. 12:12; 14:23, 26; 16:11, 14

10 Isa. 11:12; 40:3; 57:14

11 Zech. 9:9; Matt. 21:5; John 12:15; Rev. 22:12

12 Isa. 62:4

CHAPTER 62

1 For Zion's sake will I not hold my peace, and for Jerusalem's sake I will not rest, until the righteousness thereof go forth as brightness, and the salvation thereof as a lamp *that* burneth.

2 And the Gentiles shall see thy righteousness, and all kings thy glory: and thou shalt be called by a new name, which the mouth of the LORD shall name.

3 Thou shalt also be a crown of glory in the hand of the LORD, and a royal diadem in the hand of thy God.

4 Thou shalt no more be termed Forsaken; neither shall thy land any more be termed Desolate: but thou shalt be called Hephzibah, and thy land Beulah: for the LORD delighteth in thee, and thy land shall be married.

5 For *as* a young man marrieth a virgin, *so* shall thy sons marry thee: and *as* the bridegroom rejoiceth over the bride, *so* shall thy God rejoice over thee.

6 I have set watchmen upon thy walls, O Jerusalem, *which* shall never hold their peace day nor night: ye that make mention of the LORD, keep not silence,

7 And give him no rest, till he establish, and till he make Jerusalem a praise in the earth.

8 The LORD hath sworn by his right hand, and by the arm of his strength, Surely I will no more give thy corn *to be* meat for thine enemies; and the sons of the stranger shall not drink thy wine, for the which thou hast laboured:

9 But they that have gathered it shall eat it, and praise the LORD; and they that have brought it together shall drink it in the courts of my holiness.

10 Go through, go through the gates; prepare ye the way of the people; cast up, cast up the highway; gather out the stones; lift up a standard for the people.

11 Behold, the LORD hath proclaimed unto the end of the world, Say ye to the daughter of Zion, Behold, thy salvation cometh; behold, his reward *is* with him, and his work before him.

12 And they shall call them, The holy people, The redeemed of the LORD: and thou

---

62:1–12 Here we see the conditions required for the deliverance of Zion and the establishment of Messiah's kingdom. Righteousness and salvation will burst forth as a light upon the Gentiles. Moreover, the Gentiles will not merely observe this light, but will receive it. Israel will change so radically that she will be "called by a new name."

shalt be called, Sought out, A city not forsaken.

CHAPTER 63
Victory

1 Who *is* this that cometh from Edom, with dyed garments from Bozrah? this *that is* glorious in his apparel, travelling in the greatness of his strength? I that speak in righteousness, mighty to save.
2 Wherefore *art thou* red in thine apparel, and thy garments like him that treadeth in the winefat?
3 I have trodden the winepress alone; and of the people *there was* none with me: for I will tread them in mine anger, and trample them in my fury; and their blood shall be sprinkled upon my garments, and I will stain all my raiment.
4 For the day of vengeance *is* in mine heart, and the year of my redeemed is come.
5 And I looked, and *there was* none to help; and I wondered that *there was* none to uphold: therefore mine own arm brought salvation unto me; and my fury, it upheld me.
6 And I will tread down the people in mine anger, and make them drunk in my fury, and I will bring down their strength to the earth.

The Lord Is Good to Israel

7 I will mention the lovingkindnesses of the LORD, *and* the praises of the LORD, according to all that the LORD hath bestowed on us, and the great goodness toward the house of Israel, which he hath bestowed on them according to his mercies, and according to the multitude of his lovingkindnesses.
8 For he said, Surely they *are* my people, children *that* will not lie: so he was their Saviour.
9 In all their affliction he was afflicted, and the angel of his presence saved them: in his love and in his pity he redeemed them; and he bare them, and carried them all the days of old.
10 But they rebelled, and vexed his holy

Spirit: therefore he was turned to be their enemy, *and* he fought against them.
11 Then he remembered the days of old, Moses, *and* his people, *saying*, Where *is* he that brought them up out of the sea with the shepherd of his flock? where *is* he that put his holy Spirit within him?
12 That led *them* by the right hand of Moses with his glorious arm, dividing the water before them, to make himself an everlasting name?
13 That led them through the deep, as an horse in the wilderness, *that* they should not stumble?
14 As a beast goeth down into the valley, the Spirit of the LORD caused him to rest: so didst thou lead thy people, to make thyself a glorious name.

A Prayer for Vengeance

15 Look down from heaven, and behold from the habitation of thy holiness and of thy glory: where *is* thy zeal and thy strength, the sounding of thy bowels and of thy mercies toward me? are they restrained?
16 Doubtless thou *art* our father, though Abraham be ignorant of us, and Israel acknowledge us not: thou, O LORD, *art* our father, our redeemer; thy name *is* from everlasting.
17 O LORD, why hast thou made us to err from thy ways, *and* hardened our heart from thy fear? Return for thy servants' sake, the tribes of thine inheritance.
18 The people of thy holiness have possessed *it* but a little while: our adversaries have trodden down thy sanctuary.
19 We are *thine*: thou never barest rule over them; they were not called by thy name.

CHAPTER 64

1 Oh that thou wouldest rend the heavens, that thou wouldest come down, that the mountains might flow down at thy presence,
2 As *when* the melting fire burneth, the fire causeth the waters to boil, to make thy

Cross references (center column)

2 Rev. 19:13
3 Lam. 1:15; Rev. 14:19, 20; 19:15
5 Ps. 98:1; Isa. 41:28; 59:16; John 16:32
6 Rev. 16:6
9 Ex. 14:19; 19:4; 23:20, 21; 33:14; Deut. 1:31; 7:7, 8; 32:11, 12; Judg. 10:16; Isa. 46:3, 4; Zech. 2:8; Mal. 3:1; Acts 9:4; 12:11
10 Ex. 15:24; 23:21; Num. 14:11; Ps. 78:56, 40; 95:9; Acts 7:51; Eph. 4:30
11 Ex. 14:30; 32:11, 12; Num. 11:17, 25; 14:13, 14; Neh. 9:20; Ps. 77:20; Jer. 2:6; Dan. 4:8; Hag. 2:5
12 Ex. 14:21; 15:6; Josh. 3:16
13 Ps. 106:9
14 2Sam. 7:23
15 Deut. 26:15; Ps. 33:14; 80:14; Jer. 31:20; Hos. 11:8
16 Deut. 32:6; 1Chr. 29:10; Job 14:21
17 Num. 10:36; Ps. 90:13; 119:10
18 Dan. 8:24
1 Mic. 1:4

63:1–6 Isaiah has listed God's conditions for peace (chaps. 58—59), and described the nature of that peace (chaps. 60—62). He now looks to the consummation of that peace (chaps. 63—66). The garments dyed red seem to indicate the conditions noted by John in Revelation 19:13: "And he was clothed with a vesture dipped in blood: and his name is called The Word of God." The red-stained condition of His garments comes from trampling out blood in the winepress of God's judgment. The vengeance of God is a judgment so severe that the very lifeblood of the nations will be poured out on the earth. The entire passage is strikingly similar to Revelation 19, where Christ comes to "judge and make war" (v. 11), treading "the winepress of the fierceness and wrath of Almighty God" (v. 15). The flowing of the blood is similar to the description in Revelation 14:20.

name known to thine adversaries, *that* the nations may tremble at thy presence!

3 When thou didst terrible things *which* we looked not for, thou camest down, the mountains flowed down at thy presence.

4 For since the beginning of the world *men* have not heard, nor perceived by the ear, neither hath the eye seen, O God, beside thee, *what* he hath prepared for him that waiteth for him.

5 Thou meetest him that rejoiceth and worketh righteousness, *those that* remember thee in thy ways: behold, thou art wroth; for we have sinned: in those is continuance, and we shall be saved.

6 But we are all as an unclean *thing*, and all our righteousnesses *are* as filthy rags; and we all do fade as a leaf; and our iniquities, like the wind, have taken us away.

7 And *there is* none that calleth upon thy name, that stirreth up himself to take hold of thee: for thou hast hid thy face from us, and hast consumed us, because of our iniquities.

8 But now, O LORD, thou *art* our father; we *are* the clay, and thou our potter; and we all *are* the work of thy hand.

9 Be not wroth very sore, O LORD, neither remember iniquity for ever: behold, see, we beseech thee, we *are* all thy people.

10 Thy holy cities are a wilderness, Zion is a wilderness, Jerusalem a desolation.

11 Our holy and our beautiful house, where our fathers praised thee, is burned up with fire: and all our pleasant things are laid waste.

12 Wilt thou refrain thyself for these *things*, O LORD? wilt thou hold thy peace, and afflict us very sore?

CHAPTER 65
The Rebellious Will Be Punished

1 I am sought of *them that* asked not *for me*; I am found of *them that* sought me not: I said, Behold me, behold me, unto a nation *that* was not called by my name.

2 I have spread out my hands all the day unto a rebellious people, which walketh in a way *that was* not good, after their own thoughts;

Cross references (center column)

3 Ex. 34:10
4 1Cor. 2:9
6 Phil. 3:9
7 Hos. 7:7
8 Jer. 18:6; Rom. 9:20, 21; Eph. 2:10
9 Ps. 74:1, 2; 79:8, 13
10 Ps. 79:1
11 2Kgs. 25:9; 2Chr. 36:19; Ps. 74:7; Ezek. 24:21, 21
12 Ps. 83:1
1 Rom. 9:24-26, 30; 10:20; Eph. 2:12, 13
2 Rom. 10:21
3 Lev. 17:5; Deut. 32:21; Isa. 1:29; 66:17
4 Lev. 11:7; Deut. 18:11; Isa. 66:17
5 Matt. 9:11; Luke 5:30; 18:11; Jude 1:19
6 Deut. 32:34; Ps. 50:3; 79:12; Jer. 16:18; Ezek. 11:21; Mal. 3:16
7 Ex. 20:5; Ezek. 18:6; 20:27, 28
8 Joel 2:14
9 Isa. 65:15, 22; Matt. 24:22; Rom. 11:5, 7
10 Hos. 2:15
11 Ezek. 23:41; 1Cor. 10:21
12 2Chr. 36:15, 16; Matt. 21:34-43
14 Matt. 8:12; Luke 13:28

3 A people that provoketh me to anger continually to my face; that sacrificeth in gardens, and burneth incense upon altars of brick;

4 Which remain among the graves, and lodge in the monuments, which eat swine's flesh, and broth of abominable *things is in* their vessels;

5 Which say, Stand by thyself, come not near to me; for I am holier than thou. These *are* a smoke in my nose, a fire that burneth all the day.

6 Behold, *it is* written before me: I will not keep silence, but will recompense, even recompense into their bosom,

7 Your iniquities, and the iniquities of your fathers together, saith the LORD, which have burned incense upon the mountains, and blasphemed me upon the hills: therefore will I measure their former work into their bosom.

8 Thus saith the LORD, As the new wine is found in the cluster, and *one* saith, Destroy it not; for a blessing *is* in it: so will I do for my servants' sakes, that I may not destroy them all.

9 And I will bring forth a seed out of Jacob, and out of Judah an inheritor of my mountains: and mine elect shall inherit it, and my servants shall dwell there.

10 And Sharon shall be a fold of flocks, and the valley of Achor a place for the herds to lie down in, for my people that have sought me.

11 But ye *are* they that forsake the LORD, that forget my holy mountain, that prepare a table for that troop, and that furnish the drink offering unto that number.

12 Therefore will I number you to the sword, and ye shall all bow down to the slaughter: because when I called, ye did not answer; when I spake, ye did not hear; but did evil before mine eyes, and did choose *that* wherein I delighted not.

13 Therefore thus saith the Lord GOD, Behold, my servants shall eat, but ye shall be hungry: behold, my servants shall drink, but ye shall be thirsty: behold, my servants shall rejoice, but ye shall be ashamed:

14 Behold, my servants shall sing for joy of

65:1–16 I am found of them that sought me not. Responding to the prayer of the previous chapter, God speaks to the Gentiles who have come to trust in Him, referring to the unconditional election of the Gentiles (see Rom. 10:20). While the Jews themselves are called a "rebellious people," God still promises to bring a "seed out of Jacob . . . mine elect." The language here is remarkably similar to Romans 11:1–5, where Paul insists that God has not forsaken His people Israel. The references to the plain of Sharon and the valley of Achor blossoming abundantly look forward to the prosperity Israel will enjoy in the Millennium.

The New Jerusalem

By Paul Lee Tan

Revelation 21—22 describes the New Jerusalem that will be located in the new heavens and new earth. This new creation will be part of the new world created after the present heavens and earth are destroyed by fire (2 Pet. 3:10–13) at the end of history. New Jerusalem will be the eternal residence of all believers from history. John's vision of the celestial city is of a real, literal city of the future.

In the description of the New Jerusalem, all the elements of an actual city—dimensions, foundations, walls, gates, streets—are indicated. While some details of its structure may not be fully understood, none of them are wholly outside the realm of sober possibility.

The record of Scripture is definite: the length, width, and height of the city will be exactly twelve thousand furlongs long each (Rev. 21:16–17). A furlong is 582 feet; therefore the city will be 1,323 miles in all directions, giving it a total base area of 1,750,329 square miles! It has been conservatively estimated that such a city could hold a staggering 72 billion inhabitants. On the basis of the dimensions given in Revelation 21:16 alone, it is not possible to determine whether the city will be a gigantic cube or a square-based triangle.

> *John's vision is of a real, literal city of the future.*

The building components of the New Jerusalem are astounding. The wall around the city will have gates made of pearl, each with the name of one of the twelve tribes of Israel inscribed on the gates (Rev. 21:12, 17–18, 21). This wall will glitter like a bracelet of diamonds (Rev. 21:18). In connection with the pearly gates, twelve angels are said to be stationed at each gate as servants of God. The foundation of the wall is composed of twelve precious stones of various brilliant colors (Rev. 21:19–20). Each color of the precious stones represents one of the twelve apostles upon whom the Church is built. The streets are made of transparent gold (Rev. 21:18, 21), while Jesus, the Lamb, lights the city (Rev. 21:11, 23).

Hebrews 12:22–24 lists the inhabitants of the New Jerusalem to include angels, the Church, God the Judge, Old Testament saints, and Jesus, the Mediator. There will be no need of a temple, because God Almighty and the Lamb are the temple (Rev. 21:22). In the middle of the city will be a river that flows from the throne of God down through the city (Rev. 22:1–2). The tree of life will be on either side of the river bearing fruit and leaves "for the healing of the nations" (Rev. 22:2). The inhabitants of this glorious future city will enjoy each other's presence and bask under the glory of the eternal Godhead.

In the New Jerusalem there will be no more death, tears, mourning, crying, or pain (Rev. 21:4). The Lamb will remove the curse that began in the Garden of Eden, as believers dwell forever in their spotless home. Every aspect of life will bring joy and fulfillment for all eternity.

What Scripture tells us of the splendid New Jerusalem is but a pebble in the great ocean of unrevealed truths. Truly, the half has never been told in the Bible—nor could it ever be (1 Kgs. 10:7)! But what has been told, is enough to make us realize that we will stand ourselves happily in our future home—the New Jerusalem—for all eternity.

heart, but ye shall cry for sorrow of heart, and shall howl for vexation of spirit.

15 And ye shall leave your name for a curse unto my chosen: for the Lord GOD shall slay thee, and call his servants by another name:

16 That he who blesseth himself in the earth shall bless himself in the God of truth; and he that sweareth in the earth shall swear by the God of truth; because the former troubles are forgotten, and because they are hid from mine eyes.

New Heavens and a New Earth

17 For, behold, I create new heavens and a new earth: and the former shall not be remembered, nor come into mind.

18 But be ye glad and rejoice for ever in that which I create: for, behold, I create Jerusalem a rejoicing, and her people a joy.

19 And I will rejoice in Jerusalem, and joy in my people: and the voice of weeping shall be no more heard in her, nor the voice of crying.

20 There shall be no more thence an infant of days, nor an old man that hath not filled his days: for the child shall die an hundred years old; but the sinner being an hundred years old shall be accursed.

21 And they shall build houses, and inhabit them; and they shall plant vineyards, and eat the fruit of them.

22 They shall not build, and another inhabit; they shall not plant, and another eat: for as the days of a tree are the days of my people, and mine elect shall long enjoy the work of their hands.

23 They shall not labour in vain, nor bring forth for trouble; for they are the seed of the blessed of the LORD, and their offspring with them.

24 And it shall come to pass, that before they call, I will answer; and while they are yet speaking, I will hear.

25 The wolf and the lamb shall feed together, and the lion shall eat straw like the bullock: and dust shall be the serpent's meat. They shall not hurt nor destroy in all my holy mountain, saith the LORD.

CHAPTER 66
God Judges the Nations

1 Thus saith the LORD, The heaven is my throne, and the earth is my footstool: where is the house that ye build unto me? and where is the place of my rest?

2 For all those things hath mine hand made, and all those things have been, saith the LORD: but to this man will I look, even to him that is poor and of a contrite spirit, and trembleth at my word.

3 He that killeth an ox is as if he slew a man; he that sacrificeth a lamb, as if he cut off a dog's neck; he that offereth an oblation, as if he offered swine's blood; he that burneth incense, as if he blessed an idol. Yea, they have chosen their own ways, and their soul delighteth in their abominations.

4 I also will choose their delusions, and will bring their fears upon them; because when I called, none did answer; when I spake, they did not hear: but they did evil before mine eyes, and chose that in which I delighted not.

5 Hear the word of the LORD, ye that tremble at his word; Your brethren that hated you, that cast you out for my name's sake, said, Let the LORD be glorified: but he shall appear to your joy, and they shall be ashamed.

6 A voice of noise from the city, a voice from the temple, a voice of the LORD that rendereth recompence to his enemies.

7 Before she travailed, she brought forth; before her pain came, she was delivered of a man child.

8 Who hath heard such a thing? who hath

---

15 Jer. 29:22; Acts 11:26

16 Deut. 6:13; Ps. 63:11; 72:17

17 Isa. 51:16; 66:22; 2Pet. 3:13; Rev. 21:1

19 Isa. 35:10; 51:11; 62:5; Rev. 7:17; 21:4

20 Eccl. 8:12

21 Lev. 26:16; Deut. 28:30; Isa. 62:8; Amos 9:14

22 Ps. 92:12; Isa. 65:9, 15

23 Deut. 28:41; Isa. 61:9; Hos. 9:12

24 Ps. 32:5; Dan. 9:21

25 Gen. 3:14; Isa. 11:6, 7, 9

1 1Kgs. 8:27; 2Chr. 6:18; Matt. 5:34, 35; Acts 7:48, 49; 17:24

2 Ezra 9:4; 10:3; Ps. 34:18; 51:17; Prov. 28:14; Isa. 57:15; 61:1; 66:5

3 Lev. 2:2; Deut. 23:18; Isa. 1:11

4 Prov. 1:24; Isa. 65:12; Jer. 7:13

5 2Thess. 1:10; Titus 2:13

65:17–25 In an overview of the future, Isaiah speaks of the "new heavens and a new earth" (cf. Rev. 21). This seems to be a reference to the eternal state, that is, to heaven; however, the "early" death of someone at one hundred years of age (v. 20) must certainly be a reference to the earthly Millennial Kingdom. The implication is that the prophet saw a vision of both the Eternal and Millennial Kingdoms, and that the two were not clearly distinguished by Isaiah in that vision. The extended life span of men and women indicates that during the Millennium normal life spans will revert to the lengthy time periods recorded prior to the Flood. The absence of weeping and crying is reminiscent of the description of the eternal state in Revelation 21:4: "God shall wipe away all tears from their eyes," but in this context may merely be a description of the peace on earth during Christ's thousand-year reign.

66:1–16 Isaiah's final prophecy points to the magnitude and immensity of God, who is greater than all the heavens. Thus heaven is His throne and earth His footstool. He is not limited to any house (temple) made by man. Reflecting on his vision of heaven, the apostle John declares that there is no need for a temple, "for the Lord God Almighty and the Lamb are the temple of it" (Rev. 21:22).

seen such things? Shall the earth be made to bring forth in one day? *or* shall a nation be born at once? for as soon as Zion travailed, she brought forth her children.

9 Shall I bring to the birth, and not cause to bring forth? saith the LORD: shall I cause to bring forth, and shut *the womb?* saith thy God.

10 Rejoice ye with Jerusalem, and be glad with her, all ye that love her: rejoice for joy with her, all ye that mourn for her:

11 That ye may suck, and be satisfied with the breasts of her consolations; that ye may milk out, and be delighted with the abundance of her glory.

12 For thus saith the LORD, Behold, I will extend peace to her like a river, and the glory of the Gentiles like a flowing stream: then shall ye suck, ye shall be borne upon *her* sides, and be dandled upon *her* knees.

13 As one whom his mother comforteth, so will I comfort you; and ye shall be comforted in Jerusalem.

14 And when ye see *this*, your heart shall rejoice, and your bones shall flourish like an herb: and the hand of the LORD shall be known toward his servants, and *his* indignation toward his enemies.

15 For, behold, the LORD will come with fire, and with his chariots like a whirlwind, to render his anger with fury, and his rebuke with flames of fire.

16 For by fire and by his sword will the LORD plead with all flesh: and the slain of the LORD shall be many.

17 They that sanctify themselves, and purify themselves in the gardens behind one *tree* in the midst, eating swine's flesh, and the abomination, and the mouse, shall be consumed together, saith the LORD.

18 For I *know* their works and their thoughts: it shall come, that I will gather all nations and tongues; and they shall come, and see my glory.

19 And I will set a sign among them, and I will send those that escape of them unto the nations, *to* Tarshish, Pul, and Lud, that draw the bow, *to* Tubal, and Javan, *to* the isles afar off, that have not heard my fame, neither have seen my glory; and they shall declare my glory among the Gentiles.

20 And they shall bring all your brethren *for* an offering unto the LORD out of all nations upon horses, and in chariots, and in litters, and upon mules, and upon swift beasts, to my holy mountain Jerusalem, saith the LORD, as the children of Israel bring an offering in a clean vessel into the house of the LORD.

21 And I will also take of them for priests *and* for Levites, saith the LORD.

22 For as the new heavens and the new earth, which I will make, shall remain before me, saith the LORD, so shall your seed and your name remain.

23 And it shall come to pass, *that* from one new moon to another, and from one sabbath to another, shall all flesh come to worship before me, saith the LORD.

24 And they shall go forth, and look upon the carcases of the men that have transgressed against me: for their worm shall not die, neither shall their fire be quenched; and they shall be an abhorring unto all flesh.

---

9 12 Isa. 48:18; 49:22; 60:4, 5, 16

14 Ezek. 37:1

15 Isa. 9:5; 2Thess. 1:8

16 Isa. 27:1

17 Isa. 65:3, 4

19 Mal. 1:11; Luke 2:34

20 Rom. 15:16

21 Ex. 19:6; Isa. 61:6; 1Pet. 2:9; Rev. 1:6

22 Isa. 65:17; 2Pet. 3:13; Rev. 21:1

23 Ps. 65:2; Zech. 14:16

24 Isa. 66:16; Mark 9:44, 46, 48

66:17–24 The book ends with a fearful glimpse of final judgment. The prophet foresees a time when "those that escape" the Tribulation period, the converted Israelites that survive the persecution, will be sent to the nations (Gentiles) to declare God's glory among them. During the Millennial Kingdom the nations will come to Jerusalem to worship Him. The expression "all flesh" refers to the redeemed of the Lord from all nations who will gather to worship Him. The book closes with a chilling reminder that there is a real heaven to be gained and a real hell to be avoided (cf. Mark 9:44; Rev. 20:14–15). The scene described is that of the redeemed of heaven in their final glorified state and that of those who are lost forever in the lake of fire.

Jeremiah

Jeremiah's name means "exalted or appointed by the Lord." He was appointed a prophet before his birth (Jer. 1:5, cf. Paul's statement about his own call in Gal. 1:15–16). In God touching Jeremiah's mouth to give His message to him (Jer. 1:9), one is reminded of Isaiah's call (Isa. 6:6–7). Jeremiah's lack of confidence in his own abilities is reminiscent of Moses' words in Exodus 4:10.

The many prophecies given by Jeremiah are not in chronological order, but concern two conditions of his times: political and social evils in Judah and personal accounts of his relationship with the Lord. Sprinkled throughout the prophecies already fulfilled in the Old Testament times are remarkable forecasts of the coming Messiah (Jesus) and predictions of a glorious future age.

Jeremiah lived during the reigns of Josiah, Shallum, Jehoikim, Jeconiah, and Zedekiah, of whom only the first was a godly king. Rejected by the people and their rulers when he accurately predicted the fall of Jerusalem and the conquests of Nebuchadnezzar, Jeremiah suffered persecution, ridicule, and imprisonment. After Jerusalem fell in 586 B.C., he was forced to join the refugees who fled into Egypt against his advice. Succeeding generations realized what a great prophet Jeremiah was. He is quoted seven times in the New Testament.

The impending fall of Jerusalem is described in 222 verses. The Captivity (606–586 B.C.) is predicted in 25:1–14, and later, a letter is sent by Jeremiah to the exiles (29:1–23). Daniel's prophecy of the seventy weeks of years was sparked by Jeremiah's earlier prediction (Dan. 9:1–2). Messianic prophecies and blessings for Israel in the Last Days are forecast. That there will be a new covenant with Israel in the future millennial reign of Christ is evident from 31:31–40.

In this, the longest prophetic book in the Old Testament, are 1,364 verses, 812 of those being predictive in nature or 60 percent.

Author
Jeremiah

Date
629–585 B.C.

Key Truth
Sinful Israel Will Be Restored through Messiah

Historic Time
King Josiah to Destruction of Jerusalem

Key Verse
1:10
See, I have this day set thee over the nations and over the kingdoms. . . .

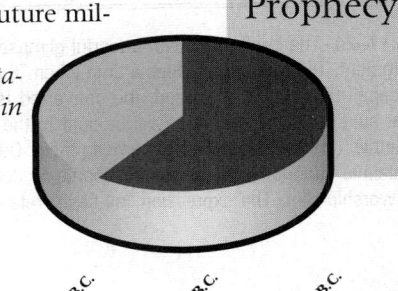

60%
Prophecy

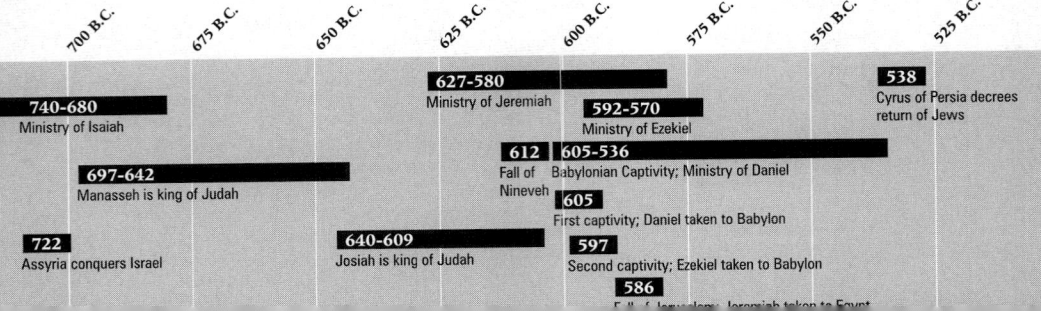

740-680
Ministry of Isaiah

722
Assyria conquers Israel

697-642
Manasseh is king of Judah

640-609
Josiah is king of Judah

627-580
Ministry of Jeremiah

612
Fall of Nineveh

605
First captivity; Daniel taken to Babylon

597
Second captivity; Ezekiel taken to Babylon

586

592-570
Ministry of Ezekiel

605-536
Babylonian Captivity; Ministry of Daniel

538
Cyrus of Persia decrees return of Jews

CHAPTER 1
Jeremiah's Call

1 The words of Jeremiah the son of Hilkiah, of the priests that *were* in Anathoth in the land of Benjamin:

2 To whom the word of the LORD came in the days of Josiah the son of Amon king of Judah, in the thirteenth year of his reign.

3 It came also in the days of Jehoiakim the son of Josiah king of Judah, unto the end of the eleventh year of Zedekiah the son of Josiah king of Judah, unto the carrying away of Jerusalem captive in the fifth month.

4 Then the word of the LORD came unto me, saying,

5 Before I formed thee in the belly I knew thee; and before thou camest forth out of the womb I sanctified thee, *and* I ordained thee a prophet unto the nations.

6 Then said I, Ah, Lord GOD! behold, I cannot speak: for I *am* a child.

7 But the LORD said unto me, Say not, I *am* a child: for thou shalt go to all that I shall send thee, and whatsoever I command thee thou shalt speak.

8 Be not afraid of their faces: for I *am* with thee to deliver thee, saith the LORD.

9 Then the LORD put forth his hand, and touched my mouth. And the LORD said unto me, Behold, I have put my words in thy mouth.

10 See, I have this day set thee over the nations and over the kingdoms, to root out, and to pull down, and to destroy, and to throw down, to build, and to plant.

11 Moreover the word of the LORD came unto me, saying, Jeremiah, what seest thou? And I said, I see a rod of an almond tree.

12 Then said the LORD unto me, Thou hast well seen: for I will hasten my word to perform it.

13 And the word of the LORD came unto me the second time, saying, What seest thou? And I said, I see a seething pot; and the face thereof *is* toward the north.

14 Then the LORD said unto me, Out of the north an evil shall break forth upon all the inhabitants of the land.

15 For, lo, I will call all the families of the kingdoms of the north, saith the LORD; and they shall come, and they shall set every one his throne at the entering of the gates of Jerusalem, and against all the walls thereof round about, and against all the cities of Judah.

16 And I will utter my judgments against them touching all their wickedness, who have forsaken me, and have burned incense unto other gods, and worshipped the works of their own hands.

17 Thou therefore gird up thy loins, and arise, and speak unto them all that I command thee: be not dismayed at their faces, lest I confound thee before them.

18 For, behold, I have made thee this day a defenced city, and an iron pillar, and brasen walls against the whole land, against the kings of Judah, against the princes thereof, against the priests thereof, and against the people of the land.

19 And they shall fight against thee; but they shall not prevail against thee; for I *am* with thee, saith the LORD, to deliver thee.

CHAPTER 2
Israel Must Repent

1 Moreover the word of the LORD came to me, saying,

Cross references

1 Josh. 21:18; 1Chr. 6:60; Jer. 32:7-9

3 2Kgs. 25:8; Jer. 39:2; 52:12, 15

5 Ex. 33:12, 17; Isa. 49:1, 5; Luke 1:15, 41; Gal. 1:15, 16

6 Ex. 4:10; 6:12, 30; Isa. 6:5

7 Num. 22:20, 38; Matt. 28:20

8 Ex. 3:12; Deut. 31:6, 8; Josh. 1:5; Jer. 1:17; 15:20; Ezek. 2:6; 3:9; Acts 26:17; Heb. 13:6

9 Isa. 6:7; 51:16; Jer. 5:14

10 1Kgs. 19:17; Jer. 18:7; 2Cor. 10:4, 5

13 Ezek. 11:3, 7; 24:3

15 Jer. 5:15; 6:22; 10:22; 25:9; 39:3; 43:10

16 Deut. 28:20; Jer. 17:13

17 Ex. 3:12; 1Kgs. 18:46; 2Kgs. 4:29

18 Isa. 50:7; Ezek. 6:27; 15:20

1:5 I ordained thee a prophet unto the nations. Jeremiah was sovereignly chosen by God before birth to be a prophet to Judah and to the nations surrounding Israel.

1:9 I have put my words in thy mouth. This is one of the many means that the Lord uses to provide direct, prophetic revelation to His prophet, making clear that God is the ultimate author of Scripture.

1:11 the word of the LORD came unto me, saying. This is yet another expression indicating the inspiration of Jeremiah when he wrote Scripture.

1:13 What seest thou? This phrase tells us that Jeremiah's prophecy on this occasion came through a vision. In the image of the "seething pot," Jeremiah sees turmoil and judgment in the future. This judgment would be coming upon Jerusalem and Judah from the north as an enemy attack; Jeremiah 20:4 identifies the enemy as Babylon. Since there is no approach to Jerusalem from the east, Babylon would have to come from the north. Nebuchadnezzar fulfilled this prophecy when he led the Babylonian attack that overran Jerusalem in 586 B.C.

1:16 I will utter my judgments against them. These judgments were predicted in Leviticus 26:27–39 and Deuteronomy 28:49–63 as the consequences of persistent disobedience toward the Lord by Israel.

1:17–19 Even though Jeremiah's nation of Judah was to be destroyed, God promises to personally protect Jeremiah from personal harm. This is significant since virtually the whole nation opposed him and his ministry. However, as God predicted, Jeremiah was not harmed (Jer. 21:1–2; 37:3, 17; 38:14; 42:1–7).

The Prophecies of Jeremiah

By Richard Patterson

Like the other Old Testament prophets, Jeremiah was set apart by God and called to proclaim His messages (1:4–19). Much of his prophecy consists of sermonic discourses designed to inform, instruct, exhort, or even confront the people of Jerusalem and Judah (1:11–19) as to their faithfulness in stewarding the high standards of God, their Redeemer (e.g., 2:1—3:5).

Many of the predictive portions of Jeremiah relate to the situation of the late seventh and early sixth centuries B.C. God tells Jeremiah to pronounce imminent judgment on His people (3:6—24:10). Matters relative not only to Judah and Jerusalem but also to the surrounding nations are dealt with in 25:16–29; 46:1—51:64.

God also delivers messages through Jeremiah, furnishing details of the distant future. Here the prophetic pronouncements take on a universal dimension. Jeremiah 25:30–38 contains a dramatic scene rich with similes, in which God is portrayed as a prosecuting attorney. Jeremiah's message is one of God's climactic judgments against an unbelieving world and its leadership. He tells of the great day of the Lord's anger against sin, a time when the Divine Warrior will come with devastating force to destroy the wickedness of the entire world.

Jeremiah's prophecies challenge all persons to live responsibly.

One of the grandest sections of the book, a collection of kingdom oracles (chaps. 30—33), deals with end-time events—mainly, oracles of judgment and the sure hope of God's salvation. In that awful "day of the LORD," God's people will be delivered out of great trouble, be restored to their land, and experience the abundant blessings of the Lord (30:1—31:28).

God will also establish a new covenant with his people (31:31–37; 32:37–44; 33:14–22), which will bring to full realization the promises made in the earlier Abrahamic and Davidic covenants (33:23–26). Not only will God's people find forgiveness and cleansing from their sins (31:34; 33:8), but also all believers everywhere will know God (31:34). Moreover, because God's moral law is written in their hearts (31:33), believers will experience the full life that comes with complete faithfulness to God.

In that regard Jeremiah speaks of a faithful remnant which God will lead back to the land of promise (e.g., 23:3; 31:7–11; 33:7–8). There they will rejoice over God's goodness and enjoy the peace and fulfillment of life that only He can give (31:12–14; 32:37–44; 33:9–14). In place of the false shepherds of Jeremiah's day, God will install faithful men who will serve as undershepherds to His flock (23:3–4; 31:10).

Jeremiah also speaks of a coming Redeemer, an heir of the line of David, through whom these promises will be realized (30:21–22). Unlike the unfaithful shepherds of Jeremiah's day, this righteous Branch will rule wisely, always doing what is just and right (23:5; 33:15). So just and fair will this One and the character of His reign be, that He will be called "THE LORD OUR RIGHTEOUSNESS" (23:6). So intimate will be the relation between that One and the people of Jerusalem, that the people will reflect His character, and Jerusalem itself will be known by His name (33:16).

These prophecies find their ultimate fulfillment in Christ, in whom the new covenant is established (Matt. 26:27–28) and through whom the hope of a believing mankind will be realized (Rev. 11:15). Jeremiah's prophecies challenge all persons to live responsibly in the certain knowledge that God will come in judgment to put away wickedness and bring in everlasting righteousness.

2 Go and cry in the ears of Jerusalem, saying, Thus saith the LORD; I remember thee, the kindness of thy youth, the love of thine espousals, when thou wentest after me in the wilderness, in a land *that was* not sown.

3 Israel *was* holiness unto the LORD, *and* the firstfruits of his increase: all that devour him shall offend; evil shall come upon them, saith the LORD.

4 Hear ye the word of the LORD, O house of Jacob, and all the families of the house of Israel:

5 Thus saith the LORD, What iniquity have your fathers found in me, that they are gone far from me, and have walked after vanity, and are become vain?

6 Neither said they, Where *is* the LORD that brought us up out of the land of Egypt, that led us through the wilderness, through a land of deserts and of pits, through a land of drought, and of the shadow of death, through a land that no man passed through, and where no man dwelt?

7 And I brought you into a plentiful country, to eat the fruit thereof and the goodness thereof; but when ye entered, ye defiled my land, and made mine heritage an abomination.

8 The priests said not, Where *is* the LORD? and they that handle the law knew me not: the pastors also transgressed against me, and the prophets prophesied by Baal, and walked after *things that* do not profit.

9 Wherefore I will yet plead with you, saith the LORD, and with your children's children will I plead.

10 For pass over the isles of Chittim, and see; and send unto Kedar, and consider diligently, and see if there be such a thing.

11 Hath a nation changed *their* gods, which *are* yet no gods? but my people have changed their glory for *that which* doth not profit.

12 Be astonished, O ye heavens, at this, and be horribly afraid, be ye very desolate, saith the LORD.

13 For my people have committed two evils; they have forsaken me the fountain of living waters, *and* hewed them out cisterns, broken cisterns, that can hold no water.

14 *Is* Israel a servant? *is* he a homeborn *slave?* why is he spoiled?

15 The young lions roared upon him, *and* yelled, and they made his land waste: his cities are burned without inhabitant.

16 Also the children of Noph and Tahapanes have broken the crown of thy head.

17 Hast thou not procured this unto thyself, in that thou hast forsaken the LORD thy God, when he led thee by the way?

18 And now what hast thou to do in the way of Egypt, to drink the waters of Sihor? or what hast thou to do in the way of Assyria, to drink the waters of the river?

19 Thine own wickedness shall correct thee, and thy backslidings shall reprove thee: know therefore and see that *it is* an evil *thing* and bitter, that thou hast forsaken the LORD thy God, and that my fear *is* not in thee, saith the Lord GOD of hosts.

20 For of old time I have broken thy yoke, *and* burst thy bands; and thou saidst, I will not transgress; when upon every high hill and under every green tree thou wanderest, playing the harlot.

21 Yet I had planted thee a noble vine, wholly a right seed: how then art thou turned into the degenerate plant of a strange vine unto me?

22 For though thou wash thee with nitre, and take thee much soap, *yet* thine iniquity is marked before me, saith the Lord GOD.

23 How canst thou say, I am not polluted, I have not gone after Baalim? see thy way in the valley, know what thou hast done: *thou art* a swift dromedary traversing her ways;

24 A wild ass used to the wilderness, *that* snuffeth up the wind at her pleasure; in her occasion who can turn her away? all they that seek her will not weary themselves; in her month they shall find her.

25 Withhold thy foot from being unshod, and thy throat from thirst: but thou saidst, There is no hope: no; for I have loved strangers, and after them will I go.

26 As the thief is ashamed when he is found, so is the house of Israel ashamed; they, their kings, their princes, and their priests, and their prophets,

27 Saying to a stock, Thou *art* my father;

---

2 Deut. 2:7
3 Ex. 19:5, 6; James 1:18; Rev. 14:4
5 2Kgs. 17:15; Isa. 5:4
6 Deut. 8:15; 32:10
7 Lev. 18:25, 27, 28
8 Jer. 2:11; 23:13; Hab. 2:18; Mal. 2:6, 7; Rom. 2:20
9 Ex. 20:5; Lev. 20:5; Ezek. 20:35, 36; Mic. 6:2
11 Ps. 106:20; 115:4; Isa. 37:19; Jer. 2:8; 16:20; Mic. 4:5; Rom. 1:23
12 Isa. 1:2; Jer. 6:19
13 Ps. 36:9; Jer. 17:13; 18:14; John 4:14
14 Ex. 4:22
15 Isa. 1:7; Jer. 4:7
16 Deut. 33:20; Isa. 8:8; Jer. 43:7-9
17 Deut. 32:10; Jer. 4:18
18 Josh. 13:3
20 Ex. 19:8; 34:15, 16; Deut. 12:2
21 Isa. 1:21; 5:1, 4; 60:21; Matt. 21:33; Mark 12:1; Luke 20:9
22 Job 9:30; 14:17
23 Prov. 30:12
27 Isa. 26:16

2:14–15 they made his land waste. Jeremiah refers to Israel, the Northern Kingdom that was judged in 722 B.C. by the "young lions" (the Assyrians). God judged Israel, and now Judah was walking down the same path to judgment and destruction.

2:16–17 have broken the crown of thy head. Noph and Tahapanes are cities in Egypt. Judah submitted to a vassal relationship with Egypt, thinking it would protect her from enemies. Instead, the alliance led to the death of Judah's King Josiah. Judah should have trusted the Lord and not other Gentile nations whom God would use to chastise His wayward people.

and to a stone, Thou hast brought me forth: for they have turned *their* back unto me, and not *their* face: but in the time of their trouble they will say, Arise, and save us.

28 But where *are* thy gods that thou hast made thee? let them arise, if they can save thee in the time of thy trouble: for *according to* the number of thy cities are thy gods, O Judah.

29 Wherefore will ye plead with me? ye all have transgressed against me, saith the LORD.

30 In vain have I smitten your children; they received no correction: your own sword hath devoured your prophets, like a destroying lion.

31 O generation, see ye the word of the LORD. Have I been a wilderness unto Israel? a land of darkness? wherefore say my people, We are lords; we will come no more unto thee?

32 Can a maid forget her ornaments, *or a* bride her attire? yet my people have forgotten me days without number.

33 Why trimmest thou thy way to seek love? therefore hast thou also taught the wicked ones thy ways.

34 Also in thy skirts is found the blood of the souls of the poor innocents: I have not found it by secret search, but upon all these.

35 Yet thou sayest, Because I am innocent, surely his anger shall turn from me. Behold, I will plead with thee, because thou sayest, I have not sinned.

36 Why gaddest thou about so much to change thy way? thou also shalt be ashamed of Egypt, as thou wast ashamed of Assyria.

37 Yea, thou shalt go forth from him, and thine hands upon thine head: for the LORD hath rejected thy confidences, and thou shalt not prosper in them.

CHAPTER 3
Unfaithfulness

1 They say, If a man put away his wife, and she go from him, and become another man's, shall he return unto her again? shall not that land be greatly polluted? but thou

hast played the harlot with many lovers; yet return again to me, saith the LORD.

2 Lift up thine eyes unto the high places, and see where thou hast not been lien with. In the ways hast thou sat for them, as the Arabian in the wilderness; and thou hast polluted the land with thy whoredoms and with thy wickedness.

3 Therefore the showers have been withholden, and there hath been no latter rain; and thou hadst a whore's forehead, thou refusedst to be ashamed.

4 Wilt thou not from this time cry unto me, My father, thou *art* the guide of my youth?

5 Will he reserve *his anger* for ever? will he keep *it* to the end? Behold, thou hast spoken and done evil things as thou couldest.

6 The LORD said also unto me in the days of Josiah the king, Hast thou seen *that* which backsliding Israel hath done? she is gone up upon every high mountain and under every green tree, and there hath played the harlot.

7 And I said after she had done all these *things*, Turn thou unto me. But she returned not. And her treacherous sister Judah saw *it*.

8 And I saw, when for all the causes whereby backsliding Israel committed adultery I had put her away, and given her a bill of divorce; yet her treacherous sister Judah feared not, but went and played the harlot also.

9 And it came to pass through the lightness of her whoredom, that she defiled the land, and committed adultery with stones and with stocks.

10 And yet for all this her treacherous sister Judah hath not turned unto me with her whole heart, but feignedly, saith the LORD.

11 And the LORD said unto me, The backsliding Israel hath justified herself more than treacherous Judah.

12 Go and proclaim these words toward the north, and say, Return, thou backsliding Israel, saith the LORD; *and* I will not cause mine anger to fall upon you: for I *am* merci-

Cross references

28 Isa. 45:20
30 2Chr. 36:16; Neh. 9:26; Matt. 23:29
32 Ps. 106:21; Jer. 13:25; Hos. 8:14
34 Ps. 106:38; Jer. 19:4
35 Prov. 28:13; Jer. 2:9, 23, 29; 1John 1:8, 10
36 2Chr. 28:16, 20, 21; Isa. 30:3; Jer. 2:18; 31:22; 37:7; Hos. 5:13; 12:1
37 Deut. 24:4; 2Sam. 13:19; Jer. 2:7, 20; 4:1; Ezek. 16:26, 28, 29; Zech. 1:3
2 Gen. 38:14; Deut. 12:2; Prov. 23:28; Jer. 2:7, 20; 3:9; Ezek. 16:24, 25
3 Lev. 26:19; Deut. 28:23, 24; Jer. 5:3; 6:15; 8:12; 9:12; 14:4; Ezek. 3:7; Zeph. 3:5
4 Prov. 2:17; Jer. 2:2; Hos. 2:15
5 Ps. 77:7; 103:9
7 2Kgs. 17:13
8 2Kgs. 17:6, 18
10 2Chr. 34:33
11 Ezek. 16:51; 23:11
12 Ps. 86:15

3:8 The Lord, through Jeremiah, uses the language of marital unfaithfulness in charging Judah with disobedience. God's punishment of the Northern Kingdom should have awakened Judah. But it did not.

3:11–14 Return . . . and I will not cause mine anger to fall upon you. Jeremiah appeals to the survivors of the Northern Kingdom. The condition for repentance was for Israel to acknowledge her iniquity. If Israel would repent, the Lord would bring her to Zion. This prophecy was fulfilled during the return of the exiles to Jerusalem (Zion) in 587–537 B.C. Some of these exiles were descendants of the tribes of the Northern Kingdom.

ful, saith the LORD, *and* I will not keep *anger* for ever.

13 Only acknowledge thine iniquity, that thou hast transgressed against the LORD thy God, and hast scattered thy ways to the strangers under every green tree, and ye have not obeyed my voice, saith the LORD.

14 Turn, O backsliding children, saith the LORD; for I am married unto you: and I will take you one of a city, and two of a family, and I will bring you to Zion:

15 And I will give you pastors according to mine heart, which shall feed you with knowledge and understanding.

16 And it shall come to pass, when ye be multiplied and increased in the land, in those days, saith the LORD, they shall say no more, The ark of the covenant of the LORD: neither shall it come to mind: neither shall they remember it; neither shall they visit *it*; neither shall *that* be done any more.

17 At that time they shall call Jerusalem the throne of the LORD; and all the nations shall be gathered unto it, to the name of the LORD, to Jerusalem: neither shall they walk any more after the imagination of their evil heart.

18 In those days the house of Judah shall walk with the house of Israel, and they shall come together out of the land of the north to the land that I have given for an inheritance unto your fathers.

19 But I said, How shall I put thee among the children, and give thee a pleasant land, a goodly heritage of the hosts of nations? and I said, Thou shalt call me, My father; and shalt not turn away from me.

20 Surely *as* a wife treacherously departeth from her husband, so have ye dealt treacherously with me, O house of Israel, saith the LORD.

21 A voice was heard upon the high places, weeping *and* supplications of the children of Israel: for they have perverted their way, *and* they have forgotten the LORD their God.

22 Return, ye backsliding children, *and* I will heal your backslidings. Behold, we come unto thee; for thou *art* the LORD our God.

23 Truly in vain *is salvation hoped for* from the hills, *and from* the multitude of mountains: truly in the LORD our God *is* the salvation of Israel.

24 For shame hath devoured the labour of our fathers from our youth; their flocks and their herds, their sons and their daughters.

25 We lie down in our shame, and our confusion covereth us: for we have sinned against the LORD our God, we and our fathers, from our youth even unto this day, and have not obeyed the voice of the LORD our God.

CHAPTER 4
Return to God!

1 If thou wilt return, O Israel, saith the LORD, return unto me: and if thou wilt put away thine abominations out of my sight, then shalt thou not remove.

2 And thou shalt swear, The LORD liveth, in truth, in judgment, and in righteousness; and the nations shall bless themselves in him, and in him shall they glory.

3 For thus saith the LORD to the men of Judah and Jerusalem, Break up your fallow ground, and sow not among thorns.

4 Circumcise yourselves to the LORD, and take away the foreskins of your heart, ye men of Judah and inhabitants of Jerusalem: lest my fury come forth like fire, and burn that none can quench *it*, because of the evil of your doings.

13 Lev. 26:40; Deut. 12:2; 30:1, 2; Prov. 28:13

14 Jer. 31:22

15 Jer. 23:4; Ezek. 34:23; Acts 20:28; Eph. 4:11

16 Isa. 65:17

17 Isa. 60:9; Jer. 11:8

18 Isa. 11:13; Jer. 3:12; 31:8; Ezek. 37:16-22; Hos. 1:11; Amos 9:15

19 Ps. 106:24; Isa. 63:16; Ezek. 20:6; Dan. 8:9; 11:16, 41, 45

20 Isa. 48:8; Jer. 5:11

21 Isa. 15:2

22 Jer. 3:14; Hos. 6:1; 14:1, 4

23 Ps. 3:8; 121:1, 2

24 Jer. 11:13; Hos. 9:10

25 Ezra 9:7; Jer. 3:1, 22; 22:21; Joel 2:12

2 Gen. 22:18; Deut. 10:20; Ps. 72:17; Isa. 45:23, 25

3 Matt. 13:7, 22

4 Rom. 2:28, 29; Col. 2:11

3:15 Full repentance in Israel and Judah will not take place until the future Millennium, at which time the Lord will send "pastors according to [His] heart." These "pastors" are those who will provide oversight to the nation in accordance with God's true will. This restoration will result in "knowledge and understanding."

3:16–17 in those days. This is a reference to Israel's future Millennial Kingdom that will be established by Jesus at the Second Coming. During the Millennium, Israel's worship will not be centered around the ark of the covenant, because the Messiah Himself will be personally present. Thus, there will be no need for the invisible presence of the Lord as the ark represented in the Taber-

nacle and Solomon's Temple. Jeremiah 31:31 tells us that in that day the Lord will give the Jews a new heart which will result in obedience to His Word.

3:18 with the house of Israel. The rift that took place between the Northern and Southern Kingdoms will no longer be in effect when the Jews return to their land for the Millennium (Hos. 1:11; 2:23).

3:19 a pleasant land. In contrast to the judgment forecast for Judah, the future millennial restoration will be a pleasant time. Why? Because the once wayward children of Israel and Judah will now address the Lord as their Father and shall not turn away from God.

5 Declare ye in Judah, and publish in Jerusalem; and say, Blow ye the trumpet in the land: cry, gather together, and say, Assemble yourselves, and let us go into the defenced cities.

6 Set up the standard toward Zion: retire, stay not: for I will bring evil from the north, and a great destruction.

7 The lion is come up from his thicket, and the destroyer of the Gentiles is on his way; he is gone forth from his place to make thy land desolate; *and* thy cities shall be laid waste, without an inhabitant.

8 For this gird you with sackcloth, lament and howl: for the fierce anger of the LORD is not turned back from us.

9 And it shall come to pass at that day, saith the LORD, *that* the heart of the king shall perish, and the heart of the princes; and the priests shall be astonished, and the prophets shall wonder.

10 Then said I, Ah, Lord GOD! surely thou hast greatly deceived this people and Jerusalem, saying, Ye shall have peace; whereas the sword reacheth unto the soul.

11 At that time shall it be said to this people and to Jerusalem, A dry wind of the high places in the wilderness toward the daughter of my people, not to fan, nor to cleanse,

12 *Even* a full wind from those *places* shall come unto me: now also will I give sentence against them.

13 Behold, he shall come up as clouds, and his chariots *shall be* as a whirlwind: his horses are swifter than eagles. Woe unto us! for we are spoiled.

14 O Jerusalem, wash thine heart from wickedness, that thou mayest be saved. How long shall thy vain thoughts lodge within thee?

15 For a voice declareth from Dan, and publisheth affliction from mount Ephraim.

16 Make ye mention to the nations; behold, publish against Jerusalem, *that* watchers come from a far country, and give out their voice against the cities of Judah.

17 As keepers of a field, are they against her round about; because she hath been rebellious against me, saith the LORD.

18 Thy way and thy doings have procured these *things* unto thee; this *is* thy wickedness, because it is bitter, because it reacheth unto thine heart.

19 My bowels, my bowels! I am pained at my very heart; my heart maketh a noise in me; I cannot hold my peace, because thou hast heard, O my soul, the sound of the trumpet, the alarm of war.

20 Destruction upon destruction is cried; for the whole land is spoiled: suddenly are my tents spoiled, *and* my curtains in a moment.

21 How long shall I see the standard, *and* hear the sound of the trumpet?

22 For my people *is* foolish, they have not known me; they *are* sottish children, and they have none understanding: they *are* wise to do evil, but to do good they have no knowledge.

23 I beheld the earth, and, lo, *it was* without form, and void; and the heavens, and they *had* no light.

24 I beheld the mountains, and, lo, they trembled, and all the hills moved lightly.

25 I beheld, and, lo, *there was* no man, and all the birds of the heavens were fled.

26 I beheld, and, lo, the fruitful place *was* a wilderness, and all the cities thereof were broken down at the presence of the LORD, *and* by his fierce anger.

Cross references:
- 5 Jer. 8:14
- 6 Jer. 1:13-15; 6:1, 22
- 7 2Kgs. 24:1; Isa. 1:7; Jer. 2:15; 5:6; 25:9; Dan. 7:4
- 8 Isa. 22:12; Jer. 6:26
- 10 Jer. 5:12; 14:13; Ezek. 14:9; 2Thess. 2:11
- 11 Jer. 51:1; Ezek. 17:10; Hos. 13:15
- 13 Deut. 28:49; Isa. 5:28; Lam. 4:19; Hos. 8:1; Hab. 1:8
- 14 Isa. 1:16; James 4:8
- 15 Jer. 8:16
- 16 Jer. 5:15
- 17 2Kgs. 25:1, 4
- 18 Ps. 107:17; Isa. 50:1; Jer. 2:17, 19
- 19 Isa. 15:5; 16:11; 21:3; 22:4; Jer. 9:1, 10; Luke 19:42
- 20 Ps. 42:7; Jer. 10:20; Ezek. 7:26
- 22 Rom. 16:19
- 23 Gen. 1:2; Isa. 24:19
- 24 Isa. 5:25
- 25 Zeph. 1:3

4:5–7 Blow ye the trumpet [Hebr. *shofar*] **in the land.** Jeremiah gave this prediction of the destruction of Jerusalem between 622 and 609 B.C. It was fulfilled in 586 B.C. Jeremiah repeats his prophecy of Babylon's invasion coming from the north. The invader is said to pounce like a lion, suddenly and without warning.

4:8 Sackcloth is a thick, course material that was often worn in conjunction with those who would "lament and howl" over an impending judgment.

4:9 At a time when Judah would need leadership and courage in the face of the attack of an enemy, her leaders will not provide it, leading to Judah's defeat.

4:19–20 My Bowels, my bowels! Since there is not a Hebrew word used in the Old Testament for emotions, the Jews often related their emotions to their bowels. Further

prophecy about Judah's destined destruction will encompass the entire land.

4:23–25 I beheld the earth [land], **and, lo, it was without form, and void.** Jeremiah uses vocabulary from the creation account in Genesis 1:2 to describe the coming devastation upon Judah. This passage is a picture of complete devastation, so much so that there were neither men nor birds in the land.

4:26–27 the fruitful place was a wilderness. Jeremiah names the different aspects of the land of Judah that will be affected by the wrath of the Lord upon His people. Every city would be impacted. In spite of the great judgment coming upon Judah, the Lord will not destroy the land so totally that it cannot be inhabited in the future.

27 For thus hath the LORD said, The whole land shall be desolate; yet will I not make a full end.

28 For this shall the earth mourn, and the heavens above be black: because I have spoken *it*, I have purposed *it*, and will not repent, neither will I turn back from it.

29 The whole city shall flee for the noise of the horsemen and bowmen; they shall go into thickets, and climb up upon the rocks: every city *shall be* forsaken, and not a man dwell therein.

30 And *when* thou *art* spoiled, what wilt thou do? Though thou clothest thyself with crimson, though thou deckest thee with ornaments of gold, though thou rentest thy face with painting, in vain shalt thou make thyself fair; *thy* lovers will despise thee, they will seek thy life.

31 For I have heard a voice as of a woman in travail, *and* the anguish as of her that bringeth forth her first child, the voice of the daughter of Zion, *that* bewaileth herself, *that* spreadeth her hands, *saying*, Woe *is* me now! for my soul is wearied because of murderers.

CHAPTER 5
The Sins of Jerusalem and Judah

1 Run ye to and fro through the streets of Jerusalem, and see now, and know, and seek in the broad places thereof, if ye can find a man, if there be *any* that executeth judgment, that seeketh the truth; and I will pardon it.

2 And though they say, The LORD liveth; surely they swear falsely.

3 O LORD, *are* not thine eyes upon the truth? thou hast stricken them, but they have not grieved; thou hast consumed them, *but* they have refused to receive correction: they have made their faces harder than a rock; they have refused to return.

4 Therefore I said, Surely these *are* poor; they are foolish: for they know not the way of the LORD, *nor* the judgment of their God.

5 I will get me unto the great men, and will speak unto them; for they have known the way of the LORD, *and* the judgment of their God: but these have altogether broken the yoke, *and* burst the bonds.

6 Wherefore a lion out of the forest shall slay them, *and* a wolf of the evenings shall spoil them, a leopard shall watch over their cities: every one that goeth out thence shall be torn in pieces: because their transgressions are many, *and* their backslidings are increased.

7 How shall I pardon thee for this? thy children have forsaken me, and sworn by *them that are* no gods: when I had fed them to the full, they then committed adultery, and assembled themselves by troops in the harlots houses.

8 They were *as* fed horses in the morning: every one neighed after his neighbour's wife.

9 Shall I not visit for these *things*? saith the LORD: and shall not my soul be avenged on such a nation as this?

10 Go ye up upon her walls, and destroy; but make not a full end: take away her battlements; for they *are* not the LORD's.

11 For the house of Israel and the house of Judah have dealt very treacherously against me, saith the LORD.

12 They have belied the LORD, and said, *It is* not he; neither shall evil come upon us; neither shall we see sword nor famine:

13 And the prophets shall become wind, and the word *is* not in them: thus shall it be done unto them.

14 Wherefore thus saith the LORD God of hosts, Because ye speak this word, behold, I will make my words in thy mouth fire, and this people wood, and it shall devour them.

15 Lo, I will bring a nation upon you from far, O house of Israel, saith the LORD: it *is* a mighty nation, it *is* an ancient nation, a nation whose language thou knowest not, neither understandest what they say.

16 Their quiver *is* as an open sepulchre, they *are* all mighty men.

17 And they shall eat up thine harvest, and

Cross references

27 Jer. 5:10, 18; 30:11; 46:28
28 Num. 23:19; Isa. 5:30; 50:3; Jer. 7:16; Hos. 4:3
30 2Kgs. 9:30; Jer. 22:20, 22; Lam. 1:2, 19; Ezek. 23:40
31 Gen. 18:23, 26; Ps. 12:1; Isa. 1:15; Lam. 1:17; Ezek. 22:30
2 Jer. 4:2; 7:9; Titus 1:16
3 2Chr. 16:9; Isa. 1:5; 9:13; Jer. 2:30; 7:28; Zeph. 3:2
4 Jer. 8:7
5 Ps. 2:3; Mic. 3:1
6 Ps. 104:20; Jer. 4:7; Hos. 13:7; Hab. 1:8; Zeph. 3:3
7 Deut. 32:15, 21; Josh. 23:7; Zeph. 1:5; Gal. 4:8
8 Jer. 13:27; Ezek. 22:11
9 Jer. 5:29; 9:9; 44:22
12 2Chr. 36:16; Isa. 28:15; Jer. 4:10; 14:13
14 Jer. 1:9
15 Deut. 28:49; Isa. 5:26; 39:3; Jer. 1:15; 4:16; 6:22
17 Lev. 26:16; Deut. 28:31, 33

4:28 I have purposed it, and will not repent. Judah's sin had progressed to the point that God's impending wrath was inevitable. He would not take pity upon them as He had done in the past. This judgment Jeremiah prophesied would surely come to pass.

5:9–10 make not a full end. God is not finished with His people. Though He will "visit" (Hebr. "punish") them, God has an ultimate plan that includes final blessing for His nation.

5:19 The Lord makes clear to Jeremiah that the reason these calamities will come upon Judah is that the people have been unfaithful to Him in the covenant relationship to which they were bound. The Lord promised that if the people disobeyed Him, then He would do these things to them (Lev. 26:27–39; Deut. 28:49–63). This judgment was fulfilled through the time of the Babylonian captivity, which took place in the sixth century B.C.

thy bread, *which* thy sons and thy daughters should eat: they shall eat up thy flocks and thine herds: they shall eat up thy vines and thy fig trees: they shall impoverish thy fenced cities, wherein thou trustedst, with the sword.

18 Nevertheless in those days, saith the LORD, I will not make a full end with you.

19 And it shall come to pass, when ye shall say, Wherefore doeth the LORD our God all these *things* unto us? then shalt thou answer them, Like as ye have forsaken me, and served strange gods in your land, so shall ye serve strangers in a land *that is* not yours.

20 Declare this in the house of Jacob, and publish it in Judah, saying,

21 Hear now this, O foolish people, and without understanding; which have eyes, and see not; which have ears, and hear not:

22 Fear ye not me? saith the LORD: will ye not tremble at my presence, which have placed the sand *for* the bound of the sea by a perpetual decree, that it cannot pass it: and though the waves thereof toss themselves, yet can they not prevail; though they roar, yet can they not pass over it?

23 But this people hath a revolting and a rebellious heart; they are revolted and gone.

24 Neither say they in their heart, Let us now fear the LORD our God, that giveth rain, both the former and the latter, in his season: he reserveth unto us the appointed weeks of the harvest.

25 Your iniquities have turned away these *things*, and your sins have withholden good *things* from you.

26 For among my people are found wicked *men*: they lay wait, as he that setteth snares; they set a trap, they catch men.

27 As a cage is full of birds, so *are* their houses full of deceit: therefore they are become great, and waxen rich.

28 They are waxen fat, they shine: yea, they overpass the deeds of the wicked: they judge not the cause, the cause of the fatherless, yet they prosper; and the right of the needy do they not judge.

29 Shall I not visit for these *things*? saith the LORD: shall not my soul be avenged on such a nation as this?

30 A wonderful and horrible thing is committed in the land;

31 The prophets prophesy falsely, and the priests bear rule by their means; and my people love *to have it* so: and what will ye do in the end thereof?

CHAPTER 6
The Siege of Jerusalem

1 O ye children of Benjamin, gather yourselves to flee out of the midst of Jerusalem, and blow the trumpet in Tekoa, and set up a sign of fire in Beth-haccerem: for evil appeareth out of the north, and great destruction.

2 I have likened the daughter of Zion to a comely and delicate *woman*.

3 The shepherds with their flocks shall come unto her; they shall pitch *their* tents against her round about; they shall feed every one in his place.

4 Prepare ye war against her; arise, and let us go up at noon. Woe unto us! for the day goeth away, for the shadows of the evening are stretched out.

5 Arise, and let us go by night, and let us destroy her palaces.

6 For thus hath the LORD of hosts said, Hew ye down trees, and cast a mount against Jerusalem: this *is* the city to be visited; she *is* wholly oppression in the midst of her.

7 As a fountain casteth out her waters, so she casteth out her wickedness: violence and spoil is heard in her; before me continually *is* grief and wounds.

8 Be thou instructed, O Jerusalem, lest my soul depart from thee; lest I make thee desolate, a land not inhabited.

9 Thus saith the LORD of hosts, They shall throughly glean the remnant of Israel as a vine: turn back thine hand as a grapegatherer into the baskets.

10 To whom shall I speak, and give warning, that they may hear? behold, their ear *is* uncircumcised, and they cannot hearken: behold, the word of the LORD is unto them a reproach; they have no delight in it.

11 Therefore I am full of the fury of the LORD; I am weary with holding in: I will

Cross references (center column)

18 Jer. 4:27
19 Deut. 28:48; 29:24; 1Kgs. 9:8, 9; Jer. 2:13; 13:22; 16:10
21 Isa. 6:9; Ezek. 12:2; Hos. 7:11; Matt. 13:14; John 12:40; Acts 28:26; Rom. 11:8
22 Job 26:10; 38:10, 11; Ps. 104:9; Prov. 8:29; Rev. 15:4
24 Gen. 8:22; Deut. 11:14; Ps. 147:8; Jer. 14:22; Joel 2:23; Matt. 5:45; Acts 14:17
25 Jer. 3:3
26 Prov. 1:11, 17, 18; Hab. 1:15
28 Deut. 32:15; Job 12:6; Ps. 73:12; Isa. 1:23; Jer. 12:1; Zech. 7:10
29 Jer. 5:9; Mal. 3:5
30 Jer. 23:14; Hos. 6:10
31 Neh. 3:14; Jer. 1:14; 4:6; 14:14; 23:25, 26; Ezek. 13:6; Mic. 2:11
3 2Kgs. 25:1, 4; Jer. 4:17
4 Jer. 15:8; 51:27; Joel 3:9
7 Ps. 55:9-11; Isa. 57:20; Jer. 20:8; Ezek. 7:11, 23
8 Ezek. 23:18

5:29 God's standard of justice is built upon the principle that just compensation is required for every unrighteous act. The time was rapidly approaching when Judah would "be avenged" by the Lord.

6:9 throughly glean. As opposed to the normal practice of leaving a small percentage of the harvest behind for gleaners, Judah would be thoroughly judged, sparing no one. The imagery of this verse indicates thorough judgment.

pour it out upon the children abroad, and upon the assembly of young men together: for even the husband with the wife shall be taken, the aged with *him that is* full of days.

12 And their houses shall be turned unto others, *with their* fields and wives together: for I will stretch out my hand upon the inhabitants of the land, saith the LORD.

13 For from the least of them even unto the greatest of them every one *is* given to covetousness; and from the prophet even unto the priest every one dealeth falsely.

14 They have healed also the hurt *of the daughter* of my people slightly, saying, Peace, peace; when *there is* no peace.

15 Were they ashamed when they had committed abomination? nay, they were not at all ashamed, neither could they blush: therefore they shall fall among them that fall: at the time *that* I visit them they shall be cast down, saith the LORD.

16 Thus saith the LORD, Stand ye in the ways, and see, and ask for the old paths, where *is* the good way, and walk therein, and ye shall find rest for your souls. But they said, We will not walk *therein.*

17 Also I set watchmen over you, *saying,* Hearken to the sound of the trumpet. But they said, We will not hearken.

18 Therefore hear, ye nations, and know, O congregation, what *is* among them.

19 Hear, O earth: behold, I will bring evil upon this people, *even* the fruit of their thoughts, because they have not hearkened unto my words, nor to my law, but rejected it.

20 To what purpose cometh there to me incense from Sheba, and the sweet cane from a far country? your burnt offerings *are* not acceptable, nor your sacrifices sweet unto me.

21 Therefore thus saith the LORD, Behold, I will lay stumblingblocks before this people, and the fathers and the sons together shall fall upon them; the neighbour and his friend shall perish.

22 Thus saith the LORD, Behold, a people cometh from the north country, and a great nation shall be raised from the sides of the earth.

23 They shall lay hold on bow and spear; they *are* cruel, and have no mercy; their voice roareth like the sea; and they ride

upon horses, set in array as men for war against thee, O daughter of Zion.

24 We have heard the fame thereof: our hands wax feeble: anguish hath taken hold of us, *and* pain, as of a woman in travail.

25 Go not forth into the field, nor walk by the way; for the sword of the enemy *and* fear *is* on every side.

26 O daughter of my people, gird *thee* with sackcloth, and wallow thyself in ashes: make thee mourning, *as for* an only son, most bitter lamentation: for the spoiler shall suddenly come upon us.

27 I have set thee *for* a tower *and* a fortress among my people, that thou mayest know and try their way.

28 They *are* all grievous revolters, walking with slanders: *they are* brass and iron; they *are* all corrupters.

29 The bellows are burned, the lead is consumed of the fire; the founder melteth in vain: for the wicked are not plucked away.

30 Reprobate silver shall *men* call them, because the LORD hath rejected them.

CHAPTER 7
Jeremiah Preaches

1 The word that came to Jeremiah from the LORD, saying,

2 Stand in the gate of the LORD's house, and proclaim there this word, and say, Hear the word of the LORD, all *ye of* Judah, that enter in at these gates to worship the LORD.

3 Thus saith the LORD of hosts, the God of Israel, Amend your ways and your doings, and I will cause you to dwell in this place.

4 Trust ye not in lying words, saying, The temple of the LORD, The temple of the LORD, The temple of the LORD, *are* these.

5 For if ye throughly amend your ways and your doings; if ye throughly execute judgment between a man and his neighbour;

6 *If* ye oppress not the stranger, the fatherless, and the widow, and shed not innocent blood in this place, neither walk after other gods to your hurt:

7 Then will I cause you to dwell in this place, in the land that I gave to your fathers, for ever and ever.

8 Behold, ye trust in lying words, that cannot profit.

9 Will ye steal, murder, and commit adul-

Cross-references (center column)

12 Deut. 28:30; Jer. 8:10

13 Isa. 56:11; Jer. 8:10; 14:18; 23:11; Mic. 3:5, 11

14 Jer. 4:10; 8:11; 14:13; 23:17; Ezek. 13:10

15 Jer. 3:3; 8:12

16 Isa. 8:20; Jer. 18:15; Mal. 4:4; Matt. 11:29; Luke 16:29

17 Isa. 21:11; 58:1; Jer. 25:4; Ezek. 3:17; Hab. 2:1

19 Prov. 1:31; Isa. 1:2

20 Ps. 40:6; 50:7-9; Isa. 1:11; 60:6; 66:3; Jer. 7:21; Amos 5:21; Mic. 6:6

22 Jer. 1:15; 5:15; 10:22; 50:41-43

23 Isa. 5:30

24 Jer. 4:31; 13:21; 49:24; 50:43

26 Jer. 4:8; 25:34; Mic. 1:10; Zech. 12:10

27 Jer. 1:18; 15:20

28 Jer. 5:23; 9:4; Ezek. 22:18

30 Isa. 1:22; Jer. 26:2

3 Jer. 18:11; 26:13

4 Mic. 3:11

5 Jer. 22:3

6 Deut. 6:14, 15; 8:19

7 Deut. 4:40; Jer. 3:18

9 Ex. 20:3; 1Kgs. 18:21; Zeph. 1:5

6:18–19 hear, ye nations . . . O earth. The Gentiles and nations of the earth are called to witness that which the Lord is about to do to the nation of Israel. The word "evil" refers to the calamities of judgment which are about to be brought upon Judah.

tery, and swear falsely, and burn incense unto Baal, and walk after other gods whom ye know not;

10 And come and stand before me in this house, which is called by my name, and say, We are delivered to do all these abominations?

11 Is this house, which is called by my name, become a den of robbers in your eyes? Behold, even I have seen *it*, saith the LORD.

12 But go ye now unto my place which *was* in Shiloh, where I set my name at the first, and see what I did to it for the wickedness of my people Israel.

13 And now, because ye have done all these works, saith the LORD, and I spake unto you, rising up early and speaking, but ye heard not; and I called you, but ye answered not;

14 Therefore will I do unto *this* house, which is called by my name, wherein ye trust, and unto the place which I gave to you and to your fathers, as I have done to Shiloh.

15 And I will cast you out of my sight, as I have cast out all your brethren, *even* the whole seed of Ephraim.

16 Therefore pray not thou for this people, neither lift up cry nor prayer for them, neither make intercession to me: for I will not hear thee.

17 Seest thou not what they do in the cities of Judah and in the streets of Jerusalem?

18 The children gather wood, and the fathers kindle the fire, and the women knead *their* dough, to make cakes to the queen of heaven, and to pour out drink offerings unto other gods, that they may provoke me to anger.

19 Do they provoke me to anger? saith the LORD: *do they* not *provoke* themselves to the confusion of their own faces?

20 Therefore thus saith the Lord GOD; Behold, mine anger and my fury shall be poured out upon this place, upon man, and

upon beast, and upon the trees of the field, and upon the fruit of the ground; and it shall burn, and shall not be quenched.

21 Thus saith the LORD of hosts, the God of Israel; Put your burnt offerings unto your sacrifices, and eat flesh.

22 For I spake not unto your fathers, nor commanded them in the day that I brought them out of the land of Egypt, concerning burnt offerings or sacrifices:

23 But this thing commanded I them, saying, Obey my voice, and I will be your God, and ye shall be my people: and walk ye in all the ways that I have commanded you, that it may be well unto you.

24 But they hearkened not, nor inclined their ear, but walked in the counsels *and* in the imagination of their evil heart, and went backward, and not forward.

25 Since the day that your fathers came forth out of the land of Egypt unto this day I have even sent unto you all my servants the prophets, daily rising up early and sending *them*:

26 Yet they hearkened not unto me, nor inclined their ear, but hardened their neck: they did worse than their fathers.

27 Therefore thou shalt speak all these words unto them; but they will not hearken to thee: thou shalt also call unto them; but they will not answer thee.

28 But thou shalt say unto them, This *is* a nation that obeyeth not the voice of the LORD their God, nor receiveth correction: truth is perished, and is cut off from their mouth.

29 Cut off thine hair, *O Jerusalem*, and cast *it* away, and take up a lamentation on high places; for the LORD hath rejected and forsaken the generation of his wrath.

30 For the children of Judah have done evil in my sight, saith the LORD: they have set their abominations in the house which is called by my name, to pollute it.

31 And they have built the high places of

Cross References

10 Ezek. 23:39
11 Isa. 56:7; Matt. 21:13; Mark 11:17; Luke 19:46
12 Josh. 18:1; Judg. 18:31; 1Sam. 4:10, 11
13 2Chr. 36:15; Prov. 1:24; Isa. 65:12; 66:4; Jer. 7:25; 11:7
14 1Sam. 4:10, 11; Ps. 78:60; Jer. 26:6
15 2Kgs. 17:23; Ps. 78:67, 68
16 Ex. 32:10; Jer. 11:14; 14:11; 15:1
18 Jer. 19:13; 44:17, 19
19 Deut. 32:16, 21
21 Isa. 1:11; Jer. 6:20; Hos. 8:13; Amos 5:21
22 1Sam. 15:22; Ps. 51:16, 17; Hos. 6:6
23 Ex. 15:26; 19:5; Lev. 26:12; Deut. 6:3; Jer. 11:4, 7
24 Deut. 29:19
25 2Chr. 36:15
27 Ezek. 2:7
29 Isa. 15:2; Jer. 16:6
31 2Kgs. 23:10

7:12 Shiloh. When Israel first entered the land of promise, the Tabernacle was set up at Shiloh for many years. Because of Israel's sin, the Lord permitted the Philistines to devastate Shiloh (1 Sam. 4). Jeremiah tells Judah that God will permit what happened to His former dwelling place, the Tabernacle, to occur to His current abode, the temple.

7:14–16 Ephraim refers to the Northern Kingdom that was judged in 722 B.C. (2 Kgs. 17:5–20). God forbids Jeremiah's intercessory prayer on behalf of Judah, for God will not listen to such requests. Judah's sin had progressed to the point of certain judgment (cf. Jer. 11:14; 14:11–12).

7:29 Cut off thine hair. This is an expression of deep mourning (cf. Ezek. 5:1–4), as is the lamentation ("funeral dirge"). Even before the actual event of destruction was to take place, lamentation should begin because the certainty of God's decree would bring it to pass.

7:31 to burn their sons and their daughters in the fire. The growth of gross idolatry in Judah is seen in the ritu-

Tophet, which *is* in the valley of the son of Hinnom, to burn their sons and their daughters in the fire; which I commanded *them* not, neither came it into my heart.

32 Therefore, behold, the days come, saith the Lord, that it shall no more be called Tophet, nor the valley of the son of Hinnom, but the valley of slaughter: for they shall bury in Tophet, till there be no place.

33 And the carcases of this people shall be meat for the fowls of the heaven, and for the beasts of the earth; and none shall fray *them* away.

34 Then will I cause to cease from the cities of Judah, and from the streets of Jerusalem, the voice of mirth, and the voice of gladness, the voice of the bridegroom, and the voice of the bride: for the land shall be desolate.

Chapter 8

1 At that time, saith the Lord, they shall bring out the bones of the kings of Judah, and the bones of his princes, and the bones of the priests, and the bones of the prophets, and the bones of the inhabitants of Jerusalem, out of their graves:

2 And they shall spread them before the sun, and the moon, and all the host of heaven, whom they have loved, and whom they have served, and after whom they have walked, and whom they have sought, and whom they have worshipped: they shall not be gathered, nor be buried; they shall be for dung upon the face of the earth.

3 And death shall be chosen rather than life by all the residue of them that remain of this evil family, which remain in all the places whither I have driven them, saith the Lord of hosts.

4 Moreover thou shalt say unto them, Thus saith the Lord; Shall they fall, and not arise? shall he turn away, and not return?

5 Why *then* is this people of Jerusalem slidden back by a perpetual backsliding? they hold fast deceit, they refuse to return.

6 I hearkened and heard, *but* they spake

not aright: no man repented him of his wickedness, saying, What have I done? every one turned to his course, as the horse rusheth into the battle.

7 Yea, the stork in the heaven knoweth her appointed times; and the turtle and the crane and the swallow observe the time of their coming; but my people know not the judgment of the Lord.

8 How do ye say, We *are* wise, and the law of the Lord *is* with us? Lo, certainly in vain made he *it*; the pen of the scribes *is* in vain.

9 The wise *men* are ashamed, they are dismayed and taken: lo, they have rejected the word of the Lord; and what wisdom *is* in them?

10 Therefore will I give their wives unto others, *and* their fields to them that shall inherit *them*: for every one from the least even unto the greatest is given to covetousness, from the prophet even unto the priest every one dealeth falsely.

11 For they have healed the hurt of the daughter of my people slightly, saying, Peace, peace; when *there is* no peace.

12 Were they ashamed when they had committed abomination? nay, they were not at all ashamed, neither could they blush: therefore shall they fall among them that fall: in the time of their visitation they shall be cast down, saith the Lord.

13 I will surely consume them, saith the Lord: *there shall be* no grapes on the vine, nor figs on the fig tree, and the leaf shall fade; and *the things that* I have given them shall pass away from them.

14 Why do we sit still? assemble yourselves, and let us enter into the defenced cities, and let us be silent there: for the Lord our God hath put us to silence, and given us water of gall to drink, because we have sinned against the Lord.

15 We looked for peace, but no good *came; and* for a time of health, and behold trouble!

16 The snorting of his horses was heard from Dan: the whole land trembled at the sound of the neighing of his strong ones; for

32 2Kgs. 23:10; Jer. 19:6, 11; Ezek. 6:5

33 Deut. 28:26; Ps. 79:2; Jer. 12:9; 16:4; 34:20

34 Lev. 26:33; 2Kgs. 9:36; 23:5; Ps. 83:10; Isa. 1:7; 3:26; 24:7, 8; Jer. 9:22; 16:4, 9; 22:19; 25:10; 33:11; Ezek. 8:16; 26:13; Hos. 2:11; Rev. 18:23

3 Job 3:21, 22; 7:15, 16; Rev. 9:6

5 Jer. 5:3; 7:24; 9:6

6 2Pet. 3:9

7 Song 2:12; Isa. 1:3; Jer. 5:4, 5

8 Isa. 10:1; Rom. 2:17

9 Jer. 6:15

10 Deut. 28:30; Isa. 56:11; Jer. 6:12, 13; Amos 5:11; Zeph. 1:13

11 Jer. 6:14; Ezek. 13:10

12 Jer. 3:3; 6:15

13 Isa. 5:1; Joel 1:7; Matt. 21:19; Luke 13:6

14 Jer. 4:5; 9:15; 23:15

15 Jer. 14:19

16 Judg. 5:22; Jer. 4:15; 47:3

---

al sacrifice of their children to the pagan god Molech. This practice was halted, at least for a time, by the good king, Josiah, when he slew the idolatrous priests (2 Kgs. 23:10, 20). This valley of slaughter became the city dump, and was used by Jesus as a picture of hell (Gr. *geena*, Gehenna [Matt. 5:29–30; 10:28]) and the eternal burning of the lake of fire (Rev. 20:15).

8:5–6 backsliding. An Old Testament term used of those

who continually disobeyed God and His Word (cf. Jer. 2:19; 3:6, 8, 11–12, 14, 22; 31:22; 49:4; Hos. 11:7; 14:4).

8:12–14 As a lawyer arguing his case before the court, Jeremiah continues to add evidence as to why Judah has merited and continues to merit God's judgment. The "time of their visitation" is the moment when Judah's judgment would arrive.

they are come, and have devoured the land, and all that is in it; the city, and those that dwell therein.

17 For, behold, I will send serpents, cockatrices, among you, which *will* not *be* charmed, and they shall bite you, saith the LORD.

Jeremiah's Sorrow

18 *When* I would comfort myself against sorrow, my heart *is* faint in me.

19 Behold the voice of the cry of the daughter of my people because of them that dwell in a far country: *Is* not the LORD in Zion? *is* not her king in her? Why have they provoked me to anger with their graven images, *and* with strange vanities?

20 The harvest is past, the summer is ended, and we are not saved.

21 For the hurt of the daughter of my people am I hurt; I am black; astonishment hath taken hold on me.

22 *Is there* no balm in Gilead; *is there* no physician there? why then is not the health of the daughter of my people recovered?

CHAPTER 9

1 Oh that my head were waters, and mine eyes a fountain of tears, that I might weep day and night for the slain of the daughter of my people!

2 Oh that I had in the wilderness a lodging place of wayfaring men; that I might leave my people, and go from them! for they *be* all adulterers, an assembly of treacherous men.

3 And they bend their tongues *like* their bow *for* lies: but they are not valiant for the truth upon the earth; for they proceed from evil to evil, and they know not me, saith the LORD.

4 Take ye heed every one of his neighbour, and trust ye not in any brother: for every brother will utterly supplant, and every neighbour will walk with slanders.

5 And they will deceive every one his neighbour, and will not speak the truth: they have taught their tongue to speak lies, *and* weary themselves to commit iniquity.

6 Thine habitation *is* in the midst of deceit; through deceit they refuse to know me, saith the LORD.

7 Therefore thus saith the LORD of hosts, Behold, I will melt them, and try them; for how shall I do for the daughter of my people?

8 Their tongue *is as* an arrow shot out; it speaketh deceit: *one* speaketh peaceably to his neighbour with his mouth, but in heart he layeth his wait.

9 Shall I not visit them for these *things?* saith the LORD: shall not my soul be avenged on such a nation as this?

10 For the mountains will I take up a weeping and wailing, and for the habitations of the wilderness a lamentation, because they are burned up, so that none can pass through *them;* neither can *men* hear the voice of the cattle; both the fowl of the heavens and the beast are fled; they are gone.

11 And I will make Jerusalem heaps, *and* a den of dragons; and I will make the cities of Judah desolate, without an inhabitant.

12 Who *is* the wise man, that may understand this? and *who is he* to whom the mouth of the LORD hath spoken, that he may declare it, for what the land perisheth *and* is burned up like a wilderness, that none passeth through?

13 And the LORD saith, Because they have forsaken my law which I set before them, and have not obeyed my voice, neither walked therein;

14 But have walked after the imagination of their own heart, and after Baalim, which their fathers taught them:

15 Therefore thus saith the LORD of hosts, the God of Israel; Behold, I will feed them, *even* this people, with wormwood, and give them water of gall to drink.

16 I will scatter them also among the heathen, whom neither they nor their fathers have known: and I will send a sword after them, till I have consumed them.

Jerusalem Cries Out for Help

17 Thus saith the LORD of hosts, Consider ye, and call for the mourning women, that they may come; and send for cunning *women,* that they may come:

18 And let them make haste, and take up a

Cross References (center column)

17 Ps. 58:4, 5; Eccl. 10:11

19 Deut. 32:21; Isa. 1:4; 39:3

21 Jer. 4:19; 9:1; 14:17; Joel 2:6; Nah. 2:10

22 Gen. 37:25; 43:11; Isa. 22:4; Jer. 4:19; 13:17; 14:17; 6:11; 51:8; Lam. 2:11; 3:48

2 Jer. 5:7, 8

3 1Sam. 2:12; Ps. 64:3; Isa. 59:4, 13, 15; Hos. 4:1

4 Jer. 6:28; 12:6; Mic. 7:5, 6

7 Isa. 1:25; Hos. 11:8; Mal. 3:3

8 Ps. 12:2; 28:3; 55:21; 120:3; Jer. 9:3

9 Jer. 5:9, 29

10 Jer. 4:25; 12:4; 23:10; Hos. 4:3

11 Isa. 13:22; 25:2; 34:13; Jer. 10:22

12 Ps. 107:43; Hos. 14:9

14 Jer. 3:17; 7:24; Gal. 1:14

15 Ps. 80:5; Jer. 8:14; 23:15; Lam. 3:15, 19

16 Lev. 26:33; Deut. 28:64; Jer. 44:27; Ezek. 5:2, 12

17 2Chr. 35:25; Matt. 9:23

9:12–16 Jeremiah seeks for at least one wise man in Judah, but none is found. Judgment is coming. Not only has Judah become disobedient, but also she has gone after "Baalim" (i.e., false gods). The bitter leaves of wormwood and the poisonous or salty drink of gall (cf. Jer. 8:14) speak of judgment.

9:17–22 Thus saith the LORD. This is an expression emphasizing the certainty of a future matter. These verses contain further prophetic statements signifying that God's impending judgment of Judah is certain, so much so, that Jeremiah advocates that the people of Judah act as if it has already happened.

wailing for us, that our eyes may run down with tears, and our eyelids gush out with waters.

19 For a voice of wailing is heard out of Zion, How are we spoiled! we are greatly confounded, because we have forsaken the land, because our dwellings have cast *us* out.

20 Yet hear the word of the LORD, O ye women, and let your ear receive the word of his mouth, and teach your daughters wailing, and every one her neighbour lamentation.

21 For death is come up into our windows, *and* is entered into our palaces, to cut off the children from without, *and* the young men from the streets.

22 Speak, Thus saith the LORD, Even the carcases of men shall fall as dung upon the open field, and as the handful after the harvest man, and none shall gather *them*.

23 Thus saith the LORD, Let not the wise *man* glory in his wisdom, neither let the mighty *man* glory in his might, let not the rich *man* glory in his riches:

24 But let him that glorieth glory in this, that he understandeth and knoweth me, that I *am* the LORD which exercise lovingkindness, judgment, and righteousness, in the earth: for in these *things* I delight, saith the LORD.

25 Behold, the days come, saith the LORD, that I will punish all *them which are* circumcised with the uncircumcised;

26 Egypt, and Judah, and Edom, and the children of Ammon, and Moab, and all *that are* in the utmost corners, that dwell in the wilderness: for all *these* nations *are* uncircumcised, and all the house of Israel *are* uncircumcised in the heart.

CHAPTER 10
The True God and Idolatry

1 Hear ye the word which the LORD speaketh unto you, O house of Israel:

2 Thus saith the LORD, Learn not the way of the heathen, and be not dismayed at the signs of heaven; for the heathen are dismayed at them.

3 For the customs of the people *are* vain:

for *one* cutteth a tree out of the forest, the work of the hands of the workman, with the axe.

4 They deck it with silver and with gold; they fasten it with nails and with hammers, that it move not.

5 They *are* upright as the palm tree, but speak not: they must needs be borne, because they cannot go. Be not afraid of them; for they cannot do evil, neither also *is it* in them to do good.

6 Forasmuch as *there is* none like unto thee, O LORD; thou *art* great, and thy name *is* great in might.

7 Who would not fear thee, O King of nations? for to thee doth it appertain: forasmuch as among all the wise *men* of the nations, and in all their kingdoms, *there is* none like unto thee.

8 But they are altogether brutish and foolish: the stock *is* a doctrine of vanities.

9 Silver spread into plates is brought from Tarshish, and gold from Uphaz, the work of the workman, and of the hands of the founder: blue and purple *is* their clothing: they *are* all the work of cunning *men*.

10 But the LORD *is* the true God, he *is* the living God, and an everlasting king: at his wrath the earth shall tremble, and the nations shall not be able to abide his indignation.

11 Thus shall ye say unto them, The gods that have not made the heavens and the earth, *even* they shall perish from the earth, and from under these heavens.

12 He hath made the earth by his power, he hath established the world by his wisdom, and hath stretched out the heavens by his discretion.

13 When he uttereth his voice, *there is* a multitude of waters in the heavens, and he causeth the vapours to ascend from the ends of the earth; he maketh lightnings with rain, and bringeth forth the wind out of his treasures.

14 Every man is brutish in *his* knowledge: every founder is confounded by the graven image: for his molten image *is* falsehood, and *there is* no breath in them.

15 They *are* vanity, *and* the work of errors: in

Cross references

19 Lev. 18:28; 20:22
21 Jer. 6:11
22 Jer. 8:2; 16:4
23 Eccl. 9:11
24 Mic. 6:8; 7:18; 1Cor. 1:31; 2Cor. 10:17
25 Rom. 2:8, 9
26 Lev. 18:3; 20:23; 26:41;Jer. 25:23; 49:32; Ezek. 44:7; Rom. 2:28, 29
3 Isa. 40:19, 20; 44:9, 10; 45:20
4 Isa. 41:7; 46:7
5 Ps. 115:5, 7; 135:16; Isa. 41:23; 46:1, 7; Hab. 2:19; 1Cor. 12:2
6 Ex. 15:11; Ps. 86:8, 10
7 Ps. 89:6; Rev. 15:4
8 Ps. 115:8; Isa. 41:29; Hab. 2:18; Zech. 13:2; Rom. 1:21, 22
9 Ps. 115:4; Dan. 10:5
10 Ps. 10:16; 31:5; 1Tim. 6:17
11 Ps. 96:5; Isa. 2:18; Jer. 10:15; Zech. 13:2
12 Gen. 1:1, 6, 9; Job 9:8; Ps. 93:1; 104:2; 136:5, 6; Isa. 40:22; Jer. 51:15
13 Job 38:34; Ps. 135:7
14 Prov. 30:2

9:25–26 Jeremiah indicates the need for a circumcised heart, which he predicts in Jeremiah 31:31 that Judah and Israel will one day have. But at this time, Judah, even though circumcised in the flesh, behaves in the same way as the Gentiles do. It should be no surprise that Judah is listed with other heathen nations such as Egypt, Edom, Ammon, and Moab.

10:10 Since Jeremiah here speaks in global terminology ("the earth shall tremble, and the nations"), he likely is referring to the future and global judgments of the Tribulation period.

the time of their visitation they shall perish.

16 The portion of Jacob is not like them: for he is the former of all *things*; and Israel is the rod of his inheritance: The LORD of hosts is his name.

The Desolation of Judah

17 Gather up thy wares out of the land, O inhabitant of the fortress.

18 For thus saith the LORD, Behold, I will sling out the inhabitants of the land at this once, and will distress them, that they may find it so.

19 Woe is me for my hurt! my wound is grievous: but I said, Truly this is a grief, and I must bear it.

20 My tabernacle is spoiled, and all my cords are broken: my children are gone forth of me, and they are not: there is none to stretch forth my tent any more, and to set up my curtains.

21 For the pastors are become brutish, and have not sought the LORD: therefore they shall not prosper, and all their flocks shall be scattered.

22 Behold, the noise of the bruit is come, and a great commotion out of the north country, to make the cities of Judah desolate, and a den of dragons.

23 O LORD, I know that the way of man is not in himself: it is not in man that walketh to direct his steps.

24 O LORD, correct me, but with judgment; not in thine anger, lest thou bring me to nothing.

25 Pour out thy fury upon the heathen that know thee not, and upon the families that call not on thy name: for they have eaten up Jacob, and devoured him, and consumed him, and have made his habitation desolate.

CHAPTER 11
The Broken Covenant

1 The word that came to Jeremiah from the LORD, saying,

2 Hear ye the words of this covenant, and speak unto the men of Judah, and to the inhabitants of Jerusalem;

3 And say thou unto them, Thus saith the

Center cross-references

16 Deut. 32:9; Ps. 16:5; 73:26; 74:2; 119:57
17 Jer. 6:1; Ezek. 12:3
18 1Sam. 25:29; Jer. 16:13; Ezek. 6:10
19 Ps. 77:10; Jer. 4:19; 8:21; 9:1; Mic. 7:9
20 Jer. 4:20
22 Jer. 1:15; 4:6; 5:15; 6:22; 9:11
23 Prov. 16:1; 20:24
24 Ps. 6:1; 38:1; Jer. 30:11
25 Deut. 27:26; Job 18:21; Ps. 79:6; Jer. 8:16; Gal. 3:10; 1Thess. 4:5; 2Thess. 1:8
4 Lev. 26:3, 12; Deut. 4:20; 1Kgs. 8:51; Jer. 7:23
5 Deut. 7:12, 13; 27:15-26; Ps. 105:9, 10
6 Rom. 2:13; James 1:22
7 Jer. 7:13, 25; 35:15
8 Jer. 3:17; 7:24, 26; 9:14
9 Ezek. 22:25; Hos. 6:9
10 Ezek. 20:18
11 Ps. 18:41; Prov. 1:28
12 Deut. 32:37, 38
13 Hos. 9:10

LORD God of Israel; Cursed be the man that obeyeth not the words of this covenant,

4 Which I commanded your fathers in the day that I brought them forth out of the land of Egypt, from the iron furnace, saying, Obey my voice, and do them, according to all which I command you: so shall ye be my people, and I will be your God:

5 That I may perform the oath which I have sworn unto your fathers, to give them a land flowing with milk and honey, as it is this day. Then answered I, and said, So be it, O LORD.

6 Then the LORD said unto me, Proclaim all these words in the cities of Judah, and in the streets of Jerusalem, saying, Hear ye the words of this covenant, and do them.

7 For I earnestly protested unto your fathers in the day that I brought them up out of the land of Egypt, even unto this day, rising early and protesting, saying, Obey my voice.

8 Yet they obeyed not, nor inclined their ear, but walked every one in the imagination of their evil heart: therefore I will bring upon them all the words of this covenant, which I commanded them to do; but they did them not.

9 And the LORD said unto me, A conspiracy is found among the men of Judah, and among the inhabitants of Jerusalem.

10 They are turned back to the iniquities of their forefathers, which refused to hear my words; and they went after other gods to serve them: the house of Israel and the house of Judah have broken my covenant which I made with their fathers.

11 Therefore thus saith the LORD, Behold, I will bring evil upon them, which they shall not be able to escape; and though they shall cry unto me, I will not hearken unto them.

12 Then shall the cities of Judah and inhabitants of Jerusalem go, and cry unto the gods unto whom they offer incense: but they shall not save them at all in the time of their trouble.

13 For according to the number of thy cities were thy gods, O Judah; and according to the number of the streets of Jerusalem have ye

---

10:17–18 Gather up thy wares out of the land. This is a description of refugees who are being taken captive into another land.

10:20 Like one who dwells in the dessert when marauders destroy one's "tabernacle" (tent), so will Judah be left with no children to restore the damage that will be done.

11:5 The Lord reminds Judah of the oath He swore unto their fathers (Gen. 12:7). In this oath, God promised His chosen people that He would give them a land of their own and an eternal kingdom. One day this will be fulfilled when Judah and all of Israel obey the Lord from a new heart (Jer. 31:31).

set up altars to *that* shameful thing, *even* altars to burn incense unto Baal.

14 Therefore pray not thou for this people, neither lift up a cry or prayer for them: for I will not hear *them* in the time that they cry unto me for their trouble.

15 What hath my beloved to do in mine house, *seeing* she hath wrought lewdness with many, and the holy flesh is passed from thee? when thou doest evil, then thou rejoicest.

16 The LORD called thy name, A green olive tree, fair, *and* of goodly fruit: with the noise of a great tumult he hath kindled fire upon it, and the branches of it are broken.

17 For the LORD of hosts, that planted thee, hath pronounced evil against thee, for the evil of the house of Israel and of the house of Judah, which they have done against themselves to provoke me to anger in offering incense unto Baal.

The Plot to Kill Jeremiah

18 And the LORD hath given me knowledge *of it*, and I know *it*: then thou shewedst me their doings.

19 But I *was* like a lamb *or* an ox *that* is brought to the slaughter; and I knew not that they had devised devices against me, *saying*, Let us destroy the tree with the fruit thereof, and let us cut him off from the land of the living, that his name may be no more remembered.

20 But, O LORD of hosts, that judgest righteously, that triest the reins and the heart, let me see thy vengeance on them: for unto thee have I revealed my cause.

21 Therefore thus saith the LORD of the men of Anathoth, that seek thy life, saying, Prophesy not in the name of the LORD, that thou die not by our hand:

22 Therefore thus saith the LORD of hosts, Behold, I will punish them: the young men shall die by the sword; their sons and their daughters shall die by famine:

23 And there shall be no remnant of them: for I will bring evil upon the men of Anathoth, *even* the year of their visitation.

CHAPTER 12
Jeremiah's Complaint and God's Answer

1 Righteous *art* thou, O LORD, when I plead with thee: yet let me talk with thee of *thy*

judgments: Wherefore doth the way of the wicked prosper? *wherefore* are all they happy that deal very treacherously?

2 Thou hast planted them, yea, they have taken root: they grow, yea, they bring forth fruit: thou *art* near in their mouth, and far from their reins.

3 But thou, O LORD, knowest me: thou hast seen me, and tried mine heart toward thee: pull them out like sheep for the slaughter, and prepare them for the day of slaughter.

4 How long shall the land mourn, and the herbs of every field wither, for the wickedness of them that dwell therein? the beasts are consumed, and the birds; because they said, He shall not see our last end.

5 If thou hast run with the footmen, and they have wearied thee, then how canst thou contend with horses? and *if* in the land of peace, *wherein* thou trustedst, *they wearied thee*, then how wilt thou do in the swelling of Jordan?

6 For even thy brethren, and the house of thy father, even they have dealt treacherously with thee; yea, they have called a multitude after thee: believe them not, though they speak fair words unto thee.

7 I have forsaken mine house, I have left mine heritage; I have given the dearly beloved of my soul into the hand of her enemies.

8 Mine heritage is unto me as a lion in the forest; it crieth out against me: therefore have I hated it.

9 Mine heritage *is* unto me *as* a speckled bird, the birds round about *are* against her; come ye, assemble all the beasts of the field, come to devour.

10 Many pastors have destroyed my vineyard, they have trodden my portion under foot, they have made my pleasant portion a desolate wilderness.

11 They have made it desolate, *and being* desolate it mourneth unto me; the whole land is made desolate, because no man layeth *it* to heart.

12 The spoilers are come upon all high places through the wilderness: for the sword of the LORD shall devour from the *one* end of the land even to the *other* end of the land: no flesh shall have peace.

13 They have sown wheat, but shall reap

Cross-references: **14** Ex. 32:10; Jer. 7:16; 14:11; 1John 5:16 • **15** Ps. 50:16; Prov. 2:14; Isa. 1:11; Ezek. 16:25; Hag. 2:12, 13, 14; Titus 1:15 • **16** Ps. 52:8; Rom. 11:17 • **17** Isa. 5:2; Jer. 2:21 • **19** Ps. 27:13; 83:4; 116:9; 142:5; Jer. 18:18 • **20** 1Sam. 16:7; 1Chr. 28:9; Ps. 7:9; Jer. 17:10; 20:12; Rev. 2:23 • **21** Isa. 30:10; Jer. 12:5, 6; Amos 2:12; 7:13, 16; Mic. 2:6 • **23** Job 12:6; 21:7; Ps. 37:1, 35; 51:4; 73:3; Hab. 1:4; Mal. 3:15; Luke 19:44 • **2** Isa. 29:13; Matt. 15:8; Mark 7:6 • **3** Ps. 17:3; 139:1; Jer. 11:20; James 5:5 • **4** Ps. 107:34; Jer. 4:25; 7:20; 9:10; 23:10; Hos. 4:3 • **5** Josh. 3:15; 1Chr. 12:15; Jer. 49:19; 50:44 • **6** Prov. 26:25; Jer. 9:4; 11:19, 21 • **9** Isa. 56:9; Jer. 7:33 • **10** Isa. 5:1, 5; 63:18; Jer. 6:3 • **13** Lev. 26:16; Deut. 28:38

11:20–21 Jeremiah appeals for God's vindication against those plotting to kill him from his hometown of Anathoth. But the Lord has promised to protect him (cf. Jer. 1:8, 18–19). The word "reins" refers to the internal organs of the body widely viewed as the seat of human emotions. The word "heart" here refers to the intellect.

thorns: they have put themselves to pain, *but* shall not profit: and they shall be ashamed of your revenues because of the fierce anger of the LORD.

14 Thus saith the LORD against all mine evil neighbours, that touch the inheritance which I have caused my people Israel to inherit; Behold, I will pluck them out of their land, and pluck out the house of Judah from among them.

15 And it shall come to pass, after that I have plucked them out I will return, and have compassion on them, and will bring them again, every man to his heritage, and every man to his land.

16 And it shall come to pass, if they will diligently learn the ways of my people, to swear by my name, The LORD liveth; as they taught my people to swear by Baal; then shall they be built in the midst of my people.

17 But if they will not obey, I will utterly pluck up and destroy that nation, saith the LORD.

CHAPTER 13
The Sign of the Marked Undergarment

1 Thus saith the LORD unto me, Go and get thee a linen girdle, and put it upon thy loins, and put it not in water.

2 So I got a girdle according to the word of the LORD, and put *it* on my loins.

3 And the word of the LORD came unto me the second time, saying,

4 Take the girdle that thou hast got, which *is* upon thy loins, and arise, go to Euphrates, and hide it there in a hole of the rock.

5 So I went, and hid it by Euphrates, as the LORD commanded me.

6 And it came to pass after many days, that the LORD said unto me, Arise, go to Euphrates, and take the girdle from thence, which I commanded thee to hide there.

7 Then I went to Euphrates, and digged, and took the girdle from the place where I had hid it: and, behold, the girdle was marred, it was profitable for nothing.

8 Then the word of the LORD came unto me, saying,

9 Thus saith the LORD, After this manner will I mar the pride of Judah, and the great pride of Jerusalem.

10 This evil people, which refuse to hear my words, which walk in the imagination of their heart, and walk after other gods, to serve them, and to worship them, shall even be as this girdle, which is good for nothing.

11 For as the girdle cleaveth to the loins of a man, so have I caused to cleave unto me the whole house of Israel and the whole house of Judah, saith the LORD; that they might be unto me for a people, and for a name, and for a praise, and for a glory: but they would not hear.

The Bottles of Wine

12 Therefore thou shalt speak unto them this word; Thus saith the LORD God of Israel, Every bottle shall be filled with wine: and they shall say unto thee, Do we not certainly know that every bottle shall be filled with wine?

13 Then shalt thou say unto them, Thus saith the LORD, Behold, I will fill all the inhabitants of this land, even the kings that sit upon David's throne, and the priests, and the prophets, and all the inhabitants of Jerusalem, with drunkenness.

14 And I will dash them one against another, even the fathers and the sons together, saith the LORD: I will not pity, nor spare, nor have mercy, but destroy them.

Jeremiah Warns against Pride

15 Hear ye, and give ear; be not proud: for the LORD hath spoken.

16 Give glory to the LORD your God, before

Cross references
14 Deut. 30:3; Jer. 32:37; Zech. 2:8
15 Ezek. 28:25; Amos 9:14
16 Jer. 4:2; Eph. 2:20, 21; 1Pet. 2:5
17 Lev. 26:19; Isa. 60:12
10 Jer. 9:14; 11:8; 16:12
11 Ex. 19:5; Jer. 33:9
13 Isa. 51:17, 21; 63:6; Jer. 25:27; 51:7
14 Ps. 2:9
16 Josh. 7:19; Ps. 44:19; Isa. 5:30; 8:22; 59:9; Amos 8:9

12:14–17 In spite of the severe judgment pending upon Judah, Jeremiah prophesies that there will come a day when the Lord will judge the nations that He is about to use against Judah. One day, Judah will learn obedience to the Lord and will be returned back to her land to receive great blessing from the Lord.

13:8–11 Jeremiah prophesies the ruin of Judah by using the symbol of a linen sash (girdle). God speaks to Jeremiah and tells him to buy a linen sash to wear around his waist. This sash was not to touch water (v. 1) and represents Judah's priestly element, while the water repre-

sents cleansing. Thus, Judah is pictured as dirty and in need of cleansing. As instructed by God, Jeremiah buried the girdle in the crevice of rocks near the Euphrates River, indicating the impending Babylonian invasion. Jeremiah's prophecy relating to the linen sash explains that God will judge Judah because "they would not hear" His word.

13:15–21 Jeremiah is told to warn the king and queen of Judah that if they do not repent and humble themselves then their "principalities shall come down." This was fulfilled in the Babylonian invasion of 586 B.C.

he cause darkness, and before your feet stumble upon the dark mountains, and, while ye look for light, he turn it into the shadow of death, *and* make *it* gross darkness.

17 But if ye will not hear it, my soul shall weep in secret places for *your* pride; and mine eye shall weep sore, and run down with tears, because the LORD's flock is carried away captive.

18 Say unto the king and to the queen, Humble yourselves, sit down: for your principalities shall come down, *even* the crown of your glory.

19 The cities of the south shall be shut up, and none shall open *them*: Judah shall be carried away captive all of it, it shall be wholly carried away captive.

20 Lift up your eyes, and behold them that come from the north: where *is* the flock *that* was given thee, thy beautiful flock?

21 What wilt thou say when he shall punish thee? for thou hast taught them *to be* captains, *and* as chief over thee: shall not sorrows take thee, as a woman in travail?

22 And if thou say in thine heart, Wherefore come these things upon me? For the greatness of thine iniquity are thy skirts discovered, *and* thy heels made bare.

23 Can the Ethiopian change his skin, or the leopard his spots? *then* may ye also do good, that are accustomed to do evil.

24 Therefore will I scatter them as the stubble that passeth away by the wind of the wilderness.

25 This *is* thy lot, the portion of thy measures from me, saith the LORD; because thou hast forgotten me, and trusted in falsehood.

26 Therefore will I discover thy skirts upon thy face, that thy shame may appear.

27 I have seen thine adulteries, and thy neighings, the lewdness of thy whoredom, *and* thine abominations on the hills in the fields. Woe unto thee, O Jerusalem! wilt thou not be made clean? when *shall it* once *be?*

CHAPTER 14
The Drought

1 The word of the LORD that came to Jeremiah concerning the dearth.

2 Judah mourneth, and the gates thereof languish; they are black unto the ground; and the cry of Jerusalem is gone up.

3 And their nobles have sent their little ones to the waters: they came to the pits, *and* found no water; they returned with their vessels empty; they were ashamed and confounded, and covered their heads.

4 Because the ground is chapt, for there was no rain in the earth, the plowmen were ashamed, they covered their heads.

5 Yea, the hind also calved in the field, and forsook *it*, because there was no grass.

6 And the wild asses did stand in the high places, they snuffed up the wind like dragons; their eyes did fail, because *there was* no grass.

7 O LORD, though our iniquities testify against us, do thou *it* for thy name's sake: for our backslidings are many; we have sinned against thee.

8 O the hope of Israel, the saviour thereof in time of trouble, why shouldest thou be as a stranger in the land, and as a wayfaring man *that* turneth aside to tarry for a night?

9 Why shouldest thou be as a man astonied, as a mighty man *that* cannot save? yet thou, O LORD, *art* in the midst of us, and we are called by thy name; leave us not.

10 Thus saith the LORD unto this people, Thus have they loved to wander, they have not refrained their feet, therefore the LORD doth not accept them; he will now remember their iniquity, and visit their sins.

11 Then said the LORD unto me, Pray not for this people for *their* good.

12 When they fast, I will not hear their cry; and when they offer burnt offering and an oblation, I will not accept them: but I will consume them by the sword, and by the famine, and by the pestilence.

13 Then said I, Ah, Lord GOD! behold, the prophets say unto them, Ye shall not see the sword, neither shall ye have famine; but I will give you assured peace in this place.

14 Then the LORD said unto me, The prophets prophesy lies in my name: I sent them not, neither have I commanded them, neither spake unto them: they prophesy unto you a false vision and divination, and a thing of nought, and the deceit of their heart.

15 Therefore thus saith the LORD concerning the prophets that prophesy in my name, and I sent them not, yet they say, Sword and famine shall not be in this land; By sword and famine shall those prophets be consumed.

16 And the people to whom they prophesy shall be cast out in the streets of Jerusalem because of the famine and the sword; and they shall have none to bury them, them, their wives, nor their sons, nor their daughters: for I will pour their wickedness upon them.

17 Therefore thou shalt say this word unto

---

17 Jer. 9:1; 14:17; Lam. 1:2, 16; 2:18
18 2Kgs. 24:12; Jer. 22:26
20 Jer. 6:22
21 Jer. 6:24
22 Isa. 3:17; 47:2, 3; Jer. 5:19; 13:26; 16:10; Ezek. 16:37-39; Nah. 3:5
24 Ps. 1:4; Hos. 13:3
25 Job 20:29; Ps. 11:6; Jer. 10:14
26 Jer. 13:2; Lam. 1:8; Ezek. 16:37; 23:29; Hos. 2:10
27 Isa. 65:7; Jer. 2:20; 3:2, 6; 5:8; Ezek. 6:13

2 1Sam. 5:12; Isa. 3:26; Jer. 8:21
3 2Sam. 15:30; Ps. 40:14
6 Jer. 2:24
7 Ps. 25:11
8 Jer. 17:13
9 Ex. 29:45, 46; Lev. 26:11, 12; Isa. 59:1; Dan. 9:18, 19
10 Jer. 2:23-25; Hos. 8:13; 9:9
11 Ex. 32:10; Jer. 7:16; 11:14
12 Prov. 1:28; Isa. 1:15; 58:3; Jer. 6:20; 7:21, 22; 9:16; 11:11; Ezek. 8:18; Mic. 3:4; Zech. 7:13
13 Jer. 4:10
14 Jer. 23:21; 27:10, 15; 29:8, 9
15 Jer. 5:12, 13
16 Ps. 79:3
17 Jer. 8:21; 9:1; 13:17; Lam. 1:16; 2:18;

them; Let mine eyes run down with tears night and day, and let them not cease: for the virgin daughter of my people is broken with a great breach, with a very grievous blow.

18 If I go forth into the field, then behold the slain with the sword! and if I enter into the city, then behold them that are sick with famine! yea, both the prophet and the priest go about into a land that they know not.

The People Plead with God

19 Hast thou utterly rejected Judah? hath thy soul lothed Zion? why hast thou smitten us, and *there is* no healing for us? we looked for peace, and *there is* no good; and for the time of healing, and behold trouble!

20 We acknowledge, O LORD, our wickedness, *and* the iniquity of our fathers: for we have sinned against thee.

21 Do not abhor *us*, for thy name's sake, do not disgrace the throne of thy glory: remember, break not thy covenant with us.

22 Are there *any* among the vanities of the Gentiles that can cause rain? or can the heavens give showers? *art* not thou he, O LORD our God? therefore we will wait upon thee: for thou hast made all these *things*.

CHAPTER 15
The Lord's Fury

1 Then said the LORD unto me, Though Moses and Samuel stood before me, *yet* my mind *could* not *be* toward this people: cast *them* out of my sight, and let them go forth.

2 And it shall come to pass, if they say unto thee, Whither shall we go forth? then thou shalt tell them, Thus saith the LORD; Such as *are* for death, to death; and such as *are* for the sword, to the sword; and such as *are* for the famine, to the famine; and such as *are* for the captivity, to the captivity.

3 And I will appoint over them four kinds, saith the LORD: the sword to slay, and the dogs to tear, and the fowls of the heaven,

and the beasts of the earth, to devour and destroy.

4 And I will cause them to be removed into all kingdoms of the earth, because of Manasseh the son of Hezekiah king of Judah, for *that* which he did in Jerusalem.

5 For who shall have pity upon thee, O Jerusalem? or who shall bemoan thee? or who shall go aside to ask how thou doest?

6 Thou hast forsaken me, saith the LORD, thou art gone backward: therefore will I stretch out my hand against thee, and destroy thee; I am weary with repenting.

7 And I will fan them with a fan in the gates of the land; I will bereave *them* of children, I will destroy my people, *since* they return not from their ways.

8 Their widows are increased to me above the sand of the seas: I have brought upon them against the mother of the young men a spoiler at noonday: I have caused *him* to fall upon it suddenly, and terrors upon the city.

9 She that hath borne seven languisheth: she hath given up the ghost; her sun is gone down while *it was* yet day: she hath been ashamed and confounded: and the residue of them will I deliver to the sword before their enemies, saith the LORD.

Jeremiah's Complaints

10 Woe is me, my mother, that thou hast borne me a man of strife and a man of contention to the whole earth! I have neither lent on usury, nor men have lent to me on usury; *yet* every one of them doth curse me.

11 The LORD said, Verily it shall be well with thy remnant; verily I will cause the enemy to entreat thee *well* in the time of evil and in the time of affliction.

12 Shall iron break the northern iron and the steel?

13 Thy substance and thy treasures will I give to the spoil without price, and *that* for all thy sins, even in all thy borders.

14 And I will make *thee* to pass with thine

18 Jer. 5:31; Ezek. 7:15
19 Jer. 8:15; 15:18; Lam. 5:22
20 Ps. 106:6; Dan. 9:8
21 Ps. 74:2, 20; 106:45
22 Ex. 32:11, 12; Deut. 32:21; 1Sam. 7:9; Ps. 99:6; 135:7; 147:8; Isa. 30:23; Jer. 5:24; 10:13; Ezek. 14:14; Zech. 10:1; 2
2 Jer. 43:11; Ezek. 5:2, 12; Zech. 11:9
3 Lev. 26:16; Deut. 28:26; Jer. 7:33
4 Deut. 28:25; 2Kgs. 21:11; 23:26; 24:3, 4; Jer. 24:9; Ezek. 23:46
5 Isa. 51:19
6 Jer. 2:13; 7:24; Hos. 13:14
7 Isa. 9:13; Jer. 5:3; Amos 4:10, 11
9 1Sam. 2:5; Amos 8:9
10 Job 3:1; Jer. 20:14
11 Jer. 39:11, 12; 40:4, 5
13 Ps. 44:12; Jer. 17:3
14 Deut. 32:22; Jer. 16:13; 17:4

14:19–22 Jeremiah intercedes on behalf of the nation and pleads to God for mercy.

15:1–7 Moses and Samuel stood before me. Moses and Samuel interceded on behalf of the nation, and God relented (Num. 14:11–25; 1 Sam. 12:19–25), but not even these two men could get Judah out of the coming judgment because the nation had become too entrenched in disobedience. The Lord would use four instruments of judgment: death, the sword, famine, and captivity. The

four types of judgment depict the completeness of the judgment God is about to send upon Judah. Specifically God will judge Judah because of the sin of King Manasseh. Manasseh led the nation into the worship of Molech, which included child sacrifice (2 Kgs. 21:1–18; Jer. 7:31).

15:6 I am weary with repenting. The Lord had relented upon His judgment in the past, but the nation continued in her sin. This time the Lord would not repent (i.e., change his mind) and would destroy His people.

enemies into a land *which* thou knowest not: for a fire is kindled in mine anger, *which* shall burn upon you.

15 O LORD, thou knowest: remember me, and visit me, and revenge me of my persecutors; take me not away in thy longsuffering: know that for thy sake I have suffered rebuke.

16 Thy words were found, and I did eat them; and thy word was unto me the joy and rejoicing of mine heart: for I am called by thy name, O LORD God of hosts.

17 I sat not in the assembly of the mockers, nor rejoiced; I sat alone because of thy hand: for thou hast filled me with indignation.

18 Why is my pain perpetual, and my wound incurable, *which* refuseth to be healed? wilt thou be altogether unto me as a liar, *and as* waters *that* fail?

19 Therefore thus saith the LORD, If thou return, then will I bring thee again, *and* thou shalt stand before me: and if thou take forth the precious from the vile, thou shalt be as my mouth: let them return unto thee; but return not thou unto them.

20 And I will make thee unto this people a fenced brasen wall: and they shall fight against thee, but they shall not prevail against thee: for I *am* with thee to save thee and to deliver thee, saith the LORD.

21 And I will deliver thee out of the hand of the wicked, and I will redeem thee out of the hand of the terrible.

CHAPTER 16
Judgment upon the People

1 The word of the LORD came also unto me, saying,

2 Thou shalt not take thee a wife, neither shalt thou have sons or daughters in this place.

3 For thus saith the LORD concerning the sons and concerning the daughters that are born in this place, and concerning their mothers that bare them, and concerning their fathers that begat them in this land;

4 They shall die of grievous deaths; they shall not be lamented; neither shall they be buried; *but* they shall be as dung upon the face of the earth: and they shall be consumed by the sword, and by famine; and their carcases shall be meat for the fowls of heaven, and for the beasts of the earth.

15 Ps. 69:7; Jer. 11:20; 12:3; 20:12

16 Job 23:12; Ps. 119:72, 111; Ezek. 3:1, 3; Rev. 10:9, 10

17 Ps. 1:1; 26:4, 5

18 Job 6:15; Jer. 1:18, 19; 30:15

19 Jer. 15:1; Ezek. 22:26; 44:23; Zech. 3:7

20 Ps. 79:2; 83:10; Jer. 1:18; 6:27; 7:33; 8:2; 9:22; 15:2; 20:11, 12; 22:18, 19; 25:33; 34:20

5 Ezek. 24:17, 22, 23

6 Lev. 19:28; Deut. 14:1; Isa. 22:12; Jer. 7:29; 22:18; 41:5; 47:5

7 Deut. 26:14; Job 42:11; Prov. 31:6, 7; Hos. 9:4

9 Isa. 24:7, 8; Jer. 7:34; 25:10; Ezek. 26:13; Hos. 2:11; Rev. 18:23

10 Deut. 29:24; Jer. 5:19; 13:22; 22:8

11 Deut. 29:25; Jer. 22:9

12 Jer. 7:26; 13:10

13 Deut. 4:26-28; 28:36, 64, 65; Jer. 15:14

14 Isa. 43:18; Jer. 23:7, 8

15 Jer. 24:6; 30:3; 32:37

5 For thus saith the LORD, Enter not into the house of mourning, neither go to lament nor bemoan them: for I have taken away my peace from this people, saith the LORD, *even* lovingkindness and mercies.

6 Both the great and the small shall die in this land: they shall not be buried, neither shall *men* lament for them: nor cut themselves, nor make themselves bald for them:

7 Neither shall *men* tear *themselves* for them in mourning, to comfort them for the dead; neither shall *men* give them the cup of consolation to drink for their father or for their mother.

8 Thou shalt not also go into the house of feasting, to sit with them to eat and to drink.

9 For thus saith the LORD of hosts, the God of Israel; Behold, I will cause to cease out of this place in your eyes, and in your days, the voice of mirth, and the voice of gladness, the voice of the bridegroom, and the voice of the bride.

10 And it shall come to pass, when thou shalt shew this people all these words, and they shall say unto thee, Wherefore hath the LORD pronounced all this great evil against us? or what *is* our iniquity? or what *is* our sin that we have committed against the LORD our God?

11 Then shalt thou say unto them, Because your fathers have forsaken me, saith the LORD, and have walked after other gods, and have served them, and have worshipped them, and have forsaken me, and have not kept my law;

12 And ye have done worse than your fathers; for, behold, ye walk every one after the imagination of his evil heart, that they may not hearken unto me:

13 Therefore will I cast you out of this land into a land that ye know not, *neither* ye nor your fathers; and there shall ye serve other gods day and night; where I will not shew you favour.

A Return Predicted

14 Therefore, behold, the days come, saith the LORD, that it shall no more be said, The LORD liveth, that brought up the children of Israel out of the land of Egypt;

15 But, The LORD liveth, that brought up the children of Israel from the land of the north,

---

16:14–15 Jeremiah prophesies that when the Lord brings the people of Judah back to their land in the Last Days that it will become a more famous phenomenon than that of the Exodus from Egypt.

and from all the lands whither he had driven them: and I will bring them again into their land that I gave unto their fathers.

16 Behold, I will send for many fishers, saith the LORD, and they shall fish them; and after will I send for many hunters, and they shall hunt them from every mountain, and from every hill, and out of the holes of the rocks.

17 For mine eyes *are* upon all their ways: they are not hid from my face, neither is their iniquity hid from mine eyes.

18 And first I will recompense their iniquity and their sin double; because they have defiled my land, they have filled mine inheritance with the carcases of their detestable and abominable things.

19 O LORD, my strength, and my fortress, and my refuge in the day of affliction, the Gentiles shall come unto thee from the ends of the earth, and shall say, Surely our fathers have inherited lies, vanity, and *things* wherein *there is* no profit.

20 Shall a man make gods unto himself, and they *are* no gods?

21 Therefore, behold, I will this once cause them to know, I will cause them to know mine hand and my might; and they shall know that my name *is* The LORD.

CHAPTER 17
The Sin of Judah

1 The sin of Judah *is* written with a pen of iron, *and* with the point of a diamond: *it is* graven upon the table of their heart, and upon the horns of your altars;

2 Whilst their children remember their altars and their groves by the green trees upon the high hills.

3 O my mountain in the field, I will give thy substance *and* all thy treasures to the spoil, *and* thy high places for sin, throughout all thy borders.

4 And thou, even thyself, shalt discontinue from thine heritage that I gave thee; and I will cause thee to serve thine enemies in the land which thou knowest not: for ye have kindled a fire in mine anger, *which* shall burn for ever.

Trust in the Lord

5 Thus saith the LORD; Cursed *be* the man that trusteth in man, and maketh flesh his arm, and whose heart departeth from the LORD.

6 For he shall be like the heath in the desert, and shall not see when good cometh; but shall inhabit the parched places in the wilderness, *in* a salt land and not inhabited.

7 Blessed *is* the man that trusteth in the LORD, and whose hope the LORD is.

8 For he shall be as a tree planted by the waters, and *that* spreadeth out her roots by the river, and shall not see when heat cometh, but her leaf shall be green; and shall not be careful in the year of drought, neither shall cease from yielding fruit.

9 The heart *is* deceitful above all *things*, and desperately wicked: who can know it?

10 I the LORD search the heart, *I* try the reins, even to give every man according to his ways, *and* according to the fruit of his doings.

11 *As* the partridge sitteth *on eggs*, and hatcheth *them* not; *so* he that getteth riches, and not by right, shall leave them in the midst of his days, and at his end shall be a fool.

12 A glorious high throne from the beginning *is* the place of our sanctuary.

13 O LORD, the hope of Israel, all that forsake thee shall be ashamed, *and* they that depart from me shall be written in the earth, because they have forsaken the LORD, the fountain of living waters.

Jeremiah Pleads with God

14 Heal me, O LORD, and I shall be healed; save me, and I shall be saved: for thou *art* my praise.

15 Behold, they say unto me, Where *is* the word of the LORD? let it come now.

16 As for me, I have not hastened from *being* a pastor to follow thee: neither have I desired the woeful day; thou knowest: that which came out of my lips was *right* before thee.

17 Be not a terror unto me: thou *art* my hope in the day of evil.

18 Let them be confounded that persecute me, but let not me be confounded: let them be dismayed, but let not me be dismayed: bring upon them the day of evil, and destroy them with double destruction.

Cross references (center column):

16 Amos 4:2; Hab. 1:15
17 Job 34:21; Prov. 5:21; 15:3; Jer. 32:19
18 Ezra 43:7, 9; Isa. 40:2; Jer. 17:18
19 Ps. 18:2; Isa. 44:10; Jer. 2:11; 10:5; 17:17
20 Isa. 37:19; Jer. 2:11; Gal. 4:8
21 Ex. 15:3; Job 19:24; Ps. 83:18; Prov. 3:3; Jer. 33:2; Amos 5:8; 2Cor. 3:3
2 Judg. 3:7; 2Chr. 24:18; 33:3, 19; Isa. 1:29; 17:8; Jer. 2:20
3 Jer. 15:13
4 Jer. 15:14; 16:13
5 Isa. 30:1, 2; 31:1
6 Deut. 29:23; Job 20:17; Jer. 48:6
7 Ps. 2:12; 34:8; 125:1; 146:5; Prov. 16:20; Isa. 30:18
8 Job 8:16; Ps. 1:3
9 1Sam. 16:7; Prov. 17:3; Rom. 2:6; 8:27
11 Ps. 55:23; Luke 12:20
13 Ps. 73:27; Isa. 1:28; Jer. 2:13; 14:8; Luke 10:20
14 Ps. 109:1; 148:14
15 Isa. 5:19; Ezek. 12:22; 2Pet. 3:4
17 Jer. 16:19

16:16–19 fishers . . . hunters. These terms refer to the Babylonians who would scour the land to find those hiding out when the invasion comes.

17:4 I will cause thee to serve thine enemies in the land which thou knowest not. Simply, if the people of Judah were not going to serve the Lord in His land, then they would become servants in the land of their enemies, whose behavior they were imitating.

The Sabbath Must Be Observed

19 Thus said the LORD unto me; Go and stand in the gate of the children of the people, whereby the kings of Judah come in, and by the which they go out, and in all the gates of Jerusalem;

20 And say unto them, Hear ye the word of the LORD, ye kings of Judah, and all Judah, and all the inhabitants of Jerusalem, that enter in by these gates:

21 Thus saith the LORD; Take heed to yourselves, and bear no burden on the sabbath day, nor bring *it* in by the gates of Jerusalem;

22 Neither carry forth a burden out of your houses on the sabbath day, neither do ye any work, but hallow ye the sabbath day, as I commanded your fathers.

23 But they obeyed not, neither inclined their ear, but made their neck stiff, that they might not hear, nor receive instruction.

24 And it shall come to pass, if ye diligently hearken unto me, saith the LORD, to bring in no burden through the gates of this city on the sabbath day, but hallow the sabbath day, to do no work therein;

25 Then shall there enter into the gates of this city kings and princes sitting upon the throne of David, riding in chariots and on horses, they, and their princes, the men of Judah, and the inhabitants of Jerusalem: and this city shall remain for ever.

26 And they shall come from the cities of Judah, and from the places about Jerusalem, and from the land of Benjamin, and from the plain, and from the mountains, and from the south, bringing burnt offerings, and sacrifices, and meat offerings, and incense, and bringing sacrifices of praise, unto the house of the LORD.

27 But if ye will not hearken unto me to hallow the sabbath day, and not to bear a burden, even entering in at the gates of Jerusalem on the sabbath day; then will I kindle a fire in the gates thereof, and it shall devour the palaces of Jerusalem, and it shall not be quenched.

CHAPTER 18
The Potter and the Clay

1 The word which came to Jeremiah from the LORD, saying,

2 Arise, and go down to the potter's house, and there I will cause thee to hear my words.

3 Then I went down to the potter's house, and, behold, he wrought a work on the wheels.

4 And the vessel that he made of clay was marred in the hand of the potter: so he made it again another vessel, as seemed good to the potter to make *it.*

5 Then the word of the LORD came to me, saying,

6 O house of Israel, cannot I do with you as this potter? saith the LORD. Behold, as the clay *is* in the potter's hand, so *are* ye in mine hand, O house of Israel.

7 *At what* instant I shall speak concerning a nation, and concerning a kingdom, to pluck up, and to pull down, and to destroy *it*;

8 If that nation, against whom I have pronounced, turn from their evil, I will repent of the evil that I thought to do unto them.

9 And *at what* instant I shall speak concerning a nation, and concerning a kingdom, to build and to plant *it*;

10 If it do evil in my sight, that it obey not my voice, then I will repent of the good, wherewith I said I would benefit them.

11 Now therefore go to, speak to the men of Judah, and to the inhabitants of Jerusalem, saying, Thus saith the LORD; Behold, I frame evil against you, and devise a device against you: return ye now every one from his evil way, and make your ways and your doings good.

12 And they said, There is no hope: but we will walk after our own devices, and we will every one do the imagination of his evil heart.

13 Therefore thus saith the LORD; Ask ye now among the heathen, who hath heard such things: the virgin of Israel hath done a very horrible thing.

14 Will *a man* leave the snow of Lebanon *which cometh* from the rock of the field? *or* shall the cold flowing waters that come from another place be forsaken?

15 Because my people hath forgotten me, they have burned incense to vanity, and they have caused them to stumble in their ways *from* the ancient paths, to walk in paths, *in* a way not cast up;

16 To make their land desolate, *and* a perpetual hissing; every one that passeth thereby shall be astonished, and wag his head.

17 I will scatter them as with an east wind before the enemy; I will shew them the

Cross references

20 Jer. 19:3; 22:2

21 Num. 15:32; Neh. 13:19

22 Ex. 20:8; 23:12; 31:13; Jer. 7:24, 26; 11:10; Ezek. 20:12

25 Jer. 22:4

26 Ps. 107:22; 116:17; Jer. 32:44; 33:13; Zech. 7:7

27 2Kgs. 25:9; Jer. 21:14; 49:27; 52:13; Lam. 4:11; Amos 1:4, 7, 10, 12; 2:2, 5

6 Isa. 45:9; 64:8; Rom. 9:20, 21

7 Jer. 1:10

8 Jer. 26:3; Ezek. 18:21; 33:11; Jon. 3:10

11 2Kgs. 17:13; Jer. 7:3; 25:5; 26:13; 35:15

12 Jer. 2:25

13 Jer. 2:10; 5:30; 1Cor. 5:1

15 Jer. 2:13, 32; 3:21; 6:16; 10:15; 13:25; 16:19; 17:13

16 1Kgs. 9:8; Jer. 19:8; 49:13; 50:13; Lam. 2:15; Mic. 6:16

17 Ps. 48:7; Jer. 2:27; 13:24

18:16–17 See similar notes on Jeremiah 4:26–28; 6:9.

back, and not the face, in the day of their calamity.

Another Plot against Jeremiah

18 Then said they, Come, and let us devise devices against Jeremiah; for the law shall not perish from the priest, nor counsel from the wise, nor the word from the prophet. Come, and let us smite him with the tongue, and let us not give heed to any of his words.

19 Give heed to me, O LORD, and hearken to the voice of them that contend with me.

20 Shall evil be recompensed for good? for they have digged a pit for my soul. Remember that I stood before thee to speak good for them, *and* to turn away thy wrath from them.

21 Therefore deliver up their children to the famine, and pour out their *blood* by the force of the sword; and let their wives be bereaved of their children, and *be* widows; and let their men be put to death; *let* their young men *be* slain by the sword in battle.

22 Let a cry be heard from their houses, when thou shalt bring a troop suddenly upon them: for they have digged a pit to take me, and hid snares for my feet.

23 Yet, LORD, thou knowest all their counsel against me to slay *me*: forgive not their iniquity, neither blot out their sin from thy sight, but let them be overthrown before thee; deal *thus* with them in the time of thine anger.

CHAPTER 19
The Broken Pot

1 Thus saith the Lord, Go and get a potter's earthen bottle, and *take* of the ancients of the people, and of the ancients of the priests;

2 And go forth unto the valley of the son of Hinnom, which *is* by the entry of the east gate, and proclaim there the words that I shall tell thee,

3 And say, Hear ye the word of the LORD, O kings of Judah, and inhabitants of Jerusalem; Thus saith the LORD of hosts, the God of Israel; Behold, I will bring evil upon this place, the which whosoever heareth, his ears shall tingle.

4 Because they have forsaken me, and have estranged this place, and have burned incense in it unto other gods, whom neither they nor their fathers have known, nor the

kings of Judah, and have filled this place with the blood of innocents;

5 They have built also the high places of Baal, to burn their sons with fire *for* burnt offerings unto Baal, which I commanded not, nor spake *it*, neither came *it* into my mind:

6 Therefore, behold, the days come, saith the LORD, that this place shall no more be called Tophet, nor The valley of the son of Hinnom, but The valley of slaughter.

7 And I will make void the counsel of Judah and Jerusalem in this place; and I will cause them to fall by the sword before their enemies, and by the hands of them that seek their lives: and their carcases will I give to be meat for the fowls of the heaven, and for the beasts of the earth.

8 And I will make this city desolate, and an hissing; every one that passeth thereby shall be astonished and hiss because of all the plagues thereof.

9 And I will cause them to eat the flesh of their sons and the flesh of their daughters, and they shall eat every one the flesh of his friend in the siege and straitness, wherewith their enemies, and they that seek their lives, shall straiten them.

10 Then shalt thou break the bottle in the sight of the men that go with thee,

11 And shalt say unto them, Thus saith the LORD of hosts; Even so will I break this people and this city, as *one* breaketh a potter's vessel, that cannot be made whole again: and they shall bury *them* in Tophet, till *there be* no place to bury.

12 Thus will I do unto this place, saith the LORD, and to the inhabitants thereof, and *even* make this city as Tophet:

13 And the houses of Jerusalem, and the houses of the kings of Judah, shall be defiled as the place of Tophet, because of all the houses upon whose roofs they have burned incense unto all the host of heaven, and have poured out drink offerings unto other gods.

14 Then came Jeremiah from Tophet, whither the LORD had sent him to prophesy; and he stood in the court of the LORD's house; and said to all the people,

15 Thus saith the LORD of hosts, the God of Israel; Behold, I will bring upon this city and upon all her towns all the evil that I have pronounced against it, because they

Cross-references

18 Lev. 10:11; Jer. 11:19; Mal. 2:7; John 7:48, 49

20 Ps. 35:7; 57:6; 109:4, 5; Jer. 18:22

21 Ps. 109:9, 10

22 Jer. 18:20

23 Josh. 15:8; 2Kgs. 23:10; Ps. 35:4; 109:14; Jer. 7:31; 11:20; 15:15

3 1Sam. 3:11; 2Kgs. 21:12; Jer. 17:20

4 Deut. 28:20; 2Kgs. 21:16; Isa. 65:11; Jer. 2:13, 17, 19, 34; 15:6; 17:13

5 Lev. 18:21; Jer. 7:31, 32; 32:35

6 Josh. 15:8

7 Lev. 26:17; Deut. 28:53; Ps. 79:2; Jer. 7:33; 16:4; 34:20

8 Jer. 18:16; 49:13; 50:13

9 Lev. 26:29; Deut. 28:53; Isa. 9:20; Lam. 4:10

10 Jer. 51:63, 64

11 Ps. 2:9; Isa. 30:14; Jer. 7:32; Lam. 4:2

13 2Kgs. 23:10, 12; Jer. 7:18; 32:29; Zeph. 1:5

14 2Chr. 20:5

15 1Chr. 24:14; Jer. 7:26; 17:23

19:8 hissing. This is a term denoting ridicule and scorn.

have hardened their necks, that they might not hear my words.

CHAPTER 20
The Curse upon Pashur

1 Now Pashur the son of Immer the priest, who *was* also chief governor in the house of the LORD, heard that Jeremiah prophesied these things.

2 Then Pashur smote Jeremiah the prophet, and put him in the stocks that *were* in the high gate of Benjamin, which *was* by the house of the LORD.

3 And it came to pass on the morrow, that Pashur brought forth Jeremiah out of the stocks. Then said Jeremiah unto him, The LORD hath not called thy name Pashur, but Magor-missabib.

4 For thus saith the LORD, Behold, I will make thee a terror to thyself, and to all thy friends: and they shall fall by the sword of their enemies, and thine eyes shall behold *it*: and I will give all Judah into the hand of the king of Babylon, and he shall carry them captive into Babylon, and shall slay them with the sword.

5 Moreover I will deliver all the strength of this city, and all the labours thereof, and all the precious things thereof, and all the treasures of the kings of Judah will I give into the hand of their enemies, which shall spoil them, and take them, and carry them to Babylon.

6 And thou, Pashur, and all that dwell in thine house shall go into captivity: and thou shalt come to Babylon, and there thou shalt die, and shalt be buried there, thou, and all thy friends, to whom thou hast prophesied lies.

Jeremiah's Lamentation

7 O LORD, thou hast deceived me, and I was deceived: thou art stronger than I, and hast prevailed: I am in derision daily, every one mocketh me.

8 For since I spake, I cried out, I cried violence and spoil; because the word of the LORD was made a reproach unto me, and a derision, daily.

9 Then I said, I will not make mention of him, nor speak any more in his name. But *his word* was in mine heart as a burning fire

shut up in my bones, and I was weary with forbearing, and I could not *stay*.

10 For I heard the defaming of many, fear on every side. Report, *say they*, and we will report it. All my familiars watched for my halting, *saying*, Peradventure he will be enticed, and we shall prevail against him, and we shall take our revenge on him.

11 But the LORD *is* with me as a mighty terrible one: therefore my persecutors shall stumble, and they shall not prevail: they shall be greatly ashamed; for they shall not prosper: *their* everlasting confusion shall never be forgotten.

12 But, O LORD of hosts, that triest the righteous, *and* seest the reins and the heart, let me see thy vengeance on them: for unto thee have I opened my cause.

13 Sing unto the LORD, praise ye the LORD: for he hath delivered the soul of the poor from the hand of evildoers.

14 Cursed *be* the day wherein I was born: let not the day wherein my mother bare me be blessed.

15 Cursed *be* the man who brought tidings to my father, saying, A man child is born unto thee; making him very glad.

16 And let that man be as the cities which the LORD overthrew, and repented not: and let him hear the cry in the morning, and the shouting at noontide;

17 Because he slew me not from the womb; or that my mother might have been my grave, and her womb *to be* always great *with me.*

18 Wherefore came I forth out of the womb to see labour and sorrow, that my days should be consumed with shame?

CHAPTER 21
Jerusalem Will Be Destroyed

1 The word which came unto Jeremiah from the LORD, when king Zedekiah sent unto him Pashur the son of Melchiah, and Zephaniah the son of Maaseiah the priest, saying,

2 Inquire, I pray thee, of the LORD for us; for Nebuchadrezzar king of Babylon maketh war against us; if so be that the LORD will deal with us according to all his wondrous works, that he may go up from us.

3 Then said Jeremiah unto them, Thus shall ye say to Zedekiah:

Cross references

3 Ps. 31:13; Jer. 6:25; 20:10; 46:5; 49:29

5 2Kgs. 20:17; 24:12-16; 25:13; Jer. 3:24

6 Jer. 14:13, 14; 28:15; 29:21

7 Jer. 1:6, 7; Lam. 3:14

8 Jer. 6:7

9 Job 32:18, 19; Ps. 39:3; Acts 18:5

10 Job 19:19; Ps. 31:13; 41:9; 55:13, 14; Luke 11:53, 54

11 Jer. 1:8, 19; 15:20; 17:18; 23:40

12 Ps. 54:7; 50:10; Jer. 11:20; 17:10

13 Ps. 35:9, 10; 109:30, 31

14 Job 3:3; Jer. 15:10

16 Gen. 19:25; Jer. 18:22

17 2Kgs. 25:18; Job 3:10, 11, 20; Jer. 29:25; 37:3; 38:1; Lam. 3:1

2 Jer. 37:3, 7

20:6 Pashur. He was apparently a false prophet in Judah who prophesied that no harm would come to Judah. Jeremiah prophesied that Pashur and all who lived in his house would not only go into captivity, they would also die in captivity. Jeremiah was vindicated through this prophecy.

4 Thus saith the Lord God of Israel; Behold, I will turn back the weapons of war that *are* in your hands, wherewith ye fight against the king of Babylon, and *against* the Chaldeans, which besiege you without the walls, and I will assemble them into the midst of this city.

5 And I myself will fight against you with an outstretched hand and with a strong arm, even in anger, and in fury, and in great wrath.

6 And I will smite the inhabitants of this city, both man and beast: they shall die of a great pestilence.

7 And afterward, saith the Lord, I will deliver Zedekiah king of Judah, and his servants, and the people, and such as are left in this city from the pestilence, from the sword, and from the famine, into the hand of Nebuchadrezzar king of Babylon, and into the hand of their enemies, and into the hand of those that seek their life: and he shall smite them with the edge of the sword; he shall not spare them, neither have pity, nor have mercy.

8 And unto this people thou shalt say, Thus saith the Lord; Behold, I set before you the way of life, and the way of death.

9 He that abideth in this city shall die by the sword, and by the famine, and by the pestilence: but he that goeth out, and falleth to the Chaldeans that besiege you, he shall live, and his life shall be unto him for a prey.

10 For I have set my face against this city for evil, and not for good, saith the Lord: it shall be given into the hand of the king of Babylon, and he shall burn it with fire.

11 And touching the house of the king of Judah, *say*, Hear ye the word of the Lord;

12 O house of David, thus saith the Lord; Execute judgment in the morning, and deliver *him that is* spoiled out of the hand of the oppressor, lest my fury go out like fire, and burn that none can quench *it*, because of the evil of your doings.

13 Behold, I *am* against thee, O inhabitant of the valley, *and* rock of the plain, saith the

Lord; which say, Who shall come down against us? or who shall enter into our habitations?

14 But I will punish you according to the fruit of your doings, saith the Lord: and I will kindle a fire in the forest thereof, and it shall devour all things round about it.

CHAPTER 22
Prophecies against the Kings of Judah

1 Thus saith the Lord; Go down to the house of the king of Judah, and speak there this word,

2 And say, Hear the word of the Lord, O king of Judah, that sittest upon the throne of David, thou, and thy servants, and thy people that enter in by these gates:

3 Thus saith the Lord; Execute ye judgment and righteousness, and deliver the spoiled out of the hand of the oppressor: and do no wrong, do no violence to the stranger, the fatherless, nor the widow, neither shed innocent blood in this place.

4 For if ye do this thing indeed, then shall there enter in by the gates of this house kings sitting upon the throne of David, riding in chariots and on horses, he, and his servants, and his people.

5 But if ye will not hear these words, I swear by myself, saith the Lord, that this house shall become a desolation.

6 For thus saith the Lord unto the king's house of Judah; Thou *art* Gilead unto me, *and* the head of Lebanon: *yet* surely I will make thee a wilderness, *and* cities *which* are not inhabited.

7 And I will prepare destroyers against thee, every one with his weapons: and they shall cut down thy choice cedars, and cast *them* into the fire.

8 And many nations shall pass by this city, and they shall say every man to his neighbour, Wherefore hath the Lord done thus unto this great city?

9 Then they shall answer, Because they have forsaken the covenant of the Lord

Cross-references (center column):

4 Isa. 13:4
5 Ex. 6:6
7 Deut. 28:50; 2Chr. 36:17; Jer. 37:17; 39:5; 52:9
8 Deut. 30:19
9 Jer. 38:2, 17, 18; 39:18; 45:5
10 Lev. 17:10; Jer. 34:2, 22; 37:10; 38:3, 18, 23; 44:11; 52:13; Amos 9:4
12 Ps. 101:8; Jer. 22:3; Zech. 7:9
13 Jer. 49:4; Ezek. 13:8
14 2Chr. 36:19; Prov. 1:31; Isa. 3:10, 11; Jer. 17:20; 52:13
3 Jer. 21:12; 22:17
4 Jer. 17:25
5 Heb. 6:13, 17
7 Isa. 37:24; Jer. 21:14
8 Deut. 29:24, 25; 1Kgs. 9:8, 9
9 2Kgs. 22:17; 2Chr. 34:25

21:7 I will deliver Zedekiah . . . into the hand of Nebuchadnezzar. King Zedekiah was captured and sent to Nebuchadnezzar at Riblah (2 Kgs. 25:6), and his sons were killed in his presence. After this, Zedekiah was blinded (Ezek. 12:12) and imprisoned for the rest of his life in Babylon.

21:10 he shall burn it with fire. This is a specific pre-

diction of the Babylonian invasion and conquering of Jerusalem that was fulfilled in history during August 586 B.C. (2 Chr. 36:15–21).

22:4–5 If Judah continues to disobey, then the "throne of David" would become a desolation. Judah did not repent, however.

their God, and worshipped other gods, and served them.

10 Weep ye not for the dead, neither bemoan him: *but* weep sore for him that goeth away: for he shall return no more, nor see his native country.

11 For thus saith the LORD touching Shallum the son of Josiah king of Judah, which reigned instead of Josiah his father, which went forth out of this place; He shall not return thither any more:

12 But he shall die in the place whither they have led him captive, and shall see this land no more.

13 Woe unto him that buildeth his house by unrighteousness, and his chambers by wrong; *that* useth his neighbour's service without wages, and giveth him not for his work;

14 That saith, I will build me a wide house and large chambers, and cutteth him out windows; and *it is* cieled with cedar, and painted with vermilion.

15 Shalt thou reign, because thou closest *thyself* in cedar? did not thy father eat and drink, and do judgment and justice, *and* then *it was* well with him?

16 He judged the cause of the poor and needy; then *it was* well *with him: was* not this to know me? saith the LORD.

17 But thine eyes and thine heart *are* not but for thy covetousness, and for to shed innocent blood, and for oppression, and for violence, to do *it.*

18 Therefore thus saith the LORD concerning Jehoiakim the son of Josiah king of Judah; They shall not lament for him, *saying*, Ah my brother! or, Ah sister! they shall not lament for him, *saying*, Ah lord! or, Ah his glory!

19 He shall be buried with the burial of an ass, drawn and cast forth beyond the gates of Jerusalem.

20 Go up to Lebanon, and cry; and lift up thy voice in Bashan, and cry from the passages: for all thy lovers are destroyed.

21 I spake unto thee in thy prosperity; *but* thou saidst, I will not hear. This *hath been* thy manner from thy youth, that thou obeyedst not my voice.

22 The wind shall eat up all thy pastors, and thy lovers shall go into captivity: surely then shalt thou be ashamed and confounded for all thy wickedness.

23 O inhabitant of Lebanon, that makest thy nest in the cedars, how gracious shalt thou be when pangs come upon thee, the pain as of a woman in travail!

24 *As* I live, saith the LORD, though Coniah the son of Jehoiakim king of Judah were the signet upon my right hand, yet would I pluck thee thence;

25 And I will give thee into the hand of them that seek thy life, and into the hand *of them* whose face thou fearest, even into the hand of Nebuchadrezzar king of Babylon, and into the hand of the Chaldeans.

26 And I will cast thee out, and thy mother that bare thee, into another country, where ye were not born; and there shall ye die.

27 But to the land whereunto they desire to return, thither shall they not return.

28 *Is* this man Coniah a despised broken idol? *is he* a vessel wherein *is* no pleasure? wherefore are they cast out, he and his seed, and are cast into a land which they know not?

29 O earth, earth, earth, hear the word of the LORD.

30 Thus saith the LORD, Write ye this man childless, a man *that* shall not prosper in his days: for no man of his seed shall prosper, sitting upon the throne of David, and ruling any more in Judah.

CHAPTER 23
The Promised Return of the Remnant

1 Woe be unto the pastors that destroy and scatter the sheep of my pasture! saith the LORD.

Cross references:

10 2Kgs. 22:20; Jer. 22:11
11 2Kgs. 23:30, 34; 1Chr. 3:15
13 Lev. 19:13; Deut. 24:14, 15; 2Kgs. 23:35; Jer. 22:18; Mic. 3:10; Hab. 2:9; James 5:4
15 2Kgs. 23:25; Ps. 128:2; Isa. 3:10
17 Ezek. 19:6
18 1Kgs. 13:30; Jer. 16:4, 6
19 2Chr. 36:6; Jer. 36:30
21 Jer. 3:25; 7:23
22 Jer. 22:20; 23:1
23 Jer. 6:24
24 2Kgs. 24:6, 8; 1Chr. 3:16; 37:1; Song 8:6; Hag. 2:23
25 Jer. 34:20
26 2Kgs. 24:15; 2Chr. 36:10
27 Jer. 44:14
28 Ps. 31:12; Jer. 48:38; Hos. 8:8
29 Deut. 32:1; Isa. 1:2; 34:1; Mic. 1:2
30 1Chr. 3:16, 17; Ezek. 34:2; Matt. 1:12

22:10–12 This prophecy speaks specifically of King Shallum whom the people called Shalom (peace), but Shallum means "retribution." This king, the fourth son of Josiah, who reigned for three months in 609 B.C. (2 Kgs. 23:31), was dethroned and taken to Egypt where he died (2 Chr. 36:1–4).

22:18–19 Jehoiakim. A wicked king who ruled Judah from 609 to 598 B.C., Jehoiakim was slain during a Babylonian siege and was not given a burial, but was left like a donkey to be eaten by the scavengers.

22:28–30 Coniah is a shortened form of Jeconiah (24:1; 27:20; Matt. 1:11–12) and was another name for King Jehoiachin (2 Kgs. 24:8–16; 25:27–30). Even though this king had seven sons (1 Chr. 3:17–18), none would ever sit on the throne. The "curse of Jehoiachin" continued down to Joseph, the stepfather of Jesus. Because of the virgin birth of Christ (Matt. 1:20–21), the bloodline of Jesus did not come through Joseph. His humanity descended through Mary (Luke 3:31–32), fulfilling the dual requirement that the Messiah descend from David, but not through Jeconiah. Jehoiachin was imprisoned during the entire reign of Nebuchadnezzar from 598 to 562 B.C.

2 Therefore thus saith the Lord God of Israel against the pastors that feed my people; Ye have scattered my flock, and driven them away, and have not visited them: behold, I will visit upon you the evil of your doings, saith the Lord.

3 And I will gather the remnant of my flock out of all countries whither I have driven them, and will bring them again to their folds; and they shall be fruitful and increase.

4 And I will set up shepherds over them which shall feed them: and they shall fear no more, nor be dismayed, neither shall they be lacking, saith the Lord.

5 Behold, the days come, saith the Lord, that I will raise unto David a righteous Branch, and a King shall reign and prosper, and shall execute judgment and justice in the earth.

6 In his days Judah shall be saved, and Israel shall dwell safely: and this is his name whereby he shall be called, THE LORD OUR RIGHTEOUSNESS.

7 Therefore, behold, the days come, saith the Lord, that they shall no more say, The Lord liveth, which brought up the children of Israel out of the land of Egypt;

8 But, The Lord liveth, which brought up and which led the seed of the house of Israel out of the north country, and from all countries whither I had driven them; and they shall dwell in their own land.

Jeremiah Preaches against Lying Prophets

9 Mine heart within me is broken because of the prophets; all my bones shake; I am like a drunken man, and like a man whom wine hath overcome, because of the Lord, and because of the words of his holiness.

10 For the land is full of adulterers; for because of swearing the land mourneth; the pleasant places of the wilderness are dried up, and their course is evil, and their force is not right.

11 For both prophet and priest are profane; yea, in my house have I found their wickedness, saith the Lord.

12 Wherefore their way shall be unto them as slippery ways in the darkness: they shall be driven on, and fall therein: for I will bring evil upon them, even the year of their visitation, saith the Lord.

13 And I have seen folly in the prophets of Samaria; they prophesied in Baal, and caused my people Israel to err.

14 I have seen also in the prophets of Jerusalem an horrible thing: they commit adultery, and walk in lies: they strengthen also the hands of evildoers, that none doth return from his wickedness: they are all of them unto me as Sodom, and the inhabitants thereof as Gomorrah.

15 Therefore thus saith the Lord of hosts concerning the prophets; Behold, I will feed them with wormwood, and make them drink the water of gall: for from the prophets of Jerusalem is profaneness gone forth into all the land.

16 Thus saith the Lord of hosts, Hearken not unto the words of the prophets that prophesy unto you: they make you vain: they speak a vision of their own heart, and not out of the mouth of the Lord.

17 They say still unto them that despise me, The Lord hath said, Ye shall have peace; and they say unto every one that walketh after the imagination of his own heart, No evil shall come upon you.

18 For who hath stood in the counsel of the Lord, and hath perceived and heard his word? who hath marked his word, and heard it?

19 Behold, a whirlwind of the Lord is gone forth in fury, even a grievous whirlwind: it shall fall grievously upon the head of the wicked.

20 The anger of the Lord shall not return, until he have executed, and till he have performed the thoughts of his heart: in the latter days ye shall consider it perfectly.

21 I have not sent these prophets, yet they

Cross references:

2 Ex. 32:34
3 Jer. 32:37; Ezek. 34:13
4 Jer. 3:15; Ezek. 34:23
5 Ps. 72:2; Isa. 4:2; 9:7; 11:1; 32:1, 18; 40:10, 11; Jer. 33:14-16; Dan. 9:24; Zech. 3:8; 6:12; John 1:45
6 Deut. 33:28; Jer. 32:37; 33:16; Zech. 14:11; 1Cor. 1:30
7 Jer. 16:14, 15
8 Isa. 43:5, 6; Jer. 23:3
9 Hab. 3:16
10 Jer. 5:7, 8; 9:2, 10; 12:4; Hos. 4:2, 3
11 Jer. 6:13; 7:30; 8:10; 11:15; 32:34; Ezek. 8:11; 23:39; Zeph. 3:4
12 Ps. 35:6; Prov. 4:19
13 Isa. 9:16; Jer. 2:8
14 Deut. 32:32; Isa. 1:9, 10; Jer. 23:26; 29:23; Ezek. 13:22
15 Jer. 8:14; 9:15
16 Jer. 14:14; 23:21
17 Jer. 6:14; 8:11; 13:10; Ezek. 13:10; Mic. 3:11; Zech. 10:2
18 Job 15:8; 1Cor. 2:16
20 Jer. 30:24

23:3–8 the remnant. This is a common Old Testament term that refers to Jews who are faithful to the Lord, usually in contrast to the nation as a whole that is disobedient (Isa. 1:9; 10:20–23; 11:16; 46:3). This remnant will be regathered from "out of all countries [where God has] driven them," and will result in the setting up of "shepherds over them which shall feed them." This will commence at the second coming of Christ (Matt. 24:29–30)

and will prepare the way for Christ's shepherding of Israel and the nations in the Millennium.

23:19–20 Even though Judah in Jeremiah's day would not respond positively to God's whirlwind of judgment, a time will come, "in the latter days," when they will heed His voice and understand it perfectly.

ran: I have not spoken to them, yet they prophesied.

22 But if they had stood in my counsel, and had caused my people to hear my words, then they should have turned them from their evil way, and from the evil of their doings.

23 *Am* I a God at hand, saith the LORD, and not a God afar off?

24 Can any hide himself in secret places that I shall not see him? saith the LORD. Do not I fill heaven and earth? saith the LORD.

25 I have heard what the prophets said, that prophesy lies in my name, saying, I have dreamed, I have dreamed.

26 How long shall *this* be in the heart of the prophets that prophesy lies? yea, *they are* prophets of the deceit of their own heart;

27 Which think to cause my people to forget my name by their dreams which they tell every man to his neighbour, as their fathers have forgotten my name for Baal.

28 The prophet that hath a dream, let him tell a dream; and he that hath my word, let him speak my word faithfully. What *is* the chaff to the wheat? saith the LORD.

29 *Is* not my word like as a fire? saith the LORD; and like a hammer *that* breaketh the rock in pieces?

30 Therefore, behold, I *am* against the prophets, saith the LORD, that steal my words every one from his neighbour.

31 Behold, I *am* against the prophets, saith the LORD, that use their tongues, and say, He saith.

32 Behold, I *am* against them that prophesy false dreams, saith the LORD, and do tell them, and cause my people to err by their lies, and by their lightness; yet I sent them not, nor commanded them: therefore they shall not profit this people at all, saith the LORD.

The Burden of the Lord

33 And when this people, or the prophet, or a priest, shall ask thee, saying, What *is* the burden of the LORD? thou shalt then say unto them, What burden? I will even forsake you, saith the LORD.

34 And *as for* the prophet, and the priest, and the people, that shall say, The burden of the LORD, I will even punish that man and his house.

35 Thus shall ye say every one to his neigh-

bour, and every one to his brother, What hath the LORD answered? and, What hath the LORD spoken?

36 And the burden of the LORD shall ye mention no more: for every man's word shall be his burden; for ye have perverted the words of the living God, of the LORD of hosts our God.

37 Thus shalt thou say to the prophet, What hath the LORD answered thee? and, What hath the LORD spoken?

38 But since ye say, The burden of the LORD; therefore thus saith the LORD; Because ye say this word, The burden of the LORD, and I have sent unto you, saying, Ye shall not say, The burden of the LORD;

39 Therefore, behold, I, even I, will utterly forget you, and I will forsake you, and the city that I gave you and your fathers, *and cast you* out of my presence:

40 And I will bring an everlasting reproach upon you, and a perpetual shame, which shall not be forgotten.

CHAPTER 24
The Good Figs and the Bad Figs

1 The LORD shewed me, and, behold, two baskets of figs *were* set before the temple of the LORD, after that Nebuchadrezzar king of Babylon had carried away captive Jeconiah the son of Jehoiakim king of Judah, and the princes of Judah, with the carpenters and smiths, from Jerusalem, and had brought them to Babylon.

2 One basket *had* very good figs, *even* like the figs *that are* first ripe: and the other basket *had* very naughty figs, which could not be eaten, they were so bad.

3 Then said the LORD unto me, What seest thou, Jeremiah? And I said, Figs; the good figs, very good; and the evil, very evil, that cannot be eaten, they are so evil.

4 Again the word of the LORD came unto me, saying,

5 Thus saith the LORD, the God of Israel; Like these good figs, so will I acknowledge them that are carried away captive of Judah, whom I have sent out of this place into the land of the Chaldeans for *their* good.

6 For I will set mine eyes upon them for good, and I will bring them again to this land: and I will build them, and not pull *them* down; and I will plant them, and not pluck *them* up.

Cross references (center column):

24 1Kgs. 8:27; Ps. 139:7; Amos 9:2, 3

27 Judg. 3:7; 8:33, 34

30 Deut. 18:20; Jer. 14:14, 15

32 Zeph. 3:4

33 Jer. 23:39; Mal. 1:1

39 Jer. 23:33; Hos. 4:6

40 2Kgs. 24:12; 2Chr. 36:10; Jer. 20:11; 22:24; 29:2; Amos 7:1, 4; 8:1

6 Jer. 12:15; 29:10; 32:41; 33:7; 42:10

23:39–40 Jeremiah once again prophesies the impending Babylonian judgment.

7 And I will give them an heart to know me, that I *am* the LORD: and they shall be my people, and I will be their God: for they shall return unto me with their whole heart.

8 And as the evil figs, which cannot be eaten, they are so evil; surely thus saith the LORD, So will I give Zedekiah the king of Judah, and his princes, and the residue of Jerusalem, that remain in this land, and them that dwell in the land of Egypt:

9 And I will deliver them to be removed into all the kingdoms of the earth for *their* hurt, *to be* a reproach and a proverb, a taunt and a curse, in all places whither I shall drive them.

10 And I will send the sword, the famine, and the pestilence, among them, till they be consumed from off the land that I gave unto them and to their fathers.

CHAPTER 25
Seventy Years of Desolation

1 The word that came to Jeremiah concerning all the people of Judah in the fourth year of Jehoiakim the son of Josiah king of Judah, that *was* the first year of Nebuchadrezzar king of Babylon;

2 The which Jeremiah the prophet spake unto all the people of Judah, and to all the inhabitants of Jerusalem, saying,

3 From the thirteenth year of Josiah the son of Amon king of Judah, even unto this day, that *is* the three and twentieth year, the word of the LORD hath come unto me, and I have spoken unto you, rising early and speaking; but ye have not hearkened.

4 And the LORD hath sent unto you all his servants the prophets, rising early and sending *them*; but ye have not hearkened, nor inclined your ear to hear.

5 They said, Turn ye again now every one from his evil way, and from the evil of your doings, and dwell in the land that the LORD hath given unto you and to your fathers for ever and ever:

6 And go not after other gods to serve them, and to worship them, and provoke

me not to anger with the works of your hands; and I will do you no hurt.

7 Yet ye have not hearkened unto me, saith the LORD; that ye might provoke me to anger with the works of your hands to your own hurt.

8 Therefore thus saith the LORD of hosts; Because ye have not heard my words,

9 Behold, I will send and take all the families of the north, saith the LORD, and Nebuchadrezzar the king of Babylon, my servant, and will bring them against this land, and against the inhabitants thereof, and against all these nations round about, and will utterly destroy them, and make them an astonishment, and an hissing, and perpetual desolations.

10 Moreover I will take from them the voice of mirth, and the voice of gladness, the voice of the bridegroom, and the voice of the bride, the sound of the millstones, and the light of the candle.

11 And this whole land shall be a desolation, *and* an astonishment; and these nations shall serve the king of Babylon seventy years.

12 And it shall come to pass, when seventy years are accomplished, *that* I will punish the king of Babylon, and that nation, saith the LORD, for their iniquity, and the land of the Chaldeans, and will make it perpetual desolations.

13 And I will bring upon that land all my words which I have pronounced against it, *even* all that is written in this book, which Jeremiah hath prophesied against all the nations.

14 For many nations and great kings shall serve themselves of them also: and I will recompense them according to their deeds, and according to the works of their own hands.

The Cup of Wrath for the Nations

15 For thus saith the LORD God of Israel unto me; Take the wine cup of this fury at my hand, and cause all the nations, to whom I send thee, to drink it.

Cross references (center column):

7 Deut. 30:6; Jer. 29:13; 30:22; 31:33; 32:38, 39; Ezek. 11:19; 36:26, 27

8 Jer. 29:17

9 Deut. 28:25, 37; 1Kgs. 9:7; 2Chr. 7:20; Ps. 44:13, 14; Jer. 15:4; 29:18, 22; 34:17; 36:1

3 Jer. 1:2; 7:13; 11:7, 8, 10; 13:10, 11; 16:12; 17:23; 18:12; 19:15; 22:21

4 Jer. 7:13, 25; 26:5; 29:19

5 2Kgs. 17:13; Jer. 18:11; 35:15; Jon. 3:8

7 Deut. 32:21; Jer. 7:19; 32:30

9 Isa. 44:28; 45:1; Jer. 1:15; 18:16; 27:6; 40:2; 43:10

10 Eccl. 12:4; Isa. 24:7; Jer. 7:34; 16:9; Ezek. 26:13; Hos. 2:11; Rev. 18:23

12 2Chr. 36:21, 22; Ezra 1:1; Isa. 13:19; 14:23; 21:1; 47:1; Jer. 29:10; 50:3, 13, 23, 39, 40, 45; 51:25, 26; Dan. 9:2

15 Job 21:20; Ps. 75:8; Isa. 51:17; Rev. 14:10

24:7 Jeremiah predicts that there will come a time in which the Lord will give Israel a heart to know God. This act of God is later called the new covenant (Jer. 31:31), and will correct the basic problem with God's people noted at the founding of the nation (Deut. 29:4).

25:12 The specific statement is made that Judah's Babylonian captivity would last seventy years. This occurred from 586 to 516 B.C. God predicted the exact number of years of Judah's captivity and this was literally fulfilled. This prophecy was made in 604 B.C. and was the passage Daniel is said to have been studying in Daniel 9:2. The reference to Babylon's future desolation and ruin is a part of the prophecy that has never been fulfilled, but will occur in the future (cf. Jer. 50—51).

25:15–26 the wine cup of this fury. The wine cup pictured in this passage is a cup full of God's wrath (cf. Rev.

16 And they shall drink, and be moved, and be mad, because of the sword that I will send among them.

17 Then took I the cup at the LORD's hand, and made all the nations to drink, unto whom the LORD had sent me:

18 *To wit,* Jerusalem, and the cities of Judah, and the kings thereof, and the princes thereof, to make them a desolation, an astonishment, an hissing, and a curse; as *it is* this day;

19 Pharaoh king of Egypt, and his servants, and his princes, and all his people;

20 And all the mingled people, and all the kings of the land of Uz, and all the kings of the land of the Philistines, and Ashkelon, and Azzah, and Ekron, and the remnant of Ashdod,

21 Edom, and Moab, and the children of Ammon,

22 And all the kings of Tyrus, and all the kings of Zidon, and the kings of the isles which *are* beyond the sea,

23 Dedan, and Tema, and Buz, and all *that are* in the utmost corners,

24 And all the kings of Arabia, and all the kings of the mingled people that dwell in the desert,

25 And all the kings of Zimri, and all the kings of Elam, and all the kings of the Medes,

26 And all the kings of the north, far and near, one with another, and all the kingdoms of the world, which *are* upon the face of the earth: and the king of Sheshach shall drink after them.

27 Therefore thou shalt say unto them, Thus saith the LORD of hosts, the God of Is-

rael; Drink ye, and be drunken, and spue, and fall, and rise no more, because of the sword which I will send among you.

28 And it shall be, if they refuse to take the cup at thine hand to drink, then shalt thou say unto them, Thus saith the LORD of hosts; Ye shall certainly drink.

29 For, lo, I begin to bring evil on the city which is called by my name, and should ye be utterly unpunished? Ye shall not be unpunished: for I will call for a sword upon all the inhabitants of the earth, saith the LORD of hosts.

30 Therefore prophesy thou against them all these words, and say unto them, The LORD shall roar from on high, and utter his voice from his holy habitation; he shall mightily roar upon his habitation; he shall give a shout, as they that tread *the grapes,* against all the inhabitants of the earth.

31 A noise shall come *even* to the ends of the earth; for the LORD hath a controversy with the nations, he will plead with all flesh; he will give them *that are* wicked to the sword, saith the LORD.

32 Thus saith the LORD of hosts, Behold, evil shall go forth from nation to nation, and a great whirlwind shall be raised up from the coasts of the earth.

33 And the slain of the LORD shall be at that day from *one* end of the earth even unto the *other* end of the earth: they shall not be lamented, neither gathered, nor buried; they shall be dung upon the ground.

34 Howl, ye shepherds, and cry; and wallow yourselves *in the ashes,* ye principal of the flock: for the days of your slaughter and of

Cross references

16 Jer. 51:7; Ezek. 23:34; Nah. 3:11
18 Jer. 24:9; 25:9, 11
19 Jer. 46:2, 25
20 Job 1:1; Isa. 20:1; Jer. 25:24; 47:1, 5, 7
21 Jer. 48:1; 49:1, 7
22 Jer. 47:4; 49:23
23 Jer. 9:26; 49:8, 32
24 2Chr. 9:14; Jer. 25:20; 49:31; 50:37; Ezek. 30:5
25 Jer. 49:34
26 Jer. 50:9; 51:41
27 Isa. 51:21; 63:6; Hab. 2:16
29 Prov. 11:31; Dan. 9:18, 19; Luke 23:31; 1Pet. 4:17
30 Ps. 11:4; 132:14; Jer. 17:12; 48:33
31 Joel 3:2; Mic. 6:2
33 Ps. 79:3; Isa. 66:16; Jer. 8:2; 16:4, 6; Rev. 11:9
34 Jer. 4:8; 6:26

16:1–21; 18:6). Notice the threefold sequence to which God's judgment moves: "drink, and be moved, and be mad." The first ones to drink of God's judgment are Jerusalem and the cities of Judah, but the Gentile nations will follow as noted in verses 19–26.

25:27–29 After the Lord punishes His own city of Jerusalem and His own people of Judah, He will surely turn His wrath upon the Gentile nations. This will take place during the future seven-year Tribulation and is one of the reasons why this time will be one of global judgment. The title, "the LORD of hosts," is a picture of the Lord leading an army in battle. This description of the Lord is often used in judgment passages indicating that God has the power and might to execute judgment.

25:30 The LORD shall roar from on high. Chapters 4 and 5 of Revelation show us that the Lord readies His battle plan of judgment from His heavenly throne room. It is

from the same place that Jeremiah also speaks of the Lord launching His judgments. The phrase "they that tread the grapes" is a picture used in Revelation 19:15 of God's intervening judgment at Armageddon during the Second Coming.

25:31 the LORD hath a controversy with the nations. This is another reference to the Great Tribulation and Armageddon (Rev. 16:16; 19:15). The Hebrew word translated "controversy" is a technical word for a legal complaint against someone in a legal setting. This means that God's controversy with the nations was one that would hold up in a court of law. The statement "he will plead with all flesh" denotes that during the process of judgment, the Lord will give individuals an opportunity to repent of their sin and trust Christ as their Savior (cf. Rev. 14:6–7; 16:9, 11, 21).

your dispersions are accomplished; and ye shall fall like a pleasant vessel.

35 And the shepherds shall have no way to flee, nor the principal of the flock to escape.

36 A voice of the cry of the shepherds, and an howling of the principal of the flock, *shall be heard*: for the LORD hath spoiled their pasture.

37 And the peaceable habitations are cut down because of the fierce anger of the LORD.

38 He hath forsaken his covert, as the lion: for their land is desolate because of the fierceness of the oppressor, and because of his fierce anger.

CHAPTER 26
Jeremiah on Trial

1 In the beginning of the reign of Jehoiakim the son of Josiah king of Judah came this word from the LORD, saying,

2 Thus saith the LORD; Stand in the court of the LORD's house, and speak unto all the cities of Judah, which come to worship in the LORD's house, all the words that I command thee to speak unto them; diminish not a word:

3 If so be they will hearken, and turn every man from his evil way, that I may repent me of the evil, which I purpose to do unto them because of the evil of their doings.

4 And thou shalt say unto them, Thus saith the LORD; If ye will not hearken to me, to walk in my law, which I have set before you,

5 To hearken to the words of my servants the prophets, whom I sent unto you, both rising up early, and sending *them*, but ye have not hearkened;

6 Then will I make this house like Shiloh, and will make this city a curse to all the nations of the earth.

7 So the priests and the prophets and all the people heard Jeremiah speaking these words in the house of the LORD.

8 Now it came to pass, when Jeremiah had made an end of speaking all that the LORD had commanded *him* to speak unto all the people, that the priests and the prophets and all the people took him, saying, Thou shalt surely die.

9 Why hast thou prophesied in the name of the LORD, saying, This house shall be like Shiloh, and this city shall be desolate without an inhabitant? And all the people were gathered against Jeremiah in the house of the LORD.

10 When the princes of Judah heard these things, then they came up from the king's house unto the house of the LORD, and sat down in the entry of the new gate of the LORD's *house*.

11 Then spake the priests and the prophets unto the princes and to all the people, saying, This man *is* worthy to die; for he hath prophesied against this city, as ye have heard with your ears.

12 Then spake Jeremiah unto all the princes and to all the people, saying, The LORD sent me to prophesy against this house and against this city all the words that ye have heard.

13 Therefore now amend your ways and your doings, and obey the voice of the LORD your God; and the LORD will repent him of the evil that he hath pronounced against you.

14 As for me, behold, I *am* in your hand: do with me as seemeth good and meet unto you.

15 But know ye for certain, that if ye put me to death, ye shall surely bring innocent blood upon yourselves, and upon this city, and upon the inhabitants thereof: for of a truth the LORD hath sent me unto you to speak all these words in your ears.

16 Then said the princes and all the people unto the priests and to the prophets; This man *is* not worthy to die: for he hath spoken to us in the name of the LORD our God.

17 Then rose up certain of the elders of the land, and spake to all the assembly of the people, saying,

18 Micah the Morasthite prophesied in the days of Hezekiah king of Judah, and spake to all the people of Judah, saying, Thus saith the LORD of hosts; Zion shall be plowed *like* a field, and Jerusalem shall become heaps, and the mountain of the house as the high places of a forest.

19 Did Hezekiah king of Judah and all Judah put him at all to death? did he not fear the LORD, and besought the LORD, and the LORD repented him of the evil which he had pronounced against them? Thus might we procure great evil against our souls.

Cross references

35 Amos 2:14

38 Ps. 76:2; Jer. 19:14; Ezek. 3:10; Matt. 28:20; Acts 20:27

3 Jer. 18:8; 36:3; Jon. 3:8, 9

4 Lev. 26:14; Deut. 28:15

5 Jer. 7:13, 25; 11:7; 25:3, 4

6 1Sam. 4:10, 11; Ps. 78:60; Isa. 65:15; Jer. 7:12, 14; 24:9

11 Jer. 38:4

13 Jer. 7:3; 26:3, 19

14 Jer. 38:5

17 Acts 5:34

18 Mic. 1:1; 3:12

19 Ex. 32:14; 2Sam. 24:16; 2Chr. 32:26; Acts 5:39

26:3 The Lord tells Judah that He will not judge them if they will repent of their sins. This gracious offer was not accepted by Judah. Instead, the princes of Judah wanted to kill Jeremiah (26:10–11).

26:6 Shiloh. See the note on Jeremiah 7:12.

20 And there was also a man that prophesied in the name of the LORD, Urijah the son of Shemaiah of Kirjath-jearim, who prophesied against this city and against this land according to all the words of Jeremiah:

21 And when Jehoiakim the king, with all his mighty men, and all the princes, heard his words, the king sought to put him to death: but when Urijah heard it, he was afraid, and fled, and went into Egypt;

22 And Jehoiakim the king sent men into Egypt, *namely*, Elnathan the son of Achbor, and *certain* men with him into Egypt.

23 And they fetched forth Urijah out of Egypt, and brought him unto Jehoiakim the king; who slew him with the sword, and cast his dead body into the graves of the common people.

24 Nevertheless the hand of Ahikam the son of Shaphan was with Jeremiah, that they should not give him into the hand of the people to put him to death.

CHAPTER 27
The Command to Serve Nebuchadnezzar

1 In the beginning of the reign of Jehoiakim the son of Josiah king of Judah came this word unto Jeremiah from the LORD, saying,

2 Thus saith the LORD to me; Make thee bonds and yokes, and put them upon thy neck,

3 And send them to the king of Edom, and to the king of Moab, and to the king of the Ammonites, and to the king of Tyrus, and to the king of Zidon, by the hand of the messengers which come to Jerusalem unto Zedekiah king of Judah;

4 And command them to say unto their masters, Thus saith the LORD of hosts, the God of Israel; Thus shall ye say unto your masters;

5 I have made the earth, the man and the beast that *are* upon the ground, by my great power and by my outstretched arm, and have given it unto whom it seemed meet unto me.

6 And now have I given all these lands into the hand of Nebuchadnezzar the king of Babylon, my servant; and the beasts of the field have I given him also to serve him.

7 And all nations shall serve him, and his son, and his son's son, until the very time of his land come: and then many nations and great kings shall serve themselves of him.

8 And it shall come to pass, *that* the nation and kingdom which will not serve the same Nebuchadnezzar the king of Babylon, and that will not put their neck under the yoke of the king of Babylon, that nation will I punish, saith the LORD, with the sword, and with the famine, and with the pestilence, until I have consumed them by his hand.

9 Therefore hearken not ye to your prophets, nor to your diviners, nor to your dreamers, nor to your enchanters, nor to your sorcerers, which speak unto you, saying, Ye shall not serve the king of Babylon:

10 For they prophesy a lie unto you, to remove you far from your land; and that I should drive you out, and ye should perish.

11 But the nations that bring their neck under the yoke of the king of Babylon, and serve him, those will I let remain still in their own land, saith the LORD; and they shall till it, and dwell therein.

12 I spake also to Zedekiah king of Judah according to all these words, saying, Bring your necks under the yoke of the king of Babylon, and serve him and his people, and live.

13 Why will ye die, thou and thy people, by the sword, by the famine, and by the pestilence, as the LORD hath spoken against the nation that will not serve the king of Babylon?

14 Therefore hearken not unto the words of the prophets that speak unto you, saying, Ye shall not serve the king of Babylon: for they prophesy a lie unto you.

15 For I have not sent them, saith the LORD, yet they prophesy a lie in my name; that I might drive you out, and that ye might perish, ye, and the prophets that prophesy unto you.

16 Also I spake to the priests and to all this people, saying, Thus saith the LORD; Hearken not to the words of your prophets that prophesy unto you, saying, Behold, the vessels of the LORD's house shall now shortly be brought again from Babylon: for they prophesy a lie unto you.

17 Hearken not unto them; serve the king of Babylon, and live: wherefore should this city be laid waste?

Cross references (center column):

24 2Kgs. 22:12, 14; Jer. 27:3, 12, 20; 28:1; 39:14

2 Jer. 28:10, 12; Ezek. 4:1; 12:3; 24:3

5 Ps. 115:15, 16; 146:6; Isa. 45:12; Dan. 4:17, 25, 32

6 Jer. 25:9; 28:14; 43:10; Ezek. 29:18, 20; Dan. 2:38

7 2Chr. 36:20; Ezek. 25:12, 14; 50:7; Dan. 5:26

10 Jer. 27:14

12 Jer. 28:1; 38:17

13 Ezek. 18:31

14 Jer. 14:14; 23:21; 29:8, 9

16 2Chr. 36:7, 10; Jer. 28:3; Dan. 1:2

26:20 Because of the opposition that Jeremiah received from the political and religious establishment of Judah, the Lord brings a second prophet on the scene with the same message of judgment that Jeremiah has brought. The Lord permits those in Judah to kill Urijah (26:23), but He protects Jeremiah (26:24).

18 But if they *be* prophets, and if the word of the LORD be with them, let them now make intercession to the LORD of hosts, that the vessels which are left in the house of the LORD, and *in* the house of the king of Judah, and at Jerusalem, go not to Babylon.

19 For thus saith the LORD of hosts concerning the pillars, and concerning the sea, and concerning the bases, and concerning the residue of the vessels that remain in this city,

20 Which Nebuchadnezzar king of Babylon took not, when he carried away captive Jeconiah the son of Jehoiakim king of Judah from Jerusalem to Babylon, and all the nobles of Judah and Jerusalem;

21 Yea, thus saith the LORD of hosts, the God of Israel, concerning the vessels that remain *in* the house of the LORD, and *in* the house of the king of Judah and of Jerusalem;

22 They shall be carried to Babylon, and there shall they be until the day that I visit them, saith the LORD; then will I bring them up, and restore them to this place.

CHAPTER 28
Hananiah's False Prophecy

1 And it came to pass the same year, in the beginning of the reign of Zedekiah king of Judah, in the fourth year, *and* in the fifth month, *that* Hananiah the son of Azur the prophet, which *was* of Gibeon, spake unto me in the house of the LORD, in the presence of the priests and of all the people, saying,

2 Thus speaketh the LORD of hosts, the God of Israel, saying, I have broken the yoke of the king of Babylon.

3 Within two full years will I bring again into this place all the vessels of the LORD's house, that Nebuchadnezzar king of Babylon took away from this place, and carried them to Babylon:

4 And I will bring again to this place Jeconiah the son of Jehoiakim king of Judah, with all the captives of Judah, that went into Babylon, saith the LORD: for I will break the yoke of the king of Babylon.

5 Then the prophet Jeremiah said unto the prophet Hananiah in the presence of the priests, and in the presence of all the people that stood in the house of the LORD,

6 Even the prophet Jeremiah said, Amen: the LORD do so: the LORD perform thy words which thou hast prophesied, to bring again the vessels of the LORD's house, and all that is carried away captive, from Babylon into this place.

7 Nevertheless hear thou now this word that I speak in thine ears, and in the ears of all the people;

8 The prophets that have been before me and before thee of old prophesied both against many countries, and against great kingdoms, of war, and of evil, and of pestilence.

9 The prophet which prophesieth of peace, when the word of the prophet shall come to pass, *then* shall the prophet be known, that the LORD hath truly sent him.

10 Then Hananiah the prophet took the yoke from off the prophet Jeremiah's neck, and brake it.

11 And Hananiah spake in the presence of all the people, saying, Thus saith the LORD; Even so will I break the yoke of Nebuchadnezzar king of Babylon from the neck of all nations within the space of two full years. And the prophet Jeremiah went his way.

12 Then the word of the LORD came unto Jeremiah *the prophet*, after that Hananiah the prophet had broken the yoke from off the neck of the prophet Jeremiah, saying,

13 Go and tell Hananiah, saying, Thus saith the LORD; Thou hast broken the yokes of wood; but thou shalt make for them yokes of iron.

14 For thus saith the LORD of hosts, the God of Israel; I have put a yoke of iron upon the neck of all these nations, that they may serve Nebuchadnezzar king of Babylon; and they shall serve him: and I have given him the beasts of the field also.

15 Then said the prophet Jeremiah unto Hananiah the prophet, Hear now, Hananiah; The LORD hath not sent thee; but thou makest this people to trust in a lie.

Cross references (center column)

19 2Kgs. 25:13; Jer. 52:17, 20, 21
20 2Kgs. 24:14, 15; Jer. 24:1
22 2Kgs. 25:13; 2Chr. 36:18, 21; Ezra 1:7; 7:19; Jer. 27:1; 29:10; 32:5
2 Jer. 27:12
3 Jer. 27:16
6 1Kgs. 1:36
9 Deut. 18:22
10 Jer. 27:2
11 Jer. 27:7
14 Deut. 28:48; Jer. 27:6, 7
15 Jer. 29:31; Ezek. 13:22

27:22 They shall be carried to Babylon. Here Jeremiah summarizes his prophecy concerning Judah and her destiny in the near future. The prophet predicts that the remaining temple vessels not already taken by the Babylonians would be carried away at that time (see 2 Kgs. 25:14–15). There is also a word of hope in this verse that Judah will be restored to the land. This prophecy was fulfilled in 516 B.C. when a remnant of 50,000 returned under the Medo-Persian Empire (see Ezra 1:7–11), and the articles were returned to the second temple.

28:15–17 Hananiah is the false prophet that came into the temple of the Lord to tell the rebellious people of Judah what they wanted to hear instead of the true message that God provided through Jeremiah. In a contest of who truly spoke for the Lord, Jeremiah was vindicated

16 Therefore thus saith the LORD; Behold, I will cast thee from off the face of the earth: this year thou shalt die, because thou hast taught rebellion against the LORD.

17 So Hananiah the prophet died the same year in the seventh month.

CHAPTER 29
Jeremiah's Letter to the Captives

1 Now these *are* the words of the letter that Jeremiah the prophet sent from Jerusalem unto the residue of the elders which were carried away captives, and to the priests, and to the prophets, and to all the people whom Nebuchadnezzar had carried away captive from Jerusalem to Babylon;

2 (After that Jeconiah the king, and the queen, and the eunuchs, the princes of Judah and Jerusalem, and the carpenters, and the smiths, were departed from Jerusalem;)

3 By the hand of Elasah the son of Shaphan, and Gemariah the son of Hilkiah, (whom Zedekiah king of Judah sent unto Babylon to Nebuchadnezzar king of Babylon) saying,

4 Thus saith the LORD of hosts, the God of Israel, unto all that are carried away captives, whom I have caused to be carried away from Jerusalem unto Babylon;

5 Build ye houses, and dwell *in them*; and plant gardens, and eat the fruit of them;

6 Take ye wives, and beget sons and daughters; and take wives for your sons, and give your daughters to husbands, that they may bear sons and daughters; that ye may be increased there, and not diminished.

7 And seek the peace of the city whither I have caused you to be carried away captives, and pray unto the LORD for it: for in the peace thereof shall ye have peace.

8 For thus saith the LORD of hosts, the God of Israel; Let not your prophets and your diviners, that *be* in the midst of you, deceive you, neither hearken to your dreams which ye cause to be dreamed.

9 For they prophesy falsely unto you in my name: I have not sent them, saith the LORD.

10 For thus saith the LORD, That after seventy years be accomplished at Babylon I will visit you, and perform my good word toward you, in causing you to return to this place.

11 For I know the thoughts that I think toward you, saith the LORD, thoughts of peace, and not of evil, to give you an expected end.

12 Then shall ye call upon me, and ye shall go and pray unto me, and I will hearken unto you.

13 And ye shall seek me, and find *me*, when ye shall search for me with all your heart.

14 And I will be found of you, saith the LORD: and I will turn away your captivity, and I will gather you from all the nations, and from all the places whither I have driven you, saith the LORD; and I will bring you again into the place whence I caused you to be carried away captive.

15 Because ye have said, The LORD hath raised us up prophets in Babylon;

16 *Know* that thus saith the LORD of the king that sitteth upon the throne of David, and of all the people that dwelleth in this city, *and* of your brethren that are not gone forth with you into captivity;

17 Thus saith the LORD of hosts; Behold, I will send upon them the sword, the famine, and the pestilence, and will make them like vile figs, that cannot be eaten, they are so evil.

18 And I will persecute them with the sword, with the famine, and with the pestilence, and will deliver them to be removed to all the kingdoms of the earth, to be a curse, and an astonishment, and an hissing, and a reproach, among all the nations whither I have driven them:

19 Because they have not hearkened to my words, saith the LORD, which I sent unto them by my servants the prophets, rising up early and sending *them*; but ye would not hear, saith the LORD.

20 Hear ye therefore the word of the LORD,

against the lie of Hananiah. The word that Jeremiah spoke came true and "Hananiah the prophet died the same year in the seventh month."

29:10–14 after seventy years be accomplished. Seventy years is the specific length of Judah's captivity. This is one of the passages that Daniel studied whereby he learned when his people would return from captivity (Dan. 9:2). This prophecy was fulfilled in 516 B.C. The

overall purpose for the exile was to woo Judah back to the Lord. Not only will the Lord return Judah from Babylon at the end of the seventy-year captivity, but God says, "I will gather you from all the nations," so there will also come a time in the future when all of Judah and Israel will be returned permanently to the land. This time will be at the second coming of Christ in preparation for the Millennial Kingdom (Dan. 12:1–4; Matt. 24:29–31).

God's Plan for Your Future

By Harold L. Willmington

A popular but totally perverted concept of heaven would describe that glorious future life in terms of some disembodied spirits piously perched on fleecy clouds and strumming their golden harps. This may be heaven according to some, but New Testament teaching it is not. Scripture would indicate that heaven will be both a place of singing and a place of fellowship (Isa. 44:23; Heb. 2:12; Rev. 14:3; 15:3).

Evidence that heaven will be a "concert hall" of singing lies in the fact that two of heaven's greatest songs will have God's two great works for their theme: the hymn praising God for his mighty work of creation (Rev. 4:11) and the hymn praising God for his mighty work of redemption (Rev. 5:9). But heaven will also be a place of fellowship. Not only will believers enjoy blessed fellowship with other believers, but, even more importantly, we shall know and be known by the Savior in a far more intimate way than ever possible here on earth. Note the things this great chief Shepherd will do for his sheep in heaven as listed by John. First, He will feed us that hidden heavenly manna; he will give us a new name (Rev. 2:17). Secondly, He will lead us beside the living waters; He will dry all our tears (Rev. 7:17). Then He will allow us to sit with Him on His throne (Rev. 3:21), and finally, He will dress us with his own righteousness (Rev. 19:8).

> *Heaven will be a place of singing, serving, and learning.*

Heaven will be a place of serving (Rev. 7:15; 22:3). While we cannot be dogmatic on the exact nature of this service, we do know from the following passages that a portion of our labor for the Lamb will be that of exercising authority and judgment over men and angels (1 Cor. 6:2–3; 2 Tim. 2:12; Rev. 22:5).

Finally, heaven will be a place of learning (1 Cor. 13:9–10) in the following areas:

1. We will learn concerning the person of God. Throughout a timeless eternity, a child of God can learn more about the Creator each year and yet never even remotely exhaust the awesome height, depth, or length of the person of God (Rom. 11:33).

2. We will learn concerning the plan of God. One of the most painful questions asked here on earth by Christians is why a loving and wise God allows certain terrible tragedies to occur. We may rest assured, however, that once we understand the reason for all our sufferings and trials, we will repeat the words once stated by a Galilean crowd in Jesus' day: "He hath done all things well" (Mark 7:37).

3. We will learn concerning the power of God. "In the beginning God created the heaven and the earth" (Gen. 1:1). The universe is so huge that it takes a beam of light (which travels some 700 million miles per hour) over ten billion years to cross the known universe! Within this universe are untold trillions of stars, planets, and other heavenly bodies. God made them all to instruct man concerning his power and glory (Ps. 19:1; 147:4; Isa. 40:26). Perhaps we shall someday visit each star and explore every corner of our Father's universe!

all ye of the captivity, whom I have sent from Jerusalem to Babylon:

21 Thus saith the LORD of hosts, the God of Israel, of Ahab the son of Kolaiah, and of Zedekiah the son of Maaseiah, which prophesy a lie unto you in my name; Behold, I will deliver them into the hand of Nebuchadrezzar king of Babylon; and he shall slay them before your eyes;

22 And of them shall be taken up a curse by all the captivity of Judah which *are* in Babylon, saying, The LORD make thee like Zedekiah and like Ahab, whom the king of Babylon roasted in the fire;

23 Because they have committed villany in Israel, and have committed adultery with their neighbours' wives, and have spoken lying words in my name, which I have not commanded them; even I know, and *am* a witness, saith the LORD.

24 *Thus* shalt thou also speak to Shemaiah the Nehelamite, saying,

25 Thus speaketh the LORD of hosts, the God of Israel, saying, Because thou hast sent letters in thy name unto all the people that *are* at Jerusalem, and to Zephaniah the son of Maaseiah the priest, and to all the priests, saying,

26 The LORD hath made thee priest in the stead of Jehoiada the priest, that ye should be officers in the house of the LORD, for every man *that is* mad, and maketh himself a prophet, that thou shouldest put him in prison, and in the stocks.

27 Now therefore why hast thou not reproved Jeremiah of Anathoth, which maketh himself a prophet to you?

28 For therefore he sent unto us *in* Babylon, saying, This *captivity is* long: build ye houses, and dwell *in them*; and plant gardens, and eat the fruit of them.

29 And Zephaniah the priest read this letter in the ears of Jeremiah the prophet.

30 Then came the word of the LORD unto Jeremiah, saying,

31 Send to all them of the captivity, saying, Thus saith the LORD concerning Shemaiah the Nehelamite; Because that Shemaiah hath prophesied unto you, and I sent him not, and he caused you to trust in a lie:

32 Therefore thus saith the LORD; Behold, I will punish Shemaiah the Nehelamite, and his seed: he shall not have a man to dwell among this people; neither shall he behold the good that I will do for my people, saith the LORD; because he hath taught rebellion against the LORD.

CHAPTER 30
Israel Will Return to the Land

1 The word that came to Jeremiah from the LORD, saying,

2 Thus speaketh the LORD God of Israel, saying, Write thee all the words that I have spoken unto thee in a book.

3 For, lo, the days come, saith the LORD, that I will bring again the captivity of my people Israel and Judah, saith the LORD: and I will cause them to return to the land that I gave to their fathers, and they shall possess it.

4 And these *are* the words that the LORD spake concerning Israel and concerning Judah.

5 For thus saith the LORD; We have heard a voice of trembling, of fear, and not of peace.

6 Ask ye now, and see whether a man doth travail with child? wherefore do I see every

Cross references:
22 Gen. 48:20; Isa. 65:15; Dan. 3:6
23 Jer. 23:14
25 2Kgs. 25:18; Jer. 21:1
26 2Kgs. 9:11; Jer. 20:1, 2; Acts 26:24
28 Jer. 29:5
31 Jer. 28:15
32 Jer. 16:15; 28:16; 29:18; 32:44; Ezek. 39:25; Amos 9:14, 15
6 Jer. 4:31; 6:24

29:21–22 Jeremiah predicted the false prophets, Ahab and Zedekiah would be burned by fire and killed by the Babylonians. We do not have an account reporting the fulfillment of this prophecy; but, since all the other prophecies have been fulfilled, it is not wrong to assume that this prophecy was fulfilled as well.

29:31–32 Shemaiah, a false prophet in the exile, apparently was continuing to declare his false message through letters. The Lord would punish Shemaiah by cutting off his descendants. It is significant that neither he nor any of his descendants are listed among those returning from this exile.

30:1–3 Jeremiah is specifically instructed by the Lord to write these things in a book. This would include a scroll, as noted in Jeremiah 36:2. This prophecy concerning the return of Israel has in mind a still-future time when both the Northern and Southern Kingdoms will be fully restored in their land (Jer. 29:10; Amos 9:14; Rom. 11:26). Israel's possession of the land in this sense refers to the nation obediently keeping the land specifications of the Mosaic covenant. This will take place during the Millennium.

30:6–9 every man with his hands on his loins, as a woman in travail. Jeremiah is communicating that just as it would be unique to see a male doubled over with the pains of child labor, so the coming time of the Tribulation period will be a unique time in the entire history of the world, "so that none is like it." Jeremiah calls the Tribulation "the time of Jacob's trouble." In addition to the judgment that God is sending through the Babylonian captivity, there is coming a future time of the greatest trouble in the history of Israel and the entire world.

man with his hands on his loins, as a woman in travail, and all faces are turned into paleness?

7 Alas! for that day *is* great, so that none *is* like it: it *is* even the time of Jacob's trouble; but he shall be saved out of it.

8 For it shall come to pass in that day, saith the LORD of hosts, *that* I will break his yoke from off thy neck, and will burst thy bonds, and strangers shall no more serve themselves of him:

9 But they shall serve the LORD their God, and David their king, whom I will raise up unto them.

10 Therefore fear thou not, O my servant Jacob, saith the LORD; neither be dismayed, O Israel: for, lo, I will save thee from afar, and thy seed from the land of their captivity; and Jacob shall return, and shall be in

7 Dan. 12:1; Joel 2:11, 31; Amos 5:18; Zeph. 1:14

9 Isa. 55:3, 4; Ezek. 34:23; 37:24; Hos. 3:5; Luke 1:69; Acts 2:30; 13:23

10 Isa. 41:13; 43:5; 44:2

11 Ps. 6:1; Isa. 27:8; Jer. 4:27; 10:24; 46:28; Amos 9:8

12 2Chr. 36:16

14 Job 13:24; 16:9

rest, and be quiet, and none shall make *him* afraid.

11 For I *am* with thee, saith the LORD, to save thee: though I make a full end of all nations whither I have scattered thee, yet will I not make a full end of thee: but I will correct thee in measure, and will not leave thee altogether unpunished.

12 For thus saith the LORD, Thy bruise *is* incurable, *and* thy wound *is* grievous.

13 *There is* none to plead thy cause, that thou mayest be bound up: thou hast no healing medicines.

14 All thy lovers have forgotten thee; they seek thee not; for I have wounded thee with the wound of an enemy, with the chastisement of a cruel one, for the multitude of thine iniquity; *because* thy sins were increased.

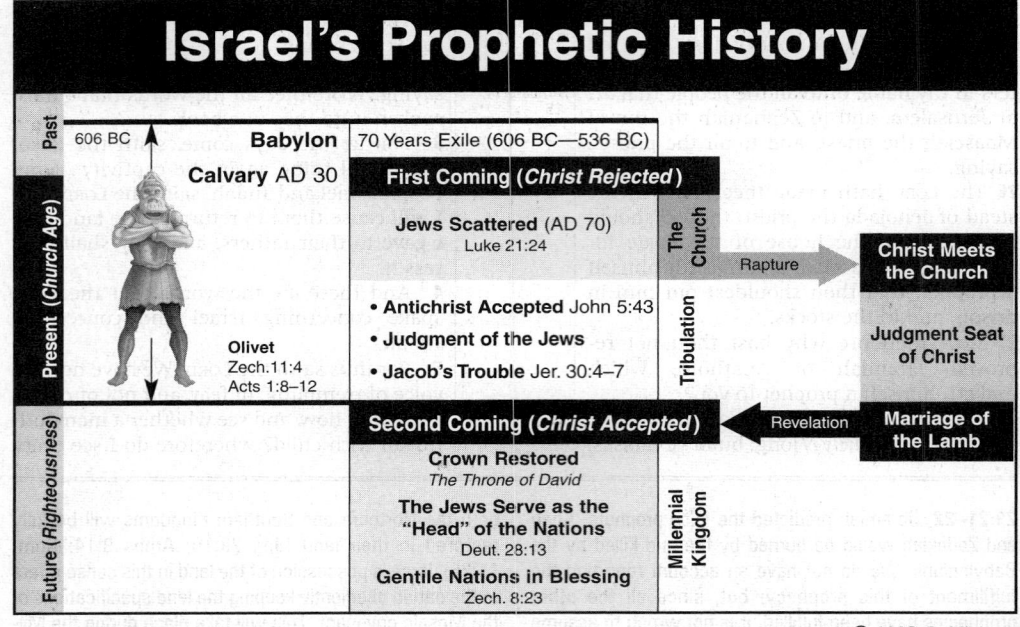

Israel's Prophetic History

Past | 606 BC **Babylon** | 70 Years Exile (606 BC—536 BC)

Calvary AD 30 | **First Coming** (*Christ Rejected*)

Present (Church Age) | **Jews Scattered** (AD 70) Luke 21:24 | The Church | Rapture → **Christ Meets the Church**

Olivet Zech.11:4 Acts 1:8–12 | • **Antichrist Accepted** John 5:43 • **Judgment of the Jews** • **Jacob's Trouble** Jer. 30:4–7 | Tribulation | **Judgment Seat of Christ**

Future (Righteousness) | **Second Coming** (*Christ Accepted*) | ← Revelation | **Marriage of the Lamb**

Crown Restored *The Throne of David*

The Jews Serve as the "Head" of the Nations Deut. 28:13 | Millennial Kingdom

Gentile Nations in Blessing Zech. 8:23

© AMG Publishers

Though Israel will experience great persecution (Dan. 9:27; 12:1; Zech. 13:8–9; Matt. 24:15–22), "he shall be saved out of it" and "shall serve the LORD" during the Millennium. The Millennium will also be a time during which the Lord will raise up unto the Israelites, David their king. While Jesus, the Messiah, will reign over the entire earth, David will be resurrected to reign with Christ as vice regent over the nation of Israel (Ezek. 34:23–24; 37:24–25; Hos. 3:5).

30:10 I will save thee from afar. After the time of the

Tribulation, the Lord will rescue Israel from her scattering throughout the entire globe. No country will be too far from which to return the Lord's scattered people.

30:14–17 Jeremiah uses the language of an unfaithful wife (Judah) who has deserted her husband (the Lord) and now, because she has lived the difficult life of a prostitute, is all battered and bruised and has lost her beauty. In this condition, none of those with whom she has been having relations are interested in her. But the mercy of the Lord comes to her rescue.

15 Why criest thou for thine affliction? thy sorrow *is* incurable for the multitude of thine iniquity: *because* thy sins were increased, I have done these things unto thee.
16 Therefore all they that devour thee shall be devoured; and all thine adversaries, every one of them, shall go into captivity; and they that spoil thee shall be a spoil, and all that prey upon thee will I give for a prey.
17 For I will restore health unto thee, and I will heal thee of thy wounds, saith the LORD; because they called thee an Outcast, *saying*, This *is* Zion, whom no man seeketh after.
18 Thus saith the LORD; Behold, I will bring again the captivity of Jacob's tents, and have mercy on his dwellingplaces; and the city shall be builded upon her own heap, and the palace shall remain after the manner thereof.
19 And out of them shall proceed thanksgiving and the voice of them that make merry: and I will multiply them, and they shall not be few; I will also glorify them, and they shall not be small.
20 Their children also shall be as aforetime, and their congregation shall be established before me, and I will punish all that oppress them.
21 And their nobles shall be of themselves, and their governor shall proceed from the midst of them; and I will cause him to draw near, and he shall approach unto me: for who *is* this that engaged his heart to approach unto me? saith the LORD.
22 And ye shall be my people, and I will be your God.
23 Behold, the whirlwind of the LORD goeth forth with fury, a continuing whirlwind: it shall fall with pain upon the head of the wicked.

24 The fierce anger of the LORD shall not return, until he have done *it*, and until he have performed the intents of his heart: in the latter days ye shall consider it.

CHAPTER 31
A Happy Return

1 At the same time, saith the Lord, will I be the God of all the families of Israel, and they shall be my people.
2 Thus saith the LORD, The people *which were* left of the sword found grace in the wilderness; *even* Israel, when I went to cause him to rest.
3 The LORD hath appeared of old unto me, *saying*, Yea, I have loved thee with an everlasting love: therefore with lovingkindness have I drawn thee.
4 Again I will build thee, and thou shalt be built, O virgin of Israel: thou shalt again be adorned with thy tabrets, and shalt go forth in the dances of them that make merry.
5 Thou shalt yet plant vines upon the mountains of Samaria: the planters shall plant, and shall eat *them* as common things.
6 For there shall be a day, *that* the watchmen upon the mount Ephraim shall cry, Arise ye, and let us go up to Zion unto the LORD our God.
7 For thus saith the LORD; Sing with gladness for Jacob, and shout among the chief of the nations: publish ye, praise ye, and say, O LORD, save thy people, the remnant of Israel.
8 Behold, I will bring them from the north country, and gather them from the coasts of the earth, *and* with them the blind and the lame, the woman with child and her that travaileth with child together: a great company shall return thither.

Cross references
15 Jer. 15:18
16 Ex. 23:22; Isa. 33:1; 41:11; Jer. 10:25
17 Jer. 33:6
18 Ps. 102:13; Jer. 30:3; 33:7, 11
19 Isa. 35:10; 51:11; Zech. 10:8
20 Isa. 1:26
22 Jer. 24:7; 31:1, 33; 32:38; Ezek. 11:20; 36:28; 37:27
23 Jer. 23:19, 20; 25:32
24 Gen. 49:1; Jer. 30:22, 24
2 Num. 10:33; Deut. 1:33; Ps. 95:11; Isa. 63:14
3 Hos. 11:4; Mal. 1:2; Rom. 11:28, 29
4 Ex. 15:20; Judg. 11:34; Ps. 149:3; Jer. 33:7
5 Deut. 20:6; 28:30; Isa. 65:21; Amos 9:14
6 Isa. 2:3; Mic. 4:2
8 Ezek. 20:34, 41; 34:13

30:18–20 During the Millennium, there "shall proceed thanksgiving and the voice of them that make merry" from the rebuilt city. Israel will experience a population explosion during the Millennium when she will be transformed from a small to a large nation. Instead of Israel and Judah being punished, as was the case in Jeremiah's day, the Lord "will punish all that oppress them."

30:24 in the latter days ye shall consider it. This phrase substantiates that the Lord is speaking of the Tribulation leading up to the Millennium, during which Israel will receive these blessings. This time is yet to come. During this time, Israel will finally obey the Lord and He will bless them (cf. 23:20).

31:1 "And ye shall be my people, and I will be your God." The purpose for which God originally chose Israel (Deut.

26:16–19; Jer. 24:7; 31:33; Ezek. 14:11; 37:23, 27; Hos. 2:23; Zech. 8:8; 13:9) will be realized during the Millennium.

31:3–14 This major prophetic passage in Jeremiah describes God's future blessings to Israel, her return to the land, her joy in serving the Lord, and the fact that she would be gathered from all over the earth. It describes many aspects of the Millennial Kingdom. This prophecy regarding the remnant cannot refer to the nation's return in 616 B.C. since it was only a partial return at that time. Therefore, this prophecy must refer to the future return spoken of in Matthew 24:31 in preparation for the Millennium. At this future time, Israel will return to her God-given land and experience great joy and bounty.

9 They shall come with weeping, and with supplications will I lead them: I will cause them to walk by the rivers of waters in a straight way, wherein they shall not stumble: for I am a father to Israel, and Ephraim *is* my firstborn.

10 Hear the word of the LORD, O ye nations, and declare *it* in the isles afar off, and say, He that scattered Israel will gather him, and keep him, as a shepherd *doth* his flock.

11 For the LORD hath redeemed Jacob, and ransomed him from the hand of *him that was* stronger than he.

12 Therefore they shall come and sing in the height of Zion, and shall flow together to the goodness of the LORD, for wheat, and for wine, and for oil, and for the young of the flock and of the herd: and their soul shall be as a watered garden; and they shall not sorrow any more at all.

13 Then shall the virgin rejoice in the dance, both young men and old together: for I will turn their mourning into joy, and will comfort them, and make them rejoice from their sorrow.

14 And I will satiate the soul of the priests with fatness, and my people shall be satisfied with my goodness, saith the LORD.

God's Mercy

15 Thus saith the LORD; A voice was heard in Ramah, lamentation, *and* bitter weeping; Rahel weeping for her children refused to be comforted for her children, because they *were* not.

16 Thus saith the LORD; Refrain thy voice from weeping, and thine eyes from tears: for thy work shall be rewarded, saith the LORD; and they shall come again from the land of the enemy.

17 And there is hope in thine end, saith the LORD, that thy children shall come again to their own border.

18 I have surely heard Ephraim bemoaning himself *thus*; Thou hast chastised me, and I was chastised, as a bullock unaccustomed *to*

the yoke: turn thou me, and I shall be turned; for thou *art* the LORD my God.

19 Surely after that I was turned, I repented; and after that I was instructed, I smote upon *my* thigh: I was ashamed, yea, even confounded, because I did bear the reproach of my youth.

20 *Is* Ephraim my dear son? *is he* a pleasant child? for since I spake against him, I do earnestly remember him still: therefore my bowels are troubled for him; I will surely have mercy upon him, saith the LORD.

21 Set thee up waymarks, make thee high heaps: set thine heart toward the highway, *even* the way *which* thou wentest: turn again, O virgin of Israel, turn again to these thy cities.

22 How long wilt thou go about, O thou backsliding daughter? for the LORD hath created a new thing in the earth, A woman shall compass a man.

23 Thus saith the LORD of hosts, the God of Israel; As yet they shall use this speech in the land of Judah and in the cities thereof, when I shall bring again their captivity; The LORD bless thee, O habitation of justice, *and* mountain of holiness.

24 And there shall dwell in Judah itself, and in all the cities thereof together, husbandmen, and they *that* go forth with flocks.

25 For I have satiated the weary soul, and I have replenished every sorrowful soul.

26 Upon this I awaked, and beheld; and my sleep was sweet unto me.

The New Covenant

27 Behold, the days come, saith the LORD, that I will sow the house of Israel and the house of Judah with the seed of man, and with the seed of beast.

28 And it shall come to pass, *that* like as I have watched over them, to pluck up, and to break down, and to throw down, and to destroy, and to afflict; so will I watch over them, to build, and to plant, saith the LORD.

29 In those days they shall say no more, The

Cross references

9 Ex. 4:22; Ps. 126:5, 6; Isa. 35:8; 43:19; 49:10, 11; Jer. 50:4; Zech. 12:10
10 Isa. 40:11; Ezek. 34:12-14
11 Isa. 44:23; 48:20; 49:24, 25
12 Isa. 35:10; 58:11; 65:19; Ezek. 17:23; 20:40; Hos. 3:5; Rev. 21:4
15 Gen. 42:13; Josh. 18:25; Matt. 2:17, 18
16 Ezra 1:5; Jer. 31:4, 5; Hos. 1:11
18 Lam. 5:21
19 Deut. 30:2
20 Deut. 32:36; Isa. 57:18; 63:15; Hos. 11:8; 14:4
21 Jer. 50:5
22 Jer. 2:18, 23, 36; 3:6, 8, 11, 12, 14, 22
23 Ps. 122:5-8; Isa. 1:26; Zech. 8:3
24 Jer. 33:12, 13
27 Ezek. 36:9-11; Hos. 2:23; Zech. 10:9
28 Jer. 1:10; 18:7; 24:6; 44:27
29 Ezek. 18:2, 3

31:27 the house of Israel and the house of Judah. This promise of the restoration of the Jewish nation applies to both the Northern and Southern Kingdoms. Thus, God's future work of restoration will include descendants from all of the twelve tribes.

31:29 The fathers have eaten a sour grape, and the children's teeth are set on edge. This was a common saying in the days of Jeremiah relating to cause and

effect, emphasizing that one generation (the fathers) would sin and the next generation (the children) would receive the judgment. During the Tribulation, the Lord will rescue the righteous remnant. It will be a time when each individual will be judged directly for his or her sin. No longer will God delay punishment and accumulate transgressions because of His mercy (Lev. 26; Deut. 28); instead, He will judge immediately.

fathers have eaten a sour grape, and the children's teeth are set on edge.

30 But every one shall die for his own iniquity: every man that eateth the sour grape, his teeth shall be set on edge.

31 Behold, the days come, saith the LORD, that I will make a new covenant with the house of Israel, and with the house of Judah:

32 Not according to the covenant that I made with their fathers in the day *that* I took them by the hand to bring them out of the land of Egypt; which my covenant they brake, although I was an husband unto them, saith the LORD:

33 But this *shall be* the covenant that I will make with the house of Israel; After those days, saith the LORD, I will put my law in their inward parts, and write it in their hearts; and will be their God, and they shall be my people.

34 And they shall teach no more every man his neighbour, and every man his brother, saying, Know the LORD: for they shall all know me, from the least of them unto the greatest of them, saith the LORD: for I will forgive their iniquity, and I will remember their sin no more.

35 Thus saith the LORD, which giveth the sun for a light by day, *and* the ordinances of the moon and of the stars for a light by night, which divideth the sea when the waves thereof roar; The LORD of hosts *is* his name:

36 If those ordinances depart from before

me, saith the LORD, *then* the seed of Israel also shall cease from being a nation before me for ever.

37 Thus saith the LORD; If heaven above can be measured, and the foundations of the earth searched out beneath, I will also cast off all the seed of Israel for all that they have done, saith the LORD.

38 Behold, the days come, saith the LORD, that the city shall be built to the LORD from the tower of Hananeel unto the gate of the corner.

39 And the measuring line shall yet go forth over against it upon the hill Gareb, and shall compass about to Goath.

40 And the whole valley of the dead bodies, and of the ashes, and all the fields unto the brook of Kidron, unto the corner of the horse gate toward the east, *shall be* holy unto the LORD; it shall not be plucked up, nor thrown down any more for ever.

CHAPTER 32
Jeremiah Buys a Field

1 The word that came to Jeremiah from the LORD in the tenth year of Zedekiah king of Judah, which *was* the eighteenth year of Nebuchadrezzar.

2 For then the king of Babylon's army besieged Jerusalem: and Jeremiah the prophet was shut up in the court of the prison, which *was* in the king of Judah's house.

3 For Zedekiah king of Judah had shut him up, saying, Wherefore dost thou prophesy, and say, Thus saith the LORD, Behold,

Cross references

30 Gal. 6:5, 7
31 Jer. 32:40; 33:14; Ezek. 37:26; Heb. 8:8-12; 10:16, 17
32 Deut. 1:31
33 Ps. 40:8; Jer. 24:7; 30:22; 32:38, 40; Ezek. 11:19, 20; 36:26, 27; 2Cor. 3:3
34 Isa. 54:13; Jer. 33:8; 50:20; Mic. 7:18; John 6:45; Acts 10:43; 13:39; Rom. 11:27; 1Cor. 2:10; 1John 2:20
35 Gen. 1:16; Ps. 72:5, 17; 89:2, 36, 37; 119:91 Isa. 51:15; Jer. 10:16
36 Ps. 148:6; Isa. 54:9, 10; Jer. 33:20
37 Jer. 33:22
38 Neh. 3:1; Zech. 14:10
39 Ezek. 40:8; Zech. 2:1
40 2Kgs. 25:1, 2; Neh. 3:28

31:31–34 The new covenant is one of the biblical covenants that God uses in His governance of humanity (see the article entitled, "God's Covenants with Man"). The new covenant provides for the future spiritual regeneration of Israel in preparation for the Millennial Kingdom. The new covenant, as stated here and in other Old Testament passages, is for Israel (Deut. 30:6; Isa. 59:20–21; Jer. 32:37–40; 50:4–5; Ezek. 34:25–26; 36:24–27; Zech. 9:11; 12:10; Heb. 8:1–13). The new covenant is also applied to the Church (Matt. 26:27–28; Luke 22:20; 2 Cor. 3:6), because it provides the forgiveness of sins and a spiritual dynamic that is not reserved exclusively for the nation of Israel.

31:35–37 This passage is an oath that the Lord swears upon Himself saying that if the sun, moon, and stars cease to exist and if the secrets of the universe can all be solved, then He "will also cast off all the seed of Israel for all that they have done." This passage clearly teaches the permanence of Israel's election as God's chosen people since the passage describes impossible human accom-

plishments. These words were intended to encourage the people in the midst of their impending judgment in the days of Jeremiah.

31:38–40 Behold, the days come. This is a prediction of a whole new era in the life of Judah, indicating a shift from a time of judgment to that of a future blessing. The specific predictions outlined in this passage were not fulfilled by the Jewish return to Jerusalem at the end of the seventh century B.C., but they will literally be fulfilled when Jesus, the Messiah, returns and begins His millennial reign from a restructured Jerusalem. That this is the time when they will be fulfilled is evidenced by the use of millennial language in verse 40.

32:2 Babylon's army besieged Jerusalem. This records the beginning of Jeremiah's prophecies about the coming judgment upon Judah. This siege was set up in January of 588 B.C. and lasted until July of 586 B.C. when the city and the temple were destroyed.

I will give this city into the hand of the king of Babylon, and he shall take it;

4 And Zedekiah king of Judah shall not escape out of the hand of the Chaldeans, but shall surely be delivered into the hand of the king of Babylon, and shall speak with him mouth to mouth, and his eyes shall behold his eyes;

5 And he shall lead Zedekiah to Babylon, and there shall he be until I visit him, saith the LORD: though ye fight with the Chaldeans, ye shall not prosper.

6 And Jeremiah said, The word of the LORD came unto me, saying,

7 Behold, Hanameel the son of Shallum thine uncle shall come unto thee, saying, Buy thee my field that is in Anathoth: for the right of redemption is thine to buy it.

8 So Hanameel mine uncle's son came to me in the court of the prison according to the word of the LORD, and said unto me, Buy my field, I pray thee, that is in Anathoth, which is in the country of Benjamin: for the right of inheritance is thine, and the redemption is thine; buy it for thyself. Then I knew that this was the word of the LORD.

9 And I bought the field of Hanameel my uncle's son, that was in Anathoth, and weighed him the money, even seventeen shekels of silver.

10 And I subscribed the evidence, and sealed it, and took witnesses, and weighed him the money in the balances.

11 So I took the evidence of the purchase, both that which was sealed according to the law and custom, and that which was open:

12 And I gave the evidence of the purchase unto Baruch the son of Neriah, the son of Maaseiah, in the sight of Hanameel mine uncle's son, and in the presence of the witnesses that subscribed the book of the purchase, before all the Jews that sat in the court of the prison.

13 And I charged Baruch before them, saying,

14 Thus saith the LORD of hosts, the God of Israel; Take these evidences, this evidence of the purchase, both which is sealed, and this evidence which is open; and put them in an earthen vessel, that they may continue many days.

15 For thus saith the LORD of hosts, the God of Israel; Houses and fields and vineyards shall be possessed again in this land.

Jeremiah Prays

16 Now when I had delivered the evidence of the purchase unto Baruch the son of Neriah, I prayed unto the LORD, saying,

17 Ah Lord GOD! behold, thou hast made the heaven and the earth by thy great power and stretched out arm, and there is nothing too hard for thee:

18 Thou shewest lovingkindness unto thousands, and recompensest the iniquity of the fathers into the bosom of their children after them: the Great, the Mighty God, the LORD of hosts, is his name,

19 Great in counsel, and mighty in work: for thine eyes are open upon all the ways of the sons of men: to give every one according to his ways, and according to the fruit of his doings:

20 Which hast set signs and wonders in the land of Egypt, even unto this day, and in Israel, and among other men; and hast made thee a name, as at this day;

21 And hast brought forth thy people Israel out of the land of Egypt with signs, and with wonders, and with a strong hand, and with a stretched out arm, and with great terror;

22 And hast given them this land, which thou didst swear to their fathers to give them, a land flowing with milk and honey;

23 And they came in, and possessed it; but they obeyed not thy voice, neither walked in thy law; they have done nothing of all that thou commandedst them to do: therefore thou hast caused all this evil to come upon them:

24 Behold the mounts, they are come unto the city to take it; and the city is given into the hand of the Chaldeans, that fight against it, because of the sword, and of the famine, and of the pestilence: and what thou hast spoken is come to pass; and, behold, thou seest it.

25 And thou hast said unto me, O Lord GOD, Buy thee the field for money, and take witnesses; for the city is given into the hand of the Chaldeans.

26 Then came the word of the LORD unto Jeremiah, saying,

Cross references (center column):

4 Jer. 34:3; 38:18, 23; 39:5; 52:9

5 Jer. 21:4; 27:22; 33:5

7 Lev. 25:24, 25, 32; Ruth 4:4

9 Gen. 23:16; Zech. 11:12

12 Isa. 8:2; Jer. 36:4

15 Jer. 32:37, 43

17 Gen. 18:14; 2Kgs. 19:15; Jer. 32:27; Luke 1:37

18 Ex. 20:6; 34:7; Deut. 5:9, 10; Isa. 9:6; Jer. 10:16

19 Job 34:21; Ps. 33:13; Prov. 5:21; Isa. 28:29; Jer. 16:17; 17:10

20 Ex. 9:16; 1Chr. 17:21; Isa. 63:12; Dan. 9:15

21 Ex. 6:6; 2Sam. 7:23; 1Chr. 17:21; Ps. 136:11, 12

22 Ex. 3:8, 17; Jer. 11:5

23 Neh. 9:26; Jer. 11:8; Dan. 9:10-14

24 Jer. 14:12; 32:25, 36; 33:4

25 Jer. 32:24

32:6–8 Then I knew that this was the word of the LORD. That this prophecy was fulfilled literally is a specific affirmation from the Lord that Jeremiah was indeed a prophet who spoke His words (cf. Deut. 18:20–22).

32:6–15 Houses and fields and vineyards shall be possessed again. Once again, the Lord tells the people of Judah that even though their immediate destiny is judgment, their future is clearly one of hope and blessing.

27 Behold, I *am* the LORD, the God of all flesh: is there any thing too hard for me?
28 Therefore thus saith the LORD; Behold, I will give this city into the hand of the Chaldeans, and into the hand of Nebuchadrezzar king of Babylon, and he shall take it:
29 And the Chaldeans, that fight against this city, shall come and set fire on this city, and burn it with the houses, upon whose roofs they have offered incense unto Baal, and poured out drink offerings unto other gods, to provoke me to anger.
30 For the children of Israel and the children of Judah have only done evil before me from their youth: for the children of Israel have only provoked me to anger with the work of their hands, saith the LORD.
31 For this city hath been to me *as* a provocation of mine anger and of my fury from the day that they built it even unto this day; that I should remove it from before my face,
32 Because of all the evil of the children of Israel and of the children of Judah, which they have done to provoke me to anger, they, their kings, their princes, their priests, and their prophets, and the men of Judah, and the inhabitants of Jerusalem.
33 And they have turned unto me the back, and not the face: though I taught them, rising up early and teaching *them*, yet they have not hearkened to receive instruction.
34 But they set their abominations in the house, which is called by my name, to defile it.
35 And they built the high places of Baal, which *are* in the valley of the son of Hinnom, to cause their sons and their daughters to pass through *the fire* unto Molech; which I commanded them not, neither came it into my mind, that they should do this abomination, to cause Judah to sin.

Hope of Restoration

36 And now therefore thus saith the LORD, the God of Israel, concerning this city, whereof ye say, It shall be delivered into the hand of the king of Babylon by the sword, and by the famine, and by the pestilence;
37 Behold, I will gather them out of all countries, whither I have driven them in mine anger, and in my fury, and in great wrath; and I will bring them again unto this place, and I will cause them to dwell safely:
38 And they shall be my people, and I will be their God:
39 And I will give them one heart, and one way, that they may fear me for ever, for the good of them, and of their children after them:
40 And I will make an everlasting covenant with them, that I will not turn away from them, to do them good; but I will put my fear in their hearts, that they shall not depart from me.
41 Yea, I will rejoice over them to do them good, and I will plant them in this land assuredly with my whole heart and with my whole soul.
42 For thus saith the LORD; Like as I have brought all this great evil upon this people, so will I bring upon them all the good that I have promised them.
43 And fields shall be bought in this land, whereof ye say, It *is* desolate without man or beast; it is given into the hand of the Chaldeans.
44 Men shall buy fields for money, and subscribe evidences, and seal *them*, and take witnesses in the land of Benjamin, and in the places about Jerusalem, and in the cities of Judah, and in the cities of the mountains, and in the cities of the valley, and in the cities of the south: for I will cause their captivity to return, saith the LORD.

Cross references

27 Num. 16:22; Jer. 32:17
28 Jer. 19:13; 21:10; 32:3; 37:8, 10; 52:13
30 Jer. 2:7; 3:25; 7:22-26; 22:21; Ezek. 20:28
31 2Kgs. 23:27; 24:3
32 Isa. 1:4, 6; Dan. 9:8
33 Jer. 2:27; 7:13, 24
34 Jer. 7:30, 31; 23:11; Ezek. 8:5, 6
35 Lev. 18:21; 1Kgs. 11:33; Jer. 7:31; 19:5
36 Jer. 32:24
37 Deut. 30:3; Jer. 23:3, 6; 29:14; 31:10; 33:16; Ezek. 37:21
38 Jer. 24:7; 30:22; 31:33
39 Jer. 24:7; Ezek. 11:19, 20
40 Isa. 55:3; Jer. 31:31, 33
41 Deut. 30:9; Jer. 24:6; 31:28; Amos 9:15; Zeph. 3:17
42 Jer. 31:28
43 Jer. 32:15; 33:10
44 Jer. 17:26; 32:2, 3; 33:7, 11, 26

32:36–44 The Lord repeats the promise of the new covenant of Jeremiah 31 (cf. Jer. 31:31–34; 50:4–5). In spite of impending, immediate judgment, in the long run, Israel's God will provide greater blessing than curse. This passage speaks of millennial blessing.

32:37 I will gather them out of all countries . . . I will bring them again unto this place. This regathering will be the one at the second coming of Christ to begin the Millennium (cf. Deut. 30:4; Isa. 11:12; Dan. 12:1; Matt. 24:31; Mark 13:27) because the remaining context is that of the new covenant and millennial blessing.

32:39 I will give them one heart, and one way, that they may fear me for ever. The act of God in carrying out this promise is the solution to the problem of fallen human nature, which is incapable apart from divine enablement to faithfully serve the Lord (cf. Deut. 29:4).

32:41 I will plant them in this land. This promise, which will be fulfilled in the future, is repeated frequently for the nation of Israel and includes promises of permanent dwelling in the land (Isa. 60:21; Jer. 23:5–6; Ezek. 28:25–26; 37:21–25; Amos 9:15; Zech. 8:7–8).

CHAPTER 33

Prosperity Will Return to Jerusalem

1 Moreover the word of the LORD came unto Jeremiah the second time, while he was yet shut up in the court of the prison, saying,

2 Thus saith the LORD the maker thereof, the LORD that formed it, to establish it; the LORD *is* his name;

3 Call unto me, and I will answer thee, and shew thee great and mighty things, which thou knowest not.

4 For thus saith the LORD, the God of Israel, concerning the houses of this city, and concerning the houses of the kings of Judah, which are thrown down by the mounts, and by the sword;

5 They come to fight with the Chaldeans, but *it is* to fill them with the dead bodies of men, whom I have slain in mine anger and in my fury, and for all whose wickedness I have hid my face from this city.

6 Behold, I will bring it health and cure, and I will cure them, and will reveal unto them the abundance of peace and truth.

7 And I will cause the captivity of Judah and the captivity of Israel to return, and will build them, as at the first.

8 And I will cleanse them from all their iniquity, whereby they have sinned against me; and I will pardon all their iniquities, whereby they have sinned, and whereby they have transgressed against me.

9 And it shall be to me a name of joy, a praise and an honour before all the nations of the earth, which shall hear all the good that I do unto them: and they shall fear and tremble for all the goodness and for all the prosperity that I procure unto it.

10 Thus saith the LORD; Again there shall be heard in this place, which ye say *shall be* desolate without man and without beast, *even* in the cities of Judah, and in the streets of Jerusalem, that are desolate, without man, and without inhabitant, and without beast,

11 The voice of joy, and the voice of gladness, the voice of the bridegroom, and the voice of the bride, the voice of them that shall say, Praise the LORD of hosts: for the LORD *is* good; for his mercy *endureth* for ever: *and* of them that shall bring the sacrifice of praise into the house of the LORD. For I will cause to return the captivity of the land, as at the first, saith the LORD.

12 Thus saith the LORD of hosts; Again in this place, which is desolate without man and without beast, and in all the cities thereof, shall be an habitation of shepherds causing *their* flocks to lie down.

13 In the cities of the mountains, in the cities of the vale, and in the cities of the south, and in the land of Benjamin, and in the places about Jerusalem, and in the cities of Judah, shall the flocks pass again under the hands of him that telleth *them*, saith the LORD.

14 Behold, the days come, saith the LORD, that I will perform that good thing which I have promised unto the house of Israel and to the house of Judah.

15 In those days, and at that time, will I

Cross references

2 Ex. 15:3; Isa. 37:26; Amos 5:8; 9:6

3 Ps. 91:15; Isa. 48:6; Jer. 29:12

6 Jer. 30:17

7 Isa. 1:26; Jer. 24:6; 30:3, 20; 31:4, 28; 32:44; 33:11; 42:10

8 Jer. 31:34; Ezek. 36:25; Mic. 7:18; Zech. 13:1; Heb. 9:13, 14

9 Isa. 60:5; 62:7; Jer. 13:11

10 Jer. 32:43

11 Lev. 7:12; 1Chr. 16:8, 34; 2Chr. 5:13; 7:3; Ezra 3:11; Ps. 107:22; 116:17; 136:1; Isa. 12:4; Jer. 7:34; 16:9; 25:10; 33:7; Rev. 18:23

12 Isa. 65:10; Jer. 31:24; 50:19

13 Lev. 27:32; Jer. 17:26; 32:44

15 Isa. 4:2; 11:1

33:1–3 and shew thee great and mighty things, which thou knowest not. Jeremiah receives a prophetic word from the Lord while still in prison. In chapter 32, God reassures Judah and Israel that He has ultimate blessing in store for them. In chapter 33, God invites the nation to call upon Him in belief, and He will hear their call. The only way we can ever know anything solid about the future is if the God who has hidden it reveals it to an individual. God desired to reveal secrets of the future through Jeremiah.

33:4–5 The first thing that God reveals through Jeremiah is the impending judgment that would come in spite of human efforts to prevent it.

33:6–9 The next revelation God discloses through Jeremiah is of a future restoration and blessing. Some students of the Bible are confused that God would promise both judgment (vv. 4–5) and blessing (vv. 6–9). However, this confusion is not hard to resolve when judgment and blessing are seen as different events. The "health" and "abundance of peace and truth" were something lacking in Jeremiah's day but would one day be found in great quantity. This abundance will come when God returns Judah (the Southern Kingdom) and Israel (the Northern Kingdom) from captivity, and at the same time cleanses the people of these two nations from all their iniquity, sin, and transgression. This prophecy will be fulfilled after the second coming of Christ.

33:10–11 At the time of the final restoration of Israel and Judah during the Millennium, the Lord will restore the fruits of righteousness so that the joys of life are restored.

33:14–16 the days come. This phrase is used here and throughout the rest of Jeremiah (16:14–15; 23:5–8; 30:3; 31:31–34, 38–40) to indicate a future time when Israel will experience blessing under the new covenant, called here by the prophet "that good thing." The title, "the Branch of righteousness," is a reference to Jesus, who was a descendant of David and is promised to sit on David's throne (cf. Jer. 23:5; Luke 1:31–33). Jesus will sit

cause the Branch of righteousness to grow up unto David; and he shall execute judgment and righteousness in the land.

16 In those days shall Judah be saved, and Jerusalem shall dwell safely: and this *is the name* wherewith she shall be called, The LORD our righteousness.

17 For thus saith the LORD; David shall never want a man to sit upon the throne of the house of Israel;

18 Neither shall the priests the Levites want a man before me to offer burnt offerings, and to kindle meat offerings, and to do sacrifice continually.

19 And the word of the LORD came unto Jeremiah, saying,

20 Thus saith the LORD; If ye can break my covenant of the day, and my covenant of the night, and that there should not be day and night in their season;

21 *Then* may also my covenant be broken with David my servant, that he should not have a son to reign upon his throne; and with the Levites the priests, my ministers.

22 As the host of heaven cannot be numbered, neither the sand of the sea measured: so will I multiply the seed of David my servant, and the Levites that minister unto me.

23 Moreover the word of the LORD came to Jeremiah, saying,

24 Considerest thou not what this people have spoken, saying, The two families which the LORD hath chosen, he hath even cast them off? thus they have despised my

people, that they should be no more a nation before them.

25 Thus saith the LORD; If my covenant *be* not with day and night, *and if* I have not appointed the ordinances of heaven and earth;

26 Then will I cast away the seed of Jacob, and David my servant, *so* that I will not take *any* of his seed *to be* rulers over the seed of Abraham, Isaac, and Jacob: for I will cause their captivity to return, and have mercy on them.

CHAPTER 34
Jeremiah's Warning to Zedekiah

1 The word which came unto Jeremiah from the LORD, when Nebuchadnezzar king of Babylon, and all his army, and all the kingdoms of the earth of his dominion, and all the people, fought against Jerusalem, and against all the cities thereof, saying,

2 Thus saith the LORD, the God of Israel; Go and speak to Zedekiah king of Judah, and tell him, Thus saith the LORD; Behold, I will give this city into the hand of the king of Babylon, and he shall burn it with fire:

3 And thou shalt not escape out of his hand, but shalt surely be taken, and delivered into his hand; and thine eyes shall behold the eyes of the king of Babylon, and he shall speak with thee mouth to mouth, and thou shalt go to Babylon.

4 Yet hear the word of the LORD, O Zedekiah king of Judah; Thus saith the LORD of thee, Thou shalt not die by the sword:

5 *But* thou shalt die in peace: and with the

Cross references
16 Jer. 23:6
17 2Sam. 7:16; 1Kgs. 2:4; Ps. 89:29, 36; Luke 1:32, 33
18 Rom. 12:1; 15:16; 1Pet. 2:5, 9; Rev. 1:6
20 Ps. 89:37; Isa. 54:9; Jer. 31:36; 33:25
21 Ps. 89:34
22 Gen. 13:16; 15:5; 22:17; Jer. 31:37
24 Jer. 33:21, 22
25 Gen. 8:22; Ps. 74:16, 17; 104:19; Jer. 31:35, 36; 33:20;
26 2Kgs. 25:1; Ezra 2:1; Jer. 1:15; 31:37; 33:7, 11; 39:1; 52:4
2 Jer. 21:10; 32:3, 28, 29; 34:22
3 Jer. 32:4
5 2Chr. 16:14; 21:19; Jer. 22:18; Dan. 2:46

---

on David's throne at His second coming and will continue to reign as king throughout the Millennium. Even though Jesus is qualified to reign as king, by virtue of the successful completion of His work at His first coming, He is not currently sitting on David's throne. Presently, He is at the Father's right hand (Rev. 3:21) and is making intercession on behalf of those who are believers in Him (Heb. 2:14–18; 1 John 2:1).

33:17–18 David shall never want a man to sit upon the throne of the house of Israel. The Lord reminds Judah of His covenant with David (2 Sam. 7:8–16; 1 Chr. 17:4–14) in relation to a political throne. There was a cessation of Davidic rulers with the Babylonian invasion of 586 B.C. However, if one examines closely the nature of the promise, it is not a promise of an unbroken line, but an unbroken line of descendants qualified to sit upon such a throne. Jesus will ultimately fulfill this promise (cf. genealogies in Matt. 1:1–17; Luke 3:23–38). Here the Lord also makes a similar promise to the priests and Levites. As with the Davidic promise, the Lord does not

promise a continual, unbroken sacrifice, but a perpetual priesthood descending from the tribe of Levi. This prophecy will ultimately be fulfilled in the Millennium with the return of a temple, temple ritual, and a priesthood (Isa. 56:7; 60:7, 13; 66:20–23; Ezek. 40—48; Zech. 14:16–21; Mal. 3:3–4).

33:20–26 This passage is yet another prophetic promise of the indestructibility and inevitability of the fulfillment of God's covenant to Judah and Israel. Indeed, this will be fulfilled at the Second Coming, when Jesus shall set up His Millennial Kingdom.

34:4–5 The Lord speaks a personal word to King Zedekiah through Jeremiah. Even though most of the inhabitants of Jerusalem were destined to die by the sword, pestilence, and famine, Zedekiah would not die in this manner. This was fulfilled when his sons were killed in front of him and subsequently his eyes were put out (2 Kgs. 24:2; 25:6–7, 27–30), but he himself did not die by the sword.

burnings of thy fathers, the former kings which were before thee, so shall they burn *odours* for thee; and they will lament thee, *saying*, Ah lord! for I have pronounced the word, saith the LORD.

6 Then Jeremiah the prophet spake all these words unto Zedekiah king of Judah in Jerusalem,

7 When the king of Babylon's army fought against Jerusalem, and against all the cities of Judah that were left, against Lachish, and against Azekah: for these defenced cities remained of the cities of Judah.

The Broken Covenant

8 *This is* the word that came unto Jeremiah from the LORD, after that the king Zedekiah had made a covenant with all the people which *were* at Jerusalem, to proclaim liberty unto them;

9 That every man should let his manservant, and every man his maidservant, *being* an Hebrew or an Hebrewess, go free; that none should serve himself of them, *to wit*, of a Jew his brother.

10 Now when all the princes, and all the people, which had entered into the covenant, heard that every one should let his manservant, and every one his maidservant, go free, that none should serve themselves of them any more, then they obeyed, and let *them* go.

11 But afterward they turned, and caused the servants and the handmaids, whom they had let go free, to return, and brought them into subjection for servants and for handmaids.

12 Therefore the word of the LORD came to Jeremiah from the LORD, saying,

13 Thus saith the LORD, the God of Israel; I made a covenant with your fathers in the day that I brought them forth out of the land of Egypt, out of the house of bondmen, saying,

14 At the end of seven years let ye go every man his brother an Hebrew, which hath been sold unto thee; and when he hath served thee six years, thou shalt let him go free from thee: but your fathers hearkened not unto me, neither inclined their ear.

15 And ye were now turned, and had done

right in my sight, in proclaiming liberty every man to his neighbour; and ye had made a covenant before me in the house which is called by my name:

16 But ye turned and polluted my name, and caused every man his servant, and every man his handmaid, whom ye had set at liberty at their pleasure, to return, and brought them into subjection, to be unto you for servants and for handmaids.

17 Therefore thus saith the LORD; Ye have not hearkened unto me, in proclaiming liberty, every one to his brother, and every man to his neighbour: behold, I proclaim a liberty for you, saith the LORD, to the sword, to the pestilence, and to the famine; and I will make you to be removed into all the kingdoms of the earth.

18 And I will give the men that have transgressed my covenant, which have not performed the words of the covenant which they had made before me, when they cut the calf in twain, and passed between the parts thereof,

19 The princes of Judah, and the princes of Jerusalem, the eunuchs, and the priests, and all the people of the land, which passed between the parts of the calf;

20 I will even give them into the hand of their enemies, and into the hand of them that seek their life: and their dead bodies shall be for meat unto the fowls of the heaven, and to the beasts of the earth.

21 And Zedekiah king of Judah and his princes will I give into the hand of their enemies, and into the hand of them that seek their life, and into the hand of the king of Babylon's army, which are gone up from you.

22 Behold, I will command, saith the LORD, and cause them to return to this city; and they shall fight against it, and take it, and burn it with fire: and I will make the cities of Judah a desolation without an inhabitant.

CHAPTER 35
The Rechabites

1 The word which came unto Jeremiah from the LORD in the days of Jehoiakim the son of Josiah king of Judah, saying,

---

Cross references (center column):

7 2Kgs. 18:13; 19:8; 2Chr. 11:5, 9

8 Ex. 21:2; Lev. 25:10; Jer. 34:14

9 Lev. 25:39-46; Neh. 5:11

11 Jer. 34:21; 37:5

14 Ex. 21:2; 23:10; Deut. 15:12

15 2Kgs. 23:3; Neh. 10:29

16 Ex. 20:7; Lev. 19:12

17 Deut. 28:25, 64; Jer. 29:18; 32:24, 36; Matt. 7:2; Gal. 6:7; James 2:13

18 Gen. 15:10, 17

20 Jer. 7:33; 16:4; 19:7

21 Jer. 37:5, 11

22 1Kgs. 6:5; 2Kgs. 10:15; 1Chr. 2:55; Jer. 9:11; 37:8, 10; 38:3; 39:1, 2, 8; 44:2, 6; 52:7, 13

34:8-11 Here is a prediction and fulfillment stated in a single passage.

34:22 cause them to return to this city. Nebuchadnezzar attacked Jerusalem in 587 B.C. and was distracted by the Egyptians from the South. Later he returned to Jerusalem in 586 B.C. and destroyed Jerusalem, fulfilling in detail this specific prophecy (cf. Jer. 37:21 with 32:1-2).

2 Go unto the house of the Rechabites, and speak unto them, and bring them into the house of the LORD, into one of the chambers, and give them wine to drink.

3 Then I took Jaazaniah the son of Jeremiah, the son of Habaziniah, and his brethren, and all his sons, and the whole house of the Rechabites;

4 And I brought them into the house of the LORD, into the chamber of the sons of Hanan, the son of Igdaliah, a man of God, which *was* by the chamber of the princes, which *was* above the chamber of Maaseiah the son of Shallum, the keeper of the door:

5 And I set before the sons of the house of the Rechabites pots full of wine, and cups, and I said unto them, Drink ye wine.

6 But they said, We will drink no wine: for Jonadab the son of Rechab our father commanded us, saying, Ye shall drink no wine, *neither* ye, nor your sons for ever:

7 Neither shall ye build house, nor sow seed, nor plant vineyard, nor have *any*: but all your days ye shall dwell in tents; that ye may live many days in the land where ye *be* strangers.

8 Thus have we obeyed the voice of Jonadab the son of Rechab our father in all that he hath charged us, to drink no wine all our days, we, our wives, our sons, nor our daughters;

9 Nor to build houses for us to dwell in: neither have we vineyard, nor field, nor seed:

10 But we have dwelt in tents, and have obeyed, and done according to all that Jonadab our father commanded us.

11 But it came to pass, when Nebuchadrezzar king of Babylon came up into the land, that we said, Come, and let us go to Jerusalem for fear of the army of the Chaldeans, and for fear of the army of the Syrians: so we dwell at Jerusalem.

12 Then came the word of the LORD unto Jeremiah, saying,

13 Thus saith the LORD of hosts, the God of Israel; Go and tell the men of Judah and the inhabitants of Jerusalem, Will ye not receive instruction to hearken to my words? saith the LORD.

14 The words of Jonadab the son of Rechab, that he commanded his sons not to drink wine, are performed; for unto this day they drink none, but obey their father's commandment: notwithstanding I have spoken unto you, rising early and speaking; but ye hearkened not unto me.

15 I have sent also unto you all my servants the prophets, rising up early and sending *them*, saying, Return ye now every man from his evil way, and amend your doings, and go not after other gods to serve them, and ye shall dwell in the land which I have given to you and to your fathers: but ye have not inclined your ear, nor hearkened unto me.

16 Because the sons of Jonadab the son of Rechab have performed the commandment of their father, which he commanded them; but this people hath not hearkened unto me:

17 Therefore thus saith the LORD God of hosts, the God of Israel; Behold, I will bring upon Judah and upon all the inhabitants of Jerusalem all the evil that I have pronounced against them: because I have spoken unto them, but they have not heard; and I have called unto them, but they have not answered.

18 And Jeremiah said unto the house of the Rechabites, Thus saith the LORD of hosts, the God of Israel; Because ye have obeyed the commandment of Jonadab your father, and kept all his precepts, and done according unto all that he hath commanded you:

19 Therefore thus saith the LORD of hosts, the God of Israel; Jonadab the son of Rechab shall not want a man to stand before me for ever.

CHAPTER 36
The Burning of the Scroll

1 And it came to pass in the fourth year of Jehoiakim the son of Josiah king of Judah, *that* this word came unto Jeremiah from the LORD, saying,

2 Take thee a roll of a book, and write therein all the words that I have spoken unto thee against Israel, and against Judah, and against all the nations, from the day I spake unto thee, from the days of Josiah, even unto this day.

3 It may be that the house of Judah will hear all the evil which I purpose to do unto them; that they may return every man from

Cross references (center column)

4 2Kgs. 12:9; 25:18; 1Chr. 9:18, 19
6 2Kgs. 10:15
7 Ex. 20:12; Eph. 6:2, 3
13 Jer. 32:33
14 2Chr. 36:15; Jer. 7:13; 25:3
15 Jer. 7:25; 18:11; 25:4, 5, 6
17 Prov. 1:24; Isa. 65:12; 66:4; Jer. 7:13
19 Isa. 8:1; Jer. 15:19; 25:3, 15; 30:2; Ezek. 2:9; Zech. 5:1
3 Jer. 18:8; 26:3; 36:7; Jon. 3:8

35:18–19 Jonadab the son of Rechab shall not want [lack] **a man to stand before me for ever.** This promise has been kept down through history wherever there has been a specific record of those serving the Lord (Neh. 3:14). This promise will likely have a future fulfillment throughout the plan of God.

his evil way; that I may forgive their iniquity and their sin.

4 Then Jeremiah called Baruch the son of Neriah: and Baruch wrote from the mouth of Jeremiah all the words of the LORD, which he had spoken unto him, upon a roll of a book.

5 And Jeremiah commanded Baruch, saying, I *am* shut up; I cannot go into the house of the LORD:

6 Therefore go thou, and read in the roll, which thou hast written from my mouth, the words of the LORD in the ears of the people in the LORD's house upon the fasting day: and also thou shalt read them in the ears of all Judah that come out of their cities.

7 It may be they will present their supplication before the LORD, and will return every one from his evil way: for great *is* the anger and the fury that the LORD hath pronounced against this people.

8 And Baruch the son of Neriah did according to all that Jeremiah the prophet commanded him, reading in the book the words of the LORD in the LORD's house.

9 And it came to pass in the fifth year of Jehoiakim the son of Josiah king of Judah, in the ninth month, *that* they proclaimed a fast before the LORD to all the people in Jerusalem, and to all the people that came from the cities of Judah unto Jerusalem.

10 Then read Baruch in the book the words of Jeremiah in the house of the LORD, in the chamber of Gemariah the son of Shaphan the scribe, in the higher court, at the entry of the new gate of the LORD's house, in the ears of all the people.

11 When Michaiah the son of Gemariah, the son of Shaphan, had heard out of the book all the words of the LORD,

12 Then he went down into the king's house, into the scribe's chamber: and, lo, all the princes sat there, *even* Elishama the scribe, and Delaiah the son of Shemaiah, and Elnathan the son of Achbor, and Gemariah the son of Shaphan, and Zedekiah the son of Hananiah, and all the princes.

13 Then Michaiah declared unto them all the words that he had heard, when Baruch read the book in the ears of the people.

14 Therefore all the princes sent Jehudi the son of Nethaniah, the son of Shelemiah, the son of Cushi, unto Baruch, saying, Take in thine hand the roll wherein thou hast read in the ears of the people, and come. So Baruch the son of Neriah took the roll in his hand, and came unto them.

15 And they said unto him, Sit down now, and read it in our ears. So Baruch read *it* in their ears.

16 Now it came to pass, when they had heard all the words, they were afraid both one and other, and said unto Baruch, We will surely tell the king of all these words.

17 And they asked Baruch, saying, Tell us now, How didst thou write all these words at his mouth?

18 Then Baruch answered them, He pronounced all these words unto me with his mouth, and I wrote *them* with ink in the book.

19 Then said the princes unto Baruch, Go, hide thee, thou and Jeremiah; and let no man know where ye be.

20 And they went in to the king into the court, but they laid up the roll in the chamber of Elishama the scribe, and told all the words in the ears of the king.

21 So the king sent Jehudi to fetch the roll: and he took it out of Elishama the scribe's chamber. And Jehudi read it in the ears of the king, and in the ears of all the princes which stood beside the king.

22 Now the king sat in the winterhouse in the ninth month: and *there was a fire* on the hearth burning before him.

23 And it came to pass, *that* when Jehudi had read three or four leaves, he cut it with the penknife, and cast *it* into the fire that *was* on the hearth, until all the roll was consumed in the fire that *was* on the hearth.

24 Yet they were not afraid, nor rent their garments, *neither* the king, nor any of his servants that heard all these words.

25 Nevertheless Elnathan and Delaiah and Gemariah had made intercession to the king that he would not burn the roll: but he would not hear them.

26 But the king commanded Jerahmeel the son of Hammelech, and Seraiah the son of Azriel, and Shelemiah the son of Abdeel, to take Baruch the scribe and Jeremiah the prophet: but the LORD hid them.

The Second Scroll

27 Then the word of the LORD came to Jeremiah, after that the king had burned the roll, and the words which Baruch wrote at the mouth of Jeremiah, saying,

28 Take thee again another roll, and write in it all the former words that were in the first roll, which Jehoiakim the king of Judah hath burned.

29 And thou shalt say to Jehoiakim king of Judah, Thus saith the LORD; Thou hast

---

4 Jer. 32:12; 45:1

6 Lev. 16:29; 23:27-32; Acts 27:9

7 Jer. 36:3

10 Jer. 26:10

22 Amos 3:15

24 2Kgs. 22:11; Isa. 36:22; 37:1

burned this roll, saying, Why hast thou written therein, saying, The king of Babylon shall certainly come and destroy this land, and shall cause to cease from thence man and beast?

30 Therefore thus saith the LORD of Jehoiakim king of Judah; He shall have none to sit upon the throne of David: and his dead body shall be cast out in the day to the heat, and in the night to the frost.

31 And I will punish him and his seed and his servants for their iniquity; and I will bring upon them, and upon the inhabitants of Jerusalem, and upon the men of Judah, all the evil that I have pronounced against them; but they hearkened not.

32 Then took Jeremiah another roll, and gave it to Baruch the scribe, the son of Neriah; who wrote therein from the mouth of Jeremiah all the words of the book which Jehoiakim king of Judah had burned in the fire: and there were added besides unto them many like words.

CHAPTER 37
Jeremiah Is Put in Prison

1 And king Zedekiah the son of Josiah reigned instead of Coniah the son of Jehoiakim, whom Nebuchadrezzar king of Babylon made king in the land of Judah.

2 But neither he, nor his servants, nor the people of the land, did hearken unto the words of the LORD, which he spake by the prophet Jeremiah.

3 And Zedekiah the king sent Jehucal the son of Shelemiah and Zephaniah the son of Maaseiah the priest to the prophet Jeremiah, saying, Pray now unto the LORD our God for us.

4 Now Jeremiah came in and went out among the people: for they had not put him into prison.

5 Then Pharaoh's army was come forth out of Egypt: and when the Chaldeans that besieged Jerusalem heard tidings of them, they departed from Jerusalem.

6 Then came the word of the LORD unto the prophet Jeremiah, saying,

7 Thus saith the LORD, the God of Israel; Thus shall ye say to the king of Judah, that sent you unto me to inquire of me; Behold, Pharaoh's army, which is come forth to help you, shall return to Egypt into their own land.

8 And the Chaldeans shall come again, and fight against this city, and take it, and burn it with fire.

9 Thus saith the LORD; Deceive not yourselves, saying, The Chaldeans shall surely depart from us: for they shall not depart.

10 For though ye had smitten the whole army of the Chaldeans that fight against you, and there remained *but* wounded men among them, *yet* should they rise every man in his tent, and burn this city with fire.

11 And it came to pass, that when the army of the Chaldeans was broken up from Jerusalem for fear of Pharaoh's army,

12 Then Jeremiah went forth out of Jerusalem to go into the land of Benjamin, to separate himself thence in the midst of the people.

13 And when he was in the gate of Benjamin, a captain of the ward *was* there, whose name *was* Irijah, the son of Shelemiah, the son of Hananiah; and he took Jeremiah the prophet, saying, Thou fallest away to the Chaldeans.

14 Then said Jeremiah, *It is* false; I fall not away to the Chaldeans. But he hearkened not to him: so Irijah took Jeremiah, and brought him to the princes.

15 Wherefore the princes were wroth with Jeremiah, and smote him, and put him in prison in the house of Jonathan the scribe: for they had made that the prison.

16 When Jeremiah was entered into the dungeon, and into the cabins, and Jeremiah had remained there many days;

17 Then Zedekiah the king sent, and took him out: and the king asked him secretly in his house, and said, Is there *any* word from the LORD? And Jeremiah said, There is: for, said he, thou shalt be delivered into the hand of the king of Babylon.

18 Moreover Jeremiah said unto king Zedekiah, What have I offended against thee, or against thy servants, or against this people, that ye have put me in prison?

19 Where *are* now your prophets which prophesied unto you, saying, The king of Babylon shall not come against you, nor against this land?

20 Therefore hear now, I pray thee, O my lord the king: let my supplication, I pray thee, be accepted before thee; that thou cause me not to return to the house of Jonathan the scribe, lest I die there.

21 Then Zedekiah the king commanded that they should commit Jeremiah into the court of the prison, and that they should give him daily a piece of bread out of the bakers' street, until all the bread in the city were spent. Thus Jeremiah remained in the court of the prison.

Cross references (center column):

30 Jer. 22:19, 30
31 Jer. 23:34
32 2Kgs. 24:17; 2Chr. 36:10; Jer. 22:24
2 2Chr. 36:12, 14
3 Jer. 21:1, 2; 29:25; 52:24
5 2Kgs. 24:7; Jer. 34:21; 37:11; Ezek. 17:15
7 Jer. 21:2
8 Jer. 34:22
10 Jer. 21:4, 5
11 Jer. 37:5
15 Jer. 38:26
16 Jer. 38:6
21 Jer. 21:1, 8; 32:2; 37:3; 38:9, 13, 28; 52:6

CHAPTER 38
Jeremiah Rescued from the Dry Well

1 Then Shephatiah the son of Mattan, and Gedaliah the son of Pashur, and Jucal the son of Shelemiah, and Pashur the son of Malchiah, heard the words that Jeremiah had spoken unto all the people, saying,
2 Thus saith the LORD, He that remaineth in this city shall die by the sword, by the famine, and by the pestilence: but he that goeth forth to the Chaldeans shall live; for he shall have his life for a prey, and shall live.
3 Thus saith the LORD, This city shall surely be given into the hand of the king of Babylon's army, which shall take it.
4 Therefore the princes said unto the king, We beseech thee, let this man be put to death: for thus he weakeneth the hands of the men of war that remain in this city, and the hands of all the people, in speaking such words unto them: for this man seeketh not the welfare of this people, but the hurt.
5 Then Zedekiah the king said, Behold, he is in your hand: for the king is not he that can do any thing against you.
6 Then took they Jeremiah, and cast him into the dungeon of Malchiah the son of Hammelech, that was in the court of the prison: and they let down Jeremiah with cords. And in the dungeon there was no water, but mire: so Jeremiah sunk in the mire.
7 Now when Ebed-melech the Ethiopian, one of the eunuchs which was in the king's house, heard that they had put Jeremiah in the dungeon; the king then sitting in the gate of Benjamin;
8 Ebed-melech went forth out of the king's house, and spake to the king, saying,
9 My lord the king, these men have done evil in all that they have done to Jeremiah the prophet, whom they have cast into the dungeon; and he is like to die for hunger in the place where he is: for there is no more bread in the city.
10 Then the king commanded Ebed-melech the Ethiopian, saying, Take from hence thirty men with thee, and take up Jeremiah the prophet out of the dungeon, before he die.

11 So Ebed-melech took the men with him, and went into the house of the king under the treasury, and took thence old cast clouts and old rotten rags, and let them down by cords into the dungeon to Jeremiah.
12 And Ebed-melech the Ethiopian said unto Jeremiah, Put now these old cast clouts and rotten rags under thine armholes under the cords. And Jeremiah did so.
13 So they drew up Jeremiah with cords, and took him up out of the dungeon: and Jeremiah remained in the court of the prison.

Zedekiah Seeks Counsel from Jeremiah

14 Then Zedekiah the king sent, and took Jeremiah the prophet unto him into the third entry that is in the house of the LORD: and the king said unto Jeremiah, I will ask thee a thing; hide nothing from me.
15 Then Jeremiah said unto Zedekiah, If I declare it unto thee, wilt thou not surely put me to death? and if I give thee counsel, wilt thou not hearken unto me?
16 So Zedekiah the king sware secretly unto Jeremiah, saying, As the LORD liveth, that made us this soul, I will not put thee to death, neither will I give thee into the hand of these men that seek thy life.
17 Then said Jeremiah unto Zedekiah, Thus saith the LORD, the God of hosts, the God of Israel; If thou wilt assuredly go forth unto the king of Babylon's princes, then thy soul shall live, and this city shall not be burned with fire; and thou shalt live, and thine house:
18 But if thou wilt not go forth to the king of Babylon's princes, then shall this city be given into the hand of the Chaldeans, and they shall burn it with fire, and thou shalt not escape out of their hand.
19 And Zedekiah the king said unto Jeremiah, I am afraid of the Jews that are fallen to the Chaldeans, lest they deliver me into their hand, and they mock me.
20 But Jeremiah said, They shall not deliver thee. Obey, I beseech thee, the voice of the LORD, which I speak unto thee: so it shall be well unto thee, and thy soul shall live.

Cross references:
2 Jer. 21:9
3 Jer. 21:10; 32:3
4 Jer. 26:11
6 Jer. 37:21
7 Jer. 39:16
13 Jer. 37:21; 38:6
16 Isa. 57:16
17 2Kgs. 24:12; Jer. 39:3
18 Jer. 32:4; 34:3; 38:23
19 1Sam. 31:4

38:20–23 Obey. Jeremiah entreats Zedekiah that if he would surrender to the invading enemy, he would personally be protected. The consequences to befall Zedekiah if he refused to surrender to Nebuchadnezzar would be that Jerusalem would be destroyed and the women and children would be taken captive. This specific prophetic fulfillment is not recorded, but we do know that the Babylonians captured Zedekiah's sons and apparently his daughters (Jer. 39:6; 43:6).

21 But if thou refuse to go forth, this *is* the word that the LORD hath shewed me:

22 And, behold, all the women that are left in the king of Judah's house *shall be* brought forth to the king of Babylon's princes, and those *women* shall say, Thy friends have set thee on, and have prevailed against thee: thy feet are sunk in the mire, *and* they are turned away back.

23 So they shall bring out all thy wives and thy children to the Chaldeans: and thou shalt not escape out of their hand, but shalt be taken by the hand of the king of Babylon: and thou shalt cause this city to be burned with fire.

24 Then said Zedekiah unto Jeremiah, Let no man know of these words, and thou shalt not die.

25 But if the princes hear that I have talked with thee, and they come unto thee, and say unto thee, Declare unto us now what thou hast said unto the king, hide it not from us, and we will not put thee to death; also what the king said unto thee:

26 Then thou shalt say unto them, I presented my supplication before the king, that he would not cause me to return to Jonathan's house, to die there.

27 Then came all the princes unto Jeremiah, and asked him: and he told them according to all these words that the king had commanded. So they left off speaking with him; for the matter was not perceived.

28 So Jeremiah abode in the court of the prison until the day that Jerusalem was taken: and he was *there* when Jerusalem was taken.

CHAPTER 39
Jerusalem Falls

1 In the ninth year of Zedekiah king of Judah, in the tenth month, came Nebuchadrezzar king of Babylon and all his army against Jerusalem, and they besieged it.

2 *And* in the eleventh year of Zedekiah, in the fourth month, the ninth *day* of the month, the city was broken up.

3 And all the princes of the king of Babylon came in, and sat in the middle gate, *even* Nergal-sharezer, Samgar-nebo, Sarsechim, Rabsaris, Nergal-sharezer, Rab-mag,

with all the residue of the princes of the king of Babylon.

4 And it came to pass, *that* when Zedekiah the king of Judah saw them, and all the men of war, then they fled, and went forth out of the city by night, by the way of the king's garden, by the gate betwixt the two walls: and he went out the way of the plain.

5 But the Chaldeans' army pursued after them, and overtook Zedekiah in the plains of Jericho: and when they had taken him, they brought him up to Nebuchadnezzar king of Babylon to Riblah in the land of Hamath, where he gave judgment upon him.

6 Then the king of Babylon slew the sons of Zedekiah in Riblah before his eyes: also the king of Babylon slew all the nobles of Judah.

7 Moreover he put out Zedekiah's eyes, and bound him with chains, to carry him to Babylon.

8 And the Chaldeans burned the king's house, and the houses of the people, with fire, and brake down the walls of Jerusalem.

9 Then Nebuzaradan the captain of the guard carried away captive into Babylon the remnant of the people that remained in the city, and those that fell away, that fell to him, with the rest of the people that remained.

10 But Nebuzaradan the captain of the guard left of the poor of the people, which had nothing, in the land of Judah, and gave them vineyards and fields at the same time.

11 Now Nebuchadnezzar king of Babylon gave charge concerning Jeremiah to Nebuzaradan the captain of the guard, saying,

12 Take him, and look well to him, and do him no harm; but do unto him even as he shall say unto thee.

13 So Nebuzaradan the captain of the guard sent, and Nebushasban, Rabsaris, and Nergal-sharezer, Rab-mag, and all the king of Babylon's princes;

14 Even they sent, and took Jeremiah out of the court of the prison, and committed him unto Gedaliah the son of Ahikam the son of Shaphan, that he should carry him home: so he dwelt among the people.

15 Now the word of the LORD came unto Jeremiah, while he was shut up in the court of the prison, saying,

---

Cross-references (center column):

23 Jer. 38:18; 39:6; 41:10

26 Jer. 37:15, 20

28 2Kgs. 37:21; 39:14; 52:4-7

3 Jer. 38:17

4 2Kgs. 25:4; Jer. 52:7

5 2Kgs. 23:33; Jer. 4:12; 32:4; 38:18, 23

7 Jer. 32:9; Ezek. 12:13

8 2Kgs. 25:9; Jer. 38:18; 52:13

9 Gen. 37:36; 2Kgs. 25:11; Jer. 39:10, 11; 52:15

14 Jer. 26:24; 38:28; 40:5

39:15–18 while he was shut up in the court of the prison. Jeremiah is imprisoned by the king because of his condemning prophecy concerning Judah. Ebedmelech the Ethiopian risked his own life by trying to help Jeremiah—a demonstration of his faith in the Lord. While most of the other prophets would be killed by the Babylonians, Jeremiah and Ebed-melech would be delivered from their wrath.

16 Go and speak to Ebed-melech the Ethiopian, saying, Thus saith the LORD of hosts, the God of Israel; Behold, I will bring my words upon this city for evil, and not for good; and they shall be *accomplished* in that day before thee.

17 But I will deliver thee in that day, saith the LORD: and thou shalt not be given into the hand of the men of whom thou *art* afraid.

18 For I will surely deliver thee, and thou shalt not fall by the sword, but thy life shall be for a prey unto thee: because thou hast put thy trust in me, saith the LORD.

CHAPTER 40
Jeremiah and Gedaliah

1 The word that came to Jeremiah from the LORD, after that Nebuzaradan the captain of the guard had let him go from Ramah, when he had taken him being bound in chains among all that were carried away captive of Jerusalem and Judah, which were carried away captive unto Babylon.

2 And the captain of the guard took Jeremiah, and said unto him, The LORD thy God hath pronounced this evil upon this place.

3 Now the LORD hath brought *it*, and done according as he hath said: because ye have sinned against the LORD, and have not obeyed his voice, therefore this thing is come upon you.

4 And now, behold, I loose thee this day from the chains which *were* upon thine hand. If it seem good unto thee to come with me into Babylon, come; and I will look well unto thee: but if it seem ill unto thee to come with me into Babylon, forbear: behold, all the land *is* before thee: whither it seemeth good and convenient for thee to go, thither go.

5 Now while he was not yet gone back, *he said*, Go back also to Gedaliah the son of Ahikam the son of Shaphan, whom the king of Babylon hath made governor over the cities of Judah, and dwell with him among the people: or go wheresoever it seemeth convenient unto thee to go. So the captain of the guard gave him victuals and a reward, and let him go.

6 Then went Jeremiah unto Gedaliah the son of Ahikam to Mizpah; and dwelt with him among the people that were left in the land.

7 Now when all the captains of the forces which *were* in the fields, *even* they and their men, heard that the king of Babylon had

made Gedaliah the son of Ahikam governor in the land, and had committed unto him men, and women, and children, and of the poor of the land, of them that were not carried away captive to Babylon;

8 Then they came to Gedaliah to Mizpah, even Ishmael the son of Nethaniah, and Johanan and Jonathan the sons of Kareah, and Seraiah the son of Tanhumeth, and the sons of Ephai the Netophathite, and Jezaniah the son of a Maachathite, they and their men.

9 And Gedaliah the son of Ahikam the son of Shaphan sware unto them and to their men, saying, Fear not to serve the Chaldeans: dwell in the land, and serve the king of Babylon, and it shall be well with you.

10 As for me, behold, I will dwell at Mizpah to serve the Chaldeans, which will come unto us: but ye, gather ye wine, and summer fruits, and oil, and put *them* in your vessels, and dwell in your cities that ye have taken.

11 Likewise when all the Jews that *were* in Moab, and among the Ammonites, and in Edom, and that *were* in all the countries, heard that the king of Babylon had left a remnant of Judah, and that he had set over them Gedaliah the son of Ahikam the son of Shaphan;

12 Even all the Jews returned out of all places whither they were driven, and came to the land of Judah, to Gedaliah, unto Mizpah, and gathered wine and summer fruits very much.

Gedaliah Is Murdered

13 Moreover Johanan the son of Kareah, and all the captains of the forces that *were* in the fields, came to Gedaliah to Mizpah,

14 And said unto him, Dost thou certainly know that Baalis the king of the Ammonites hath sent Ishmael the son of Nethaniah to slay thee? But Gedaliah the son of Ahikam believed them not.

15 Then Johanan the son of Kareah spake to Gedaliah in Mizpah secretly, saying, Let me go, I pray thee, and I will slay Ishmael the son of Nethaniah, and no man shall know *it*: wherefore should he slay thee, that all the Jews which are gathered unto thee should be scattered, and the remnant in Judah perish?

16 But Gedaliah the son of Ahikam said unto Johanan the son of Kareah, Thou shalt not do this thing: for thou speakest falsely of Ishmael.

---

16 Jer. 38:7, 12; Dan. 9:12

18 1Chr. 5:20; Ps. 37:40; Jer. 21:9; 39:14; 45:5

2 Jer. 50:7

3 Deut. 29:24, 25; Dan. 9:11

4 Gen. 20:15; Jer. 39:12

5 2Kgs. 25:22

6 Judg. 20:1; Jer. 39:14

7 2Kgs. 25:23; Jer. 39:10

8 Jer. 41:1

10 Deut. 1:38

14 2Kgs. 25:25; Jer. 40:6, 8; 41:10

CHAPTER 41

1 Now it came to pass in the seventh month, *that* Ishmael the son of Nethaniah the son of Elishama, of the seed royal, and the princes of the king, even ten men with him, came unto Gedaliah the son of Ahikam to Mizpah; and there they did eat bread together in Mizpah.

2 Then arose Ishmael the son of Nethaniah, and the ten men that were with him, and smote Gedaliah the son of Ahikam the son of Shaphan with the sword, and slew him, whom the king of Babylon had made governor over the land.

3 Ishmael also slew all the Jews that were with him, *even* with Gedaliah, at Mizpah, and the Chaldeans that were found there, *and* the men of war.

4 And it came to pass the second day after he had slain Gedaliah, and no man knew *it*,

5 That there came certain from Shechem, from Shiloh, and from Samaria, *even* fourscore men, having their beards shaven, and their clothes rent, and having cut themselves, with offerings and incense in their hand, to bring *them* to the house of the LORD.

6 And Ishmael the son of Nethaniah went forth from Mizpah to meet them, weeping all along as he went: and it came to pass, as he met them, he said unto them, Come to Gedaliah the son of Ahikam.

7 And it was *so*, when they came into the midst of the city, that Ishmael the son of Nethaniah slew them, *and cast them* into the midst of the pit, he, and the men that *were* with him.

8 But ten men were found among them that said unto Ishmael, Slay us not: for we have treasures in the field, of wheat, and of barley, and of oil, and of honey. So he forbear, and slew them not among their brethren.

9 Now the pit wherein Ishmael had cast all the dead bodies of the men, whom he had slain because of Gedaliah, *was* it which Asa the king had made for fear of Baasha king of Israel: *and* Ishmael the son of Nethaniah filled it with *them that were* slain.

10 Then Ishmael carried away captive all the residue of the people that *were* in Mizpah, *even* the king's daughters, and all the people that remained in Mizpah, whom Nebuzaradan the captain of the guard had committed to Gedaliah the son of Ahikam: and Ishmael the son of Nethaniah carried them away captive, and departed to go over to the Ammonites.

11 But when Johanan the son of Kareah, and all the captains of the forces that *were* with him, heard of all the evil that Ishmael the son of Nethaniah had done,

12 Then they took all the men, and went to fight with Ishmael the son of Nethaniah, and found him by the great waters that *are* in Gibeon.

13 Now it came to pass, *that* when all the people which *were* with Ishmael saw Johanan the son of Kareah, and all the captains of the forces that *were* with him, then they were glad.

14 So all the people that Ishmael had carried away captive from Mizpah cast about and returned, and went unto Johanan the son of Kareah.

15 But Ishmael the son of Nethaniah escaped from Johanan with eight men, and went to the Ammonites.

16 Then took Johanan the son of Kareah, and all the captains of the forces that *were* with him, all the remnant of the people whom he had recovered from Ishmael the son of Nethaniah, from Mizpah, after *that* he had slain Gedaliah the son of Ahikam, *even* mighty men of war, and the women, and the children, and the eunuchs, whom he had brought again from Gibeon:

17 And they departed, and dwelt in the habitation of Chimham, which is by Bethlehem, to go to enter into Egypt,

18 Because of the Chaldeans: for they were afraid of them, because Ishmael the son of Nethaniah had slain Gedaliah the son of Ahikam, whom the king of Babylon made governor in the land.

CHAPTER 42

Jeremiah's Message to Johanan

1 Then all the captains of the forces, and Johanan the son of Kareah, and Jezaniah the son of Hoshaiah, and all the people from the least even unto the greatest, came near,

2 And said unto Jeremiah the prophet, Let, we beseech thee, our supplication be accepted before thee, and pray for us unto the LORD thy God, *even* for all this remnant; (for we are left *but* a few of many, as thine eyes do behold us:)

3 That the LORD thy God may shew us the way wherein we may walk, and the thing that we may do.

4 Then Jeremiah the prophet said unto them, I have heard *you*; behold, I will pray unto the LORD your God according to your words; and it shall come to pass, *that* whatsoever thing the LORD shall answer you, I

Cross references: 2 2Kgs. 25:25; 5 Lev. 19:27, 28; Deut. 14:1; 1Sam. 1:7; 2Kgs. 25:9; Isa. 15:2; 9 1Kgs. 15:22; 2Chr. 16:6; 10 Jer. 40:7, 14; 43:6; 11 Jer. 40:7, 8, 13; 12 2Sam. 2:13; 17 2Sam. 19:37, 38; 18 Jer. 40:5, 8, 13; 41:11; 2 Lev. 26:22; 1Sam. 7:8; 12:19; Isa. 37:4; James 5:16; 3 Ezra 8:21; 4 1Sam. 3:18; 1Kgs. 22:14; Acts 20:20

will declare *it* unto you; I will keep nothing back from you.

5 Then they said to Jeremiah, The LORD be a true and faithful witness between us, if we do not even according to all things for the which the LORD thy God shall send thee to us.

6 Whether *it be* good, or whether *it be* evil, we will obey the voice of the LORD our God, to whom we send thee; that it may be well with us, when we obey the voice of the LORD our God.

7 And it came to pass after ten days, that the word of the LORD came unto Jeremiah.

8 Then called he Johanan the son of Kareah, and all the captains of the forces which *were* with him, and all the people from the least even to the greatest,

9 And said unto them, Thus saith the LORD, the God of Israel, unto whom ye sent me to present your supplication before him;

10 If ye will still abide in this land, then will I build you, and not pull *you* down, and I will plant you, and not pluck *you* up: for I repent me of the evil that I have done unto you.

11 Be not afraid of the king of Babylon, of whom ye are afraid; be not afraid of him, saith the LORD: for I *am* with you to save you, and to deliver you from his hand.

12 And I will shew mercies unto you, that he may have mercy upon you, and cause you to return to your own land.

13 But if ye say, We will not dwell in this land, neither obey the voice of the LORD your God,

14 Saying, No; but we will go into the land of Egypt, where we shall see no war, nor hear the sound of the trumpet, nor have hunger of bread; and there will we dwell:

15 And now therefore hear the word of the LORD, ye remnant of Judah; Thus saith the LORD of hosts, the God of Israel; If ye wholly set your faces to enter into Egypt, and go to sojourn there;

16 Then it shall come to pass, *that* the sword, which ye feared, shall overtake you there in the land of Egypt, and the famine, whereof ye were afraid, shall follow close after you there in Egypt; and there ye shall die.

17 So shall it be with all the men that set their faces to go into Egypt to sojourn there; they shall die by the sword, by the famine, and by the pestilence: and none of them shall remain or escape from the evil that I will bring upon them.

18 For thus saith the LORD of hosts, the God of Israel; As mine anger and my fury hath been poured forth upon the inhabitants of Jerusalem; so shall my fury be poured forth upon you, when ye shall enter into Egypt: and ye shall be an execration, and an astonishment, and a curse, and a reproach; and ye shall see this place no more.

19 The LORD hath said concerning you, O ye remnant of Judah; Go ye not into Egypt: know certainly that I have admonished you this day.

20 For ye dissembled in your hearts, when ye sent me unto the LORD your God, saying, Pray for us unto the LORD our God; and according unto all that the LORD our God shall say, so declare unto us, and we will do *it*.

21 And *now* I have this day declared *it* to you; but ye have not obeyed the voice of the LORD your God, nor any *thing* for the which he hath sent me unto you.

22 Now therefore know certainly that ye shall die by the sword, by the famine, and by the pestilence, in the place whither ye desire to go *and* to sojourn.

CHAPTER 43
Jeremiah Taken to Egypt

1 And it came to pass, *that* when Jeremiah had made an end of speaking unto all the people all the words of the LORD their God, for which the LORD their God had sent him to them, *even* all these words,

2 Then spake Azariah the son of Hoshaiah, and Johanan the son of Kareah, and all the proud men, saying unto Jeremiah, Thou speakest falsely: the LORD our God hath not sent thee to say, Go not into Egypt to sojourn there:

3 But Baruch the son of Neriah setteth thee on against us, for to deliver us into the hand of the Chaldeans, that they might put us to death, and carry us away captives into Babylon.

4 So Johanan the son of Kareah, and all the captains of the forces, and all the people, obeyed not the voice of the LORD, to dwell in the land of Judah.

5 But Johanan the son of Kareah, and all the captains of the forces, took all the remnant of Judah, that were returned from all nations, whither they had been driven, to dwell in the land of Judah;

6 *Even* men, and women, and children, and the king's daughters, and every person that Nebuzaradan the captain of the guard had left with Gedaliah the son of Ahikam the son of Shaphan, and Jeremiah the prophet, and Baruch the son of Neriah.

Center column references:

5 Gen. 31:50
6 Deut. 6:3; Jer. 7:23
10 Deut. 32:36; Jer. 18:8; 24:6; 31:28; 33:7
11 Isa. 43:5; Rom. 8:31
12 Ps. 106:45, 46
13 Jer. 44:16
15 Deut. 17:16; Jer. 44:12-14; Luke 9:51
16 Ezek. 11:8
17 Jer. 24:10; 42:22; 44:14, 28
18 Jer. 7:20; 18:16; 24:9; 26:6; 29:18, 22; 44:12; Zech. 8:13
19 Deut. 17:16
20 Jer. 42:2
22 Jer. 42:1, 17; Ezek. 6:11

5 Jer. 40:11, 12

6 Jer. 39:10; 40:7; 41:10

7 So they came into the land of Egypt: for they obeyed not the voice of the LORD: thus came they *even* to Tahpanhes.

8 Then came the word of the LORD unto Jeremiah in Tahpanhes, saying,

9 Take great stones in thine hand, and hide them in the clay in the brickkiln, which *is* at the entry of Pharaoh's house in Tahpanhes, in the sight of the men of Judah;

10 And say unto them, Thus saith the LORD of hosts, the God of Israel; Behold, I will send and take Nebuchadrezzar the king of Babylon, my servant, and will set his throne upon these stones that I have hid; and he shall spread his royal pavilion over them.

11 And when he cometh, he shall smite the land of Egypt, *and deliver* such *as are* for death to death; and such *as are* for captivity to captivity; and such *as are* for the sword to the sword.

12 And I will kindle a fire in the houses of the gods of Egypt; and he shall burn them, and carry them away captives: and he shall array himself with the land of Egypt, as a shepherd putteth on his garment; and he shall go forth from thence in peace.

13 He shall break also the images of Bethshemesh, that *is* in the land of Egypt; and the houses of the gods of the Egyptians shall he burn with fire.

CHAPTER 44
Jeremiah Preaches in Egypt

1 The word that came to Jeremiah concerning all the Jews which dwell in the land of Egypt, which dwell at Migdol, and at Tahpanhes, and at Noph, and in the country of Pathros, saying,

2 Thus saith the LORD of hosts, the God of Israel; Ye have seen all the evil that I have brought upon Jerusalem, and upon all the cities of Judah; and, behold, this day they *are* a desolation, and no man dwelleth therein,

3 Because of their wickedness which they have committed to provoke me to anger, in that they went to burn incense, *and* to serve other gods, whom they knew not, *neither* they, ye, nor your fathers.

4 Howbeit I sent unto you all my servants the prophets, rising early and sending *them*, saying, Oh, do not this abominable thing that I hate.

5 But they hearkened not, nor inclined their ear to turn from their wickedness, to burn no incense unto other gods.

6 Wherefore my fury and mine anger was poured forth, and was kindled in the cities of Judah and in the streets of Jerusalem; and they are wasted *and* desolate, as at this day.

7 Therefore now thus saith the LORD, the God of hosts, the God of Israel; Wherefore commit ye *this* great evil against your souls, to cut off from you man and woman, child and suckling, out of Judah, to leave you none to remain;

8 In that ye provoke me unto wrath with the works of your hands, burning incense unto other gods in the land of Egypt, whither ye be gone to dwell, that ye might cut yourselves off, and that ye might be a curse and a reproach among all the nations of the earth?

9 Have ye forgotten the wickedness of your fathers, and the wickedness of the kings of Judah, and the wickedness of their wives, and your own wickedness, and the wickedness of your wives, which they have committed in the land of Judah, and in the streets of Jerusalem?

10 They are not humbled *even* unto this day, neither have they feared, nor walked in my law, nor in my statutes, that I set before you and before your fathers.

11 Therefore thus saith the LORD of hosts, the God of Israel; Behold, I will set my face against you for evil, and to cut off all Judah.

12 And I will take the remnant of Judah, that have set their faces to go into the land of Egypt to sojourn there, and they shall all be consumed, *and* fall in the land of Egypt; they shall *even* be consumed by the sword *and* by the famine: they shall die, from the least even unto the greatest, by the sword and by the famine: and they shall be an execration, *and* an astonishment, and a curse, and a reproach.

Cross references (center column)

7 Isa. 30:4; Jer. 2:16; 44:1

10 Jer. 25:9; 27:6; Ezek. 29:18, 20

11 Jer. 15:2; 44:13; 46:13; Zech. 11:9

12 Jer. 46:25

13 Ex. 14:2; Isa. 19:13; Jer. 43:7; 46:14

2 Jer. 9:11; 34:22

3 Deut. 13:6; 32:17; Jer. 19:4

4 2Chr. 36:15; Jer. 7:25; 25:4; 26:5; 29:19

6 Jer. 42:18

7 Num. 16:38; Jer. 7:19

8 Jer. 25:6, 7; 42:18; 44:12

10 Ps. 51:17; Prov. 28:14

11 Lev. 17:10; 20:5, 6; Jer. 21:10; Amos 9:4

12 Jer. 42:15-17, 18, 22

44:2–6 After the destruction of the city of Jerusalem at the hand of Nebuchadnezzar and his Babylonian forces, Jeremiah reminds the people of Judah that it had happened just as the Lord had predicted.

44:10–14 I will punish them that dwell in the land of Egypt, as I have punished Jerusalem. In spite of God's judgment upon Judah through the Babylonians, they have not learned their lesson. A remnant of Judean Jews fled to Egypt seeking safety. In their unbelief and rebellion, the Lord declares that this remnant will suffer the same fate as those who doubted Jeremiah's divinely inspired message (cf. Jer. 42:22).

13 For I will punish them that dwell in the land of Egypt, as I have punished Jerusalem, by the sword, by the famine, and by the pestilence:

14 So that none of the remnant of Judah, which are gone into the land of Egypt to sojourn there, shall escape or remain, that they should return into the land of Judah, to the which they have a desire to return to dwell there: for none shall return but such as shall escape.

15 Then all the men which knew that their wives had burned incense unto other gods, and all the women that stood by, a great multitude, even all the people that dwelt in the land of Egypt, in Pathros, answered Jeremiah, saying,

16 *As for* the word that thou hast spoken unto us in the name of the LORD, we will not hearken unto thee.

17 But we will certainly do whatsoever thing goeth forth out of our own mouth, to burn incense unto the queen of heaven, and to pour out drink offerings unto her, as we have done, we, and our fathers, our kings, and our princes, in the cities of Judah, and in the streets of Jerusalem: for *then* had we plenty of victuals, and were well, and saw no evil.

18 But since we left off to burn incense to the queen of heaven, and to pour out drink offerings unto her, we have wanted all *things*, and have been consumed by the sword and by the famine.

19 And when we burned incense to the queen of heaven, and poured out drink offerings unto her, did we make her cakes to worship her, and pour out drink offerings unto her, without our men?

20 Then Jeremiah said unto all the people, to the men, and to the women, and to all the people which had given him *that* answer, saying,

21 The incense that ye burned in the cities of Judah, and in the streets of Jerusalem, ye, and your fathers, your kings, and your princes, and the people of the land, did not the LORD remember them, and came it *not* into his mind?

22 So that the LORD could no longer bear, because of the evil of your doings, *and* because of the abominations which ye have committed; therefore is your land a desolation, and an astonishment, and a curse, without an inhabitant, as at this day.

23 Because ye have burned incense, and because ye have sinned against the LORD, and have not obeyed the voice of the LORD, nor walked in his law, nor in his statutes, nor in his testimonies; therefore this evil is happened unto you, as at this day.

24 Moreover Jeremiah said unto all the people, and to all the women, Hear the word of the LORD, all Judah that *are* in the land of Egypt:

25 Thus saith the LORD of hosts, the God of Israel, saying; Ye and your wives have both spoken with your mouths, and fulfilled with your hand, saying, We will surely perform our vows that we have vowed, to burn incense to the queen of heaven, and to pour out drink offerings unto her: ye will surely accomplish your vows, and surely perform your vows.

26 Therefore hear ye the word of the LORD, all Judah that dwell in the land of Egypt; Behold, I have sworn by my great name, saith the LORD, that my name shall no more be named in the mouth of any man of Judah in all the land of Egypt, saying, The Lord GOD liveth.

27 Behold, I will watch over them for evil, and not for good: and all the men of Judah that *are* in the land of Egypt shall be consumed by the sword and by the famine, until there be an end of them.

28 Yet a small number that escape the sword shall return out of the land of Egypt into the land of Judah, and all the remnant of Judah, that are gone into the land of Egypt to sojourn there, shall know whose words shall stand, mine, or theirs.

29 And this *shall be* a sign unto you, saith the LORD, that I will punish you in this place, that ye may know that my words shall surely stand against you for evil:

30 Thus saith the LORD; Behold, I will give Pharaoh-hophra king of Egypt into the

---

Cross references:

13 Jer. 43:11
14 Jer. 44:28
16 Jer. 6:16
17 Num. 30:12; Deut. 23:23; Judg. 11:36; Jer. 7:18; 44:25
19 Jer. 7:18
22 Jer. 25:11, 18, 38; 44:6
23 Dan. 9:11, 12
24 Jer. 43:7; 44:15
25 Jer. 44:15
26 Gen. 22:16; Ezek. 20:39
27 Jer. 1:10; 31:28; 44:12; Ezek. 7:6
28 Isa. 27:13; Jer. 44:14, 17, 25, 26
29 Ps. 33:11
30 Jer. 36:1, 4, 32; 39:5; 46:25, 26; Ezek. 29:3; 30:21

44:20–23 Instead of the blessings the Jews had hoped to gain from their worship of the false gods, their prayers of incense only brought the wrath of the Lord. Jeremiah explains the reason for the Lord's judgment.

44:29–30 this shall be a sign unto you. The Lord seeks to vindicate Himself through a prophetic sign that comes true. This He does, but it is an unpleasant sign of punishment upon Judah. The sign was that Pharaoh-hophra king of Egypt would be handed over to his enemies, as Zedekiah king of Judah was delivered into the hand of Nebuchadnezzar king of Babylon. The Greek historian, Herodotus, tells us that Pharaoh-hophra was dethroned in 570 B.C., when one of his generals overthrew him.

hand of his enemies, and into the hand of them that seek his life; as I gave Zedekiah king of Judah into the hand of Nebuchadrezzar king of Babylon, his enemy, and that sought his life.

CHAPTER 45
Jeremiah's Message to Baruch

1 The word that Jeremiah the prophet spake unto Baruch the son of Neriah, when he had written these words in a book at the mouth of Jeremiah, in the fourth year of Jehoiakim the son of Josiah king of Judah, saying,

2 Thus saith the LORD, the God of Israel, unto thee, O Baruch;

3 Thou didst say, Woe is me now! for the LORD hath added grief to my sorrow; I fainted in my sighing, and I find no rest.

4 Thus shalt thou say unto him, The LORD saith thus; Behold, *that* which I have built will I break down, and that which I have planted I will pluck up, even this whole land.

5 And seekest thou great things for thyself? seek *them* not: for, behold, I will bring evil upon all flesh, saith the LORD: but thy life will I give unto thee for a prey in all places whither thou goest.

CHAPTER 46
The Battle of Carchemish

1 The word of the LORD which came to Jeremiah the prophet against the Gentiles;

2 Against Egypt, against the army of Pharaoh-necho king of Egypt, which was by the river Euphrates in Carchemish, which Nebuchadrezzar king of Babylon smote in the fourth year of Jehoiakim the son of Josiah king of Judah.

3 Order ye the buckler and shield, and draw near to battle.

4 Harness the horses; and get up, ye horsemen, and stand forth with *your* helmets; furbish the spears, *and* put on the brigandines.

5 Wherefore have I seen them dismayed *and* turned away back? and their mighty ones are beaten down, and are fled apace, and look not back: *for* fear *was* round about, saith the LORD.

6 Let not the swift flee away, nor the mighty man escape; they shall stumble, and fall toward the north by the river Euphrates.

7 Who *is* this *that* cometh up as a flood, whose waters are moved as the rivers?

8 Egypt riseth up like a flood, and *his* waters are moved like the rivers; and he saith, I will go up, *and* will cover the earth; I will destroy the city and the inhabitants thereof.

9 Come up, ye horses; and rage, ye chariots; and let the mighty men come forth; the Ethiopians and the Libyans, that handle the shield; and the Lydians, that handle *and* bend the bow.

10 For this *is* the day of the Lord GOD of hosts, a day of vengeance, that he may avenge him of his adversaries: and the sword shall devour, and it shall be satiate and made drunk with their blood: for the Lord GOD of hosts hath a sacrifice in the north country by the river Euphrates.

11 Go up into Gilead, and take balm, O virgin, the daughter of Egypt: in vain shalt thou use many medicines; *for* thou shalt not be cured.

12 The nations have heard of thy shame, and thy cry hath filled the land: for the mighty man hath stumbled against the mighty, *and* they are fallen both together.

Nebuchadnezzar's Coming

13 The word that the LORD spake to Jeremiah the prophet, how Nebuchadrezzar king of Babylon should come *and* smite the land of Egypt.

14 Declare ye in Egypt, and publish in Migdol, and publish in Noph and in Tahpanhes: say ye, Stand fast, and prepare thee; for the sword shall devour round about thee.

15 Why are thy valiant *men* swept away?

Cross references
4 Isa. 5:5
5 Jer. 21:9; 25:15, 26; 38:2; 39:18
2 2Kgs. 23:29; 2Chr. 35:20
3 Jer. 51:11, 12; Nah. 2:1; 3:14
5 Jer. 6:25; 49:29
6 Dan. 11:19
7 Isa. 8:7, 8; Jer. 47:2; Dan. 11:22
9 Isa. 66:19
10 Deut. 32:42; Isa. 13:6; 34:6; Ezek. 39:17; Joel 1:15; 2:1; Zeph. 1:7
11 Isa. 47:1; Jer. 8:22; 51:8; Ezek. 30:21
13 Isa. 19:1; Jer. 43:10, 11
14 Jer. 46:3, 4, 10

45:4–5 but thy life will I give unto thee for a prey in all places whither thou goest. The Lord gives a specific prophecy concerning Baruch, Jeremiah's scribe. The prophecy indicates that Baruch's life would be spared, but only through his taking flight from the coming Babylonian judgment. This was apparently fulfilled through Baruch's escaping into Egypt (Jer. 43:6–7).

46:5–6 they shall stumble, and fall toward the north by the river Euphrates. Because of Egypt's role in God's judgment upon Judah, God, through his prophet, mocks the Egyptians in a taunting way. This is a reference to the Babylonian defeat of the Egyptians and Pharaoh Necho in the famous Battle of Carchemish in October of 605 B.C. Carchemish was located near the Euphrates River. Nebuchadnezzar's victory at Carchemish set the stage for his later invasion of Jerusalem, thus being used as God's instrument against Egypt and Judah.

they stood not, because the LORD did drive them.

16 He made many to fall, yea, one fell upon another: and they said, Arise, and let us go again to our own people, and to the land of our nativity, from the oppressing sword.

17 They did cry there, Pharaoh king of Egypt *is but* a noise; he hath passed the time appointed.

18 *As* I live, saith the King, whose name *is* the LORD of hosts, Surely as Tabor *is* among the mountains, and as Carmel by the sea, *so* shall he come.

19 O thou daughter dwelling in Egypt, furnish thyself to go into captivity: for Noph shall be waste and desolate without an inhabitant.

20 Egypt *is like* a very fair heifer, *but* destruction cometh; it cometh out of the north.

21 Also her hired men *are* in the midst of her like fatted bullocks; for they also are turned back, *and* are fled away together: they did not stand, because the day of their calamity was come upon them, *and* the time of their visitation.

22 The voice thereof shall go like a serpent; for they shall march with an army, and come against her with axes, as hewers of wood.

23 They shall cut down her forest, saith the LORD, though it cannot be searched; because they are more than the grasshoppers, and *are* innumerable.

24 The daughter of Egypt shall be confounded; she shall be delivered into the hand of the people of the north.

25 The LORD of hosts, the God of Israel, saith; Behold, I will punish the multitude of No, and Pharaoh, and Egypt, with their gods, and their kings; even Pharaoh, and *all* them that trust in him:

26 And I will deliver them into the hand of those that seek their lives, and into the hand of Nebuchadrezzar king of Babylon, and into the hand of his servants: and afterward it shall be inhabited, as in the days of old, saith the LORD.

27 But fear not thou, O my servant Jacob, and be not dismayed, O Israel: for, behold, I will save thee from afar off, and thy seed from the land of their captivity; and Jacob shall return, and be in rest and at ease, and none shall make *him* afraid.

28 Fear thou not, O Jacob my servant, saith the LORD: for I *am* with thee; for I will make a full end of all the nations whither I have driven thee: but I will not make a full end of thee, but correct thee in measure; yet will I not leave thee wholly unpunished.

CHAPTER 47
The Philistines

1 The word of the LORD that came to Jeremiah the prophet against the Philistines, before that Pharaoh smote Gaza.

2 Thus saith the LORD; Behold, waters rise up out of the north, and shall be an overflowing flood, and shall overflow the land, and all that is therein; the city, and them that dwell therein: then the men shall cry, and all the inhabitants of the land shall howl.

3 At the noise of the stamping of the hoofs of his strong *horses*, at the rushing of his chariots, *and at* the rumbling of his wheels, the fathers shall not look back to *their* children for feebleness of hands;

4 Because of the day that cometh to spoil all the Philistines, *and* to cut off from Tyrus and Zidon every helper that remaineth: for the LORD will spoil the Philistines, the remnant of the country of Caphtor.

5 Baldness is come upon Gaza; Ashkelon is cut off *with* the remnant of their valley: how long wilt thou cut thyself?

6 O thou sword of the LORD, how long *will it be* ere thou be quiet? put up thyself into thy scabbard, rest, and be still.

7 How can it be quiet, seeing the LORD hath given it a charge against Ashkelon, and against the sea shore? there hath he appointed it.

CHAPTER 48
Moab

1 Against Moab thus saith the LORD of hosts, the God of Israel; Woe unto Nebo! for

Cross references (center column):

16 Lev. 26:37
18 Isa. 47:4; 48:2; Jer. 48:15
19 Isa. 20:4; Jer. 48:18
20 Hos. 10:11
21 Ps. 37:13; Jer. 50:27
22 Isa. 29:4
23 Judg. 6:5; Isa. 10:34
25 Jer. 43:12, 13; Ezek. 30:13, 14-16; Nah. 3:8
26 Jer. 44:30; Ezek. 29:11, 13, 14; 32:11
27 Isa. 41:13, 14; 43:5; 44:2; Jer. 30:10, 11
28 Jer. 10:24; 25:20; 30:11; Ezek. 25:15, 16; Amos 1:6-8; Zeph. 2:4, 5
2 Isa. 8:7; Jer. 1:14; 46:7, 8, 20
3 Jer. 8:16; Nah. 3:2
4 Gen. 10:14; Jer. 25:22; Ezek. 25:16; Amos 1:8; 9:7
5 Jer. 16:6; 25:20; 41:5; 48:37; Amos 1:7; Mic. 1:16; Zeph. 2:4, 7; Zech. 9:5
6 Deut. 32:41; Ezek. 21:3-5
7 Isa. 15:2; Ezek. 14:17; 25:9; Amos 2:1, 2; Mic. 6:9

46:26–28 afterward it shall be inhabited, as in the days of old. Fulfilled under the rule of Pharaoh Amasis after 568 B.C., this prophecy speaks of Egypt's recovery after her defeat at the hands of the Babylonians. The passage, (cf. Jer. 30:10–11), also mentions that, ultimately, the Lord will return Israel and Judah to their land, punish the Gentile nations, and bless Judah and Israel.

47:5 Baldness is come upon Gaza . . . how long wilt thou cut thyself? The heathen performed self-mutilation, mourning rituals in an effort to gain the attention of their gods. Such practices were forbidden in Israel (Lev. 19:28; 21:5; Jer. 16:6).

Prophecies of the Gentile Nations

By John F. Walvoord

The prophetic Word gives revelation in three broad areas: prophecies about the Gentile world, prophecies about Israel, and prophecies about the Church (1 Cor. 10:32). Both the Old and New Testaments contain many prophecies that affect the world as a whole.

The first eleven chapters of Genesis record broad prophecies concerning the Gentile world. Prophecy concerned all mankind as one unit until Noah and his three sons lived. The predictions of Genesis 9:24–27 are the first indication that God has differing expectations for various parts of humanity. For instance, Noah's three sons and their descendants would have different destinies. Japheth's descendants would become the largest division of the Gentiles. Shem, who would receive God's special blessing, would father a line that eventually would produce the Savior. Ham, the father of Canaan, and his descendants would bear a special curse as God's enemies.

Old Testament Scripture records six major world empires: Egypt, Assyria, Babylon, Media-Persia, Greece, and Rome, giving a prophetic outline of past and future world events as God sees them. Many of these prophecies have already been fulfilled with remarkable accuracy. Egypt is the first major country with which God chose to involve in relation to God's chosen people—Israel. Egypt is pictured as God's enemy from which He delivers Israel. Scripture predicts that Egypt will have a more respectable role in the future Millennial Kingdom. Assyria was the greatest empire of the Middle East in the seventh and eighth centuries B.C. Her armies captured the ten tribes of Israel in 722 B.C. and dominated the political scene for a century. Like Egypt, some of the prophecies concerning Assyria have not yet been fulfilled, and she is assured a place in the prophetic future. Babylon rose to power in the Middle East by conquering Assyria in 605 B.C. Although Babylon as an empire ceased to exist when the Medes and Persians conquered it in 539 B.C., I believe that the religious aspects of the Babylonian nation as well as the city of Babylon itself will reappear in the End Times. Babylon's complete devastation, in my opinion, awaits future fulfillment in connection with Christ's Second Coming (Rev. 18:1–24). Media-Persia and Greece followed Babylon as Gentile world powers during the "times of the Gentiles" (Luke 21:24). Yet these nations also passed off the scene as they fulfilled God's plan for the Gentiles. The greatest of all is the Roman Empire, whose rule extended almost seventeen hundred years. Scripture teaches that a form of this empire will be revived in a ten-nation confederacy through which the Antichrist will rise to power during the future seven-year Tribulation.

> *Throughout Gentile history, we see God revealed as sovereign.*

Matthew 25 teaches that after the second coming of Christ the nations will be judged. In this chapter, those Gentiles who are believers are called sheep; those who are unbelievers are called goats.

Throughout Gentile history, we see God revealed as sovereign. He has judged each empire in His time. The rebellion of the Gentile kingdoms described in Psalm 2 will conclude at the second coming of Christ. In dealing with the Gentile nations, God has saved and will continue to save some individuals, giving the Gentiles a time of special blessing in the body of Christ—the Church of the present age.

it is spoiled: Kiriathaim is confounded *and* taken: Misgab is confounded and dismayed.

2 *There shall be* no more praise of Moab: in Heshbon they have devised evil against it; come, and let us cut it off from *being* a nation. Also thou shalt be cut down, O Madmen; the sword shall pursue thee.

3 A voice of crying *shall be* from Horonaim, spoiling and great destruction.

4 Moab is destroyed; her little ones have caused a cry to be heard.

5 For in the going up of Luhith continual weeping shall go up; for in the going down of Horonaim the enemies have heard a cry of destruction.

6 Flee, save your lives, and be like the heath in the wilderness.

7 For because thou hast trusted in thy works and in thy treasures, thou shalt also be taken: and Chemosh shall go forth into captivity *with* his priests and his princes together.

8 And the spoiler shall come upon every city, and no city shall escape: the valley also shall perish, and the plain shall be destroyed, as the LORD hath spoken.

9 Give wings unto Moab, that it may flee and get away: for the cities thereof shall be desolate, without any to dwell therein.

10 Cursed *be* he that doeth the work of the LORD deceitfully, and cursed *be* he that keepeth back his sword from blood.

11 Moab hath been at ease from his youth, and he hath settled on his lees, and hath not been emptied from vessel to vessel, neither hath he gone into captivity: therefore his taste remained in him, and his scent is not changed.

12 Therefore, behold, the days come, saith the LORD, that I will send unto him wanderers, that shall cause him to wander, and shall empty his vessels, and break their bottles.

13 And Moab shall be ashamed of Chemosh, as the house of Israel was ashamed of Beth-el their confidence.

14 How say ye, We *are* mighty and strong men for the war?

15 Moab is spoiled, and gone up *out of* her cities, and his chosen young men are gone down to the slaughter, saith the King, whose name *is* the LORD of hosts.

16 The calamity of Moab *is* near to come, and his affliction hasteth fast.

17 All ye that are about him, bemoan him; and all ye that know his name, say, How is the strong staff broken, *and* the beautiful rod!

18 Thou daughter that dost inhabit Dibon, come down from *thy* glory, and sit in thirst; for the spoiler of Moab shall come upon thee, *and* he shall destroy thy strong holds.

19 O inhabitant of Aroer, stand by the way, and espy; ask him that fleeth, and her that escapeth, *and* say, What is done?

20 Moab is confounded; for it is broken down: howl and cry; tell ye it in Arnon, that Moab is spoiled,

21 And judgment is come upon the plain country; upon Holon, and upon Jahazah, and upon Mephaath,

22 And upon Dibon, and upon Nebo, and upon Beth-diblathaim,

23 And upon Kiriathaim, and upon Beth-gamul, and upon Bethmeon,

24 And upon Kerioth, and upon Bozrah, and upon all the cities of the land of Moab, far or near.

25 The horn of Moab is cut off, and his arm is broken, saith the LORD.

26 Make ye him drunken: for he magnified *himself* against the LORD: Moab also shall wallow in his vomit, and he also shall be in derision.

27 For was not Israel a derision unto thee? was he found among thieves? for since thou spakest of him, thou skippedst for joy.

28 O ye that dwell in Moab, leave the cities, and dwell in the rock, and be like the dove *that* maketh her nest in the sides of the hole's mouth.

29 We have heard the pride of Moab, (he is exceeding proud) his loftiness, and his arrogancy, and his pride, and the haughtiness of his heart.

30 I know his wrath, saith the LORD; but *it shall* not *be* so; his lies shall not so effect *it*.

31 Therefore will I howl for Moab, and I will cry out for all Moab; *mine heart* shall mourn for the men of Kir-heres.

32 O vine of Sibmah, I will weep for thee with the weeping of Jazer: thy plants are gone over the sea, they reach *even* to the sea of Jazer: the spoiler is fallen upon thy summer fruits and upon thy vintage.

33 And joy and gladness is taken from the plentiful field, and from the land of Moab; and I have caused wine to fail from the winepresses: none shall tread with shouting; *their* shouting *shall be* no shouting.

34 From the cry of Heshbon *even* unto Elealeh, *and even* unto Jahaz, have they uttered their voice, from Zoar *even* unto Horonaim, *as* an heifer of three years old: for the waters also of Nimrim shall be desolate.

Cross references (center column):

2 Isa. 15:1, 4; 16:14
3 Jer. 48:5
5 Isa. 15:5
6 Jer. 17:6; 51:6
7 Num. 21:29; Judg. 11:24; Isa. 46:1, 2; Jer. 43:12; 49:3
8 Jer. 6:26; 48:18
9 Ps. 55:6; Jer. 48:28
10 Judg. 5:23; 1Sam. 15:3, 9; 1Kgs. 20:42
11 Zeph. 1:12
13 Judg. 11:24; 1Kgs. 11:7; 12:29; Hos. 10:6
14 Isa. 16:6
15 Jer. 46:18; 48:8, 9, 18; 50:27; 51:57
17 Isa. 9:4; 14:4, 5
18 Num. 21:30; Isa. 15:2; 47:1; Jer. 46:19; 48:8
19 Deut. 2:36; 1Sam. 4:13, 16
20 Num. 21:13; Isa. 16:7
21 Jer. 48:8
24 Jer. 48:41; Amos 2:2
25 Ps. 75:10; Ezek. 30:21
26 Jer. 25:15, 27
27 Jer. 2:26; Zeph. 2:8
28 Ps. 55:6, 7; Song 2:14; Jer. 48:9
29 Isa. 16:6
30 Isa. 16:6; Jer. 50:36
31 Isa. 15:5; 16:7, 11
32 Isa. 16:8, 9
33 Isa. 16:10; Joel 1:12

35 Moreover I will cause to cease in Moab, saith the LORD, him that offereth in the high places, and him that burneth incense to his gods.

36 Therefore mine heart shall sound for Moab like pipes, and mine heart shall sound like pipes for the men of Kir-heres: because the riches *that* he hath gotten are perished.

37 For every head *shall be* bald, and every beard clipped: upon all the hands *shall be* cuttings, and upon the loins sackcloth.

38 *There shall be* lamentation generally upon all the housetops of Moab, and in the streets thereof: for I have broken Moab like a vessel wherein *is* no pleasure, saith the LORD.

39 They shall howl, *saying*, How is it broken down! how hath Moab turned the back with shame! so shall Moab be a derision and a dismaying to all them about him.

40 For thus saith the LORD; Behold, he shall fly as an eagle, and shall spread his wings over Moab.

41 Kerioth is taken, and the strong holds are surprised, and the mighty men's hearts in Moab at that day shall be as the heart of a woman in her pangs.

42 And Moab shall be destroyed from *being* a people, because he hath magnified *himself* against the LORD.

43 Fear, and the pit, and the snare, *shall be* upon thee, O inhabitant of Moab, saith the LORD.

44 He that fleeth from the fear shall fall into the pit; and he that getteth up out of the pit shall be taken in the snare: for I will bring upon it, *even* upon Moab, the year of their visitation, saith the LORD.

45 They that fled stood under the shadow of Heshbon because of the force: but a fire shall come forth out of Heshbon, and a flame from the midst of Sihon, and shall devour the corner of Moab, and the crown of the head of the tumultuous ones.

46 Woe be unto thee, O Moab! the people of

35 Isa. 15:2; 16:12
36 Isa. 15:5, 7; 16:11
37 Gen. 37:34; Isa. 15:2, 3; Jer. 47:5
38 Jer. 22:28
40 Deut. 28:49; Isa. 8:8; Jer. 49:22; Dan. 7:4; Hos. 8:1; Hab. 1:8
41 Isa. 13:8; 21:3; Jer. 30:6; 41:24; 49:22, 24; 50:43; 51:30; Mic. 4:9
42 Ps. 83:4; Isa. 7:8
43 Isa. 24:17, 18
44 Jer. 11:23
45 Num. 21:28; 24:17
46 Num. 21:29
47 Jer. 49:6, 39; Jer. 21:28; 25:2; Amos 1:13; Zeph. 2:8, 9
2 Ezek. 25:5; Amos 1:14
3 1Kgs. 11:5, 33; Isa. 32:11; Jer. 4:8; 6:26; 48:7; Amos 1:15
4 Jer. 3:14; 7:24; 21:13
6 Jer. 48:47; 49:39
7 Isa. 19:11; Ezek. 25:12; Amos 1:11; Obad. 1:8
8 Jer. 25:23; 49:30

Chemosh perisheth: for thy sons are taken captives, and thy daughters captives.

47 Yet will I bring again the captivity of Moab in the latter days, saith the LORD. Thus far *is* the judgment of Moab.

CHAPTER 49
The Ammonites

1 Concerning the Ammonites, thus saith the LORD; Hath Israel no sons? hath he no heir? why *then* doth their king inherit Gad, and his people dwell in his cities?

2 Therefore, behold, the days come, saith the LORD, that I will cause an alarm of war to be heard in Rabbah of the Ammonites; and it shall be a desolate heap, and her daughters shall be burned with fire: then shall Israel be heir unto them that were his heirs, saith the LORD.

3 Howl, O Heshbon, for Ai is spoiled: cry, ye daughters of Rabbah, gird you with sackcloth; lament, and run to and fro by the hedges; for their king shall go into captivity, *and* his priests and his princes together.

4 Wherefore gloriest thou in the valleys, thy flowing valley, O backsliding daughter? that trusted in her treasures, *saying*, Who shall come unto me?

5 Behold, I will bring a fear upon thee, saith the Lord GOD of hosts, from all those that be about thee; and ye shall be driven out every man right forth; and none shall gather up him that wandereth.

6 And afterward I will bring again the captivity of the children of Ammon, saith the LORD.

Edom

7 Concerning Edom, thus saith the LORD of hosts; *Is* wisdom no more in Teman? is counsel perished from the prudent? is their wisdom vanished?

8 Flee ye, turn back, dwell deep, O inhabitants of Dedan; for I will bring the calamity

---

48:47 Moab. The nation of Moab bordered the lower half of the southeastern shore of the Dead Sea in the modern state of Jordan. Moab lost its national identity to the Nabataeans in the first century B.C. and then later to the Arabs. But according to this verse, Moab will be restored during the future Millennium. The Lord will bless many Gentile nations during this time of global blessing.

49:1–6 Hath Israel no sons? When the Northern Kingdom was taken into captivity by Assyria in 722 B.C., the Ammonites came and took over much of their land. The

Hebrew word for "their king" could also be translated "Molech," who is the god of the Ammonites. Such idolatry had spread to the region of Gad and its cities. Jeremiah predicts that the day would come when an enemy would attack the Ammonite city of Rabbah. When that day comes, "then shall Israel be heir unto them." In other words, Israel will do to the Ammonites what they did to the Northern Kingdom. Yet, in the end, the Lord will one day bless even the children of Ammon (cf. Jer. 48:47; 49:39), in spite of their treatment of Israel.

of Esau upon him, the time *that* I will visit him.

9 If grapegatherers come to thee, would they not leave *some* gleaning grapes? if thieves by night, they will destroy till they have enough.

10 But I have made Esau bare, I have uncovered his secret places, and he shall not be able to hide himself: his seed is spoiled, and his brethren, and his neighbours, and he *is* not.

11 Leave thy fatherless children, I will preserve *them* alive; and let thy widows trust in me.

12 For thus saith the LORD; Behold, they whose judgment *was* not to drink of the cup have assuredly drunken; and *art* thou he *that* shall altogether go unpunished? thou shalt not go unpunished, but thou shalt surely drink *of it*.

13 For I have sworn by myself, saith the LORD, that Bozrah shall become a desolation, a reproach, a waste, and a curse; and all the cities thereof shall be perpetual wastes.

14 I have heard a rumour from the LORD, and an ambassador is sent unto the heathen, *saying*, Gather ye together, and come against her, and rise up to the battle.

15 For, lo, I will make thee small among the heathen, *and* despised among men.

16 Thy terribleness hath deceived thee, *and* the pride of thine heart, O thou that dwellest in the clefts of the rock, that holdest the height of the hill: though thou shouldest make thy nest as high as the eagle, I will bring thee down from thence, saith the LORD.

17 Also Edom shall be a desolation: every one that goeth by it shall be astonished, and shall hiss at all the plagues thereof.

18 As in the overthrow of Sodom and Gomorrah and the neighbour *cities* thereof, saith the LORD, no man shall abide there, neither shall a son of man dwell in it.

19 Behold, he shall come up like a lion from the swelling of Jordan against the habitation of the strong: but I will suddenly make him run away from her: and who *is* a chosen *man, that* I may appoint over her? for who *is* like me? and who will appoint me

the time? and who *is* that shepherd that will stand before me?

20 Therefore hear the counsel of the LORD, that he hath taken against Edom; and his purposes, that he hath purposed against the inhabitants of Teman: Surely the least of the flock shall draw them out: surely he shall make their habitations desolate with them.

21 The earth is moved at the noise of their fall, at the cry the noise thereof was heard in the Red sea.

22 Behold, he shall come up and fly as the eagle, and spread his wings over Bozrah: and at that day shall the heart of the mighty men of Edom be as the heart of a woman in her pangs.

Damascus

23 Concerning Damascus. Hamath is confounded, and Arpad: for they have heard evil tidings: they are fainthearted; *there is* sorrow on the sea; it cannot be quiet.

24 Damascus is waxed feeble, *and* turneth herself to flee, and fear hath seized on *her*: anguish and sorrows have taken her, as a woman in travail.

25 How is the city of praise not left, the city of my joy!

26 Therefore her young men shall fall in her streets, and all the men of war shall be cut off in that day, saith the LORD of hosts.

27 And I will kindle a fire in the wall of Damascus, and it shall consume the palaces of Ben-hadad.

The Tribe of Kedar and the City of Hazor

28 Concerning Kedar, and concerning the kingdoms of Hazor, which Nebuchadrezzar king of Babylon shall smite, thus saith the LORD; Arise ye, go up to Kedar, and spoil the men of the east.

29 Their tents and their flocks shall they take away: they shall take to themselves their curtains, and all their vessels, and their camels; and they shall cry unto them, Fear *is* on every side.

30 Flee, get you far off, dwell deep, O ye inhabitants of Hazor, saith the LORD; for Nebuchadrezzar king of Babylon hath taken

Center reference column

9 Obad. 1:5

10 Isa. 17:14; Mal. 1:3

12 Jer. 25:29; Obad. 1:16

13 Gen. 22:16; Isa. 34:6; 45:23; 63:1; Amos 6:8

14 Obad. 1:1-3

16 Job 39:27; Amos 9:2; Obad. 1:4

17 Jer. 18:16; 50:13

18 Gen. 19:25; Deut. 29:23; Jer. 50:40; Amos 4:11

19 Ex. 15:11; Job 41:10; Jer. 12:5; 50:44

20 Jer. 50:45

21 Jer. 50:46

22 Jer. 4:13; 48:40, 41

23 Isa. 17:1; 37:13; 57:20; Amos 1:3; Zech. 9:1, 2

24 Isa. 13:8; Jer. 4:31; 6:24; 30:6; 48:41; 49:22

25 Jer. 33:9; 51:41

26 Jer. 50:30; 51:4

27 Amos 1:4

28 Judg. 6:3; Job 1:3; Isa. 21:13

29 Ps. 120:5; Jer. 6:25; 46:5

30 Jer. 49:8

49:23–27 The city of Damascus mentioned in these verses is the same city that exists today in modern Syria. Hamath and Arpad were two other cities in Syria. As with Judah, God is pronouncing judgment upon these Syrian cities. When the Babylonians came down upon Israel, they also set siege and defeated these Syrian cities as part of God's judgment upon them. Thus, Syria also experienced the consequences of God's judgment.

counsel against you, and hath conceived a purpose against you.

31 Arise, get you up unto the wealthy nation, that dwelleth without care, saith the LORD, which have neither gates nor bars, *which* dwell alone.

32 And their camels shall be a booty, and the multitude of their cattle a spoil: and I will scatter into all winds them *that are* in the utmost corners; and I will bring their calamity from all sides thereof, saith the LORD.

33 And Hazor shall be a dwelling for dragons, *and* a desolation for ever: there shall no man abide there, nor *any* son of man dwell in it.

Elam

34 The word of the LORD that came to Jeremiah the prophet against Elam in the beginning of the reign of Zedekiah king of Judah, saying,

35 Thus saith the LORD of hosts; Behold, I will break the bow of Elam, the chief of their might.

36 And upon Elam will I bring the four winds from the four quarters of heaven, and will scatter them toward all those winds; and there shall be no nation whither the outcasts of Elam shall not come.

37 For I will cause Elam to be dismayed before their enemies, and before them that seek their life: and I will bring evil upon them, *even* my fierce anger, saith the LORD; and I will send the sword after them, till I have consumed them:

38 And I will set my throne in Elam, and will destroy from thence the king and the princes, saith the LORD.

39 But it shall come to pass in the latter days, *that* I will bring again the captivity of Elam, saith the LORD.

CHAPTER 50
Babylon

1 The word that the Lord spake against Babylon *and* against the land of the Chaldeans by Jeremiah the prophet.

2 Declare ye among the nations, and publish, and set up a standard; publish, *and* conceal not: say, Babylon is taken, Bel is confounded, Merodach is broken in pieces; her idols are confounded, her images are broken in pieces.

3 For out of the north there cometh up a nation against her, which shall make her land desolate, and none shall dwell therein: they shall remove, they shall depart, both man and beast.

4 In those days, and in that time, saith the LORD, the children of Israel shall come, they and the children of Judah together, going and weeping: they shall go, and seek the LORD their God.

5 They shall ask the way to Zion with their faces thitherward, *saying*, Come, and let us join ourselves to the LORD in a perpetual covenant *that* shall not be forgotten.

6 My people hath been lost sheep: their shepherds have caused them to go astray, they have turned them away *on* the mountains: they have gone from mountain to hill, they have forgotten their restingplace.

7 All that found them have devoured them: and their adversaries said, We offend not, because they have sinned against the LORD, the habitation of justice, even the LORD, the hope of their fathers.

8 Remove out of the midst of Babylon, and go forth out of the land of the Chaldeans, and be as the he goats before the flocks.

9 For, lo, I will raise and cause to come up against Babylon an assembly of great nations from the north country: and they shall set themselves in array against her; from thence she shall be taken: their arrows *shall be* as of a mighty expert man; none shall return in vain.

10 And Chaldea shall be a spoil: all that spoil her shall be satisfied, saith the LORD.

11 Because ye were glad, because ye rejoiced, O ye destroyers of mine heritage, because ye are grown fat as the heifer at grass, and bellow as bulls;

12 Your mother shall be sore confounded; she that bare you shall be ashamed: behold, the hindermost of the nations *shall be* a wilderness, a dry land, and a desert.

13 Because of the wrath of the LORD it shall not be inhabited, but it shall be wholly desolate: every one that goeth by Babylon shall be astonished, and hiss at all her plagues.

14 Put yourselves in array against Babylon round about: all ye that bend the bow, shoot at her, spare no arrows: for she hath sinned against the LORD.

15 Shout against her round about: she hath

Cross references (center column)

31 Num. 23:9; Deut. 33:28; Ezek. 38:11; Mic. 7:14

32 Jer. 9:26; 25:23; 49:36; Ezek. 5:10

33 Jer. 9:11; 10:22; 25:25; 49:18; Mal. 1:3

35 Isa. 22:6

36 Jer. 49:32

37 Jer. 9:16; 48:2

38 Jer. 43:10

39 Isa. 13:1; 21:1; Jer. 48:47; 49:6

2 Isa. 46:1; Jer. 43:12, 13; 51:44

3 Isa. 13:17, 18, 20; Jer. 50:39, 40; 51:48

4 Ezra 3:12, 13; Ps. 126:5, 6; Jer. 31:9; Hos. 1:11; 3:5; Zech. 12:10

5 Jer. 31:31; 32:40

6 Isa. 53:6; Jer. 2:20; 3:6, 23; 50:17; 1Pet. 2:25

7 Ps. 22:4; 79:7; 90:1; 91:1; Jer. 2:3; 40:2, 3; Dan. 9:16; Zech. 11:5

8 Isa. 48:20; Jer. 51:6, 45; Zech. 2:6, 7; Rev. 18:4

9 2Sam. 1:22; Jer. 15:14; 50:3, 14, 29, 41; 51:27

10 Rev. 17:16

11 Isa. 47:6; Hos. 10:11

13 Jer. 25:12; 49:17

15 Rev. 18:6

49:39 in the latter days. During the Millennium, the Lord will also restore Elam and bless them at that future time, as He will bless a whole host of Gentile nations. Elam was east of Babylon and would make up part of the modern country of Iran (cf. Jer. 48:47; 49:6).

given her hand: her foundations are fallen, her walls are thrown down: for it *is* the vengeance of the Lord: take vengeance upon her; as she hath done, do unto her.

16 Cut off the sower from Babylon, and him that handleth the sickle in the time of harvest: for fear of the oppressing sword they shall turn every one to his people, and they shall flee every one to his own land.

Israel Will Return

17 Israel *is* a scattered sheep; the lions have driven *him* away: first the king of Assyria hath devoured him; and last this Nebuchadrezzar king of Babylon hath broken his bones.

18 Therefore thus saith the Lord of hosts, the God of Israel; Behold, I will punish the king of Babylon and his land, as I have punished the king of Assyria.

19 And I will bring Israel again to his habitation, and he shall feed on Carmel and Bashan, and his soul shall be satisfied upon mount Ephraim and Gilead.

20 In those days, and in that time, saith the Lord, the iniquity of Israel shall be sought for, and *there shall be* none; and the sins of Judah, and they shall not be found: for I will pardon them whom I reserve.

The People of Babylon

21 Go up against the land of Merathaim, *even* against it, and against the inhabitants of Pekod: waste and utterly destroy after them, saith the Lord, and do according to all that I have commanded thee.

22 A sound of battle *is* in the land, and of great destruction.

23 How is the hammer of the whole earth cut asunder and broken! how is Babylon become a desolation among the nations!

24 I have laid a snare for thee, and thou art also taken, O Babylon, and thou wast not aware: thou art found, and also caught, because thou hast striven against the Lord.

25 The Lord hath opened his armoury, and hath brought forth the weapons of his indignation: for this *is* the work of the Lord God of hosts in the land of the Chaldeans.

26 Come against her from the utmost border, open her storehouses: cast her up as heaps, and destroy her utterly: let nothing of her be left.

27 Slay all her bullocks; let them go down to the slaughter: woe unto them! for their day is come, the time of their visitation.

28 The voice of them that flee and escape out of the land of Babylon, to declare in Zion the vengeance of the Lord our God, the vengeance of his temple.

29 Call together the archers against Babylon: all ye that bend the bow, camp against it round about; let none thereof escape: recompense her according to her work; according to all that she hath done, do unto her: for she hath been proud against the Lord, against the Holy One of Israel.

30 Therefore shall her young men fall in the streets, and all her men of war shall be cut off in that day, saith the Lord.

31 Behold, I *am* against thee, *O thou* most proud, saith the Lord God of hosts: for thy day is come, the time *that* I will visit thee.

32 And the most proud shall stumble and fall, and none shall raise him up: and I will kindle a fire in his cities, and it shall devour all round about him.

33 Thus saith the Lord of hosts; The children of Israel and the children of Judah *were* oppressed together: and all that took them captives held them fast; they refused to let them go.

34 Their Redeemer *is* strong; the Lord of hosts *is* his name: he shall throughly plead their cause, that he may give rest to the land, and disquiet the inhabitants of Babylon.

35 A sword *is* upon the Chaldeans, saith the Lord, and upon the inhabitants of Babylon, and upon her princes, and upon her wise *men*.

36 A sword *is* upon the liars; and they shall dote: a sword *is* upon her mighty men; and they shall be dismayed.

37 A sword *is* upon their horses, and upon their chariots, and upon all the mingled people that *are* in the midst of her; and they shall become as women: a sword *is* upon her treasures; and they shall be robbed.

38 A drought *is* upon her waters; and they shall be dried up: for it *is* the land of graven images, and they are mad upon *their* idols.

Cross references

16 Isa. 13:14; Jer. 51:9
17 2Kgs. 17:6; 24:10, 14; Jer. 2:15; 50:6
19 Isa. 65:10; Jer. 33:12; Ezek. 34:13, 14
20 Isa. 1:9; Jer. 31:34
21 2Sam. 16:11; 2Kgs. 18:25; 2Chr. 36:23; Isa. 10:6; 44:28; 48:14; Jer. 34:22; Ezek. 23:23
22 Jer. 51:54
23 Isa. 14:6; Jer. 51:20
24 Jer. 51:8, 31, 39, 57; Dan. 5:30, 31
25 Isa. 13:5
27 Ps. 22:12; Isa. 34:7; Jer. 46:21; 48:44; 50:31
28 Jer. 51:10, 11
29 Isa. 47:10; Jer. 50:14, 15; 51:56; Rev. 18:6
30 Jer. 49:26; 51:4
31 Jer. 50:27
32 Jer. 21:14
34 Isa. 47:4; Rev. 18:8
35 Isa. 47:13; Dan. 5:30
36 Isa. 44:25; Jer. 48:30
37 Jer. 25:20, 24; 51:30; Ezek. 30:5; Nah. 3:13
38 Isa. 44:27; Jer. 50:2; 51:32, 36, 44, 47, 52; Rev. 16:12

50:19–20 I will bring Israel again to his habitation. This is another of the many passages about the end-time restoration of the nation Israel, including both the Northern and Southern Kingdoms. The mountain of Carmel and the plains of Bashan will once again belong to Israel during this end-time restoration of God's people. This time of blessing will include Israel living in obedience to the Lord because her sins will be forgiven and pardoned.

39 Therefore the wild beasts of the desert with the wild beasts of the islands shall dwell *there*, and the owls shall dwell therein: and it shall be no more inhabited for ever; neither shall it be dwelt in from generation to generation.

40 As God overthrew Sodom and Gomorrah and the neighbour *cities* thereof, saith the LORD; *so* shall no man abide there, neither shall any son of man dwell therein.

41 Behold, a people shall come from the north, and a great nation, and many kings shall be raised up from the coasts of the earth.

42 They shall hold the bow and the lance: they *are* cruel, and will not shew mercy: their voice shall roar like the sea, and they shall ride upon horses, *every one* put in array, like a man to the battle, against thee, O daughter of Babylon.

43 The king of Babylon hath heard the report of them, and his hands waxed feeble: anguish took hold of him, *and* pangs as of a woman in travail.

44 Behold, he shall come up like a lion from the swelling of Jordan unto the habitation of the strong: but I will make them suddenly run away from her: and who *is* a chosen *man, that* I may appoint over her? for who *is* like me? and who will appoint me the time? and who *is* that shepherd that will stand before me?

45 Therefore hear ye the counsel of the LORD, that he hath taken against Babylon; and his purposes, that he hath purposed against the land of the Chaldeans: Surely the least of the flock shall draw them out: surely he shall make *their* habitation desolate with them.

46 At the noise of the taking of Babylon the earth is moved, and the cry is heard among the nations.

CHAPTER 51
God's Judgment upon Babylon

1 Thus saith the LORD; Behold, I will raise up against Babylon, and against them that dwell in the midst of them that rise up against me, a destroying wind;

2 And will send unto Babylon fanners, that shall fan her, and shall empty her land: for in the day of trouble they shall be against her round about.

3 Against *him that* bendeth let the archer bend his bow, and against *him that* lifteth himself up in his brigandine: and spare ye not her young men; destroy ye utterly all her host.

4 Thus the slain shall fall in the land of the Chaldeans, and *they that are* thrust through in her streets.

5 For Israel *hath* not *been* forsaken, nor Judah of his God, of the LORD of hosts; though their land was filled with sin against the Holy One of Israel.

6 Flee out of the midst of Babylon, and deliver every man his soul: be not cut off in her iniquity; for this *is* the time of the LORD's vengeance; he will render unto her a recompence.

7 Babylon *hath been* a golden cup in the LORD's hand, that made all the earth drunken: the nations have drunken of her wine; therefore the nations are mad.

8 Babylon is suddenly fallen and destroyed: howl for her; take balm for her pain, if so be she may be healed.

9 We would have healed Babylon, but she is not healed: forsake her, and let us go every one into his own country: for her judgment reacheth unto heaven, and is lifted up *even* to the skies.

10 The LORD hath brought forth our righteousness: come, and let us declare in Zion the work of the LORD our God.

11 Make bright the arrows; gather the shields: the LORD hath raised up the spirit of the kings of the Medes: for his device *is* against Babylon, to destroy it; because it *is* the vengeance of the LORD, the vengeance of his temple.

12 Set up the standard upon the walls of Babylon, make the watch strong, set up the watchmen, prepare the ambushes: for the LORD hath both devised and done that which he spake against the inhabitants of Babylon.

13 O thou that dwellest upon many waters, abundant in treasures, thine end is come, *and* the measure of thy covetousness.

14 The LORD of hosts hath sworn by himself, *saying*, Surely I will fill thee with men, as with caterpillers; and they shall lift up a shout against thee.

A Hymn of Praise to God

15 He hath made the earth by his power, he hath established the world by his wisdom,

---

Cross references (center column):

39 Isa. 13:20, 21, 22; 34:14; Jer. 25:12; 51:37; Rev. 18:2

40 Gen. 19:25; Isa. 13:19; Jer. 49:18; 51:26

41 Jer. 6:22; 25:14; 50:9; 51:27; Rev. 17:16

42 Isa. 5:30; 13:18; Jer. 6:23

43 Jer. 49:24

44 Job 41:10; Jer. 49:19

45 Isa. 14:24; Jer. 51:11

46 2Kgs. 19:7; Jer. 4:11; Rev. 18:9

2 Jer. 15:7; 50:14

3 Jer. 50:14, 21

4 Jer. 49:26; 50:30, 37

6 Jer. 25:14; 50:8, 15, 28; Rev. 18:4

7 Jer. 25:16; Rev. 14:8; 17:4

8 Isa. 21:9; Jer. 46:11; 48:20; Rev. 14:8; 18:2, 9, 11, 19

9 Isa. 13:14; Jer. 50:16; Rev. 18:5

10 Ps. 37:6; Jer. 50:28

11 Isa. 13:17; Jer. 46:4; 50:28, 45; 51:28

12 Nah. 2:1; 3:14

13 Rev. 17:1, 15

14 Jer. 49:13; 50:15; Amos 6:8; Nah. 3:15

15 Gen. 1:1, 6; Job 9:8; Ps. 104:2

51:5 Even though Jeremiah's message has been one of Judah's disobedience and judgment, God will never abandon nor forsake His people. In the end, God will take away their sin and bring blessing in the place of judgment.

and hath stretched out the heaven by his understanding.

16 When he uttereth *his* voice, *there is* a multitude of waters in the heavens; and he causeth the vapours to ascend from the ends of the earth: he maketh lightnings with rain, and bringeth forth the wind out of his treasures.

17 Every man is brutish by *his* knowledge; every founder is confounded by the graven image: for his molten image *is* falsehood, and *there is* no breath in them.

18 They *are* vanity, the work of errors: in the time of their visitation they shall perish.

19 The portion of Jacob *is* not like them; for he *is* the former of all things: and *Israel is* the rod of his inheritance: the LORD of hosts *is* his name.

God's Tool

20 Thou *art* my battle axe *and* weapons of war: for with thee will I break in pieces the nations, and with thee will I destroy kingdoms;

21 And with thee will I break in pieces the horse and his rider; and with thee will I break in pieces the chariot and his rider;

22 With thee also will I break in pieces man and woman; and with thee will I break in pieces old and young; and with thee will I break in pieces the young man and the maid;

23 I will also break in pieces with thee the shepherd and his flock; and with thee will I break in pieces the husbandman and his yoke of oxen; and with thee will I break in pieces captains and rulers.

24 And I will render unto Babylon and to all the inhabitants of Chaldea all their evil that they have done in Zion in your sight, saith the LORD.

25 Behold, I *am* against thee, O destroying mountain, saith the LORD, which destroyest all the earth: and I will stretch out mine hand upon thee, and roll thee down from the rocks, and will make thee a burnt mountain.

26 And they shall not take of thee a stone for a corner, nor a stone for foundations; but thou shalt be desolate for ever, saith the LORD.

27 Set ye up a standard in the land, blow the trumpet among the nations, prepare the nations against her, call together against her the kingdoms of Ararat, Minni, and Ashchenaz; appoint a captain against her; cause the horses to come up as the rough caterpillers.

28 Prepare against her the nations with the kings of the Medes, the captains thereof, and all the rulers thereof, and all the land of his dominion.

29 And the land shall tremble and sorrow: for every purpose of the LORD shall be performed against Babylon, to make the land of Babylon a desolation without an inhabitant.

30 The mighty men of Babylon have forborn to fight, they have remained in *their* holds: their might hath failed; they became as women: they have burned her dwellingplaces; her bars are broken.

31 One post shall run to meet another, and one messenger to meet another, to shew the king of Babylon that his city is taken at *one* end,

32 And that the passages are stopped, and the reeds they have burned with fire, and the men of war are affrighted.

33 For thus saith the LORD of hosts, the God of Israel; The daughter of Babylon *is* like a threshingfloor, *it is* time to thresh her: yet a little while, and the time of her harvest shall come.

34 Nebuchadrezzar the king of Babylon hath devoured me, he hath crushed me, he hath made me an empty vessel, he hath swallowed me up like a dragon, he hath filled his belly with my delicates, he hath cast me out.

35 The violence done to me and to my flesh *be* upon Babylon, shall the inhabitant of Zion say; and my blood upon the inhabitants of Chaldea, shall Jerusalem say.

God Will Rescue Israel

36 Therefore thus saith the LORD; Behold, I will plead thy cause, and take vengeance for thee; and I will dry up her sea, and make her springs dry.

37 And Babylon shall become heaps, a dwellingplace for dragons, an astonishment, and an hissing, without an inhabitant.

38 They shall roar together like lions: they shall yell as lions' whelps.

39 In their heat I will make their feasts, and I will make them drunken, that they may rejoice, and sleep a perpetual sleep, and not wake, saith the LORD.

40 I will bring them down like lambs to the slaughter, like rams with he goats.

41 How is Sheshach taken! and how is the praise of the whole earth surprised! how is Babylon become an astonishment among the nations!

Cross references (center column)

16 Ps. 135:7; Jer. 10:13
17 Jer. 10:14; 50:2
18 Jer. 10:15
19 Jer. 10:16
20 Isa. 10:5, 15; Jer. 50:23
22 2 Chr. 36:17
24 Jer. 50:15, 29
25 Isa. 13:2; Zech. 4:7; Rev. 8:8
26 Jer. 50:40
27 Isa. 13:2; Jer. 25:14; 50:41
28 Jer. 51:11
29 Jer. 50:13, 39, 40; 51:43
30 Isa. 19:16; Jer. 48:41; 50:37; Lam. 2:9; Amos 1:5; Nah. 3:13
31 Jer. 50:24
32 Jer. 50:38
33 Isa. 17:5; 21:10; 41:15; Hos. 6:11; Joel 3:13; Amos 1:3; Mic. 4:13; Hab. 3:12; Rev. 14:15, 18
34 Jer. 50:17
36 Jer. 50:34, 38
37 Isa. 13:22; Jer. 25:9, 18; 50:39; Rev. 18:2
39 Jer. 51:5, 7
41 Isa. 13:19; Jer. 25:26; 49:25; Dan. 4:30

42 The sea is come up upon Babylon: she is covered with the multitude of the waves thereof.

43 Her cities are a desolation, a dry land, and a wilderness, a land wherein no man dwelleth, neither doth *any* son of man pass thereby.

44 And I will punish Bel in Babylon, and I will bring forth out of his mouth that which he hath swallowed up: and the nations shall not flow together any more unto him: yea, the wall of Babylon shall fall.

45 My people, go ye out of the midst of her, and deliver ye every man his soul from the fierce anger of the LORD.

46 And lest your heart faint, and ye fear for the rumour that shall be heard in the land; a rumour shall both come *one* year, and after that in *another* year *shall come* a rumour, and violence in the land, ruler against ruler.

47 Therefore, behold, the days come, that I will do judgment upon the graven images of Babylon: and her whole land shall be confounded, and all her slain shall fall in the midst of her.

48 Then the heaven and the earth, and all that *is* therein, shall sing for Babylon: for the spoilers shall come unto her from the north, saith the LORD.

49 As Babylon *hath caused* the slain of Israel to fall, so at Babylon shall fall the slain of all the earth.

God Speaks to Jews in Babylon

50 Ye that have escaped the sword, go away, stand not still: remember the LORD afar off, and let Jerusalem come into your mind.

51 We are confounded, because we have heard reproach: shame hath covered our faces: for strangers are come into the sanctuaries of the LORD's house.

52 Wherefore, behold, the days come, saith the LORD, that I will do judgment upon her graven images: and through all her land the wounded shall groan.

53 Though Babylon should mount up to heaven, and though she should fortify the height of her strength, *yet* from me shall spoilers come unto her, saith the LORD.

54 A sound of a cry *cometh* from Babylon, and great destruction from the land of the Chaldeans:

55 Because the LORD hath spoiled Babylon, and destroyed out of her the great voice; when her waves do roar like great waters, a noise of their voice is uttered:

56 Because the spoiler is come upon her, *even* upon Babylon, and her mighty men are

taken, every one of their bows is broken: for the LORD God of recompences shall surely requite.

57 And I will make drunk her princes, and her wise *men*, her captains, and her rulers, and her mighty men: and they shall sleep a perpetual sleep, and not wake, saith the King, whose name *is* the LORD of hosts.

58 Thus saith the LORD of hosts; The broad walls of Babylon shall be utterly broken, and her high gates shall be burned with fire; and the people shall labour in vain, and the folk in the fire, and they shall be weary.

59 The word which Jeremiah the prophet commanded Seraiah the son of Neriah, the son of Maaseiah, when he went with Zedekiah the king of Judah into Babylon in the fourth year of his reign. And *this* Seraiah *was* a quiet prince.

60 So Jeremiah wrote in a book all the evil that should come upon Babylon, *even* all these words that are written against Babylon.

61 And Jeremiah said to Seraiah, When thou comest to Babylon, and shalt see, and shalt read all these words;

62 Then shalt thou say, O LORD, thou hast spoken against this place, to cut it off, that none shall remain in it, neither man nor beast, but that it shall be desolate for ever.

63 And it shall be, when thou hast made an end of reading this book, *that* thou shalt bind a stone to it, and cast it into the midst of Euphrates:

64 And thou shalt say, Thus shall Babylon sink, and shall not rise from the evil that I will bring upon her: and they shall be weary. Thus far *are* the words of Jeremiah.

CHAPTER 52
The Reign of Zedekiah

1 Zedekiah *was* one and twenty years old when he began to reign, and he reigned eleven years in Jerusalem. And his mother's name *was* Hamutal the daughter of Jeremiah of Libnah.

2 And he did *that which was* evil in the eyes of the LORD, according to all that Jehoiakim had done.

3 For through the anger of the LORD it came to pass in Jerusalem and Judah, till he had cast them out from his presence, that Zedekiah rebelled against the king of Babylon.

The Fall of Jerusalem

4 And it came to pass in the ninth year of his reign, in the tenth month, in the tenth

Cross references (center column)

42 Isa. 8:7, 8
43 Jer. 50:39, 40; 51:29
44 Isa. 46:1; Jer. 50:2; 51:58
45 Jer. 50:8; 51:6; Rev. 18:4
46 2Kgs. 19:7
47 Jer. 50:2; 51:52
48 Isa. 44:23; 49:13; Jer. 50:3, 41; Rev. 18:20
50 Jer. 44:28
51 Ps. 44:15, 16; 79:4
52 Jer. 51:47
53 Jer. 49:16; Amos 9:2; Obad. 1:4
54 Jer. 50:22
56 Ps. 94:1; Jer. 50:29; 51:24
57 Jer. 46:18; 48:15; 51:39
58 Jer. 51:44; Hab. 2:13
62 Jer. 50:3, 39; 51:29
63 Rev. 18:21
64 2Kgs. 24:18; Jer. 51:58
4 2Kgs. 25:1-27; Jer. 39:1; Zech. 8:19

day of the month, *that* Nebuchadrezzar king of Babylon came, he and all his army, against Jerusalem, and pitched against it, and built forts against it round about.

5 So the city was besieged unto the eleventh year of king Zedekiah.

6 And in the fourth month, in the ninth *day* of the month, the famine was sore in the city, so that there was no bread for the people of the land.

7 Then the city was broken up, and all the men of war fled, and went forth out of the city by night by the way of the gate between the two walls, which *was* by the king's garden; (now the Chaldeans *were* by the city round about:) and they went by the way of the plain.

8 But the army of the Chaldeans pursued after the king, and overtook Zedekiah in the plains of Jericho; and all his army was scattered from him.

9 Then they took the king, and carried him up unto the king of Babylon to Riblah in the land of Hamath; where he gave judgment upon him.

10 And the king of Babylon slew the sons of Zedekiah before his eyes: he slew also all the princes of Judah in Riblah.

11 Then he put out the eyes of Zedekiah; and the king of Babylon bound him in chains, and carried him to Babylon, and put him in prison till the day of his death.

The Destruction of the Temple

12 Now in the fifth month, in the tenth *day* of the month, which *was* the nineteenth year of Nebuchadrezzar king of Babylon, came Nebuzaradan, captain of the guard, *which* served the king of Babylon, into Jerusalem,

13 And burned the house of the LORD, and the king's house; and all the houses of Jerusalem, and all the houses of the great *men*, burned he with fire:

14 And all the army of the Chaldeans, that *were* with the captain of the guard, brake down all the walls of Jerusalem round about.

15 Then Nebuzaradan the captain of the guard carried away captive *certain* of the poor of the people, and the residue of the people that remained in the city, and those that fell away, that fell to the king of Babylon, and the rest of the multitude.

16 But Nebuzaradan the captain of the guard left *certain* of the poor of the land for vinedressers and for husbandmen.

17 Also the pillars of brass that *were* in the house of the LORD, and the bases, and the brasen sea that *was* in the house of the LORD, the Chaldeans brake, and carried all the brass of them to Babylon.

18 The caldrons also, and the shovels, and the snuffers, and the bowls, and the spoons, and all the vessels of brass wherewith they ministered, took they away.

19 And the basons, and the firepans, and the bowls, and the caldrons, and the candlesticks, and the spoons, and the cups; *that* which *was* of gold *in* gold, and *that* which *was* of silver *in* silver, took the captain of the guard away.

20 The two pillars, one sea, and twelve brasen bulls that *were* under the bases, which king Solomon had made in the house of the LORD: the brass of all these vessels was without weight.

21 And *concerning* the pillars, the height of one pillar *was* eighteen cubits; and a fillet of twelve cubits did compass it; and the thickness thereof *was* four fingers: *it was* hollow.

22 And a chapiter of brass *was* upon it; and the height of one chapiter *was* five cubits, with network and pomegranates upon the chapiters round about, all *of* brass. The second pillar also and the pomegranates *were* like unto these.

23 And there were ninety and six pomegranates on a side; *and* all the pomegranates upon the network *were* an hundred round about.

The Deportation

24 And the captain of the guard took Seraiah the chief priest, and Zephaniah the second priest, and the three keepers of the door:

25 He took also out of the city a eunuch, which had the charge of the men of war; and seven men of them that were near the king's person, which were found in the city; and the principal scribe of the host, who mustered the people of the land; and threescore men of the people of the land, that were found in the midst of the city.

26 So Nebuzaradan the captain of the guard took them, and brought them to the king of Babylon to Riblah.

27 And the king of Babylon smote them, and put them to death in Riblah in the land of Hamath. Thus Judah was carried away captive out of his own land.

28 This *is* the people whom Nebuchadrezzar carried away captive: in the seventh year three thousand Jews and three and twenty:

29 In the eighteenth year of Nebuchadrez-

Cross references

9 Jer. 32:4

10 Ezek. 12:13

12 Jer. 39:9; 52:29; Zech. 7:5; 8:19

15 Jer. 39:9

17 1Kgs. 7:15, 23, 27, 50; Jer. 27:19

18 Ex. 27:3; 2Kgs. 25:14-16

20 1Kgs. 7:47

21 1Kgs. 7:15; 2Kgs. 25:17; 2Chr. 3:15

23 1Kgs. 7:20

24 2Kgs. 25:18; Jer. 21:1; 29:25

28 2Kgs. 24:2, 12, 14

29 Jer. 39:9; 52:12

zar he carried away captive from Jerusalem eight hundred thirty and two persons:

30 In the three and twentieth year of Nebuchadrezzar Nebuzaradan the captain of the guard carried away captive of the Jews seven hundred forty and five persons: all the persons *were* four thousand and six hundred.

31 And it came to pass in the seven and thirtieth year of the captivity of Jehoiachin king of Judah, in the twelfth month, in the five and twentieth *day* of the month, *that* Evil-merodach king of Babylon in the *first*

31 Gen. 40:13, 20; 2Kgs. 25:27-30

33 2Sam. 9:13

year of his reign lifted up the head of Jehoiachin king of Judah, and brought him forth out of prison,

32 And spake kindly unto him, and set his throne above the throne of the kings that *were* with him in Babylon,

33 And changed his prison garments: and he did continually eat bread before him all the days of his life.

34 And *for* his diet, there was a continual diet given him of the king of Babylon, every day a portion until the day of his death, all the days of his life.

Lamentations

Lamentations was originally part of the book of Jeremiah. It was later separated because it was read publicly at one of the feasts of Israel and included in the Five Megilloth (or scrolls). Lamentations is read each year at Tisha B'av, a fast commemorating the destruction of the temple in Jerusalem in 586 B.C. Though the text of Lamentations does not specifically identify the author of the book, the mournful style and content leave little doubt that Jeremiah, "the weeping prophet," is the author.

Grieving over the fall of Jerusalem and the destruction of Solomon's four hundred-year-old temple, Jeremiah was inspired to pen these deeply moving poems that lament the end of an era. Jeremiah's lamentations also express the love and sorrow of the Lord for His people, whose wickedness and departure from truth brought on these tragic circumstances. But Jeremiah's melancholy tone is not one of hopeless despair. Because of the Lord's promises to Moses and David, the aged prophet is confident that, if Israel truly repents and returns to God, there will be mercy, forgiveness, and restoration. God "will not cast off for ever" (Lam. 3:31).

Author
Jeremiah
Date
586 B.C.
Key Truth
Mourning
Historic Time
The Fall of Jerusalem
Key Verse
3:22–23
. . . his compassions fail not. . . . great is thy faithfulness.

Lamentations consists of five poems. The first four poems are written in an acrostic style in conjunction with the Hebrew alphabet. In these acrostic poems, each of the twenty-two letters of the Hebrew alphabet is used to begin a stanza of the poem. (In the third poem, each letter begins three consecutive stanzas.) This acrostic format was a literary device of that time used mainly to make memorization simpler.

Standing amid the smoldering ruins of the old temple, Jeremiah utters his plaintive cry for God's mercy and blessing. Judah's transgressions have brought on not only the ruthless invasion by the Babylonians, but the righteous vengeance of God. Amid the darkness of despair, hope yet shines, for God's mercies and compassion never fail. As the venerable prophet says in Lamentations 3:23, "They are new every morning: great is thy faithfulness."

Lamentations contains only 4 prophecies, accounting for no more than 8 verses out of the book's 154 total verses (5%).

5%
Prophecy

---

700 B.C. 675 B.C. 650 B.C. 625 B.C. 600 B.C. 575 B.C. 550 B.C. 525 B.C. 500

740-680
Ministry of Isaiah

627-580
Ministry of Jeremiah

592-570
Ministry of Ezekiel

538
Cyrus of Persia decrees return of Jews

640-609
Josiah is king of Judah

605-536
Babylonian Captivity; Ministry of Daniel

605
First captivity; Daniel taken to Babylon

697-642
Manasseh is king of Judah

597
Second captivity; Ezekiel taken to Babylon

586
Fall of Jerusalem; Jeremiah taken to Egypt; Book of Lamentations

CHAPTER 1

The Sorrows of Jerusalem

1 How doth the city sit solitary, *that was* full of people! *how* is she become as a widow! she *that was* great among the nations, *and* princess among the provinces, *how* is she become tributary!

2 She weepeth sore in the night, and her tears *are* on her cheeks: among all her lovers she hath none to comfort *her*: all her friends have dealt treacherously with her, they are become her enemies.

3 Judah is gone into captivity because of affliction, and because of great servitude: she dwelleth among the heathen, she findeth no rest: all her persecutors overtook her between the straits.

4 The ways of Zion do mourn, because none come to the solemn feasts: all her gates are desolate: her priests sigh, her virgins are afflicted, and she *is* in bitterness.

5 Her adversaries are the chief, her enemies prosper; for the LORD hath afflicted her for the multitude of her transgressions: her children are gone into captivity before the enemy.

6 And from the daughter of Zion all her beauty is departed: her princes are become like harts *that* find no pasture, and they are gone without strength before the pursuer.

7 Jerusalem remembered in the days of her affliction and of her miseries all her pleasant things that she had in the days of old, when her people fell into the hand of the enemy, and none did help her: the adversaries saw her, *and* did mock at her sabbaths.

8 Jerusalem hath grievously sinned; therefore she is removed: all that honoured her despise her, because they have seen her nakedness: yea, she sigheth, and turneth backward.

9 Her filthiness *is* in her skirts; she remembereth not her last end; therefore she came down wonderfully: she had no comforter. O LORD, behold my affliction: for the enemy hath magnified *himself*.

10 The adversary hath spread out his hand upon all her pleasant things: for she hath seen *that* the heathen entered into her sanctuary, whom thou didst command *that* they should not enter into thy congregation.

11 All her people sigh, they seek bread; they have given their pleasant things for meat to relieve the soul: see, O LORD, and consider; for I am become vile.

12 *Is it* nothing to you, all ye that pass by? behold, and see if there be any sorrow like unto my sorrow, which is done unto me, wherewith the LORD hath afflicted *me* in the day of his fierce anger.

13 From above hath he sent fire into my bones, and it prevaileth against them: he hath spread a net for my feet, he hath turned me back: he hath made me desolate *and* faint all the day.

14 The yoke of my transgressions is bound by his hand: they are wreathed, *and* come

Cross references

1 Ezra 4:20; Isa. 47:7, 8
2 Job 7:3; Ps. 6:6; Jer. 4:30; 13:17; 30:14; Lam. 1:9, 16, 17, 21
3 Deut. 28:64, 65; Jer. 52:27; Lam. 2:9
5 Deut. 28:43, 44; Jer. 30:14, 15; Dan. 9:7, 16
7 Lam. 1:10
8 1 Kgs. 8:46; Jer. 13:22, 26; Ezek. 16:37; 23:29; Hos. 2:10
9 Deut. 32:29; Isa. 47:7; Lam. 1:2, 17, 21
10 Deut. 23:3; Neh. 13:1; Jer. 51:51; Lam. 1:7
11 Jer. 38:9; 52:6; Lam. 2:12; 4:4
12 Dan. 9:12
13 Ezek. 12:13; 17:20
14 Deut. 28:48

1:1–3 Here the prophet uses personification, picturing Jerusalem as the unfaithful wife of the Lord after her destruction and ruin in 586 B.C. The passage is a picture of a loose woman who has had sexual relations with many different men, as Judah had gone after the many different gods from the surrounding nations. When her beauty faded, no one would have anything to do with her. Though Judah once supported herself by her philandering, she has now become like a widow who has the status of a slave and is not able to support herself.

1:4 Zion. Originally referred to the hill in Jerusalem where David built his city (2 Sam. 5:7; 1 Kgs. 8:1). Later, Mount Moriah, where the temple was built, came to be known as Zion (2 Chr. 5:2, 7; Ps. 20:2; 48:2; 78:68–69). As time progressed, the word "Zion" began to be applied to the entire city of Jerusalem, emphasizing that it was there that the God of Israel dwelled. The word "Zion" is often used to emphasize the dwelling place of God, which was supposed to be in Jerusalem. Thus, in this setting, Zion, the place where God should be dwelling is empty and still. No activity that would evidence the presence of the Lord occurs. This is the reason for the lament.

1:7 the adversaries saw her, and did mock at her sabbaths. Even though Judah was at one time popular among the nations, when the time of her trouble came during the Babylonian invasion of 586 B.C., none of her "lovers" came to her rescue. Not only did her former "lovers" not help her in time of need, but also they mocked and made fun of her ways, in this case, her religious ways which were designed by God to make her different from all the nations around her (Ex. 19:6; Lev. 11:44–45; Deut. 7:6).

1:12 behold, and see if there be any sorrow like unto my sorrow. This personification asks everyone that passes by to compare Judah's sorrow with that of any other. She seeks compassion from strangers, something that is normally sought from friends and family. The mention of God's "fierce anger" is used of the Babylonian judgment of Judah (586 B.C.), but in other contexts it refers to the future time of the seven-year Tribulation (Joel 2:1–11; Zeph. 1:14–18).

up upon my neck: he hath made my strength to fall, the Lord hath delivered me into *their* hands, *from whom* I am not able to rise up.

15 The Lord hath trodden under foot all my mighty *men* in the midst of me: he hath called an assembly against me to crush my young men: the Lord hath trodden the virgin, the daughter of Judah, *as* in a winepress.

16 For these *things* I weep; mine eye, mine eye runneth down with water, because the comforter that should relieve my soul is far from me: my children are desolate, because the enemy prevailed.

17 Zion spreadeth forth her hands, *and there is* none to comfort her: the LORD hath commanded concerning Jacob, *that* his adversaries *should be* round about him: Jerusalem is as a menstruous woman among them.

18 The LORD is righteous; for I have rebelled against his commandment: hear, I pray you, all people, and behold my sorrow: my virgins and my young men are gone into captivity.

19 I called for my lovers, *but* they deceived me: my priests and mine elders gave up the ghost in the city, while they sought their meat to relieve their souls.

20 Behold, O LORD; for I *am* in distress: my bowels are troubled; mine heart is turned within me; for I have grievously rebelled: abroad the sword bereaveth, at home *there is* as death.

21 They have heard that I sigh: *there is* none to comfort me: all mine enemies have heard of my trouble; they are glad that thou hast done *it*: thou wilt bring the day *that* thou hast called, and they shall be like unto me.

22 Let all their wickedness come before thee; and do unto them, as thou hast done unto me for all my transgressions: for my sighs *are* many, and my heart *is* faint.

15 Isa. 63:3; Rev. 14:19, 20; 19:15

16 Jer. 13:17; 14:17; Lam. 1:2, 9; 2:18

17 Jer. 4:31; Lam. 1:2, 9

18 1Sam. 12:14, 15; Neh. 9:33; Dan. 9:7, 14

19 Lam. 1:2, 11; Jer. 30:14

20 Deut. 32:25; Job 30:27; Isa. 16:11; Jer. 4:19; 48:36; Lam. 2:11; Ezek. 7:15; Hos. 11:8

21 Lam. 1:2

22 2Sam. 1:19; 1Chr. 28:2; Ps. 99:5; 109:15; 132:7; Lam. 5:17; Matt. 11:23

2 Ps. 89:39; Lam. 2:17; 21; 3:43

3 Ps. 74:11; 89:46

4 Isa. 63:10; Lam. 2:5; Ezek. 24:25

5 2Kgs. 25:9; Lam. 2:4; Jer. 30:14; 52:13

6 Ps. 80:12; 89:40; Isa. 1:8; 5:5; Lam. 1:4; Zeph. 3:18

7 Ps. 74:4

CHAPTER 2
God Punished Zion

1 How hath the Lord covered the daughter of Zion with a cloud in his anger, *and* cast down from heaven unto the earth the beauty of Israel, and remembered not his footstool in the day of his anger!

2 The Lord hath swallowed up all the habitations of Jacob, and hath not pitied: he hath thrown down in his wrath the strong holds of the daughter of Judah; he hath brought *them* down to the ground: he hath polluted the kingdom and the princes thereof.

3 He hath cut off in *his* fierce anger all the horn of Israel: he hath drawn back his right hand from before the enemy, and he burned against Jacob like a flaming fire, *which* devoureth round about.

4 He hath bent his bow like an enemy: he stood with his right hand as an adversary, and slew all *that were* pleasant to the eye in the tabernacle of the daughter of Zion: he poured out his fury like fire.

5 The Lord was as an enemy: he hath swallowed up Israel, he hath swallowed up all her palaces: he hath destroyed his strong holds, and hath increased in the daughter of Judah mourning and lamentation.

6 And he hath violently taken away his tabernacle, as *if it were of* a garden: he hath destroyed his places of the assembly: the LORD hath caused the solemn feasts and sabbaths to be forgotten in Zion, and hath despised in the indignation of his anger the king and the priest.

7 The Lord hath cast off his altar, he hath abhorred his sanctuary, he hath given up into the hand of the enemy the walls of her palaces; they have made a noise in the house of the LORD, as in the day of a solemn feast.

1:16–17 Jerusalem is as a menstruous woman among them. This graphic picture explains why no one has come to comfort this tormented woman. The Lord would not comfort Judah because, like a menstruous woman, she is unclean according to the Mosaic Law, and anyone that touches one who is defiled becomes defiled themselves (Lev. 15:19–24). Just as there would be no appeal for intimacy with a woman in this condition, the nations surrounding Israel had no desire to have friendly relations with Judah.

2:1–2 his footstool. Jeremiah's lament continues as he recites further reasons for Judah's demise at the hands of the Babylonians. The reference to the footstool alludes to

the ark of the covenant, around which the Lord's special presence occasionally appeared in the form of His glory cloud (i.e., Shechinah glory [1 Sam. 4:4; 2 Sam. 6:2; 1 Chr. 28:2; Ps. 80:1; 99:1, 5; 132:7]).

2:6–7 he hath violently taken away his tabernacle. The word "tabernacle" means "booth" or "hut" and here is used as a reference to God's temple. The Hebrew word for "tabernacle" is spelled similarly to the Hebrew word for "violently taken away." The relationship of these words paints the picture of God tearing down His temple in the same way a farmer would tear down a temporary structure used to provide shade during harvest time.

8 The LORD hath purposed to destroy the wall of the daughter of Zion: he hath stretched out a line, he hath not withdrawn his hand from destroying: therefore he made the rampart and the wall to lament; they languished together.

9 Her gates are sunk into the ground; he hath destroyed and broken her bars: her king and her princes *are* among the Gentiles: the law *is no more*; her prophets also find no vision from the LORD.

10 The elders of the daughter of Zion sit upon the ground, *and* keep silence: they have cast up dust upon their heads; they have girded themselves with sackcloth: the virgins of Jerusalem hang down their heads to the ground.

11 Mine eyes do fail with tears, my bowels are troubled, my liver is poured upon the earth, for the destruction of the daughter of my people; because the children and the sucklings swoon in the streets of the city.

12 They say to their mothers, Where *is* corn and wine? when they swooned as the wounded in the streets of the city, when their soul was poured out into their mothers' bosom.

13 What thing shall I take to witness for thee? what thing shall I liken to thee, O daughter of Jerusalem? what shall I equal to thee, that I may comfort thee, O virgin daughter of Zion? for thy breach *is* great like the sea: who can heal thee?

14 Thy prophets have seen vain and foolish things for thee: and they have not discovered thine iniquity, to turn away thy captivity; but have seen for thee false burdens and causes of banishment.

15 All that pass by clap *their* hands at thee; they hiss and wag their head at the daughter of Jerusalem, *saying, Is* this the city that *men* call The perfection of beauty, The joy of the whole earth?

16 All thine enemies have opened their mouth against thee: they hiss and gnash the teeth: they say, We have swallowed *her* up: certainly this *is* the day that we looked for; we have found, we have seen *it*.

17 The LORD hath done *that* which he had devised; he hath fulfilled his word that he had commanded in the days of old: he hath thrown down, and hath not pitied: and he hath caused *thine* enemy to rejoice over

thee, he hath set up the horn of thine adversaries.

18 Their heart cried unto the Lord, O wall of the daughter of Zion, let tears run down like a river day and night: give thyself no rest; let not the apple of thine eye cease.

19 Arise, cry out in the night: in the beginning of the watches pour out thine heart like water before the face of the Lord: lift up thy hands toward him for the life of thy young children, that faint for hunger in the top of every street.

20 Behold, O LORD, and consider to whom thou hast done this. Shall the women eat their fruit, *and* children of a span long? shall the priest and the prophet be slain in the sanctuary of the Lord?

21 The young and the old lie on the ground in the streets: my virgins and my young men are fallen by the sword; thou hast slain *them* in the day of thine anger; thou hast killed, *and* not pitied.

22 Thou hast called as in a solemn day my terrors round about, so that in the day of the LORD's anger none escaped nor remained: those that I have swaddled and brought up hath mine enemy consumed.

CHAPTER 3
Repentance and Hope

1 I *am* the man *that* hath seen affliction by the rod of his wrath.

2 He hath led me, and brought *me into* darkness, but not *into* light.

3 Surely against me is he turned; he turneth his hand *against me* all the day.

4 My flesh and my skin hath he made old; he hath broken my bones.

5 He hath builded against me, and compassed *me* with gall and travail.

6 He hath set me in dark places, as *they that be* dead of old.

7 He hath hedged me about, that I cannot get out: he hath made my chain heavy.

8 Also when I cry and shout, he shutteth out my prayer.

9 He hath inclosed my ways with hewn stone, he hath made my paths crooked.

10 He *was* unto me *as* a bear lying in wait, *and as* a lion in secret places.

11 He hath turned aside my ways, and pulled me in pieces: he hath made me desolate.

---

8 2Kgs. 21:13; Isa. 34:11

9 Deut. 28:36; 2Kgs. 24:15; 25:7; Jer. 51:30

10 Isa. 3:26; 15:3; Ezek. 7:18; 27:31

11 Ps. 6:7; 22:14

13 Lam. 1:12; Dan. 9:12

14 Isa. 58:1; Jer. 2:8; 5:31; 14:14; 23:16; 27:14; 29:8, 9; Ezek. 13:2

15 1Kgs. 9:8; 2Kgs. 19:21; Ps. 44:14; 48:2; 50:2; Jer. 18:16; Ezek. 25:6; Nah. 3:19

16 Job 16:9, 10; Ps. 22:13; 35:21; 56:2; Lam. 3:46

17 Lev. 26:16; Deut. 28:15; Ps. 38:16; 89:42; Lam. 2:2

18 Jer. 14:17; Lam. 1:16; 2:8

19 Ps. 62:8; 119:147; Isa. 51:20; Lam. 2:11; 4:1; Nah. 3:10

20 Lev. 26:29; Deut. 28:52; Jer. 19:9; Lam. 4:10, 13, 16; Ezek. 5:10

21 2Chr. 36:17; Lam. 3:43

22 Job 16:8; Ps. 31:13

6 Ps. 88:5, 6; 143:3

7 Job 3:23

8 Job 30:20; Ps. 22:2

11 Hos. 6:1

3:1–3 I am the man. Jeremiah refers to himself in the singular, and later in the chapter the first person changes into the plural (vv. 22, 40–46). At these points the experience of Jeremiah and the nation overlap, and his words become a lament for the nation as a whole.

12 He hath bent his bow, and set me as a mark for the arrow.

13 He hath caused the arrows of his quiver to enter into my reins.

14 I was a derision to all my people; *and* their song all the day.

15 He hath filled me with bitterness, he hath made me drunken with wormwood.

16 He hath also broken my teeth with gravel stones, he hath covered me with ashes.

17 And thou hast removed my soul far off from peace: I forgat prosperity.

18 And I said, My strength and my hope is perished from the LORD:

19 Remembering mine affliction and my misery, the wormwood and the gall.

20 My soul hath *them* still in remembrance, and is humbled in me.

21 This I recall to my mind, therefore have I hope.

22 *It is of* the LORD's mercies that we are not consumed, because his compassions fail not.

23 *They are* new every morning: great *is* thy faithfulness.

24 The LORD *is* my portion, saith my soul; therefore will I hope in him.

25 The LORD *is* good unto them that wait for him, to the soul *that* seeketh him.

26 *It is* good that *a man* should both hope and quietly wait for the salvation of the LORD.

27 *It is* good for a man that he bear the yoke in his youth.

28 He sitteth alone and keepeth silence, because he hath borne *it* upon him.

29 He putteth his mouth in the dust; if so be there may be hope.

30 He giveth *his* cheek to him that smiteth him: he is filled full with reproach.

31 For the Lord will not cast off for ever:

32 But though he cause grief, yet will he have compassion according to the multitude of his mercies.

33 For he doth not afflict willingly nor grieve the children of men.

34 To crush under his feet all the prisoners of the earth,

35 To turn aside the right of a man before the face of the most High,

36 To subvert a man in his cause, the Lord approveth not.

37 Who *is* he *that* saith, and it cometh to pass, *when* the Lord commandeth *it* not?

38 Out of the mouth of the most High proceedeth not evil and good?

39 Wherefore doth a living man complain, a man for the punishment of his sins?

40 Let us search and try our ways, and turn again to the LORD.

41 Let us lift up our heart with *our* hands unto God in the heavens.

42 We have transgressed and have rebelled: thou hast not pardoned.

43 Thou hast covered with anger, and persecuted us: thou hast slain, thou hast not pitied.

44 Thou hast covered thyself with a cloud, that *our* prayer should not pass through.

45 Thou hast made us *as* the offscouring and refuse in the midst of the people.

46 All our enemies have opened their mouths against us.

47 Fear and a snare is come upon us, desolation and destruction.

48 Mine eye runneth down with rivers of water for the destruction of the daughter of my people.

49 Mine eye trickleth down, and ceaseth not, without any intermission,

50 Till the LORD look down, and behold from heaven.

51 Mine eye affecteth mine heart because of all the daughters of my city.

52 Mine enemies chased me sore, like a bird, without cause.

53 They have cut off my life in the dungeon, and cast a stone upon me.

54 Waters flowed over mine head; *then* I said, I am cut off.

55 I called upon thy name, O LORD, out of the low dungeon.

56 Thou hast heard my voice: hide not thine ear at my breathing, at my cry.

57 Thou drewest near in the day *that* I called upon thee: thou saidst, Fear not.

58 O Lord, thou hast pleaded the causes of my soul; thou hast redeemed my life.

59 O LORD, thou hast seen my wrong: judge thou my cause.

60 Thou hast seen all their vengeance *and* all their imaginations against me.

Cross references (center column):

12 Ps. 38:2
14 Ps. 69:12; Jer. 20:7
16 Prov. 20:17
18 Ps. 31:22
19 Jer. 9:15
22 Mal. 3:6
23 Isa. 33:2
24 Ps. 16:5; 73:26; 119:57; Jer. 10:16
25 Ps. 130:6; Isa. 30:18; Mic. 7:7
26 Ps. 37:7
27 Ps. 94:12; 119:71
28 Jer. 15:17
30 Isa. 50:6; Matt. 5:39
31 Ps. 94:14
33 Heb. 12:10
36 Hab. 1:13
37 Ps. 33:9
38 Isa. 45:7; Amos 3:6
39 Prov. 19:3; Mic. 7:9
41 Ps. 86:4
42 Dan. 9:5
45 1Cor. 4:13
46 Lam. 2:16
47 Isa. 24:17; 51:19; Jer. 48:43
48 Jer. 4:19; 9:1; 14:17
52 Ps. 35:7, 19; 69:4
53 Jer. 37:16; 38:6, 9, 10
58 Ps. 35:1; 71:23; Jer. 51:36
59 Ps. 9:4; 35:23
60 Jer. 11:19

3:31 the Lord will not cast off for ever. Out of Jeremiah's lament comes a ray of hope. The Lord will not "reject" His promises made to Judah.

3:45 offscouring. This word refers to something that has been rejected and is unfit for use (1 Cor. 4:13). Judah has been rejected and treated like refuse by her neighboring nations.

61 Thou hast heard their reproach, O LORD, *and* all their imaginations against me;
62 The lips of those that rose up against me, and their device against me all the day.
63 Behold their sitting down, and their rising up; I *am* their musick.
64 Render unto them a recompence, O LORD, according to the work of their hands.
65 Give them sorrow of heart, thy curse unto them.
66 Persecute and destroy them in anger from under the heavens of the LORD.

CHAPTER 4
The Results of the Siege

1 How is the gold become dim! how is the most fine gold changed! the stones of the sanctuary are poured out in the top of every street.
2 The precious sons of Zion, comparable to fine gold, how are they esteemed as earthen pitchers, the work of the hands of the potter!
3 Even the sea monsters draw out the breast, they give suck to their young ones: the daughter of my people *is become* cruel, like the ostriches in the wilderness.
4 The tongue of the sucking child cleaveth to the roof of his mouth for thirst: the young children ask bread, *and* no man breaketh *it* unto them.
5 They that did feed delicately are desolate in the streets: they that were brought up in scarlet embrace dunghills.
6 For the punishment of the iniquity of the daughter of my people is greater than the punishment of the sin of Sodom, that was overthrown as in a moment, and no hands stayed on her.
7 Her Nazarites were purer than snow, they were whiter than milk, they were more ruddy in body than rubies, their polishing *was* of sapphire:
8 Their visage is blacker than a coal; they are not known in the streets: their skin cleaveth to their bones; it is withered, it is become like a stick.
9 *They that be* slain with the sword are better than *they that be* slain with hunger: for

these pine away, stricken through for *want of* the fruits of the field.
10 The hands of the pitiful women have sodden their own children: they were their meat in the destruction of the daughter of my people.
11 The LORD hath accomplished his fury; he hath poured out his fierce anger, and hath kindled a fire in Zion, and it hath devoured the foundations thereof.
12 The kings of the earth, and all the inhabitants of the world, would not have believed that the adversary and the enemy should have entered into the gates of Jerusalem.
13 For the sins of her prophets, *and* the iniquities of her priests, that have shed the blood of the just in the midst of her,
14 They have wandered *as* blind *men* in the streets, they have polluted themselves with blood, so that men could not touch their garments.
15 They cried unto them, Depart ye; *it is* unclean; depart, depart, touch not: when they fled away and wandered, they said among the heathen, They shall no more sojourn *there*.
16 The anger of the LORD hath divided them; he will no more regard them: they respected not the persons of the priests, they favoured not the elders.
17 As for us, our eyes as yet failed for our vain help: in our watching we have watched for a nation *that* could not save *us*.
18 They hunt our steps, that we cannot go in our streets: our end is near, our days are fulfilled; for our end is come.
19 Our persecutors are swifter than the eagles of the heaven: they pursued us upon the mountains, they laid wait for us in the wilderness.
20 The breath of our nostrils, the anointed of the LORD, was taken in their pits, of whom we said, Under his shadow we shall live among the heathen.
21 Rejoice and be glad, O daughter of Edom, that dwellest in the land of Uz; the cup also shall pass through unto thee: thou shalt be drunken, and shalt make thyself naked.
22 The punishment of thine iniquity is

---

63 Ps. 139:2
64 Ps. 28:4; Jer. 11:20; 2Tim. 4:14
66 Ps. 8:3
2 Isa. 30:14; Jer. 19:11; 2Cor. 4:7
3 Job 39:14, 16
4 Ps. 22:15; Lam. 2:11, 12
5 Job 24:8
6 Gen. 19:25
8 Ps. 102:5; Lam. 5:10; Joel 2:6; Nah. 2:10
10 Deut. 28:57; 2Kgs. 6:29; Isa. 49:15; Lam. 2:20
11 Deut. 32:22; Jer. 7:20; 21:14
13 Jer. 5:31; 6:13; 14:14; 23:11, 21; Ezek. 22:26, 28; Zeph. 3:4; Matt. 23:31, 37
14 Num. 19:16; Jer. 2:34
15 Lev. 13:45
16 Lam. 5:12
17 2Kgs. 24:7; Isa. 20:5; 30:6, 7; Jer. 37:7; Ezek. 29:16
18 2Kgs. 25:4, 5; Ezek. 7:2, 3, 6; Amos 8:2
19 Deut. 28:49; Jer. 4:13
20 Jer. 52:9
21 Jer. 25:15, 16, 21
22 Isa. 40:2; Lam. 2:15

4:21–22 Jeremiah draws a contrast between Israel and her Gentile enemy Edom. The phrase "daughter of Edom" is used in sarcastic contrast with "daughter of Zion" both here and in Lamentations 2:1. The "cup of wrath" from which Judah is now drinking (Lam. 1:21–22) would one day pass from Judah to Edom. Jeremiah assures the "daughter of Zion" that her punishment is accomplished. Assurance of this type certainly brought relief and hope to Judah. Having finished dealing with His people, one day the Lord would turn His judgment upon Edom. Obadiah 1:5 records the destruction that fell upon Edom a few decades later.

accomplished, O daughter of Zion; he will no more carry thee away into captivity: he will visit thine iniquity, O daughter of Edom; he will discover thy sins.

CHAPTER 5
A Plea for Mercy

1 Remember, O Lord, what is come upon us: consider, and behold our reproach.
2 Our inheritance is turned to strangers, our houses to aliens.
3 We are orphans and fatherless, our mothers *are* as widows.
4 We have drunken our water for money; our wood is sold unto us.
5 Our necks *are* under persecution: we labour, *and* have no rest.
6 We have given the hand *to* the Egyptians, *and to* the Assyrians, to be satisfied with bread.
7 Our fathers have sinned, *and are* not; and we have borne their iniquities.
8 Servants have ruled over us: *there is* none that doth deliver *us* out of their hand.
9 We gat our bread with *the peril of* our lives because of the sword of the wilderness.

10 Our skin was black like an oven because of the terrible famine.
11 They ravished the women in Zion, *and* the maids in the cities of Judah.
12 Princes are hanged up by their hand: the faces of elders were not honoured.
13 They took the young men to grind, and the children fell under the wood.
14 The elders have ceased from the gate, the young men from their musick.
15 The joy of our heart is ceased; our dance is turned into mourning.
16 The crown is fallen *from* our head: woe unto us, that we have sinned!
17 For this our heart is faint; for these *things* our eyes are dim.
18 Because of the mountain of Zion, which is desolate, the foxes walk upon it.
19 Thou, O Lord, remainest for ever; thy throne from generation to generation.
20 Wherefore dost thou forget us for ever, *and* forsake us so long time?
21 Turn thou us unto thee, O Lord, and we shall be turned; renew our days as of old.
22 But thou hast utterly rejected us; thou art very wroth against us.

5 Deut. 28:48; Jer. 28:14
6 Jer. 50:15
7 Gen. 42:13; Jer. 31:29; Ezek. 18:2; Zech. 1:5
8 Neh. 5:15
10 Job 30:30; Ps. 119:83; Lam. 4:8
11 Isa. 13:16; Zech. 14:2
12 Isa. 47:6; Lam. 4:16
13 Judg. 16:21
16 Job 19:9; Ps. 89:39
17 Ps. 6:7; Lam. 1:22; 2:11
19 Ps. 9:7
21 Ps. 80:3, 7, 19; Jer. 31:18

Contrasts between Edom and Israel

EDOM	REFERENCES	ISRAEL	REFERENCES
Now joyful	Psalm 137:7 Lamentations 4:21	Now suffering	Lamentations 4:6, 11, 22 Daniel 9:12
Will be punished	Lamentations 4:21–22; Obadiah 1:1, 10–14; Malachi 1:4	Will be rejoicing	Isaiah 65:18–19; Lamentations 5:21; Zephaniah 3:14–16

Ezekiel

The name Ezekiel means "strength of God" and is a fitting name for a godly man of strong character, particularly in light of the difficulties that Ezekiel would endure during his life and ministry. Ezekiel was a priest who was called into the prophetic ministry at age thirty, some five years after being carried away captive in the second deportation to Babylon in 597 B.C. As a prophet to the exiles, he reminded them of their national sins that brought on their seventy-year captivity, and he reinforced their faith with predictions of the future national restoration. He also prophesied of the still-unfulfilled future glory of the coming Millennial Kingdom. It is believed that Ezekiel spent the rest of his life in Babylon.

Ezekiel's five sections reveal "the glory of the Lord" **1)** manifested to reveal and reprove sin (chaps. 1—8); **2)** withdrawn from the defiled Jerusalem temple (chaps. 9—11); **3)** departed, resulting in desolation and doom (chaps. 12—24); **4)** promised with divine intervention (chaps. 25—39); and **5)** restored in the new temple and the new Holy Land (chaps. 40—48). The key phrase in the book, "son of man" (Ezek. 2:1) is used ninety-three times. Jesus used the terms "Son of man" and "Son of God" to show that He had the characteristics of both deity and humanity.

Of the sixty-six specific forecasts in Ezekiel, about one fourth are classified as typology. Prophecies directly relating to Israel in the End Times begin in chapters 34 and 36. Israel's restoration is shown in chapter 37 in the vision of the "dry bones" that came to life. Chapters 38 and 39 deal with the future invasion of Israel from the North and Israel's victory over "Gog and Magog." The Millennial Temple, Israel's supremacy in the future kingdom, and the new borders of each tribe are all described, concluding with a new name for Jerusalem, *Jehovah-Shammah*, meaning "the Lord is there."

Ezekiel's 1,273 verses include 821 verses of predictions, which amount to 65 percent of the total and the largest amount of predictive prophecy to appear in any Bible book.

Author
Ezekiel

Date
593–571 B.C.

Key Truth
The Glory of the Lord

Historic Time
The Babylonian Captivity

Key Verse
3:17
Son of man, . . . hear the word at my mouth, and give them warning from me.

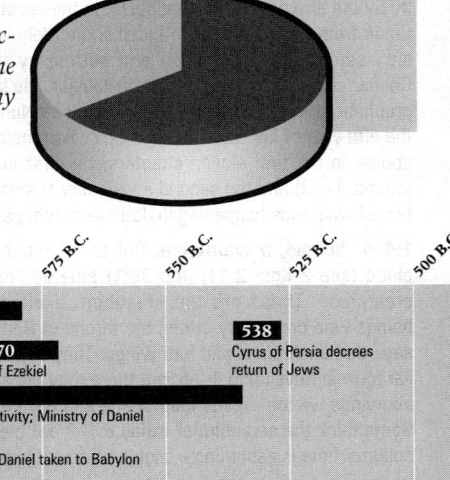

65%
Prophecy

700 B.C.   675 B.C.   650 B.C.   625 B.C.   600 B.C.   575 B.C.   550 B.C.   525 B.C.   500 B.C.

627-580
Ministry of Jeremiah

740-680
Ministry of Isaiah

592-570
Ministry of Ezekiel

538
Cyrus of Persia decrees return of Jews

722
Assyria conquers Israel

640-609
Josiah is king of Judah

605-536
Babylonian Captivity; Ministry of Daniel

605
First captivity; Daniel taken to Babylon

612
Fall of Nineveh

597
Second captivity; Ezekiel taken to Babylon

586
Fall of Jerusalem; Jeremiah taken to Egypt

CHAPTER 1

The First Vision

1 Now it came to pass in the thirtieth year, in the fourth *month*, in the fifth *day* of the month, as I *was* among the captives by the river of Chebar, *that* the heavens were opened, and I saw visions of God.
2 In the fifth *day* of the month, which *was* the fifth year of king Jehoiachin's captivity,
3 The word of the LORD came expressly unto Ezekiel the priest, the son of Buzi, in the land of the Chaldeans by the river Chebar; and the hand of the LORD was there upon him.
4 And I looked, and, behold, a whirlwind came out of the north, a great cloud, and a fire infolding itself, and a brightness *was* about it, and out of the midst thereof as the colour of amber, out of the midst of the fire.

The Four Living Creatures

5 Also out of the midst thereof *came* the likeness of four living creatures. And this *was* their appearance; they had the likeness of a man.
6 And every one had four faces, and every one had four wings.
7 And their feet *were* straight feet; and the sole of their feet *was* like the sole of a calf's foot: and they sparkled like the colour of burnished brass.
8 And *they had* the hands of a man under their wings on their four sides; and they four had their faces and their wings.
9 Their wings *were* joined one to another;

they turned not when they went; they went every one straight forward.
10 As for the likeness of their faces, they four had the face of a man, and the face of a lion, on the right side: and they four had the face of an ox on the left side; they four also had the face of an eagle.
11 Thus *were* their faces: and their wings *were* stretched upward; two *wings* of every one *were* joined one to another, and two covered their bodies.
12 And they went every one straight forward: whither the spirit was to go, they went; *and* they turned not when they went.
13 As for the likeness of the living creatures, their appearance *was* like burning coals of fire, *and* like the appearance of lamps: it went up and down among the living creatures; and the fire was bright, and out of the fire went forth lightning.
14 And the living creatures ran and returned as the appearance of a flash of lightning.

The Wheels

15 Now as I beheld the living creatures, behold one wheel upon the earth by the living creatures, with his four faces.
16 The appearance of the wheels and their work *was* like unto the colour of a beryl: and they four had one likeness: and their appearance and their work *was* as it were a wheel in the middle of a wheel.
17 When they went, they went upon their four sides: *and* they turned not when they went.

Cross references

1 Ezek. 1:3; 3:15, 23; 8:3; 10:15, 20, 22; 43:3; Matt. 3:16; Acts 7:56; 10:11; Rev. 19:11
2 2Kgs. 24:12, 15
3 1Kgs. 18:46; 2Kgs. 3:15; Ezek. 3:14, 22; 8:1; 40:1
4 Jer. 1:14; 4:6; 6:1; 23:19; 25:32
5 Ezek. 1:10; 10:14, 18, 21; Rev. 4:6
7 Dan. 10:6; Rev. 1:15
8 Ezek. 10:8, 21
9 Ezek. 1:11, 12; 10:11
10 Num. 2:3, 10, 18, 25; Rev. 4:7
11 Isa. 6:2
12 Ezek. 1:9, 17, 20; 10:22
13 Rev. 4:5
14 Zech. 4:10; Matt. 24:27
15 Ezek. 10:9
16 Ezek. 10:9, 10; Dan. 10:6
17 Ezek. 1:12

1:1 Ezekiel, son of Buzi, a priest, was carried into captivity by the armies of Nebuchadnezzar in the second deportation from Jerusalem with Judah's king Jehoichin (597 B.C., see 2 Kgs. 24:11–16), and settled by the River Chebar, a great canal southeast of Babylon. He began his prophetic ministry at the age of thirty (see Num. 4:3) in the fifth year of his captivity in 592 B.C. Two major visions appear in the first eleven chapters, the first in Babylon (chaps. 1—3) and the second a visionary spiritual revelation of what was happening in Jerusalem (chaps. 8—11).

1:4–6 behold, a whirlwind. Out of the whirlwind and cloud (see 2 Kgs. 2:11; Job 38:1) emerge "four living creatures." These are the cherubim, exalted angelic beings who constantly attend the throne of God. Verse 6 says that each angel had four wings. They appear in similar form in Revelation 4—5, but there they are seen with six wings, which means their shape and form may vary. Some think the seraphim of Isaiah 6:1–3 are these same celestial beings assuming a slightly different appearance.

1:6–14 four faces . . . four wings. The four faces may prefigure the revelation of Christ in the four gospels (**lion**—Matthew; **ox**—Mark; **man**—Luke; **eagle**—John), an idea advanced by early Christian writers. They are, however, real. Their actual wings were outstretched, one pair being linked to those of the next creature, apparently forming a close knit square. Since they were thus connected, they could fly forward without turning.

1:15–21 appearance of the wheels . . . wheel in the middle of a wheel. Each of them had a connected wheel, possibly with two intersecting at right angles. Thus they could roll in all directions without turning. Much spiritualized speculation has not solved this mystery of design. What is evident is that supernatural energy, likely angelic (cf. Heb. 1:7), at the center of each wheel caused them to rotate. Their rims, adorned by eyes (see Rev. 4:6), speak of heavenly observation from God's celestial throne.

18 As for their rings, they were so high that they were dreadful; and their rings *were* full of eyes round about them four.

19 And when the living creatures went, the wheels went by them: and when the living creatures were lifted up from the earth, the wheels were lifted up.

20 Whithersoever the spirit was to go, they went, thither *was their* spirit to go; and the wheels were lifted up over against them: for the spirit of the living creature *was* in the wheels.

21 When those went, *these* went; and when those stood, *these* stood; and when those were lifted up from the earth, the wheels were lifted up over against them: for the spirit of the living creature *was* in the wheels.

22 And the likeness of the firmament upon the heads of the living creature *was* as the colour of the terrible crystal, stretched forth over their heads above.

23 And under the firmament *were* their wings straight, the one toward the other: every one had two, which covered on this side, and every one had two, which covered on that side, their bodies.

24 And when they went, I heard the noise of their wings, like the noise of great waters, as the voice of the Almighty, the voice of speech, as the noise of an host: when they stood, they let down their wings.

25 And there was a voice from the firmament that *was* over their heads, when they stood, *and* had let down their wings.

26 And above the firmament that *was* over their heads *was* the likeness of a throne, as the appearance of a sapphire stone: and upon the likeness of the throne *was* the likeness as the appearance of a man above upon it.

27 And I saw as the colour of amber, as the appearance of fire round about within it, from the appearance of his loins even upward, and from the appearance of his loins even downward, I saw as it were the appearance of fire, and it had brightness round about.

28 As the appearance of the bow that is in the cloud in the day of rain, so *was* the appearance of the brightness round about. This *was* the appearance of the likeness of the glory of the LORD. And when I saw *it*, I fell upon my face, and I heard a voice of one that spake.

CHAPTER 2
God Calls Ezekiel

1 And he said unto me, Son of man, stand upon thy feet, and I will speak unto thee.

1:22–24 the likeness of the firmament. These four living creatures seem to be conveying, with wings outstretched, a crystalline firmament above their heads, which glitters like transparent ice. This is similar to the "sea of glass like unto crystal" before the throne of God in Revelation 4:6. In that passage, the four living creatures are not conveying, but standing upon the sparkling pavilion. Moses and more than seventy others also saw the manifestation of the God of Israel on a sapphire-like pavement, transparently clear as the heavens (Ex. 24:10).

1:25–27 likeness of a throne. Above this expanse, sparkling like ice crystals, Ezekiel then saw a sapphire-like throne upon which was seated the semblance of a man, a manifestation of God. This vision depicts God coming to earth in His moveable throne (suggested in Psalm 18:9–12) to reveal Himself to His chosen prophet, thus summoning this prophet into His special ministry. This vision, of course, is only a semblance, a likeness, because no one (John 1:18) has ever seen God in His pure essence. Only Jesus, God incarnate, could say, "He that hath seen me hath seen the Father" (John 14:8–9 [cf. John 1:14; 4:24; Col. 2:9; 1 Tim. 3:16]).

1:28 the glory of the LORD. This phrase and similar expressions occur seventeen times in the book. The word "glory" (Hebr. *kabod*) carries the idea of weight or magnitude or worthiness. When used of God, it speaks of His presence, power, splendor, and radiance, that manifestation of His divine holiness, beauty, and effulgence that reveals Him worthy of worshipful praise. Ancient rabbis also used the word *shechinah* (meaning residence) to denote the radiance, glory, or presence of God, "dwelling in the midst of His people," as in the Tabernacle (Ex. 40:34) and the temple (2 Chr. 7:1–3). The rabbinical term *shechinah* was reserved for occasions when God's glory was physically manifested. The removal and ultimate return of this "glory of the Lord" is a major theme of this prophecy.

2:1 Son of man. God addresses Ezekiel by this remarkable title some eighty-five times in the book. It suggests that in contrast to the glorious and mighty LORD and the angelic beings who convey His throne, he is a human being. Yet Ezekiel is a special "son of man," the man of the hour, chosen, spiritually endowed, and delegated by God. Jesus used this title over eighty times when speaking about Himself, indicating His true and perfect humanity. He also identified Himself with Daniel 7:13, where the "Son of man" is seen receiving universal dominion from God, the "Ancient of Days." The term appears nowhere else in the Old Testament. In Revelation 1:13, it is as "the

2 And the spirit entered into me when he spake unto me, and set me upon my feet, that I heard him that spake unto me.
3 And he said unto me, Son of man, I send thee to the children of Israel, to a rebellious nation that hath rebelled against me: they and their fathers have transgressed against me, *even* unto this very day.
4 For *they are* impudent children and stiffhearted. I do send thee unto them; and thou shalt say unto them, Thus saith the Lord GOD.
5 And they, whether they will hear, or whether they will forbear, (for they *are* a rebellious house,) yet shall know that there hath been a prophet among them.
6 And thou, son of man, be not afraid of them, neither be afraid of their words, though briers and thorns *be* with thee, and thou dost dwell among scorpions: be not afraid of their words, nor be dismayed at their looks, though they *be* a rebellious house.
7 And thou shalt speak my words unto them, whether they will hear, or whether they will forbear: for they *are* most rebellious.
8 But thou, son of man, hear what I say unto thee; Be not thou rebellious like that rebellious house: open thy mouth, and eat that I give thee.
9 And when I looked, behold, an hand *was* sent unto me; and, lo, a roll of a book *was* therein;
10 And he spread it before me; and it *was* written within and without: and *there was* written therein lamentations, and mourning, and woe.

CHAPTER 3

1 Moreover he said unto me, Son of man, eat that thou findest; eat this roll, and go speak unto the house of Israel.

2 So I opened my mouth, and he caused me to eat that roll.
3 And he said unto me, Son of man, cause thy belly to eat, and fill thy bowels with this roll that I give thee. Then did I eat *it*; and it was in my mouth as honey for sweetness.
4 And he said unto me, Son of man, go, get thee unto the house of Israel, and speak with my words unto them.
5 For thou *art* not sent to a people of a strange speech and of an hard language, *but* to the house of Israel;
6 Not to many people of a strange speech and of an hard language, whose words thou canst not understand. Surely, had I sent thee to them, they would have hearkened unto thee.
7 But the house of Israel will not hearken unto thee; for they will not hearken unto me: for all the house of Israel *are* impudent and hardhearted.
8 Behold, I have made thy face strong against their faces, and thy forehead strong against their foreheads.
9 As an adamant harder than flint have I made thy forehead: fear them not, neither be dismayed at their looks, though they *be* a rebellious house.
10 Moreover he said unto me, Son of man, all my words that I shall speak unto thee receive in thine heart, and hear with thine ears.
11 And go, get thee to them of the captivity, unto the children of thy people, and speak unto them, and tell them, Thus saith the Lord GOD; whether they will hear, or whether they will forbear.
12 Then the spirit took me up, and I heard behind me a voice of a great rushing, *saying,* Blessed *be* the glory of the LORD from his place.

Cross references

2 Ezek. 3:24
3 Jer. 3:25; Ezek. 20:18, 21, 30
4 Ezek. 3:7
5 Ezek. 3:11, 26, 27; Ezek. 33:33
6 Isa. 9:18; Jer. 1:8, 17; 6:28; Ezek. 3:9, 26, 27; Mic. 7:4; Luke 12:4; 1Pet. 3:14
7 Jer. 1:7, 17; Ezek. 2:5
8 Rev. 10:9
9 Ezek. 3:1; 8:3; Jer. 1:9
1 Ezek. 2:8, 9
3 Ps. 19:10; 119:103; Jer. 15:6; Rev. 10:9
5 Ezek. 2:6
6 Matt. 11:21, 23
7 Ezek. 2:4; John 15:20
9 Isa. 50:7; Jer. 1:8, 17, 18; 15:20; Ezek. 2:6; Mic. 3:8
11 Ezek. 2:5, 7; 3:27
12 1Kgs. 18:12; 2Kgs. 2:16; Ezek. 3:14; 8:3; Acts 8:30

Son of man" that Jesus appears in the midst of His churches. Finally, in Revelation 14:14–16 the title is applied to Jesus during the coming Tribulation and the preparations for Armageddon, leading to His dominion over the whole world (as in Dan. 7:14).

2:2 the spirit entered into me. The Spirit empowers Ezekiel to perform His ministry, as He speaks to him. Other occasions of such special empowerment are found in Numbers 24:2; Judges 3:10; 6:34; 11:29; 13:25; 1 Samuel 10:10; 16: 13–14; 19:20; 2 Chronicles 15:1; Zechariah 4:6. Before Christ's first coming, the Spirit did not indwell all believers as now, but He "moved" and "came upon them" (see 2 Pet. 1:21).

2:9–10 a roll of a book. Normally, such scrolls were written only on one side, but the message is lengthy, requiring both sides (cf. Rev. 5:1). Figuratively, he is to "eat" the roll, that is, absorb it and then relay to the people the words of God.

3:1–3 eat this roll. The words of God were "sweet as honey" to the young prophet, as John also initially experienced when he "ate" the roll the mighty angel gave him (Rev. 10:8–11). The bittersweet message of God's grace and judgment brought bitterness to John's belly. Similarly, Ezekiel became "bitter," as he began his ministry to this "rebellious nation" (see v. 14). This scroll, as in Zechariah 5:1–4 and Revelation 5—6, is symbolic of the Word itself, with the message of judgment and tribulation written therein.

The Prophecies of Ezekiel

By Kenneth Gillming

Ezekiel was one of three prophets who were also priests, the others being Jeremiah (Jer. 1:1) and Zechariah (Zech. 1:1; Neh. 12:16). He was a contemporary of Daniel, the prophet in the court of Nebuchadnezzar, and Jeremiah, who prophesied in Jerusalem before the city fell in 586 B.C. Ezekiel ministered to the people in captivity in Babylon for twenty-four years.

No prophet had a more dramatic call than Ezekiel, who saw the throne of God in a mysterious vision by the banks of the River Chebar, near the Euphrates in Babylon.

As a "watchman," he warned of Jerusalem's coming judgment. The prophet not only deals with Jerusalem and Judah prior to the destruction of the temple, but also prophesies against seven surrounding nations: Ammon, Moab, Edom, Philistia, Tyre, Sidon, Babylon and Egypt. Judgments against these nations are now recorded in history books (Ezek. 25—32).

Ezekiel contains pertinent prophecy for Jews today. In Ezekiel's book there are prophecies of the restoration of the land, the city, the temple, and the glory of the Lord in Israel's midst. Ezekiel is also relevant for Christians, for it is through this book that God reveals part of His plan for consummating history in the coming "day of the LORD" and in the glorious future world.

> *Ezekiel ministered to the people in captivity in Babylon for twenty-four years.*

Four visions are recorded in Ezekiel. The most famous of these visions is likely the picture of "the valley of dry bones," identified as the "whole house of Israel" that is restored in several stages (Ezek. 37:1–14). The other three visions are found in chapters 1—3; 8—11; and 40—48. In addition to the four visions, there are six major parables (Ezek. 15, 16, 17, 19, 23, 24) and ten symbolic actions or signs (4:1–3; 4:4–8; 4:9–17; 5:1–17; 12:1–7, 17–20; 21:1–17; 21:19–23; 22:17–31; 24:15–17; 37:15–17).

The mysterious battles of Gog and Magog describe a vast confederacy of nations, directly north of Israel, poised for an invasion in which they will suffer ignominious defeat. While difficult to define, the nations are listed. It is possible the landmass to the North includes the modern nation of Russia. Whoever these nations are, the victory will belong to God (Ezek. 38—39).

Climaxing the book is the description of a glorious temple (Ezek. 40—48). Some think this is a symbolic presentation of an ideal center of worship. Others think the prophet relates to Solomon's Temple, or Zerubbabel's Temple, which was built after the return from captivity. It has been suggested that this is Christ's heavenly temple. However, the description of this temple suggests that the magnificent structure will be the center of worldwide worship of the Lord in the coming Millennium, when Jesus reigns for a thousand years (Rev. 20:1–6).

This mighty prophet drew his strength from four sources. First, the visions of God and His throne were awesome and motivating. Secondly, "the word of the Lord" (mentioned 50 times) came to him. The "hand of the Lord" (occurs 7 times) and the "Spirit of God" (mentioned 26 times) empowered him.

The book of Ezekiel ranks with Daniel and Zechariah in the Old Testament and the Revelation in the New Testament as one of the most apocalyptic books in the Bible. It is no wonder that the book of Revelation alludes to Ezekiel sixty-four times.

13 *I heard* also the noise of the wings of the living creatures that touched one another, and the noise of the wheels over against them, and a noise of a great rushing.
14 So the spirit lifted me up, and took me away, and I went in bitterness, in the heat of my spirit; but the hand of the LORD was strong upon me.
15 Then I came to them of the captivity at Tel-abib, that dwelt by the river of Chebar, and I sat where they sat, and remained there astonished among them seven days.

Ezekiel, a Watchman

16 And it came to pass at the end of seven days, that the word of the LORD came unto me, saying,
17 Son of man, I have made thee a watchman unto the house of Israel: therefore hear the word at my mouth, and give them warning from me.
18 When I say unto the wicked, Thou shalt surely die; and thou givest him not warning, nor speakest to warn the wicked from his wicked way, to save his life; the same wicked *man* shall die in his iniquity; but his blood will I require at thine hand.
19 Yet if thou warn the wicked, and he turn not from his wickedness, nor from his wicked way, he shall die in his iniquity; but thou hast delivered thy soul.
20 Again, When a righteous *man* doth turn from his righteousness, and commit iniquity, and I lay a stumblingblock before him, he shall die: because thou hast not given him warning, he shall die in his sin, and his righteousness which he hath done shall not be remembered; but his blood will I require at thine hand.
21 Nevertheless if thou warn the righteous *man*, that the righteous sin not, and he doth not sin, he shall surely live, because he is warned; also thou hast delivered thy soul.

The Prophet Made Speechless

22 And the hand of the LORD was there upon me; and he said unto me, Arise, go forth into the plain, and I will there talk with thee.
23 Then I arose, and went forth into the plain: and, behold, the glory of the LORD stood there, as the glory which I saw by the river of Chebar: and I fell on my face.
24 Then the spirit entered into me, and set me upon my feet, and spake with me, and said unto me, Go, shut thyself within thine house.
25 But thou, O son of man, behold, they shall put bands upon thee, and shall bind thee with them, and thou shalt not go out among them:
26 And I will make thy tongue cleave to the roof of thy mouth, that thou shalt be dumb, and shalt not be to them a reprover: for they *are* a rebellious house.
27 But when I speak with thee, I will open thy mouth, and thou shalt say unto them, Thus saith the Lord GOD; He that heareth, let him hear; and he that forbeareth, let him forbear: for they *are* a rebellious house.

CHAPTER 4
The Siege of Jerusalem Portrayed

1 Thou also, son of man, take thee a tile, and lay it before thee, and pourtray upon it the city, *even* Jerusalem:
2 And lay siege against it, and build a fort against it, and cast a mount against it; set the camp also against it, and set *battering* rams against it round about.
3 Moreover take thou unto thee an iron pan, and set it *for* a wall of iron between thee and the city: and set thy face against it, and it shall be besieged, and thou shalt lay siege against it. This *shall be* a sign to the house of Israel.
4 Lie thou also upon thy left side, and lay

Cross references (center column):
14 2Kgs. 3:15; Ezek. 1:3; 3:12; 8:1, 3; 37:1
15 Job 2:13; Ps. 137:1
17 Isa. 52:8; 56:10; 62:6; Jer. 6:17; Ezek. 33:7-9
18 Ezek. 3:6; John 8:21, 24
19 Isa. 49:4, 5; Acts 20:26
20 Ezek. 18:24; 33:12, 13
22 Ezek. 1:3; 3:14; 8:4
23 Ezek. 1:1, 28
24 Ezek. 2:2
25 Ezek. 4:8
26 Ezek. 2:5-7; 24:27; Luke 1:20, 22
27 Ezek. 3:9, 11, 26; 12:2, 3; 21:22; 24:27; 33:22
3 Ezek. 12:6, 11; 24:24, 27

3:16–21 the word of the LORD came. Further confirming Ezekiel's call, God designates him as a watchman, like a sentinel on a city wall to alert the populace of danger. His responsibility is to warn the wicked of impending judgment, calling for spiritual change, but each hearer would experience the result of believing the message or the consequences for rejecting God's Word. So it has always been among hearers of divine truth. Each sinner is responsible to God for his own reaction to the proclamation of the Word. Even now, the preacher must share the gospel, or be held accountable himself for failing to warn the wicked.

4:1–3 pourtray . . . Jerusalem. In the first sign in chapters 4 and 5, the prophet constructs a small model of the city, depicting the coming siege and conquest by Nebuchadnezzar. The tile is a sizable brick, used in construction.

4:4–8 Lie . . . upon thy left side . . . right side. In the second sign, by lying on his left side for 390 days (not continually but daily), then on his right side for forty more days, Ezekiel represented, one day for each year, the previous centuries of Israel and Judah's spiritual failure. As a consequence of His people's idolatry and immorality,

the iniquity of the house of Israel upon it: *according* to the number of the days that thou shalt lie upon it thou shalt bear their iniquity.

5 For I have laid upon thee the years of their iniquity, according to the number of the days, three hundred and ninety days: so shalt thou bear the iniquity of the house of Israel.

6 And when thou hast accomplished them, lie again on thy right side, and thou shalt bear the iniquity of the house of Judah forty days: I have appointed thee each day for a year.

7 Therefore thou shalt set thy face toward the siege of Jerusalem, and thine arm *shall be* uncovered, and thou shalt prophesy against it.

8 And, behold, I will lay bands upon thee, and thou shalt not turn thee from one side to another, till thou hast ended the days of thy siege.

9 Take thou also unto thee wheat, and barley, and beans, and lentiles, and millet, and fitches, and put them in one vessel, and make thee bread thereof, *according* to the number of the days that thou shalt lie upon thy side, three hundred and ninety days shalt thou eat thereof.

10 And thy meat which thou shalt eat *shall be* by weight, twenty shekels a day: from time to time shalt thou eat it.

11 Thou shalt drink also water by measure, the sixth part of an hin: from time to time shalt thou drink.

12 And thou shalt eat it *as* barley cakes, and thou shalt bake it with dung that cometh out of man, in their sight.

13 And the LORD said, Even thus shall the children of Israel eat their defiled bread among the Gentiles, whither I will drive them.

14 Then said I, Ah Lord GOD! behold, my

soul hath not been polluted: for from my youth up even till now have I not eaten of that which dieth of itself, or is torn in pieces; neither came there abominable flesh into my mouth.

15 Then he said unto me, Lo, I have given thee cow's dung for man's dung, and thou shalt prepare thy bread therewith.

16 Moreover he said unto me, Son of man, behold, I will break the staff of bread in Jerusalem: and they shall eat bread by weight, and with care; and they shall drink water by measure, and with astonishment:

17 That they may want bread and water, and be astonied one with another, and consume away for their iniquity.

CHAPTER 5
Ezekiel Cuts His Hair as a Sign

1 And thou, son of man, take thee a sharp knife, take thee a barber's razor, and cause *it* to pass upon thine head and upon thy beard: then take thee balances to weigh, and divide the *hair.*

2 Thou shalt burn with fire a third part in the midst of the city, when the days of the siege are fulfilled: and thou shalt take a third part, *and* smite about it with a knife: and a third part thou shalt scatter in the wind; and I will draw out a sword after them.

3 Thou shalt also take thereof a few in number, and bind them in thy skirts.

4 Then take of them again, and cast them into the midst of the fire, and burn them in the fire; *for* thereof shall a fire come forth into all the house of Israel.

5 Thus saith the Lord GOD; This *is* Jerusalem: I have set it in the midst of the nations and countries *that are* round about her.

6 And she hath changed my judgments into wickedness more than the nations, and my statutes more than the countries that *are*

Cross references (center column)

5 Num. 14:34

8 Ezek. 3:25

13 Hos. 9:3

14 Ex. 22:31; Lev. 11:40; 17:15; Deut. 14:3; Isa. 65:4; Acts 10:14

16 Lev. 26:26; Ps. 105:16; Isa. 3:1; Ezek. 5:16; 12:19; 14:13

17 Lev. 21:5; 26:39; Isa. 7:20; Ezek. 24:23; 44:20

2 Ezek. 4:1, 8, 9; 5:12

3 Jer. 40:6; 52:16

4 Jer. 41:1, 2; 44:14

---

divine judgment in the destruction of Jerusalem was at hand. During the 430-year period between 1036 and 606 B.C. (when the first of the three groups of Jews were led away into captivity), the nation's history was marred by many evils, which the prophets denounced. The forty-year period, especially for Judah, may indicate the worst times under Manasseh's reign, prior to his repentance (2 Chr. 33:1–20). Ezekiel performed this symbolic act around the year 593 B.C., nearly 5 years after the second deportation of Jews to Babylon, in which he was taken, along with King Jehoiachin in 597 B.C. (Ezek. 1:1–3).

4:8–17 make thee bread. This third sign, the baking of

bread with mixed grains and preparing it over a fire kindled by burning human waste, forecast the scarcity of food in the coming eighteen-month siege of 587–586 B.C.

5:1–4 a barber's razor. This fourth sign, in which Ezekiel shaves his head and beard, demonstrated the severe humiliation to come and represented (by separate clumps of hair) the four groups among the Jerusalem populace who would experience its fall. One part would die by pestilence and starvation; another third would die in battle; and a third would be scattered and even persecuted in dispersion. A few, the hairs on Ezekiel's garment, a tiny remnant, would escape death, but experience trials.

round about her: for they have refused my judgments and my statutes, they have not walked in them.

7 Therefore thus saith the Lord GOD; Because ye multiplied more than the nations that *are* round about you, *and* have not walked in my statutes, neither have kept my judgments, neither have done according to the judgments of the nations that *are* round about you;

8 Therefore thus saith the Lord GOD; Behold, I, even I, *am* against thee, and will execute judgments in the midst of thee in the sight of the nations.

9 And I will do in thee that which I have not done, and whereunto I will not do any more the like, because of all thine abominations.

10 Therefore the fathers shall eat the sons in the midst of thee, and the sons shall eat their fathers; and I will execute judgments in thee, and the whole remnant of thee will I scatter into all the winds.

11 Wherefore, *as* I live, saith the Lord GOD; Surely, because thou hast defiled my sanctuary with all thy detestable things, and with all thine abominations, therefore will I also diminish *thee*; neither shall mine eye spare, neither will I have any pity.

12 A third part of thee shall die with the pestilence, and with famine shall they be consumed in the midst of thee: and a third part shall fall by the sword round about thee; and I will scatter a third part into all the winds, and I will draw out a sword after them.

13 Thus shall mine anger be accomplished, and I will cause my fury to rest upon them, and I will be comforted: and they shall know that I the LORD have spoken *it* in my zeal, when I have accomplished my fury in them.

14 Moreover I will make thee waste, and a reproach among the nations that *are* round about thee, in the sight of all that pass by.

15 So it shall be a reproach and a taunt, an instruction and an astonishment unto the nations that *are* round about thee, when I

Cross references

7 Jer. 2:10, 11
9 Lam. 4:6; Dan. 9:12; Amos 3:2
10 Lev. 26:29, 33; Deut. 28:53, 64
11 2Chr. 36:14; Ezek. 7: 4, 9, 20; 8:5, 18; 9:10; 11:21; 23:38
12 Lev. 26:33; Jer. 9:16; 15:2; 21:9; Ezek. 5:2, 10; 6:8, 12; 12:14
13 Deut. 32:36; Isa. 1:24; Lam. 4:11; Ezek. 6:12; 7:8; 21:17; 36:6; 38:19
14 Lev. 26:31, 32; Neh. 2:17
15 Deut. 28:37; 1Kgs. 9:7; Ps. 79:4; Jer. 24:9; Lam. 2:15; Ezek. 25:17
16 Lev. 26:26; Deut. 32:23, 24; Ezek. 4:16; 14:13
17 Lev. 26:22; Deut. 32:24; Ezek. 14:21; 20:46; 21:2; 25:2; 33:27; 34:25; 36:1; 38:22
3 Lev. 26:30
4 Lev. 26:30; Ezek. 6:6
7 Ezek. 6:6; 7:4, 9; 11:10, 12; 12:15
8 Jer. 44:28
9 Lev. 26:39; Isa. 7:13; 43:24

shall execute judgments in thee in anger and in fury and in furious rebukes. I the LORD have spoken *it*.

16 When I shall send upon them the evil arrows of famine, which shall be for *their* destruction, *and* which I will send to destroy you: and I will increase the famine upon you, and will break your staff of bread:

17 So will I send upon you famine and evil beasts, and they shall bereave thee; and pestilence and blood shall pass through thee; and I will bring the sword upon thee. I the LORD have spoken *it*.

CHAPTER 6
Idolatry Condemned

1 And the word of the LORD came unto me, saying,

2 Son of man, set thy face toward the mountains of Israel, and prophesy against them,

3 And say, Ye mountains of Israel, hear the word of the Lord GOD; Thus saith the Lord GOD to the mountains, and to the hills, to the rivers, and to the valleys; Behold, I, *even* I, will bring a sword upon you, and I will destroy your high places.

4 And your altars shall be desolate, and your images shall be broken: and I will cast down your slain *men* before your idols.

5 And I will lay the dead carcases of the children of Israel before their idols; and I will scatter your bones round about your altars.

6 In all your dwellingplaces the cities shall be laid waste, and the high places shall be desolate; that your altars may be laid waste and made desolate, and your idols may be broken and cease, and your images may be cut down, and your works may be abolished.

7 And the slain shall fall in the midst of you, and ye shall know that I *am* the LORD.

8 Yet will I leave a remnant, that ye may have *some* that shall escape the sword among the nations, when ye shall be scattered through the countries.

9 And they that escape of you shall re-

5:13 they shall know that I the LORD have spoken. This is the first of some sixty-four uses of this or similar assertions, showing that His people will respond to divine actions, if not to His word.

6:2 mountains of Israel. This message, addressed to the mountains of Israel, where vile idolatry was widely practiced, predicts the destruction of idol worshipers.

Notice the term "Israel" is used for all the land and its entire people.

6:8 a remnant. The theme of the godly Jewish remnant preserved through the ages is found throughout the prophets in the Old Testament and in New Testament prophecy as well (see Rom. 9:27; 11:5–6; Rev. 11:13; 12:17).

member me among the nations whither they shall be carried captives, because I am broken with their whorish heart, which hath departed from me, and with their eyes, which go a whoring after their idols: and they shall lothe themselves for the evils which they have committed in all their abominations.

10 And they shall know that I *am* the LORD, *and that* I have not said in vain that I would do this evil unto them.

11 Thus saith the Lord GOD; Smite with thine hand, and stamp with thy foot, and say, Alas for all the evil abominations of the house of Israel! for they shall fall by the sword, by the famine, and by the pestilence.

12 He that is far off shall die of the pestilence; and he that is near shall fall by the sword; and he that remaineth and is besieged shall die by the famine: thus will I accomplish my fury upon them.

13 Then shall ye know that I *am* the LORD, when their slain *men* shall be among their idols round about their altars, upon every high hill, in all the tops of the mountains, and under every green tree, and under every thick oak, the place where they did offer sweet savour to all their idols.

14 So will I stretch out my hand upon them, and make the land desolate, yea, more desolate than the wilderness toward Diblath, in all their habitations: and they shall know that I *am* the LORD.

CHAPTER 7
Prophecy of Pending Judgment

1 Moreover the word of the LORD came unto me, saying,

2 Also, thou son of man, thus saith the Lord GOD unto the land of Israel; An end, the end is come upon the four corners of the land.

3 Now *is* the end *come* upon thee, and I will send mine anger upon thee, and will judge thee according to thy ways, and will recompense upon thee all thine abominations.

4 And mine eye shall not spare thee, neither will I have pity: but I will recompense thy ways upon thee, and thine abomina-

tions shall be in the midst of thee: and ye shall know that I *am* the LORD.

5 Thus saith the Lord GOD; An evil, an only evil, behold, is come.

6 An end is come, the end is come: it watcheth for thee; behold, it is come.

7 The morning is come unto thee, O thou that dwellest in the land: the time is come, the day of trouble *is* near, and not the sounding again of the mountains.

8 Now will I shortly pour out my fury upon thee, and accomplish mine anger upon thee: and I will judge thee according to thy ways, and will recompense thee for all thine abominations.

9 And mine eye shall not spare, neither will I have pity: I will recompense thee according to thy ways and thine abominations *that* are in the midst of thee; and ye shall know that I *am* the LORD that smiteth.

10 Behold the day, behold, it is come: the morning is gone forth; the rod hath blossomed, pride hath budded.

11 Violence is risen up into a rod of wickedness: none of them *shall remain*, nor of their multitude, nor of any of theirs: neither *shall there be* wailing for them.

12 The time is come, the day draweth near: let not the buyer rejoice, nor the seller mourn: for wrath *is* upon all the multitude thereof.

13 For the seller shall not return to that which is sold, although they were yet alive: for the vision *is* touching the whole multitude thereof, *which* shall not return; neither shall any strengthen himself in the iniquity of his life.

14 They have blown the trumpet, even to make all ready; but none goeth to the battle: for my wrath *is* upon all the multitude thereof.

15 The sword *is* without, and the pestilence and the famine within: he that *is* in the field shall die with the sword; and he that *is* in the city, famine and pestilence shall devour him.

16 But they that escape of them shall escape, and shall be on the mountains like doves of the valleys, all of them mourning, every one for his iniquity.

Center column cross-references

11 Ezek. 5:12; 21:14

12 Ezek. 5:13

13 Isa. 57:5; Jer. 2:20; Ezek. 6:7; Hos. 4:13

14 Num. 33:46; Isa. 5:25; Jer. 48:22; Ezek. 7:3, 6; Amos 8:2; Matt. 24:6, 13, 14

3 Ezek. 7:8, 9

4 Ezek. 5:11; 6:7; 7:9, 27; 8:18; 9:10; 12:20

7 Ezek. 7:10, 12; Zeph. 1:14, 15

8 Ezek. 7:3; 20:8, 21

9 Ezek. 7:4

10 Ezek. 7:7

11 Jer. 6:7; 16:5, 6; Ezek. 24:16, 22

12 Ezek. 7:7

15 Deut. 32:25; Lam. 1:20; Ezek. 5:12

16 Ezek. 6:8

6:11 sword . . . famine . . . pestilence. These three can be instruments of divine judgment. Notice also Ezekiel 14:21, which adds another, the "noisome" or wild beasts, making a total of four sore judgments. Revelation 6:8 describes four future Tribulation judgments which will impact the fourth part of the earth.

7:12 the buyer . . . the seller. The economy is to collapse, as happens in wars. The final, future destruction of the world economic system, described in Revelation 18, will be far more severe than what happened in Jerusalem in 586 B.C.

17 All hands shall be feeble, and all knees shall be weak *as* water.

18 They shall also gird *themselves* with sackcloth, and horror shall cover them; and shame *shall be* upon all faces, and baldness upon all their heads.

19 They shall cast their silver in the streets, and their gold shall be removed: their silver and their gold shall not be able to deliver them in the day of the wrath of the LORD: they shall not satisfy their souls, neither fill their bowels: because it is the stumblingblock of their iniquity.

20 As for the beauty of his ornament, he set it in majesty: but they made the images of their abominations *and* of their detestable things therein: therefore have I set it far from them.

21 And I will give it into the hands of the strangers for a prey, and to the wicked of the earth for a spoil; and they shall pollute it.

22 My face will I turn also from them, and they shall pollute my secret *place*: for the robbers shall enter into it, and defile it.

23 Make a chain: for the land is full of bloody crimes, and the city is full of violence.

24 Wherefore I will bring the worst of the heathen, and they shall possess their houses: I will also make the pomp of the strong to cease; and their holy places shall be defiled.

25 Destruction cometh; and they shall seek peace, and *there shall be* none.

26 Mischief shall come upon mischief, and rumour shall be upon rumour; then shall they seek a vision of the prophet; but the law shall perish from the priest, and counsel from the ancients.

27 The king shall mourn, and the prince shall be clothed with desolation, and the hands of the people of the land shall be troubled: I will do unto them after their way, and according to their deserts will I judge them; and they shall know that I *am* the LORD.

17 Isa. 13:7; Jer. 6:24; Ezek. 21:7

18 Ps. 55:5; Isa. 3:24; 15:2, 3; Jer. 48:37; Amos 8:10

19 Prov. 11:4; Ezek. 14:3, 4; 44:12; Zeph. 1:18

20 Jer. 7:30

23 2Kgs. 21:16; Ezek. 9:9; 11:6

26 Deut. 32:23; Ps. 74:9; Jer. 4:20; Lam. 2:9; Ezek. 20:1, 3

27 Ezek. 1:3; 3:22; 7:4; 14:1; 20:1; 33:31

2 Ezek. 1:4, 26, 27

3 Deut. 32:16, 21; Jer. 7:30; 32:34; Ezek. 3:14; 5:11; 11:1, 24; 40:2; Dan. 5:5

4 Ezek. 1:28; 3:22, 23

CHAPTER 8
The Second Vision

1 And it came to pass in the sixth year, in the sixth *month*, in the fifth *day* of the month, *as* I sat in mine house, and the elders of Judah sat before me, that the hand of the Lord God fell there upon me.

2 Then I beheld, and lo a likeness as the appearance of fire: from the appearance of his loins even downward, fire; and from his loins even upward, as the appearance of brightness, as the colour of amber.

3 And he put forth the form of an hand, and took me by a lock of mine head; and the spirit lifted me up between the earth and the heaven, and brought me in the visions of God to Jerusalem, to the door of the inner gate that looketh toward the north; where *was* the seat of the image of jealousy, which provoketh to jealousy.

4 And, behold, the glory of the God of Israel *was* there, according to the vision that I saw in the plain.

5 Then said he unto me, Son of man, lift up thine eyes now the way toward the north. So I lifted up mine eyes the way toward the north, and behold northward at the gate of the altar this image of jealousy in the entry.

6 He said furthermore unto me, Son of man, seest thou what they do? *even* the great abominations that the house of Israel committeth here, that I should go far off from my sanctuary? but turn thee yet again, *and* thou shalt see greater abominations.

7 And he brought me to the door of the court; and when I looked, behold a hole in the wall.

8 Then said he unto me, Son of man, dig now in the wall: and when I had digged in the wall, behold a door.

9 And he said unto me, Go in, and behold the wicked abominations that they do here.

10 So I went in and saw; and behold every form of creeping things, and abominable beasts, and all the idols of the house of Israel, pourtrayed upon the wall round about.

7:27 according to their deserts will I judge. The nations of Israel and Judah at long last would receive what they deserved because of their rebellious, heinous history of sin, particularly the sin of worshiping other gods.

8:3–5 he . . . brought me in the visions of God to Jerusalem. This second vision, occurring fourteen months after the experience of chapters 1—3, takes place in Ezekiel's home, where he is meeting with the elders near Babylon. Not in body, but in spirit, he is lifted up and conveyed to Jerusalem to see the abominable idolatry being practiced in God's temple, beginning with an "image of jealousy" (5)—an evil idol at the entrance.

11 And there stood before them seventy men of the ancients of the house of Israel, and in the midst of them stood Jaazaniah the son of Shaphan, with every man his censer in his hand; and a thick cloud of incense went up.

12 Then said he unto me, Son of man, hast thou seen what the ancients of the house of Israel do in the dark, every man in the chambers of his imagery? for they say, The LORD seeth us not; the LORD hath forsaken the earth.

13 He said also unto me, Turn thee yet again, *and* thou shalt see greater abominations that they do.

14 Then he brought me to the door of the gate of the LORD's house which *was* toward the north; and, behold, there sat women weeping for Tammuz.

15 Then said he unto me, Hast thou seen *this*, O son of man? turn thee yet again, *and* thou shalt see greater abominations than these.

16 And he brought me into the inner court of the LORD's house, and, behold, at the door of the temple of the LORD, between the porch and the altar, *were* about five and twenty men, with their backs toward the temple of the LORD, and their faces toward the east; and they worshipped the sun toward the east.

17 Then he said unto me, Hast thou seen *this*, O son of man? Is it a light thing to the house of Judah that they commit the abominations which they commit here? for they have filled the land with violence, and have returned to provoke me to anger: and, lo, they put the branch to their nose.

18 Therefore will I also deal in fury: mine eye shall not spare, neither will I have pity: and though they cry in mine ears with a loud voice, *yet* will I not hear them.

CHAPTER 9
Jerusalem's Punishment

1 He cried also in mine ears with a loud voice, saying, Cause them that have charge over the city to draw near, even every man *with* his destroying weapon in his hand.

2 And, behold, six men came from the way of the higher gate, which lieth toward the north, and every man a slaughter weapon in his hand; and one man among them *was* clothed with linen, with a writer's inkhorn by his side: and they went in, and stood beside the brasen altar.

3 And the glory of the God of Israel was gone up from the cherub, whereupon he was, to the threshold of the house. And he called to the man clothed with linen, which *had* the writer's inkhorn by his side;

4 And the LORD said unto him, Go through the midst of the city, through the midst of Jerusalem, and set a mark upon the foreheads of the men that sigh and that cry for all the abominations that be done in the midst thereof.

5 And to the others he said in mine hearing, Go ye after him through the city, and smite: let not your eye spare, neither have ye pity:

6 Slay utterly old *and* young, both maids, and little children, and women: but come not near any man upon whom *is* the mark; and begin at my sanctuary. Then they began at the ancient men which *were* before the house.

7 And he said unto them, Defile the house, and fill the courts with the slain: go ye forth. And they went forth, and slew in the city.

8 And it came to pass, while they were slaying them, and I was left, that I fell upon

Cross References

12 Ezek. 9:9

16 Deut. 4:19; 2Kgs. 23:5, 11; Job 31:26; Jer. 2:27; 32:33; 44:17; Ezek. 11:1; Joel 2:17

17 Ezek. 9:9

18 Lev. 16:4; Prov. 1:28; Isa. 1:15; Jer. 11:11; 14:12; Ezek. 5:11, 13; 7:4, 9; 9:5, 10; 10:2, 6, 7; 16:42; 24:13; Mic. 3:4; Zech. 7:13; Rev. 15:6

3 Ezek. 3:23; 8:4; 10:4, 18; 11:22, 23

4 Ex. 12:7; Ps. 119:53, 136; Jer. 13:17; 2Cor. 12:21; 2Pet. 2:8; Rev. 7:3; 9:4; 13:16, 17; 20:4

5 Ezek. 5:11; 9:10

6 2Chr. 36:17; Jer. 25:29; Ezek. 8:11, 12, 16; 1Pet. 4:17; Rev. 9:4

8 Num. 14:5; 16:4, 22, 45; Josh. 7:6; Ezek. 11:13

8:14–16 women weeping for Tammuz. This Babylonian god was the husband of Ishtar, the goddess of fertility. Supposedly, he died in autumn and was raised from the underworld in the spring, when flowers and vegetation grew. Raw and degrading immoral acts were associated with worshiping him. These increasingly greater abominations culminated with the prophet seeing twenty-five men with their backs toward God's temple, facing and worshiping the sun (see 2 Kgs. 23:5, 11; Rom. 1:25).

9:1–2 behold, six men. These six men are evidently angelic beings, who symbolically slay the wicked. One is clothed in linen, with an inkhorn or writing case probably attached to his belt that contains pens for marking. Of a higher rank than the others, he may be compared to the angelic personality in Daniel 10:5; 12:6. The armies of Nebuchadnezzar literally slew multitudes of Jews in 586 B.C., fulfilling the vision.

9:3 the glory of the God of Israel was gone up. Here begins the progressive withdrawal of the glory of God, later called the *shechinah* by the rabbis, that glowing manifestation of His presence that had appeared between the golden cherubim on the ark in the Holy of Holies.

9:6 come not near any . . . upon whom is the mark. True worshipers of God, who despised idolatry, would be protected from judgment. In Revelation 7:1–4, the 144,000 Israelites in the Tribulation period are sealed in their foreheads and protected by God before the trumpet judgments occur (Rev. 8).

my face, and cried, and said, Ah Lord God! wilt thou destroy all the residue of Israel in thy pouring out of thy fury upon Jerusalem?

9 Then said he unto me, The iniquity of the house of Israel and Judah *is* exceeding great, and the land is full of blood, and the city full of perverseness: for they say, The Lord hath forsaken the earth, and the Lord seeth not.

10 And as for me also, mine eye shall not spare, neither will I have pity, *but* I will recompense their way upon their head.

11 And, behold, the man clothed with linen, which *had* the inkhorn by his side, reported the matter, saying, I have done as thou hast commanded me.

CHAPTER 10

1 Then I looked, and, behold, in the firmament that was above the head of the cherubims there appeared over them as it were a sapphire stone, as the appearance of the likeness of a throne.

2 And he spake unto the man clothed with linen, and said, Go in between the wheels, *even* under the cherub, and fill thine hand with coals of fire from between the cherubims, and scatter *them* over the city. And he went in in my sight.

3 Now the cherubims stood on the right side of the house, when the man went in; and the cloud filled the inner court.

4 Then the glory of the Lord went up from the cherub, *and stood* over the threshold of the house; and the house was filled with the cloud, and the court was full of the brightness of the Lord's glory.

5 And the sound of the cherubims' wings was heard *even* to the outer court, as the voice of the Almighty God when he speaketh.

6 And it came to pass, *that* when he had commanded the man clothed with linen, saying, Take fire from between the wheels, from between the cherubims; then he went in, and stood beside the wheels.

7 And *one* cherub stretched forth his hand from between the cherubims unto the fire that *was* between the cherubims, and took *thereof,* and put *it* into the hands of *him that was* clothed with linen: who took *it,* and went out.

8 And there appeared in the cherubims the form of a man's hand under their wings.

9 And when I looked, behold the four wheels by the cherubims, one wheel by one cherub, and another wheel by another cherub: and the appearance of the wheels *was* as the colour of a beryl stone.

10 And *as for* their appearances, they four had one likeness, as if a wheel had been in the midst of a wheel.

11 When they went, they went upon their four sides; they turned not as they went, but to the place whither the head looked they followed it; they turned not as they went.

12 And their whole body, and their backs, and their hands, and their wings, and the wheels, *were* full of eyes round about, *even* the wheels that they four had.

13 As for the wheels, it was cried unto them in my hearing, O wheel.

14 And every one had four faces: the first face *was* the face of a cherub, and the second face *was* the face of a man, and the third the face of a lion, and the fourth the face of an eagle.

15 And the cherubims were lifted up. This *is* the living creature that I saw by the river of Chebar.

16 And when the cherubims went, the wheels went by them: and when the cherubims lifted up their wings to mount up from the earth, the same wheels also turned not from beside them.

17 When they stood, *these* stood; and when they were lifted up, *these* lifted up themselves *also*: for the spirit of the living creature *was* in them.

God's Glory Departs from the Temple

18 Then the glory of the Lord departed from off the threshold of the house, and stood over the cherubims.

19 And the cherubims lifted up their wings, and mounted up from the earth in my sight: when they went out, the wheels also *were* beside them, and *every one* stood at the door of the east gate of the Lord's house; and the glory of the God of Israel *was* over them above.

20 This *is* the living creature that I saw

Cross references (center column)

9 2Kgs. 21:16; Ps. 10:11; Isa. 29:15; Ezek. 8:12, 17

10 Ezek. 5:11; 7:4; 8:18; 11:21

11 Ezek. 1:22, 26

2 Ezek. 1:13; 9:2, 3; Rev. 8:5

4 1Kgs. 8:10, 11; Ezek. 1:28; 9:3; 10:18; 43:5

5 Ps. 29:3; Ezek. 1:24

8 Ezek. 1:8; 10:21

9 Ezek. 1:15, 16

11 Ezek. 1:17

12 Ezek. 1:18

14 Ezek. 1:6, 10

15 Ezek. 1:5

16 Ezek. 1:19

17 Ezek. 1:12, 20, 21

18 Ezek. 10:4; Hos. 9:12

19 Ezek. 11:22

20 Ezek. 1:1, 22; 10:15

10:3–4 the cherubims. These four cherubim are to be distinguished from the cherub (v. 4), which was associated with the literal ark and temple worship. As in Ezekiel 9:3, the glory of God moves and hovers above the threshold of the temple, and the brightness of God's glory shines above the temple and in the inner courtyard.

10:18 the glory of the Lord departed. The progressive departure of the glory of the Lord continues with a move from above the threshold to a position above the four cherubim, no longer in contact with the temple structure.

under the God of Israel by the river of Chebar; and I knew that they *were* the cherubims.

21 Every one had four faces apiece, and every one four wings; and the likeness of the hands of a man *was* under their wings.

22 And the likeness of their faces *was* the same faces which I saw by the river of Chebar, their appearances and themselves: they went every one straight forward.

CHAPTER 11
God Condemns Jerusalem

1 Moreover the spirit lifted me up, and brought me unto the east gate of the LORD's house, which looketh eastward: and behold at the door of the gate five and twenty men; among whom I saw Jaazaniah the son of Azur, and Pelatiah the son of Benaiah, princes of the people.

2 Then said he unto me, Son of man, these *are* the men that devise mischief, and give wicked counsel in this city:

3 Which say, *It is* not near; let us build houses: this *city is* the caldron, and we *be* the flesh.

4 Therefore prophesy against them, prophesy, O son of man.

5 And the Spirit of the LORD fell upon me, and said unto me, Speak; Thus saith the LORD; Thus have ye said, O house of Israel: for I know the things that come into your mind, *every one of* them.

6 Ye have multiplied your slain in this city, and ye have filled the streets thereof with the slain.

7 Therefore thus saith the Lord GOD; Your slain whom ye have laid in the midst of it, they *are* the flesh, and this *city is* the caldron: but I will bring you forth out of the midst of it.

8 Ye have feared the sword; and I will bring a sword upon you, saith the Lord GOD.

9 And I will bring you out of the midst thereof, and deliver you into the hands of strangers, and will execute judgments among you.

10 Ye shall fall by the sword; I will judge

you in the border of Israel; and ye shall know that I *am* the LORD.

11 This *city* shall not be your caldron, neither shall ye be the flesh in the midst thereof; *but* I will judge you in the border of Israel:

12 And ye shall know that I *am* the LORD: for ye have not walked in my statutes, neither executed my judgments, but have done after the manners of the heathen that *are* round about you.

13 And it came to pass, when I prophesied, that Pelatiah the son of Benaiah died. Then fell I down upon my face, and cried with a loud voice, and said, Ah Lord GOD! wilt thou make a full end of the remnant of Israel?

God Promises Restoration

14 Again the word of the LORD came unto me, saying,

15 Son of man, thy brethren, *even* thy brethren, the men of thy kindred, and all the house of Israel wholly, *are* they unto whom the inhabitants of Jerusalem have said, Get you far from the LORD: unto us is this land given in possession.

16 Therefore say, Thus saith the Lord GOD; Although I have cast them far off among the heathen, and although I have scattered them among the countries, yet will I be to them as a little sanctuary in the countries where they shall come.

17 Therefore say, Thus saith the Lord GOD; I will even gather you from the people, and assemble you out of the countries where ye have been scattered, and I will give you the land of Israel.

18 And they shall come thither, and they shall take away all the detestable things thereof and all the abominations thereof from thence.

19 And I will give them one heart, and I will put a new spirit within you; and I will take the stony heart out of their flesh, and will give them an heart of flesh:

20 That they may walk in my statutes, and keep mine ordinances, and do them: and they shall be my people, and I will be their God.

Cross references

21 Ezek. 1:6, 8; 10:8, 14
22 Ezek. 1:10, 12; 3:12, 14; 8:3, 16; 10:19; 11:24
3 Jer. 1:13; Ezek. 12:22, 27; 24:3; 2Pet. 3:4
5 Ezek. 2:2; 3:24
6 Ezek. 7:23; 22:3, 4
7 Ezek. 11:9; 24:3, 6, 10, 11; Mic. 3:3
9 Ezek. 5:8
10 1Kgs. 8:65; 2Kgs. 14:25; 25:19-21; Ps. 9:16; Jer. 39:6; 52:10; Ezek. 6:7; 13:9, 14, 21, 23
11 Ezek. 11:3
12 Lev. 18:3, 24; Deut. 12:30, 31; Ezek. 8:10, 14, 16; 11:10
13 Ezek. 9:8; 11:1; Acts 5:5
16 Ps. 90:1; 91:9; Isa. 8:14
17 Jer. 24:5; Ezek. 28:25; 34:13; 36:24
18 Ezek. 37:23
19 Ps. 51:10; Jer. 31:33; 32:39; Ezek. 18:31; 36:26, 27; Zeph. 3:9; Zech. 7:12
20 Ps. 105:45; Jer. 24:7; Ezek. 14:11; 36:28; 37:27

11:13 Pelatiah . . . died. An indication of many deaths to come. This prince's sudden demise, as seen in the vision, caused the prophet to fear that all Jews in Jerusalem would die.

11:14–16 a little sanctuary. To the exiles in captivity in Babylon and those scattered elsewhere comes this first promise of protection. Though access to the temple will be gone, God Himself promises to be a "little sanctuary" for them wherever they go.

11:17–21 I will give you the land of Israel. This passage goes beyond the return from Babylonian captivity experienced by the Jews under the Persians (see Ezra and Nehemiah) and speaks of the ultimate, full restoration of Israel in the future Millennium, when the people will have a new heart (cf. Jer. 31:33).

21 But *as for them* whose heart walketh after the heart of their detestable things and their abominations, I will recompense their way upon their own heads, saith the Lord GOD. **22** Then did the cherubims lift up their wings, and the wheels beside them; and the glory of the God of Israel *was* over them above.

23 And the glory of the LORD went up from the midst of the city, and stood upon the mountain which *is* on the east side of the city. **24** Afterwards the spirit took me up, and brought me in a vision by the Spirit of God into Chaldea, to them of the captivity. So the vision that I had seen went up from me.

25 Then I spake unto them of the captivity all the things that the LORD had shewed me.

CHAPTER 12
Ezekiel Portrays the Deportation

1 The word of the LORD also came unto me, saying,

2 Son of man, thou dwellest in the midst of a rebellious house, which have eyes to see, and see not; they have ears to hear, and hear not: for they *are* a rebellious house.

3 Therefore, thou son of man, prepare thee stuff for removing, and remove by day in their sight; and thou shalt remove from thy place to another place in their sight: it may be they will consider, though they *be* a rebellious house.

4 Then shalt thou bring forth thy stuff by day in their sight, as stuff for removing: and thou shalt go forth at even in their sight, as they that go forth into captivity.

5 Dig thou through the wall in their sight, and carry out thereby.

6 In their sight shalt thou bear *it* upon *thy* shoulders, *and* carry *it* forth in the twilight: thou shalt cover thy face, that thou see not the ground: for I have set thee *for* a sign unto the house of Israel.

7 And I did so as I was commanded: I brought forth my stuff by day, as stuff for captivity, and in the even I digged through the wall with mine hand; I brought *it* forth in the twilight, *and* I bare *it* upon *my* shoulder in their sight.

8 And in the morning came the word of the LORD unto me, saying,

9 Son of man, hath not the house of Israel, the rebellious house, said unto thee, What doest thou?

10 Say thou unto them, Thus saith the Lord GOD; This burden *concerneth* the prince in Jerusalem, and all the house of Israel that *are* among them.

11 Say, I *am* your sign: like as I have done, so shall it be done unto them: they shall remove *and* go into captivity.

12 And the prince that *is* among them shall bear upon *his* shoulder in the twilight, and shall go forth: they shall dig through the wall to carry out thereby: he shall cover his face, that he see not the ground with *his* eyes.

13 My net also will I spread upon him, and he shall be taken in my snare: and I will bring him to Babylon *to* the land of the Chaldeans; yet shall he not see it, though he shall die there.

14 And I will scatter toward every wind all that *are* about him to help him, and all his bands; and I will draw out the sword after them.

15 And they shall know that I *am* the LORD, when I shall scatter them among the nations, and disperse them in the countries.

16 But I will leave a few men of them from the sword, from the famine, and from the pestilence; that they may declare all their abominations among the heathen whither they come; and they shall know that I *am* the LORD.

17 Moreover the word of the LORD came to me, saying,

18 Son of man, eat thy bread with quaking, and drink thy water with trembling and with carefulness;

19 And say unto the people of the land, Thus saith the Lord GOD of the inhabitants of Jerusalem, *and* of the land of Israel; They shall eat their bread with carefulness, and drink their water with astonishment, that her land may be desolate from all that is therein, because of the violence of all them that dwell therein.

Cross references

21 Ezek. 9:10; 22:31

22 Ezek. 1:19; 10:19

23 Ezek. 8:4; 9:3; 10:4, 18; 43:2, 4; Zech. 14:4

24 Isa. 6:9; 42:20; Jer. 5:21; Ezek. 2:3, 5, 6-8; 3:26, 27; 8:3; Matt. 13:13, 14

6 Isa. 8:18; Ezek. 4:3; 12:11; 24:24

9 Ezek. 2:5; 17:12; 24:19

10 Mal. 1:1

11 2Kgs. 25:4, 5, 7; Ezek. 12:6

12 Jer. 39:4

13 2Kgs. 25:7; Job 19:6; Jer. 52:9, 11; Lam. 1:13; Ezek. 17:16, 20

14 2Kgs. 25:4, 5; Ezek. 5:2, 10, 12

15 Ps. 9:16; Ezek. 6:7, 14; 11:10; 12:16, 20

16 Ezek. 6:8-10

18 Ezek. 4:16

19 Ps. 107:34; Zech. 7:14

11:22–24 the glory of the LORD went up. As the chariot-throne ascends into heaven, the glory of the Lord also rises finally from the city and stands on the Mount of Olives east of the city, then ascends and evidently disappears. Only in the Millennial Temple will this effulgence and beauty, this special presence of God, return to fill the house of God (see 43:4–6, cf. Acts 1:11–12; Zech. 14:4).

12:5–6 Dig . . . through the wall. . . in the twilight. This prophetic sign anticipates King Zedekiah's nighttime attempted escape (2 Kgs. 25:1–7). Blinded by his captors, Zedekiah did not see the ground (v. 12) when brought to Babylon where he died (Jer. 52:4–11).

20 And the cities that are inhabited shall be laid waste, and the land shall be desolate; and ye shall know that I *am* the LORD.

21 And the word of the LORD came unto me, saying,

22 Son of man, what *is* that proverb *that* ye have in the land of Israel, saying, The days are prolonged, and every vision faileth?

23 Tell them therefore, Thus saith the Lord GOD; I will make this proverb to cease, and they shall no more use it as a proverb in Israel; but say unto them, The days are at hand, and the effect of every vision.

24 For there shall be no more any vain vision nor flattering divination within the house of Israel.

25 For I *am* the LORD: I will speak, and the word that I shall speak shall come to pass; it shall be no more prolonged: for in your days, O rebellious house, will I say the word, and will perform it, saith the Lord GOD.

26 Again the word of the LORD came to me, saying,

27 Son of man, behold, *they of* the house of Israel say, The vision that he seeth *is* for many days *to come*, and he prophesieth of the times *that are* far off.

28 Therefore say unto them, Thus saith the Lord GOD; There shall none of my words be prolonged any more, but the word which I have spoken shall be done, saith the Lord GOD.

CHAPTER 13
False Prophets

1 And the word of the LORD came unto me, saying,

2 Son of man, prophesy against the prophets of Israel that prophesy, and say thou unto them that prophesy out of their own hearts, Hear ye the word of the LORD;

3 Thus saith the Lord GOD; Woe unto the foolish prophets, that follow their own spirit, and have seen nothing!

4 O Israel, thy prophets are like the foxes in the deserts.

5 Ye have not gone up into the gaps, neither made up the hedge for the house of Israel to stand in the battle in the day of the LORD.

6 They have seen vanity and lying divina-

tion, saying, The LORD saith: and the LORD hath not sent them: and they have made *others* to hope that they would confirm the word.

7 Have ye not seen a vain vision, and have ye not spoken a lying divination, whereas ye say, The LORD saith *it*; albeit I have not spoken?

8 Therefore thus saith the Lord GOD; Because ye have spoken vanity, and seen lies, therefore, behold, I *am* against you, saith the Lord GOD.

9 And mine hand shall be upon the prophets that see vanity, and that divine lies: they shall not be in the assembly of my people, neither shall they be written in the writing of the house of Israel, neither shall they enter into the land of Israel; and ye shall know that I *am* the Lord GOD.

10 Because, even because they have seduced my people, saying, Peace; and *there was* no peace; and one built up a wall, and, lo, others daubed it with untempered *morter*:

11 Say unto them which daub *it* with untempered *morter*, that it shall fall: there shall be an overflowing shower; and ye, O great hailstones, shall fall; and a stormy wind shall rend *it*.

12 Lo, when the wall is fallen, shall it not be said unto you, Where *is* the daubing wherewith ye have daubed *it*?

13 Therefore thus saith the Lord GOD; I will even rend *it* with a stormy wind in my fury; and there shall be an overflowing shower in mine anger, and great hailstones in *my* fury to consume *it*.

14 So will I break down the wall that ye have daubed with untempered *morter*, and bring it down to the ground, so that the foundation thereof shall be discovered, and it shall fall, and ye shall be consumed in the midst thereof: and ye shall know that I *am* the LORD.

15 Thus will I accomplish my wrath upon the wall, and upon them that have daubed it with untempered *morter*, and will say unto you, The wall *is* no *more*, neither they that daubed it;

16 *To wit*, the prophets of Israel which prophesy concerning Jerusalem, and which

Cross references: 22 Ezek. 11:3; 12:27; Amos 6:3; 2Pet. 3:4 · 23 Joel 2:1; Zeph. 1:14 · 24 Lam. 2:14; Ezek. 13:23 · 25 Isa. 55:11; Ezek. 12:28; Dan. 9:12; Luke 21:33 · 27 Ezek. 12:22; 2Pet. 3:4 · 28 Jer. 14:14; 23:16, 26; Ezek. 12:17, 23, 25 · 4 Song 2:15 · 5 Ps. 106:23, 30; Ezek. 22:30 · 6 Ezek. 12:24; 13:23; 22:28 · 9 Ezra 2:59, 62; Neh. 7:5; Ps. 69:28; Ezek. 11:10, 12; 20:38 · 10 Jer. 6:14; 8:11; Ezek. 22:28 · 11 Ezek. 38:22 · 14 Ezek. 13:9, 21, 23; 14:8 · 16 Jer. 6:14; 28:9

12:22–28 proverb. The popular saying (proverb) back in Israel (Judah) was that judgment was in the distant future. This saying would soon cease, as the days were at hand.

13:1–7 Woe unto the foolish prophets. Claiming the message of God, but prophesying out of their own wicked hearts, false prophets announced peace "and there was no peace" (v. 10) for the doomed city (see Jer. 6:14; 8:11; 1 Thess. 5:1–3). So it was, and so shall it be in the coming Tribulation.

see visions of peace for her, and *there is* no peace, saith the Lord GOD.

17 Likewise, thou son of man, set thy face against the daughters of thy people, which prophesy out of their own heart; and prophesy thou against them,

18 And say, Thus saith the Lord GOD; Woe to the *women* that sew pillows to all armholes, and make kerchiefs upon the head of every stature to hunt souls! Will ye hunt the souls of my people, and will ye save the souls alive *that come* unto you?

19 And will ye pollute me among my people for handfuls of barley and for pieces of bread, to slay the souls that should not die, and to save the souls alive that should not live, by your lying to my people that hear *your* lies?

20 Wherefore thus saith the Lord GOD; Behold, I *am* against your pillows, wherewith ye there hunt the souls to make *them* fly, and I will tear them from your arms, and will let the souls go, *even* the souls that ye hunt to make *them* fly.

21 Your kerchiefs also will I tear, and deliver my people out of your hand, and they shall be no more in your hand to be hunted; and ye shall know that I *am* the LORD.

22 Because with lies ye have made the heart of the righteous sad, whom I have not made sad; and strengthened the hands of the wicked, that he should not return from his wicked way, by promising him life:

23 Therefore ye shall see no more vanity, nor divine divinations: for I will deliver my people out of your hand: and ye shall know that I *am* the LORD.

CHAPTER 14
Idolaters

1 Then came certain of the elders of Israel unto me, and sat before me.

2 And the word of the LORD came unto me, saying,

3 Son of man, these men have set up their idols in their heart, and put the stumblingblock of their iniquity before their face: should I be inquired of at all by them?

4 Therefore speak unto them, and say unto them, Thus saith the Lord GOD; Every man of the house of Israel that setteth up his

idols in his heart, and putteth the stumblingblock of his iniquity before his face, and cometh to the prophet; I the LORD will answer him that cometh according to the multitude of his idols;

5 That I may take the house of Israel in their own heart, because they are all estranged from me through their idols.

6 Therefore say unto the house of Israel, Thus saith the Lord GOD; Repent, and turn *yourselves* from your idols; and turn away your faces from all your abominations.

7 For every one of the house of Israel, or of the stranger that sojourneth in Israel, which separateth himself from me, and setteth up his idols in his heart, and putteth the stumblingblock of his iniquity before his face, and cometh to a prophet to inquire of him concerning me; I the LORD will answer him by myself:

8 And I will set my face against that man, and will make him a sign and a proverb, and I will cut him off from the midst of my people; and ye shall know that I *am* the LORD.

9 And if the prophet be deceived when he hath spoken a thing, I the LORD have deceived that prophet, and I will stretch out my hand upon him, and will destroy him from the midst of my people Israel.

10 And they shall bear the punishment of their iniquity: the punishment of the prophet shall be even as the punishment of him that seeketh *unto him*;

11 That the house of Israel may go no more astray from me, neither be polluted any more with all their transgressions; but that they may be my people, and I may be their God, saith the Lord GOD.

The Surety of Judgment

12 The word of the LORD came again to me, saying,

13 Son of man, when the land sinneth against me by trespassing grievously, then will I stretch out mine hand upon it, and will break the staff of the bread thereof, and will send famine upon it, and will cut off man and beast from it:

14 Though these three men, Noah, Daniel, and Job, were in it, they should deliver *but*

Cross references (center column)
17 Ezek. 13:2; 20:46; 21:2
18 2Pet. 2:14
19 Prov. 28:21; Mic. 3:5
21 Ezek. 13:9
22 Jer. 23:14
23 Ezek. 8:1; 12:24; 13:6, 9; 14:8; 15:7; 20:1; 33:31; Mic. 3:6
3 2Kgs. 3:13; Ezek. 7:19; 14:4, 7
8 Lev. 17:10; 20:3, 5, 6; Num. 26:10; Deut. 28:37; Jer. 44:11; Ezek. 5:15; 6:7; 15:7
9 1Kgs. 22:23; Job 12:16; Jer. 4:10; 2Thess. 2:11
11 Ezek. 11:20; 37:27; 2Pet. 2:15
13 Lev. 26:26; Isa. 3:1; Ezek. 4:16; 5:16
14 Prov. 11:4; Jer. 7:16; 11:14; 14:11; 15:1; Ezek. 14:16, 18, 20

13:17–19 Woe to the women. A cult of women in Jerusalem was using supposedly magical powers, occult ceremonies, and wicked incantations, along with their false prophecies. Compare this with the story of Jezebel in Rev. 2:20, a church-age false prophetess and deceiver.

14:14 Noah, Daniel, and Job. Even if these three great men were in Jerusalem when destruction came, they would, by their own dedication to God, be the only ones worthy of deliverance. All three are known in Scripture for their righteousness.

their own souls by their righteousness, saith the Lord GOD.

15 If I cause noisome beasts to pass through the land, and they spoil it, so that it be desolate, that no man may pass through because of the beasts:

16 Though these three men *were* in it, *as* I live, saith the Lord GOD, they shall deliver neither sons nor daughters; they only shall be delivered, but the land shall be desolate.

17 Or *if* I bring a sword upon that land, and say, Sword, go through the land; so that I cut off man and beast from it:

18 Though these three men *were* in it, *as* I live, saith the Lord GOD, they shall deliver neither sons nor daughters, but they only shall be delivered themselves.

19 Or *if* I send a pestilence into that land, and pour out my fury upon it in blood, to cut off from it man and beast:

20 Though Noah, Daniel, and Job, *were* in it, *as* I live, saith the Lord GOD, they shall deliver neither son nor daughter; they shall *but* deliver their own souls by their righteousness.

21 For thus saith the Lord GOD; How much more when I send my four sore judgments upon Jerusalem, the sword, and the famine, and the noisome beast, and the pestilence, to cut off from it man and beast?

22 Yet, behold, therein shall be left a remnant that shall be brought forth, *both* sons and daughters: behold, they shall come forth unto you, and ye shall see their way and their doings: and ye shall be comforted concerning the evil that I have brought upon Jerusalem, *even* concerning all that I have brought upon it.

23 And they shall comfort you, when ye see their ways and their doings: and ye shall know that I have not done without cause all that I have done in it, saith the Lord GOD.

CHAPTER 15
A Useless Vine

1 And the word of the LORD came unto me, saying,

2 Son of man, What is the vine tree more than any tree, *or than* a branch which is among the trees of the forest?

3 Shall wood be taken thereof to do any work? or will *men* take a pin of it to hang any vessel thereon?

4 Behold, it is cast into the fire for fuel; the fire devoureth both the ends of it, and the midst of it is burned. Is it meet for *any* work?

5 Behold, when it was whole, it was meet for no work: how much less shall it be meet yet for *any* work, when the fire hath devoured it, and it is burned?

6 Therefore thus saith the Lord GOD; As the vine tree among the trees of the forest, which I have given to the fire for fuel, so will I give the inhabitants of Jerusalem.

7 And I will set my face against them; they shall go out from *one* fire, and *another* fire shall devour them; and ye shall know that I *am* the LORD, when I set my face against them.

8 And I will make the land desolate, because they have committed a trespass, saith the Lord GOD.

CHAPTER 16
The Unfaithfulness of Jerusalem

1 Again the word of the LORD came unto me, saying,

2 Son of man, cause Jerusalem to know her abominations,

3 And say, Thus saith the Lord GOD unto Jerusalem; Thy birth and thy nativity *is* of the land of Canaan; thy father *was* an Amorite, and thy mother an Hittite.

4 And *as for* thy nativity, in the day thou wast born thy navel was not cut, neither wast thou washed in water to supple *thee*; thou wast not salted at all, nor swaddled at all.

5 None eye pitied thee, to do any of these unto thee, to have compassion upon thee; but thou wast cast out in the open field, to the lothing of thy person, in the day that thou wast born.

---

15 Lev. 26:22; Ezek. 5:17

16 Ezek. 14:14, 18, 20

17 Lev. 26:25; Ezek. 5:12; 21:3, 4; 25:13; 29:8; 38:21; Zeph. 1:3

18 Ezek. 14:14

19 2Sam. 24:15; Ezek. 7:8; 38:22

20 Ezek. 14:14

21 Ezek. 5:17; 33:27

22 Ezek. 6:8; 20:43

23 Jer. 22:8, 9; John 15:6

7 Lev. 17:10; Ezek. 6:7; 7:4; 11:10; 14:8; 20:38, 42, 44

8 Ezek. 20:4; 22:2; 33:7-9

3 Ezek. 15:45; 21:30; Hos. 2:3

14:21 four sore judgments. The sword or war, famine and starvation, wild ravenous beasts, and pestilence or plagues came upon Israel. Similar but far more horrendous judgments appear in Revelation 6:1–8; 9:3–21.

15:2 What is the vine? In this parable, the vine is a type of Israel, brought out of Egypt in the Exodus (Ps. 80:8–12), called an "empty vine" (Hos. 10:1), to come under judgment (Isa. 5:1–6), to wither and be consumed

(Ezek. 17:5–10; 19:10–14). In Matthew 21:33–46, Jesus likens Israel to a vineyard whose caretakers, symbolizing the Jewish leadership, would come under judgment for rejecting their Messiah.

16:1–9 as for thy nativity. In this parable, Jerusalem is compared to an abandoned child, lovingly rescued from bleeding to death, then richly blessed.

6 And when I passed by thee, and saw thee polluted in thine own blood, I said unto thee *when thou wast* in thy blood, Live; yea, I said unto thee *when thou wast* in thy blood, Live.

7 I have caused thee to multiply as the bud of the field, and thou hast increased and waxen great, and thou art come to excellent ornaments: *thy* breasts are fashioned, and thine hair is grown, whereas thou *wast* naked and bare.

8 Now when I passed by thee, and looked upon thee, behold, thy time *was* the time of love; and I spread my skirt over thee, and covered thy nakedness: yea, I sware unto thee, and entered into a covenant with thee, saith the Lord God, and thou becamest mine.

9 Then washed I thee with water; yea, I throughly washed away thy blood from thee, and I anointed thee with oil.

10 I clothed thee also with broidered work, and shod thee with badgers' skin, and I girded thee about with fine linen, and I covered thee with silk.

11 I decked thee also with ornaments, and I put bracelets upon thy hands, and a chain on thy neck.

12 And I put a jewel on thy forehead, and earrings in thine ears, and a beautiful crown upon thine head.

13 Thus wast thou decked with gold and silver; and thy raiment *was of* fine linen, and silk, and broidered work; thou didst eat fine flour, and honey, and oil: and thou wast exceeding beautiful, and thou didst prosper into a kingdom.

14 And thy renown went forth among the heathen for thy beauty: for it *was* perfect through my comeliness, which I had put upon thee, saith the Lord God.

15 But thou didst trust in thine own beauty, and playedst the harlot because of thy renown, and pouredst out thy fornications on every one that passed by; his it was.

16 And of thy garments thou didst take, and deckedst thy high places with divers colours, and playedst the harlot thereupon: *the like things* shall not come, neither shall it be *so*.

17 Thou hast also taken thy fair jewels of my gold and of my silver, which I had given thee, and madest to thyself images of men, and didst commit whoredom with them,

18 And tookest thine broidered garments, and coveredst them: and thou hast set mine oil and mine incense before them.

19 My meat also which I gave thee, fine flour, and oil, and honey, *wherewith* I fed thee, thou hast even set it before them for a sweet savour: and *thus* it was, saith the Lord God.

20 Moreover thou hast taken thy sons and thy daughters, whom thou hast borne unto me, and these hast thou sacrificed unto them to be devoured. *Is this* of thy whoredoms a small matter,

21 That thou hast slain my children, and delivered them to cause them to pass through *the fire* for them?

22 And in all thine abominations and thy whoredoms thou hast not remembered the days of thy youth, when thou wast naked and bare, *and* wast polluted in thy blood.

23 And it came to pass after all thy wickedness, (woe, woe unto thee! saith the Lord God;)

24 *That* thou hast also built unto thee an eminent place, and hast made thee an high place in every street.

25 Thou hast built thy high place at every head of the way, and hast made thy beauty to be abhorred, and hast opened thy feet to every one that passed by, and multiplied thy whoredoms.

26 Thou hast also committed fornication with the Egyptians thy neighbours, great of flesh; and hast increased thy whoredoms, to provoke me to anger.

27 Behold, therefore I have stretched out my hand over thee, and have diminished thine ordinary *food*, and delivered thee unto the will of them that hate thee, the daughters of the Philistines, which are ashamed of thy lewd way.

28 Thou hast played the whore also with the Assyrians, because thou wast unsatiable; yea, thou hast played the harlot with them, and yet couldest not be satisfied.

29 Thou hast moreover multiplied thy fornication in the land of Canaan unto Chaldea; and yet thou wast not satisfied herewith.

30 How weak is thine heart, saith the Lord God, seeing thou doest all these *things*, the work of an imperious whorish woman;

31 In that thou buildest thine eminent place in the head of every way, and makest thine high place in every street; and hast not been as an harlot, in that thou scornest hire;

Cross references:

7 Ex. 1:7

8 Ex. 19:5; Ruth 3:9; Jer. 2:2

11 Gen. 24:22, 47; Prov. 1:9

12 Isa. 3:21

13 Deut. 32:13, 14; Ps. 48:2

14 Lam. 2:15

15 Deut. 32:15; Isa. 1:21; 57:8; Jer. 2:20; 3:2, 6, 20; 7:4; Ezek. 23:3, 8, 11, 12; Hos. 1:2; Mic. 3:11

16 2Kgs. 23:7; Ezek. 7:20; Hos. 2:8

19 Hos. 2:8

20 2Kgs. 16:3; Ps. 106:37, 38; Isa. 57:5; Jer. 7:31; 32:35; Ezek. 20:26; 23:37

22 Jer. 2:2; Ezek. 16:4-6, 43, 60; Hos. 11:1

24 Isa. 57:5, 7; Jer. 2:20; 3:2; Ezek. 16:31

25 Prov. 9:14

26 Ezek. 8:10, 14; 20:7, 8; 23:19-21

27 2Chr. 28:18, 19; Ezek. 16:57

28 2Kgs. 16:7, 10; 2Chr. 28:23; Jer. 2:18, 36; Ezek. 23:12

29 Ezek. 23:14

31 Ezek. 16:24, 39

16:15–34 playedst the harlot. The parable then depicts the city as an immoral harlot—an evil, adulterous woman.

32 *But as* a wife that committeth adultery, *which* taketh strangers instead of her husband!

33 They give gifts to all whores: but thou givest thy gifts to all thy lovers, and hirest them, that they may come unto thee on every side for thy whoredom.

34 And the contrary is in thee from *other* women in thy whoredoms, whereas none followeth thee to commit whoredoms: and in that thou givest a reward, and no reward is given unto thee, therefore thou art contrary.

The Judgment of God

35 Wherefore, O harlot, hear the word of the LORD:

36 Thus saith the Lord GOD; Because thy filthiness was poured out, and thy nakedness discovered through thy whoredoms with thy lovers, and with all the idols of thy abominations, and by the blood of thy children, which thou didst give unto them;

37 Behold, therefore I will gather all thy lovers, with whom thou hast taken pleasure, and all *them* that thou hast loved, with all *them* that thou hast hated; I will even gather them round about against thee, and will discover thy nakedness unto them, that they may see all thy nakedness.

38 And I will judge thee, as women that break wedlock and shed blood are judged; and I will give thee blood in fury and jealousy.

39 And I will also give thee into their hand, and they shall throw down thine eminent place, and shall break down thy high places: they shall strip thee also of thy clothes, and shall take thy fair jewels, and leave thee naked and bare.

40 They shall also bring up a company against thee, and they shall stone thee with stones, and thrust thee through with their swords.

41 And they shall burn thine houses with fire, and execute judgments upon thee in the sight of many women: and I will cause thee to cease from playing the harlot, and thou also shalt give no hire any more.

42 So will I make my fury toward thee to rest, and my jealousy shall depart from thee, and I will be quiet, and will be no more angry.

43 Because thou hast not remembered the days of thy youth, but hast fretted me in all these *things*; behold, therefore I also will recompense thy way upon *thine* head, saith the Lord GOD: and thou shalt not commit this lewdness above all thine abominations.

44 Behold, every one that useth proverbs shall use *this* proverb against thee, saying, As *is* the mother, *so is* her daughter.

45 Thou *art* thy mother's daughter, that lotheth her husband and her children; and thou *art* the sister of thy sisters, which lothed their husbands and their children: your mother *was* an Hittite, and your father an Amorite.

46 And thine elder sister *is* Samaria, she and her daughters that dwell at thy left hand: and thy younger sister, that dwelleth at thy right hand, *is* Sodom and her daughters.

47 Yet hast thou not walked after their ways, nor done after their abominations: but, as *if that were* a very little *thing,* thou wast corrupted more than they in all thy ways.

48 *As* I live, saith the Lord GOD, Sodom thy sister hath not done, she nor her daughters, as thou hast done, thou and thy daughters.

49 Behold, this was the iniquity of thy sister Sodom, pride, fulness of bread, and abundance of idleness was in her and in her daughters, neither did she strengthen the hand of the poor and needy.

50 And they were haughty, and committed abomination before me: therefore I took them away as I saw *good.*

51 Neither hath Samaria committed half of thy sins; but thou hast multiplied thine abominations more than they, and hast justified thy sisters in all thine abominations which thou hast done.

52 Thou also, which hast judged thy sisters, bear thine own shame for thy sins that thou hast committed more abominable than they: they are more righteous than thou: yea, be thou confounded also, and bear thy shame, in that thou hast justified thy sisters.

Sodom and Samaria

53 When I shall bring again their captivity, the captivity of Sodom and her daughters, and the captivity of Samaria and her daughters, then *will I bring again* the captivity of thy captives in the midst of them:

54 That thou mayest bear thine own shame, and mayest be confounded in all that thou hast done, in that thou art a comfort unto them.

55 When thy sisters, Sodom and her daughters, shall return to their former estate, and Samaria and her daughters shall return to their former estate, then thou and thy

---

Cross references (center column):

33 Isa. 30:6; Hos. 8:9
36 Ezek. 16:20; Jer. 2:34
37 Jer. 13:22, 26; Lam. 1:8; Ezek. 23:9, 10, 22, 29; Hos. 2:10; 8:10; Nah. 3:5
38 Gen. 9:6; Ex. 21:12; Lev. 20:10; Deut. 22:22; Ezek. 16:20, 36; 23:45
39 Ezek. 16:24, 31; 23:26; Hos. 2:3
40 Ezek. 23:46, 47; John 8:5, 7
41 Deut. 13:16; 2Kgs. 25:9; Jer. 39:8; 52:13; Ezek. 23:10, 27, 48
42 Ezek. 5:13
43 Ps. 78:42; Ezek. 9:10; 11:21; 16:22; 22:31
45 Ezek. 16:3
46 Deut. 32:32; Isa. 1:10
47 2Kgs. 21:9; Ezek. 5:6, 7; 16:48, 51
48 Matt. 10:15; 11:24
49 Gen. 13:10
50 Gen. 13:13; 18:20; 19:5, 24
51 Jer. 3:11; Matt. 12:41, 42
53 Isa. 1:9; Jer. 20:16; Ezek. 16:60, 61
54 Ezek. 14:22, 23

daughters shall return to your former estate.

56 For thy sister Sodom was not mentioned by thy mouth in the day of thy pride,

57 Before thy wickedness was discovered, as at the time of *thy* reproach of the daughters of Syria, and all *that are* round about her, the daughters of the Philistines, which despise thee round about.

58 Thou hast borne thy lewdness and thine abominations, saith the LORD.

59 For thus saith the Lord GOD; I will even deal with thee as thou hast done, which hast despised the oath in breaking the covenant.

60 Nevertheless I will remember my covenant with thee with thee in the days of thy youth, and I will establish unto thee an everlasting covenant.

61 Then thou shalt remember thy ways, and be ashamed, when thou shalt receive thy sisters, thine elder and thy younger: and I will give them unto thee for daughters, but not by thy covenant.

62 And I will establish my covenant with thee; and thou shalt know that I *am* the LORD:

63 That thou mayest remember, and be confounded, and never open thy mouth any more because of thy shame, when I am pacified toward thee for all that thou hast done, saith the Lord GOD.

CHAPTER 17
The Eagles and the Vine

1 And the word of the LORD came unto me, saying,

2 Son of man, put forth a riddle, and speak a parable unto the house of Israel;

3 And say, Thus saith the Lord GOD; A great eagle with great wings, longwinged, full of feathers, which had divers colours, came unto Lebanon, and took the highest branch of the cedar:

4 He cropped off the top of his young twigs, and carried it into a land of traffick; he set it in a city of merchants.

5 He took also of the seed of the land, and planted it in a fruitful field; he placed *it* by great waters, *and* set it *as* a willow tree.

6 And it grew, and became a spreading vine of low stature, whose branches turned toward him, and the roots thereof were under him: so it became a vine, and brought forth branches, and shot forth sprigs.

7 There was also another great eagle with great wings and many feathers: and, behold, this vine did bend her roots toward him, and shot forth her branches toward him, that he might water it by the furrows of her plantation.

8 It was planted in a good soil by great waters, that it might bring forth branches, and that it might bear fruit, that it might be a goodly vine.

9 Say thou, Thus saith the Lord GOD; Shall it prosper? shall he not pull up the roots thereof, and cut off the fruit thereof, that it wither? it shall wither in all the leaves of her spring, even without great power or many people to pluck it up by the roots thereof.

10 Yea, behold, *being* planted, shall it prosper? shall it not utterly wither, when the east wind toucheth it? it shall wither in the furrows where it grew.

11 Moreover the word of the LORD came unto me, saying,

12 Say now to the rebellious house, Know ye not what these *things mean?* tell *them,* Behold, the king of Babylon is come to Jerusalem, and hath taken the king thereof, and the princes thereof, and led them with him to Babylon;

13 And hath taken of the king's seed, and made a covenant with him, and hath taken an oath of him: he hath also taken the mighty of the land:

14 That the kingdom might be base, that it might not lift itself up, *but* that by keeping of his covenant it might stand.

15 But he rebelled against him in sending his ambassadors into Egypt, that they might give him horses and much people. Shall he prosper? shall he escape that doeth such *things*? or shall he break the covenant, and be delivered?

16 *As* I live, saith the Lord GOD, surely in the place *where* the king *dwelleth* that made him king, whose oath he despised, and whose

Cross refs: 57 2Kgs. 16:5; 2Chr. 28:18; Isa. 7:1; 14:28; Ezek. 16:27. 58 Ezek. 23:49. 59 Deut. 29:12, 14; Ezek. 17:13, 16. 60 Ps. 106:45; Jer. 32:40; 50:5. 61 Isa. 54:1; 60:4; Jer. 31:31; Ezek. 20:43; 36:31; Gal. 4:26. 62 Hos. 2:19, 20. 63 2Kgs. 24:12; Ezek. 16:61; 17:12; Rom. 3:19. 5 Deut. 8:7-9; Isa. 44:4. 6 Ezek. 17:14. 7 Ezek. 17:15. 9 2Kgs. 25:7. 10 Ezek. 19:12; Hos. 13:15. 12 2Kgs. 24:11-16; Ezek. 2:5; 12:9; 17:3. 13 2Kgs. 24:17; 2Chr. 36:13. 14 Ezek. 17:6; 29:14. 15 Deut. 17:16; 2Kgs. 24:20; 2Chr. 36:13; Isa. 31:1, 3; 36:6, 9; Ezek. 17:9. 16 Jer. 32:5; 34:3; 52:11; Ezek. 12:13.

16:60–63 I will remember . . . I will establish my covenant. In mercy, God will restore Israel under a new covenant (see Jer. 31:31). This will be gloriously fulfilled in the coming Millennial Kingdom, described in chapters 40—48.

17:1–7 In this parable of the two eagles, the first eagle is Nebuchadnezzar of Babylon, who carried away many captives both in 606 and 597 B.C., leaving only a remnant in the land. Those who were still in the land looked to Hophra, king of Egypt, to be their protector, but the Egyptians also would fall to the Babylonians. This happened in 586 B.C., the same year Jerusalem capitulated.

covenant he brake, *even* with him in the midst of Babylon he shall die.

17 Neither shall Pharaoh with *his* mighty army and great company make for him in the war, by casting up mounts, and building forts, to cut off many persons:

18 Seeing he despised the oath by breaking the covenant, when, lo, he had given his hand, and hath done all these *things*, he shall not escape.

19 Therefore thus saith the Lord GOD; *As* I live, surely mine oath that he hath despised, and my covenant that he hath broken, even it will I recompense upon his own head.

20 And I will spread my net upon him, and he shall be taken in my snare, and I will bring him to Babylon, and will plead with him there for his trespass that he hath trespassed against me.

21 And all his fugitives with all his bands shall fall by the sword, and they that remain shall be scattered toward all winds: and ye shall know that I the LORD have spoken *it*.

22 Thus saith the Lord GOD; I will also take of the highest branch of the high cedar, and will set *it*; I will crop off from the top of his young twigs a tender one, and will plant *it* upon an high mountain and eminent:

23 In the mountain of the height of Israel will I plant it: and it shall bring forth boughs, and bear fruit, and be a goodly cedar: and under it shall dwell all fowl of every wing; in the shadow of the branches thereof shall they dwell.

24 And all the trees of the field shall know that I the LORD have brought down the high tree, have exalted the low tree, have dried up the green tree, and have made the dry tree to flourish: I the LORD have spoken and have done *it*.

CHAPTER 18
"The Soul That Sinneth, It Shall Die"

1 The word of the LORD came unto me again, saying,

2 What mean ye, that ye use this proverb concerning the land of Israel, saying, The fathers have eaten sour grapes, and the children's teeth are set on edge?

3 *As* I live, saith the Lord GOD, ye shall not have *occasion* any more to use this proverb in Israel.

4 Behold, all souls are mine; as the soul of the father, so also the soul of the son is mine: the soul that sinneth, it shall die.

5 But if a man be just, and do that which is lawful and right,

6 *And* hath not eaten upon the mountains, neither hath lifted up his eyes to the idols of the house of Israel, neither hath defiled his neighbour's wife, neither hath come near to a menstruous woman,

7 And hath not oppressed any, *but* hath restored to the debtor his pledge, hath spoiled none by violence, hath given his bread to the hungry, and hath covered the naked with a garment;

8 He *that* hath not given forth upon usury, neither hath taken any increase, *that* hath withdrawn his hand from iniquity, hath executed true judgment between man and man,

9 Hath walked in my statutes, and hath kept my judgments, to deal truly; he *is* just, he shall surely live, saith the Lord GOD.

10 If he beget a son *that is* a robber, a shedder of blood, and *that* doeth the like to *any* one of these *things*,

11 And that doeth not any of those *duties*, but even hath eaten upon the mountains, and defiled his neighbour's wife,

12 Hath oppressed the poor and needy, hath spoiled by violence, hath not restored the pledge, and hath lifted up his eyes to the idols, hath committed abomination,

13 Hath given forth upon usury, and hath taken increase: shall he then live? he shall not live: he hath done all these abominations; he shall surely die; his blood shall be upon him.

14 Now, lo, *if* he beget a son, that seeth all his father's sins which he hath done, and considereth, and doeth not such like,

15 *That* hath not eaten upon the mountains, neither hath lifted up his eyes to the idols of the house of Israel, hath not defiled his neighbour's wife,

16 Neither hath oppressed any, hath not withholden the pledge, neither hath spoiled

Cross references (center column)

17 Jer. 37:7; 52:4; Ezek. 4:2

18 1Chr. 29:24; Lam. 5:6

20 Ezek. 12:13; 20:36; 32:3

21 Ezek. 12:14

22 Ps. 2:6; Isa. 11:1; 53:2; Jer. 23:5; Zech. 3:8

23 Isa. 2:2, 3; Ezek. 20:40; 31:6; Dan. 4:12; Mic. 4:1

24 Jer. 31:29; Lam. 5:7; Ezek. 22:14; 24:14; Luke 1:52

4 Ezek. 18:20; Rom. 6:23

6 Lev. 18:19, 20; 20:10, 18; Ezek. 22:9

7 Ex. 22:21, 26; Lev. 19:15; 25:14; Deut. 15:7, 8; 24:12, 13; Isa. 58:7; Matt. 25:35, 36

8 Ex. 22:25; Lev. 25:36, 37; Deut. 1:16; 23:19; Neh. 5:7; Ps. 15:5; Zech. 8:16

9 Gen. 9:6; Ex. 21:12; Num. 35:31; Ezek. 20:11; Amos 5:4

12 Ezek. 8:6, 17

13 Lev. 20:9, 11-13, 16, 27; Ezek. 3:18; 33:4; Acts 18:6

15 Ezek. 18:6

17:22–24 I will also take . . . the highest branch. God speaks here, promising to take the highest branch, one of the Davidic royal line, planting it on a high mountain, indicating the fruitful and prosperous future reign of the Messiah (cf. Isa. 4:2; 11:1; 53:2; Jer. 23:5; Zech. 3:8; 6:12; Rev. 22:16).

18:2–32 fathers have eaten sour grapes, and the children's teeth are set on edge. This saying was being used by the Israelites to lay all the blame for their misfortunes on their fathers' disobedience. In this powerful sermon, Ezekiel makes it clear that all are responsible for their own souls in their own times.

by violence, *but* hath given his bread to the hungry, and hath covered the naked with a garment,

17 *That* hath taken off his hand from the poor, *that* hath not received usury nor increase, hath executed my judgments, hath walked in my statutes; he shall not die for the iniquity of his father, he shall surely live.

18 *As for* his father, because he cruelly oppressed, spoiled his brother by violence, and did *that* which *is* not good among his people, lo, even he shall die in his iniquity.

19 Yet say ye, Why? doth not the son bear the iniquity of the father? When the son hath done that which is lawful and right, *and* hath kept all my statutes, and hath done them, he shall surely live.

20 The soul that sinneth, it shall die. The son shall not bear the iniquity of the father, neither shall the father bear the iniquity of the son: the righteousness of the righteous shall be upon him, and the wickedness of the wicked shall be upon him.

God's Way Is Just

21 But if the wicked will turn from all his sins that he hath committed, and keep all my statutes, and do that which is lawful and right, he shall surely live, he shall not die.

22 All his transgressions that he hath committed, they shall not be mentioned unto him: in his righteousness that he hath done he shall live.

23 Have I any pleasure at all that the wicked should die? saith the Lord GOD: *and* not that he should return from his ways, and live?

24 But when the righteous turneth away from his righteousness, and committeth iniquity, *and* doeth according to all the abominations that the wicked *man* doeth, shall he live? All his righteousness that he hath done shall not be mentioned: in his trespass that he hath trespassed, and in his sin that he hath sinned, in them shall he die.

25 Yet ye say, The way of the Lord is not equal. Hear now, O house of Israel; Is not my way equal? are not your ways unequal?

26 When a righteous *man* turneth away from his righteousness, and committeth in-

Cross references column:
18 Ezek. 3:18
19 Ex. 20:5; Deut. 5:9; 2Kgs. 23:26; 24:3, 4
20 Deut. 24:16; 2Kgs. 14:6; 2Chr. 25:4; Isa. 3:10, 11; Jer. 31:29, 30; Ezek. 18:4; Rom. 2:9
21 Ezek. 18:27; 33:12, 19
22 Ezek. 33:16
23 Ezek. 18:32; 33:11; 1Tim. 2:4; 2Pet. 3:9
24 Ezek. 3:20; 33:12, 13, 18; 2Pet. 2:20
25 Ezek. 18:29; 33:17, 20
26 Ezek. 18:24
27 Ezek. 18:21
28 Ezek. 18:14
29 Ezek. 18:25
30 Ezek. 7:3; 33:20; Matt. 3:2; Rev. 2:5
31 Jer. 32:39; Ezek. 11:19; 36:26; Eph. 4:22, 23
32 Lam. 3:33; Ezek. 18:23; 26:17; 27:2; 33:11; 2Pet. 3:9
3 2Kgs. 23:31, 32; Ezek. 19:6
4 2Kgs. 23:33; 2Chr. 36:4; Jer. 22:11, 12
5 2Kgs. 23:34
6 Jer. 22:13-17; Ezek. 19:3
8 2Kgs. 24:2; Ezek. 19:4

iquity, and dieth in them; for his iniquity that he hath done shall he die.

27 Again, when the wicked *man* turneth away from his wickedness that he hath committed, and doeth that which is lawful and right, he shall save his soul alive.

28 Because he considereth, and turneth away from all his transgressions that he hath committed, he shall surely live, he shall not die.

29 Yet saith the house of Israel, The way of the Lord is not equal. O house of Israel, are not my ways equal? are not your ways unequal?

30 Therefore I will judge you, O house of Israel, every one according to his ways, saith the Lord GOD. Repent, and turn *yourselves* from all your transgressions; so iniquity shall not be your ruin.

31 Cast away from you all your transgressions, whereby ye have transgressed; and make you a new heart and a new spirit: for why will ye die, O house of Israel?

32 For I have no pleasure in the death of him that dieth, saith the Lord GOD: wherefore turn *yourselves*, and live ye.

CHAPTER 19
A Lamentation

1 Moreover take thou up a lamentation for the princes of Israel,

2 And say, What *is* thy mother? A lioness: she lay down among lions, she nourished her whelps among young lions.

3 And she brought up one of her whelps: it became a young lion, and it learned to catch the prey; it devoured men.

4 The nations also heard of him; he was taken in their pit, and they brought him with chains unto the land of Egypt.

5 Now when she saw that she had waited, *and* her hope was lost, then she took another of her whelps, *and* made him a young lion.

6 And he went up and down among the lions, he became a young lion, and learned to catch the prey, *and* devoured men.

7 And he knew their desolate palaces, and he laid waste their cities; and the land was desolate, and the fulness thereof, by the noise of his roaring.

8 Then the nations set against him on

19:1–9 lamentation for the princes of Israel. This poetic lamentation likens the last two kings of Israel to a lioness and her whelps. Jehoahaz, successor to King Josiah, was taken captive by the Egyptians after a three-month reign. King Jehoiachin also ruled three months and was taken captive to Babylon (see 2 Kgs. 23:34–37; 24:6–13; 25:27–30).

every side from the provinces, and spread their net over him: he was taken in their pit.
9 And they put him in ward in chains, and brought him to the king of Babylon: they brought him into holds, that his voice should no more be heard upon the mountains of Israel.
10 Thy mother *is* like a vine in thy blood, planted by the waters: she was fruitful and full of branches by reason of many waters.
11 And she had strong rods for the sceptres of them that bare rule, and her stature was exalted among the thick branches, and she appeared in her height with the multitude of her branches.
12 But she was plucked up in fury, she was cast down to the ground, and the east wind dried up her fruit: her strong rods were broken and withered; the fire consumed them.
13 And now she *is* planted in the wilderness, in a dry and thirsty ground.
14 And fire is gone out of a rod of her branches, *which* hath devoured her fruit, so that she hath no strong rod *to be* a sceptre to rule. This *is* a lamentation, and shall be for a lamentation.

CHAPTER 20
Israel Defies God

1 And it came to pass in the seventh year, in the fifth *month*, the tenth *day* of the month, *that* certain of the elders of Israel came to inquire of the LORD, and sat before me.
2 Then came the word of the LORD unto me, saying,
3 Son of man, speak unto the elders of Israel, and say unto them, Thus saith the Lord GOD; Are ye come to inquire of me? *As* I live, saith the Lord GOD, I will not be inquired of by you.
4 Wilt thou judge them, son of man, wilt thou judge *them*? cause them to know the abominations of their fathers:
5 And say unto them, Thus saith the Lord GOD; In the day when I chose Israel, and lifted up mine hand unto the seed of the house of Jacob, and made myself known unto them in the land of Egypt, when I lifted up mine hand unto them, saying, I *am* the LORD your God;

6 In the day *that* I lifted up mine hand unto them, to bring them forth of the land of Egypt into a land that I had espied for them, flowing with milk and honey, which *is* the glory of all lands:
7 Then said I unto them, Cast ye away every man the abominations of his eyes, and defile not yourselves with the idols of Egypt: I *am* the LORD your God.
8 But they rebelled against me, and would not hearken unto me: they did not every man cast away the abominations of their eyes, neither did they forsake the idols of Egypt: then I said, I will pour out my fury upon them, to accomplish my anger against them in the midst of the land of Egypt.
9 But I wrought for my name's sake, that it should not be polluted before the heathen, among whom they *were*, in whose sight I made myself known unto them, in bringing them forth out of the land of Egypt.
10 Wherefore I caused them to go forth out of the land of Egypt, and brought them into the wilderness.
11 And I gave them my statutes, and shewed them my judgments, which *if* a man do, he shall even live in them.
12 Moreover also I gave them my sabbaths, to be a sign between me and them, that they might know that I *am* the LORD that sanctify them.
13 But the house of Israel rebelled against me in the wilderness: they walked not in my statutes, and they despised my judgments, which *if* a man do, he shall even live in them; and my sabbaths they greatly polluted: then I said, I would pour out my fury upon them in the wilderness, to consume them.
14 But I wrought for my name's sake, that it should not be polluted before the heathen, in whose sight I brought them out.
15 Yet also I lifted up my hand unto them in the wilderness, that I would not bring them into the land which I had given *them*, flowing with milk and honey, which *is* the glory of all lands;
16 Because they despised my judgments, and walked not in my statutes, but polluted my sabbaths: for their heart went after their idols.

Cross references

9 2Chr. 36:6; Jer. 22:18
10 Deut. 8:7-9; Ezek. 17:6
11 Dan. 4:11
12 Ezek. 17:10; Hos. 13:15
14 Judg. 9:15; 2Kgs. 24:20; Lam. 4:20
5 Ex. 3:8; 4:31; 6:7, 8; 20:2; Deut. 4:34; 7:6
6 Ex. 3:8, 17; Deut. 8:7-9; Ps. 48:2; Jer. 32:22; Ezek. 20:15; Dan. 8:9; 11:16, 41; Zech. 7:14
7 Lev. 17:7; 18:3; Deut. 29:16-18; Josh. 24:14; 2Chr. 15:8; Ezek. 18:31
8 Ezek. 7:8; 20:13, 21
9 Ex. 32:12; Num. 14:13; Deut. 9:28; Ezek. 20:14, 22; 36:21, 22
10 Ex. 13:18
11 Lev. 18:5; Deut. 4:8; Neh. 9:13, 14; Ps. 147:19, 20; Ezek. 20:13, 21; Rom. 10:5; Gal. 3:12
12 Ex. 20:8; 31:13; 35:2; Deut. 5:12; Neh. 9:14
13 Ex. 16:27; Num. 14:22, 29; 26:65; Ps. 78:40; 95:8-10
15 Num. 14:28
16 Num. 15:39; Amos 5:25, 26; Acts 7:42, 43

20:1–33 Then came the word of the LORD. In this long sermon to the elders of Israel, Ezekiel reviews their history from the Egyptian bondage and the Exodus through their entrance into Canaan and their continual lapses into idolatry. God preserved them in His mercy and to keep His promises, but in Ezekiel's days, the same unfaithfulness continued. God promises in this passage to chastise His people, but also to gather them again in the land, where they would serve Him and be accepted.

17 Nevertheless mine eye spared them from destroying them, neither did I make an end of them in the wilderness.

18 But I said unto their children in the wilderness, Walk ye not in the statutes of your fathers, neither observe their judgments, nor defile yourselves with their idols:

19 I *am* the Lord your God; walk in my statutes, and keep my judgments, and do them;

20 And hallow my sabbaths; and they shall be a sign between me and you, that ye may know that I *am* the Lord your God.

21 Notwithstanding the children rebelled against me: they walked not in my statutes, neither kept my judgments to do them, which *if* a man do, he shall even live in them; they polluted my sabbaths: then I said, I would pour out my fury upon them, to accomplish my anger against them in the wilderness.

22 Nevertheless I withdrew mine hand, and wrought for my name's sake, that it should not be polluted in the sight of the heathen, in whose sight I brought them forth.

23 I lifted up mine hand unto them also in the wilderness, that I would scatter them among the heathen, and disperse them through the countries;

24 Because they had not executed my judgments, but had despised my statutes, and had polluted my sabbaths, and their eyes were after their fathers' idols.

25 Wherefore I gave them also statutes *that were* not good, and judgments whereby they should not live;

26 And I polluted them in their own gifts, in that they caused to pass through *the fire* all that openeth the womb, that I might make them desolate, to the end that they might know that I *am* the Lord.

27 Therefore, son of man, speak unto the house of Israel, and say unto them, Thus saith the Lord God; Yet in this your fathers have blasphemed me, in that they have committed a trespass against me.

28 *For* when I had brought them into the land, *for* the which I lifted up mine hand to give it to them, then they saw every high hill, and all the thick trees, and they offered there their sacrifices, and there they presented the provocation of their offering:

there also they made their sweet savour, and poured out there their drink offerings.

29 Then I said unto them, What *is* the high place whereunto ye go? And the name thereof is called Bamah unto this day.

30 Wherefore say unto the house of Israel, Thus saith the Lord God; Are ye polluted after the manner of your fathers? and commit ye whoredom after their abominations?

31 For when ye offer your gifts, when ye make your sons to pass through the fire, ye pollute yourselves with all your idols, even unto this day: and shall I be inquired of by you, O house of Israel? *As* I live, saith the Lord God, I will not be inquired of by you.

32 And that which cometh into your mind shall not be at all, that ye say, We will be as the heathen, as the families of the countries, to serve wood and stone.

God Punishes but Forgives

33 *As* I live, saith the Lord God, surely with a mighty hand, and with a stretched out arm, and with fury poured out, will I rule over you:

34 And I will bring you out from the people, and will gather you out of the countries wherein ye are scattered, with a mighty hand, and with a stretched out arm, and with fury poured out.

35 And I will bring you into the wilderness of the people, and there will I plead with you face to face.

36 Like as I pleaded with your fathers in the wilderness of the land of Egypt, so will I plead with you, saith the Lord God.

37 And I will cause you to pass under the rod, and I will bring you into the bond of the covenant:

38 And I will purge out from among you the rebels, and them that transgress against me: I will bring them forth out of the country where they sojourn, and they shall not enter into the land of Israel: and ye shall know that I *am* the Lord.

39 As for you, O house of Israel, thus saith the Lord God; Go ye, serve ye every one his idols, and hereafter *also*, if ye will not hearken unto me: but pollute ye my holy name no more with your gifts, and with your idols.

40 For in mine holy mountain, in the

Cross References

17 Ps. 78:38
19 Deut. 5:32, 33
20 Jer. 17:22; Ezek. 20:12
21 Num. 25:1, 2; Deut. 9:23, 24; 31:27; Ezek. 20:8, 11, 13
22 Ps. 78:38; Ezek. 20:9, 14, 17
23 Lev. 26:33; Deut. 28:64; Ps. 106:27; Jer. 15:4
24 Ezek. 6:9; 20:13, 16
25 Ps. 81:12; Ezek. 20:39; Rom. 1:24; 2Thess. 2:11
26 2Kgs. 17:17; 21:6; 2Chr. 28:3; 33:6; Jer. 32:35; Ezek. 16:20, 21; 20:6, 7
27 Rom. 2:24
28 Isa. 57:5; Ezek. 6:13; 16:19
31 Ezek. 20:3, 26
32 Ezek. 11:5
33 Jer. 21:5
35 Jer. 2:9, 35; Ezek. 17:20
36 Num. 14:21-23, 28, 29
37 Lev. 27:32; Jer. 33:13
38 Jer. 44:14; Ezek. 6:7; 15:7; 23:49; 34:17, 20; Matt. 25:32, 33
39 Judg. 10:14; Ps. 81:12; Isa. 1:13; Ezek. 23:38, 39; Amos 4:4

20:37 under the rod. The process of Israel's ultimate restoration involves coming under the rod of future judgment, when they are regathered from all nations. After that "purging," called by Jeremiah "the time of Jacob's trouble" (Jer. 30:7) and designated by Jesus as the "great tribulation" (Matt. 24:15–21), comes the Millennial Kingdom.

mountain of the height of Israel, saith the Lord GOD, there shall all the house of Israel, all of them in the land, serve me: there will I accept them, and there will I require your offerings, and the firstfruits of your oblations, with all your holy things.

41 I will accept you with your sweet savour, when I bring you out from the people, and gather you out of the countries wherein ye have been scattered; and I will be sanctified in you before the heathen.

42 And ye shall know that I *am* the LORD, when I shall bring you into the land of Israel, into the country *for* the which I lifted up mine hand to give it to your fathers.

43 And there shall ye remember your ways, and all your doings, wherein ye have been defiled; and ye shall lothe yourselves in your own sight for all your evils that ye have committed.

44 And ye shall know that I *am* the LORD, when I have wrought with you for my name's sake, not according to your wicked ways, nor according to your corrupt doings, O ye house of Israel, saith the Lord GOD.

The Prophecy against the Forest of the South

45 Moreover the word of the LORD came unto me, saying,

46 Son of man, set thy face toward the south, and drop *thy word* toward the south, and prophesy against the forest of the south field;

47 And say to the forest of the south, Hear the word of the LORD; Thus saith the Lord GOD; Behold, I will kindle a fire in thee, and it shall devour every green tree in thee, and every dry tree: the flaming flame shall not be quenched, and all faces from the south to the north shall be burned therein.

48 And all flesh shall see that I the LORD have kindled it: it shall not be quenched.

49 Then said I, Ah Lord GOD! they say of me, Doth he not speak parables?

CHAPTER 21
The Sword of the Lord

1 And the word of the LORD came unto me, saying,

2 Son of man, set thy face toward Jerusalem, and drop *thy word* toward the holy places, and prophesy against the land of Israel,

3 And say to the land of Israel, Thus saith the LORD; Behold, I *am* against thee, and will draw forth my sword out of his sheath, and will cut off from thee the righteous and the wicked.

4 Seeing then that I will cut off from thee the righteous and the wicked, therefore shall my sword go forth out of his sheath against all flesh from the south to the north:

5 That all flesh may know that I the LORD have drawn forth my sword out of his sheath: it shall not return any more.

6 Sigh therefore, thou son of man, with the breaking of *thy* loins; and with bitterness sigh before their eyes.

7 And it shall be, when they say unto thee, Wherefore sighest thou? that thou shalt answer, For the tidings; because it cometh: and every heart shall melt, and all hands shall be feeble, and every spirit shall faint, and all knees shall be weak *as* water: behold, it cometh, and shall be brought to pass, saith the Lord GOD.

8 Again the word of the LORD came unto me, saying,

9 Son of man, prophesy, and say, Thus saith the LORD; Say, A sword, a sword is sharpened, and also furbished:

10 It is sharpened to make a sore slaughter; it is furbished that it may glitter: should we then make mirth? it contemneth the rod of my son, *as* every tree.

11 And he hath given it to be furbished, that it may be handled: this sword is sharpened, and it is furbished, to give it into the hand of the slayer.

12 Cry and howl, son of man: for it shall be upon my people, it *shall be* upon all the princes of Israel: terrors by reason of the sword shall be upon my people: smite therefore upon *thy* thigh.

13 Because *it is* a trial, and what if *the sword* contemn even the rod? it shall be no *more*, saith the Lord GOD.

14 Thou therefore, son of man, prophesy, and smite *thine* hands together, and let the

Cross references (center column)

41 Eph. 5:2; Phil. 4:18

42 Ezek. 11:17; 20:38, 44; 34:13; 36:23, 24; 38:23

43 Lev. 26:39; Ezek. 6:9; 16:61; Hos. 5:15

44 Ezek. 20:38; 24:24; 36:22

46 Ezek. 6:2; 21:2

47 Deut. 32:2; Jer. 21:14; Ezek. 20:46; 21:4; Amos 7:16; Mic. 2:6, 11; Luke 23:31

3 Job 9:22

4 Ezek. 20:47

5 Isa. 45:23; 55:11

6 Isa. 22:4

7 Ezek. 7:17

9 Deut. 32:41; Ezek. 21:15, 28

11 Ezek. 21:19

12 Jer. 31:19

13 Job 9:23; Ezek. 21:27; 2Cor. 8:2

14 Num. 24:10; 1Kgs. 20:30; 22:25; Ezek. 6:11; 21:1, 7

20:47 I will kindle a fire. This parable of the forest that is consumed by fire metaphorically speaks of fires of judgment, sweeping through the land in the form of the Babylonian invaders, like a mighty forest fire which cannot be quenched. (Compare the fiery future devastation yet to affect the Middle East and the world, as forecast in Rev. 9:14–18.)

21:2–17 prophesy against the land of Israel. This parable of the sword symbolizes the slaughter to be perpetrated by the Babylonian invaders against Israel, which would happen in 588–586 B.C.

sword be doubled the third time, the sword of the slain: it *is* the sword of the great *men that are* slain, which entereth into their privy chambers.

15 I have set the point of the sword against all their gates, that *their* heart may faint, and *their* ruins be multiplied: ah! *it is* made bright, *it is* wrapped up for the slaughter.

16 Go thee one way or other, *either* on the right hand, *or* on the left, whithersoever thy face *is* set.

17 I will also smite mine hands together, and I will cause my fury to rest: I the LORD have said *it*.

The King of Babylon

18 The word of the LORD came unto me again, saying,

19 Also, thou son of man, appoint thee two ways, that the sword of the king of Babylon may come: both twain shall come forth out of one land: and choose thou a place, choose *it* at the head of the way to the city.

20 Appoint a way, that the sword may come to Rabbath of the Ammonites, and to Judah in Jerusalem the defenced.

21 For the king of Babylon stood at the parting of the way, at the head of the two ways, to use divination: he made *his* arrows bright, he consulted with images, he looked in the liver.

22 At his right hand was the divination for Jerusalem, to appoint captains, to open the mouth in the slaughter, to lift up the voice with shouting, to appoint *battering* rams against the gates, to cast a mount, *and* to build a fort.

23 And it shall be unto them as a false divination in their sight, to them that have sworn oaths: but he will call to remembrance the iniquity, that they may be taken.

24 Therefore thus saith the Lord GOD; Because ye have made your iniquity to be remembered, in that your transgressions are discovered, so that in all your doings your sins do appear; because, *I say*, that ye are come to remembrance, ye shall be taken with the hand.

25 And thou, profane wicked prince of Israel, whose day is come, when iniquity *shall have* an end,

26 Thus saith the Lord GOD; Remove the diadem, and take off the crown: this *shall* not *be* the same: exalt *him that is* low, and abase *him that is* high.

27 I will overturn, overturn, overturn, it: and it shall be no *more*, until he come whose right it is; and I will give it *him*.

Judgment upon the Ammonites

28 And thou, son of man, prophesy and say, Thus saith the Lord GOD concerning the Ammonites, and concerning their reproach; even say thou, The sword, the sword *is* drawn: for the slaughter *it is* furbished, to consume because of the glittering:

29 Whiles they see vanity unto thee, whiles they divine a lie unto thee, to bring thee upon the necks of *them that are* slain, of the wicked, whose day is come, when their iniquity *shall have* an end.

30 Shall I cause *it* to return into his sheath? I will judge thee in the place where thou wast created, in the land of thy nativity.

31 And I will pour out mine indignation upon thee, I will blow against thee in the fire of my wrath, and deliver thee into the hand of brutish men, *and* skilful to destroy.

32 Thou shalt be for fuel to the fire; thy blood shall be in the midst of the land; thou shalt be no *more* remembered: for I the LORD have spoken *it*.

CHAPTER 22
The Sins of Jerusalem

1 Moreover the word of the LORD came unto me, saying,

2 Now, thou son of man, wilt thou judge, wilt thou judge the bloody city? yea, thou shalt shew her all her abominations.

3 Then say thou, Thus saith the Lord GOD, The city sheddeth blood in the midst of it, that her time may come, and maketh idols against herself to defile herself.

4 Thou art become guilty in thy blood that thou hast shed; and hast defiled thyself in

Cross references (center column):

15 Ezek. 21:10, 28
16 Ezek. 14:17
17 Ezek. 5:13; 21:14; 22:13
20 Jer. 49:2; Ezek. 25:5; Amos 1:14
22 Jer. 51:14; Ezek. 4:2
23 Ezek. 17:13, 15, 16, 18
25 2Chr. 36:13; Jer. 52:2; Ezek. 17:19; 21:29; 35:5
26 Ezek. 17:24; Luke 1:52
27 Gen. 49:10; Ezek. 21:13; Luke 1:32, 33; John 1:49
28 Jer. 49:1; Ezek. 21:9, 10; 25:2, 3, 6; Zeph. 2:8, 9, 10
29 Job 18:20; Ps. 37:13; Ezek. 12:24; 21:25; 22:28
30 Gen. 15:14; Jer. 47:6, 7; Ezek. 16:3, 38
31 Ezek. 7:8; 14:19; 22:20, 21, 22
32 Ezek. 16:2; 20:4; 23:36; 24:6, 9; 25:10; Nah. 3:1
4 Deut. 28:37; 1Kgs. 9:7; 2Kgs. 21:16; Ezek. 5:14; Dan. 9:16

21:19–24 king of Babylon. Nebuchadnezzar is depicted as using divination to determine whether to attack Jerusalem or Ammon.

21:25 profane wicked prince. This is the wicked King Zedekiah, the last monarch (2 Chr. 36:11–21).

21:27 until he come whose right it is. The threefold use of the term "overturn" is thought by some to refer to

1) the fall and destruction of Jerusalem in 586 B.C.; 2) the burning of Jerusalem in A.D. 70; and 3) the yet future destruction in Israel during the Tribulation (Mark 13:14–19). Beyond the fall of Zedekiah, there would be overturnings, ruins in the land, until the One comes, whose right it is to reign. Jesus, descendant of David, King of Israel, will be the ultimate sovereign.

thine idols which thou hast made; and thou hast caused thy days to draw near, and art come *even* unto thy years: therefore have I made thee a reproach unto the heathen, and a mocking to all countries.

5 *Those that be* near, and *those that be* far from thee, shall mock thee, *which art* infamous *and* much vexed.

6 Behold, the princes of Israel, every one were in thee to their power to shed blood.

7 In thee have they set light by father and mother: in the midst of thee have they dealt by oppression with the stranger: in thee have they vexed the fatherless and the widow.

8 Thou hast despised mine holy things, and hast profaned my sabbaths.

9 In thee are men that carry tales to shed blood: and in thee they eat upon the mountains: in the midst of thee they commit lewdness.

10 In thee have they discovered their fathers' nakedness: in thee have they humbled her that was set apart for pollution.

11 And one hath committed abomination with his neighbour's wife; and another hath lewdly defiled his daughter-in-law; and another in thee hath humbled his sister, his father's daughter.

12 In thee have they taken gifts to shed blood; thou hast taken usury and increase, and thou hast greedily gained of thy neighbours by extortion, and hast forgotten me, saith the Lord GOD.

13 Behold, therefore I have smitten mine hand at thy dishonest gain which thou hast made, and at thy blood which hath been in the midst of thee.

14 Can thine heart endure, or can thine hands be strong, in the days that I shall deal with thee? I the LORD have spoken *it*, and will do *it*.

15 And I will scatter thee among the heathen, and disperse thee in the countries, and will consume thy filthiness out of thee.

16 And thou shalt take thine inheritance in thyself in the sight of the heathen, and thou shalt know that I *am* the LORD.

17 And the word of the LORD came unto me, saying,

18 Son of man, the house of Israel is to me become dross: all they *are* brass, and tin,

and iron, and lead, in the midst of the furnace; they are *even* the dross of silver.

19 Therefore thus saith the Lord GOD; Because ye are all become dross, behold, therefore I will gather you into the midst of Jerusalem.

20 *As* they gather silver, and brass, and iron, and lead, and tin, into the midst of the furnace, to blow the fire upon it, to melt *it*; so will I gather *you* in mine anger and in my fury, and I will leave *you there*, and melt you.

21 Yea, I will gather you, and blow upon you in the fire of my wrath, and ye shall be melted in the midst thereof.

22 As silver is melted in the midst of the furnace, so shall ye be melted in the midst thereof; and ye shall know that I the LORD have poured out my fury upon you.

23 And the word of the LORD came unto me, saying,

24 Son of man, say unto her, Thou *art* the land that is not cleansed, nor rained upon in the day of indignation.

25 *There is* a conspiracy of her prophets in the midst thereof, like a roaring lion ravening the prey; they have devoured souls; they have taken the treasure and precious things; they have made her many widows in the midst thereof.

26 Her priests have violated my law, and have profaned mine holy things: they have put no difference between the holy and profane, neither have they shewed *difference* between the unclean and the clean, and have hid their eyes from my sabbaths, and I am profaned among them.

27 Her princes in the midst thereof *are* like wolves ravening the prey, to shed blood, *and* to destroy souls, to get dishonest gain.

28 And her prophets have daubed them with untempered *morter*, seeing vanity, and divining lies unto them, saying, Thus saith the Lord GOD, when the LORD hath not spoken.

29 The people of the land have used oppression, and exercised robbery, and have vexed the poor and needy: yea, they have oppressed the stranger wrongfully.

30 And I sought for a man among them, that should make up the hedge, and stand in the gap before me for the land, that I should not destroy it: but I found none.

Cross references (center column):

6 Isa. 1:23; Mic. 3:1-3; Zeph. 3:3
7 Deut. 27:16
8 Lev. 19:16, 30; Ezek. 22:26; 23:38
10 Lev. 18:7, 8, 19; 20:11, 18; Ezek. 18:6; 1Cor. 5:1
11 Lev. 18:9, 15, 20; Deut. 22:22; Jer. 5:8
12 Ex. 22:25; 23:8; Lev. 25:36; Deut. 16:19; 23:19; 27:25; 32:18; Jer. 3:21; Ezek. 18:13; 23:35
13 Ezek. 21:17
14 Ezek. 21:7 Ezek. 17:24
15 Deut. 4:27; 28:25, 64; Ezek. 12, 14, 15 Ezek. 23:27, 48
16 Ps. 9:16; Ezek. 6:7
18 Isa. 1:22; Jer. 6:28; Ps. 119:119
21 Ezek. 22:20-22
22 Ezek. 20:8, 33; 22:31
26 Lev. 10:10; 22:2; 1Sam. 2:29; Jer. 15:19; Ezek. 44:23
27 Isa. 1:23
29 Jer. 5:26-28

22:18 furnace. In this parable, the smelting furnace is the symbol of God's fiery indignation against the wicked city.

22:30 a man . . . [to] stand in the gap. No one was able to interpose or intercede in order to halt divine judgment. In New Testament times however, there is One who stood in the gap for sinners, Jesus Christ!

31 Therefore have I poured out mine indignation upon them; I have consumed them with the fire of my wrath: their own way have I recompensed upon their heads, saith the Lord GOD.

CHAPTER 23
The Sin of Aholah and Aholibah

1 The word of the LORD came again unto me, saying,

2 Son of man, there were two women, the daughters of one mother:

3 And they committed whoredoms in Egypt; they committed whoredoms in their youth: there were their breasts pressed, and there they bruised the teats of their virginity.

4 And the names of them were Aholah the elder, and Aholibah her sister: and they were mine, and they bare sons and daughters. Thus were their names; Samaria is Aholah, and Jerusalem Aholibah.

5 And Aholah played the harlot when she was mine; and she doted on her lovers, on the Assyrians her neighbours,

6 Which were clothed with blue, captains and rulers, all of them desirable young men, horsemen riding upon horses.

7 Thus she committed her whoredoms with them, with all them that were the chosen men of Assyria, and with all on whom she doted: with all their idols she defiled herself.

8 Neither left she her whoredoms brought from Egypt: for in her youth they lay with her, and they bruised the breasts of her virginity, and poured their whoredom upon her.

9 Wherefore I have delivered her into the hand of her lovers, into the hand of the Assyrians, upon whom she doted.

10 These discovered her nakedness: they took her sons and her daughters, and slew her with the sword: and she became famous among women; for they had executed judgment upon her.

11 And when her sister Aholibah saw this,

she was more corrupt in her inordinate love than she, and in her whoredoms more than her sister in her whoredoms.

12 She doted upon the Assyrians her neighbours, captains and rulers clothed most gorgeously, horsemen riding upon horses, all of them desirable young men.

13 Then I saw that she was defiled, that they took both one way,

14 And that she increased her whoredoms: for when she saw men pourtrayed upon the wall, the images of the Chaldeans pourtrayed with vermilion,

15 Girded with girdles upon their loins, exceeding in dyed attire upon their heads, all of them princes to look to, after the manner of the Babylonians of Chaldea, the land of their nativity:

16 And as soon as she saw them with her eyes, she doted upon them, and sent messengers unto them into Chaldea.

17 And the Babylonians came to her into the bed of love, and they defiled her with their whoredom, and she was polluted with them, and her mind was alienated from them.

18 So she discovered her whoredoms, and discovered her nakedness: then my mind was alienated from her, like as my mind was alienated from her sister.

19 Yet she multiplied her whoredoms, in calling to remembrance the days of her youth, wherein she had played the harlot in the land of Egypt.

20 For she doted upon their paramours, whose flesh is as the flesh of asses, and whose issue is like the issue of horses.

21 Thus thou calledst to remembrance the lewdness of thy youth, in bruising thy teats by the Egyptians for the paps of thy youth.

The Younger Sister

22 Therefore, O Aholibah, thus saith the Lord GOD; Behold, I will raise up thy lovers against thee, from whom thy mind is alienated, and I will bring them against thee on every side;

Cross References

31 Ezek. 9:10; 11:21; 16:43; 16:46; 22:22; Jer. 3:7, 8, 10

3 Lev. 17:7; Josh. 24:14; Ezek. 16:22; 20:8

4 1Kgs. 8:29; Ezek. 16:8, 20

5 2Kgs. 15:19; 16:7; 17:3; Hos. 8:9

8 Ezek. 23:3

9 2Kgs. 17:3-6, 23; 18:9-11

10 Ezek. 16:37, 41

11 Jer. 3:8–11; Ezek. 16:47, 51

12 2Kgs. 16:7, 10; 2Chr. 28:16-23; Ezek. 16:28; 23:6, 23

16 2Kgs. 24:1; Ezek. 16:29

17 Ezek. 23:22, 28

18 Jer. 6:8

19 Ezek. 23:3

20 Ezek. 16:26

22 Ezek. 16:37; 23:28

23:4 Aholah . . . and Aholibah her sister. The parable represents Samaria, the Northern Kingdom, and the surviving Southern Kingdom. Aholah means "her own tabernacle" and Aholibah signifies "my tabernacle is in her." This refers to Israel's total apostasy with her own false religion and Judah, where God's temple or tabernacle, though defiled, still stood in Jerusalem. Both had been guilty of spiritual prostitution and were and would be recompensed. Dramatically and retrospectively, the parable looks back at the two nations, figuratively and vividly depicting their spiritual adulteries ranging from turning against the true God of Israel to embracing evil, idolatrous practices, called "whoredoms."

23 The Babylonians, and all the Chaldeans, Pekod, and Shoa, and Koa, *and* all the Assyrians with them: all of them desirable young men, captains and rulers, great lords and renowned, all of them riding upon horses.

24 And they shall come against thee with chariots, wagons, and wheels, and with an assembly of people, *which* shall set against thee buckler and shield and helmet round about: and I will set judgment before them, and they shall judge thee according to their judgments.

25 And I will set my jealousy against thee, and they shall deal furiously with thee: they shall take away thy nose and thine ears; and thy remnant shall fall by the sword: they shall take thy sons and thy daughters; and thy residue shall be devoured by the fire.

26 They shall also strip thee out of thy clothes, and take away thy fair jewels.

27 Thus will I make thy lewdness to cease from thee, and thy whoredom *brought* from the land of Egypt: so that thou shalt not lift up thine eyes unto them, nor remember Egypt any more.

28 For thus saith the Lord GOD; Behold, I will deliver thee into the hand *of them* whom thou hatest, into the hand *of them* from whom thy mind is alienated:

29 And they shall deal with thee hatefully, and shall take away all thy labour, and shall leave thee naked and bare: and the nakedness of thy whoredoms shall be discovered, both thy lewdness and thy whoredoms.

30 I will do these *things* unto thee, because thou hast gone a whoring after the heathen, *and* because thou art polluted with their idols.

31 Thou hast walked in the way of thy sister; therefore will I give her cup into thine hand.

32 Thus saith the Lord GOD; Thou shalt drink of thy sister's cup deep and large: thou shalt be laughed to scorn and had in derision; it containeth much.

33 Thou shalt be filled with drunkenness and sorrow, with the cup of astonishment and desolation, with the cup of thy sister Samaria.

34 Thou shalt even drink it and suck *it* out, and thou shalt break the sherds thereof, and pluck off thine own breasts: for I have spoken *it*, saith the Lord GOD.

35 Therefore thus saith the Lord GOD; Because thou hast forgotten me, and cast me behind thy back, therefore bear thou also thy lewdness and thy whoredoms.

---

23 Jer. 50:21; Ezek. 23:12
26 Ezek. 16:39
27 Ezek. 16:41; 22:15; 23:3, 19
28 Ezek. 16:37; 23:17
29 Ezek. 16:39; 23:26
30 Ezek. 6:9
31 Jer. 25:15
32 Ezek. 22:4, 5
34 Ps. 75:8; Isa. 51:17
35 1Kgs. 14:9; Neh. 9:26; Jer. 2:32; 3:21; 13:25; Ezek. 22:12
36 Isa. 58:1; Ezek. 20:4; 22:2
37 Ezek. 16:20, 21, 36, 38, 45; 20:26, 31; 23:45
38 Ezek. 22:8
39 2Kgs. 21:4
40 Ruth 3:3; 2Kgs. 9:30; Esth. 1:6; Isa. 57:7, 9; Jer. 4:30; Amos 2:8; 6:4
41 Prov. 7:17; Ezek. 16:18, 19; Hos. 2:8
45 Ezek. 16:38; 23:37
46 Ezek. 16:40
47 2Chr. 36:17, 19; Ezek. 16:40; 24:21
48 Deut. 13:11; Ezek. 22:15; 23:27; 2Pet. 2:6

Judgment upon Aholah and Aholibah

36 The LORD said moreover unto me; Son of man, wilt thou judge Aholah and Aholibah? yea, declare unto them their abominations;

37 That they have committed adultery, and blood *is* in their hands, and with their idols have they committed adultery, and have also caused their sons, whom they bare unto me, to pass for them through *the fire*, to devour *them*.

38 Moreover this they have done unto me: they have defiled my sanctuary in the same day, and have profaned my sabbaths.

39 For when they had slain their children to their idols, then they came the same day into my sanctuary to profane it; and, lo, thus have they done in the midst of mine house.

40 And furthermore, that ye have sent for men to come from far, unto whom a messenger *was* sent; and, lo, they came: for whom thou didst wash thyself, paintedst thy eyes, and deckedst thyself with ornaments,

41 And satest upon a stately bed, and a table prepared before it, whereupon thou hast set mine incense and mine oil.

42 And a voice of a multitude being at ease *was* with her: and with the men of the common sort *were* brought Sabeans from the wilderness, which put bracelets upon their hands, and beautiful crowns upon their heads.

43 Then said I unto *her that was* old in adulteries, Will they now commit whoredoms with her, and she *with them*?

44 Yet they went in unto her, as they go in unto a woman that playeth the harlot: so went they in unto Aholah and unto Aholibah, the lewd women.

45 And the righteous men, they shall judge them after the manner of adulteresses, and after the manner of women that shed blood; because they *are* adulteresses, and blood *is* in their hands.

46 For thus saith the Lord GOD; I will bring up a company upon them, and will give them to be removed and spoiled.

47 And the company shall stone them with stones, and dispatch them with their swords; they shall slay their sons and their daughters, and burn up their houses with fire.

48 Thus will I cause lewdness to cease out of the land, that all women may be taught not to do after your lewdness.

49 And they shall recompense your lewdness upon you, and ye shall bear the sins of your idols: and ye shall know that I *am* the Lord GOD.

CHAPTER 24
The Boiling Pot

1 Again in the ninth year, in the tenth month, in the tenth *day* of the month, the word of the LORD came unto me, saying,
2 Son of man, write thee the name of the day, *even* of this same day: the king of Babylon set himself against Jerusalem this same day.
3 And utter a parable unto the rebellious house, and say unto them, Thus saith the Lord GOD; Set on a pot, set *it* on, and also pour water into it:
4 Gather the pieces thereof into it, *even* every good piece, the thigh, and the shoulder; fill *it* with the choice bones.
5 Take the choice of the flock, and burn also the bones under it, *and* make it boil well, and let them seethe the bones of it therein.
6 Wherefore thus saith the Lord GOD; Woe to the bloody city, to the pot whose scum *is* therein, and whose scum is not gone out of it! bring it out piece by piece; let no lot fall upon it.
7 For her blood is in the midst of her; she set it upon the top of a rock; she poured it not upon the ground, to cover it with dust;
8 That it might cause fury to come up to take vengeance; I have set her blood upon the top of a rock, that it should not be covered.
9 Therefore thus saith the Lord GOD; Woe to the bloody city! I will even make the pile for fire great.
10 Heap on wood, kindle the fire, consume the flesh, and spice it well, and let the bones be burned.
11 Then set it empty upon the coals thereof, that the brass of it may be hot, and may burn, and *that* the filthiness of it may be

molten in it, *that* the scum of it may be consumed.
12 She hath wearied *herself* with lies, and her great scum went not forth out of her: her scum *shall be* in the fire.
13 In thy filthiness *is* lewdness: because I have purged thee, and thou wast not purged, thou shalt not be purged from thy filthiness any more, till I have caused my fury to rest upon thee.
14 I the LORD have spoken *it*: it shall come to pass, and I will do *it*; I will not go back, neither will I spare, neither will I repent; according to thy ways, and according to thy doings, shall they judge thee, saith the Lord GOD.

The Death of Ezekiel's Wife

15 Also the word of the LORD came unto me, saying,
16 Son of man, behold, I take away from thee the desire of thine eyes with a stroke: yet neither shalt thou mourn nor weep, neither shall thy tears run down.
17 Forbear to cry, make no mourning for the dead, bind the tire of thine head upon thee, and put on thy shoes upon thy feet, and cover not *thy* lips, and eat not the bread of men.
18 So I spake unto the people in the morning: and at even my wife died; and I did in the morning as I was commanded.
19 And the people said unto me, Wilt thou not tell us what these *things are* to us, that thou doest *so*?
20 Then I answered them, The word of the LORD came unto me, saying,
21 Speak unto the house of Israel, Thus saith the Lord GOD; Behold, I will profane my sanctuary, the excellency of your strength, the desire of your eyes, and that which your soul pitieth; and your sons and your daughters whom ye have left shall fall by the sword.
22 And ye shall do as I have done: ye shall not cover *your* lips, nor eat the bread of men.
23 And your tires *shall be* upon your heads,

Cross References (center column)

49 2Kgs. 25:1; Jer. 39:1; 52:4; Ezek. 20:38, 42, 44; 23:35; 25:5

3 Jer. 1:13; Ezek. 11:3; 17:12

6 2Sam. 8:2; Ezek. 22:3; 23:37; 24:9; Joel 3:3; Obad. 1:11; Nah. 3:10

7 Lev. 17:13; Deut. 12:16, 24

8 Matt. 7:2

9 Ezek. 24:6; Nah. 3:1; Hab. 2:12

11 Ezek. 22:15

13 Ezek. 5:13; 8:18; 16:42

14 1Sam. 15:29; Ezek. 5:11

17 Lev. 10:6; 21:10; 2Sam. 15:30; Jer. 16:5-7; Ezek. 24:22; Mic. 3:7

19 Ezek. 12:9; 37:18

21 Ps. 27:4; Jer. 7:14; Ezek. 7:20-22; 23:47

22 Jer. 16:6, 7; Ezek. 24:17

23 Lev. 26:39; Job 27:15; Ps. 78:64; Ezek. 33:10

24:3 Set on a pot. The parable of the boiling pot follows up on Jerusalem's claim in 11:3 that the "city is the caldron, and we be the flesh," meaning they would be protected and preserved from judgment. Here the Lord tells them Jerusalem shall be the caldron, not for preservation, but for fiery judgment.

24:16–17, 24 neither shalt thou mourn. Ezekiel's wife dies suddenly, but the prophet is not to follow the usual mourning customs of the Jews. With little show of emotion, he is to be silent, "covering his lips" until news of Jerusalem's fall arrives in Babylon. As the prophet did not publicly mourn, so Israelite exiles were not to grieve outwardly over the fall of Jerusalem and divine punishment when their relatives were smitten, because their judgment was just.

and your shoes upon your feet: ye shall not mourn nor weep; but ye shall pine away for your iniquities, and mourn one toward another.

24 Thus Ezekiel is unto you a sign: according to all that he hath done shall ye do: and when this cometh, ye shall know that I *am* the Lord GOD.

25 Also, thou son of man, *shall it* not *be* in the day when I take from them their strength, the joy of their glory, the desire of their eyes, and that whereupon they set their minds, their sons and their daughters,

26 *That* he that escapeth in that day shall come unto thee, to cause *thee* to hear *it* with *thine* ears?

27 In that day shall thy mouth be opened to him which is escaped, and thou shalt speak, and be no more dumb: and thou shalt be a sign unto them; and they shall know that I *am* the LORD.

CHAPTER 25
The Ammonites

1 The word of the LORD came again unto me, saying,

2 Son of man, set thy face against the Ammonites, and prophesy against them;

3 And say unto the Ammonites, Hear the word of the Lord GOD; Thus saith the Lord GOD; Because thou saidst, Aha, against my sanctuary, when it was profaned; and against the land of Israel, when it was desolate; and against the house of Judah, when they went into captivity;

4 Behold, therefore I will deliver thee to the men of the east for a possession, and they shall set their palaces in thee, and make their dwellings in thee: they shall eat thy fruit, and they shall drink thy milk.

5 And I will make Rabbah a stable for camels, and the Ammonites a couching-place for flocks: and ye shall know that I *am* the LORD.

6 For thus saith the Lord GOD; Because thou hast clapped *thine* hands, and stamped

with the feet, and rejoiced in heart with all thy despite against the land of Israel;

7 Behold, therefore I will stretch out mine hand upon thee, and will deliver thee for a spoil to the heathen; and I will cut thee off from the people, and I will cause thee to perish out of the countries: I will destroy thee; and thou shalt know that I *am* the LORD.

Moab

8 Thus saith the Lord GOD; Because that Moab and Seir do say, Behold, the house of Judah *is* like unto all the heathen;

9 Therefore, behold, I will open the side of Moab from the cities, from his cities *which are* on his frontiers, the glory of the country, Beth-jeshimoth, Baal-meon, and Kiriathaim,

10 Unto the men of the east with the Ammonites, and will give them in possession, that the Ammonites may not be remembered among the nations.

11 And I will execute judgments upon Moab; and they shall know that I *am* the LORD.

Edom

12 Thus saith the Lord GOD; Because that Edom hath dealt against the house of Judah by taking vengeance, and hath greatly offended, and revenged himself upon them;

13 Therefore thus saith the Lord GOD; I will also stretch out mine hand upon Edom, and will cut off man and beast from it; and I will make it desolate from Teman; and they of Dedan shall fall by the sword.

14 And I will lay my vengeance upon Edom by the hand of my people Israel: and they shall do in Edom according to mine anger and according to my fury; and they shall know my vengeance, saith the Lord GOD.

The Philistines

15 Thus saith the Lord GOD; Because the Philistines have dealt by revenge, and have

Cross references

24 Isa. 20:3; Jer. 17:15; Ezek. 4:3; 6:7; 12:6, 11; 25:5; John 13:19; 14:29

25 Ezek. 24:21

26 Ezek. 33:21, 22

27 Jer. 49:1; Ezek. 3:26, 27; 6:2; 21:28; 24:24; 29:21; 33:22; 35:2; Amos 1:13; Zeph. 2:9

3 Prov. 17:5; Ezek. 26:2

4 Isa. 17:2; 32:14; Ezek. 21:20; 24:24, 26:6, 35:9; Zeph. 2:14, 15

6 Job 27:23; Lam. 2:15; Ezek. 36:5; Zeph. 2:8, 10, 15

7 Ezek. 35:3

8 Jer. 48:1; Ezek. 35:2, 5, 12; Amos 2:1

10 Ezek. 21:32; 25:4

12 2Chr. 28:17; Ps. 137:7; Jer. 49:7, 8; Ezek. 35:2; Amos 1:11; Obad. 1:10

14 Isa. 11:14; Jer. 49:2

15 2Chr. 28:18; Jer. 25:20; 47:1; Joel 3:4; Amos 1:6

24:26–27 shall thy mouth be opened. Evidently, Ezekiel continued in silence without prophesying publicly until an escapee from Jerusalem brought word of the actual fall of the city in 586 B.C. (See Ezekiel 33:22 when Ezekiel resumes his preaching.)

25:1–7 against the Ammonites. Descendants of Lot and his daughter (Gen. 19:33–38), the Ammonites are also discussed by this prophet (Ezek. 21:28–32), by Amos (Amos 1:13–15), by Jeremiah (Jer. 49:1, etc.), and

later by Ezra (Ezra 9:1) and Nehemiah (Neh. 2:19; 13:1).

25:12–14 Edom. The descendants of Esau, Jacob's brother, were closer relatives to Israel than Ammon and Moab. Israel was commanded not to "abhor an Edomite; for he is thy brother" (Deut. 23:7). Perennial enemies for centuries (Amos 1:11; Obadiah 3–5), Edom was also punished, but the Herodian kings were Idumeans (Edomites) in Jesus' and Paul's times.

taken vengeance with a despiteful heart, to destroy it for the old hatred;

16 Therefore thus saith the Lord GOD; Behold, I will stretch out mine hand upon the Philistines, and I will cut off the Cherethims, and destroy the remnant of the sea coast.

17 And I will execute great vengeance upon them with furious rebukes; and they shall know that I am the LORD, when I shall lay my vengeance upon them.

CHAPTER 26
Tyre

1 And it came to pass in the eleventh year, in the first day of the month, that the word of the LORD came unto me, saying,

2 Son of man, because that Tyrus hath said against Jerusalem, Aha, she is broken that was the gates of the people: she is turned unto me: I shall be replenished, now she is laid waste:

3 Therefore thus saith the Lord GOD; Behold, I am against thee, O Tyrus, and will cause many nations to come up against thee, as the sea causeth his waves to come up.

4 And they shall destroy the walls of Tyrus, and break down her towers: I will also scrape her dust from her, and make her like the top of a rock.

5 It shall be a place for the spreading of nets in the midst of the sea: for I have spoken it, saith the Lord GOD: and it shall become a spoil to the nations.

6 And her daughters which are in the field shall be slain by the sword; and they shall know that I am the LORD.

7 For thus saith the Lord GOD; Behold, I will bring upon Tyrus Nebuchadrezzar king of Babylon, a king of kings, from the north, with horses, and with chariots, and with horsemen, and companies, and much people.

8 He shall slay with the sword thy daughters in the field: and he shall make a fort against thee, and cast a mount against thee, and lift up the buckler against thee.

9 And he shall set engines of war against thy walls, and with his axes he shall break down thy towers.

10 By reason of the abundance of his horses their dust shall cover thee: thy walls shall

16 1Sam. 30:14; Jer. 47:4; Zeph. 2:4

17 Ps. 9:16; Jer. 25:32; 47:4; Ezek. 5:15; 25:3; 36:2; Amos 1:9; Zech. 9:2

4 Ezek. 26:14

5 Ezek. 27:32

6 Ezek. 25:5

7 Ezra 7:12; Dan. 2:37

8 Ezek. 21:22

13 Isa. 14:11; 23:16; 24:8; Jer. 7:34; 16:9; 25:10; Ezek. 28:13; Rev. 18:22

14 Ezek. 26:4, 5

15 Jer. 49:21; Ezek. 26:18; 27:28; 31:16

16 Job 2:13; Isa. 23:8; Ezek. 27:35; 32:10; Jon. 3:6

17 Isa. 23:4; Ezek. 27:32; Rev. 18:9

18 Ezek. 26:15

20 Ezek. 32:18, 23, 24, 26, 27, 32

shake at the noise of the horsemen, and of the wheels, and of the chariots, when he shall enter into thy gates, as men enter into a city wherein is made a breach.

11 With the hoofs of his horses shall he tread down all thy streets: he shall slay thy people by the sword, and thy strong garrisons shall go down to the ground.

12 And they shall make a spoil of thy riches, and make a prey of thy merchandise: and they shall break down thy walls, and destroy thy pleasant houses: and they shall lay thy stones and thy timber and thy dust in the midst of the water.

13 And I will cause the noise of thy songs to cease; and the sound of thy harps shall be no more heard.

14 And I will make thee like the top of a rock: thou shalt be a place to spread nets upon; thou shalt be built no more: for I the LORD have spoken it, saith the Lord GOD.

15 Thus saith the Lord GOD to Tyrus; Shall not the isles shake at the sound of thy fall, when the wounded cry, when the slaughter is made in the midst of thee?

16 Then all the princes of the sea shall come down from their thrones, and lay away their robes, and put off their broidered garments: they shall clothe themselves with trembling; they shall sit upon the ground, and shall tremble at every moment, and be astonished at thee.

17 And they shall take up a lamentation for thee, and say to thee, How art thou destroyed, that wast inhabited of seafaring men, the renowned city, which wast strong in the sea, she and her inhabitants, which cause their terror to be on all that haunt it!

18 Now shall the isles tremble in the day of thy fall; yea, the isles that are in the sea shall be troubled at thy departure.

19 For thus saith the Lord GOD; When I shall make thee a desolate city, like the cities that are not inhabited; when I shall bring up the deep upon thee, and great waters shall cover thee;

20 When I shall bring thee down with them that descend into the pit, with the people of old time, and shall set thee in the low parts of the earth, in places desolate of old, with them that go down to the pit, that thou be not inhabited; and I shall set glory in the land of the living;

26:1–2 Tyrus. Nebuchadnezzar conquered the mainland city, but not the island. Ezekiel's prophecy here was not fulfilled until about 260 years later, when Alexander the Great used the massive debris of the mainland portion to build a causeway to the island and overrun it (330 B.C.).

21 I will make thee a terror, and thou *shalt be* no *more*: though thou be sought for, yet shalt thou never be found again, saith the Lord GOD.

CHAPTER 27
A Funeral Dirge for Tyre

1 The word of the LORD came again unto me, saying,

2 Now, thou son of man, take up a lamentation for Tyrus;

3 And say unto Tyrus, O thou that art situate at the entry of the sea, *which art* a merchant of the people for many isles, Thus saith the Lord GOD; O Tyrus, thou hast said, I *am* of perfect beauty.

4 Thy borders *are* in the midst of the seas, thy builders have perfected thy beauty.

5 They have made all thy *ship* boards of fir trees of Senir: they have taken cedars from Lebanon to make masts for thee.

6 *Of* the oaks of Bashan have they made thine oars; the company of the Ashurites have made thy benches *of* ivory, *brought* out of the isles of Chittim.

7 Fine linen with broidered work from Egypt was that which thou spreadest forth to be thy sail; blue and purple from the isles of Elishah was that which covered thee.

8 The inhabitants of Zidon and Arvad were thy mariners: thy wise *men*, O Tyrus, *that* were in thee, were thy pilots.

9 The ancients of Gebal and the wise *men* thereof were in thee thy caulkers: all the ships of the sea with their mariners were in thee to occupy thy merchandise.

10 They of Persia and of Lud and of Phut were in thine army, thy men of war: they hanged the shield and helmet in thee; they set forth thy comeliness.

11 The men of Arvad with thine army *were* upon thy walls round about, and the Gammadims were in thy towers: they hanged their shields upon thy walls round about; they have made thy beauty perfect.

12 Tarshish *was* thy merchant by reason of the multitude of all *kind of* riches; with silver, iron, tin, and lead, they traded in thy fairs.

13 Javan, Tubal, and Meshech, they *were* thy merchants: they traded the persons of men and vessels of brass in thy market.

14 They of the house of Togarmah traded in thy fairs with horses and horsemen and mules.

15 The men of Dedan *were* thy merchants; many isles *were* the merchandise of thine hand: they brought thee *for* a present horns of ivory and ebony.

16 Syria *was* thy merchant by reason of the multitude of the wares of thy making: they occupied in thy fairs with emeralds, purple, and broidered work, and fine linen, and coral, and agate.

17 Judah, and the land of Israel, they *were* thy merchants: they traded in thy market wheat of Minnith, and Pannag, and honey, and oil, and balm.

18 Damascus *was* thy merchant in the multitude of the wares of thy making, for the multitude of all riches; in the wine of Helbon, and white wool.

19 Dan also and Javan going to and fro occupied in thy fairs: bright iron, cassia, and calamus, were in thy market.

20 Dedan *was* thy merchant in precious clothes for chariots.

21 Arabia, and all the princes of Kedar, they occupied with thee in lambs, and rams, and goats: in these *were they* thy merchants.

22 The merchants of Sheba and Raamah, they *were* thy merchants: they occupied in thy fairs with chief of all spices, and with all precious stones, and gold.

23 Haran, and Canneh, and Eden, the merchants of Sheba, Asshur, *and* Chilmad, *were* thy merchants.

24 These *were* thy merchants in all sorts of *things*, in blue clothes, and broidered work, and in chests of rich apparel, bound with cords, and made of cedar, among thy merchandise.

25 The ships of Tarshish did sing of thee in thy market: and thou wast replenished, and made very glorious in the midst of the seas.

26 Thy rowers have brought thee into great waters: the east wind hath broken thee in the midst of the seas.

27 Thy riches, and thy fairs, thy merchandise, thy mariners, and thy pilots, thy caulkers, and the occupiers of thy merchandise, and all thy men of war, that *are* in thee, and in all thy company which *is* in the midst of thee, shall fall into the midst of the seas in the day of thy ruin.

Cross references: 21 Ps. 37:36; Ezek. 19:1; 26:17; 27:36; 28:12, 19; 32:2 • 3 Isa. 23:3; Ezek. 28:2, 12 • 5 Deut. 3:9 • 6 Jer. 2:10 • 9 1Kgs. 5:18; Ps. 83:7 • 10 Jer. 46:9; Ezek. 30:5; 38:5 • 11 Ezek. 27:3 • 12 Gen. 10:4; 2Chr. 20:36 • 13 Gen. 10:2; Rev. 18:13 • 14 Gen. 10:3; Ezek. 38:6 • 15 Gen. 10:7 • 17 Judg. 11:33; 1Kgs. 5:9, 11; Ezra 3:7; Jer. 8:22; Acts 12:20 • 20 Gen. 25:3 • 21 Gen. 25:13; Isa. 60:7 • 22 Gen. 10:7; 1Kgs. 10:1, 2; Ps. 72:10, 15; Isa. 60:6 • 23 Gen. 11:31; 25:3; 2Kgs. 19:12 • 25 Ps. 48:7; Isa. 2:16; 23:14; Ezek. 27:4 • 26 Ps. 48:7 • 27 Prov. 11:4; Ezek. 27:34; Rev. 18:9

27:2 lamentation for Tyrus. This poetic elegy was appropriate for both the early conquest of the mainland city by Nebuchadnezzar and the later destruction wrought by Alexander the Great's conquering Greek armies. (Compare Rev. 18:1–24 for a future lamentation over the fall of commercial Babylon.)

28 The suburbs shall shake at the sound of the cry of thy pilots.

29 And all that handle the oar, the mariners, *and* all the pilots of the sea, shall come down from their ships, they shall stand upon the land;

30 And shall cause their voice to be heard against thee, and shall cry bitterly, and shall cast up dust upon their heads, they shall wallow themselves in the ashes:

31 And they shall make themselves utterly bald for thee, and gird them with sackcloth, and they shall weep for thee with bitterness of heart *and* bitter wailing.

32 And in their wailing they shall take up a lamentation for thee, and lament over thee, *saying,* What *city is* like Tyrus, like the destroyed in the midst of the sea?

33 When thy wares went forth out of the seas, thou filledst many people; thou didst enrich the kings of the earth with the multitude of thy riches and of thy merchandise.

34 In the time *when* thou shalt be broken by the seas in the depths of the waters thy merchandise and all thy company in the midst of thee shall fall.

35 All the inhabitants of the isles shall be astonished at thee, and their kings shall be sore afraid, they shall be troubled in *their* countenance.

36 The merchants among the people shall hiss at thee; thou shalt be a terror, and never *shalt be* any more.

CHAPTER 28
The King of Tyre

1 The word of the LORD came again unto me, saying,

2 Son of man, say unto the prince of Tyrus, Thus saith the Lord GOD; Because thine

heart *is* lifted up, and thou hast said, I *am* a God, I sit *in* the seat of God, in the midst of the seas; yet thou *art* a man, and not God, though thou set thine heart as the heart of God:

3 Behold, thou *art* wiser than Daniel; there is no secret that they can hide from thee:

4 With thy wisdom and with thine understanding thou hast gotten thee riches, and hast gotten gold and silver into thy treasures:

5 By thy great wisdom *and* by thy traffick hast thou increased thy riches, and thine heart is lifted up because of thy riches:

6 Therefore thus saith the Lord GOD; Because thou hast set thine heart as the heart of God;

7 Behold, therefore I will bring strangers upon thee, the terrible of the nations: and they shall draw their swords against the beauty of thy wisdom, and they shall defile thy brightness.

8 They shall bring thee down to the pit, and thou shalt die the deaths of *them that are* slain in the midst of the seas.

9 Wilt thou yet say before him that slayeth thee, I *am* God? but thou *shalt be* a man, and no God, in the hand of him that slayeth thee.

10 Thou shalt die the deaths of the uncircumcised by the hand of strangers: for I have spoken *it,* saith the Lord GOD.

11 Moreover the word of the LORD came unto me, saying,

12 Son of man, take up a lamentation upon the king of Tyrus, and say unto him, Thus saith the Lord GOD; Thou sealest up the sum, full of wisdom, and perfect in beauty.

13 Thou hast been in Eden the garden of God; every precious stone *was* thy covering,

Cross References

28 Ezek. 26:15, 18
29 Rev. 18:17
30 Esth. 4:1, 3; Job 2:12; Jer. 6:26; Rev. 18:19
31 Jer. 16:6; 47:5; Mic. 1:16
32 Ezek. 26:17; 27:2; Rev. 18:18
33 Rev. 18:19
34 Ezek. 26:19; 27:27
35 Ezek. 26:15, 16
36 Isa. 31:3; Jer. 18:16; Ezek. 26:21; 27:3, 4; 28:9
3 Zech. 9:2
5 Ps. 62:10; Zech. 9:3
7 Ezek. 30:11; 31:12; 32:12
9 Ezek. 28:2
10 Ezek. 31:18; 32:19, 21, 25, 27
11 Ezek. 27:2, 3; 28:3
13 Ezek. 26:13, 31:8, 9

28:2 the prince of Tyrus. Alive in Ezekiel's time, this wicked ruler known as Ethbaal claimed to be a god, but was merely a mortal man. Some think he is a type of future Antichrist. Tyrus means "rock," indicative of the rocky island which the city occupied.

28:12 lamentation upon the king of Tyrus. With the change from "prince" to "king," the prophet moves beyond a human ruler to describe the fall of the "prince of the power of the air" (Eph. 2:2), the real diabolical personality behind all wicked political and religious leaders. Here a supernatural being is addressed, first recounting his lofty heavenly position prior to his disastrous sin and rebellion against God.

28:13–15 Thou hast been in Eden. Some scholars

claim that this passage refers only to the King of Tyre and not to Satan, but consider this description: 1) He had been in Eden (Gen. 3:1–17), where he tempted Adam and Eve, as an "angel of light" (2 Cor. 11:14), the "shining one" (which is what "serpent" signifies); 2) His appearance and attire were bedecked with multi-colored jewels and gold of indescribable splendor; 3) His supernatural instruments included tabrets or timbrels (percussion instruments) probably indicating his immense musical ability; 4) He was an especially created being; 5) Only angelic beings are so designated in Scripture; 6) He was present with God; 7) He walked in the midst of "the stones of fire"; 8) As a created being he was perfect until his fall. (See Isa. 14:12–15, where he is called Lucifer, meaning "light-bearer.")

the sardius, topaz, and the diamond, the beryl, the onyx, and the jasper, the sapphire, the emerald, and the carbuncle, and gold: the workmanship of thy tabrets and of thy pipes was prepared in thee in the day that thou wast created.

14 Thou *art* the anointed cherub that covereth; and I have set thee *so*: thou wast upon the holy mountain of God; thou hast walked up and down in the midst of the stones of fire.

15 Thou *wast* perfect in thy ways from the day that thou wast created, till iniquity was found in thee.

16 By the multitude of thy merchandise they have filled the midst of thee with violence, and thou hast sinned: therefore I will cast thee as profane out of the mountain of God: and I will destroy thee, O covering cherub, from the midst of the stones of fire.

17 Thine heart was lifted up because of thy beauty, thou hast corrupted thy wisdom by reason of thy brightness: I will cast thee to the ground, I will lay thee before kings, that they may behold thee.

18 Thou hast defiled thy sanctuaries by the multitude of thine iniquities, by the iniquity of thy traffick; therefore will I bring forth a fire from the midst of thee, it shall devour thee, and I will bring thee to ashes upon the earth in the sight of all them that behold thee.

19 All they that know thee among the people shall be astonished at thee: thou shalt be a terror, and never *shalt* thou *be* any more.

Zidon

20 Again the word of the LORD came unto me, saying,

21 Son of man, set thy face against Zidon, and prophesy against it,

22 And say, Thus saith the Lord GOD; Behold, I *am* against thee, O Zidon; and I will be glorified in the midst of thee: and they shall know that I *am* the LORD, when I shall have executed judgments in her, and shall be sanctified in her.

23 For I will send into her pestilence, and blood into her streets; and the wounded shall be judged in the midst of her by the sword upon her on every side; and they shall know that I *am* the LORD.

Israel

24 And there shall be no more a pricking brier unto the house of Israel, nor *any* grieving thorn of all *that are* round about them, that despised them; and they shall know that I *am* the Lord GOD.

25 Thus saith the Lord GOD; When I shall have gathered the house of Israel from the people among whom they are scattered, and shall be sanctified in them in the sight of the heathen, then shall they dwell in their land that I have given to my servant Jacob.

26 And they shall dwell safely therein, and shall build houses, and plant vineyards; yea, they shall dwell with confidence, when I have executed judgments upon all those that despise them round about them; and they shall know that I *am* the LORD their God.

CHAPTER 29

Egypt

1 In the tenth year, in the tenth *month*, in the twelfth *day* of the month, the word of the LORD came unto me, saying,

2 Son of man, set thy face against Pharaoh king of Egypt, and prophesy against him, and against all Egypt:

3 Speak, and say, Thus saith the Lord GOD; Behold, I *am* against thee, Pharaoh king of Egypt, the great dragon that lieth in the midst of his rivers, which hath said, My river *is* mine own, and I have made *it* for myself.

4 But I will put hooks in thy jaws, and I will cause the fish of thy rivers to stick unto thy scales, and I will bring thee up out of the midst of thy rivers, and all the fish of thy rivers shall stick unto thy scales.

5 And I will leave thee *thrown* into the wilderness, thee and all the fish of thy rivers: thou shalt fall upon the open fields; thou shalt not be brought together, nor

Center column references

14 Ex. 25:20; Ezek. 20:40; 28:16
16 Ezek. 28:14
17 Ezek. 28:2, 5
19 Ezek. 26:21; 27:36
21 Isa. 23:4, 12; Jer. 25:22; 27:3; Ezek. 6:2; 25:2; 29:2; 32:30
22 Ex. 14:4, 17; Ps. 9:16; Ezek. 20:41; 28:25; 36:23; 39:13
23 Ezek. 38:22
24 Num. 33:55; Josh. 23:13
25 Isa. 11:12; Ezek. 11:17; 20:41; 28:22; 34:13; 37:21
26 Isa. 19:1; 65:21; Jer. 23:6; 25:19; 31:5; 46:2, 25; Ezek. 28:21; 36:28; Amos 9:14
3 Ps. 74:13, 14; Isa. 27:1; 51:9; Jer. 44:30; Ezek. 28:2, 22; 29:10; 32:2
4 Isa. 37:29; Ezek. 38:4
5 Jer. 7:33; 8:2; 16:4; 25:33; 34:20

28:25–26 gathered the house of Israel. This prophecy goes beyond the return of Israel in ancient times to forecast the safety and prosperity of the nation in the Millennial Kingdom. Again, during the future Tribulation, many Jews will flee (Matt. 24:16), but the Messiah, returning in glory (Matt. 24:31), will gather them all to their promised land.

29:2 Pharaoh king of Egypt. No nation in ancient times played a larger role in Israel's history than Egypt. The Pharaoh here is Hophra (Jer. 44:30). The next four chapters are devoted to the prophecy against Egypt, the last and greatest of the seven nations around ancient Israel.

gathered: I have given thee for meat to the beasts of the field and to the fowls of the heaven.

6 And all the inhabitants of Egypt shall know that I *am* the LORD, because they have been a staff of reed to the house of Israel.

7 When they took hold of thee by thy hand, thou brakest, and rend all their shoulder: and when they leaned upon thee, thou didst brake, and madest all their loins to be at a stand.

8 Therefore thus saith the Lord GOD; Behold, I will bring a sword upon thee, and cut off man and beast out of thee.

9 And the land of Egypt shall be desolate and waste; and they shall know that I *am* the LORD: because he hath said, The river *is* mine, and I have made *it*.

10 Behold, therefore I *am* against thee, and against thy rivers, and I will make the land of Egypt utterly waste *and* desolate, from the tower of Syene even unto the border of Ethiopia.

11 No foot of man shall pass through it, nor foot of beast shall pass through it, neither shall it be inhabited forty years.

12 And I will make the land of Egypt desolate in the midst of the countries *that are* desolate, and her cities among the cities *that are* laid waste shall be desolate forty years: and I will scatter the Egyptians among the nations, and will disperse them through the countries.

13 Yet thus saith the Lord GOD; At the end of forty years will I gather the Egyptians from the people whither they were scattered:

14 And I will bring again the captivity of Egypt, and will cause them to return *into* the land of Pathros, into the land of their habitation; and they shall be there a base kingdom.

15 It shall be the basest of the kingdoms; neither shall it exalt itself any more above the nations: for I will diminish them, that they shall no more rule over the nations.

16 And it shall be no more the confidence of the house of Israel, which bringeth *their* in-

iquity to remembrance, when they shall look after them: but they shall know that I *am* the Lord GOD.

Nebuchadnezzar's Conquests

17 And it came to pass in the seven and twentieth year, in the first *month*, in the first *day* of the month, the word of the LORD came unto me, saying,

18 Son of man, Nebuchadrezzar king of Babylon caused his army to serve a great service against Tyrus: every head *was* made bald, and every shoulder *was* peeled: yet had he no wages, nor his army, for Tyrus, for the service that he had served against it:

19 Therefore thus saith the Lord GOD; Behold, I will give the land of Egypt unto Nebuchadrezzar king of Babylon; and he shall take her multitude, and take her spoil, and take her prey; and it shall be the wages for his army.

20 I have given him the land of Egypt *for* his labour wherewith he served against it, because they wrought for me, saith the Lord GOD.

21 In that day will I cause the horn of the house of Israel to bud forth, and I will give thee the opening of the mouth in the midst of them; and they shall know that I *am* the LORD.

CHAPTER 30
God Will Punish Egypt

1 The word of the LORD came again unto me, saying,

2 Son of man, prophesy and say, Thus saith the Lord GOD; Howl ye, Woe worth the day!

3 For the day *is* near, even the day of the LORD *is* near, a cloudy day; it shall be the time of the heathen.

4 And the sword shall come upon Egypt, and great pain shall be in Ethiopia, when the slain shall fall in Egypt, and they shall take away her multitude, and her foundations shall be broken down.

5 Ethiopia, and Libya, and Lydia, and all the mingled people, and Chub, and the men

Cross references
6 2Kgs. 18:21; Isa. 36:6
7 Jer. 37:5, 7, 11; Ezek. 17:17
8 Ezek. 14:17; 32:11-13
10 Ex. 14:2; Jer. 44:1; Ezek. 30:6, 12
12 Ezek. 30:7, 26; 32:13
13 Isa. 19:23; Jer. 46:26
14 Ezek. 17:6, 14
16 Isa. 30:2, 3; 36:4, 6
18 Jer. 27:6; Ezek. 26:7, 8
20 Jer. 25:9
21 Ps. 132:17; Isa. 13:6; Ezek. 24:27
3 Ezek. 7:7, 12; Joel 2:1; Zeph. 1:7
4 Jer. 25:20, 24; 50:15; Ezek. 29:19
5 Ezek. 27:10

29:21 horn of the house of Israel. The horn as a symbol of power indicates that Israel would experience blessing. Evidently, when Egypt, ancient enemy of Israel, also fell, there came an unrecorded revival among the Jews, and the prophet gave his message in the midst of them.

30:3 the day of the LORD is near. The fall of Egypt and other allied nations in ancient times (568–567 B.C.) is in

view. However, the term "day of the LORD" is widely used for end-time events related to Israel; therefore, there may also be a forecast of the future incorporated here (see Isa. 2; 13:6, 9; Joel 1:15; 2:1, 11; 3:14; Amos 5:18, 20; Obad. 1:15; Zeph. 1:7, 14; Zech 14:1). In the Millennium, Egypt will enjoy the greatest blessings in worshiping the true God (see Isa. 19:19–25).

of the land that is in league, shall fall with them by the sword.

6 Thus saith the LORD; They also that uphold Egypt shall fall; and the pride of her power shall come down: from the tower of Syene shall they fall in it by the sword, saith the Lord GOD.

7 And they shall be desolate in the midst of the countries *that are* desolate, and her cities shall be in the midst of the cities *that are* wasted.

8 And they shall know that I *am* the LORD, when I have set a fire in Egypt, and *when* all her helpers shall be destroyed.

9 In that day shall messengers go forth from me in ships to make the careless Ethiopians afraid, and great pain shall come upon them, as in the day of Egypt: for, lo, it cometh.

10 Thus saith the Lord GOD; I will also make the multitude of Egypt to cease by the hand of Nebuchadrezzar king of Babylon.

11 He and his people with him, the terrible of the nations, shall be brought to destroy the land: and they shall draw their swords against Egypt, and fill the land with the slain.

12 And I will make the rivers dry, and sell the land into the hand of the wicked: and I will make the land waste, and all that is therein, by the hand of strangers: I the LORD have spoken *it*.

13 Thus saith the Lord GOD; I will also destroy the idols, and I will cause *their* images to cease out of Noph; and there shall be no more a prince of the land of Egypt: and I will put a fear in the land of Egypt.

14 And I will make Pathros desolate, and will set fire in Zoan, and will execute judgments in No.

15 And I will pour my fury upon Sin, the strength of Egypt; and I will cut off the multitude of No.

16 And I will set fire in Egypt: Sin shall have great pain, and No shall be rent asunder, and Noph *shall have* distresses daily.

17 The young men of Aven and of Pi-beseth shall fall by the sword: and these *cities* shall go into captivity.

18 At Tehaphnehes also the day shall be darkened, when I shall break there the yokes of Egypt: and the pomp of her strength shall cease in her: as for her, a cloud shall cover her, and her daughters shall go into captivity.

19 Thus will I execute judgments in Egypt: and they shall know that I *am* the LORD.

20 And it came to pass in the eleventh year, in the first *month*, in the seventh *day* of the month, *that* the word of the LORD came unto me, saying,

21 Son of man, I have broken the arm of Pharaoh king of Egypt; and, lo, it shall not be bound up to be healed, to put a roller to bind it, to make it strong to hold the sword.

22 Therefore thus saith the Lord GOD; Behold, I *am* against Pharaoh king of Egypt, and will break his arms, the strong, and that which was broken; and I will cause the sword to fall out of his hand.

23 And I will scatter the Egyptians among the nations, and will disperse them through the countries.

24 And I will strengthen the arms of the king of Babylon, and put my sword in his hand: but I will break Pharaoh's arms, and he shall groan before him with the groanings of a deadly wounded *man*.

25 But I will strengthen the arms of the king of Babylon, and the arms of Pharaoh shall fall down; and they shall know that I *am* the LORD, when I shall put my sword into the hand of the king of Babylon, and he shall stretch it out upon the land of Egypt.

26 And I will scatter the Egyptians among the nations, and disperse them among the countries; and they shall know that I *am* the LORD.

CHAPTER 31
A Warning to Pharaoh

1 And it came to pass in the eleventh year, in the third *month*, in the first *day* of the month, *that* the word of the LORD came unto me, saying,

2 Son of man, speak unto Pharaoh king of Egypt, and to his multitude; Whom art thou like in thy greatness?

3 Behold, the Assyrian *was* a cedar in Lebanon with fair branches, and with a shadowing shroud, and of an high stature; and his top was among the thick boughs.

4 The waters made him great, the deep set him up on high with her rivers running round about his plants, and sent out her little rivers unto all the trees of the field.

5 Therefore his height was exalted above all the trees of the field, and his boughs were multiplied, and his branches became long because of the multitude of waters, when he shot forth.

6 All the fowls of heaven made their nests in his boughs, and under his branches did all the beasts of the field bring forth their young, and under his shadow dwelt all great nations.

7 Thus was he fair in his greatness, in the

length of his branches: for his root was by great waters.

8 The cedars in the garden of God could not hide him: the fir trees were not like his boughs, and the chestnut trees were not like his branches; nor any tree in the garden of God was like unto him in his beauty.

9 I have made him fair by the multitude of his branches: so that all the trees of Eden, that *were* in the garden of God, envied him.

10 Therefore thus saith the Lord God; Because thou hast lifted up thyself in height, and he hath shot up his top among the thick boughs, and his heart is lifted up in his height;

11 I have therefore delivered him into the hand of the mighty one of the heathen; he shall surely deal with him: I have driven him out for his wickedness.

12 And strangers, the terrible of the nations, have cut him off, and have left him: upon the mountains and in all the valleys his branches are fallen, and his boughs are broken by all the rivers of the land; and all the people of the earth are gone down from his shadow, and have left him.

13 Upon his ruin shall all the fowls of the heaven remain, and all the beasts of the field shall be upon his branches:

14 To the end that none of all the trees by the waters exalt themselves for their height, neither shoot up their top among the thick boughs, neither their trees stand up in their height, all that drink water: for they are all delivered unto death, to the nether parts of the earth, in the midst of the children of men, with them that go down to the pit.

15 Thus saith the Lord God; In the day when he went down to the grave I caused a mourning: I covered the deep for him, and I restrained the floods thereof, and the great waters were stayed: and I caused Lebanon to mourn for him, and all the trees of the field fainted for him.

16 I made the nations to shake at the sound of his fall, when I cast him down to hell with them that descend into the pit: and all the trees of Eden, the choice and best of Lebanon, all that drink water, shall be comforted in the nether parts of the earth.

17 They also went down into hell with him unto *them that be* slain with the sword; and *they that were* his arm, *that* dwelt under his shadow in the midst of the heathen.

18 To whom art thou thus like in glory and in greatness among the trees of Eden? yet shalt thou be brought down with the trees of Eden unto the nether parts of the earth: thou shalt lie in the midst of the uncircumcised with *them that be* slain by the sword. This *is* Pharaoh and all his multitude, saith the Lord God.

CHAPTER 32
Lamentation for Pharaoh

1 And it came to pass in the twelfth year, in the twelfth month, in the first *day* of the month, *that* the word of the Lord came unto me, saying,

2 Son of man, take up a lamentation for Pharaoh king of Egypt, and say unto him, Thou art like a young lion of the nations, and thou *art* as a whale in the seas: and thou camest forth with thy rivers, and troubledst the waters with thy feet, and fouledst their rivers.

3 Thus saith the Lord God; I will therefore spread out my net over thee with a company of many people; and they shall bring thee up in my net.

4 Then will I leave thee upon the land, I will cast thee forth upon the open field, and will cause all the fowls of the heaven to remain upon thee, and I will fill the beasts of the whole earth with thee.

5 And I will lay thy flesh upon the mountains, and fill the valleys with thy height.

6 I will also water with thy blood the land wherein thou swimmest, *even* to the mountains; and the rivers shall be full of thee.

7 And when I shall put thee out, I will cover the heaven, and make the stars thereof dark; I will cover the sun with a cloud, and the moon shall not give her light.

8 All the bright lights of heaven will I make dark over thee, and set darkness upon thy land, saith the Lord God.

9 I will also vex the hearts of many people, when I shall bring thy destruction among the nations, into the countries which thou hast not known.

10 Yea, I will make many people amazed at thee, and their kings shall be horribly afraid for thee, when I shall brandish my sword before them; and they shall tremble at *every* moment, every man for his own life, in the day of thy fall.

11 For thus saith the Lord God; The sword

Cross references (center column)

8 Gen. 2:8; 13:10; Ezek. 28:13

10 Dan. 5:20

12 Ezek. 28:7; 32:5; 35:8

13 Isa. 18:6; Ezek. 32:4

14 Ps. 82:7; Ezek. 32:18

16 Isa. 14:8, 15; Ezek. 26:15; Ezek. 32:31

17 Lam. 4:20

18 Ezek. 28:10; 31:2; 32:19, 21, 24

2 Ezek. 19:3, 6; 27:2; 29:3; 32:16; 34:18; 38:13

3 Ezek. 12:13; 17:20; Hos. 7:12

4 Ezek. 29:5; 31:13

5 Ezek. 31:12

7 Isa. 13:10; Joel 2:31; 3:15; Amos 8:9; Matt. 24:29; Rev. 6:12, 13

10 Ezek. 26:16; 27:35

11 Jer. 46:26; Ezek. 30:4

32:1–32 a lamentation for Pharaoh. This dirge is addressed to Pharaoh, especially the first sixteen verses. The rest of the chapter is a lamentation for all Egyptians, for many would be slain in the Babylonian invasion of their land.

of the king of Babylon shall come upon thee.

12 By the swords of the mighty will I cause thy multitude to fall, the terrible of the nations, all of them: and they shall spoil the pomp of Egypt, and all the multitude thereof shall be destroyed.

13 I will destroy also all the beasts thereof from beside the great waters; neither shall the foot of man trouble them any more, nor the hoofs of beasts trouble them.

14 Then will I make their waters deep, and cause their rivers to run like oil, saith the Lord God.

15 When I shall make the land of Egypt desolate, and the country shall be destitute of that whereof it was full, when I shall smite all them that dwell therein, then shall they know that I *am* the Lord.

16 This *is* the lamentation wherewith they shall lament her: the daughters of the nations shall lament her: they shall lament for her, *even* for Egypt, and for all her multitude, saith the Lord God.

The Egyptians in Sheol

17 It came to pass also in the twelfth year, in the fifteenth *day* of the month, *that* the word of the Lord came unto me, saying,

18 Son of man, wail for the multitude of Egypt, and cast them down, *even* her, and the daughters of the famous nations, unto the nether parts of the earth, with them that go down into the pit.

19 Whom dost thou pass in beauty? go down, and be thou laid with the uncircumcised.

20 They shall fall in the midst of *them that are* slain by the sword: she is delivered to the sword: draw her and all her multitudes.

21 The strong among the mighty shall speak to him out of the midst of hell with them that help him: they are gone down, they lie uncircumcised, slain by the sword.

22 Asshur *is* there and all her company: his graves *are* about him: all of them slain, fallen by the sword:

23 Whose graves are set in the sides of the pit, and her company is round about her grave: all of them slain, fallen by the sword, which caused terror in the land of the living.

24 There *is* Elam and all her multitude round about her grave, all of them slain, fallen by the sword, which are gone down uncircumcised into the nether parts of the earth, which caused their terror in the land of the living; yet have they borne their shame with them that go down to the pit.

25 They have set her a bed in the midst of the slain with all her multitude: her graves *are* round about him: all of them uncircumcised, slain by the sword: though their terror was caused in the land of the living, yet have they borne their shame with them that go down to the pit: he is put in the midst of *them that be* slain.

26 There *is* Meshech, Tubal, and all her multitude: her graves *are* round about him: all of them uncircumcised, slain by the sword, though they caused their terror in the land of the living.

27 And they shall not lie with the mighty *that are* fallen of the uncircumcised, which are gone down to hell with their weapons of war: and they have laid their swords under their heads, but their iniquities shall be upon their bones, though *they were* the terror of the mighty in the land of the living.

28 Yea, thou shalt be broken in the midst of the uncircumcised, and shalt lie with *them that are* slain with the sword.

29 There *is* Edom, her kings, and all her princes, which with their might are laid by *them that were* slain by the sword: they shall lie with the uncircumcised, and with them that go down to the pit.

30 There *be* the princes of the north, all of them, and all the Zidonians, which are gone down with the slain; with their terror they are ashamed of their might; and they lie uncircumcised with *them that be* slain by the sword, and bear their shame with them that go down to the pit.

31 Pharaoh shall see them, and shall be comforted over all his multitude, *even* Pharaoh and all his army slain by the sword, saith the Lord God.

32 For I have caused my terror in the land of the living: and he shall be laid in the midst of the uncircumcised with *them that are* slain with the sword, *even* Pharaoh and all his multitude, saith the Lord God.

CHAPTER 33
The Watchman's Duty

1 Again the word of the Lord came unto me, saying,

2 Son of man, speak to the children of thy people, and say unto them, When I bring the sword upon a land, if the people of the land take a man of their coasts, and set him for their watchman:

3 If when he seeth the sword come upon the land, he blow the trumpet, and warn the people;

4 Then whosoever heareth the sound of

---

12 Ezek. 28:7; 29:19

13 Ezek. 29:11

15 Ex. 7:5; 14:4, 18; Ps. 9:16; Ezek. 6:7

16 2Sam. 1:17; 2Chr. 35:25; Ezek. 26:17; 32:2

18 Ezek. 26:20; 31:14

19 Ezek. 28:10; 31:2, 18; 32:21, 24

21 Isa. 1:31; 14:9, 10; Ezek. 32:19, 25, 27

22 Ezek. 32:24, 26, 29, 30

23 Isa. 14:15; Ezek. 26:17, 20; 32:24-27, 32

24 Jer. 49:34; Ezek. 32:21, 23

26 Gen. 10:2; Ezek. 27:13; 32:19, 20; 38:2

27 Ezek. 32:21; Isa. 14:18, 19

29 Ezek. 25:12

30 Ezek. 28:21; 38:6, 15; 39:2

31 Ezek. 31:16

1 Ezek. 3:11

2 2Sam. 18:24, 25; 2Kgs. 9:17; Ezek. 14:17; 33:7; Hos. 9:8

4 Ezek. 18:13

the trumpet, and taketh not warning; if the sword come, and take him away, his blood shall be upon his own head.

5 He heard the sound of the trumpet, and took not warning; his blood shall be upon him. But he that taketh warning shall deliver his soul.

6 But if the watchman see the sword come, and blow not the trumpet, and the people be not warned; if the sword come, and take *any* person from among them, he is taken away in his iniquity; but his blood will I require at the watchman's hand.

7 So thou, O son of man, I have set thee a watchman unto the house of Israel; therefore thou shalt hear the word at my mouth, and warn them from me.

8 When I say unto the wicked, O wicked *man*, thou shalt surely die; if thou dost not speak to warn the wicked from his way, that wicked *man* shall die in his iniquity; but his blood will I require at thine hand.

9 Nevertheless, if thou warn the wicked of his way to turn from it; if he do not turn from his way, he shall die in his iniquity; but thou hast delivered thy soul.

Personal Accountability

10 Therefore, O thou son of man, speak unto the house of Israel; Thus ye speak, saying, If our transgressions and our sins *be* upon us, and we pine away in them, how should we then live?

11 Say unto them, *As* I live, saith the Lord God, I have no pleasure in the death of the wicked; but that the wicked turn from his way and live: turn ye, turn ye from your evil ways; for why will ye die, O house of Israel?

12 Therefore, thou son of man, say unto the children of thy people, The righteousness of the righteous shall not deliver him in the day of his transgression: as for the wickedness of the wicked, he shall not fall thereby in the day that he turneth from his wickedness; neither shall the righteous be able to live for his *righteousness* in the day that he sinneth.

13 When I shall say to the righteous, *that he* shall surely live; if he trust to his own right-

eousness, and commit iniquity, all his righteousnesses shall not be remembered; but for his iniquity that he hath committed, he shall die for it.

14 Again, when I say unto the wicked, Thou shalt surely die; if he turn from his sin, and do that which is lawful and right;

15 *If* the wicked restore the pledge, give again that he had robbed, walk in the statutes of life, without committing iniquity; he shall surely live, he shall not die.

16 None of his sins that he hath committed shall be mentioned unto him: he hath done that which is lawful and right; he shall surely live.

17 Yet the children of thy people say, The way of the Lord is not equal: but as for them, their way is not equal.

18 When the righteous turneth from his righteousness, and committeth iniquity, he shall even die thereby.

19 But if the wicked turn from his wickedness, and do that which is lawful and right, he shall live thereby.

20 Yet ye say, The way of the Lord is not equal. O ye house of Israel, I will judge you every one after his ways.

The News of Jerusalem's Fall

21 And it came to pass in the twelfth year of our captivity, in the tenth *month*, in the fifth *day* of the month, *that* one that had escaped out of Jerusalem came unto me, saying, The city is smitten.

22 Now the hand of the Lord was upon me in the evening, afore he that was escaped came; and had opened my mouth, until he came to me in the morning; and my mouth was opened, and I was no more dumb.

23 Then the word of the Lord came unto me, saying,

24 Son of man, they that inhabit those wastes of the land of Israel speak, saying, Abraham was one, and he inherited the land: but we *are* many; the land is given us for inheritance.

25 Wherefore say unto them, Thus saith the Lord God; Ye eat with the blood, and lift up your eyes toward your idols, and

6 Ezek. 33:8
7 Ezek. 3:17
10 Isa. 49:14; Ezek. 24:23; 37:11
11 2Sam. 14:14; Ezek. 18:23, 31, 32; 2Pet. 3:9
12 2Chr. 7:14; Ezek. 3:20; 18:24, 26, 27
13 Ezek. 3:20; 18:24
14 Ezek. 3:18, 19; 18:27
15 Ex. 22:1, 4; Lev. 6:2, 4, 5; 18:5; Num. 5:6, 7; Ezek. 18:7; 20:11, 13, 21; Luke 19:8
16 Ezek. 18:22
17 Ezek. 18:25, 29; 33:20
18 Ezek. 18:26, 27
20 Ezek. 18:25, 29; 33:17
21 2Kgs. 25:4; Ezek. 1:2; 24:26
22 Ezek. 1:3; 24:27
24 Isa. 51:2; Ezek. 33:27; 34:2; 36:4; Mic. 3:11; Matt. 3:9; John 8:39; Acts 7:5
25 Gen. 9:4; Lev. 3:17; 7:26; 17:10; 19:26; Deut. 12:16; Ezek. 18:6; 22:6, 9

33:7–9 I have set thee a watchman unto the house of Israel. Ezekiel's ministry as a "watchman," first assigned in Ezekiel 3:16–21, is now reconfirmed, since Jerusalem has just fallen. The faithful watchman must warn of impending danger, both physical and spiritual, a responsibility that must not be taken lightly.

33:21–22 The city is smitten. News comes from an escapee from the destruction of Jerusalem in 586 B.C., resulting in Ezekiel, who had been silent since his wife died, resuming his public prophesying ministry.

shed blood: and shall ye possess the land? **26** Ye stand upon your sword, ye work abomination, and ye defile every one his neighbour's wife: and shall ye possess the land?

27 Say thou thus unto them, Thus saith the Lord GOD; As I live, surely they that are in the wastes shall fall by the sword, and him that is in the open field will I give to the beasts to be devoured, and they that be in the forts and in the caves shall die of the pestilence.

28 For I will lay the land most desolate, and the pomp of her strength shall cease; and the mountains of Israel shall be desolate, that none shall pass through.

29 Then shall they know that I am the LORD, when I have laid the land most desolate because of all their abominations which they have committed.

30 Also, thou son of man, the children of thy people still are talking against thee by the walls and in the doors of the houses, and speak one to another, every one to his brother, saying, Come, I pray you, and hear what is the word that cometh forth from the LORD.

31 And they come unto thee as the people cometh, and they sit before thee as my people, and they hear thy words, but they will not do them: for with their mouth they shew much love, but their heart goeth after their covetousness.

32 And, lo, thou art unto them as a very lovely song of one that hath a pleasant voice, and can play well on an instrument: for they hear thy words, but they do them not.

33 And when this cometh to pass, (lo, it will come,) then shall they know that a prophet hath been among them.

CHAPTER 34
The Shepherds of Israel

1 And the word of the LORD came unto me, saying,

2 Son of man, prophesy against the shepherds of Israel, prophesy, and say unto them, Thus saith the Lord GOD unto the shepherds; Woe be to the shepherds of Israel

that do feed themselves! should not the shepherds feed the flocks?

3 Ye eat the fat, and ye clothe you with the wool, ye kill them that are fed: but ye feed not the flock.

4 The diseased have ye not strengthened, neither have ye healed that which was sick, neither have ye bound up that which was broken, neither have ye brought again that which was driven away, neither have ye sought that which was lost; but with force and with cruelty have ye ruled them.

5 And they were scattered, because there is no shepherd: and they became meat to all the beasts of the field, when they were scattered.

6 My sheep wandered through all the mountains, and upon every high hill: yea, my flock was scattered upon all the face of the earth, and none did search or seek after them.

7 Therefore, ye shepherds, hear the word of the LORD;

8 As I live, saith the Lord GOD, surely because my flock became a prey, and my flock became meat to every beast of the field, because there was no shepherd, neither did my shepherds search for my flock, but the shepherds fed themselves, and fed not my flock;

9 Therefore, O ye shepherds, hear the word of the LORD;

10 Thus saith the Lord GOD; Behold, I am against the shepherds; and I will require my flock at their hand, and cause them to cease from feeding the flock; neither shall the shepherds feed themselves any more; for I will deliver my flock from their mouth, that they may not be meat for them.

The True Shepherd

11 For thus saith the Lord GOD; Behold, I, even I, will both search my sheep, and seek them out.

12 As a shepherd seeketh out his flock in the day that he is among his sheep that are scattered; so will I seek out my sheep, and will deliver them out of all places where they have been scattered in the cloudy and dark day.

13 And I will bring them out from the

Center column references:

26 Ezek. 18:6; 22:11

27 Judg. 6:2; 1Sam. 13:6; Ezek. 33:24; 39:4

28 Jer. 44:2, 6, 22; Ezek. 6:2, 3, 6; 7:24; 24:21; 30:6, 7; 36:34, 35

30 Isa. 29:13

31 Ps. 78:36, 37; Isa. 29:13; Ezek. 8:1; 14:1; 20:1; Matt. 13:22

33 1Sam. 3:20; Ezek. 2:5

2 Jer. 23:1; Ezek. 33:24; Zech. 11:17

3 Isa. 56:11; Ezek. 33:25, 26; Mic. 3:1-3; Zech. 11:5, 16

4 Ezek. 34:16; Zech. 11:16; Luke 15:4; 1Pet. 5:3

5 1Kgs. 22:17; Isa. 56:9; Jer. 12:9; Ezek. 33:21, 28; 34:8; Matt. 9:36

8 Ezek. 34:2, 5, 6, 10

10 Ezek. 3:18; 34:2, 8; Heb. 13:17

12 Ezek. 30:3; Joel 2:2

13 Isa. 65:9, 10; Jer. 23:3; Ezek. 28:25; 36:24; 37:21, 22

34:2 Woe be to the shepherds of Israel. The shepherds were the kings, princes, and priests who ruled over the nation in the last years of the kingdom, along with the many false prophets earlier condemned (see Jer. 23:1–2). They had exploited and led the people astray. God holds kings, priests, pastors, and other shepherds of people accountable for the way they lead.

34:11–16 I . . . will . . . search my sheep, and seek them. This messianic passage anticipates the coming of the Good Shepherd (John 10:1–2), who will come to gather the flock of Israel and completely restore them in the future Millennial Kingdom.

people, and gather them from the countries, and will bring them to their own land, and feed them upon the mountains of Israel by the rivers, and in all the inhabited places of the country.

14 I will feed them in a good pasture, and upon the high mountains of Israel shall their fold be: there shall they lie in a good fold, and *in* a fat pasture shall they feed upon the mountains of Israel.

15 I will feed my flock, and I will cause them to lie down, saith the Lord GOD.

16 I will seek that which was lost, and bring again that which was driven away, and will bind up *that which was* broken, and will strengthen that which was sick: but I will destroy the fat and the strong; I will feed them with judgment.

17 And *as for* you, O my flock, thus saith the Lord GOD; Behold, I judge between cattle and cattle, between the rams and the he goats.

18 *Seemeth it* a small thing unto you to have eaten up the good pasture, but ye must tread down with your feet the residue of your pastures? and to have drunk of the deep waters, but ye must foul the residue with your feet?

19 And *as for* my flock, they eat that which ye have trodden with your feet; and they drink that which ye have fouled with your feet.

20 Therefore thus saith the Lord GOD unto them; Behold, I, *even* I, will judge between the fat cattle and between the lean cattle.

21 Because ye have thrust with side and with shoulder, and pushed all the diseased with your horns, till ye have scattered them abroad;

22 Therefore will I save my flock, and they shall no more be a prey; and I will judge between cattle and cattle.

23 And I will set up one shepherd over them, and he shall feed them, *even* my servant David; he shall feed them, and he shall be their shepherd.

24 And I the LORD will be their God, and my

servant David a prince among them; I the LORD have spoken *it*.

25 And I will make with them a covenant of peace, and will cause the evil beasts to cease out of the land: and they shall dwell safely in the wilderness, and sleep in the woods.

26 And I will make them and the places round about my hill a blessing; and I will cause the shower to come down in his season; there shall be showers of blessing.

27 And the tree of the field shall yield her fruit, and the earth shall yield her increase, and they shall be safe in their land, and shall know that I *am* the LORD, when I have broken the bands of their yoke, and delivered them out of the hand of those that served themselves of them.

28 And they shall no more be a prey to the heathen, neither shall the beast of the land devour them; but they shall dwell safely, and none shall make *them* afraid.

29 And I will raise up for them a plant of renown, and they shall be no more consumed with hunger in the land, neither bear the shame of the heathen any more.

30 Thus shall they know that I the LORD their God *am* with them, and *that* they, *even* the house of Israel, *are* my people, saith the Lord GOD.

31 And ye my flock, the flock of my pasture, *are* men, *and* I *am* your God, saith the Lord GOD.

CHAPTER 35
Edom

1 Moreover the word of the LORD came unto me, saying,

2 Son of man, set thy face against mount Seir, and prophesy against it,

3 And say unto it, Thus saith the Lord GOD; Behold, O mount Seir, I *am* against thee, and I will stretch out mine hand against thee, and I will make thee most desolate.

4 I will lay thy cities waste, and thou shalt be desolate, and thou shalt know that I *am* the LORD.

5 Because thou hast had a perpetual ha-

Cross references (center column):

14 Ps. 23:2; Jer. 33:12

16 Isa. 10:16; 40:11; Jer. 10:24; Ezek. 34:4; Amos 4:1; Mic. 4:6; Matt. 18:11; Mark 2:17; Luke 5:32

17 Ezek. 20:37, 38; 34:20, 22; Zech. 10:3; Matt. 25:32, 33

20 Ezek. 34:17

22 Ezek. 34:17

23 Isa. 40:11; Jer. 23:4, 5; 30:9; Ezek. 37:24, 25; Hos. 3:5; John 10:11; Heb. 13:20; 1Pet. 2:25; 5:4

24 Ex. 29:45; Ezek. 34:30; 37:22, 27; Luke 1:32, 33

25 Lev. 26:6; Isa. 11:6-9; Jer. 23:6; Ezek. 34:28; 37:26; Hos. 2:18

26 Gen. 12:2; Lev. 26:4

27 Lev. 26:4, 13; Ps. 85:12; Isa. 4:2; Jer. 2:20; 25:14

28 Jer. 30:10; 46:27; Ezek. 34:8, 25; 36:4

29 Isa. 11:1

31 Ps. 100:3; John 10:11

2 Deut. 2:5; Jer. 49:7, 8

34:22–26 I will set up one shepherd over them. This will be David's great descendant, Jesus, the Messiah, "the root and the offspring of David" (Rev. 22:16), who will reign in the coming kingdom (see 37:24–26; Jer. 30:9; Hos. 3:5; Zech. 14:9). When Christ returns to establish His kingdom, "there shall be showers of blessing" upon Israel and the world.

35:2 mount Seir. This is another name for Edom, which,

seeing Judah's fall, sought to take over its land, but was also conquered by Babylon. Edom's capital was the great rock city of Petra, which had many inhabitants through the centuries, including the Nabateans and the Romans who garrisoned an army there in New Testament times. This chapter elaborates an earlier prophecy (Ezek. 25:12–14).

tred, and hast shed *the blood of* the children of Israel by the force of the sword in the time of their calamity, in the time *that their* iniquity *had* an end:

6 Therefore, *as* I live, saith the Lord GOD, I will prepare thee unto blood, and blood shall pursue thee: sith thou hast not hated blood, even blood shall pursue thee.

7 Thus will I make mount Seir most desolate, and cut off from it him that passeth out and him that returneth.

8 And I will fill his mountains with his slain *men*: in thy hills, and in thy valleys, and in all thy rivers, shall they fall that are slain with the sword.

9 I will make thee perpetual desolations, and thy cities shall not return: and ye shall know that I *am* the LORD.

10 Because thou hast said, These two nations and these two countries shall be mine, and we will possess it; whereas the LORD was there:

11 Therefore, *as* I live, saith the Lord GOD, I will even do according to thine anger, and according to thine envy which thou hast used out of thy hatred against them; and I will make myself known among them, when I have judged thee.

12 And thou shalt know that I *am* the LORD, *and that* I have heard all thy blasphemies which thou hast spoken against the mountains of Israel, saying, They are laid desolate, they are given us to consume.

13 Thus with your mouth ye have boasted against me, and have multiplied your words against me: I have heard *them*.

14 Thus saith the Lord GOD; When the whole earth rejoiceth, I will make thee desolate.

15 As thou didst rejoice at the inheritance of the house of Israel, because it was desolate, so will I do unto thee: thou shalt be desolate, O mount Seir, and all Idumea, *even* all of it: and they shall know that I *am* the LORD.

CHAPTER 36
The Future Restoration of Israel

1 Also, thou son of man, prophesy unto the mountains of Israel, and say, Ye mountains of Israel, hear the word of the LORD:

2 Thus saith the Lord GOD; Because the enemy hath said against you, Aha, even the ancient high places are ours in possession:

3 Therefore prophesy and say, Thus saith the Lord GOD; Because they have made *you* desolate, and swallowed you up on every side, that ye might be a possession unto the residue of the heathen, and ye are taken up in the lips of talkers, and *are* an infamy of the people:

4 Therefore, ye mountains of Israel, hear the word of the Lord GOD; Thus saith the Lord GOD to the mountains, and to the hills, to the rivers, and to the valleys, to the desolate wastes, and to the cities that are forsaken, which became a prey and derision to the residue of the heathen that *are* round about:

5 Therefore thus saith the Lord GOD; Surely in the fire of my jealousy have I spoken against the residue of the heathen, and against all Idumea, which have appointed my land into their possession with the joy of all *their* heart, with despiteful minds, to cast it out for a prey.

6 Prophesy therefore concerning the land of Israel, and say unto the mountains, and to the hills, to the rivers, and to the valleys, Thus saith the Lord GOD; Behold, I have spoken in my jealousy and in my fury, because ye have borne the shame of the heathen:

7 Therefore thus saith the Lord GOD; I have lifted up mine hand, Surely the heathen that *are* about you, they shall bear their shame.

8 But ye, O mountains of Israel, ye shall shoot forth your branches, and yield your fruit to my people of Israel; for they are at hand to come.

9 For, behold, I *am* for you, and I will turn unto you, and ye shall be tilled and sown:

10 And I will multiply men upon you, all the house of Israel, *even* all of it: and the cities shall be inhabited, and the wastes shall be builded:

11 And I will multiply upon you man and beast; and they shall increase and bring fruit: and I will settle you after your old estates, and will do better *unto you* than at your beginnings: and ye shall know that I *am* the LORD.

12 Yea, I will cause men to walk upon you, *even* my people Israel; and they shall possess

Cross References

6 Ps. 109:17
7 Judg. 5:6; Ezek. 29:11; 35:3
8 Ezek. 31:12; 32:5
9 Jer. 49:17, 18; Ezek. 6:7; 7:4, 9; 25:13; 35:4; 36:11; Mal. 1:3, 4
10 Ps. 48:1, 3; 83:4, 12; 132:13, 14; Ezek. 36:5; 48:35; Obad. 1:13
11 Matt. 7:2; James 2:13
12 Ps. 9:16; Ezek. 6:7
13 1Sam. 2:3; Rev. 13:6
14 Isa. 65:13, 14
15 Ezek. 35:3, 4; Obad. 1:12, 15

1 Ezek. 6:2, 3
2 Deut. 32:13; Ezek. 25:3; 26:2; 35:10
3 Deut. 28:37; 1Kgs. 9:7; Lam. 2:15; Dan. 9:16
4 Ps. 79:4; Ezek. 34:28
5 Deut. 4:24; Ezek. 35:10, 12; 38:19
6 Ps. 123:3, 4; Ezek. 34:29; 36:15
7 Ezek. 20:5
10 Isa. 58:12; 61:4; Ezek. 36:33; Amos 9:14
11 Jer. 31:27; 33:12; Ezek. 35:9; 37:6, 13
12 Jer. 15:7; Obad. 1:17

36:1–15 Ye mountains of Israel. Contrasted with Edom's desolation in chapter 35, Israel was destined to experience total restoration and national salvation and become like the Garden of Eden (v. 35). At the Messiah's coming, "all Israel will be saved" (Rom. 11:26), that is, all living Israelites will embrace their Messiah (Zech. 12:8–14; 13:1–6; 14:1–4; Rev. 1:7), and the thousand-year reign of Christ on earth will begin.

thee, and thou shalt be their inheritance, and thou shalt no more henceforth bereave them *of men*.

13 Thus saith the Lord GOD; Because they say unto you, Thou *land* devourest up men, and hast bereaved thy nations;

14 Therefore thou shalt devour men no more, neither bereave thy nations any more, saith the Lord GOD.

15 Neither will I cause *men* to hear in thee the shame of the heathen any more, neither shalt thou bear the reproach of the people any more, neither shalt thou cause thy nations to fall any more, saith the Lord GOD.

16 Moreover the word of the LORD came unto me, saying,

17 Son of man, when the house of Israel dwelt in their own land, they defiled it by their own way and by their doings: their way was before me as the uncleanness of a removed woman.

18 Wherefore I poured my fury upon them for the blood that they had shed upon the land, and for their idols *wherewith* they had polluted it:

19 And I scattered them among the heathen, and they were dispersed through the countries: according to their way and according to their doings I judged them.

20 And when they entered unto the heathen, whither they went, they profaned my holy name, when they said to them, These *are* the people of the LORD, and are gone forth out of his land.

21 But I had pity for mine holy name, which the house of Israel had profaned among the heathen, whither they went.

22 Therefore say unto the house of Israel, Thus saith the Lord GOD; I do not *this* for your sakes, O house of Israel, but for mine holy name's sake, which ye have profaned among the heathen, whither ye went.

23 And I will sanctify my great name, which was profaned among the heathen, which ye have profaned in the midst of them; and the heathen shall know that I *am* the LORD, saith the Lord GOD, when I shall be sanctified in you before their eyes.

24 For I will take you from among the heathen, and gather you out of all countries, and will bring you into your own land.

25 Then will I sprinkle clean water upon you, and ye shall be clean: from all your filthiness, and from all your idols, will I cleanse you.

A New Spirit and a New Heart

26 A new heart also will I give you, and a new spirit will I put within you: and I will take away the stony heart out of your flesh, and I will give you an heart of flesh.

27 And I will put my spirit within you, and cause you to walk in my statutes, and ye shall keep my judgments, and do *them*.

28 And ye shall dwell in the land that I gave to your fathers; and ye shall be my people, and I will be your God.

29 I will also save you from all your uncleannesses: and I will call for the corn, and will increase it, and lay no famine upon you.

30 And I will multiply the fruit of the tree, and the increase of the field, that ye shall receive no more reproach of famine among the heathen.

31 Then shall ye remember your own evil ways, and your doings that *were* not good, and shall lothe yourselves in your own sight for your iniquities and for your abominations.

32 Not for your sakes do I *this*, saith the Lord GOD, be it known unto you: be ashamed and confounded for your own ways, O house of Israel.

33 Thus saith the Lord GOD; In the day that I shall have cleansed you from all your iniquities I will also cause *you* to dwell in the cities, and the wastes shall be builded.

34 And the desolate land shall be tilled, whereas it lay desolate in the sight of all that passed by.

35 And they shall say, This land that was desolate is become like the garden of Eden; and the waste and desolate and ruined cities *are become* fenced, *and* are inhabited.

36 Then the heathen that are left round about you shall know that I the LORD build the ruined *places, and* plant that that was desolate: I the LORD have spoken *it*, and I will do *it*.

37 Thus saith the Lord GOD; I will yet *for* this be inquired of by the house of Israel, to

Cross references

13 Num. 13:32
15 Ezek. 34:29
17 Lev. 15:19; 18:25, 27, 28; Jer. 2:7
18 Ezek. 16:36, 38; 23:37
19 Ezek. 7:3; 18:30; 22:15; 39:24
20 Isa. 52:5; Rom. 2:24
21 Ezek. 20:9, 14
22 Ps. 106:8
23 Ezek. 20:41; 28:22
24 Ezek. 34:13; 37:21
25 Isa. 52:15; Jer. 33:8; Heb. 10:22
26 Jer. 32:39; Ezek. 11:19
27 Ezek. 11:19; 37:14
28 Jer. 30:22; Ezek. 11:20; 28:25; 37:25, 27
29 Ps. 105:16; Ezek. 34:29; Matt. 1:21; Rom. 11:26
30 Ezek. 34:27
31 Lev. 26:39; Ezek. 6:9; 16:61, 63; 20:43
32 Deut. 9:5; Ezek. 36:22
33 Ezek. 36:10
35 Isa. 51:3; Ezek. 28:13; Joel 2:3
36 Ezek. 17:24; 22:14; 37:14
37 Ezek. 14:3; 20:3, 31; 36:10

36:17–24 the house of Israel. Though the people of Israel had sinned, been scattered, and chastised, God promised for His own name's sake, not for theirs, to gather them out of all countries and bring them back into their own land. After the seventy years of captivity, multiplied thousands returned from other countries, but the vast majority dispersed. After Jerusalem's destruction in A.D. 70, most Jews fled from the city. Jews have continued to be dispersed ever since A.D. 70.

do *it* for them; I will increase them with men like a flock.
38 As the holy flock, as the flock of Jerusalem in her solemn feasts; so shall the waste cities be filled with flocks of men: and they shall know that I *am* the LORD.

CHAPTER 37
The Valley of Dry Bones

1 The hand of the LORD was upon me, and carried me out in the spirit of the LORD, and set me down in the midst of the valley which *was* full of bones,
2 And caused me to pass by them round about: and, behold, *there were* very many in the open valley; and, lo, *they were* very dry.
3 And he said unto me, Son of man, can these bones live? And I answered, O Lord GOD, thou knowest.
4 Again he said unto me, Prophesy upon these bones, and say unto them, O ye dry bones, hear the word of the LORD.
5 Thus saith the Lord GOD unto these bones; Behold, I will cause breath to enter into you, and ye shall live:
6 And I will lay sinews upon you, and will bring up flesh upon you, and cover you with skin, and put breath in you, and ye shall live; and ye shall know that I *am* the LORD.
7 So I prophesied as I was commanded: and as I prophesied, there was a noise, and behold a shaking, and the bones came together, bone to his bone.
8 And when I beheld, lo, the sinews and the flesh came up upon them, and the skin covered them above: but *there was* no breath in them.

9 Then said he unto me, Prophesy unto the wind, prophesy, son of man, and say to the wind, Thus saith the Lord GOD; Come from the four winds, O breath, and breathe upon these slain, that they may live.
10 So I prophesied as he commanded me, and the breath came into them, and they lived, and stood up upon their feet, an exceeding great army.
11 Then he said unto me, Son of man, these bones are the whole house of Israel: behold, they say, Our bones are dried, and our hope is lost: we are cut off for our parts.
12 Therefore prophesy and say unto them, Thus saith the Lord GOD; Behold, O my people, I will open your graves, and cause you to come up out of your graves, and bring you into the land of Israel.
13 And ye shall know that I *am* the LORD, when I have opened your graves, O my people, and brought you up out of your graves,
14 And shall put my spirit in you, and ye shall live, and I shall place you in your own land: then shall ye know that I the LORD have spoken *it*, and performed *it*, saith the LORD.

The Restoration of a United Kingdom

15 The word of the LORD came again unto me, saying,

Cross references
1 Ezek. 1:3; 3:14; 8:3; 11:24; Luke 4:1
3 Deut. 32:39; 1Sam. 2:6; John 5:21; Rom. 4:17; 2Cor. 1:9
5 Ps. 104:30; Ezek. 37:9
6 Ezek. 6:7; 35:12; Joel 2:27; 3:17
9 Ps. 104:30; Ezek. 37:5
10 Rev. 11:11
11 Ps. 141:7; Isa. 49:14
12 Isa. 26:19; Ezek. 36:24; 37:25; Hos. 13:14
14 Ezek. 36:27

Restoration Stages of Israel in Ezekiel 37

STAGE	HISTORICAL FULFILLMENT
Scattered bones	Israel in dispersion
Sinews connected to bones	Pre-1948 gathering
Flesh on bones	Israel becomes a nation (present status)
Skin covers body	Israel during the Tribulation
Breath in the body	Israel after national conversion

37:1–28 carried me out in the spirit of the LORD. The third major vision in the book, this vision of the "Valley of the Dry Bones" was given to Ezekiel to reassure the exiles that the promises of God regarding His people are secure. The "valley" signifies the world, where Jews have been dispersed (v. 7). After being away from their homeland so long, they are like dry bones; all their hope was gone. Nevertheless, God affirmed that He would bring them back to their homeland from wherever they were (vv. 12–14). This vision is explicitly concerned with God's renewal of His promises to Israel. God's Spirit is placed within Israel (v. 14, cf. 36:22–28), the reign of the Messiah begins (vv. 24–25), the confirmation of the new covenant with Israel is given (v. 26, cf. Jer. 31:31–34), and God's presence and identification with His redeemed people is evident (v. 27 [cf. Hos. 1:10; 2:23; Rev. 21:3–7]). The final fulfillment of this passage awaits Israel's spiritual regeneration and their political and spiritual restoration in the End Times and in the Millennium.

37:15–23 take . . . one stick. The Kingdom of David and Solomon split in 931 B.C., becoming Israel and Judah. In restored Israel, all tribes are represented and the nation will be united, as the sign of the fused stick reveals.

Israel in Two Centuries

By Jim Combs

The restoration of Israel, leading to a golden age of blessing, is a prominent theme in Scripture. No passage more graphically illustrates the process than Ezekiel 37.

This vision of the dry bones as the "whole house of Israel" has five stages: **1)** the dry bones are scattered around (v. 2); **2)** the bones come together, develop connective tissues, and are covered with flesh (vv. 7–8); **3)** the wind blows breath into these bodies (vv. 9–10); **4)** the restoration is also a spiritual one (vv. 24–28); and **5)** "David," actually Jesus Christ, the "root and offspring of David" (Rev. 22:16), will reign over the nation.

Setting no dates for specific fulfillments, but surveying the trend of Israel's resurgence in the nineteenth and twentieth centuries, it appears this divine program of restoration is in progress. The following are highlights of these two centuries:

1814—Presbyterian pastor John MacDonald in Albany, New York, began to preach on Bible prophecy and Israel's restoration, sparking an interest in the literalist interpretation of Old Testament prophecies about Israel.

It appears that the restoration of Israel is already in progress.

1878—W. E. Blackstone's book *Jesus is Coming* was published, predicting and encouraging the return of Jews in fulfillment of the prophecy.

1881–1900—The First Aliya (meaning ascent) occurred and consisted of some 30,000 Jews under persecution in Russia moving to Palestine.

1897—The First Zionist Congress, convened in Basel, Switzerland, adopted Zionism as a program, and stated, "The aim of Zionism is to create for the Jewish people a home in Palestine by public law."

1904–1914—The Second Aliya resulted in 32,000 persecuted Russian Jews moving to Palestine.

1917—The Balfour Declaration, read in part: "His majesty's government views with favor the establishment in Palestine of a national home for Jewish people."

1924–1939—The Third Aliya, when 78,000 Polish Jews moved to Palestine.

1933–1939—The Fourth Aliya, when 230,000 Jews fled from persecution in Germany and central Europe.

1940–1948—The Fifth Aliya, when 95,000 Jews escaped from central Europe. Many Jews remained in Europe, and more than six million were killed during the Holocaust led by Adolph Hitler and Nazi Germany.

1948—The Jewish Agency in what would become the new nation of Israel proclaimed nation status. On May 14, 1948, the United States President Harry Truman's administration made this announcement: "The United States recognizes the provisional government as the de-facto authority of the New State of Israel."

1967—The Six Day War, precipitated by an Arab invasion, results in Israel capturing Jerusalem and the West Bank.

1973—Another attack by Arabs was repulsed with Israeli victories.

1978–2000—Egypt recognizes Israel; the Arab-Palestinian resistance movement begins; negotiations, agreements, and tensions continue.

It seems that during these two centuries, the dry bones have come together to form a living nation, the most powerful small nation on earth (with just over five million people), but there awaits the complete spiritual awakening, when true life enters them, as prophesied here and in Joel 2:28–29.

16 Moreover, thou son of man, take thee one stick, and write upon it, For Judah, and for the children of Israel his companions: then take another stick, and write upon it, For Joseph, the stick of Ephraim, and *for* all the house of Israel his companions:

17 And join them one to another into one stick; and they shall become one in thine hand.

18 And when the children of thy people shall speak unto thee, saying, Wilt thou not shew us what thou *meanest* by these?

19 Say unto them, Thus saith the Lord GOD; Behold, I will take the stick of Joseph, which *is* in the hand of Ephraim, and the tribes of Israel his fellows, and will put them with him, *even* with the stick of Judah, and make them one stick, and they shall be one in mine hand.

20 And the sticks whereon thou writest shall be in thine hand before their eyes.

21 And say unto them, Thus saith the Lord GOD; Behold, I will take the children of Israel from among the heathen, whither they be gone, and will gather them on every side, and bring them into their own land:

22 And I will make them one nation in the land upon the mountains of Israel; and one king shall be king to them all: and they shall be no more two nations, neither shall they be divided into two kingdoms any more at all:

23 Neither shall they defile themselves any more with their idols, nor with their detestable things, nor with any of their transgressions: but I will save them out of all their dwellingplaces, wherein they have sinned, and will cleanse them: so shall they be my people, and I will be their God.

24 And David my servant *shall be* king over them; and they all shall have one shepherd: they shall also walk in my judgments, and observe my statutes, and do them.

25 And they shall dwell in the land that I have given unto Jacob my servant, wherein your fathers have dwelt; and they shall

dwell therein, *even* they, and their children, and their children's children for ever: and my servant David *shall be* their prince for ever.

An Everlasting Covenant of Peace

26 Moreover I will make a covenant of peace with them; it shall be an everlasting covenant with them: and I will place them, and multiply them, and will set my sanctuary in the midst of them for evermore.

27 My tabernacle also shall be with them: yea, I will be their God, and they shall be my people.

28 And the heathen shall know that I the LORD do sanctify Israel, when my sanctuary shall be in the midst of them for evermore.

CHAPTER 38
Gog

1 And the word of the LORD came unto me, saying,

2 Son of man, set thy face against Gog, the land of Magog, the chief prince of Meshech and Tubal, and prophesy against him,

3 And say, Thus saith the Lord GOD; Behold, I *am* against thee, O Gog, the chief prince of Meshech and Tubal:

4 And I will turn thee back, and put hooks into thy jaws, and I will bring thee forth, and all thine army, horses and horsemen, all of them clothed with all sorts *of armour, even* a great company *with* bucklers and shields, all of them handling swords:

5 Persia, Ethiopia, and Libya with them; all of them with shield and helmet:

6 Gomer, and all his bands; the house of Togarmah of the north quarters, and all his bands: *and* many people with thee.

7 Be thou prepared, and prepare for thyself, thou, and all thy company that are assembled unto thee, and be thou a guard unto them.

8 After many days thou shalt be visited: in the latter years thou shalt come into the land *that is* brought back from the sword, *and is*

16 Num. 17:2; 2Chr. 11:12, 13, 16; 15:9; 30:11, 18

19 Zech. 10:6; Ezek. 37:16, 17

22 Isa. 11:13; Jer. 3:18; 50:4; Ezek. 34:23, 24; Hos. 1:11; John 10:16

24 Isa. 40:11; Jer. 23:5; 30:9; Ezek. 34:23, 24; 36:27; 37:22; Hos. 3:5; Luke 1:32; John 10:16

25 Isa. 60:21; Ezek. 36:28; 37:24; Joel 3:20; Amos 9:15; John 12:34

26 Ps. 89:3; Isa. 55:3; Jer. 32:40; Ezek. 34:25; 36:10, 37; 2Cor. 6:16

27 Lev. 26:11, 12; Ezek. 11:20; 14:11; 36:28; 43:7; John 1:14

28 Ezek. 20:12; 36:23

4 2Kgs. 19:28; Ezek. 23:12; 29:4; 39:2

5 Ezek. 27:10; 30:5

6 Gen. 10:2; Ezek. 27:14

7 Isa. 8:9, 10; Jer. 46:3, 4, 14; 51:12

8 Jer. 23:6

38:2 Gog . . . Magog. Gog is the leader of the coalition; Magog is in the territory, identified with the vast land north of Israel beyond the Caucasus and around and above the Black Sea. The descendants of Magog (Gen. 10:2), son of Japheth, were later called Scythians, from whom the Slavic peoples may have descended.

38:3 chief prince of Meshech and Tubal. The word "chief" in Hebrew is *Rosh,* and the passage has been translated, "prince of Rosh, Meshech and Tubal," making

an identification with Russia, according to some researchers. Both Meshech and Tubal, also sons of Japheth (Gen. 10:2) probably were ancestors of peoples who settled in eastern Europe and southern Asia.

38:6 Gomer . . . Togarmah. These are thought by some to designate eastern Turkey and the Ukraine. Others associate Gomer with the Cimmerians in western Asia, who are thought to have migrated to eastern and central Europe.

Gog and Magog

By Mark Hitchcock

The prophet Ezekiel predicted 2,600 years ago that in the latter times Israel would be furiously invaded by a people "out of the north parts" (Ezek. 38:6, 15). In Ezekiel 38:2–3; 39:1, the Hebrew word *rosh,* which simply means head, top, summit, or chief, is used to identify these people from the north. The interpretive problem is that the word *rosh* can be translated as either a proper noun or an adjective. Many translations use *rosh* as an adjective and translate it as the word "chief." I believe the better translation is to interpret *rosh* as a proper noun referring to a specific place—Russia.

The fulfillment of God's most amazing prophecies concerning Russia seems more imminent than ever before. As we track this nation in the prophecies of the End Times, we discover that her footprints lead right to the land of Israel. In tracking the events that lead to this invasion, one must consider the appearance, the allies, the activity, the annihilation, and the aftermath.

A madman called Gog by Ezekiel will be the end-time leader of Russia (38:2). A host of allies will join this leader when he invades the land of Israel (Ezek. 38:9). Eight other geographical locations are mentioned in Ezekiel 38:1–6: Meshech, Tubal, Gomer, and Togarmah (Turkey); Magog (Central Asia: Islamic southern republics of the former Soviet Union); Persia (Iran); Ethiopia or Cush (Sudan); and Libya.

Ezekiel says that these nations, led by "Gog," will come against Israel "in the latter years," at a time when the people of Israel are living in peace and prosperity (38:8–12). This probably describes the first half of the Tribulation, when Israel will be living under her peace treaty with the Antichrist. Near the middle of the Tribulation, Russia and her Islamic allies will descend upon the nation of Israel "like a storm . . . and like a cloud to cover the land" (38:9).

> *Near the middle of the Tribulation, Russia and her Islamic allies will descend upon the nation of Israel.*

These nations will invade Israel 1) to cash in on the wealth of Israel (Ezek. 38:11–12), 2) to control the Middle East, 3) to crush Israel (the Islamic nations mentioned in Scripture hate Israel), and 4) to challenge the authority of Antichrist (Dan. 11:40–44). Israel will be under her peace treaty with Antichrist, so an attack against Israel is a direct challenge to Antichrist's power. After he has destroyed the armies of Ezekiel 38, Antichrist will break his covenant with Israel and invade her himself (Dan. 11:41–44).

When Antichrist assembles this strike force, it will look like Israel is finished. But God will be in full control of the entire situation. He will come to rescue His helpless people and will use four judgments to destroy the nations: 1) a great earthquake (38:19–20), 2) infighting among the troops of the various nations (38:21), 3) disease (38:22), and 4) torrential rain, hailstones, fire and burning sulfur (38:22).

The four key events that occur in the aftermath of this invasion are the call for the birds and the beasts to feast on the dead (Ezek. 39:4–5, 17–20 [cf. Rev. 19:17–18]), the burying of the dead (7 months, Ezek. 39:11–12, 14–16), the burning of the weapons (7 years, Ezek. 39:9–10), and the blessing of salvation (Ezek. 38:16, 23; 39:6–7, 21–22).

gathered out of many people, against the mountains of Israel, which have been always waste: but it is brought forth out of the nations, and they shall dwell safely all of them.

9 Thou shalt ascend and come like a storm, thou shalt be like a cloud to cover the land, thou, and all thy bands, and many people with thee.

10 Thus saith the Lord GOD; It shall also come to pass, *that* at the same time shall things come into thy mind, and thou shalt think an evil thought:

11 And thou shalt say, I will go up to the land of unwalled villages; I will go to them that are at rest, that dwell safely, all of them dwelling without walls, and having neither bars nor gates,

12 To take a spoil, and to take a prey; to turn thine hand upon the desolate places *that are now* inhabited, and upon the people *that are* gathered out of the nations, which have gotten cattle and goods, that dwell in the midst of the land.

13 Sheba, and Dedan, and the merchants of Tarshish, with all the young lions thereof, shall say unto thee, Art thou come to take a spoil? hast thou gathered thy company to take a prey? to carry away silver and gold, to take away cattle and goods, to take a great spoil?

14 Therefore, son of man, prophesy and say unto Gog, Thus saith the Lord GOD; In that day when my people of Israel dwelleth safely, shalt thou not know *it?*

15 And thou shalt come from thy place out of the north parts, thou, and many people with thee, all of them riding upon horses, a great company, and a mighty army:

16 And thou shalt come up against my people of Israel, as a cloud to cover the land; it shall be in the latter days, and I will bring thee against my land, that the heathen may know me, when I shall be sanctified in thee, O Gog, before their eyes.

17 Thus saith the Lord GOD; *Art* thou he of

whom I have spoken in old time by my servants the prophets of Israel, which prophesied in those days *many* years that I would bring thee against them?

18 And it shall come to pass at the same time when Gog shall come against the land of Israel, saith the Lord GOD, *that* my fury shall come up in my face.

19 For in my jealousy *and* in the fire of my wrath have I spoken, Surely in that day there shall be a great shaking in the land of Israel;

20 So that the fishes of the sea, and the fowls of the heaven, and the beasts of the field, and all creeping things that creep upon the earth, and all the men that *are* upon the face of the earth, shall shake at my presence, and the mountains shall be thrown down, and the steep places shall fall, and every wall shall fall to the ground.

21 And I will call for a sword against him throughout all my mountains, saith the Lord GOD: every man's sword shall be against his brother.

22 And I will plead against him with pestilence and with blood; and I will rain upon him, and upon his bands, and upon the many people that *are* with him, an overflowing rain, and great hailstones, fire, and brimstone.

23 Thus will I magnify myself, and sanctify myself; and I will be known in the eyes of many nations, and they shall know that I *am* the LORD.

CHAPTER 39

1 Therefore, thou son of man, prophesy against Gog, and say, Thus saith the Lord GOD; Behold, I *am* against thee, O Gog, the chief prince of Meshech and Tubal:

2 And I will turn thee back, and leave but the sixth part of thee, and will cause thee to come up from the north parts, and will bring thee upon the mountains of Israel:

3 And I will smite thy bow out of thy left

Cross references (center column)

9 Isa. 28:2; Jer. 4:13; Ezek. 38:16

11 Jer. 49:31; Ezek. 38:8

12 Ezek. 29:19; 36:34, 35; 38:8

13 Ezek. 19:3, 5; 27:12, 15, 20, 22, 23

14 Isa. 4:1; Ezek. 38:8

15 Ezek. 38:6; 39:2

16 Ex. 14:4; Ezek. 36:23; 38:8, 9; 39:21

19 Ps. 89:46; Ezek. 36:5, 6; 39:25; Hag. 2:6, 7; Rev. 16:18

20 Jer. 4:24; Hos. 4:3; Nah. 1:5, 6

21 Judg. 7:22; 1Sam. 14:20; 2Chr. 20:23; Ps. 105:16; Ezek. 14:17

22 Ps. 11:6; Isa. 29:6; 30:30; 66:16; Jer. 25:31; Ezek. 5:17; 13:11; Rev. 16:21

23 Ps. 9:16; Ezek. 36:23; 37:28; 38:16; 39:7

1 Ezek. 38:2, 3

2 Ezek. 38:4, 15

38:11 I will go up to . . . unwalled villages. The chief prince of Meshech and Tubal (v. 3) will lead this confederation of nations, which in the latter days invades Israel. This may take place at the end of this current age and the beginning of the seven-year Tribulation, toward the middle of the Tribulation, or in the last half of the Tribulation. The likelihood is that it will occur early, after Antichrist negotiates his treaty with Israel (Dan. 9:27).

38:13 Sheba, and Dedan, and the merchants of Tarshish. Sheba and Dedan were countries on the Arabian

Peninsula. Tarshish usually means Spain or the western extremities of the Mediterranean world, possibly including, as some think, western France and even England. These countries object to Gog's invasion.

38:17–21 Thus saith the Lord. There follows in this oracle a prediction of Gog's fall, as God sends an earthquake, confusion among the invaders, and a fiery rain.

39:3 will cause thine arrows to fall. The weaponry for the armies of the North simply fails.

hand, and will cause thine arrows to fall out of thy right hand.

4 Thou shalt fall upon the mountains of Israel, thou, and all thy bands, and the people that *is* with thee: I will give thee unto the ravenous birds of every sort, and *to* the beasts of the field to be devoured.

5 Thou shalt fall upon the open field: for I have spoken *it*, saith the Lord GOD.

6 And I will send a fire on Magog, and among them that dwell carelessly in the isles: and they shall know that I *am* the LORD.

7 So will I make my holy name known in the midst of my people Israel; and I will not *let them* pollute my holy name any more: and the heathen shall know that I *am* the LORD, the Holy One in Israel.

8 Behold, it is come, and it is done, saith the Lord GOD; this *is* the day whereof I have spoken.

9 And they that dwell in the cities of Israel shall go forth, and shall set on fire and burn the weapons, both the shields and the bucklers, the bows and the arrows, and the handstaves, and the spears, and they shall burn them with fire seven years:

10 So that they shall take no wood out of the field, neither cut down *any* out of the forests; for they shall burn the weapons with fire: and they shall spoil those that spoiled them, and rob those that robbed them, saith the Lord GOD.

11 And it shall come to pass in that day, *that* I will give unto Gog a place there of graves in Israel, the valley of the passengers on the east of the sea: and it shall stop the *noses* of the passengers: and there shall they bury Gog and all his multitude: and they shall call *it* The valley of Hamon-gog.

12 And seven months shall the house of Israel be burying of them, that they may cleanse the land.

13 Yea, all the people of the land shall bury *them*; and it shall be to them a renown the day that I shall be glorified, saith the Lord GOD.

14 And they shall sever out men of continual employment, passing through the land to bury with the passengers those that re-

main upon the face of the earth, to cleanse it: after the end of seven months shall they search.

15 And the passengers *that* pass through the land, when *any* seeth a man's bone, then shall he set up a sign by it, till the buriers have buried it in the valley of Hamon-gog.

16 And also the name of the city *shall be* Hamonah. Thus shall they cleanse the land.

17 And, thou son of man, thus saith the Lord GOD; Speak unto every feathered fowl, and to every beast of the field, Assemble yourselves, and come; gather yourselves on every side to my sacrifice that I do sacrifice for you, *even* a great sacrifice upon the mountains of Israel, that ye may eat flesh, and drink blood.

18 Ye shall eat the flesh of the mighty, and drink the blood of the princes of the earth, of rams, of lambs, and of goats, of bullocks, all of them fatlings of Bashan.

19 And ye shall eat fat till ye be full, and drink blood till ye be drunken, of my sacrifice which I have sacrificed for you.

20 Thus ye shall be filled at my table with horses and chariots, with mighty men, and with all men of war, saith the Lord GOD.

Israel Restored

21 And I will set my glory among the heathen, and all the heathen shall see my judgment that I have executed, and my hand that I have laid upon them.

22 So the house of Israel shall know that I *am* the LORD their God from that day and forward.

23 And the heathen shall know that the house of Israel went into captivity for their iniquity: because they trespassed against me, therefore hid I my face from them, and gave them into the hand of their enemies: so fell they all by the sword.

24 According to their uncleanness and according to their transgressions have I done unto them, and hid my face from them.

25 Therefore thus saith the Lord GOD; Now will I bring again the captivity of Jacob, and have mercy upon the whole house of Israel, and will be jealous for my holy name;

26 After that they have borne their shame,

Cross-references (center column)

4 Ezek. 33:27; 38:21; 39:17

6 Ps. 72:10; Ezek. 38:22; Amos 1:4

7 Lev. 18:21; Ezek. 20:39; 38:16, 23; 39:22

8 Ezek. 38:17; Rev. 16:17; 21:6

10 Isa. 14:2

12 Deut. 21:23; Ezek. 39:14, 16

13 Ezek. 28:22

14 Ezek. 39:12

16 Ezek. 39:12

17 Isa. 18:6; 34:6; Jer. 12:9; Ezek. 39:4; Zeph. 1:7; Rev. 19:17

18 Deut. 32:14; Ps. 22:12; Rev. 19:18

20 Ps. 76:6; Ezek. 38:4; Rev. 19:18

21 Ex. 7:4; Ezek. 38:16, 23

22 Ezek. 39:7, 28

23 Lev. 26:25; Deut. 31:17; Isa. 59:2; Ezek. 36:18-20, 23

24 Ezek. 36:19

25 Jer. 30:3, 18; Ezek. 20:40; 34:13; 36:24; Hos. 1:11

26 Lev. 26:5, 6; Dan. 9:16

39:6 I will send a fire. The homelands of the invaders will suffer dire consequences, as will the invading soldiers that sweep into Israel.

39:21–29 I will set my glory. The nations will acknowledge God's deliverance of His people, and Israel will better understand His protective power and plan for them.

God is going to fulfill all of His promises to Israel, especially their restoration (v. 25). Involved in this restoration is a renewed reverence for God and the forsaking of idolatry (v. 22), the regathering of God's chosen people into the land of promise (vv. 27–28), and the outpouring of God's spirit (cf. Zech 12:9—13:1; Rom. 11:26).

and all their trespasses whereby they have trespassed against me, when they dwelt safely in their land, and none made *them* afraid.

27 When I have brought them again from the people, and gathered them out of their enemies' lands, and am sanctified in them in the sight of many nations;

28 Then shall they know that I *am* the LORD their God, which caused them to be led into captivity among the heathen: but I have gathered them unto their own land, and have left none of them any more there.

29 Neither will I hide my face any more from them: for I have poured out my spirit upon the house of Israel, saith the Lord GOD.

CHAPTER 40
The Prophet's Vision of the Temple

1 In the five and twentieth year of our captivity, in the beginning of the year, in the tenth *day* of the month, in the fourteenth year after that the city was smitten, in the selfsame day the hand of the LORD was upon me, and brought me thither.

2 In the visions of God brought he me into the land of Israel, and set me upon a very high mountain, by which *was* as the frame of a city on the south.

3 And he brought me thither, and, behold, *there was* a man, whose appearance *was* like the appearance of brass, with a line of flax in his hand, and a measuring reed; and he stood in the gate.

4 And the man said unto me, Son of man, behold with thine eyes, and hear with thine ears, and set thine heart upon all that I shall shew thee; for to the intent that I might shew *them* unto thee *art* thou brought hither: declare all that thou seest to the house of Israel.

5 And behold a wall on the outside of the house round about, and in the man's hand

a measuring reed of six cubits *long* by the cubit and an handbreadth: so he measured the breadth of the building, one reed; and the height, one reed.

6 Then came he unto the gate which looketh toward the east, and went up the stairs thereof, and measured the threshold of the gate, *which was* one reed broad; and the other threshold *of the gate, which was* one reed broad.

7 And *every* little chamber *was* one reed long, and one reed broad; and between the little chambers *were* five cubits; and the threshold of the gate by the porch of the gate within *was* one reed.

8 He measured also the porch of the gate within, one reed.

9 Then measured he the porch of the gate, eight cubits; and the posts thereof, two cubits; and the porch of the gate *was* inward.

10 And the little chambers of the gate eastward *were* three on this side, and three on that side; they three *were* of one measure: and the posts had one measure on this side and on that side.

11 And he measured the breadth of the entry of the gate, ten cubits; *and* the length of the gate, thirteen cubits.

12 The space also before the little chambers *was* one cubit *on this side*, and the space *was* one cubit on that side: and the little chambers *were* six cubits on this side, and six cubits on that side.

13 He measured then the gate from the roof of *one* little chamber to the roof of another: the breadth *was* five and twenty cubits, door against door.

14 He made also posts of threescore cubits, even unto the post of the court round about the gate.

15 And from the face of the gate of the entrance unto the face of the porch of the inner gate *were* fifty cubits.

16 And *there were* narrow windows to the

Cross references (center column):

27 Ezek. 28:25, 26; 36:23, 24; 38:16

28 Ezek. 34:30; 39:22

29 Isa. 54:8; Joel 2:28; Zech. 12:10; Acts 2:17

1 Ezek. 1:3; 33:21

2 Ezek. 8:3; Rev. 21:10

3 Ezek. 1:7; 47:3; Dan. 10:6; Rev. 11:1; 21:15

4 Ezek. 43:10; 44:5

5 Ezek. 42:20

16 1Kgs. 6:4

40:2 visions of God. This is the fourth and final major vision. Here the prophet is transported to a high mountain to see the future Millennial Temple in Jerusalem.

40:3 a man. This is either a high-ranking angel (see Dan. 10; 12:6; Zech. 2:1–10; Rev. 10:1–11; 11:1–2) or possibly a pre-incarnate appearance of the "angel of the Lord," Jesus Christ. The measuring tools will be used to record specific distances and sizes in the temple area (cf. Rev. 11:1–2).

40:4–49 declare all . . . thou seest to the house of

Israel. A wall surrounded the entire temple area with a huge gateway on the east. Three little chambers (guardrooms) were situated on each side of the hall leading to the outer court of the temple, where thirty additional chambers were seen. Two more gates to the north and south and another large gate led into the inner court, where sacrificial offerings were to be prepared. Special rooms for priests and other entrances are described, all of which depict a literal structure, not an idealistic symbol.

little chambers, and to their posts within the gate round about, and likewise to the arches: and windows *were* round about inward: and upon *each* post *were* palm trees.

17 Then brought he me into the outward court, and, lo, *there were* chambers, and a pavement made for the court round about: thirty chambers *were* upon the pavement.

18 And the pavement by the side of the gates over against the length of the gates *was* the lower pavement.

19 Then he measured the breadth from the forefront of the lower gate unto the forefront of the inner court without, an hundred cubits eastward and northward.

20 And the gate of the outward court that looked toward the north, he measured the length thereof, and the breadth thereof.

21 And the little chambers thereof *were* three on this side and three on that side; and the posts thereof and the arches thereof were after the measure of the first gate: the length thereof *was* fifty cubits, and the breadth five and twenty cubits.

22 And their windows, and their arches, and their palm trees, *were* after the measure of the gate that looketh toward the east; and they went up unto it by seven steps; and the arches thereof *were* before them.

23 And the gate of the inner court *was* over against the gate toward the north, and toward the east; and he measured from gate to gate an hundred cubits.

24 After that he brought me toward the south, and behold a gate toward the south: and he measured the posts thereof and the arches thereof according to these measures.

25 And *there were* windows in it and in the arches thereof round about, like those windows: the length *was* fifty cubits, and the breadth five and twenty cubits.

26 And *there were* seven steps to go up to it, and the arches thereof *were* before them: and it had palm trees, one on this side, and another on that side, upon the posts thereof.

27 And *there was* a gate in the inner court toward the south: and he measured from gate to gate toward the south an hundred cubits.

28 And he brought me to the inner court by the south gate: and he measured the south gate according to these measures;

29 And the little chambers thereof, and the posts thereof, and the arches thereof, according to these measures: and *there were* windows in it and in the arches thereof round about: *it was* fifty cubits long, and five and twenty cubits broad.

30 And the arches round about *were* five

and twenty cubits long, and five cubits broad.

31 And the arches thereof *were* toward the utter court; and palm trees *were* upon the posts thereof: and the going up to it *had* eight steps.

32 And he brought me into the inner court toward the east: and he measured the gate according to these measures.

33 And the little chambers thereof, and the posts thereof, and the arches thereof, *were* according to these measures: and *there were* windows therein and in the arches thereof round about: *it was* fifty cubits long, and five and twenty cubits broad.

34 And the arches thereof *were* toward the outward court; and palm trees *were* upon the posts thereof, on this side, and on that side: and the going up to it *had* eight steps.

35 And he brought me to the north gate, and measured *it* according to these measures;

36 The little chambers thereof, the posts thereof, and the arches thereof, and the windows to it round about: the length *was* fifty cubits, and the breadth five and twenty cubits.

37 And the posts thereof *were* toward the utter court; and palm trees *were* upon the posts thereof, on this side, and on that side: and the going up to it *had* eight steps.

38 And the chambers and the entries thereof *were* by the posts of the gates, where they washed the burnt offering.

39 And in the porch of the gate *were* two tables on this side, and two tables on that side, to slay thereon the burnt offering and the sin offering and the trespass offering.

40 And at the side without, as one goeth up to the entry of the north gate, *were* two tables; and on the other side, which *was* at the porch of the gate, *were* two tables.

41 Four tables *were* on this side, and four tables on that side, by the side of the gate; eight tables, whereupon they slew *their sacrifices*.

42 And the four tables *were* of hewn stone for the burnt offering, of a cubit and an half long, and a cubit and an half broad, and one cubit high: whereupon also they laid the instruments wherewith they slew the burnt offering and the sacrifice.

43 And within *were* hooks, an hand broad, fastened round about: and upon the tables *was* the flesh of the offering.

44 And without the inner gate *were* the chambers of the singers in the inner court, which *was* at the side of the north gate; and their prospect *was* toward the south: one at

---

17 1Kgs. 6:5; Ezek. 45:5; Rev. 11:2

30 Ezek. 40:21, 25, 33, 36

39 Lev. 4:2, 3; 5:6; 6:6; 7:1

44 1Chr. 6:31

the side of the east gate *having* the prospect toward the north.

45 And he said unto me, This chamber, whose prospect *is* toward the south, *is* for the priests, the keepers of the charge of the house.

46 And the chamber whose prospect *is* toward the north *is* for the priests, the keepers of the charge of the altar: these *are* the sons of Zadok among the sons of Levi, which come near to the LORD to minister unto him.

47 So he measured the court, an hundred cubits long, and an hundred cubits broad, foursquare; and the altar *that was* before the house.

48 And he brought me to the porch of the house, and measured *each* post of the porch, five cubits on this side, and five cubits on that side: and the breadth of the gate *was* three cubits on this side, and three cubits on that side.

49 The length of the porch *was* twenty cubits, and the breadth eleven cubits; and *he brought me* by the steps whereby they went up to it: and *there were* pillars by the posts, one on this side, and another on that side.

CHAPTER 41

1 Afterward he brought me to the temple, and measured the posts, six cubits broad on the one side, and six cubits broad on the other side, *which was* the breadth of the tabernacle.

2 And the breadth of the door *was* ten cubits; and the sides of the door *were* five cubits on the one side, and five cubits on the other side: and he measured the length thereof, forty cubits: and the breadth, twenty cubits.

3 Then went he inward, and measured the post of the door, two cubits; and the door, six cubits; and the breadth of the door, seven cubits.

4 So he measured the length thereof, twenty cubits; and the breadth, twenty cubits, before the temple: and he said unto me, This *is* the most holy *place.*

5 After he measured the wall of the house, six cubits; and the breadth of *every* side chamber, four cubits, round about the house on every side.

6 And the side chambers *were* three, one over another, and thirty in order; and they entered into the wall which *was* of the house for the side chambers round about, that they might have hold, but they had not hold in the wall of the house.

7 And *there was* an enlarging, and a winding about still upward to the side chambers: for the winding about of the house went still upward round about the house: therefore the breadth of the house *was still* upward, and so increased *from* the lowest *chamber* to the highest by the midst.

8 I saw also the height of the house round about: the foundations of the side chambers *were* a full reed of six great cubits.

9 The thickness of the wall, which *was* for the side chamber without, *was* five cubits: and *that* which *was* left *was* the place of the side chambers that *were* within.

10 And between the chambers *was* the wideness of twenty cubits round about the house on every side.

11 And the doors of the side chambers *were* toward *the place that was* left, one door toward the north, and another door toward the south: and the breadth of the place that was left *was* five cubits round about.

12 Now the building that *was* before the separate place at the end toward the west *was* seventy cubits broad; and the wall of the building *was* five cubits thick round about, and the length thereof ninety cubits.

13 So he measured the house, an hundred cubits long; and the separate place, and the building, with the walls thereof, an hundred cubits long;

14 Also the breadth of the face of the house, and of the separate place toward the east, an hundred cubits.

15 And he measured the length of the building over against the separate place which *was* behind it, and the galleries thereof on the one side and on the other

Cross references

45 Lev. 8:35; Num. 3:27, 28, 32, 38; 18:5; 1Chr. 9:23; 2Chr. 13:11; Ps. 134:1

46 Num. 18:5; 1Kgs. 2:35; Ezek. 43:19; 44:15, 16

49 1Kgs. 6:3; 7:21

4 1Kgs. 6:20; 2Chr. 3:8

6 1Kgs. 6:5, 6

7 1Kgs. 6:8

8 Ezek. 40:5

41:1–12 he brought me to the temple. There follows an extensive description of the temple edifice, including the porch (Ezek. 40:49), the Holy Place (Ezek. 41:1–2), the Most Holy Place (vv. 3–4), the side buildings with three stories, thirty rooms on each floor (vv. 5–11), and another building behind the temple (v. 12).

41:13–26 he measured the house. The temple is then measured, the hundred cubits equaling about 170 feet.

The interior walls were wainscoted with wood. Gold and silver, so prominent in Solomon's Temple, are absent. Chief ornamentation on the walls are the palm trees and the cherubim, their two faces are that of a man and a lion, possibly typifying the humanity and the royalty of Jesus the King. The wooden altar is for incense, not for sacrifices, as in Ezekiel 43:13–17.

side, an hundred cubits, with the inner temple, and the porches of the court;

16 The door posts, and the narrow windows, and the galleries round about on their three stories, over against the door, cieled with wood round about, and from the ground up to the windows, and the windows *were* covered;

17 To that above the door, even unto the inner house, and without, and by all the wall round about within and without, by measure.

18 And *it was* made with cherubims and palm trees, so that a palm tree *was* between a cherub and a cherub; and *every* cherub had two faces;

19 So that the face of a man *was* toward the palm tree on the one side, and the face of a young lion toward the palm tree on the other side: *it was* made through all the house round about.

20 From the ground unto above the door *were* cherubims and palm trees made, and *on* the wall of the temple.

21 The posts of the temple *were* squared, *and* the face of the sanctuary; the appearance *of the one* as the appearance *of the other*.

22 The altar of wood *was* three cubits high, and the length thereof two cubits; and the corners thereof, and the length thereof, and the walls thereof, *were* of wood: and he said unto me, This *is* the table that *is* before the Lord.

23 And the temple and the sanctuary had two doors.

24 And the doors had two leaves *apiece*, two turning leaves; two *leaves* for the one door, and two leaves for the other *door*.

25 And *there were* made on them, on the doors of the temple, cherubims and palm trees, like as *were* made upon the walls; and *there were* thick planks upon the face of the porch without.

26 And *there were* narrow windows and palm trees on the one side and on the other side, on the sides of the porch, and *upon* the side chambers of the house, and thick planks.

CHAPTER 42

1 Then he brought me forth into the utter court, the way toward the north: and he brought me into the chamber that *was* over against the separate place, and which *was* before the building toward the north.

2 Before the length of an hundred cubits *was* the north door, and the breadth *was* fifty cubits.

3 Over against the twenty *cubits* which *were* for the inner court, and, over against the pavement which *was* for the utter court, *was* gallery against gallery in three *stories*.

4 And before the chambers *was* a walk of ten cubits breadth inward, a way of one cubit; and their doors toward the north.

5 Now the upper chambers *were* shorter: for the galleries were higher than these, than the lower, and than the middlemost of the building.

6 For they *were* in three *stories*, but had not pillars as the pillars of the courts: therefore *the building* was straitened more than the lowest and the middlemost from the ground.

7 And the wall that *was* without over against the chambers, toward the utter court on the forepart of the chambers, the length thereof *was* fifty cubits.

8 For the length of the chambers that *were* in the utter court *was* fifty cubits: and, lo, before the temple *were* an hundred cubits.

9 And from under these chambers *was* the entry on the east side, as one goeth into them from the utter court.

10 The chambers *were* in the thickness of the wall of the court toward the east, over against the separate place, and over against the building.

11 And the way before them *was* like the appearance of the chambers which *were* toward the north, as long as they, *and* as broad as they: and all their goings out *were* both according to their fashions, and according to their doors.

12 And according to the doors of the chambers that *were* toward the south *was* a door in the head of the way, *even* the way directly before the wall toward the east, as one entereth into them.

13 Then said he unto me, The north chambers *and* the south chambers, which *are* before the separate place, they *be* holy chambers, where the priests that approach unto the Lord shall eat the most holy things: there shall they lay the most holy things, and the meat offering, and the sin offering, and the trespass offering; for the place *is* holy.

14 When the priests enter therein, then shall they not go out of the holy *place* into the utter court, but there they shall lay their garments wherein they minister; for they *are* holy; and shall put on other garments, and shall approach to *those things* which *are* for the people.

Cross references

16 Ezek. 40:16; 41:26
18 1Kgs. 6:29
19 Ezek. 1:10
22 Ex. 30:1, 8; Ezek. 44:16; Mal. 1:7, 12
23 1Kgs. 6:31-35
26 Ezek. 40:16; 41:16
1 Ezek. 41:12, 15
3 Ezek. 41:16
11 Ezek. 42:4
13 Lev. 2:3, 10; 6:14, 16, 17, 25, 26, 29; 7:1; 10:13, 14; 24:9; Num. 18:9, 10
14 Ezek. 44:19

The Millennial Temple

By John C. Whitcomb

A careful reading of Ezekiel 40—43 confirms the impression of a literal temple because of the immense number of details concerning its dimensions, parts, and contents. The fact that its structure and ceremonies will have a symbolic significance cannot be used as an argument against its literal existence, for the Tabernacle was an actual structure, regardless of the fact of its typical significance.

All will agree that the temple of Ezekiel 8—11 was the literal temple of Ezekiel's day (Solomon's Temple), even though the prophet saw it in "visions of God" (8:3), while he himself was still exiled in Babylon. The "glory of God" is seen as progressively departing from the doomed and defiled old temple and is seen returning to the Millennial Temple (43:4, cf. 10:19), exactly as it had departed Solomon's Temple. If the Millennial Temple is not to be a reality, why insist that the return of the God of Israel is to be a reality?

Ezekiel is not the only Old Testament prophet who saw a future temple for God's chosen people, complete with animal sacrifices in the Holy Land (see Joel 3:18; Isa. 2:3; 60:13; Dan. 9:24; Hag. 2:7, 9).

> *The "glory of God" is seen returning to the Millennial Temple.*

God also definitely promised the priestly line of Zadok an everlasting priesthood (1 Sam. 2:35, cf. 1 Kgs. 2:27, 35). In view of this promise of God, it is highly significant that the Millennial Temple will have descendants of Zadok serving as priests (Ezek. 40:46; 44:15).

There is no earthly temple, altar, or animal sacrifices in Christianity or Judaism today (John 4:21; Heb. 7—10), but there will be such provisions for Israel after the rapture of the Church (Matt. 24:15; 2 Thess. 2:4; Rev. 11:1–2; cf. Hos. 3:4–5 with Dan. 9:24–27). The clear New Testament teaching of a post-rapture "holy place" and "temple of God" in Jerusalem, complete with "the altar" (Rev. 11:1) prepares us to anticipate a magnificent Millennial Temple, as Ezekiel describes. This will require topographical changes, which are prophesied (Isa. 26:15; 33:17; 54:2; Zech. 14:4–10).

Israel will have the only sanctuary and priesthood in the world during the Millennial Kingdom; thus the temple courts and sacred areas will need to be very large to accommodate the vast number of priests and Levites (Isa. 2:3; 60:14; 61:6; Zech. 14:4–10).

Concerning the sacrifices, it must be remembered there is a clear distinction between Israel and the Church. Just because God will have finished His work of sanctification and glorification of the Church at the time of the Rapture is no warrant for assuming He has finished His work of instruction, testing, and sanctification of Israel. Even in this present age, the bread and the cup at communion are a memorial to the awful price Jesus paid (1 Cor. 11:25–26). So likewise, the five different offerings in Ezekiel (43:13—46:15), four of them with bloodletting, will serve God's purposes. These offerings are not voluntary but obligatory; God will "accept" people on the basis of these animal sacrifices (43:27), which make reconciliation for the house of Israel (45:17, cf. 45:15). The offerings will not take away sin (see Heb. 10:4), but they will be effective in sanctifying Israelites ceremonially because of His infinitely holy presence in their midst. Hence, these sacrifices will serve as effective vehicles of divine instruction for Israel and the nations during the Millennial Kingdom.

15 Now when he had made an end of measuring the inner house, he brought me forth toward the gate whose prospect *is* toward the east, and measured it round about.

16 He measured the east side with the measuring reed, five hundred reeds, with the measuring reed round about.

17 He measured the north side, five hundred reeds, with the measuring reed round about.

18 He measured the south side, five hundred reeds, with the measuring reed.

19 He turned about to the west side, *and* measured five hundred reeds with the measuring reed.

20 He measured it by the four sides: it had a wall round about, five hundred *reeds* long, and five hundred broad, to make a separation between the sanctuary and the profane place.

CHAPTER 43
God's Glory Fills the Temple Again

1 Afterward he brought me to the gate, *even* the gate that looketh toward the east:

2 And, behold, the glory of the God of Israel came from the way of the east: and his voice *was* like a noise of many waters: and the earth shined with his glory.

3 And *it was* according to the appearance of the vision which I saw, *even* according to the vision that I saw when I came to destroy the city: and the visions *were* like the vision that I saw by the river Chebar; and I fell upon my face.

4 And the glory of the LORD came into the house by the way of the gate whose prospect *is* toward the east.

5 So the spirit took me up, and brought me into the inner court; and, behold, the glory of the LORD filled the house.

6 And I heard *him* speaking unto me out of the house; and the man stood by me.

7 And he said unto me, Son of man, the

place of my throne, and the place of the soles of my feet, where I will dwell in the midst of the children of Israel for ever, and my holy name, shall the house of Israel no more defile, *neither* they, nor their kings, by their whoredom, nor by the carcases of their kings in their high places.

8 In their setting of their threshold by my thresholds, and their post by my posts, and the wall between me and them, they have even defiled my holy name by their abominations that they have committed: wherefore I have consumed them in mine anger.

9 Now let them put away their whoredom, and the carcases of their kings, far from me, and I will dwell in the midst of them for ever.

10 Thou son of man, shew the house to the house of Israel, that they may be ashamed of their iniquities: and let them measure the pattern.

11 And if they be ashamed of all that they have done, shew them the form of the house, and the fashion thereof, and the goings out thereof, and the comings in thereof, and all the forms thereof, and all the ordinances thereof, and all the forms thereof, and all the laws thereof: and write *it* in their sight, that they may keep the whole form thereof, and all the ordinances thereof, and do them.

12 This *is* the law of the house; Upon the top of the mountain the whole limit thereof round about *shall be* most holy. Behold, this *is* the law of the house.

13 And these *are* the measures of the altar after the cubits: The cubit *is* a cubit and an handbreadth; even the bottom *shall be* a cubit, and the breadth a cubit, and the border thereof by the edge thereof round about *shall be* a span: and this *shall be* the higher place of the altar.

14 And from the bottom *upon* the ground *even* to the lower settle *shall be* two cubits,

Cross references (center column):

20 Ezek. 40:5; 45:2

1 Ezek. 10:19; 44:1; 46:1

2 Ezek. 1:24; 10:4; 11:23; Rev. 1:15; 14:2; 18:1; 19:1, 6

3 Jer. 1:10; Ezek. 1:3, 4, 28; 3:23; 8:4; 9:1, 5

4 Ezek. 10:19; 44:2

5 1Kgs. 8:10, 11; Ezek. 3:12, 14; 8:3; 44:4

6 Ezek. 40:3

7 Ex. 29:45; Lev. 26:30; 1Chr. 28:2; Ps. 68:16; 99:1, 5; 132:14; Jer. 16:18; Ezek. 39:7; Joel 3:17; John 1:14; 2Cor. 6:16

8 2Kgs. 16:14; 21:4, 5, 7; Ezek. 8:3; 23:39; 44:7

9 Ezek. 43:7

10 Ezek. 40:4

12 Ezek. 40:2

13 Ezek. 40:5; 41:8

42:15–20 he brought me forth toward the gate . . . east. Having measured the thickness of the walls (Ezek. 40:5), the outer court (40:6–27), the inner court and chambers (40:28—42:14), the man (angel) then measures the entire temple area to be five hundred reeds square, about one mile on each side. A change of topography in the land will make this possible (see Zech. 14:4–8).

43:1–5 behold, the glory of the God of Israel. Ezekiel now beholds the future return of the *shechinah* glory, the divine presence in the temple, progressively withdrawn before the destruction of the temple (see Ezek. 9:3; 10:4; 10:18; 11:23). It appeared in Solomon's Temple (1 Kgs.

8:10–11) at its dedication and was withdrawn 375 years later. It was never seen in the post-exilic temple or in Herod's vastly expanded temple. In the future, the glory will fill the Millennial Temple.

43:7–12 the place of my throne. God will dwell in a special, spiritual, and supernatural manner in this temple. The description, "my throne," is often used of heaven (Ps. 11:4; Isa. 66:1; cf. Ezek. 37:26–28), so this may be a vision of heaven coming down to earth.

43:13–27 measures of the altar. The measurements of the altar for burnt offerings are set forth, followed by

and the breadth one cubit; and from the lesser settle *even* to the greater settle *shall be* four cubits, and the breadth *one* cubit.

15 So the altar *shall be* four cubits; and from the altar and upward *shall be* four horns.

16 And the altar *shall be* twelve *cubits* long, twelve broad, square in the four squares thereof.

17 And the settle *shall be* fourteen *cubits* long and fourteen broad in the four squares thereof; and the border about it *shall be* half a cubit; and the bottom thereof *shall be* a cubit about; and his stairs shall look toward the east.

18 And he said unto me, Son of man, thus saith the Lord GOD; These *are* the ordinances of the altar in the day when they shall make it, to offer burnt offerings thereon, and to sprinkle blood thereon.

19 And thou shalt give to the priests the Levites that be of the seed of Zadok, which approach unto me, to minister unto me, saith the Lord GOD, a young bullock for a sin offering.

20 And thou shalt take of the blood thereof, and put *it* on the four horns of it, and on the four corners of the settle, and upon the border round about: thus shalt thou cleanse and purge it.

21 Thou shalt take the bullock also of the sin offering, and he shall burn it in the appointed place of the house, without the sanctuary.

22 And on the second day thou shalt offer a kid of the goats without blemish for a sin offering; and they shall cleanse the altar, as they did cleanse *it* with the bullock.

23 When thou hast made an end of cleansing *it*, thou shalt offer a young bullock without blemish, and a ram out of the flock without blemish.

24 And thou shalt offer them before the LORD, and the priests shall cast salt upon them, and they shall offer them up *for* a burnt offering unto the LORD.

25 Seven days shalt thou prepare every day a goat *for* a sin offering: they shall also prepare a young bullock, and a ram out of the flock, without blemish.

26 Seven days shall they purge the altar and purify it; and they shall consecrate themselves.

27 And when these days are expired, it shall be, *that* upon the eighth day, and *so* forward, the priests shall make your burnt offerings upon the altar, and your peace offerings; and I will accept you, saith the Lord GOD.

Cross references:
15 Isa. 29:1
17 Ex. 20:26
18 Lev. 1:5
19 Ex. 29:10, 12; Lev. 8:14, 15; Ezek. 44:15; 45:18, 19
21 Ex. 29:14; Heb. 13:11
24 Lev. 2:13
25 Ex. 29:35, 36; Lev. 8:33
26 Ex. 29:24
27 Lev. 9:1; Job 42:8; Ezek. 20:40, 41; Rom. 12:1; 1 Pet. 2:5

Israel's Covenant and Worship

Mosaic Laws and Observances		Millennial Practices and Observances	
Old Covenant	Exodus 21—24	New Covenant	Ezekiel 37:26–28; Jeremiah 31:31–34
Tabernacle/Temple	Exodus 26—31 2 Chronicles 3—6	New Temple	Ezekiel 40—46
Sacrifices/Offerings (pointing forward to Christ)	Leviticus 1—5, 16 Hebrews 9:12–15; 10:4–7	Sacrifices/Memorials (looking back to Christ)	Ezekiel 43:13—46:24
New Year in Abib (April)	Exodus 12:1–2; 13:4	New Year in Abib (April)	Ezekiel 45:18–20
Sabbaths	Exodus 20:8–11	Sabbaths (continued)	Ezekiel 46:1
Feast of Passover	Leviticus 23:4–5	Passover (continued)	Ezekiel 45:21–24
Feast of Unleavened Bread	Leviticus 23:6–8	Unleavened Bread (continued)	Ezekiel 45:21–24
Feast of Firstfruits	Leviticus 23:9–14	Firstfruits (fulfilled)	1 Corinthians 15:20–21
Feast of Pentecost	Leviticus 23:15–22	Pentecost (fulfilled)	Acts 2:1–20; Joel 2:28–29
Feast of Trumpets	Leviticus 23:23–25	Trumpets (fulfilled)	Isaiah 18:3; 27:13; Joel 2:15–32
Day of Atonement	Leviticus 23:26–32	Atonement (fulfilled)	Hebrews 9:1–16
Feast of Tabernacles	Leviticus 23:33–44	Tabernacles (continued)	Ezekiel 45:25; Zechariah 14:16–21

detailed directions for its consecration. The offerings will be memorial and retrospective, looking back to Christ's finished work on the cross, instead of looking forward to Christ. Old Testament offerings never actually took away sins (see Heb. 10:1–18). These Millennial Temple offerings will be administered by the descendants of the priestly line of Zadok (1 Chr. 29:22).

CHAPTER 44

1 Then he brought me back the way of the gate of the outward sanctuary which looketh toward the east; and it *was* shut.

2 Then said the LORD unto me; This gate shall be shut, it shall not be opened, and no man shall enter in by it; because the LORD, the God of Israel, hath entered in by it, therefore it shall be shut.

3 *It is* for the prince; the prince, he shall sit in it to eat bread before the LORD; he shall enter by the way of the porch of *that* gate, and shall go out by the way of the same.

4 Then brought he me the way of the north gate before the house: and I looked, and, behold, the glory of the LORD filled the house of the LORD: and I fell upon my face.

5 And the LORD said unto me, Son of man, mark well, and behold with thine eyes, and hear with thine ears all that I say unto thee concerning all the ordinances of the house of the LORD, and all the laws thereof; and mark well the entering in of the house, with every going forth of the sanctuary.

6 And thou shalt say to the rebellious, *even* to the house of Israel, Thus saith the Lord GOD; O ye house of Israel, let it suffice you of all your abominations,

7 In that ye have brought *into my sanctuary* strangers, uncircumcised in heart, and uncircumcised in flesh, to be in my sanctuary, to pollute it, *even* my house, when ye offer my bread, the fat and the blood, and they have broken my covenant because of all your abominations.

8 And ye have not kept the charge of mine holy things: but ye have set keepers of my charge in my sanctuary for yourselves.

9 Thus saith the Lord GOD; No stranger, uncircumcised in heart, nor uncircumcised in flesh, shall enter into my sanctuary, of any stranger that *is* among the children of Israel.

10 And the Levites that are gone away far from me, when Israel went astray, which went astray away from me after their idols; they shall even bear their iniquity.

11 Yet they shall be ministers in my sanctuary, *having* charge at the gates of the house, and ministering to the house: they shall slay the burnt offering and the sacrifice for the people, and they shall stand before them to minister unto them.

12 Because they ministered unto them before their idols, and caused the house of Israel to fall into iniquity; therefore have I lifted up mine hand against them, saith the Lord GOD, and they shall bear their iniquity.

13 And they shall not come near unto me, to do the office of a priest unto me, nor to come near to any of my holy things, in the most holy *place*: but they shall bear their shame, and their abominations which they have committed.

14 But I will make them keepers of the charge of the house, for all the service thereof, and for all that shall be done therein.

15 But the priests the Levites, the sons of Zadok, that kept the charge of my sanctuary when the children of Israel went astray from me, they shall come near to me to minister unto me, and they shall stand before me to offer unto me the fat and the blood, saith the Lord GOD:

16 They shall enter into my sanctuary, and they shall come near to my table, to minister unto me, and they shall keep my charge.

17 And it shall come to pass, *that* when they enter in at the gates of the inner court, they shall be clothed with linen garments; and no wool shall come upon them, whiles they minister in the gates of the inner court, and within.

18 They shall have linen bonnets upon their heads, and shall have linen breeches upon their loins; they shall not gird *themselves* with any thing that causeth sweat.

19 And when they go forth into the utter court, *even* into the utter court to the people, they shall put off their garments wherein they ministered, and lay them in the holy chambers, and they shall put on other garments; and they shall not sanctify the people with their garments.

Cross references

3 Gen. 31:54; Ezek. 46:2, 8; 1Cor. 10:18

5 Ezek. 40:4

6 Ezek. 2:5; 45:9; 1Pet. 4:3

7 Lev. 3:16; 17:11; 21:6, 8, 17, 21; 22:25; 26:41; Deut. 10:16; Ezek. 43:8; Acts 7:51; 21:28

8 Lev. 22:2; Ezek. 40:45; 44:14, 16

9 Ezek. 44:7

10 2Kgs. 23:8; 2Chr. 29:4, 5; Ezek. 48:11

11 Num. 16:9; 1Chr. 26:1; 2Chr. 29:34

12 Ps. 106:26; Isa. 9:16; Ezek. 14:3, 4; Mal. 2:8

13 Num. 18:3; 2Kgs. 23:9; Num. 32:30; 36:7

14 Num. 18:4; 1Chr. 23:28, 32

15 Deut. 10:8; 1Sam. 2:35; Ezek. 40:46; 43:19; 44:7, 10

16 Ezek. 41:22

17 Ex. 28:39, 40, 43; 39:27, 28

18 Ex. 28:40, 42; 39:28

19 Ex. 29:37; 30:29; Lev. 6:27

44:1–3 This gate shall be shut. The outward eastern gate, facing the Mount of Olives, where Jesus will return (Zech. 14:4), is said to be shut. Through an eastern gate of ancient Jerusalem, Jesus entered on Palm Sunday. When He returns, He will doubtless enter the city from the East. For hundreds of years a sealed gate has faced east, some assuming that Jesus will enter through it at His return.

44:4 glory of the LORD. Ezekiel now sees the "glory of the LORD" filling the temple as in Ezekiel 43:5.

44:5–15 ordinances of the house of the LORD. Contrary to past times, this temple's holy nature will be preserved. No foreigner who is uncircumcised in heart and flesh may enter it, neither will any descendants of the Levites conduct services, other than the godly descendants of Zadok.

20 Neither shall they shave their heads, nor suffer their locks to grow long; they shall only poll their heads.

21 Neither shall any priest drink wine, when they enter into the inner court.

22 Neither shall they take for their wives a widow, nor her that is put away: but they shall take maidens of the seed of the house of Israel, or a widow that had a priest before.

23 And they shall teach my people *the difference* between the holy and profane, and cause them to discern between the unclean and the clean.

24 And in controversy they shall stand in judgment; *and* they shall judge it according to my judgments: and they shall keep my laws and my statutes in all mine assemblies; and they shall hallow my sabbaths.

25 And they shall come at no dead person to defile themselves: but for father, or for mother, or for son, or for daughter, for brother, or for sister that hath had no husband, they may defile themselves.

26 And after he is cleansed, they shall reckon unto him seven days.

27 And in the day that he goeth into the sanctuary, unto the inner court, to minister in the sanctuary, he shall offer his sin offering, saith the Lord God.

28 And it shall be unto them for an inheritance: I *am* their inheritance: and ye shall give them no possession in Israel: I *am* their possession.

29 They shall eat the meat offering, and the sin offering, and the trespass offering; and every dedicated thing in Israel shall be theirs.

30 And the first of all the firstfruits of all *things*, and every oblation of all, of every *sort* of your oblations, shall be the priest's: ye shall also give unto the priest the first of your dough, that he may cause the blessing to rest in thine house.

31 The priests shall not eat of any thing that is dead of itself, or torn, whether it be fowl or beast.

Cross-references

20 Lev. 21:5
21 Lev. 10:9
22 Lev. 21:7, 13, 14
23 Lev. 10:10, 11; Ezek. 22:26; Mal. 2:7
24 Deut. 17:8; 2Chr. 19:8, 10; Ezek. 22:26
25 Lev. 21:1
26 Num. 6:10; 19:11
27 Lev. 4:3; Ezek. 44:17
28 Num. 18:20; Deut. 10:9; 18:1, 2; Josh. 13:14, 33
29 Lev. 6:18, 29; 7:6; 27:21, 28; Num. 18:14
30 Ex. 13:2; 22:29, 30; 23:19; Num. 3:13; 15:20; 18:12, 13; Neh. 10:37; Prov. 3:9, 10; Mal. 3:10
31 Ex. 22:31; Lev. 22:8
1 Ezek. 47:22; 48:8
2 Ezek. 42:20
3 Ezek. 48:10
4 Ezek. 45:1; 48:10
5 Ezek. 40:17; 48:13
6 Ezek. 48:15
7 Ezek. 48:21
8 Jer. 22:17; Ezek. 22:27; 46:18

Chapter 45
God's Portion of the Land

1 Moreover, when ye shall divide by lot the land for inheritance, ye shall offer an oblation unto the Lord, an holy portion of the land: the length *shall be* the length of five and twenty thousand *reeds*, and the breadth *shall be* ten thousand. This *shall be* holy in all the borders thereof round about.

2 Of this there shall be for the sanctuary five hundred *in length*, with five hundred *in breadth*, square round about; and fifty cubits round about for the suburbs thereof.

3 And of this measure shalt thou measure the length of five and twenty thousand, and the breadth of ten thousand: and in it shall be the sanctuary *and* the most holy *place*.

4 The holy *portion* of the land shall be for the priests the ministers of the sanctuary, which shall come near to minister unto the Lord: and it shall be a place for their houses, and an holy place for the sanctuary.

5 And the five and twenty thousand of length, and the ten thousand of breadth, shall also the Levites, the ministers of the house, have for themselves, for a possession for twenty chambers.

6 And ye shall appoint the possession of the city five thousand broad, and five and twenty thousand long, over against the oblation of the holy *portion*: it shall be for the whole house of Israel.

7 And a *portion shall be* for the prince on the one side and on the other side of the oblation of the holy *portion*, and of the possession of the city, before the oblation of the holy *portion*, and before the possession of the city, from the west side westward, and from the east side eastward: and the length *shall be* over against one of the portions, from the west border unto the east border.

8 In the land shall be his possession in Israel: and my princes shall no more oppress my people; and *the rest of* the land shall they

---

45:1–6 The larger boundaries around the temple and its enclosed one square mile area (Ezek. 42:16–20) are described. A portion north of the priests' area, measuring about 8.3 by 3.3 miles, will be assigned for the Levites. On the south of the city will be a section for Jerusalem, an area of about 8.3 by 1.66 miles. See the map, "The Division of Land during the Millennium."

45:7 the prince. The identity of the prince, whose office denotes a sub-ruler, is of interest. Some say he is Jesus, but his functions of service are limited in the temple and he is said to have sons (Ezek. 46:16). Evidently, he is a special vice regent, an Israelite, possibly a descendant of David, who presides over the nation under King Jesus' supervision. Some think that in his resurrected body, David will also exercise royal authority (Jer. 30:9) but would not be the prince, since in the resurrected state children are not produced.

give to the house of Israel according to their tribes.

9 Thus saith the Lord GOD; Let it suffice you, O princes of Israel: remove violence and spoil, and execute judgment and justice, take away your exactions from my people, saith the Lord GOD.

10 Ye shall have just balances, and a just ephah, and a just bath.

11 The ephah and the bath shall be of one measure, that the bath may contain the tenth part of an homer, and the ephah the tenth part of an homer: the measure thereof shall be after the homer.

12 And the shekel *shall be* twenty gerahs: twenty shekels, five and twenty shekels, fifteen shekels, shall be your maneh.

13 This *is* the oblation that ye shall offer; the sixth part of an ephah of an homer of wheat, and ye shall give the sixth part of an ephah of an homer of barley:

14 Concerning the ordinance of oil, the bath of oil, *ye shall offer* the tenth part of a bath out of the cor, *which is* an homer of ten baths; for ten baths *are* an homer:

15 And one lamb out of the flock, out of two hundred, out of the fat pastures of Israel; for a meat offering, and for a burnt offering, and for peace offerings, to make reconciliation for them, saith the Lord GOD.

16 All the people of the land shall give this oblation for the prince in Israel.

17 And it shall be the prince's part *to give* burnt offerings, and meat offerings, and drink offerings, in the feasts, and in the new moons, and in the sabbaths, in all solemnities of the house of Israel: he shall prepare the sin offering, and the meat offering, and the burnt offering, and the peace offerings, to make reconciliation for the house of Israel.

The Feast Days

18 Thus saith the Lord GOD; In the first *month*, in the first *day* of the month, thou shalt take a young bullock without blemish, and cleanse the sanctuary:

9 Jer. 22:3;
Ezek. 44:6

10 Lev. 19:35, 36;
Prov. 11:1

12 Ex. 30:13;
Lev. 27:25;
Num. 3:47

15 Lev. 1:4

18 Lev. 16:16

19 Ezek. 43:20

20 Lev. 4:27

21 Ex. 12:18;
Lev. 23:5, 6;
Num. 9:2, 3;
28:16, 17;
Deut. 16:1

22 Lev. 4:14

23 Lev. 23:8;
Num. 28:15, 22, 30; 29:5, 11, 16, 19

24 Ezek. 46:5, 7

25 Lev. 23:34; Num. 29:12; Deut. 16:13; Ezek. 44:3; 46:8

19 And the priest shall take of the blood of the sin offering, and put *it* upon the posts of the house, and upon the four corners of the settle of the altar, and upon the posts of the gate of the inner court.

20 And so thou shalt do the seventh *day* of the month for every one that erreth, and for *him that is* simple: so shall ye reconcile the house.

21 In the first *month*, in the fourteenth day of the month, ye shall have the passover, a feast of seven days; unleavened bread shall be eaten.

22 And upon that day shall the prince prepare for himself and for all the people of the land a bullock *for* a sin offering.

23 And seven days of the feast he shall prepare a burnt offering to the LORD, seven bullocks and seven rams without blemish daily the seven days; and a kid of the goats daily *for* a sin offering.

24 And he shall prepare a meat offering of an ephah for a bullock, and an ephah for a ram, and an hin of oil for an ephah.

25 In the seventh *month*, in the fifteenth day of the month, shall he do the like in the feast of the seven days, according to the sin offering, according to the burnt offering, and according to the meat offering, and according to the oil.

CHAPTER 46
The Prince and the Festivals

1 Thus saith the Lord GOD; The gate of the inner court that looketh toward the east shall be shut the six working days; but on the sabbath it shall be opened, and in the day of the new moon it shall be opened.

2 And the prince shall enter by the way of the porch of *that* gate without, and shall stand by the post of the gate, and the priests shall prepare his burnt offering and his peace offerings, and he shall worship at the threshold of the gate: then he shall go forth; but the gate shall not be shut until the evening.

3 Likewise the people of the land shall

45:18–25 first month, in the fourteenth day. The Passover will be observed during the Millennium. In the "seventh month, in the fifteenth day," the Feast of Tabernacles (booths) will likewise be observed, but both of these feasts seem renewed and changed appropriately for the Millennial Kingdom with the prince participating. These memorial feasts are most appropriate, since "Christ our Passover" (1 Cor. 5:7) is the "Lamb slain from the foundation of the world" (Rev. 13:8), the Alpha,

the beginning of God's plan of the ages (Rev. 1:8, 11; 21:6) and the Omega, the end, who rules forever (Rev. 22:12–14).

46:1–15 the prince. The prince's further participation in temple worship is described. This vice regent, which is evidently neither Jesus the King nor the resurrected David, will represent Christ in Jerusalem, serving as an example of spiritual fidelity and integrity. He participates

worship at the door of this gate before the LORD in the sabbaths and in the new moons.

4 And the burnt offering that the prince shall offer unto the LORD in the sabbath day *shall be* six lambs without blemish, and a ram without blemish.

5 And the meat offering *shall be* an ephah for a ram, and the meat offering for the lambs as he shall be able to give, and an hin of oil to an ephah.

6 And in the day of the new moon *it shall be* a young bullock without blemish, and six lambs, and a ram: they shall be without blemish.

7 And he shall prepare a meat offering, an ephah for a bullock, and an ephah for a ram, and for the lambs according as his hand shall attain unto, and an hin of oil to an ephah.

8 And when the prince shall enter, he shall go in by the way of the porch of *that* gate, and he shall go forth by the way thereof.

9 But when the people of the land shall come before the LORD in the solemn feasts, he that entereth in by the way of the north gate to worship shall go out by the way of the south gate; and he that entereth by the way of the south gate shall go forth by the way of the north gate: he shall not return by the way of the gate whereby he came in, but shall go forth over against it.

10 And the prince in the midst of them, when they go in, shall go in; and when they go forth, shall go forth.

11 And in the feasts and in the solemnities the meat offering shall be an ephah to a bullock, and an ephah to a ram, and to the lambs as he is able to give, and an hin of oil to an ephah.

12 Now when the prince shall prepare a voluntary burnt offering or peace offerings voluntarily unto the LORD, *one* shall then open him the gate that looketh toward the east, and he shall prepare his burnt offering and his peace offerings, as he did on the sabbath day: then he shall go forth; and after his going forth *one* shall shut the gate.

13 Thou shalt daily prepare a burnt offering unto the LORD *of* a lamb of the first year without blemish: thou shalt prepare it every morning.

14 And thou shalt prepare a meat offering for it every morning, the sixth part of an ephah, and the third part of an hin of oil, to

temper with the fine flour; a meat offering continually by a perpetual ordinance unto the LORD.

15 Thus shall they prepare the lamb, and the meat offering, and the oil, every morning *for* a continual burnt offering.

16 Thus saith the Lord GOD; If the prince give a gift unto any of his sons, the inheritance thereof shall be his sons'; it *shall be* their possession by inheritance.

17 But if he give a gift of his inheritance to one of his servants, then it shall be his to the year of liberty; after it shall return to the prince: but his inheritance shall be his sons' for them.

18 Moreover the prince shall not take of the people's inheritance by oppression, to thrust them out of their possession; *but* he shall give his sons inheritance out of his own possession: that my people be not scattered every man from his possession.

19 After he brought me through the entry, which *was* at the side of the gate, into the holy chambers of the priests, which looked toward the north: and, behold, there *was* a place on the two sides westward.

20 Then said he unto me, This *is* the place where the priests shall boil the trespass offering and the sin offering, where they shall bake the meat offering; that they bear *them* not out into the utter court, to sanctify the people.

21 Then he brought me forth into the utter court, and caused me to pass by the four corners of the court; and, behold, in every corner of the court *there was* a court.

22 In the four corners of the court *there were* courts joined of forty *cubits* long and thirty broad: these four corners *were* of one measure.

23 And *there was* a row of *building* round about in them, round about them four, and *it was* made with boiling places under the rows round about.

24 Then said he unto me, These *are* the places of them that boil, where the ministers of the house shall boil the sacrifice of the people.

CHAPTER 47
The Healing Waters from the Temple

1 Afterward he brought me again unto the door of the house; and, behold, waters

Cross References (center column)

4 Ezek. 45:17

5 Deut. 16:17; Ezek. 45:24; 46:7, 11

8 Ezek. 46:2

9 Ex. 23:14-17; Deut. 16:16

11 Ezek. 46:5

12 Ezek. 44:3; 46:2

13 Ex. 29:38; Num. 28:3

17 Lev. 25:10

18 Ezek. 45:8

20 Lev. 2:4, 5, 7; 2Chr. 35:13; Ezek. 44:19

24 Ezek. 24:20

1 Joel 3:18; Zech. 13:1; 14:8; Rev. 22:1

---

frequently in the religious ceremonies for Israel. The Church is not in view here at all.

47:1-12 waters issued out. This is a literal stream, flowing from the temple (as in Joel 3:18; Zech. 14:8), increasing in size and depth as it continues. Isaiah had a similar vision (Isa. 35:7; 43:19). Wherever the waters flow, verdant

issued out from under the threshold of the house eastward: for the forefront of the house *stood toward* the east, and the waters came down from under from the right side of the house, at the south *side* of the altar.

2 Then brought he me out of the way of the gate northward, and led me about the way without unto the utter gate by the way that looketh eastward; and, behold, there ran out waters on the right side.

3 And when the man that had the line in his hand went forth eastward, he measured a thousand cubits, and he brought me through the waters; the waters *were* to the ancles.

4 Again he measured a thousand, and brought me through the waters; the waters *were* to the knees. Again he measured a thousand, and brought me through; the waters *were* to the loins.

5 Afterward he measured a thousand; *and it was* a river that I could not pass over: for the waters were risen, waters to swim in, a river that could not be passed over.

6 And he said unto me, Son of man, hast thou seen *this*? Then he brought me, and caused me to return to the brink of the river.

7 Now when I had returned, behold, at the bank of the river *were* very many trees on the one side and on the other.

8 Then said he unto me, These waters issue out toward the east country, and go down into the desert, and go into the sea: *which being* brought forth into the sea, the waters shall be healed.

9 And it shall come to pass, *that* every thing that liveth, which moveth, whithersoever the rivers shall come, shall live: and there shall be a very great multitude of fish, because these waters shall come thither: for they shall be healed; and every thing shall live whither the river cometh.

10 And it shall come to pass, *that* the fishers shall stand upon it from En-gedi even unto Eneglaim; they shall be a *place* to spread forth nets; their fish shall be according to their kinds, as the fish of the great sea, exceeding many.

11 But the miry places thereof and the marishes thereof shall not be healed; they shall be given to salt.

12 And by the river upon the bank thereof, on this side and on that side, shall grow all trees for meat, whose leaf shall not fade, neither shall the fruit thereof be consumed: it shall bring forth new fruit according to his months, because their waters they issued out of the sanctuary: and the fruit thereof shall be for meat, and the leaf thereof for medicine.

The Boundaries of the Land

13 Thus saith the Lord God; This *shall be* the border, whereby ye shall inherit the land according to the twelve tribes of Israel: Joseph *shall have two* portions.

14 And ye shall inherit it, one as well as another: *concerning* the which I lifted up mine hand to give it unto your fathers: and this land shall fall unto you for inheritance.

15 And this *shall be* the border of the land toward the north side, from the great sea, the way of Hethlon, as men go to Zedad;

16 Hamath, Berothah, Sibraim, which *is* between the border of Damascus and the border of Hamath; Hazarhatticon, which *is* by the coast of Hauran.

17 And the border from the sea shall be Hazar-enan, the border of Damascus, and the north northward, and the border of Hamath. And *this is* the north side.

18 And the east side ye shall measure from Hauran, and from Damascus, and from Gilead, and from the land of Israel *by* Jordan, from the border unto the east sea. And *this is* the east side.

19 And the south side southward, from Tamar *even* to the waters of strife *in* Kadesh, the river to the great sea. And *this is* the south side southward.

20 The west side also *shall be* the great sea from the border, till a man come over against Hamath. This *is* the west side.

21 So shall ye divide this land unto you according to the tribes of Israel.

22 And it shall come to pass, *that* ye shall

3 Ezek. 40:3

7 Ezek. 47:12; Rev. 22:2

10 Num. 34:6; Josh. 23:4; Ezek. 48:28

12 Job 8:16; Ps. 1:3; Jer. 17:8; Ezek. 47:7; Rev. 22:2

13 Gen. 48:5; 1Chr. 5:1; Ezek. 48:4, 5

14 Gen. 12:7; 13:15; 15:7; 17:8; 26:3; 28:13; Ezek. 20:5, 6, 28, 42; 48:29

15 Num. 34:8; Ezek. 48:1

16 Num. 34:8; 2Sam. 8:8

17 Num. 34:9; Ezek. 48:1

19 Num. 20:13; Deut. 32:51; Ps. 81:7

22 Rom. 10:12; Gal. 3:28; Eph. 3:6; Col. 3:11; Rev. 7:9, 10

---

trees and plentiful fish may be found, the westward flowing stream even freshening the waters of the Dead Sea. Any spiritual applications of this passage, while interesting, do not nullify its literal reality. Another river in the New Jerusalem, of which the earthly city is a type, will flow from the throne of God by the street of the holy city, nourishing the tree of life (Rev. 22:1–2).

47:13–23 This shall be the border. The northern Israeli border will run from the Mediterranean above Tyre to an area near Damascus. The eastern border extends from a frontier near Damascus, down along the Jordan River to the Dead Sea and beyond. The southern boundary stretches from the Mediterranean and the River of Egypt (not the Nile, Gen. 15:18) to south of the Dead Sea. On the west is the Mediterranean Sea.

divide it by lot for an inheritance unto you, and to the strangers that sojourn among you, which shall beget children among you: and they shall be unto you as born in the country among the children of Israel; they shall have inheritance with you among the tribes of Israel.

23 And it shall come to pass, *that* in what tribe the stranger sojourneth, there shall ye give *him* his inheritance, saith the Lord GOD.

CHAPTER 48
Allotment to the Tribes

1 Now these *are* the names of the tribes. From the north end to the coast of the way of Hethlon, as one goeth to Hamath, Hazar-enan, the border of Damascus northward, to the coast of Hamath; for these are his sides east *and* west; a *portion for* Dan.

2 And by the border of Dan, from the east side unto the west side, a *portion for* Asher.

3 And by the border of Asher, from the east side even unto the west side, a *portion for* Naphtali.

4 And by the border of Naphtali, from the east side unto the west side, a *portion for* Manasseh.

5 And by the border of Manasseh, from the east side unto the west side, a *portion for* Ephraim.

6 And by the border of Ephraim, from the east side even unto the west side, a *portion for* Reuben.

7 And by the border of Reuben, from the east side unto the west side, a *portion for* Judah.

8 And by the border of Judah, from the east side unto the west side, shall be the offering which ye shall offer of five and twenty thousand *reeds in* breadth, and *in* length as one of the *other* parts, from the east side unto the west side: and the sanctuary shall be in the midst of it.

9 The oblation that ye shall offer unto the

1 Ezek. 47:15
8 Ezek. 45:1-6

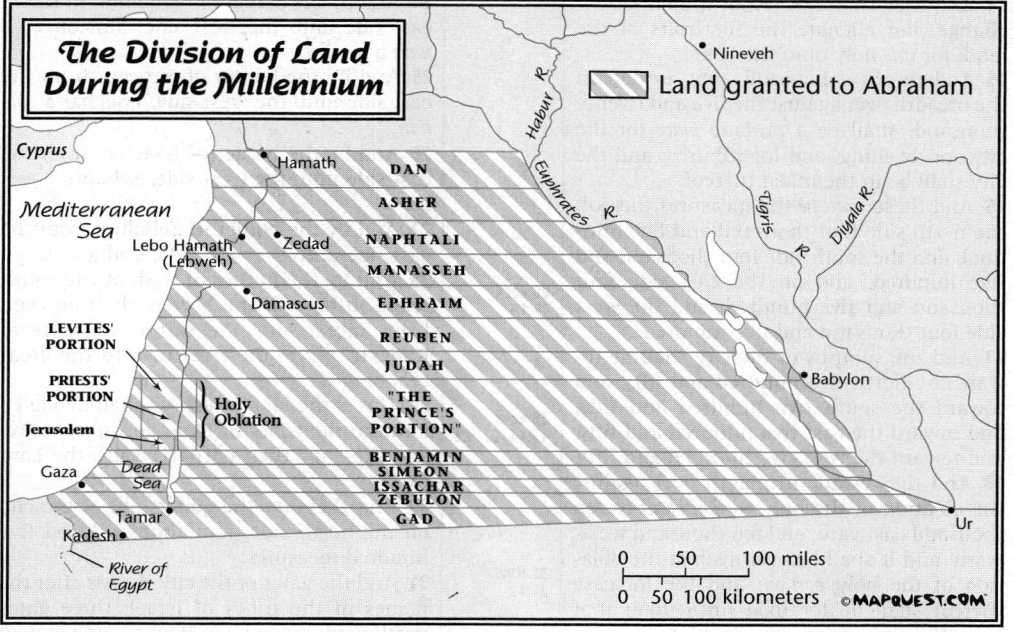

The Division of Land During the Millennium

Land granted to Abraham

Nineveh

Cyprus

Mediterranean Sea

Hamath   DAN

                ASHER

Lebo Hamath   Zedad   NAPTHALI
(Lebweh)

                MANASSEH

Damascus   EPHRAIM

LEVITES' PORTION   REUBEN

                JUDAH

PRIESTS' PORTION

Jerusalem   Holy   "THE PRINCE'S PORTION"
             Oblation

Gaza   Dead   BENJAMIN
        Sea   SIMEON
                    ISSACHAR
Tamar   ZEBULON
Kadesh   GAD   Ur

River of Egypt

Habur R.
Euphrates R.
Tigris R.
Diyala R.

Babylon

0   50   100 miles
0 50 100 kilometers ©MAPQUEST.COM

48:1–7 the names of the tribes. Different from the tribal territories of the past (Josh. 13–17), these new borders will be established in the Millennial Kingdom. North of this temple are seven tribal provinces: Judah, Reuben, Ephraim, Manasseh, Napthali, Asher and Dan, each territory a long rectangular section. Jesus promised rulership over the tribes to the twelve apostles (Matt. 19:28).

48:8–22 the sanctuary shall be in the midst. The temple complex with surrounding areas for the Levites, priests and the prince, are situated north of the city of Jerusalem and its adjoining territories.

LORD *shall be* of five and twenty thousand in length, and of ten thousand in breadth.

10 And for them, *even* for the priests, shall be *this* holy oblation; toward the north five and twenty thousand *in length*, and toward the west ten thousand in breadth, and toward the east ten thousand in breadth, and toward the south five and twenty thousand in length: and the sanctuary of the LORD shall be in the midst thereof.

11 *It shall be* for the priests that are sanctified of the sons of Zadok; which have kept my charge, which went not astray when the children of Israel went astray, as the Levites went astray.

12 And *this* oblation of the land that is offered shall be unto them a thing most holy by the border of the Levites.

13 And over against the border of the priests the Levites *shall have* five and twenty thousand in length, and ten thousand in breadth: all the length *shall be* five and twenty thousand, and the breadth ten thousand.

14 And they shall not sell of it, neither exchange, nor alienate the firstfruits of the land: for *it is* holy unto the LORD.

15 And the five thousand, that are left in the breadth over against the five and twenty thousand, shall be a profane *place* for the city, for dwelling, and for suburbs: and the city shall be in the midst thereof.

16 And these *shall be* the measures thereof; the north side four thousand and five hundred, and the south side four thousand and five hundred, and on the east side four thousand and five hundred, and the west side four thousand and five hundred.

17 And the suburbs of the city shall be toward the north two hundred and fifty, and toward the south two hundred and fifty, and toward the east two hundred and fifty, and toward the west two hundred and fifty.

18 And the residue in length over against the oblation of the holy *portion shall be* ten thousand eastward, and ten thousand westward: and it shall be over against the oblation of the holy *portion*; and the increase thereof shall be for food unto them that serve the city.

19 And they that serve the city shall serve it out of all the tribes of Israel.

20 All the oblation *shall be* five and twenty thousand by five and twenty thousand: ye shall offer the holy oblation foursquare, with the possession of the city.

21 And the residue *shall be* for the prince, on the one side and on the other of the holy oblation, and of the possession of the city, over against the five and twenty thousand of the oblation toward the east border, and westward over against the five and twenty thousand toward the west border, over against the portions for the prince: and it shall be the holy oblation; and the sanctuary of the house *shall be* in the midst thereof.

22 Moreover from the possession of the Levites, and from the possession of the city, *being* in the midst *of that* which is the prince's, between the border of Judah and the border of Benjamin, shall be for the prince.

23 As for the rest of the tribes, from the east side unto the west side, Benjamin *shall have* a *portion.*

24 And by the border of Benjamin, from the east side unto the west side, Simeon *shall have* a *portion.*

25 And by the border of Simeon, from the east side unto the west side, Issachar a *portion.*

26 And by the border of Issachar, from the east side unto the west side, Zebulun a *portion.*

27 And by the border of Zebulun, from the east side unto the west side, Gad a *portion.*

28 And by the border of Gad, at the south side southward, the border shall be even from Tamar *unto* the waters of strife *in* Kadesh, *and* to the river toward the great sea.

29 This *is* the land which ye shall divide by lot unto the tribes of Israel for inheritance, and these *are* their portions, saith the Lord GOD.

30 And these *are* the goings out of the city on the north side, four thousand and five hundred measures.

31 And the gates of the city *shall be* after the names of the tribes of Israel: three gates northward; one gate of Reuben, one gate of Judah, one gate of Levi.

32 And at the east side four thousand and

11 Ezek. 44:10, 15

14 Ex. 22:29; Lev. 27:10, 28, 33

15 Ezek. 42:20; 45:6

19 Ezek. 45:6

21 Ezek. 45:7; 48:8, 10

28 Ezek. 47:19

29 Ezek. 47:14, 21, 22

31 Rev. 21:12

48:23–29 rest of the tribes. The five tribes south of Jerusalem and the temple are Benjamin, Simeon, Issachar, Zebulun, and Gad.

48:30 the city. The core of Jerusalem will measure one and one-half miles on each side, or six miles in perimeter.

five hundred: and three gates; and one gate of Joseph, one gate of Benjamin, one gate of Dan.

33 And at the south side four thousand and five hundred measures: and three gates; one gate of Simeon, one gate of Issachar, one gate of Zebulun.

35 Ex. 17:15; Judg. 6:24; Jer. 3:17; 33:16; Joel 2:10; Rev. 21:3; 22:3

34 At the west side four thousand and five hundred, *with* their three gates; one gate of Gad, one gate of Asher, one gate of Naphtali.

35 *It was* round about eighteen thousand *measures*: and the name of the city from that day *shall be*, The Lord *is* there.

48:35 name of the city. The city's new name will be, "The Lord is there," which in Hebrew is *Jehovah Shammah*, or more correctly *Yahweh-Shammah*. This capital city of Israel and the world will be the site of the throne of David where Jesus reigns (Luke 1:32–33) and probably the twelve thrones of the apostles (Matt. 19:28). From this glorious center of divine power the whole earth will enjoy the blessings of God for a thousand years (see Isa. 65—66; Mic. 5:2; Zech. 14:20–21; Rev. 20:1–6). More glorious, however, will be the holy or new Jerusalem. In that vast, shining, eternal city, a place prepared by Christ (John 14:2–3), no temple will be needed, "for the Lord God Almighty and the Lamb are the temple of it" (Rev. 21:22).

Daniel

T he book of Daniel is one of the most significant prophecy books in the Old Testament. Taken into captivity as a fifteen-year-old youth, Daniel distinguished himself in wisdom, administration, and spiritual leadership. When all the wise men, soothsayers, and false prophets of Babylon—the cradle of world idolatry—could not recall or interpret the king's dream, Daniel, the servant of God revealed the meaning of the dream in one of the most fascinating prophecies in the Old Testament. The interpretation of the dream foretold God's dealing with both the children of Israel and the years of the so-called "times of the Gentiles" (Luke 21:24).

Author
Daniel

Date
6th Century B.C.

Key Truth
God Reigns Supreme

Historic Time
The Babylonian Captivity

Key Verse
2:44
And in the days of these kings shall . . . God . . . set up a kingdom, which shall never be destroyed. . . .

A proper understanding of Daniel assists in a proper interpretation of the book of Revelation, for many of the same symbols and parallel prophecies are used in both books. The image vision God gave to King Nebuchadnezzar is probably the seminal prophecy of the "times of the Gentiles." This prophecy details world events from Daniel's day (605 B.C.) until the kingdom of Antichrist is displaced at the second coming of Christ.

One of the distinguishing features of this book is the diverse views of government presented by God and man. The kingdom of Babylon (chap. 2), is pictured by many people to be representative of the best in human government—an image of stability, law, and order. However, God's view of government, seen through Daniel (7—12), reveals human history and empires as a series of rapacious beasts. Historically, God's view has been the most accurate, for history reveals that nothing has been more destructive of human beings than government.

Daniel does not mention the Church Age, but does allude to the "one week" (seven years) yet to come, called elsewhere the "Tribulation" (Dan. 9:27) or the "time of Jacob's trouble" (Jer. 30:7), ending with the second coming of Christ and "the end of this world" (Matt. 13:40).

Fifty-eight separate prophecies appear in the book of Daniel, involving 162 of the total 357 verses, or 45 percent.

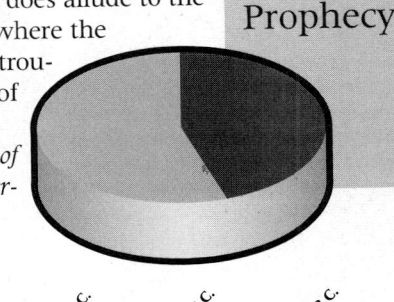

45%
Prophecy

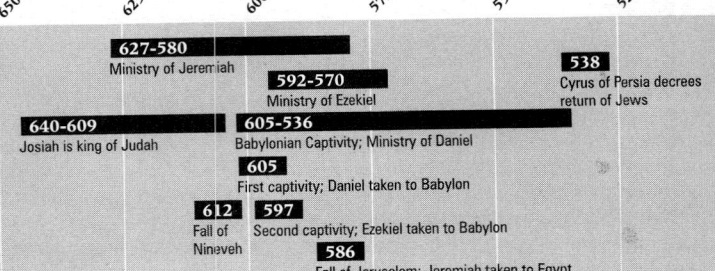

700 B.C.   675 B.C.   650 B.C.   625 B.C.   600 B.C.   575 B.C.   550 B.C.   525 B.C.   500

740–680
Ministry of Isaiah

722
Assyria conquers Israel

627–580
Ministry of Jeremiah

640–609
Josiah is king of Judah

592–570
Ministry of Ezekiel

605–536
Babylonian Captivity; Ministry of Daniel

605
First captivity; Daniel taken to Babylon

612
Fall of Nineveh

597
Second captivity; Ezekiel taken to Babylon

586
Fall of Jerusalem; Jeremiah taken to Egypt

538
Cyrus of Persia decrees return of Jews

CHAPTER 1
Dare to Stand

1 In the third year of the reign of Jehoiakim king of Judah came Nebuchadnezzar king of Babylon unto Jerusalem, and besieged it.

2 And the Lord gave Jehoiakim king of Judah into his hand, with part of the vessels of the house of God: which he carried into the land of Shinar to the house of his god; and he brought the vessels into the treasure house of his god.

3 And the king spake unto Ashpenaz the master of his eunuchs, that he should bring *certain* of the children of Israel, and of the king's seed, and of the princes;

4 Children in whom *was* no blemish, but well favoured, and skilful in all wisdom, and cunning in knowledge, and understanding science, and such as *had* ability in them to stand in the king's palace, and whom they might teach the learning and the tongue of the Chaldeans.

5 And the king appointed them a daily provision of the king's meat, and of the wine which he drank: so nourishing them three years, that at the end thereof they might stand before the king.

6 Now among these were of the children of Judah, Daniel, Hananiah, Mishael, and Azariah:

7 Unto whom the prince of the eunuchs gave names: for he gave unto Daniel *the name* of Belteshazzar; and to Hananiah, of Shadrach; and to Mishael, of Meshach; and to Azariah, of Abed-nego.

8 But Daniel purposed in his heart that he would not defile himself with the portion of the king's meat, nor with the wine which he drank: therefore he requested of the prince of the eunuchs that he might not defile himself.

9 Now God had brought Daniel into favour and tender love with the prince of the eunuchs.

10 And the prince of the eunuchs said unto Daniel, I fear my lord the king, who hath appointed your meat and your drink: for why should he see your faces worse liking than the children which *are* of your sort? then shall ye make *me* endanger my head to the king.

11 Then said Daniel to Melzar, whom the prince of the eunuchs had set over Daniel, Hananiah, Mishael, and Azariah,

12 Prove thy servants, I beseech thee, ten days; and let them give us pulse to eat, and water to drink.

13 Then let our countenances be looked upon before thee, and the countenance of the children that eat of the portion of the king's meat: and as thou seest, deal with thy servants.

14 So he consented to them in this matter, and proved them ten days.

15 And at the end of ten days their countenances appeared fairer and fatter in flesh than all the children which did eat the portion of the king's meat.

16 Thus Melzar took away the portion of their meat, and the wine that they should drink; and gave them pulse.

17 As for these four children, God gave them knowledge and skill in all learning and wisdom: and Daniel had understanding in all visions and dreams.

18 Now at the end of the days that the king had said he should bring them in, then the prince of the eunuchs brought them in before Nebuchadnezzar.

Cross References

1 2Kgs. 24:1; 2Chr. 36:6
2 Gen. 10:10; 11:2; 2Chr. 36:7; Isa. 11:11; Jer. 27:19, 20; Zech. 5:11
3 2Kgs. 20:17, 18; Isa. 39:7
4 Lev. 24:19, 20; Acts 7:22
5 Gen. 41:46; 1Kgs. 10:8; Dan. 1:19
7 Gen. 41:45; 2Kgs. 24:17; Dan. 4:8; 5:12
8 Deut. 32:38; Ezek. 4:13; Hos. 9:3
9 Gen. 39:21; Ps. 106:46; Prov. 16:7
17 Num. 12:6; 1Kgs. 3:12; 2Chr. 26:5; Dan. 5:11, 12, 14; 10:1; Acts 7:22; James 1:5, 17

1:1–2 Nebuchadnezzar king of Babylon. The Babylonian warrior Nebuchadnezzar had just won the decisive Battle of Carchemish against the Assyrians prior to his assault on Jerusalem. Daniel refers to him as "king" because his father, Nabopolassar, died on August 15, 605 B.C. while Nebuchadnezzar was in Jerusalem, leaving the son as heir to the throne.

After the Babylonians conquered Judah and Jerusalem, they confiscated some of the temple vessels in fulfillment of Isaiah's prophecy to King Hezekiah many years earlier (Isa. 39:1–6). God had already revealed this judgment on Judah through Hulda the prophetess (2 Chr. 34:22–28) and many others. Micah (Mic. 4:10), Jeremiah (Jer. 25:11), and Habakkuk (Hab. 1:5–11) all predicted the Babylonian captivity in advance.

1:6–7 Daniel, Hananiah, Mishael, and Azariah. These four men were among the teenage captives taken to Babylon as "hostages" of Nebuchadnezzar. Their original Hebrew names reflected their devotion to the Lord, whereas their Babylonian names reflected their captors' desire to honor the pagan gods of Babylon. The peer pressure placed upon these Hebrew captives was designed to program them to think and act like Babylonians.

1:21 Daniel continued. This glimpse into the future looks ahead seventy years into the reign of the Persian king, Cyrus the Great, who conquered Babylon in 539 B.C. Daniel was approximately fifteen years old when he was taken captive and lived through the entire seventy-year captivity; therefore, he would have been about eighty-five years old when the Persians captured the city (Dan. 5—6).

The Prophecies of Daniel

By Thomas S. McCall

Think of the prophecies of Daniel as the steel superstructure of a great building to which are attached walls, roof, floors, and so forth. All the subsequent Bible predictions are attached to the superstructure of Daniel. The two primary parts of the framework are the "times of the gentiles" and the "seventy weeks" concerning Israel and Jerusalem (Dan. 9:24–27). Everything else, the broad expanse of human history, the first and second comings of Christ, and all the details supplied by the Lord through His prophets and apostles are attached to this magnificent superstructure.

Already by Daniel's time, the following prophetic truths had been revealed to God's chosen nation:

1. Israel would be the channel of the Lord's great messianic kingdom on earth (the Abrahamic covenant and Jacob's prophecy concerning Judah [Gen. 49:8–10]).

2. The Davidic dynasty would be the catalyst behind the Messiah's authority, with Jerusalem and Israel the bases of His ruling operations (the Davidic covenant [2 Sam. 7:12–16] and Ps. 2).

> *All subsequent Bible predictions are attached to the superstructure of Daniel.*

3. The Suffering Servant of the Lord would make possible future blessings with His redemptive sacrifice for sins and His resurrection from the dead (Ps. 16; Isa. 53).

All of this revelation and much more may not have been fully understood by Israel. After the Babylonian destruction of Jerusalem, the entire promised program of God appeared to be in total shambles. As Jerusalem and Israel lay in ruins, the Davidic dynasty was cut off in disgrace, and the people of Israel and Judah languished in the heart of ancient paganism a thousand miles away from the land of promise. Many other prophecies about Israel's glorious future appeared to be conditioned upon the obedience of Israel to the Lord, and obedience seemed to be a rare commodity among God's chosen people in Babylon in Daniel's time.

Daniel and the people had clung to the prophecy of their contemporary Jeremiah that the Babylonian Captivity would last only seventy years, after which the people would return to Jerusalem. As the seventy years drew to a close and Daniel studied Jeremiah's prophecy even more closely, praying earnestly for the forgiveness of Israel and their restoration to Jerusalem to rebuild the sanctuary of the Lord, God sent His angel to reveal the new truth concerning the "seventy sevens" or "weeks" (Dan. 9:24–27), laying out the future schedule for Jerusalem and Israel and the coming of the Messiah.

Two great parallel events would have to transpire before the Messiah would fulfill the prophecies concerning His reign over the kingdom of God on earth: the times of the Gentiles (see the article on "The Times of the Gentiles") and the seventy weeks of Israel and Jerusalem (see the article on "Daniel's Seventy Weeks").

The end of the seventy weeks of Daniel and the times of the Gentiles is the same: the second coming of the Lord Jesus Christ. Both prophetic streams reach their zenith in the person of the "prince that shall come" (9:26), the counterfeit messiah or Antichrist, whom Christ will destroy at the time of His return.

The book of Daniel stands as a monument of predictive truth. It is often compared to the book of Revelation, and, in truth, the book of Revelation cannot be understood apart from the foundation laid in the book of Daniel. An understanding of Daniel and Revelation constitutes the basics of biblical prophecy.

19 And the king communed with them; and among them all was found none like Daniel, Hananiah, Mishael, and Azariah: therefore stood they before the king.

20 And in all matters of wisdom *and* understanding, that the king inquired of them, he found them ten times better than all the magicians *and* astrologers that *were* in all his realm.

21 And Daniel continued *even* unto the first year of king Cyrus.

CHAPTER 2
The Dream of Nebuchadnezzar

1 And in the second year of the reign of Nebuchadnezzar Nebuchadnezzar dreamed dreams, wherewith his spirit was troubled, and his sleep brake from him.

2 Then the king commanded to call the magicians, and the astrologers, and the sorcerers, and the Chaldeans, for to shew the king his dreams. So they came and stood before the king.

3 And the king said unto them, I have dreamed a dream, and my spirit was troubled to know the dream.

4 Then spake the Chaldeans to the king in Syriac, O king, live for ever: tell thy servants the dream, and we will shew the interpretation.

5 The king answered and said to the Chaldeans, The thing is gone from me: if ye will not make known unto me the dream, with the interpretation thereof, ye shall be cut in pieces, and your houses shall be made a dunghill.

6 But if ye shew the dream, and the interpretation thereof, ye shall receive of me gifts and rewards and great honour: therefore shew me the dream, and the interpretation thereof.

7 They answered again and said, Let the king tell his servants the dream, and we will shew the interpretation of it.

8 The king answered and said, I know of certainty that ye would gain the time, because ye see the thing is gone from me.

9 But if ye will not make known unto me the dream, *there is but* one decree for you: for ye have prepared lying and corrupt words to speak before me, till the time be changed: therefore tell me the dream, and I shall know that ye can shew me the interpretation thereof.

10 The Chaldeans answered before the king, and said, There is not a man upon the earth that can shew the king's matter: therefore *there is* no king, lord, nor ruler, *that* asked such things at any magician, or astrologer, or Chaldean.

11 And *it is* a rare thing that the king requireth, and there is none other that can shew it before the king, except the gods, whose dwelling is not with flesh.

12 For this cause the king was angry and very furious, and commanded to destroy all the wise *men* of Babylon.

13 And the decree went forth that the wise *men* should be slain; and they sought Daniel and his fellows to be slain.

14 Then Daniel answered with counsel and wisdom to Arioch the captain of the king's guard, which was gone forth to slay the wise *men* of Babylon:

15 He answered and said to Arioch the king's captain, Why *is* the decree *so* hasty from the king? Then Arioch made the thing known to Daniel.

16 Then Daniel went in, and desired of the king that he would give him time, and that he would shew the king the interpretation.

17 Then Daniel went to his house, and made the thing known to Hananiah, Mishael, and Azariah, his companions:

18 That they would desire mercies of the God of heaven concerning this secret; that Daniel and his fellows should not perish with the rest of the wise *men* of Babylon.

19 Then was the secret revealed unto Dan-

2:1 Nebuchadnezzar dreamed dreams. Nebuchadnezzar's vision was from God and constitutes, when interpreted by the prophet of God, the most important single prophecy in the Bible concerning Gentile nations. As such, it proves the supernatural ability of God to reveal history in advance.

2:2–4 astrologers, sorcerers, and magicians. These represented the best prophets and soothsayers of Babylon, the birthplace of all forms of paganism. It was from here that Nimrod's many forms of demon-inspired pagan idolatry spread throughout the nations of the world (Gen. 11). These "wise men" probably came from many differ-

ent nations, so they spoke in Syriac (Aramaic), a dialect related to Hebrew and the commercial language of the Near East at that time. In Daniel chapter 2, the original texts shift from Hebrew to Aramaic and remain in Aramaic through chapter 7. It seems that Daniel switched languages because he intended for the Aramaic section to be read by Gentiles as well.

2:11 The king's extraordinary demand was designed to expose the fraudulent methods of these false prophets. Even these pagan "wise men" knew that only a God "whose dwelling is not with flesh" could reveal the king's dream and its meaning.

The Future Roman Empire

By John C. Whitcomb, Th.D.

The Old Testament prophets saw six great empires which, under the control of Satan, oppressed God's chosen people, Israel. Two of these empires preceded the time of Daniel—Egypt and Assyria (see Isa. 10:14; 27:13; 52:4).

In his visions, Daniel saw four additional oppressive empires. In Daniel 8, the second and third of these empires are identified as Medo-Persia and the Greek Empire, established under Alexander the Great. Since Daniel identifies the first empire as Nebuchadnezzar's Babylonia in Daniel 2:38, there can be no doubt that the fourth empire is Rome. Daniel could have known this only by supernatural revelation, because Rome's conquest of Jerusalem (63 B.C.) occurred long after the time of this prophecy.

The New Testament book of Revelation, however, adds two more oppressive empires, for a total of eight. The apostle John, writing about A.D. 90, saw the Beast with seven "heads" (Rev. 12:3; 13:1; 17:3, 9). These "heads" or "mountains" (or empires) are represented as seven successive "kings" (Rev. 17:10), five of whom in John's day had already "fallen." These would be Egypt, Assyria, Babylonia, Medo-Persia, and Greece. The interpreting angel then explained that one empire remains (Rev. 17:10). This would be number six, namely, the great Roman Empire of New Testament times.

> *This kingdom of the Beast is the last and greatest oppressor of Israel.*

Significantly, however, the seventh and last of these kings "is not yet come; and when he comes, he must continue a short space" (17:10). This will be the revived Roman Empire, the final phase of the great image of Daniel 2 (the ten toes) and the Beast in Daniel 7 (the ten horns and the eleventh "little horn" who will arise "among them" [7:8]).

Revelation 17:8 says this Beast with seven heads suddenly "is not" (cf. Rev. 17:11). Then the Beast reappears as "an eighth" empire, though it is actually "of the seven." Evidently, the angel assumes that John remembered that the Beast-King will somehow be killed in the midst of his demonic career, descend into "the bottomless pit," ascend out of the pit (Rev. 11:7), and return to mortal life (Rev. 13:3, 12, 14) to begin his global dominion of forty-two months. This kingdom of the Beast is the last and greatest oppressor of Israel.

Daniel foresaw the beginning of this forty-two month dominion in Daniel 7:25 (note the contrast with the first phase of the career of "the little horn" in 7:24), and also in Daniel 9:27 (after the breaking of the seven-year covenant), and in Daniel 11:36–39 (the worldwide dominion of the king who will do "according to his [own] will"). The Lord Jesus described this latter part of the seven-year Tribulation period as the "great tribulation" (Matt. 24:21, 29) which would follow the setting up of the abomination of desolation (24:15), "spoken of by Daniel the prophet" (cf. Dan. 9:27; 12:11).

I believe the explanation for the first death of the final Beast-King by "the wound of a sword" (Rev. 13:14) is in Daniel. As the King of the North sweeps through "the glorious land" (Dan. 11:41) on his way to northeast Africa, he apparently kills the Beast. Then the King of the North is destroyed by the Lord with fire from heaven (cf. Ezek. 38:22) as he attempts to kill the Beast who has risen from death to mortal life again (Dan. 11:45). This leaves the Beast-King as the eighth and final oppressor of Israel, with no further threats to come from earthly kingdoms (Rev. 13:4, 13).

iel in a night vision. Then Daniel blessed the God of heaven.

20 Daniel answered and said, Blessed be the name of God for ever and ever: for wisdom and might are his:

Rulers Are Established by God

21 And he changeth the times and the seasons: he removeth kings, and setteth up kings: he giveth wisdom unto the wise, and knowledge to them that know understanding:

22 He revealeth the deep and secret things: he knoweth what *is* in the darkness, and the light dwelleth with him.

23 I thank thee, and praise thee, O thou God of my fathers, who hast given me wisdom and might, and hast made known unto me now what we desired of thee: for thou hast *now* made known unto us the king's matter.

24 Therefore Daniel went in unto Arioch, whom the king had ordained to destroy the wise *men* of Babylon: he went and said thus unto him; Destroy not the wise *men* of Babylon: bring me in before the king, and I will shew unto the king the interpretation.

25 Then Arioch brought in Daniel before the king in haste, and said thus unto him, I have found a man of the captives of Judah, that will make known unto the king the interpretation.

The Dream Revealed

26 The king answered and said to Daniel, whose name *was* Belteshazzar, Art thou

able to make known unto me the dream which I have seen, and the interpretation thereof?

27 Daniel answered in the presence of the king, and said, The secret which the king hath demanded cannot the wise *men*, the astrologers, the magicians, the soothsayers, shew unto the king;

28 But there is a God in heaven that revealeth secrets, and maketh known to the king Nebuchadnezzar what shall be in the latter days. Thy dream, and the visions of thy head upon thy bed, are these;

29 As for thee, O king, thy thoughts came *into thy mind* upon thy bed, what should come to pass hereafter: and he that revealeth secrets maketh known to thee what shall come to pass.

30 But as for me, this secret is not revealed to me for *any* wisdom that I have more than any living, but for *their* sakes that shall make known the interpretation to the king, and that thou mightest know the thoughts of thy heart.

The Dream Explained

31 Thou, O king, sawest, and behold a great image. This great image, whose brightness *was* excellent, stood before thee; and the form thereof *was* terrible.

32 This image's head *was* of fine gold, his breast and his arms of silver, his belly and his thighs of brass,

33 His legs of iron, his feet part of iron and part of clay.

Cross references (center column):

20 Ps. 113:2; 115:18; Jer. 32:19
21 1Chr. 29:30; Esth. 1:13; Job 12:18; Ps. 75:6, 7; Jer. 27:5; Dan. 4:17; 7:25; 11:6; James 1:5
22 Job 12:22; Ps. 25:14; 139:11, 12; Dan. 2:28, 29; 5:11, 14; Heb. 4:13; James 1:17
23 Dan. 2:18
28 Gen. 40:8; 41:16; 49:1; Dan. 2:18, 47; Amos 4:13
29 Dan. 2:22, 28
30 Gen. 41:16; Dan. 2:47; Acts 3:12
32 Dan. 2:38, 39

2:19 Then was the secret revealed unto Daniel in a night vision. That two people, Nebuchadnezzar and Daniel, could receive the same vision can be attributed only to the divine origin of the vision. Like Joseph's experience with Pharaoh (see Gen. 41), God gave Daniel the ability to interpret the king's dream in order to gain his attention and influence his decisions.

2:19–23 Daniel's poem not only gave praise to God for saving his life and the lives of his friends but also praised God that He has a marvelous plan for mankind's future and was ready to reveal it. This poem of praise reveals the spiritual heart of the prophet.

2:28 there is a God in heaven that revealeth secrets. This unique ability to know history in advance is proof that the God of prophecy, the God of the Bible, is indeed the omniscient (all-knowing) God! He alone is worthy of our prayer, praise, and worship. Daniel told Nebuchadnezzar that God has made "known to the king . . . what shall be in the latter days"—this vision extends from Daniel's own day (6th century B.C.) to the setting up of

the kingdom of the Messiah in the "latter days."

2:31–33 In these verses Daniel describes the terrifying metallic image the king saw in his dream. This image represents the future course of Gentile world empires. If taken symbolically, this vision of temporal governments that deteriorate in consecutive order until God Himself sets up His kingdom is easy to understand from a historical viewpoint, for there have been only four major Gentile empires since the days of Babylon.

The metals of the great image represent four Gentile empires—Gold (Babylon), Silver (Media-Persia), Brass (Greece), and Iron (Rome)—that will dominate the people of Israel until the second coming of Christ. The diminishing value of the elements in each successive section of the image suggests a decrease of absolute rule by the kings of each portion, while the increasing strength of the metals is indicative of the growing military power of each successive empire. The feet of iron and clay represent the final form of Gentile world dominion—a revived Roman or Western power led by the Antichrist.

34 Thou sawest till that a stone was cut out without hands, which smote the image upon his feet *that were* of iron and clay, and brake them to pieces.

35 Then was the iron, the clay, the brass, the silver, and the gold, broken to pieces together, and became like the chaff of the summer threshingfloors; and the wind carried them away, that no place was found for them: and the stone that smote the image became a great mountain, and filled the whole earth.

36 This *is* the dream; and we will tell the interpretation thereof before the king.

37 Thou, O king, *art* a king of kings: for the God of heaven hath given thee a kingdom, power, and strength, and glory.

38 And wheresoever the children of men dwell, the beasts of the field and the fowls of the heaven hath he given into thine hand, and hath made thee ruler over them all. Thou *art* this head of gold.

39 And after thee shall arise another kingdom inferior to thee, and another third kingdom of brass, which shall bear rule over all the earth.

40 And the fourth kingdom shall be strong as iron: forasmuch as iron breaketh in pieces and subdueth all *things*: and as iron that breaketh all these, shall it break in pieces and bruise.

41 And whereas thou sawest the feet and toes, part of potters' clay, and part of iron, the kingdom shall be divided; but there shall be in it of the strength of the iron, forasmuch as thou sawest the iron mixed with miry clay.

42 And *as* the toes of the feet *were* part of iron, and part of clay, *so* the kingdom shall be partly strong, and partly broken.

43 And whereas thou sawest iron mixed with miry clay, they shall mingle themselves with the seed of men: but they shall not cleave one to another, even as iron is not mixed with clay.

44 And in the days of these kings shall the God of heaven set up a kingdom, which shall never be destroyed: and the kingdom shall not be left to other people, *but* it shall break in pieces and consume all these kingdoms, and it shall stand for ever.

45 Forasmuch as thou sawest that the stone was cut out of the mountain without hands, and that it brake in pieces the iron, the brass, the clay, the silver, and the gold; the great God hath made known to the king what shall come to pass hereafter: and the dream *is* certain, and the interpretation thereof sure.

The King Rewards Daniel

46 Then the king Nebuchadnezzar fell upon his face, and worshipped Daniel, and commanded that they should offer an oblation and sweet odours unto him.

47 The king answered unto Daniel, and said, Of a truth *it is*, that your God *is* a God of gods, and a Lord of kings, and a revealer of secrets, seeing thou couldest reveal this secret.

48 Then the king made Daniel a great man, and gave him many great gifts, and made him ruler over the whole province of Babylon, and chief of the governors over all the wise *men* of Babylon.

Cross references

34 Dan. 2:45; 8:25; Zech. 4:6; 2Cor. 5:1; Heb. 9:24
35 Ps. 1:4; 37:10, 36; 80:9; Isa. 2:2, 3; Hos. 13:3
37 Ezra 1:2; 7:12; Isa. 47:5; Jer. 27:6, 7; Ezek. 26:7; Hos. 8:10
38 Jer. 27:6; Dan. 2:32; 4:21, 22
39 Dan. 2:32; 5:28, 31
40 Dan. 7:7, 23
41 Dan. 2:33
44 Ps. 2:9; Isa. 28:16; 60:12; Dan. 2:28, 35; 4:3, 34; 6:26; 7:14, 27; Mic. 4:7; Luke 1:32, 33; 1Cor. 15:24
46 Ezra 6:10; Acts 10:25; 14:13; 28:6
47 Dan. 2:28
48 Dan. 2:6; 4:9; 5:11

2:34–35 a stone . . . cut out without hands. The "stone" is of divine origin and is the result of supernatural activity. The "mountain" is a biblical symbol for a kingdom (cf. Isa. 2:2; Jer. 51:25; Ezek. 20:40; Zech. 8:3). Here the stone and mountain represent the kingdom of God that will eventually replace all human kingdoms (Rev. 16:13–16; 19:17). The destruction of the final Gentile power, that governed by the Antichrist, results in the establishment of Christ's Millennial Kingdom (Rev. 20:6).

2:41–44 The ten toes of the statue represent the ten kings that will rule simultaneously over the region of former Roman dominion. In 364 B.C., Emperor Valentinian divided the Roman Empire into east and west. The city of Rome became capital of the Western Roman Empire, and Constantinople (present day Istanbul) became capital of the Eastern Roman Empire. Even today, the world is largely divided between East and West and will remain so until Antichrist sets up a united government of ten kings (toes) just before the kingdom age, when Christ returns. The toes correspond to the ten horns of the "fourth beast" in Daniel 7:23–24. Many scholars think this "iron and clay" section of the image represents a very unstable form of government comparable to the social democracies that primarily exist throughout the world today. This instability will continue until the God of heaven establishes His Son's kingdom at Christ's second coming, over which the Lord will rule forever.

2:46–47 Nebuchadnezzar . . . worshipped Daniel. These verses do not mean that the king actually bowed down and worshiped Daniel, but that he worshiped Daniel's God. While Nebuchadnezzar remained unconverted at this point, he was deeply impressed by God's ability to predict the future, both accurately and literally.

49 Then Daniel requested of the king, and he set Shadrach, Meshach, and Abed-nego, over the affairs of the province of Babylon: but Daniel *sat* in the gate of the king.

CHAPTER 3
The Image of Gold

1 Nebuchadnezzar the king made an image of gold, whose height *was* threescore cubits, *and* the breadth thereof six cubits: he set it up in the plain of Dura, in the province of Babylon.

2 Then Nebuchadnezzar the king sent to gather together the princes, the governors, and the captains, the judges, the treasurers, the counsellers, the sheriffs, and all the rulers of the provinces, to come to the dedication of the image which Nebuchadnezzar the king had set up.

3 Then the princes, the governors, and captains, the judges, the treasurers, the counsellers, the sheriffs, and all the rulers of the provinces, were gathered together unto the dedication of the image that Nebuchadnezzar the king had set up; and they stood before the image that Nebuchadnezzar had set up.

4 Then an herald cried aloud, To you it is

commanded, O people, nations, and languages,

5 *That* at what time ye hear the sound of the cornet, flute, harp, sackbut, psaltery, dulcimer, and all kinds of musick, ye fall down and worship the golden image that Nebuchadnezzar the king hath set up:

6 And whoso falleth not down and worshippeth shall the same hour be cast into the midst of a burning fiery furnace.

7 Therefore at that time, when all the people heard the sound of the cornet, flute, harp, sackbut, psaltery, and all kinds of musick, all the people, the nations, and the languages, fell down *and* worshipped the golden image that Nebuchadnezzar the king had set up.

8 Wherefore at that time certain Chaldeans came near, and accused the Jews.

9 They spake and said to the king Nebuchadnezzar, O king, live for ever.

10 Thou, O king, hast made a decree, that every man that shall hear the sound of the cornet, flute, harp, sackbut, psaltery, and dulcimer, and all kinds of musick, shall fall down and worship the golden image:

11 And whoso falleth not down and worshippeth, *that* he should be cast into the midst of a burning fiery furnace.

Cross references: 49 Esth. 2:19, 21; 3:2; Dan. 3:12 · 4 Dan. 4:1; 6:25 · 6 Jer. 29:22; Rev. 13:15 · 8 Dan. 6:12 · 9 Dan. 2:4; 5:10; 6:6, 21

The Image Vision of King Nebuchadnezzar (Dan. 2:1–45)
© AMG Publishers

12 There are certain Jews whom thou hast set over the affairs of the province of Babylon, Shadrach, Meshach, and Abed-nego; these men, O king, have not regarded thee: they serve not thy gods, nor worship the golden image which thou hast set up.

13 Then Nebuchadnezzar in *his* rage and fury commanded to bring Shadrach, Meshach, and Abed-nego. Then they brought these men before the king.

The Fiery Furnace

14 Nebuchadnezzar spake and said unto them, *Is it* true, O Shadrach, Meshach, and Abed-nego, do not ye serve my gods, nor worship the golden image which I have set up?

15 Now if ye be ready that at what time ye hear the sound of the cornet, flute, harp, sackbut, psaltery, and dulcimer, and all kinds of musick, ye fall down and worship the image which I have made; *well*: but if ye worship not, ye shall be cast the same hour into the midst of a burning fiery furnace; and who *is* that God that shall deliver you out of my hands?

16 Shadrach, Meshach, and Abed-nego, answered and said to the king, O Nebuchadnezzar, we *are* not careful to answer thee in this matter.

17 If it be *so*, our God whom we serve is able to deliver us from the burning fiery furnace, and he will deliver *us* out of thine hand, O king.

18 But if not, be it known unto thee, O king, that we will not serve thy gods, nor worship the golden image which thou hast set up.

19 Then was Nebuchadnezzar full of fury, and the form of his visage was changed against Shadrach, Meshach, and Abed-nego: *therefore* he spake, and commanded that they should heat the furnace one seven times more than it was wont to be heated.

20 And he commanded the most mighty men that *were* in his army to bind Shadrach, Meshach, and Abed-nego, *and* to cast *them* into the burning fiery furnace.

21 Then these men were bound in their coats, their hosen, and their hats, and their *other* garments, and were cast into the midst of the burning fiery furnace.

22 Therefore because the king's commandment was urgent, and the furnace exceeding hot, the flame of the fire slew those men that took up Shadrach, Meshach, and Abed-nego.

23 And these three men, Shadrach, Meshach, and Abed-nego, fell down bound into the midst of the burning fiery furnace.

24 Then Nebuchadnezzar the king was astonied, and rose up in haste, *and* spake, and said unto his counsellers, Did not we cast three men bound into the midst of the fire? They answered and said unto the king, True, O king.

Four Men in the Furnace

25 He answered and said, Lo, I see four men loose, walking in the midst of the fire, and they have no hurt; and the form of the fourth is like the Son of God.

26 Then Nebuchadnezzar came near to the mouth of the burning fiery furnace, *and* spake, and said, Shadrach, Meshach, and Abed-nego, ye servants of the most high God, come forth, and come *hither*. Then Shadrach, Meshach, and Abed-nego, came forth of the midst of the fire.

27 And the princes, governors, and captains, and the king's counsellers, being gathered together, saw these men, upon whose bodies the fire had no power, nor was an hair of their head singed, neither were their coats changed, nor the smell of fire had passed on them.

28 *Then* Nebuchadnezzar spake, and said, Blessed *be* the God of Shadrach, Meshach, and Abed-nego, who hath sent his angel, and delivered his servants that trusted in him, and have changed the king's word, and yielded their bodies, that they might not serve nor worship any god, except their own God.

29 Therefore I make a decree, That every people, nation, and language, which speak any thing amiss against the God of Shadrach, Meshach, and Abed-nego, shall be cut in pieces, and their houses shall be made a dunghill: because there is no other God that can deliver after this sort.

30 Then the king promoted Shadrach, Meshach, and Abed-nego, in the province of Babylon.

Cross references:

12 Dan. 2:49
14 Ex. 21:13
15 Ex. 5:2; 32:32; 2Kgs. 18:35; Luke 13:9
16 Matt. 10:19
25 Job 1:6; 38:7; Ps. 34:7; Isa. 43:2; Dan. 3:28
27 Heb. 11:34
28 Ps. 34:7, 8; Jer. 17:7; Dan. 6:22, 23
29 Dan. 2:5; Dan. 6:26, 27

3:17–18 The refusal of the three Hebrew children to bow down and worship the king's image and their deliverance from the fiery furnace is seen by some as a type or picture of the way God will preserve the believing children of Israel during the seven-year Tribulation, when they refuse to worship the image of Antichrist (Rev. 13).

CHAPTER 4
A Second Dream

1 Nebuchadnezzar the king, unto all people, nations, and languages, that dwell in all the earth; Peace be multiplied unto you.

2 I thought it good to shew the signs and wonders that the high God hath wrought toward me.

3 How great *are* his signs! and how mighty *are* his wonders! his kingdom *is* an everlasting kingdom, and his dominion *is* from generation to generation.

4 I Nebuchadnezzar was at rest in mine house, and flourishing in my palace:

5 I saw a dream which made me afraid, and the thoughts upon my bed and the visions of my head troubled me.

6 Therefore made I a decree to bring in all the wise *men* of Babylon before me, that they might make known unto me the interpretation of the dream.

7 Then came in the magicians, the astrologers, the Chaldeans, and the soothsayers: and I told the dream before them; but they did not make known unto me the interpretation thereof.

8 But at the last Daniel came in before me, whose name *was* Belteshazzar, according to the name of my god, and in whom *is* the spirit of the holy gods: and before him I told the dream, *saying*,

9 O Belteshazzar, master of the magicians, because I know that the spirit of the holy gods *is* in thee, and no secret troubleth thee, tell me the visions of my dream that I have seen, and the interpretation thereof.

10 Thus *were* the visions of mine head in my bed; I saw, and behold a tree in the midst of the earth, and the height thereof *was* great.

11 The tree grew, and was strong, and the height thereof reached unto heaven, and the sight thereof to the end of all the earth:

12 The leaves thereof *were* fair, and the fruit thereof much, and in it *was* meat for all: the beasts of the field had shadow under it, and the fowls of the heaven dwelt in the boughs thereof, and all flesh was fed of it.

13 I saw in the visions of my head upon my bed, and, behold, a watcher and an holy one came down from heaven;

14 He cried aloud, and said thus, Hew down the tree, and cut off his branches, shake off his leaves, and scatter his fruit: let the beasts get away from under it, and the fowls from his branches:

15 Nevertheless leave the stump of his roots in the earth, even with a band of iron and brass, in the tender grass of the field; and let it be wet with the dew of heaven, and *let* his portion *be* with the beasts in the grass of the earth:

16 Let his heart be changed from man's, and let a beast's heart be given unto him; and let seven times pass over him.

17 This matter *is* by the decree of the watchers, and the demand by the word of the holy ones: to the intent that the living may know that the most High ruleth in the kingdom of men, and giveth it to whomsoever he will, and setteth up over it the basest of men.

18 This dream I king Nebuchadnezzar have seen. Now thou, O Belteshazzar, declare the interpretation thereof, forasmuch as all the wise *men* of my kingdom are not able to make known unto me the interpretation: but thou *art* able; for the spirit of the holy gods *is* in thee.

Daniel Explains the Dream

19 Then Daniel, whose name *was* Belteshazzar, was astonied for one hour, and his thoughts troubled him. The king spake, and said, Belteshazzar, let not the dream, or the interpretation thereof, trouble thee. Belteshazzar answered and said, My lord, the dream *be* to them that hate thee, and the interpretation thereof to thine enemies.

20 The tree that thou sawest, which grew, and was strong, whose height reached unto the heaven, and the sight thereof to all the earth;

21 Whose leaves *were* fair, and the fruit thereof much, and in it *was* meat for all; under which the beasts of the field dwelt, and upon whose branches the fowls of the heaven had their habitation:

22 It *is* thou, O king, that art grown and become strong: for thy greatness is grown, and reacheth unto heaven, and thy dominion to the end of the earth.

Cross references
1 Dan. 3:4; 6:25
2 Dan. 3:26
3 Dan. 2:44; 4:34; 6:26, 27
5 Dan. 2:1, 28, 29
7 Dan. 2:2
8 Isa. 63:11; Dan. 1:7; 2:11; 4:18; 5:11, 14
9 Dan. 2:48; 5:11
10 Ezek. 31:3-9; Dan. 4:20
12 Ezek. 17:23; 31:6; Lam. 4:20
13 Deut. 33:2; Ps. 103:20; Dan. 4:17, 23; 8:13; Zech. 14:5; Jude 1:14
14 Ezek. 31:12; Matt. 3:10
16 Dan. 11:13; 12:7
17 Ps. 9:16; Dan. 2:21; 4:25, 32; 5:21
18 Gen. 41:8, 15; Dan. 4:8; 5:8, 15
19 2Sam. 18:32; Jer. 29:7; Dan. 4:8
20 Dan. 4:10-12
22 Jer. 27:6-8; Dan. 2:38

4:19 Nebuchadnezzar was the man who had destroyed Jerusalem and carried Daniel away in his service. However, when Daniel received a message from God concerning judgment upon Nebuchadnezzar, he felt compelled to encourage the Babylonian king to repent (v. 27) in hopes that the consequences could be avoided. It could also be inferred that Daniel watched over the empire during the time when these consequences took place (vv. 28–37).

23 And whereas the king saw a watcher and an holy one coming down from heaven, and saying, Hew the tree down, and destroy it; yet leave the stump of the roots thereof in the earth, even with a band of iron and brass, in the tender grass of the field; and let it be wet with the dew of heaven, and *let* his portion *be* with the beasts of the field, till seven times pass over him;

24 This *is* the interpretation, O king, and this *is* the decree of the most High, which is come upon my lord the king:

25 That they shall drive thee from men, and thy dwelling shall be with the beasts of the field, and they shall make thee to eat grass as oxen, and they shall wet thee with the dew of heaven, and seven times shall pass over thee, till thou know that the most High ruleth in the kingdom of men, and giveth it to whomsoever he will.

26 And whereas they commanded to leave the stump of the tree roots; thy kingdom shall be sure unto thee, after that thou shalt have known that the heavens do rule.

27 Wherefore, O king, let my counsel be acceptable unto thee, and break off thy sins by righteousness, and thine iniquities by shewing mercy to the poor; if it may be a lengthening of thy tranquillity.

28 All this came upon the king Nebuchadnezzar.

29 At the end of twelve months he walked in the palace of the kingdom of Babylon.

30 The king spake, and said, Is not this great Babylon, that I have built for the house of the kingdom by the might of my power, and for the honour of my majesty?

31 While the word *was* in the king's mouth, there fell a voice from heaven, *saying*, O king Nebuchadnezzar, to thee it is spoken; The kingdom is departed from thee.

32 And they shall drive thee from men, and thy dwelling *shall be* with the beasts of the field: they shall make thee to eat grass as

oxen, and seven times shall pass over thee, until thou know that the most High ruleth in the kingdom of men, and giveth it to whomsoever he will.

33 The same hour was the thing fulfilled upon Nebuchadnezzar: and he was driven from men, and did eat grass as oxen, and his body was wet with the dew of heaven, till his hairs were grown like eagles' *feathers*, and his nails like birds' *claws*.

34 And at the end of the days I Nebuchadnezzar lifted up mine eyes unto heaven, and mine understanding returned unto me, and I blessed the most High, and I praised and honoured him that liveth for ever, whose dominion *is* an everlasting dominion, and his kingdom *is* from generation to generation:

35 And all the inhabitants of the earth *are* reputed as nothing: and he doeth according to his will in the army of heaven, and *among* the inhabitants of the earth: and none can stay his hand, or say unto him, What doest thou?

36 At the same time my reason returned unto me; and for the glory of my kingdom, mine honour and brightness returned unto me; and my counsellers and my lords sought unto me; and I was established in my kingdom, and excellent majesty was added unto me.

37 Now I Nebuchadnezzar praise and extol and honour the King of heaven, all whose works *are* truth, and his ways judgment: and those that walk in pride he is able to abase.

CHAPTER 5
The Handwriting on the Wall

1 Belshazzar the king made a great feast to a thousand of his lords, and drank wine before the thousand.

2 Belshazzar, whiles he tasted the wine, commanded to bring the golden and silver

Cross-references

23 Dan. 4:13; 5:21
25 Ps. 83:18; 106:20; Jer. 27:5; Dan. 4:17, 32; 5:21-31
26 Matt. 21:25; Luke 15:18, 21
27 1Kgs. 21:29; Ps. 41:1-3; 1Pet. 4:8
30 Prov. 16:18; Dan. 5:20
31 Dan. 4:24; 5:5; Luke 12:20
32 Dan. 4:25
34 Ps. 10:16; Dan. 2:44; 4:26; 7:14; 12:7; Mic. 4:7; Luke 1:33; Rev. 4:10
35 Job 9:12; 34:29; Ps. 115:3; 135:6; Isa. 40:15, 17; 45:9; Rom. 9:20
36 Job 42:12; Prov. 22:4; Dan. 4:26; Matt. 6:33
37 Ex. 18:11; Ps. 33:4; Dan. 5:20; Rev. 15:3; 16:7

1 Esth. 1:3
2 2Sam. 9:7; 2Chr. 15:16; Jer. 27:7; 52:19; Dan. 1:2; 5:11, 13

4:37 Nebuchadnezzar's precise relationship to God at the end of this chapter is a matter of dispute, but several factors suggest that he was truly converted to the worship of the God of Israel. Nebuchadnezzar speaks of his seven-year period of insanity as something God did "toward" him (4:2). Moreover, he no longer calls God "the God of Shadrach, Meshach, and Abed-nego" (cf. Dan. 3:28), but "the most High" and "King of heaven" (4:34, 37). He understood that God was able to humble anyone who has a proud heart.

5:1–9 The Aramaic word for "father" (v. 2) refers to an ancestor but not necessarily an immediate predecessor. Belshazzar was actually the grandson of Nebuchadnezzar. He shared co-regency with his father, Nabonidus, the son-in-law of Nebuchadnezzar from 553–539 B.C. Therefore, Belshazzar was actually the second highest ruler in the kingdom. His promise to make Daniel the "third ruler" was the highest position he could offer anyone else. The famous "writing on the wall" event during King Belshazzar's reign predicted his immediate fate and that of the Babylonian Empire.

vessels which his father Nebuchadnezzar had taken out of the temple which *was* in Jerusalem; that the king, and his princes, his wives, and his concubines, might drink therein.

3 Then they brought the golden vessels that were taken out of the temple of the house of God which *was* at Jerusalem; and the king, and his princes, his wives, and his concubines, drank in them.

4 They drank wine, and praised the gods of gold, and of silver, of brass, of iron, of wood, and of stone.

5 In the same hour came forth fingers of a man's hand, and wrote over against the candlestick upon the plaister of the wall of the king's palace: and the king saw the part of the hand that wrote.

6 Then the king's countenance was changed, and his thoughts troubled him, so that the joints of his loins were loosed, and his knees smote one against another.

7 The king cried aloud to bring in the astrologers, the Chaldeans, and the soothsayers. *And* the king spake, and said to the wise *men* of Babylon, Whosoever shall read this writing, and shew me the interpretation thereof, shall be clothed with scarlet, and *have* a chain of gold about his neck, and shall be the third ruler in the kingdom.

8 Then came in all the king's wise *men:* but they could not read the writing, nor make known to the king the interpretation thereof.

9 Then was king Belshazzar greatly troubled, and his countenance was changed in him, and his lords were astonied.

10 *Now* the queen, by reason of the words of the king and his lords, came into the banquet house: *and* the queen spake and said, O king, live for ever: let not thy thoughts trouble thee, nor let thy countenance be changed:

11 There is a man in thy kingdom, in whom *is* the spirit of the holy gods; and in the days of thy father light and understanding and wisdom, like the wisdom of the gods, was found in him; whom the king Nebuchadnezzar thy father, the king, *I say,* thy father, made master of the magicians, astrologers, Chaldeans, *and* soothsayers;

12 Forasmuch as an excellent spirit, and knowledge, and understanding, interpreting of dreams, and shewing of hard sentences, and dissolving of doubts, were

found in the same Daniel, whom the king named Belteshazzar: now let Daniel be called, and he will shew the interpretation.

13 Then was Daniel brought in before the king. *And* the king spake and said unto Daniel, *Art* thou that Daniel, which *art* of the children of the captivity of Judah, whom the king my father brought out of Jewry?

14 I have even heard of thee, that the spirit of the gods *is* in thee, and *that* light and understanding and excellent wisdom is found in thee.

15 And now the wise *men,* the astrologers, have been brought in before me, that they should read this writing, and make known unto me the interpretation thereof: but they could not shew the interpretation of the thing:

16 And I have heard of thee, that thou canst make interpretations, and dissolve doubts: now if thou canst read the writing, and make known to me the interpretation thereof, thou shalt be clothed with scarlet, and *have* a chain of gold about thy neck, and shalt be the third ruler in the kingdom.

17 Then Daniel answered and said before the king, Let thy gifts be to thyself, and give thy rewards to another; yet I will read the writing unto the king, and make known to him the interpretation.

18 O thou king, the most high God gave Nebuchadnezzar thy father a kingdom, and majesty, and glory, and honour:

19 And for the majesty that he gave him, all people, nations, and languages, trembled and feared before him: whom he would he slew; and whom he would he kept alive; and whom he would he set up; and whom he would he put down.

20 But when his heart was lifted up, and his mind hardened in pride, he was deposed from his kingly throne, and they took his glory from him:

21 And he was driven from the sons of men; and his heart was made like the beasts, and his dwelling *was* with the wild asses: they fed him with grass like oxen, and his body was wet with the dew of heaven; till he knew that the most high God ruled in the kingdom of men, and *that* he appointeth over it whomsoever he will.

22 And thou his son, O Belshazzar, hast not humbled thine heart, though thou knewest all this;

---

4 Rev. 9:20
5 Dan. 4:31
6 Isa. 5:27; Dan. 5:9; Nah. 2:10
7 Isa. 47:13; Dan. 2:2; 4:6; 6:2
8 Dan. 2:27; 4:7
9 Dan. 2:1; 5:6
10 Dan. 2:4; 3:9
11 Dan. 2:48; 4:8, 9, 18; 5:2
12 Dan. 1:7; 6:3
14 Dan. 5:11, 12
15 Dan. 5:7, 8
16 Dan. 5:7
17 Dan. 2:6
18 Dan. 2:37, 38; 4:17, 22, 25
19 Jer. 27:7; Dan. 3:4

20 Ex. 18:11; Dan. 4:30, 37

21 Dan. 4:17, 25, 32-37

22 2Chr. 33:23; 36:12

5:10–16 The "queen" is probably Nebuchadnezzar's wife Amytis, now the "queen mother" and Belshazzar's grandmother. Belshazzar himself did not seem to know Daniel personally (v. 13).

23 But hast lifted up thyself against the Lord of heaven; and they have brought the vessels of his house before thee, and thou, and thy lords, thy wives, and thy concubines, have drunk wine in them; and thou hast praised the gods of silver, and gold, of brass, iron, wood, and stone, which see not, nor hear, nor know: and the God in whose hand thy breath *is*, and whose *are* all thy ways, hast thou not glorified:

24 Then was the part of the hand sent from him; and this writing was written.

25 And this *is* the writing that was written, MENE, MENE, TEKEL, UPHARSIN.

26 This *is* the interpretation of the thing: MENE; God hath numbered thy kingdom, and finished it.

27 TEKEL; Thou art weighed in the balances, and art found wanting.

28 PERES; Thy kingdom is divided, and given to the Medes and Persians.

29 Then commanded Belshazzar, and they clothed Daniel with scarlet, and *put* a chain of gold about his neck, and made a proclamation concerning him, that he should be the third ruler in the kingdom.

30 In that night was Belshazzar the king of the Chaldeans slain.

31 And Darius the Median took the kingdom, *being* about threescore and two years old.

CHAPTER 6
Daniel in the Lions' Den

1 It pleased Darius to set over the kingdom an hundred and twenty princes, which should be over the whole kingdom;

2 And over these three presidents; of whom Daniel *was* first: that the princes might give accounts unto them, and the king should have no damage.

3 Then this Daniel was preferred above the presidents and princes, because an excellent spirit *was* in him; and the king thought to set him over the whole realm.

Cross references:
23 Ps. 115:5, 6; Jer. 10:23; Dan. 5:3, 4
27 Job 31:6; Ps. 62:9; Jer. 6:30
28 Isa. 21:2; Dan. 5:31; 6:28; 9:1
29 Dan. 5:7
30 Jer. 51:31, 39, 57
31 Dan. 9:1
1 Esth. 1:1
3 Dan. 5:12
4 Eccl. 4:4
6 Neh. 2:3; Dan. 2:4; 6:21
8 Esth. 1:19; 8:8
10 1 Kgs. 8:44, 48; Ps. 5:7; 55:17; Jon. 2:4; Acts 2:1, 2, 15; 3:1; 10:9
12 Dan. 3:8; 6:8
13 Dan. 1:6; 3:12; 5:13

4 Then the presidents and princes sought to find occasion against Daniel concerning the kingdom; but they could find none occasion nor fault; forasmuch as he *was* faithful, neither was there any error or fault found in him.

5 Then said these men, We shall not find any occasion against this Daniel, except we find *it* against him concerning the law of his God.

6 Then these presidents and princes assembled together to the king, and said thus unto him, King Darius, live for ever.

7 All the presidents of the kingdom, the governors, and the princes, the counsellers, and the captains, have consulted together to establish a royal statute, and to make a firm decree, that whosoever shall ask a petition of any God or man for thirty days, save of thee, O king, he shall be cast into the den of lions.

8 Now, O king, establish the decree, and sign the writing, that it be not changed, according to the law of the Medes and Persians, which altereth not.

9 Wherefore king Darius signed the writing and the decree.

10 Now when Daniel knew that the writing was signed, he went into his house; and his windows being open in his chamber toward Jerusalem, he kneeled upon his knees three times a day, and prayed, and gave thanks before his God, as he did aforetime.

11 Then these men assembled, and found Daniel praying and making supplication before his God.

12 Then they came near, and spake before the king concerning the king's decree; Hast thou not signed a decree, that every man that shall ask *a petition* of any God or man within thirty days, save of thee, O king, shall be cast into the den of lions? The king answered and said, The thing *is* true, according to the law of the Medes and Persians, which altereth not.

13 Then answered they and said before the

5:24–30 MENE . . . TEKEL . . . PERES. These are Hebrew words, unfamiliar to the Babylonians, meaning "weighed," "numbered," and "divided" respectively. Daniel interpreted these words to mean that Belshazzar's kingdom had been "weighed in the balances" of divine judgment and "found wanting"; thus the empire would be terminated and given to the Medes and Persians that very night. History records that on that very same night the great city of Babylon, under the co-regency of Nabonidus and Belshazzar was indeed conquered by the Medes and Persians without resistance.

5:31 Darius here is either another name for the Persian emperor Cyrus the Great, or another name for Gubaru, the governor appointed by Cyrus over Babylonia and Syria. Darius the Median is not the same person as Darius the Persian, who ruled Persia much later from 521–486 B.C. (see Ezra 4:5). This new king from the Medes obviously saw something special in Daniel, for he appointed the prophet, who was now about eighty-five years old, as one of the administrators in the newly formed government.

king, That Daniel, which *is* of the children of the captivity of Judah, regardeth not thee, O king, nor the decree that thou hast signed, but maketh his petition three times a day.

14 Then the king, when he heard *these* words, was sore displeased with himself, and set *his* heart on Daniel to deliver him: and he laboured till the going down of the sun to deliver him.

15 Then these men assembled unto the king, and said unto the king, Know, O king, that the law of the Medes and Persians *is*, That no decree nor statute which the king establisheth may be changed.

16 Then the king commanded, and they brought Daniel, and cast *him* into the den of lions. *Now* the king spake and said unto Daniel, Thy God whom thou servest continually, he will deliver thee.

17 And a stone was brought, and laid upon the mouth of the den; and the king sealed it with his own signet, and with the signet of his lords; that the purpose might not be changed concerning Daniel.

18 Then the king went to his palace, and passed the night fasting: neither were instruments of musick brought before him: and his sleep went from him.

19 Then the king arose very early in the morning, and went in haste unto the den of lions.

20 And when he came to the den, he cried with a lamentable voice unto Daniel: *and* the king spake and said to Daniel, O Daniel, servant of the living God, is thy God, whom thou servest continually, able to deliver thee from the lions?

21 Then said Daniel unto the king, O king, live for ever.

22 My God hath sent his angel, and hath shut the lions' mouths, that they have not hurt me: forasmuch as before him innocency was found in me; and also before thee, O king, have I done no hurt.

23 Then was the king exceeding glad for him, and commanded that they should take Daniel up out of the den. So Daniel was taken up out of the den, and no manner of hurt was found upon him, because he believed in his God.

24 And the king commanded, and they brought those men which had accused Daniel, and they cast *them* into the den of lions, them, their children, and their wives; and the lions had the mastery of them, and brake all their bones in pieces or ever they came at the bottom of the den.

25 Then king Darius wrote unto all people, nations, and languages, that dwell in all the earth; Peace be multiplied unto you.

26 I make a decree, That in every dominion of my kingdom men tremble and fear before the God of Daniel: for he *is* the living God, and stedfast for ever, and his kingdom *that* which shall not be destroyed, and his dominion *shall be even* unto the end.

27 He delivereth and rescueth, and he worketh signs and wonders in heaven and in earth, who hath delivered Daniel from the power of the lions.

28 So this Daniel prospered in the reign of Darius, and in the reign of Cyrus the Persian.

CHAPTER 7
The Four Beasts

1 In the first year of Belshazzar king of Babylon Daniel had a dream and visions of

Cross references (center column)

14 Mark 6:26
15 Dan. 6:8
17 Lam. 3:53; Matt. 27:66
18 Dan. 2:1
20 Dan. 3:15
21 Dan. 2:4
22 Dan. 3:28; Heb. 11:33
23 Heb. 11:33
24 Deut. 19:19; 24:16; 2Kgs. 14:6; Esth. 9:10
25 Dan. 4:1
26 Ps. 99:1; Dan. 2:44; 3:29; 4:3, 34; 7:14, 27; Luke 1:33
27 Dan. 4:3
28 Ezra 1:1, 2; Dan. 1:21
1 Num. 12:6; Dan. 2:28; Amos 3:7

7:1–28 Daniel himself had a dream, which was a vision of future world empires. In chapter 2, man's view of kingdoms and government is that of a beautiful image that people can worship in place of Jehovah. In this chapter we see God's view of those same kingdoms as a series of rapacious beasts ready to devour mankind. History proves God's view is the right one. This vision was actually given to Daniel some fourteen years before the Medes and Persians conquered Babylon in approximately 553 B.C. The "lion" represents Nebuchadnezzar and the Babylonian Empire. The plucking of the wings refers to his insanity, and the granting of a "human mind" refers to his conversion. The "bear" represents Media-Persia. Being "raised up on one side" (Dan. 8:8, 21–22) refers to the two unequal partners in the empire: the Persians gradually gained the supremacy over the Medes. The three ribs in the bear's mouth refer to the three provincial kingdoms conquered by the Medes and Persians: Lydia, Babylon, and Egypt. The leopard represents Greece, and its four wings and heads speak of the division of the Greek empire into four sections, following the death of Alexander the Great (cf. Dan. 8:8, 21–22). The "fourth beast" corresponds to the kingdom of iron legs in Daniel 2:33, 40 and symbolizes the Roman Empire. The "iron teeth" speak of Rome's unequalled military strength, and the trampling and crushing described in verse seven illustrate the imposition of Rome's culture and laws upon conquered peoples. The "ten horns" parallel the "ten toes" of Daniel 2:41–43 and represent the final form of Gentile power in the End Times. The kingdom of Antichrist is typified by the "little horn" that arises from the ten horns (Dan. 7:25; 8:23–26; 11:36; 2 Thess. 2:3–8; Rev. 13:5–6).

his head upon his bed: then he wrote the dream, *and* told the sum of the matters.

2 Daniel spake and said, I saw in my vision by night, and, behold, the four winds of the heaven strove upon the great sea.

3 And four great beasts came up from the sea, diverse one from another.

4 The first *was* like a lion, and had eagle's wings: I beheld till the wings thereof were plucked, and it was lifted up from the earth, and made stand upon the feet as a man, and a man's heart was given to it.

5 And behold another beast, a second, like to a bear, and it raised up itself on one side, and *it had* three ribs in the mouth of it between the teeth of it: and they said thus unto it, Arise, devour much flesh.

6 After this I beheld, and lo another, like a leopard, which had upon the back of it four wings of a fowl; the beast had also four heads; and dominion was given to it.

7 After this I saw in the night visions, and behold a fourth beast, dreadful and terrible, and strong exceedingly; and it had great iron teeth: it devoured and brake in pieces, and stamped the residue with the feet of it: and it *was* diverse from all the beasts that *were* before it; and it had ten horns.

8 I considered the horns, and, behold, there came up among them another little horn, before whom there were three of the first horns plucked up by the roots: and, behold, in this horn *were* eyes like the eyes of man, and a mouth speaking great things.

9 I beheld till the thrones were cast down, and the Ancient of days did sit, whose garment *was* white as snow, and the hair of his head like the pure wool: his throne *was like* the fiery flame, *and* his wheels *as* burning fire.

10 A fiery stream issued and came forth from before him: thousand thousands ministered unto him, and ten thousand times ten thousand stood before him: the judgment was set, and the books were opened.

11 I beheld then because of the voice of the great words which the horn spake: I beheld *even* till the beast was slain, and his body

destroyed, and given to the burning flame.

12 As concerning the rest of the beasts, they had their dominion taken away: yet their lives were prolonged for a season and time.

13 I saw in the night visions, and, behold, *one* like the Son of man came with the clouds of heaven, and came to the Ancient of days, and they brought him near before him.

14 And there was given him dominion, and glory, and a kingdom, that all people, nations, and languages, should serve him: his dominion *is* an everlasting dominion, which shall not pass away, and his kingdom *that* which shall not be destroyed.

15 I Daniel was grieved in my spirit in the midst of *my* body, and the visions of my head troubled me.

16 I came near unto one of them that stood by, and asked him the truth of all this. So he told me, and made me know the interpretation of the things.

The Four Kings

17 These great beasts, which are four, *are* four kings, *which* shall arise out of the earth.

18 But the saints of the most High shall take the kingdom, and possess the kingdom for ever, even for ever and ever.

19 Then I would know the truth of the fourth beast, which was diverse from all the others, exceeding dreadful, whose teeth *were* of iron, and his nails of brass; *which* devoured, brake in pieces, and stamped the residue with his feet;

20 And of the ten horns that *were* in his head, and *of* the other which came up, and before whom three fell; even *of* that horn that had eyes, and a mouth that spake very great things, whose look *was* more stout than his fellows.

21 I beheld, and the same horn made war with the saints, and prevailed against them;

22 Until the Ancient of days came, and judgment was given to the saints of the most High; and the time came that the saints possessed the kingdom.

Cross references

3 Rev. 13:1
4 Jer. 4:7, 13; 48:40; Ezek. 17:3
6 Dan. 8:8, 22
7 Rev. 13:1
8 Ps. 12:3; Dan. 7:20, 21, 24, 25; 8:9; Rev. 9:7; 13:5
9 Ps. 104:2; Ezek. 1:15, 16; Rev. 1:14; 20:4
10 Isa. 30:33; 66:15; Rev. 5:11; 20:4, 12
11 Rev. 19:20
13 Ezek. 1:26; Dan. 7:9; Matt. 24:30; 26:64; Rev. 1:7, 13; 14:14
14 Ps. 2:6-8; 8:6; 110:1, 2; 145:13; Dan. 2:44; 3:4; 7:27; Mic. 4:7; Matt. 11:27; 28:18; Luke 1:33; John 3:35; 12:34; 1 Cor. 15:27; Eph. 1:22; Heb. 12:28
15 Dan. 7:28
17 Dan. 7:3
18 Rev. 2:26, 27; 3:21; 20:4
19 Dan. 7:7
21 Dan. 8:12, 24; 11:31; Rev. 11:7; 13:7; 17:14; 19:19
22 Dan. 7:9, 18; 1 Cor. 6:2; Rev. 1:6; 5:10; 20:4

7:2–3 The "four great beasts" came from "the great sea," meaning the peoples around the Mediterranean Sea.

7:9–14 the Ancient of days. This title refers to God the Father, whose description is similar to John's description of the Father in Revelation 4. The "Son of Man" refers to Jesus Christ, who receives a kingdom of "everlasting

dominion" from the Father. This is a clear prediction of the Messiah's coronation to rule as King over the world during the Millennium.

7:21 saints. The "saints" referred to in this chapter are true believers in God that will rule with Christ in His future Millennial Kingdom (cf. Matt. 19:28–29; Luke 22:29–30; Rev. 20:6).

23 Thus he said, The fourth beast shall be the fourth kingdom upon earth, which shall be diverse from all kingdoms, and shall devour the whole earth, and shall tread it down, and break it in pieces.

24 And the ten horns out of this kingdom *are* ten kings *that* shall arise: and another shall rise after them; and he shall be diverse from the first, and he shall subdue three kings.

25 And he shall speak *great* words against the most High, and shall wear out the saints of the most High, and think to change times and laws: and they shall be given into his hand until a time and times and the dividing of time.

26 But the judgment shall sit, and they shall take away his dominion, to consume and to destroy *it* unto the end.

27 And the kingdom and dominion, and the greatness of the kingdom under the whole heaven, shall be given to the people of the saints of the most High, whose kingdom *is* an everlasting kingdom, and all dominions shall serve and obey him.

28 Hitherto *is* the end of the matter. As for me Daniel, my cogitations much troubled me, and my countenance changed in me: but I kept the matter in my heart.

CHAPTER 8
The Vision of the Ram and the Goat

1 In the third year of the reign of king Belshazzar a vision appeared unto me, *even unto* me Daniel, after that which appeared unto me at the first.

2 And I saw in a vision; and it came to pass, when I saw, that I *was* at Shushan *in* the palace, which *is* in the province of Elam; and I saw in a vision, and I was by the river of Ulai.

3 Then I lifted up mine eyes, and saw, and, behold, there stood before the river a ram which had *two* horns: and the *two* horns *were* high; but one *was* higher than the other, and the higher came up last.

4 I saw the ram pushing westward, and northward, and southward; so that no beasts might stand before him, neither *was there any* that could deliver out of his hand; but he did according to his will, and became great.

5 And as I was considering, behold, an he goat came from the west on the face of the

23 Dan. 2:40
24 Dan. 7:7, 8, 20; Rev. 17:12
25 Isa. 37:23; Dan. 2:21; 8:24, 25; 11:28, 30, 31, 36; 12:7; Rev. 12:14; 13:5, 6, 7; 17:6; 18:24
26 Dan. 7:10, 22
27 Isa. 60:12; Dan. 2:44; 7:14, 18, 22; Luke 1:33; John 12:34; Rev. 11:15
28 Dan. 7:15; 8:27; 10:8, 16; Luke 2:19, 51
1 Dan. 7:1
2 Esth. 1:2
4 Dan. 5:19; 11:3, 16
5 Dan. 8:21

7:23–25 The career of the Antichrist is described involving blasphemous words against God ("the most High") and an intense persecution of the Tribulation saints. The reference to "a time and times and the dividing of time" corresponds to the three and one-half years or forty-two months of the Great Tribulation, the latter half of the seven-year Tribulation period (see Rev. 12:14; 13:5).

7:26–28 Hitherto is the end of the matter. This portion of Daniel's prophecy concludes with the prediction that the Antichrist and the ten-nation confederacy will be defeated when Jesus returns to establish his Millennial Kingdom on earth. Ultimately, the greatness of this kingdom will be everlasting as the Millennial Kingdom is merged with the eternal kingdom of God (see 1 Cor. 15:24).

8:1–2 a vision appeared unto me. This vision, given to Daniel just prior to the fall of the Babylonian Empire is difficult to understand because it primarily focuses on "the time of the end," yet it mentions both the Medo-Persian and the Greek empires—empires no longer in existence. After writing in Aramaic from 2:4—7:28, Daniel returns to writing in Hebrew and continues to do so for the remainder of the book.

8:3 The "ram which had two horns" represents Media-Persia (8:20) and predicts the two-nation empire that replaced Babylon.

8:5–9, 14, 22 The male "goat" from the west refers to Greece, which conquered the Persian empire and is symbolized by the "notable horn." With lightning speed, Alexander the Great conquered the then-known world by the time he was thirty-two years old. Upon his death, the empire was divided among his four generals: Antigonus, Ptolemy, Lysimachus, and Cassander. The Syrian region of the Greek or Hellenistic empire was given control over the land of Israel ("the pleasant land"). Out of this region of the empire later arose the reign of Antiochus, symbolized in this chapter as the "little horn." Antiochus, who assumed the name "Epiphanes" or "glorious one," became a type of the Antichrist by instigating a wave of anti-Semitism that resulted in the desecration of the temple and the slaughter of thousands of Jews during a six-year period (2300 days, v. 14) from 171–165 B.C. The prediction of cleansing in verse 14 was fulfilled when Judas Maccabeus and the Jewish zealots defeated the Greeks (165 B.C.) and cleansed the temple in an elaborate ceremony of dedication known today as Hanukkah.

The accuracy of this prophecy as fulfilled in history has caused many critics to suggest that a "latter Daniel" wrote the book of Daniel because the original Daniel was dead long before the Greeks rose to prominence. However, no such evidence can be found to support this notion, and the discovery of the book of Daniel among the Dead Sea Scrolls has provided ample evidence that the book is of ancient origin and consequently, is prophetic Scripture.

whole earth, and touched not the ground: and the goat *had* a notable horn between his eyes.

6 And he came to the ram that had *two* horns, which I had seen standing before the river, and ran unto him in the fury of his power.

7 And I saw him come close unto the ram, and he was moved with choler against him, and smote the ram, and brake his two horns: and there was no power in the ram to stand before him, but he cast him down to the ground, and stamped upon him: and there was none that could deliver the ram out of his hand.

8 Therefore the he goat waxed very great: and when he was strong, the great horn was broken; and for it came up four notable ones toward the four winds of heaven.

9 And out of one of them came forth a little horn, which waxed exceeding great, toward the south, and toward the east, and toward the pleasant *land*.

10 And it waxed great, *even* to the host of heaven; and it cast down *some* of the host and of the stars to the ground, and stamped upon them.

11 Yea, he magnified *himself* even to the prince of the host, and by him the daily *sacrifice* was taken away, and the place of his sanctuary was cast down.

12 And an host was given *him* against the daily *sacrifice* by reason of transgression, and it cast down the truth to the ground; and it practised, and prospered.

13 Then I heard one saint speaking, and another saint said unto that certain *saint* which spake, How long *shall be* the vision *concerning* the daily *sacrifice*, and the transgression of desolation, to give both the sanctuary and the host to be trodden under foot?

14 And he said unto me, Unto two thousand and three hundred days; then shall the sanctuary be cleansed.

Cross references:
8 Dan. 7:6; 8:22; 11:4
9 Ps. 48:2; Ezek. 20:6, 15
10 Isa. 14:13; Dan. 11:28; Rev. 12:4
11 Jer. 48:26, 42; Ezek. 46:13; Dan. 8:25; 11:31, 36; 12:11
12 Dan. 8:4; 11:23, 31, 36
13 Dan. 4:13; 11:31; 12:6, 11; 1Pet. 1:12
15 Ezek. 1:26; Dan. 12:8; 1Pet. 1:10, 11
16 Dan. 9:21; 12:6, 7; Luke 1:19, 26
17 Ezek. 1:28; Rev. 1:17
18 Ezek. 2:2; Dan. 10:9, 10; Luke 9:32
19 Dan. 9:27; 11:27, 35, 36; 12:7; Hab. 2:3
20 Dan. 8:3
21 Dan. 8:5; 11:3
22 Dan. 8:8; 11:4
24 Dan. 11:36; Rev. 17:13, 17
25 Dan. 2:34, 45; 8:11; 11:21, 23, 24, 36

15 And it came to pass, when I, *even* I Daniel, had seen the vision, and sought for the meaning, then, behold, there stood before me as the appearance of a man.

Gabriel Is God's Messenger

16 And I heard a man's voice between *the banks of* Ulai, which called, and said, Gabriel, make this *man* to understand the vision.

17 So he came near where I stood: and when he came, I was afraid, and fell upon my face: but he said unto me, Understand, O son of man: for at the time of the end *shall be* the vision.

18 Now as he was speaking with me, I was in a deep sleep on my face toward the ground: but he touched me, and set me upright.

19 And he said, Behold, I will make thee know what shall be in the last end of the indignation: for at the time appointed the end *shall be*.

20 The ram which thou sawest having *two* horns *are* the kings of Media and Persia.

21 And the rough goat *is* the king of Grecia: and the great horn that *is* between his eyes *is* the first king.

22 Now that being broken, whereas four stood up for it, four kingdoms shall stand up out of the nation, but not in his power.

23 And in the latter time of their kingdom, when the transgressors are come to the full, a king of fierce countenance, and understanding dark sentences, shall stand up.

24 And his power shall be mighty, but not by his own power: and he shall destroy wonderfully, and shall prosper, and practise, and shall destroy the mighty and the holy people.

25 And through his policy also he shall cause craft to prosper in his hand; and he shall magnify *himself* in his heart, and by peace shall destroy many: he shall also

---

8:11–19 Biblical prophecy scholars are divided over whether this vision of Daniel focuses on Antiochus Epiphanes, or the "man of sin" described in the New Testament as the Antichrist—or both. It would seem that both men are in view since Antiochus is the prototype of the Antichrist who is yet to come. Gabriel (mentioned by name for the first time in Scripture) explicitly said that the vision refers to the "time of the end," and that he was making known to him "what shall be in the last end of the indignation" (v. 19). In the meantime, Gabriel identifies the "ram" as Media-Persia (v. 20) and the "goat" as Greece (v. 21) in the coming military confrontation for control of the Near East.

8:23–26 king of fierce countenance. These verses look ahead to the rise of the Antichrist "when the transgressors" have reached their "fullness." The fact that the Antichrist rules by a power "not . . . his own" indicates that he will be Satan-incarnate and have satanic supernatural wisdom and powers ascribed to him (Rev. 13). He will even dare to rise against the "Prince of Princes"— Jesus Christ. But God Almighty will soundly defeat the Antichrist and the satanic forces that power him (see Rev. 19:11–16, 18–21, 20:10).

stand up against the Prince of princes; but he shall be broken without hand.

26 And the vision of the evening and the morning which was told *is* true: wherefore shut thou up the vision; for it *shall be* for many days.

27 And I Daniel fainted, and was sick *certain* days; afterward I rose up, and did the king's business; and I was astonished at the vision, but none understood *it*.

CHAPTER 9
Daniel Prays for His People

1 In the first year of Darius the son of Ahasuerus, of the seed of the Medes, which was made king over the realm of the Chaldeans;

2 In the first year of his reign I Daniel un-

26	Ezek. 12:27; Dan. 10:1, 14; 12:4, 9; Rev. 22:10
27	Dan. 6:2, 3; 7:28; 8:16; 10:8, 16
1	Dan. 1:21; 5:31; 6:28
2	2Chr. 36:21; Jer. 25:11, 12; 29:10
3	Neh. 1:4; Jer. 29:12, 13; Dan. 6:10; James 4:8-10

derstood by books the number of the years, whereof the word of the LORD came to Jeremiah the prophet, that he would accomplish seventy years in the desolations of Jerusalem.

3 And I set my face unto the Lord God, to seek by prayer and supplications, with fasting, and sackcloth, and ashes:

4 And I prayed unto the LORD my God, and made my confession, and said, O Lord, the great and dreadful God, keeping the covenant and mercy to them that love him, and to them that keep his commandments;

5 We have sinned, and have committed iniquity, and have done wickedly, and have rebelled, even by departing from thy precepts and from thy judgments:

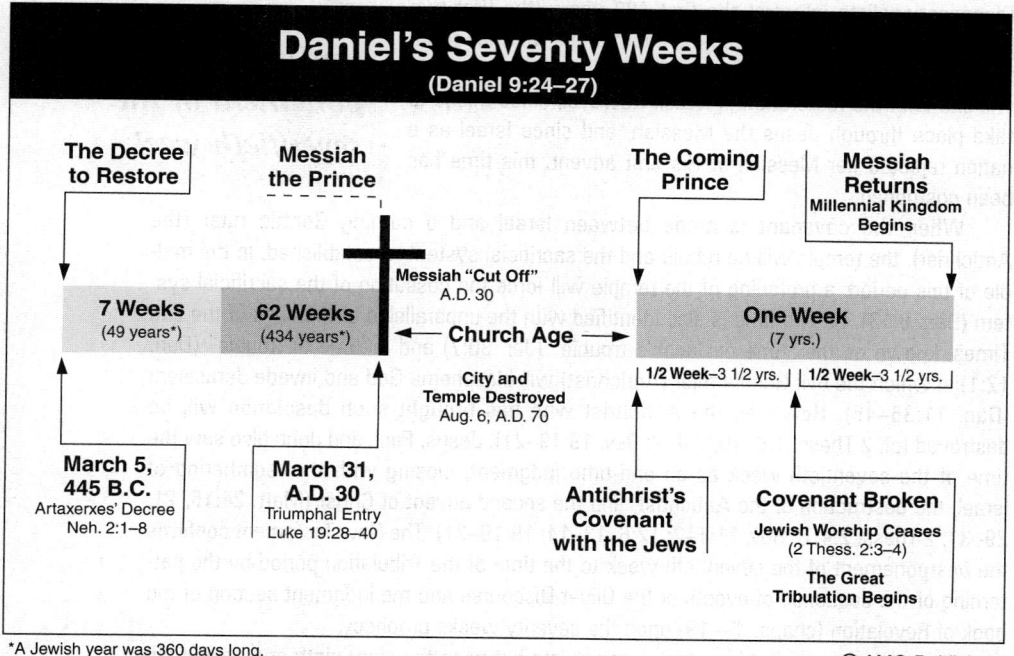

Daniel's Seventy Weeks
(Daniel 9:24–27)

The Decree to Restore — **Messiah the Prince** — **The Coming Prince** — **Messiah Returns** — Millennial Kingdom Begins

Messiah "Cut Off" A.D. 30

7 Weeks (49 years*) — **62 Weeks** (434 years*) — ◄— **Church Age** —► — **One Week** (7 yrs.)

City and Temple Destroyed Aug. 6, A.D. 70

1/2 Week–3 1/2 yrs. | 1/2 Week–3 1/2 yrs.

March 5, 445 B.C. Artaxerxes' Decree Neh. 2:1–8

March 31, A.D. 30 Triumphal Entry Luke 19:28–40

Antichrist's Covenant with the Jews

Covenant Broken Jewish Worship Ceases (2 Thess. 2:3–4)

The Great Tribulation Begins

*A Jewish year was 360 days long.

© AMG Publishers

8:26, 27 The angel Gabriel's message made Daniel sick. Daniel was apparently overwhelmed by the events foretold in the visions he witnessed. The emotional drain that Daniel suffered may also suggest that the prophets did not always fully understand the things that they recorded. The admonition for Daniel to "shut . . . up the vision" indicates that the prophecies would be fulfilled long after Daniel's time. Daniel's faintheartedness also confirms that he knew how tragic the prophetic events would be for his people, the Jews.

9:1–2 seventy years in the desolations of Jerusalem. Chapter 9 begins with Daniel's realization that the seventy years of the Babylonian captivity, predicted in Jeremiah 25:11–12, were coming to an end. The fact that he understood this "by books" points out the importance of studying the prophetic passages of Scripture.

9:3–19 This prayer of Daniel's is the longest prayer in the Old Testament and was used as a model for other prayers in the Bible (cf. Neh. 1:4–11). It is based on promises he had found in Scripture (Jer. 29:10–11).

Daniel's Seventy Weeks

By Randall Price

Daniel's prophecy of the seventy weeks (Dan. 9:24–27) is in the portion of his book (chaps. 7—12) that reveals God's divine program for the kingdoms of this world. Finding that Jeremiah had prophesied that Israel's exile would last for seventy years (Jer. 25:11–12; 29:10), Daniel interceded for Israel in order to realize the fulfillment of the prophecy with the restoration of Jerusalem and the temple (Dan. 9:3–19). The archangel Gabriel was sent to explain to Daniel the "seventy weeks" of years (a total of 490 years), the time necessary to compensate for Israel's violation of her sabbatical law (2 Chr. 36:21).

According to verses 25–27, this period is divided into three periods consisting of seven weeks (49 years), sixty-two weeks (434 years), and one week (7 years). The time would not be completed until six restoration goals were realized (Dan. 9:24), including a time of tribulation for Israel (Dan. 12:1, cf. Matt. 24:21) and the end of the Gentile world domination (Dan. 12:1 [cf. 9:27; Matt. 24:31; Luke 21:24, 28]). Dispensationalists interpret the first 483 years (the first two periods) as being fulfilled before the death of the Messiah (Dan. 9:26). The remaining week of seven years, the seventieth week, will end with the restoration of Israel. However, since this is to take place through Jesus the Messiah, and since Israel as a nation rejected her Messiah at His first advent, this time has been postponed.

> *The New Testament confirms the postponement of the seventieth week.*

When the covenant is made between Israel and a coming Gentile ruler (the Antichrist), the temple will be rebuilt and the sacrificial system re-established. In the middle of this period, a profaning of the temple will force the cessation of the sacrificial system (Dan. 8:13). Such a time is also identified with the unparalleled birth pangs of the End Times, known as the "time of Jacob's trouble" (Jer. 30:7) and a "time of trouble" (Dan. 12:1) in which the evil Gentile ruler (Antichrist) will blaspheme God and invade Jerusalem (Dan. 11:36–45). However, the Antichrist who has brought such desolation will be destroyed (cf. 2 Thess. 1:6–10; 2:4–9; Rev. 19:19–21). Jesus, Paul, and John also saw the time of the seventieth week as an end-time judgment, closing with the regathering of Israel, the destruction of the Antichrist, and the second advent of Christ (Matt. 24:15, 21, 29–31; 2 Thess. 2:4, 8; Rev. 11:1–2; 12:6, 13–14; 19:19–21). The New Testament confirms the postponement of the seventieth week to the time of the Tribulation period by the patterning of the sequence of events of the Olivet Discourse and the judgment section of the book of Revelation (chaps. 4—19) upon the seventy weeks prophecy.

There are those who deny that a gap exists between the sixty-ninth and seventieth weeks. They wrongly assert that such a long prophetic postponement would be inconsistent with other passages of predictive Scripture. However, prophetic delays are really not uncommon at all. For instance, in some passages, both advents of Christ are mentioned practically in the same breath, yet we know that an indeterminate period of time exists between them (e.g., Gen. 49:10–12; 2 Sam. 7:13–16; Ps. 2:7–8 [cf. Acts 13:33; Heb. 1:5; 5:5]; 22:1–31; 34:14, 16; Isa. 9:1–7; 11:1–2, 11; 52:13—59:21; 61:1–11 [cf. Luke 4:16–19; 7:22]; Joel 2:28, cf. Acts 2:17; Mic. 5:2–15; Zeph. 2:13—3:20; Zech. 9:9–10; Mal. 3:1–3; 4:5–6).

6 Neither have we hearkened unto thy servants the prophets, which spake in thy name to our kings, our princes, and our fathers, and to all the people of the land.

7 O Lord, righteousness *belongeth* unto thee, but unto us confusion of faces, as at this day; to the men of Judah, and to the inhabitants of Jerusalem, and unto all Israel, *that are* near, and *that are* far off, through all the countries whither thou hast driven them, because of their trespass that they have trespassed against thee.

8 O Lord, to us *belongeth* confusion of face, to our kings, to our princes, and to our fathers, because we have sinned against thee.

9 To the Lord our God *belong* mercies and forgivenesses, though we have rebelled against him;

10 Neither have we obeyed the voice of the Lord our God, to walk in his laws, which he set before us by his servants the prophets.

11 Yea, all Israel have transgressed thy law, even by departing, that they might not obey thy voice; therefore the curse is poured upon us, and the oath that *is* written in the law of Moses the servant of God, because we have sinned against him.

12 And he hath confirmed his words, which he spake against us, and against our judges that judged us, by bringing upon us a great evil: for under the whole heaven hath not been done as hath been done upon Jerusalem.

13 As *it is* written in the law of Moses, all this evil is come upon us: yet made we not our prayer before the Lord our God, that we might turn from our iniquities, and understand thy truth.

14 Therefore hath the Lord watched upon the evil, and brought it upon us: for the Lord our God *is* righteous in all his works which he doeth: for we obeyed not his voice.

15 And now, O Lord our God, that hast brought thy people forth out of the land of Egypt with a mighty hand, and hast gotten

thee renown, as at this day; we have sinned, we have done wickedly.

16 O Lord, according to all thy righteousness, I beseech thee, let thine anger and thy fury be turned away from thy city Jerusalem, thy holy mountain: because for our sins, and for the iniquities of our fathers, Jerusalem and thy people *are become* a reproach to all *that are* about us.

17 Now therefore, O our God, hear the prayer of thy servant, and his supplications, and cause thy face to shine upon thy sanctuary that is desolate, for the Lord's sake.

18 O my God, incline thine ear, and hear; open thine eyes, and behold our desolations, and the city which is called by thy name: for we do not present our supplications before thee for our righteousnesses, but for thy great mercies.

19 O Lord, hear; O Lord, forgive; O Lord, hearken and do; defer not, for thine own sake, O my God: for thy city and thy people are called by thy name.

The Seventy Weeks

20 And whiles I *was* speaking, and praying, and confessing my sin and the sin of my people Israel, and presenting my supplication before the Lord my God for the holy mountain of my God;

21 Yea, whiles I *was* speaking in prayer, even the man Gabriel, whom I had seen in the vision at the beginning, being caused to fly swiftly, touched me about the time of the evening oblation.

22 And he informed *me*, and talked with me, and said, O Daniel, I am now come forth to give thee skill and understanding.

23 At the beginning of thy supplications the commandment came forth, and I am come to shew *thee*; for thou *art* greatly beloved: therefore understand the matter, and consider the vision.

24 Seventy weeks are determined upon thy people and upon thy holy city, to finish the

Cross References

6 2Chr. 36:15, 16; Dan. 9:10
7 Neh. 9:33
11 Lev. 26:14-46; Deut. 27:15-26; 28:15-68; Isa. 1:4-6; Jer. 8:5, 10; Lam. 2:17
12 Lam. 1:12; 2:13; Ezek. 5:9; Amos 3:2; Zech. 1:6
13 Lev. 26:14-46; Deut. 28:15; Isa. 9:13; Jer. 2:30; 5:3; Lam. 2:17; Hos. 7:7, 10
14 Neh. 9:33; Jer. 31:28; 44:27; Dan. 9:7, 10
15 Ex. 6:1, 6; 14:18; 32:11; 1Kgs. 8:51; Neh. 1:10; 9:10; Jer. 32:20, 21; Dan. 9:5
16 Ex. 20:5; 1Sam. 12:7; Ps. 31:1; 44:13, 14; 71:2; 79:4; Lam. 2:15, 16; Dan. 9:20; Mic. 6:4, 5; Zech. 8:3
17 Num. 6:25; Ps. 67:1; 80:3, 7, 19
18 Ps. 80:14-19
24 Isa. 53:10, 11; Jer. 23:5, 6; Ezek. 4:6; Rev. 14:6

9:24 Seventy weeks. The prophecy of the "seventy weeks" is the major biblical prophecy about future events related to the nation of Israel—from the decree to rebuild the walls of Jerusalem to the first and second comings of the Messiah. Each "week" (Hebr., *shavuah*) is a unit of seven years, thus the seventy "sevens" constitute a total of 490 years. Six things are predicted regarding the Jews that will occur during these 490 years: 1) Their "transgression" will be finished; 2) their "sins" will end; 3) "reconciliation for iniquity" will be made; 4) "everlasting righteousness" will become a reality; 5) prophecy will be sealed up; and 6) the "most Holy" will be anointed. These six things will not be completely fulfilled until the entire 490 years transpire. Some biblical scholars suggest that the first sixty-nine "weeks" (483 years) began with the decree that was issued to Nehemiah to rebuild Jerusalem in 445–444 B.C. and ended during the week of Jesus' crucifixion. A gap apparently exists in this prophecy between the sixty-ninth and seventieth weeks. Many prophecy scholars believe that this gap corresponds with the Church Age; therefore, as long as the Church Age continues, the "seventieth week of Daniel" will remain

transgression, and to make an end of sins, and to make reconciliation for iniquity, and to bring in everlasting righteousness, and to seal up the vision and prophecy, and to anoint the most Holy.

25 Know therefore and understand, *that* from the going forth of the commandment to restore and to build Jerusalem unto the Messiah the Prince *shall be* seven weeks, and threescore and two weeks: the street shall

be built again, and the wall, even in troublous times.

26 And after threescore and two weeks shall Messiah be cut off, but not for himself: and the people of the prince that shall come shall destroy the city and the sanctuary; and the end thereof *shall be* with a flood, and unto the end of the war desolations are determined.

27 And he shall confirm the covenant with

25 Ezra 4:24; 6:1, 15; Neh. 2:1, 3, 5, 6, 8; Matt. 24:15

26 Isa. 8:7, 8; 53:8; Luke 19:44; 24:26

27 Matt. 24:15; 26:28

Daniel's Outline of the Future

THE EVENTS THAT WILL OCCUR	REFERENCES
To finish "the transgression"	Matt. 1:21; 1 John 3:8
To make an end of sins	Lam. 4:22; Col. 2:14; Heb. 9:26; 10:14
To make reconciliation for iniquity	Lev. 8:15; 2 Chr. 29:24; Isa. 53:10; Rom. 5:10; 2 Cor. 5:18–20; Col. 1:20; Heb. 2:17
To bring in everlasting righteousness	Isa. 51:6, 8; 53:11; 56:1; Jer. 23:5–6; Rom. 3:21–22; 1 Cor. 1:30; 2 Cor. 5:21; Phil. 3:9; Heb. 9:12–14; 2 Pet. 1:1; Rev. 14:6
To seal up the vision and prophecy	Matt. 11:13; Luke 24:25–27, 44–45; John 19:28–30
To anoint the most Holy	Ps. 2:6; 45:7; Isa. 61:1; Mark 1:24; Luke 1:35; 4:18–21; John 1:41; 3:34; Acts 3:14; Heb. 1:8–9; 7:26; 9:11; Rev. 3:7

All these events point to and are dependent on the death of Messiah to atone for sin and the eventual establishment of His righteous kingdom, when the will of God for man—since God put Adam and Eve in the garden of Eden—will finally be accomplished forever.

future. According to this teaching, after Christ raptures His Church, the clock of God's judgment will count off the final "week" of Daniel. This "seventieth week" of Daniel (v. 27) then is synonymous with the seven-year Tribulation. For more information on this subject, see the article by Randall Price entitled "Daniel's Seventy Weeks."

9:26 shall Messiah be cut off, but not for himself. The end of the period of "threescore and two [62] weeks" or 434 years added to the 7 "weeks" or 49 years that already had transpired during the restoration of Jerusalem total 69 "weeks" or 483 years. This 483-year period concluded when Messiah was "cut off," a clear prophecy of the day that Jesus was crucified. Only a supernatural God could make such an accurate prediction of the crucifixion of Christ.

9:26 the prince that shall come. This phrase does not refer to the Messiah, but is rather a clear reference to a future "prince" or ruler who will come on the scene during Daniel's "seventieth week." This "prince" is referred to in Daniel 8:23 as "the king of fierce countenance"; the apostle Paul calls him "the man of sin" and "the son of perdition" (2 Thess. 2:1–8). John calls him "the Antichrist" (1 John 2:18). Verse 26 also contains a definitive clue for determining the nationality of the Antichrist, for it says he will be of "the people . . . that shall . . . destroy the city and the sanctuary." Many believe the

term, "the people" refers to the Romans, who destroyed the city of Jerusalem in A.D. 70. This observation, along with the fact that the Antichrist will rule the Gentile nations of the Western world, seems to indicate that he is of European descent.

9:27 he shall confirm the covenant with many for one week [seven years]. This important phrase indicates that the event that starts the "seventieth week" (of years) is the signing of a seven-year covenant between "the prince" (Antichrist) of the people who destroyed the city of Jerusalem and the Jews. This event is yet to come. The significance of this seven-year period is seen by the fact that more space is given in Scripture to the Tribulation than any other comparable period of time. It is described by Jesus in the Olivet Discourse (Matt. 24—25), by the apostle Paul in 2 Thessalonians 2:1–12, and by John in Revelation 6—19.

The Antichrist will break his covenant with Israel and desecrate the temple. "In the midst of the week" indicates this will occur at the midpoint of the Tribulation, or after only three and one-half years. Jesus called this event of desecration "the abomination of desolation, spoken of by Daniel the prophet" (Matt. 24:15). At the end of the "seventieth week," "the consummation" will occur; that is, Christ will return in power to rule this world as king (cf. Dan. 2:35, 45).

many for one week: and in the midst of the week he shall cause the sacrifice and the oblation to cease, and for the overspreading of abominations he shall make *it* desolate, even until the consummation, and that determined shall be poured upon the desolate.

CHAPTER 10
Daniel's Terrifying Vision

1   In the third year of Cyrus king of Persia a thing was revealed unto Daniel, whose name was called Belteshazzar; and the thing *was* true, but the time appointed *was* long: and he understood the thing, and had understanding of the vision.

2   In those days I Daniel was mourning three full weeks.

3   I ate no pleasant bread, neither came flesh nor wine in my mouth, neither did I anoint myself at all, till three whole weeks were fulfilled.

4   And in the four and twentieth day of the first month, as I was by the side of the great river, which *is* Hiddekel;

5   Then I lifted up mine eyes, and looked, and behold a certain man clothed in linen, whose loins *were* girded with fine gold of Uphaz:

6   His body also *was* like the beryl, and his face as the appearance of lightning, and his eyes as lamps of fire, and his arms and his feet like in colour to polished brass, and the voice of his words like the voice of a multitude.

7   And I Daniel alone saw the vision: for the men that were with me saw not the vision; but a great quaking fell upon them, so that they fled to hide themselves.

8   Therefore I was left alone, and saw this great vision, and there remained no strength in me: for my comeliness was turned in me into corruption, and I retained no strength.

9   Yet heard I the voice of his words: and when I heard the voice of his words, then was I in a deep sleep on my face, and my face toward the ground.

10   And, behold, an hand touched me, which set me upon my knees and *upon* the palms of my hands.

11   And he said unto me, O Daniel, a man greatly beloved, understand the words that I speak unto thee, and stand upright: for unto thee am I now sent. And when he had spoken this word unto me, I stood trembling.

12   Then said he unto me, Fear not, Daniel: for from the first day that thou didst set thine heart to understand, and to chasten thyself before thy God, thy words were heard, and I am come for thy words.

13   But the prince of the kingdom of Persia withstood me one and twenty days: but, lo, Michael, one of the chief princes, came to help me; and I remained there with the kings of Persia.

14   Now I am come to make thee understand what shall befall thy people in the latter days: for yet the vision *is* for *many* days.

15   And when he had spoken such words unto me, I set my face toward the ground, and I became dumb.

16   And, behold, *one* like the similitude of the sons of men touched my lips: then I opened my mouth, and spake, and said unto him that stood before me, O my lord, by the vision my sorrows are turned upon me, and I have retained no strength.

17   For how can the servant of this my lord talk with this my lord? for as for me, straightway there remained no strength in me, neither is there breath left in me.

18   Then there came again and touched me *one* like the appearance of a man, and he strengthened me,

19   And said, O man greatly beloved, fear

Cross references

1 Dan. 1:7, 17; 8:16, 26; 10:14; Rev. 19:9

3 Matt. 6:17

4 Gen. 2:14

5 Josh. 5:13; Jer. 10:9; Dan. 12:6, 7; Rev. 1:13-15; 15:6

6 Ezek. 1:7, 14, 16, 24; Rev. 1:14, 15; 19:12

7 2Kgs. 6:17; Acts 9:7

8 Dan. 7:28; 8:27

9 Dan. 8:18

10 Jer. 1:9; Dan. 9:21; Rev. 1:17

11 Dan. 9:23

12 Dan. 9:3, 4, 22, 23; Acts 10:4; Rev. 1:17

13 Dan. 10:20, 21; Jude 1:9; Rev. 12:7

14 Gen. 49:1; Dan. 2:28; 8:26; 10:1; Hab. 2:3

15 Dan. 8:18, 10:9

16 Jer. 1:9; Dan. 8:15; Dan. 10:8, 10

19 Judg. 6:23; Dan. 10:11

10:4–6 a certain man. By this time, Daniel was at least eighty-five years old, having lived through the entire seventy years of the Babylonian/Persian captivity. This vision of a "certain man" may have been a glimpse of Christ Himself, since it parallels the description of Jesus in Revelation 1:13–16. If this "certain man" is indeed Jesus Christ, then a glimpse of the Son of God is befitting for this last vision given to Daniel, for it is a most significant prophecy of the End Times (Dan. 10—12).

10:12–21 Daniel's prayers were heard from the first day he uttered them, but the spiritual warfare between Satan's demons and the angelic hosts delayed their

coming. The announcing angel, who came in response to Daniel's earnest prayers for Israel and her future, was probably Gabriel, but he needed the help of Michael the archangel to "fight with the prince of Persia" (v. 20). This suggests the very real possibility that Satan, who is "the prince of the power of the air" (Eph. 2:2) may well have his demons currently indwelling world rulers, attempting to thwart the plans of God for mankind. This scene should alert all believers that we are indeed in a great spiritual conflict in which we need to walk holy before God in order to enjoy His supernatural protection.

not: peace *be* unto thee, be strong, yea, be strong. And when he had spoken unto me, I was strengthened, and said, Let my lord speak; for thou hast strengthened me.

20 Then said he, Knowest thou wherefore I come unto thee? and now will I return to fight with the prince of Persia: and when I am gone forth, lo, the prince of Grecia shall come.

21 But I will shew thee that which is noted in the Scripture of truth: and *there is* none that holdeth with me in these things, but Michael your prince.

CHAPTER 11
The Kingdoms of Egypt and Syria

1 Also I in the first year of Darius the Mede, *even* I, stood to confirm and to strengthen him.

2 And now will I shew thee the truth. Behold, there shall stand up yet three kings in Persia; and the fourth shall be far richer than *they* all: and by his strength through his riches he shall stir up all against the realm of Grecia.

3 And a mighty king shall stand up, that shall rule with great dominion, and do according to his will.

4 And when he shall stand up, his kingdom shall be broken, and shall be divided toward the four winds of heaven; and not to his posterity, nor according to his dominion which he ruled: for his kingdom shall

be plucked up, even for others beside those.

5 And the king of the south shall be strong, and *one* of his princes; and he shall be strong above him, and have dominion; his dominion *shall be* a great dominion.

6 And in the end of years they shall join themselves together; for the king's daughter of the south shall come to the king of the north to make an agreement: but she shall not retain the power of the arm; neither shall he stand, nor his arm: but she shall be given up, and they that brought her, and he that begat her, and he that strengthened her in *these* times.

7 But out of a branch of her roots shall *one* stand up in his estate, which shall come with an army, and shall enter into the fortress of the king of the north, and shall deal against them, and shall prevail:

8 And shall also carry captives into Egypt their gods, with their princes, *and* with their precious vessels of silver and of gold; and he shall continue *more* years than the king of the north.

9 So the king of the south shall come into *his* kingdom, and shall return into his own land.

10 But his sons shall be stirred up, and shall assemble a multitude of great forces: and *one* shall certainly come, and overflow, and pass through: then shall he return, and be stirred up, *even* to his fortress.

Marginal references:
20 Dan. 10:13
21 Dan. 10:13; Jude 1:9; Rev. 12:7
1 Dan. 5:31; 9:1
3 Dan. 7:6; 8:4, 5; 11:16, 36
4 Dan. 8:8, 22
7 Dan. 11:20
10 Isa. 8:8; Dan. 9:26; 11:7

11:1–20 will I show thee the truth. The prophecies that follow so carefully describe the historical details of world events as they relate to Israel that many skeptics have tried to insist they were written after the events transpired. However, Daniel was reassured in advance that these events would be fulfilled just as they were revealed. Verses 1–20 give the prediction of the events of world history from approximately 500–175 B.C. The kings of "the north" and "the south" (v. 5, 13) refer to the succeeding rulers of the Ptolemaic and Seleucid dynasties of the Hellenistic empire. Two generals (Ptolemy I and Seleucus I), who were among the four generals that divided the Hellenistic Empire upon the death of Alexander the Great, founded these two dynasties.

11:2 Three kings in Persia and the fourth . . . shall stir up . . . the realm of Grecia. The "three kings" likely refer to Cambyses (530–522 B.C.), Pseudo–Smerdis (522–521 B.C.), and Darius I (521–486 B.C.). The "fourth" king refers to Xerxes I (486–465 B.C. [also known as Ahasuerus, Ezra 4:6; Esth. 1:1]). Xerxes I angered the Greeks by conquering Athens, which paved the way for Alexander the Great to avenge the Greek nation.

11:3–6 divided toward the four winds. These verses

describe in uncannily accurate detail Alexander the Great's lightning-fast conquest of the world. Alexander conquered the known world by age 32 but died prematurely without designating a successor. The empire was then divided among his four generals. Two of the four generals, Ptolemy and Seleucus, became known respectively as the "king of the south" (Egypt) and "the king of the north" (Syria). These two empires fought each other during the Intertestamental Period (the time from the closing of the Old Testament to the opening of the New Testament). The land of Israel geographically served as a bridge between the two empires and was used as a battleground that was repeatedly attacked from both directions.

11:6–16 These prophecies correspond precisely to the history of the period, describing a series of conflicts between the Seleucid and the Ptolemaic dynasties. The term, "the glorious land" refers to Israel and predicts she will be controlled by the "king of the north" (v. 15). This was fulfilled when Antiochus the Great (a monarch in the Seleucid Dynasty) conquered and overran the land in 199–198 B.C.

11 And the king of the south shall be moved with choler, and shall come forth and fight with him, *even* with the king of the north: and he shall set forth a great multitude; but the multitude shall be given into his hand.

12 *And* when he hath taken away the multitude, his heart shall be lifted up; and he shall cast down *many* ten thousands: but he shall not be strengthened *by it.*

13 For the king of the north shall return, and shall set forth a multitude greater than the former, and shall certainly come after certain years with a great army and with much riches.

14 And in those times there shall many stand up against the king of the south: also the robbers of thy people shall exalt themselves to establish the vision; but they shall fall.

15 So the king of the north shall come, and cast up a mount, and take the most fenced cities: and the arms of the south shall not withstand, neither his chosen people, neither *shall there be any* strength to withstand.

16 But he that cometh against him shall do according to his own will, and none shall stand before him: and he shall stand in the glorious land, which by his hand shall be consumed.

17 He shall also set his face to enter with the strength of his whole kingdom, and upright ones with him; thus shall he do: and he shall give him the daughter of women, corrupting her: but she shall not stand *on his side*, neither be for him.

18 After this shall he turn his face unto the isles, and shall take many: but a prince for his own behalf shall cause the reproach offered by him to cease; without his own reproach he shall cause *it* to turn upon him.

19 Then he shall turn his face toward the fort of his own land: but he shall stumble and fall, and not be found.

20 Then shall stand up in his estate a raiser of taxes *in* the glory of the kingdom: but within few days he shall be destroyed, neither in anger, nor in battle.

21 And in his estate shall stand up a vile person, to whom they shall not give the honour of the kingdom: but he shall come in peaceably, and obtain the kingdom by flatteries.

22 And with the arms of a flood shall they be overflown from before him, and shall be broken; yea, also the prince of the covenant.

23 And after the league *made* with him he shall work deceitfully: for he shall come up, and shall become strong with a small people.

24 He shall enter peaceably even upon the fattest places of the province; and he shall do *that* which his fathers have not done, nor his fathers' fathers; he shall scatter among them the prey, and spoil, and riches: *yea,* and he shall forecast his devices against the strong holds, even for a time.

25 And he shall stir up his power and his courage against the king of the south with a great army; and the king of the south shall be stirred up to battle with a very great and mighty army; but he shall not stand: for they shall forecast devices against him.

26 Yea, they that feed of the portion of his meat shall destroy him, and his army shall overflow: and many shall fall down slain.

27 And both these kings' hearts *shall be* to do mischief, and they shall speak lies at one table; but it shall not prosper: for yet the end *shall be* at the time appointed.

28 Then shall he return into his land with great riches; and his heart *shall be* against the holy covenant; and he shall do *exploits,* and return to his own land.

29 At the time appointed he shall return, and come toward the south; but it shall not be as the former, or as the latter.

30 For the ships of Chittim shall come against him: therefore he shall be grieved, and return, and have indignation against the holy covenant: so shall he do; he shall even return, and have intelligence with them that forsake the holy covenant.

31 And arms shall stand on his part, and they shall pollute the sanctuary of strength, and shall take away the daily *sacrifice,* and they shall place the abomination that maketh desolate.

---

13 Dan. 4:16; 12:7

16 Josh. 1:5; Dan. 8:4, 7, 9; 11:3, 36, 41, 45

17 2Chr. 20:3; Dan. 9:26

19 Job 20:8; Ps. 37:36; Ezek. 26:21

20 Dan. 11:7

21 Dan. 7:8; 8:9, 23, 25

22 Dan. 8:10, 11, 25; 11:10

23 Dan. 8:25

26 Dan. 11:10, 22

27 Dan. 8:19; 11:29, 35, 40

28 Dan. 11:22

29 Dan. 11:23, 25

30 Num. 24:24; Jer. 2:10; Dan. 11:28

31 Dan. 8:11; 12:11

11:21–31 a vile person. In many aspects, these verses refer to Antiochus Epiphanes, one of the most wicked kings of that period. He is the one Daniel says "shall pollute the sanctuary . . . take away the daily sacrifice, and . . . place the abomination that maketh desolate" (v. 31). This is a most enigmatic section, for Jesus referred to this in Matthew 24:15 as yet future. For this reason many prophecy scholars believe this particular prediction bears dual reference. Antiochus indeed fits the description of this prophecy, for he desecrated the temple in his day by sacrificing a pig's blood on the holy altar in 168 B.C. Yet a similar event will transpire during the Tribulation when the Antichrist will desecrate the temple and claim to be God.

32 And such as do wickedly against the covenant shall he corrupt by flatteries: but the people that do know their God shall be strong, and do *exploits*.
33 And they that understand among the people shall instruct many: yet they shall fall by the sword, and by flame, by captivity, and by spoil, *many* days.
34 Now when they shall fall, they shall be holpen with a little help: but many shall cleave to them with flatteries.
35 And *some* of them of understanding shall fall, to try them, and to purge, and to make *them* white, *even* to the time of the end: because *it is* yet for a time appointed.
36 And the king shall do according to his will; and he shall exalt himself, and magnify himself above every god, and shall speak marvellous things against the God of gods, and shall prosper till the indignation be accomplished: for that that is determined shall be done.
37 Neither shall he regard the God of his fathers, nor the desire of women, nor regard any god: for he shall magnify himself above all.
38 But in his estate shall he honour the God of forces: and a god whom his fathers knew not shall he honour with gold, and silver, and with precious stones, and pleasant things.
39 Thus shall he do in the most strong holds with a strange god, whom he shall acknowledge *and* increase with glory: and he shall cause them to rule over many, and shall divide the land for gain.

33 Mal. 2:7; Heb. 11:35-40
35 Dan. 8:17, 19; 11:29, 40; 12:10; 1Pet. 1:7
36 Dan. 7:8, 25; 8:11, 24, 25; 9:27; 11:16; 2Thess. 2:4; Rev. 13:5, 6
37 Isa. 14:13; 2Thess. 2:4; 1Tim. 4:3
38 Isa. 44:9
40 Isa. 21:1; Ezek. 38:4, 15; Dan. 11:10, 22, 35; Zech. 9:14; Rev. 9:16
41 Isa. 11:14; Dan. 11:16
43 Ex. 11:8; Judg. 4:10
45 Ps. 48:2; Dan. 11:16, 41; 2Thess. 2:4, 8; Rev. 19:20
1 Ex. 32:32; Ps. 56:8; 69:28; Isa. 26:20, 21; Jer. 30:7; Ezek. 13:9; Dan. 10:13, 21; Matt. 24:21

40 And at the time of the end shall the king of the south push at him: and the king of the north shall come against him like a whirlwind, with chariots, and with horsemen, and with many ships; and he shall enter into the countries, and shall overflow and pass over.
41 He shall enter also into the glorious land, and many *countries* shall be overthrown: but these shall escape out of his hand, *even* Edom, and Moab, and the chief of the children of Ammon.
42 He shall stretch forth his hand also upon the countries: and the land of Egypt shall not escape.
43 But he shall have power over the treasures of gold and of silver, and over all the precious things of Egypt: and the Libyans and the Ethiopians *shall be* at his steps.
44 But tidings out of the east and out of the north shall trouble him: therefore he shall go forth with great fury to destroy, and utterly to make away many.
45 And he shall plant the tabernacles of his palace between the seas in the glorious holy mountain; yet he shall come to his end, and none shall help him.

CHAPTER 12
The Time of the End

1 And at that time shall Michael stand up, the great prince which standeth for the children of thy people: and there shall be a time of trouble, such as never was since there was a nation *even* to that same time: and at that time thy people shall be delivered,

11:36 At this point, the prophecy seems to go beyond Antiochus Epiphanes, the prototype, to refer to the Antichrist himself as the "willful king" described in this passage. Verse 40 indicates this person is neither the "king of the north" (Syria), nor the "king of the south" (Egypt), suggesting that the last ten verses of chapter 11 is yet future, particularly what Jesus described as "the abomination of desolation" (Matt. 24:15 [cf. 2 Thess. 2:3–8; Rev. 13]). The fact that the "willful king" is defeated in Israel (v. 45) also indicates this is the Antichrist, since Antiochus Epiphanes died in Persia. If the Antichrist is in view in verses 36–45, he is then the king who will "exalt himself, and magnify himself above every god [until] the indignation [or time of God's wrath, i.e., the Tribulation period] be accomplished" (v. 35).

11:37–38 nor the desire of women. This phrase has been taken by some to suggest that the Antichrist will be a homosexual. However, it only means that he will be unmarried. Some believe the phrase "desire of women"

means that he will have no regard for what most Jewish women yearn—to be the mother of the Messiah. The main point of this verse is that the Antichrist will have no respect for Judeo-Christian beliefs or practices and will totally disregard the God of the Bible.

11:40 at the time of the end. In the Tribulation, the kings of the North and South have broader significance and refer to the alliances of nations that will gather in "the glorious land" (v. 41) for the final battle of all time—the Battle of Armageddon, which Antichrist will lose at the second coming of Jesus Christ (see Rev. 19:11–21).

12:1–4 This passage is the clearest Old Testament reference to the resurrection of the dead. The setting is the Great Tribulation or "time of trouble." Here two different resurrections are discussed—one for dead believers, and one for the unbelieving dead. Compare these verses with the teaching of Jesus on the end-time resurrections in John 5:28–29 and that of John in Revelation 19—22.

The Signs of the Times

By David R. Reagan

The prophet Daniel was told by the Lord that many of the Bible's end-time prophecies would remain mysterious in their meaning until the time came for them to be understood (Dan. 12:8–9). An indication that we are now living in the final days before the Lord's return is to be found in the fact that we are understanding prophecies that have never been understood before. Our understanding is based upon two factors: historical developments and technological innovations.

An example of an historical development is the re-establishment of the nation of Israel on May 14, 1948. The Bible is full of prophecies that the Jews will be regathered to their land in the End Times, right before the return of the Messiah (Isa. 11:10–12). For almost 2,000 years, the Jews were dispersed all over the world, with seemingly no hope of ever existing again as a nation. Because of this dispersion, the prophecies concerning the end-time existence of Israel were not understandable. The same was true of the prophecies (Zech. 12:1–6; Luke 21:24) regarding the Jewish reoccupation of Jerusalem which occurred on June 7, 1967.

> *We are understanding prophecies that have never been understood before.*

The book of Revelation contains several examples of prophecies that have never been understood until recently:

1. The Magnitude of the Tribulation Slaughter—Revelation 6—9 says that one-half the population of the world will die during the initial Tribulation judgments (1/4 in the seal judgments and 1/3 of those remaining in the trumpet judgments). Such carnage has never been possible through natural means until the development of nuclear weapons (1945) and intercontinental ballistic missiles (in the '60s).

2. The Asian Army of 200 Million—Revelation says an army of 200 million will march across Asia toward Israel during the Tribulation (Rev. 9:13–16; 16:12). At the time the book of Revelation was written, the total population of the world was only 200 million. It took until A.D. 1650 for the world's population to double in size, reaching 400 million. Unprecedented population growth took place during the twentieth century because of the development of modern medicine. For example, the first antibiotic, penicillin, was not developed until 1927.

3. The Two Witnesses in Jerusalem—In Revelation 11, we are told that two witnesses of God will serve during the Tribulation as prophets calling, the world to repentance. The Antichrist will kill them in the middle of the Tribulation, and their bodies will lie in the streets of Jerusalem for three and one-half days while the whole world looks upon them.

4. The Image of the Antichrist—Revelation 13 tells us that the False Prophet will make an image of the Antichrist and then will appear to give it life. Since Satan cannot give life, this will have to be a deception.

5. The Mark of the Beast—Revelation 13 also says that the Antichrist will control all buying and selling worldwide through a mark on the right hand or forehead of each person. Such control was never a possibility before the invention of laser and computer technology.

These are only a few examples of prophecies that we now understand for the first time, clearly indicating that we are living in the season of the Lord's return.

every one that shall be found written in the book.

2 And many of them that sleep in the dust of the earth shall awake, some to everlasting life, and some to shame *and* everlasting contempt.

3 And they that be wise shall shine as the brightness of the firmament; and they that turn many to righteousness as the stars for ever and ever.

4 But thou, O Daniel, shut up the words, and seal the book, *even* to the time of the end: many shall run to and fro, and knowledge shall be increased.

5 Then I Daniel looked, and, behold, there stood other two, the one on this side of the bank of the river, and the other on that side of the bank of the river.

2 Isa. 66:24; Matt. 25:46; John 5:28, 29; Acts 24:15; Rom. 9:21

3 Prov. 4:18; Dan. 11:33, 35; Matt. 13:43; 1Cor. 15:41, 42; James 5:20

4 Dan. 8:26; 10:1; 12:9; Rev. 10:4; 22:10

6 Dan. 8:13; 10:5

7 Luke 21:24; Rev. 10:5, 6, 7; 12:14

6 And *one* said to the man clothed in linen, which *was* upon the waters of the river, How long *shall it be to* the end of these wonders?

7 And I heard the man clothed in linen, which *was* upon the waters of the river, when he held up his right hand and his left hand unto heaven, and sware by him that liveth for ever that *it shall be* for a time, times, and an half; and when he shall have accomplished to scatter the power of the holy people, all these *things* shall be finished.

8 And I heard, but I understood not: then said I, O my Lord, what *shall be* the end of these *things*?

9 And he said, Go thy way, Daniel: for the words *are* closed up and sealed till the time of the end.

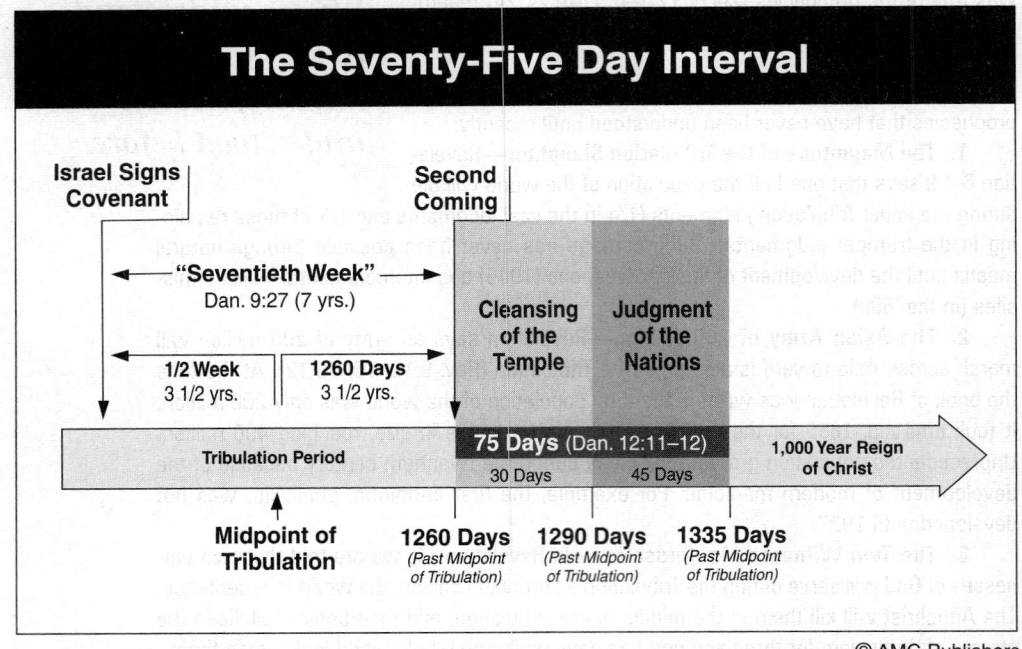

The Seventy-Five Day Interval

Israel Signs Covenant

Second Coming

◄──── "Seventieth Week" ────►
Dan. 9:27 (7 yrs.)

1/2 Week
3 1/2 yrs.

1260 Days
3 1/2 yrs.

Cleansing of the Temple

Judgment of the Nations

Tribulation Period

75 Days (Dan. 12:11–12)
30 Days   45 Days

1,000 Year Reign of Christ

Midpoint of Tribulation

1260 Days
(Past Midpoint of Tribulation)

1290 Days
(Past Midpoint of Tribulation)

1335 Days
(Past Midpoint of Tribulation)

© AMG Publishers

12:4 many shall run to and fro, and knowledge shall be increased. Some interpret this verse to mean that travel and intellectual knowledge will be immeasurably increased among mankind during the latter days. Others suggest that the verse refers to an increase in the study of prophecy, signified by eyes running "to and fro" or racing through the prophetic Scriptures, therefore increasing overall knowledge of prophetic events. In a vital sense, both interpretations are representative of the approach of the Last Days as the stage is set for the Rapture, the

Tribulation, the glorious appearance of Christ, and the Millennial Kingdom.

12:6–7 How long . . . to the end? This question and its corresponding answer by "the man clothed in linen" refer to the final three and one-half years of the Tribulation. This coincides with the three and one-half years after the desecration of the temple and scattering of Israel during the middle of the Tribulation (Rev. 12:13–17).

12:9 Daniel was told to "seal the book" (v. 4) until "the time of the end" (v. 9). The sealing of the scroll indicates

10 Many shall be purified, and made white, and tried; but the wicked shall do wickedly: and none of the wicked shall understand; but the wise shall understand.

11 And from the time *that* the daily *sacrifice* shall be taken away, and the abomination that maketh desolate set up, *there shall be*

10 Hos. 14:9; John 7:17; Rev. 9:20; 22:11

11 Dan. 8:11; 11:31

13 Rev. 14:13

a thousand two hundred and ninety days.

12 Blessed *is* he that waiteth, and cometh to the thousand three hundred and five and thirty days.

13 But go thou thy way till the end *be*: for thou shalt rest, and stand in thy lot at the end of the days.

---

the words of the prophecy were complete and should remain unaltered until the time of their fulfillment. By contrast, John was told not to seal the scroll of the Revelation (Rev. 22:10), indicating that human understanding of Christ's second coming would be more clear after His first coming had occurred. The key to understanding Daniel's prophecies is found in Revelation 6—20, chapters that essentially detail Daniel's "seventieth week" of years, better known as the Tribulation.

12:11–12 In these verses, the extra days added to the established 1,260 days for the Tribulation probably include thirty days for the Judgment of the nations (Matt.

25:31–46) and a forty-five-day restoration period, when God renovates the entire world in preparation for the millennial reign of Christ (see Isa. 65:17–21; 2 Pet. 3:10–13).

12:13 The book of Daniel ends on a note of great promise that is often overlooked. Daniel, who had lived almost his entire life in Babylon, is promised that he will receive his "lot." This refers to that portion of the promised land allocated to Daniel's family. This final verse also states that Daniel, like all Old Testament believers, will be resurrected at the "end of the days" to personally participate in the kingdom of Christ on earth.

Hosea

Hosea is the first of the books the Jews call "The Twelve," which are otherwise referred to as the Minor Prophets. Judging by the time period of the kings during whose reigns he prophesied (Hos. 1:1), Hosea's ministry extended from about 770–725 B.C. The name Hosea means "salvation," and his prophecy was directed to the Kingdom of Israel (Northern Kingdom) in the days of Jeroboam (782–753 B.C.) and during the reigns of Uzziah, Jothan, Ahaz, and Hezekiah, whose times spanned the entire 8th century B.C. Both Amos and Isaiah were contemporaries of Hosea.

After Israel divided, the Northern Kingdom sank into pagan religion and idolatry until 722 B.C., when they were overrun by Assyria. Continually warning the people to repent of their "backslidings," Hosea reminded them of God's undying love. Hosea was specifically called by God to exemplify the relationship between God and Israel through his marriage to a prostitute (Gomer). With his own marriage and family as a tragic illustration, Hosea weaves the theme of God's love for His chosen people, depicted as the Lord's adulterous wife who is put away temporarily, but eventually cleansed and restored. Closing the book of prophecy with a note of hope and reconciliation after punishment, God's own promise shines forth: "I will heal their backsliding. I will love them freely: for mine anger is turned away from them" (14:4).

Author	Hosea
Date	8th Century B.C.
Key Truth	Redemptive Love
Historic Time	Reign of Jeroboam II
Key Verse	13:9–10 O Israel . . . in me is thine help. . . .

Of special interest is chapter 3, which sets forth Israel's past, present, and future. Illustrating Israel's idolatrous past is Gomer's unfaithfulness to Hosea, who buys her back out of her enslavement to prostitution. Israel's long history and present era is prophesied and illustrated in verses 3–4. In the future Millennial Kingdom age, all Israel will return, seeking the Lord and turning to David whose descendent is Jesus the King (3:5).

No less than 28 specific predictions involve 111 out of the book's 197 verses, or 56 percent.

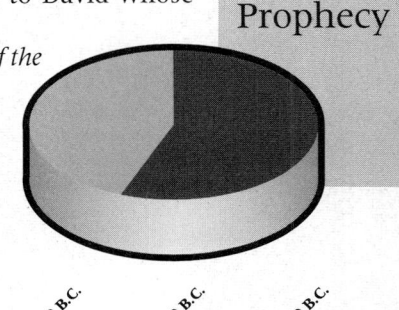

56%
Prophecy

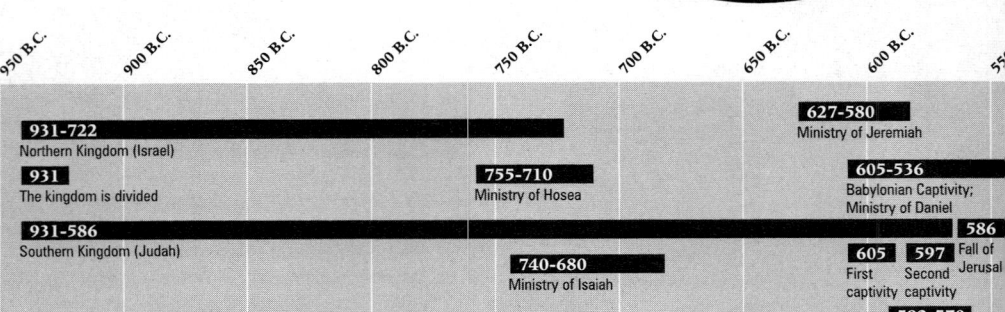

950 B.C.	900 B.C.	850 B.C.	800 B.C.	750 B.C.	700 B.C.	650 B.C.	600 B.C.	55

931–722
Northern Kingdom (Israel)

931
The kingdom is divided

931–586
Southern Kingdom (Judah)

755–710
Ministry of Hosea

740–680
Ministry of Isaiah

627–580
Ministry of Jeremiah

605–536
Babylonian Captivity;
Ministry of Daniel

586
Fall of Jerusal

605 First captivity   **597** Second captivity

592–570
Ministry of Ezekiel

CHAPTER 1
Hosea Marries

1 The word of the LORD that came unto Hosea, the son of Beeri, in the days of Uzziah, Jotham, Ahaz, *and* Hezekiah, kings of Judah, and in the days of Jeroboam the son of Joash, king of Israel.

2 The beginning of the word of the LORD by Hosea. And the LORD said to Hosea, Go, take unto thee a wife of whoredoms and children of whoredoms: for the land hath committed great whoredom, *departing* from the LORD.

3 So he went and took Gomer the daughter of Diblaim; which conceived, and bare him a son.

4 And the LORD said unto him, Call his name Jezreel; for yet a little *while*, and I will avenge the blood of Jezreel upon the house of Jehu, and will cause to cease the kingdom of the house of Israel.

5 And it shall come to pass at that day, that I will break the bow of Israel in the valley of Jezreel.

6 And she conceived again, and bare a daughter. And *God* said unto him, Call her name Lo-ruhamah: for I will no more have mercy upon the house of Israel; but I will utterly take them away.

7 But I will have mercy upon the house of Judah, and will save them by the LORD their God, and will not save them by bow, nor by sword, nor by battle, by horses, nor by horsemen.

8 Now when she had weaned Lo-ruhamah, she conceived, and bare a son.

9 Then said *God*, Call his name Lo-ammi: for ye *are* not my people, and I will not be your *God*.

Israel Comes Back

10 Yet the number of the children of Israel shall be as the sand of the sea, which cannot be measured nor numbered; and it shall come to pass, *that* in the place where it was said unto them, Ye *are* not my people, *there* it shall be said unto them, *Ye are* the sons of the living God.

11 Then shall the children of Judah and the children of Israel be gathered together, and appoint themselves one head, and they shall come up out of the land: for great *shall be* the day of Jezreel.

CHAPTER 2

1 Say ye unto your brethren, Ammi; and to your sisters, Ruhamah.

2 Plead with your mother, plead: for she *is* not my wife, neither *am* I her husband: let

Cross references:
2 Deut. 31:16; Ps. 73:27; Jer. 2:13; Ezek. 23:3-21; Hos. 3:1
4 2Kgs. 10:11; 15:10, 12
5 2Kgs. 15:29
6 2Kgs. 17:6, 23
7 2Kgs. 19:35; Zech. 4:6; 9:10
10 Gen. 32:12; Hos. 2:23; John 1:12; Rom. 9:25, 26, 27, 28; 1Pet. 2:10; 1John 3:1
11 Isa. 11:12, 13; Jer. 3:18; Ezek. 34:23; 37:16-24
2 Isa. 50:1; Ezek. 16:25

1:2 Go, take unto thee a wife of whoredoms. Great controversy surrounds this passage. Would God really tell His prophet to marry a prostitute? The text says just that. Hosea is called to make the same choice that was before God. God commands Hosea to marry a woman who was a prostitute, just as the Lord's wife, Israel, was committing spiritual adultery by "departing from the LORD" to worship idols. This setting forms the basis for the whole prophecy. Jezreel, Hosea's first son, was legitimate (1:3). The other two children are identified as "children of whoredoms," and are pictures of Israel's illegitimate unions with strange gods.

1:4 Call his name Jezreel. The name of Gomer's first child literally means, "God sows," and conveys the image of God as the giver of life. It was also the name of the valley-plain between the mountain ranges of Samaria and Galilee and of a city at the valley's southern edge at the foot of Mount Galboa. These locations were the scene of many bloody atrocities by the wicked king of Israel, Ahab, and God's servant Jehu. In this verse, Hosea unveils the prophecy about the impending destruction of the Northern Kingdom (Israel) at the hand of the Assyrian Empire.

1:7 I will have mercy upon the house of Judah. Judah, the Southern Kingdom, will be spared from the coming Assyrian invasion. This prophecy was fulfilled in 701 B.C.,

when the Assyrian king, Sennacherib, invaded the land of Israel but did not conquer Judah or Jerusalem.

1:10-11 Yet the number of the children of Israel shall be as the sand of the sea. This phrase and the phrase "Ye are the sons of the living God," are also used in Joshua 3:10 in reference to the Lord's mighty deliverance of the nation. Even though Israel is currently in disobedience, this will not continue and the nation will eventually prosper and be blessed by many offspring (cf. Gen. 22:17; 32:12). This deliverance will take place during the second coming of Jesus to rescue His people (Israel) when they will occupy the Promised Land for a thousand years. There is also a prophetic reference to the end-time regathering of the Northern and Southern Kingdoms at Christ's second coming. Verse 11 states that the children of Israel will "appoint themselves one head," a clear reference to the future rule of Jesus as their eventual King in the Millennium (Ezek. 37:22; Hos. 3:5; Isa. 9:6-7; Amos 9:11; Mic. 5:2).

2:1-3 Ammi. This literally means, "My people," and "Ruhamah" literally means, "My loved one." The phrase, "your brethren . . . your sisters," refers to other Israelites. This section refers to a future time when Israel will be restored during the Millennium (cf. Deut. 30:1-7; Rom. 11:25-26).

her therefore put away her whoredoms out of her sight, and her adulteries from between her breasts;

3 Lest I strip her naked, and set her as in the day that she was born, and make her as a wilderness, and set her like a dry land, and slay her with thirst.

4 And I will not have mercy upon her children; for they *be* the children of whoredoms.

5 For their mother hath played the harlot: she that conceived them hath done shamefully: for she said, I will go after my lovers, that give *me* my bread and my water, my wool and my flax, mine oil and my drink.

6 Therefore, behold, I will hedge up thy way with thorns, and make a wall, that she shall not find her paths.

7 And she shall follow after her lovers, but she shall not overtake them; and she shall seek them, but shall not find *them*: then shall she say, I will go and return to my first husband; for then *was it* better with me than now.

8 For she did not know that I gave her corn, and wine, and oil, and multiplied her silver and gold, *which* they prepared for Baal.

9 Therefore will I return, and take away my corn in the time thereof, and my wine in the season thereof, and will recover my wool and my flax *given* to cover her nakedness.

10 And now will I discover her lewdness in the sight of her lovers, and none shall deliver her out of mine hand.

11 I will also cause all her mirth to cease, her feast days, her new moons, and her sabbaths, and all her solemn feasts.

12 And I will destroy her vines and her fig trees, whereof she hath said, These *are* my rewards that my lovers have given me: and I will make them a forest, and the beasts of the field shall eat them.

13 And I will visit upon her the days of Baalim, wherein she burned incense to them, and she decked herself with her earrings and her jewels, and she went after her lovers, and forgat me, saith the LORD.

God Loves His Unfaithful People

14 Therefore, behold, I will allure her, and bring her into the wilderness, and speak comfortably unto her.

15 And I will give her her vineyards from thence, and the valley of Achor for a door of hope: and she shall sing there, as in the days of her youth, and as in the day when she came up out of the land of Egypt.

16 And it shall be at that day, saith the LORD, *that* thou shalt call me Ishi; and shalt call me no more Baali.

17 For I will take away the names of Baalim out of her mouth, and they shall no more be remembered by their name.

18 And in that day will I make a covenant for them with the beasts of the field, and

Cross references

3 Jer. 13:22, 26; Ezek. 19:13; Amos 8:11, 13
4 John 8:41
5 Jer. 3:1, 6, 8, 9; 44:17
6 Job 3:23; 19:8; Lam. 3:7, 9
7 Ezek. 16:8; Hos. 5:15; Luke 15:18
8 Isa. 1:3; Ezek. 16:17-19; Hos. 8:4
9 Hos. 2:3
10 Ezek. 16:37; 23:29
11 1Kgs. 12:32; Amos 8:5, 10
12 Ps. 80:12, 13; Isa. 5:5; Hos. 2:5
13 Ezek. 23:40, 42
14 Ezek. 20:35
15 Ex. 15:1; Josh. 7:26; Isa. 65:10; Jer. 2:2
17 Ex. 23:13
18 Ezek. 34:25; 39:9, 10; Zech. 9:10

2:6–13 These verses anticipate the coming exile at the hands of the Assyrians that will begin in 722 B.C. The term "lovers" refers to the pagan gods of the Canaanites. The worship of Baal involved the worship of the forces of nature that were believed to control different areas of life, including agricultural prosperity. Since the people in the Northern Kingdom chose to believe that their abundance came from the gods of Baal, God destroyed their prosperity.

2:14–16 I will betroth thee unto me for ever. This passage speaks of Israel's eventual restoration as a new, permanent betrothal to God (vv. 19–20). Jeremiah likened the future relationship to Israel's relationship to God in the wilderness (Jer. 2:2–37), except that in the future, Israel will be faithful. God had been removing the material aspects of Israel's prosperity, but when He regathers the nation, He will grant a new prosperity and reverse the significance of Jezreel, Hosea's first child. While the name, "Jezreel," had previously connoted judgment (1:5), the new meaning of the name, "God sows," points to God's millennial blessings upon Israel (v. 22). It is during the Millennium that Israel will experience her great end-time conversion to Jesus as her Messiah.

2:18–22 covenant. Hosea has the new covenant in mind (Deut. 29:4; 30:6; Isa. 59:20–21; 61:8–9; Jer. 31:31–34; 32:37–40; 50:4–5; Ezek. 11:19–20; 16:60–63; 34:25–26; 36:24–27; 37:21–28; Zech. 9:11; 12:10; Heb. 8:1–13; 10:15–18). He is emphasizing that aspect of the new covenant that will remove the curse in relation to the animal and plant kingdoms during the Millennium (Isa. 11:6–9). Betrothal in Israel was a much more legally binding arrangement than the traditional engagement process in many nations today. It meant that a couple was legally married, but had yet to consummate the relationship. Involved in a betrothal was payment to the bride's family. The payment in this allegorical case is eternal righteousness, judgment, lovingkindness, and mercy. This time, during the Millennium, there will be no unfaithfulness leading to a break in relations. The word "Jezreel" in verse 22 means "God plants." Here it is used for the nation of Israel as a whole (not just Hosea's son) because God will plant Israel in her land during the Millennium, and the result will be great agricultural productivity.

with the fowls of heaven, and *with* the creeping things of the ground: and I will break the bow and the sword and the battle out of the earth, and will make them to lie down safely.

19 And I will betroth thee unto me for ever; yea, I will betroth thee unto me in righteousness, and in judgment, and in lovingkindness, and in mercies.

20 I will even betroth thee unto me in faithfulness: and thou shalt know the LORD.

21 And it shall come to pass in that day, I will hear, saith the LORD, I will hear the heavens, and they shall hear the earth;

22 And the earth shall hear the corn, and the wine, and the oil; and they shall hear Jezreel.

23 And I will sow her unto me in the earth; and I will have mercy upon her that had not obtained mercy; and I will say to *them which were* not my people, Thou *art* my people; and they shall say, *Thou art* my God.

CHAPTER 3
Hosea Takes Back
His Unfaithful Wife

1 Then said the LORD unto me, Go yet, love a woman beloved of *her* friend, yet an adulteress, according to the love of the LORD toward the children of Israel, who look to other gods, and love flagons of wine.

2 So I bought her to me for fifteen *pieces* of silver, and *for* an homer of barley, and an half homer of barley:

3 And I said unto her, Thou shalt abide for me many days; thou shalt not play the harlot, and thou shalt not be for *another* man: so *will* I also *be* for thee.

4 For the children of Israel shall abide

many days without a king, and without a prince, and without a sacrifice, and without an image, and without an ephod, and *without* teraphim:

5 Afterward shall the children of Israel return, and seek the LORD their God, and David their king; and shall fear the LORD and his goodness in the latter days.

CHAPTER 4
God Blames Israel

1 Hear the word of the LORD, ye children of Israel: for the LORD hath a controversy with the inhabitants of the land, because *there is* no truth, nor mercy, nor knowledge of God in the land.

2 By swearing, and lying, and killing, and stealing, and committing adultery, they break out, and blood toucheth blood.

3 Therefore shall the land mourn, and every one that dwelleth therein shall languish, with the beasts of the field, and with the fowls of heaven; yea, the fishes of the sea also shall be taken away.

4 Yet let no man strive, nor reprove another: for thy people *are* as they that strive with the priest.

5 Therefore shalt thou fall in the day, and the prophet also shall fall with thee in the night, and I will destroy thy mother.

6 My people are destroyed for lack of knowledge: because thou hast rejected knowledge, I will also reject thee, that thou shalt be no priest to me: seeing thou hast forgotten the law of thy God, I will also forget thy children.

7 As they were increased, so they sinned against me: *therefore* will I change their glory into shame.

Cross-references

20 Jer. 31:33, 34; John 17:3
21 Zech. 8:12
22 Hos. 1:4
23 Jer. 31:27; Hos. 1:6, 10; Zech. 10:9; 13:9; Rom. 9:26; 1Pet. 2:10

1 Jer. 3:20; Hos. 1:2
3 Deut. 21:13
4 Ex. 28:6; Judg. 17:5; Isa. 19:19; Hos. 10:3
5 Isa. 2:2; Jer. 30:9, 24; 50:4, 5; Ezek. 34:23, 24; 37:22, 24; 38:8, 16; Dan. 2:28; Hos. 5:6; Mic. 4:1

1 Isa. 1:18; 3:13, 14; Jer. 4:22; 5:4; 25:31; Hos. 12:2; Mic. 6:2
3 Jer. 4:28; 12:4; Amos 5:16; Zeph. 1:3
4 Deut. 17:12
5 Jer. 6:4, 5; 15:8
6 Isa. 5:13

3:1–5 according to the love of the LORD toward the children of Israel. God's love for Israel is endless even though Israel was guilty of loving other gods (cf. Isa. 49:14–16; Zech. 2:8). Hosea acts out God's redemption of His strayed people. The normal price for a slave was 30 pieces of silver. It is not coincidence that the value of the silver and other items Hosea paid to regain his own wife added up to thirty shekels (cf. Zech. 11:12–13; Matt. 26:15). Verse 4 describes the present state of the Jewish people since the destruction of the temple in A.D. 70: Israel has no king and no temple at which to offer sacrifices. Since their years of captivity the Jews, by and large, have not had a problem with the kind of idolatry that is seen in Hosea. After going so long without a king or prince, Jesus the Messiah will rule the world from Jerusalem during the thousand-year kingdom, and David will take his rightful place as prince over Israel (Jer. 30:9;

Ezek. 34:23–24; 37:24–25) under the overall authority of Messiah. Verse five refers to the "latter days," a term used throughout the Old Testament to refer to the time of Tribulation, the Millennium, or both (Deut. 4:30; 31:29; Isa. 2:2; Jer. 23:20; 30:24; 48:47; Ezek. 38:16; Dan. 2:28; 10:14).

4:1–6 The Lord declares specific charges against Israel, explaining why she will be taken into captivity in 722 B.C. by the Assyrians. The result of God's judgment will be degradation to the land of Israel. Judgment would come upon the people because of a failure of Israel's religious leaders to steer them in the right direction. Most of their prophets and priests had failed. Since the priests had failed to teach God's law, the people did not understand what the Lord was doing with the nation. God was going to reject these priests by terminating the priestly line.

8 They eat up the sin of my people, and they set their heart on their iniquity.

9 And there shall be, like people, like priest: and I will punish them for their ways, and reward them their doings.

10 For they shall eat, and not have enough: they shall commit whoredom, and shall not increase: because they have left off to take heed to the LORD.

11 Whoredom and wine and new wine take away the heart.

12 My people ask counsel at their stocks, and their staff declareth unto them: for the spirit of whoredoms hath caused *them* to err, and they have gone a whoring from under their God.

13 They sacrifice upon the tops of the mountains, and burn incense upon the hills, under oaks and poplars and elms, because the shadow thereof *is* good: therefore your daughters shall commit whoredom, and your spouses shall commit adultery.

14 I will not punish your daughters when they commit whoredom, nor your spouses when they commit adultery: for themselves are separated with whores, and they sacrifice with harlots: therefore the people *that* doth not understand shall fall.

15 Though thou, Israel, play the harlot, *yet* let not Judah offend; and come not ye unto Gilgal, neither go ye up to Beth-aven, nor swear, The LORD liveth.

16 For Israel slideth back as a backsliding heifer: now the LORD will feed them as a lamb in a large place.

17 Ephraim *is* joined to idols: let him alone.

18 Their drink is sour: they have committed whoredom continually: her rulers *with* shame do love, Give ye.

19 The wind hath bound her up in her wings, and they shall be ashamed because of their sacrifices.

Cross references

9 Isa. 24:2; Jer. 5:31
10 Lev. 26:26; Mic. 6:14; Hag. 1:6
11 Isa. 28:7; Eccl. 7:7
12 Isa. 44:20; Jer. 2:27; Hos. 5:4; Hab. 2:19
13 Isa. 1:29; 57:5, 7; Ezek. 6:13; 20:28; Amos 7:17; Rom. 1:28
14 Hos. 4:1, 6
15 1Kgs. 12:29; Hos. 9:15; 10:5; 12:11; Amos 4:4; 5:5; 8:14; Zeph. 1:5
16 Jer. 3:6; 7:24; 8:5; Zech. 7:11
17 Matt. 15:14
18 Ps. 47:9; Mic. 3:11; 7:3
19 Isa. 1:29; Jer. 2:26; 4:11, 12; 51:1
2 Isa. 29:15
3 Ezek. 23:5; Hos. 4:17; Amos 3:2
6 Isa. 1:15; Jer. 11:11; John 7:34
7 Jer. 3:20
11 Deut. 28:33
12 Prov. 12:4

CHAPTER 5

God Punishes Israel

1 Hear ye this, O priests; and hearken, ye house of Israel; and give ye ear, O house of the king; for judgment *is* toward you, because ye have been a snare on Mizpah, and a net spread upon Tabor.

2 And the revolters are profound to make slaughter, though I *have been* a rebuker of them all.

3 I know Ephraim, and Israel is not hid from me: for now, O Ephraim, thou committest whoredom, *and* Israel is defiled.

4 They will not frame their doings to turn unto their God: for the spirit of whoredoms *is* in the midst of them, and they have not known the LORD.

5 And the pride of Israel doth testify to his face: therefore shall Israel and Ephraim fall in their iniquity; Judah also shall fall with them.

6 They shall go with their flocks and with their herds to seek the LORD; but they shall not find *him*; he hath withdrawn himself from them.

7 They have dealt treacherously against the LORD: for they have begotten strange children: now shall a month devour them with their portions.

8 Blow ye the cornet in Gibeah, *and* the trumpet in Ramah: cry aloud *at* Beth-aven, after thee, O Benjamin.

9 Ephraim shall be desolate in the day of rebuke: among the tribes of Israel have I made known that which shall surely be.

10 The princes of Judah were like them that remove the bound: *therefore* I will pour out my wrath upon them like water.

11 Ephraim *is* oppressed *and* broken in judgment, because he willingly walked after the commandment.

12 Therefore *will* I *be* unto Ephraim as a

4:9 like people, like priest. An idiom meaning that the people and the priests have become the same. The priests were supposed to be separated from the rest of the nation so they could live as unto the Lord (Lev. 8—10). But since the priests were in this instance no different from the people, then they would experience the coming judgment just like the nation as a whole.

4:19 The wind hath bound her up in her wings. A prophecy that Ephraim (a prominent tribe in the Northern Kingdom) was about to find herself swallowed up among the nations. This occurs during the impending Assyrian invasion and through the subsequent years of dispersion among the Gentile nations (cf. 2 Kgs. 17:6; 18:11).

5:5 Judah also shall fall with them. This is not saying that Israel and Judah would fall at the same time, but from the same cause—pride. The fall of Judah in this verse is not a prediction of Sennacherib's desolations of Judah in 701 B.C., after he had conquered Israel in 722 B.C., but of Judah's fall to Nebuchadnezzar and Babylon in 586 B.C.

5:9 in the day of rebuke. This is a reference to the purpose of the impending Assyrian judgment.

5:12 as a moth. As the moth slowly destroys clothing, so the Lord would destroy Israel (Job 13:28; Isa. 50:9; 51:8). Similarly, the Hebrew word translated "rottenness"

moth, and to the house of Judah as rottenness.

13 When Ephraim saw his sickness, and Judah *saw* his wound, then went Ephraim to the Assyrian, and sent to king Jareb: yet could he not heal you, nor cure you of your wound.

14 For I *will be* unto Ephraim as a lion, and as a young lion to the house of Judah: I, *even* I, will tear and go away; I will take away, and none shall rescue *him*.

15 I will go *and* return to my place, till they acknowledge their offence, and seek my face: in their affliction they will seek me early.

CHAPTER 6
Israel Isn't Sincere

1 Come, and let us return unto the LORD: for he hath torn, and he will heal us; he hath smitten, and he will bind us up.

2 After two days will he revive us: in the third day he will raise us up, and we shall live in his sight.

3 Then shall we know, *if* we follow on to know the LORD: his going forth is prepared as the morning; and he shall come unto us as the rain, as the latter *and* former rain unto the earth.

4 O Ephraim, what shall I do unto thee? O Judah, what shall I do unto thee? for your goodness *is* as a morning cloud, and as the early dew it goeth away.

5 Therefore have I hewed *them* by the prophets; I have slain them by the words of my mouth: and thy judgments *are as* the light *that* goeth forth.

6 For I desired mercy, and not sacrifice; and the knowledge of God more than burnt offerings.

7 But they like men have transgressed the covenant: there have they dealt treacherously against me.

8 Gilead *is* a city of them that work iniquity, *and is* polluted with blood.

9 And as troops of robbers wait for a man, *so* the company of priests murder in the way by consent: for they commit lewdness.

10 I have seen an horrible thing in the house of Israel: there *is* the whoredom of Ephraim, Israel is defiled.

11 Also, O Judah, he hath set an harvest for thee, when I returned the captivity of my people.

CHAPTER 7
Israel Rebels

1 When I would have healed Israel, then the iniquity of Ephraim was discovered, and the wickedness of Samaria: for they commit falsehood; and the thief cometh in, *and the* troop of robbers spoileth without.

2 And they consider not in their hearts *that* I remember all their wickedness: now their own doings have beset them about; they are before my face.

3 They make the king glad with their wickedness, and the princes with their lies.

4 They *are* all adulterers, as an oven heated by the baker, *who* ceaseth from raising after he hath kneaded the dough, until it be leavened.

5 In the day of our king the princes have

Cross references (center column)

13 2Kgs. 15:19; Jer. 30:12; Hos. 7:11; 10:6; 12:1
14 Ps. 50:22; Lam. 3:10; Hos. 13:7, 8
15 Lev. 26:40, 41; Ps. 78:34; Jer. 29:12, 13; Ezek. 6:9; 20:43; 36:31
1 Deut. 32:39
2 1Cor. 15:4
3 2Sam. 23:4; Job 29:23; Ps. 72:6; Isa. 54:13
4 Hos. 11:8; 13:3
5 Jer. 1:10; 5:14; 23:29; Heb. 4:12
6 1Sam. 15:22; Isa. 1:11; Matt. 9:13; 12:7; John 17:3
7 Job 31:33; Hos. 5:7; 8:1
8 Hos. 12:11
10 Jer. 5:30
11 Rev. 14:15
2 Ps. 9:16
3 Rom. 1:32
4 Jer. 9:2

---

usually refers to the slow decay of bones or teeth (Prov. 12:4; Hab. 3:16).

5:14 as a young lion to the house of Judah. A young lion paints a picture of judgment that was still developing. Such was the case with the Southern Kingdom—its judgment would not come from the Assyrians, but from the Babylonians (2 Kgs. 25), whose kingdom had not yet come to power.

5:15 I will go and return to my place. The description is much like a lion returning to his den (see v. 14) until he is ready to seek new prey. The Lord's place is heaven (cf. Acts 3:19–21). The Lord would not hear Israel's prayers until they underwent the punishment of the dispersion. Here is one of the passages that teach that a condition for the second coming of Christ is the national regeneration of Israel and her call for Messiah to return and rescue her (cf. Lev. 26:40–42; Jer. 3:11–18; Zech. 12:10; Matt. 23:37–39). Since the nation did not seek the Lord at the time of the Assyrian captivity, this must refer to that time

when the nation will turn to the Lord during the Tribulation. This will be fulfilled in the future.

6:1–3 After two days will he revive us. In chapter 4, the priests and prophets were said to be the ones leading the nation downward. In the future time of repentance, they will lead the nation back to the Lord. During this time of repentance during the Tribulation, Israel will experience a national confession of sin for a period of two days. On the third day of this process, the entire nation of Israel will become regenerated and saved. The wonderful result of this time will be that Israel will live with her Lord during the entire thousand years of His kingdom.

6:11 O Judah, he hath set an harvest for thee. Just as the Lord has had a word of judgment for the Southern Kingdom, so now there is a forecast of blessing. The time of this blessing will be during the restoration and regathering at the second coming of Christ in preparation for the Millennial Kingdom.

made *him* sick with bottles of wine; he stretched out his hand with scorners.

6 For they have made ready their heart like an oven, whiles they lie in wait: their baker sleepeth all the night; in the morning it burneth as a flaming fire.

7 They are all hot as an oven, and have devoured their judges; all their kings are fallen: *there is* none among them that calleth unto me.

8 Ephraim, he hath mixed himself among the people; Ephraim is a cake not turned.

9 Strangers have devoured his strength, and he knoweth *it* not: yea, gray hairs are here and there upon him, yet he knoweth not.

10 And the pride of Israel testifieth to his face: and they do not return to the LORD their God, nor seek him for all this.

11 Ephraim also is like a silly dove without heart: they call to Egypt, they go to Assyria.

12 When they shall go, I will spread my net upon them; I will bring them down as the fowls of the heaven; I will chastise them, as their congregation hath heard.

13 Woe unto them! for they have fled from me: destruction unto them! because they have transgressed against me: though I have redeemed them, yet they have spoken lies against me.

14 And they have not cried unto me with their heart, when they howled upon their beds: they assemble themselves for corn and wine, *and* they rebel against me.

15 Though I have bound *and* strengthened their arms, yet do they imagine mischief against me.

16 They return, *but* not to the most High: they are like a deceitful bow: their princes shall fall by the sword for the rage of their tongue: this *shall be* their derision in the land of Egypt.

CHAPTER 8
Israel Continues to Worship Idols

1 *Set* the trumpet to thy mouth. *He shall come* as an eagle against the house of the LORD, because they have transgressed my covenant, and trespassed against my law.

2 Israel shall cry unto me, My God, we know thee.

3 Israel hath cast off *the thing that is* good: the enemy shall pursue him.

4 They have set up kings, but not by me: they have made princes, and I knew *it* not: of their silver and their gold have they made them idols, that they may be cut off.

5 Thy calf, O Samaria, hath cast *thee* off; mine anger is kindled against them: how long *will it be* ere they attain to innocency?

6 For from Israel *was* it also: the workman made it; therefore it *is* not God: but the calf of Samaria shall be broken in pieces.

7 For they have sown the wind, and they shall reap the whirlwind: it hath no stalk: the bud shall yield no meal: if so be it yield, the strangers shall swallow it up.

8 Israel is swallowed up: now shall they be among the Gentiles as a vessel wherein *is* no pleasure.

9 For they are gone up to Assyria, a wild ass alone by himself: Ephraim hath hired lovers.

10 Yea, though they have hired among the nations, now will I gather them, and they shall sorrow a little for the burden of the king of princes.

11 Because Ephraim hath made many altars to sin, altars shall be unto him to sin.

12 I have written to him the great things of my law, *but* they were counted as a strange thing.

13 They sacrifice flesh *for* the sacrifices of mine offerings, and eat *it; but* the LORD accepteth them not; now will he remember their iniquity, and visit their sins: they shall return to Egypt.

14 For Israel hath forgotten his Maker, and buildeth temples; and Judah hath multiplied fenced cities: but I will send a fire upon his cities, and it shall devour the palaces thereof.

CHAPTER 9
God Keeps on Punishing Israel

1 Rejoice not, O Israel, for joy, as *other* people: for thou hast gone a whoring from thy God, thou hast loved a reward upon every cornfloor.

7 2Kgs. 15:10, 25, 30; Isa. 64:7; Hos. 8:4
8 Ps. 106:35
9 Hos. 8:7
10 Isa. 9:13; Hos. 5:5
11 2Kgs. 15:19; 17:4; Hos. 5:13; 9:3; 11:11; 12:1
12 Lev. 26:14; Deut. 28:15; 2Kgs. 17:13, 18; Ezek. 12:13
13 Mic. 6:4
14 Job 35:9, 10; Ps. 78:36; Jer. 3:10; Zech. 7:5
16 Ps. 73:9; 78:57; Hos. 9:3, 6; 11:7
1 Deut. 28:49; Jer. 4:13
2 Ps. 78:34; Hos. 5:15; Titus 1:16
4 2Kgs. 15:13, 17, 25
5 Jer. 13:27
7 Prov. 10:12, 13; 22:8; Hos. 7:9
8 2Kgs. 17:6; Jer. 22:28; 48:38
9 2Kgs. 15:19; Isa. 30:6; Jer. 2:24; Ezek. 16:33, 34
10 Isa. 10:8; Ezek. 26:7; Dan. 2:37; Hag. 2:6
13 Jer. 7:21; 14:10, 12
14 Jer. 17:27
1 Jer. 44:17

8:8 Israel is swallowed up. Here is the image of Israel's neighboring enemies trying to surround and devour her. Now she has no appeal "among the Gentiles as a vessel wherein is no pleasure."

9:1–3 They shall not dwell in the LORD's land. The land of Israel belongs to the Lord (cf. Ex. 15:17; Lev. 25:23), who is responsible for its fertility (cf. Deut. 11:10–12).

When the people of Israel attributed the productivity of the land to pagan deities, they forfeited the blessing of living on it in peace and prosperity (Deut. 11:8–21). The word Egypt is used only as a symbol for the slavery of captivity. Assyria would be the actual country to which Israel would become enslaved in 722 B.C.

2 The floor and the winepress shall not feed them, and the new wine shall fail in her.

3 They shall not dwell in the LORD's land; but Ephraim shall return to Egypt, and they shall eat unclean *things* in Assyria.

4 They shall not offer wine *offerings* to the LORD, neither shall they be pleasing unto him: their sacrifices *shall be* unto them as the bread of mourners; all that eat thereof shall be polluted: for their bread for their soul shall not come into the house of the LORD.

5 What will ye do in the solemn day, and in the day of the feast of the LORD?

6 For, lo, they are gone because of destruction: Egypt shall gather them up, Memphis shall bury them: the pleasant *places* for their silver, nettles shall possess them: thorns *shall be* in their tabernacles.

7 The days of visitation are come, the days of recompence are come; Israel shall know *it*: the prophet *is* a fool, the spiritual man *is* mad, for the multitude of thine iniquity, and the great hatred.

8 The watchman of Ephraim *was* with my God: *but* the prophet *is* a snare of a fowler in all his ways, *and* hatred in the house of his God.

9 They have deeply corrupted *themselves*, as in the days of Gibeah: *therefore* he will remember their iniquity, he will visit their sins.

10 I found Israel like grapes in the wilderness; I saw your fathers as the firstripe in the fig tree at her first time: *but* they went to Baal-peor, and separated themselves unto *that* shame; and *their* abominations were according as they loved.

11 *As for* Ephraim, their glory shall fly away like a bird, from the birth, and from the womb, and from the conception.

12 Though they bring up their children, yet will I bereave them, *that there shall* not *be* a man *left*: yea, woe also to them when I depart from them!

13 Ephraim, as I saw Tyrus, *is* planted in a

pleasant place: but Ephraim shall bring forth his children to the murderer.

14 Give them, O LORD: what wilt thou give? give them a miscarrying womb and dry breasts.

15 All their wickedness *is* in Gilgal: for there I hated them: for the wickedness of their doings I will drive them out of mine house, I will love them no more: all their princes *are* revolters.

16 Ephraim is smitten, their root is dried up, they shall bear no fruit: yea, though they bring forth, yet will I slay *even* the beloved *fruit* of their womb.

17 My God will cast them away, because they did not hearken unto him: and they shall be wanderers among the nations.

CHAPTER 10

1 Israel *is* an empty vine, he bringeth forth fruit unto himself: according to the multitude of his fruit he hath increased the altars; according to the goodness of his land they have made goodly images.

2 Their heart is divided; now shall they be found faulty: he shall break down their altars, he shall spoil their images.

3 For now they shall say, We have no king, because we feared not the LORD; what then should a king do to us?

4 They have spoken words, swearing falsely in making a covenant: thus judgment springeth up as hemlock in the furrows of the field.

5 The inhabitants of Samaria shall fear because of the calves of Beth-aven: for the people thereof shall mourn over it, and the priests thereof *that* rejoiced on it, for the glory thereof, because it is departed from it.

6 It shall be also carried unto Assyria *for* a present to king Jareb: Ephraim shall receive shame, and Israel shall be ashamed of his own counsel.

7 *As for* Samaria, her king is cut off as the foam upon the water.

8 The high places also of Aven, the sin of Israel, shall be destroyed: the thorn and the

Cross references (center column)

2 Hos. 2:9, 12

3 Lev. 25:23; 2Kgs. 17:6; Jer. 2:7; 16:18; Ezek. 4:13; Dan. 1:8; Hos. 8:13; 11:5, 11

4 Lev. 17:11; Deut. 26:14; Jer. 6:20; Hos. 3:4; 8:13

5 Hos. 2:11

6 Isa. 5:6; 32:13; 34:13; Hos. 7:16; 9:3; 10:8

7 Ezek. 13:3-16; Mic. 2:11; Zeph. 3:4

8 Jer. 6:17; 31:6; Ezek. 3:17; 33:7

9 Judg. 19:22; Isa. 31:6; Hos. 8:13; 10:9

10 Num. 25:3; Judg. 6:32; Ps. 81:12; 106:28; Isa. 28:4; Jer. 11:13; Ezek. 20:8; Hos. 2:15; 4:14; Amos 4:5; Mic. 7:1

12 Deut. 28:41, 62; 31:17; 1Sam. 28:15, 16; 2Kgs. 17:18; Job 27:14; Hos. 5:6

14 Luke 23:29

15 Isa. 1:23

17 Deut. 28:64, 65

1 Nah. 2:2

8 Luke 23:30; Rev. 6:16; 9:6

9:6 Egypt is used figuratively here as in verse 3. The Egyptian city of Memphis is used as a symbol for a burial place.

9:14 Hosea prays that the children of Israel will be miscarried or die in the process of God's impending judgment.

9:17 they shall be wanderers among the nations. This is a forecast of Israel's dispersion among the Gentile nations (cf. Deut. 28:64–67) until the ultimate time of ingathering at the Second Coming (Deut. 30:7; Isa. 11:12; Dan. 12:1; Matt. 24:31; Mark 13:27).

10:7 her king is cut off as the foam upon the water. This is a prediction that Israel's king would be swept away by invading forces like a piece of wood is swept away by a powerful stream of water. This occurred in the Assyrian invasion of 722 B.C.

thistle shall come up on their altars; and they shall say to the mountains, Cover us; and to the hills, Fall on us.

9 O Israel, thou hast sinned from the days of Gibeah: there they stood: the battle in Gibeah against the children of iniquity did not overtake them.

10 *It is* in my desire that I should chastise them; and the people shall be gathered against them, when they shall bind themselves in their two furrows.

11 And Ephraim *is as* an heifer *that is* taught, *and* loveth to tread out *the corn;* but I passed over upon her fair neck: I will make Ephraim to ride; Judah shall plow, *and* Jacob shall break his clods.

12 Sow to yourselves in righteousness, reap in mercy; break up your fallow ground: for *it is* time to seek the LORD, till he come and rain righteousness upon you.

13 Ye have plowed wickedness, ye have reaped iniquity; ye have eaten the fruit of lies: because thou didst trust in thy way, in the multitude of thy mighty men.

14 Therefore shall a tumult arise among thy people, and all thy fortresses shall be spoiled, as Shalman spoiled Beth-arbel in the day of battle: the mother was dashed in pieces upon *her* children.

15 So shall Beth-el do unto you because of your great wickedness: in a morning shall the king of Israel utterly be cut off.

CHAPTER 11
God Still Loves His Sinful Children

1 When Israel *was* a child, then I loved him, and called my son out of Egypt.

2 *As* they called them, so they went from them: they sacrificed unto Baalim, and burned incense to graven images.

3 I taught Ephraim also to go, taking them by their arms; but they knew not that I healed them.

4 I drew them with cords of a man, with bands of love: and I was to them as they that take off the yoke on their jaws, and I laid meat unto them.

5 He shall not return into the land of Egypt, but the Assyrian shall be his king, because they refused to return.

6 And the sword shall abide on his cities,

and shall consume his branches, and devour *them*, because of their own counsels.

7 And my people are bent to backsliding from me: though they called them to the most High, none at all would exalt *him*.

8 How shall I give thee up, Ephraim? *how* shall I deliver thee, Israel? how shall I make thee as Admah? *how* shall I set thee as Zeboim? mine heart is turned within me, my repentings are kindled together.

9 I will not execute the fierceness of mine anger, I will not return to destroy Ephraim: for I *am* God, and not man; the Holy One in the midst of thee: and I will not enter into the city.

10 They shall walk after the LORD: he shall roar like a lion: when he shall roar, then the children shall tremble from the west.

11 They shall tremble as a bird out of Egypt, and as a dove out of the land of Assyria: and I will place them in their houses, saith the LORD.

12 Ephraim compasseth me about with lies, and the house of Israel with deceit: but Judah yet ruleth with God, and is faithful with the saints.

CHAPTER 12
Ephraim Is a Liar

1 Ephraim feedeth on wind, and followeth after the east wind: he daily increaseth lies and desolation; and they do make a covenant with the Assyrians, and oil is carried into Egypt.

2 The LORD hath also a controversy with Judah, and will punish Jacob according to his ways; according to his doings will he recompense him.

3 He took his brother by the heel in the womb, and by his strength he had power with God:

4 Yea, he had power over the angel, and prevailed: he wept, and made supplication unto him: he found him *in* Beth-el, and there he spake with us;

5 Even the LORD God of hosts; the LORD *is* his memorial.

6 Therefore turn thou to thy God: keep mercy and judgment, and wait on thy God continually.

7 *He is* a merchant, the balances of deceit *are* in his hand: he loveth to oppress.

Cross references

10 Deut. 28:63; Jer. 16:16; Ezek. 23:46, 47

12 Prov. 11:18; Jer. 4:3

13 Job 4:8; Prov. 22:8; Gal. 6:7, 8

14 2Kgs. 18:34; 19:13

1 Ex. 4:22, 23

2 2Kgs. 17:16

3 Ex. 15:26; Deut. 1:31; 32:10-12; Isa. 46:3

4 Ps. 78:25

5 2Kgs. 17:13, 14; Hos. 8:13; 9:3

6 Hos. 10:6

7 Jer. 3:6-18; 8:5; Hos. 4:16; 7:16

8 Gen. 14:8; 19:24, 25; Deut. 29:23; 32:36; Isa. 63:15; Jer. 9:7; 31:20; Amos 4:11

9 Num. 23:19; Isa. 55:8, 9; Mal. 3:6

10 Isa. 31:4; Joel 3:16; Amos 1:2; Zech. 8:7

11 Isa. 60:8; Ezek. 28:25, 26

1 2Kgs. 17:4

3 Gen. 25:26; 32:24-26

4 Gen. 28:12, 19; 35:9, 10, 15

6 Ps. 37:7; Hos. 14:1; Mic. 6:8

7 Prov. 11:1; Ezek. 16:3; Amos 8:5, 8

11:1 called my son out of Egypt. While the context of this statement refers historically to the Exodus, Matthew applies the passage to Jesus' return from Egypt with His parents after the death of Herod (Matt. 2:15).

12:2 The LORD hath also a controversy with Judah. The word controversy is the Hebrew word that means a "legal complaint." The Southern Kingdom is often seen throughout Hosea as a brother watching his brother receive punishment. The lesson for the observer is that their punishment is coming in the future.

8 And Ephraim said, Yet I am become rich, I have found me out substance: *in* all my labours they shall find none iniquity in me that *were* sin.

9 And I *that am* the LORD thy God from the land of Egypt will yet make thee to dwell in tabernacles, as in the days of the solemn feast.

10 I have also spoken by the prophets, and I have multiplied visions, and used similitudes, by the ministry of the prophets.

11 *Is there* iniquity *in* Gilead? surely they are vanity: they sacrifice bullocks in Gilgal; yea, their altars *are* as heaps in the furrows of the fields.

12 And Jacob fled into the country of Syria, and Israel served for a wife, and for a wife he kept *sheep*.

13 And by a prophet the LORD brought Israel out of Egypt, and by a prophet was he preserved.

14 Ephraim provoked *him* to anger most bitterly: therefore shall he leave his blood upon him, and his reproach shall his Lord return unto him.

CHAPTER 13
The Lord Is Angry with Israel

1 When Ephraim spake trembling, he exalted himself in Israel; but when he offended in Baal, he died.

2 And now they sin more and more, and have made them molten images of their silver, *and* idols according to their own understanding, all of it the work of the craftsmen: they say of them, Let the men that sacrifice kiss the calves.

3 Therefore they shall be as the morning cloud, and as the early dew that passeth away, as the chaff *that* is driven with the whirlwind out of the floor, and as the smoke out of the chimney.

4 Yet I *am* the LORD thy God from the land of Egypt, and thou shalt know no god but me: for *there is* no saviour beside me.

5 I did know thee in the wilderness, in the land of great drought.

6 According to their pasture, so were they filled; they were filled, and their heart was exalted; therefore have they forgotten me.

7 Therefore I will be unto them as a lion: as a leopard by the way will I observe *them*:

8 I will meet them as a bear *that is* bereaved *of her whelps*, and will rend the caul of their heart, and there will I devour them like a lion: the wild beast shall tear them.

9 O Israel, thou hast destroyed thyself; but in me *is* thine help.

10 I will be thy king: where *is any other* that may save thee in all thy cities? and thy judges of whom thou saidst, Give me a king and princes?

11 I gave thee a king in mine anger, and took *him* away in my wrath.

12 The iniquity of Ephraim *is* bound up; his sin *is* hid.

13 The sorrows of a travailing woman shall come upon him: he *is* an unwise son; for he should not stay long in *the place of* the breaking forth of children.

14 I will ransom them from the power of the grave; I will redeem them from death: O death, I will be thy plagues; O grave, I will be thy destruction: repentance shall be hid from mine eyes.

15 Though he be fruitful among *his* brethren, an east wind shall come, the wind of the LORD shall come up from the wilderness, and his spring shall become dry, and his fountain shall be dried up: he shall spoil the treasure of all pleasant vessels.

16 Samaria shall become desolate; for she hath rebelled against her God: they shall fall by the sword: their infants shall be dashed in pieces, and their women with child shall be ripped up.

CHAPTER 14
Hosea Begs Israel to Come Back

1 O Israel, return unto the LORD thy God; for thou hast fallen by thine iniquity.

9 Lev. 23:42, 43
12 Gen. 28:5; 29:20, 28; Deut. 26:5
13 Ex. 12:50, 51; 13:3
14 Deut. 28:37; 2Kgs. 17:11-18; Ezek. 18:13; 24:7, 8; Dan. 11:18
1 2Kgs. 17:16, 18; Hos. 11:2
2 1Kgs. 19:18; Hos. 2:8; 8:4
3 Dan. 2:35; Hos. 6:4
4 Isa. 43:11; 45:21; Hos. 12:9
5 Deut. 2:7; 8:15; 32:10
6 Deut. 8:12, 14; 32:15; Hos. 8:14
7 Jer. 5:6; Lam. 3:10; Hos. 5:14
8 2Sam. 17:8; Prov. 17:12
9 Prov. 6:32
10 1Sam. 8:5, 19
11 1Sam. 8:7
13 Jer. 30:6
14 Rom. 11:29; 1Cor. 15:54, 55
15 Ezek. 17:10; 19:12
16 2Kgs. 8:12; 15:16; 17:6; 18:12; Isa. 13:16
1 Hos. 12:6; 13:9; Joel 2:13

12:9 will yet make thee to dwell in tabernacles. Here the Lord has in mind the Feast of Tabernacles (cf. Lev. 23:33–43), which will be fulfilled prophetically for Israel during the yet future Millennium.

13:13–14 sorrows of a travailing woman. In this description of the impending judgment upon the Northern Kingdom, Israel is likened to a baby who does not come forth in spite of the vigorous efforts of the mother in labor. Despite such stubbornness, the Lord will one day bring back the nation from the dead (cf. Ezek. 37) as well as

resurrect individuals unto glory (cf. Dan. 12:2–3). Paul quotes the last half of this verse in 1 Corinthians 15:55–56 in his description of the resurrection of believers.

13:16 Hosea describes some of the graphic details that will occur when the Northern Kingdom is taken into captivity by the Assyrians. The Assyrians were one of the cruelest nations of this time in their treatment of a conquered foe. Israel was about to experience such travesty firsthand.

2 Take with you words, and turn to the LORD: say unto him, Take away all iniquity, and receive *us* graciously: so will we render the calves of our lips.

3 Asshur shall not save us; we will not ride upon horses: neither will we say any more to the work of our hands, *Ye are* our gods: for in thee the fatherless findeth mercy.

4 I will heal their backsliding, I will love them freely: for mine anger is turned away from him.

5 I will be as the dew unto Israel: he shall grow as the lily, and cast forth his roots as Lebanon.

6 His branches shall spread, and his beauty shall be as the olive tree, and his smell as Lebanon.

7 They that dwell under his shadow shall return; they shall revive *as* the corn, and grow as the vine: the scent thereof *shall be* as the wine of Lebanon.

8 Ephraim *shall say*, What have I to do any more with idols? I have heard *him*, and observed him: I *am* like a green fir tree. From me is thy fruit found.

9 Who *is* wise, and he shall understand these *things*? prudent, and he shall know them? for the ways of the LORD *are* right, and the just shall walk in them: but the transgressors shall fall therein.

Cross references:

2 Heb. 13:15
3 Isa. 30:2, 16; 31:1; Jer. 31:18
4 Jer. 5:6; 14:7; Hos. 11:7; Eph. 1:6
5 Job 29:19; Prov. 19:12
6 Ps. 52:8; 128:3; Song 4:11
8 Jer. 31:18; James 1:17
9 Prov. 10:29

14:4–8 I will heal. The Lord will one day heal Israel's backsliding with the new heart of the new covenant (Deut. 29:4; 30:6; Isa. 59:20–21; 61:8–9; Jer. 31:31–34; 32:37–40; 50:4–5; Ezek. 11:19–20; 16:60–63; 34:25–26; 36:24–27; 37:21–28; Zech. 9:11; 12:10; Heb. 8:1–13; 10:15–18). This will occur during the Millennium, after the second coming of Christ, when the extent of Israel's blessings will be grand in magnitude.

Joel

J oel, whose name means "Jehovah is God," portrays a historical and horrendous plague of locusts, a judgment from God on the kingdom of Judah, followed by a severe drought. This prophecy of spiritual revival calls for the nation's leaders to proclaim a solemn assembly for national sorrow, repentance, and deliverance.

Some of the prophetic statements in the book of Joel are typical in nature and others are of the specific-prediction variety that are already fulfilled, but the future "day of the Lord" is the emphasis. The prophecies in this book can be divided into four sections: **1)** a prophetic type of the day of the Lord (Joel 1:1–20); **2)** the direct prophecy of the day of the Lord itself (Joel 2:1–32); **3)** the prophecy of the judgment of the nations (Joel 3:1–17); and **4)** a prophecy of the full kingdom blessing of Israel (Joel 3:18–21).

Author
Joel

Date
9th Century B.C.

Key Truth
The Day of the Lord

Historic Time
The Reign of Joash

Key Verse
1:15
Alas for the day! for the day of the Lord is at hand. . . .

The prophetic type of the day of the Lord in Joel 1:1–20 is a declaration of God's judgment upon Judah that took place during Joel's own lifetime. Then, using the locust calamity as a powerful illustration, Joel expands his message to predict events of the Last Days. This prophet of Pentecost foresees the outpouring of the Holy Spirit, applied by Peter to Pentecost (Acts 2) and to be perfectly fulfilled at the second coming of Christ. Both the judgment of the nations and the battle of "that great day of God Almighty" (Armageddon) are within the scope of this book (see Rev. 16:14).

The expression "day of the Lord," mentioned some twenty times in the Old Testament by eight prophets, can occasionally refer to divine judgments in Israel's history which may foreshadow the future, but usually connotes the Lord's direct intervention on earth in the Last Days, including the millennial reign of Christ. The book climaxes with a description of the messianic reign in Jerusalem and the blessings that will characterize Christ's kingdom.

Prophecies occur in 50 of the 73 verses, or 68 percent of the book, and encompass 25 specific predictions.

68%
Prophecy

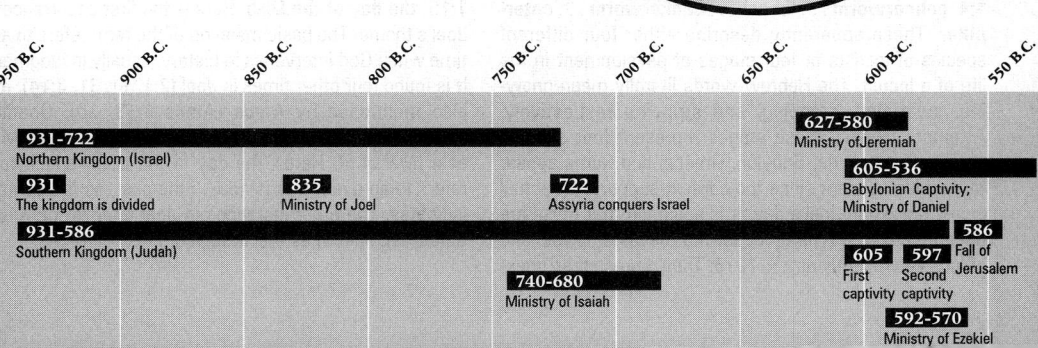

950 B.C.	900 B.C.	850 B.C.	800 B.C.	750 B.C.	700 B.C.	650 B.C.	600 B.C.	550 B.C.

627-580
Ministry of Jeremiah

931-722
Northern Kingdom (Israel)

931
The kingdom is divided

835
Ministry of Joel

722
Assyria conquers Israel

605-536
Babylonian Captivity;
Ministry of Daniel

931-586
Southern Kingdom (Judah)

586
Fall of
Jerusalem

605
First
captivity

597
Second
captivity

740-680
Ministry of Isaiah

592-570
Ministry of Ezekiel

CHAPTER 1
Locusts Destroy the Crops

1 The word of the Lord that came to Joel the son of Pethuel.
2 Hear this, ye old men, and give ear, all ye inhabitants of the land. Hath this been in your days, or even in the days of your fathers?
3 Tell ye your children of it, and *let* your children *tell* their children, and their children another generation.
4 That which the palmerworm hath left hath the locust eaten; and that which the locust hath left hath the cankerworm eaten; and that which the cankerworm hath left hath the caterpiller eaten.
5 Awake, ye drunkards, and weep; and howl, all ye drinkers of wine, because of the new wine; for it is cut off from your mouth.
6 For a nation is come up upon my land, strong, and without number, whose teeth *are* the teeth of a lion, and he hath the cheek teeth of a great lion.
7 He hath laid my vine waste, and barked my fig tree: he hath made it clean bare, and cast *it* away; the branches thereof are made white.
8 Lament like a virgin girded with sackcloth for the husband of her youth.
9 The meat offering and the drink offering is cut off from the house of the Lord; the priests, the Lord's ministers, mourn.
10 The field is wasted, the land mourneth;

for the corn is wasted: the new wine is dried up, the oil languisheth.
11 Be ye ashamed, O ye husbandmen; howl, O ye vinedressers, for the wheat and for the barley; because the harvest of the field is perished.
12 The vine is dried up, and the fig tree languisheth; the pomegranate tree, the palm tree also, and the apple tree, *even* all the trees of the field, are withered: because joy is withered away from the sons of men.
13 Gird yourselves, and lament, ye priests: howl, ye ministers of the altar: come, lie all night in sackcloth, ye ministers of my God: for the meat offering and the drink offering is withholden from the house of your God.
14 Sanctify ye a fast, call a solemn assembly, gather the elders *and* all the inhabitants of the land *into* the house of the Lord your God, and cry unto the Lord,
15 Alas for the day! for the day of the Lord *is* at hand, and as a destruction from the Almighty shall it come.
16 Is not the meat cut off before our eyes, *yea*, joy and gladness from the house of our God?
17 The seed is rotten under their clods, the garners are laid desolate, the barns are broken down; for the corn is withered.
18 How do the beasts groan! the herds of cattle are perplexed, because they have no pasture; yea, the flocks of sheep are made desolate.
19 O Lord, to thee will I cry: for the fire

Cross references (center column)
2 Joel 2:2
3 Ps. 78:4
4 Deut. 28:38; Joel 2:25
5 Isa. 32:10
6 Prov. 30:25, 26, 27; Joel 2:2, 11, 25; Rev. 9:8
7 Isa. 5:6
8 Prov. 2:17; Isa. 22:12; Jer. 3:4
9 Joel 1:13; 2:14
10 Isa. 24:7; Jer. 12:11; 14:2; Joel 1:12
11 Jer. 14:3, 4
12 Ps. 4:7; Isa. 9:3; 24:11; Jer. 48:33; Joel 1:10
13 Jer. 4:8; Joel 1:8, 9
14 Lev. 23:36; 2Chr. 20:3, 4, 13; Joel 2:15, 16
15 Isa. 13:6, 9; Jer. 30:7; Joel 2:1
16 Deut. 12:6, 7; 16:11, 14, 15

1:2–20 Joel reveals a message concerning "the day of the Lord" that took place in his own lifetime. This small-scale and local "day of the Lord" is prophetically important because it becomes a pattern for the future "day of the Lord" which will be global and large in scale. (See the article on "The Day of the Lord" for more information.) God's judgment upon Judah is forecast to be a swarm of locusts in successive stages. Such judgments were forecast for Israel in Deuteronomy 28:38–42 (see Isa. 33:4; Amos 7:1; Rev. 9:1–12).

1:4 palmerworm . . . locust . . . cankerworm . . . caterpiller. These apparently describe either four different species of locusts or four stages of development in the life of a locust. The Hebrew words literally mean gnawing, swarming, creeping, and stripping respectively. Attempts to have these stages represent four specific nations like Assyria, Babylon, Greece, and Rome appear to be without merit since the context supports an actual locust swarm in Joel's day. It is assumed that these are desert locusts, a type of locust that devastated the land of Israel as recently as A.D. 1915. They represent an unex-

plained metamorphoses from grasshoppers to their locust form. Furthermore, when their density reaches a certain level, the swarm of insects will devour any plants in its path. Just as the plague of locusts mocked the Egyptians' pride in the fertility of their land (see Ex. 10:1–19), so this locust invasion would rebuke God's people, who had forgotten that their prosperity came from God. The locust swarm then becomes a historical pattern for future times of God's judgment as described in Joel 1:6–7.

1:15 the day of the Lord. Here is the first occurrence of Joel's theme. The basic meaning of the term refers to any time when God intervenes in history, usually in judgment. It is found four other times in Joel (2:1, 11, 31; 3:14). It is also mentioned by Amos (Amos 5:18, 20), Obadiah (Obad. 1:15), Zephaniah (Zeph. 1:7, 14, 18; 2:2) and Malachi (Mal. 4:5). Here, "the day of the Lord" specifically refers to an event that is now in the past, as the context indicates. The other instances in Joel refer to the future time often known as the Tribulation.

hath devoured the pastures of the wilderness, and the flame hath burned all the trees of the field.

20 The beasts of the field cry also unto thee: for the rivers of waters are dried up, and the fire hath devoured the pastures of the wilderness.

CHAPTER 2
The Locusts Warn about the Day of the Lord

1 Blow ye the trumpet in Zion, and sound an alarm in my holy mountain: let all the inhabitants of the land tremble: for the day of the LORD cometh, for *it is* nigh at hand;

2 A day of darkness and of gloominess, a day of clouds and of thick darkness, as the morning spread upon the mountains: a great people and a strong; there hath not been ever the like, neither shall be any more after it, *even* to the years of many generations.

3 A fire devoureth before them; and behind them a flame burneth: the land *is* as the garden of Eden before them, and behind them a desolate wilderness; yea, and nothing shall escape them.

4 The appearance of them *is* as the appearance of horses; and as horsemen, so shall they run.

5 Like the noise of chariots on the tops of mountains shall they leap, like the noise of a flame of fire that devoureth the stubble, as a strong people set in battle array.

6 Before their face the people shall be much pained: all faces shall gather blackness.

7 They shall run like mighty men; they shall climb the wall like men of war; and they shall march every one on his ways, and they shall not break their ranks:

8 Neither shall one thrust another; they shall walk every one in his path: and *when* they fall upon the sword, they shall not be wounded.

9 They shall run to and fro in the city; they shall run upon the wall, they shall climb up upon the houses; they shall enter in at the windows like a thief.

10 The earth shall quake before them; the heavens shall tremble: the sun and the moon shall be dark, and the stars shall withdraw their shining:

11 And the LORD shall utter his voice before his army: for his camp *is* very great: for *he is* strong that executeth his word: for the day of the LORD *is* great and very terrible; and who can abide it?

The Lord's Mercy

12 Therefore also now, saith the LORD, turn ye *even* to me with all your heart, and with fasting, and with weeping, and with mourning:

13 And rend your heart, and not your garments, and turn unto the LORD your God: for he *is* gracious and merciful, slow to anger, and of great kindness, and repenteth him of the evil.

14 Who knoweth *if* he will return and repent, and leave a blessing behind him; *even* a meat offering and a drink offering unto the LORD your God?

15 Blow the trumpet in Zion, sanctify a fast, call a solemn assembly:

Cross references (center column)

20 1Kgs. 17:7; 18:5; Job 38:41; Ps. 104:21; 145:15

1 Num. 10:5, 9; Jer. 4:5; Joel 1:15; 2:15; Obad. 1:15; Zeph. 1:14, 15

2 Ex. 10:14; Amos 5:18, 20

3 Gen. 2:8; 13:10; Isa. 51:3; Zech. 7:14

4 Rev. 9:7

5 Joel 2:2; Rev. 9:9

6 Jer. 8:21; Lam. 4:8; Nah. 2:10

9 Jer. 9:21; John 10:1

10 Isa. 13:10; Ezek. 32:7; Matt. 24:29

11 Joel 2:25; 3:16; Amos 1:2; Rev. 18:8

13 Ps. 34:18; 51:17; Jon. 4:2

14 Isa. 65:8; Amos 5:15

15 Num. 10:3; Joel 1:14; 2:1

2:1–11 Having introduced a past "day of the LORD" judgment in chapter 1, Joel's use of the term in this passage refers to the future time often called "the seven-year Tribulation." The context supports a future understanding of the "day of the LORD" in this passage, which can be seen in Joel 2:2, when it is said that "there hath not been ever the like, neither shall be any more after it, even to the years of many generations." Here and in the remainder of Joel's references to the "day of the LORD" (2:31; 3:14) we see various references to the future Tribulation period.

2:1 cometh . . . nigh at hand. A term that denotes imminence. The day of the LORD could arrive without warning; there are no gradual steps or signs preceding it.

2:2 Darkness . . . gloominess . . . clouds . . . thick darkness. This prophecy describes the affective impact upon those who will experience the "day of the LORD." This is the language of a locust swarm. However, in contrast to Joel 1, this plague appears to be the one described in John's vision from Revelation 9:1–21 which depicts unique demonic creatures carrying out the fifth trumpet judgment of the Tribulation.

2:11 the LORD shall utter his voice before his army. Although this is likely the demonic army of Revelation 9, God is sovereign over evil as well as good, even though He is righteous in every way. In fact, if one exercises ultimate control over his enemies, then he is indeed a sovereign. This is one of the things that prophecy demonstrates in history—that God is in control. If He is in control of the geopolitical affairs, then it is comforting for individuals to realize that He is also in control of their lives.

2:15–17 One of the conditions of Israel's special blessing is national repentance toward God and His plan for the nation (Lev. 26:40–45; Deut. 4:29–31; 30:1–10; Matt. 23:37–39).

Israel in Tribulation

By David Allen Lewis

Israel has always been a troubled people, her existence threatened, her survival hanging by the slenderest of threads. Surrounded by hostile neighbors, who have sworn themselves to her destruction, she is presently beset by malicious media, greedy politicians, manipulators, and opportunists, and holds onto life with the most tenuous grasp.

Will this wife of Jehovah survive? Will the days of rest and restoration come at last, or is the modern state of Israel only a momentary aberration upon the pages of history?

Having passed through the furnace of affliction, the Jews are now hounded by revisionists, who accuse the survivors of Nazi Germany of inventing the Holocaust to win sympathy.

The Church would do well to rediscover the biblical meaning of Zion. We should rediscover those heroic Christians who have a zeal and compassion for Jerusalem, who battle racism, prejudice, and hatred for the Jews. Above all, let the Word of God convince us of what the Lord has at stake in Israel (Ezek. 36). The holiness of God and the return of the Jews to the land should captivate every believer in Christ. Shades of blindness should be removed from the eyes of the uninformed and the misinformed.

> *Only Jerusalem has been promised continued existence.*

This task of informing others about the tribulations of the nation and people of Israel is not for the fainthearted, the bigot, nor the ignorant. Our purpose is to help serious, thoughtful people get an insight into the major issues of our times. Christians who are lovers of Zion deal with the most serious of problems and the darkest of fears, yet their message is one of hope, both for the present and the future. Will Israel survive in this hostile environment? The answer is yes, but everyone has serious choices before him or her. The Church, the Jewish people, politicians, and the nations of the world are undergoing a litmus test. Under God's watchful eye, performances are evaluated and futures predicated, based not only on the exercise of our faith, but also on our relationship to the Jewish people.

The ultimate outcome of these choices is yet to come. The worst of times ever faced by humanity may be near at hand. Called the "time of Jacob's trouble" 2,600 years ago, it can now be labeled the "time of Gentile trouble" as well. The book of Revelation states that at least fifty percent of earth's population will die during those horrendous seven years of the Tribulation (Rev 6:8; 9:15–18). Only Israel is promised survival. Other nations may survive, in reduced capacity, but only Jerusalem has been promised continued existence.

At the end of the Tribulation, all Gentile nations will come against Jerusalem to make war against God's chosen people (Zech. 12—14). This will be the final provocation of divine anger. Our Lord, Messiah Himself, will lead heaven's hosts for the final conflict of this age. The Battle of Armageddon shall be fought and won by the Son of God. Only Judah is seen as standing on God's side against Antichrist and his band of incorrigible rebels (Zech. 14:14). All Israel shall be saved (Rom. 11:26–27), and God will remove iniquity from the land in a single day (Zech. 3:9). God will demonstrate His sovereignty (Isa. 43:25; 48:11), as Jesus will return to Jerusalem and reign over all the earth (Zech. 14:1–3).

16 Gather the people, sanctify the congregation, assemble the elders, gather the children, and those that suck the breasts: let the bridegroom go forth of his chamber, and the bride out of her closet.

17 Let the priests, the ministers of the LORD, weep between the porch and the altar, and let them say, Spare thy people, O LORD, and give not thine heritage to reproach, that the heathen should rule over them: wherefore should they say among the people, Where *is* their God?

18 Then will the LORD be jealous for his land, and pity his people.

19 Yea, the LORD will answer and say unto his people, Behold, I will send you corn, and wine, and oil, and ye shall be satisfied therewith: and I will no more make you a reproach among the heathen:

20 But I will remove far off from you the northern *army*, and will drive him into a land barren and desolate, with his face toward the east sea, and his hinder part toward the utmost sea, and his stink shall come up, and his ill savour shall come up, because he hath done great things.

21 Fear not, O land; be glad and rejoice: for the LORD will do great things.

22 Be not afraid, ye beasts of the field: for the pastures of the wilderness do spring, for the tree beareth her fruit, the fig tree and the vine do yield their strength.

23 Be glad then, ye children of Zion, and rejoice in the LORD your God: for he hath given you the former rain moderately, and he will cause to come down for you the rain, the former rain, and the latter rain in the first *month*.

24 And the floors shall be full of wheat, and the fats shall overflow with wine and oil.

25 And I will restore to you the years that the locust hath eaten, the cankerworm, and the caterpiller, and the palmerworm, my great army which I sent among you.

26 And ye shall eat in plenty, and be satisfied, and praise the name of the LORD your God, that hath dealt wondrously with you: and my people shall never be ashamed.

27 And ye shall know that I *am* in the midst of Israel, and *that* I *am* the LORD your God, and none else: and my people shall never be ashamed.

28 And it shall come to pass afterward, *that*

16 Ex. 19:10, 22; 2Chr. 20:13; Joel 1:14; 1Cor. 7:5
17 Ex. 32:11, 12; Deut. 9:26-29; Ps. 42:10; 79:10; 115:2; Ezek. 8:16; Mic. 7:10; Matt. 23:35
18 Deut. 32:36; Isa. 60:10; Zech. 1:14; 8:2
19 Joel 1:10; Mal. 3:10-12
20 Ex. 10:19; Deut. 11:24; Jer. 1:14; Ezek. 47:18; Zech. 14:8
22 Joel 1:18, 19, 20; Zech. 8:12
26 Mic. 6:14
27 Lev. 26:11, 12

2:18 Even though the condition for millennial blessing is obedience (cf. 2:15–17), God insures the nation that one day the people will repent and He will respond in pity. God's pity will take two directions: 1) toward His land, indicating that the land of Israel will be involved in millennial blessing and 2) toward His people. The Jewish people still have a future destiny that includes a great time of blessing because of God's pity upon them.

2:20 the northern army. Almost all of Israel's enemies invaded from the North (i.e., Assyria and Babylon). During the time of the Tribulation, of which this passage is set, Israel will also experience invasion from the North. First, before the Tribulation, Israel will be invaded from the north by Gog and Magog (Ezek. 38—39). Second, toward the end of the Tribulation, the assembly of armies for Armageddon will arrive via the north. Revelation 16:12–16 tells us that the Euphrates River (north of Israel) will be dried up to make way for the armies of the world to invade Israel, but God will destroy them all (Rev. 19:11–21). The context indicates that this carnage will take place at Armageddon.

2:23 the former rain, and the latter rain. This agricultural illustration was first used in Deuteronomy 11:13–17; 28:11–24 as a promise that God would send rain at the right time to bless an obedient Israel, but would withhold rainfall from a disobedient nation. Passages like these are sometimes used to support a revival of the Church before Christ can return. However, the context of these references relates to Israel and not the

Church. When used of Israel, it does not denote the harvest of souls; instead, as noted above, it is a reference to agricultural blessing, in this case, the blessings on Israel during the Millennium.

2:28–32 These events will occur in conjunction with the second coming of Christ to earth. Peter in Acts 2:17–21 almost entirely quotes this passage during his sermon on the Day of Pentecost. Many believe that at least part of Joel 2 was fulfilled in Acts 2. However, a close look at Peter's reference to Joel is not that of fulfillment (the word "fulfill" is not used in Acts 2), but one of noting similarity ("this is that," i.e., *like* that in Acts 2:16) between the working of God's Spirit in the future—as noted in Joel—and what the Holy Spirit was doing at the nativity of the Church. The question posed by the mockers on the Day of Pentecost was that the disciples were "full of new wine" (Acts 2:13). Peter answered this specific question by declaring that "these are not drunken, as ye suppose. . . . But this is that (*like*) which was spoken by the prophet Joel" (Acts 2:15–16). What does Joel describe in these five verses? Joel describes the activity of God's Spirit at work in events surrounding the second coming of Christ. Thus, Peter's point is that of similarity between what the Holy Spirit will do in the future with the nation of Israel and what He was doing at Pentecost.

2:28 Peter, under the inspiration of the Holy Spirit, changes the word "afterward" in Joel 2:28 to "in the last days" (Acts 2:17), underscoring the fact that his citation of the Joel passage was not being fulfilled in his day, but

I will pour out my spirit upon all flesh; and your sons and your daughters shall prophesy, your old men shall dream dreams, your young men shall see visions:

29 And also upon the servants and upon the handmaids in those days will I pour out my spirit.

30 And I will shew wonders in the heavens and in the earth, blood, and fire, and pillars of smoke.

31 The sun shall be turned into darkness, and the moon into blood, before the great and the terrible day of the LORD come.

32 And it shall come to pass, *that* whosoever shall call on the name of the LORD shall be delivered: for in mount Zion and in Jerusalem shall be deliverance, as the LORD hath said, and in the remnant whom the LORD shall call.

CHAPTER 3
The Lord Will Judge the Nations

1 For, behold, in those days, and in that time, when I shall bring again the captivity of Judah and Jerusalem,

2 I will also gather all nations, and will bring them down into the valley of Jehoshaphat, and will plead with them there for my people and *for* my heritage Israel, whom

29 1Cor. 12:13; Gal. 3:28; Col. 3:11

30 Matt. 24:29; Mark 13:24; Luke 21:11, 25

31 Isa. 13:9, 10; Matt. 24:29; Mark 13:24; Luke 21:25; Rev. 6:12

32 Rom. 9:27; 10:13; 11:5, 7, 26

1 Jer. 30:3; Ezek. 38:14

2 2Chr. 20:26; Isa. 66:16; Ezek. 38:22; Joel 3:12; Zech. 14:2-4

3 Obad. 1:11; Nah. 3:10

4 Ezek. 25:15-17

5 Dan. 11:38

7 Isa. 43:5, 6; 49:12

8 Jer. 6:20; Ezek. 23:42

9 Ezek. 38:7

they have scattered among the nations, and parted my land.

3 And they have cast lots for my people; and have given a boy for an harlot, and sold a girl for wine, that they might drink.

4 Yea, and what have ye to do with me, O Tyre, and Zidon, and all the coasts of Palestine? will ye render me a recompence? and if ye recompence me, swiftly *and* speedily will I return your recompence upon your own head;

5 Because ye have taken my silver and my gold, and have carried into your temples my goodly pleasant things:

6 The children also of Judah and the children of Jerusalem have ye sold unto the Grecians, that ye might remove them far from their border.

7 Behold, I will raise them out of the place whither ye have sold them, and will return your recompence upon your own head:

8 And I will sell your sons and your daughters into the hand of the children of Judah, and they shall sell them to the Sabeans, to a people far off: for the LORD hath spoken *it*.

9 Proclaim ye this among the Gentiles; Prepare war, wake up the mighty men, let all the men of war draw near; let them come up:

must await the time of the Last Days, which, as used by Peter, refers to the Tribulation (cf. Deut. 4:30; 31:29; Isa. 2:2; Jer. 23:20; 30:24; 48:47; Ezek. 38:16; Dan. 2:28; 10:14; Mic. 4:1).

2:30–31 wonders in the heavens and in the earth. This phrase likely refers to the seal, trumpet, and vial judgments of Revelation 6, 8—9, 16 that transpire throughout much of the seven-year Tribulation period. However, Joel 2:31 likely refers to a blackout at the end of the Tribulation, right before the second coming of Christ to the earth. This is supported by Matthew 24:29 which says, "Immediately after the tribulation of those days shall the sun be darkened, and the moon shall not give her light."

While some say the phrase, "before the great and the terrible day of the Lord," refers to the Tribulation period, the context indicates that it describes the actual second advent of Christ, when our Lord comes to earth to personally judge all unbelievers (Mal. 3:1–3; 4:1, 3, 5; Rev. 19:11–21).

2:32 whosoever shall call on the name of the LORD shall be delivered. Deliverance in this context means physical rescue from Israel's enemies that have gathered for this phase of Armageddon against Jerusalem. The

phrase is quoted in Romans 10:13, where the context indicates that only believing Israel will be willing to call upon the Lord for deliverance. Matthew 24:22 says of the Great Tribulation, "except those days should be shortened, there should no flesh be saved," speaking of the Jews in Jerusalem.

3:1–17 The judgment of the Tribulation precedes and prepares the way for peace and rest in the kingdom (Joel 3:18–21). Perhaps Joel 3:1–3 speaks of a judgment after the Second Coming similar to that described in Matthew 25:31–46.

3:2 I will also gather all nations. Not only will Israel be regathered to the land of Israel, but the Gentile nations will be gathered into Israel for judgment (cf. Rev. 16:12–16). "The valley of Jehoshaphat" will be the assembly area for the Gentiles and their armies at Armageddon. Jehoshaphat means "Yahweh judges." This valley is named for a king of Judah by the name of Jehoshaphat (875–859 B.C.) where he experienced military victory over his enemies when the Lord caused them to fight amongst themselves. Here the Lord indicts the Gentiles for their treatment of His people, Israel. It is only fitting that the Lord brings the nations to the homeland of the people they intend to destroy and then "turns the tables" on them.

10 Beat your plowshares into swords, and your pruninghooks into spears: let the weak say, I *am* strong.

11 Assemble yourselves, and come, all ye heathen, and gather yourselves together round about: thither cause thy mighty ones to come down, O LORD.

12 Let the heathen be wakened, and come up to the valley of Jehoshaphat: for there will I sit to judge all the heathen round about.

13 Put ye in the sickle, for the harvest is ripe: come, get you down; for the press is full, the fats overflow; for their wickedness *is* great.

14 Multitudes, multitudes in the valley of decision: for the day of the LORD *is* near in the valley of decision.

15 The sun and the moon shall be darkened, and the stars shall withdraw their shining.

Blessings for the Lord's People

16 The LORD also shall roar out of Zion, and utter his voice from Jerusalem; and the heavens and the earth shall shake: but the LORD *will be* the hope of his people, and the strength of the children of Israel.

17 So shall ye know that I *am* the LORD your God dwelling in Zion, my holy mountain: then shall Jerusalem be holy, and there shall no strangers pass through her any more.

18 And it shall come to pass in that day, *that* the mountains shall drop down new wine, and the hills shall flow with milk, and all the rivers of Judah shall flow with waters, and a fountain shall come forth of the house of the LORD, and shall water the valley of Shittim.

19 Egypt shall be a desolation, and Edom shall be a desolate wilderness, for the violence *against* the children of Judah, because they have shed innocent blood in their land.

20 But Judah shall dwell for ever, and Jerusalem from generation to generation.

21 For I will cleanse their blood *that* I have not cleansed: for the LORD dwelleth in Zion.

10 Isa. 2:4; Zech. 12:8
11 Ps. 103:20
12 Ps. 96:13; 98:9; 110:6; Isa. 2:4; 3:13; Joel 3:2; Mic. 4:3
13 Matt. 13:39; Rev. 14:15, 18, 19, 20
16 Isa. 51:5, 6; Jer. 25:30; Amos 1:2; Hag. 2:6
17 Rev. 21:27
18 Ezek. 47:1; Zech. 14:8; Rev. 22:1
19 Jer. 49:17
20 Amos 9:15

3:15–16 The earthquake and blackout seem parallel with events described in Zechariah 14:4–5, which describes an earthquake that restructures a valley near the Mount of Olives in Jerusalem. This remodeling of Jerusalem will be accompanied by signs in the heavens, as God powerfully defends and vindicates His people Israel.

3:17 the LORD your God dwelling in Zion, my holy mountain. As the Millennium begins in Israel, Messiah will dwell with the nation, personally ruling from Jerusalem. Only those known by the Lord will be allowed to "pass through" the city.

3:18 The Judean wilderness will be no more, as Messiah will provide the blessing of new water sources for His people. Originating from within the Millennial Temple that will exist in that day, this new source of water will spur great agricultural productivity (cf. Ezek. 47:1–8; Zech. 13:1).

3:20 Judah . . . Jerusalem. In contrast to Israel's enemies like Egypt and Edom, Judah and Jerusalem have an eternal destiny of blessing from the Lord. Future prophecies such as this passage have never been literally fulfilled.

Amos

The name Amos means "burden," which is a key word in this prophetic book. Amos is an appropriate name for one suddenly taken from his humble rural roots, since he was a rough shepherd who lived in the desert of Tekoa, south of Jerusalem. His visits to the great cities of Israel had shown him the sin, corruption, and idolatry especially prevalent in the Northern Kingdom. Amos is believed to have prophesied during the reign of Jeroboam II, between the years 765–755 B.C. Upon receiving a call from God, Amos became a prophet of social justice, and he preached in dramatic language, boldly condemning external and idolatrous religion that embraced moral corruption. In the first two chapters of his book, he pronounced judgments on nations surrounding Israel and Judah by using a Hebrew poetic device of repetition. Using this method and the phrase "three transgressions . . . and for four," the prophet introduces each judgment prediction. Chapters 3—6 focus on Israel, admonishing the people against false worship, sinful corruption, and excessive love of luxury and pleasure. Warning of the future defeats and captivity, chapters 7—9 contain five visions (locusts, fire, the plumbline, the basket of ripe fruit, and impending judgment).

Some profound quotes from the graphic sermons delivered by Amos are found in 3:3 ("Can two walk together except they be agreed?"); 4:12 ("Prepare to meet thy God, O Israel"); 5:1 ("Seek good and not evil that ye may live"); and 6:1 ("Woe to them that are at ease in Zion").

Author	Amos
Date	8th Century B.C.
Key Truth	National Sin and National Judgment
Historic Time	Reign of Jeroboam II
Key Verse	3:1–2 The LORD hath spoken against you, O children of Israel. . . .

Yet unfulfilled is the marvelous passage in 9:8–15, which predicts severe destruction, but not the utter end of Israel. After decrying the many sins of His people, Amos describes the ultimate restoration and prosperity of Israel in the Millennial Kingdom age, when the great "Son of David," Jesus, the Messiah, reigns in splendor.

Out of 146 verses, 85 are predictive, or 58 percent of the book. Many predictions among the 25 separate forecasts are already fulfilled.

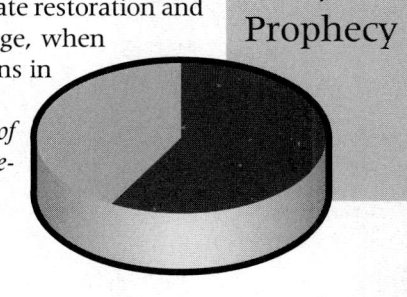

58%
Prophecy

950 B.C.	900 B.C.	850 B.C.	800 B.C.	750 B.C.	700 B.C.	650 B.C.	600 B.C.	550

931-722
Northern Kingdom (Israel)

931
The kingdom is divided

835
Ministry of Joel

793-753
Reign of Jeroboam II over Israel

627-580
Ministry of Jeremiah

605-536
Babylonian Captivity;
Ministry of Daniel

931-586
Southern Kingdom (Judah)

586

760-753
Ministry of Amos

605 First captivity **597** Second captivity **Fall of Jerusalem**

796-767
Reign of Amaziah over Judah

740-680
Ministry of Isaiah

592-570
Ministry of Ezekiel

CHAPTER 1

God Judges Israel's Neighbors

1 The words of Amos, who was among the herdmen of Tekoa, which he saw concerning Israel in the days of Uzziah king of Judah, and in the days of Jeroboam the son of Joash king of Israel, two years before the earthquake.

2 And he said, The LORD will roar from Zion, and utter his voice from Jerusalem; and the habitations of the shepherds shall mourn, and the top of Carmel shall wither.

3 Thus saith the LORD; For three transgressions of Damascus, and for four, I will not turn away *the punishment* thereof; because they have threshed Gilead with threshing instruments of iron:

4 But I will send a fire into the house of Hazael, which shall devour the palaces of Ben-hadad.

5 I will break also the bar of Damascus, and cut off the inhabitant from the plain of Aven, and him that holdeth the sceptre from the house of Eden: and the people of Syria shall go into captivity unto Kir, saith the LORD.

6 Thus saith the LORD; For three transgressions of Gaza, and for four, I will not turn away *the punishment* thereof; because they carried away captive the whole captivity, to deliver *them* up to Edom:

7 But I will send a fire on the wall of Gaza, which shall devour the palaces thereof:

8 And I will cut off the inhabitant from Ashdod, and him that holdeth the sceptre from Ashkelon, and I will turn mine hand against Ekron: and the remnant of the Philistines shall perish, saith the Lord GOD.

9 Thus saith the LORD; For three transgressions of Tyrus, and for four, I will not turn away *the punishment* thereof; because they delivered up the whole captivity to Edom,

and remembered not the brotherly covenant:

10 But I will send a fire on the wall of Tyrus, which shall devour the palaces thereof.

11 Thus saith the LORD; For three transgressions of Edom, and for four, I will not turn away *the punishment* thereof; because he did pursue his brother with the sword, and did cast off all pity, and his anger did tear perpetually, and he kept his wrath for ever:

12 But I will send a fire upon Teman, which shall devour the palaces of Bozrah.

13 Thus saith the LORD; For three transgressions of the children of Ammon, and for four, I will not turn away *the punishment* thereof; because they have ripped up the women with child of Gilead, that they might enlarge their border:

14 But I will kindle a fire in the wall of Rabbah, and it shall devour the palaces thereof, with shouting in the day of battle, with a tempest in the day of the whirlwind:

15 And their king shall go into captivity, he and his princes together, saith the LORD.

CHAPTER 2

1 Thus saith the LORD; For three transgressions of Moab, and for four, I will not turn away *the punishment* thereof; because he burned the bones of the king of Edom into lime:

2 But I will send a fire upon Moab, and it shall devour the palaces of Kerioth: and Moab shall die with tumult, with shouting, *and* with the sound of the trumpet:

3 And I will cut off the judge from the midst thereof, and will slay all the princes thereof with him, saith the LORD.

4 Thus saith the LORD; For three transgressions of Judah, and for four, I will not turn away *the punishment* thereof; because they have despised the law of the LORD, and have

Cross references

1 Zech. 14:5
2 Joel 3:16
3 2Kgs. 10:33; 13:7
4 Jer. 17:27; 49:27
5 2Kgs. 16:9; Jer. 51:30; Lam. 2:9; Amos 9:7
6 2Chr. 21:16, 17; 28:18; Isa. 14:29; Jer. 47:4, 5; Ezek. 25:15; Joel 3:6; Amos 1:9; Zeph. 2:4
7 Jer. 47:1
8 Ps. 81:14; Jer. 47:4; Ezek. 25:16; Zeph. 2:4; Zech. 9:5, 6
9 2Sam. 5:11; 1Kgs. 5:1; 9:11-14; Isa. 23:1; Jer. 47:4; Joel 3:4, 5; Amos 1:6
10 Amos 1:4, 7-9
11 Gen. 27:41; Deut. 23:7
13 Jer. 49:1, 2
15 Jer. 49:3
1 2Kgs. 3:27
2 Jer. 48:41
4 Lev. 26:14, 15; Neh. 1:7; Isa. 28:15; Jer. 16:19, 20; Ezek. 20:13, 16, 18, 24, 30; Dan. 9:11; Rom. 1:25

1:1 Amos and most of the other prophets stressed three basic points: 1) the world in which they lived and ministered was wicked and corrupt; 2) a just God would administer judgment against this sinful world; and 3) a golden age of blessing under divine royal rule that exalts Israel would follow that judgment.

1:2 roar from Zion. This expression is used in connection with God's judgment on Gentile nations (cf. Isa. 42:13; Jer. 25:30–33; Hos. 11:10–12; Joel 3:16). What happened to Damascus and the hostile nations in the area seems to look beyond ancient times to the future "day of the LORD," the Tribulation that precedes the establishment of Christ's kingdom on earth.

1:3 three transgressions . . . and for four. Amos uses this rhetorical expression, called a Hebrew numeric parallelism, not for a specific limitation, but to signify that the sins of Damascus were innumerable. He employs the attention-getting literary device eight times (concerning Damascus/Syria, Gaza/Philistia, Tyrus/Phoenicia, Edom, Ammon, Moab, Judah, and Israel). Seven times he speaks of sending "a fire" upon these lands, indicating fiery destruction from invading armies. All these regions came under attack by the Assyrians and the Babylonians from the North and the Egyptians from the South. These prophecies were literally fulfilled during the two hundred years that followed Amos' predictions.

not kept his commandments, and their lies caused them to err, after the which their fathers have walked:

5 But I will send a fire upon Judah, and it shall devour the palaces of Jerusalem.

He Will Judge Israel Too

6 Thus saith the LORD; For three transgressions of Israel, and for four, I will not turn away *the punishment* thereof; because they sold the righteous for silver, and the poor for a pair of shoes;

7 That pant after the dust of the earth on the head of the poor, and turn aside the way of the meek: and a man and his father will go in unto the *same* maid, to profane my holy name:

8 And they lay *themselves* down upon clothes laid to pledge by every altar, and they drink the wine of the condemned *in* the house of their god.

9 Yet destroyed I the Amorite before them, whose height *was* like the height of the cedars, and he *was* strong as the oaks; yet I destroyed his fruit from above, and his roots from beneath.

10 Also I brought you up from the land of Egypt, and led you forty years through the wilderness, to possess the land of the Amorite.

11 And I raised up of your sons for prophets, and of your young men for Nazarites. *Is it* not even thus, O ye children of Israel? saith the LORD.

12 But ye gave the Nazarites wine to drink; and commanded the prophets, saying, Prophesy not.

13 Behold, I am pressed under you, as a cart is pressed *that is* full of sheaves.

14 Therefore the flight shall perish from the swift, and the strong shall not strengthen his force, neither shall the mighty deliver himself:

15 Neither shall he stand that handleth the bow; and *he that is* swift of foot shall not deliver *himself*: neither shall he that rideth the horse deliver himself.

16 And *he that is* courageous among the mighty shall flee away naked in that day, saith the LORD.

CHAPTER 3
The Work of a Prophet

1 Hear this word that the LORD hath spoken against you, O children of Israel, against the whole family which I brought up from the land of Egypt, saying,

2 You only have I known of all the families of the earth: therefore I will punish you for all your iniquities.

3 Can two walk together, except they be agreed?

4 Will a lion roar in the forest, when he hath no prey? will a young lion cry out of his den, if he have taken nothing?

5 Can a bird fall in a snare upon the earth, where no gin *is* for him? shall *one* take up a snare from the earth, and have taken nothing at all?

6 Shall a trumpet be blown in the city, and the people not be afraid? shall there be evil in a city, and the LORD hath not done *it*?

7 Surely the Lord GOD will do nothing, but he revealeth his secret unto his servants the prophets.

8 The lion hath roared, who will not fear? the Lord GOD hath spoken, who can but prophesy?

Samaria Is Doomed

9 Publish in the palaces at Ashdod, and in the palaces in the land of Egypt, and say, Assemble yourselves upon the mountains of Samaria, and behold the great tumults in the midst thereof, and the oppressed in the midst thereof.

10 For they know not to do right, saith the LORD, who store up violence and robbery in their palaces.

11 Therefore thus saith the Lord GOD; An

Cross references

5 Jer. 17:27; Hos. 8:14
6 Lev. 25:35-40; Deut. 24:7; 1Sam. 29:21; Amos 8:6
7 Lev. 18:6-20; 19:29; 20:3, 10; Isa. 10:2; Ezek. 22:11; 36:20; Amos 5:12; Rom. 2:24
8 Ex. 22:26; Deut. 24:13; Ezek. 23:41; 1Cor. 8:10; 10:21
9 Deut. 2:31; Josh. 24:8; Isa. 5:24; Mal. 4:1
10 Ex. 12:51; Deut. 2:7; 8:2; Mic. 6:4
11 Num. 6:2; Judg. 13:5
12 Isa. 30:10; Jer. 11:21; Amos 7:12, 13; Mic. 2:6
13 Isa. 1:14
14 Ps. 33:16; Jer. 9:23; Amos 9:1-4
15 Ps. 33:17
2 Dan. 9:12; Matt. 11:22; Luke 12:47; Rom. 2:9; 1Pet. 4:17
6 Isa. 45:7
7 Gen. 6:13; 18:17; Ps. 25:14; John 15:15
8 Amos 1:2; Acts 4:20; 5:20, 29; 1Cor. 9:16
10 Jer. 4:22

2:5 fire . . . devour the palaces of Jerusalem. Literally fulfilled in 586 B.C., when Jerusalem was destroyed on the ninth of Av (Jewish calendar). Curiously, the burning of Jerusalem in A.D. 70 also occured on the ninth of Av (a summer month).

3:1 children of Israel . . . whole family. The ten tribes (Israel) were carried away into captivity in 722 B.C. (see 2 Kgs. 17:18–23), while Judah was progressively overrun by the Babylonians in 606, 597, and 586 B.C.

3:3–6 Notice the seven rhetorical questions posed in these verses. These questions are illustrations to drive home the truth that God sends "evil" (v. 6)—which, in this case, does not mean iniquity but disaster or calamity as a consequence (i.e., a judgment) of sin. A similar scenario would be the Lord sending the curse upon Adam and Eve as a result of their fall into sin (Gen. 3:13–19).

3:11–15 These verses summarize Amos' message of judgment. The two evils of which Israel was most guilty were false worship at Bethel (1 Kgs. 12:25–30) and worldly materialism.

adversary *there shall be* even round about the land; and he shall bring down thy strength from thee, and thy palaces shall be spoiled.
12 Thus saith the LORD; As the shepherd taketh out of the mouth of the lion two legs, or a piece of an ear; so shall the children of Israel be taken out that dwell in Samaria in the corner of a bed, and in Damascus *in* a couch.
13 Hear ye, and testify in the house of Jacob, saith the Lord GOD, the God of hosts,
14 That in the day that I shall visit the transgressions of Israel upon him I will also visit the altars of Beth-el: and the horns of the altar shall be cut off, and fall to the ground.
15 And I will smite the winter house with the summer house; and the houses of ivory shall perish, and the great houses shall have an end, saith the LORD.

CHAPTER 4

1 Hear this word, ye kine of Bashan, that *are* in the mountain of Samaria, which oppress the poor, which crush the needy, which say to their masters, Bring, and let us drink.
2 The Lord GOD hath sworn by his holiness, that, lo, the days shall come upon you, that he will take you away with hooks, and your posterity with fishhooks.
3 And ye shall go out at the breaches, every *cow at that which is* before her; and ye shall cast *them* into the palace, saith the LORD.

Israel Will Not Learn the Lesson

4 Come to Beth-el, and transgress; at Gilgal multiply transgression; and bring your sacrifices every morning, *and* your tithes after three years:
5 And offer a sacrifice of thanksgiving with leaven, and proclaim *and* publish the free offerings: for this liketh you, O ye children of Israel, saith the Lord GOD.
6 And I also have given you cleanness of teeth in all your cities, and want of bread in all your places: yet have ye not returned unto me, saith the LORD.
7 And also I have withholden the rain from you, when *there were* yet three months to the harvest: and I caused it to rain upon one city, and caused it not to rain upon another city: one piece was rained upon, and

the piece whereupon it rained not withered.
8 So two *or* three cities wandered unto one city, to drink water; but they were not satisfied: yet have ye not returned unto me, saith the LORD.
9 I have smitten you with blasting and mildew: when your gardens and your vineyards and your fig trees and your olive trees increased, the palmerworm devoured *them*: yet have ye not returned unto me, saith the LORD.
10 I have sent among you the pestilence after the manner of Egypt: your young men have I slain with the sword, and have taken away your horses; and I have made the stink of your camps to come up unto your nostrils: yet have ye not returned unto me, saith the LORD.
11 I have overthrown *some* of you, as God overthrew Sodom and Gomorrah, and ye were as a firebrand plucked out of the burning: yet have ye not returned unto me, saith the LORD.
12 Therefore thus will I do unto thee, O Israel: *and* because I will do this unto thee, prepare to meet thy God, O Israel.
13 For, lo, he that formeth the mountains, and createth the wind, and declareth unto man what *is* his thought, that maketh the morning darkness, and treadeth upon the high places of the earth, The LORD, The God of hosts, *is* his name.

CHAPTER 5
Come Back, Israel!

1 Hear ye this word which I take up against you, *even* a lamentation, O house of Israel.
2 The virgin of Israel is fallen; she shall no more rise: she is forsaken upon her land; *there is* none to raise her up.
3 For thus saith the Lord GOD; The city that went out *by* a thousand shall leave an hundred, and that which went forth *by* an hundred shall leave ten, to the house of Israel.
4 For thus saith the LORD unto the house of Israel, Seek ye me, and ye shall live:
5 But seek not Beth-el, nor enter into Gilgal, and pass not to Beer-sheba: for Gilgal shall surely go into captivity, and Beth-el shall come to nought.
6 Seek the LORD, and ye shall live; lest he break out like fire in the house of Joseph,

Cross references

15 Judg. 3:20; 1Kgs. 22:39; Jer. 36:22

1 Ps. 22:12;

2 Ps. 89:35; Jer. 16:16; Hab. 1:15

3 Ezek. 12:5, 12

4 Num. 28:3, 4; Deut. 14:28; Ezek. 20:39; Hos. 4:15; 12:11

5 Lev. 7:13; 22:18, 21; 23:17; Deut. 12:6; Ps. 81:12

6 Isa. 26:11; Jer. 5:3; Hag. 2:17

8 Amos 4:6, 10, 11

9 Deut. 28:22; Joel 1:4; 2:25; Hag. 2:17

10 Ex. 9:3, 6; 12:29; Deut. 28:27, 60; 2Kgs. 13:7; Ps. 78:50; Amos 4:6

11 Gen. 19:24, 25; Isa. 13:19; Jer. 49:18; Amos 4:6; Zech. 3:2; Jude 1:23

12 Ezek. 13:5; 22:30; Luke 14:31, 32

13 Deut. 32:13; 33:29; Ps. 139:2; Isa. 47:4; Jer. 10:16; Dan. 2:28; Amos 5:8; 8:9; 9:6; Mic. 1:3

1 Jer. 7:29; Ezek. 19:1; 27:2

4 2Chr. 15:2; Isa. 55:3

5 Hos. 4:15; 10:8; Amos 4:4; 8:14

6 Amos 5:4

4:1–3 kine [cows] **of Bashan.** Bashan, east of the Sea of Galilee, was known for the fine quality of cattle raised in the area. Metaphorically, they refer to upper class women of Samaria who felt no remorse in oppressing the poor. Amos warned that they would be treated like cattle when the captors of Samaria sorted them out for slavery.

and devour *it*, and *there be* none to quench *it* in Beth-el.

7 Ye who turn judgment to wormwood, and leave off righteousness in the earth,

8 *Seek him* that maketh the seven stars and Orion, and turneth the shadow of death into the morning, and maketh the day dark with night: that calleth for the waters of the sea, and poureth them out upon the face of the earth: The LORD *is* his name:

9 That strengtheneth the spoiled against the strong, so that the spoiled shall come against the fortress.

10 They hate him that rebuketh in the gate, and they abhor him that speaketh uprightly.

11 Forasmuch therefore as your treading *is* upon the poor, and ye take from him burdens of wheat: ye have built houses of hewn stone, but ye shall not dwell in them; ye have planted pleasant vineyards, but ye shall not drink wine of them.

12 For I know your manifold transgressions and your mighty sins: they afflict the just, they take a bribe, and they turn aside the poor in the gate *from their right*.

13 Therefore the prudent shall keep silence in that time; for it *is* an evil time.

14 Seek good, and not evil, that ye may live: and so the LORD, the God of hosts, shall be with you, as ye have spoken.

15 Hate the evil, and love the good, and establish judgment in the gate: it may be that the LORD God of hosts will be gracious unto the remnant of Joseph.

16 Therefore the LORD, the God of hosts, the Lord, saith thus; Wailing *shall be* in all streets; and they shall say in all the highways, Alas! alas! and they shall call the husbandman to mourning, and such as are skilful of lamentation to wailing.

17 And in all vineyards *shall be* wailing: for I will pass through thee, saith the LORD.

18 Woe unto you that desire the day of the LORD! to what end *is* it for you? the day of the LORD *is* darkness, and not light.

19 As if a man did flee from a lion, and a bear met him; or went into the house, and leaned his hand on the wall, and a serpent bit him.

20 *Shall* not the day of the LORD *be* darkness, and not light? even very dark, and no brightness in it?

21 I hate, I despise your feast days, and I will not smell in your solemn assemblies.

22 Though ye offer me burnt offerings and your meat offerings, I will not accept *them*: neither will I regard the peace offerings of your fat beasts.

23 Take thou away from me the noise of thy songs; for I will not hear the melody of thy viols.

24 But let judgment run down as waters, and righteousness as a mighty stream.

25 Have ye offered unto me sacrifices and offerings in the wilderness forty years, O house of Israel?

26 But ye have borne the tabernacle of your Moloch and Chiun your images, the star of your god, which ye made to yourselves.

27 Therefore will I cause you to go into captivity beyond Damascus, saith the LORD, whose name *is* The God of hosts.

CHAPTER 6
Israel Will Be Destroyed

1 Woe to them *that are* at ease in Zion, and trust in the mountain of Samaria, *which are* named chief of the nations, to whom the house of Israel came!

2 Pass ye unto Calneh, and see; and from thence go ye to Hamath the great: then go down to Gath of the Philistines: *be they* better than these kingdoms? or their border greater than your border?

3 Ye that put far away the evil day, and cause the seat of violence to come near;

4 That lie upon beds of ivory, and stretch themselves upon their couches, and eat the lambs out of the flock, and the calves out of the midst of the stall;

5 That chant to the sound of the viol, *and*

Cross references

8 Ps. 104:20; Job 9:9; 38:31, 34
11 Deut. 28:30, 38, 39
12 Isa. 29:21; Amos 2:6, 7
14 Mic. 3:11
15 Ex. 32:30; 2Kgs. 19:4; Ps. 34:14; 97:10; Joel 2:14; Rom. 12:9
16 Jer. 9:17
17 Ex. 12:12; Nah. 1:12
18 Isa. 5:19; Jer. 17:15; 30:7; Ezek. 12:22, 27; Joel 2:2; Zeph. 1:15; 2Pet. 3:4
19 Jer. 48:44
21 Lev. 26:31; Jer. 6:20
22 Isa. 66:3; Mic. 6:6, 7
24 Hos. 6:6; Mic. 6:8
25 Deut. 32:17; Josh. 24:14; Isa. 43:23; Ezek. 20:8, 16, 24; Acts 7:42, 43;
26 1Kgs. 11:33
27 2Kgs. 17:6
2 2Kgs. 18:34; Isa. 10:9; Jer. 2:10
3 Ps. 94:20; Ezek. 12:27; Amos 5:12, 18; 6:12; 9:10
5 1Chr. 23:5; Isa. 5:12

5:8 that maketh the seven stars and Orion. Amos pleads with Israel to seek the great Creator who placed the Pleiades (a cluster of several hundred stars, of which only 12 or less are visible to the naked eye in the autumn and winter sky) in the heavens and formed Orion, the most magnificent of the constellations in the winter sky. God is the universal and all-powerful Designer and Administrator of the heavens, the seas, and the earth.

5:18–20 the day of the LORD is darkness, and not light. The "day of the LORD" is the ultimate time when God man-

ifests His power and glory, vindicating His claim over the earth. In Amos' time, some longed for that glorious day, but did not realize that it included divine judgment. Amos is anticipating an imminent and decisive judgment upon Israel, glimpses of the defining events of the Last Days. (For uses of the expression in ancient times and future apocalyptic times, see Isa. 2:12; 13:6; Jer. 46:10; Lam. 2:22; Ezek. 13:5; 30:3; Joel 1:15; 2:1; Obad. 1:15; Zeph. 1:7–8, 18; 2:2–3; Zech. 14:1; and Mal. 4:5.)

invent to themselves instruments of music, like David;

6 That drink wine in bowls, and anoint themselves with the chief ointments: but they are not grieved for the affliction of Joseph.

7 Therefore now shall they go captive with the first that go captive, and the banquet of them that stretched themselves shall be removed.

8 The Lord GOD hath sworn by himself, saith the LORD the God of hosts, I abhor the excellency of Jacob, and hate his palaces: therefore will I deliver up the city with all that is therein.

9 And it shall come to pass, if there remain ten men in one house, that they shall die.

10 And a man's uncle shall take him up, and he that burneth him, to bring out the bones out of the house, and shall say unto him that is by the sides of the house, Is there yet any with thee? and he shall say, No. Then shall he say, Hold thy tongue: for we may not make mention of the name of the LORD.

11 For, behold, the LORD commandeth, and he will smite the great house with breaches, and the little house with clefts.

12 Shall horses run upon the rock? will one plow there with oxen? for ye have turned judgment into gall, and the fruit of righteousness into hemlock:

13 Ye which rejoice in a thing of nought, which say, Have we not taken to us horns by our own strength?

14 But, behold, I will raise up against you a nation, O house of Israel, saith the LORD the God of hosts; and they shall afflict you from the entering in of Hemath unto the river of the wilderness.

CHAPTER 7
Three Visions: How Israel Will Be Destroyed

1 Thus hath the Lord GOD shewed unto me; and, behold, he formed grasshoppers in the beginning of the shooting up of the latter growth; and, lo, it was the latter growth after the king's mowings.

2 And it came to pass, that when they had made an end of eating the grass of the land, then I said, O Lord GOD, forgive, I beseech thee: by whom shall Jacob arise? for he is small.

3 The LORD repented for this: It shall not be, saith the LORD.

4 Thus hath the Lord GOD shewed unto me: and, behold, the Lord GOD called to contend by fire, and it devoured the great deep, and did eat up a part.

5 Then said I, O Lord GOD, cease, I beseech thee: by whom shall Jacob arise? for he is small.

6 The LORD repented for this: This also shall not be, saith the Lord GOD.

7 Thus he shewed me: and, behold, the Lord stood upon a wall made by a plumbline, with a plumbline in his hand.

8 And the LORD said unto me, Amos, what seest thou? And I said, A plumbline. Then said the Lord, Behold, I will set a plumbline in the midst of my people Israel: I will not again pass by them any more:

9 And the high places of Isaac shall be desolate, and the sanctuaries of Israel shall be laid waste; and I will rise against the house of Jeroboam with the sword.

Amos and Amaziah

10 Then Amaziah the priest of Beth-el sent to Jeroboam king of Israel, saying, Amos hath conspired against thee in the midst of the house of Israel: the land is not able to bear all his words.

11 For thus Amos saith, Jeroboam shall die by the sword, and Israel shall surely be led away captive out of their own land.

12 Also Amaziah said unto Amos, O thou seer, go, flee thee away into the land of Judah, and there eat bread, and prophesy there:

13 But prophesy not again any more at

Cross references:

6 Gen. 37:25
8 Ps. 47:4; Jer. 51:14; Ezek. 24:21; Amos 8:7; Heb. 6:13, 17
10 Amos 5:13; 8:3
11 Isa. 55:11; Amos 3:15
12 Hos. 10:4; Amos 5:7
14 Num. 34:8; 1Kgs. 8:65; Jer. 5:15
2 Isa. 51:19
3 Deut. 32:36; Amos 7:6; Jon. 3:10; James 5:16
5 Amos 7:2, 3
8 2Kgs. 21:13; Isa. 28:17; 34:11; Lam. 2:8; Amos 8:2; Mic. 7:18
9 Gen. 26:23; 46:1; 2Kgs. 15:10; Amos 5:5; 8:14; Beer-sheba
10 1Kgs. 12:32; 2Kgs. 14:23
13 1Kgs. 12:32; 13:1; Amos 2:12

7:8 The "plumbline" was to serve as the measure of Israel's sin to reveal how far she had gone astray. Despite the fact that the Lord complied with Amos' first two requests to stay His judgment, destruction is now imminent, and captivity by the Assyrians certain.

7:10 the land is not able to bear all his words. This phrase referred to Amos' preaching, which was intolerable to those who held positions of leadership. Amos spoke out against the unfair practices used by the rich to oppress the poor. When Amos said that the rich would be judged for their injustices, the poor people began to support Amos' message. Amaziah and other leaders in the Northern Kingdom saw this as a direct threat to their authority.

7:12–17 Amos affirms his divine call (vv. 14–15), as he predicts that Amaziah and his family would suffer in future invasions, and that Israel would indeed go into captivity (see 2 Kgs. 14:28—17:6).

Beth-el: for it *is* the king's chapel, and it *is* the king's court.

14 Then answered Amos, and said to Amaziah, I *was* no prophet, neither *was* I a prophet's son; but I *was* an herdman, and a gatherer of sycomore fruit:

15 And the LORD took me as I followed the flock, and the Lord said unto me, Go, prophesy unto my people Israel.

16 Now therefore hear thou the word of the LORD: Thou sayest, Prophesy not against Israel, and drop not *thy word* against the house of Isaac.

17 Therefore thus saith the LORD; Thy wife shall be an harlot in the city, and thy sons and thy daughters shall fall by the sword, and thy land shall be divided by line; and thou shalt die in a polluted land: and Israel shall surely go into captivity forth of his land.

CHAPTER 8
A Basket of Ripe Fruit

1 Thus hath the Lord GOD shewed unto me: and behold a basket of summer fruit.

2 And he said, Amos, what seest thou? And I said, A basket of summer fruit. Then said the LORD unto me, The end is come upon my people of Israel; I will not again pass by them any more.

3 And the songs of the temple shall be howlings in that day, saith the Lord GOD: *there shall be* many dead bodies in every place; they shall cast *them* forth with silence.

Israel's Doom Is Near

4 Hear this, O ye that swallow up the needy, even to make the poor of the land to fail,

5 Saying, When will the new moon be gone, that we may sell corn? and the sabbath, that we may set forth wheat, making the ephah small, and the shekel great, and falsifying the balances by deceit?

6 That we may buy the poor for silver, and the needy for a pair of shoes; *yea*, and sell the refuse of the wheat?

7 The LORD hath sworn by the excellency of Jacob, Surely I will never forget any of their works.

8 Shall not the land tremble for this, and every one mourn that dwelleth therein? and it shall rise up wholly as a flood; and it shall be cast out and drowned, as *by* the flood of Egypt.

9 And it shall come to pass in that day, saith the Lord GOD, that I will cause the sun to go down at noon, and I will darken the earth in the clear day:

10 And I will turn your feasts into mourning, and all your songs into lamentation; and I will bring up sackcloth upon all loins, and baldness upon every head; and I will make it as the mourning of an only *son*, and the end thereof as a bitter day.

11 Behold, the days come, saith the Lord GOD, that I will send a famine in the land, not a famine of bread, nor a thirst for water, but of hearing the words of the LORD:

12 And they shall wander from sea to sea, and from the north even to the east, they shall run to and fro to seek the word of the LORD, and shall not find *it*.

13 In that day shall the fair virgins and young men faint for thirst.

14 They that swear by the sin of Samaria, and say, Thy god, O Dan, liveth; and, The manner of Beer-sheba liveth; even they shall fall, and never rise up again.

CHAPTER 9
Israel Can't Escape the Lord

1 I saw the Lord standing upon the altar: and he said, Smite the lintel of the door, that the posts may shake: and cut them in the head, all of them; and I will slay the last of them with the sword: he that fleeth of them shall not flee away, and he that escapeth of them shall not be delivered.

2 Though they dig into hell, thence shall mine hand take them; though they climb up to heaven, thence will I bring them down:

3 And though they hide themselves in the top of Carmel, I will search and take them out thence; and though they be hid from my

Cross references (center column)

14 1Kgs. 20:35; 2Kgs. 2:5; 4:38; 6:1; Amos 1:1; Zech. 13:5

16 Ezek. 21:2; Mic. 2:6

17 Isa. 13:16; Jer. 28:12; 29:21, 25, 31, 32; Lam. 5:11; Hos. 4:13; Zech. 14:2

2 Ezek. 7:2; Amos 7:8

3 Amos 5:33; 6:9, 10

4 Ps. 14:4; Prov. 30:14

5 Neh. 13:15, 16; Hos. 12:7; Mic. 6:10, 11

6 Amos 2:6

7 Hos. 8:13; 9:9; Amos 6:8

8 Hos. 4:3; Amos 9:5

9 Job 5:14; Isa. 13:10; 59:9, 10; Jer. 15:9; Mic. 3:6

10 Isa. 15:2, 3; Jer. 6:26; 48:37; Ezek. 7:18; 27:31; Zech. 12:10

11 1Sam. 3:1; Ps. 74:9; Ezek. 7:26

14 Deut. 9:21; Hos. 4:15; Amos 5:5

1 Ps. 68:21; Amos 2:14; Hab. 3:13

2 Job 20:6; Ps. 139:8-14; Jer. 51:53; Obad. 1:4

Study notes (bottom)

8:1 basket of summer fruit. This term symbolized that the sinful kingdom was ripe for ruin.

8:4–14 Israel not only wallowed in false worship and idolatry, but dishonest merchants complained of a lull in their financial dealings because of sacred seasons and the Sabbath. Their sin included oppression of the poor. Part of divine judgment was a "famine of hearing the words of the LORD," not a lack of divine truth, but a failure to bring a true message. This could be said of the situation in the world today—many voices claim to speak for God, but few are faithful to His holy Word.

9:3–10 though they hide themselves. Amos in these verses warns the Israelites that there will be no place to hide, that divine judgment will be inescapable, and that widespread dispersion will be certain. However, Amos also declares that God will not utterly destroy Israel.

sight in the bottom of the sea, thence will I command the serpent, and he shall bite them:

4 And though they go into captivity before their enemies, thence will I command the sword, and it shall slay them: and I will set mine eyes upon them for evil, and not for good.

5 And the Lord God of hosts *is* he that toucheth the land, and it shall melt, and all that dwell therein shall mourn: and it shall rise up wholly like a flood; and shall be drowned, as *by* the flood of Egypt.

6 *It is* he that buildeth his stories in the heaven, and hath founded his troop in the earth; he that calleth for the waters of the sea, and poureth them out upon the face of the earth: The Lord *is* his name.

7 *Are* ye not as children of the Ethiopians unto me, O children of Israel? saith the Lord. Have not I brought up Israel out of the land of Egypt? and the Philistines from Caphtor, and the Syrians from Kir?

8 Behold, the eyes of the Lord God *are* upon the sinful kingdom, and I will destroy it from off the face of the earth; saving that I will not utterly destroy the house of Jacob, saith the Lord.

9 For, lo, I will command, and I will sift the house of Israel among all nations, like as *corn* is sifted in a sieve, yet shall not the least grain fall upon the earth.

10 All the sinners of my people shall die by the sword, which say, The evil shall not overtake nor prevent us.

Israel Will Come Back

11 In that day will I raise up the tabernacle of David that is fallen, and close up the breaches thereof; and I will raise up his ruins, and I will build it as in the days of old:

12 That they may possess the remnant of Edom, and of all the heathen, which are called by my name, saith the Lord that doeth this.

13 Behold, the days come, saith the Lord, that the plowman shall overtake the reaper, and the treader of grapes him that soweth seed; and the mountains shall drop sweet wine, and all the hills shall melt.

14 And I will bring again the captivity of my people of Israel, and they shall build the waste cities, and inhabit *them*; and they shall plant vineyards, and drink the wine thereof; they shall also make gardens, and eat the fruit of them.

15 And I will plant them upon their land, and they shall no more be pulled up out of their land which I have given them, saith the Lord thy God.

Cross references

4 Lev. 17:10; 26:33; Deut. 28:65; Jer. 44:11; Ezek. 5:12
5 Amos 8:8; Mic. 1:4
6 Ps. 104:3, 13; Amos 4:13; 5:8
7 Deut. 2:23; Jer. 47:4; Amos 1:5
8 Jer. 30:11; 31:35, 36; Amos 9:4; Obad. 1:16, 17
10 Amos 6:3
11 Acts 15:16, 17
12 Num. 24:18; Obad. 1:19
13 Lev. 26:5; Joel 3:18
14 Isa. 61:4; 65:21; Jer. 30:3; Ezek. 36:33-36
15 Isa. 60:21; Jer. 32:41; Ezek. 34:28; Joel 3:20

9:10–11 Amos is using the illustration of a "sieve" to show how God will sift out every evil thing that has been committed, and not one deed will pass through this judgment. The people are proud of their sin (v. 10), not realizing that God will ultimately judge them for all their wicked deeds.

9:11 In that day will I raise up the tabernacle of David. Amos now looks far beyond the fall of Israel as a nation and their dispersion to a future glorious age of restoration and blessing. The fallen tabernacle (tent) or hut of David, a metaphor for the Davidic dynasty, would be raised up and fully restored when the Messiah comes. There may also be a suggestion of David, as resurrected, occupying a place of leadership in "that day," the Millennial Kingdom (see Jer. 30:9; Ezek. 34:23–24).

9:12 possess the remnant of Edom, and of all the heathen [Gentiles]. Israel will absorb Edom (Obad. 1:21) and exercise authority over all Gentile nations.

9:13 plowman shall overtake the reaper. During the Millennium, great prosperity, plenty, and beauty will spring forth in the land of Israel, as this poetic passage indicates. Another description of the Millennium in Joel 3:18 pictures a land flowing with God's blessings, a land made fruitful by the stream that shall come forth from the house of the Lord (see Ezek. 47:1–12; Zech. 14:8).

9:15 no more be pulled up. When Israel is finally completely restored and the world capital is Jerusalem with the Messiah Jesus reigning, never again will the people of Israel be dislodged, carried into captivity, or endangered. Compare Hosea 2:23 as to when the promises of Genesis 15:18; Isaiah 2:1–5; 19:23–25; and Ezekiel 48:35 are all fulfilled.

Obadiah

Obadiah's name means "servant and worshiper of Jehovah." Containing only one chapter for a total of twenty-one verses, the book of Obadiah is the shortest book in the Old Testament. Obadiah prophesies the events regarding the destruction of the Edomites. Since Edom is mentioned by Obadiah as having more than one ally, the most likely time this prophecy occurred was during the reign of King Jehoram (853–842 B.C.). While Jehoram was king of Judah, the Edomites, the descendents of Esau, Jacob's brother, were allied with the Philistines and the Arabians, who overran Jerusalem. The Edomites' persecution of Jerusalem prompted this prophecy, which focuses solely on this bitter foe of Israel.

Author	Obadiah
Date	8th–9th Century B.C.
Key Truth	The Doom of Edom
Historic Time	Reign of Jehu
Key Verse	10

For thy violence against thy brother Jacob . . . thou shalt be cut off for ever.

The Edomites were a proud, bitter, resentful people, ever seeking to harm the Israelites. They had refused to let Israel pass through their land after the Exodus (Num. 20:14–21). Throughout the centuries that followed, the Edomites were never Israel's friends, although King David's empire once controlled the land of Edom. Frequently at war with Israel, Edom rejoiced over Jerusalem's downfall, cruelly taking part in the plundering and massacre when Nebuchadnezzar captured Jerusalem. Other prophets in other times had forecast Edom's ultimate punishment for their wickedness and opposition to God's chosen people—godly spokesmen like Jeremiah, Ezekiel, Joel, Amos, and Malachi.

Following Jerusalem's destruction, many Edomites left the mountains and the red rock city, known later as Petra, to settle in southern Judea, becoming known as Idumeans. Herod the Great, who received his crown from Caesar, was an Idumean who professed Judaism but sought to slay the infant Jesus (Matt. 2:16). Thus the conflict between Jacob and Esau culminated in the clash between Christ the King and Herod the King. After New Testament times, the Idumeans faded from history.

Awaiting fulfillment is the "day of the Lord" passage (vv. 15–21), when millennial Israel will "possess their possessions," populate their territory, and "the kingdom shall be the Lord's."

Out of 21 verses, 17 are prophetic (approximately 81%), most of which have been fulfilled.

81%
Prophecy

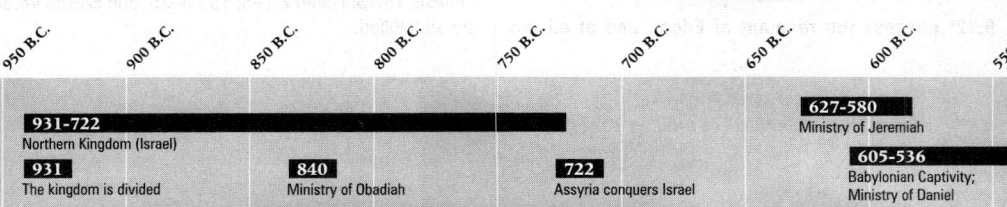

| 950 B.C. | 900 B.C. | 850 B.C. | 800 B.C. | 750 B.C. | 700 B.C. | 650 B.C. | 600 B.C. | 550 |

627-580
Ministry of Jeremiah

931-722
Northern Kingdom (Israel)

931
The kingdom is divided

840
Ministry of Obadiah

722
Assyria conquers Israel

605-536
Babylonian Captivity; Ministry of Daniel

931-586
Southern Kingdom (Judah)

586

841-814
Reign of Jehu over Israel

740-680
Ministry of Isaiah

605 **597** Fall of
First Second Jerusalem
captivity captivity

852-841
Reign of Jehorom over Israel

592-570
Ministry of Ezekiel

CHAPTER 1
Edom Will Be Humbled

1 The vision of Obadiah. Thus saith the Lord GOD concerning Edom; We have heard a rumour from the LORD, and an ambassador is sent among the heathen, Arise ye, and let us rise up against her in battle.

2 Behold, I have made thee small among the heathen: thou art greatly despised.

3 The pride of thine heart hath deceived thee, thou that dwellest in the clefts of the rock, whose habitation *is* high; that saith in his heart, Who shall bring me down to the ground?

4 Though thou exalt *thyself* as the eagle, and though thou set thy nest among the stars, thence will I bring thee down, saith the LORD.

5 If thieves came to thee, if robbers by night, (how art thou cut off!) would they not have stolen till they had enough? if the grapegatherers came to thee, would they not leave *some* grapes?

6 How are *the things* of Esau searched out! *how* are his hidden things sought up!

7 All the men of thy confederacy have brought thee *even* to the border: the men that were at peace with thee have deceived thee, *and* prevailed against thee; *they that eat* thy bread have laid a wound under thee: *there is* none understanding in him.

8 Shall I not in that day, saith the LORD, even destroy the wise *men* out of Edom, and understanding out of the mount of Esau?

9 And thy mighty *men*, O Teman, shall be dismayed, to the end that every one of the mount of Esau may be cut off by slaughter.

10 For *thy* violence against thy brother Jacob shame shall cover thee, and thou shalt be cut off for ever.

11 In the day that thou stoodest on the other side, in the day that the strangers carried away captive his forces, and foreigners entered into his gates, and cast lots upon Jerusalem, even thou *wast* as one of them.

12 But thou shouldest not have looked on the day of thy brother in the day that he became a stranger; neither shouldest thou have rejoiced over the children of Judah in the day of their destruction; neither shouldest thou have spoken proudly in the day of distress.

13 Thou shouldest not have entered into the gate of my people in the day of their calamity; yea, thou shouldest not have looked on their affliction in the day of their calamity, nor have laid *hands* on their substance in the day of their calamity;

14 Neither shouldest thou have stood in the crossway, to cut off those of his that did escape; neither shouldest thou have delivered up those of his that did remain in the day of distress.

Israel Will Win!

15 For the day of the LORD *is* near upon all the heathen: as thou hast done, it shall be done unto thee: thy reward shall return upon thine own head.

16 For as ye have drunk upon my holy mountain, *so* shall all the heathen drink continually, yea, they shall drink, and they shall swallow down, and they shall be as though they had not been.

17 But upon mount Zion shall be deliverance, and there shall be holiness; and the house of Jacob shall possess their possessions.

18 And the house of Jacob shall be a fire, and the house of Joseph a flame, and the house of Esau for stubble, and they shall

Cross references (center column)

1 Isa. 21:11; 34:5; Jer. 49:14-20; Ezek. 25:12-14; Joel 3:19; Mal. 1:3

3 2Kgs. 14:7; Isa. 14:13-15; Rev. 18:7

4 Job 20:6; Jer. 49:16; 51:53; Amos 9:2; Hab. 2:9

5 Deut. 24:21; Isa. 17:6; 24:13; Jer. 49:9

7 Isa. 19:11, 12; Jer. 38:22

8 Job 5:12, 13; Isa. 29:14; Jer. 49:7

9 Ps. 76:5; Jer. 49:7; Amos 2:16

10 Gen. 27:41; Amos 1:11

11 Joel 3:3; Nah. 3:10

12 Job 31:29; Mic. 4:11; 7:8, 10

14 Ps. 31:8

15 Ezek. 30:3; 35:15; Joel 3:14; Hab. 2:8

16 Jer. 25:28, 29

17 Joel 2:32; 3:17; Amos 9:8

18 Isa. 10:17; Zech. 12:6

---

1 Obadiah's vision predicts the destruction of Edom. This prophecy is focused on the nation of the descendants of Esau, Jacob's twin brother. The hostility between the brothers began in Genesis 27 and continued over the centuries in the hostilities between their descendants, Israel and Edom.

3–4 clefts of the rock. The territory of Edom is southeast of the Dead Sea. In biblical times, it was a mountain fortress in the rocky canyons of that region. The Hebrew word translated "rock" is from the word *sela* and was the name of the Edomite capital, Petra. From this invincible standpoint, Edom controlled the desert trade routes between Babylon and Arabia and met with few military challenges. But Obadiah predicted that God would deal with Edom's pride and bring her down. This prophecy

was fulfilled when Petra was destroyed by the Moslems in A.D. 629–632 and never inhabited again. To this day, ancient Edom is a wilderness, and the Edomites have totally disappeared from human history.

15–17 the day of the LORD is near. In contrast to Edom's destruction, Obadiah predicted the ultimate deliverance of Jerusalem in the coming "day of the LORD." Unlike the mountains of Edom, from which no one will escape, there will be a remnant of survivors on Mount Zion in the day of trouble that is coming during the Tribulation period. In the end, Israel will regain her possessions and reclaim her land. The houses of Jacob (Judah) and Joseph (Ephraim) will unite and form one kingdom in the future to execute God's judgment on the "house of Esau" (v. 18).

kindle in them, and devour them; and there shall not be *any* remaining of the house of Esau; for the LORD hath spoken *it*.

19 And *they of* the south shall possess the mount of Esau; and *they of* the plain the Philistines: and they shall possess the fields of Ephraim, and the fields of Samaria: and Benjamin *shall possess* Gilead.

19 Amos 9:12; Zeph. 2:7

20 1Kgs. 17:9, 10; Jer. 32:44

21 Zech. 14:9; Luke 1:33; Rev. 11:15; 19:6

20 And the captivity of this host of the children of Israel *shall possess* that of the Canaanites, *even* unto Zarephath; and the captivity of Jerusalem, which *is* in Sepharad, shall possess the cities of the south.

21 And saviours shall come up on mount Zion to judge the mount of Esau; and the kingdom shall be the LORD's.

Jonah

J onah, whose name means "dove," lived during the reign of wicked king Jeroboam II (793–753 B.C.). Jonah's active prophetic ministry is mentioned in 2 Kings 14:23–29. It is from this passage that we learn that Jonah was from the town of Gath-hepher, approximately two miles northeast of Nazareth.

Jonah's experiences prove to be quite interesting, and insightful. God commanded Jonah to prophesy against Nineveh, the capital of Assyria, at the time when the power of the Assyrian Empire posed an ominous threat to Israel's security. For this reason, Jonah was unwilling to travel to Nineveh to speak of their impending judgment.

Author
Jonah

Date
8th Century B.C.

Key Truth
God's Mercy on the Gentiles

Historic Time
Reign of Jeroboam II

Key Verse
2:2
. . . out of the belly of hell cried I, and thou heardest my voice.

The book of Jonah is highly significant, because it shows that God is willing to show mercy on all (including Gentile peoples) who seek Him in humility and sincerity. Jonah wrote his book upon his return from Nineveh. Belatedly obedient to his mission, Jonah preaches to Nineveh, "Forty days and Nineveh shall be overthrown" (3:4). Much to his surprise (and dismay), the king and the whole population repent of their sins, initiating the greatest revival in history that prompted God to refrain from immediately destroying the city. This stay of execution was short lived; however, as the Ninevites gradually returned to their decadent lifestyles and their city was ransacked by the Medo-Persian Empire in 612 B.C.

Many critics dismiss the miraculous account of Jonah and the great fish as being a myth or a fable because they sadly reject the supernatural nature of the God of the Bible. But Jesus treats the story as a historically accurate one, comparing Jonah's time in the belly of the fish to His own time in the tomb (Matt. 12:40). Therefore, Jonah prefigures Christ as the Sent One, suffering death, being buried, and raised from death after three days, then ministering salvation to the Gentiles (Matt. 12:39–41; Luke 11:29–32).

A total of 4 predictive statements appear in Jonah that comprise only 5 out of the book's 48 total verses (approximately 10%).

10%
Prophecy

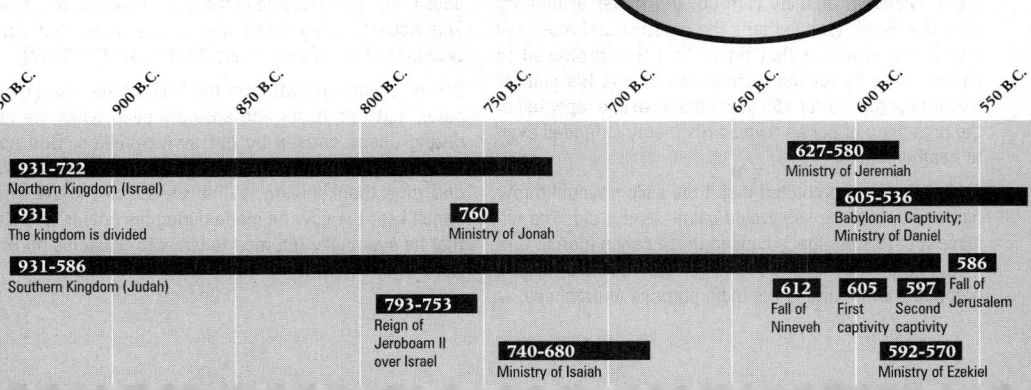

950 B.C.	900 B.C.	850 B.C.	800 B.C.	750 B.C.	700 B.C.	650 B.C.	600 B.C.	550 B.C.

931-722
Northern Kingdom (Israel)

931
The kingdom is divided

760
Ministry of Jonah

627-580
Ministry of Jeremiah

605-536
Babylonian Captivity;
Ministry of Daniel

931-586
Southern Kingdom (Judah)

586
Fall of Jerusalem

793-753
Reign of Jeroboam II over Israel

740-680
Ministry of Isaiah

612
Fall of Nineveh

605
First captivity

597
Second captivity

592-570
Ministry of Ezekiel

CHAPTER 1
Jonah Runs Away

1 Now the word of the LORD came unto Jonah the son of Amittai, saying,

2 Arise, go to Nineveh, that great city, and cry against it; for their wickedness is come up before me.

3 But Jonah rose up to flee unto Tarshish from the presence of the LORD, and went down to Joppa; and he found a ship going to Tarshish: so he paid the fare thereof, and went down into it, to go with them unto Tarshish from the presence of the LORD.

4 But the LORD sent out a great wind into the sea, and there was a mighty tempest in the sea, so that the ship was like to be broken.

5 Then the mariners were afraid, and cried every man unto his god, and cast forth the wares that were in the ship into the sea, to lighten it of them. But Jonah was gone down into the sides of the ship; and he lay, and was fast asleep.

6 So the shipmaster came to him, and said unto him, What meanest thou, O sleeper? arise, call upon thy God, if so be that God will think upon us, that we perish not.

7 And they said every one to his fellow, Come, and let us cast lots, that we may know for whose cause this evil is upon us. So they cast lots, and the lot fell upon Jonah.

8 Then said they unto him, Tell us, we pray thee, for whose cause this evil is upon us; What is thine occupation? and whence comest thou? what is thy country? and of what people art thou?

9 And he said unto them, I am an Hebrew; and I fear the LORD, the God of heaven, which hath made the sea and the dry land.

10 Then were the men exceedingly afraid, and said unto him, Why hast thou done this? For the men knew that he fled from the presence of the LORD, because he had told them.

11 Then said they unto him, What shall we do unto thee, that the sea may be calm unto us? for the sea wrought, and was tempestuous.

12 And he said unto them, Take me up, and cast me forth into the sea; so shall the sea be calm unto you: for I know that for my sake this great tempest is upon you.

13 Nevertheless the men rowed hard to bring it to the land; but they could not: for the sea wrought, and was tempestuous against them.

14 Wherefore they cried unto the LORD, and said, We beseech thee, O LORD, we beseech thee, let us not perish for this man's life, and lay not upon us innocent blood: for thou, O LORD, hast done as it pleased thee.

15 So they took up Jonah, and cast him forth into the sea: and the sea ceased from her raging.

16 Then the men feared the LORD exceedingly, and offered a sacrifice unto the LORD, and made vows.

17 Now the LORD had prepared a great fish to swallow up Jonah. And Jonah was in the belly of the fish three days and three nights.

CHAPTER 2
Jonah Is Thankful

1 Then Jonah prayed unto the LORD his God out of the fish's belly,

2 And said, I cried by reason of mine affliction unto the LORD, and he heard me; out of the belly of hell cried I, and thou heardest my voice.

---

1 2Kgs. 14:25; Matt. 12:39

2 Gen. 10:11, 12; 18:20, 21; Ezra 9:6; Jon. 3:2, 3; 4:11; James 5:4; Rev. 18:5

3 Gen. 4:16; Josh. 19:46; 2Chr. 2:16; Job 1:12; 2:7; Jon. 4:2; Acts 9:36

4 Ps. 107:25

5 1Sam. 24:3; Acts 27:18, 19, 38

6 Ps. 107:28; Joel 2:14

7 Josh. 7:14, 16; 1Sam. 10:20, 21; 14:41, 42; Prov. 16:33; Acts 1:26

8 Josh. 7:19; 1Sam. 14:43

9 Ps. 146:6; Acts 17:24

12 John 11:50

13 Prov. 21:30

14 Deut. 21:8; Ps. 115:3

15 Ps. 89:9; Luke 8:24

16 Mark 4:41; Acts 5:11

17 Matt. 12:40; 16:4; Luke 11:30

1:2 The fact that God chooses to withhold judgment on men and nations hardly means that He does not see their sinful deeds and will not eventually judge and punish them. Nineveh, built by Nimrod, the father of idolatry after the Flood, was perhaps the greatest and most evil city in the world at that time. That God promised to destroy the city for her wickedness shows His justice; that He spared her for 150 years because she repented at the preaching of Jonah reveals His mercy extended even to heathen cities.

1:12–15 Jonah predicted that if the sailors would throw him overboard, the sea would calm—and it did. The fulfillment of this prophecy caused these pagan men to turn to the Lord and recognize Him, for only God can inspire prophecy. Such faith is the main purpose of prophecy.

1:17 It was from Jesus some eight hundred years later that we find that the three days and nights Jonah spent in the belly of the fish was a prophetic type of the three days Christ would spend in the grave after His crucifixion. This became a legitimate sign to the Jews that Jesus was indeed the Christ. (Matt. 16:4; Luke 11:29–32).

2:1–9 Jonah's prayer from the "fish's belly" (v. 1), indicates that God hears and answers even when we pray during chaos caused by our own rebellion. God gave Jonah prophetic insight that he would yet live to sacrifice and give thanksgiving. While we do not know when Jonah kept the vow he made during his prayer, it is clear that he eventually returned to Israel to finish his ministry (cf. 2 Kgs. 14:25).

History's Coming Capstone

By Earl Radmacher

The ultimate purpose for the history of the earth is to graphically demonstrate the glory of God by showing that God alone is sovereign Ruler over all creation. This is why Jesus taught His disciples to pray after this manner: "Thy kingdom come. Thy will be done in earth, as it is in heaven" (Matt. 6:10). The ultimate display of God's will is coming, when Jesus Christ, together with His saints, will bring the first perfect government to this earth (1 Cor. 15:20–28). God has allowed the usurper, Satan, to reign thousands of years as the "god of this world" (2 Cor. 4:4) and the "prince of the power of the air" (Eph. 2:2), but Satan's control will come to an abrupt end. Satan's last government will be a mighty, hands-on, desperate effort to succeed in his rebellion against God (Rev. 12—13).

The first prophetic declaration of the supremacy of God over Satan came very early in Scripture when the Lord God declared to the serpent "It [i.e., Christ] shall bruise thy head, and thou shalt bruise his heel" (Gen. 3:15). Several thousand years later, Jesus vividly portrayed the breaking of Satan's power: "I beheld Satan fall like lightning from heaven" (Luke 10:18). Thus, Jesus set His face like a flint toward the cross, where the curse of sin and death that Satan introduced through his deception in Genesis 3 would be reversed. Satan was judged at the cross (John 16:11), but the execution of the judgment is yet to come (Rev. 20:10).

> *God's grace determines where we go at the end of this earthly sojourn.*

The destruction that will take place on earth after the Rapture will be so intense that Jesus characterized it as "great tribulation, such as has not been since the beginning of the world until this time, no, nor ever shall be" (Matt. 24:21; cf. Dan. 12:1). Jesus prophesied that, "Immediately after the tribulation of those days . . . shall appear the sign of the Son of man in heaven: and then shall all the tribes of the earth mourn, and they shall see the Son of man coming in the clouds of heaven with power and great glory" (Matt. 24:29–30).

We must not confuse the gift of redeeming grace with the reward or prize that may cost us our very lives. God's grace determines where we go at the end of this earthly sojourn. The rewards that Christians receive for their obedience to Christ determine the position of service that they will have in Christ's kingdom. Paul succinctly summarizes the concepts of grace and rewards for Timothy in poetry that became a first-century hymn:

For if we died with *Him,* we shall also live with *Him* [cf. Rom. 6:1–8].

If we endure, we shall also reign with *Him* [cf. Rev. 2:26–28].

If we deny *Him,* He will also deny us [cf. Matt. 10:32–33].

If we are faithless, He remains faithful. "He cannot deny Himself" [2 Tim. 2:11–13].

Ninety-three times in the New Testament our Lord and the apostles use descriptions of service in the coming messianic kingdom to move Christians out of infancy into faithful service. In summary, our future is determined by what we do with what God has given us.

3 For thou hadst cast me into the deep, in the midst of the seas; and the floods compassed me about: all thy billows and thy waves passed over me.

4 Then I said, I am cast out of thy sight; yet I will look again toward thy holy temple.

5 The waters compassed me about, *even* to the soul: the depth closed me round about, the weeds were wrapped about my head.

6 I went down to the bottoms of the mountains; the earth with her bars *was* about me for ever: yet hast thou brought up my life from corruption, O LORD my God.

7 When my soul fainted within me I remembered the LORD: and my prayer came in unto thee, into thine holy temple.

8 They that observe lying vanities forsake their own mercy.

9 But I will sacrifice unto thee with the voice of thanksgiving; I will pay *that* that I have vowed. Salvation *is* of the LORD.

10 And the LORD spake unto the fish, and it vomited out Jonah upon the dry *land*.

CHAPTER 3
Jonah Finally Obeys

1 And the word of the LORD came unto Jonah the second time, saying,

2 Arise, go unto Nineveh, that great city, and preach unto it the preaching that I bid thee.

3 So Jonah arose, and went unto Nineveh, according to the word of the LORD. Now Nineveh was an exceeding great city of three days' journey.

4 And Jonah began to enter into the city a day's journey, and he cried, and said, Yet forty days, and Nineveh shall be overthrown.

5 So the people of Nineveh believed God, and proclaimed a fast, and put on sackcloth, from the greatest of them even to the least of them.

6 For word came unto the king of Nineveh, and he arose from his throne, and he laid his robe from him, and covered *him* with sackcloth, and sat in ashes.

7 And he caused *it* to be proclaimed and published through Nineveh by the decree of the king and his nobles, saying, Let neither man nor beast, herd nor flock, taste any

thing: let them not feed, nor drink water:

8 But let man and beast be covered with sackcloth, and cry mightily unto God: yea, let them turn every one from his evil way, and from the violence that *is* in their hands.

9 Who can tell *if* God will turn and repent, and turn away from his fierce anger, that we perish not?

10 And God saw their works, that they turned from their evil way; and God repented of the evil, that he had said that he would do unto them; and he did *it* not.

CHAPTER 4
Jonah Is Angry

1 But it displeased Jonah exceedingly, and he was very angry.

2 And he prayed unto the LORD, and said, I pray thee, O LORD, *was* not this my saying, when I was yet in my country? Therefore I fled before unto Tarshish: for I knew that thou *art* a gracious God, and merciful, slow to anger, and of great kindness, and repentest thee of the evil.

3 Therefore now, O LORD, take, I beseech thee, my life from me; for *it is* better for me to die than to live.

4 Then said the LORD, Doest thou well to be angry?

5 So Jonah went out of the city, and sat on the east side of the city, and there made him a booth, and sat under it in the shadow, till he might see what would become of the city.

6 And the LORD God prepared a gourd, and made *it* to come up over Jonah, that it might be a shadow over his head, to deliver him from his grief. So Jonah was exceeding glad of the gourd.

7 But God prepared a worm when the morning rose the next day, and it smote the gourd that it withered.

8 And it came to pass, when the sun did arise, that God prepared a vehement east wind; and the sun beat upon the head of Jonah, that he fainted, and wished in himself to die, and said, *It is* better for me to die than to live.

9 And God said to Jonah, Doest thou well to be angry for the gourd? And he said, I do well to be angry, *even* unto death.

10 Then said the LORD, Thou hast had pity

---

3 Ps. 42:7; 88:6

4 1Kgs. 8:38; Ps. 31:22

5 Ps. 69:1; Lam. 3:54

6 Ps. 16:10

7 Ps. 18:6

8 2Kgs. 17:15; Ps. 31:6; Jer. 10:8; 16:19

9 Ps. 3:8; 50:14, 23; 116:17, 18; Hos. 14:2; Heb. 13:15

3 Gen. 30:8; Ps. 36:6; 80:10

4 Deut. 18:22

5 Matt. 12:41; Luke 11:32

6 Job 2:8

7 2Chr. 20:3; Joel 2:15

8 Isa. 58:6; 59:6

9 2Sam. 12:22; Joel 2:14

10 Jer. 18:8; Amos 7:3, 6

2 Ex. 34:6; Ps. 86:5; Joel 2:13; Jon. 1:3

3 1Kgs. 19:4; Jon. 4:8

8 Jon. 4:3

9 11 Deut. 1:39; Ps. 36:6; 145:9; Ezek. 1:2; 3:2, 3

3:10—4:2 While Jonah's reaction to the repentance of the Ninevites shows his animosity toward the people of Nineveh and the Assyrians, this act of forgiveness shows the nature of God, that he is "a gracious God, and merciful, slow to anger, and of great kindness." This story does not cast the prophet in a good light, but it gives us a sublime picture of the graciousness and longsuffering of God. For he is willing to forgive all who call upon Him in sincere repentance, both Gentile idol worshipers and rebellious believers.

on the gourd, for the which thou hast not laboured, neither madest it grow; which came up in a night, and perished in a night: **11** And should not I spare Nineveh, that

11 Isa. 1:18;
Matt. 18:33

great city, wherein are more than sixscore thousand persons that cannot discern between their right hand and their left hand; and *also* much cattle?

4:11 persons that cannot discern between their right hand and their left. As we will see in Nahum, this entire generation was spared, and the ultimate destruction God predicted on the city and country was not fulfilled until 150 years later, when a subsequent generation fell into the same idolatry and ritual killing of human beings and did not repent. The city was so utterly destroyed that its ruins were completely covered for 2,600 years.

Micah

M icah's name is a contraction of Micaiah, meaning "who is like Jehovah?" He apparently makes a word play on his name in verse 18 of chapter 7 where he asks, "Who is a God like unto thee?" Micah ministered during the reigns of Jotham, Ahaz, and Hezekiah—a period of about fifty years. Contemporary with Isaiah in Judah and Hosea and Amos in Israel, his ministry impacted both nations. Although Micah came from the seemingly insignificant city of Moresheth, a village bordering on the Philistine territory, his prophecy relates to the sins and judgments on the capital cities of Israel and Judah. The destruction of Samaria and Jerusalem, the return of the Jews from a future captivity, and the punishment of their enemies are all foretold.

Author
Micah

Date
8th Century B.C.

Key Truth
Judgments and Promises

Historic Time
Reigns of Jotham, Ahaz, and Hezekiah

Key Verse
7:18
Who is a God like unto thee, that pardoneth iniquity. . . ?

Micah prophesies that God will raise up a loyal remnant who will follow their king and God. He proclaims the coming of the Messiah as the foundation of hope for the blessed and glorious future he describes, even specifying Bethlehem as the place where Messiah would be born (see Matt. 2:1–6). The great ethical statement as to what God "requires" is found in 6:8: "to do justly, and to love mercy, and to walk humbly with thy God."

A century later, Jeremiah's life was saved by an appeal from his friends, quoting Micah 3:12 (Jer. 26:17–19). Jesus alludes to Micah 7:6 in his instructions to the apostles in Matthew 10:35–36.

The book has three major sections (1:2—2:13; 3:1—5:13; 6:1—7:20), each introduced by the word "Hear." The remarkable prophecy about the Messiah being born in Bethlehem is powerful proof of divine inspiration and the value of biblical predictions. Many predictions in Micah will be fulfilled in the coming Millennial Kingdom age. As in Isaiah, both comings of Christ are prophesied.

With a total of 40 separate prophetic subjects scattered through the book, 73 verses out of 105, or 70 percent of the content, are predictive in nature.

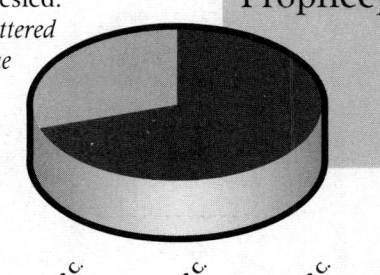

70%
Prophecy

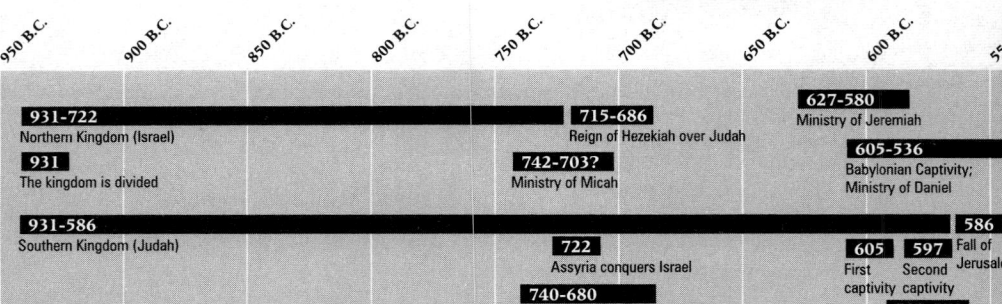

950 B.C.   900 B.C.   850 B.C.   800 B.C.   750 B.C.   700 B.C.   650 B.C.   600 B.C.   55

627-580
Ministry of Jeremiah

931-722
Northern Kingdom (Israel)

715-686
Reign of Hezekiah over Judah

931
The kingdom is divided

742-703?
Ministry of Micah

605-536
Babylonian Captivity; Ministry of Daniel

931-586
Southern Kingdom (Judah)

722
Assyria conquers Israel

586
Fall of Jerusalem

605 First captivity   **597** Second captivity

740-680
Ministry of Isaiah

592-570
Ministry of Ezekiel

CHAPTER 1
The Lord Will Judge

1 The word of the LORD that came to Micah the Morasthite in the days of Jotham, Ahaz, *and* Hezekiah, kings of Judah, which he saw concerning Samaria and Jerusalem.

2 Hear, all ye people; hearken, O earth, and all that therein is: and let the Lord GOD be witness against you, the Lord from his holy temple.

3 For, behold, the LORD cometh forth out of his place, and will come down, and tread upon the high places of the earth.

4 And the mountains shall be molten under him, and the valleys shall be cleft, as wax before the fire, *and as* the waters that *are* poured down a steep place.

5 For the transgression of Jacob *is* all this, and for the sins of the house of Israel. What *is* the transgression of Jacob? *is it* not Samaria? and what *are* the high places of Judah? *are they* not Jerusalem?

6 Therefore I will make Samaria as an heap of the field, *and* as plantings of a vineyard: and I will pour down the stones thereof into the valley, and I will discover the foundations thereof.

7 And all the graven images thereof shall be beaten to pieces, and all the hires thereof shall be burned with the fire, and all the idols thereof will I lay desolate: for she gathered *it* of the hire of an harlot, and they shall return to the hire of an harlot.

8 Therefore I will wail and howl, I will go stripped and naked: I will make a wailing like the dragons, and mourning as the owls.

9 For her wound *is* incurable; for it is come unto Judah; he is come unto the gate of my people, *even* to Jerusalem.

10 Declare ye *it* not at Gath, weep ye not at all: in the house of Aphrah roll thyself in the dust.

11 Pass ye away, thou inhabitant of Saphir, having thy shame naked: the inhabitant of Zaanan came not forth in the mourning of Beth-ezel; he shall receive of you his standing.

12 For the inhabitant of Maroth waited carefully for good: but evil came down from the LORD unto the gate of Jerusalem.

13 O thou inhabitant of Lachish, bind the chariot to the swift beast: she *is* the beginning of the sin to the daughter of Zion: for the transgressions of Israel were found in thee.

14 Therefore shalt thou give presents to Moresheth-gath: the houses of Achzib *shall be* a lie to the kings of Israel.

15 Yet will I bring an heir unto thee, O inhabitant of Mareshah: he shall come unto Adullam the glory of Israel.

16 Make thee bald, and poll thee for thy delicate children; enlarge thy baldness as the eagle; for they are gone into captivity from thee.

CHAPTER 2
What Will Happen to Those Who Hurt the Poor

1 Woe to them that devise iniquity, and work evil upon their beds! when the morning is light, they practise it, because it is in the power of their hand.

2 And they covet fields, and take *them* by violence; and houses, and take *them* away: so they oppress a man and his house even a man and his heritage.

3 Therefore thus saith the LORD; Behold, against this family do I devise an evil, from which ye shall not remove your necks; neither shall ye go haughtily: for this time *is* evil.

4 In that day shall *one* take up a parable against you, and lament with a doleful lamentation, *and* say, We be utterly spoiled: he hath changed the portion of my people: how

---

1 Jer. 26:18
2 Isa. 1:2; Jon. 2:7; Hab. 2:20; Mal. 3:5
3 Deut. 32:13; 33:29; Ps. 115:3; Isa. 26:21; Amos 4:13
4 Judg. 5:5; Ps. 97:5; Isa. 64:1-3; Amos 9:5; Hab. 3:6, 10
6 2Kgs. 19:25; Ezek. 13:14
7 Hos. 2:5, 12
8 Job 30:29; Ps. 102:6; Isa. 20:2-4; 21:3; 22:4; Jer. 4:19
9 2Kgs. 18:13; Isa. 8:7, 8
10 2Sam. 1:20; Jer. 6:26
11 Isa. 20:4; 47:2, 3; Jer. 13:22; Nah. 3:5
12 Amos 3:6
13 2Kgs. 18:14, 17
14 Josh. 15:44; 2Sam. 8:2; 2Kgs. 18:14-16
15 Josh. 15:44; 2Chr. 11:7
16 Job 1:20; Isa. 15:2; 22:12; Jer. 7:29; 16:6
1 Ps. 36:4
2 Isa. 5:8
4 Hab. 2:6

1:1–7 Samaria and Jerusalem. Micah, a contemporary of Isaiah and Hosea, prophesies against Samaria and Jerusalem, the capitals of the Northern and Southern kingdoms (Israel and Judah). He pictures the Lord coming down to tread upon the mountains and valleys that will melt and split apart. Samaria will become a heap, and "all the graven images" (idols) will be destroyed.

1:8–16 gone into captivity from thee. Micah foresees the coming destruction of Samaria by the Assyrians (see 2 Kgs. 17:1–18). He even acted out part of the prophecy to depict Samaria's coming captivity. His prophecy was fulfilled in 722 B.C., when the Assyrians conquered the Northern Kingdom and destroyed Samaria. Micah also predicted this evil (Assyria) would come "unto the gate of Jerusalem" (v. 12) but not into the city itself. In the days of King Hezekiah of Judah, the Assyrians, led by Sennacherib, surrounded the city of Jerusalem (701 B.C.) but did not conquer it (cf. 2 Kgs. 18—19; Isa. 36—37).

2:1–5 Micah pronounces a "woe" (lit. "doom") upon those who "devise iniquity, and work evil" (v. 1). He is especially critical of the materialistic covetousness of greedy people who steal their wealth from others. The prophet predicts that all their wealth will be lost in the coming Assyrian invasion.

hath he removed *it* from me! turning away he hath divided our fields.

5 Therefore thou shalt have none that shall cast a cord by lot in the congregation of the LORD.

6 Prophesy ye not, *say they to them that* prophesy: they shall not prophesy to them, *that* they shall not take shame.

7 O *thou that art* named the house of Jacob, is the spirit of the LORD straitened? *are* these his doings? do not my words do good to him that walketh uprightly?

8 Even of late my people is risen up as an enemy: ye pull off the robe with the garment from them that pass by securely as men averse from war.

9 The women of my people have ye cast out from their pleasant houses; from their children have ye taken away my glory for ever.

10 Arise ye, and depart; for this *is* not *your* rest: because it is polluted, it shall destroy *you*, even with a sore destruction.

11 If a man walking in the spirit and falsehood do lie, *saying*, I will prophesy unto thee of wine and of strong drink; he shall even be the prophet of this people.

12 I will surely assemble, O Jacob, all of thee; I will surely gather the remnant of Israel; I will put them together as the sheep of Bozrah, as the flock in the midst of their fold: they shall make great noise by reason of *the multitude of* men.

13 The breaker is come up before them: they have broken up, and have passed through the gate, and are gone out by it: and their king shall pass before them, and the LORD on the head of them.

CHAPTER 3
God Blames Israel's Leaders

1 And I said, Hear, I pray you, O heads of Jacob, and ye princes of the house of Israel; *Is it* not for you to know judgment?

2 Who hate the good, and love the evil; who pluck off their skin from off them, and their flesh from off their bones;

---

5 Deut. 32:8, 9
6 Isa. 30:10; Ezek. 21:2; Amos 2:12; 7:16
8 10 Lev. 18:25, 28; Deut. 12:9; Jer. 3:2
11 Ezek. 13:3
12 Jer. 31:10; Ezek. 36:37; Mic. 4:6, 7
13 Isa. 52:12; Hos. 3:5
1 Jer. 5:4, 5
3 Ps. 14:4; Ezek. 11:3, 7
4 Ps. 18:41; Prov. 1:28; Isa. 1:15; Ezek. 8:18; Zech. 7:13
5 Isa. 56:10, 11; Ezek. 13:10, 18, 19; 22:25; Mic. 2:11; Matt. 7:15
6 Isa. 8:20, 22; Ezek. 13:23; Amos 8:9; Zech. 13:4
7 Ps. 74:9; Amos 8:11
8 Isa. 58:1
10 Jer. 22:13; Ezek. 22:27; Hab. 2:12; Zeph. 3:3
11 Isa. 1:23; 48:2; Jer. 6:13; 7:4; Ezek. 22:12; Hos. 4:18; Mic. 7:3; Rom. 2:17
12 Ps. 79:1; Jer. 26:18; Mic. 1:6; 4:2
1 Ezek. 17:22, 23

---

3 Who also eat the flesh of my people, and flay their skin from off them; and they break their bones, and chop them in pieces, as for the pot, and as flesh within the caldron.

4 Then shall they cry unto the LORD, but he will not hear them: he will even hide his face from them at that time, as they have behaved themselves ill in their doings.

5 Thus saith the LORD concerning the prophets that make my people err, that bite with their teeth, and cry, Peace; and he that putteth not into their mouths, they even prepare war against him.

6 Therefore night *shall be* unto you, that ye shall not have a vision; and it shall be dark unto you, that ye shall not divine; and the sun shall go down over the prophets, and the day shall be dark over them.

7 Then shall the seers be ashamed, and the diviners confounded: yea, they shall all cover their lips; for *there is* no answer of God.

8 But truly I am full of power by the spirit of the LORD, and of judgment, and of might, to declare unto Jacob his transgression, and to Israel his sin.

9 Hear this, I pray you, ye heads of the house of Jacob, and princes of the house of Israel, that abhor judgment, and pervert all equity.

10 They build up Zion with blood, and Jerusalem with iniquity.

11 The heads thereof judge for reward, and the priests thereof teach for hire, and the prophets thereof divine for money: yet will they lean upon the LORD, and say, *Is* not the LORD among us? none evil can come upon us.

12 Therefore shall Zion for your sake be plowed *as* a field, and Jerusalem shall become heaps, and the mountain of the house as the high places of the forest.

CHAPTER 4
The Lord Will Rule Everywhere

1 But in the last days it shall come to pass, *that* the mountain of the house of the LORD

2:12 I will surely gather the remnant. Despite this dark picture of judgment, God promises to regather "the remnant of Israel . . . as [lost] sheep." Micah's imagery is similar to that of Jesus when He referred to the "lost sheep of the house of Israel" (Matt. 10:6; Luke 15:3–7) and pictured Himself as the Good Shepherd of God's people (John 10:1–30). Micah looks beyond the return from the Babylonian captivity and foresees a complete restoration of all of Jacob, or all the tribes, during the Millennial

Kingdom, when all Israel will be completely restored.

2:13 The breaker is come up. The breaker is the Messiah, Jesus Christ, who will remove all the obstacles to Israel's regathering when He returns as her rightful King (cf. Isa. 11:15–16).

3:1–8 flay their skin from off them. This reference to flaying skin may be a reference to the Assyrians, who were notorious for flaying their captives alive.

shall be established in the top of the mountains, and it shall be exalted above the hills; and people shall flow unto it.

2 And many nations shall come, and say, Come, and let us go up to the mountain of the LORD, and to the house of the God of Jacob; and he will teach us of his ways, and we will walk in his paths: for the law shall go forth of Zion, and the word of the LORD from Jerusalem.

3 And he shall judge among many people, and rebuke strong nations afar off; and they shall beat their swords into plowshares, and their spears into pruninghooks: nation shall not lift up a sword against nation, neither shall they learn war any more.

4 But they shall sit every man under his vine and under his fig tree; and none shall make *them* afraid: for the mouth of the LORD of hosts hath spoken *it*.

5 For all people will walk every one in the name of his god, and we will walk in the name of the LORD our God for ever and ever.

Israel Will Return from Captivity

6 In that day, saith the LORD, will I assemble her that halteth, and I will gather her that is driven out, and her that I have afflicted;

7 And I will make her that halted a remnant, and her that was cast far off a strong nation: and the LORD shall reign over them in mount Zion from henceforth, even for ever.

8 And thou, O tower of the flock, the strong hold of the daughter of Zion, unto

thee shall it come, even the first dominion; the kingdom shall come to the daughter of Jerusalem.

9 Now why dost thou cry out aloud? *is there* no king in thee? is thy counsellor perished? for pangs have taken thee as a woman in travail.

10 Be in pain, and labour to bring forth, O daughter of Zion, like a woman in travail: for now shalt thou go forth out of the city, and thou shalt dwell in the field, and thou shalt go *even* to Babylon; there shalt thou be delivered; there the LORD shall redeem thee from the hand of thine enemies.

11 Now also many nations are gathered against thee, that say, Let her be defiled, and let our eye look upon Zion.

12 But they know not the thoughts of the LORD, neither understand they his counsel: for he shall gather them as the sheaves into the floor.

13 Arise and thresh, O daughter of Zion: for I will make thine horn iron, and I will make thy hoofs brass: and thou shalt beat in pieces many people: and I will consecrate their gain unto the LORD, and their substance unto the Lord of the whole earth.

CHAPTER 5
God Promises a Ruler from Bethlehem

1 Now gather thyself in troops, O daughter of troops: he hath laid siege against us: they shall smite the judge of Israel with a rod upon the cheek.

2 But thou, Beth-lehem Ephratah, *though*

Cross references:

3 Ps. 72:7; Isa. 2:4; Joel 3:10
4 1Kgs. 4:25; Zech. 3:10
5 Jer. 2:11; Zech. 10:12
6 Ps. 147:2; Ezek. 34:13, 16; 37:21; Zeph. 3:19
7 Isa. 9:6; 24:23; Dan. 7:14, 27; Mic. 2:12; 5:3, 7, 8; 7:18; Luke 1:33; Rev. 11:15
8 Gen. 35:21
9 Isa. 13:8; 21:3; Jer. 8:19; 30:6; 50:43
11 Lam. 2:16; Obad. 1:12; Mic. 7:10
12 Isa. 21:10; 55:8; Rom. 11:33
13 Isa. 18:7; 23:18; 41:15, 16; 60:6, 9; Jer. 51:33; Dan. 2:44; Zech. 4:14; 6:5
1 Lam. 3:30; Matt. 5:39; 27:30
2 Matt. 2:6; John 1:1; 7:42

4:1–8 they shall beat their swords into plowshares. Micah's focus now shifts from the nation's current problems to her prophetic destiny. He sees a brilliant future for Israel "in the last days." The prophet foresees the establishment of the kingdom of God as a great mountain (v. 1). His symbolism is similar to that of Daniel 2:34–35, 44–45, where the mountain represents God's kingdom on earth. Micah foresees the Messiah's kingdom as a universal kingdom in which the nations of the world will come to Jerusalem to worship God. The prophet pictures this future kingdom as one of peace (v. 3) and prosperity (v. 4).

4:9–13 thou shalt go even to Babylon. In contrast to the glorious days of the future Millennium, the prophet again shifts his attention to the problems of his own day. While the ultimate picture of Israel's future is bright, the immediate forecast is dark. Israel is in pain, like a woman experiencing labor pains (v. 10). In this context, Micah specifically predicts that Judah will go into captivity to Babylon. His prediction was fulfilled in the years from

605–586 B.C., when Nebuchadnezzar conquered Jerusalem three times, sending various people into captivity each time until the land of Judah was desolate and Jerusalem was completely destroyed (cf. 2 Kgs. 24; 2 Chr. 36; Dan. 1).

5:2–5 whose goings forth have been from of old. More than seven hundred years before the birth of Christ, Micah predicted the Messiah, the "ruler in Israel," would be born in the town of Bethlehem (v. 2). It was this passage that the scribes quoted to King Herod about the birthplace of the Messiah (cf. Matt. 2:3–6). Micah's prophecy is so specific that it actually designates Bethlehem Ephratah in Judah as the birthplace of the Messiah to distinguish it from any other towns with a similar name. Only David, the progenitor of the Davidic line, and Jesus the culmination of that line, were actually born in the little village of Bethlehem, five miles south of Jerusalem. Micah predicts that Israel's future will be left in the hands of her enemies until the birth of the Messiah (cf. also Isa. 7:14; 9:6).

thou be little among the thousands of Judah, *yet* out of thee shall he come forth unto me *that is* to be ruler in Israel; whose goings forth *have been* from of old, from everlasting.

3 Therefore will he give them up, until the time *that* she which travaileth hath brought forth: then the remnant of his brethren shall return unto the children of Israel.

4 And he shall stand and feed in the strength of the LORD, in the majesty of the name of the LORD his God; and they shall abide: for now shall he be great unto the ends of the earth.

5 And this *man* shall be the peace, when the Assyrian shall come into our land: and when he shall tread in our palaces, then shall we raise against him seven shepherds, and eight principal men.

6 And they shall waste the land of Assyria with the sword, and the land of Nimrod in the entrances thereof: thus shall he deliver *us* from the Assyrian, when he cometh into our land, and when he treadeth within our borders.

7 And the remnant of Jacob shall be in the midst of many people as a dew from the LORD, as the showers upon the grass, that tarrieth not for man, nor waiteth for the sons of men.

8 And the remnant of Jacob shall be among the Gentiles in the midst of many people as a lion among the beasts of the forest, as a young lion among the flocks of sheep: who, if he go through, both treadeth down, and teareth in pieces, and none can deliver.

9 Thine hand shall be lifted up upon thine adversaries, and all thine enemies shall be cut off.

10 And it shall come to pass in that day, saith the LORD, that I will cut off thy horses

3 Mic. 4:7, 10
4 Ps. 72:8; Isa. 40:11; 49:10; 52:13; Ezek. 34:23; Mic. 7:14; Zech. 9:10; Luke 1:32
5 Ps. 72:7; Isa. 9:6; Zech. 9:10; Luke 2:14; Eph. 2:14
6 Gen. 10:8, 10, 11; Luke 1:71
7 Deut. 32:2; Ps. 72:6; 110:3; Mic. 5:3
8 Or, *goats*
10 Zech. 9:10
12 Isa. 2:6
13 Isa. 2:8; Zech. 13:2
15 Ps. 149:7; Mic. 5:8; 2Thess. 1:8
2 Deut. 32:1; Ps. 50:1, 4; Isa. 1:2, 18; 5:3, 4; 43:26; Hos. 4:1; 12:2
3 Jer. 2:5, 31
4 Ex. 12:51; 14:30; 20:2; Deut. 4:20; Amos 2:10
5 Num. 22:5; 23:7; 24:10, 11; 25:1; 33:49; Deut. 23:4, 5; Josh. 4:19; 5:10; 24:9, 10; Judg. 5:11; Rev. 2:14

out of the midst of thee, and I will destroy thy chariots:

11 And I will cut off the cities of thy land, and throw down all thy strong holds:

12 And I will cut off witchcrafts out of thine hand; and thou shalt have no *more* soothsayers:

13 Thy graven images also will I cut off, and thy standing images out of the midst of thee; and thou shalt no more worship the work of thine hands.

14 And I will pluck up thy groves out of the midst of thee: so will I destroy thy cities.

15 And I will execute vengeance in anger and fury upon the heathen, such as they have not heard.

CHAPTER 6
The Lord's Case against Israel

1 Hear ye now what the Lord saith; Arise, contend thou before the mountains, and let the hills hear thy voice.

2 Hear ye, O mountains, the LORD's controversy, and ye strong foundations of the earth: for the LORD hath a controversy with his people, and he will plead with Israel.

3 O my people, what have I done unto thee? and wherein have I wearied thee? testify against me.

4 For I brought thee up out of the land of Egypt, and redeemed thee out of the house of servants; and I sent before thee Moses, Aaron, and Miriam.

5 O my people, remember now what Balak king of Moab consulted, and what Balaam the son of Beor answered him from Shittim unto Gilgal; that ye may know the righteousness of the LORD.

6 Wherewith shall I come before the LORD, *and* bow myself before the high God? shall I come before him with burnt offerings, with calves of a year old?

5:6–7 shall waste the land of Assyria with the sword. The Assyrians were Israel's major enemy in the days of Micah. The reference is best understood as a symbolic representation of all of Israel's enemies. The title, Nimrod, is sometimes applied to the Antichrist because of the proximity of Assyria to Babylon (cf. Isa. 10:5; 14:4). By referring to Nimrod (see Gen. 10:8–13), Micah depicts Babylon and Assyria as a single foe in the future. This future end-times enemy of Israel will be defeated by the Messiah at the Battle of Armageddon (cf. Dan. 11:36–45; Rev. 19:14–21).

5:11–15 In the Millennial Kingdom, God's people will be secure in His presence and will no longer depend on either weapons of war or pagan idols. Redeemed Israel

will trust only in the Lord and His power to sustain them. The Lord will remove every other thing in which the people might place their trust during that time.

6:1–8 the LORD hath a controversy with his people. God calls Israel to accountability. Though the people of Israel have disowned Him, He still calls them "my people" (v. 3). He reminds them of the historical record of His grace and power on their behalf. It is their hearts that He desires, not their burnt offerings. He is not content with merely the external formalities of their religion. Instead, He calls for internal sincerity and integrity, asking them "to do justly, and to love mercy, and to walk humbly" before Him (v. 8).

7 Will the LORD be pleased with thousands of rams, *or* with ten thousands of rivers of oil? shall I give my firstborn *for* my transgression, the fruit of my body *for* the sin of my soul?

8 He hath shewed thee, O man, what *is* good; and what doth the LORD require of thee, but to do justly, and to love mercy, and to walk humbly with thy God?

9 The LORD'S voice crieth unto the city, and *the man of* wisdom shall see thy name: hear ye the rod, and who hath appointed it.

10 Are there yet the treasures of wickedness in the house of the wicked, and the scant measure *that is* abominable?

11 Shall I count *them* pure with the wicked balances, and with the bag of deceitful weights?

12 For the rich men thereof are full of violence, and the inhabitants thereof have spoken lies, and their tongue *is* deceitful in their mouth.

13 Therefore also will I make *thee* sick in smiting thee, in making *thee* desolate because of thy sins.

14 Thou shalt eat, but not be satisfied; and thy casting down *shall be* in the midst of thee; and thou shalt take hold, but shalt not deliver; and *that* which thou deliverest will I give up to the sword.

15 Thou shalt sow, but thou shalt not reap; thou shalt tread the olives, but thou shalt not anoint thee with oil; and sweet wine, but shalt not drink wine.

16 For the statutes of Omri are kept, and all the works of the house of Ahab, and ye walk in their counsels; that I should make thee a desolation, and the inhabitants thereof an hissing: therefore ye shall bear the reproach of my people.

CHAPTER 7
Israel Is Corrupt

1 Woe is me! for I am as when they have gathered the summer fruits, as the grape-gleanings of the vintage: *there is* no cluster to eat: my soul desired the firstripe fruit.

2 The good *man* is perished out of the earth: and *there is* none upright among men: they all lie in wait for blood; they hunt every man his brother with a net.

3 That they may do evil with both hands

earnestly, the prince asketh, and the judge *asketh* for a reward; and the great *man,* he uttereth his mischievous desire: so they wrap it up.

4 The best of them *is* as a brier: the most upright *is sharper* than a thorn hedge: the day of thy watchmen *and* thy visitation cometh; now shall be their perplexity.

5 Trust ye not in a friend, put ye not confidence in a guide: keep the doors of thy mouth from her that lieth in thy bosom.

6 For the son dishonoureth the father, the daughter riseth up against her mother, the daughter-in-law against her mother-in-law; a man's enemies *are* the men of his own house.

7 Therefore I will look unto the LORD; I will wait for the God of my salvation: my God will hear me.

8 Rejoice not against me, O mine enemy: when I fall, I shall arise; when I sit in darkness, the LORD *shall be* a light unto me.

9 I will bear the indignation of the LORD, because I have sinned against him, until he plead my cause, and execute judgment for me: he will bring me forth to the light, *and* I shall behold his righteousness.

10 Then *she that is* mine enemy shall see *it,* and shame shall cover her which said unto me, Where is the LORD thy God? mine eyes shall behold her: now shall she be trodden down as the mire of the streets.

11 *In* the day that thy walls are to be built, *in* that day shall the decree be far removed.

12 *In* that day *also* he shall come even to thee from Assyria, and *from* the fortified cities, and from the fortress even to the river, and from sea to sea, and *from* mountain to mountain.

13 Notwithstanding the land shall be desolate because of them that dwell therein, for the fruit of their doings.

The Lord Loves Israel

14 Feed thy people with thy rod, the flock of thine heritage, which dwell solitarily *in* the wood, in the midst of Carmel: let them feed *in* Bashan and Gilead, as in the days of old.

15 According to the days of thy coming out of the land of Egypt will I shew unto him marvellous *things.*

16 The nations shall see and be confounded

Cross references

7 2Kgs. 16:3; 21:6; 23:10
8 Gen. 18:19; Deut. 10:12; 1Sam. 15:22; Isa. 1:17; Hos. 6:6; 12:6
10 Deut. 25:13-16
11 Hos. 12:7
12 Jer. 9:3, 5, 6, 8
14 Lev. 26:26; Hos. 4:10
15 Deut. 28:38-40; Amos 5:11; Zeph. 1:13; Hag. 1:6
16 1Kgs. 9:8; 16:25, 26, 30; 21:25, 26; 2Kgs. 21:3; Isa. 25:8; Jer. 19:8; 51:51; Lam. 5:1, 2; Hos. 5:11
1 Isa. 17:6; 24:13; 28:4; Hos. 9:10
2 Ps. 12:1; 14:1, 3; Isa. 57:1; Hab. 1:15
3 Isa. 1:23; Hos. 4:18; Mic. 3:11
4 2Sam. 23:6, 7; Isa. 55:13; Ezek. 2:6
5 Jer. 9:4
6 Ezek. 22:7; Matt. 10:21, 35, 36; Luke 12:53; 21:16; 2Tim. 3:2, 3
7 Isa. 8:17
8 Ps. 27:1
9 Ps. 35:26
11 Amos 9:11
12 Isa. 11:16; 19:23
13 Jer. 21:14
14 Ps. 28:9; Isa. 37:24; Mic. 5:4

7:5–15 Micah looks ahead to the ultimate victory of the kingdom of God. In contrast to those who look to men for advice, the prophet announces, "I will look unto the LORD" and "wait for the God of my salvation" (v. 7). His prophecy ends with great messianic expectation. God will again do great things (miracles) for Israel "as in the days of old" (vv. 14–15).

at all their might: they shall lay *their* hand upon *their* mouth, their ears shall be deaf.

17 They shall lick the dust like a serpent, they shall move out of their holes like worms of the earth: they shall be afraid of the LORD our God, and shall fear because of thee.

18 Who *is* a God like unto thee, that pardoneth iniquity, and passeth by the transgression of the remnant of his heritage? he

17 Isa. 49:23; Jer. 33:9

18 Ex. 15:11; 34:6, 7; Ps. 103:9; Isa. 57:16; Jer. 3:5; 50:20; Mic. 4:7; 5:3

20 Ps. 105:9, 10; Luke 1:72, 73

retaineth not his anger for ever, because he delighteth *in* mercy.

19 He will turn again, he will have compassion upon us; he will subdue our iniquities; and thou wilt cast all their sins into the depths of the sea.

20 Thou wilt perform the truth to Jacob, *and* the mercy to Abraham, which thou hast sworn unto our fathers from the days of old.

7:18–20 he will subdue our iniquities. The closing words of Micah's prophecy praise the Lord for His compassion, mercy, and forgiveness, based on God's covenant promises to Abraham and Jacob. Thus, the prophecy concludes as it began, with a word from the Lord. In the beginning, it was a word of impending doom for Israel, but, in the end, it is a word of hope and assurance that God will keep His promises to His people.

Nahum

Nahum, meaning "consolation or comfort," wrote this descriptive poem of the grandeur, power, and justice of God and the approaching fall of the cruel and defiant Assyrians. His entire message concerns the destruction of Nineveh. In 722 B.C., Hoshea, last of the monarchs of the Kingdom of Israel (Northern Kingdom), was overwhelmed and the Israelites were carried into captivity by Assyrian forces. Written some 100–150 years after Jonah's prophecy concerning Nineveh, Nahum probably penned this bold, majestic book shortly after God miraculously delivered Judah from the Assyrian armies led by Sennacherib (see Isa. 37). In 612 B.C., the Medes and Babylonians destroyed Nineveh, fulfilling Nahum and Jonah's prophecy. Since there are no references to contemporary kings, some scholars believe that Nahum prophesied in the 7th century B.C., not long before Nineveh fell.

There is but one theme, the destruction of Nineveh, but many principles of divine justice and sovereignty appear. God does not allow sin and injustice to go unpunished. His majesty and glory are exalted in chapter 1. In chapter 2, the invasion and plundering of Nineveh is colorfully described. Chapter 3 expresses the causes and consequences of the city's demise.

A most interesting application of Isaiah 52:7 is made by the apostle Paul in Romans, which also may be application of Nahum 1:15. Romans 10:15 says, "How beautiful are the feet of them that preach the gospel of peace, and bring glad tidings of good things!" The similarly-worded statements of Nahum and Isaiah are a clear prediction of Jesus' ministry. Nahum's poetic portrayal of the ruin of Ninevah is similar to John's very vivid description of Babylon's future destruction (see Rev. 18).

Of the 47 verses, 35 of them, or 74 percent, are predictive with 33 devoted to Nineveh's fall and only 2 related to Israel. All of the prophecies concerning Nineveh have been fulfilled. There are no messianic prophecies in the book, and only 1 verse (1:15) contains a prediction of end-time events.

Author
Nahum

Date
6th or 7th Century B.C.

Key Truth
The Doom of Nineveh

Historic Time
Reign of Josiah

Key Verse
1:2
. . . the LORD will take vengeance on his adversaries. . . .

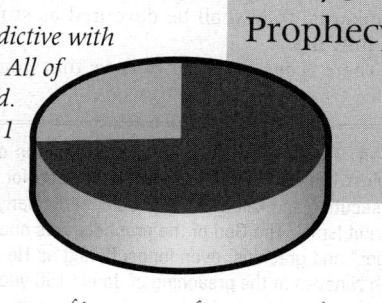

74%
Prophecy

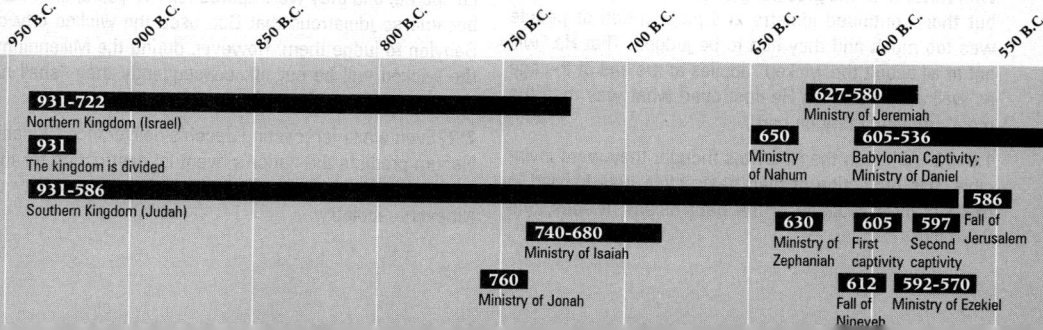

950 B.C.	900 B.C.	850 B.C.

931-722
Northern Kingdom (Israel)

931
The kingdom is divided

931-586
Southern Kingdom (Judah)

627-580
Ministry of Jeremiah

650
Ministry of Nahum

605-536
Babylonian Captivity; Ministry of Daniel

586
Fall of Jerusalem

740-680
Ministry of Isaiah

630
Ministry of Zephaniah

605
First captivity

597
Second captivity

760
Ministry of Jonah

612
Fall of Nineveh

592-570
Ministry of Ezekiel

CHAPTER 1
The Lord Is Angry with Nineveh

1 The burden of Nineveh. The book of the vision of Nahum the Elkoshite.

2 God *is* jealous, and the LORD revengeth; the LORD revengeth, and *is* furious; the LORD will take vengeance on his adversaries, and he reserveth *wrath* for his enemies.

3 The LORD *is* slow to anger, and great in power, and will not at all acquit *the wicked*: the LORD hath his way in the whirlwind and in the storm, and the clouds *are* the dust of his feet.

4 He rebuketh the sea, and maketh it dry, and drieth up all the rivers: Bashan languisheth, and Carmel, and the flower of Lebanon languisheth.

5 The mountains quake at him, and the hills melt, and the earth is burned at his presence, yea, the world, and all that dwell therein.

6 Who can stand before his indignation? and who can abide in the fierceness of his anger? his fury is poured out like fire, and the rocks are thrown down by him.

7 The LORD *is* good, a strong hold in the day of trouble; and he knoweth them that trust in him.

8 But with an overrunning flood he will make an utter end of the place thereof, and darkness shall pursue his enemies.

9 What do ye imagine against the LORD? he will make an utter end: affliction shall not rise up the second time.

10 For while *they be* folded together *as* thorns, and while they are drunken *as* drunkards, they shall be devoured as stubble fully dry.

11 There is *one* come out of thee, that imag-ineth evil against the LORD, a wicked counseller.

12 Thus saith the LORD; Though *they be* quiet, and likewise many, yet thus shall they be cut down, when he shall pass through. Though I have afflicted thee, I will afflict thee no more.

13 For now will I break his yoke from off thee, and will burst thy bonds in sunder.

14 And the LORD hath given a commandment concerning thee, *that* no more of thy name be sown: out of the house of thy gods will I cut off the graven image and the molten image: I will make thy grave; for thou art vile.

15 Behold upon the mountains the feet of him that bringeth good tidings, that publisheth peace! O Judah, keep thy solemn feasts, perform thy vows: for the wicked shall no more pass through thee; he is utterly cut off.

CHAPTER 2
Nineveh Will Fall

1 He that dasheth in pieces is come up before thy face: keep the munition, watch the way, make *thy* loins strong, fortify *thy* power mightily.

2 For the LORD hath turned away the excellency of Jacob, as the excellency of Israel: for the emptiers have emptied them out, and marred their vine branches.

3 The shield of his mighty men is made red, the valiant men *are* in scarlet: the chariots *shall be* with flaming torches in the day of his preparation, and the fir trees shall be terribly shaken.

4 The chariots shall rage in the streets, they shall justle one against another in the

Cross references
1 Zeph. 2:13
2 Ex. 20:5; 34:14; Deut. 4:24; 32:35
3 Ex. 34:6, 7; Job 9:4
4 Ps. 106:9; Isa. 33:9; 50:2; Matt. 8:26
5 Judg. 5:5; Ps. 68:8; 97:5; Mic. 1:4; 2Pet. 3:10
6 Mal. 3:2; Rev. 16:1
7 1Chr. 16:34; Ps. 1:6; 100:5; Jer. 33:11; Lam. 3:25; 2Tim. 2:19
8 Dan. 9:26; 11:10, 22, 40
9 1Sam. 3:12; Ps. 2:1
10 2Sam. 23:6, 7; Nah. 3:11; Mal. 4:1
11 2Kgs. 19:22, 23
12 2Kgs. 19:35, 37; Isa. 8:8; Dan. 11:10
13 Jer. 2:20; 30:8
15 Isa. 52:7
2 Ps. 80:12; Isa. 10:12; Jer. 25:29; Hos. 10:1
3 Isa. 63:2, 3

1:1–4 The burden of Nineveh. This burden of Nahum against Nineveh was the judgment of God for viciously persecuting and killing many people, particularly the children of Israel. The God of the prophets was one "slow to anger" and gracious, even longsuffering as He had been with Nineveh at the preaching of Jonah 150 years earlier, but their continued idolatry and persecution of people was too much and they had to be judged. That He "will not at all acquit the wicked" applies at the end of the age as well as it did when He destroyed what was then the most prominent city on earth.

1:5–12 Although the Ninevites thought they were invincible, this prediction of their destruction was fulfilled in 612 B.C. by a coalition of the Babylonians, Medes, and Scythians.

1:7 the day of trouble. This may be a reference to the Tribulation period that is yet to come, which Jesus mentioned in Matthew 24:21.

1:15 While the prophet was predicting the total destruction of this great city, he also forecast that Judah would be spared, and they were spared for 137 years, until they became so idolatrous that God used the wicked city of Babylon to judge them. However, during the Millennium, the wicked will be cut off; consequently they "shall no more pass through" Judah.

2:2 Even while forecasting Jacob's deliverance (Judah), Nahum predicts the nation's eventual destruction for the same sin that led to the judgment of the pagan city of Nineveh—idolatry.

broad ways: they shall seem like torches, they shall run like the lightnings.

5 He shall recount his worthies: they shall stumble in their walk; they shall make haste to the wall thereof, and the defence shall be prepared.

6 The gates of the rivers shall be opened, and the palace shall be dissolved.

7 And Huzzab shall be led away captive, she shall be brought up, and her maids shall lead *her* as with the voice of doves, tabering upon their breasts.

8 But Nineveh *is* of old like a pool of water: yet they shall flee away. Stand, stand, *shall they cry*; but none shall look back.

9 Take ye the spoil of silver, take the spoil of gold: for *there is* none end of the store *and* glory out of all the pleasant furniture.

10 She is empty, and void, and waste: and the heart melteth, and the knees smite together, and much pain *is* in all loins, and the faces of them all gather blackness.

11 Where *is* the dwelling of the lions, and the feedingplace of the young lions, where the lion, *even* the old lion, walked, *and* the lion's whelp, and none made *them* afraid?

12 The lion did tear in pieces enough for his whelps, and strangled for his lionesses, and filled his holes with prey, and his dens with ravin.

13 Behold, I *am* against thee, saith the LORD of hosts, and I will burn her chariots in the smoke, and the sword shall devour thy young lions: and I will cut off thy prey from the earth, and the voice of thy messengers shall no more be heard.

CHAPTER 3
Woe to Nineveh

1 Woe to the bloody city! it *is* all full of lies *and* robbery; the prey departeth not;

2 The noise of a whip, and the noise of the rattling of the wheels, and of the pransing horses, and of the jumping chariots.

3 The horseman lifteth up both the bright sword and the glittering spear: and *there is* a multitude of slain, and a great number of carcases; and *there is* none end of *their* corpses; they stumble upon their corpses:

4 Because of the multitude of the whore-

doms of the wellfavoured harlot, the mistress of witchcrafts, that selleth nations through her whoredoms, and families through her witchcrafts.

5 Behold, I *am* against thee, saith the LORD of hosts; and I will discover thy skirts upon thy face, and I will shew the nations thy nakedness, and the kingdoms thy shame.

6 And I will cast abominable filth upon thee, and make thee vile, and will set thee as a gazingstock.

7 And it shall come to pass, *that* all they that look upon thee shall flee from thee, and say, Nineveh is laid waste: who will bemoan her? whence shall I seek comforters for thee?

8 Art thou better than populous No, that was situate among the rivers, *that had* the waters round about it, whose rampart *was* the sea, *and* her wall *was* from the sea?

9 Ethiopia and Egypt *were* her strength, and *it was* infinite; Put and Lubim were thy helpers.

10 Yet *was* she carried away, she went into captivity: her young children also were dashed in pieces at the top of all the streets: and they cast lots for her honourable men, and all her great men were bound in chains.

11 Thou also shalt be drunken: thou shalt be hid, thou also shalt seek strength because of the enemy.

12 All thy strong holds *shall be like* fig trees with the firstripe figs: if they be shaken, they shall even fall into the mouth of the eater.

13 Behold, thy people in the midst of thee *are* women: the gates of thy land shall be set wide open unto thine enemies: the fire shall devour thy bars.

14 Draw thee waters for the siege, fortify thy strong holds: go into clay, and tread the morter, make strong the brickkiln.

15 There shall the fire devour thee; the sword shall cut thee off, it shall eat thee up like the cankerworm: make thyself many as the cankerworm, make thyself many as the locusts.

16 Thou hast multiplied thy merchants above the stars of heaven: the cankerworm spoileth, and flieth away.

Center column references

7 Isa. 38:14; 59:11

10 Isa. 13:7, 8; Jer. 30:6; Dan. 5:6; Joel 2:6

11 Job 4:10, 11; Ezek. 19:2-7

13 2Kgs. 18:17, 19; Ezek. 29:3; 38:3; 39:1; Nah. 3:5

1 Ezek. 22:2, 3; 24:6, 9; Hab. 2:12

2 Jer. 47:3

4 Isa. 47:9, 12; Rev. 18:2, 3

5 Isa. 47:2, 3; Jer. 13:22, 26; Ezek. 16:37; Mic. 1:11; Nah. 2:13; Hab. 2:16

6 Mal. 2:9; Heb. 10:33

7 Jer. 15:5; Rev. 18:10

8 Jer. 46:25, 26; Ezek. 30:14-16; Amos 6:2

10 Ps. 137:9; Isa. 13:16; Lam. 2:19; Hos. 13:16; Joel 3:3; Obad. 1:11

11 Jer. 25:17, 27; Nah. 1:10

12 Rev. 6:13

13 Ps. 147:13; Jer. 50:37; 51:30

14 Nah. 2:1

15 Joel 1:4

3:7 Nineveh is laid waste. The final destruction of this city-state was indeed fulfilled, to the extent that for 2,600 years it was buried under so much debris and dirt that it was unknown to historians, many of whom were denying it ever existed. Now, thanks to the archeologist's spade, it is evident that Nineveh was all that the prophets said it was. The message of Nahum is that God's prophecies of judgment may, as an act of mercy, be delayed, but ultimately will be fulfilled in every detail upon an unrepentant people, confirming the supernatural hand of God in the Scriptures.

17 Thy crowned *are* as the locusts, and thy captains as the great grasshoppers, which camp in the hedges in the cold day, *but* when the sun ariseth they flee away, and their place is not known where they *are*.

18 Thy shepherds slumber, O king of Assyria: thy nobles shall dwell *in the dust*: thy people is scattered upon the mountains, and no man gathereth *them*.

19 *There is* no healing of thy bruise; thy wound is grievous: all that hear the bruit of thee shall clap the hands over thee: for upon whom hath not thy wickedness passed continually?

17 Rev. 9:7
18 Ex. 15:16; 1Kgs. 22:17; Ps. 76:6; Jer. 50:18; Ezek. 31:3
19 Isa. 14:8; Lam. 2:15

Habakkuk

Very little is known about Habakkuk other than his name, which means "embrace." In this book, Habakkuk wrestles with the question of why God would seemingly let evil go unpunished among the surrounding heathen nations and at the same time bring calamity and judgment upon His own people through such nations. Habakkuk was probably a contemporary of Zephaniah and Jeremiah, who lived during the time of the godly king Josiah but saw the revival fires ebb after the king's death. His prophecies were directed to Judah during a time of serious apostasy, and they forecast the impending invasion of the Chaldeans (Babylonians). In spite of Judah's wickedness, the prophet seems bewildered. Why should Judah, faced with critical conditions, continue in glaring sin? Why would God send even more wicked people to conquer a nation that at least had a remnant of faithful believers?

Author	Habakkuk
Date	607 B.C.
Key Truth	From Inquiry to Faith
Historic Time	Josiah's Reign
Key Verse	2:4 — The just shall live by his faith.

In answer to these and other questions, God and the prophet have a dialogue about injustice. That the Chaldeans will likewise face divine wrath is stated in five "woes" on the invaders for their sins, and before eighty years had passed, mighty, wealthy, violent, and immoral Babylon would also come under judgment. Habakkuk, with prayer and praise, expresses his enduring faith in the glorious magnificence of God and His power to conquer, resolving to rejoice in Him whatever the circumstance (chap. 3).

Habakkuk contains four separate predictions that were mostly fulfilled in Judah's succeeding years or in the 6th century B.C., when Babylon was defeated and absorbed into Medo-Persia. While not directly prophetic, the principle of justification by faith is clearly introduced in 2:4, "the just shall live by his faith" (see Rom. 1:17; Gal. 3:11; Heb. 10:38). The description of God coming in glory and power (Hab. 3:3–15) harks back to Israel's ancient victories in Canaan, but may suggest something of the splendor of Christ's return (see Isa. 63:4).

God's answer to Habakkuk's questions is basically predictive, involving 23 out the 56 verses, or 41 percent of the book.

41%
Prophecy

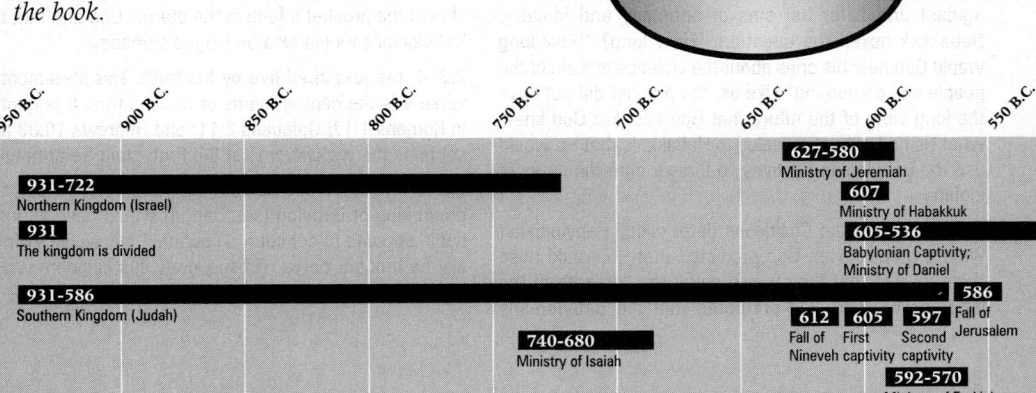

950 B.C.	900 B.C.	850 B.C.	800 B.C.	750 B.C.	700 B.C.	650 B.C.	600 B.C.	550 B.C.

627-580
Ministry of Jeremiah
607
Ministry of Habakkuk
605-536
Babylonian Captivity; Ministry of Daniel

931-722
Northern Kingdom (Israel)
931
The kingdom is divided

931-586
Southern Kingdom (Judah)

586
Fall of Jerusalem

612 Fall of Nineveh   **605** First captivity   **597** Second captivity

740-680
Ministry of Isaiah

592-570
Ministry of Ezekiel

CHAPTER 1
Habakkuk Complains about Injustice

1 The burden which Habakkuk the prophet did see.

2 O LORD, how long shall I cry, and thou wilt not hear! *even* cry out unto thee *of* violence, and thou wilt not save!

3 Why dost thou shew me iniquity, and cause *me* to behold grievance? for spoiling and violence *are* before me: and there are *that* raise up strife and contention.

4 Therefore the law is slacked, and judgment doth never go forth: for the wicked doth compass about the righteous; therefore wrong judgment proceedeth.

5 Behold ye among the heathen, and regard, and wonder marvellously: for *I* will work a work in your days, *which* ye will not believe, though it be told *you*.

6 For, lo, I raise up the Chaldeans, *that* bitter and hasty nation, which shall march through the breadth of the land, to possess the dwellingplaces *that are* not theirs.

7 They *are* terrible and dreadful: their judgment and their dignity shall proceed of themselves.

8 Their horses also are swifter than the leopards, and are more fierce than the evening wolves: and their horsemen shall spread themselves, and their horsemen shall come from far; they shall fly as the eagle *that* hasteth to eat.

9 They shall come all for violence: their faces shall sup up *as* the east wind, and they shall gather the captivity as the sand.

10 And they shall scoff at the kings, and the princes shall be a scorn unto them: they shall deride every strong hold; for they shall heap dust, and take it.

11 Then shall *his* mind change, and he shall pass over, and offend, *imputing* this his power unto his god.

Cross references (center column):

2 Lam. 3:8
4 Job 21:7; Ps. 94:3; Jer. 12:1
5 Isa. 29:14; Acts 13:41
6 Deut. 28:49, 50; Jer. 5:15
8 Jer. 4:13; 5:6; Zeph. 3:3
11 Dan. 5:4
12 Deut. 32:4; 2Kgs. 19:25; Ps. 17:13; 90:2; 93:2; Isa. 10:5-7; Lam. 5:19; Ezek. 30:25
13 Ps. 5:5; Jer. 12:1
15 Jer. 16:6; Amos 4:2
16 Deut. 8:17; Isa. 10:13; 37:24, 25

1 Ps. 85:8; Isa. 21:8, 11

2 Isa. 8:1; 30:8

3 Dan. 10:14; 11:27, 35; Heb. 10:37

4 John 3:36; Rom. 1:17; Gal. 3:11; Heb. 10:38

5 Prov. 27:20; 30:16

---

12 *Art* thou not from everlasting, O LORD my God, mine Holy One? we shall not die. O LORD, thou hast ordained them for judgment; and, O mighty God, thou hast established them for correction.

13 *Thou art* of purer eyes than to behold evil, and canst not look on iniquity: wherefore lookest thou upon them that deal treacherously, *and* holdest thy tongue when the wicked devoureth *the man that is* more righteous than he?

14 And makest men as the fishes of the sea, as the creeping things, *that have* no ruler over them?

15 They take up all of them with the angle, they catch them in their net, and gather them in their drag: therefore they rejoice and are glad.

16 Therefore they sacrifice unto their net, and burn incense unto their drag; because by them their portion *is* fat, and their meat plenteous.

17 Shall they therefore empty their net, and not spare continually to slay the nations?

CHAPTER 2
The Lord Answers Habakkuk

1 I will stand upon my watch, and set me upon the tower, and will watch to see what he will say unto me, and what I shall answer when I am reproved.

2 And the LORD answered me, and said, Write the vision, and make *it* plain upon tables, that he may run that readeth it.

3 For the vision *is* yet for an appointed time, but at the end it shall speak, and not lie: though it tarry, wait for it; because it will surely come, it will not tarry.

4 Behold, his soul *which* is lifted up is not upright in him: but the just shall live by his faith.

5 Yea also, because he transgresseth by

1:1–4 Before he wrote the prophecy God gave him against Judah for her sins of apostasy and idolatry, Habakkuk asked the question, "How long?" How long would God hear his cries about the violence and sin of the people and do nothing? Like us, the prophet did not have the long view of the future that God has. For God knew what He had not yet revealed to Habakkuk, that He would use the Babylonian captivity to forever cure the Jews of idolatry.

1:5–12 Before the Chaldeans (later called Babylonians) were a great power, God predicted that He would raise them up and that they would cover the "breadth of the land" (v. 6). God also predicted that the Babylonians would attribute their success to their god. Verse 12 shows the prophet's faith in the eternal God and that the Babylonians would also be judged someday.

2:3–4 the just shall live by his faith. This statement in verse 4 is the central theme of all Scripture. It is quoted in Romans 1:17; Galatians 3:11; and Hebrews 10:38 and contains the watchwords of the Protestant Reformation.

2:5–8 These verses contain a clear prediction that the proud king of Babylon (see Dan. 4) would have an insatiable appetite to conquer "all nations" but would eventually be brought down; subsequently, his kingdom would be conquered, as it was in 539 B.C.

wine, *he is* a proud man, neither keepeth at home, who enlargeth his desire as hell, and *is* as death, and cannot be satisfied, but gathereth unto him all nations, and heapeth unto him all people:

6 Shall not all these take up a parable against him, and a taunting proverb against him, and say, Woe to him that increaseth *that which is* not his! how long? and to him that ladeth himself with thick clay!

7 Shall they not rise up suddenly that shall bite thee, and awake that shall vex thee, and thou shalt be for booties unto them?

8 Because thou hast spoiled many nations, all the remnant of the people shall spoil thee; because of men's blood, and *for* the violence of the land, of the city, and of all that dwell therein.

9 Woe to him that coveteth an evil covetousness to his house, that he may set his nest on high, that he may be delivered from the power of evil!

10 Thou hast consulted shame to thy house by cutting off many people, and hast sinned *against* thy soul.

11 For the stone shall cry out of the wall, and the beam out of the timber shall answer it.

12 Woe to him that buildeth a town with blood, and stablisheth a city by iniquity!

13 Behold, *is it* not of the LORD of hosts that the people shall labour in the very fire, and the people shall weary themselves for very vanity?

14 For the earth shall be filled with the knowledge of the glory of the LORD, as the waters cover the sea.

15 Woe unto him that giveth his neighbour drink, that puttest thy bottle *to him*, and makest *him* drunken also, that thou mayest look on their nakedness!

16 Thou art filled with shame for glory: drink thou also, and let thy foreskin be uncovered: the cup of the LORD's right hand shall be turned unto thee, and shameful spewing *shall be* on thy glory.

17 For the violence of Lebanon shall cover thee, and the spoil of beasts, *which* made them afraid, because of men's blood, and for the violence of the land, of the city, and of all that dwell therein.

18 What profiteth the graven image that the maker thereof hath graven it; the molten image, and a teacher of lies, that the maker of his work trusteth therein, to make dumb idols?

19 Woe unto him that saith to the wood, Awake; to the dumb stone, Arise, it shall teach! Behold, it *is* laid over with gold and silver, and *there is* no breath at all in the midst of it.

20 But the LORD *is* in his holy temple: let all the earth keep silence before him.

CHAPTER 3
Habakkuk's Prayer

1 A prayer of Habakkuk the prophet upon Shigionoth.

2 O LORD, I have heard thy speech, *and* was afraid: O LORD, revive thy work in the midst of the years, in the midst of the years make known; in wrath remember mercy.

3 God came from Teman, and the Holy One from mount Paran. Selah. His glory covered the heavens, and the earth was full of his praise.

4 And *his* brightness was as the light; he had horns *coming* out of his hand: and there *was* the hiding of his power.

5 Before him went the pestilence, and burning coals went forth at his feet.

6 He stood, and measured the earth: he beheld, and drove asunder the nations; and the everlasting mountains were scattered, the perpetual hills did bow: his ways *are* everlasting.

7 I saw the tents of Cushan in affliction: *and* the curtains of the land of Midian did tremble.

8 Was the LORD displeased against the rivers? *was* thine anger against the rivers? *was* thy wrath against the sea, that thou didst ride upon thine horses *and* thy chariots of salvation?

9 Thy bow was made quite naked, *according* to the oaths of the tribes, *even thy* word. Selah. Thou didst cleave the earth with rivers.

10 The mountains saw thee, *and* they trembled: the overflowing of the water passed by: the deep uttered his voice, *and* lifted up his hands on high.

11 The sun *and* moon stood still in their habitation: at the light of thine arrows they

Center reference column

6 Mic. 2:4
8 Isa. 33:1; Hab. 2:17
9 Jer. 22:13; 49:16; Obad. 1:4
12 Jer. 22:13; Ezek. 24:9; Mic. 3:10; Nah. 3:1
13 Jer. 51:58
14 Isa. 11:9
15 Gen. 9:22; Hos. 7:5
16 Jer. 25:26, 27; 51:57
17 Hab. 2:8
18 Ps. 115:5; Isa. 44:9, 10; 46:2; Jer. 10:8, 14; Zech. 10:2; 1Cor. 12:2
19 Ps. 135:17
20 Ps. 11:4; Zeph. 1:7; Zech. 2:13
2 Ps. 85:6
3 Deut. 33:2; Judg. 5:4; Ps. 68:7
5 Deut. 32:24; Ps. 18:8; Nah. 1:3
6 Gen. 49:26; Nah. 1:5
8 Deut. 33:26, 27; Ps. 68:4; 104:3; Hab. 3:15
9 Ps. 78:15, 16; 105:41
10 Ex. 14:22; 19:16, 18; Josh. 3:16; Judg. 5:4, 5; Ps. 68:8; 77:18; 114:4
11 Josh. 10:11, 12, 13; Ps. 18:14; 77:17, 18

2:14 Long after the "Nebuchadnezzars" of this world have passed away, "the earth shall be filled with the knowledge of the glory of the LORD." This will be fulfilled during the Millennial Kingdom.

3:3–4 This vision of the glorified Lord will have its literal fulfillment in the glorious appearing of Christ upon earth and the setting up of His kingdom (see Rev. 19:11–16; 21:23).

went, *and* at the shining of thy glittering spear.

12 Thou didst march through the land in indignation, thou didst thresh the heathen in anger.

13 Thou wentest forth for the salvation of thy people, *even* for salvation with thine anointed; thou woundedst the head out of the house of the wicked, by discovering the foundation unto the neck. Selah.

14 Thou didst strike through with his staves the head of his villages: they came out as a whirlwind to scatter me: their rejoicing *was* as to devour the poor secretly.

15 Thou didst walk through the sea with thine horses, *through* the heap of great waters.

16 When I heard, my belly trembled; my lips quivered at the voice: rottenness entered into my bones, and I trembled in myself, that I might rest in the day of trouble: when he cometh up unto the people, he will invade them with his troops.

17 Although the fig tree shall not blossom, neither *shall* fruit *be* in the vines; the labour of the olive shall fail, and the fields shall yield no meat; the flock shall be cut off from the fold, and *there shall be* no herd in the stalls:

18 Yet I will rejoice in the LORD, I will joy in the God of my salvation.

19 The LORD God *is* my strength, and he will make my feet like hinds' *feet*, and he will make me to walk upon mine high places. To the chief singer on my stringed instruments.

12 Jer. 51:33; Amos 1:3; Mic. 4:13

13 Josh. 10:24; 11:8, 12; Ps. 68:21

15 Ps. 77:19

16 Ps. 119:120; Jer. 23:9

18 Job 13:15; Isa. 41:16; 61:10

19 Deut. 32:13; 33:29; 2Sam. 22:34; Ps. 18:33; 27:1

3:11–17 The prophet rehearses the miraculous ways of old when God preserved His people, and saw in a vision when He will do even greater exploits during the Tribulation period, culminating in the kingdom of Christ.

3:18–19 The conclusion of the book is a challenge for those who live in times of the judgment of God to look forward by faith to the day when Christ shall again establish the Edenic-like conditions of His kingdom.

Zephaniah

Zephaniah, whose name means "hidden of the Lord," was the great grandson of King Hezekiah. The superscription dates his ministry to the reign of King Josiah (640–609 B.C.), and he likely produced this book in 630 B.C., prior to the spiritual revival and reforms in 621 B.C. Zephaniah's noble ancestry may have given him access to the palace and made it possible for him to effectively reach the heart of young Josiah with his prophecies. A contemporary of Habakkuk and Jeremiah, Zephaniah was aware of military threats from the North, and in his book he warns of coming dangers (2:1–3).

Author	Zephaniah
Date	7th Century B.C.
Key Truth	The Day of the Lord
Historic Time	Reign of Josiah
Key Verse	1:14

1:14
The great day of the LORD is near,
it is near, and hasteth greatly.

Zephaniah was commissioned to proclaim the enormity of Judah's wickedness and to announce the imminent desolation that lay ahead, but also to stir them to repentance, to foretell the destruction of their enemies, and to comfort the faithful with the promise of future blessings. Like Isaiah fifty years before him, the inspired prophet looks beyond the immediate situation to focus frequently on the future "day of the LORD," which events in Judah would soon foreshadow. Another key element of Zephaniah's teaching is the concept of a "remnant" that is protected in the "day of the LORD" (Zeph. 2:7–9; 3:13).

Most of the book concerns events and conditions that were still yet to happen at the time the book was written. Zephaniah contains twenty separate prophetic subjects, most of which relate to Jerusalem's troubles and final defeat to Babylon in 586 B.C. or judgments on surrounding nations. Initial prophecies of "utter consumption" all over Judah (1:2–4) were fulfilled by the Babylonian invasion, but these prophecies may also suggest similar devastation in the future Tribulation. The "day of the LORD" prophecies in 1:14–18 will be fulfilled at the second coming of Christ. Divine judgment on the nations is forecast (3:8), followed by the supremacy of Israel in the Millennial Kingdom (3:9–13) and Israel's comfort, healing, and glorious restoration to their land (3:14–20).

Out of 53 verses, 47 (89%) are predictive.

89%
Prophecy

950 B.C.	900 B.C.	850 B.C.	800 B.C.	750 B.C.	700 B.C.	650 B.C.	600 B.C.	550 B.C.

931-722
Northern Kingdom (Israel)

931
The kingdom is divided

931-586
Southern Kingdom (Judah)

740-680
Ministry of Isaiah

627-580
Ministry of Jeremiah

630
Ministry of Zephaniah

605-536
Babylonian Captivity;
Ministry of Daniel

586
Fall of Jerusalem

605
First captivity

597
Second captivity

612
Fall of Nineveh

592-570
Ministry of Ezekiel

CHAPTER 1

The Day of God's Anger Is Coming

1 The word of the LORD which came unto Zephaniah the son of Cushi, the son of Gedaliah, the son of Amariah, the son of Hizkiah, in the days of Josiah the son of Amon, king of Judah.

2 I will utterly consume all *things* from off the land, saith the LORD.

3 I will consume man and beast; I will consume the fowls of the heaven, and the fishes of the sea, and the stumblingblocks with the wicked; and I will cut off man from off the land, saith the LORD.

4 I will also stretch out mine hand upon Judah, and upon all the inhabitants of Jerusalem; and I will cut off the remnant of Baal from this place, *and* the name of the Chemarims with the priests;

5 And them that worship the host of heaven upon the housetops; and them that worship *and* that swear by the LORD, and that swear by Malcham;

6 And them that are turned back from the LORD; and *those* that have not sought the LORD, nor inquired for him.

7 Hold thy peace at the presence of the Lord GOD: for the day of the LORD *is* at hand: for the LORD hath prepared a sacrifice, he hath bid his guests.

8 And it shall come to pass in the day of the LORD's sacrifice, that I will punish the princes, and the king's children, and all such as are clothed with strange apparel.

9 In the same day also will I punish all those that leap on the threshold, which fill their masters' houses with violence and deceit.

10 And it shall come to pass in that day,

saith the LORD, *that there shall be* the noise of a cry from the fish gate, and an howling from the second, and a great crashing from the hills.

11 Howl, ye inhabitants of Maktesh, for all the merchant people are cut down; all they that bear silver are cut off.

12 And it shall come to pass at that time, *that* I will search Jerusalem with candles, and punish the men that are settled on their lees: that say in their heart, The LORD will not do good, neither will he do evil.

13 Therefore their goods shall become a booty, and their houses a desolation: they shall also build houses, but not inhabit *them*; and they shall plant vineyards, but not drink the wine thereof.

14 The great day of the LORD *is* near, *it is* near, and hasteth greatly, *even* the voice of the day of the LORD: the mighty man shall cry there bitterly.

15 That day *is* a day of wrath, a day of trouble and distress, a day of wasteness and desolation, a day of darkness and gloominess, a day of clouds and thick darkness,

16 A day of the trumpet and alarm against the fenced cities, and against the high towers.

17 And I will bring distress upon men, that they shall walk like blind men, because they have sinned against the LORD: and their blood shall be poured out as dust, and their flesh as the dung.

18 Neither their silver nor their gold shall be able to deliver them in the day of the LORD's wrath; but the whole land shall be devoured by the fire of his jealousy: for he shall make even a speedy riddance of all them that dwell in the land.

Cross references:
3 Ezek. 7:19; 14:3, 4, 7; Hos. 4:3; Matt. 13:41
4 2Kgs. 23:4, 5; Hos. 10:5
5 Josh. 23:7; 2Kgs. 17:33, 41; 23:12; Jer. 19:13; Hos. 4:15
6 Isa. 1:4; Jer. 2:13, 17; Hos. 7:7
7 Isa. 13:6; 34:6; Ezek. 39:17; Hab. 2:20; Rev. 19:17
8 Jer. 39:6
10 2Chr. 33:14
12 Ps. 94:7; Jer. 48:11; Amos 6:1
13 Deut. 28:30, 39; Amos 5:11; Mic. 6:15
14 Joel 2:1, 11
15 Isa. 22:5; Jer. 30:7; Joel 2:2, 11; Zeph. 1:18
16 Jer. 4:19
17 Deut. 28:29; Ps. 79:3; 83:10; Isa. 59:10; Jer. 9:22; 16:4
18 Prov. 11:4; Ezek. 7:19; Zeph. 1:2, 3; 3:8

1:2–4 Zephaniah opens his prophecy with a declaration of global judgment that will take place during the future seven-year Tribulation period. Literally, a "stumblingblock" (v. 3) refers to anything that causes "ruin," thus, an "obstacle." In this context, the stumblingblock is the idolatry of Judah worshiping the idols of Baal. Zephaniah now predicts the immediate judgment upon Judah and Jerusalem that is to come at the hands of the Babylonians in 586 B.C.

1:7 the day of the LORD. This phrase refers to the times that God manifests Himself as judge (Isa. 2:12; 13:6, 9; Ezek. 13:5; 30:3; Joel 1:15; 2:1, 11, 31; 3:14; Amos 5:18, 20; Obad. 1:15; Zeph. 1:14; Zech. 14:1). (See the article on "The Day of the Lord" for more information.) No longer does God allow things to continue on the path that they are on; He comes to earth and personally interjects Himself into the affairs of man. The "day of the LORD" may also

designate the "seventieth week of Daniel," a future seven-year period of judgment (Dan. 9:24–27) often called the Tribulation.

1:14–18 This section of Zephaniah's prophecy contains a great number of terms describing the future seven-year Tribulation period. It stresses, with words like "near" and "hasteth," that the Tribulation is imminent, meaning the end-time events could begin at any time. God's judgment is ready to fall. Zephaniah is calling on the people to hear what is going to happen in the "day of the LORD." The description that follows describes the "day of the LORD" militarily, cosmically, physically, psychologically, and emotionally. God's judgment will occur so suddenly and without warning that no one will be prepared for it. Men will lose their orientation and be like blind men stumbling around in a strange place.

Israel Today

By Jimmy DeYoung

Although the regathering of a people once scattered among the nations of the world is evidence that God is at work in fulfilling His prophetic word, this is only the beginning of a most marvelous story for Israel. The continuing immigration of Jews to their ancient homeland has earned the attention of the entire world, as well as students of biblical prophecy. This ingathering, each stage of which is known among the Jewish people as an *aliya*, has populated a young nation with the cross-section of humankind needed to build, plant, harvest, educate, and even defend themselves from the surrounding nations that are determined to destroy regathered Israel.

An alignment of nations described in the Bible, who will come against Israel in the Last Days, is placing the actors on the stage in possible preparation for the final act to begin. Syria, Egypt, Iran, Libya, Sudan, and Russia have formed loose alliances that may become the fulfillment of the prophecies of both Daniel and Ezekiel. The European Union, Iraq, and the nations of the "Far East" are all in position to be at least the foundational "infrastructures" of the prophesied revived Roman Empire, Babylon, and the "kings of the east" respectively (Rev. 16:12).

> *God is at work in fulfilling His prophetic word.*

Because of the desire of many international leaders to remove the Jewish people from the land of their forefathers, some have been doing all they can to put together comprehensive peace agreements for the region; namely, the Camp David accords between Egypt and Israel during the late '70s and the 1993 Oslo Accord, a peace agreement between the Palestinians and the Israelis. None of these treaties are working as they were intended. The impasse in peace negotiations sets the stage for a world personality to come on the scene to enforce these and other agreements. Daniel 9:27 says the Antichrist will eventually "confirm" the agreements (covenants), evidently making them stronger, and giving him a sense of legitimacy. The peace will not last long, however, as Antichrist will violate his own covenant with Israel.

The most exciting, documented evidence that the Lord's return could be close at hand is the activity surrounding preparations for the rebuilding of the temple on the Temple Mount in Jerusalem. There are Jewish men who now believe they are qualified to serve as "priests." Their priestly garments are made and in storage; all the implements to be used for the sacrifices and worship at the temple are ready; biblical harps are being handmade for the Levite orchestra; and a "red heifer" is even available for the "purification" of everything for the temple.

Ezekiel 40 to 46 gives detailed instructions for the temple that will stand on the Temple Mount during the Millennium. However, Daniel 9:27 states that an earlier temple, preparations for which are in process, will exist in Jerusalem during the Tribulation period.

These four major trends—the *aliya* of the Jewish people, alignment of the nations, anticipation for peace, and arrangements for the temple—were actually mentioned by the ancient Jewish prophets up to 2,500 years ago. These are the "signposts" along the way that the prophets and Jesus alerted the Jewish people to anticipate at the time of the end, the time of the second coming of Jesus Christ. Since Christ's return takes place only seven years after the Rapture, how close must the Rapture be?

CHAPTER 2
Israel's Neighbors Are Doomed

1 Gather yourselves together, yea, gather together, O nation not desired;

2 Before the decree bring forth, *before* the day pass as the chaff, before the fierce anger of the LORD come upon you, before the day of the LORD's anger come upon you.

3 Seek ye the LORD, all ye meek of the earth, which have wrought his judgment; seek righteousness, seek meekness: it may be ye shall be hid in the day of the LORD's anger.

4 For Gaza shall be forsaken, and Ashkelon a desolation: they shall drive out Ashdod at the noon day, and Ekron shall be rooted up.

5 Woe unto the inhabitants of the sea coast, the nation of the Cherethites! the word of the LORD *is* against you; O Canaan, the land of the Philistines, I will even destroy thee, that there shall be no inhabitant.

6 And the sea coast shall be dwellings *and* cottages for shepherds, and folds for flocks.

7 And the coast shall be for the remnant of the house of Judah; they shall feed there-

1 Joel 2:16
2 Job 21:18; Ps. 1:4; Hos. 13:3
3 Ps. 76:9; 105:4; Joel 2:14; Amos 5:6, 15; Jon. 3:9
4 Jer. 6:4; 15:8; 47:4, 5; Ezek. 25:15
5 Josh. 13:3; Ezek. 25:16

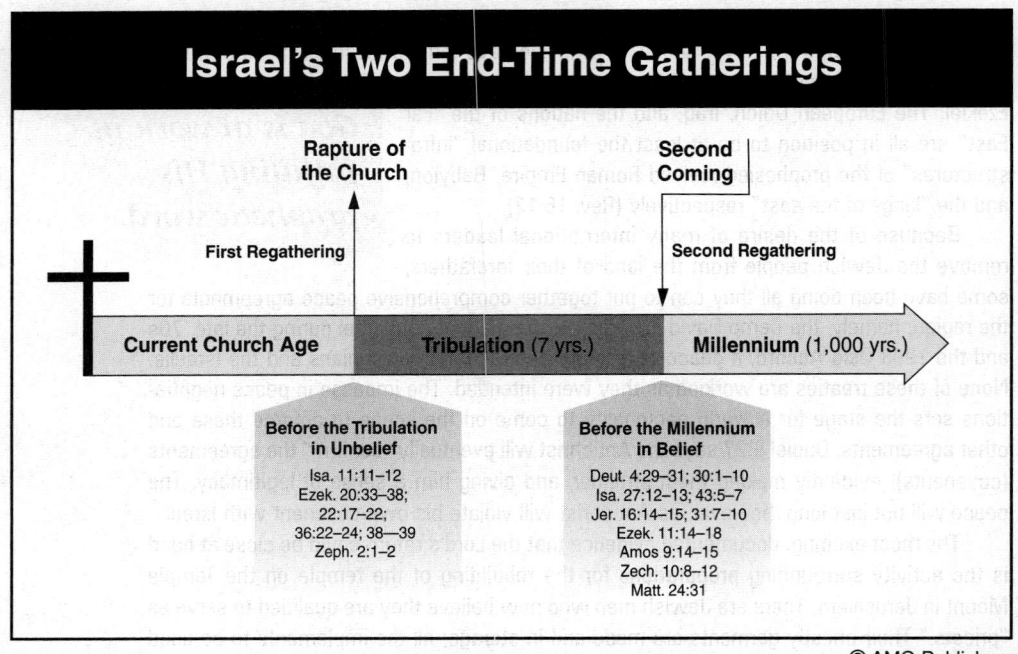

Israel's Two End-Time Gatherings

Rapture of the Church

Second Coming

First Regathering

Second Regathering

Current Church Age · Tribulation (7 yrs.) · Millennium (1,000 yrs.)

Before the Tribulation in Unbelief
Isa. 11:11–12
Ezek. 20:33–38;
22:17–22;
36:22–24; 38—39
Zeph. 2:1–2

Before the Millennium in Belief
Deut. 4:29–31; 30:1–10
Isa. 27:12–13; 43:5–7
Jer. 16:14–15; 31:7–10
Ezek. 11:14–18
Amos 9:14–15
Zech. 10:8–12
Matt. 24:31

© AMG Publishers

2:1–3 Gather yourselves together, yea, gather together. Zephaniah uses a rare verb that derives from gathering chaff or stubble, meaning to "gather that which is small and insignificant." The prophet repeats this word twice for emphasis. Having spelled out the judgment up to this point, Zephaniah now begins a call to repentance. That which is to take place once they are gathered is described as "the decree . . . the day . . . the fierce anger of the LORD" and "the day of the LORD's anger." These descriptions are all references to Israel's regathering into the land of Israel before the seven-year Tribulation period is to begin (cf. Isa. 11:11–12; Ezek. 20:33–38; 22:17–22; 38—39). It is especially significant that Israel was re-established as a political entity in A.D. 1948. The current nation of Israel is now back in its land, in unbelief, yet

positioned to fulfill what the prophets have predicted will happen during the Tribulation. What is the purpose of this regathering before the Tribulation? It is so that Israel may seek the Lord. The Lord will offer protection during the Tribulation to the elect remnant who will submit to Him (Isa. 26:20).

2:4–7 Gaza . . . Ashkelon . . . Ashdod . . . Ekron. Four of the five major cities of Philistia, mentioned in order from south to north, are singled out by the Lord for destruction. Here we have specific lists of prophecies against many of the Gentiles surrounding Judah.

2:7 the LORD their God shall visit them. Earlier, Zephaniah had spoken of a visitation of the Lord in judgment (Zeph. 1:8–9); now he speaks of a future visit for blessing.

upon: in the houses of Ashkelon shall they lie down in the evening: for the LORD their God shall visit them, and turn away their captivity.

8 I have heard the reproach of Moab, and the revilings of the children of Ammon, whereby they have reproached my people, and magnified *themselves* against their border.

9 Therefore *as* I live, saith the LORD of hosts, the God of Israel, Surely Moab shall be as Sodom, and the children of Ammon as Gomorrah, *even* the breeding of nettles, and salt-pits, and a perpetual desolation: the residue of my people shall spoil them, and the remnant of my people shall possess them.

10 This shall they have for their pride, because they have reproached and magnified *themselves* against the people of the LORD of hosts.

11 The LORD *will be* terrible unto them: for he will famish all the gods of the earth; and *men* shall worship him, every one from his place, *even* all the isles of the heathen.

12 Ye Ethiopians also, ye *shall be* slain by my sword.

13 And he will stretch out his hand against the north, and destroy Assyria; and will make Nineveh a desolation, *and* dry like a wilderness.

14 And flocks shall lie down in the midst of her, all the beasts of the nations: both the cormorant and the bittern shall lodge in the upper lintels of it; *their* voice shall sing in the windows; desolation *shall be* in the thresholds: for he shall uncover the cedar work.

15 This *is* the rejoicing city that dwelt carelessly, that said in her heart, I *am*, and *there is* none beside me: how is she become a desolation, a place for beasts to lie down in!

every one that passeth by her shall hiss, *and* wag his hand.

CHAPTER 3
Jerusalem Will Be Saved

1 Woe to her that is filthy and polluted, to the oppressing city!

2 She obeyed not the voice; she received not correction; she trusted not in the LORD; she drew not near to her God.

3 Her princes within her *are* roaring lions; her judges *are* evening wolves; they gnaw not the bones till the morrow.

4 Her prophets *are* light *and* treacherous persons: her priests have polluted the sanctuary, they have done violence to the law.

5 The just LORD *is* in the midst thereof; he will not do iniquity: every morning doth he bring his judgment to light, he faileth not; but the unjust knoweth no shame.

6 I have cut off the nations: their towers are desolate; I made their streets waste, that none passeth by: their cities are destroyed, so that there is no man, that there is none inhabitant.

7 I said, Surely thou wilt fear me, thou wilt receive instruction; so their dwelling should not be cut off, howsoever I punished them: but they rose early, *and* corrupted all their doings.

8 Therefore wait ye upon me, saith the LORD, until the day that I rise up to the prey: for my determination *is* to gather the nations, that I may assemble the kingdoms, to pour upon them mine indignation, *even* all my fierce anger: for all the earth shall be devoured with the fire of my jealousy.

9 For then will I turn to the people a pure language, that they may all call upon the name of the LORD, to serve him with one consent.

Cross references (center column):

8 Jer. 48:27; 49:1; Ezek. 25:3, 6, 8
9 Gen. 19:25; Deut. 29:23; Ezek. 25:9; Amos 1:13; 2:1; Zeph. 2:7
10 Isa. 16:6; Jer. 48:29
11 Gen. 10:5; Mal. 1:11; John 4:21
12 Ps. 17:13; Isa. 18:1; 20:4; Jer. 46:9; Ezek. 30:9
13 Isa. 10:12; Ezek. 31:3; Nah. 1:1; 2:10; 3:15, 18
14 Isa. 13:21, 22; 34:11, 14; Jer. 22:14; Zeph. 2:6
15 Isa. 47:8; Lam. 2:15; Ezek. 27:36
2 Jer. 5:3; 22:21
3 Ezek. 22:27; Mic. 3:9-11; Hab. 1:8
4 Jer. 23:11, 32; Hos. 9:7
5 Deut. 32:4; Lam. 3:22
7 Gen. 6:12; Jer. 8:6
8 Joel 3:2; Zeph. 1:18
9 Isa. 19:18

2:8–9 they have reproached my people. Moab and Ammon were descendants of Lot by his daughters' incest (Gen. 19:30–38). Occupying land to the east of Judah, they have a long history of opposition and resistance to God's people (cf. Num. 22; 24:17; Judg. 3:12–14; 10:7–9; 11:4–6). Since the boundaries of Israel and Judah are divinely decreed by God for His people (cf. Num. 34—36), the fact that Moab and Ammon tried to capture part of Judah's land was a crime against God Himself. Just as God totally annihilated Sodom and Gomorrah (Gen. 18—19), so also would He do to Moab and Ammon (cf. Isa. 15—16; Jer. 48—49; Ezek. 25:1–11; Amos 1:13–15; 2:1–5). The area of Moab and Ammon—today known as southern Jordan—was over-run by the Babylonians in 582–581 B.C. and has by-and-large been a desolate area ever since. The absorption of the territories of Ammon and Moab is clearly presupposed in the millennial land allocations (Ezek. 45:1–25; 47:13—48:35).

3:8 wait ye upon me. The Lord appeals to the faithful remnant of Judah to be patient until God executes global judgment upon all of mankind who rebel against Him. This will occur during the Tribulation period. The gathering of nations and outpouring of God's wrath are references to the Battle of Armageddon (cf. Joel 3:2, 13–14; Zech. 14:4–5; Rev. 14:14–20; 16:12–16; 19:11–21), a time of judgment for the nations.

10 From beyond the rivers of Ethiopia my suppliants, *even* the daughter of my dispersed, shall bring mine offering.

11 In that day shalt thou not be ashamed for all thy doings, wherein thou hast transgressed against me: for then I will take away out of the midst of thee them that rejoice in thy pride, and thou shalt no more be haughty because of my holy mountain.

12 I will also leave in the midst of thee an afflicted and poor people, and they shall trust in the name of the LORD.

13 The remnant of Israel shall not do iniquity, nor speak lies; neither shall a deceitful tongue be found in their mouth: for they shall feed and lie down, and none shall make *them* afraid.

14 Sing, O daughter of Zion; shout, O Israel; be glad and rejoice with all the heart, O daughter of Jerusalem.

15 The LORD hath taken away thy judgments, he hath cast out thine enemy: the

king of Israel, *even* the LORD, *is* in the midst of thee: thou shalt not see evil any more.

16 In that day it shall be said to Jerusalem, Fear thou not: *and to* Zion, Let not thine hands be slack.

17 The LORD thy God in the midst of thee *is* mighty; he will save, he will rejoice over thee with joy; he will rest in his love, he will joy over thee with singing.

18 I will gather *them that are* sorrowful for the solemn assembly, *who* are of thee, *to whom* the reproach of it *was* a burden.

19 Behold, at that time I will undo all that afflict thee: and I will save her that halteth, and gather her that was driven out; and I will get them praise and fame in every land where they have been put to shame.

20 At that time will I bring you *again*, even in the time that I gather you: for I will make you a name and a praise among all people of the earth, when I turn back your captivity before your eyes, saith the LORD.

Cross references:
11 Jer. 7:4; Mic. 3:11; Matt. 3:9
12 Isa. 14:32; Zech. 11:11; Matt. 5:3; James 2:5
13 Isa. 60:21; 63:8; Rev. 14:5
14 Isa. 12:6; 54:1; Zech. 2:10; 9:9
15 Ezek. 48:35; Rev. 7:15; 21:3, 4
16 Isa. 35:3, 4; Heb. 12:12
17 Deut. 30:9; Isa. 62:5; 65:19; Jer. 32:41; Zeph. 3:15
18 Lam. 2:6

3:11 In that day. These things will all take place during the Millennium, after the Lord has purged out global unbelief, pride, and rebellion. The phrase, "my holy mountain," is a popular term used to refer to Jerusalem, especially to the reconstructed Jerusalem during the Millennial Kingdom (Isa. 11:9; 56:7; 57:13; 65:11, 25; 66:20; Ezek. 20:40; 28:14; Dan. 11:45; Joel 3:17; Obad. 1:16; Zech. 8:3).

3:13 The remnant of Israel shall not do iniquity. This will be a future time, during the Millennium, when the Lord will effect a greater change in the hearts of men than we see today.

3:14–20 In contrast to the cry of lament that Jeremiah

advocates to the nation because of impending judgment (Lam. 2:18–19; 3:48–54), Zephaniah now inspires Judah to be glad. This passage states that the very presence of Jesus the Messiah will dwell within Jerusalem during the Millennial Kingdom. As a result of the Lord dwelling in favor with the nation of Israel, He too will express joy over the nation with singing. During the Millennium, the Lord will bless the nation and remove any curse that may have been upon its people from the past. With this millennial blessing, national Israel will go from being the most hated nation in the world today, to being the most admired and looked-up-to nation. Anti-Semitism will be a thing of the past. During the Millennium, Israel and Judah will fulfill the destiny for which God chose them.

Haggai

The name Haggai means "festival of the Lord." Because of the precise dates given for each prophetic message, the events of this book may be more accurately dated than perhaps any other book in the whole Bible. Darius, who is mentioned for the first two dates, was the Babylonian king that removed the law that prohibited the Jews from reconstructing the temple. Haggai was the first of the prophets who spoke to the exiles after they had returned to Palestine. An older man, he labored with the younger Zechariah, encouraging the Jews who had returned from the seventy-year captivity to finish rebuilding the temple. The temple rebuilding project had been started, but adversaries stifled the construction, and work stopped. The book of Ezra contains an account of what happened between 536 and 516 B.C., and how Haggai and Zechariah challenged the leaders and the people to complete the building program.

The temple was important to the Jewish people as the center of worship, but to those who remembered the original temple, this first phase of the Second Temple must have seemed a far cry from Solomon's masterpiece. With the purpose of encouraging the disheartened exiles, the book consists of five motivating messages given over a period of four months.

Haggai's prediction that God would "shake the heavens and the nations" (2:6, 21) is referenced in Hebrews 12:25–29 regarding the passing of this world order and the coming of a "kingdom which cannot be moved [shaken]." That the glory of the reconstructed or "latter" house would be greater than Solomon's Temple (Hag. 2:9) was true of the temple in Jesus' time. The expression "desire of all nations" (2:7) refers to the nations' most desirable treasures being brought to the temple, as partially illustrated by the gifts of the wise men (Matt. 2). These prophecies will finally be fulfilled in the glorious future with the Millennial Temple.

Of 38 verses, 15 are prophetic, which amounts to 39 percent of the book. Some seemingly fulfilled prophecies occasionally have long-range applications.

Author
Haggai

Date
520 B.C.

Key Truth
Rebuilding the Temple

Historic Time
After First Return from the Babylonian Captivity

Key Verse
2:9
The glory of this latter house shall be greater than of the former.

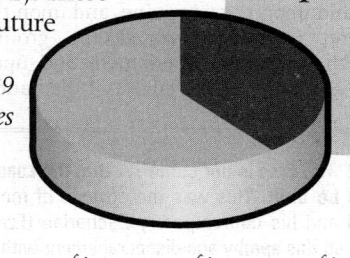

39%
Prophecy

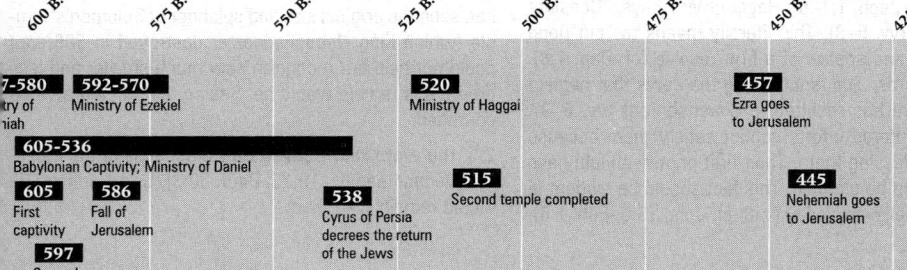

600 B.C.	575 B.C.	550 B.C.	525 B.C.	500 B.C.	475 B.C.	450 B.C.	425 B.C.	400 B.C.

597-580
try of ...iah

592-570
Ministry of Ezekiel

520
Ministry of Haggai

457
Ezra goes to Jerusalem

605-536
Babylonian Captivity; Ministry of Daniel

605
First captivity

586
Fall of Jerusalem

538
Cyrus of Persia decrees the return of the Jews

515
Second temple completed

445
Nehemiah goes to Jerusalem

597
Second captivity

CHAPTER 1

The Appeal to Rebuild the Temple

1 In the second year of Darius the king, in the sixth month, in the first day of the month, came the word of the LORD by Haggai the prophet unto Zerubbabel the son of Shealtiel, governor of Judah, and to Joshua the son of Josedech, the high priest, saying,

2 Thus speaketh the LORD of hosts, saying, This people say, The time is not come, the time that the LORD's house should be built.

3 Then came the word of the LORD by Haggai the prophet, saying,

4 Is it time for you, O ye, to dwell in your cieled houses, and this house lie waste?

5 Now therefore thus saith the LORD of hosts; Consider your ways.

6 Ye have sown much, and bring in little; ye eat, but ye have not enough; ye drink, but ye are not filled with drink; ye clothe you, but there is none warm; and he that earneth wages earneth wages to put it into a bag with holes.

7 Thus saith the LORD of hosts; Consider your ways.

8 Go up to the mountain, and bring wood, and build the house; and I will take pleasure in it, and I will be glorified, saith the LORD.

9 Ye looked for much, and, lo, it came to little; and when ye brought it home, I did blow upon it. Why? saith the LORD of hosts. Because of mine house that is waste, and ye run every man unto his own house.

10 Therefore the heaven over you is stayed from dew, and the earth is stayed from her fruit.

11 And I called for a drought upon the land, and upon the mountains, and upon the corn, and upon the new wine, and upon the oil, and upon that which the ground bringeth forth, and upon men, and upon cattle, and upon all the labour of the hands.

12 Then Zerubbabel the son of Shealtiel, and Joshua the son of Josedech, the high priest, with all the remnant of the people, obeyed the voice of the LORD their God, and the words of Haggai the prophet, as the LORD their God had sent him, and the people did fear before the LORD.

13 Then spake Haggai the LORD's messenger in the LORD's message unto the people, saying, I am with you, saith the LORD.

14 And the LORD stirred up the spirit of Zerubbabel the son of Shealtiel, governor of Judah, and the spirit of Joshua the son of Josedech, the high priest, and the spirit of all the remnant of the people; and they came and did work in the house of the LORD of hosts, their God,

15 In the four and twentieth day of the sixth month, in the second year of Darius the king.

CHAPTER 2

God's Glory Will Again Fill the Temple

1 In the seventh month, in the one and twentieth day of the month, came the word of the LORD by the prophet Haggai, saying,

2 Speak now to Zerubbabel the son of Shealtiel, governor of Judah, and to Joshua the son of Josedech, the high priest, and to the residue of the people, saying,

3 Who is left among you that saw this house in her first glory? and how do ye see it now? is it not in your eyes in comparison of it as nothing?

4 Yet now be strong, O Zerubbabel, saith the LORD; and be strong, O Joshua, son of Josedech, the high priest; and be strong, all ye people of the land, saith the LORD, and work: for I am with you, saith the LORD of hosts:

5 According to the word that I covenanted

Cross references (center column):

1 1Chr. 3:17, 19; 6:15; Ezra 3:2; 4:24; 5:1, 2; Zech. 1:1; Matt. 1:12; Luke 3:27
3 Ezra 5:1
4 2Sam. 7:2; Ps. 132:3
5 Lam. 3:40; Hag. 1:7
6 Deut. 28:38; Hos. 4:10; Mic. 6:14, 15; Hag. 2:16; Zech. 8:10
9 Hag. 2:16, 17
10 Lev. 26:19; Deut. 28:23; 1Kgs. 8:35
11 1Kgs. 17:1; 2Kgs. 8:1; Hag. 2:17
12 Ezra 5:2
13 Matt. 28:20; Rom. 8:31
14 2Chr. 36:22; Ezra 1:1; 5:2, 8; Hag. 2:21
3 Ezra 3:12; Zech. 4:10
4 Zech. 8:9
5 Ex. 29:45, 46; Neh. 9:20; Isa. 63:11

1:2–12 The time is not come . . . that the LORD's house should be built. This was the attitude of most Jews. Haggai and his contemporary Zechariah (Ezra 5:1–6) countered this apathy and discouragement with dynamic appeals (see Zech. 1:1–6). Haggai twice says, "Consider your ways" (vv. 5–9). This literally means to "put upon your heart," and speaks of a firm resolve (cf. Dan. 1:8). By these words, God is informing the Jews that neglect of the temple has resulted in chastisement (vv. 6–9). Their self-centered efforts cannot satisfy them because God is not blessing them. Their first priority should have been that God be glorified. This fact should be evident in the lives of believers today (v. 8, cf. John 15:8; Eph. 1:6).

2:1 This was the seventh day of the Feast of Tabernacles (Lev. 23:39–44).

2:2–4 Obviously, the problem at this time was similar to the situation in Ezra 3:8–13. Those older survivors who had seen the original size and splendor of Solomon's Temple (which King Nebuchadnezzar destroyed in 586 B.C.) could not help but recognize how much smaller and less ornate this temple would be. Seeing this, they grew discouraged.

2:5 the word that I covenanted. Because of the Mosaic covenant (see Ex. 19:25; Deut. 30:3), God promised He would remain with them.

with you when ye came out of Egypt, so my spirit remaineth among you: fear ye not.

6 For thus saith the LORD of hosts; Yet once, it *is* a little while, and I will shake the heavens, and the earth, and the sea, and the dry *land*;

7 And I will shake all nations, and the desire of all nations shall come: and I will fill this house with glory, saith the LORD of hosts.

8 The silver *is* mine, and the gold *is* mine, saith the LORD of hosts.

9 The glory of this latter house shall be greater than of the former, saith the LORD of hosts: and in this place will I give peace, saith the LORD of hosts.

10 In the four and twentieth *day* of the ninth *month*, in the second year of Darius, came the word of the LORD by Haggai the prophet, saying,

11 Thus saith the LORD of hosts; Ask now the priests *concerning* the law, saying,

12 If one bear holy flesh in the skirt of his garment, and with his skirt do touch bread, or pottage, or wine, or oil, or any meat, shall it be holy? And the priests answered and said, No.

13 Then said Haggai, If *one that is* unclean by a dead body touch any of these, shall it be unclean? And the priests answered and said, It shall be unclean.

14 Then answered Haggai, and said, So *is* this people, and so *is* this nation before me, saith the LORD; and so *is* every work of their hands; and that which they offer there *is* unclean.

15 And now, I pray you, consider from this day and upward, from before a stone was laid upon a stone in the temple of the LORD:

16 Since those *days* were, when *one* came to an heap of twenty *measures*, there were *but* ten: when *one* came to the pressfat for to draw out fifty *vessels* out of the press, there were *but* twenty.

17 I smote you with blasting and with mildew and with hail in all the labours of your hands; yet ye *turned* not to me, saith the LORD.

18 Consider now from this day and upward, from the four and twentieth day of the ninth *month, even* from the day that the foundation of the LORD's temple was laid, consider *it*.

19 Is the seed yet in the barn? yea, as yet the vine, and the fig tree, and the pomegranate, and the olive tree, hath not brought forth: from this day will I bless *you*.

20 And again the word of the Lord came unto Haggai in the four and twentieth day of the month, saying,

21 Speak to Zerubbabel, governor of Judah,

Cross references

6 Joel 3:16; Hag. 2:21; Heb. 12:26
7 Gen. 49:10; Mal. 3:1
9 Ps. 85:8, 9; Luke 2:14; John 1:14; Eph. 2:14
11 Lev. 10:10, 11; Deut. 33:10; Mal. 2:7
13 Num. 19:11
14 Titus 1:15
15 Hag. 1:5
16 Hag. 1:6, 9; Zech. 8:10
17 Deut. 28:22; 1Kgs. 8:37; Jer. 5:3; Amos 4:6, 8-11; Hag. 1:9, 11
18 Zech. 8:9
19 Zech. 8:12
21 Hag. 1:14; 2:6, 7; Heb. 12:26

2:6–7 Yet once . . . and I will shake the heavens. The "shaking" of the nations goes beyond the conditions of the Persian Empire and refers to the future Tribulation and the coming of the "kingdom which cannot be moved" (Heb. 12:26–28).

2:7 the desire of all nations. Some commentators see this as a prophecy of Christ, the supremely desirable Person, who will bring peace to the nations. However, the Hebrew word is in the feminine gender, and the verb translated "shall come" is plural, which seems inconsistent with that interpretation. Other authorities translate the passage to mean that desirable delights and treasures will be brought from all nations to Jerusalem and the temple, as demonstrated by the magi from the East who brought gifts to Jesus (Matt. 2:11, cf. Zech. 14:16).

2:9 The glory of this latter house . . . greater than of the former. This prediction, comparing Solomon's Temple to a future temple, goes beyond this second temple under construction at the time, and is thought by some to mean the vast temple complex of Jesus' time that would be viewed as having a greater glory because of the presence of Jesus. The wicked king Herod, seeking to curry favor with the Jews and to build a monument, inaugurated a huge expansion program for the temple forty-six years before Jesus began His ministry (John 2:20), but construction for this temple was not completed until A.D. 64. Herod's Temple was the largest religious center in the world at the time. However, only the Millennial Temple of Ezekiel's vision (Ezek. 40—47) will fulfill this far-reaching prophecy.

2:10–19 This third message of encouragement and exhortation deals with the importance of personal holiness. The people's failure to be truly holy in their lives had affected their activities. Now they had repented and laid the foundation for the temple in obedience to Haggai's message. Here God asks them if they are ready for a harvest, because He is now ready to bless their fields and orchards (v. 19).

2:18 Consider now from this day. Haggai appeals to the people to keep in mind the motives for their labor. Previously they had been slothful in their service (vv. 14–16). Consequently, God's chastisement came (v. 17). Believers today should remember to perform every task conscious that God desires diligence and integrity (Eph. 6:5–6).

2:21–22 shake the heavens. This fifth and final excerpt from Haggai's sermons is still entirely unfulfilled prophecy.

saying, I will shake the heavens and the earth;

22 And I will overthrow the throne of kingdoms, and I will destroy the strength of the kingdoms of the heathen; and I will overthrow the chariots, and those that ride in them; and the horses and their riders shall

come down, every one by the sword of his brother.

23 In that day, saith the LORD of hosts, will I take thee, O Zerubbabel, my servant, the son of Shealtiel, saith the LORD, and will make thee as a signet: for I have chosen thee, saith the LORD of hosts.

22 Dan. 2:44; Mic. 5:10; Zech. 4:6; 9:10; Matt. 24:7	
23 Song 8:6; Isa. 42:1; 43:10; Jer. 22:24	

The shaking of the heavens and the earth and the overthrow of the nations refer to the future Tribulation. Forecasting the concluding wars of the Tribulation (see Zech. 14:13; Heb. 12:26; Rev. 16:16), Haggai joins his compatriot Zechariah in looking toward a glorious victory over the armies of the wicked.

2:23 will make thee as a signet. This prophecy to Zerubbabel, the representative of the Davidic dynasty, which was promised an eternal royal line (2 Sam. 7:16), goes beyond his own governorship to that day when the Messiah receives the throne. The term "servant" is a messianic title (Is. 42:1–4; 49:1–7; 50:4–10; 52:13—53:13). The signet was a portable instrument, sometimes a ring, used to stamp a document to make it official, legal,

and authentic. Because Zerubbabel was the grandson of Jehoichin (a.k.a. Jeconiah and Coniah), he surely would have known of Jeremiah's prophecy (Jer. 22:24–30), that announced God's curse upon the Davidic line as a result of the wickedness of Judah's last kings. The prophecy of Haggai assures the godly Zerubbabel that though he would not rule as king, he would serve as the signet and seal of royal authority. He would be blessed, and the royal authority of the Davidic line of kings would be preserved and authenticated through him. While these words applied initially to Zerubbabel, the promise is a renewal of the Davidic dynasty. In that future day, Jesus, Son of David, will reign (Isa. 11:10).

Zechariah

Z echariah, whose name means "Jehovah remembers," was a priest and prophet, who joined Haggai in 520 B.C., urging the completion of the Jewish temple following the captivity. Zechariah's ministry overlapped that of Haggai but continued long after Haggai ceased to prophesy. Like Haggai, Zechariah had a ministry of encouragement. However, while Haggai focuses on the immediate blessings of rebuilding the temple with only brief allusions to future blessings of ultimate glory, Zechariah contains words of encouragement primarily centered on the ultimate blessing coming upon Israel through the first and second comings of Christ.

Author
Zechariah

Date
6th Century B.C.

Key Truth
God's Future Plans for His People

Historic Time
First Return from the Babylonian Captivity

Key Verse
14:9
And the LORD shall be king over all the earth.

In the first six chapters, eight visions encompass both near and distant prophetic truth, reminding the reader that God is the Sovereign Ruler of His people and the world. God's servant, the Branch, is a strong messianic prediction of Jesus (Zech. 3:8; 6:12).

Chapters 9—14 are full of promises concerning the second coming of the Messiah and a worldwide kingdom. He shall come the first time however as the Lowly One, riding on a beast (9:9, cf. Matt. 21:1–11). Then we see Him as a mighty Sovereign (14:8–11), when He comes the second time to reign (cf. Rev. 19:11).

Chapter 11 describes the Shepherd who would seek to save Israel, but is rejected (11:12–13, cf. Matt. 26:15; 27:1–10). In chapter 12, a future invasion of Jerusalem during the Tribulation is foreseen, followed by the Jews' repentance as they look on the returning Messiah whom they pierced (12:10, cf. Rev. 1:7; 19:11–21), touching down on the Mount of Olives from which He ascended (14:4). Finally, Christ shall be King over all the earth (14:9–20).

To gain a full picture of end-time events, these last chapters should be compared with Isaiah 2, 11—12, 24—25, 35, 62—66; Ezekiel 34—38; Daniel 7, 9, 12; Matthew 24—25 and Revelation 6—20.

A full 144 verses in Zechariah are predictive out of a total of 211, or 69 percent.

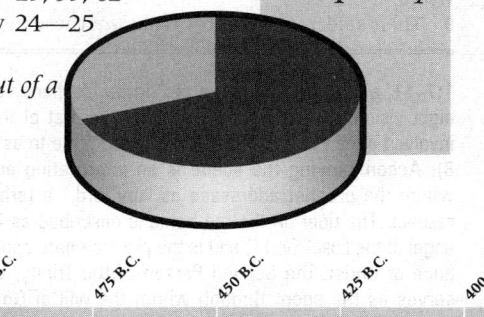

69% Prophecy

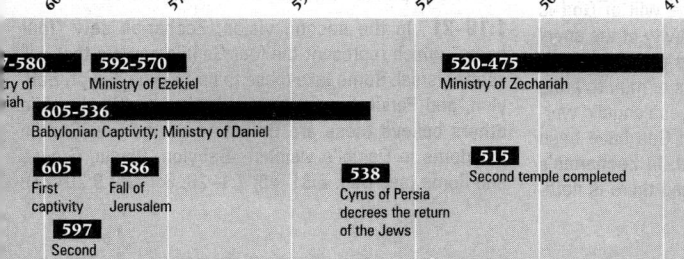

600 B.C.	575 B.C.	550 B.C.	525 B.C.	500 B.C.	475 B.C.	450 B.C.	425 B.C.	400 B.C.

7-580
ry of
iah

592-570
Ministry of Ezekiel

605-536
Babylonian Captivity; Ministry of Daniel

520-475
Ministry of Zechariah

457
Ezra goes
to Jerusalem

605
First
captivity

586
Fall of
Jerusalem

538
Cyrus of Persia
decrees the return
of the Jews

515
Second temple completed

445
Nehemiah goes
to Jerusalem

597
Second
captivity

CHAPTER 1
A Call to Come Back to the Lord

1 In the eighth month, in the second year of Darius, came the word of the LORD unto Zechariah, the son of Berechiah, the son of Iddo the prophet, saying,

2 The LORD hath been sore displeased with your fathers.

3 Therefore say thou unto them, Thus saith the LORD of hosts; Turn ye unto me, saith the LORD of hosts, and I will turn unto you, saith the LORD of hosts.

4 Be ye not as your fathers, unto whom the former prophets have cried, saying, Thus saith the LORD of hosts; Turn ye now from your evil ways, and *from* your evil doings: but they did not hear, nor hearken unto me, saith the LORD.

5 Your fathers, where *are* they? and the prophets, do they live for ever?

6 But my words and my statutes, which I commanded my servants the prophets, did they not take hold of your fathers? and they returned and said, Like as the LORD of hosts thought to do unto us, according to our ways, and according to our doings, so hath he dealt with us.

7 Upon the four and twentieth day of the eleventh month, which *is* the month Sebat, in the second year of Darius, came the word of the LORD unto Zechariah, the son of Berechiah, the son of Iddo the prophet, saying,

8 I saw by night, and behold a man riding upon a red horse, and he stood among the myrtle trees that *were* in the bottom; and behind him *were there* red horses, speckled, and white.

9 Then said I, O my lord, what *are* these? And the angel that talked with me said unto me, I will shew thee what these *be*.

10 And the man that stood among the myrtle trees answered and said, These *are they* whom the LORD hath sent to walk to and fro through the earth.

11 And they answered the angel of the LORD that stood among the myrtle trees, and said, We have walked to and fro through the earth, and, behold, all the earth sitteth still, and is at rest.

12 Then the angel of the LORD answered and said, O LORD of hosts, how long wilt thou not have mercy on Jerusalem and on the cities of Judah, against which thou hast had indignation these threescore and ten years?

13 And the LORD answered the angel that talked with me *with* good words *and* comfortable words.

14 So the angel that communed with me said unto me, Cry thou, saying, Thus saith the LORD of hosts; I am jealous for Jerusalem and for Zion with a great jealousy.

15 And I am very sore displeased with the heathen *that are* at ease: for I was but a little displeased, and they helped forward the affliction.

16 Therefore thus saith the LORD; I am returned to Jerusalem with mercies: my house shall be built in it, saith the LORD of hosts, and a line shall be stretched forth upon Jerusalem.

17 Cry yet, saying, Thus saith the LORD of hosts; My cities through prosperity shall yet be spread abroad; and the LORD shall yet comfort Zion, and shall yet choose Jerusalem.

18 Then lifted I up mine eyes, and saw, and behold four horns.

Cross References

1 Ezra 4:24; 5:1; Hag. 1:1; Matt. 23:35

3 Jer. 25:5; 35:15; Mic. 7:19; Mal. 3:7; Luke 15:20; James 4:8

4 2Chr. 36:15, 16; Isa. 31:6; Jer. 3:12; 18:11; Ezek. 18:30; Hos. 14:1

6 Isa. 55:1; Lam. 1:18; 2:17

8 Josh. 5:13; Zech. 6:2-7; Rev. 6:4

10 Heb. 1:14

11 Ps. 103:20, 21

12 Ps. 102:13; Jer. 25:11, 12; Dan. 9:2; Zech. 7:5; Rev. 6:10

13 Jer. 29:10

14 Joel 2:18; Zech. 8:2

15 Isa. 47:6

16 Isa. 12:1; 54:8; Zech. 2:1, 2, 10; 8:3

17 Isa. 14:1; 51:3; Zech. 2:12; 3:2

1:7–11 a man riding upon a red horse. Zechariah saw eight visions in one night (1:7—6:8). The first of these involved a man who stands "among the myrtle trees" (v. 8). Accompanying the scene is an interpreting angel whom the prophet addresses as "my lord," a term of respect. The rider on the red horse is described as "the angel of the LORD" (v. 11) and is the pre-incarnate appearance of Christ, the Second Person of the Trinity, who serves as the agent through whom the will of God is accomplished. The description of the activity of the angel of the Lord and the other riders suggests they were constantly on patrol intervening in the affairs of men to bring to pass the will of God for His people. These angelic warriors under the command of the Son of God have been victorious in their deliverance of Israel. In Zechariah's vision, the world is in a relative calm, and there is nothing to hinder the rebuilding of the temple.

1:12–17 angel of the LORD. God the Son intercedes for Jerusalem, pleading with the "LORD of hosts" (God the Father) on behalf of Judah (v. 12), which has suffered the ravages of the seventy-year Babylonian captivity (cf. Jer. 25:11; Dan. 9:2). This passage clearly distinguishes between the first and second members of the Godhead as the Son pleads with the Father to restore Jerusalem.

1:18–21 In the second vision, Zechariah saw "four horns" which represent the four Gentile powers that will scatter Israel. Some take these to be Assyria, Egypt, Babylon, and Persia (up to the prophet's own time), while others believe these are the same as the four Gentile kingdoms in Daniel's visions—Babylon, Persia, Greece and Rome (see Dan. 2:31–45; 7:1–28; 8:1–25; 9:20–27).

19 And I said unto the angel that talked with me, What *be* these? And he answered me, These *are* the horns which have scattered Judah, Israel, and Jerusalem.
20 And the LORD shewed me four carpenters.
21 Then said I, What come these to do? And he spake, saying, These *are* the horns which have scattered Judah, so that no man did lift up his head: but these are come to fray them, to cast out the horns of the Gentiles, which lifted up *their* horn over the land of Judah to scatter it.

CHAPTER 2
A Man with a Measuring Line

1 I lifted up mine eyes again, and looked, and behold a man with a measuring line in his hand.
2 Then said I, Whither goest thou? And he said unto me, To measure Jerusalem, to see what *is* the breadth thereof, and what *is* the length thereof.
3 And, behold, the angel that talked with me went forth, and another angel went out to meet him,
4 And said unto him, Run, speak to this young man, saying, Jerusalem shall be inhabited *as* towns without walls for the multitude of men and cattle therein:
5 For I, saith the LORD, will be unto her a wall of fire round about, and will be the glory in the midst of her.
6 Ho, ho, *come forth*, and flee from the land of the north, saith the LORD: for I have spread you abroad as the four winds of the heaven, saith the LORD.

7 Deliver thyself, O Zion, that dwellest *with* the daughter of Babylon.
8 For thus saith the LORD of hosts; After the glory hath he sent me unto the nations which spoiled you: for he that toucheth you toucheth the apple of his eye.
9 For, behold, I will shake mine hand upon them, and they shall be a spoil to their servants: and ye shall know that the LORD of hosts hath sent me.
10 Sing and rejoice, O daughter of Zion: for, lo, I come, and I will dwell in the midst of thee, saith the LORD.
11 And many nations shall be joined to the LORD in that day, and shall be my people: and I will dwell in the midst of thee, and thou shalt know that the LORD of hosts hath sent me unto thee.
12 And the LORD shall inherit Judah his portion in the holy land, and shall choose Jerusalem again.
13 Be silent, O all flesh, before the LORD: for he is raised up out of his holy habitation.

CHAPTER 3
Clean Clothes for the High Priest

1 And he shewed me Joshua the high priest standing before the angel of the LORD, and Satan standing at his right hand to resist him.
2 And the LORD said unto Satan, The LORD rebuke thee, O Satan; even the LORD that hath chosen Jerusalem rebuke thee: *is* not this a brand plucked out of the fire?
3 Now Joshua was clothed with filthy garments, and stood before the angel.
4 And he answered and spake unto those

Cross References

19 Ezra 4:1, 4, 7; 5:3
21 Ps. 75:4
1 Ezek. 40:3
2 Rev. 11:1; 21:15, 16
4 Jer. 31:27; Ezek. 36:10
5 Isa. 26:1; 60:19; Zech. 9:8; Rev. 21:23
6 Deut. 28:64; Isa. 48:20; 52:11
7 Rev. 18:4
8 Deut. 32:10; Ps. 17:8; 2 Thess. 1:6
9 Isa. 11:15; 19:16; Zech. 4:9
10 Lev. 26:12; Isa. 12:6; 54:1; John 1:14; 2 Cor. 6:16
11 Ex. 12:49; Isa. 2:2, 3; 49:22; 60:3; Ezek. 33:33
13 Ps. 68:5; Hab. 2:20; Zeph. 1:7
1 Ps. 109:6; Hag. 1:1; Rev. 12:10
2 Amos 4:11; Jude 1:9, 23
4 Isa. 61:10; Luke 15:22; Rev. 19:8

Zechariah also saw "four carpenters" (v. 20) who were called to whittle the four horns down to size, reminding God's people that He would take care of their future destiny.

2:1–5 In the third vision, the prophet sees the Jerusalem of the future as a town without walls, dwelling in peace and safety because the Lord Himself will be "a wall of fire" around her (v. 5). Here it seems the prophet sees beyond the immediate rebuilding of Jerusalem into the distant future of the days when the Messiah will rule Jerusalem during the Millennial Kingdom.

2:6–13 The prophet sounds four warnings to the Jewish exiles remaining in Babylon: 1) He calls them to come forth and return to Zion (Jerusalem); 2) He announces that God will judge the nations that have scattered Israel, the "apple of his eye"; 3) God will bless the nations by blessing Israel; and 4) All mankind should be silent and reverence God. Zechariah foresees the Millennial King-

dom when many nations will be joined together and become God's people (v. 11).

3:1–8. In the fourth vision, we are given a behind-the-scenes look into spiritual warfare in heavenly places. Joshua, a fallible human priest stands accused by Satan in the presence of Christ (the angel of the Lord). It is clear that Joshua is a symbol of what God is going to do in the future cleansing of Israel under the ministry of the Messiah, designated in verse 8 as "my servant the BRANCH [a sprout]." This is a proper name for the Messiah (cf. Isa. 11:1; Jer. 23:5; Zech. 6:12) used to indicate that He is a descendant of the Davidic line and grows up like a "shoot" or "sprout" out of the "root of Jesse [David's father]" (Rom. 15:12). Joshua's high priestly ministry prefigures the ministry of the Messiah who is both the Priest and King over God's people, although the Messiah will not have Joshua's filthy garments and will be qualified to make a proper sacrifice.

that stood before him, saying, Take away the filthy garments from him. And unto him he said, Behold, I have caused thine iniquity to pass from thee, and I will clothe thee with change of raiment.

5 And I said, Let them set a fair mitre upon his head. So they set a fair mitre upon his head, and clothed him with garments. And the angel of the LORD stood by.

6 And the angel of the LORD protested unto Joshua, saying,

7 Thus saith the LORD of hosts; If thou wilt walk in my ways, and if thou wilt keep my charge, then thou shalt also judge my house, and shalt also keep my courts, and I will give thee places to walk among these that stand by.

8 Hear now, O Joshua the high priest, thou, and thy fellows that sit before thee: for they *are* men wondered at: for, behold, I will bring forth my servant the BRANCH.

9 For behold the stone that I have laid before Joshua; upon one stone *shall be* seven eyes: behold, I will engrave the graving thereof, saith the LORD of hosts, and I will remove the iniquity of that land in one day.

10 In that day, saith the LORD of hosts, shall ye call every man his neighbour under the vine and under the fig tree.

CHAPTER 4
The Lampstand and the Olive Trees

1 And the angel that talked with me came again, and waked me, as a man that is wakened out of his sleep,

2 And said unto me, What seest thou? And I said, I have looked, and behold a candlestick all *of* gold, with a bowl upon the top of it, and his seven lamps thereon, and seven pipes to the seven lamps, which *are* upon the top thereof:

3 And two olive trees by it, one upon the right *side* of the bowl, and the other upon the left *side* thereof.

4 So I answered and spake to the angel

that talked with me, saying, What *are* these, my lord?

5 Then the angel that talked with me answered and said unto me, Knowest thou not what these be? And I said, No, my lord.

6 Then he answered and spake unto me, saying, This *is* the word of the LORD unto Zerubbabel, saying, Not by might, nor by power, but by my spirit, saith the LORD of hosts.

7 Who *art* thou, O great mountain? before Zerubbabel *thou shalt become* a plain: and he shall bring forth the headstone *thereof* with shoutings, *crying*, Grace, grace unto it.

8 Moreover the word of the LORD came unto me, saying,

9 The hands of Zerubbabel have laid the foundation of this house; his hands shall also finish it; and thou shalt know that the LORD of hosts hath sent me unto you.

10 For who hath despised the day of small things? for they shall rejoice, and shall see the plummet in the hand of Zerubbabel *with* those seven; they *are* the eyes of the LORD, which run to and fro through the whole earth.

11 Then answered I, and said unto him, What *are* these two olive trees upon the right *side* of the candlestick and upon the left *side* thereof?

12 And I answered again, and said unto him, What *be these* two olive branches which through the two golden pipes empty the golden *oil* out of themselves?

13 And he answered me and said, Knowest thou not what these *be*? And I said, No, my lord.

14 Then said he, These *are* the two anointed ones, that stand by the Lord of the whole earth.

CHAPTER 5
The Flying Scroll

1 Then I turned, and lifted up mine eyes, and looked, and behold a flying roll.

Cross references (center column)

5 Ex. 29:6; Zech. 6:11

7 Lev. 8:35; Deut. 17:9; 1Kgs. 2:3; Mal. 2:7

8 Ps. 71:7; Isa. 4:2; 8:18; 11:1; 20:3; 42:1; 49:3, 5; 52:13; 53:11

9 Ps. 118:22; Jer. 31:34; 50:20; Mic. 7:18, 19; Zech. 4:10; 13:1; Rev. 5:6

10 1Kgs. 4:25; Isa. 36:16; Mic. 4:4; Zech. 2:11

1 Dan. 8:18; Zech. 2:3

2 Ex. 25:31, 37; Rev. 1:12; 4:5

3 Zech. 4:11, 12; Rev. 11:4

6 Hos. 1:7

7 Ezra 3:11, 13; Ps. 118:22; Jer. 51:25; Matt. 21:21

9 Ezra 3:10; 6:15; Isa. 48:16; Zech. 2:8, 9, 11; 6:15

10 2Chr. 16:9; Prov. 15:3; Hag. 2:3; Zech. 3:9

11 Zech. 4:3

14 Josh. 3:11, 13; Zech. 3:7; 6:5; Luke 1:19; Rev. 11:4

1 Ezek. 2:9

3:9 The "stone" is often used in the Bible as a symbol of the Messiah (Gen. 49:24; Ps. 118:22; Isa. 28:16; Dan. 2:34–35, 44–45; Matt. 21:42; Acts 4:11) and pictures the eternality of His kingdom. The "seven eyes" represent omniscient intelligence and probably refer to the seven spirits or characteristics of God (cf. Isa. 11:2; 1 Cor. 12:4–11; Rev. 3:1; 4:5; 5:6).

4:1–14 The fifth vision describes the golden candlestick and seven lamps (cf. Rev. 1:12–20). It is in the shape of a menorah, which gave light in the temple of God. The two olive trees are pictured as the sources from which

the oil flows into the bowl through the pipes into the seven lamps. In verse 14, the two olive trees are identified as the "two anointed ones," referring to Zerubbabel the governor and Joshua the high priest. They will lead the people in rebuilding the temple, which will reflect the light and glory of God. The symbolism also points to the future ministry of the two witnesses who will be empowered by the Holy Spirit during the Tribulation period to call Israel back to God (see Rev. 11:3–12).

5:1–4 The sixth vision is that of a "flying roll" (or scroll). The size of the scroll, twenty cubits (30 feet) by ten

2 And he said unto me, What seest thou? And I answered, I see a flying roll; the length thereof *is* twenty cubits, and the breadth thereof ten cubits.

3 Then said he unto me, This *is* the curse that goeth forth over the face of the whole earth: for every one that stealeth shall be cut off *as* on this side according to it; and every one that sweareth shall be cut off *as* on that side according to it.

4 I will bring it forth, saith the LORD of hosts, and it shall enter into the house of the thief, and into the house of him that sweareth falsely by my name: and it shall remain in the midst of his house, and shall consume it with the timber thereof and the stones thereof.

5 Then the angel that talked with me went forth, and said unto me, Lift up now thine eyes, and see what *is* this that goeth forth.

6 And I said, What *is* it? And he said, This *is* an ephah that goeth forth. He said moreover, This *is* their resemblance through all the earth.

7 And, behold, there was lifted up a talent of lead: and this *is* a woman that sitteth in the midst of the ephah.

8 And he said, This *is* wickedness. And he cast it into the midst of the ephah; and he cast the weight of lead upon the mouth thereof.

9 Then lifted I up mine eyes, and looked, and, behold, there came out two women, and the wind *was* in their wings; for they had wings like the wings of a stork: and they lifted up the ephah between the earth and the heaven.

10 Then said I to the angel that talked with me, Whither do these bear the ephah?

3 Mal. 4:6
4 Lev. 14:45; 19:12; Zech. 8:17; Mal. 3:5
11 Gen. 10:10; Jer. 29:5, 28
2 Zech. 1:8; Rev. 6:4, 5
3 Rev. 6:2
4 Zech. 5:10
5 1Kgs. 22:19; Ps. 104:4; Dan. 7:10; Zech. 4:14; Luke 1:19; Heb. 1:7, 14
6 Jer. 1:14
7 Gen. 13:17; Zech. 1:10
8 Judg. 8:3; Eccl. 10:4

11 And he said unto me, To build it an house in the land of Shinar: and it shall be established, and set there upon her own base.

CHAPTER 6
The Four Chariots

1 And I turned, and lifted up mine eyes, and looked, and, behold, there came four chariots out from between two mountains; and the mountains *were* mountains of brass.

2 In the first chariot *were* red horses; and in the second chariot black horses;

3 And in the third chariot white horses; and in the fourth chariot grisled and bay horses.

4 Then I answered and said unto the angel that talked with me, What *are* these, my lord?

5 And the angel answered and said unto me, These *are* the four spirits of the heavens, which go forth from standing before the Lord of all the earth.

6 The black horses which *are* therein go forth into the north country; and the white go forth after them; and the grisled go forth toward the south country.

7 And the bay went forth, and sought to go that they might walk to and fro through the earth: and he said, Get you hence, walk to and fro through the earth. So they walked to and fro through the earth.

8 Then cried he upon me, and spake unto me, saying, Behold, these that go toward the north country have quieted my spirit in the north country.

9 And the word of the LORD came unto me, saying,

10 Take of *them of* the captivity, *even of*

cubits (15 feet), and the speed of its flight indicates this is ominous news that is about to burst on the scene quickly. As the scroll flies over the land, the indictment of its curse is pronounced against all those who hinder the work of God. This symbolism is similar to that of Christ opening the seven seals of the scroll of God's judgment in Revelation 6:1—8:1.

5:5–11 The seventh night vision is that of the woman in an "ephah" (basket). The woman symbolizes all the evil that must be removed from the land of Israel (like the bread at Passover) in order for the nation to be purified. In this case, the evil will be taken to Babylon, where it originated, and will be permanently deposited there. During the Tribulation period (Daniel's seventieth "week"), God will remove every form of wickedness in preparation for the Millennial Kingdom of the redeemed. Babylon (the

world system) will be destroyed and Jesus will reign on David's throne (see Rev. 14:8; 17—18).

6:1–8 The eighth and final night vision was of four chariots and red, black, white, and spotted horses, reminiscent of the four horses of the Apocalypse (Rev. 6:2–8). These are divine messengers who are instruments of God's judgment on the earth. They reveal the fact that God's enemies must be judged so that none can rise up against His authority.

6:9–11 The crowning of Joshua as the high priest symbolized the future crowning of the Messiah, the Branch, as both King and Priest over Israel. This prophecy foresees the building of the Millennial Temple with the help of the Gentiles (those who are "far off"). It looks beyond the rebuilding of the second temple or even the Tribulation temple and pictures the glories of the millennial age.

Heldai, of Tobijah, and of Jedaiah, which are come from Babylon, and come thou the same day, and go into the house of Josiah the son of Zephaniah;

11 Then take silver and gold, and make crowns, and set *them* upon the head of Joshua the son of Josedech, the high priest;

12 And speak unto him, saying, Thus speaketh the LORD of hosts, saying, Behold the man whose name *is* The BRANCH; and he shall grow up out of his place, and he shall build the temple of the LORD:

13 Even he shall build the temple of the LORD; and he shall bear the glory, and shall sit and rule upon his throne; and he shall be a priest upon his throne: and the counsel of peace shall be between them both.

14 And the crowns shall be to Helem, and to Tobijah, and to Jedaiah, and to Hen the son of Zephaniah, for a memorial in the temple of the LORD.

15 And they *that are* far off shall come and build in the temple of the LORD, and ye shall know that the LORD of hosts hath sent me unto you. And *this* shall come to pass, if ye will diligently obey the voice of the LORD your God.

CHAPTER 7
Insincere Fasting Reproved

1 And it came to pass in the fourth year of king Darius, *that* the word of the LORD came unto Zechariah in the fourth *day* of the ninth month, *even* in Chisleu;

2 When they had sent unto the house of God Sherezer and Regem-melech, and their men, to pray before the LORD,

3 *And* to speak unto the priests which *were* in the house of the LORD of hosts, and to the prophets, saying, Should I weep in the fifth month, separating myself, as I have done these so many years?

4 Then came the word of the LORD of hosts unto me, saying,

5 Speak unto all the people of the land, and to the priests, saying, When ye fasted and mourned in the fifth and seventh *month*, even those seventy years, did ye at all fast unto me, *even* to me?

6 And when ye did eat, and when ye did drink, did not ye eat *for yourselves*, and drink *for yourselves*?

7 *Should* ye not *hear* the words which the

LORD hath cried by the former prophets, when Jerusalem was inhabited and in prosperity, and the cities thereof round about her, when *men* inhabited the south and the plain?

8 And the word of the LORD came unto Zechariah, saying,

9 Thus speaketh the LORD of hosts, saying, Execute true judgment, and shew mercy and compassions every man to his brother:

10 And oppress not the widow, nor the fatherless, the stranger, nor the poor; and let none of you imagine evil against his brother in your heart.

11 But they refused to hearken, and pulled away the shoulder, and stopped their ears, that they should not hear.

12 Yea, they made their hearts *as* an adamant stone, lest they should hear the law, and the words which the LORD of hosts hath sent in his spirit by the former prophets: therefore came a great wrath from the LORD of hosts.

13 Therefore it is come to pass, *that* as he cried, and they would not hear; so they cried, and I would not hear, saith the LORD of hosts:

14 But I scattered them with a whirlwind among all the nations whom they knew not. Thus the land was desolate after them, that no man passed through nor returned: for they laid the pleasant land desolate.

CHAPTER 8
Jerusalem Will Be Blessed

1 Again the word of the Lord of hosts came *to me*, saying,

2 Thus saith the LORD of hosts; I was jealous for Zion with great jealousy, and I was jealous for her with great fury.

3 Thus saith the LORD; I am returned unto Zion, and will dwell in the midst of Jerusalem: and Jerusalem shall be called a city of truth; and the mountain of the LORD of hosts the holy mountain.

4 Thus saith the LORD of hosts; There shall yet old men and old women dwell in the streets of Jerusalem, and every man with his staff in his hand for very age.

5 And the streets of the city shall be full of boys and girls playing in the streets thereof.

6 Thus saith the LORD of hosts; If it be marvellous in the eyes of the remnant of

Center reference column

11 Ex. 28:36; 29:6; Lev. 8:9; Zech. 3:5

12 Zech. 3:8; 4:9; Matt. 16:18; Eph. 2:20-22; Heb. 3:3

13 Ps. 110:4; Isa. 22:24; Heb. 3:1

14 Ex. 12:14; Mark 14:9

15 Isa. 57:19; 60:10

3 Deut. 17:9-11; 33:10; Jer. 52:12; Zech. 8:19; Mal. 2:7

5 Jer. 41:1; Zech. 1:12; 8:19; Rom. 14:6

7 Jer. 17:26

9 Isa. 58:6, 7; Jer. 7:23; Mic. 6:8; Zech. 8:16; Matt. 23:23

10 Ex. 22:21, 22; Deut. 24:17; Jer. 5:28; Zech. 8:17

11 Neh. 9:29; Jer. 7:24; Hos. 4:16; Acts 7:57

12 Ezek. 11:19; 36:26; Dan. 9:11

13 Prov. 1:24-28; Jer. 11:11; 14:12

14 Lev. 26:22; Deut. 4:27; 28:33, 64; Ezek. 36:19

2 Nah. 1:2; Zech. 1:14

3 Jer. 31:23; Zech. 1:16; 2:10

4 1Sam. 2:31; Lam. 2:20; 5:11-14

6 Luke 1:37; 18:27; Rom. 4:21

8:1–8 God promised to restore Jerusalem to her intended greatness in the future. Jerusalem will be called "a city of truth" and "the holy mountain" (v. 3). The city is pictured as a place of peace and safety for both the elderly and for children (vv. 4–5). This wonderful restoration of the city will take place at Christ's return (Matt. 24:31).

this people in these days, should it also be marvellous in mine eyes? saith the LORD of hosts.

7 Thus saith the LORD of hosts; Behold, I will save my people from the east country, and from the west country;

8 And I will bring them, and they shall dwell in the midst of Jerusalem: and they shall be my people, and I will be their God, in truth and in righteousness.

9 Thus saith the LORD of hosts; Let your hands be strong, ye that hear in these days these words by the mouth of the prophets, which *were* in the day *that* the foundation of the house of the LORD of hosts was laid, that the temple might be built.

10 For before these days there was no hire for man, nor any hire for beast; neither *was there any* peace to him that went out or came in because of the affliction: for I set all men every one against his neighbour.

11 But now I *will* not *be* unto the residue of this people as in the former days, saith the LORD of hosts.

12 For the seed *shall be* prosperous; the vine shall give her fruit, and the ground shall give her increase, and the heavens shall give their dew; and I will cause the remnant of this people to possess all these *things*.

13 And it shall come to pass, *that* as ye were a curse among the heathen, O house of Judah, and house of Israel; so will I save you, and ye shall be a blessing: fear not, *but* let your hands be strong.

14 For thus saith the LORD of hosts; As I thought to punish you, when your fathers provoked me to wrath, saith the LORD of hosts, and I repented not:

15 So again have I thought in these days to do well unto Jerusalem and to the house of Judah: fear ye not.

16 These *are* the things that ye shall do; Speak ye every man the truth to his neighbour; execute the judgment of truth and peace in your gates:

17 And let none of you imagine evil in your hearts against his neighbour; and love no false oath: for all these *are things* that I hate, saith the LORD.

18 And the word of the LORD of hosts came unto me, saying,

19 Thus saith the LORD of hosts; The fast of the fourth *month,* and the fast of the fifth, and the fast of the seventh, and the fast of the tenth, shall be to the house of Judah joy and gladness, and cheerful feasts; therefore love the truth and peace.

20 Thus saith the LORD of hosts; *It shall* yet *come to pass,* that there shall come people, and the inhabitants of many cities:

21 And the inhabitants of one *city* shall go to another, saying, Let us go speedily to pray before the LORD, and to seek the LORD of hosts: I will go also.

22 Yea, many people and strong nations shall come to seek the LORD of hosts in Jerusalem, and to pray before the LORD.

23 Thus saith the LORD of hosts; In those days *it shall come to pass,* that ten men shall take hold out of all languages of the nations, even shall take hold of the skirt of him that is a Jew, saying, We will go with you: for we have heard *that* God *is* with you.

CHAPTER 9
Judgment on Israel's Enemies

1 The burden of the word of the LORD in the land of Hadrach, and Damascus *shall be* the rest thereof: when the eyes of man, as of all the tribes of Israel, *shall be* toward the LORD.

2 And Hamath also shall border thereby; Tyrus, and Zidon, though it be very wise.

3 And Tyrus did build herself a strong hold, and heaped up silver as the dust, and fine gold as the mire of the streets.

4 Behold, the Lord will cast her out, and he will smite her power in the sea; and she shall be devoured with fire.

5 Ashkelon shall see *it,* and fear; Gaza also *shall see it,* and be very sorrowful, and Ekron; for her expectation shall be ashamed; and the king shall perish from Gaza, and Ashkelon shall not be inhabited.

6 And a bastard shall dwell in Ashdod, and I will cut off the pride of the Philistines.

7 And I will take away his blood out of his mouth, and his abominations from between his teeth: but he that remaineth, even he, *shall be* for our God, and he shall be as a governor in Judah, and Ekron as a Jebusite.

8 And I will encamp about mine house

Cross references

7 Ps. 50:1; 113:3; Isa. 11:11, 12; 43:5, 6; Ezek. 37:21

8 Jer. 4:2; 30:22; 31:1, 33; Zech. 13:9

9 Ezra 5:1, 2; Hag. 2:4, 18; Zech. 8:18

10 2Chr. 15:5; Hag. 1:6, 9, 10; 2:16

12 Ps. 67:6; Hos. 2:21, 22; Joel 2:22; Hag. 1:10; 2:19

13 Gen. 12:2; Isa. 19:24, 25; Jer. 42:18; Zech. 8:9

14 2Chr. 36:16; Jer. 31:28; Zech. 1:6

16 Zech. 7:9; 8:19; Eph. 4:25

17 Prov. 3:29; Zech. 5:3, 4; 7:10

19 2Kgs. 25:25; Esth. 8:17; Jer. 41:1, 2; 52:4, 6, 7, 12, 13

21 Isa. 2:3; Mic. 4:1, 2

22 Isa. 60:3; 66:23

23 Isa. 3:6; 4:1; 1Cor. 14:25

1 Jer. 23:33; Amos 1:3

2 Ezek. 28:3, 21; Amos 1:9; Obad. 1:20

3 Job 27:16; Ezek. 28:4, 5

4 Isa. 23:1; Ezek. 26:17

5 Jer. 47:1, 5; Zeph. 2:4

6 Amos 1:8

8:20–23 Zechariah also predicts a time when the Gentiles will seek the Lord during the Millennial Kingdom. Many people and nations will come to Jerusalem seeking the Lord because they have heard that God is there.

9:1–8 God's prophet pronounces judgment on Israel's enemies. Damascus, Hamath, Tyre, Zidon, Gaza, Ekron, Ashkelon, and Ashdod will all be destroyed. These cities fell to Alexander the Great in 333 B.C., but Jerusalem was spared during his invasion of the Holy Land.

because of the army, because of him that passeth by, and because of him that returneth: and no oppressor shall pass through them any more: for now have I seen with mine eyes.

A King in Zion

9 Rejoice greatly, O daughter of Zion; shout, O daughter of Jerusalem: behold, thy King cometh unto thee: he *is* just, and having salvation; lowly, and riding upon an ass, and upon a colt the foal of an ass.

10 And I will cut off the chariot from Ephraim, and the horse from Jerusalem, and the battle bow shall be cut off: and he shall speak peace unto the heathen: and his dominion *shall be* from sea *even* to sea, and from the river *even* to the ends of the earth.

11 As for thee also, by the blood of thy covenant I have sent forth thy prisoners out of the pit wherein *is* no water.

12 Turn you to the strong hold, ye prisoners of hope: even today do I declare *that* I will render double unto thee;

13 When I have bent Judah for me, filled the bow with Ephraim, and raised up thy sons, O Zion, against thy sons, O Greece, and made thee as the sword of a mighty man.

14 And the LORD shall be seen over them, and his arrow shall go forth as the lightning: and the Lord GOD shall blow the trumpet, and shall go with whirlwinds of the south.

15 The LORD of hosts shall defend them; and they shall devour, and subdue with slingstones; and they shall drink, *and* make a noise as through wine; and they shall be filled like bowls, *and* as the corners of the altar.

16 And the LORD their God shall save them in that day as the flock of his people: for they *shall be as* the stones of a crown, lifted up as an ensign upon his land.

17 For how great *is* his goodness, and how great *is* his beauty! corn shall make the

young men cheerful, and new wine the maids.

CHAPTER 10
The Lord Will Deliver

1 Ask ye of the LORD rain in the time of the latter rain; *so* the LORD shall make bright clouds, and give them showers of rain, to every one grass in the field.

2 For the idols have spoken vanity, and the diviners have seen a lie, and have told false dreams; they comfort in vain: therefore they went their way as a flock, they were troubled, because *there was* no shepherd.

3 Mine anger was kindled against the shepherds, and I punished the goats: for the LORD of hosts hath visited his flock the house of Judah, and hath made them as his goodly horse in the battle.

4 Out of him came forth the corner, out of him the nail, out of him the battle bow, out of him every oppressor together.

5 And they shall be as mighty *men*, which tread down *their enemies* in the mire of the streets in the battle: and they shall fight, because the LORD *is* with them, and the riders on horses shall be confounded.

6 And I will strengthen the house of Judah, and I will save the house of Joseph, and I will bring them again *to place them*; for I have mercy upon them: and they shall be as though I had not cast them off: for I *am* the LORD their God, and will hear them.

7 And *they of* Ephraim shall be like a mighty *man*, and their heart shall rejoice as through wine: yea, their children shall see *it*, and be glad; their heart shall rejoice in the LORD.

8 I will hiss for them, and gather them; for I have redeemed them: and they shall increase as they have increased.

9 And I will sow them among the people: and they shall remember me in far countries; and they shall live with their children, and turn again.

10 I will bring them again also out of the

Cross references

8 Isa. 60:18; Ezek. 28:24
9 Zech. 2:10; Matt. 21:5; Luke 19:38; John 1:49; 12:15
10 Ps. 72:8; Hos. 1:7; 2:18; Mic. 5:10
11 Ex. 24:8; Isa. 42:7; 51:14; 61:1
12 Isa. 49:9; 61:7
14 Ps. 18:14; 77:17; 144:6
15 Lev. 4:18, 25; Deut. 12:27
16 Isa. 11:12; 62:3; Mal. 3:17
17 Ps. 31:19; Joel 3:18; Amos 9:14
1 Job 29:23; Joel 2:23
2 Judg. 17:5; Jer. 10:8; Ezek. 34:5; Hab. 2:18
3 Ezek. 34:17; Luke 1:68
4 Num. 24:17; 1Sam. 14:38; Isa. 19:13; 22:23
6 Jer. 3:18; Ezek. 37:21; Hos. 1:7; Zech. 13:9
7 Ps. 104:15; Zech. 9:15
8 Isa. 5:26; 49:19; Ezek. 36:37
9 Deut. 30:1; Hos. 2:23
10 Isa. 11:11, 16; 49:20

9:9–10 Zechariah predicts the coming of the Messiah riding into Jerusalem on a donkey just as David had done centuries before (see 2 Sam. 18:9; 1 Kgs. 1:33). Over five hundred years ahead of time, the prophet sees the King riding in His royal procession into Jerusalem (v. 9). This prophecy was fulfilled when Jesus entered Jerusalem on Palm Sunday in His triumphal entry to present Himself officially as Israel's Messiah (cf. Matt. 21:4–5; John 12:15). This prophecy depicts Jesus as both King and Savior. When it was fulfilled, the people shouted, "Hosanna (meaning "save now") to the son of David!" (Matt. 21:9; cf. Ps. 118:25–26). The response of the crowd made it clear that they recognized Him as the Messiah, even though they rejected Him.

10:6–8 God promised to regather both Judah (the Southern Kingdom) and Joseph also called Ephraim (the Northern Kingdom) into one nation in the future. He will "hiss" ("whistle") at them, and they will come running together at God's appointed time.

land of Egypt, and gather them out of Assyria; and I will bring them into the land of Gilead and Lebanon; and *place* shall not be found for them.

11 And he shall pass through the sea with affliction, and shall smite the waves in the sea, and all the deeps of the river shall dry up: and the pride of Assyria shall be brought down, and the sceptre of Egypt shall depart away.

12 And I will strengthen them in the LORD; and they shall walk up and down in his name, saith the LORD.

CHAPTER 11
The Foolish Shepherds

1 Open thy doors, O Lebanon, that the fire may devour thy cedars.

2 Howl, fir tree; for the cedar is fallen; because the mighty are spoiled: howl, O ye oaks of Bashan; for the forest of the vintage is come down.

3 *There is* a voice of the howling of the shepherds; for their glory is spoiled: a voice of the roaring of young lions; for the pride of Jordan is spoiled.

4 Thus saith the LORD my God; Feed the flock of the slaughter;

5 Whose possessors slay them, and hold themselves not guilty: and they that sell them say, Blessed *be* the LORD; for I am rich: and their own shepherds pity them not.

6 For I will no more pity the inhabitants of the land, saith the LORD: but, lo, I will deliver the men every one into his neighbour's hand, and into the hand of his king: and they shall smite the land, and out of their hand I will not deliver *them*.

7 And I will feed the flock of slaughter, *even* you, O poor of the flock. And I took unto me two staves; the one I called Beauty, and the other I called Bands; and I fed the flock.

8 Three shepherds also I cut off in one

month; and my soul lothed them, and their soul also abhorred me.

9 Then said I, I will not feed you: that that dieth, let it die; and that that is to be cut off, let it be cut off; and let the rest eat every one the flesh of another.

10 And I took my staff, *even* Beauty, and cut it asunder, that I might break my covenant which I had made with all the people.

11 And it was broken in that day: and so the poor of the flock that waited upon me knew that it *was* the word of the LORD.

12 And I said unto them, If ye think good, give *me* my price; and if not, forbear. So they weighed for my price thirty *pieces* of silver.

13 And the LORD said unto me, Cast it unto the potter: a goodly price that I was prised at of them. And I took the thirty *pieces* of silver, and cast them to the potter in the house of the LORD.

14 Then I cut asunder mine other staff, *even* Bands, that I might break the brotherhood between Judah and Israel.

15 And the LORD said unto me, Take unto thee yet the instruments of a foolish shepherd.

16 For, lo, I will raise up a shepherd in the land, *which* shall not visit those that be cut off, neither shall seek the young one, nor heal that that is broken, nor feed that that standeth still: but he shall eat the flesh of the fat, and tear their claws in pieces.

17 Woe to the idol shepherd that leaveth the flock! the sword *shall be* upon his arm, and upon his right eye: his arm shall be clean dried up, and his right eye shall be utterly darkened.

CHAPTER 12
Jerusalem's Enemies to Be Destroyed

1 The burden of the word of the LORD for Israel, saith the LORD, which stretcheth

Cross References

11 Isa. 11:15, 16; 14:25; Ezek. 30:13
12 Mic. 4:5
1 Zech. 10:10
2 Isa. 32:19
4 Zech. 11:7
5 Deut. 29:19; Jer. 2:3; 50:7; Hos. 12:8
7 Zeph. 3:12; 11:4; Matt. 11:5
8 Hos. 5:7
9 Jer. 15:2; 43:11
11 Zeph. 3:12; Zech. 11:7
12 Ex. 21:32; Matt. 26:15
13 Matt. 27:9, 10
15 Ezek. 34:2-4
17 Jer. 23:1; Ezek. 34:2; John 10:12, 13
1 Num. 16:22; Eccl. 12:7; Isa. 57:16; 42:5; 44:24; 45:12, 18; 48:13; Heb. 12:9

11:9–10 Israel's rejection of the Messiah will have devastating consequences for the nation and her shepherds (religious leaders).

11:12–13 thirty pieces of silver. Zechariah acts out the part of a shepherd of Israel, but he was rejected. When he asked for his pay, he was given only thirty pieces of silver, the price of a common slave (see Ex. 21:32) and an insult to his worth. Zechariah's actions, including throwing the money into the temple, prefigured the betrayal of Christ by Judas Iscariot for thirty pieces of silver (see Matt. 26:14–16). Zechariah's prediction was fulfilled when Judas returned the betrayal money to the priests and they used it to purchase the "potter's field"

(Matt. 27:7).

11:15–17 Since Israel will refuse her good shepherd, Jesus Christ, He will be replaced by a "foolish (lit. 'worthless') shepherd"—the Antichrist. This idle shepherd will neither heal nor feed God's people. In fact, he will be the exact opposite of Jesus, the Good Shepherd (see John 10). Instead of feeding the flock, he will fleece and flay the flock mercilessly.

12:1–9 Zechariah foresees a day when Jerusalem will become "a cup of trembling" and "a burdensome stone" to those who dare invade her (vv. 2–3). The expression "in that day" occurs sixteen times in Zechariah pointing

forth the heavens, and layeth the foundation of the earth, and formeth the spirit of man within him.

2 Behold, I will make Jerusalem a cup of trembling unto all the people round about, when they shall be in the siege both against Judah *and* against Jerusalem.

3 And in that day will I make Jerusalem a burdensome stone for all people: all that burden themselves with it shall be cut in pieces, though all the people of the earth be gathered together against it.

4 In that day, saith the LORD, I will smite every horse with astonishment, and his rider with madness: and I will open mine eyes upon the house of Judah, and will smite every horse of the people with blindness.

5 And the governors of Judah shall say in their heart, The inhabitants of Jerusalem *shall be* my strength in the LORD of hosts their God.

6 In that day will I make the governors of Judah like an hearth of fire among the wood, and like a torch of fire in a sheaf; and they shall devour all the people round about, on the right hand and on the left: and Jerusalem shall be inhabited again in her own place, *even* in Jerusalem.

7 The LORD also shall save the tents of Judah first, that the glory of the house of David and the glory of the inhabitants of Jerusalem do not magnify *themselves* against Judah.

8 In that day shall the LORD defend the inhabitants of Jerusalem; and he that is feeble among them at that day shall be as David;

and the house of David *shall be* as God, as the angel of the LORD before them.

9 And it shall come to pass in that day, *that* I will seek to destroy all the nations that come against Jerusalem.

10 And I will pour upon the house of David, and upon the inhabitants of Jerusalem, the spirit of grace and of supplications: and they shall look upon me whom they have pierced, and they shall mourn for him, as one mourneth for *his* only *son*, and shall be in bitterness for him, as one that is in bitterness for *his* firstborn.

11 In that day shall there be a great mourning in Jerusalem, as the mourning of Hadadrimmon in the valley of Megiddon.

12 And the land shall mourn, every family apart; the family of the house of David apart, and their wives apart; the family of the house of Nathan apart, and their wives apart;

13 The family of the house of Levi apart, and their wives apart; the family of Shimei apart, and their wives apart;

14 All the families that remain, every family apart, and their wives apart.

CHAPTER 13

1 In that day there shall be a fountain opened to the house of David and to the inhabitants of Jerusalem for sin and for uncleanness.

2 And it shall come to pass in that day, saith the LORD of hosts, *that* I will cut off the names of the idols out of the land, and they shall no more be remembered: and also I will cause the prophets and the unclean spirit to pass out of the land.

Cross references

2 Isa. 51:17, 22, 23
3 Ezek. 12:4, 6, 8, 9, 11; 13:1; 14:4, 6, 8, 9, 13; Matt. 21:44
4 Ps. 76:6; Ezek. 38:4
5 Joel 3:16
6 Obad. 1:18
8 Joel 3:10
9 Hag. 2:22; Zech. 12:3
10 Jer. 6:26; 31:9; 50:4; Ezek. 39:29; Joel 2:28; Amos 8:10; John 19:34, 37; Rev. 1:7
11 2Kgs. 23:29; 2Chr. 35:24; Acts 2:37
12 2Sam. 5:14; Matt. 24:30; Luke 3:31; Rev. 1:7
1 Zech. 12:3; Heb. 9:14; 1Pet. 1:19; Rev. 1:5
2 Ex. 23:13; 30:13; Josh. 23:7; Ps. 16:4; Hos. 2:17; Mic. 5:12, 13; 2Pet. 2:1

---

to the "day of the LORD," which appears seventeen times. These events look ahead to the Tribulation period when the Antichrist will invade the land of Israel and bring all the nations of the earth (Gentiles) against it. The prophet predicts this great invasion, which will culminate in the Battle of Armageddon (see Rev. 16:16—19:21), will end in defeat for Israel's enemies because of the supernatural intervention of God. In no way does this passage relate to the Roman invasion of Jerusalem in A.D. 70. This prophecy predicts victory, not defeat, for Jerusalem. It looks ahead to the triumphal return of Christ at Armageddon (Rev. 19:11—21).

12:10–14 the spirit of grace and of supplications. In addition to Israel's physical deliverance, she will also experience a spiritual regeneration. The "spirit of grace" refers to the ministry of the Holy Spirit to bring about the conversion of the nation by drawing them to Jesus Christ, their true Messiah. As a result of the Spirit's min-

istry, the Jews will "look upon" (Hebr., *nabat*, "look attentively" or "come to realize") the One whom they "have pierced" (Hebr., *daqar*, "to pierce through") and will mourn for Him with godly repentance, sorrow, and contrition. There can be no doubt the phrase, "whom they have pierced," is talking about the crucifixion of Jesus Christ (John 19:34–37 [cf. Luke 2:35; Rev. 1:7]). Zechariah foretells Israel's rejection of the Messiah at His first coming and their reception of Him at His second coming. The New Testament attributes this change of heart to the preaching of the "two witnesses" (see Rev. 11:3–12).

13:1–7 there shall be a fountain opened. Zechariah predicts a national conversion of the Jewish people and their spiritual regeneration and renewal by the atonement of the Messiah. After Israel's conversion and divine rescue, the nation will be cleansed in preparation for the millennial reign of Christ (see Rom. 11:26–27).

3 And it shall come to pass, *that* when any shall yet prophesy, then his father and his mother that begat him shall say unto him, Thou shalt not live; for thou speakest lies in the name of the LORD: and his father and his mother that begat him shall thrust him through when he prophesieth.

4 And it shall come to pass in that day, *that* the prophets shall be ashamed every one of his vision, when he hath prophesied; neither shall they wear a rough garment to deceive:

5 But he shall say, I *am* no prophet, I *am* an husbandman; for man taught me to keep cattle from my youth.

6 And *one* shall say unto him, What *are* these wounds in thine hands? Then he shall answer, *Those* with which I was wounded *in* the house of my friends.

The Lord's Shepherd Will Be Struck Down

7 Awake, O sword, against my shepherd, and against the man *that is* my fellow, saith the LORD of hosts: smite the shepherd, and the sheep shall be scattered: and I will turn mine hand upon the little ones.

8 And it shall come to pass, *that* in all the land, saith the LORD, two parts therein shall be cut off *and* die; but the third shall be left therein.

9 And I will bring the third part through the fire, and will refine them as silver is refined, and will try them as gold is tried: they shall call on my name, and I will hear them: I will say, It *is* my people: and they shall say, The LORD *is* my God.

CHAPTER 14
The Lord Will Rule

1 Behold, the day of the Lord cometh, and thy spoil shall be divided in the midst of thee.

2 For I will gather all nations against Jerusalem to battle; and the city shall be taken, and the houses rifled, and the women ravished; and half of the city shall go forth into captivity, and the residue of the people shall not be cut off from the city.

3 Then shall the LORD go forth, and fight against those nations, as when he fought in the day of battle.

4 And his feet shall stand in that day upon the mount of Olives, which *is* before Jerusalem on the east, and the mount of Olives shall cleave in the midst thereof toward the east and toward the west, *and there shall be* a very great valley; and half of the mountain shall remove toward the north, and half of it toward the south.

5 And ye shall flee *to* the valley of the mountains; for the valley of the mountains shall reach unto Azal: yea, ye shall flee, like as ye fled from before the earthquake in the days of Uzziah king of Judah: and the LORD my God shall come, *and* all the saints with thee.

6 And it shall come to pass in that day, *that* the light shall not be clear, *nor* dark:

7 But it shall be one day which shall be known to the LORD, not day, nor night: but it shall come to pass, *that* at evening time it shall be light.

8 And it shall be in that day, *that* living waters shall go out from Jerusalem; half of them toward the former sea, and half of them toward the hinder sea: in summer and in winter shall it be.

9 And the LORD shall be king over all the earth: in that day shall there be one LORD, and his name one.

10 All the land shall be turned as a plain from Geba to Rimmon south of Jerusalem: and it shall be lifted up, and inhabited in

Cross-references
3 Deut. 13:6, 8; 18:20
4 2Kgs. 1:8; Isa. 20:2; Mic. 3:6, 7; Matt. 3:4
5 Amos 7:14
7 Isa. 40:11; Matt. 26:31; Mark 14:27; Luke 12:32; John 10:30
8 Rom. 11:5
9 Ps. 50:15; 91:15; 144:15; Isa. 48:10; Jer. 30:22; Ezek. 11:20; Hos. 2:23
1 Isa. 13:9; Joel 2:31; Acts 2:20
2 Isa. 13:16; Joel 3:2
4 Ezek. 11:23; Joel 3:12, 14
5 Joel 3:11; Amos 1:1; Matt. 16:27; 24:30, 31; 25:31; Jude 1:14
7 Isa. 30:26; 60:19, 20; Matt. 24:36; Rev. 21:23; 22:5
8 Ezek. 47:1; Joel 2:20; 3:18; Rev. 22:1
9 Dan. 2:44; Eph. 4:5, 6; Rev. 11:15
10 Neh. 3:1; 12:39; Jer. 31:38; Zech. 12:6

13:7–9 Prior to Israel's conversion, Zechariah predicts that two-thirds ("two parts") of the Jewish people in the land will perish during the Tribulation period. Only one third of the Jewish population will survive until Christ comes to establish His kingdom on earth.

14:1–8 day of the LORD. This is one of many Old Testament terms for the Tribulation period. In other passages it is referred to as the "time of Jacob's trouble" (cf. Isa. 24:1–20; Jer. 30:7; Dan. 12:1; Zeph. 1:14–18; Matt. 24:22). In its concluding vision, Zechariah predicts the ultimate triumph of the Messiah at the Battle of Armageddon when the Gentile nations, led by the Antichrist, will be defeated at the second coming of Jesus Christ. Zechariah sees the Lord standing on the Mount of Olives when He returns (v. 4). From the very place where Jesus ascended back into heaven (Acts 1:11–12), He will again return, and this time the mountain shall split in half, creating a rift valley from the Mediterranean to the Dead Sea (v. 8).

14:9–21 the LORD shall be king over all the earth. The closing verses of Zechariah's prophecy foresee the Millennial Kingdom when Christ will reign supreme (v. 9). The topography of the land will be changed, and Jerusalem will be elevated to even greater prominence (v. 10). Prosperity and security will prevail, and Jerusalem will finally know true peace for the first time. The survivors of the Tribulation period will go up to Jerusalem annually to worship the King and keep the Feast of Tabernacles (v. 16) because it commemorates the culmination of God's promises to Israel and His plan of the ages.

her place, from Benjamin's gate unto the place of the first gate, unto the corner gate, and *from* the tower of Hananeel unto the king's winepresses.

11 And *men* shall dwell in it, and there shall be no more utter destruction; but Jerusalem shall be safely inhabited.

12 And this shall be the plague wherewith the LORD will smite all the people that have fought against Jerusalem; Their flesh shall consume away while they stand upon their feet, and their eyes shall consume away in their holes, and their tongue shall consume away in their mouth.

13 And it shall come to pass in that day, *that* a great tumult from the LORD shall be among them; and they shall lay hold every one on the hand of his neighbour, and his hand shall rise up against the hand of his neighbour.

14 And Judah also shall fight at Jerusalem; and the wealth of all the heathen round about shall be gathered together, gold, and silver, and apparel, in great abundance.

15 And so shall be the plague of the horse, of the mule, of the camel, and of the ass, and of all the beasts that shall be in these tents, as this plague.

16 And it shall come to pass, *that* every one that is left of all the nations which came against Jerusalem shall even go up from year to year to worship the King, the LORD of hosts, and to keep the feast of tabernacles.

17 And it shall be, *that* whoso will not come up of *all* the families of the earth unto Jerusalem to worship the King, the LORD of hosts, even upon them shall be no rain.

18 And if the family of Egypt go not up, and come not, that *have* no rain; there shall be the plague, wherewith the LORD will smite the heathen that come not up to keep the feast of tabernacles.

19 This shall be the punishment of Egypt, and the punishment of all nations that come not up to keep the feast of tabernacles.

20 In that day shall there be upon the bells of the horses, HOLINESS UNTO THE LORD; and the pots in the LORD's house shall be like the bowls before the altar.

21 Yea, every pot in Jerusalem and in Judah shall be holiness unto the LORD of hosts: and all they that sacrifice shall come and take of them, and seethe therein: and in that day there shall be no more the Canaanite in the house of the LORD of hosts.

11 Jer. 23:6; 31:40

13 Judg. 7:22; 1Sam. 14:15, 20; 2Chr. 20:23; Zech. 38:21

14 Zech. 39:10, 17

15 Zech. 14:12

16 Lev. 23:34, 43; Neh. 8:14; Isa. 60:6, 7, 9; 66:23; Hos. 12:9; John 7:2

17 Isa. 60:12

18 Deut. 11:10

20 Isa. 23:18

21 Isa. 35:8; Joel 3:17; Eph. 2:19-22; Rev. 21:27; 22:15

The Campaign of Armageddon

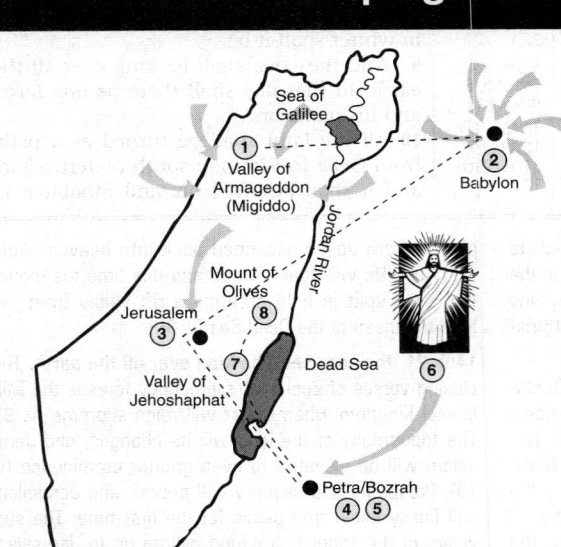

The Eight Stages
1. Gathering of the Armies of the Antichrist
2. Destruction of Babylon
3. The Fall of Jerusalem
4. The Armies of the Antichrist at Bosrah
5. Israel's Regeneration
6. Second Coming of Christ
7. End of Fighting at the Valley of Jehoshaphat
8. Victory Ascent upon the Mount of Olives

By Arnold Fruchtenbaum. Used by permission

Malachi

Malachi, whose name means "messenger," is the last of the Old Testament prophets. By the time Malachi wrote his prophecy, a century had passed since the first Jews returned to Jerusalem after the Babylonian captivity.

The prophecy is clearly later than those of Haggai and Zechariah. The reconstruction of the temple had been complete long enough for abuses to creep into the sacrificial system. A short-lived spiritual revival under Ezra and Nehemiah was followed by a lapse into empty religious formalism. Corruption, mixed marriages, and neglect of tithing, combined with a caustic, questioning attitude of denial were predominant trends during this time.

Malachi chides negligent and indifferent Jews, but offers God's promises of present blessings for the faithful and the hope of a new "messenger" to come, the rising of the Sun of Righteousness, with healing for Israel (4:2). Referring to Israel's special, blessed future, Malachi writes of them being "refined as silver," called blessed by all nations and a "delightsome land," and accepted by the Lord as His "jewels" (3:12, 17). As for the wicked of the world, the "day of the LORD" would consume them.

The closing prophecy of the Old Testament speaks of the return of Elijah the prophet, partially fulfilled by John the Baptist, but the literal return of Elijah is yet to come. Very significant is the prophecy of the "messenger" (3:1), fulfilled by John the Baptist, the forerunner of the Messiah. Following Malachi's stinging, condemning prophecy, Israel went through a period of four hundred years in which God was silent towards His people. Malachi's prediction of John the Baptist (3:1, cf. Mark 1:2) marks the last time God spoke to His people through a prophet until John the Baptist came to "prepare the way" of Christ.

Thirty-one of the 55 verses are predictive, or 56 percent of the content. Of 19 prophetic subjects, about half are either conditional or fulfilled in Old Testament times.

Author
Malachi

Date
450–400 B.C.

Key Truth
Religious Formalism without Dedication

Historic Time
After the Return from the Babylonian Captivity

Key Verse
3:6
For I am the LORD, I change not.

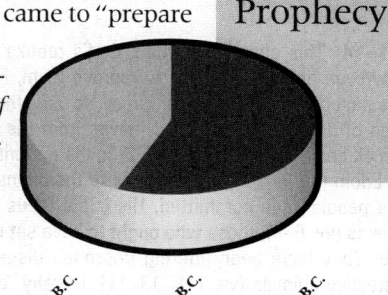

56%
Prophecy

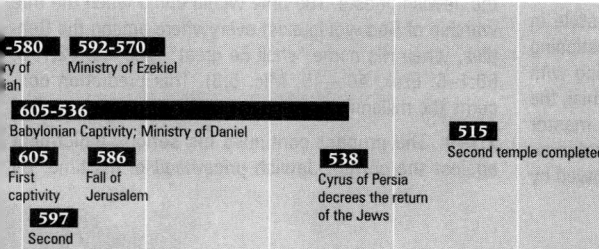

600 B.C.	575 B.C.	550 B.C.	525 B.C.	500 B.C.	475 B.C.	450 B.C.	425 B.C.	400 B.C.

-580
...ry of ...iah

592-570
Ministry of Ezekiel

605-536
Babylonian Captivity; Ministry of Daniel

457
Ezra goes to Jerusalem

515
Second temple completed

445
Nehemiah goes to Jerusalem

605
First captivity

586
Fall of Jerusalem

538
Cyrus of Persia decrees the return of the Jews

597
Second captivity

433
Ministry of Malachi

CHAPTER 1
The Lord Loves Jacob

1 The burden of the word of the LORD to Israel by Malachi.

2 I have loved you, saith the LORD. Yet ye say, Wherein hast thou loved us? *Was* not Esau Jacob's brother? saith the LORD: yet I loved Jacob,

3 And I hated Esau, and laid his mountains and his heritage waste for the dragons of the wilderness.

4 Whereas Edom saith, We are impoverished, but we will return and build the desolate places; thus saith the LORD of hosts, They shall build, but I will throw down; and they shall call them, The border of wickedness, and, The people against whom the LORD hath indignation for ever.

5 And your eyes shall see, and ye shall say, The LORD will be magnified from the border of Israel.

6 A son honoureth *his* father, and a servant his master: if then I *be* a father, where *is* mine honour? and if I *be* a master, where *is* my fear? saith the LORD of hosts unto you, O priests, that despise my name. And ye say, Wherein have we despised thy name?

7 Ye offer polluted bread upon mine altar; and ye say, Wherein have we polluted thee? In that ye say, The table of the LORD *is* contemptible.

8 And if ye offer the blind for sacrifice, *is it* not evil? and if ye offer the lame and sick, *is it* not evil? offer it now unto thy governor; will he be pleased with thee, or accept thy person? saith the LORD of hosts.

9 And now, I pray you, beseech God that he will be gracious unto us: this hath been by your means: will he regard your persons? saith the LORD of hosts.

10 Who *is there* even among you that would shut the doors *for nought*? neither do ye kindle *fire* on mine altar for nought. I have no pleasure in you, saith the LORD of hosts, neither will I accept an offering at your hand.

11 For from the rising of the sun even unto the going down of the same my name *shall be* great among the Gentiles; and in every place incense *shall be* offered unto my name, and a pure offering: for my name *shall be* great among the heathen, saith the LORD of hosts.

12 But ye have profaned it, in that ye say, The table of the LORD *is* polluted; and the fruit thereof, *even* his meat, *is* contemptible.

13 Ye said also, Behold, what a weariness *is it*! and ye have snuffed at it, saith the LORD of hosts; and ye brought *that which was* torn, and the lame, and the sick; thus ye brought an offering: should I accept this of your hand? saith the LORD.

14 But cursed *be* the deceiver, which hath in his flock a male, and voweth, and sacrificeth unto the Lord a corrupt thing: for I *am* a great King, saith the LORD of hosts, and my name *is* dreadful among the heathen.

CHAPTER 2
Israel Is Unfaithful

1 And now, O ye priests, this commandment *is* for you.

2 If ye will not hear, and if ye will not lay

Cross references
2 Deut. 7:8; 10:15; Rom. 9:13
3 Jer. 49:18; Ezek. 35:3, 4, 7, 9, 14, 15; Obad. 1:10
5 Ps. 35:27
6 Ex. 20:12; Mal. 2:14, 17; 3:7, 8, 13; Luke 6:46
7 Deut. 15:21; Ezek. 41:22; Mal. 1:12
8 Lev. 22:22; Deut. 15:21; Job 42:8; Mal. 8:14
9 Hos. 13:9
10 Isa. 1:11; Jer. 6:20; Amos 5:21; 1Cor. 9:13
11 Ps. 113:3; Isa. 59:19; 60:3, 5; 66:19, 20; John 4:21, 23; 1Tim. 2:8; Rev. 8:3
12 Mal. 1:7
13 Lev. 22:20
14 Ps. 47:2; 1Tim. 6:15; Mal. 1:8
2 Lev. 26:14; Deut. 28:15

1:1–14 This chapter contains God's rebuke of Israel. However, before He begins to reprove them, He affirms His past and present love for Israel. He uses the comparison of Jacob and Esau, and moves from His choice of Jacob and rejection of Esau (v. 2) to the current situation of Edom (vv. 3–4). God then turns to the offenses which His people have committed. His initial focus is on the priests (vv. 6–9), those who ought to have set the example. They have been offering improper, diseased, and defective animals (vv. 7–8, 13–14), thereby "despising" God and His table (vv. 6–7, 12).

1:2 Malachi launches into an argumentative style in which he presents a truth, then records the questioning negative response of the people, usually beginning with "Wherein?" Skeptical, almost tantamount to a denial, the word means "How and in what way?" The master debater takes each objection and answers it before moving to another. This pattern of stating a truth, followed by an objection from the Jewish people, and then a reply with an explanation and an application of his original point, is used seven times in the book (1:2, 6–7; 2:14, 17; 3:8, 13–14).

1:5 This far-reaching prophecy looks beyond Edom's attempts to regain the mountainous area and forecasts the climactic triumph which concludes the future Tribulation (see Isa. 34; 63:1–6; Jer. 49:7–22; Ezek. 25:12–14).

1:11 great among the Gentiles. A nugget of prophetic truth appears in the midst of Malachi's charges against the Jewish priests. The time would come when the true worship of God would exist everywhere among the Gentiles, when His name "shall be great" (see Isa. 42:1, 6; 60:1–5; Ezek. 40—48; Mic. 5:8). This prediction concerns the millennial age.

2:1–9 The prophet continues his serious indictment against the corrupt Jewish priesthood of his time. By

it to heart, to give glory unto my name, saith the Lord of hosts, I will even send a curse upon you, and I will curse your blessings: yea, I have cursed them already, because ye do not lay *it* to heart.

3 Behold, I will corrupt your seed, and spread dung upon your faces, *even* the dung of your solemn feasts; and *one* shall take you away with it.

4 And ye shall know that I have sent this commandment unto you, that my covenant might be with Levi, saith the Lord of hosts.

5 My covenant was with him of life and peace; and I gave them to him *for* the fear wherewith he feared me, and was afraid before my name.

6 The law of truth was in his mouth, and iniquity was not found in his lips: he walked with me in peace and equity, and did turn many away from iniquity.

7 For the priest's lips should keep knowledge, and they should seek the law at his mouth: for he *is* the messenger of the Lord of hosts.

8 But ye are departed out of the way; ye have caused many to stumble at the law; ye have corrupted the covenant of Levi, saith the Lord of hosts.

9 Therefore have I also made you contemptible and base before all the people, according as ye have not kept my ways, but have been partial in the law.

10 Have we not all one father? hath not one God created us? why do we deal treacherously every man against his brother, by profaning the covenant of our fathers?

11 Judah hath dealt treacherously, and an abomination is committed in Israel and in Jerusalem; for Judah hath profaned the holiness of the Lord which he loved, and hath married the daughter of a strange god.

12 The Lord will cut off the man that doeth

this, the master and the scholar, out of the tabernacles of Jacob, and him that offereth an offering unto the Lord of hosts.

13 And this have ye done again, covering the altar of the Lord with tears, with weeping, and with crying out, insomuch that he regardeth not the offering any more, or receiveth *it* with good will at your hand.

14 Yet ye say, Wherefore? Because the Lord hath been witness between thee and the wife of thy youth, against whom thou hast dealt treacherously: yet *is* she thy companion, and the wife of thy covenant.

15 And did not he make one? Yet had he the residue of the spirit. And wherefore one? That he might seek a godly seed. Therefore take heed to your spirit, and let none deal treacherously against the wife of his youth.

16 For the Lord, the God of Israel, saith that he hateth putting away: for *one* covereth violence with his garment, saith the Lord of hosts: therefore take heed to your spirit, that ye deal not treacherously.

The Judgment Day Is Near

17 Ye have wearied the Lord with your words. Yet ye say, Wherein have we wearied *him*? When ye say, Every one that doeth evil *is* good in the sight of the Lord, and he delighteth in them; or, Where *is* the God of judgment?

CHAPTER 3

1 Behold, I will send my messenger, and he shall prepare the way before me: and the Lord, whom ye seek, shall suddenly come to his temple, even the messenger of the covenant, whom ye delight in: behold, he shall come, saith the Lord of hosts.

2 But who may abide the day of his coming? and who shall stand when he

3 1Kgs. 14:10

5 Num. 25:12; Deut. 33:8, 9; Ezek. 34:25; 37:26

6 Deut. 33:10; Jer. 23:22; James 5:20

7 Lev. 10:11; Deut. 17:9, 10; 24:8; Hag. 2:11, 12; Gal. 4:14

8 1Sam. 2:17; Neh. 13:29; Jer. 18:15

9 1Sam. 2:30

10 Job 31:15; 1Cor. 8:6; Eph. 4:6

11 Ezra 9:1; 10:2; Neh. 13:23

12 Neh. 13:28, 29

14 Prov. 2:17; 5:18

15 Ezra 9:2; Matt. 19:4, 5; 1Cor. 7:14

16 Deut. 24:1; Matt. 5:32; 19:8

17 Isa. 43:24; Amos 2:13; Mal. 3:13-15

1 Isa. 40:3; 63:9; Matt. 11:10; Mark 1:2; Luke 1:76; 7:27

2 Isa. 4:4; Mal. 4:1; Matt. 3:10-12; Rev. 6:17

---

their attitude and their actions, both corrupt and contemptible in the eyes of God, they were violating the covenant of Levi, the divinely selected and designated priestly tribe (vv. 4, 5, 8). Similar corruption among the pastors and teachers of this present age deserves the same condemnation.

2:10 one father. This verse has been misused to overemphasize the concept of the universal fatherhood of God. This is a Jewish passage and refers to the special relationship all Israelites had with God.

3:1 Behold, I will send my messenger. The writer is the last messenger in the Old Testament; the next messenger

would be John the Baptist, the first prophet of the New Testament, over four centuries later. This was fulfilled as recorded in Matthew 11:10; Mark 1:2–3; Luke 1:76; 7:26–27. Following the description of John's ministry, the announcement of the one for whom John ministered is given: "the Lord . . . shall suddenly come to his temple." "Suddenly" means instantly or with surprise. Jesus came to the temple at age twelve (Luke 2:46), again at the beginning of His public ministry (John 2:13–21), and at the close of His public ministry (Luke 19:45–48); but none of these were the final fulfillment of this prophecy. The Lord Jesus will fulfill this prophecy once and for all at His second coming.

appeareth? for he *is* like a refiner's fire, and like fullers' soap:

3 And he shall sit *as* a refiner and purifier of silver: and he shall purify the sons of Levi, and purge them as gold and silver, that they may offer unto the LORD an offering in righteousness.

4 Then shall the offering of Judah and Jerusalem be pleasant unto the LORD, as in the days of old, and as in former years.

5 And I will come near to you to judgment; and I will be a swift witness against the sorcerers, and against the adulterers, and against false swearers, and against those that oppress the hireling in *his* wages, the widow, and the fatherless, and that turn aside the stranger *from his right*, and fear not me, saith the LORD of hosts.

Robbing God

6 For I *am* the LORD, I change not; therefore ye sons of Jacob are not consumed.

7 Even from the days of your fathers ye are gone away from mine ordinances, and have not kept *them*. Return unto me, and I will return unto you, saith the LORD of hosts. But ye said, Wherein shall we return?

8 Will a man rob God? Yet ye have robbed me. But ye say, Wherein have we robbed thee? In tithes and offerings.

9 Ye *are* cursed with a curse: for ye have robbed me, *even* this whole nation.

10 Bring ye all the tithes into the storehouse, that there may be meat in mine house, and prove me now herewith, saith the LORD of hosts, if I will not open you the windows of heaven, and pour you out a blessing, that *there shall* not *be room* enough *to receive it*.

11 And I will rebuke the devourer for your sakes, and he shall not destroy the fruits of your ground; neither shall your vine cast her fruit before the time in the field, saith the LORD of hosts.

12 And all nations shall call you blessed: for ye shall be a delightsome land, saith the LORD of hosts.

13 Your words have been stout against me, saith the LORD. Yet ye say, What have we spoken *so much* against thee?

14 Ye have said, It *is* vain to serve God: and what profit *is it* that we have kept his ordinance, and that we have walked mournfully before the LORD of hosts?

15 And now we call the proud happy; yea, they that work wickedness are set up; yea, *they that* tempt God are even delivered.

16 Then they that feared the LORD spake often one to another: and the LORD hearkened, and heard *it*, and a book of remembrance was written before him for them that feared the LORD, and that thought upon his name.

17 And they shall be mine, saith the LORD of hosts, in that day when I make up my jewels; and I will spare them, as a man spareth his own son that serveth him.

18 Then shall ye return, and discern between the righteous and the wicked, between him that serveth God and him that serveth him not.

CHAPTER 4
The Lord's Day Is Coming

1 For, behold, the day cometh, that shall burn as an oven; and all the proud, yea, and all that do wickedly, shall be stubble: and the day that cometh shall burn them up, saith the LORD of hosts, that it shall leave them neither root nor branch.

2 But unto you that fear my name shall the Sun of righteousness arise with healing in his wings; and ye shall go forth, and grow up as calves of the stall.

Cross references
3 Isa. 1:25; Zech. 13:9; 1Pet. 2:5
4 Mal. 1:11
5 Zech. 5:4; James 5:4, 12
6 Num. 23:19; Lam. 3:22; Rom. 11:29; James 1:17
7 Zech. 1:3; Mal. 1:6; Acts 7:51
8 Neh. 13:10, 12
10 Gen. 7:11; 2Kgs. 7:2; 1Chr. 26:20; 2Chr. 31:10, 11
11 Amos 4:9
12 Dan. 8:9
13 Mal. 2:17
14 Job 21:14, 15; 22:17; Ps. 73:13; Zeph. 1:12
15 Ps. 73:12; 95:9; Mal. 2:17
16 Ps. 56:8; Rev. 20:12
17 Ex. 19:5; Deut. 7:6; Ps. 103:13; 135:4; Isa. 62:3; Titus 2:14; 1Pet. 2:9
18 Ps. 58:11
1 Joel 2:31; Mal. 3:2, 18; 2Pet. 3:7
2 Mal. 3:16; Luke 1:78; Rev. 2:28

3:3 he shall purify the sons of Levi. As in Zechariah, the priestly tribe that will serve in the millennial age will first repent and embrace their Messiah (Zech. 12:11–14; 13:1). The Levites have a great destiny and ministry in the Millennial Temple during the kingdom age (see Ezek. 43:19–27; 44:10–31; 48:10–20, 22).

3:4 offering . . . pleasant. These are the memorial sacrifices to be offered in the Millennial Temple (Ezek. 43:19–27).

3:12 all nations shall call you blessed. This will fulfill God's promise to Abraham (Gen. 12:2–3) and the prophecy of Isaiah (Isa. 61:9).

3:6–17 when I make up my jewels. As the Millennium begins, King Jesus will gather the faithful repenting Jews unto Himself, record their dedication in the scroll of remembrance and regard them as His "jewels," His treasured possessions forever.

4:1 the day cometh. This is a reference to the "day of the LORD," a much used expression in Scripture, usually describing the Tribulation and the dawn of the Kingdom Age.

4:2 Sun of righteousness. This is a symbol of Jesus, who comes with "healing in His wings" to establish His righteous kingdom, bringing health and prosperity and blessing to this world (cf. "Jesus, the bright and morning star" in Rev. 22:16).

The Messianic Hope

By Warren Baker

From the fall of Adam and Eve in the garden of Eden to the events of our own day, all of human history sheds light on the ultimate need of the human race—the need to be made righteous before a holy God. Beginning with the promise in Genesis 3:15 of the seed that would crush the serpent's head and ending with the promise in Malachi 4:2 that the Sun of righteousness would come, God has revealed to man, and particularly to the nation of Israel, that He would meet the ultimate need of man through His Servant, the Messiah. The covenants with Abraham, Moses, and David, the sacrifices in the Tabernacle and temple, the promises of an eternal priest, an everlasting throne, and an ultimate prophet all point to the Messiah.

The book of Malachi was the last book of the Old Testament to be written. Following the writing of this book in about 433 B.C., Israel went over four hundred years without a writing prophet, without a revelation from God until the announcement of the birth of John the Baptist (Luke 1:13). The canon of the Old Testament was completed, and the people of God were left to search the Scriptures and await the coming of Messiah. The book of Malachi serves as a bridge across those silent years, instructing the people on how to live while they waited, preparing the people for the announcement of the birth of Christ.

> *The messianic hope of Israel answers the question, "What is life all about?"*

Malachi promises that the Sun of Righteousness, the Messiah, brings hope to the people of God—a hope of righteousness, a hope of healing, and a hope of victory over their enemies (Mal. 4:2–3). The hope of righteousness is twofold—a hope of salvation through His righteousness being applied to us by faith and a hope of being made righteous when we go to be with Him. The term, "Sun of righteousness," brings to mind the picture John paints of the New Jerusalem in Revelation 21:23, "And the city had no need of the sun, neither of the moon, to shine in it: for the glory of God did lighten it, and the Lamb is the light thereof."

The hope of "healing in his wings" (Mal. 4:2), though it symbolizes the eternal spiritual healing that comes from faith in Christ, is indicative, in context, of God protecting the Jews from the heat of His wrath during the "day" that is coming (Mal. 4:1), the seven-year Tribulation period. The hope of victory, when the people of Israel will "tread down the wicked" (Mal. 4:3), is a prophetic promise regarding the Lord's deliverance of Israel and the Millennial Kingdom that follows.

The other side of Malachi's message was the warning, "Lest I come and smite the earth with a curse" (Mal. 4:6). Unless the Messiah comes to fulfill the Old Testament promises, there is no hope for the future.

As the Jews waited for the advent of Messiah they were instructed to "remember . . . the law of Moses my servant . . . with the statutes and judgments" (Mal. 4:4). The messianic hope of Israel, like the hope of the Church for the Rapture, answers the question, "What is life all about?" It is about putting our faith in God, obeying His word, receiving the completion of our faith, and enjoying Him forever.

3 And ye shall tread down the wicked; for they shall be ashes under the soles of your feet in the day that I shall do *this*, saith the LORD of hosts.

4 Remember ye the law of Moses my servant, which I commanded unto him in Horeb for all Israel, *with* the statutes and judgments.

3 Zech. 10:5
5 Matt. 11:14; 17:11; Mark 9:11; Luke 1:17
6 Zech. 5:3; 14:12

5 Behold, I will send you Elijah the prophet before the coming of the great and dreadful day of the LORD:

6 And he shall turn the heart of the fathers to the children, and the heart of the children to their fathers, lest I come and smite the earth with a curse.

4:5 Behold, I will send you Elijah the prophet. Preceding Jesus' first coming was John the Baptist, who came in "the spirit and power" of Elijah (Luke 1:13–17). Had Jesus been accepted by His people, John would have fulfilled the prophecy completely (Matt. 11:13–14); but since He was rejected, this prophecy awaits a future Elijah (Matt. 17:11–12). John did not claim to be Elijah; in fact, he specifically denied it (John 1:21), but he did fill the role of the forerunner for Messiah's first coming. Elijah, who appeared on the Mount of Transfiguration (Matt. 17:4), may be one of the two witnesses forecast in Revelation 11:1–3 who will prophesy during three and one-half years of the Tribulation in Jerusalem. Orthodox Jews at the Passover set an empty chair for Elijah in every home observance as a result of this verse. Jesus affirmed, "Elias truly shall first come and restore all things" (Matt. 17:11).

4:6 curse. The last sentence in the Old Testament mentions the word "curse" (see also Gen. 3:14, 17), which is the result of sin. The last sentence in the New Testament (Rev. 22:21) uses the word "grace," the wonderful result of God's love and forgiveness through Christ.

The Apocryphal Literature

By Mal Couch

The word *apocrypha* is of Greek origin, meaning "concealed," or "hidden." Narrowly defined, the apocryphal literature is a term often used to categorize fourteen documents written from 200 B.C. to A.D. 100. The adjective "apocryphal" has also been used to describe dozens of books labeled as Gospels, Acts, Epistles, and Apocalypses written in competition with the books of the New Testament. These books are officially called New Testament Apocrypha. This article, however, seeks only to deal with the books of the intertestamental period known as Old Testament Apocrypha.

Though often embellished with exaggeration and perhaps pure fiction, the Apocrypha still gives a panoramic view of Jewish belief regarding the first advent of the Messiah and the Jewish hopes concerning Messiah's coming kingdom reign. The core of messianic belief in the Apocrypha is based upon Old Testament prophetic books.

Since the Greek Septuagint Bible (the Old Testament of the early Church) contained apocryphal writings from its inception, while the Hebrew Old Testament did not, it is only natural that some people would eventually lay claim to the Apocrypha's canonicity. Though objections were raised, the Greek Orthodox Church and the Roman Catholic Church generally accepted certain apocryphal books as inspired Scripture. These books, with a couple of exceptions, make up the fourteen books commonly called the Apocrypha: 1 and 2 Esdras, Tobit, Judith, Additions to the Book of Esther, The Wisdom of Solomon, Ecclesiasticus, Baruch, The Song of the Three Young Men, The History of Susanna, Bel and the Dragon, the Prayer of Manasseh, and 1 and 2 Maccabees.

> *It is in the area of prophecy that the Apocrypha is of utmost importance.*

Interestingly, it is in the area of prophecy that this body of literature is of utmost importance. In the Apocalypse of Baruch (ca. A.D. 70), the writer shows the Tribulation period divided into twelve parts in which the Messiah destroys the last empire, which is the Roman Empire. Though the style of Baruch is steeped in heavy symbolism, the influence of the earlier Hebrew prophets cannot be ignored.

While not included in the fourteen traditional books of the Apocrypha, other intertestamental documents have uncanny allusions to Old Testament prophecy. For instance, in the books of Enoch (first century B.C.), this pre-Flood Old Testament character sees future messianic visions of judgment. In the second volume, he envisions the world from the Flood down to the messianic kingdom. The Sibylline Oracles (ca. fifth century B.C. to the Christian era) is a broad collection of Jewish and Christian materials that seem to bind together beliefs about the Messiah's return. The book gives a complete picture of the Messiah, who brings in prosperity for the righteous. It closes with the sons of God dwelling around the rebuilt temple in Jerusalem.

The Protestant Reformation encouraged many people to carefully consider which books were indeed authoritative and essential for the establishment of doctrine, leading to a gradual dismissal of the Apocrypha as inspired Scripture. Perhaps the most outspoken Protestant declaration concerning the Apocrypha is found in the Westminster Confession of Faith (1643), which states: "The books commonly called Apocrypha, not being of divine inspiration, are no part of the canon of Scripture, and therefore are of no authority in the Church of God." From 1629 onward, the Apocrypha were omitted from many English Bible editions, and, since 1827, few editions of the Bible have included these disputed books.

THE
NEW TESTAMENT
OF
OUR LORD AND SAVIOR JESUS CHRIST

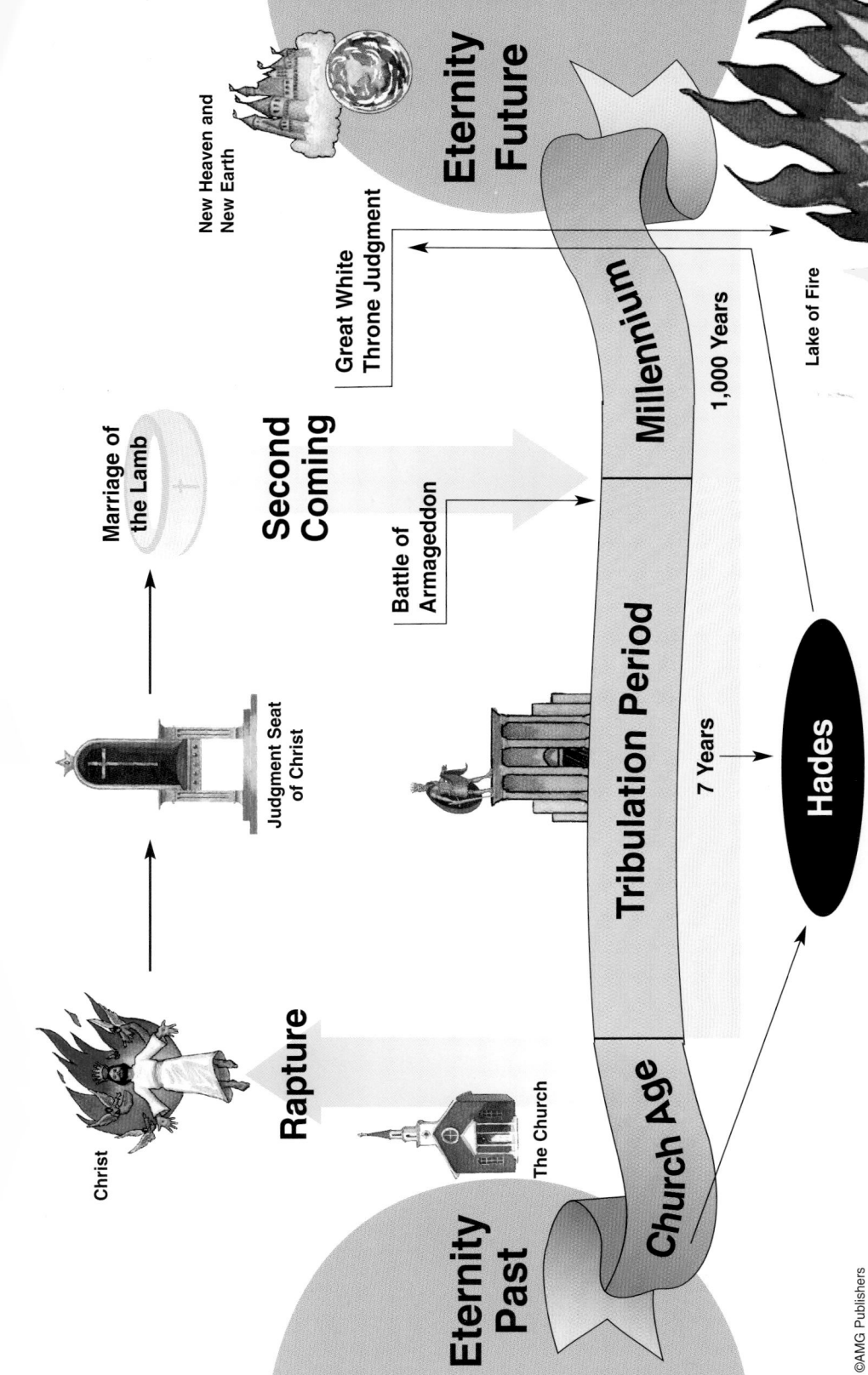

Eternity Past

Eternity Future

Second Coming

Rapture

Christ

Marriage of the Lamb

Judgment Seat of Christ

New Heaven and New Earth

Great White Throne Judgment

Battle of Armageddon

Millennium

1,000 Years

Lake of Fire

Tribulation Period

7 Years

Hades

Church Age

The Church

©AMG Publishers

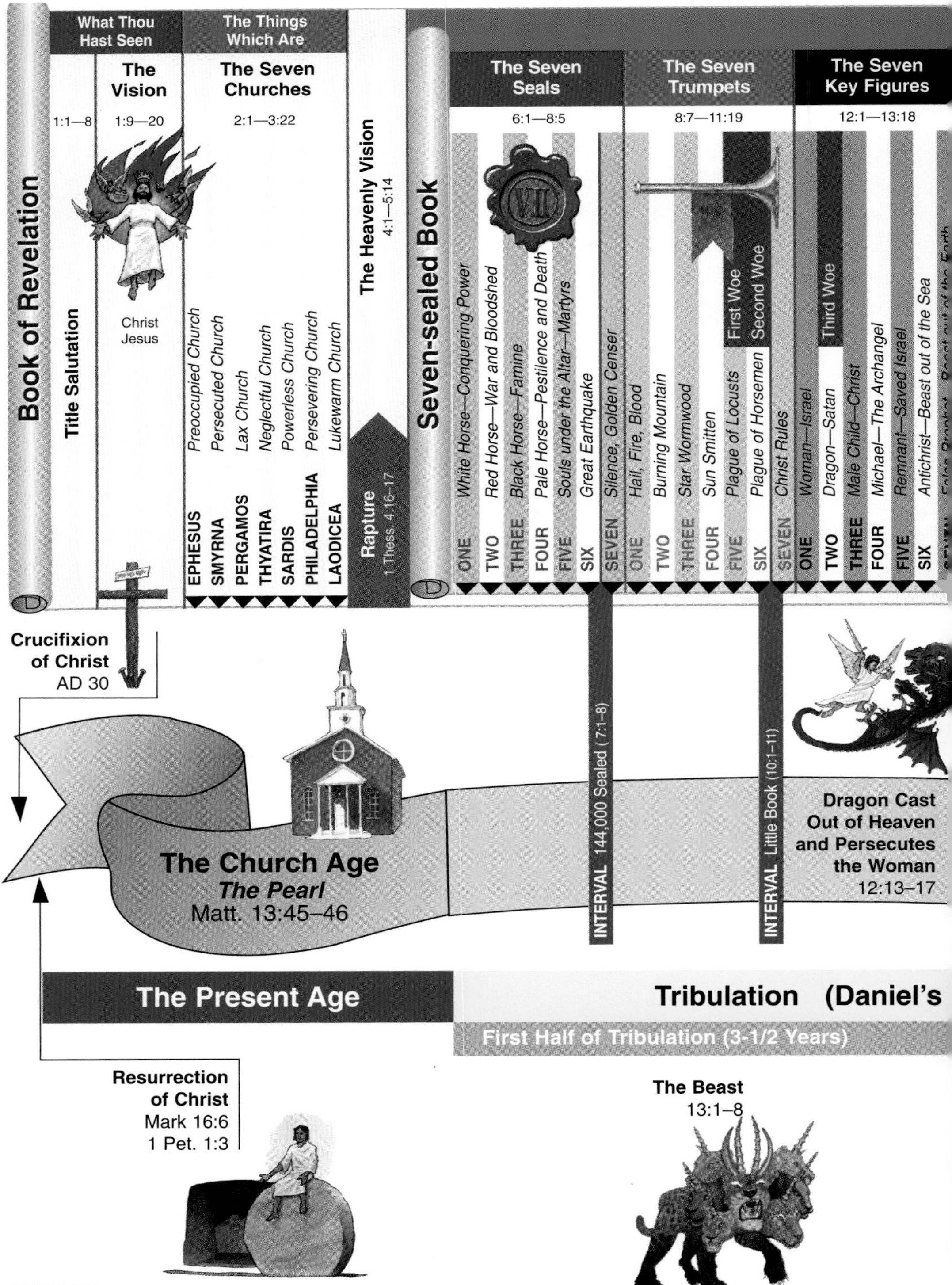

Book of Revelation

What Thou Hast Seen

The Vision
1:1—8   1:9—20

Title Salutation

Christ Jesus

The Things Which Are

The Seven Churches
2:1—3:22

EPHESUS	Preoccupied Church
SMYRNA	Persecuted Church
PERGAMOS	Lax Church
THYATIRA	Neglectful Church
SARDIS	Powerless Church
PHILADELPHIA	Persevering Church
LAODICEA	Lukewarm Church

The Heavenly Vision
4:1—5:14

Rapture
1 Thess. 4:16—17

Seven-sealed Book

The Seven Seals
6:1—8:5

- ONE — White Horse—Conquering Power
- TWO — Red Horse—War and Bloodshed
- THREE — Black Horse—Famine
- FOUR — Pale Horse—Pestilence and Death
- FIVE — Souls under the Altar—Martyrs
- SIX — Great Earthquake
- SEVEN — Silence, Golden Censer

The Seven Trumpets
8:7—11:19

- ONE — Hail, Fire, Blood
- TWO — Burning Mountain
- THREE — Star Wormwood
- FOUR — Sun Smitten
- FIVE — Plague of Locusts — First Woe
- SIX — Plague of Horsemen — Second Woe
- SEVEN — Christ Rules

The Seven Key Figures
12:1—13:18

- ONE — Woman—Israel
- TWO — Dragon—Satan — Third Woe
- THREE — Male Child—Christ
- FOUR — Michael—The Archangel
- FIVE — Remnant—Saved Israel
- SIX — Antichrist—Beast out of the Sea

Crucifixion of Christ
AD 30

The Church Age
The Pearl
Matt. 13:45—46

INTERVAL 144,000 Sealed (7:1—8)

INTERVAL Little Book (10:1—11)

Dragon Cast Out of Heaven and Persecutes the Woman
12:13—17

The Present Age

Tribulation (Daniel's

First Half of Tribulation (3-1/2 Years)

Resurrection of Christ
Mark 16:6
1 Pet. 1:3

The Beast
13:1—8

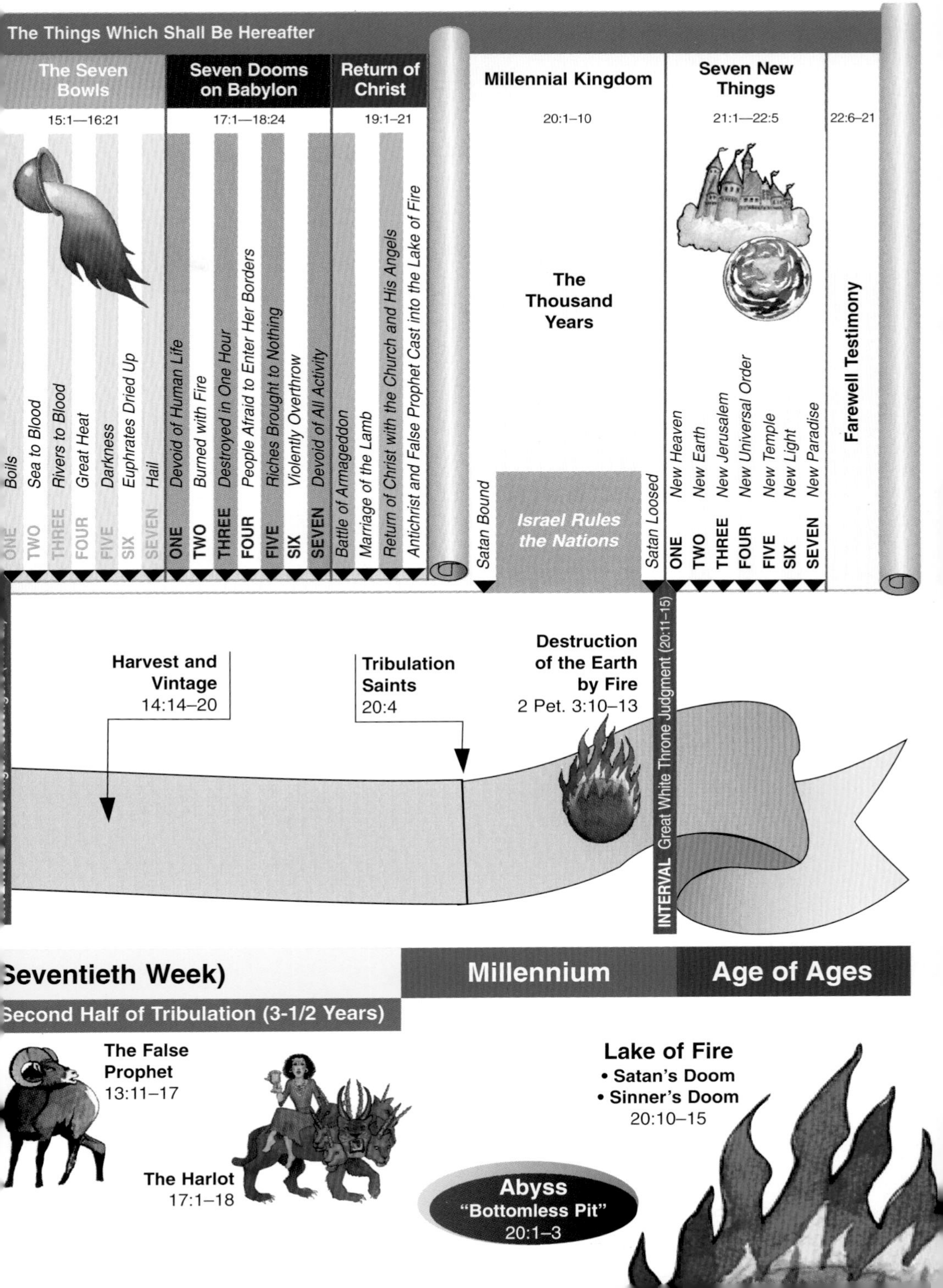

The Things Which Shall Be Hereafter

The Seven Bowls	Seven Dooms on Babylon	Return of Christ	Millennial Kingdom	Seven New Things	
15:1—16:21	17:1—18:24	19:1–21	20:1–10	21:1—22:5	22:6–21

The Seven Bowls

- ONE — Boils
- TWO — Sea to Blood
- THREE — Rivers to Blood
- FOUR — Great Heat
- FIVE — Darkness
- SIX — Euphrates Dried Up
- SEVEN — Hail

Seven Dooms on Babylon

- ONE — Devoid of Human Life
- TWO — Burned with Fire
- THREE — Destroyed in One Hour
- FOUR — People Afraid to Enter Her Borders
- FIVE — Riches Brought to Nothing
- SIX — Violently Overthrow
- SEVEN — Devoid of All Activity

Return of Christ

- Battle of Armageddon
- Marriage of the Lamb
- Return of Christ with the Church and His Angels
- Antichrist and False Prophet Cast into the Lake of Fire

Millennial Kingdom

The Thousand Years

Satan Bound — *Israel Rules the Nations* — Satan Loosed

Seven New Things

- ONE — New Heaven
- TWO — New Earth
- THREE — New Jerusalem
- FOUR — New Universal Order
- FIVE — New Temple
- SIX — New Light
- SEVEN — New Paradise

Farewell Testimony

Harvest and Vintage
14:14–20

Tribulation Saints
20:4

Destruction of the Earth by Fire
2 Pet. 3:10–13

INTERVAL — Great White Throne Judgment (20:11–15)

(Seventieth Week)

Second Half of Tribulation (3-1/2 Years)

Millennium

Age of Ages

The False Prophet
13:11–17

The Harlot
17:1–18

Lake of Fire
- Satan's Doom
- Sinner's Doom
20:10–15

Abyss
"Bottomless Pit"
20:1–3

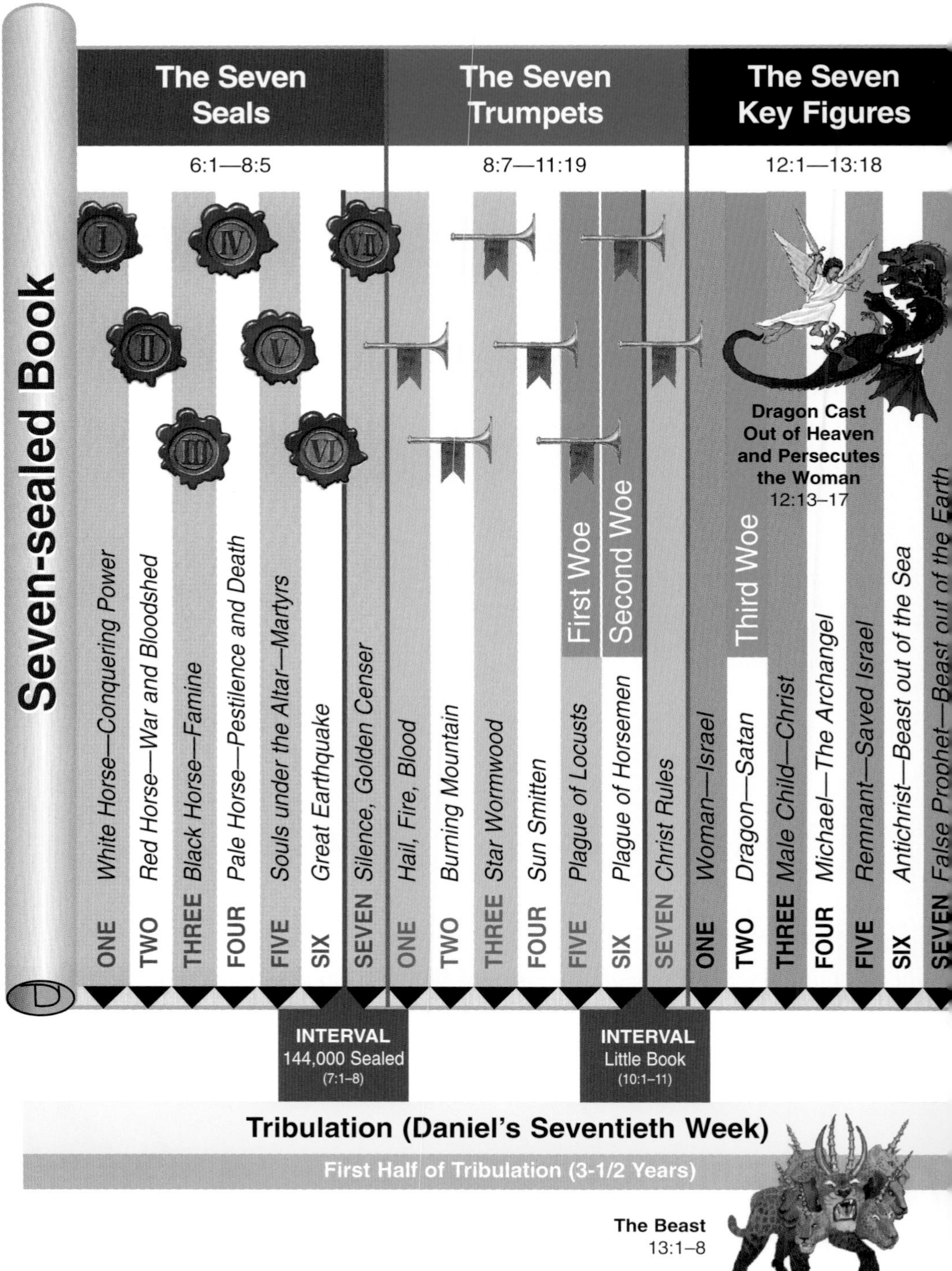

Seven-sealed Book

The Seven Seals
6:1—8:5

The Seven Trumpets
8:7—11:19

The Seven Key Figures
12:1—13:18

Dragon Cast Out of Heaven and Persecutes the Woman
12:13–17

The Seven Seals

- ONE — White Horse—Conquering Power
- TWO — Red Horse—War and Bloodshed
- THREE — Black Horse—Famine
- FOUR — Pale Horse—Pestilence and Death
- FIVE — Souls under the Altar—Martyrs
- SIX — Great Earthquake
- SEVEN — Silence, Golden Censer

The Seven Trumpets

- ONE — Hail, Fire, Blood
- TWO — Burning Mountain
- THREE — Star Wormwood
- FOUR — Sun Smitten
- FIVE — Plague of Locusts — First Woe
- SIX — Plague of Horsemen — Second Woe
- SEVEN — Christ Rules

The Seven Key Figures

- ONE — Woman—Israel
- TWO — Dragon—Satan — Third Woe
- THREE — Male Child—Christ
- FOUR — Michael—The Archangel
- FIVE — Remnant—Saved Israel
- SIX — Antichrist—Beast out of the Sea
- SEVEN — False Prophet—Beast out of the Earth

INTERVAL 144,000 Sealed (7:1–8)

INTERVAL Little Book (10:1–11)

Tribulation (Daniel's Seventieth Week)

First Half of Tribulation (3-1/2 Years)

The Beast 13:1–8

Matthew

Matthew, whose name means "gift of Jehovah," left his occupation of gathering taxes (Matt. 9:9–13) in order to follow Jesus. Luke 5:27–32 describes Matthew giving a banquet for Jesus before he became one of the Twelve Apostles (Matt. 10:3).

The four Gospels (Matthew, Mark, Luke, and John) form a unique kind of written document. Each Gospel presents a different view or perspective of the life of Jesus Christ. Aside from historical documents by Josephus and Tacitus, no other writings exist that document the life and times of Jesus.

Author
Matthew the Apostle

Date
A.D. 50

Key Truth
Jesus, the "Son of David," is the Messiah

Historic Time
Birth of Christ to His Resurrection

Key Verse
5:17
I am not come to destroy, but to fulfil.

The gospel of Matthew begins by identifying Jesus as "the son of Abraham," "the son of David," and heir to the royal throne of Israel, the rightful King. Written especially for the Jews to prove that Jesus is the predicted Messiah or Christ (anointed one), Matthew reveals Him against the background of Old Testament promise, prophecy, type, and symbol, emphasizing His royalty. The book lays a foundation for the transition from the old Dispensation of Law (the Jewish Age), to the new dispensation, known as the Church Age (13; 16:18).

Within the book are five discourses (5—7; 10; 13; 23; 24—25), twenty-five parables, and seventeen specific miracles. Out of sixty-six references and allusions to the Old Testament, forty-one are specific quotations by Christ. Like all the four Gospels, major emphasis is placed on Christ's last week of earthly ministry, from His triumphal entry into Jerusalem on Palm Sunday (chap. 21), through the Crucifixion, to the Resurrection (chap. 28).

Prophecies appear throughout the first Gospel, some of which are fulfilled while others are yet to transpire. Of special significance are predictions to the Twelve Apostles (chap. 10); the prophetic parables (chaps. 13; 20; 22); the announcement concerning the Church (16:18); the Olivet Discourse (24—25).

There are 81 specific predictions in 278 out of 1,067 verses, or 26 percent of the book. Forty-seven Old Testament passages are quoted in Matthew.

26%
Prophecy

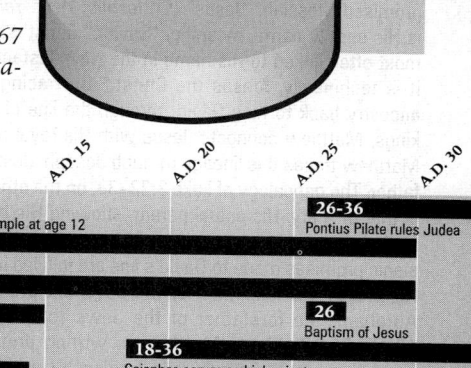

10 B.C.	5 B.C.	A.D. 1	A.D. 5	A.D. 10	A.D. 15	A.D. 20	A.D. 25	A.D. 30

9
Jesus in the temple at age 12

26-36
Pontius Pilate rules Judea

6 B.C.-A.D. 30
Events of the Gospel of Matthew

5 B.C.-A.D. 30
Life of Christ

6-15
Annas serves as high priest

26
Baptism of Jesus

18-36
Caiaphas serves as high priest

7 B.C.-A.D. 14
stus is Emperor of Rome

14-37
Tiberius is Emperor of Rome

4 B.C.-A.D. 39
Herod Antipas rules over Galilee

6 B.C.-A.D. 28
Life of John the Baptist

26-30

CHAPTER 1
The Genealogy of Jesus

1 The book of the generation of Jesus Christ, the son of David, the son of Abraham.

2 Abraham begat Isaac; and Isaac begat Jacob; and Jacob begat Judas and his brethren;

3 And Judas begat Phares and Zara of Tamar; and Phares begat Esrom; and Esrom begat Aram;

4 And Aram begat Aminadab; and Aminadab begat Naasson; and Naasson begat Salmon;

5 And Salmon begat Booz of Rahab; and Booz begat Obed of Ruth; and Obed begat Jesse;

6 And Jesse begat David the king; and David the king begat Solomon of her *that had been the wife* of Uriah;

7 And Solomon begat Roboam; and Roboam begat Abia; and Abia begat Asa;

8 And Asa begat Jehoshaphat; and Jehoshaphat begat Joram; and Joram begat Ozias;

9 And Ozias begat Joatham; and Joatham begat Achaz; and Achaz begat Ezekias;

10 And Ezekias begat Manasses; and Manasses begat Amon; and Amon begat Josias;

11 And Josias begat Jechoniah and his brethren, about the time they were carried away to Babylon:

12 And after they were brought to Babylon, Jechoniah begat Shealtiel; and Shealtiel begat Zorobabel;

13 And Zorobabel begat Abiud; and Abiud begat Eliakim; and Eliakim begat Azor;

14 And Azor begat Sadoc; and Sadoc begat Achim; and Achim begat Eliud;

15 And Eliud begat Eleazar; and Eleazar begat Matthan; and Matthan begat Jacob;

16 And Jacob begat Joseph the husband of Mary, of whom was born Jesus, who is called Christ.

17 So all the generations from Abraham to David *are* fourteen generations; and from David until the carrying away into Babylon *are* fourteen generations; and from the carrying away into Babylon unto Christ *are* fourteen generations.

The Birth of Jesus

18 Now the birth of Jesus Christ was on this wise: When as his mother Mary was espoused to Joseph, before they came together, she was found with child of the Holy Ghost.

19 Then Joseph her husband, being a just *man*, and not willing to make her a publick example, was minded to put her away privily.

20 But while he thought on these things, behold, the angel of the Lord appeared unto him in a dream, saying, Joseph, thou son of David, fear not to take unto thee Mary thy wife; for that which is conceived in her is of the Holy Ghost.

21 And she shall bring forth a son, and thou shalt call his name JESUS: for he shall save his people from their sins.

1 Gen. 12:3; 22:18; Ps. 132:11; Isa. 11:1; Jer. 23:5; Acts 2:30; 13:23; Rom. 1:3; Gal. 3:16

2 Gen. 21:2, 3; 25:26; 29:35

3 Gen. 38:27-30; Ruth 4:18-22; 1Chr. 2:5, 9-16

6 1Sam. 16:1; 17:12; 2Sam. 12:24

7 1Chr. 3:10

10 2Kgs. 20:21; 1Chr. 3:13

11 2Kgs. 24:14-16; 25:11; 1Chr. 3:15, 16; 2Chr. 36:10, 20; Dan. 1:2

12 1Chr. 3:17, 19; Ezra 3:2; 5:2; Neh. 12:1

18 Luke 1:27, 35

19 Deut. 24:1

20 Luke 1:35

21 Luke 1:31; Acts 4:12; 5:31; 13:23, 38

1:1-2 The book of the generation. *Christos* is the Greek translation for "Messiah" or "Anointed." The genealogy of Christ opens by connecting Jesus to the family line of the promised Messiah. "Jesus" (Gr. *Iesous*; Hebr. *Yehoshua*) is His earthly name, meaning, "Savior." Christ is the title most often linked to His name in the New Testament. So it is technically, "Jesus the Christ." By tracing Jesus' ancestry back to King David, through the line of Davidic kings, Matthew connects Jesus with His royal heritage. Matthew traces this lineage through Joseph, Jesus' legal father. The genealogy of Luke 3:23-38, on the other hand, is that of Mary, His actual parent, showing His bloodline back to David. Here the purpose is to show that the messianic promises made to David's line are fulfilled in Jesus. He is also the fulfillment of the covenant promises to Abraham, the forefather of the Jews (cf. Gen. 12:3; 13:15; 22:18). Since Matthew is writing primarily to Jewish readers, he naturally begins by emphasizing Jesus' Jewish parentage.

1:3 Judas. This is the Greek form of Judah, Jacob's son,

through whom it was promised that the leadership of the twelve tribes would come (cf. Gen. 49:3-12).

1:11 Jechoniah. Called "Coniah" in Jeremiah 22:24-30, he is the cursed descendant of David from whom no future king could come. Had Jesus been the "natural" son of Joseph, He could not have reigned on David's throne. However, since His natural lineage is through Mary, and His legal authority is granted through His adoptive relationship to Joseph's line, this curse does not apply to Him.

1:21-22 call his name JESUS. The name of the child Jesus (Hebr. *Yehoshua*) means "Jehovah Saves." Placed early in the New Testament, this statement becomes the foundational concept of the gospel. Jesus, by His very name and nature, is the Savior. The phrase "that it might be fulfilled" (Gr. *pleroō*) indicates the inevitability of the fulfillment of the words of Isaiah the prophet (Isa. 7:14), as well as the fact that Matthew saw the fulfillment in the birth of Christ.

22 Now all this was done, that it might be fulfilled which was spoken of the Lord by the prophet, saying,
23 Behold, a virgin shall be with child, and shall bring forth a son, and they shall call his name Emmanuel, which being interpreted is, God with us.
24 Then Joseph being raised from sleep did as the angel of the Lord had bidden him, and took unto him his wife:
25 And knew her not till she had brought forth her firstborn son: and he called his name JESUS.

CHAPTER 2
The Visit of the Magi

1 Now when Jesus was born in Bethlehem of Judea in the days of Herod the king, behold, there came wise men from the east to Jerusalem,
2 Saying, Where is he that is born King of the Jews? for we have seen his star in the east, and are come to worship him.
3 When Herod the king had heard *these things,* he was troubled, and all Jerusalem with him.
4 And when he had gathered all the chief priests and scribes of the people together, he demanded of them where Christ should be born.
5 And they said unto him, In Bethlehem of Judea: for thus it is written by the prophet,
6 And thou Bethlehem, *in* the land of Judah, art not the least among the princes of Judah: for out of thee shall come a Governor, that shall rule my people Israel.
7 Then Herod, when he had privily called the wise men, inquired of them diligently what time the star appeared.
8 And he sent them to Bethlehem, and said, Go and search diligently for the young child; and when ye have found *him,* bring me word again, that I may come and worship him also.
9 When they had heard the king, they departed; and, lo, the star, which they saw in the east, went before them, till it came and stood over where the young child was.
10 When they saw the star, they rejoiced with exceeding great joy.
11 And when they were come into the house, they saw the young child with Mary his mother, and fell down, and worshipped him: and when they had opened their treasures, they presented unto him gifts; gold, and frankincense, and myrrh.
12 And being warned of God in a dream that they should not return to Herod, they departed into their own country another way.

God Warns Joseph

13 And when they were departed, behold, the angel of the Lord appeareth to Joseph in a dream, saying, Arise, and take the young child and his mother, and flee into Egypt,

Cross references:
23 Isa. 7:14
25 Ex. 13:2; Luke 2:7, 21
1 Gen. 10:30; 25:6; 1Kgs. 4:30; Luke 2:4, 6, 7
2 Num. 24:17; Isa. 60:3; Luke 2:11
4 2Chr. 34:13; 36:14; Mal. 2:7
6 Mic. 5:2; John 7:42; Rev. 2:27
11 Ps. 72:10; Isa. 60:6
12 Matt. 1:20

1:23–25 a virgin. This relates Mary, the mother of Jesus, to the prediction found in Isaiah 7:14. Matthew used the Greek word *parthenos* to translate the Hebrew word *almah.* The quotation of Isaiah 7:14 follows the Septuagint (LXX) rendering where *parthenos* is also used to translate the Hebrew *almah.* There can be no doubt that the Greek term *parthenos* is always to be translated "virgin." The Hebrew *almah* is the most accurate and precise term for virgin used in the Old Testament. Therefore, Matthew is clearly correct in quoting Isaiah 7:14 as being fulfilled in the virgin birth of Christ. "Emmanuel" is a title describing the deity of the person of the Son of God rather than a name actually used by Him. It asserts that God will come to dwell among His own people, which He did in the person of Christ.

2:1–2 Bethlehem of Judea. This town, also called Ephratah, is located five miles south of Jerusalem. Its name in Hebrew means "House of Bread." It was the birthplace of King David and the original city of Joseph's ancestors. According to Luke 2:1–7, Joseph and Mary traveled there from Nazareth, and Jesus was born in a stable after they arrived. Herod the king was known as Herod the Great. He was the son of Antipater, an Edomite, who was appointed procurator of Judea by Julius Caesar in 43 B.C. Wise men were originally a priestly caste among the Persians and Babylonians. These Magi "from the East" were experts in the study of the stars. They naturally came to Jerusalem, the royal capital of Israel, seeking one whom they thought was to be born "King of the Jews." The star could not have been merely a natural phenomenon, since it led the wise men to Jerusalem and later to Bethlehem. The star almost certainly was a divine manifestation used by God to indicate the fact and place of the Messiah's birth.

2:12–18 The death of Herod occurred in the spring of 4 B.C. Our present calendar is off in its calculation by about six years. (This would place the birth of Christ at 6/5 B.C.) The phrase "Rachel weeping for her children" (v. 18) is a quotation of Jeremiah 31:15. The calamity of Israel's mourning at the time of the Exile is correlated here to this renewed calamity brought on by Herod. Rachel refers to Benjamin's mother, who died outside Bethlehem (Gen. 35:19), the eventual birthplace of the Messiah.

Fulfilled Messianic Prophecies

By John F. Ankerberg

Think how difficult it would be for someone to predict the exact city in which the birth of a future U.S. president would take place seven hundred years from now. The prophet Micah accurately predicted similar information—the birthplace and birth date of the Messiah seven hundred years prior to the event (Mic. 5:2). How difficult do you think it would be to indicate the precise form of death that a new, unknown religious leader would experience a thousand years from today? Could you predict a new method of execution not currently known—one that will not even be invented for hundreds of years? That's what David did in 1000 B.C. when he wrote Psalm 22.

On the other hand, if you were able to think up fifty specific prophecies about some man in the future you will never meet, how difficult do you think it would be for that man to fulfill all fifty of your predictions?

For example, how could someone "arrange" to be born into a specific family (Gen. 12:2–3; 17:1, 5–7; 22:18; Matt. 1; Gal. 3:15–16) in a specified city, which is not even the family's hometown (Mic. 5:2; Matt. 2:5–6; Luke 2:1–7)? How does one "arrange" to be virgin born (Isa. 7:14; Matt. 1:18–24; Luke 1:26–35)? How does one "arrange" to have God inform and send a proper messenger to go before him (Mal. 3:1; Matt. 11:10)? How does one arrange to be considered a prophet "like Moses" (Deut. 18:15; John 1:45; 5:46; 6:14; 7:40; Acts 3:17–26; 7:37)?

> *Jesus of Nazareth is the predicted Messiah of the Old Testament.*

How does one "arrange" to be betrayed for a specific amount of money, 30 pieces of silver (Zech. 11:13; Matt. 27:3–10)? How does someone orchestrate his own death, which included being put to death by the strange method of crucifixion, and then arrange to have his executioners gamble for his clothes during the execution (Ps. 22; Isa. 53; Matt. 27:31–38)? How does one plan in advance that his executioners will carry out their regular practice of breaking the legs of the two victims on either side of him, but not his own (Ps. 34:20; John 19:33)? Finally, how does a pretender to being the Messiah "arrange" to be God (Isa. 9:6; Zech. 12:10; John 1:1; 10:30; 14:6), and how could he possibly escape from a grave and appear to people after he has been killed (Ps. 22; Isa. 53:9, 11; Luke 24; 1 Cor. 15:3–8)?

It might be possible to fake one or two of these predictions, but it would be impossible for any man to arrange and fulfill all these predictions (and many others) in advance. So, if it can be proven that such prophecies were predicted about the Messiah hundreds of years in advance, and one man fulfilled all of them, then that man would logically have to be this predicted Messiah of the Old Testament.

God gave hundreds of prophecies about the Messiah for at least two reasons: to make identifying the Messiah obvious, and to make an imposter's task impossible. With all the identifying characteristics in the Old Testament that point to one man, the science of probability tells us that, not only is this particular man the Messiah, but also that God indeed exists.

and be thou there until I bring thee word: for Herod will seek the young child to destroy him.

14 When he arose, he took the young child and his mother by night, and departed into Egypt:

15 And was there until the death of Herod: that it might be fulfilled which was spoken of the Lord by the prophet, saying, Out of Egypt have I called my son.

16 Then Herod, when he saw that he was mocked of the wise men, was exceeding wroth, and sent forth, and slew all the children that were in Bethlehem, and in all the coasts thereof, from two years old and under, according to the time which he had diligently inquired of the wise men.

17 Then was fulfilled that which was spoken by Jeremy the prophet, saying,

18 In Ramah was there a voice heard, lamentation, and weeping, and great mourning, Rachel weeping *for* her children, and would not be comforted, because they are not.

19 But when Herod was dead, behold, an angel of the Lord appeareth in a dream to Joseph in Egypt,

20 Saying, Arise, and take the young child and his mother, and go into the land of Israel: for they are dead which sought the young child's life.

21 And he arose, and took the young child and his mother, and came into the land of Israel.

22 But when he heard that Archelaus did reign in Judea in the room of his father Herod, he was afraid to go thither: notwithstanding, being warned of God in a dream, he turned aside into the parts of Galilee:

23 And he came and dwelt in a city called Nazareth: that it might be fulfilled which

15 Hos. 11:1
17 Jer. 31:15
22 Matt. 3:13; Luke 2:39
23 Judg. 13:5; 1Sam. 1:11; John 1:45
1 Mark 1:4, 15; Luke 3:2, 3; John 1:28
2 Dan. 2:44; Matt. 4:17; 10:7
3 Isa. 40:3; Mark 1:3; Luke 1:76; 3:4; John 1:23
4 Lev. 11:22; 1Sam. 14:25, 26; 2Kgs. 1:8; Zech. 13:4; Mark 1:6
5 Mark 1:5; Luke 3:7
6 Acts 19:4, 18
7 Matt. 12:34; 23:33; Luke 3:7-9; Rom. 5:9; 1Thess. 1:10
9 John 8:33, 39; Acts 13:26; Rom. 4:1, 11, 16
10 Matt. 7:19; Luke 13:7, 9; John 15:6
11 Mark 1:8; Luke 3:16; John 1:15, 26, 33; 1Cor. 12:13

was spoken by the prophets, He shall be called a Nazarene.

CHAPTER 3
John the Baptist Preaches

1 In those days came John the Baptist, preaching in the wilderness of Judea,

2 And saying, Repent ye: for the kingdom of heaven is at hand.

3 For this is he that was spoken of by the prophet Esaias, saying, The voice of one crying in the wilderness, Prepare ye the way of the Lord, make his paths straight.

4 And the same John had his raiment of camel's hair, and a leather girdle about his loins; and his meat was locusts and wild honey.

5 Then went out to him Jerusalem, and all Judea, and all the region round about Jordan,

6 And were baptized of him in Jordan, confessing their sins.

7 But when he saw many of the Pharisees and Sadducees come to his baptism, he said unto them, O generation of vipers, who hath warned you to flee from the wrath to come?

8 Bring forth therefore fruits meet for repentance:

9 And think not to say within yourselves, We have Abraham to *our* father: for I say unto you, that God is able of these stones to raise up children unto Abraham.

10 And now also the axe is laid unto the root of the trees: therefore every tree which bringeth not forth good fruit is hewn down, and cast into the fire.

11 I indeed baptize you with water unto repentance: but he that cometh after me is mightier than I, whose shoes I am not wor-

---

2:15 out of Egypt. This is a fulfillment of Hosea 11:1 that Messiah would be called out of Egypt.

2:19–23 when Herod was dead. Herod was succeeded by his son Archelaus, the son of his Samaritan wife, Malthace. Archelaus was as brutal as his father. Joseph, again warned in a dream, returned to Nazareth, avoiding any further residence in Judea. The phrase "He shall be called a Nazarene" is a reference to Christ's coming from the city of Nazareth. It should not be taken to mean that He was a Nazarite (see Num. 6).

3:1 John the Baptist. John was the forerunner of Christ, the son of Zechariah and Elizabeth, and a cousin of the Lord (cf. Luke 1:5–80). His birth was accompanied by the promise: "He shall be great in the sight of the Lord . . . and he shall be filled with the Holy Ghost" (Luke 1:15). Jesus

later said of him that there were none "greater than John" (Matt. 11:11–13). John the Baptist was the last and greatest epitome of the Old Testament prophets. Matthew's reference to John assumes that his readers were familiar with him. He is presented as the prophet sent in the spirit of Elijah "before the coming of the great and dreadful day of the LORD" (Mal. 4:5). Jesus would later say of him, "I say unto you, That Elias [Elijah] is come already" (Matt. 17:12).

3:11–12 I indeed baptize . . . with water. John's baptism in water was not Christian baptism. The death and resurrection of Christ had not yet occurred in order to be depicted by this baptism. John's baptism was similar to the Old Testament "washings" that symbolized a cleansing associated with repentance on the part of a contrite

thy to bear: he shall baptize you with the Holy Ghost, and *with* fire:

12 Whose fan *is* in his hand, and he will throughly purge his floor, and gather his wheat into the garner; but he will burn up the chaff with unquenchable fire.

John Baptizes Jesus

13 Then cometh Jesus from Galilee to Jordan unto John, to be baptized of him.

14 But John forbad him, saying, I have need to be baptized of thee, and comest thou to me?

15 And Jesus answering said unto him, Suffer *it to be so* now: for thus it becometh us to fulfil all righteousness. Then he suffered him.

16 And Jesus, when he was baptized, went up straightway out of the water: and, lo, the heavens were opened unto him, and he saw the Spirit of God descending like a dove, and lighting upon him:

17 And lo a voice from heaven, saying, This is my beloved Son, in whom I am well pleased.

CHAPTER 4
The Devil Tempts Jesus

1 Then was Jesus led up of the spirit into the wilderness to be tempted of the devil.

2 And when he had fasted forty days and forty nights, he was afterward an hungred.

3 And when the tempter came to him, he said, If thou be the Son of God, command that these stones be made bread.

4 But he answered and said, It is written, Man shall not live by bread alone, but by every word that proceedeth out of the mouth of God.

12 Mal. 3:3; 4:1; Matt. 13:30
13 Matt. 2:22; Mark 1:9; Luke 3:21
16 Isa. 11:2; 42:1; Mark 1:10; Luke 3:22; John 1:32, 33
17 Ps. 2:7; Matt. 12:18; 17:5; Mark 1:11; Luke 9:35; John 12:28
1 Mark 1:12, 13; Luke 4:1-13; Acts 8:39
4 Deut. 8:3
5 Neh. 11:1, 18; Isa. 48:2; 52:1; Matt. 27:53; Rev. 11:2
6 Ps. 91:11, 12
7 Deut. 6:16
10 Deut. 6:13; 10:20; Josh. 24:14; 1Sam. 7:3
11 Heb. 1:14
12 Mark 1:14; Luke 3:20; 4:14, 31; John 4:43
15 Isa. 9:1, 2

5 Then the devil taketh him up into the holy city, and setteth him on a pinnacle of the temple,

6 And saith unto him, If thou be the Son of God, cast thyself down: for it is written, He shall give his angels charge concerning thee: and in *their* hands they shall bear thee up, lest at any time thou dash thy foot against a stone.

7 Jesus said unto him, It is written again, Thou shalt not tempt the Lord thy God.

8 Again, the devil taketh him up into an exceeding high mountain, and sheweth him all the kingdoms of the world, and the glory of them;

9 And saith unto him, All these things will I give thee, if thou wilt fall down and worship me.

10 Then saith Jesus unto him, Get thee hence, Satan: for it is written, Thou shalt worship the Lord thy God, and him only shalt thou serve.

11 Then the devil leaveth him, and, behold, angels came and ministered unto him.

Jesus Preaches Repentance

12 Now when Jesus had heard that John was cast into prison, he departed into Galilee;

13 And leaving Nazareth, he came and dwelt in Capernaum, which is upon the sea coast, in the borders of Zebulun and Nephthalim:

14 That it might be fulfilled which was spoken by Esaias the prophet, saying,

15 The land of Zebulun, and the land of Nephthalim, *by* the way of the sea, beyond Jordan, Galilee of the Gentiles;

---

believer. Neither should this be confused with the baptism with the Holy Spirit that refers to the spiritual rebirth of the believer who shall receive the baptism of the Spirit. This baptism of the Spirit first occurred at Pentecost (Acts 1) and was repeated upon every new group of converts (Samaritans [Acts 8], Gentiles [Acts 10], John's disciples [Acts 19]) until it became normative for all Christian believers, corresponding to their entrance into the body of Christ (cf. 1 Cor. 12:13).

3:15 Suffer it to be so. This phrase means "allow it to be" or "let it happen." Jesus sought this outward identification with John's ministry not because he needed to repent from sin, but in order to fulfill all righteousness.

3:16–17 the Spirit of God descending. The descending of the Spirit of God fulfilled the predicted sign to John to indicate the true Messiah (cf. John 1:33; Isa. 11:2). The dove was a symbol of innocence and purity (cf. 10:16)

and served as an ideal, symbolic representation of the Holy Spirit. The "voice from heaven" is that of the Father. This is one of those rare occasions where all three persons of the Trinity are represented together: the Father speaks, the Spirit descends, and the Son is baptized.

4:12–16 The author omits some of the early Judean ministry and begins with Jesus at Capernaum in Galilee where he first met Christ (cf. 9:9). Capernaum was a Roman settlement near the Sea of Galilee that served as the center of the Roman government in the northern provinces of Israel. It also became the headquarters of Jesus' ministry to the house of Israel. This fulfilled the prophecy of Isaiah 9:1–2, "beyond Jordan, in Galilee of the nations. The people that walked in darkness have seen a great light." Jesus Himself was that "great light" that shone forth in His earthly ministry to the people of Galilee.

16 The people which sat in darkness saw great light; and to them which sat in the region and shadow of death light is sprung up. **17** From that time Jesus began to preach, and to say, Repent: for the kingdom of heaven is at hand.

Jesus Calls Four Fishermen

18 And Jesus, walking by the sea of Galilee, saw two brethren, Simon called Peter, and Andrew his brother, casting a net into the sea: for they were fishers. **19** And he saith unto them, Follow me, and I will make you fishers of men. **20** And they straightway left *their* nets, and followed him. **21** And going on from thence, he saw other two brethren, James *the son* of Zebedee, and John his brother, in a ship with Zebedee their father, mending their nets; and he called them. **22** And they immediately left the ship and their father, and followed him.

Jesus Ministers to a Great Multitude

23 And Jesus went about all Galilee, teaching in their synagogues, and preaching the gospel of the kingdom, and healing all manner of sickness and all manner of disease among the people. **24** And his fame went throughout all Syria: and they brought unto him all sick people that were taken with divers diseases and torments, and those which were possessed with devils, and those which were lunatic, and those that had the palsy; and he healed them. **25** And there followed him great multitudes of people from Galilee, and *from* Decapolis, and *from* Jerusalem, and *from* Judea, and *from* beyond Jordan.

CHAPTER 5
The Beatitudes

1 And seeing the multitudes, he went up into a mountain: and when he was set, his disciples came unto him:

2 And he opened his mouth, and taught them, saying, **3** Blessed are the poor in spirit: for theirs is the kingdom of heaven. **4** Blessed are they that mourn: for they shall be comforted. **5** Blessed are the meek: for they shall inherit the earth. **6** Blessed are they which do hunger and thirst after righteousness: for they shall be filled. **7** Blessed are the merciful: for they shall obtain mercy. **8** Blessed are the pure in heart: for they shall see God. **9** Blessed are the peacemakers: for they shall be called the children of God. **10** Blessed are they which are persecuted for righteousness' sake: for theirs is the kingdom of heaven. **11** Blessed are ye, when men shall revile you, and persecute you, and shall say all manner of evil against you falsely, for my sake. **12** Rejoice, and be exceeding glad: for great is your reward in heaven: for so persecuted they the prophets which were before you.

Salt and Light

13 Ye are the salt of the earth: but if the salt have lost his savour, wherewith shall it be salted? it is thenceforth good for nothing, but to be cast out, and to be trodden under foot of men. **14** Ye are the light of the world. A city that is set on an hill cannot be hid. **15** Neither do men light a candle, and put it under a bushel, but on a candlestick; and it giveth light unto all that are in the house. **16** Let your light so shine before men, that they may see your good works, and glorify your Father which is in heaven.

Teaching about the Law

17 Think not that I am come to destroy the law, or the prophets: I am not come to destroy, but to fulfil. **18** For verily I say unto you, Till heaven and

Cross references

16 Isa. 42:7; Luke 2:32
17 Matt. 3:2; 10:7; Mark 1:14, 15
18 Mark 1:16-18; Luke 5:2; John 1:42
19 Luke 5:10, 11
20 Mark 10:28; Luke 18:28
21 Mark 1:19, 20; Luke 5:10
25 Mark 3:7
1 Mark 3:13
3 Ps. 51:17; Luke 6:20
4 John 16:2
5 Ps. 37:11; Rom. 4:13
6 Isa. 55:1; 65:13
7 Matt. 6:14; Mark 11:25
8 Ps. 15:2
10 2Cor. 4:17; 2Tim. 2:12; 1Pet. 3:14
11 Luke 6:22; 1Pet. 4:14
12 2Chr. 36:16; Luke 6:23; Acts 5:41; 7:52
13 Mark 9:50; Luke 14:34, 35
14 Prov. 4:18; Phil. 2:15
15 Mark 4:21; Luke 8:16; 11:33
16 John 15:8; 1Pet. 2:12
17 Rom. 3:31; 10:4; Gal. 3:24

5:1–2 In the Sermon on the Mount, Jesus states the spiritual character and quality of the kingdom He would establish. Virtually every section of this message is repeated in substance elsewhere in the New Testament, showing that this message is not to be limited in its application to the people of Israel.

5:17 not . . . come to destroy the law. Having laid the foundation of the message in the summary statements of the Beatitudes, Jesus now proceeds to show the superiority of His message to that of the law of Moses. The New Testament gospel is not contradictory to the Old Testament Law; rather it is the fulfillment of the spiritual intention of that law through the person and work of Jesus Christ.

earth pass, one jot or one tittle shall in no wise pass from the law, till all be fulfilled.

19 Whosoever therefore shall break one of these least commandments, and shall teach men so, he shall be called the least in the kingdom of heaven: but whosoever shall do and teach them, the same shall be called great in the kingdom of heaven.

20 For I say unto you, That except your righteousness shall exceed the righteousness of the scribes and Pharisees, ye shall in no case enter into the kingdom of heaven.

Teaching about Anger

21 Ye have heard that it was said by them of old time, Thou shalt not kill; and whosoever shall kill shall be in danger of the judgment:

22 But I say unto you, That whosoever is angry with his brother without a cause shall be in danger of the judgment: and whosoever shall say to his brother, Raca, shall be in danger of the council: but whosoever shall say, Thou fool, shall be in danger of hell fire.

23 Therefore if thou bring thy gift to the altar, and there rememberest that thy brother hath ought against thee;

24 Leave there thy gift before the altar, and go thy way; first be reconciled to thy brother, and then come and offer thy gift.

25 Agree with thine adversary quickly, whiles thou art in the way with him; lest at any time the adversary deliver thee to the judge, and the judge deliver thee to the officer, and thou be cast into prison.

26 Verily I say unto thee, Thou shalt by no means come out thence, till thou hast paid the uttermost farthing.

Sin Begins in the Heart

27 Ye have heard that it was said by them of old time, Thou shalt not commit adultery:

28 But I say unto you, That whosoever looketh on a woman to lust after her hath committed adultery with her already in his heart.

29 And if thy right eye offend thee, pluck it out, and cast it from thee: for it is profitable for thee that one of thy members should perish, and not that thy whole body should be cast into hell.

30 And if thy right hand offend thee, cut it off, and cast it from thee: for it is profitable for thee that one of thy members should perish, and not that thy whole body should be cast into hell.

18 Luke 16:17
19 James 2:10
20 Rom. 9:31; 10:3
21 Ex. 20:13; Deut. 5:17
22 2 Sam. 6:20; 1 John 3:15; James 2:20
23 Matt. 8:4; 23:19
24 Job 42:8; Matt. 18:19; 1 Tim. 2:8; 1 Pet. 3:7
25 Ps. 32:6; Prov. 25:8; Isa. 55:6; Luke 12:58, 59
27 Ex. 20:14; Deut. 5:18
28 Gen. 34:2; Prov. 6:25
29 Matt. 18:8, 9; 19:12; Mark 9:43-47
31 Deut. 24:1; Jer. 3:1; Matt. 19:3-12; Mark 10:2-12
32 Matt. 19:9; Luke 16:18; Rom. 7:3; 1 Cor. 7:10, 11
33 Ex. 20:7; Lev. 19:12; Num. 30:2; Deut. 5:11
34 Isa. 66:1; Matt. 23:16, 18, 22; James 5:12
35 Ps. 48:2; 87:3
37 Col. 4:6; James 5:12
38 Ex. 21:24; Lev. 24:20; Deut. 19:21
39 Luke 6:29; 1 Pet. 3:9
41 Matt. 27:32; Mark 15:21
43 Lev. 19:18; Deut. 23:6
45 Job 25:3
46 Luke 6:32

Divorce

31 It hath been said, Whosoever shall put away his wife, let him give her a writing of divorcement:

32 But I say unto you, That whosoever shall put away his wife, saving for the cause of fornication, causeth her to commit adultery: and whosoever shall marry her that is divorced committeth adultery.

Oaths

33 Again, ye have heard that it hath been said by them of old time, Thou shalt not forswear thyself, but shalt perform unto the Lord thine oaths:

34 But I say unto you, Swear not at all; neither by heaven; for it is God's throne:

35 Nor by the earth; for it is his footstool: neither by Jerusalem; for it is the city of the great King.

36 Neither shalt thou swear by thy head, because thou canst not make one hair white or black.

37 But let your communication be, Yea, yea; Nay, nay: for whatsoever is more than these cometh of evil.

Retaliation

38 Ye have heard that it hath been said, An eye for an eye, and a tooth for a tooth:

39 But I say unto you, That ye resist not evil: but whosoever shall smite thee on thy right cheek, turn to him the other also.

40 And if any man will sue thee at the law, and take away thy coat, let him have thy cloke also.

41 And whosoever shall compel thee to go a mile, go with him twain.

42 Give to him that asketh thee, and from him that would borrow of thee turn not thou away.

Enemies

43 Ye have heard that it hath been said, Thou shalt love thy neighbour, and hate thine enemy.

44 But I say unto you, Love your enemies, bless them that curse you, do good to them that hate you, and pray for them which despitefully use you, and persecute you;

45 That ye may be the children of your Father which is in heaven: for he maketh his sun to rise on the evil and on the good, and sendeth rain on the just and on the unjust.

46 For if ye love them which love you, what reward have ye? do not even the publicans the same?

47 And if ye salute your brethren only, what do ye more than others? do not even the publicans so?

48 Be ye therefore perfect, even as your Father which is in heaven is perfect.

CHAPTER 6
The Proper Manner of Almsgiving

1 Take heed that ye do not your alms before men, to be seen of them: otherwise ye have no reward of your Father which is in heaven.

2 Therefore when thou doest thine alms, do not sound a trumpet before thee, as the hypocrites do in the synagogues and in the streets, that they may have glory of men. Verily I say unto you, They have their reward.

3 But when thou doest alms, let not thy left hand know what thy right hand doeth:

4 That thine alms may be in secret: and thy Father which seeth in secret himself shall reward thee openly.

Prayer

5 And when thou prayest, thou shalt not be as the hypocrites are: for they love to pray standing in the synagogues and in the corners of the streets, that they may be seen of men. Verily I say unto you, They have their reward.

6 But thou, when thou prayest, enter into thy closet, and when thou hast shut thy door, pray to thy Father which is in secret; and thy Father which seeth in secret shall reward thee openly.

7 But when ye pray, use not vain repetitions, as the heathen do: for they think that they shall be heard for their much speaking.

8 Be not ye therefore like unto them: for your Father knoweth what things ye have need of, before ye ask him.

9 After this manner therefore pray ye: Our Father which art in heaven, Hallowed be thy name.

10 Thy kingdom come. Thy will be done in earth, as it is in heaven.

11 Give us this day our daily bread.

12 And forgive us our debts, as we forgive our debtors.

13 And lead us not into temptation, but deliver us from evil: For thine is the kingdom,

and the power, and the glory, for ever. Amen.

14 For if ye forgive men their trespasses, your heavenly Father will also forgive you:

15 But if ye forgive not men their trespasses, neither will your Father forgive your trespasses.

Fasting

16 Moreover when ye fast, be not, as the hypocrites, of a sad countenance: for they disfigure their faces, that they may appear unto men to fast. Verily I say unto you, They have their reward.

17 But thou, when thou fastest, anoint thine head, and wash thy face;

18 That thou appear not unto men to fast, but unto thy Father which is in secret: and thy Father, which seeth in secret, shall reward thee openly.

Treasures in Heaven

19 Lay not up for yourselves treasures upon earth, where moth and rust doth corrupt, and where thieves break through and steal:

20 But lay up for yourselves treasures in heaven, where neither moth nor rust doth corrupt, and where thieves do not break through nor steal:

21 For where your treasure is, there will your heart be also.

The Light of the World

22 The light of the body is the eye: if therefore thine eye be single, thy whole body shall be full of light.

23 But if thine eye be evil, thy whole body shall be full of darkness. If therefore the light that is in thee be darkness, how great is that darkness!

Put God's Kingdom First

24 No man can serve two masters: for either he will hate the one, and love the other; or else he will hold to the one, and despise the other. Ye cannot serve God and mammon.

25 Therefore I say unto you, Take no thought for your life, what ye shall eat, or what ye shall drink; nor yet for your body, what ye shall put on. Is not the life more than meat, and the body than raiment?

26 Behold the fowls of the air: for they sow

Cross-references (center column):

48 Luke 6:36; Eph. 5:1; Col. 1:28; 4:12; James 1:4; 1Pet. 1:15, 16

1 Deut. 24:13; Ps. 112:9; Dan. 4:27; 2Cor. 9:9, 10

2 Rom. 12:8

4 Luke 14:14

6 2Kgs. 4:33

7 1Kgs. 18:26, 29; Eccl. 5:2

9 Luke 11:2-4

10 Ps. 103:20, 21; Matt. 26:39, 42; Acts 21:14

11 Job 23:12; Prov. 30:8

12 Matt. 18:21, 22

13 Matt. 26:41; Luke 22:40, 46; John 17:15; Rev. 3:10

14 Mark 11:25, 26; Eph. 4:32; Col. 3:13

15 Matt. 18:35; James 2:13

16 Isa. 58:5

17 Ruth 3:3; Dan. 10:3

19 Prov. 23:4; 1Tim. 6:17

20 Matt. 19:21; Luke 12:33, 34; 18:22; 1Tim. 6:19

22 Luke 11:34, 36

24 Luke 16:13; 1Tim. 6:17

25 Luke 12:22, 23; Phil. 4:6

6:10 The phrase "Thy kingdom come" refers to the end-time nature of this prayer. Notice that this kingdom is to be prayed **for**, implying that it has not yet arrived. The recognition of "Thy will be done" emphasizes the idea that prayer conforms the will of the believer to the will of God. Prayer as an act of spiritual expression is one of the means by which believers are brought into conformity to the very nature and purpose of God.

not, neither do they reap, nor gather into barns; yet your heavenly Father feedeth them. Are ye not much better than they?

27 Which of you by taking thought can add one cubit unto his stature?

28 And why take ye thought for raiment? Consider the lilies of the field, how they grow; they toil not, neither do they spin:

29 And yet I say unto you, That even Solomon in all his glory was not arrayed like one of these.

30 Wherefore, if God so clothe the grass of the field, which today is, and to morrow is cast into the oven, shall he not much more clothe you, O ye of little faith?

31 Therefore take no thought, saying, What shall we eat? or, What shall we drink? or, Wherewithal shall we be clothed?

32 (For after all these things do the Gentiles seek:) for your heavenly Father knoweth that ye have need of all these things.

33 But seek ye first the kingdom of God, and his righteousness; and all these things shall be added unto you.

34 Take therefore no thought for the morrow: for the morrow shall take thought for the things of itself. Sufficient unto the day is the evil thereof.

CHAPTER 7
Judging Others

1 Judge not, that ye be not judged.

2 For with what judgment ye judge, ye shall be judged: and with what measure ye mete, it shall be measured to you again.

3 And why beholdest thou the mote that is in thy brother's eye, but considerest not the beam that is in thine own eye?

4 Or how wilt thou say to thy brother, Let me pull out the mote out of thine eye; and, behold, a beam is in thine own eye?

5 Thou hypocrite, first cast out the beam

out of thine own eye; and then shalt thou see clearly to cast out the mote out of thy brother's eye.

6 Give not that which is holy unto the dogs, neither cast ye your pearls before swine, lest they trample them under their feet, and turn again and rend you.

Asking and Seeking

7 Ask, and it shall be given you; seek, and ye shall find; knock, and it shall be opened unto you:

8 For every one that asketh receiveth; and he that seeketh findeth; and to him that knocketh it shall be opened.

9 Or what man is there of you, whom if his son ask bread, will he give him a stone?

10 Or if he ask a fish, will he give him a serpent?

11 If ye then, being evil, know how to give good gifts unto your children, how much more shall your Father which is in heaven give good things to them that ask him?

12 Therefore all things whatsoever ye would that men should do to you, do ye even so to them: for this is the law and the prophets.

The Narrow Way

13 Enter ye in at the strait gate: for wide is the gate, and broad is the way, that leadeth to destruction, and many there be which go in thereat:

14 Because strait is the gate, and narrow is the way, which leadeth unto life, and few there be that find it.

Behavior and Belief

15 Beware of false prophets, which come to you in sheep's clothing, but inwardly they are ravening wolves.

---

26 Job 38:41; Ps. 147:9; Luke 12:24-34

33 Mark 10:30; Luke 12:31; 1Tim. 4:8

1 Luke 6:37; Rom. 2:1; 14:3, 4, 10, 13; 1Cor. 4:3, 5; James 4:11, 12

2 Mark 4:24; Luke 6:38

3 Luke 6:41, 42

6 Prov. 9:7, 8; 23:9; Acts 13:45, 46

7 Matt. 21:22; Mark 11:24; Luke 11:9, 10; 18:1; John 14:13; 15:7; 16:23, 24

8 Prov. 8:17; Jer. 29:12, 13

9 Luke 11:11-13

11 Gen. 6:5; 8:21

12 Lev. 19:18; Matt. 22:40; Luke 6:31; Rom. 13:8-10; Gal. 5:14; 1Tim. 1:5

13 Luke 13:24

15 Deut. 13:3; Jer. 23:16; Matt. 24:4, 5, 11, 24; Mark 13:22

6:33–34 This portion of the Sermon on the Mount is summarized by the statement "Seek ye first the kingdom of God." The disciples who have pledged their allegiance to the King must continue seeking the kingdom and its righteousness. The present imperative form of the verb (Gr. *zeteo*) indicates a continual or constant seeking. The believer is to seek first the righteousness that is characteristic of God's kingdom and then "all these things" (material things—cf. vv. 25–32) shall be added to him. When our priority is God, then He will take care of things.

6:33 The phrase "kingdom of heaven" is featured in the Gospel of Matthew and seems to be based on similar references in the book of Daniel (cf. Dan. 2:44; 4:25, 52).

The phrase "kingdom of heaven" is essentially synonymous with the more common phrase, "kingdom of God" used in the other Gospels. Matthew's use of this latter expression (6:33) has particular reference to God's earthly (Davidic) kingdom.

7:15 Beware the false prophets. This warning fits appropriately with the concept of the two ways that lead to eternity. Since many are being led in the wrong way, they are obviously being led by the wrong people. False prophets were prevalent in the Old Testament, whereas God's true prophets were often in the minority. False prophets appear "in sheep's clothing" but are in reality "ravening wolves." This is a perfect description of those

16 Ye shall know them by their fruits. Do men gather grapes of thorns, or figs of thistles?

17 Even so every good tree bringeth forth good fruit; but a corrupt tree bringeth forth evil fruit.

18 A good tree cannot bring forth evil fruit, neither can a corrupt tree bring forth good fruit.

19 Every tree that bringeth not forth good fruit is hewn down, and cast into the fire.

20 Wherefore by their fruits ye shall know them.

"I Never Knew You"

21 Not every one that saith unto me, Lord, Lord, shall enter into the kingdom of heaven; but he that doeth the will of my Father which is in heaven.

22 Many will say to me in that day, Lord, Lord, have we not prophesied in thy name and in thy name have cast out devils? and in thy name done many wonderful works?

23 And then will I profess unto them, I never knew you: depart from me, ye that work iniquity.

Build on a Firm Foundation

24 Therefore whosoever heareth these sayings of mine, and doeth them, I will liken him unto a wise man, which built his house upon a rock:

25 And the rain descended, and the floods came, and the winds blew, and beat upon that house; and it fell not: for it was founded upon a rock.

26 And every one that heareth these sayings of mine, and doeth them not, shall be likened unto a foolish man, which built his house upon the sand:

27 And the rain descended, and the floods came, and the winds blew, and beat upon

that house; and it fell: and great was the fall of it.

28 And it came to pass, when Jesus had ended these sayings, the people were astonished at his doctrine:

29 For he taught them as *one* having authority, and not as the scribes.

CHAPTER 8
Jesus Heals Leprosy

1 When he was come down from the mountain, great multitudes followed him.

2 And, behold, there came a leper and worshipped him, saying, Lord, if thou wilt, thou canst make me clean.

3 And Jesus put forth *his* hand, and touched him, saying, I will; be thou clean. And immediately his leprosy was cleansed.

4 And Jesus saith unto him, See thou tell no man; but go thy way, shew thyself to the priest, and offer the gift that Moses commanded, for a testimony unto them.

Healing a Centurion's Servant

5 And when Jesus was entered into Capernaum, there came unto him a centurion, beseeching him,

6 And saying, Lord, my servant lieth at home sick of the palsy, grievously tormented.

7 And Jesus saith unto him, I will come and heal him.

8 The centurion answered and said, Lord, I am not worthy that thou shouldest come under my roof: but speak the word only, and my servant shall be healed.

9 For I am a man under authority, having soldiers under me: and I say to this *man,* Go, and he goeth; and to another, Come, and he cometh; and to my servant, Do this, and he doeth *it.*

10 When Jesus heard *it,* he marvelled, and said to them that followed, Verily I say unto

Cross references (center column):

16 Matt. 7:20; 12:30; Luke 6:43, 44

17 Jer. 11:19; Matt. 12:33

19 Matt. 3:10; Luke 3:9; John 15:2, 6

21 Hos. 8:2; Matt. 25:11, 12; Luke 6:46; 13:25; Acts 19:13; Rom. 2:13; James 1:22

22 Num. 24:4; John 11:51; 1Cor. 13:2

23 Ps. 5:5; 6:8; Matt. 25:12, 41; Luke 13:25, 27; 2Tim. 2:19

24 Luke 6:46-49

28 Matt. 13:54; Mark 1:22; 6:2; Luke 4:32

29 John 7:46

2 Mark 1:40-45; Luke 5:12-16

4 Lev. 14:3, 4, 10; Matt. 9:30; Mark 5:43; Luke 5:14

5 Luke 7:1-10

8 Ps. 107:20; Luke 15:19, 21

---

religious leaders of Jesus' day who denied or distorted the truth. They looked like lambs but acted like wolves. Prophetically, they anticipate the False Prophet in Revelation 13:11.

7:16–20 One test of a true prophet was the conformity of his doctrine to the Scriptures (cf. 1 Cor. 14:37; Deut. 13:1–5). "Their fruits" refers not only to actions of their lives, but also to the doctrines they proclaim. The two trees are contrasted in relation to the fruit they produce. "Every good tree bringeth forth good fruit" consistently, while a "corrupt tree bringeth forth evil fruit" continually. Therefore, the normal and consistent production of fruit,

whether good or evil, in a person's life will bear evidence whether or not that life is of God. Verse 19 illustrates the unfruitful of the unregenerate who is "cast into the fire." This is a common warning from Jesus (cf. John 15:6) and from later texts of the New Testament (cf. Heb. 6:7–9). Sometimes the distinction between fruit as works and fruitbearers as persons is blurred. Works that are "wood, hay, and stubble" will be burned (1 Cor. 3:12–13). "Workers of iniquity" will also be burned in "hell fire." This latter sense seems to be in view here (cf. 7:21–23; 8:12).

you, I have not found so great faith, no, not in Israel.

11 And I say unto you, That many shall come from the east and west, and shall sit down with Abraham, and Isaac, and Jacob, in the kingdom of heaven.

12 But the children of the kingdom shall be cast out into outer darkness: there shall be weeping and gnashing of teeth.

13 And Jesus said unto the centurion, Go thy way; and as thou hast believed, so be it done unto thee. And his servant was healed in the selfsame hour.

Peter's Mother-in-law Is Healed

14 And when Jesus was come into Peter's house, he saw his wife's mother laid, and sick of a fever.

15 And he touched her hand, and the fever left her: and she arose, and ministered unto them.

16 When the even was come, they brought unto him many that were possessed with devils: and he cast out the spirits with *his* word, and healed all that were sick:

17 That it might be fulfilled which was spoken by Esaias the prophet, saying, Himself took our infirmities, and bare *our* sicknesses.

Following Jesus

18 Now when Jesus saw great multitudes about him, he gave commandment to depart unto the other side.

19 And a certain scribe came, and said unto him, Master, I will follow thee whithersoever thou goest.

20 And Jesus saith unto him, The foxes have holes, and the birds of the air have nests; but the Son of man hath not where to lay his head.

21 And another of his disciples said unto him, Lord, suffer me first to go and bury my father.

22 But Jesus said unto him, Follow me; and let the dead bury their dead.

Calming a Storm

23 And when he was entered into a ship, his disciples followed him,

24 And, behold, there arose a great tempest in the sea, insomuch that the ship was covered with the waves: but he was asleep.

25 And his disciples came to *him* and awoke him, saying, Lord, save us: we perish.

26 And he saith unto them, Why are ye fearful, O ye of little faith? Then he arose, and rebuked the winds and the sea; and there was a great calm.

27 But the men marvelled, saying, What manner of man is this, that even the winds and the sea obey him!

Healing the Demon-Possessed at Gergesenes

28 And when he was come to the other side into the country of the Gergesenes, there met him two possessed with devils, coming out of the tombs, exceeding fierce, so that no man might pass by that way.

29 And, behold, they cried out, saying, What have we to do with thee, Jesus, thou Son of God? art thou come hither to torment us before the time?

30 And there was a good way off from them an herd of many swine feeding.

31 So the devils besought him, saying, If thou cast us out, suffer us to go away into the herd of swine.

32 And he said unto them, Go. And when they were come out, they went into the herd of swine: and, behold, the whole herd of swine ran violently down a steep place into the sea, and perished in the waters.

33 And they that kept them fled, and went their ways into the city, and told every thing, and what was befallen to the possessed of the devils.

34 And, behold, the whole city came out to meet Jesus: and when they saw him, they besought *him* that he would depart out of their coasts.

CHAPTER 9
Jesus Heals a Crippled Man

1 And he entered into a ship, and passed over, and came into his own city.

2 And, behold, they brought to him a man sick of the palsy, lying on a bed: and Jesus seeing their faith said unto the sick of the

Cross references (center column)

11 Gen. 12:3; Isa. 2:2, 3; 11:10; Mal. 1:11; Luke 13:29; Acts 10:45; 11:18; 14:27; Rom. 15:9; Eph. 3:6

12 Matt. 13:42, 50; 21:43; 22:13; 24:51; 25:30; Luke 13:28; 2Pet. 2:17; Jude 1:13

14 Mark 1:29-31; Luke 4:38, 39; 1Cor. 9:5

16 Mark 1:32-34; Luke 4:40, 41

17 Isa. 53:4; 1Pet. 2:24

19 Luke 9:57, 58

21 1Kgs. 19:20; Luke 9:59, 60

24 Mark 4:37-41; Luke 8:23-25

26 Ps. 65:7; 89:9; 107:29

28 Mark 5:1-20; Luke 8:26-36

34 Deut. 5:25; 1Kgs. 17:18; Luke 5:8; Acts 16:39

1 Matt. 4:13

2 Matt. 8:10; Mark 2:3; Luke 5:18

8:10–13 from the east and west. These words are taken from Psalm 107 (with allusions also to Isa. 49:12; 59:19; Mal. 1:11). Here Christ is referring to the ingathering of the Gentiles through the preaching of the gospel, culminating in their final gathering at the time of His second coming. "The children of the kingdom" refers to those to whom the kingdom really belongs. "Outer darkness" refers to the condemnation of the second death. Even though the servant was a Gentile, he was healed because of the faith of the centurion. The contrast to this incident drawn by Jesus emphasizes the foolishness of Israel's rejection of Him as the Messiah.

palsy; Son, be of good cheer; thy sins be forgiven thee.

3 And, behold, certain of the scribes said within themselves, This *man* blasphemeth.

4 And Jesus knowing their thoughts said, Wherefore think ye evil in your hearts?

5 For whether is easier, to say, Thy sins be forgiven thee; or to say, Arise, and walk?

6 But that ye may know that the Son of man hath power on earth to forgive sins, (then saith he to the sick of the palsy,) Arise, take up thy bed, and go unto thine house.

7 And he arose, and departed to his house.

8 But when the multitudes saw *it*, they marvelled, and glorified God, which had given such power unto men.

Jesus Calls Matthew

9 And as Jesus passed forth from thence, he saw a man, named Matthew, sitting at the receipt of custom: and he saith unto him, Follow me. And he arose, and followed him.

10 And it came to pass, as Jesus sat at meat in the house, behold, many publicans and sinners came and sat down with him and his disciples.

11 And when the Pharisees saw *it*, they said unto his disciples, Why eateth your Master with publicans and sinners?

12 But when Jesus heard *that*, he said unto them, They that be whole need not a physician, but they that are sick.

13 But go ye and learn what that meaneth, I will have mercy, and not sacrifice: for I am not come to call the righteous, but sinners to repentance.

Fasting

14 Then came to him the disciples of John, saying, Why do we and the Pharisees fast oft, but thy disciples fast not?

15 And Jesus said unto them, Can the children of the bridechamber mourn, as long as the bridegroom is with them? but the days will come, when the bridegroom shall be taken from them, and then shall they fast.

16 No man putteth a piece of new cloth unto an old garment, for that which is put in to fill it up taketh from the garment, and the rent is made worse.

4 Ps. 139:2; Matt. 12:25; Mark 12:15; Luke 5:22; 6:8; 9:47; 11:17

9 Mark 2:14; Luke 5:27

10 Mark 2:15-17; Luke 5:29-32

11 Matt. 11:19; Luke 5:30; 15:2; Gal. 2:15

13 Hos. 6:6; Mic. 6:6-8; Matt. 12:7; 1Tim. 1:15

14 Mark 2:18-22; Luke 5:33-35; 18:12

15 John 3:29; Acts 13:2, 3; 14:23; 1Cor. 7:5

18 Mark 5:22-24; Luke 8:41, 42

20 Mark 5:25; Luke 8:43

22 Luke 7:50; 8:48; 17:19; 18:42

23 2Chr. 35:25; Mark 5:38; Luke 8:51

24 Acts 20:10

27 Matt. 15:22; 20:30, 31; Mark 10:47, 48; Luke 18:38, 39

30 Matt. 8:4; 12:16; 17:9; Luke 5:14

31 Mark 7:36

17 Neither do men put new wine into old bottles: else the bottles break, and the wine runneth out, and the bottles perish: but they put new wine into new bottles, and both are preserved.

Jesus Raises Jairus' Daughter

18 While he spake these things unto them, behold, there came a certain ruler, and worshipped him, saying, My daughter is even now dead: but come and lay thy hand upon her, and she shall live.

19 And Jesus arose, and followed him, and *so did* his disciples.

20 And, behold, a woman, which was diseased with an issue of blood twelve years, came behind *him*, and touched the hem of his garment:

21 For she said within herself, If I may but touch his garment, I shall be whole.

22 But Jesus turned him about, and when he saw her, he said, Daughter, be of good comfort; thy faith hath made thee whole. And the woman was made whole from that hour.

23 And when Jesus came into the ruler's house, and saw the minstrels and the people making a noise,

24 He said unto them, Give place: for the maid is not dead, but sleepeth. And they laughed him to scorn.

25 But when the people were put forth, he went in, and took her by the hand, and the maid arose.

26 And the fame hereof went abroad into all that land.

Jesus Heals Two Blind Men

27 And when Jesus departed thence, two blind men followed him, crying, and saying, *Thou* son of David, have mercy on us.

28 And when he was come into the house, the blind men came to him: and Jesus saith unto them, Believe ye that I am able to do this? They said unto him, Yea, Lord.

29 Then touched he their eyes, saying, According to your faith be it unto you.

30 And their eyes were opened; and Jesus straitly charged them, saying, See that no man know it.

31 But they, when they were departed, spread abroad his fame in all that country.

9:27–32 two blind men followed him. This incident is peculiar to Matthew's gospel (cf. Luke 11:14–26). These men call out, "Thou son of David," a messianic designation. The form of their address seems to indicate that they had put their faith in Jesus as the Messiah.

Jesus Heals a Mute

32 As they went out, behold, they brought to him a dumb man possessed with a devil.
33 And when the devil was cast out, the dumb spake: and the multitudes marvelled, saying, It was never so seen in Israel.
34 But the Pharisees said, He casteth out devils through the prince of the devils.

Jesus' Compassion

35 And Jesus went about all the cities and villages, teaching in their synagogues, and preaching the gospel of the kingdom, and healing every sickness and every disease among the people.
36 But when he saw the multitudes, he was moved with compassion on them, because they fainted, and were scattered abroad, as sheep having no shepherd.
37 Then saith he unto his disciples, The harvest truly is plenteous, but the labourers are few;
38 Pray ye therefore the Lord of the harvest, that he will send forth labourers into his harvest.

CHAPTER 10
Jesus Chooses Twelve Apostles

1 And when he had called unto *him* his twelve disciples, he gave them power *against* unclean spirits, to cast them out, and to heal all manner of sickness and all manner of disease.
2 Now the names of the twelve apostles are these; The first, Simon, who is called Peter, and Andrew his brother; James *the son* of Zebedee, and John his brother;
3 Philip, and Bartholomew; Thomas, and Matthew the publican; James the *son* of Alphaeus, and Lebbaeus whose surname was Thaddaeus;
4 Simon the Canaanite, and Judas Iscariot, who also betrayed him.

5 These twelve Jesus sent forth, and commanded them, saying, Go not into the way of the Gentiles, and into any city of the Samaritans enter ye not:
6 But go rather to the lost sheep of the house of Israel.
7 And as ye go, preach, saying, The kingdom of heaven is at hand.
8 Heal the sick, cleanse the lepers, raise the dead, cast out devils: freely ye have received, freely give.
9 Provide neither gold, nor silver, nor brass in your purses,
10 Nor scrip for your journey, neither two coats, neither shoes, nor yet staves: for the workman is worthy of his meat.
11 And into whatsoever city or town ye shall enter, inquire who in it is worthy; and there abide till ye go thence.
12 And when ye come into an house, salute it.
13 And if the house be worthy, let your peace come upon it: but if it be not worthy, let your peace return to you.
14 And whosoever shall not receive you, nor hear your words, when ye depart out of that house or city, shake off the dust of your feet.
15 Verily I say unto you, It shall be more tolerable for the land of Sodom and Gomorrah in the day of judgment, than for that city.

The Disciples Should Expect Persecution

16 Behold, I send you forth as sheep in the midst of wolves: be ye therefore wise as serpents, and harmless as doves.
17 But beware of men: for they will deliver you up to the councils, and they will scourge you in their synagogues;
18 And ye shall be brought before governors and kings for my sake, for a testimony against them and the Gentiles.
19 But when they deliver you up, take no

Cross references

32 Matt. 12:22; Luke 11:14
35 Matt. 4:23; Mark 6:6; Luke 13:22
36 Mark 6:34
37 Luke 10:2; John 4:35
38 2Thess. 3:1
1 Mark 3:13, 14; 6:7; Luke 6:13; 9:1
4 Luke 6:15; John 13:26; Acts 1:13
5 2Kgs. 17:24; Matt. 4:15; John 4:9, 20
6 Matt. 15:24; Acts 13:46
7 Matt. 3:2; 4:17; Luke 9:2; 10:9
9 Mark 6:8; Luke 9:3; 10:4; 22:35
13 Ps. 35:13; Luke 10:5
14 Mark 6:11; Luke 9:5; 10:10, 11
15 Matt. 11:22, 24
16 Luke 10:3; Phil. 2:15
17 Matt. 24:9; Mark 13:9; Luke 12:11; 21:12
18 Acts 12:1; 2Tim. 4:16

9:34–36 casteth out devils through the prince of the devils. The "prince of the devils" is Satan himself. The connection between spiritual evil and physical illness is clearly illustrated in this incident. That they "fainted" means they were distressed. Christ views the people "as sheep having no shepherd," an idea taken from the Septuagint translation of Numbers 27:17. From this point on there is a subtle shift in Jesus' teaching as He begins to prepare His followers for rejection and a later "coming" to establish His kingdom (cf. 10:23–25; 13:1–50; Luke 17:25).

10:1–4 twelve disciples. These twelve had been

formed as a group some time previously. Now after a period of instruction and training, they were sent on their first mission. They were also given "power," or authority, over demons and disease. Their miracle-working ministry was to attest the legitimate claim of Jesus to be the Messiah. The word "apostles" (Gr. *apostoloi*) is the technical term that later came to be applied to the twelve disciples, meaning literally "Sent Ones." In this passage their twelve names are arranged in six pairs, which probably corresponded to the lists of the disciples found elsewhere (cf. Mark 3:16; Luke 6:14; Acts 1:13).

thought how or what ye shall speak: for it shall be given you in that same hour what ye shall speak.

20 For it is not ye that speak, but the Spirit of your Father which speaketh in you.

21 And the brother shall deliver up the brother to death, and the father the child: and the children shall rise up against their parents, and cause them to be put to death.

22 And ye shall be hated of all men for my name's sake: but he that endureth to the end shall be saved.

23 But when they persecute you in this city, flee ye into another: for verily I say unto you, Ye shall not have gone over the cities of Israel, till the Son of man be come.

24 The disciple is not above his master, nor the servant above his lord.

25 It is enough for the disciple that he be as his master, and the servant as his lord. If they have called the master of the house Beelzebub, how much more shall they call them of his household?

Admonitions against Fear

26 Fear them not therefore: for there is nothing covered, that shall not be revealed; and hid, that shall not be known.

27 What I tell you in darkness, that speak ye in light: and what ye hear in the ear, that preach ye upon the housetops.

28 And fear not them which kill the body, but are not able to kill the soul: but rather fear him which is able to destroy both soul and body in hell.

29 Are not two sparrows sold for a farthing? and one of them shall not fall on the ground without your Father.

30 But the very hairs of your head are all numbered.

31 Fear ye not therefore, ye are of more value than many sparrows.

Confessing Christ before Men

32 Whosoever therefore shall confess me before men, him will I confess also before my Father which is in heaven.

33 But whosoever shall deny me before men, him will I also deny before my Father which is in heaven.

The Cost of Discipleship

34 Think not that I am come to send peace on earth: I came not to send peace, but a sword.

35 For I am come to set a man at variance against his father, and the daughter against her mother, and the daughter-in-law against her mother-in-law.

36 And a man's foes shall be they of his own household.

37 He that loveth father or mother more than me is not worthy of me: and he that loveth son or daughter more than me is not worthy of me.

38 And he that taketh not his cross, and followeth after me, is not worthy of me.

39 He that findeth his life shall lose it: and he that loseth his life for my sake shall find it.

Rewards for Service

40 He that receiveth you receiveth me, and he that receiveth me receiveth him that sent me.

41 He that receiveth a prophet in the name of a prophet shall receive a prophet's reward; and he that receiveth a righteous man in the name of a righteous man shall receive a righteous man's reward.

42 And whosoever shall give to drink unto one of these little ones a cup of cold water only in the name of a disciple, verily I say unto you, he shall in no wise lose his reward.

CHAPTER 11

Messengers from John the Baptist

1 And it came to pass, when Jesus had made an end of commanding his twelve disciples, he departed thence to teach and to preach in their cities.

2 Now when John had heard in the prison

Cross references (center column)

20 Acts 4:8; 6:10
21 Matt. 10:35, 36; Luke 21:16
22 Matt. 24:13; Mark 13:13; Luke 21:17
23 Acts 8:1
24 Luke 6:40; John 13:16; 15:20
25 Mark 3:22; Luke 11:15; John 8:48, 52
26 Mark 4:22; Luke 8:17; 12:2, 3
28 Isa. 8:12, 13; Luke 12:4; 1Pet. 3:14
30 Luke 21:18; Acts 27:34
32 Luke 12:8; Rom. 10:9, 10; Rev. 3:5
33 Mark 8:38; Luke 9:26; 2Tim. 2:12
34 Luke 12:49, 51-53
35 Mic. 7:6
36 Ps. 41:9; 55:13; Mic. 7:6; John 13:18
38 Matt. 16:24; Mark 8:34; Luke 9:23; 14:27
39 Matt. 16:25; Luke 17:33; John 12:25
41 1Kgs. 17:10; 18:4; 2Kgs. 4:8
42 Mark 9:41

10:23–24 Son of man. Some have claimed that this phrase refers to a forerunner of the yet-coming Messiah. Such a claim contradicts all the statements made earlier in the Gospel of Matthew concerning who Jesus is—the Messiah, Himself. With the context being the Tribulation, the second coming of Christ is in view here.

10:41–42 in the name of a prophet (i.e., "as a prophet"). The meaning of this statement is that those who are

not prophets themselves may share in the labor and reward of the prophets by willingly supporting the ministry of the prophets. "One of these little ones" is a reference to the fact that even the smallest service done to the most insignificant of Christ's servants shall be rewarded by the Lord Himself.

11:1–7 This imprisonment has already been mentioned in Matthew 4:12, but the circumstances leading up to it

the works of Christ, he sent two of his disciples,

3 And said unto him, Art thou he that should come, or do we look for another?

4 Jesus answered and said unto them, Go and shew John again those things which ye do hear and see:

5 The blind receive their sight, and the lame walk, the lepers are cleansed, and the deaf hear, the dead are raised up, and the poor have the gospel preached to them.

6 And blessed is he, whosoever shall not be offended in me.

7 And as they departed, Jesus began to say unto the multitudes concerning John, What went ye out into the wilderness to see? A reed shaken with the wind?

8 But what went ye out for to see? A man clothed in soft raiment? behold, they that wear soft clothing are in kings' houses.

9 But what went ye out for to see? A prophet? yea, I say unto you, and more than a prophet.

10 For this is he, of whom it is written, Behold, I send my messenger before thy face, which shall prepare thy way before thee.

11 Verily I say unto you, Among them that are born of women there hath not risen a greater than John the Baptist: notwithstanding he that is least in the kingdom of heaven is greater than he.

12 And from the days of John the Baptist until now the kingdom of heaven suffereth violence, and the violent take it by force.

13 For all the prophets and the law prophesied until John.

14 And if ye will receive it, this is Elias, which was for to come.

15 He that hath ears to hear, let him hear.

16 But whereunto shall I liken this generation? It is like unto children sitting in the markets, and calling unto their fellows,

17 And saying, We have piped unto you, and ye have not danced; we have mourned unto you, and ye have not lamented.

18 For John came neither eating nor drinking, and they say, He hath a devil.

19 The Son of man came eating and drinking, and they say, Behold a man gluttonous, and a winebibber, a friend of publicans and sinners. But wisdom is justified of her children.

Jesus Condemns Certain Cities

20 Then began he to upbraid the cities wherein most of his mighty works were done, because they repented not:

21 Woe unto thee, Chorazin! woe unto thee, Bethsaida! for if the mighty works, which were done in you, had been done in Tyre and Sidon, they would have repented long ago in sackcloth and ashes.

22 But I say unto you, It shall be more tolerable for Tyre and Sidon at the day of judgment, than for you.

23 And thou, Capernaum, which art exalted unto heaven, shalt be brought down to hell: for if the mighty works, which have been done in thee, had been done in Sodom, it would have remained until this day.

24 But I say unto you, That it shall be more tolerable for the land of Sodom, in the day of judgment, than for thee.

Cross references (center column)

3 Gen. 49:10; Num. 24:17; Dan. 9:24; John 6:14

5 Isa. 29:18; Luke 4:18; James 2:5

6 Isa. 8:14, 15; 13:57; 24:10; 26:31; Gal. 5:11; 1Pet. 2:8

7 Luke 7:24; Eph. 4:14

9 Matt. 14:5; 21:26; Luke 1:76; 7:26

10 Mal. 3:1; Mark 1:2; Luke 1:76; 7:27

12 Luke 16:16

13 Mal. 4:6

14 Mal. 4:5; Matt. 17:12; Luke 1:17

15 Matt. 13:9; Luke 8:8; Rev. 2:7, 11, 17, 29; 3:6, 13, 22

16 Luke 7:31

19 Luke 7:35

20 Luke 10:13-16

21 Jon. 3:7, 8

23 Isa. 14:13; Lam. 2:1

24 Matt. 10:15

---

are not described in detail until 14:3–12, where the manner of John's death is also recounted. "The works of Christ" refer to His miracles. "He that should come" refers to the predicted Messiah of Old Testament prophecy whose coming had already been proclaimed by John. The blind receiving their sight is an allusion to Isaiah 35:5 and 61:1, where it is stated that this will be one of the works performed by the Messiah. Hence, Jesus was clearly vindicating His messiahship to John, who may have begun to wonder about his own circumstances. (For a parallel account to verses 2–19, see Luke 7:18–35.)

11:8–11 But what went ye out for to see? A prophet? . . . more. Actually, the Greek (*perissoteron*) is more emphatic, "much more." The quotation in verse 10 is from Malachi 3:1. John was recognized as the foreordained messenger of the Savior and, technically, the last of the Old Testament prophets. The weakest believer who has the knowledge of the glory of God in the face of the risen Christ, will be in a more privileged position than the greatest of the Old Testament prophets. "Them that are born of women" means mortal men, the idea being that the greatest of all in this life cannot be compared with the glory of the life to come.

11:12–15 the kingdom of heaven suffereth violence (Gr. *biazomai*). The meaning of this saying, and the connection of verses 12–14 with preceding and following contexts, indicates that John became the culminating point of Old Testament witness. Jesus' statement that "this is Elias [Elijah]" indicates the ministry predicted by Malachi 4:5–6.

11:20–24 The denunciation of Galilean cities that follows is recorded also by Luke, but in a different context (see Luke 10:13–16). "Shalt be brought down to hell" is an allusion to Isaiah 14:13, 15, where it is spoken of the king of Babylon with a symbolic reference to Satan himself.

Jesus Praises God

25 At that time Jesus answered and said, I thank thee, O Father, Lord of heaven and earth, because thou hast hid these things from the wise and prudent, and hast revealed them unto babes.

26 Even so, Father: for so it seemed good in thy sight.

27 All things are delivered unto me of my Father: and no man knoweth the Son, but the Father; neither knoweth any man the Father, save the Son, and he to whomsoever the Son will reveal him.

Rest in Jesus

28 Come unto me, all ye that labour and are heavy laden, and I will give you rest.

29 Take my yoke upon you, and learn of me; for I am meek and lowly in heart: and ye shall find rest unto your souls.

30 For my yoke is easy, and my burden is light.

CHAPTER 12
Jesus Is Lord over the Sabbath Day

1 At that time Jesus went on the sabbath day through the corn; and his disciples were an hungred, and began to pluck the ears of corn, and to eat.

2 But when the Pharisees saw it, they said unto him, Behold, thy disciples do that which is not lawful to do upon the sabbath day.

3 But he said unto them, Have ye not read what David did, when he was an hungred, and they that were with him;

4 How he entered into the house of God, and did eat the shewbread, which was not lawful for him to eat, neither for them which were with him, but only for the priests?

5 Or have ye not read in the law, how that on the sabbath days the priests in the temple profane the sabbath, and are blameless?

6 But I say unto you, That in this place is one greater than the temple.

7 But if ye had known what this meaneth, I will have mercy, and not sacrifice, ye would not have condemned the guiltless.

8 For the Son of man is Lord even of the sabbath day.

Jesus Heals a Man with a Withered Hand

9 And when he was departed thence, he went into their synagogue:

10 And, behold, there was a man which had

25 Ps. 8:2;
Matt. 16:17;
Luke 10:21;
1Cor. 1:19,
27; 2:8;
2Cor. 3:14

27 Matt.
28:18; Luke
10:22; John
1:18; 3:35;
6:46; 10:15;
13:3; 17:2;
1Cor. 15:27

29 Jer. 6:16;
Zech. 9:9;
John 13:15

30 1John 5:3

1 Deut.
23:25; Mark
2:23; Luke
6:1

3 1Sam.
21:6

4 Ex. 25:30;
29:32, 33;
Lev. 8:31;
24:5, 9

5 Num. 28:9;
John 7:22

6 2Chr. 6:18;
Mal. 3:1

7 Hos. 6:6;
Mic. 6:6-8;
Matt. 9:13

9 Mark 3:1;
Luke 6:6

10 Luke
13:14; 14:3;
John 9:16

11 Ex. 23:4,
5; Deut. 22:4

14 Mark 3:6;
Luke 6:11;
John 5:18;
10:39; 11:53

15 Matt.
10:23; 19:2;
Mark 3:7

16 Matt.
9:30

18 Isa. 42:1;
Matt. 3:17;
17:5

22 Matt.
9:32; Mark
3:11; Luke
11:14

24 Matt.
9:34; Mark
3:22; Luke
11:15

25 Matt. 9:4;
John 2:25;
Rev. 2:23

28 Dan.
2:44; 7:14;
Luke 1:33;
11:20; 17:20,
21

his hand withered. And they asked him, saying, Is it lawful to heal on the sabbath days? that they might accuse him.

11 And he said unto them, What man shall there be among you, that shall have one sheep, and if it fall into a pit on the sabbath day, will he not lay hold on it, and lift it out?

12 How much then is a man better than a sheep? Wherefore it is lawful to do well on the sabbath days.

13 Then saith he to the man, Stretch forth thine hand. And he stretched it forth; and it was restored whole, like as the other.

14 Then the Pharisees went out, and held a council against him, how they might destroy him.

God's Servant

15 But when Jesus knew it, he withdrew himself from thence: and great multitudes followed him, and he healed them all;

16 And charged them that they should not make him known:

17 That it might be fulfilled which was spoken by Esaias the prophet, saying,

18 Behold my servant, whom I have chosen; my beloved, in whom my soul is well pleased: I will put my spirit upon him, and he shall shew judgment to the Gentiles.

19 He shall not strive, nor cry; neither shall any man hear his voice in the streets.

20 A bruised reed shall he not break, and smoking flax shall he not quench, till he send forth judgment unto victory.

21 And in his name shall the Gentiles trust.

The Power of God over the Devil

22 Then was brought unto him one possessed with a devil, blind, and dumb: and he healed him, insomuch that the blind and dumb both spake and saw.

23 And all the people were amazed, and said, Is not this the son of David?

24 But when the Pharisees heard it, they said, This fellow doth not cast out devils, but by Beelzebub the prince of the devils.

25 And Jesus knew their thoughts, and said unto them, Every kingdom divided against itself is brought to desolation; and every city or house divided against itself shall not stand:

26 And if Satan cast out Satan, he is divided against himself; how shall then his kingdom stand?

27 And if I by Beelzebub cast out devils, by whom do your children cast them out? therefore they shall be your judges.

28 But if I cast out devils by the Spirit of

God, then the kingdom of God is come unto you.

29 Or else how can one enter into a strong man's house, and spoil his goods, except he first bind the strong man? and then he will spoil his house.

30 He that is not with me is against me; and he that gathereth not with me scattereth abroad.

Blasphemy against the Holy Spirit

31 Wherefore I say unto you, All manner of sin and blasphemy shall be forgiven unto men: but the blasphemy against the Holy Ghost shall not be forgiven unto men.

32 And whosoever speaketh a word against the Son of man, it shall be forgiven him: but whosoever speaketh against the Holy Ghost, it shall not be forgiven him, neither in this world, neither in the world to come.

A Tree Is Known by Its Fruit

33 Either make the tree good, and his fruit good; or else make the tree corrupt, and his fruit corrupt: for the tree is known by his fruit.

34 O generation of vipers, how can ye, being evil, speak good things? for out of the abundance of the heart the mouth speaketh.

35 A good man out of the good treasure of the heart bringeth forth good things: and an evil man out of the evil treasure bringeth forth evil things.

36 But I say unto you, That every idle word that men shall speak, they shall give account thereof in the day of judgment.

37 For by thy words thou shalt be justified, and by thy words thou shalt be condemned.

The Desire for Signs Is Rebuked

38 Then certain of the scribes and of the Pharisees answered, saying, Master, we would see a sign from thee.

39 But he answered and said unto them, An

29 Isa. 49:24; Luke 11:21-23

31 Mark 3:28; Luke 12:10; Acts 7:51; Heb. 6:4-6; 10:26, 29; 1John 5:16

32 Matt. 11:19; 13:55; John 7:12, 52; 1Tim. 1:13

33 Matt. 7:17; Luke 6:43, 44

34 Matt. 3:7; 23:33; Luke 6:45

38 Mark 8:11; Luke 11:16, 29; John 2:18; 1Cor. 1:22

39 Isa. 57:3; Matt. 16:4; Mark 8:38; John 4:48

40 Jon. 1:17

41 Jer. 3:11; Ezek. 16:51, 52; Jon. 3:5; Luke 11:32; Rom. 2:27

42 1Kgs. 10:1; 2Chr. 9:1; Luke 11:31

43 Job 1:7; Luke 11:24; 1Pet. 5:8

45 Heb. 6:4; 10:26; 2Pet. 2:20-22

46 Mark 3:31; 6:3; Luke 8:19-21; John 2:12; 7:3, 5

evil and adulterous generation seeketh after a sign; and there shall no sign be given to it, but the sign of the prophet Jonas:

40 For as Jonas was three days and three nights in the whale's belly; so shall the Son of man be three days and three nights in the heart of the earth.

41 The men of Nineveh shall rise in judgment with this generation, and shall condemn it: because they repented at the preaching of Jonas; and, behold, a greater than Jonas is here.

42 The queen of the south shall rise up in the judgment with this generation, and shall condemn it: for she came from the uttermost parts of the earth to hear the wisdom of Solomon; and, behold, a greater than Solomon is here.

The Unclean Spirit Returns

43 When the unclean spirit is gone out of a man, he walketh through dry places, seeking rest, and findeth none.

44 Then he saith, I will return into my house from whence I came out; and when he is come, he findeth it empty, swept, and garnished.

45 Then goeth he, and taketh with himself seven other spirits more wicked than himself, and they enter in and dwell there: and the last state of that man is worse than the first. Even so shall it be also unto this wicked generation.

The True Family of Jesus

46 While he yet talked to the people, behold, *his* mother and his brethren stood without, desiring to speak with him.

47 Then one said unto him, Behold, thy mother and thy brethren stand without, desiring to speak with thee.

48 But he answered and said unto him that told him, Who is my mother? and who are my brethren?

49 And he stretched forth his hand toward

12:28–30 the kingdom of God. Matthew's usual expression is the "kingdom of heaven" (3:2). Some have attempted to distinguish between the meaning of the two, but they likely mean the same thing. "Is come unto you" (lit., "has come upon you") affirms that the Lord's power over demons was enough evidence to prove that He was the Messiah. Hence the phrase, "spoil his goods" refers to Satan being defeated or ruined by the capture of souls from him by Christ.

12:39–42 the prophet Jonas. Jesus uses Jonah's bur-

ial in the fish for "three days and three nights" as an illustration of the three days and three nights that Christ would spend in the grave Himself. The Greek word *ketos*, translated "whale's belly," actually means "a great sea creature," not necessarily a whale. The Old Testament references are to a "great fish" (Jonah 1:17). Notice that the Lord referred to this incident as a historical reality, linking it to the people of Nineveh, the Queen of Sheba, Solomon, and Christ Himself.

his disciples, and said, Behold my mother and my brethren!

50 For whosoever shall do the will of my Father which is in heaven, the same is my brother, and sister, and mother.

CHAPTER 13
The Parable of the Sower

1 The same day went Jesus out of the house, and sat by the sea side.

2 And great multitudes were gathered together unto him, so that he went into a ship, and sat; and the whole multitude stood on the shore.

3 And he spake many things unto them in parables, saying, Behold, a sower went forth to sow;

4 And when he sowed, some seeds fell by the way side, and the fowls came and devoured them up:

5 Some fell upon stony places, where they had not much earth: and forthwith they sprung up, because they had no deepness of earth:

6 And when the sun was up, they were scorched; and because they had no root, they withered away.

7 And some fell among thorns; and the thorns sprung up, and choked them:

8 But other fell into good ground, and brought forth fruit, some an hundredfold, some sixtyfold, some thirtyfold.

9 Who hath ears to hear, let him hear.

The Reason for Parables

10 And the disciples came, and said unto him, Why speakest thou unto them in parables?

11 He answered and said unto them, Because it is given unto you to know the mysteries of the kingdom of heaven, but to them it is not given.

12 For whosoever hath, to him shall be

50 John 15:14; Gal. 5:6; 6:15; Col. 3:11; Heb. 2:11

1 Mark 4:1
2 Luke 5:3; 8:4
3 Luke 8:5
8 Gen. 26:12
11 Matt. 11:25; 16:17; Mark 4:11; 1Cor. 2:10; 1John 2:27
12 Matt. 25:29; Mark 4:25; Luke 8:18; 19:26
14 Isa. 6:9; Ezek. 12:2; Mark 4:12; Luke 8:10; John 12:40; Acts 28:26, 27; Rom. 11:8; 2Cor. 3:14, 15
15 Heb. 5:11
16 Matt. 16:17; Luke 10:23, 24; John 20:29
17 Heb. 11:13; 1Pet. 1:10, 11
18 Mark 4:14; Luke 8:11
20 Isa. 58:2; Ezek. 33:31, 32; John 5:35
21 Matt. 11:6; 2Tim. 1:15
22 Jer. 4:3; Matt. 19:23; Mark 10:23; Luke 18:24; 1Tim. 6:9; 2Tim. 4:10

given, and he shall have more abundance: but whosoever hath not, from him shall be taken away even that he hath.

13 Therefore speak I to them in parables: because they seeing see not; and hearing they hear not, neither do they understand.

14 And in them is fulfilled the prophecy of Esaias, which saith, By hearing ye shall hear, and shall not understand; and seeing ye shall see, and shall not perceive:

15 For this people's heart is waxed gross, and their ears are dull of hearing, and their eyes they have closed; lest at any time they should see with their eyes, and hear with their ears, and should understand with their heart, and should be converted, and I should heal them.

16 But blessed are your eyes, for they see: and your ears, for they hear.

17 For verily I say unto you, That many prophets and righteous men have desired to see those things which ye see, and have not seen them; and to hear those things which ye hear, and have not heard them.

The Parable of the Sower Explained

18 Hear ye therefore the parable of the sower.

19 When any one heareth the word of the kingdom, and understandeth it not, then cometh the wicked one, and catcheth away that which was sown in his heart. This is he which received seed by the way side.

20 But he that received the seed into stony places, the same is he that heareth the word, and anon with joy receiveth it;

21 Yet hath he not root in himself, but dureth for a while: for when tribulation or persecution ariseth because of the word, by and by he is offended.

22 He also that received seed among the thorns is he that heareth the word; and the care of this world, and the deceitfulness of

---

13:1–3 This is the turning point in the Gospel of Matthew. Already sensing His impending rejection, Jesus now expresses the mysteries of the kingdom that will explain the function of the kingdom between the two advents of Christ. His early ministry involved a proclamation of the spiritual principles of the kingdom. To bring in a political kingdom before men were redeemed would be a travesty. Therefore, an interval is now announced between the Messiah's original appearance and His final return. That interval will include the Church Age and the Tribulation. During the Church Age, believers are citizens of the kingdom that is "within" them (Luke 17:21), while they await the establishment of the Millennial Kingdom at the second coming of Christ.

13:11–13 Jesus explained that only the disciples are to know the "mysteries of the kingdom of heaven." A "mystery" in the Bible implies a sacred secret into which one must be initiated in order to understand it. The mystery revealed would be the new form of the kingdom during the interval between the first and second advents (cf. Rom. 16:25–26).

13:14 the prophecy of Esaias. This description of people in the Last Days addresses the fulfillment of Isaiah 6:9–10.

The Kingdom of God

By Stanley D. Toussaint

The kingdom of God is a theme that embraces the entire Bible. It includes the Lord's eternal sovereign reign over all creation (Ps. 10:16; 29:10; 103:19; Dan. 4:35) and the temporal and local reign of God known as His theocratic kingdom.

God's earthly theocratic kingdom began with the creation of Adam and Eve and the authority God delegated to them (Gen. 1:26–28). They were to reign over the earth under the authority of God even after the Fall. However, because of Adam's sin God's reign on earth over an earthly kingdom was brought to an abrupt halt.

From Adam to Moses, God reigned over the world through various agencies, but not through a theocratic kingdom on this earth. All of this changed at Mount Sinai, where God entered into a covenant relationship with Israel (formalized in Ex. 24:1–8), and that nation became God's kingdom on earth with the land of Canaan as its manifest destiny. For the first time, the word "kingdom" is used of God's kingdom in the Bible (cf. Ex. 19:4–6). God mediated His rule over Israel first through Moses, then Joshua and then through the judges. Eventually, the people demanded a king, a request God granted (1 Sam. 8:9–22). The first king, Saul, proved to be disobedient, and God terminated that dynasty. God then chose David to be king and gave him promises and a covenant in which He committed to give David an eternal throne, kingdom, and house (2 Sam. 7:12–16; Ps. 89:3–4, 28–37). The glory of the Davidic house reached its apex with David's son and heir, Solomon.

> *With John we pray, "Even so, come, Lord Jesus."*

After Solomon's son, Rehoboam, inherited the throne, the northern tribes, under the leadership of Jeroboam, seceded from the kingdom of Rehoboam. Only Judah remained as the nation over which the line of David ruled. The Northern Kingdom failed spiritually and was deported to Assyria in 722 B.C. Tiny Judah continued to be God's theocratic kingdom in spite of the apostasy of so many of its kings and the increasingly rampant idolatry practiced there. Finally, the painful, tragic, and deliberate departure of God's glory from His chosen people took place (Ezek. 10:4, 18–19; 11:23), and Jerusalem and the temple were destroyed in 586 B.C. God's theocracy on earth was terminated. The "times of the Gentiles" had begun (Luke 21:24).

The New Testament opens with the message of John the Baptist, Jesus Christ, and the twelve apostles that electrified Israel—"the kingdom of God (heaven) has drawn near!" Israel was called upon to respond in repentance in preparation for its arrival. Of course, the kingdom was to come by way of Christ's crucifixion. Because of Israel's rejection the kingdom still has not come and is yet future. God is today ruling over His universe, and He is calling out people for Himself, but the kingdom is not present in any form.

But one day there will be a massive turning to God by Israel (Zech. 12:10–14; Matt. 23:39; Rom. 11:25–27). Then the Lord will restore Israel (cf. Acts 1:6). The kingdom will come, first, in the form of the millennial reign of Christ and, finally, in its eternal form. When the Lord returns to reign, there will come to pass the shout of the heavenly host (see Rev. 11:15). And so with John we pray, "Even so, come, Lord Jesus" (Rev. 22:20).

riches, choke the word, and he becometh unfruitful.

23 But he that received seed into the good ground is he that heareth the word, and understandeth it; which also beareth fruit, and bringeth forth, some an hundredfold some sixty, some thirty.

The Wheat and Tares

24 Another parable put he forth unto them, saying, The kingdom of heaven is likened unto a man which sowed good seed in his field:

25 But while men slept, his enemy came and sowed tares among the wheat, and went his way.

26 But when the blade was sprung up, and brought forth fruit, then appeared the tares also.

27 So the servants of the householder came and said unto him, Sir, didst not thou sow good seed in thy field? from whence then hath it tares?

28 He said unto them, An enemy hath done this. The servants said unto him, Wilt thou then that we go and gather them up?

29 But he said, Nay; lest while ye gather up the tares, ye root up also the wheat with them.

30 Let both grow together until the harvest: and in the time of harvest I will say to the reapers, Gather ye together first the tares, and bind them in bundles to burn them: but gather the wheat into my barn.

A Mustard Seed

31 Another parable put he forth unto them, saying, The kingdom of heaven is like to a grain of mustard seed, which a man took, and sowed in his field:

32 Which indeed is the least of all seeds: but when it is grown, it is the greatest among herbs, and becometh a tree, so that

the birds of the air come and lodge in the branches thereof.

Leaven

33 Another parable spake he unto them; The kingdom of heaven is like unto leaven, which a woman took, and hid in three measures of meal, till the whole was leavened.

Parables Explained

34 All these things spake Jesus unto the multitude in parables; and without a parable spake he not unto them:

35 That it might be fulfilled which was spoken by the prophet, saying, I will open my mouth in parables; I will utter things which have been kept secret from the foundation of the world.

36 Then Jesus sent the multitude away, and went into the house: and his disciples came unto him, saying, Declare unto us the parable of the tares of the field.

37 He answered and said unto them, He that soweth the good seed is the Son of man;

38 The field is the world; the good seed are the children of the kingdom; but the tares are the children of the wicked one;

39 The enemy that sowed them is the devil; the harvest is the end of the world; and the reapers are the angels.

40 As therefore the tares are gathered and burned in the fire; so shall it be in the end of this world.

41 The Son of man shall send forth his angels, and they shall gather out of his kingdom all things that offend, and them which do iniquity;

42 And shall cast them into a furnace of fire: there shall be wailing and gnashing of teeth.

43 Then shall the righteous shine forth as the sun in the kingdom of their Father. Who hath ears to hear, let him hear.

Center column references:

30 Matt. 3:12
31 Isa. 2:2, 3; Mic. 4:1; Mark 4:30-32; Luke 13:18, 19
33 Luke 13:20, 21
34 Mark 4:33, 34
35 Ps. 78:2; Rom. 16:25, 26; 1Cor. 2:7; Eph. 3:9; Col. 1:26
38 Gen. 3:15; Matt. 24:14; 28:19; Mark 16:15, 20; Luke 24:47; John 8:44; Acts 13:10; Rom. 10:18; Col. 1:6; 1John 3:8
39 Joel 3:13; Rev. 14:15
41 Matt. 18:7; 2Pet. 2:1, 2
42 Matt. 3:12; 8:12; 13:50; Rev. 19:20; 20:10
43 Dan. 12:3; Matt. 13:9; 1Cor. 15:42, 43, 58

13:24–27 a man which sowed . . . seed. This parable serves as a warning to the laborers in the field (the world, v. 38). During the national form of the kingdom in the Old Testament, citizens of Israel could be easily recognized. During the Church Age converts will be made from all over the world and received upon their profession of faith. Thus, it will be easier for counterfeits to slip in. The enemy is Satan and the "tares" (Gr. *zizanion*, "darnel") are these false converts. Darnel is a weed that resembles wheat but does not come to fruition. The good seed that "sprung up, and brought forth fruit" emphasizes that true converts live fruitful lives. By contrast, false converts produce no lasting fruit.

13:33–35 kingdom of heaven. This is the spiritual form of the kingdom. Leaven is a lump of old dough in a state of fermentation, which makes the bread dough rise. In Scripture, leaven is virtually always used as a symbol of evil (cf. Matt. 16:6–12; Mark 8:15; Gal. 5:9). The leaven here seems to refer to the false doctrine that lost souls will attempt to introduce and spread among others (cf. the note on Luke 13:21).

A Buried Treasure

44 Again, the kingdom of heaven is like unto treasure hid in a field; the which when a man hath found, he hideth, and for joy thereof goeth and selleth all that he hath, and buyeth that field.

The Pearl of Great Price

45 Again, the kingdom of heaven is like unto a merchant man, seeking goodly pearls:
46 Who, when he had found one pearl of great price, went and sold all that he had, and bought it.

A Large Net

47 Again, the kingdom of heaven is like unto a net, that was cast into the sea, and gathered of every kind:
48 Which, when it was full, they drew to shore, and sat down, and gathered the good into vessels, but cast the bad away.
49 So shall it be at the end of the world: the angels shall come forth, and sever the wicked from among the just,
50 And shall cast them into the furnace of fire: there shall be wailing and gnashing of teeth.

The Householder's Treasure

51 Jesus saith unto them, Have ye understood all these things? They say unto him, Yea, Lord.
52 Then said he unto them, Therefore every scribe which is instructed unto the kingdom of heaven is like unto a man that is an householder, which bringeth forth out of his treasure things new and old.

Jesus Rejected at Nazareth

53 And it came to pass, *that* when Jesus had finished these parables, he departed thence.
54 And when he was come into his own country, he taught them in their synagogue, insomuch that they were astonished, and said, Whence hath this *man* this wisdom, and *these* mighty works?
55 Is not this the carpenter's son? is not his mother called Mary? and his brethren, James, and Joses, and Simon, and Judas?
56 And his sisters, are they not all with us?

Whence then hath this *man* all these things?
57 And they were offended in him. But Jesus said unto them, A prophet is not without honour, save in his own country, and in his own house.
58 And he did not many mighty works there because of their unbelief.

Chapter 14
The Death of John the Baptist

1 At that time Herod the tetrarch heard of the fame of Jesus,
2 And said unto his servants, This is John the Baptist; he is risen from the dead; and therefore mighty works do shew forth themselves in him.
3 For Herod had laid hold on John, and bound him, and put *him* in prison for Herodias' sake, his brother Philip's wife.
4 For John said unto him, It is not lawful for thee to have her.
5 And when he would have put him to death, he feared the multitude, because they counted him as a prophet.
6 But when Herod's birthday was kept, the daughter of Herodias danced before them, and pleased Herod.
7 Whereupon he promised with an oath to give her whatsoever she would ask.
8 And she, being before instructed of her mother, said, Give me here John Baptist's head in a charger.
9 And the king was sorry: nevertheless for the oath's sake, and them which sat with him at meat, he commanded *it* to be given *her*.
10 And he sent, and beheaded John in the prison.
11 And his head was brought in a charger, and given to the damsel: and she brought *it* to her mother.
12 And his disciples came, and took up the body, and buried it, and went and told Jesus.

Jesus Feeds the Five Thousand

13 When Jesus heard *of it,* he departed thence by ship into a desert place apart: and when the people had heard *thereof,* they followed him on foot out of the cities.

Cross references (center column)

44 Isa. 55:1; Phil. 3:7, 8; Rev. 3:18
46 Prov. 2:4; 3:14, 15; 8:10, 19
47 Matt. 22:10
49 Matt. 25:32
50 Matt. 13:42
52 Song 7:13
54 Matt. 2:23; Mark 6:1; Luke 4:16, 23
55 Isa. 49:7; Matt. 12:46; Mark 6:3; 15:40; Luke 3:23; John 6:42
57 Matt. 11:6; Mark 6:3, 4; Luke 4:24; John 4:44
58 Mark 6:5, 6
1 Mark 6:14; Luke 9:7
3 Mark 6:17; Luke 3:19, 20
4 Lev. 18:16; 20:21
5 Matt. 21:26; Luke 20:6
13 Matt. 10:23; 12:15; Mark 6:32; Luke 9:10; John 6:1, 2

14:1–2 The occasion of John's death signaled a time for Jesus to retreat in order to prevent His own death before the appointed time. "Herod the tetrarch" is Herod Antipas, the son of Herod the Great. His obvious ignorance of Jesus prior to this time suggests how little he knew of his subjects, and is probably due to his self-indulgent, luxurious lifestyle that afforded little contact with the average person. His guilty conscience over John's death caused him to think Jesus was John the Baptist "risen from the dead."

14 And Jesus went forth, and saw a great multitude, and was moved with compassion toward them, and he healed their sick.

15 And when it was evening, his disciples came to him, saying, This is a desert place, and the time is now past; send the multitude away, that they may go into the villages, and buy themselves victuals.

16 But Jesus said unto them, They need not depart; give ye them to eat.

17 And they say unto him, We have here but five loaves, and two fishes.

18 He said, Bring them hither to me.

19 And he commanded the multitude to sit down on the grass, and took the five loaves, and the two fishes, and looking up to heaven, he blessed, and brake, and gave the loaves to *his* disciples, and the disciples to the multitude.

20 And they did all eat, and were filled: and they took up of the fragments that remained twelve baskets full.

21 And they that had eaten were about five thousand men, beside women and children.

Walking on Water

22 And straightway Jesus constrained his disciples to get into a ship, and to go before him unto the other side, while he sent the multitudes away.

23 And when he had sent the multitudes away, he went up into a mountain apart to pray: and when the evening was come, he was there alone.

24 But the ship was now in the midst of the sea, tossed with waves: for the wind was contrary.

25 And in the fourth watch of the night Jesus went unto them, walking on the sea.

26 And when the disciples saw him walking on the sea, they were troubled, saying, It is a spirit; and they cried out for fear.

27 But straightway Jesus spake unto them, saying, Be of good cheer; it is I; be not afraid.

28 And Peter answered him and said, Lord, if it be thou, bid me come unto thee on the water.

29 And he said, Come. And when Peter was come down out of the ship, he walked on the water, to go to Jesus.

30 But when he saw the wind boisterous, he was afraid; and beginning to sink, he cried, saying, Lord, save me.

31 And immediately Jesus stretched forth *his* hand, and caught him, and said unto him, O thou of little faith, wherefore didst thou doubt?

32 And when they were come into the ship, the wind ceased.

33 Then they that were in the ship came and worshipped him, saying, Of a truth thou art the Son of God.

Jesus Heals the Sick at Gennesaret

34 And when they were gone over, they came into the land of Gennesaret.

35 And when the men of that place had knowledge of him, they sent out into all that country round about, and brought unto him all that were diseased;

36 And besought him that they might only touch the hem of his garment: and as many as touched were made perfectly whole.

CHAPTER 15
God's Command or Man's Tradition?

1 Then came to Jesus scribes and Pharisees, which were of Jerusalem, saying,

2 Why do thy disciples transgress the tradition of the elders? for they wash not their hands when they eat bread.

3 But he answered and said unto them, Why do ye also transgress the commandment of God by your tradition?

4 For God commanded, saying, Honour thy father and mother: and, He that curseth father or mother, let him die the death.

5 But ye say, Whosoever shall say to his father or his mother, It is a gift, by whatsoever thou mightest be profited by me;

6 And honour not his father or his mother, he shall be free. Thus have ye made the commandment of God of none effect by your tradition.

7 Ye hypocrites, well did Esaias prophesy of you, saying,

8 This people draweth nigh unto me with their mouth, and honoureth me with their lips; but their heart is far from me.

9 But in vain they do worship me, teaching for doctrines the commandments of men.

10 And he called the multitude, and said unto them, Hear, and understand:

11 Not that which goeth into the mouth defileth a man; but that which cometh out of the mouth, this defileth a man.

12 Then came his disciples, and said unto him, Knowest thou that the Pharisees were offended, after they heard this saying?

13 But he answered and said, Every plant, which my heavenly Father hath not planted, shall be rooted up.

14 Let them alone: they be blind leaders of

Cross References

14 Matt. 9:36; Mark 6:34

15 Mark 6:35; Luke 9:12; John 6:5

19 Matt. 15:36

23 Mark 6:46; John 6:16

26 Job 9:8

33 Ps. 2:7; Matt. 16:16; 26:63; Mark 1:1; Luke 4:41; John 1:49; 6:69; 11:27; Acts 8:37; Rom. 1:4

34 Mark 6:53

36 Matt. 9:20; Mark 3:10; Luke 6:19; Acts 19:12

1 Mark 7:1

2 Mark 7:5; Col. 2:8

4 Ex. 20:12; 21:17; Lev. 19:3; 20:9; Deut. 5:16; 27:16; Prov. 20:20; 23:22; 30:17; Eph. 6:2

5 Mark 7:11, 12

7 Mark 7:6

8 Isa. 29:13; Ezek. 33:31

9 Isa. 29:13; Col. 2:18-22; Titus 1:14

10 Mark 7:14

11 Acts 10:15; Rom. 14:14, 17, 20; 1Tim. 4:4; Titus 1:15

13 John 15:2; 1Cor. 3:12-15

14 Isa. 9:16; Mal. 2:8; Matt. 23:16; Luke 6:39

the blind. And if the blind lead the blind, both shall fall into the ditch.

15 Then answered Peter and said unto him, Declare unto us this parable.

16 And Jesus said, Are ye also yet without understanding?

17 Do not ye yet understand, that whatsoever entereth in at the mouth goeth into the belly, and is cast out into the draught?

18 But those things which proceed out of the mouth come forth from the heart; and they defile the man.

19 For out of the heart proceed evil thoughts, murders, adulteries, fornications, thefts, false witness, blasphemies:

20 These are the things which defile a man: but to eat with unwashen hands defileth not a man.

The Faith of a Gentile Woman

21 Then Jesus went thence, and departed into the coasts of Tyre and Sidon.

22 And, behold, a woman of Canaan came out of the same coasts, and cried unto him, saying, Have mercy on me, O Lord, *thou* son of David; my daughter is grievously vexed with a devil.

23 But he answered her not a word. And his disciples came and besought him, saying, Send her away; for she crieth after us.

24 But he answered and said, I am not sent but unto the lost sheep of the house of Israel.

25 Then came she and worshipped him, saying, Lord, help me.

26 But he answered and said, It is not meet to take the children's bread, and to cast it to dogs.

27 And she said, Truth, Lord: yet the dogs eat of the crumbs which fall from their masters' table.

28 Then Jesus answered and said unto her, O woman, great is thy faith: be it unto thee even as thou wilt. And her daughter was made whole from that very hour.

Jesus Heals Many

29 And Jesus departed from thence, and came nigh unto the sea of Galilee; and went up into a mountain, and sat down there.

30 And great multitudes came unto him, having with them *those that were* lame, blind,

dumb, maimed, and many others, and cast them down at Jesus' feet; and he healed them:

31 Insomuch that the multitude wondered, when they saw the dumb to speak, the maimed to be whole, the lame to walk, and the blind to see: and they glorified the God of Israel.

Jesus Feeds Four Thousand

32 Then Jesus called his disciples *unto him,* and said, I have compassion on the multitude, because they continue with me now three days, and have nothing to eat: and I will not send them away fasting, lest they faint in the way.

33 And his disciples say unto him, Whence should we have so much bread in the wilderness, as to fill so great a multitude?

34 And Jesus saith unto them, How many loaves have ye? And they said, Seven, and a few little fishes.

35 And he commanded the multitude to sit down on the ground.

36 And he took the seven loaves and the fishes, and gave thanks, and brake *them,* and gave to his disciples, and the disciples to the multitude.

37 And they did all eat, and were filled: and they took up of the broken *meat* that was left seven baskets full.

38 And they that did eat were four thousand men, beside women and children.

39 And he sent away the multitude, and took ship, and came into the coasts of Magdala.

CHAPTER 16
Understanding the Times

1 The Pharisees also with the Sadducees came, and tempting desired him that he would shew them a sign from heaven.

2 He answered and said unto them, When it is evening, ye say, It will be fair weather: for the sky is red.

3 And in the morning, It will be foul weather today: for the sky is red and lowering. O ye hypocrites, ye can discern the face of the sky; but can ye not discern the signs of the times?

4 A wicked and adulterous generation seeketh after a sign; and there shall no sign

Cross-references (center column):
- **15** Mark 7:17
- **16** Matt. 16:9; Mark 7:18
- **17** 1Cor. 6:13
- **18** James 3:6
- **19** Gen. 6:5; 8:21; Prov. 6:14; Jer. 17:9; Mark 7:21
- **21** Mark 7:24
- **24** Matt. 10:5, 6; Acts 3:25, 26; 13:46; Rom. 15:8
- **26** Matt. 7:6; Phil. 3:2
- **29** Matt. 4:18; Mark 7:31
- **30** Isa. 35:5, 6; Matt. 11:5; Luke 7:22
- **32** Mark 8:1
- **33** 2Kgs. 4:43
- **36** 1Sam. 9:13; Matt. 14:19; Luke 22:19
- **39** Mark 8:10
- **1** Matt. 12:38; Mark 8:11; Luke 11:16; 12:54-56; 1Cor. 1:22
- **4** Matt. 12:39

16:1–12 The unbelieving leaders came seeking a "sign from heaven," that is, an outward miraculous manifestation. Notice that miracles alone never save anyone. They serve only to give supernatural authentication to the truth of the message. Instead of another miracle, Jesus points them to the "signs of the times." The "sign of the prophet Jonas [Jonah]" relates to Christ's resurrection (see 12:38–40; John 2:18–22).

be given unto it, but the sign of the prophet Jonas. And he left them, and departed.

Pharisees and Sadducees and Their Influence

5 And when his disciples were come to the other side, they had forgotten to take bread.
6 Then Jesus said unto them, Take heed and beware of the leaven of the Pharisees and of the Sadducees.
7 And they reasoned among themselves, saying, *It is* because we have taken no bread.
8 *Which* when Jesus perceived, he said unto them, O ye of little faith, why reason ye among yourselves, because ye have brought no bread?
9 Do ye not yet understand, neither remember the five loaves of the five thousand, and how many baskets ye took up?
10 Neither the seven loaves of the four thousand, and how many baskets ye took up?
11 How is it that ye do not understand that I spake it not to you concerning bread, that ye should beware of the leaven of the Pharisees and of the Sadducees?
12 Then understood they how that he bade *them* not beware of the leaven of bread, but of the doctrine of the Pharisees and of the Sadducees.

Jesus Is the Messiah

13 When Jesus came into the coasts of Caesarea Philippi, he asked his disciples,

saying, Whom do men say that I the Son of man am?
14 And they said, Some *say that thou art* John the Baptist: some, Elias; and others, Jeremias, or one of the prophets.
15 He saith unto them, But whom say ye that I am?
16 And Simon Peter answered and said, Thou art the Christ, the Son of the living God.
17 And Jesus answered and said unto him, Blessed art thou, Simon Bar-jona: for flesh and blood hath not revealed it unto thee, but my Father which is in heaven.
18 And I say also unto thee, That thou art Peter, and upon this rock I will build my church; and the gates of hell shall not prevail against it.
19 And I will give unto thee the keys of the kingdom of heaven: and whatsoever thou shalt bind on earth shall be bound in heaven: and whatsoever thou shalt loose on earth shall be loosed in heaven.
20 Then charged he his disciples that they should tell no man that he was Jesus the Christ.

Jesus Foretells His Death

21 From that time forth began Jesus to shew unto his disciples, how that he must go unto Jerusalem, and suffer many things of the elders and chief priests and scribes, and be killed, and be raised again the third day.

Cross-references (center column):

5 Mark 8:14
6 Luke 12:1
9 Matt. 14:17; John 6:9
10 Matt. 15:34
13 Mark 8:27; Luke 9:18
14 Matt. 14:2; Luke 9:7-9
16 Matt. 14:33; Mark 8:29; Luke 9:20; John 6:69; 11:27
17 1Cor. 2:10; Gal. 1:16; Eph. 2:8
18 Isa. 38:10; John 1:42; Eph. 2:20; Rev. 21:14
19 Matt. 18:18; John 20:23
20 Matt. 17:9; Mark 8:30; Luke 9:21
21 Matt. 20:17; Mark 8:31; 9:31; 10:33; Luke 9:22; 18:31; 24:6, 7

16:13–17 Caesarea Philippi was a town in the extreme northeast of Galilee, near the head of the Jordan. Verse 14 shows that public opinion placed our Lord on the highest human pedestal by identifying Him with one of the national heroes of the past, such as Elijah, Jeremiah, or, more recently, John the Baptist. Herod himself was a victim of this particular superstition (see 14:2). In Matthew 21:15 we read that Jesus was held in high esteem as a prophet by the people. Simon Peter recognized that Jesus was greater than all of the prophets when he said, "Thou art the Christ, the Son of the living God." He may have been speaking for all the disciples (cf. v. 20), but it is evident that God revealed this truth to him. (For parallel accounts, see Mark 8:27–33; Luke 9:19–21.)

16:18 The Greek word used for "rock" (*petra*) is played against the name *Peter* (Gr. *Petros*). Peter may well be the rock, but he is not the exclusive foundation. (For the twelve-fold foundation of the apostles of the Church, see Eph. 2:20 and Rev. 21:14.) The same words that are spoken to Simon Peter in 16:19 are spoken to all the disciples

in Matthew 18:18. The rock or foundation of the Church is the confession (ultimately, the doctrine) of the apostles who played a foundational role in establishing the Church and writing the New Testament.

16:19–20 the keys of the kingdom. This means that Peter will have the right to enter the kingdom himself, and that preaching the gospel would be the means of opening the kingdom to others. The book of Acts shows us this process at work. The expressions "bound" and "loose" (see also Matt. 18:18) were common in Jewish legal phraseology, meaning to declare forbidden or to declare allowed. Peter and the other disciples were to continue the work of Christ on earth by preaching the gospel and declaring God's will to men.

16:21 From that time forth. From this point onward, the Lord's ministry seeks to prepare His followers for the suffering that awaited Him and that would so disappoint their hopes. The words "killed" and "raised again the third day" clearly indicate the Messiah's awareness of His earthly mission and destiny.

22 Then Peter took him, and began to rebuke him, saying, Be it far from thee, Lord: this shall not be unto thee.

23 But he turned, and said unto Peter, Get thee behind me, Satan: thou art an offence unto me: for thou savourest not the things that be of God, but those that be of men.

Take Up Your Cross

24 Then said Jesus unto his disciples, If any man will come after me, let him deny himself, and take up his cross, and follow me.

25 For whosoever will save his life shall lose it: and whosoever will lose his life for my sake shall find it.

26 For what is a man profited, if he shall gain the whole world, and lose his own soul? or what shall a man give in exchange for his soul?

27 For the Son of man shall come in the glory of his Father with his angels; and then he shall reward every man according to his works.

28 Verily I say unto you, There be some standing here, which shall not taste of death, till they see the Son of man coming in his kingdom.

CHAPTER 17
The Transfiguration

1 And after six days Jesus taketh Peter, James, and John his brother, and bringeth them up into an high mountain apart,

2 And was transfigured before them: and his face did shine as the sun, and his raiment was white as the light.

3 And, behold, there appeared unto them Moses and Elias talking with him.

4 Then answered Peter, and said unto Jesus, Lord, it is good for us to be here: if thou wilt, let us make here three tabernacles; one for thee, and one for Moses, and one for Elias.

5 While he yet spake, behold, a bright cloud overshadowed them: and behold a voice out of the cloud, which said, This is my beloved Son, in whom I am well pleased; hear ye him.

6 And when the disciples heard *it*, they fell on their face, and were sore afraid.

7 And Jesus came and touched them, and said, Arise, and be not afraid.

8 And when they had lifted up their eyes, they saw no man, save Jesus only.

9 And as they came down from the mountain, Jesus charged them, saying, Tell the vision to no man, until the Son of man be risen again from the dead.

10 And his disciples asked him, saying, Why then say the scribes that Elias must first come?

11 And Jesus answered and said unto them, Elias truly shall first come, and restore all things.

12 But I say unto you, That Elias is come already, and they knew him not, but have done unto him whatsoever they listed. Likewise shall also the Son of man suffer of them.

13 Then the disciples understood that he spake unto them of John the Baptist.

Jesus Heals a Boy Possessed with a Demon

14 And when they were come to the multitude, there came to him a *certain* man, kneeling down to him, and saying,

15 Lord, have mercy on my son: for he is lunatic, and sore vexed: for ofttimes he falleth into the fire, and oft into the water.

16 And I brought him to thy disciples, and they could not cure him.

17 Then Jesus answered and said, O faithless and perverse generation, how long shall I be with you? how long shall I suffer you? bring him hither to me.

18 And Jesus rebuked the devil; and he de-

Cross references

23 2Sam. 19:22; Rom. 8:7
24 Matt. 10:38; Mark 8:34; Luke 9:23; 14:27; 2Tim. 3:12
25 Luke 17:33; John 12:25
26 Ps. 49:7, 8
27 Dan. 7:10; Zech. 14:5; Matt. 25:31; 26:64; Mark 8:38; Luke 9:26; Rom. 2:6; 1Pet. 1:17; Jude 1:14; Rev. 2:23; 22:12
28 Mark 9:1; Luke 9:27
1 Mark 9:2; Luke 9:28
5 Matt. 3:17; Mark 1:11; Luke 3:22; 2Pet. 1:17
6 2Pet. 1:18
7 Dan. 8:18; 9:21; 10:10, 18
9 Matt. 16:20; Mark 8:30; 9:9
10 Mal. 4:5; Matt. 11:14; Mark 9:11
11 Mal. 4:6; Luke 1:16
12 Matt. 11:14; 14:3, 10; 16:21; Mark 9:12
13 Matt. 11:14
14 Mark 9:14; Luke 9:37

16:27–28 the Son of man shall come. Verse 27 speaks of the second coming of Christ. In order to encourage His disciples to keep a heavenly perspective, Jesus promises to demonstrate a glimpse of His second coming to some of them. This promise was fulfilled in the Transfiguration (Matt. 17:1–8).

17:1–9 Peter, James, and John represent the "inner circle" of leadership among the disciples (cf. Matt. 26:37; Luke 8:51) and serve here as ample witnesses according to Mosaic Law. Tradition claims this took place at Mount Tabor, but a more probable location would be Mount Her-

mon, near Caesarea Philippi. That Jesus was "transfigured" (Gr. *metamorphoo*) indicates a transformation of essential form, proceeding from within. In Romans 12:2 and 2 Corinthians 3:18, a spiritual transformation of the believer's new nature is explained. The testimony of Peter in 2 Peter 1:17–18 verifies the testimony that this was a real experience, not a vision. (For parallel accounts, see Mark 9:2–13; Luke 9:28–36.)

17:10–13 Elias must first come. The Lord's answer is a quotation from Malachi 4:5–6, where the coming of Elijah is prophesied.

parted out of him: and the child was cured from that very hour.

19 Then came the disciples to Jesus apart, and said, Why could not we cast him out?

20 And Jesus said unto them, Because of your unbelief: for verily I say unto you, If ye have faith as a grain of mustard seed, ye shall say unto this mountain, Remove hence to yonder place; and it shall remove; and nothing shall be impossible unto you.

21 Howbeit this kind goeth not out but by prayer and fasting.

Jesus Prophesies of His Death and Resurrection

22 And while they abode in Galilee, Jesus said unto them, The Son of man shall be betrayed into the hands of men:

23 And they shall kill him, and the third day he shall be raised again. And they were exceeding sorry.

Tax Money in the Mouth of a Fish

24 And when they were come to Capernaum, they that received tribute *money* came to Peter, and said, Doth not your master pay tribute?

25 He saith, Yes. And when he was come into the house, Jesus prevented him, saying, What thinkest thou, Simon? of whom do the kings of the earth take custom or tribute? of their own children, or of strangers?

26 Peter saith unto him, Of strangers. Jesus saith unto him, Then are the children free.

27 Notwithstanding, lest we should offend them, go thou to the sea, and cast an hook, and take up the fish that first cometh up; and when thou hast opened his mouth, thou shalt find a piece of money: that take, and give unto them for me and thee.

CHAPTER 18
Humble Yourself as a Little Child

1 At the same time came the disciples unto Jesus, saying, Who is the greatest in the kingdom of heaven?

2 And Jesus called a little child unto him, and set him in the midst of them,

3 And said, Verily I say unto you, Except ye be converted, and become as little children, ye shall not enter into the kingdom of heaven.

4 Whosoever therefore shall humble himself as this little child, the same is greatest in the kingdom of heaven.

5 And whoso shall receive one such little child in my name receiveth me.

Stumblingblocks

6 But whoso shall offend one of these little ones which believe in me, it were better for him that a millstone were hanged about his neck, and that he were drowned in the depth of the sea.

7 Woe unto the world because of offences! for it must needs be that offences come; but woe to that man by whom the offence cometh!

8 Wherefore if thy hand or thy foot offend thee, cut them off, and cast them from thee: it is better for thee to enter into life halt or maimed, rather than having two hands or two feet to be cast into everlasting fire.

9 And if thine eye offend thee, pluck it out, and cast it from thee: it is better for thee to enter into life with one eye, rather than having two eyes to be cast into hell fire.

Parable of a Lost Sheep

10 Take heed that ye despise not one of these little ones; for I say unto you, That in heaven their angels do always behold the face of my Father which is in heaven.

11 For the Son of man is come to save that which was lost.

12 How think ye? if a man have an hundred sheep, and one of them be gone astray, doth he not leave the ninety and nine, and goeth into the mountains, and seeketh that which is gone astray?

13 And if so be that he find it, verily I say unto you, he rejoiceth more of that sheep, than of the ninety and nine which went not astray.

14 Even so it is not the will of your Father which is in heaven, that one of these little ones should perish.

When One Brother Sins against Another

15 Moreover if thy brother shall trespass against thee, go and tell him his fault between thee and him alone: if he shall hear thee, thou hast gained thy brother.

16 But if he will not hear thee, then take with thee one or two more, that in the mouth of two or three witnesses every word may be established.

17 And if he shall neglect to hear them, tell it unto the church: but if he neglect to hear the church, let him be unto thee as an heathen man and a publican.

18 Verily I say unto you, Whatsoever ye shall bind on earth shall be bound in

---

20 Matt. 21:21; Mark 11:23; Luke 17:6; 1Cor. 12:9; 13:2

22 Matt. 16:21; 20:17; Mark 8:31; 9:30, 31; 10:33; Luke 9:22, 44; 18:31; 24:6, 7

24 Mark 9:33

1 Mark 9:33; Luke 9:46; 22:24

3 Ps. 131:2; Matt. 19:14; Mark 10:14; Luke 18:16; 1Cor. 14:20; 1Pet. 2:2

4 Matt. 20:27; 23:11

5 Matt. 10:42; Luke 9:48

6 Mark 9:42; Luke 17:1, 2

7 Matt. 26:24; Luke 17:1; 1Cor. 11:19

8 Matt. 5:29, 30; Mark 9:43, 45

10 Esth. 1:14; Ps. 34:7; Zech. 13:7; Luke 1:19; Heb. 1:14

11 Luke 9:56; 19:10; John 3:17; 12:47

12 Luke 15:4

15 Lev. 19:17; Luke 17:3; James 5:20; 1Pet. 3:1

16 Deut. 17:6; 19:15; John 8:17; 2Cor. 13:1; Heb. 10:28

17 Rom. 16:17; 1Cor. 5:9; 2Thess. 3:6, 14; 2John 1:10

18 Matt. 16:19; John 20:23; 1Cor. 5:4

heaven: and whatsoever ye shall loose on earth shall be loosed in heaven.

19 Again I say unto you, That if two of you shall agree on earth as touching any thing that they shall ask, it shall be done for them of my Father which is in heaven.

20 For where two or three are gathered together in my name, there am I in the midst of them.

Forgiving Others

21 Then came Peter to him, and said, Lord, how oft shall my brother sin against me, and I forgive him? till seven times?

22 Jesus saith unto him, I say not unto thee, Until seven times: but, Until seventy times seven.

23 Therefore is the kingdom of heaven likened unto a certain king, which would take account of his servants.

24 And when he had begun to reckon, one was brought unto him, which owed him ten thousand talents.

25 But forasmuch as he had not to pay, his lord commanded him to be sold, and his wife, and children, and all that he had, and payment to be made.

26 The servant therefore fell down, and worshipped him, saying, Lord, have patience with me, and I will pay thee all.

27 Then the lord of that servant was moved with compassion and loosed him, and forgave him the debt.

28 But the same servant went out, and found one of his fellow servants, which owed him an hundred pence: and he laid hands on him, and took him by the throat, saying, Pay me that thou owest.

29 And his fellowservant fell down at his feet, and besought him, saying, Have patience with me, and I will pay thee all.

30 And he would not: but went and cast him into prison, till he should pay the debt.

31 So when his fellowservants saw what was done, they were very sorry, and came and told their lord all that was done.

32 Then his lord, after that he had called him, said unto him, O thou wicked servant, I forgave thee all that debt, because thou desiredst me:

33 Shouldest not thou also have had compassion on thy fellow servant, even as I had pity on thee?

34 And his lord was wroth, and delivered him to the tormentors, till he should pay all that was due unto him.

35 So likewise shall my heavenly Father do

19 Matt. 5:24; 1 John 3:22; 5:14

21 Luke 17:4

22 Matt. 6:14; Mark 11:25; Col. 3:13

25 2 Kgs. 4:1; Neh. 5:8

35 Prov. 21:13; Matt. 6:12; Mark 11:26; James 2:13

1 Mark 10:1; John 10:40

2 Matt. 12:15

4 Gen. 1:27; 5:2; Mal. 2:15

5 Gen. 2:24; Mark 10:5-9; 1 Cor. 6:16; 7:2; Eph. 5:31

7 Deut. 24:1; Matt. 5:31

9 Matt. 5:32; Mark 10:11; Luke 16:18; 1 Cor. 7:10, 11

10 Prov. 21:19

11 1 Cor. 7:2, 7, 9, 17

12 1 Cor. 7:32, 34; 9:5, 15

13 Mark 10:13; Luke 18:15

14 Matt. 18:3

also unto you, if ye from your hearts forgive not every one his brother their trespasses.

CHAPTER 19
Divorce

1 And it came to pass, *that* when Jesus had finished these sayings, he departed from Galilee, and came into the coasts of Judea beyond Jordan;

2 And great multitudes followed him; and he healed them there.

3 The Pharisees also came unto him, tempting him, and saying unto him, Is it lawful for a man to put away his wife for every cause?

4 And he answered and said unto them, Have ye not read, that he which made them at the beginning made them male and female,

5 And said, For this cause shall a man leave father and mother, and shall cleave to his wife: and they twain shall be one flesh

6 Wherefore they are no more twain, but one flesh. What therefore God hath joined together, let not man put asunder.

7 They say unto him, Why did Moses then command to give a writing of divorcement, and to put her away

8 He saith unto them, Moses because of the hardness of your hearts suffered you to put away your wives: but from the beginning it was not so.

9 And I say unto you, Whosoever shall put away his wife, except it be for fornication, and shall marry another, committeth adultery: and whoso marrieth her which is put away doth commit adultery.

10 His disciples say unto him, If the case of the man be so with *his* wife, it is not good to marry.

11 But he said unto them, All men cannot receive this saying, save they to whom it is given.

12 For there are some eunuchs, which were so born from their mother's womb: and there are some eunuchs, which were made eunuchs of men: and there be eunuchs, which have made themselves eunuchs for the kingdom of heaven's sake. He that is able to receive it, let him receive it.

Who Will Enter God's Kingdom?

13 Then were there brought unto him little children, that he should put *his* hands on them, and pray: and the disciples rebuked them.

14 But Jesus said, Suffer little children, and

forbid them not, to come unto me: for of such is the kingdom of heaven.

15 And he laid *his* hands on them, and departed thence.

The Rich Young Man

16 And, behold, one came and said unto him, Good Master, what good thing shall I do, that I may have eternal life?

17 And he said unto him, Why callest thou me good? there is none good but one, that is, God: but if thou wilt enter into life, keep the commandments.

18 He saith unto him, Which? Jesus said, Thou shalt do no murder, Thou shalt not commit adultery, Thou shalt not steal, Thou shalt not bear false witness,

19 Honour thy father and thy mother: and, Thou shalt love thy neighbour as thyself.

20 The young man saith unto him, All these things have I kept from my youth up: what lack I yet?

21 Jesus said unto him, If thou wilt be perfect, go and sell that thou hast, and give to the poor, and thou shalt have treasure in heaven: and come and follow me.

22 But when the young man heard that saying, he went away sorrowful: for he had great possessions.

23 Then said Jesus unto his disciples, Verily I say unto you, That a rich man shall hardly enter into the kingdom of heaven.

24 And again I say unto you, It is easier for a camel to go through the eye of a needle, than for a rich man to enter into the kingdom of God.

25 When his disciples heard *it,* they were exceedingly amazed, saying, Who then can be saved?

26 But Jesus beheld *them,* and said unto them, With men this is impossible; but with God all things are possible.

27 Then answered Peter and said unto him, Behold, we have forsaken all, and followed thee; what shall we have therefore?

28 And Jesus said unto them, Verily I say unto you, That ye which have followed me, in the regeneration when the Son of man shall sit in the throne of his glory, ye also shall sit upon twelve thrones, judging the twelve tribes of Israel.

29 And every one that hath forsaken houses, or brethren, or sisters, or father, or mother, or wife, or children, or lands, for my name's sake, shall receive an hundredfold, and shall inherit everlasting life.

30 But many that are first shall be last; and the last shall be first.

CHAPTER 20
The Parable of the Laborers

1 For the kingdom of heaven is like unto a man that is an householder, which went out early in the morning to hire labourers into his vineyard.

2 And when he had agreed with the labourers for a penny a day, he sent them into his vineyard.

3 And he went out about the third hour, and saw others standing idle in the marketplace,

4 And said unto them; Go ye also into the vineyard, and whatsoever is right I will give you. And they went their way.

5 Again he went out about the sixth and ninth hour, and did likewise.

6 And about the eleventh hour he went out, and found others standing idle, and saith unto them, Why stand ye here all the day idle?

7 They say unto him, Because no man hath hired us. He saith unto them, Go ye also into the vineyard; and whatsoever is right, that shall ye receive.

8 So when even was come, the lord of the vineyard saith unto his steward, Call the labourers, and give them their hire, beginning from the last unto the first.

9 And when they came that were hired about the eleventh hour, they received every man a penny.

10 But when the first came, they supposed that they should have received more; and they likewise received every man a penny.

11 And when they had received it, they murmured against the goodman of the house,

12 Saying, These last have wrought but one hour, and thou hast made them equal unto us, which have borne the burden and heat of the day.

13 But he answered one of them, and said, Friend, I do thee no wrong: didst not thou agree with me for a penny?

14 Take that thine is, and go thy way: I will give unto this last, even as unto thee.

Cross references (center column):

16 Mark 10:17; Luke 10:25; 18:18

18 Ex. 20:13; Deut. 5:17

19 Lev. 19:18; Matt. 15:4; 22:39; Rom. 13:9; Gal. 5:14; James 2:8

21 Matt. 6:20; Luke 12:33; 16:9; Acts 2:45; 4:34, 35; 1Tim. 6:18, 19

23 Matt. 13:22; Mark 10:24; 1Cor. 1:26; 1Tim. 6:9, 10

26 Gen. 18:14; Job 42:2; Jer. 32:17; Zech. 8:6; Luke 1:37; 18:27

27 Deut. 33:9; Matt. 4:20; Mark 10:28; Luke 5:11; 18:28

28 Matt. 20:21; Luke 22:28, 29, 30; 1Cor. 6:2, 3; Rev. 2:26

29 Mark 10:29, 30; Luke 18:29, 30

30 Matt. 20:16; 21:31, 32; Mark 10:31; Luke 13:30

19:27–30 In the regeneration. The word "regeneration" refers to the renewed world of the future, the kingdom of righteousness yet to come (Isa. 11:6–9; Rom. 8:19–23). While the term is used for individual rebirth in Titus 3:5, here it looks to the future Millennial Kingdom where the apostles will literally judge Israel.

15 Is it not lawful for me to do what I will with mine own? Is thine eye evil, because I am good?

16 So the last shall be first, and the first last: for many be called, but few chosen.

Jesus Will Rise from the Dead

17 And Jesus going up to Jerusalem took the twelve disciples apart in the way, and said unto them,

18 Behold, we go up to Jerusalem: and the Son of man shall be betrayed unto the chief priests and unto the scribes, and they shall condemn him to death,

19 And shall deliver him to the Gentiles to mock, and to scourge, and to crucify him: and the third day he shall rise again.

The Request of the Mother of James and John

20 Then came to him the mother of Zebedee's children with her sons, worshipping *him*, and desiring a certain thing of him.

21 And he said unto her, What wilt thou? She saith unto him, Grant that these my two sons may sit, the one on thy right hand, and the other on the left, in thy kingdom.

22 But Jesus answered and said, Ye know not what ye ask. Are ye able to drink of the cup that I shall drink of, and to be baptized with the baptism that I am baptized with? They say unto him, We are able.

23 And he saith unto them, Ye shall drink indeed of my cup, and be baptized with the baptism that I am baptized with: but to sit on my right hand, and on my left, is not mine to give, but it shall be given to them for whom it is prepared of my Father.

24 And when the ten heard *it*, they were moved with indignation against the two brethren.

25 But Jesus called them *unto him*, and said, Ye know that the princes of the Gentiles exercise dominion over them, and they that are great exercise authority upon them.

26 But it shall not be so among you: but whosoever will be great among you, let him be your minister;

27 And whosoever will be chief among you, let him be your servant:

28 Even as the Son of man came not to be ministered unto, but to minister, and to give his life a ransom for many.

Jesus Heals Two Blind Men

29 And as they departed from Jericho, a great multitude followed him.

30 And, behold, two blind men sitting by the way side, when they heard that Jesus passed by, cried out, saying, Have mercy on us, O Lord, *thou* son of David.

31 And the multitude rebuked them, because they should hold their peace: but they cried the more, saying, Have mercy on us, O Lord, *thou* son of David.

32 And Jesus stood still, and called them, and said, What will ye that I shall do unto you?

33 They say unto him, Lord, that our eyes may be opened.

34 So Jesus had compassion *on them*, and touched their eyes: and immediately their eyes received sight, and they followed him.

CHAPTER 21
Jesus' Triumphal Entry into Jerusalem

1 And when they drew nigh unto Jerusalem, and were come to Bethphage, unto the mount of Olives, then sent Jesus two disciples,

2 Saying unto them, Go into the village over against you, and straightway ye shall find an ass tied, and a colt with her: loose them, and bring them unto me.

3 And if any man say ought unto you, ye shall say, The Lord hath need of them; and straightway he will send them.

4 All this was done, that it might be fulfilled which was spoken by the prophet, saying,

5 Tell ye the daughter of Sion, Behold, thy king cometh unto thee, meek, and sitting upon an ass, and a colt the foal of an ass.

6 And the disciples went, and did as Jesus commanded them,

7 And brought the ass, and the colt, and

Cross references

15 Deut. 15:9; Prov. 23:6; Matt. 6:23; Rom. 9:21

16 Matt. 19:30; 22:14

17 Mark 10:32; Luke 18:31; John 12:12

18 Matt. 16:21

19 Matt. 27:2; Mark 15:1, 16; Luke 23:1; John 18:28-37

20 Matt. 4:21; Mark 10:35

21 Matt. 19:28

22 Mark 14:36; Luke 12:50; 22:42; John 18:11

23 Matt. 25:34; Acts 12:2; Rom. 8:17; 2Cor. 1:7; Rev. 1:9

24 Mark 10:41; Luke 22:24, 25

26 Matt. 23:11; Mark 9:35; 10:43; 1Pet. 5:3

27 Matt. 18:4

28 Isa. 53:10, 11; Luke 22:27; John 11:51, 52; 13:4, 14; Rom. 5:15, 19; Phil. 2:7

30 Matt. 9:27

1 Zech. 14:4; Mark 11:1; Luke 19:29

5 Isa. 62:11; Zech. 9:9; John 12:15

6 Mark 11:4

7 2Kgs. 9:13

21:1–9 they drew nigh unto Jerusalem. This event is traditionally known as the Triumphal Entry. However, in many ways it was far from triumphant. Before the day ended, Jesus publicly predicts His ultimate rejection by His own people (see Mark 11:1–10; Luke 19:29–38; John 12:12–15). The quotation in verse 5 is a combination of Isaiah 62:11 and Zechariah 9:9. "Hosanna" is the transliteration of a Hebrew term meaning "please save," and occurs in 2 Samuel 14:4 and Psalm 118:25. (See the note on Mark 11:1–11.) From the following verse of this psalm the acclamation "Blessed is he that cometh in the name of the Lord" is taken. Riding on the colt of an ass marked the official entry of Israel's kings. Thus Jesus arrives in the full declaration of His royal status.

put on them their clothes, and they set *him* thereon.

8 And a very great multitude spread their garments in the way; others cut down branches from the trees, and strawed *them* in the way.

9 And the multitudes that went before, and that followed, cried, saying, Hosanna to the son of David: Blessed *is* he that cometh in the name of the Lord; Hosanna in the highest.

10 And when he was come into Jerusalem, all the city was moved, saying, Who is this?

11 And the multitude said, This is Jesus the prophet of Nazareth of Galilee.

Jesus Cleanses the Temple

12 And Jesus went into the temple of God, and cast out all them that sold and bought in the temple, and overthrew the tables of the moneychangers, and the seats of them that sold doves,

13 And said unto them, It is written, My house shall be called the house of prayer; but ye have made it a den of thieves.

14 And the blind and the lame came to him in the temple; and he healed them.

15 And when the chief priests and scribes saw the wonderful things that he did, and the children crying in the temple, and saying, Hosanna to the son of David; they were sore displeased,

16 And said unto him, Hearest thou what these say? And Jesus saith unto them, Yea; have ye never read, Out of the mouth of babes and sucklings thou hast perfected praise?

17 And he left them, and went out of the city into Bethany; and he lodged there.

Jesus and the Unfruitful Fig Tree

18 Now in the morning as he returned into the city, he hungered.

19 And when he saw a fig tree in the way, he came to it, and found nothing thereon, but leaves only, and said unto it, Let no fruit

grow on thee henceforward for ever. And presently the fig tree withered away.

20 And when the disciples saw *it,* they marvelled, saying, How soon is the fig tree withered away!

21 Jesus answered and said unto them, Verily I say unto you, If ye have faith, and doubt not, ye shall not only do this which is done to the fig tree, but also if ye shall say unto this mountain, Be thou removed, and be thou cast into the sea; it shall be done.

22 And all things, whatsoever ye shall ask in prayer, believing, ye shall receive.

The Chief Priests Inquire about Jesus' Authority

23 And when he was come into the temple, the chief priests and the elders of the people came unto him as he was teaching, and said, By what authority doest thou these things? and who gave thee this authority?

24 And Jesus answered and said unto them, I also will ask you one thing, which if ye tell me, I in likewise will tell you by what authority I do these things.

25 The baptism of John, whence was it? from heaven, or of men? And they reasoned with themselves, saying, If we shall say, From heaven; he will say unto us, Why did ye not then believe him?

26 But if we shall say, Of men; we fear the people; for all hold John as a prophet.

27 And they answered Jesus, and said, We cannot tell. And he said unto them, Neither tell I you by what authority I do these things.

The Parable of the Two Sons

28 But what think ye? A certain man had two sons; and he came to the first, and said, Son, go work today in my vineyard.

29 He answered and said, I will not: but afterward he repented, and went.

30 And he came to the second, and said likewise. And he answered and said, I go, sir: and went not.

31 Whether of them twain did the will of

Cross-references

8 Lev. 23:40; John 12:13
9 Ps. 118:25, 26; Matt. 23:39
10 Mark 11:15; Luke 19:45; John 2:13, 15
11 Matt. 2:23; Luke 7:16; John 6:14; 7:40; 9:17
12 Deut. 14:25; Mark 11:11; Luke 19:45; John 2:15
13 Isa. 56:7; Jer. 7:11; Mark 11:17; Luke 19:46
16 Ps. 8:2
17 Mark 11:11; John 11:18
18 Mark 11:12
19 Mark 11:13
20 Mark 11:20
21 Matt. 17:20; Luke 17:6; 1Cor. 13:2; James 1:6
22 Matt. 7:7; Mark 11:24; Luke 11:9; James 5:16; 1John 3:22; 5:14
23 Ex. 2:14; Mark 11:27; Luke 20:1; Acts 4:7; 7:27
26 Matt. 14:5; Mark 6:20; Luke 20:6
31 Luke 7:29, 50

21:18–22 he saw a fig tree. Figs generally appear on the trees in February, followed by leaves, which are not formed until late spring. So there should normally have been some fruit on the tree. The fig tree is often used as a symbol of the nation of Israel (cf. Hos. 9:10; Joel 1:7); and when Jesus actually came upon a barren fig tree, He used the tree to fully illustrate Israel's desperate condition. The curse, "Let no fruit grow . . . for ever," results in the almost immediate withering of the entire tree. Here Jesus provides a vivid demonstration of His earlier statement in Matthew 7:17–19. Political and religious Israel had not produced fruit and would come under divine judgment. Forty years later Jerusalem was destroyed, just as Jesus predicted (Luke 21:20–24). (For a parallel account, see Mark 11:12–14, 20–26.)

his father? They say unto him, The first. Jesus saith unto them, Verily I say unto you, That the publicans and the harlots go into the kingdom of God before you.

32 For John came unto you in the way of righteousness, and ye believed him not; but the publicans and the harlots believed him: and ye, when ye had seen it, repented not afterward, that ye might believe him.

The Wicked Husbandmen

33 Hear another parable: There was a certain householder, which planted a vineyard, and hedged it round about, and digged a winepress in it, and built a tower, and let it out to husbandmen, and went into a far country:

34 And when the time of the fruit drew near, he sent his servants to the husbandmen, that they might receive the fruits of it.

35 And the husbandmen took his servants, and beat one, and killed another, and stoned another.

36 Again, he sent other servants more than the first: and they did unto them likewise.

37 But last of all he sent unto them his son, saying, They will reverence my son.

38 But when the husbandmen saw the son, they said among themselves, This is the heir; come, let us kill him, and let us seize on his inheritance.

39 And they caught him, and cast him out of the vineyard, and slew him.

40 When the lord therefore of the vineyard cometh, what will he do unto those husbandmen?

41 They say unto him, He will miserably destroy those wicked men, and will let out *his* vineyard unto other husbandmen, which shall render him the fruits in their seasons.

42 Jesus saith unto them, Did ye never read in the scriptures, The stone which the builders rejected, the same is become the head of the corner: this is the Lord's doing, and it is marvellous in our eyes?

43 Therefore say I unto you, The kingdom of God shall be taken from you, and given to a nation bringing forth the fruits thereof.

44 And whosoever shall fall on this stone shall be broken: but on whomsoever it shall fall, it will grind him to powder.

45 And when the chief priests and Pharisees had heard his parables, they perceived that he spake of them.

46 But when they sought to lay hands on him, they feared the multitude, because they took him for a prophet.

CHAPTER 22
The Wedding Banquet

1 And Jesus answered and spake unto them again by parables, and said,

2 The kingdom of heaven is like unto a certain king, which made a marriage for his son.

3 And sent forth his servants to call them

Cross references:

32 Matt. 3:1-3; Luke 3:12
33 Mark 12:1; Luke 20:9
35 Matt. 5:12; 23:34
38 John 11:53; Acts 4:27; Heb. 1:2
39 Mark 14:46-49; Luke 22:54-62; John 18:12-14
41 Acts 13:46; 15:7; 18:6; 28:28; Heb. 2:3
42 Ps. 118:22; Isa. 28:16; Mark 12:10; Luke 20:17
43 Matt. 8:12
44 Isa. 8:14, 15; 60:12; Luke 20:18; Rom. 9:33; 1Pet. 2:8
46 Matt. 21:11; Luke 7:16; John 7:40
1 Luke 14:16; Rev. 19:7, 9

21:33–39 In the parable of the wicked "husbandmen" (tenant farmers), the "householder" represents God the Father, and the "vineyard" is a picture of Israel, a symbol of the theocracy that was familiar to the Jewish leaders (cf. Ps. 80:8–16; Isa. 5:1–7). The "servants" sent by the owner that were beaten and killed represent the Old Testament prophets who were rejected and mistreated by the Jews. "Last of all" indicates that Jesus was God's final emissary to Israel. None has ever appeared since Him, and none will appear again until His people recognize Christ as their final Prophet and Messiah. Jesus clearly foretells His imminent rejection and death with the fateful statement, "They . . . slew him." (For a parallel account, see Mark 12:2–7.)

21:40–43 what will he do unto those husbandmen? The Pharisees' reply again unwittingly condemns their own attitude of rejection toward Jesus. The "other husbandmen" are the Gentiles (v. 43). Jesus quotes Psalm 118:22–23, relating His present rejection to His ultimate triumph (cf. Acts 4:11; 1 Pet. 2:6–7). The builders of Israel's religion rejected Jesus, the true Cornerstone and

Foundation of the Church.

21:43–46 The kingdom of God shall be taken from you. This generation of Israelites would have the kingdom removed from them and given to a future generation of Israel at the start of the Millennium. Yet, within this warning of judgment, Jesus offers mercy to these falling "on this stone," meaning, falling upon Him in repentance and faith. But His falling upon man in judgment will "grind him to powder."

22:1–3 In preparation for the major confrontation that was coming, Jesus tells the parable of the marriage supper. While similar to the parable in Luke 14, this one differs in its occasion and details. Here, the "kingdom of heaven" refers to its "mystery" form as the Church. The "king" is the Father, and Christ is the "son." Rejection of the invitation to attend his wedding celebration constitutes disloyalty to the king and discourtesy to the son, and accounts for the severe treatment of the rebels (vv. 6–7), which includes their city being "burned up," an obvious reference to the coming destruction of Jerusalem in A.D. 70.

that were bidden to the wedding: and they would not come.

4 Again, he sent forth other servants, saying, Tell them which are bidden, Behold, I have prepared my dinner: my oxen and my fatlings are killed, and all things are ready: come unto the marriage.

5 But they made light of it, and went their ways, one to his farm, another to his merchandise:

6 And the remnant took his servants, and entreated them spitefully, and slew them.

7 But when the king heard thereof, he was wroth: and he sent forth his armies, and destroyed those murderers, and burned up their city.

8 Then saith he to his servants, The wedding is ready, but they which were bidden were not worthy.

9 Go ye therefore into the highways, and as many as ye shall find, bid to the marriage.

10 So those servants went out into the highways, and gathered together all as many as they found, both bad and good: and the wedding was furnished with guests.

11 And when the king came in to see the guests, he saw there a man which had not on a wedding garment:

12 And he saith unto him, Friend, how camest thou in hither not having a wedding garment? And he was speechless.

13 Then said the king to the servants, Bind him hand and foot, and take him away, and cast him into outer darkness; there shall be weeping and gnashing of teeth.

14 For many are called, but few are chosen.

Jesus and Taxes

15 Then went the Pharisees, and took counsel how they might entangle him in *his* talk.

16 And they sent out unto him their disciples with the Herodians, saying, Master, we know that thou art true, and teachest the way of God in truth, neither carest thou for any *man*: for thou regardest not the person of men.

17 Tell us therefore, What thinkest thou? Is it lawful to give tribute unto Caesar, or not?

18 But Jesus perceived their wickedness, and said, Why tempt ye me, ye hypocrites?

19 Shew me the tribute money. And they brought unto him a penny.

20 And he saith unto them, Whose is this image and superscription?

21 They say unto him, Caesar's. Then saith he unto them, Render therefore unto Caesar the things which are Caesar's; and unto God the things that are God's.

22 When they had heard *these words,* they marvelled, and left him, and went their way.

Questions Concerning the Resurrection

23 The same day came to him the Sadducees, which say that there is no resurrection, and asked him,

24 Saying, Master, Moses said, If a man die, having no children, his brother shall marry his wife, and raise up seed unto his brother.

25 Now there were with us seven brethren: and the first, when he had married a wife, deceased, and, having no issue, left his wife unto his brother:

26 Likewise the second also, and the third, unto the seventh.

27 And last of all the woman died also.

28 Therefore in the resurrection whose wife shall she be of the seven? for they all had her.

29 Jesus answered and said unto them, Ye do err, not knowing the scriptures, nor the power of God.

30 For in the resurrection they neither marry, nor are given in marriage, but are as the angels of God in heaven.

31 But as touching the resurrection of the

Cross References

4	Prov. 9:2
7	Dan. 9:26; Luke 19:27
8	Matt. 10:11, 13; Acts 13:46
10	Matt. 13:38, 47
11	2Cor. 5:3; Eph. 4:24; Col. 3:10, 12; Rev. 3:4; 16:15; 19:8
13	Matt. 8:12
14	Matt. 20:16
15	Mark 12:13; Luke 20:20
21	Matt. 17:25; Rom. 13:7
23	Mark 12:18; Luke 20:27; Acts 23:8
24	Deut. 25:5
29	John 20:9
30	1John 3:2

22:4–14 The "bidden" or invited guests are the people of Israel, whereas those in the highways are the Gentiles. "Both bad and good" refers to moral and immoral sinners who alike are extended God's gracious invitation. The man without the wedding garment attempted to come to the feast on his own terms, disregarding the propriety of the king's provision, since such garments were normally supplied by the host. The reference seems to be to the "robe of righteousness" (Isa. 61:10), which we must receive from the Lord in order to attend the marriage feast. Casting the unclad guest into "outer darkness" symbolizes the eternal judgment of the lost.

22:31–34 Jesus confronts the Sadducees' unbelief in a resurrection of the dead with Exodus 3:6, a text that the Sadducees unquestionably accepted (the Pentateuch). He related the eternal "I AM" of God to the patriarchs (Abraham, Isaac, and Jacob) to demonstrate that they were still "of the living" (a fact unlikely to be denied by the Sadducees in a public dispute). The statement "God is not the God of the dead" does not mean that He has no relationship to those believers who have died; it means that the deceased have never ceased to exist. They are still responsible to the living God (cf. Heb. 10:31).

dead, have ye not read that which was spoken unto you by God, saying,

32 I am the God of Abraham, and the God of Isaac, and the God of Jacob God is not the God of the dead, but of the living.

33 And when the multitude heard *this,* they were astonished at his doctrine.

The Great Commandment

34 But when the Pharisees had heard that he had put the Sadducees to silence, they were gathered together.

35 Then one of them, *which was* a lawyer, asked *him* a *question,* tempting him, and saying,

36 Master, which *is* the great commandment in the law?

37 Jesus said unto him, Thou shalt love the Lord thy God with all thy heart, and with all thy soul, and with all thy mind.

38 This is the first and great commandment.

39 And the second is like unto it, Thou shalt love thy neighbour as thyself.

40 On these two commandments hang all the law and the prophets.

David's Lord

41 While the Pharisees were gathered together, Jesus asked them,

42 Saying, What think ye of Christ? whose son is he? They say unto him, *The son* of David.

43 He saith unto them, How then doth David in spirit call him Lord, saying,

44 The LORD said unto my Lord, Sit thou on my right hand, till I make thine enemies thy footstool?

45 If David then call him, Lord, how is he his son?

46 And no man was able to answer him a word, neither durst any *man* from that day forth ask him any more *questions.*

CHAPTER 23

Jesus Condemns the Scribes and Pharisees

1 Then spake Jesus to the multitude, and to his disciples,

---

32 Ex. 3:6, 16; Mark 12:26; Luke 20:37; Acts 7:32; Heb. 11:16

34 Mark 12:28

35 Luke 10:25

37 Deut. 6:5; 10:12; 30:6; Luke 10:27

39 Lev. 19:18; Mark 12:31; Luke 10:27; Rom. 13:9

40 Matt. 7:12

44 Ps. 110:1

46 Mark 12:34; Luke 14:6; 20:40

2 Neh. 8:4, 8; Mal. 2:7; Mark 12:38; Luke 20:45

3 Rom. 2:17-24

4 Luke 11:46; Acts 15:10; Gal. 6:13

5 Num. 15:38; Matt. 6:1, 2, 5, 16

6 Mark 12:38, 39; Luke 11:43; 20:46

8 2Cor. 1:24; James 3:1; 1Pet. 5:3

9 Mal. 1:6

11 Matt. 20:26, 27

12 Job 22:29; Prov. 15:33; 29:23; Luke 14:11; 18:14

13 Luke 11:52

16 Matt. 5:33, 34; 15:14; 23:24

17 Ex. 30:29

---

2 Saying, The scribes and the Pharisees sit in Moses' seat:

3 All therefore whatsoever they bid you observe, that observe and do; but do not ye after their works: for they say, and do not.

4 For they bind heavy burdens and grievous to be borne, and lay them on men's shoulders; but they themselves will not move them with one of their fingers.

5 But all their works they do for to be seen of men: they make broad their phylacteries, and enlarge the borders of their garments,

6 And love the uppermost rooms at feasts, and the chief seats in the synagogues,

7 And greetings in the markets, and to be called of men, Rabbi, Rabbi.

8 But be not ye called Rabbi: for one is your Master, even Christ; and all ye are brethren.

9 And call no man your father upon the earth: for one is your Father, which is in heaven.

10 Neither be ye called masters: for one is your Master, even Christ.

11 But he that is greatest among you shall be your servant.

12 And whosoever shall exalt himself shall be abased; and he that shall humble himself shall be exalted.

13 But woe unto you, scribes and Pharisees, hypocrites! for ye shut up the kingdom of heaven against men: for ye neither go in yourselves, neither suffer ye them that are entering to go in.

14 Woe unto you, scribes and Pharisees, hypocrites! for ye devour widows' houses, and for a pretence make long prayer: therefore ye shall receive the greater damnation.

15 Woe unto you, scribes and Pharisees, hypocrites! for ye compass sea and land to make one proselyte, and when he is made, ye make him twofold more the child of hell than yourselves.

16 Woe unto you, ye blind guides, which say, Whosoever shall swear by the temple, it is nothing; but whosoever shall swear by the gold of the temple, he is a debtor!

17 Ye fools and blind: for whether is greater,

22:41–46 What think ye of Christ? whose son is he? By asking this of the Pharisees, Jesus gives them a clear opportunity to acknowledge Him. The question is similar to that asked of the disciples earlier in 16:15, where they gave the correct answer. The Pharisees' response, "The son of David," reflected the common teaching of the scribes of their day (cf. Mark 12:35). Jesus then calls their attention to Psalm 110, which they already recognized as messianic. This psalm, written by David "in spirit," that is, by inspiration of the Holy Spirit, refers to the Messiah as his Lord. Jesus totally stumps his detractors, who wanted to believe in a human Messiah but not a divine Messiah.

the gold, or the temple that sanctifieth the gold?

18 And, Whosoever shall swear by the altar, it is nothing; but whosoever sweareth by the gift that is upon it, he is guilty.

19 Ye fools and blind: for whether is greater, the gift, or the altar that sanctifieth the gift

20 Whoso therefore shall swear by the altar, sweareth by it, and by all things thereon.

21 And whoso shall swear by the temple, sweareth by it, and by him that dwelleth therein.

22 And he that shall swear by heaven, sweareth by the throne of God, and by him that sitteth thereon.

23 Woe unto you, scribes and Pharisees, hypocrites! for ye pay tithe of mint and anise and cummin, and have omitted the weightier matters of the law, judgment, mercy, and faith: these ought ye to have done, and not to leave the other undone.

24 Ye blind guides, which strain at a gnat, and swallow a camel.

25 Woe unto you, scribes and Pharisees, hypocrites! for ye make clean the outside of the cup and of the platter, but within they are full of extortion and excess.

26 Thou blind Pharisee, cleanse first that which is within the cup and platter, that the outside of them may be clean also.

27 Woe unto you, scribes and Pharisees, hypocrites! for ye are like unto whited sepulchres, which indeed appear beautiful outward, but are within full of dead men's bones, and of all uncleanness.

28 Even so ye also outwardly appear righteous unto men, but within ye are full of hypocrisy and iniquity.

29 Woe unto you, scribes and Pharisees, hypocrites! because ye build the tombs of the prophets, and garnish the sepulchres of the righteous,

30 And say, If we had been in the days of our fathers, we would not have been partakers with them in the blood of the prophets.

31 Wherefore ye be witnesses unto your-

selves, that ye are the children of them which killed the prophets.

32 Fill ye up then the measure of your fathers.

33 Ye serpents, ye generation of vipers, how can ye escape the damnation of hell?

34 Wherefore, behold, I send unto you prophets, and wise men, and scribes: and some of them ye shall kill and crucify; and some of them shall ye scourge in your synagogues, and persecute them from city to city:

35 That upon you may come all the righteous blood shed upon the earth, from the blood of righteous Abel unto the blood of Zacharias son of Barachias, whom ye slew between the temple and the altar.

36 Verily I say unto you, All these things shall come upon this generation.

Christ Weeps over Jerusalem

37 O Jerusalem, Jerusalem, thou that killest the prophets, and stonest them which are sent unto thee, how often would I have gathered thy children together, even as a hen gathereth her chickens under her wings, and ye would not!

38 Behold, your house is left unto you desolate.

39 For I say unto you, Ye shall not see me henceforth, till ye shall say, Blessed is he that cometh in the name of the Lord.

CHAPTER 24
The Destruction of the Temple and the Last Days

1 And Jesus went out, and departed from the temple: and his disciples came to *him* for to shew him the buildings of the temple.

2 And Jesus said unto them, See ye not all these things? verily I say unto you, There shall not be left here one stone upon another, that shall not be thrown down.

Signs of the End Times

3 And as he sat upon the mount of Olives, the disciples came unto him privately,

---

Cross references (center column):

19 Ex. 29:37
21 1Kgs. 8:13; 2Chr. 6:2; Ps. 26:8; 132:14
22 Ps. 11:4; Matt. 5:34; Acts 7:49
23 1Sam. 15:22; Hos. 6:6; Mic. 6:8; Matt. 9:13; 12:7; Luke 11:42
25 Mark 7:4; Luke 11:39
27 Luke 11:44; Acts 23:3
29 Luke 11:47
31 Acts 7:51, 52; 1Thess. 2:15
32 Gen. 15:16; 1Thess. 2:16
33 Matt. 3:7; 12:34
34 Matt. 10:17; 21:34, 35; Luke 11:49; Acts 5:40; 7:58, 59; 22:19; 2Cor. 11:24, 25
35 Gen. 4:8; 2Chr. 24:20, 21; 1John 3:12; Rev. 18:24
37 Deut. 32:11, 12; 2Chr. 24:21; Ps. 17:8; 91:4; Luke 13:34
39 Ps. 118:26; Matt. 21:9
2 1Kgs. 9:7; Jer. 26:18; Mic. 3:12; Luke 19:44
3 Mark 13:3; 1Thess. 5:1

24:1–25:46 This section, referred to as the Olivet Discourse, forms Jesus' last major discourse and His most prophetic sermon. While the message includes a prediction of the imminent fall of Jerusalem (24:2, cf. 23:38), it also looks to the distant future of the "times of the Gentiles" (Luke 21:24), which will continue until the end of the Great Tribulation. Jesus went east of Jerusalem onto the Mount of Olives from which He could look down on the temple courtyard. Here His disciples asked Him three questions: 1) "when shall these things be?" (the destruction of the temple); 2) "what shall be the sign of thy coming [Gr. *parousia*, technical term for His coming]?"; 3) "and [what] of the end of the world [Gr. *aion*, "the age"]?". Therefore, the entire discourse must be looked upon as answering all three of these questions.

saying, Tell us, when shall these things be? and what *shall be* the sign of thy coming, and of the end of the world?

4 And Jesus answered and said unto them, Take heed that no man deceive you.

5 For many shall come in my name, saying, I am Christ; and shall deceive many.

6 And ye shall hear of wars and rumours of wars: see that ye be not troubled: for all these things must come to pass, but the end is not yet.

7 For nation shall rise against nation, and kingdom against kingdom: and there shall be famines, and pestilences, and earthquakes, in divers places.

8 All these are the beginning of sorrows.

9 Then shall they deliver you up to be afflicted, and shall kill you: and ye shall be hated of all nations for my name's sake.

4 Eph. 5:6; Col. 2:8, 18
5 John 5:43
7 2Chr. 15:6; Isa. 19:2; Hag. 2:22; Zech. 14:13
9 Luke 21:12; John 15:20; 16:2
11 1Tim. 4:1; 2Pet. 2:1
13 Mark 13:13; Heb. 3:6, 14; Rev. 2:10
14 Rom. 10:18; Col. 1:6, 23
15 Dan. 9:23, 25, 27; 12:11

10 And then shall many be offended, and shall betray one another, and shall hate one another.

11 And many false prophets shall rise, and shall deceive many.

12 And because iniquity shall abound, the love of many shall wax cold.

13 But he that shall endure unto the end, the same shall be saved.

14 And this gospel of the kingdom shall be preached in all the world for a witness unto all nations; and then shall the end come.

The Great Tribulation

15 When ye therefore shall see the abomination of desolation, spoken of by Daniel the prophet, stand in the holy place, (whoso readeth, let him understand:)

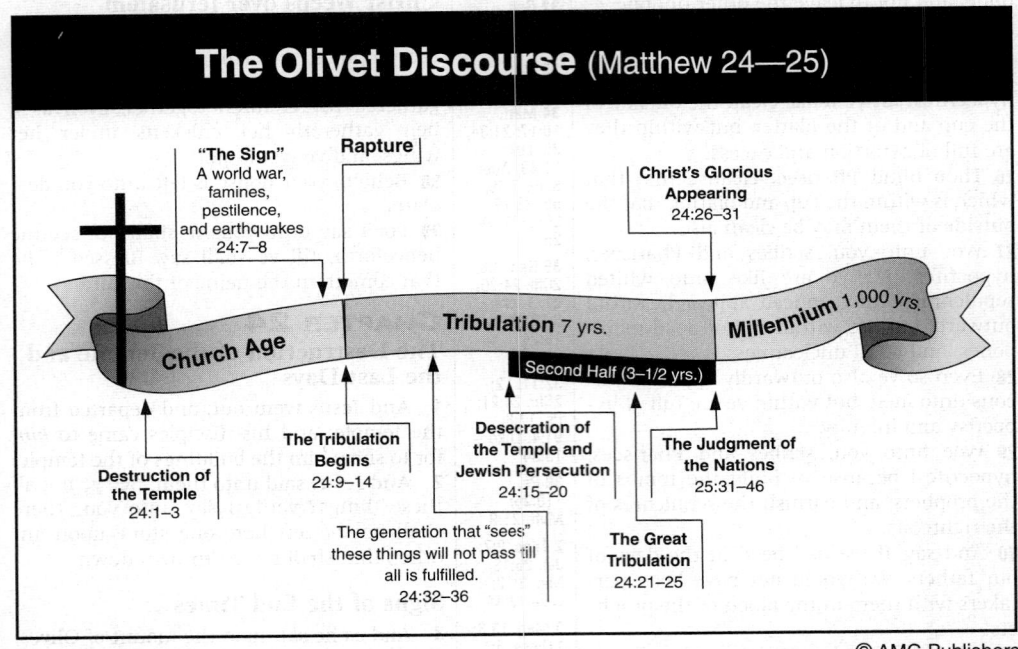

The Olivet Discourse (Matthew 24—25)

"The Sign" A world war, famines, pestilence, and earthquakes 24:7–8

Rapture

Christ's Glorious Appearing 24:26–31

Church Age

Tribulation 7 yrs.

Second Half (3–1/2 yrs.)

Millennium 1,000 yrs.

Destruction of the Temple 24:1–3

The Tribulation Begins 24:9–14

Desecration of the Temple and Jewish Persecution 24:15–20

The Judgment of the Nations 25:31–46

The generation that "sees" these things will not pass till all is fulfilled. 24:32–36

The Great Tribulation 24:21–25

© AMG Publishers

24:5–14 many shall come. Jesus anticipates the host of false messiahs who have now spanned the centuries of church history and have lead many astray into false religious cults. "Wars and rumors of wars" will mark the "age of the Gentiles." The famines and pestilences characterize only the "beginning of sorrows" (Gr. *odin*) or "birth pangs." These "birth pangs" will be followed by the martyrdom of true believers in Christ, the rise of false prophets, and an abundance of iniquity. The "gospel of the kingdom" refers to the evangelistic expansion of the

gospel "in all the world." The gospel shall be preached unto "all nations" (Gr. *ethnos*), that is the Gentile nations, as contrasted with the Jews. The declaration, "Then shall the end come" refers to the end of the Tribulation.

24:15 The word "ye" must be taken generically as "you" of the Jewish nation." "The abomination of desolation" recalls Daniel 9:27; 11:31 and Antiochus Epiphanes' profanation of the Jewish temple. The act of desecration by Antiochus will be repeated in the future by the Antichrist

The Olivet Discourse

By Jim Combs

The most complete account of the Olivet Discourse is recorded for us in Matthew 24 and 25. These two chapters were primarily written to show Jesus' offer of the kingdom to Israel, their rejection of it, and why Jesus did not usher in the kingdom at that time.

After Christ predicted that the temple complex would be torn down stone by stone, Peter, James, John, and Andrew approached Jesus privately, posing two questions (24:1–3): **1)** when will the temple complex be destroyed? and **2)** what will be the sign of Christ's coming (Gr. *parousia*) and the end of the world or age (Gr. *aion*)? The first question is answered in Luke's account and was fulfilled in A.D. 70 (Luke 21:20–24).

Many Bible scholars believe that the answers to the second question, concerning the "coming" and the end of the age should be viewed in an entirely Jewish context. In other words, the disciples were asking questions as Jews—not as "the foundation of the Church"—while they were thinking of the end of the age (Eph. 2:20).

According to this widely accepted interpretation, Jesus' analogy of the signs and "the beginning of sorrows" (Gr. "birth pangs" ["sorrows" in Matt. 24:8]) relates solely to the first half of the coming seven-year Tribulation. The disciples would understand "the gospel of the kingdom" as being a proclamation that the Messiah was coming to reveal Himself fully as Israel's king.

> *These "signs" culminate during the first half of the Tribulation.*

Premillennial prophetic thought generally agrees that the "signs" culminate during the first half of the Tribulation, leading up to the abomination of desolation, or the Antichrist claiming to be God inside the rebuilt Jerusalem temple. Unquestionably, the last half of the Tribulation is described in verses 15–26, leading up to the Glorious Coming which ends the Tribulation and introduces the Millennial Kingdom.

Some interpreters, however, say verses 4–8 also forecast the course of this entire present dispensation, the age often referred to as the Church Age. As incidents of false christs, worldwide wars, famines, and earthquakes are believed to have increased and intensified in recent times, some see these signs to indicate that the whole process of the Rapture, the Tribulation, and the glorious return of Christ are imminent and near.

According to some prophetic writers, the illustrations and thrust of verses 32–51 deal with the godly believers and the wicked at the end of the Tribulation and therefore do not apply to the Rapture. Others suggest that, beginning in verse 32, Jesus fills in further details of the end of the present age and describes the Rapture. Even if the latter half of Matthew 24 does not specifically speak of the Rapture, the appeals to "watch" and "be ready" for a sudden coming of Christ are applicable to believers today (Matt. 24:42, 44, 46; 25:13). Therefore the Church Age (Matt. 13; 25:1–13) would also be in view in this part of the Olivet Discourse.

The Olivet Discourse may be outlined as follows: **1)** signs of the latter days, including the first half (1260 days) of the Tribulation (Matt. 24:4–14), **2)** the second half of the Tribulation (Matt. 24:15–26), **3)** the glorious return of Christ (Matt. 24:27–31), **4)** parables stressing watchfulness, preparedness and faithfulness in the light of His Return (Matt. 24:32–51), and **5)** parables and predictions dealing with judgment and the end of the age (Matt. 25:1–46).

16 Then let them which be in Judea flee into the mountains:

17 Let him which is on the housetop not come down to take any thing out of his house:

18 Neither let him which is in the field return back to take his clothes.

19 And woe unto them that are with child, and to them that give suck in those days!

20 But pray ye that your flight be not in the winter, neither on the sabbath day:

21 For then shall be great tribulation, such as was not since the beginning of the world to this time, no, nor ever shall be.

22 And except those days should be shortened, there should no flesh be saved: but for the elect's sake those days shall be shortened.

23 Then if any man shall say unto you, Lo, here is Christ, or there; believe it not.

24 For there shall arise false Christs, and false prophets, and shall shew great signs and wonders; insomuch that, if it were possible, they shall deceive the very elect.

25 Behold, I have told you before.

26 Wherefore if they shall say unto you, Behold, he is in the desert; go not forth: behold, he is in the secret chambers; believe it not.

27 For as the lightning cometh out of the east, and shineth even unto the west; so shall also the coming of the Son of man be.

28 For wheresoever the carcase is, there will the eagles be gathered together.

Christ Is Coming Again

29 Immediately after the tribulation of those days shall the sun be darkened, and the moon shall not give her light, and the stars shall fall from heaven, and the powers of the heavens shall be shaken:

30 And then shall appear the sign of the Son of man in heaven: and then shall all the tribes of the earth mourn, and they shall see the Son of man coming in the clouds of heaven with power and great glory.

31 And he shall send his angels with a great sound of a trumpet, and they shall gather together his elect from the four winds, from one end of heaven to the other.

The Lesson of the Fig Tree

32 Now learn a parable of the fig tree; When his branch is yet tender, and putteth forth leaves, ye know that summer is nigh:

33 So likewise ye, when ye shall see all these things, know that it is near, even at the doors.

34 Verily I say unto you, This generation shall not pass, till all these things be fulfilled.

35 Heaven and earth shall pass away, but my words shall not pass away.

21 Dan. 9:26; 12:1; Joel 2:2
22 Isa. 65:8, 9; Zech. 14:2, 3
24 John 6:37; 10:28, 29; 2Thess. 2:9–11; 2Tim. 2:19; Rev. 13:13
27 Luke 17:24
28 Job 39:30; Luke 17:37
29 Isa. 13:10; Ezek. 32:7; Mark 13:24; Luke 21:25; Rev. 6:12
30 Dan. 7:13; Matt. 16:27; Mark 13:26; Rev. 1:7
31 1Cor. 15:52; 1Thess. 4:16
34 Mark 13:30; Luke 21:32
35 Ps. 102:26; Mark 13:31; Luke 21:33

---

to mark, as Daniel had predicted, the breaking of the covenant "in the midst" of Daniel's "seventieth week" (Dan. 9:27), and the beginning of the Great Tribulation, which is the second half of the Tribulation. The length of the final half of Daniel's "seventieth week" is confirmed to be forty-two months (Rev. 11:2), 1,260 days (Rev. 12:6), or "times, and times, and half a time" (Dan. 7:25; Rev. 12:14).

24:16–28 flee into the mountains. This warning looks beyond the first century to the Jews' flight from the intense persecution of the Antichrist (cf. Rev. 12:6–14). The reference to the "sabbath" indicates that these events will occur in a Jewish area, where such restrictions would be observed. Jesus makes it clear that the "time of trouble" of Daniel 12:1 takes place just prior to the resurrection "to everlasting life" in Daniel 12:2, a reference to the resurrection of the just at the Rapture. The terrible days of that time shall be "shortened" by the sudden return of Christ to destroy the "Wicked" one (2 Thess. 2:8). The lightning shining from "the east . . . even unto the west" suggests the final aspect of Christ's return (not the Rapture) in judgment upon the earth. In 1 Thessalonians 4, He comes in the clouds **for** the Church; in 2 Thessalonians 1 and 2, He comes to the

earth **with** the Church to judge the world.

24:29–31 The reference to the events immediately after the Tribulation, such as the sun being darkened and the stars falling, refer to the cataclysmic events that will accompany Christ's Millennial Kingdom on earth. Christ's return will be marked by the "sign of the Son of man." The "clouds of heaven" reveal that Christ will come from heaven to the earth (cf. Dan. 7:13–14; 2 Thess. 1:7–9). The "elect" are the saved of the Tribulation period who have come to faith in Christ by the grace of God and are gladly anticipating their Lord's return.

24:32–33 In these verses, the fig tree is not symbolic of the nation of Israel (as in chap. 21), but an example of how quickly all these final events will come to pass once they have begun. There will be no lengthy gaps of time to delay the consummation of Christ's coming. As the budding of the fig tree is a sign that summer is near, so the appearance of "all these things" is a clear sign that the end "is near" (cf. Luke 21:20).

24:34 This generation shall not pass. This is a reference to the future generation that will live to see all the signs listed in the previous verses fulfilled in their lifetime.

24:35–38 Verses 35 and 36, by implication, warn

The Time of Christ's Coming Is Unknown

36 But of that day and hour knoweth no man, no, not the angels of heaven, but my Father only.

37 But as the days of Noe were, so shall also the coming of the Son of man be.

38 For as in the days that were before the flood they were eating and drinking, marrying and giving in marriage, until the day that Noe entered into the ark,

39 And knew not until the flood came, and took them all away; so shall also the coming of the Son of man be.

40 Then shall two be in the field; the one shall be taken, and the other left.

41 Two women shall be grinding at the mill; the one shall be taken, and the other left.

42 Watch therefore: for ye know not what hour your Lord doth come.

43 But know this, that if the goodman of the house had known in what watch the thief would come, he would have watched, and would not have suffered his house to be broken up.

44 Therefore be ye also ready: for in such an hour as ye think not the Son of man cometh.

Faithful and Unfaithful Servants

45 Who then is a faithful and wise servant, whom his lord hath made ruler over his household, to give them meat in due season?

46 Blessed is that servant, whom his lord when he cometh shall find so doing.

47 Verily I say unto you, That he shall make him ruler over all his goods.

48 But and if that evil servant shall say in his heart, My lord delayeth his coming;

49 And shall begin to smite his fellow servants, and to eat and drink with the drunken;

50 The lord of that servant shall come in a day when he looketh not for him, and in an hour that he is not aware of,

51 And shall cut him asunder, and appoint him his portion with the hypocrites: there shall be weeping and gnashing of teeth.

CHAPTER 25

The Ten Virgins

1 Then shall the kingdom of heaven be likened unto ten virgins, which took their lamps, and went forth to meet the bridegroom.

2 And five of them were wise, and five were foolish.

3 They that were foolish took their lamps, and took no oil with them:

4 But the wise took oil in their vessels with their lamps.

5 While the bridegroom tarried, they all slumbered and slept.

6 And at midnight there was a cry made, Behold, the bridegroom cometh; go ye out to meet him.

7 Then all those virgins arose, and trimmed their lamps.

8 And the foolish said unto the wise, Give us of your oil; for our lamps are gone out.

9 But the wise answered, saying, Not so; lest there be not enough for us and you: but go ye rather to them that sell, and buy for yourselves.

10 And while they went to buy, the bridegroom came; and they that were ready went in with him to the marriage: and the door was shut.

11 Afterward came also the other virgins, saying, Lord, Lord, open to us.

12 But he answered and said, Verily I say unto you, I know you not.

13 Watch therefore, for ye know neither the day nor the hour wherein the Son of man cometh.

Cross references (center column)

36 Mark 13:32; Acts 1:7; 1Thess. 5:2
38 Gen. 6:3, 4, 5; 7:5; Luke 17:26; 1Pet. 3:20
40 Luke 17:34-37
43 Luke 12:3
44 Matt. 25:13; 1Thess. 5:6
45 Luke 12:42; Acts 20:28; 1Cor. 4:2; Heb. 3:5
46 Rev. 16:15
47 Matt. 25:21, 23; Luke 22:29
51 Matt. 8:12; 25:30
1 Eph. 5:29, 30; Rev. 19:7; 21:2, 9
2 Matt. 13:47; 22:10
5 1Thess. 5:6
6 Matt. 24:31; 1Thess. 4:16
7 Luke 12:35
10 Luke 13:25
11 Matt. 7:21-23
12 John 9:31
13 Mark 13:33, 35; Luke 21:36; 1Cor. 16:13; 1Thess. 5:6; Rev. 16:15

---

against attempts to set an exact date for the Rapture. Only the Father knows the time of this event since it has been set by His authority (cf. Acts 1:7).

24:39–42 The reference to two being in the field or at work at the time of Christ's return implies the suddenness of His coming to separate the lost and the saved.

24:43–51 The parable of the two servants illustrates the seriousness of Christ's second coming, a fact that Jesus never allegorized or spiritualized.

25:1–13 The parable of the "ten virgins" explains the place of Israel's true converts of the Great Tribulation period in relation to the Church. These "virgins" are the attendants at the wedding. The bride of Christ, though not identified here, is the Church (Eph. 5:31–32), and John the Baptist is the "best man," or the "friend of the bridegroom" (John 3:29). The prepared virgins here are the Jews saved during the Great Tribulation. The "lamps" refer to their lives, which are either prepared or unprepared. The "oil" refers to that which prepares them to give forth light, illustrative of the regeneration of the Holy Spirit. The fact that they all slept "while the bridegroom tarried" implies a period of Jewish inactivity during the Church Age, while the bride is gathered.

The Talents

14 For the kingdom of heaven is as a man travelling into a far country, who called his own servants, and delivered unto them his goods.

15 And unto one he gave five talents, to another two, and to another one; to every man according to his several ability; and straightway took his journey.

16 Then he that had received the five talents went and traded with the same, and made them other five talents.

17 And likewise he that had received two, he also gained other two.

18 But he that had received one went and digged in the earth, and hid his lord's money.

19 After a long time the lord of those servants cometh, and reckoneth with them.

20 And so he that had received five talents came and brought other five talents, saying, Lord, thou deliveredst unto me five talents: behold, I have gained beside them five talents more.

21 His lord said unto him, Well done, thou good and faithful servant: thou hast been faithful over a few things, I will make thee ruler over many things: enter thou into the joy of thy lord.

22 He also that had received two talents came and said, Lord, thou deliveredst unto me two talents: behold, I have gained two other talents beside them.

23 His lord said unto him, Well done, good and faithful servant; thou hast been faithful over a few things, I will make thee ruler over many things: enter thou into the joy of thy lord.

24 Then he which had received the one talent came and said, Lord, I knew thee that thou art an hard man, reaping where thou hast not sown, and gathering where thou hast not strawed:

25 And I was afraid, and went and hid thy talent in the earth: lo, there thou hast that is thine.

26 His lord answered and said unto him, Thou wicked and slothful servant, thou knewest that I reap where I sowed not, and gather where I have not strawed:

27 Thou oughtest therefore to have put my money to the exchangers, and then at my coming I should have received mine own with usury.

28 Take therefore the talent from him, and give it unto him which hath ten talents.

29 For unto everyone that hath shall be given, and he shall have abundance: but from him that hath not shall be taken away even that which he hath.

30 And cast ye the unprofitable servant into outer darkness: there shall be weeping and gnashing of teeth.

Concerning the Future Judgment

31 When the Son of man shall come in his glory, and all the holy angels with him, then shall he sit upon the throne of his glory:

32 And before him shall be gathered all nations: and he shall separate them one from another, as a shepherd divideth his sheep from the goats:

33 And he shall set the sheep on his right hand, but the goats on the left.

34 Then shall the King say unto them on his right hand, Come, ye blessed of my Fa-

Cross references

14 Matt. 21:33; Luke 19:12
15 Rom. 12:6; 1Cor. 12:7, 11, 29; Eph. 4:11
21 Matt. 24:47; 25:34, 46; Luke 12:44; 22:29, 30; 2Tim. 2:12; Heb. 12:2; 1Pet. 1:8
23 Matt. 25:21
29 Matt. 13:12; Mark 4:25; Luke 8:18; 19:26; John 15:2
30 Matt. 8:12; 24:51
31 Zech. 14:5; Matt. 16:27; 19:28; Mark 8:38; Acts 1:11; 1Thess. 4:16; 2Thess. 1:7; Jude 1:14; Rev. 1:7
32 Ezek. 20:38; 34:17, 20; Matt. 13:49; Rom. 14:10; 2Cor. 5:10; Rev. 20:12
34 Matt. 20:23; Mark 10:40; Rom. 8:17; 1Cor. 2:9; Heb. 11:16; 1Pet. 1:4, 9; 3:9; Rev. 21:7

25:14–23 The parable of the "talents" further emphasizes personal preparation and faithful service to the Master (see also Luke 19:11–28). The talents are large units of money that are distributed according to ability (v. 15). "Far country" indicates the heavenly abode of Jesus between His first coming and His final return. Not all are expected to produce the same results, but all are to be faithful with what they have. The phrase "after a long time" gives a veiled indication of the length of Christ's session in heaven during the present age. Each of those producing results is commended by the Master and promised that he will be a "ruler over many things," with a view to continued service in the Millennial Kingdom.

25:26–30 The fact that the latter man is called "wicked and slothful" and an "unprofitable servant" (v. 30), who is cast into "outer darkness," indicates that he is not a true disciple of the master.

25:31–46 The judgment of the nations concludes our Lord's prophetic discourse. This judgment of "all nations" must be distinguished from the Great White Throne Judgment at the end of the Millennium. The "nations" (Gr. *ethnos*) are those peoples living through the Great Tribulation on earth at the time of Christ's return. This is a judgment of separation: "sheep on his right . . . goats on the left." At this judgment, all nations (better, "all Gentiles") stand before Christ, who then separates the "sheep" (the saved) from the "goats" (the lost) in a manner reminiscent of the wheat and tares parable. Note that these are living nations. The saved are invited to come and share the blessings of Christ's Millennial Kingdom. The acceptable evidence of their faith seems to be their treatment of the "least of these my brethren," the Jews saved during the Great Tribulation.

ther, inherit the kingdom prepared for you from the foundation of the world:

35 For I was an hungred, and ye gave me meat: I was thirsty, and ye gave me drink: I was a stranger, and ye took me in:

36 Naked, and ye clothed me: I was sick, and ye visited me: I was in prison, and ye came unto me.

37 Then shall the righteous answer him, saying, Lord, when saw we thee an hungred, and fed thee? or thirsty, and gave thee drink?

38 When saw we thee a stranger, and took thee in? or naked, and clothed thee?

39 Or when saw we thee sick, or in prison, and came unto thee?

40 And the King shall answer and say unto them, Verily I say unto you, Inasmuch as ye have done it unto one of the least of these my brethren, ye have done it unto me.

41 Then shall he say also unto them on the left hand, Depart from me, ye cursed, into everlasting fire, prepared for the devil and his angels:

42 For I was an hungred, and ye gave me no meat: I was thirsty, and ye gave me no drink:

43 I was a stranger, and ye took me not in: naked, and ye clothed me not: sick, and in prison, and ye visited me not.

44 Then shall they also answer him, saying, Lord, when saw we thee an hungred, or athirst, or a stranger, or naked, or sick, or in prison, and did not minister unto thee?

45 Then shall he answer them, saying, Verily I say unto you, Inasmuch as ye did it not to one of the least of these, ye did it not to me.

46 And these shall go away into everlasting punishment: but the righteous into life eternal.

CHAPTER 26
The Leaders Plot to Kill Jesus

1 And it came to pass, when Jesus had finished all these sayings, he said unto his disciples,

2 Ye know that after two days is the feast of the passover, and the Son of man is betrayed to be crucified.

3 Then assembled together the chief priests, and the scribes, and the elders of the people, unto the palace of the high priest, who was called Caiaphas,

4 And consulted that they might take Jesus by subtilty, and kill *him*.

5 But they said, Not on the feast *day*, lest there be an uproar among the people.

Jesus Anointed at Bethany

6 Now when Jesus was in Bethany, in the house of Simon the leper,

7 There came unto him a woman having an alabaster box of very precious ointment, and poured it on his head, as he sat *at meat*.

8 But when his disciples saw *it*, they had indignation, saying, To what purpose *is* this waste?

9 For this ointment might have been sold for much, and given to the poor.

10 When Jesus understood *it*, he said unto them, Why trouble ye the woman? for she hath wrought a good work upon me.

11 For ye have the poor always with you; but me ye have not always.

12 For in that she hath poured this ointment on my body, she did it for my burial.

13 Verily I say unto you, Wheresoever this gospel shall be preached in the whole world, there shall also this, that this woman hath done, be told for a memorial of her.

Judas Agrees to Betray Jesus

14 Then one of the twelve, called Judas Iscariot, went unto the chief priests,

15 And said *unto them*, What will ye give me, and I will deliver him unto you? And they covenanted with him for thirty pieces of silver.

16 And from that time he sought opportunity to betray him.

Cross references

35 Isa. 58:7; Ezek. 18:7; Heb. 13:2; James 1:27; 3John 1:5

36 2Tim. 1:16; James 2:15, 16

40 Prov. 14:31; 19:17; Matt. 10:42; Mark 9:41; Heb. 6:10

41 Ps. 6:8; Matt. 7:23; 13:40, 42; Luke 13:27; 2Pet. 2:4; Jude 1:6

45 Prov. 14:31; 17:5; Zech. 2:8; Acts 9:5

46 Dan. 12:2; John 5:29

2 Mark 14:1; Luke 22:1; John 13:1

3 Ps. 2:2; John 11:47; Acts 4:25-28

6 Matt. 21:17; Mark 14:3; John 11:1, 2; 12:3

8 John 12:4

11 Deut. 15:11; Matt. 18:20; 28:20; John 12:8; 13:33; 14:19; 16:5, 28; 17:11

14 Matt. 10:4; Mark 14:10; Luke 22:3; John 13:2, 30

15 Zech. 11:12; Matt. 27:3

26:1–2 Jesus makes a final prediction of His death two days before Passover. The feast of Passover was the first feast on the Jewish yearly calendar, celebrating the deliverance of the Jews from Egypt during the Exodus. Passover takes its name from the Hebrew term related to the passing over of those who had applied the blood to their homes (see Ex. 12). (For parallel accounts, see Mark 14:1–2; Luke 22:1–2.)

26:2–5 Jesus also predicts His betrayal. The title, "Son of man" is His favorite designation of Himself. The word "betrayed" is better translated here as "delivered up" or

"handed over." The assemblage of the Sanhedrin takes place at the palace (Gr. *aule*, "the courtyard of the High Priest"). Caiaphas was a Sadducee who had been appointed high priest a few years earlier, about A.D. 18, just before Christ's earthly ministry began. In 1990, a small coffin (ossuary) was found in Jerusalem containing the bones of Caiaphas, verifying his historicity.

26:6–16 And they covenanted with him [Judas Iscariot, see Mark 3:19] **for thirty pieces of silver.** This was about a month's wages for a general laborer, or the price of a common slave (see the footnote on Zech. 11:11–12).

Jesus Eats the Passover with His Disciples

17 Now the first *day* of the *feast of* unleavened bread the disciples came to Jesus, saying unto him, Where wilt thou that we prepare for thee to eat the passover?

18 And he said, Go into the city to such a man, and say unto him, The Master saith, My time is at hand; I will keep the passover at thy house with my disciples.

19 And the disciples did as Jesus had appointed them; and they made ready the passover.

20 Now when the even was come, he sat down with the twelve.

21 And as they did eat, he said, Verily I say unto you, that one of you shall betray me.

22 And they were exceeding sorrowful, and began every one of them to say unto him, Lord, is it I?

23 And he answered and said, He that dippeth his hand with me in the dish, the same shall betray me.

24 The Son of man goeth as it is written of him: but woe unto that man by whom the Son of man is betrayed! it had been good for that man if he had not been born.

25 Then Judas, which betrayed him, answered and said, Master, is it I? He said unto him, Thou hast said.

The Lord's Supper

26 And as they were eating, Jesus took bread, and blessed *it*, and brake *it*, and gave *it* to the disciples, and said, Take, eat; this is my body.

27 And he took the cup, and gave thanks, and gave *it* to them, saying, Drink ye all of it;

28 For this is my blood of the new testament, which is shed for many for the remission of sins.

29 But I say unto you, I will not drink henceforth of this fruit of the vine, until that day when I drink it new with you in my Father's kingdom.

30 And when they had sung an hymn, they went out into the mount of Olives.

Jesus Predicts Peter's Denial

31 Then saith Jesus unto them, All ye shall be offended because of me this night: for it is written, I will smite the shepherd, and the sheep of the flock shall be scattered abroad.

32 But after I am risen again, I will go before you into Galilee.

33 Peter answered and said unto him, Though all *men* shall be offended because of thee, *yet* will I never be offended.

34 Jesus said unto him, Verily I say unto thee, That this night, before the cock crow, thou shalt deny me thrice.

35 Peter said unto him, Though I should die with thee, yet will I not deny thee. Likewise also said all the disciples.

Jesus Prays in Gethsemane

36 Then cometh Jesus with them unto a place called Gethsemane, and saith unto the disciples, Sit ye here, while I go and pray yonder.

37 And he took with him Peter and the two

Cross-references

17 Ex. 12:6, 18; Mark 14:12; Luke 22:7
20 Mark 14:17-21; Luke 22:14; John 13:21
23 Ps. 41:9; Luke 22:21; John 13:18
24 Ps. 22; Isa. 53; Mark 9:12; Luke 24:25, 26, 46; John 17:12
26 Mark 6:41; 14:22; Luke 22:19; 1Cor. 10:16; 11:23-25
28 Ex. 24:8; Lev. 17:11; Jer. 31:31; Heb. 9:22
29 Mark 14:25; Luke 22:18; Acts 10:41
31 Zech. 13:7; Matt. 11:6; Mark 14:27; John 16:32
32 Mark 14:28; 16:7
34 Mark 14:30; Luke 22:34; John 13:38
36 Mark 14:32-35; Luke 22:39; John 18:1

26:17–22 the first day . . . of unleavened bread (fourteenth of Nisan [cf. Mark 14:12; Luke 22:7]). While Jesus said, "I will keep the passover," the cross-reference in Luke 22:16 notes He added, "I will not any more eat thereof," implying an interruption. Jesus is alone with the twelve disciples. (The Last Supper is also related in Mark 14:12–26; Luke 22:7–23; and John 13:1–29.) At this crucial time Jesus announced, "One of you shall betray me." For the first time, Jesus predicted that the betrayer would be one of His closest followers.

26:26 this is my body. During the Passover feast, the Jewish householder took bread in his hand and said, "This is the bread of affliction that our fathers ate in the land of Egypt," meaning, of course, that the one represented the other. By His words the Lord changed the whole significance and emphasis of the feast from looking back to redemption from Egypt to the redemption from sin soon to be accomplished by His death. The bread and wine were outward symbols of our Lord's

death for our sins.

26:27–28 he took the cup. The Jewish householder passed around three cups during the Passover meal. The third, which is probably the cup referred to here, was known as "the cup of blessing." The phrase, "my blood of the new testament" is taken from the Septuagint rendering of Exodus 24:8, with allusions to Jeremiah 31:31 and Zechariah 9:11. The covenant in Exodus 24:8 was sealed with blood. The word "testament" (Gr. *diatheke*) can also mean "a covenant."

26:29 in my Father's kingdom. This is a reference to the Marriage Supper of the Lamb, which takes place after the Rapture.

26:36–39 My soul is exceeding sorrowful. This phrase is found in the Septuagint translation of Psalm 43:5. Gethsemane ("olive press") was a lush olive garden east of the city near the slopes of the Mount of Olives. Jesus often resorted there for peace and quiet (Luke 22:39;

sons of Zebedee, and began to be sorrowful and very heavy.
38 Then saith he unto them, My soul is exceeding sorrowful, even unto death: tarry ye here, and watch with me.
39 And he went a little farther, and fell on his face, and prayed, saying, O my Father, if it be possible, let this cup pass from me: nevertheless not as I will, but as thou wilt.
40 And he cometh unto the disciples, and findeth them asleep, and saith unto Peter, What, could ye not watch with me one hour?
41 Watch and pray, that ye enter not into temptation: the spirit indeed is willing, but the flesh is weak.
42 He went away again the second time, and prayed, saying, O my Father, if this cup may not pass away from me, except I drink it, thy will be done.
43 And he came and found them asleep again: for their eyes were heavy.
44 And he left them, and went away again, and prayed the third time, saying the same words.
45 Then cometh he to his disciples, and saith unto them, Sleep on now, and take your rest: behold, the hour is at hand, and the Son of man is betrayed into the hands of sinners.
46 Rise, let us be going: behold, he is at hand that doth betray me.

Judas Betrays the Lord

47 And while he yet spake, lo, Judas, one of the twelve, came, and with him a great multitude with swords and staves, from the chief priests and elders of the people.
48 Now he that betrayed him gave them a sign, saying, Whomsoever I shall kiss, that same is he: hold him fast.
49 And forthwith he came to Jesus, and said, Hail, master; and kissed him.
50 And Jesus said unto him, Friend, wherefore art thou come? Then came they, and laid hands on Jesus, and took him.
51 And, behold, one of them which were with Jesus stretched out *his* hand, and drew his sword, and struck a servant of the high priest's, and smote off his ear.

38 John 12:27
39 Mark 14:36; Luke 22:42; John 5:30; 6:38; 12:27; Phil. 2:8
41 Mark 13:33; 14:38; Luke 22:40, 46; Eph. 6:18
47 Mark 14:43; Luke 22:47; John 18:3; Acts 1:16
49 2Sam. 20:9
50 Ps. 41:9; 55:13
51 John 18:10
52 Gen. 9:6; Rev. 13:10
53 2Kgs. 6:17; Dan. 7:10
54 Isa. 53:7; Matt. 26:24; Luke 24:25, 44, 46
56 Lam. 4:20; Matt. 26:54; John 18:15
57 Mark 14:53; Luke 22:54; John 18:12, 13, 24
60 Ps. 27:12; 35:11; Matt. 27:40; Mark 14:55; John 2:19
62 Mark 14:60
63 Lev. 5:1; 1Sam. 14:24, 26; Isa. 53:7; Matt. 27:12, 14
64 Ps. 110:1; Dan. 7:13; Matt. 16:27; 24:30; 25:31; Luke 21:27; John 1:51; 1Thess. 4:16; Rev. 1:7

52 Then said Jesus unto him, Put up again thy sword into his place: for all they that take the sword shall perish with the sword.
53 Thinkest thou that I cannot now pray to my Father, and he shall presently give me more than twelve legions of angels?
54 But how then shall the scriptures be fulfilled, that thus it must be?
55 In that same hour said Jesus to the multitudes, Are ye come out as against a thief with swords and staves for to take me? I sat daily with you teaching in the temple, and ye laid no hold on me.
56 But all this was done, that the scriptures of the prophets might be fulfilled. Then all the disciples forsook him, and fled.

Jesus Is Brought before Caiaphas

57 And they that had laid hold on Jesus led *him* away to Caiaphas the high priest, where the scribes and the elders were assembled.
58 But Peter followed him afar off unto the high priest's palace, and went in, and sat with the servants, to see the end.
59 Now the chief priests, and elders, and all the council, sought false witness against Jesus, to put him to death;
60 But found none: yea, though many false witnesses came, *yet* found they none. At the last came two false witnesses,
61 And said, this *fellow* said, I am able to destroy the temple of God, and to build it in three days.
62 And the high priest arose, and said unto him, Answerest thou nothing? what *is it which* these witness against thee?
63 But Jesus held his peace. And the high priest answered and said unto him, I adjure thee by the living God, that thou tell us whether thou be the Christ, the Son of God.
64 Jesus saith unto him, Thou hast said: nevertheless I say unto you, Hereafter shall ye see the Son of man sitting on the right hand of power, and coming in the clouds of heaven.
65 Then the high priest rent his clothes, saying, He hath spoken blasphemy; what further need have we of witnesses? behold, now ye have heard his blasphemy.

John 18:2). He took with Him the same inner circle that witnessed the Transfiguration (Peter, James, and John). The prayer for the cup to pass is not due to Jesus' fear of death; rather, He asks the will of the Father as to the necessity of drinking the cup. While this cup may refer to death (he did "taste death" [Heb. 2:9]) it is more likely that it represents the wrath of God against sin that Christ would incur on the cross as man's sin-bearer. In the awful anguish of that moment, the sin of the world was poured on Christ, and He became "sin for us," (2 Cor. 5:21) dying a substitutionary death for guilty mankind.

66 What think ye? They answered and said, He is guilty of death.

67 Then did they spit in his face, and buffeted him; and others smote *him* with the palms of their hands,

68 Saying, Prophesy unto us, thou Christ, Who is he that smote thee?

Peter Denies Jesus

69 Now Peter sat without in the palace: and a damsel came unto him, saying, Thou also wast with Jesus of Galilee.

70 But he denied before *them* all, saying, I know not what thou sayest.

71 And when he was gone out into the porch, another *maid* saw him, and said unto them that were there, This *fellow* was also with Jesus of Nazareth.

72 And again he denied with an oath, I do not know the man.

73 And after a while came unto *him* they that stood by, and said to Peter, Surely thou also art *one* of them; for thy speech bewrayeth thee.

74 Then began he to curse and to swear, *saying*, I know not the man. And immediately the cock crew.

75 And Peter remembered the word of Jesus, which said unto him, Before the cock crow, thou shalt deny me thrice. And he went out, and wept bitterly.

CHAPTER 27
Jesus Is Brought before Pilate

1 When the morning was come, all the chief priests and elders of the people took counsel against Jesus to put him to death:

2 And when they had bound him, they led *him* away, and delivered him to Pontius Pilate the governor.

The Death of Judas

3 Then Judas, which had betrayed him, when he saw that he was condemned, repented himself, and brought again the thirty pieces of silver to the chief priests and elders,

4 Saying, I have sinned in that I have betrayed the innocent blood. And they said, What *is that* to us? see thou *to that.*

5 And he cast down the pieces of silver in the temple, and departed, and went and hanged himself.

6 And the chief priests took the silver pieces, and said, It is not lawful for to put them into the treasury, because it is the price of blood.

7 And they took counsel, and bought with them the potter's field, to bury strangers in.

8 Wherefore that field was called, The field of blood, unto this day.

9 Then was fulfilled that which was spoken by Jeremy the prophet, saying, And they took the thirty pieces of silver, the price of him that was valued, whom they of the children of Israel did value;

10 And gave them for the potter's field, as the Lord appointed me.

Jesus Questioned by Pilate

11 And Jesus stood before the governor: and the governor asked him, saying, Art thou the King of the Jews? And Jesus said unto him, Thou sayest.

12 And when he was accused of the chief priests and elders, he answered nothing.

13 Then said Pilate unto him, Hearest thou not how many things they witness against thee?

14 And he answered him to never a word; insomuch that the governor marvelled greatly.

Jesus Sentenced to Death

15 Now at *that* feast the governor was wont to release unto the people a prisoner, whom they would.

16 And they had then a notable prisoner, called Barabbas.

17 Therefore when they were gathered together, Pilate said unto them, Whom will ye that I release unto you? Barabbas, or Jesus which is called Christ?

18 For he knew that for envy they had delivered him.

19 When he was set down on the judgment seat, his wife sent unto him, saying, Have thou nothing to do with that just man: for I have suffered many things this day in a dream because of him.

20 But the chief priests and elders per-

Cross references (center column)

66 Lev. 24:16; John 19:7
67 Isa. 50:6; 53:3; Matt. 27:30; Luke 22:63; John 19:3
68 Mark 14:65; Luke 22:64
69 Mark 14:66; Luke 22:55; John 18:16, 17, 25
73 Luke 22:59
74 Mark 14:71
75 Matt. 26:34; Mark 14:30; Luke 22:61, 62; John 13:38
1 Ps. 2:2; Mark 15:1; Luke 22:66; 23:1; John 18:28
2 Matt. 20:19; Acts 3:13
3 Matt. 26:14, 15
5 2Sam. 17:23; Acts 1:18
8 Acts 1:19
9 Zech. 11:12, 13
11 Mark 15:2; Luke 23:3; John 18:33, 37; 1Tim. 6:13
12 Matt. 26:63; John 19:9
13 Matt. 26:62; John 19:10
15 Mark 15:6; Luke 23:17; John 18:39
20 Mark 15:11; Luke 23:18; John 18:40; Acts 3:14

27:1–2 Pontius Pilate was the Roman procurator of Judea from A.D. 26–36, holding his office under the prefect of Syria. His usual place of residence was Caesarea, but he was in Jerusalem during the feast to deal with any possible insurrection or trouble that might arise. In 1961, an inscription containing his name was found at Caesarea, the first archaeological evidence of his rule. (For parallel accounts, see Mark 15:1–15; Luke 23:1–25; John 18:28—19:16.)

suaded the multitude that they should ask Barabbas, and destroy Jesus.
21 The governor answered and said unto them, Whether of the twain will ye that I release unto you? They said, Barabbas.
22 Pilate saith unto them, What shall I do then with Jesus which is called Christ? *They* all say unto him, Let him be crucified.
23 And the governor said, Why, what evil hath he done? But they cried out the more, saying, Let him be crucified.
24 When Pilate saw that he could prevail nothing, but *that* rather a tumult was made, he took water, and washed *his* hands before the multitude, saying, I am innocent of the blood of this just person: see ye *to it*.
25 Then answered all the people, and said, His blood *be* on us, and on our children.
26 Then released he Barabbas unto them: and when he had scourged Jesus, he delivered *him* to be crucified.

Jesus Is Mocked by the Soldiers

27 Then the soldiers of the governor took Jesus into the common hall, and gathered unto him the whole band *of soldiers*.
28 And they stripped him, and put on him a scarlet robe.
29 And when they had platted a crown of thorns, they put *it* upon his head, and a reed in his right hand: and they bowed the knee before him, and mocked him, saying, Hail, King of the Jews!
30 And they spit upon him, and took the reed, and smote him on the head.
31 And after that they had mocked him, they took the robe off from him, and put his own raiment on him, and led him away to crucify *him*.

Jesus' Crucifixion

32 And as they came out, they found a man of Cyrene, Simon by name: him they compelled to bear his cross.

33 And when they were come unto a place called Golgotha, that is to say, a place of a skull,
34 They gave him vinegar to drink mingled with gall: and when he had tasted *thereof*, he would not drink.
35 And they crucified him, and parted his garments, casting lots: that it might be fulfilled which was spoken by the prophet, They parted my garments among them, and upon my vesture did they cast lots.
36 And sitting down they watched him there;
37 And set up over his head his accusation written, THIS IS JESUS THE KING OF THE JEWS.
38 Then were there two thieves crucified with him, one on the right hand, and another on the left.
39 And they that passed by reviled him, wagging their heads,
40 And saying, Thou that destroyest the temple, and buildest *it* in three days, save thyself. If thou be the Son of God, come down from the cross.
41 Likewise also the chief priests mocking *him*, with the scribes and elders, said,
42 He saved others; himself he cannot save. If he be the King of Israel, let him now come down from the cross, and we will believe him.
43 He trusted in God; let him deliver him now, if he will have him: for he said, I am the Son of God.
44 The thieves also, which were crucified with him, cast the same in his teeth.

Jesus' Death

45 Now from the sixth hour there was darkness over all the land unto the ninth hour.
46 And about the ninth hour Jesus cried with a loud voice, saying, Eli, Eli, lama sabachthani? that is to say, My God, my God, why hast thou forsaken me?

27:32–35 vinegar to drink mingled with gall. This act is a fulfillment of Psalm 69:21. It was literally a medicated "wine" (Gr. *oinon*), which was customarily given to condemned prisoners to serve as a kind of anesthetic or anodyne. The statement that "he would not drink" indicates that Jesus refused any mitigation of His sufferings on our behalf.

27:36–44 THIS IS JESUS THE KING OF THE JEWS. Little did Pilate realize how true this intended mockery of Jesus really was. Indeed, as Matthew shows, Jesus was the King of the Jews, whom they had rejected. The

"thieves" (Gr. *lestes*) were robbers, perhaps cohorts of Barabbas. The statement "cast the same in his teeth" means they repeated similar taunts to Him.

27:45–50 from the sixth hour . . . unto the ninth hour. This darkness lasted from noon until 3:00 P.M. Mark (15:25) indicates Jesus had been placed on the cross at the third hour (9:00 A.M.). This darkness was supernatural, since an eclipse of the sun at full noon is impossible. God's wrath was poured upon His Son during this time of darkness.

47 Some of them that stood there, when they heard *that,* said, This *man* calleth for Elias.

48 And straightway one of them ran, and took a sponge, and filled *it* with vinegar, and put *it* on a reed, and gave him to drink.

49 The rest said, Let be, let us see whether Elias will come to save him.

50 Jesus, when he had cried again with a loud voice, yielded up the ghost.

51 And, behold, the veil of the temple was rent in twain from the top to the bottom; and the earth did quake, and the rocks rent;

52 And the graves were opened; and many bodies of the saints which slept arose,

53 And came out of the graves after his resurrection, and went into the holy city, and appeared unto many.

54 Now when the centurion, and they that were with him, watching Jesus, saw the earthquake, and those things that were done, they feared greatly, saying, Truly this was the Son of God.

55 And many women were there beholding afar off, which followed Jesus from Galilee, ministering unto him:

56 Among which was Mary Magdalene, and Mary the mother of James and Joses, and the mother of Zebedee's children.

The Burial of Jesus

57 When the even was come, there came a rich man of Arimathaea, named Joseph, who also himself was Jesus' disciple:

58 He went to Pilate, and begged the body of Jesus. Then Pilate commanded the body to be delivered.

59 And when Joseph had taken the body, he wrapped it in a clean linen cloth,

60 And laid it in his own new tomb, which he had hewn out in the rock: and he rolled a great stone to the door of the sepulchre, and departed.

61 And there was Mary Magdalene, and the other Mary, sitting over against the sepulchre.

62 Now the next day, that followed the day of the preparation, the chief priests and Pharisees came together unto Pilate,

63 Saying, Sir, we remember that that deceiver said, while he was yet alive, After three days I will rise again.

64 Command therefore that the sepulchre be made sure until the third day, lest his disciples come by night, and steal him away, and say unto the people, He is risen from the dead: so the last error shall be worse than the first.

65 Pilate said unto them, Ye have a watch: go your way, make *it* as sure as ye can.

66 So they went, and made the sepulchre sure, sealing the stone, and setting a watch.

CHAPTER 28
Jesus Is Risen

1 In the end of the sabbath, as it began to dawn toward the first *day* of the week, came Mary Magdalene and the other Mary to see the sepulchre.

2 And, behold, there was a great earthquake: for the angel of the Lord descended from heaven, and came and rolled back the stone from the door, and sat upon it.

Cross references (center column):

48 Ps. 69:21; Mark 15:36; Luke 23:36; John 19:29

50 Mark 15:37; Luke 23:46

51 Ex. 26:31; 2Chr. 3:14; Mark 15:38; Luke 23:45

54 Matt. 27:36; Mark 15:39; Luke 23:47

55 Luke 8:2, 3

56 Mark 15:40

57 Mark 15:42; Luke 23:50; John 19:38

60 Isa. 53:9

63 Matt. 16:21; 17:23; 20:19; 26:61; Mark 8:31; 10:34; Luke 9:22; 18:33; 24:6, 7; John 2:19

66 Dan. 6:17

1 Matt. 27:56; Mark 16:1; Luke 24:1; John 20:1

2 Mark 16:5; Luke 24:4; John 20:12

27:51–53 the veil of the temple. This could refer to the curtain over the entrance to the Holy Place (which could be viewed from the porch), but probably refers to the curtain separating the Holy Place from the Holy of Holies (cf. Ex. 26:31). This symbolizes the permanent opening of God's presence to us, giving us direct access to God through the atoning death of Christ (Heb. 10:19–20).

27:57–61 rich man of Arimathaea, named Joseph. In fulfillment of Isaiah 53:9, Jesus made His death with the rich. A recent disciple of Christ, Joseph was a member of the Sanhedrin. His wealth enabled him to own a tomb at Jerusalem, even though he lived nearly twenty miles away.

27:62–66 the day of the preparation. Some question whether this was Saturday (the Sabbath), following a Friday crucifixion. John 19:14, 31 indicates that this "preparation" day was the day before the Passover feast day. In modern Greek, the word here translated "preparation"

(*paraskeue*) is the word for Friday.

28:1–7 All four Gospels agree in reporting the facts of the Resurrection. The variety of details in each account supplement rather than contradict one another. The empty tomb was discovered "in the end [Gr. *opsē,* "after"] of the sabbath," agreeing with the other evangelists. By Jewish reckoning, the day ended at sunset and the new day began at the same time. Saturday night by modern reckoning was actually Sunday by their calendar. Accordingly, the Resurrection actually occurred sometime during the night, for by the time the women arrived "as it began to dawn," He had already risen from the dead. The "earthquake" and the "angel" ("man . . . clothed in a long white garment" [Mark 16:5]) who rolled the stone away did not come to let Jesus out of the tomb, but to reveal that it was empty and that He was already gone. (For parallel accounts, see Mark 16:1–20; Luke 24:1–12; John 20:1–31.)

3 His countenance was like lightning, and his raiment white as snow:

4 And for fear of him the keepers did shake, and became as dead *men*.

5 And the angel answered and said unto the women, Fear not ye: for I know that ye seek Jesus, which was crucified.

6 He is not here: for he is risen, as he said. Come, see the place where the Lord lay.

7 And go quickly, and tell his disciples that he is risen from the dead; and, behold, he goeth before you into Galilee; there shall ye see him: lo, I have told you.

8 And they departed quickly from the sepulchre with fear and great joy; and did run to bring his disciples word.

9 And as they went to tell his disciples, behold, Jesus met them, saying, All hail. And they came and held him by the feet, and worshipped him.

10 Then said Jesus unto them, Be not afraid: go tell my brethren that they go into Galilee, and there shall they see me.

11 Now when they were going, behold, some of the watch came into the city, and shewed unto the chief priests all the things that were done.

12 And when they were assembled with the elders, and had taken counsel, they gave large money unto the soldiers,

13 Saying, Say ye, His disciples came by night, and stole him *away* while we slept.

14 And if this come to the governor's ears, we will persuade him, and secure you.

15 So they took the money, and did as they were taught: and this saying is commonly reported among the Jews until this day.

The Great Commission

16 Then the eleven disciples went away into Galilee, into a mountain where Jesus had appointed them.

17 And when they saw him, they worshipped him: but some doubted.

18 And Jesus came and spake unto them, saying, All power is given unto me in heaven and in earth.

19 Go ye therefore, and teach all nations, baptizing them in the name of the Father, and of the Son, and of the Holy Ghost:

20 Teaching them to observe all things whatsoever I have commanded you: and, lo, I am with you alway, even unto the end of the world. Amen.

Cross references:

3 Dan. 10:6
6 Matt. 12:40; 16:21; 17:23; 20:19
7 Matt. 26:32; Mark 16:7
9 Mark 16:9; John 20:14
10 John 20:17; Rom. 8:29; Heb. 2:11
16 Matt. 26:32; 28:7
18 Matt. 11:27; 16:28; Luke 1:32; 10:22; John 3:35; 5:22; 13:3; 17:2; Acts 2:36; Phil. 2:9, 10; Rev. 17:14
19 Mark 16:15; Luke 24:47; Acts 2:38, 39
20 Acts 2:42

28:16–17 This appearance in Galilee is not to be confused with the appearances at Jerusalem, but is probably the same as the appearance to "above five hundred brethren" (cf. 1 Cor. 15:6), with the eleven remaining apostles being among them.

28:18–20 Instead of sending His disciples back to the house of Israel, they were sent into all the world. The kingdom rejected by the Jews is now offered to the Gentiles in accordance with Jesus' earlier parables. The Great Commission brings the Gospel of Matthew to its grand finale. The triumphant, living Lord sends forth His ambassadors to proclaim His gospel throughout the entire world. The Great Commission is not just an order but a pronouncement of victory by the risen Savior through His disciples. Christ's empowerment of the Church to evangelize the world is available to every generation of believers.

Mark

The name Mark is actually a surname, his common name being John (see Acts 12:12; 13:5; 2 Tim. 4:11). Mark was a nephew of Barnabas and a fellow teacher who traveled with Paul and Barnabas on their first missionary journey (Acts 12:25) but chose to abandon them (Acts 13:13). For this reason, Paul refused to consider taking him along on the second missionary journey (Acts 15:36–39). Paul's unwillingness to give Mark opportunity to redeem himself led to such a strong dispute with Barnabas that the two decided to minister in different directions—Paul with Silas and Barnabas with Mark. (see Col. 4:10; 2 Tim. 4:11; Phile. 1:24).

Author
Mark

Date
A.D. 67

Key Truth
Jesus Is the Servant-Son of God

Historic Time
Ministry of John the Baptist to Christ's Ascension

Key Verse
10:45
The Son of man came not to be ministered unto, but to minister.

As tradition suggests, this shortest Gospel may have been composed in Rome with Peter, since it was written to Gentiles—especially Romans. While Matthew stresses Christ's teachings, Mark, in quick-paced style, focuses on His actions, frequently using terms like *forthwith*, *straightway*, and *immediately* (all the same word in Greek). The gospel of Mark is simple, clear, and concise, and abounds in little nuances and details that give readers the feeling that Mark was a key eyewitness to the accounts that he mentions.

Jesus is introduced initially as the "Son of God" (1:1) whose message is good news. The aim of this book is to present Him as the humble Servant, constantly doing His Father's business. The book begins with the preaching of John the Baptist and proceeds with Christ's baptism and the start of His ministry in Galilee.

The book contains fifty distinct predictions, including the prophetic mysteries of the kingdom (chap. 4), the parable of the vineyard farmers who killed the owner's son (chap. 12), and the condensed version of the Olivet Discourse (cf. Matt. 24—25) relate to this current dispensation and to the End Times.

Predictive matter is contained in 125 of 662 verses, or 19 percent of the whole. There are 22 Old Testament quotations in Mark, most by Jesus Himself.

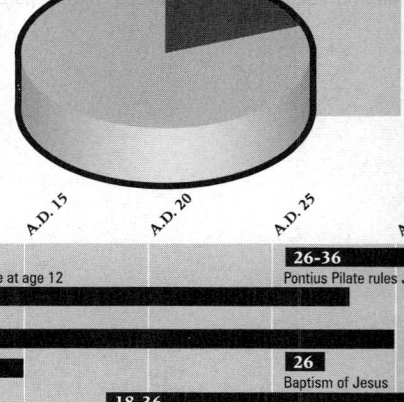

19%
Prophecy

10 B.C.	5 B.C.	A.D. 1	A.D. 5	A.D. 10	A.D. 15	A.D. 20	A.D. 25

9
Jesus in the temple at age 12

26-36
Pontius Pilate rules J

6 B.C.-A.D. 28
Life of John the Baptist

5 B.C.-A.D. 30
Life of Christ

6-15
Annas serves as high priest

26
Baptism of Jesus

18-36
Caiaphas serves as high priest

27 B.C.-A.D. 14
Agustus is Emperor of Rome

14-37
Tiberius is Emperor of Rome

4 B.C.-A.D. 39
Herod Antipas rules over Galilee

26-30
Events of Mark's Gos

CHAPTER 1

John the Baptist Preaches

1 The beginning of the gospel of Jesus Christ, the Son of God;

2 As it is written in the prophets, Behold, I send my messenger before thy face, which shall prepare thy way before thee.

3 The voice of one crying in the wilderness, Prepare ye the way of the Lord, make his paths straight.

4 John did baptize in the wilderness, and preach the baptism of repentance for the remission of sins.

5 And there went out unto him all the land of Judea, and they of Jerusalem, and were all baptized of him in the river of Jordan, confessing their sins.

6 And John was clothed with camel's hair, and with a girdle of a skin about his loins; and he did eat locusts and wild honey;

7 And preached, saying, There cometh one mightier than I after me, the latchet of whose shoes I am not worthy to stoop down and unloose.

8 I indeed have baptized you with water: but he shall baptize you with the Holy Ghost.

John Baptizes Jesus

9 And it came to pass in those days, that Jesus came from Nazareth of Galilee, and was baptized of John in Jordan.

10 And straightway coming up out of the water, he saw the heavens opened, and the Spirit like a dove descending upon him:

11 And there came a voice from heaven, *saying*, Thou art my beloved Son, in whom I am well pleased.

The Devil Tempts Jesus

12 And immediately the Spirit driveth him into the wilderness.

13 And he was there in the wilderness forty days, tempted of Satan; and was with the wild beasts; and the angels ministered unto him.

Jesus Preaches Repentance

14 Now after that John was put in prison, Jesus came into Galilee, preaching the gospel of the kingdom of God,

15 And saying, The time is fulfilled, and the kingdom of God is at hand: repent ye, and believe the gospel.

Jesus Calls Four Fishermen

16 Now as he walked by the sea of Galilee, he saw Simon and Andrew his brother casting a net into the sea: for they were fishers.

17 And Jesus said unto them, Come ye after me, and I will make you to become fishers of men.

18 And straightway they forsook their nets, and followed him.

19 And when he had gone a little farther thence, he saw James the *son* of Zebedee,

Cross references

2 Mal. 3:1; Matt. 11:10; Luke 7:27
3 Isa. 40:3; Matt. 3:3; Luke 3:4; John 1:15, 23
4 Matt. 3:1; Luke 3:3; John 3:23
5 Matt. 3:5
6 Lev. 11:22; Matt. 3:4
7 Matt. 3:11; John 1:27; Acts 13:25
8 Joel 2:28; Acts 1:5; 2:4
9 Matt. 3:13; Luke 3:21
10 Matt. 3:16; John 1:32
11 Matt. 3:17; Mark 9:7
12 Matt. 4:1; Luke 4:1
14 Matt. 4:12, 23
15 Matt. 3:2; 4:17
16 Matt. 4:18; Luke 5:4
18 Matt. 19:27; Luke 5:11

1:1 Son of God. Mark immediately introduces the facts and personalities initially involved in spreading the good news about Jesus. The title, "Son of God," expresses the relation of the Son to the Father, emphasizing His deity as God "manifest in the flesh" (1 Tim. 3:16). Seven aspects of Christ's sonship are mentioned in the Gospel of Mark: 1) "Son of God" (cf. 3:11; 15:39); 2) "Son of man," used fifteen times, stressing His humanity; 3) "my beloved Son" (1:10–11), revealing Him as within the Trinity (Father-Son-Spirit); 4) "Son of the Most High God" (5:7), used by demons acknowledging His authority; 5) "son of Mary" (6:3), identifying Him with His human family; 6) "Son of David" (10:47–48; 12:35), denoting His royalty; and 7) "Son of the Blessed" (14:61), used by the high priest at Jesus' trial in connection with His messiahship.

1:2–3 Behold . . . my messenger. A quotation of a prophecy by Isaiah (40:3), it is literally fulfilled in the well-publicized ministry of John the Baptist. Except for Jesus' own quotations from the Old Testament, this is the only quotation of the Old Testament in the Gospel of Mark. This gospel was originally intended for the Romans, who would have little knowledge of the Old Testament. Therefore, Mark focuses on the public ministry and miracles of Jesus, not on the Old Testament background of Messiah (as does Matthew).

1:4 baptism of repentance. John baptized people only as they confessed and repented, in preparation for them to receive the Messiah. There is no evidence that Jesus rebaptized John's disciples, but after the Resurrection and Ascension, twelve disciples who had received only the baptism of John were again baptized (Acts 19:1–5).

1:9 Jesus . . . baptized. By this action, Jesus identified Himself with John and his teaching, fulfilling all righteousness as the Son of God (Matt. 3:15).

1:14–15 the gospel of the kingdom of God. The time fulfilled may refer to the 483 years (69 weeks of years) which Daniel prophesied would end with the first advent of the Messiah (see the notes on Daniel 9:24; 9:26; and 9:27). The "kingdom" here is concerned with the dominion of the Messiah over Israel.

and John his brother, who also were in the ship mending their nets.

20 And straightway he called them: and they left their father Zebedee in the ship with the hired servants, and went after him.

The Man with an Unclean Spirit

21 And they went into Capernaum; and straightway on the sabbath day he entered into the synagogue, and taught.

22 And they were astonished at his doctrine: for he taught them as one that had authority, and not as the scribes.

23 And there was in their synagogue a man with an unclean spirit; and he cried out,

24 Saying, Let *us* alone; what have we to do with thee, thou Jesus of Nazareth? art thou come to destroy us? I know thee who thou art, the Holy One of God.

25 And Jesus rebuked him, saying, Hold thy peace, and come out of him.

26 And when the unclean spirit had torn him, and cried with a loud voice, he came out of him.

27 And they were all amazed, insomuch that they questioned among themselves saying, What thing is this? what new doctrine *is* this? for with authority commandeth he even the unclean spirits, and they do obey him.

28 And immediately his fame spread abroad throughout all the region round about Galilee.

Jesus Heals Many

29 And forthwith, when they were come out of the synagogue, they entered into the house of Simon and Andrew, with James and John.

30 But Simon's wife's mother lay sick of a fever, and anon they tell him of her.

31 And he came and took her by the hand, and lifted her up; and immediately the fever left her, and she ministered unto them.

32 And at even, when the sun did set, they brought unto him all that were diseased, and them that were possessed with devils.

33 And all the city was gathered together at the door.

34 And he healed many that were sick of divers diseases, and cast out many devils; and suffered not the devils to speak, because they knew him.

Jesus Ministers in All of Galilee

35 And in the morning, rising up a great while before day, he went out, and departed into a solitary place, and there prayed.

36 And Simon and they that were with him followed after him.

37 And when they had found him, they said unto him, All *men* seek for thee.

38 And he said unto them, Let us go into the next towns, that I may preach there also: for therefore came I forth.

39 And he preached in their synagogues throughout all Galilee, and cast out devils.

Jesus Cleanses a Leper

40 And there came a leper to him, beseeching him, and kneeling down to him, and saying unto him, If thou wilt, thou canst make me clean.

41 And Jesus, moved with compassion, put forth *his* hand, and touched him, and saith unto him, I will; be thou clean.

42 And, as soon as he had spoken, immediately the leprosy departed from him, and he was cleansed.

43 And he straitly charged him, and forthwith sent him away;

44 And saith unto him, See thou say nothing to any man: but go thy way, shew thyself to the priest, and offer for thy cleansing those things which Moses commanded, for a testimony unto them.

45 But he went out, and began to publish *it* much, and to blaze abroad the matter, insomuch that Jesus could no more openly enter into the city, but was without in desert places: and they came to him from every quarter.

CHAPTER 2

Jesus Heals a Crippled Man

1 And again he entered into Capernaum after *some* days; and it was noised that he was in the house.

2 And straightway many were gathered together, insomuch that there was no room to receive *them*, no, not so much as about the door: and he preached the word unto them.

3 And they come unto him, bringing one sick of the palsy, which was borne of four.

4 And when they could not come nigh unto him for the press, they uncovered the roof where he was: and when they had broken *it* up, they let down the bed wherein the sick of the palsy lay.

5 When Jesus saw their faith, he said unto the sick of the palsy, Son, thy sins be forgiven thee.

6 But there were certain of the scribes sitting there, and reasoning in their hearts,

21 Matt. 4:13; Luke 4:31

22 Matt. 7:28

23 Luke 4:33

24 Matt. 8:29

25 Mark 1:34

26 Mark 9:20

29 Matt. 8:14; Luke 4:38

32 Matt. 8:16; Luke 4:40

34 Mark 3:12; Luke 4:41, 42; Acts 16:17, 18

38 Isa. 61:1; Luke 4:43; John 16:28; 17:4

39 Matt. 4:23; Luke 4:44

40 Matt. 8:2; Luke 5:12

44 Lev. 14:3, 4, 10; Luke 5:14

45 Mark 2:13; Luke 5:15

1 Matt. 9:1; Luke 5:18

7 Why doth this *man* thus speak blasphemies? who can forgive sins but God only?

8 And immediately when Jesus perceived in his spirit that they so reasoned within themselves, he said unto them, Why reason ye these things in your hearts?

9 Whether is it easier to say to the sick of the palsy, Thy sins be forgiven thee; or to say, Arise, and take up thy bed, and walk?

10 But that ye may know that the Son of man hath power on earth to forgive sins, (he saith to the sick of the palsy,)

11 I say unto thee, Arise, and take up thy bed, and go thy way into thine house.

12 And immediately he arose, took up the bed, and went forth before them all; insomuch that they were all amazed, and glorified God, saying, We never saw it on this fashion.

Jesus Calls Levi

13 And he went forth again by the sea side; and all the multitude resorted unto him, and he taught them.

14 And as he passed by, he saw Levi the *son* of Alphaeus sitting at the receipt of custom, and said unto him, Follow me. And he arose and followed him.

15 And it came to pass, that, as Jesus sat at meat in his house, many publicans and sinners sat also together with Jesus and his disciples: for there were many, and they followed him.

16 And when the scribes and Pharisees saw him eat with publicans and sinners, they said unto his disciples, How is it that he eateth and drinketh with publicans and sinners?

17 When Jesus heard *it*, he saith unto them, They that are whole have no need of the physician, but they that are sick: I came not to call the righteous, but sinners to repentance.

7 Job 14:4; Isa. 43:25
8 Matt. 9:4
9 Matt. 9:5
13 Matt. 9:9
14 Matt. 9:9; Luke 5:27
15 Matt. 9:10
17 Matt. 9:12, 13; 18:11; Luke 5:31, 32; 19:10; 1Tim. 1:15
18 Matt. 9:14; Luke 5:33

Jesus' Teaching on Fasting

18 And the disciples of John and of the Pharisees used to fast: and they come and say unto him, Why do the disciples of John and of the Pharisees fast, but thy disciples fast not?

19 And Jesus said unto them, Can the children of the bridechamber fast, while the bridegroom is with them? as long as they have the bridegroom with them, they cannot fast.

20 But the days will come, when the bridegroom shall be taken away from them, and then shall they fast in those days.

21 No man also seweth a piece of new cloth on an old garment: else the new piece that filled it up taketh away from the old, and the rent is made worse.

22 And no man putteth new wine into old bottles: else the new wine doth burst the bottles, and the wine is spilled, and the bottles will be marred: but new wine must be put into new bottles.

Jesus Is Lord over the Sabbath Day

23 And it came to pass, that he went through the corn fields on the sabbath day; and his disciples began, as they went, to pluck the ears of corn.

24 And the Pharisees said unto him, Behold, why do they on the sabbath day that which is not lawful?

25 And he said unto them, Have ye never read what David did, when he had need, and was an hungred, he, and they that were with him?

26 How he went into the house of God in the days of Abiathar the high priest, and did eat the shewbread, which is not lawful to eat but for the priests, and gave also to them which were with him?

27 And he said unto them, The sabbath was made for man, and not man for the sabbath:

28 Therefore the Son of man is Lord also of the sabbath.

23 Deut. 23:25; Matt. 12:1; Luke 6:1
25 1Sam. 21:6
26 Ex. 29:32, 33; Lev. 24:9
28 Matt. 12:8

2:10 Son of man. This is the first of fifteen instances where this title appears in the Gospel of Mark (cf. Dan. 7:13–14). The term identifies Christ as truly human, but since He is God, the only individual qualified to be Messiah-king. It also implies Jesus' prophetic office, as the Jews must have realized, remembering it was a title bestowed upon Ezekiel, the great prophet of things regarding the future kingdom age.

2:19 the bridegroom is with them. John the Baptist called himself "the friend of the bridegroom" (John 3:26–30). In this and other passages, the bride is the Church, and Jesus is the bridegroom (cf. Matt. 25:1; Eph. 5:25–32).

2:21–22 new cloth . . . new wine . . . new bottles. Jesus begins to contrast His teaching with legalistic Judaism, an initial prediction that the Christian faith that would develop from His teachings would not be merely a reform of traditional Judaism. At this stage it was not revealed that these events would introduce a whole new dispensation (see Gal. 2:15–21; Eph. 3:1–11).

CHAPTER 3

Jesus Heals a Man on the Sabbath Day

1 And he entered again into the synagogue; and there was a man there which had a withered hand.

2 And they watched him, whether he would heal him on the sabbath day; that they might accuse him.

3 And he saith unto the man which had the withered hand, Stand forth.

4 And he saith unto them, Is it lawful to do good on the sabbath days, or to do evil? to save life, or to kill? But they held their peace.

5 And when he had looked round about on them with anger, being grieved for the hardness of their hearts, he saith unto the man, Stretch forth thine hand. And he stretched *it* out: and his hand was restored whole as the other.

6 And the Pharisees went forth, and straightway took counsel with the Herodians against him, how they might destroy him.

A Multitude Follows Jesus to the Sea

7 But Jesus withdrew himself with his disciples to the sea: and a great multitude from Galilee followed him, and from Judea,

8 And from Jerusalem, and from Idumea, and *from* beyond Jordan; and they about Tyre and Sidon, a great multitude, when they had heard what great things he did, came unto him.

9 And he spake to his disciples, that a small ship should wait on him because of the multitude, lest they should throng him.

10 For he had healed many; insomuch that they pressed upon him for to touch him, as many as had plagues.

11 And unclean spirits, when they saw him, fell down before him, and cried, saying, Thou art the Son of God.

12 And he straitly charged them that they should not make him known.

Jesus Chooses Twelve Apostles

13 And he goeth up into a mountain, and calleth *unto him* whom he would: and they came unto him.

14 And he ordained twelve, that they should be with him, and that he might send them forth to preach,

15 And to have power to heal sicknesses, and to cast out devils:

16 And Simon he surnamed Peter;

17 And James the *son* of Zebedee, and John the brother of James; and he surnamed them Boanerges, which is, The sons of thunder:

18 And Andrew, and Philip, and Bartholomew, and Matthew, and Thomas, and James the *son* of Alphaeus, and Thaddaeus, and Simon the Canaanite,

19 And Judas Iscariot, which also betrayed him: and they went into an house.

Jesus Accused of Being Beelzebub

20 And the multitude cometh together again, so that they could not so much as eat bread.

21 And when his friends heard *of it,* they went out to lay hold on him: for they said, He is beside himself.

22 And the scribes which came down from Jerusalem said, He hath Beelzebub, and by the prince of the devils casteth he out devils.

23 And he called them *unto him,* and said unto them in parables, How can Satan cast out Satan?

24 And if a kingdom be divided against itself, that kingdom cannot stand.

25 And if a house be divided against itself, that house cannot stand.

26 And if Satan rise up against himself, and be divided, he cannot stand, but hath an end.

27 No man can enter into a strong man's house, and spoil his goods, except he will first bind the strong man; and then he will spoil his house.

Cross references

1 Matt. 12:9; Luke 6:6
6 Matt. 12:14; 22:16
7 Luke 6:17
11 Matt. 14:33; Mark 1:1, 23, 24; Luke 4:41
12 Matt. 12:16; Mark 1:25, 34
13 Matt. 10:1; Luke 6:12; 9:1
16 John 1:42
20 Mark 6:31
21 John 7:5; 10:20
22 Matt. 9:34; 10:25; Luke 11:15; John 7:20; 8:48, 52; 10:20
23 Matt. 12:25
27 Isa. 49:24; Matt. 12:29

3:6 The Pharisees were a strict Jewish sect, which observed not only the letter of the law, but a vast array of traditions, some of which nullified the Mosaic Law (Matt. 15:2–6; Mark 7:9). These joined with the Herodians, a Jewish political group, which supported the Herodian family of rulers and favored cooperation with Rome. Already, plots of violence against Jesus had begun.

3:13–19 Four lists of apostles appear in the New Testament (Matt. 10:1–4; Luke 6:13–16; Acts 1:13), and several have more than one name. The apostles are destined to sit on thrones, judging the twelve tribes of Israel in the Millennium (Matt. 19:28). Their names are to be inscribed on the twelve foundations of the New Jerusalem (Rev. 21:14).

Blasphemy against the Holy Spirit

28 Verily I say unto you, All sins shall be forgiven unto the sons of men, and blasphemies wherewith soever they shall blaspheme:

29 But he that shall blaspheme against the Holy Ghost hath never forgiveness, but is in danger of eternal damnation:

30 Because they said, He hath an unclean spirit.

Jesus' Mother and Brothers

31 There came then his brethren and his mother, and, standing without, sent unto him, calling him.

32 And the multitude sat about him, and they said unto him, Behold, thy mother and thy brethren without seek for thee.

33 And he answered them, saying, Who is my mother, or my brethren?

34 And he looked round about on them which sat about him, and said, Behold my mother and my brethren!

35 For whosoever shall do the will of God, the same is my brother, and my sister, and mother.

CHAPTER 4
The Parable of the Sower

1 And he began again to teach by the sea side: and there was gathered unto him a great multitude, so that he entered into a ship, and sat in the sea; and the whole multitude was by the sea on the land.

2 And he taught them many things by parables, and said unto them in his doctrine,

3 Hearken; Behold, there went out a sower to sow:

4 And it came to pass, as he sowed, some fell by the way side, and the fowls of the air came and devoured it up.

5 And some fell on stony ground, where it had not much earth; and immediately it sprang up, because it had no depth of earth:

6 But when the sun was up, it was scorched; and because it had no root, it withered away.

7 And some fell among thorns, and the thorns grew up, and choked it, and it yielded no fruit.

8 And other fell on good ground, and did yield fruit that sprang up and increased; and brought forth, some thirty, and some sixty, and some an hundred.

9 And he said unto them, He that hath ears to hear, let him hear.

Why Jesus Taught in Parables

10 And when he was alone, they that were about him with the twelve asked of him the parable.

11 And he said unto them, Unto you it is given to know the mystery of the kingdom of God: but unto them that are without, all these things are done in parables:

12 That seeing they may see, and not perceive; and hearing they may hear, and not understand; lest at any time they should be converted, and their sins should be forgiven them.

Explanation of the Parable of the Sower

13 And he said unto them, Know ye not this parable? and how then will ye know all parables?

14 The sower soweth the word.

15 And these are they by the way side, where the word is sown; but when they have heard, Satan cometh immediately, and taketh away the word that was sown in their hearts.

Cross-references (center column)

28 Matt. 12:31; Luke 12:10; 1John 5:16

31 Matt. 12:46; Luke 8:19

1 Matt. 13:1; Luke 8:4

2 Mark 12:38

8 John 15:5; Col. 1:6

10 Matt. 13:10; Luke 8:9, 10

11 1Cor. 5:12; Col. 4:5; 1Thess. 4:12; 1Tim. 3:7

12 Isa. 6:9; Matt. 13:14; Luke 8:10; John 12:40; Acts 28:26; Rom. 11:8

14 Matt. 13:19

3:35 the will of God. Both then and now, those who do the will of God by believing and following Jesus become His spiritual extended family. Some of Jesus' "friends" (v. 21), which encompassed close friends and His brothers, thought He was out of His mind. Jesus was not being unkind, but knew their thoughts at this particular time, and alluded to the new concept of the great, close-knit spiritual family of all believers (see Eph. 3:15).

4:1–20 Of the seven parables in Matthew 13, only the parable of the sower and the parable of the mustard seed (Mark 4:30–32) appear in the Gospel of Mark (see Matt. 13:1–53, cf. Luke 8:4–15). The kingdom of God (or heaven) spoken of here is not the coming Millennial Kingdom (see Luke 19:11; Acts 1:6; Rev. 12:10), but rather this present age. These parables speak of the time between the two comings of Christ, but particularly denote the people and the areas where the Christian religion has spread, including both the "saved" and the "lost" ("tares" and "wheat," Matt. 13:24–30).

4:15–20 This parable uses four kinds of soil to represent people who hear the gospel: 1) wayside hearers, who are unresponsive and susceptible to satanic interference; 2) stony ground hearers, who quickly make profession but lack true conversion; 3) hearers among thorns, who are so enmeshed in worldly concerns, money-making, and self-centered desires, that they are unfruitful; 4) responsive hearers, who heed God's message and bring forth fruit (see John 15:1–8).

16 And these are they likewise which are sown on stony ground; who, when they have heard the word, immediately receive it with gladness;

17 And have no root in themselves, and so endure but for a time: afterward, when affliction or persecution ariseth for the word's sake, immediately they are offended.

18 And these are they which are sown among thorns; such as hear the word,

19 And the cares of this world, and the deceitfulness of riches, and the lusts of other things entering in, choke the word, and it becometh unfruitful.

20 And these are they which are sown on good ground; such as hear the word, and receive it, and bring forth fruit, some thirtyfold, some sixty, and some an hundred.

A Light under a Bushel

21 And he said unto them, Is a candle brought to be put under a bushel, or under a bed? and not to be set on a candlestick?

22 For there is nothing hid, which shall not be manifested; neither was any thing kept secret, but that it should come abroad.

23 If any man have ears to hear, let him hear.

24 And he said unto them, Take heed what ye hear: with what measure ye mete, it shall be measured to you: and unto you that hear shall more be given.

25 For he that hath, to him shall be given: and he that hath not, from him shall be taken even that which he hath.

The Parable of the Growth of the Seed

26 And he said, So is the kingdom of God, as if a man should cast seed into the ground;

27 And should sleep, and rise night and day, and the seed should spring and grow up, he knoweth not how.

28 For the earth bringeth forth fruit of herself; first the blade, then the ear, after that the full corn in the ear.

29 But when the fruit is brought forth, immediately he putteth in the sickle, because the harvest is come.

The Parable of the Mustard Seed

30 And he said, Whereunto shall we liken the kingdom of God? or with what comparison shall we compare it?

31 It is like a grain of mustard seed, which, when it is sown in the earth, is less than all the seeds that be in the earth:

32 But when it is sown, it groweth up, and becometh greater than all herbs, and shooteth out great branches; so that the fowls of the air may lodge under the shadow of it.

Jesus' Use of Parables

33 And with many such parables spake he the word unto them, as they were able to hear *it*.

34 But without a parable spake he not unto them: and when they were alone, he expounded all things to his disciples.

Jesus Calms a Storm

35 And the same day, when the even was come, he saith unto them, Let us pass over unto the other side.

36 And when they had sent away the multitude, they took him even as he was in the ship. And there were also with him other little ships.

37 And there arose a great storm of wind, and the waves beat into the ship, so that it was now full.

38 And he was in the hinder part of the ship, asleep on a pillow: and they awake him, and say unto him, Master, carest thou not that we perish?

39 And he arose, and rebuked the wind, and said unto the sea, Peace, be still. And the wind ceased, and there was a great calm.

40 And he said unto them, Why are ye so fearful? how is it that ye have no faith?

41 And they feared exceedingly, and said one to another, What manner of man is this, that even the wind and the sea obey him?

CHAPTER 5
Healing the Gadarene Demoniac

1 And they came over unto the other side of the sea, into the country of the Gadarenes.

Cross-references

19 1Tim. 6:9, 17
21 Matt. 5:15; Luke 8:16; 11:33
22 Matt. 10:26; Luke 12:2
23 Matt. 11:15; Mark 4:9
24 Matt. 7:2; Luke 6:38
25 Matt. 13:12; 25:29; Luke 8:18; 19:26
26 Matt. 13:24
29 Rev. 14:15
30 Matt. 13:31; Luke 13:18; Acts 2:41; 4:4; 5:14; 19:20
33 Matt. 13:34; John 16:12
35 Matt. 8:18, 23; Luke 8:22
1 Matt. 8:28; Luke 8:26

4:26–29 It was supposed by many that the messianic kingdom would suddenly appear, which it will at the glorious appearing of Christ (2 Thess. 1:7–10; Titus 2:13). But, in this age, the gospel that began as a seed will grow until the return of Christ and the "harvest" (cf. Matt. 13:24–30, 47–50).

4:31–34 grain of mustard seed. This parable also relates to this present age, symbolizing the rapid spread of the Christian religion over the world (see the note on Luke 13:19).

5:1–20 Jesus frees a deranged victim of "unclean

2 And when he was come out of the ship, immediately there met him out of the tombs a man with an unclean spirit,
3 Who had *his* dwelling among the tombs; and no man could bind him, no, not with chains:
4 Because that he had been often bound with fetters and chains, and the chains had been plucked asunder by him, and the fetters broken in pieces: neither could any *man* tame him.
5 And always, night and day, he was in the mountains, and in the tombs, crying, and cutting himself with stones.
6 But when he saw Jesus afar off, he ran and worshipped him,
7 And cried with a loud voice, and said, What have I to do with thee, Jesus, *thou* Son of the most high God? I adjure thee by God, that thou torment me not.
8 For he said unto him, Come out of the man, thou unclean spirit.
9 And he asked him, What is thy name? And he answered, saying, My name *is* Legion: for we are many.
10 And he besought him much that he would not send them away out of the country.
11 Now there was there nigh unto the mountains a great herd of swine feeding.
12 And all the devils besought him, saying, Send us into the swine, that we may enter into them.
13 And forthwith Jesus gave them leave. And the unclean spirits went out, and entered into the swine: and the herd ran violently down a steep place into the sea, (they were about two thousand;) and were choked in the sea.
14 And they that fed the swine fled, and told *it* in the city, and in the country. And they went out to see what it was that was done.
15 And they come to Jesus, and see him that was possessed with the devil, and had the legion, sitting, and clothed, and in his right mind: and they were afraid.

17 Matt. 8:34; Luke 8:38; Acts 16:39
21 Matt. 9:1; Luke 8:40
22 Matt. 9:18; Luke 8:41
25 Lev. 15:25; Matt. 9:20

16 And they that saw *it* told them how it befell to him that was possessed with the devil, and *also* concerning the swine.
17 And they began to pray him to depart out of their coasts.
18 And when he was come into the ship, he that had been possessed with the devil prayed him that he might be with him.
19 Howbeit Jesus suffered him not, but saith unto him, Go home to thy friends, and tell them how great things the Lord hath done for thee, and hath had compassion on thee.
20 And he departed, and began to publish in Decapolis how great things Jesus had done for him: and all *men* did marvel.

Jesus Raises Jairus' Daughter

21 And when Jesus was passed over again by ship unto the other side, much people gathered unto him: and he was nigh unto the sea.
22 And, behold, there cometh one of the rulers of the synagogue, Jairus by name; and when he saw him, he fell at his feet,
23 And besought him greatly, saying, My little daughter lieth at the point of death: *I pray thee,* come and lay thy hands on her, that she may be healed; and she shall live.
24 And *Jesus* went with him; and much people followed him, and thronged him.
25 And a certain woman, which had an issue of blood twelve years,
26 And had suffered many things of many physicians, and had spent all that she had, and was nothing bettered, but rather grew worse,
27 When she had heard of Jesus, came in the press behind, and touched his garment.
28 For she said, If I may touch but his clothes, I shall be whole.
29 And straightway the fountain of her blood was dried up; and she felt in *her* body that she was healed of that plague.

spirits," or demons. Demons are unclean spirits, fallen angels, responsible to Beelzebub, the prince of demons (Satan), the one actual devil (Gr. *diabolos*). Satan is at work, using his fallen angels (see Eph. 6:11–12), demonic beings, and demon-possessed people to foster violence, immorality, and occultism. Some demons are imprisoned and will be loosed from the bottomless pit to torment men during the Tribulation (see Rev. 9:1–12). Others are free, but seem to seek embodiment (Matt.

12:45). Every time Jesus confronted demons they recognized Him and admitted that He was the Son of the Most High God.

5:9 Legion. The vocal demon was a representative of a "legion" of demons, indwelling and tormenting this tragic victim. While its usage here is expressive of a huge number, an actual Roman legion could number six thousand soldiers.

30 And Jesus, immediately knowing in himself that virtue had gone out of him, turned him about in the press, and said, Who touched my clothes?

31 And his disciples said unto him, Thou seest the multitude thronging thee, and sayest thou, Who touched me?

32 And he looked round about to see her that had done this thing.

33 But the woman fearing and trembling, knowing what was done in her, came and fell down before him, and told him all the truth.

34 And he said unto her, Daughter, thy faith hath made thee whole; go in peace, and be whole of thy plague.

35 While he yet spake, there came from the ruler of the synagogue's *house certain* which said, Thy daughter is dead: why troublest thou the Master any further?

36 As soon as Jesus heard the word that was spoken, he saith unto the ruler of the synagogue, Be not afraid, only believe.

37 And he suffered no man to follow him, save Peter, and James, and John the brother of James.

38 And he cometh to the house of the ruler of the synagogue, and seeth the tumult, and them that wept and wailed greatly.

39 And when he was come in, he saith unto them, Why make ye this ado, and weep? the damsel is not dead, but sleepeth.

40 And they laughed him to scorn. But when he had put them all out, he taketh the father and the mother of the damsel, and them that were with him, and entereth in where the damsel was lying.

41 And he took the damsel by the hand, and said unto her, Talitha cumi; which is, being interpreted, Damsel, I say unto thee, arise.

42 And straightway the damsel arose, and walked; for she was *of the age* of twelve years. And they were astonished with a great astonishment.

43 And he charged them straitly that no man should know it; and commanded that something should be given her to eat.

Cross references

30 Luke 6:19; 8:46
34 Matt. 9:22; Mark 10:52; Acts 14:9
35 Luke 8:49
39 John 11:11
40 Acts 9:40
43 Matt. 8:4; 9:30; 12:16; 17:9; Mark 3:12; Luke 5:14
1 Matt. 13:54; Luke 4:16
2 John 6:42
3 Matt. 11:6; 12:46; Gal. 1:19
4 Matt. 13:57; John 4:44
5 Gen. 19:22; 32:25; Matt. 13:58; Mark 9:23
6 Isa. 59:16; Matt. 9:35; Luke 13:22
7 Matt. 10:1; Mark 3:13, 14; Luke 9:1
9 Acts 12:8
10 Matt. 10:11; Luke 9:4; 10:7, 8
11 Matt. 10:14; Luke 10:10; Acts 13:51; 18:6

CHAPTER 6
Jesus Is Rejected in His Own Home Town

1 And he went out from thence, and came into his own country; and his disciples follow him.

2 And when the sabbath day was come, he began to teach in the synagogue: and many hearing *him* were astonished, saying, From whence hath this *man* these things? and what wisdom *is* this which is given unto him, that even such mighty works are wrought by his hands?

3 Is not this the carpenter, the son of Mary, the brother of James, and Joses, and of Juda, and Simon? and are not his sisters here with us? And they were offended at him.

4 But Jesus said unto them, A prophet is not without honour, but in his own country, and among his own kin, and in his own house.

5 And he could there do no mighty work, save that he laid his hands upon a few sick folk, and healed *them.*

6 And he marvelled because of their unbelief. And he went round about the villages, teaching.

The Mission of the Twelve

7 And he called *unto him* the twelve, and began to send them forth by two and two; and gave them power over unclean spirits;

8 And commanded them that they should take nothing for *their* journey, save a staff only; no scrip, no bread, no money in *their* purse;

9 But *be* shod with sandals; and not put on two coats.

10 And he said unto them, In what place soever ye enter into an house, there abide till ye depart from that place.

11 And whosoever shall not receive you, nor hear you, when ye depart thence, shake off the dust under your feet for a testimony against them. Verily I say unto you, It shall be more tolerable for Sodom and

---

5:30 virtue had gone out of him. When the woman with this serious illness touched Jesus' garment, virtue (Gr. *dunamis,* "dynamic power") flowed from His divine person, healing the woman (cf. Lev. 15:5–27).

6:7 the twelve . . . send them forth. Jesus sends forth His twelve apostles and summarizes their activities on several occasions. They were heralds of the King and the kingdom, which was rejected by the Jews (John 1:11–12). Jesus called the Twelve to be apostles and trained them to proclaim His gospel after His ascension. Hence, they were to become the twelve foundation stones of the Church (Eph. 2:20; Rev. 21:14).

Gomorrah in the day of judgment, than for that city.

12 And they went out, and preached that men should repent.

13 And they cast out many devils, and anointed with oil many that were sick, and healed *them*.

Herod Is Confused about Jesus

14 And king Herod heard *of him*; (for his name was spread abroad:) and he said, That John the Baptist was risen from the dead, and therefore mighty works do shew forth themselves in him.

15 Others said, That it is Elias. And others said, That it is a prophet, or as one of the prophets.

16 But when Herod heard *thereof*, he said, It is John, whom I beheaded: he is risen from the dead.

17 For Herod himself had sent forth and laid hold upon John, and bound him in prison for Herodias' sake, his brother Philip's wife: for he had married her.

18 For John had said unto Herod, It is not lawful for thee to have thy brother's wife.

19 Therefore Herodias had a quarrel against him, and would have killed him; but she could not:

20 For Herod feared John, knowing that he was a just man and an holy, and observed him; and when he heard him, he did many things, and heard him gladly.

21 And when a convenient day was come, that Herod on his birthday made a supper to his lords, high captains, and chief *estates* of Galilee;

22 And the daughter of the said Herodias came in, and danced, and pleased Herod and them that sat with him, the king said unto the damsel, Ask of me whatsoever thou wilt, and I will give *it* thee.

23 And he sware unto her, Whatsoever thou shalt ask of me, I will give *it* thee, unto the half of my kingdom.

24 And she went forth, and said unto her mother, What shall I ask? And she said, The head of John the Baptist.

25 And she came in straightway with haste unto the king, and asked, saying, I will that thou give me by and by in a charger the head of John the Baptist.

26 And the king was exceeding sorry; *yet* for his oath's sake, and for their sakes which sat with him, he would not reject her.

27 And immediately the king sent an executioner, and commanded his head to be

brought: and he went and beheaded him in the prison,

28 And brought his head in a charger, and gave it to the damsel: and the damsel gave it to her mother.

29 And when his disciples heard *of it*, they came and took up his corpse, and laid it in a tomb.

The Feeding of the Five Thousand

30 And the apostles gathered themselves together unto Jesus, and told him all things, both what they had done, and what they had taught.

31 And he said unto them, Come ye yourselves apart into a desert place, and rest a while: for there were many coming and going, and they had no leisure so much as to eat.

32 And they departed into a desert place by ship privately.

33 And the people saw them departing, and many knew him, and ran afoot thither out of all cities, and outwent them, and came together unto him.

34 And Jesus, when he came out, saw much people, and was moved with compassion toward them, because they were as sheep not having a shepherd: and he began to teach them many things.

35 And when the day was now far spent, his disciples came unto him, and said, This is a desert place, and now the time is far passed:

36 Send them away, that they may go into the country round about, and into the villages, and buy themselves bread: for they have nothing to eat.

37 He answered and said unto them, Give ye them to eat. And they say unto him, Shall we go and buy two hundred pennyworth of bread, and give them to eat?

38 He saith unto them, How many loaves have ye? go and see. And when they knew, they say, Five, and two fishes.

39 And he commanded them to make all sit down by companies upon the green grass.

40 And they sat down in ranks, by hundreds, and by fifties.

41 And when he had taken the five loaves and the two fishes, he looked up to heaven, and blessed, and brake the loaves, and gave *them* to his disciples to set before them; and the two fishes divided he among them all.

42 And they did all eat, and were filled.

43 And they took up twelve baskets full of the fragments, and of the fishes.

Cross references (center column)

13 James 5:14

14 Matt. 14:1; Luke 9:7

15 Matt. 16:14; Mark 8:28

16 Matt. 14:2; Luke 3:19

18 Lev. 18:16; 20:21

20 Matt. 14:5; 21:26

21 Gen. 40:20; Matt. 14:6

23 Esth. 5:3, 6; 7:2

26 Matt. 14:9

30 Luke 9:10

31 Matt. 14:13; Mark 3:20

32 Matt. 14:13

34 Matt. 9:36; 14:14; Luke 9:11

35 Matt. 14:15; Luke 9:12

37 Num. 11:13, 22; 2Kgs. 4:43

38 Matt. 14:17; 15:34; Mark 8:5; Luke 9:13; John 6:9

41 1Sam. 9:13; Matt. 26:26

44 And they that did eat of the loaves were about five thousand men.

Jesus Walks on Water

45 And straightway he constrained his disciples to get into the ship, and to go to the other side before unto Bethsaida, while he sent away the people.

46 And when he had sent them away, he departed into a mountain to pray.

47 And when even was come, the ship was in the midst of the sea, and he alone on the land.

48 And he saw them toiling in rowing; for the wind was contrary unto them: and about the fourth watch of the night he cometh unto them, walking upon the sea, and would have passed by them.

49 But when they saw him walking upon the sea, they supposed it had been a spirit, and cried out:

50 For they all saw him, and were troubled. And immediately he talked with them, and saith unto them, Be of good cheer: it is I; be not afraid.

51 And he went up unto them into the ship; and the wind ceased: and they were sore amazed in themselves beyond measure, and wondered.

52 For they considered not *the miracle* of the loaves: for their heart was hardened.

Jesus Heals in Gennesaret

53 And when they had passed over, they came into the land of Gennesaret, and drew to the shore.

54 And when they were come out of the ship, straightway they knew him,

55 And ran through that whole region round about, and began to carry about in beds those that were sick, where they heard he was.

56 And whithersoever he entered, into villages, or cities, or country, they laid the sick in the streets, and besought him that they might touch if it were but the border of his garment: and as many as touched him were made whole.

Cross References (center column)
45 Matt. 14:22; John 6:17
47 Matt. 14:23; John 6:16, 17
48 Luke 24:28
52 Mark 3:5; 8:17, 18; 16:14
53 Matt. 14:34
56 Matt. 9:20; Mark 5:27, 28; Acts 19:12
1 Matt. 15:1
5 Matt. 15:2
6 Isa. 29:13; Matt. 15:8
10 Ex. 20:12; 21:17; Lev. 20:9; Deut. 5:16; Prov. 20:20; Matt. 15:4
11 Matt. 15:5; 23:18

CHAPTER 7
God's Command or Man's Tradition?

1 Then came together unto him the Pharisees, and certain of the scribes, which came from Jerusalem.

2 And when they saw some of his disciples eat bread with defiled, that is to say, with unwashen, hands, they found fault.

3 For the Pharisees, and all the Jews, except they wash *their* hands oft, eat not, holding the tradition of the elders.

4 And *when they come* from the market, except they wash, they eat not. And many other things there be, which they have received to hold, *as* the washing of cups, and pots, brasen vessels, and of tables.

5 Then the Pharisees and scribes asked him, Why walk not thy disciples according to the tradition of the elders, but eat bread with unwashen hands?

6 He answered and said unto them, Well hath Esaias prophesied of you hypocrites, as it is written, This people honoureth me with their lips, but their heart is far from me.

7 Howbeit in vain do they worship me, teaching for doctrines the commandments of men.

8 For laying aside the commandment of God, ye hold the tradition of men, as the washing of pots and cups: and many other such like things ye do.

9 And he said unto them, Full well ye reject the commandment of God, that ye may keep your own tradition.

10 For Moses said, Honour thy father and thy mother; and, Whoso curseth father or mother, let him die the death:

11 But ye say, If a man shall say to his father or mother, It is Corban, that is to say, a gift, by whatsoever thou mightest be profited by me; he shall be free.

12 And ye suffer him no more to do ought for his father or his mother;

13 Making the word of God of none effect through your tradition, which ye have delivered: and many such like things do ye.

6:56 as many as touched him were made whole. Although the chapter opens with His being rejected at Nazareth, it closes with a grand reception in Gennesaret. In a similar fashion, when He comes again, the Son of Man in humiliation will, as the Son of Man with power and glory, be known to all. Then the earth as a whole will be blessed as Gennesaret was here.

7:2–9 Well hath Esaias prophesied. Citing Isaiah 29:13, Jesus rebukes these legalistic teachers, who practiced religiosity, but in their hearts were far from God. Substituting religious practices or humanistic philosophy for the divinely revealed, literal truth of God's word leads to false and erroneous teaching.

Evil Comes from the Heart

14 And when he had called all the people *unto him,* he said unto them, Hearken unto me every one of you, and understand:

15 There is nothing from without a man, that entering into him can defile him: but the things which come out of him, those are they that defile the man.

16 If any man have ears to hear, let him hear.

17 And when he was entered into the house from the people, his disciples asked him concerning the parable.

18 And he saith unto them, Are ye so without understanding also? Do ye not perceive, that whatsoever thing from without entereth into the man, it cannot defile him;

19 Because it entereth not into his heart, but into the belly, and goeth out into the draught, purging all meats?

20 And he said, That which cometh out of the man, that defileth the man.

21 For from within, out of the heart of men, proceed evil thoughts, adulteries, fornications, murders,

22 Thefts, covetousness, wickedness, deceit, lasciviousness, an evil eye, blasphemy, pride, foolishness:

23 All these evil things come from within, and defile the man.

Jesus Honors a Syrophenician Woman's Faith

24 And from thence he arose, and went into the borders of Tyre and Sidon, and entered into an house, and would have no man know *it,* but he could not be hid.

25 For a *certain* woman, whose young daughter had an unclean spirit, heard of him, and came and fell at his feet:

26 The woman was a Greek, a Syrophenician by nation; and she besought him that he would cast forth the devil out of her daughter.

27 But Jesus said unto her, Let the children first be filled: for it is not meet to take the children's bread, and to cast it unto the dogs.

28 And she answered and said unto him, Yes, Lord: yet the dogs under the table eat of the children's crumbs.

29 And he said unto her, For this saying go thy way; the devil is gone out of thy daughter.

30 And when she was come to her house, she found the devil gone out, and her daughter laid upon the bed.

Jesus Heals a Deaf and Dumb Man

31 And again, departing from the coasts of Tyre and Sidon, he came unto the sea of Galilee, through the midst of the coasts of Decapolis.

32 And they bring unto him one that was deaf, and had an impediment in his speech; and they beseech him to put his hand upon him.

33 And he took him aside from the multitude, and put his fingers into his ears, and he spit, and touched his tongue;

34 And looking up to heaven, he sighed, and saith unto him, Ephphatha, that is, Be opened.

35 And straightway his ears were opened, and the string of his tongue was loosed, and he spake plain.

36 And he charged them that they should tell no man: but the more he charged them, so much the more a great deal they published *it;*

37 And were beyond measure astonished, saying, He hath done all things well: he maketh both the deaf to hear, and the dumb to speak.

CHAPTER 8
Jesus Feeds the Four Thousand

1 In those days the multitude being very great, and having nothing to eat, Jesus called his disciples *unto him,* and saith unto them,

2 I have compassion on the multitude, because they have now been with me three days, and have nothing to eat:

3 And if I send them away fasting to their own houses, they will faint by the way: for divers of them came from far.

4 And his disciples answered him, From whence can a man satisfy these *men* with bread here in the wilderness?

Cross references (margin)

14 Matt. 15:10
16 Matt. 11:15
17 Matt. 15:15
21 Gen. 6:5; 8:21; Matt. 15:19
24 Matt. 15:21
31 Matt. 15:29
32 Matt. 9:32; Luke 11:14
33 Mark 8:23; John 9:6
34 Mark 6:41; John 11:33, 38, 41; 17:1
35 Isa. 35:5, 6; Matt. 11:5
36 Mark 5:43
1 Matt. 15:32

7:14–23 Jesus here emphasizes that spiritual defilement was not a matter of external things—food intake or ceremonies for outward cleansing (Matt. 15:20). Spiritual defilement arises out of a wicked heart (see Jer. 17:9).

7:27 Let the children first be filled. The gospel was to be taken first to the Jews, later to the Gentiles. Jesus' healing of the Syrophenician woman's daughter is a portent of the time that followed the Resurrection, when the gospel and its power would spread rapidly among the Gentiles.

5 And he asked them, How many loaves have ye? And they said, Seven.
6 And he commanded the people to sit down on the ground: and he took the seven loaves, and gave thanks, and brake, and gave to his disciples to set before *them*; and they did set *them* before the people.
7 And they had a few small fishes: and he blessed, and commanded to set them also before *them*.
8 So they did eat, and were filled: and they took up of the broken *meat* that was left seven baskets.
9 And they that had eaten were about four thousand: and he sent them away.
10 And straightway he entered into a ship with his disciples, and came into the parts of Dalmanutha.

The Pharisees Demand a Sign

11 And the Pharisees came forth, and began to question with him, seeking of him a sign from heaven, tempting him.
12 And he sighed deeply in his spirit, and saith, Why doth this generation seek after a sign? verily I say unto you, There shall no sign be given unto this generation.
13 And he left them, and entering into the ship again departed to the other side.

The Leaven of the Pharisees and of Herod

14 Now *the disciples* had forgotten to take bread, neither had they in the ship with them more than one loaf.
15 And he charged them, saying, Take heed, beware of the leaven of the Pharisees, and of the leaven of Herod.
16 And they reasoned among themselves, saying, *It is* because we have no bread.
17 And when Jesus knew *it,* he saith unto them, Why reason ye, because ye have no bread? perceive ye not yet, neither understand? have ye your heart yet hardened?
18 Having eyes, see ye not? and having ears, hear ye not? and do ye not remember?
19 When I brake the five loaves among five thousand, how many baskets full of fragments took ye up? They say unto him, Twelve.
20 And when the seven among four thousand, how many baskets full of fragments took ye up? And they said, Seven.

21 And he said unto them, How is it that ye do not understand?

Jesus Heals a Blind Man at Bethsaida

22 And he cometh to Bethsaida: and they bring a blind man unto him, and besought him to touch him.
23 And he took the blind man by the hand, and led him out of the town; and when he had spit on his eyes, and put his hands upon him, he asked him if he saw ought.
24 And he looked up, and said, I see men as trees, walking.
25 After that he put *his* hands again upon his eyes, and made him look up: and he was restored, and saw every man clearly.
26 And he sent him away to his house, saying, Neither go into the town, nor tell it to any in the town.

Peter's Declaration That Jesus Is the Messiah

27 And Jesus went out, and his disciples, into the towns of Caesarea Philippi: and by the way he asked his disciples, saying unto them, Whom do men say that I am?
28 And they answered, John the Baptist: but some *say,* Elias; and others, One of the prophets.
29 And he saith unto them, But whom say ye that I am? And Peter answereth and saith unto him, Thou art the Christ.
30 And he charged them that they should tell no man of him.

Jesus Predicts His Death and Resurrection

31 And he began to teach them, that the Son of man must suffer many things, and be rejected of the elders, and *of* the chief priests, and scribes, and be killed, and after three days rise again.
32 And he spake that saying openly. And Peter took him, and began to rebuke him.
33 But when he had turned about and looked on his disciples, he rebuked Peter, saying, Get thee behind me, Satan: for thou savourest not the things that be of God, but the things that be of men.

Take Up Your Cross

34 And when he had called the people *unto him* with his disciples also, he said unto

Cross-references (center column):
5 Matt. 15:34; Mark 6:38
7 Matt. 14:19; Mark 6:41
10 Matt. 15:39
11 Matt. 12:38; 16:1; John 6:30
14 Matt. 16:5
15 Matt. 16:6; Luke 12:1
16 Matt. 16:7
17 Mark 6:52
19 Matt. 14:20; Mark 6:43; Luke 9:17; John 6:13
20 Matt. 15:37; Mark 8:8
21 Mark 6:52; 8:17
23 Mark 7:33
26 Matt. 5:43; 8:4
27 Matt. 16:13; Luke 9:18
28 Matt. 14:2
29 Matt. 16:16; John 6:69; 11:27
30 Matt. 16:20
31 Matt. 16:21; 17:22; Luke 9:22
34 Matt. 10:38; 16:24; Luke 9:23; 14:27

8:29 Thou art the Christ [the Messiah]. Peter's confession (see also Matt. 16:13–16) affirms what most of the apostles already had begun to believe. Addressing Jesus as Messiah ("the anointed one") referred to Jesus being the predicted "Prophet" (Deut. 18:18), the "priest" (Ps. 110:1–4), and "King" (Matt. 2:1–6).

them, Whosoever will come after me, let him deny himself, and take up his cross, and follow me.

35 For whosoever will save his life shall lose it; but whosoever shall lose his life for my sake and the gospel's, the same shall save it.

36 For what shall it profit a man, if he shall gain the whole world, and lose his own soul?

37 Or what shall a man give in exchange for his soul?

38 Whosoever therefore shall be ashamed of me and of my words in this adulterous and sinful generation; of him also shall the Son of man be ashamed, when he cometh in the glory of his Father with the holy angels.

CHAPTER 9

1 And he said unto them, Verily I say unto you, That there be some of them that stand here, which shall not taste of death, till they have seen the kingdom of God come with power.

The Transfiguration

2 And after six days Jesus taketh *with him* Peter, and James, and John, and leadeth them up into an high mountain apart by themselves: and he was transfigured before them.

3 And his raiment became shining, exceeding white as snow; so as no fuller on earth can white them.

4 And there appeared unto them Elias with Moses: and they were talking with Jesus.

5 And Peter answered and said to Jesus, Master, it is good for us to be here: and let us make three tabernacles; one for thee, and one for Moses, and one for Elias.

6 For he wist not what to say; for they were sore afraid.

7 And there was a cloud that overshadowed them: and a voice came out of the cloud, saying, This is my beloved Son: hear him.

8 And suddenly, when they had looked round about, they saw no man any more, save Jesus only with themselves.

9 And as they came down from the mountain, he charged them that they should tell no man what things they had seen, till the Son of man were risen from the dead.

10 And they kept that saying with themselves, questioning one with another what the rising from the dead should mean.

11 And they asked him, saying, Why say the scribes that Elias must first come?

12 And he answered and told them, Elias verily cometh first, and restoreth all things; and how it is written of the Son of man, that he must suffer many things, and be set at nought.

13 But I say unto you, That Elias is indeed come, and they have done unto him

Cross references

35 John 12:25
38 Matt. 10:33; Luke 9:26; 12:9; Rom. 1:16; 2Tim. 1:8; 2:12
1 Matt. 16:28; 24:30; 25:31; Luke 9:27; 22:18
2 Matt. 17:1; Luke 9:28
3 Dan. 7:9; Matt. 28:3
9 Matt. 17:9
11 Mal. 4:5; Matt. 17:10
12 Ps. 22:6; Isa. 53:2-9; Dan. 9:26; Luke 23:11; Phil. 2:7
13 Matt. 11:14; 17:12; Luke 1:17

8:38 when he cometh. This is the first mention in Mark of the second coming of Christ. When He returns with His holy angels (see 2 Thess. 1:7–10), those who have been ashamed of Jesus will experience a deep sense of disgrace over their failure to stand up and confess Him before men (cf. Matt. 10:32).

9:1 seen the kingdom of God. Jesus positively affirms that some of the disciples would not taste death until they saw the kingdom of God come with power. He was referring to the event know as the Transfiguration, which was a glimpse of what the kingdom will be like when Jesus reigns. Jesus is seen as the glorified King, who will reign in the Millennium.

9:2 transfigured before them. Jesus was transformed (Gr. *metamorphoo*, "changed in form and appearance"), radiating from His person His perfect humanity and His sovereign deity. This was a confirmation and climactic proof that He is the Messiah, the Anointed One forecast more than 109 times in the Old Testament (see Rev. 1:12–16; 2 Pet. 1:16–20).

9:4–5 Moses and Elijah's appearance confirms that the Law and the prophets endorse Jesus, not the views of the scribes and Pharisees. The three disciples thought

that the kingdom might be established almost immediately and were ready for the Feast of Tabernacles (Zech. 14:16).

9:7 This is my beloved Son. The Father's voice is heard a second time, affirming Jesus' Sonship. God spoke from heaven at Christ's baptism, as His ministry began, and on a third occasion shortly before His crucifixion in Jerusalem (John 12:27–28).

9:9 risen from the dead. Jesus predicted His resurrection, but the disciples did not grasp the significance of His words until after it had occurred.

9:12 Elias verily cometh. Jesus does not nullify Malachi 4:5–6, but expressly says Elias will restore all things. Many premillennialists believe that Elijah will be one of the two witnesses during the Tribulation (Rev. 11:3–12).

9:13 Elias is indeed come. Jesus refers here to John the Baptist (see Luke 1:13–17; John 1:19–21; Matt. 11:11–15). Had Israel received John the Baptist's message and Jesus as the promised King, John would have been the fulfillment of Malachi's prophecy (see v. 12). Since they did not receive it, the final fulfillment of Malachi's prophecy is yet future.

whatsoever they listed, as it is written of him.

Jesus Heals a Boy with an Unclean Spirit

14 And when he came to *his* disciples, he saw a great multitude about them, and the scribes questioning with them.

15 And straightway all the people, when they beheld him, were greatly amazed, and running to *him* saluted him.

16 And he asked the scribes, What question ye with them?

17 And one of the multitude answered and said, Master, I have brought unto thee my son, which hath a dumb spirit;

18 And wheresoever he taketh him, he teareth him: and he foameth, and gnasheth with his teeth, and pineth away: and I spake to thy disciples that they should cast him out; and they could not.

19 He answereth him, and saith, O faithless generation, how long shall I be with you? how long shall I suffer you? bring him unto me.

20 And they brought him unto him: and when he saw him, straightway the spirit tare him; and he fell on the ground, and wallowed foaming.

21 And he asked his father, How long is it ago since this came unto him? And he said, Of a child.

22 And ofttimes it hath cast him into the fire, and into the waters, to destroy him: but if thou canst do any thing, have compassion on us, and help us.

23 Jesus said unto him, If thou canst believe, all things are possible to him that believeth.

24 And straightway the father of the child cried out, and said with tears, Lord, I believe; help thou mine unbelief.

25 When Jesus saw that the people came running together, he rebuked the foul spirit, saying unto him, Thou dumb and deaf spirit, I charge thee, come out of him, and enter no more into him.

26 And *the spirit* cried, and rent him sore, and came out of him: and he was as one dead; insomuch that many said, He is dead.

27 But Jesus took him by the hand, and lifted him up; and he arose.

28 And when he was come into the house,

his disciples asked him privately, Why could not we cast him out?

29 And he said unto them, This kind can come forth by nothing, but by prayer and fasting.

Jesus Predicts His Death and Resurrection

30 And they departed thence, and passed through Galilee; and he would not that any man should know *it*.

31 For he taught his disciples, and said unto them, The Son of man is delivered into the hands of men, and they shall kill him; and after that he is killed, he shall rise the third day.

32 But they understood not that saying, and were afraid to ask him.

The Greatness of Humility

33 And he came to Capernaum: and being in the house he asked them, What was it that ye disputed among yourselves by the way?

34 But they held their peace: for by the way they had disputed among themselves, who *should be* the greatest.

35 And he sat down, and called the twelve, and saith unto them, If any man desire to be first, the same shall be last of all, and servant of all.

36 And he took a child, and set him in the midst of them: and when he had taken him in his arms, he said unto them,

37 Whosoever shall receive one of such children in my name, receiveth me: and whosoever shall receive me, receiveth not me, but him that sent me.

Others Who Work in the Name of Christ

38 And John answered him, saying, Master, we saw one casting out devils in thy name, and he followeth not us: and we forbad him, because he followeth not us.

39 But Jesus said, Forbid him not: for there is no man which shall do a miracle in my name, that can lightly speak evil of me.

40 For he that is not against us is on our part.

41 For whosoever shall give you a cup of water to drink in my name, because ye

Cross-references

14	Matt. 17:14; Luke 9:37
17	Matt. 17:14; Luke 9:38
20	Mark 1:26; Luke 9:42
23	Matt. 17:20; Mark 11:23; Luke 17:6; John 11:40
28	Matt. 17:19
29	Matt. 17:22; Luke 9:44
33	Matt. 18:1; Luke 9:46; 22:24
35	Matt. 20:26, 27; Mark 10:43
36	Matt. 18:2; Mark 10:16
37	Matt. 10:40; Luke 9:48
38	Num. 11:28; Luke 9:49
39	1Cor. 12:3
40	Matt. 12:30
41	Matt. 10:42

9:31 after that he is killed. This is the second time in the Gospel of Mark that Jesus predicts His approaching death and resurrection.

9:41 he shall not lose his reward. At the judgment seat of Christ (Rom. 14:9–12; 2 Cor. 5:10), where only believers appear after the rapture and the resurrection of the

The Glorious Appearing of Christ

By J. Dwight Pentecost

The transfiguration of Jesus (Matt. 17:1–8; Mark 9:1–8) was a miniature and premature revelation to three of the apostles of the essential glory which belongs to Jesus (Heb. 10:20) that will be displayed to the world at His Second Advent. The second coming of Christ will be heralded by the appearance of the "sign of the Son of man in heaven" (Matt. 24:30). Thus these three apostles were given a revelation at the Transfiguration as to who this Person actually is (Matt. 12:24).

At His ascension, the veil was removed and the Son appeared in glory (Acts 7:55–56), never to have that glory veiled again. When He returns to this earth to set His feet on the Mount of Olives (Zech. 14:4), all who dwell on the earth "shall see the Son of man coming in the clouds of heaven with power and great glory" (Matt. 24:30; [cf. Rev. 19:11–16]).

When the Son returns in glory (Rev. 1:13–16), He is fulfilling His God-given role as Judge (John 5:27). He is portrayed in that role throughout the book of Revelation. Christ is the one (Rev. 5:5) who looses the series of judgments described in the breaking of the seals (Rev. 6:1–17) and the blowing of the trumpets (Rev. 8:2—9:21). The seventh trumpet is actually the Second Advent of the Judge back to the earth (Rev. 11:15). The form of the judgment associated with His advent is revealed in the emptying of the vials in judgment (Rev. 16:1–21). His right to judge is vindicated (John 5:27). Upon the Second Coming, He will assemble living Israel for judgment (Matt. 24:31; 25:1–30) and will judge living Gentiles to determine who will enter the covenanted kingdom. His glory will be revealed through His judgments.

> *Believers anticipate the glory that will be revealed at Christ's coming.*

Also upon the Second Coming, Christ will fulfil the role of a Savior or Deliverer (Rom. 11:26–27). Because of lawlessness and idolatry, Israel was delivered into the hand of Gentile oppressors who would rule over them and their land until "the times of the Gentiles" (Luke 21:24) should be fulfilled (See the article, "The Times of the Gentiles" by David Breese). The Son's glory will be revealed as a Savior, and the nation of Israel shall look in faith upon the One whom they rejected and will give Him the glory due Him (Zech. 12:10).

Christ returns the second time to fulfil His God-given role as King, a role appointed to him by His Father at His ascension (Ps. 2:6–7; 110:1). He was introduced in that role by His appointed forerunner, John (Matt. 3:2), and claimed that right Himself (Matt. 4:17). When the multitudes witnessed a spectacular miracle, they acknowledged that Christ was the Messiah, the son of David (Matt. 12:23). At the Second Advent, He appears as "KING OF KINGS AND LORD OF LORDS" (Rev. 19:16). His glory will be revealed throughout the thousand years of His reign here on earth (Rev. 20:2–3) as David's "son" in David's kingdom as covenanted by God with Israel (2 Sam. 7:16; Ps. 89:3–4).

The believer anticipates the glory that will be revealed at His coming (see Titus 2:13), for we will share His glory. This hope (settled assurance) is a source of blessing while we await the revelation of His glory: His glory as a Judge, His glory as a Deliverer, and His glory as King.

belong to Christ, verily I say unto you, he shall not lose his reward.

Entrapments

42 And whosoever shall offend one of these little ones that believe in me, it is better for him that a millstone were hanged about his neck, and he were cast into the sea.
43 And if thy hand offend thee, cut it off: it is better for thee to enter into life maimed, than having two hands to go into hell, into the fire that never shall be quenched:
44 Where their worm dieth not, and the fire is not quenched.
45 And if thy foot offend thee, cut it off: it is better for thee to enter halt into life, than having two feet to be cast into hell, into the fire that never shall be quenched:
46 Where their worm dieth not, and the fire is not quenched.
47 And if thine eye offend thee, pluck it out: it is better for thee to enter into the kingdom of God with one eye, than having two eyes to be cast into hell fire:
48 Where their worm dieth not, and the fire is not quenched.
49 For every one shall be salted with fire, and every sacrifice shall be salted with salt.
50 Salt is good: but if the salt have lost his saltness, wherewith will ye season it? Have salt in yourselves, and have peace one with another.

CHAPTER 10
Divorce

1 And he arose from thence, and cometh into the coasts of Judea by the farther side of Jordan: and the people resort unto him again; and, as he was wont, he taught them again.
2 And the Pharisees came to him, and asked him, Is it lawful for a man to put away *his* wife? tempting him.

3 And he answered and said unto them, What did Moses command you?
4 And they said, Moses suffered to write a bill of divorcement, and to put *her* away.
5 And Jesus answered and said unto them, For the hardness of your heart he wrote you this precept.
6 But from the beginning of the creation God made them male and female.
7 For this cause shall a man leave his father and mother, and cleave to his wife;
8 And they twain shall be one flesh: so then they are no more twain, but one flesh.
9 What therefore God hath joined together, let not man put asunder.
10 And in the house his disciples asked him again of the same *matter*.
11 And he saith unto them, Whosoever shall put away his wife, and marry another, committeth adultery against her.
12 And if a woman shall put away her husband, and be married to another, she committeth adultery.

Who Will Enter God's Kingdom?

13 And they brought young children to him, that he should touch them: and *his* disciples rebuked those that brought *them*.
14 But when Jesus saw *it*, he was much displeased, and said unto them, Suffer the little children to come unto me, and forbid them not: for of such is the kingdom of God.
15 Verily I say unto you, Whosoever shall not receive the kingdom of God as a little child, he shall not enter therein.
16 And he took them up in his arms, put *his* hands upon them, and blessed them.

The Rich Man Tested

17 And when he was gone forth into the way, there came one running, and kneeled to him, and asked him, Good Master, what

Cross-references

42 Matt. 18:6; Luke 17:1
43 Deut. 13:6; Matt. 5:29; 18:8
44 Isa. 66:24
49 Lev. 2:13; Ezek. 43:24
50 Matt. 5:13; Luke 14:34; Rom. 12:18; 14:19; 2Cor. 13:11; Eph. 4:29; Col. 4:6; Heb. 12:14
1 Matt. 19:1; John 10:40; 11:7
2 Matt. 19:3
4 Deut. 24:1; Matt. 5:31; 19:7
6 Gen. 1:27; 5:2
7 Gen. 2:24; 1Cor. 6:16; Eph. 5:31
11 Matt. 5:32; 19:9; Luke 16:18; Rom. 7:3; 1Cor. 7:10, 11
13 Matt. 19:13; Luke 18:15
14 1Cor. 14:20; 1Pet. 2:2
15 Matt. 18:3
17 Matt. 19:16; Luke 18:18

---

dead in Christ (1 Thess. 4:11–18), rewards will be bestowed for faithful service, including even the simplest of godly deeds.

9:42–48 their worm dieth not. Some have attempted to spiritualize this "worm" as a description of the guilt-ridden conscience of those who are without Christ for eternity. However, based on the prophecy of Isaiah 66:24, the text seems to be a literal picture of the real "living hell." The bodies of those in hell are being consumed but never die, so that the worms that consume them never die. The torture of hell is eternal; there is no exit, no way of escape for those who are cast into the lake of fire. Jesus warns that whatever prevents a person from coming to

Christ, anything that offends, should be "cut . . . off." This strong teaching does not encourage actual amputation, but powerfully suggests that even so dire an act would not be as severe as dying and going to hell, where the fire is not quenched.

9:50 salt in yourselves. Jesus is here emphasizing the savory nature of salt. Believers are to have salt in themselves, by their presence bringing out the flavor of the truth of God. Christians are to be "the salt of the earth" (Matt. 5:13), not losing their savory influence, lest they fail to be a force for God and goodness on earth.

shall I do that I may inherit eternal life?
18 And Jesus said unto him, Why callest thou me good? there is none good but one, that is, God.

19 Thou knowest the commandments, Do not commit adultery, Do not kill, Do not steal, Do not bear false witness, Defraud not, Honour thy father and mother.

20 And he answered and said unto him, Master, all these have I observed from my youth.

21 Then Jesus beholding him loved him, and said unto him, One thing thou lackest: go thy way, sell whatsoever thou hast, and give to the poor, and thou shalt have treasure in heaven: and come, take up the cross, and follow me.

22 And he was sad at that saying, and went away grieved: for he had great possessions.

23 And Jesus looked round about, and saith unto his disciples, How hardly shall they that have riches enter into the kingdom of God!

24 And the disciples were astonished at his words. But Jesus answereth again, and saith unto them, Children, how hard is it for them that trust in riches to enter into the kingdom of God!

25 It is easier for a camel to go through the eye of a needle, than for a rich man to enter into the kingdom of God.

26 And they were astonished out of measure, saying among themselves, Who then can be saved?

27 And Jesus looking upon them saith, With men it is impossible, but not with God: for with God all things are possible.

28 Then Peter began to say unto him, Lo, we have left all, and have followed thee.

29 And Jesus answered and said, Verily I say unto you, There is no man that hath left house, or brethren, or sisters, or father, or mother, or wife, or children, or lands, for my sake, and the gospel's,

30 But he shall receive an hundredfold now

19 Ex. 20;
Rom. 13:9

21 Matt.
6:19, 20;
19:21; Luke
12:33; 16:9

22 Matt.
19:23; Luke
18:24

24 Job
31:24; Ps.
52:7; 62:10;
1Tim. 6:17

27 Jer.
32:17; Matt.
19:26; Luke
1:37

28 Matt.
19:27; Luke
18:28

30 2Chr.
25:9; Luke
18:30

31 Matt.
19:30; 20:16;
Luke 13:30

32 Matt.
20:17; Mark
8:31; 9:31;
Luke 9:22;
18:31

35 Matt.
20:20

in this time, houses, and brethren, and sisters, and mothers, and children, and lands, with persecutions; and in the world to come eternal life.

31 But many that are first shall be last; and the last first.

Jesus Will Rise from the Dead

32 And they were in the way going up to Jerusalem; and Jesus went before them: and they were amazed; and as they followed, they were afraid. And he took again the twelve, and began to tell them what things should happen unto him,

33 *Saying,* Behold, we go up to Jerusalem; and the Son of man shall be delivered unto the chief priests, and unto the scribes; and they shall condemn him to death, and shall deliver him to the Gentiles:

34 And they shall mock him, and shall scourge him, and shall spit upon him, and shall kill him: and the third day he shall rise again.

James and John Request Special Positions

35 And James and John, the sons of Zebedee, come unto him, saying, Master, we would that thou shouldest do for us whatsoever we shall desire.

36 And he said unto them, What would ye that I should do for you?

37 They said unto him, Grant unto us that we may sit, one on thy right hand, and the other on thy left hand, in thy glory.

38 But Jesus said unto them, Ye know not what ye ask: can ye drink of the cup that I drink of? and be baptized with the baptism that I am baptized with?

39 And they said unto him, We can. And Jesus said unto them, Ye shall indeed drink of the cup that I drink of; and with the baptism that I am baptized withal shall ye be baptized:

40 But to sit on my right hand and on my

10:34 shall kill him. Very explicitly now, the Lord begins to explain the future trial, mocking, death, and resurrection, all of which are only a few weeks away. His prediction that these things would happen, and that He would rise again after three days are in keeping with the supernatural element of prophecy, that it is God alone who accurately predicts the future, because it is God alone who controls it all.

10:35–40 While Jesus is speaking of dying on a cross, two of the leading apostles, James and John, speak of

sitting on thrones, one on each side when He reigns. Christ challenges them about passing through a "baptism," which symbolically predicted His suffering, death, and resurrection. The implication is given that these disciples would indeed drink of that baptism of suffering and death. James was the first apostle to be martyred (Acts 12:1–2), and John suffered terrible persecution and exile (see Rev. 1:9–10), but even that "baptism" did not necessarily qualify them for the positions they requested.

left hand is not mine to give; but *it shall be given to them* for whom it is prepared.

41 And when the ten heard *it*, they began to be much displeased with James and John.

42 But Jesus called them *to him*, and saith unto them, Ye know that they which are accounted to rule over the Gentiles exercise lordship over them; and their great ones exercise authority upon them.

43 But so shall it not be among you: but whosoever will be great among you, shall be your minister:

44 And whosoever of you will be the chiefest shall be servant of all.

45 For even the Son of man came not to be ministered unto, but to minister, and to give his life a ransom for many.

The Healing of Blind Bartimaeus

46 And they came to Jericho: and as he went out of Jericho with his disciples and a great number of people, blind Bartimaeus, the son of Timaeus, sat by the highway side begging.

47 And when he heard that it was Jesus of Nazareth, he began to cry out, and say, Jesus, *thou* son of David, have mercy on me.

48 And many charged him that he should hold his peace: but he cried the more a great deal, *Thou* son of David, have mercy on me.

49 And Jesus stood still, and commanded him to be called. And they call the blind man, saying unto him, Be of good comfort, rise; he calleth thee.

50 And he, casting away his garment, rose, and came to Jesus.

51 And Jesus answered and said unto him, What wilt thou that I should do unto thee?

The blind man said unto him, Lord, that I might receive my sight.

52 And Jesus said unto him, Go thy way; thy faith hath made thee whole. And immediately he received his sight, and followed Jesus in the way.

Cross references

41 Matt. 20:24
42 Luke 22:25
43 Matt. 20:26, 28; Mark 9:35; Luke 9:48
45 Matt. 20:28; John 13:14; Phil. 2:7; 1Tim. 2:6; Titus 2:14
46 Matt. 20:29; Luke 18:35
52 Matt. 9:22; Mark 5:34
1 Matt. 21:1; Luke 19:29; John 12:14
8 Matt. 21:8
9 Ps. 118:26
10 Ps. 148:1
11 Matt. 21:12
12 Matt. 21:18

CHAPTER 11
Jesus' Triumphal Entry into Jerusalem

1 And when they came nigh to Jerusalem, unto Bethphage and Bethany, at the mount of Olives, he sendeth forth two of his disciples,

2 And saith unto them, Go your way into the village over against you: and as soon as ye be entered into it, ye shall find a colt tied, whereon never man sat; loose him, and bring him.

3 And if any man say unto you, Why do ye this? say ye that the Lord hath need of him; and straightway he will send him hither.

4 And they went their way, and found the colt tied by the door without in a place where two ways met; and they loose him.

5 And certain of them that stood there said unto them, What do ye, loosing the colt?

6 And they said unto them even as Jesus had commanded: and they let them go.

7 And they brought the colt to Jesus, and cast their garments on him; and he sat upon him.

8 And many spread their garments in the way: and others cut down branches off the trees, and strawed *them* in the way.

9 And they that went before, and they that followed, cried, saying, Hosanna; Blessed *is* he that cometh in the name of the Lord:

10 Blessed *be* the kingdom of our father David, that cometh in the name of the Lord: Hosanna in the highest.

11 And Jesus entered into Jerusalem, and into the temple: and when he had looked round about upon all things, and now the eventide was come, he went out unto Bethany with the twelve.

The Fruitless Fig Tree

12 And on the morrow, when they were come from Bethany, he was hungry:

11:1–11 The triumphal entry of Jesus into Jerusalem on "Palm Sunday" is His final offer of Himself before His death as the promised Messiah. (See the note on Matt. 21:1–9.) Here he directly fulfills Zechariah 9:9. The word "hosanna" is the transliteration of a Hebrew expression meaning "Please save" taken from Psalm 118:25–26. This psalm was a part of the Hallel, consisting of Psalms 113—118, which was recited by the priests and others at the Passover season. Just as the Passover celebrates the sprinkled blood that saved Israel's firstborn in the plague in Egypt, so God's "only begotten son" shed his blood, in fulfillment of prophecy, to save those who trust in Him (see Isa. 53). As evidenced by verse 10, the crowd believed that Jesus the son of David and royal heir to his throne would immediately establish the messianic kingdom, prophesied in the Old Testament. Indeed Christ will establish the kingdom, but not until the Millennium.

11:12–14 The fig tree is used in both testaments as a type of Israel (Judg. 9:10–11; 1 Kgs. 4:25; 2 Kgs. 18:31; Isa. 34:4; Jer. 8:13; Hos. 9:10; Joel 1:7; Mic. 4:4; Hab. 3:17; Zech. 3:10; Luke 13:6–9). See the note on Matthew 21:18–22.

13 And seeing a fig tree afar off having leaves, he came, if haply he might find anything thereon: and when he came to it, he found nothing but leaves; for the time of figs was not *yet.*
14 And Jesus answered and said unto it, No man eat fruit of thee hereafter for ever. And his disciples heard *it.*

Jesus Cleanses the Temple

15 And they come to Jerusalem: and Jesus went into the temple, and began to cast out them that sold and bought in the temple, and overthrew the tables of the moneychangers, and the seats of them that sold doves;
16 And would not suffer that any man should carry *any* vessel through the temple.
17 And he taught, saying unto them, Is it not written, My house shall be called of all nations the house of prayer? but ye have made it a den of thieves.
18 And the scribes and chief priests heard *it,* and sought how they might destroy him: for they feared him, because all the people was astonished at his doctrine.
19 And when even was come, he went out of the city.

"Have Faith in God"

20 And in the morning, as they passed by, they saw the fig tree dried up from the roots.
21 And Peter calling to remembrance saith unto him, Master, behold, the fig tree which thou cursedst is withered away.
22 And Jesus answering saith unto them, Have faith in God.
23 For verily I say unto you, That whosoever shall say unto this mountain, Be thou removed, and be thou cast into the sea; and shall not doubt in his heart, but shall believe that those things which he saith shall come to pass; he shall have whatsoever he saith.
24 Therefore I say unto you, What things soever ye desire, when ye pray, believe that ye receive them, and ye shall have them.
25 And when ye stand praying, forgive, if ye have ought against any: that your Father

also which is in heaven may forgive you your trespasses.
26 But if ye do not forgive, neither will your Father which is in heaven forgive your trespasses.

Where Did Christ's Authority Come from?

27 And they come again to Jerusalem: and as he was walking in the temple, there come to him the chief priests, and the scribes, and the elders,
28 And say unto him, By what authority doest thou these things? and who gave thee this authority to do these things?
29 And Jesus answered and said unto them, I will also ask of you one question, and answer me, and I will tell you by what authority I do these things.
30 The baptism of John, was it from heaven, or of men? answer me.
31 And they reasoned with themselves, saying, If we shall say, From heaven; he will say, Why then did ye not believe him?
32 But if we shall say, Of men; they feared the people: for all *men* counted John, that he was a prophet indeed.
33 And they answered and said unto Jesus, We cannot tell. And Jesus answering saith unto them, Neither do I tell you by what authority I do these things.

CHAPTER 12
The Parable of the Vineyard and the Tenants

1 And he began to speak unto them by parables. A *certain* man planted a vineyard, and set an hedge about *it,* and digged *a place for* the winefat, and built a tower, and let it out to husbandmen, and went into a far country.
2 And at the season he sent to the husbandmen a servant, that he might receive from the husbandmen of the fruit of the vineyard.
3 And they caught him, and beat him, and sent him away empty.
4 And again he sent unto them another servant; and at him they cast stones, and

Cross references

13 Matt. 21:19
15 Matt. 21:12; Luke 19:45; John 2:14
17 Isa. 56:7; Jer. 7:11
18 Matt. 7:28; 21:45, 46; Mark 1:22; Luke 4:32; 19:47
20 Matt. 21:19
23 Matt. 17:20; 21:21; Luke 17:6
24 Matt. 7:7; Luke 11:9; John 14:13; 15:7; 16:24; James 1:5, 6
25 Matt. 6:14; Col. 3:13
26 Matt. 18:35
27 Matt. 21:23; Luke 20:1
32 Matt. 3:5; 14:5; Mark 6:20
1 Matt. 21:33; Luke 20:9

11:15–19 Christ's first ministry in Jerusalem began with the cleansing of the temple (John 2:13–25). Three years later, also at the Passover season, He again comes to the temple, this time quoting Isaiah 56:7 and Jeremiah 7:11, driving out the merchants and moneychangers, whom he called "thieves."

12:2–7 God's spokesmen have often been beaten and killed: Isaiah is said to have been sawn asunder; Jeremiah was imprisoned; John the Baptist was beheaded; and many others suffered ridicule and persecution (see Luke 13:34; Matt. 23:29–34; 37–39). For an explanation of this parable, see the note on Matthew 21:33–41.

wounded him in the head, and sent him away shamefully handled.

5 And again he sent another; and him they killed, and many others; beating some, and killing some.

6 Having yet therefore one son, his well-beloved, he sent him also last unto them, saying, They will reverence my son.

7 But those husbandmen said among themselves, This is the heir; come, let us kill him, and the inheritance shall be ours.

8 And they took him, and killed him, and cast him out of the vineyard.

9 What shall therefore the lord of the vineyard do? he will come and destroy the husbandmen, and will give the vineyard unto others.

10 And have ye not read this scripture; The stone which the builders rejected is become the head of the corner:

11 This was the Lord's doing, and it is marvellous in our eyes?

12 And they sought to lay hold on him, but feared the people: for they knew that he had spoken the parable against them: and they left him, and went their way.

Jesus and Taxes

13 And they send unto him certain of the Pharisees and of the Herodians, to catch him in *his* words.

14 And when they were come, they say unto him, Master, we know that thou art true, and carest for no man: for thou regardest not the person of men, but teachest the way of God in truth: Is it lawful to give tribute to Caesar, or not?

15 Shall we give, or shall we not give? But he, knowing their hypocrisy, said unto them, Why tempt ye me? bring me a penny, that I may see it.

16 And they brought *it*. And he saith unto them, Whose is this image and superscription? And they said unto him, Caesar's.

17 And Jesus answering said unto them, Render to Caesar the things that are Caesar's, and to God the things that are God's. And they marvelled at him.

Life after the Resurrection

18 Then come unto him the Sadducees, which say there is no resurrection; and they asked him, saying,

19 Master, Moses wrote unto us, If a man's brother die, and leave *his* wife *behind him*, and leave no children, that his brother should take his wife, and raise up seed unto his brother.

20 Now there were seven brethren: and the first took a wife, and dying left no seed.

21 And the second took her, and died, neither left he any seed: and the third likewise.

22 And the seven had her, and left no seed: last of all the woman died also.

23 In the resurrection therefore, when they shall rise, whose wife shall she be of them? for the seven had her to wife.

24 And Jesus answering said unto them, Do ye not therefore err, because ye know not the scriptures, neither the power of God?

25 For when they shall rise from the dead, they neither marry, nor are given in marriage; but are as the angels which are in heaven.

26 And as touching the dead, that they rise: have ye not read in the book of Moses, how in the bush God spake unto him, saying, I am the God of Abraham, and the God of Isaac, and the God of Jacob?

27 He is not the God of the dead, but the God of the living: ye therefore do greatly err.

The Great Commandment

28 And one of the scribes came, and having heard them reasoning together, and perceiving that he had answered them well, asked him, Which is the first commandment of all?

29 And Jesus answered him, The first of all the commandments is, Hear, O Israel; The Lord our God is one Lord:

30 And thou shalt love the Lord thy God with all thy heart, and with all thy soul, and with all thy mind, and with all thy strength: this is the first commandment.

31 And the second is like, namely this, Thou shalt love thy neighbour as thyself. There is

Cross references

10 Ps. 118:22

12 Matt. 21:45, 46; Mark 11:18; John 7:25, 30, 44

13 Matt. 22:15; Luke 20:20

18 Matt. 22:23; Luke 20:27; Acts 23:8

19 Deut. 25:5

25 1Cor. 15:42, 49, 52

26 Ex. 3:6

28 Matt. 22:35

29 Deut. 6:4; Luke 10:27

31 Lev. 19:18; Matt. 22:39; Rom. 13:9; Gal. 5:14; James 2:8

12:10–11 The stone. This messianic prophecy was commonly recited at Passover (see Ps. 118:22–23 and 1 Pet. 2:8). Jesus alluded to the Jewish story that the builders of Solomon's Temple, not realizing the stone they rejected was indeed the cornerstone, had initially cast it aside. Jesus' words here also encompass the destruction of Jerusalem and the giving of God's blessings to the Gentiles during this Church Age (see Eph. 2:19–20). When He returns as the smiting stone (Dan. 2:34–35, 44–45), He will become the cornerstone of millennial Israel to rule the world.

none other commandment greater than these.

32 And the scribe said unto him, Well, Master, thou hast said the truth: for there is one God; and there is none other but he:

33 And to love him with all the heart and with all the understanding, and with all the soul, and with all the strength, and to love *his* neighbour as himself, is more than all whole burnt offerings and sacrifices.

34 And when Jesus saw that he answered discreetly he said unto him, Thou art not far from the kingdom of God. And no man after that durst ask him *any question.*

David's Lord

35 And Jesus answered and said, while he taught in the temple, How say the scribes that Christ is the son of David?

36 For David himself said by the Holy Ghost, the LORD said to my LORD, Sit thou on my right hand, till I make thine enemies thy footstool.

37 David therefore himself calleth him Lord; and whence is he then his son? And the common people heard him gladly.

Jesus Denounces the Scribes

38 And he said unto them in his doctrine, Beware of the scribes, which love to go in long clothing, and love salutations in the marketplaces,

39 And the chief seats in the synagogues, and the uppermost rooms at feasts:

40 Which devour widows' houses, and for a pretence make long prayers: these shall receive greater damnation.

The Widow's Offering

41 And Jesus sat over against the treasury, and beheld how the people cast money into the treasury: and many that were rich cast in much.

42 And there came a certain poor widow,

and she threw in two mites, which make a farthing.

43 And he called *unto him* his disciples, and saith unto them, Verily I say unto you, That this poor widow hath cast more in, than all they which have cast into the treasury:

44 For all they did cast in of their abundance; but she of her want did cast in all that she had, even all her living.

CHAPTER 13
The Destruction of the Temple and the Last Days

1 And as he went out of the temple, one of his disciples saith unto him, Master, see what manner of stones and what buildings *are here!*

2 And Jesus answering said unto him, Seest thou these great buildings? there shall not be left one stone upon another, that shall not be thrown down.

Forthcoming Woes

3 And as he sat upon the mount of Olives over against the temple, Peter and James and John and Andrew asked him privately,

4 Tell us, when shall these things be? and what *shall be* the sign when all these things shall be fulfilled?

5 And Jesus answering them began to say, Take heed lest any man deceive you:

6 For many shall come in my name, saying, I am Christ; and shall deceive many.

7 And when ye shall hear of wars and rumours of wars, be ye not troubled: for such things must needs be; but the end shall not be yet.

8 For nation shall rise against nation, and kingdom against kingdom: and there shall be earthquakes in divers places, and there shall be famines and troubles: these are the beginnings of sorrows.

9 But take heed to yourselves: for they shall deliver you up to councils; and in the

Center cross-reference column

32 Deut. 4:39; Isa. 45:6, 14; 46:9

33 1Sam. 15:22; Hos. 6:6; Mic. 6:6-8

34 Matt. 22:46

35 Matt. 22:41; Luke 20:41

36 2Sam. 23:2; Ps. 110:1

38 Matt. 23:1-12; Mark 4:2; Luke 11:43; 20:46

40 Matt. 23:14

41 2Kgs. 12:9; Luke 21:1

43 2Cor. 8:12

44 Deut. 24:6; 1John 3:17

1 Matt. 24:1; Luke 21:5

2 Luke 19:44

4 Matt. 24:3; Luke 21:7

5 Jer. 29:8; Eph. 5:6; 1Thess. 2:3

8 Matt. 24:8

9 Matt. 10:17, 18; 24:9; Rev. 2:10

12:35–36 Quoting from Psalm 110:1, Jesus indicates that the Messiah is more than the Son of David; He is God, here distinguished as the LORD (the Father) speaking to the Lord (Christ). Yet future is the glorious return, when His enemies will be made His footstool (cf. Luke 20:42; Acts 2:34; Heb. 10:13). See the notes on Psalm 110:1 and Matthew 22:44.

13:1–37 Commonly called the Olivet Discourse, because it was spoken while Jesus sat on the Mount of Olives, Mark presents a shorter account of the events of the End Times (see the notes on Matt. 24—25 and Luke

21:5–36). Jesus' prediction of the destruction of Jerusalem (v. 2) provoked questions from the four apostles regarding the time and sign of these events. The two parts of the Olivet sermon refer to separate future events: the fall of Jerusalem (A.D. 70, see Luke 21:20–24) and the events related to the Tribulation and the second coming of Christ. While verses 5–9 may provide insight into past and present-day false christs, wars, earthquakes, famines and troubles, the first half of the seven-year Tribulation (Dan. 9:27) will see the fulfillment of these predictions.

The Imminent Coming of Christ

By Renald Showers

The English word "imminent" means "hanging over one's head, ready to befall or over-take one; close at hand in its incidence" (*The Oxford English Dictionary*, 1901, V, 66). Thus, an imminent event is one that is always hanging overhead, is always close at hand in the sense that it could happen at any moment. If something else must take place before an event can happen, that event is not imminent.

One never knows exactly when an imminent event will happen. Because of this, three things are true. First, one cannot count on a certain amount of time transpiring before an imminent event occurs. Thus, one should always be prepared for it to happen at any moment. Second, it is not legitimate to set a date for the occurrence of an imminent event. Date setting insinuates that the event cannot take place until that date. It thereby destroys the concept of imminency. Third, it is not legitimate to say that, because an event is imminent, it will happen soon. The Bible indicates that the second coming of Christ was imminent when the New Testament was written. However, it is obvious that Christ's return would not be a soon-coming event for those in apostolic times.

> *Christ's imminent coming should motivate believers to live as if the Rapture could happen any day.*

The concept of the imminent return of Christ is as follows: His second coming is always hanging overhead, is constantly ready to befall or overtake us, and is always close at hand in the sense that it could happen at any moment. Other things may happen before Christ's return, but nothing else biblically must happen before it takes place. If something else must happen first, then Christ's second coming would not be imminent.

Because we do not know exactly when Christ will return, three things are true. First, we cannot count on a certain amount of time transpiring before His return; therefore, we should always be ready for Him to come at any moment. Second, we cannot legitimately set a date for Christ's return. Third, we cannot necessarily say that just because Christ's second coming is imminent it will happen soon. It may happen soon, but it does not have to be soon.

A significant contrast exists in the Bible. It teaches an imminent return of Christ, but it also teaches a return of Christ that is not imminent—a return that cannot take place until after the "great tribulation" (Matt. 24:21, 29–30). This contrast prompts the conclusion that the Bible teaches two future comings of Christ—the imminent one to rapture the Church and the non-imminent one to rule the world after the Great Tribulation.

The biblical concept of the imminent return of Christ carries a strong implication concerning the time of Christ's coming to rapture the Church. (See the articles, "The Rapture and the Return of Christ" by Ed Hindson and "The Timing of the Rapture" by Paul Benware.) Any view other than the pretribulational rapture view conflicts with the biblical concept of the imminent return of Christ.

The pretribulational rapture view teaches that Christ will come to rapture the Church before Daniel's "seventieth week" begins, that nothing else must happen before that coming, and that Christ's coming could take place at any moment. Christ's imminent coming should motivate believers to live their lives as if the Rapture could happen on any given day (1 John 2:28; 3:2–3).

synagogues ye shall be beaten: and ye shall be brought before rulers and kings for my sake, for a testimony against them.

10 And the gospel must first be published among all nations.

11 But when they shall lead you, and deliver you up, take no thought beforehand what ye shall speak, neither do ye premeditate: but whatsoever shall be given you in that hour, that speak ye: for it is not ye that speak, but the Holy Ghost.

12 Now the brother shall betray the brother to death, and the father the son; and children shall rise up against their parents, and shall cause them to be put to death.

13 And ye shall be hated of all men for my name's sake: but he that shall endure unto the end, the same shall be saved.

The Great Tribulation

14 But when ye shall see the abomination of desolation, spoken of by Daniel the prophet, standing where it ought not, let (him that readeth understand,) then let them that be in Judea flee to the mountains:

10 Matt. 24:14
11 Matt. 10:19; Luke 12:11; 21:14; Acts 2:4; 4:8, 31
12 Mic. 7:6; Matt. 10:21; 24:10; Luke 21:16
13 Dan. 12:12; Matt. 10:22; 24:9, 13; Luke 21:17; Rev. 2:10
14 Dan. 9:27; Matt. 24:15; Luke 21:21
17 Luke 21:23; 23:29
19 Dan. 9:26; 12:1; Joel 2:2; Matt. 24:21
21 Matt. 24:23; Luke 17:23; 21:8
23 2Pet. 3:17

15 And let him that is on the housetop not go down into the house, neither enter therein, to take any thing out of his house:

16 And let him that is in the field not turn back again for to take up his garment.

17 But woe to them that are with child, and to them that give suck in those days!

18 And pray ye that your flight be not in the winter.

19 For in those days shall be affliction, such as was not from the beginning of the creation which God created unto this time, neither shall be.

20 And except that the Lord had shortened those days, no flesh should be saved: but for the elect's sake, whom he hath chosen, he hath shortened the days.

21 And then if any man shall say to you, Lo, here is Christ; or, lo, he is there; believe him not:

22 For false Christs and false prophets shall rise, and shall shew signs and wonders, to seduce, if it were possible, even the elect.

23 But take ye heed: behold, I have foretold you all things.

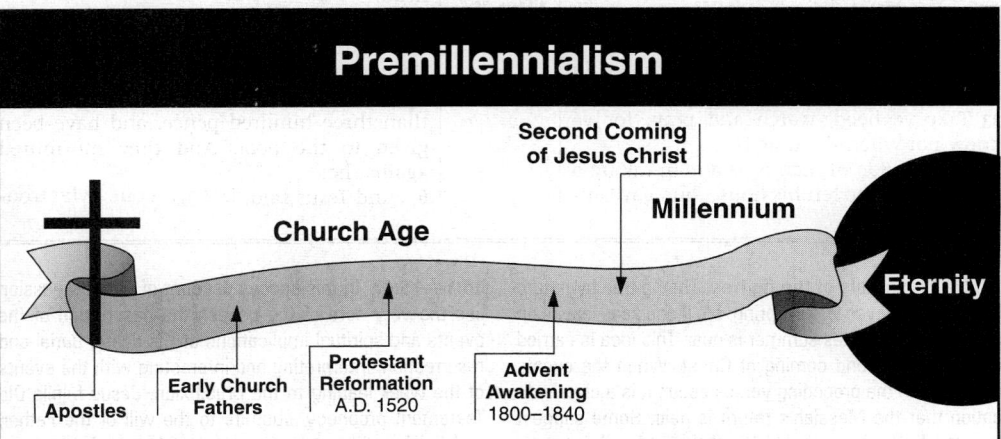

Premillennialism

Second Coming of Jesus Christ

Church Age

Millennium

Eternity

Apostles | Early Church Fathers | Protestant Reformation A.D. 1520 | Advent Awakening 1800–1840

Premillennialists believe that Christ will return at the end of the Church Age and establish a physical kingdom on earth for a literal thousand years. Most premillennialists believe that the return of Christ is preceded by the seventieth week (of years) of Daniel (Dan. 9:27) which includes a seven-year Tribulation. Premillennialists disagree as to whether the Church will be raptured before (pretribulationalism), in the middle of (mid-), or after (post-) the Tribulation. Dispensational premillennialists do not hold that Old Testament promises to Israel apply to the Church, but rather that the nation of Israel will one day be restored and converted to faith in Christ during the Tribulation.

© AMG Publishers

13:20 for the elect's sake, whom he hath chosen. This is a reference to the elect remnant of Israel during the Tribulation, who will be spared from utter destruction by the return of Christ.

The Second Coming of Christ

24 But in those days, after that tribulation, the sun shall be darkened, and the moon shall not give her light,

25 And the stars of heaven shall fall, and the powers that are in heaven shall be shaken.

26 And then shall they see the Son of man coming in the clouds with great power and glory.

27 And then shall he send his angels, and shall gather together his elect from the four winds, from the uttermost part of the earth to the uttermost part of heaven.

The Parable of the Fig Tree

28 Now learn a parable of the fig tree; When her branch is yet tender, and putteth forth leaves, ye know that summer is near:

29 So ye in like manner, when ye shall see these things come to pass, know that it is nigh, even at the doors.

30 Verily I say unto you, that this generation shall not pass, till all these things be done.

31 Heaven and earth shall pass away: but my words shall not pass away.

Time of Christ's Coming Unknown

32 But of that day and that hour knoweth no man, no, not the angels which are in heaven, neither the Son, but the Father.

33 Take ye heed, watch and pray: for ye know not when the time is.

34 For the Son of man is as a man taking a far journey, who left his house, and gave au-thority to his servants, and to every man his work, and commanded the porter to watch.

35 Watch ye therefore: for ye know not when the master of the house cometh, at even, or at midnight, or at the cockcrowing, or in the morning:

36 Lest coming suddenly he find you sleeping.

37 And what I say unto you I say unto all, Watch.

CHAPTER 14
The Plot to Kill Jesus

1 After two days was *the feast of* the passover, and of unleavened bread: and the chief priests and the scribes sought how they might take him by craft, and put *him* to death.

2 But they said, Not on the feast *day,* lest there be an uproar of the people.

The Anointing of Jesus at Bethany

3 And being in Bethany in the house of Simon the leper, as he sat at meat, there came a woman having an alabaster box of ointment of spikenard very precious; and she brake the box, and poured *it* on his head.

4 And there were some that had indignation within themselves, and said, Why was this waste of the ointment made?

5 For it might have been sold for more than three hundred pence, and have been given to the poor. And they murmured against her.

6 And Jesus said, Let her alone; why trou-

Cross references

24 Dan. 7:10; Zeph. 1:15; Matt. 24:29-31; Luke 21:25
26 Dan. 7:13, 14; Matt. 16:27; 24:30; Mark 14:62; Acts 1:11; 1 Thess. 4:16; 2 Thess. 1:7, 10; Rev. 1:7
28 Matt. 24:32; Luke 21:29-33
31 Isa. 40:8
33 Matt. 24:42; 25:13; Luke 12:40; 21:34; Rom. 13:11; 1 Thess. 5:6
34 Matt. 24:45; 25:14
35 Matt. 24:42, 44
1 Matt. 26:2; Luke 22:1; John 11:55; 13:1
3 Matt. 26:6; Luke 7:37; John 12:1, 3

13:28–29 parable of the fig tree. The fig tree by nature brings forth leaves late in spring; so, if one sees leaves on a fig tree, it indicates summer is near. This idea is carried over to the second coming of Christ. When the events described in the preceding verses occur, it is a clear indication that the Messiah's return is near. Some suggest that the fig tree represents Israel (see related notes on Matt. 24:32 and Mark 11:12–14).

13:30 this generation. The word "generation" (Gr. *genea,* "race" or "people") here refers to the Jewish people. Christ is saying that the generation of people living when the signs begin will not all perish before the events of the Tribulation are completely fulfilled.

13:34–37 far journey. Jesus is forecasting the present dispensation, when He is away in heaven, leaving His servants to watch for His return. Since Mark wrote to the Gentiles, the admonition to "watch" is applicable "unto all," throughout this present age.

14:1—15:47 In this serious account of Christ's passion lies the very core of the gospel, the description of the events and spiritual implications of His death, burial and resurrection. Interpreting and interacting with the events of the week leading to the Crucifixion, Jesus fulfills Old Testament prophecy, submits to the will of the Father, and finishes the work of atonement for sin. It has been estimated that Jesus fulfilled over fifty Old Testament prophecies in His death alone.

14:1 passover, and [feast] of unleavened bread. The connection of these two festivals is indicated in Exodus 12:3–20; Leviticus 23:4–8; and Deuteronomy 16:1–8. The Passover reflected redemption from bondage and deliverance from death through the application of the Lamb's blood. The annual commemoration occurred on the 14th of Nisan (mid-spring), continuing with the eating of unleavened bread through the 21st of Nisan.

ble ye her? she hath wrought a good work on me.

7 For ye have the poor with you always, and whensoever ye will ye may do them good: but me ye have not always.

8 She hath done what she could: she is come aforehand to anoint my body to the burying.

9 Verily I say unto you, Wheresoever this gospel shall be preached throughout the whole world, this also that she hath done shall be spoken of for a memorial of her.

Judas Agrees to Betray Jesus

10 And Judas Iscariot, one of the twelve, went unto the chief priests, to betray him unto them.

11 And when they heard it, they were glad, and promised to give him money. And he sought how he might conveniently betray him.

Jesus Eats the Passover with His Disciples

12 And the first day of unleavened bread, when they killed the passover, his disciples said unto him, Where wilt thou that we go and prepare that thou mayest eat the passover?

13 And he sendeth forth two of his disciples, and saith unto them, Go ye into the city, and there shall meet you a man bearing a pitcher of water: follow him.

14 And wheresoever he shall go say ye to the goodman of the house, The Master saith, Where is the guestchamber, where I shall eat the passover with my disciples?

15 And he will shew you a large upper room furnished and prepared: there make ready for us.

16 And his disciples went forth, and came into the city, and found as he had said unto them: and they made ready the passover.

17 And in the evening he cometh with the twelve.

18 And as they sat and did eat, Jesus said,

Verily I say unto you, One of you which eateth with me shall betray me.

19 And they began to be sorrowful, and to say unto him one by one, Is it I? and another said, Is it I?

20 And he answered and said unto them, It is one of the twelve, that dippeth with me in the dish.

21 The Son of man indeed goeth, as it is written of him: but woe to that man by whom the Son of man is betrayed! good were it for that man if he had never been born.

The Lord's Supper

22 And as they did eat, Jesus took bread, and blessed, and brake it, and gave to them, and said, Take, eat: this is my body.

23 And he took the cup, and when he had given thanks, he gave it to them: and they all drank of it.

24 And he said unto them, This is my blood of the new testament, which is shed for many.

25 Verily I say unto you, I will drink no more of the fruit of the vine, until that day that I drink it new in the kingdom of God.

26 And when they had sung an hymn, they went out into the mount of Olives.

Jesus Predicts Peter's Denial

27 And Jesus saith unto them, All ye shall be offended because of me this night: for it is written, I will smite the shepherd, and the sheep shall be scattered.

28 But after that I am risen, I will go before you into Galilee.

29 But Peter said unto him, Although all shall be offended, yet will not I.

30 And Jesus saith unto him, Verily I say unto thee, That this day, even in this night, before the cock crow twice, thou shalt deny me thrice.

31 But he spake the more vehemently, If I should die with thee, I will not deny thee in any wise. Likewise also said they all.

Cross-references

7 Deut. 15:11

10 Matt. 26:14; Luke 22:3, 4

12 Matt. 26:17; Luke 22:7

17 Matt. 26:20-25

21 Matt. 26:24; Luke 22:22

22 Matt. 26:26; Luke 22:19; 1Cor. 11:23

26 Matt. 26:30

27 Zech. 13:7; Matt. 26:31

28 Mark 16:7

29 Matt. 26:33, 34; Luke 22:33, 34; John 13:37, 38

14:18 One . . . shall betray me. Jesus prophesied the betrayal by Judas (John 13:18–19, 26–27 [cf. Ps. 41:9]).

14:22, 25 this is my body. After observance of the Passover, Jesus institutes a new observance with the bread symbolizing His body and the wine His blood, under the new covenant. Jesus indicates that the Passover as an official celebration, now superceded for New Testament believers by the Lord's Supper, will not be observed by Him until the joy of the messianic feast takes place

after the Glorious Appearing (Ezek. 45:21).

14:26 sung an hymn. Psalms 114—118 were customarily sung at the Passover celebration.

14:27 smite the shepherd. Jesus refers to Zechariah 13:7, applying the verse to Himself and His disciples.

14:28 after that I am risen. Jesus reassures His apostles of the Resurrection and appearances thereafter in Galilee (see Matt. 28:7, 10, 16; Mark 16:7; John 21).

Jesus Prays in Gethsemane

32 And they came to a place which was named Gethsemane: and he saith to his disciples, Sit ye here, while I shall pray.
33 And he taketh with him Peter and James and John, and began to be sore amazed, and to be very heavy;
34 And saith unto them, My soul is exceeding sorrowful unto death: tarry ye here, and watch.
35 And he went forward a little, and fell on the ground, and prayed that, if it were possible, the hour might pass from him.
36 And he said, Abba, Father, all things are possible unto thee; take away this cup from me: nevertheless not what I will, but what thou wilt.
37 And he cometh, and findeth them sleeping, and saith unto Peter, Simon, sleepest thou? couldest not thou watch one hour?
38 Watch ye and pray, lest ye enter into temptation. The spirit truly is ready, but the flesh is weak.
39 And again he went away, and prayed, and spake the same words.
40 And when he returned, he found them asleep again, (for their eyes were heavy,) neither wist they what to answer him.
41 And he cometh the third time, and saith unto them, Sleep on now, and take your rest; it is enough, the hour is come; behold, the Son of man is betrayed into the hands of sinners.
42 Rise up, let us go; lo, he that betrayeth me is at hand.

Judas Betrays the Lord

43 And immediately, while he yet spake, cometh Judas, one of the twelve, and with him a great multitude with swords and staves, from the chief priests and the scribes and the elders.
44 And he that betrayed him had given them a token, saying, Whomsoever I shall kiss, that same is he; take him, and lead *him* away safely.
45 And as soon as he was come, he goeth straightway to him, and saith, Master, master; and kissed him.
46 And they laid their hands on him, and took him.
47 And one of them that stood by drew a sword, and smote a servant of the high priest, and cut off his ear.
48 And Jesus answered and said unto them, Are ye come out, as against a thief, with swords and with staves to take me?
49 I was daily with you in the temple teaching, and ye took me not: but the scriptures must be fulfilled.
50 And they all forsook him, and fled.
51 And there followed him a certain young man, having a linen cloth cast about *his* naked *body*; and the young men laid hold on him:
52 And he left the linen cloth, and fled from them naked.

Jesus Is Brought to Caiaphas

53 And they led Jesus away to the high priest: and with him were assembled all the chief priests and the elders and the scribes.
54 And Peter followed him afar off, even into the palace of the high priest: and he sat with the servants, and warmed himself at the fire.
55 And the chief priests and all the council sought for witness against Jesus to put him to death; and found none.
56 For many bare false witness against him, but their witness agreed not together.
57 And there arose certain, and bare false witness against him, saying,
58 We heard him say, I will destroy this temple that is made with hands, and within three days I will build another made without hands.
59 But neither so did their witness agree together.

Cross-references

32 Matt. 26:36; Luke 22:39; John 18:1
34 John 12:27
36 John 5:30; 6:38; Rom. 8:15; Gal. 4:6; Heb. 5:7
38 Rom. 7:23; Gal. 5:17
41 John 13:1
42 Matt. 26:46; John 18:1, 2
43 Matt. 26:47; Luke 22:47; John 18:3
48 Matt. 26:55; Luke 22:52
49 Ps. 22:6; Isa. 53:7-10; Luke 22:37; 24:44
50 Ps. 88:8; Mark 14:27
53 Matt. 26:57; Luke 22:54; John 18:13
55 Matt. 26:59
58 Mark 15:29; John 2:19

14:36 Abba, Father. This is an Aramaic word, translated as "Father" by Mark, and used in a special sense of close intimacy (cf. Rom. 8:15). Jesus completely surrenders His human will to the divine will of the Father, showing there was no other way to atone for sin but by the vicarious sacrifice of Himself on the cross for us.

14:51 a certain young man. Many think this young man was Mark himself.

14:53–54 This inquest is held before Caiaphas and the Sanhedrin. Jesus appeared five separate times before religious and civil authorities: 1) before Annas (John 18:12–14; 19:19–23); 2) before Caiaphas and the Sanhedrin (here and Matt. 26:57–68); 3) before Pilate (Matt. 27:2, 11–14); 4) before Herod (Luke 23:7–12); 5) before Pilate one final time (Luke 23:13–25).

14:58 destroy this temple. The false witness against Jesus distorts Jesus' statement (John 2:19–21), alleging that Jesus spoke of Herod's Temple. But Jesus had spoken of the "temple of his body," a prophecy fulfilled in His resurrection.

60 And the high priest stood up in the midst, and asked Jesus, saying, Answerest thou nothing? what is it which these witness against thee?

61 But he held his peace, and answered nothing. Again the high priest asked him, and said unto him, Art thou the Christ, the Son of the Blessed?

62 And Jesus said, I am: and ye shall see the Son of man sitting on the right hand of power, and coming in the clouds of heaven.

63 Then the high priest rent his clothes, and saith, What need we any further witnesses?

64 Ye have heard the blasphemy: what think ye? And they all condemned him to be guilty of death.

65 And some began to spit on him, and to cover his face, and to buffet him, and to say unto him, Prophesy: and the servants did strike him with the palms of their hands.

Peter Denies Jesus

66 And as Peter was beneath in the palace, there cometh one of the maids of the high priest:

67 And when she saw Peter warming himself, she looked upon him, and said, And thou also wast with Jesus of Nazareth.

68 But he denied, saying, I know not, neither understand I what thou sayest. And he went out into the porch; and the cock crew.

69 And a maid saw him again, and began to say to them that stood by, This is one of them.

70 And he denied it again. And a little after, they that stood by said again to Peter, Surely thou art one of them: for thou art a Galilaean, and thy speech agreeth thereto.

71 But he began to curse and to swear, saying, I know not this man of whom ye speak.

72 And the second time the cock crew. And Peter called to mind the word that Jesus said unto him, Before the cock crow twice, thou shalt deny me thrice. And when he thought thereon, he wept.

CHAPTER 15
Jesus Is Brought to Pilate

1 And straightway in the morning the chief priests held a consultation with the

---

Cross-references column:

60 Matt. 26:62
61 Isa. 53:7; Matt. 26:63
62 Matt. 24:30; 26:64; Luke 22:69
66 Matt. 26:58, 69; Luke 22:55; John 18:16
69 Matt. 26:71; Luke 22:58; John 18:25
70 Matt. 26:73; Luke 22:59; John 18:26; Acts 2:7
72 Matt. 26:75
1 Ps. 2:2; Matt. 27:1; Luke 22:66; 23:1; John 18:28; Acts 3:13; 4:26
2 Matt. 27:11
4 Matt. 27:13
5 Isa. 53:7; John 19:9
6 Matt. 27:15; Luke 23:17; John 18:39
11 Matt. 27:20; Acts 3:14
15 Matt. 27:26; John 19:1, 16
16 Matt. 27:27

---

elders and scribes and the whole council, and bound Jesus, and carried him away, and delivered him to Pilate.

2 And Pilate asked him, Art thou the King of the Jews? And he answering said unto him, Thou sayest it.

3 And the chief priests accused him of many things: but he answered nothing.

4 And Pilate asked him again, saying, Answerest thou nothing? behold how many things they witness against thee.

5 But Jesus yet answered nothing; so that Pilate marvelled.

Jesus Sentenced to Death

6 Now at that feast he released unto them one prisoner, whomsoever they desired.

7 And there was one named Barabbas, which lay bound with them that had made insurrection with him, who had committed murder in the insurrection.

8 And the multitude crying aloud began to desire him to do as he had ever done unto them.

9 But Pilate answered them, saying, Will ye that I release unto you the King of the Jews?

10 For he knew that the chief priests had delivered him for envy.

11 But the chief priests moved the people, that he should rather release Barabbas unto them.

12 And Pilate answered and said again unto them, What will ye then that I shall do unto him whom ye call the King of the Jews?

13 And they cried out again, Crucify him.

14 Then Pilate said unto them, Why, what evil hath he done? And they cried out the more exceedingly, Crucify him.

15 And so Pilate, willing to content the people, released Barabbas unto them, and delivered Jesus, when he had scourged him, to be crucified.

The Soldiers Mock Jesus

16 And the soldiers led him away into the hall, called Praetorium; and they call together the whole band.

17 And they clothed him with purple, and

14:63 high priest rent his clothes. The high priest's garment was not to be rent (Ex. 28:32). This defiant act and his rejection of the Messiah terminated the official status of the Aaronic priesthood at the time. Jesus, a priest forever after the order of Melchizedek (Heb. 5:6, 10; 6:20; 7:11, 15–17, 21–28 [cf. Ps. 110:4]) then enters into the exercise of His high priesthood, offering "himself without spot to God" (see Heb. 9:11–15). The renting of the veil (Mark 15:38) later that day signified the opening of direct access to God through Christ's blood (see Heb. 10:19–22). Thus the Dispensation of Law came to an end.

platted a crown of thorns, and put it about his *head,*

18 And began to salute him, Hail, King of the Jews!

19 And they smote him on the head with a reed, and did spit upon him, and bowing *their* knees worshipped him.

20 And when they had mocked him, they took off the purple from him, and put his own clothes on him, and led him out to crucify him.

Jesus Is Crucified

21 And they compel one Simon a Cyrenian, who passed by, coming out of the country, the father of Alexander and Rufus, to bear his cross.

22 And they bring him unto the place Golgotha, which is, being interpreted, The place of a skull.

23 And they gave him to drink wine mingled with myrrh: but he received *it* not.

24 And when they had crucified him, they parted his garments, casting lots upon them, what every man should take.

25 And it was the third hour, and they crucified him.

26 And the superscription of his accusation was written over, THE KING OF THE JEWS.

27 And with him they crucify two thieves; the one on his right hand, and the other on his left.

28 And the scripture was fulfilled, which saith, And he was numbered with the transgressors.

29 And they that passed by railed on him, wagging their heads, and saying, Ah, thou that destroyest the temple, and buildest *it* in three days,

30 Save thyself, and come down from the cross.

31 Likewise also the chief priests mocking said among themselves with the scribes, He saved others; himself he cannot save.

32 Let Christ the King of Israel descend now from the cross, that we may see and believe. And they that were crucified with him reviled him.

Cross references (center column)
21 Matt. 27:32; Luke 23:26
22 Matt. 27:33; Luke 23:33; John 19:17
24 Ps. 22:18; Luke 23:34; John 19:23
25 Matt. 27:45; Luke 23:44; John 19:14
26 Matt. 27:37; John 19:19
27 Matt. 27:38
28 Isa. 53:12
29 Ps. 22:7; Mark 14:58; John 2:19
32 Matt. 27:44; Luke 23:39
33 Matt. 27:45; Luke 23:44
34 Ps. 22:1; Matt. 27:46
36 Ps. 69:21; Matt. 27:48; John 19:29
37 Matt. 27:50; Luke 23:46; John 19:30
38 Matt. 27:51; Luke 23:45
39 Matt. 27:54; Luke 23:47
40 Matt. 27:55; Luke 23:49
42 Matt. 27:57; Luke 23:50; John 19:38
43 Luke 2:25, 38
46 Matt. 27:59, 60; Luke 23:53; John 19:40

The Death of Jesus

33 And when the sixth hour was come, there was darkness over the whole land until the ninth hour.

34 And at the ninth hour Jesus cried with a loud voice, saying, Eloi, Eloi, lama sabachthani? which is, being interpreted, My God, my God, why hast thou forsaken me?

35 And some of them that stood by, when they heard *it,* said, Behold, he calleth Elias.

36 And one ran and filled a sponge full of vinegar, and put *it* on a reed, and gave him to drink, saying, Let alone; let us see whether Elias will come to take him down.

37 And Jesus cried with a loud voice, and gave up the ghost.

38 And the veil of the temple was rent in twain from the top to the bottom.

39 And when the centurion, which stood over against him, saw that he so cried out, and gave up the ghost, he said, Truly this man was the Son of God.

40 There were also women looking on afar off: among whom was Mary Magdalene, and Mary the mother of James the less and of Joses, and Salome;

41 (Who also, when he was in Galilee, followed him, and ministered unto him;) and many other women which came up with him unto Jerusalem.

Joseph of Arimathea

42 And now when the even was come, because it was the preparation, that is, the day before the sabbath,

43 Joseph of Arimathaea, an honourable counsellor, which also waited for the kingdom of God, came, and went in boldly unto Pilate, and craved the body of Jesus.

44 And Pilate marvelled if he were already dead: and calling *unto him* the centurion, he asked him whether he had been any while dead.

45 And when he knew *it* of the centurion, he gave the body to Joseph.

46 And he bought fine linen, and took him down, and wrapped him in the linen, and

---

15:25 third hour. A time of nine o'clock in the morning is indicated.

15:28 numbered with the transgressors. This is a reference to the fulfillment of Isaiah 53:12.

15:34 Eloi, Eloi, lama sabachthani. Here Mark uses Aramaic, while Matthew (27:46) employed the Hebrew in this quotation from Psalm 22:1. Jesus suffers a sense of aban-

donment by God, as He becomes sin for us (2 Cor. 5:21), experiencing divine judgment for all sin as our substitute.

15:46 laid him in a sepulchre. No further indignities were perpetrated against Jesus' body, but rather with respect and reverence did Joseph and Nicodemus, both secret disciples, wrap the body and place it in Joseph's own newly hewn tomb (Matt. 27:59–61; John 3:1–16).

laid him in a sepulchre which was hewn out of a rock, and rolled a stone unto the door of the sepulchre.

47 And Mary Magdalene and Mary *the mother* of Joses beheld where he was laid.

CHAPTER 16
Jesus Is Risen

1 And when the sabbath was past, Mary Magdalene, and Mary the *mother* of James, and Salome, had bought sweet spices, that they might come and anoint him.

2 And very early in the morning the first *day* of the week, they came unto the sepulchre at the rising of the sun.

3 And they said among themselves, Who shall roll us away the stone from the door of the sepulchre?

4 And when they looked, they saw that the stone was rolled away: for it was very great.

5 And entering into the sepulchre, they saw a young man sitting on the right side, clothed in a long white garment; and they were affrighted.

6 And he saith unto them, Be not affrighted: Ye seek Jesus of Nazareth, which was crucified: he is risen; he is not here: behold the place where they laid him.

7 But go your way, tell his disciples and Peter that he goeth before you into Galilee: there shall ye see him, as he said unto you.

8 And they went out quickly, and fled from the sepulchre; for they trembled and were amazed: neither said they any thing to any *man*; for they were afraid.

Jesus Appears to Mary Magdalene

9 Now when *Jesus* was risen early the first *day* of the week, he appeared first to Mary Magdalene, out of whom he had cast seven devils.

10 *And* she went and told them that had been with him, as they mourned and wept.

11 And they, when they had heard that he was alive, and had been seen of her, believed not.

The Appearance to Two Disciples

12 After that he appeared in another form unto two of them, as they walked, and went into the country.

13 And they went and told *it* unto the residue: neither believed they them.

The Great Commission

14 Afterward he appeared unto the eleven as they sat at meat, and upbraided them with their unbelief and hardness of heart, because they believed not them which had seen him after he was risen.

15 And he said unto them, Go ye into all the world, and preach the gospel to every creature.

16 He that believeth and is baptized shall be saved; but he that believeth not shall be damned.

17 And these signs shall follow them that believe; In my name shall they cast out devils; they shall speak with new tongues;

18 They shall take up serpents; and if they drink any deadly thing, it shall not hurt them; they shall lay hands on the sick, and they shall recover.

The Ascension of Jesus

19 So then after the Lord had spoken unto them, he was received up into heaven, and sat on the right hand of God.

20 And they went forth, and preached every where, the Lord working with *them,* and confirming the word with signs following. Amen.

Cross references: 1 Matt. 28:1; Luke 23:56; 24:1; John 20:1 · 2 Luke 24:1; John 20:1 · 5 Luke 24:3; John 20:11, 12 · 6 Matt. 28:5-7 · 7 Matt. 26:32; Mark 14:28 · 8 Matt. 28:8; Luke 24:9 · 10 Luke 24:10; John 20:18 · 11 Luke 24:11 · 12 Luke 24:13 · 14 Luke 24:36; John 20:19 · 15 Matt. 28:19; John 15:16 · 16 John 3:18, 36; 12:48; Rom. 10:9; 1Pet. 3:21 · 17 Luke 10:17; Acts 2:4; 5:16; 8:7; 10:46; 16:18; 19:6, 12; 1Cor. 12:10, 28 · 18 Luke 10:19; Acts 28:5, 8 · 19 Ps. 110:1; Luke 24:51; Acts 1:2, 3

16:15–16 preach the gospel. Like the other three Gospels, a commission to preach and witness appears toward the close of Mark (see Matt. 28:18–20; Luke 24:46–48; John 20:21).

16:19 received up into heaven. The ascension of Christ forty days after His resurrection (Luke 24:49–52; Acts 1:1–11; Eph. 4:10; Heb. 1:3) brought Him to the heavenly throne, where He fulfilled the portion of Psalm 110:1 that predicted that He would sit at the right hand of God the Father (see Acts 2:32–36; Heb. 10:12–13). Christ is in a place of preeminent honor until He comes again.

Luke

The gospel of Luke was written by a man with a scientific mind who carefully collected and combined facts, then arranged his material in chronological order. Called "the beloved physician" by the apostle Paul (Col. 4:14), Luke the historian dedicated this work and the book of Acts to his friend, Theophilus (1:1–4; Acts 1:1–3).

Luke accompanied Paul from Troas on Paul's second missionary journey, but remained in Philippi until Paul returned there on his last known missionary expedition (Acts 20:6). Paul and Luke seem to have been longtime companions, as evidenced by the fact that Luke was the only one with Paul near the time of Paul's execution (2 Tim. 4:11).

Apparently, as Luke gathered a wealth of information from eyewitnesses of Christ, the Holy Spirit impressed upon him the need to compose another gospel narrative. The gospel of Luke begins with a short prologue, followed by the events leading up to the births of John the Baptist and Jesus Christ. Luke's genealogy of Christ differs from Matthew's in that it traces Mary's ancestry from her father all the way to Adam rather than tracing Joseph's lineage beginning with Abraham. The unique aspect of both genealogy lists is that Christ can be traced to David through the lineage of both Joseph and Mary, emphasizing Christ's humanity.

Prophecy in the gospel of Luke includes Christ's prediction of His death and resurrection and His second coming (9:22–26, cf. 17:20–37). The second coming of Christ is again mentioned in 21:8–36, along with predictions of Jerusalem's destruction, the "times of the Gentiles," and the coming Tribulation (cf. Matt. 24; Mark 13). After the Resurrection, Jesus appeared to two disciples and explained how He had fulfilled much prophecy (24:26–27).

There are 75 distinct prophecies in 250 out of a total of 1,146 verses, or 22 percent of the content. There are 24 Old Testament quotations in Luke.

Author
Luke

Date
A.D. 60

Key Truth
Jesus Is the Son of Man

Historic Time
Announcement of John the Baptist's Birth to Christ's Ascension

Key Verse
19:10
For the Son of man is come to seek and to save that which was lost.

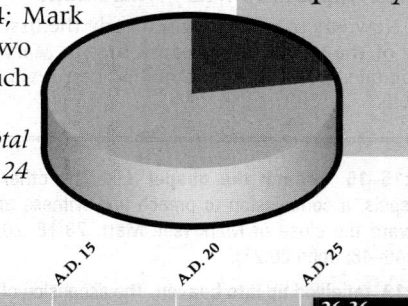

22%
Prophecy

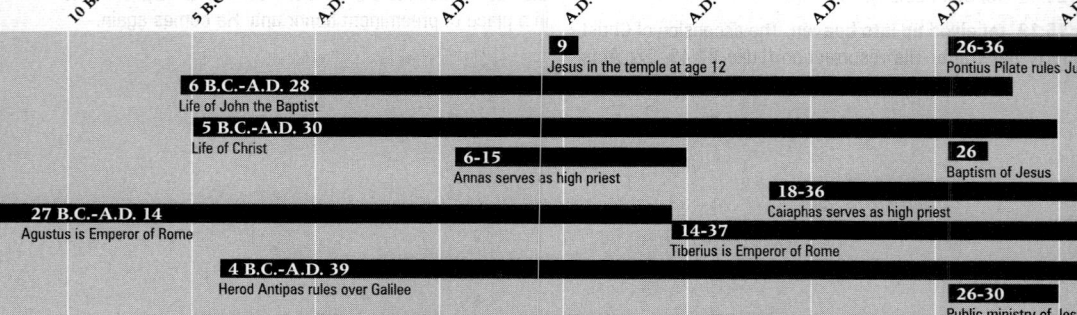

10 B.C. — 5 B.C. — A.D. 1 — A.D. 5 — A.D. 10 — A.D. 15 — A.D. 20 — A.D. 25 — A.D.

9
Jesus in the temple at age 12

26-36
Pontius Pilate rules Ju

6 B.C.-A.D. 28
Life of John the Baptist

5 B.C.-A.D. 30
Life of Christ

6-15
Annas serves as high priest

26
Baptism of Jesus

18-36
Caiaphas serves as high priest

27 B.C.-A.D. 14
Agustus is Emperor of Rome

14-37
Tiberius is Emperor of Rome

4 B.C.-A.D. 39
Herod Antipas rules over Galilee

26-30
Public ministry of Jesu

6 B.C.-30 A.D.
Events of the Gospel of Luke

CHAPTER 1

1 Forasmuch as many have taken in hand to set forth in order a declaration of those things which are most surely believed among us,

2 Even as they delivered them unto us, which from the beginning were eyewitnesses, and ministers of the word;

3 It seemed good to me also, having had perfect understanding of all things from the very first, to write unto thee in order, most excellent Theophilus,

4 That thou mightest know the certainty of those things, wherein thou hast been instructed.

The Birth of John the Baptist

5 There was in the days of Herod, the king of Judea, a certain priest named Zacharias, of the course of Abijah: and his wife *was* of the daughters of Aaron, and her name *was* Elisabeth.

6 And they were both righteous before God, walking in all the commandments and ordinances of the Lord blameless.

7 And they had no child, because that Elisabeth was barren, and they both were *now* well stricken in years.

8 And it came to pass, that while he executed the priest's office before God in the order of his course,

9 According to the custom of the priest's office, his lot was to burn incense when he went into the temple of the Lord.

10 And the whole multitude of the people were praying without at the time of incense.

11 And there appeared unto him an angel of the Lord standing on the right side of the altar of incense.

12 And when Zacharias saw *him,* he was troubled, and fear fell upon him.

13 But the angel said unto him, Fear not, Zacharias: for thy prayer is heard; and thy wife Elisabeth shall bear thee a son, and thou shalt call his name John.

14 And thou shalt have joy and gladness; and many shall rejoice at his birth.

15 For he shall be great in the sight of the Lord, and shall drink neither wine nor strong drink; and he shall be filled with the Holy Ghost, even from his mother's womb.

16 And many of the children of Israel shall he turn to the Lord their God.

Cross references:
2 Mark 1:1; John 15:27; Heb. 2:3;
3 Acts 1:1; 11:4; 15:19, 25, 28; 1Cor. 7:40
4 John 20:31
5 Neh. 12:4, 17; Matt. 2:1
6 Job 1:1; Acts 23:1; 24:16; Phil. 3:6
8 1Chr. 24:19; 2Chr. 8:14; 31:2
9 Ex. 30:7, 8; 1Sam. 2:28; 1Chr. 23:13; 2Chr. 29:11
10 Lev. 16:17; Rev. 8:3, 4
12 Luke 1:29; 2:9
13 Luke 1:60, 63
15 Num. 6:3; Judg. 13:4
16 Mal. 4:5, 6

The Career of Messiah the King

OT REFERENCE	PROPHECY FULFILLED IN JESUS	NT REFERENCE
Micah 5:2	Always Existed	John 1:1–2
Psalm 2:7	The Son of God	Luke 9:35
Micah 5:2	Born in Bethlehem	Luke 2:4–7
Isaiah 40:3	Public Ministry Is Preceded by a Messenger	Luke 1:17
Isaiah 35:5–6	Performed Many Miracles	Luke 7:22
Psalm 41:9	Betrayed by a Friend	John 13:18, 26–27
Psalm 22:16	Died on a Cross	Luke 23:33
Isaiah 53:9	Buried with the Rich	Matthew 27:57–60
Hosea 6:2	Raised from the Dead	Luke 24:6–8
Psalm 110:1	Seated at the Right Hand of God	Romans 8:34

1:13 Elisabeth shall bear thee a son. The first prophecy in Luke is to a childless older couple (Zacharias and Elisabeth). This prophecy was fulfilled according to Luke 1:24, 57–66.

1:14 many shall rejoice at his birth. The joy of the nation, for a while, described in John 5:35 is a fulfillment of this prophecy.

1:15 He shall be great in the sight of the Lord. The fulfillment of this prophecy is evidenced when Christ stated that there had been no one greater up until John's appearing (7:28). That he would "drink neither wine nor

strong drink" means that John would, like Samson and Samuel, live under the constraints of the Nazarite vow (Num. 6; Judg. 13:5–7; 16:17; Amos 2:11–12; see Luke 7:33). That he would "be filled with the Holy Ghost, even from his mother's womb" was fulfilled six months later when Elisabeth visited Mary (v. 41).

1:16 many of the children of Israel shall he turn to the Lord their God. This was fulfilled in Luke 3:1–20 as John directed many within the nation of Israel to Jesus, their Messiah.

17 And he shall go before him in the spirit and power of Elias, to turn the hearts of the fathers to the children, and the disobedient to the wisdom of the just; to make ready a people prepared for the Lord.

18 And Zacharias said unto the angel, Whereby shall I know this? for I am an old man and my wife well stricken in years.

19 And the angel answering said unto him, I am Gabriel, that stand in the presence of God; and am sent to speak unto thee, and to shew thee these glad tidings.

20 And, behold, thou shalt be dumb, and not able to speak, until the day that these things shall be performed, because thou believest not my words, which shall be fulfilled in their season.

21 And the people waited for Zacharias, and marvelled that he tarried so long in the temple.

22 And when he came out, he could not speak unto them: and they perceived that he had seen a vision in the temple: for he beckoned unto them, and remained speechless.

23 And it came to pass, that, as soon as the days of his ministration were accomplished, he departed to his own house.

24 And after those days his wife Elisabeth conceived, and hid herself five months, saying,

25 Thus hath the Lord dealt with me in the days wherein he looked on *me,* to take away my reproach among men.

An Angel Appears to Mary

26 And in the sixth month the angel Gabriel was sent from God unto a city of Galilee, named Nazareth,

27 To a virgin espoused to a man whose name was Joseph, of the house of David; and the virgin's name *was* Mary.

28 And the angel came in unto her, and said, Hail, *thou that art* highly favoured, the Lord *is* with thee: blessed *art* thou among women.

29 And when she saw *him,* she was troubled at his saying, and cast in her mind what manner of salutation this should be.

30 And the angel said unto her, Fear not, Mary: for thou hast found favour with God.

31 And, behold, thou shalt conceive in thy womb, and bring forth a son, and shalt call his name JESUS.

32 He shall be great, and shall be called the Son of the Highest: and the Lord God shall give unto him the throne of his father David:

33 And he shall reign over the house of Jacob for ever; and of his kingdom there shall be no end.

Cross references
17 Mal. 4:5; Matt. 11:14; Mark 9:12
18 Gen. 17:17
19 Dan. 8:16; 9:21-23; Matt. 18:10
23 2Kgs. 11:5; 1Chr. 9:25
25 Gen. 30:23; Isa. 4:1; 54:1, 4
27 Matt. 1:18; Luke 2:4, 5
28 Dan. 9:23; 10:29; Luke 1:3
29 Luke 1:12
31 Isa. 7:14; Matt. 1:21; Luke 2:21
32 Ps. 132:11; Isa. 9:6, 7; 16:5; Mark 5:7; Rev. 3:7
33 Dan. 2:44; 7:14, 27; Mic. 4:7; John 12:34

1:17 he shall go before him. This speaks of John being the forerunner of Jesus (3:1–22). Malachi 4:5 predicted that the Lord would send Elijah to the nation "before the coming of the great and dreadful day of the LORD." When asked by Israel's religious leaders "Art thou Elias?" John answered clearly, "I am not" (John 1:21), but John did come in the spirit and power of Elijah. He would fulfill an Elijah-like ministry of turning "the heart of the fathers to the children, and the heart of the children to their fathers" (Mal. 4:6, cf. Luke 1:77). Later, John says of himself, quoting Isaiah 40:3, that he was "The voice of one crying in the wilderness, Prepare ye the way of the Lord, make his paths straight" (Luke 3:7). Christ, when discussing John the Baptist, said, "If ye will receive it, this is Elias, which was for to come" (Matt. 11:14). The people did not receive it, thus John the Baptist turns out not to be the Elijah prophesied in Malachi (Matt. 17:11–12). Therefore, we conclude that Elijah is yet to come and will likely be one of the two witnesses during the Tribulation (Rev. 11:4–13), when the nation of Israel will receive Jesus as their Messiah.

1:30–31 thou shalt conceive in thy womb, and bring forth a son. The Old Testament predicted that a virgin would conceive and give birth to Messiah (Isa. 7:14). Mary was selected as that virgin not because she was better than others or deserving of the position, but merely because she "found favour with God." This prophecy was fulfilled according to Luke 2:1–20.

1:32 Gabriel provides Mary with a prophetic profile of her Son-to-be—Messiah. He, in essence, tells Mary that her Son is equal to God, and thus, is God. This was also predicted often in the Old Testament (2 Sam. 7:8–16; 1 Kgs. 2:24–25; Ps. 2:1–12; 89:14, 19–29, 35–37; 110:1–7; 132:11–12; Isa. 9:6–7; 11:1–5, 10; Jer. 23:5–6). The Old Testament also predicted that the Messiah would be given "the throne of his father David" (2 Sam. 7:13–16; Ps. 2:6; 89:26–29). Christ makes note of this promise in Luke 20:41–44. Luke, more than the other Gospels, is concerned with the kingdom of God, i.e., the throne of David. While Christ has already fulfilled the necessary requirements to ascend that throne, He will actually sit upon David's throne after His second coming.

1:33 of his kingdom there shall be no end. Two points are being made here. First, Mary's son, Jesus the Messiah, will reign over Israel forever. Since His ascension Christ reigns in heaven, but He will not reign over Israel until He sets up the Millennial Kingdom after His second coming. Secondly, Jesus will reign over His people Israel forever (2 Sam 7:16).

The Reliability of the New Testament

By Josh McDowell

Can you really trust the New Testament, a collection of documents written around two thousand years ago? The historical reliability of the Scripture should be tested by the same criteria by which all historical documents are tested. Military historian C. Sanders lists three basic principles of historiography: the **bibliographical test**, the **internal evidence test**, and the **external evidence test**.[1]

The **bibliographical test** is an examination of the textual transmission by which documents reach us. How reliable are the extant copies of the original manuscripts? We can answer this question by examining the time interval between the original and extant copy. Over twenty thousand copies of New Testament manuscripts are in existence today, with the earliest copy dating 130 A.D.—less than one hundred years after it was originally penned! The New Testament has more manuscript authority than any piece of literature from antiquity.

The bibliographical test has determined that the words of the earliest manuscripts we have available are exactly what were originally recorded. But are the original manuscripts credible? The author's credibility is determined by the **internal evidence test**.

Dr. Louis Gottschalk, former professor of history at the University of Chicago, points out that the ability of the writer or the witness to tell the truth is helpful to the historian to determine credibility.[2] This "ability to tell the truth" is closely related to the witness's nearness both geographically and chronologically to the events recorded. The New Testament accounts of the life and teaching of Jesus were recorded by men who had been either eyewitnesses or those who related the accounts of eyewitnesses of the actual events and teachings of Christ (Luke 1:1–3).

> *Can we be certain that today's Scripture is reliable, without errors and discrepancies?*

This closeness to the recorded accounts is an extremely effective means of certifying the accuracy of what is retained by a witness. The historian, however, also has to deal with the eyewitness who either consciously or unconsciously tells falsehoods, even though he is near to the event and is competent to tell the truth. The New Testament accounts of Christ were being circulated within the lifetimes of those alive at the time of Christ. These people could certainly confirm or deny the accuracy of the accounts.

The third test of historicity is the **external evidence test**. What secondary sources are there that substantiate the work's accuracy and authenticity? Gottschalk argues that "conformity or agreement with other known historical or scientific facts is often the decisive test of evidence, whether of one or of more witnesses."[3] For instance, a friend of the apostle John confirms the internal evidence from John's accounts. Polycarp, Bishop of Smyrna (ca. A.D. 70–160), was a disciple of John who testified that John penned the Gospel of John while in Ephesus. Polycarp's testimony regarding John is recorded in the treatise, *Against Heresies,* written by Irenaeus, Bishop of Lyon (ca. A.D. 140–200).

Therefore, if a person discards the Scripture as unreliable, then he or she must discard almost all the literature of antiquity. The New Testament is indeed trustworthy and historically reliable in its witness about Jesus.

[1] C. Sanders, *Introduction to Research in English Literary History*. (New York: MacMillan Company, 1952), pp. 143 ff.
[2] Louis R. Gottschalk, *Understanding History* (New York: Knopf, 1969, 2nd ed.), p. 150; p. 161; p. 168.
[3] Ibid.

34 Then said Mary unto the angel, How shall this be, seeing I know not a man?

35 And the angel answered and said unto her, The Holy Ghost shall come upon thee, and the power of the Highest shall overshadow thee: therefore also that holy thing which shall be born of thee shall be called the Son of God.

36 And, behold, thy cousin Elisabeth, she hath also conceived a son in her old age: and this is the sixth month with her, who was called barren.

37 For with God nothing shall be impossible.

38 And Mary said, Behold the handmaid of the Lord; be it unto me according to thy word. And the angel departed from her.

Mary Visits Elisabeth

39 And Mary arose in those days, and went into the hill country with haste, into a city of Judah;

40 And entered into the house of Zacharias, and saluted Elisabeth.

41 And it came to pass, that, when Elisabeth heard the salutation of Mary, the babe leaped in her womb; and Elisabeth was filled with the Holy Ghost:

42 And she spake out with a loud voice, and said, Blessed *art* thou among women, and blessed *is* the fruit of thy womb.

43 And whence *is* this to me, that the mother of my Lord should come to me?

44 For, lo, as soon as the voice of thy salutation sounded in mine ears, the babe leaped in my womb for joy.

45 And blessed *is* she that believed for there shall be a performance of those things which were told her from the Lord.

Mary's Song of Praise

46 And Mary said, My soul doth magnify the Lord,

47 And my spirit hath rejoiced in God my Saviour.

48 For he hath regarded the low estate of his handmaiden: for, behold, from henceforth all generations shall call me blessed.

49 For he that is mighty hath done to me great things; and holy *is* his name.

50 And his mercy *is* on them that fear him from generation to generation.

51 He hath shewed strength with his arm; he hath scattered the proud in the imagination of their hearts.

52 He hath put down the mighty from *their* seats, and exalted them of low degree.

53 He hath filled the hungry with good things; and the rich he hath sent empty away.

54 He hath holpen his servant Israel, in remembrance of *his* mercy;

55 As he spake to our fathers, to Abraham, and to his seed for ever.

56 And Mary abode with her about three months, and returned to her own house.

The Birth of John the Baptist

57 Now Elisabeth's full time came that she should be delivered; and she brought forth a son.

58 And her neighbours and her cousins heard how the Lord had shewed great mercy upon her; and they rejoiced with her.

59 And it came to pass, that on the eighth day they came to circumcise the child; and they called him Zacharias, after the name of his father.

60 And his mother answered and said, Not *so;* but he shall be called John.

61 And they said unto her, There is none of thy kindred that is called by this name.

62 And they made signs to his father, how he would have him called.

63 And he asked for a writing table, and

Cross References
- **35** Matt. 1:20; Mark 1:1; John 1:34; 20:31; Acts 8:37
- **37** Gen. 18:14; Jer. 32:17; Matt. 19:26; Mark 10:27; Luke 18:27
- **42** Judg. 5:24; Luke 1:28
- **46** 1Sam. 2:1; Ps. 34:2, 3; 35:9; Hab. 3:18
- **48** 1Sam. 1:11; Ps. 138:6; Mal. 3:12; Luke 11:27
- **49** Ps. 71:19; 111:9; 126:2, 3
- **50** Gen. 17:7; Ex. 20:6; Ps. 103:17, 18
- **51** Ps. 33:10; 98:1; 118:15; Isa. 40:10; 51:9; 52:10; 1Pet. 5:5
- **52** 1Sam. 2:6-10; Job 5:11; Ps. 113:6
- **53** 1Sam. 2:5; Ps. 34:10
- **54** Ps. 98:3; Jer. 31:3, 20
- **55** Gen. 17:19
- **58** Luke 1:14
- **59** Gen. 17:12; Lev. 12:3
- **60** Luke 1:13

1:34 How shall this be, seeing I know not a man? "Know" in this context means sexual relations. Mary is a virgin as predicted of Messiah's mother in Isaiah 7:14. This is not a question of unbelief or doubt (cf. 1:38), but she does not comprehend how this prophecy can be fulfilled. The virgin birth—actually conception—is clearly described here as a direct miracle similar to original creation in Genesis 1 and 2. Jesus is the only person in history besides Adam to have been created directly from the hand of God. However, Adam led us in to sin, while Jesus provides the way out of sin.

1:42–43 Elisabeth, under the inspiration of the Holy Spirit provides a prophetic recognition that the child in Mary's womb is Israel's Messiah. She calls Him "my Lord" (cf. Psalm 110:1).

1:46–55 Mary's prophecy about her Son, Jesus the Messiah, is called the Magnificat and is filled with Old Testament allusions and quotations.

1:54–55 his servant Israel. Israel as God's servant is found often in Isaiah (Isa. 41:8–9; 44:1–2, 21; 48:20; 49:3). God's actions with Mary were the beginning of the fulfillment of prophecies made many centuries earlier (Gen. 12:1–3; 22:16–18).

1:59–64 This is the completion of Gabriel's prophecy in verse 20 that Zacharias would be mute until John's birth.

wrote, saying, His name is John. And they marvelled all.

64 And his mouth was opened immediately, and his tongue *loosed,* and he spake, and praised God.

65 And fear came on all that dwelt round about them: and all these sayings were noised abroad throughout all the hill country of Judea.

66 And all they that heard *them* laid *them* up in their hearts, saying, What manner of child shall this be! And the hand of the Lord was with him.

The Prophecy of Zacharias

67 And his father Zacharias was filled with the Holy Ghost, and prophesied, saying,

68 Blessed *be* the Lord God of Israel; for he hath visited and redeemed his people,

69 And hath raised up an horn of salvation for us in the house of his servant David;

70 As he spake by the mouth of his holy prophets, which have been since the world began:

71 That we should be saved from our enemies, and from the hand of all that hate us;

72 To perform the mercy *promised* to our fathers, and to remember his holy covenant;

73 The oath which he sware to our father Abraham,

74 That he would grant unto us, that we being delivered out of the hand of our enemies might serve him without fear,

75 In holiness and righteousness before him, all the days of our life.

76 And thou, child, shalt be called the prophet of the Highest: for thou shalt go before the face of the Lord to prepare his ways;

77 To give knowledge of salvation unto his people by the remission of their sins,

78 Through the tender mercy of our God; whereby the dayspring from on high hath visited us,

79 To give light to them that sit in darkness and *in* the shadow of death, to guide our feet into the way of peace.

66 Luke 2:19, 51
67 Joel 2:28
68 Ex. 3:16; 4:31; 1Kgs. 1:48; Luke 7:16
69 Ps. 132:17
70 Jer. 23:5, 6; 30:10; Dan. 9:24
72 Lev. 26:42; Ps. 98:3; 105:8, 9; 106:45
73 Gen. 12:3; 17:4; 22:16, 17
74 Rom. 6:18, 22; Heb. 9:14
75 Jer. 32:39, 40; 1Pet. 1:15; 2Pet. 1:4
76 Isa. 40:3; Mal. 3:1; 4:5; Matt. 11:10; Luke 1:17
77 Mark 1:4; Luke 3:3
79 Isa. 9:2; Matt. 4:16
2 Acts 5:37
4 1Sam. 16:1, 4; Matt. 1:16; Luke 1:27; John 7:42
5 Matt. 1:18; Luke 1:27
7 Matt. 1:25
10 Matt. 28:19; Mark 1:15; Luke 2:31, 32
11 Isa. 9:6; Matt. 1:16, 21; Luke 1:43
13 Gen. 28:12; Dan. 7:10; Rev. 5:11

80 And the child grew, and waxed strong in spirit, and was in the deserts till the day of his shewing unto Israel.

CHAPTER 2
The Birth of Jesus

1 And it came to pass in those days, that there went out a decree from Caesar Augustus, that all the world should be taxed.

2 (*And* this taxing was first made when Cyrenius was governor of Syria.)

3 And all went to be taxed, every one into his own city.

4 And Joseph also went up from Galilee, out of the city of Nazareth, into Judea, unto the city of David, which is called Bethlehem; because (he was of the house and lineage of David:)

5 To be taxed with Mary his espoused wife, being great with child.

6 And so it was, that, while they were there, the days were accomplished that she should be delivered.

7 And she brought forth her firstborn son, and wrapped him in swaddling clothes, and laid him in a manger; because there was no room for them in the inn.

The Shepherds and the Angels

8 And there were in the same country shepherds abiding in the field, keeping watch over their flock by night.

9 And, lo, the angel of the Lord came upon them, and the glory of the Lord shone round about them: and they were sore afraid.

10 And the angel said unto them, Fear not: for, behold, I bring you good tidings of great joy, which shall be to all people.

11 For unto you is born this day in the city of David a Saviour, which is Christ the Lord.

12 And this *shall be* a sign unto you; Ye shall find the babe wrapped in swaddling clothes, lying in a manger.

13 And suddenly there was with the angel a multitude of the heavenly host praising God, and saying,

---

1:68–79 Zacharias' prophecy is known as the Benedictus. Zacharias speaks about the coming ministry of John the Baptist in preparation for the ministry of Jesus the Messiah.

1:76 the prophet of the Highest. This not only tells us something about the coming ministry of John the Baptist, but also implies that Jesus is God, since He is called "the Highest." The primary ministry of John was to prepare the way for Christ by preaching a message of repentance

(Luke 3:1–22).

2:1–20 The prediction of the birth of Jesus in Luke 1:31 is fulfilled in these verses.

2:14 good will toward men. This is an angelic prophecy about the Messiah, demonstrating that heaven was very pleased. Literally the original Greek reads: "And on earth peace among men with whom He is pleased."

14 Glory to God in the highest, and on earth peace, good will toward men.

15 And it came to pass, as the angels were gone away from them into heaven, the shepherds said one to another, Let us now go even unto Bethlehem, and see this thing which is come to pass, which the Lord hath made known unto us.

16 And they came with haste, and found Mary, and Joseph, and the babe lying in a manger.

17 And when they had seen *it*, they made known abroad the saying which was told them concerning this child.

18 And all they that heard *it* wondered at those things which were told them by the shepherds.

19 But Mary kept all these things, and pondered *them* in her heart.

20 And the shepherds returned, glorifying and praising God for all the things that they had heard and seen, as it was told unto them.

21 And when eight days were accomplished for the circumcising of the child, his name was called JESUS, which was so named of the angel before he was conceived in the womb.

Jesus Is Dedicated in the Temple

22 And when the days of her purification according to the law of Moses were accomplished, they brought him to Jerusalem, to present *him* to the Lord;

23 (As it is written in the law of the Lord, Every male that openeth the womb shall be called holy to the Lord;)

24 And to offer a sacrifice according to that which is said in the law of the Lord, A pair of turtledoves, or two young pigeons.

25 And, behold, there was a man in Jerusalem, whose name *was* Simeon; and the same man *was* just and devout, waiting for the consolation of Israel: and the Holy Ghost was upon him.

26 And it was revealed unto him by the Holy Ghost, that he should not see death, before he had seen the Lord's Christ.

27 And he came by the Spirit into the temple: and when the parents brought in the child Jesus, to do for him after the custom of the law,

28 Then took he him up in his arms, and blessed God, and said,

29 Lord, now lettest thou thy servant depart in peace, according to thy word:

30 For mine eyes have seen thy salvation,

31 Which thou hast prepared before the face of all people;

32 A light to lighten the Gentiles, and the glory of thy people Israel.

33 And Joseph and his mother marvelled at those things which were spoken of him.

34 And Simeon blessed them, and said unto Mary his mother, Behold, this *child* is set for the fall and rising again of many in Israel; and for a sign which shall be spoken against;

35 (Yea, a sword shall pierce through thy own soul also,) that the thoughts of many hearts may be revealed.

36 And there was one Anna, a prophetess, the daughter of Phanuel, of the tribe of Asher: she was of a great age, and had lived with an husband seven years from her virginity;

37 And she *was* a widow of about fourscore and four years, which departed not from the temple, but served *God* with fastings and prayers night and day.

38 And she coming in that instant gave thanks likewise unto the Lord, and spake of him to all them that looked for redemption in Jerusalem.

Cross-references

14 Isa. 57:19; Luke 1:79; John 3:16; Eph. 1:6; 2:4, 2Thess. 2:16; 1John 4:9, 10; Rev. 5:13
19 Gen. 37:11; Luke 1:66; 2:51
21 Gen. 17:12; Lev. 12:3; Matt. 1:21, 25; Luke 1:31, 59
22 Lev. 12:2-4, 6
23 Ex. 13:2; 22:29; 34:19; Num. 3:13; 8:17; 18:15
24 Lev. 12:2, 6, 8
25 Isa. 40:1; Mark 15:43; Luke 2:38
26 Ps. 89:48; Heb. 11:5
27 Matt. 4:1
29 Gen. 46:30; Phil. 1:23
30 Isa. 52:10; Luke 3:6
32 Isa. 9:2; 42:6; 49:6; 60:1-3; Matt. 4:16
34 Isa. 8:14; Matt. 21:44; Rom. 9:32, 33; 1Pet. 2:7
35 Ps. 42:10; John 19:25
38 Mark 15:43; Luke 1:25; 24:21

2:25–26 waiting for the consolation of Israel. Simeon prophetically signified that Jesus, even in infancy, was the promised Messiah (see Isa. 25:9). Even though there was prophetic expectation in Israel in general, perhaps because the time of Daniel's seventy weeks was drawing seemingly to a close (see the notes on Dan. 9:24; 9:26; and 9:27), Simeon had received direct revelation through the Holy Spirit that he would live to see the Lord's Christ, that is, the Messiah.

2:30–32 For mine eyes have seen thy salvation. Simeon's prophecy declares that Jesus would be "a light to lighten the Gentiles," that is, the source of revelation to them (Isa. 42:6; 49:6), and "the glory of thy people Israel," the Messiah who would bring fame to Israel.

2:34 the fall and rising again of many in Israel. This prophecy relates to the judgment aspect of Christ's future ministry (Isa. 8:14–15; Hos. 14:9). For the opponents of Jesus, He will not be a source of hope; instead He will be the focus of opposition.

2:35 a sword shall pierce through thy own soul. This was fulfilled by the rejection and crucifixion of Jesus by Israel (Luke 12:50; 13:31–32; 17:25; 18:32–33; 22:15, 63–64; 23:11; John 19:25–27). The "thoughts of many hearts" continue to be revealed because He brings the truth to mankind.

The Return to Nazareth

39 And when they had performed all things according to the law of the Lord, they returned into Galilee, to their own city Nazareth.

40 And the child grew, and waxed strong in spirit, filled with wisdom: and the grace of God was upon him.

Jesus Speaks with the Leaders in the Temple

41 Now his parents went to Jerusalem every year at the feast of the passover.

42 And when he was twelve years old, they went up to Jerusalem after the custom of the feast.

43 And when they had fulfilled the days, as they returned, the child Jesus tarried behind in Jerusalem; and Joseph and his mother knew not *of it*.

44 But they, supposing him to have been in the company, went a day's journey; and they sought him among *their* kinsfolk and acquaintance.

45 And when they found him not, they turned back again to Jerusalem, seeking him.

46 And it came to pass, that after three days they found him in the temple, sitting in the midst of the doctors, both hearing them, and asking them questions.

47 And all that heard him were astonished at his understanding and answers.

48 And when they saw him, they were amazed: and his mother said unto him, Son, why hast thou thus dealt with us? behold, thy father and I have sought thee sorrowing.

49 And he said unto them, How is it that ye sought me? wist ye not that I must be about my Father's business?

50 And they understood not the saying which he spake unto them.

51 And he went down with them, and came to Nazareth, and was subject unto them: but his mother kept all these sayings in her heart.

52 And Jesus increased in wisdom and stature, and in favour with God and man.

CHAPTER 3
John the Baptist Preaches

1 Now in the fifteenth year of the reign of Tiberius Caesar, Pontius Pilate being gover-

---

40 Luke 1:80; 2:52
41 Ex. 23:15, 17; 34:23; Deut. 16:1, 16
47 Matt. 7:28; Mark 1:22; Luke 4:22, 32; John 7:15, 46
49 John 2:16
50 Luke 9:45; 18:34
51 Dan. 7:28; Luke 2:40
52 1Sam. 2:26; Luke 2:40
2 John 11:49, 51; 18:13; Acts 4:6
3 Matt. 3:1; Mark 1:4; Luke 1:77
4 Isa. 40:3; Matt. 3:3; Mark 1:3; John 1:23
6 Ps. 98:2; Isa. 52:10; Luke 2:10
7 Matt. 3:7
9 Matt. 7:19
10 Acts 2:37
11 Luke 11:41; 2Cor. 8:14; James 2:15, 16; 1John 3:17; 4:20
12 Matt. 21:32; Luke 7:29
13 Luke 19:8
14 Ex. 23:1; Lev. 19:11

---

nor of Judea, and Herod being tetrarch of Galilee, and his brother Philip tetrarch of Ituraea and of the region of Trachonitis, and Lysanias the tetrarch of Abilene,

2 Annas and Caiaphas being the high priests, the word of God came unto John the son of Zacharias in the wilderness.

3 And he came into all the country about Jordan, preaching the baptism of repentance for the remission of sins;

4 As it is written in the book of the words of Esaias the prophet, saying, The voice of one crying in the wilderness, Prepare ye the way of the Lord, make his paths straight.

5 Every valley shall be filled, and every mountain and hill shall be brought low; and the crooked shall be made straight, and the rough ways *shall be* made smooth;

6 And all flesh shall see the salvation of God.

7 Then said he to the multitude that came forth to be baptized of him, O generation of vipers, who hath warned you to flee from the wrath to come?

8 Bring forth therefore fruits worthy of repentance, and begin not to say within yourselves, We have Abraham to *our* father: for I say unto you, That God is able of these stones to raise up children unto Abraham.

9 And now also the axe is laid unto the root of the trees: every tree therefore which bringeth not forth good fruit is hewn down, and cast into the fire.

10 And the people asked him, saying, What shall we do then?

11 He answereth and saith unto them, He that hath two coats, let him impart to him that hath none; and he that hath meat, let him do likewise.

12 Then came also publicans to be baptized, and said unto him, Master, what shall we do?

13 And he said unto them, Exact no more than that which is appointed you.

14 And the soldiers likewise demanded of him, saying, And what shall we do? And he said unto them, Do violence to no man, neither accuse *any* falsely; and be content with your wages.

15 And as the people were in expectation, and all men mused in their hearts of John, whether he were the Christ, or not;

3:2 the word of God came unto John. This means that John the Baptist began prophesying. The essence of his prophecy is stated in verses 4–6.

3:5–6 These verses are a quotation from Isaiah 40:3–5, speaking of the ancient custom of preparation that precedes an important dignitary. The glory of Jesus and the salvation He would bring would not be limited to Israel alone.

16 John answered, saying unto *them* all, I indeed baptize you with water; but one mightier than I cometh, the latchet of whose shoes I am not worthy to unloose: he shall baptize you with the Holy Ghost and with fire:

17 Whose fan *is* in his hand, and he will throughly purge his floor, and will gather the wheat into his garner; but the chaff he will burn with fire unquenchable.

18 And many other things in his exhortation preached he unto the people.

19 But Herod the tetrarch, being reproved by him for Herodias his brother Philip's wife, and for all the evils which Herod had done,

20 Added yet this above all, that he shut up John in prison.

John Baptizes Jesus

21 Now when all the people were baptized, it came to pass, that Jesus also being baptized, and praying, the heaven was opened,

22 And the Holy Ghost descended in a bodily shape like a dove upon him, and a voice came from heaven, which said, Thou art my beloved Son; in thee I am well pleased.

The Genealogy of Jesus

23 And Jesus himself began to be about thirty years of age being (as was supposed) the son of Joseph, which was *the son* of Heli,

24 Which was *the son* of Matthat, which was *the son* of Levi, which was *the son* of Melchi, which was *the son* of Janna, which was *the son* of Joseph,

25 Which was *the son* of Mattathias, which was *the son* of Amos, which was *the son* of Naum, which was *the son* of Esli, which was *the son* of Nagge,

26 Which was *the son* of Maath, which was *the son* of Mattathias, which was *the son* of Semei, which was *the son* of Joseph, which was *the son* of Judah,

27 Which was *the son* of Joanna, which was *the son* of Rhesa, which was *the son* of Zorobabel, which was *the son* of Shealtiel, which was *the son* of Neri,

28 Which was *the son* of Melchi, which was

the son of Addi, which was *the son* of Cosam, which was *the son* of Elmodam, which was *the son* of Er,

29 Which was *the son* of Jose, which was *the son* of Eliezer, which was *the son* of Jorim, which was *the son* of Matthat, which was *the son* of Levi,

30 Which was *the son* of Simeon, which was *the son* of Judah, which was *the son* of Joseph, which was *the son* of Jonan, which was *the son* of Eliakim,

31 Which was *the son* of Melea, which was *the son* of Menan, which was *the son* of Mattatha, which was *the son* of Nathan, which was *the son* of David,

32 Which was *the son* of Jesse, which was *the son* of Obed, which was *the son* of Booz, which was *the son* of Salmon, which was *the son* of Naasson,

33 Which was *the son* of Aminadab, which was *the son* of Aram, which was *the son* of Esrom, which was *the son* of Phares, which was *the son* of Judah,

34 Which was *the son* of Jacob, which was *the son* of Isaac, which was *the son* of Abraham, which was *the son* of Thara, which was *the son* of Nachor,

35 Which was *the son* of Serug, which was *the son* of Reu, which was *the son* of Phalec, which was *the son* of Heber, which was *the son* of Sala,

36 Which was *the son* of Cainan, which was *the son* of Arphaxad, which was *the son* of Sem, which was *the son* of Noe, which was *the son* of Lamech,

37 Which was *the son* of Methuselah, which was *the son* of Enoch, which was *the son* of Jared, which was *the son* of Maleleel, which was *the son* of Cainan,

38 Which was *the son* of Enos, which was *the son* of Seth, which was *the son* of Adam, which was *the son* of God.

CHAPTER 4
The Devil Tempts Jesus

1 And Jesus being full of the Holy Ghost returned from Jordan, and was led by the Spirit into the wilderness,

2 Being forty days tempted of the devil.

Cross references (center column):

16 Matt. 3:11
17 Mic. 4:12; Matt. 13:30
19 Matt. 14:3; Mark 6:17
21 Matt. 3:13; John 1:32
23 Num. 4:3, 35, 39, 43, 47; Matt. 13:55; John 6:42
31 2Sam. 5:14; 1Chr. 3:5; Zech. 12:12
32 Ruth 4:18-22; 1Chr. 2:10-12
34 Gen. 11:24, 26
36 Gen. 5:6-26; 11:10-26
38 Gen. 5:1, 2
1 Matt. 4:1; Mark 1:12; Luke 2:27; 4:14
2 Ex. 34:28; 1Kgs. 19:8

3:16–17 with fire. This symbol represents the fire of judgment at Christ's second coming, though it is often misapplied as a reference to the power of the Holy Spirit. The next phrase, "The chaff he will burn with fire unquenchable," is clearly an image of judgment.

3:23–38 This genealogy of Jesus serves a prophetic purpose in that it provides further witness that Jesus is indeed the Messiah, as John the Baptist claims. This genealogy traces His line through Joseph all the way back to Adam, "the son of God." (See Matthew 1:1–17 for the other genealogy of Jesus in the New Testament.)

And in those days he did eat nothing: and when they were ended, he afterward hungered.

3 And the devil said unto him, If thou be the Son of God, command this stone that it be made bread.

4 And Jesus answered him, saying, It is written, That man shall not live by bread alone, but by every word of God.

5 And the devil, taking him up into an high mountain, shewed unto him all the kingdoms of the world in a moment of time.

6 And the devil said unto him, All this power will I give thee, and the glory of them: for that is delivered unto me; and to whomsoever I will I give it.

7 If thou therefore wilt worship me, all shall be thine.

8 And Jesus answered and said unto him, Get thee behind me, Satan: for it is written, Thou shalt worship the Lord thy God, and him only shalt thou serve.

9 And he brought him to Jerusalem, and set him on a pinnacle of the temple, and said unto him, If thou be the Son of God, cast thyself down from hence:

10 For it is written, He shall give his angels charge over thee, to keep thee:

Cross-references:
4 Deut. 8:3
6 John 12:31; 14:30; Rev. 13:2, 7
8 Deut. 6:13; 10:20
9 Matt. 4:5
10 Ps. 91:11
12 Deut. 6:16
13 John 14:30; Heb. 4:15
14 Matt. 4:12; Luke 4:1; John 4:43; Acts 10:37
16 Matt. 2:23; 13:54; Mark 6:1; Acts 13:14; 17:2
18 Isa. 61:1

11 And in *their* hands they shall bear thee up, lest at any time thou dash thy foot against a stone.

12 And Jesus answering said unto him, It is said, Thou shalt not tempt the Lord thy God.

13 And when the devil had ended all the temptation, he departed from him for a season.

Jesus Teaches the People

14 And Jesus returned in the power of the Spirit into Galilee: and there went out a fame of him through all the region round about.

15 And he taught in their synagogues, being glorified of all.

Jesus' Rejection at Nazareth

16 And he came to Nazareth, where he had been brought up: and, as his custom was, he went into the synagogue on the sabbath day, and stood up for to read.

17 And there was delivered unto him the book of the prophet Esaias. And when he had opened the book, he found the place where it was written,

18 The Spirit of the Lord *is* upon me, because he hath anointed me to preach the

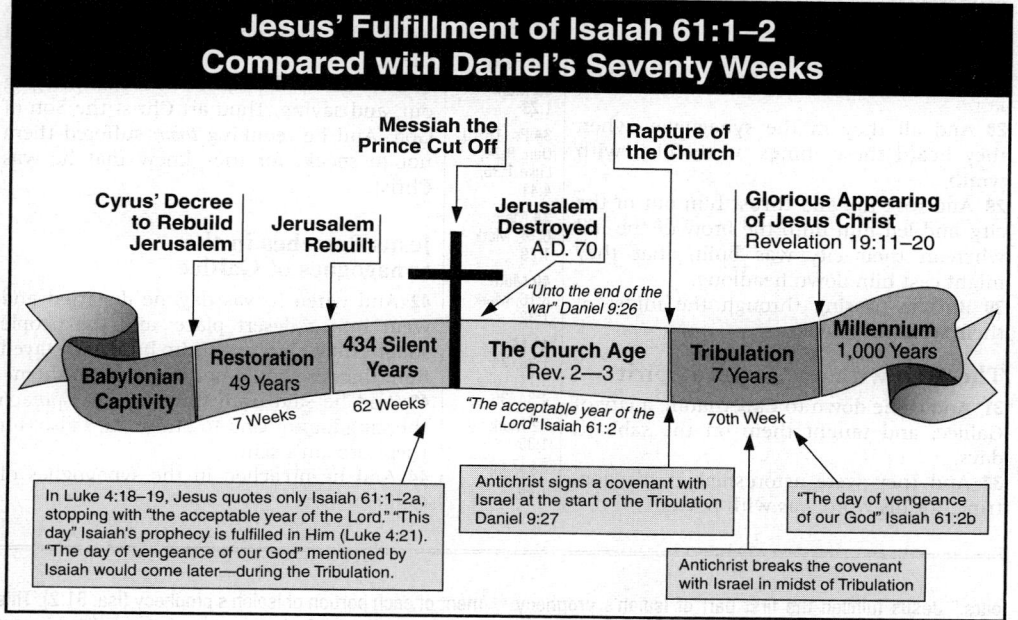

Jesus' Fulfillment of Isaiah 61:1–2 Compared with Daniel's Seventy Weeks

Messiah the Prince Cut Off

Rapture of the Church

Cyrus' Decree to Rebuild Jerusalem

Jerusalem Rebuilt

Jerusalem Destroyed A.D. 70

Glorious Appearing of Jesus Christ Revelation 19:11–20

"Unto the end of the war" Daniel 9:26

Babylonian Captivity | **Restoration** 49 Years | **434 Silent Years** | **The Church Age** Rev. 2–3 | **Tribulation** 7 Years | **Millennium** 1,000 Years

7 Weeks   62 Weeks   *"The acceptable year of the Lord" Isaiah 61:2*   70th Week

In Luke 4:18–19, Jesus quotes only Isaiah 61:1–2a, stopping with "the acceptable year of the Lord." "This day" Isaiah's prophecy is fulfilled in Him (Luke 4:21). "The day of vengeance of our God" mentioned by Isaiah would come later—during the Tribulation.

Antichrist signs a covenant with Israel at the start of the Tribulation Daniel 9:27

"The day of vengeance of our God" Isaiah 61:2b

Antichrist breaks the covenant with Israel in midst of Tribulation

© AMG Publishers

4:18–22 To preach the acceptable year of the Lord. Christ stood up and read Isaiah 61:1–2a. He stopped reading as He was in the middle of a sentence. He said, concerning the part He read, "This day is this scripture fulfilled in your

gospel to the poor; he hath sent me to heal the brokenhearted, to preach deliverance to the captives, and recovering of sight to the blind, to set at liberty them that are bruised,

19 To preach the acceptable year of the Lord.

20 And he closed the book, and he gave *it* again to the minister, and sat down. And the eyes of all them that were in the synagogue were fastened on him.

21 And he began to say unto them, This day is this scripture fulfilled in your ears.

22 And all bare him witness, and wondered at the gracious words which proceeded out of his mouth. And they said, Is not this Joseph's son?

23 And he said unto them, Ye will surely say unto me this proverb, Physician, heal thyself: whatsoever we have heard done in Capernaum, do also here in thy country.

24 And he said, Verily I say unto you, No prophet is accepted in his own country,

25 But I tell you of a truth, many widows were in Israel in the days of Elias, when the heaven was shut up three years and six months, when great famine was throughout all the land;

26 But unto none of them was Elias sent, save unto Sarepta, *a city* of Sidon, unto a woman *that was* a widow.

27 And many lepers were in Israel in the time of Eliseus the prophet; and none of them was cleansed, saving Naaman the Syrian.

28 And all they in the synagogue, when they heard these things, were filled with wrath,

29 And rose up, and thrust him out of the city, and led him unto the brow of the hill whereon their city was built, that they might cast him down headlong.

30 But he passing through the midst of them went his way,

The Man with an Unclean Spirit

31 And came down to Capernaum, a city of Galilee, and taught them on the sabbath days.

32 And they were astonished at his doctrine: for his word was with power.

33 And in the synagogue there was a man, which had a spirit of an unclean devil, and cried out with a loud voice,

34 Saying, Let *us* alone; what have we to do with thee, *thou* Jesus of Nazareth? art thou come to destroy us? I know thee who thou art; the Holy One of God.

35 And Jesus rebuked him, saying, Hold thy peace, and come out of him. And when the devil had thrown him in the midst, he came out of him, and hurt him not.

36 And they were all amazed, and spake among themselves, saying, What a word *is* this! for with authority and power he commandeth the unclean spirits, and they come out.

37 And the fame of him went out into every place of the country round about.

Jesus Heals Many

38 And he arose out of the synagogue, and entered into Simon's house. And Simon's wife's mother was taken with a great fever; and they besought him for her.

39 And he stood over her, and rebuked the fever; and it left her: and immediately she arose and ministered unto them.

40 Now when the sun was setting, all they that had any sick with divers diseases brought them unto him; and he laid his hands on every one of them, and healed them.

41 And devils also came out of many, crying out, and saying, Thou art Christ the Son of God. And he rebuking *them* suffered them not to speak: for they knew that he was Christ.

Jesus Preaches in the Synagogues of Galilee

42 And when it was day, he departed and went into a desert place: and the people sought him, and came unto him, and stayed him, that he should not depart from them.

43 And he said unto them, I must preach the kingdom of God to other cities also: for therefore am I sent.

44 And he preached in the synagogues of Galilee.

22 Ps. 45:2; Matt. 13:54; Mark 6:2; Luke 2:47; John 6:42

23 Matt. 4:13; 11:23; 13:54; Mark 6:1

24 Matt. 13:57; Mark 6:4; John 4:44

25 1 Kgs. 17:9; 18:1; James 5:17

27 2 Kgs. 5:14

30 John 8:59; 10:39

31 Matt. 4:13; Mark 1:21

32 Matt. 7:28, 29; Titus 2:15

33 Mark 1:23

34 Ps. 16:10; Dan. 9:24; Luke 1:35; 4:41

38 Matt. 8:14; Mark 1:29

40 Matt. 8:16; Mark 1:32

41 Mark 1:25, 34; 3:11; Luke 4:34, 35

42 Mark 1:35

44 Mark 1:39

---

ears." Jesus fulfilled the first part of Isaiah's prophecy during His first coming. Had Jesus read on He would have read a passage about the "day of vengeance of our God" (Isa. 61:2b), the beginning of the Tribulation. This signifies that there is a gap of time between the fulfill-

ment of each portion of Isaiah's prophecy (Isa. 61:2). This is an example of a Scripture verse that is fulfilled in part by Christ's first advent, with the rest of the verse to be fulfilled later, in conjunction with His second coming.

CHAPTER 5
Jesus Calls Four Fishermen

1 And it came to pass, that, as the people pressed upon him to hear the word of God, he stood by the lake of Gennesaret,

2 And saw two ships standing by the lake: but the fishermen were gone out of them, and were washing *their* nets.

3 And he entered into one of the ships, which was Simon's, and prayed him that he would thrust out a little from the land. And he sat down, and taught the people out of the ship.

4 Now when he had left speaking, he said unto Simon, Launch out into the deep, and let down your nets for a draught.

5 And Simon answering said unto him, Master, we have toiled all the night, and have taken nothing: nevertheless at thy word I will let down the net.

6 And when they had this done, they inclosed a great multitude of fishes: and their net brake.

7 And they beckoned unto *their* partners, which were in the other ship, that they should come and help them. And they came, and filled both the ships, so that they began to sink.

8 When Simon Peter saw *it,* he fell down at Jesus' knees, saying, Depart from me; for I am a sinful man, O Lord.

9 For he was astonished, and all that were with him, at the draught of the fishes which they had taken:

10 And so *was* also James, and John, the sons of Zebedee, which were partners with Simon. And Jesus said unto Simon, Fear not; from henceforth thou shalt catch men.

11 And when they had brought their ships to land, they forsook all, and followed him.

Jesus Cleanses a Leper

12 And it came to pass, when he was in a certain city, behold a man full of leprosy: who seeing Jesus fell on *his* face, and besought him, saying, Lord, if thou wilt, thou canst make me clean.

13 And he put forth *his* hand, and touched him, saying, I will: be thou clean. And immediately the leprosy departed from him.

14 And he charged him to tell no man: but go, and shew thyself to the priest, and offer for thy cleansing, according as Moses commanded, for a testimony unto them.

15 But so much the more went there a fame abroad of him: and great multitudes came

together to hear, and to be healed by him of their infirmities.

16 And he withdrew himself into the wilderness, and prayed.

Jesus Heals a Paralytic

17 And it came to pass on a certain day, as he was teaching, that there were Pharisees and doctors of the law sitting by, which were come out of every town of Galilee, and Judea, and Jerusalem: and the power of the Lord was *present* to heal them.

18 And, behold, men brought in a bed a man which was taken with a palsy: and they sought *means* to bring him in, and to lay *him* before him.

19 And when they could not find by what *way* they might bring him in because of the multitude, they went upon the housetop, and let him down through the tiling with *his* couch into the midst before Jesus.

20 And when he saw their faith, he said unto him, Man, thy sins are forgiven thee.

21 And the scribes and the Pharisees began to reason, saying, Who is this which speaketh blasphemies? Who can forgive sins, but God alone?

22 But when Jesus perceived their thoughts, he answering said unto them, What reason ye in your hearts?

23 Whether is easier, to say, Thy sins be forgiven thee; or to say, Rise up and walk?

24 But that ye may know that the Son of man hath power upon earth to forgive sins, (he said unto the sick of the palsy,) I say unto thee, Arise, and take up thy couch, and go into thine house.

25 And immediately he rose up before them, and took up that whereon he lay, and departed to his own house, glorifying God.

26 And they were all amazed, and they glorified God, and were filled with fear, saying, We have seen strange things today.

Jesus Calls Levi

27 And after these things he went forth, and saw a publican, named Levi, sitting at the receipt of custom: and he said unto him, Follow me.

28 And he left all, rose up, and followed him.

29 And Levi made him a great feast in his own house: and there was a great company of publicans and of others that sat down with them.

30 But their scribes and Pharisees murmured against his disciples, saying, Why do

---

Cross references (center column):

1 Matt. 4:18; Mark 1:16

4 John 21:6

8 2Sam. 6:9; 1Kgs. 17:18

10 Matt. 4:19; Mark 1:17

11 Matt. 4:20; 19:27; Mark 1:18; Luke 18:28

12 Matt. 8:2; Mark 1:40

14 Lev. 14:4, 10, 21, 22; Matt. 8:4

15 Matt. 4:25; Mark 3:7; John 6:2

16 Matt. 14:23; Mark 6:46

18 Matt. 9:2; Mark 2:3

21 Ps. 32:5; Isa. 43:25; Matt. 9:3; Mark 2:6, 7

27 Matt. 9:9; Mark 2:13, 14

29 Matt. 9:10; Mark 2:15; Luke 15:1

ye eat and drink with publicans and sinners?

31 And Jesus answering said unto them, They that are whole need not a physician: but they that are sick.

32 I came not to call the righteous, but sinners to repentance.

The Question Concerning Fasting

33 And they said unto him, Why do the disciples of John fast often, and make prayers, and likewise *the disciples* of the Pharisees; but thine eat and drink?

34 And he said unto them, Can ye make the children of the bridechamber fast, while the bridegroom is with them?

35 But the days will come, when the bridegroom shall be taken away from them, and then shall they fast in those days.

36 And he spake also a parable unto them; No man putteth a piece of a new garment upon an old; if otherwise, then both the new maketh a rent, and the piece that was *taken* out of the new agreeth not with the old.

37 And no man putteth new wine into old bottles; else the new wine will burst the bottles, and be spilled, and the bottles shall perish.

38 But new wine must be put into new bottles; and both are preserved.

39 No man also having drunk old *wine* straightway desireth new: for he saith, The old is better.

CHAPTER 6
Jesus Is Lord over the Sabbath

1 And it came to pass on the second sabbath after the first, that he went through the corn fields; and his disciples plucked the ears of corn, and did eat, rubbing *them* in *their* hands.

2 And certain of the Pharisees said unto them, Why do ye that which is not lawful to do on the sabbath days?

3 And Jesus answering them said, Have ye not read so much as this, what David did, when himself was an hungred, and they which were with him;

4 How he went into the house of God, and did take and eat the shewbread, and gave also to them that were with him; which it is not lawful to eat but for the priests alone?

5 And he said unto them, That the Son of man is Lord also of the sabbath.

The Man with a Withered Hand

6 And it came to pass also on another sabbath, that he entered into the synagogue

and taught: and there was a man whose right hand was withered.

7 And the scribes and Pharisees watched him, whether he would heal on the sabbath day; that they might find an accusation against him.

8 But he knew their thoughts, and said to the man which had the withered hand, Rise up, and stand forth in the midst. And he arose and stood forth.

9 Then said Jesus unto them, I will ask you one thing; Is it lawful on the sabbath days to do good, or to do evil? to save life, or to destroy *it*?

10 And looking round about upon them all, he said unto the man, Stretch forth thy hand. And he did so: and his hand was restored whole as the other.

11 And they were filled with madness; and communed one with another what they might do to Jesus.

Jesus Chooses the Twelve Disciples

12 And it came to pass in those days, that he went out into a mountain to pray, and continued all night in prayer to God.

13 And when it was day, he called *unto him* his disciples: and of them he chose twelve, whom also he named apostles;

14 Simon, (whom he also named Peter,) and Andrew his brother, James and John, Philip and Bartholomew,

15 Matthew and Thomas, James the *son* of Alphaeus, and Simon called Zelotes,

16 And Judas *the brother* of James, and Judas Iscariot, which also was the traitor.

Jesus Ministers to a Great Multitude

17 And he came down with them, and stood in the plain, and the company of his disciples, and a great multitude of people out of all Judea and Jerusalem, and from the sea coast of Tyre and Sidon, which came to hear him, and to be healed of their diseases;

18 And they that were vexed with unclean spirits: and they were healed.

19 And the whole multitude sought to touch him: for there went virtue out of him, and healed *them* all.

Blessings and Woes

20 And he lifted up his eyes on his disciples, and said, Blessed *be ye* poor: for yours is the kingdom of God.

21 Blessed *are ye* that hunger now: for ye shall be filled. Blessed *are ye* that weep now: for ye shall laugh.

Center column cross-references:

32 Matt. 9:13; 1Tim. 1:15

33 Matt. 9:14; Mark 2:18

36 Matt. 9:16, 17; Mark 2:21, 22

1 Matt. 12:1; Mark 2:23

2 Ex. 20:10

3 1Sam. 21:6

4 Lev. 24:9

6 Matt. 12:9; Mark 3:1; Luke 13:14; 14:3; John 9:16

12 Matt. 14:23

13 Matt. 10:1

14 John 1:42

16 Jude 1:1

17 Matt. 4:25; Mark 3:7

19 Matt. 14:36; Mark 5:30; Luke 8:46

20 Matt. 5:3; 11:5; James 2:5

21 Isa. 55:1; 61:3; 65:13; Matt. 5:4, 6

22 Blessed are ye, when men shall hate you, and when they shall separate you *from their company,* and shall reproach *you,* and cast out your name as evil, for the Son of man's sake.

23 Rejoice ye in that day, and leap for joy: for, behold, your reward *is* great in heaven: for in the like manner did their fathers unto the prophets.

24 But woe unto you that are rich! for ye have received your consolation.

25 Woe unto you that are full! for ye shall hunger. Woe unto you that laugh now! for ye shall mourn and weep.

26 Woe unto you, when all men shall speak well of you! for so did their fathers to the false prophets.

Love Your Enemies

27 But I say unto you which hear, Love your enemies, do good to them which hate you,

28 Bless them that curse you, and pray for them which despitefully use you.

29 And unto him that smiteth thee on the *one* cheek offer also the other; and him that taketh away thy cloke forbid not *to take thy* coat also.

30 Give to every man that asketh of thee; and of him that taketh away thy goods ask *them* not again.

31 And as ye would that men should do to you, do ye also to them likewise.

32 For if ye love them which love you, what thank have ye? for sinners also love those that love them.

33 And if ye do good to them which do good to you, what thank have ye? for sinners also do even the same.

34 And if ye lend *to them* of whom ye hope to receive, what thank have ye? for sinners also lend to sinners, to receive as much again.

35 But love ye your enemies, and do good, and lend, hoping for nothing again; and your reward shall be great, and ye shall be the children of the Highest: for he is kind unto the unthankful and *to* the evil.

36 Be ye therefore merciful, as your Father also is merciful.

Judging Others

37 Judge not, and ye shall not be judged: condemn not, and ye shall not be condemned: forgive, and ye shall be forgiven:

38 Give, and it shall be given unto you; good measure, pressed down, and shaken together, and running over, shall men give into your bosom. For with the same mea-

sure that ye mete withal it shall be measured to you again.

39 And he spake a parable unto them, Can the blind lead the blind? shall they not both fall into the ditch?

40 The disciple is not above his master: but every one that is perfect shall be as his master.

41 And why beholdest thou the mote that is in thy brother's eye, but perceivest not the beam that is in thine own eye?

42 Either how canst thou say to thy brother, Brother, let me pull out the mote that is in thine eye, when thou thyself beholdest not the beam that is in thine own eye? Thou hypocrite, cast out first the beam out of thine own eye, and then shalt thou see clearly to pull out the mote that is in thy brother's eye.

Bearing Fruit

43 For a good tree bringeth not forth corrupt fruit; neither doth a corrupt tree bring forth good fruit.

44 For every tree is known by his own fruit. For of thorns men do not gather figs, nor of a bramble bush gather they grapes.

45 A good man out of the good treasure of his heart bringeth forth that which is good; and an evil man out of the evil treasure of his heart bringeth forth that which is evil: for of the abundance of the heart his mouth speaketh.

The Two Foundations

46 And why call ye me, Lord, Lord, and do not the things which I say?

47 Whosoever cometh to me, and heareth my sayings, and doeth them, I will shew you to whom he is like:

48 He is like a man which built an house, and digged deep, and laid the foundation on a rock: and when the flood arose, the stream beat vehemently upon that house, and could not shake it: for it was founded upon a rock.

49 But he that heareth, and doeth not, is like a man that without a foundation built an house upon the earth; against which the stream did beat vehemently, and immediately it fell; and the ruin of that house was great.

CHAPTER 7
Jesus Heals the Centurion's Servant

1 Now when he had ended all his sayings in the audience of the people, he entered into Capernaum.

Cross-references

22 Matt. 5:11; John 16:2; 1Pet. 2:19; 3:14; 4:14
23 Matt. 5:12; Acts 5:41; 7:51
24 Matt. 6:2, 5, 16; Luke 12:21; 16:25; James 5:1
25 Prov. 14:13; Isa. 65:13
26 John 15:19; 1John 4:5
27 Ex. 23:4; Prov. 25:21; Matt. 5:44; Luke 6:35
28 Luke 23:34; Acts 7:60
29 Matt. 5:39; 1Cor. 6:7
30 Deut. 15:7, 8, 10; Prov. 21:26; Matt. 5:42
31 Matt. 7:12
32 Matt. 5:46
34 Matt. 5:42
35 Ps. 37:26; Matt. 5:45; Luke 6:27, 30
36 Matt. 5:48
37 Matt. 7:1
38 Matt. 7:2; Mark 4:24
39 Matt. 15:14
40 Matt. 10:24; John 13:16; 15:20
41 Matt. 7:3
42 Prov. 18:17
43 Matt. 7:16, 17
44 Matt. 12:33
45 Matt. 12:34, 35
46 Matt. 7:21; 25:11; Luke 13:25
47 Matt. 7:24
1 Matt. 8:5

2 And a certain centurion's servant, who was dear unto him, was sick, and ready to die.

3 And when he heard of Jesus, he sent unto him the elders of the Jews, beseeching him that he would come and heal his servant.

4 And when they came to Jesus, they besought him instantly, saying, That he was worthy for whom he should do this:

5 For he loveth our nation, and he hath built us a synagogue.

6 Then Jesus went with them. And when he was now not far from the house, the centurion sent friends to him, saying unto him, Lord, trouble not thyself: for I am not worthy that thou shouldest enter under my roof:

7 Wherefore neither thought I myself worthy to come unto thee: but say in a word, and my servant shall be healed.

8 For I also am a man set under authority, having under me soldiers, and I say unto one, Go, and he goeth; and to another, Come, and he cometh; and to my servant, Do this, and he doeth it.

9 When Jesus heard these things, he marvelled at him, and turned him about, and said unto the people that followed him, I say unto you, I have not found so great faith, no, not in Israel.

10 And they that were sent, returning to the house, found the servant whole that had been sick.

The Raising of the Widow's Son at Nain

11 And it came to pass the day after, that he went into a city called Nain; and many of his disciples went with him, and much people.

12 Now when he came nigh to the gate of the city, behold, there was a dead man carried out, the only son of his mother, and she was a widow: and much people of the city was with her.

13 And when the Lord saw her, he had compassion on her, and said unto her, Weep not.

14 And he came and touched the bier: and they that bare him stood still. And he said, Young man, I say unto thee, Arise.

15 And he that was dead sat up, and began to speak. And he delivered him to his mother.

16 And there came a fear on all: and they glorified God, saying, That a great prophet is risen up among us; and, That God hath visited his people.

17 And this rumour of him went forth throughout all Judea, and throughout all the region round about.

Jesus Talks about John the Baptist

18 And the disciples of John shewed him of all these things.

19 And John calling *unto him* two of his disciples sent *them* to Jesus, saying, Art thou he that should come or look we for another?

20 When the men were come unto him, they said, John Baptist hath sent us unto thee, saying, Art thou he that should come or look we for another?

21 And in that same hour he cured many of *their* infirmities and plagues, and of evil spirits; and unto many *that were* blind he gave sight.

22 Then Jesus answering said unto them, Go your way, and tell John what things ye have seen and heard; how that the blind see, the lame walk, the lepers are cleansed, the deaf hear, the dead are raised, to the poor the gospel is preached.

23 And blessed is *he*, whosoever shall not be offended in me.

24 And when the messengers of John were departed, he began to speak unto the people concerning John, What went ye out into the wilderness for to see? A reed shaken with the wind?

25 But what went ye out for to see? A man clothed in soft raiment? Behold, they which are gorgeously apparelled, and live delicately, are in kings' courts.

26 But what went ye out for to see? A prophet? Yea, I say unto you, and much more than a prophet.

27 This is *he*, of whom it is written, Behold, I send my messenger before thy face, which shall prepare thy way before thee.

28 For I say unto you, Among those that are born of women there is not a greater prophet than John the Baptist: but he that is least in the kingdom of God is greater than he.

29 And all the people that heard *him*, and the publicans, justified God, being baptized with the baptism of John.

30 But the Pharisees and lawyers rejected the counsel of God against themselves, being not baptized of him.

31 And the Lord said, Whereunto then shall I liken the men of this generation? and to what are they like?

32 They are like unto children sitting in the marketplace, and calling one to another, and saying, We have piped unto you, and ye

14 Luke 8:54; John 11:43; Acts 9:40; Rom. 4:17

16 Luke 1:65, 68; 24:19; John 4:19; 6:14; 9:17

18 Matt. 11:2

22 Isa. 35:5; Matt. 11:4; Luke 4:18

24 Matt. 11:7

27 Mal. 3:1

29 Matt. 3:5; Luke 3:12

30 Acts 20:27

31 Matt. 11:16

have not danced; we have mourned to you, and ye have not wept.

33 For John the Baptist came neither eating bread nor drinking wine; and ye say, He hath a devil.

34 The Son of man is come eating and drinking; and ye say, Behold a gluttonous man, and a winebibber, a friend of publicans and sinners!

35 But wisdom is justified of all her children.

Jesus Forgives a Sinful Woman

36 And one of the Pharisees desired him that he would eat with him. And he went into the Pharisee's house, and sat down to meat.

37 And, behold, a woman in the city, which was a sinner, when she knew that *Jesus* sat at meat in the Pharisee's house, brought an alabaster box of ointment,

38 And stood at his feet behind *him* weeping, and began to wash his feet with tears, and did wipe *them* with the hairs of her head, and kissed his feet, and anointed *them* with the ointment.

39 Now when the Pharisee which had bidden him saw *it,* he spake within himself, saying, This man, if he were a prophet, would have known who and what manner of woman *this is* that toucheth him: for she is a sinner.

40 And Jesus answering said unto him, Simon, I have somewhat to say unto thee. And he saith, Master, say on.

41 There was a certain creditor which had two debtors: the one owed five hundred pence, and the other fifty.

42 And when they had nothing to pay, he frankly forgave them both. Tell me therefore, which of them will love him most?

43 Simon answered and said, I suppose that *he,* to whom he forgave most. And he said unto him, Thou hast rightly judged.

44 And he turned to the woman, and said unto Simon, Seest thou this woman? I entered into thine house, thou gavest me no water for my feet: but she hath washed my feet with tears, and wiped *them* with the hairs of her head.

45 Thou gavest me no kiss: but this woman since the time I came in hath not ceased to kiss my feet.

46 My head with oil thou didst not anoint: but this woman hath anointed my feet with ointment.

47 Wherefore I say unto thee, Her sins, which are many, are forgiven; for she loved

much: but to whom little is forgiven, *the same* loveth little.

48 And he said unto her, Thy sins are forgiven.

49 And they that sat at meat with him began to say within themselves, Who is this that forgiveth sins also?

50 And he said to the woman, Thy faith hath saved thee; go in peace.

CHAPTER 8

1 And it came to pass afterward, that he went throughout every city and village, preaching and shewing the glad tidings of the kingdom of God: and the twelve *were* with him,

2 And certain women, which had been healed of evil spirits and infirmities, Mary called Magdalene, out of whom went seven devils,

3 And Joanna the wife of Chuza Herod's steward, and Susanna, and many others, which ministered unto him of their substance.

The Parable of the Sower

4 And when much people were gathered together, and were come to him out of every city, he spake by a parable:

5 A sower went out to sow his seed: and as he sowed, some fell by the way side; and it was trodden down, and the fowls of the air devoured it.

6 And some fell upon a rock; and as soon as it was sprung up, it withered away, because it lacked moisture.

7 And some fell among thorns; and the thorns sprang up with it, and choked it.

8 And other fell on good ground, and sprang up, and bare fruit an hundredfold. And when he had said these things, he cried, He that hath ears to hear, let him hear.

The Reason for Parables

9 And his disciples asked him, saying, What might this parable be?

10 And he said, Unto you it is given to know the mysteries of the kingdom of God: but to others in parables; that seeing they might not see, and hearing they might not understand.

Explanation of the Parable of the Sower

11 Now the parable is this: The seed is the word of God.

12 Those by the way side are they that hear;

Cross references (center column):

33 Matt. 3:4; Mark 1:6; Luke 1:15

35 Matt. 11:19

36 Matt. 26:6; Mark 14:3; John 11:2

39 Luke 15:2

41 Matt. 18:28

46 Ps. 23:5

47 1 Tim. 1:14

48 Matt. 9:2; Mark 2:5

49 Matt. 9:3; Mark 2:7

50 Matt. 9:22; Mark 5:34; 10:52; Luke 8:48; 18:42

2 Matt. 27:55, 56; Mark 16:9

4 Matt. 13:2; Mark 4:1

9 Matt. 13:10; Mark 4:10

10 Isa. 6:9; Mark 4:12

11 Matt. 13:18; Mark 4:14

then cometh the devil, and taketh away the word out of their hearts, lest they should believe and be saved.

13 They on the rock *are they,* which, when they hear, receive the word with joy; and these have no root, which for a while believe, and in time of temptation fall away.

14 And that which fell among thorns are they, which, when they have heard, go forth, and are choked with cares and riches and pleasures of *this* life, and bring no fruit to perfection.

15 But that on the good ground are they, which in an honest and good heart, having heard the word, keep *it,* and bring forth fruit with patience.

A Light Hidden

16 No man, when he hath lighted a candle, covereth it with a vessel, or putteth *it* under a bed; but setteth *it* on a candlestick, that they which enter in may see the light.

17 For nothing is secret, that shall not be made manifest; neither *any thing* hid, that shall not be known and come abroad.

18 Take heed therefore how ye hear: for whosoever hath, to him shall be given; and whosoever hath not, from him shall be taken even that which he seemeth to have.

Jesus' Mother and Brothers

19 Then came to him *his* mother and his brethren, and could not come at him for the press.

20 And it was told him *by certain* which said, Thy mother and thy brethren stand without, desiring to see thee.

21 And he answered and said unto them, My mother and my brethren are these which hear the word of God, and do it.

Jesus Calms a Storm

22 Now it came to pass on a certain day, that he went into a ship with his disciples: and he said unto them, Let us go over unto the other side of the lake. And they launched forth.

23 But as they sailed he fell asleep: and there came down a storm of wind on the lake; and they were filled *with water,* and were in jeopardy.

24 And they came to him, and awoke him, saying, Master, master, we perish. Then he arose, and rebuked the wind and the raging of the water: and they ceased, and there was a calm.

25 And he said unto them, Where is your faith? And they being afraid wondered, say-

ing one to another, What manner of man is this! for he commandeth even the winds and water, and they obey him.

Jesus Heals the Gadarene Demoniac

26 And they arrived at the country of the Gadarenes, which is over against Galilee.

27 And when he went forth to land, there met him out of the city a certain man, which had devils long time, and ware no clothes, neither abode in *any* house, but in the tombs.

28 When he saw Jesus, he cried out, and fell down before him, and with a loud voice said, What have I to do with thee, Jesus, *thou* Son of God most high? I beseech thee, torment me not.

29 (For he had commanded the unclean spirit to come out of the man. For oftentimes it had caught him: and he was kept bound with chains and in fetters; and he brake the bands, and was driven of the devil into the wilderness.)

30 And Jesus asked him, saying, What is thy name? And he said, Legion: because many devils were entered into him.

31 And they besought him that he would not command them to go out into the deep.

32 And there was there an herd of many swine feeding on the mountain: and they besought him that he would suffer them to enter into them. And he suffered them.

33 Then went the devils out of the man, and entered into the swine: and the herd ran violently down a steep place into the lake, and were choked.

34 When they that fed *them* saw what was done, they fled, and went and told *it* in the city and in the country.

35 Then they went out to see what was done; and came to Jesus, and found the man, out of whom the devils were departed, sitting at the feet of Jesus, clothed, and in his right mind: and they were afraid.

36 They also which saw *it* told them by what means he that was possessed of the devils was healed.

37 Then the whole multitude of the country of the Gadarenes round about besought him to depart from them; for they were taken with great fear: and he went up into the ship, and returned back again.

38 Now the man out of whom the devils were departed besought him that he might be with him: but Jesus sent him away, saying,

39 Return to thine own house, and shew how great things God hath done unto thee.

Cross references

16 Matt. 5:15; Mark 4:21; Luke 11:33

17 Matt. 10:26; Luke 12:2

18 Matt. 13:12; 25:29; Luke 19:26

19 Matt. 12:46; Mark 3:31

22 Matt. 8:23; Mark 4:35

26 Matt. 8:28; Mark 5:1

31 Rev. 20:3

37 Matt. 8:34; Acts 16:39

38 Mark 5:18

And he went his way, and published throughout the whole city how great things Jesus had done unto him.

Jesus Raises Jairus' Daughter

40 And it came to pass, that, when Jesus was returned, the people *gladly* received him: for they were all waiting for him.

41 And, behold, there came a man named Jairus, and he was a ruler of the synagogue: and he fell down at Jesus' feet, and besought him that he would come into his house:

42 For he had one only daughter, about twelve years of age, and she lay a dying. But as he went the people thronged him.

43 And a woman having an issue of blood twelve years, which had spent all her living upon physicians, neither could be healed of any,

44 Came behind *him,* and touched the border of his garment: and immediately her issue of blood stanched.

45 And Jesus said, Who touched me? When all denied, Peter and they that were with him said, Master, the multitude throng thee and press *thee,* and sayest thou, Who touched me?

46 And Jesus said, Somebody hath touched me: for I perceive that virtue is gone out of me.

47 And when the woman saw that she was not hid, she came trembling, and falling down before him, she declared unto him before all the people for what cause she had touched him, and how she was healed immediately.

48 And he said unto her, Daughter, be of good comfort: thy faith hath made thee whole; go in peace.

49 While he yet spake, there cometh one from the ruler of the synagogue's *house,* saying to him, Thy daughter is dead; trouble not the Master.

50 But when Jesus heard *it,* he answered him, saying, Fear not: believe only, and she shall be made whole.

51 And when he came into the house, he suffered no man to go in, save Peter, and James, and John, and the father and the mother of the maiden.

52 And all wept, and bewailed her: but he said, Weep not; she is not dead, but sleepeth.

53 And they laughed him to scorn, knowing that she was dead.

54 And he put them all out, and took her by the hand, and called, saying, Maid, arise.

55 And her spirit came again, and she arose straightway: and he commanded to give her meat.

56 And her parents were astonished: but he charged them that they should tell no man what was done.

CHAPTER 9

The Twelve Apostles Are Sent Forth

1 Then he called his twelve disciples together, and gave them power and authority over all devils, and to cure diseases.

2 And he sent them to preach the kingdom of God, and to heal the sick.

3 And he said unto them, Take nothing for *your* journey, neither staves, nor scrip, neither bread, neither money; neither have two coats apiece.

4 And whatsoever house ye enter into, there abide, and thence depart.

5 And whosoever will not receive you, when ye go out of that city, shake off the very dust from your feet for a testimony against them.

6 And they departed, and went through the towns, preaching the gospel, and healing everywhere.

Herod Disturbed

7 Now Herod the tetrarch heard of all that was done by him: and he was perplexed, because that it was said of some, that John was risen from the dead;

8 And of some, that Elias had appeared; and of others, that one of the old prophets was risen again.

9 And Herod said, John have I beheaded: but who is this, of whom I hear such things? And he desired to see him.

Jesus Feeds Five Thousand People

10 And the apostles, when they were returned, told him all that they had done. And he took them, and went aside privately into a desert place belonging to the city called Bethsaida.

11 And the people, when they knew *it,* followed him: and he received them, and spake unto them of the kingdom of God, and healed them that had need of healing.

12 And when the day began to wear away, then came the twelve, and said unto him, Send the multitude away, that they may go into the towns and country round about, and lodge, and get victuals: for we are here in a desert place.

13 But he said unto them, Give ye them to eat. And they said, We have no more but

Cross references (center column)

41 Matt. 9:18; Mark 5:22

43 Matt. 9:20

46 Mark 5:30; Luke 6:19

49 Mark 5:35

52 John 11:11, 13

54 Luke 7:14; John 11:43

56 Matt. 8:4; 9:30; Mark 5:43

1 Matt. 10:1; Mark 3:13; 6:7

2 Matt. 10:7, 8; Mark 6:12; Luke 10:1, 9

3 Matt. 10:9; Mark 6:8; Luke 10:4; 22:35

4 Matt. 10:11; Mark 6:10

5 Matt. 10:14; Acts 13:51

6 Mark 6:12

7 Matt. 14:1; Mark 6:14

9 Luke 23:8

10 Matt. 14:13; Mark 6:30

12 Matt. 14:15; Mark 6:35; John 6:1, 5

five loaves and two fishes; except we should go and buy meat for all this people.

14 For they were about five thousand men. And he said to his disciples, Make them sit down by fifties in a company.

15 And they did so, and made them all sit down.

16 Then he took the five loaves and the two fishes, and looking up to heaven, he blessed them, and brake, and gave to the disciples to set before the multitude.

17 And they did eat, and were all filled: and there was taken up of fragments that remained to them twelve baskets.

Peter's Confession

18 And it came to pass, as he was alone praying, his disciples were with him: and he asked them, saying, Whom say the people that I am?

19 They answering said, John the Baptist; but some *say*, Elias; and others *say*, that one of the old prophets is risen again.

20 He said unto them, But whom say ye that I am? Peter answering said, The Christ of God.

Jesus Predicts His Death and Resurrection

21 And he straitly charged them, and commanded *them* to tell no man that thing;

22 Saying, The Son of man must suffer many things, and be rejected of the elders and chief priests and scribes, and be slain, and be raised the third day.

Take Up Your Cross

23 And he said to *them* all, If any *man* will come after me, let him deny himself, and take up his cross daily, and follow me.

24 For whosoever will save his life shall lose

it: but whosoever will lose his life for my sake, the same shall save it.

25 For what is a man advantaged, if he gain the whole world, and lose himself, or be cast away?

26 For whosoever shall be ashamed of me and of my words, of him shall the Son of man be ashamed, when he shall come in his own glory, and *in his* Father's, and of the holy angels.

27 But I tell you of a truth, there be some standing here, which shall not taste of death, till they see the kingdom of God.

The Transfiguration

28 And it came to pass about eight days after these sayings, he took Peter and John and James, and went up into a mountain to pray.

29 And as he prayed, the fashion of his countenance was altered, and his raiment *was* white *and* glistering.

30 And, behold, there talked with him two men, which were Moses and Elias:

31 Who appeared in glory, and spake of his decease which he should accomplish at Jerusalem.

32 But Peter and they that were with him were heavy with sleep: and when they were awake, they saw his glory, and the two men that stood with him.

33 And it came to pass, as they departed from him, Peter said unto Jesus, Master, it is good for us to be here: and let us make three tabernacles; one for thee, and one for Moses, and one for Elias: not knowing what he said.

34 While he thus spake, there came a cloud, and overshadowed them: and they feared as they entered into the cloud.

35 And there came a voice out of the cloud,

Cross-references

18 Matt. 16:13; Mark 8:27

19 Matt. 14:2; Luke 9:7, 8

20 Matt. 16:16; John 6:69

21 Matt. 16:20

22 Matt. 16:21; 17:22

23 Matt. 10:38; 16:24; Mark 8:34; Luke 14:27

25 Matt. 16:26; Mark 8:36

26 Matt. 10:33; Mark 8:38; 2Tim. 2:12

27 Matt. 16:28; Mark 9:1

28 Matt. 17:1; Mark 9:2

32 Dan. 8:18; 10:9

35 Matt. 3:17; Acts 3:22

9:22 Christ plainly predicts His death and resurrection for the first time to the disciples.

9:26 This verse is a prediction about the blessings for believers at Christ's second coming, but judgment for those who are "ashamed of [Christ] and of [His] words" in this life.

9:27 there be some standing here, which shall not taste of death, till they see the kingdom of God. Christ has just spoken of His death and the future deaths of the disciples for following Him (vv. 23–26). Now He tells them that they will get a glimpse of what they had wanted since following Him—a view of the kingdom of God. This is fulfilled in the very next section (vv. 28–36) to Peter, James, and John in the Transfiguration.

9:28–36 The fashion of his countenance was altered. Somehow Jesus was changed physically. His altered appearance is similar to that described by John in Revelation 1:13–16. Christ bears evidence of the physical characteristics of God, which throughout the Bible are exhibited as the Shechinah glory (Ex. 3:1–5; 13:21–22; 14:19–20, 24; 16:6–12; 29:42–46; 33:17–23; 34:5–9; 40:34–38; Ezek. 1:28; 3:12, 23; 8:3–4; 9:3; 10:4, 18–19; 11:22–23). By communicating with Moses, who represents the Law, and Elijah, who represents the prophets, Christ demonstrates His continuity with trusted Old Testament personalities. Because Moses and Elijah appear here together, many believe they will be the two witnesses in Revelation 11:3–6.

saying, This is my beloved Son: hear him.
36 And when the voice was past, Jesus was found alone. And they kept *it* close, and told no man in those days any of those things which they had seen.

Jesus Heals a Boy with an Unclean Spirit

37 And it came to pass, that on the next day, when they were come down from the hill, much people met him.
38 And, behold, a man of the company cried out, saying, Master, I beseech thee, look upon my son: for he is mine only child.
39 And, lo, a spirit taketh him, and he suddenly crieth out; and it teareth him that he foameth again, and bruising him hardly departeth from him.
40 And I besought thy disciples to cast him out; and they could not.
41 And Jesus answering said, O faithless and perverse generation, how long shall I be with you, and suffer you? Bring thy son hither.
42 And as he was yet a coming, the devil threw him down, and tare *him*. And Jesus rebuked the unclean spirit, and healed the child, and delivered him again to his father.

Jesus Again Foretells His Death

43 And they were all amazed at the mighty power of God. But while they wondered every one at all things which Jesus did, he said unto his disciples,
44 Let these sayings sink down into your ears: for the Son of man shall be delivered into the hands of men.
45 But they understood not this saying, and it was hid from them, that they perceived it not: and they feared to ask him of that saying.

Jesus Sets a Child before His Disciples

46 Then there arose a reasoning among them, which of them should be greatest.
47 And Jesus, perceiving the thought of their heart, took a child, and set him by him,
48 And said unto them, Whosoever shall receive this child in my name receiveth me: and whosoever shall receive me receiveth him that sent me: for he that is least among you all, the same shall be great.

Others Who Work in Christ's Name

49 And John answered and said, Master, we saw one casting out devils in thy name; and

we forbad him, because he followeth not with us.
50 And Jesus said unto him, Forbid *him* not: for he that is not against us is for us.

A Samaritan Village Refuses to Receive Jesus

51 And it came to pass, when the time was come that he should be received up, he stedfastly set his face to go to Jerusalem,
52 And sent messengers before his face: and they went, and entered into a village of the Samaritans, to make ready for him.
53 And they did not receive him, because his face was as though he would go to Jerusalem.
54 And when his disciples James and John saw *this*, they said, Lord, wilt thou that we command fire to come down from heaven, and consume them, even as Elias did?
55 But he turned, and rebuked them, and said, Ye know not what manner of spirit ye are of.
56 For the Son of man is not come to destroy men's lives, but to save *them*. And they went to another village.

God's Kingdom Must Be First

57 And it came to pass, that, as they went in the way, a certain *man* said unto him, Lord, I will follow thee whithersoever thou goest.
58 And Jesus said unto him, Foxes have holes, and birds of the air *have* nests; but the Son of man hath not where to lay *his* head.
59 And he said unto another, Follow me. But he said, Lord, suffer me first to go and bury my father.
60 Jesus said unto him, Let the dead bury their dead: but go thou and preach the kingdom of God.
61 And another also said, Lord, I will follow thee; but let me first go bid them farewell, which are at home at my house.
62 And Jesus said unto him, No man, having put his hand to the plow, and looking back, is fit for the kingdom of God.

CHAPTER 10
Jesus Sends the Seventy

1 After these things the Lord appointed other seventy also, and sent them two and two before his face into every city and place, whither he himself would come.
2 Therefore said he unto them, The harvest truly *is* great, but the labourers *are* few: pray ye therefore the Lord of the harvest,

---

Cross references (center column):

36 Matt. 17:9
37 Matt. 17:14; Mark 9:14, 17
44 Matt. 17:22
45 Mark 9:32; Luke 2:50; 18:34
46 Matt. 18:1; Mark 9:34
48 Matt. 10:40; 18:5; 23:11, 12; Mark 9:37; John 12:44; 13:20
49 Num. 11:28; Mark 9:38
50 Matt. 12:30; Luke 11:23
51 Mark 16:19; Acts 1:2
53 John 4:4, 9
54 2Kgs. 1:10, 12
56 John 3:17; 12:47
57 Matt. 8:19
59 Matt. 8:21
61 1Kgs. 19:20
1 Matt. 10:1; Mark 6:7
2 Matt. 9:37, 38; John 4:35; 2Thess. 3:1

that he would send forth labourers into his harvest.

3 Go your ways: behold, I send you forth as lambs among wolves.

4 Carry neither purse, nor scrip, nor shoes: and salute no man by the way.

5 And into whatsoever house ye enter, first say, Peace *be* to this house.

6 And if the son of peace be there, your peace shall rest upon it: if not, it shall turn to you again.

7 And in the same house remain, eating and drinking such things as they give: for the labourer is worthy of his hire. Go not from house to house.

8 And into whatsoever city ye enter, and they receive you, eat such things as are set before you:

9 And heal the sick that are therein, and say unto them, The kingdom of God is come nigh unto you.

10 But into whatsoever city ye enter, and they receive you not, go your ways out into the streets of the same, and say,

11 Even the very dust of your city, which cleaveth on us, we do wipe off against you: notwithstanding be ye sure of this, that the kingdom of God is come nigh unto you.

12 But I say unto you, that it shall be more tolerable in that day for Sodom, than for that city.

Jesus Condemns Certain Cities

13 Woe unto thee, Chorazin! woe unto thee, Bethsaida! for if the mighty works had been done in Tyre and Sidon, which have been done in you, they had a great while ago repented, sitting in sackcloth and ashes.

14 But it shall be more tolerable for Tyre and Sidon at the judgment, than for you.

15 And thou, Capernaum, which art exalted to heaven, shalt be thrust down to hell.

16 He that heareth you heareth me; and he that despiseth you despiseth me; and he that despiseth me despiseth him that sent me.

The Return of the Seventy

17 And the seventy returned again with joy, saying, Lord, even the devils are subject unto us through thy name.

18 And he said unto them, I beheld Satan as lightning fall from heaven.

19 Behold, I give unto you power to tread on serpents and scorpions, and over all the power of the enemy: and nothing shall by any means hurt you.

20 Notwithstanding in this rejoice not, that the spirits are subject unto you; but rather rejoice, because your names are written in heaven.

Jesus Praises God

21 In that hour Jesus rejoiced in spirit, and said, I thank thee, O Father, Lord of heaven and earth, that thou hast hid these things from the wise and prudent, and hast revealed them unto babes: even so, Father; for so it seemed good in thy sight.

22 All things are delivered to me of my Father: and no man knoweth who the Son is, but the Father; and who the Father is, but the Son, and *he* to whom the Son will reveal *him*.

23 And he turned him unto *his* disciples, and said privately, Blessed *are* the eyes which see the things that ye see:

24 For I tell you, that many prophets and kings have desired to see those things which ye see, and have not seen *them*; and to hear those things which ye hear, and have not heard *them*.

A Good Samaritan

25 And, behold, a certain lawyer stood up, and tempted him, saying, Master, what shall I do to inherit eternal life?

26 He said unto him, What is written in the law? how readest thou?

27 And he answering said, Thou shalt love the Lord thy God with all thy heart, and with all thy soul, and with all thy strength, and with all thy mind; and thy neighbour as thyself.

28 And he said unto him, Thou hast answered right: this do, and thou shalt live.

29 But he, willing to justify himself, said unto Jesus, And who is my neighbour?

30 And Jesus answering said, A certain *man* went down from Jerusalem to Jericho, and fell among thieves, which stripped him of his raiment, and wounded *him*, and departed, leaving *him* half dead.

31 And by chance there came down a cer-

Cross references

3 Matt. 10:16
4 Matt. 10:9, 10; Mark 6:8; Luke 9:3
5 Matt. 10:12
7 Matt. 10:10, 11
9 Matt. 3:2; 4:17; 10:7; Luke 9:2
11 Matt. 10:14; Luke 9:5; Acts 13:51; 18:6
12 Matt. 10:15; Mark 6:11
13 Ezek. 3:6; Matt. 11:21
15 Matt. 11:23
16 Matt. 10:40; Mark 9:37; John 5:23; 13:20
18 John 12:31; 16:11; Rev. 9:1; 12:8, 9
19 Mark 16:18; Acts 28:5
20 Ps. 69:28; Isa. 4:3; Dan. 12:1; Phil. 4:3; Heb. 12:23; Rev. 13:8; 20:12; 21:27
21 Matt. 11:25
22 Matt. 28:18; John 1:18; 3:35; 5:27; 6:44, 46; 17:2
23 Matt. 13:16
24 1Pet. 1:10
25 Matt. 19:16; 22:35
27 Lev. 19:18; Deut. 6:5
28 Lev. 18:5; Rom. 10:5
29 Luke 16:15
31 Ps. 38:11

10:12–16 more tolerable in that day for Sodom, than for that city. This passage implies that there will be degrees of punishment in hell since both Sodom and the Galilean cities of which Christ spoke were known for unbelief. The reason that the Galilean cities will receive a stricter judgment is that they saw God's Son face to face and still rejected him.

tain priest that way: and when he saw him, he passed by on the other side.

32 And likewise a Levite, when he was at the place, came and looked *on him,* and passed by on the other side.

33 But a certain Samaritan, as he journeyed, came where he was: and when he saw him, he had compassion *on him,*

34 And went to *him,* and bound up his wounds, pouring in oil and wine, and set him on his own beast, and brought him to an inn, and took care of him.

35 And on the morrow when he departed, he took out two pence, and gave *them* to the host, and said unto him, Take care of him; and whatsoever thou spendest more, when I come again, I will repay thee.

36 Which now of these three, thinkest thou, was neighbour unto him that fell among the thieves?

37 And he said, He that shewed mercy on him. Then said Jesus unto him, Go, and do thou likewise.

Visiting Martha and Mary

38 Now it came to pass, as they went, that he entered into a certain village: and a certain woman named Martha received him into her house.

39 And she had a sister called Mary, which also sat at Jesus' feet, and heard his word.

40 But Martha was encumbered about much serving, and came to him, and said, Lord, dost thou not care that my sister hath left me to serve alone? bid her therefore that she help me.

41 And Jesus answered and said unto her, Martha, Martha, thou art careful and troubled about many things:

42 But one thing is needful: and Mary hath chosen that good part, which shall not be taken away from her.

CHAPTER 11
Jesus Teaches the Disciples How to Pray

1 And it came to pass, that, as he was praying in a certain place, when he ceased, one of his disciples said unto him, Lord, teach us to pray, as John also taught his disciples.

2 And he said unto them, When ye pray, say, Our Father which art in heaven, Hal-

lowed be thy name. Thy kingdom come. Thy will be done, as in heaven, so in earth.

3 Give us day by day our daily bread.

4 And forgive us our sins; for we also forgive every one that is indebted to us. And lead us not into temptation; but deliver us from evil.

5 And he said unto them, Which of you shall have a friend, and shall go unto him at midnight, and say unto him, Friend, lend me three loaves;

6 For a friend of mine in his journey is come to me, and I have nothing to set before him?

7 And he from within shall answer and say, Trouble me not: the door is now shut, and my children are with me in bed; I cannot rise and give thee.

8 I say unto you, Though he will not rise and give him, because he is his friend, yet because of his importunity he will rise and give him as many as he needeth.

9 And I say unto you, Ask, and it shall be given you; seek, and ye shall find; knock, and it shall be opened unto you.

10 For every one that asketh receiveth; and he that seeketh findeth; and to him that knocketh it shall be opened.

11 If a son shall ask bread of any of you that is a father, will he give him a stone? or if *he* ask a fish, will he for a fish give him a serpent?

12 Or if he shall ask an egg, will he offer him a scorpion?

13 If ye then, being evil, know how to give good gifts unto your children: how much more shall *your* heavenly Father give the Holy Spirit to them that ask him?

Jesus Accused of Being Beelzebub

14 And he was casting out a devil, and it was dumb. And it came to pass, when the devil was gone out, the dumb spake; and the people wondered.

15 But some of them said, He casteth out devils through Beelzebub the chief of the devils.

16 And others, tempting *him,* sought of him a sign from heaven.

17 But he, knowing their thoughts, said unto them, Every kingdom divided against itself is brought to desolation; and a house *divided* against an house falleth.

18 If Satan also be divided against himself,

---

33 John 4:9
35 Matt. 20:2
38 John 11:1; 12:2, 3
39 Luke 8:35; Acts 22:3; 1Cor. 7:32-34;
42 Ps. 27:4
2 Matt. 6:9

8 Luke 18:1

9 Matt. 7:7; 21:22; Mark 11:24; John 15:7; James 1:6; 1John 3:22
11 Matt. 7:9

14 Matt. 9:32; 12:22

15 Matt. 9:34; 12:24; Luke 11:18, 19
16 Matt. 12:38; 16:1
17 Matt. 12:25; Mark 3:24; John 2:25

11:2 Thy kingdom come. This prayer will be fulfilled at the end of the seven-year Tribulation when our Lord will bring in His Millennial Kingdom.

how shall his kingdom stand? because ye say that I cast out devils through Beelzebub. **19** And if I by Beelzebub cast out devils, by whom do your sons cast *them* out? therefore shall they be your judges. **20** But if I with the finger of God cast out devils, no doubt the kingdom of God is come upon you. **21** When a strong man armed keepeth his palace, his goods are in peace: **22** But when a stronger than he shall come upon him, and overcome him, he taketh from him all his armour wherein he trusted, and divideth his spoils. **23** He that is not with me is against me: and he that gathereth not with me scattereth.

The Return of the Unclean Spirit

24 When the unclean spirit is gone out of a man, he walketh through dry places, seeking rest; and finding none, he saith, I will return unto my house whence I came out. **25** And when he cometh, he findeth *it* swept and garnished. **26** Then goeth he, and taketh *to him* seven other spirits more wicked than himself; and they enter in, and dwell there: and the last *state* of that man is worse than the first.

True Blessedness

27 And it came to pass, as he spake these things, a certain woman of the company lifted up her voice, and said unto him, Blessed *is* the womb that bare thee, and the paps which thou hast sucked. **28** But he said, Yea rather, blessed *are* they that hear the word of God, and keep it.

The Demand for a Sign

29 And when the people were gathered thick together, he began to say, This is an evil generation: they seek a sign; and there shall no sign be given it, but the sign of Jonas the prophet. **30** For as Jonas was a sign unto the Ninevites, so shall also the Son of man be to this generation. **31** The queen of the south shall rise up in the judgment with the men of this generation, and condemn them: for she came from the utmost parts of the earth to hear the

wisdom of Solomon; and, behold, a greater than Solomon *is* here. **32** The men of Nineve shall rise up in the judgment with this generation, and shall condemn it: for they repented at the preaching of Jonas; and, behold, a greater than Jonas *is* here.

Light Should Not Be Hidden

33 No man, when he hath lighted a candle, putteth *it* in a secret place, neither under a bushel, but on a candlestick, that they which come in may see the light. **34** The light of the body is the eye: therefore when thine eye is single, thy whole body also is full of light; but when *thine eye* is evil, thy body also *is* full of darkness. **35** Take heed therefore that the light which is in thee be not darkness. **36** If thy whole body therefore *be* full of light, having no part dark, the whole shall be full of light, as when the bright shining of a candle doth give thee light.

Jesus Denounces the Pharisees and Lawyers

37 And as he spake, a certain Pharisee besought him to dine with him: and he went in, and sat down to meat. **38** And when the Pharisee saw *it*, he marvelled that he had not first washed before dinner. **39** And the Lord said unto him, Now do ye Pharisees make clean the outside of the cup and the platter; but your inward part is full of ravening and wickedness. **40** *Ye* fools, did not he that made that which is without make that which is within also? **41** But rather give alms of such things as ye have; and, behold, all things are clean unto you. **42** But woe unto you, Pharisees! for ye tithe mint and rue and all manner of herbs, and pass over judgment and the love of God: these ought ye to have done, and not to leave the other undone. **43** Woe unto you, Pharisees! for ye love the uppermost seats in the synagogues, and greetings in the markets. **44** Woe unto you, scribes and Pharisees, hypocrites! for ye are as graves which ap-

Cross references

20 Ex. 8:19
21 Matt. 12:29; Mark 3:27
22 Isa. 53:12; Col. 2:15
23 Matt. 12:30
24 Matt. 12:43
26 John 5:14; Heb. 6:4; 10:26; 2Pet. 2:20
27 Luke 1:28, 48
28 Matt. 7:21; Luke 8:21; James 1:25
29 Matt. 12:38, 39
30 Jon. 1:17; 2:10
31 1Kgs. 10:1
32 Jon. 3:5
33 Matt. 5:15; Mark 4:21; Luke 8:16
34 Matt. 6:22
38 Mark 7:3
39 Matt. 23:25; Titus 1:15
41 Isa. 58:7; Dan. 4:27; Luke 12:33
42 Matt. 23:23
43 Matt. 23:6; Mark 12:38, 39
44 Ps. 5:9; Matt. 23:27

11:29 This is an evil generation: they seek a sign. Jesus always declined to give a sign when asked. He did give signs, but only on His timetable. Why was it evil for Israel to ask for a sign? They were to believe on the basis of the Word of God. Besides, they never believed even when He did a sign. This will be demonstrated in Luke 16:19–31. The "sign of Jonas the prophet" refers to his prophetic call for Nineveh to repent.

pear not, and the men that walk over *them* are not aware *of them.*

45 Then answered one of the lawyers, and said unto him, Master, thus saying thou reproachest us also.

46 And he said, Woe unto you also, ye lawyers! for ye lade men with burdens grievous to be borne, and ye yourselves touch not the burdens with one of your fingers.

47 Woe unto you! for ye build the sepulchres of the prophets, and your fathers killed them.

48 Truly ye bear witness that ye allow the deeds of your fathers: for they indeed killed them, and ye build their sepulchres.

49 Therefore also said the wisdom of God, I will send them prophets and apostles, and *some* of them they shall slay and persecute:

50 That the blood of all the prophets, which was shed from the foundation of the world, may be required of this generation;

51 From the blood of Abel unto the blood of Zacharias, which perished between the altar and the temple: verily I say unto you, It shall be required of this generation.

52 Woe unto you, lawyers! for ye have taken away the key of knowledge: ye entered not in yourselves, and them that were entering in ye hindered.

53 And as he said these things unto them, the scribes and the Pharisees began to urge *him* vehemently, and to provoke him to speak of many things:

54 Laying wait for him, and seeking to catch something out of his mouth, that they might accuse him.

CHAPTER 12
Hypocrisy Will Be Revealed

1 In the mean time, when there were gathered together an innumerable multitude of people, insomuch that they trode one upon another, he began to say unto his disciples first of all, Beware ye of the leaven of the Pharisees, which is hypocrisy.

2 For there is nothing covered, that shall not be revealed; neither hid, that shall not be known.

3 Therefore whatsoever ye have spoken in darkness shall be heard in the light; and that which ye have spoken in the ear in closets shall be proclaimed upon the housetops.

Fear God

4 And I say unto you my friends, Be not afraid of them that kill the body, and after that have no more that they can do.

5 But I will forewarn you whom ye shall fear: Fear him, which after he hath killed hath power to cast into hell; yea, I say unto you, Fear him.

6 Are not five sparrows sold for two farthings, and not one of them is forgotten before God?

7 But even the very hairs of your head are all numbered. Fear not therefore: ye are of more value than many sparrows.

Confessing Christ before Men

8 Also I say unto you, Whosoever shall confess me before men, him shall the Son of man also confess before the angels of God:

9 But he that denieth me before men shall be denied before the angels of God.

Blasphemy against the Holy Spirit

10 And whosoever shall speak a word against the Son of man, it shall be forgiven him: but unto him that blasphemeth against the Holy Ghost it shall not be forgiven.

11 And when they bring you unto the synagogues, and *unto* magistrates, and powers, take ye no thought how or what thing ye shall answer, or what ye shall say:

12 For the Holy Ghost shall teach you in the same hour what ye ought to say.

A Prosperous Farmer

13 And one of the company said unto him, Master, speak to my brother, that he divide the inheritance with me.

---

46 Matt. 23:4
47 Matt. 23:29
49 Matt. 23:34
51 Gen. 4:8; 2Chr. 24:20, 21
52 Matt. 23:13
54 Mark 12:13
1 Matt. 16:6, 12; Mark 8:15
2 Matt. 10:26; Mark 4:22; Luke 8:17
4 Isa. 51:7, 8, 12, 13; Jer. 1:8; Matt. 10:28; John 15:14, 15
6 Matt. 10:29
8 Matt. 10:32; Mark 8:38; 2Tim. 2:12; 1John 2:23
10 Matt. 12:31, 32; Mark 3:28; 1John 5:16
11 Matt. 10:19; Mark 13:11; Luke 21:14

11:49 and some of them they shall slay and persecute. This prophecy was fulfilled in the death of Christ Himself and most of the twelve apostles through persecution because of the gospel message.

11:50–51 From the blood of Abel unto the blood of Zacharias. These are the first and last martyrs mentioned in the Old Testament. Thus, the generation of Jews that saw and rejected Jesus will receive maximum pun-

ishment on the judgment day, as if they had been responsible for killing every martyred representative of God. Judgment came upon this generation of Jews during the siege and destruction of Jerusalem and the temple in A.D. 70 when, according to Josephus, more than a million Jews were killed and many were enslaved (Luke 21:20–24).

14 And he said unto him, Man, who made me a judge or a divider over you?
15 And he said unto them, Take heed, and beware of covetousness: for a man's life consisteth not in the abundance of the things which he possesseth.
16 And he spake a parable unto them, saying, The ground of a certain rich man brought forth plentifully:
17 And he thought within himself, saying, What shall I do, because I have no room where to bestow my fruits?
18 And he said, This will I do: I will pull down my barns, and build greater; and there will I bestow all my fruits and my goods.
19 And I will say to my soul, Soul, thou hast much goods laid up for many years; take thine ease, eat, drink, *and* be merry.
20 But God said unto him, *Thou* fool, this night thy soul shall be required of thee: then whose shall those things be, which thou hast provided?
21 So *is* he that layeth up treasure for himself, and is not rich toward God.

Christ Warns against Earthly Anxiety

22 And he said unto his disciples, Therefore I say unto you, Take no thought for your life, what ye shall eat; neither for the body, what ye shall put on.
23 The life is more than meat, and the body *is more* than raiment.
24 Consider the ravens: for they neither sow nor reap; which neither have storehouse nor barn; and God feedeth them: how much more are ye better than the fowls?
25 And which of you with taking thought can add to his stature one cubit?
26 If ye then be not able to do that thing which is least, why take ye thought for the rest?

27 Consider the lilies how they grow: they toil not, they spin not; and yet I say unto you, that Solomon in all his glory was not arrayed like one of these.
28 If then God so clothe the grass, which is today in the field, and to morrow is cast into the oven; how much more *will he clothe* you, O ye of little faith?
29 And seek not ye what ye shall eat, or what ye shall drink, neither be ye of doubtful mind.
30 For all these things do the nations of the world seek after: and your Father knoweth that ye have need of these things.
31 But rather seek ye the kingdom of God; and all these things shall be added unto you.
32 Fear not, little flock; for it is your Father's good pleasure to give you the kingdom.
33 Sell that ye have, and give alms; provide yourselves bags which wax not old, a treasure in the heavens that faileth not, where no thief approacheth, neither moth corrupteth.
34 For where your treasure is, there will your heart be also.

Watchful Servants

35 Let your loins be girded about, and *your* lights burning;
36 And ye yourselves like unto men that wait for their lord, when he will return from the wedding; that when he cometh and knocketh, they may open unto him immediately.
37 Blessed *are* those servants, whom the lord when he cometh shall find watching: verily I say unto you, that he shall gird himself, and make them to sit down to meat, and will come forth and serve them.
38 And if he shall come in the second watch, or come in the third watch, and find *them* so, blessed are those servants.

Cross references

14 John 18:36
15 1Tim. 6:7-10
19 Eccl. 11:9; 1Cor. 15:32; James 5:5
20 Job 20:22; 27:8; Ps. 39:6; 52:7; Jer. 17:11; James 4:14
21 Matt. 6:20; Luke 12:33; 1Tim. 6:18, 19; James 2:5
22 Matt. 6:25
24 Job 38:41; Ps. 147:9
31 Matt. 6:33
32 Matt. 11:25, 26
33 Matt. 6:20; 19:21; Luke 16:9; Acts 2:45; 4:34; 1Tim. 6:19
35 Matt. 25:1-13; Eph. 6:14; 1Pet. 1:13
37 Matt. 24:46

12:32 it is your Father's good pleasure to give you the kingdom. The kingdom spoken of here is the future, thousand-year rule of Christ upon earth from Jerusalem. The Gospels know nothing of an immaterial, mystical kingdom in the heart of an individual, as some suggest of this passage.

12:35–48 This is one of the many passages in the New Testament that express a clear relationship between expectation of the Lord's return and one's behavior during His absence (cf. 2 Pet. 3:1–9). Faithful service for the Lord in His absence will be rewarded with a position of responsibility during the next phase of earth's history,

known as the Millennial Kingdom. Watchful anticipation of one's coming Lord stands in opposition to the belief of the first century nation of Israel as a whole, though there were some in Israel who believed (see Luke 1—2).

12:35 Let your loins be girded about, and your lights burning. This is an expression of anticipation. In Christ's day, the girding of the loins would take place in preparation to work or perform a task.

12:38 The second watch is the time period from 9:00 P.M. to midnight, while the third watch is from midnight to 3:00 A.M.

39 And this know, that if the goodman of the house had known what hour the thief would come, he would have watched, and not have suffered his house to be broken through.

40 Be ye therefore ready also: for the Son of man cometh at an hour when ye think not.

The Duties of Christ's Ministers

41 Then Peter said unto him, Lord, speakest thou this parable unto us, or even to all?

42 And the Lord said, Who then is that faithful and wise steward, whom *his* lord shall make ruler over his household, to give *them their* portion of meat in due season?

43 Blessed *is* that servant, whom his lord when he cometh shall find so doing.

44 Of a truth I say unto you, that he will make him ruler over all that he hath.

45 But and if that servant say in his heart, My lord delayeth his coming; and shall begin to beat the menservants and maidens, and to eat and drink, and to be drunken;

46 The lord of that servant will come in a day when he looketh not for *him,* and at an hour when he is not aware, and will cut him in sunder, and will appoint him his portion with the unbelievers.

47 And that servant, which knew his lord's will, and prepared not *himself,* neither did according to his will, shall be beaten with many *stripes.*

48 But he that knew not, and did commit things worthy of stripes, shall be beaten with few *stripes.* For unto whomsoever much is given, of him shall be much required: and to whom men have committed much, of him they will ask the more.

No Compromise

49 I am come to send fire on the earth; and what will I, if it be already kindled?

50 But I have a baptism to be baptized with; and how am I straitened till it be accomplished!

51 Suppose ye that I am come to give peace on earth? I tell you, Nay; but rather division:

52 For from henceforth there shall be five in one house divided, three against two, and two against three.

53 The father shall be divided against the son, and the son against the father; the mother against the daughter, and the daughter against the mother; the mother in law against her daughter in law, and the daughter in law against her mother in law.

39 Matt. 24:43; 1Thess. 5:2; 2Pet. 3:10; Rev. 3:3; 16:15

40 Matt. 24:44; 25:13; Mark 13:33; Luke 21:34, 36; 1Thess. 5:6; 2Pet. 3:12

42 Matt. 24:45; 25:21; 1Cor. 4:2

44 Matt. 24:47

45 Matt. 24:48

46 Matt. 24:51

47 Num. 15:30; Deut. 25:2; John 9:41; 15:22; Acts 17:30; James 4:17

48 Lev. 5:17; 1Tim. 1:13

49 Luke 12:51

50 Matt. 20:22; Mark 10:38

51 Mic. 7:6; Matt. 10:34; Luke 12:49; John 7:43; 9:16; 10:19

52 Matt. 10:35

54 Matt. 16:2

58 Ps. 32:6; Prov. 25:8; Isa. 55:6; Matt. 5:25

4 Matt. 18:24; Luke 11:4

6 Isa. 5:2; Matt. 21:19

Discerning the Time

54 And he said also to the people, When ye see a cloud rise out of the west, straightway ye say, There cometh a shower; and so it is.

55 And when *ye see* the south wind blow, ye say, There will be heat; and it cometh to pass.

56 *Ye* hypocrites, ye can discern the face of the sky and of the earth; but how is it that ye do not discern this time?

Being Reconciled with Your Accuser

57 Yea, and why even of yourselves judge ye not what is right?

58 When thou goest with thine adversary to the magistrate, *as thou art* in the way, give diligence that thou mayest be delivered from him; lest he hale thee to the judge, and the judge deliver thee to the officer, and the officer cast thee into prison.

59 I tell thee, thou shalt not depart thence, till thou hast paid the very last mite.

CHAPTER 13
A Call to Repentance

1 There were present at that season some that told him of the Galilaeans, whose blood Pilate had mingled with their sacrifices.

2 And Jesus answering said unto them, Suppose ye that these Galilaeans were sinners above all the Galilaeans, because they suffered such things?

3 I tell you, Nay: but, except ye repent, ye shall all likewise perish.

4 Or those eighteen, upon whom the tower in Siloam fell, and slew them, think ye that they were sinners above all men that dwelt in Jerusalem?

5 I tell you, Nay: but, except ye repent, ye shall all likewise perish.

The Parable of the Barren Fig Tree

6 He spake also this parable; A certain *man* had a fig tree planted in his vineyard; and he came and sought fruit thereon, and found none.

7 Then said he unto the dresser of his vineyard, Behold, these three years I come seeking fruit on this fig tree, and find none: cut it down; why encumbereth it the ground?

8 And he answering said unto him, Lord, let it alone this year also, till I shall dig about it, and dung *it:*

9 And if it bear fruit, *well:* and if not, *then* after that thou shalt cut it down.

The Healing of a Crippled Woman on the Sabbath

10 And he was teaching in one of the synagogues on the sabbath.

11 And, behold, there was a woman which had a spirit of infirmity eighteen years, and was bowed together, and could in no wise lift up *herself*.

12 And when Jesus saw her, he called *her to him*, and said unto her, Woman, thou art loosed from thine infirmity.

13 And he laid *his* hands on her: and immediately she was made straight, and glorified God.

14 And the ruler of the synagogue answered with indignation, because that Jesus had healed on the sabbath day, and said unto the people, There are six days in which men ought to work: in them therefore come and be healed, and not on the sabbath day.

15 The Lord then answered him, and said, *Thou* hypocrite, doth not each one of you on the sabbath loose his ox or *his* ass from the stall, and lead *him* away to watering?

16 And ought not this woman, being a daughter of Abraham, whom Satan hath bound, lo, these eighteen years, be loosed from this bond on the sabbath day?

17 And when he had said these things, all his adversaries were ashamed: and all the people rejoiced for all the glorious things that were done by him.

The Parables of the Mustard Seed and the Leaven

18 Then said he, Unto what is the kingdom of God like? and whereunto shall I resemble it?

19 It is like a grain of mustard seed, which a man took, and cast into his garden; and it grew, and waxed a great tree; and the fowls of the air lodged in the branches of it.

13 Mark 16:18; Acts 9:17

14 Ex. 20:9; Matt. 12:10; Mark 3:2; Luke 6:7; 14:13

15 Luke 14:5

16 Luke 19:9

18 Matt. 13:31; Mark 4:30

22 Matt. 9:35; Mark 6:6

24 Matt. 7:13; John 7:34; 8:21; 13:33; Rom. 9:31

25 Ps. 32:6; Isa. 55:6; Matt. 7:23; 25:10, 12; Luke 6:46

27 Ps. 6:8; Matt. 7:23; 25:41; Luke 13:25

28 Matt. 8:11, 12; 13:42; 21:51

30 Matt. 19:30; 20:16; Mark 10:31

20 And again he said, Whereunto shall I liken the kingdom of God?

21 It is like leaven, which a woman took and hid in three measures of meal, till the whole was leavened.

"The Strait Gate"

22 And he went through the cities and villages, teaching, and journeying toward Jerusalem.

23 Then said one unto him, Lord, are there few that be saved? And he said unto them,

24 Strive to enter in at the strait gate: for many, I say unto you, will seek to enter in, and shall not be able.

25 When once the master of the house is risen up, and hath shut to the door, and ye begin to stand without, and to knock at the door, saying, Lord, Lord, open unto us; and he shall answer and say unto you, I know you not whence ye are:

26 Then shall ye begin to say, We have eaten and drunk in thy presence, and thou hast taught in our streets.

27 But he shall say, I tell you, I know you not whence ye are; depart from me, all *ye* workers of iniquity.

28 There shall be weeping and gnashing of teeth, when ye shall see Abraham, and Isaac, and Jacob, and all the prophets, in the kingdom of God, and you *yourselves* thrust out.

29 And they shall come from the east, and *from* the west, and from the north, and *from* the south, and shall sit down in the kingdom of God.

30 And, behold, there are last which shall be first, and there are first which shall be last.

Jesus Laments over Jerusalem

31 The same day there came certain of the Pharisees, saying unto him, Get thee out,

13:18 See the note on Mark 4:26–29.

13:19 the fowls of the air lodged in the branches of it. The growth is such that it is able to accommodate birds, emphasizing the external growth of the kingdom. This image is found in the Old Testament (Ps. 104:12; Ezek. 17:22–24; 31:6; Dan. 4:10–12).

13:21 leaven. Often symbolizing evil in other passages (Ex. 12:15; Lev. 2:11; Matt. 16:6; 1 Cor. 5:6–8; Gal. 5:9 [cf. 1 Tim. 4:1; Jude 1:12]), here leaven has a good sense, depicting the internal growth of the kingdom because the leaven is said to be "hid" (cf. the note on Matt. 13:33–35).

13:23 are there few that be saved? Jesus is teaching that many from Israel will not be part of His future kingdom (cf. v. 28).

13:29–30 Many Gentiles will be included in the future Millennial Kingdom (Ps. 22:29; Isa. 25:6). Matthew 8:11 adds that these Gentiles "shall sit down with Abraham, and Isaac and Jacob." The Greek for "sit down" refers to gathering for a meal. Eating with one another in the ancient world indicates equality and acceptance. In the kingdom, Christ will reverse the order of His day. Many Jews, who thought themselves to be first will be last, while many Gentiles, thought to be last, will become first.

and depart hence: for Herod will kill thee.
32 And he said unto them, Go ye, and tell that fox, Behold, I cast out devils, and I do cures today and to morrow, and the third *day* I shall be perfected.
33 Nevertheless I must walk today, and to morrow, and the *day* following: for it cannot be that a prophet perish out of Jerusalem.
34 O Jerusalem, Jerusalem, which killest the prophets, and stonest them that are sent unto thee; how often would I have gathered thy children together, as a hen *doth gather* her brood under *her* wings, and ye would not!
35 Behold, your house is left unto you desolate: and verily I say unto you, Ye shall not see me, until *the time* come when ye shall say, Blessed *is* he that cometh in the name of the Lord.

CHAPTER 14
Jesus Heals a Man on the Sabbath Day

1 And it came to pass, as he went into the house of one of the chief Pharisees to eat bread on the sabbath day, that they watched him.
2 And, behold, there was a certain man before him which had the dropsy.
3 And Jesus answering spake unto the lawyers and Pharisees, saying, Is it lawful to heal on the sabbath day?
4 And they held their peace. And he took *him,* and healed him, and let him go;
5 And answered them, saying, Which of you shall have an ass or an ox fallen into a pit, and will not straightway pull him out on the sabbath day?
6 And they could not answer him again to these things.

32 Heb. 2:10
34 Matt. 23:37
35 Lev. 26:31, 32; Ps. 69:25; 118:26; Isa. 1:7; Dan. 9:27; Mic. 3:12; Matt. 21:9; Mark 11:10; Luke 19:38; John 12:13
3 Matt. 12:10
5 Ex. 23:5; Deut. 22:4; Luke 13:15
10 Prov. 25:6, 7
11 Job 22:29; Ps. 18:27; Prov. 29:23; Matt. 23:12; Luke 18:14; James 4:6; 1Pet. 5:5

13 Neh. 8:10, 12

15 Rev. 19:9

Jesus Teaches Humility

7 And he put forth a parable to those which were bidden, when he marked how they chose out the chief rooms; saying unto them,
8 When thou art bidden of any *man* to a wedding, sit not down in the highest room; lest a more honourable man than thou be bidden of him;
9 And he that bade thee and him come and say to thee, Give this man place; and thou begin with shame to take the lowest room.
10 But when thou art bidden, go and sit down in the lowest room; that when he bade thee cometh, he may say unto thee, Friend, go up higher: then shalt thou have worship in the presence of them that sit at meat with thee.
11 For whosoever exalteth himself shall be abased; and he that humbleth himself shall be exalted.
12 Then said he also to him that bade him, When thou makest a dinner or a supper, call not thy friends, nor thy brethren, neither thy kinsmen, nor *thy* rich neighbours; lest they also bid thee again, and a recompence be made thee.
13 But when thou makest a feast, call the poor, the maimed, the lame, the blind:
14 And thou shalt be blessed; for they cannot recompense thee: for thou shalt be recompensed at the resurrection of the just.

The Parable of the Great Banquet

15 And when one of them that sat at meat with him heard these things, he said unto him, Blessed *is* he that shall eat bread in the kingdom of God.

13:34 gathered thy children together, as a hen doth gather her brood under her wings. Israel refused Christ at His first coming, but they will have a change of heart in conjunction with His second coming (Zech. 12:10). Matthew 24:31 says that Christ "shall send his angels . . . and they shall gather together his elect." The same Greek word for "gathering" (*episunago*) is used here and in Matthew.

13:35 your house. The desolation of the temple was fulfilled in the A.D. 70 destruction of Jerusalem and the temple by the Roman army (Luke 21:20–24). At the Second Coming, the nation of Israel will see Christ again and say, "Blessed is he that cometh in the name of the Lord" (cf. Lev. 26:40–42; Jer. 3:11–18; Hos. 5:15; Zech. 12:10—13:1; Rom. 10:13–15; 11:25–26).

14:14 for thou shalt be recompensed at the resurrection of the just. This is a prediction that those who have died as believers during the Church Age will be resurrected at the Rapture (1 Thess. 4:12–18). Christ will reward Church-Age believers at the bema judgment (Rom. 14:10; 1 Cor. 3:10–15; 2 Cor. 5:10).

14:15–24 Go out into the highways and hedges, and compel them to come in, that my house may be filled. This parable speaks of an invitation to those who were rejected by Jewish society and to the Gentiles to enter Christ's kingdom. Thus, Christ demonstrates that those who were thought to have prominence in Jewish society were not recognized in the eyes of God. This parable serves as a prophecy that Gentiles will have a part in the Millennial Kingdom.

16 Then said he unto him, A certain man made a great supper, and bade many:
17 And sent his servant at supper time to say to them that were bidden, Come; for all things are now ready.
18 And they all with one *consent* began to make excuse. The first said unto him, I have bought a piece of ground, and I must needs go and see it: I pray thee have me excused.
19 And another said, I have bought five yoke of oxen, and I go to prove them: I pray thee have me excused.
20 And another said, I have married a wife, and therefore I cannot come.
21 So that servant came, and shewed his lord these things. Then the master of the house being angry said to his servant, Go out quickly into the streets and lanes of the city, and bring in hither the poor, and the maimed, and the halt, and the blind.
22 And the servant said, Lord, it is done as thou hast commanded, and yet there is room.
23 And the lord said unto the servant, Go out into the highways and hedges, and compel *them* to come in, that my house may be filled.
24 For I say unto you, That none of those men which were bidden shall taste of my supper.

Love Jesus More Than Yourself

25 And there went great multitudes with him: and he turned, and said unto them,
26 If any *man* come to me, and hate not his father, and mother, and wife, and children, and brethren, and sisters, yea, and his own life also, he cannot be my disciple.
27 And whosoever doth not bear his cross, and come after me, cannot be my disciple.
28 For which of you, intending to build a tower, sitteth not down first, and counteth the cost, whether he have *sufficient* to finish *it*?
29 Lest haply, after he hath laid the foundation, and is not able to finish *it*, all that behold *it* begin to mock him,
30 Saying, This man began to build, and was not able to finish.
31 Or what king, going to make war against another king, sitteth not down first, and consulteth whether he be able with ten thousand to meet him that cometh against him with twenty thousand?
32 Or else, while the other is yet a great way off, he sendeth an ambassage, and desireth conditions of peace.
33 So likewise, whosoever he be of you that

16 Matt. 22:2

17 Prov. 9:2, 5

24 Matt. 21:43; 22:8; Acts 13:46

26 Deut. 13:6; 33:9; Matt. 10:37; Rom. 9:13; Rev. 12:11

27 Matt. 16:24; Mark 8:34; Luke 9:23; 2Tim. 3:12

28 Prov. 24:27

34 Matt. 5:13; Mark 9:50

1 Matt. 9:10

2 Acts 11:3; Gal. 2:12

4 Matt. 18:12

6 1Pet. 2:10, 25

7 Luke 5:32

12 Mark 12:44

forsaketh not all that he hath, he cannot be my disciple.

Salt

34 Salt *is* good: but if the salt have lost his savour, wherewith shall it be seasoned?
35 It is neither fit for the land, nor yet for the dunghill; *but* men cast it out. He that hath ears to hear, let him hear.

CHAPTER 15
The Lost Sheep

1 Then drew near unto him all the publicans and sinners for to hear him.
2 And the Pharisees and scribes murmured, saying, This man receiveth sinners, and eateth with them.
3 And he spake this parable unto them, saying,
4 What man of you, having an hundred sheep, if he lose one of them, doth not leave the ninety and nine in the wilderness, and go after that which is lost, until he find it?
5 And when he hath found *it*, he layeth *it* on his shoulders, rejoicing.
6 And when he cometh home, he calleth together *his* friends and neighbours, saying unto them, Rejoice with me; for I have found my sheep which was lost.
7 I say unto you, that likewise joy shall be in heaven over one sinner that repenteth, more than over ninety and nine just persons, which need no repentance.

The Lost Coin

8 Either what woman having ten pieces of silver, if she lose one piece, doth not light a candle, and sweep the house, and seek diligently till she find *it*?
9 And when she hath found *it*, she calleth *her* friends and *her* neighbours together, saying, Rejoice with me; for I have found the piece which I had lost.
10 Likewise, I say unto you, there is joy in the presence of the angels of God over one sinner that repenteth.

The Lost Son

11 And he said, A certain man had two sons:
12 And the younger of them said to *his* father, Father, give me the portion of goods that falleth *to me*. And he divided unto them *his* living.
13 And not many days after the younger son gathered all together, and took his journey into a far country, and there wasted his substance with riotous living.

14 And when he had spent all, there arose a mighty famine in that land; and he began to be in want.

15 And he went and joined himself to a citizen of that country; and he sent him into his fields to feed swine.

16 And he would fain have filled his belly with the husks that the swine did eat: and no man gave unto him.

17 And when he came to himself, he said, How many hired servants of my father's have bread enough and to spare, and I perish with hunger!

18 I will arise and go to my father, and will say unto him, Father, I have sinned against heaven, and before thee,

19 And am no more worthy to be called thy son: make me as one of thy hired servants.

20 And he arose, and came to his father. But when he was yet a great way off, his father saw him, and had compassion, and ran, and fell on his neck, and kissed him.

21 And the son said unto him, Father, I have sinned against heaven, and in thy sight, and am no more worthy to be called thy son.

22 But the father said to his servants, Bring forth the best robe, and put *it* on him; and put a ring on his hand, and shoes on *his* feet:

23 And bring hither the fatted calf, and kill *it*; and let us eat, and be merry:

24 For this my son was dead, and is alive again; he was lost, and is found. And they began to be merry.

25 Now his elder son was in the field: and as he came and drew nigh to the house, he heard musick and dancing.

26 And he called one of the servants, and asked what these things meant.

27 And he said unto him, Thy brother is come; and thy father hath killed the fatted calf, because he hath received him safe and sound.

28 And he was angry, and would not go in: therefore came his father out, and intreated him.

29 And he answering said to *his* father, Lo, these many years do I serve thee, neither transgressed I at any time thy commandment: and yet thou never gavest me a kid, that I might make merry with my friends:

30 But as soon as this thy son was come, which hath devoured thy living with harlots, thou hast killed for him the fatted calf.

31 And he said unto him, Son, thou art ever with me, and all that I have is thine.

32 It was meet that we should make merry,

and be glad: for this thy brother was dead, and is alive again; and was lost, and is found.

CHAPTER 16
The Parable of the Unrighteous Steward

1 And he said also unto his disciples, There was a certain rich man, which had a steward; and the same was accused unto him that he had wasted his goods.

2 And he called him, and said unto him, How is it that I hear this of thee? give an account of thy stewardship; for thou mayest be no longer steward.

3 Then the steward said within himself, What shall I do? for my lord taketh away from me the stewardship: I cannot dig; to beg I am ashamed.

4 I am resolved what to do, that, when I am put out of the stewardship, they may receive me into their houses.

5 So he called every one of his lord's debtors *unto him,* and said unto the first, how much owest thou unto my lord?

6 And he said, an hundred measures of oil. And he said unto him, Take thy bill, and sit down quickly, and write fifty.

7 Then said he to another, And how much owest thou? And he said, an hundred measures of wheat. And he said unto him, Take thy bill, and write fourscore.

8 And the lord commended the unjust steward, because he had done wisely: for the children of this world are in their generation wiser than the children of light.

9 And I say unto you, Make to yourselves friends of the mammon of unrighteousness; that, when ye fail, they may receive you into everlasting habitations.

10 He that is faithful in that which is least is faithful also in much: and he that is unjust in the least is unjust also in much.

11 If therefore ye have not been faithful in the unrighteous mammon, who will commit to your trust the true *riches*?

12 And if ye have not been faithful in that which is another man's, who shall give you that which is your own?

13 No servant can serve two masters: for either he will hate the one, and love the other; or else he will hold to the one, and despise the other. Ye cannot serve God and mammon.

14 And the Pharisees also, who were covetous, heard all these things: and they derided him.

15 And he said unto them, Ye are they

Cross references

20 Acts 2:39; Eph. 2:13, 17
21 Ps. 51:4
24 Luke 15:32; Eph. 2:1; 5:14; Rev. 3:1
32 Luke 15:24
8 John 12:36; Eph. 5:8; 1Thess. 5:5
9 Dan. 4:27; Matt. 6:19; 19:21; Luke 11:41; 1Tim. 6:17-19
10 Matt. 25:21; Luke 19:17
13 Matt. 6:24
14 Matt. 23:14
15 1Sam. 16:7; Ps. 7:9; Luke 10:29

which justify yourselves before men; but God knoweth your hearts: for that which is highly esteemed among men is abomination in the sight of God.

The Law and the Kingdom of God

16 The law and the prophets *were* until John: since that time the kingdom of God is preached, and every man presseth into it.
17 And it is easier for heaven and earth to pass, than one tittle of the law to fail.

Divorce

18 Whosoever putteth away his wife, and marrieth another, committeth adultery: and whosoever marrieth her that is put away from *her* husband committeth adultery.

The Rich Man and Lazarus

19 There was a certain rich man, which was clothed in purple and fine linen, and fared sumptuously every day:
20 And there was a certain beggar named Lazarus, which was laid at his gate, full of sores,
21 And desiring to be fed with the crumbs

which fell from the rich man's table: moreover the dogs came and licked his sores.
22 And it came to pass, that the beggar died, and was carried by the angels into Abraham's bosom: the rich man also died, and was buried;
23 And in hell he lift up his eyes, being in torments, and seeth Abraham afar off, and Lazarus in his bosom.
24 And he cried and said, Father Abraham, have mercy on me, and send Lazarus, that he may dip the tip of his finger in water, and cool my tongue; for I am tormented in this flame.
25 But Abraham said, Son, remember that thou in thy lifetime receivedst thy good things, and likewise Lazarus evil things: but now he is comforted, and thou art tormented.
26 And beside all this, between us and you there is a great gulf fixed: so that they which would pass from hence to you cannot; neither can they pass to us, that *would* come from thence.
27 Then he said, I pray thee therefore, father, that thou wouldest send him to my father's house:

16 Matt. 4:17; 11:12, 13; Luke 7:29

17 Ps. 102:26, 27; Isa. 40:8; 51:6; Matt. 5:18; 1Pet. 1:25

18 Matt. 5:32; 19:9; Mark 10:11; 1Cor. 7:10, 11

24 Isa. 66:24; Zech. 14:12; Mark 9:44-50

25 Job 21:13; Luke 6:24

Where the Dead Are Now

© AMG Publishers

16:23–25 I am tormented in this flame. The torments listed in these verses are presented by Christ as a literal description of what hell is like.

28 For I have five brethren; that he may testify unto them, lest they also come into this place of torment.

29 Abraham saith unto him, They have Moses and the prophets; let them hear them.

30 And he said, Nay, father Abraham: but if one went unto them from the dead, they will repent.

31 And he said unto him, If they hear not Moses and the prophets, neither will they be persuaded, though one rose from the dead.

CHAPTER 17
Always Forgive

1 Then said he unto the disciples, It is impossible but that offences will come: but woe *unto* him, through whom they come!

2 It were better for him that a millstone were hanged about his neck, and he cast into the sea, than that he should offend one of these little ones.

3 Take heed to yourselves: If thy brother trespass against thee, rebuke him; and if he repent, forgive him.

4 And if he trespass against thee seven times in a day, and seven times in a day turn again to thee, saying, I repent; thou shalt forgive him.

5 And the apostles said unto the Lord, Increase our faith.

6 And the Lord said, If ye had faith as a grain of mustard seed, ye might say unto this sycamine tree, Be thou plucked up by the root, and be thou planted in the sea; and it should obey you.

7 But which of you, having a servant plowing or feeding cattle, will say unto him by and by, when he is come from the field, Go and sit down to meat?

8 And will not rather say unto him, Make ready wherewith I may sup, and gird thyself, and serve me, till I have eaten and drunken; and afterward thou shalt eat and drink?

9 Doth he thank that servant because he did the things that were commanded him? I trow not.

10 So likewise ye, when ye shall have done all those things which are commanded you, say, We are unprofitable servants: we have done that which was our duty to do.

Jesus Cleanses Ten Lepers

11 And it came to pass, as he went to Jerusalem, that he passed through the midst of Samaria and Galilee.

12 And as he entered into a certain village, there met him ten men that were lepers, which stood afar off:

13 And they lifted up *their* voices, and said, Jesus, Master, have mercy on us.

14 And when he saw *them,* he said unto them, Go shew yourselves unto the priests. And it came to pass, that, as they went, they were cleansed.

15 And one of them, when he saw that he was healed, turned back, and with a loud voice glorified God,

16 And fell down on *his* face at his feet, giving him thanks: and he was a Samaritan.

17 And Jesus answering said, Were there not ten cleansed? but where *are* the nine?

18 There are not found that returned to give glory to God, save this stranger.

19 And he said unto him, Arise, go thy way: thy faith hath made thee whole.

The Kingdom of God

20 And when he was demanded of the Pharisees, when the kingdom of God should come, he answered them and said, The kingdom of God cometh not with observation:

29 Isa. 8:20; 34:16; John 5:39, 45; Acts 15:21; 17:11

31 John 12:10, 1:11

1 Matt. 18:6, 7; Mark 9:42; 1Cor. 11:19

3 Lev. 19:17; Prov. 17:10; Matt. 18:15, 21; James 5:19

6 Matt. 17:20; 21:21; Mark 9:23; 11:23

8 Luke 12:37

10 Job 22:3; 35:7; Ps. 16:2; Matt. 25:30; Rom. 3:12; 11:35; 1Cor. 9:16, 17; Phile. 1:11

11 Luke 9:51, 52; John 4:4

12 Lev. 13:46

14 Lev. 13:2; 14:2; Matt. 8:4; Luke 5:14

19 Matt. 9:22; Mark 5:34; 10:52; Luke 7:50; 8:48; 18:42

16:29 They have Moses and the prophets; let them hear them. In context, the point is that the Old Testament taught generosity and care for the disabled poor (Deut. 14:28–29; Isa. 3:14–15; Mic. 6:10–11), but that did not impact the rich man. In principle, as taught in Romans 1:18—2:16, if an individual does not respond positively to God's revelation, then more revelation will not help them believe. In this case, if a Jew does not believe the Old Testament, then it makes sense that they would not believe in Jesus, the Messiah to whom it pointed.

16:31 neither will they be persuaded, though one rose from the dead. This was proven later when Jesus raised another man named Lazarus from the dead (John 11:1–44). While "many" believed (John 11:45), "some" did not (John 11:46). Jesus Himself rose from the dead (Luke 24:1–12), yet Israel remained primarily in unbelief.

17:20 The kingdom of God cometh not with observation. The kingdom of God would not come in the way that the Pharisees expected it to come. This is vindicated by the fact that the King of the kingdom was the one with whom they were talking, yet they did not recognize Him.

Hell

By Jack Van Impe

Hell is the biblical term for the place of those who are eternally lost. The two Greek words used for "hell" in the New Testament are *Hades* and *Gehenna.* The temporary holding place is Hades, while Gehenna refers to the final "penitentiary" for lost souls. The lake of fire is synonymous with Gehenna, which differs from Hades in that Gehenna is a place where there are degrees of suffering. Thus, the final hell will differ depending on one's evil deeds and the number of times he rejected Christ (Rom. 2:5; Matt. 11:23–24; 23:14).

Hades was the place where the souls and the spirits of all humans went until the Cross. *Sheol* (Old Testament) and *Hades* (New Testament) are one and the same. In Sheol or Hades there were two compartments, one for the wicked, and the other for the righteous . . . one for suffering, and the other for comfort. The area of comfort was known as Paradise or "Abraham's Bosom" (Luke 16:22–23). The thief on the cross went to Paradise, as promised by Christ (Luke 23:43). This is where Christ went upon His death (Eph. 4:8–10), releasing and transporting the entire righteous dead into the "third heaven" of 2 Corinthians 12:2. That is why Paradise is referred to as "up" (Rev. 2:7, 2 Cor. 12:4). So presently, the comfort side of Hades (Paradise) has been emptied by Him who has the keys of death and hell (Rev. 20:13).

> *Hell is the biblical term for the place of those who are eternally lost.*

Of course, the suffering side of Hades still teems with the wicked, as the unregenerate continue to die day by day and are added to its population. They have joined the rich man of Luke 16:23 and will not come out again until Judgment Day, when they will meet Christ at their trial and be transferred to the final penitentiary of lost souls, Gehenna (Rev. 20:13–14). Christ describes Hades eleven times in the New Testament (Matt. 11:23; 16:18; Luke 10:15; 16:22–23; Acts 2:27, 31; Rev. 1:18; 6:8; 20:13–14).

The word "Gehenna" is used twelve times in the New Testament. It takes its name from the "Valley of Hinnom," a place where King Ahaz introduced the sacrifice of little children to the god, Molech (1 Kgs. 11:7). This place became so detested that it was used as a dump for all kinds of refuse that burned continually. Therefore, Gehenna is equivalent to the "lake of fire." In the following scriptures, Christ refers to Gehenna, translated "hell" or "hell fire": Matthew 5:22, 29–30; 10:28; 18:9; 23:15; 23:33; Mark 9:43-47.

The lake of fire, or Gehenna, is the final place of punishment and torment for all those who reject Christ (Rev. 19:20; 20:10, 14–15). Those consigned there are all whose names are not found in the book of life (Rev. 20:15), including worshipers of Antichrist and the False Prophet (Rev. 19:20), the devil (Rev. 20:10, Matt. 24:42), and the devil's angels (Matt. 25:41; Rev. 19:20; 20:10). They are all forever separated from God (2 Thess. 1:9).

The lake of fire is described in Scripture as a place "where their worm dieth not" (Mark 9:44), as a place of outer "darkness" (Matt. 8:12), as a place of "everlasting fire" (Matt. 18:8), where "the smoke of their torment ascendeth" (Rev. 14:11), and where the "second death occurs" (eternal separation from God) in "fire and brimstone" (Rev. 20:14; 21:8).

21 Neither shall they say, Lo here! or, lo there! for, behold, the kingdom of God is within you.

22 And he said unto the disciples, The days will come, when ye shall desire to see one of the days of the Son of man, and ye shall not see *it*.

23 And they shall say to you, See here; or, see there: go not after *them*, nor follow *them*.

When Jesus Comes Again

24 For as the lightning, that lighteneth out of the one *part* under heaven, shineth unto the other *part* under heaven; so shall also the Son of man be in his day.

25 But first must he suffer many things, and be rejected of this generation.

26 And as it was in the days of Noe, so shall it be also in the days of the Son of man.

27 They did eat, they drank, they married wives, they were given in marriage, until the day that Noe entered into the ark, and the flood came, and destroyed them all.

28 Likewise also as it was in the days of Lot; they did eat, they drank, they bought, they sold, they planted, they builded;

29 But the same day that Lot went out of Sodom it rained fire and brimstone from heaven, and destroyed *them* all.

30 Even thus shall it be in the day when the Son of man is revealed.

31 In that day, he which shall be upon the housetop, and his stuff in the house, let him not come down to take it away: and he that is in the field, let him likewise not return back.

32 Remember Lot's wife.

33 Whosoever shall seek to save his life

shall lose it; and whosoever shall lose his life shall preserve it.

34 I tell you, in that night there shall be two *men* in one bed; the one shall be taken, and the other shall be left.

35 Two *women* shall be grinding together; the one shall be taken, and the other left.

36 Two *men* shall be in the field; the one shall be taken, and the other left.

37 And they answered and said unto him, Where, Lord? And he said unto them, Wheresoever the body *is*, thither will the eagles be gathered together.

CHAPTER 18

The Importunate Widow: A Lesson in Prayer

1 And he spake a parable unto them *to this end*, that men ought always to pray, and not to faint;

2 Saying, There was in a city a judge, which feared not God, neither regarded man:

3 And there was a widow in that city; and she came unto him, saying, Avenge me of mine adversary.

4 And he would not for a while: but afterward he said within himself, Though I fear not God, nor regard man;

5 Yet because this widow troubleth me, I will avenge her, lest by her continual coming she weary me.

6 And the Lord said, Hear what the unjust judge saith.

7 And shall not God avenge his own elect, which cry day and night unto him, though he bear long with them?

8 I tell you that he will avenge them

Cross References

21 Luke 17:23; John 1:26
22 Matt. 9:15; John 17:12
23 Matt. 24:23; Mark 13:21; Luke 21:8
24 Matt. 24:27
25 Mark 8:31; 9:31; 10:33; Luke 9:22
26 Gen. 7; Matt. 24:37
29 Gen. 19:16, 24
30 2 Thess. 1:7
31 Matt. 24:17; Mark 13:15
32 Gen. 19:26
33 Matt. 10:39; 16:25; Mark 8:35; Luke 9:24; John 12:25
34 Matt. 24:40, 41; 1 Thess. 4:17
37 Job 39:30; Matt. 24:28
1 Rom. 12:12; Col. 4:2; 1 Thess. 5:17
5 Luke 11:8
7 Rev. 6:10

17:21 within you. A better translation is "in your midst." Jesus was not teaching that there was a spiritual kingdom within the hearts of the unbelieving Pharisees who were plotting to kill Him. Instead, He told them that the kingdom was standing right in front of them, in their midst. The kingdom was possible because the King was there, but it did not come at that time because of Jewish unbelief, led by the Pharisees.

17:25 first must he suffer many things. This is a prediction of Jesus' death.

17:26–32 in the days of Noe. The days of Noah prefigure the conditions of the Tribulation leading up to the second coming of Jesus to earth, "the days of the Son of man." As those in Noah's day went about normal pursuits, not paying attention to God's Word, and the declared judgment of God came upon them suddenly, and "destroyed them all," so unbelievers during the Tribulation

will be unprepared for the return of Christ and the start of the Millennial Kingdom. A similar illustration is given, comparing the mind-set of unbelievers in the Tribulation to "the days of Lot."

17:34–36 the one shall be taken, and the other shall be left. This is not a reference to the Rapture, which will have taken place at least seven years before the Second Coming. Instead, these three illustrations speak of unbelievers who are taken in judgment. Believers are left at the Second Coming to enter into Christ's Millennial Kingdom.

18:7–8 he will avenge them speedily. One of the purposes of the Tribulation is that it will be a time in which God will exercise vengeance upon those who have persecuted His people (Deut. 30:7; 2 Thess. 1:5–10). God's judgment will come in a swift or speedy manner (Rom. 16:20; Rev. 1:1). In context, "the elect" here refers to the

speedily. Nevertheless when the Son of man cometh, shall he find faith on the earth?

The Parable of the Pharisee and the Tax Collector

9 And he spake this parable unto certain which trusted in themselves that they were righteous, and despised others:

10 Two men went up into the temple to pray; the one a Pharisee, and the other a publican.

11 The Pharisee stood and prayed thus with himself, God, I thank thee, that I am not as other men *are*, extortioners, unjust, adulterers, or even as this publican.

12 I fast twice in the week, I give tithes of all that I possess.

13 And the publican, standing afar off, would not lift up so much as *his* eyes unto heaven, but smote upon his breast, saying, God be merciful to me a sinner.

14 I tell you, this man went down to his house justified *rather* than the other: for every one that exalteth himself shall be abased; and he that humbleth himself shall be exalted.

Jesus Blesses Little Children

15 And they brought unto him also infants, that he would touch them: but when *his* disciples saw *it*, they rebuked them.

16 But Jesus called them *unto him*, and said, Suffer little children to come unto me, and forbid them not: for of such is the kingdom of God.

17 Verily I say unto you, Whosoever shall not receive the kingdom of God as a little child shall in no wise enter therein.

How to Inherit Eternal Life

18 And a certain ruler asked him, saying, Good Master, what shall I do to inherit eternal life?

19 And Jesus said unto him, Why callest thou me good? none is good, save one, *that is*, God.

20 Thou knowest the commandments, Do not commit adultery, Do not kill, Do not steal, Do not bear false witness, Honour thy father and thy mother.

21 And he said, All these have I kept from my youth up.

22 Now when Jesus heard these things, he said unto him, Yet lackest thou one thing: sell all that thou hast, and distribute unto the poor, and thou shalt have treasure in heaven: and come, follow me.

23 And when he heard this, he was very sorrowful: for he was very rich.

24 And when Jesus saw that he was very sorrowful, he said, How hardly shall they that have riches enter into the kingdom of God!

25 For it is easier for a camel to go through a needle's eye, than for a rich man to enter into the kingdom of God.

26 And they that heard *it* said, Who then can be saved?

27 And he said, The things which are impossible with men are possible with God.

28 Then Peter said, Lo, we have left all, and followed thee.

29 And he said unto them, Verily I say unto you, There is no man that hath left house, or parents, or brethren, or wife, or children, for the kingdom of God's sake,

30 Who shall not receive manifold more in this present time, and in the world to come life everlasting.

Jesus Foretells His Resurrection

31 Then he took *unto him* the twelve, and said unto them, Behold, we go up to Jerusalem, and all things that are written by the prophets concerning the Son of man shall be accomplished.

32 For he shall be delivered unto the Gentiles, and shall be mocked, and spitefully entreated, and spitted on:

33 And they shall scourge *him*, and put him to death: and the third day he shall rise again.

34 And they understood none of these things: and this saying was hid from them, neither knew they the things which were spoken.

Jesus Heals a Blind Beggar Near Jericho

35 And it came to pass, that as he was come nigh unto Jericho, a certain blind man sat by the way side begging:

36 And hearing the multitude pass by, he asked what it meant.

37 And they told him, that Jesus of Nazareth passeth by.

Cross references
9 Luke 10:29; 16:15
11 Ps. 135:2; Isa. 1:15; 58:2; Rev. 3:17
14 Job 22:29; Matt. 23:12; Luke 14:11; James 4:6; 1Pet. 5:5, 6
15 Matt. 19:13; Mark 10:13
16 1Cor. 14:20; 1Pet. 2:2
17 Mark 10:15
18 Matt. 19:16; Mark 10:17
20 Ex. 20:12, 16; Deut. 5:16-20; Rom. 13:9; Eph. 6:2; Col. 3:20
22 Matt. 6:19, 20; 19:21; 1Tim. 6:19
24 Prov. 11:28; Matt. 19:23; Mark 10:23
27 Jer. 32:17; Zech. 8:6; Matt. 19:26; Luke 1:37
28 Matt. 19:27
29 Deut. 33:9
30 Job 42:10
31 Matt. 16:21; 17:22; 20:17; Mark 10:32
32 Matt. 27:2; 23:1; John 18:28; Acts 3:13
34 Mark 9:32; Luke 2:50; 9:45; John 10:6; 12:16
35 Matt. 20:29; Mark 10:46

---

remnant of believers in Israel during the Tribulation who will call out to the Lord, upon their repentance, leading to the Second Coming and Israel's rescue (see also Matt. 24:22–31; Mark 13:20, 22, 27). Though there will be an elect remnant in Israel, the general condition throughout the earth will be one of unbelief.

38 And he cried, saying, Jesus, *thou* son of David, have mercy on me.

39 And they which went before rebuked him, that he should hold his peace: but he cried so much the more, *Thou* son of David, have mercy on me.

40 And Jesus stood, and commanded him to be brought unto him: and when he was come near, he asked him,

41 Saying, What wilt thou that I shall do unto thee? And he said, Lord, that I may receive my sight.

42 And Jesus said unto him, Receive thy sight: thy faith hath saved thee.

43 And immediately he received his sight, and followed him, glorifying God: and all the people, when they saw *it,* gave praise unto God.

CHAPTER 19
The Conversion of Zacchaeus

1 And *Jesus* entered and passed through Jericho.

2 And, behold, *there was* a man named Zacchaeus, which was the chief among the publicans, and he was rich.

3 And he sought to see Jesus who he was; and could not for the press, because he was little of stature.

4 And he ran before, and climbed up into a sycomore tree to see him: for he was to pass that *way.*

5 And when Jesus came to the place, he looked up, and saw him, and said unto him, Zacchaeus, make haste, and come down; for today I must abide at thy house.

6 And he made haste, and came down, and received him joyfully.

7 And when they saw *it,* they all murmured, saying, That he was gone to be guest with a man that is a sinner.

8 And Zacchaeus stood, and said unto the Lord; Behold, Lord, the half of my goods I give to the poor; and if I have taken any

thing from any man by false accusation, I restore *him* fourfold.

9 And Jesus said unto him, This day is salvation come to this house forsomuch as he also is a son of Abraham.

10 For the Son of man is come to seek and to save that which was lost.

The Parable of the Ten Pound

11 And as they heard these things, he added and spake a parable, because he was nigh to Jerusalem, and because they thought that the kingdom of God should immediately appear.

12 He said therefore, A certain noble man went into a far country to receive for himself a kingdom, and to return.

13 And he called his ten servants, and delivered them ten pounds, and said unto them, Occupy till I come.

14 But his citizens hated him, and sent a message after him, saying, We will not have this *man* to reign over us.

15 And it came to pass, that when he was returned, having received the kingdom, then he commanded these servants to be called unto him, to whom he had given the money, that he might know how much every man had gained by trading.

16 Then came the first, saying, Lord, thy pound hath gained ten pounds.

17 And he said unto him, Well, thou good servant: because thou hast been faithful in a very little, have thou authority over ten cities.

18 And the second came, saying, Lord, thy pound hath gained five pounds.

19 And he said likewise to him, Be thou also over five cities.

20 And another came, saying, Lord, behold, *here is* thy pound, which I have kept laid up in a napkin:

21 For I feared thee, because thou art an austere man: thou takest up that thou

42 Luke 17:19

43 Luke 5:26; Acts 4:21; 11:18

7 Matt. 9:11; Luke 5:30

8 Ex. 22:1; 1Sam. 12:3; 2Sam. 12:6; Luke 3:14

9 Luke 13:16; Rom. 4:11, 12, 16; Gal. 3:7

10 Matt. 10:6; 15:24; 18:11

11 Acts 1:6

12 Matt. 25:14; Mark 13:34

14 John 1:11

17 Matt. 25:21; Luke 16:10

21 Matt. 25:24

19:11 they thought that the kingdom of God should immediately appear. Christ's disciples thought Jesus was heading to Jerusalem to establish His earthly kingdom, when in reality He was going there to die for the sins of the world.

19:13 Occupy till I come. This passage does not mean that believers are to rule over this present world until Christ's return, as some suggest. The phrase literally means, "Keep busy till I come."

19:14 We will not have this man to reign over us. This parable, like all parables, relates to the nation of Israel.

The rejection of Jesus is the clear conclusion reached by the majority of the citizens of Israel at Christ's first coming.

19:16–26 These verses demonstrate that a believer's performance during the absence of the King will determine one's position and responsibility when the kingdom does arrive at the return of Jesus. They also clearly teach that God will reward the faithful use of the resources He gives His people while He is gone. To be active in this way demonstrates that the servant believed his master's word and expected him to return and reward him.

layedst not down, and reapest that thou didst not sow.

22 And he saith unto him, Out of thine own mouth will I judge thee, *thou* wicked servant. Thou knewest that I was an austere man, taking up that I laid not down, and reaping that I did not sow:

23 Wherefore then gavest not thou my money into the bank, that at my coming I might have required mine own with usury?

24 And he said unto them that stood by, Take from him the pound, and give *it* to him that hath ten pounds.

25 (And they said unto him, Lord, he hath ten pounds.)

26 For I say unto you, That unto every one which hath shall be given; and from him that hath not, even that he hath shall be taken away from him.

27 But those mine enemies, which would not that I should reign over them, bring hither, and slay *them* before me.

Jesus' Triumphal Entry into Jerusalem

28 And when he had thus spoken, he went before, ascending up to Jerusalem.

29 And it came to pass, when he was come nigh to Bethphage and Bethany, at the mount called *the mount* of Olives, he sent two of his disciples,

30 Saying, Go ye into the village over against *you;* in the which at your entering ye shall find a colt tied, whereon yet never man sat: loose him, and bring *him hither.*

31 And if any man ask you, Why do ye loose *him?* thus shall ye say unto him, Because the Lord hath need of him.

32 And they that were sent went their way, and found even as he had said unto them.

33 And as they were loosing the colt, the owners thereof said unto them, Why loose ye the colt?

34 And they said, The Lord hath need of him.

35 And they brought him to Jesus: and they cast their garments upon the colt, and they set Jesus thereon.

36 And as he went, they spread their clothes in the way.

37 And when he was come nigh, even now at the descent of the mount of Olives, the whole multitude of the disciples began to rejoice and praise God with a loud voice for all the mighty works that they had seen;

38 Saying, Blessed *be* the King that cometh in the name of the Lord: peace in heaven, and glory in the highest.

39 And some of the Pharisees from among the multitude said unto him, Master, rebuke thy disciples.

40 And he answered and said unto them, I tell you that, if these should hold their peace, the stones would immediately cry out.

41 And when he was come near, he beheld the city, and wept over it,

42 Saying, If thou hadst known, even thou, at least in this thy day, the things *which belong* unto thy peace! but now they are hid from thine eyes.

43 For the days shall come upon thee, that thine enemies shall cast a trench about thee, and compass thee round, and keep thee in on every side,

44 And shall lay thee even with the ground, and thy children within thee; and they shall not leave in thee one stone upon another; because thou knewest not the time of thy visitation.

The Cleansing of the Temple

45 And he went into the temple, and began to cast out them that sold therein, and them that bought;

46 Saying unto them, It is written, My

Cross references (center column)

22 2Sam. 1:16; Job 15:6; Matt. 12:37; 25:26

26 Matt. 13:12; 25:29; Mark 4:25; Luke 8:18

28 Mark 10:32

29 Matt. 21:1; Mark 11:1

35 2Kgs. 9:13; Matt. 21:7; Mark 11:7; John 12:14

36 Matt. 21:8

38 Ps. 118:26; Luke 2:14; 13:35; Eph. 2:14

40 Hab. 2:11

41 John 11:35

43 Isa. 29:3, 4; Jer. 6:3, 6; Luke 21:20

44 1Kgs. 9:7, 8; Dan. 9:24; Mic. 3:12; Matt. 24:2; Mark 13:2; Luke 1:68, 78; 21:6; 1Pet. 2:12

45 Matt. 21:12; Mark 11:11, 15; John 2:14, 15

46 Isa. 56:7; Jer. 7:11

19:41–42 he beheld the city, and wept over it. Jesus, knowing the certainty of Jerusalem's destruction because of their disobedience, weeps over their future. The prophecy in this passage was fulfilled in A.D. 70 when the Romans destroyed the temple and Jerusalem. Christ had told them about these things previously (Luke 13:34–35; 17:20–37), but they were not heeded by the Jewish people.

19:43 thine enemies shall cast a trench about thee, and compass thee round, and keep thee in on every side. This is an exact description of the kind of siege that the Romans executed in events leading up to the A.D. 70 destruction of Jerusalem, some forty years after Christ's

prophecy.

19:44 because thou knewest not the time of thy visitation. A devout Jew that knew his Old Testament, especially the prediction of the "seventy weeks" of years in Daniel 9:24–27, would have known that the time of Messiah had arrived in their day (see the notes on Daniel 9:24; 9:26; and 9:27). The literal fulfillment of the first sixty-nine weeks of years (483 years) came to completion on the very day of Christ's triumphal entry, which takes place in this passage. This is why Israel should have known the "time" of her visitation.

19:46 My house is the house of prayer. This is a cita-

house is the house of prayer: but ye have made it a den of thieves.

47 And he taught daily in the temple. But the chief priests and the scribes and the chief of the people sought to destroy him,

48 And could not find what they might do: for all the people were very attentive to hear him.

CHAPTER 20
Jesus' Authority Questioned

1 And it came to pass, *that* on one of those days, as he taught the people in the temple, and preached the gospel, the chief priests and the scribes came upon *him* with the elders,

2 And spake unto him, saying, Tell us, by what authority doest thou these things? or who is he that gave thee this authority?

3 And he answered and said unto them, I will also ask you one thing; and answer me:

4 The baptism of John, was it from heaven, or of men?

5 And they reasoned with themselves, saying, If we shall say, From heaven; he will say, Why then believed ye him not?

6 But and if we say, Of men; all the people will stone us: for they be persuaded that John was a prophet.

7 And they answered, that they could not tell whence *it was*.

8 And Jesus said unto them, Neither tell I you by what authority I do these things.

The Parable of the Husbandmen

9 Then began he to speak to the people this parable; A certain man planted a vineyard, and let it forth to husbandmen,

and went into a far country for a long time.

10 And at the season he sent a servant to the husbandmen, that they should give him of the fruit of the vineyard: but the husbandmen beat him, and sent *him* away empty.

11 And again he sent another servant: and they beat him also, and entreated *him* shamefully, and sent *him* away empty.

12 And again he sent a third: and they wounded him also, and cast *him* out.

13 Then said the lord of the vineyard, What shall I do? I will send my beloved son: it may be they will reverence *him* when they see him.

14 But when the husbandmen saw him, they reasoned among themselves, saying, This is the heir: come, let us kill him, that the inheritance may be ours.

15 So they cast him out of the vineyard, and killed *him*. What therefore shall the lord of the vineyard do unto them?

16 He shall come and destroy these husbandmen, and shall give the vineyard to others. And when they heard *it*, they said, God forbid.

17 And he beheld them, and said, What is this then that is written, The stone which the builders rejected, the same is become the head of the corner?

18 Whosoever shall fall upon that stone shall be broken; but on whomsoever it shall fall, it will grind him to powder.

19 And the chief priests and the scribes the same hour sought to lay hands on him; and they feared the people: for they perceived that he had spoken this parable against them.

Cross references (center column):

47 Mark 11:18; John 7:19; 8:37

48 Acts 16:14

1 Matt. 21:23

2 Acts 4:7; 7:27

6 Matt. 14:5; 21:26; Luke 7:29

9 Matt. 21:33; Mark 12:1

17 Ps. 118:22; Matt. 21:42

18 Dan. 2:34, 35; Matt. 21:44

---

tion from Isaiah 56:7, which is in the context of the Millennial Kingdom. In that verse, the prophet predicts that during the Millennium, people from all the nations will flock to the temple to pray. Jesus' citation of the passage in this context is a prophecy about what that temple (His house) will become.

20:9–18 This parable is a prophecy of Israel's treatment of Jesus and the prophets. Repeatedly in the Gospels, Christ tells the nation of Israel that they are treating Him the same way they had treated all of God's other messengers (i.e., the prophets). (For parallel accounts, see Matt. 21:33–41; Mark 12:1–9.)

20:17 The stone which the builders rejected, the same is become the head of the corner. This is a quotation of Psalm 118:22. In the ancient world, the best stone would be used as the cornerstone of the building.

The cornerstone would mark the reference points for both the foundation and the superstructure. The rejection of Jesus by His own nation, Israel, was predicted in the Old Testament (Ps. 118:22; Isa. 28:16; Zech. 3:9); in their misguided discernment they are rejecting perfection. (For parallel accounts, see Matt. 21:42; Mark 12:10.)

20:18 Whosoever shall fall upon that stone shall be broken. This prediction speaks of one falling upon the stone as a picture of salvation from one's sin. The following prediction, "On whomsoever it shall fall, it will grind him to powder," speaks of judgment upon those who do not look to Jesus for salvation. Since earlier predictions in this section of Luke have looked to the A.D. 70 judgment at the hands of the Romans, it seems plausible that this passage also alludes to that event.

Paying Tribute

20 And they watched *him*, and sent forth spies, which should feign themselves just men, that they might take hold of his words, that so they might deliver him unto the power and authority of the governor.
21 And they asked him, saying, Master, we know that thou sayest and teachest rightly, neither acceptest thou the person *of any*, but teachest the way of God truly:
22 Is it lawful for us to give tribute unto Caesar, or no?
23 But he perceived their craftiness, and said unto them, Why tempt ye me?
24 Shew me a penny. Whose image and superscription hath it? They answered and said, Caesar's.
25 And he said unto them, Render therefore unto Caesar the things which be Caesar's and unto God the things which be God's.
26 And they could not take hold of his words before the people: and they marvelled at his answer, and held their peace.

Is There a Resurrection?

27 Then came to *him* certain of the Sadducees, which deny that there is any resurrection: and they asked him,
28 Saying, Master, Moses wrote unto us, If any man's brother die, having a wife, and he die without children, that his brother should take his wife, and raise up seed unto his brother.
29 There were therefore seven brethren: and the first took a wife, and died without children.
30 And the second took her to wife, and he died childless.
31 And the third took her; and in like manner the seven also: and they left no children, and died.
32 Last of all the woman died also.
33 Therefore in the resurrection whose wife of them is she? for seven had her to wife.
34 And Jesus answering said unto them, The children of this world marry, and are given in marriage:

35 But they which shall be accounted worthy to obtain that world, and the resurrection from the dead, neither marry, nor are given in marriage:
36 Neither can they die any more: for they are equal unto the angels; and are the children of God, being the children of the resurrection.
37 Now that the dead are raised, even Moses shewed at the bush, when he calleth the Lord the God of Abraham, and the God of Isaac, and the God of Jacob.
38 For he is not a God of the dead, but of the living: for all live unto him.
39 Then certain of the scribes answering said, Master, thou hast well said.
40 And after that they durst not ask him any *question at all*.

David's Lord

41 And he said unto them, How say they that Christ is David's son?
42 And David himself saith in the book of Psalms, The Lord said unto my Lord, Sit thou on my right hand,
43 Till I make thine enemies thy footstool.
44 David therefore calleth him Lord, how is he then his son?

Jesus Denounces the Scribes

45 Then in the audience of all the people he said unto his disciples,
46 Beware of the scribes, which desire to walk in long robes, and love greetings in the markets, and the highest seats in the synagogues, and the chief rooms at feasts;
47 Which devour widows' houses, and for a shew make long prayers: the same shall receive greater damnation.

CHAPTER 21
The Widow's Offering

1 And he looked up, and saw the rich men casting their gifts into the treasury.
2 And he saw also a certain poor widow casting in thither two mites.
3 And he said, Of a truth I say unto you,

Cross references

20 Matt. 22:15
21 Matt. 22:16; Mark 12:14
24 Matt. 18:28
27 Matt. 22:23; Mark 12:18; Acts 23:6, 8
28 Deut. 25:5
36 1Cor. 15:42, 49, 52; Rom. 8:23; 1John 3:2
37 Ex. 3:6
38 Rom. 6:10, 11
41 Matt. 22:42; Mark 12:35
42 Ps. 110:1; Acts 2:34
45 Matt. 23:1; Mark 12:38
46 Matt. 23:5; Luke 11:43
47 Matt. 23:14
1 Mark 12:41
2 Mark 12:42
3 2Cor. 8:12

20:27–38 Jesus believed in and taught the resurrection from the dead. The Sadducees were a Jewish sect that did not believe in the resurrection of the dead. They formulated a question involving the resurrection in the hopes of making Jesus look bad. As always, Jesus "turned the tables" on them by showing the fallacy of the question. One of their premises was wrong: there will not be marriage in heaven among resurrected humans.

20:41–44 Jesus refers to Psalm 110:1. Christ's enemies will be made His footstool during the Tribulation, after which time Christ will reign on His messianic throne in Jerusalem for one thousand years (Ps. 2; Rev. 20:6). Since Jesus is God, He is David's Lord. He existed before David and all mankind, yet He came into this world as a descendant of David. (For parallel accounts, see Matt. 22:41–46; Mark 12:35–37.)

that this poor widow hath cast in more than they all:

4 For all these have of their abundance cast in unto the offerings of God: but she of her penury hath cast in all the living that she had.

The Temple Will Be Destroyed

5 And as some spake of the temple, how it was adorned with goodly stones and gifts, he said,

6 *As for* these things which ye behold, the days will come, in the which there shall not be left one stone upon another, that shall not be thrown down.

Signs and Persecutions

7 And they asked him, saying, Master, but when shall these things be? and what sign *will there be* when these things shall come to pass?

8 And he said, Take heed that ye be not deceived: for many shall come in my name, saying, I am *Christ*; and the time draweth near: go ye not therefore after them.

9 But when ye shall hear of wars and commotions, be not terrified: for these things must first come to pass; but the end *is* not by and by.

10 Then said he unto them, Nation shall rise against nation, and kingdom against kingdom:

---

5 Matt. 24:1; Mark 13:1

6 Luke 19:44

8 Matt. 3:2; 4:17; 24:4; Mark 13:5; Eph. 5:6; 2Thess. 2:3

10 Matt. 24:7

12 Mark 13:9; Acts 4:3; 5:18; 12:4; 16:24; 25:23; 1Pet. 2:13; Rev. 2:10

13 Phil. 1:28; 2Thess. 1:5

14 Matt. 10:19; Mark 13:11; Luke 12:11

15 Acts 6:10

16 Mic. 7:6; Mark 13:12; Acts 7:59; 12:2

17 Matt. 10:22

18 Matt. 10:30

20 Matt. 24:15; Mark 13:14

---

11 And great earthquakes shall be in divers places, and famines, and pestilences; and fearful sights and great signs shall there be from heaven.

12 But before all these, they shall lay their hands on you, and persecute *you*, delivering *you* up to the synagogues, and into prisons, being brought before kings and rulers for my name's sake.

13 And it shall turn to you for a testimony.

14 Settle *it* therefore in your hearts, not to meditate before what ye shall answer:

15 For I will give you a mouth and wisdom, which all your adversaries shall not be able to gainsay nor resist.

16 And ye shall be betrayed both by parents, and brethren, and kinsfolks, and friends; and *some* of you shall they cause to be put to death.

17 And ye shall be hated of all *men* for my name's sake.

18 But there shall not an hair of your head perish.

19 In your patience possess ye your souls.

The Destruction of Jerusalem Foretold

20 And when ye shall see Jerusalem compassed with armies, then know that the desolation thereof is nigh.

21 Then let them which are in Judea flee to

21:5–36 This is Luke's account of the Olivet Discourse. Unlike Matthew and Mark, which speak exclusively of yet future Tribulation events, Luke deals with both the destruction of Jerusalem in A.D. 70 (Luke 21:5–7, 12–24) and future Tribulation events leading up to Christ's second coming (Luke 21:8–11, 25–36). (For parallel accounts, see Matt. 24—25; Mark 13.)

21:5–6 spake of the temple. Jesus once again predicts the destruction of the temple (19:44) during the A.D. 70 Roman conquest.

21:7 The disciples ask Jesus two questions: 1) "When shall these things be?" and 2) "What sign will there be when these things shall come to pass?" The first question relates to when these things will take place, while the second question asks about signs that will precede this event. It appears that the disciples thought that these things—the destruction of the temple and the return of Christ—would occur simultaneously. However, the temple of Christ's time was destroyed in the A.D. 70 judgment, while the Tribulation with signs leading up to Christ's return has yet to occur.

21:8–11 earthquakes . . . famines . . . pestilences. The items mentioned in these verses parallel the first four seal

judgments of Revelation 6:1–8 and thus refer to events that will take place at the beginning of the Tribulation. While isolated catastrophic events such as the ones listed in this passage occur today with alarming frequency, they do not constitute the global events that will occur during the Tribulation. (For parallel accounts, see Matt. 24:7–8; Mark 13:8.)

21:8 Christ's first warning and sign is about protecting oneself from spiritual deception. The time of the Tribulation will be the greatest time of spiritual deception because of the activities of the Antichrist.

21:11 great earthquakes shall be in divers places. This passage refers to earthquakes all around the globe that will occur throughout the Tribulation (Rev. 6:12; 8:5; 11:13, 19; 16:18), as well as other sorrows inflicted upon humanity during this time.

21:12 But before all these. Before the future Tribulation, Christ's disciples would experience persecution and imprisonment because of their testimony to the name of Christ. This took place before the A.D. 70 judgment upon Jerusalem.

21:20–21 Jerusalem compassed with armies. History

the mountains; and let them which are in the midst of it depart out; and let not them that are in the countries enter thereinto.

22 For these be the days of vengeance, that all things which are written may be fulfilled.

23 But woe unto them that are with child, and to them that give suck, in those days! for there shall be great distress in the land, and wrath upon this people.

24 And they shall fall by the edge of the sword, and shall be led away captive into all nations: and Jerusalem shall be trodden down of the Gentiles, until the times of the Gentiles be fulfilled.

Jesus Will Return

25 And there shall be signs in the sun, and in the moon, and in the stars; and upon the earth distress of nations, with perplexity; the sea and the waves roaring;

26 Men's hearts failing them for fear, and for looking after those things which are

coming on the earth: for the powers of heaven shall be shaken.

27 And then shall they see the Son of man coming in a cloud with power and great glory.

28 And when these things begin to come to pass, then look up, and lift up your heads; for your redemption draweth nigh.

The Parable of the Fig Tree

29 And he spake to them a parable; Behold the fig tree, and all the trees;

30 When they now shoot forth, ye see and know of your own selves that summer is now nigh at hand.

31 So likewise ye, when ye see these things come to pass, know ye that the kingdom of God is nigh at hand.

32 Verily I say unto you, This generation shall not pass away, till all be fulfilled.

33 Heaven and earth shall pass away: but my words shall not pass away.

Cross references (center column):

22 Dan. 9:26; 27; Zech. 11:1
23 Matt. 24:19
24 Dan. 9:27; 12:7; Rom. 11:25
25 Matt. 24:29; Mark 13:24; 2Pet. 3:10, 12
26 Matt. 24:29
27 Matt. 24:30; Rev. 1:7; 14:14
28 Rom. 8:10, 23
29 Matt. 24:32; Mark 13:28
33 Matt. 24:35

---

tells us that the Roman General Vespasian set siege to Jerusalem and then lifted it when he was called back to Rome to become emperor upon the death of Nero. Vespasian's son, Titus, later returned, applied another siege and overthrew the city in A.D. 70. History also records that between sieges, those who had become believers in Jesus as their Messiah heeded Jesus' warning and fled from Jerusalem to the wilderness city of Pella, where they were protected, and not one Christian was killed because they believed this prophecy.

21:22 that all things which are written may be fulfilled. All prophecy about this judgment would be literally fulfilled. This judgment was prophesied throughout the ministry of Christ (Luke 13:9, 34–35; 19:41–44). Such vengeance was also predicted in Leviticus 26:27–39; Deuteronomy 28:49–68; 32:35; Jeremiah 6:1–8; 26:1–9; and Hosea 9:7.

21:23 there shall be great distress in the land. This distress emphasizes the human response to the days of vengeance. God's wrath fell upon the nation of Israel for their rejection of Jesus as their Messiah.

21:24 shall be led away captive into all nations. According to the historian Josephus, the Romans took over 100,000 Jewish captives to Egypt and sold them as slaves to the merchants of the world (see the prediction in Deut. 28:68). The Jewish people will remain an oppressed, scattered people throughout the nations until "the times of the Gentiles" comes to its end. The times of the Gentiles is likely a reference to the prophecy in Daniel 2 and 7 which teaches that history will be dominated by various Gentile powers until the coming of Messiah's

kingdom. Even though many Jews have returned back to their land, Scripture is clear that the times of the Gentiles will not come to an end until Messiah returns and begins His millennial reign.

21:25–26 These two verses summarize the physical judgments of the Tribulation period that lead up to the second coming of Christ as the climax of such events. These global disturbances will cause unbelieving mankind to react in distress, perplexity, and fear. Similar responses are noted in Revelation 6:15–17; 9:20–21; 16:9.

21:27 the Son of man coming. This refers to the bodily, second coming of Christ to the earth at the end of the Tribulation. Jesus does not return to earth in the weakness and obscurity that marked His first coming. Instead, He returns with great power "in a cloud," which is related to His Shechinah glory that has appeared throughout history.

21:28 your redemption draweth nigh. Here, "redemption" refers to physical deliverance; Jewish believers will be rescued out of the final events of the seven-year Tribulation (vv. 25–27) by Christ's glorious appearing.

21:32 This generation shall not pass away, till all be fulfilled. Christ is saying that the generation that sees all "these things" occur—the generation that will go through the Tribulation—will not cease to exist until all the events are literally fulfilled. Christ is telling us that the events of the Tribulation, start to finish, will occur within one generation (17:22–24). (For parallel accounts, see Matt. 24:34; Mark 13:30.)

The Times of the Gentiles

By David W. Breese

Knowing the teaching of Holy Scripture makes life understandable; knowing the content of history can give us a growing appreciation of the Word of God. To aid our understanding, God divides history into different eras. One such era is "the times of the Gentiles" (Luke 21:24), a period of time in which the leadership of the nations has no longer been in the hands of Israel but rather Gentile empires. This period began with the captivity of Judah under the Babylonian King Nebuchadnezzar (2 Chr. 36:21). Since that time, the world has been "trodden down of the Gentiles" (Luke 21:24) and will continue to be until Christ returns for the Church.

This Gentile era has been characterized by many developments: **1)** the emergence of Gentile world power and control (Luke 21:24); **2)** the disappearance of Israel as a world power (Matt. 21:18–20); **3)** the emergence of the Church (Eph. 1:20–23); **4)** the renewal of Israel (Matt. 24:39); **5)** pronouncement of the futility of temple worship (Matt. 24:2); **6)** the Jews being called "lost sheep" by Christ Himself (Matt. 15:24); and **7)** attempted domination by Gentile power over the entire world under the leadership of the Antichrist.

> *Only Christ, returning in power and great glory, can bring to pass a beneficial society.*

The Bible then indicates that the massive force of Gentile world power will be destroyed. The commercial world, centered in the city of Babylon, will be in control for a limited time. The Scriptures announce the devastation of the world's commerce and currency (see Rev. 18:2–3, 9).

When we consider the conditions that characterize the times of the Gentiles, we come to the conclusion that man without God, whatever his abilities may be, cannot succeed. The result of merely human activity, however impressive, will be failure, loss, and final devastation. The world has long boasted that it has no need of God. It has insisted on its own ability to govern by making mere human wisdom as its guide. During the times of the Gentiles, the world will believe many religions, many philosophies, and set many goals. These may be temporarily impressive but, in the last analysis, they will amount to nothing. We do well, therefore, to conclude that the culture can be improved only by divine intervention. Only Christ, returning in power and great glory, can bring to pass a beneficial society. Such a society, as the Scripture clearly teaches, can only exist by altering human nature itself. The world is sinful and, during the times of the Gentiles, is controlled by a fallen human race, which, having steeped itself in sin, has lost its spiritual status. It has "come short of the glory of God" (Rom. 3:23). Man cannot, therefore, trust in "humanity." He must build his life on the one foundation—faith in Jesus Christ, the eternal Son of God.

The final condition of the wealth, the values of the world, is summed up in the Word of God (see Rev. 18:14–15). In the revelation picture, the times of the Gentiles are temporarily magnificent but morally blind. What unbelievers can do in the world may be momentarily attractive but ultimately and totally consumed with devastating fire from heaven. We are to learn then that neither Jew nor Gentile, without God, can produce anything but devastation. We are invited to be aware of, but not in cooperation with, that world program, the times of the Gentiles.

Be Watchful

34 And take heed to yourselves, lest at any time your hearts be overcharged with surfeiting, and drunkenness, and cares of this life, and *so* that day come upon you unawares.

35 For as a snare shall it come on all them that dwell on the face of the whole earth.

36 Watch ye therefore, and pray always, that ye may be accounted worthy to escape all these things that shall come to pass, and to stand before the Son of man.

37 And in the daytime he was teaching in the temple; and at night he went out, and abode in the mount that is called *the mount* of Olives.

38 And all the people came early in the morning to him in the temple, for to hear him.

CHAPTER 22

Passover Is Near

1 Now the feast of unleavened bread drew nigh, which is called the Passover.

2 And the chief priests and scribes sought how they might kill him; for they feared the people.

3 Then entered Satan into Judas surnamed Iscariot, being of the number of the twelve.

4 And he went his way, and communed with the chief priests and captains, how he might betray him unto them.

5 And they were glad, and covenanted to give him money.

6 And he promised, and sought opportunity to betray him unto them in the absence of the multitude.

The Preparation of the Passover

7 Then came the day of unleavened bread, when the passover must be killed.

8 And he sent Peter and John, saying, Go and prepare us the passover, that we may eat.

9 And they said unto him, Where wilt thou that we prepare?

10 And he said unto them, Behold, when ye are entered into the city, there shall a man

meet you, bearing a pitcher of water; follow him into the house where he entereth in.

11 And ye shall say unto the goodman of the house, The Master saith unto thee, Where is the guestchamber, where I shall eat the passover with my disciples?

12 And he shall shew you a large upper room furnished: there make ready.

13 And they went, and found as he had said unto them: and they made ready the passover.

The True Meaning of the Passover Meal

14 And when the hour was come, he sat down, and the twelve apostles with him.

15 And he said unto them, With desire I have desired to eat this passover with you before I suffer:

16 For I say unto you, I will not any more eat thereof, until it be fulfilled in the kingdom of God.

17 And he took the cup, and gave thanks, and said, Take this, and divide *it* among yourselves:

18 For I say unto you, I will not drink of the fruit of the vine, until the kingdom of God shall come.

19 And he took bread, and gave thanks, and brake *it*, and gave unto them, saying, This is my body which is given for you: this do in remembrance of me.

20 Likewise also the cup after supper, saying, This cup *is* the new testament in my blood, which is shed for you.

21 But, behold, the hand of him that betrayeth me *is* with me on the table.

22 And truly the Son of man goeth, as it was determined: but woe unto that man by whom he is betrayed!

23 And they began to inquire among themselves, which of them it was that should do this thing.

Who Is the Greatest?

24 And there was also a strife among them, which of them should be accounted the greatest.

Cross references:

34 Rom. 13:13; 1Pet. 4:7
35 1Thess. 5:2; 2Pet. 3:10; Rev. 3:3; 16:15
36 Ps. 1:5; Matt. 24:42; 25:13; Mark 13:33; Luke 18:1
37 Luke 22:39; John 8:1, 2
1 Matt. 26:2; Mark 14:1
2 Ps. 2:2; John 11:47
3 Matt. 26:14; Mark 14:10; John 13:2, 27
5 Zech. 11:12
7 Matt. 26:17; Mark 14:12
14 Matt. 26:20; Mark 14:17
16 Luke 14:15; Acts 10:41; Rev. 19:9
18 Matt. 26:29; Mark 14:25
19 Matt. 26:26; Mark 14:22; 1Cor. 11:24
20 1Cor. 10:16
21 Ps. 41:9; Matt. 26:21, 23; Mark 14:18; John 13:21, 26
22 Matt. 26:24; Acts 2:23; 4:28
23 Matt. 26:22; John 13:22, 25
24 Mark 9:34; Luke 9:46

22:10–12 Christ predicts details related to the disciples' preparation of the last Passover until His death. This prophecy is fulfilled in the following context (22:13–15).

22:15 before I suffer. This is another prediction by Jesus of His impending death.

22:16–18 This prophecy indicates that the kingdom of God did not arrive at Christ's first coming. Paul, in

1 Corinthians 11:26, builds upon this passage when he says, "As often as you eat this bread . . . you proclaim the Lord's death until He comes."

22:21–23 Christ predicts His betrayal by one of the disciples and speaks a "woe" to him—Judas (cf. Ps. 41:9). This is fulfilled in verses 47–48.

25 And he said unto them, The kings of the Gentiles exercise lordship over them; and they that exercise authority upon them are called benefactors.

26 But ye *shall* not *be* so: but he that is greatest among you, let him be as the younger; and he that is chief, as he that doth serve.

27 For whether *is* greater, he that sitteth at meat, or he that serveth? *is* not he that sitteth at meat? but I am among you as he that serveth.

28 Ye are they which have continued with me in my temptations.

29 And I appoint unto you a kingdom, as my Father hath appointed unto me;

30 That ye may eat and drink at my table in my kingdom, and sit on thrones judging the twelve tribes of Israel.

Jesus Predicts Peter's Denial

31 And the Lord said, Simon, Simon, behold, Satan hath desired *to have* you, that he may sift *you* as wheat:

32 But I have prayed for thee, that thy faith fail not: and when thou art converted, strengthen thy brethren.

33 And he said unto him, Lord, I am ready to go with thee, both into prison, and to death.

34 And he said, I tell thee, Peter, the cock shall not crow this day, before that thou shalt thrice deny that thou knowest me.

Christ's Servants Will Lack Nothing

35 And he said unto them, When I sent you without purse, and scrip, and shoes, lacked ye any thing? And they said, Nothing.

36 Then said he unto them, But now, he that hath a purse, let him take *it*, and likewise *his* scrip: and he that hath no sword, let him sell his garment, and buy one.

37 For I say unto you, that this that is written must yet be accomplished in me, And he was reckoned among the transgressors: for the things concerning me have an end.

38 And they said, Lord, behold, here *are* two swords. And he said unto them, It is enough.

Jesus Prays on the Mount of Olives

39 And he came out, and went, as he was wont, to the mount of Olives; and his disciples also followed him.

40 And when he was at the place, he said unto them, Pray that ye enter not into temptation.

41 And he was withdrawn from them about a stone's cast, and kneeled down, and prayed,

42 Saying, Father, if thou be willing, remove this cup from me: nevertheless not my will, but thine, be done.

43 And there appeared an angel unto him from heaven, strengthening him.

44 And being in an agony he prayed more earnestly: and his sweat was as it were great drops of blood falling down to the ground.

45 And when he rose up from prayer, and was come to his disciples, he found them sleeping for sorrow,

46 And said unto them, Why sleep ye? rise and pray, lest ye enter into temptation.

Judas Betrays the Lord

47 And while he yet spake, behold a multitude, and he that was called Judas, one of the twelve, went before them, and drew near unto Jesus to kiss him.

48 But Jesus said unto him, Judas, betrayest thou the Son of man with a kiss?

49 When they which were about him saw what would follow, they said unto him, Lord, shall we smite with the sword?

50 And one of them smote the servant of the high priest, and cut off his right ear.

51 And Jesus answered and said, Suffer ye thus far. And he touched his ear, and healed him.

52 Then Jesus said unto the chief priests, and captains of the temple, and the elders,

---

Cross references:
25 Matt. 20:25; Mark 10:42
26 Matt. 20:26; Luke 9:48
27 Matt. 20:28; Luke 12:37; John 13:13, 14
29 Matt. 24:47; Luke 12:32
30 Ps. 49:14; Matt. 8:11; 19:28; Luke 14:15; Rev. 3:21; 19:9
32 John 17:9, 11, 15; 21:15-17
34 Matt. 26:34; Mark 14:30; John 13:38
35 Matt. 10:9; Luke 9:3; 10:4
37 Isa. 53:12; Mark 15:28
39 Matt. 26:36; Mark 14:32; Luke 21:37; John 18:1
41 Matt. 26:39; Mark 14:35
42 John 5:30; 6:38
43 Matt. 4:11
44 John 12:27; Heb. 5:7
47 Matt. 26:47; Mark 14:43; John 18:3
50 Matt. 26:51; Mark 14:47; John 18:10

22:29–30 I appoint unto you a kingdom. Christ's disciples, devoid of understanding that Jesus would soon be crucified, are anticipating their various roles in Christ's kingdom, which they think is just days away. Jesus promises His disciples that they will indeed have lofty positions in His future Millennial Kingdom (cf. Rev. 3:21). The disciples are also promised a personal relationship with Jesus in this future kingdom (see also Matt. 19:28) and will have some role in judging or ruling over the twelve tribes of Israel (see Rev. 20:4).

22:31–35 before that thou shalt thrice deny that thou knowest me. This prophecy was fulfilled a few hours later when Peter denied his Lord (vv. 54–62; cf. John 21:15–25).

22:37 Jesus quotes from Isaiah 53:12 concerning the death that He would die on behalf of sinners. In fulfillment of that prophecy, He would be "reckoned among the transgressors."

which were come to him, Be ye come out, as against a thief, with swords and staves?

53 When I was daily with you in the temple, ye stretched forth no hands against me: but this is your hour, and the power of darkness.

Peter's Denial of Jesus

54 Then took they him, and led *him,* and brought him into the high priest's house. And Peter followed afar off.

55 And when they had kindled a fire in the midst of the hall, and were set down together, Peter sat down among them.

56 But a certain maid beheld him as he sat by the fire, and earnestly looked upon him, and said, This man was also with him.

57 And he denied him, saying, Woman, I know him not.

58 And after a little while another saw him, and said, Thou art also of them. And Peter said, Man, I am not.

59 And about the space of one hour after another confidently affirmed, saying, Of a truth this *fellow* also was with him: for he is a Galilaean.

60 And Peter said, Man, I know not what thou sayest. And immediately, while he yet spake, the cock crew.

61 And the Lord turned, and looked upon Peter. And Peter remembered the word of the Lord, how he had said unto him, Before the cock crow, thou shalt deny me thrice.

62 And Peter went out, and wept bitterly.

Mocking and Beating of Jesus

63 And the men that held Jesus mocked him, and smote him.

64 And when they had blindfolded him, they struck him on the face, and asked him, saying, Prophesy, who is it that smote thee?

65 And many other things blasphemously spake they against him.

Jesus before the Council

66 And as soon as it was day, the elders of the people and the chief priests and the scribes came together, and led him into their council, saying,

67 Art thou the Christ? tell us. And he said unto them, If I tell you, ye will not believe:

68 And if I also ask *you,* ye will not answer me, nor let *me* go.

69 Hereafter shall the Son of man sit on the right hand of the power of God.

70 Then said they all, Art thou then the Son of God? And he said unto them, Ye say that I am.

71 And they said, What need we any further witness? for we ourselves have heard of his own mouth.

CHAPTER 23
Jesus Brought before Pilate

1 And the whole multitude of them arose, and led him unto Pilate.

2 And they began to accuse him, saying, We found this *fellow* perverting the nation, and forbidding to give tribute to Caesar, saying that he himself is Christ a King.

3 And Pilate asked him, saying, Art thou the King of the Jews? And he answered him and said, Thou sayest *it.*

4 Then said Pilate to the chief priests and *to* the people, I find no fault in this man.

5 And they were the more fierce, saying, He stirreth up the people, teaching throughout all Jewry, beginning from Galilee to this place.

Jesus before Herod

6 When Pilate heard of Galilee, he asked whether the man were a Galilaean.

7 And as soon as he knew that he belonged unto Herod's jurisdiction, he sent him to Herod, who himself also was at Jerusalem at that time.

8 And when Herod saw Jesus, he was exceeding glad: for he was desirous to see him of a long *season,* because he had heard many things of him; and he hoped to have seen some miracle done by him.

9 Then he questioned with him in many words; but he answered him nothing.

10 And the chief priests and scribes stood and vehemently accused him.

11 And Herod with his men of war set him at nought, and mocked *him,* and arrayed him in a gorgeous robe, and sent him again to Pilate.

12 And the same day Pilate and Herod were made friends together: for before they were at enmity between themselves.

Jesus Sentenced to Die

13 And Pilate, when he had called together the chief priests and the rulers and the people,

---

22:69 Jesus references Psalm 110:1 before the religious leaders. This passage speaks of His future second coming in judgment.

14 Said unto them, Ye have brought this man unto me, as one that perverteth the people: and, behold, I, having examined *him* before you, have found no fault in this man touching those things whereof ye accuse him:
15 No, nor yet Herod: for I sent you to him; and, lo, nothing worthy of death is done unto him.
16 I will therefore chastise him, and release *him.*
17 (For of necessity he must release one unto them at the feast.)
18 And they cried out all at once, saying, Away with this *man,* and release unto us Barabbas:
19 (Who for a certain sedition made in the city, and for murder, was cast into prison.)
20 Pilate therefore, willing to release Jesus, spake again to them.
21 But they cried, saying, Crucify *him,* crucify him.
22 And he said unto them the third time, Why, what evil hath he done? I have found no cause of death in him: I will therefore chastise him, and let *him* go.
23 And they were instant with loud voices, requiring that he might be crucified. And the voices of them and of the chief priests prevailed.
24 And Pilate gave sentence that it should be as they required.
25 And he released unto them him that for sedition and murder was cast into prison, whom they had desired; but he delivered Jesus to their will.

The Way to the Cross

26 And as they led him away, they laid hold upon one Simon, a Cyrenian, coming out of the country, and on him they laid the cross, that he might bear *it* after Jesus.
27 And there followed him a great company of people, and of women, which also bewailed and lamented him.
28 But Jesus turning unto them said,

Daughters of Jerusalem, weep not for me, but weep for yourselves, and for your children.
29 For, behold, the days are coming, in the which they shall say, Blessed *are* the barren, and the wombs that never bare, and the paps which never gave suck.
30 Then shall they begin to say to the mountains, Fall on us; and to the hills, Cover us.
31 For if they do these things in a green tree, what shall be done in the dry?
32 And there were also two other, malefactors, led with him to be put to death.
33 And when they were come to the place, which is called Calvary, there they crucified him, and the malefactors, one on the right hand, and the other on the left.
34 Then said Jesus, Father, forgive them; for they know not what they do. And they parted his raiment, and cast lots.
35 And the people stood beholding. And the rulers also with them derided *him,* saying, He saved others; let him save himself, if he be Christ, the chosen of God.
36 And the soldiers also mocked him, coming to him, and offering him vinegar,
37 And saying, If thou be the king of the Jews, save thyself.
38 And a superscription also was written over him in letters of Greek, and Latin, and Hebrew, THIS IS THE KING OF THE JEWS.
39 And one of the malefactors which were hanged railed on him, saying, If thou be Christ, save thyself and us.
40 But the other answering rebuked him, saying, Dost not thou fear God, seeing thou art in the same condemnation?
41 And we indeed justly; for we receive the due reward of our deeds: but this man hath done nothing amiss.
42 And he said unto Jesus, Lord, remember me when thou comest into thy kingdom.
43 And Jesus said unto him, Verily I say unto thee, Today shalt thou be with me in paradise.

14 Luke 23:1, 2, 4
16 Matt. 27:26; John 19:1
17 Matt. 27:15; Mark 15:6; John 18:39
18 Acts 3:14
24 Ex. 23:2; Matt. 27:26; Mark 15:15; John 19:16
26 Matt. 27:32; Mark 15:21; John 19:17
29 Matt. 24:19; Luke 21:23
30 Isa. 2:19; Hos. 10:8; Rev. 6:16; 9:6
31 Prov. 11:31; Jer. 25:29; Ezek. 20:47; 21:3, 4; 1Pet. 4:17
32 Isa. 53:12; Matt. 27:38
33 Matt. 27:33; Mark 15:22; John 19:17, 18
34 Matt. 5:44; 27:35; Mark 15:24; John 19:23; Acts 3:17; 7:60; 1Cor. 4:12
35 Ps. 22:17; Zech. 12:10; Matt. 27:39; Mark 15:29
38 Matt. 27:37; Mark 15:26; John 19:19
39 Matt. 27:44; Mark 15:32

23:28 Daughters of Jerusalem. In the ancient world women were often hired to weep and wail at a funeral or tragedy. Some were weeping for Him, but as Jesus looks ahead to the coming judgment in A.D. 70, He tells them to mourn for their own tragedy to come.

23:37–38 THIS IS THE KING OF THE JEWS. In their unbelief and sarcasm the Romans put this sign above Jesus on the cross, which in an ironic sense is prophetic

of His future millennial reign and eternal glory. (For parallel accounts, see Matt. 27:27; Mark 15:26.)

23:42–43 Today shalt thou be with me in paradise. Jesus made this promise to the repentant thief. Each person's eternal destiny is based upon whether his or her sins are forgiven by the Lord of the universe—Jesus Christ. When an individual dies as a believer in Christ, he or she joins Jesus instantly in paradise.

The Death of Jesus

44 And it was about the sixth hour, and there was a darkness over all the earth until the ninth hour.

45 And the sun was darkened, and the veil of the temple was rent in the midst.

46 And when Jesus had cried with a loud voice, he said, Father, into thy hands I commend my spirit: and having said thus, he gave up the ghost.

47 Now when the centurion saw what was done, he glorified God, saying, Certainly this was a righteous man.

48 And all the people that came together to that sight, beholding the things which were done, smote their breasts, and returned.

49 And all his acquaintance, and the women that followed him from Galilee, stood afar off, beholding these things.

The Burial of Jesus

50 And, behold, *there was* a man named Joseph, a counsellor; *and he was* a good man, and a just:

51 (The same had not consented to the counsel and deed of them;) *he was* of Arimathaea, a city of the Jews: who also himself waited for the kingdom of God.

52 This *man* went unto Pilate, and begged the body of Jesus.

53 And he took it down, and wrapped it in linen, and laid it in a sepulchre that was hewn in stone, wherein never man before was laid.

54 And that day was the preparation, and the sabbath drew on.

55 And the women also, which came with him from Galilee, followed after, and beheld the sepulchre, and how his body was laid.

56 And they returned, and prepared spices and ointments; and rested the sabbath day according to the commandment.

CHAPTER 24
The Resurrection of Jesus

1 Now upon the first *day* of the week, very early in the morning, they came unto the sepulchre, bringing the spices which they had prepared, and certain *others* with them.

2 And they found the stone rolled away from the sepulchre.

3 And they entered in, and found not the body of the Lord Jesus.

4 And it came to pass, as they were much perplexed thereabout, behold, two men stood by them in shining garments:

5 And as they were afraid, and bowed down *their* faces to the earth, they said unto them, Why seek ye the living among the dead?

6 He is not here, but is risen: remember how he spake unto you when he was yet in Galilee,

7 Saying, the Son of man must be delivered into the hands of sinful men, and be crucified, and the third day rise again.

8 And they remembered his words,

9 And returned from the sepulchre, and told all these things unto the eleven, and to all the rest.

10 It was Mary Magdalene and Joanna, and Mary *the mother* of James, and other *women that were* with them, which told these things unto the apostles.

11 And their words seemed to them as idle tales, and they believed them not.

12 Then arose Peter, and ran unto the sepulchre; and stooping down, he beheld the linen clothes laid by themselves, and departed, wondering in himself at that which was come to pass.

The Road to Emmaus

13 And, behold, two of them went that same day to a village called Emmaus, which was from Jerusalem *about* threescore furlongs.

14 And they talked together of all these things which had happened.

15 And it came to pass, that, while they communed *together* and reasoned, Jesus himself drew near, and went with them.

16 But their eyes were holden that they should not know him.

17 And he said unto them, What manner of communications *are* these that ye have one to another, as ye walk, and are sad?

18 And the one of them, whose name was Cleopas, answering said unto him, Art thou only a stranger in Jerusalem, and hast not known the things which are come to pass there in these days?

19 And he said unto them, What things? And they said unto him, Concerning Jesus of Nazareth, which was a prophet mighty in deed and word before God and all the people:

20 And how the chief priests and our rulers delivered him to be condemned to death, and have crucified him.

---

44 Matt. 27:45; Mark 15:33
45 Matt. 27:51; Mark 15:38
46 Ps. 31:5; Matt. 27:50; Mark 15:37; John 19:30
47 Matt. 27:54; Mark 15:39
49 Ps. 38:11; Matt. 27:55; Mark 15:40; John 19:25
50 Matt. 27:57; Mark 15:42; John 19:38
51 Mark 15:43; Luke 2:25, 38
53 Matt. 27:59; Mark 15:46
54 Matt. 27:62
55 Mark 15:47
56 Ex. 20:10; Mark 16:1
1 Matt. 28:1; Mark 16:1; John 20:1
2 Matt. 28:2; Mark 16:4
3 Mark 16:5
4 John 20:12; Acts 1:10
6 Matt. 16:21; 17:23; Mark 8:31; 9:31; Luke 9:22
9 Matt. 28:8; Mark 16:10
11 Mark 16:11
12 John 20:3, 6
13 Mark 16:12
15 Matt. 18:20; Luke 24:36
16 John 20:14; 21:4
18 John 19:25
19 Matt. 21:11
20 Luke 23:1; Acts 13:27, 28

The Signs of Our Lord's Return

By David R. Reagan

Jesus said we cannot know the date of His return (Matt. 24:36). But the signs we are told to look for make it possible for believers to know the season of the Lord's return. Paul makes this clear in 1 Thessalonians 5:2, 4–6 where he says, "For yourselves know perfectly that the day of the Lord so cometh as a thief in the night. But ye, brethren, are not in darkness, that that day should overtake you as a thief. Ye are all the children of light, and the children of the day: we are not of the night, nor of darkness. Therefore let us not sleep, as do others; but let us watch and be sober."

There are many more signs about Christ's second coming than His first because God knew that untold millions would be reading His Word long after the first advent; therefore, He wanted information regarding Christ's return to encourage multitudes to repent and trust in the name of Jesus (see 2 Pet. 3:9). Jesus said that when we see the signs being fulfilled, we can "know that it [His second coming] is near, even at the doors" (Matt. 24:33). Below is a comprehensive list of some of these signs.

Certain signs make it possible for believers to know the season of our Lord's return.

Signs of Nature (Matt. 24:7): famine, earthquakes, plagues, signs in the heavens.

Signs of Society (2 Tim. 3:1–4): lawlessness, violence, immorality, greed, selfishness, hedonism, rebellion, despair.

Negative Spiritual Signs: false christs and prophets and their cultic groups (Matt. 24:24), apostasy and widespread heresy in the Church (2 Tim. 3:5; 4:1–4), religious and economic globalism (Rev. 17—18), persecution of believers (Matt. 24:9–10; Mark 13:9, 11–13; Luke 21:12–19), outbreak of demonic and occult activity (1 Tim. 4:1).

Positive Spiritual Signs: outpouring of the Holy Spirit (Joel 2:28–29), revival of Davidic-style worship (Amos 9:11), worldwide evangelism (Mark 13:10), understanding of Bible prophecy (Dan. 12:4, 8–9).

World Political Signs: Arab hostility toward Israel (Ezek. 35:1—36:7), military powers to the "far north" (perhaps Russia) threatening Israel (Ezek. 38:1—39:16), Asian nations capable of fielding an army of two hundred million (Rev. 9:15–16; 16:12), wars and rumors of wars (Matt. 24:6–7; Mark 13:7–8; Luke 21:10), reunification of Europe (Dan. 2:41–44; 7:8, 24–25; 9:26).

The Accelerator Signs: population explosion (Rev. 9:15–16), increase in knowledge (Dan. 12:4), increase in violence (Matt. 24:12).

Signs of Israel: regathering of the people (Isa. 11:10–12; Ezek. 37:1–12), re-establishment of the state (Zech. 12:1–6; Matt. 24:32–35), reclamation of the land (Isa. 35:1–2, 7), resurgence of the military (Zech. 12:6), re-occupation of Jerusalem (Zech. 12:2–6).

The signs of Israel are more important than all the rest put together, for the Jews are God's prophetic time clock. Jesus Himself states in Luke 21:24 that we are to watch Jerusalem, and that when we see the city no longer under Gentile domination, we will know that the time has come for Him to return. All of these signs point to the beginning of the Tribulation and the second coming of Jesus. However, when we see the signs, we can be sure that the Rapture is imminent, for it will occur before the Tribulation begins.

21 But we trusted that it had been he which should have redeemed Israel: and beside all this, today is the third day since these things were done.

22 Yea, and certain women also of our company made us astonished, which were early at the sepulchre;

23 And when they found not his body, they came, saying, that they had also seen a vision of angels, which said that he was alive.

24 And certain of them which were with us went to the sepulchre, and found *it* even so as the women had said: but him they saw not.

25 Then he said unto them, O fools, and slow of heart to believe all that the prophets have spoken:

26 Ought not Christ to have suffered these things, and to enter into his glory?

27 And beginning at Moses and all the prophets, he expounded unto them in all the scriptures the things concerning himself.

28 And they drew nigh unto the village, whither they went: and he made as though he would have gone further.

29 But they constrained him, saying, Abide with us: for it is toward evening, and the day is far spent. And he went in to tarry with them.

30 And it came to pass, as he sat at meat with them, he took bread, and blessed *it*, and brake, and gave to them.

31 And their eyes were opened, and they knew him; and he vanished out of their sight.

32 And they said one to another, Did not our heart burn within us, while he talked with us by the way, and while he opened to us the scriptures?

33 And they rose up the same hour, and returned to Jerusalem, and found the eleven gathered together, and them that were with them,

34 Saying, The Lord is risen indeed, and hath appeared to Simon.

35 And they told what things *were done* in the way, and how he was known of them in breaking of bread.

21 Luke 1:68; 2:38; Acts 1:6

22 Matt. 28:8; Mark 16:10; Luke 24:9, 10; John 20:18

27 Gen. 3:15; 49:10; Num. 21:9; Deut. 18:15; Ps. 16:9, 10; 22; 132:11; Isa. 7:14; Jer. 23:5; Ezek. 34:23; 37:25; Dan. 9:24; Mic. 7:20; Mal. 3:1; 4:2

31 Luke 4:30; John 8:59

34 1Cor. 15:5

36 Mark 16:14

37 Mark 6:49

39 John 20:20, 27

41 Gen. 45:26; John 21:5

44 Matt. 16:21; 17:22; 20:18; Mark 8:31

46 Isa. 50:6; 53:2-12; Acts 17:3

47 Isa. 49:6, 22; Acts 13:38, 46

48 John 15:27; Acts 1:8, 22; 2:32; 3:15

49 Isa. 44:3; John 14:16, 26; 15:26; 16:7; Acts 1:4; 2:1-4

50 Acts 1:12

51 Mark 16:19; John 20:17; Acts 1:9

52 Matt. 28:9, 17

Jesus Appears to the Disciples

36 And as they thus spake, Jesus himself stood in the midst of them, and saith unto them, Peace *be* unto you.

37 But they were terrified and affrighted, and supposed that they had seen a spirit.

38 And he said unto them, Why are ye troubled? and why do thoughts arise in your hearts?

39 Behold my hands and my feet, that it is I myself: handle me, and see; for a spirit hath not flesh and bones, as ye see me have.

40 And when he had thus spoken, he shewed them *his* hands and *his* feet.

41 And while they yet believed not for joy, and wondered, he said unto them, Have ye here any meat?

42 And they gave him a piece of a broiled fish, and of an honeycomb.

43 And he took *it*, and did eat before them.

44 And he said unto them, These *are* the words which I spake unto you, while I was yet with you, that all things must be fulfilled, which were written in the law of Moses, and *in* the prophets, and *in* the psalms, concerning me.

45 Then opened he their understanding, that they might understand the scriptures,

46 And said unto them, Thus it is written, and thus it behoved Christ to suffer, and to rise from the dead the third day:

47 And that repentance and remission of sins should be preached in his name among all nations, beginning at Jerusalem.

48 And ye are witnesses of these things.

49 And, behold, I send the promise of my Father upon you: but tarry ye in the city of Jerusalem, until ye be endued with power from on high.

The Ascension of Jesus

50 And he led them out as far as to Bethany, and he lifted up his hands, and blessed them.

51 And it came to pass, while he blessed them, he was parted from them, and carried up into heaven.

52 And they worshipped him, and returned to Jerusalem with great joy:

53 And were continually in the temple, praising and blessing God. Amen.

24:21 But we trusted that it had been he which should have redeemed Israel. As these two men walked on the road to Emmaus and talked with the resurrected Christ, they did not realize how His death had accomplished the redemption of Israel they longed to see. Since they were talking to the resurrected Jesus on the third day after His crucifixion, this passage is proof that His prophecy about the Resurrection had been fulfilled.

John

The apostle John is believed to have written this book while in the city of Ephesus. Though John's name is never mentioned in the gospel of John, it is assumed that he is referring to himself when he speaks of the disciple "whom Jesus loved." He was the youngest of the original Twelve Disciples and the brother of James. Because of the zeal shown by James and John, Jesus nicknamed them the "sons of thunder." The book reveals Jesus as the Light and Life, and the Father as the Loving God.

Beginning with a prologue that affirms Jesus as the Word (the *Logos*) of God, John sets forth seven miracles/signs showing Christ's supernatural power (see 2:1–11; 4:46–54; 5:1–47; 6:1–14; 6:15–21; 9:1–41; 11:1–57). Seven times Jesus announces that He is the "I AM" (6:35; 8:12; 8:58; 10:11; 11:25; 14:6; 15:1; cf. Exodus 3:14). Christ's sublime deity is the emphasis of John.

Almost half of the verses in the gospel of John contain words spoken by Jesus, more than any other Gospel. The Upper Room Discourse (14—17), spoken the night before the Crucifixion, is found only in John. As a historian, theologian, and personal disciple, John goes beyond a mere biographical picture to present Christ's unique, glowing personality and divinity with the aim of convincing the lost to believe in Jesus.

Along with Christ's rejection, death, and resurrection, many other prophetic statements have been fulfilled, such as the coming of the Holy Spirit. Jesus' first clear prediction about the Rapture appears in 14:2–3 in which He promises, "I will come again, and receive you unto myself." That all believers will be one in heaven (17:20–23) is an event that is yet to happen. The last prediction contains a hint that believers would be alive when Christ comes (21:18, 22) and suggests the martyr's death of Peter.

There are 45 separate predictions found in 180 verses out of a total of 866, or 20 percent of the content. John contains 25 quotations from the Old Testament.

Author
John the Apostle

Date
A.D. 90

Key Truth
Jesus Is the Son of God

Historic Time
Preincarnate Work of Christ to His Post-Resurrection Appearances

Key Verse
20:31
But these are written, that ye might believe that Jesus is the Christ.

20% Prophecy

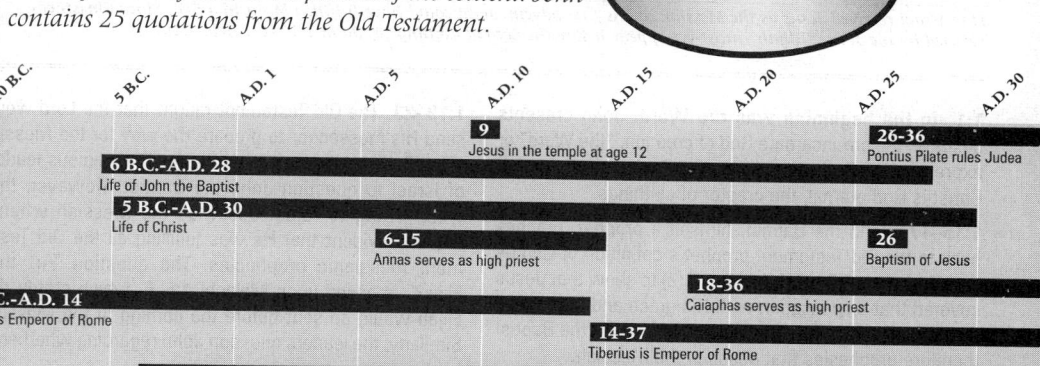

10 B.C.	5 B.C.	A.D. 1	A.D. 5	A.D. 10	A.D. 15	A.D. 20	A.D. 25	A.D. 30

9
Jesus in the temple at age 12

26-36
Pontius Pilate rules Judea

6 B.C.-A.D. 28
Life of John the Baptist

5 B.C.-A.D. 30
Life of Christ

6-15
Annas serves as high priest

26
Baptism of Jesus

18-36
Caiaphas serves as high priest

B.C.-A.D. 14
us is Emperor of Rome

14-37
Tiberius is Emperor of Rome

4 B.C.-A.D. 39
Herod Antipas rules over Galilee

26-30
Events of the Gospel of John

CHAPTER 1
The Word Became Flesh

1 In the beginning was the Word, and the Word was with God, and the Word was God.
2 The same was in the beginning with God.
3 All things were made by him; and without him was not any thing made that was made.
4 In him was life; and the life was the light of men.
5 And the light shineth in darkness; and the darkness comprehended it not.
6 There was a man sent from God, whose name *was* John.
7 The same came for a witness, to bear witness of the Light, that all *men* through him might believe.
8 He was not that Light, but *was sent* to bear witness of that Light.
9 *That* was the true Light, which lighteth every man that cometh into the world.
10 He was in the world, and the world was made by him, and the world knew him not.
11 He came unto his own, and his own received him not.

12 But as many as received him, to them gave he power to become the sons of God, *even* to them that believe on his name:
13 Which were born, not of blood, nor of the will of the flesh, nor of the will of man, but of God.
14 And the Word was made flesh, and dwelt among us, (and we beheld his glory, the glory as of the only begotten of the Father,) full of grace and truth.
15 John bare witness of him, and cried, saying, This was he of whom I spake, He that cometh after me is preferred before me: for he was before me.
16 And of his fulness have all we received, and grace for grace.
17 For the law was given by Moses, *but* grace and truth came by Jesus Christ.
18 No man hath seen God at any time; the only begotten Son, which is in the bosom of the Father, he hath declared *him*.

The Testimony of John the Baptist

19 And this is the record of John, when the Jews sent priests and Levites from Jerusalem to ask him, Who art thou?

Cross references

1 1John 1:1, 2; 5:7; Rev. 1:2; 19:13
2 Gen. 1:1
3 Ps. 33:6
4 John 5:26; 1John 5:11
5 John 3:19
6 Mal. 3:1
9 1John 2:8
12 Isa. 56:5; Rom. 8:15; Gal. 3:26
14 Isa. 40:5; 1Tim. 3:16; Heb. 2:11, 14, 16, 17; 2Pet. 1:17
15 Matt. 3:11; Mark 1:7; Luke 3:16
16 Eph. 1:6-8
17 Ex. 20:1-17; Deut. 4:44; 5:1; 33:4; John 8:32
18 Ex. 33:20; Deut. 4:12

Elijah and John the Baptist in Scripture

1 and 2 Kings	Malachi	Gospels	Jesus' Words	Revelation
Elijah was a historical prophet ca. 874 B.C.	Elijah's return is prophesied ca. 430 B.C.	John was a chosen prophet 7 B.C. to A.D. 29	Elijah and John are compared A.D. 29	Is Elijah one of two future witnesses? Rev. 11:3–12
Sudden appearance 1 Kgs. 17:1	Sudden appearance Mal. 4:5	Sudden appearance Matt. 3:1–12; Luke 3:1–18	Elijah has come Matt. 11:14	Sudden appearance Rev. 11:3, cf. James 5:17
Ministry and miracles 1 Kgs. 17—2 Kgs. 1	Ministry of restoration Mal. 4:6; Matt. 17:11	Ministry of preparation Luke 1:13–17	Elijah will come Matt. 17:10–11 Luke 9:27–30	Ministry of warning and judgment Rev. 11:3–6
Translation into heaven 2 Kings 2	At each Passover the Jews still await his coming	Imprisonment and martyrdom Mark 6:14–30	Elijah at the Transfiguration Matt. 17:1–9 Luke 9:27–30	Slain by the Beast, rises and ascends Rev. 11:7–12

Had Israel received Jesus as the Messiah at His first advent, John could have fulfilled Malachi 4:5–6. Since Christ was rejected by the Jews, "Elijah" must yet appear before the Second Coming (cf. John 1:11–13; Heb. 9:28).

1:1 In the beginning was the Word. John presents Jesus as the pre-incarnate God of creation, "the Word" or expression of God, as well as the Savior of the world. Christ is God eternal, the creator of all things.

1:15–17 John the Baptist, himself a prophet, reaches back to the Old Testament prophet's definition of God as gracious, merciful, and kind (Jon. 4:2) to show that Jesus covered that dispensation with His grace and introduced the new dispensation, "grace and truth." John the Baptist therefore prophesies that Jesus is the Messiah.

1:19–23 The Old Testament taught that the Lord would send His messenger to prepare the way for the Messiah (Mal. 3:1), so it was not wrong for the religious leaders of Israel to question John the Baptist. However, they were wrong to reject Jesus as the Messiah when it became evident that He was fulfilling all the Old Testament messianic prophecies. The question "Art thou Elias?" is based upon Malachi 4:5–6, which states that Elijah would be sent before the coming of the Messiah. Similarly, the leaders question John regarding whether he

20 And he confessed, and denied not; but confessed, I am not the Christ.

21 And they asked him, What then? Art thou Elias? And he saith, I am not. Art thou that Prophet? And he answered, No.

22 Then said they unto him, Who art thou? that we may give an answer to them that sent us. What sayest thou of thyself?

23 He said, I *am* the voice of one crying in the wilderness, Make straight the way of the Lord, as said the prophet Esaias.

24 And they which were sent were of the Pharisees.

25 And they asked him, and said unto him, Why baptizest thou then, if thou be not that Christ, nor Elias, neither that prophet?

26 John answered them, saying, I baptize with water: but there standeth one among you, whom ye know not;

27 He it is, who coming after me is preferred before me, whose shoe's latchet I am not worthy to unloose.

28 These things were done in Bethabara beyond Jordan, where John was baptizing.

The Lamb of God

29 The next day John seeth Jesus coming unto him, and saith, Behold the Lamb of God, which taketh away the sin of the world.

30 This is he of whom I said, After me cometh a man which is preferred before me: for he was before me.

31 And I knew him not: but that he should be made manifest to Israel, therefore am I come baptizing with water.

32 And John bare record, saying, I saw the Spirit descending from heaven like a dove, and it abode upon him.

33 And I knew him not: but he that sent me to baptize with water, the same said unto me, Upon whom thou shalt see the Spirit descending, and remaining on him, the same is he which baptizeth with the Holy Ghost.

34 And I saw, and bare record that this is the Son of God.

The First Disciples

35 Again the next day after John stood, and two of his disciples;

36 And looking upon Jesus as he walked, he saith, Behold the Lamb of God!

37 And the two disciples heard him speak, and they followed Jesus.

38 Then Jesus turned, and saw them following, and saith unto them, What seek ye? They said unto him, Rabbi, (which is to say, being interpreted, Master,) where dwellest thou?

39 He saith unto them, Come and see. They came and saw where he dwelt, and abode with him that day: for it was about the tenth hour.

40 One of the two which heard John *speak,* and followed him, was Andrew, Simon Peter's brother.

41 He first findeth his own brother Simon, and saith unto him, We have found the Messias, which is, being interpreted, the Christ.

42 And he brought him to Jesus. And when Jesus beheld him, he said, Thou art Simon the son of Jona: thou shalt be called Cephas, which is by interpretation, A stone.

Jesus Calls Philip and Nathanael

43 The day following Jesus would go forth into Galilee, and findeth Philip, and saith unto him, Follow me.

44 Now Philip was of Bethsaida, the city of Andrew and Peter.

45 Philip findeth Nathanael, and saith unto him, We have found him, of whom Moses in

Cross-references

20 Luke 3:15; John 3:28
21 Deut. 18:15, 18; Mal. 4:5; Matt. 17:10
23 Isa. 40:3; Matt. 3:3; Mark 1:3; Luke 3:4; John 3:28
26 Mal. 3:1; Matt. 3:11
27 John 1:15, 30
28 Judg. 7:24; John 10:40
29 Ex. 12:3; Isa. 53:7, 11; John 1:36; Heb. 1:3; 2:17; 9:28; Rev. 1:5; 5:6-10
30 John 1:15, 27
31 Matt. 3:6; Luke 1:17, 76, 77; 3:3, 4
32 Matt. 3:16; Mark 1:10; Luke 3:22
33 Matt. 3:11; Acts 1:5; 2:4; 10:44; 19:6
40 Matt. 4:18
42 Matt. 16:18
44 John 12:21
45 Gen. 3:15; 49:10; Deut. 18:18; Isa. 4:2; 7:14; 9:6; 53:2

---

is "that Prophet," the messianic prophet that Moses said God would raise up (Deut. 18:15). John the Baptist denied he was the prophesied Messiah, but declared himself to be the fulfillment of the prophecy of Isaiah 40:3 as the herald or "voice" who announces the Messiah.

1:29, 36 the Lamb of God, which taketh away the sin of the world. This designates Jesus as the sin-bearer of the world that fulfills all the sacrifices of the Old Testament sacrificial system. Only the blood of God's own Son could possibly cleanse the whole world from its sins. This statement also attests to Jesus' moral and personal perfection, for John knew that only the lamb "without blemish and without spot" (1 Pet. 1:19) could be the Lamb of God.

1:33 Upon whom thou shalt see the Spirit descending, and remaining. The Lord had revealed to John the Baptist that the Messiah would be known by this event. The fulfillment of this prophecy in Jesus is attested to by John the Baptist: "I saw, and bare record that this is the Son of God" (v. 34).

1:45 Philip tells Nathanael that Jesus is the One "of whom Moses in the law (Deut. 18:15–19), and the prophets did write" (Isa. 52:13—53:12; Dan. 7:13; Micah 5:2; Zech. 9:9). Both of these men became members of the twelve apostles. The fact that Philip could recognize that Jesus was the Messiah is proof that he had studied these Old Testament prophecies.

the law, and the prophets, did write, Jesus of Nazareth, the son of Joseph.

46 And Nathanael said unto him, Can there any good thing come out of Nazareth? Philip saith unto him, Come and see.

47 Jesus saw Nathanael coming to him, and saith of him, Behold an Israelite indeed, in whom is no guile!

48 Nathanael saith unto him, Whence knowest thou me? Jesus answered and said unto him, Before that Philip called thee, when thou wast under the fig tree, I saw thee.

49 Nathanael answered and saith unto him, Rabbi, thou art the Son of God; thou art the King of Israel.

50 Jesus answered and said unto him, Because I said unto thee, I saw thee under the fig tree, believest thou? thou shalt see greater things than these.

51 And he saith unto him, Verily, verily, I say unto you, Hereafter ye shall see heaven open, and the angels of God ascending and descending upon the Son of man.

CHAPTER 2
The First Miracle

1 And the third day there was a marriage in Cana of Galilee; and the mother of Jesus was there:

2 And both Jesus was called, and his disciples, to the marriage.

3 And when they wanted wine, the mother of Jesus saith unto him, They have no wine.

4 Jesus saith unto her, Woman, what have I to do with thee? mine hour is not yet come.

5 His mother saith unto the servants, Whatsoever he saith unto you, do *it*.

6 And there were set there six waterpots of stone, after the manner of the purifying of the Jews, containing two or three firkins apiece.

7 Jesus saith unto them, Fill the waterpots with water. And they filled them up to the brim.

8 And he saith unto them, Draw out now, and bear unto the governor of the feast. And they bare *it*.

9 When the ruler of the feast had tasted the water that was made wine, and knew not whence it was: (but the servants which drew the water knew;) the governor of the feast called the bridegroom,

10 And saith unto him, Every man at the beginning doth set forth good wine; and when men have well drunk, then that which is worse: *but* thou hast kept the good wine until now.

11 This beginning of miracles did Jesus in Cana of Galilee, and manifested forth his glory; and his disciples believed on him.

12 After this he went down to Capernaum, he, and his mother, and his brethren, and his disciples: and they continued there not many days.

Jesus Goes to the Temple

13 And the Jews' passover was at hand, and Jesus went up to Jerusalem,

14 And found in the temple those that sold oxen and sheep and doves, and the changers of money sitting:

15 And when he had made a scourge of small cords, he drove them all out of the temple, and the sheep, and the oxen; and poured out the changers' money, and overthrew the tables;

16 And said unto them that sold doves, Take these things hence; make not my Father's house an house of merchandise.

17 And his disciples remembered that it was written, The zeal of thine house hath eaten me up.

18 Then answered the Jews and said unto him, What sign shewest thou us, seeing that thou doest these things?

Cross references (center column)

46 John 7:41, 42, 52
47 Ps. 32:2; 73:1; John 8:39; Rom. 2:28, 29; 9:6
49 Matt. 14:33; 21:5; 27:11, 42; John 18:37; 19:3
51 Gen. 28:12; Matt. 4:11; Luke 2:9, 13; 22:43; 24:4; Acts 1:10
1 Josh. 19:28
4 2Sam. 16:10; 19:22; John 7:6; 19:26
6 Mark 7:3
9 John 4:46
11 John 1:14
12 Matt. 12:46
13 Ex. 12:14; Deut. 16:1, 16; John 1:23; 5:1; 6:4; 11:55
14 Matt. 21:12; Mark 11:15; Luke 19:45
16 Luke 2:49
17 Ps. 69:9
18 Matt. 12:38; John 6:30

1:49 Nathanael is apparently convinced that Jesus is the Son of God by His miraculous ability to know his inner thoughts and character (cf. John 16:30; 21:17).

1:51 ye shall see heaven open, and the angels of God ascending and descending upon the Son of man. This statement is reminiscent of Jacob's vision of angels ascending and descending on a ladder from heaven (Gen. 28:12). Jesus declares that, as the Son of man, He will be the vehicle for communication between heaven and earth. The expression "son of man" was sometimes used in the Old Testament to designate the common human

nature of the prophets (Ezek. 2:1; Dan. 8:17). Christ often referred to Himself as "the Son of man" (Matt. 8:20; John 6:27, 53), emphasizing His role as a vehicle for divine revelation to humanity.

2:18–22 Destroy this temple, and in three days I will raise it up. Jesus explains what He means by this statement two verses later—the resurrection of His body. The supreme sign of Jesus' deity and His coming again was His bodily resurrection from the dead after three days. All believers rest on the foundation of His resurrection, which guarantees His future second coming.

19 Jesus answered and said unto them, Destroy this temple, and in three days I will raise it up.

20 Then said the Jews, Forty and six years was this temple in building, and wilt thou rear it up in three days?

21 But he spake of the temple of his body.

22 When therefore he was risen from the dead, his disciples remembered that he had said this unto them; and they believed the scripture, and the word which Jesus had said.

23 Now when he was in Jerusalem at the passover, in the feast *day*, many believed in his name, when they saw the miracles which he did.

24 But Jesus did not commit himself unto them, because he knew all *men*,

25 And needed not that any should testify of man: for he knew what was in man.

CHAPTER 3
Nicodemus

1 There was a man of the Pharisees, named Nicodemus, a ruler of the Jews:

2 The same came to Jesus by night, and said unto him, Rabbi, we know that thou art a teacher come from God: for no man can do these miracles that thou doest, except God be with him.

3 Jesus answered and said unto him, Verily, verily, I say unto thee, Except a man be born again, he cannot see the kingdom of God.

4 Nicodemus saith unto him, How can a man be born when he is old? can he enter the second time into his mother's womb, and be born?

5 Jesus answered, Verily, verily, I say unto thee, Except a man be born of water and of the Spirit, he cannot enter into the kingdom of God.

6 That which is born of the flesh is flesh; and that which is born of the Spirit is spirit.

7 Marvel not that I said unto thee, Ye must be born again.

8 The wind bloweth where it listeth, and thou hearest the sound thereof, but canst not tell whence it cometh, and whither it goeth: so is every one that is born of the Spirit.

9 Nicodemus answered and said unto him, How can these things be?

10 Jesus answered and said unto him, Art thou a master of Israel, and knowest not these things?

11 Verily, verily, I say unto thee, We speak that we do know, and testify that we have seen; and ye receive not our witness.

12 If I have told you earthly things, and ye believe not, how shall ye believe, if I tell you of heavenly things?

13 And no man hath ascended up to heaven, but he that came down from heaven, even the Son of man which is in heaven.

14 And as Moses lifted up the serpent in the wilderness, even so must the Son of man be lifted up:

15 That whosoever believeth in him should not perish, but have eternal life.

16 For God so loved the world, that he gave his only begotten Son, that whosoever believeth in him should not perish, but have everlasting life.

17 For God sent not his Son into the world to condemn the world; but that the world through him might be saved.

18 He that believeth on him is not condemned: but he that believeth not is condemned already, because he hath not believed in the name of the only begotten Son of God.

19 And this is the condemnation, that light is come into the world, and men loved darkness rather than light, because their deeds were evil.

20 For every one that doeth evil hateth the light, neither cometh to the light, lest his deeds should be reproved.

21 But he that doeth truth cometh to the light, that his deeds may be made manifest, that they are wrought in God.

Jesus Is Greater Than John

22 After these things came Jesus and his disciples into the land of Judea; and there he tarried with them, and baptized.

23 And John also was baptizing in Aenon near to Salim, because there was much water there: and they came, and were baptized.

24 For John was not yet cast into prison.

Cross references:

19 Matt. 26:61; 27:40; Mark 14:58; 15:29

21 1Cor. 3:16; 6:19; Heb. 8:2

22 Luke 24:8

25 1Sam. 16:7; Matt. 9:4; Mark 2:8; John 6:64; 16:30; Rev. 2:23

2 John 7:50; 9:16, 33; 19:39; Acts 2:22; 10:38

3 John 1:13; Gal. 6:15; Titus 3:5; James 1:18; 1Pet. 1:23; 1John 3:9

5 Mark 16:16; Acts 2:38

8 Eccl. 11:5; 1Cor. 2:11

11 John 1:18; 3:32; 7:16; 8:28

13 Prov. 30:4; John 6:33, 38, 51, 62; 16:28

14 Num. 21:9; John 8:28; 12:32

15 John 3:36; 6:47

16 Rom. 5:8; 1John 4:9

17 Luke 9:56; John 5:45; 8:15; 12:47; 1John 4:14

18 John 5:24; 6:40, 47; 20:31

19 John 1:4, 9-11; 8:12

20 Job 24:13, 17; Eph. 5:13

22 John 4:2

23 Matt. 3:5, 6

24 Matt. 14:3

3:3–7 the kingdom of God. See the note on John 18:36.

3:14–18 lifted up the serpent. Jesus predicted that just as Moses lifted the serpent in the wilderness for the people to look at in faith to be healed, He would be lifted up as the supreme expression of God's love for mankind. He was lifted up on the cross, and since His resurrection, millions have looked to the empty cross and tomb and have been saved by faith in the finished work of Christ.

God's Plan of Salvation

By Adrian Rogers

"**A**nd they said, Believe on the Lord Jesus Christ, and thou shalt be saved, and thy house" (Acts 16:31). A great truth and eternal blessing is that we can be saved.

We are saved **from** certain things. Sin is a debt against Almighty God (Matt. 6:12). Salvation means that we are delivered from that debt and will not be cast into debtor's prison, that is, eternal hell. Sin is also defilement (Jer. 17:9). Our hearts (inner nature) have been defiled by sin. By salvation we are made pure and righteous in the sight of a holy God. Sin also brings dominion (Rom. 6:16). By nature, we are slaves to sin; but salvation breaks the power of sin and brings liberty.

Not only are we saved **from** these things, but we are saved **unto** certain things. We are saved to a life of fullness. Jesus came to bring abundant life (John 10:10). We are saved to a life of fruitfulness (John 15:5), not life devoid of meaning and worthwhileness. We are also saved to a life of eternal fellowship with God through Jesus Christ and with our brothers and sisters in Christ (1 John 1:3).

> *Our salvation was purchased by the Lord Jesus with His precious blood on the cross.*

Salvation was purchased by the Lord Jesus with His precious blood on the cross. God's nature is holiness and righteousness; He cannot merely overlook our sins; even His love will not permit that. Sin must be punished or God would contradict His holiness. Sin will be pardoned in Christ or punished in hell; but it can never be overlooked by a holy God.

Since all have sinned (Rom. 3:23), all must be saved. None is so good he need not be saved, and none is so bad he cannot be saved.

There are three key prepositions in Ephesians 2:8–10 that clearly tell how to be saved.

1. Salvation is "**by** grace." Grace means that God saves us apart from any merit of our own. Grace is the unmerited love and favor of God shown to sinners.

2. Salvation is "**through** faith." No one is saved by good works. Salvation is a gift that is totally by grace and must be received totally by faith.

3. Salvation is "**unto** good works." We are not saved by good works, but we are saved to do good works. Good works are not the root of our salvation, but the fruits of salvation.

In order to be saved, one may sincerely pray a prayer like this:

Dear God, I know that You love me, and want to save me. I am a sinner, and my sin deserves judgment, but I need mercy. Jesus, You died to save me and promised to save me if I would trust You. I do trust You. I believe that You are the Son of God. I believe that You paid for my sin with Your blood on the cross. I believe that God raised You from the dead. I now receive You by faith into my life as my Lord and Savior. Forgive my sin, cleanse me, and begin now to make me the person that You want me to be. Because You died for me, I will live for You. I do this not in order to be saved but because I have been saved by Your grace. You are now my Lord, my Master, my Savior, and my Friend. In Your name I pray. Amen.

25 Then there arose a question between *some* of John's disciples and the Jews about purifying.

26 And they came unto John, and said unto him, Rabbi, he that was with thee beyond Jordan, to whom thou barest witness, behold, the same baptizeth, and all *men* come to him.

27 John answered and said, A man can receive nothing, except it be given him from heaven.

28 Ye yourselves bear me witness, that I said, I am not the Christ, but that I am sent before him.

29 He that hath the bride is the bridegroom: but the friend of the bridegroom, which standeth and heareth him, rejoiceth greatly because of the bridegroom's voice: this my joy therefore is fulfilled.

30 He must increase, but I *must* decrease.

31 He that cometh from above is above all: he that is of the earth is earthly, and speaketh of the earth: he that cometh from heaven is above all.

32 And what he hath seen and heard, that he testifieth; and no man receiveth his testimony.

33 He that hath received his testimony hath set to his seal that God is true.

34 For he whom God hath sent speaketh the words of God: for God giveth not the Spirit by measure *unto him*.

35 The Father loveth the Son, and hath given all things into his hand.

36 He that believeth on the Son hath everlasting life: and he that believeth not the Son shall not see life; but the wrath of God abideth on him.

CHAPTER 4
A Samaritan Woman

1 When therefore the Lord knew how the Pharisees had heard that Jesus made and baptized more disciples than John,

2 (Though Jesus himself baptized not, but his disciples,)

3 He left Judea, and departed again into Galilee.

4 And he must needs go through Samaria.

5 Then cometh he to a city of Samaria, which is called Sychar, near to the parcel of ground that Jacob gave to his son Joseph.

6 Now Jacob's well was there. Jesus therefore, being wearied with *his* journey, sat thus on the well: *and* it was about the sixth hour.

7 There cometh a woman of Samaria to draw water: Jesus saith unto her, Give me to drink.

26 John 1:7, 15, 27, 34

27 1Cor. 4:7; Heb. 5:4; James 1:17

28 Mal. 3:1; Mark 1:2; Luke 1:17; John 1:20, 27

29 Song 5:1; Matt. 22:2; 2Cor. 11:2; Eph. 5:25, 27; Rev. 21:9

31 John 1:13, 15, 27; 6:33; 8:23; Rom. 9:5; Phil. 2:9

32 John 1:11; 8:26; 15:15

33 Rom. 3:4; 1John 5:10

34 John 1:16; 7:16

35 Matt. 11:27; 28:18; Luke 10:22; John 5:20, 22; 13:3

36 John 1:12, 15, 16; 6:47; Rom. 1:17

1 John 3:22, 26

5 Gen. 33:19; 48:22

9 2Kgs. 17:24; Luke 9:52, 53

10 Isa. 12:3; 44:3

14 John 6:35, 58

15 John 6:34; 17:2, 3; 1John 5:20

19 Luke 7:16; 24:19; John 6:14; 7:40

20 Deut. 12:5, 11; Judg. 9:7; 1Kgs. 9:3; 2Chr. 7:12

21 Mal. 1:11; 1Tim. 2:8

22 2Kgs. 17:29; Isa. 2:3

23 John 1:17; Phil. 3:3

24 2Cor. 3:17

8 (For his disciples were gone away unto the city to buy meat.)

9 Then saith the woman of Samaria unto him, How is it that thou, being a Jew, askest drink of me, which am a woman of Samaria? for the Jews have no dealings with the Samaritans.

10 Jesus answered and said unto her, If thou knewest the gift of God, and who it is that saith to thee, Give me to drink; thou wouldest have asked of him, and he would have given thee living water.

11 The woman saith unto him, Sir, thou hast nothing to draw with, and the well is deep: from whence then hast thou that living water?

12 Art thou greater than our father Jacob, which gave us the well, and drank thereof himself, and his children, and his cattle?

13 Jesus answered and said unto her, Whosoever drinketh of this water shall thirst again:

14 But whosoever drinketh of the water that I shall give him shall never thirst; but the water that I shall give him shall be in him a well of water springing up into everlasting life.

15 The woman saith unto him, Sir, give me this water, that I thirst not, neither come hither to draw.

16 Jesus saith unto her, Go, call thy husband, and come hither.

17 The woman answered and said, I have no husband. Jesus said unto her, Thou hast well said, I have no husband:

18 For thou hast had five husbands; and he whom thou now hast is not thy husband: in that saidst thou truly.

19 The woman saith unto him, Sir, I perceive that thou art a prophet.

20 Our fathers worshiped in this mountain; and ye say, that in Jerusalem is the place where men ought to worship.

21 Jesus saith unto her, Woman, believe me, the hour cometh, when ye shall neither in this mountain, nor yet at Jerusalem, worship the Father.

22 Ye worship ye know not what: we know what we worship: for salvation is of the Jews.

23 But the hour cometh, and now is, when the true worshippers shall worship the Father in spirit and in truth: for the Father seeketh such to worship him.

24 God is a Spirit: and they that worship him must worship him in spirit and in truth.

25 The woman saith unto him, I know that

Messias cometh, which is called Christ: when he is come, he will tell us all things.

26 Jesus saith unto her, I that speak unto thee am he.

27 And upon this came his disciples, and marvelled that he talked with the woman: yet no man said, What seekest thou? or, Why talkest thou with her?

28 The woman then left her waterpot, and went her way into the city, and saith to the men,

29 Come, see a man, which told me all things that ever I did: is not this the Christ?

30 Then they went out of the city, and came unto him.

31 In the mean while his disciples prayed him, saying, Master, eat.

32 But he said unto them, I have meat to eat that ye know not of.

33 Therefore said the disciples one to another, Hath any man brought him *ought* to eat?

34 Jesus saith unto them, My meat is to do the will of him that sent me, and to finish his work.

35 Say not ye, There are yet four months, and then cometh harvest? behold, I say unto you, Lift up your eyes, and look on the fields; for they are white already to harvest.

36 And he that reapeth receiveth wages, and gathereth fruit unto life eternal: that both he that soweth and he that reapeth may rejoice together.

37 And herein is that saying true, One soweth, and another reapeth.

38 I sent you to reap that whereon ye bestowed no labour: other men laboured, and ye are entered into their labours.

39 And many of the Samaritans of that city believed on him for the saying of the woman, which testified, He told me all that ever I did.

40 So when the Samaritans were come unto him, they besought him that he would tarry with them: and he abode there two days.

41 And many more believed because of his own word;

42 And said unto the woman, Now we believe, not because of thy saying: for we have heard *him* ourselves, and know that this is indeed the Christ, the Saviour of the world.

Jesus Heals an Official's Son

43 Now after two days he departed thence, and went into Galilee.

44 For Jesus himself testified, that a prophet hath no honour in his own country.

45 Then when he was come into Galilee, the

Galilaeans received him, having seen all the things that he did at Jerusalem at the feast: for they also went unto the feast.

46 So Jesus came again into Cana of Galilee, where he made the water wine. And there was a certain nobleman, whose son was sick at Capernaum.

47 When he heard that Jesus was come out of Judea into Galilee, he went unto him, and besought him that he would come down, and heal his son: for he was at the point of death.

48 Then said Jesus unto him, Except ye see signs and wonders, ye will not believe.

49 The nobleman saith unto him, Sir, come down ere my child die.

50 Jesus saith unto him, Go thy way; thy son liveth. And the man believed the word that Jesus had spoken unto him, and he went his way.

51 And as he was now going down, his servants met him, and told *him,* saying, Thy son liveth.

52 Then inquired he of them the hour when he began to amend. And they said unto him, Yesterday at the seventh hour the fever left him.

53 So the father knew that *it was* at the same hour, in the which Jesus said unto him, Thy son liveth: and himself believed, and his whole house.

54 This *is* again the second miracle *that* Jesus did, when he was come out of Judea into Galilee.

CHAPTER 5
Jesus Heals a Sick Man on the Sabbath Day

1 After this there was a feast of the Jews; and Jesus went up to Jerusalem.

2 Now there is at Jerusalem by the sheep *market* a pool, which is called in the Hebrew tongue Bethesda, having five porches.

3 In these lay a great multitude of impotent folk, of blind, halt, withered, waiting for the moving of the water.

4 For an angel went down at a certain season into the pool, and troubled the water: whosoever then first after the troubling of the water stepped in was made whole of whatsoever disease he had.

5 And a certain man was there, which had an infirmity thirty and eight years.

6 When Jesus saw him lie, and knew that he had been now a long time *in that case*, he saith unto him, Wilt thou be made whole?

7 The impotent man answered him, Sir, I have no man, when the water is troubled, to

26 Matt. 26:63, 64; Mark 14:61, 62; John 9:37

29 John 4:25

34 Job 23:12; John 6:38; 17:4; 19:30

35 Matt. 9:37; Luke 10:2

36 Dan. 12:3

39 John 4:29

42 John 17:8; 1John 4:14

44 Matt. 13:57; Mark 6:4; Luke 4:24

45 Deut. 16:16; John 2:23; 3:2

46 John 2:1, 11

48 1Cor. 1:22

1 Lev. 23:2; Deut. 16:1; John 2:13

2 Neh. 3:1; 12:39

put me into the pool: but while I am coming, another steppeth down before me.

8 Jesus saith unto him, Rise, take up thy bed, and walk.

9 And immediately the man was made whole, and took up his bed, and walked: and on the same day was the sabbath.

10 The Jews therefore said unto him that was cured, It is the sabbath day: it is not lawful for thee to carry *thy* bed.

11 He answered them, He that made me whole, the same said unto me, Take up thy bed, and walk.

12 Then asked they him, What man is that which said unto thee, Take up thy bed, and walk?

13 And he that was healed wist not who it was: for Jesus had conveyed himself away, a multitude being in *that* place.

14 Afterward Jesus findeth him in the temple, and said unto him, Behold, thou art made whole: sin no more, lest a worse thing come unto thee.

15 The man departed, and told the Jews that it was Jesus, which had made him whole.

16 And therefore did the Jews persecute Jesus, and sought to slay him, because he had done these things on the sabbath day.

17 But Jesus answered them, My Father worketh hitherto, and I work.

18 Therefore the Jews sought the more to kill him, because he not only had broken the sabbath, but said also that God was his Father, making himself equal with God.

The Father and the Son

19 Then answered Jesus and said unto them, Verily, verily, I say unto you, The Son can do nothing of himself, but what he seeth the Father do: for what things soever he doeth, these also doeth the Son likewise.

20 For the Father loveth the Son, and sheweth him all things that himself doeth: and he will shew him greater works than these, that ye may marvel.

21 For as the Father raiseth up the dead,

and quickeneth *them;* even so the Son quickeneth whom he will.

22 For the Father judgeth no man, but hath committed all judgment unto the Son:

23 That all men should honour the Son, even as they honour the Father. He that honoureth not the Son honoureth not the Father which hath sent him.

24 Verily, verily, I say unto you, He that heareth my word, and believeth on him that sent me, hath everlasting life, and shall not come into condemnation; but is passed from death unto life.

25 Verily, verily, I say unto you, The hour is coming, and now is, when the dead shall hear the voice of the Son of God: and they that hear shall live.

26 For as the Father hath life in himself; so hath he given to the Son to have life in himself;

27 And hath given him authority to execute judgment also, because he is the Son of man.

28 Marvel not at this: for the hour is coming, in the which all that are in the graves shall hear his voice,

29 And shall come forth; they that have done good, unto the resurrection of life; and they that have done evil, unto the resurrection of damnation.

30 I can of mine own self do nothing: as I hear, I judge: and my judgment is just; because I seek not mine own will, but the will of the Father which hath sent me.

31 If I bear witness of myself, my witness is not true.

32 There is another that beareth witness of me; and I know that the witness which he witnesseth of me is true.

33 Ye sent unto John, and he bare witness unto the truth.

34 But I receive not testimony from man: but these things I say, that ye might be saved.

35 He was a burning and a shining light: and ye were willing for a season to rejoice in his light.

Cross-references

10 Ex. 20:10
14 Matt. 12:45; John 8:11
17 John 9:4; 14:10
18 Phil. 2:6
19 John 5:30; 9:4; 12:49; 14:10
20 Matt. 3:17; 2Pet. 1:17
21 Luke 7:14; 8:54; John 11:25, 43
22 Matt. 11:27; 28:18; John 5:27; 3:35; 17:2
23 1John 2:23
24 John 3:16, 18; 6:40, 47; 8:51; 20:31; 1John 3:14
25 John 5:28; Eph. 2:1, 5; 5:14; Col. 2:13
27 Dan. 7:13, 14; John 5:22; Acts 10:42; 17:31
29 Isa. 26:19; Dan. 12:2; Matt. 25:32, 33, 46; 1Cor. 15:52; 1Thess. 4:16
30 Matt. 26:39; John 4:34; 5:19; 6:38
31 John 8:14; Rev. 3:14
32 Matt. 3:17; 17:5
35 Matt. 13:20; 21:26; Mark 6:20

5:21 Jesus had power to raise the dead, and did so on three occasions in His ministry (Matt. 9:18–26 [cf. Mark 5:22–43; Luke 8:41–56]; Luke 7:11–17; John 11:1–44), and He will raise all men in the future (vv. 28–29).

5:22 Jesus declared that He will be the judge of all men: of Christians at the judgment seat of Christ (Rom. 14:10–11; 2 Cor. 5:10) and of the unsaved at the Great White Throne Judgment after the Millennium

(Rev. 20:11–15).

5:25–29 Christ teaches the concept of bodily resurrection from the dead. Other passages teach a sequential order of resurrections (cf. Dan. 12:1–3; 1 Cor. 15:51–58; 1 Thess. 4:13–18; Rev. 20:4–6). Jesus also teaches that there are two kinds of resurrections: a resurrection to life (the saved) and a resurrection to judgment (the lost).

36 But I have greater witness than that of John: for the works which the Father hath given me to finish, the same works that I do, bear witness of me, that the Father hath sent me.

37 And the Father himself, which hath sent me, hath borne witness of me. Ye have neither heard his voice at any time, nor seen his shape.

38 And ye have not his word abiding in you: for whom he hath sent, him ye believe not.

39 Search the scriptures; for in them ye think ye have eternal life: and they are they which testify of me.

40 And ye will not come to me, that ye might have life.

41 I receive not honour from men.

42 But I know you, that ye have not the love of God in you.

43 I am come in my Father's name, and ye receive me not: if another shall come in his own name, him ye will receive.

44 How can ye believe, which receive honour one of another, and seek not the honour that cometh from God only?

45 Do not think that I will accuse you to the Father: there is one that accuseth you, even Moses, in whom ye trust.

46 For had ye believed Moses, ye would have believed me: for he wrote of me.

47 But if ye believe not his writings, how shall ye believe my words?

CHAPTER 6
Jesus Feeds the Five Thousand

1 After these things Jesus went over the sea of Galilee, which is *the sea of* Tiberias.

2 And a great multitude followed him, because they saw his miracles which he did on them that were diseased.

3 And Jesus went up into a mountain, and there he sat with his disciples.

4 And the passover, a feast of the Jews, was nigh.

5 When Jesus then lifted up *his* eyes, and saw a great company come unto him, he saith unto Philip, Whence shall we buy bread, that these may eat?

6 And this he said to prove him: for he himself knew what he would do.

7 Philip answered him, Two hundred pennyworth of bread is not sufficient for them, that every one of them may take a little.

8 One of his disciples, Andrew, Simon Peter's brother, saith unto him,

9 There is a lad here, which hath five barley loaves, and two small fishes: but what are they among so many?

10 And Jesus said, Make the men sit down. Now there was much grass in the place. So the men sat down, in number about five thousand.

11 And Jesus took the loaves; and when he had given thanks, he distributed to the disciples, and the disciples to them that were set down; and likewise of the fishes as much as they would.

12 When they were filled, he said unto his disciples, Gather up the fragments that remain, that nothing be lost.

13 Therefore they gathered *them* together, and filled twelve baskets with the fragments of the five barley loaves, which remained over and above unto them that had eaten.

14 Then those men, when they had seen the miracle that Jesus did, said, This is of a truth that prophet that should come into the world.

15 When Jesus therefore perceived that they would come and take him by force, to make him a king, he departed again into a mountain himself alone.

Jesus Walks on Water

16 And when even was *now* come, his disciples went down unto the sea,

17 And entered into a ship, and went over the sea toward Capernaum. And it was now dark, and Jesus was not come to them.

18 And the sea arose by reason of a great wind that blew.

19 So when they had rowed about five and

Cross references:

36 John 3:2; 10:25; 15:24; 1John 5:9
37 Deut. 4:12; Matt. 3:17; 17:5; John 1:18; 6:27; 8:18; 1Tim. 1:17; 1John 4:12
39 Deut. 18:15; Isa. 8:20; 34:16; Luke 16:29; 24:27; John 1:45; 5:46; Acts 17:11
40 John 1:11; 3:19
41 John 5:34; 1Thess. 2:6
44 John 12:43; Rom. 2:29
45 Rom. 2:12
46 Gen. 3:15; 12:3; 18:18; 22:18; 49:10; Deut. 18:15, 18; John 1:45; Acts 26:22
1 Matt. 14:15; Mark 6:35; Luke 9:10, 12
4 Lev. 23:5, 7; Deut. 16:1; John 2:13; 5:1
5 Matt. 14:14; Mark 6:35; Luke 9:12
9 2Kgs. 4:43
14 Gen. 49:10; Deut. 18:15, 18; Matt. 11:3; John 1:21; 4:19, 25; 7:40
16 Matt. 14:23; Mark 6:47

5:39 the scriptures . . . testify of me. This is a reference to the many messianic prophecies (ca. 109 of them) Jesus fulfilled in His first advent (see the table "Prophecies of the First Coming of Christ"). Jesus appeals to Scripture to vindicate His claim that He is the Messiah. We should point people to the same Scriptures when proclaiming Jesus as the Messiah. No other person who ever lived or will live could have fulfilled more than a few of such prophecies—Jesus fulfilled them all!

5:46 Moses . . . wrote of me. Moses wrote the first five books of the Bible which contain many predictions of the Messiah (Gen. 3:15; 22:18; 49:10; Num. 24:17; Deut. 18:15 [cf. Luke 24:25–26]). Christ is prophetically pictured in typological symbols found in the Pentateuch, such as the Passover, the manna, the rock, the offerings, and the high priesthood.

twenty or thirty furlongs, they see Jesus walking on the sea, and drawing nigh unto the ship: and they were afraid.

20 But he saith unto them, It is I; be not afraid.

21 Then they willingly received him into the ship: and immediately the ship was at the land whither they went.

22 The day following, when the people which stood on the other side of the sea saw that there was none other boat there, save that one whereinto his disciples were entered, and that Jesus went not with his disciples into the boat, but *that* his disciples were gone away alone;

23 (Howbeit there came other boats from Tiberias nigh unto the place where they did eat bread, after that the Lord had given thanks:)

24 When the people therefore saw that Jesus was not there, neither his disciples, they also took shipping, and came to Capernaum, seeking for Jesus.

Everlasting Food: Jesus the Bread of Life

25 And when they had found him on the other side of the sea, they said unto him, Rabbi, when camest thou hither?

26 Jesus answered them and said, Verily, verily, I say unto you, Ye seek me, not because ye saw the miracles, but because ye did eat of the loaves, and were filled.

27 Labour not for the meat which perisheth, but for that meat which endureth unto everlasting life, which the Son of man shall give unto you: for him hath God the Father sealed.

28 Then said they unto him, What shall we do, that we might work the works of God?

29 Jesus answered and said unto them, This is the work of God, that ye believe on him whom he hath sent.

30 They said therefore unto him, What sign shewest thou then, that we may see, and believe thee? what dost thou work?

31 Our fathers did eat manna in the desert; as it is written, He gave them bread from heaven to eat.

32 Then Jesus said unto them, Verily, verily, I say unto you, Moses gave you not that bread from heaven; but my Father giveth you the true bread from heaven.

33 For the bread of God is he which cometh down from heaven, and giveth life unto the world.

34 Then said they unto him, Lord, evermore give us this bread.

35 And Jesus said unto them, I am the bread of life: he that cometh to me shall never hunger; and he that believeth on me shall never thirst.

36 But I said unto you, That ye also have seen me, and believe not.

37 All that the Father giveth me shall come to me; and him that cometh to me I will in no wise cast out.

38 For I came down from heaven, not to do mine own will, but the will of him that sent me.

39 And this is the Father's will which hath sent me, that of all which he hath given me I should lose nothing, but should raise it up again at the last day.

40 And this is the will of him that sent me, that every one which seeth the Son, and believeth on him, may have everlasting life: and I will raise him up at the last day.

41 The Jews then murmured at him, because he said, I am the bread which came down from heaven.

42 And they said, Is not this Jesus, the son of Joseph, whose father and mother we know? how is it then that he saith, I came down from heaven?

43 Jesus therefore answered and said unto them, Murmur not among yourselves.

44 No man can come to me, except the Father which hath sent me draw him: and I will raise him up at the last day.

45 It is written in the prophets, And they shall be all taught of God. Every man therefore that hath heard, and hath learned of the Father, cometh unto me.

46 Not that any man hath seen the Father, save he which is of God, he hath seen the Father.

Cross references

27 Matt. 3:17; 17:5; Mark 1:11; 9:7; Luke 3:22; 9:35; John 1:33; 4:14; 5:37; 6:54; 8:18; Acts 2:22; 2Pet. 1:17

29 1John 3:23

30 Matt. 12:38; 16:1; Mark 8:11; 1Cor. 1:22

31 Ex. 16:15; Num. 11:7; Neh. 9:15; Ps. 78:24, 25; 1Cor. 10:3

34 John 4:15

35 John 4:14; 6:48, 58; 7:37

36 John 6:26, 64

37 Matt. 24:24; John 6:45; 10:28, 29; 2Tim. 2:19; 1John 2:19

38 Matt. 26:39; John 4:34; 5:30

39 John 10:28; 17:12; 18:9

40 John 3:15, 16; 4:14; 6:27, 47, 54

42 Matt. 13:55; Mark 6:3; Luke 4:22

44 Song 1:4; John 6:65

45 Isa. 54:13; Jer. 31:34; Mic. 4:2; John 6:37; Heb. 8:10; 10:16

46 Matt. 11:27; Luke 10:22; John 1:18; 5:37; 7:29; 8:19

6:33–35 I am the bread of life. Jesus teaches that the manna provided by God to His people in the wilderness, following their exodus from Egypt, was not "from heaven." Though the Father in heaven provided the manna to them, the manna did not provide eternal life. Christ, however, affirms that He is the true bread "from heaven" that gives eternal life.

6:39–40 I will raise him up at the last day. Jesus clearly promises that He will resurrect all those who believe in Him (see vv. 44, 54). This promise will be fulfilled "at the last day," at the rapture of the Church before the Tribulation (see 1 Thess. 4:14).

47 Verily, verily, I say unto you, He that believeth on me hath everlasting life.

48 I am that bread of life.

49 Your fathers did eat manna in the wilderness, and are dead.

50 This is the bread which cometh down from heaven, that a man may eat thereof, and not die.

51 I am the living bread which came down from heaven: if any man eat of this bread, he shall live for ever: and the bread that I will give is my flesh, which I will give for the life of the world.

52 The Jews therefore strove among themselves, saying, How can this man give us *his* flesh to eat?

53 Then Jesus said unto them, Verily, verily, I say unto you, Except ye eat the flesh of the Son of man, and drink his blood, ye have no life in you.

54 Whoso eateth my flesh, and drinketh my blood, hath eternal life; and I will raise him up at the last day.

55 For my flesh is meat indeed, and my blood is drink indeed.

56 He that eateth my flesh, and drinketh my blood, dwelleth in me, and I in him.

57 As the living Father hath sent me, and I live by the Father: so he that eateth me, even he shall live by me.

58 This is that bread which came down from heaven: not as your fathers did eat manna, and are dead: he that eateth of this bread shall live for ever.

59 These things said he in the synagogue, as he taught in Capernaum.

Many Disciples Stop Following Jesus

60 Many therefore of his disciples, when they had heard *this*, said, This is an hard saying; who can hear it?

61 When Jesus knew in himself that his disciples murmured at it, he said unto them, Doth this offend you?

62 What and if ye shall see the Son of man ascend up where he was before?

63 It is the spirit that quickeneth; the flesh profiteth nothing: the words that I speak unto you, they are spirit, and they are life.

64 But there are some of you that believe not. For Jesus knew from the beginning who they were that believed not, and who should betray him.

65 And he said, Therefore said I unto you, that no man can come unto me, except it were given unto him of my Father.

66 From that *time* many of his disciples went back, and walked no more with him.

67 Then said Jesus unto the twelve, Will ye also go away?

68 Then Simon Peter answered him, Lord, to whom shall we go? thou hast the words of eternal life.

69 And we believe and are sure that thou art that Christ, the Son of the living God.

70 Jesus answered them, Have not I chosen you twelve, and one of you is a devil?

71 He spake of Judas Iscariot *the son* of Simon: for he it was that should betray him, being one of the twelve.

CHAPTER 7
Jesus at the Feast of Tabernacles

1 After these things Jesus walked in Galilee: for he would not walk in Jewry, because the Jews sought to kill him.

2 Now the Jews' feast of tabernacles was at hand.

3 His brethren therefore said unto him, Depart hence, and go into Judea, that thy disciples also may see the works that thou doest.

4 For *there is* no man *that* doeth any thing in secret, and he himself seeketh to be known openly. If thou do these things, shew thyself to the world.

5 For neither did his brethren believe in him.

6 Then Jesus said unto them, My time is not yet come: but your time is alway ready.

7 The world cannot hate you; but me it hateth, because I testify of it, that the works thereof are evil.

8 Go ye up unto this feast: I go not up yet unto this feast; for my time is not yet full come.

9 When he had said these words unto them, he abode *still* in Galilee.

10 But when his brethren were gone up, then went he also up unto the feast, not openly, but as it were in secret.

11 Then the Jews sought him at the feast, and said, Where is he?

12 And there was much murmuring among the people concerning him: for some said,

---

Cross references (center column):

47 John 3:16, 18, 36; 6:40

48 John 6:33, 35

49 John 6:31

50 John 6:51, 58

51 John 3:13; Heb. 10:5, 10

52 John 3:9; 7:43; 9:16; 10:19

53 Matt. 26:26, 28

54 John 4:14; 6:27, 40, 63

56 1 John 3:24; 4:15, 16

58 John 6:49-51

60 Matt. 11:6; John 6:66

62 Mark 16:19

63 2 Cor. 3:6

64 John 2:24, 25; 6:36; 13:11

65 John 6:44, 45

69 Matt. 16:16; Mark 8:29; Luke 9:20; John 1:49; 11:27

70 Luke 6:13; John 13:27

1 John 5:16, 18

2 Lev. 23:34

3 Matt. 12:46; Mark 3:31

5 Mark 3:21

6 John 2:4; 7:8, 30; 8:20

7 John 3:19; 15:19

8 John 7:6; 8:20

12 Matt. 21:46; Luke 7:16; John 6:14; 7:40

6:62 Jesus fulfilled this implied prediction of His ascension in Acts 1:8–12 when He went up to heaven (cf. Eph. 1:20–23; Heb. 4:14). Following Pentecost His followers no longer saw Him in the flesh, but His Holy Spirit was given to help them continue to grow.

He is a good man: others said, Nay; but he deceiveth the people.

13 Howbeit no man spake openly of him for fear of the Jews.

14 Now about the midst of the feast Jesus went up into the temple, and taught.

15 And the Jews marvelled, saying, How knoweth this man letters, having never learned?

16 Jesus answered them, and said, My doctrine is not mine, but his that sent me.

17 If any man will do his will, he shall know of the doctrine, whether it be of God, or whether I speak of myself.

18 He that speaketh of himself seeketh his own glory: but he that seeketh his glory that sent him, the same is true, and no unrighteousness is in him.

19 Did not Moses give you the law, and yet none of you keepeth the law? Why go ye about to kill me?

20 The people answered and said, Thou hast a devil: who goeth about to kill thee?

21 Jesus answered and said unto them, I have done one work, and ye all marvel.

22 Moses therefore gave unto you circumcision; (not because it is of Moses, but of the fathers;) and ye on the sabbath day circumcise a man.

23 If a man on the sabbath day receive circumcision, that the law of Moses should not be broken; are ye angry at me, because I have made a man every whit whole on the sabbath day?

24 Judge not according to the appearance, but judge righteous judgment.

Divisions Concerning Who Christ Is

25 Then said some of them of Jerusalem, Is not this he, whom they seek to kill?

26 But, lo, he speaketh boldly, and they say nothing unto him. Do the rulers know indeed that this is the very Christ?

27 Howbeit we know this man whence he is: but when Christ cometh, no man knoweth whence he is.

28 Then cried Jesus in the temple as he taught, saying, Ye both know me, and ye

know whence I am: and I am not come of myself, but he that sent me is true, whom ye know not.

29 But I know him: for I am from him, and he hath sent me.

30 Then they sought to take him: but no man laid hands on him, because his hour was not yet come.

31 And many of the people believed on him, and said, When Christ cometh, will he do more miracles than these which this *man* hath done?

Officers Sent to Arrest Jesus

32 The Pharisees heard that the people murmured such things concerning him; and the Pharisees and the chief priests sent officers to take him.

33 Then said Jesus unto them, Yet a little while am I with you, and then I go unto him that sent me.

34 Ye shall seek me, and shall not find me: and where I am, thither ye cannot come.

35 Then said the Jews among themselves, Whither will he go, that we shall not find him? will he go unto the dispersed among the Gentiles, and teach the Gentiles?

36 What *manner of* saying is this that he said, Ye shall seek me, and shall not find *me*: and where I am, *thither* ye cannot come?

"Rivers of Living Water"

37 In the last day, that great *day* of the feast, Jesus stood and cried, saying, If any man thirst, let him come unto me, and drink.

38 He that believeth on me, as the scripture hath said, out of his belly shall flow rivers of living water.

39 (But this spake he of the Spirit, which they that believe on him should receive: for the Holy Ghost was not yet *given*; because that Jesus was not yet glorified.)

Division among the People

40 Many of the people therefore, when they heard this saying, said, Of a truth this is the Prophet.

Cross references:

15 Matt. 13:54; Mark 6:2; Luke 4:22
16 John 3:11; 8:28; 12:49; 14:10, 24
19 Ex. 24:3; Deut. 33:4
20 John 8:48, 52; 10:20
22 Gen. 17:10; Lev. 12:3
23 John 5:8, 9, 16
24 Deut. 1:16, 17
27 Matt. 13:55; Mark 6:3; Luke 4:22
28 John 1:18; 5:32, 43; 8:14, 26, 42, 55
29 Matt. 11:27; John 10:15
30 Mark 11:18; Luke 19:47; 20:19; John 7:19, 44; 8:20, 37
31 Matt. 12:23; John 3:2; 8:30
33 John 13:33; 16:16
34 Hos. 5:6
35 Isa. 11:12; 1Pet. 1:1
37 Isa. 55:1; Rev. 22:17
38 Prov. 18:4; Isa. 12:3; 44:3; John 4:14
39 Isa. 44:3; Joel 2:28; Acts 2:17, 33, 38
40 Deut. 18:15, 18

7:40–42 the Prophet. This discussion raises many questions about the origin of the Messiah. Moses predicted that the Lord would raise up for Israel "a Prophet from the midst of thee, of thy brethren, like unto me; unto him ye shall hearken" (Deut. 18:15). The singular pronoun "him" in Deuteronomy 18 emphasizes the ultimate Prophet who was to come. According to Acts 3:20–24; 7:37, Jesus is the fulfillment of this prophecy. Like Moses, Jesus would receive and preach God's revelation and lead people to the truth. Some wondered if Jesus might be the Prophet that Moses had spoken about. However, in their mingling of truth and error, the people demonstrate that they did not take the time to investigate who Jesus was and where He came from. If they had, they would have discovered that Jesus was a descendant of David (Matt. 1:1–17; Luke 3:23–38) and that He was

41 Others said, This is the Christ. But some said, Shall Christ come out of Galilee?

42 Hath not the scripture said, That Christ cometh of the seed of David, and out of the town of Bethlehem, where David was?

43 So there was a division among the people because of him.

44 And some of them would have taken him; but no man laid hands on him.

Unbelieving Rulers

45 Then came the officers to the chief priests and Pharisees; and they said unto them, Why have ye not brought him?

46 The officers answered, Never man spake like this man.

47 Then answered them the Pharisees, Are ye also deceived?

48 Have any of the rulers or of the Pharisees believed on him?

49 But this people who knoweth not the law are cursed.

50 Nicodemus saith unto them, (he that came to Jesus by night, being one of them,)

51 Doth our law judge *any* man, before it hear him, and know what he doeth?

52 They answered and said unto him, Art thou also of Galilee? Search, and look: for out of Galilee ariseth no prophet.

53 And every man went unto his own house.

CHAPTER 8
A Woman Taken in Adultery

1 Jesus went unto the mount of Olives.

2 And early in the morning he came again into the temple, and all the people came unto him; and he sat down, and taught them.

3 And the scribes and Pharisees brought unto him a woman taken in adultery; and when they had set her in the midst,

4 They say unto him, Master, this woman was taken in adultery, in the very act.

5 Now Moses in the law commanded us, that such should be stoned: but what sayest thou?

6 This they said, tempting him, that they might have to accuse him. But Jesus stooped down, and with *his* finger wrote on the ground, *as though* he *heard them not.*

7 So when they continued asking him, he lifted up himself, and said unto them, He

that is without sin among you, let him first cast a stone at her.

8 And again he stooped down, and wrote on the ground.

9 And they which heard *it,* being convicted by *their own* conscience, went out one by one, beginning at the eldest, *even* unto the last: and Jesus was left alone, and the woman standing in the midst.

10 When Jesus had lifted up himself, and saw none but the woman, he said unto her, Woman, where are those thine accusers? hath no man condemned thee?

11 She said, No man, Lord. And Jesus said unto her, Neither do I condemn thee: go, and sin no more.

Jesus Is the True Light

12 Then spake Jesus again unto them, saying, I am the light of the world: he that followeth me shall not walk in darkness, but shall have the light of life.

13 The Pharisees therefore said unto him, Thou bearest record of thyself; thy record is not true.

14 Jesus answered and said unto them, Though I bear record of myself, yet my record is true: for I know whence I came, and whither I go; but ye cannot tell whence I come, and whither I go.

15 Ye judge after the flesh; I judge no man.

16 And yet if I judge, my judgment is true: for I am not alone, but I and the Father that sent me.

17 It is also written in your law, that the testimony of two men is true.

18 I am one that bear witness of myself, and the Father that sent me beareth witness of me.

19 Then said they unto him, Where is thy Father? Jesus answered, Ye neither know me, nor my Father: if ye had known me, ye should have known my Father also.

20 These words spake Jesus in the treasury, as he taught in the temple: and no man laid hands on him; for his hour was not yet come.

21 Then said Jesus again unto them, I go my way, and ye shall seek me, and shall die in your sins: whither I go, ye cannot come.

22 Then said the Jews, Will he kill himself? because he saith, Whither I go, ye cannot come.

23 And he said unto them, Ye are from be-

Cross references

41 John 1:46; 4:42; 6:69; 7:52
42 1Sam. 16:1, 4; Ps. 132:11; Jer. 23:5; Mic. 5:2; Matt. 2:5; Luke 2:4
44 John 7:30
46 Matt. 7:29
48 John 12:42; Acts 6:7; 1Cor. 1:20, 26; 2:8
50 John 3:2
51 Deut. 1:17; 17:8-13; 19:15
52 Isa. 9:1, 2; Matt. 4:15; John 1:46; 7:41
5 Lev. 20:10; Deut. 22:22
7 Deut. 17:7; Rom. 2:1
9 Rom. 2:22
11 Luke 9:56; 12:14; John 3:17; 5:14
12 John 1:4, 5, 9; 3:19; 9:5; 12:35, 36, 46
13 John 5:31
14 John 7:28; 9:29
15 John 3:17; 7:24; 12:47; 18:36
16 John 8:29; 16:32
17 Deut. 17:6; 19:15; Matt. 18:16; 2Cor. 13:1; Heb. 10:28
18 John 5:37
19 John 8:55; 14:7; 16:3
20 Mark 12:41; John 7:8, 30
21 John 7:34; 8:24; 13:33
23 John 3:31; 15:19; 17:16; 1John 4:5

---

born in Bethlehem (Matt. 2:6; Luke 2:4), the city where the Old Testament proclaimed the Messiah would be born (Micah 5:2).

neath; I am from above: ye are of this world; I am not of this world.

24 I said therefore unto you, that ye shall die in your sins: for if ye believe not that I am he, ye shall die in your sins.

25 Then said they unto him, Who art thou? And Jesus saith unto them, Even the same that I said unto you from the beginning.

26 I have many things to say and to judge of you: but he that sent me is true; and I speak to the world those things which I have heard of him.

27 They understood not that he spake to them of the Father.

28 Then said Jesus unto them, When ye have lifted up the Son of man, then shall ye know that I am he, and that I do nothing of myself; but as my Father hath taught me, I speak these things.

29 And he that sent me is with me: the Father hath not left me alone; for I do always those things that please him.

30 As he spake these words, many believed on him.

The Truth Frees You

31 Then said Jesus to those Jews which believed on him, If ye continue in my word, then are ye my disciples indeed;

32 And ye shall know the truth, and the truth shall make you free.

33 They answered him, We be Abraham's seed, and were never in bondage to any man: how sayest thou, Ye shall be made free?

34 Jesus answered them, Verily, verily, I say unto you, Whosoever committeth sin is the servant of sin.

35 And the servant abideth not in the house for ever: but the Son abideth ever.

36 If the Son therefore shall make you free, ye shall be free indeed.

37 I know that ye are Abraham's seed; but ye seek to kill me, because my word hath no place in you.

38 I speak that which I have seen with my Father: and ye do that which ye have seen with your father.

39 They answered and said unto him, Abraham is our father. Jesus saith unto them, If ye were Abraham's children, ye would do the works of Abraham.

40 But now ye seek to kill me, a man that hath told you the truth, which I have heard of God: this did not Abraham.

41 Ye do the deeds of your father. Then said they to him, We be not born of fornication; we have one Father, *even* God.

42 Jesus said unto them, If God were your Father, ye would love me: for I proceeded forth and came from God; neither came I of myself, but he sent me.

43 Why do ye not understand my speech? even because ye cannot hear my word.

44 Ye are of your father the devil, and the lusts of your father ye will do. He was a murderer from the beginning, and abode not in the truth, because there is no truth in him. When he speaketh a lie, he speaketh of his own: for he is a liar, and the father of it.

45 And because I tell you the truth, ye believe me not.

46 Which of you convinceth me of sin? And if I say the truth, why do ye not believe me?

47 He that is of God heareth God's words: ye therefore hear them not, because ye are not of God.

48 Then answered the Jews, and said unto him, Say we not well that thou art a Samaritan, and hast a devil?

49 Jesus answered, I have not a devil; but I honour my Father, and ye do dishonour me.

50 And I seek not mine own glory: there is one that seeketh and judgeth.

51 Verily, verily, I say unto you, If a man keep my saying, he shall never see death.

52 Then said the Jews unto him, Now we know that thou hast a devil. Abraham is dead, and the prophets; and thou sayest, If a man keep my saying, he shall never taste of death.

53 Art thou greater than our father Abraham, which is dead? and the prophets are dead: whom makest thou thyself?

54 Jesus answered, If I honour myself, my honour is nothing: it is my Father that honoureth me; of whom ye say, that he is your God:

55 Yet ye have not known him; but I know him: and if I should say, I know him not, I shall be a liar like unto you: but I know him, and keep his saying.

56 Your father Abraham rejoiced to see my day: and he saw it, and was glad.

Cross references

24 Mark 16:16; John 8:21
26 John 3:32; 7:28; 15:15
28 Rom. 1:4
30 John 7:31; 10:42; 11:45
32 Rom. 6:14, 18, 22; 8:2; James 1:25; 2:12
33 Lev. 25:42; Matt. 3:9
34 Rom. 6:16, 20
35 Gal. 4:30
36 Rom. 8:2; Gal. 5:1
38 John 3:32; 5:19, 30; 14:10, 24
39 Matt. 3:9; John 8:33; Rom. 2:28
40 John 8:26, 37
41 Isa. 63:16; 64:8; Mal. 1:6
42 John 5:43; 7:28, 29; 16:27; 17:8, 25; 1John 5:1
44 Matt. 13:38; 1John 3:8; Jude 1:6
47 John 10:26, 27; 1John 4:6
48 John 7:20; 8:52; 10:20
50 John 5:41; 7:18
51 John 5:24; 11:26
52 Zech. 1:5; Heb. 11:13
54 John 5:31, 41; 16:14; 17:1
55 John 7:28, 29
56 Luke 10:24; Heb. 11:13

8:56 Abraham rejoiced to see my day. The Abraham of which Jesus speaks is the same one that is the physical father of those to whom He spoke, even though they were not related to Abraham spiritually. Jesus declares that Abraham prophetically saw His day, meaning that Abraham prophetically saw the day of Messiah. Jesus claims that He is the Messiah that Abraham prophetically saw (Gen. 12:3).

57 Then said the Jews unto him, Thou art not yet fifty years old, and hast thou seen Abraham?

58 Jesus said unto them, Verily, verily, I say unto you, Before Abraham was, I am.

59 Then took they up stones to cast at him: but Jesus hid himself, and went out of the temple, going through the midst of them, and so passed by.

CHAPTER 9
A Man Born Blind

1 And as *Jesus* passed by, he saw a man which was blind from *his* birth.

2 And his disciples asked him, saying, Master, who did sin, this man, or his parents, that he was born blind?

3 Jesus answered, Neither hath this man sinned, nor his parents: but that the works of God should be made manifest in him.

4 I must work the works of him that sent me, while it is day: the night cometh, when no man can work.

5 As long as I am in the world, I am the light of the world.

6 When he had thus spoken, he spat on the ground, and made clay of the spittle, and he anointed the eyes of the blind man with the clay,

7 And said unto him, Go, wash in the pool of Siloam, (which is by interpretation, Sent.) He went his way therefore, and washed, and came seeing.

8 The neighbours therefore, and they which before had seen him that he was blind, said, Is not this he that sat and begged?

9 Some said, This is he: others *said,* He is like him: *but* he said, I am *he.*

10 Therefore said they unto him, How were thine eyes opened?

11 He answered and said, A man that is called Jesus made clay, and anointed mine eyes, and said unto me, Go to the pool of Siloam, and wash: and I went and washed, and I received sight.

12 Then said they unto him, Where is he? He said, I know not.

13 They brought to the Pharisees him that aforetime was blind.

14 And it was the sabbath day when Jesus made the clay, and opened his eyes.

15 Then again the Pharisees also asked him how he had received his sight. He said unto them, He put clay upon mine eyes, and I washed, and do see.

16 Therefore said some of the Pharisees, This man is not of God, because he keepeth not the sabbath day. Others said, How can a man that is a sinner do such miracles? And there was a division among them.

17 They say unto the blind man again, What sayest thou of him, that he hath opened thine eyes? He said, He is a prophet.

18 But the Jews did not believe concerning him, that he had been blind, and received his sight, until they called the parents of him that had received his sight.

19 And they asked them, saying, Is this your son, who ye say was born blind? how then doth he now see?

20 His parents answered them and said, We know that this is our son, and that he was born blind:

21 But by what means he now seeth, we know not; or who hath opened his eyes, we know not: he is of age; ask him: he shall speak for himself.

22 These *words* spake his parents, because they feared the Jews: for the Jews had agreed already, that if any man did confess that he was Christ, he should be put out of the synagogue.

23 Therefore said his parents, He is of age; ask him.

24 Then again called they the man that was blind, and said unto him, Give God the praise: we know that this man is a sinner.

25 He answered and said, Whether he be a sinner *or no,* I know not: one thing I know, that, whereas I was blind, now I see.

26 Then said they to him again, What did he to thee? how opened he thine eyes?

27 He answered them, I have told you already, and ye did not hear: wherefore would ye hear *it* again? will ye also be his disciples?

28 Then they reviled him, and said, Thou art his disciple; but we are Moses' disciples.

29 We know that God spake unto Moses: *as for* this *fellow,* we know not from whence he is.

30 The man answered and said unto them, Why herein is a marvellous thing, that ye

---

Cross references:

58 Ex. 3:14; Isa. 43:13; John 17:5, 24; Col. 1:17; Rev. 1:8

59 Luke 4:30; John 10:31, 39; 11:8

2 John 9:34

3 John 11:4

4 John 4:34; 5:19, 36; 11:9; 12:35; 17:4

5 John 1:5, 9; 3:19; 8:12; 12:35, 46

6 Mark 7:33; 8:23

7 2Kgs. 5:14; Neh. 3:15

11 John 9:6, 7

16 John 3:2; 7:12, 43; 9:33; 10:19

17 John 4:19; 6:14

22 John 7:13; 9:34; 12:42; 16:2; 19:38; Acts 5:13

24 Josh. 7:19; 1Sam. 6:5; John 9:16

29 John 8:14

30 John 3:10

9:29–30 God spake unto Moses. Both Moses and Jesus performed miracles. In this instance, Jesus heals a blind man both physically and spiritually. The formerly blind man could now see that Jesus was the Messiah that Moses pointed to in his writings. Yet Jesus' critics separated his power to heal physically from any spiritual authority to forgive sin. Even though Jesus, the light of the world, shone brightly in the faces of those critics, they could not see the truth and refused to acknowledge Him.

know not from whence he is, and *yet* he hath opened mine eyes.

31 Now we know that God heareth not sinners: but if any man be a worshipper of God, and doeth his will, him he heareth.

32 Since the world began was it not heard that any man opened the eyes of one that was born blind.

33 If this man were not of God, he could do nothing.

34 They answered and said unto him, Thou wast altogether born in sins, and dost thou teach us? And they cast him out.

35 Jesus heard that they had cast him out; and when he had found him, he said unto him, Dost thou believe on the Son of God?

36 He answered and said, Who is he, Lord, that I might believe on him?

37 And Jesus said unto him, Thou hast both seen him, and it is he that talketh with thee.

38 And he said, Lord, I believe. And he worshipped him.

39 And Jesus said, For judgment I am come into this world, that they which see not might see; and that they which see might be made blind.

40 And *some* of the Pharisees which were with him heard these words and said unto him, Are we blind also?

41 Jesus said unto them, If ye were blind, ye should have no sin: but now ye say, We see; therefore your sin remaineth.

CHAPTER 10
Jesus Is the Good Shepherd

1 Verily, verily, I say unto you, He that entereth not by the door into the sheepfold, but climbeth up some other way, the same is a thief and a robber.

2 But he that entereth in by the door is the shepherd of the sheep.

3 To him the porter openeth; and the sheep hear his voice: and he calleth his own sheep by name, and leadeth them out.

4 And when he putteth forth his own sheep, he goeth before them, and the sheep follow him: for they know his voice.

5 And a stranger will they not follow, but will flee from him: for they know not the voice of strangers.

6 This parable spake Jesus unto them: but

31 Job 27:9; 35:12; Ps. 18:41; 34:15; 66:18; Prov. 1:28; 15:29; 28:9; Isa. 1:15; Jer. 11:11; 14:12; Ezek. 8:18; Mic. 3:4; Zech. 7:13
33 John 9:16
34 John 9:2, 22
35 Matt. 14:33; 16:16; Mark 1:1; John 10:36; 1John 5:13
37 John 4:26
39 Matt. 13:13; John 3:17; 5:22, 27; 12:47
40 Rom. 2:19
41 John 15:22, 24
9 John 14:6; Eph. 2:18
11 Isa. 40:11; Ezek. 34:12, 23; 37:24; Heb. 13:20; 1Pet. 2:25; 5:4
12 Zech. 11:16, 17
14 2Tim. 2:19
15 Matt. 11:27; John 15:13
16 Isa. 56:8; Ezek. 37:22; Eph. 2:14; 1Pet. 2:25
17 Isa. 53:7, 8, 12; Heb. 2:9
18 John 2:19; 6:38; 15:10; Acts 2:24, 32
19 John 7:43; 9:16
20 John 7:20; 8:48
21 Ex. 4:11; Ps. 94:9; 146:8; John 9:6, 7, 32, 33

they understood not what things they were which he spake unto them.

7 Then said Jesus unto them again, Verily, verily, I say unto you, I am the door of the sheep.

8 All that ever came before me are thieves and robbers: but the sheep did not hear them.

9 I am the door: by me if any man enter in, he shall be saved, and shall go in and out, and find pasture.

10 The thief cometh not, but for to steal, and to kill, and to destroy: I am come that they might have life, and that they might have it more abundantly.

11 I am the good shepherd: the good shepherd giveth his life for the sheep.

12 But he that is an hireling, and not the shepherd, whose own the sheep are not, seeth the wolf coming, and leaveth the sheep, and fleeth: and the wolf catcheth them, and scattereth the sheep.

13 The hireling fleeth, because he is an hireling, and careth not for the sheep.

14 I am the good shepherd, and know my sheep, and am known of mine.

15 As the Father knoweth me, even so know I the Father: and I lay down my life for the sheep.

16 And other sheep I have, which are not of this fold: them also I must bring, and they shall hear my voice; and there shall be one fold, and one shepherd.

17 Therefore doth my Father love me, because I lay down my life, that I might take it again.

18 No man taketh it from me, but I lay it down of myself. I have power to lay it down, and I have power to take it again. This commandment have I received of my Father.

19 There was a division therefore again among the Jews for these sayings.

20 And many of them said, He hath a devil, and is mad; why hear ye him?

21 Others said, These are not the words of him that hath a devil. Can a devil open the eyes of the blind?

The Believer's Assurance

22 And it was at Jerusalem the feast of the dedication, and it was winter.

10:16 other sheep I have. Christ alludes to the Church, which will be revealed later in the book (chaps. 13—17), begun in Acts 2, and explained in Paul's Epistles. The promise of one fold and one shepherd is a prediction of the unity of Jewish and Gentile believers through the single Shepherd—Christ. Implicitly, Jesus prays for this in His high priestly prayer (John 17:6–26) and Paul explains this mystery (Eph. 2—3).

23 And Jesus walked in the temple in Solomon's porch.

24 Then came the Jews round about him, and said unto him, How long dost thou make us to doubt? If thou be the Christ, tell us plainly.

25 Jesus answered them, I told you, and ye believed not: the works that I do in my Father's name, they bear witness of me.

26 But ye believe not, because ye are not of my sheep, as I said unto you.

27 My sheep hear my voice, and I know them, and they follow me:

28 And I give unto them eternal life; and they shall never perish, neither shall any man pluck them out of my hand.

29 My Father, which gave them me, is greater than all; and no man is able to pluck them out of my Father's hand.

30 I and my Father are one.

31 Then the Jews took up stones again to stone him.

32 Jesus answered them, Many good works have I shewed you from my Father; for which of those works do ye stone me?

33 The Jews answered him, saying, For a good work we stone thee not; but for blasphemy; and because that thou, being a man, makest thyself God.

34 Jesus answered them, Is it not written in your law, I said, Ye are gods?

35 If he called them gods, unto whom the word of God came, and the scripture cannot be broken;

36 Say ye of him, whom the Father hath sanctified, and sent into the world, Thou blasphemest; because I said, I am the Son of God?

37 If I do not the works of my Father, believe me not.

38 But if I do, though ye believe not me, believe the works: that ye may know, and believe, that the Father is in me, and I in him.

39 Therefore they sought again to take him: but he escaped out of their hand,

40 And went away again beyond Jordan into the place where John at first baptized; and there he abode.

41 And many resorted unto him, and said, John did no miracle: but all things that John spake of this man were true.

42 And many believed on him there.

CHAPTER 11
The Death of Lazarus

1 Now a certain *man* was sick, *named* Lazarus, of Bethany, the town of Mary and her sister Martha.

2 (It was *that* Mary which anointed the Lord with ointment, and wiped his feet with her hair, whose brother Lazarus was sick.)

3 Therefore his sisters sent unto him, saying, Lord, behold, he whom thou lovest is sick.

4 When Jesus heard *that*, he said, This sickness is not unto death, but for the glory of God, that the Son of God might be glorified thereby.

5 Now Jesus loved Martha, and her sister, and Lazarus.

6 When he had heard therefore that he was sick, he abode two days still in the same place where he was.

7 Then after that saith he to *his* disciples, Let us go into Judea again.

8 *His* disciples say unto him, Master, the Jews of late sought to stone thee; and goest thou thither again?

9 Jesus answered, Are there not twelve hours in the day? If any man walk in the day, he stumbleth not, because he seeth the light of this world.

10 But if a man walk in the night, he stumbleth, because there is no light in him.

11 These things said he: and after that he saith unto them, Our friend Lazarus sleepeth; but I go, that I may awake him out of sleep.

12 Then said his disciples, Lord, if he sleep, he shall do well.

13 Howbeit Jesus spake of his death: but they thought that he had spoken of taking of rest in sleep.

14 Then said Jesus unto them plainly, Lazarus is dead.

15 And I am glad for your sakes that I was not there, to the intent ye may believe; nevertheless let us go unto him.

16 Then said Thomas, which is called Didymus, unto his fellow disciples, Let us also go, that we may die with him.

17 Then when Jesus came, he found that he had *lain* in the grave four days already.

18 Now Bethany was nigh unto Jerusalem, about fifteen furlongs off:

19 And many of the Jews came to Martha and Mary, to comfort them concerning their brother.

20 Then Martha, as soon as she heard that Jesus was coming, went and met him: but Mary sat *still* in the house.

21 Then said Martha unto Jesus, Lord, if thou hadst been here, my brother had not died.

22 But I know, that even now, whatsoever thou wilt ask of God, God will give *it* thee.

Cross references:

23 Acts 3:11; 5:12
25 John 3:2; 5:36; 10:38
26 John 8:47; 1 John 4:6
27 John 10:4, 14
28 John 6:37; 17:11, 12; 18:9
29 John 14:28; 17:2, 6-10
30 John 8:59; 17:11, 22
33 John 5:18
34 Ps. 82:6
35 Rom. 13:1
36 Luke 1:35; John 3:17; 5:17, 18, 36, 37; 6:27; 8:42; 9:35, 37; 10:30
37 John 15:24
38 John 5:36; 14:10, 11; 17:21
39 John 7:30, 44; 8:59
40 John 1:28
41 John 3:30
42 John 8:30; 11:45
1 Luke 10:38, 39
2 Matt. 26:7; Mark 14:3; John 12:3
4 John 9:3; 11:40
6 John 10:40
8 John 10:31
9 John 9:4
10 John 12:35
11 Deut. 31:16; Dan. 12:2; Matt. 9:24; Acts 7:60; 1 Cor. 15:18, 51
22 John 9:31

23 Jesus saith unto her, Thy brother shall rise again.

24 Martha saith unto him, I know that he shall rise again in the resurrection at the last day.

25 Jesus said unto her, I am the resurrection, and the life: he that believeth in me, though he were dead, yet shall he live:

26 And whosoever liveth and believeth in me shall never die. Believest thou this?

27 She saith unto him, Yea, Lord: I believe that thou art the Christ, the Son of God, which should come into the world.

28 And when she had so said, she went her way, and called Mary her sister secretly, saying, The Master is come, and calleth for thee.

29 As soon as she heard *that*, she arose quickly, and came unto him.

30 Now Jesus was not yet come into the town, but was in that place where Martha met him.

31 The Jews then which were with her in the house, and comforted her, when they saw Mary, that she rose up hastily and went out, followed her, saying, She goeth unto the grave to weep there.

32 Then when Mary was come where Jesus was, and saw him, she fell down at his feet, saying unto him, Lord, if thou hadst been here, my brother had not died.

33 When Jesus therefore saw her weeping, and the Jews also weeping which came with her, he groaned in the spirit, and was troubled.

34 And said, Where have ye laid him? They said unto him, Lord, come and see.

35 Jesus wept.

36 Then said the Jews, Behold how he loved him!

37 And some of them said, Could not this man, which opened the eyes of the blind, have caused that even this man should not have died?

Jesus Brings Lazarus Back to Life

38 Jesus therefore again groaning in himself cometh to the grave. It was a cave, and a stone lay upon it.

39 Jesus said, Take ye away the stone. Martha, the sister of him that was dead, saith unto him, Lord, by this time he stinketh: for he hath been *dead* four days.

40 Jesus saith unto her, Said I not unto thee, that, if thou wouldest believe, thou shouldest see the glory of God?

41 Then they took away the stone *from the place* where the dead was laid. And Jesus lifted up *his* eyes, and said, Father, I thank thee that thou hast heard me.

42 And I knew that thou hearest me always: but because of the people which stand by I said it, that they may believe that thou hast sent me.

43 And when he thus had spoken, he cried with a loud voice, Lazarus, come forth.

44 And he that was dead came forth, bound hand and foot with graveclothes: and his face was bound about with a napkin. Jesus saith unto them, Loose him, and let him go.

45 Then many of the Jews which came to Mary, and had seen the things which Jesus did, believed on him.

46 But some of them went their ways to the Pharisees, and told them what things Jesus had done.

47 Then gathered the chief priests and the Pharisees a council, and said, What do we? for this man doeth many miracles.

48 If we let him thus alone, all *men* will believe on him: and the Romans shall come and take away both our place and nation.

49 And one of them, *named* Caiaphas, being the high priest that same year, said unto them, Ye know nothing at all,

50 Nor consider that it is expedient for us, that one man should die for the people, and that the whole nation perish not.

51 And this spake he not of himself: but being high priest that year, he prophesied that Jesus should die for that nation;

52 And not for that nation only, but that also he should gather together in one the children of God that were scattered abroad.

53 Then from that day forth they took counsel together for to put him to death.

54 Jesus therefore walked no more openly among the Jews; but went thence unto a

24 Luke 14:14; John 5:29

25 John 1:4; 3:36; 5:21; 6:35, 39, 40, 44; 14:6; Col. 3:4; 1John 1:1, 2; 5:10-12

27 Matt. 4:42; 16:16; John 6:14, 69

31 John 11:19

32 John 11:21

35 Luke 19:41

37 John 9:6

40 John 11:4, 23

42 John 12:30

44 John 20:7

45 John 2:23; 10:42; 12:11, 18

47 Ps. 2:2; Matt. 26:3; Mark 14:1; Luke 22:2; John 12:19; Acts 4:16

49 Luke 3:2; John 18:14; Acts 4:6

50 John 18:14

52 Isa. 49:6; John 10:16; Eph. 2:14-17; 1John 2:2

54 2Chr. 13:19; John 4:1, 3; 7:1

11:23–26 Thy brother shall rise again. Just as Christ had the power to raise Lazarus, even so He will raise all believers in Him at the Rapture. Their souls, meanwhile, are present with the Lord immediately at death, awaiting the resurrection. The same Lord who guaranteed the resurrection of Lazarus and made it happen guarantees to raise all believers!

11:40–42 if thou wouldest believe, thou shouldest see the glory of God? Jesus reminds Martha of His earlier promise (verses 4, 25–26). Martha's trust is certainly expressed in her granting permission for the tomb to be opened. She saw the glory of God when Jesus raised her brother. God's glory is expressed through miracles, particularly through the miracle of resurrecting the dead.

country near to the wilderness, into a city called Ephraim, and there continued with his disciples.

55 And the Jews' passover was nigh at hand: and many went out of the country up to Jerusalem before the passover, to purify themselves.

56 Then sought they for Jesus, and spake among themselves, as they stood in the temple, What think ye, that he will not come to the feast?

57 Now both the chief priests and the Pharisees had given a commandment, that, if any man knew where he were, he should shew *it*, that they might take him.

CHAPTER 12
Mary Anoints Jesus at Bethany

1 Then Jesus six days before the passover came to Bethany, where Lazarus was which had been dead, whom he raised from the dead.

2 There they made him a supper; and Martha served: but Lazarus was one of them that sat at the table with him.

3 Then took Mary a pound of ointment of spikenard, very costly, and anointed the feet of Jesus, and wiped his feet with her hair: and the house was filled with the odour of the ointment.

4 Then saith one of his disciples, Judas Iscariot, Simon's *son*, which should betray him,

5 Why was not this ointment sold for three hundred pence, and given to the poor?

6 This he said, not that he cared for the poor; but because he was a thief, and had the bag, and bare what was put therein.

7 Then said Jesus, Let her alone: against the day of my burying hath she kept this.

8 For the poor always ye have with you; but me ye have not always.

9 Much people of the Jews therefore knew that he was there: and they came not for Jesus' sake only, but that they might see Lazarus also, whom he had raised from the dead.

10 But the chief priests consulted that they might put Lazarus also to death;

11 Because that by reason of him many of the Jews went away, and believed on Jesus.

Jesus' Triumphal Entry into Jerusalem

12 On the next day much people that were come to the feast, when they heard that Jesus was coming to Jerusalem,

13 Took branches of palm trees, and went forth to meet him, and cried, Hosanna: Blessed *is* the King of Israel that cometh in the name of the Lord.

14 And Jesus, when he had found a young ass, sat thereon; as it is written,

15 Fear not, daughter of Sion; behold, thy King cometh, sitting on an ass's colt.

16 These things understood not his disciples at the first: but when Jesus was glorified, then remembered they that these things were written of him, and *that* they had done these things unto him.

17 The people therefore that was with him when he called Lazarus out of his grave, and raised him from the dead, bare record.

18 For this cause the people also met him, for that they heard that he had done this miracle.

19 The Pharisees therefore said among themselves, Perceive ye how ye prevail nothing? behold, the world is gone after him.

Christ's Final Discourse to the People

20 And there were certain Greeks among them that came up to worship at the feast:

21 The same came therefore to Philip, which was of Bethsaida of Galilee, and desired him, saying, Sir, we would see Jesus.

22 Philip cometh and telleth Andrew: and again Andrew and Philip tell Jesus.

23 And Jesus answered them, saying, The hour is come, that the Son of man should be glorified.

24 Verily, verily, I say unto you, Except a corn of wheat fall into the ground and die, it abideth alone: but if it die, it bringeth forth much fruit.

25 He that loveth his life shall lose it; and he that hateth his life in this world shall keep it unto life eternal.

---

55 John 2:13; 5:1; 6:4
56 John 7:11
1 John 11:1, 43
2 Matt. 26:6; Mark 14:3
3 Luke 10:38, 39; John 11:2
6 John 13:29
8 Matt. 26:11; Mark 14:7
9 John 11:43, 44
10 Luke 16:31
11 John 11:45; 12:18
12 Matt. 21:8; Mark 11:8; Luke 19:35-38
13 Ps. 118:25, 26
14 Matt. 21:7
15 Zech. 9:9
16 Luke 18:34; John 7:39; 14:26
18 John 12:11
19 John 11:47, 48
20 1Kgs. 8:41, 42; Acts 8:27; 17:4
21 John 1:44
23 John 13:32; 17:1
24 1Cor. 15:36
25 Matt. 10:39; 16:25; Mark 8:35; Luke 9:24; 17:33

12:13–15 This event is called the "triumphal entry" because the Jewish crowd received Jesus as their king. Amazingly, this was only hours before they would be calling out for Him to be crucified. The crowd directed the words from Psalm 118:25–26 toward Jesus. But in light of His upcoming rejection by the Jewish leaders, Jesus announced a future fulfillment of this praise at His second coming in conjunction with the conversion of Israel (Matt. 23:39; Luke 13:35). (See the footnotes on Daniel 9:24; 9:26; and 9:27. For parallel accounts, see Matt. 21:1–10; Mark 11:1–10.)

26 If any man serve me, let him follow me; and where I am, there shall also my servant be: if any man serve me, him will my Father honour.

27 Now is my soul troubled; and what shall I say? Father, save me from this hour: but for this cause came I unto this hour.

28 Father, glorify thy name. Then came there a voice from heaven, *saying,* I have both glorified *it,* and will glorify *it* again.

29 The people therefore, that stood by, and heard *it,* said that it thundered: others said, An angel spake to him.

30 Jesus answered and said, This voice came not because of me, but for your sakes.

31 Now is the judgment of this world: now shall the prince of this world be cast out.

32 And I, if I be lifted up from the earth, will draw all men unto me.

33 This he said, signifying what death he should die.

34 The people answered him, We have heard out of the law that Christ abideth for ever: and how sayest thou, The Son of man must be lifted up? who is this Son of man?

35 Then Jesus said unto them, Yet a little while is the light with you. Walk while ye have the light, lest darkness come upon you: for he that walketh in darkness knoweth not whither he goeth.

36 While ye have light, believe in the light, that ye may be the children of light. These things spake Jesus, and departed, and did hide himself from them.

Many People Believe, but Are Afraid

37 But though he had done so many miracles before them, yet they believed not on him:

38 That the saying of Esaias the prophet might be fulfilled, which he spake, Lord, who hath believed our report? and to whom hath the arm of the Lord been revealed?

39 Therefore they could not believe, because that Esaias said again,

40 He hath blinded their eyes, and hardened their heart; that they should not see with *their* eyes, nor understand with *their* heart, and be converted, and I should heal them.

41 These things said Esaias, when he saw his glory, and spake of him.

42 Nevertheless among the chief rulers also many believed on him; but because of the Pharisees they did not confess *him,* lest they should be put out of the synagogue:

43 For they loved the praise of men more than the praise of God.

44 Jesus cried and said, He that believeth on me, believeth not on me, but on him that sent me.

45 And he that seeth me seeth him that sent me.

46 I am come a light into the world, that whosoever believeth on me should not abide in darkness.

47 And if any man hear my words, and believe not, I judge him not: for I came not to judge the world, but to save the world.

48 He that rejecteth me, and receiveth not my words, hath one that judgeth him: the word that I have spoken, the same shall judge him in the last day.

49 For I have not spoken of myself; but the Father which sent me, he gave me a commandment, what I should say, and what I should speak.

50 And I know that his commandment is life everlasting: whatsoever I speak therefore, even as the Father said unto me, so I speak.

CHAPTER 13
Jesus Washes His Disciples' Feet

1 Now before the feast of the passover, when Jesus knew that his hour was come

---

Cross-references:

26 John 14:3; 17:24; 1Thess. 4:17
27 Matt. 26:38, 39; Luke 12:50; 22:53; John 13:21; 18:37
28 Matt. 3:17
30 John 11:42
31 Matt. 12:29; Luke 10:18
32 John 3:14; 8:28
33 John 18:32
34 Isa. 9:7; 53:8; Ezek. 37:25; Dan. 2:44; 7:14, 27; Mic. 4:7
35 Jer. 13:16; John 1:9; 8:12; 9:5; 11:10
36 Luke 16:8; John 8:59; 11:54; Eph. 5:8; 1John 2:9; 10:11
38 Isa. 53:1; Rom. 10:16
40 Isa. 6:9, 10; Matt. 13:14
41 Isa. 6:1
44 Mark 9:37
46 John 3:19; 8:12; 9:5, 39; 12:35, 36
48 Deut. 18:19; Mark 16:16; Luke 10:16

12:26 if any man serve me, him will my Father honour. Anyone truly saved by faith is willing to serve His Master, Jesus, and will be exalted in the next life with either rewards or crowns or both, forever. This willingness to serve is a divinely enabled evidence of salvation.

12:37–43 In spite of the incredible miracles that Jesus did many Jews did not believe or commit themselves to Him because they "loved the praise of men" (v. 43). This is another fulfillment of Isaiah 6:9–10, where Isaiah is commanded to proclaim God's message to the people of Judah, to the hardening of the hearts of the rebellious.

12:41 These things said Esaias [Isaiah], **when he saw his glory, and spake of him.** The Jewish leaders of Jesus' day did not recognize in themselves the same blind insensitivity to God's Word that existed in the days of Isaiah. Isaiah often spoke of the Messiah in his prophecies (Isa. 4:2; 7:14; 9:6–7; 11:1–5, 10; 32:1; 42:1–4; 49:1–7; 52:13—53:12; 61:1–3). These prophecies were fulfilled in Jesus, the Son of God (cf. John 5:46; 8:46).

13:1—17:26 This is one of the most sublime teachings Jesus gave to the twelve. Spoken the night before He was crucified, it contains instructions on life, love, service, and also a prophecy of His imminent death on the cross.

that he should depart out of this world unto the Father, having loved his own which were in the world, he loved them unto the end.

2 And supper being ended, the devil having now put into the heart of Judas Iscariot, Simon's *son*, to betray him;

3 Jesus knowing that the Father had given all things into his hands, and that he was come from God, and went to God;

4 He riseth from supper, and laid aside his garments; and took a towel, and girded himself.

5 After that he poureth water into a bason, and began to wash the disciples' feet, and to wipe *them* with the towel wherewith he was girded.

6 Then cometh he to Simon Peter: and Peter saith unto him, Lord, dost thou wash my feet?

7 Jesus answered and said unto him, What I do thou knowest not now; but thou shalt know hereafter.

8 Peter saith unto him, Thou shalt never wash my feet. Jesus answered him, If I wash thee not, thou hast no part with me.

9 Simon Peter saith unto him, Lord, not my feet only, but also *my* hands and *my* head.

10 Jesus saith to him, He that is washed needeth not save to wash his feet, but is clean every whit: and ye are clean, but not all.

11 For he knew who should betray him; therefore said he, Ye are not all clean.

12 So after he had washed their feet, and had taken his garments, and was set down again, he said unto them, Know ye what I have done to you?

13 Ye call me Master and Lord: and ye say well; for so I am.

14 If I then, your Lord and Master, have washed your feet; ye also ought to wash one another's feet.

15 For I have given you an example, that ye should do as I have done to you.

16 Verily, verily, I say unto you, The servant is not greater than his lord; neither he that is sent greater than he that sent him.

17 If ye know these things, happy are ye if ye do them.

18 I speak not of you all: I know whom I have chosen: but that the scripture may be fulfilled, He that eateth bread with me hath lifted up his heel against me.

19 Now I tell you before it come, that, when it is come to pass, ye may believe that I am he.

20 Verily, verily, I say unto you, He that receiveth whomsoever I send receiveth me; and he that receiveth me receiveth him that sent me.

Jesus Foretells His Betrayal

21 When Jesus had thus said, he was troubled in spirit, and testified, and said, Verily, verily, I say unto you, that one of you shall betray me.

22 Then the disciples looked one on another, doubting of whom he spake.

23 Now there was leaning on Jesus' bosom one of his disciples, whom Jesus loved.

24 Simon Peter therefore beckoned to him, that he should ask who it should be of whom he spake.

25 He then lying on Jesus' breast saith unto him, Lord, who is it?

26 Jesus answered, He it is, to whom I shall give a sop, when I have dipped it. And when he had dipped the sop, he gave *it* to Judas Iscariot, *the son* of Simon.

27 And after the sop Satan entered into him. Then said Jesus unto him, That thou doest, do quickly.

28 Now no man at the table knew for what intent he spake this unto him.

29 For some *of them* thought, because Judas had the bag, that Jesus had said unto him, Buy *those things* that we have need of against the feast; or, that he should give something to the poor.

30 He then having received the sop went immediately out: and it was night.

"Love One Another"

31 Therefore, when he was gone out, Jesus said, Now is the Son of man glorified, and God is glorified in him.

32 If God be glorified in him, God shall also glorify him in himself, and shall straightway glorify him.

33 Little children, yet a little while I am with you. Ye shall seek me: and as I said unto the Jews, Whither I go, ye cannot come; so now I say to you.

34 A new commandment I give unto you, That ye love one another; as I have loved you, that ye also love one another.

35 By this shall all men know that ye are my disciples, if ye have love one to another.

Cross References

2 Luke 22:3; John 13:27
3 Matt. 11:27; 28:18; John 3:35; 8:42; 16:28; 17:2; Acts 2:36; 1Cor. 15:27; Heb. 2:8
4 Luke 22:27; Phil. 2:7, 8
6 Matt. 3:14
7 John 13:12
8 1Cor. 6:11; Titus 3:5
10 John 15:3
11 John 6:64
13 Matt. 23:8, 10; Luke 6:46
14 Luke 22:27; Rom. 12:10; Gal. 6:1, 2; 1Pet. 5:5
15 Matt. 11:29; Phil. 2:5; 1Pet. 2:21; 1John 2:6
16 Matt. 10:24; Luke 6:40; John 15:20
17 James 1:25
18 Ps. 41:9; Matt. 26:23; John 13:21
19 John 14:29; 16:4
20 Matt. 10:40; 25:40; Luke 10:16
21 Matt. 26:21; Mark 14:18; Luke 22:21; Acts 1:17
23 John 19:26; 20:2
27 Luke 6:70; 22:3
29 John 12:6
31 John 12:23; 14:13; 1Pet. 4:11
34 Lev. 19:15:12, 17; 18; Eph. 5:2
35 1John 2:5; 4:20

13:21 one of you shall betray me. Jesus was not surprised by Judas' betrayal; it had been predicted (see vv. 18, 26 and Ps. 41:9). (For parallel accounts, see Matt. 26:16, 21–25, 46; Mark 14:10–11, 18; Luke 22:46.)

Jesus Predicts Peter's Denial

36 Simon Peter said unto him, Lord, whither goest thou? Jesus answered him, Whither I go, thou canst not follow me now; but thou shalt follow me afterwards.

37 Peter said unto him, Lord, why cannot I follow thee now? I will lay down my life for thy sake.

38 Jesus answered him, Wilt thou lay down thy life for my sake? Verily, verily, I say unto thee, The cock shall not crow, till thou hast denied me thrice.

CHAPTER 14
"I Go to Prepare a Place"

1 Let not your heart be troubled: ye believe in God, believe also in me.

2 In my Father's house are many mansions: if it were not so, I would have told you. I go to prepare a place for you.

3 And if I go and prepare a place for you, I will come again, and receive you unto myself; that where I am, there ye may be also.

4 And whither I go ye know, and the way ye know.

5 Thomas saith unto him, Lord, we know not whither thou goest; and how can we know the way?

6 Jesus saith unto him, I am the way, the truth, and the life: no man cometh unto the Father, but by me.

7 If ye had known me, ye should have known my Father also: and from henceforth ye know him, and have seen him.

8 Philip saith unto him, Lord, shew us the Father, and it sufficeth us.

9 Jesus saith unto him, Have I been so long time with you, and yet hast thou not known me, Philip? he that hath seen me hath seen the Father; and how sayest thou then, Shew us the Father?

10 Believest thou not that I am in the Father, and the Father in me? the words that I speak unto you I speak not of myself: but the Father that dwelleth in me, he doeth the works.

11 Believe me that I am in the Father, and the Father in me: or else believe me for the very works' sake.

12 Verily, verily, I say unto you, He that believeth on me, the works that I do shall he

Cross references:
36 John 21:18; 2Pet. 1:14
37 Matt. 26:33-35; Mark 14:29-31; Luke 22:33, 34
2 John 13:33, 36
3 Acts 1:11
6 John 1:4, 17; 8:32; 10:9; 11:25; Heb. 9:8
7 John 8:19
9 John 12:45; Col. 1:15; Heb. 1:3
10 John 5:19; 7:16; 8:28; 10:38; 12:49; 14:20; 17:21, 23
11 John 5:36; 10:38
12 Matt. 21:21; Mark 16:17; Luke 10:17

The Rapture in John 14

Terms Used in John 14	Terms Used in 1 Thessalonians 4
Trouble (v. 1)	Sorrow (v. 13)
Believe (v. 1)	Believe (v. 14)
God, me (v. 1)	Jesus, God (v. 14)
Told you (v. 2)	Say to you (v. 15)
Come again (v. 3)	Coming of the Lord (v. 15)
Receive you (v. 3)	Caught up (v. 17)
Unto myself (v. 3)	To meet the Lord (v. 17)
Be where I am (v. 3)	Ever be with the Lord (v. 17)

13:38 The cock shall not crow, till thou hast denied me thrice. Jesus knew of Peter's denial in advance, because He was God and God declares the end from the beginning (Isa. 46:10). The fulfillment of this prophecy is recorded in John 18:16–27. (For parallel accounts, see Matt. 26:34, 74–75; Mark 14:30, 68–72; Luke 22:34, 60–61.)

14:1–3 I will come again, and receive you unto myself. This is the first teaching on the Rapture in Scripture. After predicting that He was going to return to His "Father's house" (see also v. 28) "to prepare a place for [His followers]" (a mansion or dwelling place), He promised that He would come again. Verse 3 is a reference to the Rapture, when Jesus takes His "bride" the Church up to the Father's house to be with Him. Verse 3 does not refer to the glorious appearing of Christ at the end of the Tribulation, when Jesus brings His saints with Him to the earth and sets up His kingdom (Matt. 24:27–31; Rev. 19:11–16). That this is a reference to the Rapture is supported by its similarity to Paul's more detailed teaching (1 Thess. 4:13–18). In contrast, a comparison of these verses with the description of the Second Coming in Revelation 19:11–21 shows no parallel themes.

14:12 greater works than these shall he do. Even though Jesus will be absent from them, the apostles and all believers throughout the Church Age will continue His ministry. The apostles will do no more spectacular miracles than Jesus, but their outreach will be much greater than Jesus' human outreach. Christ's return to His Father at His ascension ("because I go unto my Father") will result in the sending of the Holy Spirit that is needed to open the depraved eyes and minds of fallen mankind. This will result in a greater, global extension of the gospel (cf. John 14:16–18, 26; 15:26–27; 16:5–15).

The Rapture

By John F. Walvoord

The central theme of prophecy for believers today is the coming of Christ for His own in what is called the Rapture, or the "catching up" of the Church. The one single purpose of the Rapture is to take the Church from earth to heaven. The Rapture is never mentioned in the Old Testament and was first revealed by Christ to His disciples on the last night before His crucifixion (John 14:1–3).

The major passage on the Rapture is 1 Thessalonians 4:13–18. Paul describes the scene as the Lord coming bodily from heaven to the air above the earth and issuing a trumpet call that will be the signal for Christians who have died to be resurrected. A moment later, Christians still living will also be raptured with those who have been resurrected to meet the Lord in the air. Once they meet the Lord in the air, they go to heaven in fulfillment of the prophecy of going to the Father's house (John 14:2–3). First Corinthians 15 reveals more about the Rapture, saying that the human bodies of both those who have died and those who are living will be transformed instantly into bodies suited for heaven (15:51–52).

> *The one single purpose of the Rapture is to take the Church from earth to heaven.*

The New Testament indicates that the Rapture is different than the Second Coming. First, the Rapture is a movement from earth to heaven that will occur before the Tribulation, while the Second Coming is a movement from heaven to earth that takes place at the end of the Tribulation.

Second, the doctrine of the Rapture is a simple one. Prophecies regarding the Rapture make no mention of angels or attending hosts, and no mention of a judgment on earth to follow. The Second Coming, however, is a complex event that, as described in Revelation 19:11–16, will take place over many hours as a gigantic procession of millions of saints and angels move from heaven to earth.

Finally, in all the passages concerning the Rapture, a preceding event is never mentioned. In fact, the only reference to the timing of the Rapture is that it must occur before the Tribulation (the "wrath" of God, 1 Thess. 1:10; 5:9). Yet those passages that describe Christ's return describe many events that must take place before the Second Coming can occur. Christ's description of His second coming is recorded in Matthew 24, and Revelation 6—18 provides many details regarding the events of the Tribulation that precede it. Scripture uniformly presents the Rapture as an imminent event, one that can occur at any time, though that time is not known. (See the article, "The Imminent Coming of Christ" by Renald Showers.) The Second Coming, on the other hand, is by no means imminent; the prophecies of events described as preceding the Second Coming must first be literally fulfilled.

The imminent nature of the Rapture not only confronts individuals with the challenge to receive Christ before it is too late; it also challenges Christians to live with eternal values in view. Since the Rapture can occur at any moment and believers' lives on earth will thus be cut short, we need to maximize our commitment to Christ, doing all we can for the Lord in upright living and service to Him and others. While many future prophetic events are of great importance, the Rapture is perhaps the most important to the believer in Christ.

do also; and greater works than these shall he do; because I go unto my Father.

Praying in Jesus' Name

13 And whatsoever ye shall ask in my name, that will I do, that the Father may be glorified in the Son.

14 If ye shall ask any thing in my name, I will do it.

The Holy Spirit Will Come

15 If ye love me, keep my commandments.

16 And I will pray the Father, and he shall give you another Comforter, that he may abide with you for ever;

17 Even the Spirit of truth; whom the world cannot receive, because it seeth him not, neither knoweth him: but ye know him; for he dwelleth with you, and shall be in you.

18 I will not leave you comfortless: I will come to you.

19 Yet a little while, and the world seeth me no more; but ye see me: because I live, ye shall live also.

20 At that day ye shall know that I am in my Father, and ye in me, and I in you.

21 He that hath my commandments, and keepeth them, he it is that loveth me: and he that loveth me shall be loved of my Father, and I will love him, and will manifest myself to him.

22 Judas saith unto him, not Iscariot, Lord, how is it that thou wilt manifest thyself unto us, and not unto the world?

23 Jesus answered and said unto him, If a man love me, he will keep my words: and my Father will love him, and we will come unto him, and make our abode with him.

24 He that loveth me not keepeth not my sayings: and the word which ye hear is not mine, but the Father's which sent me.

25 These things have I spoken unto you, being yet present with you.

26 But the Comforter, which is the Holy Ghost, whom the Father will send in my name, he shall teach you all things, and bring all things to your remembrance, whatsoever I have said unto you.

Jesus Will Go to the Father

27 Peace I leave with you, my peace I give unto you: not as the world giveth, give I unto you. Let not your heart be troubled, neither let it be afraid.

28 Ye have heard how I said unto you, I go away, and come again unto you. If ye loved me, ye would rejoice, because I said, I go unto the Father: for my Father is greater than I.

29 And now I have told you before it come to pass, that, when it is come to pass, ye might believe.

30 Hereafter I will not talk much with you: for the prince of this world cometh, and hath nothing in me.

31 But that the world may know that I love the Father; and as the Father gave me commandment, even so I do. Arise, let us go hence.

CHAPTER 15
Jesus Is the True Vine

1 I am the true vine, and my Father is the husbandman.

2 Every branch in me that beareth not fruit he taketh away: and every branch that beareth fruit, he purgeth it, that it may bring forth more fruit.

3 Now ye are clean through the word which I have spoken unto you.

4 Abide in me, and I in you. As the branch cannot bear fruit of itself, except it abide in the vine; no more can ye, except ye abide in me.

13 Matt. 7:7; 21:22; Mark 11:24; Luke 11:9; John 15:7, 16

15 1John 5:3

17 1Cor. 2:14

18 Matt. 28:20; John 14:3, 28

19 John 16:16

20 John 10:38; 14:10; 17:21, 23, 26

21 John 14:15, 23; 1John 2:5; 5:3

22 Luke 6:16

23 John 14:15; 1John 2:24; Rev. 3:20

24 John 5:19, 38; 7:16; 8:28; 12:49; 14:10

25 Luke 24:49

26 John 14:16; 15:26; 16:7, 13; 1John 2:20, 27

28 John 5:18; 10:30; 14:3, 12, 18

29 John 13:19; 16:4

30 John 12:31; 16:11

31 Phil. 2:8

1 Matt. 15:13

3 Eph. 5:26

4 Col. 1:23; 1John 2:6

14:16–18 he shall give you another Comforter . . . the Spirit of truth. This prophecy is fulfilled in the coming of the Holy Spirit to indwell all believers during the Church Age, starting on the Day of Pentecost (Acts 2:1–13). Christ goes on to say, "I will come to you." What does He mean? The next couple of verses make it clear that Christ will be present in the Church and individual believers during the interim of His absence through the indwelling ministry of the Holy Spirit.

14:26 bring all things to your remembrance. Jesus predicts that the Holy Spirit will come and help His disciples recall His words. This was accomplished in Acts 2,

after Jesus had ascended into heaven (Acts 1:9–11). The Spirit of truth assures us that the words of Jesus in the New Testament are accurate and dependable. They are not the product of the belated human memories, but rather of the Holy Spirit's inspiration.

14:28 I go away [His ascension, Acts 1], **and come again unto you.** The second clause speaks of the rapture of the Church when Jesus takes believers to His Father's house. Jesus' challenge to all Christians should not be overlooked. The truth of Christ's return comforts and assures the hearts of all believers.

5 I am the vine, ye are the branches: He that abideth in me, and I in him, the same bringeth forth much fruit: for without me ye can do nothing.

6 If a man abide not in me, he is cast forth as a branch, and is withered; and men gather them, and cast them into the fire, and they are burned.

7 If ye abide in me, and my words abide in you, ye shall ask what ye will, and it shall be done unto you.

8 Herein is my Father glorified, that ye bear much fruit; so shall ye be my disciples.

9 As the Father hath loved me, so have I loved you: continue ye in my love.

10 If ye keep my commandments, ye shall abide in my love; even as I have kept my Father's commandments, and abide in his love.

11 These things have I spoken unto you, that my joy might remain in you, and that your joy might be full.

12 This is my commandment, That ye love one another, as I have loved you.

13 Greater love hath no man than this, that a man lay down his life for his friends.

14 Ye are my friends, if ye do whatsoever I command you.

15 Henceforth I call you not servants; for the servant knoweth not what his lord doeth: but I have called you friends; for all things that I have heard of my Father I have made known unto you.

16 Ye have not chosen me, but I have chosen you, and ordained you, that ye should go and bring forth fruit, and that your fruit should remain: that whatsoever ye shall ask of the Father in my name, he may give it you.

17 These things I command you, that ye love one another.

The Disciple of Christ Should Expect Persecution

18 If the world hate you, ye know that it hated me before it hated you.

19 If ye were of the world, the world would love his own: but because ye are not of the world, but I have chosen you out of the world, therefore the world hateth you.

20 Remember the word that I said unto you, The servant is not greater than his lord. If they have persecuted me, they will also persecute you; if they have kept my saying, they will keep yours also.

21 But all these things will they do unto you for my name's sake, because they know not him that sent me.

22 If I had not come and spoken unto them, they had not had sin: but now they have no cloke for their sin.

23 He that hateth me hateth my Father also.

24 If I had not done among them the works which none other man did, they had not had sin: but now have they both seen and hated both me and my Father.

25 But this cometh to pass, that the word might be fulfilled that is written in their law, They hated me without a cause.

26 But when the Comforter is come, whom I will send unto you from the Father, even the Spirit of truth, which proceedeth from the Father, he shall testify of me:

27 And ye also shall bear witness, because ye have been with me from the beginning.

CHAPTER 16

1 These things have I spoken unto you, that ye should not be offended.

2 They shall put you out of the synagogues: yea, the time cometh, that whosoever killeth you will think that he doeth God service.

3 And these things will they do unto you, because they have not known the Father, nor me.

4 But these things have I told you, that when the time shall come, ye may remember that I told you of them. And these things I said not unto you at the beginning, because I was with you.

Cross references:
5 Hos. 14:8
6 Matt. 3:10; 7:19
7 John 14:13, 14; 15:16; 16:23
8 Matt. 5:16
11 John 16:24; 17:13; 1 John 1:4
12 1 John 3:11; 4:21
13 John 10:11, 15; 1 John 3:16
14 Matt. 12:50; John 14:15, 23
16 Matt. 28:19; Mark 16:15
18 John 3:1, 13
19 John 17:14; 1 John 4:5,
20 Matt. 10:24; Luke 6:40; John 13:16
21 Matt. 10:22; 24:9; John 16:3
22 John 9:41; James 4:17
23 1 John 2:23
24 John 3:2; 7:31; 9:32
25 Ps. 35:19; 69:4
26 Acts 2:33
27 Luke 24:48
1 Matt. 11:6; 24:10; 26:31
2 John 9:22, 34; 12:42; Acts 8:1; 9:1; 26:9-11
4 Matt. 9:1

15:6 cast *them* into the fire, and they are burned. This is the language of future judgment.

15:20 If they have persecuted me, they will also persecute you. This prophecy has been fulfilled millions of times down through church history. The reason why fallen humanity opposes and persecutes the Church is that it hates and opposes our Head—Jesus Christ. Because He gave His life for us, we should be willing to give our lives for Him (2 Tim. 3:12).

15:25 that the word might be fulfilled. This fulfills the prophecy of Psalm 69:4, which says, "They that hate me without a cause are more than the hairs of mine head."

16:2–3 Christ builds upon the prophecy in John 15:20 that His followers will suffer persecution. In these verses, Jesus emphasizes the religious nature of the persecution they will endure (cf. Acts 7:59; 9:1–4; 12:2; see the note on 15:20).

The Work of the Holy Spirit

5 But now I go my way to him that sent me; and none of you asketh me, Whither goest thou?

6 But because I have said these things unto you, sorrow hath filled your heart.

7 Nevertheless I tell you the truth; It is expedient for you that I go away: for if I go not away, the Comforter will not come unto you; but if I depart, I will send him unto you.

8 And when he is come, he will reprove the world of sin, and of righteousness, and of judgment:

9 Of sin, because they believe not on me;

10 Of righteousness, because I go to my Father, and ye see me no more;

11 Of judgment, because the prince of this world is judged.

12 I have yet many things to say unto you, but ye cannot bear them now.

13 Howbeit when he, the Spirit of truth, is come, he will guide you into all truth: for he shall not speak of himself; but whatsoever he shall hear, that shall he speak: and he will shew you things to come.

14 He shall glorify me: for he shall receive of mine, and shall shew it unto you.

15 All things that the Father hath are mine: therefore said I, that he shall take of mine, and shall shew it unto you.

16 A little while, and ye shall not see me: and again, a little while, and ye shall see me, because I go to the Father.

17 Then said *some* of his disciples among themselves, What is this that he saith unto us, A little while, and ye shall not see me: and again, a little while, and ye shall see me: and, Because I go to the Father?

18 They said therefore, What is this that he saith, A little while? we cannot tell what he saith.

19 Now Jesus knew that they were desirous to ask him, and said unto them, Do ye inquire among yourselves of that I said, A little while, and ye shall not see me: and again, a little while, and ye shall see me?

20 Verily, verily, I say unto you, That ye shall weep and lament, but the world shall rejoice: and ye shall be sorrowful, but your sorrow shall be turned into joy.

21 A woman when she is in travail hath sorrow, because her hour is come: but as soon as she is delivered of the child, she remembereth no more the anguish, for joy that a man is born into the world.

22 And ye now therefore have sorrow: but I will see you again, and your heart shall rejoice, and your joy no man taketh from you.

23 And in that day ye shall ask me nothing. Verily, verily, I say unto you, Whatsoever ye shall ask the Father in my name, he will give it you.

24 Hitherto have ye asked nothing in my name: ask, and ye shall receive, that your joy may be full.

Jesus Will Return to Heaven

25 These things have I spoken unto you in proverbs: but the time cometh, when I shall no more speak unto you in proverbs, but I shall shew you plainly of the Father.

26 At that day ye shall ask in my name: and I say not unto you, that I will pray the Father for you:

27 For the Father himself loveth you, because ye have loved me, and have believed that I came out from God.

28 I came forth from the Father, and am come into the world: again, I leave the world, and go to the Father.

29 His disciples said unto him, Lo, now speakest thou plainly, and speakest no proverb.

Cross references

7 John 7:39; 14:16, 26; 15:26; Acts 2:33

10 John 3:14; 5:32; Acts 2:32

11 Luke 10:18; Eph. 2:2; Heb. 2:14

12 Mark 4:33

13 John 14:17, 26; 15:26; 1John 2:20, 27

15 Matt. 11:27; John 3:35; 13:3; 17:10

16 John 7:33; 13:3, 33; 14:19; 16:10, 28

21 Isa. 26:17

22 Luke 24:41, 52; John 14:1, 27; 16:6; 1Pet. 1:8

23 Matt. 7:7; John 14:13; 15:16

24 John 15:11

26 John 16:23

27 John 3:13; 14:21, 23; 16:30; 17:8

28 John 13:3

16:8–13 Jesus declares that the Holy Spirit convicts the world of sin and guides believers "into all truth." Believers are comforted by the provision of the New Testament that God provided through the Spirit's inspiration to His apostles. The Holy Spirit continues to comfort believers, who know that when they proclaim the gospel, the Holy Spirit is working in the hearts of hearers to bring some to faith in Christ.

16:16–24 Jesus predicts that after His departure the immediate life of His disciples will be characterized by great sorrow (16:20). Worse, while they are in sorrow "the world shall rejoice." But the believers' sorrow will be temporary, lasting only until Christ's resurrection, at which time their "sorrow shall be turned into joy." Later, simply knowing that Christ is alive and at the right hand of the Father will provide a new basis for joy and a new incentive to pray to the Father in His name. This promise continues to be fulfilled in our own day.

16:22 I will see you again. The antidote to sorrow is the promise of Christ's future return. Right-thinking believers realize that in spite of present sorrow and pain, there is a present joy in knowing that Christ will return to this world to take them to be with Him ("your heart shall rejoice," cf. John 14:3). This hope of joy, Jesus adds, "no man taketh from you."

30 Now are we sure that thou knowest all things, and needest not that any man should ask thee: by this we believe that thou camest forth from God.

31 Jesus answered them, Do ye now believe?

32 Behold, the hour cometh, yea, is now come, that ye shall be scattered, every man to his own, and shall leave me alone: and yet I am not alone, because the Father is with me.

33 These things I have spoken unto you, that in me ye might have peace. In the world ye shall have tribulation: but be of good cheer; I have overcome the world.

CHAPTER 17
Jesus' Intercessory Prayer

1 These words spake Jesus, and lifted up his eyes to heaven, and said, Father, the hour is come; glorify thy Son, that thy Son also may glorify thee:

2 As thou hast given him power over all flesh, that he should give eternal life to as many as thou hast given him.

3 And this is life eternal, that they might know thee the only true God, and Jesus Christ, whom thou hast sent.

4 I have glorified thee on the earth: I have finished the work which thou gavest me to do.

5 And now, O Father, glorify thou me with thine own self with the glory which I had with thee before the world was.

6 I have manifested thy name unto the men which thou gavest me out of the world: thine they were, and thou gavest them me; and they have kept thy word.

7 Now they have known that all things whatsoever thou hast given me are of thee.

8 For I have given unto them the words which thou gavest me; and they have received them, and have known surely that I came out from thee, and they have believed that thou didst send me.

9 I pray for them: I pray not for the world, but for them which thou hast given me; for they are thine.

10 And all mine are thine, and thine are mine; and I am glorified in them.

11 And now I am no more in the world, but these are in the world, and I come to thee. Holy Father, keep through thine own name those whom thou hast given me, that they may be one, as we are.

12 While I was with them in the world, I kept them in thy name: those that thou gavest me I have kept, and none of them is lost, but the son of perdition; that the scripture might be fulfilled.

13 And now come I to thee; and these things I speak in the world, that they might have my joy fulfilled in themselves.

14 I have given them thy word; and the world hath hated them, because they are not of the world, even as I am not of the world.

15 I pray not that thou shouldest take them out of the world, but that thou shouldest keep them from the evil.

16 They are not of the world, even as I am not of the world.

17 Sanctify them through thy truth: thy word is truth.

18 As thou hast sent me into the world, even so have I also sent them into the world.

19 And for their sakes I sanctify myself, that they also might be sanctified through the truth.

20 Neither pray I for these alone, but for them also which shall believe on me through their word;

21 That they all may be one; as thou, Father, art in me, and I in thee, that they also may be one in us: that the world may believe that thou hast sent me.

22 And the glory which thou gavest me I have given them; that they may be one, even as we are one:

23 I in them, and thou in me, that they may be made perfect in one; and that the world may know that thou hast sent me, and hast loved them, as thou hast loved me.

24 Father, I will that they also, whom thou hast given me, be with me where I am; that they may behold my glory, which thou hast given me: for thou lovedst me before the foundation of the world.

25 O righteous Father, the world hath not known thee: but I have known thee, and

32 Matt. 26:31; Mark 14:27

33 Isa. 9:6; 1John 4:4; 5:4

2 Matt. 11:27; 28:18

3 Isa. 53:11; Jer. 9:24

4 John 19:30

5 John 1:1, 2; 10:30; 14:9; Phil. 2:6; Col. 1:15; Heb. 1:3, 10

6 Ps. 22:22; John 6:37, 39; 10:29; 15:19; 16:26; 17:2, 9, 11

8 John 8:28; 12:49; 14:10; 16:27, 30; 17:25

9 1John 5:19

10 John 16:15

11 John 10:30; 13:1; 16:28; 17:21-23; 1Pet. 1:5; Jude 1:1

12 Ps. 109:8; John 18:9; Acts 1:20

14 1John 3:13

15 Matt. 6:13; Gal. 1:4; 2Thess. 3:3; 1John 5:18

17 2Sam. 7:28; Ps. 119:142, 151; Eph. 5:26

18 John 20:21

19 1Cor. 1:2, 30

21 John 10:16

24 John 14:3 1Thess. 4:17

16:32 ye shall be scattered. This is a fulfillment of Zechariah's prophecy (13:7) that the Shepherd (the Messiah) will be smitten and the sheep (the disciples) scattered. This was fulfilled in the disciples' general desertion of Jesus at His trial and crucifixion and Peter's particular denial (Matt. 26:56; John 18:17, 25–26).

17:12 but the son of perdition. This is a reference to Judas (John 13:2, 11, 27; 15:2, 6; 1 John 2:19). The Old Testament predicted that one disciple, Judas in this case, would defect and betray Jesus (Ps. 41:9; 109:8; John 18:1–11).

these have known that thou hast sent me.
26 And I have declared unto them thy name, and will declare it: that the love wherewith thou hast loved me may be in them, and I in them.

CHAPTER 18
Jesus Prays in the Garden

1 When Jesus had spoken these words, he went forth with his disciples over the brook Cedron, where was a garden, into the which he entered, and his disciples.
2 And Judas also, which betrayed him, knew the place: for Jesus ofttimes resorted thither with his disciples.

Judas Betrays the Lord

3 Judas then, having received a band of men and officers from the chief priests and Pharisees, cometh thither with lanterns and torches and weapons.
4 Jesus therefore, knowing all things that should come upon him, went forth, and said unto them, Whom seek ye?
5 They answered him, Jesus of Nazareth. Jesus saith unto them, I am he. And Judas also, which betrayed him, stood with them.
6 As soon then as he had said unto them, I am he, they went backward, and fell to the ground.
7 Then asked he them again, Whom seek ye? And they said, Jesus of Nazareth.
8 Jesus answered, I have told you that I am he: if therefore ye seek me, let these go their way:
9 That the saying might be fulfilled, which he spake, Of them which thou gavest me have I lost none.
10 Then Simon Peter having a sword drew it, and smote the high priest's servant, and cut off his right ear. The servant's name was Malchus.
11 Then said Jesus unto Peter, Put up thy sword into the sheath: the cup which my Father hath given me, shall I not drink it?

Jesus before the High Priest

12 Then the band and the captain and officers of the Jews took Jesus, and bound him,

13 And led him away to Annas first; for he was father in law to Caiaphas, which was the high priest that same year.
14 Now Caiaphas was he, which gave counsel to the Jews, that it was expedient that one man should die for the people.

Peter Denies Jesus

15 And Simon Peter followed Jesus, and so did another disciple: that disciple was known unto the high priest, and went in with Jesus into the palace of the high priest.
16 But Peter stood at the door without. Then went out that other disciple, which was known unto the high priest, and spake unto her that kept the door, and brought in Peter.
17 Then saith the damsel that kept the door unto Peter, Art not thou also one of this man's disciples? He saith, I am not.
18 And the servants and officers stood there, who had made a fire of coals; for it was cold: and they warmed themselves: and Peter stood with them, and warmed himself.

The High Priest Questions Jesus

19 The high priest then asked Jesus of his disciples, and of his doctrine.
20 Jesus answered him, I spake openly to the world; I ever taught in the synagogue, and in the temple, whither the Jews always resort; and in secret have I said nothing.
21 Why askest thou me? ask them which heard me, what I have said unto them: behold, they know what I said.
22 And when he had thus spoken, one of the officers which stood by struck Jesus with the palm of his hand, saying, Answerest thou the high priest so?
23 Jesus answered him, If I have spoken evil, bear witness of the evil: but if well, why smitest thou me?
24 Now Annas had sent him bound unto Caiaphas the high priest.

Peter Denies Jesus Again

25 And Simon Peter stood and warmed himself. They said therefore unto him, Art

Cross-references: 2 Luke 21:37; 22:39 · 9 John 17:12 · 10 Matt. 26:51; Mark 14:47; Luke 22:49, 50 · 11 Matt. 20:22; 26:39, 42 · 13 Matt. 26:57; Luke 3:2 · 14 John 11:50 · 15 Matt. 26:58; Mark 14:54; Luke 22:54 · 16 Matt. 26:69; Mark 14:66; Luke 22:54 · 20 Matt. 26:55; Luke 4:15; John 7:14, 26, 28; 8:2 · 22 Jer. 20:2; Acts 23:2 · 24 Matt. 26:57 · 25 Matt. 26:69, 71; Mark 14:69; Luke 22:58

18:11 Psalm 40:8 prophesies the obedience of Messiah when it says, "I delight to do thy will, O my God." The full extent of this obedience is predicted here when Jesus asks Peter, "The cup which my Father hath given me, shall I not drink it?" See the note on Matthew 26:36–39.

18:14 it was expedient that one man should die for the people. Caiaphas, the rebellious high priest, here predicts that one man must die for all the rest. Caiaphas may have been hoping for a way to placate the anger of the Romans against Israel, and probably did not connect this to any atonement for sins. Nevertheless, the words are true of Christ, whose death on the cross paid the penalty necessary to appease God's anger for those who trust in Him.

not thou also *one* of his disciples? He denied *it,* and said, I am not.

26 One of the servants of the high priest, being *his* kinsman whose ear Peter cut off, saith, Did not I see thee in the garden with him?

27 Peter then denied again: and immediately the cock crew.

Jesus Is Brought to Pilate

28 Then led they Jesus from Caiaphas unto the hall of judgment: and it was early; and they themselves went not into the judgment hall, lest they should be defiled; but that they might eat the passover.

29 Pilate then went out unto them, and said, What accusation bring ye against this man?

30 They answered and said unto him, If he were not a malefactor, we would not have delivered him up unto thee.

31 Then said Pilate unto them, Take ye him, and judge him according to your law. The Jews therefore said unto him, It is not lawful for us to put any man to death:

32 That the saying of Jesus might be fulfilled, which he spake, signifying what death he should die.

33 Then Pilate entered into the judgment hall again, and called Jesus, and said unto him, Art thou the King of the Jews?

34 Jesus answered him, Sayest thou this thing of thyself, or did others tell it thee of me?

35 Pilate answered, Am I a Jew? Thine own nation and the chief priests have delivered thee unto me: what hast thou done?

36 Jesus answered, My kingdom is not of this world: if my kingdom were of this world, then would my servants fight, that I should not be delivered to the Jews: but now is my kingdom not from hence.

37 Pilate therefore said unto him, Art thou a king then? Jesus answered, Thou sayest

that I am a king. To this end was I born, and for this cause came I into the world, that I should bear witness unto the truth. Every one that is of the truth heareth my voice.

Jesus Sentenced to Die

38 Pilate saith unto him, What is truth? And when he had said this, he went out again unto the Jews, and saith unto them, I find in him no fault *at all.*

39 But ye have a custom, that I should release unto you one at the passover: will ye therefore that I release unto you the King of the Jews?

40 Then cried they all again, saying, Not this man, but Barabbas. Now Barabbas was a robber.

CHAPTER 19
Jesus Is Sent to Die on the Cross

1 Then Pilate therefore took Jesus, and scourged *him.*

2 And the soldiers platted a crown of thorns, and put *it* on his head, and they put on him a purple robe,

3 And said, Hail, King of the Jews! and they smote him with their hands.

4 Pilate therefore went forth again, and saith unto them, Behold, I bring him forth to you, that ye may know that I find no fault in him.

5 Then came Jesus forth, wearing the crown of thorns, and the purple robe. And *Pilate* saith unto them, Behold the man!

6 When the chief priests therefore and officers saw him, they cried out, saying, Crucify *him,* crucify *him.* Pilate saith unto them, Take ye him, and crucify *him:* for I find no fault in him.

7 The Jews answered him, We have a law, and by our law he ought to die, because he made himself the Son of God.

8 When Pilate therefore heard that saying, he was the more afraid;

27 Matt. 26:74; Mark 14:72; Luke 22:60; John 13:38

28 Matt. 27:2, 27; Mark 15:1; Luke 23:1; Acts 3:13; 10:28; 11:3

32 Matt. 29:19; John 12:32, 33

33 Matt. 27:11

36 Dan. 2:44; 7:14; Luke 12:14; John 6:15; 8:15; 1Tim. 6:13

37 John 8:47; 1John 3:19; 4:6

38 Matt. 27:24; Luke 23:4; John 19:4, 6

39 Matt. 27:15; Mark 15:6; Luke 23:17

40 Luke 23:19; Acts 3:14

1 Matt. 20:19; 27:26; Mark 15:15; Luke 18:33

4 John 18:38; 19:6

6 Acts 3:13

7 Lev. 24:16; Matt. 26:65; John 5:18; 10:33

18:36 My kingdom is not of this world. Jesus' first coming, according to prophecy, was to suffer for the sins of the world so those who received Him could enter the spiritual kingdom He offered to Nicodemus (John 3). That spiritual kingdom can be entered by anyone at any time simply by placing faith in Christ. Later in the verse, however, Christ refers to the physical kingdom He will establish "in" this world when He comes in power and great glory. The Millennial Kingdom will not be "of" this world in the sense of originating from or out of the present world system (see John 15:19; 1 John 2:16; 4:5); instead, it will be a kingdom of righteousness.

19:1 scourged. This punishment of the Messiah, the Suffering Servant, was predicted in Isaiah 53:5.

19:6 Crucify him. Crucifixion was first developed by the Phoenicians and Persians in the fifth century B.C., years after Isaiah's prophetic description (Isa. 53). It was not practiced by the Jews, but by the Romans, who ruled Israel for less than 150 years. Jesus' death is the fulfillment of Isaiah's prophecy—a prophecy only crucifixion could literally fulfill. (For parallel accounts, see Mark 15:13–14; Luke 23:21.)

9 And went again into the judgment hall, and saith unto Jesus, Whence art thou? But Jesus gave him no answer.

10 Then saith Pilate unto him, Speakest thou not unto me? knowest thou not that I have power to crucify thee, and have power to release thee?

11 Jesus answered, Thou couldest have no power at all against me, except it were given thee from above: therefore he that delivered me unto thee hath the greater sin.

12 And from thenceforth Pilate sought to release him: but the Jews cried out, saying, If thou let this man go, thou art not Caesar's friend: whosoever maketh himself a king speaketh against Caesar.

13 When Pilate therefore heard that saying, he brought Jesus forth, and sat down in the judgment seat in a place that is called the Pavement, but in the Hebrew, Gabbatha.

14 And it was the preparation of the passover, and about the sixth hour: and he saith unto the Jews, Behold your King!

15 But they cried out, Away with *him,* away with *him,* crucify him. Pilate saith unto them, Shall I crucify your King? The chief priests answered, We have no king but Caesar.

16 Then delivered he him therefore unto them to be crucified. And they took Jesus, and led *him* away.

Jesus on the Cross

17 And he bearing his cross went forth into a place called *the place* of a skull, which is called in the Hebrew Golgotha:

18 Where they crucified him, and two other with him, on either side one, and Jesus in the midst.

19 And Pilate wrote a title, and put *it* on the cross. And the writing was, JESUS OF NAZARETH THE KING OF THE JEWS.

20 This title then read many of the Jews: for the place where Jesus was crucified was nigh to the city: and it was written in Hebrew, *and* Greek, *and* Latin.

21 Then said the chief priests of the Jews to Pilate, Write not, The King of the Jews; but that he said, I am King of the Jews.

22 Pilate answered, What I have written I have written.

23 Then the soldiers, when they had crucified Jesus, took his garments, and made four parts, to every soldier a part; and also *his* coat: now the coat was without seam, woven from the top throughout.

24 They said therefore among themselves, Let us not rend it, but cast lots for it, whose it shall be: that the scripture might be fulfilled, which saith, They parted my raiment among them, and for my vesture they did cast lots. These things therefore the soldiers did.

25 Now there stood by the cross of Jesus his mother, and his mother's sister, Mary the *wife* of Cleophas, and Mary Magdalene.

26 When Jesus therefore saw his mother, and the disciple standing by, whom he loved, he saith unto his mother, Woman, behold thy son!

27 Then saith he to the disciple, Behold thy mother! And from that hour that disciple took her unto his own *home.*

The Death of Jesus

28 After this, Jesus knowing that all things were now accomplished, that the scripture might be fulfilled, saith, I thirst.

29 Now there was set a vessel full of vinegar: and they filled a sponge with vinegar, and put *it* upon hyssop, and put *it* to his mouth.

30 When Jesus therefore had received the vinegar, he said, It is finished: and he bowed his head, and gave up the ghost.

31 The Jews therefore, because it was the preparation, that the bodies should not remain upon the cross on the sabbath day,

Cross references: 9 Isa. 53:7; Matt. 27:12, 14 · 11 Luke 22:53; John 7:30 · 12 Luke 23:2; Acts 17:7 · 14 Matt. 27:62 · 15 Gen. 49:10 · 16 Matt. 27:26, 31; Mark 15:15; Luke 23:24 · 17 Num. 15:36; Matt. 27:31, 33; Mark 15:21, 22; Luke 23:26, 33; Heb. 13:12 · 19 Matt. 27:37; Mark 15:26; Luke 23:38 · 23 Matt. 27:35; Mark 15:24; Luke 23:34 · 24 Ps. 22:18 · 25 Matt. 27:55; Mark 15:40; Luke 23:49; 24:18 · 26 John 2:4; 13:23; 20:2; 21:7, 20, 24 · 27 John 1:11; 16:32 · 28 Ps. 69:21 · 29 Matt. 27:48 · 30 John 17:4 · 31 Deut. 21:23; Mark 15:42; John 19:42

19:9 Jesus gave him no answer. This fulfills Isaiah 53:7, which says, "He was oppressed, and he was afflicted, yet he opened not his mouth."

19:18 This verse fulfills prophecy from Isaiah 53:12 which says, "He was numbered with the transgressors." Jesus is crucified between two criminals.

19:24 that the scripture might be fulfilled. John quotes from Psalm 22:18 which says, "They part my garments among them, and cast lots upon my vesture." The Roman soldiers unwittingly fulfilled this ancient prophecy of the Messiah's suffering.

19:28–29 Jesus . . . saith, I thirst. This is a reference to Psalm 69:21 which says, "In my thirst they gave me vinegar to drink." Jesus fulfilled this and every other detail predicted of His life and death. (For parallel accounts, see Matt. 27:48; Mark 15:36.)

19:30 It is finished. Having fulfilled every prophetic detail related to His life and death, Jesus dies of His own volition (John 10:18). More than twenty-five prophecies were fulfilled in Christ's death, further confirming that He was anointed by God the Father to take away "the sin of the world" (John 1:29).

(for that sabbath day was an high day,) besought Pilate that their legs might be broken, and *that* they might be taken away.

32 Then came the soldiers, and brake the legs of the first, and of the other which was crucified with him.

33 But when they came to Jesus, and saw that he was dead already, they brake not his legs:

34 But one of the soldiers with a spear pierced his side, and forthwith came there out blood and water.

35 And he that saw *it* bare record, and his record is true: and he knoweth that he saith true, that ye might believe.

36 For these things were done, that the scripture should be fulfilled, A bone of him shall not be broken.

37 And again another scripture saith, They shall look on him whom they pierced.

The Burial of Jesus

38 And after this Joseph of Arimathaea, being a disciple of Jesus, but secretly for fear of the Jews, besought Pilate that he might take away the body of Jesus: and Pilate gave *him* leave. He came therefore, and took the body of Jesus.

39 And there came also Nicodemus, which at the first came to Jesus by night, and brought a mixture of myrrh and aloes, about an hundred pound *weight*.

40 Then took they the body of Jesus, and wound it in linen clothes with the spices, as the manner of the Jews is to bury.

41 Now in the place where he was crucified there was a garden; and in the garden a new sepulchre, wherein was never man yet laid.

42 There laid they Jesus therefore because of the Jews' preparation *day*; for the sepulchre was nigh at hand.

34 1John 5:6, 8

36 Ex. 12:46; Num. 9:12; Ps. 34:20

37 Ps. 22:16, 17; Zech. 12:10; Rev. 1:7

38 Matt. 27:57; Mark 15:42; Luke 23:50; John 9:22; 12:42

39 John 3:1, 2; 7:50

40 Acts 5:6

42 Isa. 53:9; John 19:31

1 Matt. 28:1; Mark 16:1; Luke 24:1

2 John 13:23; 19:26; 21:7, 20, 24

3 Luke 24:12

5 John 19:40

7 John 11:44

9 Ps. 16:10; Acts 2:25-31; 13:34, 35

11 Mark 16:5

CHAPTER 20
The Resurrection of Jesus

1 The first *day* of the week cometh Mary Magdalene early, when it was yet dark, unto the sepulchre, and seeth the stone taken away from the sepulchre.

2 Then she runneth, and cometh to Simon Peter, and to the other disciple, whom Jesus loved, and saith unto them, They have taken away the Lord out of the sepulchre, and we know not where they have laid him.

3 Peter therefore went forth, and that other disciple, and came to the sepulchre.

4 So they ran both together: and the other disciple did outrun Peter and came first to the sepulchre.

5 And he stooping down, *and looking in,* saw the linen clothes lying; yet went he not in.

6 Then cometh Simon Peter following him, and went into the sepulchre, and seeth the linen clothes lie,

7 And the napkin, that was about his head, not lying with the linen clothes, but wrapped together in a place by itself.

8 Then went in also that other disciple, which came first to the sepulchre, and he saw, and believed.

9 For as yet they knew not the scripture, that he must rise again from the dead.

10 Then the disciples went away again unto their own home.

Jesus Appears to Mary Magdalene

11 But Mary stood without at the sepulchre weeping: and as she wept, she stooped down, *and looked* into the sepulchre,

12 And seeth two angels in white sitting, the one at the head, and the other at the feet, where the body of Jesus had lain.

13 And they say unto her, Woman, why weepest thou? She saith unto them, Be-

---

19:33, 36 they brake not his legs. The normal Roman custom during crucifixion was to break the legs of the subject, as noted in verse 32. By going against the standard procedure, the prophecy of Psalm 34:20 was fulfilled: "He keepeth all his bones: not one of them is broken." In His death, Jesus fulfills the role of the Passover lamb in the Mosaic Law (Ex. 12:46; Num. 9:12). The Passover lamb was not to have any broken bones.

19:34, 37 with a spear pierced his side. The Roman soldiers continue to fulfill prophecy, even after Jesus has died. This act fulfills Zechariah 12:10, which says, "They shall look upon me whom they have pierced" (cf. Rev.

1:7). The observation that "forthwith came there out blood and water" fulfills Psalm 22:14 which prophesied "I am poured out like water . . . my heart is like wax; it is melted in the midst of my bowels." The soldiers pierced Christ's side to make sure He had died.

19:38–42 Even though Jesus was destitute concerning the things of this world, Isaiah 53:9 predicted that "he made his grave . . . with the rich in his death." The body of Jesus was placed into the tomb of a wealthy man named Joseph of Arimathaea, thus fulfilling Isaiah's prophecy. (For parallel accounts, see Matt. 27:57–60; Mark 15:43–46; Luke 23:50–53.)

cause they have taken away my Lord, and I know not where they have laid him.

14 And when she had thus said, she turned herself back, and saw Jesus standing, and knew not that it was Jesus.

15 Jesus saith unto her, Woman, why weepest thou? whom seekest thou? She, supposing him to be the gardener, saith unto him, Sir, if thou have borne him hence, tell me where thou hast laid him, and I will take him away.

16 Jesus saith unto her, Mary. She turned herself, and saith unto him, Rabboni; which is to say, Master.

17 Jesus saith unto her, Touch me not; for I am not yet ascended to my Father: but go to my brethren, and say unto them, I ascend unto my Father, and your Father; and to my God, and your God.

18 Mary Magdalene came and told the disciples that she had seen the Lord, and *that* he had spoken these things unto her.

Jesus Appears to the Disciples

19 Then the same day at evening, being the first *day* of the week, when the doors were shut where the disciples were assembled for fear of the Jews, came Jesus and stood in the midst, and saith unto them, Peace be unto you.

20 And when he had so said, he shewed unto them *his* hands and his side. Then were the disciples glad, when they saw the Lord.

21 Then said Jesus to them again, Peace be unto you: as my Father hath sent me, even so send I you.

22 And when he had said this, he breathed on *them,* and saith unto them, Receive ye the Holy Ghost:

23 Whose soever sins ye remit, they are remitted unto them; and whose soever sins ye retain, they are retained.

Thomas Doubts

24 But Thomas, one of the twelve, called Didymus, was not with them when Jesus came.

25 The other disciples therefore said unto him, We have seen the Lord. But he said unto them, Except I shall see in his hands the print of the nails, and put my finger into

the print of the nails, and thrust my hand into his side, I will not believe.

26 And after eight days again his disciples were within, and Thomas with them: *then* came Jesus, the doors being shut, and stood in the midst, and said, Peace, be unto you.

27 Then saith he to Thomas, Reach hither thy finger, and behold my hands; and reach hither thy hand, and thrust it into my side: and be not faithless, but believing.

28 And Thomas answered and said unto him, My Lord and my God.

29 Jesus saith unto him, Thomas, because thou hast seen me, thou hast believed: blessed are they that have not seen, and yet have believed.

The Purpose of John's Gospel

30 And many other signs truly did Jesus in the presence of his disciples, which are not written in this book:

31 But these are written, that ye might believe that Jesus is the Christ, the Son of God; and that believing ye might have life through his name.

CHAPTER 21
Jesus Appears in Galilee

1 After these things Jesus shewed himself again to the disciples at the sea of Tiberias; and on this wise shewed he *himself.*

2 There were together Simon Peter, and Thomas called Didymus, and Nathanael of Cana in Galilee, and the *sons* of Zebedee, and two other of his disciples.

3 Simon Peter saith unto them, I go a fishing. They say unto him, We also go with thee. They went forth, and entered into a ship immediately: and that night they caught nothing.

4 But when the morning was now come, Jesus stood on the shore: but the disciples knew not that it was Jesus.

5 Then Jesus saith unto them, Children, have ye any meat? They answered him, No.

6 And he said unto them, Cast the net on the right side of the ship, and ye shall find. They cast therefore, and now they were not able to draw it for the multitude of fishes.

7 Therefore that disciple whom Jesus loved saith unto Peter, It is the Lord. Now

Cross-reference column

14 Matt. 28:9; Mark 16:9; Luke 24:16, 31; John 21:4

17 Ps. 22:22; Matt. 28:10; John 16:28; Rom. 8:29; Eph. 1:17; Heb. 2:11

18 Matt. 28:10; Luke 24:10

19 Mark 16:14; Luke 24:36; 1Cor. 15:5

20 John 16:22

21 Matt. 28:18; John 17:18, 19; 2Tim. 2:2; Heb. 3:1

23 Matt. 16:19; 18:18

24 John 11:16

27 1John 1:1

29 2Cor. 5:7; 1Pet. 1:8

30 John 21:25

31 Luke 1:4; John 3:15, 16; 5:24; 1Pet. 1:8, 9

1 Matt. 4:21; John 1:45

4 John 20:14

5 Luke 24:41

6 Luke 5:4, 6, 7

7 John 13:23; 20:2

21:6 Cast the net on the right side of the ship, and ye shall find [fish]. Following this prophecy, Peter obeyed the Lord and caught 153 fish in a single haul. This event no doubt reminded the disciples of a similar experience three years earlier when Jesus called them to be "fishers of men." The abundant catch stresses that they have the potential in Christ to win souls in every country of the world to Christ.

when Simon Peter heard that it was the Lord, he girt *his* fisher's coat *unto him,* (for he was naked,) and did cast himself into the sea.

8 And the other disciples came in a little ship; (for they were not far from land, but as it were two hundred cubits,) dragging the net with fishes.

9 As soon then as they were come to land, they saw a fire of coals there, and fish laid thereon, and bread.

10 Jesus saith unto them, Bring of the fish which ye have now caught.

11 Simon Peter went up, and drew the net to land full of great fishes, an hundred and fifty and three: and for all there were so many, yet was not the net broken.

12 Jesus saith unto them, Come and dine. And none of the disciples durst ask him, Who art thou? knowing that it was the Lord.

13 Jesus then cometh, and taketh bread, and giveth them, and fish likewise.

14 This is now the third time that Jesus shewed himself to his disciples, after that he was risen from the dead.

"Lovest Thou Me?"

15 So when they had dined, Jesus saith to Simon Peter, Simon, son of Jona, lovest thou me more than these? He saith unto him, Yea, Lord; thou knowest that I love thee. He saith unto him, Feed my lambs.

16 He saith to him again the second time, Simon, son of Jona, lovest thou me? He saith unto him, Yea, Lord; thou knowest that I love thee. He saith unto him, Feed my sheep.

17 He saith unto him the third time, Simon, son of Jona, lovest thou me? Peter was grieved because he said unto him the third time, Lovest thou me? And he said unto him, Lord, thou knowest all things; thou knowest that I love thee. Jesus saith unto him, Feed my sheep.

18 Verily, verily, I say unto thee, When thou wast young, thou girdedst thyself, and walkedst whither thou wouldest: but when thou shalt be old, thou shalt stretch forth thy hands, and another shall gird thee, and carry *thee* whither thou wouldest not.

19 This spake he, signifying by what death he should glorify God. And when he had spoken this, he saith unto him, Follow me.

20 Then Peter, turning about, seeth the disciple whom Jesus loved following; which also leaned on his breast at supper, and said, Lord, which is he that betrayeth thee?

21 Peter seeing him saith to Jesus, Lord, and what *shall* this man *do?*

22 Jesus saith unto him, If I will that he tarry till I come, what is that to thee? follow thou me.

23 Then went this saying abroad among the brethren, that that disciple should not die: yet Jesus said not unto him, He shall not die; but, If I will that he tarry till I come, what *is that* to thee?

24 This is the disciple which testifieth of these things, and wrote these things: and we know that his testimony is true.

25 And there are also many other things which Jesus did, the which, if they should be written every one, I suppose that even the world itself could not contain the books that should be written. Amen.

12 Acts 10:41

14 John 20:19; 26

16 Acts 20:28; Heb. 13:20; 1Pet. 2:25; 5:2, 4

17 John 2:24, 25; 16:30

18 John 13:36; Acts 12:3, 4

19 2Pet. 1:14

20 John 13:23, 25; 20:2

22 Matt. 16:27, 28; 25:31; 1Cor. 4:5; 11:26; Rev. 2:25; 3:11; 22:7, 20

24 John 19:35; 3John 1:12

25 Amos 7:10; John 20:30

21:18 Another shall gird thee, and carry thee whither thou wouldest not. After lovingly forgiving Peter for denying Him (as He had predicted), Jesus tells him how he will die. Peter lived for about thirty-five years after the death of Christ at which time, according to tradition, he was crucified upside down at his own request, because he felt unworthy to be crucified in the same manner as his Lord.

21:22–23 If I will that he tarry till I come. This is another reminder of the imminence of Christ's return for His followers. The word for "if" in the Greek (*ean*) implies that Jesus is not prophesying that John will be alive when He returns. It is interesting, however, that John outlived the other disciples. In fact, all of the others were probably dead by the time John wrote this book (vv. 23–24). Some view this verse as a prediction of Christ's appearance to John on the island of Patmos (Rev. 1:10–18). However, in spite of the mysteries opened to John and recorded for us in the book of Revelation, his soul is with Christ awaiting the day of resurrection.

Acts

Luke the physician wrote the book of Acts to Theophilus as a sequel to the gospel of Luke. As the continuing account of the results of Jesus' ministry, Luke's Gospel is followed by this fast-moving historical account of the beginnings of the Christian movement. While the gospel of Luke relates "all that Jesus began both to do and teach" (Acts 1:1), the Acts of the Apostles begins with the ascension of Jesus and tells the story of how the gospel was spread far beyond the confines of the Jewish community to the whole world. The statement of Jesus in Acts 1:8, "and ye shall be witnesses unto me both in Jerusalem, . . . and unto the uttermost part of the earth," provides an excellent framework for the entire book.

Author	Luke
Date	A.D. 62
Key Truth	The Church Is Growing
Historic Time	From Christ's Post-Resurrection Appearances to Paul's Imprisonment in Rome
Key Verse	1:8 . . . ye shall be witnesses unto me . . .

Following the coming of the Holy Spirit on the Day of Pentecost, the apostles are supernaturally empowered. Peter's ministry is emphasized in Jerusalem and Judea (chaps. 2—7; 10—12). Phillip's ministry in Samaria is also presented (chap. 8) along with the conversion of an Ethiopian official who took the gospel to Africa. Paul's ministry begins with his dramatic conversion on the Damascus Road and continues through three major missionary journeys in the Roman Empire (chaps. 13—21). At Jerusalem, Paul is attacked by Jewish religious leaders, imprisoned by the Roman government, and is eventually transported to Rome for a hearing before Caesar. Paul never ceases to witness, even while under house arrest in Rome (28:30–31).

Some have called the book the Acts of the Holy Spirit, for this person of the Trinity is mentioned seventy-one times. Important future prophecies include the promise of Christ's return (1:11; 3:18–26) and the times of "refreshing" and "restitution" for Israel and the resurrection and Day of Judgment (17:30–32).

About half of the 63 distinct prophecies were fulfilled in contemporary times. They involve 125 of 1,003 verses or 13 percent of the content. The book of Acts contains 31 quotations from the Old Testament.

13% Prophecy

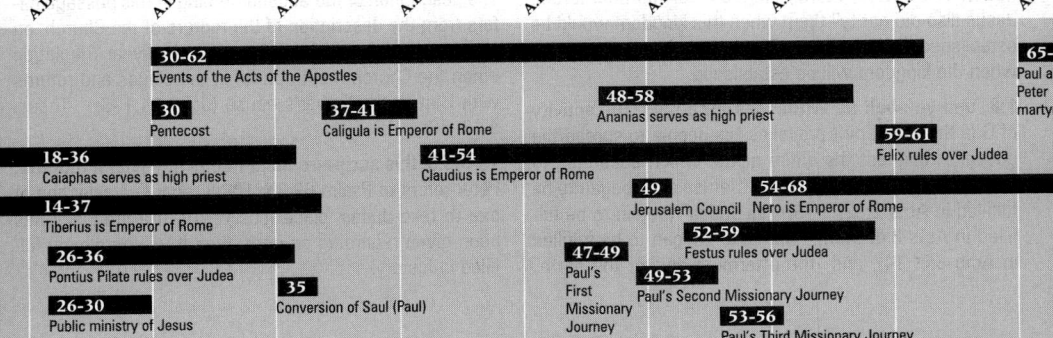

Timeline (A.D. 25 – A.D. 65):

- **30-62** Events of the Acts of the Apostles
- **30** Pentecost
- **37-41** Caligula is Emperor of Rome
- **48-58** Ananias serves as high priest
- **65-68** Paul and Peter martyred
- **18-36** Caiaphas serves as high priest
- **41-54** Claudius is Emperor of Rome
- **59-61** Felix rules over Judea
- **14-37** Tiberius is Emperor of Rome
- **49** Jerusalem Council
- **54-68** Nero is Emperor of Rome
- **26-36** Pontius Pilate rules over Judea
- **52-59** Festus rules over Judea
- **35** Conversion of Saul (Paul)
- **47-49** Paul's First Missionary Journey
- **49-53** Paul's Second Missionary Journey
- **26-30** Public ministry of Jesus
- **53-56** Paul's Third Missionary Journey

CHAPTER 1

1 The former treatise have I made, O Theophilus, of all that Jesus began both to do and teach,

2 Until the day in which he was taken up, after that he through the Holy Ghost had given commandments unto the apostles whom he had chosen:

3 To whom also he shewed himself alive after his passion by many infallible proofs, being seen of them forty days, and speaking of the things pertaining to the kingdom of God:

4 And, being assembled together with *them*, commanded them that they should not depart from Jerusalem, but wait for the promise of the Father, which, *saith he*, ye have heard of me.

5 For John truly baptized with water; but ye shall be baptized with the Holy Ghost not many days hence.

6 When they therefore were come together, they asked of him, saying, Lord, wilt thou at this time restore again the kingdom to Israel?

7 And he said unto them, It is not for you to know the times or the seasons, which the Father hath put in his own power.

The Holy Spirit Promised

8 But ye shall receive power, after that the Holy Ghost is come upon you: and ye shall be witnesses unto me both in Jerusalem, and in all Judea, and in Samaria, and unto the uttermost part of the earth.

9 And when he had spoken these things,

while they beheld, he was taken up; and a cloud received him out of their sight.

10 And while they looked stedfastly toward heaven as he went up, behold, two men stood by them in white apparel;

11 Which also said, Ye men of Galilee, why stand ye gazing up into heaven? this same Jesus, which is taken up from you into heaven, shall so come in like manner as ye have seen him go into heaven.

Matthias Replaces Judas

12 Then returned they unto Jerusalem from the mount called Olivet, which is from Jerusalem a sabbath day's journey.

13 And when they were come in, they went up into an upper room, where abode both Peter, and James, and John, and Andrew, Philip, and Thomas, Bartholomew, and Matthew, James *the son* of Alphaeus, and Simon Zelotes, and Judas *the brother* of James.

14 These all continued with one accord in prayer and supplication, with the women, and Mary the mother of Jesus, and with his brethren.

15 And in those days Peter stood up in the midst of the disciples, and said, (the number of names together were about an hundred and twenty,)

16 Men *and* brethren, this scripture must needs have been fulfilled, which the Holy Ghost by the mouth of David spake before concerning Judas, which was guide to them that took Jesus.

Cross-references

1 Luke 1:3
2 Matt. 28:19; Mark 16:15, 19
3 Luke 24:36; John 20:19, 26; 1Cor. 15:5
4 John 14:16, 26, 27; 15:26; 16:7; Acts 2:33
5 Joel 3:18; Matt. 3:11; Acts 2:4; 11:15, 16; 19:4
6 Isa. 1:26; Matt. 24:3
7 Matt. 24:36; Mark 13:32; 1Thess. 5:1
8 Luke 24:48, 49
10 Matt. 28:3; Mark 16:5
11 Dan. 7:13; Luke 21:27; John 14:3
14 Matt. 13:55; Luke 23:49, 55; 24:10; Acts 2:1, 46
16 Ps. 41:9; Luke 22:47; John 13:18; 18:3

1:4–5 ye shall be baptized with the Holy Ghost not many days hence. Jesus makes reference to His own previous prediction (Luke 24:49) that the disciples would receive the baptism by God's Holy Spirit. This prophecy would shortly be fulfilled on the Day of Pentecost as recorded in Acts 2.

1:6–7 Lord, wilt thou at this time restore again the kingdom to Israel? The Lord did not correct the disciples' notion of a future, literal, kingdom for national Israel. Jesus also did not tell them when this kingdom would be established. Even believers in our own day cannot know when the kingdom will be established.

1:8 and ye shall be witnesses unto me. The activity of God the Holy Spirit provokes His people to spread the gospel throughout the entire globe, which according to this verse included the areas of "Jerusalem" (began to be fulfilled in Acts 2:32; 3:15), "all Judea" (began to be fulfilled in Acts 8:4; 9:32), "Samaria" (began to be fulfilled in Acts 8:5, 14), and "the uttermost part of the earth"

(began to be fulfilled in Acts 13).

1:11 in like manner as ye have seen him go into heaven. The return of Christ at the end of the seven-year Tribulation will occur in the same manner as Jesus ascended: physically, visibly, and in the clouds as He descends upon the Mount of Olives. This passage is consistent with the way other passages depict Christ's second coming (Dan. 7:13; Zech. 14:4; Matt. 24:29–31; Rev. 1:8; 19:11–16). The description of the Second Coming in this passage differs from the description of the rapture of the Church, an event which takes place before the seven-year Tribulation when the Church meets Christ in the clouds and returns with Him to the Father's house (John 14:1–3; 1 Thess. 4:13–18).

1:16, 20 this scripture must needs have been fulfilled. Peter refers to Psalm 69:25; 109:8 regarding selection of one to take Judas' place (see v. 20). If a prophecy has been given regarding an item, then it will be clearly fulfilled in history.

17 For he was numbered with us, and had obtained part of this ministry.

18 Now this man purchased a field with the reward of iniquity; and falling headlong, he burst asunder in the midst, and all his bowels gushed out.

19 And it was known unto all the dwellers at Jerusalem; insomuch as that field is called in their proper tongue, Aceldama, that is to say, The field of blood.

20 For it is written in the book of Psalms, Let his habitation be desolate, and let no man dwell therein: and his bishopric let another take.

21 Wherefore of these men which have companied with us all the time that the Lord Jesus went in and out among us,

22 Beginning from the baptism of John, unto that same day that he was taken up from us, must one be ordained to be a witness with us of his resurrection.

23 And they appointed two, Joseph called Barsabas, who was surnamed Justus, and Matthias.

24 And they prayed, and said, Thou, Lord, which knowest the hearts of all *men*, shew whether of these two thou hast chosen,

25 That he may take part of this ministry and apostleship, from which Judas by transgression fell, that he might go to his own place.

26 And they gave forth their lots; and the lot fell upon Matthias; and he was numbered with the eleven apostles.

CHAPTER 2
The Baptism of the Holy Spirit

1 And when the day of Pentecost was fully come, they were all with one accord in one place.

2 And suddenly there came a sound from heaven as of a rushing mighty wind, and it filled all the house where they were sitting.

3 And there appeared unto them cloven tongues like as of fire, and it sat upon each of them.

4 And they were all filled with the Holy Ghost, and began to speak with other tongues, as the Spirit gave them utterance.

5 And there were dwelling at Jerusalem Jews, devout men, out of every nation under heaven.

6 Now when this was noised abroad, the multitude came together, and were confounded, because that every man heard them speak in his own language.

7 And they were all amazed and marvelled, saying one to another, Behold, are not all these which speak Galilaeans?

8 And how hear we every man in our own tongue, wherein we were born?

9 Parthians, and Medes, and Elamites, and the dwellers in Mesopotamia, and in Judea, and Cappadocia, in Pontus, and Asia,

10 Phrygia, and Pamphylia, in Egypt, and in the parts of Libya about Cyrene, and strangers of Rome, Jews and proselytes,

11 Cretes and Arabians, we do hear them speak in our tongues the wonderful works of God.

12 And they were all amazed, and were in doubt, saying one to another, What meaneth this?

13 Others mocking said, These men are full of new wine.

Peter's Sermon

14 But Peter, standing up with the eleven, lifted up his voice, and said unto them, Ye

---

Cross references:

17 Matt. 10:4; Luke 6:16; Acts 1:25; 12:25; 20:24; 21:19

18 Matt. 26:15; 27:5, 7, 8; 2Pet. 2:15

20 Ps. 69:25; 109:8

22 Mark 1:1; John 15:27; Acts 1:8, 9; 4:33

23 Acts 15:22

24 1Sam. 16:7; 1Chr. 28:9; 29:17; Jer. 11:20; 17:10; Acts 15:8; Rev. 2:23

25 Acts 1:17

1 Lev. 23:15; Deut. 16:9; Acts 1:14; 20:16

2 Acts 4:31

4 Mark 16:17; Acts 1:5; 10:46; 19:6; 1Cor. 12:10, 28, 30; 13:1; 14:2

7 Acts 1:11

1:17–19 This passage relates the fulfillment of the prophecy from Zechariah 11:12–13 concerning the betrayal of Jesus by Judas.

2:1 day of Pentecost The word "pentecost" means fifty and was the Greek name for the Jewish Feasts of Weeks (Ex. 34:22–23) or Harvest (Lev. 23:15–22). Pentecost was after seven sevens (i.e., Feasts of Weeks), thus fifty days after the Feast of Firstfruits (Ex. 23:16). While the Church began on this day in the Jewish Calendar, the Old Testament significance of this feast does not relate to the founding of the Church (Rom. 16:25; Eph. 3:4–5, 9; Col. 1:25–27).

2:2–4 The Church Age began with the baptism of the Holy Spirit (1 Cor. 12:13) which had been predicted by John the Baptist (Matt. 3:11) and Jesus (Acts 1:5). The Church Age is a time in which the gospel is preached throughout the whole earth (Matt. 28:19–20; Mark 16:15–16), leading to the worldwide growth of the Church (Matt. 13:1–52). Man's responsibility in this current age is to believe the gospel, preach the gospel to all creation, and live a life pleasing to Christ (Matt. 28:19–20; Mark 16:15–16; Acts 17:30). The consequences for any individual who does not believe the gospel are that such a person will spend eternity in the lake of fire (Rev. 20:11–15). The Church Age will be brought to an end by the rapture of the Church (John 14:1–3; 1 Cor. 15:51–54; 1 Thess. 4:12–17), which will come suddenly, without signs or warning (1 Cor. 1:7; 16:22; Phil. 3:20; 4:5; Titus 2:13; Jude 21). The Rapture precedes the seven-year Tribulation, also known as the "seventieth week" of Daniel and the time of God's wrath (Dan. 9:24–27; Rom. 5:9; 1 Thess. 1:10; 5:9; Rev. 3:10).

The Church Age

By Earl Radmacher

The first mention of the word "church" in Scripture is by Jesus Christ. There is no record of Christ using the word anywhere in the four Gospels except the three occurrences in Matthew (16:18; 18:17). In contrast, however, Christ regularly referred to the coming kingdom, the focal point of His teaching, in continuation with the unanimous proclamation of the Old Testament prophets and the forerunner of Jesus, John the Baptist (cf. Matt. 3:1–2).

When Jesus stood in Caesarea Philippi at the foot of Mount Hermon and made the remarkable prophetic claim, "I will build my church; and the gates of hell shall not prevail against it" (Matt. 16:18), His description went beyond any visible, physical organization on earth. This prophecy of Christ's Church is carefully defined by the apostle Paul as a "mystery, which from the beginning of the world [i.e., eternity past] hath been hid in God" (Eph. 3:9). Thus, the Church is not a continuation of Judaism, nor is it to be identified with Israel.

The future tense (Matt. 16:18) and the "mystery" (Eph. 3:1–10) require the establishment of the Church to commence after the earthly life of Christ. But where can we place the beginning historically?

The Lord Jesus, who was designated to be the Head of the Church, had commissioned the Holy Spirit to be the key to the beginning of the Church, the body of Christ. In the upper room, during His passion week, Jesus taught His disciples concerning the Holy Spirit (John 14:17). Just a few days before the Feast of Pentecost, the resurrected Christ reminded the apostles of the Father's promise that "ye shall be baptized with the Holy [Spirit] not many days hence" (Acts 1:5). Shortly after, God breathed on these same disciples in special preparation for their upcoming ministry as the foundation of the Church that was to come (cf. Eph. 2:20) and said to them: "Receive ye the Holy [Spirit]" (John 20:22).

> *There is no prophesied event that must take place before the Lord Jesus returns.*

Therefore, the precise event that inaugurated the Church on earth was the advent of the Holy Spirit on the day of Pentecost. On this day, the resurrected Lord Jesus Christ, from His position of authority as Head of the Church, joined all believers into one body and placed them in the care and safekeeping of the Holy Spirit during their sojourn on earth (1 Cor. 12:13). This event was celebrated with miraculous signs and wonders appropriate for such an awesome occasion (Acts 2:1–12).

Just as the beginning of the Church was the object of significant prophecies, so the completion of the Church will be supernatural and spectacular. Also, just as the Church itself was a mystery hidden in God until the revelation in the New Testament, so the completion of the Church is a mystery (1 Cor. 15:51–52). About five years earlier, Paul had stated the same truth to the Thessalonians concerning the rapture of the Church (1 Thess. 4:15–17). "Our gathering together unto Him" (2 Thess. 2:1) will include all who by faith are in Christ Jesus. It may occur at any moment. There is no prophesied event that must take place before the Lord Jesus returns for all believers—those who are ready and those who are not (cf. Matt. 25:1–13). Thus, the apostle John exhorts, "And now, little children, abide in him; that, when he shall appear, we may have confidence, and not be ashamed before him at his coming" (1 John 2:28).

men of Judea, and all *ye* that dwell at Jerusalem, be this known unto you, and hearken to my words:

15 For these are not drunken, as ye suppose, seeing it is *but* the third hour of the day.

16 But this is that which was spoken by the prophet Joel;

17 And it shall come to pass in the last days, saith God, I will pour out of my Spirit upon all flesh: and your sons and your daughters shall prophesy, and your young men shall see visions, and your old men shall dream dreams:

18 And on my servants and on my handmaidens I will pour out in those days of my Spirit; and they shall prophesy:

19 And I will shew wonders in heaven above, and signs in the earth beneath; blood, and fire, and vapour of smoke:

20 The sun shall be turned into darkness, and the moon into blood, before that great and notable day of the Lord come:

21 And it shall come to pass, *that* whosoever shall call on the name of the Lord shall be saved.

22 Ye men of Israel, hear these words; Jesus of Nazareth, a man approved of God among you by miracles and wonders and signs, which God did by him in the midst of you, as ye yourselves also know:

23 Him, being delivered by the determinate counsel and foreknowledge of God, ye have

15 1Thess. 5:7
17 Joel 2:28, 29
18 Acts 21:4, 9, 10
19 Joel 2:30, 31
20 Matt. 24:29; Mark 13:24; Luke 21:25
23 Matt. 26:24
24 Acts 2:32; 3:15; 4:10; 10:40; Eph. 1:20; Col. 2:12; 1Thess. 1:10; Heb. 13:20; 1Pet. 1:21
25 Ps. 16:8
29 1Kgs. 2:10; Acts 13:36
30 2Sam. 7:12, 13; Ps. 132:11; Luke 1:32, 69; Rom. 1:3; 2Tim. 2:8
31 Ps. 16:10; Acts 13:35
32 Acts 1:8; 2:24

taken, and by wicked hands have crucified and slain:

24 Whom God hath raised up, having loosed the pains of death: because it was not possible that he should be holden of it.

25 For David speaketh concerning him, I foresaw the Lord always before my face, for he is on my right hand, that I should not be moved:

26 Therefore did my heart rejoice, and my tongue was glad; moreover also my flesh shall rest in hope:

27 Because thou wilt not leave my soul in hell, neither wilt thou suffer thine Holy One to see corruption.

28 Thou hast made known to me the ways of life; thou shalt make me full of joy with thy countenance.

29 Men *and* brethren, let me freely speak unto you of the patriarch David, that he is both dead and buried, and his sepulchre is with us unto this day.

30 Therefore being a prophet, and knowing that God had sworn with an oath to him, that of the fruit of his loins, according to the flesh, he would raise up Christ to sit on his throne;

31 He seeing this before spake of the resurrection of Christ, that his soul was not left in hell, neither his flesh did see corruption.

32 This Jesus hath God raised up, whereof we all are witnesses.

2:16 But this is [like] that which was spoken by the prophet Joel. The text of Joel 2:28–32 describes the activity of God's Spirit at work in events surrounding the second coming of Christ. Peter's point is that of similarity between what the Holy Spirit will do in the future with the nation of Israel and what He was doing at the opening of the Church age. The Spirit's activity in Joel is linked to the events that will transpire during the Tribulation; thus, it could not have been fulfilled in Acts 2. The unique statement of Peter ("this is that") is in the language of comparison and similarity, not fulfillment. See the notes on Joel 2:28–32 for further explanation of Joel's prophecy.

2:17–21 it shall come to pass in the last days. Peter, under the inspiration of the Holy Spirit, changes the word "afterward" in Joel 2:28 to "in the last days" (v. 17), underscoring the fact that the Joel passage was not being fulfilled in his day, but must await the time of the Tribulation. The term "last days," as used by Peter, refers to the Tribulation (cf. Deut. 4:30; 31:29; Isa. 2:2; Jer. 23:20; 30:24; 48:47; Ezek. 38:16; Dan. 2:28; 10:14; Mic. 4:1). Accordingly, it seems that the Tribulation will be a period of new revelation from God.

2:19–20 before that great and notable day of the Lord

come. While the term "day of the Lord" is usually synonymous with the Tribulation period, in this instance it is likely a reference to the Second Coming because of the phrase "great and notable." (See the note on Joel 2:30–31.)

2:21 whosoever shall call on the name of the Lord shall be saved. The context of this statement that also appears in Joel 2:32 likely refers to the physical rescue of the Jews from their enemies right before the Second Coming. The statement is also quoted in Romans 10:13 in a context indicating that only believing Israel will be willing to call upon the Lord for deliverance. Peter likely ends His quote from Joel 2 here as a transition into preaching the gospel to his fellow countrymen, emphasizing spiritual salvation from their sins recently provided by Jesus the Messiah.

2:25–28 Peter quotes from Psalm 16:8–11, a passage that speaks of resurrection. Christ fulfilled this prophecy of the psalmist at His resurrection.

2:29–31 Peter explains why Psalm 16 was fulfilled by Jesus and not David. The fact that Jesus was raised from the dead is proof that Jesus was the Messiah of Israel.

33 Therefore being by the right hand of God exalted, and having received of the Father the promise of the Holy Ghost, he hath shed forth this, which ye now see and hear.

34 For David is not ascended into the heavens: but he saith himself, The Lord said unto my Lord, Sit thou on my right hand,

35 Until I make thy foes thy footstool.

36 Therefore let all the house of Israel know assuredly, that God hath made that same Jesus, whom ye have crucified, both Lord and Christ.

37 Now when they heard *this,* they were pricked in their heart, and said unto Peter and to the rest of the apostles, Men *and* brethren, what shall we do?

38 Then Peter said unto them, Repent, and be baptized every one of you in the name of Jesus Christ for the remission of sins, and ye shall receive the gift of the Holy Ghost.

39 For the promise is unto you, and to your children, and to all that are afar off, *even* as many as the Lord our God shall call.

40 And with many other words did he testify and exhort, saying, Save yourselves from this untoward generation.

41 Then they that gladly received his word were baptized: and the same day there were added *unto them* about three thousand souls.

42 And they continued stedfastly in the apostles' doctrine and fellowship, and in breaking of bread, and in prayers.

"All Things Common"

43 And fear came upon every soul: and many wonders and signs were done by the apostles.

44 And all that believed were together, and had all things common;

45 And sold their possessions and goods, and parted them to all *men,* as every man had need.

46 And they, continuing daily with one accord in the temple, and breaking bread from house to house, did eat their meat with gladness and singleness of heart,

47 Praising God, and having favour with all

the people. And the Lord added to the church daily such as should be saved.

CHAPTER 3
The Healing of the Lame Man

1 Now Peter and John went up together into the temple at the hour of prayer, *being* the ninth *hour.*

2 And a certain man lame from his mother's womb was carried, whom they laid daily at the gate of the temple which is called Beautiful, to ask alms of them that entered into the temple;

3 Who seeing Peter and John about to go into the temple asked an alms.

4 And Peter, fastening his eyes upon him with John, said, Look on us.

5 And he gave heed unto them, expecting to receive something of them.

6 Then Peter said, Silver and gold have I none; but such as I have give I thee: In the name of Jesus Christ of Nazareth rise up and walk.

7 And he took him by the right hand, and lifted *him* up: and immediately his feet and ancle bones received strength.

8 And he leaping up stood, and walked, and entered with them into the temple, walking, and leaping, and praising God.

9 And all the people saw him walking and praising God:

10 And they knew that it was he which sat for alms at the Beautiful gate of the temple: and they were filled with wonder and amazement at that which had happened unto him.

Peter Addresses the People

11 And as the lame man which was healed held Peter and John, all the people ran together unto them in the porch that is called Solomon's, greatly wondering.

12 And when Peter saw *it,* he answered unto the people, Ye men of Israel, why marvel ye at this? or why look ye so earnestly on us, as though by our own power or holiness we had made this man to walk?

---

33 John 14:26; 15:26; 16:7, 13; Acts 1:4; 5:31; 10:45; Eph. 4:8; Phil. 2:9; Heb. 10:12

34 Ps. 110:1; Matt. 22:44; 1Cor. 15:25; Eph. 1:20; Heb. 1:13

36 Acts 5:31

37 Zech. 12:10; Luke 3:10; Acts 9:6; 16:30

38 Luke 24:47; Acts 3:19

39 Joel 2:28; Acts 3:25; 10:45; 11:15, 18; 14:27; 15:3, 8, 14; Eph. 2:13, 17

42 Acts 1:14; 2:46; Rom. 12:12; Eph. 6:18; Col. 4:2; Heb. 10:25

43 Mark 16:17; Acts 4:33; 5:12

44 Acts 4:32, 34

45 Isa. 58:7

46 Luke 24:53; Acts 1:14; 5:42; 20:7

47 Luke 2:52; Acts 4:33; 5:14; 11:24; Rom. 14:18

1 Ps. 55:17; Acts 2:46

2 John 9:8; Acts 14:8

6 Acts 4:10

8 Isa. 35:6

9 Acts 4:16, 21

10 John 9:8

2:33 Peter explains that the phenomena they are witnessing are produced by the Holy Spirit, who has been sent by the resurrected and ascended Jesus in order to show the Jewish people that Christ was the promised Messiah of Israel.

2:34–35 Sit thou on my right hand, Until I make thy foes thy footstool. Peter quotes Psalm 110:1 (the most quoted Old Testament passage in the New Testament)

and notes that this prediction was not fulfilled by David, but by Jesus in relation to the events taking place on that day. Christ is presently seated at the right hand of God the Father, until the events of the Tribulation result in the conquest of His enemies in preparation for the Millennial Kingdom (1 Cor. 15:24–28; Rev. 4——5). Along the same lines, Acts 3:19–21 tells us that Christ remains in the heavens until "the times of restitution of all things."

13 The God of Abraham, and of Isaac, and of Jacob, the God of our fathers, hath glorified his Son Jesus; whom ye delivered up, and denied him in the presence of Pilate, when he was determined to let *him* go.
14 But ye denied the Holy One and the Just, and desired a murderer to be granted unto you;
15 And killed the Prince of life, whom God hath raised from the dead; whereof we are witnesses.
16 And his name through faith in his name hath made this man strong, whom ye see and know: yea, the faith which is by him hath given him this perfect soundness in the presence of you all.
17 And now, brethren, I wot that through ignorance ye did *it*, as *did* also your rulers.
18 But those things, which God before had shewed by the mouth of all his prophets, that Christ should suffer, he hath so fulfilled.
19 Repent ye therefore, and be converted, that your sins may be blotted out, when the times of refreshing shall come from the presence of the Lord;
20 And he shall send Jesus Christ, which before was preached unto you:
21 Whom the heaven must receive until the times of restitution of all things, which God hath spoken by the mouth of all his holy prophets since the world began.
22 For Moses truly said unto the fathers, A prophet shall the Lord your God raise up unto you of your brethren, like unto me;

13 Matt. 27:2, 20; Mark 15:11; Luke 23:18, 20, 21; John 18:40; 19:15
14 Ps. 16:10; Mark 1:24; Luke 1:35
15 Heb. 2:10, 24, 32; 5:9
17 Luke 23:34; John 16:3; 1Cor. 2:8
18 Ps. 22; Isa. 50:6; 53:5; Dan. 9:26
19 Acts 2:38
21 Matt. 17:11; Luke 1:70; Acts 1:11
22 Deut. 18:15, 18, 19
25 Gen. 12:3; 18:18; Rom. 9:4, 8; 15:8
26 Luke 24:47
1 Luke 22:4; Acts 5:24
2 Matt. 22:23; Acts 23:8
6 Luke 3:2; John 11:49; 18:13

him shall ye hear in all things whatsoever he shall say unto you.
23 And it shall come to pass, *that* every soul, which will not hear that prophet, shall be destroyed from among the people.
24 Yea, and all the prophets from Samuel and those that follow after, as many as have spoken, have likewise foretold of these days.
25 Ye are the children of the prophets, and of the covenant which God made with our fathers, saying unto Abraham, And in thy seed shall all the kindreds of the earth be blessed.
26 Unto you first God, having raised up his Son Jesus, sent him to bless you, in turning away every one of you from his iniquities.

CHAPTER 4
Peter and John Are Brought before the Jewish Leaders

1 And as they spake unto the people, the priests, and the captain of the temple, and the Sadducees, came upon them,
2 Being grieved that they taught the people, and preached through Jesus the resurrection from the dead.
3 And they laid hands on them, and put *them* in hold unto the next day: for it was now eventide.
4 Howbeit many of them which heard the word believed; and the number of the men was about five thousand.
5 And it came to pass on the morrow, that their rulers, and elders, and scribes,
6 And Annas the high priest, and Caiaphas,

3:18 that Christ should suffer, he hath so fulfilled. For general prophecies of Messiah coming as a Suffering Servant, see Genesis 3:15; Psalm 22; 69; Isaiah 42:1–9; 49:1–13; 52:13—53:12; Zechariah 12:10.

3:19–21 the times of refreshing . . . the times of restitution of all things. Christ's return will bring about the repentance and conversion of the Jewish people (Zech. 12:10; Matt. 23:39; Rom. 10:8–21), so that they believe in the death of Jesus in order to take away their sins. This will result in the return of Christ and His millennial reign.

3:22–23 A prophet shall the Lord your God raise up unto you of your brethren, like unto me. In Deuteronomy 18:15, Moses made this prediction of Jesus' first coming. At Christ's first coming, Israel failed to hear and obey the words of Christ. The prediction is that Jesus will return again and that all who do not believe "shall be destroyed from among the people." This will occur during the Tribulation when the Lord will cause Israel "to pass under the rod," so that He "will purge out from among you the rebels" (Ezek. 20:37–38). Two-thirds

of Israel will be destroyed during the Tribulation, leaving a believing remnant of one-third (Zech. 13:9).

3:25 of the covenant which God made with our fathers. Peter preaches to the Jewish people and thus clearly states that the children of Israel, not the Church, are the descendants of the Hebrew prophets. Israel has not been disinherited, even after Christ came and was rejected by them. Israel, as a nation, cannot be blessed until they respond nationally with trust in Jesus as their Messiah, but this will come in the future, during the Tribulation period.

4:2 the resurrection from the dead. Literally translated, this phrase would read, "the resurrection from out of the dead ones." This defines a partial group out of a total body. The apostles were teaching the first resurrection, or resurrection of believers, as opposed to the general resurrection of unbelievers at the end of history. This first resurrection takes place a number of times throughout history (see the article "The Resurrections" by Gary Frazier).

and John, and Alexander, and as many as were of the kindred of the high priest, were gathered together at Jerusalem.

7 And when they had set them in the midst, they asked, By what power, or by what name, have ye done this?

8 Then Peter, filled with the Holy Ghost, said unto them, Ye rulers of the people, and elders of Israel,

9 If we this day be examined of the good deed done to the impotent man, by what means he is made whole;

10 Be it known unto you all, and to all the people of Israel, that by the name of Jesus Christ of Nazareth, whom ye crucified, whom God raised from the dead, *even* by him doth this man stand here before you whole.

11 This is the stone which was set at nought of you builders, which is become the head of the corner.

12 Neither is there salvation in any other: for there is none other name under heaven given among men, whereby we must be saved.

13 Now when they saw the boldness of Peter and John, and perceived that they were unlearned and ignorant men, they marvelled; and they took knowledge of them, that they had been with Jesus.

14 And beholding the man which was healed standing with them, they could say nothing against it.

15 But when they had commanded them to go aside out of the council, they conferred among themselves,

16 Saying, What shall we do to these men? for that indeed a notable miracle hath been done by them *is* manifest to all them that dwell in Jerusalem; and we cannot deny *it*.

17 But that it spread no further among the people, let us straitly threaten them, that they speak henceforth to no man in this name.

18 And they called them, and commanded them not to speak at all nor teach in the name of Jesus.

19 But Peter and John answered and said unto them, Whether it be right in the sight of God to hearken unto you more than unto God, judge ye.

20 For we cannot but speak the things which we have seen and heard.

21 So when they had further threatened them, they let them go, finding nothing how they might punish them, because of the people: for all *men* glorified God for that which was done.

22 For the man was above forty years old, on whom this miracle of healing was shewed.

The Apostles Seek Courage from God in Prayer

23 And being let go, they went to their own company, and reported all that the chief priests and elders had said unto them.

24 And when they heard that, they lifted up their voice to God with one accord, and said, Lord, thou *art* God, which hast made heaven, and earth, and the sea, and all that in them is:

25 Who by the mouth of thy servant David hast said, Why did the heathen rage, and the people imagine vain things?

26 The kings of the earth stood up, and the rulers were gathered together against the Lord, and against his Christ.

27 For of a truth against thy holy child Jesus, whom thou hast anointed, both Herod, and Pontius Pilate, with the Gentiles, and the people of Israel, were gathered together,

28 For to do whatsoever thy hand and thy counsel determined before to be done.

29 And now, Lord, behold their threatenings: and grant unto thy servants, that with all boldness they may speak thy word,

30 By stretching forth thine hand to heal; and that signs and wonders may be done by the name of thy holy child Jesus.

31 And when they had prayed, the place was shaken where they were assembled together; and they were all filled with the Holy Ghost, and they spake the word of God with boldness.

The Believers Had All Things Common

32 And the multitude of them that believed were of one heart and of one soul: neither said any *of them* that ought of the things which he possessed was his own; but they had all things common.

33 And with great power gave the apostles witness of the resurrection of the Lord Jesus: and great grace was upon them all.

Cross references

7 Ex. 2:14; Matt. 21:23; Acts 7:27
8 Luke 12:11, 12
10 Acts 2:24; 3:6, 16
11 Ps. 118:22; Isa. 28:16; Matt. 21:42
12 Matt. 1:21; Acts 10:43; 1Tim. 2:5, 6
13 Matt. 11:25; 1Cor. 1:27
14 Acts 3:11
16 John 11:47; Acts 3:9, 10
18 Acts 5:40
19 Acts 5:29
20 Acts 1:8; 2:32; 22:15; 1John 1:1, 3
21 Matt. 21:26; Luke 20:6, 19; 22:2; Acts 3:7, 8; 5:26
23 Acts 12:12
24 2Kgs. 19:15
25 Ps. 2:1
27 Matt. 26:3; Luke 1:35; 4:18; 22:2; 23:1, 8; John 10:36
28 Acts 2:23; 3:18
29 Acts 4:13, 31; 9:27; 13:46; 14:3; 19:8; 26:26; 28:31; Eph. 6:19
30 Acts 2:43; 3:6, 16; 4:27; 5:12
31 Acts 2:2, 4; 16:26
32 Acts 2:44; 5:12; Rom. 15:5, 6; 2Cor. 13:11; Phil. 1:27; 2:2; 1Pet. 3:8
33 Acts 1:8, 22; 2:47

4:25–26 This is a citation from Psalm 2:1–2, not as a fulfillment, but because the initial human response of rulers to the newly revealed gospel (see verse 27) is similar to that recorded in Psalm 2.

34 Neither was there any among them that lacked: for as many as were possessors of lands or houses sold them, and brought the prices of the things that were sold,

35 And laid *them* down at the apostles' feet: and distribution was made unto every man according as he had need.

36 And Joses, who by the apostles was surnamed Barnabas, (which is, being interpreted, The son of consolation,) a Levite, *and* of the country of Cyprus,

37 Having land, sold *it,* and brought the money, and laid *it* at the apostles' feet.

CHAPTER 5
Ananias and Sapphira

1 But a certain man named Ananias, with Sapphira his wife, sold a possession,

2 And kept back *part* of the price, his wife also being privy *to it,* and brought a certain part, and laid *it* at the apostles' feet.

3 But Peter said, Ananias, why hath Satan filled thine heart to lie to the Holy Ghost, and to keep back *part* of the price of the land?

4 Whiles it remained, was it not thine own? and after it was sold, was it not in thine own power? why hast thou conceived this thing in thine heart? thou hast not lied unto men, but unto God.

5 And Ananias hearing these words fell down, and gave up the ghost: and great fear came on all them that heard these things.

6 And the young men arose, wound him up, and carried *him* out, and buried *him*.

7 And it was about the space of three hours after, when his wife, not knowing what was done, came in.

8 And Peter answered unto her, Tell me whether ye sold the land for so much? And she said, Yea, for so much.

9 Then Peter said unto her, How is it that ye have agreed together to tempt the Spirit of the Lord? behold, the feet of them which have buried thy husband *are* at the door, and shall carry thee out.

10 Then fell she down straightway at his feet, and yielded up the ghost: and the young men came in, and found her dead, and, carrying *her* forth, buried *her* by her husband.

11 And great fear came upon all the church, and upon as many as heard these things.

34 Acts 2:45
35 Acts 2:45; 4:37; 5:2; 6:1
37 Acts 4:34, 35; 5:1, 2
2 Acts 4:37
3 Num. 30:2; Deut. 23:21; Eccl. 5:4; Luke 22:3; Acts 5:9
5 Acts 5:10, 11
6 John 19:40
9 Matt. 4:7; Acts 5:3
10 Acts 5:5
11 Acts 2:43; 5:5; 19:17
12 Acts 2:43; 3:11; 4:32; 14:3; 19:11; Rom. 15:19; 2Cor. 12:12; Heb. 2:4
13 John 9:22; 12:42; 19:38; Acts 2:47; 4:21
15 Matt. 9:21; 14:36; Acts 19:12
16 Mark 16:17, 18; John 14:12
17 Acts 4:1, 2, 6
18 Luke 21:12
19 Acts 12:7; 16:26
20 John 6:68; 17:3; 1John 5:11
21 Acts 4:5, 6
24 Luke 22:4; Acts 4:1

"Many Signs and Wonders"

12 And by the hands of the apostles were many signs and wonders wrought among the people; (and they were all with one accord in Solomon's porch.

13 And of the rest durst no man join himself to them: but the people magnified them.

14 And believers were the more added to the Lord, multitudes both of men and women.)

15 Insomuch that they brought forth the sick into the streets, and laid *them* on beds and couches, that at the least the shadow of Peter passing by might overshadow some of them.

16 There came also a multitude *out* of the cities round about unto Jerusalem, bringing sick folks, and them which were vexed with unclean spirits: and they were healed every one.

The Apostles Are Arrested

17 Then the high priest rose up, and all they that were with him, (which is the sect of the Sadducees,) and were filled with indignation,

18 And laid their hands on the apostles, and put them in the common prison.

19 But the angel of the Lord by night opened the prison doors, and brought them forth, and said,

20 Go, stand and speak in the temple to the people all the words of this life.

21 And when they heard *that,* they entered into the temple early in the morning, and taught. But the high priest came, and they that were with him, and called the council together, and all the senate of the children of Israel, and sent to the prison to have them brought.

22 But when the officers came, and found them not in the prison, they returned, and told,

23 Saying, The prison truly found we shut with all safety, and the keepers standing without before the doors: but when we had opened, we found no man within.

24 Now when the high priest and the captain of the temple and the chief priests heard these things, they doubted of them whereunto this would grow.

25 Then came one and told them, saying, Behold, the men whom ye put in prison are

---

5:9–10 Peter's prediction to Sapphira is that she, like her husband, would die for lying to God. It is immediately fulfilled.

standing in the temple, and teaching the people.

26 Then went the captain with the officers, and brought them without violence: for they feared the people, lest they should have been stoned.

27 And when they had brought them, they set *them* before the council: and the high priest asked them,

28 Saying, Did not we straitly command you that ye should not teach in this name? and, behold, ye have filled Jerusalem with your doctrine, and intend to bring this man's blood upon us.

29 Then Peter and the *other* apostles answered and said, We ought to obey God rather than men.

30 The God of our fathers raised up Jesus, whom ye slew and hanged on a tree.

31 Him hath God exalted with his right hand *to be* a Prince and a Saviour, for to give repentance to Israel, and forgiveness of sins.

32 And we are his witnesses of these things; and *so is* also the Holy Ghost, whom God hath given to them that obey him.

33 When they heard *that,* they were cut *to the heart,* and took counsel to slay them.

34 Then stood there up one in the council, a Pharisee, named Gamaliel, a doctor of the law, had in reputation among all the people, and commanded to put the apostles forth a little space;

35 And said unto them, Ye men of Israel, take heed to yourselves what ye intend to do as touching these men.

36 For before these days rose up Theudas, boasting himself to be somebody; to whom a number of men, about four hundred, joined themselves: who was slain; and all, as many as obeyed him, were scattered, and brought to nought.

37 After this man rose up Judas of Galilee in the days of the taxing, and drew away much people after him: he also perished; and all, *even* as many as obeyed him, were dispersed.

38 And now I say unto you, Refrain from these men, and let them alone: for if this counsel or this work be of men, it will come to nought:

39 But if it be of God, ye cannot overthrow it; lest haply ye be found even to fight against God.

40 And to him they agreed: and when they

had called the apostles, and beaten *them,* they commanded that they should not speak in the name of Jesus, and let them go.

41 And they departed from the presence of the council, rejoicing that they were counted worthy to suffer shame for his name.

42 And daily in the temple, and in every house, they ceased not to teach and preach Jesus Christ.

CHAPTER 6
Seven Are Chosen

1 And in those days, when the number of the disciples was multiplied, there arose a murmuring of the Grecians against the Hebrews, because their widows were neglected in the daily ministration.

2 Then the twelve called the multitude of the disciples *unto them,* and said, It is not reason that we should leave the word of God, and serve tables.

3 Wherefore, brethren, look ye out among you seven men of honest report, full of the Holy Ghost and wisdom, whom we may appoint over this business.

4 But we will give ourselves continually to prayer, and to the ministry of the word.

5 And the saying pleased the whole multitude: and they chose Stephen, a man full of faith and of the Holy Ghost, and Philip, and Prochorus, and Nicanor, and Timon, and Parmenas, and Nicolas a proselyte of Antioch:

6 Whom they set before the apostles: and when they had prayed, they laid *their* hands on them.

7 And the word of God increased; and the number of the disciples multiplied in Jerusalem greatly; and a great company of the priests were obedient to the faith.

Stephen Taken Prisoner

8 And Stephen, full of faith and power, did great wonders and miracles among the people.

9 Then there arose certain of the synagogue, which is called *the synagogue* of the Libertines, and Cyrenians, and Alexandrians, and of them of Cilicia and of Asia, disputing with Stephen.

10 And they were not able to resist the wisdom and the spirit by which he spake.

11 Then they suborned men, which said,

26 Matt. 21:26

28 Acts 2:23, 36; 3:15; 4:18; 7:52

30 Acts 3:13, 15; Gal. 3:13; 1Pet. 2:24

31 Matt. 1:21; Luke 24:47; Acts 3:15, 26; 13:38; Heb. 2:10; 12:2

32 John 15:26, 27; Acts 2:4; 10:44

34 Acts 22:3

38 Prov. 21:30; Isa. 8:10

39 Luke 21:15

41 Matt. 5:12; 2Cor. 12:10; Phil. 1:29; Heb. 10:34

42 Acts 2:46; 4:20, 29

1 Acts 2:41; 4:4, 35; 5:14; 6:7; 9:29; 11:20

2 Ex. 18:17

3 Deut. 1:13; Acts 1:21; 16:2; 1Tim. 3:7

4 Acts 2:42

5 Acts 8:5, 26; 11:24; 21:8; Rev. 2:6, 15

6 Acts 1:24; 8:17; 9:17; 13:3; 1Tim. 4:14; 5:22; 2Tim. 1:6

7 John 12:42; Acts 12:24; 19:20; Col. 1:6

10 Ex. 4:12; Isa. 54:17; Luke 21:15; Acts 5:39

11 1Kgs. 21:10, 13; Matt. 26:59, 60

5:38–39 Gamaliel's wise counsel becomes a prophecy that is being fulfilled throughout the Church Age as the gospel message spreads and can never be suppressed.

We have heard him speak blasphemous words against Moses, and *against* God.

12 And they stirred up the people, and the elders, and the scribes, and came upon *him*, and caught him, and brought *him* to the council,

13 And set up false witnesses, which said, This man ceaseth not to speak blasphemous words against this holy place, and the law:

14 For we have heard him say, that this Jesus of Nazareth shall destroy this place, and shall change the customs which Moses delivered us.

15 And all that sat in the council, looking stedfastly on him, saw his face as it had been the face of an angel.

CHAPTER 7
Stephen's Sermon

1 Then said the high priest, Are these things so?

2 And he said, Men, brethren, and fathers, hearken; The God of glory appeared unto our father Abraham, when he was in Mesopotamia, before he dwelt in Haran,

3 And said unto him, Get thee out of thy country, and from thy kindred, and come into the land which I shall shew thee.

4 Then came he out of the land of the Chaldeans, and dwelt in Haran: and from thence, when his father was dead, he removed him into this land, wherein ye now dwell.

5 And he gave him none inheritance in it, no, not *so much as* to set his foot on: yet he promised that he would give it to him for a possession, and to his seed after him, when *as yet* he had no child.

6 And God spake on this wise, That his seed should sojourn in a strange land; and that they should bring them into bondage, and entreat *them* evil four hundred years.

7 And the nation to whom they shall be in bondage will I judge, said God: and after that shall they come forth, and serve me in this place.

---

14 Dan. 9:26; Acts 25:8

2 Acts 22:1

3 Gen. 12:1

4 Gen. 11:31; 12:4, 5

5 Gen. 12:7; 13:15; 15:3, 18; 17:8; 26:3

6 Gen. 15:13, 16; Ex. 12:40; Gal. 3:17

7 Ex. 3:12

8 Gen. 17:9-11; 21:2-4; 25:26; 29:31; 30:5; 35:18, 23

9 Gen. 37:4, 11, 28; 39:2, 21, 23; Ps. 105:17

10 Gen. 41:37; 42:6

11 Gen. 41:54

12 Gen. 42:1

13 Gen. 45:4, 16

14 Gen. 45:9, 27; 46:27; Deut. 10:22

15 Gen. 46:5; 49:33; Ex. 1:6

16 Gen. 23:16; 33:19; Ex. 13:19; Josh. 24:32

17 Gen. 15:13; Ex. 1:7, 8, 9; Ps. 105:24, 25; Acts 7:6

19 Ex. 1:22

20 Ex. 2:2; Heb. 11:23

21 Ex. 2:3-10

---

8 And he gave him the covenant of circumcision: and so *Abraham* begat Isaac, and circumcised him the eighth day; and Isaac *begat* Jacob; and Jacob *begat* the twelve patriarchs.

9 And the patriarchs, moved with envy, sold Joseph into Egypt: but God was with him,

10 And delivered him out of all his afflictions, and gave him favour and wisdom in the sight of Pharaoh king of Egypt; and he made him governor over Egypt and all his house.

11 Now there came a dearth over all the land of Egypt and Canaan, and great affliction: and our fathers found no sustenance.

12 But when Jacob heard that there was corn in Egypt, he sent out our fathers first.

13 And at the second *time* Joseph was made known to his brethren; and Joseph's kindred was made known unto Pharaoh.

14 Then sent Joseph, and called his father Jacob to *him*, and all his kindred, threescore and fifteen souls.

15 So Jacob went down into Egypt, and died, he, and our fathers,

16 And were carried over into Shechem, and laid in the sepulchre that Abraham bought for a sum of money of the sons of Hamor *the father* of Shechem.

17 But when the time of the promise drew nigh, which God had sworn to Abraham, the people grew and multiplied in Egypt,

18 Till another king arose, which knew not Joseph.

19 The same dealt subtilly with our kindred, and evil entreated our fathers, so that they cast out their young children, to the end they might not live.

20 In which time Moses was born, and was exceeding fair, and nourished up in his father's house three months:

21 And when he was cast out, Pharaoh's daughter took him up, and nourished him for her own son.

22 And Moses was learned in all the

6:14 this Jesus of Nazareth shall destroy this place. Those arresting Stephen misrepresent Jesus' statement about destroying His own body as a prediction of the destruction of the temple (John 2:19). Jesus did predict the destruction of Herod's Temple (Matt. 23:38; Luke 21:20–24) which was fulfilled by the Romans in A.D. 70. Likewise, despite the statements made by Stephen's accusers, Jesus did not change the Mosaic customs; He fulfilled them (Matt. 5:17).

7:5 yet he promised that he would give it to him for a possession, and to his seed after him. This promise to Abraham is found in passages like Genesis 12:7; 17:8; 48:4. The promise will be fulfilled during the millennial reign of Christ when Israel will be given and possess her full land grant.

7:6–7 His seed should sojourn in a strange land. This is taken directly from Genesis 15:13 and refers to Egypt from the time of Joseph to the ten plagues and the Exodus. Stephen rounds off the exact number of years Israel sojourned in Egypt (see Ex. 12:40).

wisdom of the Egyptians, and was mighty in words and in deeds.

23 And when he was full forty years old, it came into his heart to visit his brethren the children of Israel.

24 And seeing one *of them* suffer wrong, he defended *him,* and avenged him that was oppressed, and smote the Egyptian:

25 For he supposed his brethren would have understood how that God by his hand would deliver them: but they understood not.

26 And the next day he shewed himself unto them as they strove, and would have set them at one again, saying, Sirs, ye are brethren; why do ye wrong one to another?

27 But he that did his neighbour wrong thrust him away, saying, Who made thee a ruler and a judge over us?

28 Wilt thou kill me, as thou diddest the Egyptian yesterday?

29 Then fled Moses at this saying, and was a stranger in the land of Midian, where he begat two sons.

30 And when forty years were expired, there appeared to him in the wilderness of mount Sina an angel of the Lord in a flame of fire in a bush.

31 When Moses saw *it,* he wondered at the sight: and as he drew near to behold *it,* the voice of the Lord came unto him,

32 *Saying,* I *am* the God of thy fathers, the God of Abraham, and the God of Isaac, and the God of Jacob. Then Moses trembled, and durst not behold.

33 Then said the Lord to him, Put off thy shoes from thy feet: for the place where thou standest is holy ground.

34 I have seen, I have seen the affliction of my people which is in Egypt, and I have heard their groaning, and am come down to deliver them. And now come, I will send thee into Egypt.

35 This Moses whom they refused, saying, Who made thee a ruler and a judge? the same did God send *to be* a ruler and a deliv-

erer by the hand of the angel which appeared to him in the bush.

36 He brought them out, after that he had shewed wonders and signs in the land of Egypt, and in the Red sea, and in the wilderness forty years.

37 This is that Moses, which said unto the children of Israel, A prophet shall the Lord your God raise up unto you of your brethren, like unto me; him shall ye hear.

38 This is he, that was in the church in the wilderness with the angel which spake to him in the mount Sina, and *with* our fathers: who received the lively oracles to give unto us:

39 To whom our fathers would not obey, but thrust *him* from them, and in their hearts turned back again into Egypt,

40 Saying unto Aaron, Make us gods to go before us: for *as for* this Moses, which brought us out of the land of Egypt, we wot not what is become of him.

41 And they made a calf in those days, and offered sacrifice unto the idol, and rejoiced in the works of their own hands.

42 Then God turned, and gave them up to worship the host of heaven; as it is written in the book of the prophets, O ye house of Israel, have ye offered to me slain beasts and sacrifices *by the space of* forty years in the wilderness?

43 Yea, ye took up the tabernacle of Moloch, and the star of your god Remphan, figures which ye made to worship them: and I will carry you away beyond Babylon.

44 Our fathers had the tabernacle of witness in the wilderness, as he had appointed, speaking unto Moses, that he should make it according to the fashion that he had seen.

45 Which also our fathers that came after brought in with Jesus into the possession of the Gentiles, whom God drave out before the face of our fathers, unto the days of David;

46 Who found favour before God, and de-

23 Ex. 2:11, 12
26 Ex. 2:13
27 Luke 12:14; Acts 4:7
29 Ex. 2:15, 22; 4:20; 18:3, 4
30 Ex. 3:2
32 Matt. 22:32; Heb. 11:16
33 Ex. 3:5; Josh. 5:15
34 Ex. 3:7
35 Ex. 14:19; Num. 20:16
36 Ex. 12:41; 14:21, 27, 28, 29; 16:1, 35; 33:1
37 Deut. 18:15, 18
38 Ex. 19:3, 17; 21:1; Deut. 5:27, 31; 33:4; Isa. 63:9
40 Ex. 32:1
41 Deut. 9:16; Ps. 106:19
42 Deut. 4:19; 17:3; Ps. 81:12; Ezek. 20:25, 39
44 Ex. 25:40; 26:30; Heb. 8:5
45 Josh. 3:14; Neh. 9:24; Ps. 44:2; 78:55; Acts 13:19
46 1Sam. 16:1; 2Sam. 7:1; 1Kgs. 8:17; 1Chr. 22:7; Ps. 89:19; 132:4, 5; Acts 13:22

7:37–38 A prophet shall the Lord your God raise up unto you of your brethren. Stephen, like Peter in Acts 3:22–23, argues that Jesus fulfilled the prediction of Moses (Deut. 18:15), yet the nation did not listen and obey Him. The use of "church" in the phrase "church in the wilderness" carries a general meaning of "assembly," and hence refers to the assembly of Israelites in the wilderness. The distinct New Testament meaning of the word "church," used as a reference to all believers in Christ from the Day of Pentecost until the Rapture, was

developed later (Col. 1:18). The word "church" is also used in Acts (19:32, 39, 41) as a reference to another assembly of people.

7:42–43 Stephen quotes prophecy from Amos 5:25, which was fulfilled when the Northern Kingdom was carried away into captivity. God has a precedent of turning aside from a disobedient people, as He was doing with the current generation of Israel that had rejected Jesus as their Messiah.

sired to find a tabernacle for the God of Jacob.

47 But Solomon built him an house.

48 Howbeit the most High dwelleth not in temples made with hands; as saith the prophet,

49 Heaven *is* my throne, and earth *is* my footstool: what house will ye build me? saith the Lord: or what *is* the place of my rest?

50 Hath not my hand made all these things?

51 Ye stiffnecked and uncircumcised in heart and ears, ye do always resist the Holy Ghost: as your fathers *did,* so *do* ye.

52 Which of the prophets have not your fathers persecuted? and they have slain them which shewed before of the coming of the Just One; of whom ye have been now the betrayers and murderers:

53 Who have received the law by the disposition of angels, and have not kept *it.*

Stephen Is Put to Death

54 When they heard these things, they were cut to the heart, and they gnashed on him with *their* teeth.

55 But he, being full of the Holy Ghost, looked up stedfastly into heaven, and saw the glory of God, and Jesus standing on the right hand of God,

56 And said, Behold, I see the heavens opened, and the Son of man standing on the right hand of God.

57 Then they cried out with a loud voice, and stopped their ears, and ran upon him with one accord,

58 And cast *him* out of the city, and stoned *him*: and the witnesses laid down their clothes at a young man's feet, whose name was Saul.

59 And they stoned Stephen, calling upon *God,* and saying, Lord Jesus, receive my spirit.

60 And he kneeled down, and cried with a loud voice, Lord, lay not this sin to their charge. And when he had said this, he fell asleep.

CHAPTER 8
The Congregation Is Persecuted

1 And Saul was consenting unto his death. And at that time there was a great persecution against the church which was at Jerusalem; and they were all scattered abroad throughout the regions of Judea and Samaria, except the apostles.

2 And devout men carried Stephen *to his*

burial, and made great lamentation over him.

3 As for Saul, he made havoc of the church, entering into every house, and haling men and women committed *them* to prison.

The Gospel Proclaimed in Samaria

4 Therefore they that were scattered abroad went every where preaching the word.

5 Then Philip went down to the city of Samaria, and preached Christ unto them.

6 And the people with one accord gave heed unto those things which Philip spake, hearing and seeing the miracles which he did.

7 For unclean spirits, crying with loud voice, came out of many that were possessed *with them*: and many taken with palsies, and that were lame, were healed.

8 And there was great joy in that city.

9 But there was a certain man, called Simon, which beforetime in the same city used sorcery, and bewitched the people of Samaria, giving out that himself was some great one:

10 To whom they all gave heed, from the least to the greatest, saying, This man is the great power of God.

11 And to him they had regard, because that of long time he had bewitched them with sorceries.

12 But when they believed Philip preaching the things concerning the kingdom of God, and the name of Jesus Christ, they were baptized, both men and women.

13 Then Simon himself believed also: and when he was baptized, he continued with Philip, and wondered, beholding the miracles and signs which were done.

14 Now when the apostles which were at Jerusalem heard that Samaria had received the word of God, they sent unto them Peter and John:

15 Who, when they were come down, prayed for them, that they might receive the Holy Ghost:

16 (For as yet he was fallen upon none of them: only they were baptized in the name of the Lord Jesus.)

17 Then laid they *their* hands on them, and they received the Holy Ghost.

18 And when Simon saw that through laying on of the apostles' hands the Holy Ghost was given, he offered them money,

19 Saying, Give me also this power, that on whomsoever I lay hands, he may receive the Holy Ghost.

47 1Kgs. 6:1; 8:20; 1Chr. 17:12; 2Chr. 3:1

48 1Kgs. 8:27; 2Chr. 2:6; 6:18; Acts 17:24

49 Isa. 66:1, 2; Matt. 5:34, 35; 23:22

51 Ex. 32:9; 33:3; Lev. 26:41; Isa. 48:4

52 2Chr. 36:16; Matt. 21:35; 23:34, 37

53 Ex. 20:1; Gal. 3:19; Heb. 2:2

54 Acts 5:33

55 Acts 6:5

56 Ezek. 1:1; Dan. 7:13; Matt. 3:16; Acts 10:11

58 Lev. 24:16

59 Ps. 31:5; Luke 23:46; Acts 9:14

60 Matt. 5:44; Luke 6:28; 23:34; Acts 9:40; 20:36; 21:5

1 Acts 7:58; 11:19; 22:20

2 Gen. 23:2; 50:10; 2Sam. 3:31

3 Acts 9:1, 13, 21; 22:4; 26:10, 11; 1Cor. 15:9; Gal. 1:13

4 Matt. 10:23; Acts 11:19

5 Acts 6:5

7 Mark 16:17

9 Acts 5:36; 13:6

12 Acts 1:3

15 Acts 2:38

16 Matt. 28:19; Acts 2:38; 10:48; 19:2, 5

17 Acts 6:6; 19:6; Heb. 6:2

20 But Peter said unto him, Thy money perish with thee, because thou hast thought that the gift of God may be purchased with money.

21 Thou hast neither part nor lot in this matter: for thy heart is not right in the sight of God.

22 Repent therefore of this thy wickedness, and pray God, if perhaps the thought of thine heart may be forgiven thee.

23 For I perceive that thou art in the gall of bitterness, and *in* the bond of iniquity.

24 Then answered Simon, and said, Pray ye to the Lord for me, that none of these things which ye have spoken come upon me.

25 And they, when they had testified and preached the word of the Lord, returned to Jerusalem, and preached the gospel in many villages of the Samaritans.

Philip and the Ethiopian Eunuch

26 And the angel of the Lord spake unto Philip, saying, Arise, and go toward the south unto the way that goeth down from Jerusalem unto Gaza, which is desert.

27 And he arose and went: and, behold, a man of Ethiopia, an eunuch of great authority under Candace queen of the Ethiopians, who had the charge of all her treasure, and had come to Jerusalem for to worship,

28 Was returning, and sitting in his chariot read Esaias the prophet.

29 Then the Spirit said unto Philip, Go near, and join thyself to this chariot.

30 And Philip ran thither to *him*, and heard him read the prophet Esaias, and said, Understandest thou what thou readest?

31 And he said, How can I, except some man should guide me? And he desired Philip that he would come up and sit with him.

32 The place of the scripture which he read was this, He was led as a sheep to the slaughter; and like a lamb dumb before his shearer, so opened he not his mouth:

33 In his humiliation his judgment was taken away: and who shall declare his generation? for his life is taken from the earth.

34 And the eunuch answered Philip, and said, I pray thee, of whom speaketh the prophet this? of himself, or of some other man?

35 Then Philip opened his mouth, and began at the same scripture, and preached unto him Jesus.

36 And as they went on *their* way, they came unto a certain water: and the eunuch said, See, *here is* water; what doth hinder me to be baptized?

37 And Philip said, If thou believest with all thine heart, thou mayest. And he answered and said, I believe that Jesus Christ is the Son of God.

38 And he commanded the chariot to stand still: and they went down both into the water, both Philip and the eunuch; and he baptized him.

39 And when they were come up out of the water, the Spirit of the Lord caught away Philip, that the eunuch saw him no more: and he went on his way rejoicing.

40 But Philip was found at Azotus: and passing through he preached in all the cities, till he came to Caesarea.

CHAPTER 9
Paul's Conversion

1 And Saul, yet breathing out threatenings and slaughter against the disciples of the Lord, went unto the high priest,

2 And desired of him letters to Damascus to the synagogues, that if he found any of this way, whether they were men or women, he might bring them bound unto Jerusalem.

3 And as he journeyed, he came near Damascus: and suddenly there shined round about him a light from heaven:

4 And he fell to the earth, and heard a voice saying unto him, Saul, Saul, why persecutest thou me?

5 And he said, Who art thou, Lord? And the Lord said, I am Jesus whom thou persecutest: *it is* hard for thee to kick against the pricks.

6 And he trembling and astonished said, Lord, what wilt thou have me to do? And the Lord *said* unto him, Arise, and go into the city, and it shall be told thee what thou must do.

7 And the men which journeyed with him stood speechless, hearing a voice, but seeing no man.

8 And Saul arose from the earth; and when his eyes were opened, he saw no man: but they led him by the hand, and brought *him* into Damascus.

9 And he was three days without sight, and neither did eat nor drink.

Cross-references

20 2Kgs. 5:16; Matt. 10:8; Acts 2:38; 10:45; 11:17
22 Dan. 4:27; 2Tim. 2:25
23 Heb. 12:15
24 Gen. 20:7, 17; Ex. 8:8; Num. 21:7; 1Kgs. 13:6; Job 42:8; James 5:16
27 Zeph. 3:10; John 12:20
32 Isa. 53:7, 8
35 Luke 24:27; Acts 18:28
36 Acts 10:47
37 Matt. 16:16; 28:19; Mark 16:16; John 6:69; 9:35, 38; 11:27; Acts 9:20; 1John 4:15; 5:5, 13
39 1Kgs. 18:12; 2Kgs. 2:16; Ezek. 3:12, 14
1 Acts 8:3; Gal. 1:13; 1Tim. 1:13
2 Acts 19:9, 23
3 Acts 22:6; 26:12; 1Cor. 15:8
4 Matt. 25:40
5 Acts 5:39
6 Luke 3:10; Acts 2:37; 16:30
7 Dan. 10:7; Acts 22:9; 26:13

8:32–35 The place of the scripture which he read. This quote from Isaiah 53:7–8 was a prophecy fulfilled by Jesus at His death, as preached to the eunuch by Philip.

10 And there was a certain disciple at Damascus named Ananias; and to him said the Lord in a vision, Ananias. And he said, Behold, I *am here*, Lord.

11 And the Lord *said* unto him, Arise, and go into the street which is called Straight, and inquire in the house of Judas for *one* called Saul of Tarsus: for, behold, he prayeth,

12 And hath seen in a vision a man named Ananias coming in, and putting *his* hand on him, that he might receive his sight.

13 Then Ananias answered, Lord, I have heard by many of this man, how much evil he hath done to thy saints at Jerusalem:

14 And here he hath authority from the chief priests to bind all that call on thy name.

15 But the Lord said unto him, Go thy way: for he is a chosen vessel unto me, to bear my name before the Gentiles, and kings, and the children of Israel:

16 For I will shew him how great things he must suffer for my name's sake.

17 And Ananias went his way, and entered into the house; and putting his hands on him said, Brother Saul, the Lord, *even* Jesus, that appeared unto thee in the way as thou camest, hath sent me, that thou mightest receive thy sight, and be filled with the Holy Ghost.

18 And immediately there fell from his eyes as it had been scales: and he received sight forthwith, and arose, and was baptized.

19 And when he had received meat, he was strengthened. Then was Saul certain days with the disciples which were at Damascus.

Paul Preaches at Damascus

20 And straightway he preached Christ in the synagogues, that he is the Son of God.

21 But all that heard *him* were amazed, and said; Is not this he that destroyed them which called on this name in Jerusalem, and came hither for that intent, that he might bring them bound unto the chief priests?

22 But Saul increased the more in strength, and confounded the Jews which dwelt at Damascus, proving that this is very Christ.

Paul's Escape

23 And after that many days were fulfilled, the Jews took counsel to kill him:

24 But their laying await was known of Saul. And they watched the gates day and night to kill him.

25 Then the disciples took him by night, and let *him* down by the wall in a basket.

Paul Goes to Jerusalem

26 And when Saul was come to Jerusalem, he assayed to join himself to the disciples: but they were all afraid of him, and believed not that he was a disciple.

27 But Barnabas took him, and brought *him* to the apostles, and declared unto them how he had seen the Lord in the way, and that he had spoken to him, and how he had preached boldly at Damascus in the name of Jesus.

28 And he was with them coming in and going out at Jerusalem.

29 And he spake boldly in the name of the Lord Jesus, and disputed against the Grecians: but they went about to slay him.

30 *Which* when the brethren knew, they brought him down to Caesarea, and sent him forth to Tarsus.

31 Then had the churches rest throughout all Judea and Galilee and Samaria, and were edified; and walking in the fear of the Lord, and in the comfort of the Holy Ghost, were multiplied.

Aeneas Healed

32 And it came to pass, as Peter passed throughout all *quarters,* he came down also to the saints which dwelt at Lydda.

33 And there he found a certain man named Aeneas, which had kept his bed eight years, and was sick of the palsy.

34 And Peter said unto him, Aeneas, Jesus

Cross references

10 Acts 22:12
11 Acts 21:39; 22:3
13 Acts 9:1
14 Acts 7:59; 9:21; 22:16; 1Cor. 1:2; 2Tim. 2:22
15 Acts 13:2; 22:21; 25:22, 23; 26:1, 17; Rom. 1:1, 5; 11:13; 1Cor. 15:10; Gal. 1:15; 2:7, 8; Eph. 3:7, 8; 1Tim. 2:7; 2Tim. 1:11
16 Acts 20:23; 21:11; 2Cor. 11:23
17 Acts 2:4; 4:31; 8:17; 13:52; 22:12, 13
19 Acts 26:20
20 Acts 8:37
21 Acts 8:3; 9:1; Gal. 1:13, 23
22 Acts 18:28
23 Acts 23:12; 25:3; 2Cor. 11:26
24 2Cor. 11:32
25 Josh. 2:15; 1Sam. 19:12
26 Acts 22:17; Gal. 1:17, 18
27 Acts 4:36; 9:20, 22; 13:2
28 Gal. 1:18
29 Acts 6:1; 11:20; 2Cor. 11:26
31 Acts 8:1

9:11–12 Ananias is given a direct revelation from God about Saul's conversion and given the power to heal his blindness and provide God's explanation of what was happening to Saul.

9:15–16 a chosen vessel unto me. Saul was chosen to fulfill a special mission in relation to the founding of the Church. His mission to the Gentiles is recorded in the remainder of the book of Acts (see also Rom. 1:5; 11:13; Gal. 2:9). Saul's approach to preaching the gospel in any new community was to go to the Jews first (Rom. 1:16) as his springboard to the Gentile community (Acts 13:14; 17:2; 18:4; 19:8). The prophecy that Saul would be shown "how great things he must suffer for my name's sake" was fulfilled throughout his life as noted in the remainder of Acts (see 2 Cor. 11:23–28).

Christ maketh thee whole: arise, and make thy bed. And he arose immediately.

35 And all that dwelt at Lydda and Sharon saw him, and turned to the Lord.

Peter Raises Dorcas to Life

36 Now there was at Joppa a certain disciple named Tabitha, which by interpretation is called Dorcas: this woman was full of good works and almsdeeds which she did.

37 And it came to pass in those days, that she was sick, and died: whom when they had washed, they laid *her* in an upper chamber.

38 And forasmuch as Lydda was nigh to Joppa, and the disciples had heard that Peter was there, they sent unto him two men, desiring *him* that he would not delay to come to them.

39 Then Peter arose and went with them. When he was come, they brought him into the upper chamber: and all the widows stood by him weeping, and shewing the coats and garments which Dorcas made, while she was with them.

40 But Peter put them all forth, and kneeled down, and prayed; and turning *him* to the body said, Tabitha, arise. And she opened her eyes: and when she saw Peter, she sat up.

41 And he gave her *his* hand, and lifted her up, and when he had called the saints and widows, presented her alive.

42 And it was known throughout all Joppa; and many believed in the Lord.

43 And it came to pass, that he tarried many days in Joppa with one Simon a tanner.

CHAPTER 10
The Conversion of Cornelius

1 There was a certain man in Caesarea called Cornelius, a centurion of the band called the Italian *band,*

2 A devout *man,* and one that feared God with all his house, which gave much alms to the people, and prayed to God alway.

3 He saw in a vision evidently about the ninth hour of the day an angel of God coming in to him, and saying unto him, Cornelius.

4 And when he looked on him, he was afraid, and said, What is it, Lord? And he said unto him, Thy prayers and thine alms are come up for a memorial before God.

5 And now send men to Joppa, and call for *one* Simon, whose surname is Peter:

6 He lodgeth with one Simon a tanner, whose house is by the sea side: he shall tell thee what thou oughtest to do.

7 And when the angel which spake unto Cornelius was departed, he called two of his household servants, and a devout soldier of them that waited on him continually;

8 And when he had declared all *these* things unto them, he sent them to Joppa.

9 On the morrow, as they went on their journey, and drew nigh unto the city, Peter went up upon the housetop to pray about the sixth hour:

10 And he became very hungry, and would have eaten: but while they made ready, he fell into a trance,

11 And saw heaven opened, and a certain vessel descending unto him, as it had been a great sheet knit at the four corners, and let down to the earth:

12 Wherein were all manner of fourfooted beasts of the earth, and wild beasts, and creeping things, and fowls of the air.

13 And there came a voice to him, Rise, Peter; kill, and eat.

14 But Peter said, Not so, Lord; for I have never eaten any thing that is common or unclean.

15 And the voice *spake* unto him again the second time, What God hath cleansed, *that* call not thou common.

16 This was done thrice: and the vessel was received up again into heaven.

17 Now while Peter doubted in himself what this vision which he had seen should mean, behold, the men which were sent from Cornelius had made inquiry for Simon's house, and stood before the gate,

18 And called, and asked whether Simon, which was surnamed Peter, were lodged there.

19 While Peter thought on the vision, the Spirit said unto him, Behold, three men seek thee.

20 Arise therefore, and get thee down, and go with them, doubting nothing: for I have sent them.

21 Then Peter went down to the men which were sent unto him from Cornelius; and said, Behold, I am he whom ye seek: what *is* the cause wherefore ye are come?

22 And they said, Cornelius the centurion, a

Cross-references (center column):

35 1Chr. 5:16; Acts 11:21
36 1Tim. 2:10; Titus 3:8
37 Acts 1:13
40 Matt. 9:25; Mark 5:41, 42; John 11:43; Acts 7:60
42 John 11:45; 12:11
43 Acts 10:6
2 Acts 8:2; 10:22, 35; 22:12
3 Acts 10:30; 11:13
6 Acts 9:43; 11:14
9 Acts 11:5
11 Acts 7:56; Rev. 19:11
14 Lev. 11:4; 20:25; Deut. 14:3, 7; Ezek. 4:14
15 Matt. 15:11; Acts 10:28; Rom. 14:14, 17, 20; 1Cor. 10:25; 1Tim. 4:4; Titus 1:15
19 Acts 11:12
20 Acts 15:7
22 Acts 10:1-8; 22:12

10:19–20 Peter receives a direct prophecy from the Lord about certain men who were sent from Cornelius. This was fulfilled through the events of Acts 10:21–33.

just man, and one that feareth God, and of good report among all the nation of the Jews, was warned from God by an holy angel to send for thee into his house, and to hear words of thee.

23 Then called he them in, and lodged *them*. And on the morrow Peter went away with them, and certain brethren from Joppa accompanied him.

24 And the morrow after they entered into Caesarea. And Cornelius waited for them, and had called together his kinsmen and near friends.

25 And as Peter was coming in, Cornelius met him, and fell down at his feet, and worshipped *him*.

26 But Peter took him up, saying, Stand up; I myself also am a man.

27 And as he talked with him, he went in, and found many that were come together.

28 And he said unto them, Ye know how that it is an unlawful thing for a man that is a Jew to keep company, or come unto one of another nation; but God hath shewed me that I should not call any man common or unclean.

29 Therefore came I *unto you* without gainsaying, as soon as I was sent for: I ask therefore for what intent ye have sent for me?

30 And Cornelius said, Four days ago I was fasting until this hour; and at the ninth hour I prayed in my house, and, behold, a man stood before me in bright clothing,

31 And said, Cornelius, thy prayer is heard, and thine alms are had in remembrance in the sight of God.

32 Send therefore to Joppa, and call hither Simon, whose surname is Peter; he is lodged in the house of *one* Simon a tanner by the sea side: who, when he cometh, shall speak unto thee.

33 Immediately therefore I sent to thee; and thou hast well done that thou art come. Now therefore are we all here present before God, to hear all things that are commanded thee of God.

34 Then Peter opened *his* mouth, and said, Of a truth I perceive that God is no respecter of persons:

35 But in every nation he that feareth him, and worketh righteousness, is accepted with him.

36 The word which *God* sent unto the chil-

dren of Israel, preaching peace by Jesus Christ: (he is Lord of all:)

37 That word, *I say,* ye know, which was published throughout all Judea, and began from Galilee, after the baptism which John preached;

38 How God anointed Jesus of Nazareth with the Holy Ghost and with power: who went about doing good, and healing all that were oppressed of the devil; for God was with him.

39 And we are witnesses of all things which he did both in the land of the Jews, and in Jerusalem; whom they slew and hanged on a tree:

40 Him God raised up the third day, and shewed him openly;

41 Not to all the people, but unto witnesses chosen before of God, *even* to us, who did eat and drink with him after he rose from the dead.

42 And he commanded us to preach unto the people, and to testify that it is he which was ordained of God *to be* the Judge of quick and dead.

43 To him give all the prophets witness, that through his name whosoever believeth in him shall receive remission of sins.

The Gentiles Receive the Holy Spirit

44 While Peter yet spake these words, the Holy Ghost fell on all them which heard the word.

45 And they of the circumcision which believed were astonished, as many as came with Peter, because that on the Gentiles also was poured out the gift of the Holy Ghost.

46 For they heard them speak with tongues, and magnify God. Then answered Peter,

47 Can any man forbid water, that these should not be baptized, which have received the Holy Ghost as well as we?

48 And he commanded them to be baptized in the name of the Lord. Then prayed they him to tarry certain days.

CHAPTER 11
Peter Reports to the Jerusalem Church

1 And the apostles and brethren that were in Judea heard that the Gentiles had also received the word of God.

Cross references (center column)

23 Acts 10:45; 11:12
26 Acts 14:14, 15; Rev. 19:10; 22:9
28 John 4:9; 18:28; Gal. 2:12, 14; Eph. 3:6
30 Matt. 28:3; Mark 16:5; Luke 24:4; Acts 1:10
31 Dan. 10:12; Acts 10:4-8; Heb. 6:10
34 Deut. 10:17; Job 34:19; Col. 3:25; 1Pet. 1:17
35 Rom. 2:13, 27; 3:22, 29; 10:12, 13; Gal. 3:28
36 Isa. 57:19; Matt. 28:18; Eph. 1:20; 2:14, 16, 17; 1Pet. 3:22
37 Luke 4:14
38 Luke 4:18; John 3:2; Acts 2:22; 4:27; Heb. 1:9
41 Luke 24:30, 43; John 14:17, 22; 21:13; Acts 13:31
42 Matt. 28:19, 20; John 5:22, 27; Rom. 14:9, 10; 2Cor. 5:10
43 Isa. 53:11; Jer. 31:34; Mal. 4:2
44 Acts 4:31; 8:15-17; 11:15
45 Acts 10:23; 11:18; Gal. 3:14
47 Acts 11:17; 15:8, 9; Rom. 10:12

10:42 the Judge of quick [living] **and dead.** A common prediction throughout Acts was that Jesus will be the One who renders final judgment (Acts 16:31; 24:25; see 2 Tim. 4:1).

2 And when Peter was come up to Jerusalem, they that were of the circumcision contended with him,

3 Saying, Thou wentest in to men uncircumcised, and didst eat with them.

4 But Peter rehearsed *the matter* from the beginning, and expounded *it* by order unto them, saying,

5 I was in the city of Joppa praying: and in a trance I saw a vision, A certain vessel descend, as it had been a great sheet, let down from heaven by four corners; and it came even to me:

6 Upon the which when I had fastened mine eyes, I considered, and saw fourfooted beasts of the earth, and wild beasts, and creeping things, and fowls of the air.

7 And I heard a voice saying unto me, Arise, Peter; slay and eat.

8 But I said, Not so, Lord: for nothing common or unclean hath at any time entered into my mouth.

9 But the voice answered me again from heaven, What God hath cleansed, *that* call not thou common.

10 And this was done three times: and all were drawn up again into heaven.

11 And, behold, immediately there were three men already come unto the house where I was, sent from Caesarea unto me.

12 And the Spirit bade me go with them, nothing doubting. Moreover these six brethren accompanied me, and we entered into the man's house:

13 And he shewed us how he had seen an angel in his house, which stood and said unto him, Send men to Joppa, and call for Simon, whose surname is Peter;

14 Who shall tell thee words, whereby thou and all thy house shall be saved.

15 And as I began to speak, the Holy Ghost fell on them, as on us at the beginning.

16 Then remembered I the word of the Lord, how that he said, John indeed baptized with water; but ye shall be baptized with the Holy Ghost.

17 Forasmuch then as God gave them the like gift as *he did* unto us, who believed on the Lord Jesus Christ; what was I, that I could withstand God?

18 When they heard these things, they held their peace, and glorified God, saying, Then hath God also to the Gentiles granted repentance unto life.

The New Believers in Antioch

19 Now they which were scattered abroad upon the persecution that arose about Stephen travelled as far as Phoenicia, and Cyprus, and Antioch, preaching the word to none but unto the Jews only.

20 And some of them were men of Cyprus and Cyrene, which, when they were come to Antioch, spake unto the Grecians, preaching the Lord Jesus.

21 And the hand of the Lord was with them: and a great number believed, and turned unto the Lord.

22 Then tidings of these things came unto the ears of the church which was in Jerusalem: and they sent forth Barnabas, that he should go as far as Antioch.

23 Who, when he came, and had seen the grace of God, was glad, and exhorted them all, that with purpose of heart they would cleave unto the Lord.

24 For he was a good man, and full of the Holy Ghost and of faith: and much people was added unto the Lord.

25 Then departed Barnabas to Tarsus, for to seek Saul:

26 And when he had found him, he brought him unto Antioch. And it came to pass, that a whole year they assembled themselves with the church, and taught much people. And the disciples were called Christians first in Antioch.

27 And in these days came prophets from Jerusalem unto Antioch.

28 And there stood up one of them named Agabus, and signified by the spirit that there should be great dearth throughout all the world: which came to pass in the days of Claudius Caesar.

29 Then the disciples, every man according to his ability, determined to send relief unto the brethren which dwelt in Judea:

30 Which also they did, and sent it to the elders by the hands of Barnabas and Saul.

CHAPTER 12
Peter Is Imprisoned

1 Now about that time Herod the king stretched forth *his* hands to vex certain of the church.

2 And he killed James the brother of John with the sword.

3 And because he saw it pleased the Jews,

Cross references (center column):

2 Acts 10:45; Gal. 2:12
3 Acts 10:28; Gal. 2:12
4 Luke 1:3
5 Acts 10:9
12 John 16:13; Acts 10:19, 23; 15:7
13 Acts 10:30
15 Acts 2:4
16 Isa. 44:3; Joel 2:28; 3:18; Matt. 3:11; John 1:26, 33; Acts 1:5; 19:4
17 Acts 10:47; 15:8, 9
18 Rom. 10:12, 13; 15:9, 16
19 Acts 8:1
20 Acts 6:1; 9:29
21 Luke 1:66; Acts 2:47; 9:35
22 Acts 9:27
23 Acts 13:43; 14:22
24 Acts 5:14; 6:5; 11:21
25 Acts 9:30
27 Acts 2:17; 13:1; 15:32; 21:9; 1Cor. 12:28; Eph. 4:11
28 Acts 21:10
29 Rom. 15:26; 1Cor. 16:1; 2Cor. 9:1
30 Acts 12:25

2 Matt. 4:21; 20:23
3 Ex. 12:14, 15; 23:15

11:27–28 Because the early Church was spreading throughout the Roman world, church members were able to participate in helping feed many of those in need during the famine predicted by Agabus (Acts 11:30; 12:25).

he proceeded further to take Peter also. (Then were the days of unleavened bread.)

4 And when he had apprehended him, he put *him* in prison, and delivered *him* to four quaternions of soldiers to keep him; intending after Easter to bring him forth to the people.

5 Peter therefore was kept in prison: but prayer was made without ceasing of the church unto God for him.

Peter Delivered from Prison

6 And when Herod would have brought him forth, the same night Peter was sleeping between two soldiers, bound with two chains: and the keepers before the door kept the prison.

7 And, behold, the angel of the Lord came upon *him*, and a light shined in the prison: and he smote Peter on the side, and raised him up, saying, Arise up quickly. And his chains fell off from *his* hands.

8 And the angel said unto him, Gird thyself, and bind on thy sandals. And so he did. And he saith unto him, Cast thy garment about thee, and follow me.

9 And he went out, and followed him; and wist not that it was true which was done by the angel; but thought he saw a vision.

10 When they were past the first and the second ward, they came unto the iron gate that leadeth unto the city; which opened to them of his own accord: and they went out, and passed on through one street; and forthwith the angel departed from him.

11 And when Peter was come to himself, he said, Now I know of a surety, that the Lord hath sent his angel, and hath delivered me out of the hand of Herod, and *from* all the expectation of the people of the Jews.

12 And when he had considered *the thing*, he came to the house of Mary the mother of John, whose surname was Mark; where many were gathered together praying.

13 And as Peter knocked at the door of the gate, a damsel came to hearken, named Rhoda.

14 And when she knew Peter's voice, she opened not the gate for gladness, but ran in, and told how Peter stood before the gate.

15 And they said unto her, Thou art mad. But she constantly affirmed that it was even so. Then said they, It is his angel.

16 But Peter continued knocking: and when they had opened *the door*, and saw him, they were astonished.

17 But he, beckoning unto them with the hand to hold their peace, declared unto

them how the Lord had brought him out of the prison. And he said, Go shew these things unto James, and to the brethren. And he departed, and went into another place.

18 Now as soon as it was day, there was no small stir among the soldiers, what was become of Peter.

19 And when Herod had sought for him, and found him not, he examined the keepers, and commanded that *they* should be put to death. And he went down from Judea to Caesarea, and *there* abode.

Herod Dies

20 And Herod was highly displeased with them of Tyre and Sidon: but they came with one accord to him, and, having made Blastus the king's chamberlain their friend, desired peace; because their country was nourished by the king's *country*.

21 And upon a set day Herod, arrayed in royal apparel, sat upon his throne, and made an oration unto them.

22 And the people gave a shout, *saying*, It is the voice of a god, and not of a man.

23 And immediately the angel of the Lord smote him, because he gave not God the glory: and he was eaten of worms, and gave up the ghost.

24 But the word of God grew and multiplied.

25 And Barnabas and Saul returned from Jerusalem, when they had fulfilled *their* ministry, and took with them John, whose surname was Mark.

CHAPTER 13
Paul and Barnabas Are Chosen

1 Now there were in the church that was at Antioch certain prophets and teachers; as Barnabas, and Simeon that was called Niger, and Lucius of Cyrene, and Manaen, which had been brought up with Herod the tetrarch, and Saul.

2 As they ministered to the Lord, and fasted, the Holy Ghost said, Separate me Barnabas and Saul for the work whereunto I have called them.

3 And when they had fasted and prayed, and laid *their* hands on them, they sent *them* away.

Ministry on Cyprus

4 So they, being sent forth by the Holy Ghost, departed unto Seleucia; and from thence they sailed to Cyprus.

5 And when they were at Salamis, they

Cross References

4 John 21:18

5 2Cor. 1:11; Eph. 6:18; 1Thess. 5:17

7 Acts 5:19

9 Ps. 126:1; Acts 10:3, 17; 11:5

10 Acts 16:26

11 Job 5:19; Ps. 33:18, 19; 34:7, 22; 41:2; 97:10; Dan. 3:28; 6:22; 2Cor. 1:10; Heb. 1:14; 2Pet. 2:9

12 Acts 4:23; 12:5; 15:37

15 Gen. 48:16; Matt. 18:10

17 Acts 13:16; 19:33; 21:40

20 1Kgs. 5:9, 11; Ezek. 27:17

23 1Sam. 25:38; 2Sam. 24:17; Ps. 115:1

24 Isa. 55:11; Acts 6:7; 19:20; Col. 1:6

25 Acts 11:29, 30; 12:12; 13:5, 13; 15:37

1 Acts 11:22-26, 27; 14:26; 15:35; Rom. 16:21

2 Num. 8:14; Matt. 9:38; Acts 9:15; 14:26; 22:21; Rom. 1:1; 10:15; Gal. 1:15; 2:9; Eph. 3:7, 8; 1Tim. 2:7; 2Tim. 1:11; Heb. 5:4

3 Acts 6:6

4 Acts 4:36

5 Acts 12:25; 13:46; 15:37

preached the word of God in the synagogues of the Jews: and they had also John to *their* minister.

6 And when they had gone through the isle unto Paphos, they found a certain sorcerer, a false prophet, a Jew, whose name *was* Barjesus:

7 Which was with the deputy of the country, Sergius Paulus, a prudent man; who called for Barnabas and Saul, and desired to hear the word of God.

8 But Elymas the sorcerer (for so is his name by interpretation) withstood them, seeking to turn away the deputy from the faith.

9 Then Saul, (who also *is called* Paul,) filled with the Holy Ghost, set his eyes on him,

10 And said, O full of all subtilty and all mischief, *thou* child of the devil, *thou* enemy of all righteousness, wilt thou not cease to pervert the right ways of the Lord?

11 And now, behold, the hand of the Lord *is* upon thee, and thou shalt be blind, not seeing the sun for a season. And immediately there fell on him a mist and a darkness; and he went about seeking some to lead him by the hand.

12 Then the deputy, when he saw what was done, believed, being astonished at the doctrine of the Lord.

In Antioch of Pisidia

13 Now when Paul and his company loosed from Paphos, they came to Perga in Pamphylia: and John departing from them returned to Jerusalem.

14 But when they departed from Perga, they came to Antioch in Pisidia, and went into the synagogue on the sabbath day, and sat down.

15 And after the reading of the law and the prophets the rulers of the synagogue sent unto them, saying, *Ye* men *and* brethren, if ye have any word of exhortation for the people, say on.

16 Then Paul stood up, and beckoning with *his* hand said, Men of Israel, and ye that fear God, give audience.

17 The God of this people of Israel chose our fathers, and exalted the people when they dwelt as strangers in the land of Egypt, and with an high arm brought he them out of it.

18 And about the time of forty years suffered he their manners in the wilderness.

19 And when he had destroyed seven nations in the land of Canaan, he divided their land to them by lot.

20 And after that he gave *unto them* judges about the space of four hundred and fifty years, until Samuel the prophet.

21 And afterward they desired a king: and God gave unto them Saul the son of Kish, a man of the tribe of Benjamin, by the space of forty years.

22 And when he had removed him, he raised up unto them David to be their king; to whom also he gave testimony, and said, I have found David the *son* of Jesse, a man after mine own heart, which shall fulfil all my will.

23 Of this man's seed hath God according to *his* promise raised unto Israel a Saviour, Jesus:

24 When John had first preached before his coming the baptism of repentance to all the people of Israel.

25 And as John fulfilled his course, he said, Whom think ye that I am? I am not *he*. But, behold, there cometh one after me, whose shoes of *his* feet I am not worthy to loose.

26 Men *and* brethren, children of the stock of Abraham, and whosoever among you feareth God, to you is the word of this salvation sent.

27 For they that dwell at Jerusalem, and their rulers, because they knew him not, nor yet the voices of the prophets which are read every sabbath day, they have fulfilled *them* in condemning *him*.

28 And though they found no cause of death *in him*, yet desired they Pilate that he should be slain.

29 And when they had fulfilled all that was written of him, they took *him* down from the tree, and laid *him* in a sepulchre.

30 But God raised him from the dead:

31 And he was seen many days of them which came up with him from Galilee to Jerusalem, who are his witnesses unto the people.

32 And we declare unto you glad tidings, how that the promise which was made unto the fathers,

33 God hath fulfilled the same unto us their children, in that he hath raised up Jesus again; as it is also written in the second psalm, Thou art my Son, this day have I begotten thee.

Cross references:

10 Matt. 13:38; John 8:44
13 Acts 15:38
15 Luke 4:16; Acts 13:27
16 Acts 12:17, 26, 42, 43
17 Ex. 1:1; 6:6; 13:14, 16; Deut. 7:6, 7
18 Ex. 16:35; Num. 14:33, 34; Deut. 1:31
19 Deut. 7:1; Josh. 14:1, 2; Ps. 78:55
20 Judg. 2:16; 1Sam. 3:20
21 1Sam. 8:5; 10:1
22 1Sam. 13:14; 15:23, 26, 28; 16:1, 13; Ps. 89:20
23 2Sam. 7:12; Ps. 132:11; Isa. 11:1; Luke 1:32, 69
25 Matt. 3:11; Mark 1:7; Luke 3:16; John 1:20, 27
27 Luke 23:34; 24:20, 44
28 Matt. 27:22; Mark 15:13, 14; Luke 23:21, 22; John 19:6, 15
29 Luke 18:31; 23:53; 24:44
30 Matt. 28:6; Acts 2:24; 3:13, 15, 26; 5:30
31 Matt. 28:16; Acts 1:3, 8, 11; 2:32
32 Gen. 3:15; 12:3; 22:18
33 Ps. 2:7; Heb. 1:5; 5:5

13:11 the hand of the Lord is upon thee, and thou shalt be blind. Paul predicts that Elymas the magician would be blinded. After the utterance by Paul "there fell on him [Elymas] a mist and a darkness."

34 And as concerning that he raised him up from the dead, *now* no more to return to corruption, he said on this wise, I will give you the sure mercies of David.

35 Wherefore he saith also in another *psalm,* Thou shalt not suffer thine Holy One to see corruption.

36 For David, after he had served his own generation by the will of God, fell on sleep, and was laid unto his fathers, and saw corruption:

37 But he, whom God raised again, saw no corruption.

38 Be it known unto you therefore, men *and* brethren, that through this man is preached unto you the forgiveness of sins:

39 And by him all that believe are justified from all things, from which ye could not be justified by the law of Moses.

40 Beware therefore, lest that come upon you, which is spoken of in the prophets;

41 Behold, ye despisers, and wonder, and perish: for I work a work in your days, a work which ye shall in no wise believe, though a man declare it unto you.

42 And when the Jews were gone out of the synagogue, the Gentiles besought that these words might be preached to them the next sabbath.

43 Now when the congregation was broken up, many of the Jews and religious proselytes followed Paul and Barnabas: who, speaking to them, persuaded them to continue in the grace of God.

44 And the next sabbath day came almost the whole city together to hear the word of God.

45 But when the Jews saw the multitudes, they were filled with envy, and spake against those things which were spoken by Paul, contradicting and blaspheming.

46 Then Paul and Barnabas waxed bold, and said, It was necessary that the word of God should first have been spoken to you: but seeing ye put it from you, and judge yourselves unworthy of everlasting life, lo, we turn to the Gentiles.

47 For so hath the Lord commanded us, *saying,* I have set thee to be a light of the Gentiles, that thou shouldest be for salvation unto the ends of the earth.

48 And when the Gentiles heard this, they were glad, and glorified the word of the Lord: and as many as were ordained to eternal life believed.

49 And the word of the Lord was published throughout all the region.

50 But the Jews stirred up the devout and honourable women, and the chief men of the city, and raised persecution against Paul and Barnabas, and expelled them out of their coasts.

51 But they shook off the dust of their feet against them, and came unto Iconium.

52 And the disciples were filled with joy, and with the Holy Ghost.

CHAPTER 14
Paul and Barnabas in Iconium

1 And it came to pass in Iconium, that they went both together into the synagogue of the Jews, and so spake, that a great multitude both of the Jews and also of the Greeks believed.

2 But the unbelieving Jews stirred up the Gentiles, and made their minds evil affected against the brethren.

3 Long time therefore abode they speaking boldly in the Lord, which gave testimony unto the word of his grace, and granted signs and wonders to be done by their hands.

4 But the multitude of the city was divided: and part held with the Jews, and part with the apostles.

5 And when there was an assault made both of the Gentiles, and also of the Jews with their rulers, to use *them* despitefully, and to stone them,

6 They were ware of *it,* and fled unto Lystra and Derbe, cities of Lycaonia, and into the region that lieth round about:

7 And there they preached the gospel.

In Lystra

8 And there sat a certain man at Lystra, impotent in his feet, being a cripple from his mother's womb, who never had walked:

9 The same heard Paul speak: who stedfastly beholding him, and perceiving that he had faith to be healed,

10 Said with a loud voice, Stand upright on thy feet. And he leaped and walked.

11 And when the people saw what Paul had done, they lifted up their voices, saying in the speech of Lycaonia, The gods are come down to us in the likeness of men.

12 And they called Barnabas, Jupiter; and

Cross references (center column)

34 Isa. 55:3
35 Ps. 16:10; Acts 2:31
36 1Kgs. 2:10; Ps. 78:72; Acts 2:29; 13:22
38 Jer. 31:34; Dan. 9:24; Luke 24:47; 1John 2:12
39 Isa. 53:11; Rom. 3:28; 8:3; Heb. 7:19
40 Isa. 29:14; Hab. 1:5
43 Acts 11:23; 14:22; Titus 2:11; Heb. 12:15; 1Pet. 5:12
45 Acts 18:6; 1Pet. 4:4; Jude 1:10
46 Ex. 32:10; Deut. 32:21; Isa. 55:5; Matt. 10:6; 21:43; Acts 3:26; 13:26; 18:6; 28:28; Rom. 1:16; 10:19
47 Isa. 42:6; 49:6; Luke 2:32
50 2Tim. 3:11
51 Matt. 10:14; Mark 6:11; Luke 9:5; Acts 18:6
52 Matt. 5:12; John 16:22; Acts 2:46
3 Mark 16:20; Heb. 2:4
4 Acts 13:3
5 2Tim. 3:11
6 Matt. 10:23
8 Acts 3:2
9 Matt. 8:10; 9:28, 29
10 Isa. 35:6
11 Acts 8:10; 28:6

13:47 Paul refers to Isaiah 49:6 in conjunction with the fact that the gospel was going around the world and reaching all peoples.

Paul, Mercurius, because he was the chief speaker.

13 Then the priest of Jupiter, which was before their city, brought oxen and garlands unto the gates, and would have done sacrifice with the people.

14 *Which* when the apostles, Barnabas and Paul, heard *of,* they rent their clothes, and ran in among the people, crying out,

15 And saying, Sirs, why do ye these things? We also are men of like passions with you, and preach unto you that ye should turn from these vanities unto the living God, which made heaven, and earth, and the sea, and all things that are therein:

16 Who in times past suffered all nations to walk in their own ways.

17 Nevertheless he left not himself without witness, in that he did good, and gave us rain from heaven, and fruitful seasons, filling our hearts with food and gladness.

18 And with these sayings scarce restrained they the people, that they had not done sacrifice unto them.

19 And there came thither *certain* Jews from Antioch and Iconium, who persuaded the people, and, having stoned Paul, drew *him* out of the city, supposing he had been dead.

20 Howbeit, as the disciples stood round about him, he rose up, and came into the city: and the next day he departed with Barnabas to Derbe.

Returning to Antioch in Syria

21 And when they had preached the gospel to that city, and had taught many, they returned again to Lystra, and *to* Iconium, and Antioch,

22 Confirming the souls of the disciples, *and* exhorting them to continue in the faith, and that we must through much tribulation enter into the kingdom of God.

23 And when they had ordained them elders in every church, and had prayed with fasting, they commended them to the Lord, on whom they believed.

24 And after they had passed throughout Pisidia, they came to Pamphylia.

25 And when they had preached the word in Perga, they went down into Attalia:

26 And thence sailed to Antioch, from whence they had been recommended to the

grace of God for the work which they fulfilled.

27 And when they were come, and had gathered the church together, *they* rehearsed all that God had done with them, and how he had opened the door of faith unto the Gentiles.

28 And there they abode long time with the disciples.

CHAPTER 15
The Debate over Circumcision

1 And certain men which came down from Judea taught the brethren, *and said,* Except ye be circumcised after the manner of Moses, ye cannot be saved.

2 When therefore Paul and Barnabas had no small dissension and disputation with them, they determined that Paul and Barnabas, and certain other of them, should go up to Jerusalem unto the apostles and elders about this question.

3 And being brought on their way by the church, they passed through Phenicia and Samaria, declaring the conversion of the Gentiles: and they caused great joy unto all the brethren.

4 And when they were come to Jerusalem, they were received of the church, and of the apostles and elders, and they declared all things that God had done with them.

5 But there rose up certain of the sect of the Pharisees which believed, saying, That it was needful to circumcise them, and to command *them* to keep the law of Moses.

6 And the apostles and elders came together for to consider of this matter.

7 And when there had been much disputing, Peter rose up, and said unto them, Men *and* brethren, ye know how that a good while ago God made choice among us, that the Gentiles by my mouth should hear the word of the gospel, and believe.

8 And God, which knoweth the hearts, bare them witness, giving them the Holy Ghost, even as *he* did unto us;

9 And put no difference between us and them, purifying their hearts by faith.

10 Now therefore why tempt ye God, to put a yoke upon the neck of the disciples, which neither our fathers nor we were able to bear?

Cross references (center column)

13 Dan. 2:46
14 Matt. 26:65
15 Gen. 1:1; 1Sam. 12:21; Ps. 33:6; 146:6; Rev. 14:7; 19:10
16 Ps. 81:12; Acts 17:30; 1Pet. 4:3
17 Lev. 26:4; Deut. 11:14; 28:12; Job 5:10; Ps. 65:10; 68:9; 147:8
19 Acts 13:45; 2Cor. 11:25; 2Tim. 3:11
21 Matt. 28:19
22 Matt. 10:38; 16:24; Luke 22:28, 29; 2Tim. 2:11, 12; 3:12
23 Titus 1:5
26 Acts 13:1, 3; 15:40
27 Acts 21:19; Rev. 3:8
1 Gen. 17:10; Lev. 12:3; Gal. 2:12; Phil. 3:2; Col. 2:8, 11, 16
2 Gal. 2:1
3 Rom. 15:24; 1Cor. 16:6, 11
4 Acts 14:27; 15:12; 21:19
5 Acts 15:1
7 Acts 10:20; 11:12
8 1Chr. 28:9; Acts 1:24; 10:44
9 Acts 10:15, 28, 43; 1Cor. 1:2
10 Matt. 23:4; Gal. 5:1

14:27 how he had opened the door of faith unto the Gentiles. The Lord is working out the prophecy of Acts 1:8 and the expansion of the gospel beyond the borders of Israel and throughout the Gentile world.

15:7 God made choice among us. Peter speaks of God's eternal plan, in which He chose to include Gentiles, not just Jews, to become recipients of God's blessing through "the word of the gospel."

11 But we believe that through the grace of the Lord Jesus Christ we shall be saved, even as they.

12 Then all the multitude kept silence, and gave audience to Barnabas and Paul, declaring what miracles and wonders God had wrought among the Gentiles by them.

13 And after they had held their peace, James answered, saying, Men *and* brethren, hearken unto me:

14 Simeon hath declared how God at the first did visit the Gentiles, to take out of them a people for his name.

15 And to this agree the words of the prophets; as it is written,

16 After this I will return, and will build again the tabernacle of David, which is fallen down; and I will build again the ruins thereof, and I will set it up:

17 That the residue of men might seek after the Lord, and all the Gentiles, upon whom my name is called, saith the Lord, who doeth all these things.

18 Known unto God are all his works from the beginning of the world.

19 Wherefore my sentence is, that we trouble not them, which from among the Gentiles are turned to God:

20 But that we write unto them, that they abstain from pollutions of idols, and *from* fornication, and *from* things strangled, and *from* blood.

21 For Moses of old time hath in every city them that preach him, being read in the synagogues every sabbath day.

The Letter to Antioch

22 Then pleased it the apostles and elders, with the whole church, to send chosen men of their own company to Antioch with Paul and Barnabas: *namely,* Judas surnamed Barsabas, and Silas, chief men among the brethren:

23 And they wrote *letters* by them after this manner; The apostles and elders and brethren *send* greeting unto the brethren which are of the Gentiles in Antioch and Syria and Cilicia.

24 Forasmuch as we have heard, that cer-

tain which went out from us have troubled you with words, subverting your souls, saying, *Ye must* be circumcised, and keep the law: to whom we gave no *such* commandment:

25 It seemed good unto us, being assembled with one accord, to send chosen men unto you with our beloved Barnabas and Paul,

26 Men that have hazarded their lives for the name of our Lord Jesus Christ.

27 We have sent therefore Judas and Silas, who shall also tell *you* the same things by mouth.

28 For it seemed good to the Holy Ghost, and to us, to lay upon you no greater burden than these necessary things;

29 That ye abstain from meats offered to idols, and from blood, and from things strangled, and from fornication: from which if ye keep yourselves, ye shall do well. Fare ye well.

30 So when they were dismissed, they came to Antioch: and when they had gathered the multitude together, they delivered the epistle:

31 *Which* when they had read, they rejoiced for the consolation.

32 And Judas and Silas, being prophets also themselves, exhorted the brethren with many words, and confirmed *them.*

33 And after they had tarried *there* a space, they were let go in peace from the brethren unto the apostles.

34 Notwithstanding it pleased Silas to abide there still.

35 Paul also and Barnabas continued in Antioch, teaching and preaching the word of the Lord, with many others also.

Paul and Barnabas Separate

36 And some days after Paul said unto Barnabas, Let us go again and visit our brethren in every city where we have preached the word of the Lord, *and see* how they do.

37 And Barnabas determined to take with them John, whose surname was Mark.

38 But Paul thought not good to take him with them, who departed from them from

Cross references (center column)

11 Rom. 3:24; Eph. 2:8; Titus 2:11; 3:4, 5

12 Acts 14:27

13 Acts 12:17

14 Acts 15:7

16 Amos 9:11, 12

19 Acts 15:28; 1Thess. 1:9

20 Ex. 20:3, 23; Lev. 3:17; 1Cor. 6:9, 18; 8:1; 10:20, 28; Gal. 5:19; Eph. 5:3; Col. 3:5; 1Thess. 4:3; 1Pet. 4:3; Rev. 2:14, 20

21 Acts 13:15, 27

22 Acts 1:23

24 Acts 15:1; Gal. 2:4; 5:12; Titus 1:10

26 Acts 13:50; 14:19; 1Cor. 15:30; 2Cor. 11:23, 26

29 Lev. 17:14; Acts 15:20; 21:25; Rev. 2:14, 20

32 Acts 14:22; 18:23

33 1Cor. 16:11; Heb. 11:31

35 Acts 13:1

36 Acts 13:4, 13, 14, 51; 14:1, 6, 24, 25

37 Acts 12:12, 25; 13:5; Col. 4:10; 2Tim. 4:11; Phile. 1:24

38 Acts 13:13

15:14–35 God at the first did visit the Gentiles, to take out of them a people for his name. James explains how the decision of the counsel at Jerusalem was an outworking of God's purpose for this age. God's plan for history relates to the past ages with Israel and to Israel's role in the coming age (the Millennium), but the current Church Age would center around the Gentiles. After the Church age is concluded, the Lord will return, and "will build again the tabernacle of David" ([v. 16] i.e., the nation of Israel). This Old Testament reference is from Amos 9:11–12. During the Tribulation the Lord will work to convert the nation of Israel to Himself, ending with the second coming and the millennial reign of Christ. God's plans for history will come to pass just as He ordained.

Pamphylia, and went not with them to the work.

39 And the contention was so sharp between them, that they departed asunder one from the other: and so Barnabas took Mark, and sailed unto Cyprus;

40 And Paul chose Silas, and departed, being recommended by the brethren unto the grace of God.

41 And he went through Syria and Cilicia, confirming the churches.

CHAPTER 16
Timothy Joins Paul

1 Then came he to Derbe and Lystra: and, behold, a certain disciple was there, named Timotheus, the son of a certain woman, which was a Jewess, and believed; but his father was a Greek:

2 Which was well reported of by the brethren that were at Lystra and Iconium.

3 Him would Paul have to go forth with him; and took and circumcised him because of the Jews which were in those quarters: for they knew all that his father was a Greek.

4 And as they went through the cities, they delivered them the decrees for to keep, that were ordained of the apostles and elders which were at Jerusalem.

Paul's Vision of the Man of Macedonia

5 And so were the churches established in the faith, and increased in number daily.

6 Now when they had gone throughout Phrygia and the region of Galatia, and were forbidden of the Holy Ghost to preach the word in Asia,

7 After they were come to Mysia, they assayed to go into Bithynia: but the Spirit suffered them not.

8 And they passing by Mysia came down to Troas.

9 And a vision appeared to Paul in the night; there stood a man of Macedonia, and prayed him, saying, Come over into Macedonia, and help us.

10 And after he had seen the vision, immediately we endeavoured to go into Macedonia, assuredly gathering that the Lord had called us for to preach the gospel unto them.

In Philippi

11 Therefore loosing from Troas, we came with a straight course to Samothracia, and the next day to Neapolis;

12 And from thence to Philippi, which is the chief city of that part of Macedonia, and a colony: and we were in that city abiding certain days.

13 And on the sabbath we went out of the city by a river side, where prayer was wont to be made; and we sat down, and spake unto the women which resorted thither.

14 And a certain woman named Lydia, a seller of purple, of the city of Thyatira, which worshipped God, heard us: whose heart the Lord opened, that she attended unto the things which were spoken of Paul.

15 And when she was baptized, and her household, she besought us, saying, If ye have judged me to be faithful to the Lord, come into my house, and abide there. And she constrained us.

Paul and Silas Imprisoned

16 And it came to pass, as we went to prayer, a certain damsel possessed with a spirit of divination met us, which brought her masters much gain by soothsaying:

17 The same followed Paul and us, and cried, saying, These men are the servants of the most high God, which shew unto us the way of salvation.

18 And this did she many days. But Paul, being grieved, turned and said to the spirit, I command thee in the name of Jesus Christ to come out of her. And he came out the same hour.

19 And when her masters saw that the hope of their gains was gone, they caught Paul and Silas, and drew them into the marketplace unto the rulers,

20 And brought them to the magistrates, saying, These men, being Jews, do exceedingly trouble our city,

21 And teach customs, which are not lawful for us to receive, neither to observe, being Romans.

22 And the multitude rose up together against them: and the magistrates rent off their clothes, and commanded to beat them.

23 And when they had laid many stripes upon them, they cast them into prison, charging the jailer to keep them safely:

24 Who, having received such a charge, thrust them into the inner prison, and made their feet fast in the stocks.

25 And at midnight Paul and Silas prayed, and sang praises unto God: and the prisoners heard them.

26 And suddenly there was a great earthquake, so that the foundations of the prison were shaken: and immediately all the doors

---

Cross references (center column):

40 Acts 14:26

41 Acts 16:5

1 Acts 14:6; 19:22; Rom. 16:21; 1Cor. 4:17; Phil. 2:19; 1Thess. 3:2; 1Tim. 1:2; 2Tim. 1:2, 5

2 Acts 6:3

3 1Cor. 9:20; Gal. 2:3; 5:2

4 Acts 15:28, 29

5 Acts 15:41

8 2Cor. 2:12; 2Tim. 4:13

9 Acts 10:30

10 2Cor. 2:13

12 Phil. 1:1

14 Luke 24:45

15 Gen. 19:3; 33:11; Judg. 19:21; Luke 24:29; Heb. 13:2

16 1Sam. 28:7; Acts 19:24

18 Mark 1:25, 34; 16:17

19 Matt. 10:18; Acts 19:25, 26; 2Cor. 6:5

20 1Kgs. 18:17; Acts 17:6

22 2Cor. 6:5; 11:23, 25; 1Thess. 2:2

26 Acts 4:31; 5:19; 12:7, 10

were opened, and every one's bands were loosed.

27 And the keeper of the prison awaking out of his sleep, and seeing the prison doors open, he drew out his sword, and would have killed himself, supposing that the prisoners had been fled.

28 But Paul cried with a loud voice, saying, Do thyself no harm: for we are all here.

29 Then he called for a light, and sprang in, and came trembling, and fell down before Paul and Silas,

30 And brought them out, and said, Sirs, what must I do to be saved?

31 And they said, Believe on the Lord Jesus Christ, and thou shalt be saved, and thy house.

32 And they spake unto him the word of the Lord, and to all that were in his house.

33 And he took them the same hour of the night, and washed *their* stripes; and was baptized, he and all his, straightway.

34 And when he had brought them into his house, he set meat before them, and rejoiced, believing in God with all his house.

35 And when it was day, the magistrates sent the serjeants, saying, Let those men go.

36 And the keeper of the prison told this saying to Paul, The magistrates have sent to let you go: now therefore depart, and go in peace.

37 But Paul said unto them, They have beaten us openly uncondemned, being Romans, and have cast *us* into prison; and now do they thrust us out privily? nay verily; but let them come themselves and fetch us out.

38 And the serjeants told these words unto the magistrates: and they feared, when they heard that they were Romans.

39 And they came and besought them, and brought *them* out, and desired *them* to depart out of the city.

40 And they went out of the prison, and entered into *the house of* Lydia: and when they had seen the brethren, they comforted them, and departed.

CHAPTER 17
In Thessalonica

1 Now when they had passed through Amphipolis and Apollonia, they came to Thessalonica, where was a synagogue of the Jews:

2 And Paul, as his manner was, went in unto them, and three sabbath days reasoned with them out of the scriptures,

3 Opening and alleging, that Christ must needs have suffered, and risen again from the dead; and that this Jesus, whom I preach unto you, is Christ.

4 And some of them believed, and consorted with Paul and Silas; and of the devout Greeks a great multitude, and of the chief women not a few.

5 But the Jews which believed not, moved with envy, took unto them certain lewd fellows of the baser sort, and gathered a company, and set all the city on an uproar, and assaulted the house of Jason, and sought to bring them out to the people.

6 And when they found them not, they drew Jason and certain brethren unto the rulers of the city, crying, These that have turned the world upside down are come hither also;

7 Whom Jason hath received: and these all do contrary to the decrees of Caesar, saying that there is another king, *one* Jesus.

8 And they troubled the people and the rulers of the city, when they heard these things.

9 And when they had taken security of Jason, and of the other, they let them go.

In Berea

10 And the brethren immediately sent away Paul and Silas by night unto Berea: who coming *thither* went into the synagogue of the Jews.

11 These were more noble than those in Thessalonica, in that they received the word with all readiness of mind, and searched the scriptures daily, whether those things were so.

12 Therefore many of them believed; also of honourable women which were Greeks, and of men, not a few.

13 But when the Jews of Thessalonica had knowledge that the word of God was preached of Paul at Berea, they came thither also, and stirred up the people.

14 And then immediately the brethren sent away Paul to go as it were to the sea: but Silas and Timotheus abode there still.

15 And they that conducted Paul brought him unto Athens: and receiving a commandment unto Silas and Timotheus for to come to him with all speed, they departed.

In Athens

16 Now while Paul waited for them at Athens, his spirit was stirred in him, when he saw the city wholly given to idolatry.

17 Therefore disputed he in the synagogue with the Jews, and with the devout persons,

---

30 Luke 3:10; Acts 2:37; 9:6

31 John 3:16, 36; 6:47; 1John 5:10

34 Luke 5:29; 19:6

37 Acts 22:25

39 Matt. 8:34

40 Acts 16:14

2 Luke 4:16; Acts 9:20; 13:5, 14; 14:1; 16:13; 19:8

3 Luke 24:26, 46; Acts 18:28; Gal. 3:1

4 Acts 15:22, 27, 32, 40; 28:34

5 Rom. 16:21

6 Acts 16:20

7 Luke 23:2; John 19:12; 1Pet. 2:13

10 Acts 9:25; 17:14

11 Isa. 34:16; Luke 16:29; John 5:39

14 Matt. 10:23

15 Acts 18:5

16 2Pet. 2:8

and in the market daily with them that met with him.

18 Then certain philosophers of the Epicureans, and of the Stoics, encountered him. And some said, What will this babbler say? other some, He seemeth to be a setter forth of strange gods: because he preached unto them Jesus, and the resurrection.

19 And they took him, and brought him unto Areopagus, saying, May we know what this new doctrine, whereof thou speakest, *is*?

20 For thou bringest certain strange things to our ears: we would know therefore what these things mean.

21 (For all the Athenians and strangers which were there spent their time in nothing else, but either to tell, or to hear some new thing.)

22 Then Paul stood in the midst of Mars' hill, and said, *Ye* men of Athens, I perceive that in all things ye are too superstitious.

23 For as I passed by, and beheld your devotions, I found an altar with this inscription, TO THE UNKNOWN GOD. Whom therefore ye ignorantly worship, him declare I unto you.

24 God that made the world and all things therein, seeing that he is Lord of heaven and earth, dwelleth not in temples made with hands;

25 Neither is worshipped with men's hands, as though he needed any thing, seeing he giveth to all life, and breath, and all things;

26 And hath made of one blood all nations of men for to dwell on all the face of the earth, and hath determined the times before appointed, and the bounds of their habitation;

27 That they should seek the Lord, if haply they might feel after him, and find him,

though he be not far from every one of us:

28 For in him we live, and move, and have our being; as certain also of your own poets have said, For we are also his offspring.

29 Forasmuch then as we are the offspring of God, we ought not to think that the Godhead is like unto gold, or silver, or stone, graven by art and man's device.

30 And the times of this ignorance God winked at; but now commandeth all men every where to repent:

31 Because he hath appointed a day, in the which he will judge the world in righteousness by *that* man whom he hath ordained; *whereof* he hath given assurance unto all *men*, in that he hath raised him from the dead.

32 And when they heard of the resurrection of the dead, some mocked: and others said, We will hear thee again of this *matter*.

33 So Paul departed from among them.

34 Howbeit certain men clave unto him, and believed: among the which *was* Dionysius the Areopagite, and a woman named Damaris, and others with them.

CHAPTER 18
In Corinth

1 After these things Paul departed from Athens and came to Corinth;

2 And found a certain Jew named Aquila, born in Pontus, lately come from Italy, with his wife Priscilla; because that (Claudius had commanded all Jews to depart from Rome:) and came unto them.

3 And because he was of the same craft, he abode with them, and wrought: for by their occupation they were tentmakers.

4 And he reasoned in the synagogue every sabbath, and persuaded the Jews and the Greeks.

5 And when Silas and Timotheus were

Cross references

23 2Thess. 2:4
24 Matt. 11:25; Acts 7:48; 14:15
25 Gen. 2:7; Num. 16:22; Job 12:10; 27:3; 33:4; Ps. 50:8; Isa. 42:5; 57:16; Zech. 12:1
26 Deut. 32:8
27 Acts 14:17; Rom. 1:20
28 Col. 1:17; Titus 1:12; Heb. 1:3
29 Isa. 40:18
30 Luke 24:47; Acts 14:16; Rom. 3:25; Titus 2:11, 12; 1Pet. 1:14; 4:3
31 Acts 2:24; 10:42; Rom. 2:16; 14:10
2 Rom. 16:3; 1Cor. 16:19; 2Tim. 4:19
3 Acts 20:34; 1Cor. 4:12; 1Thess. 2:9; 2Thess. 3:8
4 Acts 17:2
5 Job 32:18; Acts 17:3, 14, 15; 18:28

17:18 He seemeth to be a setter forth of strange gods. Apparently some of the philosophers on Mars Hill believed that Paul was advocating the worship of strange gods called "Jesus" and "Resurrection." The goal within Greek philosophy was to escape the physical realm, because it was believed to be inherently evil. Therefore, the resurrection of the physical body would have been offensive to their ideals and presuppositions. As Paul here advocates, the Bible teaches the future resurrection of both Christians and non-Christians, though at different times and to different ends.

17:26 determined the times before appointed. God has determined both the timing of history (Dan. 2:36–45;

Heb. 11:3) and the boundaries of nations (Deut. 32:8). When and where key events relating to Bible prophecy will occur in history are set in stone by God's eternal decree.

17:31 he hath appointed a day. In conjunction with verse 26, it is clear that God has a specific day fixed on His calendar when "he will judge the world in righteousness." That day will be the day of the Great White Throne Judgment at the end of history following the Millennium (Rev. 20:11–15). Jesus will judge humanity because, while He is God, He is also a human being like those whom He will judge (John 5:22–27).

come from Macedonia, Paul was pressed in the spirit, and testified to the Jews *that* Jesus *was* Christ.

6 And when they opposed themselves, and blasphemed, he shook *his* raiment, and said unto them, Your blood *be* upon your own heads; I *am* clean: from henceforth I will go unto the Gentiles.

7 And he departed thence, and entered into a certain *man's* house, named Justus, *one* that worshipped God, whose house joined hard to the synagogue.

8 And Crispus, the chief ruler of the synagogue, believed on the Lord with all his house; and many of the Corinthians hearing believed, and were baptized.

9 Then spake the Lord to Paul in the night by a vision, Be not afraid, but speak, and hold not thy peace:

10 For I am with thee, and no man shall set on thee to hurt thee: for I have much people in this city.

11 And he continued *there* a year and six months, teaching the word of God among them.

12 And when Gallio was the deputy of Achaia, the Jews made insurrection with one accord against Paul, and brought him to the judgment seat,

13 Saying, This *fellow* persuadeth men to worship God contrary to the law.

14 And when Paul was now about to open *his* mouth, Gallio said unto the Jews, If it were a matter of wrong or wicked lewdness, O *ye* Jews, reason would that I should bear with you:

15 But if it be a question of words and names, and *of* your law, look ye *to it*; for I will be no judge of such *matters*.

16 And he drave them from the judgment seat.

17 Then all the Greeks took Sosthenes, the chief ruler of the synagogue, and beat *him* before the judgment seat. And Gallio cared for none of those things.

Paul Sails for Syria

18 And Paul *after this* tarried *there* yet a good while, and then took his leave of the brethren, and sailed thence into Syria, and with him Priscilla and Aquila; having shorn *his* head in Cenchrea: for he had a vow.

19 And he came to Ephesus, and left them

there: but he himself entered into the synagogue, and reasoned with the Jews.

20 When they desired *him* to tarry longer time with them, he consented not;

21 But bade them farewell, saying, I must by all means keep this feast that cometh in Jerusalem: but I will return again unto you, if God will. And he sailed from Ephesus.

22 And when he had landed at Caesarea, and gone up, and saluted the church, he went down to Antioch.

23 And after he had spent some time *there*, he departed, and went over *all* the country of Galatia and Phrygia in order, strengthening all the disciples.

Apollos Preaches at Ephesus

24 And a certain Jew named Apollos, born at Alexandria, an eloquent man, *and* mighty in the scriptures, came to Ephesus.

25 This man was instructed in the way of the Lord; and being fervent in the spirit, he spake and taught diligently the things of the Lord, knowing only the baptism of John.

26 And he began to speak boldly in the synagogue: whom when Aquila and Priscilla had heard, they took him unto *them*, and expounded unto him the way of God more perfectly.

27 And when he was disposed to pass into Achaia, the brethren wrote, exhorting the disciples to receive him: who, when he was come, helped them much which had believed through grace:

28 For he mightily convinced the Jews, *and that* publickly, shewing by the scriptures that Jesus was Christ.

CHAPTER 19
In Ephesus

1 And it came to pass, that, while Apollos was at Corinth, Paul having passed through the upper coasts came to Ephesus: and finding certain disciples,

2 He said unto them, Have ye received the Holy Ghost since ye believed? And they said unto him, We have not so much as heard whether there be any Holy Ghost.

3 And he said unto them, Unto what then were ye baptized? And they said, Unto John's baptism.

4 Then said Paul, John verily baptized with the baptism of repentance, saying unto the

Center reference column

6 Lev. 20:9, 11, 12; 2Sam. 1:16; Neh. 5:13; Ezek. 3:18, 19; 18:13; 33:4, 9; Matt. 10:14; Acts 13:45, 46, 51; 20:26; 28:28; 1Pet. 4:4

8 1Cor. 1:14

9 Acts 23:11

10 Jer. 1:18, 19; Matt. 28:20

14 Acts 23:29; 25:11, 19

17 1Cor. 1:1

18 Num. 6:18; Acts 21:24; Rom. 16:1

21 Acts 19:21; 20:16; 1Cor. 4:19; Heb. 6:3; James 4:15

23 Acts 14:22; 15:32, 41; Gal. 1:2; 4:14

24 1Cor. 1:12; 3:5, 6; 4:6; Titus 3:13

25 Acts 19:3; Rom. 12:11

27 1Cor. 3:6

28 Acts 9:22; 17:3; 18:5

1 1Cor. 1:12; 3:5, 6

2 1Sam. 3:7; Acts 8:16

3 Acts 18:25

4 Matt. 3:11; John 1:15, 27, 30; Acts 1:5; 11:16; 13:24, 25

18:9–11 Then spake the Lord to Paul in the night by a vision. Paul, as an apostle of the Lord, was the recipient of direct, verbal revelation from Christ, who in this instance gives Paul assurance and direction as to what he should do in light of hostility from opponents.

people, that they should believe on him which should come after him, that is, on Christ Jesus.

5 When they heard *this,* they were baptized in the name of the Lord Jesus.

6 And when Paul had laid *his* hands upon them, the Holy Ghost came on them; and they spake with tongues, and prophesied.

7 And all the men were about twelve.

8 And he went into the synagogue, and spake boldly for the space of three months, disputing and persuading the things concerning the kingdom of God.

9 But when divers were hardened, and believed not, but spake evil of that way before the multitude, he departed from them, and separated the disciples, disputing daily in the school of one Tyrannus.

10 And this continued by the space of two years; so that all they which dwelt in Asia heard the word of the Lord Jesus, both Jews and Greeks.

The Sons of Sceva

11 And God wrought special miracles by the hands of Paul:

12 So that from his body were brought unto the sick handkerchiefs or aprons, and the diseases departed from them, and the evil spirits went out of them.

13 Then certain of the vagabond Jews, exorcists, took upon them to call over them which had evil spirits the name of the Lord Jesus, saying, We adjure you by Jesus whom Paul preacheth.

14 And there were seven sons of *one* Sceva, a Jew, *and* chief of the priests, which did so.

15 And the evil spirit answered and said, Jesus I know, and Paul I know; but who are ye?

16 And the man in whom the evil spirit was leaped on them, and overcame them, and prevailed against them, so that they fled out of that house naked and wounded.

17 And this was known to all the Jews and Greeks also dwelling at Ephesus; and fear fell on them all, and the name of the Lord Jesus was magnified.

18 And many that believed came, and confessed, and shewed their deeds.

19 Many of them also which used curious arts brought their books together, and burned them before all *men:* and they counted the price of them, and found *it* fifty thousand *pieces* of silver.

20 So mightily grew the word of God and prevailed.

21 After these things were ended, Paul pur-

posed in the spirit, when he had passed through Macedonia and Achaia, to go to Jerusalem, saying, After I have been there, I must also see Rome.

22 So he sent into Macedonia two of them that ministered unto him, Timotheus and Erastus; but he himself stayed in Asia for a season.

The Riot at Ephesus

23 And the same time there arose no small stir about that way.

24 For a certain *man* named Demetrius, a silversmith, which made silver shrines for Diana, brought no small gain unto the craftsmen;

25 Whom he called together with the workmen of like occupation, and said, Sirs, ye know that by this craft we have our wealth.

26 Moreover ye see and hear, that not alone at Ephesus, but almost throughout all Asia, this Paul hath persuaded and turned away much people, saying that they be no gods, which are made with hands:

27 So that not only this our craft is in danger to be set at nought; but also that the temple of the great goddess Diana should be despised, and her magnificence should be destroyed, whom all Asia and the world worshippeth.

28 And when they heard *these sayings,* they were full of wrath, and cried out, saying, Great *is* Diana of the Ephesians.

29 And the whole city was filled with confusion: and having caught Gaius and Aristarchus, men of Macedonia, Paul's companions in travel, they rushed with one accord into the theatre.

30 And when Paul would have entered in unto the people, the disciples suffered him not.

31 And certain of the chief of Asia, which were his friends, sent unto him, desiring *him* that he would not adventure himself into the theatre.

32 Some therefore cried one thing, and some another: for the assembly was confused; and the more part knew not wherefore they were come together.

33 And they drew Alexander out of the multitude, the Jews putting him forward. And Alexander beckoned with the hand, and would have made his defence unto the people.

34 But when they knew that he was a Jew, all with one voice about the space of two hours cried out, Great *is* Diana of the Ephesians.

Cross references

5 Acts 8:16

6 Acts 2:4; 6:6; 8:17; 10:46

8 Acts 1:3; 17:2; 18:4; 28:23

9 Acts 9:2; 22:4; 24:14; 2Tim. 1:15; 2Pet. 2:2; Jude 1:10

10 Acts 20:31

11 Mark 16:20; Acts 14:3

12 2Kgs. 4:29; Acts 5:15

13 Matt. 12:27; Mark 9:38; Luke 9:49

17 Luke 1:65; 7:16; Acts 2:43; 5:5, 11

18 Matt. 3:6

20 Acts 6:7; 12:24

21 Acts 18:21; 20:22; 23:11; Rom. 15:24-28; Gal. 2:1

22 Acts 13:5; Rom. 16:23; 2Tim. 4:20

23 Acts 9:2; 2Cor. 1:8

24 Acts 16:16, 19

26 Ps. 115:4; Isa. 44:10-20; Jer. 10:3

29 Acts 20:4; 27:2; Rom. 16:23; 1Cor. 1:14; Col. 4:10; Phile. 1:24

33 Acts 12:17; 1Tim. 1:20; 2Tim. 4:14

35 And when the town clerk had appeased the people, he said, *Ye* men of Ephesus, what man is there that knoweth not how that the city of the Ephesians is a worshipper of the great goddess Diana, and of the *image* which fell down from Jupiter?

36 Seeing then that these things cannot be spoken against, ye ought to be quiet, and to do nothing rashly.

37 For ye have brought hither these men, which are neither robbers of churches, nor yet blasphemers of your goddess.

38 Wherefore if Demetrius, and the craftsmen which are with him, have a matter against any man, the law is open, and there are deputies: let them implead one another.

39 But if ye inquire any thing concerning other matters, it shall be determined in a lawful assembly.

40 For we are in danger to be called in question for this day's uproar, there being no cause whereby we may give an account of this concourse.

41 And when he had thus spoken, he dismissed the assembly.

Chapter 20
Paul's Journey to Macedonia and Greece

1 And after the uproar was ceased, Paul called unto *him* the disciples, and embraced *them,* and departed for to go into Macedonia.

2 And when he had gone over those parts, and had given them much exhortation, he came into Greece,

3 And *there* abode three months. And when the Jews laid wait for him, as he was about to sail into Syria, he purposed to return through Macedonia.

4 And there accompanied him into Asia Sopater of Berea; and of the Thessalonians, Aristarchus and Secundus; and Gaius of Derbe, and Timotheus; and of Asia, Tychicus and Trophimus.

5 These going before tarried for us at Troas.

6 And we sailed away from Philippi after the days of unleavened bread, and came unto them to Troas in five days; where we abode seven days.

Paul's Farewell Visit to Troas

7 And upon the first *day* of the week, when the disciples came together to break bread, Paul preached unto them, ready to depart

on the morrow; and continued his speech until midnight.

8 And there were many lights in the upper chamber, where they were gathered together.

9 And there sat in a window a certain young man named Eutychus, being fallen into a deep sleep: and as Paul was long preaching, he sunk down with sleep, and fell down from the third loft, and was taken up dead.

10 And Paul went down, and fell on him, and embracing *him* said, Trouble not yourselves; for his life is in him.

11 When he therefore was come up again, and had broken bread, and eaten, and talked a long while, even till break of day, so he departed.

12 And they brought the young man alive, and were not a little comforted.

From Troas to Miletus

13 And we went before to ship, and sailed unto Assos, there intending to take in Paul: for so had he appointed, minding himself to go afoot.

14 And when he met with us at Assos, we took him in, and came to Mitylene.

15 And we sailed thence, and came the next *day* over against Chios; and the next *day* we arrived at Samos, and tarried at Trogyllium; and the next *day* we came to Miletus.

16 For Paul had determined to sail by Ephesus, because he would not spend the time in Asia: for he hasted, if it were possible for him, to be at Jerusalem the day of Pentecost.

Paul Meets with the Ephesian Elders

17 And from Miletus he sent to Ephesus, and called the elders of the church.

18 And when they were come to him, he said unto them, Ye know, from the first day that I came into Asia, after what manner I have been with you at all seasons,

19 Serving the Lord with all humility of mind, and with many tears, and temptations, which befell me by the lying in wait of the Jews:

20 *And* how I kept back nothing that was profitable *unto* you, but have shewed you, and have taught you publickly, and from house to house,

21 Testifying both to the Jews, and also to the Greeks, repentance toward God, and faith toward our Lord Jesus Christ.

3 Acts 9:23; 23:12; 25:3; 2Cor. 11:26

4 Acts 16:1; 19:29; 21:29; 27:2; Eph. 6:21; Col. 4:7, 10; 2Tim. 4:12, 20; Titus 3:12

6 Ex. 12:14, 15; 23:15; Acts 16:8; 2Cor. 2:12; 2Tim. 4:13

7 Acts 2:42, 46; 1Cor. 10:16; 11:20; 16:2; Rev. 1:10

8 Acts 1:13

10 1Kgs. 17:21; 2Kgs. 4:34; Matt. 9:24

16 Acts 2:1; 18:21; 19:21; 21:4, 12; 24:17; 1Cor. 16:8

18 Acts 18:19; 19:1, 10

19 Acts 20:3

20 Acts 20:27

21 Mark 1:15; Luke 24:47; Acts 2:38; 18:5

Four Approaches to Prophetic Fulfillment

By Thomas Ice

When it comes to the study of biblical prophecy and when events will be fulfilled in history, four distinct approaches have been prevalent. The four views are simple in the sense that they reflect the only four possible ways that one can relate to time: past, present, future, and timeless. When speaking of the fulfillment of Bible prophecy, we identify these four timing approaches as preterism, historicism, futurism, and idealism.

The **preterist** (Latin for "past") believes that most, if not all prophecy, has already been fulfilled, usually in relation to the destruction of Jerusalem in A.D. 70. The **historicist** (present) sees much of the current Church Age as equal to the Tribulation period and claims that prophecy has been and will continue to be fulfilled during the Church Age, with few events remaining for the future. The **idealist** (timeless) does not believe either that the Bible indicates the timing of events or that we can determine their timing in advance. **Futurists** (future) usually believe that almost no prophetic events are occurring in the Church Age, but will take place in the following future episodes: the Tribulation, the Second Coming, the Millennium, and the eternal state.

> *Futurism is the only approach that can consistently apply literal interpretation.*

Preterism is divided into at least two kinds. Moderate preterists see the Tribulation and the bulk of prophetic occurrences as fulfilled in events surrounding the destruction of Jerusalem and the temple in A.D. 70. They still hold to a future second coming of Christ, a physical resurrection of the dead, an end to temporal history, and the establishment of the consummate new heavens and earth. Extreme preterists hold that **all** Bible prophecy has been fulfilled and that we are currently in the new heavens and new earth. Since extreme preterists deny a future Second Coming and the resurrection of believers in conjunction with a future return, their views place them outside the realm of orthodox Christianity.

Historicism, once the dominant view of Protestants from the Reformation until the nineteenth century, appears to exert little attraction outside Seventh-Day Adventist circles today. It is a system of prophetic interpretation known for date-setting, equating the Roman Catholic pope with the Antichrist, and identifying the seal, trumpet, and vial judgments of Revelation with the last two thousand years of European history.

Idealism is the belief that certain prophetic passages serve only as a teacher of great ideas or truths about God to be applied to our present lives. This opinion is rarely followed outside of scholarly and liberal circles.

Futurism is the prophetic approach taken by all contributors to this study Bible. It is the only approach that can consistently apply literal interpretation. The other three approaches must spiritually allegorize the text at key points. The prophecies of Christ's first coming were fulfilled literally; therefore, prophecy related to His return will be fulfilled in the same way. Since prophecy related to the Tribulation, the Second Coming, the Millennium, and the eternal state have not yet been fulfilled historically, then these prophecies are still future to our time. Such a literal approach to prophecy maintains a distinction between God's prophetic plan for Israel and the Church. Futurism harmonizes a literal fulfillment of God's promises to Israel in a future millennial glory, where God's chosen people will reign with Jesus the Messiah over all the nations. But futurists also literally interpret the scriptural promises for the Church. The futurist understanding of different historical ages maintains consistent literal interpretation.

22 And now, behold, I go bound in the spirit unto Jerusalem, not knowing the things that shall befall me there:

23 Save that the Holy Ghost witnesseth in every city, saying that bonds and afflictions abide me.

24 But none of these things move me, neither count I my life dear unto myself, so that I might finish my course with joy, and the ministry, which I have received of the Lord Jesus, to testify the gospel of the grace of God.

25 And now, behold, I know that ye all, among whom I have gone preaching the kingdom of God, shall see my face no more.

26 Wherefore I take you to record this day, that I *am* pure from the blood of all *men*.

27 For I have not shunned to declare unto you all the counsel of God.

28 Take heed therefore unto yourselves, and to all the flock, over the which the Holy Ghost hath made you overseers, to feed the church of God, which he hath purchased with his own blood.

29 For I know this, that after my departing shall grievous wolves enter in among you, not sparing the flock.

30 Also of your own selves shall men arise, speaking perverse things, to draw away disciples after them.

31 Therefore watch, and remember, that by the space of three years I ceased not to warn every one night and day with tears.

32 And now, brethren, I commend you to God, and to the word of his grace, which is able to build you up, and to give you an inheritance among all them which are sanctified.

33 I have coveted no man's silver, or gold, or apparel.

34 Yea, ye yourselves know, that these hands have ministered unto my necessities, and to them that were with me.

35 I have shewed you all things, how that so labouring ye ought to support the weak, and to remember the words of the Lord Jesus, how he said, It is more blessed to give than to receive.

36 And when he had thus spoken, he kneeled down, and prayed with them all.

37 And they all wept sore, and fell on Paul's neck, and kissed him,

38 Sorrowing most of all for the words which he spake, that they should see his face no more. And they accompanied him unto the ship.

CHAPTER 21
Paul's Voyage to Jerusalem

1 And it came to pass, that after we were gotten from them, and had launched, we came with a straight course unto Coos, and the *day* following unto Rhodes, and from thence unto Patara:

2 And finding a ship sailing over unto Phoenicia, we went aboard, and set forth.

3 Now when we had discovered Cyprus, we left it on the left hand, and sailed into Syria, and landed at Tyre: for there the ship was to unlade her burden.

4 And finding disciples we tarried there seven days: who said to Paul through the Spirit, that he should not go up to Jerusalem.

5 And when we had accomplished those days, we departed and went our way; and they all brought us on our way, with wives and children, till *we were* out of the city: and we kneeled down on the shore, and prayed.

6 And when we had taken our leave one of another, we took ship; and they returned home again.

7 And when we had finished *our* course from Tyre, we came to Ptolemais, and saluted the brethren, and abode with them one day.

Cross-references

23 Acts 21:4, 11; 1Thess. 3:3
24 Acts 1:17; 21:13; 2Cor. 4:1, 16; 2Tim. 4:7; Titus 1:3
25 Acts 20:38; Rom. 15:23
26 Acts 18:6; 2Cor. 7:2
27 Luke 7:30; John 15:15; Acts 20:20; Eph. 1:11
28 1Cor. 12:28; Eph. 1:7, 14; Col. 1:14; Rev. 5:9
29 Matt. 7:15; 2Pet. 2:1
30 1Tim. 1:20; 1John 2:19
32 Acts 9:31; 26:18; 1Pet. 1:4
33 1Cor. 9:12; 2Cor. 7:2; 11:9; 12:17
34 Acts 18:3; 1Cor. 4:12; 1Thess. 2:9; 2Thess. 3:8
35 1Cor. 9:12; 2Cor. 11:9, 12; 12:13; Eph. 4:28
37 Gen. 45:14; 46:29
5 Acts 20:36
6 John 1:11

20:22–23 I go bound in the spirit unto Jerusalem. This is an expression of Paul's strong devotion to the Lord and His will for his life. Though details were not given, the Holy Spirit had revealed to Paul that in every city where he would go to preach the gospel, he would be persecuted.

20:25 I know that ye all . . . shall see my face no more. Paul never returned to Ephesus, a city in Asia Minor (modern Turkey) and the site where he had ministered for three years (v. 31).

20:28–30 after my departing shall grievous wolves enter in among you, not sparing the flock. Paul predicts

that apostasy will arise even within the Ephesian church that he had spent so much time nurturing. Paul further predicts that it will spring up from within the congregation. This warning was fulfilled in the Ephesian church as indicated from 1 Timothy 1:3–7; 6:21; 2 Timothy 3:6; and Revelation 2:2.

21:4 who said to Paul through the Spirit, that he should not go up to Jerusalem. In this instance, Paul is warned not to go to Jerusalem through the prophetic agency of other disciples. This prophecy was heeded by Paul who went to Caesarea instead of Jerusalem (Acts 21:8).

8 And the next *day* we that were of Paul's company departed, and came unto Caesarea: and we entered into the house of Philip the evangelist, which was *one* of the seven; and abode with him.

9 And the same man had four daughters, virgins, which did prophesy.

10 And as we tarried *there* many days, there came down from Judea a certain prophet, named Agabus.

11 And when he was come unto us, he took Paul's girdle, and bound his own hands and feet, and said, Thus saith the Holy Ghost, So shall the Jews at Jerusalem bind the man that owneth this girdle, and shall deliver *him* into the hands of the Gentiles.

12 And when we heard these things, both we, and they of that place, besought him not to go up to Jerusalem.

13 Then Paul answered, What mean ye to weep and to break mine heart? for I am ready not to be bound only, but also to die at Jerusalem for the name of the Lord Jesus.

14 And when he would not be persuaded, we ceased, saying, The will of the Lord be done.

15 And after those days we took up our carriages, and went up to Jerusalem.

16 There went with us also *certain* of the disciples of Caesarea, and brought with them one Mnason of Cyprus, an old disciple, with whom we should lodge.

Paul Arrives in Jerusalem

17 And when we were come to Jerusalem, the brethren received us gladly.

18 And the *day* following Paul went in with us unto James; and all the elders were present.

19 And when he had saluted them, he declared particularly what things God had wrought among the Gentiles by his ministry.

20 And when they heard *it,* they glorified the Lord, and said unto him, Thou seest, brother, how many thousands of Jews there are which believe; and they are all zealous of the law:

21 And they are informed of thee, that thou teachest all the Jews which are among the Gentiles to forsake Moses, saying that they ought not to circumcise *their* children, neither to walk after the customs.

22 What is it therefore? the multitude must needs come together: for they will hear that thou art come.

23 Do therefore this that we say to thee: We have four men which have a vow on them;

24 Them take, and purify thyself with them, and be at charges with them, that they may shave *their* heads: and all may know that those things, whereof they were informed concerning thee, are nothing; but *that* thou thyself also walkest orderly, and keepest the law.

25 As touching the Gentiles which believe, we have written *and* concluded that they observe no such thing, save only that they keep themselves from *things* offered to idols, and from blood, and from strangled, and from fornication.

26 Then Paul took the men, and the next day purifying himself with them entered into the temple, to signify the accomplishment of the days of purification, until that an offering should be offered for every one of them.

The Riot and Paul's Arrest in the Temple

27 And when the seven days were almost ended, the Jews which were of Asia, when they saw him in the temple, stirred up all the people, and laid hands on him,

28 Crying out, Men of Israel, help: This is the man, that teacheth all *men* every where against the people, and the law, and this place: and further brought Greeks also into the temple, and hath polluted this holy place.

29 (For they had seen before with him in the city Trophimus an Ephesian, whom they supposed that Paul had brought into the temple.)

30 And all the city was moved, and the people ran together: and they took Paul, and drew him out of the temple: and forthwith the doors were shut.

31 And as they went about to kill him, tidings came unto the chief captain of the

Cross References

8 Acts 6:5; 8:26, 40; Eph. 4:11; 2Tim. 4:5

9 Joel 2:28; Acts 2:17

10 Acts 11:28

11 Acts 20:23; 21:33

13 Acts 20:24

14 Matt. 6:10; 26:42; Luke 11:2; 22:42

17 Acts 15:4

18 Acts 15:13; Gal. 1:19; 2:9

19 Acts 1:17; 15:4, 12; 20:24; Rom. 15:18, 19

20 Acts 22:3; Rom. 10:2; Gal. 1:14

24 Num. 6:2, 13, 18; Acts 18:18

25 Acts 15:20, 29

26 Num. 6:13; Acts 24:18

27 Acts 24:18; 26:21

28 Acts 24:5, 6

29 Acts 20:4

30 Acts 26:21

21:11–14 Agabus, a New Testament prophet (see 11:28), uses a colorful means to predict the specific persecution that Paul will experience if he does go to Jerusalem. In fact, Paul was attacked by a Jewish mob (Acts 21:30–31) and rescued by intervention of the Romans who bound him (Acts 21:33). When Paul was brought before the chief captain, this leader sought to scourge Paul (Acts 22:24) until Paul revealed his Roman citizenship. Later the Jews plotted to have Paul murdered (Acts 23:14). These incidents left Paul in a prison for two years in Caesarea (Acts 24:27).

band, that all Jerusalem was in an uproar.

32 Who immediately took soldiers and centurions, and ran down unto them: and when they saw the chief captain and the soldiers, they left beating of Paul.

33 Then the chief captain came near, and took him, and commanded *him* to be bound with two chains; and demanded who he was, and what he had done.

34 And some cried one thing, some another, among the multitude: and when he could not know the certainty for the tumult, he commanded him to be carried into the castle.

35 And when he came upon the stairs, so it was, that he was borne of the soldiers for the violence of the people.

36 For the multitude of the people followed after, crying, Away with him.

Paul's Defense before the Jews

37 And as Paul was to be led into the castle, he said unto the chief captain, May I speak unto thee? Who said, Canst thou speak Greek?

38 Art not thou that Egyptian, which before these days madest an uproar, and leddest out into the wilderness four thousand men that were murderers?

39 But Paul said, I am a man *which am* a Jew of Tarsus, *a city* in Cilicia, a citizen of no mean city: and, I beseech thee, suffer me to speak unto the people.

40 And when he had given him licence, Paul stood on the stairs, and beckoned with the hand unto the people. And when there was made a great silence, he spake unto *them* in the Hebrew tongue, saying,

CHAPTER 22

1 Men, brethren, and fathers, hear ye my defence *which I make* now unto you.

2 (And when they heard that he spake in the Hebrew tongue to them, they kept the more silence: and he saith,)

3 I am verily a man *which am* a Jew, born in Tarsus, *a city* in Cilicia, yet brought up in this city at the feet of Gamaliel, *and* taught according to the perfect manner of the law of the fathers, and was zealous toward God, as ye all are this day.

4 And I persecuted this way unto the

death, binding and delivering into prisons both men and women.

5 As also the high priest doth bear me witness, and all the estate of the elders: from whom also I received letters unto the brethren, and went to Damascus, to bring them which were there bound unto Jerusalem, for to be punished.

Paul's Testimony of His Conversion

6 And it came to pass, that, as I made my journey, and was come nigh unto Damascus about noon, suddenly there shone from heaven a great light round about me.

7 And I fell unto the ground, and heard a voice saying unto me, Saul, Saul, why persecutest thou me?

8 And I answered, Who art thou, Lord? And he said unto me, I am Jesus of Nazareth, whom thou persecutest.

9 And they that were with me saw indeed the light, and were afraid; but they heard not the voice of him that spake to me.

10 And I said, What shall I do, Lord? And the Lord said unto me, Arise, and go into Damascus; and there it shall be told thee of all things which are appointed for thee to do.

11 And when I could not see for the glory of that light, being led by the hand of them that were with me, I came into Damascus.

12 And one Ananias, a devout man according to the law, having a good report of all the Jews which dwelt *there,*

13 Came unto me, and stood, and said unto me, Brother Saul, receive thy sight. And the same hour I looked up upon him.

14 And he said, The God of our fathers hath chosen thee, that thou shouldest know his will, and see that Just One, and shouldest hear the voice of his mouth.

15 For thou shalt be his witness unto all men of what thou hast seen and heard.

16 And now why tarriest thou? arise, and be baptized, and wash away thy sins, calling on the name of the Lord.

Paul Sent to the Gentiles

17 And it came to pass, that, when I was come again to Jerusalem, even while I prayed in the temple, I was in a trance;

18 And saw him saying unto me, Make

Cross-references

32 Acts 23:27; 24:7
33 Acts 20:23; 21:11
36 Luke 23:18; John 19:15; Acts 22:22
38 Acts 5:36
39 Acts 9:11; 22:3
40 Acts 12:17
1 Acts 7:2
3 Deut. 33:3; 2Kgs. 4:38; Luke 10:39; Acts 5:34; 21:20, 39; 26:5; Rom. 10:2; 2Cor. 11:22; Gal. 1:14; Phil. 3:5
4 Acts 8:3; 26:9, 10, 11; Phil. 3:6; 1Tim. 1:13
5 Luke 22:66; Acts 4:5; 9:2; 26:10, 12
6 Acts 9:3; 26:12, 13
9 Dan. 10:7; Acts 9:7
12 Acts 9:17; 10:22; 1Tim. 3:7
14 Acts 3:13, 14; 5:30; 7:52; 9:15; 26:16; 1Cor. 9:1; 11:23; 15:8; Gal. 1:12
15 Acts 4:20; 23:11; 26:16
16 Acts 2:38; 9:14; Rom. 10:13; Heb. 10:22
17 Acts 9:26; 2Cor. 12:2
18 Matt. 10:14; Acts 22:14

22:17–18 I was in a trance. In this instance a trance was the means the Lord used to provide a prophetic message to Paul, which he is retelling as part of his defense. In this trance, Paul was told by the Lord to leave Jerusalem.

haste, and get thee quickly out of Jerusalem: for they will not receive thy testimony concerning me.

19 And I said, Lord, they know that I imprisoned and beat in every synagogue them that believed on thee:

20 And when the blood of thy martyr Stephen was shed, I also was standing by, and consenting unto his death, and kept the raiment of them that slew him.

21 And he said unto me, Depart: for I will send thee far hence unto the Gentiles.

Paul before the Roman Court

22 And they gave him audience unto this word, and *then* lifted up their voices, and said, Away with such a *fellow* from the earth: for it is not fit that he should live.

23 And as they cried out, and cast off *their* clothes, and threw dust into the air,

24 The chief captain commanded him to be brought into the castle, and bade that he should be examined by scourging; that he might know wherefore they cried so against him.

25 And as they bound him with thongs, Paul said unto the centurion that stood by, Is it lawful for you to scourge a man that is a Roman, and uncondemned?

26 When the centurion heard *that,* he went and told the chief captain, saying, Take heed what thou doest: for this man is a Roman.

27 Then the chief captain came, and said unto him, Tell me, art thou a Roman? He said, Yea.

28 And the chief captain answered, With a great sum obtained I this freedom. And Paul said, But I was *free* born.

29 Then straightway they departed from him which should have examined him: and the chief captain also was afraid, after he knew that he was a Roman, and because he had bound him.

30 On the morrow, because he would have known the certainty wherefore he was accused of the Jews, he loosed him from *his* bands, and commanded the chief priests and all their council to appear, and brought Paul down, and set him before them.

CHAPTER 23
Paul Speaks to the Sanhedrin

1 And Paul, earnestly beholding the council, said, Men *and* brethren, I have lived in all good conscience before God unto this day.

2 And the high priest Ananias commanded them that stood by him to smite him on the mouth.

3 Then said Paul unto him, God shall smite thee, *thou* whited wall: for sittest thou to judge me after the law, and commandest me to be smitten contrary to the law?

4 And they that stood by said, Revilest thou God's high priest?

5 Then said Paul, I wist not, brethren, that he was the high priest: for it is written, Thou shalt not speak evil of the ruler of thy people.

6 But when Paul perceived that the one part were Sadducees, and the other Pharisees, he cried out in the council, Men *and* brethren, I am a Pharisee, the son of a Pharisee: of the hope and resurrection of the dead I am called in question.

7 And when he had so said, there arose a dissension between the Pharisees and the Sadducees: and the multitude was divided.

8 For the Sadducees say that there is no resurrection, neither angel, nor spirit: but the Pharisees confess both.

9 And there arose a great cry: and the scribes *that were* of the Pharisees' part arose, and strove, saying, We find no evil in this man: but if a spirit or an angel hath spoken to him, let us not fight against God.

10 And when there arose a great dissension, the chief captain, fearing lest Paul should have been pulled in pieces of them, commanded the soldiers to go down, and to take him by force from among them, and to bring *him* into the castle.

11 And the night following the Lord stood by him, and said, Be of good cheer, Paul: for as thou hast testified of me in Jerusalem, so must thou bear witness also at Rome.

A Plot to Kill Paul

12 And when it was day, certain of the Jews banded together, and bound themselves

19 Matt. 10:17; Acts 8:3; 22:4
20 Luke 11:48; Acts 7:58; 8:1; Rom. 1:32
21 Acts 9:15; 13:2, 46, 47; 18:6; 26:17; Rom. 1:5; 11:13; 15:16; Gal. 1:15, 16; 2:7, 8; Eph. 3:7, 8; 1Tim. 2:7; 2Tim. 1:11
22 Acts 21:36; 25:24
25 Acts 16:37
1 Acts 24:16; 1Cor. 4:4; 2Cor. 1:12; 4:2; 2Tim. 1:3; Heb. 13:18
2 1Kgs. 22:24; Jer. 20:2; John 18:22
3 Lev. 19:35; Deut. 25:1, 2; John 7:51
5 Ex. 22:28; Eccl. 10:20; Acts 24:17; 2Pet. 2:10; Jude 1:8
6 Acts 24:15, 21; 26:5, 6; 28:20; Phil. 3:5
8 Matt. 22:23; Mark 12:18; Luke 20:27
9 Acts 5:39; 22:7, 17, 18; 25:25; 26:31
11 Acts 18:9; 27:23, 24
12 Acts 22:21, 30; 25:3

23:3 God shall smite thee. This prophecy was fulfilled in A.D. 66 when, as reported by Josephus, Ananias the high priest was assassinated by thieves, who were likely Jewish Zealots at the beginning of their war with Rome.

23:11 as thou hast testified of me in Jerusalem, so

must thou bear witness also at Rome. This is a clear prophecy by the Lord that Paul would not only be delivered from his current difficulty, but would make it to Rome in order to bring the gospel there. This was fulfilled in Acts 28:17–31.

under a curse, saying that they would neither eat nor drink till they had killed Paul.

13 And they were more than forty which had made this conspiracy.

14 And they came to the chief priests and elders, and said, We have bound ourselves under a great curse, that we will eat nothing until we have slain Paul.

15 Now therefore ye with the council signify to the chief captain that he bring him down unto you to morrow, as though ye would inquire something more perfectly concerning him: and we, or ever he come near, are ready to kill him.

16 And when Paul's sister's son heard of their lying in wait, he went and entered into the castle, and told Paul.

17 Then Paul called one of the centurions unto *him,* and said, Bring this young man unto the chief captain: for he hath a certain thing to tell him.

18 So he took him, and brought *him* to the chief captain, and said, Paul the prisoner called me unto *him,* and prayed me to bring this young man unto thee, who hath something to say unto thee.

19 Then the chief captain took him by the hand, and went *with him* aside privately, and asked *him,* What is that thou hast to tell me?

20 And he said, The Jews have agreed to desire thee that thou wouldest bring down Paul to morrow into the council, as though they would inquire somewhat of him more perfectly.

21 But do not thou yield unto them: for there lie in wait for him of them more than forty men, which have bound themselves with an oath, that they will neither eat nor drink till they have killed him: and now are they ready, looking for a promise from thee.

22 So the chief captain *then* let the young man depart, and charged *him,* See *thou* tell no man that thou hast shewed these things to me.

23 And he called unto *him* two centurions, saying, Make ready two hundred soldiers to go to Caesarea, and horsemen threescore and ten, and spearmen two hundred, at the third hour of the night;

24 And provide *them* beasts, that they may set Paul on, and bring *him* safe unto Felix the governor.

25 And he wrote a letter after this manner:

26 Claudius Lysias unto the most excellent governor Felix *sendeth* greeting.

27 This man was taken of the Jews, and should have been killed of them: then came

I with an army, and rescued him, having understood that he was a Roman.

28 And when I would have known the cause wherefore they accused him, I brought him forth into their council:

29 Whom I perceived to be accused of questions of their law, but to have nothing laid to his charge worthy of death or of bonds.

30 And when it was told me how that the Jews laid wait for the man, I sent straightway to thee, and gave commandment to his accusers also to say before thee what *they had* against him. Farewell.

31 Then the soldiers, as it was commanded them, took Paul, and brought *him* by night to Antipatris.

32 On the morrow they left the horsemen to go with him, and returned to the castle:

33 Who, when they came to Caesarea, and delivered the epistle to the governor, presented Paul also before him.

34 And when the governor had read *the letter,* he asked of what province he was. And when he understood that *he was* of Cilicia;

35 I will hear thee, said he, when thine accusers are also come. And he commanded him to be kept in Herod's judgment hall.

CHAPTER 24
In Caesarea

1 And after five days Ananias the high priest descended with the elders, and *with* a certain orator *named* Tertullus, who informed the governor against Paul.

2 And when he was called forth, Tertullus began to accuse *him,* saying, Seeing that by thee we enjoy great quietness, and that very worthy deeds are done unto this nation by thy providence,

3 We accept *it* always, and in all places, most noble Felix, with all thankfulness.

4 Notwithstanding, that I be not further tedious unto thee, I pray thee that thou wouldest hear us of thy clemency a few words.

5 For we have found this man *a pestilent fellow,* and a mover of sedition among all the Jews throughout the world, and a ringleader of the sect of the Nazarenes:

6 Who also hath gone about to profane the temple: whom we took, and would have judged according to our law.

7 But the chief captain Lysias came *upon us,* and with great violence took *him* away out of our hands,

8 Commanding his accusers to come unto thee: by examining of whom thyself mayest

20 Acts 22:12

27 Acts 21:33; 24:7

28 Acts 22:30

29 Acts 18:15; 25:19; 26:31

30 Acts 24:8, 20; 25:6

34 Acts 21:39

35 Matt. 27:27; Acts 24:1, 10; 25:16

1 Acts 21:27; 23:2, 30, 35; 25:2

5 Luke 23:2; Acts 6:13; 16:20; 17:6; 21:28; 1Pet. 2:12, 15

6 John 18:31; Acts 21:28

7 Acts 21:33

8 Acts 23:30

take knowledge of all these things, whereof we accuse him.

9 And the Jews also assented, saying that these things were so.

10 Then Paul, after that the governor had beckoned unto him to speak, answered, Forasmuch as I know that thou hast been of many years a judge unto this nation, I do the more cheerfully answer for myself:

11 Because that thou mayest understand, that there are yet but twelve days since I went up to Jerusalem for to worship.

12 And they neither found me in the temple disputing with any man, neither raising up the people, neither in the synagogues, nor in the city:

13 Neither can they prove the things whereof they now accuse me.

14 But this I confess unto thee, that after the way which they call heresy, so worship I the God of my fathers, believing all things which are written in the law and in the prophets:

15 And have hope toward God, which they themselves also allow, that there shall be a resurrection of the dead, both of the just and unjust.

16 And herein do I exercise myself, to have always a conscience void of offence toward God, and *toward* men.

17 Now after many years I came to bring alms to my nation, and offerings.

18 Whereupon certain Jews from Asia found me purified in the temple, neither with multitude, nor with tumult.

19 Who ought to have been here before thee, and object, if they had ought against me.

20 Or else let these same *here* say, if they have found any evil doing in me, while I stood before the council,

21 Except it be for this one voice, that I cried standing among them, Touching the resurrection of the dead I am called in question by you this day.

22 And when Felix heard these things, having more perfect knowledge of *that* way, he deferred them, and said, When Lysias the chief captain shall come down, I will know the uttermost of your matter.

23 And he commanded a centurion to keep

Paul, and to let *him* have liberty, and that he should forbid none of his acquaintance to minister or come unto him.

Felix and Drusilla

24 And after certain days, when Felix came with his wife Drusilla, which was a Jewess, he sent for Paul, and heard him concerning the faith in Christ.

25 And as he reasoned of righteousness, temperance, and judgment to come, Felix trembled, and answered, Go thy way for this time; when I have a convenient season, I will call for thee.

26 He hoped also that money should have been given him of Paul, that he might loose him: wherefore he sent for him the more often, and communed with him.

27 But after two years Porcius Festus came into Felix' room: and Felix, willing to shew the Jews a pleasure, left Paul bound.

CHAPTER 25
Paul Appears before Festus

1 Now when Festus was come into the province, after three days he ascended from Caesarea to Jerusalem.

2 Then the high priest and the chief of the Jews informed him against Paul, and besought him,

3 And desired favour against him, that he would send for him to Jerusalem, laying wait in the way to kill him.

4 But Festus answered, that Paul should be kept at Caesarea, and that he himself would depart shortly *thither.*

5 Let them therefore, said he, which among you are able, go down with *me,* and accuse this man, if there be any wickedness in him.

6 And when he had tarried among them more than ten days, he went down unto Caesarea; and the next day sitting on the judgment seat commanded Paul to be brought.

7 And when he was come, the Jews which came down from Jerusalem stood round about, and laid many and grievous complaints against Paul, which they could not prove.

8 While he answered for himself, Neither

Cross references (center column)

11 Acts 21:26; 24:17

12 Acts 25:8; 28:17

14 Amos 8:14; Acts 9:2; 26:22; 28:23; 2Tim. 1:3

15 Dan. 12:2; John 5:28, 29; Acts 23:6; 26:6, 7; 28:20

16 Acts 23:1

17 Acts 11:29, 30; 20:16; Rom. 15:25; 2Cor. 8:4; Gal. 2:10

18 Acts 21:26, 27; 26:21

19 Acts 23:30; 25:16

21 Acts 23:6; 28:20

22 Acts 24:7

23 Acts 27:3; 28:16

26 Ex. 23:8

27 Ex. 23:2; Acts 12:3; 25:9, 14

2 Acts 24:1; 25:15

3 Acts 23:12, 15

5 Acts 18:14; 25:18

7 Mark 15:3; Luke 23:2, 10; Acts 24:5, 13

8 Acts 6:13; 24:12; 28:17

24:15 a resurrection of the dead, both of the just and unjust. The resurrection of the just will take place at various times throughout the future. Christians will be resurrected at the Rapture (1 Thess. 4:13–18, see 1 Cor. 15:51–56). All Old Testament saints will be raised at the end of the Tribulation (Dan. 12:1–4), as will all the saints from the Tribulation (Rev. 20:4). The resurrection of the unjust will occur at the end of the Millennium (Rev. 20:5, 11–15).

against the law of the Jews, neither against the temple, nor yet against Caesar, have I offended any thing at all.

9 But Festus, willing to do the Jews a pleasure, answered Paul, and said, Wilt thou go up to Jerusalem, and there be judged of these things before me?

10 Then said Paul, I stand at Caesar's judgment seat, where I ought to be judged: to the Jews have I done no wrong, as thou very well knowest.

11 For if I be an offender, or have committed any thing worthy of death, I refuse not to die: but if there be none of these things whereof these accuse me, no man may deliver me unto them. I appeal unto Caesar.

12 Then Festus, when he had conferred with the council, answered, Hast thou appealed unto Caesar? unto Caesar shalt thou go.

Agrippa and Bernice

13 And after certain days king Agrippa and Bernice came unto Caesarea to salute Festus.

14 And when they had been there many days, Festus declared Paul's cause unto the king, saying, There is a certain man left in bonds by Felix:

15 About whom, when I was at Jerusalem, the chief priests and the elders of the Jews informed *me*, desiring *to have* judgment against him.

16 To whom I answered, It is not the manner of the Romans to deliver any man to die, before that he which is accused have the accusers face to face, and have licence to answer for himself concerning the crime laid against him.

17 Therefore, when they were come hither, without any delay on the morrow I sat on the judgment seat, and commanded the man to be brought forth.

18 Against whom when the accusers stood up, they brought none accusation of such things as I supposed:

19 But had certain questions against him of their own superstition, and of one Jesus, which was dead, whom Paul affirmed to be alive.

20 And because I doubted of such manner of questions, I asked *him* whether he would go to Jerusalem, and there be judged of these matters.

21 But when Paul had appealed to be reserved unto the hearing of Augustus, I commanded him to be kept till I might send him to Caesar.

22 Then Agrippa said unto Festus, I would also hear the man myself. To morrow, said he, thou shalt hear him.

23 And on the morrow, when Agrippa was come, and Bernice, with great pomp, and was entered into the place of hearing, with the chief captains, and principal men of the city, at Festus' commandment Paul was brought forth.

24 And Festus said, King Agrippa, and all men which are here present with us, ye see this man, about whom all the multitude of the Jews have dealt with me, both at Jerusalem, and *also* here, crying that he ought not to live any longer.

25 But when I found that he had committed nothing worthy of death, and that he himself hath appealed to Augustus, I have determined to send him.

26 Of whom I have no certain thing to write unto my lord. Wherefore I have brought him forth before you, and specially before thee, O king Agrippa, that, after examination had, I might have somewhat to write.

27 For it seemeth to me unreasonable to send a prisoner, and not withal to signify the crimes *laid* against him.

Chapter 26
Paul Defends Himself before Agrippa

1 Then Agrippa said unto Paul, Thou art permitted to speak for thyself. Then Paul stretched forth the hand, and answered for himself:

2 I think myself happy, king Agrippa, because I shall answer for myself this day before thee touching all the things whereof I am accused of the Jews:

3 Especially *because I know* thee to be expert in all customs and questions which are among the Jews: wherefore I beseech thee to hear me patiently.

4 My manner of life from my youth, which was at the first among mine own nation at Jerusalem, know all the Jews;

5 Which knew me from the beginning, if they would testify, that after the most straitest sect of our religion I lived a Pharisee.

6 And now I stand and am judged for the hope of the promise made of God unto our fathers:

7 Unto which *promise* our twelve tribes, instantly serving *God* day and night, hope to come. For which hope's sake, king Agrippa, I am accused of the Jews.

8 Why should it be thought a thing

9 Acts 24:27; 25:20
11 Acts 18:14; 23:29; 25:25; 26:31, 32; 28:19
14 Acts 24:27
15 Acts 25:2, 3
16 Acts 25:4, 5
17 Acts 25:6
19 Acts 18:15; 23:29
22 Acts 9:15
24 Acts 22:22; 25:2, 3, 7
25 Acts 23:9, 29; 25:11, 12; 26:31
5 Acts 22:3; 23:6; 24:15, 21; Phil. 3:5
6 Gen. 3:15; 22:18; 26:4; 49:10; Deut. 18:15; 2Sam. 7:12; Ps. 132:11; Isa. 4:2; 7:14; 9:6; 40:10; Jer. 23:5; 33:14-16; Ezek. 34:23; 37:24; Dan. 9:24; Mic. 7:20; Acts 13:32; 23:6; Rom. 15:8; Titus 2:13
7 Luke 2:37; Phil. 3:11; 1Thess. 3:10; 1Tim. 5:5; James 1:1

incredible with you, that God should raise the dead?

9 I verily thought with myself, that I ought to do many things contrary to the name of Jesus of Nazareth.

10 Which thing I also did in Jerusalem: and many of the saints did I shut up in prison, having received authority from the chief priests; and when they were put to death, I gave my voice against *them*.

11 And I punished them oft in every synagogue, and compelled *them* to blaspheme; and being exceedingly mad against them, I persecuted *them* even unto strange cities.

Paul Preaches to King Agrippa

12 Whereupon as I went to Damascus with authority and commission from the chief priests,

13 At midday, O king, I saw in the way a light from heaven, above the brightness of the sun, shining round about me and them which journeyed with me.

14 And when we were all fallen to the earth, I heard a voice speaking unto me, and saying in the Hebrew tongue, Saul, Saul, why persecutest thou me? *it is* hard for thee to kick against the pricks.

15 And I said, Who art thou, Lord? And he said, I am Jesus whom thou persecutest.

16 But rise, and stand upon thy feet: for I have appeared unto thee for this purpose, to make thee a minister and a witness both of these things which thou hast seen, and of those things in the which I will appear unto thee;

17 Delivering thee from the people, and *from* the Gentiles, unto whom now I send thee,

18 To open their eyes, *and* to turn *them* from darkness to light, and *from* the power of Satan unto God, that they may receive forgiveness of sins, and inheritance among them which are sanctified by faith that is in me.

19 Whereupon, O king Agrippa, I was not disobedient unto the heavenly vision:

20 But shewed first unto them of Damascus, and at Jerusalem, and throughout all the coasts of Judea, and *then* to the Gentiles,

that they should repent and turn to God, and do works meet for repentance.

21 For these causes the Jews caught me in the temple, and went about to kill *me*.

22 Having therefore obtained help of God, I continue unto this day, witnessing both to small and great, saying none other things than those which the prophets and Moses did say should come:

23 That Christ should suffer, *and* that he should be the first that should rise from the dead, and should shew light unto the people, and to the Gentiles.

24 And as he thus spake for himself, Festus said with a loud voice, Paul, thou art beside thyself; much learning doth make thee mad.

25 But he said, I am not mad, most noble Festus; but I speak forth the words of truth and soberness.

26 For the king knoweth of these things, before whom also I speak freely: for I am persuaded that none of these things are hidden from him; for this thing was not done in a corner.

27 King Agrippa, believest thou the prophets? I know that thou believest.

28 Then Agrippa said unto Paul, Almost thou persuadest me to be a Christian.

29 And Paul said, I would to God, that not only thou, but also all that hear me this day, were both almost, and altogether such as I am, except these bonds.

30 And when he had thus spoken, the king rose up, and the governor, and Bernice, and they that sat with them:

31 And when they were gone aside, they talked between themselves, saying, This man doeth nothing worthy of death or of bonds.

32 Then said Agrippa unto Festus, This man might have been set at liberty, if he had not appealed unto Caesar.

CHAPTER 27
Paul and Other Prisoners Sail for Italy

1 And when it was determined that we should sail into Italy, they delivered Paul and certain other prisoners unto *one* named Julius, a centurion of Augustus' band.

Cross references (center column)

9 John 16:2; 1Tim. 1:13

10 Acts 8:3; 9:14, 21; 22:5; Gal. 1:13

11 Acts 22:19

12 Acts 9:3; 22:6

16 Acts 22:15

17 Acts 22:21

18 Isa. 35:5; 42:7; Luke 1:77, 79; John 8:12; Acts 20:32; 2Cor. 4:4; 6:14; Eph. 1:11, 18; 4:18; 5:8; Col. 1:12, 13; 1Thess. 5:5; 1Pet. 2:9, 25

20 Matt. 3:8; Acts 9:20, 22, 29; 11:26; 13, 14, 16-21

21 Acts 21:30, 31

22 Luke 24:27, 44; John 5:46; Acts 24:14; 28:23; Rom. 3:21

23 Luke 2:32; 24:26, 46; 1Cor. 15:20; Col. 1:18; Rev. 1:5

24 2Kgs. 9:11; John 10:20; 1Cor. 1:23; 2:13, 14; 4:10

29 1Cor. 7:7

31 Acts 23:9, 29; 25:25

32 Acts 25:11

1 Acts 25:12, 25

26:17 Christ promised that He would deliver Paul "from the people," that is, Israel, and "from the Gentiles." This was fulfilled on a number of occasions leading to Paul's journey to Rome (cf. Acts 9:23–25; 23:20; 25:11–12; 26:22).

26:22–23 Paul declares before Agrippa that Jesus ful-

filled prophecy from "Moses," the Law or Torah, and the "prophets" by His death and resurrection. These events would be a "light unto the people [Israel], and to the Gentiles." Gentiles have been and continue to come to Christ during the Church Age, while Israel specifically will be redeemed during the Tribulation.

2 And entering into a ship of Adramyttium, we launched, meaning to sail by the coasts of Asia; *one* Aristarchus, a Macedonian of Thessalonica, being with us.

3 And the next *day* we touched at Sidon. And Julius courteously entreated Paul, and gave *him* liberty to go unto his friends to refresh himself.

4 And when we had launched from thence, we sailed under Cyprus, because the winds were contrary.

5 And when we had sailed over the sea of Cilicia and Pamphylia, we came to Myra, *a city* of Lycia.

6 And there the centurion found a ship of Alexandria sailing into Italy; and he put us therein.

7 And when we had sailed slowly many days, and scarce were come over against Cnidus, the wind not suffering us, we sailed under Crete, over against Salmone;

8 And, hardly passing it, came unto a place which is called The fair havens; nigh whereunto was the city *of* Lasea.

9 Now when much time was spent, and when sailing was now dangerous, because the fast was now already past, Paul admonished *them,*

10 And said unto them, Sirs, I perceive that this voyage will be with hurt and much damage, not only of the lading and ship, but also of our lives.

11 Nevertheless the centurion believed the master and the owner of the ship, more than those things which were spoken by Paul.

12 And because the haven was not commodious to winter in, the more part advised to depart thence also, if by any means they might attain to Phenice, *and there* to winter; *which is* an haven of Crete, and lieth toward the southwest and northwest.

The Storm

13 And when the south wind blew softly, supposing that they had obtained *their* purpose, loosing *thence,* they sailed close by Crete.

14 But not long after there arose against it a tempestuous wind, called Euroclydon.

15 And when the ship was caught, and could not bear up into the wind, we let *her* drive.

16 And running under a certain island which is called Clauda, we had much work to come by the boat:

17 Which when they had taken up, they used helps, undergirding the ship; and, fearing lest they should fall into the quicksands, strake sail, and so were driven.

18 And we being exceedingly tossed with a tempest, the next *day* they lightened the ship;

19 And the third *day* we cast out with our own hands the tackling of the ship.

20 And when neither sun nor stars in many days appeared, and no small tempest lay on *us,* all hope that we should be saved was then taken away.

21 But after long abstinence Paul stood forth in the midst of them, and said, Sirs, ye should have hearkened unto me, and not have loosed from Crete, and to have gained this harm and loss.

22 And now I exhort you to be of good cheer: for there shall be no loss of *any man's* life among you, but of the ship.

23 For there stood by me this night the angel of God, whose I am, and whom I serve,

24 Saying, Fear not, Paul; thou must be brought before Caesar: and, lo, God hath given thee all them that sail with thee.

25 Wherefore, sirs, be of good cheer: for I believe God, that it shall be even as it was told me.

26 Howbeit we must be cast upon a certain island.

27 But when the fourteenth night was come, as we were driven up and down in Adria, about midnight the shipmen deemed that they drew near to some country;

28 And sounded, and found *it* twenty fathoms: and when they had gone a little further, they sounded again, and found *it* fifteen fathoms.

29 Then fearing lest we should have fallen upon rocks, they cast four anchors out of the stern, and wished for the day.

30 And as the shipmen were about to flee out of the ship, when they had let down the boat into the sea, under colour as though they would have cast anchors out of the foreship,

31 Paul said to the centurion and to the soldiers, Except these abide in the ship, ye cannot be saved.

Cross references (center column):

2 Acts 19:29
3 Acts 24:23; 28:16
9 Lev. 23:27, 29
19 Jon. 1:5
23 Dan. 6:16; Acts 23:11; Rom. 1:9; 2Tim. 1:3
25 Luke 1:45; Rom. 4:20, 21; 2Tim. 1:12
26 Acts 28:1

27:24 thou must be brought before Caesar: and, lo, God hath given thee all them that sail with thee. These two prophecies were fulfilled when no lives were lost after the ship ran aground on an island (Acts 27:39—28:1, cf. 27:26) and later when Paul arrived in Rome (Acts 28:14, 17–19, 30).

32 Then the soldiers cut off the ropes of the boat, and let her fall off.

33 And while the day was coming on, Paul besought *them* all to take meat, saying, This day is the fourteenth day that ye have tarried and continued fasting, having taken nothing.

34 Wherefore I pray you to take *some* meat: for this is for your health: for there shall not an hair fall from the head of any of you.

35 And when he had thus spoken, he took bread, and gave thanks to God in presence of them all: and when he had broken *it*, he began to eat.

36 Then were they all of good cheer, and they also took *some* meat.

37 And we were in all in the ship two hundred threescore and sixteen souls.

38 And when they had eaten enough, they lightened the ship, and cast out the wheat into the sea.

Shipwreck

39 And when it was day, they knew not the land: but they discovered a certain creek with a shore, into the which they were minded, if it were possible, to thrust in the ship.

40 And when they had taken up the anchors, they committed *themselves* unto the sea, and loosed the rudder bands, and hoised up the mainsail to the wind, and made toward shore.

41 And falling into a place where two seas met, they ran the ship aground; and the forepart stuck fast, and remained unmoveable, but the hinder part was broken with the violence of the waves.

42 And the soldiers' counsel was to kill the prisoners, lest any of them should swim out, and escape.

43 But the centurion, willing to save Paul, kept them from *their* purpose; and commanded that they which could swim should cast *themselves* first *into* the *sea*, and get to land:

44 And the rest, some on boards, and some on *broken pieces* of the ship. And so it came to pass, that they escaped all safe to land.

CHAPTER 28
On Malta

1 And when they were escaped, then they knew that the island was called Melita.

2 And the barbarous people shewed us no little kindness: for they kindled a fire, and received us every one, because of the present rain, and because of the cold.

3 And when Paul had gathered a bundle of sticks, and laid *them* on the fire, there came a viper out of the heat, and fastened on his hand.

4 And when the barbarians saw the *venomous* beast hang on his hand, they said among themselves, No doubt this man is a murderer, whom, though he hath escaped the sea, yet vengeance suffereth not to live.

5 And he shook off the beast into the fire, and felt no harm.

6 Howbeit they looked when he should have swollen, or fallen down dead suddenly: but after they had looked a great while, and saw no harm come to him, they changed their minds, and said that he was a god.

7 In the same quarters were possessions of the chief man of the island, whose name was Publius; who received us, and lodged us three days courteously.

8 And it came to pass, that the father of Publius lay sick of a fever and of a bloody flux: to whom Paul entered in, and prayed, and laid his hands on him, and healed him.

9 So when this was done, others also, which had diseases in the island, came, and were healed:

10 Who also honoured us with many honours; and when we departed, they laded *us* with such things as were necessary.

11 And after three months we departed in a ship of Alexandria, which had wintered in the isle, whose sign was Castor and Pollux.

12 And landing at Syracuse, we tarried *there* three days.

13 And from thence we fetched a compass, and came to Rhegium: and after one day the south wind blew, and we came the next day to Puteoli:

14 Where we found brethren, and were desired to tarry with them seven days: and so we went toward Rome.

15 And from thence, when the brethren heard of us, they came to meet us as far as Appii Forum, and The Three Taverns: whom when Paul saw, he thanked God, and took courage.

Cross-references

34 1Kgs. 1:52; Matt. 10:30; Luke 12:7; 21:18
35 1Sam. 9:13; Matt. 15:36; Mark 8:6; John 6:11; 1Tim. 4:3, 4
37 Acts 2:41; 7:14; Rom. 13:1; 1Pet. 3:20
41 2Cor. 11:25
44 Acts 27:22
1 Acts 27:26
2 Rom. 1:14; 1Cor. 14:11; Col. 3:11
5 Mark 16:18; Luke 10:19
6 Acts 14:11
8 Mark 6:5; 7:32; 16:18; Luke 4:40; Acts 19:11, 12; 1Cor. 12:9, 28; James 5:14, 15
10 Matt. 15:6; 1Tim. 5:17

28:3–6 Had Paul died from the snakebite, the prophecy about his going to Rome to appear before Caesar could not have been fulfilled (27:24). However, God did not allow him to even get sick from the incident, let alone die.

Arrival in Rome

16 And when we came to Rome, the centurion delivered the prisoners to the captain of the guard: but Paul was suffered to dwell by himself with a soldier that kept him.

17 And it came to pass, that after three days Paul called the chief of the Jews together: and when they were come together, he said unto them, Men *and* brethren, though I have committed nothing against the people, or customs of our fathers, yet was I delivered prisoner from Jerusalem into the hands of the Romans.

18 Who, when they had examined me, would have let *me* go, because there was no cause of death in me.

19 But when the Jews spake against *it,* I was constrained to appeal unto Caesar; not that I had ought to accuse my nation of.

20 For this cause therefore have I called for you, to see *you,* and to speak with *you:* because that for the hope of Israel I am bound with this chain.

21 And they said unto him, We neither received letters out of Judea concerning thee, neither any of the brethren that came shewed or spake any harm of thee.

22 But we desire to hear of thee what thou thinkest: for as concerning this sect, we know that every where it is spoken against.

23 And when they had appointed him a day, there came many to him into *his* lodging; to whom he expounded and testified the kingdom of God, persuading them concerning Jesus, both out of the law of Moses, and *out of* the prophets, from morning till evening.

24 And some believed the things which were spoken, and some believed not.

25 And when they agreed not among themselves, they departed, after that Paul had spoken one word, Well spake the Holy Ghost by Esaias the prophet unto our fathers,

26 Saying, Go unto this people, and say, Hearing ye shall hear, and shall not understand; and seeing ye shall see, and not perceive:

27 For the heart of this people is waxed gross, and their ears are dull of hearing, and their eyes have they closed; lest they should see with *their* eyes, and hear with *their* ears, and understand with *their* heart, and should be converted, and I should heal them.

28 Be it known therefore unto you, that the salvation of God is sent unto the Gentiles, and *that* they will hear it.

29 And when he had said these words, the Jews departed, and had great reasoning among themselves.

30 And Paul dwelt two whole years in his own hired house, and received all that came in unto him,

31 Preaching the kingdom of God, and teaching those things which concern the Lord Jesus Christ, with all confidence, no man forbidding him.

Cross references

16 Acts 24:25; 27:3
17 Acts 21:33; 24:12, 13; 25:8
18 Acts 22:24; 24:10; 25:8; 26:31
19 Acts 25:11
20 Eph. 3:1; 4:1; 6:20; 2Tim. 1:16; 2:9
22 Luke 2:34; Acts 24:5, 14; 1Pet. 2:12; 4:14
23 Luke 24:27; Acts 17:3; 19:8; 26:6, 22
24 Acts 14:4; 17:4; 19:9
26 Isa. 6:9; Matt. 13:14, 15; Mark 4:12; Luke 8:10; John 12:40
28 Matt. 21:41, 43; Acts 13:46, 47; 18:6
31 Acts 4:31; Eph. 6:19

28:20 the hope of Israel. This phrase refers to fulfillment of the Old Testament promises made to national Israel and the patriarchs (cf. Acts 26:6–7). These promises (cf. Acts 23:6; 24:15; 26:6–7) will be realized during the Tribulation and especially during the Millennial Kingdom.

28:25–28 The sad prophecy of Isaiah 6:9–10 that the Jewish people would reject Jesus as their Messiah is fulfilled and recorded throughout the book of Acts. Yet, the joyous prophecy, "that the salvation of God is sent unto the Gentiles, and that they will hear it" has been demonstrated throughout Acts and continues even into our own day.

Romans

Paul wrote the book of Romans from the city of Corinth shortly after he wrote 2 Corinthians, presumably in the spring of A.D. 57. The style and character of Romans differ from Paul's earlier epistles (Galatians and Corinthians), which were responses to particular needs. The epistle to the Romans is Paul's theological masterpiece. It presents Paul's view of the gospel and his teachings about God, Christ, and the Holy Spirit. The doctrines of grace, faith, justification, sanctification, sin, and atonement for sin are explained in persuasive detail. Teachings on the subjects of death, resurrection, and divine punishment are also prevalent.

The theology of redemption appears in the first eight chapters, arising from the axiom, "The just shall live by faith" (see Hab. 2:4; Gal. 3:11; Heb. 10:38). Vindicating God's dealings with Israel, Paul explains the temporary blindness of the Jews and predicts their eventual restoration (chaps. 9—11). The practical exhortations from chapter 12 to the end are consistent with Jesus' teaching.

Author	Paul
Date	A.D. 57
Key Truth	God's Righteousness
Historic Time	Early Church Growth in Rome
Key Verse	1:17 — The just shall live by faith.

Future prophecies focus on the judgments of God (1:18; 2:1–16), the return of Christ (13:11–13), the manifestation of the sons of God, the redemption of the body, and the deliverance of creation from the curse of sin (8:19–23). The ultimate triumph of believers (8:28–39) and the salvation of national Israel after a long period of blindness (9–11) are other prophecies that will be fulfilled in the future. Over half of the prophecies include citations of Old Testament passages. The judgment seat of Christ (not to be confused with God's judgment on the ungodly [1:18]) is the place where only believers appear after the Rapture (14:7–12) for rewards and not for condemnation (8:1). Paul cites several verses in 15:8–13, showing that the Gentiles would one day praise the Lord. In part fulfilled today, the ultimate reign of Christ over the whole world will be the final and glorious fulfillment.

Predictions on 29 subjects involve 91 of 433 verses, or 21 percent. Romans contains 58 quotations from the Old Testament, more than any other New Testament book.

21% Prophecy

A.D. 25	A.D. 30	A.D. 35	A.D. 40	A.D. 45	A.D. 50	A.D. 55	A.D. 60	A.D.

37-41 Caligula is Emperor of Rome

57 Romans is written

14-37 Tiberius is Emperor of Rome

41-54 Claudius is Emperor of Rome

59-62 Paul is in Rome

54-68 Nero is Emperor of Rome

35 Conversion of Saul (Paul)

47-49 Paul's First Missionary Journey

64 Great fire in Rome

49-53 Paul's Second Missionary Journey

26-30 Public ministry of Jesus

53-56 Paul's Third Missionary Journey

CHAPTER 1

1 Paul, a servant of Jesus Christ, called *to be* an apostle, separated unto the gospel of God,

2 (Which he had promised afore by his prophets in the holy scriptures,)

3 Concerning his Son, Jesus Christ our Lord, which was made of the seed of David according to the flesh;

4 And declared *to be* the Son of God with power, according to the spirit of holiness, by the resurrection from the dead:

5 By whom we have received grace and apostleship, for obedience to the faith among all nations, for his name;

6 Among whom are ye also the called of Jesus Christ:

7 To all that be in Rome, beloved of God, called *to be* saints: Grace to you and peace from God our Father, and the Lord Jesus Christ.

The Gentiles' Need of Righteousness

8 First, I thank my God through Jesus Christ for you all, that your faith is spoken of throughout the whole world.

9 For God is my witness, whom I serve with my spirit in the gospel of his Son, that without ceasing I make mention of you always in my prayers;

10 Making request, if by any means now at length I might have a prosperous journey by the will of God to come unto you.

11 For I long to see you, that I may impart unto you some spiritual gift, to the end ye may be established;

12 That is, that I may be comforted together with you by the mutual faith both of you and me.

13 Now I would not have you ignorant,

brethren, that oftentimes I purposed to come unto you, (but was let hitherto,) that I might have some fruit among you also, even as among other Gentiles.

14 I am debtor both to the Greeks, and to the Barbarians; both to the wise, and to the unwise.

15 So, as much as in me is, I am ready to preach the gospel to you that are at Rome also.

16 For I am not ashamed of the gospel of Christ: for it is the power of God unto salvation to every one that believeth; to the Jew first, and also to the Greek.

17 For therein is the righteousness of God revealed from faith to faith: as it is written, The just shall live by faith.

Sin Will Be Punished

18 For the wrath of God is revealed from heaven against all ungodliness and unrighteousness of men, who hold the truth in unrighteousness;

19 Because that which may be known of God is manifest in them; for God hath shewed *it* unto them.

20 For the invisible things of him from the creation of the world are clearly seen, being understood by the things that are made, *even* his eternal power and Godhead; so that they are without excuse:

21 Because that, when they knew God, they glorified *him* not as God, neither were thankful; but became vain in their imaginations, and their foolish heart was darkened.

22 Professing themselves to be wise, they became fools,

23 And changed the glory of the uncorruptible God into an image made like to corruptible man, and to birds, and fourfooted beasts, and creeping things.

Cross references:

1 Acts 9:15; 13:2; 22:21

2 Acts 26:6; Rom. 3:21; 16:26; Gal. 3:8; Titus 1:2

3 Matt. 1:6, 16; Luke 1:32; John 1:14

4 Acts 13:33; Heb. 9:14

5 Acts 6:7

7 Gal. 1:3

8 Rom. 16:19

9 Rom. 9:1; 2Cor. 1:23; Phil. 1:8

10 Rom. 15:23, 32; 1Thess. 3:10

12 Titus 1:4; 2Pet. 1:1

13 Rom. 15:23; 1Thess. 2:18

16 Ps. 40:9, 10; Acts 3:26; 13:26, 46; 2Tim. 1:8

17 Hab. 2:4; Heb. 10:38

18 Eph. 5:6; Col. 3:6

19 John 1:9

20 Ps. 19:14; Acts 14:17; 17:27

21 Jer. 2:5; Eph. 4:17, 18

22 Jer. 10:14

23 Deut. 4:16; Ps. 106:20; Jer. 2:11; Ezek. 8:10

1:2 promised afore by his prophets in the holy scriptures. Fulfilled prophecy, relating and contrasting the Old Testament and the Dispensation of Law with the New Testament and the Dispensation of the Church, is an underlying theme throughout this epistle. More quotations from the Old Testament appear in Romans than in any other New Testament book, as Paul quotes from fifty-eight different Old Testament passages and refers to Adam, Abraham, Moses, and David, each of whom is associated with covenants in the Old Testament.

1:3 seed of David. Jesus is introduced as "his [God's] Son, Jesus Christ our Lord," indicating that He is Messiah, Savior, and Deity. As David's royal descendent, both His humanity and future kingship are implied.

1:17–18 Notice the two revelations in these verses. The righteousness of God is revealed in the gospel of salvation, whereby Jesus' vicarious death for sin means that God can be just in punishing sin and can also be the justifier of those who believe (3:26). Secondly, the wrath of God is revealed against all ungodliness of those who repress the truth and reject both an inner consciousness of His existence and the evidences of His power in the Creation. This wrath against all evil is demonstrated by the universality of death plus the consequences of idolatry, immorality, violence, and all other kinds of sins. This wrath of God will culminate in the future Great Tribulation, when the "the great day of His wrath is come" (Rev. 6:17).

24 Wherefore God also gave them up to uncleanness through the lusts of their own hearts, to dishonour their own bodies between themselves:

25 Who changed the truth of God into a lie, and worshipped and served the creature more than the Creator, who is blessed for ever. Amen.

26 For this cause God gave them up unto vile affections: for even their women did change the natural use into that which is against nature:

27 And likewise also the men, leaving the natural use of the woman, burned in their lust one toward another; men with men working that which is unseemly, and receiving in themselves that recompence of their error which was meet.

28 And even as they did not like to retain God in *their* knowledge, God gave them over to a reprobate mind, to do those things which are not convenient;

29 Being filled with all unrighteousness, fornication, wickedness, covetousness, maliciousness; full of envy, murder, debate, deceit, malignity; whisperers,

30 Backbiters, haters of God, despiteful, proud, boasters, inventors of evil things, disobedient to parents,

31 Without understanding, covenant breakers, without natural affection, implacable, unmerciful:

32 Who knowing the judgment of God, that they which commit such things are worthy of death, not only do the same, but have pleasure in them that do them.

CHAPTER 2
God's Law

1 Therefore thou art inexcusable, O man, whosoever thou art that judgest: for wherein thou judgest another, thou con-

24 Lev. 18:22; Acts 7:42; 1Cor. 6:18; Eph. 4:18, 19

25 Isa. 44:20; Jer. 10:14; 13:25

26 Lev. 18:22, 23

28 Eph. 5:4

32 Ps. 50:18; Hos. 7:3

1 2Sam. 12:5, 6, 7; Matt. 7:1, 2; John 8:9; Rom. 1:20

4 Ex. 34:6; Isa. 30:18; Rom. 3:25; 9:23; Eph. 1:7; 2:4, 7; 2Pet. 3:9, 15

5 Deut. 32:34; James 5:3

6 Job 34:11; Ps. 62:12; Prov. 24:12; Jer. 17:10; 32:19; Matt. 16:27; Rev. 2:23; 20:12; 22:12

8 Job 24:13; Rom. 1:18; 2Thess. 1:8

9 Amos 3:2; Luke 12:47, 48; 1Pet. 4:17

10 1Pet. 1:7

11 Deut. 10:17; Job 34:19; Eph. 6:9

13 Matt. 7:21; James 1:22, 23, 25; 1John 3:7

demnest thyself; for thou that judgest doest the same things.

2 But we are sure that the judgment of God is according to truth against them which commit such things.

3 And thinkest thou this, O man, that judgest them which do such things, and doest the same, that thou shalt escape the judgment of God?

4 Or despisest thou the riches of his goodness and forbearance and longsuffering; not knowing that the goodness of God leadeth thee to repentance?

5 But after thy hardness and impenitent heart treasurest up unto thyself wrath against the day of wrath and revelation of the righteous judgment of God;

6 Who will render to every man according to his deeds:

7 To them who by patient continuance in well doing seek for glory and honour and immortality, eternal life:

8 But unto them that are contentious, and do not obey the truth, but obey unrighteousness, indignation and wrath,

9 Tribulation and anguish, upon every soul of man that doeth evil, of the Jew first, and also of the Gentile;

10 But glory, honour, and peace, to every man that worketh good, to the Jew first, and also to the Gentile:

11 For there is no respect of persons with God.

12 For as many as have sinned without law shall also perish without law: and as many as have sinned in the law shall be judged by the law;

13 (For not the hearers of the law *are* just before God, but the doers of the law shall be justified.

14 For when the Gentiles, which have not the law, do by nature the things contained

---

2:1 thou art inexcusable, O man. In Romans 1:18—3:20, the ungodly and unrighteous state of the entire human family is demonstrated. Their need of salvation through Christ is seen in the immoral state of the world (1:18–32), the lost state of the cultured and moralistic Gentiles (2:1–16), the lost state of religious Jews who were practicing the letter not the spirit of the Law (2:17–29), and a universal indictment of all mankind (3:1–20).

2:2–16 the judgment of God. Five principles of divine judgment are expressed by Paul, who also indicates (14:10) that all must eventually stand before the judgment bar of God: 1) God's judgment is according to truth (v. 2), that is, in accordance with the Word of truth in the

Bible and the true nature and actions of every person; 2) God's judgment is inescapable (v. 3); 3) God will "render to every man according to his deeds" (v. 6); 4) with God "there is no respect of persons" (v. 11); 5) God will judge the "secrets of men" according to the gospel (v. 16).

Faith in the gospel of Jesus Christ and His atoning death is the great determining factor in judgment. These principles will apply at the judgment seat of Christ, where all believers will appear (1 Cor. 3:11–15; 2 Cor. 5:10). The principles will also be operative at the Great White Throne Judgment, where all the lost will appear at "the resurrection of damnation [condemnation]" (see John 5:28–29).

in the law, these, having not the law, are a law unto themselves:

15 Which shew the work of the law written in their hearts, their conscience also bearing witness, and *their* thoughts the mean while accusing or else excusing one another;)

16 In the day when God shall judge the secrets of men by Jesus Christ according to my gospel.

Obeying God's Law

17 Behold, thou art called a Jew, and restest in the law, and makest thy boast of God,

18 And knowest *his* will, and approvest the things that are more excellent, being instructed out of the law;

19 And art confident that thou thyself art a guide of the blind, a light of them which are in darkness,

20 An instructor of the foolish, a teacher of babes, which hast the form of knowledge and of the truth in the law.

21 Thou therefore which teachest another, teachest thou not thyself? thou that preachest a man should not steal, dost thou steal?

22 Thou that sayest a man should not commit adultery, dost thou commit adultery? thou that abhorrest idols, dost thou commit sacrilege?

23 Thou that makest thy boast of the law, through breaking the law dishonourest thou God?

24 For the name of God is blasphemed among the Gentiles through you, as it is written.

25 For circumcision verily profiteth, if thou keep the law: but if thou be a breaker of the law, thy circumcision is made uncircumcision.

26 Therefore if the uncircumcision keep the righteousness of the law, shall not his uncircumcision be counted for circumcision?

27 And shall not uncircumcision which is by nature, if it fulfil the law, judge thee, who by the letter and circumcision dost transgress the law?

28 For he is not a Jew, which is one outwardly; neither *is that* circumcision, which is outward in the flesh:

29 But he *is* a Jew, which is one inwardly; and circumcision *is that* of the heart, in the spirit, *and* not in the letter; whose praise *is* not of men, but of God.

16 Eccl. 12:14; Matt. 25:31; John 5:22; 12:48; 1Tim. 1:11; Rev. 20:12

17 Isa. 45:25; 48:2; Mic. 3:11; 2Cor. 11:22

18 Deut. 4:8; Ps. 147:19, 20; Phil. 1:10

19 John 9:34, 40, 41

20 Rom. 6:17; 2Tim. 1:13; 3:5

21 Ps. 50:16-22; Matt. 23:3-6

22 Mal. 3:8

24 2Sam. 12:14; Isa. 52:5; Ezek. 36:20, 23

25 Gal. 5:3

27 Matt. 12:41, 42

28 Matt. 3:9; Rev. 2:9

29 Rom. 7:6; Phil. 3:3; 1Pet. 3:4

2 Deut. 4:7, 8; Ps. 147:19, 20

3 Num. 23:19; Rom. 9:6; 10:16; 11:29

4 Job 40:8; Ps. 51:4; 62:9; 116:11

5 Rom. 6:19; Gal. 3:15

8 Rom. 5:20; 6:1, 15

9 Rom. 1:28—2:4; 3:23

10 Ps. 14:1-3; 53:1

13 Ps. 5:9; 140:3; Jer. 5:16

14 Ps. 10:7

15 Prov. 1:16; Isa. 59:7, 8

18 Ps. 36:1

CHAPTER 3

1 What advantage then hath the Jew? or what profit *is there* of circumcision?

2 Much every way: chiefly, because that unto them were committed the oracles of God.

3 For what if some did not believe? shall their unbelief make the faith of God without effect?

4 God forbid: yea, let God be true, but every man a liar; as it is written, That thou mightest be justified in thy sayings, and mightest overcome when thou art judged.

5 But if our unrighteousness commend the righteousness of God, what shall we say? *Is* God unrighteous who taketh vengeance? I (speak as a man)

6 God forbid: for then how shall God judge the world?

7 For if the truth of God hath more abounded through my lie unto his glory; why yet am I also judged as a sinner?

8 And not *rather,* (as we be slanderously reported, and as some affirm that we say,) Let us do evil, that good may come? whose damnation is just.

"All Have Sinned"

9 What then? are we better *than they*? No, in no wise: for we have before proved both Jews and Gentiles, that they are all under sin;

10 As it is written, There is none righteous, no, not one:

11 There is none that understandeth, there is none that seeketh after God.

12 They are all gone out of the way, they are together become unprofitable; there is none that doeth good, no, not one.

13 Their throat *is* an open sepulchre; with their tongues they have used deceit; the poison of asps *is* under their lips:

14 Whose mouth *is* full of cursing and bitterness:

15 Their feet *are* swift to shed blood:

16 Destruction and misery *are* in their ways:

17 And the way of peace have they not known:

18 There is no fear of God before their eyes.

19 Now we know that what things soever the law saith, it saith to them who are under the law: that every mouth may be

---

2:24 name of God is blasphemed. Paul describes the religious Jews who profess to keep the letter of the law but break it and dishonor God, thus revealing their hypocrisy to the Gentiles, who would consequently blaspheme and ridicule God (see Isa. 52:5 [cf. Ezek. 36:20–21]).

stopped, and all the world may become guilty before God.

20 Therefore by the deeds of the law there shall no flesh be justified in his sight: for by the law *is* the knowledge of sin.

The Only Way of Salvation

21 But now the righteousness of God without the law is manifested, being witnessed by the law and the prophets;

22 Even the righteousness of God *which is* by faith of Jesus Christ unto all and upon all them that believe: for there is no difference:

23 For all have sinned, and come short of the glory of God;

24 Being justified freely by his grace through the redemption that is in Christ Jesus:

25 Whom God hath set forth *to be* a propitiation through faith in his blood, to declare his righteousness for the remission of sins that are past, through the forbearance of God;

26 To declare, *I say,* at this time his righteousness: that he might be just, and the justifier of him which believeth in Jesus.

27 Where *is* boasting then? It is excluded. By what law? of works? Nay: but by the law of faith.

28 Therefore we conclude that a man is justified by faith without the deeds of the law.

29 *Is he* the God of the Jews only? *is he* not also of the Gentiles? Yes, of the Gentiles also:

30 Seeing *it is* one God, which shall justify the circumcision by faith, and uncircumcision through faith.

31 Do we then make void the law through faith? God forbid: yea, we establish the law.

CHAPTER 4

1 What shall we say then that Abraham our father, as pertaining to the flesh, hath found?

2 For if Abraham were justified by works,

he hath *whereof* to glory; but not before God.

3 For what saith the scripture? Abraham believed God, and it was counted unto him for righteousness.

4 Now to him that worketh is the reward not reckoned of grace, but of debt.

5 But to him that worketh not, but believeth on him that justifieth the ungodly, his faith is counted for righteousness.

6 Even as David also describeth the blessedness of the man, unto whom God imputeth righteousness without works,

7 *Saying,* Blessed *are* they whose iniquities are forgiven, and whose sins are covered.

8 Blessed *is* the man to whom the Lord will not impute sin.

9 *Cometh* this blessedness then upon the circumcision *only,* or upon the uncircumcision also? for we say that faith was reckoned to Abraham for righteousness.

10 How was it then reckoned? when he was in circumcision, or in uncircumcision? Not in circumcision, but in uncircumcision.

11 And he received the sign of circumcision, a seal of the righteousness of the faith which *he had yet* being uncircumcised: that he might be the father of all them that believe, though they be not circumcised; that righteousness might be imputed unto them also:

12 And the father of circumcision to them who are not of the circumcision only, but who also walk in the steps of that faith of our father Abraham, which *he had* being *yet* uncircumcised.

God's Promise

13 For the promise, that he should be the heir of the world, *was* not to Abraham, or to his seed, through the law, but through the righteousness of faith.

14 For if they which are of the law *be* heirs, faith is made void, and the promise made of none effect:

Cross references (center column):

20 Ps. 143:2; Eph. 2:8, 9
21 Rom. 1:2, 17; Heb. 11:4-22
22 Rom. 10:12; Gal. 3:28; Col. 3:11
23 Rom. 3:9; 11:32; Gal. 3:22
24 Rom. 4:16; Eph. 1:7; 2:8; Col. 1:14; 1 Pet. 1:18, 19
25 Lev. 16:15; Col. 1:20; Heb. 9:15
27 Rom. 2:17, 23; 4:2; 1 Cor. 1:29, 31; Eph. 2:9
28 Acts 13:38, 39; Rom. 3:20-22; 8:3; Gal. 2:16
30 Rom. 10:12, 13; Gal. 3:8, 20, 28
1 Isa. 51:2; Matt. 3:9; John 8:33, 39
3 Gen. 15:6; Gal. 3:6; James 2:23
4 Rom. 11:6
5 Josh. 24:2
7 Ps. 32:1, 2
11 Gen. 17:10; Luke 19:9
13 Gen. 17:4-9; Gal. 3:29
14 Gal. 3:18

3:21–31 the righteousness of God. This is a term of broad significance. Here it means a righteousness divinely provided, a perfect standing before God for those whose guilt was transferred to Christ on the cross, when He became the satisfying sacrifice, the propitiation for all sin (see 2 Cor. 5:21). The blessing thus secured for the believer is justification, wherein God legally declares that the repenting sinner is righteous before Him. This righteousness comes by faith, not by works of the law; by grace, or the extension of His unmerited favor upon believers; through the redemptive blood of Jesus. Not only did Christ take our sins upon Himself, but He also imputed His perfect righteousness to us (4:3, 22–25).

4:13–14 promise, that he should be heir of the world. No single verse in Genesis is worded exactly in that manner; this is a summary of a number of promises. Genesis 12:3 states, "In thee [Abraham] shall all families of the earth be blessed." Romans 4:13–14 states that Christ, "the son of Abraham" (Matt. 1:1), the "seed," as in Genesis 13:15, was indeed the heir of the world (see also Gal. 3:6–9, 16). Thus through Jesus and His ministry, not only are the Jews to be blessed, but the Gentile families who believe in Him are also encompassed by God's promise to Abraham.

15 Because the law worketh wrath: for where no law is, *there is* no transgression.

16 Therefore *it is* of faith, that *it might be* by grace; to the end the promise might be sure to all the seed; not to that only which is of the law, but to that also which is of the faith of Abraham; who is the father of us all,

17 (As it is written, I have made thee a father of many nations,) before him whom he believed, *even* God, who quickeneth the dead, and calleth those things which be not as though they were.

18 Who against hope believed in hope, that he might become the father of many nations, according to that which was spoken, So shall thy seed be.

19 And being not weak in faith, he considered not his own body now dead, when he was about an hundred years old, neither yet the deadness of Sarah's womb:

20 He staggered not at the promise of God through unbelief; but was strong in faith, giving glory to God;

21 And being fully persuaded that, what he had promised, he was able also to perform.

22 And therefore it was imputed to him for righteousness.

23 Now it was not written for his sake alone, that it was imputed to him;

24 But for us also, to whom it shall be imputed, if we believe on him that raised up Jesus our Lord from the dead;

25 Who was delivered for our offences, and was raised again for our justification.

CHAPTER 5
The Results of Justification

1 Therefore being justified by faith, we have peace with God through our Lord Jesus Christ:

2 By whom also we have access by faith into this grace wherein we stand, and rejoice in hope of the glory of God.

3 And not only *so*, but we glory in tribulations also: knowing that tribulation worketh patience;

4 And patience, experience; and experience, hope:

5 And hope maketh not ashamed; because the love of God is shed abroad in our hearts by the Holy Ghost which is given unto us.

6 For when we were yet without strength, in due time Christ died for the ungodly.

7 For scarcely for a righteous man will one die: yet peradventure for a good man some would even dare to die.

8 But God commendeth his love toward us, in that, while we were yet sinners, Christ died for us.

9 Much more then, being now justified by his blood, we shall be saved from wrath through him.

10 For if, when we were enemies, we were reconciled to God by the death of his Son, much more, being reconciled, we shall be saved by his life.

11 And not only *so*, but we also joy in God through our Lord Jesus Christ, by whom we have now received the atonement.

Christ and Adam Contrasted

12 Wherefore, as by one man sin entered into the world, and death by sin; and so death passed upon all men, for that all have sinned:

13 (For until the law sin was in the world: but sin is not imputed when there is no law.

14 Nevertheless death reigned from Adam to Moses, even over them that had not sinned after the similitude of Adam's

15 1Cor. 15:56; 2Cor. 3:7, 9
16 Isa. 51:2; Gal. 3:22
17 Gen. 17:5; 1Pet. 2:10
18 Gen. 15:5
19 Heb. 11:11, 12
21 Ps. 115:3
23 Rom. 15:4
24 Acts 2:24; 13:30
25 Isa. 53:5, 6; Gal. 1:4; Heb. 9:28
1 John 16:33; Eph. 2:14; Col. 1:20
2 John 10:9; 14:6; Eph. 2:18; 3:12
3 Matt. 5:11, 12; Acts 5:41; James 1:2, 3, 12
5 Gal. 4:6; Phil. 1:20
8 1Pet. 3:18; 1John 3:16; 4:9, 10
9 Eph. 2:13; 1Thess. 1:10
11 Gal. 4:9
12 Gen. 2:17; 3:6; Rom. 6:23
13 1John 3:4

4:17 a father of many nations. This is a reference not only to lineal, physical descendants who fathered nations, but through Christ the "seed," those who are saved in this Church Age share in the fulfillment of this prophecy (see Gen. 15:5; 17:5; 21:12). Believers, or the Church, do not replace Israel either in their history or their destiny. It is through Jesus, the "seed," that blessings accrue to New Testament believers, who are separate and distinct from racial or national Israel both throughout this age and in the glorious Millennium to come.

5:9–11 saved from wrath through him. After demonstrating the need for salvation in the light of universal condemnation (1:18–20) and then explaining the doctrine of justification (3—4), Paul touches on the reconciliation provided by our great salvation. Because of justification by the shed blood of Christ, who reconciled us to God by

His death, Christians shall be saved from all God's wrath against sin. Of course, this means that Christians will be delivered from the coming Tribulation period, when the "day of wrath" prophecies are fulfilled (Rom. 2:5; Rev. 6:16–17; 11:18; 14:10, 19; 15:1, 7; 16:1, 19; 19:15). At the Rapture, prior to the final seven years or final "week" of Daniel's prophecy (Dan. 9:27; 12:1), living believers will join the resurrected New Testament saints with Christ, escaping these things which shall come to pass (Luke 21:36).

5:14–19 Paul contrasts the disobedience of one man, Adam, and the consequent reign of death over the human race, with the obedience of one man, Jesus Christ, and the resulting justification of believers and the reign of grace through righteousness unto eternal life.

transgression, who is the figure of him that was to come.

15 But not as the offence, so also *is* the free gift. For if through the offence of one many be dead, much more the grace of God, and the gift by grace, *which is* by one man, Jesus Christ, hath abounded unto many.

16 And not as *it was* by one that sinned, *so is* the gift: for the judgment *was* by one to condemnation, but the free gift *is* of many offences unto justification.

17 For if by one man's offence death reigned by one; much more they which receive abundance of grace and of the gift of righteousness shall reign in life by one, Jesus Christ.)

18 Therefore as by the offence of one *judgment came* upon all men to condemnation; even so by the righteousness of one *the free gift came* upon all men unto justification of life.

19 For as by one man's disobedience many were made sinners, so by the obedience of one shall many be made righteous.

20 Moreover the law entered, that the offence might abound. But where sin abounded, grace did much more abound:

21 That as sin hath reigned unto death, even so might grace reign through righteousness unto eternal life by Jesus Christ our Lord.

CHAPTER 6
Dead to Sin

1 What shall we say then? Shall we continue in sin, that grace may abound?

2 God forbid. How shall we, that are dead to sin, live any longer therein?

3 Know ye not, that so many of us as were baptized into Jesus Christ were baptized into his death?

4 Therefore we are buried with him by baptism into death: that like as Christ was raised up from the dead by the glory of the Father, even so we also should walk in newness of life.

5 For if we have been planted together in

---

15 Isa. 53:11; Matt. 20:28; 26:28

18 John 12:32; Heb. 2:9

20 Rom. 3:20; 4:15; 7:8; Gal. 3:19, 23

1 Rom. 3:8; 6:11, 15; 7:4; Gal. 2:19; 6:14; Col. 3:3; 1Pet. 2:24

3 1Cor. 15:29; Gal. 3:27

4 John 2:11; 11:40; 1Cor. 6:14; 2Cor. 13:14; Eph. 4:22-24

5 Phil. 3:10, 11

6 Gal. 2:20; 5:24; 6:14; Eph. 4:22

7 1Pet. 4:1

8 2Tim. 2:11

9 Rev. 1:18

10 Luke 20:38; Heb. 9:27, 28

11 Rom. 6:2; Gal. 2:19

12 Ps. 19:13; 119:133

13 Col. 3:5; James 4:1

14 Rom. 7:4, 6; 8:2; Gal. 5:18

15 1Cor. 9:21

16 Matt. 6:24; John 8:34; 2Pet. 2:19

17 2Tim. 1:13

18 John 8:32; 1Cor. 7:22; Gal. 5:1; 1Pet. 2:16

---

the likeness of his death, we shall be also *in the likeness* of *his* resurrection:

6 Knowing this, that our old man is crucified with *him,* that the body of sin might be destroyed, that henceforth we should not serve sin.

7 For he that is dead is freed from sin.

8 Now if we be dead with Christ, we believe that we shall also live with him:

9 Knowing that Christ being raised from the dead dieth no more; death hath no more dominion over him.

10 For in that he died, he died unto sin once: but in that he liveth, he liveth unto God.

11 Likewise reckon ye also yourselves to be dead indeed unto sin, but alive unto God through Jesus Christ our Lord.

12 Let not sin therefore reign in your mortal body, that ye should obey it in the lusts thereof.

13 Neither yield ye your members *as* instruments of unrighteousness unto sin: but yield yourselves unto God, as those that are alive from the dead, and your members *as* instruments of righteousness unto God.

14 For sin shall not have dominion over you: for ye are not under the law, but under grace.

Servants to God

15 What then? shall we sin, because we are not under the law, but under grace? God forbid.

16 Know ye not, that to whom ye yield yourselves servants to obey, his servants ye are to whom ye obey; whether of sin unto death, or of obedience unto righteousness?

17 But God be thanked, that ye were the servants of sin, but ye have obeyed from the heart that form of doctrine which was delivered you.

18 Being then made free from sin, ye became the servants of righteousness.

19 I speak after the manner of men because of the infirmity of your flesh: for as ye have yielded your members servants to uncleanness and to iniquity unto iniquity; even so

---

6:8 we believe that we shall also live with him. Since Christ died for us, we as Christians are identified with Him in death (6:2–7). Spiritually, we have been raised with Him (see Eph. 2:5–6; Col. 3:1–4), identified with Him in newness of life. This present spiritual resurrection will result in the future physical resurrection, when at the Rapture (1 Cor. 15:51–55), we begin a new phase of our eternal life in glorified bodies, like that of Jesus (1 John 3:2–3). In this newly resurrected state, we are caught up to "meet the Lord in the air" (1 Thess. 4:16–17) where He takes us to His "Father's house" (John 14:1–3). We will stay there during the Tribulation on earth and experience the judgment seat of Christ (1 Cor. 3:9–15) and the marriage of the Lamb (Rev. 19:3–9). Then we will join with Christ for His glorious appearing (Rev. 19:11–21) and Millennial Kingdom (Rev. 20).

now yield your members servants to right-eousness unto holiness.

20 For when ye were the servants of sin, ye were free from righteousness.

21 What fruit had ye then in those things whereof ye are now ashamed? for the end of those things *is* death.

22 But now being made free from sin, and become servants to God, ye have your fruit unto holiness, and the end everlasting life.

23 For the wages of sin *is* death; but the gift of God *is* eternal life through Jesus Christ our Lord.

CHAPTER 7
Released from the Law

1 Know ye not, brethren, (for I speak to them that know the law,) how that the law hath dominion over a man as long as he liveth?

2 For the woman which hath an husband is bound by the law to *her* husband so long as he liveth; but if the husband be dead, she is loosed from the law of *her* husband.

3 So then if, while *her* husband liveth, she be married to another man, she shall be called an adulteress: but if her husband be dead, she is free from that law; so that she is no adulteress, though she be married to another man.

4 Wherefore, my brethren, ye also are become dead to the law by the body of Christ; that ye should be married to another, *even* to him who is raised from the dead, that we should bring forth fruit unto God.

5 For when we were in the flesh, the motions of sins, which were by the law, did work in our members to bring forth fruit unto death.

6 But now we are delivered from the law, that being dead wherein we were held; that we should serve in newness of spirit, and not *in* the oldness of the letter.

7 What shall we say then? *Is* the law sin? God forbid. Nay, I had not known sin, but by the law: for I had not known lust, except the law had said, Thou shalt not covet.

8 But sin, taking occasion by the commandment, wrought in me all manner of concupiscence. For without the law sin *was* dead.

9 For I was alive without the law once: but when the commandment came, sin revived, and I died.

10 And the commandment, which *was ordained* to life, I found *to be* unto death.

11 For sin, taking occasion by the commandment, deceived me, and by it slew *me*.

12 Wherefore the law *is* holy, and the commandment holy, and just, and good.

13 Was then that which is good made death unto me? God forbid. But sin, that it might appear sin, working death in me by that which is good; that sin by the commandment might become exceeding sinful.

The Sin Nature Still Remains

14 For we know that the law is spiritual: but I am carnal, sold under sin.

15 For that which I do I allow not: for what I would, that do I not; but what I hate, that do I.

16 If then I do that which I would not, I consent unto the law that *it is* good.

17 Now then it is no more I that do it, but sin that dwelleth in me.

18 For I know that in me (that is, in my flesh,) dwelleth no good thing: for to will is present with me; but *how* to perform that which is good I find not.

19 For the good that I would I do not: but the evil which I would not, that I do.

20 Now if I do that I would not, it is no more I that do it, but sin that dwelleth in me.

21 I find then a law, that, when I would do good, evil is present with me.

22 For I delight in the law of God after the inward man:

23 But I see another law in my members, warring against the law of my mind, and bringing me into captivity to the law of sin which is in my members.

20 John 8:34
21 Rom. 1:32; 7:5
22 John 8:32
23 Gen. 2:17; Rom. 2:7; 5:12, 17, 21; James 1:15; 1Pet. 1:4
2 1Cor. 7:39
3 Matt. 5:32
4 Rom. 8:2; Gal. 2:19; 5:18, 22; Eph. 2:15; Col. 2:14
5 Rom. 6:13, 21; Gal. 5:19; James 1:15
6 Rom. 2:29; 6:2; 7:4; 2Cor. 3:6
7 Ex. 20:17; Deut. 5:21; Acts 20:33; Rom. 3:20; 13:9
8 Rom. 4:15; 5:20; 1Cor. 15:56
10 Lev. 18:5; Ezek. 20:11, 13, 21; 2Cor. 3:7
12 Ps. 19:8; 119:38, 137; 1Tim. 1:8
13 1Kgs. 21:20, 25; 2Kgs. 17:17
15 Ps. 1:6; Gal. 5:17
17 Gen. 6:5; 8:21
22 Ps. 1:2; 2Cor. 4:16; Eph. 3:16; Col. 3:9, 10
23 Rom. 6:13, 19; Gal. 5:17

7:1–6 Paul shows the fact that New Testament believers have a different understanding of the Law because of faith in Christ. Law binds the living, not the dead, as exemplified in marriage, which binds in life, but is dissolved at death. This illustrates the truth that New Testament believers have died with Christ, are dead to sin (6:2), and are therefore free from the law that dealt with transgressions that produced death. Believers are not under Law, but are joined now to Christ, whose resurrec-tion power makes it possible to serve God in newness of spirit, rather than in the oldness of simply following the letter of the Law.

7:15–25 This passage describes the inner conflict between the old nature, carnal and fleshly and inherited from Adam, and the new spiritual nature received through the new birth (Gal. 2:20; 5:16–24; Col. 1:27; 2 Pet. 1:4).

24 O wretched man that I am! who shall deliver me from the body of this death?

25 I thank God through Jesus Christ our Lord. So then with the mind I myself serve the law of God; but with the flesh the law of sin.

CHAPTER 8
No Condemnation Now

1 *There is* therefore now no condemnation to them which are in Christ Jesus, who walk not after the flesh, but after the Spirit.

2 For the law of the Spirit of life in Christ Jesus hath made me free from the law of sin and death.

3 For what the law could not do, in that it was weak through the flesh, God sending his own Son in the likeness of sinful flesh, and for sin, condemned sin in the flesh:

4 That the righteousness of the law might be fulfilled in us, who walk not after the flesh, but after the Spirit.

5 For they that are after the flesh do mind the things of the flesh; but they that are after the Spirit the things of the Spirit.

6 For to be carnally minded *is* death; but to be spiritually minded *is* life and peace.

7 Because the carnal mind *is* enmity against God: for it is not subject to the law of God, neither indeed can be.

8 So then they that are in the flesh cannot please God.

9 But ye are not in the flesh, but in the Spirit, if so be that the Spirit of God dwell in you. Now if any man have not the Spirit of Christ, he is none of his.

10 And if Christ *be* in you, the body *is* dead because of sin; but the Spirit *is* life because of righteousness.

11 But if the Spirit of him that raised up Jesus from the dead dwell in you, he that raised up Christ from the dead shall also quicken your mortal bodies by his Spirit that dwelleth in you.

12 Therefore, brethren, we are debtors, not to the flesh, to live after the flesh.

13 For if ye live after the flesh, ye shall die: but if ye through the Spirit do mortify the deeds of the body, ye shall live.

14 For as many as are led by the Spirit of God, they are the sons of God.

15 For ye have not received the spirit of bondage again to fear; but ye have received the Spirit of adoption, whereby we cry, Abba, Father.

16 The Spirit itself beareth witness with our spirit, that we are the children of God:

17 And if children, then heirs; heirs of God, and joint-heirs with Christ; if so be that we suffer with *him,* that we may be also glorified together.

The Revelation of God's Glory through Believers

18 For I reckon that the sufferings of this present time *are* not worthy *to* be *compared* with the glory which shall be revealed in us.

19 For the earnest expectation of the creature waiteth for the manifestation of the sons of God.

20 For the creature was made subject to vanity, not willingly, but by reason of him who hath subjected *the same* in hope,

21 Because the creature itself also shall be delivered from the bondage of corruption into the glorious liberty of the children of God.

22 For we know that the whole creation groaneth and travaileth in pain together until now.

23 And not only *they,* but ourselves also, which have the firstfruits of the Spirit, even we ourselves groan within ourselves, waiting for the adoption, *to wit,* the redemption of our body.

24 For we are saved by hope: but hope that is seen is not hope: for what a man seeth, why doth he yet hope for?

Cross references:

25 1Cor. 15:57

1 Rom. 8:4; Gal. 5:16, 25

2 John 8:36; 1Cor. 15:45; Gal. 2:19; 5:1

3 Rom. 3:20; Heb. 7:18, 19

5 John 3:6; Gal. 5:22, 25

7 1Cor. 2:14; James 4:4

9 John 3:34; 1Cor. 3:16; 6:19

11 Acts 2:24; Rom. 6:4, 5; Eph. 2:5

12 Rom. 6:7, 14

13 Rom. 8:6; Gal. 6:8; Eph. 4:22; Col. 3:5

14 Gal. 5:18

15 Isa. 56:5; 1Cor. 2:12; Gal. 4:5, 6; Heb. 2:15

16 Eph. 1:13

17 Acts 14:22; 26:18

18 2Cor. 4:17; 1Pet. 1:6, 7; 4:13

19 2Pet. 3:13; 1John 3:2

20 Gen. 3:19; Rom. 8:22

22 Jer. 12:11; Mark 16:15; Col. 1:23

23 Luke 20:36; 21:28

24 2Cor. 5:7; Heb. 11:1

8:17 heirs of God. All believers are the children of God our Father (Gal. 3:23; Eph. 1:11; Col. 1:12; 3:24; 1 Pet. 1:4), and all sons and daughters of God are heirs of God through Christ (Gal. 4:7). We inherit eternal salvation (Titus 3:7), God Himself (Rev. 21:3), and all things with Christ (1 Cor. 3:21–23). Our inheritance is based on both the new birth, which makes us children of God, and the adoption of grace (v. 15; Gal. 4:4–6). Under Roman law an adoption ceremony officially and openly designated a person as a full heir. Hence, all children, even adopted ones, shared an inheritance, though Hebrew law gave the firstborn a double portion.

8:21 the creature itself also shall be delivered. The universe is affected by sin in both the spiritual and material realms, but the ultimate deliverance will occur after the Millennium and the last judgment (Rev. 20), when God makes all things new (Rev. 21:5—22:5).

8:23 waiting for the adoption . . . the redemption of our body. We are already adopted children, but the outward manifestation corresponding to this relationship is not yet complete. Full glorification awaits the coming of Christ.

25 But if we hope for that we see not, *then* do we with patience wait for *it*.

26 Likewise the Spirit also helpeth our infirmities: for we know not what we should pray for as we ought: but the Spirit itself maketh intercession for us with groanings which cannot be uttered.

27 And he that searcheth the hearts knoweth what *is* the mind of the Spirit, because he maketh intercession for the saints according to *the will of* God.

28 And we know that all things work together for good to them that love God, to them who are the called according to *his* purpose.

29 For whom he did foreknow, he also did predestinate *to be* conformed to the image of his Son, that he might be the firstborn among many brethren.

30 Moreover whom he did predestinate, them he also called: and whom he called, them he also justified: and whom he justified, them he also glorified.

Nothing Separates the Believer from God's Love

31 What shall we then say to these things? If God *be* for us, who *can be* against us?

32 He that spared not his own Son, but delivered him up for us all, how shall he not with him also freely give us all things?

33 Who shall lay any thing to the charge of God's elect? *It is* God that justifieth.

34 Who *is* he that condemneth? *It is* Christ that died, yea rather, that is risen again, who is even at the right hand of God, who also maketh intercession for us.

35 Who shall separate us from the love of Christ? *shall* tribulation, or distress, or persecution, or famine, or nakedness, or peril, or sword?

36 As it is written, For thy sake we are

26 Zech. 12:10; Eph. 6:18; James 4:3
27 1Chr. 28:9; Ps. 7:9; Prov. 17:3; Rev. 2:23
28 Rom. 9:11, 23, 24; 2Tim. 1:9
29 Ex. 33:12, 17; Ps. 1:5; Jer. 1:5; Eph. 1:5, 11; 1Pet. 1:2
30 Rom. 1:6; Heb. 9:15; 1Pet. 2:9
31 Num. 14:9; Ps. 118:6
33 Isa. 50:8, 9; Rev. 12:10, 11
34 Mark 16:19; Heb. 1:3; 7:25
36 Ps. 44:22
37 1Cor. 15:57; Rev. 12:11
3 Ex. 32:32
4 Ex. 4:22; Deut. 7:6 Heb. 8:8-10; 9:1
5 Deut. 10:15; Jer. 23:6
6 Num. 23:19; John 8:39
7 Gen. 21:12; Gal. 4:23; Heb. 11:18
9 Gen. 18:10, 14
10 Gen. 25:21

killed all the day long; we are accounted as sheep for the slaughter.

37 Nay, in all these things we are more than conquerors through him that loved us.

38 For I am persuaded, that neither death, nor life, nor angels, nor principalities, nor powers, nor things present, nor things to come,

39 Nor height, nor depth, nor any other creature, shall be able to separate us from the love of God, which is in Christ Jesus our Lord.

CHAPTER 9
God's Mercy on His Children

1 I say the truth in Christ, I lie not, my conscience also bearing me witness in the Holy Ghost,

2 That I have great heaviness and continual sorrow in my heart.

3 For I could wish that myself were accursed from Christ for my brethren, my kinsmen according to the flesh:

4 Who are Israelites; to whom *pertaineth* the adoption, and the glory, and the covenants, and the giving of the law, and the service *of God*, and the promises;

5 Whose *are* the fathers, and of whom as concerning the flesh Christ *came*, who is over all, God blessed for ever. Amen.

6 Not as though the word of God hath taken none effect. For they *are* not all Israel, which are of Israel:

7 Neither, because they are the seed of Abraham, *are they* all children: but, In Isaac shall thy seed be called.

8 That is, They which are the children of the flesh, these *are* not the children of God: but the children of the promise are counted for the seed.

9 For this *is* the word of promise, At this time will I come, and Sara shall have a son.

10 And not only *this*; but when Rebecca also

8:25 with patience wait for it. The idea is that of steadfastness, composure and patience. The believer's hope furnishes a strong motive for patient endurance of the sufferings of this present time.

8:30 glorified. So certain is this destiny that Paul writes of it in the past tense, as if it were already accomplished.

9:1—11:36 This portion of the book sets forth God's past dealings with Israel (chap. 9), God's present dealings with Israel during the Church Age (chap. 10), and God's future dealings in fulfilling prophetic promises (chap. 11). Thus Paul recounts Israel's past, emphasizing God selecting the descendants of Abraham, Isaac, and

Jacob to become His chosen people; Israel's rejection of the Messiah Savior, whereby the gospel is spread to the whole world; and Messiah's millennial reign, during which all living Israelites will be saved and worship the King (see also Zech. 14:9, 16–17).

9:3 accursed from Christ. Paul's profound love for his people caused him to contemplate the impossible, that he was willing to become accursed (Gr. *anathema*), which means he was willing to give himself over to divine condemnation, if by so doing he might bring his people to Jesus. Compare Moses (Ex. 32:31–34). This is the ultimate example of a passion for the lost souls of the world.

had conceived by one, *even* by our father Isaac;

11 (For *the children* being not yet born, neither having done any good or evil, that the purpose of God according to election might stand, not of works, but of him that calleth;)

12 It was said unto her, The elder shall serve the younger.

13 As it is written, Jacob have I loved, but Esau have I hated.

14 What shall we say then? *Is there* unrighteousness with God? God forbid.

15 For he saith to Moses, I will have mercy on whom I will have mercy, and I will have compassion on whom I will have compassion.

16 So then *it is* not of him that willeth, nor of him that runneth, but of God that sheweth mercy.

17 For the scripture saith unto Pharaoh, Even for this same purpose have I raised thee up, that I might shew my power in thee, and that my name might be declared throughout all the earth.

18 Therefore hath he mercy on whom he will *have mercy,* and whom he will he hardeneth.

19 Thou wilt say then unto me, Why doth he yet find fault? For who hath resisted his will?

20 Nay but, O man, who art thou that repliest against God? Shall the thing formed say to him that formed *it,* Why hast thou made me thus?

21 Hath not the potter power over the clay, of the same lump to make one vessel unto honour, and another unto dishonour?

22 *What* if God, willing to shew *his* wrath, and to make his power known, endured with much longsuffering the vessels of wrath fitted to destruction:

23 And that he might make known the riches of his glory on the vessels of mercy, which he had afore prepared unto glory,

24 Even us, whom he hath called, not of the Jews only, but also of the Gentiles?

25 As he saith also in Osee, I will call them my people, which were not my people; and her beloved, which was not beloved.

26 And it shall come to pass, *that* in the place where it was said unto them, Ye *are* not my people; there shall they be called the children of the living God.

27 Esaias also crieth concerning Israel, Though the number of the children of Israel be as the sand of the sea, a remnant shall be saved:

28 For he will finish the work, and cut *it* short in righteousness: because a short work will the Lord make upon the earth.

29 And as Esaias said before, Except the Lord of Sabaoth had left us a seed, we had been as Sodoma, and been made like unto Gomorrha.

The Gentiles Are Called

30 What shall we say then? That the Gentiles, which followed not after righteousness, have attained to righteousness, even the righteousness which is of faith.

31 But Israel, which followed after the law of righteousness, hath not attained to the law of righteousness.

32 Wherefore? Because *they sought it* not by faith, but as it were by the works of the law. For they stumbled at that stumblingstone;

33 As it is written, Behold, I lay in Sion a stumblingstone and rock of offence: and whosoever believeth on him shall not be ashamed.

CHAPTER 10

1 Brethren, my heart's desire and prayer to God for Israel is, that they might be saved.

2 For I bear them record that they have a zeal of God, but not according to knowledge.

3 For they being ignorant of God's righteousness, and going about to establish their own righteousness, have not submitted themselves unto the righteousness of God.

Cross References

11 Rom. 4:17; 8:28
12 Gen. 25:23
13 Mal. 1:2, 3
14 Deut. 32:4; Job 8:3; 34:10; Ps. 92:15
15 Ex. 33:19
17 Ex. 9:16; Gal. 3:8, 22
19 2Chr. 20:6; Job 9:12; 23:13; Dan. 4:35
20 Job 33:13
21 Prov. 16:4; Jer. 18:6; 2Tim. 2:20
22 1Thess. 5:9; 1Pet. 2:8; Jude 1:4
23 Rom. 2:4; 8:28-30; Eph. 1:7; Col. 1:27
24 Rom. 3:29
25 Hos. 2:23
26 Hos. 1:10
27 Isa. 10:22, 23; Rom. 11:5
28 Isa. 28:22
29 Isa. 1:9; 13:19
30 Rom. 1:17; 4:11; 10:20
31 Rom. 10:2; 11:7; Gal. 5:4
32 Luke 2:34; 1Cor. 1:23
33 Ps. 118:22; Isa. 8:14; 28:16; Matt. 21:42
2 Rom. 9:31
3 Phil. 3:9

9:27 a remnant shall be saved. Although Isaiah 10:22, the Old Testament reference cited, refers to the remnant of Israel returning from exile (Hag. 1:12), Paul applies the verse to believing, redeemed Jews of the future.

9:30–31 Gentiles . . . Israel. This is not a replacement of Israel by the predominantly Gentile Church, but rather the formation of a new body of believers consisting of Jews and Gentiles, a mystery foreseen and planned by God from the foundation of the world (Eph. 3:3–11). No specific promises to Israel have ever been abrogated, but must and will be fulfilled during the Millennial Kingdom.

10:1 prayer to God for Israel. The apostle's expression of affection here is very strong, as he points out again that attempting to establish one's own righteousness, as did the Jew, meant the Jew had not submitted to the righteousness of God, which came only through Jesus.

4 For Christ *is* the end of the law for righteousness to every one that believeth.

The Method of Justification

5 For Moses describeth the righteousness which is of the law, That the man which doeth those things shall live by them.
6 But the righteousness which is of faith speaketh on this wise, Say not in thine heart, Who shall ascend into heaven? (that is, to bring Christ down *from above:*)
7 Or, Who shall descend into the deep? (that is, to bring up Christ again from the dead.)
8 But what saith it? The word is nigh thee, *even* in thy mouth, and in thy heart: that is, the word of faith, which we preach;
9 That if thou shalt confess with thy mouth the Lord Jesus, and shalt believe in thine heart that God hath raised him from the dead, thou shalt be saved.
10 For with the heart man believeth unto righteousness; and with the mouth confession is made unto salvation.
11 For the scripture saith, Whosoever believeth on him shall not be ashamed.
12 For there is no difference between the Jew and the Greek: for the same Lord over all is rich unto all that call upon him.
13 For whosoever shall call upon the name of the Lord shall be saved.
14 How then shall they call on him in whom they have not believed? and how shall they believe in him of whom they have not heard? and how shall they hear without a preacher?
15 And how shall they preach, except they be sent? as it is written, How beautiful are the feet of them that preach the gospel of peace, and bring glad tidings of good things!
16 But they have not all obeyed the gospel. For Esaias saith, Lord, who hath believed our report?
17 So then faith *cometh* by hearing, and hearing by the word of God.
18 But I say, Have they not heard? Yes verily, their sound went into all the earth, and their words unto the ends of the world.
19 But I say, Did not Israel know? First

Cross references

4 Matt. 5:17; Gal. 3:24
5 Lev. 18:5; Gal. 3:12
6 Deut. 30:12, 13
9 Acts 8:37
11 Isa. 28:16; 49:23; Jer. 17:7
12 Rom. 3:22, 29; Gal. 3:28
13 Joel 2:32; Acts 2:21; 9:14
14 Titus 1:3
15 Isa. 52:7; Nah. 1:15
16 Isa. 53:1; John 12:38; Rom. 3:3; Heb. 4:2
18 Matt. 4:8; 24:14; 28:19
19 Deut. 32:21

The History and Future of Israel

The Book of Romans	Old Testament	New Testament
Chosen by God to be His people (9:9–16)	Deut. 9:4–6; 10:15	2 Tim. 1:9
Blessed by God throughout their history (9:3–5)	Deut. 4:32–34; 1 Chr. 17:20–22; Isa. 5:1–4; Hos. 11:1	Luke 1:54–55; Acts 13:26; Heb. 8:6–10
Disobedient to God and His Law (10:21)	Neh. 9:26–30; Isa. 65:2–5	Matt. 23:34–37; Acts 7:51–60
Rejected Jesus their Messiah (9:31–32)	Ps. 118:22; Isa. 8:14–15; 28:16	Luke 2:34; 1 Pet. 2:6–8
Righteous only by faith in Christ (4:13–25; 10:11–13)	Isa. 53:5–6, 10–12; Jer. 23:5–6	Acts 5:30–31; 1 Cor. 15:3–4
Gentiles blessed by Israel's rejection (9:30; 10:20; 11:11)	Isa. 55:4–5; Hos. 2:23	Eph. 2:12; 1 Pet. 2:10
Remnant still enjoys His blessing (9:27; 11:5–8)	Isa. 10:20–23	2 Cor. 3:13–14
Restored by God in the future (11:25)	Isa. 66:12; Jer. 31:33; Zech. 14:9–21	Luke 21:24; 2 Cor. 3:14–16

By Warren Baker

10:4 Christ is the end of the law. Faith in Christ as Savior eliminates attempts to gain salvation by personal merit, endeavoring to be righteous by keeping the Law. Only Christ met all the requirements of the holy Law. He died under its penalty, though innocent; He has risen and is Himself the righteousness which all need (1 Cor. 1:30).

10:13 call upon the name of the Lord. This citation from Joel 2:32 speaks of divine deliverance for Israel's godly saved remnant during the future Tribulation. Paul applies it to motivate a response to the gospel in this present age, as did Peter (Acts 2:21).

10:16 who hath believed our report? Citing Isaiah 53:1, Paul identifies the suffering Servant of that prophecy (Jesus and His gospel) as being rejected by Israel.

10:19 provoke you to jealousy. Quoted from Deuteronomy 32:21, this prophecy foresees Israel's rejection of the Messiah and the Jew's resentment of those who believe in Jesus.

Israel and the Church

By Arnold G. Fruchtenbaum

There is no biblical evidence that the Church began either with Adam or Abraham, or that it existed in the Old Testament or during the earthly life of Christ (Matt. 16:18). The first evidence that the Church is distinct from Israel is the fact that the Church was born at Pentecost. This is based on the relationship of Spirit-baptism to the Church. According to Colossians 1:18, the Church is the body of Christ. First Corinthians 12:13 teaches that entrance into this body is by Spirit-baptism. But Acts 11:15–16 teaches that Spirit-baptism was not instituted until the Holy Spirit came upon the Jewish believers in Acts 2:1–4.

The second evidence of distinction between the Church and Israel is that three specific events in the life of the Messiah were prerequisites to the establishment of the Church, and so the Church could not have come into being until these events had taken place:

1) His death by which the atonement was provided. (Matt. 16:18–21).

2) The resurrection of Jesus (see Eph. 1:20–23).

3) The ascension of Jesus (Eph. 4:7–11). The Holy Spirit was not provided until after Christ's ascension.

The third evidence that shows distinction between the Church and Israel is the "mystery" characteristics of the Church. In biblical terminology, the word "mystery" is often used to describe a New Testament truth not revealed in the Old Testament (Eph. 3:3–5, 9; Col. 1:26–27). Four features of the Church exist that were never revealed in the Old Testament: **1)** the concept of Jewish and Gentile believers united into one body (Eph. 3:1–12); **2)** the doctrine of Messiah indwelling every believer (Col. 1:24–27; 2:10–19; 3:4, 11); **3)** the Church as the bride of Messiah (Eph. 5:22–32); and **4)** the Rapture, with its corollary events of the resurrection of the "dead in Christ" and the transition into heaven of the living believers (1 Cor. 15:50–58).

> *Jesus' death, resurrection, and ascension were prerequisites to the establishment of the Church.*

The fourth evidence that the Church is distinct from Israel is the concept of the "one new man" in Ephesians 2:15. This "one new man" is distinguished from both Israel and the Gentiles and is comprised of believing members from both, identified as the Church in Ephesians 2:16 ("the body") and Ephesians 3:6 ("same body").

The fifth evidence is that the same three groups are distinguished from each other in 1 Corinthians 10:32: "Give none offence, neither to the Jews, nor to the Gentiles, nor to the church of God." This verse is a contrast made well after the Church had been established.

The sixth evidence is the fact that the term "Israel" is never used of the Church. In the New Testament it is either used of Jews in general or Jewish believers in particular. Galatians 6:16 speaks about the subject of Jewish believers. "Judaizers," or Jews who demanded adherence to the Law of Moses, were deceiving Gentiles to obtain salvation through the Law. To them, a Gentile had to convert to Judaism before he qualified for salvation through Christ. In verse 15, Paul states that the important thing for salvation is faith, resulting in the "new man." He also mentions two elements of the Church: circumcision and uncircumcision. These two elements refer to two groups of people: believing Jews and believing Gentiles. These two entities of the Church are also identified by these very same terms in Galatians 2:7–9.

Moses saith, I will provoke you to jealousy by *them that are* no people, *and* by a foolish nation I will anger you.

20 But Esaias is very bold, and saith, I was found of them that sought me not; I was made manifest unto them that asked not after me.

21 But to Israel he saith, All day long I have stretched forth my hands unto a disobedient and gainsaying people.

CHAPTER 11
God's Chosen People

1 I say then, Hath God cast away his people? God forbid. For I also am an Israelite, of the seed of Abraham, *of* the tribe of Benjamin.

2 God hath not cast away his people which he foreknew. Wot ye not what the scripture saith of Elias? how he maketh intercession to God against Israel, saying,

3 Lord, they have killed thy prophets, and digged down thine altars; and I am left alone, and they seek my life.

4 But what saith the answer of God unto him? I have reserved to myself seven thousand men, who have not bowed the knee to *the image of* Baal.

5 Even so then at this present time also there is a remnant according to the election of grace.

6 And if by grace, then *is it* no more of works: otherwise grace is no more grace. But if *it be* of works, then is it no more grace: otherwise work is no more work.

7 What then? Israel hath not obtained that which he seeketh for; but the election hath obtained it, and the rest were blinded.

8 (According as it is written, God hath given them the spirit of slumber, eyes that

Cross references

20 Isa. 65:1; Rom. 9:30
21 Isa. 65:2
1 1Sam. 12:22; Jer. 31:37; 2Cor. 11:22; Phil. 3:5
2 Rom. 8:29
3 1Kgs. 19:10, 14
4 1Kgs. 19:18
5 Rom. 9:27
6 Deut. 9:4, 5; Rom. 4:4, 5; Gal. 5:4
7 Rom. 9:31; 10:3; 2Cor. 3:14
8 Deut. 29:4; Isa. 6:9; 29:10; Jer. 5:21; Ezek. 12:2
9 Ps. 69:22
10 Ps. 69:23
11 Acts 13:46; 18:6; 22:18, 21; 28:24, 28; Rom. 10:19
13 Acts 9:15; 13:2; 22:21; 1Tim. 2:7; 2Tim. 1:11
16 Lev. 23:10; Num. 15:18-21
17 Jer. 11:16; Acts 2:39; Eph. 2:12, 13
18 1Cor. 10:12

they should not see, and ears that they should not hear;) unto this day.

9 And David saith, Let their table be made a snare, and a trap, and a stumbling block, and a recompence unto them:

10 Let their eyes be darkened, that they may not see, and bow down their back alway.

11 I say then, Have they stumbled that they should fall? God forbid: but *rather* through their fall salvation *is come* unto the Gentiles, for to provoke them to jealousy.

12 Now if the fall of them *be* the riches of the world, and the diminishing of them the riches of the Gentiles; how much more their fulness?

Israel and the Gentiles

13 For I speak to you Gentiles, inasmuch as I am the apostle of the Gentiles, I magnify mine office:

14 If by any means I may provoke to emulation *them which are* my flesh, and might save some of them.

15 For if the casting away of them *be* the reconciling of the world, what *shall* the receiving *of them be,* but life from the dead?

16 For if the firstfruit *be* holy, the lump *is* also *holy*: and if the root *be* holy, so *are* the branches.

17 And if some of the branches be broken off, and thou, being a wild olive tree, wert graffed in among them, and with them partakest of the root and fatness of the olive tree;

18 Boast not against the branches. But if thou boast, thou bearest not the root, but the root thee.

19 Thou wilt say then, The branches were broken off, that I might be graffed in.

20 Well; because of unbelief they were

10:21 stretched forth my hands. Paul cites Isaiah 65:2, showing that God still reaches out to Israel with His truth, as He did in the past and does now during this Church Age. A remnant does respond (11:5).

11:1 cast away his people. In spite of Israel's disobedience, God has not absolutely thrust them away from Himself, nor has He nullified His covenants with them.

11:5 a remnant according to the election of grace. In Old Testament times of deep spiritual apostasy in Israel, a remnant always remained loyal to Jehovah. During the first century, the remnant of Jews accepting the Messiah spread the gospel to the Gentiles. In the future Tribulation, after the Rapture, a remnant of messianic Jews will preach the gospel (see Rev. 7:3–8; 11:13; 12:17).

11:12 how much more their fulness? If the diminishing of Israel through unbelief had the blessed result of bringing the gospel and salvation to the Gentiles, how much more blessed will the future be, when Israel becomes a nation of believers and worshipers of Jesus the Messiah–King!

11:17 the olive tree. A religious symbol of Israel (Hos. 14:4–6), the olive tree here depicts the plan, purpose, and program which God began with Israel. Their rejection of Christ resulted in some of their branches being broken off, severing them from the spiritual nourishment they had long enjoyed. After Pentecost, the Gentiles were grafted into the same "tree," and became connected with the Old Testament and God's plan for the ages.

broken off, and thou standest by faith. Be not highminded, but fear:

21 For if God spared not the natural branches, *take heed* lest he also spare not thee.

22 Behold therefore the goodness and severity of God: on them which fell, severity; but toward thee, goodness, if thou continue in *his* goodness: otherwise thou also shalt be cut off.

23 And they also, if they abide not still in unbelief, shall be graffed in: for God is able to graff them in again.

24 For if thou wert cut out of the olive tree which is wild by nature, and wert graffed contrary to nature into a good olive tree: how much more shall these, which be the natural *branches,* be graffed into their own olive tree?

Israel's Future Restoration

25 For I would not, brethren, that ye should be ignorant of this mystery, lest ye should be wise in your own conceits; that blindness in part is happened to Israel, until the fulness of the Gentiles be come in.

26 And so all Israel shall be saved: as it is written, There shall come out of Sion the Deliverer, and shall turn away ungodliness from Jacob:

27 For this *is* my covenant unto them, when I shall take away their sins.

28 As concerning the gospel, *they are* enemies for your sakes: but as touching the election, *they are* beloved for the fathers' sakes.

29 For the gifts and calling of God *are* without repentance.

30 For as ye in times past have not believed God, yet have now obtained mercy through their unbelief:

31 Even so have these also now not believed, that through your mercy they also may obtain mercy.

32 For God hath concluded them all in unbelief, that he might have mercy upon all.

33 O the depth of the riches both of the wisdom and knowledge of God! how unsearchable *are* his judgments, and his ways past finding out!

34 For who hath known the mind of the Lord? or who hath been his counseller?

35 Or who hath first given to him, and it shall be recompensed unto him again?

36 For of him, and through him, and to him, *are* all things: to whom *be* glory for ever. Amen.

CHAPTER 12
Exhortation to Practical Living

1 I beseech you therefore, brethren, by the mercies of God, that ye present your bodies a living sacrifice, holy, acceptable unto God, *which is* your reasonable service.

2 And be not conformed to this world: but be ye transformed by the renewing of your mind, that ye may prove what *is* that good, and acceptable, and perfect, will of God.

3 For I say, through the grace given unto me, to every man that is among you, not to think *of himself* more highly than he ought to think; but to think soberly, according as God hath dealt to every man the measure of faith.

Cross references (center column)

22 John 15:2; 1Cor. 15:2; Heb. 3:6, 14
25 Luke 21:24; Rev. 7:9
26 Isa. 59:20; Ps. 14:7
27 Isa. 27:9; Jer. 31:31-34; Heb. 8:8; 10:16
28 Deut. 7:8; 9:5; 10:15
29 Num. 23:19
32 Rom. 3:9; Gal. 3:22
33 Job 11:7; Ps. 36:6; 92:5
34 Job 15:8; 36:22; Isa. 40:13; Jer. 23:18; 1Cor. 2:16
35 Job 35:7; 41:11
36 1Cor. 8:6; Gal. 1:5; Col. 1:16
1 1Cor. 6:13-20
2 Eph. 4:23; 5:10, 17
3 Prov. 25:27

11:24 natural branches . . . graffed into their own olive tree. At the second coming of Christ, the natural branches, Israel, will be grafted back into a right relationship to God and their true heritage, when they embrace Jesus as their Messiah (Zech. 12:10; Rev. 1:7).

11:25 this mystery. In this present dispensation, only a remnant of Israel has accepted Jesus as the Messiah. After the grand purpose of God for His Church has been fulfilled (Eph. 3:2–11), God will deliver Israel. Prior to this deliverance, the nation will experience a "hardening of the heart," with most turning away from the gospel. This rejection will continue until God's purpose for the mostly Gentile Church is complete. The fullness of the Gentiles thus presented is to be distinguished from the "times of the Gentiles" (Luke 21:24).

11:26 all Israel shall be saved . . . There shall come . . . the Deliverer. This deliverance is twofold, indicating rescue from the Gentile armies of the Antichrist (Isa. 59:20–21; Zech. 13:1, 6, 8–9; 14:1–14) and spiritual conversion, when the new covenant is established with His people (Jer. 31:33–34).

11:29 gifts and calling . . . without repentance. God's sovereign election of Israel is unchangeable and irrevocable. Nowhere in Scripture is the elimination of Israel as His earthly chosen people ever expressed or implied. Israel's promised destiny is as certain as the promises of God; the promises to Israel will be experienced by Israel.

12:1–2 present your bodies . . . prove what is that good and acceptable, and perfect, will of God. God will show His will to those who are completely committed and surrendered to Him. This presenting or yielding (6:13) of one's faculties as a living sacrifice is the logical, spiritual and worshipful service of the Christian. Rather than being conformed to the world's philosophy or standard, the yielded believer will be transformed through a mental renewal to experience God's will in his life.

4 For as we have many members in one body, and all members have not the same office:

5 So we, *being* many, are one body in Christ, and every one members one of another.

Spiritual Gifts

6 Having then gifts differing according to the grace that is given to us, whether prophecy, *let us prophesy* according to the proportion of faith;

7 Or ministry, *let us wait* on *our* ministering: or he that teacheth, on teaching;

8 Or he that exhorteth, on exhortation: he that giveth, *let him do it* with simplicity; he that ruleth, with diligence; he that sheweth mercy, with cheerfulness.

9 *Let* love be without dissimulation. Abhor that which is evil; cleave to that which is good.

10 *Be* kindly affectioned one to another with brotherly love; in honour preferring one another;

11 Not slothful in business; fervent in spirit; serving the Lord;

12 Rejoicing in hope; patient in tribulation; continuing instant in prayer;

13 Distributing to the necessity of saints; given to hospitality.

14 Bless them which persecute you: bless, and curse not.

15 Rejoice with them that do rejoice, and weep with them that weep.

16 *Be* of the same mind one toward another. Mind not high things, but condescend to men of low estate. Be not wise in your own conceits.

17 Recompense to no man evil for evil. Provide things honest in the sight of all men.

18 If it be possible, as much as lieth in you, live peaceably with all men.

19 Dearly beloved, avenge not yourselves, but *rather* give place unto wrath: for it is written, Vengeance *is* mine; I will repay, saith the Lord.

20 Therefore if thine enemy hunger, feed him; if he thirst, give him drink: for in so doing thou shalt heap coals of fire on his head.

21 Be not overcome of evil, but overcome evil with good.

CHAPTER 13
"Subject unto the Higher Powers"

1 Let every soul be subject unto the higher powers. For there is no power but of God: the powers that be are ordained of God.

2 Whosoever therefore resisteth the power, resisteth the ordinance of God: and they that resist shall receive to themselves damnation.

3 For rulers are not a terror to good works, but to the evil. Wilt thou then not be afraid of the power? do that which is good, and thou shalt have praise of the same:

4 For he is the minister of God to thee for good. But if thou do that which is evil, be afraid; for he beareth not the sword in vain: for he is the minister of God, a revenger to *execute* wrath upon him that doeth evil.

5 Wherefore *ye* must needs be subject, not only for wrath, but also for conscience sake.

6 For for this cause pay ye tribute also: for they are God's ministers, attending continually upon this very thing.

7 Render therefore to all their dues: tribute to whom tribute *is due*; custom to whom custom; fear to whom fear; honour to whom honour.

8 Owe no man any thing, but to love one another: for he that loveth another hath fulfilled the law.

9 For this, Thou shalt not commit adultery, Thou shalt not kill, Thou shalt not steal, Thou shalt not bear false witness, Thou shalt not covet; and if *there be* any other commandment, it is briefly comprehended in this saying, namely, Thou shalt love thy neighbour as thyself.

10 Love worketh no ill to his neighbour: therefore love *is* the fulfilling of the law.

Cross-references

4 Eph. 4:16
5 1Cor. 10:17; 12:20, 27
6 1Cor. 12:4, 10, 28
8 1Cor. 14:3; 2Cor. 9:7
9 Ps. 34:14; 36:4; 97:10
10 Phil. 2:3; 1Pet. 1:22; 2Pet. 1:7
12 Luke 10:20; 18:1; 21:19; Acts 2:42; 1Tim. 6:11; Heb. 3:6; James 1:4
13 Titus 1:8
14 Matt. 5:44; Luke 6:28; 23:34
15 1Cor. 12:26
16 Phil. 2:2; 3:16; 1Pet. 3:8
17 Prov. 20:22; Matt. 5:39
18 Mark 9:50
19 Lev. 19:18; Deut. 32:35; Prov. 24:29
20 Matt. 5:44
1 Dan. 2:21; 4:32
2 Titus 3:1
7 Matt. 22:21; Mark 12:17; Luke 20:25
8 Gal. 5:14
9 Ex. 20:13-17; Lev. 19:18; Deut. 5:17-21; Matt. 19:18; 22:39

12:6 whether prophecy. Some view this gift of prophecy as the ability merely to interpret the Scriptures (cf. 1 Cor. 14:1–3). If this is the case, then it is a gift that continues even today. Others believe the gift of prophecy is the continuation of the Old Testament office, including as part of the gift the ability to receive new revelation from God and to predict future events. This "office" was still functioning when Paul wrote Romans. However, since the canon of Scripture closed with the book of Revelation, no additional prophecies are necessary. Hence, the office, when defined in this way, is obsolete. It is wise to beware of any religious teacher who claims to be a divinely called prophet with a special mission; Jesus warned that there would be an increasing number of false prophets in the Last Days (Matt. 24:11, 24; Mark 13:22). In the case of either interpretation regarding the gift of prophecy, we are encouraged to study prophetic truth in the Scriptures.

11 And that, knowing the time, that now *it is* high time to awake out of sleep: for now *is* our salvation nearer than when we believed.

12 The night is far spent, the day is at hand: let us therefore cast off the works of darkness, and let us put on the armour of light.

13 Let us walk honestly, as in the day; not in rioting and drunkenness, not in chambering and wantonness, not in strife and envying.

14 But put ye on the Lord Jesus Christ, and make not provision for the flesh, to *fulfil* the lusts *thereof.*

CHAPTER 14
"Why Dost Thou Judge Thy Brother?"

1 Him that is weak in the faith receive ye, *but* not to doubtful disputations.

2 For one believeth that he may eat all things: another, who is weak, eateth herbs.

3 Let not him that eateth despise him that eateth not; and let not him which eateth not judge him that eateth: for God hath received him.

4 Who art thou that judgest another man's servant? to his own master he standeth or falleth. Yea, he shall be holden up: for God is able to make him stand.

5 One man esteemeth one day above another: another esteemeth every day *alike.* Let every man be fully persuaded in his own mind.

6 He that regardeth the day, regardeth *it* unto the Lord; and he that regardeth not the day, to the Lord he doth not regard *it.* He that eateth, eateth to the Lord, for he giveth

God thanks; and he that eateth not to the Lord he eateth not, and giveth God thanks.

7 For none of us liveth to himself, and no man dieth to himself.

8 For whether we live, we live unto the Lord; and whether we die, we die unto the Lord: whether we live therefore, or die, we are the Lord's.

9 For to this end Christ both died, and rose, and revived, that he might be Lord both of the dead and living.

10 But why dost thou judge thy brother? or why dost thou set at nought thy brother? for we shall all stand before the judgment seat of Christ.

11 For it is written, *As* I live, saith the Lord, every knee shall bow to me, and every tongue shall confess to God.

12 So then every one of us shall give account of himself to God.

The Christian's Liberty

13 Let us not therefore judge one another any more: but judge this rather, that no man put a stumblingblock or an occasion to fall in *his* brother's way.

14 I know, and am persuaded by the Lord Jesus, that *there is* nothing unclean of itself: but to him that esteemeth any thing to be unclean, to him *it is* unclean.

15 But if thy brother be grieved with *thy* meat, now walkest thou not charitably. Destroy not him with thy meat, for whom Christ died.

16 Let not then your good be evil spoken of:

17 For the kingdom of God is not meat and drink; but righteousness, and peace, and joy in the Holy Ghost.

Cross-references:

11 1Cor. 15:34; Eph. 5:14; 1Thess. 5:5, 6

12 Eph. 5:11; 6:13; Col. 3:8; 1Thess. 5:8

13 Prov. 23:20; 1Cor. 6:9

14 Gal. 3:27; 5:16; Eph. 4:24

1 Rom. 15:1, 7; 1Cor. 8:9, 11; 9:22

2 1Cor. 10:25; 1Tim. 4:4

5 Col. 2:16

6 1Cor. 10:31; Gal. 4:10; 1Tim. 4:3

7 1Cor. 6:19, 20; Gal. 2:20; 1Thess. 5:10; 1Pet. 4:2

9 Acts 10:36; 2Cor. 5:15

10 Matt. 25:31, 32; 2Cor. 5:10

11 Isa. 45:23; Phil. 2:10

12 Matt. 12:36

13 1Cor. 8:9, 13; 10:32

17 1Cor. 8:8

13:11–12 salvation nearer than when we believed. The reference is to the messianic salvation in its full scope, as introduced by the second coming of Christ. Paul and other first century Christians maintained a keen sense of watchfulness and anticipation, believing the Rapture could occur in their lifetimes. This attitude of expectancy should characterize all believers, spurring them on to "cast off the works of darkness," live godly lives and "put on the whole armor of God" (see Eph. 6:11–18).

14:9 Lord both of the dead and living. The "dead" refers to those who are physically dead but spiritually alive with Christ. When Jesus returns, these souls will be brought by the Lord to the proximity of the earth for the resurrection (1 Thess. 4:13–17). The "living" refers to those who are living worshipers of Christ.

14:10 we shall all stand before the judgment seat. Further information concerning the judgment seat of

Christ can be found in 1 Corinthians 3:11–15; 9:24–27 and 2 Corinthians 5:10. Christians should be more concerned about the sin in their own hearts, avoiding judgmental attitudes toward other believers, especially in the matter of marginal customs or traditions.

14:11 As I live ... every knee shall bow. The certainty of this judgment is emphasized by a quotation from Isaiah 45:23, which is also referenced in Philippians 2:10–11.

14:12 give account of himself to God. The primary reference here is to the judgment of believers, as the use of "us" indicates. However, every person who ever lives has an ultimate appointment with God for judgment (Eccl. 11:9; Matt. 12:36; 16:27; Heb. 9:27; 1 Pet. 4:4–5). The saved shall appear before the judgment seat of Christ. The lost will stand before the great white throne (Rev. 20:11–15).

18 For he that in these things serveth Christ *is* acceptable to God, and approved of men.
19 Let us therefore follow after the things which make for peace, and things wherewith one may edify another.
20 For meat destroy not the work of God. All things indeed *are* pure; but *it is* evil for that man who eateth with offence.
21 *It is* good neither to eat flesh, nor to drink wine, nor *any thing* whereby thy brother stumbleth, or is offended, or is made weak.
22 Hast thou faith? have *it* to thyself before God. Happy *is* he that condemneth not himself in that thing which he alloweth.
23 And he that doubteth is damned if he eat, because *he eateth* not of faith: for whatsoever *is* not of faith is sin.

CHAPTER 15
Edify One Another

1 We then that are strong ought to bear the infirmities of the weak, and not to please ourselves.
2 Let every one of us please *his* neighbour for *his* good to edification.
3 For even Christ pleased not himself: but, as it is written, The reproaches of them that reproached thee fell on me.
4 For whatsoever things were written aforetime were written for our learning, that we through patience and comfort of the scriptures might have hope.
5 Now the God of patience and consolation grant you to be likeminded one toward another according to Christ Jesus:
6 That ye may with one mind *and* one mouth glorify God, even the Father of our Lord Jesus Christ.
7 Wherefore receive ye one another, as Christ also received us to the glory of God.
8 Now I say that Jesus Christ was a minister of the circumcision for the truth of God, to confirm the promises *made* unto the fathers:
9 And that the Gentiles might glorify God for *his* mercy; as it is written, For this cause I will confess to thee among the Gentiles, and sing unto thy name.
10 And again he saith, Rejoice, ye Gentiles, with his people.

18 2Cor. 8:21
19 Ps. 34:14; 1Cor. 14:12
20 1Cor. 8:9-12; Titus 1:15
21 1Cor. 8:13
23 Titus 1:15
1 Gal. 6:1
2 Phil. 2:4, 5
3 Matt. 26:39; Ps. 69:9
4 Rom. 4:23, 24
5 Rom. 12:16; 1Cor. 1:10; Phil. 3:16
6 Acts 4:24, 32
7 Rom. 5:2; 14:1, 3
8 Matt. 15:24; John 1:11
9 Ps. 18:49; John 10:16; Rom. 9:23
10 Deut. 32:43
11 Ps. 117:1
12 Isa. 11:1, 10; Rev. 5:5; 22:16
13 Rom. 12:12; 14:17
14 2Pet. 1:12; 1John 2:21
15 Rom. 1:5; 12:3; Gal. 1:15; Eph. 3:7, 8
16 Isa. 66:20; Rom. 11:13
18 Acts 21:19; Gal. 2:8
19 Acts 19:11; 2Cor. 12:12
20 2Cor. 10:13, 15, 16
21 Isa. 52:15

11 And again, Praise the Lord, all ye Gentiles; and laud him, all ye people.
12 And again, Esaias saith, There shall be a root of Jesse, and he that shall rise to reign over the Gentiles; in him shall the Gentiles trust.
13 Now the God of hope fill you with all joy and peace in believing, that ye may abound in hope, through the power of the Holy Ghost.

Paul's Diligence in Preaching the Gospel

14 And I myself also am persuaded of you, my brethren, that ye also are full of goodness, filled with all knowledge, able also to admonish one another.
15 Nevertheless, brethren, I have written the more boldly unto you in some sort, as putting you in mind, because of the grace that is given to me of God,
16 That I should be the minister of Jesus Christ to the Gentiles, ministering the gospel of God, that the offering up of the Gentiles might be acceptable, being sanctified by the Holy Ghost.
17 I have therefore whereof I may glory through Jesus Christ in those things which pertain to God.
18 For I will not dare to speak of any of those things which Christ hath not wrought by me, to make the Gentiles obedient, by word and deed,
19 Through mighty signs and wonders, by the power of the Spirit of God; so that from Jerusalem, and round about unto Illyricum, I have fully preached the gospel of Christ.
20 Yea, so have I strived to preach the gospel, not where Christ was named, lest I should build upon another man's foundation:
21 But as it is written, To whom he was not spoken of, they shall see: and they that have not heard shall understand.
22 For which cause also I have been much hindered from coming to you.
23 But now having no more place in these parts, and having a great desire these many years to come unto you;
24 Whensoever I take my journey into Spain, I will come to you: for I trust to see

---

15:8–13 These verses reveal that God did have a purpose in history to call the Gentiles as well as Jews to form the body of Christ. Though the Old Testament did not forecast the special features of the body of Christ, it did make promises to the Gentiles. They are depicted as worshiping and singing praises to God (Deut. 32:43; 2 Sam. 22:50; Ps. 18:49; Ps 117:1; Isa. 11:10). These promises may be fulfilled to a certain extent in this present age, but will be ultimately fulfilled in the Millennial Kingdom (see Zech. 14:16; Mal. 1:11).

you in my journey, and to be brought on my way thitherward by you, if first I be somewhat filled with your *company.*

25 But now I go unto Jerusalem to minister unto the saints.

26 For it hath pleased them of Macedonia and Achaia to make a certain contribution for the poor saints which are at Jerusalem.

27 It hath pleased them verily; and their debtors they are. For if the Gentiles have been made partakers of their spiritual things, their duty is also to minister unto them in carnal things.

28 When therefore I have performed this, and have sealed to them this fruit, I will come by you into Spain.

29 And I am sure that, when I come unto you, I shall come in the fulness of the blessing of the gospel of Christ.

30 Now I beseech you, brethren, for the Lord Jesus Christ's sake, and for the love of the Spirit, that ye strive together with me in your prayers to God for me;

31 That I may be delivered from them that do not believe in Judea; and that my service which I *have* for Jerusalem may be accepted of the saints;

32 That I may come unto you with joy by the will of God, and may with you be refreshed.

33 Now the God of peace *be* with you all. Amen.

CHAPTER 16

Greetings

1 I commend unto you Phebe our sister, which is a servant of the church which is at Cenchrea:

2 That ye receive her in the Lord, as becometh saints, and that ye assist her in whatsoever business she hath need of you: for she hath been a succourer of many, and of myself also.

3 Greet Priscilla and Aquila my helpers in Christ Jesus:

4 Who have for my life laid down their own necks: unto whom not only I give thanks, but also all the churches of the Gentiles.

5 Likewise *greet* the church that is in their house. Salute my wellbeloved Epaenetus,

25 Acts 19:21; 20:22; 24:17

26 1Cor. 16:1, 2; 2Cor. 8:1; 9:2, 12

27 Rom. 11:17; 1Cor. 9:11; Gal. 6:6

28 Phil. 4:17

29 Rom. 1:11

30 2Cor. 1:11; Phil. 2:1; Col. 4:12

31 2Cor. 8:4; 2Thess. 3:2

32 Rom. 1:10; Phile. 1:7, 20; James 4:15

33 Phil. 4:9; 1Thess. 5:23;

1 Acts 18:18

2 Phil. 2:29; 3John 1:5, 6

3 Acts 18:2, 18, 26; 2Tim. 4:19

5 1Cor. 16:15, 19; Col. 4:15; Phile. 1:2

7 Gal. 1:22

13 2John 1:1

16 1Cor. 16:20; 1Thess. 5:26

17 Acts 15:1, 5, 24; 1Cor. 5:9, 11

18 Phil. 3:19; Col. 2:4

19 Matt. 10:16; Rom. 1:8; 1Cor. 14:20

20 Gen. 3:15; Phil. 4:23; Rev. 22:21

21 Acts 13:1; 16:1; 17:5; 20:4; Phil. 2:19; Col. 1:1; 1Thess. 3:2; 1Tim. 1:2; Heb. 13:23

who is the firstfruits of Achaia unto Christ.

6 Greet Mary, who bestowed much labour on us.

7 Salute Andronicus and Junia, my kinsmen, and my fellow prisoners, who are of note among the apostles, who also were in Christ before me.

8 Greet Amplias my beloved in the Lord.

9 Salute Urbane, our helper in Christ, and Stachys my beloved.

10 Salute Apelles approved in Christ. Salute them which are of Aristobulus' *household.*

11 Salute Herodion my kinsman. Greet them that be of the *household* of Narcissus, which are in the Lord.

12 Salute Tryphena and Tryphosa, who labour in the Lord. Salute the beloved Persis, which laboured much in the Lord.

13 Salute Rufus chosen in the Lord, and his mother and mine.

14 Salute Asyncritus, Phlegon, Hermas, Patrobas, Hermes, and the brethren which are with them.

15 Salute Philologus, and Julia, Nereus, and his sister, and Olympas, and all the saints which are with them.

16 Salute one another with an holy kiss. The churches of Christ salute you.

Exhortation to Unity

17 Now I beseech you, brethren, mark them which cause divisions and offences contrary to the doctrine which ye have learned; and avoid them.

18 For they that are such serve not our Lord Jesus Christ, but their own belly; and by good words and fair speeches deceive the hearts of the simple.

19 For your obedience is come abroad unto all *men.* I am glad therefore on your behalf: but yet I would have you wise unto that which is good, and simple concerning evil.

20 And the God of peace shall bruise Satan under your feet shortly. The grace of our Lord Jesus Christ *be* with you. Amen.

21 Timotheus my workfellow, and Lucius, and Jason, and Sosipater, my kinsmen, salute you.

22 I Tertius, who wrote *this* epistle, salute you in the Lord.

16:20 the God of peace shall bruise Satan under your feet shortly. While the Roman believers may have experienced a spiritual victory against satanic attack in Paul's time, the larger implication is that Christians may be certain that Satan's defeat will happen. Since no one knows the date of Christ's imminent return, the continual expectancy of Satan's bruising is always in order. Satan's destiny is clear: imprisonment in the bottomless pit for a thousand years (Rev. 20:3) and everlasting torment in the lake of fire (Rev. 20:10).

23 Gaius mine host, and of the whole church, saluteth you. Erastus the chamberlain of the city saluteth you, and Quartus a brother.

24 The grace of our Lord Jesus Christ *be* with you all. Amen.

Doxology

25 Now to him that is of power to stablish you according to my gospel, and the preach-

ing of Jesus Christ, according to the revelation of the mystery, which was kept secret since the world began,

26 But now is made manifest, and by the scriptures of the prophets, according to the commandment of the everlasting God, made known to all nations for the obedience of faith:

27 To God only wise, *be* glory through Jesus Christ for ever. Amen.

23 Acts 19:22; 1Cor. 1:14; 2Tim. 4:20	
25 Rom. 2:16; Col. 1:26, 27	
26 Acts 6:7; Rom. 1:5	
27 1Tim. 1:17; 6:16; Jude 1:25	

1 Corinthians

C orinth was an important cosmopolitan city located in the southern part of modern-day Greece approximately fifty miles west of Athens. Due to its prime port location, Corinth became one of the largest and richest cities in the Roman Empire and a tourist hub for many travelers from the world over. Its multicultural society made the city a strategic center of influence for the gospel. In approximately A.D. 52–53, Paul established the church at Corinth during his second missionary journey (Acts 18).

While in Ephesus during his third missionary journey (Acts 19), Paul learned that the congregation at Corinth was bitterly divided. As a result of their divisions and because of influences from the heathen city, Paul dispatched young Titus to Corinth (ca. A.D. 56) with this epistle of instruction, warning, and encouragement to live godly lives. The first part (chaps. 1—6) deals with divisions and immoral conduct, while the last part (chaps. 7—15) answers questions about marriage, consumption of meat dedicated to idols, Paul's apostleship, and the Lord's Supper. Spiritual gifts are explained in chapters 12 and 14, with the "Lyric of Love" (chap. 13) describing the greatest gift of all. Paul clearly describes the first Resurrection and the Rapture (chap. 15).

Of particular interest are several references to Christ's return (1:7–8; 4:5; 11:26; 16:22). Chapter three contains a description of the judgment seat of Christ, and chapter 6 asserts that believers will judge angels (vv. 1–3). Prophetic types are cited in chapters five and ten, where Old Testament events prefigure New Testament truths. The doctrine of bodily resurrection is explained in chapter 15, which concludes by predicting the "last trump" (15:52), when all living believers will be "changed" at the Rapture, and the dead in Christ will be raised "incorruptible."

Predictive material is in 85 of the book's 437 verses (19 percent). There are 17 quotations from the Old Testament in the book.

Author
Paul

Date
A.D. 55

Key Truth
Christian Conduct

Historic Time
The Early Growth of the Church in Corinth

Key Verse
6:20
For ye are bought with a price: therefore glorify God in your body.

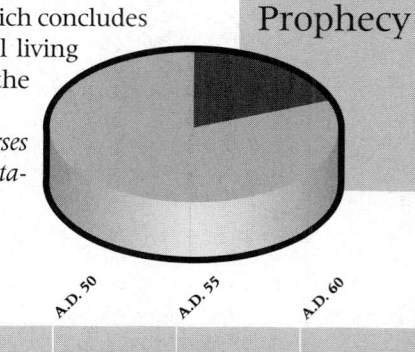

19%
Prophecy

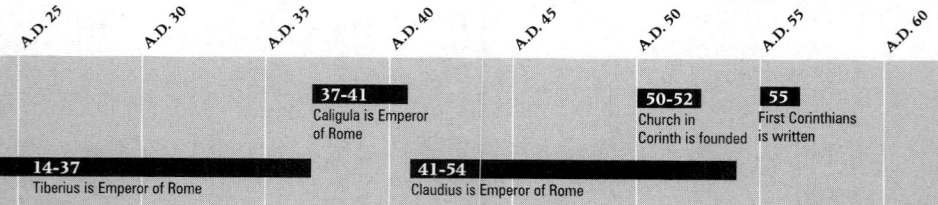

14-37 Tiberius is Emperor of Rome

37-41 Caligula is Emperor of Rome

41-54 Claudius is Emperor of Rome

50-52 Church in Corinth is founded

55 First Corinthians is written

54-68 Nero is Emperor of Rome

35 Conversion of Saul (Paul)

47-49 Paul's First Missionary Journey

49-53 Paul's Second Missionary Journey

53-56 Paul's Third Missionary Journey

A.D. 25 · A.D. 30 · A.D. 35 · A.D. 40 · A.D. 45 · A.D. 50 · A.D. 55 · A.D. 60

CHAPTER 1

1 Paul called *to be* an apostle of Jesus Christ through the will of God, and Sosthenes *our* brother,

2 Unto the church of God which is at Corinth, to them that are sanctified in Christ Jesus, called *to be* saints, with all that in every place call upon the name of Jesus Christ our Lord, both theirs and ours:

3 Grace *be* unto you, and peace, from God our Father, and *from* the Lord Jesus Christ.

4 I thank my God always on your behalf, for the grace of God which is given you by Jesus Christ;

5 That in every thing ye are enriched by him, in all utterance, and *in* all knowledge;

6 Even as the testimony of Christ was confirmed in you:

7 So that ye come behind in no gift; waiting for the coming of our Lord Jesus Christ:

8 Who shall also confirm you unto the end, *that ye may be* blameless in the day of our Lord Jesus Christ.

9 God *is* faithful, by whom ye were called unto the fellowship of his Son Jesus Christ our Lord.

Exhortation to Unity

10 Now I beseech you, brethren, by the name of our Lord Jesus Christ, that ye all speak the same thing, and *that* there be no divisions among you; but *that* ye be perfectly joined together in the same mind and in the same judgment.

11 For it hath been declared unto me of you, my brethren, by them *which are of the house* of Chloe, that there are contentions among you.

12 Now this I say, that every one of you saith, I am of Paul; and I of Apollos; and I of Cephas; and I of Christ.

13 Is Christ divided? was Paul crucified for you? or were ye baptized in the name of Paul?

14 I thank God that I baptized none of you, but Crispus and Gaius;

15 Lest any should say that I had baptized in mine own name.

16 And I baptized also the household of Stephanas: besides, I know not whether I baptized any other.

17 For Christ sent me not to baptize, but to preach the gospel: not with wisdom of words, lest the cross of Christ should be made of none effect.

Paul Defends His Manner of Preaching

18 For the preaching of the cross is to them that perish foolishness; but unto us which are saved it is the power of God.

19 For it is written, I will destroy the wisdom of the wise, and will bring to nothing the understanding of the prudent.

20 Where *is* the wise? where *is* the scribe? where *is* the disputer of this world? hath not God made foolish the wisdom of this world?

21 For after that in the wisdom of God the world by wisdom knew not God, it pleased God by the foolishness of preaching to save them that believe.

22 For the Jews require a sign, and the Greeks seek after wisdom:

23 But we preach Christ crucified, unto the Jews a stumblingblock, and unto the Greeks foolishness;

24 But unto them which are called, both Jews and Greeks, Christ the power of God, and the wisdom of God.

25 Because the foolishness of God is wiser than men; and the weakness of God is stronger than men.

26 For ye see your calling, brethren, how that not many wise men after the flesh, not many mighty, not many noble, *are called*:

27 But God hath chosen the foolish things

Cross References

1 Acts 18:17
2 John 17:19; Acts 9:14, 21; 15:9; 22:16; 1Cor. 8:6
3 Rom. 1:7
5 1Cor. 12:8
6 2Tim. 1:8
7 Phil. 3:20; Col. 3:4; 2Pet. 3:12
8 1Thess. 3:13; 5:23
9 Isa. 49:7; 1Cor. 10:13; 1Thess. 5:24; 1John 1:3; 4:13
10 1Cor. 11:18; 2Cor. 13:11; Phil. 2:2; 3:16
12 Acts 18:24; 19:1
13 2Cor. 11:4
14 Acts 18:8
18 Acts 17:19; Rom. 1:16
19 Job 5:12, 13; Isa. 29:14; Jer. 8:9
20 Job 12:17, 20
21 Matt. 11:25; Luke 10:21
22 Matt. 12:38; 16:1; Mark 8:11; Luke 11:16; John 4:48
23 Isa. 8:14; John 6:60, 66
24 Rom. 1:4, 16; Col. 2:3
26 John 7:48

1:7 waiting for the coming of our Lord Jesus Christ. This is a reference to the Rapture when Christ reveals Himself to His Church. Paul challenges believers to live in the light of Jesus' sudden unannounced coming. This cannot be the Glorious Appearing, for that will occur at a set time—seven years after the Tribulation begins.

1:8 blameless in the day of our Lord Jesus Christ. This is a clear challenge to carnal Christians to clean up their lifestyle in view of Christ's coming for His Church. The term "day of . . . Christ" must be examined in context to determine if it refers to the Rapture or the Glorious

Appearing. In this instance the term refers to the Rapture, because it could occur at any moment.

1:18–19 I will destroy the wisdom of the wise. This quote from Isaiah 29:14 is both a prediction and reminder that ultimately, man's wisdom that excludes the reality of God will one day be destroyed, and what man thinks is foolish, the preaching of the cross, will triumph. In all of life there are essentially just two kinds of wisdom, man's wisdom and God's wisdom, with the cross in between. What man thinks about the cross (either "foolishness" or "the power of God") determines his eternal destiny.

of the world to confound the wise; and God hath chosen the weak things of the world to confound the things which are mighty;

28 And base things of the world, and things which are despised, hath God chosen, *yea,* and things which are not, to bring to nought things that are:

29 That no flesh should glory in his presence.

30 But of him are ye in Christ Jesus, who of God is made unto us wisdom, and righteousness, and sanctification, and redemption:

31 That, according as it is written, He that glorieth, let him glory in the Lord.

CHAPTER 2
The Power of God

1 And I, brethren, when I came to you, came not with excellency of speech or of wisdom, declaring unto you the testimony of God.

2 For I determined not to know any thing among you, save Jesus Christ, and him crucified.

3 And I was with you in weakness, and in fear, and in much trembling.

4 And my speech and my preaching *was* not with enticing words of man's wisdom, but in demonstration of the Spirit and of power:

5 That your faith should not stand in the wisdom of men, but in the power of God.

True Wisdom

6 Howbeit we speak wisdom among them that are perfect: yet not the wisdom of this world, nor of the princes of this world, that come to nought:

7 But we speak the wisdom of God in a mystery, *even* the hidden *wisdom,* which God ordained before the world unto our glory:

8 Which none of the princes of this world knew: for had they known *it,* they would not have crucified the Lord of glory.

9 But as it is written, Eye hath not seen, nor ear heard, neither have entered into the heart of man, the things which God hath prepared for them that love him.

10 But God hath revealed *them* unto us by his Spirit: for the Spirit searcheth all things, yea, the deep things of God.

11 For what man knoweth the things of a man, save the spirit of man which is in him? even so the things of God knoweth no man, but the Spirit of God.

12 Now we have received, not the spirit of the world, but the Spirit which is of God; that we might know the things that are freely given to us of God.

13 Which things also we speak, not in the words which man's wisdom teacheth, but which the Holy Ghost teacheth; comparing spiritual things with spiritual.

14 But the natural man receiveth not the things of the Spirit of God: for they are foolishness unto him: neither can he know *them,* because they are spiritually discerned.

15 But he that is spiritual judgeth all things, yet he himself is judged of no man.

16 For who hath known the mind of the Lord, that he may instruct him? But we have the mind of Christ.

CHAPTER 3
Jesus Is the Foundation

1 And I, brethren, could not speak unto you as unto spiritual, but as unto carnal, *even* as unto babes in Christ.

2 I have fed you with milk, and not with meat: for hitherto ye were not able *to bear* it, neither yet now are ye able.

3 For ye are yet carnal: for whereas *there is* among you envying, and strife, and divisions, are ye not carnal, and walk as men?

4 For while one saith, I am of Paul; and another, I *am* of Apollos; are ye not carnal?

5 Who then is Paul, and who *is* Apollos, but ministers by whom ye believed, even as the Lord gave to every man?

6 I have planted, Apollos watered; but God gave the increase.

7 So then neither is he that planteth any thing, neither he that watereth; but God that giveth the increase.

8 Now he that planteth and he that watereth are one: and every man shall receive his own reward according to his own labour.

9 For we are labourers together with God: ye are God's husbandry, *ye are* God's building.

10 According to the grace of God which is given unto me, as a wise masterbuilder, I have laid the foundation, and another buildeth thereon. But let every man take heed how he buildeth thereupon.

Cross references

28 Rom. 4:17
29 Eph. 2:9
30 Jer. 23:5, 6; Rom. 4:25
31 Jer. 9:23, 24
2 Gal. 6:14; Phil. 3:8
4 Rom. 15:19; 2Pet. 1:16
7 Eph. 3:5, 9; 2Tim. 1:9
8 Luke 23:34; 2Cor. 3:14
9 Isa. 64:4
10 John 14:26; 16:13; 1John 2:27
11 Prov. 20:27; 27:19
12 Rom. 8:15
13 1Cor. 1:17; 2:4; 2Pet. 1:16
14 Matt. 16:23; Rom. 8:5-7
15 Prov. 28:5; 1Thess. 5:21
16 Job 15:8; Isa. 40:13; Phil. 2:5
2 John 16:12; Heb. 5:12, 13; 1Pet. 2:2
3 Gal. 5:20, 21; James 3:16
5 Rom. 12:3, 6; 1Cor. 4:1
6 2Cor. 3:5; 10:14, 15
7 2Cor. 12:11; Gal. 6:3
8 Ps. 62:12; 1Cor. 2:23; Rev. 2:23; 22:12
9 2Cor. 6:1; Col. 2:7; Heb. 3:3, 4
10 Rom. 1:5; 12:3; 15:20; 1Pet. 4:11

2:9–10 the things which God hath prepared for them that love him. Many of the things that Isaiah had in mind (Isa. 64:4) have been revealed "by his [God's] Spirit" in prophetic portions of the New Testament (1 Cor. 15; 1 Thess. 4; Rev. 21—22). Yet those who love God will doubtless be amazed at the extent of those preparations.

11 For other foundation can no man lay than that is laid, which is Jesus Christ.

12 Now if any man build upon this foundation gold, silver, precious stones, wood, hay, stubble;

13 Every man's work shall be made manifest: for the day shall declare it, because it shall be revealed by fire; and the fire shall try every man's work of what sort it is.

14 If any man's work abide which he hath built thereupon, he shall receive a reward.

15 If any man's work shall be burned, he shall suffer loss: but he himself shall be saved; yet so as by fire.

16 Know ye not that ye are the temple of God, and *that* the Spirit of God dwelleth in you?

17 If any man defile the temple of God, him shall God destroy; for the temple of God is holy, which *temple* ye are.

18 Let no man deceive himself. If any man among you seemeth to be wise in this world, let him become a fool, that he may be wise.

19 For the wisdom of this world is foolishness with God. For it is written, He taketh the wise in their own craftiness.

20 And again, The Lord knoweth the thoughts of the wise, that they are vain.

21 Therefore let no man glory in men. For all things are yours;

22 Whether Paul, or Apollos, or Cephas, or the world, or life, or death, or things present, or things to come; all are yours;

23 And ye are Christ's; and Christ *is* God's.

CHAPTER 4
Ministers Should Be Faithful

1 Let a man so account of us, as of the ministers of Christ, and stewards of the mysteries of God.

2 Moreover it is required in stewards, that a man be found faithful.

3 But with me it is a very small thing that I should be judged of you, or of man's judgment: yea, I judge not mine own self.

4 For I know nothing by myself; yet am I not hereby justified: but he that judgeth me is the Lord.

5 Therefore judge nothing before the time, until the Lord come, who both will bring to light the hidden things of darkness, and will make manifest the counsels of the hearts: and then shall every man have praise of God.

Ministers Are Servants

6 And these things, brethren, I have in a figure transferred to myself and *to* Apollos for your sakes; that ye might learn in us not to think *of men* above that which is written, that no one of you be puffed up for one against another.

7 For who maketh thee to differ *from another?* and what hast thou that thou didst not receive? now if thou didst receive *it,* why dost thou glory, as if thou hadst not received *it?*

8 Now ye are full, now ye are rich, ye have reigned as kings without us: and I would to God ye did reign, that we also might reign with you.

9 For I think that God hath set forth us the apostles last, as it were appointed to death: for we are made a spectacle unto the world, and to angels, and to men.

10 We *are* fools for Christ's sake, but ye *are* wise in Christ; we *are* weak, but ye *are* strong; ye *are* honourable, but we *are* despised.

11 Even unto this present hour we both hunger, and thirst, and are naked, and are buffeted, and have no certain dwelling place;

12 And labour, working with our own hands: being reviled, we bless; being persecuted, we suffer it:

13 Being defamed, we intreat: we are made as the filth of the world, *and are* the offscouring of all things unto this day.

14 I write not these things to shame you, but as my beloved sons I warn *you.*

Cross references

11 Isa. 28:16; Matt. 16:18

13 Luke 2:35; 1Cor. 4:5

16 1Cor. 6:19; 2Cor. 6:16

18 Prov. 3:7; Isa. 5:21

19 Job 5:13; 1Cor. 1:20; 2:6

20 Ps. 94:11

21 2Cor. 4:5, 15

23 Rom. 14:8; 1Cor. 11:3; 2Cor. 10:7

1 Matt. 24:45; Luke 12:42; 2Cor. 6:4; Titus 1:7

3 1Cor. 3:13

4 Prov. 21:2; Rom. 3:20; 4:2

5 Rom. 2:1, 16, 29; 14:4; 10, 13; Rev. 20:12

6 Rom. 12:3

7 James 1:17; 1Pet. 4:10

8 Rev. 3:17

9 Ps. 44:22; Rom. 8:36; 2Cor. 4:11; 6:9

10 Acts 17:18; 26:24; 2Cor. 13:9

11 Job 22:6; Acts 23:2; 2Cor. 4:8; Phil. 4:12

12 Rom. 12:14, 20

13 Lam. 3:45

14 1Thess. 2:11

3:11–15 the fire shall try every man's work. This is the most detailed description of the judgment seat of Christ found in Scripture (Rom. 14:10; 2 Cor. 5:10). The wood or dross (probably good works done with a proud or selfish motive) will be burned up. One whose works are consumed shall be saved but will have no rewards for eternity. Faithful believers' works for Christ will be rewarded, forever, an obvious appeal to Christians to accept Jesus' challenge to "lay up for yourselves treasures in heaven" (Matt. 6:20), for "the day [of judgment] shall declare it" (1 Cor. 3:13). Paul yearned for these saints to live godly lives so they would receive a full reward. It should be noted that it is not salvation that will be lost at this judgment, but rewards (see Rev. 1:14).

4:5 will bring to light the hidden things of darkness. The timing of this judgment, "until the Lord come," obviously refers to the Rapture, when He takes us to the Father's house.

15 For though ye have ten thousand instructors in Christ, yet *have ye* not many fathers: for in Christ Jesus I have begotten you through the gospel.

16 Wherefore I beseech you, be ye followers of me.

17 For this cause have I sent unto you Timotheus, who is my beloved son, and faithful in the Lord, who shall bring you into remembrance of my ways which be in Christ, as I teach every where in every church.

18 Now some are puffed up, as though I would not come to you.

19 But I will come to you shortly, if the Lord will, and will know, not the speech of them which are puffed up, but the power.

20 For the kingdom of God *is* not in word, but in power.

21 What will ye? shall I come unto you with a rod, or in love, and *in* the spirit of meekness?

CHAPTER 5
Concerning Church Discipline

1 It is reported commonly *that there is* fornication among you, and such fornication as is not so much as named among the Gentiles, that one should have his father's wife.

2 And ye are puffed up, and have not rather mourned, that he that hath done this deed might be taken away from among you.

3 For I verily, as absent in body, but present in spirit, have judged already, as though I were present, *concerning* him that hath so done this deed,

4 In the name of our Lord Jesus Christ, when ye are gathered together, and my spirit, with the power of our Lord Jesus Christ,

5 To deliver such a one unto Satan for the destruction of the flesh, that the spirit may be saved in the day of the Lord Jesus.

6 Your glorying *is* not good. Know ye not that a little leaven leaveneth the whole lump?

7 Purge out therefore the old leaven, that ye may be a new lump, as ye are unleavened. For even Christ our passover is sacrificed for us:

8 Therefore let us keep the feast, not with old leaven, neither with the leaven of malice and wickedness; but with the unleavened *bread* of sincerity and truth.

9 I wrote unto you in an epistle not to company with fornicators:

10 Yet not altogether with the fornicators of this world, or with the covetous, or extortioners, or with idolaters; for then must ye needs go out of the world.

11 But now I have written unto you not to keep company, if any man that is called a brother be a fornicator, or covetous, or an idolater, or a railer, or a drunkard, or an extortioner; with such a one no not to eat.

12 For what have I to do to judge them also that are without? do not ye judge them that are within?

13 But them that are without God judgeth. Therefore put away from among yourselves that wicked person.

CHAPTER 6
Concerning Believers and Legal Matters

1 Dare any of you, having a matter against another, go to law before the unjust, and not before the saints?

2 Do ye not know that the saints shall judge the world? and if the world shall be judged by you, are ye unworthy to judge the smallest matters?

3 Know ye not that we shall judge angels? how much more things that pertain to this life?

4 If then ye have judgments of things pertaining to this life, set them to judge who are least esteemed in the church.

5 I speak to your shame. Is it so, that there is not a wise man among you? no, not one that shall be able to judge between his brethren?

6 But brother goeth to law with brother, and that before the unbelievers.

7 Now therefore there is utterly a fault among you, because ye go to law one with another. Why do ye not rather take wrong? why do ye not rather *suffer yourselves* to be defrauded?

8 Nay, ye do wrong, and defraud, and that *your* brethren.

9 Know ye not that the unrighteous shall not inherit the kingdom of God? Be not deceived: neither fornicators, nor idolaters, nor adulterers, nor effeminate, nor abusers of themselves with mankind,

10 Nor thieves, nor covetous, nor drunk-

Cross References

15 Acts 18:11; Rom. 15:20; Gal. 4:19; James 1:18

16 1Cor. 11:1; Phil. 3:17

17 Acts 19:22; 1Cor. 7:17; 11:2; 14:33; 16:10; Phil. 2:19; 1Thess. 3:2; 1Tim. 1:2; 2Tim. 1:2

20 1Cor. 2:4; 1Thess. 1:5

21 Lev. 18:8; Deut. 22:30; 27:20

3 Col. 2:5

5 Job 2:6; Ps. 109:6

6 Gal. 5:9; 2Tim. 2:17; James 4:16

7 Isa. 53:7; John 1:29; 19:14; 1Cor. 15:3

8 Ex. 12:15; 13:6; Deut. 16:3; Matt. 16:6, 12

9 2Cor. 6:1

11 Matt. 18:17; Rom. 16:17

12 Col. 4:5; 1Thess. 4:12; 1Tim. 3:7

13 Deut. 13:5; 17:7; 21:21; 22:21, 22, 24

2 Dan. 7:22; Matt. 19:28; Rev. 2:26; 3:21; 20:4

3 2Pet. 2:4; Jude 1:6

4 1Cor. 5:12

7 Prov. 20:22; Matt. 5:39, 40

8 1Thess. 4:6

9 1Cor. 15:50; Gal. 5:21; Rev. 22:15

6:2–4 The saints shall judge the world. We know God will judge the world and has already condemned "to hell" the angels "which kept not their first estate" and are now "reserved unto judgment" (2 Pet. 2:4, Jude 1:6). Yet somehow we will share in that judgment as we will share in His rule of the kingdom (Rev. 20:4).

ards, nor revilers, nor extortioners, shall inherit the kingdom of God.

11 And such were some of you: but ye are washed, but ye are sanctified, but ye are justified in the name of the Lord Jesus, and by the Spirit of our God.

Abuses of Christian Liberty

12 All things are lawful unto me, but all things are not expedient: all things are lawful for me, but I will not be brought under the power of any.

13 Meats for the belly, and the belly for meats: but God shall destroy both it and them. Now the body *is* not for fornication, but for the Lord; and the Lord for the body.

14 And God hath both raised up the Lord, and will also raise up us by his own power.

15 Know ye not that your bodies are the members of Christ? shall I then take the members of Christ, and make *them* the members of an harlot? God forbid.

16 What? know ye not that he which is joined to an harlot is one body? for two, saith he, shall be one flesh.

17 But he that is joined unto the Lord is one spirit.

18 Flee fornication. Every sin that a man doeth is without the body; but he that committeth fornication sinneth against his own body.

19 What? know ye not that your body is the temple of the Holy Ghost *which is* in you, which ye have of God, and ye are not your own?

20 For ye are bought with a price: therefore glorify God in your body, and in your spirit, which are God's.

CHAPTER 7
Concerning Marriage

1 Now concerning the things whereof ye wrote unto me: *It is* good for a man not to touch a woman.

2 Nevertheless, *to avoid* fornication, let every man have his own wife, and let every woman have her own husband.

3 Let the husband render unto the wife due benevolence: and likewise also the wife unto the husband.

4 The wife hath not power of her own body, but the husband: and likewise also the husband hath not power of his own body, but the wife.

5 Defraud ye not one the other, except *it be* with consent for a time, that ye may give yourselves to fasting and prayer; and come

together again, that Satan tempt you not for your incontinency.

6 But I speak this by permission, *and* not of commandment.

7 For I would that all men were even as I myself. But every man hath his proper gift of God, one after this manner, and another after that.

8 I say therefore to the unmarried and widows, It is good for them if they abide even as I.

9 But if they cannot contain, let them marry: for it is better to marry than to burn.

10 And unto the married I command, *yet* not I, but the Lord, Let not the wife depart from *her* husband:

11 But and if she depart, let her remain unmarried, or be reconciled to *her* husband: and let not the husband put away *his* wife.

12 But to the rest speak I, not the Lord: If any brother hath a wife that believeth not, and she be pleased to dwell with him, let him not put her away.

13 And the woman which hath an husband that believeth not, and if he be pleased to dwell with her, let her not leave him.

14 For the unbelieving husband is sanctified by the wife, and the unbelieving wife is sanctified by the husband: else were your children unclean; but now are they holy.

15 But if the unbelieving depart, let him depart. A brother or a sister is not under bondage in such *cases*: but God hath called us to peace.

16 For what knowest thou, O wife, whether thou shalt save *thy* husband? or how knowest thou, O man, whether thou shalt save *thy* wife?

17 But as God hath distributed to every man, as the Lord hath called every one, so let him walk. And so ordain I in all churches.

18 Is any man called being circumcised? let him not become uncircumcised. Is any called in uncircumcision? let him not be circumcised.

19 Circumcision is nothing, and uncircumcision is nothing, but the keeping of the commandments of God.

20 Let every man abide in the same calling wherein he was called.

21 Art thou called *being* a servant? care not for it: but if thou mayest be made free, use *it* rather.

22 For he that is called in the Lord, *being* a servant, is the Lord's freeman: likewise also he that is called, *being* free, is Christ's servant.

---

11 1Cor. 1:30; 12:2; Col. 3:7; Heb. 10:22

12 1Cor. 10:23

13 Matt. 15:17; Eph. 5:23; Col. 2:22, 23

14 Rom. 6:5, 8; 8:11; 2Cor. 4:14; Eph. 1:19, 20

15 1Cor. 12:27; Eph. 4:12, 15, 16

16 Gen. 2:24; Matt. 19:5; Eph. 5:31

17 John 17:21-23; Eph. 4:4; 5:30

18 Rom. 1:24; 6:12, 13; 1Thess. 4:4

19 1Cor. 3:16; 2Cor. 6:16

20 Acts 20:28; 1Cor. 7:23

3 Ex. 21:10; 1Pet. 3:7

5 Ex. 19:15; Zech. 7:3; 1Thess. 3:5

6 2Cor. 8:8; 11:17

7 Matt. 19:12; Acts 26:29; 1Cor. 9:5; 12:11

10 Mal. 2:14, 16; Matt. 5:32; 19:6, 9; Mark 10:11, 12; Luke 16:18

14 Mal. 2:15

15 1Cor. 14:33

16 1Pet. 3:1

18 Acts 15:1, 5, 19, 24, 28; Gal. 5:2

19 John 15:14; Gal. 5:6; 6:15

22 John 8:36; Gal. 5:13; Eph. 6:6; Phile. 1:16; 1Pet. 2:16

23 Ye are bought with a price; be not ye the servants of men.

24 Brethren, let every man, wherein he is called, therein abide with God.

Concerning Virgins

25 Now concerning virgins I have no commandment of the Lord: yet I give my judgment, as one that hath obtained mercy of the Lord to be faithful.

26 I suppose therefore that this is good for the present distress, *I say*, that *it is* good for a man so to be.

27 Art thou bound unto a wife? seek not to be loosed. Art thou loosed from a wife? seek not a wife.

28 But and if thou marry, thou hast not sinned; and if a virgin marry, she hath not sinned. Nevertheless such shall have trouble in the flesh: but I spare you.

29 But this I say, brethren, the time *is* short: it remaineth, that both they that have wives be as though they had none;

30 And they that weep, as though they wept not; and they that rejoice, as though they rejoiced not; and they that buy, as though they possessed not;

31 And they that use this world, as not abusing *it:* for the fashion of this world passeth away.

32 But I would have you without carefulness. He that is unmarried careth for the things that belong to the Lord, how he may please the Lord:

33 But he that is married careth for the things that are of the world, how he may please *his* wife.

34 There is difference *also* between a wife and a virgin. The unmarried woman careth for the things of the Lord, that she may be holy both in body and in spirit: but she that is married careth for the things of the world, how she may please *her* husband.

35 And this I speak for your own profit; not that I may cast a snare upon you, but for that which is comely, and that ye may attend upon the Lord without distraction.

36 But if any man think that he behaveth himself uncomely toward his virgin, if she pass the flower of *her* age, and need so require, let him do what he will, he sinneth not: let them marry.

37 Nevertheless he that standeth stedfast in his heart, having no necessity, but hath power over his own will, and hath so decreed in his heart that he will keep his virgin, doeth well.

38 So then he that giveth *her* in marriage doeth well; but he that giveth *her* not in marriage doeth better.

39 The wife is bound by the law as long as her husband liveth; but if her husband be dead, she is at liberty to be married to whom she will; only in the Lord.

40 But she is happier if she so abide, after my judgment: and I think also that I have the Spirit of God.

CHAPTER 8
Things Offered to Idols

1 Now as touching things offered unto idols, we know that we all have knowledge. Knowledge puffeth up, but charity edifieth.

2 And if any man think that he knoweth any thing, he knoweth nothing yet as he ought to know.

3 But if any man love God, the same is known of him.

4 As concerning therefore the eating of those things that are offered in sacrifice unto idols, we know that an idol *is* nothing in the world, and that *there is* none other God but one.

5 For though there be that are called gods, whether in heaven or in earth, (as there be gods many, and lords many,)

6 But to us *there is but* one God, the Father, of whom *are* all things, and we in him; and one Lord Jesus Christ, by whom *are* all things, and we by him.

7 Howbeit *there is* not in every man that knowledge: for some with conscience of the idol unto this hour eat *it* as a thing offered unto an idol; and their conscience being weak is defiled.

8 But meat commendeth us not to God: for neither, if we eat, are we the better; neither, if we eat not, are we the worse.

9 But take heed lest by any means this liberty of yours become a stumblingblock to them that are weak.

10 For if any man see thee which hast knowledge sit at meat in the idol's temple, shall not the conscience of him which is weak be emboldened to eat those things which are offered to idols;

11 And through thy knowledge shall the weak brother perish, for whom Christ died?

12 But when ye sin so against the brethren, and wound their weak conscience, ye sin against Christ.

13 Wherefore, if meat make my brother to offend, I will eat no flesh while the world standeth, lest I make my brother to offend.

---

23 Lev. 25:42; 1Cor. 6:20

24 1Cor. 7:20

25 1Cor. 4:2; 7:6, 10, 40; 1Tim. 1:12, 16

26 1Cor. 7:1, 8

29 1Pet. 4:7; 2Pet. 3:8, 9

31 Ps. 39:6; 1Cor. 9:18; 1Pet. 1:24; 4:7; 1John 2:17

34 Luke 10:40

38 Heb. 13:4

39 2Cor. 6:14; Rom. 7:2

40 1Cor. 7:25; 1Thess. 4:8

1 Acts 15:20, 29; Rom. 14:3, 10, 14, 22; 1Cor. 10:19

2 Gal. 6:3; 1Tim. 6:4

3 Ex. 33:12, 17; Nah. 1:7; Gal. 4:9

4 Deut. 4:39; 6:4; Isa. 41:24; 44:8 Mark 12:29; 1Tim. 2:5

5 John 10:34

6 Mal. 2:10; John 1:3; 13:13; Acts 2:36; 17:28; 1Cor. 12:3; Phil. 2:11

7 Rom. 14:14, 23; 1Cor. 10:28, 29

8 Rom. 14:17

9 Rom. 14:13, 20; Gal. 5:13

10 1Cor. 10:28, 32

11 Rom. 14:15, 20

12 Matt. 25:40, 45

13 Rom. 14:21; 2Cor. 11:29

CHAPTER 9
The Necessity of Self-denial

1 Am I not an apostle? am I not free? have I not seen Jesus Christ our Lord? are not ye my work in the Lord?

2 If I be not an apostle unto others, yet doubtless I am to you: for the seal of mine apostleship are ye in the Lord.

3 Mine answer to them that do examine me is this,

4 Have we not power to eat and to drink?

5 Have we not power to lead about a sister, a wife, as well as other apostles, and *as* the brethren of the Lord, and Cephas?

6 Or I only and Barnabas, have not we power to forbear working?

7 Who goeth a warfare any time at his own charges? who planteth a vineyard, and eateth not of the fruit thereof? or who feedeth a flock, and eateth not of the milk of the flock?

8 Say I these things as a man? or saith not the law the same also?

9 For it is written in the law of Moses, Thou shalt not muzzle the mouth of the ox that treadeth out the corn. Doth God take care for oxen?

10 Or saith he *it* altogether for our sakes? For our sakes, no doubt, *this* is written: that he that ploweth should plow in hope; and that he that thresheth in hope should be partaker of his hope.

11 If we have sown unto you spiritual things, *is it* a great thing if we shall reap your carnal things?

12 If others be partakers of *this* power over you, *are* not we rather? Nevertheless we have not used this power; but suffer all things, lest we should hinder the gospel of Christ.

13 Do ye not know that they which minister about holy things live *of the things* of the temple? and they which wait at the altar are partakers with the altar?

14 Even so hath the Lord ordained that they which preach the gospel should live of the gospel.

15 But I have used none of these things: neither have I written these things, that it should be so done unto me: for *it were* better for me to die, than that any man should make my glorying void.

16 For though I preach the gospel, I have nothing to glory of: for necessity is laid upon me; yea, woe is unto me, if I preach not the gospel!

17 For if I do this thing willingly, I have a reward: but if against my will, a dispensation *of the gospel* is committed unto me.

18 What is my reward then? *Verily* that, when I preach the gospel, I may make the gospel of Christ without charge, that I abuse not my power in the gospel.

19 For though I be free from all *men,* yet have I made myself servant unto all, that I might gain the more.

20 And unto the Jews I became as a Jew, that I might gain the Jews; to them that are under the law, as under the law, that I might gain them that are under the law;

21 To them that are without law, as without law, (being not without law to God, but under the law to Christ,) that I might gain them that are without law.

22 To the weak became I as weak, that I might gain the weak: I am made all things to all *men,* that I might by all means save some.

23 And this I do for the gospel's sake, that I might be partaker thereof with *you.*

24 Know ye not that they which run in a race run all, but one receiveth the prize? So run, that ye may obtain.

25 And every man that striveth for the mastery is temperate in all things. Now they *do it* to obtain a corruptible crown; but we an incorruptible.

26 I therefore so run, not as uncertainly; so fight I, not as one that beateth the air:

27 But I keep under my body, and bring *it* into subjection: lest that by any means, when I have preached to others, I myself should be a castaway.

CHAPTER 10
Admonitions from Israel's History

1 Moreover, brethren, I would not that ye should be ignorant, how that all our fathers were under the cloud, and all passed through the sea;

2 And were all baptized unto Moses in the cloud and in the sea;

3 And did all eat the same spiritual meat;

4 And did all drink the same spiritual drink: for they drank of that spiritual Rock that followed them: and that Rock was Christ.

5 But with many of them God was not well pleased: for they were overthrown in the wilderness.

6 Now these things were our examples, to the intent we should not lust after evil things, as they also lusted.

7 Neither be ye idolaters, as *were* some of

1 Acts 9:3, 15, 17; 13:2; 18:9; 22:14, 18; 23:11; 26:17

2 2Cor. 3:2; 12:12

4 1Thess. 2:6

5 Matt. 8:14; 13:55; Mark 6:3; Luke 6:15

7 Deut. 20:6; Prov. 27:18; John 21:15

9 Deut. 25:4; 1Tim. 5:18

11 Rom. 15:27; Gal. 6:6

12 Acts 20:33; 1Thess. 2:6

13 Lev. 6:16, 26; 7:6

14 Matt. 10:10

15 Acts 18:3; 20:34; 1Thess. 2:9

16 Rom. 1:14

17 Phil. 1:17

19 Matt. 18:15

20 Acts 16:3; 18:18; 21:23

21 Rom. 2:12, 14; Gal. 3:2

22 Rom. 11:14; 15:1

24 Phil. 2:16; 3:14; 2Tim. 4:7

25 Eph. 6:12; 1Tim. 6:12; 2Tim. 2:5

1 Ex. 13:21; 14:22; 40:34

3 Ex. 16:15, 35; Neh. 9:15, 20; Ps. 78:24

4 Ex. 17:6; Ps. 78:15; 105:41

5 Num. 14:29, 32, 35; 26:64, 65

6 Num. 11:4, 33, 34; Ps. 106:14

7 Ex. 32:6; 1Cor. 10:14

them; as it is written, The people sat down to eat and drink, and rose up to play.

8 Neither let us commit fornication, as some of them committed, and fell in one day three and twenty thousand.

9 Neither let us tempt Christ, as some of them also tempted, and were destroyed of serpents.

10 Neither murmur ye, as some of them also murmured, and were destroyed of the destroyer.

11 Now all these things happened unto them for ensamples: and they are written for our admonition, upon whom the ends of the world are come.

12 Wherefore let him that thinketh he standeth take heed lest he fall.

13 There hath no temptation taken you but such as is common to man: but God *is* faithful, who will not suffer you to be tempted above that ye are able; but will with the temptation also make a way to escape, that ye may be able to bear *it*.

14 Wherefore, my dearly beloved, flee from idolatry.

15 I speak as to wise men; judge ye what I say.

16 The cup of blessing which we bless, is it not the communion of the blood of Christ? The bread which we break, is it not the communion of the body of Christ?

17 For we *being* many are one bread, *and* one body: for we are all partakers of that one bread.

18 Behold Israel after the flesh: are not they which eat of the sacrifices partakers of the altar?

19 What say I then? that the idol is any thing, or that which is offered in sacrifice to idols is any thing?

20 But *I say,* that the things which the Gentiles sacrifice, they sacrifice to devils, and not to God: and I would not that ye should have fellowship with devils.

21 Ye cannot drink the cup of the Lord, and the cup of devils: ye cannot be partakers of the Lord's table, and of the table of devils.

22 Do we provoke the Lord to jealousy? are we stronger than he?

23 All things are lawful for me, but all things are not expedient: all things are lawful for me, but all things edify not.

24 Let no man seek his own, but every man another's *wealth*.

25 Whatsoever is sold in the shambles, *that* eat, asking no question for conscience sake:

26 For the earth *is* the Lord's, and the fulness thereof.

27 If any of them that believe not bid you *to* a feast, and ye be disposed to go; whatsoever is set before you, eat, asking no question for conscience sake.

8 Num. 25:1, 9
9 Ex. 17:2, 7; Num. 21:5, 6; Deut. 6:16
10 Ex. 12:23; 16:2; 17:2
11 Phil. 4:5
13 Ps. 125:3
14 2Cor. 6:17; 1John 5:21
16 Matt. 26:26, 28; 1Cor. 11:23, 24
18 Lev. 3:3; 7:15; Rom. 4:1, 12; 9:3, 5
20 Ps. 106:37; Rev. 9:20
21 Deut. 32:38; 2Cor. 6:15, 16
23 1Cor. 6:12
24 Rom. 15:1, 2; Phil. 2:4, 21
25 1Tim. 4:4
26 Ps. 24:1; 50:12
27 Luke 10:7

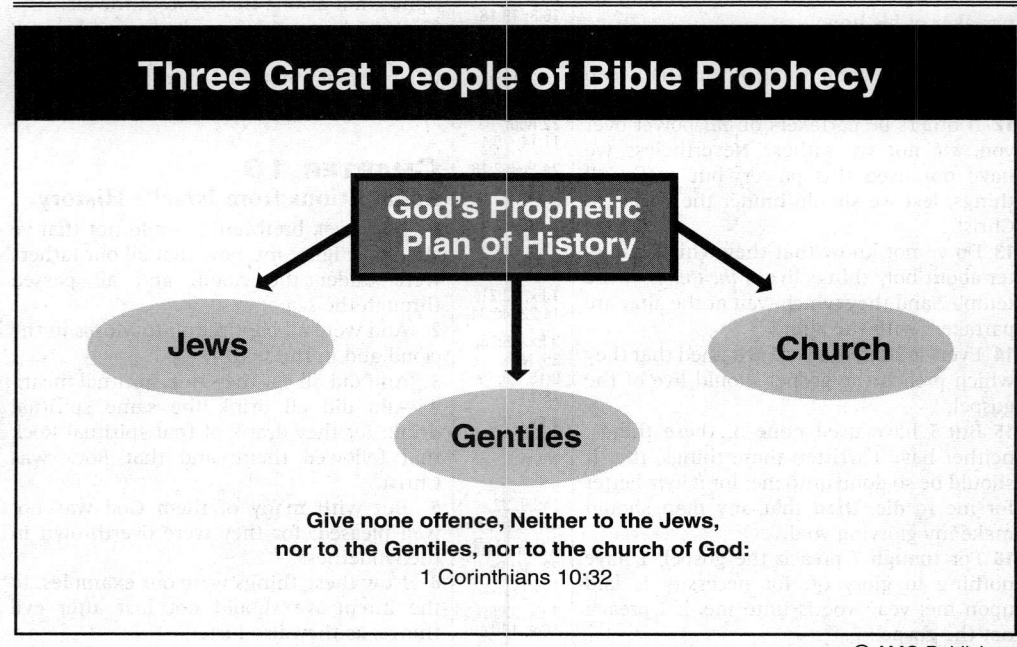

Three Great People of Bible Prophecy

God's Prophetic Plan of History

Jews

Gentiles

Church

Give none offence, Neither to the Jews, nor to the Gentiles, nor to the church of God:
1 Corinthians 10:32

28 But if any man say unto you, This is offered in sacrifice unto idols, eat not for his sake that shewed it, and for conscience sake: for the earth *is* the Lord's, and the fulness thereof:

29 Conscience, I say, not thine own, but of the other: for why is my liberty judged of another *man's* conscience?

30 For if I by grace be a partaker, why am I evil spoken of for that for which I give thanks?

31 Whether therefore ye eat, or drink, or whatsoever ye do, do all to the glory of God.

32 Give none offence, neither to the Jews, nor to the Gentiles, nor to the church of God:

33 Even as I please all *men* in all *things*, not seeking mine own profit, but the *profit* of many, that they may be saved.

CHAPTER 11

1 Be ye followers of me, even as I also *am* of Christ.

God's Ordained Order

2 Now I praise you, brethren, that ye remember me in all things, and keep the ordinances, as I delivered *them* to you.

3 But I would have you know, that the head of every man is Christ; and the head of the woman *is* the man; and the head of Christ *is* God.

4 Every man praying or prophesying, having *his* head covered, dishonoureth his head.

5 But every woman that prayeth or prophesieth with *her* head uncovered dishonoureth her head: for that is even all one as if she were shaven.

6 For if the woman be not covered, let her also be shorn: but if it be a shame for a woman to be shorn or shaven, let her be covered.

7 For a man indeed ought not to cover *his* head, forasmuch as he is the image and glory of God: but the woman is the glory of the man.

8 For the man is not of the woman; but the woman of the man.

9 Neither was the man created for the woman; but the woman for the man.

10 For this cause ought the woman to have power on *her* head because of the angels.

28 Ps. 24:1;
1Cor. 8:10,
12

31 Col. 3:17;
1Pet. 4:11

32 Acts
20:28; 1Cor.
8:13

33 Rom.
15:2; 1Cor.
9:19, 22;
10:24

2 1Cor. 4:17;
7:17;
2Thess.
2:15; 3:6

3 Gen. 3:16;
Eph. 5:23;
1Pet. 3:1, 5,
6

4 1Cor.
12:10, 28;
14:1

5 Deut.
21:12; Acts
21:9

6 Num. 5:18;
Deut. 22:5

7 Gen. 1:26,
27; 5:1; 9:6

8 Gen. 2:21,
22

9 Gen. 2:18,
21, 23

10 Gen.
24:65; Eccl.
5:6

11 Gal. 3:28

12 Rom.
11:36

16 1Cor.
7:17; 14:33;
1Tim. 6:4

18 1Cor.
1:10-12; 3:3

19 Matt.
18:7; Luke
2:35; 17:1;
1Tim. 4:1;
2Pet. 2:1, 2

21 2Pet.
2:13; Jude
1:12

22 1Cor.
10:32;
James 2:6

23 Matt.
26:26; Mark
14:22; Luke
22:19

26 John
14:3; 21:22;
Rev. 1:7

11 Nevertheless neither is the man without the woman, neither the woman without the man, in the Lord.

12 For as the woman *is* of the man, even so *is* the man also by the woman; but all things of God.

13 Judge in yourselves: is it comely that a woman pray unto God uncovered?

14 Doth not even nature itself teach you, that, if a man have long hair, it is a shame unto him?

15 But if a woman have long hair, it is a glory to her: for *her* hair is given her for a covering.

16 But if any man seem to be contentious, we have no such custom, neither the churches of God.

The Lord's Supper

17 Now in this that I declare *unto you* I praise *you* not, that ye come together not for the better, but for the worse.

18 For first of all, when ye come together in the church, I hear that there be divisions among you; and I partly believe it.

19 For there must be also heresies among you, that they which are approved may be made manifest among you.

20 When ye come together therefore into one place, *this* is not to eat the Lord's supper.

21 For in eating every one taketh before *other* his own supper: and one is hungry, and another is drunken.

22 What? have ye not houses to eat and to drink in? or despise ye the church of God, and shame them that have not? What shall I say to you? shall I praise you in this? I praise *you* not.

23 For I have received of the Lord that which also I delivered unto you, That the Lord Jesus the *same* night in which he was betrayed took bread:

24 And when he had given thanks, he brake *it,* and said, Take, eat: this is my body, which is broken for you: this do in remembrance of me.

25 After the same manner also *he took* the cup, when he had supped, saying, This cup is the new testament in my blood: this do ye, as oft as ye drink *it,* in remembrance of me.

26 For as often as ye eat this bread, and

11:26 ye do shew the Lord's death till he come. The ordinance of communion is, among other things, a testimony that shows a Christian's belief in the return of Christ. If He were not coming again there would be no real purpose in observing the Lord's table.

Rewards for Christians

By Tony Evans

The city of Corinth was famous for the Isthmian Games, a festival of athletic contests and events similar to the Olympic games. At the end of each contest or event, the athletes would appear before a large, ornately decorated platform called the *bema*. On this platform, the emperor sat on the judgment seat and gave out rewards to the victorious athletes for their years of dedicated and disciplined training and their perseverance and endurance in the heat of competition and battle.

In 2 Corinthians 5:10, Paul gives the Corinthians a similar image of the *bema* in relation to the future judgment of Christians when he states, "For we must all appear before the judgment seat (*bematos*) of Christ; that every one may receive the things done in his body, according to that he hath done, whether it be good or bad." Paul is saying that all Christians will stand before the *bema* seat of Christ. At the *bema* seat, Jesus Christ will bring to light every deed, good or bad that each believer has done on earth since he or she became a Christian. Every Christian will be rewarded based on his words, deeds, and faithfulness (see 1Cor. 3:11–14).

> *Serve God faithfully now, and you will be rewarded later.*

Jesus illustrates judgment and rewards in the parable He gives in Matthew 25:14–30. A man who is about to go on a journey entrusts his possessions to three of his servants, each according to his ability. These three servants represent Christians; the master represents Christ; and the possessions represent the time, talent, and treasures that Christ gives every Christian. In the parable, two of the servants are faithful with what the master gives them, but one is unfaithful. When the master returns and calls his servants before him, the two faithful servants are rewarded with more and are given rule or charge over many things. However, the unfaithful servant loses what he had been given and is cast into "outer darkness" (Matt. 25:30).

In this parable, those who are faithful with the time, talent, and treasures that Christ gives them will be rewarded with crowns (1 Cor. 9:24–27) and the opportunity to assist Christ in governing the Millennial Kingdom (Rev. 20:4). But those Christians who are unfaithful (Matt. 25:28–30) will have their rewards taken from them and given to those who were faithful, and they will be cast into "outer darkness," the place where there shall be "weeping and gnashing of teeth." The "outer darkness" described in this passage is not a description of hell, but is likely a lesser status in God's kingdom. Unfaithful Christians will see more diligent Christians rule and reign with Christ. Realizing that they could have had much greater reward and prominence in God's kingdom, these unfaithful stewards will weep and gnash their teeth in deep remorse and regret.

In Revelation 22:12, Jesus Christ says, "I come quickly and my reward is with me, to give every man according as his work shall be." Are you ready to stand before the *bema* seat of Christ? Out of your love for Christ and appreciation for the gift of salvation, serve God faithfully now, and you will be rewarded later. The hope of winning crowns from Jesus Christ and reigning with Him should convince a Christian that running a faithful race is worth the effort. Being awarded any one of these crowns or opportunities to rule will be an honor beyond anything we can imagine. Let's go for it!

drink this cup, ye do shew the Lord's death till he come.

27 Wherefore whosoever shall eat this bread, and drink *this* cup of the Lord, unworthily, shall be guilty of the body and blood of the Lord.

28 But let a man examine himself, and so let him eat of *that* bread, and drink of *that* cup.

29 For he that eateth and drinketh unworthily, eateth and drinketh damnation to himself, not discerning the Lord's body.

30 For this cause many *are* weak and sickly among you, and many sleep.

31 For if we would judge ourselves, we should not be judged.

32 But when we are judged, we are chastened of the Lord, that we should not be condemned with the world.

33 Wherefore, my brethren, when ye come together to eat, tarry one for another.

34 And if any man hunger, let him eat at home; that ye come not together unto condemnation. And the rest will I set in order when I come.

CHAPTER 12
Spiritual Gifts

1 Now concerning spiritual *gifts,* brethren, I would not have you ignorant.

2 Ye know that ye were Gentiles, carried away unto these dumb idols, even as ye were led.

3 Wherefore I give you to understand, that no man speaking by the Spirit of God calleth Jesus accursed: and *that* no man can say that Jesus is the Lord, but by the Holy Ghost.

4 Now there are diversities of gifts, but the same Spirit.

5 And there are differences of administrations, but the same Lord.

6 And there are diversities of operations, but it is the same God which worketh all in all.

7 But the manifestation of the Spirit is given to every man to profit withal.

8 For to one is given by the Spirit the word of wisdom; to another the word of knowledge by the same Spirit;

9 To another faith by the same Spirit; to another the gifts of healing by the same Spirit;

10 To another the working of miracles; to another prophecy; to another discerning of spirits; to another *divers* kinds of tongues; to another the interpretation of tongues:

11 But all these worketh that one and the

selfsame Spirit, dividing to every man severally as he will.

One Body, Many Members

12 For as the body is one, and hath many members, and all the members of that one body, being many, are one body: so also *is* Christ.

13 For by one Spirit are we all baptized into one body, whether *we be* Jews or Gentiles, whether *we be* bond or free; and have been all made to drink into one Spirit.

14 For the body is not one member, but many.

15 If the foot shall say, Because I am not the hand, I am not of the body; is it therefore not of the body?

16 And if the ear shall say, Because I am not the eye, I am not of the body; is it therefore not of the body?

17 If the whole body *were* an eye, where *were* the hearing? If the whole *were* hearing, where *were* the smelling?

18 But now hath God set the members every one of them in the body, as it hath pleased him.

19 And if they were all one member, where *were* the body?

20 But now *are they* many members, yet but one body.

21 And the eye cannot say unto the hand, I have no need of thee: nor again the head to the feet, I have no need of you.

22 Nay, much more those members of the body, which seem to be more feeble, are necessary:

23 And those *members* of the body, which we think to be less honourable, upon these we bestow more abundant honour; and our uncomely *parts* have more abundant comeliness.

24 For our comely *parts* have no need: but God hath tempered the body together, having given more abundant honour to that *part* which lacked:

25 That there should be no schism in the body; but *that* the members should have the same care one for another.

26 And whether one member suffer, all the members suffer with it; or one member be honoured, all the members rejoice with it.

27 Now ye are the body of Christ, and members in particular.

28 And God hath set some in the church, first apostles, secondarily prophets, thirdly teachers, after that miracles, then gifts of healings, helps, governments, diversities of tongues.

---

27 Num. 9:10, 13; John 13:27; 1Cor. 10:21

28 2Cor. 13:5; Gal. 6:4

29 Rom. 13:2

31 Ps. 32:5

32 Heb. 12:5-11

34 1Cor. 4:19; 7:17

2 Eph. 2:11, 12; 1Thess. 1:9

3 Matt. 16:17; Mark 9:39; John 15:26

4 Heb. 2:4; 1Pet. 4:10

5 Rom. 12:6-8; Eph. 4:11

6 Eph. 1:23

7 1Cor. 14:26; 1Pet. 4:10, 11

8 1Cor. 1:5; 2:6, 7; 13:2

9 Matt. 17:19, 20; 1Cor. 13:2; 2Cor. 4:13

10 Mark 16:17; Acts 2:4; 10:46; 1John 4:1

11 John 3:8; Rom. 12:6; 2Cor. 10:13; Eph. 4:7

12 Rom. 12:4, 5; 1Cor. 12:27; Gal. 3:16; Eph. 4:4, 16

13 John 6:63; 7:37-39; Rom. 6:5; Gal. 3:28; Eph. 2:13, 14, 16; Col. 3:11

18 Rom. 12:3; 1Cor. 3:5; 12:11, 28

27 Rom. 12:5; Eph. 1:23; 4:12; 5:23, 30; Col. 1:24

28 Acts 13:1; Rom. 12:6, 8; Eph. 2:20; 3:5; 4:11

29 *Are* all apostles? *are* all prophets? *are* all teachers? *are* all workers of miracles?
30 Have all the gifts of healing? do all speak with tongues? do all interpret?

Love

31 But covet earnestly the best gifts: and yet shew I unto you a more excellent way.

CHAPTER 13

1 Though I speak with the tongues of men and of angels, and have not charity, I am become *as* sounding brass, or a tinkling cymbal.
2 And though I have *the gift of* prophecy, and understand all mysteries, and all knowledge; and though I have all faith, so that I could remove mountains, and have not charity, I am nothing.
3 And though I bestow all my goods to feed *the poor,* and though I give my body to be burned, and have not charity, it profiteth me nothing.
4 Charity suffereth long, *and* is kind; charity envieth not; charity vaunteth not itself, is not puffed up,
5 Doth not behave itself unseemly, seeketh not her own, is not easily provoked, thinketh no evil;
6 Rejoiceth not in iniquity, but rejoiceth in the truth;
7 Beareth all things, believeth all things, hopeth all things, endureth all things.
8 Charity never faileth: but whether *there be* prophecies, they shall fail; whether *there be* tongues, they shall cease; whether *there be* knowledge, it shall vanish away.
9 For we know in part, and we prophesy in part.
10 But when that which is perfect is come, then that which is in part shall be done away.
11 When I was a child, I spake as a child, I understood as a child, I thought as a child: but when I became a man, I put away childish things.
12 For now we see through a glass, darkly; but then face to face: now I know in part; but then shall I know even as also I am known.
13 And now abideth faith, hope, charity, these three; but the greatest of these *is* charity.

Cross References

31 1Cor. 14:1, 39

2 Matt. 7:22; 17:20; Mark 11:23; Luke 17:6; 1Cor. 12:8-10; 14:1

3 Matt. 6:1, 2

4 Prov. 10:12; 1Pet. 4:8

5 1Cor. 10:24; Phil. 2:4

6 Ps. 10:3; Rom. 1:32; 2John 1:4

7 Rom. 15:1; Gal. 6:2; 2Tim. 2:24

9 1Cor. 8:2

12 Matt. 18:10; 2Cor. 3:18; 5:7; Phil. 3:12; 1John 3:2

1 Num. 11:25, 29; 1Cor. 12:31

2 Acts 2:4; 10:46; 22:9

6 1Cor. 14:26

15 Ps. 47:7; Eph. 5:19; Col. 3:16

CHAPTER 14
Concerning Speaking in Tongues

1 Follow after charity, and desire spiritual *gifts,* but rather that ye may prophesy.
2 For he that speaketh in an *unknown* tongue speaketh not unto men, but unto God: for no man understandeth *him;* howbeit in the spirit he speaketh mysteries.
3 But he that prophesieth speaketh unto men *to* edification, and exhortation, and comfort.
4 He that speaketh in an *unknown* tongue edifieth himself; but he that prophesieth edifieth the church.
5 I would that ye all spake with tongues, but rather that ye prophesied: for greater *is* he that prophesieth than he that speaketh with tongues, except he interpret, that the church may receive edifying.
6 Now, brethren, if I come unto you speaking with tongues, what shall I profit you, except I shall speak to you either by revelation, or by knowledge, or by prophesying, or by doctrine?
7 And even things without life giving sound, whether pipe or harp, except they give a distinction in the sounds, how shall it be known what is piped or harped?
8 For if the trumpet give an uncertain sound, who shall prepare himself to the battle?
9 So likewise ye, except ye utter by the tongue words easy to be understood, how shall it be known what is spoken? for ye shall speak into the air.
10 There are, it may be, so many kinds of voices in the world, and none of them *is* without signification.
11 Therefore if I know not the meaning of the voice, I shall be unto him that speaketh a barbarian, and he that speaketh *shall be* a barbarian unto me.
12 Even so ye, forasmuch as ye are zealous of spiritual *gifts,* seek that ye may excel to the edifying of the church.
13 Wherefore let him that speaketh in an *unknown* tongue pray that he may interpret.
14 For if I pray in an *unknown* tongue, my spirit prayeth, but my understanding is unfruitful.
15 What is it then? I will pray with the spirit, and I will pray with the understand-

---

13:12 now we see through a glass, darkly. Our present knowledge of God's plan for the future is limited, but in eternity, we shall know even as we are known, indicating a thorough knowledge. Even with the extended knowledge given in the book of Revelation, our knowledge of heavenly things is very limited.

ing also: I will sing with the spirit, and I will sing with the understanding also.

16 Else when thou shalt bless with the spirit, how shall he that occupieth the room of the unlearned say Amen at thy giving of thanks, seeing he understandeth not what thou sayest?

17 For thou verily givest thanks well, but the other is not edified.

18 I thank my God, I speak with tongues more than ye all:

19 Yet in the church I had rather speak five words with my understanding, that *by my voice* I might teach others also, than ten thousand words in an *unknown* tongue.

20 Brethren, be not children in understanding: howbeit in malice be ye children, but in understanding be men.

21 In the law it is written, With *men of* other tongues and other lips will I speak unto this people; and yet for all that will they not hear me, saith the Lord.

22 Wherefore tongues are for a sign, not to them that believe, but to them that believe not: but prophesying *serveth* not for them that believe not, but for them which believe.

23 If therefore the whole church be come together into one place, and all speak with tongues, and there come in *those that are* unlearned, or unbelievers, will they not say that ye are mad?

24 But if all prophesy, and there come in one that believeth not, or *one* unlearned, he is convinced of all, he is judged of all:

25 And thus are the secrets of his heart made manifest; and so falling down on *his* face he will worship God, and report that God is in you of a truth.

Do Things Properly and Orderly

26 How is it then, brethren? when ye come together, every one of you hath a psalm, hath a doctrine, hath a tongue, hath a revelation, hath an interpretation. Let all things be done unto edifying.

27 If any man speak in an *unknown* tongue, *let it be* by two, or at the most *by* three, and *that* by course; and let one interpret.

28 But if there be no interpreter, let him keep silence in the church; and let him speak to himself, and to God.

29 Let the prophets speak two or three, and let the other judge.

16 1Cor. 11:24

20 Ps. 131:2; Matt. 11:25; 18:3; 19:14; Rom. 16:19

21 Isa. 28:11, 12; John 10:34

23 Acts 2:13

25 Isa. 45:14; Zech. 8:23

26 2Cor. 12:19; Eph. 4:12

29 1Cor. 12:10

30 1Thess. 5:19, 20

32 1John 4:1

33 1Cor. 11:16

34 1Cor. 11:3; Eph. 5:22; 1Tim. 2:11, 12; 1Pet. 3:1

37 2Cor. 10:7; 1John 4:6

39 1Cor. 12:31; 1Thess. 5:20

40 Rom. 5:2; 1Cor. 14:33; Gal. 1:11

2 Rom. 1:16; 1Cor. 1:21; Gal. 3:4

3 Ps. 22:15; Isa. 53:5, 6; Dan. 9:26; Zech. 13:7; Luke 24:26, 46

4 Ps. 2:7; 16:10; Isa. 53:10; Hos. 6:2; Luke 24:26, 46

5 Matt. 28:17; Mark 16:14; Luke 24:34, 36; John 20:19, 26; Acts 10:41

7 Luke 24:50; Acts 1:3, 4

8 Acts 9:4, 17; 22:14, 18; 1Cor. 9:1

30 If *any thing* be revealed to another that sitteth by, let the first hold his peace.

31 For ye may all prophesy one by one, that all may learn, and all may be comforted.

32 And the spirits of the prophets are subject to the prophets.

33 For God is not *the author* of confusion, but of peace, as in all churches of the saints.

34 Let your women keep silence in the churches: for it is not permitted unto them to speak; but *they are commanded* to be under obedience, as also saith the law.

35 And if they will learn any thing, let them ask their husbands at home: for it is a shame for women to speak in the church.

36 What? came the word of God out from you? or came it unto you only?

37 If any man think himself to be a prophet, or spiritual, let him acknowledge that the things that I write unto you are the commandments of the Lord.

38 But if any man be ignorant, let him be ignorant.

39 Wherefore, brethren, covet to prophesy, and forbid not to speak with tongues.

40 Let all things be done decently and in order.

CHAPTER 15
A Summary of the Gospel

1 Moreover, brethren, I declare unto you the gospel which I preached unto you, which also ye have received, and wherein ye stand;

2 By which also ye are saved, if ye keep in memory what I preached unto you, unless ye have believed in vain.

3 For I delivered unto you first of all that which I also received, how that Christ died for our sins according to the scriptures;

4 And that he was buried, and that he rose again the third day according to the scriptures:

5 And that he was seen of Cephas, then of the twelve:

6 After that, he was seen of above five hundred brethren at once; of whom the greater part remain unto this present, but some are fallen asleep.

7 After that, he was seen of James; then of all the apostles.

8 And last of all he was seen of me also, as of one born out of due time.

15:1–4 according to the scriptures. The three scriptural elements of the gospel that fulfilled prophecy were: 1) "Christ died for our sins," 2) "He was buried," 3) "He rose again the third day"—all according to the Scriptures. Any gospel that omits one of these three prophetic principles is not the true gospel that is required for salvation.

9 For I am the least of the apostles, that am not meet to be called an apostle, because I persecuted the church of God.

10 But by the grace of God I am what I am: and his grace which *was bestowed* upon me was not in vain; but I laboured more abundantly than they all: yet not I, but the grace of God which was with me.

11 Therefore whether *it were* I or they, so we preach, and so ye believed.

12 Now if Christ be preached that he rose from the dead, how say some among you that there is no resurrection of the dead?

13 But if there be no resurrection of the dead, then is Christ not risen:

14 And if Christ be not risen, then *is* our preaching vain, and your faith *is* also vain.

15 Yea, and we are found false witnesses of God; because we have testified of God that he raised up Christ: whom he raised not up, if so be that the dead rise not.

16 For if the dead rise not, then is not Christ raised:

17 And if Christ be not raised, your faith *is* vain; ye are yet in your sins.

18 Then they also which are fallen asleep in Christ are perished.

19 If in this life only we have hope in Christ, we are of all men most miserable.

20 But now is Christ risen from the dead, *and* become the firstfruits of them that slept.

21 For since by man *came* death, by man *came* also the resurrection of the dead.

22 For as in Adam all die, even so in Christ shall all be made alive.

23 But every man in his own order: Christ the firstfruits; afterward they that are Christ's at his coming.

24 Then *cometh* the end, when he shall have delivered up the kingdom to God, even the Father; when he shall have put down all rule and all authority and power.

25 For he must reign, till he hath put all enemies under his feet.

9 Acts 8:3; 9:1; Phil. 3:6
10 Rom. 15:18, 19; 2Cor. 3:5; 11:23; 12:11; Phil. 2:13
13 1Thess. 4:14
17 Rom. 4:25
20 Acts 26:23; 1Pet. 1:3; Rev. 1:5
21 John 11:25
23 1Cor. 15:20; 1Thess. 4:15-17
24 Dan. 7:14, 27
25 Ps. 110:1; Acts 2:34, 35
26 2Tim. 1:10; Rev. 20:14
27 Ps. 8:6; Matt. 28:18; Heb. 2:8; 1Pet. 3:22
28 1Cor. 3:23; 11:3; Phil. 3:21
30 2Cor. 11:26
31 2Cor. 4:10, 11; 11:23; 1Thess. 2:19
32 Eccl. 2:24; Isa. 22:13; 56:12; Luke 12:19
33 1Cor. 5:6
34 Rom. 13:11; 1Thess. 4:5
35 Ezek. 37:3
36 John 12:24

26 The last enemy *that* shall be destroyed *is* death.

27 For he hath put all things under his feet. But when he saith all things are put under *him, it is* manifest that he is excepted, which did put all things under him.

28 And when all things shall be subdued unto him, then shall the Son also himself be subject unto him that put all things under him, that God may be all in all.

29 Else what shall they do which are baptized for the dead, if the dead rise not at all? why are they then baptized for the dead?

30 And why stand we in jeopardy every hour?

31 I protest by your rejoicing which I have in Christ Jesus our Lord, I die daily.

32 If after the manner of men I have fought with beasts at Ephesus, what advantageth it me, if the dead rise not? let us eat and drink; for to morrow we die.

33 Be not deceived: evil communications corrupt good manners.

34 Awake to righteousness, and sin not; for some have not the knowledge of God: I speak *this* to your shame.

Resurrection Promised

35 But some *man* will say, How are the dead raised up? and with what body do they come?

36 *Thou* fool, that which thou sowest is not quickened, except it die:

37 And that which thou sowest, thou sowest not that body that shall be, but bare grain, it may chance of wheat, or of some other *grain*:

38 But God giveth it a body as it hath pleased him, and to every seed his own body.

39 All flesh *is* not the same flesh: but *there is* one *kind of* flesh of men, another flesh of beasts, another of fishes, *and* another of birds.

40 *There are* also celestial bodies, and bodies

15:20 the firstfruits of them that slept. Just as the firstfruits of crops secure the promise for harvest, so Christ's resurrection secures, even predicts, our own.

15:23–27 This description, having to do with resurrection, does not discuss either the Rapture or the Tribulation period, but describes the resurrection at the glorious appearing (Rev 20:4) when Christ sets up His kingdom, which is the climax of the magnificent plan God has for mankind prior to heaven.

15:29 why are they then baptized for the dead? This

is the only verse in Scripture that says anything about baptizing for the dead. It has never been practiced or endorsed by the Church; even now it is practiced only by cults. Paul doesn't commend the practice but may be referring to the symbolism of resurrection in baptism. When one is baptized, that person is identified by faith with the risen Jesus and then is raised to walk a new life in Him. Certainly there would be no need for such a baptism if a resurrection were not in the prophetic plan of God for believers.

The Resurrections

By Gary Frazier

Physical death does not end human existence. Jesus said, "Because I live, ye shall live also" (John 14:19). Without a doubt, one of the most comforting and reassuring, yet perhaps, confusing teachings of God's word is found in the doctrine of the resurrection. The questions surrounding this great truth usually have to do with *who* will be resurrected and *when* this will take place.

The doctrine of the resurrection is easily understood when one recognizes there is a series of resurrections that occur in Scripture. In each case it is quite clear who is being resurrected and when. Revelation 20:5 speaks of "the first resurrection" in relation to the faithful martyrs who gave their lives for Christ during the Tribulation. The context implies that the second resurrection will be for unbelievers at the end of history. Thus, we see that "the first resurrection" is a qualitative distinction that refers to the resurrection of believers. The second resurrection is likewise a qualitative description referring to the resurrection of the unsaved.

The first resurrection, which is the resurrection of believers, will occur at various times throughout history. Let's examine briefly the various episodes of this resurrection.

> *Physical death does not end human existence.*

THE SAVIOR: The resurrection of Jesus becomes the pattern and firstfruits for the first resurrection (1 Cor. 15:20, 23).

SELECTED OLD TESTAMENT SAINTS: At the death of Christ, the tombs of selected Old Testament believers were opened. Then, after the resurrection of Jesus, these people appeared in the city to many people as a confirming sign that Jesus was the Messiah (Matt. 27:50–53).

THE SAVED: The redeemed of the Lord who will become the Bride of Christ and have fallen asleep "in Christ" are resurrected in the event called "the rapture" of the Church. Paul clearly states, "We shall not all sleep" (1 Cor. 15:51), meaning some will die, and those who do will be raised "in a flash." Therefore we are told we are not to grieve for our saved loved ones who have gone on to heaven before us, because we are confident they will be resurrected (1 Thess. 4:13–18).

THE SERVANTS: Revelation 11 recounts how two servants of the Lord will be witnesses in Jerusalem during the first three and one half years of the Tribulation. These two will ultimately be killed and resurrected for the entire world to see just three and one half days later (Rev. 11:8).

THE SLAIN: Revelation 20:4–6 identifies the martyred dead of the Tribulation as those who will be resurrected at the second coming of Christ in order to reign with Him for a thousand years.

THE OLD TESTAMENT SAINTS: Daniel 12:1 makes it clear that these saints will be resurrected at the close of the Tribulation period in order to reign with Messiah in His kingdom.

There will be a final resurrection of the unsaved at the end of history (Rev. 20:11–15). The lost of all the ages will be collected from the place of the dead (Hades) and brought before the great white throne (Rev. 20:11–15) where they will be condemned to spend eternity in the lake of fire (Rev. 20:15).

The resurrections of Scripture are divided into two classes: the resurrection of the saved and the resurrection of the lost. The promise of the resurrection for any believer is a comforting and reassuring promise while for the unbeliever it is yet a promise of eternal separation and suffering.

terrestrial: but the glory of the celestial *is* one, and the *glory* of the terrestrial *is* another.

41 *There is* one glory of the sun, and another glory of the moon, and another glory of the stars: for *one* star differeth from *another* star in glory.

42 So also *is* the resurrection of the dead. It is sown in corruption; it is raised in incorruption:

43 It is sown in dishonour; it is raised in glory: it is sown in weakness; it is raised in power:

44 It is sown a natural body; it is raised a spiritual body. There is a natural body, and there is a spiritual body.

45 And so it is written, The first man Adam was made a living soul; the last Adam *was* made a quickening spirit.

46 Howbeit that *was* not first which is spiritual, but that which is natural; and afterward that which is spiritual.

47 The first man *is* of the earth, earthy: the second man *is* the Lord from heaven.

48 As *is* the earthy, such *are* they also that are earthy: and as *is* the heavenly, such *are* they also that are heavenly.

49 And as we have borne the image of the earthy, we shall also bear the image of the heavenly.

50 Now this I say, brethren, that flesh and blood cannot inherit the kingdom of God; neither doth corruption inherit incorruption.

51 Behold, I shew you a mystery; We shall not all sleep, but we shall all be changed,

52 In a moment, in the twinkling of an eye, at the last trump: for the trumpet shall sound, and the dead shall be raised incorruptible, and we shall be changed.

Cross references:
42 Dan. 12:3; Matt. 13:43
43 Phil. 3:21
45 Gen. 2:7; Phil. 3:21; Col. 3:4
47 Gen. 2:7; 3:19; John 3:13, 31
49 Rom. 8:29; Phil. 3:21
50 Matt. 16:17; John 3:3, 5
51 Phil. 3:21; 1Thess. 4:15-17
52 Zech. 9:14; Matt. 24:31; John 5:25; 1Thess. 4:16

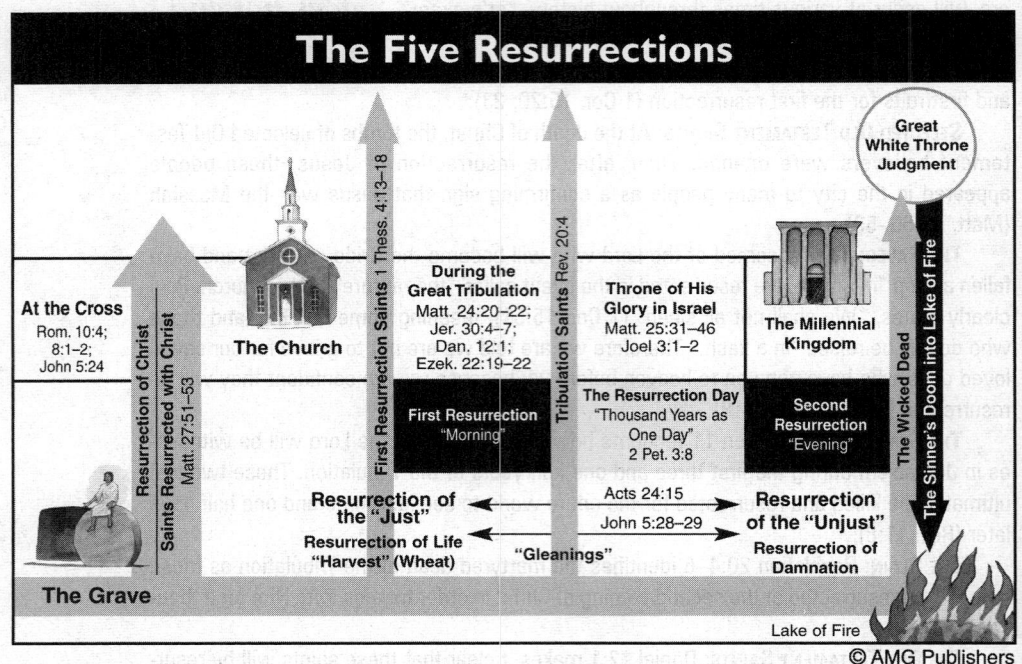

The Five Resurrections

© AMG Publishers

15:51 We shall not all sleep, but we shall all be changed. The "mystery" of the Rapture described here should be studied along with 1 Thessalonians 4:15–17. When Christ comes to rapture His saints, some will still be alive (not sleeping). Just as Enoch was taken into the very presence of God (Gen. 5:24), so living believers will be taken to be with Christ.

15:52 in the twinkling of an eye, at the last trump. This should not be confused with the trumpet judgments of Revelation 9, but is the last trumpet for the Church. When Christ is finished preparing His Father's house as He promised (John 14:1–3) He will call all believers (both dead and living) with the blast of the trumpet. They will suddenly receive their resurrected and incorruptible bodies and be raptured to the Father's house, long before the seven trumpet judgments come.

53 For this corruptible must put on incorruption, and this mortal *must* put on immortality.

54 So when this corruptible shall have put on incorruption, and this mortal shall have put on immortality, then shall be brought to pass the saying that is written, Death is swallowed up in victory.

55 O death, where *is* thy sting? O grave, where *is* thy victory?

56 The sting of death *is* sin; and the strength of sin *is* the law.

57 But thanks *be* to God, which giveth us the victory through our Lord Jesus Christ.

58 Therefore, my beloved brethren, be ye stedfast, unmoveable, always abounding in the work of the Lord, forasmuch as ye know that your labour is not in vain in the Lord.

CHAPTER 16
Concerning the Collection from the Churches

1 Now concerning the collection for the saints, as I have given order to the churches of Galatia, even so do ye.

2 Upon the first *day* of the week let every one of you lay by him in store, as *God* hath prospered him, that there be no gatherings when I come.

3 And when I come, whomsoever ye shall approve by *your* letters, them will I send to bring your liberality unto Jerusalem.

4 And if it be meet that I go also, they shall go with me.

5 Now I will come unto you, when I shall pass through Macedonia: for I do pass through Macedonia.

6 And it may be that I will abide, yea, and winter with you, that ye may bring me on my journey whithersoever I go.

7 For I will not see you now by the way; but I trust to tarry a while with you, if the Lord permit.

8 But I will tarry at Ephesus until Pentecost.

9 For a great door and effectual is opened unto me, and *there are* many adversaries.

10 Now if Timotheus come, see that he may be with you without fear: for he worketh the work of the Lord, as I also *do*.

11 Let no man therefore despise him: but conduct him forth in peace, that he may come unto me: for I look for him with the brethren.

12 As touching *our* brother Apollos, I greatly desired him to come unto you with the brethren: but his will was not at all to come at this time; but he will come when he shall have convenient time.

13 Watch ye, stand fast in the faith, quit you like men, be strong.

14 Let all your things be done with charity.

15 I beseech you, brethren, ye (know the house of Stephanas, that it is the firstfruits of Achaia, and *that* they have addicted themselves to the ministry of the saints,)

16 That ye submit yourselves unto such, and to every one that helpeth with *us,* and laboureth.

17 I am glad of the coming of Stephanas and Fortunatus and Achaicus: for that which was lacking on your part they have supplied.

18 For they have refreshed my spirit and yours: therefore acknowledge ye them that are such.

19 The churches of Asia salute you. Aquila and Priscilla salute you much in the Lord, with the church that is in their house.

20 All the brethren greet you. Greet ye one another with an holy kiss.

21 The salutation of *me* Paul with mine own hand.

22 If any man love not the Lord Jesus Christ, let him be Anathema Maranatha.

23 The grace of our Lord Jesus Christ *be* with you.

24 My love *be* with you all in Christ Jesus. Amen.

Cross References

53 2Cor. 5:4
54 Isa. 25:8; Heb. 2:14, 15; Rev. 20:14
55 Hos. 13:14
58 1Cor. 3:8; 2Pet. 3:14
1 Acts 11:29; 24:17; Gal. 2:10
2 Acts 20:7; Rev. 1:10
3 2Cor. 8:4, 6, 19
4 2Cor. 8:4, 19
5 Acts 19:21; 2Cor. 1:16
6 Acts 15:3; 17:15; 21:5
7 Acts 18:21; 1Cor. 4:19
9 Acts 14:27; 19:9; 2Cor. 2:12
10 Acts 19:22; Phil. 2:19–22; 1Thess. 3:2
11 Acts 15:33; 1Tim. 4:12
12 1Cor. 1:12; 3:5
13 Matt. 24:42; 25:13; Eph. 6:10; 1Thess. 3:8; 5:6; 2Thess. 2:15
14 1Cor. 14:1; 1Pet. 4:8
20 Rom. 16:16
21 Col. 4:18; 2Thess. 3:17
23 Rom. 16:20

15:54–57 God, which giveth us the victory through our Lord Jesus Christ. What a triumphant prophecy when "death is swallowed up in victory" at the Rapture for all believers throughout all of Church history.

15:58 be ye stedfast, unmoveable, always abounding in the work of the Lord. Now is the time to serve the Lord, for the Rapture is coming and our efforts will earn an eternal reward (cf. Eph. 2:8–9; James 3:13).

16:22 Anathema Maranatha. This concluding expression is a curse on those who "love not the Lord Jesus" when He comes, for then it will be too late for them to turn to Christ. But for those who have put their faith in Him, Christ's return is a great blessing, for they will be with the Lord. "Maranatha" is made up of two Aramaic words, *maran,* which means "the Lord," and *atha,* which means "comes." Later in the first century, "Maranatha" became a Christian greeting, a reminder that all believers should live every day in the light of His coming.

2 Corinthians

While Paul traveled through Macedonia on his way to Corinth, he met with Titus and discovered that his first letter to the Corinthian church had been received and that it accomplished much good. (See introduction to 1 Corinthians.) Nevertheless, there were still some serious problems in the church at Corinth, and this epistle, largely autobiographical, is a defense of the great apostle's ministry against repeated attacks directed toward him by some carnal professing believers at Corinth. In this letter, Paul demonstrates from his own ministry the source and impulse of all true Christian living and service—total dedication to God in all circumstances.

Author
Paul
Date
A.D. 56
Key Truth
Paul's Authority Defended
Historic Time
The Extent of Paul's Ministry to Corinth
Key Verse
4:5
For we preach not ourselves, but Christ Jesus the Lord.

Only in this most personal and revealing letter does Paul express his own strong emotions as a very loving, but sensitive person. Replying to his critics, he describes his travels, hardships, persecutions, and disappointments, but also recounts his own spiritual triumphs (chap. 12). These personal testimonies are mingled with great theological concepts, touching on the differences between the old dispensation of law, characterized by sin and death, and the new dispensation of righteousness and glory (chap. 3). Other concepts taught by Paul include information on the evil work of Satan in the blinding of sinners (chap. 4), the immortality of the soul, the judgment seat of Christ, the atonement, and the Christian's responsibility to share the gospel message (chap. 5). The book closes with a graphic but humble display of Paul's own courage in the midst of adversity. Only in this epistle (chap. 12) does Paul mention his supernatural experience in being caught up to the third heaven.

The primary prophetic passage is in chapter five, which discusses our being present with the Lord after death, but reminds us that we must all appear before the judgment seat of Christ (5:10).

Only 7 separate prophetic ideas appear in just 12 of the 257 verses, or 5 percent. The book of 2 Corinthians has 9 quotations from the Old Testament.

5% Prophecy

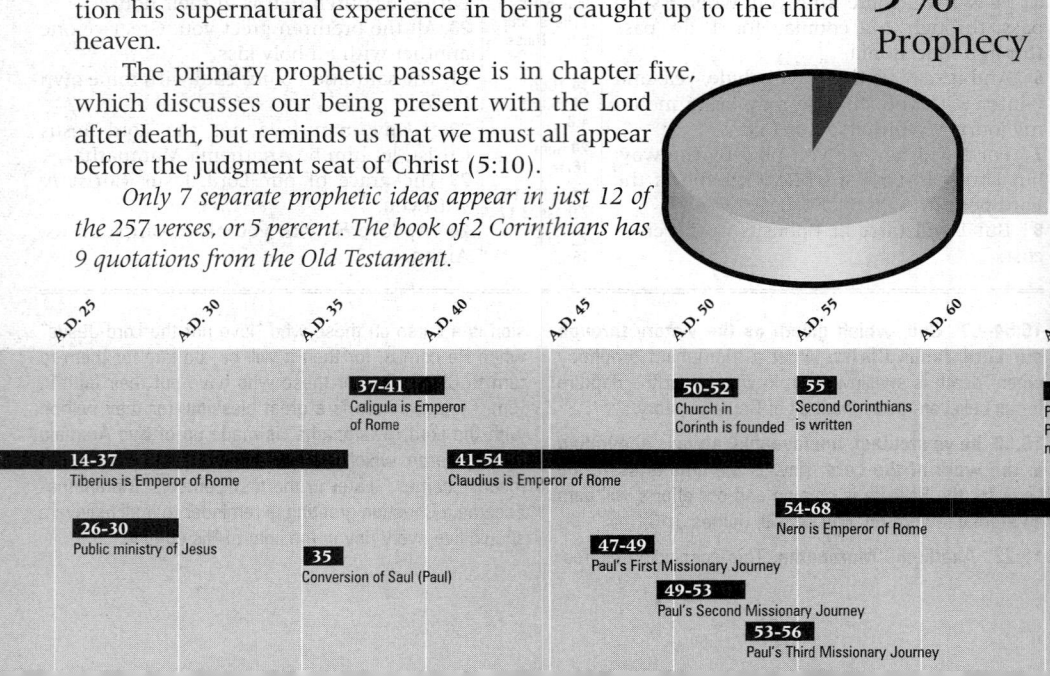

CHAPTER 1

1 Paul, an apostle of Jesus Christ by the will of God, and Timothy *our* brother, unto the church of God which is at Corinth, with all the saints which are in all Achaia:

2 Grace *be* to you and peace from God our Father, and *from* the Lord Jesus Christ.

"The God of All Comfort"

3 Blessed *be* God, even the Father of our Lord Jesus Christ, the Father of mercies, and the God of all comfort;

4 Who comforteth us in all our tribulation, that we may be able to comfort them which are in any trouble, by the comfort wherewith we ourselves are comforted of God.

5 For as the sufferings of Christ abound in us, so our consolation also aboundeth by Christ.

6 And whether we be afflicted, *it is* for your consolation and salvation, which is effectual in the enduring of the same sufferings which we also suffer: or whether we be comforted, *it is* for your consolation and salvation.

7 And our hope of you *is* stedfast, knowing, that as ye are partakers of the sufferings, so *shall ye be* also of the consolation.

8 For we would not, brethren, have you ignorant of our trouble which came to us in Asia, that we were pressed out of measure, above strength, insomuch that we despaired even of life:

9 But we had the sentence of death in ourselves, that we should not trust in ourselves, but in God which raiseth the dead:

10 Who delivered us from so great a death, and doth deliver: in whom we trust that he will yet deliver *us;*

11 Ye also helping together by prayer for us, that for the gift *bestowed* upon us by the means of many persons thanks may be given by many on our behalf.

Paul's Sincerity

12 For our rejoicing is this, the testimony of our conscience, that in simplicity and godly sincerity, not with fleshly wisdom, but by the grace of God, we have had our conversation in the world, and more abundantly to you-ward.

13 For we write none other things unto you, than what ye read or acknowledge; and I

trust ye shall acknowledge even to the end;

14 As also ye have acknowledged us in part, that we are your rejoicing, even as ye also *are* ours in the day of the Lord Jesus.

15 And in this confidence I was minded to come unto you before, that ye might have a second benefit;

16 And to pass by you into Macedonia, and to come again out of Macedonia unto you, and of you to be brought on my way toward Judea.

17 When I therefore was thus minded, did I use lightness? or the things that I purpose, do I purpose according to the flesh, that with me there should be yea yea, and nay nay?

18 But *as* God *is* true, our word toward you was not yea and nay.

19 For the Son of God, Jesus Christ, who was preached among you by us, *even* by me and Silvanus and Timotheus, was not yea and nay, but in him was yea.

20 For all the promises of God in him *are* yea, and in him Amen, unto the glory of God by us.

21 Now he which stablisheth us with you in Christ, and hath anointed us, *is* God;

22 Who hath also sealed us, and given the earnest of the Spirit in our hearts.

23 Moreover I call God for a record upon my soul, that to spare you I came not as yet unto Corinth.

24 Not for that we have dominion over your faith, but are helpers of your joy: for by faith ye stand.

CHAPTER 2

1 But I determined this with myself, that I would not come again to you in heaviness.

2 For if I make you sorry, who is he then that maketh me glad, but the same which is made sorry by me?

3 And I wrote this same unto you, lest, when I came, I should have sorrow from them of whom I ought to rejoice; having confidence in you all, that my joy is *the joy* of you all.

4 For out of much affliction and anguish of heart I wrote unto you with many tears; not that ye should be grieved, but that ye might know the love which I have more abundantly unto you.

Cross references:

1 1Cor. 1:1; Eph. 1:1; Phil. 1:1; Col. 1:1, 2; 1Tim. 1:1; 2Tim. 1:1
2 Rom. 1:7; 1Cor. 1:3
3 Eph. 1:3; 1Pet. 1:3
5 Acts 9:4; 2Cor. 4:10; Col. 1:24
6 2Cor. 4:15
7 Rom. 8:17; 2Tim. 2:12
8 Acts 19:23; 1Cor. 15:32; 16:9
9 Jer. 17:5, 7
11 Rom. 15:30; Phil. 1:19
12 1Cor. 2:4, 13; 2Cor. 2:17; 4:2
14 2Cor. 5:12; Phil. 2:16; 4:1
15 Rom. 1:11; 1Cor. 4:19
16 1Cor. 16:5, 6
17 2Cor. 10:2
19 Mark 1:1; Luke 1:35
20 Rom. 15:8, 9
21 1John 2:20, 27
22 2Cor. 5:5; Eph. 1:13, 14; 4:30
23 1Cor. 4:21; 2Cor. 2:3; Phil. 1:8
24 Rom. 11:20; 1Cor. 3:5; 15:1; 1Pet. 5:3
1 2Cor. 1:23; 12:20, 21; 13:10
3 2Cor. 7:16; 8:22; 12:21; Gal. 5:10
4 2Cor. 7:8, 9, 12

1:14 the day of the Lord Jesus. This phrase alludes to the judgment seat of Christ, and therefore is a clear reference to the Rapture. The main cause for rejoicing in that judgment for all Christians is in the souls we have led to Christ or in those we have influenced spiritually.

Forgiveness for a Penitent Man

5 But if any have caused grief, he hath not grieved me, but in part: that I may not overcharge you all.

6 Sufficient to such a man *is* this punishment, which *was inflicted* of many.

7 So that contrariwise ye *ought* rather to forgive *him,* and comfort *him,* lest perhaps such a one should be swallowed up with overmuch sorrow.

8 Wherefore I beseech you that ye would confirm *your* love toward him.

9 For to this end also did I write, that I might know the proof of you, whether ye be obedient in all things.

10 To whom ye forgive any thing, I *forgive* also: for if I forgave any thing, to whom I forgave *it,* for your sakes *forgave I it* in the person of Christ;

11 Lest Satan should get an advantage of us: for we are not ignorant of his devices.

12 Furthermore, when I came to Troas to *preach* Christ's gospel, and a door was opened unto me of the Lord,

13 I had no rest in my spirit, because I found not Titus my brother: but taking my leave of them, I went from thence into Macedonia.

Victory in Christ

14 Now thanks be unto God, which always causeth us to triumph in Christ, and maketh manifest the savour of his knowledge by us in every place.

15 For we are unto God a sweet savour of Christ, in them that are saved, and in them that perish:

16 To the one *we are* the savour of death unto death; and to the other the savour of life unto life. And who *is* sufficient for these things?

17 For we are not as many, which corrupt the word of God: but as of sincerity, but as of God, in the sight of God speak we in Christ.

CHAPTER 3
A New Ministry

1 Do we begin again to commend ourselves? or need we, as some *others,* epistles of commendation to you, or *letters* of commendation from you?

2 Ye are our epistle written in our hearts, known and read of all men:

3 *Forasmuch as ye are* manifestly declared to be the epistle of Christ ministered by us, written not with ink, but with the Spirit of

---

5 1Cor. 5:1; Gal. 4:12
6 1Cor. 5:4, 5; 1Tim. 5:20
7 Gal. 6:1
9 2Cor. 7:15; 10:6
12 Acts 16:8; 20:6; 1Cor. 16:9
13 2Cor. 7:5, 6
15 1Cor. 1:18; 2Cor. 4:3
16 John 9:39; 1Cor. 15:10
17 2Pet. 2:3
1 Acts 18:27; 2Cor. 5:12; 10:8, 12; 12:11
2 1Cor. 9:2
3 Ex. 24:12; 34:1; Ps. 40:8; 1Cor. 3:5
5 John 15:5; 1Cor. 3:5; 15:10; Phil. 2:13; 1Tim. 1:11, 12; 2Tim. 1:11
6 Matt. 26:28; Rom. 2:27, 29; 3:20
7 Ex. 34:1, 28, 29, 30, 35
8 Gal. 3:5
9 Rom. 1:17; 3:21
12 2Cor. 7:4; Eph. 6:19
13 Ex. 34:33, 35; Rom. 10:4; Gal. 3:23
14 Isa. 6:10; John 12:40; Rom. 11:7, 8, 25
16 Ex. 34:34; Isa. 25:7; Rom. 11:23, 26
17 1Cor. 15:45
18 1Cor. 13:12
1 1Cor. 7:25; 1Tim. 1:13
2 Rom. 1:16; 6:21; 2Cor. 2:17; 5:11; 6:4, 7; 7:14

---

the living God; not in tables of stone, but in fleshy tables of the heart.

4 And such trust have we through Christ to God-ward:

5 Not that we are sufficient of ourselves to think any thing as of ourselves; but our sufficiency *is* of God;

6 Who also hath made us able ministers of the new testament; not of the letter, but of the spirit: for the letter killeth, but the spirit giveth life.

7 But if the ministration of death, written *and* engraven in stones, was glorious, so that the children of Israel could not stedfastly behold the face of Moses for the glory of his countenance; which *glory* was to be done away:

8 How shall not the ministration of the spirit be rather glorious?

9 For if the ministration of condemnation *be* glory, much more doth the ministration of righteousness exceed in glory.

10 For even that which was made glorious had no glory in this respect, by reason of the glory that excelleth.

11 For if that which is done away *was* glorious, much more that which remaineth *is* glorious.

12 Seeing then that we have such hope, we use great plainness of speech:

13 And not as Moses, *which* put a vail over his face, that the children of Israel could not stedfastly look to the end of that which is abolished:

14 But their minds were blinded: for until this day remaineth the same vail untaken away in the reading of the old testament; which *vail* is done away in Christ.

15 But even unto this day, when Moses is read, the vail is upon their heart.

16 Nevertheless when it shall turn to the Lord, the vail shall be taken away.

17 Now the Lord is that Spirit: and where the Spirit of the Lord *is,* there *is* liberty.

18 But we all, with open face beholding as in a glass the glory of the Lord, are changed into the same image from glory to glory, *even* as by the Spirit of the Lord.

CHAPTER 4
Never Give Up

1 Therefore seeing we have this ministry, as we have received mercy, we faint not;

2 But have renounced the hidden things of dishonesty, not walking in craftiness, nor handling the word of God deceitfully; but by manifestation of the truth commending

ourselves to every man's conscience in the sight of God.

3 But if our gospel be hid, it is hid to them that are lost:

4 In whom the god of this world hath blinded the minds of them which believe not, lest the light of the glorious gospel of Christ, who is the image of God, should shine unto them.

5 For we preach not ourselves, but Christ Jesus the Lord; and ourselves your servants for Jesus' sake.

6 For God, who commanded the light to shine out of darkness, hath shined in our hearts, to *give* the light of the knowledge of the glory of God in the face of Jesus Christ.

7 But we have this treasure in earthen vessels, that the excellency of the power may be of God, and not of us.

8 *We are* troubled on every side, yet not distressed; *we are* perplexed, but not in despair;

9 Persecuted, but not forsaken; cast down, but not destroyed;

10 Always bearing about in the body the dying of the Lord Jesus, that the life also of Jesus might be made manifest in our body.

11 For we which live are alway delivered unto death for Jesus' sake, that the life also of Jesus might be made manifest in our mortal flesh.

12 So then death worketh in us, but life in you.

13 We having the same spirit of faith, according as it is written, I believed, and therefore have I spoken; we also believe, and therefore speak;

14 Knowing that he which raised up the Lord Jesus shall raise up us also by Jesus, and shall present *us* with you.

15 For all things *are* for your sakes, that the abundant grace might through the thanksgiving of many redound to the glory of God.

16 For which cause we faint not; but though our outward man perish, yet the inward *man* is renewed day by day.

17 For our light affliction, which is but for a moment, worketh for us a far more exceeding *and* eternal weight of glory;

18 While we look not at the things which are seen, but at the things which are not seen: for the things which are seen *are* temporal; but the things which are not seen *are* eternal.

CHAPTER 5

1 For we know that if our earthly house of *this* tabernacle were dissolved, we have a building of God, an house not made with hands, eternal in the heavens.

2 For in this we groan, earnestly desiring to be clothed upon with our house which is from heaven:

3 If so be that being clothed we shall not be found naked.

4 For we that are in *this* tabernacle do groan, being burdened: not for that we would be unclothed, but clothed upon, that mortality might be swallowed up of life.

5 Now he that hath wrought us for the selfsame thing *is* God, who also hath given unto us the earnest of the Spirit.

6 Therefore *we are* always confident, knowing that, whilst we are at home in the body, we are absent from the Lord:

7 (For we walk by faith, not by sight:)

8 We are confident, *I say,* and willing rather to be absent from the body, and to be present with the Lord.

9 Wherefore we labour, that, whether present or absent, we may be accepted of him.

10 For we must all appear before the judgment seat of Christ; that every one may receive the things *done* in *his* body, according

3 1Cor. 1:18; 2Cor. 2:15

4 Isa. 6:10; John 1:18; Eph. 6:12; Phil. 2:6

5 1Cor. 1:13, 23; 9:19; 10:33; 2Cor. 1:24

6 Gen. 1:3; 2Cor. 4:4; 1Pet. 2:9

8 2Cor. 7:5

9 Ps. 37:24

10 Rom. 8:17; 1Cor. 15:31; Phil. 3:10

11 Ps. 44:22; Rom. 8:36

12 2Cor. 13:9

13 Ps. 116:10; Rom. 1:12

14 Rom. 8:11; 1Cor. 6:14

15 1Cor. 3:21

16 Rom. 7:22

17 1Pet. 1:6; 5:10

18 Job 4:19; Heb. 11:1

3 Rev. 3:18; 16:15

4 1Cor. 15:53, 54

5 Rom. 8:23; 2Cor. 1:22

7 Heb. 11:1

8 Phil. 1:23

10 Matt. 25:31, 32; Rev. 22:12

4:14 he which raised up the Lord Jesus shall raise up us also by Jesus. The resurrection unto eternal life was anticipated and longed for by the early Christians, and should be our desire as well. This resurrection of believers is certain, not only because Christ was raised, or because the Father has promised to raise us in like manner, but because our "life is hid with Christ in God" (Col. 3:3). The life of believers is so united with Christ that if He lives, we must also live (Eph. 2:4–7).

5:5–7 Paul's confidence was that "whilst we are at home in the body, we are absent from the Lord," because this earthly life is inferior to the life and body we as Christians will have when the Lord comes.

5:8–9 that . . . we may be accepted of him. Paul's goal was to so live that when Christ comes to transform his earthly body to his heavenly body to be with Christ that he would be well-pleasing to Him, which should be the goal of all believers.

5:10 we must all appear before the judgment seat of Christ. The judgment seat of Christ should concern all of us who are Christians and influence and prioritize our lifestyle, because we shall give an account of how we have lived "whether it be good or bad" (see Rom. 14:10–11; 1 Cor. 3:11–15).

to that he hath done, whether *it be* good or bad.

Paul Defends Himself

11 Knowing therefore the terror of the Lord, we persuade men; but we are made manifest unto God; and I trust also are made manifest in your consciences.

12 For we commend not ourselves again unto you, but give you occasion to glory on our behalf, that ye may have somewhat to *answer* them which glory in appearance, and not in heart.

13 For whether we be beside ourselves, *it is* to God: or whether we be sober, *it is* for your cause.

14 For the love of Christ constraineth us; because we thus judge, that if one died for all, then were all dead:

15 And *that* he died for all, that they which live should not henceforth live unto themselves, but unto him which died for them, and rose again.

16 Wherefore henceforth know we no man after the flesh: yea, though we have known Christ after the flesh, yet now henceforth know we *him* no more.

17 Therefore if any man *be* in Christ, *he is* a new creature: old things are passed away; behold, all things are become new.

18 And all things *are* of God, who hath reconciled us to himself by Jesus Christ, and hath given to us the ministry of reconciliation;

19 To wit, that God was in Christ, reconciling the world unto himself, not imputing their trespasses unto them; and hath committed unto us the word of reconciliation.

20 Now then we are ambassadors for Christ, as though God did beseech *you* by us; we pray *you* in Christ's stead, be ye reconciled to God.

21 For he hath made him *to be* sin for us, who knew no sin; that we might be made the righteousness of God in him.

Chapter 6
The Apostle's Fidelity and Love

1 We then, as workers together *with him,* beseech *you* also that ye receive not the grace of God in vain.

2 (For he saith, I have heard thee in a time accepted, and in the day of salvation have I succoured thee: behold, now *is* the accepted time; behold, now *is* the day of salvation.)

3 Giving no offence in any thing, that the ministry be not blamed:

4 But in all *things* approving ourselves as the ministers of God, in much patience, in afflictions, in necessities, in distresses,

Cross references:
11 Job 31:2
13 2Cor. 11:1, 16, 17; 12:6, 11
14 Rom. 5:15
15 Rom. 6:11, 12; 14:7, 8; 1Cor. 6:19
16 Matt. 12:50; John 6:63; 15:14
17 Isa. 43:18, 19; 65:17; Rom. 8:9; 16:7
18 Rom. 5:10
19 Rom. 3:24, 25
20 Mal. 2:7; Eph. 6:20
21 Isa. 53:6, 9, 12; Rom. 1:17; 5:19; 10:3
1 1Cor. 3:9; Heb. 12:15
2 Isa. 49:8
3 Rom. 14:13; 1Cor. 9:12; 10:32
4 1Cor. 4:1; 2Cor. 4:2

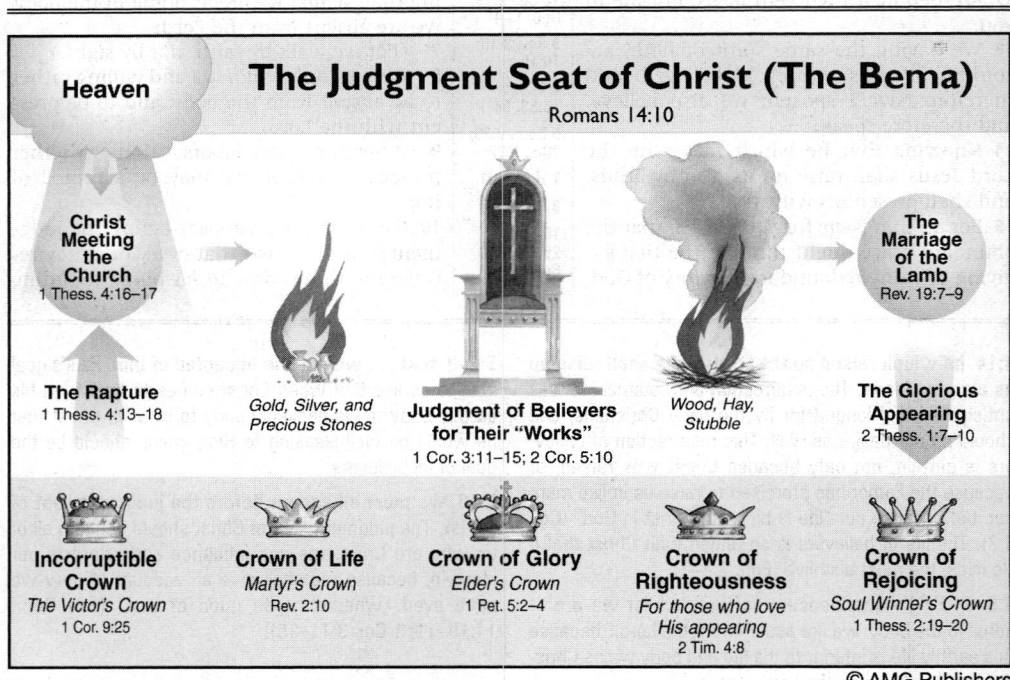

The Judgment Seat of Christ (The Bema)
Romans 14:10

Heaven

Christ Meeting the Church
1 Thess. 4:16–17

The Marriage of the Lamb
Rev. 19:7–9

The Rapture
1 Thess. 4:13–18

Gold, Silver, and Precious Stones

Judgment of Believers for Their "Works"
1 Cor. 3:11–15; 2 Cor. 5:10

Wood, Hay, Stubble

The Glorious Appearing
2 Thess. 1:7–10

Incorruptible Crown
The Victor's Crown
1 Cor. 9:25

Crown of Life
Martyr's Crown
Rev. 2:10

Crown of Glory
Elder's Crown
1 Pet. 5:2–4

Crown of Righteousness
For those who love His appearing
2 Tim. 4:8

Crown of Rejoicing
Soul Winner's Crown
1 Thess. 2:19–20

The Judgment Seat of Christ

By Erwin Lutzer

The judgment seat of Christ is often called the *bema* (the Greek word translated "judgment seat" in 2 Cor. 5:10), and in early times referred to a raised platform where speeches were given and crowns were awarded to the winners of athletic contests. The *bema* of Christ, which dwarfs all other tribunals, is not a judgment that determines salvation, for here only Christians shall be called into account before the all-knowing Judge. This event must be distinguished from the Great White Throne Judgment, to which only unbelievers of all eras shall be summoned (Rev. 20:11–15). The two judgments have these similarities: attendance is required, and all facts will be taken into consideration; thus all participants will agree that God acts with wisdom and meticulous justice.

At the judgment seat of Christ, He who died to save us will stand to judge us. The terms of this judgment are detailed in 1 Corinthians 3:9–15, indicating that "every man's work shall be made manifest: for the day shall declare it, because it shall be revealed by fire." After Paul says that "every [Christian shall] receive the things done in his body, according to that he hath done, whether it be good or bad" he adds, "Knowing therefore the terror of the Lord, we persuade men" (2 Cor. 5:10–11). Our Savior and Brother will administer that which is right and just, but He will not wink at our disobedience.

> *He who died to save us will stand to judge us.*

Theologically, a difficulty is posed by this judgment: since all believers are "in Christ" and have been declared legally righteous in God's sight, how can we be judged "for the things done in [the] body . . . whether . . . good or bad"? Some theologians thereby conclude that all believers will hear "Well done" from the lips of Christ. These people believe that the judgment, at most, may result in a loss of some potential rewards, but will make no distinction between the faithful and the unfaithful. This view is often connected with the teaching that all Christians are overcomers who will persevere in faithfulness. Thus, proponents of this view believe that the judgment seat is primarily a time of affirmation—not rebuke, nor serious loss of rewards.

However, if we take Paul's words at face value (quoted above), we must face the possibility of a serious rebuke by Christ and a loss of rewards or privileges. John warned that we should live so that we will not "be ashamed before Him at His coming" (1 John 2:28). The fact that God disciplines His children in this life, is proof that we will not be able to hide behind our justification to escape a thorough judicial review.

Paul reminded slaves to serve their masters as they would Christ, "knowing that of the Lord ye shall receive the reward of the inheritance." Then he adds, "But he that doeth wrong shall receive for the wrong which he hath done; and there is no respect of persons" (Col. 3:24–25). Those who are faithful will have the privilege of ruling with Christ (Rev. 3:21); those who are not will be rebuked and given lesser responsibilities. This does not mean that there will be two classes of people in heaven, for despite these distinctions, all will enjoy the eternal state and contribute to the honor and praise of our Lord.

5 In stripes, in imprisonments, in tumults, in labours, in watchings, in fastings;

6 By pureness, by knowledge, by longsuffering, by kindness, by the Holy Ghost, by love unfeigned,

7 By the word of truth, by the power of God, by the armour of righteousness on the right hand and on the left,

8 By honour and dishonour, by evil report and good report: as deceivers, and *yet* true;

9 As unknown, and *yet* well known; as dying, and, behold, we live; as chastened, and not killed;

10 As sorrowful, yet alway rejoicing; as poor, yet making many rich; as having nothing, and *yet* possessing all things.

11 O *ye* Corinthians, our mouth is open unto you, our heart is enlarged.

12 Ye are not straitened in us, but ye are straitened in your own bowels.

13 Now for a recompence in the same, I (speak as unto *my* children,) be ye also enlarged.

14 Be ye not unequally yoked together with unbelievers: for what fellowship hath righteousness with unrighteousness? and what communion hath light with darkness?

15 And what concord hath Christ with Belial? or what part hath he that believeth with an infidel?

16 And what agreement hath the temple of God with idols? for ye are the temple of the living God; as God hath said, I will dwell in them, and walk in *them*; and I will be their God, and they shall be my people.

17 Wherefore come out from among them, and be ye separate, saith the Lord, and touch not the unclean *thing*; and I will receive you.

18 And will be a Father unto you, and ye shall be my sons and daughters, saith the Lord Almighty.

CHAPTER 7

1 Having therefore these promises, dearly beloved, let us cleanse ourselves from all filthiness of the flesh and spirit, perfecting holiness in the fear of God.

The Former Letter

2 Receive us; we have wronged no man, we have corrupted no man, we have defrauded no man.

5 2Cor. 11:23
7 1Cor. 2:4; 2Cor. 4:2; 7:14; 10:4; Eph. 6:11, 13; 2Tim. 4:7
9 Ps. 118:18; 1Cor. 4:9; 2Cor. 1:9; 4:2, 10, 11; 5:11; 11:6
11 2Cor. 7:3
12 2Cor. 12:15
13 1Cor. 4:14
14 Deut. 7:2, 3; 1Sam. 5:2, 3; 1Kgs. 18:21; 1Cor. 5:9; 7:39; 10:21; Eph. 5:7, 11
16 Ex. 29:45; Lev. 26:12; Jer. 31:33; 32:38; Ezek. 11:20; 36:28
17 Isa. 52:11; 2Cor. 7:1; Rev. 18:4
18 Jer. 31:1, 9; Rev. 21:7
1 2Cor. 6:17, 18; 1John 3:3
2 Acts 20:33; 2Cor. 12:17
3 2Cor. 6:11, 12
4 1Cor. 1:4; 2Cor. 1:4, 14; 3:12; Phil. 2:17; Col. 1:24
5 Deut. 32:25; 2Cor. 2:13; 4:8
6 2Cor. 1:4; 2:13
8 2Cor. 2:4
10 2Sam. 12:13; Prov. 17:22; Matt. 26:75
12 2Cor. 2:4
13 Rom. 15:32

3 I speak not *this* to condemn *you*: for I have said before, that ye are in our hearts to die and live with *you*.

4 Great *is* my boldness of speech toward you, great *is* my glorying of you: I am filled with comfort, I am exceeding joyful in all our tribulation.

5 For, when we were come into Macedonia, our flesh had no rest, but we were troubled on every side; without *were* fightings, within *were* fears.

6 Nevertheless God, that comforteth those that are cast down, comforted us by the coming of Titus;

7 And not by his coming only, but by the consolation wherewith he was comforted in you, when he told us your earnest desire, your mourning, your fervent mind toward me; so that I rejoiced the more.

8 For though I made you sorry with a letter, I do not repent, though I did repent: for I perceive that the same epistle hath made you sorry, though *it were* but for a season.

9 Now I rejoice, not that ye were made sorry, but that ye sorrowed to repentance: for ye were made sorry after a godly manner, that ye might receive damage by us in nothing.

10 For godly sorrow worketh repentance to salvation not to be repented of: but the sorrow of the world worketh death.

11 For behold this selfsame thing, that ye sorrowed after a godly sort, what carefulness it wrought in you, yea, *what* clearing of yourselves, yea, *what* indignation, yea, *what* fear, yea, *what* vehement desire, yea, *what* zeal, yea, *what* revenge! In all *things* ye have approved yourselves to be clear in this matter.

12 Wherefore, though I wrote unto you, *I* did *it* not for his cause that had done the wrong, nor for his cause that suffered wrong, but that our care for you in the sight of God might appear unto you.

13 Therefore we were comforted in your comfort: yea, and exceedingly the more joyed we for the joy of Titus, because his spirit was refreshed by you all.

14 For if I have boasted any thing to him of you, I am not ashamed; but as we spake all things to you in truth, even so our boasting, which *I made* before Titus, is found a truth.

6:16–18 ye are the temple of the living God. This challenge to make our bodies temples of the Holy Spirit is based on the Old Testament prophecy that the people of Israel will one day live that way during the kingdom age when they convert to Him as He becomes their God and they become His people (Ezek. 37:27)—further evidence that if anyone has the Spirit of Christ, he should live like it.

15 And his inward affection is more abundant toward you, whilst he remembereth the obedience of you all, how with fear and trembling ye received him.

16 I rejoice therefore that I have confidence in you in all *things.*

CHAPTER 8
The Macedonian Saints

1 Moreover, brethren, we do you to wit of the grace of God bestowed on the churches of Macedonia;

2 How that in a great trial of affliction the abundance of their joy and their deep poverty abounded unto the riches of their liberality.

3 For to *their* power, I bear record, yea, and beyond *their* power *they were* willing of themselves;

4 Praying us with much intreaty that we would receive the gift, and *take upon us* the fellowship of the ministering to the saints.

5 And *this they did,* not as we hoped, but first gave their own selves to the Lord, and unto us by the will of God.

6 Insomuch that we desired Titus, that as he had begun, so he would also finish in you the same grace also.

7 Therefore, as ye abound in every *thing, in* faith, and utterance, and knowledge, and *in* all diligence, and *in* your love to us, *see* that ye abound in this grace also.

8 I speak not by commandment, but by occasion of the forwardness of others, and to prove the sincerity of your love.

9 For ye know the grace of our Lord Jesus Christ, that, though he was rich, yet for your sakes he became poor, that ye through his poverty might be rich.

10 And herein I give *my* advice: for this is expedient for you, who have begun before, not only to do, but also to be forward a year ago.

11 Now therefore perform the doing *of it;* that as *there was* a readiness to will, so *there may be* a performance also out of that which ye have.

12 For if there be first a willing mind, *it is* accepted according to that a man hath, *and* not according to that he hath not.

13 For *I mean* not that other men be eased, and ye burdened:

14 But by an equality, *that* now at this time your abundance *may be a supply* for their want, that their abundance also may be *a supply* for your want: that there may be equality:

15 As it is written, He that *had gathered* much had nothing over; and he that *had gathered* little had no lack.

Paul Receives a Report from Titus and Another Brother

16 But thanks *be* to God, which put the same earnest care into the heart of Titus for you.

17 For indeed he accepted the exhortation; but being more forward, of his own accord he went unto you.

18 And we have sent with him the brother, whose praise *is* in the gospel throughout all the churches;

19 And not *that* only, but who was also chosen of the churches to travel with us with this grace, which is administered by us to the glory of the same Lord, and *declaration of* your ready mind:

20 Avoiding this, that no man should blame us in this abundance which is administered by us:

21 Providing for honest things, not only in the sight of the Lord, but also in the sight of men.

22 And we have sent with them our brother, whom we have oftentimes proved diligent in many things, but now much more diligent, upon the great confidence which *I have* in you.

23 Whether *any do inquire* of Titus, *he is* my partner and fellowhelper concerning you: or our brethren *be inquired of, they are* the messengers of the churches, *and* the glory of Christ.

24 Wherefore shew ye to them, and before the churches, the proof of your love, and of our boasting on your behalf.

CHAPTER 9
Free and Cheerful Giving

1 For as touching the ministering to the saints, it is superfluous for me to write to you:

2 For I know the forwardness of your mind, for which I boast of you to them of

Cross references (center column)

15 2Cor. 2:9; 6:12; Phil. 2:12
16 2Thess. 3:4; Phile. 1:8, 21
2 Mark 12:44; 2Cor. 9:11
4 Acts 11:29; 24:17; Rom. 15:25, 26; 1Cor. 16:1, 3, 4; 2Cor. 9:1
6 2Cor. 8:4, 17, 19; 12:18
7 1Cor. 1:5; 12:13; 2Cor. 9:8
8 1Cor. 7:6
9 Matt. 8:20; Luke 9:58; Phil. 2:6, 7
10 Prov. 19:17; Matt. 10:42; 1Cor. 7:25; 2Cor. 9:2; 1Tim. 6:18, 19; Heb. 13:16
12 Mark 12:43, 44; Luke 21:3
15 Ex. 16:18
17 2Cor. 8:6
18 2Cor. 12:18
19 1Cor. 16:3, 4; 2Cor. 4:15; 8:4, 6, 7; 9:8
21 Rom. 12:17; Phil. 4:8; 1Pet. 2:12
23 Phil. 2:25
24 2Cor. 7:14; 9:2
1 Acts 11:29; Rom. 15:26; 1Cor. 16:1; 2Cor. 8:4; Gal. 2:10
2 2Cor. 8:10, 19, 24

8:9 that ye through his poverty might be rich. By His humiliation and suffering, the Lord Jesus has shared with us the riches of the glory that He left behind to come to earth (John 17:22; Rom. 8:17; 2 Pet. 1:4). The riches of Christ that are promised here are the subject of many prophetic passages in the New Testament (1 Cor. 15; 1 Thess. 4; Rev. 21—22).

Macedonia, that Achaia was ready a year ago; and your zeal hath provoked very many.

3 Yet have I sent the brethren, lest our boasting of you should be in vain in this behalf; that, as I said, ye may be ready:

4 Lest haply if they of Macedonia come with me, and find you unprepared, we (that we say not, ye) should be ashamed in this same confident boasting.

5 Therefore I thought it necessary to exhort the brethren, that they would go before unto you, and make up beforehand your bounty, whereof ye had notice before, that the same might be ready, as *a matter of* bounty, and not as *of* covetousness.

6 But this *I say,* He which soweth sparingly shall reap also sparingly; and he which soweth bountifully shall reap also bountifully.

7 Every man according as he purposeth in his heart, *so let him give*; not grudgingly, or of necessity: for God loveth a cheerful giver.

8 And God *is* able to make all grace abound toward you; that ye, always having all sufficiency in all *things,* may abound to every good work:

9 (As it is written, He hath dispersed abroad; he hath given to the poor: his righteousness remaineth for ever.

10 Now he that ministereth seed to the sower both minister bread for *your* food, and multiply your seed sown, and increase the fruits of your righteousness;)

11 Being enriched in every thing to all bountifulness, which causeth through us thanksgiving to God.

12 For the administration of this service not only supplieth the want of the saints, but is abundant also by many thanksgivings unto God;

13 Whiles by the experiment of this ministration they glorify God for your professed subjection unto the gospel of Christ, and for *your* liberal distribution unto them, and unto all *men*;

14 And by their prayer for you, which long after you for the exceeding grace of God in you.

15 Thanks *be* unto God for his unspeakable gift.

CHAPTER 10
Paul's Self-vindication

1 Now I Paul myself beseech you by the meekness and gentleness of Christ, who in presence *am* base among you, but being absent am bold toward you:

3 2Cor. 8:6, 17, 18, 22
5 Gen. 33:11; 1Sam. 25:27; 2Kgs. 5:15
6 Ex. 25:2; 35:5; Deut. 15:7; Prov. 11:24, 25; 19:17; 22:9; Rom. 12:8; 2Cor. 8:12; Gal. 6:7, 9
8 Prov. 11:24, 25; 28:27; Phil. 4:19
9 Ps. 112:9
10 Isa. 55:10; Hos. 10:12; Matt. 6:1
11 2Cor. 1:11; 4:15; 8:2
12 2Cor. 8:14
13 Matt. 5:16; Heb. 13:16
14 2Cor. 8:1; James 1:17
1 Rom. 12:1; 2Cor. 10:10; 12:5, 7, 9
2 1Cor. 4:21; 2Cor. 13:2, 10
4 Acts 7:22; Eph. 6:13
5 1Cor. 1:19; 3:19
6 2Cor. 2:9; 7:15; 13:2, 10
7 John 7:24; 1Cor. 3:23; 9:1; 14:37; 2Cor. 5:12; 11:18, 23; 1John 4:6
8 2Cor. 7:14; 12:6; 13:10
10 1Cor. 1:17; 2:1, 3, 4; 2Cor. 10:1; 11:6; 12:5, 7, 9; Gal. 4:13
12 2Cor. 3:1; 5:12
13 2Cor. 10:15
14 1Cor. 3:5, 10; 4:15; 9:1
15 Rom. 15:20

2 But I beseech *you*, that I may not be bold when I am present with that confidence, wherewith I think to be bold against some, which think of us as if we walked according to the flesh.

3 For though we walk in the flesh, we do not war after the flesh:

4 (For the weapons of our warfare *are* not carnal, but mighty through God to the pulling down of strong holds;)

5 Casting down imaginations, and every high thing that exalteth itself against the knowledge of God, and bringing into captivity every thought to the obedience of Christ;

6 And having in a readiness to revenge all disobedience, when your obedience is fulfilled.

7 Do ye look on things after the outward appearance? If any man trust to himself that he is Christ's, let him of himself think this again, that, as he *is* Christ's, even so *are* we Christ's.

8 For though I should boast somewhat more of our authority, which the Lord hath given us for edification, and not for your destruction, I should not be ashamed:

9 That I may not seem as if I would terrify you by letters.

10 For *his* letters, say they, *are* weighty and powerful; but *his* bodily presence *is* weak, and *his* speech contemptible.

11 Let such a one think this, that, such as we are in word by letters when we are absent, such *will we be* also in deed when we are present.

12 For we dare not make ourselves of the number, or compare ourselves with some that commend themselves: but they measuring themselves by themselves, and comparing themselves among themselves, are not wise.

13 But we will not boast of things without *our* measure, but according to the measure of the rule which God hath distributed to us, a measure to reach even unto you.

14 For we stretch not ourselves beyond *our measure*, as though we reached not unto you: for we are come as far as to you also in *preaching* the gospel of Christ:

15 Not boasting of things without *our* measure, *that is,* of other men's labours; but having hope, when your faith is increased, that we shall be enlarged by you according to our rule abundantly,

16 To preach the gospel in the *regions* beyond you, *and* not to boast in another man's line of things made ready to our hand.

17 But he that glorieth, let him glory in the Lord.

18 For not he that commendeth himself is approved, but whom the Lord commendeth.

CHAPTER 11

1 Would to God ye could bear with me a little in *my* folly: and indeed bear with me.

2 For I am jealous over you with godly jealousy: for I have espoused you to one husband, that I may present *you as* a chaste virgin to Christ.

3 But I fear, lest by any means, as the serpent beguiled Eve through his subtilty, so your minds should be corrupted from the simplicity that is in Christ.

4 For if he that cometh preacheth another Jesus, whom we have not preached, or *if ye* receive another spirit, which ye have not received, or another gospel, which ye have not accepted, ye might well bear with *him.*

5 For I suppose I was not a whit behind the very chiefest apostles.

6 But though *I be* rude in speech, yet not in knowledge; but we have been throughly made manifest among you in all things.

7 Have I committed an offence in abasing myself that ye might be exalted, because I have preached to you the gospel of God freely?

8 I robbed other churches, taking wages *of them,* to do you service.

9 And when I was present with you, and wanted, I was chargable to no man: for that which was lacking to me the brethren which came from Macedonia supplied: and in all *things* I have kept myself from being burdensome unto you, and *so* will I keep *myself.*

10 As the truth of Christ is in me, no man shall stop me of this boasting in the regions of Achaia.

11 Wherefore? because I love you not? God knoweth.

12 But what I do, that I will do, that I may cut off occasion from them which desire occasion; that wherein they glory, they may be found even as we.

13 For such *are* false apostles, deceitful workers, transforming themselves into the apostles of Christ.

14 And no marvel; for Satan himself is transformed into an angel of light.

15 Therefore *it is* no great thing if his ministers also be transformed as the ministers of righteousness; whose end shall be according to their works.

Paul's Apostolic Labors and Sufferings

16 I say again, Let no man think me a fool; if otherwise, yet as a fool receive me, that I may boast myself a little.

17 That which I speak, I speak *it* not after the Lord, but as it were foolishly, in this confidence of boasting.

18 Seeing that many glory after the flesh, I will glory also.

19 For ye suffer fools gladly, seeing ye *yourselves* are wise.

20 For ye suffer, if a man bring you into bondage, if a man devour *you,* if a man take *of you,* if a man exalt himself, if a man smite you on the face.

21 I speak as concerning reproach, as though we had been weak. Howbeit whereinsoever any is bold, (I speak foolishly,) I am bold also.

22 Are they Hebrews? so *am* I. Are they Israelites? so *am* I. Are they the seed of Abraham? so *am* I.

23 Are they ministers of Christ? (I speak as a fool) I *am* more; in labours more abundant, in stripes above measure, in prisons more frequent, in deaths oft.

24 Of the Jews five times received I forty *stripes* save one.

25 Thrice was I beaten with rods, once was I stoned, thrice I suffered shipwreck, a night and a day I have been in the deep;

26 *In* journeyings often, *in* perils of waters, *in* perils of robbers, *in* perils by *mine own* countrymen, *in* perils by the heathen, *in* perils in the city, *in* perils in the wilderness, *in* perils in the sea, *in* perils among false brethren;

27 In weariness and painfulness, in watchings often, in hunger and thirst, in fastings often, in cold and nakedness.

28 Beside those things that are without, that which cometh upon me daily, the care of all the churches.

29 Who is weak, and I am not weak? who is offended, and I burn not?

30 If I must needs glory, I will glory of the things which concern mine infirmities.

31 The God and Father of our Lord Jesus Christ, which is blessed for evermore, knoweth that I lie not.

32 In Damascus the governor under Aretas the king kept the city of the Damascenes with a garrison, desirous to apprehend me:

33 And through a window in a basket was I let down by the wall, and escaped his hands.

CHAPTER 12
Paul's Vision

1 It is not expedient for me doubtless to glory. I will come to visions and revelations of the Lord.

2 I knew a man in Christ above fourteen years ago, (whether in the body, I cannot tell; or whether out of the body, I cannot tell: God knoweth;) such a one caught up to the third heaven.

3 And I knew such a man, (whether in the body, or out of the body, I cannot tell: God knoweth;)

4 How that he was caught up into paradise, and heard unspeakable words, which it is not lawful for a man to utter.

5 Of such a one will I glory: yet of myself I will not glory, but in mine infirmities.

6 For though I would desire to glory, I shall not be a fool; for I will say the truth: but *now* I forbear, lest any man should think of me above that which he seeth me *to be,* or *that* he heareth of me.

Evidences of Paul's Apostleship

7 And lest I should be exalted above measure through the abundance of the revelations, there was given to me a thorn in the flesh, the messenger of Satan to buffet me, lest I should be exalted above measure.

8 For this thing I besought the Lord thrice, that it might depart from me.

9 And he said unto me, My grace is sufficient for thee: for my strength is made perfect in weakness. Most gladly therefore will I rather glory in my infirmities, that the power of Christ may rest upon me.

10 Therefore I take pleasure in infirmities, in reproaches, in necessities, in persecutions, in distresses for Christ's sake: for when I am weak, then am I strong.

11 I am become a fool in glorying; ye have compelled me: for I ought to have been commended of you: for in nothing am I behind the very chiefest apostles, though I be nothing.

12 Truly the signs of an apostle were wrought among you in all patience, in signs, and wonders, and mighty deeds.

13 For what is it wherein ye were inferior to other churches, except *it be* that I myself was not burdensome to you? forgive me this wrong.

14 Behold, the third time I am ready to come to you; and I will not be burdensome to you: for I seek not yours, but you: for the children ought not to lay up for the parents, but the parents for the children.

15 And I will very gladly spend and be spent for you; though the more abundantly I love you, the less I be loved.

16 But be it so, I did not burden you: nevertheless, being crafty, I caught you with guile.

17 Did I make a gain of you by any of them whom I sent unto you?

18 I desired Titus, and with *him* I sent a brother. Did Titus make a gain of you? walked we not in the same spirit? *walked we* not in the same steps?

19 Again, think ye that we excuse ourselves unto you? we speak before God in Christ: but *we do* all things, dearly beloved, for your edifying.

20 For I fear, lest when I come, I shall not find you such as I would, and *that* I shall be found unto you such as ye would not: lest *there be* debates, envyings, wraths, strifes, backbitings, whisperings, swellings, tumults:

21 *And* lest, when I come again, my God will humble me among you, and *that* I shall bewail many which have sinned already, and have not repented of the uncleanness and fornication and lasciviousness which they have committed.

CHAPTER 13
Paul's Desire to Visit Corinth Again

1 This *is* the third *time* I am coming to you. In the mouth of two or three witnesses shall every word be established.

2 I told you before, and foretell you, as if I were present, the second time; and being absent now I write to them which heretofore have sinned, and to all other, that, if I come again, I will not spare:

3 Since ye seek a proof of Christ speaking in me, which to you-ward is not weak, but is mighty in you.

4 For though he was crucified through weakness, yet he liveth by the power of God. For we also are weak in him, but we shall live with him by the power of God toward you.

5 Examine yourselves, whether ye be in the faith; prove your own selves. Know ye not your own selves, how that Jesus Christ is in you, except ye be reprobates?

6 But I trust that ye shall know that we are not reprobates.

7 Now I pray to God that ye do no evil; not that we should appear approved, but that ye should do that which is honest, though we be as reprobates.

8 For we can do nothing against the truth, but for the truth.

9 For we are glad, when we are weak, and

Cross references (center column)

2 Acts 22:17; Rom. 16:7; 2Cor. 5:17; Gal. 1:22

4 Luke 23:43

5 2Cor. 11:30

6 2Cor. 10:8; 11:16

7 Job 2:7; Luke 13:16

8 Deut. 3:23-27; Matt. 26:44

9 2Cor. 11:30; 1Pet. 4:14

10 Rom. 5:3; 2Cor. 7:4; 13:4

11 1Cor. 3:7; 15:8, 9; Gal. 2:6-8

12 1Cor. 9:2

13 1Cor. 1:7; 9:12; 2Cor. 11:7, 9

14 Acts 20:33; 1Cor. 4:14, 15; 10:33; 2Cor. 13:1

15 John 10:11; 2Cor. 1:6; 6:12, 13; Phil. 2:17

16 2Cor. 11:9

17 2Cor. 7:2

18 2Cor. 8:6, 16, 18, 22

20 1Cor. 4:21; 2Cor. 10:2; 13:2, 10

21 1Cor. 5:1; 2Cor. 2:1, 4; 13:2

1 Num. 35:30; Deut. 17:6; 19:15; Matt. 18:16

2 2Cor. 1:23; 10:2; 12:21

3 Matt. 10:20; 1Cor. 5:4; 9:2; 2Cor. 2:10

4 Rom. 6:4; 2Cor. 10:3, 4; Phil. 2:7, 8; 1Pet. 3:18

5 1Cor. 9:27; 11:28

7 2Cor. 6:9

ye are strong: and this also we wish, *even* your perfection.

10 Therefore I write these things being absent, lest being present I should use sharpness, according to the power which the Lord hath given me to edification, and not to destruction.

11 Finally, brethren, farewell. Be perfect, be

10 1Cor. 4:21; 2Cor. 2:3; 10:2, 8; 12:20, 21	
11 Phil. 2:2; 3:16	
14 Rom. 16:24; Phil. 2:1	

of good comfort, be of one mind, live in peace; and the God of love and peace shall be with you.

12 Greet one another with an holy kiss.

13 All the saints salute you.

14 The grace of the Lord Jesus Christ, and the love of God, and the communion of the Holy Ghost, *be* with you all. Amen.

Galatians

There are two prominent theories that present differing views of the location and identification of the Galatian believers. The North Galatia Theory maintains that the Galatians referred to in this epistle lived in north central Asia Minor and north of the cities where Paul ministered during his first missionary journey. This area was the first area known as Galatia, for the area was conquered by the Gauls in the third century B.C. Proponents of this theory believe that Paul wrote this letter to the Galatians while in Ephesus or Corinth during the years A.D. 53–56. The South Galatia Theory states that the Galatians to which Paul wrote were part of the Roman province called Galatia that had been established in 25 B.C.—an area in south central Asia Minor where Paul and Barnabas ministered on their first missionary journey. Thus, Paul's letter could have been written from Corinth or Syrian Antioch in A.D. 49.

Regardless of which theory is correct, the Galatian church faced a worldly threat involving purity of doctrine and purity of practice. Some professing Christian Jews (called "Judaizers") were insisting that only those who first became Jewish proselytes and kept the law were eligible to follow the Messiah. In this letter to the Galatians, Paul champions a wider view of true Christianity as distinct from being merely a messianic branch of Judaism. He defends his apostolic authority, even rebukes Peter for his apparent wavering in the debate, and insists that Christians are free from Judaism's laws, customs, and ceremonies.

Insisting that spiritual maturity is not attained by mere conformity to rules and regulations as dictated by the Law, Paul teaches that true holiness comes by walking "in the spirit" and cooperating with God in producing the "fruit of the Spirit," which is true godly living (see Gal. 5:16, 22, 25).

Seven distinct (now fulfilled) predictions appear in 16 out of 149 verses, or only 11 percent of the verse total. Galatians contains 10 quotations from the Old Testament.

Author
Paul

Date
A.D. 49

Key Truth
Justified by Faith

Historic Time
During and Shortly after Paul's First Missionary Journey

Key Verse
2:16
. . . by the faith of Jesus Christ . . . and not by the works of the law.

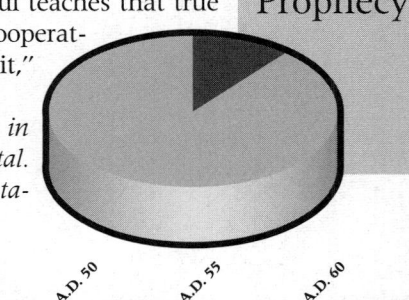

11%
Prophecy

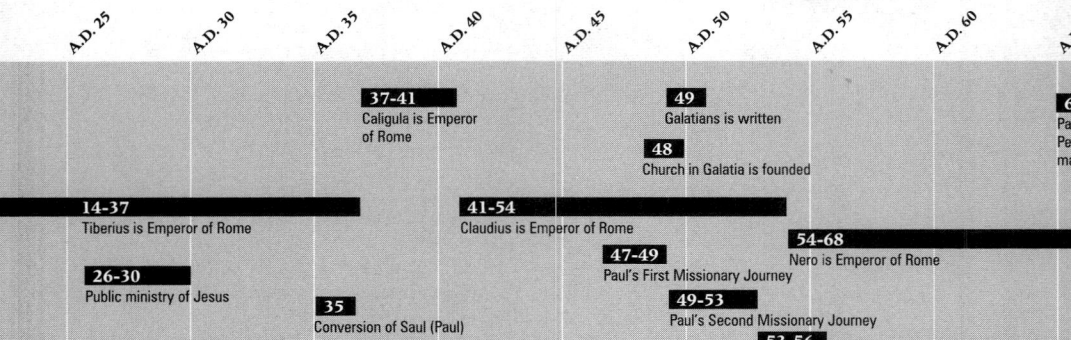

| A.D. 25 | A.D. 30 | A.D. 35 | A.D. 40 | A.D. 45 | A.D. 50 | A.D. 55 | A.D. 60 |

37-41
Caligula is Emperor of Rome

49
Galatians is written

48
Church in Galatia is founded

14-37
Tiberius is Emperor of Rome

41-54
Claudius is Emperor of Rome

54-68
Nero is Emperor of Rome

26-30
Public ministry of Jesus

47-49
Paul's First Missionary Journey

35
Conversion of Saul (Paul)

49-53
Paul's Second Missionary Journey

53-56
Paul's Third Missionary Journey

CHAPTER 1

1 Paul, an apostle, (not of men, neither by man, but by Jesus Christ, and God the Father, who raised him from the dead;)

2 And all the brethren which are with me, unto the churches of Galatia:

3 Grace *be* to you and peace from God the Father, and *from* our Lord Jesus Christ,

4 Who gave himself for our sins, that he might deliver us from this present evil world, according to the will of God and our Father:

5 To whom *be* glory for ever and ever. Amen.

The One True Gospel

6 I marvel that ye are so soon removed from him that called you into the grace of Christ unto another gospel:

7 Which is not another; but there be some that trouble you, and would pervert the gospel of Christ.

8 But though we, or an angel from heaven, preach any other gospel unto you than that which we have preached unto you, let him be accursed.

9 As we said before, so say I now again, if any *man* preach any other gospel unto you than that ye have received, let him be accursed.

10 For do I now persuade men, or God? or do I seek to please men? for if I yet pleased men, I should not be the servant of Christ.

Paul's Call to the Ministry

11 But I certify you, brethren, that the gospel which was preached of me is not after man.

12 For I neither received it of man, neither was I taught *it*, but by the revelation of Jesus Christ.

13 For ye have heard of my conversation in time past in the Jews' religion, how that beyond measure I persecuted the church of God, and wasted it:

14 And profited in the Jews' religion above many my equals in mine own nation, being more exceedingly zealous of the traditions of my fathers.

15 But when it pleased God, who separated me from my mother's womb, and called *me* by his grace,

16 To reveal his Son in me, that I might preach him among the heathen; immediately I conferred not with flesh and blood:

17 Neither went I up to Jerusalem to them which were apostles before me; but I went

into Arabia, and returned again unto Damascus.

18 Then after three years I went up to Jerusalem to see Peter, and abode with him fifteen days.

19 But other of the apostles saw I none, save James the Lord's brother.

20 Now the things which I write unto you, behold, before God, I lie not.

21 Afterwards I came into the regions of Syria and Cilicia;

22 And was unknown by face unto the churches of Judea which were in Christ:

23 But they had heard only, That he which persecuted us in times past now preacheth the faith which once he destroyed.

24 And they glorified God in me.

CHAPTER 2

In Jerusalem

1 Then fourteen years after I went up again to Jerusalem with Barnabas, and took Titus with *me* also.

2 And I went up by revelation, and communicated unto them that gospel which I preach among the Gentiles, but privately to them which were of reputation, lest by any means I should run, or had run, in vain.

3 But neither Titus, who was with me, being a Greek, was compelled to be circumcised:

4 And that because of false brethren unawares brought in, who came in privily to spy out our liberty which we have in Christ Jesus, that they might bring us into bondage:

5 To whom we gave place by subjection, no, not for an hour; that the truth of the gospel might continue with you.

6 But of these who seemed to be somewhat, (whatsoever they were, it maketh no matter to me: God accepteth no man's person;) for they who seemed *to be somewhat* in conference added nothing to me:

7 But contrariwise, when they saw that the gospel of the uncircumcision was committed unto me, as *the gospel* of the circumcision *was* unto Peter;

8 (For he that wrought effectually in Peter to the apostleship of the circumcision, the same was mighty in me toward the Gentiles:)

9 And when James, Cephas, and John, who seemed to be pillars, perceived the grace that was given unto me, they gave to me and Barnabas the right hands of fellowship; that we *should go* unto the heathen, and they unto the circumcision.

1 Acts 9:6; 22:10, 15, 21; 26:16

2 1Cor. 16:1; Phil. 2:22; 4:21

3 Rom. 1:7

4 Isa. 65:17; Matt. 20:28; John 15:19; 17:14

7 2Cor. 2:17; 11:4, 13; Gal. 5:10, 12

8 1Cor. 16:22

9 Rev. 22:18

13 Acts 8:3; 9:1; 22:4; 26:11

14 Acts 22:3; 26:9; Phil. 3:6

15 Jer. 1:5; Acts 9:15; Rom. 1:1

16 Eph. 3:8; 6:12

18 Acts 9:26

19 Matt. 13:55; Mark 6:3; 1Cor. 9:5

20 Rom. 9:1

21 Acts 9:30

22 Acts 15:2; Rom. 16:7; 1Thess. 2:14

2 Acts 15:12; Phil. 2:16; 1Thess. 3:5

4 Acts 15:1, 24; 2Cor. 11:20, 26

5 Gal. 2:14; 3:1; 4:16

6 Acts 10:34; Rom. 2:11; 2Cor. 12:11; Gal. 6:3

7 Acts 13:46; Rom. 1:5; 11:13

8 Acts 9:15; 13:2; 22:21; 26:17, 18

9 Matt. 16:18; Rom. 1:5; 12:3, 6; 15:15; 1Cor. 15:10; Eph. 2:20; 3:8; Rev. 21:14

10 Only *they would* that we should remember the poor; the same which I also was forward to do.

Paul Confronts Peter

11 But when Peter was come to Antioch, I withstood him to the face, because he was to be blamed.

12 For before that certain came from James, he did eat with the Gentiles: but when they were come, he withdrew and separated himself, fearing them which were of the circumcision.

13 And the other Jews dissembled likewise with him; insomuch that Barnabas also was carried away with their dissimulation.

14 But when I saw that they walked not uprightly according to the truth of the gospel, I said unto Peter before *them* all, If thou, being a Jew, livest after the manner of Gentiles, and not as do the Jews, why compellest thou the Gentiles to live as do the Jews?

15 We *who are* Jews by nature, and not sinners of the Gentiles,

16 Knowing that a man is not justified by the works of the law, but by the faith of Jesus Christ, even we have believed in Jesus Christ, that we might be justified by the faith of Christ, and not by the works of the law: for by the works of the law shall no flesh be justified.

17 But if, while we seek to be justified by Christ, we ourselves also are found sinners, *is* therefore Christ the minister of sin? God forbid.

18 For if I build again the things which I destroyed, I make myself a transgressor.

19 For I through the law am dead to the law, that I might live unto God.

20 I am crucified with Christ: nevertheless I live; yet not I, but Christ liveth in me: and the life which I now live in the flesh I live by the faith of the Son of God, who loved me, and gave himself for me.

21 I do not frustrate the grace of God: for if righteousness *come* by the law, then Christ is dead in vain.

CHAPTER 3
The Experience of the Galatians

1 O foolish Galatians, who hath bewitched you, that ye should not obey the truth, be-

fore whose eyes Jesus Christ hath been evidently set forth, crucified among you?

2 This only would I learn of you, Received ye the Spirit by the works of the law, or by the hearing of faith?

3 Are ye so foolish? having begun in the Spirit, are ye now made perfect by the flesh?

4 Have ye suffered so many things in vain? if *it be* yet in vain.

5 He therefore that ministereth to you the Spirit, and worketh miracles among you, *doeth he it* by the works of the law, or by the hearing of faith?

6 Even as Abraham believed God, and it was accounted to him for righteousness.

7 Know ye therefore that they which are of faith, the same are the children of Abraham.

8 And the scripture, foreseeing that God would justify the heathen through faith, preached before the gospel unto Abraham, *saying*, In thee shall all nations be blessed.

9 So then they which be of faith are blessed with faithful Abraham.

10 For as many as are of the works of the law are under the curse: for it is written, Cursed *is* every one that continueth not in all things which are written in the book of the law to do them.

11 But that no man is justified by the law in the sight of God, *it is* evident: for, The just shall live by faith.

12 And the law is not of faith: but, The man that doeth them shall live in them.

13 Christ hath redeemed us from the curse of the law, being made a curse for us: for it is written, Cursed *is* every one that hangeth on a tree:

14 That the blessing of Abraham might come on the Gentiles through Jesus Christ; that we might receive the promise of the Spirit through faith.

15 Brethren, I speak after the manner of men; Though *it be* but a man's covenant, yet *if it be* confirmed, no man disannulleth, or addeth thereto.

16 Now to Abraham and his seed were the promises made. He saith not, And to seeds, as of many; but as of one, And to thy seed, which is Christ.

17 And this I say, *that* the covenant, that was confirmed before of God in Christ, the law, which was four hundred and thirty

Cross references (center column)

10 Acts 11:30; 24:17; Rom. 15:25; 1Cor. 16:1

12 Acts 10:28; 11:3

14 Gal. 2:5; 1Tim. 5:20

15 Matt. 9:11; Acts 15:10, 11

16 Eph. 2:8–9

17 1John 3:8, 9

19 Rom. 6:11, 14; 7:4, 6; 8:2

20 Rom. 6:6; Titus 2:14; 1Pet. 4:2

21 Rom. 11:6; Heb. 7:11

2 Rom. 10:16, 17; Eph. 1:13;

4 Heb. 10:35, 36

6 Gen. 15:6; Rom. 4:3, 9, 21, 22

7 John 8:39

8 Gen. 12:3; 18:18; 22:18

10 Deut. 27:26; Jer. 11:3

11 Hab. 2:4; Rom. 1:17; Heb. 10:38

12 Ezek. 20:11; Rom. 4:4, 5; 10:5, 6; 11:6

13 Deut. 21:33; Rom. 8:3; 2Cor. 5:21; Gal. 4:5

14 Isa. 32:15; 44:3; Jer. 31:33; 32:40; Joel 2:28, 29; Acts 2:3

15 Heb. 9:17

16 Gen. 12:3, 7; 17:7

17 Ex. 12:40, 41; Rom. 4:13, 14

3:8 In thee shall all nations be blessed. This verse clearly affirms that salvation of the Gentiles through faith in Christ was a literal fulfillment of the Abrahamic covenant.

3:14 The indwelling of the Spirit in the believer is part of the fulfillment of the promise in the Abrahamic covenant that Christ would be a blessing to the nations.

years after, cannot disannul, that it should make the promise of none effect.

18 For if the inheritance *be* of the law, *it is* no more of promise: but God gave *it* to Abraham by promise.

The Purpose of the Law

19 Wherefore then *serveth* the law? It was added because of transgressions, till the seed should come to whom the promise was made; *and it was* ordained by angels in the hand of a mediator.

20 Now a mediator is not *a mediator* of one, but God is one.

21 *Is* the law then against the promises of God? God forbid: for if there had been a law given which could have given life, verily righteousness should have been by the law.

22 But the scripture hath concluded all under sin, that the promise by faith of Jesus Christ might be given to them that believe.

23 But before faith came, we were kept under the law, shut up unto the faith which should afterwards be revealed.

24 Wherefore the law was our schoolmaster *to bring us* unto Christ, that we might be justified by faith.

25 But after that faith is come, we are no longer under a schoolmaster.

26 For ye are all the children of God by faith in Christ Jesus.

27 For as many of you as have been baptized into Christ have put on Christ.

28 There is neither Jew nor Greek, there is neither bond nor free, there is neither male nor female: for ye are all one in Christ Jesus.

29 And if ye *be* Christ's, then are ye Abraham's seed, and heirs according to the promise.

CHAPTER 4
The Believer's Inheritance

1 Now I say, *That* the heir, as long as he is a child, differeth nothing from a servant, though he be lord of all;

2 But is under tutors and governors until the time appointed of the father.

3 Even so we, when we were children, were in bondage under the elements of the world:

4 But when the fulness of the time was

come, God sent forth his Son, made of a woman, made under the law,

5 To redeem them that were under the law, that we might receive the adoption of sons.

6 And because ye are sons, God hath sent forth the Spirit of his Son into your hearts, crying, Abba, Father.

7 Wherefore thou art no more a servant, but a son; and if a son, then an heir of God through Christ.

8 Howbeit then, when ye knew not God, ye did service unto them which by nature are no gods.

9 But now, after that ye have known God, or rather are known of God, how turn ye again to the weak and beggarly elements, whereunto ye desire again to be in bondage?

10 Ye observe days, and months, and times, and years.

11 I am afraid of you, lest I have bestowed upon you labour in vain.

12 Brethren, I beseech you, be as I *am*; for I *am* as ye *are*: ye have not injured me at all.

13 Ye know how through infirmity of the flesh I preached the gospel unto you at the first.

14 And my temptation which was in my flesh ye despised not, nor rejected; but received me as an angel of God, *even* as Christ Jesus.

15 Where is then the blessedness ye spake of? for I bear you record, that, if *it had been* possible, ye would have plucked out your own eyes, and have given them to me.

16 Am I therefore become your enemy, because I tell you the truth?

17 They zealously affect you, *but* not well; yea, they would exclude you, that ye might affect them.

18 But *it is* good to be zealously affected always in *a* good *thing*, and not only when I am present with you.

19 My little children, of whom I travail in birth again until Christ be formed in you,

20 I desire to be present with you now, and to change my voice; for I stand in doubt of you.

Isaac and Ishmael

21 Tell me, ye that desire to be under the law, do ye not hear the law?

---

18 Rom. 4:14; 8:17

19 Ex. 20:19, 21, 22; Deut. 5:5, 22, 23, 27, 31; John 1:17; 15:22; Rom. 4:15; 5:20; 7:8, 13

20 Rom. 3:29, 30

21 Gal. 2:21

24 Rom. 10:4; Heb. 9:9, 10

26 John 1:12; 1John 3:1, 2

27 Rom. 6:3

28 John 10:16; 17:20, 21; Rom. 10:12

29 Gen. 21:10, 12; Rom. 8:17; 9:7; Gal. 4:7, 28

3 Gal. 2:4; 4:9; 5:1; Col. 2:8, 20; Heb. 9:10

4 Gen. 3:15; 49:10; Isa. 7:14; Dan. 9:24; Matt. 1:23; 5:17; Luke 1:31; 2:7, 27

5 Matt. 20:28; John 1:12; Gal. 3:13, 26

6 Rom. 5:5; 8:15

8 Eph. 2:11, 12

10 Rom. 14:5; Col. 2:16

11 Gal. 2:2; 5:2, 4; 1Thess. 3:5

12 2Cor. 2:5

13 1Cor. 2:3; Gal. 1:6

17 Rom. 10:2; 2Cor. 11:2

19 Phile. 1:10; James 1:18

3:19 till the seed should come to whom the promise was made. This verse clearly proclaims that Jesus Christ is the fulfillment of the promise made to the seed of Abraham (cf. Gen. 3:15).

4:4 the fullness of the time. The messianic prophecies of the Old Testament are fulfilled in Jesus Christ. That Jesus was "made of a woman" is a fulfillment of Genesis 3:15 regarding the "seed of the woman."

22 For it is written, that Abraham had two sons, the one by a bondmaid, the other by a freewoman.

23 But he *who was* of the bondwoman was born after the flesh; but he of the freewoman *was* by promise.

24 Which things are an allegory: for these are the two covenants; the one from the mount Sinai, which gendereth to bondage, which is Hagar.

25 For this Hagar is mount Sinai in Arabia, and answereth to Jerusalem which now is, and is in bondage with her children.

26 But Jerusalem which is above is free, which is the mother of us all.

27 For it is written, Rejoice, *thou* barren that bearest not; break forth and cry, thou that travailest not; for the desolate hath many more children than she which hath an husband.

28 Now we, brethren, as Isaac was, are the children of promise.

29 But as then he that was born after the flesh persecuted him *that was born* after the Spirit, even so *it is* now.

30 Nevertheless what saith the scripture? Cast out the bondwoman and her son: for the son of the bondwoman shall not be heir with the son of the freewoman.

31 So then, brethren, we are not children of the bondwoman, but of the free.

CHAPTER 5
The Privileges of Christian Liberty

1 Stand fast therefore in the liberty wherewith Christ hath made us free, and be not entangled again with the yoke of bondage.

2 Behold, I Paul say unto you, that if ye be circumcised, Christ shall profit you nothing.

3 For I testify again to every man that is circumcised, that he is a debtor to do the whole law.

4 Christ is become of no effect unto you, whosoever of you are justified by the law; ye are fallen from grace.

5 For we through the Spirit wait for the hope of righteousness by faith.

6 For in Jesus Christ neither circumcision availeth any thing, nor uncircumcision; but faith which worketh by love.

7 Ye did run well; who did hinder you that ye should not obey the truth?

8 This persuasion *cometh* not of him that calleth you.

9 A little leaven leaveneth the whole lump.

10 I have confidence in you through the Lord, that ye will be none otherwise minded: but he that troubleth you shall bear his judgment, whosoever he be.

11 And I, brethren, if I yet preach circumcision, why do I yet suffer persecution? then is the offence of the cross ceased.

12 I would they were even cut off which trouble you.

13 For, brethren, ye have been called unto liberty; only *use* not liberty for an occasion to the flesh, but by love serve one another.

14 For all the law is fulfilled in one word, *even* in this; Thou shalt love thy neighbour as thyself.

15 But if ye bite and devour one another, take heed that ye be not consumed one of another.

16 *This* I say then, Walk in the Spirit, and ye shall not fulfil the lust of the flesh.

17 For the flesh lusteth against the Spirit, and the Spirit against the flesh: and these are contrary the one to the other: so that ye cannot do the things that ye would.

18 But if ye be led of the Spirit, ye are not under the law.

19 Now the works of the flesh are manifest, which are *these*; adultery, fornication, uncleanness, lasciviousness,

20 Idolatry, witchcraft, hatred, variance,

Cross references

22 Gen. 16:15; 21:2
23 Gen. 18:10, 14; 21:1, 2
24 Deut. 33:2
26 Isa. 2:2; Rev. 3:12; 21:2, 10
27 Isa. 54:1
29 Gen. 21:9
30 Gen. 21:10, 12
31 John 8:36; Gal. 5:1, 13
1 Rom. 6:18; Gal. 2:4; 4:9
2 Acts 15:1; 16:3
4 Rom. 9:31, 32; Gal. 2:21; Heb. 12:15
6 Gal. 3:28; James 2:18, 20, 22
8 Gal. 1:6
9 1Cor. 5:6; 15:33
10 2Cor. 2:3; 8:22; 10:6; Gal. 1:7
11 1Cor. 1:23; 15:30
13 1Cor. 8:9; 9:19; Jude 1:4
14 Lev. 19:18; Matt. 7:12; 22:39, 40
16 Rom. 6:12; 8:1, 4, 12; 13:14
17 Rom. 7:15, 19, 23; 8:6, 7
18 Rom. 6:14; 8:2

4:23 he of the freewoman was by promise. Isaac, not Ishmael, was the fulfillment of the promise that Abraham and Sarah would have a son (Gen. 18:10).

4:26–27 the desolate hath many more children. The children of the "desolate" seems to be a reference to the Gentiles, particularly to the descendants of Ishmael. Paul indicates that growth in the church is the fulfillment of this prophecy from Isaiah 54:1.

5:5 the hope of righteousness by faith. Even the best Christian is not perfect while in this natural body. Only

when Christ comes to rapture His Church and transforms us, or, in the case of dead believers, resurrects us, will we truly be "righteous, even as he [Christ] is righteous" (1 John 3:7). In the meantime we "wait for the hope," or the realization of the "hope" of the Christian which is the second coming of Christ. The Bible's use of "hope" is a confident expectation that Christ will come, and all the blessings He has planned for our future will commence (see 1 Cor. 15:51–14; 1 Thess. 4:13–18).

emulations, wrath, strife, seditions, heresies,

21 Envyings, murders, drunkenness, revellings, and such like: of the which I tell you before, as I have also told *you* in time past, that they which do such things shall not inherit the kingdom of God.

"The Fruit of the Spirit"

22 But the fruit of the Spirit is love, joy, peace, longsuffering, gentleness, goodness, faith,

23 Meekness, temperance: against such there is no law.

24 And they that are Christ's have crucified the flesh with the affections and lusts.

25 If we live in the Spirit, let us also walk in the Spirit.

26 Let us not be desirous of vain glory, provoking one another, envying one another.

CHAPTER 6
The Practice of Love

1 Brethren, if a man be overtaken in a fault, ye which are spiritual, restore such a one in the spirit of meekness; considering thyself, lest thou also be tempted.

2 Bear ye one another's burdens, and so fulfil the law of Christ.

3 For if a man think himself to be something, when he is nothing, he deceiveth himself.

4 But let every man prove his own work, and then shall he have rejoicing in himself alone, and not in another.

5 For every man shall bear his own burden.

6 Let him that is taught in the word communicate unto him that teacheth in all good things.

21 1Cor. 6:9
22 John 15:2; Eph. 5:9; James 3:17
23 1Tim. 1:9
24 Rom. 6:6; 13:14; Gal. 2:20; 1Pet. 2:11
25 Rom. 8:4, 5; Gal. 5:16
26 Phil. 2:3
1 Rom. 14:1; 15:1; 1Cor. 2:15; 3:1; 4:21; 7:5; 10:12
2 John 13:14, 15, 34; 15:12
4 Luke 18:11
5 Rom. 2:6; 1Cor. 3:8
6 Rom. 15:27; 1Cor. 9:11, 14
7 Luke 16:25; Rom. 2:6
8 Job 4:8; Prov. 11:18; 22:8
9 Matt. 24:13; 1Cor. 15:58
10 1Thess. 5:15
12 Gal. 2:3, 14; 5:11
14 Rom. 6:6; Gal. 2:20; Phil. 3:3, 7, 8
16 Ps. 125:5; Phil. 3:3, 16
17 2Cor. 1:5; 4:10; 11:28

The Law of Sowing and Reaping

7 Be not deceived; God is not mocked: for whatsoever a man soweth, that shall he also reap.

8 For he that soweth to his flesh shall of the flesh reap corruption; but he that soweth to the Spirit shall of the Spirit reap life everlasting.

9 And let us not be weary in well doing: for in due season we shall reap, if we faint not.

10 As we have therefore opportunity, let us do good unto all *men*, especially unto them who are of the household of faith.

Paul's Closing Remarks

11 Ye see how large a letter I have written unto you with mine own hand.

12 As many as desire to make a fair shew in the flesh, they constrain you to be circumcised; only lest they should suffer persecution for the cross of Christ.

13 For neither they themselves who are circumcised keep the law; but desire to have you circumcised, that they may glory in your flesh.

14 But God forbid that I should glory, save in the cross of our Lord Jesus Christ, by whom the world is crucified unto me, and I unto the world.

15 For in Christ Jesus neither circumcision availeth any thing, nor uncircumcision, but a new creature.

16 And as many as walk according to this rule, peace *be* on them, and mercy, and upon the Israel of God.

17 From henceforth let no man trouble me: for I bear in my body the marks of the Lord Jesus.

18 Brethren, the grace of our Lord Jesus Christ *be* with your spirit. Amen.

Ephesians

Located only a mile from the Aegean Sea, Ephesus was the capital of the chief province of Asia. The great number of pilgrims that journeyed to Ephesus to worship at the pagan temple of Diana (Artemis) was important to the city's economy, making it the center of commerce for all of Asia Minor.

Imprisoned in Rome (see Acts 28:30–31), Paul wrote this first "prison epistle" around A.D. 61 to declare the believer's position in Christ and his obligations to walk worthy of that high calling. Paul had spent three years at Ephesus during the third missionary journey (Acts 20:31) founding and pastoring this church and leaving it in the care of Timothy. A major theme, described as a mystery now revealed, was that Jews and Gentiles would come together in one body and be "partakers of his promise in Christ by the gospel" (3:1–12).

The first half of this epistle reveals our position in Christ, while the second half is devoted to practical Christian living. Five times the word "riches" appears in connection with our enjoyment of Christ's spiritual blessings and the anticipation of a glorious future (1:7, 18; 2:7; 3:8, 16). But the key chapter in Ephesians is chapter six. Though Paul asserts in this letter that every Christian is blessed "with all spiritual blessings in heavenly places in Christ" (1:3), intense spiritual warfare is still a daily reality for every believer. However, the believer clad in the "whole armour of God" will be able to stand against Satan's attacks (6:11–18).

Prophetic statements in Ephesians include the future gathering according to the mystery of God's will (1:9–10), our inheritance in Christ (1:13–14, 18–19), the riches to be bestowed in ages to come (2:7), our being "sealed unto the day of redemption" (4:30), and our position as the Bride of Christ awaiting His return (5:25–27). Chapter 6:8–9 is an intimation of future rewards.

Eight of the 155 total verses, or 5 percent are prophetic. The book contains 4 quotations from the Old Testament.

Author
Paul

Date
A.D. 61

Key Truth
Spiritual Growth and Maturity

Historic Time
Paul's Imprisonment

Key Verse
4:1
. . . that ye walk worthy of the vocation wherewith are called.

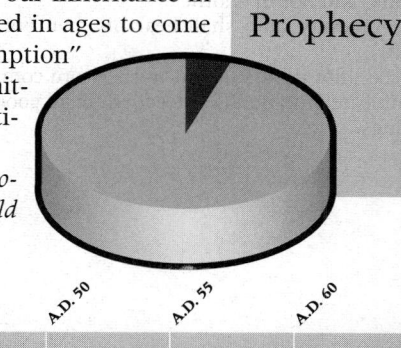

5%
Prophecy

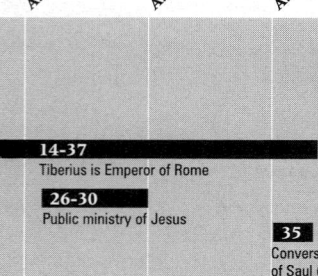

A.D. 25   A.D. 30   A.D. 35   A.D. 40   A.D. 45   A.D. 50   A.D. 55   A.D. 60

37-41
Caligula is Emperor of Rome

52-55
Church in Ephesus is founded

61
Ephesians is written

Pa Pe ma

14-37
Tiberius is Emperor of Rome

41-54
Claudius is Emperor of Rome

26-30
Public ministry of Jesus

35
Conversion of Saul (Paul)

47-49
Paul's First Missionary Journey

54-68
Nero is Emperor of Rome

49-53
Paul's Second Missionary Journey

53-56
Paul's Third Missionary Journey

CHAPTER 1

1 Paul, an apostle of Jesus Christ by the will of God, to the saints which are at Ephesus, and to the faithful in Christ Jesus:
2 Grace *be* to you, and peace, from God our Father, and *from* the Lord Jesus Christ.

The Blessings of Redemption

3 Blessed *be* the God and Father of our Lord Jesus Christ, who hath blessed us with all spiritual blessings in heavenly *places* in Christ:
4 According as he hath chosen us in him before the foundation of the world, that we should be holy and without blame before him in love:
5 Having predestinated us unto the adoption of children by Jesus Christ to himself, according to the good pleasure of his will,
6 To the praise of the glory of his grace, wherein he hath made us accepted in the beloved.
7 In whom we have redemption through his blood, the forgiveness of sins, according to the riches of his grace;
8 Wherein he hath abounded toward us in all wisdom and prudence;
9 Having made known unto us the mystery of his will, according to his good pleasure which he hath purposed in himself:
10 That in the dispensation of the fulness of times he might gather together in one all

3 2Cor. 1:3
4 Eph. 2:10; 5:27; Col. 1:22
5 Matt. 11:26; Rom. 8:15, 29, 30
6 John 3:35; 10:17
7 Acts 20:28; Rom. 2:4; 3:24; 9:23
9 Rom. 16:25; Eph. 3:4, 9, 11
10 Gal. 4:4; Eph. 2:15; 3:15; Col. 1:20
11 Rom. 8:17; Col. 1:12; 3:24
13 John 1:17
14 Luke 21:24; 1Pet. 2:9
16 Rom. 1:9; Phil. 1:3, 4; Col. 1:3; 1Thess. 1:2; 2Thess. 1:3
17 John 20:17; Col. 1:9; 2:2
19 Eph. 3:7; Col. 1:29; 2:12

things in Christ, both which are in heaven, and which are on earth; *even* in him:
11 In whom also we have obtained an inheritance, being predestinated according to the purpose of him who worketh all things after the counsel of his own will:
12 That we should be to the praise of his glory, who first trusted in Christ.
13 In whom ye also *trusted,* after that ye heard the word of truth, the gospel of your salvation: in whom also after that ye believed, ye were sealed with that holy Spirit of promise,
14 Which is the earnest of our inheritance until the redemption of the purchased possession, unto the praise of his glory.
15 Wherefore I also, after I heard of your faith in the Lord Jesus, and love unto all the saints,
16 Cease not to give thanks for you, making mention of you in my prayers,
17 That the God of our Lord Jesus Christ, the Father of glory, may give unto you the spirit of wisdom and revelation in the knowledge of him:
18 The eyes of your understanding being enlightened; that ye may know what is the hope of his calling, and what the riches of the glory of his inheritance in the saints,
19 And what *is* the exceeding greatness of his power to us-ward who believe, according to the working of his mighty power,

---

1:3–14 A threefold structure is discernible, successively focusing on God the Father (vv. 3–6, 8, 11); Christ (vv. 3, 5, 7–10, 12); and the Spirit (vv. 13–14). This passage may have been sung repetitiously in poetic stanzas as a hymn of praise, magnifying God's will (vv. 5, 9, 11).

1:3 spiritual blessings in heavenly places. The expression "heavenly places" is used four times in the epistle (1:3, 20; 2:6; 3:10) and only in Ephesians. Literally, the Greek word *epouranios* is "the heavenlies" meaning the heavenly realm where God rules and reigns (cf. Rev. 4—5). At least seven blessings appear relating to the great salvation believers enjoy (vv. 4–14). Believers are chosen in love (v. 4), predestinated for Jesus (v. 5), adopted as children (v. 5), accepted in the beloved (v. 6), redeemed through blood (v. 7), forgiven of sins (v. 7), and sealed with the Holy Spirit (v. 13).

1:9 mystery of his will. This previously unrevealed secret is God's master plan for the climax of history in the universal triumph of Christ.

1:10 dispensation of the fulness of times. A biblical dispensation is not merely a period of time; it is a period of administrative arrangement, a distinguishable system

or order in the outworking of God's purpose and plan for history, as Israel under the Law. The final dispensation here will include the millennial reign of Christ, after which God will gather together in one unified realm all things under Christ in one universal and everlasting administration. All past "times," then completed, will merge and culminate in that eternal kingdom which cannot be moved (Heb. 12:28).

1:14 the earnest of our inheritance. Being sealed by the Holy Spirit is the advance installment (earnest) of our inheritance (v. 11) in anticipation of its full redemption for which we will eternally praise God. Our inheritance includes eternal life, the "riches of His glory" (v. 18), the final redemption of the body at the resurrection (Rom. 8:23; 1 Cor. 15:50, 53), and all that will be included in the "riches of His grace" (2:6–7).

1:18 his inheritance in the saints. Believers are to know not only the "riches of His grace" in salvation (v. 7), but the "riches of His glory" in which the saints may be regarded as God's inheritance, even as He is ours. When He takes possession of His redeemed universe, the saints will "inherit all things" (Rev. 21:7).

20 Which he wrought in Christ, when he raised him from the dead, and set *him* at his own right hand in the heavenly *places,*
21 Far above all principality, and power, and might, and dominion, and every name that is named, not only in this world, but also in that which is to come:
22 And hath put all *things* under his feet, and gave him *to be* the head over all *things* to the church,
23 Which is his body, the fulness of him that filleth all in all.

CHAPTER 2
Salvation from Sin

1 And you *hath he quickened,* who were dead in trespasses and sins
2 Wherein in time past ye walked according to the course of this world, according to the prince of the power of the air, the spirit that now worketh in the children of disobedience:
3 Among whom also we all had our con-

20 Ps. 110:1; Acts 2:24
21 Rom. 8:38; Phil. 2:9, 10
22 Ps. 8:6; Matt. 28:18
23 Rom. 12:5; 1Cor. 12:6, 12, 27
1 John 5:24
2 Eph. 4:22; 5:6; 6:12
3 Ps. 51:5; Rom. 5:12
5 Rom. 5:6, 8, 10; 6:4, 5
6 Eph. 1:20
7 Titus 3:4
8 Rom. 3:24; 4:16; 10:14, 15, 17
9 Rom. 3:20, 27, 28; 4:2
10 Deut. 32:6; Ps. 100:3

versation in times past in the lusts of our flesh, fulfilling the desires of the flesh and of the mind; and were by nature the children of wrath, even as others.
4 But God, who is rich in mercy, for his great love wherewith he loved us,
5 Even when we were dead in sins, hath quickened us together with Christ, (by grace ye are saved;)
6 And hath raised *us* up together, and made *us* sit together in heavenly *places* in Christ Jesus:
7 That in the ages to come he might shew the exceeding riches of his grace in *his* kindness toward us through Christ Jesus.
8 For by grace are ye saved through faith; and that not of yourselves: *it is* the gift of God:
9 Not of works, lest any man should boast.
10 For we are his workmanship, created in Christ Jesus unto good works, which God hath before ordained that we should walk in them.

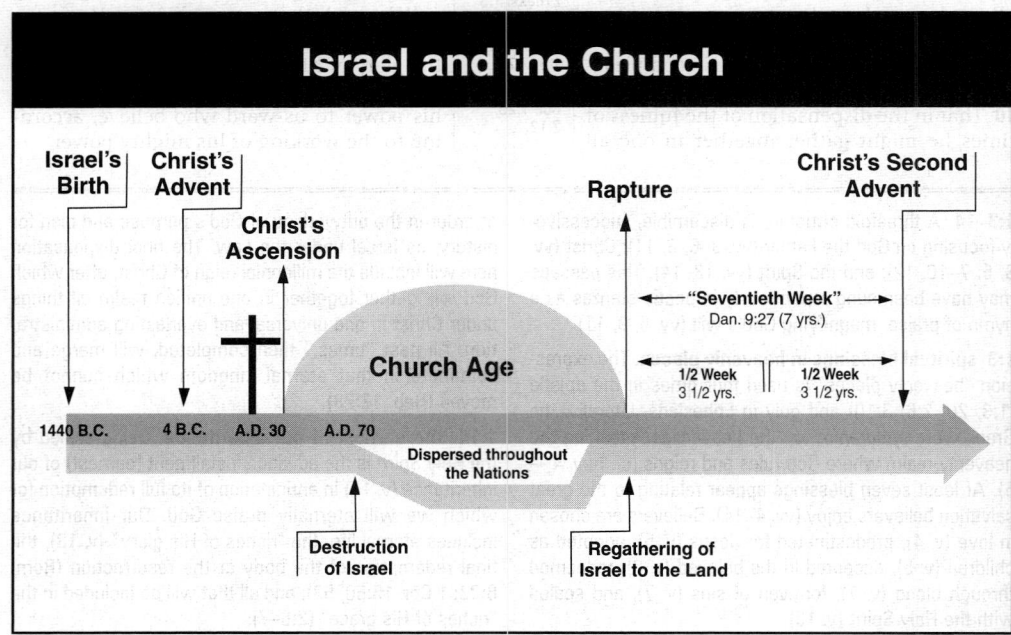

Israel and the Church

Israel's Birth — Christ's Advent — Christ's Ascension — Church Age — Rapture — Christ's Second Advent

"Seventeenth Week" Dan. 9:27 (7 yrs.)

1/2 Week 3 1/2 yrs. | 1/2 Week 3 1/2 yrs.

1440 B.C. — 4 B.C. — A.D. 30 — A.D. 70

Dispersed throughout the Nations

Destruction of Israel

Regathering of Israel to the Land

© AMG Publishers

2:7 ages to come. Beyond the Rapture, the Tribulation, the Millennium, and the unveiling of the new heaven and new earth, through all the ceaseless ages of the ages, God is going to shower the exceeding riches of His grace with untold blessings and indescribable joys on all those who put their trust in Him. No earth-bound believer can begin to imagine the wondrous things God has prepared for them who love Him (Isa. 64:4; 65:17; 1 Cor. 2:9).

Salvation Freely by Grace

By William T. James

Two blind men who found themselves near the presence of Jesus shouted to Him to get His attention when He passed by. When the Lord asked, "What will ye that I shall do unto you?" (Matt. 20:32), the men who recognized Him as Christ pleaded earnestly, "Lord, that our eyes may be opened" (v. 33).

Blindness afflicts many people within all races, cultures, languages, and socioeconomic classes throughout the world.* Those who have their sight wince in near-agony when they merely contemplate what adverse effects could enter their lives should they for some reason lose their sight. They imagine stumbling through life trapped within cerebral darkness that suffocates personality, creativity, and all hope for their future. They fear that the worst effects might be the helplessness and the humiliation that would come with their loss of independence.

Today, billions of people suffer from blindness far worse than any physical blindness so innately feared by mankind. Yet these same people scarcely turn a thought towards their terrible disability, a much more profound, inherited affliction, curable only by the saving grace of Jesus Christ (see Eph. 2:8–9).

> *Even the vilest of sinners can be saved from the wrath of God.*

Because Adam, the flesh–father of the human race, succumbed to temptation in the garden of Eden, all of us are fallen; that is, we were born into sin. Therefore, we can be saved from that sin curse only by "being justified freely by his [God's] grace through the redemption that is in Christ Jesus" (Rom. 3:24). The same Jesus who healed the two blind men is the "Lamb slain from the foundation of the world" (Rev. 13:8). He alone has the power to instantly and forever heal the poor, wretched, blind soul who confesses with his mouth the Lord Jesus and believes in his heart that God has raised him from the dead (Rom. 10:9).

When Jesus opens the eyes of the spiritually blind through the "new birth" experience (see John 3), the child of God begins a phenomenal journey that is limited in its vistas only by that person's willingness to obey his heavenly Father (Prov. 3:5–6).

Mankind's attempts throughout the centuries to predict the future have not only been futile but often destructive. When God opens the spiritual eyes of His children through salvation by grace, they can know a great deal about the future and rest assured He is in complete control. Yet, for the time being, God has chosen to keep to Himself many stupendous wonders with which He apparently plans to one day thrill believers (see 1 Cor. 2:9).

Even the vilest of sinners can be saved from the wrath of God, which ultimately must fall in judgment on all who will not repent. God's salvation by grace freely and unconditionally covers all of His children's sins from the past, present, and future (see 1 Thess. 5:9). Christians of the Church Age will be kept out of the Tribulation of Revelation 6—19 (see Rev. 3:10). What a glorious prospect awaits just ahead for those who have opened spiritual eyes and ears (see 1 Thess. 4:13–18; 1 Cor. 15:51–55; John 14:1–6).

*Incidentally, the author, William T. James, has been blind since 1993 due to a retinal disease. He received his spiritual sight as a very young boy.

No Longer Strangers

11 Wherefore remember, that ye *being* in time past Gentiles in the flesh, who are called Uncircumcision by that which is called the Circumcision in the flesh made by hands;

12 That at that time ye were without Christ, being aliens from the commonwealth of Israel, and strangers from the covenants of promise, having no hope, and without God in the world:

13 But now in Christ Jesus ye who sometimes were far off are made nigh by the blood of Christ.

14 For he is our peace, who hath made both one, and hath broken down the middle wall of partition *between us*;

15 Having abolished in his flesh the enmity, *even* the law of commandments *contained* in ordinances; for to make in himself of twain one new man, *so* making peace;

16 And that he might reconcile both unto God in one body by the cross, having slain the enmity thereby:

17 And came and preached peace to you which were afar off, and to them that were nigh.

18 For through him we both have access by one Spirit unto the Father.

19 Now therefore ye are no more strangers and foreigners, but fellow citizens with the saints, and of the household of God;

20 And are built upon the foundation of the apostles and prophets, Jesus Christ himself being the chief corner *stone*;

21 In whom all the building fitly framed together groweth unto an holy temple in the Lord:

22 In whom ye also are builded together for an habitation of God through the Spirit.

CHAPTER 3
God's Eternal Purpose in Christ

1 For this cause I Paul, the prisoner of Jesus Christ for you Gentiles,

2 If ye have heard of the dispensation of the grace of God which is given me to you-ward:

3 How that by revelation he made known unto me the mystery; (as I wrote afore in few words,

4 Whereby, when ye read, ye may understand my knowledge in the mystery of Christ)

5 Which in other ages was not made known unto the sons of men, as it is now revealed unto his holy apostles and prophets by the Spirit;

6 That the Gentiles should be fellow heirs, and of the same body, and partakers of his promise in Christ by the gospel:

7 Whereof I was made a minister, according to the gift of the grace of God given unto me by the effectual working of his power.

8 Unto me, who am less than the least of all saints, is this grace given, that I should preach among the Gentiles the unsearchable riches of Christ;

9 And to make all *men* see what *is* the fellowship of the mystery, which from the beginning of the world hath been hid in God, who created all things by Jesus Christ:

10 To the intent that now unto the principalities and powers in heavenly *places* might

Cross references

11 Rom. 2:28, 29
12 Eph. 4:18
13 Gal. 3:28
14 Mic. 5:5
15 2Cor. 5:17; Gal. 6:15
17 Ps. 148:14; Isa. 57:19
19 Gal. 6:10; Phil. 3:20
20 Ps. 118:22; Isa. 28:16
21 1Cor. 3:17; 6:19; 2Cor. 6:16; Eph. 4:15, 16
22 1Pet. 2:5
1 Acts 21:33; 28:17, 20
2 Acts 9:15; 13:2; Rom. 1:5; 11:13
3 Acts 22:17, 21; 26:17, 18
4 1Cor. 4:1; Eph. 6:19
5 Acts 10:28
6 Gal. 3:14, 28, 29
7 Rom. 1:5; 15:16, 18
8 Gal. 1:16; 2:8; Eph. 1:7
9 Ps. 33:6; 1Cor. 2:7

3:2 dispensation of the grace of God. The special stewardship and administrative responsibility to explain God's grace to the Gentiles was given to Paul. God's grace was being extended beyond Jews to all Gentiles (non-Jew). By faith in Christ they were brought together into one spiritual body—the Church (1 Cor. 10:32).

3:3–6 revelation . . . mystery. A mystery or hidden secret in the biblical sense was something in the mind and plan of God but unknown to mankind until it was revealed in the New Testament. Here the mystery is not merely that Gentiles would be blessed (Isa. 42:6–7; Matt. 4:14–16; Acts 9:15; 10:34–48; 11:18; 15:7, 13–14), which was predicted and well known. The mystery, not known in Old Testament times, was that believing Jews and believing Gentiles would be united as fellow heirs within the same body, to be sharers of God's promise in Christ through the gospel. In the body of Christ there are no racial or social distinctions.

3:7–9 I was made a minister. As the unique herald of the new promises to Gentiles and Jews together in Christ, Paul emphasizes his call, his ministry, and his gift from God to preach to the Gentiles, attributing these privileges with deep humility to the grace of God. Paul's special stewardship enabled him to enlighten everyone about this mystery, this master plan, hidden in God from the beginning of the ages. The formation of the Church was no afterthought with God, but was always a supreme and eternal purpose.

3:10–11 the manifold wisdom of God. In contrast to ages past, the manifold (Gr. *polupoikilos*, "many sided") wisdom of God may now, through the Church, be known in the angelic and spiritual realm, as God fulfills the various dimensions of His divine program. Eternally redeemed and glorified, the Church will be God's most privileged and preeminent assembly forever.

be known by the church the manifold wisdom of God,

11 According to the eternal purpose which he purposed in Christ Jesus our Lord:

12 In whom we have boldness and access with confidence by the faith of him.

13 Wherefore I desire that ye faint not at my tribulations for you, which is your glory.

Paul's Prayer for the Ephesians

14 For this cause I bow my knees unto the Father of our Lord Jesus Christ,

15 Of whom the whole family in heaven and earth is named,

16 That he would grant you, according to the riches of his glory, to be strengthened with might by his Spirit in the inner man;

17 That Christ may dwell in your hearts by faith; that ye, being rooted and grounded in love,

18 May be able to comprehend with all saints what *is* the breadth, and length, and depth, and height;

19 And to know the love of Christ, which passeth knowledge, that ye might be filled with all the fulness of God.

20 Now unto him that is able to do exceeding abundantly above all that we ask or think, according to the power that worketh in us,

21 Unto him *be* glory in the church by Christ Jesus throughout all ages, world without end. Amen.

CHAPTER 4
Oneness in Christ

1 I therefore, the prisoner of the Lord, beseech you that ye walk worthy of the vocation wherewith ye are called,

2 With all lowliness and meekness, with longsuffering, forbearing one another in love;

3 Endeavouring to keep the unity of the Spirit in the bond of peace.

4 *There is* one body, and one Spirit, even as ye are called in one hope of your calling;

5 One Lord, one faith, one baptism,

6 One God and Father of all, who *is* above all, and through all, and in you all.

11 Eph. 1:9

13 Phil. 1:14

16 Rom. 7:22; 9:23; 2Cor. 4:16

17 John 14:23

18 Rom. 10:3, 11, 12; Eph. 1:18

19 John 1:16

20 Rom. 16:25; Col. 1:29

21 Rom. 11:36; 16:27; Heb. 13:21

1 Phil. 1:27; Col. 1:10; Phile. 1:1, 9

2 Gal. 5:22, 23; Col. 3:12, 13

4 1Cor. 12:4, 11, 12, 13

5 1Cor. 1:13; 8:6; 12:5

7 Rom. 12:3, 6

8 Judg. 5:12; Ps. 68:18

9 John 3:13; 6:33, 62

10 Acts 1:9, 11; 2:33

11 1Cor. 12:28; 2Tim. 4:5

12 Eph. 1:23; Col. 1:24

14 1Cor. 14:20; Heb. 13:9

15 Col. 1:18; 1John 3:18

16 Col. 2:19

17 Rom. 1:21; 1Pet. 4:3

18 Eph. 2:12; 1Thess. 4:5

19 Rom. 1:24, 26; 1Tim. 4:2; 1Pet. 4:3

7 But unto every one of us is given grace according to the measure of the gift of Christ.

8 Wherefore he saith, When he ascended up on high, he led captivity captive, and gave gifts unto men.

9 (Now that he ascended, what is it but that he also descended first into the lower parts of the earth?

10 He that descended is the same also that ascended up far above all heavens, that he might fill all things.)

11 And he gave some, apostles; and some, prophets; and some, evangelists; and some, pastors and teachers;

12 For the perfecting of the saints, for the work of the ministry, for the edifying of the body of Christ:

13 Till we all come in the unity of the faith, and of the knowledge of the Son of God, unto a perfect man, unto the measure of the stature of the fulness of Christ:

14 That we *henceforth* be no more children, tossed to and fro, and carried about with every wind of doctrine, by the sleight of men, *and* cunning craftiness, whereby they lie in wait to deceive;

15 But speaking the truth in love, may grow up into him in all things, which is the head, *even* Christ:

16 From whom the whole body fitly joined together and compacted by that which every joint supplieth, according to the effectual working in the measure of every part, maketh increase of the body unto the edifying of itself in love.

A New Way of Thinking

17 This I say therefore, and testify in the Lord, that ye henceforth walk not as other Gentiles walk, in the vanity of their mind,

18 Having the understanding darkened, being alienated from the life of God through the ignorance that is in them, because of the blindness of their heart:

19 Who being past feeling have given themselves over unto lasciviousness, to work all uncleanness with greediness.

20 But ye have not so learned Christ;

4:8 ascended up on high. Quoting and using as an illustration Psalm 68:18, Paul adapts the passage relating to a victorious Israelite warrior and king returning from his conquests with hosts of prisoners, both receiving and bestowing gifts. Paul then applies the passage to Jesus' ascension after conquering Satan and all that had conquered us.

4:9 into the lower parts of the earth. Jesus descended into Hades/Abraham's bosom (Luke 16:19–31), transferring Old Testament saints up into the third heaven (2 Cor. 12:1–4). This also denotes the contrast between the place from which Christ came—the highest realm of heaven—and the place to which He came—earth, the lowest place.

21 If so be that ye have heard him, and have been taught by him, as the truth is in Jesus:
22 That ye put off concerning the former conversation the old man, which is corrupt according to the deceitful lusts;
23 And be renewed in the spirit of your mind;
24 And that ye put on the new man, which after God is created in righteousness and true holiness.
25 Wherefore putting away lying, speak every man truth with his neighbour: for we are members one of another.
26 Be ye angry, and sin not: let not the sun go down upon your wrath:
27 Neither give place to the devil.
28 Let him that stole steal no more: but rather let him labour, working with *his* hands the thing which is good, that he may have to give to him that needeth.
29 Let no corrupt communication proceed out of your mouth, but that which is good to the use of edifying, that it may minister grace unto the hearers.
30 And grieve not the holy Spirit of God, whereby ye are sealed unto the day of redemption.
31 Let all bitterness, and wrath, and anger, and clamour, and evil speaking, be put away from you, with all malice:
32 And be ye kind one to another, tenderhearted, forgiving one another, even as God for Christ's sake hath forgiven you.

CHAPTER 5
Walk in Love

1 Be ye therefore followers of God as dear children:
2 And walk in love, as Christ also hath loved us, and hath given himself for us an offering and a sacrifice to God for a sweet-smelling savour.
3 But fornication, and all uncleanness, or covetousness, let it not be once named among you, as becometh saints;
4 Neither filthiness, nor foolish talking, nor jesting, which are not convenient: but rather giving of thanks.
5 For this ye know, that no whoremonger, nor unclean person, nor covetous man, who is an idolater, hath any inheritance in the kingdom of Christ and of God.

22 Rom. 6:6; Eph. 2:2, 3
23 Rom. 12:2
24 Rom. 6:4; 2Cor. 5:17
26 Ps. 4:4; 37:8
27 1Pet. 5:9
28 Luke 3:11
29 Matt. 12:36
30 Luke 21:28
31 Titus 3:2, 3; James 4:11
32 Matt. 6:14; Mark 11:25
2 John 13:34; Gal. 1:4; 2:20
3 Rom. 6:13
5 1Cor. 6:9; Gal. 5:19, 21
6 2Thess. 2:3
8 Isa. 9:2; 1John 2:9
9 Gal. 5:22
12 Eph. 5:3
13 John 3:20, 21
14 Isa. 60:1
15 Col. 4:5
16 Eccl. 11:2; 12:1
19 1Cor. 14:26; Col. 3:16; James 5:13
20 Ps. 34:1
21 1Pet. 5:5
22 1Pet. 3:1
23 1Cor. 11:3
24 Col. 3:20, 22; Titus 2:9
25 Acts 20:28; Gal. 1:4; 2:20; Eph. 5:2; Col. 3:19; 1Pet. 3:7

6 Let no man deceive you with vain words: for because of these things cometh the wrath of God upon the children of disobedience.
7 Be not ye therefore partakers with them.
8 For ye were sometimes darkness, but now *are ye* light in the Lord: walk as children of light:
9 (For the fruit of the Spirit *is* in all goodness and righteousness and truth;)
10 Proving what is acceptable unto the Lord.
11 And have no fellowship with the unfruitful works of darkness, but rather reprove *them*.
12 For it is a shame even to speak of those things which are done of them in secret.
13 But all things that are reproved are made manifest by the light: for whatsoever doth make manifest is light.
14 Wherefore he saith, Awake thou that sleepest, and arise from the dead, and Christ shall give thee light.
15 See then that ye walk circumspectly, not as fools, but as wise,
16 Redeeming the time, because the days are evil.
17 Wherefore be ye not unwise, but understanding what the will of the Lord *is*.
18 And be not drunk with wine, wherein is excess; but be filled with the Spirit;
19 Speaking to yourselves in psalms and hymns and spiritual songs, singing and making melody in your heart to the Lord;
20 Giving thanks always for all things unto God and the Father in the name of our Lord Jesus Christ;

Husbands and Wives

21 Submitting yourselves one to another in the fear of God.
22 Wives, submit yourselves unto your own husbands, as unto the Lord.
23 For the husband is the head of the wife, even as Christ is the head of the church: and he is the saviour of the body.
24 Therefore as the church is subject unto Christ, so *let* the wives *be* to their own husbands in every thing.
25 Husbands, love your wives, even as Christ also loved the church, and gave himself for it;

4:30 sealed unto the day of redemption. Believers have been sealed by the Spirit who indwells them. Referring to an official mark or stamp on a document or contract, a seal represents authority, security, authenticity, and ownership. Officially and eternally the Spirit of God seals the believer "unto the day of redemption." That day will occur when the body is redeemed at the Rapture, when we are glorified (Rom. 8:23; 1 Cor. 15:42–49).

26 That he might sanctify and cleanse it with the washing of water by the word,

27 That he might present it to himself a glorious church, not having spot, or wrinkle, or any such thing; but that it should be holy and without blemish.

28 So ought men to love their wives as their own bodies. He that loveth his wife loveth himself.

29 For no man ever yet hated his own flesh; but nourisheth and cherisheth it, even as the Lord the church:

30 For we are members of his body, of his flesh, and of his bones.

31 For this cause shall a man leave his father and mother, and shall be joined unto his wife, and they two shall be one flesh.

32 This is a great mystery: but I speak concerning Christ and the church.

33 Nevertheless let every one of you in particular so love his wife even as himself; and the wife *see* that she reverence *her* husband.

CHAPTER 6
Children and Parents

1 Children, obey your parents in the Lord: for this is right.

2 Honour thy father and mother; which is the first commandment with promise;

3 That it may be well with thee, and thou mayest live long on the earth.

4 And, ye fathers, provoke not your children to wrath: but bring them up in the nurture and admonition of the Lord.

Servants and Masters

5 Servants, be obedient to them that are *your* masters according to the flesh, with fear and trembling, in singleness of your heart, as unto Christ;

6 Not with eyeservice, as menpleasers; but as the servants of Christ, doing the will of God from the heart;

7 With good will doing service, as to the Lord, and not to men:

8 Knowing that whatsoever good thing

any man doeth, the same shall he receive of the Lord, whether *he be* bond or free.

9 And, ye masters, do the same things unto them, forbearing threatening: knowing that your Master also is in heaven; neither is there respect of persons with him.

The Christian's Armor

10 Finally, my brethren, be strong in the Lord, and in the power of his might.

11 Put on the whole armour of God, that ye may be able to stand against the wiles of the devil.

12 For we wrestle not against flesh and blood, but against principalities, against powers, against the rulers of the darkness of this world, against spiritual wickedness in high *places.*

13 Wherefore take unto you the whole armour of God, that ye may be able to withstand in the evil day, and having done all, to stand.

14 Stand therefore, having your loins girt about with truth, and having on the breastplate of righteousness;

15 And your feet shod with the preparation of the gospel of peace;

16 Above all, taking the shield of faith, wherewith ye shall be able to quench all the fiery darts of the wicked.

17 And take the helmet of salvation, and the sword of the Spirit, which is the word of God:

18 Praying always with all prayer and supplication in the Spirit, and watching thereunto with all perseverance and supplication for all saints;

19 And for me, that utterance may be given unto me, that I may open my mouth boldly, to make known the mystery of the gospel,

20 For which I am an ambassador in bonds: that therein I may speak boldly, as I ought to speak.

Benediction

21 But that ye also may know my affairs, *and* how I do, Tychicus, a beloved brother

Cross References

26 John 3:5; 15:3; 17:17
27 Song 4:7
30 Gen. 2:23; Rom. 12:5; 1Cor. 6:15; 12:27
31 Gen. 2:24
33 Col. 3:19
1 Prov. 23:22
2 Ex. 20:12; Deut. 5:16; 27:16
4 Gen. 18:19; Deut. 4:9; 6:7, 20; 11:19
5 Phil. 2:12; 1Tim. 6:1; Titus 2:9
8 Rom. 2:6; Gal. 3:28
9 Lev. 25:43
10 Eph. 1:19; Col. 1:11
11 Eph. 6:13; 1Thess. 5:8
12 Matt. 16:17
13 2Cor. 10:4
14 Isa. 11:5; 59:17
15 Isa. 52:7; Rom. 10:15
16 1John 5:4
17 Isa. 59:17
18 Phil. 1:4; Col. 4:2
19 2Thess. 3:1
20 Acts 26:29; 28:20
21 Acts 20:4; Col. 4:7; 2Tim. 4:12; Titus 3:12

5:27 not having spot, or wrinkle . . . holy and without blemish. After the judgment seat of Christ, which follows the Rapture (Rom. 14:10; 1 Cor. 3:11–15; 4:5; 2 Cor. 5:10), this joyful presentation will occur. By God's grace, Christ's Church, which on earth has its imperfections and limitations, will be an assembly of glorified saints, cleansed individually and collectively of all moral and spiritual blemishes, sanctified and made holy forever. The Bride will be consecrated and made faultless (Jude 1:24–25). Then the marriage of the Lamb, with the Bride elevated to the highest rank with Christ, will be celebrated in heaven (Rev. 19:7–11).

6:7–9 receive of the Lord. Christians are challenged to serve the Lord, even as slaves serve their masters. They are to serve wholeheartedly, as though it were for the Lord and not for men, fulfilling assigned tasks and doing the will of God from their hearts. All believers will receive rewards for whatever good things they have done, regardless of their social status.

and faithful minister in the Lord, shall make known to you all things:
22 Whom I have sent unto you for the same purpose, that ye might know our affairs, and *that* he might comfort your hearts.

23 Peace *be* to the brethren, and love with faith, from God the Father and the Lord Jesus Christ.
24 Grace *be* with all them that love our Lord Jesus Christ in sincerity. Amen.

22 Col. 4:8
23 1Pet. 5:14
24 Titus 2:7

Philippians

The city of Philippi was named for Philip of Macedon, the father of Alexander the Great, who captured the city in 358 B.C. from the Thracians. Philippi later became a Roman colony, whose port location made it a prime Mediterranean trade center, and thus, a strategic locale for the spread of the gospel.

Written during Paul's second imprisonment around A.D. 62, this epistle is an exposition of Christianity as a personal experience. It is written in immediate response to an offering sent from the Philippian church that had been delivered by Epaphroditus to Paul, who was by this time a prisoner in Rome. The letter to the Philippians overflows with joy and love, reflecting Paul's deep, heartfelt relationship with Christ and his abiding faith in Him.

Author
Paul
Date
A.D. 62
Key Truth
"To Live Is Christ"
Historic Time
From Philippian Aid to Epaphroditus' Recovery
Key Verse
1:21
For to me to live is Christ, and to die is gain.

The most important theological passage is 2:5–11, which expresses the following primary truths about Christ: **1)** His divine pre-existence, **2)** His abasement or emptying of Himself, **3)** His humble humanity, **4)** His humiliating but redemptive death on the cross, **5)** His exaltation by the Father, **6)** His supreme name, and **7)** His future universal rulership.

Because we are "in Christ" (1:1), we know He is in us living through us (1:21). Therefore, Paul declares the essence of being a Christian in this brief statement: "To live is Christ and to die is gain." At death we as Christians depart to be with Christ, but He is our example while we are alive (2:5) as well as our rejoicing (3:3), our aim and goal (3:10–14), our expectation at the Rapture (3:20–21), our source of peace (4:6–7), our inner dynamic strength (4:13), and our provider and supplier (4:19).

Five prophecies include information on the second coming of Christ (1:6, 10; 3:20–21), the future reign of Jesus (2:10–11), an allusion to circumcision that is typical of God's special selection (3:3–6), attainment of the resurrection (3:11, 21), and the affirmation that the Lord is coming again (4:5).

Only 10 of the 104 verses (about 10%) are prophetic. Only 1 Old Testament quotation appears in Philippians.

10%
Prophecy

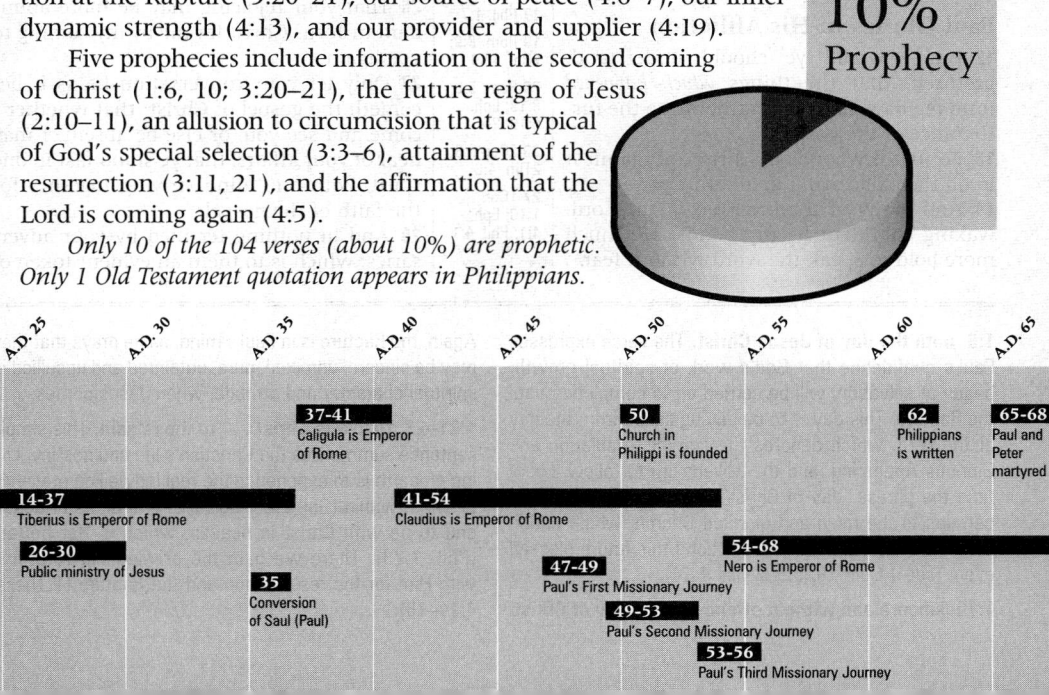

A.D. 25	A.D. 30	A.D. 35	A.D. 40	A.D. 45	A.D. 50	A.D. 55	A.D. 60	A.D. 65

37-41 Caligula is Emperor of Rome

50 Church in Philippi is founded

62 Philippians is written

65-68 Paul and Peter martyred

14-37 Tiberius is Emperor of Rome

41-54 Claudius is Emperor of Rome

26-30 Public ministry of Jesus

35 Conversion of Saul (Paul)

47-49 Paul's First Missionary Journey

54-68 Nero is Emperor of Rome

49-53 Paul's Second Missionary Journey

53-56 Paul's Third Missionary Journey

CHAPTER 1

1 Paul and Timotheus, the servants of Jesus Christ, to all the saints in Christ Jesus which are at Philippi, with the bishops and deacons:
2 Grace *be* unto you, and peace, from God our Father, and *from* the Lord Jesus Christ.
3 I thank my God upon every remembrance of you,
4 Always in every prayer of mine for you all making request with joy,
5 For your fellowship in the gospel from the first day until now;
6 Being confident of this very thing, that he which hath begun a good work in you will perform *it* until the day of Jesus Christ:
7 Even as it is meet for me to think this of you all, because I have you in my heart; inasmuch as both in my bonds, and in the defence and confirmation of the gospel, ye all are partakers of my grace.
8 For God is my record, how greatly I long after you all in the bowels of Jesus Christ.
9 And this I pray, that your love may abound yet more and more in knowledge and *in* all judgment;
10 That ye may approve things that are excellent; that ye may be sincere and without offence till the day of Christ;
11 Being filled with the fruits of righteousness, which are by Jesus Christ, unto the glory and praise of God.

Paul Glories in His Affliction

12 But I would ye should understand, brethren, that the things *which happened* unto me have fallen out rather unto the furtherance of the gospel;
13 So that my bonds in Christ are manifest in all the palace, and in all other *places*;
14 And many of the brethren in the Lord, waxing confident by my bonds, are much more bold to speak the word without fear.

1 1Cor. 1:2
2 Rom. 1:7; 2Cor. 1:2; 1Pet. 1:2
3 Rom. 1:8, 9; 1Cor. 1:4; Eph. 1:15, 16; Col. 1:3; 1Thess. 1:2; 2Thess. 1:3
5 Rom. 12:13; 15:26; 2Cor. 8:1; Phil. 4:14, 15
6 John 6:29; Phil. 1:10; 1Thess. 1:3
7 2Cor. 3:2; 7:3; Eph. 3:1; 6:20; Phil. 1:17; 4:14; Col. 4:3, 18; 2Tim. 1:8
8 Rom. 1:9; 9:1; Gal. 1:20; Phil. 2:26; 4:1; 1Thess. 2:5
9 1Thess. 3:12; Phile. 1:6
10 Rom. 2:18; 12:2; 1Cor. 1:8
11 John 15:4, 5, 8; Eph. 1:12, 14; 2:10; Col. 1:6
13 Phil. 4:22
15 Phil. 2:3
17 Phil. 1:7
19 Rom. 8:9; 2Cor. 1:11
20 Rom. 5:5; 8:19; Eph. 6:19, 20
23 2Cor. 5:8; 2Tim. 4:6
27 1Cor. 1:10; Eph. 4:1; Phil. 4:1

15 Some indeed preach Christ even of envy and strife; and some also of good will:
16 The one preach Christ of contention, not sincerely, supposing to add affliction to my bonds:
17 But the other of love, knowing that I am set for the defence of the gospel.
18 What then? notwithstanding, every way, whether in pretense, or in truth, Christ is preached; and I therein do rejoice, yea, and will rejoice.
19 For I know that this shall turn to my salvation through your prayer, and the supply of the Spirit of Jesus Christ,
20 According to my earnest expectation and *my* hope, that in nothing I shall be ashamed, but *that* with all boldness, as always, *so* now also Christ shall be magnified in my body, whether *it be* by life, or by death.
21 For to me to live *is* Christ, and to die *is* gain.
22 But if I live in the flesh, this *is* the fruit of my labour: yet what I shall choose I wot not.
23 For I am in a strait betwixt two, having a desire to depart, and to be with Christ; which is far better:
24 Nevertheless to abide in the flesh *is* more needful for you.
25 And having this confidence, I know that I shall abide and continue with you all for your furtherance and joy of faith;
26 That your rejoicing may be more abundant in Jesus Christ for me by my coming to you again.
27 Only let your conversation be as it becometh the gospel of Christ: that whether I come and see you, or else be absent, I may hear of your affairs, that ye stand fast in one spirit, with one mind striving together for the faith of the gospel;
28 And in nothing terrified by your adversaries: which is to them an evident token of

---

1:6 until the day of Jesus Christ. The verse expresses Paul's confidence that God's work of spiritual growth, begun at salvation, will be carried on to completion until the Rapture. This day is to be distinguished from the day of the Lord, which denotes the coming Tribulation and Glorious Appearing, and the Millennium to follow. Every time the phrase "day of Christ" is found in Scripture, it pertains to the risen and glorified Church, which anticipates with holy joy and fervent hope this future blessed event (see 1 Cor. 1:8; 5:5; 2 Cor. 1:14).

1:10 sincere and without offence till the day of Christ.

Again, the Rapture is in Paul's mind, as he prays that they may be sincere, unmixed, pure, untainted and unsullied in spiritual character and attitude, when Jesus comes.

1:21–23 to live is Christ . . . to die is gain. This simple sentence summarizes the Christian's life and destiny. Living on earth is to experience the real indwelling presence of Christ within (Gal. 2:20; Col. 1:27); to die is to depart and to be with Christ in heaven, which is "far better" (Phil. 1:23). There we gain the privilege of returning with Him for the resurrection and the Rapture (1 Thess. 4:14–16).

Heaven

By Joseph Stowell

An oft-repeated description of life in Narnia in C. S. Lewis' *The Lion, The Witch and The Wardrobe* is that it is "always winter but never Christmas." It is Lewis' profound way of describing life without hope.

If it weren't for heaven, life would be just that—"always winter but never Christmas." Heaven is the inevitable reality that is coming which gives us not only something to live for but also something to live toward in the midst of earthside realities that so often disappoint and defeat us. Heaven is the reality that someday we will escape the grip of our adversary and the defeating blows of this fallen world for a place that is far better . . . forever!

In fact that is exactly how the apostle Paul describes heaven (Phil. 1:21–23). Paul's picture of the wonder of heaven is so simple that its profundity just might escape us. For all of us who think that heaven will be about singing in a choir, cloud-sitting, and flying around with angel wings—think again. An eternity of that could get rather boring.

Heaven is far better—far better, period. Note that Paul did not qualify the "far better" description (v. 23). It simply will be far better than anything we have ever experienced in this world—certainly far better than the pain, despair, and crying that we have experienced here. Think of the most exhilarating, joy-producing, satisfying experiences that you have ever enjoyed. Heaven will be far better! And the "farbetterness" of heaven is the undiminished eternal joy of a relationship. We have all learned by now that good and rewarding relationships

> *Christians will escape the defeating blows of this fallen world for a place that is far better!*

are really the best part of life. All that the world offers in material or self-centered pursuit cannot compare to the richness of heaven. Paul's great anticipation is an unhindered face-to-face eternity with Christ. Now, as Paul states in 1 Corinthians 13:12, we see Him through a glass darkly, one smudged by the shallow and fleeting distractions of life in this present world, smudged by our failures and disappointments in a world that promised what it cannot deliver. But Paul also notes in the same verse that one day we will see Him face to face.

Heaven is a reunion with the Lover of our souls. There we will be individually and perfectly loved forever. While heaven will be full of reunions with loved ones already there and privileged encounters with the likes of Moses, Luke, and Timothy, the old gospel song has it right when it says, ". . . I want to see Jesus, He's the one who died for me."

I like the detail that John adds to the picture when he writes that heaven is about God dwelling with His people in an environment unfettered by the "stuff" that clogs us up in this fallen world (see Rev. 21:2–4). John then concludes with this intriguing thought: "And He that sat upon the throne said, Behold, I make all things new" (Rev. 21:5).

This is why Paul says that to die is gain. Unfortunately, most of us live for gain in this world while true gain is what is in store for us in the world to come. Living in this world is about living for Christ in anticipation of the unimaginable gain of seeing and experiencing Him on the other side.

perdition, but to you of salvation, and that of God.

29 For unto you it is given in the behalf of Christ, not only to believe on him, but also to suffer for his sake;

30 Having the same conflict which ye saw in me, and now hear *to be* in me.

CHAPTER 2
Exhortation to Be Like Christ

1 If *there be* therefore any consolation in Christ, if any comfort of love, if any fellowship of the Spirit, if any bowels and mercies,

2 Fulfil ye my joy, that ye be likeminded, having the same love, *being* of one accord, of one mind.

3 *Let* nothing *be done* through strife or vainglory; but in lowliness of mind let each esteem other better than themselves.

4 Look not every man on his own things, but every man also on the things of others.

5 Let this mind be in you, which was also in Christ Jesus:

The Humility of Christ

6 Who, being in the form of God, thought it not robbery to be equal with God:

7 But made himself of no reputation, and took upon him the form of a servant, and was made in the likeness of men:

8 And being found in fashion as a man, he humbled himself, and became obedient unto death, even the death of the cross.

9 Wherefore God also hath highly exalted

Cross-references:

29 Rom. 5:3
2 John 3:29; Phil. 3:16; 4:2
3 Rom. 12:10; Gal. 5:26
5 Matt. 11:29; John 13:15
6 John 1:1, 2; 5:18; 10:33; 17:5; 2Cor. 4:4
7 Ps. 22:6; Isa. 53:3, 11; Ezek. 34:23, 24; Dan. 9:26; Matt. 20:28
8 Matt. 26:39, 42
9 John 17:1, 2, 5; Heb. 1:4; 2:9
10 Isa. 45:23; Rev. 5:13
11 John 13:13
12 Eph. 6:5; Phil. 1:5
13 2Cor. 3:5; Heb. 13:21
14 1Cor. 10:10
15 Matt. 5:14, 16, 45
17 Rom. 15:16; Col. 1:24

him, and given him a name which is above every name:

10 That at the name of Jesus every knee should bow, of *things* in heaven, and *things* in earth, and *things* under the earth;

11 And *that* every tongue should confess that Jesus Christ *is* Lord, to the glory of God the Father.

"Work Out Your Own Salvation"

12 Wherefore, my beloved, as ye have always obeyed, not as in my presence only, but now much more in my absence, work out your own salvation with fear and trembling.

13 For it is God which worketh in you both to will and to do of *his* good pleasure.

14 Do all things without murmurings and disputings:

15 That ye may be blameless and harmless, the sons of God, without rebuke, in the midst of a crooked and perverse nation, among whom ye shine as lights in the world;

16 Holding forth the word of life; that I may rejoice in the day of Christ, that I have not run in vain, neither laboured in vain.

17 Yea, and if I be offered upon the sacrifice and service of your faith, I joy, and rejoice with you all.

18 For the same cause also do ye joy, and rejoice with me.

19 But I trust in the Lord Jesus to send Timotheus shortly unto you, that I also may be of good comfort, when I know your state.

2:6 in the form of God. Before His incarnation, the eternal Word existed in that mode of being in which He gives outward expression of His essential nature, His deity. He did not consider being of the same infinite essence as God the Father something to be clutched, embraced, or grasped, since there was total equality.

2:7–8 made himself of no reputation. A more literal translation of this phrase is that Christ emptied (Gr. *kenosis*) Himself. He could not cease to be God, but chose to set aside the outward manifestation of His glory, voluntarily relinquishing the total display of His divine attributes. He took upon Himself humanity in all of its fullness, yet without sin (John 1:14; 1 Tim. 3:16; Heb. 4:15). Notice the sevenfold self-humbling of the Savior who 1) emptied Himself; 2) took upon him the form of a slave; 3) was made in the likeness of man; 4) was found in outward guise as a man; 5) humbled himself, stooping very low; 6) became obedient even when it meant death; and 7) died in humiliation on the cross.

2:9–11 God also hath highly exalted him. In the past,

God exalted Christ. The Greek verb means "lifted Him up above," not merely above earth level but to the highest realm in the universe (Eph. 1:2–23). In the present Jesus has "a name which is above every name." His name is the sum of His fame, known to all the angels of heaven (see Rev. 5:11–12), while on earth His name, Jesus, is the most widely spoken on this planet (oftentimes without reverence). In the Bible over 250 different titles and expressions name and describe Him, a list unduplicated by any human in history. As verses 10 and 11 state, in the future, every knee shall bow and every tongue confess that Jesus Christ is Lord. (cf. Isa. 45:23). Universal salvation is not taught here. At the Great White Throne Judgment, even the lost will have to acknowledge Him as Lord (Rev. 20:11–15). It will be too late, however, for them to receive Him as Savior.

2:16 day of Christ. Paul anticipates that he can rejoice concerning the Rapture, beholding the consecrated children of God, who were saved as a result of his ministry.

20 For I have no man likeminded, who will naturally care for your state.
21 For all seek their own, not the things which are Jesus Christ's.
22 But ye know the proof of him, that, as a son with the father, he hath served with me in the gospel.
23 Him therefore I hope to send presently, so soon as I shall see how it will go with me.
24 But I trust in the Lord that I also myself shall come shortly.
25 Yet I supposed it necessary to send to you Epaphroditus, my brother, and companion in labour, and fellow soldier, but your messenger, and he that ministered to my wants.
26 For he longed after you all, and was full of heaviness, because that ye had heard that he had been sick.
27 For indeed he was sick nigh unto death: but God had mercy on him; and not on him only, but on me also, lest I should have sorrow upon sorrow.
28 I sent him therefore the more carefully, that, when ye see him again, ye may rejoice, and that I may be the less sorrowful.
29 Receive him therefore in the Lord with all gladness; and hold such in reputation:
30 Because for the work of Christ he was nigh unto death, not regarding his life, to supply your lack of service toward me.

CHAPTER 3
Count All Gain as Loss

1 Finally, my brethren, rejoice in the Lord. To write the same things to you, to me indeed *is* not grievous, but for you *it is* safe.
2 Beware of dogs, beware of evil workers, beware of the concision.
3 For we are the circumcision, which worship God in the spirit, and rejoice in Christ Jesus, and have no confidence in the flesh.
4 Though I might also have confidence in the flesh. If any other man thinketh that he hath whereof he might trust in the flesh, I more:
5 Circumcised the eighth day, of the stock of Israel, *of* the tribe of Benjamin, an He-

brew of the Hebrews; as touching the law, a Pharisee;
6 Concerning zeal, persecuting the church; touching the righteousness which is in the law, blameless.
7 But what things were gain to me, those I counted loss for Christ.
8 Yea doubtless, and I count all things *but* loss for the excellency of the knowledge of Christ Jesus my Lord: for whom I have suffered the loss of all things, and do count them *but* dung, that I may win Christ,
9 And be found in him, not having mine own righteousness, which is of the law, but that which is through the faith of Christ, the righteousness which is of God by faith:
10 That I may know him, and the power of his resurrection, and the fellowship of his sufferings, being made conformable unto his death;
11 If by any means I might attain unto the resurrection of the dead.

"The High Calling of God"

12 Not as though I had already attained, either were already perfect: but I follow after, if that I may apprehend that for which also I am apprehended of Christ Jesus.
13 Brethren, I count not myself to have apprehended: but *this* one thing I *do*, forgetting those things which are behind, and reaching forth unto those things which are before,
14 I press toward the mark for the prize of the high calling of God in Christ Jesus.
15 Let us therefore, as many as be perfect, be thus minded: and if in any thing ye be otherwise minded, God shall reveal even this unto you.
16 Nevertheless, whereto we have already attained, let us walk by the same rule, let us mind the same thing.
17 Brethren, be followers together of me, and mark them which walk so as ye have us for an ensample.
18 (For many walk, of whom I have told you often, and now tell you even weeping,

Cross references

21	1Cor. 10:24, 33; 13:5
22	1Cor. 4:17; 1Tim. 1:2; 2Tim. 1:2
25	2Cor. 8:23; 11:9
30	1Cor. 16:17
1	Phil. 4:4
2	Isa. 56:10; Rom. 2:28; Gal. 5:2, 15
3	Rom. 2:29; 4:11, 12; 7:6; Gal. 6:14; Col. 2:11
5	Acts 23:6; 26:4, 5; Rom. 11:1
6	Acts 8:3; 9:1; 22:3
8	1Cor. 2:2
9	Rom. 1:17; 3:21, 22; 9:30
10	Rom. 6:3-5; 8:17; 1Pet. 4:13
11	Acts 26:7
12	1Tim. 6:12
14	2Tim. 4:7, 8; Heb. 3:1; 12:1
15	1Cor. 2:6; 14:20; Gal. 5:10
16	Rom. 12:16; 15:5
17	1Cor. 4:16; 11:1
18	Gal. 1:7; 2:21; 6:12; Phil. 1:15, 16

3:10–14 power of his resurrection. Paul's goal was to know Christ more intimately, more deeply as he ran his life-race, desiring to experience that resurrection power in his life that would enable Him to be more Christlike, as he pressed toward the goal of fulfilling God's purpose for him (v. 14). Willing to die to reach the lost, he anticipated attaining unto the resurrection "out from among the dead" (as the Greek implies). New Testament believers will be raised at the time of the Rapture and first resur-

rection, while the rest of the dead await the final resurrection unto damnation (John 5:29). Paul then declares he has not attained that goal, nor achieved all that God "apprehended" or laid hold on him to accomplish (v. 13). He urges believers to attain the highest spiritual level possible, knowing that perfect Christ-likeness will not be reached until each one is gloriously changed (Col. 3:4; 1 John 3:2).

that they are the enemies of the cross of Christ:

19 Whose end *is* destruction, whose God *is their* belly, and *whose* glory *is* in their shame, who mind earthly things.)

20 For our conversation is in heaven; from whence also we look for the Saviour, the Lord Jesus Christ:

21 Who shall change our vile body, that it may be fashioned like unto his glorious body, according to the working whereby he is able even to subdue all things unto himself.

CHAPTER 4
"Rejoice in the Lord"

1 Therefore, my brethren dearly beloved and longed for, my joy and crown, so stand fast in the Lord, *my* dearly beloved.

2 I beseech Euodias, and beseech Syntyche, that they be of the same mind in the Lord.

3 And I intreat thee also, true yokefellow, help those women which laboured with me in the gospel, with Clement also, and *with* other my fellow labourers, whose names *are* in the book of life.

4 Rejoice in the Lord alway: *and* again I say, Rejoice.

5 Let your moderation be known unto all men. The Lord *is* at hand.

6 Be careful for nothing; but in every thing by prayer and supplication with thanksgiving let your requests be made known unto God.

7 And the peace of God, which passeth all understanding, shall keep your hearts and minds through Christ Jesus.

8 Finally, brethren, whatsoever things are true, whatsoever things *are* honest, whatso-

19 Hos. 4:7; Rom. 8:5; 16:18; Gal. 6:13; Titus 1:11; 2Pet. 2:1
20 Eph. 2:6, 19; Col. 3:1
21 1Cor. 15:26, 27, 43, 48, 49; 1John 3:2
1 Phil. 1:8, 27; 2:16; 1Thess. 2:19, 20
2 Phil. 2:2; 3:16
3 Ex. 32:32; Ps. 69:28; Dan. 12:1; Luke 10:20; Rev. 3:5; 13:8; 20:12; 21:27
4 Phil. 3:1
5 James 5:8, 9; 1Pet. 4:7; 2Pet. 3:8, 9
6 Matt. 6:25; Luke 12:22
7 John 14:27; Rom. 5:1; Col. 3:15
8 1Thess. 5:22
9 1Cor. 14:33; 2Cor. 13:11
10 2Cor. 11:9
13 John 15:5
14 Phil. 1:7
15 2Cor. 11:8, 9
17 Rom. 15:28
18 2Cor. 9:1

ever things *are* just, whatsoever things *are* pure, whatsoever things *are* lovely, whatsoever things *are* of good report; if *there be* any virtue, and if *there be* any praise, think on these things.

9 Those things, which ye have both learned, and received, and heard, and seen in me, do: and the God of peace shall be with you.

Contentment

10 But I rejoiced in the Lord greatly, that now at the last your care of me hath flourished again; wherein ye were also careful, but ye lacked opportunity.

11 Not that I speak in respect of want: for I have learned, in whatsoever state I am, *therewith* to be content.

12 I know both how to be abased, and I know how to abound: every where and in all things I am instructed both to be full and to be hungry, both to abound and to suffer need.

13 I can do all things through Christ which strengtheneth me.

14 Notwithstanding ye have well done, that ye did communicate with my affliction.

15 Now ye Philippians know also, that in the beginning of the gospel, when I departed from Macedonia, no church communicated with me as concerning giving and receiving, but ye only.

16 For even in Thessalonica ye sent once and again unto my necessity.

17 Not because I desire a gift: but I desire fruit that may abound to your account.

18 But I have all, and abound: I am full, having received of Epaphroditus the things *which were sent* from you, an odour of a sweet smell, a sacrifice acceptable, well-pleasing to God.

3:20–21 our conversation is in heaven. The Greek word translated "conversation" (*politeuma*) implies a commonwealth or citizenship. Philippi was a Roman colony with its inhabitants enjoying the privileges of Roman citizenship. Though Christians are still on earth, our citizenship is in heaven and we are governed by the invisible power of God working in our lives. The phrase "look for the Saviour" is also a reference to the Rapture (Heb. 9:28). The Greek word here translated "change our vile body" means "change our low estate" (Luke 1:48), "change our humiliation" (Acts 8:33), or "made low" (James 1:10). Our fleshly bodies experience weakness, sickness, and death. They are corruptible (1 Cor. 15:42, 50, 53), decaying and returning to dust. At the Rapture, our bodies will be changed and glorified, patterned after

Jesus' resurrection body, a transformation whereby "this corruptible" (the dead in Christ) puts on incorruption, and "this mortal" (the living believers) puts on immortality (1 Cor. 15:51–54).

4:5 moderation. This word conveys the idea of gentleness, not being unduly rigorous, exercising forbearance, being considerate, equitable, and fair. The word "moderation" also implies all proper spiritual manifestations of character and godliness. The phrase "The Lord is at hand" reminds us that while He is constantly present with us, the nearness of His coming should be a motive for godly living (1 John 3:3). All Christians should live every day as though it were the last day before He comes to take them to be with Him in His Father's house.

19 But my God shall supply all your need according to his riches in glory by Christ Jesus.
20 Now unto God and our Father *be* glory for ever and ever. Amen.
21 Salute every saint in Christ Jesus. The

19 Ps. 23:1
22 Phil. 1:13
23 Rom. 16:24

brethren which are with me greet you.
22 All the saints salute you, chiefly they that are of Caesar's household.
23 The grace of our Lord Jesus Christ *be* with you all. Amen.

Colossians

The city of Colosse was located in central Asia Minor. Epaphras and Timothy established churches here and in the neighboring cities of Laodicea and Hierapolis, but Paul never had the opportunity to visit the believers in these areas. Epaphras came to visit Paul in prison and gave him a report not only of the progress being made there, but also of the problem of false teachers who had gained a foothold in the church.

From his prison chamber in Rome (A.D. 61), Paul wrote this epistle to the Colossians to refute the errors of Gnosticism and "Judaized" Christianity. Dealing with "Judaizers," Paul warns against bringing Christians under Old Testament ceremonial law and Jewish tradition that do not bring honor to God, but merely satisfy the flesh.

Gnosticism was the "New Age" thought of the times. Its philosophy consisted of rigorous disciplines (2:20–23) and the worship of angels as intermediaries between God and man (2:18–19). This heresy taught that one could achieve perfection by progressing through a series of initiations and levels of mystical experiences to approach spiritual realms.

Instead of refuting this error point by point, Paul shows in this epistle that Christ is the Creator and Sustainer of the universe, the redeemer of sinners and the Head of the Church. Yet there is a glorious, previously unrevealed mystery in the reality that Christ actually dwells in every believer as the "hope of glory" (1:16–18, 20–23, 25–28). In Christ's preeminence, the fullness of the Godhead dwells in Him in whom are hid all the treasures of wisdom and knowledge (see 2:9).

That believers will appear with the risen Christ in glory (3:4) is a powerful incentive for godly living. Then, as prophesied, we shall receive from the Lord the "reward of the inheritance" (3:24).

A total of 9 verses out of 95 have prophetic overtones, or 9 percent of the epistle. There are no direct Old Testament quotations, but there are allusions to Old Testament types (2:11–14, 16–17),

Author
Paul

Date
A.D. 61

Key Truth
Christ's Preeminence

Historic Time
Founding of the Church in Colosse by Epaphras to Onesimus' Return

Key Verse
2:9
For in him dwelleth all the fulness of the Godhead bodily.

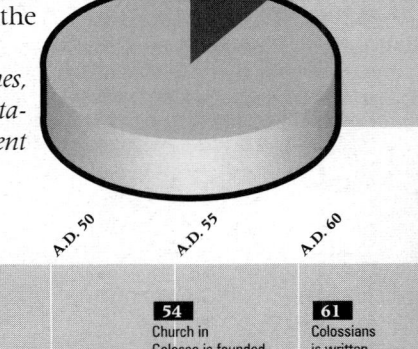

9%
Prophecy

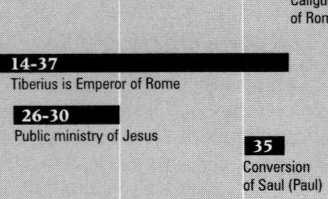

| A.D. 25 | A.D. 30 | A.D. 35 | A.D. 40 | A.D. 45 | A.D. 50 | A.D. 55 | A.D. 60 |

37-41
Caligula is Emperor of Rome

54
Church in Colosse is founded

61
Colossians is written

14-37
Tiberius is Emperor of Rome

41-54
Claudius is Emperor of Rome

26-30
Public ministry of Jesus

35
Conversion of Saul (Paul)

47-49
Paul's First Missionary Journey

54-68
Nero is Emperor of Rome

49-53
Paul's Second Missionary Journey

53-56
Paul's Third Missionary Journey

CHAPTER 1

1 Paul, an apostle of Jesus Christ by the will of God, and Timotheus *our* brother,

2 To the saints and faithful brethren in Christ which are at Colosse: Grace *be* unto you, and peace, from God our Father and the Lord Jesus Christ.

The Progress of the Gospel

3 We give thanks to God and the Father of our Lord Jesus Christ, praying always for you,

4 Since we heard of your faith in Christ Jesus, and of the love *which ye have* to all the saints.

5 For the hope which is laid up for you in heaven, whereof ye heard before in the word of the truth of the gospel;

6 Which is come unto you, as *it is* in all the world; and bringeth forth fruit, as *it doth* also in you, since the day ye heard *of it,* and knew the grace of God in truth:

7 As ye also learned of Epaphras our dear fellow servant, who is for you a faithful minister of Christ;

8 Who also declared unto us your love in the Spirit.

9 For this cause we also, since the day we heard *it,* do not cease to pray for you, and to desire that ye might be filled with the knowledge of his will in all wisdom and spiritual understanding;

10 That ye might walk worthy of the Lord unto all pleasing, being fruitful in every good work, and increasing in the knowledge of God;

11 Strengthened with all might, according to his glorious power, unto all patience and longsuffering with joyfulness;

12 Giving thanks unto the Father, which hath made us meet to be partakers of the inheritance of the saints in light:

13 Who hath delivered us from the power of darkness, and hath translated *us* into the kingdom of his dear Son:

14 In whom we have redemption through his blood, *even* the forgiveness of sins:

The Preeminence of Christ

15 Who is the image of the invisible God, the firstborn of every creature:

16 For by him were all things created, that are in heaven, and that are in earth, visible and invisible, whether *they be* thrones, or dominions, or principalities, or powers: all things were created by him, and for him:

17 And he is before all things, and by him all things consist.

18 And he is the head of the body, the church: who is the beginning, the firstborn from the dead; that in all *things* he might have the preeminence.

19 For it pleased *the Father* that in him should all fulness dwell;

20 And, having made peace through the blood of his cross, by him to reconcile all things unto himself; by him, *I say,* whether *they be* things in earth, or things in heaven.

21 And you, that were sometime alienated and enemies in *your* mind by wicked works, yet now hath he reconciled

22 In the body of his flesh through death, to present you holy and unblameable and unreproveable in his sight:

23 If ye continue in the faith grounded and settled, and *be* not moved away from the hope of the gospel, which ye have heard, *and* which was preached to every creature which is under heaven; whereof I Paul am made a minister;

Exhortation to Faithfulness

24 Who now rejoice in my sufferings for you, and fill up that which is behind of the afflictions of Christ in my flesh for his body's sake, which is the church:

25 Whereof I am made a minister, according to the dispensation of God which is given to me for you, to fulfil the word of God;

26 *Even* the mystery which hath been hid from ages and from generations, but now is made manifest to his saints:

27 To whom God would make known what *is* the riches of the glory of this mystery among the Gentiles; which is Christ in you, the hope of glory:

28 Whom we preach, warning every man, and teaching every man in all wisdom; that we may present every man perfect in Christ Jesus:

29 Whereunto I also labour, striving according to his working, which worketh in me mightily.

3 1Cor. 1:4; Eph. 1:16; Phil. 1:3; 4:6
4 Eph. 1:15; Phile. 1:5
5 2Tim. 4:8; 1Pet. 1:4
6 Matt. 24:14; Mark 4:8; 16:15; John 15:16
10 John 15:16
12 Acts 26:18
13 Matt. 3:17; Eph. 1:6; 6:12
14 Eph. 1:7
16 John 1:3; Rom. 8:38; 11:36; 1Pet. 3:22
18 1Cor. 11:3; 15:20, 23; Rev. 1:5
20 2Cor. 5:18; Eph. 1:10; 2:14-16
21 Titus 1:15, 16
22 Luke 1:75, Eph. 1:4; 2:15, 16; Jude 1:24
23 John 15:6; Acts 1:17; Rom. 10:18
24 2Cor. 1:5, 6; 7:4; Phil. 3:10; 2Tim. 1:8; 2:10
25 Gal. 2:7; Eph. 3:2; Col. 1:23
26 Matt. 13:11; Rom. 16:25
27 Rom. 9:23; 2Cor. 2:14; Eph. 1:7; 3:8
28 Acts 20:20, 27, 31; Eph. 5:27; Col. 1:22
29 1Cor. 15:10; Eph. 1:19; 3:7, 20; Col. 2:1

1:26–27 the mystery which hath been hid from ages and from generations. This mystery is "Christ in you, the hope of glory." This does not mean that Old Testament prophecies regarding salvation through Jesus, the Messiah, were hidden and unknowable. Instead, these verses are a reference to the historical realization of all that had been promised regarding the death of Christ for the sin of man.

Mysteries in The New Testament

By Jim Combs

The word "mystery" (Gr. *musterion*), appearing twenty-seven times in the New Testament, does not refer to some mysterious event or phenomena waiting to be solved, but rather previously hidden truth now revealed by God, known only by divine revelation.

Although now perceived by believers, these wondrous mysteries will not be fully understood until they are fulfilled as prophecies or until "we know even as we are known" and are in our glorified state with Christ. Major important mysteries are:

1. Mysteries of the Kingdom of Heaven (Matt. 13:3–50 and Mark 4:26–29). These parables of Jesus (seven in Matt.) cover the period of time between His first advent and His second coming, when God's gospel is carried throughout the world. This Church Age is "the kingdom of heaven in mystery form," involving the areas on earth where Christianity has spread.

2. Mystery of Israel's Blindness during the Church Age (Rom. 11:25–26): As God works out His plan for Israel and the Church, most Jews will not come to the Messiah, "until the fullness of the Gentiles be come in," when the divine program to call out Gentiles to be His people in this age ends at the Rapture.

> *The word "mystery" refers to hidden truth now revealed by God.*

3. Mystery of the Rapture (1 Cor. 15:51–52; 1 Thess. 4:14, 16), We look now for the blessed hope (Titus 2:13).

4. Mystery of His Will (Eph. 1:9–11) From eternity past God's plan has been to gather all things in Christ, both in heaven and earth in the dispensation of the fullness of times. This begins in the Millennium and continues forever.

5. Mystery of the Union of Jews and Gentiles in One Body (Eph. 3:3–4, 9). Unknown to Israel before Christ, the revelation of this truth was given to Paul and is being fulfilled in the Church Age (see Rom. 16:25).

6. Mystery of the Bride of Christ (Eph. 5:28–32). This culminates the previous mystery (see Rev. 19:7–9; 21:9).

7. Mystery of the Indwelling Christ in Believers (John 15:4; Gal. 2:20; Phil 1:21; Col. 1:26–27). Only true Christianity provides this wonderful reality.

8. Mystery of God, Even Christ (Col. 2:2, 9, 1 Cor. 2:7). This relates to the infinite knowledge of God incarnate in Christ.

9. Mystery of Iniquity/Lawlessness (2 Thess. 2:7). Dealing with Satan's ongoing master plan to bring forth the Antichrist in the End Times, the outcome is clear.

10. Mystery of Godliness (1 Tim. 3:16). Including the Incarnation, Christ's ministry and results are in view.

11. Mystery of the Seven Stars/Candlesticks (Rev. 1:20). Jesus explains they are His messenger/ministers and churches.

12. Mystery, Babylon the Great (Rev. 17:5, 7). This forecasts the final world apostate church in the Tribulation (after the Rapture).

13. Mystery of God (Rev.10:7). This mystery announces the conclusion of God's program to consummate history during "the last days of the voice of the seventh angel," a period encompassing the last half of the Tribulation Period and beyond. All the mysterious prophecies concerning the kingdom of Christ will be fulfilled, relevant to Israel and the world, leading to the reign of the Messiah (cf. Rev. 19:7–8; 20:4–6).

CHAPTER 2
Warnings against Errors

1 For I would that ye knew what great conflict I have for you, and *for* them at Laodicea, and *for* as many as have not seen my face in the flesh;

2 That their hearts might be comforted, being knit together in love, and unto all riches of the full assurance of understanding, to the acknowledgement of the mystery of God, and of the Father, and of Christ;

3 In whom are hid all the treasures of wisdom and knowledge.

4 And this I say, lest any man should beguile you with enticing words.

5 For though I be absent in the flesh, yet am I with you in the spirit, joying and beholding your order, and the stedfastness of your faith in Christ.

6 As ye have therefore received Christ Jesus the Lord, *so* walk ye in him:

7 Rooted and built up in him, and stablished in the faith, as ye have been taught, abounding therein with thanksgiving.

8 Beware lest any man spoil you through philosophy and vain deceit, after the tradition of men, after the rudiments of the world, and not after Christ.

9 For in him dwelleth all the fulness of the Godhead bodily.

Completeness in Christ

10 And ye are complete in him, which is the head of all principality and power:

11 In whom also ye are circumcised with the circumcision made without hands, in putting off the body of the sins of the flesh by the circumcision of Christ:

12 Buried with him in baptism, wherein also ye are risen with *him* through the faith of the operation of God, who hath raised him from the dead.

13 And you, being dead in your sins and the uncircumcision of your flesh, hath he quickened together with him, having forgiven you all trespasses;

14 Blotting out the handwriting of ordinances that was against us, which was contrary to us, and took it out of the way, nailing it to his cross;

15 *And* having spoiled principalities and

powers, he made a shew of them openly, triumphing over them in it.

16 Let no man therefore judge you in meat, or in drink, or in respect of an holy day, or of the new moon, or of the sabbath *days*:

17 Which are a shadow of things to come; but the body *is* of Christ.

18 Let no man beguile you of your reward in a voluntary humility and worshipping of angels, intruding into those things which he hath not seen, vainly puffed up by his fleshly mind,

19 And not holding the Head, from which all the body by joints and bands having nourishment ministered, and knit together, increaseth with the increase of God.

Legalism

20 Wherefore if ye be dead with Christ from the rudiments of the world, why, as though living in the world, are ye subject to ordinances,

21 (Touch not; taste not; handle not;

22 Which all are to perish with the using;) after the commandments and doctrines of men?

23 Which things have indeed a shew of wisdom in will-worship, and humility, and neglecting of the body; not in any honour to the satisfying of the flesh.

CHAPTER 3
"Renewed in Knowledge"

1 If ye then be risen with Christ, seek those things which are above, where Christ sitteth on the right hand of God.

2 Set your affection on things above, not on things on the earth.

3 For ye are dead, and your life is hid with Christ in God.

4 When Christ, *who is* our life, shall appear, then shall ye also appear with him in glory.

5 Mortify therefore your members which are upon the earth; fornication, uncleanness, inordinate affection, evil concupiscence, and covetousness, which is idolatry:

6 For which things' sake the wrath of God cometh on the children of disobedience:

7 In the which ye also walked some time, when ye lived in them.

8 But now ye also put off all these; anger,

Cross-references

1 Col. 1:29
2 2Cor. 1:6; Phil. 3:8
3 Eph. 1:8
4 Rom. 16:18; 2Cor. 11:13
5 1Cor. 5:3; 14:40
6 1Thess. 4:1; Jude 1:3
7 Eph. 2:21, 22; 3:17; Col. 1:23
8 Jer. 29:8; Matt. 15:2
9 John 1:14
10 John 1:16; Eph. 1:20, 21
11 Deut. 10:16; 30:6; Rom. 2:29; 6:6
12 Rom. 6:4
13 Eph. 2:1, 5, 6, 11
15 Gen. 3:15; Ps. 68:18; Isa. 53:12; Matt. 12:29
16 Rom. 14:2, 3, 5, 10, 13, 17; 1Cor. 8:8
18 Ezek. 13:1
19 Eph. 4:15, 16
20 Rom. 6:3, 5; 7:4, 6
21 1Tim. 4:3
22 Isa. 29:13; Matt. 15:9
23 Col. 2:18; 1Tim. 4:8
1 Rom. 6:5; 8:34; Eph. 1:20; 2:6
3 Rom. 6:2; Gal. 2:20
4 John 11:25; 14:6; 1John 3:2
5 Rom. 6:13; 8:13
6 Rom. 1:18

3:4 Paul encourages believers to set their minds on "things above" (v. 2) since they are already in Christ who is seated on the throne of heaven. Next, the apostle predicts that we will appear with Him when He appears or "shows" Himself to the world. The reference here is to the return of Christ with the raptured Church at the Second Coming.

wrath, malice, blasphemy, filthy communication out of your mouth.

9 Lie not one to another, seeing that ye have put off the old man with his deeds;

10 And have put on the new *man,* which is renewed in knowledge after the image of him that created him:

11 Where there is neither Greek nor Jew, circumcision nor uncircumcision, Barbarian, Scythian, bond *nor* free: but Christ *is* all, and in all.

12 Put on therefore, as the elect of God, holy and beloved, bowels of mercies, kindness, humbleness of mind, meekness, longsuffering;

13 Forbearing one another, and forgiving one another, if any man have a quarrel against any: even as Christ forgave you, so also *do* ye.

14 And above all these things *put on* charity, which is the bond of perfectness.

15 And let the peace of God rule in your hearts, to the which also ye are called in one body; and be ye thankful.

16 Let the word of Christ dwell in you richly in all wisdom; teaching and admonishing one another in psalms and hymns and spiritual songs, singing with grace in your hearts to the Lord.

17 And whatsoever ye do in word or deed, *do* all in the name of the Lord Jesus, giving thanks to God and the Father by him.

Family Relationships

18 Wives, submit yourselves unto your own husbands, as it is fit in the Lord.

19 Husbands, love *your* wives, and be not bitter against them.

20 Children, obey *your* parents in all things: for this is well pleasing unto the Lord.

21 Fathers, provoke not your children *to* anger, lest they be discouraged.

22 Servants, obey in all things *your* masters according to the flesh; not with eyeservice, as menpleasers; but in singleness of heart, fearing God:

23 And whatsoever ye do, do *it* heartily, as to the Lord, and not unto men;

24 Knowing that of the Lord ye shall receive the reward of the inheritance; for ye serve the Lord Christ.

25 But he that doeth wrong shall receive for

the wrong which he hath done; and there is no respect of persons.

CHAPTER 4
Admonitions for Christian Living

1 Masters, give unto *your* servants that which is just and equal; knowing that ye also have a Master in heaven.

2 Continue in prayer, and watch in the same with thanksgiving;

3 Withal praying also for us, that God would open unto us a door of utterance, to speak the mystery of Christ, for which I am also in bonds:

4 That I may make it manifest, as I ought to speak.

5 Walk in wisdom toward them that are without, redeeming the time.

6 Let your speech *be* alway with grace, seasoned with salt, that ye may know how ye ought to answer every man.

7 All my state shall Tychicus declare unto you, *who is* a beloved brother, and a faithful minister and fellow servant in the Lord:

8 Whom I have sent unto you for the same purpose, that he might know your estate, and comfort your hearts;

9 With Onesimus, a faithful and beloved brother, who is *one* of you. They shall make known unto you all things which *are done* here.

10 Aristarchus my fellow prisoner saluteth you, and Mark, sister's son to Barnabas, (touching whom ye received commandments: if he come unto you, receive him;)

11 And Jesus, which is called Justus, who are of the circumcision. These only *are my* fellow workers unto the kingdom of God, which have been a comfort unto me.

12 Epaphras, who is *one* of you, a servant of Christ, saluteth you, always labouring fervently for you in prayers, that ye may stand perfect and complete in all the will of God.

13 For I bear him record, that he hath a great zeal for you, and them *that are* in Laodicea, and them in Hierapolis.

14 Luke, the beloved physician, and Demas, greet you.

15 Salute the brethren which are in Laodicea, and Nymphas, and the church which is in his house.

Cross-references

9 Lev. 19:11
10 Rom. 12:2; Eph. 2:10; 4:23, 24
11 Gal. 3:28; 5:6; Eph. 1:23; 6:8
12 Eph. 4:2, 24, 32; 1Thess. 1:4
13 Mark 11:25; Eph. 4:2, 32
14 John 13:34; 1John 3:23; 4:21
15 Phil. 4:7
17 Rom. 1:8; Eph. 5:20; 1Thess. 5:18
18 Eph. 5:3, 22; Titus 2:5; 1Pet. 3:1
19 Eph. 4:31; 5:25, 28, 33; 1Pet. 3:7
20 Eph. 5:24; 6:1; Titus 2:9
21 Eph. 6:4
22 Eph. 6:5; Phile. 1:16; 1Pet. 2:18
24 1Cor. 7:22
25 Deut. 10:17; Rom. 2:11
1 Eph. 6:9
2 Luke 18:1; Eph. 6:18; 1Thess. 5:17, 18
3 1Cor. 4:1; 16:9; 2Cor. 2:12
5 Eph. 5:15, 16; 1Thess. 4:12
6 Eccl. 10:12; Mark 9:50
9 Phile. 1:10
10 Acts 15:37; 19:29; 20:4; 27:2
14 2Tim. 4:10, 11; Phile. 1:24
15 Rom. 16:5; 1Cor. 16:19

3:23–24 Having exhorted believers to live out their faith in their daily lives, Paul reminds us that we will receive the "reward of the inheritance" that is ours in Christ. This promise looks ahead to the rewards believers will receive for faithful service at the judgment seat of Christ (cf. Rom. 14:10; 2 Cor. 5:10).

16 And when this epistle is read among you, cause that it be read also in the church of the Laodiceans; and that ye likewise read the *epistle* from Laodicea.

17 And say to Archippus, Take heed to the

16 1Thess. 5:27

17 1Tim. 4:6; Phile. 1:2

18 1Cor. 16:21

ministry which thou hast received in the Lord, that thou fulfil it.

18 The salutation by the hand of me Paul. Remember my bonds. Grace *be* with you. Amen.

1 Thessalonians

The city of Thessalonica was the chief seaport of ancient Macedonia and an important commercial and military center. During the second missionary journey, Paul and Silas traveled to Thessalonica (Acts 16:39—17:1) where Paul taught in the synagogue for three sabbaths. Antagonistic Jews fomented an angry mob situation that forced Paul and Silas to leave. Paul was intent on returning to Thessalonica, but was hindered by Satan (1 Thess. 2:17–18). Instead, he sent Timothy (1 Thess. 3:1–2).

Author	Paul
Date	A.D. 51
Key Truth	Waiting for the Return of Christ
Historic Time	Paul's Second Missionary Journey to Timothy's Report
Key Verse	4:18 Wherefore comfort one another with these words.

The occasion of this letter to the Thessalonians, Paul's very first epistle, was the return of Timothy from Thessalonica to Paul's residence in Corinth (Acts 18:5). The church in Thessalonica was founded in an atmosphere of controversy and persecution (Acts 17:1–9), but the fledgling congregation was growing, prompting Timothy to bring to Paul an encouraging report.

Though Paul could not return to Thessalonica, he writes to these believers to encourage them in their faith, instruct them in godly living and, most of all, reinforce their new hope of the return of Christ. Likewise, he emphasizes the importance of leading a godly life of faith, hope, and love, and of avoiding all forms of paganism and immorality.

The epistle contains nine separate prophecies, six of them, in 4:13–18, concerning the Rapture and resurrection. The two Thessalonian epistles contain twenty different references to the second coming of Christ, as this event is mentioned in every chapter. Some statements concerning Christ's coming include "In the presence of our Lord Jesus Christ at his coming" (2:19); "At the coming of the Lord Jesus with all his saints" (3:13); "Caught up together with them in the clouds to meet the Lord in the air" (4:17); and in the last chapter, "I pray God your whole spirit and soul and body be preserved blameless unto the coming of our Lord Jesus Christ" (5:23).

Of the 89 verses, 16 are prophetic or 18 percent. There are no direct quotations of the Old Testament in the book.

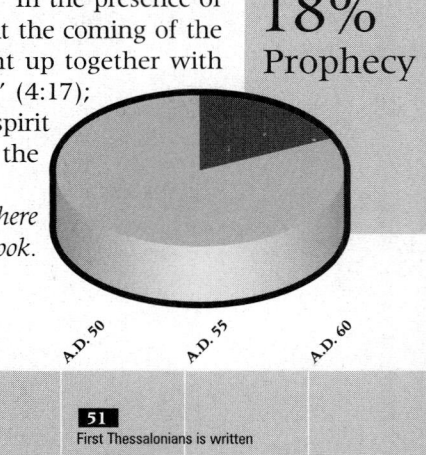

18% Prophecy

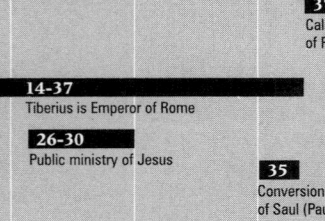

A.D. 25	A.D. 30	A.D. 35	A.D. 40	A.D. 45	A.D. 50	A.D. 55	A.D. 60

37-41
Caligula is Emperor of Rome

41-54
Claudius is Emperor of Rome

51
First Thessalonians is written

14-37
Tiberius is Emperor of Rome

26-30
Public ministry of Jesus

50
Church in Thessalonica is founded

54-68
Nero is Emperor of Rome

35
Conversion of Saul (Paul)

47-49
Paul's First Missionary Journey

49-53
Paul's Second Missionary Journey

53-56
Paul's Third Missionary Journey

CHAPTER 1

1 Paul, and Silvanus, and Timotheus, unto the church of the Thessalonians *which is* in God the Father and *in* the Lord Jesus Christ: Grace *be* unto you, and peace, from God our Father, and the Lord Jesus Christ.

The Power of the Gospel

2 We give thanks to God always for you all, making mention of you in our prayers;

3 Remembering without ceasing your work of faith, and labour of love, and patience of hope in our Lord Jesus Christ, in the sight of God and our Father;

4 Knowing, brethren beloved, your election of God.

5 For our gospel came not unto you in word only, but also in power, and in the Holy Ghost, and in much assurance; as ye know what manner of men we were among you for your sake.

6 And ye became followers of us, and of the Lord, having received the word in much affliction, with joy of the Holy Ghost:

7 So that ye were ensamples to all that believe in Macedonia and Achaia.

8 For from you sounded out the word of the Lord not only in Macedonia and Achaia, but also in every place your faith to Godward is spread abroad; so that we need not to speak any thing.

9 For they themselves shew of us what manner of entering in we had unto you, and how ye turned to God from idols to serve the living and true God;

10 And to wait for his Son from heaven, whom he raised from the dead, *even* Jesus, which delivered us from the wrath to come.

CHAPTER 2

1 For yourselves, brethren, know our entrance in unto you, that it was not in vain:

2 But even after that we had suffered before, and were shamefully entreated, as ye know, at Philippi, we were bold in our God to speak unto you the gospel of God with much contention.

3 For our exhortation *was* not of deceit, nor of uncleanness, nor in guile:

4 But as we were allowed of God to be put in trust with the gospel, even so we speak; not as pleasing men, but God, which trieth our hearts.

5 For neither at any time used we flattering words, as ye know, nor a cloke of covetousness; God *is* witness:

6 Nor of men sought we glory, neither of you, nor *yet* of others, when we might have been burdensome, as the apostles of Christ.

7 But we were gentle among you, even as a nurse cherisheth her children:

8 So being affectionately desirous of you, we were willing to have imparted unto you, not the gospel of God only, but also our own souls, because ye were dear unto us.

9 For ye remember, brethren, our labour and travail: for labouring night and day, because we would not be chargable unto any of you, we preached unto you the gospel of God.

10 Ye *are* witnesses, and God *also,* how holily and justly and unblameably we behaved ourselves among you that believe:

"Walk Worthy of God"

11 As ye know how we exhorted and comforted and charged every one of you, as a father *doth* his children,

12 That ye would walk worthy of God, who hath called you unto his kingdom and glory.

13 For this cause also thank we God without ceasing, because, when ye received the word of God which ye heard of us, ye received *it* not *as* the word of men, but as it is

Cross references

1 2Cor. 1:19; Eph. 1:2; 2Thess. 1:1; 1Pet. 5:12

3 Gal. 5:6; 1Thess. 2:13; 3:6; Heb. 6:10

4 Col. 3:12; 2Thess. 2:13

5 Mark 16:20; 1Cor. 2:4; 4:20; Col. 2:2; 2Thess. 3:7

6 Acts 5:41

8 2Thess. 1:4

10 Matt. 3:7; Acts 1:11; 2:24; Phil. 3:20; 1Thess. 4:16; 5:9

1 1Thess. 1:5, 9

2 Acts 16:22; 17:2

4 Prov. 17:3; Rom. 8:27

5 Acts 20:33; Rom. 1:9

6 John 5:41, 44; 12:43; 1Cor. 9:1, 2, 4–6, 12, 18

7 1Cor. 2:3; 9:22

9 Acts 20:34; 1Cor. 4:12; 2Cor. 11:9; 12:13, 14

10 2Cor. 7:2; 1Thess. 1:5; 2Thess. 3:7

12 1Cor. 1:9; Eph. 4:1

13 Gal. 4:14

1:3 hope in our Lord Jesus Christ. The "hope" we have in Christ is the confident expectation we have that Christ will return for all believers and take them to His Father's house (John 14:1–3). This "hope" was the driving, motivating force of the early Church.

1:10 to wait for His Son from heaven. This does not mean that Christians are to idly await the Second Coming. It means Christians are to live in such anticipation of the Savior's soon return that our daily decisions and service to our Lord will find us "not ashamed" when He comes.

1:10 Jesus, which delivered us from the wrath to come. This "wrath to come" can only mean the seven-year Tribulation (Rev. 6:16), from which believers are

"delivered" or exempt. It is one of four such promises that exempt Christians from that future time of "wrath" that Jesus said "shall come upon all the world, to try them that dwell upon the earth" (Rev. 3:10, cf. 1 Thess. 5:9; Rom. 5:9). This worldwide time of wrath has not yet occurred. The Church or Bride of Christ is "delivered" by the Rapture—before the Tribulation begins (see 1 Thess. 4:15–17).

2:12 As believers we are "called . . . unto his kingdom and glory," suggesting that we should walk now as children of the King, even before we are glorified by the resurrection, and occupy with Him when He sets up His kingdom after His return.

in truth, the word of God, which effectually worketh also in you that believe.

14 For ye, brethren, became followers of the churches of God which in Judea are in Christ Jesus: for ye also have suffered like things of your own countrymen, even as they *have* of the Jews:

15 Who both killed the Lord Jesus, and their own prophets, and have persecuted us; and they please not God, and are contrary to all men:

16 Forbidding us to speak to the Gentiles that they might be saved, to fill up their sins alway: for the wrath is come upon them to the uttermost.

17 But we, brethren, being taken from you for a short time in presence, not in heart, endeavoured the more abundantly to see your face with great desire.

18 Wherefore we would have come unto you, even I Paul, once and again; but Satan hindered us.

19 For what *is* our hope, or joy, or crown of rejoicing? *Are* not even ye in the presence of our Lord Jesus Christ at his coming?

20 For ye are our glory and joy.

CHAPTER 3
"Stand Fast in the Lord"

1 Wherefore when we could no longer forbear, we thought it good to be left at Athens alone;

2 And sent Timotheus, our brother, and minister of God, and our fellow labourer in the gospel of Christ, to establish you, and to comfort you concerning your faith:

3 That no man should be moved by these afflictions: for yourselves know that we are appointed thereunto.

4 For verily, when we were with you, we told you before that we should suffer tribulation; even as it came to pass, and ye know.

5 For this cause, when I could no longer forbear, I sent to know your faith, lest by some means the tempter have tempted you, and our labour be in vain.

6 But now when Timotheus came from you unto us, and brought us good tidings of your faith and charity, and that ye have good remembrance of us always, desiring greatly to see us, as we also *to see* you:

7 Therefore, brethren, we were comforted over you in all our affliction and distress by your faith:

8 For now we live, if ye stand fast in the Lord.

9 For what thanks can we render to God again for you, for all the joy wherewith we joy for your sakes before our God;

10 Night and day praying exceedingly that we might see your face, and might perfect that which is lacking in your faith?

11 Now God himself and our Father, and our Lord Jesus Christ, direct our way unto you.

12 And the Lord make you to increase and abound in love one toward another, and toward all *men*, even as we *do* toward you:

13 To the end he may stablish your hearts unblameable in holiness before God, even our Father, at the coming of our Lord Jesus Christ with all his saints.

CHAPTER 4
Sanctification

1 Furthermore then we beseech you, brethren, and exhort *you* by the Lord Jesus, that as ye have received of us how ye ought to walk and to please God, *so* ye would abound more and more.

2 For ye know what commandments we gave you by the Lord Jesus.

3 For this is the will of God, *even* your sanctification, that ye should abstain from fornication:

4 That every one of you should know how to possess his vessel in sanctification and honour;

5 Not in the lust of concupiscence, even as the Gentiles which know not God:

6 That no *man* go beyond and defraud his brother in *any* matter: because that the Lord

Cross references

14 Acts 17:5, 13
15 Matt. 23:34, 37; Acts 2:23; 3:15; 5:30; 7:52
16 Gen. 15:16; Luke 11:52; Acts 13:50; 14:5, 19; 17:5, 13; 18:12; 19:9; 22:21, 22
18 Rom. 1:13; 15:22
19 Prov. 16:31; Phil. 2:16; 4:1; 1Thess. 3:13; Rev. 1:7; 22:12
1 Acts 17:15
2 Rom. 16:21; 1Cor. 16:10; 2Cor. 1:19
3 Acts 9:16; 14:22; 20:23; 21:11
4 Acts 20:24
6 Acts 18:1, 5
8 Phil. 4:1
10 Acts 26:7; 1Thess. 2:17
13 Zech. 14:5; 1Thess. 5:23; 2Thess. 2:17; 1John 3:20, 21
3 Rom. 12:2; 1Cor. 6:15, 18
4 Rom. 6:19
5 Rom. 1:24, 26; 2Thess. 1:8
6 Lev. 19:11, 13

2:19–20 Paul saw these maturing young converts as his "crown of rejoicing" because they had followed his teaching and come to Christ. This is one of five crowns, called by some "the soul winner's crown," reserved for those who dedicate their lives to personal evangelism. These crowns will be given at the judgment seat of Christ "at his coming" (see also Dan. 12:3).

3:13 The believer with an established heart is one who knows the Scripture and the God it reveals in such a personal way that he is motivated to live "unblameable in holiness before God." This person will not be caught unaware "at the coming of our Lord." "With all his saints" is thought by some to be angels who attend Christ in His glorious appearing. However, since the context of this passage is the Rapture, it refers to the gathering together at the Rapture of all the saints of the Church Age, both living and dead.

The Rapture Compared to the Return of Christ

By Edward Hindson

The New Testament clearly teaches that Jesus Christ will "come again" (John 14:3) and "appear the second time" (Heb. 9:28). "I go to prepare a place for you," the Lord told His disciples, "and if I go and prepare a place for you, I will come again, and receive you unto myself" (John 14:2–3). John 14 contains our Lord's first indication that He will return specifically for His own.

Most evangelicals agree as to the nature of Christ's coming, but there is substantial disagreement about the timing. There are certain similarities between the Rapture passages and the Glorious Appearance (return) passages since they both refer to future events related to the Lord's return. But similarity does not mean they refer to the same event. Pretribulationalists believe that there are enough substantial differences between the two aspects of Christ's coming to render them as two separate and distinct events. Just as the Scripture predicted two aspects of Christ's first coming (His birth in Bethlehem and His death on the cross), so it predicts two aspects of His second coming (the Rapture and the Return).

> *The seven-year Tribulation comes between the Rapture and the Return.*

Pretribulationalists divide the second coming of Christ into two main phases: the rapture of the Church and the glorious appearing or return of Christ. In the first phase, our Lord comes to take His own (both the living and the dead) to be with Him. (See article by Renald Showers entitled "The Imminent Coming of Christ.") In the second phase, He returns with His own to win the Battle of Armageddon and establish His kingdom on earth (Rev. 19—20). (See article by J. Dwight Pentecost entitled "The Glorious Appearing of Christ.")

The Rapture is characterized as a "transformation" coming, in which Christ comes for His Bride and takes her to His Father's house (John 14:3; 1 Thess. 4:13–17; 1 Cor. 15:51–52). Here, He claims the Church as His Bride, and the Marriage Supper of the Lamb begins. Notice that this marriage feast occurs in heaven before the triumphal return of Christ (Rev. 19:7–9, 11–16). Those who do not follow a pretribulational scheme are at a loss to explain how the Church got to heaven prior to its return with Christ at the Battle of Armageddon.

Pretribulationalists place the seven-year Tribulation period between the Rapture and the glorious appearing of Christ. Such placement allows for the proper fulfillment of the seven years of Daniel's "seventieth week," and it clearly separates the two phases of the Second Coming (see Dan. 9:24–27). The concept of the Rapture is expressed by the biblical terms "caught up" (Gr. *harpazo* [1 Thess. 4:17]) and "gathered together" (Gr. *episunagoges* [1 Cor. 5:4]). The Rapture involves the "snatching away" of the Church to be with the Lord (as in Acts 8:39; 2 Cor. 12:2–4; Rev. 12:5). By contrast, *episunagoges* refers to that which results from the "catching up" (*harpazo*). Once Christians are caught up into the clouds, they shall be "gathered together" with the Lord. (See the table "Comparisons between the Rapture and the Glorious Appearance.")

There can be no valid system of biblical prophecy without a belief in the Rapture. The Church will be "caught up" and "gathered together" with her Lord. The Church's future hope is the Rapture! She awaits the Savior who is coming for her, His "Bride."

is the avenger of all such, as we also have forewarned you and testified.

7 For God hath not called us unto uncleanness, but unto holiness.

8 He therefore that despiseth, despiseth not man, but God, who hath also given unto us his holy Spirit.

9 But as touching brotherly love ye need not that I write unto you: for ye yourselves are taught of God to love one another.

10 And indeed ye do it toward all the brethren which are in all Macedonia: but we beseech you, brethren, that ye increase more and more;

7 Lev. 11:44; 19:2; 1Cor. 1:2; Heb. 12:14; 1Pet. 1:14, 15
8 Luke 10:16; 1Cor. 2:10; 7:40; 1John 3:24
9 John 6:45; 13:34; 1John 2:20, 27; 3:11, 23; 4:21
13 Eph. 2:12
14 1Cor. 15:13, 18, 23

11 And that ye study to be quiet, and to do your own business, and to work with your own hands, as we commanded you;

12 That ye may walk honestly toward them that are without, and *that* ye may have lack of nothing.

The Rapture of the Church

13 But I would not have you to be ignorant, brethren, concerning them which are asleep, that ye sorrow not, even as others which have no hope.

14 For if we believe that Jesus died and rose

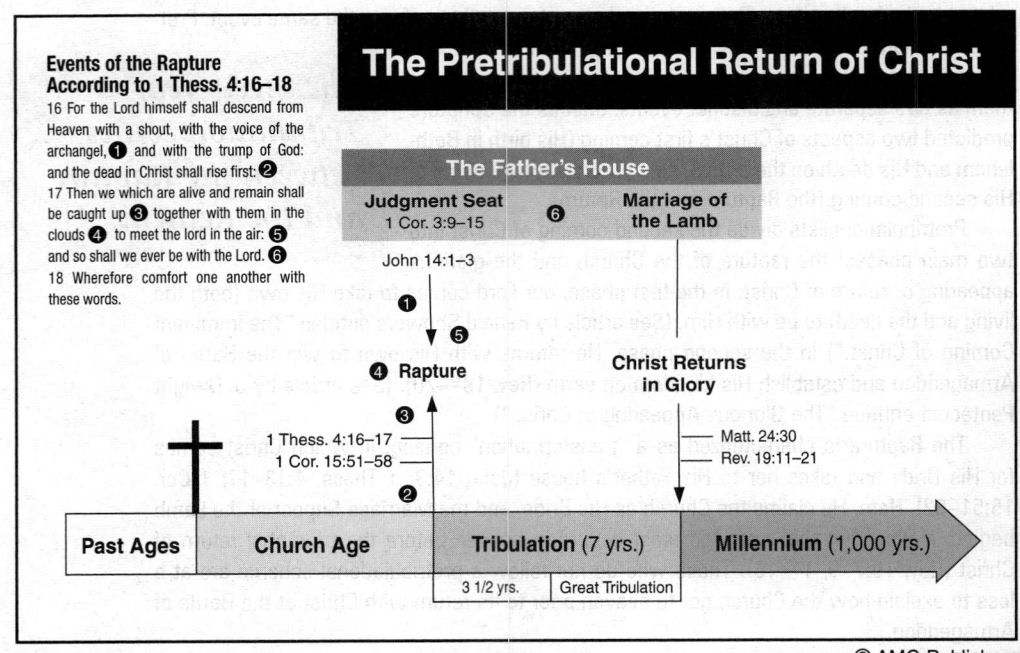

Events of the Rapture According to 1 Thess. 4:16–18

16 For the Lord himself shall descend from Heaven with a shout, with the voice of the archangel, ❶ and with the trump of God: and the dead in Christ shall rise first: ❷
17 Then we which are alive and remain shall be caught up ❸ together with them in the clouds ❹ to meet the lord in the air: ❺ and so shall we ever be with the Lord. ❻
18 Wherefore comfort one another with these words.

The Pretribulational Return of Christ

The Father's House

Judgment Seat — 1 Cor. 3:9–15 — ❻ — Marriage of the Lamb

John 14:1–3

❶
❺
❹ **Rapture** — Christ Returns in Glory
❸
1 Thess. 4:16–17 — Matt. 24:30
1 Cor. 15:51–58 — Rev. 19:11–21
❷

| Past Ages | Church Age | Tribulation (7 yrs.) | Millennium (1,000 yrs.) |
| | | 3 1/2 yrs. | Great Tribulation | |

© AMG Publishers

4:13–18 This is the seminal teaching on the rapture of the Church and should be studied in conjunction with John 14:1–3 and 1 Corinthians 15:51–54. This passage of Scripture is an answer to questions these young believers had regarding their loved ones who had died in the six or so months since Paul led them to Christ. Paul had promised that Christ would return for them to go with Him to His Father's house in heaven. They naturally wanted to know what would happen to their deceased loved ones when Christ returned. Paul's answer in the following verses is a classic description of the rapture of the Church.

4:13 Paul did not want these new Christians to be igno-

rant (lit., "uninformed") concerning the rapture phase of our Lord's second coming. Consequently, they "sorrow . . . as others which have no hope" at the time they lose loved ones in death.

4:14 The great condition to that confidence about death is whether a person has "believed" or committed himself by faith to the redemptive act of Christ Jesus—His death, burial, and resurrection. The phrase, "which sleep in Jesus" refers to the state at death when a believer's soul goes to be with Christ (see Phil. 1:23), while his body awaits the resurrection at Christ's coming. The word "sleep" does not refer to "soul sleep," but implies a conscious state "with the Lord" at death.

again, even so them also which sleep in Jesus will God bring with him.

15 For this we say unto you by the word of the Lord, that we which are alive *and* remain unto the coming of the Lord shall not prevent them which are asleep.

16 For the Lord himself shall descend from heaven with a shout, with the voice of the archangel, and with the trump of God: and the dead in Christ shall rise first:

17 Then we which are alive *and* remain shall be caught up together with them in the clouds to meet the Lord in the air: and so shall we ever be with the Lord.

18 Wherefore comfort one another with these words.

CHAPTER 5
"A Thief in the Night"

1 But of the times and the seasons, brethren, ye have no need that I write unto you.

2 For yourselves know perfectly that the day of the Lord so cometh as a thief in the night.

3 For when they shall say, Peace and safety; then sudden destruction cometh upon them, as travail upon a woman with child; and they shall not escape.

4 But ye, brethren, are not in darkness, that that day should overtake you as a thief.

5 Ye are all the children of light, and the children of the day: we are not of the night, nor of darkness.

6 Therefore let us not sleep, as *do* others; but let us watch and be sober.

7 For they that sleep sleep in the night; and they that be drunken are drunken in the night.

8 But let us, who are of the day, be sober, putting on the breastplate of faith and love; and for an helmet, the hope of salvation.

9 For God hath not appointed us to wrath, but to obtain salvation by our Lord Jesus Christ,

10 Who died for us, that, whether we wake or sleep, we should live together with him.

Cross references

15 1Cor. 15:51
16 Matt. 24:30, 31; Acts 1:11; 1Cor. 15:23, 52
17 John 14:3; Acts 1:9; 1Cor. 15:51; Rev. 11:12
2 Matt. 24:43, 44; 25:13; Luke 12:39, 40; Rev. 3:3; 16:15
3 Isa. 13:6-9; Jer. 13:21; Hos. 13:13
5 Eph. 5:8
6 Matt. 24:42; 25:5, 13
8 Eph. 6:14, 16, 17
9 Rom. 9:22
10 Rom. 14:8, 9

4:15 For this we say unto you by the word of the Lord. Paul was given divine revelation concerning this rapture truth he had taught them earlier and is about to describe now. "We which are alive and remain unto the coming of the Lord" refers to believers at the time of His return. They "shall not prevent" or go before those believers who are dead. Both dead and living Christians shall all go together!

4:16–17 Several specific events occur at the rapture of the Church. "The Lord himself shall descend from heaven with a shout." This is the shout of resurrection. "The voice of an archangel" is signaling that Michael is to lead Israel for the seven-year Tribulation as he did in the Old Testament (Dan. 10:13). The statement, "the dead in Christ rise first" indicates that dead believers of the Church Age will be resurrected in a "twinkling of an eye" (1 Cor. 15:52). "Then we which are alive and remain shall be caught up [to meet them] in the clouds." The phrase "caught up" (Gr. *harpazo*) means "snatch up" suddenly without warning. This "rapture" will unite all believers from Pentecost to the time of Christ's coming for His Church. It will constitute everyone who has ever been in the Church or, as some call it, "the body of Christ." There was nothing that needed to take place during Paul's life before the Rapture, so it is today for us. This is why the Glorious Appearing cannot occur for at least seven years, but the Rapture can occur at any moment. There is no more comforting message in the hours of the death of a loved believer than this rapture truth. It is both the comfort and the hope of the Church.

5:1 times and the seasons. Jesus did not teach His disciples the timing of future events (Acts 1:7) like the Rapture. The apostle Paul, however, had taught these young believers this truth of the "blessed hope" (Titus 2:13). This again suggests he had already taught them this truth about the Rapture so thoroughly that they had "no need that [Paul] write."

5:2 the day of the Lord. This is not a single day but a period of time filled with many prophetic events. The context must be considered to determine what time or event is considered. Here the context is that of the Tribulation, confirmed by it overtaking some who are unprepared as a "thief." Events classified as "the day of the Lord" appear over thirty times in the Old Testament and refer to any time God intervenes in judgment in the affairs of men. This verse is the first place it is used in the New Testament and refers to the Tribulation and end-time events that lead up to the physical coming of Christ.

5:3 Peace and safety. The sudden destruction or Tribulation which follows the Rapture will occur at a time when the world is obsessed with a false sense of "peace and safety." Paul is reiterating Jesus' teaching to "watch and be ready" lest that day should overtake them "as a thief" (v. 4).

5:9 God hath not appointed us to wrath. The wrath under consideration is the time of wrath, the Tribulation period, that shall try the whole world. Believers are not appointed to that "wrath," for they will escape it either by death or by rapture.

11 Wherefore comfort yourselves together, and edify one another, even as also ye do.

Final Instructions

12 And we beseech you, brethren, to know them which labour among you, and are over you in the Lord, and admonish you;

13 And to esteem them very highly in love for their work's sake. *And* be at peace among yourselves.

14 Now we exhort you, brethren, warn them that are unruly, comfort the feeble-minded, support the weak, be patient toward all *men*.

15 See that none render evil for evil unto any *man*; but ever follow that which is good, both among yourselves, and to all *men*.

16 Rejoice evermore.

17 Pray without ceasing.

18 In every thing give thanks: for this is the will of God in Christ Jesus concerning you.

19 Quench not the Spirit.

20 Despise not prophesyings.

21 Prove all things; hold fast that which is good.

22 Abstain from all appearance of evil.

23 And the very God of peace sanctify you wholly; and *I pray God* your whole spirit and soul and body be preserved blameless unto the coming of our Lord Jesus Christ.

24 Faithful *is* he that calleth you, who also will do *it*.

25 Brethren, pray for us.

26 Greet all the brethren with an holy kiss.

27 I charge you by the Lord that this epistle be read unto all the holy brethren.

28 The grace of our Lord Jesus Christ *be* with you. Amen.

Cross references:
- **12** 1Cor. 16:18; Phil. 2:29
- **14** Rom. 14:1; 15:1; Gal. 5:22; Heb. 12:12
- **15** Lev. 19:18; Prov. 20:22; 24:29; Matt. 5:39, 44
- **16** Phil. 4:4
- **17** Luke 18:1; 21:36
- **18** Eph. 5:20
- **19** 1Cor. 14:30
- **20** 1Cor. 14:1, 39
- **23** Phil. 4:9

5:20 Despise not prophesyings. We do not need new prophecies; we need instead to learn, live, and teach those prophecies we have in the Scriptures.

2 Thessalonians

This second letter of Paul to the Thessalonians was written about A.D. 51–52 and was sent from Corinth soon after his first letter. Apparently, Paul's first epistle disturbed some Thessalonians. His presentation of the resurrection of the saved dead and the rapture of the living believers caused some to think that the "Day of the Lord" was already in progress. The "Day of the Lord" is a major theme in Old Testament prophecy that includes the coming Tribulation and the establishment of the Millennial Kingdom. The misunderstanding among those in Thessalonica stemmed from the intense persecution that afflicted the believers in that city. Evidently, some believers equated the persecution with the prophesied events of the "Day of the Lord." They thought that since they had somehow missed Christ's return, there was no point in continuing the Lord's work.

In this epistle, Paul emphasizes Christ's glorious return (chap. 1). But he insists that the "Day of the Lord" has not yet come and must be preceded by **1)** believers being gathered "together unto him" (2:1) and **2)** the unveiling of Antichrist. Therefore, with this letter, Paul inspired those believers in Thessalonica to persevere in prayer and good works until Christ comes.

The grand unveiling of Christ to execute judgment is set forth in 2 Thessalonians 1:7–10 (cf. Jude 1:14–15; Rev. 19:11–20). Preceded by "our gathering together" (2:1) at the Rapture, the "falling away" (2:3) or departure (Gr. *apostasia*) finally results in the unveiling of the man of sin, Antichrist. A restraining power, evidently the ministry of the Holy Spirit, has prevented the consummation of the satanic "mystery of iniquity" (2:7), until it is "taken out of the way" (2:7). The Church as a "withholding" influence likewise is to be withdrawn at the Rapture (2:1–12).

Of 47 verses, 19 are prophetic or 40 percent of the whole. Twelve prophetic ideas are mentioned, but there are no direct Old Testament quotations.

Author
Paul

Date
A.D. 51

Key Truth
The Day of the Lord Is Still to Come

Historic Time
A Short Period after First Thessalonians

Key Verse
3:5   . . . into the love of God, and into the patient waiting for Christ.

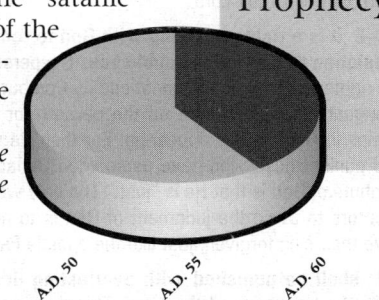

40%
Prophecy

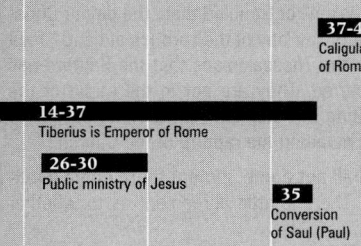

A.D. 25   A.D. 30   A.D. 35   A.D. 40   A.D. 45   A.D. 50   A.D. 55   A.D. 60   A.D. 65

37-41
Caligula is Emperor of Rome

41-54
Claudius is Emperor of Rome

51
Second Thessalonians is written

65-68
Paul and Peter martyred

14-37
Tiberius is Emperor of Rome

50
Church in Thessalonica is founded

54-68
Nero is Emperor of Rome

26-30
Public ministry of Jesus

35
Conversion of Saul (Paul)

47-49
Paul's First Missionary Journey

49-53
Paul's Second Missionary Journey

53-56
Paul's Third Missionary Journey

CHAPTER 1

1 Paul, and Silvanus, and Timotheus, unto the church of the Thessalonians in God our Father and the Lord Jesus Christ:
2 Grace unto you, and peace, from God our Father and the Lord Jesus Christ.

We Know You Are Suffering

3 We are bound to thank God always for you, brethren, as it is meet, because that your faith groweth exceedingly, and the charity of every one of you all toward each other aboundeth;
4 So that we ourselves glory in you in the churches of God for your patience and faith in all your persecutions and tribulations that ye endure:
5 *Which is* a manifest token of the righteous judgment of God, that ye may be counted worthy of the kingdom of God, for which ye also suffer:
6 Seeing *it is* a righteous thing with God to recompense tribulation to them that trouble you;
7 And to you who are troubled rest with us, when the Lord Jesus shall be revealed from heaven with his mighty angels,
8 In flaming fire taking vengeance on them that know not God, and that obey not the gospel of our Lord Jesus Christ:
9 Who shall be punished with everlasting destruction from the presence of the Lord, and from the glory of his power;
10 When he shall come to be glorified in his saints, and to be admired in all them that believe (because our testimony among you was believed) in that day.
11 Wherefore also we pray always for you, that our God would count you worthy of *this* calling, and fulfil all the good pleasure of *his* goodness, and the work of faith with power:
12 That the name of our Lord Jesus Christ may be glorified in you, and ye in him, according to the grace of our God and the Lord Jesus Christ.

CHAPTER 2

The Day of the Lord

1 Now we beseech you, brethren, by the coming of our Lord Jesus Christ, and *by* our gathering together unto him,
2 That ye be not soon shaken in mind, or be troubled, neither by spirit, nor by word, nor by letter as from us, as that the day of Christ is at hand.
3 Let no man deceive you by any means:

Cross-references

1 1Thess. 1:1
3 1Thess. 1:2, 3; 3:6, 9
5 Phil. 1:28
6 Rev. 6:10
7 1Thess. 4:16; Rev. 14:13
8 Ps. 79:6; Rev. 21:8
9 Isa. 2:19; 2Thess. 2:8
10 Ps. 68:35; 89:7
11 2Thess. 1:5
12 Matt. 24:31; Mark. 13:27

2 Matt. 24:4
3 Dan. 7:25; Matt. 24:4; John 17:12; 1John 2:18; Rev. 13:11

1:4 in all your persecutions and tribulations. It is important to note that not all tribulation and persecution of Christians is future or tied to the Tribulation period to come. Many early Christians thought they were already in the Tribulation because they suffered persecution and even death for their Lord.

1:6–8 it is a righteous thing with God to recompense tribulation to them that trouble you. The persecution of the righteous does not go unnoticed by God but will bring "vengeance" or judgment on the perpetrator when He comes in His glorious appearing. For then He will judge and punish those who have persecuted Christians. One attribute of God is that He is "just." The only way for persecutors to avoid the judgment of God is to repent and have their sins forgiven, just like the apostle Paul.

1:9 shall be punished with everlasting destruction from the presence of the Lord. This does not suggest annihilation of the lost, who, after this event, will yet be judged (Rev. 20:11–15) and cast into the lake of fire. Of course, such unsaved souls will not enjoy any of the blessings God has for those who accept Him. This verse may also suggest, however, that greater punishment is in store for the unsaved who persecute believers in this life.

1:10 When he shall come to be glorified in his saints, and to be admired in all them that believe. This verse effectively eliminates the possibility of a partial Rapture, for all believers will be taken up at the same time. Some carnal believers will be "saved; yet so as by fire" (1 Cor. 3:15) but will receive no rewards. However, all believers will be included in the Rapture.

2:1 References in Scripture to the "coming" of Jesus can refer to either the Rapture or the Glorious Appearing, or, as in this case, both. The context must be examined to determine which is in view. This chapter includes both phases of His coming separated by the revelation of the man of sin, who appears during the Tribulation. (For a complete list of the more than 300 Scripture references that speak of the second coming of Christ, see the table "Prophecies of the Second Coming of Christ.")

2:1 and by our gathering together unto him. This is a clear reference to the Rapture, the gathering of believers unto Christ as described by Paul in 1 Thessalonians 4:15–17.

2:2 Don't be "shaken" or troubled that "the day of Christ (some manuscripts say 'day of the Lord') is at hand." Paul wants to assure the Thessalonians that the Rapture has not already occurred. They are not in the midst of the Tribulation awaiting the Glorious Appearance, but in the Church Age still awaiting the rapture of the Church.

2:3 That day shall not come, except there come a falling away first. There is little agreement as to whether

The Antichrist

By Edward Hindson

The Bible clearly portrays the coming of a world leader who will negotiate a peace treaty with Israel in the Last Days. Ironically, the term "antichrist" appears only in 1 John 2:18–22; 4:3; and 2 John 1:7. The apostle John indicates that the Antichrist of the apocalyptic era is coming in the future. But he also adds that many "antichrists" (false teachers) have already come.

In the broadest sense, the "spirit of antichrist" is already at work in the world and has been since the beginning of time (1 John 4:3). This spirit is the anti-Christian spirit that opposes everything that is true about Jesus Christ. However, from the very beginning of the Christian era, believers were convinced that a world leader would come on the scene that would be the embodiment of Satan (Rev. 12—13). Thus, the real power behind the Antichrist is Satan himself.

The person we commonly refer to as the Antichrist is actually known by several names and titles throughout the Bible. Each of these provides a glimpse into the many facets of his diabolical character and name: "the beast" (Rev. 13:1), "man of

> ## The real power behind the Antichrist is Satan himself.

sin" (2 Thess. 2:3), "wicked one" (2 Thess. 2:8), "abomination" (Matt. 24:15), "little horn" (Dan. 7:8), "fierce king" (Dan. 8:23), "prince that shall come" (Dan. 9:26), "vile person" (Dan. 11:21), and "strong-willed king" (Dan. 11:36).

Much has been written about the prefix "anti" in connection with the Antichrist. It can mean either "against" (in opposition of) or "instead of" (in place of). It is best to understand that he is both "against" Christ and that he may well perpetrate himself as a "false" Christ. His rule will forge an alliance of Gentile powers and will be part of the "times of the Gentiles" (Luke 21:24).

The Antichrist will be the most incredible human leader the world has ever known. He will be the epitome of human genius and power and a master of deception, empowered by the "father of lies" (Dan. 11:21). Promising peace, he pushes the world into war.

At least ten factors will identify the Antichrist when he comes to power. Only one person in history will fit every one of these factors. There have been many prototypes, but there will only be one Antichrist.

1. He will rise to power in the Last Days (Dan. 8:19–23).
2. He will not come on the world scene until after the Rapture (2 Thess. 2:3–8).
3. He will rule the entire world (Rev. 13:7).
4. He will rule by international consent (Rev. 17:12–13).
5. He will rule by deception (Dan. 8:24–25).
6. He will be intelligent and persuasive (Dan. 7:20).
7. He will control the global economy (Rev. 13:16–17).
8. He will be assisted by the False Prophet (Rev. 13:11–18).
9. He will make and break a peace treaty with Israel (Dan. 9:26–27).
10. He will claim to be God (2 Thess. 2:4).

There are many other details given in the Bible regarding the Antichrist. Whether he is Jewish or Gentile is not entirely clear. What is clear, however, is that he will control the last great bastion of Gentile world power and will extend his control over the entire world, promising to ensure world peace through a series of international treaties, agreements, and alliances. Despite his promises of world peace, he will inevitably plunge the world into the most catastrophic war of all time.

for *that day shall not come*, except there come a falling away first, and that man of sin be revealed, the son of perdition;

4 Who opposeth and exalteth himself above all that is called God, or that is worshipped; so that he as God sitteth in the temple of God, shewing himself that he is God.

5 Remember ye not, that, when I was yet with you, I told you these things?

4 Isa. 14:13; Ezek. 28:2, 6, 9; Dan. 7:25; 11:36; Rev. 13:6

7 1 John 2:18; 4:3

8 Isa. 11:4; Dan. 7:10, 11; Hos. 6:5; Rev. 19:15, 20, 21

6 And now ye know what withholdeth that he might be revealed in his time.

"The Mystery of Iniquity"

7 For the mystery of iniquity doth already work: only he who now letteth *will let*, until he be taken out of the way.

8 And then shall that Wicked be revealed, whom the Lord shall consume with the

Comparisons between the Rapture and the Glorious Appearance

RAPTURE	GLORIOUS APPEARANCE
1. Christ comes for His own (John 14:3; 1 Thess. 4:17).	1. Christ comes with His own (Rev. 19:14).
2. He comes in the air (1 Thess. 4:17).	2. He comes to the earth (Zech. 14:4–5; Acts 1:11).
3. He comes to claim His Bride (1 Thess. 4:16–17).	3. He comes with His Bride (Rev. 19:6–14).
4. Removal of believers (1 Thess. 4:17).	4. Manifestation of Christ (Mal. 4:2).
5. Only His own see Him (1 Thess. 4:13–18).	5. Every eye shall see Him (Rev. 1:7; Matt. 24:30).
6. Tribulation begins (2 Thess. 1:6–9).	6. Millennial Kingdom begins (Rev. 20:1–7).
7. Saved are delivered from wrath (1 Thess. 1:10; 5:9; Rev. 3:10).	7. Unsaved experience the wrath of God (Rev. 6:12–17).
8. No signs precede the Rapture (1 Thess. 5:1–3).	8. Signs precede the Second Coming (Luke 21:11–28).
9. Focus: Lord and Church (1 Thess. 4:13–18).	9. Focus: Israel and kingdom (Matt. 24).
10. World is deceived (2 Thess. 2:3–12).	10. Satan is bound (Rev. 20:1–2).

the Greek word *apostesia* ("falling away") refers to a physical departure (the Rapture) or a metaphorical one (departure from the faith). The first seven translations of the English Bible translated it "departure." No one knows why the translators of the King James Version rendered it "falling away" or why others translate it "rebellion." A case can be made that all seven of the earliest translations of the English Bible were right in rendering it "departure," which could mean a physical departure or rapture. If the meaning of "departure" is the more accurate translation, this chapter would leave no doubt regarding a pretribulation Rapture, for it places the Rapture prior to the revelation of the man of sin. However, if the more popular view of "falling away" or "rebellion" is the true meaning, *apostesia* would refer to the career of Antichrist during the Tribulation. The important truth here is "that day," the Glorious Appearing, will not occur until the "son of perdition" has been revealed (see Rev. 12—13).

2:4 so that he as God sitteth in the temple of God. When Satan is cast out of heaven and actually indwells the body of Antichrist, the leader of the Tribulation, he will do what he has always wanted to do—demand that he be worshiped as God.

2:6–7 The general consensus of the identity of "he who

now letteth" is the Holy Spirit in the Church, who will "be taken out of the way" in the Rapture. When the Church is raptured, the world will be plunged into lawlessness and chaos (Rev. 9:20–21), for the restrainer will be gone. This does not mean the Holy Spirit will not be here to "reprove the world of sin" (John 16:8). According to Joel 2:28–32, He will be poured out in great measure and "a great multitude which no man could number" (Rev. 7:9) will come to faith in Christ as a result. However, there will be no restraining force against lawlessness and sin as exists today, which keeps the Antichrist from arriving on the scene.

2:8 then shall that Wicked be revealed. When? After the Holy Spirit's presence in the Church is raptured or "taken out of the way," after which Christ will destroy this Satan-filled Antichrist who demands mankind worship him by "the brightness of His coming." Note the chronology of these events before Christ can come in power. First, a falling away, or apostasy, or "departing" must occur, followed by the departure of the Holy Spirit as a restraining force (during the Rapture). Then "that man of sin" will be revealed and he will demand to be worshiped in the temple. Finally, the Antichrist will be destroyed by Christ in His second coming, which effec-

spirit of his mouth, and shall destroy with the brightness of his coming:

9 *Even him,* whose coming is after the working of Satan with all power and signs and lying wonders,

10 And with all deceivableness of unrighteousness in them that perish; because they received not the love of the truth, that they might be saved.

11 And for this cause God shall send them strong delusion, that they should believe a lie:

12 That they all might be damned who believed not the truth, but had pleasure in unrighteousness.

Stand Firm

13 But we are bound to give thanks alway to God for you, brethren beloved of the Lord, because God hath from the beginning chosen you to salvation through sanctification of the Spirit and belief of the truth:

14 Whereunto he called you by our gospel, to the obtaining of the glory of our Lord Jesus Christ.

15 Therefore, brethren, stand fast, and hold the traditions which ye have been taught, whether by word, or our epistle.

16 Now our Lord Jesus Christ himself, and God, even our Father, which hath loved us, and hath given *us* everlasting consolation and good hope through grace,

17 Comfort your hearts, and stablish you in every good word and work.

9 Deut. 13:1;
Matt. 24:24;
John 8:41;
Eph. 2:2;
Rev. 13:13;
19:20

11 1Kgs.
22:22; Ezek.
14:9; Matt.
24:5, 11;
Rom. 1:24;
1Tim. 4:1

12 Rom.
1:32

13 Luke
1:75; Eph.
1:4

14 1Thess.
2:12

17 1Cor. 1:8;
Eph. 6:19;
Col. 4:3

2 Rom.
10:16; 15:31

5 1Thess.
1:3

6 Rom.
16:17; 1Cor.
5:11, 13

7 1Cor. 4:16;
11:1;
1Thess. 1:6,
7; 2:10

8 Acts 18:3;
20:34; 2Cor.
11:9;
1Thess. 2:9

9 1Cor. 9:6;
1Thess. 2:6;
2Thess. 3:7

10 Gen.
3:19;
1Thess. 4:11

CHAPTER 3

1 Finally, brethren, pray for us, that the word of the Lord may have *free* course, and be glorified, even as *it is* with you:

2 And that we may be delivered from unreasonable and wicked men: for all *men* have not faith.

3 But the Lord is faithful, who shall stablish you, and keep *you* from evil.

4 And we have confidence in the Lord touching you, that ye both do and will do the things which we command you.

5 And the Lord direct your hearts into the love of God, and into the patient waiting for Christ.

"Be Not Weary in Well Doing"

6 Now we command you, brethren, in the name of our Lord Jesus Christ, that ye withdraw yourselves from every brother that walketh disorderly, and not after the tradition which he received of us.

7 For yourselves know how ye ought to follow us: for we behaved not ourselves disorderly among you;

8 Neither did we eat any man's bread for nought; but wrought with labour and travail night and day, that we might not be chargable to any of you:

9 Not because we have not power, but to make ourselves an ensample unto you to follow us.

10 For even when we were with you, this we commanded you, that if any would not work, neither should he eat.

---

tively ends the Tribulation. This is the most detailed account found in a single chapter of Scripture of the two phases of Christ's return, separated by the Tribulation. This same order of prophetic events is detailed in the book of Revelation.

2:9 During the last three and one-half years of the Tribulation, the Antichrist will have power to perform "signs and lying wonders" so that he can deceive millions. This period of Antichrist's deception was called by Jesus "the great tribulation," and He also warned of "false Christs" or "false prophets" who will show "great signs and wonders," so as to deceive, "if . . . possible . . . the very elect" (Matt. 24:24). The level of satanic influence in the Tribulation period will mark it as a very deceptive period of time.

2:10 The Great Tribulation (the last half of the seven years) will feature a titanic battle in the conflict of the ages between God and Satan for the souls of men. Satan will use every "unrighteous" deception he can to get

people to take his mark (Rev. 13:17–18), and once they do, they are doomed forever. God will send two special witnesses with supernatural powers (Rev. 11:3–12), the 144,000 "servants of God" (Rev. 14:1–13), the outpouring of the Holy Spirit as in the day of Pentecost, and even the "angel [with] the everlasting gospel" (Rev. 14:6). While "a great multitude, which no man could number" (Rev. 7:9) will come to faith in Christ, they will not constitute the majority of those living at that time.

2:11–12 To those who will be deceived by Antichrist into rejecting "the love of the truth," God evidently will send "strong delusion, that they should believe a lie." The only way people who live during the Tribulation period can avoid the deception of Satan is to love the truth. The primary purpose of this seven-year period, which takes up so much space in the plan of God for the future (Rev. 6—19), is to force people living at the time to make their decision for or against Christ in preparation for the kingdom age and eternity.

11 For we hear that there are some which walk among you disorderly, working not at all, but are busybodies.

12 Now them that are such we command and exhort by our Lord Jesus Christ, that with quietness they work, and eat their own bread.

13 But ye, brethren, be not weary in well doing.

14 And if any man obey not our word by this epistle, note that man, and have no com-

pany with him, that he may be ashamed.

15 Yet count *him* not as an enemy, but admonish *him* as a brother.

16 Now the Lord of peace himself give you peace always by all means. The Lord *be* with you all.

17 The salutation of Paul with mine own hand, which is the token in every epistle: so I write.

18 The grace of our Lord Jesus Christ *be* with you all. Amen.

11 1Tim. 5:13; 1Pet. 4:15
12 Eph. 4:28
13 Gal. 6:9
14 1Cor. 5:9
15 Lev. 19:17
16 Rom. 15:33; 16:20
17 1Cor. 16:21

1 Timothy

Written during the last few years of Paul's life, this epistle is one of the three Pastoral Epistles, along with 2 Timothy and Titus. Paul was very concerned with the false doctrines being espoused by some Gentiles and professing Jewish Christians. In an effort to record his thoughts on this subject as he prepared to pass his ministry on to others, Paul used these epistles to give instructions for internal operation and order in the local church. If Paul was released in Rome after two years of house arrest (Acts 28:30–31; 2 Tim. 4:17), then this epistle was written during his fifth journey, as some believe, only a few years before he was arrested for the final time and executed.

Author
Paul

Date
A.D. 64

Key Truth
Guidelines for Church Order

Historic Time
Paul's Ministry after His First Roman Imprisonment

Key Verse
3:15
. . . know how thou oughtest to behave thyself in the house of God.

Timothy, who was converted as a lad while Paul was at Lystra in the first missionary journey (Acts 14:6–22; 16:1–5), had a Jewish mother and a Greek father. He was highly esteemed by his Christian brethren both in Lystra and Iconium and became a constant and trusted follower and companion to Paul. Eventually, Paul left Timothy in Ephesus (1:3) to deal with false teachers, supervise public worship, and guide the church in the appointment of leaders. Paul's loving advice and counsel in many areas of personal life and ministry are applicable to Christian leaders today.

A prime doctrinal sequence is found in "the mystery of godliness" (3:16), teaching the incarnation of Christ and summarizing the Lord's ministry on earth. Portions of this verse were sung as a hymn in apostolic times. Paul deals with the rise of false teachers in the "latter times," but also confronts the false teaching prevalent in that day (4:1–3). Since similar departures "from the faith" have continued, the widespread development of erroneous concepts has intensified throughout the centuries.

4% Prophecy

A key prophetic passage is found in 1 Timothy 6:15–16. These two verses refer to Christ's glorious appearing and future universal dominion.

Only 2 predictions appear in 5 of the 115 verses, or 4 percent. Second Timothy has 2 Old Testament quotations.

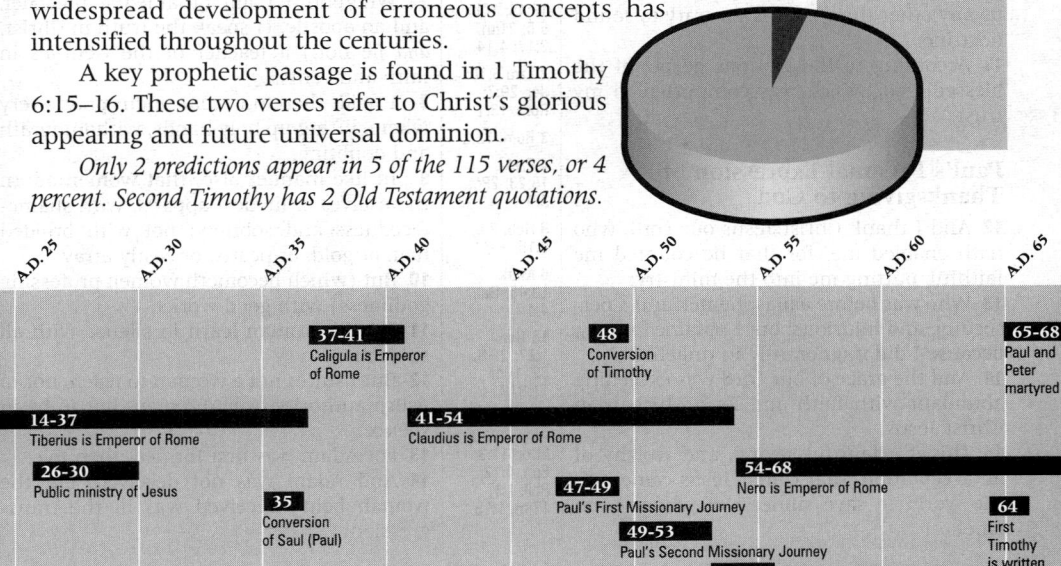

A.D. 25   A.D. 30   A.D. 35   A.D. 40   A.D. 45   A.D. 50   A.D. 55   A.D. 60   A.D. 65

37–41
Caligula is Emperor of Rome

48
Conversion of Timothy

65–68
Paul and Peter martyred

14–37
Tiberius is Emperor of Rome

41–54
Claudius is Emperor of Rome

26–30
Public ministry of Jesus

35
Conversion of Saul (Paul)

47–49
Paul's First Missionary Journey

54–68
Nero is Emperor of Rome

49–53
Paul's Second Missionary Journey

53–56
Paul's Third Missionary Journey

64
First Timothy is written

CHAPTER 1

1 Paul, an apostle of Jesus Christ by the commandment of God our Saviour, and Lord Jesus Christ, *which is* our hope;

2 Unto Timothy, *my* own son in the faith: Grace, mercy, *and* peace, from God our Father and Jesus Christ our Lord.

False Doctrine

3 As I besought thee to abide still at Ephesus, when I went into Macedonia, that thou mightest charge some that they teach no other doctrine,

4 Neither give heed to fables and endless genealogies, which minister questions, rather than godly edifying which is in faith: *so do.*

5 Now the end of the commandment is charity out of a pure heart, and *of* a good conscience, and *of* faith unfeigned:

6 From which some having swerved have turned aside unto vain jangling;

7 Desiring to be teachers of the law; understanding neither what they say, nor whereof they affirm.

8 But we know that the law *is* good, if a man use it lawfully;

9 Knowing this, that the law is not made for a righteous man, but for the lawless and disobedient, for the ungodly and for sinners, for unholy and profane, for murderers of fathers and murderers of mothers, for manslayers,

10 For whoremongers, for them that defile themselves with mankind, for menstealers, for liars, for perjured persons, and if there be any other thing that is contrary to sound doctrine;

11 According to the glorious gospel of the blessed God, which was committed to my trust.

Paul's Personal Expression of Thanksgiving to God

12 And I thank Christ Jesus our Lord, who hath enabled me, for that he counted me faithful, putting me into the ministry;

13 Who was before a blasphemer, and a persecutor, and injurious: but I obtained mercy, because I did *it* ignorantly in unbelief.

14 And the grace of our Lord was exceeding abundant with faith and love which is in Christ Jesus.

15 This *is* a faithful saying, and worthy of all acceptation, that Christ Jesus came into the world to save sinners; of whom I am chief.

16 Howbeit for this cause I obtained mercy, that in me first Jesus Christ might shew forth all longsuffering, for a pattern to them which should hereafter believe on him to life everlasting.

17 Now unto the King eternal, immortal, invisible, the only wise God, *be* honour and glory for ever and ever. Amen.

18 This charge I commit unto thee, son Timothy, according to the prophecies which went before on thee, that thou by them mightest war a good warfare;

19 Holding faith, and a good conscience; which some having put away concerning faith have made shipwreck:

20 Of whom is Hymenaeus and Alexander; whom I have delivered unto Satan, that they may learn not to blaspheme.

CHAPTER 2

Pray for Those in Authority

1 I exhort therefore, that, first of all, supplications, prayers, intercessions, *and* giving of thanks, be made for all men;

2 For kings, and *for* all that are in authority; that we may lead a quiet and peaceable life in all godliness and honesty.

3 For this *is* good and acceptable in the sight of God our Saviour;

4 Who will have all men to be saved, and to come unto the knowledge of the truth.

5 For *there is* one God, and one mediator between God and men, the man Christ Jesus;

6 Who gave himself a ransom for all, to be testified in due time.

7 Whereunto I am ordained a preacher, and an apostle, (I speak the truth in Christ, *and* lie not;) a teacher of the Gentiles in faith and verity.

8 I will therefore that men pray every where, lifting up holy hands, without wrath and doubting.

9 In like manner also, that women adorn themselves in modest apparel, with shamefacedness and sobriety; not with broided hair, or gold, or pearls, or costly array.

10 But (which becometh women professing godliness) with good works.

11 Let the woman learn in silence with all subjection.

12 But I suffer not a woman to teach, nor to usurp authority over the man, but to be in silence.

13 For Adam was first formed, then Eve.

14 And Adam was not deceived, but the woman being deceived was in the transgression.

Cross References

1 Col. 1:27
2 Acts 16:1; 1Cor. 4:17; 1Thess. 3:2
3 Acts 20:1, 3; Gal. 1:6, 7
4 1Tim. 4:7; 6:4, 20
5 Rom. 13:8, 10; Gal. 5:14
7 1Tim. 6:4
8 Rom. 7:12
9 Gal. 3:19; 5:23
12 1Cor. 7:25
13 Acts 3:17; 8:3; 9:1; 26:9
14 Luke 7:47; Rom. 5:20
15 Matt. 9:13; Mark 2:17; Luke 5:32; 19:10; Rom. 5:8
16 Acts 13:39; 2Cor. 4:1
17 1Chr. 29:11; Dan. 7:14; John 1:18; Rom. 1:23; 16:27
18 1Tim. 4:14; 6:12, 13, 14, 20; 2Tim. 2:2, 3; 4:7
19 1Tim. 3:9; 6:9
20 Acts 13:45; 1Cor. 5:5; 2Tim. 2:17; 4:14
2 Ezra 6:10; Jer. 29:7; Rom. 13:1
3 Rom. 12:2
4 Ezek. 18:23; 2Pet. 3:9
5 Heb. 8:6; 9:15
6 Mark 10:45; Gal. 4:4
13 Gen. 1:27; 2:18, 22; 1Cor. 11:8, 9
14 Gen. 3:6; Acts 20:28; 2Cor. 11:3; Eph. 4:12; Phil. 1:1; 1Tim. 1:15

15 Notwithstanding she shall be saved in childbearing, if they continue in faith and charity and holiness with sobriety.

CHAPTER 3
Qualifications of a Bishop

1 This *is* a true saying, If a man desire the office of a bishop, he desireth a good work.
2 A bishop then must be blameless, the husband of one wife, vigilant, sober, of good behaviour, given to hospitality, apt to teach;
3 Not given to wine, no striker, not greedy of filthy lucre; but patient, not a brawler, not covetous;
4 One that ruleth well his own house, having his children in subjection with all gravity;
5 (For if a man know not how to rule his own house, how shall he take care of the church of God?)
6 Not a novice, lest being lifted up with pride he fall into the condemnation of the devil.
7 Moreover he must have a good report of them which are without; lest he fall into reproach and the snare of the devil.

Qualifications of a Deacon

8 Likewise *must* the deacons *be* grave, not doubletongued, not given to much wine, not greedy of filthy lucre;
9 Holding the mystery of the faith in a pure conscience.
10 And let these also first be proved; then let them use the office of a deacon, being *found* blameless.
11 Even so *must their* wives *be* grave, not slanderers, sober, faithful in all things.
12 Let the deacons be the husbands of one wife, ruling their children and their own houses well.
13 For they that have used the office of a deacon well purchase to themselves a good

---

2 1Tim. 5:9; Titus 1:6
3 2Tim. 2:24; 1Pet. 5:2
6 Isa. 14:12
7 Acts 22:12
11 Titus 2:3
13 Matt. 25:21
15 Eph. 2:21, 22; 2Tim. 2:20
16 Matt. 3:16; 28:2; Mark 16:5; Luke 2:13; 24:4, 51; John 1:14, 32, 33; 15:26; 16:8, 9; 20:12; Acts 1:9; 10:34; 13:46, 48
1 Dan. 11:35, 37, 38; John 16:13; 2Thess. 2:3; Rev. 9:20; 16:14
2 Matt. 7:15; Rom. 16:18
3 Gen. 1:29; 9:3; Rom. 14:3, 6, 17; 1Cor. 7:28, 36, 38; 8:8; 10:30
4 1Cor. 10:25
6 2Tim. 3:14, 15
8 Ps. 37:4; 84:11; 112:2, 3; 145:19; Matt. 6:33; 19:29; Mark 10:30; Rom. 8:28; 1Cor. 8:8; Col. 2:23; 1Tim. 6:6

---

degree, and great boldness in the faith which is in Christ Jesus.
14 These things write I unto thee, hoping to come unto thee shortly:
15 But if I tarry long, that thou mayest know how thou oughtest to behave thyself in the house of God, which is the church of the living God, the pillar and ground of the truth.
16 And without controversy great is the mystery of godliness: God was manifest in the flesh, justified in the Spirit, seen of angels, preached unto the Gentiles, believed on in the world, received up into glory.

CHAPTER 4
Apostasy

1 Now the Spirit speaketh expressly, that in the latter times some shall depart from the faith, giving heed to seducing spirits, and doctrines of devils;
2 Speaking lies in hypocrisy; having their conscience seared with a hot iron;
3 Forbidding to marry, *and commanding* to abstain from meats, which God hath created to be received with thanksgiving of them which believe and know the truth.
4 For every creature of God *is* good, and nothing to be refused, if it be received with thanksgiving:
5 For it is sanctified by the word of God and prayer.

Be an Example

6 If thou put the brethren in remembrance of these things, thou shalt be a good minister of Jesus Christ, nourished up in the words of faith and of good doctrine, whereunto thou hast attained.
7 But refuse profane and old wives' fables, and exercise thyself *rather* unto godliness.
8 For bodily exercise profiteth little: but godliness is profitable unto all things, having

---

4:1–2 the Spirit speaketh expressly. In clear fashion, Paul strongly emphasizes the message that is to follow about apostasy, apparently via direct revelation from the Holy Spirit. Paul emphasizes that this is not just his human opinion derived from sociological analysis, but clearly a divine prophecy. Since phrases like "latter days" and "latter times" are used in different contexts, they may refer to differing time periods, depending on their contexts. Hebrews 1:2 is a clear reference to the entire Church Age. However, since Paul writes 1 Timothy in relation to the Church (1 Tim. 3:15), "latter times" in this context refers to the end of the current Church Age. Paul's continues his message with the warning that some within the Church will become apostate. The source of their false teaching will come from "seducing spirits, and doctrines of devils." The means through which apostasy will spread is through the human false teachers who are "having their conscience seared with a hot iron," a metaphorical allusion to cauterization, a medical practice of burning as a means to prevent infection. False teachers can propagate their false teachings because they are void of a conscience that responds to God's word. This passage characterizes the way things will be during the last days of the Church Age, an apt description of the times in which we currently live.

promise of the life that now is, and of that which is to come.

9 This *is* a faithful saying and worthy of all acceptation.

10 For therefore we both labour and suffer reproach, because we trust in the living God, who is the Saviour of all men, specially of those that believe.

11 These things command and teach.

12 Let no man despise thy youth; but be thou an example of the believers, in word, in conversation, in charity, in spirit, in faith, in purity.

13 Till I come, give attendance to reading, to exhortation, to doctrine.

14 Neglect not the gift that is in thee, which was given thee by prophecy, with the laying on of the hands of the presbytery.

15 Meditate upon these things; give thyself wholly to them; that thy profiting may appear to all.

16 Take heed unto thyself, and unto the doctrine; continue in them: for in doing this thou shalt both save thyself, and them that hear thee.

CHAPTER 5
More Instructions

1 Rebuke not an elder, but intreat *him* as a father; *and* the younger men as brethren;

2 The elder women as mothers; the younger as sisters, with all purity.

3 Honour widows that are widows indeed.

4 But if any widow have children or nephews, let them learn first to shew piety at home, and to requite their parents: for that is good and acceptable before God.

5 Now she that is a widow indeed, and desolate, trusteth in God, and continueth in supplications and prayers night and day.

6 But she that liveth in pleasure is dead while she liveth.

7 And these things give in charge, that they may be blameless.

8 But if any provide not for his own, and specially for those of his own house, he hath denied the faith, and is worse than an infidel.

9 Let not a widow be taken into the number under threescore years old, having been the wife of one man,

10 Well reported of for good works; if she have brought up children, if she have lodged strangers, if she have washed the saints' feet, if she have relieved the afflicted, if she have diligently followed every good work.

11 But the younger widows refuse: for

when they have begun to wax wanton against Christ, they will marry;

12 Having damnation, because they have cast off their first faith.

13 And withal they learn *to be* idle, wandering about from house to house; and not only idle, but tattlers also and busybodies, speaking things which they ought not.

14 I will therefore that the younger women marry, bear children, guide the house, give none occasion to the adversary to speak reproachfully.

15 For some are already turned aside after Satan.

16 If any man or woman that believeth have widows, let them relieve them, and let not the church be charged; that it may relieve them that are widows indeed.

Good Elders Receive Double Honor

17 Let the elders that rule well be counted worthy of double honour, especially they who labour in the word and doctrine.

18 For the scripture saith, Thou shalt not muzzle the ox that treadeth out the corn. And, The labourer *is* worthy of his reward.

19 Against an elder receive not an accusation, but before two or three witnesses.

20 Them that sin rebuke before all, that others also may fear.

21 I charge *thee* before God, and the Lord Jesus Christ, and the elect angels, that thou observe these things without preferring one before another, doing nothing by partiality.

22 Lay hands suddenly on no man, neither be partaker of other men's sins: keep thyself pure.

23 Drink no longer water, but use a little wine for thy stomach's sake and thine often infirmities.

24 Some men's sins are open beforehand, going before to judgment; and some *men* they follow after.

25 Likewise also the good works *of some* are manifest beforehand; and they that are otherwise cannot be hid.

CHAPTER 6

1 Let as many servants as are under the yoke count their own masters worthy of all honour, that the name of God and *his* doctrine be not blasphemed.

2 And they that have believing masters, let them not despise *them,* because they are brethren; but rather do *them* service, because they are faithful and beloved, partak-

---

9 1Tim. 1:15

10 Ps. 36:6; 107:2, 6

12 Titus 2:7, 15; 1Pet. 5:3

14 Acts 6:6; 8:17; 13:3; 19:6

16 Ezek. 33:9; Rom. 11:14; 1Cor. 9:22

1 Lev. 19:32

4 Gen. 45:10, 11; Eph. 6:1, 2

5 Acts 26:7

6 James 5:5

8 Isa. 58:7; Matt. 18:17

9 Luke 2:36

10 Luke 7:38, 44; John 13:5; 14; Acts 16:15

13 2Thess. 3:11

14 1Cor. 7:9

17 Acts 28:10; Heb. 13:7, 17

18 Lev. 19:13; Deut. 24:14, 15; 25:4; Matt. 10:10; Luke 10:7; 1Cor. 9:9

19 Deut. 19:15

20 Deut. 13:11; Gal. 2:11, 14; Titus 1:13

21 1Tim. 6:13; 2Tim. 2:14; 4:1

22 Acts 6:6; 13:3; 1Tim. 4:14; 2Tim. 1:6; 2John 1:11

23 Ps. 104:15

24 Gal. 5:19

1 Isa. 52:5; Rom. 2:24; Eph. 6:5; Col. 3:22; Titus 2:5, 8, 9; 1Pet. 2:18

2 Col. 4:1; 1Tim. 4:11

ers of the benefit. These things teach and exhort.

Healthy Teaching

3 If any man teach otherwise, and consent not to wholesome words, *even* the words of our Lord Jesus Christ, and to the doctrine which is according to godliness;
4 He is proud, knowing nothing, but doting about questions and strifes of words, whereof cometh envy, strife, railings, evil surmisings.
5 Perverse disputings of men of corrupt minds, and destitute of the truth, supposing that gain is godliness: from such withdraw thyself.
6 But godliness with contentment is great gain.
7 For we brought nothing into *this* world, *and it is* certain we can carry nothing out.
8 And having food and raiment let us be therewith content.
9 But they that will be rich fall into temptation and a snare, and *into* many foolish and hurtful lusts, which drown men in destruction and perdition.
10 For the love of money is the root of all evil: which while some coveted after, they have erred from the faith, and pierced themselves through with many sorrows.

"Fight the Good Fight"

11 But thou, O man of God, flee these things; and follow after righteousness, godliness, faith, love, patience, meekness.
12 Fight the good fight of faith, lay hold on

eternal life, whereunto thou art also called, and hast professed a good profession before many witnesses.
13 I give thee charge in the sight of God, who quickeneth all things, and *before* Christ Jesus, who before Pontius Pilate witnessed a good confession;

The Second Coming of Christ

14 That thou keep *this* commandment without spot, unrebukeable, until the appearing of our Lord Jesus Christ:
15 Which in his times he shall shew, *who is* the blessed and only Potentate, the King of kings, and Lord of lords;
16 Who only hath immortality, dwelling in the light which no man can approach unto; whom no man hath seen, nor can see: to whom *be* honour and power everlasting. Amen.
17 Charge them that are rich in this world, that they be not highminded; nor trust in uncertain riches, but in the living God, who giveth us richly all things to enjoy;
18 That they do good, that they be rich in good works, ready to distribute, willing to communicate;
19 Laying up in store for themselves a good foundation against the time to come, that they may lay hold on eternal life.
20 O Timothy, keep that which is committed to thy trust, avoiding profane *and* vain babblings, and oppositions of science falsely so called:
21 Which some professing have erred concerning the faith. Grace *be* with thee. Amen.

Cross references

5 1Cor. 11:16
6 Ps. 37:16; Prov. 15:16; 16:8
7 Job. 1:21; Ps. 49:17; Prov. 27:24; Eccl. 5:15
8 Gen. 28:20; Heb. 13:5
9 Matt. 13:22
10 Ex. 23:8; Deut. 16:19
11 Deut. 33:1; 2Tim. 2:22; 3:17
12 1Tim. 1:18; 6:19; 2Tim. 4:7
13 Matt. 27:11; John 5:21; 18:37
14 Phil. 1:6, 10; 1Thess. 3:13; 5:23
15 1Tim. 1:11, 17; Rev. 17:14; 19:16
16 Ex. 33:20; Eph. 3:21; Phil. 4:20
17 Job 31:24; Ps. 52:7; 62:10; Prov. 23:5
20 1Tim. 1:4, 6; 4:7; 2Tim. 1:14; 2:14, 16, 23

6:13–14 until the appearing of our Lord Jesus Christ. The specific instructions given by Paul in the immediate context (1 Tim. 6:11–12), as well as in all New Testament teachings on the End Times, are meant to tell believers how to live between the time of Christ's first and second advents.

6:15 in his times. The New Testament teaches us that the times of future events are in the hand of God (Dan. 2:36–45; Acts 1:7; 17:26; Heb. 11:3), but when the time does arrive "he shall shew, who is the blessed and only Potentate, the King of kings, and Lord of lords." Paul speaks here of the second coming of Christ (Rev. 19:16).

2 Timothy

Paul wrote this second letter to Timothy (see introduction to 1 Timothy) from a prison cell, shortly before his martyrdom in Rome around A.D. 67. This second installment of the so-called Pastoral Epistles contains the last words of the apostle which inspiration has preserved.

The book of Acts concludes with Paul being placed under house arrest, but this epistle to Timothy suggests that Paul was imprisoned a second time (2 Tim. 4:16–18). Many scholars believe that Paul was acquitted in the first trial and subsequently returned to Greece and Asia Minor to continue his missionary work. It is believed that prior to this epistle, Paul was arrested again, taken back to Rome, and imprisoned in what is known as the Mamertine Prison. Since Emperor Nero had recently started a full-fledged state persecution of Christians, Paul sensed that his death was near. However, he was satisfied that he had done his best for Christ (4:6–8).

Author
Paul

Date
A.D. 67

Key Truth
Faithful Ministry

Historic Time
Paul's Imprisonment Shortly before His Death

Key Verse
1:13
Hold fast the form of sound words.

Paul longs to see the face of his beloved Timothy as he urges Timothy to come to him four times (1:4; 4:9, 11, 21). "Only Luke" is with him these last days of a tremendous but arduous ministry, which began in Damascus thirty-five years earlier (4:11). In this letter to Timothy, he encourages his "son in the faith" (1 Tim. 1:2; 2 Tim. 2:1) to be a "good soldier of Jesus Christ" (2:3), to oppose false doctrine and refute errors, to be a model of spiritual virtue, and to be a faithful preacher of the gospel. This encouragement was beneficial to Timothy, for he also would soon face persecution.

There are eight predictive topics: **1)** the day of reward, consummation and glory (1:12, 18; 4:8); **2)** reigning with Christ (2:12); **3)** resurrection and judgment future (2:18); **4)** perilous times in the Last Days (3:1–9); **5)** Christ as Judge (4:1); **6)** Christ's appearance (4:1); **7)** Christ's reign (4:1); and **8)** the era of false doctrine (4:3–4).

Seventeen verses out of 83 involve prophetic thought, or 20 percent. There are no Old Testament quotations in 2 Timothy.

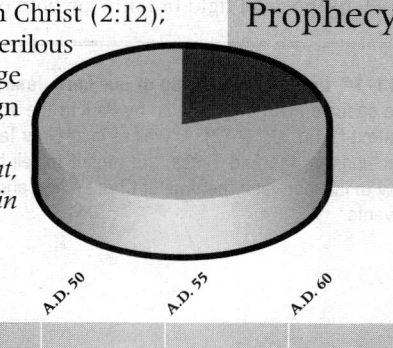

20%
Prophecy

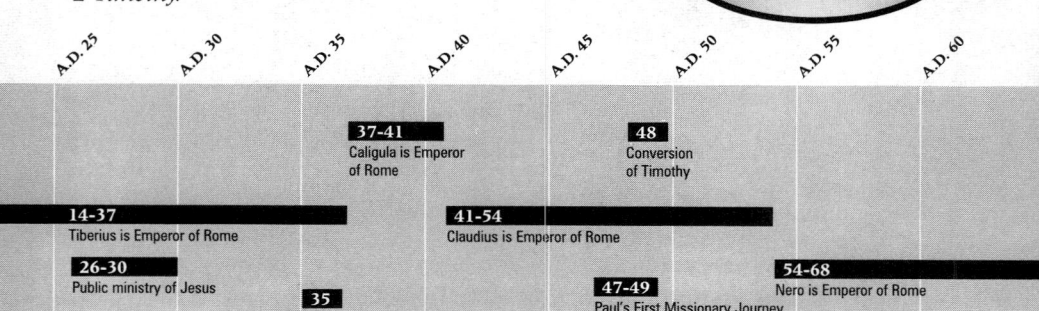

A.D. 25   A.D. 30   A.D. 35   A.D. 40   A.D. 45   A.D. 50   A.D. 55   A.D. 60

37-41
Caligula is Emperor of Rome

48
Conversion of Timothy

14-37
Tiberius is Emperor of Rome

41-54
Claudius is Emperor of Rome

26-30
Public ministry of Jesus

35
Conversion of Saul (Paul)

47-49
Paul's First Missionary Journey

54-68
Nero is Emperor of Rome

49-53
Paul's Second Missionary Journey

53-56
Paul's Third Missionary Journey

CHAPTER 1

1 Paul, an apostle of Jesus Christ by the will of God, according to the promise of life which is in Christ Jesus,

2 To Timothy, *my* dearly beloved son: Grace, mercy, *and* peace, from God the Father and Christ Jesus our Lord.

"Stir Up the Gift of God"

3 I thank God, whom I serve from *my* forefathers with pure conscience, that without ceasing I have remembrance of thee in my prayers night and day;

4 Greatly desiring to see thee, being mindful of thy tears, that I may be filled with joy;

5 When I call to remembrance the unfeigned faith that is in thee, which dwelt first in thy grandmother Lois, and thy mother Eunice; and I am persuaded that in thee also.

6 Wherefore I put thee in remembrance that thou stir up the gift of God, which is in thee by the putting on of my hands.

7 For God hath not given us the spirit of fear; but of power, and of love, and of a sound mind.

8 Be not thou therefore ashamed of the testimony of our Lord, nor of me his prisoner: but be thou partaker of the afflictions of the gospel according to the power of God;

9 Who hath saved us, and called *us* with an holy calling, not according to our works, but according to his own purpose and grace, which was given us in Christ Jesus before the world began,

10 But is now made manifest by the appearing of our Saviour Jesus Christ, who hath abolished death, and hath brought life and immortality to light through the gospel:

11 Whereunto I am appointed a preacher, and an apostle, and a teacher of the Gentiles.

12 For the which cause I also suffer these things: nevertheless I am not ashamed: for I know whom I have believed, and am persuaded that he is able to keep that which I have committed unto him against that day.

13 Hold fast the form of sound words,

which thou hast heard of me, in faith and love which is in Christ Jesus.

14 That good thing which was committed unto thee keep by the Holy Ghost which dwelleth in us.

15 This thou knowest, that all they which are in Asia be turned away from me; of whom are Phygellus and Hermogenes.

16 The Lord give mercy unto the house of Onesiphorus; for he oft refreshed me, and was not ashamed of my chain:

17 But, when he was in Rome, he sought me out very diligently, and found *me*.

18 The Lord grant unto him that he may find mercy of the Lord in that day: and in how many things he ministered unto me at Ephesus, thou knowest very well.

CHAPTER 2

The Christian Warfare

1 Thou therefore, my son, be strong in the grace that is in Christ Jesus.

2 And the things that thou hast heard of me among many witnesses, the same commit thou to faithful men, who shall be able to teach others also.

3 Thou therefore endure hardness, as a good soldier of Jesus Christ.

4 No man that warreth entangleth himself with the affairs of *this* life; that he may please him who hath chosen him to be a soldier.

5 And if a man also strive for masteries, *yet* is he not crowned, except he strive lawfully.

6 The husbandman that laboureth must be first partaker of the fruits.

7 Consider what I say; and the Lord give thee understanding in all things.

8 Remember that Jesus Christ of the seed of David was raised from the dead according to my gospel:

9 Wherein I suffer trouble, as an evil doer, *even* unto bonds; but the word of God is not bound.

10 Therefore I endure all things for the elect's sakes, that they may also obtain the salvation which is in Christ Jesus with eternal glory.

Cross References

12 1Tim. 1:2
3 Acts 22:3; 23:1; 24:14; 27:23
5 Acts 16:1; 1Tim. 1:5; 4:6
6 1Thess. 5:19
7 Luke 24:49
8 Rom. 1:16; Eph. 3:1; Phil. 1:7
9 Rom. 3:20; 8:28; 9:11; 16:25; Eph. 1:4; 3:11
10 Rom. 16:26; Heb. 2:14
11 Acts 9:15
12 Eph. 3:1; 1Tim. 6:20; 2Tim. 1:18; 4:8
13 Rom. 2:20; 6:17; Titus 1:9; Heb. 10:23; Rev. 2:25
15 Acts 19:10; 2Tim. 4:10, 16
16 Phile. 1:7
1 Eph. 6:10
2 1Tim. 1:18; Titus 1:9
5 1Cor. 9:25, 26
6 1Cor. 9:10
8 Acts 2:30; 13:23; Rom. 1:3, 4; 2:16; 1Cor. 15:1, 4, 20
9 Acts 9:16; 28:31; Eph. 3:1; 6:19, 20; Phil. 1:7, 13, 14; Col. 4:3, 18; 2Tim. 1:12
10 2Cor. 1:6; Eph. 3:13; Col. 1:24

1:12 that day. This is a reference to the day when present-age believers will be judged at the judgment seat of Christ (Rom. 14:10; 1 Cor. 3:13; 2 Cor. 5:10). This will be a day of judgment and reward for the Church. It will take place in heaven, after the Rapture, while the seven-year Tribulation takes place on earth. When complete, the Bride of Christ (the Church) will be prepared to return with Christ at the Second Coming (Rev. 19:1–16). A few verses later

Paul references "that day" again (1:18; also in 4:8).

1:18 that day. Paul's reference to Onesiphorus finding mercy at the judgment seat of Christ indicates what will be available for believers at that time. This judgment does not relate to salvation from one's sins, but instead to the rewarding of believers. (See the note on verse 12.)

11 *It is* a faithful saying: For if we be dead with *him*, we shall also live with *him*:

12 If we suffer, we shall also reign with *him*: if we deny *him*, he also will deny us:

13 If we believe not, *yet* he abideth faithful: he cannot deny himself.

Be a Good Example

14 Of these things put *them* in remembrance, charging *them* before the Lord that they strive not about words to no profit, *but* to the subverting of the hearers.

15 Study to shew thyself approved unto God, a workman that needeth not to be ashamed, rightly dividing the word of truth.

16 But shun profane *and* vain babblings: for they will increase unto more ungodliness.

17 And their word will eat as doth a canker: of whom is Hymenaeus and Philetus;

18 Who concerning the truth have erred, saying that the resurrection is past already; and overthrow the faith of some.

19 Nevertheless the foundation of God standeth sure, having this seal, The Lord knoweth them that are his. And, Let every one that nameth the name of Christ depart from iniquity.

20 But in a great house there are not only vessels of gold and of silver, but also of wood and of earth; and some to honour, and some to dishonour.

21 If a man therefore purge himself from these, he shall be a vessel unto honour, sanctified, and meet for the master's use, *and* prepared unto every good work.

22 Flee also youthful lusts: but follow righteousness, faith, charity, peace, with them that call on the Lord out of a pure heart.

23 But foolish and unlearned questions avoid, knowing that they do gender strifes.

24 And the servant of the Lord must not

strive; but be gentle unto all *men*, apt to teach, patient,

25 In meekness instructing those that oppose themselves; if God peradventure will give them repentance to the acknowledging of the truth;

26 And *that* they may recover themselves out of the snare of the devil, who are taken captive by him at his will.

Chapter 3
The Last Times

1 This know also, that in the last days perilous times shall come.

2 For men shall be lovers of their own selves, covetous, boasters, proud, blasphemers, disobedient to parents, unthankful, unholy,

3 Without natural affection, trucebreakers, false accusers, incontinent, fierce, despisers of those that are good,

4 Traitors, heady, highminded, lovers of pleasures more than lovers of God;

5 Having a form of godliness, but denying the power thereof: from such turn away.

6 For of this sort are they which creep into houses, and lead captive silly women laden with sins, led away with divers lusts,

7 Ever learning, and never able to come to the knowledge of the truth.

8 Now as Jannes and Jambres withstood Moses, so do these also resist the truth: men of corrupt minds, reprobate concerning the faith.

9 But they shall proceed no further: for their folly shall be manifest unto all *men*, as theirs also was.

Live a Godly Life

10 But thou hast fully known my doctrine, manner of life, purpose, faith, longsuffering, charity, patience,

Cross-references

11 Rom. 6:5, 8
12 Matt. 10:33; Mark 8:38; Luke 12:9
14 1Tim. 1:4; 5:21; 6:4, 13
16 1Tim. 4:7; 6:20
17 1Tim. 1:20
18 1Cor. 15:12; 1Tim. 6:21
19 Nah. 1:7; Matt. 24:24; John 10:14, 27
20 Rom. 9:21
21 Isa. 52:11
22 1Cor. 1:2; 1Tim. 1:5; 4:12; 6:11
23 1Tim. 1:4; 4:7; 6:4; Titus 3:9
25 Gal. 6:1
26 1Tim. 3:7
1 2Pet. 3:3
2 Jude 1:10, 16
3 Rom. 1:31
4 Jude 1:4, 19
5 2Thess. 3:6
6 Titus 1:11
7 1Tim. 2:4
9 Ex. 7:12; 8:18; 9:11
10 Phil. 2:22; 1Tim. 4:6

2:12 we shall also reign with him. One of the things that God has in store for believers is that we will reign with Christ during the Millennial Kingdom (Rev. 1:6; 3:21; 5:10; 20:4, 6).

2:17–18 saying that the resurrection is past already. Paul mentions the specific false teaching of Hymenaeus and Philetus, which likely sprang from an early form of Gnostic teaching that the resurrection ("rapture" of the dead saints) was spiritual, not physical, and thus past. It is impossible for there to be a spiritual resurrection since "resurrection" by definition always refers to the raising of the body. In our own day, those known as "full preterists" also teach a past, spiritual resurrection. (See the article, "Four Approaches to Prophetic Fulfillment" by Thomas Ice.)

3:1–9 the last days. Since phrases like "latter days," "latter times" are used in different contexts they may refer to differing time periods, depending on their contexts. "Last days" in this context refers to the end of the current Church Age. The perilous times that Paul speaks of do not refer to behavior in the world, since the world in many regards has always been this way. Instead, Paul speaks of these characteristics that have infiltrated into the Church from the world. This is one of the major New Testament passages that teach a spreading apostasy throughout the Church in the Last Days. Paul's instruction to true believers concerning apostate people is to "turn away," which means to disregard and disassociate with them. God has set a limit as to how much apostasy and unbelief He will allow to spread within His Church.

Deception in the Last Days

By Dave Hunt

The Bible tells us that God, through His prophets, provides signs of the times (Isa. 7:14). Jesus rebuked the Pharisees for not knowing and recognizing the prophetic signs of the Messiah's first coming (see Luke 12:56). It was therefore reasonable for Christ's disciples to ask Him, "What shall be the sign of thy coming?" (Matt. 24:3). In response, Christ gave a number of signs that would herald the nearness of His second coming.

The very first sign He offered was religious deception, and He emphasized this sign above all others: "Take heed that no man deceive you. For many shall come in my name, saying, I am Christ; and shall deceive many. And many false prophets shall rise, and shall deceive many. For there shall arise false christs, and false prophets, and shall shew great signs and wonders; insomuch that, if it were possible, they shall deceive the very elect" (Matt. 24:4–5, 11, 24).

Christ is not referring to this worldwide deception coming from rival religions such as Buddhism, Hinduism, or Islam. The "false christs, and false prophets" are professing Christians inasmuch as they claim to have done miracles in Christ's name. Not only do these false prophets deceive others, but they also seem themselves to be deceived. These "false christs" could include some contemporary religious leaders who major in the "miraculous."

> *"Take heed that no man deceive you."*

This Scripture passage adds insight into a major sign of the nearness of the Second Coming, as the deception by false prophets will involve an improper emphasis upon the seemingly miraculous. Christ's warning of a false signs and wonders movement in the Last Days was repeated by the apostle Paul, using similar language: "Let no man deceive you by any means: for that day [the day of Christ] shall not come, except there come a falling away [apostasy] first . . ." (2 Thess. 2:3). Paul explained the nature of this apostasy to Timothy as he compared the apostate church to that of Jannes and Jambres (see 2 Tim. 3:1, 8). Jannes and Jambres were the magicians in Pharaoh's court who, through the power of Satan, duplicated to a point the miracles that God did through Moses and Aaron. As in the days of Moses, the major opposition to the truth in the Last Days will neither be atheists nor skeptics, but those deceiving multitudes through signs and wonders.

That this movement which perverts the truth through false signs and wonders will help to prepare an apostate church to embrace the Antichrist seems clear: "Even him, whose coming is after the working of Satan with all power and signs and lying wonders . . . God shall send them strong delusion . . . That they all might be damned who believed not the truth" (2 Thess. 2:9, 11–12).

Paul's final warning to Timothy leaves no doubt that the Church at Christ's return will have been corrupted through the rejection of sound doctrine both by the many false prophets and those who love their ways and encourage and support them (see 2 Tim. 4:2–4).

Remember the exhortation of the Holy Spirit through Jude, which is all the more urgent in our day: "Beloved . . . earnestly contend for the faith which was once delivered unto the saints. For there are certain men crept in [to the church] unawares . . . denying the only Lord God, and our Lord Jesus Christ" (Jude 1:3–4).

11 Persecutions, afflictions, which came unto me at Antioch, at Iconium, at Lystra; what persecutions I endured: but out of *them* all the Lord delivered me.

12 Yea, and all that will live godly in Christ Jesus shall suffer persecution.

13 But evil men and seducers shall wax worse and worse, deceiving, and being deceived.

14 But continue thou in the things which thou hast learned and hast been assured of, knowing of whom thou hast learned *them*;

15 And that from a child thou hast known the holy scriptures, which are able to make thee wise unto salvation through faith which is in Christ Jesus.

The Scriptures Are Inspired

16 All scripture *is* given by inspiration of God, and *is* profitable for doctrine, for reproof, for correction, for instruction in righteousness:

17 That the man of God may be perfect, throughly furnished unto all good works.

CHAPTER 4

1 I charge *thee* therefore before God, and the Lord Jesus Christ, who shall judge the quick and the dead at his appearing and his kingdom;

2 Preach the word; be instant in season, out of season; reprove, rebuke, exhort with all longsuffering and doctrine.

3 For the time will come when they will not endure sound doctrine; but after their own lusts shall they heap to themselves teachers, having itching ears;

4 And they shall turn away *their* ears from the truth, and shall be turned unto fables.

5 But watch thou in all things, endure afflictions, do the work of an evangelist, make full proof of thy ministry.

6 For I am now ready to be offered, and the time of my departure is at hand.

7 I have fought a good fight, I have finished *my* course, I have kept the faith:

8 Henceforth there is laid up for me a crown of righteousness, which the Lord, the righteous judge, shall give me at that day: and not to me only, but unto all them also that love his appearing.

Paul's Personal Closing Words

9 Do thy diligence to come shortly unto me:

10 For Demas hath forsaken me, having loved this present world, and is departed unto Thessalonica; Crescens to Galatia, Titus unto Dalmatia.

11 Only Luke is with me. Take Mark, and bring him with thee: for he is profitable to me for the ministry.

12 And Tychicus have I sent to Ephesus.

13 The cloke that I left at Troas with Carpus, when thou comest, bring *with thee,* and the books, *but* especially the parchments.

Cross references

11 Ps. 34:19; Acts 13:45, 50; 14:2, 5, 19; 2Cor. 1:10
12 Ps. 34:19; Matt. 16:24; John 17:14; Acts 14:22
13 2Thess. 2:11; 1Tim. 4:1; 2Tim. 2:16
16 Rom. 15:4; 2Pet. 1:20, 21
1 Acts 10:42
2 Titus 1:13; 2:15
4 Titus 1:14
5 Rom. 15:19; Col. 1:25; 4:17
6 Phil. 1:23; 2:17
7 Phil. 3:14
8 1Pet. 5:4; Rev. 2:10
10 Col. 4:14; Phile. 1:24; 1John 2:15
11 Acts 12:25; 15:37; Col. 4:10, 14; 2Tim. 1:15; Phile. 1:24
12 Acts 20:4; Eph. 6:21; Col. 4:7; Titus 3:12

3:12 Paul predicts that the entire Church Age will be a time of persecution of the world toward believers (John 15:18–26; 16:33). The only way to avoid such persecution is to not openly live a life pleasing to the Lord. This prophecy has been fulfilled throughout the present age as millions of believers have given their lives for Christ in the face of a hostile world.

3:13 evil men and seducers shall wax worse and worse. The course of the Church Age will be one in which there will always be apostates and false doctrine. With the passing of time, such apostasy will grow increasingly worse.

4:1 at his appearing and his kingdom. Christ's kingdom will not arrive until He personally returns to earth to first judge unbelievers and gather believers in Him into His Millennial Kingdom.

4:3–4 the time will come when they will not endure sound doctrine. Paul resumes the theme of apostasy from chapter three and provides further warnings for the last days of the Church Age. The word "endure" has the basic meaning of "to support" or "hold up," as a foundation sustains the superstructure. Thus, there will come a time when the majority within the Church will not support the teaching of sound or healthy doctrine. The word "lust" means simply "strong desire," but in this context it has a negative connotation. A tolerance of false doctrine originates from the desires or feelings of people who do not want to follow God's Word. These church members are said by Paul to have "itching ears," which means that they want their preachers to speak only pleasantries. They will not want to hear the instruction of sound doctrine, nor will they be satisfied by the Word of God, so they will be attracted to human ideas and fables to fill the void.

4:6 I am now ready to be offered. This is a reference to Paul's impending execution because of His service for Christ. Tradition tells us that the Romans executed Paul within a year after he wrote 2 Timothy, his final epistle.

14 Alexander the coppersmith did me much evil: the Lord reward him according to his works:

15 Of whom be thou ware also; for he hath greatly withstood our words.

16 At my first answer no man stood with me, but all *men* forsook me: *I pray God* that it may not be laid to their charge.

17 Notwithstanding the Lord stood with me, and strengthened me; that by me the preaching might be fully known, and *that* all the Gentiles might hear: and I was delivered out of the mouth of the lion.

14 Acts 19:33
16 Acts 7:60
17 Ps. 22:21
18 Ps. 121:7
19 Acts 18:2

21 2Tim. 4:9

18 And the Lord shall deliver me from every evil work, and will preserve *me* unto his heavenly kingdom: to whom *be* glory for ever and ever. Amen.

19 Salute Prisca and Aquila, and the household of Onesiphorus.

20 Erastus abode at Corinth: but Trophimus have I left at Miletum sick.

21 Do thy diligence to come before winter. Eubulus greeteth thee and Pudens, and Linus, and Claudia, and all the brethren.

22 The Lord Jesus Christ *be* with thy spirit. Grace *be* with you. Amen.

4:14 Paul looks to a future day of judgment when God will right all wrongs.

Titus

Titus was most likely a Gentile from Macedonia (Gal. 2:3) who was led to Christ by Paul (Titus 1:4). Titus was with Paul in Jerusalem (Gal. 2:1) when some dogmatic Jewish brethren insisted that Titus should be circumcised. Paul would not allow Titus to be circumcised (Gal. 2:3–5) because this would have suggested that all non-Jewish Christians were second-class citizens in the Church.

Written between Paul's first and second imprisonments in Rome, this epistle to Titus deals with conditions in the churches on the island of Crete. Titus was left by Paul on the island to "set in order the things that [were] lacking" (1:5) while he went on to Nicopolis on the coast of Greece. Although his name is mentioned thirteen times in other Pauline epistles, Titus is not mentioned in Acts. At varying times, he seems to have been Paul's associate, courier, and representative, and he may have been the leader of the churches on Crete. Later Paul sent him to Dalmatia, the area now known as the Balkan Peninsula (2 Tim. 4:10).

In similar language as 1 Timothy, Paul describes the qualities which should characterize the bishops and elders (1:5–9). These church leaders are to be models for other believers, who are able to stem the tide of error and false doctrines (1:10–16). Two times Paul uses the words "sound doctrine" (1:9; 2:1); twice he uses the phrase, "sound in the faith" (1:13; 2:2), and on one occasion he cites the words, "sound speech" (2:8). An important doctrinal summary appears in 3:4–8, touching on God's mercy, salvation, regeneration, justification, and good works.

Only one verse (2:13) is truly prophetic, speaking of the "blessed hope" of our Lord's return. This verse refers generally to the second coming of Christ, but some see the "blessed hope" as the Rapture and "the glorious appearing" as His descent in glory after the coming Tribulation.

One verse of the 46 verses, or 2 percent of the book is prophetic. No Old Testament quotations appear in Titus.

Author
Paul

Date
A.D. 65

Key Truth
Teaching Sound Doctrine

Historic Time
The Early Growth of the Church in Crete

Key Verse
2:1
But speak thou the things which become sound doctrine.

2%
Prophecy

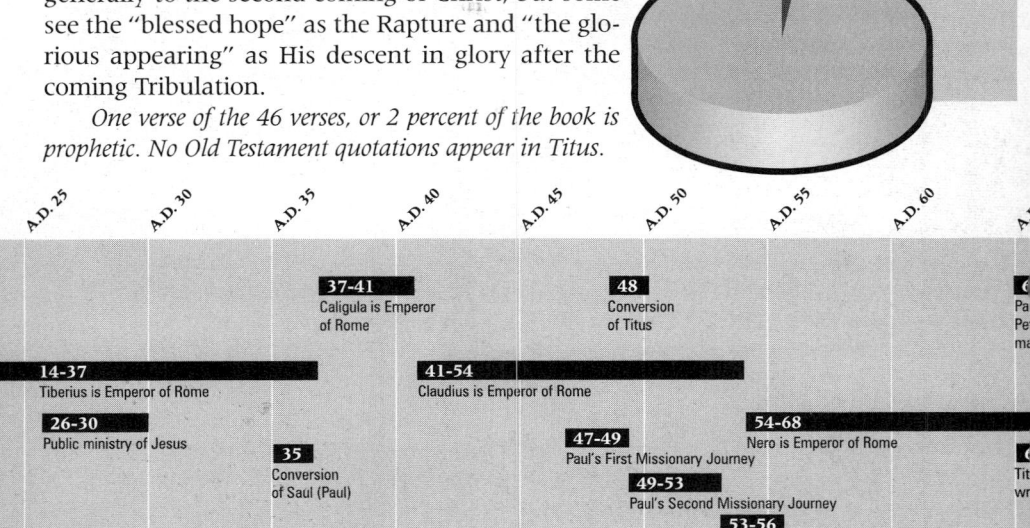

A.D. 25 A.D. 30 A.D. 35 A.D. 40 A.D. 45 A.D. 50 A.D. 55 A.D. 60 A

37-41
Caligula is Emperor of Rome

48
Conversion of Titus

14-37
Tiberius is Emperor of Rome

41-54
Claudius is Emperor of Rome

26-30
Public ministry of Jesus

35
Conversion of Saul (Paul)

47-49
Paul's First Missionary Journey

54-68
Nero is Emperor of Rome

49-53
Paul's Second Missionary Journey

53-56
Paul's Third Missionary Journey

6
Pa
Pe
ma

6
Tit
wr

CHAPTER 1

1 Paul, a servant of God, and an apostle of Jesus Christ, according to the faith of God's elect, and the acknowledging of the truth which is after godliness;

2 In hope of eternal life, which God, that cannot lie, promised before the world began;

3 But hath in due times manifested his word through preaching, which is committed unto me according to the commandment of God our Saviour;

4 To Titus, *mine* own son after the common faith: Grace, mercy, *and* peace, from God the Father and the Lord Jesus Christ our Saviour.

The Qualifications of an Elder

5 For this cause left I thee in Crete, that thou shouldest set in order the things that are wanting, and ordain elders in every city, as I had appointed thee:

6 If any be blameless, the husband of one wife, having faithful children not accused of riot or unruly.

7 For a bishop must be blameless, as the steward of God; not self-willed, not soon angry, not given to wine, no striker, not given to filthy lucre;

8 But a lover of hospitality, a lover of good men, sober, just, holy, temperate;

9 Holding fast the faithful word as he hath been taught, that he may be able by sound doctrine both to exhort and to convince the gainsayers.

10 For there are many unruly and vain talkers and deceivers, specially they of the circumcision:

11 Whose mouths must be stopped, who subvert whole houses, teaching things which they ought not, for filthy lucre's sake.

12 One of themselves, *even* a prophet of their own, said, The Cretians *are* alway liars, evil beasts, slow bellies.

13 This witness is true. Wherefore rebuke them sharply, that they may be sound in the faith;

14 Not giving heed to Jewish fables, and commandments of men, that turn from the truth.

15 Unto the pure all things *are* pure: but unto them that are defiled and unbelieving *is* nothing pure; but even their mind and conscience is defiled.

16 They profess that they know God; but in works they deny *him,* being abominable, and disobedient, and unto every good work reprobate.

CHAPTER 2
Teach Sound Doctrine

1 But speak thou the things which become sound doctrine:

2 That the aged men be sober, grave, temperate, sound in faith, in charity, in patience.

3 The aged women likewise, that *they be* in behaviour as becometh holiness, not false accusers, not given to much wine, teachers of good things;

4 That they may teach the young women to be sober, to love their husbands, to love their children,

5 *To be* discreet, chaste, keepers at home, good, obedient to their own husbands, that the word of God be not blasphemed.

6 Young men likewise exhort to be sober minded.

7 In all things shewing thyself a pattern of good works: in doctrine *shewing* uncorruptness, gravity, sincerity,

8 Sound speech, that cannot be condemned; that he that is of the contrary part may be ashamed, having no evil thing to say of you.

9 *Exhort* servants to be obedient unto their own masters, *and* to please *them* well in all *things*; not answering again;

10 Not purloining, but shewing all good fidelity; that they may adorn the doctrine of God our Saviour in all things.

11 For the grace of God that bringeth salvation hath appeared to all men,

12 Teaching us that, denying ungodliness

---

1 1Tim. 3:16; 6:3; 2Tim. 2:25
2 Num. 23:19; Rom. 16:25
3 1Thess. 2:4; 1Tim. 1:1, 11; 2:3
4 Rom. 1:2; 2Cor. 2:13; 4:13; 7:13; 8:6, 16, 23; 12:18
5 Acts 14:23
6 1Tim. 3:2, 4, 12
7 Lev. 10:9; Eph. 5:18; 1Tim. 3:3, 8
7 1Tim. 3:3, 8; 1Pet. 5:2
10 Acts 15:1; Rom. 16:18
12 Acts 17:28
13 2Cor. 13:10
15 Luke 11:39-41; Rom. 14:14, 20, 23
16 Rom. 1:28
1 1Tim. 1:10; 6:3; 2Tim. 1:13; Titus 1:9
3 1Tim. 2:9, 10; 3:11; 1Pet. 3:3, 4
5 1Cor. 14:34; Rom. 2:24; 1Pet. 3:1, 5
7 Eph. 6:24
8 Neh. 5:9; 2Thess. 3:14
9 1Pet. 2:18
10 Matt. 5:16
11 Luke 3:6; John 1:9; Rom. 5:15

2:11 appeared. Twice in this context Paul speaks of Christ's appearance in history. The first time Christ came in grace to save men from their sins; the second time He will come in glory (v. 13) to reign.

2:12–13 The appearance of the grace of God is to produce two results in the lives of believers: First, we are to resist the evil temptations of this world, living godly lives in this present age. Second, we are to look for Christ's return at the Rapture. Paul reminded Timothy that there is a special crown waiting for "all them also that love his appearing" (see 2 Tim. 4:8). Believers who are looking for Christ, Paul says, will be motivated to live a godly life in the present. The "blessed hope" is a reference to the rapture of the Church that could come at any moment. That Christ could return without warning, at any moment is indeed the "blessed hope" of the Church. It will be

The Timing of the Rapture

By Paul Benware

The "Rapture" is a marvelous meeting in the air when the Lord Jesus Christ returns from heaven and removes the true Church from the world (1 Thess. 4:13–18). When will the Rapture take place? Five prominent viewpoints have attempted to answer this question. These arguments place the Rapture in varying relationships to the Tribulation period.

First, there is the **pretribulational rapture** view, which places the Rapture before the Tribulation period begins. This view declares that the Church will not experience any part of the seven years of Tribulation since it will be with the Lord. Pretribulationalists arrive at this position by maintaining a clear distinction between God's dealings with Christ's Church and with the nation of Israel. Supporters of this view believe that God will remove the Church from the world, and then His focus will return to Israel and the Old Testament covenants He made with that nation. Furthermore, pretribulationalists conclude that since the Church is exempt from the wrath of God (1 Thess. 1:9–10; 5:9), it will not be on earth during those seven years of the Tribulation. This view also holds to the concept of the imminent ("any moment") return of the Lord Jesus to remove the Church out of the world, meaning that there are no signs or events that must take place prior to the Rapture. Hence, the pretribulational timing of the Rapture is more consistent with the texts of Scripture than the other views.

> *There are no signs or events that must take place prior to the Rapture.*

A second view concerning the timing of the Rapture is the **posttribulational rapture** view. Those holding to this view believe that the Rapture will occur after the Tribulation comes upon the world. Therefore, this view teaches the Church is on the earth during the Tribulation and will experience the tragic events of that period. Posttribulationalists do not see the Rapture and the second coming of Christ as two separate events. They teach that since the Church is told in Scripture to anticipate persecution and trouble, it should not expect to be exempted from the Tribulation period. Generally, this view denies Christ's imminent return and does not make a clear distinction between the Church and the nation of Israel.

A third view is the **midtribulational rapture** view, which places the Rapture at the halfway point of the Tribulation; or, three and one-half years into that period. It holds that the Church is exempt from the wrath of God, but that this wrath will only occur during the last half of the Tribulation. Midtribulationalists see the Rapture as a distinct event from the Second Coming, but deny the doctrine of the imminent return of Christ.

A fourth rapture interpretation is sometimes called the **partial rapture** view. This view claims that the rapture of the Church will occur before the Tribulation. Partial rapture supporters do not believe that all Christians will be taken out of the world by the Lord Jesus at the Rapture, but that the Lord will remove only the righteous, faithful Christians. According to this view, carnal believers will be left on the earth to experience the Tribulation.

The fifth view of the Rapture is often referred to as the **pre-wrath rapture** view. This more recent view holds that the Church is exempt from the wrath of God but limits the time of wrath to a short period of time near the end of the Tribulation period, perhaps lasting only a year and a half. Supporters of this view believe that the Rapture will take place about three fourths of the way through the seven-year Tribulation period.

and worldly lusts, we should live soberly, righteously, and godly, in this present world;

The Rapture of the Church

13 Looking for that blessed hope, and the glorious appearing of the great God and our Saviour Jesus Christ;

14 Who gave himself for us, that he might redeem us from all iniquity, and purify unto himself a peculiar people, zealous of good works.

15 These things speak, and exhort, and rebuke with all authority. Let no man despise thee.

CHAPTER 3

Exhortation to Good Works

1 Put them in mind to be subject to principalities and powers, to obey magistrates, to be ready to every good work,

2 To speak evil of no man, to be no brawlers, *but* gentle, shewing all meekness unto all men.

3 For we ourselves also were sometimes foolish, disobedient, deceived, serving divers lusts and pleasures, living in malice and envy, hateful, *and* hating one another.

4 But after that the kindness and love of God our Saviour toward man appeared,

5 Not by works of righteousness which we have done, but according to his mercy he saved us, by the washing of regeneration, and renewing of the Holy Ghost;

13 Phil. 3:20; Col. 1:5, 23; 3:4; Titus 1:2; 3:7; Heb. 9:28; 1Pet. 1:7; 2Pet. 3:12

14 Ex. 15:16; 19:5; Deut. 7:6; 14:2; 26:18; Gal. 1:4; 2:20

1 Rom. 13:1; Col. 1:10

2 Eph. 4:2, 31; Phil. 4:5

4 1Tim. 2:3; Titus 2:11

5 John 3:3, 5; Rom. 3:20 Eph. 2:4, 8, 9

6 John 1:16

7 Gal. 2:16

9 1Tim. 1:4

10 Matt. 18:17; Rom. 16:17; 2Cor. 13:2

12 Acts 20:4; 2Tim. 4:12

13 Acts 18:24

14 Rom. 15:28; Eph. 4:28; Phil. 1:11; 4:17; Col. 1:10; Titus 3:8; 2Pet. 1:8

6 Which he shed on us abundantly through Jesus Christ our Saviour;

7 That being justified by his grace, we should be made heirs according to the hope of eternal life.

8 *This is* a faithful saying, and these things I will that thou affirm constantly, that they which have believed in God might be careful to maintain good works. These things are good and profitable unto men.

9 But avoid foolish questions, and genealogies, and contentions, and strivings about the law; for they are unprofitable and vain.

10 A man that is an heretick after the first and second admonition reject;

11 Knowing that he that is such is subverted, and sinneth, being condemned of himself.

Conclusion

12 When I shall send Artemas unto thee, or Tychicus, be diligent to come unto me to Nicopolis: for I have determined there to winter.

13 Bring Zenas the lawyer and Apollos on their journey diligently, that nothing be wanting unto them.

14 And let ours also learn to maintain good works for necessary uses, that they be not unfruitful.

15 All that are with me salute thee. Greet them that love us in the faith. Grace *be* with you all. Amen.

---

glorious for the Church because that will be the moment when we will be glorified, thus receiving the transformation of our resurrected bodies in order to be made like Christ (1 John 3:2).

Philemon

The epistle to Philemon is one of four Pauline epistles addressed to an individual rather than a church. (The others are 1 and 2 Timothy and Titus.) The focus of the letter is to give a proper understanding of the Hebrew fugitive law found in Deuteronomy 23:15. The epistle reveals how Paul acted in strict accordance with the requirements of the law in dealing with Onesimus, a slave who had run away from his master, Philemon.

Written by Paul during his first imprisonment in Rome (A.D. 61), this letter was intimately connected with the Epistle to the Colossians, and was sent to the same city. Philemon, a wealthy merchant in Colosse, had been converted through an encounter with Paul in nearby Ephesus during Paul's third missionary journey (Acts 19). The gospel reached the city of Colosse, perhaps through the ministry of Epaphras, who was a resident of the city (Col. 1:7; 4:12).

Onesimus had stolen something from his master (Philemon) and fled to Rome, where he came in contact with the jailed apostle Paul, repented, and was converted. Paul sent him back to Philemon with this letter, in which Paul asks him to forgive and welcome Onesimus as a brother in Christ. The name "Onesimus" means "profitable," and Paul uses a play on words (vv. 10–11), affirming that he was at one time unprofitable but now would be profitable to the cause of Christ because of his conversion. In suggesting that any debt Onesimus might owe be charged to Paul's account, the apostle wisely reminds Philemon that he too had come to Christ through Paul's apostolic ministry (vv. 15–20).

The epistle demonstrates the courtesy, graciousness, and tact of the aging apostle; and we can easily believe that the letter attained its objective. It also reveals the manner in which the early Church operated (in houses) and practiced true Christian brotherhood.

Only this personal epistle and 3 John do not contain references to future events or any other prophetic overtones. Philemon also contains no Old Testament quotations, though it does contain an allusion to Deuteronomy 23:15.

Author
Paul

Date
A.D. 61

Key Truth
From Slave to Fellow Servant

Historic Time
Conversion of Onesimus in Rome to His Return to Colosse

Key Verse
1:16
Not now as a servant, but above a servant, a brother beloved.

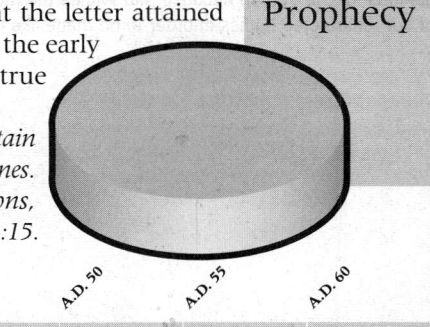

0%
Prophecy

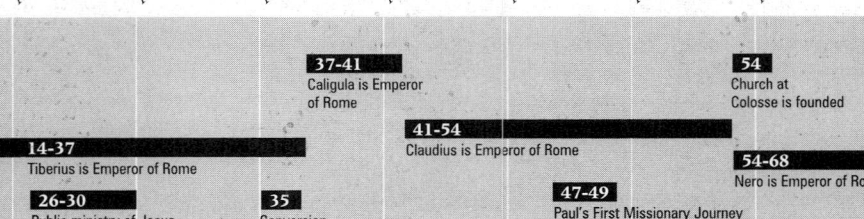

A.D. 25 A.D. 30 A.D. 35 A.D. 40 A.D. 45 A.D. 50 A.D. 55 A.D. 60

37-41
Caligula is Emperor of Rome

54
Church at Colosse is founded

61
Philemon is written

41-54
Claudius is Emperor of Rome

14-37
Tiberius is Emperor of Rome

54-68
Nero is Emperor of Rome

26-30
Public ministry of Jesus

35
Conversion of Saul (Paul)

47-49
Paul's First Missionary Journey

49-53
Paul's Second Missionary Journey

53-56
Paul's Third Missionary Journey

CHAPTER 1

1 Paul, a prisoner of Jesus Christ, and Timothy *our* brother, unto Philemon our dearly beloved, and fellow labourer,
2 And to *our* beloved Apphia, and Archippus our fellow soldier, and to the church in thy house:
3 Grace to you, and peace, from God our Father and the Lord Jesus Christ.

Paul's Expression of Thanksgiving

4 I thank my God, making mention of thee always in my prayers,
5 Hearing of thy love and faith, which thou hast toward the Lord Jesus, and toward all saints;
6 That the communication of thy faith may become effectual by the acknowledging of every good thing which is in you in Christ Jesus.
7 For we have great joy and consolation in thy love, because the bowels of the saints are refreshed by thee, brother.

Onesimus

8 Wherefore, though I might be much bold in Christ to enjoin thee that which is convenient,
9 Yet for love's sake I rather beseech *thee*, being such a one as Paul the aged, and now also a prisoner of Jesus Christ.
10 I beseech thee for my son Onesimus, whom I have begotten in my bonds:
11 Which in time past was to thee unprofitable, but now profitable to thee and to me:

1 Phil. 2:25; 2Tim. 1:8; Phile. 1:9

2 Rom. 16:5; Phil. 2:25; Col. 4:17

5 Eph. 1:15; Col. 1:4

6 Phil. 1:9, 11

7 2Cor. 7:13; 2Tim. 1:16

8 1Thess. 2:6

13 1Cor. 16:17; Phil. 2:30

14 2Cor. 9:7

15 Gen. 45:5, 8

16 1Tim. 6:2

21 2Cor. 7:16

22 2Cor. 1:11; Phil. 1:25; 2:24

23 Col. 1:7; 4:12

24 Acts 12:12, 25; 19:29; 27:2; Col. 4:10, 14; 2Tim. 4:11

25 2Tim. 4:22

12 Whom I have sent again: thou therefore receive him, that is, mine own bowels:
13 Whom I would have retained with me, that in thy stead he might have ministered unto me in the bonds of the gospel:
14 But without thy mind would I do nothing; that thy benefit should not be as it were of necessity, but willingly.
15 For perhaps he therefore departed for a season, that thou shouldest receive him for ever;
16 Not now as a servant, but above a servant, a brother beloved, specially to me, but how much more unto thee, both in the flesh and in the Lord?
17 If thou count me therefore a partner, receive him as myself.
18 If he hath wronged thee, or oweth *thee* ought, put that on mine account;
19 I Paul have written *it* with mine own hand, I will repay *it*: albeit I do not say to thee how thou owest unto me even thine own self besides.
20 Yea, brother, let me have joy of thee in the Lord: refresh my bowels in the Lord.
21 Having confidence in thy obedience I wrote unto thee, knowing that thou wilt also do more than I say.
22 But withal prepare me also a lodging: for I trust that through your prayers I shall be given unto you.
23 There salute thee Epaphras, my fellow prisoner in Christ Jesus;
24 Mark, Aristarchus, Demas, Luke, my fellow labourers.
25 The grace of our Lord Jesus Christ *be* with your spirit. Amen.

Hebrews

The author of the epistle to the Hebrews is uncertain. Martin Luther suggested that Apollos is the author. Tertullian (writing in A.D. 150–230) said that Hebrews is a letter penned by Barnabas. Others have even suggested that Priscilla (Prisca) or Philip may have drafted this epistle. However, the consensus opinion is that the apostle Paul is the author. Nonetheless, if Paul wrote Hebrews, he went against the pattern of the rest of his epistles by not including his customary salutation and his name.

Author	Uncertain
Date	A.D. 68
Key Truth	Christ Is the Perfect Priest
Historic Time	Church Growth among the Jews Prior to A.D. 70
Key Verse	12:2 Looking unto Jesus the author and finisher of our faith . . .

The purpose of this letter was to reassure first-century Hebrew Christians that their faith in Jesus the Messiah was based on Old Testament prophecies, types, and figures which Jesus fulfilled. The central truth of the message is the priesthood of Christ, which superseded the whole sacrificial system of Judaism. The impending fall of Jerusalem (A.D. 70) and the end of temple sacrifice and worship were literally only months away.

The first section of Hebrews deals with doctrinal truth (chaps. 1—10). Using 102 Old Testament references, two major comparisons are made between Christ and the agents of divine revelation (i.e., prophets and angels) and the agents of redemption (Moses and Aaron). Jesus' high priesthood, based on His own sacrifice, would endure forever. His high priesthood, "after the order of Melchizedek" (5:6, 10; 6:20; 7:11, 17, 21), was not the Levitical order under Aaron, but an eternal priesthood. This priesthood is foreshadowed in Genesis 14:17–20 and prophesied in Psalm 110:1–4.

The remainder of the book of Hebrews is historical and practical, referring back to the great faith victories in the Old Testament and its recurring prophetic theme, "The just shall live by faith" (10:38, cf. Hab. 2:4).

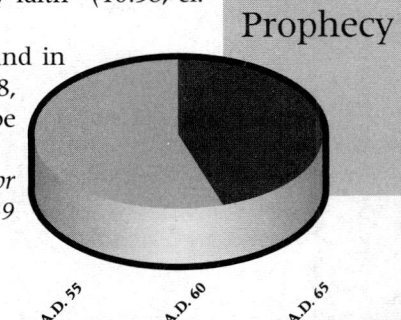

45% Prophecy

Passages dealing with future events are found in Hebrews 9:27–28; 10:14–18, 37; 12:25–29; and 13:8, the last passage indicating that Jesus is and shall be the "same yesterday, and today, and for ever."

Hebrews covers 52 prophetic topics in 137 verses, or 45 percent of its 303 total verses. Hebrews contains 39 direct quotations from the Old Testament.

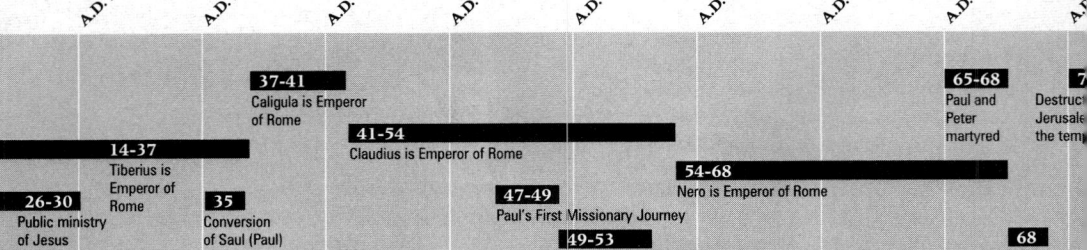

A.D. 30 A.D. 35 A.D. 40 A.D. 45 A.D. 50 A.D. 55 A.D. 60 A.D. 65

37-41 Caligula is Emperor of Rome

14-37 Tiberius is Emperor of Rome

41-54 Claudius is Emperor of Rome

54-68 Nero is Emperor of Rome

26-30 Public ministry of Jesus

35 Conversion of Saul (Paul)

47-49 Paul's First Missionary Journey

49-53 Paul's Second Missionary Journey

53-56 Paul's Third Missionary Journey

65-68 Paul and Peter martyred

68 Hebrews is written

Destruct Jerusale the temp

CHAPTER 1

God Has Spoken through His Son

1 God who at sundry times and in divers manners spake in time past unto the fathers by the prophets,

2 Hath in these last days spoken unto us by *his* Son, whom he hath appointed heir of all things, by whom also he made the worlds;

3 Who being the brightness of *his* glory, and the express image of his person, and upholding all things by the word of his power, when he had by himself purged our sins, sat down on the right hand of the Majesty on high;

Christ's Superiority to Angels

4 Being made so much better than the angels, as he hath by inheritance obtained a more excellent name than they.

5 For unto which of the angels said he at any time, Thou art my son, this day have I begotten thee? And again, I will be to him a Father, and he shall be to me a Son?

6 And again, when he bringeth in the first begotten into the world, he saith, And let all the angels of God worship him.

7 And of the angels he saith, Who maketh his angels spirits, and his ministers a flame of fire.

8 But unto the Son *he saith,* Thy throne, O God, *is* for ever and ever: a sceptre of righteousness *is* the sceptre of thy kingdom.

9 Thou hast loved righteousness, and hated iniquity; therefore God, *even* thy God, hath anointed thee with the oil of gladness above thy fellows.

---

1 Num. 12:6, 8

2 Deut. 4:30; Ps. 2:8; John 1:3, 17; 3:35; 15:15; Rom. 8:17; Eph. 1:10

3 Ps. 110:1; John 1:4, 14; 14:9; Eph. 1:20; Heb. 7:27; 8:1; 9:12, 14, 26; 10:2; 12:2; Rev. 4:11

4 Eph. 1:21; Phil. 2:9, 10

5 Ps. 2:7. 89:26, 27

6 Ps. 97:7; Rev. 1:5

7 Ps. 104:4

8 Ps. 45:6, 7

9 Isa. 61:1

10 Ps. 102:25-28

11 Isa. 34:4; 51:6; Matt. 24:35

13 Ps. 110:1

14 Gen. 19:16; 32:1, 2, 24; Ps. 34:7; 91:11; 103:20, 21; Matt. 18:10

3 Matt. 4:17; Mark 1:14; Luke 1:2

4 Mark 16:20; Acts 2:22, 43

---

10 And, Thou, Lord, in the beginning hast laid the foundation of the earth; and the heavens are the works of thine hands:

11 They shall perish; but thou remainest; and they all shall wax old as doth a garment;

12 And as a vesture shalt thou fold them up, and they shall be changed: but thou art the same, and thy years shall not fail.

13 But to which of the angels said he at any time, Sit on my right hand, until I make thine enemies thy footstool?

14 Are they not all ministering spirits, sent forth to minister for them who shall be heirs of salvation?

CHAPTER 2

1 Therefore we ought to give the more earnest heed to the things which we have heard, lest at any time we should let *them* slip.

2 For if the word spoken by angels was stedfast, and every transgression and disobedience received a just recompence of reward;

3 How shall we escape, if we neglect so great salvation; which at the first began to be spoken by the Lord, and was confirmed unto us by them that heard *him*;

4 God also bearing *them* witness, both with signs and wonders, and with divers miracles, and gifts of the Holy Ghost, according to his own will?

Christ Is Preeminent

5 For unto the angels hath he not put in subjection the world to come, whereof we speak.

1:1–2 The book of Hebrews opens with a powerful statement of Jesus' deity. The author emphasizes that the same God who spoke to the Old Testament prophets has now spoken by His Son, Jesus Christ. By referring to Him as the "appointed heir" of the Father and the one who "made the worlds" (v. 2), the author places Jesus on the same level as the Father. The language of these verses is similar to Psalm 2, to which the author refers in verse 5. In this Psalm, God places His Anointed One upon the messianic throne and grants Him the earth and its people for His inheritance. Thus, the One through whom God has given His final message is also the heir to God's final program for the earth.

1:3 Christ is described by three relative clauses which express the significance of His deity. His alone is the reflection of God's glory, the "express image of his person," and the one who upholds all things by the "word of his power." Each of these is a quality of deity and under-

scores a divine attribute of Jesus. The fact that He is seated at the right hand of God the Father does not imply inactivity but emphasizes the completion of His redemptive work, which is in direct contrast to the Old Testament priest, whose work was never complete.

1:8–13 The author continues to quote from Psalm 45:6–7 and 102:25–27 to emphasize the superiority of Christ. He is the One who fulfills these messianic predictions. Jesus is pictured as sharing in the creation of the world with the Father. John 1:1–2 tells us that He was "in the beginning" with God. Colossians 1:16 emphasizes that all things "in heaven and that are in earth, visible and invisible" were made by Him. Hebrews 1:8–13 focuses on the fact that Jesus is superior to anyone or anything, including angels, in the created realm.

2:5–10 Jesus is pictured as the one who is the fulfillment of David's prophecy in Psalm 8:4–6, which is

6 But one in a certain place testified, saying, What is man, that thou art mindful of him? or the son of man, that thou visitest him?

7 Thou madest him a little lower than the angels; thou crownedst him with glory and honour, and didst set him over the works of thy hands:

8 Thou hast put all things in subjection under his feet. For in that he put all in subjection under him, he left nothing *that is* not put under him. But now we see not yet all things put under him.

9 But we see Jesus, who was made a little lower than the angels for the suffering of death, crowned with glory and honour; that he by the grace of God should taste death for every man.

10 For it became him, for whom *are* all things, and by whom *are* all things, in bringing many sons unto glory, to make the captain of their salvation perfect through sufferings.

11 For both he that sanctifieth and they who are sanctified *are* all of one: for which cause he is not ashamed to call them brethren,

12 Saying, I will declare thy name unto my brethren, in the midst of the church will I sing praise unto thee.

13 And again, I will put my trust in him. And again, Behold I and the children which God hath given me.

14 Forasmuch then as the children are partakers of flesh and blood, he also himself likewise took part of the same; that through death he might destroy him that had the power of death, that is, the devil;

15 And deliver them who through fear of death were all their lifetime subject to bondage.

16 For verily he took not on *him the nature of* angels; but he took on *him* the seed of Abraham.

17 Wherefore in all things it behoved him to be made like unto *his* brethren, that he might be a merciful and faithful high priest in things *pertaining* to God, to make reconciliation for the sins of the people.

18 For in that he himself hath suffered being tempted, he is able to succour them that are tempted.

Chapter 3
Superior to Moses

1 Wherefore, holy brethren, partakers of the heavenly calling, consider the Apostle and High Priest of our profession, Christ Jesus;

2 Who was faithful to him that appointed him, as also Moses *was faithful* in all his house.

3 For this *man* was counted worthy of more glory than Moses, inasmuch as he who hath builded the house hath more honour than the house.

4 For every house is builded by some *man*; but he that built all things *is* God.

5 And Moses verily *was* faithful in all his house, as a servant, for a testimony of those things which were to be spoken after;

6 But Christ as a son over his own house; whose house are we, if we hold fast the confidence and the rejoicing of the hope firm unto the end.

7 Wherefore (as the Holy Ghost saith, Today if ye will hear his voice,

8 Harden not your hearts, as in the provocation, in the day of temptation in the wilderness:

9 When your fathers tempted me, proved me, and saw my works forty years.

10 Wherefore I was grieved with that generation, and said, They do alway err in *their* heart; and they have not known my ways.

11 So I sware in my wrath, They shall not enter into my rest.)

12 Take heed, brethren, lest there be in any of you an evil heart of unbelief, in departing from the living God.

13 But exhort one another daily, while it is called Today; lest any of you be hardened through the deceitfulness of sin.

14 For we are made partakers of Christ, if we hold the beginning of our confidence stedfast unto the end;

15 While it is said, Today if ye will hear his

Cross references:
6 Job 7:17; Ps. 8:4; 144:3
8 Matt. 28:18
9 John 3:16; 12:32; Acts 2:33; Phil. 2:7, 8, 9
10 Luke 13:32; 24:46; Acts 3:15; 5:31; Rom. 11:36
11 Matt. 28:10; Acts 17:26
12 Ps. 22:22, 25
13 Ps. 18:2; Isa. 8:18; 12:2; John 10:29; 17:6, 9-12
14 John 1:14; Rom. 8:3; 1Cor. 15:54, 55; Phil. 2:7; Col. 2:15; 2Tim. 1:10
17 Phil. 2:7; Heb. 4:15; 5:1, 2
18 Heb. 4:15, 16; 5:2; 7:25
1 Rom. 1:7; 15:8; Phil. 3:14; 2Pet. 1:10
3 Zech. 6:12; Matt. 16:18
4 Eph. 2:10; 3:9; Heb. 1:2
5 Ex. 14:31; Num. 12:7; Deut. 3:24; 18:15, 18, 19; Josh. 1:2; 8:31
6 Matt. 10:22; 24:13; Rom. 5:2; 1Pet. 2:5
7 Ps. 95:7; Acts 1:16
15 Heb. 3:7

---

quoted here. The author points out that angels will not be in positions of leadership in the "world to come" (v. 5). In the age to come, angels will have no authority over believers. In fact, we will judge angels (1 Cor. 6:3). Mankind in general was made "lower than the angels" but will be exalted above the angels. Likewise, Jesus assumed a position lower than that of the angels when

He became incarnate as a man. He then makes Psalm 8 a future reality by conquering death for all men. Jesus' humanity does not make Him inferior to the angels. To the contrary, it makes Him superior. Jesus is the "captain" (Gr. *archegos*, "author" or "leader") of our salvation, which He secures by this suffering for our sins.

voice, harden not your hearts, as in the provocation.

16 For some, when they had heard, did provoke: howbeit not all that came out of Egypt by Moses.

17 But with whom was he grieved forty years? *was it* not with them that had sinned, whose carcases fell in the wilderness?

18 And to whom sware he that they should not enter into his rest, but to them that believed not?

19 So we see that they could not enter in because of unbelief.

CHAPTER 4
The Saints' Everlasting Rest

1 Let us therefore fear, lest, a promise being left *us* of entering into his rest, any of you should seem to come short of it.

2 For unto us was the gospel preached, as well as unto them: but the word preached did not profit them, not being mixed with faith in them that heard *it*.

3 For we which have believed do enter into rest, as he said, As I have sworn in my wrath, if they shall enter into my rest: although the works were finished from the foundation of the world.

4 For he spake in a certain place of the seventh *day* on this wise, And God did rest the seventh day from all his works.

5 And in this *place* again, If they shall enter into my rest.

6 Seeing therefore it remaineth that some must enter therein, and they to whom it was first preached entered not in because of unbelief:

7 Again, he limiteth a certain day, saying in David, Today, after so long a time; as it is said, Today if ye will hear his voice, harden not your hearts.

8 For if Jesus had given them rest, then would he not afterward have spoken of another day.

9 There remaineth therefore a rest to the people of God.

10 For he that is entered into his rest, he also hath ceased from his own works, as God *did* from his.

11 Let us labour therefore to enter into that rest, lest any man fall after the same example of unbelief.

12 For the word of God *is* quick, and powerful, and sharper than any two-edged sword, piercing even to the dividing asunder of soul and spirit, and of the joints and marrow, and *is* a discerner of the thoughts and intents of the heart.

13 Neither is there any creature that is not manifest in his sight: but all things *are* naked and opened unto the eyes of him with whom we have to do.

Jesus, the Great High Priest

14 Seeing then that we have a great high priest, that is passed into the heavens, Jesus the Son of God, let us hold fast *our* profession.

15 For we have not an high priest which cannot be touched with the feeling of our infirmities; but was in all points tempted like as *we are, yet* without sin.

16 Let us therefore come boldly unto the throne of grace, that we may obtain mercy, and find grace to help in time of need.

CHAPTER 5

1 For every high priest taken from among men is ordained for men in things *pertaining* to God, that he may offer both gifts and sacrifices for sins:

2 Who can have compassion on the ignorant, and on them that are out of the way; for that he himself also is compassed with infirmity.

3 And by reason hereof he ought, as for the people, so also for himself, to offer for sins.

4 And no man taketh this honour unto himself, but he that is called of God, as *was* Aaron.

5 So also Christ glorified not himself to be made an high priest; but he that said unto him, Thou art my Son, today have I begotten thee.

6 As he saith also in another *place,* Thou *art* a priest for ever after the order of Melchizedek.

7 Who in the days of his flesh, when he had offered up prayers and supplications with strong crying and tears unto him that was able to save him from death, and was heard in that he feared;

8 Though he were a Son, yet learned he obedience by the things which he suffered;

9 And being made perfect, he became the author of eternal salvation unto all them that obey him;

10 Called of God an high priest after the order of Melchizedek.

11 Of whom we have many things to say, and hard to be uttered, seeing ye are dull of hearing.

12 For when for the time ye ought to be teachers, ye have need that one teach you again which *be* the first principles of the

---

16 Num. 14:2, 4, 11, 24, 30; Deut. 1:34, 36, 38

17 Num. 14:22, 29; 26:65; Jude 1:5

18 Num. 14:30; Deut. 1:34, 35

19 Heb. 4:6

1 Heb. 12:15

3 Ps. 95:11

4 Gen. 2:2; Ex. 20:11; 31:17

6 Heb. 3:19

7 Ps. 95:7; Heb. 3:7

12 Prov. 5:4; Isa. 49:2; Jer. 23:29; Rev. 1:16; 2:16

13 Job 26:6; 34:21; Ps. 33:13, 14; 90:8; 139:11, 12; Prov. 15:11

14 Heb. 3:1; 7:26; 9:12, 24; 10:23

15 Isa. 53:3; Luke 22:28; Heb. 2:18; 7:26

16 Eph. 2:18; 3:12; Heb. 10:19, 21, 22

3 Lev. 4:3; 9:7; 16:6, 15, 16, 17; Heb. 7:27; 9:7

4 Ex. 28:1; Num. 16:5, 40; John 3:27

5 Ps. 2:7; John 8:54; Heb. 1:5

6 Ps. 110:4

7 Ps. 22:1; Matt. 26:37, 39, 42, 44, 53; 27:46, 50; Mark 14:33, 36, 39; 15:34, 37; Luke 22:43; John 12:27; 17:1

8 Phil. 2:8

11 Matt. 13:15; John 16:12

12 1Cor. 3:1-3; Heb. 6:1

oracles of God; and are become such as have need of milk, and not of strong meat.

13 For every one that useth milk *is* unskillfull in the word of righteousness: for he is a babe.

14 But strong meat belongeth to them that are of full age, *even* those who by reason of use have their senses exercised to discern both good and evil.

CHAPTER 6

1 Therefore leaving the principles of the doctrine of Christ, let us go on unto perfection; not laying again the foundation of repentance from dead works, and of faith toward God,

2 Of the doctrine of baptisms, and of laying on of hands, and of resurrection of the dead, and of eternal judgment.

3 And this will we do, if God permit.

4 For *it is* impossible for those who were once enlightened, and have tasted of the heavenly gift, and were made partakers of the Holy Ghost,

5 And have tasted the good word of God, and the powers of the world to come,

6 If they shall fall away, to renew them again unto repentance; seeing they crucify to themselves the Son of God afresh, and put *him* to an open shame.

7 For the earth which drinketh in the rain that cometh oft upon it, and bringeth forth herbs meet for them by whom it is dressed, receiveth blessing from God:

8 But that which beareth thorns and briars *is* rejected, and *is* nigh unto cursing; whose end *is* to be burned.

9 But, beloved, we are persuaded better things of you, and things that accompany salvation, though we thus speak.

10 For God *is* not unrighteous to forget your work and labour of love, which ye have shewed toward his name, in that ye have ministered to the saints, and do minister.

11 And we desire that every one of you do shew the same diligence to the full assurance of hope unto the end:

12 That ye be not slothful, but followers of

13 1Cor. 13:11; 14:20; Eph. 4:14; 1Pet. 2:2

14 Isa. 7:15

1 Phil. 3:12-14

2 Acts 8:14-17; 19:4, 6, 6; 17:31, 32; 24:25; Rom. 2:16

3 Acts 18:21; 1Cor. 4:19

4 Matt. 12:31, 32; John 4:10; 6:32; Gal. 3:2, 5; Eph. 2:8

Heb. 2:4; 10:26, 32; 2Pet. 2:20, 21; 1John 5:16

5 Heb. 2:5

6 Heb. 10:29

7 Ps. 65:10

8 Isa. 5:6

10 Prov. 14:31; Matt. 10:42; 25:40; John 13:20; 1Thess. 1:3; 2Thess. 1:6, 7

11 Col. 2:2; Heb. 3:6, 14

12 Heb. 10:36

13 Gen. 22:16, 17; Ps. 105:9; Luke 1:73

16 Ex. 22:11

17 Rom. 11:29; Heb. 11:9

19 Lev. 16:15

1 Gen. 14:18

4 Gen. 14:20

5 Num. 18:21, 26

them who through faith and patience inherit the promises.

God Keeps His Promises

13 For when God made promise to Abraham, because he could swear by no greater, he sware by himself,

14 Saying, Surely blessing I will bless thee, and multiplying I will multiply thee.

15 And so, after he had patiently endured, he obtained the promise.

16 For men verily swear by the greater: and an oath for confirmation *is* to them an end of all strife.

17 Wherein God, willing more abundantly to shew unto the heirs of promise the immutability of his counsel, confirmed *it* by an oath:

18 That by two immutable things, in which *it was* impossible for God to lie, we might have a strong consolation, who have fled for refuge to lay hold upon the hope set before us:

19 Which *hope* we have as an anchor of the soul, both sure and stedfast, and which entereth into that within the veil;

20 Whither the forerunner is for us entered, *even* Jesus, made an high priest for ever after the order of Melchizedek.

CHAPTER 7
Superior to Melchizedec

1 For this Melchizedek, king of Salem, priest of the most high God, who met Abraham returning from the slaughter of the kings, and blessed him;

2 To whom also Abraham gave a tenth part of all; first being by interpretation King of righteousness, and after that also King of Salem, which is, King of peace;

3 Without father, without mother, without descent, having neither beginning of days, nor end of life; but made like unto the Son of God; abideth a priest continually.

4 Now consider how great this man *was*, unto whom even the patriarch Abraham gave the tenth of the spoils.

5 And verily they that are of the sons of

7:1–3 Melchizedek. This individual appears briefly in the Old Testament as a prophetic type of Christ. His name, "King of righteousness," and his title, "King of peace," both picture the ministry of Christ. By emphasizing the silence of the Old Testament passage (Gen. 14:18–20), the author establishes many of the parallels within the typology. Since there was no record of Melchizedek's parents or descendents, he serves as a picture of the priesthood of Christ which was promised in Psalm 110:4. Normally, genealogy was essential to a priest (cf. Ezra 2:62; Neh. 7:64). Melchizedek was without beginning or ending due to silence. Christ is such due to His divine and eternal nature. Melchizedek was "made like," or resembles, the Son of God in that he pictures Him in advance as a prophetic type of Christ.

Levi, who receive the office of the priesthood, have a commandment to take tithes of the people according to the law, that is, of their brethren, though they come out of the loins of Abraham:

6 But he whose descent is not counted from them received tithes of Abraham, and blessed him that had the promises.

7 And without all contradiction the less is blessed of the better.

8 And here men that die receive tithes; but there he *receiveth them,* of whom it is witnessed that he liveth.

9 And as I may so say, Levi also, who receiveth tithes, payed tithes in Abraham.

10 For he was yet in the loins of his father, when Melchizedek met him.

11 If therefore perfection were by the Levitical priesthood, (for under it the people received the law,) what further need *was there* that another priest should rise after the order of Melchizedek, and not be called after the order of Aaron?

12 For the priesthood being changed, there is made of necessity a change also of the law.

13 For he of whom these things are spoken pertaineth to another tribe, of which no man gave attendance at the altar.

14 For *it is* evident that our Lord sprang out of Judah; of which tribe Moses spake nothing concerning priesthood.

15 And it is yet far more evident: for that after the similitude of Melchizedek there ariseth another priest,

16 Who is made, not after the law of a carnal commandment, but after the power of an endless life.

17 For he testifieth, Thou *art* a priest for ever after the order of Melchizedek.

18 For there is verily a disannulling of the commandment going before for the weakness and unprofitableness thereof.

19 For the law made nothing perfect, but the bringing in of a better hope *did;* by the which we draw nigh unto God.

20 And inasmuch as not without an oath *he was made priest:*

21 (For those priests were made without an oath; but this with an oath by him that said unto him, The Lord sware and will not repent, Thou *art* a priest for ever after the order of Melchizedek:)

22 By so much was Jesus made a surety of a better testament.

23 And they truly were many priests, because they were not suffered to continue by reason of death:

24 But this *man,* because he continueth ever, hath an unchangeable priesthood.

25 Wherefore he is able also to save them to the uttermost that come unto God by him, seeing he ever liveth to make intercession for them.

26 For such an high priest became us, *who is* holy, harmless, undefiled, separate from sinners, and made higher than the heavens;

27 Who needeth not daily, as those high priests, to offer up sacrifice, first for his own sins, and then for the people's: for this he did once, when he offered up himself.

28 For the law maketh men high priests

Cross-references

6 Gen. 14:19; Rom. 4:13; Gal. 3:16
8 Heb. 5:6; 6:20
11 Gal. 2:21; Heb. 7:18, 19; 8:7
14 Isa. 11:1; Matt. 1:3; Luke 3:33; Rom. 1:3; Rev. 5:5
17 Ps. 110:4; Heb. 5:6, 10; 6:20
18 Rom. 8:3; Gal. 4:9
19 Acts 13:39; Rom. 3:20, 21, 28; 5:2; 8:3
21 Ps. 110:4
22 Heb. 8:6; 9:15; 12:24
25 Rom. 8:34; 1Tim. 2:5; Heb. 9:24; 1John 2:1
26 Eph. 1:20; 4:10; Heb. 4:15; 8:1
27 Lev. 9:7; 16:6, 11, 15; Rom. 6:10; Heb. 5:3; 9:7, 12, 28; 10:12
28 Heb. 2:10; 5:1, 2, 9

The Priesthood of Christ

The author of Hebrews emphasizes the distinctions between the Old Testament sacrifices and the sacrifice of Christ (Melchizedek's priesthood).

AARONIC PRIESTHOOD	MELCHIZEDEK'S PRIESTHOOD
Temporary Priesthood	Permanent Priesthood
Old Covenant	New Covenant
Daily Sacrifices	One-time Sacrifice
Yearly Atonement	Eternal Atonement

7:11–17 Both Aaron and Moses were chosen by God to serve as priests before the Law was given, and Jesus Christ was chosen after the Law was given. The fact that Jesus was from the tribe of Judah would have precluded this serving as a priest except that the completion of the Mosaic Law meant the passing of the levitical priesthood. The Law itself promised another priesthood after the "order of Melchizedek" which would permanently replace the temporary Levitical system (Ps. 110:4).

7:20–21 Jesus is pictured as both the ultimate exception and the ultimate completion of God's promise to raise up an eternal priest (Ps. 110:4) who would offer the ultimate sacrifice for our sins (Heb. 9:11–15; 10:5–14).

7:22 The new covenant is "better" than the old (see 1:4; 7:7, 19; 8:6; 9:23; 10:34; 11:16, 35, 40; 12:24).

which have infirmity; but the word of the oath, which was since the law, *maketh* the Son, who is consecrated for evermore.

CHAPTER 8
Christ Supercedes the Levitical System

1 Now of the things which we have spoken *this is* the sum: We have such an high priest, who is set on the right hand of the throne of the Majesty in the heavens;

2 A minister of the sanctuary, and of the true tabernacle, which the Lord pitched, and not man.

3 For every high priest is ordained to offer gifts and sacrifices: wherefore *it is* of necessity that this man have somewhat also to offer.

4 For if he were on earth, he should not be a priest, seeing that there are priests that offer gifts according to the law:

5 Who serve unto the example and shadow of heavenly things, as Moses was admonished of God when he was about to make the tabernacle: for, See, saith he, *that* thou make all things according to the pattern shewed to thee in the mount.

6 But now hath he obtained a more excellent ministry, by how much also he is the mediator of a better covenant, which was established upon better promises.

Better Promises

7 For if that first *covenant* had been faultless, then should no place have been sought for the second.

8 For finding fault with them, he saith, Behold, the days come, saith the Lord, when I will make a new covenant with the house of Israel and with the house of Judah:

9 Not according to the covenant that I made with their fathers in the day when I took them by the hand to lead them out of the land of Egypt; because they continued

not in my covenant, and I regarded them not, saith the Lord.

10 For this *is* the covenant that I will make with the house of Israel after those days, saith the Lord; I will put my laws into their mind, and write them in their hearts: and I will be to them a God, and they shall be to me a people:

11 And they shall not teach every man his neighbour, and every man his brother, saying, Know the Lord: for all shall know me, from the least to the greatest.

12 For I will be merciful to their unrighteousness, and their sins and their iniquities will I remember no more.

13 In that he saith, A new *covenant,* he hath made the first old. Now that which decayeth and waxeth old *is* ready to vanish away.

CHAPTER 9
A New Covenant

1 Then verily the first *covenant* had also ordinances of divine service, and a worldly sanctuary.

2 For there was a tabernacle made; the first, wherein *was* the candlestick, and the table, and the shewbread; which is called the sanctuary.

3 And after the second veil, the tabernacle which is called the holiest of all;

4 Which had the golden censer, and the ark of the covenant overlaid round about with gold, wherein *was* the golden pot that had manna, and Aaron's rod that budded, and the tables of the covenant;

5 And over it the cherubim of glory shadowing the mercy seat; of which we cannot now speak particularly.

6 Now when these things were thus ordained, the priests went always into the first tabernacle, accomplishing the service *of* God.

7 But into the second *went* the high priest

Cross references (center column)

1 Eph. 1:20; Col. 3:1; Heb. 1:3; 10:12; 12:2

2 Heb. 9:8, 11, 12, 24

3 Eph. 5:2; Heb. 5:1; 9:14

5 Ex. 25:40; 26:30; 27:8; Num. 8:4

6 2Cor. 3:6, 8, 9; Heb. 7:22

8 Jer. 31:31-34

10 Zech. 8:8

11 Isa. 54:13; 1John 6:45; 1John 2:27

12 Rom. 11:27; Heb. 10:17

13 2Cor. 5:17

1 Ex. 25:8

2 Ex. 25:23, 30, 31; 26:1, 35; 40:4; Lev. 24:5, 6

3 Ex. 26:31, 33; 40:3, 21

4 Ex. 16:33, 34; 25:10, 16, 21; 26:33; 34:29; 40:3, 20, 21; Num. 17:10; Deut. 10:2, 5

5 Ex. 25:18, 22; Lev. 16:2; 1Kgs. 8:6, 7

6 Num. 28:3; Dan. 8:11

7 Ex. 30:10; Lev. 16:2, 11, 12, 15, 34; Heb. 5:3; 7:27; 9:25

8:6–13 The superiority of Jesus Christ is further emphasized by the superiority of the new covenant of which He is the Mediator. The new covenant is the last of the biblical covenants and finalizes God's plan of salvation for mankind. The Mosaic covenant was incomplete and could not provide permanent atonement like the eternal atonement of Jesus' blood shed on the cross for our sins. By Christ's sacrifice, the old covenant (Mosaic) was fulfilled and the new covenant was established. The Law was never intended to be God's final program of redemption. Paul says, "It was added...till the seed should come

to whom the promise was made" (Gal. 3:19). This final covenant includes conversion and the ultimate redemption of Israel (cf. Rom. 11:25–26).

9:4 The contents of the ark are symbols of Christ. The table of the Law represents Christ as the only one who fulfilled its precepts perfectly (Matt. 5:17; Rom. 10:4). Aaron's rod that budded foreshadowed the resurrection of Christ (Num. 17:1–10; Heb. 10:4). The pot of manna speaks of Christ as the Bread of Life come down from heaven (John 6:33–35).

alone once every year, not without blood, which he offered for himself, and *for* the errors of the people:

8 The Holy Ghost this signifying, that the way into the holiest of all was not yet made manifest, while as the first tabernacle was yet standing:

9 Which *was* a figure for the time then present, in which were offered both gifts and sacrifices, that could not make him that did the service perfect, as pertaining to the conscience;

10 *Which stood* only in meats and drinks, and divers washings, and carnal ordinances, imposed *on them* until the time of reformation.

The Blood of Christ

11 But Christ being come an high priest of good things to come, by a greater and more perfect tabernacle, not made with hands, that is to say, not of this building;

12 Neither by the blood of goats and calves, but by his own blood he entered in once into the holy place, having obtained eternal redemption *for us.*

13 For if the blood of bulls and of goats, and the ashes of an heifer sprinkling the unclean, sanctifieth to the purifying of the flesh:

14 How much more shall the blood of Christ, who through the eternal Spirit offered himself without spot to God, purge your conscience from dead works to serve the living God?

15 And for this cause he is the mediator of the new testament, that by means of death, for the redemption of the transgressions *that were* under the first testament, they which are called might receive the promise of eternal inheritance.

16 For where a testament *is,* there must also of necessity be the death of the testator.

17 For a testament *is* of force after men are dead: otherwise it is of no strength at all while the testator liveth.

18 Whereupon neither the first *testament* was dedicated without blood.

19 For when Moses had spoken every precept to all the people according to the law, he took the blood of calves and of goats, with water, and scarlet wool, and hyssop, and sprinkled both the book, and all the people,

20 Saying, This *is* the blood of the testament which God hath enjoined unto you.

21 Moreover he sprinkled with blood both the tabernacle, and all the vessels of the ministry.

22 And almost all things are by the law purged with blood; and without shedding of blood is no remission.

A Better Sacrifice

23 *It was* therefore necessary that the patterns of things in the heavens should be purified with these; but the heavenly things themselves with better sacrifices than these.

24 For Christ is not entered into the holy places made with hands, *which are* the figures of the true; but into heaven itself, now to appear in the presence of God for us:

25 Nor yet that he should offer himself often, as the high priest entereth into the holy place every year with blood of others;

26 For then must he often have suffered since the foundation of the world: but now once in the end of the world hath he appeared to put away sin by the sacrifice of himself.

27 And as it is appointed unto men once to die, but after this the judgment:

28 So Christ was once offered to bear the sins of many; and unto them that look for him shall he appear the second time without sin unto salvation.

Cross references

8 John 14:6; Heb. 10:20
9 Gal. 3:21; Heb. 7:18, 19; 10:1, 11
10 Lev. 11:2; Num. 19:7; Eph. 2:15; Col. 2:16, 20
11 Heb. 3:1; 8:2; 10:1
12 Dan. 9:24; Zech. 3:9; Acts 20:28
13 Lev. 16:14, 16; Num. 19:2
14 Luke 1:74; Rom. 1:4; 6:13, 22; Eph. 5:2; Titus 2:14
15 Rom. 3:25; 5:6; 1Tim. 2:5; Heb. 3:1; 1Pet. 3:18
17 Gal. 3:15
19 Ex. 24:5, 6, 8; Lev. 14:4, 6, 7, 49, 51, 52; 16:14, 15, 18
20 Ex. 24:8; Matt. 26:28
21 Ex. 29:12, 36; Lev. 8:15, 19; 16:14-16, 18, 19
26 1Cor. 10:11; Eph. 1:10
27 Gen. 3:19; Eccl. 3:20; Rev. 20:12, 13
28 Matt. 26:28; Rom. 5:15; 6:10; 1Pet. 2:24

9:11–15 In contrast to the closed sanctuary of the earthly temple, Jesus opened the inner sanctuary of the heavenly temple. The reference to the "holy place" should be understood as the Holy of Holies. This passage emphasizes the essentials of the new covenant—a superior temple and an infinitely superior sacrifice. The "ashes of an heifer" (v. 13) refer to the ceremony of cleansing that involved the red heifer (Num. 19). The author's point is that if the rituals of the Old Testament sacrificial system provided ceremonial cleansing, how much more superior was the cleansing provided by Jesus' blood!

9:24–28 Under the Mosaic covenant, the Israelites put away sin by sending the scapegoat out of the camp into the wilderness (cf. Lev. 16:21–22). Under the new covenant, Jesus becomes the fulfillment of this symbolic imagery. He actually takes away the sins of the world by sacrificial death on the cross. The phrase "end of world" refers to the "end of the age," which is contrasted with the "foundation of the world" at creation. Three "appearings" of Christ are noted here: verse 25 refers to His appearing in heaven presently on our behalf; verse 26 refers to His former appearance on earth to bear our sins; and verse 28 refers to His future appearing at the time of His second coming.

CHAPTER 10
Christ's Sacrifice Once for All

1 For the law having a shadow of good things to come, *and* not the very image of the things, can never with those sacrifices which they offered year by year continually make the comers thereunto perfect.

2 For then would they not have ceased to be offered? because that the worshippers once purged should have had no more conscience of sins.

3 But in those *sacrifices there is* a remembrance again *made* of sins every year.

4 For *it is* not possible that the blood of bulls and of goats should take away sins.

5 Wherefore when he cometh into the world, he saith, Sacrifice and offering thou wouldest not, but a body hast thou prepared me:

6 In burnt offerings and *sacrifices* for sin thou hast had no pleasure.

7 Then said I, Lo, I come (in the volume of the book it is written of me,) to do thy will, O God.

8 Above when he said, Sacrifice and offering and burnt offerings and *offering* for sin thou wouldest not, neither hadst pleasure *therein*; which are offered by the law;

9 Then said he, Lo, I come to do thy will, O God. He taketh away the first, that he may establish the second.

10 By the which will we are sanctified through the offering of the body of Jesus Christ once *for all*.

11 And every priest standeth daily ministering and offering oftentimes the same sacrifices, which can never take away sins:

12 But this man, after he had offered one sacrifice for sins for ever, sat down on the right hand of God;

13 From henceforth expecting till his enemies be made his footstool.

14 For by one offering he hath perfected for ever them that are sanctified.

15 *Whereof* the Holy Ghost also is a witness to us: for after that he had said before,

16 This *is* the covenant that I will make with them after those days, saith the Lord, I will put my laws into their hearts, and in their minds will I write them;

17 And their sins and iniquities will I remember no more.

18 Now where remission of these *is*, there *is* no more offering for sin.

The Believer's Access to God

19 Having therefore, brethren, boldness to enter into the holiest by the blood of Jesus,

20 By a new and living way, which he hath consecrated for us, through the veil, that is to say, his flesh;

21 And *having* an high priest over the house of God;

22 Let us draw near with a true heart in full assurance of faith, having our hearts sprinkled from an evil conscience, and our bodies washed with pure water.

23 Let us hold fast the profession of *our* faith without wavering; (for he *is* faithful that promised;)

24 And let us consider one another to provoke unto love and to good works:

25 Not forsaking the assembling of ourselves together, as the manner of some *is*; but exhorting *one another*: and so much the more, as ye see the day approaching.

26 For if we sin wilfully after that we have received the knowledge of the truth, there remaineth no more sacrifice for sins,

27 But a certain fearful looking for of judgment and fiery indignation, which shall devour the adversaries.

28 He that despised Moses' law died without mercy under two or three witnesses:

1 Col. 2:17; Heb. 10:14
3 Lev. 16:21
4 Mic. 6:6, 7
5 Ps. 40:6; 50:8; Isa. 1:11; Jer. 6:20; Amos 5:21, 22
10 John 17:19; Heb. 9:12; 13:12
11 Num. 28:3
12 Col. 3:1; Heb. 1:3
13 Ps. 110:1
14 Heb. 10:1
16 Jer. 31:33, 34
19 Rom. 5:2; Eph. 2:18; 3:12
20 John 10:9; 14:6
22 Ezek. 36:25; 2Cor. 7:1; Eph. 3:12; James 1:6; 1John 3:21
23 1Thess. 5:24; 2Thess. 3:3
25 Acts 2:42; Rom. 13:11; Phil. 4:5
26 Num. 15:30; 2Pet. 2:20, 21
27 Ezek. 36:5; Zeph. 1:18; 3:8; 2Thess. 1:8; Heb. 12:29
28 Deut. 17:2, 6; 19:15; Matt. 18:16; John 8:17

10:5–13 The superiority of Jesus' sacrifice to the Old Testament sacrifices is shown from the prophecy of Psalm 40:6–7, in which the words of David are used typologically of Christ as a conversation between Himself and the Father. The incarnation of Christ in a human body allowed Him to literally die for our sins without corrupting His divine nature. The fact that Jesus "sat down" (v. 12) indicates the finished nature of His sacrificial atonement for our sins. Verses 12–13 are a quotation from Psalm 110:1, which looks forward to the ultimate triumph of the Messiah over His enemies.

10:15–18 Jeremiah 31:33–34 is quoted and attributed to the inspiration of the Holy Spirit as the divine author of the prediction of the new covenant. Since the new covenant promises the removal of sins and the changing of hearts, there is no more need of any further sacrifice. The death of Christ is sufficient forever.

10:25 as ye see the day approaching. The regular and consistent assembling of believers is urged in light of the truth of Jesus' second coming. The regular gathering of the Church is intended to provide encouragement, strength, and a mutual exhortation in view of the day approaching. Our commitment to assemble together as believers testifies to our confidence in Christ's return.

Animal Sacrifices: Past and Future

By John C. Whitcomb

Though commanded by God, animal sacrifices in Israel could never remove spiritual guilt from the offerer (Heb. 10:4, 11). But it is equally erroneous to say that the sacrifices were only teaching symbols given by God to prepare the nation for Messiah and His infinite atonement. From God's perspective, such teaching surely was a major purpose in the sacrificial system; but it could not have been the exclusive purpose from the perspective of Mosaic covenant Israelites.

The Scriptures tell us that something really did happen to the Israelite offerer when he came to the right altar with the appropriate sacrifice and he was expected to know what would happen to him (Lev. 1:4). What happened was temporal, finite, external, and legal; personally and immediately significant, not simply symbolic and/or prophetic.

Now what does all of this indicate with regard to animal sacrifices in the Millennial Temple for Israel under the new covenant? It indicates that future sacrifices will have nothing to do with eternal salvation that comes only through true faith in God. It also indicates that future animal sacrifices will be "effectual" and "expiatory" only in terms of the strict provision for ceremonial (and thus temporal) forgiveness within the theocracy of Israel. Such sacrifices, then, will not be memorial (like the bread and the cup in church communion services), any more than sacrifices in the age of the Mosaic covenant were primarily prospective or prophetic in the understanding of the offerer. The vast majority of people born during the Millennial Age will remain unbelievers (Rev. 20:7–9), needing the protection from the immediate wrath of a holy God that animal sacrifices will provide in accordance with their divine design and function in the Mosaic Law. Ezekiel foresaw, by the Spirit of God, that offerings would remain (Ezek. 45:17), and God told Jeremiah that the Levitical priests would never "want [lack] a man before me to offer burnt offerings, and to kindle [grain] offerings, and to do sacrifice continually" (Jer. 33:18).

> *Animal sacrifices in Israel could never remove spiritual guilt from the offerer.*

How can vital spiritual instruction be accomplished for citizens of the Millennial Kingdom through a system of animal sacrifices? It will be possible for regenerated Israel to attain the divinely intended balance between form and content, lip and heart, hand and soul, within the structures of the new covenant. It is not only possible, but prophetically certain, that millennial animal sacrifices will be used in a God-honoring way (e.g., Ps. 51:15–19; Heb. 11:4) by a regenerated, chosen nation.

Before the heavens and the earth flee away from Him who sits upon the great white throne (Rev. 20:11), God will provide a final demonstration of the validity of animal sacrifices as an instructional and disciplinary instrument for Israel. The entire world will see the true purpose of this system, one that never has and never will function on the level of Calvary's cross, where infinite and eternal guilt was dealt with once and for all. But the sacrificial system did accomplish some very important instructional and disciplinary purposes for Israel under the Mosaic covenant (Gal. 4:1–7), and there is good reason to believe that it will yet again function on the level of purely temporal cleansing and forgiveness during the Millennium under the new covenant (cf. Heb. 9:13).

29 Of how much sorer punishment, suppose ye, shall he be thought worthy, who hath trodden under foot the Son of God, and hath counted the blood of the covenant, wherewith he was sanctified, an unholy thing, and hath done despite unto the Spirit of grace?

30 For we know him that hath said, Vengeance *belongeth* unto me, I will recompense, saith the Lord. And again, The Lord shall judge his people.

31 *It is* a fearful thing to fall into the hands of the living God.

32 But call to remembrance the former days, in which, after ye were illuminated, ye endured a great fight of afflictions;

33 Partly, whilst ye were made a gazingstock both by reproaches and afflictions; and partly, whilst ye became companions of them that were so used.

34 For ye had compassion of me in my bonds, and took joyfully the spoiling of your goods, knowing in yourselves that ye have in heaven a better and an enduring substance.

35 Cast not away therefore your confidence, which hath great recompence of reward.

36 For ye have need of patience, that, after ye have done the will of God, ye might receive the promise.

37 For yet a little while, and he that shall come will come, and will not tarry.

38 Now the just shall live by faith: but if *any man* draw back, my soul shall have no pleasure in him.

39 But we are not of them who draw back unto perdition; but of them that believe to the saving of the soul.

29 Matt. 12:31, 32; 1Cor. 11:29
30 Deut. 32:35, 36
31 Luke 12:5
32 Gal. 3:4; Heb. 6:4; 2John 1:8
32 Phil. 1:29, 30; Col. 2:1
33 Phil. 1:7; 4:14
34 Acts 5:41
35 Matt. 5:12; 10:32
36 Luke 21:19; Gal. 6:9; 1Pet. 1:9
37 Hab. 2:3, 4; Luke 18:8; 2Pet. 3:9
38 Rom. 1:17; Gal. 3:11
39 Acts 16:30, 31
1 Rom. 8:24, 25
3 Gen. 1:1; Ps. 33:6; John 1:3
4 Gen. 4:4, 10
5 Gen. 5:22, 24
7 Gen. 6:13, 22
8 Gen. 12:1, 4
9 Gen. 12:8; 13:3, 18; 18:1, 9

Chapter 11
"By Faith"

1 Now faith is the substance of things hoped for, the evidence of things not seen.

2 For by it the elders obtained a good report.

3 Through faith we understand that the worlds were framed by the word of God, so that things which are seen were not made of things which do appear.

4 By faith Abel offered unto God a more excellent sacrifice than Cain, by which he obtained witness that he was righteous, God testifying of his gifts: and by it he being dead yet speaketh.

5 By faith Enoch was translated that he should not see death; and was not found, because God had translated him: for before his translation he had this testimony, that he pleased God.

6 But without faith *it is* impossible to please *him*: for he that cometh to God must believe that he is, and *that* he is a rewarder of them that diligently seek him.

7 By faith Noah, being warned of God of things not seen as yet, moved with fear, prepared an ark to the saving of his house; by the which he condemned the world, and became heir of the righteousness which is by faith.

8 By faith Abraham, when he was called to go out into a place which he should after receive for an inheritance, obeyed; and he went out, not knowing whither he went.

9 By faith he sojourned in the land of promise, as *in* a strange country, dwelling in tabernacles with Isaac and Jacob, the heirs with him of the same promise:

10:30 The certainty of future judgment is emphasized by quoting Deuteronomy 32:35–36. This was part of Moses' final warning to the Israelites before he died. By repeating this warning to his Jewish readers, the author of Hebrews reminds them of the seriousness of rejecting God's gracious offer of salvation.

10:37 Christians sometimes use the phrase "if the Lord tarry" to refer to the fact that He may not come immediately. But the author of Hebrews emphasizes that Christ "will not tarry" when He comes. While the return of Jesus Christ seems indefinitely delayed, it will occur, suddenly and instantaneously when the time is right for His return.

11:1–3 Faith is described as "substance" and "evidence," not a blind leap into the dark. Biblical faith involves a complete confidence in God. He is pictured here as the One who controls both history and our prophetic destiny. The "worlds" (Gr. *aiona*) refer to the eons of time. God is described as the One who frames time and space. He created the world out of nothing and spoke it into existence instantaneously by His word. By faith, we understand that God is the creator of the universe, the Lord of history, and the author of our prophetic destiny.

11:5 The "translation" of Enoch prefigures the rapture of the believers (cf. Gen. 5:21–24; 1 Thess. 4:13–17). Enoch was taken away instantaneously and dramatically. The Old Testament simply states that he "was not; for God took him" (Gen. 5:24). Others who experienced forms of a rapture in the Bible include Elijah (2 Kings 2:11), Paul (2 Cor. 12:2), and John (Rev. 4:1).

10 For he looked for a city which hath foundations, whose builder and maker *is* God.

11 Through faith also Sara herself received strength to conceive seed, and was delivered of a child when she was past age, because she judged him faithful who had promised.

12 Therefore sprang there even of one, and him as good as dead, *so many* as the stars of the sky in multitude, and as the sand which is by the sea shore innumerable.

13 These all died in faith, not having received the promises, but having seen them afar off, and were persuaded of *them,* and embraced *them,* and confessed that they were strangers and pilgrims on the earth.

14 For they that say such things declare plainly that they seek a country.

15 And truly, if they had been mindful of that *country* from whence they came out, they might have had opportunity to have returned.

16 But now they desire a better *country,* that is, an heavenly: wherefore God is not ashamed to be called their God: for he hath prepared for them a city.

17 By faith Abraham, when he was tried, offered up Isaac: and he that had received the promises offered up his only begotten *son,*

18 Of whom it was said, That in Isaac shall thy seed be called:

19 Accounting that God *was* able to raise *him* up, even from the dead; from whence also he received him in a figure.

20 By faith Isaac blessed Jacob and Esau concerning things to come.

21 By faith Jacob, when he was a dying, blessed both the sons of Joseph; and worshipped, *leaning* upon the top of his staff.

22 By faith Joseph, when he died, made mention of the departing of the children of Israel; and gave commandment concerning his bones.

23 By faith Moses, when he was born, was hid three months of his parents, because they saw *he was* a proper child; and they were not afraid of the king's commandment.

24 By faith Moses, when he was come to years, refused to be called the son of Pharaoh's daughter;

25 Choosing rather to suffer affliction with the people of God, than to enjoy the pleasures of sin for a season;

26 Esteeming the reproach of Christ greater riches than the treasures in Egypt: for he had respect unto the recompence of the reward.

27 By faith he forsook Egypt, not fearing the wrath of the king: for he endured, as seeing him who is invisible.

28 Through faith he kept the passover, and the sprinkling of blood, lest he that destroyed the firstborn should touch them.

29 By faith they passed through the Red sea as by dry *land:* which the Egyptians assaying to do were drowned.

30 By faith the walls of Jericho fell down, after they were compassed about seven days.

31 By faith the harlot Rahab perished not with them that believed not, when she had received the spies with peace.

32 And what shall I more say? for the time would fail me to tell of Gedeon, and *of* Barak, and *of* Samson, and *of* Jephthah; *of* David also, and Samuel, and *of* the prophets:

33 Who through faith subdued kingdoms, wrought righteousness, obtained promises, stopped the mouths of lions,

34 Quenched the violence of fire, escaped the edge of the sword, out of weakness were made strong, waxed valiant in fight, turned to flight the armies of the aliens.

35 Women received their dead raised to life again: and others were tortured, not accepting deliverance; that they might obtain a better resurrection:

36 And others had trial of *cruel* mockings and scourgings, yea, moreover of bonds and imprisonment:

37 They were stoned, they were sawn asunder, were tempted, were slain with the sword: they wandered about in sheepskins and goatskins; being destitute, afflicted, tormented;

38 (Of whom the world was not worthy:) they wandered in deserts, and *in* mountains, and *in* dens and caves of the earth.

39 And these all, having obtained a good

11 Gen. 17:19; 18:11, 14; 21:2
12 Gen. 22:17
13 Gen. 23:4; 47:9; 1Chr. 29:15; Ps. 39:12; 119:19; 1Pet. 1:17; 2:11
16 Phil. 3:20
17 Gen. 22:1, 9; James 2:21
18 Gen. 21:12
20 Gen. 27:27, 39
21 Gen. 47:31; 48:5, 16, 20
22 Gen. 50:24, 25; Ex. 13:19
23 Ex. 1:16, 22; 2:2
24 Ex. 2:10, 11
25 Ps. 84:10
27 Ex. 10:28, 29; 12:37; 13:17, 18
28 Ex. 12:21
29 Ex. 14:22, 29
30 Josh. 6:20
31 Josh. 2:1; 6:23
32 Judg. 4:6; 6:11; 11:1; 12:7; 13:24; 1Sam. 1:20; 12:20; 16:1, 13; 17:45
33 1Sam. 17:34, 35; 2Sam. 7:11; Dan. 6:22
36 Jer. 20:2; 37:15
37 Zech. 13:4; Matt. 3:4; Acts 7:58; 14:19
38 1Kgs. 18:4; 19:9

11:35–40 The "better resurrection" refers to the first resurrection that includes all believers, including both Old Testament and New Testament saints. Old Testament believers look forward to the same resurrection that we do as New Testament believers. While there is a common destiny of all believers at the resurrection, this passage also makes it clear that God's plan for humankind was not complete without New Testament believers for whom He has provided "some better thing" (v. 40). This certainly indicates the unique position of the New Testament believers (the Church) in God's eternal plan of redemption.

report through faith, received not the promise:

40 God having provided some better thing for us, that they without us should not be made perfect.

CHAPTER 12
Exhortations to Follow Christ

1 Wherefore seeing we also are compassed about with so great a cloud of witnesses, let us lay aside every weight, and the sin which doth so easily beset *us*, and let us run with patience the race that is set before us,

2 Looking unto Jesus the author and finisher of *our* faith; who for the joy that was set before him endured the cross, despising the shame, and is set down at the right hand of the throne of God.

3 For consider him that endured such contradiction of sinners against himself, lest ye be wearied and faint in your minds.

4 Ye have not yet resisted unto blood, striving against sin.

5 And ye have forgotten the exhortation which speaketh unto you as unto children, My son, despise not thou the chastening of the Lord, nor faint when thou art rebuked of him:

6 For whom the Lord loveth he chasteneth, and scourgeth every son whom he receiveth.

7 If ye endure chastening, God dealeth with you as with sons; for what son is he whom the father chasteneth not?

8 But if ye be without chastisement, whereof all are partakers, then are ye bastards, and not sons.

9 Furthermore we have had fathers of our flesh which corrected *us*, and we gave *them* reverence: shall we not much rather be in subjection unto the Father of spirits, and live?

10 For they verily for a few days chastened *us* after their own pleasure; but he for *our* profit, that *we* might be partakers of his holiness.

11 Now no chastening for the present seemeth to be joyous, but grievous: nevertheless afterward it yieldeth the peaceable fruit of righteousness unto them which are exercised thereby.

Exhortations to Holiness

12 Wherefore lift up the hands which hang down, and the feeble knees;

13 And make straight paths for your feet, lest that which is lame be turned out of the way; but let it rather be healed.

14 Follow peace with all *men*, and holiness, without which no man shall see the Lord:

15 Looking diligently lest any man fail of the grace of God; lest any root of bitterness springing up trouble *you*, and thereby many be defiled;

16 Lest there *be* any fornicator, or profane person, as Esau, who for one morsel of meat sold his birthright.

17 For ye know how that afterward, when he would have inherited the blessing, he was rejected: for he found no place of repentance, though he sought it carefully with tears.

18 For ye are not come unto the mount that might be touched, and that burned with fire, nor unto blackness, and darkness, and tempest,

19 And the sound of a trumpet, and the voice of words; which *voice* they that heard intreated that the word should not be spoken to them any more:

20 (For they could not endure that which was commanded, And if so much as a beast touch the mountain, it shall be stoned, or thrust through with a dart:

21 And so terrible was the sight, *that* Moses said, I exceedingly fear and quake:)

22 But ye are come unto mount Sion, and unto the city of the living God, the heavenly Jerusalem, and to an innumerable company of angels,

23 To the general assembly and church of the firstborn, which are written in heaven, and to God the Judge of all, and to the spirits of just men made perfect,

"The Mediator of the New Covenant"

24 And to Jesus the mediator of the new covenant, and to the blood of sprinkling, that speaketh better things than *that of* Abel.

25 See that ye refuse not him that speaketh. For if they escaped not who refused him that spake on earth, much more *shall not* we *escape*, if we turn away from him that *speaketh* from heaven:

26 Whose voice then shook the earth: but now he hath promised, saying, Yet once more I shake not the earth only, but also heaven.

Cross references

40 Rev. 6:11
1 Rom. 12:12; Phil. 3:13, 14
2 Ps. 110:1; Phil. 2:8; 1Pet. 1:11; 3:22
3 Matt. 10:24, 25; John 15:20
4 1Cor. 10:13
5 Job 5:17; Prov. 3:11
6 Ps. 94:12; 119:75; Prov. 3:12; James 1:12
7 Prov. 13:24; 19:18; 23:13
8 Ps. 73:15
9 Num. 16:22; 27:16; Eccl. 12:7; Isa. 42:5; 57:16; Zech. 12:1
11 James 3:18
12 Job 4:3, 4; Isa. 35:3
13 Prov. 4:26, 27
14 Ps. 34:14; Matt. 5:8
16 Gen. 25:33
17 Gen. 27:34, 36, 38
18 Ex. 19:12, 18, 19; 20:18; Deut. 4:11; 5:22
19 Ex. 20:19; Deut. 5:5, 25; 18:16
20 Ex. 19:13
21 Ex. 19:16
22 Deut. 33:2; Ps. 68:17; Gal. 4:26
23 Rev. 13:8; 14:4
24 Gen. 4:10; Ex. 24:8
26 Ex. 19:18; Hag. 2:6

12:26–29 Exodus 19:18 tells us that God's voice then "shook the earth." Haggai 2:6 adds that God will again shake both earth and heaven. This shaking will happen "once more" at the time of Jesus' second coming. In the place of unstable human kingdoms, God will establish this unshakeable kingdom on earth.

27 And this *word,* Yet once more, signifieth the removing of those things that are shaken, as of things that are made, that those things which cannot be shaken may remain.

28 Wherefore we receiving a kingdom which cannot be moved, let us have grace, whereby we may serve God acceptably with reverence and godly fear:

29 For our God *is* a consuming fire.

CHAPTER 13
Social and Religious Duties

1 Let brotherly love continue.

2 Be not forgetful to entertain strangers: for thereby some have entertained angels unawares.

3 Remember them that are in bonds, as bound with them; *and* them which suffer adversity, as being yourselves also in the body.

4 Marriage *is* honourable in all, and the bed undefiled: but whoremongers and adulterers God will judge.

5 *Let your* conversation *be* without covetousness; *and be* content with such things as ye have: for he hath said, I will never leave thee, nor forsake thee.

6 So that we may boldly say, The Lord *is* my helper, and I will not fear what man shall do unto me.

7 Remember them which have the rule over you, who have spoken unto you the word of God: whose faith follow, considering the end of *their* conversation.

8 Jesus Christ the same yesterday, and today, and for ever.

9 Be not carried about with divers and strange doctrines. For *it is* a good thing that the heart be established with grace; not with meats, which have not profited them that have been occupied therein.

10 We have an altar, whereof they have no right to eat which serve the tabernacle.

11 For the bodies of those beasts, whose blood is brought into the sanctuary by the

high priest for sin, are burned without the camp.

12 Wherefore Jesus also, that he might sanctify the people with his own blood, suffered without the gate.

13 Let us go forth therefore unto him without the camp, bearing his reproach.

14 For here have we no continuing city, but we seek one to come.

15 By him therefore let us offer the sacrifice of praise to God continually, that is, the fruit of *our* lips giving thanks to his name.

16 But to do good and to communicate forget not: for with such sacrifices God is well pleased.

17 Obey them that have the rule over you, and submit yourselves: for they watch for your souls, as they that must give account, that they may do it with joy, and not with grief: for that *is* unprofitable for you.

18 Pray for us: for we trust we have a good conscience, in all things willing to live honestly.

19 But I beseech *you* the rather to do this, that I may be restored to you the sooner.

"Jesus, the Great Shepherd"

20 Now the God of peace, that brought again from the dead our Lord Jesus, that great shepherd of the sheep, through the blood of the everlasting covenant,

21 Make you perfect in every good work to do his will, working in you that which is wellpleasing in his sight, through Jesus Christ; to whom *be* glory for ever and ever. Amen.

22 And I beseech you, brethren, suffer the word of exhortation: for I have written a letter unto you in few words.

23 Know ye that *our* brother Timothy is set at liberty; with whom, if he come shortly, I will see you.

24 Salute all them that have the rule over you, and all the saints. They of Italy salute you.

25 Grace *be* with you all. Amen.

---

27 Ps. 102:26; Matt. 24:35; Rev. 21:1

29 2Thess. 1:8; Heb. 10:27

1 2Pet. 1:7; 1John 3:11; 4:7, 20, 21

2 Matt. 25:35; 1Tim. 3:2; 1Pet. 4:9

3 Matt. 25:36; 1Cor. 12:26

5 Gen. 28:15; Deut. 31:6, 8; Josh. 1:5; Ps. 37:25; Matt. 6:25, 34

6 Ps. 27:1; 56:4, 11, 12; 118:6

8 John 8:58; Rev. 1:4

9 Rom. 14:17

11 Ex. 29:14

12 John 19:17, 18; Acts 7:58

15 Ps. 50:14, 23; 69:30, 31; 107:22; 116:17; Hos. 14:2

17 Ezek. 3:17; 33:2, 7; 1Tim. 5:17; Heb. 13:7

20 Isa. 40:11; Ezek. 34:23; 37:24; Zech. 9:11; John 10:11, 14

21 Gal. 1:5; Phil. 2:13

22 1Pet. 5:12

23 1Thess. 3:2; 1Tim. 6:12

James

Though four men are named James in the New Testament, the author of this "general epistle" was most likely James, the half-brother of Jesus, who became an apostle and leader of the Jerusalem church (see Matt. 13:55; Gal. 1:19). James probably witnessed Christ's appearance following His resurrection (1 Cor. 15:7), and he was among those who assembled together following Christ's Ascension (Acts 1:14) to await the coming of the Holy Spirit. Later James became a leader of the believers in Jerusalem (Acts 12:17; Gal. 1:18–19). He kept control of a potentially volatile debate over the evangelization of Gentiles and helped draft a very tolerant letter to the Gentile Christians in Antioch regarding their status in the Church (Acts 15:13–19).

Author	James the Lord's Half-Brother
Date	A.D. 49
Key Truth	Faith Accompanied by Works
Historic Time	Early Church Growth among the Jews
Key Verse	2:17 Even so faith, if it hath not works, is dead, being alone.

Written initially to Jewish believers who were dispersed throughout the Roman Empire, this epistle is about practical Christian living. The style is sharp, incisive, and strikingly similar to the wisdom literature of the Old Testament. Quotations and references to the Old Testament are numerous, and perhaps the most famous quotation comes from Leviticus 19:18, which James calls "the royal law" (2:8) that states, "Thou shalt love thy neighbor as thyself."

James emphasizes that true saving faith produces works (2:14–26). Instructions are plentiful on how to endure temptations, to be doers of the Word rather than just hearers, and to have right use of our speech. Words of wisdom flow on topics ranging from spiritual love, prayer, patience, and humility.

Four distinct prophecies appear in the book of James: 1:12; 2:12–13; 5:2–3, 7–9. The first prophecy is the promise of a crown of life to be awarded in heaven at the judgment seat of Christ for those who were faithful to the Lord on this earth or were martyred for their commitment to Christ (see Rev. 2:10). Statements concerning the second coming of Christ are found in James 5:7–8, where James urges believers to be patient unto the coming of the Lord.

Of 108 verses, 7 verses (6 percent) are prophetic. There are 5 Old Testament quotations in James.

6% Prophecy

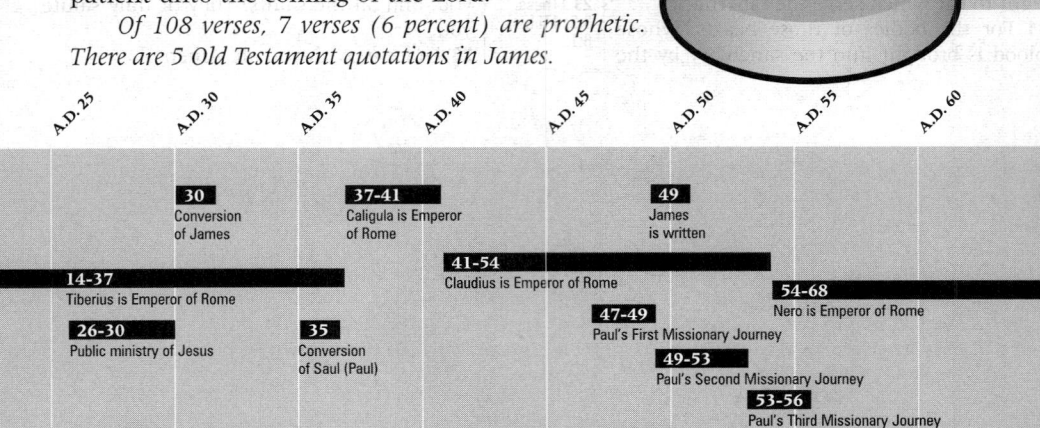

A.D. 25   A.D. 30   A.D. 35   A.D. 40   A.D. 45   A.D. 50   A.D. 55   A.D. 60   A.

30 Conversion of James

37-41 Caligula is Emperor of Rome

49 James is written

14-37 Tiberius is Emperor of Rome

41-54 Claudius is Emperor of Rome

54-68 Nero is Emperor of Rome

26-30 Public ministry of Jesus

35 Conversion of Saul (Paul)

47-49 Paul's First Missionary Journey

49-53 Paul's Second Missionary Journey

53-56 Paul's Third Missionary Journey

6 Pau Pet ma

CHAPTER 1

1 James, a servant of God and of the Lord Jesus Christ, to the twelve tribes which are scattered abroad, greeting.

The Prayer of Faith

2 My brethren, count it all joy when ye fall into divers temptations;

3 Knowing *this,* that the trying of your faith worketh patience.

4 But let patience have *her* perfect work, that ye may be perfect and entire, wanting nothing.

5 If any of you lack wisdom, let him ask of God, that giveth to all *men* liberally, and upbraideth not; and it shall be given him.

6 But let him ask in faith, nothing wavering. For he that wavereth is like a wave of the sea driven with the wind and tossed.

7 For let not that man think that he shall receive any thing of the Lord.

8 A double minded man *is* unstable in all his ways.

9 Let the brother of low degree rejoice in that he is exalted:

10 But the rich, in that he is made low: because as the flower of the grass he shall pass away.

11 For the sun is no sooner risen with a burning heat, but it withereth the grass, and the flower thereof falleth, and the grace of the fashion of it perisheth: so also shall the rich man fade away in his ways.

Enduring Tests

12 Blessed *is* the man that endureth temptation: for when he is tried, he shall receive the crown of life, which the Lord hath promised to them that love him.

13 Let no man say when he is tempted, I am tempted of God: for God cannot be tempted with evil, neither tempteth he any man:

14 But every man is tempted, when he is drawn away of his own lust, and enticed.

15 Then when lust hath conceived, it bringeth forth sin: and sin, when it is finished, bringeth forth death.

16 Do not err, my beloved brethren.

17 Every good gift and every perfect gift is from above, and cometh down from the Father of lights, with whom is no variableness, neither shadow of turning.

18 Of his own will begat he us with the word of truth, that we should be a kind of firstfruits of his creatures.

Be Doers of the Word

19 Wherefore, my beloved brethren, let every man be swift to hear, slow to speak, slow to wrath:

20 For the wrath of man worketh not the righteousness of God.

21 Wherefore lay apart all filthiness and superfluity of naughtiness, and receive with meekness the engrafted word, which is able to save your souls.

22 But be ye doers of the word, and not hearers only, deceiving your own selves.

23 For if any be a hearer of the word, and not a doer, he is like unto a man beholding his natural face in a glass:

24 For he beholdeth himself, and goeth his way, and straightway forgetteth what manner of man he was.

25 But whoso looketh into the perfect law of liberty, and continueth *therein,* he being not a forgetful hearer, but a doer of the work, this man shall be blessed in his deed.

26 If any man among you seem to be religious, and bridleth not his tongue, but deceiveth his own heart, this man's religion *is* vain.

27 Pure religion and undefiled before God

Cross references

1 Deut. 32:26; John 7:35; Acts 2:5; 8:1; 12:17; 15:13; 26:7
2 Matt. 5:12; Heb. 10:34
3 Rom. 5:3
5 Prov. 2:3; Jer. 29:12
6 Mark 11:24
10 Job 14:2; Ps. 90:5, 6; 103:15; Isa. 40:6
12 Job 5:17; Prov. 3:11, 12; Heb. 12:5; Rev. 2:10; 3:19
15 Job 15:35; Ps. 7:14; Rom. 6:21, 23
17 Mal. 3:6; John 3:27
18 Jer. 2:3; John 1:13; 3:3; 1Pet. 1:23; Rev. 14:4
19 Prov. 10:19; 17:27; Eccl. 5:1, 2
21 Rom. 1:16; 1Cor. 15:2; Heb. 2:3
22 Luke 6:46; 11:28
25 John 13:17
26 Ps. 34:13; 39:1; 1Pet. 3:10
27 Isa. 1:16, 17; 58:6, 7; Matt. 25:36

1:12 endureth temptation. This means those who persevere patiently and stand firm under trial, victoriously passing the test of such pressure, will receive due reward for their faithfulness. The "crown of life" mentioned here and in Revelation 2:10 is the special crown for martyrs. In the ancient world, the term "crown" refers to a wreath of flowers presented to winners in athletic games and to special awards bestowed on statesmen, soldiers and distinguished citizens. At the judgment seat of Christ, this promised crown will be awarded both to the martyrs and those who are victorious over severe temptations, persecutions, and adversities through faith and dedication (see also 1 Cor. 9:24–27; Phil. 4:1; 1 Thess. 2:19; 2 Tim. 4:8;

1 Pet. 5:4; Rev. 2:10; 3:11; 4:4, 10).

1:26–27 seem to be religious. . . . Pure religion. These two verses are the only places in the New Testament where the Greek word *threskos,* "external or outward religiosity," is used. Pure religion is outwardly characterized by sincere acts of kindness, compassion, and personal purity, keeping one's self uncontaminated by the world system. Paul describes the actions of Christians as "charity out of a pure heart, and of a good conscience" (1 Tim. 1:5), but there adds, "and of faith unfeigned." Sincere faith in Jesus Christ is the only way of salvation, but sincere acts of love and kindness, along with personal piety, are the discernible fruits of true faith.

and the Father is this, To visit the fatherless and widows in their affliction, *and* to keep himself unspotted from the world.

CHAPTER 2
Respect for Others

1 My brethren, have not the faith of our Lord Jesus Christ, *the Lord* of glory, with respect of persons.

2 For if there come unto your assembly a man with a gold ring, in goodly apparel, and there come in also a poor man in vile raiment;

3 And ye have respect to him that weareth the gay clothing, and say unto him, Sit thou here in a good place; and say to the poor, Stand thou there, or sit here under my footstool:

4 Are ye not then partial in yourselves, and are become judges of evil thoughts?

5 Hearken, my beloved brethren, Hath not God chosen the poor of this world rich in faith, and heirs of the kingdom which he hath promised to them that love him?

6 But ye have despised the poor. Do not rich men oppress you, and draw you before the judgment seats?

7 Do not they blaspheme that worthy name by the which ye are called?

8 If ye fulfil the royal law according to the scripture, Thou shalt love thy neighbour as thyself, ye do well:

9 But if ye have respect to persons, ye commit sin, and are convinced of the law as transgressors.

10 For whosoever shall keep the whole law, and yet offend in one *point,* he is guilty of all.

11 For he that said, Do not commit adultery, said also, Do not kill. Now if thou commit no adultery, yet if thou kill, thou art become a transgressor of the law.

12 So speak ye, and so do, as they that shall be judged by the law of liberty.

13 For he shall have judgment without mercy, that hath shewed no mercy; and mercy rejoiceth against judgment.

"Faith without Works Is Dead"

14 What *doth it* profit, my brethren, though a man say he hath faith, and have not works? can faith save him?

15 If a brother or sister be naked, and destitute of daily food,

16 And one of you say unto them, Depart in peace, be ye warmed and filled; notwithstanding ye give them not those things which are needful to the body; what *doth it* profit?

17 Even so faith, if it hath not works, is dead, being alone.

18 Yea, a man may say, Thou hast faith, and I have works: shew me thy faith without thy works, and I will shew thee my faith by my works.

19 Thou believest that there is one God; thou doest well: the devils also believe, and tremble.

20 But wilt thou know, O vain man, that faith without works is dead?

21 Was not Abraham our father justified by works, when he had offered Isaac his son upon the altar?

22 Seest thou how faith wrought with his works, and by works was faith made perfect?

23 And the scripture was fulfilled which saith, Abraham believed God, and it was imputed unto him for righteousness: and he was called the Friend of God.

24 Ye see then how that by works a man is justified, and not by faith only.

25 Likewise also was not Rahab the harlot justified by works, when she had received the messengers, and had sent *them* out another way?

26 For as the body without the spirit is dead, so faith without works is dead also.

CHAPTER 3
Control the Tongue

1 My brethren, be not many masters, knowing that we shall receive the greater condemnation.

2 For in many things we offend all. If any man offend not in word, the same *is* a per-

---

Cross references

1 Lev. 19:15; Deut. 1:17; 16:19

5 Ex. 20:6; 1Sam. 2:30; Matt. 5:3; Luke 6:20; 12:21, 32; John 7:48

6 Acts 13:50; 17:6; 18:12

8 Lev. 19:18; Matt. 22:39

10 Deut. 27:26; Matt. 5:19; Gal. 3:10

11 Ex. 20:13, 14

14 Matt. 7:26

15 Job 31:19, 20; Luke 3:11

16 1John 3:18

19 Matt. 8:29; Mark 1:24; 5:7; Luke 4:34

21 Gen. 22:9, 12

22 Heb. 11:17

23 Gen. 15:6; Rom. 4:3

25 Josh. 2:1; Heb. 11:31

1 Matt. 23:8, 14; Luke 6:37

2 1Kgs. 8:46; 2Chr. 6:36; Ps. 34:13; Prov. 20:9; Eccl. 7:20; Matt. 12:37; James 1:26; 1Pet. 3:10; 1John 1:8

2:8 royal law. This principle of unselfish love is quoted from Moses (Lev. 19:18), quoted by Christ (Matt. 19:19; 22:39; Luke 10:27), referred to by Paul (Rom. 13:8; Gal. 5:14), and fully described in 1 Corinthians 13.

2:12 judged by the law of liberty. This prediction reminds the reader that all "will give an account to God" (cf. 2 Cor. 5:10; Rom. 14:7–10).

3:1 masters. The Greek root word here is *didasko,* meaning "pertaining to teaching," from which we get the English word "didactic." The passage refers to teachers or instructors. Those who teach the Word have a great responsibility, as they influence so many. Hence they have greater accountability and will be so considered at the judgment seat of Christ (2 Cor. 5:10).

fect man, *and* able also to bridle the whole body.
3 Behold, we put bits in the horses' mouths, that they may obey us; and we turn about their whole body.
4 Behold also the ships, which though *they be* so great, and *are* driven of fierce winds, yet are they turned about with a very small helm, whithersoever the governor listeth.
5 Even so the tongue is a little member, and boasteth great things. Behold, how great a matter a little fire kindleth!
6 And the tongue *is* a fire, a world of iniquity; so is the tongue among our members, that it defileth the whole body, and setteth on fire the course of nature; and it is set on fire of hell.
7 For every kind of beasts, and of birds, and of serpents, and of things in the sea, is tamed, and hath been tamed of mankind:
8 But the tongue can no man tame; *it is* an unruly evil, full of deadly poison.
9 Therewith bless we God, even the Father; and therewith curse we men, which are made after the similitude of God.
10 Out of the same mouth proceedeth blessing and cursing. My brethren, these things ought not so to be.
11 Doth a fountain send forth at the same place sweet *water* and bitter?
12 Can the fig tree, my brethren, bear olive berries? either a vine, figs? so *can* no fountain both yield salt water and fresh.

True Wisdom Comes from God

13 Who *is* a wise man and endued with knowledge among you? let him shew out of a good conversation his works with meekness of wisdom.
14 But if ye have bitter envying and strife in your hearts, glory not, and lie not against the truth.
15 This wisdom descendeth not from above, but *is* earthly, sensual, devilish.
16 For where envying and strife *is,* there *is* confusion and every evil work.
17 But the wisdom that is from above is first pure, then peaceable, gentle, *and* easy to be intreated, full of mercy and good fruits, without partiality, and without hypocrisy.
18 And the fruit of righteousness is sown in peace of them that make peace.

3 Ps. 32:9

5 Ps. 12:3; 73:8, 9; Prov. 12:18; 15:2

6 Prov. 16:27; Matt. 15:11, 18-20; Mark 7:15, 20, 23

8 Ps. 140:3

14 Rom. 2:17, 23; 13:13

15 Phil. 3:19

16 1Cor. 3:3; Gal. 5:20

17 1Pet. 1:22; 2:1; 1John 3:18

18 Prov. 11:18; Hos. 10:12; Matt. 5:9

1 Rom. 7:23; 1Pet. 2:11

3 Job 27:9; 35:12; Ps. 18:41; 66:18; Prov. 1:28; Isa. 1:15; Jer. 11:11; 1John 3:22; 5:14

4 Ps. 73:27; John 15:19; 17:14

5 Num. 11:29; Prov. 21:10

6 Job 22:29; Ps. 138:6; Prov. 3:34; 29:23

7 Eph. 4:27; 6:11; 1Pet. 5:9

9 Matt. 5:4

10 Job 22:29; Matt. 23:12; Luke 14:11; 18:14

11 Matt. 7:1; Luke 6:37

12 Matt. 10:28; Rom. 14:4, 13

13 Job 7:7; Ps. 102:3; Prov. 27:1; Luke 12:18; James 1:10; 1Pet. 1:24; 1John 2:17

Chapter 4
Warnings against Loving the Things of the World

1 From whence *come* wars and fightings among you? *come they* not hence, *even* of your lusts that war in your members?
2 Ye lust, and have not: ye kill, and desire to have, and cannot obtain: ye fight and war, yet ye have not, because ye ask not.
3 Ye ask, and receive not, because ye ask amiss, that ye may consume *it* upon your lusts.
4 Ye adulterers and adulteresses, know ye not that the friendship of the world is enmity with God? whosoever therefore will be a friend of the world is the enemy of God.
5 Do ye think that the scripture saith in vain, The spirit that dwelleth in us lusteth to envy?
6 But he giveth more grace. Wherefore he saith, God resisteth the proud, but giveth grace unto the humble.
7 Submit yourselves therefore to God. Resist the devil, and he will flee from you.
8 Draw nigh to God, and he will draw nigh to you. Cleanse *your* hands, *ye* sinners; and purify *your* hearts, *ye* double minded.
9 Be afflicted, and mourn, and weep: let your laughter be turned to mourning, and *your* joy to heaviness.
10 Humble yourselves in the sight of the Lord, and he shall lift you up.

Cautions Concerning Criticism

11 Speak not evil one of another, brethren. He that speaketh evil of *his* brother, and judgeth his brother, speaketh evil of the law, and judgeth the law: but if thou judge the law, thou art not a doer of the law, but a judge.
12 There is one lawgiver, who is able to save and to destroy: who art thou that judgest another?

"If the Lord Will"

13 Go to now, ye that say, Today or to morrow we will go into such a city, and continue there a year, and buy and sell, and get gain:
14 Whereas ye know not what *shall be* on the morrow. For what *is* your life? It is even a vapour, that appeareth for a little time, and then vanisheth away.

4:7 Resist the devil, and he will flee. This prophetic promise is restated in 1 Peter 5:9. This does not exempt believers from temptations and persecutions but, as in Revelation 12:11, teaches that victory over Satan himself is attainable—even in martyrdom. Tribulation saints will experience both persecution and spiritual victory (Rev. 20:4).

15 For that ye *ought* to say, If the Lord will, we shall live, and do this, or that.

16 But now ye rejoice in your boastings: all such rejoicing is evil.

17 Therefore to him that knoweth to do good, and doeth *it* not, to him it is sin.

CHAPTER 5
Warnings to the Rich

1 Go to now, *ye* rich men, weep and howl for your miseries that shall come upon *you*.

2 Your riches are corrupted, and your garments are motheaten.

3 Your gold and silver is cankered; and the rust of them shall be a witness against you, and shall eat your flesh as it were fire. Ye have heaped treasure together for the last days.

4 Behold, the hire of the labourers who have reaped down your fields, which is of you kept back by fraud, crieth: and the cries of them which have reaped are entered into the ears of the Lord of Sabaoth.

5 Ye have lived in pleasure on the earth, and been wanton; ye have nourished your hearts, as in a day of slaughter.

6 Ye have condemned *and* killed the just; *and* he doth not resist you.

Patience Exhorted

7 Be patient therefore, brethren, unto the coming of the Lord. Behold, the husbandman waiteth for the precious fruit of the earth, and hath long patience for it, until he receive the early and latter rain.

8 Be ye also patient; stablish your hearts: for the coming of the Lord draweth nigh.

9 Grudge not one against another, brethren, lest ye be condemned: behold, the judge standeth before the door.

17 Luke 12:47; John 9:41; 15:22; Rom. 1:20, 21, 32

1 Prov. 11:28; Luke 6:24; 1Tim. 6:9

2 Job 13:28; Matt. 6:20

4 Lev. 19:13; Deut. 24:15; Jer. 22:13

5 Job 21:13; Amos 6:1, 4; Luke 16:19, 25

7 Deut. 11:14; Jer. 5:24; Hos. 6:3; Joel 2:23; Zech. 10:1

8 Matt. 24:33; 1Pet. 4:7

10 Matt. 5:12

11 Job 1:21, 22; 2:10; 42:10; Ps. 94:12; 103:8

12 Matt. 5:34

14 Mark 6:13; 16:18

16 Josh. 10:12; Ps. 34:15; 145:18

17 1Kgs. 17:1

18 1Kgs. 18:42, 45

19 Matt. 18:15

20 Prov. 10:12

10 Take, my brethren, the prophets, who have spoken in the name of the Lord, for an example of suffering affliction, and of patience.

11 Behold, we count them happy which endure. Ye have heard of the patience of Job, and have seen the end of the Lord; that the Lord is very pitiful, and of tender mercy.

12 But above all things, my brethren, swear not, neither by heaven, neither by the earth, neither by any other oath: but let your yea be yea; and *your* nay, nay; lest ye fall into condemnation.

13 Is any among you afflicted? let him pray. Is any merry? let him sing psalms.

14 Is any sick among you? let him call for the elders of the church; and let them pray over him, anointing him with oil in the name of the Lord:

15 And the prayer of faith shall save the sick, and the Lord shall raise him up; and if he have committed sins, they shall be forgiven him.

16 Confess *your* faults one to another, and pray one for another, that ye may be healed. The effectual fervent prayer of a righteous man availeth much.

17 Elias was a man subject to like passions as we are, and he prayed earnestly that it might not rain: and it rained not on the earth by the space of three years and six months.

18 And he prayed again, and the heaven gave rain, and the earth brought forth her fruit.

19 Brethren, if any of you do err from the truth, and one convert him;

20 Let him know, that he which converteth the sinner from the error of his way shall save a soul from death, and shall hide a multitude of sins.

5:3 last days. Some think this term refers to the latter aging years of the selfish rich, who care not for God. Others view the expression as indicative of the End Times, prior to Christ's return, when excessive capitalism and crass materialism overshadow spiritual concerns in the Christian community. The latter view seems correct.

5:7 patient. Literally "longsuffering," this attitude of anticipation of Christ's return furnishes comfort in difficult times, for the believer knows a great and wonderful event is nearing. Paul expresses a similar sentiment in 2 Thessalonians 3:5. The context shows that James uses the phrase "coming of the Lord" in reference to Christ's coming both as the judge of the wicked and the rewarder of the righteous. The "early and latter rain" is an illustra-

tion drawn from agriculture to indicate spring and fall rains, expected and anticipated. Like the farmer, true believers know that certain things will occur, but cannot set a precise date.

5:8 stablish your hearts. Strengthening and confirming in our hearts that Christ's return is "drawing nigh," that is, always imminent and could occur at any time, results in truly loving His appearing (cf. 2 Tim. 4:8).

5:9 behold, the judge standeth before the door. Christ's coming in judgment is compared to an official standing before a door and about to enter with authority. This general illustration may be applied to any aspect or phase of Christ's future dealings with His people or this earth.

1 Peter

P eter, the author of this epistle, is one of the outstanding personalities of the Gospels and the first part of the book of Acts. In fact, the first twelve chapters of Acts are devoted to his ministry and to the development of the church in the East where he was the dominant figure. Paul talks about Peter in 1 Corinthians (1 Cor. 1:12; 3:22; 9:5; 15:5) and Galatians (Gal. 1:18; 2:7–9, 11, 14). Earlier, Peter's prime ministry was to the Jews, but he "opened the door of the gospel" to the Gentiles when he led the Roman centurion, Cornelius, to Christ (Acts 10; Gal. 2:7–10). Addressed to the "elect" (1:2) scattered throughout the five Roman provinces of Asia Minor (Turkey), this letter was intended for both Jewish and Gentile Christians.

Author
Peter the Apostle

Date
A.D. 65

Key Truth
Suffering for Christ

Historic Time
Beginning of Persecution under Nero

Key Verse
4:16
Yet if any man suffer as a Christian, let him not be ashamed.

A concise manual of biblical doctrine and godly living, the epistle is filled with the hope of a glorious eternal future. Under Emperor Nero's reign, Christians were beginning to experience "fiery trial[s]" (1:6–7; 4:12). Designed to encourage Christians to be steadfast under these persecutions, this epistle mentions a form of the word "suffering" sixteen times. Peter writes of the divine preservation of the saints, the second coming of Christ, salvation, the eternal endurance of God's Word, and the believers' sacred and high calling as a chosen generation, "a royal priesthood, an holy nation" (2:9). Building his epistle on the doctrinal foundation of our high calling as Christians, the apostle sets forth spiritual guidelines for all believers, but includes special instructions for servants, husbands, wives, godly leaders, and youth.

First Peter contains numerous references to the Old Testament relating to prophecies that pertain to the second coming of Christ (1:3, 7, 11; 2:12; 4:5, 7, 18; 5:1, 4). Other fulfilled passages and typical prophecies (3:18–22) also appear in references to Old Testament passages (see 1:24–25; 2:6–8, 22; 3:10–12; 4:18).

Matters of a prophetic nature appear in 21 of the epistle's 105 verses, or 20 percent of the whole. The book of 1 Peter has 11 direct quotations from the Old Testament.

20% Prophecy

| A.D. 25 | A.D. 30 | A.D. 35 | A.D. 40 | A.D. 45 | A.D. 50 | A.D. 55 | A.D. 60 | A.D. 65 |

26 Conversion of Peter

37–41 Caligula is Emperor of Rome

65–68 Paul and Peter martyred

14–37 Tiberius is Emperor of Rome

41–54 Claudius is Emperor of Rome

26–30 Public ministry of Jesus

35 Conversion of Saul (Paul)

54–68 Nero is Emperor of Rome

47–49 Paul's First Missionary Journey

49–53 Paul's Second Missionary Journey

65 First Peter is written

53–56 Paul's Third Missionary Journey

CHAPTER 1

1 Peter, an apostle of Jesus Christ, to the strangers scattered throughout Pontus, Galatia, Cappadocia, Asia, and Bithynia,
2 Elect according to the foreknowledge of God the Father, through sanctification of the Spirit, unto obedience and sprinkling of the blood of Jesus Christ: Grace unto you, and peace, be multiplied.

"Kept by the Power of God"

3 Blessed *be* the God and Father of our Lord Jesus Christ, which according to his abundant mercy hath begotten us again unto a lively hope by the resurrection of Jesus Christ from the dead,
4 To an inheritance incorruptible, and undefiled, and that fadeth not away, reserved in heaven for you,
5 Who are kept by the power of God through faith unto salvation ready to be revealed in the last time.
6 Wherein ye greatly rejoice, though now for a season, if need be, ye are in heaviness through manifold temptations:
7 That the trial of your faith, being much more precious than of gold that perisheth, though it be tried with fire, might be found unto praise and honour and glory at the appearing of Jesus Christ:
8 Whom having not seen, ye love; in whom, though now ye see *him* not, yet believing, ye rejoice with joy unspeakable and full of glory:
9 Receiving the end of your faith, *even* the salvation of *your* souls.

10 Of which salvation the prophets have inquired and searched diligently, who prophesied of the grace *that should come* unto you:
11 Searching what, or what manner of time the Spirit of Christ which was in them did signify, when it testified beforehand the sufferings of Christ, and the glory that should follow.
12 Unto whom it was revealed, that not unto themselves, but unto us they did minister the things, which are now reported unto you by them that have preached the gospel unto you with the Holy Ghost sent down from heaven; which things the angels desire to look into.

Exhortation to Holiness

13 Wherefore gird up the loins of your mind, be sober, and hope to the end for the grace that is to be brought unto you at the revelation of Jesus Christ;
14 As obedient children, not fashioning yourselves according to the former lusts in your ignorance:
15 But as he which hath called you is holy, so be ye holy in all manner of conversation;
16 Because it is written, Be ye holy; for I am holy.
17 And if ye call on the Father, who without respect of persons judgeth according to every man's work, pass the time of your sojourning *here* in fear:
18 Forasmuch as ye know that ye were not redeemed with corruptible things, *as* silver and gold, from your vain conversation *received* by tradition from your fathers;

1 John 7:35; Acts 2:5, 9, 10
2 Rom. 1:7; 8:29; Titus 3:5; Heb. 10:22; 12:24; 1 Pet. 2:9; 3:21
4 Col. 1:5
5 John 17:11, 12, 15
6 Matt. 5:12; 1 Pet. 4:13; 5:10
7 Job 23:10; Ps. 66:10; Prov. 17:3; Isa. 48:10; Rom. 2:7, 10; 2 Thess. 1:7-12
8 John 20:29
10 Gen. 49:10; Dan. 2:44
11 Ps. 22:6; Isa. 53:3; Dan. 9:26
13 Luke 12:35; 17:30; Eph. 6:14
14 Rom. 12:2
15 Luke 1:74, 75
16 Lev. 11:44; 19:2
17 Deut. 10:17
18 1 Cor. 6:20; 7:23; 1 Pet. 4:3

1:3 lively hope. Because of the new birth, the believer anticipates a literal, bodily resurrection, even as Jesus was raised from the dead (see 1 Cor. 15:23). This living, blessed, purifying hope will be realized at the Rapture and resurrection of the "dead in Christ" (1 Thess. 4:16; Titus 2:13; 1 John 3:3).

1:4 inheritance incorruptible . . . reserved in heaven. In keeping with this "living hope," believers have a future inheritance, already reserved in heaven (Acts 26:18; Eph. 1:11, 14, 18; Col. 1:12; 3:24). An inheritance comes by virtue of relationship, to be distinguished from rewards, which are granted for obedience and good works (1 Cor. 3:13–14; 2 Cor. 5:10).

1:5 kept by the power of God. Nothing can steal the believer's heavenly inheritance, although disobedience can mean a loss of rewards (2 John 8). The final consummation of our salvation will be revealed and experienced in glorification with Christ at His return (Rom. 8:17; 2 Thess. 1:10).

1:7 appearing of Jesus Christ. The Greek word for "appearing" is *apokalupsis*, or "revelation" of Christ, a term sometimes used to encompass the whole sequence of future events from the Rapture to the Glorious Appearing at the close of the intervening Tribulation (1 Cor. 1:7; 2 Thess. 1:7). Though persecutions and suffering may befall believers, such trials will not be "worthy to be compared with the glory that shall be revealed in us" (Rom. 8:18).

1:11 sufferings of Christ . . . glory that should follow. The Old Testament prophets foresaw both the first coming, with the Messiah suffering (Isa. 53), and the Second Coming, with Messiah reigning (Isa. 32:1), without understanding the long interval of this current dispensation.

1:13 revelation of Jesus Christ. The Greek word for "revelation" is the same word that is translated "appearing" (v. 7), meaning the whole sequence of end-time events centered around the Second Coming.

The Last Days

By Robert Gromacki

Many expressions in Scripture point to the "End Times," sometimes called the "Last Days," "Latter Days," "Last Time or Times," "Last Day," or "Last Hour." The various expressions are all related to the creative-redemptive program of God for this time-space universe, and they point to a specific time period—the termination of God's purpose for a special group of people. At least four major time periods can be designated with the descriptive title of "the last days."

1. The Incarnation of Jesus Christ. Peter claimed that Jesus Christ "was manifest in these last times" to die for the sins of the world (1 Pet. 1:20). This statement corresponds to the "fullness of the time" when God sent His Son to be the Savior (Gal. 4:4). In a similar concept, God has "in these last days spoken unto us by His Son" (Heb. 1:2).

2. The Last Days of Israel, or the Final Days before the New Covenant. God's program for Israel began with His covenant promise to Abraham that He would make out of the patriarch a "great nation" (Gen. 12:1–3). For the next 2000 years, God worked out His creative-redemptive program in and through the people of Israel. That phase ended with the death, resurrection, and ascension of Jesus Christ. In the last days of Israel, the nation will experience unprecedented distress, trouble, or tribulation (Deut. 4:30; 31:29; Jer. 30:24) occurring during the predicted "seventieth week of Daniel" (Dan. 9:24–27) and an invasion from a northern confederation of armies that will be destroyed directly by God (Ezek. 38:16). At this time, Israel will go through national repentance and conversion (Deut. 4:30; Hos. 3:4–5; Rom. 11:26–27) and will enter into the full blessings of the new covenant during the Millennial Kingdom (Jer. 31:31–37). The Kingdom of God, ruled by Jesus Christ on the throne of David in Jerusalem, will be established with Israel as the dominant nation (Dan. 2:44–45). Israel will thus experience the total fulfillment of all the divine unconditional covenants: Abrahamic, Land, Davidic, and New (Deut. 4:30). The blessings of Jacob upon his twelve sons will thus be finalized.

> *At least four major time periods can be designated with the title of "the last days."*

3. The Last Days of Gentile World Dominion. This time period, called "the times of the Gentiles" by Jesus Christ (Luke 21:24), began with the destruction of the Jewish kingdom by the Babylonian king Nebuchadnezzar in 586 B.C. and essentially involves the dominion of Gentile nations over the world and over Israel from the destruction of the ancient Jewish kingdom to its reestablishment when Jesus Christ returns to earth. The Battle of Armageddon will end Gentile rule forever and will usher in the millennial and eternal reign of Christ (Dan. 2:28; Rev. 16:13–21).

4. The Last Days of the Church Age. The apostles warned that the last days of the Church Age would be marked by doctrinal apostasy (1 Tim. 4:1–3; 2 Pet. 3:3–4; Jude 1:17–19), moral deterioration (James 5:3; 2 Pet. 3:3), and the rise of many antichrists (1 John 2:18–19). The apostles also warned their readers that the features of the Last Days were present in their own day (2 Tim. 3:1–5; Jude 1:4, 17–19). Thus, the last days for the Church Age were as imminent as the Rapture itself. Whenever the Rapture occurs, the climax of personal salvation will happen, and the Church Age will end (1 Pet. 1:5).

19 But with the precious blood of Christ, as of a lamb without blemish and without spot:

20 Who verily was foreordained before the foundation of the world, but was manifest in these last times for you,

21 Who by him do believe in God, that raised him up from the dead, and gave him glory; that your faith and hope might be in God.

22 Seeing ye have purified your souls in obeying the truth through the Spirit unto unfeigned love of the brethren, *see that ye* love one another with a pure heart fervently:

23 Being born again, not of corruptible seed, but of incorruptible, by the word of God, which liveth and abideth for ever.

24 For all flesh *is* as grass, and all the glory of man as the flower of grass. The grass withereth, and the flower thereof falleth away:

25 But the word of the Lord endureth for ever. And this is the word which by the gospel is preached unto you.

CHAPTER 2
The People of God

1 Wherefore laying aside all malice, and all guile, and hypocrisies, and envies, and all evil speakings,

2 As newborn babes, desire the sincere milk of the word, that ye may grow thereby:

3 If so be ye have tasted that the Lord *is* gracious.

4 To whom coming, *as unto* a living stone, disallowed indeed of men, but chosen of God, *and* precious,

5 Ye also, as lively stones, are built up a spiritual house, an holy priesthood, to offer up spiritual sacrifices, acceptable to God by Jesus Christ.

6 Wherefore also it is contained in the scripture, Behold, I lay in Sion a chief corner stone, elect, precious: and he that believeth on him shall not be confounded.

7 Unto you therefore which believe *he is* precious: but unto them which be disobedient, the stone which the builders disal-

lowed, the same is made the head of the corner,

8 And a stone of stumbling, and a rock of offence, *even to them* which stumble at the word, being disobedient: whereunto also they were appointed.

9 But ye *are* a chosen generation, a royal priesthood, an holy nation, a peculiar people; that ye should shew forth the praises of him who hath called you out of darkness into his marvellous light:

10 Which in time past *were* not a people, but *are* now the people of God: which had not obtained mercy, but now have obtained mercy.

11 Dearly beloved, I beseech *you* as strangers and pilgrims, abstain from fleshly lusts, which war against the soul;

12 Having your conversation honest among the Gentiles: that, whereas they speak against you as evildoers, they may by *your* good works, which they shall behold, glorify God in the day of visitation.

Subjection to Human Government

13 Submit yourselves to every ordinance of man for the Lord's sake: whether it be to the king, as supreme;

14 Or unto governors, as unto them that are sent by him for the punishment of evildoers, and for the praise of them that do well.

15 For so is the will of God, that with well doing ye may put to silence the ignorance of foolish men:

16 As free, and not using *your* liberty for a cloke of maliciousness, but as the servants of God.

17 Honour all *men*. Love the brotherhood. Fear God. Honour the king.

Subjection to Authority

18 Servants, *be* subject to *your* masters with all fear; not only to the good and gentle, but also to the froward.

19 For this *is* thankworthy, if a man for conscience toward God endure grief, suffering wrongfully.

20 For what glory *is it*, if, when ye be buffeted for your faults, ye shall take it pa-

Cross References

19 Ex. 12:5; Isa. 53:7
20 Rom. 3:25; 16:25, 26; Eph. 1:10; 3:9, 11; Heb. 1:2; 9:26
21 Matt. 28:18; Acts 2:24, 33
22 1Pet. 2:17; 3:8; 4:8; 1John 3:18; 4:7, 21
23 John 1:13; 3:5
24 Ps. 103:15; Isa. 40:6; 51:12
1 Eph. 4:22, 25, 31
2 Rom. 6:4; 1Cor. 3:2; 14:20
3 Ps. 34:8
4 Ps. 118:22
5 Isa. 61:6; 66:21
6 Isa. 28:16; Rom. 9:33
7 Ps. 118:22; Matt. 21:42
8 Ex. 9:16; Isa. 8:14
9 Ex. 19:5, 6; Deut. 4:20; 7:6; 10:15; 14:2; 26:18, 19; Eph. 1:14; 5:8; Col. 1:13
11 Rom. 13:14; Gal. 5:16; Heb. 11:13
12 Matt. 5:16; Luke 19:44; Rom. 12:17
13 Matt. 22:21
15 Titus 2:8; 1Pet. 2:12
17 Matt. 22:21
18 Eph. 6:5; Col. 3:22

1:20 manifest in these last times. This expression refers to the first coming of Jesus. In this context, "last times" describes the period between the first and second comings, in which the Rapture is always imminent (see 1 Tim. 4:1; 1 John 2:18).

2:9–10 should shew forth the praises of him who

hath called you. Not only are New Testament believers a "chosen generation" and a "royal priesthood" to show forth His praises now, but they will continue to hold these "offices" in the everlasting future as well (Eph. 1:6, 12, 14; Rev. 1:6; 5:10).

tiently? but if, when ye do well, and suffer *for it*, ye take it patiently, this *is* acceptable with God.

21 For even hereunto were ye called: because Christ also suffered for us, leaving us an example, that ye should follow his steps:

22 Who did no sin, neither was guile found in his mouth:

23 Who, when he was reviled, reviled not again; when he suffered, he threatened not; but committed *himself* to him that judgeth righteously:

24 Who his own self bare our sins in his own body on the tree, that we, being dead to sins, should live unto righteousness: by whose stripes ye were healed.

25 For ye were as sheep going astray; but are now returned unto the Shepherd and Bishop of your souls.

CHAPTER 3
Advice to Wives and Husbands

1 Likewise, ye wives, *be* in subjection to your own husbands; that, if any obey not the word, they also may without the word be won by the conversation of the wives;

2 While they behold your chaste conversation *coupled* with fear.

3 Whose adorning let it not be that outward *adorning* of plaiting the hair, and of wearing of gold, or of putting on of apparel;

4 But *let it be* the hidden man of the heart, in that which is not corruptible, *even the ornament* of a meek and quiet spirit, which is in the sight of God of great price.

5 For after this manner in the old time the holy women also, who trusted in God, adorned themselves, being in subjection unto their own husbands:

6 Even as Sara obeyed Abraham, calling him lord: whose daughters ye are, as long as ye do well, and are not afraid with any amazement.

7 Likewise, ye husbands, dwell with *them* according to knowledge, giving honour unto the wife, as unto the weaker vessel,

and as being heirs together of the grace of life; that your prayers be not hindered.

The Blessedness of Suffering for Righteousness' Sake

8 Finally, *be ye* all of one mind, having compassion one of another, love as brethren, *be* pitiful, *be* courteous:

9 Not rendering evil for evil, or railing for railing: but contrariwise blessing; knowing that ye are thereunto called, that ye should inherit a blessing.

10 For he that will love life, and see good days, let him refrain his tongue from evil, and his lips that they speak no guile:

11 Let him eschew evil, and do good; let him seek peace, and ensue it.

12 For the eyes of the Lord *are* over the righteous, and his ears *are open* unto their prayers: but the face of the Lord *is* against them that do evil.

13 And who *is* he that will harm you, if ye be followers of that which is good?

14 But and if ye suffer for righteousness' sake, happy *are ye*: and be not afraid of their terror, neither be troubled;

"Having a Good Conscience"

15 But sanctify the Lord God in your hearts: and *be* ready always to *give* an answer to every man that asketh you a reason of the hope that is in you with meekness and fear:

16 Having a good conscience; that, whereas they speak evil of you, as of evildoers, they may be ashamed that falsely accuse your good conversation in Christ.

17 For *it is* better, if the will of God be so, that ye suffer for well doing, than for evil doing.

18 For Christ also hath once suffered for sins, the just for the unjust, that he might bring us to God, being put to death in the flesh, but quickened by the Spirit:

19 By which also he went and preached unto the spirits in prison;

20 Which sometime were disobedient,

Cross references

21 Matt. 16:24; John 13:15
22 Isa. 53:9; Luke 23:41; John 8:46; 2Cor. 5:21; Heb. 4:15
23 Isa. 53:7; Matt. 27:39; Luke 23:46
24 Isa. 53:4-6, 11; Matt. 8:17; Rom. 6:2, 11; 7:6
25 Isa. 53:6; John 10:11, 14, 16
1 1Cor. 7:16; 9:19-22; 14:34
3 1Tim. 2:9; Titus 2:3
4 2Cor. 4:16
6 Gen. 18:12
7 1Cor. 7:3; 12:23; Eph. 5:25
8 Rom. 12:10, 16; 15:5; Eph. 4:32
9 Prov. 17:13; 20:22; Matt. 5:39; 25:34
10 Ps. 34:12; James 1:26
11 Ps. 37:27; Isa. 1:16, 17
14 Isa. 8:12, 13; Jer. 1:8; Matt. 5:10-12
15 Col. 4:6; 2Tim. 2:25
16 Titus 2:8; Heb. 13:18; 1Pet. 2:12
18 Rom. 1:4; 5:6; 8:11; 2Cor. 13:4
19 Isa. 42:7; 49:9; 61:1

3:19–20 He went and preached unto the spirits in prison. The preincarnate Christ, by the Holy Spirit, preached through Noah to those who lived before the Flood, to those who were disobedient and who rejected the proclaimed truth. Consequently, since these rebellious people refused the message, they then died in the Flood and are now in hell, existing as "spirits in prison," awaiting judgment and everlasting punishment in the lake of fire (John 5:28–29; Rev. 20:11–15). Christ, between His death and resurrection, descended into the area of Hades and Abraham's bosom (Luke 16:22–23). Removing the Old Testament saints from a temporary Paradise and transferring them to the "third heaven" or "paradise" (see 2 Cor. 12:1–3), Jesus also proclaimed His victory over sin to the lost spirits in prison, who remained in hell. The "spirits in prison" may also refer to those fallen angels or demons (see Gen. 6:2–3; 2 Pet. 2:4; Jude 1:6), to whom Christ, between His death and resurrection, made some proclamation, the content of which is unrevealed.

when once the longsuffering of God waited in the days of Noah, while the ark was a preparing, wherein few, that is, eight souls were saved by water.

21 The like figure whereunto *even* baptism doth also now save us (not the putting away of the filth of the flesh, but the answer of a good conscience toward God,) by the resurrection of Jesus Christ:

22 Who is gone into heaven, and is on the right hand of God; angels and authorities and powers being made subject unto him.

CHAPTER 4

1 Forasmuch then as Christ hath suffered for us in the flesh, arm yourselves likewise with the same mind: for he that hath suffered in the flesh hath ceased from sin;

2 That he no longer should live the rest of *his* time in the flesh to the lusts of men, but to the will of God.

3 For the time past of *our* life may suffice us to have wrought the will of the Gentiles, when we walked in lasciviousness, lusts, excess of wine, revellings, banquetings, and abominable idolatries:

4 Wherein they think it strange that ye run not with *them* to the same excess of riot, speaking evil of *you*:

5 Who shall give account to him that is ready to judge the quick and the dead.

6 For for this cause was the gospel preached also to them that are dead, that they might be judged according to men in the flesh, but live according to God in the spirit.

7 But the end of all things is at hand: be ye therefore sober, and watch unto prayer.

8 And above all things have fervent charity among yourselves: for charity shall cover the multitude of sins.

21 Rom. 10:10; 1Pet. 1:3

22 Ps. 110:1

1 Rom. 6:2, 7

2 2Cor. 5:15; Gal. 2:20

3 Ezek. 44:6; 45:9

4 Acts 13:45; 18:6

5 Acts 10:42; 17:31; Rom. 14:10, 12; 1Cor. 15:51, 52

7 Matt. 24:13, 14; 26:41; Luke 21:34

8 1Cor. 13:7

10 Matt. 24:45; 25:14, 21; 1Cor. 4:1, 2, 7; 12:4

11 Jer. 23:22; 1Cor. 3:10

12 1Pet. 1:7

13 Phil. 3:10

14 Matt. 5:11; 1Pet. 2:12, 19, 20

15 1Thess. 4:11

17 Isa. 10:12; Jer. 25:29; 49:12; Ezek. 9:6

18 Prov. 11:31; Luke 23:31

19 Ps. 31:5; Luke 23:46; 2Tim. 1:12

9 Use hospitality one to another without grudging.

10 As every man hath received the gift, *even so* minister the same one to another, as good stewards of the manifold grace of God.

11 If any man speak, *let him speak* as the oracles of God; if any man minister, *let him do it* as of the ability which God giveth: that God in all things may be glorified through Jesus Christ, to whom be praise and dominion for ever and ever. Amen.

Believers Should Not Be Ashamed

12 Beloved, think it not strange concerning the fiery trial which is to try you, as though some strange thing happened unto you:

13 But rejoice, inasmuch as ye are partakers of Christ's sufferings; that, when his glory shall be revealed, ye may be glad also with exceeding joy.

14 If ye be reproached for the name of Christ, happy *are ye*; for the Spirit of glory and of God resteth upon you: on their part he is evil spoken of, but on your part he is glorified.

15 But let none of you suffer as a murderer, or *as* a thief, or *as* an evildoer, or as a busybody in other men's matters.

16 Yet if *any man suffer* as a Christian, let him not be ashamed; but let him glorify God on this behalf.

17 For the time *is come* that judgment must begin at the house of God: and if *it* first *begin* at us, what shall the end *be* of them that obey not the gospel of God?

18 And if the righteous scarcely be saved, where shall the ungodly and the sinner appear?

19 Wherefore let them that suffer according to the will of God commit the keeping of

---

4:5 give account to him that is ready to judge the quick [living] **and the dead.** God is prepared in His time to bring the living and the dead, all generations, before Him to give an account of their deeds (Rom. 14:12). All the unsaved, those guilty of walking in wickedness (v. 3) will be summoned before the Great White Throne to face the Judge, Jesus Christ (John 5:22; Rev. 20:11–15).

4:6 gospel preached. . . to them that are dead. This refers to those who had responded to the gospel while alive but now had died, many as martyrs. They had been judged and condemned to martyrdom in the flesh by Roman law, but were alive in spirit, living with God.

4:7 be ye therefore sober, and watch unto prayer. In the Apostolic Age, as now, there was a constant expec-

tation that the consummation, or the end of the age, was at hand. That is as it should be. Believers should always conduct their lives with seriousness, watchfulness and prayer, for no one knows the day or the hour when Christ may return.

4:13 when his glory shall be revealed. Believers who are persecuted for their faith are partakers of the same kind of suffering the Savior endured for obeying and serving God with faithfulness, loyalty and love. When Christ returns, we shall "appear with him in glory" (Col. 3:4). All will rejoice, but especially those who have been persecuted and martyred will more fully understand "that the sufferings of this present time are not worthy to be compared with the glory which shall be revealed in us" (Rom. 8:18).

their souls *to him* in well doing, as unto a faithful Creator.

CHAPTER 5
Exhortations to Elders

1 The elders which are among you I exhort, who am also an elder, and a witness of the sufferings of Christ, and also a partaker of the glory that shall be revealed:
2 Feed the flock of God which is among you, taking the oversight *thereof,* not by constraint, but willingly; not for filthy lucre, but of a ready mind;
3 Neither as being lords over *God's* heritage, but being ensamples to the flock.
4 And when the chief Shepherd shall appear, ye shall receive a crown of glory that fadeth not away.
5 Likewise, ye younger, submit yourselves unto the elder. Yea, all *of you* be subject one to another, and be clothed with humility: for God resisteth the proud, and giveth grace to the humble.
6 Humble yourselves therefore under the mighty hand of God, that he may exalt you in due time:

7 Casting all your care upon him; for he careth for you.
8 Be sober, be vigilant; because your adversary the devil, as a roaring lion, walketh about, seeking whom he may devour:
9 Whom resist stedfast in the faith, knowing that the same afflictions are accomplished in your brethren that are in the world.
10 But the God of all grace, who hath called us unto his eternal glory by Christ Jesus, after that ye have suffered a while, make you perfect, stablish, strengthen, settle *you.*
11 To him *be* glory and dominion for ever and ever. Amen.
12 By Silvanus, a faithful brother unto you, as I suppose, I have written briefly, exhorting, and testifying that this is the true grace of God wherein ye stand.
13 The *church that is* at Babylon, elected together with *you,* saluteth you; and *so doth* Mark my son.
14 Greet ye one another with a kiss of charity. Peace *be* with you all that are in Christ Jesus. Amen.

1 Luke 24:48; Acts 1:8, 22; 5:32; 10:39
2 Matt. 20:25, 26; John 21:15, 16, 17; 1Cor. 3:9; 9:17; Titus 1:7; 2:7
4 1Cor. 9:25; Heb. 13:20
5 Isa. 57:15; 66:2
7 Ps. 37:5; 55:22; Matt. 6:25; Luke 12:11, 22
8 Job 1:7; 2:2
10 2Thess. 2:17; 3:3; 1Tim. 6:12; Heb. 13:21
12 Acts 20:24
13 Acts 12:12, 25
14 Rom. 16:16; 1Cor. 16:20

5:1 partaker of the glory that shall be revealed. Peter, apostle, elder (pastor), and eyewitness of Jesus' sufferings, had also briefly beheld the transfigured person of Jesus Christ, His face shining as the sun and His garment as white as the light (Matt. 17:2). He, with James and John, had a fleeting glimpse of Jesus' effulgent majesty. When His glory is fully revealed at His return, those who have suffered for Him and those who have faithfully served Him will share forever His eternal glory (cf. Rev. 2:10; 3:12, 21).

5:4 chief Shepherd shall appear. Jesus Christ, the "chief Shepherd" (cf. John 10:11; Heb. 13:20), will return to reward His faithful undershepherds with "a crown of glory that fadeth not away." This special reward for faithful, godly spiritual leaders is one of five crowns mentioned in Scripture for loving, faithful service (see 1 Cor. 9:25; 1 Thess. 2:19; 2 Tim. 4:8; James 1:12; Rev. 2:10; 3:11).

2 Peter

T he second epistle of Peter, was written not long before the writer's martyrdom (1:14). Two major themes contrast the true knowledge of God through Scripture and the heretical doctrines of false teachers. The issue of false teachers in 2 Peter is similar to the content in the Epistle of Jude. Peter, however, issues a warning concerning the false teachers that eventually would come, while Jude states that they were already present. The overarching truth of Peter's second epistle is that Jesus is coming again!

As in his first epistle, Peter exhorts his readers to spiritual living, reminding them that God's divine power has provided all things necessary for "life and godliness through the knowledge of" Christ, who has "called us to glory and virtue" (1:3).

Concerned about false prophets, Peter draws on the Old Testament in the second chapter for dramatic illustrations of the divine punishment awaiting those who are purveyors of false doctrines on this earth— those who have professed Christ, but reveal their true evil nature by returning to practice wickedness. These deceivers teach that God's grace made the requirements of the Law completely irrelevant, thus giving believers a license to sin without consequence.

In the last chapter, Peter counters and refutes the arguments of those who deny the second coming of Christ. Today, as in this epistle, many still ask "Where is the promise of his coming?" (3:4), insisting that time has simply run its course from the beginning of creation. In their minds, Christ's return is an unrealistic hope. Those who popularize this error reject the plain and historical fact that first century believers and millions throughout the centuries have taught that Jesus will come back to earth. The truth is an integral and irremovable part of the Word of God and historic and contemporary Christianity.

Of the 61 verses in the epistle, 25 verses (41%) are related to prophetic themes with 11 separate forecasts. Some of these are fulfilled; however, most refer to end-time events. There is only 1 quotation from the Old Testament.

Author
Peter the Apostle

Date
A.D. 66

Key Truth
True Knowledge vs. False Teachings

Historic Time
Nero's Persecution of Christians

Key Verse
1:19 We have also a more sure word of prophecy.

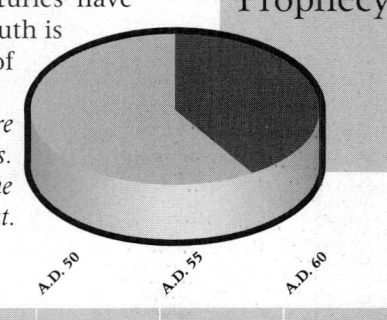

41%
Prophecy

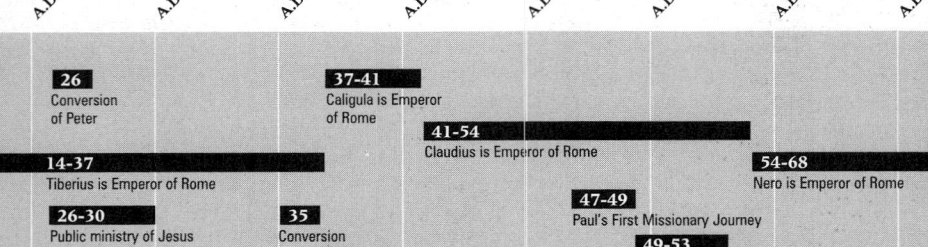

A.D. 25   A.D. 30   A.D. 35   A.D. 40   A.D. 45   A.D. 50   A.D. 55   A.D. 60   A.

26
Conversion of Peter

37-41
Caligula is Emperor of Rome

41-54
Claudius is Emperor of Rome

14-37
Tiberius is Emperor of Rome

54-68
Nero is Emperor of Rome

26-30
Public ministry of Jesus

35
Conversion of Saul (Paul)

47-49
Paul's First Missionary Journey

49-53
Paul's Second Missionary Journey

53-56
Paul's Third Missionary Journey

6
Pau
Pet
ma

Se
Pet
is

CHAPTER 1

1 Simon Peter, a servant and an apostle of Jesus Christ, to them that have obtained like precious faith with us through the righteousness of God and our Saviour Jesus Christ:

2 Grace and peace be multiplied unto you through the knowledge of God, and of Jesus our Lord,

"Great and Precious Promises"

3 According as his divine power hath given unto us all things that *pertain* unto life and godliness, through the knowledge of him that hath called us to glory and virtue:

4 Whereby are given unto us exceeding great and precious promises: that by these ye might be partakers of the divine nature, having escaped the corruption that is in the world through lust.

5 And beside this, giving all diligence, add to your faith virtue; and to virtue knowledge;

6 And to knowledge temperance; and to temperance patience; and to patience godliness;

7 And to godliness brotherly kindness; and to brotherly kindness charity.

8 For if these things be in you, and abound, they make *you that ye shall* neither *be* barren nor unfruitful in the knowledge of our Lord Jesus Christ.

9 But he that lacketh these things is blind, and cannot see afar off, and hath forgotten that he was purged from his old sins.

10 Wherefore the rather, brethren, give diligence to make your calling and election

sure: for if ye do these things, ye shall never fall:

11 For so an entrance shall be ministered unto you abundantly into the everlasting kingdom of our Lord and Saviour Jesus Christ.

12 Wherefore I will not be negligent to put you always in remembrance of these things, though ye know *them,* and be established in the present truth.

13 Yea, I think it meet, as long as I am in this tabernacle, to stir you up by putting *you* in remembrance;

14 Knowing that shortly I must put off *this* my tabernacle, even as our Lord Jesus Christ hath shewed me.

15 Moreover I will endeavour that ye may be able after my decease to have these things always in remembrance.

"A More Sure Word of Prophecy"

16 For we have not followed cunningly devised fables, when we made known unto you the power and coming of our Lord Jesus Christ, but were eyewitnesses of his majesty.

17 For he received from God the Father honour and glory, when there came such a voice to him from the excellent glory, This is my beloved Son, in whom I am well pleased.

18 And this voice which came from heaven we heard, when we were with him in the holy mount.

19 We have also a more sure word of prophecy; whereunto ye do well that ye take heed, as unto a light that shineth in a dark place, until the day dawn, and the day star arise in your hearts:

20 Knowing this first, that no prophecy of

Cross references (center column)

1 Acts 15:14
3 John 17:3; 1Thess. 2:12; 4:7
4 2Cor. 3:18; Heb. 12:10; 2Pet 2:18, 20
5 1Pet. 3:7; 2Pet. 3:18
7 Gal. 6:10
8 John 15:2
9 1John 1:7; 2:9, 11
10 2Pet. 3:17
12 Rom. 15:14, 15; 2Pet. 3:1, 17; Jude 1:5
13 2Cor. 5:1, 4
14 Deut. 4:21, 22; 31:14; John 21:18, 19
16 Matt. 17:1, 2; Mark 9:2; John 1:14
17 Matt. 3:17; 17:5; Mark 1:11; 9:7; Luke 3:22; 9:35
18 Ex. 3:5; Josh. 5:15; Matt. 17:6
19 Ps. 119:105; John 5:35
20 Rom. 12:6

1:11 entrance . . . ministered unto you abundantly into the everlasting kingdom. Dedicated Christians, who grow and become fruitful, cultivating through God's provision and power the prime qualities of faith—virtue, knowledge, self-control, patience, godliness, brotherly kindness, and brotherly love—will never stumble or fall. Not only will they enjoy assurance on earth, but their entrance into heaven will be rich and abundant. A full reward awaits the faithful, godly believer in Christ's everlasting kingdom (see Eph. 2:6–7).

1:16 power and coming of the our Lord Jesus Christ. Peter reminds his readers that at the Transfiguration, they beheld Christ's dynamic power and majestic "coming" (Gr. *parousia,* the same word used for both the Rapture and the Glorious Appearing). This scene was a foretaste of His glory to be revealed at His second coming.

1:19 more sure word of prophecy. God's prophetic Word is more complete, authoritative, and permanent than the most profound spiritual experiences, even than the Transfiguration beheld by Peter. The Word of God is the light and lamp of divine revelation, shining in a world filled with spiritual darkness (Eph. 5:11; 6:12; Col. 1:13; 1 Thess. 5:4–5; 1 Pet. 2:9). Believers will have a new understanding in their hearts of the magnitude of His future revelation in glory, as represented by the arising of "the day dawn, and the day star," clear expressions of the coming of Christ.

1:20 prophecy of the scripture. This phrase includes not only specific prophetic teachings, but the totality of God's grand revelation of Himself and His plan for time and eternity in the entire Word of God. No Scripture was privately originated in human will, released from a mere human mind, or understood by one's own power. Scripture is not the product of mere human interpretation of historical events, but the result of God's own initiative.

the scripture is of any private interpretation. **21** For the prophecy came not in old time by the will of man: but holy men of God spake *as they were* moved by the Holy Ghost.

CHAPTER 2
Warnings against False Teachers

1 But there were false prophets also among the people, even as there shall be false teachers among you, who privily shall bring in damnable heresies, even denying the Lord that bought them, and bring upon themselves swift destruction.

2 And many shall follow their pernicious ways; by reason of whom the way of truth shall be evil spoken of.

3 And through covetousness shall they with feigned words make merchandise of you: whose judgment now of a long time lingereth not, and their damnation slumbereth not.

4 For if God spared not the angels that sinned, but cast *them* down to hell, and delivered *them* into chains of darkness, to be reserved unto judgment;

5 And spared not the old world, but saved Noah the eighth *person,* a preacher of righteousness, bringing in the flood upon the world of the ungodly;

6 And turning the cities of Sodom and Gomorrah into ashes condemned *them* with an overthrow, making *them* an ensample unto those that after should live ungodly;

7 And delivered just Lot, vexed with the filthy conversation of the wicked:

8 (For that righteous man dwelling among them, in seeing and hearing, vexed *his* righteous soul from day to day with *their* unlawful deeds);

9 The Lord knoweth how to deliver the godly out of temptations, and to reserve the unjust unto the day of judgment to be punished:

10 But chiefly them that walk after the flesh in the lust of uncleanness, and despise government. Presumptuous *are they,* selfwilled, they are not afraid to speak evil of dignities.

11 Whereas angels, which are greater in power and might, bring not railing accusation against them before the Lord.

12 But these, as natural brute beasts, made to be taken and destroyed, speak evil of the things that they understand not; and shall utterly perish in their own corruption;

13 And shall receive the reward of unrighteousness, *as* they that count it pleasure to riot in the day time. Spots *they are* and blemishes, sporting themselves with their own deceivings while they feast with you;

14 Having eyes full of adultery, and that cannot cease from sin; beguiling unstable souls: an heart they have exercised with covetous practices; cursed children:

15 Which have forsaken the right way, and are gone astray, following the way of Balaam *the son* of Bosor, who loved the wages of unrighteousness;

16 But was rebuked for his iniquity: the dumb ass speaking with man's voice forbad the madness of the prophet.

17 These are wells without water, clouds that are carried with a tempest: to whom the mist of darkness is reserved for ever.

18 For when they speak great swelling *words* of vanity, they allure through the lusts of the flesh, *through much* wantonness, those that were clean escaped from them who live in error.

19 While they promise them liberty, they

Cross references (center column):

21 2Sam. 23:2; Luke 1:70; Acts 1:16; 3:18

1 Deut. 13:1; Matt. 24:11; 1Pet. 1:18; 1John 4:1; Jude 1:4, 18; Rev. 5:9

3 Deut. 32:35; 2Pet. 1:16; Jude 1:4, 15

4 Job 4:18; Luke 8:31; John 8:44; Jude 1:6; Rev. 20:2, 3

5 Gen. 7:1, 7, 23; Heb. 11:7; 1Pet. 3:19, 20; 2Pet. 3:6

6 Gen. 19:24

7 Gen. 19:16

8 Ps. 119:139, 158

9 1Cor. 10:13

10 Jude 1:4, 7, 8, 10, 16

11 Jude 1:9

12 Jer. 12:3; Jude 1:10

13 Rom. 13:13; Jude 1:12

14 Jude 1:11

15 Num. 22:5, 7, 21, 23, 28; Jude 1:11

17 Jude 1:12, 13

18 Jude 1:16

1:21 moved by the Holy Ghost. The inspired writers of the sacred Scripture were "holy men of God" who were moved, borne along, guided, and impelled by the Holy Spirit. The Spirit so guided their thoughts and writings, without suppressing their individual styles and vocabularies, that they composed and recorded (without error) in their original manuscripts the exact words God intended (2 Tim. 3:16).

2:1–22 This chapter is very similar to the book of Jude. So serious is the danger from false prophets and false teachers in this current dispensation that the Holy Spirit inspired both men to address these issues near the end of their lives, as if to warn their generation and all generations that would follow.

2:4 reserved unto judgment. Fallen angels are destined to be released from their present hell (Gr. *tartarus*) to be judged and then consigned to the lake of fire, the final hell, a place "prepared for the devil and his angels" (Matt. 25:41).

2:9 deliver the godly out of temptations. The Greek word translated "temptations" implies an attack with intent to destroy, but from which God can deliver the godly before judgment falls on the wicked. This kind of deliverance will occur prior to the Tribulation, when the Church will be kept "from the hour of temptation, which shall come upon all the world, to try them that dwell upon the earth" (Rev. 3:10). All of the wicked of ages past, having already been in hell following death, will one day stand before the Great White Throne in the day of final judgment and eternal doom (Rev. 20:11–15).

themselves are the servants of corruption: for of whom a man is overcome, of the same is he brought in bondage.

20 For if after they have escaped the pollutions of the world through the knowledge of the Lord and Saviour Jesus Christ, they are again entangled therein, and overcome, the latter end is worse with them than the beginning.

21 For it had been better for them not to have known the way of righteousness, than, after they have known *it*, to turn from the holy commandment delivered unto them.

22 But it is happened unto them according to the true proverb, The dog *is* turned to his own vomit again; and the sow that was washed to her wallowing in the mire.

20 Matt. 12:45; Luke 11:26; Heb. 6:4-8; 10:26, 27; 2Pet. 1:2, 4; 2:18

21 Luke 12:47, 48; John 9:41; 15:22

22 Prov. 26:11

1 2Pet. 1:13

2 Jude 1:17

3 1Tim. 4:1; 2Tim. 3:1; 2Pet. 2:10; Jude 1:18

4 Isa. 5:19; Jer. 17:15

CHAPTER 3
Exhortations to Faithfulness

1 This second epistle, beloved, I now write unto you; in *both* which I stir up your pure minds by way of remembrance:

2 That ye may be mindful of the words which were spoken before by the holy prophets, and of the commandment of us the apostles of the Lord and Saviour:

3 Knowing this first, that there shall come in the last days scoffers, walking after their own lusts,

4 And saying, Where is the promise of his coming? for since the fathers fell asleep, all things continue as *they were* from the beginning of the creation.

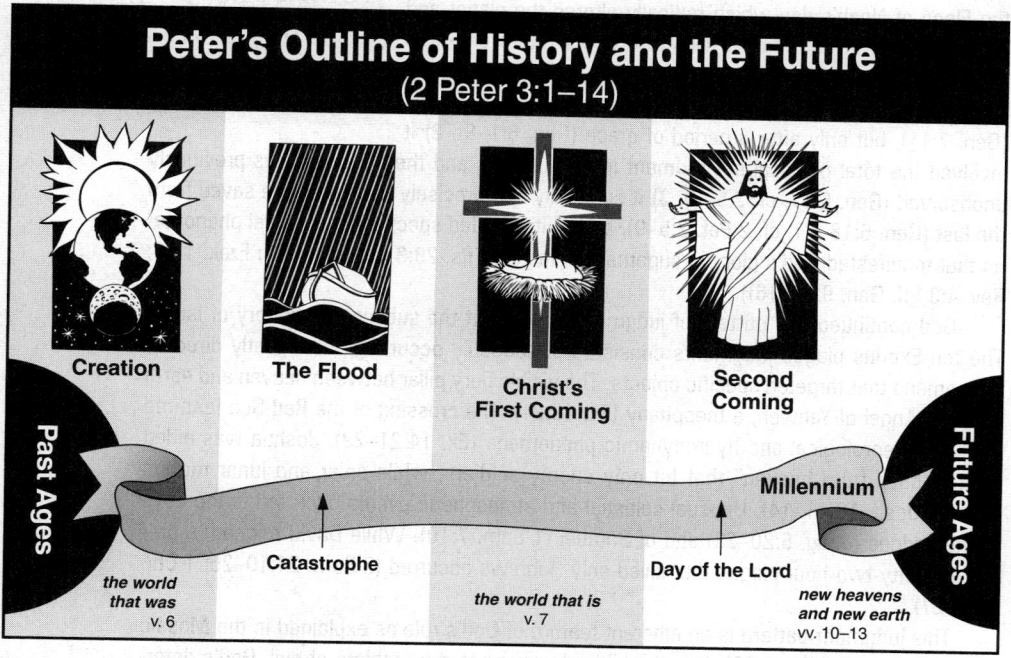

Peter's Outline of History and the Future
(2 Peter 3:1–14)

Creation | The Flood | Christ's First Coming | Second Coming

Past Ages | Future Ages

Millennium

the world that was v. 6 | Catastrophe | the world that is v. 7 | Day of the Lord | new heavens and new earth vv. 10–13

© AMG Publishers

3:3–6 Knowing this first. After describing the proliferation of false teachers to take place during this dispensation, Peter then stresses the importance of being aware of "scoffers," or those who would cast doubt on whether the Second Coming will truly happen. While the expression "in the last days" is used to characterize the entire period between Jesus' first and second advents, scoffers of our own time fit Peter's description particularly well. Ridicule and mockery arise from willful rejection of truth rather than any presentation of facts. The present popular theory of history is based on the supposedly scientific idea of uniformitarianism, which teaches that geological and biological phenomena have operated uniformly since the universe began. Peter accuses such scoffers of ignoring the biblical account of the original creation (Gen. 1), when the earth was formed out of water and in the water. Those same waters prominent in the original creation also covered the earth and destroyed it in the Noahic Flood (v. 6, cf. Gen. 6—8).

God's Pattern of Judgment

By Charles Clough

How are biblical descriptions of God's judgments such as "stars falling from heaven," "the moon turning red," and "great earthquakes" to be understood? Do they refer to literal astronomical and geophysical events, or are they merely exaggerated forms of speech and mere metaphors?

The proper way to understand prophecies of catastrophes is to follow the apostle Peter's approach and look at the true record of God's past historical judgments (2 Pet. 3:5–7). The universe, including all astronomical and geophysical processes, runs under the control of the Word of God rather than being the product of hypothesized natural laws (Col. 1:17; Heb.1:3; 11:3). God has preserved in the Bible eyewitness observations that testify to sudden, precisely-designed catastrophes affecting the celestial heavens as well as planet earth.

The most catastrophic judgment ever to befall mankind is the Flood of Noah's day which radically altered the planet and which is used in Scripture to illustrate God's future end-time judgments (Matt. 24:37–39; Luke 17:26–27). The flood judgment had a specific pattern: **1)** the judgment came suddenly (Gen. 7:11), but only after a period of grace (Gen. 6:1–8), **2)** it involved the total physical environment in the heavens and the earth in ways previously unobserved (Gen. 6:17, cf. 2:5–6), **3)** it surgically and precisely separated the saved from the lost (Gen. 6:18–21, cf. 2 Pet. 2:5–9), and **4)** it included specific geophysical phenomena that manifested God's glory in supernatural fashion (Ps. 29:3 [cf. Gen. 8:1]; Ezek. 1:28; Rev. 4:3 [cf. Gen. 9:13–16]).

> *God's past judgments model His future judgments.*

God continued this pattern of judgment throughout the subsequent history of Israel. The ten Exodus plague judgments consisted of suddenly occurring, intelligently directed phenomena that targeted specific objects. The visible fiery pillar between heaven and earth was the Angel of Yahweh, a theophany (Ex. 13:21). The crossing of the Red Sea featured unique meteorological and hydrodynamic phenomena (Ex. 14:21–29). Joshua was aided with "stones from heaven" that hit only enemy soldiers, while solar and lunar motion ceased (Josh. 10:11–14). Unusual celestial and atmospheric events occurred in the days of the Judges (Judg. 5:20–23) and of Samuel (1 Sam. 7:10). While David reigned, a precise seventy-two-hour plague that killed only Hebrews occurred (2 Sam. 24:10–25; 1 Chr. 21:9–27).

This judgment pattern is an inherent feature of God's rule as explained in the Mosaic covenant (Lev. 26; Deut. 28). It is the biblical answer to the problem of evil. God's determination to deal with the consequences of the fall extends not only to Israel but also to all nations (Deut. 30:7; 32:43; Isa. 34). The Old Testament prophets announced coming judgments within this pattern. Their prophecies of future judgments, therefore, use the vocabulary of these past judgments (e.g., Isa. 10:26; 11:15; 28:21; 29:6; Zech. 14:4–8).

The New Testament continues the Old Testament view that God judges with awesome power. Jesus and the apostle John repeat the familiar prophetic language of unprecedented physical judgments accompanied by theophanies (Matt. 24:29–30; Rev. 16:18). The same fire, smoke, hail, thunder, plague, and earthquake of the Old Testament judgments once again appear in Revelation 6—18. These terms are not exaggerations and metaphors. They point to a final culmination in God's program of separating good from evil throughout all creation. God's past judgments thus model His future judgments.

5 For this they willingly are ignorant of, that by the word of God the heavens were of old, and the earth standing out of the water and in the water:

6 Whereby the world that then was, being overflowed with water, perished.

7 But the heavens and the earth, which are now, by the same word are kept in store, reserved unto fire against the day of judgment and perdition of ungodly men.

8 But, beloved, be not ignorant of this one thing, that one day *is* with the Lord as a thousand years, and a thousand years as one day.

9 The Lord is not slack concerning his promise, as some men count slackness; but is longsuffering to us-ward, not willing that any should perish, but that all should come to repentance.

The End of Christ's Millennial Kingdom

10 But the day of the Lord will come as a thief in the night; in the which the heavens shall pass away with a great noise, and the elements shall melt with fervent heat, the earth also and the works that are therein shall be burned up.

11 *Seeing* then *that* all these things shall be

dissolved, what manner *of persons* ought ye to be in *all* holy conversation and godliness,

12 Looking for and hasting unto the coming of the day of God, wherein the heavens being on fire shall be dissolved, and the elements shall melt with fervent heat?

13 Nevertheless we, according to his promise, look for new heavens and a new earth, wherein dwelleth righteousness.

14 Wherefore, beloved, seeing that ye look for such things, be diligent that ye may be found of him in peace, without spot, and blameless.

15 And account *that* the longsuffering of our Lord *is* salvation; even as our beloved brother Paul also according to the wisdom given unto him hath written unto you;

16 As also in all *his* epistles, speaking in them of these things; in which are some things hard to be understood, which they that are unlearned and unstable wrest, as *they do* also the other scriptures, unto their own destruction.

17 Ye therefore, beloved, seeing ye know these things before, beware lest ye also, being led away with the error of the wicked, fall from your own stedfastness.

18 But grow in grace, and *in* the knowledge of our Lord and Saviour Jesus Christ. To him *be* glory both now and for ever. Amen.

Cross References

5 Gen. 1:6, 9; Ps. 24:2; 33:6; 136:6
6 Gen. 7:11, 21-23
7 Matt. 25:41; 2Thess. 1:8
8 Ps. 90:4
9 Isa. 30:18; Ezek. 18:23, 32; 33:11
10 Isa. 51:6; Matt. 24:35, 43; Mark 13:31; Rev. 3:3; 16:15; 20:11
11 1Pet. 1:15
12 Isa. 34:4; Mic. 1:4
13 Isa. 65:17; 66:22; Rev. 21:1, 27
14 1Cor. 1:8; 15:58
15 Rom. 2:4
16 Rom. 8:19; 1Cor. 15:24; 1Thess. 4:15
17 2Pet. 1:10, 11, 12; 2:18
18 Eph. 4:15

3:7 by the same word. The same Word of God that predicted the Flood and fulfilled it, also has predicted the future destruction of this world in the day of judgment and the destruction of the ungodly.

3:8 one day is with the Lord as a thousand years. God is present everywhere, and is not limited by time and space. He is not bound by the normal flow of time, as humans experience it. A thousand years is but a brief span to One who inhabits eternity; conversely, a day with the One who knows all things at all times might seem like a thousand years to finite mankind.

3:9 not slack concerning his promise. God is not late in consummating this age, since to Him it is but a brief span of time, but in His longsuffering He continues His plan to save the lost. In patience He allows time for people to repent, "not willing that any should perish, but that all should come to repentance."

3:10 day of the Lord. This term points to the special intervention of God in history involving both judgment and blessings. It is used of the End Times in general, but can also be used with reference to the key events of that time, such as the Rapture, the Tribulation, the Millennial Kingdom, or the Great White Throne Judgment. In this

verse, the emphasis is on the final end of the Millennial Kingdom (Rev. 20:7–15).

3:12 Looking for and hasting unto the coming of the day of God. With a continuing expectancy in our hearts, believers should continue looking for the "grand finale" of history, as divinely planned and set forth in prophetic Scripture. "Hasting" means eagerly desiring or enthusiastically anticipating the coming of the "day of God." This is not the second coming of Christ, but rather the arrival and presence of the day when God dissolves the heavens as we know them, the earth is burned up and the elements melt with fervent heat in a fiery cataclysmic event. This earth will be completely consumed, and a new earth, fresh from the Creator's hand, will replace the old one (Rev. 21—22).

3:13 look for new heavens and a new earth. This is not the millennial earth, but a promised eternal realm consisting of new heavenly creations, pure from sin. These consist of a new earth as described in Rev. 21:1–6, and a new city, where the Bride of Christ will live forever, the place Jesus went to prepare for us (John 14:2–3; Heb. 11:16; 12:22–24; Rev. 21:9–14).

1 John

This first of three epistles attributed to the apostle John, and the last epistle to the churches, is similar in style and vocabulary to the gospel of John. The elderly John wrote the letter primarily to those who were members of the churches of Asia Minor toward the end of the first century. Because the letter addresses such broad moral topics, it is clear that John's goal was to provide direction for those Christians who faced new challenges to their faith. At this time, there was an emergence of various groups whose teachings opposed Christianity. These people infiltrated the church, and there were many that gave in to their denial of the key fundamentals of Christianity.

Author	John the Apostle
Date	A.D. 90
Key Truth	Knowing God
Historic Time	John's Sixty Years of Life in Christ
Key Verse	1:3 — That which we have seen and heard declare we unto you.

This first epistle of John was apparently a circular letter sent to a group of churches of which Ephesus was the center, possibly the seven churches of Asia (Rev. 1:4) where John ministered. Emphasizing beautifully the spiritual truths of "light, love, and life" and warmly appealing for deeper fellowship with God and believers, this epistle is one of certainty. The word "know" in a positive sense appears some thirty times.

The purpose of the epistle is expressed in five reasons: **1)** "that your joy may be full" (1:4); **2)** "that ye sin not" (2:1); **3)** that you not be deceived by false teaching (2:26); **4)** "that ye may know that ye have eternal life" (5:13); and **5)** "that ye may believe on the name of the son of God" (5:13, cf. John 20:31). Abiding in Christ, remaining and continuing in close, intimate, prayerful fellowship with Jesus, is a strong underlying theme in the epistle, where the word "abide" appears eleven times in various contexts.

Important passages about the future include the coming of the Antichrist (2:18, 22); the coming of Christ for his saints (2:28; 3:1–3); and our preparation for the believers' judgment day (4:17).

Prophetic content involves only 4 subjects and 6 verses out of 105, or about 6 percent of the epistle. First John has no Old Testament quotations, but refers once to Cain (3:12).

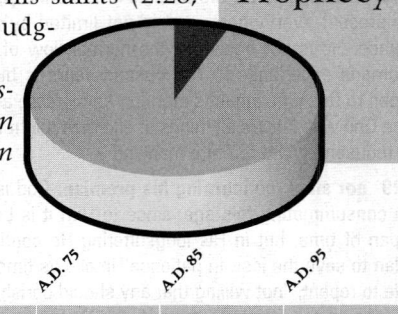

6% Prophecy

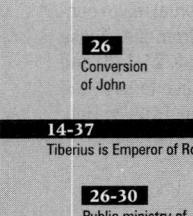
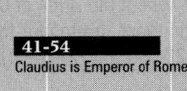
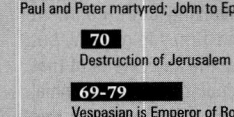
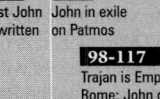

A.D. 25 A.D. 35 A.D. 45 A.D. 55 A.D. 65 A.D. 75 A.D. 85 A.D. 95 A.D.

26 Conversion of John

37-41 Caligula is Emperor of Rome

65-68 Paul and Peter martyred; John to Ephesus

90 First John is written

95 John in exile on Patmos

70 Destruction of Jerusalem

14-37 Tiberius is Emperor of Rome

41-54 Claudius is Emperor of Rome

69-79 Vespasian is Emperor of Rome

98-117 Trajan is Emperor of Rome; John dies of natural causes early in Trajan's reign

26-30 Public ministry of Jesus

54-68 Nero is Emperor of Rome

81-96 Domitian is Emperor of Rome

96-98 John returns to Ephesus when Nerva is Emperor of Rome

CHAPTER 1

1 That which was from the beginning, which we have heard, which we have seen with our eyes, which we have looked upon, and our hands have handled, of the Word of life;

2 (For the life was manifested, and we have seen *it,* and bear witness, and shew unto you that eternal life, which was with the Father, and was manifested unto us;)

3 That which we have seen and heard declare we unto you, that ye also may have fellowship with us: and truly our fellowship *is* with the Father, and with his Son Jesus Christ.

4 And these things write we unto you, that your joy may be full.

"Walk in the Light"

5 This then is the message which we have heard of him, and declare unto you, that God is light, and in him is no darkness at all.

6 If we say that we have fellowship with him, and walk in darkness, we lie, and do not the truth:

7 But if we walk in the light, as he is in the light, we have fellowship one with another, and the blood of Jesus Christ his Son cleanseth us from all sin.

8 If we say that we have no sin, we deceive ourselves, and the truth is not in us.

9 If we confess our sins, he is faithful and just to forgive us *our* sins, and to cleanse us from all unrighteousness.

10 If we say that we have not sinned, we make him a liar, and his word is not in us.

CHAPTER 2

1 My little children, these things write I unto you, that ye sin not. And if any man sin, we have an advocate with the Father, Jesus Christ the righteous:

2 And he is the propitiation for our sins: and not for ours only, but also for *the sins of* the whole world.

The Believer's Assurance

3 And hereby we do know that we know him, if we keep his commandments.

4 He that saith, I know him, and keepeth not his commandments, is a liar, and the truth is not in him.

5 But whoso keepeth his word, in him verily is the love of God perfected: hereby know we that we are in him.

6 He that saith he abideth in him ought himself also so to walk, even as he walked.

Exhortations to Brotherly Love

7 Brethren, I write no new commandment unto you, but an old commandment which ye had from the beginning. The old commandment is the word which ye have heard from the beginning.

8 Again, a new commandment I write unto you, which thing is true in him and in you: because the darkness is past, and the true light now shineth.

9 He that saith he is in the light, and hateth his brother, is in darkness even until now.

10 He that loveth his brother abideth in the light, and there is none occasion of stumbling in him.

11 But he that hateth his brother is in darkness, and walketh in darkness, and knoweth not whither he goeth, because that darkness hath blinded his eyes.

12 I write unto you, little children, because your sins are forgiven you for his name's sake.

13 I write unto you, fathers, because ye have known him *that is* from the beginning. I write unto you, young men, because ye have overcome the wicked one. I write unto you, little children, because ye have known the Father.

14 I have written unto you, fathers, because ye have known him *that is* from the beginning. I have written unto you, young men, because ye are strong, and the word of God abideth in you, and ye have overcome the wicked one.

"Love Not the World"

15 Love not the world, neither the things *that are* in the world. If any man love the world, the love of the Father is not in him.

16 For all that *is* in the world, the lust of the flesh, and the lust of the eyes, and the pride of life, is not of the Father, but is of the world.

17 And the world passeth away, and the lust thereof: but he that doeth the will of God abideth for ever.

Cross-references

1 Luke 24:39; John 1:1, 14; 20:27; 1John 4:14

2 John 1:1, 2, 4; 11:25; 14:6; 21:24; Acts 2:32; 1John 3:5; 5:20

3 John 17:21

4 John 15:11; 16:24; 2John 1:12

5 John 1:9; 8:12; 9:5; 12:35, 36; 1John 3:11

7 Eph. 1:7; 1Pet. 1:19; 1John 2:2

8 Prov. 20:9; Eccl. 7:20; 1John 2:4

9 Ps. 32:5; 51:2; Prov. 28:13

1 Rom. 8:34

2 John 1:29; 4:42; 11:51, 52; Rom. 3:25

5 John 14:21, 23; 1John 4:12, 13

6 Matt. 11:29; John 13:15

7 1John 3:11

8 John 1:9; 8:12; 12:35; 13:34; 15:12

9 1John 3:14, 15

10 2Pet. 1:10; 1John 3:14

11 John 12:35

12 Luke 24:47; 1John 1:7

15 Matt. 6:24; Rom. 12:2; Gal. 1:10; James 4:4

16 Eccl. 5:11

17 1Cor. 7:31; James 1:10; 4:14; 1Pet. 1:24

2:17 John predicts that the temporal world (Gr. *kosmos*) will pass away but that believers who do the will of God will live forever in the age to come. This prophecy foresees the coming destruction of the earth (cf. 2 Peter 3:7–13; Rev. 20:7–10).

The Promise of Eternal Life

18 Little children, it is the last time: and as ye have heard that antichrist shall come, even now are there many antichrists; whereby we know that it is the last time.

19 They went out from us, but they were not of us: for if they had been of us, they would *no doubt* have continued with us: but *they went out,* that they might be made manifest that they were not all of us.

20 But ye have an unction from the Holy One, and ye know all things.

21 I have not written unto you because ye know not the truth, but because ye know it, and that no lie is of the truth.

22 Who is a liar but he that denieth that Jesus is the Christ? He is antichrist, that denieth the Father and the Son.

23 Whosoever denieth the Son, the same hath not the Father: but he that acknowledgeth the Son hath the Father also.

24 Let that therefore abide in you, which ye have heard from the beginning. If that which ye have heard from the beginning shall remain in you, ye also shall continue in the Son, and in the Father.

25 And this is the promise that he hath promised us, *even* eternal life.

26 These *things* have I written unto you concerning them that seduce you.

27 But the anointing which ye have received of him abideth in you, and ye need not that any man teach you: but as the same anointing teacheth you of all things, and is truth, and is no lie, and even as it hath taught you, ye shall abide in him.

28 And now, little children, abide in him; that, when he shall appear, we may have confidence, and not be ashamed before him at his coming.

29 If ye know that he is righteous, ye know that every one that doeth righteousness is born of him.

CHAPTER 3
Evidences of a True Believer

1 Behold, what manner of love the Father hath bestowed upon us, that we should be called the sons of God: therefore the world knoweth us not, because it knew him not.

2 Beloved, now are we the sons of God, and it doth not yet appear what we shall be: but we know that, when he shall appear, we shall be like him; for we shall see him as he is.

3 And every man that hath this hope in him purifieth himself, even as he is pure.

4 Whosoever committeth sin transgresseth also the law: for sin is the transgression of the law.

5 And ye know that he was manifested to take away our sins; and in him is no sin.

6 Whosoever abideth in him sinneth not: whosoever sinneth hath not seen him, neither known him.

7 Little children, let no man deceive you: he that doeth righteousness is righteous, even as he is righteous.

Cross references

18 Matt. 24:5, 24; 2Thess. 2:3; 2Pet. 2:1; 1John 4:3; 2John 1:7

19 Deut. 13:13; Ps. 41:9; Matt. 24:24; John 6:37; 10:28

20 John 10:4, 5; 14:26; 16:13

22 1John 4:3; 2John 1:7

23 John 14:7, 9, 10; 14:23; 15:23

25 John 17:3

27 Jer. 31:33, 34; John 14:26; 16:13

1 John 1:12; 15:18, 19; 16:3; 17:25

2 Ps. 16:11; Isa. 56:5; Matt. 5:8; Phil. 3:21; 1John 5:1

3 1John 4:17

4 Rom. 4:15

5 Isa. 53:5, 6, 11; 1Pet. 2:22, 24

6 1John 2:4; 4:8; 3John 1:11

2:18 antichrist. This is the first appearance of this term in the Bible. It is one of several biblical designations for the end-times ruler who will appear on the world scene after the Rapture (see 2 Thess. 2:3–10). In this passage, John reminds his readers that the Antichrist is coming in the future. Then, he adds that many antichrists have already come. These are Christ-denying, false teachers who prefigure the ultimate Antichrist yet to come in the future. The "last time" refers to the period of time between the first and second comings of Christ (cf. 1 Tim. 4:1; 1 Pet. 4:7; 2 Pet. 3:3; Jude 1:18).

2:22–23 John defines the anti-Christian spirit of false prophets and false teachers by explaining that they deny that Jesus is the Christ. Their blatant rejection of Him as the Messiah is also a rejection of His incarnate deity.

2:27–28 The anointing of the Holy Spirit both guards the believer from error and guides him into truth (cf. John 14:26; 16:13). John warns of a coming apostasy of unbelief and urges true believers to hold to the truth until Jesus returns to take His Church at the Rapture. John promises us that we can have confidence (or assurance) that we will not be ashamed at Christ's coming.

3:2–3 John points to the second coming of Christ as both our future hope and our present motivation. We have been adopted into God's family and are already called the sons (lit. "children") of God. In the meantime, our future glory is not yet fully revealed to us, but we can be confident that when Jesus comes for us in the Rapture we will be completely transformed. We will become like Him in that we will be totally changed into the moral image and likeness of Christ (cf. Rom. 8:29; 1 Cor. 15:42–49; Phil. 3:21). At the Rapture, believers who have died will be resurrected and "caught up" with living believers in the air to meet the Lord (1 Thess. 4:16–17). This transformation will take place sometime during the Rapture, the judgment seat of Christ, or the Marriage Supper of the Lamb (cf. Rev. 19:7–9). John challenges his readers to purify their lives in the meantime in anticipation of Jesus' coming.

Living in the Light of His Coming

By Edward Hindson

The tension between living for today and looking for tomorrow is one of the realities of the Christian life. We often find ourselves caught between the here-and-now and the hereafter. On the one hand, we need to be ready for Jesus to come at any moment. On the other hand, we have God-given responsibilities to fulfill in this world in the meantime.

Preparing for Christ's return is something each one of us must do for ourselves. No one else can get our hearts ready to meet God. You and I must do that for ourselves. Jesus, in view of His second coming, urges us to keep watching (Matt. 24:42), be ready (Matt. 24:44), and keep serving (Matt. 24:46). He left specific instructions about what we ought to be doing while we await His coming.

1. Witness for Him everywhere you go. Our Lord taught His disciples to be His witnesses everywhere—even to the farthest ends of the earth (Acts 1:8).

2. "Go ye into all the world, and preach the gospel" (Mark 16:15). This command emphasizes the evangelistic and missionary nature of the ministry of the Church during the present era. We are to take the gospel to the whole world.

3. "Repentance and remission of sins should be preached . . . among all nations," our Lord declared in Luke 24:47. Calling men and women to repent and believe the gospel is the twofold nature of the evangelistic enterprise.

> *The balance of expectation and participation is what the Christian life is all about.*

4. "Teach all nations, baptizing them," Jesus said in Matthew 28:19. Making converts and discipling them in their walk with God is a major emphasis of the Church's mission.

5. Build the Church, in every generation. Jesus told His disciples that He would build His Church with such power that "the gates of hell shall not prevail against it" (Matt. 16:18). Jesus pictured the Church being on the march until He calls her home.

6. "Occupy till I come," Jesus said in the parable of the talents (Luke 19:13). In this parable, the servants were to "put this money to work" until their master returned. We are to be busy about the Master's business until He returns.

7. Remain faithful until He returns. Our Lord concluded His prophetic message in the Olivet Discourse by reminding His disciples to continue in faithful and wise service even though He might be gone a long time (Matt. 24:45; 25:14–21).

In the meantime, we can live with our eyes on the skies, watching for Christ to come, and with our feet on the earth, working for Him until He comes. This balance of *expectation* (that Jesus could come at any moment) and *participation* (serving Him faithfully until He comes) is what the Christian life is really all about. Living in the light of His coming keeps us focused on what is really important in life. It also keeps our attention on the balance between our present responsibilities and our future expectations.

8 He that committeth sin is of the devil; for the devil sinneth from the beginning. For this purpose the Son of God was manifested, that he might destroy the works of the devil.

9 Whosoever is born of God doth not commit sin; for his seed remaineth in him: and he cannot sin, because he is born of God.

10 In this the children of God are manifest, and the children of the devil: whosoever doeth not righteousness is not of God, neither he that loveth not his brother.

Love in Deed and Truth

11 For this is the message that ye heard from the beginning, that we should love one another.

12 Not as Cain, *who* was of that wicked one, and slew his brother. And wherefore slew he him? Because his own works were evil, and his brother's righteous.

13 Marvel not, my brethren, if the world hate you.

14 We know that we have passed from death unto life, because we love the brethren. He that loveth not *his* brother abideth in death.

15 Whosoever hateth his brother is a murderer: and ye know that no murderer hath eternal life abiding in him.

16 Hereby perceive we the love *of God,* because he laid down his life for us: and we ought to lay down *our* lives for the brethren.

17 But whoso hath this world's good, and seeth his brother have need, and shutteth up his bowels *of compassion* from him, how dwelleth the love of God in him?

18 My little children, let us not love in word, neither in tongue; but in deed and in truth.

19 And hereby we know that we are of the truth, and shall assure our hearts before him.

20 For if our heart condemn us, God is greater than our heart, and knoweth all things.

21 Beloved, if our heart condemn us not, *then* have we confidence toward God.

22 And whatsoever we ask, we receive of him, because we keep his commandments, and do those things that are pleasing in his sight.

23 And this is his commandment, That we should believe on the name of his Son Jesus Christ, and love one another, as he gave us commandment.

24 And he that keepeth his commandments dwelleth in him, and he in him. And hereby we know that he abideth in us, by the Spirit which he hath given us.

Chapter 4
"Try the Spirits"

1 Beloved, believe not every spirit, but try the spirits whether they are of God: because many false prophets are gone out into the world.

2 Hereby know ye the Spirit of God: Every spirit that confesseth that Jesus Christ is come in the flesh is of God:

3 And every spirit that confesseth not that Jesus Christ is come in the flesh is not of God: and this is that *spirit* of antichrist, whereof ye have heard that it should come; and even now already is it in the world.

4 Ye are of God, little children, and have overcome them: because greater is he that is in you, than he that is in the world.

5 They are of the world: therefore speak they of the world, and the world heareth them.

6 We are of God: he that knoweth God heareth us; he that is not of God heareth not us. Hereby know we the spirit of truth, and the spirit of error.

"God Is Love"

7 Beloved, let us love one another: for love is of God; and every one that loveth is born of God, and knoweth God.

8 He that loveth not knoweth not God; for God is love.

9 In this was manifested the love of God toward us, because that God sent his only begotten Son into the world, that we might live through him.

10 Herein is love, not that we loved God, but that he loved us, and sent his Son *to be* the propitiation for our sins.

11 Beloved, if God so loved us, we ought also to love one another.

12 No man hath seen God at any time. If we love one another, God dwelleth in us, and his love is perfected in us.

Cross references:

8 Gen. 3:15
9 1Pet. 1:23; 1John 5:18
11 John 13:34; 15:12
12 Gen. 4:4, 8
13 John 15:18, 19; 17:14
15 Matt. 5:21, 22; 1John 4:20
16 John 3:16; 15:13
17 Luke 3:11
18 Rom. 12:9; Eph. 4:15
19 John 18:37; 1John 1:8
21 Heb. 10:22
22 Matt. 7:8; 21:22; Mark 11:24; John 8:29; 9:31; 14:13; 15:7
23 Matt. 22:39; John 6:29; 13:34; 15:12; 17:3
24 John 14:23; 15:10; 17:21; 1John 4:12, 13
1 Jer. 29:8; Matt. 24:4, 5, 24; Rev. 2:2
3 2Thess. 2:7; 2John 1:7
4 John 12:31; 14:30; 16:11
6 John 8:47; 10:27; 14:17
8 1John 2:4; 3:6; 4:16
9 John 3:16
10 John 15:16
11 Matt. 18:33; John 15:12, 13

4:3 already is it in the world. Again, John points to the Antichrist who will come in the future, but then reminds us that the anti-Christian spirit is already at work in the world. This important passage indicates that Satan is always at work, opposing the work of God and the person of Christ. Therefore, it should not surprise us that there is a growing outburst of anti-Christian sentiment in secular society. Such sentiment will reach its peak after the Rapture, when the Antichrist will finally rise to power over the world (see 2 Thess. 2:3–10).

13 Hereby know we that we dwell in him, and he in us, because he hath given us of his Spirit.

14 And we have seen and do testify that the Father sent the Son *to be* the Saviour of the world.

15 Whosoever shall confess that Jesus is the Son of God, God dwelleth in him, and he in God.

16 And we have known and believed the love that God hath to us. God is love; and he that dwelleth in love dwelleth in God, and God in him.

17 Herein is our love made perfect, that we may have boldness in the day of judgment: because as he is, so are we in this world.

18 There is no fear in love; but perfect love casteth out fear: because fear hath torment. He that feareth is not made perfect in love.

19 We love him, because he first loved us.

20 If a man say, I love God, and hateth his brother, he is a liar: for he that loveth not his brother whom he hath seen, how can he love God whom he hath not seen?

21 And this commandment have we from him, That he who loveth God love his brother also.

CHAPTER 5
The Believer's Victory

1 Whosoever believeth that Jesus is the Christ is born of God: and every one that loveth him that begat loveth him also that is begotten of him.

2 By this we know that we love the children of God, when we love God, and keep his commandments.

3 For this is the love of God, that we keep his commandments: and his commandments are not grievous.

4 For whatsoever is born of God overcometh the world: and this is the victory that overcometh the world, *even* our faith.

5 Who is he that overcometh the world, but he that believeth that Jesus is the Son of God?

6 This is he that came by water and blood, *even* Jesus Christ; not by water only, but by water and blood. And it is the Spirit that beareth witness, because the Spirit is truth.

7 For there are three that bear record in

13 John 14:20
14 John 1:14; 3:17
15 Rom. 10:9
16 1John 3:24; 4:8, 12
21 Matt. 22:37, 39; John 13:34; 15:12
1 John 1:12, 13; 15:23
3 Mic. 6:8; Matt. 11:30
5 1Cor. 15:57; 1John 4:15
6 John 14:17; 15:26; 16:13; 19:34
7 John 1:1; 10:30; Rev. 19:13
9 Matt. 3:16, 17; 17:5; John 8:17, 18
10 John 3:33; 5:38
11 John 1:4
12 John 3:36; 5:24
14 1John 3:22
16 Job 42:8; Jer. 7:16; 14:11; Matt. 12:31, 32; Mark 3:29; Luke 12:10; John 17:9
17 1John 3:4
18 James 1:27; 1Pet. 1:23; 1John 3:9
19 Gal. 1:4
20 Isa. 9:6; 44:6; 54:5; Luke 24:45; John 17:3; 20:28; Acts 20:28; Rom. 9:5; 1Tim. 3:16; Titus 2:13; Heb. 1:8; 1John 5:11, 12, 13
21 1Cor. 10:14

heaven, the Father, the Word, and the Holy Ghost: and these three are one.

8 And there are three that bear witness in earth, the spirit, and the water, and the blood: and these three agree in one.

9 If we receive the witness of men, the witness of God is greater: for this is the witness of God which he hath testified of his Son.

10 He that believeth on the Son of God hath the witness in himself: he that believeth not God hath made him a liar; because he believeth not the record that God gave of his Son.

11 And this is the record, that God hath given to us eternal life, and this life is in his Son.

12 He that hath the Son hath life: *and* he that hath not the Son of God hath not life.

God Answers Prayer

13 These things have I written unto you that believe on the name of the Son of God; that ye may know that ye have eternal life, and that ye may believe on the name of the Son of God.

14 And this is the confidence that we have in him, that, if we ask any thing according to his will, he heareth us:

15 And if we know that he hear us, whatsoever we ask, we know that we have the petitions that we desired of him.

16 If any man see his brother sin a sin *which is* not unto death, he shall ask, and he shall give him life for them that sin not unto death. There is a sin unto death: I do not say that he shall pray for it.

17 All unrighteousness is sin: and there is a sin not unto death.

18 We know that whosoever is born of God sinneth not; but he that is begotten of God keepeth himself, and that wicked one toucheth him not.

19 *And* we know that we are of God, and the whole world lieth in wickedness.

20 And we know that the Son of God is come, and hath given us an understanding, that we may know him that is true, and we are in him that is true, *even* in his Son Jesus Christ. This is the true God, and eternal life.

21 Little children, keep yourselves from idols. Amen.

4:17 John predicts that true Christian believers can have "boldness" (lit. "confidence") in the day of judgment because they are in Christ. This prophecy looks forward to the Great White Throne Judgment, when unbelievers will be cast into the lake of fire (Rev. 20:11–15). Christians need not fear this judgment because they have accepted the atonement of Christ on the cross, which appeased the wrath of God against our sins (Rom. 8:1).

2 John

The apostle John is unmistakably the author of this letter. (See Introduction to 1 John.) It was probably written about the same time as the First Epistle of John (around A.D. 90) and may have been addressed to some of the same people

This personal epistle of John is addressed to "the elect lady and her children" (v. 1). Some think this refers to a dedicated Christian woman with her own family and perhaps others she influenced for Christ. Others suppose that the term, "the elect lady" is a cryptic way of addressing the letter to a local church in order to safeguard that church in case the letter fell into the hands of those hostile to Christianity. If the "lady" spoken of in verse 1 is indeed an actual woman, then she was likely a spiritual leader who was greatly respected by the apostle. If the "literal woman" theory is true, then this is the only book in the Bible that is addressed to a woman.

In the first three verses, John greets the recipients of the letter and then expresses thanks that they are "walking" (1:4), living, and serving in faithfulness to the truth of God as revealed in Scripture and in Jesus, who is the Way, the Truth, and the Life. Five times John uses the Greek word *aletheia*, "truth." The other key word, "love," appears some four times.

John addresses the dangers of spiritual deception by warning of deceivers, antichrists, and transgressors who abide not in the true "doctrine" (1:9) of Christ. Those not biblically and doctrinally correct on the incarnation, the person, and work of Christ are not to be bidden "Godspeed" (1:10). In verse seven, believers are taught that there will be many antichrists in the coming days. Throughout the centuries following John's writing of this letter, the world has seen many deceivers "who confess not that Jesus Christ is come in the flesh" (1:7). This verse also alludes to the final Antichrist (discussed elsewhere in Scripture) that will come.

Two prophetic allusions appear in verses 7–8 and amount to 15 percent of the 13 total verses. In 2 John there are no direct quotations of the Old Testament.

Author
John the Apostle
Date
A.D. 90
Key Truth
Walking in the Truth
Historic Time
John's Steadfastness for More Than Sixty Years
Key Verse
1:4
I rejoiced greatly that I found of thy children walking in truth.

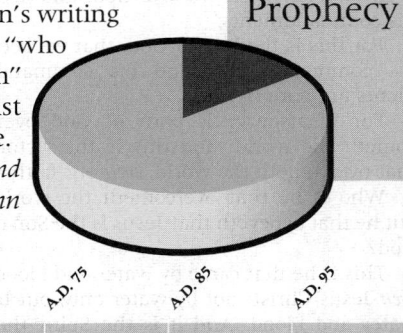

15% Prophecy

A.D. 25   A.D. 35   A.D. 45   A.D. 55   A.D. 65   A.D. 75   A.D. 85   A.D. 95

26
Conversion of John

37-41
Caligula is Emperor of Rome

65-68
Paul and Peter martyred; John to Ephesus

90
Second John is written

95
John in exile on Patmos

70
Destruction of Jerusalem

14-37
Tiberius is Emperor of Rome

41-54
Claudius is Emperor of Rome

69-79
Vespasian is Emperor of Rome

98-117
Trajan is Emperor Rome; John dies natural causes ea. in Trajan's reign

26-30
Public ministry of Jesus

54-68
Nero is Emperor of Rome

81-96
Domitian is Emperor of Rome

96-98
John returns to Ephe when Nerva is Emperor of Rome

CHAPTER 1

1 The elder unto the elect lady and her children, whom I love in the truth; and not I only, but also all they that have known the truth;
2 For the truth's sake, which dwelleth in us, and shall be with us for ever.
3 Grace be with you, mercy, *and* peace, from God the Father, and from the Lord Jesus Christ, the Son of the Father, in truth and love.

"Love One Another"

4 I rejoiced greatly that I found of thy children walking in truth, as we have received a commandment from the Father.
5 And now I beseech thee, lady, not as though I wrote a new commandment unto thee, but that which we had from the beginning, that we love one another.
6 And this is love, that we walk after his commandments. This is the commandment, That, as ye have heard from the beginning, ye should walk in it.

Exhortation to Faithfulness

7 For many deceivers are entered into the world, who confess not that Jesus Christ is come in the flesh. This is a deceiver and an antichrist.
8 Look to yourselves, that we lose not those things which we have wrought, but that we receive a full reward.
9 Whosoever transgresseth, and abideth not in the doctrine of Christ, hath not God. He that abideth in the doctrine of Christ, he hath both the Father and the Son.
10 If there come any unto you, and bring not this doctrine, receive him not into *your* house, neither bid him Godspeed:
11 For he that biddeth him Godspeed is partaker of his evil deeds.
12 Having many things to write unto you, I would not *write* with paper and ink: but I trust to come unto you, and speak face to face, that our joy may be full.
13 The children of thy elect sister greet thee. Amen.

1 John 8:32; 1John 3:18
3 1Tim. 1:2; 2John 1:1
4 3John 1:3
5 John 13:34; 15:12
6 John 14:15, 21; 15:10
7 1John 2:22; 4:1–3
8 Mark 13:9; Gal. 3:4
9 1John 2:23
10 Rom. 16:17; 1Cor. 5:11; 16:22; Gal. 1:8, 9; 2Tim. 3:5; Titus 3:10
12 John 17:13; 1John 1:4; 3John 1:13
13 1Pet. 5:13

7 John warns of "deceivers" who deny the incarnation of Christ. He reminds us that the doctrine of Christ is fundamental to true Christianity. Deceivers who deny that Christ came "in the flesh" have the spirit of antichrist. This is one of the key areas where genuine Christianity parts company with false cults. Cults inevitably deny the basic Christian belief that Jesus was God the Son incarnate in human flesh. Both the deity and humanity of Jesus Christ are essential to a biblical view of the person and nature of Christ.

3 John

The apostle John, who calls himself "the elder" (1:1), wrote the third epistle of John. This epistle is closely related to the epistles of 1 and 2 John in that they deal with similar subjects and were all written close to the same time.

Possibly written after his Patmos experience, John addresses this letter to Gaius, who may have been a pastor, but more likely was a layman. John commends Gaius for his hospitality, a virtue much prized in the early church. There were many itinerant ministers spreading the gospel in those days, dependent on churches and lay-Christians for missionary support. Again one of John's favorite words, "truth," appears five times in the first eight verses, as he commends Gaius for "walking in truth."

John strongly criticizes Diotrephes for rejecting his authority and refusing to welcome missionary evangelists. John's message includes both the duty of hospitality in the church and the danger of dictatorial, arrogant leadership.

Diotrephes seems to have risen to such power in the church that he could repudiate the authority of the oldest surviving apostle, suppress a letter written by John, refuse to receive traveling missionaries, prevent other members from so doing, and even ventured to "cast out" or exclude those who did. Following that which is evil, Diotrephes contrasts with the well-loved and faithful Demetrius, whose reputation appears unimpeachable. The apostle indicates his intention to visit this church soon and set matters straight.

Throughout history and in churches today, men much like the three mentioned in this epistle may be found. First, there is the consistent Gaius, to whom John wishes material prosperity, physical health, and spiritual prosperity. Then there is the carnal, caustic church leader, Diotrephes, who loves to have preeminence, and finally, Demetrius, the quiet faithful believer who was loved and respected by all, including other spiritual leaders.

No specific prophecy is recorded in this book, nor are there any quotations from the Old Testament.

Author
John the Apostle

Date
A.D. 90

Key Truth
Christian Hospitality

Historic Time
The Years of Ministry by Those under John's Oversight

Key Verse
1:8 . . . that we might be fellowhelpers to the truth.

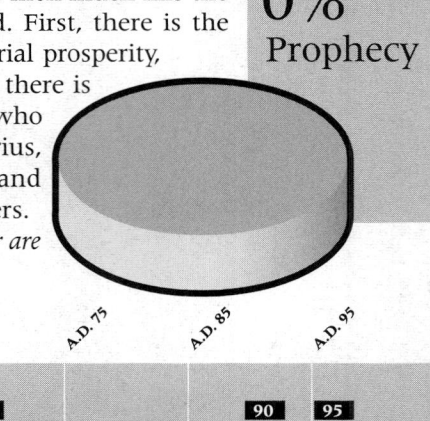

0% Prophecy

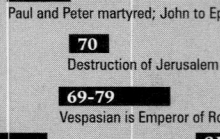

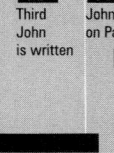

A.D. 25　A.D. 35　A.D. 45　A.D. 55　A.D. 65　A.D. 75　A.D. 85　A.D. 95　A.D.

26
Conversion of John

37-41
Caligula is Emperor of Rome

65-68
Paul and Peter martyred; John to Ephesus

90
Third John is written

95
John in exile on Patmos

14-37
Tiberius is Emperor of Rome

41-54
Claudius is Emperor of Rome

70
Destruction of Jerusalem

98-117
Trajan is Emperor of Rome; John dies of natural causes early in Trajan's reign

69-79
Vespasian is Emperor of Rome

26-30
Public ministry of Jesus

54-68
Nero is Emperor of Rome

81-96
Domitian is Emperor of Rome

96-98
John returns to Ephesus when Nerva is Emperor of Rome

CHAPTER 1

1 The elder unto the wellbeloved Gaius, whom I love in the truth.

2 Beloved, I wish above all things that thou mayest prosper and be in health, even as thy soul prospereth.

3 For I rejoiced greatly, when the brethren came and testified of the truth that is in thee, even as thou walkest in the truth.

4 I have no greater joy than to hear that my children walk in truth.

Concerning Helping Others

5 Beloved, thou doest faithfully whatsoever thou doest to the brethren, and to strangers;

6 Which have borne witness of thy charity before the church: whom if thou bring forward on their journey after a godly sort, thou shalt do well:

7 Because that for his name's sake they went forth, taking nothing of the Gentiles.

8 We therefore ought to receive such, that we might be fellow helpers to the truth.

1 2John 1:1
3 2John 1:4
4 1Cor. 4:15; Phile. 1:10
7 1Cor. 9:12, 15
11 Ps. 37:27; Isa. 1:16, 17; 1Pet. 3:11; 1John 2:29; 3:6, 9
12 John 21:24; 1Tim. 3:7
13 2John 1:12

9 I wrote unto the church: but Diotrephes, who loveth to have the preeminence among them, receiveth us not.

10 Wherefore, if I come, I will remember his deeds which he doeth, prating against us with malicious words: and not content therewith, neither doth he himself receive the brethren, and forbiddeth them that would, and casteth *them* out of the church.

11 Beloved, follow not that which is evil, but that which is good. He that doeth good is of God: but he that doeth evil hath not seen God.

12 Demetrius hath good report of all *men*, and of the truth itself: yea, and we *also* bear record; and ye know that our record is true.

Benediction

13 I had many things to write, but I will not with ink and pen write unto thee:

14 But I trust I shall shortly see thee, and we shall speak face to face. Peace *be* to thee. *Our* friends salute thee. Greet the friends by name.

Jude

The author of this letter is identified as "Jude, the servant of Jesus Christ, and brother of James" (1:1). Depending on the identification of James in verse one, Jude is either a half-brother of Jesus and not an apostle, or he is a cousin of Jesus and the apostle also known as Lebbaeus Thaddaeus (see Matt. 10:3; Luke 6:16). Some scholars feel that Jude wrote to the believers in the churches of Asia Minor, while others believe that he wrote to Jewish Christians in Roman-occupied Israel who would have been familiar with the references to Jewish history (1:7–11). The date of the letter is uncertain, but many believe that Jude wrote the epistle after Peter's death but before the destruction of Jerusalem (A.D. 70).

Author	Jude the Brother of James
Date	A.D. 68–75
Key Truth	Contending for the Faith
Historic Time	The Rise of Apostate Teachers around Jerusalem's Destruction
Key Verse	1:3 . . . ye should earnestly contend for the faith.

Writing to warn believers of false teachers, Jude uses similar material as in 2 Peter 2. Both Jude and Peter were alarmed about the rapid rise of false doctrines and the subsequent prevailing attitude of apostasy, and both men addressed these issues in their epistles.

Evidently, Jude's original intent for his letter was to discuss truths of the common salvation that both Jews and Gentiles received, but he was led of the Spirit to exhort believers to defend the truth and contend for the faith. He reminds his readers that God punishes violations of His law, citing Old Testament examples of Cain, Sodom and Gomorrah, the Egyptians, Balaam, and the rebellion of Korah (see Num. 16).

Several verses in this short epistle relate to future judgment, Christ's return, the Last Days, and the believer's destiny in the presence of His glory. An interesting tidbit of prophecy is seen in verses 14–16, where Jude quotes from ancient Jewish literature (ca. 200 B.C.). This prophecy, not recorded in the Old Testament, is from the extra-biblical book of 1 Enoch (1.9). Jude uses it to emphatically illustrate the second coming of Christ.

In the 25 verses of this short epistle, there are 8 distinct predictions in 10 verses, 40 percent of the whole. Jude has no Old Testament quotations, but contains several allusions.

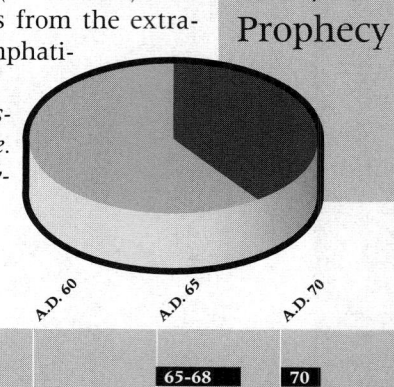

40%
Prophecy

A.D. 35 • A.D. 40 • A.D. 45 • A.D. 50 • A.D. 55 • A.D. 60 • A.D. 65 • A.D. 70 • A.

30
Conversion of James

41–54
Claudius is Emperor of Rome

37–41
Caligula is Emperor of Rome

47–49
Paul's First Missionary Journey

14–37
Tiberius is Emperor of Rome

49–53
Paul's Second Missionary Journey

35
Conversion of Saul (Paul)

53–56
Paul's Third Missionary Journey

54–68
Nero is Emperor of Rome

65–68
Paul and Peter martyred; John to Ephesus

70
Destruction of Jerusalem and the temple

7
Juc writ

69–79
Vespasian is Emperor of R

CHAPTER 1

1 Jude, the servant of Jesus Christ, and brother of James, to them that are sanctified by God the Father, and preserved in Jesus Christ, *and* called.
2 Mercy unto you, and peace, and love, be multiplied.

Warnings from History to the Ungodly

3 Beloved, when I gave all diligence to write unto you of the common salvation, it was needful for me to write unto you, and exhort *you* that ye should earnestly contend for the faith which was once delivered unto the saints.
4 For there are certain men crept in unawares, who were before of old ordained to this condemnation, ungodly men, turning the grace of our God into lasciviousness, and denying the only Lord God, and our Lord Jesus Christ.
5 I will therefore put you in remembrance, though ye once knew this, how that the Lord, having saved the people out of the land of Egypt, afterward destroyed them that believed not.
6 And the angels which kept not their first estate, but left their own habitation, he hath reserved in everlasting chains under darkness unto the judgment of the great day.
7 Even as Sodom and Gomorrah, and the cities about them in like manner, giving themselves over to fornication, and going after strange flesh, are set forth for an example, suffering the vengeance of eternal fire.

8 Likewise also these *filthy* dreamers defile the flesh, despise dominion, and speak evil of dignities.
9 Yet Michael the archangel, when contending with the devil he disputed about the body of Moses, durst not bring against him a railing accusation, but said, The Lord rebuke thee.
10 But these speak evil of those things which they know not: but what they know naturally, as brute beasts, in those things they corrupt themselves.
11 Woe unto them! for they have gone in the way of Cain, and ran greedily after the error of Balaam for reward, and perished in the gainsaying of Korah.
12 These are spots in your feasts of charity, when they feast with you, feeding themselves without fear: clouds *they are* without water, carried about of winds; trees whose fruit withereth, without fruit, twice dead, plucked up by the roots;
13 Raging waves of the sea, foaming out their own shame; wandering stars, to whom is reserved the blackness of darkness for ever.

The Second Coming of Christ

14 And Enoch also, the seventh from Adam, prophesied of these, saying, Behold, the Lord cometh with ten thousands of his saints,
15 To execute judgment upon all, and to convince all that are ungodly among them of all their ungodly deeds which they have ungodly committed, and of all their hard *speeches* which ungodly sinners have spoken against him.

Cross references:
1 Luke 6:16; John 17:11, 12, 15; Acts 1:13
3 Phil. 1:27; 1Tim. 1:18; 6:12; 2Tim. 1:13; 4:7; Titus 1:4
4 Rom. 9:21, 22; Gal. 2:4; Titus 1:16; 2:11
5 Num. 14:29, 37; 26:64
6 John 8:44; Rev. 20:10
7 Gen. 19:24
8 2Pet. 2:10
9 Dan. 10:13; 12:1; Rev. 12:7
9 Zech. 3:2; 2Pet. 2:11
10 2Pet. 2:12
11 Gen. 4:5; Num. 16:1; 22:7, 21
12 Prov. 25:14
13 Isa. 57:20
14 Gen. 5:18; Deut. 33:2; Dan. 7:10; Zech. 14:5; Matt. 25:31; 2Thess. 1:7; Rev. 1:7
15 1Sam. 2:3; Ps. 31:18; 94:4; Mal. 3:13

---

4 ordained to this condemnation. False teachers and apostates have been generally condemned as early as Old Testament times (1 Kings 18; Isa. 8:19–21; Jer. 29:9, 31; Hos. 9:9; Zeph. 3:1–8). The Scriptures condemn in the most forceful terms those who twist the doctrine of God's grace to allow and approve gross sexual immorality and those who deny the deity, atonement, and miracles of Jesus Christ.

6 the judgment of the great day. The angels who sinned (fallen angels) are currently imprisoned and destined to continue in everlasting chains through the final judgment. Some say these are "the sons of God" in Genesis 6:2, angels who assumed physical form, and cohabited with "the daughters of men," resulting in a species of "giants" (Hebr. *nephilim*) that inhabited the earth before the Flood. These "angels that sinned" by leaving their first estate or heaven are presently enchained in darkness.

10–13 blackness of darkness for ever. False teachers within the Church, themselves actually lost and without Christ, will suffer the fate of everlasting separation from God, pictured also as "the lake of fire" (Rev. 20:14–15).

14 Enoch. This patriarch was raptured long before the Flood (Gen. 5:18–24). Although a similar statement is recorded in a noncanonical ancient work known as First Enoch (I.9), the Spirit of God, inspiring Jude, is the real source of the prophecy. By the phrase "behold the Lord cometh" it seems evident that though Enoch prophesied of judgment to come in ancient times, this yet to be fulfilled prophecy relates to the Second Coming (see 2 Thess. 1:7–10).

15 To execute judgment. That Jesus is both Savior and Judge is evident (see Matt. 13:47–50; Rev. 1:7; 14:14–15; 19:11–21; 20:11–15). The final sentence is eternal hell.

16 These are murmurers, complainers, walking after their own lusts; and their mouth speaketh great swelling *words,* having men's persons in admiration because of advantage.

"Keep Yourselves in the Love of God"

17 But, beloved, remember ye the words which were spoken before of the apostles of our Lord Jesus Christ;
18 How that they told you there should be mockers in the last time, who should walk after their own ungodly lusts.
19 These be they who separate themselves, sensual, having not the Spirit.
20 But ye, beloved, building up yourselves

16 Prov. 28:21
18 2Pet. 2:1; 3:3
19 Prov. 18:1; 1Cor. 2:14
20 Rom. 8:26; Eph. 6:18
23 Amos 4:11; Zech. 3:2, 4, 5; Rom. 11:14
24 Rom. 16:25
25 Rom. 16:27; 1Tim. 1:17; 2:3

on your most holy faith, praying in the Holy Ghost,
21 Keep yourselves in the love of God, looking for the mercy of our Lord Jesus Christ unto eternal life.
22 And of some have compassion, making a difference:
23 And others save with fear, pulling *them* out of the fire; hating even the garment spotted by the flesh.
24 Now unto him that is able to keep you from falling, and to present *you* faultless before the presence of his glory with exceeding joy,
25 To the only wise God our Saviour, *be* glory and majesty, dominion and power, both now and ever. Amen.

---

18 in the last time. While throughout this present dispensation, between the first advent and the second coming of Christ, there have been those who ridicule true believers, the scoffers doubtless multiply toward the close of the age. Immoral and amoral, they seek their own unholy sensual desires, following "after their own ungodly lusts."

20–21 In the light of the fact that Jesus is coming again and that He will judge all men, Jude challenges believers to build themselves up in the Scriptures (study the Bible), to pray, to "keep . . . in the love of God" (largely by loving others), and to compassionately seek to warn the lost of their future condition.

24–25 present you faultless before the presence of his glory. This great doxology (vv. 24–25) looks forward to those heavenly scenes, when the raptured and resurrected saints are presented as a glorious Bride, holy and blameless before the true God. The names of those in this "church of the firstborn" (Heb. 12:23) are written in heaven (Eph. 5:25–27; Col. 1:22; 1 Thess. 3:13; Rev. 19:7–8; 21:9—22:5). Traditional Hebrew weddings involved three stages: 1) the betrothal; 2) the presentation, often a celebration lasting several days, suggesting the joyful assembly of all New Testament saints with Jesus (John 14:2–3); and 3) the ceremony or exchange of vows, concluding with a great final supper.

Revelation

The book of Revelation is the message from Jesus Christ to His Church in which He outlines the climax of human history. The book begins with the glorious appearance of Jesus Christ to His aged servant John, in which Christ commissions John to write down what he has seen and the things that were about to be revealed to him. The visions in the book were revealed to John while he was imprisoned "for the testimony of Jesus" on the Island of Patmos during the reign of Domitian (A.D. 81–96). Perhaps the most venerated church leader of his day, John was the only one of the twelve apostles still alive at the time he wrote this book. The book of Revelation was immediately and universally accepted as the last of the inspired writings. Neither its authorship by John nor the late date of its writing (A.D. 95) has ever been seriously questioned by those who interpret the Bible literally. Not until the third century was the suggestion launched that "another John" may have written it, and such a notion has no credibility in history.

Christ gave this vision to John and to all believers to comfort them in their trials. He assures them that there will be a day of rest for those who love God, that He will meet them in the air, and that while the Church is with Him in heaven the terrible Tribulation of which He spoke will occur on earth (see Mark 13:19). The importance of the Tribulation period is confirmed in the fact that twelve chapters of the book are devoted to describing over fifty details about it. When combined with the many Old Testament passages that mention the Tribulation, more prophecy is devoted to that brief period of time than any other comparable period in history.

However, a grim portrayal of the future days of the Tribulation is not all that Revelation contains. For instance, the glorious rapture of the Church is detailed in 4:1–2. The Church is mentioned nineteen times in chapters 1—3, but in the twelve chapters that describe the Tribulation period, it is not mentioned once. That omission can easily be explained when you understand that the Church is taken to heaven prior to the beginning of the Tribulation (4:1–2; 5:9). A study of other passages on the Rapture (e.g., 1 Thess. 4:13–18; 1 Cor. 15:50–58) clearly demonstrates that the Church escapes that time of tribulation predicted exclusively for Israel and the unbelieving world by the Hebrew prophets. Following the Tribulation, Christ and His saints will return

Author
John the Apostle

Date
A.D. 95

Key Truth
Future Things

Historic Time
John's Vision to Its Fulfillment

Key Verse
1:19
and the things which shall be hereafter.

95%
Prophecy

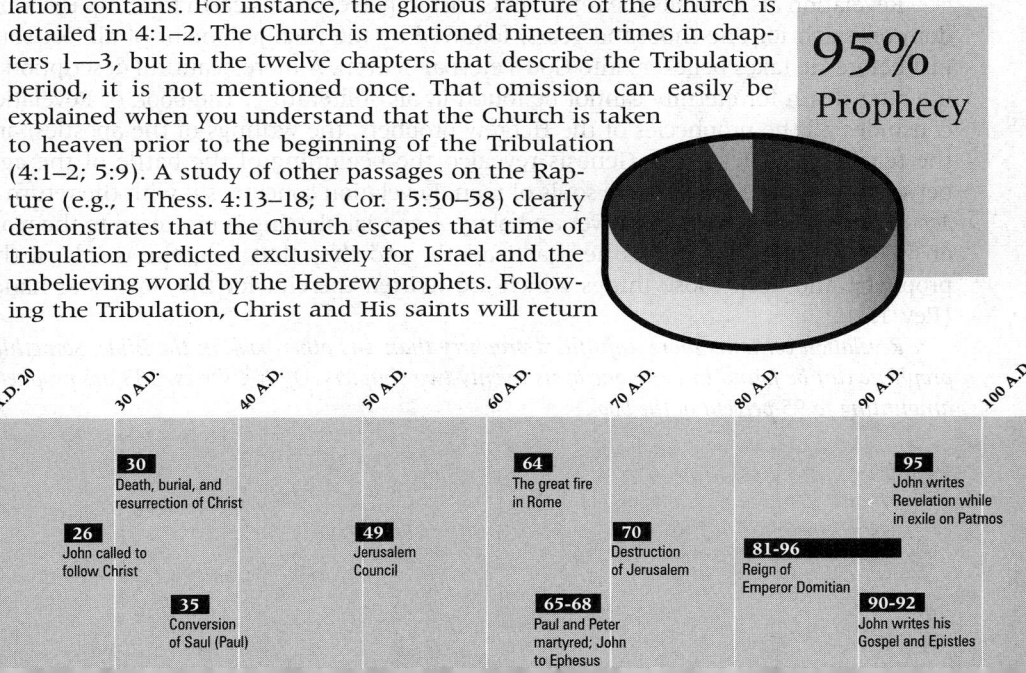

A.D. 20 | 30 A.D. | 40 A.D. | 50 A.D. | 60 A.D. | 70 A.D. | 80 A.D. | 90 A.D. | 100 A.D.

30
Death, burial, and resurrection of Christ

26
John called to follow Christ

35
Conversion of Saul (Paul)

49
Jerusalem Council

64
The great fire in Rome

70
Destruction of Jerusalem

65-68
Paul and Peter martyred; John to Ephesus

81-96
Reign of Emperor Domitian

95
John writes Revelation while in exile on Patmos

90-92
John writes his Gospel and Epistles

to earth to rule for a thousand years, followed by a day when evil will be vanquished forever and Satan and his minions and all who have spurned the Lord Jesus will be cast into eternal hell.

Revelation 1:19 provides a three-fold outline of the entire book. The book flows chronologically along these lines, with the exception of chapter 12, which is a parenthetical flashback that culminates in the middle of the Tribulation.

AN OUTLINE OF REVELATION

I. **The Things Which Thou Hast Seen . . .**
   The introduction and description of the resurrected Christ (chap. 1)

II. **The Things Which Are . . .**
   The outline of church history (chaps. 2—3)

III. **The Things Which Shall Be Hereafter . . .**
   A. The rapture of the Church and a scene in heaven (chaps. 4—5)
   B. The seven-year Tribulation; seal, trumpet, and vial judgments; the short reign of Antichrist; and the destruction of Babylon (chaps. 6—18)
   C. The glorious appearing of Christ (chap. 19)
   D. The binding of Satan, the Millennial Kingdom of Christ, and the final judgment (20)
   E. The eternal order called heaven (chaps. 21—22)

The book of Revelation relates the events of John's visions through the use of symbols, many of which are unique to the book and some of which are not explained. The key to understanding the book and the visions is to understand what is literal and what is symbolic, and to realize that even the symbols (trumpets, vials, the Beast, etc.) represent real events and real people. If you do not interpret the book literally, you will fail to understand its real meaning, and the blessing of the realities it portrays will be diminished.

Revelation also unveils the return of Christ in power to this earth to set up His kingdom on earth for one thousand years, followed by the final judgment of all lost souls just before He takes believers into God's eternal heaven. A more beautiful description of life after death for eternity cannot be found in all of literature. The book of Revelation concludes all the prophecies of the Hebrew prophets, the writings of the apostles, and the teachings of Jesus. As Genesis revealed the beginning of the battle of the ages between God and Satan for the souls of men, Revelation concludes it with the return of Jesus Christ to this earth in power and glory. A special blessing is promised to the reader of Revelation: "Blessed is he that readeth, and they that hear the words of this prophecy, and keep those things which are written therein: for the time is at hand" (Rev. 1:3).

Revelation contains more unfulfilled prophecy than any other book in the Bible. Something prophetic can be found in every one of its twenty-two chapters. Of 404 verses, 383 are prophetic, amounting to 95 percent of the book.

CHAPTER 1

1 The Revelation of Jesus Christ, which God gave unto him, to shew unto his servants things which must shortly come to pass; and he sent and signified *it* by his angel unto his servant John:

2 Who bare record of the word of God, and of the testimony of Jesus Christ, and of all things that he saw.

3 Blessed *is* he that readeth, and they that hear the words of this prophecy, and keep those things which are written therein: for the time *is* at hand.

1 John 3:32
3 Luke 11:28; 1Pet. 4:7
4 Ex. 3:14; Zech. 3:9; Rev. 1:8; 3:1; 4:5; 5:6
5 John 8:14; 13:34; 15:9
6 1Tim. 6:16; Heb. 13:21; 1Pet. 2:5, 9; 4:11; 5:11; Rev. 5:10; 20:6

"To the Seven Churches"

4 John to the seven churches which are in Asia: Grace *be* unto you, and peace, from him which is, and which was, and which is to come; and from the seven Spirits which are before his throne;

5 And from Jesus Christ, *who is* the faithful witness, *and* the first begotten of the dead, and the prince of the kings of the earth. Unto him that loved us, and washed us from our sins in his own blood,

6 And hath made us kings and priests unto God and his Father; to him *be* glory

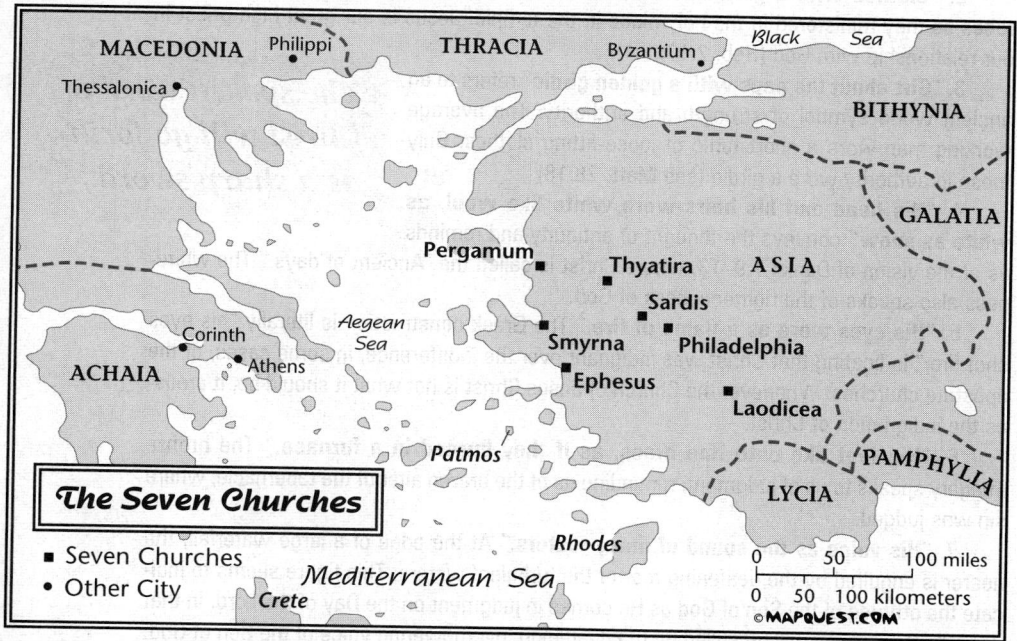

The Seven Churches

- Seven Churches
- Other City

©MAPQUEST.COM

1:1–2 Revelation (Gr. *apokalupsis*) means to "reveal" or "unveil" that which is hidden. The term "signified" does not mean that this is a book of unknowable signs, but that God signified by the miraculous presence of the announcing angel that the message was from Him. Much of this revelation was visual; thus, John wrote down what he saw (v. 2).

1:3 A special blessing is offered to those who read, hear, and obey the teachings of this book. The message is that Jesus is coming again, and we should live every day in anticipation of that coming. It is important to keep in mind that this book must be understandable or it could not provide the reader with the promised "blessing." When taken in its entirety, this book gives us hope for the future. Spiritualizing or allegorizing the book, as some

interpreters tend to do, destroys its intended meaning.

1:4 This is the first of fifty-four uses of the word "seven" in the book of Revelation. While these are symbolic of "completion," they are also literal references to various series of sevens that transpire in this prophecy. The book was a blessing to the seven churches of Asia to whom it was written. But it also has meaning for all churches throughout history. It is thought by many that these specific churches were selected because they typify the seven stages of Church history.

1:6 Our current status as sons of God by faith in the gospel also includes our becoming "kings and priests unto God," forever when Christ comes to reign.

John's Vision of Christ

By Tim LaHaye

As John turned to see who was speaking to him (Rev. 1:12), he saw seven golden candlesticks and a person in their midst, for whom he lists ten very descriptive details.
Nothing about the person of Christ is interpreted because the Holy Spirit has interpreted
these details on other occasions in the Scriptures. Each of these characteristics of John's
vision are noted along with their meaning from Scripture:

1. **"One like unto the Son of man"** indicates that this person was not a grotesque
supernatural creature; rather, His appearance was human. "Son of man," a title Jesus frequently applied to Himself, is used of the Messiah in all four Gospels and in Daniel 7:13.

2. **"Clothed with a garment down to the foot."** Typically high priests wore long
robes as they ministered in the holy place in the temple. Jesus is our great high priest in
our relationship with God (Heb. 2:17; 3:1).

3. **"Girt about the paps with a golden girdle"** refers to an
ancient world symbol of strength and authority. The average
working man wore a short tunic of loose-fitting clothes. Only
those in authority wore a girdle (see Matt. 28:18).

> *The spoken word of Christ will go forth as a sharp sword.*

4. **"His head and his hairs were white like wool, as
white as snow"** conveys the thought of antiquity and reminds
us of the vision of Daniel 7:9–13, where Christ is called the "Ancient of days." The white-
ness also speaks of the righteousness of God.

5. **"His eyes were as a flame of fire."** The Greek construction is literally "his eyes
shot fire," indicating that Christ was indignant over the indifference, in some cases, of the
apostate churches. Whenever the Church of Jesus Christ is not what it should be, it arous-
es the indignation of Christ.

6. **"His feet like unto fine brass, as if they burned in a furnace."** The bronze
imagery speaks to us of judgment, reminding us of the brazen altar of the tabernacle, where
sin was judged.

7. **"His voice as the sound of many waters."** At the edge of a large waterfall, the
hearer is engulfed by the deafening roar of the turbulent waters. This figure seems to indicate the attitude of the Son of God as He comes in judgment on the Day of the Lord. In that
day, all other voices will be stilled by the deafening, overpowering voice of the Son of God.

8. **"He had in his right hand seven stars."** The Lord Himself interpreted this in verse
20, "The seven stars are the angels of the seven churches." The Greek word translated
"angels" is literally "messengers." Some believe the word "angels" here refers to the messengers (pastors) appointed by God to lead local congregations. Another view is that each
messenger is an actual angel especially assigned to that church. This could mean that all
churches have guardian angels, just as Christ indicated that little children have guardian
angels (Matt. 18:10).

9. **"Out of his mouth went a sharp two-edged sword."** Hebrews 4:12 tells us that
the Word of God is "sharper than any two-edged sword." Evidently the spoken word of
Christ will go forth as a sharp sword against which there will be no defense in the day of
judgment.

10. **"His countenance was as the sun shineth in his strength"** speaks of the divine
nature of Christ and reminds us of the description of Christ on the Mount of Transfiguration
(Matt. 17:2).

and dominion for ever and ever. Amen.

7 Behold, he cometh with clouds; and every eye shall see him, and they *also* which pierced him: and all kindreds of the earth shall wail because of him. Even so, Amen.

8 I am Alpha and Omega, the beginning and the ending, saith the Lord, which is, and which was, and which is to come, the Almighty.

John on the Isle of Patmos

9 I John, who also am your brother, and companion in tribulation, and in the kingdom and patience of Jesus Christ, was in the isle that is called Patmos, for the word of God, and for the testimony of Jesus Christ.

10 I was in the Spirit on the Lord's day, and heard behind me a great voice, as of a trumpet,

11 Saying, I am Alpha and Omega, the first and the last: and, What thou seest, write in a book, and send *it* unto the seven churches which are in Asia; unto Ephesus, and unto

7 Dan. 7:13;
Zech. 12:10

8 Rev. 2:8;
4:8; 11:17;
16:5; 21:6;
22:13

9 Rom. 8:17;
Phil. 1:7;
4:14; 2Tim.
1:8; 2:12;
Rev. 1:2; 6:9

10 John
20:26; Rev.
4:1, 2; 10:8;
17:3; 21:10

12 Ex. 25:37

13 Ezek.
1:26; Dan.
7:13

14 Dan. 7:9;
10:6; Rev.
2:18; 19:12

15 Ezek. 1:7;
43:2

16 Isa. 49:2;
Acts 26:13

17 Ezek.
1:28; Dan.
8:18; 10:10

Smyrna, and unto Pergamos, and unto Thyatira, and unto Sardis, and unto Philadelphia, and unto Laodicea.

12 And I turned to see the voice that spake with me. And being turned, I saw seven golden candlesticks;

13 And in the midst of the seven candlesticks *one* like unto the Son of man, clothed with a garment down to the foot, and girt about the paps with a golden girdle.

14 His head and *his* hairs *were* white like wool, as white as snow; and his eyes *were* as a flame of fire;

15 And his feet like unto fine brass, as if they burned in a furnace; and his voice as the sound of many waters.

16 And he had in his right hand seven stars: and out of his mouth went a sharp two-edged sword and his countenance *was* as the sun shineth in his strength.

17 And when I saw him, I fell at his feet as dead. And he laid his right hand upon me, saying unto me, Fear not; I am the first and the last:

1:7 Behold, he cometh with clouds ... every eye shall see him, and they also which pierced him: and all kindreds shall wail because of him. This guarantee that Jesus is coming again literally and physically accords with 317 other promises of His coming again. The second coming of Jesus is mentioned more frequently than any other subject, except salvation itself. It was mentioned by the prophets, apostles, angels, and even Jesus Himself (see John 14:1–4; Matt. 24:27–30). Jesus will return, and all who have received Him by faith will join Him. Those who reject Him will mourn or "wail" at His coming.

1:8 The first words of Jesus to John personally identify Him with the "I AM" of Scripture, for He calls Himself the "Alpha and Omega." These are the first and last letters of the Greek alphabet. The title signifies, in the language of communication, the completeness with which God revealed Himself to mankind through Christ. This is nothing less than an official affirmation by Jesus of His personal deity. No ordinary human would ever say of himself, "I am the first and last."

1:9 companion in tribulation. This is not the Great Tribulation mentioned by Jesus in Matthew 24 and described in Revelation 6—18. That Tribulation will last only seven years and is yet to happen. The "tribulation" John had in mind was the suffering that he was currently experiencing as a disciple of Jesus Christ. Becoming a Christian does not exempt one from the tribulations of this world, but it does exempt believers

from the seven-year Tribulation intended for Israel and unbelieving Gentiles (see Rom. 5:9; 1 Thess. 1:10; 5:9; Rev. 3:10).

1:9 for the word of God, and for the testimony of Jesus Christ. John received this revelation while confined on the Isle of Patmos. External evidence points to the writing of Revelation by John when he was banished to Patmos during the reign of Roman emperor Domitian (A.D. 81–96). Evidence has been found that Patmos was used to incarcerate prisoners at that period of history. That would make the writing of Revelation in and around the traditionally accepted date of A.D. 95, near the very end of John's life (see article on Preterism and the Date of Revelation).

1:10 This is the first use of "the Lord's Day" in the New Testament. By A.D. 95, Christians were accustomed to meeting to read Scripture, teach, and pray on the first day of the week, which they called "the Lord's Day." This was their testimony, that their Lord rose from the dead on the first day of the week.

1:11 John is commissioned by the voice of the Lord Himself to send this message to "the seven churches" of Asia, all of which he probably knew personally. The prophetic message of Revelation was intended for much broader distribution than these seven churches. Many believe that these churches were selected by Christ as typical of the seven stages of Church history (see article on the seven churches).

The Book of Revelation

By Robert Thomas

How do you strengthen people who are persecuted for being Christians? How do you motivate God-rejecting people to repent and turn to Him? God's answer to both questions is the same: by telling them what is to happen in the future, the very thing He does in the final book of the Bible.

That book, Revelation (sometimes called the Apocalypse), centers around prophetic predictions of the future (Rev. 1:3; 10:11; 18:20; 19:10; 22:6–7, 9–10, 18–19). Revelation plays a significant role in biblical prophecy as a whole. John, one of Jesus' twelve apostles, wrote the book in about A.D. 95 while in exile on a small Mediterranean island off the coast of Asia Minor (1:9). The resurrected Jesus appeared to him there and gave him information about the future for him to deliver to messengers from seven churches of the nearby Roman province located in the western portion of what is today the country of Turkey.

Revelation deals with the return of Jesus Christ.

The announced subject of the book is "things that must happen soon" (Rev. 1:1), the highlight of which is stated in the book's theme verse, "Behold, He (Jesus) will come with the clouds" (1:7). Revelation deals with the return of Jesus Christ and all the events accompanying His return. In instructing John to write the book, Jesus appeared to the Apostle in a glorified state (1:12–16) and gave him an advance outline of the prophecy (1:19). It included the vision of Jesus he had just seen (1:12–16), a message to each of the seven churches (Rev. 2—3), and events that were to transpire on earth after the faithful in the churches are taken away to heaven at Jesus' promised coming (Rev. 4—22).

Two themes recur in Jesus' messages to the churches, one of threat and one of encouragement. He issued threats to those in the churches whose relationship to Himself was only superficial. He promised to come and judge these people because of their empty profession (2:5; 3:11, 16). For them an unparalleled hour of trial is imminent (3:10). His words of encouragement went to the faithful who had stood firm in the face of persecution caused by their faith in Him. For these He promised His imminent return to deliver them from adversity (2:25; 3:11, 20). Chapters 2 and 3 advise the churches about needed adjustments in their lives in view of the outpouring of God's wrath that is described in chapters 4 and following.

Jesus devoted the bulk of His revelation to John to describing judgments about to fall on an unrepentant world because of its rebellion against God. Through prophetic vision, He first allowed John to visit the heavenly throne-room from which the judgments will proceed (Revelation 4—5). There the prophet encountered the Father, seated on His throne and the slain Lamb, Jesus, who was the only one worthy to open a seven-sealed scroll that the Father gave Him.

As it turns out, that seven-sealed scroll contained the remainder of Revelation except for some concluding remarks in chapter 22. John saw the breaking of the first six seals (Rev. 6) portrayed as a drama before his eyes. First came four different-colored horses with riders depicting peaceful conquest of the world (white horse), warfare and bloodshed (red horse), widespread famine (black horse), and death to one-quarter of earth's population (pale horse). Then he witnessed martyred saints in heaven praying for God to avenge their blood by punishing people responsible for their deaths. Next, the sixth seal divulged various cosmic and terrestrial disturbances that unmistakably signal to earth's inhabitants that

the seal judgments have initiated the predicted wrath of God against rebellious humanity.

The breaking of the seventh seal (8:1) resulted in the sounding of seven trumpets (8:7—11:15), in themselves seven physical judgments additional to and more severe than those of the first six seals. The first six trumpets were prophetic of **1)** the burning up of a third of earth's vegetation, **2)** destruction of a third of sea life, **3)** poisoning of a third of earth's fresh water, **4)** darkening of a third of the heavenly bodies, **5)** a pain-inflicting demonic locust plague, and **6)** death to a third of earth's inhabitants through another demonic visitation.

The blowing of the seventh trumpet (11:15) ushered in another series of judgments predicting God's future visitations against rebellious mankind, the seven vials of God's wrath (15:7). The seven vials represented to John what will be the seven last plagues that will complete God's wrath (15:1) against creatures who have rebelled against Him. The first six of those plagues will produce **1)** the afflicting of false-christ worshipers with incurable sores (16:2), **2)** death to all sea life (16:3), **3)** transformation of all fresh water into blood (16:4–7), **4)** scorching of all rebels because of superheat from the sun (16:8–9), **5)** darkening of the false-christ's kingdom (16:10–11), and **6)** battle preparation for the doom of earth's kings (16:12–16).

The prophetic message of the seventh vial of God's wrath carries forward into the eternal state (16:17—22:5). It will include eight main events: the second coming of Christ to conquer His enemies, a summons of birds to feast on conquered humans, the slaughter of Christ's human opponents, Satan's imprisonment, Satan's release and final defeat, the setting of the Great White Throne Judgment, sentencing of lost people to the lake of fire, and a sketch of the New Jerusalem and those excluded from it (19:11—21:8).

Along with his description of the seals, trumpets, and vials, John's visions also furnish supplemental data (7:1–17: 10:1—14:20; 17:1—18:24; 21:9—22:5) to give readers details of the future judgments that will occupy seven years (the Tribulation), one thousand years (the Millennium), and eternity future as this present creation of God runs its course and steps aside to be replaced by His new creation.

Revelation's picture of the future is more than sufficient to strike terror in the thoughts of any person who has not made his/her peace with God through a personal invitation to Christ for salvation from sin and its punishment. But that picture is also more than sufficient to offer incentive to the faithful believer in Christ to persevere through present trials, awaiting His imminent coming to deliver from those trials to a future of unparalleled joy.

18 I am he that liveth, and was dead; and, behold, I am alive for evermore, Amen; and have the keys of hell and of death.

19 Write the things which thou hast seen, and the things which are, and the things which shall be hereafter;

20 The mystery of the seven stars which thou sawest in my right hand, and the seven golden candlesticks. The seven stars

18 Ps. 68:20; Rom. 6:9; Rev. 4:9; 5:14; 20:1
19 Rev. 1:12
19 Rev. 2:1; 4:1
20 Zech. 4:2; Mal. 2:7; Matt. 5:15

are the angels of the seven churches: and the seven candlesticks which thou sawest are the seven churches.

CHAPTER 2
Christ's Message to the Church of Ephesus

1 Unto the angel of the church of Ephesus write; These things saith he that holdeth

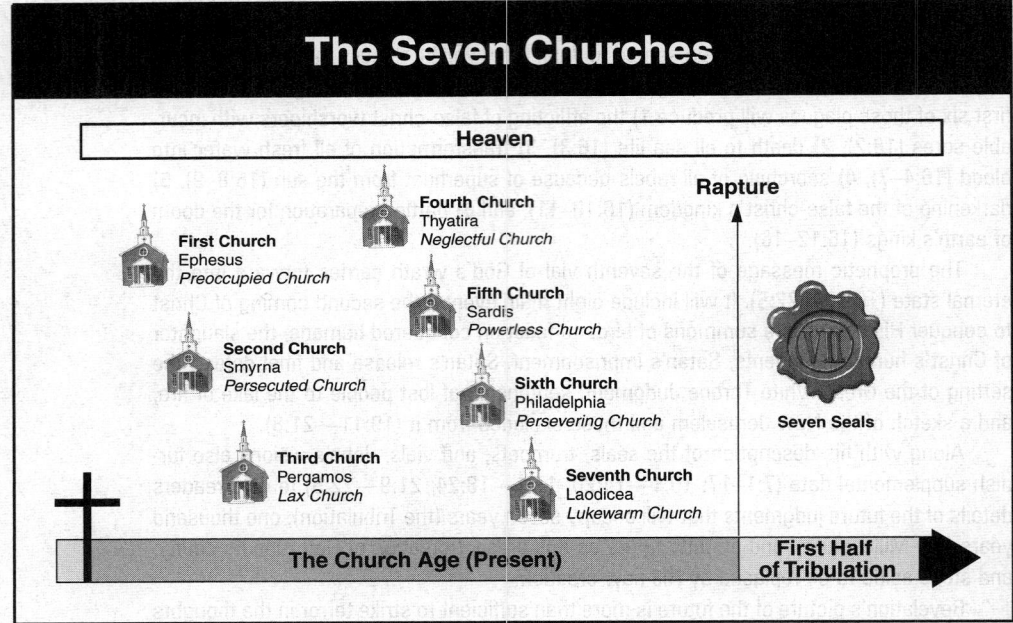

© AMG Publishers

1:18 and have the keys of hell and of death. Jesus refers to His death, resurrection, and eternity. This is an important statement because the greatest fear of mankind is death and hell, the place of the dead. Not to worry! Jesus has the keys! This makes knowing Him by faith the most important thing in this life.

1:19 Here we have the outline of the entire book which John is commanded to "write": 1) *the things John has seen* (1:1–19), 2) *the things which are* (1:20—3:22), and 3) *the things which shall be hereafter* (4:1—22:21). The basic intent of the book is to reveal the future.

1:20 This verse provides an example from Christ Himself on how to interpret the symbols in Revelation. The immediate context surrounding a symbol or previous prophetic symbols provides the key to understanding these symbols. In this case, Christ defines the identity of the key symbols, the stars in His hand as "angels" or messengers. The seven candlesticks are the "seven churches." The obvious meaning then is that churches, which

are "the light of the world" (Matt. 5:14), are the candlesticks that hold forth the light of the gospel, and the stars are angels or special messengers of Christ sent to protect the churches. Throughout its history, the Church has served as the candlestick of God in a dark and depraved world.

2:1 The church at Ephesus may have been one of the finest churches of the first century. Founded by Paul (see Acts 20) and pastored by John for many years after Paul's death, it was a church spiritually "on fire" in the midst of one of the most pagan cities of Asia. Christ commended them for their good works, patience (endurance), hatred of evil, for their testing of those who claimed to be apostles, and for their labor for Christ's name's sake (Rev. 2:2–3). He also condemned them for leaving their first love. During Paul's lifetime they had preached the gospel to every creature under heaven (Col. 1:6, 23), but over the years their priorities had gradually shifted away from their original zeal.

The Seven Churches

By Elmer Towns

When Jesus appeared to John on the Isle of Patmos, the first part of His revelation was seven letters to the messengers of seven specifically named churches in Asia with which John was familiar, for much of his ministry had been conducted throughout that area of Asia (Rev. 2—3). There were more than seven churches in that region, but only seven were chosen by Christ to receive messages. The order in which the messages are presented is not likely to be the order in which these churches would be visited by a traveler. Many dispensational scholars believe Christ selected these seven churches in this particular order to prophetically suggest the major trends in church history, but this is not a universal belief. A study of history reveals that the Church has gone through seven basic periods or stages: **1)** Ephesus—Apostolic church (Pentecost, A.D. 100), **2)** Smyrna—Persecuted church (A.D. 100–316), **3)** Pergamos—World church (A.D. 316–800), **4)** Thyatira—Medieval church (A.D. 800–1517), **5)** Sardis—Rise of the state church (A.D. 1517–1750), **6)** Philadelphia—Missionary church (A.D. 1750–1900), **7)** Laodicea—Apostate church (A.D. 1900–?).

Both the kingdom parables (Matt. 13) and church epistles (Rev. 2—3) describe the course of this present age, suggesting a relationship between these two sections of Scripture. The parable of the sower and the church at Ephesus represent the age of the apostles, and portray the failure of leaving one's first love.

> *These seven churches comprise seven methods of attack by Satan on the Church.*

The parable of the evil seed and the church at Smyrna show the full persecution by the enemy. The parable of the mustard seed and the church at Pergamos reflect the professing church becoming a state institution under Constantine the Great. The unclean birds (nations) find shelter there. The parable of the leaven and the church at Thyatira are the medieval church. Her abominations are a reflection of the woman Jezebel, the harlot who corresponds to the woman in the parable of the leaven. The parable of the hid treasure and the church of Sardis, having a reputation of being alive but being dead, reflect the age of the state church where the church belongs to the One who has purchased the field. The parable of the pearl and the church at Philadelphia show the ideal church, and the one pearl being the ideal body of Christ. The parable of the dragnet and the church at Laodicea reflect the judgment of God to come.

One could argue that some parables or epistles may overlap, but the major themes illustrate the course of this present age. As one surveys the history of the last two millennia, it is possible to see how these prophetic allusions may have been fulfilled. One sign of Christ's soon return is the fact that we are at the end of the age according to these two passages. The rapture of the Church and God's final judgment are the only prophetic events that remain to be fulfilled in this age.

A practical application of the message to the seven churches can be made on an individual basis. We can readily see that these seven churches comprise seven methods of attack by Satan on the Church or on individual Christians within the Church. In whatever age the Christian may live, he should take unto himself "the whole armor of God" (Eph. 6:10–18) and "resist the devil" (James 4:7, cf. 1 Pet. 5:9).

the seven stars in his right hand who walketh in midst of the seven golden candlesticks;

2 I know thy works, and thy labour, and thy patience, and how thou canst not bear them which are evil: and thou hast tried them which say they are apostles, and are not, and hast found them liars:

3 And hast borne, and hast patience, and for my name's sake hast laboured, and hast not fainted.

4 Nevertheless I have *somewhat* against thee, because thou hast left thy first love.

5 Remember therefore from whence thou art fallen, and repent, and do the first works; or else I will come unto thee quickly, and will remove thy candlestick out of his place, except thou repent.

6 But this thou hast, that thou hatest the deeds of the Nicolaitanes, which I also hate.

7 He that hath an ear, let him hear what the Spirit saith unto the churches; To him that overcometh will I give to eat of the tree

of life, which is in the midst of the paradise of God.

Christ's Message to the Church of Smyrna

8 And unto the angel of the church in Smyrna write; These things saith the first and the last, which was dead, and is alive;

9 I know thy works, and tribulation, and poverty, (but thou art rich) and *I know* the blasphemy of them which say they are Jews, and are not, but *are* the synagogue of Satan.

10 Fear none of those things which thou shalt suffer: behold, the devil shall cast *some* of you into prison, that ye may be tried; and ye shall have tribulation ten days: be thou faithful unto death, and I will give thee a crown of life.

11 He that hath an ear, let him hear what the Spirit saith unto the churches; He that overcometh shall not be hurt of the second death.

Cross references:

2 Ps. 1:6; 2Cor. 11:13; 2Pet. 2:1; 1John 4:1; Rev. 2:9, 13, 19; 3:1, 8, 15

3 Gal. 6:9; Heb. 12:3, 5

5 Matt. 21:41, 43

7 Gen. 2:9; Matt. 11:15; 13:9, 43; Rev. 2:11, 17, 29; 3:6, 13, 22; 13:9; 22:2, 14

8 Rev. 1:8, 17, 18

9 Luke 12:21; Rom. 2:17, 28, 29; 9:6; 1Tim. 6:18; James 2:5; Rev. 2:2; 3:9

10 Matt. 10:22; 24:13

2:2 thou hast tried them which say they are apostles. By the end of the first century, all of the apostles, except John, had given their lives in testimony to their faith in Jesus Christ. Over the centuries, the Church has suffered from many false teachers who have sought to corrupt its doctrine. A true teacher of God welcomes the testing of his teachings by the Scriptures.

2:6 Nicolaitanes. This word is made up of two Greek words: *Nico* meaning "overcome" and *laitanes* meaning "lay people." Right from the first century there were those who wanted to become "overcomers" of the people and build a hierarchy within the Church. The sin of fornication was also prevalent among the leaders of these Nicolaitanes. The church of Ephesus was commended by our Lord for guarding against such leaders who wanted to lord it over the common people.

2:7 unto the churches. Apparently the Lord wanted all the churches to read all of these messages to the seven churches. There are obviously principles in each letter that are helpful for all churches.

2:7 To him that overcometh will I give to eat of the tree of life. See 1 John 5:4. A believer automatically "overcomes" because of the Holy Spirit within him as a result of being born again by faith. Consequently, he will enter the Millennial Kingdom which Christ has prepared and heaven, where the "tree of life" is restored (22:1–2). This is the same tree that was in the Garden of Eden from which, because of their fall, Adam and Eve were forbidden to eat. Believers in heaven will have access to that tree forever.

2:8 The name Smyrna refers to myrrh, and the crushing process used to release its fragrance symbolizes the persecution of believers. The local church by that name and the Church age it represents (the second and third centuries) were among the most persecuted in all of Church history. Roman dictators from Nero to Diocletian mounted various waves of persecution, using governmental power in their attempts to destroy the Church. It is a miracle of God that the Church not only survived that period but that it also thrived, grew, and spread across the Roman Empire. Just like myrrh, when the Church is crushed with trials, the fragrance of her faith is released.

2:8 the church in Smyrna. Not one word of condemnation was issued by our Lord against this church. He did, however, honor and commend them for their suffering and poverty. This city today is called Izmir, in modern Turkey. Polycarp, a convert of John, pastored the church there until he was martyred in A.D. 155.

2:9 the synagogue of Satan. Some believe this was a group who tried to pervert the gospel of free grace through faith alone by requiring the adoption of Jewish law for salvation. Others suggest this group fostered the idea of apostolic succession and the building of a hierarchy of leaders, similar to the practice of the Nicolaitanes, which was condemned by the Lord (vv. 6, 15).

2:10 I will give thee a crown of life. This is one of two places where a martyr's crown is mentioned as a special reward in eternity for those who sacrifice their lives for the gospel (James 1:12). Most martyrs were killed either by false religious leaders or by pagan governments that opposed their message.

Christ's Message to the Church of Pergamos

12 And to the angel of the church in Pergamos write; These things saith he which hath the sharp sword with two edges;

13 I know thy works, and where thou dwellest, *even* where Satan's seat *is:* and thou holdest fast my name, and hast not denied my faith, even in those days wherein Antipas *was* my faithful martyr, who was slain among you, where Satan dwelleth.

14 But I have a few things against thee, because thou hast there them that hold the doctrine of Balaam, who taught Balac to cast a stumblingblock before the children of Israel, to eat things sacrificed unto idols, and to commit fornication.

15 So hast thou also them that hold the doctrine of the Nicolaitanes, which thing I hate.

16 Repent; or else I will come unto thee quickly, and will fight against them with the sword of my mouth.

17 He that hath an ear, let him hear what the Spirit saith unto the churches; To him that overcometh will I give to eat of the hidden manna, and will give him a white stone, and in the stone a new name written, which no man knoweth saving he that receiveth *it.*

12 Rev. 1:16
13 Rev. 2:2, 9
14 Num. 24:14; 25:1; 31:16; Acts 15:29; 1Cor. 6:13; 8:9, 10; 10:19, 20; 2Pet. 2:15; Jude 1:11; Rev. 2:20
15 Rev. 2:6
16 Isa. 11:4; 2Thess. 2:8; Rev. 1:16; 19:15, 21
17 Rev. 2:7, 11; 3:12; 19:12
20 1Kgs. 16:31; 21:25; Acts 15:20, 29; 1Cor. 10:19, 20
21 Rom. 2:4; Rev. 9:20
23 1Sam. 16:7; Ps. 7:9; 62:12; Matt. 16:27; Rev. 20:12

Christ's Message to the Church of Thyatira

18 And unto the angel of the church in Thyatira write; These things saith the Son of God, who hath his eyes like unto a flame of fire, and his feet *are* like fine brass;

19 I know thy works, and charity, and service, and faith, and thy patience, and thy works; and the last *to be* more than the first.

20 Notwithstanding I have a few things against thee, because thou sufferest that woman Jezebel, which calleth herself a prophetess, to teach and to seduce my servants to commit fornication, and to eat things sacrificed unto idols.

21 And I gave her space to repent of her fornication; and she repented not.

22 Behold, I will cast her into a bed, and them that commit adultery with her into great tribulation, except they repent of their deeds.

23 And I will kill her children with death; and all the churches shall know that I am he which searcheth the reins and hearts: and I will give unto every one of you according to your works.

24 But unto you I say, and unto the rest in Thyatira, as many as have not this doctrine, and which have not known the depths of

---

2:12–13 the church in Pergamos. Pergamos was located about sixty miles north of Smyrna. It was a hotbed of pagan idolatry and was plagued by both false apostles and those who were in favor of an extremely powerful hierarchy of "apostles" and priests (the Nicolaitanes). Pergamos was the Roman capital in Asia and the seat of pagan authority; thus, "Satan's seat" was there. The church at Pergamos was guilty of seeking to please the society around them rather than the Lord, which later paved the way for the paganization of the Church in the centuries that followed. All commendations aside, our Lord indicts them for indulging false teachers like the Nicolaitanes (vv. 6, 15) and those who taught the doctrines of Balaam (see Num. 22—24). Pergamos also had the largest altar in the world, to Zeus. In a very real sense, it may have been the devil's capital for the propagation of paganism. Many pagan doctrines were brought into the Church during this period of history.

2:15 which thing I hate. Jesus takes doctrine seriously. He hates all compromise with immorality (Balaamism, v. 14). He hates those who would lord it over the common people as the Nicolaitanes did (see the note on 2:6). Doctrinal purity should never be compromised for political or social acceptance. With the elevation of Christianity as the state religion in A.D. 325, the church became rich and powerful. It was suggested at that time that the world was getting better and better, that Christ's kingdom had already begun, and that Jesus would come at the end of the next thousand years.

2:18–20 the church in Thyatira. The letter to Thyatira, a city about forty miles east of Pergamos, is the longest of the seven letters. This church seemed to have a woman like Jezebel of the Old Testament, who brought pagan worship and gross sexual immorality into the church (cf. 1 Kgs. 18—19). The identity of this local woman of Thyatira is not known except that she was Jezebel-like. The pagan practices brought into this church typify the excessive paganism and superstitions that often influenced the medieval churches.

2:22 This church was condemned by our Lord for both sexual immorality and idolatry. Unless they repent, those in this current age, of which the church in Thyatira is a symbol, will live right on into the Great Tribulation which Jesus predicted and John describes in 6:1–17. The fact that all true believers in Jesus Christ will be raptured before the Tribulation begins will make it easy for the unsaved leadership that remains in the churches to formulate the global religion of the last days.

2:24–25 which have not known the depths of Satan. These verses further clarify the fact that there will be, right up to the coming of Christ, some in the church who

Satan, as they speak; I will put upon you none other burden.

25 But that which ye have *already* hold fast till I come.

26 And he that overcometh, and keepeth my works unto the end, to him will I give power over the nations:

27 And he shall rule them with a rod of iron; as the vessels of a potter shall they be broken to shivers: even as I received of my Father.

28 And I will give him the morning star.

29 He that hath an ear, let him hear what the Spirit saith unto the churches.

CHAPTER 3
Christ's Message to the Church of Sardis

1 And unto the angel of the church in Sardis write; These things saith he that hath

25	Rev. 3:11
26	Matt. 19:28; Luke 22:29, 30
27	Ps. 2:8, 9; 49:14
28	Rev. 22:16
1	Eph. 2:1, 5; 1Tim. 5:6
3	Matt. 24:42, 43; 25:13; Mark 13:33; Luke 12:39, 40; 1Thess. 5:2
4	Rev. 4:4; 6:11; 7:9, 13
5	Ex. 32:32; Matt. 10:32; Rev. 13:8; 17:8; 19:8; 20:12, 21:27

the seven Spirits of God, and the seven stars; I know thy works, that thou hast a name that thou livest, and art dead.

2 Be watchful, and strengthen the things which remain that are ready to die: for I have not found thy works perfect before God.

3 Remember therefore how thou hast received and heard, and hold fast, and repent. If therefore thou shalt not watch, I will come on thee as a thief, and thou shalt not know what hour I will come upon thee.

4 Thou hast a few names even in Sardis which have not defiled their garments; and they shall walk with me in white: for they are worthy.

5 He that overcometh, the same shall be clothed in white raiment; and I will not blot out his name out of the book of life, but I will confess his name before my Father, and before his angels.

do not adhere to pagan doctrines and practices. It is encouraging to note that "he which searcheth the reins and hearts" (v. 23) will be the one who truly knows who is trusting the finished work of Christ for salvation as opposed to those who are trusting their church to give them salvation. It should always be remembered that salvation is not a corporate experience. It is an intensely individual matter of personal faith in Christ alone that guarantees our being taken in the Rapture (see John 14:1–2; 1 Thess. 4:13–18).

2:26–27 shall rule them with a rod of iron. Overcomers even in this unfaithful church are promised to be a part of that kingdom over which Jesus shall reign when He comes again. Further evidence that these churches mentioned in the book of Revelation refer not just to first-century churches, but to periods of Church history, is that the overcomers in the church of Thyatira will still be alive and functioning in His name when He comes. Since He has not yet come, it is obvious that the primary message to these seven churches is to the ages, not just to the churches themselves, most of which have long become extinct. Of the seven churches, the last four will symbolically be alive and functioning when Jesus returns, and He will rescue or save the faithful out of them all.

2:28 I will give him the morning star. Some think this and the reference to the morning star mentioned in 2 Peter 1:19 may indicate that those who are alive just before His return and who study the prophetic Scriptures will have that "morning" or "daystar" arise and give them spiritual insight that the time is at hand. Simeon and Anna had such a spiritual premonition; consequently, they were able to see the Christ child in His first coming. It is possible that such a spirit of anticipation may spring up in the hearts of many just before He returns for His Church.

2:29 hear what the Spirit saith unto the churches. Those who would overcome are challenged by this phrase seven times in the book of Revelation. His faithful "overcomers" will be ready for His return, regardless of the condition of the church of which they are a part. Hearing and obeying God's Word is essential if we are to overcome the enemy.

3:1 the church in Sardis. Sardis was a wealthy city thirty miles southeast of Thyatira. In the sixth century B.C., it was one of the great cities of the world, ruled by the fabled Croesus, called Midas by the Greeks and known for his golden treasures. However, the glory of Sardis was past, for the city had fallen to the Persians in 546 B.C. and to the Greeks in 334 B.C. In A.D. 17, Sardis was destroyed by an earthquake and rebuilt by Tiberius Caesar. The church in Sardis, like the city, was in constant danger of internal decay and collapse. Its inclusion in the seven can best be attributed to the fact that many local churches are similar to it, and it best typifies the churches that start out well but lose their spiritual fervency after a generation or two and begin to live on their past laurels. Such was the case of the dying church at Sardis. By the time John wrote the Revelation, the local church that had been started on the gospel was spiritually "dead." This clearly indicates that John wrote this message long after this church was founded, an important consideration in dating the book of Revelation.

3:3 I will come on thee as a thief. His challenge to them is universal to all whose love for Christ has cooled: "Repent, turn around, and remember how you received the gospel by grace through faith, or I will come and judge you."

3:4 shall walk with me in white: for they are worthy. Fortunately, like all churches, there are people in this one

6 He that hath an ear, let him hear what the Spirit saith unto the churches.

Christ's Message to the Church of Philadelphia

7 And to the angel of the church in Philadelphia write; These things saith he that is holy, he that is true, he that hath the

6 Rev. 2:7
7 Job 12:14;
Isa. 22:22;
Matt. 16:19;
1 John 5:20;
Rev. 1:5, 18;
3:14; 6:10;
19:11
9 Isa. 49:23

key of David, he that openeth, and no man shutteth; and shutteth, and no man openeth;

8 I know thy works: behold, I have set before thee an open door, and no man can shut it: for thou hast a little strength, and hast kept my word, and hast not denied my name.

9 Behold, I will make them of the synagogue

The Seven Churches of Revelation

	Meaning	Characteristics	Rebuke/ Exhortation	Promise
Ephesus	Desirable	Faith and patience Doctrinal truth	You have strayed from your love for Christ	I will let you eat of the Tree of Life
Smyrna	Myrrh	Martyrdom Persecution	Have no fear in the midst of tribulation; be faithful	I will give you a crown of life
Pergamos	Height, Elevation of power	Worldly alliance Great external growth	You are holding to false doctrines	I will give you hidden manna and a white stone with a new name
Thyatira	Sweet smell, Sacrifice of labor	False teachers Doctrinal corruption	You have some committing fornication; you who are faithful, hold fast till I come	I will give you power over the nations and the morning star
Sardis	Prince of joy	Dying Faith Ritualism	You appear to be alive, but in your heart you are dying, and your works are imperfect	I will dress you in white raiment and confess your name before My Father
Philadelphia	Brotherly love	Evangelism Missions	Hold fast and continue to keep My Word	I will make you a pillar in the house of God
Laodicea	Laypeople	Apostasy	Your material riches have blinded you to your spiritual shame	I will allow you to sit with Me on My throne

who have not bent their knees to unscriptural traditionalism but truly worship the living Christ. When Christ raptures His Church, there will be millions of true believers taken to be with Him. These will be clothed in the white garments of heaven.

3:5 He that overcometh [a believer in Christ] **. . . I will not blot out his name out of the book of life.** This promise is very significant! At the Great White Throne Judgment, this "book of life" will be used as a final check to see if a sinner should be cast into the lake of fire (20:15). All true believers will be raptured, and their names will remain in the book of life forever! These names will be confessed by Jesus before the Father, which is the ultimate guarantee of salvation for ALL who call on the name of Christ.

3:7 the church in Philadelphia. The city of Philadelphia was located twenty-eight miles from Sardis. This city was founded by King Attalus in honor of his brother and is known as the "city of brotherly love." It seems to have been a faithful church, for the Lord gave them much praise and no condemnation whatsoever.

3:8 I know thy works . . . I have set before thee an open door, and no man can shut it. Both the local church and the Church age it represents are characterized by "the open door." Many believe this refers to world evangelism that characterizes Bible-believing, missionary-minded churches. Of the seven churches described, Philadelphia is the most ideal model of the true church.

3:8 thou hast a little strength. This indicates that the churches do not depend on themselves but, in humility, depend on the Holy Spirit. To enjoy His blessing, they know they must teach holy living and evangelism. Like their predecessors in the early Church era, they have proclaimed the second coming of Christ.

3:9 "Judaizers" or legalists have plagued the Church in every age. Evidently they also hampered the church of Philadelphia. Those who would add legalism or works to the free gift of salvation destroy "the gift of God," which is "not of works, lest any man should boast" (Eph. 2:8–9).

of Satan, which say they are Jews, and are not, but do lie; behold, I will make them to come and worship before thy feet, and to know that I have loved thee.

10 Because thou hast kept the word of my patience, I also will keep thee from the hour of temptation, which shall come upon all the world, to try them that dwell upon the earth.

11 Behold, I come quickly: hold that fast which thou hast, that no man take thy crown.

12 Him that overcometh will I make a pillar in the temple of my God, and he shall go no more out: and I will write upon him the name of my God, and the name of the city of my God, *which is* new Jerusalem, which cometh down out of heaven from my God: and *I will write upon him* my new name.

13 He that hath an ear, let him hear what the Spirit saith unto the churches.

Christ's Message to the Church of Laodicea

14 And unto the angel of the church of the Laodiceans write; These things saith the

Amen, the faithful and true witness, the beginning of the creation of God;

15 I know thy works, that thou art neither cold nor hot: I would thou wert cold or hot.

16 So then because thou art lukewarm, and neither cold nor hot, I will spue thee out of my mouth.

17 Because thou sayest, I am rich, and increased with goods, and have need of nothing; and knowest not that thou art wretched, and miserable, and poor, and blind, and naked:

18 I counsel thee to buy of me gold tried in the fire, that thou mayest be rich; and white raiment, that thou mayest be clothed, and *that* the shame of thy nakedness do not appear; and anoint thine eyes with eyesalve, that thou mayest see.

19 As many as I love, I rebuke and chasten: be zealous therefore, and repent.

20 Behold, I stand at the door, and knock: if any man hear my voice, and open the door, I will come in to him, and will sup with him, and he with me.

21 To him that overcometh will I grant to sit with me in my throne, even as I also over-

Cross references (center column)

10 Isa. 24:17; Luke 2:1; 2Pet. 2:9

11 Rev. 22:7, 12, 20

12 1Kgs. 7:21; Rev. 2:17; 14:1; 21:2, 10; 22:4

14 Isa. 65:16; Col. 1:15; Rev. 1:5; 3:7; 19:11; 22:6

17 Hos. 12:8; 1Cor. 4:8

18 Isa. 55:1; Matt. 13:44; 25:9; 2Cor. 5:3; Rev. 7:13; 16:15; 19:8

19 Job 5:17; Prov. 3:11, 12

20 Song 5:2; Luke 12:37; John 14:23

21 Matt. 19:28; Rev. 2:26, 27

3:10 I also will keep thee from the hour of temptation. This is the most specific guarantee from our Lord Himself that Christian believers will not go into that seven-year Tribulation period He is about to unveil (Rev. 6—18). Revelation 3:10 should be studied in the light of Romans 5:9 and 1 Thessalonians 1:10; 5:9. After giving this assurance that believers would be kept out of the hour of trial, it is no accident that the very next chapter begins with a picture of the Rapture, when John is seen taken up to heaven just before the Tribulation begins.

3:11 I come quickly. Christ wants all believers to live every day as if this is the day He will come. There will be absolutely no warning when Christ comes for His Church. He challenges believers to "hold . . . fast" to the faith in both belief and practice. It is very important that Christians not only start well but also finish well, as did Paul who said, "I have kept the faith" (2 Tim. 4:7). Sin has crept into many believers' lives, and because of this sin they will not "receive a full reward" at the judgment seat of Christ (2 John 1:8).

3:12 him that overcometh. The eternal promises mentioned here are offered to those who have faith in Christ (see 1 John 5:1–5).

3:14 the church of the Laodiceans. This church was located about forty miles from Philadelphia in a wealthy city filled with Greek culture and learning. Christian tradition points out the early relationship of Laodicea to the church at Colossae. The apostle Paul wrote a letter,

which was apparently lost, to the church at Laodicea (cf. Col. 4:16). The designation of the church as "lukewarm" is taken from the contrasting hot springs of nearby Hierapolis and the pure, cold waters of Colossae. There are no words of positive commendation for the lukewarm Laodiceans. Today's "Laodicean" churches have "a form of godliness, but [deny] the power thereof" (2 Tim. 3:5). In such churches, the Bible is rarely taught, and sinners are rarely converted.

3:14 the faithful and true witness. Christ threatens to reject this apostate church, as noted by the picture of vomiting from the mouth. While the church is rejected, those individuals who believe are not.

3:16 I will spue thee out of my mouth. A lukewarm church claims to be Christian, but preaches another gospel, often one based on good works. In this fashion they mislead men about the person of Christ and the salvation He bought for man.

3:17–18 and have need of nothing. Unlike Philadelphia, which recognized it was of "little strength" (v. 8) and must depend on the power and Spirit of God, the Laodicean church was proud of its riches, mistaking material success for the approval of God. Consequently, they didn't realize that without the truth of the Word of God they were wretched, miserable, poor, blind, and naked.

3:20 Though some have been encouraged by this verse

came, and am set down with my Father in his throne.

22 He that hath an ear, let him hear what the Spirit saith unto the churches.

CHAPTER 4
John Caught Up to Heaven

1 After this I looked, and, behold, a door *was* opened in heaven: and the first voice which I heard *was* as it were of a trumpet talking with me; which said, Come up hither, and I will shew thee things which must be hereafter.

2 And immediately I was in the spirit: and, behold, a throne was set in heaven, and *one* sat on the throne.

3 And he that sat was to look upon like a jasper and a sardine stone: and *there was* a rainbow round about the throne, in sight like unto an emerald.

4 And round about the throne *were* four and twenty seats: and upon the seats I saw four and twenty elders sitting, clothed in white raiment; and they had on their heads crowns of gold.

5 And out of the throne proceeded lightnings and thunderings and voices: and *there were* seven lamps of fire burning before the throne, which are the seven Spirits of God.

6 And before the throne *there was* a sea of glass like unto crystal: and in the midst of the throne, and round about the throne, *were* four beasts full of eyes before and behind.

7 And the first beast *was* like a lion, and the second beast like a calf, and the third beast had a face as a man, and the fourth beast *was* like a flying eagle.

8 And the four beasts had each of them six wings about *him*; and *they were* full of eyes within: and they rest not day and night, saying, Holy, holy, holy, Lord God Almighty, which was, and is, and is to come.

9 And when those beasts give glory and honour and thanks to him that sat on the throne, who liveth for ever and ever,

---

Cross-references:

1 Rev. 1:10, 19

2 Isa. 6:1; Jer. 17:12; Ezek. 1:26; 10:1; Dan. 7:9; Rev. 1:10; 17:3; 21:10

3 Ezek. 1:28

4 Rev. 3:4, 5; 4:10; 6:11; 7:9, 13, 14; 11:16; 19:14

5 Ezek. 1:13; Rev. 1:4; 3:1; 5:6; 8:5; 16:18

6 Ex. 38:8; Ezek. 1:5; Rev. 4:8; 15:2

7 Num. 2:2; Ezek. 1:10; 10:14

8 Isa. 6:2, 3

---

to receive the resurrected Christ as Savior, it is not actually a presentation of the gospel. Since the church of Laodicea is the recipient of this message, it seems to be a call for Christians who are cold and indifferent to spiritual things to repent and "open the door" of their hearts to the resurrected Christ. This is a beautiful picture of Christ's invitation to His Bride to come to the marriage supper of the Lamb.

3:22 Although the words "church" or "churches" have been used nineteen times by this point in the book, these words are not mentioned again until 22:16, long after the Tribulation. The absence of any mention of the Church reinforces the fact that the Church will be raptured before the Tribulation takes place.

4:1–2 immediately I was in the spirit. The transition that occurs in verse 1 shifts our focus into the future. This is emphasized by the words "after this" (Gr. *meta tauta*), which indicate a sequence of events that follow. John was taken by the Spirit into heaven. It was no coincidence that the first thing to happen after John described the seven churches was his conveyance into heaven. John's perspective of the Tribulation is the same as the Church—in heaven. The invitation comes from Christ himself, who is the One who spoke to John "as of a trumpet" (Rev. 1:10). Note the similarity of this event to the promise of our Lord near the end of His life to His disciples about taking them to His Father's house (John 14:2–3).

4:1 shew thee things which must be hereafter. This statement marks a distinct change in the book. The message of Christ to the seven churches is complete. Now He addresses what will take place after the time of the seven churches, namely the seven-year Tribulation period. But first, we are shown a scene in heaven (Rev. 4—5). It is important for the reader to examine the context of each passage to determine whether an event is pictured in heaven or on earth.

4:4–5 The identity of the twenty-four elders refers to redeemed men. Since these same elders are mentioned in 5:9 as having come "out of every kindred, and tongue, and people," they are probably representative of the saved people of the Church age.

4:5 the seven spirits of God. This refers to the seven eyes of the Lord or characteristics of God (cf. Zech. 4:10 and Isa. 11:2).

4:6 a sea of glass. This description of the sea in heaven and around the throne suggests the calm and tranquility there in contrast to the turmoil of the earth from which the martyred saints have just departed. The "four living creatures" that worship God continually are best considered in the light of Ezekiel's vision of heaven (Ezek. 1:5–25; cf. Isa. 6:1–4), showing the awesome view of God that the heavenly seraphim have.

4:8 Holy, holy, holy. This is the cry of these heavenly creatures who know God as He really is. It has been suggested that each "holy" is directed to one of the members of the Trinity. Then these creatures remind us of the One who "is to come." The return of Christ is guaranteed in the words of these heavenly hosts. In Acts 1:9–11 angelic beings describe how Christ will literally return "in like manner as ye have seen him go." Here these angels in heaven reaffirm that promise.

10 The four and twenty elders fall down before him that sat on the throne, and worship him that liveth for ever and ever, and cast their crowns before the throne, saying, **11** Thou art worthy, O Lord, to receive glory and honour and power: for thou hast created all things, and for thy pleasure they are and were created.

CHAPTER 5
The Seven-sealed Book

1 And I saw in the right hand of him that sat on the throne a book written within and on the backside, sealed with seven seals.
2 And I saw a strong angel proclaiming with a loud voice, Who is worthy to open the book, and to loose the seals thereof?
3 And no man in heaven, nor in earth, neither under the earth, was able to open the book, neither to look thereon.
4 And I wept much, because no man was found worthy to open and to read the book, neither to look thereon.
5 And one of the elders saith unto me, Weep not: behold, the Lion of the tribe of Judah, the Root of David, hath prevailed to open the book, and to loose the seven seals thereof.
6 And I beheld, and, lo, in the midst of the throne and of the four beasts, and in the midst of the elders, stood a Lamb as it had been slain, having seven horns and seven eyes, which are the seven Spirits of God sent forth into all the earth.
7 And he came and took the book out of the right hand of him that sat upon the throne.
8 And when he had taken the book, the

10 Rev. 4:4, 9; 5:8, 14
1 Isa. 29:11; Ezek. 2:9, 10; Dan. 12:4
5 Gen. 49:9, 10; Isa. 11:1, 10; Rom. 15:12; Heb. 7:14; Rev. 5:1; 6:1; 22:16
6 Isa. 53:7; Zech. 3:9; 4:10; John 1:29, 36; 1Pet. 1:19; Rev. 4:5; 5:9, 12; 13:8
7 Rev. 4:2
8 Ps. 141:2; Rev. 4:8, 10; 8:3, 4; 14:2; 15:2
9 Ps. 40:3; Dan. 4:1; 6:25; Acts 20:28; Rom. 3:24; 1Cor. 6:20; 7:23; Eph. 1:7; Col. 1:14; Heb. 9:12; 1Pet. 1:18, 19; 2Pet. 2:1; 1John 1:7; Rev. 4:11; 5:6; 7:9; 11:9; 14:3, 4, 6
10 Ex. 19:6; 1Pet. 2:5, 9; Rev. 1:6; 20:6; 22:5
12 Rev. 4:11
13 Rev. 1:6; 5:3; 6:16; 7:10

four beasts and four *and* twenty elders fell down before the Lamb, having every one of them harps, and golden vials full of odours, which are the prayers of saints.
9 And they sung a new song, saying, Thou art worthy to take the book, and to open the seals thereof: for thou wast slain, and hast redeemed us to God by thy blood out of every kindred, and tongue, and people, and nation;
10 And hast made us unto our God kings and priests: and we shall reign on the earth.
11 And I beheld, and I heard the voice of many angels round about the throne and the beasts and the elders: and the number of them was ten thousand times ten thousand, and thousands of thousands;
12 Saying with a loud voice, Worthy is the Lamb that was slain to receive power, and riches, and wisdom, and strength, and honour, and glory, and blessing.
13 And every creature which is in heaven, and on the earth, and under the earth, and such as are in the sea, and all that are in them, heard I saying, Blessing, and honour, and glory, and power, *be* unto him that sitteth upon the throne, and unto the Lamb for ever and ever.
14 And the four beasts said, Amen. And the four *and* twenty elders fell down and worshipped him that liveth for ever and ever.

CHAPTER 6
Christ Opens the Seven-sealed Scroll

1 And I saw when the Lamb opened one of the seals, and I heard, as it were the noise of

---

4:11 The twenty-four elders who represent the redeemed in heaven acknowledge that humans were created by God for His good pleasure. Their response of praise recognizes the sovereignty of God over our lives.

5:1 The seven-sealed scroll is thought to be the title deed to the earth. In practical terms, it seems God the Father holds this title deed, awaiting the return of His Son, Jesus Christ, to the earth. This powerful scene in heaven indicates that only Christ, who died to redeem mankind back to God, is qualified to open the seals of this scroll and claim His kingdom over all the earth.

5:9 John observes these events just prior to the beginning of the Tribulation. Whether these men represent Israel or the Church, they are redeemed saints who are in heaven just before the revelation of the Tribulation period, confirming a pretribulation rapture.

5:10 we shall reign on the earth. A similar promise is given to that "multitude, which no man could number" (Rev. 7:9) when resurrected after the Tribulation (Rev. 20:4). Together the Christians, who were saved before the Tribulation, along with the saints saved out of the Tribulation will "rule and reign" during Christ's one thousand-year kingdom.

5:11 ten thousand times ten thousand, and thousands of thousands. An incredible number of souls have been saved during the history of man and, at this point in John's vision, are in heaven. Then there is the "innumerable" host (Heb. 12:22) from the seven-year Tribulation's soul harvest.

6:1 Come and see. From his vantage point in heaven, John is invited to look down and see the judgment of God on all those left behind after the Rapture. As Christ, the

thunder, one of the four beasts saying, Come and see.

2 And I saw, and behold a white horse: and he that sat on him had a bow; and a crown was given unto him: and he went forth conquering, and to conquer.

3 And when he had opened the second seal, I heard the second beast say, Come and see.

4 And there went out another horse *that was* red: and *power* was given to him that sat thereon to take peace from the earth, and that they should kill one another: and

there was given unto him a great sword.

5 And when he had opened the third seal, I heard the third beast say, Come and see. And I beheld, and lo a black horse; and he that sat on him had a pair of balances in his hand.

6 And I heard a voice in the midst of the four beasts say, A measure of wheat for a penny, and three measures of barley for a penny; and *see* thou hurt not the oil and the wine.

7 And when he had opened the fourth seal, I heard the voice of the fourth beast say, Come and see.

Cross-references:
2 Ps. 45:4, 5; Zech. 6:3, 11; Rev. 14:14; 19:11
3 Rev. 4:7
4 Zech. 6:2
5 Zech. 6:2; Rev. 4:7
6 Rev. 9:4
7 Rev. 4:7

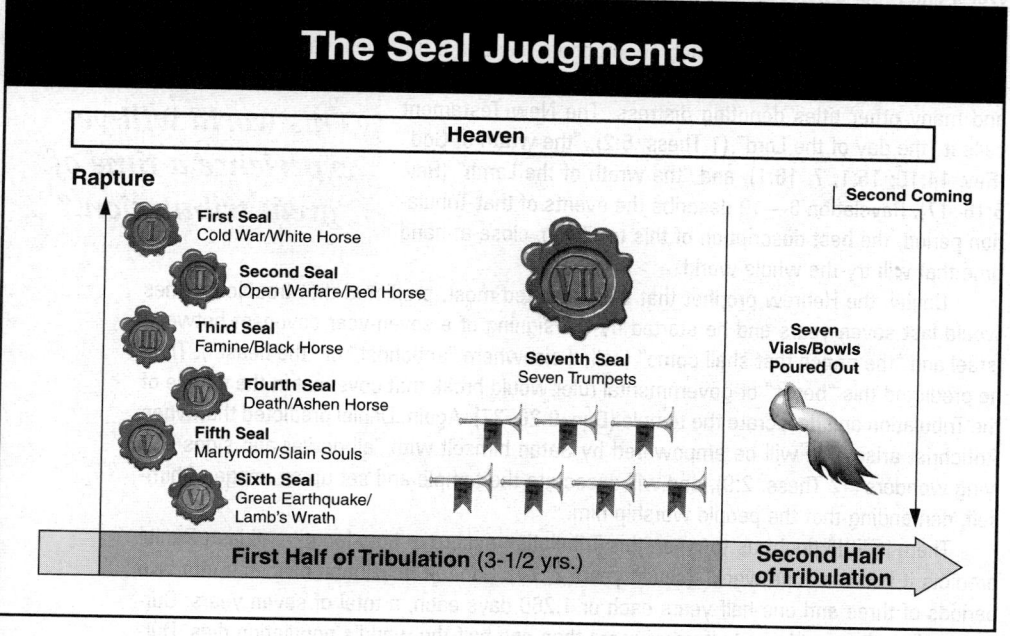

The Seal Judgments

Heaven

Rapture

Second Coming

First Seal — Cold War/White Horse
Second Seal — Open Warfare/Red Horse
Third Seal — Famine/Black Horse
Fourth Seal — Death/Ashen Horse
Fifth Seal — Martyrdom/Slain Souls
Sixth Seal — Great Earthquake/Lamb's Wrath

Seventh Seal — Seven Trumpets

Seven Vials/Bowls Poured Out

First Half of Tribulation (3-1/2 yrs.)

Second Half of Tribulation

© AMG Publishers

reigning Lord of heaven, opens each seal, this opening triggers an action that takes place on the earth. The first four seals introduce the "four horsemen" of the Apocalypse—conquest, war, famine, and death. The seven seals (Rev. 6:1—8:1), probably cover the first twenty-one months of the Tribulation.

6:2 The first horseman reveals a rider with a crown, indicating authority, and a bow without arrows, suggesting that he conquers the world by diplomatically offering peace (1 Thess. 5:1–3). We see here the Antichrist (1 John 4:3), or "man of sin" (2 Thess. 2:3), who will arise at that time. (See the article entitled "The Antichrist" by Edward Hindson).

6:3–4 take peace from the earth. Like all man-made, false promises of "peace," the promised peace of the

Antichrist fails. The world erupts into war, and peace is taken away by the "great sword."

6:5–6 for a penny. The third seal introduces a worldwide famine when a quart of wheat is sold for the equivalent of a full day's work. The food of the rich, however, the "oil and wine," will not be hurt, showing the continued injustice of man to his fellow.

6:7–8 The breaking of the fourth seal will result in the deaths of one quarter of the earth by the "sword . . . hunger . . . and [by] the beasts of the earth." Evidently there will be a rampage of wild animal attacks on humans at the same time the world is plunged into a worldwide war. Since hell followed death here, and since believers will not go to hell, these dead are those who have rejected the gospel and chose to follow Antichrist.

The Tribulation

By Tim LaHaye

There is no question this world will yet experience a time of "great tribulation, such as was not since the beginning of the world to this time" as predicted by our Lord (Matt. 24:21). In Revelation 3:10, He promised to keep believers from "the hour of temptation which shall come upon all the world, to try them that dwell upon the earth."

Such a time will have to be worse than anything ever known in human history; far worse than the destruction of Jerusalem in A.D. 70 (1 million casualties), than the Black Plague (9 million killed), than World War I (20 million killed), than the devastation of World War II and Hitler's holocaust (6 million Jews and at least 4 million Christians killed).

The Scriptures give more space to describing the coming Tribulation period than to any other prophetic event. The Hebrew prophets mention it 39 times, calling it a "time of Jacob's trouble" (Jer. 30:7), "tribulation" (distress, Deut. 4:30), and many other titles denoting distress. The New Testament calls it "the day of the Lord" (1 Thess. 5:2), "the wrath of God" (Rev. 14:10; 15:1, 7; 16:1), and "the wrath of the Lamb" (Rev. 6:16–17). Revelation 6—19 describe the events of that Tribulation period, the best description of this terrifying, close-at-hand time that will try the whole world.

> *This world will yet experience a time of "great tribulation."*

Daniel, the Hebrew prophet that Jesus quoted most, predicted that troublous times would last seven years and be started by the signing of a seven-year covenant between Israel and "the prince that shall come" (called elsewhere "antichrist" or "the beast"). Then he predicted this "beast" or governmental ruler would break that covenant in the middle of the Tribulation and desecrate the temple (Dan. 9:26–27). Again, Daniel predicted that when Antichrist arises, he will be empowered by Satan himself with "all power and signs and lying wonders" (2 Thess. 2:9), and will desecrate the temple and set up an image of himself, demanding that the people worship him.

There is little doubt as to when this Tribulation occurs or how long it will last. Daniel predicts it will last "one week" (seven years, 9:27). John in Revelation divides it into two periods of three and one-half years each or 1,260 days each, a total of seven years. During the first three and one-half years more than one-half the world's population dies. During the second half, conditions get even worse after Satan is cast out of heaven and indwells the Antichrist's body and demands the world worship him. Our Lord Jesus predicted this Tribulation would end immediately prior to His return to this earth to set up His earthly kingdom for 1000 years (Matt. 24:29, see Dan. 9:24).

We should never lose sight of the true purpose of that Tribulation period: a divine expression of His mercy and grace. For in that brief seven-year period, at a time when the world's population is at its largest, God will shake the earth in an attempt to lessen man's false sense of security. He will send 144,000 Jewish witnesses filled with the Holy Spirit (Rev. 7; Joel 2:28–32) and other witnesses. God will go to the most extreme measures in all of history during the final days of man's life on earth to bring a massive number of souls to faith in Him so multitudes of people may enjoy the blessings He has prepared for their eternal future.

8 And I looked, and behold a pale horse: and his name that sat on him was Death, and Hell followed with him. And power was given unto them over the fourth part of the earth, to kill with sword, and with hunger, and with death, and with the beasts of the earth.

9 And when he had opened the fifth seal, I saw under the altar the souls of them that were slain for the word of God, and for the testimony which they held:

10 And they cried with a loud voice, saying, How long, O Lord, holy and true, dost thou not judge and avenge our blood on them that dwell on the earth?

11 And white robes were given unto every one of them; and it was said unto them, that they should rest yet for a little season, until their fellow servants also and their brethren, that should be killed as they *were*, should be fulfilled.

12 And I beheld when he had opened the sixth seal, and, lo, there was a great earthquake; and the sun became black as sackcloth of hair, and the moon became as blood;

13 And the stars of heaven fell unto the earth, even as a fig tree casteth her untimely figs, when she is shaken of a mighty wind.

14 And the heaven departed as a scroll when it is rolled together; and every mountain and island were moved out of their places.

15 And the kings of the earth, and the great men, and the rich men, and the chief cap-

tains, and the mighty men, and every bondman, and every free man, hid themselves in the dens and in the rocks of the mountains;

16 And said to the mountains and rocks, Fall on us, and hide us from the face of him that sitteth on the throne, and from the wrath of the Lamb:

17 For the great day of his wrath is come; and who shall be able to stand?

CHAPTER 7
Sealing the 144,000 Tribulation Evangelists

1 And after these things I saw four angels standing on the four corners of the earth, holding the four winds of the earth, that the wind should not blow on the earth, nor on the sea, nor on any tree.

2 And I saw another angel ascending from the east, having the seal of the living God: and he cried with a loud voice to the four angels, to whom it was given to hurt the earth and the sea,

3 Saying, Hurt not the earth, neither the sea, nor the trees, till we have sealed the servants of our God in their foreheads.

4 And I heard the number of them which were sealed: *and there were* sealed an hundred *and* forty *and* four thousand of all the tribes of the children of Israel.

5 Of the tribe of Juda *were* sealed twelve thousand. Of the tribe of Reuben *were* sealed twelve thousand. Of the tribe of Gad *were* sealed twelve thousand.

6 Of the tribe of Aser *were* sealed twelve

Cross references

8 Lev. 26:22; Ezek. 14:21; Zech. 6:3
9 2Tim. 1:8; Rev. 1:9; 8:3; 9:13; 12:17; 14:18; 19:10; 20:4
10 Zech. 1:12; Rev. 3:7; 11:18; 19:2
11 Heb. 11:40; Rev. 3:4, 5; 7:9, 14; 14:13
12 Joel 2:10, 31; 3:15; Matt. 24:29; Acts 2:20; Rev. 16:18
13 Rev. 8:10; 9:1
14 Ps. 102:26; Isa. 34:4; Jer. 3:23; 4:24; Heb. 1:12, 13; Rev. 16:20
15 Isa. 2:19
16 Hos. 10:8; Luke 23:30; Rev. 9:6
17 Isa. 13:6; Zeph. 1:14
1 Dan. 7:2; Rev. 9:4
3 Ezek. 9:4
4 Rev. 9:16; 14:1

6:9–11 The fifth seal shows the souls "under the altar" who were martyred for their faith. These martyrs are those who accepted Christ by faith during the early days of the Tribulation and were beheaded for their faith. They will not receive their resurrected bodies until Christ returns at the end of the Tribulation (Rev. 20:4–5).

6:11 The earth's population during the Tribulation will be reduced enormously. God will slay those who follow the Antichrist and take his mark (Rev. 13), and Antichrist, the official tool of Satan, will slay many tribulation believers who refuse to worship him. Half of the world's population will be dead by the middle of the Tribulation.

6:12–17 hide us from the face of him that sitteth on the throne. The sixth seal signals that the wrath of God is being poured out on the earth. In all probability (though millions have died in earthquakes past) this will be the most devastating quake since the flood. It will be so bad that even the kings of the earth and all men will call on the rocks to hide them. Even the lost know these judgments are from the Christ they have rejected.

7:1–8 Between the opening of the sixth and seventh seals, we are given an insight into the divine protection of the earth from powerful winds by the assignment of powerful angels and the sealing and ministry of the 144,000 witnesses. This chapter shows the supernatural efforts to which God will go during that time to bring a maximum number of souls to faith in Christ.

God will select 12,000 Jews from each of the twelve tribes of Israel to be His special servants throughout the Tribulation. We are not told what the seal is that He places on their foreheads, but whatever it is, it endows them with both protection and power from on high. The fact that these are Jewish groups indicates that there will be many Jews who come to accept Christ as their Messiah at the outset of the Tribulation. We can only imagine what evangelistic success these 144,000 servants of God will have. They are often likened to the zeal of the apostle Paul and those anointed with the outpouring of the Holy Spirit on the day of Pentecost (Joel 2:28–32; Acts 2:1–40).

thousand. Of the tribe of Nepthalim *were* sealed twelve thousand. Of the tribe of Manasses *were* sealed twelve thousand.

7 Of the tribe of Simeon *were* sealed twelve thousand. Of the tribe of Levi *were* sealed twelve thousand. Of the tribe of Issachar *were* sealed twelve thousand.

8 Of the tribe of Zebulun *were* sealed twelve thousand. Of the tribe of Joseph *were* sealed twelve thousand. Of the tribe of Benjamin *were* sealed twelve thousand.

The Congregation in Heaven

9 After this I beheld, and, lo, a great multitude, which no man could number, of all nations, and kindreds, and people, and tongues, stood before the throne, and before the Lamb, clothed with white robes, and palms in their hands;

10 And cried with a loud voice, saying, Salvation to our God which sitteth upon the throne, and unto the Lamb.

11 And all the angels stood round about the throne, and *about* the elders and the four beasts, and fell before the throne on their faces, and worshipped God,

12 Saying, Amen: Blessing, and glory, and wisdom, and thanksgiving, and honour, and power, and might, *be* unto our God for ever and ever. Amen.

13 And one of the elders answered, saying unto me, What are these which are arrayed in white robes? and whence came they?

14 And I said unto him, Sir, thou knowest. And he said to me, These are they which came out of great tribulation, and have

9 Rom. 11:25; Rev. 3:5, 18; 4:4; 5:9; 6:11; 7:14

10 Ps. 3:8; Isa. 43:11; Jer. 3:23; Hos. 13:4; Rev. 5:13; 19:1

11 Rev. 4:6

12 Rev. 5:13, 14

14 Isa. 1:18; Zech. 3:3-5; Heb. 9:14; 1John 1:7; Rev. 1:5; 6:9; 17:6

15 Isa. 4:5, 6; Rev. 21:3

16 Ps. 121:6; Isa. 49:10; Rev. 21:4

17 Ps. 23:1; 36:8; Isa. 25:8; John 10:11, 14; Rev. 21:4

1 Rev. 6:1

2 2Chr. 29:25-28; Matt. 18:10; Luke 1:19

3 Ex. 30:1; Rev. 5:8; 6:9

4 Ps. 141:2; Luke 1:10

5 2Sam. 22:8; Acts 4:31; Rev. 16:18

washed their robes, and made them white in the blood of the Lamb.

15 Therefore are they before the throne of God, and serve him day and night in his temple: and he that sitteth on the throne shall dwell among them.

16 They shall hunger no more, neither thirst any more; neither shall the sun light on them, nor any heat.

17 For the Lamb which is in the midst of the throne shall feed them, and shall lead them unto living fountains of waters: and God shall wipe away all tears from their eyes.

CHAPTER 8
Christ Opens the Seventh Seal

1 And when he had opened the seventh seal, there was silence in heaven about the space of half an hour.

2 And I saw the seven angels which stood before God; and to them were given seven trumpets.

3 And another angel came and stood at the altar, having a golden censer; and there was given unto him much incense, that he should offer *it* with the prayers of all saints upon the golden altar which was before the throne.

4 And the smoke of the incense, *which came* with the prayers of the saints, ascended up before God out of the angel's hand.

5 And the angel took the censer, and filled it with fire of the altar, and cast *it* into the earth: and there were voices, and thunderings, and lightnings, and an earthquake.

7:9–14 a great multitude, which no man could number. After their sealing and doubtless as a result of their ministry, John sees a multitude from all nations, tongues, and tribes standing "before the throne, and before the Lamb." This indicates there will be a great soul harvest during the Tribulation that is so enormous it cannot even be counted.

Who are these people standing before the throne? John asked that same question, and the angel said, "These are they who came out of the great tribulation." The 144,000 witnesses will be so effective during that chaotic time that an innumerable host of people will be saved. Note that the song of salvation sung by the angelic beings in heaven (vv. 11–12) is in accord with the Scripture that tells us angels rejoice over each soul that comes to faith (Luke 15:10).

7:16–17 Here we are given insights of the kind of suffering the martyrs of the Tribulation will experience: hunger, sun, and heat, indicating they will probably have

to flee from the Antichrist's population centers for safety and live as vagabonds before being killed.

8:1 silence in heaven. The next set of judgments, which shall cover the second quarter of the Tribulation, will be so catastrophic that heaven is silent in anticipation. Many see a parallel between this period of silence and the time of silence during the solemn ceremony of the temple worship.

8:2 The breaking of the seventh seal judgment does nothing on the earth except introduce the seven trumpet judgments, which describe what conditions on earth will be like during the next twenty-one months of the Tribulation. This is one reason for believing these three sets of judgments (seals, trumpets, and vial judgments) are chronological, each following the other.

8:3–5 the prayers of the saints. This prelude in heaven before the first trumpet on earth reflects on all the prayers of the people of God through the ages.

The Seven Trumpets

6 And the seven angels which had the seven trumpets prepared themselves to sound.

7 The first angel sounded, and there followed hail and fire mingled with blood, and they were cast upon the earth: and the third part of trees was burnt up, and all green grass was burnt up.

8 And the second angel sounded, and as it were a great mountain burning with fire was cast into the sea: and the third part of the sea became blood;

9 And the third part of the creatures which were in the sea, and had life, died; and the third part of the ships were destroyed.

10 And the third angel sounded, and there fell a great star from heaven, burning as it were a lamp, and it fell upon the third part of the rivers, and upon the fountains of waters;

11 And the name of the star is called Wormwood: and the third part of the waters became wormwood; and many men died of the waters, because they were made bitter.

12 And the fourth angel sounded, and the third part of the sun was smitten, and the third part of the moon, and the third part of

---

7 Isa. 2:13; Ezek. 38:22; Rev. 9:4; 16:2
8 Jer. 51:25; Ezek. 14:19; Amos 7:4; Rev. 16:3
9 Rev. 16:3
10 Isa. 14:12; Rev. 9:1; 16:4
11 Ex. 15:23
12 Isa. 13:10; Amos 8:9

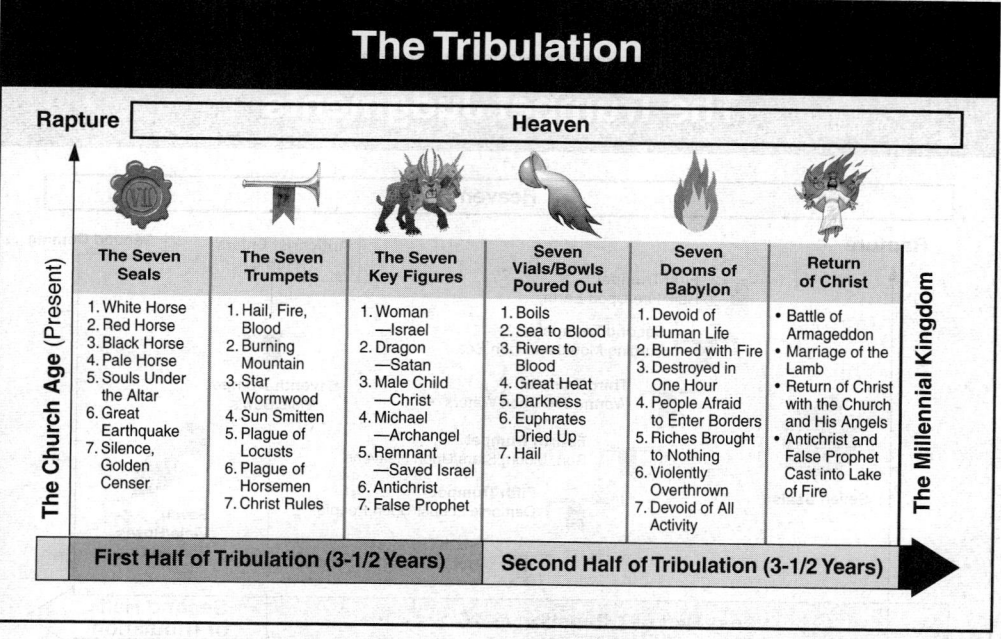

The Tribulation

Rapture	Heaven						The Millennial Kingdom
The Church Age (Present)	**The Seven Seals**	**The Seven Trumpets**	**The Seven Key Figures**	**Seven Vials/Bowls Poured Out**	**Seven Dooms of Babylon**	**Return of Christ**	
	1. White Horse 2. Red Horse 3. Black Horse 4. Pale Horse 5. Souls Under the Altar 6. Great Earthquake 7. Silence, Golden Censer	1. Hail, Fire, Blood 2. Burning Mountain 3. Star Wormwood 4. Sun Smitten 5. Plague of Locusts 6. Plague of Horsemen 7. Christ Rules	1. Woman —Israel 2. Dragon —Satan 3. Male Child —Christ 4. Michael —Archangel 5. Remnant —Saved Israel 6. Antichrist 7. False Prophet	1. Boils 2. Sea to Blood 3. Rivers to Blood 4. Great Heat 5. Darkness 6. Euphrates Dried Up 7. Hail	1. Devoid of Human Life 2. Burned with Fire 3. Destroyed in One Hour 4. People Afraid to Enter Borders 5. Riches Brought to Nothing 6. Violently Overthrown 7. Devoid of All Activity	• Battle of Armageddon • Marriage of the Lamb • Return of Christ with the Church and His Angels • Antichrist and False Prophet Cast into Lake of Fire	
	First Half of Tribulation (3-1/2 Years)			**Second Half of Tribulation (3-1/2 Years)**			

© AMG Publishers

8:7 hail and fire mingled with blood. John the revelator sees a picture of a vast global conflagration in which one third of the vegetation of earth is burned up. This is a literal experience that shall terrify the whole earth (Joel 1:18–20). The very fact that the Bible predicts such massive global destruction at the end of human history ought to challenge each one of us to live godly lives on a daily basis in light of the fact that we live in a time when such destruction is possible.

8:8–9 a great mountain burning with fire was cast into the sea. This may refer to nuclear devastation or a giant asteroid or meteor that comes from outer space, killing one-third of the aquatic life.

8:10–11 The third trumpet calls forth "Wormwood," which in Greek is *apsinthos*, a bitter, often poisonous herb or drug that will pollute one third of the fresh water on earth. The desperation of mankind in that day will be unbelievable.

8:12 The fourth trumpet reveals that the sun, moon, and stars will literally be darkened; thus the world will experience a one-third increase in darkness. This will have a devastating effect on crops, the food supply, and everyone's lifestyle. The hardship that results will no doubt contribute to many calling on the name of the Lord (Rev. 7:9).

the stars; so as the third part of them was darkened, and the day shone not for a third part of it, and the night likewise.

13 And I beheld, and heard an angel flying through the midst of heaven, saying with a loud voice, Woe, woe, woe, to the inhabiters of the earth by reason of the other voices of the trumpet of the three angels, which are yet to sound!

CHAPTER 9

1 And the fifth angel sounded, and I saw a star fall from heaven unto the earth: and to him was given the key of the bottomless pit.

2 And he opened the bottomless pit; and there arose a smoke out of the pit, as the smoke of a great furnace; and the sun and

13 Rev. 9:12; 11:14; 14:6; 19:17

1 Rev. 8:10; 9:2, 11; 17:8; 20:1

2 Joel 2:2, 10

3 Rev. 9:10

4 Ex. 12:23; Ezek. 9:4; Rev. 6:6; 7:3; 8:7

5 Rev. 9:10; 11:7

6 Job 3:21; Isa. 2:19; Jer. 8:3; Rev. 6:16

the air were darkened by reason of the smoke of the pit.

3 And there came out of the smoke locusts upon the earth: and unto them was given power, as the scorpions of the earth have power.

4 And it was commanded them that they should not hurt the grass of the earth, neither any green thing, neither any tree; but only those men which have not the seal of God in their foreheads.

5 And to them it was given that they should not kill them, but that they should be tormented five months: and their torment *was* the torment of a scorpion, when he striketh a man.

6 And in those days shall men seek death,

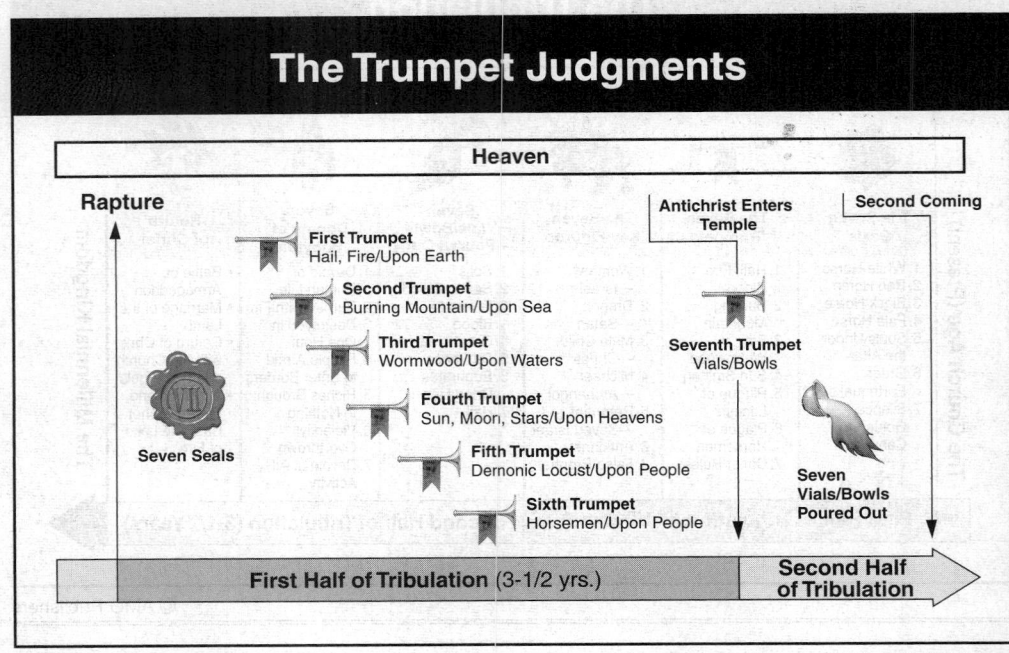

The Trumpet Judgments

Heaven

Rapture

Second Coming

Antichrist Enters Temple

First Trumpet
Hail, Fire/Upon Earth

Second Trumpet
Burning Mountain/Upon Sea

Third Trumpet
Wormwood/Upon Waters

Fourth Trumpet
Sun, Moon, Stars/Upon Heavens

Seven Seals

Fifth Trumpet
Demonic Locust/Upon People

Sixth Trumpet
Horsemen/Upon People

Seventh Trumpet
Vials/Bowls

Seven Vials/Bowls Poured Out

First Half of Tribulation (3-1/2 yrs.)

Second Half of Tribulation

© AMG Publishers

8:13 An angel announces in heaven that the next three judgments (two trumpets and the vial judgments) will be even worse than the first, which is what the three "woes" mean—the worst is yet to come!

9:1–11 angel of the bottomless pit. The fifth trumpet produces an angel that opens that hellish place to permit poisonous "locusts," creatures who sting like scorpions, whose stings hurt people five months . . . but in mercy cannot kill them. They have a king over them called Apollyon ("destroyer"). Many believe this is a horde of demons who will plague people during the Tribulation.

9:4 which have not the seal of God in their foreheads. It is very interesting that this judgment was only for those who did not have that seal. Those with the seal of God likely include the 144,000 witnesses, and probably the innumerable multitude which will be converted through their preaching.

9:5 The fact that they could not kill these unsaved souls may indicate that the purpose of this judgment is to lead the undecided to faith in Christ.

and shall not find it; and shall desire to die, and death shall flee from them.

7 And the shapes of the locusts *were* like unto horses prepared unto battle; and on their heads *were* as it were crowns like gold, and their faces *were* as the faces of men.

8 And they had hair as the hair of women, and their teeth were as *the teeth* of lions.

9 And they had breastplates, as it were breastplates of iron; and the sound of their wings *was* as the sound of chariots of many horses running to battle.

10 And they had tails like unto scorpions, and there were stings in their tails: and their power *was* to hurt men five months.

11 And they had a king over them, *which is* the angel of the bottomless pit, whose name in the Hebrew tongue *is* Abaddon, but in the Greek tongue hath *his* name Apollyon.

12 One woe is past; *and,* behold, there come two woes more hereafter.

13 And the sixth angel sounded, and I heard a voice from the four horns of the golden altar which is before God,

14 Saying to the sixth angel which had the trumpet, Loose the four angels which are bound in the great river Euphrates.

15 And the four angels were loosed, which were prepared for an hour, and a day, and a month, and a year, for to slay the third part of men.

16 And the number of the army of the horsemen *were* two hundred thousand thousand: and I heard the number of them.

17 And thus I saw the horses in the vision, and them that sat on them, having breastplates of fire, and of jacinth, and brimstone:

and the heads of the horses *were* as the heads of lions; and out of their mouths issued fire and smoke and brimstone.

18 By these three was the third part of men killed, by the fire, and by the smoke, and by the brimstone, which issued out of their mouths.

19 For their power is in their mouth, and in their tails: for their tails *were* like unto serpents, and had heads, and with them they do hurt.

20 And the rest of the men which were not killed by these plagues yet repented not of the works of their hands, that they should not worship devils, and idols of gold, and silver, and brass, and stone, and of wood: which neither can see, nor hear, nor walk:

21 Neither repented they of their murders, nor of their sorceries, nor of their fornication, nor of their thefts.

CHAPTER 10
Opening the Little Book

1 And I saw another mighty angel come down from heaven, clothed with a cloud: and a rainbow *was* upon his head, and his face *was* as it were the sun, and his feet as pillars of fire:

2 And he had in his hand a little book open: and he set his right foot upon the sea, and his left *foot* on the earth,

3 And cried with a loud voice, as *when* a lion roareth: and when he had cried, seven thunders uttered their voices.

4 And when the seven thunders had uttered their voices, I was about to write: and I heard a voice from heaven saying unto me,

Cross references: 7 Dan. 7:8; Joel 2:4; Nah. 3:17 | 8 Joel 1:6 | 9 Joel 2:5, 7 | 10 Rev. 9:5 | 11 Eph. 2:2; Rev. 9:1 | 12 Rev. 8:13 | 14 Rev. 16:12 | 16 Ps. 68:17; Ezek. 38:4; Dan. 7:10; Rev. 7:4 | 17 1Chr. 12:8; Isa. 5:28, 29 | 19 Isa. 9:15 | 20 Lev. 17:7; Deut. 31:29; 32:17; Ps. 106:37; 115:4; 135:15; Dan. 5:23; 1Cor. 10:20 | 21 Rev. 22:15 | 1 Ezek. 1:28; Matt. 17:2; Rev. 1:15, 16 | 2 Matt. 28:18 | 3 Rev. 8:5 | 4 Dan. 8:26; 12:4, 9

9:13–16 the army of the horsemen. The sixth angel introduces an awesome army of two hundred million riding on horses.

9:14 Loose the four angels. The fact that this army is released by these four angels (demons) indicates that God has kept these angels who followed Satan from hurting mankind. It is Satan, not God, that dictates their evil work, for as soon as they are released they seek to kill mankind.

9:17–19 The description of these fearful creatures must so terrify mankind that many die of fright; however, it is assumed that they have no power over believers living in that period. It would seem that only the Antichrist and his human followers have the capability of actually killing the "saints."

9:20–21 One would think that in the midst of this great battle for the souls of mankind that the majority would

turn to the Lord. Not so; "a great multitude, which no man could number" does receive Christ (Rev. 7:9), but even after all these catastrophic judgments designed to make men turn to God, a majority rebel against Him. Note the sins that are rampant in that day that keep men from Christ: 1) worship of demons and idols, 2) murders, 3) sorceries (Gr. *pharmakon*, or drugs), 4) sexual immorality of all kinds, 5) theft and robbery.

The conclusion of Chapter 9 marks the half-way point of the Tribulation period. "The Great Tribulation" follows immediately.

10:1 At no other time does Christ appear as an angel or created being after His resurrection. This angel is most likely Michael, Gabriel, or an angel equal to them who swears an oath by Jesus Christ, indicating something significant is about to happen. Angels play a prominent role in the Apocalypse, being mentioned sixty-six times.

Seal up those things which the seven thunders uttered, and write them not.

5 And the angel which I saw stand upon the sea and upon the earth lifted up his hand to heaven,

6 And sware by him that liveth for ever and ever, who created heaven, and the things that therein are, and the earth, and the things that therein are, and the sea, and the things which are therein, that there should be time no longer:

7 But in the days of the voice of the seventh angel, when he shall begin to sound, the mystery of God should be finished, as he hath declared to his servants the prophets.

8 And the voice which I heard from heaven spake unto me again, and said, Go *and* take the little book which is open in the hand of the angel which standeth upon the sea and upon the earth.

9 And I went unto the angel, and said unto him, Give me the little book. And he said unto me, Take *it,* and eat it up; and it shall make thy belly bitter, but it shall be in thy mouth sweet as honey.

10 And I took the little book out of the angel's hand, and ate it up; and it was in my

5 Ex. 6:8;
Dan. 12:7

6 Neh. 9:6;
Dan. 12:7;
Rev. 4:11;
14:7; 16:17

7 Rev. 11:15

8 Rev. 10:4

9 Jer. 15:16;
Ezek. 2:8;
3:1-3

10 Ezek. 3:3

10 Ezek. 2:10

1 Num.
23:18; Ezek.
40:3; Zech.
2:1; Rev.
21:15

2 Ps. 79:1;
Ezek. 40:17,
20; Dan.
8:10; Luke
21:24; Rev.
13:5

3 Rev. 12:6;
19:10; 20:4

4 Ps. 52:8;
Jer. 11:16;
Zech. 4:3,
11, 14

5 Num.
16:29

mouth sweet as honey: and as soon as I had eaten it, my belly was bitter.

11 And he said unto me, Thou must prophesy again before many peoples, and nations, and tongues, and kings.

CHAPTER 11
The Temple and God's Two Witnesses

1 And there was given me a reed like unto a rod: and the angel stood, saying, Rise, and measure the temple of God, and the altar, and them that worship therein.

2 But the court which is without the temple leave out, and measure it not; for it is given unto the Gentiles: and the holy city shall they tread under foot forty *and* two months.

3 And I will give *power* unto my two witnesses, and they shall prophesy a thousand two hundred *and* threescore days, clothed in sackcloth.

4 These are the two olive trees, and the two candlesticks standing before the God of the earth.

5 And if any man will hurt them, fire proceedeth out of their mouth, and devoureth

---

10:6 time no longer. This literally means "delay no longer" and indicates that the time of the end is rapidly approaching. From the sounding of the seventh angel's trumpet, the world will move relentlessly toward the fulfillment of all the prophecies of the Bible, culminating in the coming of Christ to the earth.

10:7 the mystery of God should be finished. The culmination of the conflict of the ages is about to take place with the sounding of the seventh angel's trumpet. This trumpet introduces the seven vial judgments that will cover the events of the last three and one-half years of the Tribulation described in chapter 16. In the meantime, most of what occurs from chapter 12—15 are scenes in heaven describing events which will occur on earth.

10:8–10 but it shall be in thy mouth sweet as honey. The "little book" that was seen in heaven in verse 2 has a similar mission as that given to Ezekiel (3:1–3) and Jeremiah (15:16). The prophetic Word, which is what the "little book" is, contains the "sweet" message of God's wonderful plan for mankind including the coming of Christ, the Millennial Kingdom, and heaven, but it also contains the judgment of God on sinners who do not repent and come to Him, and their ultimate consignment to hell.

10:11 Thou must prophesy again. John's task of communicating prophecy was not complete, but the message of God's grace and judgment must still be communicated

until He completes God's final plan to consummate end-time events which are rapidly approaching.

11:1–2 The temple John is commissioned to "measure" is probably a reference to the temple that the orthodox Jews will build during the Tribulation. This refers to the temple that Daniel predicted would be desecrated during the Tribulation (Dan. 9:27). Antichrist will make a covenant with Israel, which he breaks in the middle of the seven-year period (Dan. 9:27).

11:2 the holy city shall they tread under foot. This event cannot happen in the first half of the Tribulation, for the Jews control the city and worship in their temple during that time. This indicates that the Gentiles, under the leadership of Antichrist, will control the city during the last half of those seven years. In fact, we find that Antichrist not only desecrates the temple, but also sets himself up as God to be worshiped in that temple (2 Thess. 2:4; Rev. 13).

11:3–4 I will give power unto my two witnesses. God's two powerful witnesses will prophesy 1260 days. These two witnesses with supernatural powers will warn Israel and the world, right at the temple site, that the coming judgment is about to fall upon the world. These witnesses will not only attempt to call Israel to repentance by proclaiming the gospel, they will also urge her to accept her Messiah.

The Two Witnesses

By Tim LaHaye

Two of the most colorful characters in all of biblical prophecy may be the supernatural prophets that burst on the scene during the first half of the Tribulation. According to the eleventh chapter of Revelation, these two characters dress in sackcloth, prophesy, dispense astonishing miracles, and witness to the grace of God in the most evil culture known to mankind. There is much speculation as to the identity of the two witnesses.

Though some believe Elijah and Enoch are the two witnesses, most Bible scholars consider them to be Moses and Elijah. Proponents of the Moses and Elijah argument point out that these two Old Testament characters were the most influential Hebrew men of their respective times—Moses introduced God's written Law to Israel, while Elijah was the first of the writing prophets and even started the school for the prophets. In fact, whenever the Jews said, "Moses and Elijah," they usually meant "the law and the prophets." One factor that may suggest Moses and Elijah will be the two witnesses mentioned in Revelation is that the two men accompanied Jesus at the Transfiguration (Matt. 17). Another element is that the miracles the witnesses are to produce have striking similarities to the judgment plagues initiated by Moses and Elijah in the Old Testament (see Ex. 7—12; 1 Kgs. 17:1).

> *God will raise two prophets from the dead.*

Together with the 144,000 witnesses, the two witnesses of Revelation 11 will have awesome power and impact in producing the enormous soul harvest of the first forty-two months of the Tribulation described in Revelation 7. They will provide the millions of Jews in the Holy Land a spiritual bridge to the Christian gospel. God will demonstrate His mighty power and existence through these two prophets over whom the Antichrist will have no power until the God-appointed time. Before that designated time, the two witnesses will be untouchable, and anyone who threatens them will be killed (Rev. 11:5).

The two prophets make mortal enemies of the Antichrist and those who reject Christ and worship the Beast during the first half (or 1,260 days) of the Tribulation. For reasons known only to God, the Lord will allow the Antichrist to overcome and kill the two witnesses once they have "finished their testimony" (Rev. 11:7).

Then the unsaved people of the world who so despise the witnesses will refuse to bury them, leaving their dead bodies to decay in the streets of Jerusalem. They will even make a Christmas-like celebration out of their murders by sending and receiving gifts "in honor" of the occasion. John prophesies that, "they of the people and kindreds and tongues and nations *shall see their dead bodies three days and an half*" (Rev. 11:9, emphasis added). How could the whole world see their dead bodies? Only a short time ago, it would have been humanly inconceivable for the entire world to witness such an event, but today, with rapid advancements in communication technology, such a spectacle is not so difficult to imagine.

But the most incredible aspect of Revelation 11 is that the story doesn't end with the deaths of the two witnesses! God predicted that while the world is watching, He will do a mighty miracle—He will raise the two prophets from the dead and take them up to heaven (Rev. 11:11–13). This event will be a loving gesture by God Almighty, not only to resurrect and take to heaven His two prophets, but also to make His existence and power known around the world.

their enemies: and if any man will hurt them, he must in this manner be killed.

6 These have power to shut heaven, that it rain not in the days of their prophecy: and have power over waters to turn them to blood, and to smite the earth with all plagues, as often as they will.

7 And when they shall have finished their testimony, the beast that ascendeth out of the bottomless pit shall make war against them, and shall overcome them, and kill them.

8 And their dead bodies *shall lie* in the street of the great city, which spiritually is called Sodom and Egypt, where also our Lord was crucified.

9 And they of the people and kindreds and tongues and nations shall see their dead bodies three days and an half, and shall not suffer their dead bodies to be put in graves.

10 And they that dwell upon the earth shall rejoice over them, and make merry, and shall send gifts one to another; because these two prophets tormented them that dwelt on the earth.

11 And after three days and an half the Spirit of life from God entered into them, and they stood upon their feet; and great fear fell upon them which saw them.

12 And they heard a great voice from heaven saying unto them, Come up hither. And they ascended up to heaven in a cloud; and their enemies beheld them.

13 And the same hour was there a great earthquake, and the tenth part of the city fell, and in the earthquake were slain of men seven thousand: and the remnant were affrighted, and gave glory to the God of heaven.

The Seventh Angel Introduces the Last Half of the Tribulation

14 The second woe is past; *and*, behold, the third woe cometh quickly.

15 And the seventh angel sounded; and there were great voices in heaven, saying, The kingdoms of this world are become *the kingdoms* of our Lord, and of his Christ; and he shall reign for ever and ever.

16 And the four and twenty elders, which

Cross references:
6 Ex. 7:19; 1Kgs. 17:1
7 Dan. 7:21; Zech. 14:2
8 Heb. 13:12; Rev. 14:8; 17:1, 5; 18:10, 24
10 Rev. 12:12; 13:8; 16:10
11 Ezek. 37:5, 9, 10, 14; Rev. 11:9
12 2Kgs. 2:1, 5, 7; Isa. 14:13; 60:8; Acts 1:9; Rev. 12:5
13 Rev. 3:4; 6:12; 14:7; 15:4; 16:19
15 Isa. 27:13; Dan. 2:44; 7:14, 18, 27; Rev. 10:7; 12:10; 16:17; 19:6

11:5–6 Even the Antichrist cannot touch these witnesses during their mission period of 1260 days, for they have the power to devour their enemies with fire. These witnesses will exhibit three supernatural acts so that all should know that they come from God. They will exhibit power to stop the rain from falling, power to turn the water to blood, and power to bring a plague on earth as they see fit. The powers of these two witnesses are similar to those that Elijah and Moses had in Old Testament times. For this reason and the fact that Moses and Elijah appeared on the Mount of Transfiguration (Matt. 17:9), many scholars think Moses and Elijah also are indeed the two witnesses who will appear during this time. The Jews refer to the Old Testament as "Moses and the prophets." Moses represents the first five books of the law, and Elijah, who started the school of the prophets, represents the other writers of Scripture.

11:7 the beast that ascendeth. While these two prophets are supernaturally protected during their 1260 days of ministry, in the middle of the Tribulation, "the Beast" or Antichrist is finally permitted to kill them. He then leaves their bodies in the street for three days. This is the first of thirty-four uses in Revelation of the title "the Beast" to describe the Antichrist. From this midpoint of the Tribulation, he becomes the dominant personality on earth and the embodiment of evil.

11:8 where also our Lord was crucified. The moral depravity of Jerusalem ("the holy city") is seen in the imagery of Sodom and Egypt to depict its spiritual state. During the first half of the Tribulation there will be two

kinds of Jews in that ancient city: the God-fearing orthodox Jews who rebuild their temple and worship without faith in their Messiah, and the sinners who reject anything spiritual, live totally depraved lives, and are open followers of Antichrist.

11:9 This is a significant verse for it indicates the use of technology that has only recently become available. Only in the last decade or so of the twentieth century did global television news coverage and the Internet make this possible.

11:10 The pent-up hatred toward these two witnesses and the God they represent erupts into a global celebration over the deaths of the men who had consistently warned the people of the world to repent.

11:11–12 The Spirit of God enters these two witnesses; they are supernaturally resurrected, and "they ascended up to heaven in a cloud." They experience a personal rapture here. God is showing His supremacy over anything that Antichrist can do.

11:13 This act of God's judgment causes great "fear" or awe of God, so that many glorify God. This implies that thousands of rebellious Jews, many of whom rejoiced at the killing of the two witnesses, will turn to God in faith at this point—just prior to Antichrist's desecration of the temple.

11:15–18 God meant this earth to be a rich source of blessing to mankind, but Satan, the Antichrist, and thousands of their false prophets have led mankind to rebel

sat before God on their seats, fell upon their faces, and worshipped God,

17 Saying, We give thee thanks, O Lord God Almighty, which art, and wast, and art to come; because thou hast taken to thee thy great power, and hast reigned.

18 And the nations were angry, and thy wrath is come, and the time of the dead, that they should be judged, and that thou shouldest give reward unto thy servants the prophets, and to the saints, and them that fear thy name, small and great; and shouldest destroy them which destroy the earth.

19 And the temple of God was opened in heaven, and there was seen in his temple the ark of his testament: and there were lightnings, and voices, and thunderings, and an earthquake, and great hail.

CHAPTER 12
A Recap of Israel's History and Prophecy of Her Future

1 And there appeared a great wonder in heaven; a woman clothed with the sun, and the moon under her feet, and upon her head a crown of twelve stars:

2 And she being with child cried, travailing in birth, and pained to be delivered.

3 And there appeared another wonder in

17	Rev. 1:4, 8; 4:8; 16:5
17	Rev. 19:6
18	Dan. 7:9, 10; Rev. 6:10; 11:2, 9; 13:10; 18:6; 19:5
19	Rev. 8:5; 15:5, 8; 16:18, 21
2	Isa. 66:7; Gal. 4:19
3	Rev. 13:1; 17:3, 9, 10
4	Ex. 1:16; Dan. 8:10; Rev. 9:10, 19; 12:2; 17:18
5	Ps. 2:9; Rev. 2:27; 19:15
6	Rev. 11:3; 12:4
7	Dan. 10:13, 21; 12:1; Rev. 12:3; 20:2
9	Gen. 3:1, 4; Luke 10:18; John 12:31; Rev. 9:1; 20:2, 3
10	Job 1:9

heaven; and behold a great red dragon, having seven heads and ten horns, and seven crowns upon his heads.

4 And his tail drew the third part of the stars of heaven, and did cast them to the earth: and the dragon stood before the woman which was ready to be delivered, for to devour her child as soon as it was born.

5 And she brought forth a man child, who was to rule all nations with a rod of iron: and her child was caught up unto God, and to his throne.

6 And the woman fled into the wilderness, where she hath a place prepared of God, that they should feed her there a thousand two hundred and threescore days.

7 And there was war in heaven: Michael and his angels fought against the dragon; and the dragon fought and his angels,

8 And prevailed not; neither was their place found any more in heaven.

9 And the great dragon was cast out, that old serpent, called the Devil, and Satan, which deceiveth the whole world: he was cast out into the earth, and his angels were cast out with him.

10 And I heard a loud voice saying in heaven, Now is come salvation, and strength, and the kingdom of our God, and the power of his Christ: for the accuser of

---

against God, causing this earth to be a place of great suffering. The elders in heaven rejoice because the time of God's judgment and rectification of all things is only three and one-half years away.

11:19 the ark of his testament. This is a reference to the heavenly ark of the covenant, after which the earthly ark of the covenant was patterned.

12:1–2 This review of the conflict of the ages between God and Satan is used to show how Satan's past enmity to God, mankind, and Israel fits in with God's consummation of all things (see chaps. 16—22).

12:1–5 a great wonder in heaven. This great sign must be Israel, for she is seen as Joseph saw her in a vision (Gen. 37:9–10). Her identity is crucial to the interpretation of Revelation. It is the remnant of Israel, not the Church, that is persecuted by the Antichrist. The manchild that Satan tries to devour could only be Christ, the chosen child of Israel who will one day soon "rule all nations with a rod of iron" (v. 5, cf. Acts 1:9–11). It is Christ who Satan has tried to kill many times during His life, and failing in that, Satan tried to destroy His Church.

12:3 The red dragon is unquestionably a reference to Satan. "The seven heads" refer to the seven world king-

doms that have existed from Egypt, Assyria, Babylon, Medo-Persia, Greece, Rome, and the end-time government of Antichrist made up of the ten horns (Dan. 7—8; Rev. 13; 17).

12:6 a place prepared of God. During this time, Satan will unleash the persecution of Israel that will be more heinous than that of the Holocaust. The Hebrew prophets foretold that coming time of tribulation or distress (Lev. 26:40–45; Deut. 30:1–5; Isa. 11:10–16; 27:6–13; Jer. 23:3–8; 30:3–11). There in that wilderness setting, thought to be Edom, God will feed the Jews supernaturally as He fed the children of Israel in the wilderness.

12:7 there was war in heaven. One can only imagine what this war between the forces of Satan and Michael the archangel entails. This is a description of the effects of Satan's fall, centuries ago, which left him limited access to God, during which time he accuses the brethren as he accused Job and doubtless many other believers to this day (v. 10).

12:9 that old serpent. This phrase calls to remembrance Satan's temptation of Eve in the garden (Gen. 3:1–6), the beginning of Satan's work to deceive the world. He is clearly identified as "Satan" and the "devil."

our brethren is cast down, which accused them before our God day and night.

11 And they overcame him by the blood of the Lamb, and by the word of their testimony; and they loved not their lives unto the death.

12 Therefore rejoice, *ye* heavens, and ye that dwell in them. Woe to the inhabitants of the earth and of the sea! for the devil is come down unto you, having great wrath, because he knoweth that he hath but a short time.

13 And when the dragon saw that he was cast unto the earth, he persecuted the woman which brought forth the man *child*.

14 And to the woman were given two wings of a great eagle, that she might fly into the wilderness, into her place, where she is nourished for a time, and times, and half a time, from the face of the serpent.

15 And the serpent cast out of his mouth water as a flood after the woman, that he might cause her to be carried away of the flood.

16 And the earth helped the woman, and the earth opened her mouth, and swallowed up the flood which the dragon cast out of his mouth.

17 And the dragon was wroth with the woman, and went to make war with the remnant of her seed, which keep the commandments of God, and have the testimony of Jesus Christ.

CHAPTER 13
The End-time Beast

1 And I stood upon the sand of the sea, and saw a beast rise up out of the sea, having seven heads and ten horns, and upon his horns ten crowns, and upon his heads the name of blasphemy.

2 And the beast which I saw was like unto a leopard, and his feet were as *the feet* of a bear, and his mouth as the mouth of a lion: and the dragon gave him his power, and his seat, and great authority.

3 And I saw one of his heads as it were wounded to death; and his deadly wound was healed: and all the world wondered after the beast.

4 And they worshipped the dragon which gave power unto the beast: and they worshipped the beast, saying, Who *is* like unto the beast? who is able to make war with him?

---

11 Luke 14:26; Rom. 8:33, 34, 37; 16:20

12 Ps. 96:11; Isa. 49:13; Rev. 8:13; 10:6; 11:10; 18:20

13 Rev. 12:5

14 Ex. 19:4; Dan. 7:25; 12:7; Rev. 12:6; 17:3

15 Isa. 59:19

17 Gen. 3:15; 1Cor. 2:1; 1John 5:10; Rev. 1:2, 9; 6:9; 11:7; 13:7; 14:12; 20:4

1 Dan. 7:2, 7; Rev. 12:3; 17:3, 9, 12

2 Dan. 7:4, 5, 6; Rev. 12:4, 9; 16:10

3 Rev. 13:12, 14; 17:8

4 Rev. 18:18

12:11 loved not their lives unto the death. Note how dying as a martyr for Christ is seen as a victory to God— the only way that can be so is that resurrection and life after death is a practical fact.

12:12 he knoweth that he hath but a short time. Satan's most savage attack on mankind will be in the last three and one-half years of the Tribulation that are about to be unveiled. Jesus warned that this would be the greatest time of tribulation (Matt. 24:21).

12:15–16 cast out of his mouth water as a flood. Since the serpent is symbolic of the devil and the woman is symbolic of the Israelites who have accepted their Messiah and fled from Antichrist, the flood that flows from Satan's "mouth" must also be symbolic, signifying that whatever he does to try to destroy Israel will come to naught.

12:17 the remnant of her seed. This seed of the woman that Satan and the Antichrist try to destroy from the middle of the Tribulation throughout the days that follow represents Jews who have trusted Jesus as Savior. God will protect those who keep His commandments, and many Jews in that day will follow the Messiah, Jesus Christ. When the Antichrist breaks his covenant with the Jews and desecrates their temple, they will reject him and turn to Jesus Christ in saving faith.

13:1 Beast . . . out of the sea. This Beast out of the sea is the most dominant personality to arise during the last

three and one-half years of the Tribulation. The sea here may have reference to the peoples of the Mediterranean region. The name "blasphemy" indicates that the kingdom of Antichrist during the Tribulation will be an anti-God and anti-Christ type of kingdom.

13:2 the beast which I saw. The description of this Beast is similar to that of the dragon in chapter 12. Since beasts, when used symbolically, refer either to a king or a kingdom, it would seem that this "beast" is the embodiment of all the beastly governments of man that have ruled the world. All the empires represented by the Beast have had one thing in common: they were indwelt by the dragon, that serpent the devil—Satan himself.

13:3 wounded to death. In the middle of the Tribulation, the Antichrist will be killed, lie in state briefly, and then actually be indwelt personally by Satan, who was cast out of heaven in the previous chapter. Satan will indwell Antichrist and imitate Christ's resurrection. This wondering (or marveling) at the Beast indicates that he may claim to have seen things in the nether world that contradict the Bible to give lost sinners a false sense of security about eternity.

13:4 who is able to make war with him? This confirms the absolute power that Satan will have over the world at this time. No one else will be able to stop the rise of the Beast to world dominion.

5 And there was given unto him a mouth speaking great things and blasphemies; and power was given unto him to continue forty *and* two months.

6 And he opened his mouth in blasphemy against God, to blaspheme his name, and his tabernacle, and them that dwell in heaven.

7 And it was given unto him to make war with the saints, and to overcome them: and power was given him over all kindreds, and tongues, and nations.

8 And all that dwell upon the earth shall worship him, whose names are not written in the book of life of the Lamb slain from the foundation of the world.

9 If any man have an ear, let him hear.

10 He that leadeth into captivity shall go into captivity: he that killeth with the sword must be killed with the sword. Here is the patience and the faith of the saints.

The False Prophet

11 And I beheld another beast coming up out of the earth; and he had two horns like a lamb, and he spake as a dragon.

12 And he exerciseth all the power of the first beast before him, and causeth the earth and them which dwell therein to worship the first beast, whose deadly wound was healed.

Cross references:

5 Dan. 7:8, 11, 25; 11:36; Rev. 11:2; 12:6
7 Dan. 7:21; Rev. 11:7, 18; 12:17; 17:15
8 Ex. 32:32; Dan. 12:1; Phil. 4:3; Rev. 3:5; 17:8; 20:12, 15; 21:27
9 Rev. 2:7
10 Gen. 9:6; Isa. 33:1; Rev. 14:12
11 Rev. 11:7

The Lamb versus the Beast

The Lamb—Jesus Christ	The Beast—Antichrist
A slain Lamb (Rev. 5:6)	A ferocious beast (Rev. 13:2)
Seven horns, eyes, and Spirits (Rev. 5:6)	Seven heads, ten horns, and ten crowns (Rev. 13:1)
Four heavenly creatures and twenty-four elders fell down before the Lamb (Rev. 5:8)	All the world worshiped the Beast and Dragon (Rev. 13:3–4)
Worship saying, "Worthy is the Lamb" (Rev. 5:12)	Worship saying, "Who is like unto the Beast?" (Rev. 13:4)
All heaven, earth, under the earth, and in the sea worship the Lamb (Rev. 5:13)	The earth and almost all those that dwell upon the earth worship the Beast (Rev. 13:12, cf. v. 8)
A great redeemed multitude standing before the Lamb (Rev. 7:9)	The Beast deceives all them (except believers, v. 8) that dwell upon the earth (Rev. 13:14)
The Lamb comforts and nourishes His followers (Rev. 7:17)	One may not buy or sell unless one has the mark of the Beast (Rev. 13:17)
The 144,000 witnesses of the Lamb, having His Father's name written in their foreheads (Rev. 14:1)	Almost all them that dwell upon the earth have the mark of the Beast upon their right hand or forehead (Rev. 13:16)
The 144,000 freely follow the Lamb wherever He goes (Rev. 14:4)	Imposes the mark of the Beast upon his followers (Rev. 13:17)
Those following the Lamb dwell eternally in the New Jerusalem (Rev. 22:5)	Those following the Beast shall dwell eternally in the lake of fire (Rev. 14:9–10)

13:5–6 them that dwell in heaven. This "beast," the Antichrist, blasphemes not only God, but those that dwell in heaven. Satan blasphemes God and every object of God's gracious mercy.

13:8 Satan's "authority" will be all but unlimited, and almost everyone on earth will worship him. This is the very thing Satan has sought from the beginning, worship from angels and men. Of course, believers in Christ will not worship Antichrist, because they will have their names written "in the book of life of the Lamb." This book of the Lamb contains the names of all those who have called on the Lamb of God for salvation.

13:10 the patience and the faith of the saints. This refers to the endurance of the saints in the face of unprecedented persecution for their faith.

13:11 another beast coming out of the earth. This second "beast" is also referred to as "the false prophet" (Rev. 16:13; 19:20; 20:10). He is the alter ego of the Antichrist. He will take charge of the religions of the world after the "harlot" religion is destroyed during the middle of the Tribulation (Rev. 17). Some scholars suggest that because this False Prophet comes from the "earth," he might be an apostate Jew from Israel or a Gentile of Mediterranean ancestry. That he has "two horns like a lamb" indicates he will appear as a gentle lamb to deceive, but his false gospel will be supportive of Antichrist's doctrine. He will speak "as a dragon," a supreme destroyer of the truth and the souls of men.

13:12 exerciseth all the power of the first beast before him. The False Prophet will be the second highest ranking world leader during the Tribulation, and he will force the whole world to worship the Antichrist.

The False Prophet

By Edward Hindson

The ultimate deception of the End Times will involve the worldwide worship of the Antichrist. But the Antichrist will not rise to power alone. His success will result from a worldwide spiritual deception perpetrated by the False Prophet. This prophet's ability to perform miraculous signs will enable him to convince the public that the Antichrist is the leader for whom they have been searching.

Revelation 13 presents ten identifying features of the False Prophet: **1)** rises out of the earth (13:11), **2)** controls religious affairs (13:11), **3)** is motivated by Satan (13:11), **4)** promotes the worship of the Beast (13:12), **5)** performs signs and miracles (13:13), **6)** deceives the whole world (13:14), **7)** empowers the image of the Beast (13:15), **8)** kills all who refuse to worship (13:15), **9)** controls all economic commerce (13:17), and **10)** controls the marks of the Beast (13:17–18).

Together, Satan (dragon), Antichrist (beast of sea), and the False Prophet (beast of earth) comprise an "unholy trinity" that is a counterfeit of the Holy Trinity. Satan opposes the Father; Antichrist opposes the Son; and the False Prophet opposes the Holy Spirit. This ungodly alliance is Satan's final attempt to overthrow the work of God on earth.

> *The False Prophet will arise to prepare for the coming of the Antichrist.*

The method of their diabolical attempt is explained in the biblical record. The Antichrist dares not appear until after the "falling away" of apostasy (2 Thess. 2:3). In the meantime, the spirit of Antichrist (lawlessness) is already at work, attempting to pervert the gospel and to corrupt the true Church. When this process is sufficiently established, the False Prophet will arise to prepare for the coming of the Antichrist.

The False Prophet is depicted as having "two horns like a lamb," and one who speaks as a dragon (Rev. 13:11). He looks religious, but he talks like the devil. He counterfeits true religion in order to hide his real identity. Just as the Holy Spirit is dedicated to bringing the world to Jesus Christ, the False Prophet is dedicated to bringing all men into spiritual allegiance with the Antichrist.

It should not surprise us then that the False Prophet represents the apostate religion of the End Times. If his rise to power parallels that of the Antichrist, he will preside over apostate Christendom after the rapture of true believers to heaven. All who are left behind, whatever their denomination, will be unbelievers. In such an environment, the False Prophet will have no problem deceiving the whole world.

The False Prophet is presented in Revelation as an individual who is empowered by Satan (13:11, 12). However, the religious system that he represents is called the "great whore" (17:1) who is drunk with the "blood of the saints" (17:6). Therefore, the final phase of apostasy is epitomized by a religious system and the individual who leads it. Later, the False Prophet is personally cast into the lake of fire (19:20; 20:10).

Spiritual deception is the goal of the False Prophet as he encourages people to embrace the social, economic, and religious programs of the Antichrist. As we approach the end of the age, false prophets, new religions, and spiritual darkness will engulf the world, preparing the world for the rise of these great deceivers—the Antichrist and the False Prophet.

13 And he doeth great wonders, so that he maketh fire come down from heaven on the earth in the sight of men,

14 And deceiveth them that dwell on the earth by *the means of* those miracles which he had power to do in the sight of the beast; saying to them that dwell on the earth, that they should make an image to the beast, which had the wound by a sword, and did live.

15 And he had power to give life unto the image of the beast, that the image of the beast should both speak, and cause that as many as would not worship the image of the beast should be killed.

The Mark

16 And he causeth all, both small and great, rich and poor, free and bond, to receive a mark in their right hand, or in their foreheads:

17 And that no man might buy or sell, save he that had the mark, or the name of the beast, or the number of his name.

18 Here is wisdom. Let him that hath understanding count the number of the beast: for it is the number of a man; and his number *is* Six hundred threescore *and* six.

13 Deut. 13:1-3; 1Kgs. 18:38; 2Kgs. 1:10, 12; Matt. 24:24; 2Thess. 2:9; Rev. 16:14
14 2Kgs. 20:7; 2Thess. 2:9, 10; Rev. 12:9; 19:20
15 Rev. 16:2; 19:20; 20:4
16 Rev. 14:9; 19:20; 20:4
17 Rev. 14:11; 15:2
18 Rev. 15:2; 17:9; 21:17
1 Rev. 5:6; 7:3, 4; 13:16
2 Rev. 1:15; 5:8; 19:6
3 Rev. 5:9; 14:1; 15:3
4 2Cor. 11:2; James 1:18; Rev. 3:4; 5:9; 7:15, 17; 17:14
5 Ps. 32:2; Zeph. 3:13; Eph. 5:27; Jude 1:24

CHAPTER 14

144,000 Servants of God

1 And I looked, and, lo, a Lamb stood on the mount Sion, and with him an hundred forty *and* four thousand, having his Father's name written in their foreheads.

2 And I heard a voice from heaven, as the voice of many waters, and as the voice of a great thunder: and I heard the voice of harpers harping with their harps:

3 And they sung as it were a new song before the throne, and before the four beasts, and the elders: and no man could learn that song but the hundred *and* forty *and* four thousand, which were redeemed from the earth.

4 These are they which were not defiled with women; for they are virgins. These are they which follow the Lamb whithersoever he goeth. These were redeemed from among men, *being* the firstfruits unto God and to the Lamb.

5 And in their mouth was found no guile: for they are without fault before the throne of God.

6 And I saw another angel fly in the midst of heaven, having the everlasting gospel to preach unto them that dwell on the earth,

---

13:13–14 he maketh fire come down from heaven. Among the False Prophet's supernatural powers will be his ability to call down fire from heaven in order to deceive those who dwell on the earth. His power exceeds that of the false prophets of Baal, who were unable to call down fire in the days of Elijah (1 Kgs. 18:36–38). Many will believe on the Antichrist during that time because the False Prophet possesses this power.

13:15 power to give life unto the image of the beast. In a manner similar to Nebuchadnezzar, the False Prophet will set up an image of the Antichrist and demand that people worship the image which will appear to be alive.

13:16 The "mark of the beast," which the False Prophet will require of all people, will bring the entire world into a global economy, a world government, and a world religion. In order to buy or sell, every person will have to have this mark on his or her forehead or right hand for identification. In Revelation 13:8, we are told that some will refuse to worship Antichrist, and it appears that these will not have the mark upon them.

13:17 The mark must be the equivalent of the name of the beast. Evidently the Greek equivalent of the Antichrist's name will in some way equal the number 666.

This second half of the Tribulation will be an awful time for believers who refuse the mark. They will have to flee for safety, and it will be almost impossible to feed their families without the mark of the Beast.

14:1–5 firstfruits unto God and to the Lamb. The last half of the Tribulation opens with an overview of what follows in chapters 15–19. The fourteenth chapter opens with the 144,000 and proceeds to four climactic announcements: 1) the proclamation of the everlasting gospel, 2) the fall of Babylon, 3) the judgment of the lost, and 4) the blessedness of the saved. The whole chapter surveys the final states of blessing and judgment that are coming in the future.

14:6–7 having the everlasting gospel. This is the first of four special angelic messengers who appear during this time to reveal the compassionate heart of God. This is the only time in the history of the world that God uses angels to proclaim the one true gospel (see 1 Cor. 15:1–4; Gal. 1:8–9). In the midst of the Tribulation, when Satan is actively seeking to destroy all faith in Christ, God sends an angel to proclaim to all the people on earth that personal faith in Jesus' death and resurrection can save them.

and to every nation, and kindred, and tongue, and people,

7 Saying with a loud voice, Fear God, and give glory to him; for the hour of his judgment is come: and worship him that made heaven, and earth, and the sea, and the fountains of waters.

8 And there followed another angel, saying, Babylon is fallen, is fallen, that great city, because she made all nations drink of the wine of the wrath of her fornication.

9 And the third angel followed them, saying with a loud voice, If any man worship the beast and his image, and receive *his* mark in his forehead, or in his hand,

10 The same shall drink of the wine of the wrath of God, which is poured out without mixture into the cup of his indignation; and he shall be tormented with fire and brim-

stone in the presence of the holy angels, and in the presence of the Lamb:

11 And the smoke of their torment ascendeth up for ever and ever: and they have no rest day nor night, who worship the beast and his image, and whosoever receiveth the mark of his name.

12 Here is the patience of the saints: here *are* they that keep the commandments of God, and the faith of Jesus.

13 And I heard a voice from heaven saying unto me, Write, Blessed *are* the dead which die in the Lord from henceforth: Yea, saith the Spirit, that they may rest from their labours; and their works do follow them.

The Time for Judgment

14 And I looked, and behold a white cloud, and upon the cloud *one* sat like unto the Son

Cross-references:
7 Neh. 9:6; Ps. 33:6; 124:8; 146:5, 6
8 Isa. 21:9; Jer. 51:7, 8
9 Rev. 13:14-16
10 Ps. 75:8; Isa. 51:17; Jer. 25:15; Rev. 16:19; 18:6; 19:20; 20:10
11 Isa. 34:10; Rev. 19:3
13 Eccl. 4:1, 2; 1Thess. 4:16
14 Ezek. 1:26; Dan. 7:13

Biblical Terms for the Tribulation

Terms from the Old Testament	
The Tribulation	Deuteronomy 4:30
The day of Israel's calamity	Deuteronomy 32:35; Obad. 1:12–14
The indignation	Isaiah 26:20; Dan. 11:36
The overflowing scourge	Isaiah 28:15, 18
The Lord's strange work	Isaiah 28:21
The year of recompence	Isaiah 34:8
The day of vengeance	Isaiah 34:8; 35:4; 61:2
The time of Jacob's Trouble	Jeremiah 30:7
The seventieth week of Daniel	Daniel 9:27
The time of trouble	Daniel 12:1; Zephaniah 1:15
The day of darkness	Joel 2:2; Amos 5:18, 20; Zephaniah 1:15
The day of wrath	Zephaniah 1:15
The day of distress	Zephaniah 1:15
The day of wasteness and desolation	Zephaniah 1:15
The day of gloominess	Zephaniah 1:15; Joel 2:2
The day of clouds and thick darkness	Zephaniah 1:15; Joel 2:2
The day of the trumpet and alarm	Zephaniah 1:16

14:8 This second angel pronounces a doom judgment on Babylon, the source of all religious false teaching from Nimrod to Antichrist and the False Prophet (cf. Rev. 17—18).

14:9–10 The third angel warns the people of the earth about believing the lies of Satan and his False Prophet and receiving the mark of the Beast. Certain judgment will follow those who take that mark!

14:10–11 they have no rest day nor night. These verses clearly teach eternal punishment in the next life. The punishment of the lost continues forever and ever. Their restless souls continue to experience the wrath of God forever.

14:12–13 Blessed are the dead which die in the Lord. This is one of the most comforting promises of God to the Tribulation saints. What a contrast from physical torment and persecution here on earth to "rest" in heaven with the Lord!

14:14–19 her grapes are fully ripe. These verses describe a scene of Jesus Christ in heaven just before He descends to the earth for the Battle of Armageddon and His glorious appearing. This harvest of judgment on the Christ-rejecting souls and nations who gather against Him in Armageddon coincides with the seventh vial judgment of Revelation 16:17. When the "grapes are fully ripe" (at the end of the Great Tribulation) denotes the time

of man, having on his head a golden crown, and in his hand a sharp sickle.

15 And another angel came out of the temple, crying with a loud voice to him that sat on the cloud, Thrust in thy sickle, and reap: for the time is come for thee to reap; for the harvest of the earth is ripe.

16 And he that sat on the cloud thrust in his sickle on the earth; and the earth was reaped.

17 And another angel came out of the temple which is in heaven, he also having a sharp sickle.

18 And another angel came out from the altar, which had power over fire; and cried with a loud cry to him that had the sharp sickle, saying, Thrust in thy sharp sickle, and gather the clusters of the vine of the earth; for her grapes are fully ripe.

19 And the angel thrust in his sickle into the earth, and gathered the vine of the earth, and cast *it* into the great winepress of the wrath of God.

15 Jer. 51:33; Joel 3:13; Matt. 13:39; Rev. 13:12; 16:17

18 Joel 3:13; Rev. 16:8

19 Rev. 19:15

20 Isa. 63:3; Lam. 1:15; Heb. 13:12; Rev. 11:8

1 Rev. 12:1, 3; 14:10; 16:1; 21:9

2 Matt. 3:11; Rev. 4:6; 5:8; 13:15-17; 14:2; 21:18

3 Ex. 15:1; Deut. 31:30; 32:4; Ps. 111:2; 139:14; 145:17; Hos. 14:9; Rev. 14:3; 16:7

20 And the winepress was trodden without the city, and blood came out of the winepress, even unto the horse bridles, by the space of a thousand *and* six hundred furlongs.

CHAPTER 15
Another Glimpse of Heaven Just Before the Great Tribulation

1 And I saw another sign in heaven, great and marvellous, seven angels having the seven last plagues; for in them is filled up the wrath of God.

2 And I saw as it were a sea of glass mingled with fire: and them that had gotten the victory over the beast, and over his image, and over his mark, *and* over the number of his name, stand on the sea of glass, having the harps of God.

3 And they sing the song of Moses the servant of God, and the song of the Lamb, saying, Great and marvellous *are* thy works, Lord God Almighty; just and true *are* thy ways, thou King of saints.

Biblical Terms for the Tribulation

Terms from the New Testament	
The great Tribulation	Matthew 24:21; Revelation 2:22; 7:14
The Tribulation	Matthew 24:29
The wrath to come	1 Thessalonians 1:10
The day of the Lord	1 Thessalonians 5:2
The wrath	1 Thessalonians 5:9; Revelation 11:18
The hour of trial	Revelation 3:10
The great day of the wrath of the Lamb of God	Revelation 6:16–17
The hour of judgment	Revelation 14:7
The wrath of God	Revelation 14:10, 19; 15:1, 7; 16:1

after every living soul has made his choice to worship either Christ or Antichrist.

14:20 blood came out of the winepress. This verse can be understood only in the light of the enormous army that will come against Christ in the Battle of Armageddon (Isa. 34:6; 63:1–4; Joel 3:12–13; Ps. 105—106; Rev. 19:11–19). Christ will slay with the word of His mouth these rebellious millions who will comprise the greatest array of troops ever mustered in one place. Hailstones weighing "a talent [ca. 100 pounds]" will fall from heaven (Rev. 16:21) which, with the blood of this massive army, will create a river of blood that reaches up to the horses' bridles.

15:1 another sign in heaven. This chapter in the book of Revelation sets the stage for the last seven vial judgments that cover the last three and one-half years of the Tribulation which are described in 16:1—19:21. These

plagues will conclude with the wrath of God on sinful mankind for rejecting His Son, the Lord Jesus Christ.

15:2 them that had gotten the victory. These who stand on the sea of glass (cf. 4:6) are the souls of the martyrs who were killed by Antichrist. They had "victory" over Satan because his persecution sent them to heaven where they await the resurrection, just three and one-half years away.

15:3–4 the song of Moses. This refers to the victory God gave the children of Israel over Pharaoh and his army at the Red Sea (Ex. 15:1–3; 17—18). The Lamb's song avows their faith in Christ, who gave them victory over Antichrist by taking them to heaven. This is similar to the song of the "elders" in heaven in 5:9. Note how they sing praise to God exalting His creation, justice, worship, holiness, omnipotence, and eternity.

4 Who shall not fear thee, O Lord, and glorify thy name? for *thou* only *art* holy: for all nations shall come and worship before thee; for thy judgments are made manifest.

5 And after that I looked, and, behold, the temple of the tabernacle of the testimony in heaven was opened:

6 And the seven angels came out of the temple, having the seven plagues, clothed in pure and white linen, and having their breasts girded with golden girdles.

7 And one of the four beasts gave unto the seven angels seven golden vials full of the wrath of God, who liveth for ever and ever.

8 And the temple was filled with smoke from the glory of God, and from his power; and no man was able to enter into the temple, till the seven plagues of the seven angels were fulfilled.

CHAPTER 16
The Great Tribulation

1 And I heard a great voice out of the temple saying to the seven angels, Go your ways, and pour out the vials of the wrath of God upon the earth.

2 And the first went, and poured out his vial upon the earth; and there fell a noisome and grievous sore upon the men which had the mark of the beast, and *upon* them which worshipped his image.

3 And the second angel poured out his vial

4 Ex. 15:14-16
5 Num. 1:50
6 Rev. 1:13; 15:1
7 1Thess. 1:9; Rev. 4:6, 9; 10:6
8 Ex. 40:34; 1Kgs. 8:10; 2Chr. 5:14; Isa. 6:4; 2Thess. 1:9
1 Rev. 14:10; 15:1, 7
2 Ex. 9:9-11; Rev. 8:7; 13:14, 16, 17
3 Ex. 7:17, 20; Rev. 8:8
4 Ex. 7:20
5 Rev. 1:4, 8; 4:8; 11:17; 15:3
6 Isa. 49:26; Matt. 23:34, 35; Rev. 11:18; 13:15; 18:20
7 Rev. 13:10
8 Rev. 8:12; 9:17, 18; 14:18
9 Dan. 5:22, 23
12 Jer. 50:38; 51:36

upon the sea; and it became as the blood of a dead *man*: and every living soul died in the sea.

4 And the third angel poured out his vial upon the rivers and fountains of waters; and they became blood.

5 And I heard the angel of the waters say, Thou art righteous, O Lord, which art, and wast, and shalt be, because thou hast judged thus.

6 For they have shed the blood of saints and prophets, and thou hast given them blood to drink; for they are worthy.

7 And I heard another out of the altar say, Even so, Lord God Almighty, true and righteous *are* thy judgments.

8 And the fourth angel poured out his vial upon the sun; and power was given unto him to scorch men with fire.

9 And men were scorched with great heat, and blasphemed the name of God, which hath power over these plagues: and they repented not to give him glory.

10 And the fifth angel poured out his vial upon the seat of the beast; and his kingdom was full of darkness; and they gnawed their tongues for pain,

11 And blasphemed the God of heaven because of their pains and their sores, and repented not of their deeds.

12 And the sixth angel poured out his vial upon the great river Euphrates; and the

---

15:7 seven golden vials full of the wrath of God. These are the "plagues" (v. 6) that will strike the earth in the last three and one-half years to punish those who have chosen to serve the Antichrist, doing his bidding to persecute the saints for their faith in Christ.

15:8 no man was able to enter. The cloud of God's glory (see 2 Chr. 7:2; Ezek. 43:5; 44:4) fills the heavenly temple for this entire period of three and one-half years on earth until the judgments of the seven angels (described in the next chapter) have run their course. God is both holy and just, even when wreaking judgment on those who have deceived mankind.

16:1 This chapter unveils the seven final and most severe judgments of the Great Tribulation. This period lasts three and one-half years and prepares the world for the coming of Christ in power to establish His kingdom. The vials that are poured out by these seven angels are literal plagues or catastrophes that will come on the earth.

16:2 a noisome and grievous sore. The first vial that is poured out affects only those who have the mark of the Beast. The plague that results is similar to the plagues of

Egypt (see Ex. 8—12).

16:3 The second angel's vial is poured upon the sea and turns it to blood. This terrible pollution will kill all creatures in the sea.

16:4–6 Since the followers of Antichrist lusted so after the blood of the saints, all the rivers and springs will be turned to blood.

16:8–9 scorch men with fire. The fourth angel's vial results in an increase of heat produced by the sun. Men will know this is God acting in judgment, but instead of repenting, as is His desire, they will become angry and curse Him.

16:10–11 upon the seat of the beast. The fifth angel's vial results in a judgment on the throne of the Beast and his kingdom. This plague may affect only the capital of the world at that time. There will be untold suffering for the followers of Antichrist even during the last months of the Tribulation. Yet with all this suffering they still will not repent.

16:12 the water thereof was dried up. The sixth angel's vial dries up the great river Euphrates, which was

water thereof was dried up, that the way of the kings of the east might be prepared.

13 And I saw three unclean spirits like frogs *come* out of the mouth of the dragon, and out of the mouth of the beast, and out of the mouth of the false prophet.

14 For they are the spirits of devils, working miracles, *which* go forth unto the kings of the earth and of the whole world, to gather them to the battle of that great day of God Almighty.

15 Behold, I come as a thief. Blessed *is* he that watcheth, and keepeth his garments, lest he walk naked, and they see his shame.

16 And he gathered them together into a place called in the Hebrew tongue Armageddon.

17 And the seventh angel poured out his

vial into the air; and there came a great voice out of the temple of heaven, from the throne, saying, It is done.

18 And there were voices, and thunders, and lightnings; and there was a great earthquake, such as was not since men were upon the earth, so mighty an earthquake, *and* so great.

19 And the great city was divided into three parts, and the cities of the nations fell: and great Babylon came in remembrance before God, to give unto her the cup of the wine of the fierceness of his wrath.

20 And every island fled away, and the mountains were not found.

21 And there fell upon men a great hail out of heaven, *every stone* about the weight of a talent: and men blasphemed God because of

13 1John 4:1-3; Rev. 12:3, 9; 19:20; 20:10

14 2Thess. 2:9; Rev. 13:13, 14; 17:14; 19:19, 20; 20:8

15 Matt. 24:43; 1Thess. 5:2

16 Rev. 19:19

17 Rev. 21:6

18 Dan. 12:1

19 Isa. 51:17, 22

21 Ex. 9:23-25

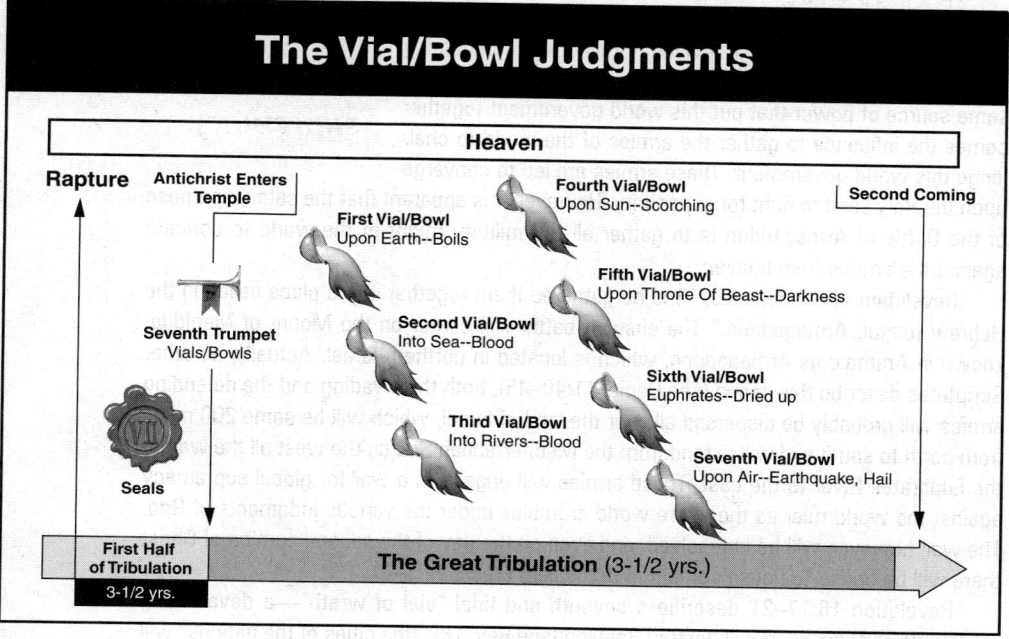

The Vial/Bowl Judgments

Heaven

Rapture

Antichrist Enters Temple

First Vial/Bowl
Upon Earth--Boils

Fourth Vial/Bowl
Upon Sun--Scorching

Second Coming

Fifth Vial/Bowl
Upon Throne Of Beast--Darkness

Seventh Trumpet
Vials/Bowls

Second Vial/Bowl
Into Sea--Blood

Sixth Vial/Bowl
Euphrates--Dried up

Third Vial/Bowl
Into Rivers--Blood

Seventh Vial/Bowl
Upon Air--Earthquake, Hail

Seals

VII

First Half of Tribulation
3-1/2 yrs.

The Great Tribulation (3-1/2 yrs.)

© AMG Publishers

the eastern limit of the old Roman Empire and has served as a natural boundary between East and West for centuries. The drying up of this natural border clears the way for the eastern "kings" to join their western cohorts in the Battle of Armageddon.

16:13–14 three unclean spirits like frogs. The satanic trinity (Satan, Beast, and False Prophet) will send these spirits (probably the chief fallen angels in Satan's hierarchy) "out of the mouth" of Satan himself to deceive the kings of the world into gathering their armies to prepare

for what is best known as the Battle of Armageddon. They will gather in the valley of Megiddo, which Napoleon proclaimed to be the most ideal battlefield in the world.

16:17–20 The seventh angel's vial introduces the most violent earthquake in the history of the world. This earthquake, which destroys the cities of the nations, is so extensive John takes the next two chapters to describe it. All the mountains and islands of the world will be leveled. This earthquake will flatten the entire surface of the earth, making it ready for the Millennial Kingdom.

The Battle of Armageddon

By John F. Walvoord

The so-called Battle of Armageddon will occur during the final days of the Great Tribulation. As revealed in Revelation 16, God will pour out a series of seven devastating judgments on the earth called "vials of wrath." The first six vials God's wrath will serve as an introduction to what the Bible refers to as Armageddon. When the sixth vial is poured out (v. 12), the time of the second coming of Christ is very near. Verse 12 says that the waters of the Euphrates River will be dried up to prepare the way for a military invasion of Israel by the kings of the East.

As John contemplated this end-time scene, he recorded, "And I saw three unclean spirits like frogs come out of the mouth of the Dragon, and out of the mouth of the Beast, and out of the mouth of the False Prophet. For they are the spirits of devils, working miracles, which go forth unto the kings of the earth and of the whole world, to gather them to the battle of that great day of God Almighty" (vv. 13–14).

At the beginning of the Great Tribulation, through satanic deception and power, a world government is formed, with the ruler of the ten nations of the revived Roman Empire becoming a dictator over the entire globe (cf. Rev. 13:7). Now from the same source of power that put this world government together comes the influence to gather the armies of the world to challenge this world government. These armies are led to converge

> *The armies of the world will engage in a war for global supremacy.*

upon the Holy Land to fight for superiority. However, it is apparent that the satanic purpose of the Battle of Armageddon is to gather all the military might of the world to contend against the armies from heaven.

Revelation 16:16 declares, "And he gathered them together into a place called in the Hebrew tongue Armageddon." The ensuing battle will center on the Mount of Megiddo, known in Aramaic as Armageddon, which is located in northern Israel. Actually, as other Scriptures describe this scene (see Daniel 11:40–45), both the invading and the defending armies will probably be dispersed all over the land of Israel, which will be some 200 miles from north to south and will extend from the Mediterranean Sea on the west all the way to the Euphrates River to the east. These armies will engage in a war for global supremacy against the world ruler as the entire world crumbles under the various judgments of God. The war, however, will be unresolved, and even on the day of the second coming of Christ there will be house-to-house combat in Jerusalem (Zech. 14:1–3).

Revelation 16:17–21 describe a seventh and final "vial of wrath"—a devastating worldwide earthquake. It will destroy Babylon (see Rev. 18); "the cities of the nations" will collapse (vv. 16–19); and islands and mountains will disappear (v. 20). The judgment of the earthquake will climax in a supernatural hailstorm in which the hailstones will weigh approximately one hundred pounds each (v. 21). The world will be left in shambles and its cities will be in ruins. Apparently, only Jerusalem and the cities of Israel will be left unscathed. It is to this scene that Christ will return in power and glory, as described in Revelation 19:11–16.

the plague of the hail; for the plague thereof was exceeding great.

CHAPTER 17
The Destruction of Religious Babylon

1 And there came one of the seven angels which had the seven vials, and talked with me, saying unto me, Come hither; I will shew unto thee the judgment of the great whore that sitteth upon many waters:
2 With whom the kings of the earth have committed fornication, and the inhabitants of the earth have been made drunk with the wine of her fornication.
3 So he carried me away in the spirit into the wilderness: and I saw a woman sit upon a scarlet coloured beast, full of names of blasphemy, having seven heads and ten horns.
4 And the woman was arrayed in purple and scarlet colour, and decked with gold and precious stones and pearls, having a golden cup in her hand full of abominations and filthiness of her fornication:
5 And upon her forehead was a name written, MYSTERY, BABYLON THE GREAT, THE MOTHER OF HARLOTS AND ABOMINATIONS OF THE EARTH.
6 And I saw the woman drunken with the blood of the saints, and with the blood of the martyrs of Jesus: and when I saw her, I wondered with great admiration.

7 And the angel said unto me, Wherefore didst thou marvel? I will tell thee the mystery of the woman, and of the beast that carrieth her, which hath the seven heads and ten horns.
8 The beast that thou sawest was, and is not; and shall ascend out of the bottomless pit, and go into perdition: and they that dwell on the earth shall wonder, whose names were not written in the book of life from the foundation of the world, when they behold the beast that was, and is not, and yet is.
9 And here is the mind which hath wisdom. The seven heads are seven mountains, on which the woman sitteth.
10 And there are seven kings: five are fallen, and one is, and the other is not yet come; and when he cometh, he must continue a short space.
11 And the beast that was, and is not, even he is the eighth, and is of the seven, and goeth into perdition.
12 And the ten horns which thou sawest are ten kings, which have received no kingdom as yet; but receive power as kings one hour with the beast.
13 These have one mind, and shall give their power and strength unto the beast.
14 These shall make war with the Lamb, and the Lamb shall overcome them: for he is Lord of lords, and King of kings: and they that are with him are called, and chosen, and faithful.

Cross references: 1 Jer. 51:13; Nah. 3:4; Rev. 16:19; 17:15; 18:16, 17, 19; 19:2; 21:9 • 2 Jer. 51:7; Rev. 14:8; 18:3 • 3 Rev. 12:3, 6, 14; 13:1; 17:9, 12 • 4 Jer. 51:7; Dan. 11:38; Rev. 14:8; 18:6, 12, 16 • 5 2 Thess. 2:7; Rev. 11:8; 14:8; 16:19; 18:2, 9, 10, 21; 19:2 • 6 Rev. 6:9, 10; 12:11; 13:15; 16:6; 18:24 • 8 Rev. 11:7; 13:1, 3, 8, 10; 17:11 • 9 Rev. 13:1, 18 • 12 Dan. 7:20; Zech. 1:18, 19, 21; Rev. 13:1 • 14 Deut. 10:17; Jer. 50:44, 45; 1 Tim. 6:15; Rev. 14:4; 16:14; 19:16, 19

17:1 the judgment of the great whore. Revelation 17—18 describes the judgments of God at the end of the Tribulation on the age-old enemy "Babylon the great" in all of its forms. Satan has used idolatrous religion, government, and commerce as his chief agents to deceive mankind. All will be destroyed just before Christ returns to this earth. The fall of "Babylon" has already been announced in Revelation 14:8. Its doom has already been certified. Now, John fills in the details as both political and ecclesiastical "Babylon" come into view. The "beast" represents government, and "the woman" is religion. Both are opposed to Christ and His kingdom.

17:8 whose names were not written in the book of life. The false religious system of the end times will be very convincing and popular among the unsaved, but those who have committed themselves to Christ will understand that anything idolatrous is not of God.

17:10—11 seven kings. These probably refer to the seven world empires that have influenced human government throughout history—Egypt, Assyria, Babylon, Medo-Persia, Greece and Rome. The Roman government system of religious and political imperialism that has continued in various forms is the seventh, and the dominion of Antichrist will be the eighth. The fact that the Beast "was, and is not" may refer to the assassination of the Antichrist, who is indwelled by Satan himself in the midst of the Tribulation and continues for three and one-half years before eventually going to destruction.

17:12—13 the ten horns which thou sawest. These correspond to the ten horns of Daniel 7—8 and the ten toes of Daniel 2. They are the leaders appointed by Antichrist to whom he gives authority to govern the world. These are "of one mind" and do the bidding of the Beast.

17:14 These shall make war with the Lamb. This will occur when these kings kill His faithful followers and come out to fight against Christ in the Battle of Armageddon. Those who join with Christ to overcome them are called "chosen, and faithful," titles used in other Scriptures to describe true believers (1 Pet. 2:9).

15 And he saith unto me, The waters which thou sawest, where the whore sitteth, are peoples, and multitudes, and nations, and tongues.

16 And the ten horns which thou sawest upon the beast, these shall hate the whore, and shall make her desolate and naked, and shall eat her flesh, and burn her with fire.

17 For God hath put in their hearts to fulfil his will, and to agree, and give their kingdom unto the beast, until the words of God shall be fulfilled.

18 And the woman which thou sawest is that great city, which reigneth over the kings of the earth.

CHAPTER 18
God's Judgment on Babylon

1 And after these things I saw another angel come down from heaven, having great power; and the earth was lightened with his glory.

2 And he cried mightily with a strong voice, saying, Babylon the great is fallen, is fallen, and is become the habitation of devils, and the hold of every foul spirit, and a cage of every unclean and hateful bird.

3 For all nations have drunk of the wine of the wrath of her fornication, and the kings of the earth have committed fornication with her, and the merchants of the earth are waxed rich through the abundance of her delicacies.

4 And I heard another voice from heaven, saying, Come out of her, my people, that ye be not partakers of her sins, and that ye receive not of her plagues.

5 For her sins have reached unto heaven, and God hath remembered her iniquities.

6 Reward her even as she rewarded you, and double unto her double according to her works: in the cup which she hath filled fill to her double.

7 How much she hath glorified herself, and lived deliciously, so much torment and sorrow give her: for she saith in her heart, I sit a queen, and am no widow, and shall see no sorrow.

8 Therefore shall her plagues come in one day, death, and mourning, and famine; and she shall be utterly burned with fire: for strong *is* the Lord God who judgeth her.

9 And the kings of the earth, who have committed fornication and lived deliciously with her, shall bewail her, and lament for her, when they shall see the smoke of her burning,

10 Standing afar off for the fear of her torment, saying, Alas, alas that great city Babylon, that mighty city! for in one hour is thy judgment come.

11 And the merchants of the earth shall weep and mourn over her; for no man buyeth their merchandise any more:

12 The merchandise of gold, and silver, and precious stones, and of pearls, and fine linen, and purple, and silk, and scarlet, and all thyine wood, and all manner vessels of ivory, and all manner vessels of most precious wood, and of brass, and iron, and marble,

13 And cinnamon, and odours, and ointments, and frankincense, and wine, and oil, and fine flour, and wheat, and beasts, and

Cross references

15 Isa. 8:7
16 Rev. 16:12; 18:8, 16
17 2Thess. 2:11
18 Rev. 12:4; 16:19;
2 Isa. 13:19, 21; 14:23; 21:8, 9; 34:11, 14; Rev. 14:8
3 Rev. 14:8; 17:2
3 Isa. 47:15; Rev. 18:11, 15
4 Isa. 48:20; 52:11; Jer. 50:8; 51:6, 45; 2Cor. 6:17
5 Gen. 18:20, 21; Jer. 51:9; Jon. 1:2; Rev. 16:19
6 Ps. 137:8; Jer. 50:15, 29; 51:24, 49; 2Tim. 4:14; Rev. 13:10; 14:10; 16:19
8 Isa. 47:9
9 Ezek. 26:16, 17
10 Isa. 21:9; Rev. 14:8
11 Ezek. 27:27-36

17:15–17 peoples, and multitudes, and nations, and tongues. This is an apt description of the idolatrous global religion that will engulf the world after the rapture of the Church. For the first half of the Tribulation, this false religion will globalize all traditional religions and actually "ride the beast," or dominate him politically. Finally, in the midst of the Tribulation, in a struggle for power, the ten kings will "kill her [the religious whore]"; and the False Prophet will take over the direction of all religious practice in the world.

18:1–4 Babylon the great. No longer does the seer have the ecclesiastical religious system in view but now turns the spotlight of God's judgment on the commercial and governmental systems that originated there. Babylon has had the most harmful effect on mankind of all the cities of the world. For all idolatrous religion, greed-based commerce, and secular government were begun there. At the end of the Tribulation, God will destroy them all in the seventh or last vial judgment in fulfillment of the prophecy in Isaiah 47:1–9 (cf. Isa. 21:9).

18:4 Come out of her, my people. It is difficult to know if these people are worldly-minded believers living in the capital city of commerce and government for material reasons or dedicated believers dwelling there for witnessing opportunities. The latter seems more likely for two reasons: first, that all "believers" will know the end is at hand. Second, since Antichrist will require the mark of the Beast for all that work for him, believers living at that time would be in danger.

18:5–8 The righteous God of the universe has not overlooked the sins of the elite power brokers who have used commerce and government for centuries to live luxuriously at the expense of others. The commercial, social, and political systems of the Antichrist will receive double judgment for their sins.

The Marriage of the Lamb

By Paul Benware

The "marriage of the Lamb" (Rev. 19:7) is a phrase that beautifully describes the final and complete union of Jesus Christ and true believers. It communicates an intimacy of relationship between Christ and believers that in this life has never been experienced and one that will never be compromised or broken. From the time of the "marriage" onward, the bride and Christ are inseparable.

The phrase is built on the imagery of marriage used by both Old and New Testament writers to communicate something of God's relationship with those who are His people. Weddings were used by Jesus in His teaching about spiritual relationships (e.g., Matt. 22:2–14; 25:1–13), and Christ is viewed on several occasions as the Bridegroom (e.g., Matt. 9:15; Mark 2:19–20; John 3:29). The apostle Paul spoke of the Church's relationship with Christ as a "bride" (Eph. 5:23–27) and declared that he had betrothed the Church to her one and only heavenly Husband, Jesus Christ (2 Cor. 11:1–3). At the marriage of the Lamb, the days of temptation and the struggle with sin are over, and the Bride is presented to Christ in total and complete purity.

Revelation 19 places the marriage of the Lamb in heaven. The chapter records the joyful celebration over the judgment of the great harlot and the vindication of God and His people. The marriage of the Lamb (Rev. 19:7–9) takes place immediately before the second coming of Christ to the earth (Rev. 19:11–16).

> *The Marriage of the Lamb communicates an intimacy between Christ and believers.*

It is best to identify the Bride as the true Church of Jesus Christ. The Church is clearly so identified in the New Testament (Eph. 5:23ff.; 2 Cor. 11:1–3). When the marriage takes place, the Bride is seen as resurrected and rewarded, a situation which would mean that the Bride has been raptured and rewarded (at the Judgment Seat of Christ). But this view of the Bride would seem to exclude saints from the Old Testament and Tribulation periods since they are raised and rewarded in connection with the Second Coming itself. However, it is possible that the bride might grow to include other redeemed people in the days of the kingdom (cf. Rev. 21:1–3, 10–14).

An emphasis is placed on the beautiful garments of the Bride (Rev. 19:8). These garments are a brilliant white, representing her glory and purity. Specifically, the garments are said to be her righteous deeds, the result of human effort as she labored for Christ in the contrary circumstances of a sin-cursed world. Yet, the garments are said to be given to her (see Rev. 19:8), which reveals that ultimately her righteous acts are the result of God's gracious working in and through her. Thus, she is rewarded, and God receives great glory.

As is the case in most of our weddings, a distinction should be made between the marriage and the marriage supper. The marriage which unites is followed by a time of celebration of that uniting (Rev. 19:7, 9). The marriage takes place in heaven, but the feast takes place on the earth. This great wedding feast is the picture of the Millennial Kingdom of Christ and perhaps the eternal kingdom that follows. It is a picture of the great joy that will permeate the reign of the Lord Jesus over all the redeemed of all ages.

sheep, and horses, and chariots, and slaves, and souls of men.

14 And the fruits that thy soul lusted after are departed from thee, and all things which were dainty and goodly are departed from thee, and thou shalt find them no more at all.

15 The merchants of these things, which were made rich by her, shall stand afar off for the fear of her torment, weeping and wailing,

16 And saying, Alas, alas that great city, that was clothed in fine linen, and purple, and scarlet, and decked with gold, and precious stones, and pearls!

17 For in one hour so great riches is come to nought. And every shipmaster, and all the company in ships, and sailors, and as many as trade by sea, stood afar off,

18 And cried when they saw the smoke of her burning, saying, What *city is* like unto this great city!

19 And they cast dust on their heads, and cried, weeping and wailing, saying, Alas, alas, that great city, wherein were made rich all that had ships in the sea by reason of her costliness! for in one hour is she made desolate.

20 Rejoice over her, *thou* heaven, and *ye* holy apostles and prophets; for God hath avenged you on her.

21 And a mighty angel took up a stone like a great millstone, and cast *it* into the sea, saying, Thus with violence shall that great city Babylon be thrown down, and shall be found no more at all.

22 And the voice of harpers, and musicians, and of pipers, and trumpeters, shall be heard no more at all in thee; and no craftsman, of whatsoever craft *he be,* shall be found any more in thee; and the sound of a millstone shall be heard no more at all in thee;

23 And the light of a candle shall shine no more at all in thee; and the voice of the bridegroom and of the bride shall be heard no more at all in thee: for thy merchants were the great men of the earth; for by thy sorceries were all nations deceived.

24 And in her was found the blood of prophets, and of saints, and of all that were slain upon the earth.

CHAPTER 19
Praise in Heaven

1 And after these things I heard a great voice of much people in heaven, saying, Alleluia; Salvation, and glory, and honour, and power, unto the Lord our God:

2 For true and righteous *are* his judgments: for he hath judged the great whore, which did corrupt the earth with her fornication, and hath avenged the blood of his servants at her hand.

3 And again they said, Alleluia. And her smoke rose up for ever and ever.

4 And the four and twenty elders and the four beasts fell down and worshipped God that sat on the throne, saying, Amen; Alleluia.

5 And a voice came out of the throne, saying, Praise our God, all ye his servants, and ye that fear him, both small and great.

6 And I heard as it were the voice of a great multitude, and as the voice of many waters, and as the voice of mighty thunderings, saying, Alleluia: for the Lord God omnipotent reigneth.

The Marriage of the Lamb

7 Let us be glad and rejoice, and give honour to him: for the marriage of the Lamb is

Marginal refs: 16 Rev. 17:4; 17 Isa. 23:14; 18 Ezek. 27:30, 31; 19 Ezek. 27:30; 20 Isa. 44:23; 49:13; Jer. 51:48; Rev. 19:2; 21 Jer. 51:64; Rev. 12:8; 16:20; 22 Isa. 24:8; Jer. 7:34; 16:9; 25:10; Ezek. 26:13; 23 2Kgs. 9:22; Isa. 23:8; Jer. 7:34; 16:9; 25:10; 33:11; Nah. 3:4; Rev. 17:2, 5; 24 Jer. 51:49; Rev. 17:6; 1 Rev. 4:11; 7:10, 12; 11:15; 12:10; 2 Deut. 32:43; Rev. 6:10; 15:3; 16:7; 18:20; 3 Isa. 34:10; Rev. 14:11; 18:9, 18; 4 Rev. 4:4, 6, 10; 5:14; 6 Ezek. 1:24; 43:2; 7 Matt. 22:2; 25:10

18:20–23 by thy sorceries were all nations deceived. The word "sorceries" (Gr. *pharmakeia*) is used here to describe a lifestyle of drug-induced occult practices. The angel cast a millstone into the sea as an example of how the kingdom of Antichrist will be utterly destroyed in that moment. This judgment will target those who, while they lived, traded their soul for material possessions.

19:1–6 This chapter is one of the most dramatic in all the Bible. In it, the Church, the Bride of Christ, is the guest of honor at the marriage of the Lamb in heaven (vv. 1–10) and returns with Christ in His triumphal Second Coming (vv. 11–21). It is the only chapter in the New Testament where this word "Alleluia" is found, and it appears four times. The people mentioned here are distinct from the other beings in heaven, for they are singing a song that includes mention of salvation. This scene incorporates all believers—the Old Testament saints, the Church-age saints, and the Tribulation saints. Together they join in this great chorus proclaiming, "Alleluia!"

19:7–10 The marriage of the Lamb and the marriage supper of the Lamb "in heaven" (19:1) are evidence of the Church being in heaven prior to the return of Christ to earth. Christ is the Bridegroom at the marriage and His Church is the Bride. The word "church" (Gr. *ekklesia*) appears nineteen times in Revelation 1–3, and does not appear again until Revelation 22:16, emphasizing the absence of the Church from the earth during the judgments of Rev. 4—18.

come, and his wife hath made herself ready. **8** And to her was granted that she should be arrayed in fine linen, clean and white: for the fine linen is the righteousness of saints. **9** And he saith unto me, Write, Blessed *are* they which are called unto the marriage supper of the Lamb. And he saith unto me, These are the true sayings of God.

10 And I fell at his feet to worship him. And he said unto me, See *thou do it* not: I am thy fellow servant, and of thy brethren that have the testimony of Jesus: worship God: for the testimony of Jesus is the spirit of prophecy.

The Glorious Appearing of Jesus

11 And I saw heaven opened, and behold a white horse; and he that sat upon him *was* called Faithful and True, and in right-

eousness he doth judge and make war. **12** His eyes *were* as a flame of fire, and on his head *were* many crowns; and he had a name written, that no man knew, but he himself.

13 And he *was* clothed with a vesture dipped in blood: and his name is called The Word of God.

14 And the armies *which were* in heaven followed him upon white horses, clothed in fine linen, white and clean.

15 And out of his mouth goeth a sharp sword, that with it he should smite the nations: and he shall rule them with a rod of iron: and he treadeth the winepress of the fierceness and wrath of Almighty God.

16 And he hath on *his* vesture and on his thigh a name written, KING OF KINGS, AND LORD OF LORDS.

Cross-references:
9 Rev. 21:5; 22:6
10 Acts 10:26; 14:14, 15
11 Isa. 11:4; Rev. 3:14; 6:2; 15:5
12 Rev. 1:14; 2:17, 18; 6:2; 19:16
13 Isa. 63:2, 3; John 1:1
14 Matt. 28:3
15 Isa. 11:4; 63:3; 2Thess. 2:8
16 Dan. 2:47

The Triumphal Return of Christ

CHARACTERISTIC	DESCRIPTION	REFERENCE
His code	Secret name	Judges 13:18
His command	Rod of iron	Psalms 2:9
His conquest	Winepress of God	Isaiah 63:3
His celebration	Lord of kings	Daniel 2:47
His confirmation	Called Word of God	John 1:1
His commission	Judges and makes war	2 Thessalonians 1:7–8
His communication	Sword of His mouth	Hebrews 4:12
His clarity	Eyes as a flame of fire	Revelation 1:14
His character	Faithful and true	Revelation 3:14
His charge	White horse	Revelation 6:2
His coronation	Wears many crowns	Revelation 19:12
His clothing	Vesture dipped in blood	Revelation 19:13

19:10 for the testimony of Jesus is the spirit of prophecy. Everything about Jesus is prophetic: His birth (109 prophecies), His life, His death (Isa. 53), His Resurrection, His Church (Matt. 16), His Second Coming (see the table entitled "Prophecies of the Second Coming of Christ"), and the wonderful future He has planned for those who love Him.

19:11–16 Faithful and True. In these six verses, we are swept up into the triumphal entourage of redeemed saints in the heavenly procession with the King of kings. Jesus Christ comes to make war on Satan, the Antichrist, the False Prophet, and the kings of the earth. He rides on a white horse and has on His head "many crowns." When this war with Satan is over, He becomes the absolute ruler of the earth.

19:13 the Word of God. This reminds us of Christ's eternity and His identity as God (cf. John 1:1). His twelve-fold description emphasizes His role as prophet,

priest, and king.

19:14 the armies in heaven. These are the saints who come with Christ (Zech. 14:5; 1 Thess. 3:13; 4:14; Jude 1:14). This is the Church, His Bride. She is dressed in white, which she received at the marriage supper (vv. 7–14). In reality, the saints are only observers and attendants to Christ, who wages and wins this war by Himself.

19:15 out of his mouth goeth a sharp sword. If Christ could call this world into being (John 1:1–3) with the power of His Word, then the armies of Satan are no match for Him. No human weapons are necessary. No tanks, no rockets, no planes—He conquers the world with His word, proving that He is God.

19:16 KING OF KINGS, AND LORD OF LORDS. This is the name on Christ's vesture, indicating He will be above all natural and supernatural beings. His title clearly indicates the coming triumph as He returns to set up His Millennial Kingdom on earth.

The Millennial Views

By Mal Couch

The word "millennium" in Greek (*chilia*) means one thousand as in one thousand years and is used six times in Revelation 20:2–7. The word clearly defines the length of the earthly kingdom reign of Christ. Three views have dominated Christianity as to what constitutes the Millennium or kingdom.

Premillennialism. The early church was "pre" millennial and expected Christ to return and establish the throne of David, as promised in the Old Testament. Premillennialism holds to the literal promises of an earthly kingdom and cites how the apostle Peter referred to 2 Samuel 7:12. "[David was] a prophet, and [knew] that God had sworn with an oath to him . . . he would raise up Christ to sit on his throne" (Acts 2:30). Many references describe this coming blessed, earthly period. For example, the Anointed King will have the nations for His inheritance (Ps. 2:8), and He will gather "the dispersed of Judah from the four corners of the earth" (Isa. 11:12) and exercise justice in the land of Israel (Isa. 9:7). "The wolf also will dwell with the lamb" (Isa. 11:6) and "the earth will be full of the knowledge of the Lord" (Isa. 11:9).

> *Premillennialism holds to the literal promises of an earthly kingdom.*

In time, the Church departed from Premillennialism, though there is some evidence that the teaching lingered for some centuries among certain groups. For example, Antioch in Syria was a great Christian teaching center that appears to have made known a literal understanding of Scripture for generations. At the beginning of the nineteenth century in England, a natural and normal approach to biblical interpretation was revived, accompanied by an explosion of interest in Premillennialism. Premillennialism grew even more rapidly during the twentieth century.

Amillennialism. Early on, interpretation in the Church began to shift away from belief in Premillennialism. Clement of Alexandria (ca. A.D. 155–220), believing in the divine origin of Greek philosophy, taught that all Scripture must be allegorically understood. This idea began to slowly grow and was systematized and propounded by Origen of Alexandria (A.D. 185–254) and further propagated by Augustine of Hippo (A.D. 354–430) who made the view popular. With the Greek negative "a" in front of the word "millennium," this view says that there will not be a literal, earthly kingdom established.

The Reformers restored Bible interpretation to a more literal approach, except in the area of Bible prophecy. Many still took an allegorical approach when teaching about the kingdom. They taught that the literal promises to Israel were passed on to the Church in a spiritualized way and that there would be no regathering of the Jews to the land and no literal one thousand year reign of Christ.

Postmillennialism. This view was first propagated by Daniel Whitby (A.D. 1638–1726), a Unitarian. Postmillennialists hold that the Church is progressively building and bettering itself.

World War I, and finally World War II, virtually ended the hopes of the postmillennialists. Mankind's cruelty was made evident and things were not getting better, as was being taught. However, there are some indications that Postmillennialism is returning in new forms. Some are teaching that if the Church restores all the demands of the Old Testament Law, then it could conquer society and restore righteousness, making it possible for the promised kingdom to be realized.

17 And I saw an angel standing in the sun; and he cried with a loud voice, saying to all the fowls that fly in the midst of heaven, Come and gather yourselves together unto the supper of the great God;
18 That ye may eat the flesh of kings, and the flesh of captains, and the flesh of mighty men, and the flesh of horses, and of them that sit on them, and the flesh of all *men, both* free and bond, both small and great.
19 And I saw the beast, and the kings of the earth, and their armies, gathered together to make war against him that sat on the horse, and against his army.
20 And the beast was taken, and with him the false prophet that wrought miracles before him, with which he deceived them that had received the mark of the beast, and them that worshipped his image. These both were cast alive into a lake of fire burning with brimstone.
21 And the remnant were slain with the sword of him that sat upon the horse, which *sword* proceeded out of his mouth: and all the fowls were filled with their flesh.

17 Ezek. 39:17; Rev. 19:21
18 Ezek. 39:18, 20
19 Rev. 16:16; 17:13, 14
20 Dan. 7:11Rev. 13:12, 15; 14:10; 16:13, 14; 20:10; 21:8
21 Rev. 17:16; 19:15, 17, 18
1 Rev. 1:18; 9:1
2 2Pet. 2:4; Jude 1:6; Rev. 12:9
3 Dan. 6:17; Rev. 16:14, 16; 20:8
4 Dan. 7:9, 22, 27; Matt. 19:28; Luke 22:30; Rom. 8:17; 1Cor. 6:2, 3; 2Tim. 2:12

CHAPTER 20
The Binding of Satan

1 And I saw an angel come down from heaven, having the key of the bottomless pit and a great chain in his hand.
2 And he laid hold on the dragon, that old serpent, which is the Devil, and Satan, and bound him a thousand years,
3 And cast him into the bottomless pit, and shut him up, and set a seal upon him, that he should deceive the nations no more, till the thousand years should be fulfilled: and after that he must be loosed a little season.
4 And I saw thrones, and they sat upon them, and judgment was given unto them: and *I saw* the souls of them that were beheaded for the witness of Jesus, and for the word of God, and which had not worshipped the beast, neither his image, neither had received *his* mark upon their foreheads, or in their hands; and they lived and reigned with Christ a thousand years.
5 But the rest of the dead lived not again until the thousand years were finished. This *is* the first resurrection.

19:20 the beast . . . and . . . the false prophet. These two great deceivers, members of the satanic trinity, who were used by the devil to deceive men about God during the Tribulation, are conquered by Jesus Christ, who will cast them "alive into a lake of fire." They are the first to be cast into this lake of fire, which is really the eternal hell which God has "prepared for the devil and his angels" (Matt. 25:41, see the article entitled "Hell" by Jack Van Impe). These two men do not go to judgment; rather they will go straight to hell. One thousand years later, when Satan is also cast into the lake of fire, these men are still there and still alive, indicating their punishment is eternal (cf. Rev. 20:10).

19:21 In the concluding verse about the Battle of Armageddon, Christ slays all who rebelled against Him in anticipation of setting up His kingdom. The bodies left on the earth will become food for the birds. The souls of these rebels against God will go, just as all sinners before them, to the place of torment where they await the Great White Throne Judgment after the Millennium.

20:1–2 The introduction to Christ's Millennial Kingdom begins with Satan being bound for a thousand years in the bottomless pit (Gr. *abyss*) by an angel, probably the one who opened the pit in Revelation 9:1. Some think that Christ is the angel with "the key of the bottomless pit," for in Revelation 1:18, Christ holds the keys "of hell and of death" where the pit is located. However, since

Christ is nowhere seen as an angel after His Ascension to heaven, it would seem more likely that He will empower an angel such as Michael to bind Satan.

20:2 a thousand years. This reference is the first time in the Bible that the length of the messianic kingdom of Christ is given. Scores of passages in the Bible teach a coming literal kingdom on earth when the Messiah will reign (Isa. 2:2–4; Ezek. 37:21–28; Zech. 9:10; 14:9). This chapter is the only one that mentions "the thousand years," but it does so six times, indicating the length of time is literal and specific. The Latin word *mille,* meaning thousand, is the basis of the word "millennium." A premillennialist is one who believes that Christ will come before He sets up His millennial reign on this earth (see the article entitled "The Millennial Views" by Mal Couch).

20:3 To deceive the nations no more. One of the factors that makes the Millennium such a utopian kingdom is that Satan will not be present to tempt or deceive mankind. Christ will reign supreme during the one thousand-year period following Satan's imprisonment.

20:4–5 them that were beheaded for the witness of Jesus. Revelation 6:9–11 speaks of many who will be slain by Antichrist during the Tribulation for refusing to take his mark. Here they will be resurrected so they can reign with Christ during His one thousand-year kingdom on earth.

6 Blessed and holy *is* he that hath part in the first resurrection: on such the second death hath no power, but they shall be priests of God and of Christ, and shall reign with him a thousand years.

7 And when the thousand years are expired, Satan shall be loosed out of his prison,

8 And shall go out to deceive the nations which are in the four quarters of the earth, Gog and Magog, to gather them together to battle: the number of whom *is* as the sand of the sea.

9 And they went up on the breadth of the earth, and compassed the camp of the saints about, and the beloved city: and fire came down from God out of heaven, and devoured them.

10 And the devil that deceived them was cast into the lake of fire and brimstone, where the beast and the false prophet *are*,

6 1Pet. 2:9
8 Ezek. 38:2; 39:1
9 Isa. 8:8; Ezek. 38:9, 16
10 Rev. 14:10, 11; 19:20; 20:8
11 Dan. 2:35; 2Pet. 3:7, 10, 11; Rev. 21:1
12 Ps. 69:28; Jer. 17:10; 32:19; Dan. 7:10; 12:1; Matt. 16:27; Rev. 2:23; 3:5; 13:8; 19:5; 22:12
14 1Cor. 15:26, 54, 55; Rev. 20:6; 21:8

and shall be tormented day and night for ever and ever

The Great White Throne Judgment

11 And I saw a great white throne, and him that sat on it, from whose face the earth and the heaven fled away; and there was found no place for them.

12 And I saw the dead, small and great, stand before God; and the books were opened: and another book was opened, which is *the book* of life: and the dead were judged out of those things which were written in the books, according to their works.

13 And the sea gave up the dead which were in it; and death and hell delivered up the dead which were in them: and they were judged every man according to their works.

14 And death and hell were cast into the lake of fire. This is the second death.

20:6 he that hath part in the first resurrection. The "first resurrection" is for believers and takes place in installments: 1) Christ as the firstfruits (1 Cor. 15:20); 2) the rapture of the Church (1 Cor. 15:23, 1 Thess. 4:13–18); 3) Tribulation saints are raised before the kingdom along with the Old Testament saints (Ps. 50:1–6). This resurrection includes all believing dead up to the time of Christ's return. The second resurrection is exclusively for unbelievers. The "second death" is the final death or incarceration into the lake of fire for all that have rejected God's great salvation (Rev. 21:8).

20:7–8 Gog and Magog. The use of these names here and in Ezekiel 38—39 has confused some readers. A thorough reading of the two passages will reveal that the events are not the same. The one thing these events have in common is that both national entities (Gog and Magog) are driven by the spirit of rebellion against God. In these two cases, God uses the same names because of the deceptively satanic spirit that motivates them both.

20:8 as the sand of the sea. This expression proves that the world's population will be enormous at the end of the Millennium. This multitude that follows Satan appears to be made up of only those who are less than one hundred years of age (see Isa. 65:20). The second issue here is the depravity and rebellion of the human heart. Even under the ideal conditions of Christ's reign on earth, unregenerate hearts will rebel against him. That men could live under the righteous reign of Jesus the Messiah and then, as soon as Satan is released, follow him in rebellion indicates that Jeremiah was right when he said, "The heart is deceitful above all things, and desperately wicked: who can know it?" (Jer. 17:9).

20:9 the beloved city. The city that this army of rebels

surrounds is the millennial Jerusalem. That Satan, even after being bound for a thousand years in the bottomless pit, would still think he could lead one last triumph over God is incredible. God sends fire down from heaven and devours Satan and all his followers.

20:10 cast into the lake of fire. This is the final destiny of Satan and all unbelievers. As far as unbelievers are concerned, the saddest aspect of this lake of fire is that it was not designed for man, but for Satan and his angels (Matt. 25:41). The price of rebellion against God is eternal. There is no escape nor release, which is why the consignment is referred to as "the second death" (v. 14).

20:11–12 At the end of the Millennium, all those who have rejected Christ must "stand before God" (v. 12). The "dead" are those who are spiritually dead because of their rejection of Christ. They will stand in their resurrected state before Jesus to be judged by Him (cf. John 5:22).

20:12 the books were opened. The dead are those who have been kept in hell (Hebr. *Sheol;* Gr. *Hades*), the temporary place for the souls of unbelievers until judgment day (see the article entitled "Hell" by Jack Van Impe). From Cain to the final rebellion, all unbelievers are there. They will be judged "according to their works." This is not a judgment for believers in Christ. Every single soul at this judgment is an unbeliever.

20:13–14 gave up the dead. There is no hiding place from God's final judgment. Consignment to the lake of fire will be forever. The sea, the graves, and death and hell will all surrender the unsaved dead. These people will be resurrected, then judged and cast into the lake of fire. This casting of souls into the lake of fire is called the second death, for it involves the permanent condemnation of all unbelievers.

The Great White Throne Judgment

By Tim LaHaye

Mankind's eventual meeting with God on judgment day is stamped indelibly on the human heart. Recognition of this eventual meeting is one of the things that distinguishes man from animals and seems part of the human conscience. More importantly, such an encounter with God is mentioned many times in Scripture and occurs immediately after the Millennial Kingdom, after Christ extinguishes man's final rebellion, and just before the beginning of the new eternity, which God has prepared for those who love and accept Him.

"The dead, small and great, stand[ing] before God" (Rev. 20:12) indicates that all those "dead" toward God and living in the place of torment where they went upon their earthly deaths are resurrected (as Dan. 12:2 promised) to appear before God, who will judge them "according to their works" (v. 12). Evidently there are books of man's works kept in heaven that will be revealed at this judgment. The "dead" mentioned here are people who had never received Christ before their first death. After the Millennium, they will be resurrected to appear before God. The books of their works will be opened, none of which have been erased through the forgiving blood of Jesus, because they rejected Him in their earthly lives. Therefore, they stand condemned by their own works.

> *The Great White Throne Judgment is not for Christians.*

That there will be degrees of punishment in eternity seems both biblical and just. Many believe the reason for this specific judgment is to determine the degrees of suffering in the lake of fire. It is before this throne that the prediction of Philippians 2:9–11 will be fulfilled, that there is an appointed day when every man and woman will bend his or her knees to worship Jesus Christ and "confess that Jesus Christ is Lord, to the glory of God the Father." If we repent and confess Christ now, of course, we will be excluded from that judgment and have our names written in the "book of life of the Lamb" (Rev. 13:8). This guarantees our names will remain in the "book of life," a separate book from which everyone's name is blotted out if he or she dies without a saving relationship with Christ (Rev. 3:5). According to Revelation 20:15, after a final check in this book of life, anyone whose name is missing is cast into the lake of fire.

The greatness of this throne is not in the size of it, nor is it in the number of the multitude who stand convicted before it, but in the greatness of the Judge who presides over it—the Lord Jesus Christ. The white color is representative of His holiness and purity, and of how fitting it is that He should judge mankind (see John 5:22, 27–29; 2 Tim. 4:1). He is the eternal word (John 1:1), come to give life, a life free from the power and wages of sin (Luke 19:10; Rom. 6:23; Heb. 12:9). Those who refuse the free gift wrought by the Lamb of God, will find that it is truly "a fearful thing to fall into the hands of the living God" (Heb. 10:29–31).

The Great White Throne Judgment is *not* for Christians. It is only for those who refuse to accept Jesus Christ in this earthly life. To avoid this judgment, all one must do is repent and believe in the name of the Lord Jesus Christ and invite Him to become his or her Lord and Savior.

15 And whosoever was not found written in the book of life was cast into the lake of fire.

CHAPTER 21
Heaven on Earth

1 And I saw a new heaven and a new earth: for the first heaven and the first earth were passed away; and there was no more sea.

2 And I John saw the holy city, new Jerusalem, coming down from God out of heaven, prepared as a bride adorned for her husband.

3 And I heard a great voice out of heaven saying, Behold, the tabernacle of God *is* with men, and he will dwell with them, and they shall be his people, and God himself shall be with them, *and be* their God.

4 And God shall wipe away all tears from their eyes; and there shall be no more death, neither sorrow, nor crying, neither shall there be any more pain: for the former things are passed away.

5 And he that sat upon the throne said, Behold, I make all things new. And he said unto me, Write: for these words are true and faithful.

6 And he said unto me, It is done. I am Alpha and Omega, the beginning and the end. I will give unto him that is athirst of the fountain of the water of life freely.

7 He that overcometh shall inherit all

References column:
15 Rev. 19:20
1 Isa. 65:17; 66:22; 2Pet. 3:13
2 Isa. 52:1; 54:5; 61:10
3 Ezek. 43:7
4 Isa. 25:8; 35:10; 61:3; 65:19
5 Isa. 43:19
6 Isa. 12:3; 55:1; Rev. 1:8
7 Zech. 8:8

The New Heaven and the New Jerusalem

CHARACTERISTIC	REFERENCES	OLD TESTAMENT PROPHECIES
God Will Dwell with Us	Rev. 7:15; 21:3	Isa. 12:6; Ezek. 43:7; 48:35
We Shall Be His People	Rev. 21:3, 7	Jer. 31:33; Zech. 13:9
He Will Be Our God	Rev. 21:3	Ezek. 37:27; Zech. 8:8
God Will Wipe Away Our Tears	Rev. 7:17; 21:4	Isa. 25:8; 35:10
There Will Be No More Death	Rev. 20:14; 21:4	Isa. 25:8; Hos. 13:14
There Will Be No More Mourning	Rev. 21:4	Isa. 35:10; Jer. 31:13
There Will Be No More Weeping	Rev. 21:4	Isa. 30:19; 65:18–19
There Will Be No More Night	Rev. 18:23; 21:23, 25; 22:5	Isa. 60:19–20; Zech. 2:5
There Will Be No More Curse	Rev. 22:3	Ezek. 37:26; Zech. 14:11

20:15 Typical of the loving nature of God, He reviews the "book of life" one final time, to see if the names of anyone at this final judgment are there. This affirms the justice of God's judgment on the unsaved. Except for the mercy of the living Christ, we would all perish, forever separated from the presence of God.

21:1 a new heaven and a new earth. The "new heaven" is the atmospheric heaven around and above the earth. This area has been the domain of Satan (see Eph. 2:2) and must be purified before the heaven of God can come down to the new earth. This new earth will be a perfect environment similar to that of the Garden of Eden. A unique distinctive of this new earth will be that the vast oceans of water that now cover three fourths of the world's surface will not be included, leaving much more inhabitable land for the population of the redeemed.

21:2 as a bride adorned for her husband. The Father's house to which Jesus ascended is heaven. There Christ has been building mansions or living quarters for His Bride, the Church (see John 14:1–4). In this magnificent prophecy, which will be fulfilled after the Millennium, Christ will bring that "city" to the new beautified earth where He will set up His capital for eternity. This city will be prepared as a wedding gift for the "bride" of Christ, which is His Church.

21:3 the tabernacle of God is with men. The Tabernacle was the original symbol of God dwelling with His people. In eternity, mankind will dwell with God. In that eternal state, we will not only enjoy fellowship with our redeemed loved ones but will also have actual fellowship with God Himself.

21:4–5 All tears, pain, sorrow, and death will be removed in that heavenly New Jerusalem where Christians will live. This is the exact opposite of the curse that resulted from Adam's sin (see Gen. 3:16–19). The effects of the curse are removed, and all things are made new. God does not merely repair the creation, He re-creates it for His children to enjoy for all eternity.

21:6 It is done. This is a statement (Gr. *gegonan*) of divine finality. It represents God's promise that this new state will be forever. Alpha and Omega are the first and last letters of the Greek alphabet. Hence, this phrase represents the sum of all things. In Revelation 1:11 and 22:12–13 it is used of Christ. Here it is used of God the Father ("he that sat on the throne"), indicating the deity of both the Father and the Son.

things; and I will be his God, and he shall be my son.

8 But the fearful, and unbelieving, and abominable, and murderers, and whoremongers, and sorcerers, and idolaters, and all liars, shall have their part in the lake which burneth with fire and brimstone: which is the second death.

The City Walls

9 And there came unto me one of the seven angels which had the seven vials full of the seven last plagues, and talked with me, saying, Come hither, I will shew thee the bride, the Lamb's wife.

10 And he carried me away in the spirit to a great and high mountain, and shewed me that great city, the holy Jerusalem, descending out of heaven from God,

11 Having the glory of God: and her light was like unto a stone most precious, even like a jasper stone, clear as crystal;

12 And had a wall great and high, and had twelve gates, and at the gates twelve angels, and names written thereon, which are the names of the twelve tribes of the children of Israel:

13 On the east three gates; on the north three gates; on the south three gates; and on the west three gates.

14 And the wall of the city had twelve foundations, and in them the names of the twelve apostles of the Lamb.

15 And he that talked with me had a golden reed to measure the city, and the gates thereof, and the wall thereof.

16 And the city lieth foursquare, and the length is as large as the breadth: and he measured the city with the reed, twelve thousand furlongs. The length and the breadth and the height of it are equal.

17 And he measured the wall thereof, an hundred and forty and four cubits, according to the measure of a man, that is, of the angel.

18 And the building of the wall of it was of jasper: and the city was pure gold, like unto clear glass.

19 And the foundations of the wall of the city were garnished with all manner of precious stones. The first foundation was jasper; the second, sapphire; the third, a chalcedony; the fourth, an emerald;

20 The fifth, sardonyx; the sixth, sardius; the seventh, chrysolyte; the eighth, beryl; the ninth, a topaz; the tenth, a chrysoprasus; the eleventh, a jacinth; the twelfth, an amethyst.

21 And the twelve gates were twelve pearls; every several gate was of one pearl: and the street of the city was pure gold, as it were transparent glass.

Cross references (center column)

8 1Cor. 6:9, 10; Gal. 5:19-21; Eph. 5:5; 1Tim. 1:9; Heb. 12:14; Rev. 20:14, 15; 22:15

9 Rev. 15:1, 6, 7; 19:7; 21:2

10 Ezek. 48; Rev. 1:10; 17:3; 21:2

11 Rev. 21:23; 22:5

12 Ezek. 48:31-34

13 Ezek. 48:31-34

14 Matt. 16:18; Gal. 2:9; Eph. 2:20

15 Ezek. 40:3; Zech. 2:1; Rev. 11:1

19 Isa. 54:11

21 Rev. 22:2

21:7 Just as a bride is an equal inheritor of all that is her husband's, so the Church, the Bride of Christ, will inherit all that is His. He even promises that He will be our God and we shall be His son. These terms of endearment are experiences we as Christians shall enjoy forever.

21:8 The contrasts between verses seven and eight are graphic. They represent the age-old concept that there are only two kinds of people with God, believers and unbelievers. They experience two different lifestyles on earth and go to two different eternal destinies. Believers go to "eternal life" while unbelievers experience "the second death," which is the lake of fire.

21:9-11 that great city, the holy Jerusalem. The Lamb's wife is described as the new city of Jerusalem. This magnificent city is where the Bride of Christ (the Church) will live forever. The most dominant characteristic of the holy city is the presence of God's glory, which personifies God's presence with His people. The glory that departed from the Old Jerusalem (see Ezek. 8—11) is restored to the New Jerusalem of the future.

21:12-14 The inclusion of the names of the twelve tribes of Israel and the twelve apostles in the foundations and gates of the city indicates that both Jewish and Gentile believers will all be part of the family of God and share eternity as one. Although it would seem that the Jews are distinct from the Church during the Millennium, they will all be one as children of the living God for eternity.

21:16 the city lieth foursquare. The size of this city indicates that each border is approximately fifteen hundred miles long. Thus the dimensions of the city would be equal to the area from the eastern seaboard of the United States to the Mississippi River on one side and from the Canadian border to the Gulf of Mexico on the other. In addition to the length and breadth, the city will be fifteen hundred miles high. This great size will afford sufficient space for the habitation of the saints from all ages of history.

21:17-21 the twelve gates were twelve pearls. Every gate will be one pearl, each large enough to cover the gateway to this huge city. In addition, the street of the city will be "pure gold, like unto clear glass," indicating that believers will walk on golden streets. The holy city of God will be so magnificent that believers will literally walk on precious metals that today are used for costly adornments.

22 And I saw no temple therein: for the Lord God Almighty and the Lamb are the temple of it.

23 And the city had no need of the sun, neither of the moon, to shine in it: for the glory of God did lighten it, and the Lamb *is* the light thereof.

24 And the nations of them which are saved shall walk in the light of it: and the kings of the earth do bring their glory and honour into it.

25 And the gates of it shall not be shut at all by day: for there shall be no night there.

26 And they shall bring the glory and honour of the nations into it.

27 And there shall in no wise enter into it any thing that defileth, neither *whatsoever* worketh abomination, or *maketh* a lie: but they which are written in the Lamb's book of life.

CHAPTER 22

1 And he shewed me a pure river of water of life, clear as crystal, proceeding out of the throne of God and of the Lamb.

2 In the midst of the street of it, and on either side of the river, *was there* the tree of life, which bare twelve *manner of* fruits, *and* yielded her fruit every month: and the leaves of the tree *were* for the healing of the nations.

23 Isa. 24:23; 60:19, 20

24 Isa. 60:3, 5, 11; 66:12

25 Isa. 60:11, 20; Rev. 22:5

27 Rev. 3:5; 13:8; 20:12; 22:14, 15

1 Ezek. 47:1; Zech. 14:8

2 Gen. 2:9; Ezek. 47:12; Rev. 2:7; 21:21, 24

3 Ezek. 48:35; Zech. 14:11

4 Matt. 5:8; 1Cor. 13:12; 1John 3:2; Rev. 3:12; 14:1

5 Dan. 7:27; Rev. 21:23, 25

6 Rev. 1:1

9 Rev. 19:10

10 Dan. 8:26; 12:4, 9

3 And there shall be no more curse: but the throne of God and of the Lamb shall be in it; and his servants shall serve him:

4 And they shall see his face; and his name *shall be* in their foreheads.

5 And there shall be no night there; and they need no candle, neither light of the sun; for the Lord God giveth them light: and they shall reign for ever and ever.

Christ Is Coming Quickly

6 And he said unto me, These sayings *are* faithful and true: and the Lord God of the holy prophets sent his angel to shew unto his servants the things which must shortly be done.

7 Behold, I come quickly: blessed *is* he that keepeth the saying of the prophecy of this book.

8 And I John saw these things, and heard *them.* And when I had heard and seen, I fell down to worship before the feet of the angel which shewed me these things.

9 Then saith he unto me, See *thou do it* not: for I am thy fellow servant, and of thy brethren the prophets, and of them which keep the sayings of this book: worship God.

10 And he saith unto me, Seal not the sayings of the prophecy of this book: for the time is at hand.

11 He that is unjust, let him be unjust still:

21:22 no temple therein. There will be no need for a temple in heaven to provide a means for a man to fellowship with God. Because of Jesus' sacrificial death on the cross, sin will not exist there. God and the Lamb are the temple of the eternal city. This clearly emphasizes the deity of Christ as equal in essence to that of the Father.

21:24 The reference to "nations" reminds us that our national distinctions, like our personal appearances, are God-given. Revelation 7:9 refers to "a great multitude . . . of all nations," and Revelation 5:10 refers to believers as "kings and priests" who reign with Christ.

21:27 Once again, we are confronted with the significance of having our names written in the Lamb's book of life, assuring us that Christ knows each believer personally, by name.

22:1 pure river of water of life. In one final glimpse into the future, John sees this river flowing from the throne of God. It is the source of eternal life that emanates from God. Even in heaven, we will drink water and eat food, probably not out of necessity for our health, but because of the pleasure and fellowship it will give us.

22:2 Here at the close of the Bible we are reintroduced to the tree of life, which has not been mentioned in the

Bible since Genesis 3, where Adam and Eve sinned in the Garden of Eden. Paradise is restored in the eternal state. All that was lost in the fall is redeemed by the Lamb. The leaves of this tree will be used to heal the relationships of the nations toward each other so that we might live equitably and fairly in eternity.

22:3–5 The picture of eternal life in these verses indicates that we will be busy serving God for all eternity. We will both serve Him (v. 3) and reign with Him (v. 5). Since He is an infinite God, we can be sure He will have infinite things for us to do as we reign there forever. The phrase, "they shall see his face," means that, as believers, we will be granted an audience with the King on a regular basis.

22:7 Behold, I come quickly. Jesus did not say He was "coming soon," but "suddenly" (Gr. *taxis*), which is why we should be ready for His return every day of our lives. When He comes to rapture us to heaven, He will come "suddenly," in the "twinkling of an eye" (1 Cor. 15:51–52).

22:10 The command not to seal this prophetic message is quite different than what the Lord told Daniel, "But thou, O Daniel, shut up the words, and seal the book,

and he which is filthy, let him be filthy still: and he that is righteous, let him be righteous still: and he that is holy, let him be holy still. **12** And, behold, I come quickly; and my reward *is* with me, to give every man according as his work shall be. **13** I am Alpha and Omega, the beginning and the end, the first and the last. **14** Blessed *are* they that do his commandments, that they may have right to the tree of life, and may enter in through the gates into the city. **15** For without *are* dogs, and sorcerers, and whoremongers, and murderers, and idolaters, and whosoever loveth and maketh a lie. **16** I Jesus have sent mine angel to testify unto you these things in the churches. I am the root and the offspring of David, *and* the bright and morning star.

12 Isa. 40:10; 62:11; Rom. 2:6; 14:12; Rev. 20:12; 22:7

13 Isa. 41:4; 44:6; 48:12; Rev. 1:8, 11; 21:6

14 Dan. 12:12; 1John 3:24; Rev. 2:7; 21:27; 22:2

16 Zech. 6:12; 2Pet. 1:19; Rev. 1:1; 2:28; 5:5

17 Isa. 55:1

19 Rev. 3:5; 13:8; 21:2

17 And the Spirit and the bride say, Come. And let him that heareth say, Come. And let him that is athirst come. And whosoever will, let him take the water of life freely. **18** For I testify unto every man that heareth the words of the prophecy of this book, If any man shall add unto these things, God shall add unto him the plagues that are written in this book: **19** And if any man shall take away from the words of the book of this prophecy, God shall take away his part out of the book of life, and out of the holy city, and *from* the things which are written in this book. **20** He which testifieth these things saith, Surely I come quickly. Amen. Even so, come, Lord Jesus. **21** The grace of our Lord Jesus Christ *be* with you all. Amen.

---

even to the time of the end" (Dan. 12:4). The reason for the difference in the instructions is simply stated, "the time is at hand." Until the death and resurrection of Christ, the time for this prophecy had not come. Since Jesus already opened the seven seals prophetically (Rev. 5—6) to reveal the future, it is only appropriate that the entire book remain open for us to read as well.

22:10–11 let him be filthy still. This suggests that in eternity unregenerate man will not experience a second chance for a changed nature. Once people are condemned at the Great White Throne Judgment, they will remain lost forever.

22:12 my reward is with me. After the Rapture, all believers will face the judgment seat of Christ. He will hold us accountable for the way we have served Him in this life. We shall enter into heaven by faith in Christ, but faithful service in this life is the basis for how we will be rewarded by Him for eternity.

22:16 I Jesus have sent mine angel to testify. This verse is Jesus' seal of approval on the whole book of Revelation. It marks the first use of the word "church" since chapter three. Why is there no reference to the Church during the time of tribulation on earth described in chapters 6—18? Because the Church, having been raptured to heaven, will not be on earth! Jesus is the Lord

and offspring of David, who gives us a shining hope because He is coming again and will triumph over Satan, suffering, and death.

22:17 The Spirit and the bride say, Come. Jesus clarifies the primary mission of the Spirit and the Church (His Bride) during this entire Church age, which is to invite lost men and women to come to Him for salvation before it is too late.

22:18–19 The Greek word *biblion,* translated "book," is where we get our word "Bible." John warns against any who would deliberately "add unto these things" (meaning the prophecies of this book) or "take away" any of its revealed truth. Since Revelation is the culmination of all Bible prophecy, we have no need for additional prophecy. Instead, we need to study and teach the prophecies that have already been revealed in the text of Scripture.

22:20 Surely I come quickly. Christ will come "suddenly" and without warning (vv. 7, 12). Every believer should live in anticipation that Christ's "coming again" is imminent. Christians from every generation should live their lives as though Jesus could come at any moment. "Even so, come, Lord Jesus" is the attitude of the Christian whose mind is filled with the "spirit of prophecy" (Rev. 19:10). Let us exhort one another as Paul did in 1 Corinthians 16:22: "Maranatha," meaning "the Lord is coming."

Glossary of Prophetic Terms

Abomination of Desolation—The expression used to describe the act of setting up an idolatrous image in the Holy Place, thus defiling or "making desolate" the Jewish Temple, and ending the offering of all sacrifices. This was done in the past by Antiochus Epiphanes (Dan. 11:31), whose act reflects the future defilement by the Antichrist (Dan. 9:27). Both Daniel and Jesus indicated that this future act would signal the start of the great tribulation (Dan. 12:11; Matt. 24:15; Mark 13:14).

Antichrist—Antichrist (1 John 2:2) is the individual who arises at the beginning of the seven-year tribulation and gains worldwide power for the last three and a half years. He is the imitator of the program of Jesus Christ and is known by many names throughout the Bible.

Amillennialism—(Latin, "no millennium"): The theological view that Christ and His saints will *not* reign personally upon the earth for a thousand years after His Second Coming.

Apocalyptic—Adj., prophetic; n., prophetic literature.

Apostasy—(Greek, "departure"): The term used for the condition of those who once professed the Christian faith but have since departed from its doctrine or practice.

Armageddon—(Hebrew, "mountain of Magedon"): The military campaign at the end of the tribulation in which the Antichrist's global army is assembled in Israel and defeated by Jesus Christ at His Second Coming (Dan. 11:40–45; Joel 3:9–17; Zech. 14:1–3; Rev. 16:14, 16; 19:11–21).

Bema—(Greek, "raised platform"): The transliteration of a Greek word used in the New Testament as a technical term to distinguish the event of rewards for believers from the final judgment of unbelievers, known as the Great White Throne judgment of Revelation 20:11–15. In the Roman world of New Testament times, there was a raised platform in the city square or at the coliseums where a dignitary would sit to hear civil matters or hand out rewards, usually a wreath, for competitive accomplishment. The Church will appear at Christ's bema in heaven in order to be evaluated during the Tribulation (Rom. 14:10; 1 Cor. 3:11–16; 4:1–5; 9:24–27; 2 Cor. 5:10; Rev. 19:1–10).

Chiliasm—(Greek, "one thousand"): This is the oldest term for Christ's one thousand-year kingdom in Revelation 20:1–7.

Covenant Theology—A system of theology that interprets Scripture from the perspective of salvation covenants between God and humanity. It is not a system of theology developed from the biblical covenants. Instead it is based upon two theorized covenants called the covenant of works and the covenant of grace.

Day of the Lord—Involves God's direct intervention in human affairs and history. This phrase is one of numerous terms and phrases used throughout the Bible to refer to a time of judgment (such as the Tribulation). In the Old Testament, the phrase was used by the prophets to refer to a coming time of judgment. In some cases, that judgment is now past, and, in others, it is yet future. As a future time of judgment, the day of the Lord is a time of devastation and destruction (Zech. 12—14).

Dispensationalism—A system of theology that interprets Scripture literally and from the perspective of God's interaction with humanity through successive ages. This view of biblical history maintains one plan of salvation in which God reveals Himself to man and deals with humanity in different ways in each successive period of their relationship or economy (dispensation) of time.

Eschatology—(Greek, "study of last things"): The study of things relating to the end of the world, the final judgment, and the life and world to come.

End Times—There are a number of different biblical expressions that appear to speak of the end times. In the Bible "end times" may refer to the end of the current church age or it may refer to other times, such as the end of the Tribulation that is followed by the second coming of Christ. Often the seven-year Tribulation is called the "end times."

False Prophet—The religious miracle worker, who is the Antichrist's minister of propaganda during the Tribulation (Revelation 16:13; 19:20; 20:10). He is called the "beast out of the earth" and shares the beastly nature of the Antichrist.

Futurism—The belief that major prophetic events such as the Rapture, the Tribulation, the Second Coming, and the Millennium are yet future.

Great Tribulation—The last half of the seven-year period also known as the 70th-week of Daniel or the Tribulation.

Great White Throne Judgment—The term pertains to the judgment that is recorded in Revelation 20:11–15. All who experience this judgment are there because they have rejected Jesus Christ during their lifetimes. Because of their rejection of Christ's substitutionary work, God will judge them on the basis of their own works, which fail utterly to measure up at any point to His holy standard. In this judgment, their works are judged to show that the punishment is deserved, and as a result, everyone in this judgment is thrown into the lake of fire.

Hermeneutic—One's method of interpreting literature, especially Scripture.

Historicism—The belief that the Tribulation and the present Church Age are generally the same. Historicists see the Second Coming and possibly the Millennium as yet future to the current age. They also hold that the Antichrist is the Pope and Roman Catholicism.

Idealism—The belief that the timing of major prophetic events is undetermined.

Imminency—(Latin, "any moment"): A term used to describe the Rapture and emphasizes that it could happen at any moment, without prior signs or warning.

Kingdom—A term used throughout the Bible to often refer to the time when Jesus the Messiah will return to earth and reign from Jerusalem for a thousand years.

Lake of Fire—The final eternal abode of all unbelievers throughout history. It is the proper name for what is popularly thought of as hell (Rev. 19:20; 20:14–15; 21:8).

Last Days— There are a number of different biblical expressions that appear to speak of the last days. In the Bible, "last days" may refer to the end of the current Church Age or it may refer to other times, such as the end of the Tribulation that is followed by the Second Coming. Often the seven-year Tribulation is called the "last days."

Maranatha—(Aramaic, "our Lord come"): A greeting often used in the first century church reflecting the eager expectation and hope that the Lord could return at any moment (1 Cor. 16:22).

Mark of the Beast—A mark that will be given by the Antichrist and False Prophet during the last three and a half years of the Tribulation (Rev. 13:16–17; 14:9; 20:4). Anyone receiving this mark (the number 666) on the right hand or forehead will be destined for the Lake of Fire for all eternity.

Marriage Supper of the Lamb—The time of celebrating the relationship between Christ and the Church called the marriage of the Lamb (Rev. 19:8), which will probably take place at the beginning of the Millennium (Rev. 19:9).

New Earth—The new planet that God will create to replace earth after He destroys the current one with fire at the end of history (2 Pet. 3:10–12; Rev. 22:3).

New Heaven—The new creation that God will create to replace the present heaven after He destroys the current one with fire at the end of the Millennium (2 Pet. 3:10–13; Rev. 21:1).

New Jerusalem—The eternal city that God will create as the eternal residence for believers throughout history after He destroys the current heaven and earth with fire at the end of history (Heb. 11:8–10; 12:22–25; Rev. 3:12; 21—22).

Midtribulationalism—A type of premillennialism in which the rapture of the Church will occur in the middle of the seven-year Tribulation.

Millennium—The future thousand-year reign of Christ on earth.

Olivet Discourse—Christ's prophetic sermon which is found in the following passages: Matthew 24—25; Mark 13; Luke 21:5–38.

Postmillennialism—(Latin, "after millennium"): The belief that the second coming of Christ follows the Millennium. Before Christ's return, the Church will have converted a majority of the world to Christ, resulting in the righteous rule of believers throughout the world.

Posttribulationalism—A type of premillennialism in which the rapture of the Church is said to occur after the seven-year Tribulation, in conjunction with the Second Coming.

Premillennialism—(Latin, "before millennium"): The belief that the second coming of Christ occurs before the Millennium, in which Christ personally reigns from Jerusalem for one thousand years.

Preterism—(Latin, "gone by," or "past"): The belief that most, if not all, major prophetic events have already been fulfilled in history.

Pretribulationalism—A type of premillennialism in which the rapture of the Church will occur before the seven-year Tribulation.

Rapture—The coming of the Lord to meet the Church in the air and His return with them to heaven.

Remnant—The saved Israelites throughout the entire history of Israel.

Replacement Theology—A theological view among both Catholics and Protestants that the Jews have been rejected and replaced by "the true Israel," the Church. Those who espouse this view disavow any distinct ethnic future for the Jewish people in connection with the biblical covenants, believing that their only spiritual destiny is either to perish or become a part of the Christian Church.

Revelation—(Greek, "to reveal"): God's act of telling humanity about Himself and His view of things. The Bible is God's revelation of His spoken word.

Second Coming—The physical, bodily return of Jesus Christ to earth at the end of the seven-year tribulation period.

Tribulation—That period of time, according to the premillennial interpretation of prophecy, which follows the rapture of the Church. Lasting for seven years, the first three and one-half years are a time of peace, which witness the rise of Antichrist and the rebuilding of the Jewish temple. The last three and one-half years are a time of divine judgment known in the Old Testament as "the time of Jacob's trouble." At the end of this period, climaxed by the Battle of Armageddon, Christ returns to rescue Israel and set up His Millennial Kingdom.

Old Testament Types of Christ Fulfilled in the New Testament

The Old Testament presents many types or "figures" (Rom. 5:14; Heb. 9:9; 11:19) of Christ and the Gospel. These are divinely-intended prophetic foregleams, based on real, historical people, actual spiritual ceremonies, religious institutions, artifacts and general objects. The Old Testament "figure" is in Greek a *tupos* or TYPE (Rom. 5:14). The New Testament application of the "figure" is an *antitupos* or ANTITYPE (Heb. 9:9). Out of the twenty-seven percent of Scripture that is predictive, nearly half of that amount, over four thousand verses, is typical in nature. These primary types are cited in the New Testament, usually by comparison, sometimes by contrast, and illustrate the unique ministry of the Messiah and Savior. Although these types are beautiful, illustrative applications, no doctrine can be based solely on a type. However, these prophetic, typical forecasts clearly demonstrate that "the Old Testament is the New Testament concealed, and the New Testament is the Old Testament revealed."

Aaron: Ex. 28:1; 40:12–15
  compare: Lev. 16:14–16; Heb. 4:25; 5:4–6; 9:7–14

Abel: Gen. 4:4, 8, 10; Heb. 11:4
  COMPARE: Eph. 5:2; Heb. 12:24

Abraham: Gen. 17:5
  COMPARE: Eph. 3:15

Adam: Gen. 2:7
  COMPARE: Rom. 5:14–19; 1 Cor. 15:45–47

Ark: Gen. 7:16
  COMPARE: 1 Pet. 3:20–21

Brazen Serpent: Num. 21:8–9
  COMPARE: John 3:14–15

Burnt Offering and All Other Sacrifices for Sin: Lev. 1:1–17; 4:22–35; 6:1–30
  COMPARE: Isa. 53:10; Eph. 5:2; Heb. 9:26; 10:1–12

Cities of Refuge: Num. 35:6, 11–15
  COMPARE: Isa. 4:6; Heb. 6:18

Daily Sacrifices: Ex. 29:38–41
  COMPARE: John 1:29, 36

David: Ps. 89:19–29
  COMPARE: Jer. 30:9; Ezek. 34:23; 37:24; Acts 2:25–31

Eliakim: Isa. 22:20–22
  COMPARE: Rev. 3:7

Isaac: Gen. 22:2–12; Heb. 11:17
  COMPARE: John 3:16; 1 John 4:9

Jacob's Plea: Gen. 32:24–28
  COMPARE: Luke 22:41–44; Heb. 5:7; 2 John 11:42

Jacob's Ladder: Gen. 28:12
  COMPARE: John 1:51; Eph. 1:10; Col. 1:20

Jonah: Jon. 1:17
  COMPARE: Matt. 12:39–40; Luke 11:29–30

Joseph: Gen. 45:5–7; 50:19–20
  COMPARE: Acts 5:30–31; Heb. 7:25

Joshua: Deut. 31:23; Josh. 1:5–6; 11:23
  COMPARE: John 14:2–3; Heb. 4:8–9, 14

Laver of Brass: Ex. 30:18–21
  COMPARE: Zech. 13:1; John 13:8; 1 Cor. 6:11; Eph 5:26–27; Rev. 1:5

Light: Gen. 1:3; Ps. 27:1
  COMPARE: John 1:5–10; 8:12; 2 Cor. 4:6; 1 John 1:5

Manna: Ex. 16:11–15; Ps. 78:24
  COMPARE: John 6:32–35, 48–51

Meal Offering: Lev. 2:1–11
  COMPARE: 1 Cor. 5:8; 11:23–24

Melchizedek: Gen. 14:18–20
  COMPARE: Ps. 110:4; Heb. 5:6; 6:20; 7:1–21

Mercy Seat: Ex. 25:17–22
  COMPARE: Eph. 2:18; 3:12; Heb. 4:16; 10:19

Moses: Num. 12:7
  COMPARE: Heb. 3:2; Deut. 18:15; Acts 3:22; 7:37

Paschal Lamb or Passover: Ex. 12:3–13
  COMPARE: Isa. 53:7; John 1:29, 36; Acts 8:32; 1 Cor. 5:7; 1 Pet. 1:19; Rev. 5:6, 12; 7:14

Peace Offering: Lev. 3:1–17
  COMPARE: Rom. 5:1; Eph. 2:14, 17; Col. 1:20

Red Heifer: Num. 19:2–10
  COMPARE: Heb. 9:13–14

Rock of Horeb: Ex. 17:6; Ps. 78:15–16
  COMPARE: 1 Cor. 10:4

Sacrifice on the Day of Atonement: Ex. 30:10; Lev. 16:15–18, 30–34
  COMPARE: Heb. 9:7, 12–14

Scapegoat: Lev. 16:20–22
  COMPARE: Isa. 53:6, 12; 2 Cor. 5:21; 1 Pet. 2:24

Sin offering: Lev. 4:2–21
  COMPARE: Heb. 13:11–13

Solomon: 2 Sam 7:12–16; 1 Chr. 22:9–10; 29:23–25
  COMPARE: Isa. 9:7; Dan. 7:14; Luke 1:32–33

OT Types of Christ Fulfilled in the New Testament

Tabernacle: Lev. 16:2–16
COMPARE: Heb. 8:2–6; 9:6–14
Temple of Jerusalem: 1 Kgs. 6
COMPARE: John 2:19–21

Veil of the Tabernacle: Ex. 40:21; 2 Chr. 3:14
COMPARE: Matt. 27:51; Mark 15:38; Luke 23:45; Heb. 10:20

Jesus the Prophet

Jesus was the Prophet like unto Moses (Deut. 18:17–19 [cf. John 1:21; Acts 3:22; 7:37]), who spoke words given to Him by the Father. Exercising that office during His earthly ministry, Jesus cited, referred to, or expressed parallel truths from at least 125 Old Testament passages, drawn from 24 of the 39 books. He came to fulfill the law (Matt. 5:17), but also to stress the spirit over the letter in many cases. Not only did he interpret and explain many Old Testament passages, but He prophesied of His death and resurrection, His return to the Father, this present age, and His second coming and subsequent reign. Listed below are Old Testament passages with New Testament quotations, allusions, or similar statements expressed by Jesus the Prophet.

The testimony of Jesus is the spirit of prophecy.
Revelation 19:10

Genesis
1:27	Matt. 19:4; Mark 10:6
2:24	Matt. 19:5; Mark 10:7
4:8	Matt. 23:35; Luke 11:51
5:2	Matt. 19:4; Mark 10:6
7:10	Matt. 24:38; Luke 17:26
9:6	Matt. 26:52
14:19, 22	Matt. 11:25
17:1	Matt. 5:48
17:10	John 7:22
18:14	Matt. 19:26; Mark 10:27
19:24	Luke 17:29
19:26	Luke 17:32
28:12	John 1:51

Exodus
3:6	Matt. 22:32; Mark 12:26; Luke 20:37
12:8	Matt. 26:18; Mark 14:14; Luke 22:11
16:4, 14	John 6:32
16:35	John 6:49, 58
20:12	Matt. 15:4; 19:19; Mark 7:10; 10:19; Luke 18:20
20:13–16	Matt. 19:18; Mark 10:19; Luke 18:20
20:14	Matt. 5:27
21:17	Matt. 15:4; Mark 7:10
21:24	Matt. 5:38
24:8	Matt. 26:28; Mark 14:24
29:32	Matt. 12:4

Leviticus
2:13	Mark 9:49
12:3	John 7:22–23
14:2	Matt. 8:4; Mark 1:44; Luke 5:14; 17:14
18:5	Luke 10:28
19:2	Matt. 5:48

19:12	Matt. 5:33
19:11, 13	Matt. 19:18–19; Mark 10:19; Luke 18:20
19:18	Matt. 5:43; 22:39; Mark 12:31
20:9	Matt. 15:4; Mark 7:10
22:32	Matt. 6:9; Luke 11:2
24:9	Matt. 12:4; Mark 2:26; Luke 6:4
24:20	Matt. 5:38; 7:2

Numbers
21:9	John 3:14–15
28:9–10	Matt. 12:5
30:2	Matt. 5:33

Deuteronomy
5:16	Matt. 15:4; Mark 7:10
5:16–20	Matt. 19:18–19; Mark 10:19; Luke 18:20
5:18	Matt. 5:27
6:4–5	Matt. 22:37; Mark 12:29
6:13	Matt. 4:10; Luke 4:8
6:16	Matt. 4:7; Luke 4:12
8:3	Matt. 4:4; Luke 4:4
10:12	Matt. 22:37
10:20	Matt. 4:10; Luke 4:8
15:11	Matt. 26:11; Mark 14:7; John 12:8
17:6	Matt. 18:16; John 8:17
18:18	John 12:49–50
19:15	Matt. 18:16; John 8:17
19:21	Matt. 5:38
23:21	Matt. 5:33
24:1	Matt. 5:31; 19:8; Mark 10:5

1 Samuel
7:3	Matt. 4:10; Luke 4:8
21:6	Matt. 12:3–4; Mark 2:25–26; Luke 6:3–4

2 Samuel

22:26	Matt. 5:7
22:27	Matt. 5:8

1 Kings

10:1	Matt. 12:42; Luke 11:31
17:1	Luke 4:25
17:9	Luke 4:26

2 Kings

5:14	Luke 4:27

2 Chronicles

9:1	Matt. 12:42; Luke 11:31
24:21	Matt. 23:35; Luke 11:51
36:16	Matt. 5:12

Nehemiah

9:26	Matt. 5:12

Job

34:11	Matt. 16:27
39:30	Luke 17:37
42:2	Matt. 19:26; Mark 10:27; 14:36; Luke 18:27

Psalms

2:9	Rev. 2:27
6:8	Matt. 7:23; 25:41; Luke 13:27
8:2	Matt. 21:16
22:1	Matt. 27:46; Mark 15:34
24:4	Matt. 5:8
31:5	Luke 23:46
35:19	John 15:25
37:11	Matt. 5:5
41:9	Mark 14:18; John 13:18
48:2	Matt. 5:35
69:4	John 15:25
82:6	John 10:34
110:1	Matt. 22:44; Mark 12:36; Luke 20:42
118:22–23	Matt. 21:42; Mark 12:10; Luke 20:17
118:26	Matt. 23:39; Luke 13:35

Proverbs

20:20	Matt. 15:4; Mark 7:10
25:6–7	Luke 14:8–10
25:9	Matt. 18:15

Isaiah

6:9–10	Matt. 13:14; Mark 4:12; Luke 8:10
8:14–15	Matt. 21:44; Luke 20:18

13:9–10	Matt. 24:29; Mark 13:24–25; Luke 21:25
29:13	Matt. 15:8–9; Mark 7:6–7
35:5–6	Matt. 11:5; Luke 7:22
40:8	Mark 13:31
42:7	Luke 4:18
53:12	Luke 22:37
54:13	John 6:45
55:1	John 7:37
56:7	Matt. 21:13; Mark 11:17; Luke 19:46
61:1	Luke 4:18
66:1	Matt. 5:34–35
66:24	Mark 9:44, 46, 48

Jeremiah

5:21	Mark 8:18
7:11	Matt. 21:13; Mark 11:17; Luke 19:46
22:5	Matt. 23:38
32:17	Matt. 19:26; Mark 10:27

Ezekiel

12:2	Matt. 13:13; Mark 8:18

Daniel

7:13	Matt. 24:30; 26:64; Mark 13:26; 14:62; Luke 21:27
9:27	Matt. 24:15; Mark 13:14
11:31	Matt. 24:15; Mark 13:14
12:1–2	Matt. 24:21
12:11	Matt. 24:15; Mark 13:14

Hosea

6:6	Matt. 9:13; 12:7
10:8	Luke 23:30

Joel

2:10	Matt. 24:29
3:15	Matt. 24:29

Jonah

1:17	Matt. 12:40; 16:4; Luke 11:30
3:5	Matt. 12:41; Luke 11:32

Micah

6:6–8	Matt. 12:7
7:6	Matt. 10:35; Luke 12:53

Zechariah

13:7	Matt. 26:31; Mark 14:27

Malachi

3:1	Matt. 11:10; Luke 7:27

Prophecies of the First Coming of Christ

No	OT text	Description	NT text	Topic
1	Genesis 3:15	Born of the seed of the woman	Matthew 1:20; Galatians 4:4	Birth
2	Genesis 14:18	Priest after order of Melchizedek	Hebrews 3:1; 5:5; 7:1–28	Priest
3	Genesis 17:19	Son of Isaac	Matthew 1:2; Luke 3:23–34	Ancestry
4	Genesis 21:12	Son of Isaac	Matthew 1:2; Luke 3:23–34	Ancestry
5	Genesis 22:18	Seed of Abraham	Matthew 1:1; Galatians 3:16	Ancestry
6	Genesis 35:10–12	Son of Jacob	Matthew 1:2; Luke 1:33; 3:32–34	Ancestry
7	Genesis 49:10	Tribe of Judah	Matthew 1:2; Luke 3:23–24; Hebrews 7:14	Ancestry
8	Exodus 12:1–46	Messiah the Passover Lamb	John 19:31–36; 1 Corinthians 5:7; 1 Peter 1:19	Sacrifice
9	Exodus 24:8	Messiah to shed blood as a sacrifice	Hebrews 9:11–28	Sacrifice
10	Numbers 21:8–9	Look at One on a Cross to live	John 3:14–15	Sacrifice
11	Numbers 24:17	Son of Jacob	Matthew 1:2; Luke 1:33; 3:32–34	Ancestry
12	Deuteronomy 18:17	God to send the Prophet	John 6:14; 12:49–50; Acts 3:22–23	Prophet
13	Deuteronomy 18:18	Prophet like Moses	Matthew 21:11; Luke 7:16; John 4:19	Prophet
14	Deuteronomy 21:22–23	Death by crucifixion	Matthew 27:35	Death
15	Deuteronomy 21:23	Cursed for hanging on a tree	Galatians 3:13	Death/Rejected
16	2 Samuel 7:14	Messiah to be God's Son	Hebrews 1:5	Deity
17	2 Samuel 7:16	David's son as Eternal King	Luke 1:32–33; Revelation 19:11–16	Ancestry
18	1 Chronicles 17:13	Messiah to be God's Son	Hebrews 1:5	Deity
19	1 Chronicles 17:14	David's son the Eternal King	Luke 1:32–33; Revelation 19:11–16	Ancestry
20	Psalm 2:6	King upon the holy hill	Matthew 27:37; John 18:33–38	King
21	Psalm 2:7	Son of God	Matthew 3:17	Deity
22	Psalm 8:2	Adored by infants	Matthew 21:15–16	Honored
23	Psalm 8:6	Everything subject to God's Son	1 Corinthians 15:27–28; Ephesians 1:22	Sovereign
24	Psalm 16:10	Not to see corruption	Matthew 28:6; Acts 2:31; 13:33	Resurrected

No	OT text	Description	NT text	Topic
25	Psalm 22:1	Forsaken by God	Matthew 27:46	Rejected
26	Psalm 22:7	People to shake their heads	Matthew 27:39	Mocked
27	Psalm 22:7–8	Scorned and mocked	Matthew 27:31; Luke 23:35	Mocked
28	Psalm 22:14	His heart broken	John 19:34	Death
29	Psalm 22:15	Messiah to suffer thirst	John 19:28	Death
30	Psalm 22:16–18	Soldiers to gamble for His clothes	Matthew 27:35–36	Mocked
31	Psalm 22:17	Stared upon by the people	Luke 23:35	Mocked
32	Psalm 30:3	Soul brought from grave	Matthew 28:6; Acts 2:31; 13:33	Resurrected
33	Psalm 31:5	Committed Himself to God	Luke 23:46	Death
34	Psalm 34:20	Bones not to be broken	John 19:32–33; 36	Death
35	Psalm 35:11	Accused by false witnesses	Matthew 26:59–61	Rejected
36	Psalm 35:19	People to hate without reason	John 15:24–25	Rejected
37	Psalm 38:11	Friends to stand afar off	Mark 15:40; Luke 23:49	Rejected
38	Psalm 40:6–8	Messiah to do God's perfect will	John 6:48; Hebrews 10:5–9	Obedience
39	Psalm 41:9	Close friend to betray	Matthew 10:4; Luke 22:47–48	Rejected
40	Psalm 45:6–7	Anointed and Eternal	Hebrews 1:8–12	Sovereign
41	Psalm 69:4	People to hate without reason	John 15:24–25	Rejected
42	Psalm 69:9	Zeal for God's house	John 2:15–17	Obedience
43	Psalm 69:9	Reproaches upon Him	Romans 15:3	Rejected
44	Psalm 69:21	Soldiers to offer Him gall and vinegar	Matthew 27:34	Death
45	Psalm 69:21	Messiah to suffer thirst	John 19:28	Death
46	Psalm 72:10	Wise men to bring gifts	Matthew 2:1, 11	Honored
47	Psalm 78:2	Teacher of parables	Matthew 13:34	Ministry
48	Psalm 102:25–27	Characteristics of the coming King	Hebrews 1:10–12	King
49	Psalm 109:4	Prayed for His enemies	Luke 23:34	Death
50	Psalm 109:24–25	Fell under the cross	Luke 23:26; John 19:17	Death

No	OT text	Description	NT text	Topic
51	Psalm 109:25	People to shake their heads	Matthew 27:39	Rejected
52	Psalm 110:1	Seated at the right hand of God	Mark 16:19; Hebrews 1:3	Ascension
53	Psalm 110:1	Messiah to sit at the right hand of God	Acts 1:9	Ascension
54	Psalm 110:1	Messiah to be called Lord	Luke 2:11; 20:41–44	Sovereign
55	Psalm 110:4	Priest after order of Melchizedek	Hebrews 3:1; 5:5; 7	Priest
56	Psalm 118:22	Stone of stumbling to the Jews	Romans 9:32–33; 1 Peter 2:7	Rejected
57	Psalm 118:26	Messiah to come in the name of the Lord	Matthew 21:9; Mark 11:9; John 12:13	Rejected
58	Isaiah 4:2	Messiah to be a Righteous Branch	John 8:46	Deity
59	Isaiah 6:9–10	Hearts to be closed to the gospel	Matthew 13:14–15; Mark 4:12; Luke 10:8	Obedience
60	Isaiah 7:14	Born of a virgin	Matthew 1:18, 24–25; Luke 1:26–35	Rejected
61	Isaiah 7:14	Name to be Immanuel	Matthew 1:23; Luke 7:16	Birth
62	Isaiah 8:14	Stone of stumbling to the Jews	Romans 9:32–33; 1 Peter 2:7	Birth
63	Isaiah 9:1	Ministry to begin in Galilee	Matthew 4:12–13, 17	Rejected
64	Isaiah 9:7	Messiah to be God	John 1:1, 18	Ministry
65	Isaiah 11:1, 10	Family line of Jesse	Matthew 1:6; Luke 3:23, 32	Deity
66	Isaiah 11:2	Special anointment of the Holy Spirit	Matthew 3:16–17; Mark 1:10–11	Ancestry
67	Isaiah 11:10	Salvation to be available to the Gentiles	Romans 15:12	Deity
68	Isaiah 22:22	Jesus to receive the key of David	Revelation 3:7	Sovereign
69	Isaiah 25:8	Death to be swallowed up in victory	1 Corinthians 15:54	King
70	Isaiah 28:16	Messiah to be the Chief Cornerstone	Romans 9:32–33; 1 Peter 2:6	Sacrifice
71	Isaiah 32:3–4	Ministry of miracles	Matthew 9:35; John 5:5–9	Honored
72	Isaiah 33:22	Messiah to rule over him	John 5:30; 2 Timothy 4:1	Ministry
73	Isaiah 35:6	Ministry of miracles	Matthew 9:35; John 5:5–9	Sovereign
74	Isaiah 40:3	Preceded by messenger	Matthew 3:1–2; John 1:23	Ministry
75	Isaiah 40:3–5	Way to be prepared	Luke 3:3–6	Ministry
76	Isaiah 42:1–4	Messiah as the chosen Servant of the Lord	Matthew 12:15–21	Obedience

No	OT text	Description	NT text	Topic
77	Isaiah 50:6	Messiah to be smitten and spat upon	Matthew 26:67	Rejected
78	Isaiah 53:1	Not believed upon by people	John 12:37–38	Rejected
79	Isaiah 53:3	Men to despise and reject Him	John 1:11	Rejected
80	Isaiah 53:4	Messiah to bear our griefs and sorrows	Matthew 8:17	Sacrifice
81	Isaiah 53:5	Wounded for our transgressions	Matthew 27:26; John 19:34	Sacrifice
82	Isaiah 53:5	Bruised for our iniquities	1 Peter 2:24	Sacrifice
83	Isaiah 53:5	Sacrifice to be vicarious	Romans 5:6, 8	Sacrifice
84	Isaiah 53:6	Iniquities to be laid on Him	1 Peter 2:25; 3:18	Sacrifice
85	Isaiah 53:7	Silent before His accusers	Matthew 27:12–19	Obedience
86	Isaiah 53:8	Messiah "The Anointed One" to be cut off	Acts 3:14–15, 26	Rejected
87	Isaiah 53:8	Christ is to be taken from prison and from judgment	Matthew 26:54–57	Death
88	Isaiah 53:9	Made His grave with the wicked	Matthew 27:38	Death
89	Isaiah 53:9	Buried with the rich	Matthew 27:57–60	Death
90	Isaiah 53:9	Sinless Servant of God	Hebrews 4:15; 1 Peter 2:22	Obedience
91	Isaiah 53:10	His soul an offering for sin	2 Corinthians 5:21	Sacrifice
92	Isaiah 53:12	Numbered with the Transgressors	Matthew 27:38	Rejected
93	Isaiah 55:3	Blessing of David given to the Messiah	Acts 13:33	King
94	Isaiah 59:20–21	Israel's Deliverer comes from Zion	Romans 11:26–27	Ancestry
95	Isaiah 60:1–3	Light to the Gentiles	Acts 13:47–48a; 26:23; 28:28	Compassion
96	Isaiah 60:6	Presented with gifts	Matthew 2:1, 11	Honored
97	Isaiah 61:1–2	Heals the brokenhearted	Luke 4:18–19	Compassion
98	Isaiah 65:1	Gentiles to believe in the Messiah	Acts 15:13–18; Romans 10:20	Compassion
99	Isaiah 65:2	Israel to reject the Messiah	Romans 10:21	Rejected
100	Jeremiah 23:5–6	Messiah to be a Righteous Branch	John 8:46	Obedience
101	Jeremiah 23:6	Messiah to be named "Our Righteousness"	1 Corinthians 1:30	Sacrifice
102	Jeremiah 23:6	David's Son to be Savior	Matthew 1:21	King

No	OT text	Description	NT text	Topic
103	Jeremiah 31:15	Slaughter of children	Matthew 2:16–18	Birth
104	Jeremiah 31:31–34	Mediator of the new covenant	Luke 22:20; 1 Corinthians 11:25; Hebrews 8:8	Priest
105	Jeremiah 33:16	Messiah to be "Our Righteousness"	1 Corinthians 1:30	Obedience
106	Ezekiel 34:23–24	The Good Shepherd to come	John 10:11, 14, 16; Hebrews 13:20	Sovereign
107	Ezekiel 37:24–25	The Good Shepherd to come	John 10:11, 14, 16; Hebrews 13:20	Sovereign
108	Daniel 9:24–27	Messiah "The Anointed One" to be cut off	Acts 3:14–15, 26	Death
109	Daniel 9:25	Time of His birth	Luke 2:1–2	Rejected
110	Hosea 6:2	Messiah to rise up on the third day	Matthew 28:6; Acts 2:31; 13:33	Resurrection
111	Hosea 11:1	Flight to Egypt implied	Matthew 2:14–15	Birth
112	Hosea 11:1	Jesus to return from Egypt	Matthew 2:14–15	Birth
113	Amos 9:11–12	Gentiles to believe in the Messiah	Acts 15:13–18; Romans 10:20	Compassion
114	Jonah 1:17	Messiah to be three days and nights in grave	Matthew 12:39–40	Resurrection
115	Micah 5:2	Born at Bethlehem	Matthew 2:1; John 7:42	Birth
116	Micah 5:4	The coming Shepherd of God's flock	John 10:11	Sovereign
117	Micah 5:5	Messiah to be our peace	Ephesians 2:14	Sacrifice
118	Zechariah 9:9	Messiah to enter Jerusalem on a donkey	Matthew 21:6–11; Luke 19:35–37a	Sovereign
119	Zechariah 11:12	Betrayed for thirty pieces of silver	Matthew 26:14–15	Rejected
120	Zechariah 11:13b	Price for a potter's field	Matthew 27:7	Death
121	Zechariah 12:10	Pierced through His hands and feet	John 20:27	Death
122	Zechariah 12:10	Messiah's side to be pierced	John 19:34	Death
123	Zechariah 13:7	Forsaken by His disciples	Mark 14:50	Rejected
124	Malachi 3:1	Messiah to enter the temple	Matthew 21:12	Priest
125	Malachi 3:1	Preceded by messenger	Matthew 3:1–2; John 1:23	Ministry

Prophecies of the Second Coming of Christ

PROMISES OF CHRIST'S RETURN IN THE OLD TESTAMENT

No.	Reference	Excerpt (KJV)	Description	Topic
1	Gen 5:24	And Enoch walked with God: and he was not; for God took him	Type of the Rapture	Rapture
2	Gen 17:7	And I will establish my covenant between me and thee and thy seed after thee in their generations for an everlasting covenant, to be a God unto thee, and to thy seed after thee	Everlasting covenant with Israel	Glorious Appearing
3	Gen 17:8	all the land of Canaan, for an everlasting possession; and I will be their God	Everlasting possession of the land of Canaan	Glorious Appearing
4	Gen 49:10	The sceptre shall not depart from Judah, nor a lawgiver from between his feet, until Shiloh come	Messiah to rule	Glorious Appearing
5	Num 24:17	there shall come a Star out of Jacob, and a Sceptre shall rise out of Israel, and shall smite the corners of Moab, and destroy all the children of Sheth	Messiah to destroy all enemies	Glorious Appearing
6	Num 24:19	Out of Jacob shall come he that shall have dominion, and shall destroy him that remaineth of the city	Messiah to destroy all enemies	Glorious Appearing
7	Deut 30:5	And the LORD thy God will bring thee into the land which thy fathers possessed, and thou shalt possess it	Israel to return to its land	Glorious Appearing
8	Ps 2:6	Yet have I set my king upon my holy hill of Zion	Messiah to rule in Jerusalem	Glorious Appearing
9	Ps 2:8	and I shall give thee the heathen for thine inheritance, and the uttermost parts of the earth for thy possession	Messiah to rule the nations	Glorious Appearing
10	Ps 2:9	Thou shalt break them with a rod of iron; thou shalt dash them in pieces like a potter's vessel	Messiah to conquer the nations	Glorious Appearing

No.	Reference	Excerpt (KJV)	Description	Topic
11	Ps 45:6	Thy throne, O God, is for ever and ever: the sceptre of thy kingdom is a right sceptre	Messiah to rule forever	Glorious Appearing
12	Ps 72:5	They shall fear thee as long as the sun and moon endure, throughout all generations	Messiah to rule forever	Glorious Appearing
13	Ps 72:8	He shall have dominion also from sea to sea, and from the river unto the ends of the earth	Messiah to rule over all	Glorious Appearing
14	Ps 72:17	His name shall endure for ever: his name shall be continued as long as the sun	Messiah to rule forever	Glorious Appearing
15	Ps 96:13	for he cometh, for he cometh to judge the earth	Messiah to judge the earth	Glorious Appearing
16	Ps 110:1	The Lord said unto my Lord, Sit thou at my right hand, until I make thine enemies thy footstool	Messiah to have all enemies subjected to Him	Glorious Appearing
17	Ps 110:2	The Lord shall send the rod of thy strength out of Zion: rule thou in the midst of thine enemies	Messiah to rule all enemies	Glorious Appearing
18	Ps 110:5	The Lord at thy right hand shall strike through kings in the day of his wrath	Messiah to destroy all enemies	Glorious Appearing
19	Ps 110:6	He shall judge among the heathen, he shall fill the places with the dead bodies, he shall wound the heads over many countries	Messiah to destroy all enemies	Glorious Appearing
20	Isa 9:4	For thou hast broken the yoke of his burden, and the staff of his shoulder, the rod of his oppressor	Messiah to defeat His enemies	Glorious Appearing
21	Isa 9:7	Of the increase of his government and peace there shall be no end, upon the throne of David, and upon his kingdom	Messiah to reign permanently	Glorious Appearing
22	Isa 11:4	and he shall smite the earth with the rod of his mouth, and with the breath of his lips shall he slay the wicked	Messiah to smite His enemies	Glorious Appearing
23	Isa 13:19	And Babylon, the glory of kingdoms, the beauty of the Chaldees' excellency, shall be as when God overthrew Sodom and Gomorrah	Babylon to be utterly destroyed	Glorious Appearing

No.	Reference	Excerpt (KJV)	Description	Topic
24	Isa 25:9	we have waited for him, we will be glad and rejoice in his salvation	Israel to be saved	Glorious Appearing
25	Isa 26:19	Thy dead men shall live, together with my dead body shall they arise	Israel's resurrection	Glorious Appearing
26	Isa 26:21	For, behold, the LORD cometh out of his place to punish the inhabitants of the earth	Messiah to punish the wicked	Glorious Appearing
27	Isa 40:10	the Lord GOD will come with strong hand, and his arm shall rule for him	Messiah to conquer His enemies	Glorious Appearing
28	Isa 55:3	and I will make an everlasting covenant with you	Everlasting covenant with Israel	Glorious Appearing
29	Isa 59:20	And the Redeemer shall come to Zion	Messiah to return to Jerusalem	Glorious Appearing
30	Isa 63:1	Who is this that cometh from Edom, with dyed garments from Bozrah? this that is glorious in his apparel, travelling in the greatness of his strength?	Messiah to return in glory	Glorious Appearing
31	Isa 63:2	Wherefore art thou red in thine apparel, and thy garments like him that treadeth in the winefat?	Messiah to return with blood-stained garments	Glorious Appearing
32	Isa 63:4	For the day of vengeance is in mine heart, and the year of my redeemed is come	Messiah to appear as Israel's redeemer	Glorious Appearing
33	Isa 63:5	therefore mine own arm brought salvation unto me	Messiah to conquer by His own might	Glorious Appearing
34	Isa 64:2	As when the melting fire burneth, the fire causeth the waters to boil, to make thy name known to thine adversaries, that the nations may tremble at thy presence!	Messiah's power to be feared	Glorious Appearing
35	Isa 66:15	For, behold, the LORD will come with fire, and with his chariots like a whirlwind, to render his anger with fury, and his rebuke with flames of fire	Messiah's fury to destroy enemies	Glorious Appearing
36	Jer 23:5	the days come, saith the LORD, that I will raise unto David a righteous Branch	Messiah to be raised up as a righteous king	Glorious Appearing
37	Jer 23:5	and a King shall reign and prosper, and shall execute judgment and justice in the earth	Messiah to rule with justice	Glorious Appearing
38	Jer 23:6	In his days Judah shall be saved, and Israel shall dwell safely	Judah and Israel to live in peace	Glorious Appearing

No.	Reference	Excerpt (KJV)	Description	Topic
39	Jer 25:30	The LORD shall roar from on high, and utter his voice from his holy habitation . . . he shall give a shout, as they that tread the grapes, against all the inhabitants of the earth	Messiah to defeat His enemies	Glorious Appearing
40	Jer 25:33	And the slain of the LORD shall be at that day from one end of the earth even unto the other end of the earth	Messiah's enemies to be destroyed	Glorious Appearing
41	Jer 30:7	Alas! for that day is great, so that none is like it: it is even the time of Jacob's trouble	Time of Jacob's trouble	Glorious Appearing
42	Jer 30:7	but he shall be saved out of it	Israel to be saved	Glorious Appearing
43	Jer 31:31	Behold, the days come, saith the LORD, that I will make a new covenant with the house of Israel, and with the house of Judah	A new covenant with Israel	Glorious Appearing
44	Ezek 34:23	my servant David; he shall feed them, and he shall be their shepherd	Messiah to shepherd His people	Glorious Appearing
45	Ezek 34:24	And I the LORD will be their God, and my servant David a prince among them	Messiah to reign as Israel's God	Glorious Appearing
46	Ezek 37:22	And I will make them one nation in the land upon the mountains of Israel; and one king shall be king to them all	Israel and Judah to be united	Glorious Appearing
47	Ezek 37:24	And David my servant shall be king over them; and they all shall have one shepherd	Messiah to reign as Israel's shepherd	Glorious Appearing
48	Ezek 37:25	and my servant David shall be their prince for ever	Messiah to reign permanently	Glorious Appearing
49	Ezek 43:7	Son of man, the place of my throne, and the place of the soles of my feet, where I will dwell in the midst of the children of Israel for ever	Messiah to reign permanently	Glorious Appearing
50	Dan 2:44	in the days of these kings shall the God of heaven set up a kingdom	God to set up His kingdom	Glorious Appearing
51	Dan 2:45	Forasmuch as thou sawest that the stone was cut out of the mountain without hands, and that it brake in pieces the iron, the brass, the clay, the silver, and the gold	Messiah to destroy His enemies	Glorious Appearing

No.	Reference	Excerpt (KJV)	Description	Topic
52	Dan 7:9	I beheld till the thrones were cast down, and the Ancient of days did sit	Messiah to cast down all other thrones	Glorious Appearing
53	Dan 7:13	the Son of man came with the clouds of heaven	Messiah to come in the clouds	Glorious Appearing
54	Dan 7:14	And there was given him dominion, and glory, and a kingdom, that all people, nations, and languages, should serve him	Messiah to reign over all	Glorious Appearing
55	Dan 7:26	But the judgment shall sit, and they shall take away his dominion, to consume and to destroy it unto the end	Antichrist to be destroyed	Glorious Appearing
56	Dan 7:27	the most High, whose kingdom is an everlasting kingdom, and all dominions shall serve and obey him	Messiah to reign permanently	Glorious Appearing
57	Dan 9:24	and to bring in everlasting righteousness, and to seal up the vision and prophecy, and to anoint the most Holy	Messiah to be anointed to reign in everlasting righteousness	Glorious Appearing
58	Dan 12:1	And at that time shall Michael stand up . . . and at that time thy people shall be delivered	Israel to be delivered	Glorious Appearing
59	Dan 12:2	many of them that sleep in the dust of the earth shall awake, some to everlasting life, and some to shame and everlasting contempt	Old Testament saints to be resurrected	Glorious Appearing
60	Dan 12:13	But go thou thy way till the end be: for thou shalt rest, and stand in thy lot at the end of the days	Daniel to be resurrected	Glorious Appearing
61	Hosea 1:11	Then shall the children of Judah and the children of Israel be gathered together, and appoint themselves one head, and they shall come up out of the land	David's house to be a protector	Glorious Appearing
62	Hosea 2:18	And in that day will I make a covenant for them with the beasts of the field, and with the fowls of heaven, and with the creeping things of the ground	All animals to live in safety	Glorious Appearing
63	Hosea 2:20	I will even betroth thee unto me in faithfulness: and thou shalt know the Lord	God to renew His vows with Israel	Glorious Appearing
64	Hosea 3:5	Afterward shall the children of Israel return, and seek the Lord their God, and David their king; and shall fear the Lord and his goodness in the latter days	Israel to return to God	Glorious Appearing

No.	Reference	Excerpt (KJV)	Description	Topic
65	Joel 2:31	The sun shall be turned into darkness, and the moon into blood, before the great and the terrible day of the LORD come	Signs in heaven	Glorious Appearing
66	Joel 2:32	for in mount Zion and in Jerusalem shall be deliverance	Jerusalem to be delivered	Glorious Appearing
67	Joel 3:1	in those days, and in that time, when I shall bring again the captivity of Judah and Jerusalem	God's people to be delivered	Glorious Appearing
68	Joel 3:2	I will also gather all nations	The nations to be gathered for judgment	Glorious Appearing
69	Joel 3:10	Beat your plowshares into swords, and your pruning-hooks into spears	Peace to be enforced	Glorious Appearing
70	Joel 3:12	Let the heathen be wakened, and come up to the valley of Jehoshaphat: for there will I sit to judge all the heathen round about	The nations to be judged	Glorious Appearing
71	Joel 3:14	Multitudes, multitudes in the valley of decision: for the day of the LORD is near in the valley of decision	Messiah to judge the Gentiles	Glorious Appearing
72	Joel 3:16	The LORD also shall roar out of Zion, and utter his voice from Jerusalem; and the heavens and the earth shall shake	Signs to occur in heaven	Glorious Appearing
73	Joel 3:17	So shall ye know that I am the LORD your God dwelling in Zion	Messiah to dwell in Jerusalem	Glorious Appearing
74	Joel 3:20	But Judah shall dwell for ever, and Jerusalem from generation to generation	God's people to live forever	Glorious Appearing
75	Joel 3:21	For I will cleanse their blood that I have not cleansed: for the LORD dwelleth in Zion	Messiah to forgive His people	Glorious Appearing
76	Amos 5:18	Woe unto you that desire the day of the LORD! to what end is it for you? the day of the LORD is darkness, and not light	The day of the LORD to bring judgment	Glorious Appearing
77	Amos 5:20	Shall not the day of the LORD be darkness, and not light?	The day of the LORD to bring judgment	Glorious Appearing
78	Amos 9:14	And I will bring again the captivity of my people of Israel, and they shall build the waste cities, and inhabit them	Israel to be regathered	Glorious Appearing

No.	Reference	Excerpt (KJV)	Description	Topic
79	Micah 1:3	the LORD cometh forth out of his place, and will come down, and tread upon the high places of the earth	Messiah to come in judgment	Glorious Appearing
80	Micah 2:12	I will surely assemble, O Jacob, all of thee; I will surely gather the remnant of Israel	Messiah to gather Israel's scattered	Glorious Appearing
81	Micah 2:13	their king shall pass before them, and the LORD on the head of them	Messiah to come as king and judge	Glorious Appearing
82	Micah 4:1	in the last days it shall come to pass, that the mountain of the house of the LORD shall be established in the top of the mountains	Jerusalem to be exalted	Glorious Appearing
83	Micah 4:2	for the law shall go forth of Zion, and the word of the LORD from Jerusalem	God's Word to be established	Glorious Appearing
84	Micah 4:3	he shall judge among many people	Messiah to reign over many	Glorious Appearing
85	Micah 4:3	they shall beat their swords into plowshares, and their spears into pruninghooks: nation shall not lift up a sword against nation, neither shall they learn war any more	Messiah to establish peace	Glorious Appearing
86	Micah 4:5	we will walk in the name of the LORD our God for ever and ever	God's people to walk in His name forever	Glorious Appearing
87	Micah 4:7	the LORD shall reign over them in mount Zion from henceforth, even for ever	Messiah to reign over His people forever	Glorious Appearing
88	Micah 4:8	the kingdom shall come to the daughter of Jerusalem	Messiah to come to Jerusalem to reign	Glorious Appearing
89	Micah 4:10	the LORD shall redeem thee from the hand of thine enemies	Messiah to deliver His people	Glorious Appearing
90	Micah 5:3	then the remnant of his brethren shall return unto the children of Israel	Israel to be converted	Glorious Appearing
91	Habakkuk 2:14	the earth shall be filled with the knowledge of the glory of the LORD, as the waters cover the sea	All earth to recognize His glory	Glorious Appearing
92	Zeph 1:14	The great day of the LORD is near, it is near, and hasteth greatly, even the voice of the day of the LORD	Messiah to come in power	Glorious Appearing
93	Zeph 1:15	That day is a day of wrath, a day of trouble and distress	Messiah to come with vengeance	Glorious Appearing

No.	Reference	Excerpt (KJV)	Description	Topic
94	Zeph 3:8	wait ye upon me, saith the LORD, until the day that I rise up to the prey: for my determination is to gather the nations, that I may assemble the kingdoms, to pour upon them mine indignation	Messiah to come with vengeance	Glorious Appearing
95	Zeph 3:20	At that time will I bring you again, even in the time that I gather you: for I will make you a name and a praise among all people of the earth	Messiah to gather His people	Glorious Appearing
96	Haggai 2:7	I will shake all nations, and the desire of all nations shall come	Messiah to shake the world	Glorious Appearing
97	Haggai 2:21	I will shake the heavens and the earth;	Messiah to shake all of creation	Glorious Appearing
98	Haggai 2:22	I will overthrow the throne of kingdoms, and I will destroy the strength of the kingdoms of the heathen	Messiah to overthrow all enemies	Glorious Appearing
99	Zech 2:10	Sing and rejoice, O daughter of Zion: for, lo, I come, and I will dwell in the midst of thee, saith the LORD	Messiah to come to His people	Glorious Appearing
100	Zech 2:11	And many nations shall be joined to the LORD in that day, and shall be my people: and I will dwell in the midst of thee, and thou shalt know that the LORD of hosts hath sent me unto thee	Many nations to be converted	Glorious Appearing
101	Zech 2:12	And the LORD shall inherit Judah his portion in the holy land, and shall choose Jerusalem again	Messiah to choose Judah as His own	Glorious Appearing
102	Zech 3:8	behold, I will bring forth my servant the BRANCH	Messiah to come as the Branch of David	Glorious Appearing
103	Zech 6:12	Behold the man whose name is The BRANCH; and he shall grow up out of his place, and he shall build the temple of the LORD	Messiah, as the Branch of David, to build temple	Glorious Appearing
104	Zech 8:3	Thus saith the LORD; I am returned unto Zion, and will dwell in the midst of Jerusalem	Messiah to return and to reign in Jerusalem	Glorious Appearing
105	Zech 8:7	Thus saith the LORD of hosts; Behold, I will save my people from the east country, and from the west country	Messiah to deliver His people from all enemies	Glorious Appearing
106	Zech 8:12	For the seed shall be prosperous; the vine shall give her fruit, and the ground shall give her increase, and the heavens shall give their dew; and I will cause the remnant of this people to possess all these things	Messiah's people to prosper	Glorious Appearing

No.	Reference	Excerpt (KJV)	Description	Topic
107	Zech 8:13	so will I save you, and ye shall be a blessing	Messiah to make Israel a blessing to others	Glorious Appearing
108	Zech 12:6	In that day . . . Jerusalem shall be inhabited again in her own place, even in Jerusalem	Messiah to reestablish Jerusalem	Glorious Appearing
109	Zech 12:8	In that day shall the LORD defend the inhabitants of Jerusalem	Messiah to defend Jerusalem	Glorious Appearing
110	Zech 12:8	and the house of David shall be as God, as the angel of the LORD before them	David's house to be a protector	Glorious Appearing
111	Zech 12:9	And it shall come to pass in that day, that I will seek to destroy all the nations that come against Jerusalem	Messiah to destroy all Jerusalem's enemies	Glorious Appearing
112	Zech 12:10	and they shall look upon me whom they have pierced	Pierced Messiah to be seen by all	Glorious Appearing
113	Zech 13:2	And it shall come to pass in that day, saith the LORD of hosts, that I will cut off the names of the idols out of the land	Messiah to remove idolatry	Glorious Appearing
114	Zech 13:8	And it shall come to pass, that in all the land, saith the LORD, two parts therein shall be cut off and die; but the third shall be left therein	Messiah to destroy two thirds of all Israel	Glorious Appearing
115	Zech 13:9	And I will bring the third part through the fire, and will refine them as silver is refined, and will try them as gold is tried: they shall call on my name	Messiah to refine the remaining one third of Israel	Glorious Appearing
116	Zech 14:1	the day of the LORD cometh	Jerusalem to be plundered initially	Glorious Appearing
117	Zech 14:4	his feet shall stand in that day upon the mount of Olives . . . and the mount of Olives shall cleave in the midst	Messiah to split the mount of Olives to form a valley	Glorious Appearing
118	Zech 14:5	ye shall flee to the valley of the mountains	Jerusalem to escape through the valley	Glorious Appearing
119	Zech 14:5	and the LORD my God shall come, and all the saints with thee	Messiah to return with resurrected saints	Glorious Appearing
120	Zech 14:9	And the LORD shall be king over all the earth	Messiah to reign over all the earth	Glorious Appearing
121	Zech 14:12	Their flesh shall consume away while they stand upon their feet	Messiah to consume His enemies	Glorious Appearing
122	Zech 14:20	In that day shall there be upon the bells of the horses, HOLINESS UNTO THE LORD	All of Jerusalem to be sanctified	Glorious Appearing

No.	Reference	Excerpt (KJV)	Description	Topic
123	Zech 14:21	and in that day there shall be no more the Canaanite in the house of the LORD of hosts	No unbelievers to enter the temple	Glorious Appearing
124	Mal 3:1	Behold, I will send my messenger, and he shall prepare the way before me	His return to be announced	Glorious Appearing
125	Mal 3:1	and the Lord, whom ye seek, shall suddenly come to his temple, even the messenger of the covenant	Messiah to return to His temple	Glorious Appearing
126	Mal 3:2	But who may abide the day of his coming? and who shall stand when he appeareth? for he is like a refiner's fire	All unbelievers to be destroyed	Glorious Appearing
127	Mal 3:5	And I will come near to you to judgment	Messiah to judge His people	Glorious Appearing
128	Mal 4:1	For, behold, the day cometh, that shall burn as an oven	All enemies to be consumed	Glorious Appearing
129	Mal 4:2	But unto you that fear my name shall the Sun of righteousness arise with healing in his wings; and ye shall go forth	Messiah to bring healing for His people	Glorious Appearing

PROMISES OF CHRIST'S RETURN IN THE GOSPELS AND ACTS

No.	Reference	Excerpt (KJV)	Description	Topic
130	Matt 10:23	Ye shall not have gone over the cities of Israel, till the Son of man be come	Jesus to return before evangelization is complete	Glorious Appearing
131	Matt 16:27	the Son of man shall come in the glory of his Father with his angels	Jesus to return in glory	Glorious Appearing
132	Matt 19:28	when the Son of man shall sit in the throne of his glory, ye shall also sit upon twelve thrones, judging the twelve tribes of Israel	Apostles also to rule	Glorious Appearing
133	Matt 24:15	When ye therefore shall see the abomination of desolation, spoken of by Daniel the prophet	The only "time" sign given by Jesus: the Abomination of Desolation	Glorious Appearing
134	Matt 24:27	For as the lightning cometh out of the east, and shineth even unto the west; so shall also the coming of the Son of man be	Jesus to return suddenly and obviously	Glorious Appearing
135	Matt 24:29	Immediately after the tribulation of those days shall the sun be darkened, and the moon shall not give her light	Jesus to return with cataclysmic signs	Glorious Appearing

No.	Reference	Excerpt (KJV)	Description	Topic
136	Matt 24:30	And then shall appear the sign of the Son of man in heaven: and then shall all the tribes of the earth mourn	All the earth to see and mourn	Glorious Appearing
137	Matt 24:30	they shall see the Son of man coming in the clouds of heaven with power and great glory	Jesus to come in glory	Glorious Appearing
138	Matt 24:31	And he shall send his angels with a great sound of a trumpet, and they shall gather together his elect	Angels to gather the elect	Glorious Appearing
139	Matt 24:32	a parable of the fig tree; When his branch is yet tender, and putteth forth leaves, ye know that summer is nigh	Jesus' return to be accompanied by signs	Glorious Appearing
140	Matt 24:36	But of that day and hour knoweth no man, no, not the angels of heaven, but my Father only	The exact time know only by the Father	Glorious Appearing
141	Matt 24:37	as the days of Noe were, so shall also the coming of the Son of man be	Jesus' coming to be totally unexpected	Glorious Appearing
142	Matt 24:39	And knew not until the flood came, and took them all away; so shall also the coming of the Son of man be	Unbelievers to be unexpectedly swept away	Glorious Appearing
143	Matt 24:40	Then shall two be in the field; the one shall be taken, and the other left	Only the saved to be left	Glorious Appearing
144	Matt 24:41	Two women shall be grinding at the mill; the one shall be taken, and the other left	Only the saved to be left	Glorious Appearing
145	Matt 24:42	Watch therefore: for ye know not what hour your Lord doth come	The uncertainty of the time of His coming	Glorious Appearing
146	Matt 24:44	Therefore be ye also ready: for in such an hour as ye think not the Son of man cometh	The uncertainty of the time of His coming	Glorious Appearing
147	Matt 24:46	Blessed is that servant, whom his lord when he cometh shall find so doing	Those who watch to be rewarded	Glorious Appearing
148	Matt 24:50	The lord of that servant shall come in a day when he looketh not for him, and in an hour that he is not aware of	Scoffers to be surprised and cut asunder	Glorious Appearing
149	Matt 25:1	the kingdom of heaven be likened unto ten virgins, which took their lamps, and went forth to meet the bridegroom	Necessity of being prepared	Glorious Appearing

No.	Reference	Excerpt (KJV)	Description	Topic
150	Matt 25:10	the bridegroom came; and they that were ready went in with him to the marriage: and the door was shut	Those who are prepared allowed to enter	Glorious Appearing
151	Matt 25:12	But he answered and said, Verily I say unto you, I know you not	Unbelievers to be rejected	Glorious Appearing
152	Matt 25:13	Watch therefore, for ye know neither the day nor the hour wherein the Son of man cometh	The uncertainty of the time of His coming	Glorious Appearing
153	Matt 25:21	His lord said unto him, Well done, thou good and faithful servant	Faithful service to be rewarded	Glorious Appearing
154	Matt 25:23	His lord said unto him, Well done, thou good and faithful servant	Faithful service to be rewarded	Glorious Appearing
155	Matt 25:30	And cast ye the unprofitable servant into outer darkness: there shall be weeping and gnashing of teeth	Unbelief to be punished with destruction	Glorious Appearing
156	Matt 25:31	the Son of man shall come in his glory, and all the holy angels with him, and then shall he sit upon the throne of his glory	Jesus to sit in judgment	Glorious Appearing
157	Matt 25:32	And before him shall be gathered all nations: and he shall separate them one from another, as a shepherd divideth his sheep from the goats	Judgment of the nations	Glorious Appearing
158	Matt 25:34	Then shall the King say unto them on his right hand, Come, ye blessed of my Father	Those who help God's people are to be rewarded	Glorious Appearing
159	Matt 25:41	Then shall he say also unto them on the left hand, Depart from me, ye cursed, into everlasting fire, prepared for the devil and his angels	Those who do not help God's people are to be punished	Glorious Appearing
160	Matt 26:29	I will not drink henceforth of the fruit of the vine, until that day when I drink it new with you in my Father's kingdom	Jesus to drink wine again only in the kingdom	Glorious Appearing
161	Matt 26:64	Hereafter shall ye see the Son of man sitting on the right hand of power, and coming in the clouds of heaven	Jesus to come in glory	Glorious Appearing
162	Mark 8:38	when he cometh in the glory of his Father with the holy angels	Jesus to come in glory	Glorious Appearing

No.	Reference	Excerpt (KJV)	Description	Topic
163	Mark 13:26	And then shall they see the Son of man coming in the clouds with great power and glory	Jesus to come in glory	Glorious Appearing
164	Mark 13:32	But of that day and that hour knoweth no man	The uncertainty of the time of His coming	Glorious Appearing
165	Mark 13:33	Take ye heed, watch and pray: for ye know not when the time is	The uncertainty of the time of His coming	Glorious Appearing
166	Mark 14:25	I will drink no more of the fruit of the vine, until that day that I drink it new in the kingdom of God	Jesus to drink wine again only in the kingdom	Glorious Appearing
167	Mark 14:62	and ye shall see the Son of man sitting on the right hand of power, and coming in the clouds of heaven	Coming in the clouds	Glorious Appearing
168	Luke 1:32	and the Lord God shall give unto him the throne of his father David	Jesus to reign on David's throne	Glorious Appearing
169	Luke 1:33	And he shall reign over the house of Jacob for ever; and of his kingdom there shall be no end	Jesus to reign forever	Glorious Appearing
170	Luke 9:26	when he shall come in his own glory, and in his Father's, and of the holy angels	Jesus to appear in glory	Glorious Appearing
171	Luke 12:37	Blessed are those servants, whom the lord when he cometh shall find watching	Those who watch to be rewarded	Glorious Appearing
172	Luke 12:40	for the Son of man cometh at an hour when ye think not	The uncertainty of the time of His coming	Glorious Appearing
173	Luke 12:43	Blessed is that servant, whom his lord when he cometh shall find so doing	Faithful watching to be rewarded	Glorious Appearing
174	Luke 12:46	The lord of that servant will come in a day when he looketh not for him . . . and at an hour when he is not aware, and will cut him in sunder	Unbelievers will be destroyed	Glorious Appearing
175	Luke 13:35	Ye shall not see me, until the time come when ye shall say, Blessed is he that cometh in the name of the Lord	Israel to be desolate until Messiah returns	Glorious Appearing
176	Luke 17:24	For as the lightning, that lighteneth out of the one part under heaven, shineth unto the other part under heaven; so shall also the Son of man be in his day	Jesus to return suddenly and obviously	Glorious Appearing
177	Luke 17:26	And as it was in the days of Noe, so shall it be also in the days of the Son of man	Jesus to come unexpectedly	Glorious Appearing

No.	Reference	Excerpt (KJV)	Description	Topic
178	Luke 17:28-30	as it was in the days of Lot . . . Even thus shall it be in the day when the Son of man is revealed	Jesus to come unexpectedly	Glorious Appearing
179	Luke 17:34	in that night there shall be two men in one bed; the one shall be taken, and the other left	Only the saved to be left	Glorious Appearing
180	Luke 17:35	Two women shall be grinding together; the one shall be taken, and the other left	Only the saved to be left	Glorious Appearing
181	Luke 17:36	Two men shall be in the field; the one shall be taken, and the other left	Only the saved to be left	Glorious Appearing
182	Luke 17:37	Wheresoever the body is, thither will the eagles be gathered together	Bodies of the slain at Armageddon	Glorious Appearing
183	Luke 18:8	I tell you that he will avenge them speedily	Jesus to avenge the abused elect	Glorious Appearing
184	Luke 19:15	when he was returned, having received the kingdom	Jesus to return as accepted king	Glorious Appearing
185	Luke 19:17	And he said unto him, Well, thou good servant: because thou hast been faithful in a very little, have thou authority over ten cities	Jesus to reward the faithful	Glorious Appearing
186	Luke 19:19	And he said likewise to him, Be thou also over five cities	Jesus to reward the faithful	Glorious Appearing
187	Luke 19:24	And he said unto them that stood by, Take from him the pound, and give it to him that hath ten pounds	Jesus to judge the unfaithful	Glorious Appearing
188	Luke 21:20	when ye shall see Jerusalem compassed with armies, then know that the desolation thereof is nigh	Jerusalem to be surrounded when Messiah comes	Glorious Appearing
189	Luke 21:24	Jerusalem shall be trodden down of the Gentiles, until the times of the Gentiles be fulfilled	Jerusalem to be trodden down until Messiah comes	Glorious Appearing
190	Luke 21:25	And there shall be signs in the sun, and in the moon, and in the stars	Jesus' return to be accompanied by signs	Glorious Appearing
191	Luke 21:26	Men's hearts failing them for fear, and for looking after those things which are coming on the earth	Unbelievers to fear at His coming	Glorious Appearing
192	Luke 21:27	then shall they see the Son of man coming in a cloud with power and great glory	Jesus to come in glory	Glorious Appearing
193	Luke 21:28	And when these things begin to come to pass, then look up, and lift up your heads; for your redemption draweth nigh	Jesus to bring redemption	Glorious Appearing

No.	Reference	Excerpt (KJV)	Description	Topic
194	Luke 21:31	So likewise ye, when ye see these things come to pass, know ye that the kingdom of God is nigh at hand	Jesus' coming preceded by signs	Glorious Appearing
195	Luke 21:34	and so that day come upon you unawares	Many to be surprised	Glorious Appearing
196	Luke 21:36	that ye may be accounted worthy to escape all these things that shall come to pass, and to stand before the Son of man	The faithful to escape judgment	Glorious Appearing
197	Luke 22:18	For I say unto you, I will not drink of the fruit of the vine, until the kingdom of God shall come	Jesus to drink wine again only in the kingdom	Glorious Appearing
198	John 14:3	I will come again, and receive you unto myself; that where I am, there ye may be also	Jesus to return to receive believers	Rapture
199	John 14:28	Ye have heard how I said unto you, I go away, and come again unto you	Jesus to come again	Rapture
200	Acts 1:11	this same Jesus, which is taken up from you into heaven, shall so come in like manner as ye have seen him go into heaven	Jesus to come in the clouds	Rapture
201	Acts 2:20	The sun shall be turned into darkness, and the moon into blood, before that great and notable day of the Lord come	Jesus' return to be accompanied by signs	Glorious Appearing
202	Acts 3:19	Repent ye therefore, and be converted, that your sins may be blotted out, when the times of refreshing shall come	The kingdom to be received only when Israel repents	Glorious Appearing
203	Acts 3:20–21	send Jesus Christ . . . Whom the heaven must receive until the times of restitution of all things	Jesus to restore Israel's kingdom in due time	Glorious Appearing
204	Acts 3:23	every soul, which will not hear that prophet, shall be destroyed from among the people	Unbelievers to be cut off	Glorious Appearing

PROMISES OF CHRIST'S RETURN IN THE PAULINE EPISTLES

No.	Reference	Excerpt (KJV)	Description	Topic
205	Rom 8:19	For the earnest expectation of the creature waiteth for the manifestation of the sons of God	Our bodies to be redeemed	Rapture
206	Rom 8:23	waiting for the adoption, to wit, the redemption of our body	Our bodies to be redeemed	Rapture

No.	Reference	Excerpt (KJV)	Description	Topic
207	Rom 11:25	that blindness in part is happened to Israel, until the fulness of the Gentiles be come in	Israel to be converted	Glorious Appearing
208	Rom 11:26	And so all Israel shall be saved: as it is written, There shall come out of Sion the Deliverer	Israel to be delivered by Jesus	Glorious Appearing
209	Rom 11:27	For this is my covenant unto them, when I shall take away their sins	Israel's sins to be forgiven	Glorious Appearing
210	Rom 14:10	for we shall all stand before the judgment seat of Christ	All Christians to be judged	Rapture
211	Rom 14:11	As I live, saith the Lord, every knee shall bow to me, and every tongue shall confess to God	All men to confess God's majesty	Rapture
212	1 Cor 1:7	waiting for the coming of our Lord Jesus Christ	Jesus' return a motive to faithfulness	Rapture
213	1 Cor 1:8	Who shall also confirm you unto the end, that ye may be blameless in the day of our Lord Jesus Christ	Christians deemed blameless at His coming	Rapture
214	1 Cor 3:14	If any man's work abide which he hath built thereupon, he shall receive a reward	The faithful to be rewarded	Rapture
215	1 Cor 3:15	If any man's work shall be burned, he shall suffer loss: but he himself shall be saved; yet so as by fire	The careless to lose rewards	Rapture
216	1 Cor 4:5	until the Lord come, who both will bring to light the hidden things of darkness, and will make manifest the counsels of the hearts	Jesus to reveal and judge all things	Rapture
217	1 Cor 9:25	Now they do it to obtain a corruptible crown; but we an incorruptible	The faithful obtain an incorruptible crown	Rapture
218	1 Cor 11:26	ye do shew the Lord's death till he come	The Lord's supper as pointing toward Jesus' coming	Rapture
219	1 Cor 13:10	But when that which is perfect is come, then that which is in part shall be done away	Temporary gifts to be set aside	Rapture
220	1 Cor 15:23	Christ the firstfruits; afterward they that are Christ's at his coming	All Christians who have died to be resurrected	Rapture
221	1 Cor 15:24	Then cometh the end, when he shall have delivered up the kingdom to God	The kingdom of God to rule forever	Glorious Appearing

No.	Reference	Excerpt (KJV)	Description	Topic
222	1 Cor 15:42	So also is the resurrection of the dead. It is sown in corruption; it is raised in incorruption	The resurrection body to be incorruptible	Rapture
223	1 Cor 15:43	It is sown in dishonour; it is raised in glory: it is sown in weakness; it is raised in power	The resurrection body to be glorious	Rapture
224	1 Cor 15:44	It is sown a natural body; it is raised a spiritual body	The resurrection body to be immaterial	Rapture
225	1 Cor 15:51	Behold, I shew you a mystery; We shall not all sleep, but we shall all be changed	Those still alive to be raptured	Rapture
226	1 Cor 15:52	In a moment, in the twinkling of an eye, at the last trump. . . the dead shall be raised incorruptible, and we shall be changed	Resurrection and Rapture to be instantaneous	Rapture
227	1 Cor 15:53	For this corruptible must put on incorruption, and this mortal must put on immortality	The resurrection body to be incorruptible and immortal	Rapture
228	1 Cor 15:54	then shall be brought to pass the saying that is written, Death is swallowed up in victory	The resurrection to conquer death	Rapture
229	1 Cor 16:22	If any man love not the Lord Jesus Christ, let him be Anathema Maranatha	Maranatha is a prayer for the Lord's return	Rapture
230	2 Cor 4:14	Knowing that he which raised up the Lord Jesus shall raise up us also by Jesus, and shall present us with you	Resurrection at His coming	Rapture
231	2 Cor 5:10	For we must all appear before the judgment seat of Christ	All Christians to have their works judged	Rapture
232	Phil 2:10	That at the name of Jesus every knee should bow, of things in heaven, and things in earth, and things under the earth	All to worship Jesus	Glorious Appearing
233	Phil 2:11	And that every tongue should confess that Jesus Christ is Lord, to the glory of God the Father	All to confess Jesus as Lord	Glorious Appearing
234	Phil 3:20	our conversation is in heaven; from whence also we look for the Saviour, the Lord Jesus Christ	Jesus to return from heaven	Rapture
235	Phil 3:21	Who shall change our vile body, that it may be fashioned like unto his glorious body	Christians to receive glorified bodies	Rapture
236	Phil 4:5	Let your moderation be known unto all men. The Lord is at hand	Jesus' return a motive to Christian living	Rapture

No.	Reference	Excerpt (KJV)	Description	Topic
237	Col 3:4	When Christ, who is our life, shall appear, then shall ye also appear with him in glory	The saints to be glorified with Christ	Rapture
238	1 Thess 1:10	And to wait for his Son from heaven, whom he raised from the dead, even Jesus	Jesus to come from heaven	Rapture
239	1 Thess 1:10	which delivered us from the wrath to come	Christians to be delivered from the coming wrath	Rapture
240	1 Thess 2:19	For what is our hope, or joy, or crown of rejoicing? Are not even ye in the presence of our Lord Jesus Christ at his coming?	Present converts to be our crown of reward	Rapture
241	1 Thess 3:13	To the end he may stablish your hearts unblameable in holiness before God, even our Father, at the coming of our Lord Jesus Christ with all his saints	Faithful saints to be deemed blameless	Glorious Appearing
242	1 Thess 4:15	For this we say unto you by the word of the Lord, that we which are alive and remain unto the coming of the Lord shall not prevent them which are asleep	The living not to precede the dead	Rapture
243	1 Thess 4:16	For the Lord himself shall descend from heaven	Jesus to descend from heaven	Rapture
244	1 Thess 4:16	with a shout, with the voice of the archangel, and with the trump of God	The trumpet to sound	Rapture
245	1 Thess 4:16	and the dead in Christ shall rise first	The dead to rise first	Rapture
246	1 Thess 4:17	Then we which are alive and remain shall be caught up together with them in the clouds, to meet the Lord in the air	All Christians to be caught up together	Rapture
247	1 Thess 4:17	and so shall we ever be with the Lord	Christians to be with Jesus permanently	Rapture
248	1 Thess 5:2	the day of the Lord so cometh as a thief in the night	The day of the Lord to begin unexpectedly	Glorious Appearing
249	1 Thess 5:3	For when they shall say, Peace and safety; then sudden destruction cometh upon them, . . . and they shall not escape	Destruction to come upon the unsaved	Glorious Appearing
250	1 Thess 5:4	But ye, brethren, are not in darkness, that that day should overtake you as a thief	Christians not to be overtaken	Rapture
251	1 Thess 5:9	For God hath not appointed us to wrath, but to obtain salvation by our Lord Jesus Christ	Christians to be delivered from wrath	Rapture

No.	Reference	Excerpt (KJV)	Description	Topic
252	1 Thess 5:23	I pray God your whole spirit and soul and body be preserved blameless unto the coming of our Lord Jesus Christ	Christians to be preserved blameless	Rapture
253	2 Thess 1:7	When the Lord Jesus shall be revealed from heaven with his mighty angels	Jesus to come with the angels	Glorious Appearing
254	2 Thess 1:8	In flaming fire taking vengeance on them that know not God	Jesus to destroy the unsaved with fire	Glorious Appearing
255	2 Thess 1:10	When he shall come to be glorified in his saints	Jesus to be admired by the saints	Glorious Appearing
256	2 Thess 2:1	by the coming of our Lord Jesus Christ, and by our gathering together unto him	The saints to be gathered	Rapture
257	2 Thess 2:2	be not soon shaken in mind . . . as that the day of Christ is at hand	Christ's return is imminent and unmistakable	Glorious Appearing
258	2 Thess 2:3	for that day shall not come, except there come a falling away first	Second Coming preceded by a "falling away"	Glorious Appearing
259	2 Thess. 2:3–4	and that man of sin be revealed, the son of perdition; Who opposeth and exalteth himself above all that is called God	Antichrist to rise up first	Glorious Appearing
260	2 Thess 2:7	only he who now letteth will let, until he be taken out of the way	The Holy Spirit to be removed first	Rapture
261	2 Thess 2:8	And then shall that Wicked be revealed, whom the Lord shall consume with the spirit of His mouth	Antichrist to be destroyed	Glorious Appearing
262	2 Thess 2:11	And for this cause God shall send them strong delusion, that they should believe a lie	Delusion to precede the Second Coming	Glorious Appearing
263	1 Tim 4:1	in the latter times some shall depart from the faith, giving heed to seducing spirits, and doctrines of devils	Signs of the Last Days	Rapture
264	1 Tim 6:14	until the appearing of our Lord Jesus Christ: Which in his times he shall shew	Jesus to return in His own time	Rapture
265	2 Tim 1:18	The Lord grant unto him that he may find mercy of the Lord in that day	All faithful deeds to be rewarded	Rapture
266	2 Tim 3:1	This know also, that in the last days perilous times shall come	Signs of the Last Days	Rapture

No.	Reference	Excerpt (KJV)	Description	Topic
267	2 Tim 4:1	God, and the Lord Jesus Christ, who shall judge the quick and the dead at his appearing and his kingdom	God to judge all Christians	Rapture
268	2 Tim 4:8	There is laid up for me a crown of righteousness, which the Lord, the righteous judge, shall give me at that day	The faithful to be rewarded	Rapture
269	2 Tim 4:8	and not to me only, but unto all them also that love his appearing	The faithful to be rewarded	Rapture
270	Titus 2:13	Looking for that blessed hope, and the glorious appearing of the great God and our Saviour Jesus Christ	Jesus' return a motive to Christian living	Rapture
271	Heb 1:8	But unto the Son he saith, Thy throne, O God, is for ever and ever: a scepter of righteousness is	Jesus will reign in righteousness	Glorious Appearing
272	Heb 1:8	the scepter of thy kingdom	Heaven and earth will perish	Glorious Appearing
273	Heb 1:12	they shall be changed: but thou art the same, and thy years shall not fail	His throne will last forever	Glorious Appearing
274	Heb 8:8	Behold, the days come, saith the Lord, when I will make a new covenant with the house of Israel	God to make a new covenant with Israel	Glorious Appearing
275	Heb 8:10	I will put my laws into their mind, and write them in their hearts: and I will be to them a God, and they shall be to me a people	New covenant with Israel based on personal relationship with God	Glorious Appearing
276	Heb 9:28	unto them that look for him shall he appear the second time without sin unto salvation	Jesus' return will complete our salvation	Rapture
277	Heb 10:37	For yet a little while, and he that shall come will come, and will not tarry	Jesus to return at the proper time	Rapture
278	Heb 12:25	much more shall not we escape, if we turn away from him that speaketh from heaven	No one rejecting Jesus will escape	Glorious Appearing
279	Heb 12:26	Yet once more I shake not the earth only, but also heaven	This material universe to be shaken	Glorious Appearing
280	Heb 12:28	Wherefore we receiving a kingdom which cannot be moved, let us have grace, whereby we may serve God acceptably with reverence and godly fear	Believers are warned	Glorious Appearing

PROMISES OF CHRIST'S RETURN IN THE GENERAL EPISTLES

No.	Reference	Excerpt (KJV)	Description	Topic
281	James 1:12	Blessed is the man that endureth temptation: for when he is tried, he shall receive the crown of life, which the Lord hath promised to them that love him	The faithful to be rewarded	Rapture
282	James 5:7	Be patient therefore, brethren, unto the coming of the Lord	Christians to be patient	Rapture
283	James 5:8	for the coming of the Lord draweth nigh	Imminent return	Rapture
284	1 Pet 1:4	To an inheritance incorruptible, and undefiled, and that fadeth not away, reserved in heaven for you	Incorruptible inheritance	Rapture
285	1 Pet 1:7	That the trial of your faith, . . . might be found unto praise and honour and glory at the appearing of Jesus Christ	Faithfulness to Christ to be rewarded	Rapture
286	1 Pet 1:13	Be sober, and hope to the end for the grace that is to be brought unto you at the revelation of Jesus Christ	Rewards at His coming	Rapture
287	1 Pet 4:13	when his glory shall be revealed, ye may be glad also with exceeding joy	His glory shall be revealed	Glorious Appearing
288	1 Pet 5:4	And when the chief Shepherd shall appear, ye shall receive a crown of glory that fadeth not away	Faithful church leaders to receive a crown of glory	Rapture
289	2 Pet 1:16	For we have not followed cunningly devised fables, when we made known unto you the power and coming of our Lord Jesus Christ	He is coming in power	Glorious Appearing
290	2 Pet 2:1	there shall be false teachers among you, who privily shall bring in damnable heresies	Signs of the Last Days	Rapture
291	2 Pet 3:3	Knowing this first, that there shall come in the last days scoffers, walking after their own lusts	Signs of the Last Days	Rapture
292	2 Pet 3:4	And saying, Where is the promise of his coming?	Mockers to deny His return	Rapture
293	2 Pet 3:10	the day of the Lord will come as a thief in the night	Jesus to come unexpectedly	Rapture
294	2 Pet 3:12	Looking for and hasting unto the coming of the day of God	Jesus' return a motive to Christian living	Glorious Appearing
295	2 Pet 3:13	Nevertheless we, according to his promise, look for new heavens and a new earth	New heavens and new earth to appear	Glorious Appearing

No.	Reference	Excerpt (KJV)	Description	Topic
296	2 Pet 3:14	seeing that ye look for such things, be diligent that ye may be found of him in peace, without spot, and blameless	Jesus' return a motive to purity	Rapture
297	1 John 2:28	when he shall appear, we may have confidence, and not be ashamed before him at his coming	Jesus' return a motive to purity	Rapture
298	1 John 3:2	when he shall appear, we shall be like him; for we shall see him as he is	Christians to become like Jesus	Rapture
299	1 John 3:3	And every man that hath this hope in him purifieth himself, even as he is pure	Jesus' return a motive to purity	Rapture
300	1 John 4:17	Herein is our love made perfect, that we may have boldness in the day of judgment	Confidence if we dwell in love	Rapture
301	2 John 1:8	that we lose not those things which we have wrought, but that we receive a full reward	Faithful Christians to be rewarded	Rapture
302	Jude 1:14	the Lord cometh with ten thousands of his saints	Jesus to return with His saints	Glorious Appearing
303	Jude 1:15	To execute judgment upon all	Jesus to judge sinners	Glorious Appearing
304	Jude 1:21	Keep yourselves in the love of God, looking for the mercy of our Lord Jesus Christ unto eternal life	Christians to be granted eternal life	Rapture
305	Jude 1:24	Now unto him that is able . . . to present you faultless before the presence of his glory with exceeding joy	Christians to be presented to the Father as righteous	Rapture

PROMISES OF CHRIST'S RETURN IN THE REVELATION

No.	Reference	Excerpt (KJV)	Description	Topic
306	Rev 1:7	Behold, he cometh with clouds	Jesus to come in the clouds	Glorious Appearing
307	Rev 1:7	and every eye shall see him	Jesus to be seen by everyone	Glorious Appearing
308	Rev 2:10	that ye may be tried; and ye shall have tribulation ten days: be thou faithful unto death, and I will give thee a crown of life	Martyrs to receive a special crown	Rapture
309	Rev 2:25	But that which ye have already hold fast till I come	Christians to endure until the Rapture	Rapture
310	Rev 3:3	If therefore thou shalt not watch, I will come on thee as a thief, and thou shalt not know what hour I will come upon thee	Jesus to catch the careless unprepared	Rapture

No.	Reference	Excerpt (KJV)	Description	Topic
311	Rev 3:10	I also will keep thee from the hour of temptation, which shall come upon all the world	Rapture to precede the Tribulation	Rapture
312	Rev 3:11	Behold, I come quickly	Jesus to come suddenly	Rapture
313	Rev 3:12	Him that overcometh will I make a pillar in the temple of my God, . . . and I will write upon him my new name	He who overcomes is to be honored	Rapture
314	Rev 4:8	Holy, holy, holy, Lord God Almighty, which was, and is, and is to come	Jesus to come again	Glorious Appearing
315	Rev 5:13	And every creature which is in heaven, and on the earth, and under the earth . . . saying, Blessing, and honour, and glory, and power, be unto him that sitteth upon the throne, and unto the Lamb for ever and ever	All to worship Jesus	Glorious Appearing
316	Rev 6:17	For the great day of his wrath is come; and who is able to stand	None able to stand His wrath	Glorious Appearing
317	Rev 11:17	We give thee thanks, O Lord God Almighty, which art, and wast, and art to come	Jesus to come again	Glorious Appearing
318	Rev 11:18	thy wrath is come, and the time of the dead, that they should be judged	God's enemies to be judged	Glorious Appearing
319	Rev 12:10	the kingdom of our God, and the power of his Christ: for the accuser of our brethren is cast down	Satan to be defeated	Glorious Appearing
320	Rev 14:7	for the hour of his judgment is come	Babylon and God's enemy to be judged	Glorious Appearing
321	Rev 16:15	Behold, I come as a thief	Jesus to come unexpectedly	Glorious Appearing
322	Rev 19:7	for the marriage of the Lamb is come	Marriage of the Lamb to come	Glorious Appearing
323	Rev 19:11	And I saw heaven opened, and behold a white horse; and he that sat upon him was called Faithful and True	Jesus is to come triumphantly	Glorious Appearing
324	Rev 19:14	And the armies which were in heaven followed him upon white horses	His saints to come with Him	Glorious Appearing
325	Rev 20:6	he that hath part in the first resurrection: on such the second death hath no power	Saints resurrected to die no more	Glorious Appearing
326	Rev 22:7	Behold, I come quickly	Jesus to come suddenly	Glorious Appearing

No.	Reference	Excerpt (KJV)	Description	Topic
327	Rev 22:12	I come quickly; and my reward is with me	Jesus to come suddenly with rewards	Glorious Appearing
328	Rev 22:20	Surely I come quickly. Amen	Jesus to come suddenly	Glorious Appearing
329	Rev 22:20	Even so, come, Lord Jesus	Jesus to come quickly	Glorious Appearing

Twenty Major Prophetic Events Yet To Be Fulfilled

1. The Church is raptured to the Father's house before Christ comes to set up His kingdom (John 14:1–3; 1 Cor. 15:51–58; 1 Thess. 4:13–18).

2. Gog and Magog will be destroyed on the mountains of Israel (Ezek. 38—39).

3. Antichrist sets up a one-world government (Rev. 6:2; 13:1–8).

4. Antichrist, "the prince that shall come," establishes a seven-year covenant of peace with Israel (Isa. 28:15; Dan. 9:24–27).

5. A global apostate church established (Rev. 17:1–15).

6. Two witnesses with supernatural powers like Moses and Elijah preach and prophesy in Jerusalem (Rev. 11:1–6).

7. The 144,000 Jewish witnesses lead a multitude "which no man could number." They will come from all nations, tribes, peoples, and tongues (Rev. 7:1–15).

8. Seven seal judgments of worldwide magnitude will include a world war that kills twenty-five percent of the population, an unprecedented martyrdom of believers, and a great earthquake (Rev. 6:1–17)

9. Seven trumpet judgments disrupt the earth, producing the death of one-third of the population of unbelievers (Rev. 8—9).

10. The two witnesses are killed, and their bodies are seen lying in the streets by the entire world. After three and one-half days they are resurrected and caught up to heaven (Rev. 11:7–13).

11. Antichrist desecrates the temple, setting up his image in the midst of it. He threatens death to all who refuse to worship him (Dan. 9:27b; Matt. 24:15; 2 Thess. 2:1–8).

12. Antichrist breaks his covenant with Israel three and one-half years into the Tribulation (Dan. 9:27).

13. The False Prophet arises, and the mark of a beast is required of the entire world in order to buy, sell, or work (Rev. 13:11–18).

14. Antichrist persecutes the Jews, killing two-thirds of them. The remaining Jews flee to Edom (Petra) where they are preserved (Zech. 13:8–9; Rev. 12:13–17).

15. Seven vial (bowl) judgments produce a "great tribulation, such as was not since the beginning of the world" (Matt. 24:21, cf. Rev. 16:1–21).

16. The Battle of Armageddon takes place (Rev. 16:12–16).

17. The destruction (political, commercial, and religious) of Babylon (Rev. 17—18).

18. The literal, physical second coming of Jesus Christ as promised in Acts 1:9–11 (see also Matt. 24:22–31; Rev. 19:11–21).

19. The Millennial Kingdom of Christ is established on earth (Rev. 20:1–7).

20. The New Heavens and the New Earth are created; the New Jerusalem descends from heaven (Rev. 21—22).

Master Index to Bible Prophecy

There are over 8300 verses in the Bible that contain predictive prophecy. The following index lists the most significant of these prophecies, totaling over 700 prophecies. The index is divided into five sections:

I.   Prophecies Fulfilled from the Beginning to the Exile of Judah
II. Prophecies Fulfilled from the Exile of Judah to the First Coming of Christ
III. Prophecies Fulfilled at the First Coming of Christ
IV. Prophecies Fulfilled during the Church Age
V.   Prophecies to Be Fulfilled after the Rapture of the Church

Within each of these five sections the named prophecies are listed in biblical order. Each entry includes the prophecy's biblical reference together with a brief description of the prophecy and a notation regarding its fulfillment.

I. PROPHECIES FULFILLED FROM THE BEGINNING TO THE EXILE OF JUDAH

Reference	Prophecy	Fulfillment
Gen. 2:17	Death to be normal lot of mankind	Gen. 3:19; 5:5
Gen. 6:7, 17	Flood to destroy the entire earth	Gen. 7:11–24
Gen. 6:18	God to establish His covenant with Noah	Gen. 9:9–17
Gen. 9:25, 27	Canaan to serve Shem	Josh. 6—12; 2 Chr. 2:17–18
Gen. 9:26	God to choose the Semites	Gen. 12:1–3
Gen. 12:1	God to show Abram a new land	Gen. 12:5–9
Gen. 12:2a; 13:15–16	Abram to become the father of a great nation	Deut. 26:5
Gen. 12:2b	God to bless Abram	Gen. 24:1
Gen. 12:2c	Abram's name to be made great	Gen. 23:6
Gen. 12:2d	Abram to be a blessing	Gen. 28:4
Gen. 15:13	Israel to be slaves in Egypt for four hundred years	Ex. 12:40–41

Reference	Prophecy	Fulfillment
Gen. 15:14a	Egypt to be judged	Ex. 7:1—15:21
Gen. 15:14b	Israel to despoil Egypt	Ex. 12:35–36
Gen. 15:15	Abram to die in peace at an old age	Gen. 25:7–8
Gen. 15:16	Israel to return to their land from Egypt	Josh. 3:14–17
Gen. 16:10	Hagar to have many descendants	Gen. 25:13–18; Ps. 83:6
Gen. 16:11	Hagar to bear a son	Gen. 16:15
Gen. 16:12	Ishmael to be "a wild man"	Gen. 21:20–21
Gen. 17:4–6	Abram to be the father of many nations	Gen. 21:1–3; 25:1–4; cf. Gal. 3:29
Gen. 17:16; 18:10	Sarah to bear a son	Gen. 21:1–3
Gen. 17:19, 21	God to establish His covenant with Isaac	Gen. 26:1–3, 24
Gen. 22:8	God to provide a sacrifice for Abraham	Gen. 22:13
Gen. 28:15	Jacob to return to his land	Gen. 33:18
Gen. 37:7–10	Joseph's family to bow down to him	Gen. 42:6; 47:12
Gen. 40:13	Pharaoh's butler to be restored to position	Gen. 40:21
Gen. 40:19	Pharaoh's baker to be executed	Gen. 40:22
Gen. 41:26–32	Egypt to have seven years of plenty, seven years of famine	Gen. 41:47–57
Gen. 49:3–27	Future of the twelve tribes in their land described	Pre-exilic period
Ex. 3:8a; 6:6	Israel to be delivered from Egyptian bondage	Ex. 12:41
Ex. 3:8b	Israel to return to their land from Egypt	Josh. 3:14–17
Ex. 3:12	Israel to worship God on Mt. Sinai	Ex. 19:2, 17
Ex. 4:12–16	Moses and Aaron to be empowered to speak	Ex. 11:3; 12:31
Ex. 7:5a	Egypt to recognize God as the Lord	Ex. 10:7; 12:31–36
Ex. 15:14–16	Canaanites to "melt away" before Israel	Josh. 2:9–11
Ex. 15:17	Israel to live securely around the temple	1 Kgs. 4 — 8
Ex. 16:6–8	Israel to see God's glory, quail, and manna	Ex. 16:10–15
Ex. 17:14–16	Amalek to perish	1 Sam. 15:2–9, 32–34; 1 Chr. 4:43

Reference	Prophecy	Fulfillment
Ex. 23:29–30	Israel to drive out Canaanites "by little and little"	Judg. 1:1–36; 2:23
Num. 11:18–23	Israel to eat meat	Num. 11:31–34
Num. 14:23, 32–35	Israel to wander in the wilderness for forty years	Num. 26:63–65; 32:13
Num. 14:24, 30; 32:12	Joshua and Caleb to enter the land	Josh. 14:6–15; 19:49–50
Num. 14:43	Israel to be defeated by Amalek and Canaan	Num. 14:45
Num. 21:33–34	Israel to defeat Og, king of Bashan	Num. 21:35
Num. 24:20	Amalek to perish	1 Sam. 15:2–9, 32–34; 1 Chr. 4:43
Num. 24:22	Assyria to deport the Kenite	2 Kgs. 15:29
Deut. 12:5	God to choose a place for His habitation	2 Chr. 6:6
Deut. 17:14	Israel to demand a king	1 Sam. 8:4–20
Deut. 31:16	Israel to forsake God	Judg. 2:11–13
Deut. 33:6–25	Future of the twelve tribes in their land described	Pre-exilic period
Josh. 1:6	Joshua to conquer and apportion the land	Josh. 11:23
Josh. 6:2–5	Jericho to fall to Israel	Josh. 6:20–21
Josh. 6:26	Sons of the rebuilder of Jericho to die	1 Kgs. 16:34
Josh. 8:1–2	Ai to fall to Israel	Josh. 8:19–29
Josh. 10:8	Israel to defeat the southern confederacy	Josh. 10:10–42
Josh. 10:12	Sun to stand still	Josh. 10:13
Josh. 11:6	Israel to defeat the northern confederacy	Josh. 11:7–14
Judg. 1:2	Judah to possess its land	Judg. 1:4–20
Judg. 2:3, 21	Canaanites to continue to oppress Israel	Judg. 2:23
Judg. 7:13–14	Gideon to defeat Midian	Judg. 7:21–23
Judg. 9:15, 20	Abimelech and Shechem to "devour" one another	Judg. 9:22–57
Judg. 13:3, 7	Manoah's wife to bear a son	Judg. 13:24
Judg. 13:5b	Samson to begin to deliver Israel from Philistines	Judg. 15:20
1 Sam. 2:31–34; 3:11–14	House of Eli to be punished	1 Sam. 4:11–21

Reference	Prophecy	Fulfillment
1 Sam. 2:32a	Tabernacle in Shiloh to be destroyed	Jer. 7:12
1 Sam. 2:35–36	God to raise up "a faithful priest"	1 Kgs. 2:27, 35
1 Sam. 9:16	Samuel to anoint Saul	1 Sam. 10:1
1 Sam. 10:2–8	Certain men to encounter Saul	1 Sam. 10:9
1 Sam. 12:16–17	Unexpected thunderstorm to occur	1 Sam. 12:18
1 Sam. 13:14; 15:23	Saul's kingdom to end	2 Sam. 3:1; 5:1–3
1 Sam. 17:37	David to defeat Goliath	1 Sam. 17:50
2 Sam. 3:18	David to defeat Philistines	2 Sam. 5:17–25
2 Sam. 7:12	David's son to succeed him as king	1 Kgs. 8:20a
2 Sam. 7:13a	David's son to build the temple	1 Kgs. 5—8
2 Sam. 7:14–15	David's sons to be chastened for their sins	All royal descendants chastened
2 Sam. 12:10–12	David's house to suffer violence and humiliation	2 Sam. 13—20
2 Sam. 12:14	David's son by Bathsheba to die	2 Sam. 12:18
1 Kgs. 3:12	Solomon to become the wisest of men	1 Kgs. 4:30–31
1 Kgs. 3:13	Solomon to become the richest king of his time	1 Kgs. 10:23
1 Kgs. 11:11–13, 32	Solomon's son to reign over only one tribe	1 Kgs. 12:20b
1 Kgs. 11:30–31	Jeroboam to reign over ten tribes	1 Kgs. 12:16–20a
1 Kgs. 13:2–3	Josiah to break down the altars of Jeroboam	2 Kgs. 23:15–20
1 Kgs. 14:10–11	Jeroboam's dynasty to end	1 Kgs. 15:27–29
1 Kgs. 14:12	Jeroboam's son to die	1 Kgs. 14:17
1 Kgs. 14:15–16	Israel to be deported to Assyria	2 Kgs. 17:5–7
1 Kgs. 16:3–4	Baasha's dynasty to end	1 Kgs. 16:11–13
1 Kgs. 17:1	Land to have no rain or dew for three years	1 Kgs. 18:1–2
1 Kgs. 17:14	Widow of Zeraphath to have sufficient food	1 Kgs. 17:15–16
1 Kgs. 18:1	Land to have rain	1 Kgs. 18:45
1 Kgs. 20:13–14	Ahab to defeat Syrians	1 Kgs. 20:20–21

Reference	Prophecy	Fulfillment
1 Kgs. 20:28	Ahab to defeat Syrians a second time	1 Kgs. 20:29–30
1 Kgs. 21:19	Ahab to be killed	1 Kgs. 22:37–38
1 Kgs. 21:21–22	Ahab's dynasty to end	2 Kgs. 10:11, 17
1 Kgs. 21:23	Jezebel to be eaten by dogs	2 Kgs. 9:30–37
2 Kgs. 1:4	Ahaziah to die from a fall	2 Kgs. 1:17
2 Kgs. 2:9–10	Elisha to receive a double portion of Elijah's spirit	2 Kgs. 2:12–15
2 Kgs. 3:17–19	Moab to be defeated	2 Kgs. 3:20–25
2 Kgs. 4:16	Shunammite woman to bear a son	2 Kgs. 4:17
2 Kgs. 7:1	Syrian siege to be lifted	2 Kgs. 7:6–7, 16–20
2 Kgs. 8:1	Israel to suffer a seven-year famine	2 Kgs. 8:2–3
2 Kgs. 8:13	Hazael to become king of Syria	2 Kgs. 8:15
2 Kgs. 10:30	Jehu's dynasty to end after four generations	2 Kgs. 15:8–12
2 Kgs. 13:19	Joash to smite but not destroy Syria	2 Kgs. 13:25
2 Kgs. 14:25	Jeroboam to restore the borders of Israel	2 Kgs. 14:25
2 Kgs. 19:29–31	Land to be productive again	Mid-7th century B.C.
2 Kgs. 19:32–34	Sennacherib to not enter Jerusalem	2 Kgs. 19:35–36
2 Kgs. 20:5–6	Hezekiah to live an additional fifteen years	2 Chr. 32:24
2 Kgs. 22:20	Josiah to die before the Babylonian captivity	2 Kgs. 23:29
2 Chr. 20:37	Jehoshaphat's ships to be wrecked	2 Chr. 20:37
2 Chr. 21:15	Jehoram to die of an intestinal disease	2 Chr. 21:18–19
2 Chr. 25:16	Amaziah to be defeated and killed	2 Chr. 25:23, 27
Isa. 7:7–9, 16	Judah to survive attack by Israel and Syria	2 Kgs. 16:5–9
Isa. 7:9b	Ahaz to "not be established"	2 Chr. 28:5–21
Isa. 7:17–25; 8:7–10	Assyria to nearly defeat Judah	2 Kgs. 18:13; 19:35–36
Isa. 10:12–19	King of Assyria to be punished by God	2 Kgs. 19:35–37
Isa. 17:4–8	Remnant from Israel to become faithful	2 Chr. 30:11; 34:9

Reference	Prophecy	Fulfillment
Isa. 39:6–7	Leaders of Judah to be taken away	2 Kgs. 24:14; 25:11–12
Jer. 2:16–19	Judah to fall to Egypt	2 Kgs. 23:29–35
Jer. 5:19; 7:15	Judah to go into exile	2 Kgs. 24:14; 25:11
Jer. 22:10–12	Shallum (Jehoahaz) to die in exile	2 Kgs. 23:33–34
Jer. 25:14–33	Many nations to be defeated	Late 7th—early 6th centuries B.C.
Jer. 28:15–16	Hananiah the prophet to die within the year	Jer. 28:17
Jer. 46:1–12	Egypt to be defeated at Carchemish	605 B.C.
Hos. 1:4a	Jehu's dynasty to end	2 Kgs. 15:8–12
Hos. 1:4b–6; 10:1–8	Israel to be destroyed by Assyria	2 Kgs. 17:5–23
Hos. 1:7; 8:14	Judah to be devastated but saved	2 Kgs. 18:13; 19:35–36
Joel 1:15	Judah to be invaded and devastated	2 Kgs. 18:13
Joel 2:19–26	Land of Judah to again be productive	Mid-7th century B.C.
Amos 1:3–5	Damascus to be defeated and exiled	2 Kgs. 16:9
Amos 3:11–12; 4:3; 6:7–8	Israel to be defeated and exiled	2 Kgs. 17:5–6
Amos 7:7–9	Jeroboam's dynasty to end	2 Kgs. 15:8–12
Mic. 1:3–7	Samaria to be destroyed	2 Kgs. 17:5–6
Mic. 1:9—2:4	Israel and Judah to be devastated	2 Kgs. 18:13
Nah. 1:12–14; 2:13	Nineveh to be destroyed	612 B.C.
Hab. 1:5–11	Chaldeans to devastate Judah	2 Kgs. 24–25
Zeph. 2:13–15	Nineveh to be destroyed	612 B.C.

II. PROPHECIES FULFILLED FROM THE EXILE OF JUDAH TO THE FIRST COMING OF CHRIST

Reference	Prophecy	Fulfillment
Lev. 26:33b–35	Land to "enjoy her sabbaths" during the exile	2 Chr. 36:21
Deut. 28:15–68	Israel comprehensively cursed and exiled for disobeying the Law	2 Kgs. 25:1–21
Deut. 28:64b	Some Jews to lapse into idolatry while in exile	Jer. 44:15; Ezek. 14:1–7

Reference	Prophecy	Fulfillment
Deut. 28:65–67	Jews to not have rest in exile	Descriptive of the Exile and Diaspora
Deut. 28:68	Israel to return to Egypt	Descriptive of the Exile and Diaspora
Deut. 29:22–28	Jewish people to go into exile	2 Kgs. 25:1–21
Esth. 6:13	Haman to fall before Mordecai does	Esth. 7:10
Isa. 2:6–21; 5:5–6; 6:11–12	Judah to be "wasted without inhabitant"	2 Kgs. 25:1–21
Isa. 6:13	God to preserve a faithful remnant of Israel	Preserved throughout the ages
Isa. 13:1–18	Babylon to fall to the Medes	539 B.C.
Isa. 14:28–31	Philistia to be "dissolved"	Gradual decline and destruction
Isa. 15:1—16:14	Moab to be virtually destroyed	Gradual decline and destruction
Isa. 19:1–17	Egypt to be weakened	Gradual decline
Isa. 43:5–7	Jews to return to their land after the exile	Ezra 1—2; 7—8
Isa. 45:1–2	Cyrus to "subdue nations"	Mid-sixth century B.C.
Jer. 4:27b; 31:7	God to preserve a faithful remnant of Israel	Preserved throughout the ages
Jer. 6:9	Judah to suffer multiple exiles to Babylon	Jer. 52:28–30
Jer. 7:13–14	Temple to be destroyed	2 Kgs. 25:9
Jer. 9:11; 32:28–29	Jerusalem and Judah to be destroyed	2 Kgs. 25:1–21
Jer. 21:7; 32:4–5	Zedekiah to be captured and exiled	2 Kgs. 25:4–7
Jer. 22:24–28	Coniah (Jehoiachin) to die in exile	2 Kgs. 25:27–30
Jer. 25:11; 29:10	Judah to serve Babylon for "seventy years"	2 Chr. 36:20–21; 605—536 B.C.
Jer. 25:12; 50:1–3a, 9–10	Babylon to be defeated	539 B.C.
Jer. 27:21–22a	Temple vessels to be taken to Babylon	2 Kgs. 25:14–15
Jer. 27:22b	Temple vessels to be returned to Jerusalem	Ezra 1:7–11
Jer. 32:37	Israel to be regathered into its land	Ezra 1—2; 7—8
Jer. 32:38–40	Israel to be spiritually regenerated	Neh. 9–10
Jer. 43:8–13; 46:13–26a	Nebuchadnezzar to defeat Egypt	568–567 B.C.
Jer. 44:30	Pharaoh Hophra to be killed by enemies	569 B.C.

Reference	Prophecy	Fulfillment
Jer. 46:26b	Egypt to recover from Babylonian invasion	Gradual recovery after 567 B.C.
Ezek. 5:12–17; 7:1–27	Judah to be decimated and exiled	2 Kgs. 25:1–21
Ezek. 6:8–10; 12:16	God to preserve a faithful remnant of Israel	Preserved throughout the ages
Ezek. 12:4–12	Zedekiah to try to escape Jerusalem	2 Kgs. 25:4–5
Ezek. 12:13; 17:18–20	Zedekiah to be captured and exiled	2 Kgs. 25:6–7
Ezek. 17:17	Egypt to be unsuccessful in aiding Judah	2 Kgs. 25:8–9; Jer. 37:5
Ezek. 22:15	Israel to be scattered among the nations	Descriptive of the exile and Diaspora
Ezek. 24:21	Temple to be profaned	2 Kgs. 25:9
Ezek. 25:1–7	Ammon to be overrun and cut off	Gradual decline and destruction
Ezek. 25:8–11	Moab to be overrun and cut off	Gradual decline and destruction
Ezek. 25:12–14; 35:1–15	Edom to become desolate	Gradual decline and destruction
Ezek. 25:15–17	Philistia to be destroyed	Gradual decline and destruction
Ezek. 26:1—28:19	Tyre to be destroyed	332 B.C. by Alexander the Great
Ezek. 29:1—32:32	Nebuchadnezzar to devastate Egypt	568–567 B.C.
Ezek. 33:27–29	Judah to become desolate during exile	2 Kgs. 25:11–12; Jer. 39:10
Ezek. 34:10	Israel's civil leaders to be removed	Israel under foreign control from 586 B.C.
Ezek. 36:5–7	Nations to be conquered by Babylon	Sixth century B.C.
Dan. 2:32a	A head of gold	Dan. 2:37–38 Babylonian Empire
Dan. 2:32b	Chest and arms of silver	Dan. 2:39a Medo-Persian Empire
Dan. 2:32c	Belly and thighs of bronze	Dan. 2:39b Greek Empire
Dan. 2:33	Legs of iron	Dan. 2:40–41 Roman Empire
Dan. 4:10–27	Nebuchadnezzar to suffer an animal-like madness	Dan. 4:28–33
Dan. 5:5–29	Babylon to be defeated	Dan. 5:30–31; Oct. 12, 539 B.C.
Dan. 7:4, 17	A beast like a lion	Babylonian Empire
Dan. 7:5, 17	A beast like a bear	Medo-Persian Empire
Dan. 7:6, 17	A beast like a leopard	Greek Empire

Reference	Prophecy	Fulfillment
Dan. 7:7a, 17	A "dreadful and terrible" beast	Roman Empire
Dan. 8:3–4	An overpowering ram with two horns	Dan. 8:20 Medo-Persian Empire
Dan. 8:5–8a	A male goat with a single horn	Dan. 8:21 Greek Empire of Alexander
Dan. 8:8b, 22	Four horns replace the single horn	Division of Alexander's Empire
Dan. 8:9–12, 23–25	A self-exultant little horn	Antiochus IV
Dan. 11:2	Four Persian kings to arise in succession	Cambyses, Bardiya, Darius I, Xerxes I
Dan. 11:3	A mighty king to arise	Alexander the Great
Dan. 11:4	Alexander's kingdom to be divided into four parts	Division of Alexander's Empire
Dan. 11:5a	King of the South to arise	Ptolemy I
Dan. 11:5b	A prince to eclipse the king of the South	Seleucus I
Dan. 11:6	South and North to form an alliance	Ptolemy II and Antiochus I
Dan. 11:7–8	South to defeat the North	Ptolemy III
Dan. 11:9	North to invade the South, but fail	Seleucus II
Dan. 11:10–13	North to successfully invade the South	Antiochus III
Dan. 11:14–17	North to conquer "the Glorious Land"	Antiochus III conquered Israel
Dan. 11:18–19	North to be defeated in the coastlands	Rome defeated Antiochus III
Dan. 11:20	Attempt to tax Israel to fail	Seleucus IV
Dan. 11:21–30a	A "vile person" to defeat the South	Antiochus IV
Dan. 11:30b–31	This "vile person" to desecrate the temple	Dec. 16, 167 B.C. by Antiochus IV
Dan. 11:32–35	Jews to fight against the "vile person"	Maccabean revolt beginning 166 B.C.
Amos 1:6–8	Philistines to perish	Gradual decline and destruction
Amos 1:9–10	Tyre to be defeated	332 B.C. by Alexander the Great
Amos 1:11–12	Edom to be defeated	Gradual decline and destruction
Amos 1:13–15	Ammon to be defeated	Gradual decline and destruction
Amos 2:1–3	Moab to be defeated	Gradual decline and destruction
Amos 2:4–5	Judah to be defeated	2 Kgs. 25:1–21

Reference	Prophecy	Fulfillment
Obad. 1:2, 4	Edom to be made small	Gradual decline
Obad. 1:5, 9–10	Edom to be "cut off forever"	Mal. 1:3
Mic. 3:9–12	Israel and Judah to be destroyed	2 Kgs. 25:1–21
Mic. 4:9–10a	Jews to mourn in exile	Descriptive of the Exile
Mic. 4:10b	Jews to return to their homeland	Ezra 1—2; 7—8
Mic. 7:8–10	Israel to wait in humiliation	Descriptive of the Exile and Diaspora
Hab. 2:6–13, 15–19	Chaldeans to be destroyed	539 B.C.
Zeph. 1:4–18	Judah to be destroyed	2 Kgs. 25:1–21
Zeph. 2:4–6	Philistia to be destroyed	Gradual decline and destruction
Zeph. 2:8–9a, 10	Moab and Ammon to be destroyed	Gradual decline and destruction
Zech. 1:16; 4:8–10; 8:9	Zerubbabel to rebuild the temple	Ezra 6:13–18
Zech. 1:18–21	Four world powers to be defeated	Assyria, Egypt, Babylon, Medo-Persia
Zech. 9:1–8	Army to destroy Syria, Tyre and Philistia, but spare Jerusalem	332 B.C. by Alexander the Great
Zech. 9:13–17	Jews to be delivered from Greece	Maccabean revolt against Antiochus IV

III. PROPHECIES FULFILLED AT THE FIRST COMING OF CHRIST

Reference	Prophecy	Fulfillment
Gen. 3:15b	The Messiah to be a man, from the seed of a woman	Luke 1:31–33
Gen. 3:15c	The Seed of Eve to be harmed	Matt. 27:27–50
Gen. 49:10a	The Messiah to descend from the line of Judah	Matt. 1:1–16
Deut. 18:15, 18–19	A Prophet like Moses to arise	John 3:34; Acts 3:20–23
1 Sam. 2:35–36	God to raise up a "faithful priest"	Heb. 2:17
2 Sam. 7:12a	The Messiah to come from the line of David	Matt. 1:1–16
2 Sam. 7:14a	The Messiah to be God's Son	Matt. 3:17; Luke 1:35
Ps. 2:1–3	People and kings to plot against the Messiah	Luke 23:1–25; Acts 4:25–28
Ps. 2:7	The Messiah to be God's begotten Son	Matt. 3:17; Luke 1:35; Acts 13:33

Reference	Prophecy	Fulfillment
Ps. 16:10	The Messiah to be raised from the dead	Acts 2:22–32; 13:35
Ps. 22:1–2	The Messiah to be forsaken and abandoned by God	Matt. 27:46
Ps. 22:6	The Messiah to be despised	Matt. 26:67; John 1:10–11
Ps. 22:7–8	The Messiah to be scorned and mocked	Matt. 27:27–31, 39–44; Luke 23:35
Ps. 22:9–10	The Messiah to trust in God from birth	Luke 2:40
Ps. 22:12–13, 16a, 20–21a	The Messiah's enemies to surround Him	Matt. 27:27–50
Ps. 22:14–15, 17	The Messiah to suffer greatly	Matt. 27:27–50; John 19:28; 1 Pet. 4:1a
Ps. 22:16b	The Messiah's hands and feet to be pierced	John 19:18; 20:25, 27
Ps. 22:18	The Messiah's garments to be divided by lot	Matt. 27:35
Ps. 34:20	None of the Messiah's bones to be broken	John 19:31–36
Ps. 35:11	The Messiah to be accused by false witnesses	Mark 14:57–58
Ps. 35:19	The Messiah to be hated without cause	John 15:24–25
Ps. 40:6–8	The Messiah to do God's will	John 6:38; Heb. 10:5–9
Ps. 41:9	The Messiah to be betrayed by a friend	Luke 22:47; John 13:18, 21–30
Ps. 68:18a	The Messiah to ascend to God's right hand	Mark 16:19; Acts 1:9; 2:34
Ps. 69:4a	The Messiah to be hated without cause	John 15:25
Ps. 69:7, 20	The Messiah to bear the reproach of others	Rom. 15:3
Ps. 69:8	The Messiah to be rejected by His own family	Mark 3:21
Ps. 69:9	The Messiah to be consumed by His zeal for God's house	John 2:13–17
Ps. 69:21	The Messiah to be given gall and vinegar	Matt. 27:34, 48
Ps. 69:25	The habitation of the enemies of the Messiah to become desolate	Matt. 23:38; Acts 1:16–20a
Ps. 78:2	The Messiah to speak in parables	Matt. 13:34–35
Ps. 89:26–27	The Messiah to be made the firstborn Son of God the Father	John 3:16, 35
Ps. 109:3	The Messiah to be hated without a cause	John 15:24–25
Ps. 109:4	The Messiah to pray for His enemies	Luke 23:34
Ps. 109:6–19	The enemy of the Messiah (Judas) to be destroyed	John 17:12; Acts 1:16, 20b

Reference	Prophecy	Fulfillment
Ps. 110:1a	The Messiah to be deity, Lord	Matt. 22:41–45
Ps. 110:1b	The Messiah to ascend to God's right hand	Mark 16:19; Acts 1:9; 2:34
Ps. 110:4	The Messiah to be a priest after the order of Melchizedek	Heb. 5:6, 10; 6:20
Ps. 118:22a	The Messiah to be rejected	Matt. 21:42a; John 1:11–12; 1 Pet. 2:7a
Ps. 118:25–26	The Messiah to come in the name of the Lord with blessings	Matt. 21:9; Luke 19:38
Isa. 7:14	A virgin to conceive and bear a son, Immanuel	Matt. 1:22–23; Luke 2:6–7
Isa. 8:14	The Messiah to be a stumbling stone for Israel	Luke 2:34; 1 Pet. 2:8
Isa. 9:1–2	The Messiah to bring light to Galilee	Matt. 4:12–17
Isa. 9:6a	The Messiah to be born as a child	Luke 2:6–7
Isa. 11:1	The Messiah to be a Branch from the root of Jesse	Matt. 2:23 Jesus from Nazareth, "branch-town"
Isa. 11:2	The Spirit of the Lord to rest on the Messiah	John 1:32
Isa. 40:3–5	A voice in the wilderness to announce the coming Messiah	Luke 3:3–6; John 1:23–27
Isa. 42:1–3	The Messiah to be anointed for unpretentious yet effective service	Matt. 12:15–21
Isa. 49:4	The Messiah initially to labor in vain	John 1:10–11
Isa. 49:7a	The Messiah to be abhorred and despised	Matt. 26:67; John 1:11
Isa. 50:5	The Messiah to be obedient	Matt. 26:39; John 14:31
Isa. 50:6	The Messiah to be struck and spit at	Matt. 26:67; 27:30
Isa. 52:14	The Messiah to be seen as physically undesirable	Mark 15:32
Isa. 52:15a	The Messiah to sprinkle (purify) many nations	John 1:29; 3:15–18; Heb. 12:24; 1 John 1:7
Isa. 53:1	The Messiah's work to be disbelieved	John 12:38; Rom. 10:16
Isa. 53:2a	The Messiah to grow up in insignificance	Luke 2:40, 52
Isa. 53:2b	The Messiah to be seen as physically undesirable	Mark 15:32
Isa. 53:3	The Messiah to be despised and rejected	Matt. 26:67; John 1:10–11
Isa. 53:4a	The Messiah to carry others' griefs (sicknesses) and sorrows	Matt. 8:16–17
Isa. 53:4b, 10a	The Messiah to be smitten by God	Matt. 26:42; 27:46

Reference	Prophecy	Fulfillment
Isa. 53:5–6, 12c	The Messiah to be killed for the sins of others	Rom. 4:25a; Heb. 9:28; 1 Pet. 2:24–25
Isa. 53:7	The Messiah to remain silent before His accusers	Matt. 27:11–50; Acts 8:32
Isa. 53:8	The Messiah to be killed	Matt. 27:50; Acts 8:33; 1 Cor. 15:3
Isa. 53:9a	The Messiah to be with the wicked and the rich in death	Matt. 27:38, 57–60; John 19:38–42
Isa. 53:9b	The Messiah to commit no sin	2 Cor. 5:21; 1 John 3:5
Isa. 53:10b	God to prolong the days of the Messiah	Luke 24:5–7; Acts 2:24
Isa. 53:11	The Messiah to justify many through His suffering	Rom. 15:18–19
Isa. 53:12b	The Messiah to be numbered with sinners	Matt. 27:38; Luke 22:37
Isa. 61:1–2a	The Messiah to be anointed for service	Luke 4:16–21
Jer. 31:15	Weeping to be heard over the children of Rachel	Matt. 2:16–18
Dan. 9:25	Sixty-nine "weeks" to pass until the coming of the Messiah	Fulfilled with Christ's Triumphal Entry
Dan. 9:26a	The Messiah to be killed	Matt. 27:50; Acts 8:33; 1 Cor. 15:3
Hos. 11:1	The Messiah to be called out of Egypt	Matt. 2:15
Mic. 5:1	The judge of Israel to be struck on the cheek	Mark 15:19
Mic. 5:2	The Messiah to be born in Bethlehem of Judah	Matt. 2:1–6; Luke 2:4–6; John 7:42
Zech. 9:9a	The Messiah to have salvation for others	John 12:47; Acts 4:12
Zech. 9:9b	The Messiah to arrive riding a donkey	Matt. 21:5, 7; John 12:12–16
Zech. 11:12	Zechariah enacted the "sale" of Jesus by the Jews	Matt. 26:15
Zech. 11:13	Zechariah enacted the purchase of the potter's field	Matt. 27:3–10
Zech. 12:10b	The Messiah to be pierced	John 19:37
Zech. 13:7	The Messiah's sheep to be scattered	Matt. 26:31, 56, 69–75; Mark 14:27, 50–52
Mal. 3:1a	God's messenger to prepare the way for the Messiah	Matt. 11:7–10
Mal. 3:1b	The Lord to suddenly come to His temple	Matt. 21:12–13
Mal. 4:5–6	Elijah to come and effect repentance	Matt. 11:2–15; 17:9–13; Luke 3:1–17
Matt. 1:21a	Mary to bear a son, Jesus	Matt. 1:25; Luke 2:6–7
Matt. 2:13	Herod to seek to kill Jesus	Matt. 2:16

Reference	Prophecy	Fulfillment
Matt. 26:32	Jesus to meet His disciples in Galilee after His Resurrection	Matt. 28:16–17; John 21:1–23
Mark 11:1–3	Jesus' disciples to acquire a colt for His use	Mark 11:4–6
Mark 14:3–8	Mary enacted the anointing of Jesus' body for burial	John 19:40–42
Mark 14:13–15	Jesus' disciples to be led to the room for His Last Supper	Mark 14:16
Mark 14:30	Peter to deny Jesus three times	Mark 14:66–72; Luke 22:54–62
Luke 1:13	Elizabeth to bear a son, John	Luke 1:36, 57
Luke 1:14b	Many to rejoice at the birth of John	John 5:35
Luke 1:15a	John to be great	Luke 7:28
Luke 1:15b	John to be a Nazarite	Luke 7:33
Luke 1:16–17	John to effect repentance among many	Matt. 17:9–13; Luke 3:1–17
Luke 1:20	Zechariah to be mute until the birth of John	Luke 1:63–64
Luke 1:31	Mary to bear a son, Jesus	Luke 2:6–7
Luke 1:32b	Jesus to be called the Son of the Highest	Mark 5:7; John 3:16, 35
Luke 1:48	All generations to call Mary blessed	Luke 11:27 and all future generations
Luke 2:26	Simeon to live to see the Messiah	Luke 2:27–32
Luke 5:4	Peter to catch a large number of fish	Luke 5:6
John 2:19–21	Jesus to be raised in three days	Acts 10:40
John 6:62	Jesus to ascend into heaven	Acts 1:9
John 11:23	Lazarus to be raised to life	John 11:43–44
John 13:21	One of Jesus' disciples to betray Him	John 18:2–5
John 21:6a	The disciples to catch a large number of fish a second time	John 21:6b, 8–11

IV. PROPHECIES FULFILLED DURING THE CHURCH AGE

Reference	Prophecy	Fulfillment
Gen. 12:3	All nations to be blessed through Abraham	Acts 1:8
2 Sam. 22:50	The Lord to be spoken of among the Gentiles	Rom. 15:9

Reference	Prophecy	Fulfillment
Ps. 18:49	The Lord to be spoken of among the Gentiles	Rom. 15:9
Ps. 22:22–25	The Messiah to call believers "brethren"	Heb. 2:11–12
Ps. 68:18b	The Messiah to receive (and redistribute) gifts to men	Eph. 4:8–12
Ps. 117:1	Gentiles to praise the Lord	Rom. 15:11
Isa. 8:18	God to bring people to Himself	Heb. 2:13b
Isa. 11:10	Gentiles to seek the Messiah	Rom. 15:12
Isa. 28:16	The Messiah to be a precious cornerstone in which people must believe	1 Pet. 2:4–6
Isa. 42:6b	The Messiah to be a light of salvation to Gentiles	Luke 2:32; Acts 13:47–48
Isa. 49:6b	The Messiah to be a light of salvation to Gentiles	Luke 2:32; Acts 13:47–48
Isa. 49:8	An acceptable day of salvation to come	2 Cor. 6:2
Isa. 52:7a	Messengers to bring good news	Rom. 10:15
Isa. 52:15b	Gentiles to hear of the Messiah	Rom. 15:21
Dan. 9:26b	Jerusalem and the temple to be destroyed	A.D. 70 by Titus
Amos 9:11–12	Gentiles to be saved	Acts 15:14–17
Matt. 16:18	The church to be built	Acts 2
Matt. 23:38	The temple to be destroyed	A.D. 70 by Titus
Mark 1:17	Peter to become a fisher of men	Acts 2:14–41
Mark 10:39	James and John to suffer as did Jesus	Acts 12:2; Rev. 1:9
Luke 12:11	The Jews to arrest Jesus' disciples	Acts 4:1–3; 7:58–60
Luke 12:12	The disciples to be given words for their own defense	Acts 4:8
Luke 18:8	Widespread apostasy to occur on earth	End of the Church Age
Luke 19:42–44	The temple to be destroyed	A.D. 70 by Titus
John 14:2	Jesus to prepare a place for His followers	Church Age
John 14:3	Jesus to return bodily for His followers	Rapture
Acts 1:8a	Jesus' disciples to receive power to be His witnesses	Acts 2:1–13; 3:15

Reference	Prophecy	Fulfillment
Acts 1:8b	Jesus' disciples to be witnesses in Jerusalem	Acts 2—7
Acts 1:8c	Jesus' disciples to be witnesses in all Judea	Acts 8:1, 4
Acts 1:8d	Jesus' disciples to be witnesses in Samaria	Acts 8:1, 5, 14
Acts 1:8e	Jesus' disciples to be witnesses to the ends of the earth	Phil. 4:22 and the missions movement
Acts 5:9	Sapphira to die	Acts 5:10
Acts 9:15a	Paul to be a witness to the Gentiles	Gal. 2:9
Acts 9:15b	Paul to be a witness to kings	Acts 26; Phil. 4:22
Acts 9:15c	Paul to be a witness to Israel	Acts 13:14–43; 21:40—22:21
Acts 11:28a	A great famine to occur	Acts 11:28b
Acts 18:10	Paul to preach without harm in Corinth	Acts 18:11
Acts 20:22–23	Paul to be arrested upon returning to Jerusalem	Acts 21:27—26:32
Acts 20:29–30	The church at Ephesus to be attacked by false teachers	Rev. 2:2
Acts 21:11	Paul to be arrested by Jews and turned over to Gentiles	Acts 21:27—26:32
Acts 23:3	Ananias to be struck by God	Assassinated in A.D. 66
Acts 23:11	Paul to testify of Jesus in Rome	Acts 28:17–31; 2 Tim. 4:17
Acts 26:17a	Paul to be delivered from the Jews	Acts 9:23–25; 25:11–12
Acts 26:17b	Paul to be delivered from the Gentiles	Acts 16:35–40; 20:1
Acts 27:22–26	All passengers to survive shipwreck	Acts 27:42–44
1 Cor. 15:51, 52b, 53	Persons alive to receive heavenly bodies	Rapture
1 Cor. 15:52a	The dead (in Christ) to be raised at the last trumpet	Rapture
1 Thess. 4:16a	Christ to return with trumpet sound and a shout	Rapture
1 Thess. 4:16b	The dead in Christ to be raised	Rapture
1 Thess. 4:17a	All believers to meet Jesus in the air	Rapture
1 Thess. 4:17b	All believers to be with the Lord	Rapture
1 Tim. 4:1–3	The church to undergo apostasy	End of the Church Age
2 Tim. 3:1–7; 4:3–4	The church to undergo apostasy	End of the Church Age

Reference	Prophecy	Fulfillment
2 Pet. 2:1–3	The church to undergo apostasy	End of the Church Age
2 Pet. 3:3–4	Mockers to deny Christ's return	End of the Church Age
1 John 3:2	Believers to see God and be like Him	Rapture and following
Rev. 2:10	The church at Smyrna to suffer persecution	First century under Nero and Domitian

V. PROPHECIES TO BE FULFILLED AFTER THE RAPTURE OF THE CHURCH

Reference	Prophecy	Fulfillment
Gen. 12:1–3	All nations to be blessed through Abraham	Millennium
Gen. 17:7	God to establish an everlasting covenant with Israel	Millennium and eternal state
Gen. 17:8	Israel to have everlasting possession of its land	Millennium
Gen. 49:8–12	Future of the 12 tribes in their land described	Millennium
Gen. 49:10b	The Messiah to rule all people	Millennium and eternal state
Num. 24:17–19	The Messiah to rule all people	Millennium and eternal state
Deut. 33:6–25	Future of the 12 tribes in their land described	Millennium
Deut. 30:5	Israel to return to its land	Second Coming of Christ
Deut. 30:6, 8	Israel to be spiritually regenerated	After the Second Coming of Christ
Deut. 30:9	Israel to be blessed abundantly	Millennium and eternal state
Deut. 32:43a	Gentiles to rejoice together with Jews	Millennium
2 Sam. 7:13a	David's son to build the temple	Millennium
2 Sam. 7:13, 16	The Messiah's kingdom to be established forever	Millennium and eternal state
Ps. 2:6	The Messiah to rule from Mt. Zion	Millennium
Ps. 2:8	The Messiah to rule over the nations	Millennium and eternal state
Ps. 2:9	The Messiah to judge the nations	Second Coming of Christ
Ps. 8:6	The Messiah to have dominion over all things	Millennium and eternal state
Ps. 45:6	The Messiah to reign forever	Millennium and eternal state
Ps. 72:1–5, 7, 12–14	The Messiah to reign in righteousness forever	Millennium and eternal state

Reference	Prophecy	Fulfillment
Ps. 72:8–11, 15, 17	The Messiah to rule over all people	Millennium and eternal state
Ps. 72:6, 16, 18–19	The Messiah's kingdom to be abundantly blessed	Millennium and eternal state
Isa. 1:26	Israel's leadership to be restored	Millennium
Isa. 2:2	The Jerusalem temple to be exalted among the nations	Millennium
Isa. 2:3	Gentiles to worship at the Jerusalem temple	Millennium
Isa. 2:4	All nations to live in peace in the Messiah's kingdom	Millennium
Isa. 4:3–4	Israel to be holy	Millennium and eternal state
Isa. 9:3	Israel to experience great joy	Millennium and eternal state
Isa. 9:4–5	Israel's enemies to be defeated	Battle of Armageddon
Isa. 9:6–7	The Messiah to reign in righteousness forever	Millennium and eternal state
Isa. 11:3–5	The Messiah to reign in righteousness forever	Millennium and eternal state
Isa. 11:6–9a	All animals and people to live in peaceful harmony on earth	Millennium
Isa. 11:9b	The earth to be full of the knowledge of the glory of the Lord	Millennium
Isa. 11:10	Gentiles to come to the Messiah	Millennium
Isa. 11:11–13, 16	Israel to be regathered into its land	After the Second Coming of Christ
Isa. 11:14–15	Israel's enemies to be defeated	Battle of Armageddon
Isa. 12:3–6	Israel to joyfully worship God	Millennium and eternal state
Isa. 13:19–22	Babylon to be utterly destroyed	Battle of Armageddon
Isa. 24:1–23	The earth to become desolate and its people mourn	Great Tribulation
Isa. 25:6	Israel to feast on the mountain of the Lord	Millennium and eternal state
Isa. 25:7	Veil covering the nations to be removed	Second Coming of Christ
Isa. 25:8	Death, pain and sorrow to be no more	Millennium and eternal state
Isa. 25:9	Conversion of Israel	Second Coming of Christ
Isa. 26:12	All nations to live in peace	Millennium and eternal state
Isa. 26:15	Israel to have expanded borders	Millennium
Isa. 26:19	Old Testament believers to be raised	Second Coming of Christ

Reference	Prophecy	Fulfillment
Isa. 26:20–21	God to judge the earth	Great Tribulation
Isa. 30:23–26	The land to have abundant water and sunlight	Millennium
Isa. 32:18	Israel to live in peace and security	Millennium and eternal state
Isa. 33:24	Sickness to be removed from Israel	Millennium and eternal state
Isa. 35:1–2, 6b–9	The land to be abundantly fertile	Millennium
Isa. 35:3, 5–6a	All physical ailments to be healed	Millennium and eternal state
Isa. 35:10	Israel to be regathered into its land	After the Second Coming of Christ
Isa. 41:17–20	Israel to know and understand God	Millennium and eternal state
Isa. 42:4	The Messiah to establish justice throughout the earth	Millennium
Isa. 45:23	All people to worship the Lord	Millennium and eternal state
Isa. 49:7b–13	The Messiah to reign over all forever	Millennium and eternal state
Isa. 49:18	Israel to be regathered into its land	After the Second Coming of Christ
Isa. 49:19–23	Israel to prosper in its land	Millennium
Isa. 54:1–17	Israel to be prosperous and cared for by God	Millennium and eternal state
Isa. 55:3	God to establish an everlasting covenant with Israel	Millennium and eternal state
Isa. 55:12	The land of Israel to experience peace and joy	Millennium
Isa. 55:13	The land to be abundantly fertile	Millennium
Isa. 56:6–8	Gentiles to worship at the Jerusalem temple	Millennium
Isa. 60:3–6, 8–14	Gentiles to pay homage to Israel	Millennium
Isa. 60:7	Gentiles to worship at the Jerusalem temple	Millennium
Isa. 63:1–6	The nations to be judged and destroyed	Second Coming of Christ
Isa. 64:1–2	The Messiah to return and defeat Israel's enemies	Second Coming of Christ
Isa. 65:8–9	A renewed and numerous Israel to inhabit its land	Millennium
Isa. 65:17–19	God to create a new heaven and a new earth	Eternal state
Isa. 65:20	Human longevity to be restored	Millennium
Isa. 65:21–23	Israel to work in productive and satisfying labor	Millennium

Reference	Prophecy	Fulfillment
Isa. 65:25	All animals and people to live in peaceful harmony	Millennium and eternal state
Isa. 66:12	Israel to experience peace like a river	Millennium and eternal state
Isa. 66:15–17	The unrighteous to be destroyed	Second Coming of Christ
Isa. 66:20–23	All nations to worship the Lord	Millennium and eternal state
Jer. 3:18a	Israel to be reunited as a nation	Second Coming of Christ
Jer. 3:18b	Israel to return to its land	Second Coming of Christ
Jer. 4:2	Gentiles to be blessed because of Israel	Millennium
Jer. 16:14–15	Israel to be regathered into its land	After the Second Coming of Christ
Jer. 23:5–6	The Messiah to reign in righteousness over Israel	Millennium
Jer. 25:30–38	Multitudes to be slain	Second Coming
Jer. 30:7	Israel (Jacob) to suffer great trouble, but be saved	Great Tribulation
Jer. 30:17a	Israel to be healed of wounds and sicknesses	Millennium and eternal state
Jer. 31:13–14	Israel to experience great joy and rejoicing	Millennium and eternal state
Jer. 31:31–34	God to establish a new covenant with Israel	Millennium and eternal state
Jer. 31:38–40	The city of Jerusalem to be rebuilt to its former limits	Millennium
Jer. 33:17–18	Sacrifices to be offered in the Jerusalem temple	Millennium
Jer. 33:20–26	God to establish an everlasting covenant with Israel	Millennium and eternal state
Ezek. 11:17	Israel to be regathered into its land	After the Second Coming of Christ
Ezek. 11:18–20	Israel to be spiritually regenerated	After the Second Coming of Christ
Ezek. 16:60–63	God to establish an everlasting covenant with Israel	Millennium and eternal state
Ezek. 20:37	Believing Israel to enter the millennial kingdom	Second Coming of Christ
Ezek. 20:38	Unbelieving Israel to be purged out	Second Coming of Christ
Ezek. 28:25–26	Israel to dwell in its land in security and peace	Millennium
Ezek. 34:11–16	Israel to be regathered into its land	After the Second Coming of Christ
Ezek. 34:25, 28	All animals and people to live in peaceful harmony	Millennium and eternal state
Ezek. 34:26–27	The land to be abundantly fertile	Millennium

Reference	Prophecy	Fulfillment
Ezek. 36:24	Israel to be regathered into its land	After the Second Coming of Christ
Ezek. 36:25—29a	Israel to be spiritually regenerated	After the Second Coming of Christ
Ezek. 36:29b, 30	The land to be abundantly fertile	Millennium
Ezek. 37:1—13, 21	Israel to be regathered into its land	After the Second Coming of Christ
Ezek. 37:14, 23	Israel to be spiritually regenerated	After the Second Coming of Christ
Ezek. 37:25	Israel to dwell securely forever	Millennium and eternal state
Ezek. 37:26	God to establish an eternal covenant with Israel	Millennium and eternal state
Ezek. 37:27—28	God to dwell with His people	Millennium and eternal state
Ezek. 38:1—16	A northern confederacy led by Gog of Magog to attack Israel	Just before the middle of the Tribulation
Ezek. 38:17—39:16	The northern confederacy to be defeated	Just before the middle of the Tribulation
Ezek. 39:22—29	Israel begins to turn toward God	Just before the middle of the Tribulation
Ezek. 40:5—43:27	The Temple to be rebuilt in Jerusalem	Millennium
Ezek. 43:1—5	The glory of the Lord to inhabit the temple	Millennium
Ezek. 44:1—45:8	The temple priesthood to be restored	Millennium
Ezek. 45:9—46:24	The sacrificial system to be reinstituted	Millennium
Ezek. 47:1—12	A river to flow eastward out of the temple in Jerusalem	Millennium
Ezek. 47:13—48:29	The land to be reapportioned among the 12 tribes of Israel	Millennium
Dan. 2:33	Feet of iron and clay, revived Roman Empire	Tribulation
Dan. 2:44a	God's kingdom to destroy all other kingdoms	Second Coming of Christ
Dan. 2:44b	God's kingdom to be established forever	Millennium and eternal state
Dan. 7:7b, 24a	A ten-nation confederacy to arise	Great Tribulation
Dan. 7:8, 24b	The Antichrist to arise	Great Tribulation
Dan. 7:13	The Son of Man to come with the clouds of heaven	Second Coming of Christ
Dan. 7:14	The Son of Man to reign forever	Millennium and eternal state
Dan. 7:18, 22, 27	Believing Israel to reign with the Son of Man	Millennium
Dan. 7:25a	The Antichrist to institute false religious and legal systems	Great Tribulation

Reference	Prophecy	Fulfillment
Dan. 7:25b	The Antichrist to persecute "the saints" for three and one half years	Great Tribulation
Dan. 7:26	The Antichrist to be destroyed	Second Coming of Christ
Dan. 9:26b	The Antichrist to rise from the people of the revived Roman Empire	Tribulation
Dan. 9:27a	The Antichrist to make, then break, a covenant with Israel	Tribulation
Dan. 9:27b	The Antichrist to institute false worship	Great Tribulation
Dan. 11:36–39	The Antichrist to exalt himself until the wrath is completed	Great Tribulation
Dan. 11:40	Kings of the South and North to attack Israel	Battle of Armageddon
Dan. 11:41–45	The Antichrist to invade Israel but be defeated	Battle of Armageddon
Dan. 12:1	Israel to experience great trouble, but be saved	Great Tribulation
Dan. 12:2–3	Resurrection of the Old Testament saints	Second Coming of Christ
Dan. 12:13	Resurrection of the Old Testament saints	Second Coming of Christ
Hos. 1:11	Israel to be reunited as a nation	Second Coming of Christ
Hos. 2:18	All animals to live in peaceful harmony	Millennium and eternal state
Hos. 14:5–7	Israel to be revived and bless others	Millennium
Joel 2:1–11	Land of Israel to be invaded and devastated	Tribulation
Joel 2:30–31	Cataclysmic, cosmic events to occur	Great Tribulation
Joel 2:32	All who call on the Lord to be saved	Great Tribulation
Joel 3:1	Israel to be regathered into its land	After the Second Coming of Christ
Joel 3:2–16	The nations to be judged and destroyed	Second Coming of Christ
Joel 3:18	The land to be abundantly fertile	Millennium
Joel 3:20	Judah and Jerusalem to abide forever	Millennium and eternal state
Amos 9:13	The land to be abundantly fertile	Millennium
Amos 9:14a	Israel to be regathered into its land	After the Second Coming of Christ
Amos 9:14b, 15	Israel to prosper in its land	Millennium
Obad. 1:17a	Israel to be holy on Mt. Zion	Millennium and eternal state

Reference	Prophecy	Fulfillment
Obad. 1:17b–21a	Israel to possess the land of its neighbors	Millennium
Obad. 1:21b	The kingdom to belong to the Lord	Millennium and eternal state
Mic. 12:a	Israel to be regathered into its land	After the Second Coming of Christ
Mic. 2:12b, 13	A strong leader to lead Israel	Millennium
Mic. 4:1	The Jerusalem temple to be exalted among the nations	Millennium
Mic. 4:2	Gentiles to worship at the Jerusalem temple	Millennium
Mic. 4:3–4	Nations to live in peace in the Messiah's kingdom	Millennium
Mic. 5:2b–4	The Messiah to be ruler in Israel	Millennium and eternal state
Mic. 5:5–6	The Messiah to defeat the enemies of Israel	Battle of Armageddon
Nah. 1:15b	Israel to worship in the Jerusalem temple	Millennium
Nah. 2:2a	Israel to be restored	Millennium
Hab. 2:14	The earth to be filled with the knowledge of the glory of the Lord	Millennium
Hab. 3:19	Israel to live securely	Millennium and eternal state
Zeph. 2:7	Israel to possess the land of its neighbors	Millennium
Zeph. 2:11a	God to defeat the powers of the earth	Battle of Armageddon
Zeph. 2:11b	All peoples to worship God	Millennium and eternal state
Zeph. 3:8	The nations to be judged and destroyed	Second Coming of Christ
Zeph. 3:9–13a	All peoples to be purified and worship God	Millennium and eternal state
Zeph. 3:13b–19	Israel to live securely in its land	Millennium
Zeph. 3:20	Israel to be regathered into its land	After the Second Coming of Christ
Hag. 2:7c, 9	The glory of the latter temple to exceed that of the former	Millennium
Hag. 2:21–22	The strength of all kingdoms to be destroyed	Battle of Armageddon
Zech. 1:17	Judah to expand and prosper	Millennium and eternal state
Zech. 2:1–5	God to inhabit and protect an expanding Jerusalem	Millennium and eternal state
Zech. 2:10–13	God to dwell in the midst of His people in the Holy Land	Millennium and eternal state
Zech. 3:9	Israel to be spiritually regenerated	After the Second Coming of Christ

Reference	Prophecy	Fulfillment
Zech. 6:11–13	The Messiah to rebuild the temple and reign as priest and king	Millennium
Zech. 6:15	The nations to help rebuild the temple	Millennium
Zech. 8:3	Jerusalem to be a city of truth and holiness	Millennium and eternal state
Zech. 8:7–8	Israel to be regathered to its land	After the Second Coming of Christ
Zech. 8:12	The land to be abundantly fertile	Millennium and eternal state
Zech. 8:19	Israel to experience great joy and celebration	Millennium and eternal state
Zech. 8:20–23	Gentiles to worship the Lord in Jerusalem	Millennium
Zech. 10:11	An army from the east to advance on Israel	Great Tribulation
Zech. 11:15–17a	The Antichrist to persecute Israel	Great Tribulation
Zech. 11:17b	The Antichrist to be destroyed	Second Coming of Christ
Zech. 12:10	Israel to look on the one whom they pierced and mourn	Second Coming of Christ
Zech. 13:8–9	Many from Israel to die, but some to be saved	Great Tribulation
Zech. 14:1–3	The nations to attack Jerusalem but be destroyed	Battle of Armageddon
Zech. 14:4	The Messiah to stand on the Mt. of Olives, which will then split in two	Second Coming of Christ
Zech. 14:6–7	Cataclysmic cosmic events to occur	Great Tribulation
Zech. 14:9	The Messiah to be king over all the earth	Millennium
Zech. 14:10–11	Jerusalem to be elevated among the hills of Judah	Millennium
Zech. 14:16–19	Gentiles to celebrate the Feast of Tabernacles in Jerusalem	Millennium
Zech. 14:20–21	Israel to be spiritually regenerated	After the Second Coming of Christ
Mal. 1:11	The Lord to be worshiped among all nations	Millennium
Mal. 3:4	Acceptable offerings to be offered to God	Millennium
Mal. 3:17	Israel to be God's special treasure	Millennium and eternal state
Mal. 4:1	The unrighteous to be burned	After the Millennium
Matt. 13:30, 47–50	Believers to be separated from unbelievers	Second Coming of Christ
Matt. 13:41–42	The unrighteous to be cast into fire	After the Millennium

Reference	Prophecy	Fulfillment
Matt. 24:5	False messiahs and prophets to arise	First half of Tribulation
Matt. 24:6–8	Wars and natural disasters to increase	First half of Tribulation
Matt. 24:9–10, 12	Individual Jews to be persecuted	Great Tribulation
Matt. 24:14	Believing Israel to proclaim the gospel	Great Tribulation
Matt. 24:15	The Antichrist to institute false worship	Great Tribulation
Matt. 24:16–20	Israel to flee the Antichrist's false worship	Great Tribulation
Matt. 24:21–22	Great tribulation to come	Great Tribulation
Matt. 24:27–30, 36–44	Christ to return suddenly and bodily to earth	Second Coming of Christ
Matt. 24:31	Israel to be regathered into its land	After the Second Coming of Christ
Matt. 24:35	Heaven and earth to pass away	After the Millennium
Matt. 25:1–30	Israel to be judged by Christ	After the Second Coming of Christ
Matt. 25:31–33	Living Gentiles to be judged by Christ	After the Second Coming of Christ
Matt. 25:34–40	Believing Gentiles to enter the millennial kingdom	After the Second Coming of Christ
Matt. 25:41–46	Unbelieving Gentiles to be cast into everlasting fire	Second Coming of Christ
Acts 1:11	Jesus to return bodily from heaven	Second Coming of Christ
Rom. 8:20–22	Creation to be renewed	Millennium and eternal state
Rom. 11:25–27	Israel to be spiritually regenerated	After the Second Coming of Christ
Rom. 14:10	Believers to stand before the judgment seat of Christ	Following the Rapture
1 Cor. 3:14	Believers to be rewarded for good works done	Following the Rapture
1 Cor. 3:15	Believers to lose reward for bad works done	Following the Rapture
1 Cor. 9:25	Believers to receive an imperishable crown	Following the Rapture
1 Cor. 13:12	Believers to know God intimately	Following their resurrection
1 Cor. 15:24, 28	Christ to submit His kingdom to God	After the Millennium
1 Cor. 15:25–26	Christ to defeat all enemies, including death	After the Millennium
2 Cor. 5:9–10	Believers to stand before the judgment seat of Christ	Following the Rapture
1 Thess. 4:16a	Christ to return with a shout and trumpet call	Rapture

Reference	Prophecy	Fulfillment
1 Thess. 4:16b	The church-age believers who have died to be raised	Rapture
1 Thess. 4:17	All believers to meet the Lord in the air	Rapture
1 Thess. 5:3	Sudden destruction to come, with no escape	Great Tribulation
2 Thess. 2:3–4a	The Antichrist to exalt himself	Great Tribulation
2 Thess. 2:4b	The Antichrist to institute false worship	Great Tribulation
2 Thess. 2:8	The Antichrist to be destroyed	Second Coming of Christ
2 Tim. 4:8	Believers to receive a crown of righteousness	Following the Rapture
James 1:12	Believers to receive a crown of life	Following the Rapture
1 Pet. 5:4	Believers to receive a crown of glory	Following the Rapture
2 Pet. 2:4	Fallen angels to be judged	After the Millennium
2 Pet. 3:7, 10, 12	The earth to be burned up with fire	After the Millennium
2 Pet. 3:13	God to create a new heaven and a new earth	After the Millennium
Jude 1:6	Fallen angels to be judged	After the Millennium
Rev. 1:7	Every eye to see Christ return to earth	Second Coming of Christ
Rev. 4:10–11	Believers to cast their crowns before God	Following the Rapture and for eternity
Rev. 5:9–14	All nations to worship the Lord	Millennium and eternal state
Rev. 6:1–2	First seal; Antichrist to conquer	First half of the Tribulation
Rev. 6:3–4	Second seal; world-wide warfare	First half of the Tribulation
Rev. 6:5–6	Third seal; famine and death	First half of the Tribulation
Rev. 6:7–8	Fourth seal; one fourth of world's population to die	First half of the Tribulation
Rev. 6:9–11	Fifth seal; many to be saved, then martyred	First half of the Tribulation
Rev. 6:12–16	Sixth seal; great earthquake and cosmic disruptions	First half of the Tribulation
Rev. 7:1–8	A believing remnant of Israel (144,000 persons) to be sealed and saved	Beginning of the Tribulation
Rev. 7:9–17	Martyred Gentiles to worship around God's throne	Great Tribulation and eternal state
Rev. 8:1–5	Seventh seal; silence in heaven	First half of the Tribulation

Reference	Prophecy	Fulfillment
Rev. 8:6–7	First trumpet; hail and fire with blood	Great Tribulation
Rev. 8:8–9	Second trumpet; sea to turn to blood	Great Tribulation
Rev. 8:10–11	Third trumpet; fresh water fouled	Great Tribulation
Rev. 8:12	Fourth trumpet; cosmic lights darkened	Great Tribulation
Rev. 9:1–12	Fifth trumpet; demons to afflict the earth for five months	Great Tribulation
Rev. 9:13–19	Sixth trumpet; a huge army from the east to invade and kill	Great Tribulation
Rev. 9:20–21	Those afflicted in the Tribulation to not repent	Great Tribulation
Rev. 11:1–6	Two miracle-working witnesses to testify of God's kingdom	Tribulation
Rev. 11:7–13	The two witnesses to be killed, raised and ascend to heaven	Middle of the Tribulation
Rev. 11:15–19	Seventh trumpet; additional judgments announced	Great Tribulation
Rev. 12:1–17	Israel to be persecuted by the Antichrist	Great Tribulation
Rev. 13:1–10	A ten-nation alliance led by the Antichrist to make a covenant with Israel	Tribulation
Rev. 13:11–15	The False Prophet to institute a false religious system	Great Tribulation
Rev. 13:16–18	The False Prophet to control the world's economy	Great Tribulation
Rev. 16:2	First bowl; Followers of the Antichrist to be inflicted by sores	Great Tribulation
Rev. 16:3	Second bowl; seas to turn to blood	Great Tribulation
Rev. 16:4–7	Third bowl; fresh water to turn to blood	Great Tribulation
Rev. 16:8–9	Fourth bowl; sun to scorch the earth	Great Tribulation
Rev. 16:10–11	Fifth bowl; the earth to become darkened	Great Tribulation
Rev. 16:12–16	Sixth bowl; invasion from the east to Armageddon	Battle of Armageddon
Rev. 16:17–21	Seventh bowl; earthquake and hail to destroy world's cities	Battle of Armageddon
Rev. 17:1–6	A wealthy and apostate church to arise	Tribulation
Rev. 17:9	The Antichrist to rule from Rome	Tribulation
Rev. 17:12–13	Ten kings to submit to the Antichrist	Tribulation
Rev. 17:14	Christ to defeat the Antichrist	Second Coming of Christ

Views of Christ's Future Kingdom

By Tim LaHaye

One future event which many Christians anticipate is the second coming of Jesus Christ to this earth where He will "rule and reign" in power and great glory. The Second Coming was taught by the apostles, believed by the early church, and has been acknowledged by all the creeds and councils of Christendom. However, there is little agreement concerning the timing of His coming.

Since the fourth century, an increasing number of people have interpreted Christ's kingdom as a spiritual experience that is already taking place. According to this view, known as amillennialism (see the chart below), the book of Revelation is a collection of spiritual experiences of the past. This position is still held today by many Catholics and some reformed Protestants.

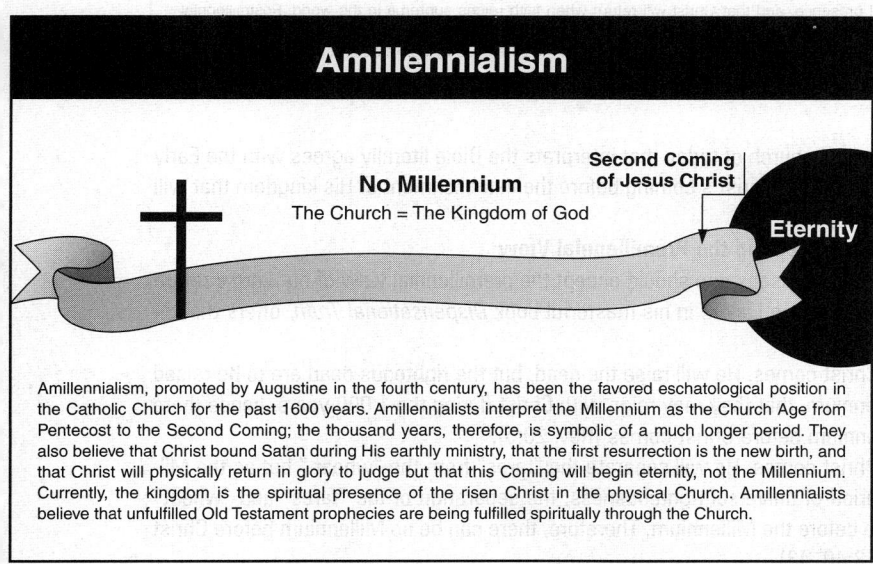

Amillennialism

No Millennium
The Church = The Kingdom of God

Second Coming of Jesus Christ

Eternity

Amillennialism, promoted by Augustine in the fourth century, has been the favored eschatological position in the Catholic Church for the past 1600 years. Amillennialists interpret the Millennium as the Church Age from Pentecost to the Second Coming; the thousand years, therefore, is symbolic of a much longer period. They also believe that Christ bound Satan during His earthly ministry, that the first resurrection is the new birth, and that Christ will physically return in glory to judge but that this Coming will begin eternity, not the Millennium. Currently, the kingdom is the spiritual presence of the risen Christ in the physical Church. Amillennialists believe that unfulfilled Old Testament prophecies are being fulfilled spiritually through the Church.

In the sixteenth century a new theory known as postmillennialism (see chart below), was developed, which states that the world will largely be converted to Christianity and work to prepare a "Christianized" world for Christ's return. Although this view was given some impetus during the great revival movements of John and Charles Wesley, Charles Finney, and others, and was popular before the turn of the twentieth century, it has been almost eliminated due to the catastrophic results of two world wars, the Great Depression, and an overwhelming rise in moral decay. Postmillennialism has experienced limited resurgence among a group of intellectuals known as theonomists. One theology professor I remember from years ago observed, "The postmillennialist does not have a post to lean on. Many of those who once held the postmillennial view have changed to the amillennial position."

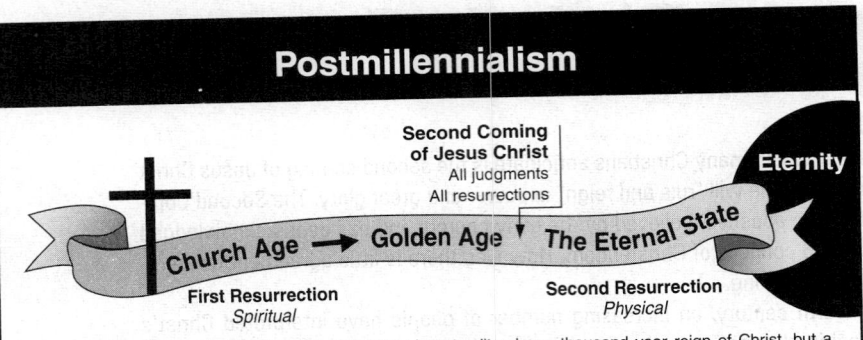

Postmillennialism

Second Coming
of Jesus Christ
All judgments
All resurrections

Eternity

Church Age → Golden Age ▼ The Eternal State

First Resurrection
Spiritual

Second Resurrection
Physical

Most postmillennialists believe that the Millennium is not a literal one thousand year reign of Christ, but a period of time that begins during the Church Age and extends to the Second Coming. The Millennium, according to postmillennialists, is that latter part of the Church Age characterized by revival—the successful permeation of the Gospel throughout the earth. According to postmillennialists, kingdom analogies like the mustard seed's growth into a tree (Matt. 13:31–32) and leaven leavening an entire lump (Matt. 13:33) are said to imply that Christ returns to a world that has responded to the gospel. Therefore, to postmillennialists, the Church's call to conquer unbelief, therefore, is accompanied by the assurance that it will succeed without Jesus' physical presence, and that Christ will return when faith reigns supreme in the world. Postmillennial writing diminished after World War II, but there is a renewed interest today that is often conjoined with preterism (the belief that most prophecies were fulfilled at the time of Jerusalem's destruction in 70 A.D.).

© AMG Publishers

The evangelical church of today that interprets the Bible literally agrees with the Early Church Fathers in seeing Christ's coming before the establishment of His kingdom that will last one thousand years.

Reasons for Accepting the Premillennial View

There are many reasons one should accept the premillennial view of our Lord's return to this earth. Dr. Clarence Larkin, in his masterful book *Dispensational Truth,* offers the following evidences:

1. When Christ comes, He will raise the dead, but the righteous dead are to be raised before the Millennium, that they may reign with Christ during the 1,000 years, hence there can be no Millennium before Christ comes (Rev. 20:5).

2. When Christ comes, He will separate the "tares" from the "wheat," but as the Millennium is a period of universal righteousness, the separation of the "tares" and "wheat" must take place before the Millennium. Therefore, there can be no Millennium before Christ comes (Matt. 13:40–43).

3. When Christ comes, Satan shall be bound, but as Satan is to be bound during the Millennium, there can be no Millennium until Christ comes (Rev. 20:1–3).

4. When Christ comes, Antichrist is to be destroyed, but as Antichrist is to come before the Millennium, there can be no Millennium until Christ comes (2 Thess. 2:8; Rev. 19:20).

5. When Christ comes, the Jews are to be restored to their own land, but as they are to be restored to their own land before the Millennium, there can be no Millennium before Christ comes (Ezek. 36:24–28; Rev. 1:7; Zech. 12:10).

6. When Christ comes, it will be unexpectedly, and we are commanded to watch lest He take us unawares. Now if He is not coming until after the Millennium, and the Millennium is not yet here, why are we commanded to watch for an event that is over one thousand years away?

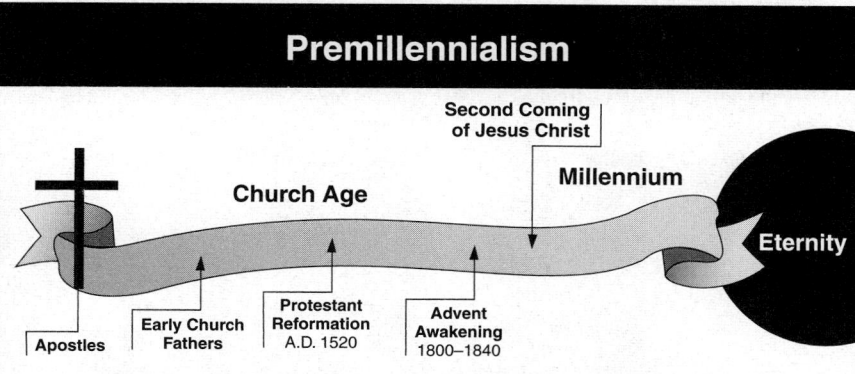

Premillennialism

Second Coming of Jesus Christ

Church Age

Millennium

Eternity

Apostles | Early Church Fathers | Protestant Reformation A.D. 1520 | Advent Awakening 1800–1840

Premillennialists believe that Christ will return at the end of the Church Age and establish a physical kingdom on earth for a literal thousand years. Most premillennialists believe that the return of Christ is preceded by the seventieth week (of years) of Daniel (Dan. 9:27) which includes a seven-year Tribulation. Premillennialists disagree as to whether the Church will be raptured before (pretribulationalism), in the middle of (mid-), or after (post-) the Tribulation. Dispensational premillennialists do not hold that Old Testament promises to Israel apply to the Church, but rather that the nation of Israel will one day be restored and converted to faith in Christ during the Tribulation.

© AMG Publishers

These are only some of the reasons why we should anticipate the coming of Christ before the Millennium. After Satan is bound, Christ will rule with His saints for one thousand years. A literal interpretation of Scripture will invariably point one to the premillennial return of Christ to the earth. Revelation 19 pictures Christ coming literally to the earth, slaying Antichrist, and casting him alive into the lake of fire.

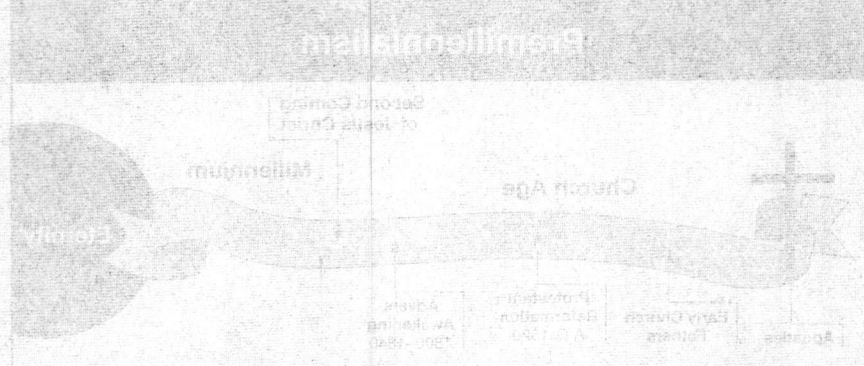

Reasons for a Pretribulation Rapture

By Tim LaHaye

Among the many who believe that the return of Christ will take place before the Millennium, there are at least five groups that teach different views of the timing of the Rapture. The prevailing view is the one we present in this study Bible, called the pretribulational Rapture. In short, this belief indicates that Christ will rapture His Church to His Father's house prior to the seven-year Tribulation. (See our study notes on 1 Thess. 4:13–18, 1 Cor. 15:50–58, John 14:1–3 and Rev. 4:1–3.) There are, however, many very fine Christians who long for the Savior's return, but see it differently. Some of these people are called midtribulationalists; some posttribulationalists; some believe in a partial rapture (that Christ will return in several stages); and some believe in the most recent view, the pre-wrath rapture, that places all of the apocalyptic wrath in the last quarter of the Tribulation and places Christ's return just before the judgment begins.

The editors and contributors of this prophecy study Bible believe two things about the Rapture: 1) The timing of the Rapture is not a cardinal doctrine over which Christians should argue and become divisive, and 2) we believe there are more than adequate reasons for believing that when all second-coming texts are considered carefully, there is more reason for believing that the Rapture will be pretribulational. Here are some of those reasons:

1. Both Jesus and the apostle Paul (under inspiration of the Holy Spirit) promised believers they would be saved from the "wrath to come" (Matt. 3:7; Luke 3:7; 1 Thess. 1:10), and kept from "the hour of trial that shall come upon the whole world, to test those who dwell on the earth" (Rev. 3:10). Such a "trial" has not yet occurred, and we have Jesus' unconditional promise to keep believers out of that trial (Rev. 3:10). Paul gave that same promise in Romans 5:9; 1 Thessalonians 1:10; and 1 Thessalonians 5:9. The Hebrew prophets referred to that future time of "wrath" or "trouble" for Israel over fifty times, and although Israel has suffered much throughout it's tragic history, those prophecies will not be fulfilled until the Tribulation. All the other interpretations have at least a portion of the Church experiencing all or some of the Tribulation period, which we believe, contradicts the above scriptures.

2. The pretribulational view is the most logical view of second-coming Scriptures when taken for their plain, literal meaning whenever possible.

Many of the details of the Second Coming must be pieced together from various passages of Scripture, no matter what view you take. The pretribulational position finds a logical place for every second-coming passage. Like a completed puzzle, all the pieces fit.

3. The pretribulational position clearly and logically untangles the contrasting details of Christ's second coming.

The Scriptures say that Jesus will come in the air secretly to rapture His Church, yet He will also come to the earth publicly. According to the pretribulational view, the coming of Christ in blessing for His Church and His return to the earth in judgment are two distinct events separated by time. The book of Revelation and 2 Thessalonians 2 clarify what takes place between those two events.

4. The pretribulational-rapture position is the only view that makes a clear distinction between Israel and the Church.

The lack of a proper understanding of the relationship between Israel and the Church in Bible prophecy is one of the major causes of confusion, as illustrated in the teachings of amillennialism and posttribulationalism. Pretribulationalism is the only position that clearly outlines the program of the Church (see the article entitled "Israel and the Church" by Arnold Fruchtenbaum).

5. Pretribulationalism is the only view that makes "that blessed hope" (Titus 2:13) truly a blessed hope.

Few Bible doctrines have brought more hope to grieving souls during the past two thousand years than the doctrine of this "blessed hope," the teaching that Christ will return for His Church, resurrect the dead, and transport living believers to be with Himself while the world endures the Tribulation.

The midtribulational position destroys that hope by forcing the Christian to anticipate the trauma of at least part of the Tribulation. Posttribulationalism further destroys such optimism in that it propels us through the entire Tribulation period. No proper reading of Bible prophecy gives credence to the idea that the Church will be on earth during that seven-year period. The judgment pictured in Revelation is clearly intended for Israel and the Gentile world.

Keep in mind that the teaching on the Rapture was given to comfort those who mourn! The threat of experiencing the Tribulation is hardly a doctrine of comfort to the saints.

6. Pretribulationalism allows sufficient time for important end-time events to occur.

The pretribulational view allows adequate time for Christians to be taken to the Father's house, experience the judgment seat of Christ ("every one of us shall give account of himself to God" [Rom. 14:12]), yet the view still provides time for the Marriage Supper events in heaven before He comes "with power and great glory" to the earth (Matt. 24:30; Luke 21:27). Other viewpoints offer various periods of time for these events to take place, but all are too brief to allow adequate time for important events listed in Revelation.

7. Only the pretribulational view preserves the motivating power of the imminent return of Christ that was such a challenge to the early Church.

In John 14:1–3, Acts 1:11, 1 Corinthians 15:51–52, Philippians 3:20, Colossians 3:4, and many other passages, the apostles taught that Christ could come at any moment. When the Church loses this form of anticipation, she tends to become carnal and spiritually dead.

8. Pretribulational Christians are looking for the coming of the Lord.

Other views have Christians awaiting the Tribulation, Antichrist, and great suffering. In fact, only the Rapture could occur as soon as today—the Glorious Appearing cannot occur for at least seven or more years.

9. Pretribulationalism emphasizes the magnitude of the Rapture.

Since at least four passages of Scripture describe the Rapture, it must be a significant event. The posttribulational view trivializes the Rapture, treating it as an express-elevator trip—zip up and right back down! The pretribulational view treats it as a dignified, blessed event commensurate with a heavenly Bridegroom who comes to take His Bride to His Father's house for their wedding.

10. Pretribulationalism most clearly fits the flow of the Book of Revelation.

Revelation 4:1–2 by itself never could unlock the mystery of the Rapture, but since that event is revealed in other passages (1 Thess. 4:13–18, 1 Cor. 15:50–58, John 14:1–3), one may appropriately identify John's call up to heaven as a rapture event that unfolds before the Tribulation period.

11. The pretribulational view explains why the Church is not mentioned from Revelation 4:3—18:24.

There must be a reason why the Church is so central in the first three chapters of Revelation but disappears until the Glorious Appearing. Pretribulationalists insist that the Church has already been raptured before the events of this passage of Revelation. Midtribulationalists and posttribulationalists would ask us to find the Church in the Tribulation even though she is not mentioned in Revelation 4—18.

12. Pretribulationalism preserves the credibility of Christ's word that Christians will be kept from the Tribulation.

The pretribulational view is the only one that resolves the contrasting difficulties of Revelation 3:10 and 7:14. For if Church members will be among the martyrs of 7:14 who are killed during the Tribulation, then the Lord will not have kept His Word in 3:10. Pretribulationalists explain that there will be no person from the Church on the earth during the Tribulation. The Church will be raptured before it begins—fulfilling the Lord's promise.

13. Pretribulationalism explains why there is no Bible instruction on preparation for the Tribulation.

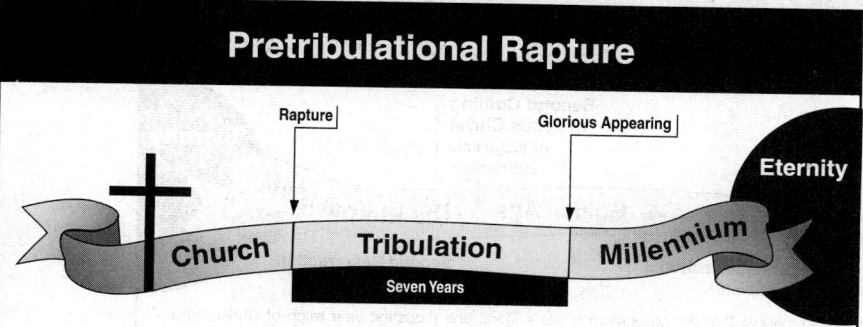

Pretribulational Rapture

Pretribulationialists hold to the future fulfillment of the seventieth week of Daniel in which the Antichrist makes a covenant with the nation of Israel, which is followed by the seven-year Tribulation period. Prior to this entire seven-year period, the Church will be resurrected, raptured with living saints, taken to the Father's house (John 14:1–3), and judged/rewarded for good works done in the body (2 Cor. 5:10) following their conversion to Christ. After the seven years, Christ will return in glory, destroy the Antichrist and the False Prophet, bind Satan, and cast him into the "bottomless pit" (Rev. 20:3). Christ will then set up a physical kingdom of His saints who will rule with Him over the world. This view is characterized by a belief in the literal thousand-year Millennium, a physical distinction between Israel and the Church, a differentiation between the Rapture and the Second Coming, and the imminence of Christ's return.

© AMG Publishers

Doesn't it seem strange that although the Bible advises Christians how to face ordinary, everyday troubles, it submits absolutely no instructions related to the worst time the world will ever face, a period filled with frightening events that have never come close to being fulfilled? Pretribulationalists have a simple answer. The Church will not be there!

The apostle Paul presented the Rapture as a treasured truth that was to bring comfort to believers. Just as Paul intended it to (1 Thess. 4:18), the pretribulational Rapture doctrine has comforted millions of Christians in their hours of grief.

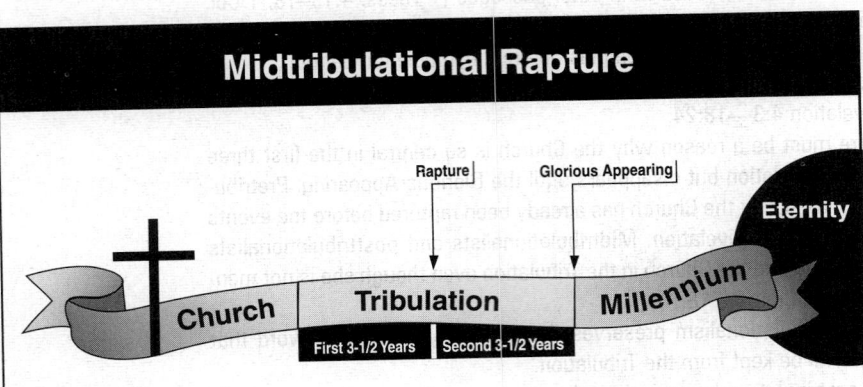

Midtribulational Rapture

Rapture | Glorious Appearing

Church | Tribulation | Millennium | Eternity

First 3-1/2 Years | Second 3-1/2 Years

The midtribulational view is similar to the pretribulational view, except that midtribulationalists believe that the Rapture (1 Cor. 15:52; 1 Thess. 4:16–17) takes place in the middle (Matt. 24:15, 21; Rev. 11:12) of the Tribulation. Proponents of this view state that the first half of the Tribulation is characterized by the persecuting, local wrath of the Antichrist on the Church while the second half begins the universal and inescapable wrath of God. The prophecy of the Two Witnesses (Rev. 11) is used by midtribulationalists as evidence for the Church's rapture prior to God's wrath.

© AMG Publishers

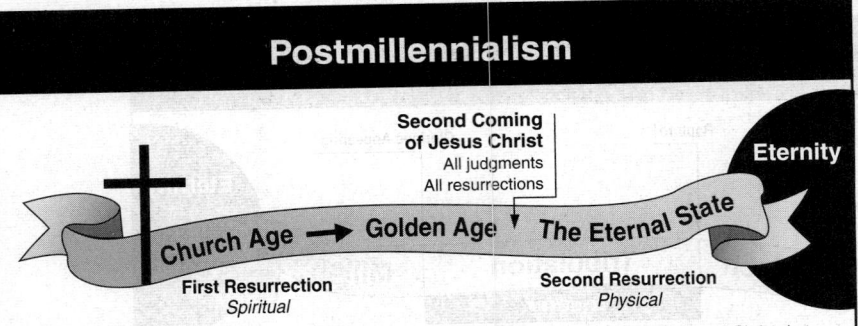

Postmillennialism

Second Coming
of Jesus Christ
All judgments
All resurrections

Church Age → Golden Age → The Eternal State | Eternity

First Resurrection
Spiritual

Second Resurrection
Physical

Most postmillennialists believe that the Millennium is not a literal one thousand year reign of Christ, but a period of time that begins during the Church Age and extends to the Second Coming. The Millennium, according to postmillennialists, is that latter part of the Church Age characterized by revival—the successful permeation of the Gospel throughout the earth. According to postmillennialists, kingdom analogies like the mustard seed's growth into a tree (Matt. 13:31–32) and leaven leavening an entire lump (Matt. 13:33) are said to imply that Christ returns to a world that has responded to the gospel. Therefore, to postmillennialists, the Church's call to conquer unbelief, therefore, is accompanied by the assurance that it will succeed without Jesus' physical presence, and that Christ will return when faith reigns supreme in the world. Postmillennial writing diminished after World War II, but there is a renewed interest today that is often conjoined with preterism (the belief that most prophecies were fulfilled at the time of Jerusalem's destruction in 70 A.D.).

© AMG Publishers

Preterism and the Date of Revelation

By Thomas Ice

Preterism (Latin for "past") teaches that most, if not all prophecy, has already been fulfilled, and that most apocalyptic prophecy relates to the destruction of Jerusalem in A.D. 70. Preterists teach that the book of Revelation is primarily a prophecy about the Roman war against the Jews in Israel, a war that began in A.D. 67 and ended with the destruction of the Temple in A.D. 70. In order for Revelation to be a prediction of the future (Rev. 1:1, 3, 11, 19; 22:6–10, 16, 18–20), and in order for it to be fulfilled by August A.D. 70, then the book had to have been written by A.D. 67 for the preterist interpretation to be even a remote possibility. For futurists (those who believe that the fulfillment of the events in Revelation has yet to occur, which is the view of the editors and contributors of this study Bible), the date when Revelation was written does not matter since these events are still future to our own time. If Revelation was written after A.D. 70, then the preterist interpretation is impossible.

Today, the overwhelming consensus of scholarship believes that Revelation was written well after A.D. 70. In fact, most have concluded that Revelation was written around A.D. 95, primarily because of a statement made by Irenaeus (A.D. 120–202), one of the early church fathers, around A.D. 180.

> "We will not, however, incur the risk of pronouncing positively as to the name of Antichrist; for if it were necessary that his name should be distinctly revealed in this present time, it would have been announced by him who beheld the apocalyptic vision. For that was seen not very long time since, but almost in our day, towards the end of Domitian's reign." (*Against Heresies*, v.xxx.3)

It is important to note that Irenaeus was from Asia Minor (modern Turkey). The Apostle John was from Ephesus, which is also in Asia Minor. Irenaeus was discipled in the faith by Polycarp, who was discipled by the Apostle John. Thus, there is a direct link between the one who wrote Revelation and Irenaeus. This link strongly supports the credibility of Irenaeus and his statement. No other tradition relating to the date of Revelation developed or gained a following in Asia Minor, the very area in which the Revelation was given. Later, other traditions developed in the territories of Christendom that suggested a different time for the writing of Revelation. However, these were areas where Revelation was not interpreted as literally as it was in Asia Minor. It appears logical that if the theory of an earlier date for Revelation were indeed genuine, then it should have had a witness to that fact in Asia Minor, and such a tradition would have begun earlier than the fifth and sixth centuries, when preterist teachings first surfaced.

Preterists contend that Irenaeus' statement is not clear and should be doubted, yet support for Irenaeus' statement is seen in some of the writings of the early enemies of his interpretation of Revelation. Clement of Alexandria, Origen, and Eusebius, to name just a few, supported Irenaeus' statement of a Domitian-era date.

Many preterists contend that there are two major evidences from the book of Revelation that provide proof for their assertion of an earlier date for the book. Their first argument states that since John mentions a temple in Jerusalem (Rev. 11:1–2), then such a building must have been standing at the time of writing. If it were still standing, then

Revelation was written before A.D. 70. Next, preterists contend that the seven kings of Revelation 17:1–16 refer to a succession of Roman kings in the first century. Preterists argue that the phrase "one is" in Revelation 17:10 is a reference to the Roman emperor Nero, and they also mention that the phrase "the other is not yet come" in that same verse is a reference to the Roman emperor Galba. Therefore, preterists maintain that when John wrote, Nero was still alive, and Galba's reign was looming in the near future.

In rebuttal to the preterists' temple argument, it must first be remembered that the book of Revelation is a vision John received about future things. John is clearly transported in some way to a future time in order to view the events as they will unfold. This is why the word "saw" is used 49 times in 46 different verses in Revelation because John witnessed future events. Whether the temple is standing in Jerusalem at the time that John sees the vision is irrelevant, since the existence of the temple would not have any bearing upon a vision. John is told by the angel accompanying him during the vision to "measure the temple" (Rev. 11:1), but what temple is he told to measure, the one in Jerusalem or the one in his vision? This must be a reference to the temple in John's vision. In fact, Ezekiel, during a similar vision of a temple (Ezek. 40—48) was told to measure that same temple. Preterists agree that when Ezekiel saw and was told to measure a temple, there was not one standing in Jerusalem. Thus, there is no compulsion whatsoever to conclude that just because a temple is referenced in Revelation 11 that it implies that there had to be a physical temple standing in Jerusalem at the same time.

The preterist argument regarding the seven kings of Revelation 17:1–16 is polluted by the same assumption that underlies their position regarding the temple. Preterists assume that the line of kings refers to a first century succession of Roman kings, and then they pronounce Nero as the one to which Revelation 17:10 refers. But preterists provide no proof to establish their assumption. In Revelation 17, John is obviously seeing, recording, and commenting on a vision of the future. Thus, the time frame that he references would be the time frame of his vision of the future. The references to the kings cannot be used as a proof that he was viewing a particular time frame, without having previously, by some other internal evidence, established the period of time that he views in the vision. Preterists have not previously established when the time frame of John's vision is to take place. Hence, their time frame is not a valid proof for a Neronian date for Revelation. In fact, we are finding that all of their evidence presupposes a preterist interpretation, which certainly has not been established, in order to make their points valid.

Regardless of the interpretation of Rev. 17:1–16, it cannot be used as a proof for when Revelation was written. A better interpretation of this passage would be to view the kings as providing a landscape of biblical history. The five which are fallen refer to the kingdoms of Egypt, Assyria, Babylon, Persia, and Greece. The sixth empire that was reigning at the time when John wrote was Rome. The seventh that is to come will be the future kingdom of the Antichrist, known in Revelation as the Beast. Such an understanding is consistent with the way in which kings are used throughout both Daniel and Revelation. The various kings refer to the heads of diverse empires, rather than the succession of kings within a single empire. According to Revelation 17:10, the future leader and his empire will have a short life . . . "when he cometh, he must continue a short space." The adjective "short" has the idea of brevity (Rev. 12:12). Here God says that He has decreed that the time of this final empire will be shorter than the previous six. This factor alone would eliminate the possibility of the seven kings being first-century Roman emperors.

All of the "proofs" offered by the preterists to support their claims presuppose that

their preterist interpretation of the events in Revelation is accurate. Therefore, they do not provide objective evidence upon which one could build such a view. Since a preterist interpretation of Revelation requires an early date of the final book of the Bible, preterists go to great lengths in their attempts to make their view appear viable. The Domitian-era date for the writing of Revelation is the overwhelmingly accepted view of scholarship in our day, and nothing in Revelation itself contradicts such a conclusion. It appears the major reason that preterists believe in an early date for Revelation is that their system of interpretation requires it.

Concordance

to the Old and New Testaments

This concordance is a compilation of **key words** found in Scripture. **Key words** are followed by portions of Scripture, along with their references, designed to give an example of how the word is used in its context. These words are abbreviated to their first letter in the Scripture portions (e.g., "wash" is **"w"** [in boldface]). Verbs that occur in different forms will appear under the root of that word (e.g., "worked" will be under "work").

A

ABADDON
whose name in the Hebrew
tongue is **A** . . . . Rev 9:11

ABHOR
I hate and **a** lying . . . . Ps 119:163

ABIDE
shall **a** under the shadow . . . . Ps 91:1

A with us . . . . Luke 24:29

Comforter, that he may **a** . . . . John 14:16

A in me . . . . John 15:4

a in my love . . . . John 15:10

now **a** faith, hope, charity . . . . 1 Cor 13:13

ABLE
a to separate us . . . . Rom 8:39

tempted above that ye are **a** . . . . 1 Cor 10:13

a ministers of the new
testament . . . . 2 Cor 3:6

a to comprehend with all
saints . . . . Eph 3:18

a to keep you from falling . . . . Jude 1:24

a to open the book . . . . Rev 5:3

ABODE (n)
make our **a** with him . . . . John 14:23

ABODE (v)
and it **a** upon him . . . . John 1:32

ABOLISH
a in his flesh the enmity . . . . Eph 2:15

Christ, who hath **a** death . . . . 2 Tim 1:10

ABOMINATION
a to the Lord . . . . Prov 3:32; 11:20

sacrifice of the wicked is **a** . . . . . Prov 15:8; 21:27

overspreading of **a** . . . . Dan 9:27

a that maketh desolate . . . . Dan 11:31; 12:11

the **a** of desolation . . . . . Matt 24:15; Mark 13:14

ABOUND
faithful man shall **a** . . . . Prov 28:20

that ye may **a** in hope . . . . Rom 15:13

always **a** in the work . . . . 1 Cor 15:58

sufferings of Christ **a** . . . . 2 Cor 1:5

ABRAHAM
Jesus Christ . . . the son of **A** . . . . Matt 1:1

shall sit down with **A** . . . in the
kingdom . . . . Matt 8:11

I am the God of **A** . . . . Matt 22:32

if **A** were justified by works . . . . Rom 4:2

A believed God, and it was
counted . . . righteousness . . . . Rom 4:3
(See also Gal 3:6; James 2:23.)

of faith, the same are the children
of **A** . . . . Gal 3:7

by faith **A** . . . obeyed; and he
went out . . . . Heb 11:8

by faith **A,** when he was tried,
offered up Isaac . . . . Heb 11:17

Was not **A** our father justified
by works? . . . . James 2:21

Even as Sara obeyed **A** . . . . 1 Pet 3:6

ABSENT
a in body . . . . 1 Cor 5:3

a from the Lord . . . . 2 Cor 5:6

ABSTAIN
a from pollutions of idols . . . . Acts 15:20

A from all appearance of evil . . . . . . 1 Thess 5:22

a from fleshly lusts. . . . . 1 Pet 2:11

ABUNDANCE
out of the **a** of the heart . . . . Matt 12:34

have of their **a** cast in unto the
    offerings. Luke 21:4

ACCESS
we have **a** by faith . . . . Rom 5:2

both have **a** by one Spirit. . . . . Eph 2:18

have boldness and **a** . . . . Eph 3:12

ACCORD
being of one **a** . . . . Phil 2:2

ACCOUNT (n)
give **a** thereof in the day. . . . . Matt 12:36

give an **a** of thy stewardship . . . . Luke 16:2

give **a** of himself to God . . . . Rom 14:12

as they that must give **a**. . . . . Heb 13:17

ACCOUNT (v)
a to him for righteousness . . . . Gal 3:6

ACCURSED
wish that myself were **a** . . . . Rom 9:3

let him be **a**. . . . . Gal 1:8, 9

ACCUSATION
receive not an **a**. . . . . 1 Tim 5:19

bring against him a railing **a** . . . . Jude 1:9

ACKNOWLEDGE
in all thy ways **a** him . . . . Prov 3:6

he that **a** the Son. . . . . 1 John 2:23

ACQUAINT
and **a** with grief. . . . . Isa 53:3

ADMONISH
a one another. . . . . Rom 15:14; Col 3:16

a him as a brother . . . . 2 Thess 3:15

ADOPTION
received the Spirit of **a** . . . . Rom 8:15

to whom pertaineth the **a**. . . . . Rom 9:4

receive the **a** of sons . . . . Gal 4:5

unto the **a** of children . . . . Eph 1:5

ADVANTAGE
Lest Satan should get an **a**. . . . . 2 Cor 2:11

ADVERSARY
give none occasion to the **a**. . . . . 1 Tim 5:14

your **a** the devil, as a roaring lion. . . . . . 1 Pet 5:8

ADVOCATE
we have an **a** with the Father . . . . 1 John 2:1

AFAR OFF
promise . . . to all that are **a** . . . . Acts 2:39

peace to you which were **a**. . . . . Eph 2:17

having seen them **a** . . . . Heb 11:13

AFFECTION
gave them up unto vile **a** . . . . Rom 1:26

without natural **a**. . . . . Rom 1:31;
    2 Tim 3:3

crucified the flesh with the **a** . . . . Gal 5:24

Set your **a** on things above . . . . Col 3:2

inordinate **a**. . . . . Col 3:5

AFFLICT
smitten of God, and **a** . . . . Isa 53:4

he was **a**, yet he opened not
    his mouth . . . . Isa 53:7

Is any among you **a**? . . . . James 5:13

AFFLICTION
seen the **a** of my people . . . . . . Ex 3:7; Acts 7:34

For our light **a** . . . . 2 Cor 4:17

and widows in their **a** . . . . James 1:27

AFRAID
What time I am **a** . . . . Ps 56:3

I will not be **a** what man can do. . . . . . . Ps 56:11

not be **a** for the terror. . . . . Ps 91:5

be not **a** . . . . Matt 14:27;
Mark 5:36; 6:50; John 6:20

AFRESH
the Son of God **a** . . . . Heb 6:6

AGE
in the **a** to come. . . . . Eph 2:7

hath been hid from **a** . . . . Col 1:26

AGONY
being in an **a** he prayed . . . . Luke 22:44

AGREE
two of you shall **a** . . . . Matt 18:19

AIR
prince of the power of the **a** . . . . Eph 2:2

to meet the Lord in the **a** . . . . 1 Thess 4:17

ALIEN
being **a** from the commonwealth
of Israel. . . . . Eph 2:12

ALIVE
son was dead, and is **a** . . . . Luke 15:24

angels, which said that he was **a** . . . . Luke 24:23

a unto God . . . . Rom 6:11

I am **a** for evermore . . . . Rev 1:18

ALMS
do not your **a** before men. . . . . Matt 6:1

ALONE
not live by bread **a** . . . . Matt 4:4; Luke 4:4

ALPHA
I am **A** and Omega . . . . . Rev 1:8, 11; 21:6; 22:13

ALTAR
bring thy gift to the **a**. . . . . Matt 5:23

found an **a** . . . TO
THE UNKNOWN GOD . . . . Acts 17:23

wait at the **a**. . . . . 1 Cor 9:13
(See also 1 Cor 10:18.)

We have an **a** . . . . Heb 13:10

I saw under the **a** the souls . . . . Rev 6:9

ALWAY
I am with you **a** . . . . Matt 28:20

Rejoice in the Lord **a** . . . . Phil 4:4

ALWAYS
the poor **a** with you . . . . Matt 26:11

me ye have not **a** . . . . Mark 14:7; John 12:8

AMBASSADOR
we are **a** for Christ. . . . . 2 Cor 5:20

AMEN
These things saith the **A** . . . . Rev 3:14

ANATHEMA
let him be **A** Maranatha . . . . 1 Cor 16:22

ANCHOR
we have as an **a** of the soul . . . . Heb 6:19

ANCIENT
the **A** of days . . . . Dan 7:9, 13, 22

ANGEL
a little lower than the **a** . . . . Ps 8:5; Heb 2:7

we shall judge **a**. . . . . 1 Cor 6:3

transformed into an **a** of light . . . . . 2 Cor 11:14

word spoken by **a**. . . . . Heb 2:2

entertained **a** unawares . . . . Heb 13:2

a desire to look into . . . . 1 Pet 1:12

the **a** that sinned . . . . 2 Pet 2:4

ANGER
a endureth but a moment . . . . Ps 30:5

grievous words stir up **a** . . . . Prov 15:1

a, wrath, malice . . . . Col 3:8

ANGRY
Doest thou well to be **a**?. . . . . Jon 4:4

are ye **a** at me? . . . . John 7:23

ANOINT
Touch not mine **a**. . . . . 1 Chr 16:22

thou **a** my head with oil . . . . Ps 23:5

the same **a** teacheth you . . . . 1 John 2:27

ANSWER (n)
A soft **a** turneth. . . . . Prov 15:1

be ready always to give an **a**. . . . . 1 Pet 3:15

ANSWER (v)
A not a fool. . . . . Prov 26:4

how ye ought to **a** every man . . . . Col 4:6

ANTICHRIST
heard that **a** shall come. . . . . 1 John 2:18

he is **a,** that denieth . . . . 1 John 2:22

this is that spirit of **a**. . . . . 1 John 4:3

APOLLYON
angel of the bottomless pit,
　　　his name . . . **A** . . . . Rev 9:11

APOSTLE
he gave some, **a**; some. . . . . Eph 4:11

APPEAR
then shall **a** the sign. . . . . Matt 24:30

we must all **a** before . . . . 2 Cor 5:10

who is our life, shall **a**. . . . . Col 3:4

doth not yet **a** what we
　　　shall be. . . . . 1 John 3:2

APPEARANCE
man looketh on the outward **a**. . . . . . 1 Sam 16:7

Abstain from all **a** of evil . . . . 1 Thess 5:22

APPREHEND
that I may **a**. . . . . Phil 3:12

APPROACH
as ye see the day **a** . . . . Heb 10:25

APPROVE
a man **a** of God . . . . Acts 2:22

a things that are excellent . . . . Phil 1:10

shew thyself **a** unto God . . . . 2 Tim 2:15

ARCHANGEL
the voice of the **a** . . . . 1 Thess 4:16

Michael the **a** . . . . Jude 1:9

ARISE
shall the Sun of righteousness **a** . . . . Mal 4:2

the day star **a** in your hearts . . . . 2 Pet 1:19

ARRAY
not **a** like one of these. . . . . Matt 6:29;
　　　　　　　　　　　　　　　　　　　　Luke 12:27

a in white robes . . . . Rev 7:13

ASHAMED
not **a** of the gospel . . . . Rom 1:16

hope maketh not **a** . . . . Rom 5:5

needeth not to be **a**. . . . . 2 Tim 2:15

not **a** to be called their God . . . . Heb 11:16

ASK
A, and it shall be given . . . . Matt 7:7;
　　　　　　　　　　　　　　　　　　　　Luke 11:9

whatsoever ye shall **a** in prayer . . . . . Matt 21:22

A of me whatsoever. . . . . Mark 6:22

a in my name . . . . John 14:13

let him **a** of God. . . . . James 1:5

ASLEEP
some are fallen **a** . . . . 1 Cor 15:6

them which are **a** . . . . 1 Thess 4:13, 15

ASS
and sitting upon an **a**. . . . . Matt 21:5

ASSURANCE
full **a** of hope . . . . Heb 6:11

ATTAIN
I might **a** . . . . Phil 3:11

AUTHOR
not the **a** of confusion . . . . 1 Cor 14:33

became the **a** of eternal salvation . . . . . . Heb 5:9

Jesus the **a** and finisher. . . . . Heb 12:2

AUTHORITY
as one having **a**. . . . . Matt 7:29

By what **a?**. . . . . Matt 21:23

power and **a** over all devils. . . . . Luke 9:1

and for all that are in **a**. . . . . 1 Tim 2:2

AVAILETH
righteous man **a** much. . . . . James 5:16

AVOID
a profane and vain babblings . . . . 1 Tim 6:20

AWAKE
A thou that sleepest. . . . . Eph 5:14

B

BABBLING
profane and vain **b**. . . . . . 1 Tim 6:20; 2 Tim 2:16

BABE
out of the mouth of **b** . . . . Ps 8:2; Matt 21:16

b in Christ . . . . 1 Cor 3:1

newborn **b** . . . . 1 Pet 2:2

BABYLON
the church that is at **B** . . . saluteth . . . 1 Pet 5:13

saying, **B** is fallen, is fallen. . . . . Rev 14:8

MYSTERY, **B** THE GREAT. . . . . Rev 17:5

Saying, **B** the great is fallen, is fallen. . . Rev 18:2

BAPTISM
b of John. . . . . Matt 21:25; Mark 11:30;
Luke 7:29; 20:4;
Acts 1:22; 18:25

b of repentance. . . . . Mark 1:4; Luke 3:3;
Acts 13:24; 19:4

buried with him by **b** . . . . Rom 6:4

One Lord, one faith, one **b**. . . . . Eph 4:5

BAPTIZE
b you with the Holy Ghost . . . . Matt 3:11;
Mark 1:8; Luke 3:16

I have need to be **b**. . . . . Matt 3:14

Jesus, when he was **b,** went up . . . . . . Matt 3:16

He that believeth and is **b** . . . . Mark 16:16

that came forth to be **b**. . . . . Luke 3:7

publicans to be **b** . . . . Luke 3:12

Jesus also being **b,** and praying . . . . . Luke 3:21

being not **b** of him . . . . Luke 7:30

he that sent me to **b**. . . . . John 1:33

tarried with them, and **b** . . . . John 3:22

Jesus made and **b** more disciples . . . . . John 4:1

Jesus himself **b** not . . . . John 4:2

Repent, and be **b** . . . . Acts 2:38

gladly received his word were **b** . . . . . Acts 2:41

b, both men and women. . . . . Acts 8:12

b in the name of the Lord Jesus . . . . . Acts 8:16

what doth hinder me to be **b?**. . . . . . . Acts 8:36

arose, and was **b** . . . . Acts 9:18

that these should not be **b**. . . . . Acts 10:47

b, and her household. . . . . Acts 16:15

believed, and were **b** . . . . Acts 18:8

be **b,** and wash away thy sins . . . . . . Acts 22:16

were **b** into Jesus . . . . Rom 6:3

b in the name of Paul . . . . 1 Cor 1:13

were all **b** unto Moses . . . . 1 Cor 10:2

all **b** into one body. . . . . 1 Cor 12:13

b for the dead . . . . 1 Cor 15:29

BARE (v)
b you on eagles' wings. . . . . Ex 19:4

his own self **b** our sins . . . . 1 Pet 2:24

BASE
b things of the world. . . . . 1 Cor 1:28

BASKET
twelve **b**. . . . . Matt 14:20; Mark 6:43;
Luke 9:17; John 6:13

seven **b**. . . . . Matt 15:37; Mark 8:8

how many **b?**. . . . . Matt 16:9; Mark 8:19

BATTLE
the **b** is the LORD'S . . . . 1 Sam 17:47

when kings go forth to **b** . . . . 2 Sam 11:1

BEAM
cast out the **b** . . . . Matt 7:5

BEAR (v)
b his cross . . . . Matt 27:32; Mark 15:21

b the infirmities of the weak . . . . Rom 15:1

b all things. 1 Cor 13:7

b his own burden . . . . Gal 6:5

b in my body. . . . . Gal 6:17

BEARING
b his cross. John 19:17

b about in the body . . . . 2 Cor 4:10

b his reproach . . . . Heb 13:13

BEASTS
four **b** . . . . Rev 4:6; 5:6; 6:1; 7:11;
14:3; 15:7; 19:4

BEAT
b with many stripes . . . . Luke 12:47

as one that **b** the air. . . . . 1 Cor 9:26

BEAUTIFUL
B for situation. . . . . Ps 48:2

How **b** upon the mountains are
the feet . . . . Isa 52:7
(See also Rom 10:15.)

BEGOTTEN
this day have I **b** thee . . . . . . Ps 2:7; Acts 13:33;
. . . . Heb 1:5

that he gave his only **b** son . . . . John 3:16

BEGUN
hath **b** a good work . . . . Phil 1:6

BEHAVE
I will **b** myself wisely . . . . Ps 101:2

BEHOLD
their angels do always **b** . . . . Matt 18:10

BELIEVE
I **b** Satan as lightning . . . . Luke 10:18

b as in a glass . . . . 2 Cor 3:18

B, what manner of love. . . . . 1 John 3:1

BELIEVE
come down from the cross,
and we will **b**. . . . . Matt 27:42

If thou canst **b**, all things are
possible. . . . . Mark 9:23

slow of heart to **b** . . . . Luke 24:25

all men through him might **b** . . . . John 1:7

seen me, and **b** not. . . . . John 6:36

b the works. John 10:38

b in me shall never die . . . . John 11:26

have not seen, and yet have **b** . . . . . . John 20:29

all that **b** are justified . . . . Acts 13:39

father of all them that **b** . . . . Rom 4:11

against hope **b** in hope . . . . Rom 4:18

how shall they **b**? . . . . Rom 10:14

we also **b,** and therefore speak . . . . . 2 Cor 4:13

must **b** that he is . . . . Heb 11:6

devils also **b,** and tremble. . . . . James 2:19

BELLY
upon thy **b** shalt thou go . . . . Gen 3:14

out of his **b** shall flow . . . . John 7:38

whose God is their **b** . . . . Phil 3:19

BELOVED
giveth his **b** sleep . . . . Ps 127:2

b Son . . . . Matt 3:17; 17:5;
. . . . Mark 1:11; 9:7;
. . . . Luke 3:22; 9:35; 2 Pet 1:17

compassed the . . . **b** city . . . . Rev 20:9

BESET
sin which doth so easily **b** us. . . . . Heb 12:1

BEST
covet earnestly the **b** gifts . . . . 1 Cor 12:31

BETRAY
opportunity to **b** . . . . Matt 26:16

brother shall **b** the brother . . . . Mark 13:12

night in which he was **b** . . . . 1 Cor 11:23

BETTER
to obey is **b** than sacrifice. . . . . 1 Sam 15:22

Two are **b** than one . . . . Eccl 4:9

each esteem other **b** than . . . . Phil 2:3

much **b** than the angels. . . . . Heb 1:4

desire a **b** country . . . . Heb 11:16

BEWARE
b of the leaven . . . . Matt 16:6; Mark 8:15

B of the scribes. . . . . Mark 12:38; Luke 20:46

b of covetousness . . . . Luke 12:15

b of dogs, **b** of evil workers . . . . Phil 3:2

BEWITCHED
who hath **b** you . . . . Gal 3:1

BIND
B them continually upon
    thine heart . . . . Prov 6:21

b up the brokenhearted . . . . Isa 61:1

b the strong man . . . . Matt 12:29; Mark 3:27

b on earth . . . . Matt 16:19; 18:18

BIRTHRIGHT
Sell me this day thy **b** . . . . Gen 25:31

he took away my **b**. . . . . Gen 27:36

morsel of meat sold his **b**. . . . . Heb 12:16

BISHOP
If a man desire the office of a **b** . . . . . . 1 Tim 3:1

b must be blameless. . . . . Titus 1:7

BITTERNESS
all **b** . . . be put away . . . . Eph 4:31

lest any root of **b** springing up. . . . . . . Heb 12:15

BLAME (n)
be holy and without **b** . . . . Eph 1:4

BLASPHEME
b against the Holy Ghost. . . . . Mark 3:29

BLEMISH
holy and without **b** . . . . Eph 5:27

a lamb without **b** . . . . 1 Pet 1:19

BLESS
b them that curse . . . . Matt 5:44; Luke 6:28

BLESSED
more **b** to give than to receive . . . . . . Acts 20:35

Looking for that **b** hope . . . . Titus 2:13

B are the dead which die in the Lord. . Rev 14:13

BLIND (n)
the **b** lead the **b**. . . . . Matt 15:14; Luke 6:39

BLOOD
precious shall their **b** be in his sight. . . . Ps 72:14

turned into darkness, and the moon
    into **b** . . . . Joel 2:31
    (See also Acts 2:20.)

flesh and **b** hath not revealed. . . . . . . Matt 16:17

His **b** be on us, and on our
    children . . . . Matt 27:25

b of the new testament . . . . Mark 14:24

new testament in my **b** . . . . Luke 22:20;
                                  1 Cor 11:25

great drops of **b** falling . . . . Luke 22:44

born, not of **b** . . . . John 1:13

drinketh my **b**. . . . . John 6:54, 56

purchased with his own **b** . . . . Acts 20:28

through faith in his **b** . . . . Rom 3:25

justified by his **b** . . . . Rom 5:9

guilty of the body and **b**. . . . . 1 Cor 11:27

flesh and **b** cannot inherit . . . . 1 Cor 15:50

redemption through his **b**. . . . . Eph 1:7; Col 1:14

without shedding of **b** . . . . Heb 9:22

b of the covenant. . . . . Heb 10:29

precious **b** of Christ . . . . 1 Pet 1:19

moon became as **b** . . . . Rev 6:12

white in the **b** of the Lamb. . . . . Rev 7:14
    (See also Rev 12:11.)

BLOT

that your sins may be **b** out. . . . . Acts 3:19

BOAST (v)

that I may **b** myself a little . . . . 2 Cor 11:16

lest any man should **b** . . . . Eph 2:9

BODILY

fulness of the Godhead **b** . . . . Col 2:9

b exercise profiteth little . . . . 1 Tim 4:8

BODY

b should be cast into hell . . . . Matt 5:29

b shall be full of light . . . . Matt 6:22

the temple of his **b** . . . . John 2:21

b of sin might be destroyed . . . . Rom 6:6

b of this death. . . . . Rom 7:24

your **b** a living sacrifice. . . . . Rom 12:1

many members in one **b** . . . . Rom 12:4

though I give my **b** to be burned . . . . . 1 Cor 13:3

absent from the **b** . . . . 2 Cor 5:8

whether in the **b** . . . . 2 Cor 12:2

I bear in my **b** the marks . . . . Gal 6:17

like unto his glorious **b** . . . . Phil 3:21

in his own **b** on the tree. . . . . 1 Pet 2:24

BOLDLY

Let us therefore come **b** unto
  the throne. Heb 4:16

BOLDNESS

we have **b** and access. . . . . Eph 3:12

BOOK

b of life . . . . Phil 4:3; Rev 3:5;
  13:8; 17:8; 20:12; 21:27

if any man shall take away from
  the words of the **b**. . . . . Rev 22:19

BORN

b of a woman . . . . Job 14:1; 15:14; 25:4
  (See also Matt 11:11.)

unto us a child is **b** . . . . Isa 9:6

b of God . . . . 1 John 4:7; 5:1, 4, 18

b again . . . . John 3:3; 1 Pet 1:23

b of the Spirit . . . . John 3:6, 8

as of one **b** out of due time . . . . 1 Cor 15:8

BOTTLE

new wine into old **b** . . . . Matt 9:17;
  Mark 2:22; Luke 5:37

BOUGHT

ye are **b** with a price . . . . 1 Cor 6:20; 7:23

BOWELS

straitened in your own **b** . . . . 2 Cor 6:12

b of mercies. Col 3:12

b of compassion. . . . . 1 John 3:17

BREAD

not live by **b** . . . . . . Deut 8:3; Matt 4:4; Luke 4:4

Cast thy **b** upon the waters . . . . Eccl 11:1

money for that which is not **b** . . . . Isa 55:2

stones be made **b** . . . . Matt 4:3

our daily **b** . . . . Matt 6:11

breaking of **b**. . . . . Acts 2:42
  (See also Acts 20:7; 27:35.)

BREATHE

he **b** on them, and saith. . . . . John 20:22

BRIDE

as a **b** adorneth herself . . . . Isa 61:10

a **b** her attire . . . . Jer 2:32

b adorned for her husband. . . . . Rev 21:2

BRIDLE

b not his tongue. . . . . James 1:26

able also to **b** the whole body. . . . . . . James 3:2

BROKEN

scripture cannot be **b** . . . . John 10:35

b down the middle wall. . . . . Eph 2:14

BROOK

panteth after the water **b** . . . . Ps 42:1

C

BROTHER
b offended is harder to be won . . . . . . Prov 18:19

closer than a **b**. . . . . Prov 18:24

b shall deliver up the **b**. . . . . Matt 10:21

BROTHERLY
b love . . . . Rom 12:10; 1 Thess 4:9; Heb 13:1

BRUISE (v)
b reed shall he not break . . . Isa 42:3; Matt 12:20

b for our iniquities. . . . . Isa 53:5

BUFFET
messenger of Satan to **b** me . . . . 2 Cor 12:7

BUILD
b his house upon a rock . . . . Matt 7:24
 (See also Luke 6:48.)

lest I should **b** upon another
 man's foundation. . . . . Rom 15:20

BUILDER
b rejected . . . . Mark 12:10; Luke 20:17
 (See also Acts 4:11; 1 Pet 2:7.)

whose **b** and maker is God. . . . . Heb 11:10

BURDEN
Cast thy **b** upon the Lord . . . . Ps 55:22

my **b** is light . . . . Matt 11:30

bear his own **b** . . . . Gal 6:5

BURN
Did not our heart **b**? . . . . Luke 24:32

give my body to be **b** . . . . 1 Cor 13:3

into a lake of fire **b** . . . . Rev 19:20

BURY
let the dead **b** their dead . . . Matt 8:22; Luke 9:60

b with him by baptism . . . . Rom 6:4

he was **b,** and that he rose again . . . . . 1 Cor 15:4

BUSINESS
about my Father's **b** . . . . Luke 2:49

CALLING
prize of the high **c** . . . . Phil 3:14

partakers of the heavenly **c** . . . . Heb 3:1

make your **c** and election sure . . . . 2 Pet 1:10

CAPTIVITY
bringing into **c** every thought . . . . 2 Cor 10:5

led **c** captive. Eph 4:8

CARE (n)
Casting all your **c** upon him. . . . . 1 Pet 5:7

CARNAL
the **c** mind is enmity against God. . . . . . Rom 8:7

ye are yet **c**. 1 Cor 3:3

weapons of our warfare are not **c** . . . . 2 Cor 10:4

CAST
C all your care upon him . . . . 1 Pet 5:7

love **c** out fear . . . . 1 John 4:18

CATTLE
c upon a thousand hills . . . . Ps 50:10

CAUGHT
ram **c** in a thicket by his horns . . . . . . Gen 22:13

c up to the third heaven . . . . 2 Cor 12:2

be **c** up together with them . . . . 1 Thess 4:17

CEASE
tongues, they shall **c** . . . . 1 Cor 13:8

Pray without **c** . . . . 1 Thess 5:17

CHANGE (v)
I am the Lord, I **c** not. . . . . Mal 3:6

c the glory of the uncorruptible God. . . Rom 1:23

we shall all be **c** . . . . 1 Cor 15:51

are **c** into the same image . . . . 2 Cor 3:18

CHARITY
put on **c**. . . . . Col 3:14

faith, **c,** peace . . . . 2 Tim 2:22

sound in faith, in **c** . . . . Titus 2:2

c shall cover the multitude of sins . . . . . 1 Pet 4:8

to brotherly kindness **c** . . . . 2 Pet 1:

CHASTE

To be discreet, **c**, keepers at home . . . . . Titus 2:5

CHASTEN

C thy son while there is hope . . . . Prov 19:18

whom the Lord loveth he **c** . . . . Heb 12:6

CHEEK

smite thee on thy right **c** . . . . Matt 5:39
     (See also Luke 6:29.)

CHEERFUL

God loveth a **c** giver . . . . 2 Cor 9:7

CHILD

Train up a **c** in the way . . . . Prov 22:6

Foolishness is bound in the heart
     of a **c** . . . . Prov 22:15

unto us a **c** is born . . . . Isa 9:6

When I was a **c** . . . . 1 Cor 13:11

CHILDREN

Suffer little **c** . . . . Matt 19:14; Luke 18:16

c of God . . . . Luke 20:36

c of light . . . . . . John 12:36; Eph 5:8; 1 Thess 5:5

the **c** of God . . . . Rom 8:16; Gal 3:26;
                                 1 John 3:10

c of disobedience . . . . Eph 5:6; Col 3:6

C, obey your parents . . . . Eph 6:1; Col 3:20

CHOSE

called, but few **c** . . . . Matt 20:16; 22:14

Ye have not **c** me . . . . John 15:16

c in the Lord . . . . Rom 16:13

God hath **c** the foolish things . . . . 1 Cor 1:27

as he hath **c** us . . . . Eph 1:4

c of God, and precious . . . . 1 Pet 2:4

a **c** generation . . . . 1 Pet 2:9

CHRIST

where **C** should be born . . . . Matt 2:4

Thou art the **C** . . . . Matt 16:16

C died for the ungodly . . . . Rom 5:6

while we were yet sinners, **C** died f
     or us . . . . Rom 5:8

if any man be in **C**, ... 2 Cor 5:17

created in **C** Jesus unto good works . . . Eph 2:10

as **C** is the head of the church . . . . Eph 5:23

to me to live is **C**, and to die . . . . Phil 1:21

I can do all things through **C** . . . . Phil 4:13

the dead in **C** shall rise first . . . . 1 Thess 4:16

Jesus **C** the same yesterday . . . . Heb 13:8

CHRISTIAN

called **C** first in Antioch . . . . Acts 11:26

persuadest me to be a **C** . . . . Acts 26:28

man suffer as a **C** . . . . 1 Pet 4:16

CHRISTS

shall arise false **C**, and false
     prophets . . . . Matt 24:24
     (See also Mark 13:22.)

CHURCH

tell it unto the **c** . . . . Matt 18:17

added to the **c** daily . . . . Acts 2:47

keep silence in the **c** . . . . 1 Cor 14:28, 34

the **c** is subject unto Christ . . . . Eph 5:24

as Christ also loved the **c** . . . . Eph 5:25

head of the body, the **c** . . . . Col 1:18

c of the firstborn . . . . Heb 12:23

CIRCUMCISION

what profit is there of **c**? . . . . Rom 3:1

Jesus Christ was a minister of the **c** . . . Rom 15:8

neither **c** availeth any thing . . . . . . Gal 5:6; 6:15

the **c**, which worship God . . . . Phil 3:3

c made without hands . . . . Col 2:11

c nor uncircumcision . . . . Col 3:11

CITY

make glad the **c** of God. . . . . Ps 46:4

c that is set on a hill. . . . . Matt 5:14

a **c** which hath foundations. . . . . Heb 11:10

the **c** of the living God . . . . Heb 12:22

no continuing **c** . . . . Heb 13:14

CLAY

out of the miry **c**. . . . . Ps 40:2

power over the **c** . . . . Rom 9:21

CLEAN

He that hath **c** hands . . . . Ps 24:4

Create in me a **c** heart. . . . . Ps 51:10

c through word. . . . . John 15:3

CLEANSE

C your hands, ye sinners . . . . James 4:8

c us from all sin. . . . . 1 John 1:7

CLEARLY

creation of the world are **c** seen . . . . . . Rom 1:20

CLOKE (CLOAK)

let him have thy **c**. . . . . Matt 5:40

CLOSET

enter into thy **c**. . . . . Matt 6:6

CLOTH

a piece of new **c** . . . . Matt 9:16; Mark 2:21

CLOTHE

c the grass. . . . . Matt 6:30; Luke 12:28

c with camel's hair . . . . Mark 1:6

be **c** with humility . . . . 1 Pet 5:5

CLOTHES

in swaddling **c** . . . . Luke 2:7

laid down their **c** at a young
    man's feet. Acts 7:58

CLOUD

in the **c**. . . . . 1 Thess 4:17

so great a **c** of witnesses . . . . Heb 12:1

he cometh with **c** . . . . Rev 1:7

COAL

Can one go upon hot **c?** . . . . Prov 6:28

heap **c** of fire upon his head. . . . . Prov 25:22;
                               Rom 12:20

COCK

before the **c** crow . . . . . . Matt 26:34; Mark 14:30

the **c** shall not crow . . . . Luke 22:34

COLD

cup of **c** water only in the name
    of a disciple . . . . Matt 10:42

love of many shall wax **c** . . . . Matt 24:12

neither **c** nor hot. . . . . Rev 3:15

COMFORT (n)

c of the Holy Ghost . . . . Acts 9:31

God of all **c** . . . . 2 Cor 1:3

COMFORT (v)

rod and thy staff they **c** . . . . Ps 23:4

c one another with these words. . . . 1 Thess 4:18

COMFORTER

another **C** . . . . John 14:16

when the **C** is come . . . . John 15:26

the **C** will not come . . . . John 16:7

COMMANDMENT

the first and great **c** . . . . Matt 22:38

A new **c** I give unto you . . . . John 13:34

COMMEND

into thy hands I **c** . . . . Luke 23:46

c ourselves to every man's. . . . . 2 Cor 4:2

COMMON

had all things **c** . . . . Acts 2:44

What God hath cleansed, that call
    not thou **c**. . . . . Acts 10:15

Temptation taken you but such
    as is **c** to man . . . . 1 Cor 10:13

COMMUNICATION

let your **c** be . . . . Matt 5:37

Let no corrupt **c** proceed . . . . Eph 4:29

COMPARE

not worthy to be **c** with the glory . . . . . Rom 8:18

c spiritual things with spiritual . . . . . . 1 Cor 2:13

COMPASS (v)

c about with so great a cloud . . . . Heb 12:1

COMPASSION

I will have **c** on whom I will . . . . Rom 9:15

of one mind, having **c** . . . . 1 Pet 3:8

COMPLETE

ye are **c** in him . . . . Col 2:10

stand perfect and **c** in all . . . . Col 4:12

COMPREHEND

able to **c** with all saints . . . . Eph 3:18

CONDEMN

by thy words thou shalt be **c** . . . . Matt 12:37

c not, and ye shall not be **c** . . . . Luke 6:37

his Son into the world to **c** . . . . John 3:17

believeth not is **c** . . . . John 3:18

hath no man **c** thee? . . . . John 8:10

Neither do I **c** thee . . . . John 8:11

Who is he that **c**? . . . . Rom 8:34

lest ye be **c** . . . . James 5:9

if our heart **c** us not. . . . . 1 John 3:21

CONFESS

c me before men . . . . Matt 10:32; Luke 12:8

shalt **c** with thy mouth . . . . Rom 10:9

every tongue shall **c** . . . . Rom 14:11

C your faults one to another . . . . James 5:16

If we **c** our sins . . . . 1 John 1:9

Every spirit that **c** that Jesus Christ . . 1 John 4:2

c that Jesus is the Son of God . . . . . . 1 John 4:15

CONFESSION

with the month **c** is made unto
  salvation. Rom 10:10

witnessed a good **c**. . . . . I Tim 6:13

CONFIDENCE

access with **c** by the faith . . . . Eph 3:12

no **c** in the flesh. . . . . Phil 3:3

hold fast the **c** . . . . Heb 3:6

Cast not away therefore your **c** . . . . . . Heb 10:35

have we **c** toward God. . . . . 1 John 3:21

CONFIDENT

Being **c** of this very thing. . . . . Phil 1:6

CONFORM

also did predestinate to be **c** . . . . Rom 8:29

be not **c** to this world . . . . Rom 12:2

CONFUSION

God is not the author of **c** . . . . 1 Cor 14:33

CONQUERORS

more than **c** through him . . . . Rom 8:37

CONSCIENCE

a good **c** . . . . 1 Tim 1:5, 19;
  Heb 13:18; 1 Pet 3:16

faith in a pure **c**. . . . . 1 Tim 3:9

purge your **c** from dead works. . . . . . . Heb 9:14

hearts sprinkled from an evil **c** . . . . . . Heb 10:22

CONSIDER

When I **c** thy heavens. . . . . Ps 8:3

C the lilies . . . . Matt 6:28; Luke 12:27

c not the beam . . . . Matt 7:3

C the ravens . . . . Luke 12:24

c one another to provoke . . . . Heb 10:24

c him that endured . . . . Heb 12:3

CONSOLATION

If there be therefore any **c** . . . . Phil 2:1

CONSTRAIN
the love of Christ **c** us . . . . 2 Cor 5:14

CONSUME
bush was not **c**. . . . . Ex 3:2

take heed that ye be not **c**. . . . . Gal 5:15

that ye may **c** it upon your lusts . . . . . James 4:3

CONTENT
to be **c** . . . . Phil 4:11

let us be therewith **c** . . . . 1 Tim 6:8

be **c** with such things as ye have . . . . . . Heb 13:5

CONTINUALLY
give ourselves **c** to prayer . . . . Acts 6:4

abideth a priest **c** . . . . Heb 7:3

CONTINUE
If ye **c** in my word . . . . John 8:31

c ye in my love . . . . John 15:9

Shall we **c** in sin? . . . . Rom 6:1

If ye **c** in the faith . . . . Col 1:23

here have we no **c** city . . . . Heb 13:14

and **c** there a year. . . . . James 4:13

CONTRITE
a broken and a **c** heart . . . . Ps 51:17

CONVERT
perfect, **c** the soul . . . . Ps 19:7

Except ye be **c**. . . . . Matt 18:3

Repent ye therefore, and be **c** . . . . Acts 3:19

CORD
a threefold **c**. Eccl 4:12

CORRECT
whom the Lᴏʀᴅ loveth he **c**. . . . . Prov 3:12

C thy son. . . . . Prov 29:17

CORRECTION
is profitable for doctrine,
 for reproof, for **c** . . . . 2 Tim 3:16

CORRUPT (adj)
off . . . the old man, which is **c** . . . . . . Eph 4:22

Let no **c** communication . . . . Eph 4:29

CORRUPTIBLE
image made like to **c** man. . . . . Rom 1:23

this **c** must put on . . . . 1 Cor 15:53

not redeemed with **c** things . . . . 1 Pet 1:18

CORRUPTION
Holy One to see **c**. . . . . Ps 16:10; Acts 2:27; 13:35

of the flesh reap **c**. . . . . Gal 6:8

COUNSEL
c of the ungodly . . . . Ps 1:1

determinate **c** and foreknowledge. . . . . Acts 2:23

after the **c** of his own will . . . . Eph 1:11

COUNSELLER
in the multitude of **c** . . . . Prov 11:14; 15:22; 24:6

who hath been his **c**? . . . . Rom 11:34

COUNT
c unto him for righteousness . . . . Rom 4:3

I **c** loss for Christ . . . . Phil 3:7

do **c** them but dung. . . . . Phil 3:8

I **c** not myself to have apprehended. . . . Phil 3:13

c it all joy . . . . James 1:2

COUNTRY
into a far **c** . . . . Matt 21:33; 25:14;
            Mark 12:1

sojourned in the land of promise,
 as in a strange **c** . . . . Heb 11:9

desire a better **c** . . . . Heb 11:16

COVENANT
I will make a new **c**. . . . . Jer 31:31

to whom pertaineth the adoption,
 and the glory, and the **c**. . . . . Rom 9:4

mediator of a better **c** . . . . Heb 8:6

mediator of the new **c** . . . . Heb 12:24

blood of the everlasting **c**. . . . . Heb 13:20

COVER

that **c** his sins shall not prosper . . . . . Prov 28:13

there is nothing **c** . . . . Matt 10:26; Luke 12:2

if the woman be not **c** . . . . 1 Cor 11:6

charity shall **c** the multitude of sins. . . . 1 Pet 4:8

COVETOUSNESS

c, wickedness, deceit, lasciviousness,
    and evil eye. . . . . Mark 7:22

wickedness, **c**, maliciousness . . . . Rom 1:29

c, let it not be once named . . . . Eph 5:3

conversation be without **c** . . . . Heb 13:5

CREATE

after God is **c** in righteousness . . . . Eph 4:24

by him were all things **c** . . . . Col 1:16

CREATION

from the **c** of the world. . . . . Rom 1:20

the whole **c** groaneth . . . . Rom 8:22

from the beginning of the **c** . . . . 2 Pet 3:4

CREATOR

Remember now thy **C** . . . . Eccl 12:1

served the creature more
    than the **C** . . . . Rom 1:25

CREATURE

new **c** . . . . 2 Cor 5:17; Gal 6:15

firstborn of every **c** . . . . Col 1:15

CREW

the cock **c** . . . . Matt 26:74; Mark 14:68;
    Luke 22:60

CRIMSON

though they be red like **c** . . . . Isa 1:18

CROSS

take up his **c** . . . . Matt 16:24;
    Mark 8:34; Luke 9:23

come down from the **c**. . . . . Matt 27:40;
    Mark 15:30

c of Christ. . . . . 1 Cor 1:17;
    Gal 6:12; Phil 3:18

offence of the **c** . . . . Gal 5:11

glory, save in the **c** . . . . Gal 6:14

in one body by the **c** . . . . Eph 2:16

the death of the **c**. . . . . Phil 2:8

peace through the blood of his **c** . . . . . . Col 1:20

nailing it to his **c** . . . . Col 2:14

endured the **c**. . . . . Heb 12:2

CROWN (n)

A virtuous woman is a **c** . . . . Prov 12:4

to obtain a corruptible **c**. . . . . 1 Cor 9:25

my joy and **c** . . . . Phil 4:1

a **c** of righteousness . . . . 2 Tim 4:8

shall receive the **c** of life. . . . . James 1:12

a **c** of glory . . . . 1 Pet 5:4

that no man take thy **c**. . . . . Rev 3:11

cast their **c** before the throne . . . . Rev 4:10

CRUCIFY

C him . . . . Mark 15:13; Luke 23:21;
    John 19:6, 15

we preach Christ **c**. . . . . 1 Cor 1:23

save Jesus Christ, and him **c** . . . . 1 Cor 2:2

I am **c** with Christ. . . . . Gal 2:20

have **c** the flesh. . . . . Gal 5:24

the world is **c** unto me . . . . Gal 6:14

c to themselves . . . . Heb 6:6

CRYSTAL

a sea of glass like unto **c**. . . . . Rev 4:6

light . . . clear as **c**. . . . . Rev 21:11

river of water of life, clear as **c** . . . . Rev 22:1

CUBIT

can add one **c** unto his stature . . . . Matt 6:27

add to his stature one **c** . . . . Luke 12:25

CUP

drink of the **c** . . . . Matt 20:22; Mark 10:39

took the **c** . . . . Matt 26:27; Mark 14:23;
    Luke 22:17; 1 Cor 11:25

let this **c** pass . . . . Matt 26:39

This **c** is the new testament. . . . . . . Luke 22:20;
1 Cor 11:25

drink this **c** of the Lord,
unworthily . . . . 1 Cor 11:27

CURSE (v)

I will not again **c** the ground . . . . Gen 8:21

I will . . . **c** him that curseth thee . . . . . Gen 12:3

bless them that **c** you . . . . . Matt 5:44; Luke 6:28

fig tree which thou **c** . . . . Mark 11:21

CURSE (n)

of the law are under the **c**. . . . . Gal 3:10

being made a **c** for us . . . . Gal 3:13

shall be no more **c** . . . . Rev 22:3

CYRUS

saith of **C,** He is my shepherd . . . . Isa 44:28

to his anointed, to **C** . . . . Isa 45:1

D

DAILY

our **d** bread . . . . Matt 6:11; Luke 11:3

take up his cross **d** . . . . Luke 9:23

increased in number **d**. . . . . Acts 16:5

searched the scriptures **d**. . . . . Acts 17:11

I die **d**. . . . . 1 Cor 15:31

DAMNED

he that believeth not shall be **d** . . . . Mark 16:16

he that doubteth is **d** if he eat . . . . . Rom 14:23

That they all might be **d** who
believed not . . . . 2 Thess 2:12

DAMNATION

the resurrection of **d**. . . . . John 5:29

eateth and drinketh **d** . . . . 1 Cor 11:29

DARKNESS

d and the light are both alike . . . . Ps 139:12

sun shall be turned into **d** . . . . Joel 2:31

body shall be full of **d**. . . . . Matt 6:23

outer **d** . . . . Matt 8:12; 22:13; 25:30

What I tell you in **d** . . . . Matt 10:27

the power of **d** . . . . Luke 22:53; Col 1:13

d comprehended it not. . . . . John 1:5

loved **d** rather than light . . . . John 3:19

what communion hath light
with **d** ? . . . . 2 Cor 6:14

rulers of the **d** of this world. . . . . Eph 6:12

out of **d** into his marvellous light. . . . . 1 Pet 2:9

in him is no **d** at all. . . . . 1 John 1:5

hateth his brother, is in **d** . . . . 1 John 2:9

DART

quench all the fiery **d**. . . . . Eph 6:16

DAY

teach us to number our **d** . . . . Ps 90:12

length of **d**. . . . . Prov 3:2, 16

Many will say to me in that **d** . . . . . . Matt 7:22

that **d** and hour knoweth no man . . . Matt 24:36

the **d** nor the hour . . . . Matt 25:13

he hath shortened the **d** . . . . Mark 13:20

Abraham rejoiced to see my **d** . . . . . . John 8:56

wrath against the **d** of wrath . . . . Rom 2:5

sealed unto the **d** of redemption . . . . . Eph 4:30

perform it until the **d** of Jesus Christ . . . Phil 1:6

d of the Lord. . . . . 1 Thess 5:2; 2 Pet 3:10

a thousand years as one **d** . . . . 2 Pet 3:8

DEAD

let the **d** bury their **d** . . . . Matt 8:22

not **d**, but sleepeth . . . . Matt 9:24;
Mark 5:39; Luke 8:52

deaf hear, the **d** are raised. . Matt 11:5; Luke 7:22

d, and is alive again . . . . Luke 15:24, 32

d shall hear. John 5:25

though he were **d**, yet shall
he live . . . . John 11:25

Judge of quick and **d** . . . . Acts 10:42

first that should rise from the **d** . . . . . Acts 26:23

d to sin . . . . Rom 6:2; 1 Pet 2:24

d to the law . . . . Rom 7:4; Gal 2:19

How are the **d** raised? . . . . 1 Cor 15:35

d in trespasses and sins . . . . Eph 2:1

firstborn from the **d** . . . . Col 1:18

you, being **d** in your sins. . . . . Col 2:13

d with Christ. . . . . Col 2:20

d in Christ shall rise first . . . . 1 Thess 4:16

For if we be **d** with him . . . . 2 Tim 2:11

quick and the **d** at his appearing . . . . . 2 Tim 4:1

brought again from the **d**. . . . . Heb 13:20

faith without works is **d** . . . . James 2:20, 26

preached also to them that are **d** . . . . . . 1 Pet 4:6

DEAF

in that day shall the **d** hear . . . . Isa 29:18

ears of the **d** shall be unstopped . . . . . . Isa 35:5

the **d** hear, the dead are raised . . . . . Matt 11:5;
Luke 7:22

DEAR

kingdom of his **d** Son . . . . Col 1:13

DEATH

shadow of **d** . . . . Ps 23:4; Ps 107:10;
Isa 9:2; Jer 2:6

let him die the **d** . . . . Matt 15:4; Mark 7:10

not taste of **d** . . . . Matt 16:28;
Mark 9:1; Luke 9:27

My soul is exceeding sorrowful,
even unto **d** . . . . Matt 26:38; Mark 14:34

passed from **d** unto life . . . . John 5:24;
1 John 3:14

shall never see **d**. . . . . John 8:51

sickness is not unto **d**. . . . . John 11:4

reconciled to God by the **d** . . . . Rom 5:10

d by sin, and so **d** passed . . . . Rom 5:12

d reigned from Adam to Moses . . . . . Rom 5:14

in the likeness of his **d** . . . . Rom 6:5

end of those things is **d** . . . . Rom 6:21

wages of sin is **d** . . . . Rom 6:23

law of sin and **d** . . . . Rom 8:2

life, or **d** . . . . 1 Cor 3:22

shew the Lord's **d** till he come. . . . . . 1 Cor 11:26

O **d**, where is thy sting?. . . . . 1 Cor 15:55

even the **d** of the cross. . . . . Phil 2:8

taste **d** for every man. . . . . Heb 2:9

bringeth forth **d** . . . . James 1:15

a sin unto **d**. . . . . 1 John 5:16

his name that sat on him was **D** . . . . Rev 6:8

DEBTOR

forgive us our debts as we forgive
our **d** . . . . Matt 6:12

I am **d** both to the Greeks. . . . . Rom 1:14

DECEITFUL

The heart is **d** above all things . . . . Jer 17:9

DECEIVE

d the very elect. . . . . Matt 24:24

Be not **d** . . . . 1 Cor 6:9; 15:33; Gal 6:7

Adam was not **d** . . . . 1 Tim 2:14

we **d** ourselves. . . . . 1 John 1:8

DECENTLY

all things be done **d** and in order. . . . 1 Cor 14:40

DECISION

multitudes in the valley of **d** . . . . Joel 3:14

DECREASE

the waters **d** continually . . . . Gen 8:5

He must increase, but I must **d** . . . . . . John 3:30

DEED

because their **d** were evil . . . . John 3:19

mighty in words and in **d** . . . . Acts 7:22

put off the old man with his **d** . . . . Col 3:9

whatsoever ye do in word or **d** . . . . . . Col 3:17

but in **d** and in truth. . . . . 1 John 3:18

DEFILE

If any man **d** the temple of God . . . . . 1 Cor 3:17

conscience being weak is **d** . . . . 1 Cor 8:7

DELAY

My lord **d** his coming . . . Matt 24:48; Luke 12:45

DELIVER

d us from evil . . . . Matt 6:13; Luke 11:4

was **d** for our offences . . . . Rom 4:25

d unto death for Jesus' sake . . . . 2 Cor 4:11

faith which was once **d** unto
    the saints. Jude 1:3

DELIVERANCE

preach **d** to the captives . . . . Luke 4:18

DELUSION

I also will choose their **d** . . . . Isa 66:4

shall send them strong **d** . . . . 2 Thess 2:11

DEPART

when he is old, he will not **d**
    from it . . . . Prov 22:6

D from me, ye cursed . . . . Matt 25:41

that he should **d** out of this world . . . . John 13:1

having a desire to **d** . . . . Phil 1:23

DEPTH

the **d** of the riches. . . . . Rom 11:33

DESCEND

angels of God ascending and **d** . . . . . . Gen 28:12

Lord himself shall **d** . . . . 1 Thess 4:16

holy Jerusalem, **d** . . . . Rev 21:10

DESERT

the **d** shall rejoice, and blossom . . . . Isa 35:1

I will even make . . . rivers in the **d** . . . . Isa 43:19

they wandered in **d** . . . . Heb 11:38

DESIRE (n)

he shall give thee the **d** of thine heart . . . Ps 37:4

the **d** of all nations shall come. . . . . Hag 2:7

having a **d** to depart. . . . . Phil 1:23

DESIRE (v)

More to be **d** are they than gold . . . . . . Ps 19:10

One thing have I **d** of the LORD. . . . . Ps 27:4

I **d** mercy, and not sacrifice . . . . Hos 6:6

If any man **d** to be first . . . . Mark 9:35

Satan hath **d** to have you . . . . Luke 22:31

and **d** spiritual gifts . . . . 1 Cor 14:1

they **d** a better country . . . . Heb 11:16

the angels **d** to look into . . . . 1 Pet 1:12

As newborn babes, **d** the
    sincere milk. . . . . 1 Pet 2:2

DESOLATE

abominations he shall make it **d** . . . . . . Dan 9:27

abomination that maketh **d** . . . Dan 11:31; 12:11

DESOLATION

transgression of **d** . . . . Dan 8:13

seventy years in the **d**
    of Jerusalem . . . . Dan 9:2

abomination of **d** . . . . . . Matt 24:15; Mark 13:14

DESPISE

d not thou the chastening . . . Job 5:17; Heb 12:5

fools **d** wisdom . . . . Prov 1:7

hold to the one, and **d**
    the other . . . . Matt 6:24; Luke 16:13

d not one of these little ones . . . . Matt 18:10

he that **d** me **d** him that sent me . . . . Luke 10:16

D not prophesyings . . . . 1 Thess 5:20

Let no man **d** thee . . . . Titus 2:15

endured the cross, **d** the shame. . . . . . . Heb 12:2

DESPITEFULLY

which **d** use you . . . . Matt 5:44; Luke 6:28

DESTROY

d the righteous with the wicked . . . . . Gen 18:23

one sinner **d** much good . . . . Eccl 9:18

fear him which is able to **d**. . . . . Matt 10:28

they might **d** him . . . . Matt 12:14;
Mark 3:6; 11:18

art thou come to **d** us?. . . . Mark 1:24; Luke 4:34

say, I will **d** this temple . . . . Mark 14:58

thou that **d** the temple . . . . Mark 15:29

to save life, or to **d** it . . . . Luke 6:9

flood came, and **d** them all. . . . . Luke 17:27

D this temple . . . . John 2:19

able to save and to **d** . . . . James 4:12

d the works of the devil . . . . 1 John 3:8

DESTRUCTION
Pride goeth before **d** . . . . Prov 16:18

broad is the way, that leadeth to **d** . . . . Matt 7:13

vessels of wrath fitted to **d** . . . . Rom 9:22

Whose end is **d** . . . . Phil 3:19

DEVIL
(Jesus) tempted of the **d** . . . . Matt 4:1; Luke 4:2

enemy that sowed them is the **d** . . . . Matt 13:39

everlasting fire, prepared for the **d** . . . Matt 25:41

thou hast a **d** . . . . John 7:20

Ye are of your father the **d** . . . . John 8:44

fall into the condemnation of the **d** . . . 1 Tim 3:6

the **d** also believe, and tremble. . . . . . James 2:19

Resist the **d**, and he will flee . . . . James 4:7

your adversary the **d,** as a roaring . . . . . 1 Pet 5:8

Michael the archangel, when
contending with the **d**. . . . . Jude 1:9

DIE
thou shalt surely **d**. . . . . Gen 2:17

Ye shall not surely **d**. . . . . Gen 3:4

Let me **d** the death of righteous. . . . . Num 23:10

curse God, and **d**. . . . . Job 2:9

my brother had not **d** . . . . John 11:21, 32

that Jesus should **d** for
that nation. . . . . John 11:51

for a righteous man will one **d** . . . . Rom 5:7

It is Christ that **d** . . . . Rom 8:34

Christ **d** for our sins. . . . . 1 Cor 15:3

as in Adam all **d**. . . . . 1 Cor 15:22

I **d** daily . . . . 1 Cor 15:31

appointed unto men once to **d**. . . . . . . Heb 9:27

DIP
d his hand with me in the dish . . . . Matt 26:23

DIRECT
he shall **d** thy paths . . . . Prov 3:6

DISCERN
d the face of the sky . . . . . Matt 16:3; Luke 12:56

they are spiritually **d** . . . . 1 Cor 2:14

a **d** of the thoughts and intents. . . . . . . Heb 4:12

exercised to **d** both good and evil . . . . . Heb 5:14

DISCIPLE
called unto him his
twelve **d** . . . . Matt 10:1; Luke 6:13

d is not above his
master . . . . Matt 10:24; Luke 6:40

thy **d** do that which is not lawful. . . . . Matt 12:2

Why do thy **d** transgress the
tradition?. . . . . Matt 15:2

brought him to thy **d,** and they
could not cure . . . . Matt 17:16

the **d** rebuked them . . . . Matt 19:13

took the twelve **d** apart. . . . . Matt 20:17

sent out unto him their **d**. . . . . Matt 22:16

all the **d** forsook him, and fled. . . . . . Matt 26:56

tell his **d** that he is risen. . . . . Matt 28:7

Why do the **d** of John . . . . Mark 2:18; Luke 5:33

he expounded all things to his **d** . . . . . Mark 4:34

d eat bread with defiled . . . . Mark 7:2

Why walk not thy **d** according
to the tradition? . . . . Mark 7:5

Pharisees murmured against his **d** . . . . Luke 5:30

as John also taught his **d** . . . . Luke 11:1

cannot be my **d** . . . . Luke 14:26, 27, 33

d began to rejoice and praise God . . . Luke 19:37

Master, rebuke thy **d**. . . . . Luke 19:39

his **d** believed on him. . . . . John 2:11

Jesus himself baptized not, but his **d**. . . John 4:2

thy **d** also may see the works. . . . . John 7:3

then are ye my **d** indeed. . . . . John 8:31

will ye also be his **d**? . . . . John 9:27

began to wash the **d** feet . . . . John 13:5

so shall ye be my **d**. . . . . John 15:8

that **d** was known . . . . John 18:15

one of this man's **d**?. . . . . John 18:17

a **d** of Jesus, but secretly for fear . . . . John 19:38

told the **d** that she had seen
 the Lord. . . . . John 20:18

d whom Jesus loved . . . . John 21:7, 20

that that **d** should not die . . . . John 21:23

This is the **d** which testifieth . . . . . . John 21:24

d were called Christians first. . . . . . . Acts 11:26

d came together to break bread. . . . . Acts 20:7

DISOBEDIENCE

by one man's **d** many were
 made sinners . . . . Rom 5:19

children of **d** . . . . Eph 2:2; 5:6; Col 3:6

DISPENSATION

a **d** of the gospel . . . . 1 Cor 9:17

in the **d** of the fulness of times . . . . . . Eph 1:10

the **d** of the grace of God. . . . . Eph 3:2

minister according the **d** of God . . . . . Col 1:25

DIVIDE

D the living child in two . . . . 1 Kgs 3:25

kingdom **d**. . . . . Matt 12:25; Luke 11:17

d against himself. . . . . . Matt 12:26; Luke 11:18

Is Christ **d**? . . . . 1 Cor 1:13

rightly **d** the word of truth . . . . 2 Tim 2:15

piercing even to the **d** asunder . . . . . . Heb 4:12

DIVINE (adj)

his **d** power. 2 Pet 1:3

partakers of the **d** nature1504 . . . . 2 Pet 1:4

DO

this **d**, and thou shalt live. . . . . Luke 10:28

this **d** in remembrance . . . . Luke 22:19;
           1 Cor 11:24

without me ye can **d** nothing. . . . . . . John 15:5

I can **d** all things through Christ . . . . . Phil 4:13

DOCTRINE

continued stedfastly in
 the apostles' **d** . . . . Acts 2:42

every wind of **d** . . . . Eph 4:14

contrary to sound **d**. . . . . 1 Tim 1:10

in the words of faith and of good **d** . . . 1 Tim 4:6

to reading, to exhortation, to **d**. . . . . . 1 Tim 4:13

Take heed unto thyself,
 and unto the **d**. . . . . 1 Tim 4:16

is profitable for **d**. . . . . 2 Tim 3:16

DOG

As a **d** returneth . . . . Prov 26:11

the **d** eat of the crumbs . . . . Matt 15:27

Beware of **d** . . . . Phil 3:2

DOMINION

let not any iniquity have **d**
 over me . . . . Ps 119:133

sin shall not have **d**. . . . . Rom 6:14

law hath **d** over a man . . . . Rom 7:1

all principality, and power,
 and might, and **d** . . . . Eph 1:21

whether they be thrones, or **d**. . . . . . . Col 1:16

DOOR

near, even at the **d** . . . . Matt 24:33
 (See also Mark 13:29.)

I am the **d**. John 10:7, 9

great **d** and effectual . . . . 1 Cor 16:9

judge standeth before the **d** . . . . James 5:9

set before thee an open **d** . . . . Rev 3:8

I stand at the **d**, and knock . . . . Rev 3:20

behold, a **d** was opened in heaven . . . . . Rev 4:1

DOORKEEPER
rather be a **d** in the house of my God, . . Ps 84:10

DOUBLE
worthy of **d** honour. . . . . 1 Tim 5:17

purify your hearts, ye **d** minded. . . . . . James 4:8

DOVE
and harmless as **d**. . . . . Matt 10:16

them that sold **d**. . . . . . Matt 21:12; Mark 11:15

DRAGON
Pharaoh king of Egypt, the great **d** . . . Ezek 29:3

a great red **d**. Rev 12:3

the **d** gave him his power. . . . . Rev 13:2

they worshipped the **d**. . . . . Rev 13:4

DRAW
people **d** nigh unto me with
    their mouth. . . . . Matt 15:8

your redemption **d** nigh . . . . Luke 21:28

will **d** all men unto me. . . . . John 12:32

d near with a true heart. . . . . Heb 10:22

D nigh to God, and he will **d** . . . . James 4:8

DREAM (v)
old men shall **d** dreams. . . . . Joel 2:28; Acts 2:17

DRINK (n)
thirsty, and ye gave me **d** . . . . Matt 25:35

the kingdom of God is not
    meat and **d**. . . . . Rom 14:17

same spiritual **d**. . . . . 1 Cor 10:4

judge you in meat, or in **d**. . . . . Col 2:16

DRINK (v)
Are ye able to **d**?. . . . . Matt 20:22

except I **d** it. . . . . Matt 26:42

can ye **d** of the cup?. . . . . Mark 10:38

let him come unto me, and **d**. . . . . . . John 7:37

as oft as ye **d** it. . . . . 1 Cor 11:25

DRUNK
be not **d** with wine . . . . Eph 5:18

DUE
meat in **d** season. . . . . Ps 104:27; 145:15;
                Matt 24:45; Luke 12:42

word spoken in **d** season. . . . . Prov 15:23

in **d** time Christ died. . . . . Rom 5:6

in **d** season we shall reap . . . . Gal 6:9

DUMB
as a sheep before her shearers is **d** . . . . . Isa 53:7

a lamb **d** before his shearer . . . . Acts 8:32

DUST
formed man of the **d** . . . . Gen 2:7

d shalt thou eat . . . . Gen 3:14

d thou art, and unto **d**. . . . . Gen 3:19

Shall the **d** praise thee? . . . . Ps 30:9

lick the **d** like a serpent . . . . Mic 7:17

shake off the **d** of your feet . . . . Matt 10:14

DWELL
for brethren to **d** together in unity . . . . . Ps 133:1

d in me, and I in him. . . . . John 6:56

sin that **d** in me . . . . Rom 7:17

in him **d** all the fulness of Godhead . . . . . Col 2:9

word of Christ **d** in you richly. . . . . Col 3:16

d in the light. . . . . 1 Tim 6:16

E

EAGLE
how I bare you on **e** wings. . . . . Ex 19:4

youth is renewed like the **e**. . . . . Ps 103:5

mount up with wings as **e**. . . . . Isa 40:31

EAR (n)
e are dull of hearing. . . . . Matt 13:15; Acts 28:27

smote off his **e** . . . . Matt 26:51

nor **e** heard . . . . 1 Cor 2:9

if the **e** shall say, Because I am
    not the eye . . . . 1 Cor 12:16

having itching **e** . . . . 2 Tim 4:3

EARTH

Judge of all the **e** do right . . . . Gen 18:25

excellent is thy name in all the **e** . . . . Ps 8:1

shall inherit the **e** . . . . Ps 37:9, 11, 22

glory be above all the **e** . . . . Ps 57:5

a God that judgeth in the **e** . . . . Ps 58:11

most high over all the **e** . . . . Ps 83:18

laid the foundation of the **e** . . . Ps 102:25; 104:5; Isa 48:13

the **e** is full of thy riches . . . . Ps 104:24

treasures upon **e** . . . . Matt 6:19

power upon **e** to forgive . . . Matt 9:6; Mark 2:10; Luke 5:24

to send peace on **e** . . . . Matt 10:34

shalt bind on **e** . . . . Matt 16:19; 18:18

on **e** peace . . . . Luke 2:14

darkness over all the **e** . . . . Luke 23:44

I have glorified thee on the **e** . . . . John 17:4

treasure in **e** vessels . . . . 2 Cor 4:7

not on things on the **e** . . . . Col 3:2

EAT

Why **e** your Master with publicans and sinners? . . . . Matt 9:11

give ye them to **e** . . . . Matt 14:16; Mark 6:37; Luke 9:13

to **e** with unwashen hands . . . . Matt 15:20

dogs **e** of the crumbs . . . . Matt 15:27

That ye may **e** and drink at my table . . . . Luke 22:30

he took it, and did **e** before them . . . . Luke 24:43

e to the Lord . . . . Rom 14:6

e it as a thing offered unto an idol . . . . 1 Cor 8:7

if we **e,** are we the better . . . . 1 Cor 8:8

all **e** the same spiritual meat . . . . 1 Cor 10:3

Whether therefore ye **e** . . . . 1 Cor 10:31

he that **e** and drinketh unworthily . . . . 1 Cor 11:29

EFFECTUAL

e fervent prayer of a righteous man . . . . James 5:16

EFFEMINATE

adulterers, nor **e**, nor abusers of themselves . . . . 1 Cor 6:9

ELDER

Ordained them **e** in every church . . . . Acts 14:23

Rebuke not an **e** . . . . 1 Tim 5:1

Against an **e** receive not . . . . 1 Tim 5:19

the **e** obtained a good report . . . . Heb 11:2

let (the sick) call for the **e** . . . . James 5:14

ELECT

deceive the very **e** . . . . Matt 24:24

gather together his **e** . . . Matt 24:31; Mark 13:27

avenge his own **e** . . . . Luke 18:7

to the charge of God's **e** . . . . Rom 8:33

as the **e** of God . . . . Col 3:12

E according to the foreknowledge . . . . . 1 Pet 1:2

corner stone, **e**, precious . . . . 1 Pet 2:6

ELECTION

purpose of God according to **e** . . . . Rom 9:11

according to the **e** of grace . . . . Rom 11:5

your **e** of God . . . . 1 Thess 1:4

make your calling and **e** sure . . . . 2 Pet 1:10

ELIAS

this is **E**, which was for to come . . . . . Matt 11:14

some say that thou art John the Baptist; some **E,** . . . . Matt 16:14 (See also Mark 8:28; Luke 9:19.)

appeared unto them Moses and **E** . . . . Matt 17:3

E truly shall first come, and restore . . . . Matt 17:11

appeared unto them **E** and Moses . . . . . Mark 9:4

This man calleth for **E** . . . . Matt 27:47 (See also Mark 15:35.)

let us see whether **E** will come . . . . . Matt 27:49; Mark 15:36

in the spirit and power of **E** . . . . Luke 1:17

ELIJAH

I will send you **E** the prophet . . . . Mal 4:5

EMMANUEL

shall call his name **E**. . . . . Matt 1:23

END

Better is the **e** of a thing . . . . Eccl 7:8

gather together . . . from one
    e of heaven . . . . Matt 24:31

I am with you alway, even unto
    the **e** . . . . Matt 28:20

of his kingdom there shall be no **e**. . . . Luke 1:33

Whose **e** is destruction. . . . . Phil 3:19

the **e** of all things is at hand . . . . 1 Pet 4:7

ENDEAVOUR

E to keep the unity . . . . Eph 4:3

ENDURE

his mercy **e** for ever. . . . . Ps 106:1; 107:1;
    118:1; 136:1; Jer 33:11

his righteousness **e** for ever . . . Ps 111:3; 112:3, 9

Thy name, O Lᴏʀᴅ, **e** for ever . . . . Ps 135:13

e all things. . . . . 1 Cor 13:7

e hardness, as a good soldier . . . . 2 Tim 2:3

they will not **e** sound doctrine . . . . 2 Tim 4:3

watch thou in all things, **e** afflictions. . 2 Tim 4:5

in heaven a better and an
    e substance. . . . . Heb 10:34

If ye **e** chastening. . . . . Heb 12:7

Blessed is the man that
    e temptation . . . . James 1:12

the word of the Lord **e** for ever . . . . . . 1 Pet 1:25

ENEMY

in the presence of mine **e** . . . . Ps 23:5

wiser than mine **e** . . . . Ps 119:98

Rejoice not when thine **e** falleth . . . . . Prov 24:17

hate thine **e** . . . . Matt 5:43

But I say unto you, Love your **e** . . . . . Matt 5:44

if thine **e** hunger, feed him . . . . Rom 12:20

the **e** of the cross . . . . Phil 3:18

friend of the world is the **e** of God. . . . James 4:4

ENLIGHTEN

commandment of the Lᴏʀᴅ is pure,
    e the eyes. Ps 19:8

eyes of your understanding being **e** . . . . Eph 1:18

those who were once **e** . . . . Heb 6:4

ENMITY

I will put **e** between. . . . . Gen 3:15

carnal mind is **e** against God . . . . Rom 8:7

abolished in his flesh the **e** . . . . Eph 2:15

ENOCH

E walked with God: and he was not . . . Gen 5:24

By faith **E** was translated. . . . . Heb 11:5

E . . . prophesied of these saying,
    Behold, the Lord cometh . . . . Jude 1:14

ENTER

E ye in at the strait gate . . . . Matt 7:13;
    Luke 13:24

better for thee to **e** into life . . . . Matt 18:8;
    Mark 9:43

we may **e** into them. . . . . Mark 5:12

lest ye **e** into temptation. . . . . Mark 14:38;
    Luke 22:46

sin **e** into the world . . . . Rom 5:12

neither have **e** into the heart of man. . . 1 Cor 2:9

shall not **e** into my rest . . . . Heb 3:11

ENTIRE

that ye may be perfect and **e** . . . . James 1:4

ENVY (n)

full of **e**, murder . . . . Rom 1:29

preach Christ even of **e** . . . . Phil 1:15

living in malice and **e**. . . . . Titus 3:3

ENVYING

not in strife and **e**. . . . . Rom 13:13

among you **e**, and strife. . . . . 1 Cor 3:3

lest there be debates, **e**, wraths . . . . . 2 Cor 12:20

E, murders, drunkenness . . . . Gal 5:21

EQUAL

are **e** unto the angel . . . . Luke 20:36

making himself **e** with God . . . . John 5:18

not robbery to be **e** with God. . . . . Phil 2:6

ESCAPE

How shall we **e**, if we neglect . . . . Heb 2:3

e the corruption that is in the world . . . 2 Pet 1:4

ESPECIALLY

men, **e** unto them who are . . . . Gal 6:10

ESTEEM

did **e** him smitten . . . . Isa 53:4

One man **e** one day above another . . . . Rom 14:5

let each **e** other better . . . . Phil 2:3

E the reproach of Christ greater
    riches. . . . . Heb 11:26

ETERNAL

righteous into life **e** . . . . Matt 25:46

is in danger of **e** damnation . . . . Mark 3:29

that I may inherit **e** life . . . . Mark 10:17
    (See also Luke 10:25; 18:18.)

in the world to come **e** life. . . . . Mark 10:30

not perish, but have **e** life . . . . John 3:15

gathereth fruit unto life **e**. . . . . John 4:36

in them ye think ye have **e** life. . . . . . John 5:39

drinketh my blood, hath **e** life . . . . . . John 6:54

thou hast the words of **e** life . . . . John 6:68

give unto them **e** life . . . . John 10:28

shall keep it unto life **e**. . . . . John 12:25

give **e** life to as many . . . . John 17:2

this is life **e**, that they might
    know thee . . . . John 17:3

many as were ordained to **e** life . . . . . Acts 13:48

for glory and honour and
    immortality, **e** life . . . . Rom 2:7

grace reign through righteousness
    unto **e** life . . . . Rom 5:21

gift of God is **e** life . . . . Rom 6:23

and **e** weight of glory. . . . . 2 Cor 4:17

things which are not seen are **e**. . . . . . 2 Cor 4:18

According to the **e** purpose . . . . Eph 3:11

lay hold on **e** life . . . . 1 Tim 6:12, 19

In hope of **e** life . . . . Titus 1:2
    (See also Titus 3:7.)

author of **e** salvation . . . . Heb 5:9

e judgment. . . . . Heb 6:2

promise of **e** inheritance . . . . Heb 9:15

called us unto his **e** glory by Christ . . . 1 Pet 5:10

e life, which was with the Father . . . . 1 John 1:2

hath promised us, even **e** life . . . . . . 1 John 2:25

no murderer hath **e** life . . . . 1 John 3:15

know that ye have **e** life . . . . 1 John 5:13

This is the true God, and **e** life . . . . . 1 John 5:20

EVANGELIST

some, **e**; and some, pastors . . . . Eph 4:11

do the work of an **e**. . . . . 2 Tim 4:5

EVER

my sin is **e** before me . . . . Ps 51:3

trust in the mercy of God for
    ever and **e** . . . . Ps 52:8

so shall we **e** be with the Lord . . . . . 1 Thess 4:17

he **e** liveth to make . . . . Heb 7:25

EVERLASTING

an **e** priesthood. . . . . Ex 40:15; Num 25:13

from **e** to **e**, thou art God . . . . Ps 90:2

lead me in the way **e**. . . . . Ps 139:24

righteous is an **e** foundation. . . . . Prov 10:25

The **e** Father . . . . Isa 9:6

in the Lord JEHOVAH is **e** strength . . . . Isa 26:4

e joy . . . . Isa 35:10; 51:11; 61:7

with an **e** salvation . . . . Isa 45:17

an **e** light . . . . Isa 60:19

into **e** fire . . . . Matt 18:8; 25:41

inherit **e** life . . . . Matt 19:29

into **e** punishment . . . . Matt 25:46

but have **e** life. John 3:16
  (See also John 3:36.)

water springing up into **e** life. . . . . . . John 4:14

may have **e** life. . . . . John 6:40

Spirit reap life **e** . . . . Gal 6:8

EVERY
e knee shall bow to me, and **e**
  tongue shall confess. . . . . Rom 14:11

bringing into captivity **e** thought. . . . . 2 Cor 10:5

e name. . . . . Eph 1:21; Phil 2:9

E good gift and **e** perfect gift . . . . James 1:17

believe not **e** spirit. . . . . 1 John 4:1

EVIDENCE
the **e** of things not seen. . . . . Heb 11:1

EVIL
Depart from **e** . . . . Ps 34:14; 37:27; Prov 3:7

that call **e** good, and good **e** . . . . Isa 5:20

Sufficient unto the day is the
  e thereof . . . . Matt 6:34

If ye then, being **e**. . . . . . Matt 7:11; Luke 11:13

Abhor that which is **e**. . . . . Rom 12:9

Recompense to no man **e** for **e** . . . . . . Rom 12:17

overcome **e** with good. . . . . Rom 12:21

appearance of **e** . . . . 1 Thess 5:22

the root of all **e** . . . . 1 Tim 6:10

speak **e** of no man . . . . Titus 3:2

Not rendering **e** for **e** . . . . 1 Pet 3:9

EXALT
let us **e** his name together . . . . Ps 34:3

e far above all gods. . . . . Ps 97:9

Righteousness **e** a nation . . . . Prov 14:34

e himself shall be abased. . . . . Matt 23:12;
  Luke 14:11; 18:14

if a man **e** himself . . . . 2 Cor 11:20

e above measure . . . . 2 Cor 12:7

God also hath highly **e** him . . . . Phil 2:9

e himself above all that is called . . . . 2 Thess 2:4

he may **e** you in due time . . . . 1 Pet 5:6

EXAMINE
E me, O Lord . . . . Ps 26:2

let a man **e** himself . . . . 1 Cor 11:28

E yourselves. . . . . 2 Cor 13:5

EXAMPLE
Christ also suffered for us, leaving
  us an **e**. . . . . 1 Pet 2:21

EXCEEDING
e and eternal weight of glory. . . . . . . 2 Cor 4:17

able to do **e** abundantly. . . . . Eph 3:20

e great and precious promises . . . . 2 Pet 1:4

EXCELLENCY
loss for the **e** of the knowledge
  of Christ . . . . Phil 3:8

EXCELLENT
a more **e** way. . . . . 1 Cor 12:31

EXCEPT
E the Lord build the house. . . . . Ps 127:1

e your righteousness shall exceed . . . . Matt 5:20

e those days should be shortened. . . . Matt 24:22

E a man be born of water and of
  the Spirit . . . . John 3:5

E I shall see in his hands . . . . John 20:25

how shall they preach, **e** they
  be sent? . . . . Rom 10:15

EXCUSE (n)
they are without **e** . . . . Rom 1:20

EXHORT
he that **e**, on exhortation . . . . Rom 12:8

These things teach and **e** . . . . 1 Tim 6:2

may be able by sound doctrine
  both to **e** . . . . Titus 1:9

e, and rebuke with all authority. . . . . . Titus 2:15

e one another . . . . Heb 3:13; 10:25

EXPRESS

the **e** image of his person . . . . Heb 1:3

EYE

right in his own **e**. . . Deut 12:8; Judg 17:6; 21:25

kept him as the apple of his **e** . . . . . . Deut 32:10

e of the LORD are upon the righteous . . . Ps 34:15

no fear of God before his **e** . . . . Ps 36:1

if thy right **e** offend thee . . . . Matt 5:29

Having **e**, see ye not?. . . . . Mark 8:18

The **e** of your understanding . . . . Eph 1:18

e of the LORD are over the righteous. . . 1 Pet 3:12

the lust of the **e**. . . . . 1 John 2:16

F

FABLES

refuse profane and old wives' **f**. . . . . . 1 Tim 4:7

cunningly devised **f** . . . . 2 Pet 1:16

FACE

LORD spake unto Moses **f** to **f**. . . . . Ex 33:11

skin of his **f** shone . . . . Ex 34:29

put a vail on his **f**. . . . . Ex 34:33

wash thy **f**. . . . . Matt 6:17

discern the **f** of the sky . . . Matt 16:3; Luke 12:56

his **f** did shine as the sun . . . . Matt 17:2

angels do always behold the **f** of
my Father . . . . Matt 18:10

set his **f** to go to Jerusalem. . . . . Luke 9:51

struck him on the **f**. . . . . Luke 22:64

then **f** to **f**. 1 Cor 13:12

But we all, with open **f** . . . . 2 Cor 3:18

withstood him to the **f** . . . . Gal 2:11

beholding his natural **f** in a glass . . . . James 1:23

FAIL

the grass **f** . . . . Isa 15:6

his compassions **f** not . . . . Lam 3:22

Charity never **f**. . . . . 1 Cor 13:8

FAINT (v)

shall walk, and not **f** . . . . Isa 40:31

pray, and not to **f** . . . . Luke 18:1

we shall reap, if we **f** not . . . . Gal 6:9

FAITH

ye of little **f** . . . Matt 6:30; 8:26; 16:8; Luke 12:28

so great **f**. . . . . Matt 8:10; Luke 7:9

seeing their **f**. . . . . Matt 9:2
(See also Mark 2:5; Luke 5:20.)

thy **f** hath made thee whole . . . . Matt 9:22;
Mark 5:34; 10:52; Luke 8:48; 17:19

According to your **f**. . . . . Matt 9:29

great is thy **f**. . . . . Matt 15:28

f as a grain of mustard seed . . . . Matt 17:20

If ye have **f**, and doubt not, ye shall
not only do this . . . . Matt 21:21

judgment, mercy, and **f**. . . . . Matt 23:23

how is it that ye have no **f**? . . . . Mark 4:40

Have **f** in God. . . . . Mark 11:22

Thy **f** hath saved thee. . . . . Luke 7:50

Where is your **f**? . . . . Luke 8:25

Increase our **f** . . . . Luke 17:5

shall he find **f** on the earth?. . . . . Luke 18:8

that thy **f** fail not . . . . Luke 22:32

the **f** which is by him . . . . Acts 3:16

a man full of **f** . . . . Acts 6:5

perceiving that he had **f** to be healed . . Acts 14:9

opened the door of **f** . . . . Acts 14:27

purifying their hearts by **f** . . . . Acts 15:9

established in the **f** . . . . Acts 16:5

sanctified by **f** . . . . Acts 26:18

for obedience to the **f** . . . . Rom 1:5

revealed from **f** to **f**. . . . . Rom 1:17

by the law of **f**. . . . . Rom 3:27

justified by **f**. . . . . Rom 3:28; 5:1
(See also Gal 2:16.)

f is counted for righteousness. . . . . Rom 4:5

of the **f** of Abraham . . . . Rom 4:16

being not weak in **f**. . . . . Rom 4:19

strong in **f** . . . . Rom 4:20

we have access by **f**. . . . . Rom 5:2

the word of **f**, which we preach . . . . . . Rom 10:8

f cometh by hearing . . . . Rom 10:17

the measure of **f** . . . . Rom 12:3

prophesy according to the
    proportion of **f** . . . . Rom 12:6

weak in the **f** receive ye . . . . Rom 14:1

Hast thou **f**? . . . . Rom 14:22

whatsoever is not of **f** is sin . . . . Rom 14:23

your **f** should not stand in
    the wisdom. 1 Cor 2:5

though I have all **f** . . . . 1 Cor 13:2

now abideth **f**. . . . . 1 Cor 13:13

and your **f** is also vain . . . . 1 Cor 15:14

stand fast in the **f** . . . . 1 Cor 16:13

same spirit of **f**. . . . . 2 Cor 4:13

we walk by **f** . . . . 2 Cor 5:7

whether ye be in the **f** . . . . 2 Cor 13:5

I live by the **f** of Son of God . . . . Gal 2:20

by the hearing of **f** . . . . Gal 3:2

law is not of **f** . . . . Gal 3:12

before **f** came . . . . Gal 3:23

f which worketh by love . . . . Gal 5:6

the household of **f**. . . . . Gal 6:10

access with confidence
    by the **f** of him . . . . Eph 3:12

dwell in your hearts by **f** . . . . Eph 3:17

One Lord, one **f** . . . . Eph 4:5

in the unity of the **f** . . . . Eph 4:13

the shield of **f**. . . . . Eph 6:16

striving together for the **f** of
    the gospel . . . . Phil 1:27

If ye continue in the **f** . . . . Col 1:23

the stedfastness of your **f** . . . . Col 2:5

work of **f**. . . . . 1 Thess 1:3; 2 Thess 1:11

the breastplate of **f** . . . . 1 Thess 5:8

all men have not **f** . . . . 2 Thess 3:2

my own son in the **f** . . . . 1 Tim 1:2

f unfeigned . . . . 1 Tim 1:5

if they continue in **f** . . . . 1 Tim 2:15

great boldness in the **f**. . . . . 1 Tim 3:13

shall depart from the **f** . . . . 1 Tim 4:1

he hath denied the **f** . . . . 1 Tim 5:8

erred from the **f**. . . . . 1 Tim 6:10

Fight the good fight of **f** . . . . 1 Tim 6:12

reprobate concerning the **f** . . . . 2 Tim 3:8

I have kept the **f** . . . . 2 Tim 4:7

the **f** of God's elect . . . . Titus 1:1

not being mixed with **f** . . . . Heb 4:2

of **f** toward God . . . . Heb 6:1

through **f** and patience inherit
    the promises . . . . Heb 6:12

in full assurance of **f** . . . . Heb 10:22

f is the substance of things
    hoped for. . . . . Heb 11:1

By **f**. . . . . Heb 11:4, 5, 7, 8, 9

without **f** it is impossible . . . . Heb 11:6

These all died in **f**. . . . . Heb 11:13

through **f** subdued kingdoms. . . . . Heb 11:33

a good report through **f** . . . . Heb 11:39

author and finisher of our **f** . . . . Heb 12:2

whose **f** follow . . . . Heb 13:7

the trying of your **f**. . . . . James 1:3

let him ask in **f**. . . . . James 1:6

My brethren, have not the **f** . . . . James 2:1

rich in **f**. . . . . James 2:5

man say he hath **f**, and have
    not works . . . . James 2:14

f, if it hath not works, is dead . . . . . . James 2:17

Thou hast **f**, and I have works . . . . . . James 2:18

f wrought with his works. . . . . James 2:22

the prayer of **f** shall save . . . . James 5:15

the end of your **f**. . . . . 1 Pet 1:9

resist stedfast in the **f**. . . . . 1 Pet 5:9

like precious **f**. . . . . 2 Pet 1:1

add to your **f** virtue . . . . 2 Pet 1:5

overcometh the world, even our **f** . . . . 1 John 5:4

earnestly contend for the **f** . . . . Jude 1:3

your most holy **f** . . . . Jude 1:20

hast not denied my **f** . . . . Rev 2:13

FAITHFUL

F are the wounds of a friend . . . . Prov 27:6

good and **f** servant . . . . Matt 25:21

f over a few things . . . . Matt 25:23

f also in much . . . . Luke 16:10

F is he that calleth you . . . . 1 Thess 5:24

a **f** saying . . . . 1 Tim 1:15; 4:9;
2 Tim 2:11; Titus 3:8

f in all things . . . . 1 Tim 3:11

f high priest . . . . Heb 2:17

he is **f** that promised . . . . Heb 10:23

he is **f** and just to forgive . . . . 1 John 1:9

FALL (v)

my feet from **f** . . . . Ps 56:13; 116:8

F on us . . . . Hos 10:8; Luke 23:30; Rev 6:16

shall **f** into the ditch . . . . Matt 15:14
(See also Luke 6:39.)

in time of temptation **f** away . . . . Luke 8:13

Satan as lightning **f** from heaven . . . . Luke 10:18

take heed lest he **f** . . . . 1 Cor 10:12

are **f** asleep . . . . 1 Cor 15:6, 18

If they shall **f** away . . . . Heb 6:6

to **f** into the hands of the living God . . Heb 10:31

FALLING

able to keep you from **f** . . . . Jude 1:24

FALSE

A **f** balance is abomination . . . . Prov 11:1

bear **f** witness . . . . Ex 20:16; Deut 5:20;
Matt 19:18

f Christs, and **f** prophets . . . . Matt 24:24;
Mark 13:22

are **f** apostles . . . . 2 Cor 11:13

among **f** brethren . . . . 2 Cor 11:26

FAR

Be not **f** from me . . . . Ps 22:11; 35:22;
38:21; 71:12

f above all gods . . . . Ps 97:9

f as the east is from the west . . . . Ps 103:12

F above all principality . . . . Eph 1:21

f above all heavens . . . . Eph 4:10

which is **f** better . . . . Phil 1:23

FAST

when he had **f** forty days . . . . Matt 4:2

not out but by prayer and **f** . . . . Matt 17:21

I **f** twice in the week . . . . Luke 18:12

may give yourselves to **f** . . . . 1 Cor 7:5

FATHER

a **f** of many nations . . . . Gen 17:4; Rom 4:17

my **f** God, and I will exalt him . . . . Ex 15:2

he that curseth his **f** . . . . Ex 21:17

f of the fatherless . . . . Ps 68:5

as a **f** pitieth his children . . . . Ps 103:13

The everlasting **F** . . . . Isa 9:6

I am a **f** to Israel . . . . Jer 31:9

your **F** which is in heaven . . . . . Matt 5:16, 45, 48

your **F** knoweth . . . . Matt 6:8, 32; Luke 12:30

Our **F** which art in heaven . . . . Matt 6:9;
Luke 11:2

the will of my **F** . . . . Matt 7:21; 12:50

behold the face of my **F** . . . . Matt 18:10

ye blessed of my **F** . . . . Matt 25:34

Abba, **F** . . . . Mark 14:36; Rom 8:15; Gal 4:6

about my **F** business . . . . Luke 2:49

as your **F** also is merciful . . . . Luke 6:36

it is your **F** good pleasure . . . . Luke 12:32

F, I have sinned . . . . Luke 15:21

F, if thou be willing . . . . Luke 22:42

F, forgive them . . . . Luke 23:34

F, into thy hands . . . . Luke 23:46

as of the only begotten of the **F** . . . . . . John 1:14

the **F** judgeth no man . . . . John 5:22

the **F** himself, which hath sent me . . . John 5:37

all that the **F** giveth me . . . . John 6:37

hath seen the **F** . . . . John 6:46
(See also John 14:9.)

we have one **F**, even God . . . . John 8:41

F, save me from this hour . . . . John 12:27

F, glorify thy name . . . . John 12:28

should depart out of this world
unto the **F** . . . . John 13:1

no man cometh unto the **F**, but
by me . . . . John 14:6

I will pray the **F** . . . . John 14:16; 16:26

my **F** is the husbandman . . . . John 15:1

whatsoever ye shall ask
of the **F** . . . . John 15:16

because I go to the **F** . . . . John 16:16

I came forth from the **F** . . . . John 16:28

the **F** is with me . . . . John 16:32

F, the hour is come . . . . John 17:1

I ascend unto my **F**, and
your **F** . . . . John 20:17

F of mercies, and the God of
all comfort . . . . 2 Cor 1:3

One God and **F** of all . . . . Eph 4:6

f, provoke not your children . . . . Eph 6:4

to the glory of God the **F** . . . . Phil 2:11

I will be to him a **F** . . . . Heb 1:5

fellowship is with the **F** . . . . 1 John 1:3

an advocate with the **F** . . . . 1 John 2:1

what manner of love the **F** hath . . . . . 1 John 3:1

the **F**, the Word, and the
Holy Ghost . . . . 1 John 5:7

FAULT
go and tell him his **f** . . . . Matt 18:15

I find no **f** in this man . . . . Luke 23:4

if a man be overtaken in a **f** . . . . Gal 6:1

confess your **f** one to . . . . James 5:16

FAULTLESS
present you **f** before the presence . . . . . Jude 1:24

FEAR (n)
f of the LORD is the beginning
of wisdom . . . . Ps 111:10; Prov 9:10

with **f** and trembling . . . . Eph 6:5; Phil 2:12

FEAR (v)
Doth Job **f** God for nought? . . . . Job 1:9

F God, and keep his
commandments . . . . Eccl 12:13

F not, little flock . . . . Luke 12:32

I will not **f** what man . . . . Heb 13:6

FEED
f me with food convenient . . . . Prov 30:8

your heavenly Father **f** them . . . . Matt 6:26

F my lambs . . . . John 21:15

if thine enemy hunger, **f** him . . . . Rom 12:20

FEET
all things under his **f** . . . . Ps 8:6;
1 Cor 15:27; Eph 1:22

pierced my hands and my **f** . . . . Ps 22:16

my **f** upon a rock . . . . Ps 40:2

my **f** from falling . . . . Ps 56:13; 116:8

a lamp unto my **f** . . . . Ps 119:105

How beautiful upon the mountains
are the **f** . . . . Isa 52:7

trample them under their **f** . . . . Matt 7:6

dust of your **f** . . . . Matt 10:14
(See also Mark 6:11; Luke 9:5.)

rather than having two hands
or two **f** . . . . Matt 18:8

kissed his **f**, and anointed them . . . . . . Luke 7:38

sitting at the **f** of Jesus . . . . Luke 8:35

Mary, which also sat at Jesus' **f** . . . . . Luke 10:39

Behold my hands and my **f** . . . . Luke 24:39

anointed the **f** of Jesus . . . . John 12:3

began to wash the disciples' **f** . . . . John 13:5

dost thou wash my **f**? . . . . John 13:6

at the apostles' **f** . . . . Acts 4:35, 37; 5:2

bruise Satan under your **f** . . . . Rom 16:20

your **f** shod with the preparation . . . . . . Eph 6:15

FELLOWSHIP
in the apostles' doctrine and **f** . . . . Acts 2:42

what **f** hath righteousness . . . . 2 Cor 6:14

your **f** in the gospel . . . . Phil 1:5

if any **f** of the Spirit . . . . Phil 2:1

the **f** of his sufferings . . . . Phil 3:10

our **f** is with the Father . . . . 1 John 1:3

we have **f** one with another . . . . 1 John 1:7

FERVENT
f in the spirit . . . . Acts 18:25

f in spirit . . . . Rom 12:11

f prayer of a righteous man . . . . James 5:16

with a pure heart **f** . . . . 1 Pet 1:22

melt with **f** heat . . . . 2 Pet 3:10, 12

FEW
let thy words be **f** . . . . Eccl 5:2

f there be that find it . . . . Matt 7:14

the labourers are **f** . . . . Matt 9:37; Luke 10:2

many be called, but **f** chosen . . . . . . Matt 20:16

faithful over a **f** things . . . . Matt 25:21

laid his hands upon a **f** sick folk . . . . . Mark 6:5

FIGHT (v)
so **f** I , not as one . . . . 1 Cor 9:26

F the good **f** of faith . . . . 1 Tim 6:12

I have **f** a good **f** . . . . 2 Tim 4:7

FILL
shall be **f** . . . . Matt 5:6; Luke 6:21

f with the Holy Ghost . . . . Luke 1:15;
　　　　　　　　　　　　　　　　Acts 4:8; 9:17; 13:9

him that **f** all in all . . . . Eph 1:23

be **f** with the Spirit . . . . Eph 5:18

FIND
f a wife **f** a good thing . . . . Prov 18:22

thy hand **f** to do, do it . . . . Eccl 9:10

seek, and ye shall **f** . . . . Matt 7:7; Luke 11:9

few there be that **f** it . . . . Matt 7:14

loseth his life for my sake shall **f** it. . . Matt 10:39

as many as ye shall **f** . . . . Matt 22:9

FINGER
little **f** shall be thicker . . 1 Kgs 12:10; 2 Chr 10:10

the tip of his **f** . . . . Luke 16:24

with his **f** wrote on the ground . . . . John 8:6

put my **f** into the print of the nails . . John 20:25

FINISH
So the wall was **f** . . . . Neh 6:15

which the Father hath
　　given me to **f** . . . . John 5:36

I have **f** the work . . . . John 17:4

It is **f** . . . . John 19:30

f my course . . . . Acts 20:24; 2 Tim 4:7

sin, when it is **f** . . . . James 1:15

FIRE
bush burned with **f** . . . . Ex 3:2

the LORD was not in the **f** . . . . 1 Kgs 19:12

Can a man take **f** . . . . Prov 6:27

cast into the **f** . . . . Matt 3:10; 7:19; Luke 3:9

baptize you with the Holy Ghost,
　　and with **f** . . . . Matt 3:11; Luke 3:16

everlasting **f** . . . . Matt 18:8; 25:41

rained **f** and brimstone . . . . Luke 17:29

cloven tongues like as of **f** . . . . Acts 2:3

saved; yet so as by **f** . . . . 1 Cor 3:15

his ministers a flame of **f** . . . . Heb 1:7

a little **f** kindleth . . . . James 3:5

the tongue is a **f** . . . . James 3:6

though it be tried with **f** . . . . 1 Pet 1:7

reserved unto **f** . . . . 2 Pet 3:7

cast into the lake of **f** . . . . Rev 20:10, 14

FIRST
seek ye **f** the kingdom . . . . Matt 6:33

f cast out the beam . . . . Matt 7:5

f bind the strong man . . . Matt 12:29; Mark 3:27

the **f** and great commandment . . . . . . Matt 22:38

But **f** must he suffer many things . . . Luke 17:25

let him **f** cast a stone . . . . John 8:7

called Christians **f** in Antioch . . . . Acts 11:26

The **f** man Adam was made a
  living soul . . . . 1 Cor 15:45

dead in Christ shall rise **f** . . . . 1 Thess 4:16

learn **f** to shew piety at home . . . . 1 Tim 5:4

f for his own sins . . . . Heb 7:27

f pure, then peaceable . . . . James 3:17

because he **f** loved us. . . . . 1 John 4:19

left thy **f** love . . . . Rev 2:4

f heaven and the **f** earth were
  passed away. . . . . Rev 21:1

FIRSTBORN

brought forth her **f** son . . . . . Matt 1:25; Luke 2:7

f among many brethren . . . . Rom 8:29

f of every creature . . . . Col 1:15

f from the dead . . . . Col 1:18

church of the **f** . . . . Heb 12:23

FISHERS

I will make you **f** of men . . . . Matt 4:19
  (See also Mark 1:17.)

FITLY

word **f** spoken is like apples . . . . Prov 25:11

all the building **f** framed . . . . Eph 2:21

whole body **f** joined together . . . . Eph 4:16

FLEE

man of God, **f** these things . . . . 1 Tim 6:11

F also youthful lusts . . . . 2 Tim 2:22

and he will **f** from you . . . . James 4:7

FLESH

yet in my **f** shall I see God . . . . Job 19:26

pour out my spirit upon all **f**. . . . . Joel 2:28;
  Acts 2:17

but the **f** is weak . . . . . . Matt 26:41; Mark 14:38

and the Word was made **f** . . . . John 1:14

and the bread that I will
  give is my **f** . . . . John 6:51

not in the **f**, but in the Spirit . . . . Rom 8:9

make not provision for the **f** . . . . Rom 13:14

was given to me a thorn in the **f** . . . . . 2 Cor 12:7

life which I now live in the **f** . . . . Gal 2:20

For the **f** lusteth against the Spirit . . . . . Gal 5:17

have no confidence in the **f** . . . . Phil 3:3

FLESHLY

not with **f** wisdom . . . . 2 Cor 1:12

abstain from **f** lusts . . . . 1 Pet 2:11

FLOCK

Fear not, little **f**. . . . . Luke 12:32

Feed the **f** of God . . . . 1 Pet 5:2

being ensamples to the **f** . . . . 1 Pet 5:3

FOLLOW

F me . . . . Matt 4:19; 8:22; 9:9; 16:24; 19:21;
  Mark 2:14; 8:34; 10:21;
  Luke 5:27; 9:23, 59; John 1:43

we have left all, and have **f** thee. . . . Mark 10:28;
  Luke 18:28

f after the things which make
  for peace. . . . . Rom 14:19

FOOL

way of a **f** is right in his own eyes . . . Prov 12:15

F make a mock at sin . . . . Prov 14:9

FOOLISHNESS

F is bound in the heart of a child . . . . Prov 22:15

to them that perish **f** . . . . 1 Cor 1:18

FOOT

thy **f** shall not stumble . . . . Prov 3:23

if thy hand or thy **f** offend thee . . . . . . Matt 18:8

If the **f** shall say, Because. . . . . 1 Cor 12:15

FOREKNOW

whom he did **f** . . . . Rom 8:29

his people which he **f** . . . . Rom 11:2

FOREKNOWLEDGE
the determinate counsel
and **f** of God . . . . Acts 2:23

according to the **f** of God . . . . 1 Pet 1:2

FOREORDAINED
f before the foundation
of the world. . . . . 1 Pet 1:20

FORERUNNER
Whither the **f** is entered. . . . . Heb 6:20

FOR EVER
F, O Lᴏʀᴅ, thy word is settled . . . . Ps 119:89

word of our God shall stand **f** . . . . Isa 40:8

abide with you **f** . . . . John 14:16

same yesterday, and to day, and **f** . . . . . Heb 13:8

FORGET
not **f** the works of God . . . . Ps 78:7

f those things which are behind . . . . . . Phil 3:13

not **f** to entertain . . . . Heb 13:2

FORGIVE
whose transgression is **f** . . . . Ps 32:1

f us our debts, as we **f** . . . . Matt 6:12

if ye **f** . . . . Matt 6:14

if ye **f** not . . . . Matt 6:15

power on earth to **f** sins . . . . Matt 9:6; Mark 2:10

faithful and just to **f** . . . . 1 John 1:9

FORGOTTEN
Hath God **f** to be gracious? . . . . Ps 77:9

f that he was purged from his
old sins . . . . 2 Pet 1:9

FORM (n)
the earth was without **f** . . . . Gen 1:2
(See also Jer 4:23.)

Who, being in the **f** of God . . . . Phil 2:6

took upon him the **f** of a servant . . . . . . Phil 2:7

Hold fast the **f** of sound words . . . . . . 2 Tim 1:13

Having a **f** of godliness . . . . 2 Tim 3:5

FORSAKE
why hast thou **f** me? . . . . Ps 22:1;
Matt 27:46; Mark 15:34

yet have I not seen the righteous **f** . . . . . Ps 37:25

the Lᴏʀᴅ loveth judgment, and **f** not
his saints . . . . Ps 37:28

Persecuted, but not **f** . . . . 2 Cor 4:9

Demas hath **f** me. . . . . 2 Tim 4:10

Not **f** the assembling of ourselves . . . . Heb 10:25

FOUND
f one pearl of great price. . . . . Matt 13:46

they **f** him in the temple. . . . . Luke 2:46

f the stone rolled away . . . . Luke 24:2

we have **f** the Messias . . . . John 1:41

f in fashion as a man . . . . Phil 2:8

FOUNDATION
upon another man's **f** . . . . Rom 15:20

other **f** can no man lay. . . . . 1 Cor 3:11

upon the **f** of the apostles and
prophets . . . . Eph 2:20

not laying again the **f** of repentance . . . . Heb 6:1

a city which hath **f** . . . . Heb 11:10

FREE
and the truth shall make you **f**. . . . . . . John 8:32

If the Son therefore shall
make you **f**. . . . . John 8:36

FREELY
Being justified **f** by his grace. . . . . Rom 3:24

how shall he not with him also
f give us all things . . . . Rom 8:32

FRIEND
f loveth at all times . . . . Prov 17:17

a **f** that sticketh closer than
a brother. Prov 18:24

Faithful are the wounds of a **f**. . . . . Prov 27:6

lay down his life for his **f** . . . . John 15:13

I have called you **f** . . . . John 15:15

FRUIT

by their **f** ye shall know them . . . . Matt 7:20

make the tree good, and
    his **f** good. . . . . Matt 12:33

f of the vine . . . . Matt 26:29; Mark 14:25

the **f** of the Spirit . . . . Gal 5:22; Eph 5:9

FULFIL

love is the **f** of the law . . . . Rom 13:10

so **f** the law of Christ . . . . Gal 6:2

f the desires of the flesh . . . . Eph 2:3

FULL

f of grace and truth . . . . John 1:14

f of the Holy Ghost . . . . . . Acts 6:3; 7:55; 11:24

G

GABRIEL

G, make this man to understand. . . . . . Dan 8:16

even the man **G**, whom I had seen . . . . Dan 9:21

I am **G**, that stand . . . . Luke 1:19

the angel **G** was sent . . . unto
    Nazareth . . . . Luke 1:26

GAIN (n)

to die is **g** . . . . Phil 1:21

g to me, those I counted loss . . . . Phil 3:7

GAVE

God **g** them over . . . . Rom 1:28

g gifts unto men . . . . Eph 4:8

he **g** some, apostles . . . . Eph 4:11

GENERATION

a perverse and crooked **g** . . . . Deut 32:5

g of vipers . . . . . Matt 3:7; 12:34; 23:33; Luke 3:7

perverse **g** . . . . Matt 17:17

this **g** shall not pass . . . Matt 24:34; Mark 13:30;
    Luke 21:32

a chosen **g** . . . . 1 Pet 2:9

GENTILES

we turn to the **G** . . . . Acts 13:46

is he not also [God] of the **G**?. . . . . . . Rom 3:29

salvation is come unto the **G** . . . . Rom 11:11

until the fulness of the **G** be
    come in . . . . Rom 11:25

That the **G** should be fellowheirs. . . . . . Eph 3:6

walk not as other **G** . . . . Eph 4:17

GENTLE

g, shewing all meekness. . . . . Titus 3:2

is first pure, then peaceable, **g** . . . . . James 3:17

GETHSEMANE

a place called **G**. . . . . Matt 26:36
    (See also Mark 14:32.)

GIFT

bring thy **g** to the altar . . . . Matt 5:23

know how to give good **g** . . . . Matt 7:11;
    Luke 11:13

g differing according to the grace . . . . . Rom 12:6

covet earnestly the best **g**. . . . . 1 Cor 12:31

desire spiritual **g** . . . . 1 Cor 14:1

unspeakable **g** . . . . 2 Cor 9:15

Neglect not the **g**. . . . . 1 Tim 4:14

stir up the **g**. . . . . 2 Tim 1:6

good gift and every perfect **g** . . . . James 1:17

GIVE

G to him that asketh . . . . Matt 5:42

G us this day our daily bread . . . . Matt 6:11

will he **g** him a stone? . . . . Matt 7:9

freely **g** . . . . Matt 10:8

G, and it shall be **g** . . . . Luke 6:38

G me to drink. . . . . John 4:7, 10

God loveth a cheerful **g** . . . . 2 Cor 9:7

that **g** to all men liberally. . . . . James 1:5

g grace unto the humble . . . . James 4:6

GLORIFY

g your Father which is in heaven . . . . . Matt 5:16

but when Jesus was **g**, then
remembered they . . . . John 12:16

Father, **g** thy name . . . . John 12:28

Herein is my Father **g** . . . . John 15:8

g thy Son . . . . John 17:1

I have **g** thee on the earth . . . . John 17:4

they **g** him not as God . . . . Rom 1:21

g God in your body, and in
your spirit . . . . 1 Cor 6:20

GLORIOUS

make his praise **g** . . . . Ps 66:2

blessed be his **g** name . . . . Ps 72:19

G things are spoken . . . . Ps 87:3

a **g** church . . . . Eph 5:27

GLORY

shew me thy **g** . . . . Ex 33:18

this King of **g**? . . . . Ps 24:8, 10

the whole earth is full of his **g** . . . . Isa 6:3

Solomon in all his **g** . . . . . Matt 6:29; Luke 12:27

G to God in the highest . . . . Luke 2:14

we beheld his **g** . . . . John 1:14

I seek not mine own **g** . . . . John 8:50

not worthy to be compared with
the **g**. . . . . Rom 8:18

crucified the Lord of **g** . . . . 1 Cor 2:8

woman is the **g** of the man . . . . 1 Cor 11:7

eternal weight of **g**. . . . . 2 Cor 4:17

Christ in you, the hope of **g** . . . . Col 1:27

the brightness of his **g** . . . . Heb 1:3

this man was counted worthy of
more **g**. . . . . Heb 3:3

called us unto his eternal **g** . . . . 1 Pet 5:10

worthy, O Lord, to receive **g** . . . . Rev 4:11

GOD

G is not a man, that he should lie . . . Num 23:19

if the Lord be **G**, follow him . . . . 1 Kgs 18:21

in his heart, There is no **G** . . . . Ps 14:1; 53:1

My **G**, my **G**, why hast thou
forsaken me? . . . . Ps 22:1; Matt 27:46

for I am **G**, and there is
none else . . . . Isa 45:22; 46:9

and to walk humbly with thy **G** . . . . Mic 6:8

G is a Spirit. John 4:24

If **G** be for us. . . . . Rom 8:31

For **G** is not the author
of confusion . . . . 1 Cor 14:33

G is not mocked . . . . Gal 6:7

No man hath seen **G** . . . . 1 John 4:12

And **G** shall wipe away all tears . . . . . . Rev 21:4

GODLINESS

the mystery of **g** . . . . 1 Tim 3:16

exercise thyself rather unto **g** . . . . 1 Tim 4:7

g is profitable . . . . 1 Tim 4:8

a form of **g** . . . . 2 Tim 3:5

pertain unto life and **g** . . . . 2 Pet 1:3

GOLD

I shall come forth as **g** . . . . Job 23:10

More to be desired are they than **g** . . . . . Ps 19:10

like apples of **g** . . . . Prov 25:11

being much more precious than of **g** . . . 1 Pet 1:7

corruptible things, as silver and **g** . . . . 1 Pet 1:18

city was pure **g** . . . . Rev 21:18

GOOD (adj)

The Lord is **g** to all . . . . Ps 145:9

how to give **g** gifts. . . . . . . Matt 7:11; Luke 11:13

g and faithful servant. . . . . Matt 25:21

Salt is **g**, but. . . . . Mark 9:50; Luke 14:34

g measure, pressed down . . . . Luke 6:38

I am the **g** shepherd . . . . John 10:11

that **g**, and acceptable, and perfect,
will of God . . . . Rom 12:2

hath begun a **g** work . . . . Phil 1:6

the law is **g** . . . . 1 Tim 1:8

Every **g** gift. . . . . James 1:17

GOOD (n)

God meant it unto **g** . . . . Gen 50:20

none that doeth **g** . . . . . . Ps 14:1; 53:1; Rom 3:12

work together for **g** . . . . Rom 8:28

bestow all my **g** to feed . . . . 1 Cor 13:3

GOODNESS

g and mercy shall follow . . . . Ps 23:6

earth is full of the **g** of the Lord . . . . Ps 33:5

the **g** and severity of God . . . . Rom 11:22

GOSPEL

not ashamed of the **g** of Christ . . . . Rom 1:16

according to my **g** . . . . Rom 2:16

if our **g** be hid . . . . 2 Cor 4:3

any other **g** . . . . Gal 1:8, 9

our **g** came not unto you in
    word only . . . . 1 Thess 1:5

GOVERNMENT

the **g** shall be upon his shoulder . . . . Isa 9:6

Of the increase of his **g** and peace
    there shall be no end . . . . Isa 9:7

gifts of healings, helps, **g** . . . . 1 Cor 12:28

(they that) despise **g** . . . . 2 Pet 2:10

GRACE

full of **g** and truth. . . . . John 1:14

justified freely by his **g** . . . . Rom 3:24

access by faith into this **g** . . . . Rom 5:2

where sin abounded, **g** did much
    more abound . . . . Rom 5:20

My **g** is sufficient . . . . 2 Cor 12:9

by **g** ye are saved . . . . Eph 2:5, 8

Let your speech be alway with **g** . . . . Col 4:6

he giveth more **g** . . . . James 4:6

heirs together of the **g** . . . . 1 Pet 3:7

grow in **g** . . . . 2 Pet 3:18

GRAFF

thou, being a wild olive tree,
    wert **g** in . . . . Rom 11:17

able to **g** them (Israel) in again . . . . . Rom 11:23

GRASS

days are as **g** . . . . Ps 103:15

if God so clothe the **g** . . . . Matt 6:30; Luke 12:28

GRAVE (n)

the **g** cannot praise thee . . . . Isa 38:18

O **g**, I will be thy destruction . . . . Hos 13:14

O **g**, where is thy victory? . . . . 1 Cor 15:55

GREAT

g is your reward . . . . Matt 5:12

called **g** in the kingdom
    of heaven. . . . . Matt 5:19

pearl of **g** price . . . . Matt 13:46

g is thy faith. . . . . Matt 15:28

whosoever will be **g** among you . . . . . Matt 20:26

the **g** commandment . . . . Matt 22:36
    (See also Matt 22:38.)

a **g** gulf fixed. . . . . Luke 16:26

so **g** salvation. Heb 2:3

so **g** a cloud of witnesses . . . . Heb 12:1

GREATER

Art thou **g** than our father . . . . . John 4:12; 8:53

servant is not **g** than
    his lord . . . . John 13:16; 15:20

G love hath no man . . . . John 15:13

God is **g** than our heart . . . . 1 John 3:20

g is he that is in you, than he
    that is in the world. . . . . 1 John 4:4

GROAN (v)

whole creation **g** . . . . Rom 8:22

we that are in this tabernacle
    do **g** . . . . 2 Cor 5:4

GROUND

holy **g** . . . . Ex 3:5; Acts 7:33

with his finger wrote on the **g** . . . . John 8:6

H

HAND

at thy right **h** there are pleasures
for evermore. . . . . Ps 16:11

none can stay his **h** . . . . Dan 4:35

kingdom of heaven is at **h**. . . . . Matt 3:2;
4:17; 10:7

My time is at **h** . . . . Matt 26:18

sitting on the right **h** of power . . . . . Mark 14:62

sat on the right **h** of God . . . . Mark 16:19

pluck them out of my **h** . . . . John 10:28

my Father's **h** . . . . John 10:29

an house not made with **h** . . . . 2 Cor 5:1

lifting up holy **h** . . . . 1 Tim 2:8

our **h** have handled, of the
Word of life. . . . . 1 John 1:1

HANDLE

nor **h** the word of God deceitfully . . . . 2 Cor 4:2

taste not; **h** not . . . . Col 2:21

have **h,** of the Word of life . . . . 1 John 1:1

HANG

went and **h** himself . . . . Matt 27:5

Cursed is every one that **h** on a tree . . . . Gal 3:13

HARD

Is any thing too **h** for the LORD? . . . . . Gen 18:14

Is there any thing too **h** for me? . . . . . . Jer 32:27

it is **h** for thee to kick against
the pricks. . . . . Acts 9:5; 26:14

HARDEN

I will **h** his heart . . . . Ex 4:21

I will **h** Pharaoh's heart . . . . Ex 7:3; 14:4

h the hearts of the Egyptians. . . . . Ex 14:17

whom he will he **h** . . . . Rom 9:18

HARVEST

The **h** is past, the summer is ended. . . . . Jer 8:20

The **h** is plenteous . . . . Matt 9:37

the Lord of the **h**. . . . . Matt 9:38; Luke 10:2

the **h** is the end of the world . . . . Matt 13:39

they are white already to **h** . . . . John 4:35

HATE

And I **h** Esau . . . . Mal 1:3
(See also Rom 9:13.)

do good to them that **h** you. . . . . Matt 5:44;
Luke 6:27

either he will **h** the one . . . . Matt 6:24

Blessed are ye, when men shall
h you . . . . Luke 6:22

he that **h** his life. . . . . John 12:25

If the world **h** you . . . . . John 15:18; 1 John 3:13

HEAD

it shall bruise thy **h** . . . . Gen 3:15

lift up your **h** . . . . Luke 21:28

helmet of salvation upon his **h** . . . . . . Isa 59:17
(See also Eph 6:17.)

the **h** of every man is Christ . . . . 1 Cor 11:3

husband is the **h** of the wife . . . . Eph 5:23

h of the . . . church. . . . . Eph 5:23; Col 1:18

HEAL

with his stripes we are **h**. . . . . Isa 53:5

H the sick. . . . . Matt 10:8; Luke 9:2; 10:9

to **h** the brokenhearted. . . . . Luke 4:18

Physician, **h** thyself . . . . Luke 4:23

pray for one another,
that ye may be **h**. . . . . James 5:16

by whose stripes ye were **h**. . . . . 1 Pet 2:24

HEAR

He that is of God **h** God's words . . . . . John 8:47

h without a preacher. . . . . Rom 10:14

save thyself, and them that **h** . . . . 1 Tim 4:16

swift to **h** . . . . James 1:19

HEARD

which we have seen and **h**. . . . . Acts 4:20;
1 John 1:3

whom they have not **h** . . . . Rom 10:14

Eye hath not seen, nor ear **h** . . . . 1 Cor 2:9

learned, and received, and **h** . . . . Phil 4:9

we have **h,** which we have seen . . . . . 1 John 1:1

I **h** a voice from heaven . . . . Rev 10:4; 14:2

HEARER
grace unto the **h.** . . . . Eph 4:29

a **h** of the word. . . . . James 1:23

HEARING
faith cometh by **h** . . . . Rom 10:17

ye are dull of **h.** . . . . Heb 5:11

HEART
love the Lord your God
    with all your **h** . . . . . . Deut 13:3; Matt 22:37;
                      Mark 12:30; Luke 10:27

the LORD looketh on the **h** . . . . 1 Sam 16:7

The fool hath said in his **h** . . . . Ps 14:1

Search me, O God, and know my **h** . . . Ps 139:23

The king's **h** is in the hand of
    the LORD . . . . Prov 21:1

The **h** is deceitful above all things . . . . . . Jer 17:9

Blessed are the pure in **h** . . . . Matt 5:8

I am meek and lowly in **h** . . . . Matt 11:29

out of the **h** proceed evil thoughts . . . Matt 15:19

Let not your **h** be troubled . . . . . . John 14:1, 27

That Christ may dwell in your **h**
    by faith . . . . Eph 3:17

making melody in your **h** . . . . Eph 5:19

in singleness of **h** . . . . Col 3:22

draw near with a true **h.** . . . . Heb 10:22

sanctify the Lord God in your **h** . . . . . 1 Pet 3:15

HEAVEN
Whom have I in **h** but thee?. . . . . Ps 73:25

thy word is settled in **h.** . . . . Ps 119:89

God is in **h.** . . . . Eccl 5:2

new **h** and a new earth . . . . . Isa 65:17; Rev 21:1

Do not I fill **h** and earth?. . . . . Jer 23:24

bread from **h.** . . . . John 6:31, 32

none other name under **h** . . . . Acts 4:12

whole family in **h.** . . . . Eph 3:15

Lord himself shall descend
    from **h** . . . . 1 Thess 4:16

written in **h** . . . . Heb 12:23

HEAVENLY
partakers of the **h** calling . . . . Heb 3:1

shadow of **h** things . . . . Heb 8:5

a better country, that is, an **h.** . . . . Heb 11:16

HEEL
thou shalt bruise his **h.** . . . . Gen 3:15

lifted up his **h** against me . . . Ps 41:9; John 13:18

HELL
not leave my soul in **h** . . . . . . Ps 16:10; Acts 2:27

in danger of **h** fire . . . . Matt 5:22

whole body should be
    cast into **h** . . . . Matt 5:29, 30

destroy both soul and body in **h.** . . . . Matt 10:28

gates of **h** shall not prevail . . . . Matt 16:18

two eyes to be cast into **h** . . . . Matt 18:9;
                              Mark 9:47

hath power to cast into **h** . . . . Luke 12:5

cast them down to **h** . . . . 2 Pet 2:4

HELP (n)
an **h** meet for him . . . . Gen 2:18, 20

he is our **h** and our shield. . . . . Ps 33:20

a very present **h** in trouble . . . . Ps 46:1

the hills, from whence cometh my **h** . . . Ps 121:1

HID
Thy word have I **h** in mine heart . . . . . Ps 119:11

Nothing . . . **h,** that shall not
    be known. . . . . Matt 10:26

if our gospel be **h,** it is **h** to . . . . 2 Cor 4:3

your life is **h** with Christ. . . . . Col 3:3

the **h** man of the heart. . . . . 1 Pet 3:4

HIGH
as the heaven is **h** above the earth . . . . Ps 103:11

it is **h,** I cannot attain unto it . . . . Ps 139:6

for prize of the **h** calling. . . . . Phil 3:14

HIGHER
heavens are **h** than the earth. . . . . Isa 55:9

HINDER
but Satan **h** us . . . . 1 Thess 2:18

that your prayers be not **h** . . . . 1 Pet 3:7

HOLD
H forth the word of life . . . . Phil 2:16

h such in reputation . . . . Phil 2:29

h fast that which is good . . . . 1 Thess 5:21

H faith, and a good conscience . . . . . . 1 Tim 1:19

H the mystery of the faith . . . . 1 Tim 3:9

H fast the form of sound words . . . . . 2 Tim 1:13

H fast the faithful word . . . . Titus 1:9

h the beginning of our confidence. . . . . Heb 3:14

h fast our profession . . . . Heb 4:14; 10:23

thou **h** fast my name . . . . Rev 2:13

HOLINESS
beauty of **h**. . . . . 1 Chr 16:29; 2 Chr 20:21;
Ps 29:2; 96:9; 110:3

created in righteousness and true **h** . . . Eph 4:24

continue in faith and charity and **h** . . 1 Tim 2:15

partakers of his **h**. . . . . Heb 12:10

h, without which no man . . . . Heb 12:14

HOLY
is **h** ground. . . . . Ex 3:5

by ye **h** . . . . Lev 20:7

H, **h**, **h**, is the Lord . . . . Isa 6:3

baptize you with the **H** Ghost . . . . . . Matt 3:11;
Mark 1:8; Luke 3:16
(See also John 1:33; Acts 1:5.)

shall be filled with the **H** Ghost . . . . . Luke 1:15

commandment **h**, and just,
and good . . . . Rom 7:12

a living sacrifice, **h**, acceptable
unto God . . . . Rom 12:1

with an **h** kiss . . . . Rom 16:16; 1 Cor 16:20;
2 Cor 13:12; 1 Thess 5:26

present you **h** and unblameable . . . . Col 1:22

lifting up **h** hands . . . . 1 Tim 2:8

h in all manner of conversation . . . . . . 1 Pet 1:15
(See also 1 Pet 1:16.)

an **h** priesthood . . . . 1 Pet 2:5

with him in the **h** mount . . . . 2 Pet 1:18

HOME
ask their husbands at **h**. . . . . 1 Cor 14:35

at **h** in the body. . . . . 2 Cor 5:6

let [children] learn first to show
piety at **h** . . . . 1 Tim 5:4

young women to be . . . keepers at **h** . . . Tit 2:4, 5

HONOUR (n)
crowned him with glory and **h**. . . Ps 8:5; Heb 2:7

in **h** preferring one another . . . . Rom 12:10

h to whom **h**. . . . . Rom 13:7

counted worthy of double **h** . . . . 1 Tim 5:17

worthy, O Lord, to receive glory
and **h** and power. . . . . Rev 4:11
(See also Rev 5:12.)

HONOUR (v)
H thy father and thy mother . . . . Ex 20:12;
Deut 5:16; Matt 19:19;
Mark 7:10; Luke 18:20

h me with their lips . . . . Matt 15:8

H all men. . . . . 1 Pet 2:17

HOPE (n)
h deferred maketh the heart sick . . . . Prov 13:12

who against **h** believed in **h** . . . . Rom 4:18

Rejoicing in **h** . . . . Rom 12:12

abideth faith, **h**, charity. . . . . 1 Cor 13:13

Christ in you, the **h** of glory . . . . Col 1:27

even as others which have no **h** . . . . 1 Thess 4:13

for an helmet, the **h** of salvation . . . . 1 Thess 5:8

the **h** of eternal life. . . . . Titus 3:7

lay hold upon the **h** set before us . . . . . Heb 6:18

begotten us again unto a lively **h**......1 Pet 1:3

a reason of the **h** that is in you ......1 Pet 3:15

HORSE
Be ye not as the **h,** or as the mule ......Ps 32:9

An **h** is a vain thing for safety ....Ps 33:17

behold a white **h** ....Rev 6:2; 19:11

another **h** that was red.............Rev 6:4

and lo a black **h** ....Rev 6:5

and behold a pale **h** ....Rev 6:8

HOSPITALITY
given to **h**.............Rom 12:13; 1 Tim 3:2

a lover of **h**......................Titus 1:8

Use **h** one to another ....1 Pet 4:9

HOUR
h knoweth no man.....Matt 24:36; Mark 13:32

watch with me one **h** ....Matt 26:40

mine **h** is not yet come.............John 2:4

The **h** is coming, and now is ....John 5:25

save me from this **h** ....John 12:27

thou shalt not know what **h** ....Rev 3:3

keep thee from the **h** of temptation ....Rev 3:10

HOUSE
Why is the **h** of God forsaken? ......Neh 13:11

h divided...................Matt 12:25
  (See also Mark 3:25.)

In my Father's **h** are many
  mansions...................John 14:2

h not made with hands............2 Cor 5:1

ruleth well his own **h** ....1 Tim 3:4

specially for those of his own **h** ......1 Tim 5:8

HOUSEHOLD
a man's foes shall be they of his
  own **h** ....Matt 10:36

the **h** of faith..................Gal 6:10

of the **h** of God.................Eph 2:19

HUMBLE (adj)
forgetteth not the cry of the **h** ....Ps 9:12

the **h** shall hear thereof ....Ps 34:2

be of an **h** spirit..................Prov 16:19

contrite and **h** spirit................Isa 57:15

giveth grace unto the **h** ....James 4:6; 1 Pet 5:5

HUMBLE (v)
h himself........Matt 18:4; 23:12; Luke 14:11;
  18:14; Phil 2:8

H yourselves therefore under the mighty hand of
  God ....1 Pet 5:6

HUSBAND
Go, call thy **h** ....John 4:16

Wives, submit yourselves unto
  your own **h**...................Eph 5:22

H, love your wives ....Eph 5:25; Col 3:19

the **h** of one wife.................1 Tim 3:12

to love their **h**..................Titus 2:4

obedient to their own **h** ....Titus 2:5

be in subjection to your own **h**........1 Pet 3:1

HYPOCRITE
ye **h** ....Matt 15:7; 16:3; 22:18;
  Mark 7:6; Luke 12:56

woe unto you, scribes and
  Pharisees **h**........Matt 23:13, Luke 11:44

I

IDLE
eateth not the bread of **i** ....Prov 31:27

every **i** word that men shall speak ...Matt 12:36

IDOL
touching things offered unto **i**........1 Cor 8:1

an **i** is nothing in the world.........1 Cor 8:4

ye turned to God from **i** ....1 Thess 1:9

keep yourselves from **i**.............1 John 5:21

IMMANUEL
shall call his name **I**................Isa 7:14

IMMORTALITY
this mortal must put on **i**. . . . . 1 Cor 15:53
  (See also 1 Cor 15:54)

IMPOSSIBLE
nothing shall be **i** unto you . . . . Matt 17:20

With men this is **i**. . . . . Matt 19:26
  (See also Mark 10:27.)

with God nothing shall be **i** . . . . Luke 1:37

it was **i** for God to lie . . . . Heb 6:18

without faith it is **i** to please him . . . . . Heb 11:6

INCORRUPTIBLE
But we an **i** (crown) . . . . 1 Cor 9:25

dead shall be raised **i** . . . . 1 Cor 15:52

To an inheritance **i** . . . . 1 Pet 1:4

born again, not of corruptible seed,
  but of **i** (seed) . . . . 1 Pet 1:23

INCORRUPTION
sown in corruption; it is raised in **i** . . 1 Cor 15:42

neither doth corruption inherit **i** . . . . 1 Cor 15:50

this corruption must put on **i**. . . . . . . 1 Cor 15:53

this corruptible shall have
  put on **i**. . . . . 1 Cor 15:54

INDEED
The Lord is risen **i**. . . . . Luke 24:34

ye shall be free **i**. . . . . John 8:36

INFIRMITY
Himself took our **i**. . . . . Matt 8:17

the Spirit also helpeth our **i** . . . . Rom 8:26

glory, but in mine **i**. . . . . 2 Cor 12:5
  (See also 2 Cor 12:10.)

INHERIT
the meek shall **i** the earth. . . . . Ps 37:11

shall **i** everlasting life . . . . Matt 19:29

i the kingdom prepared . . . . Matt 25:34

i eternal life . . . . . Mark 10:17; Luke 10:25; 18:18

not **i** the kingdom . . . . 1 Cor 6:9
  (See also 15:50; Gal 5:21.)

INIQUITY
visiting the **i** of the fathers. . . . . . . Ex 20:5; 34:7;
  Num 14:18; Deut 5:9

If I regard **i** in my heart . . . . Ps 66:18

If thou, LORD, shouldest mark **i** . . . . Ps 130:3

he was bruised for our **i**. . . . . Isa 53:5

depart from **i**. . . . . 2 Tim 2:19

INSPIRATION
All scripture is given by **i** of God. . . . . 2 Tim 3:16

INSTRUCTION
fools despise wisdom and **i** . . . . Prov 1:7

A fool despiseth his father's **i** . . . . Prov 15:5

for **i** in righteousness. . . . . 2 Tim 3:16

INTERCESSION
the Spirit itself maketh **i**. . . . . Rom 8:26

ever liveth to make **i** . . . . Heb 7:25

INTREAT
but **i** him as a father . . . . 1 Tim 5:1

INVISIBLE
the **i** things of him . . . are
  clearly seen . . . . Rom 1:20

image of the **i** God . . . . Col 1:15

the King eternal, immortal, **i** . . . . 1 Tim 1:17

as seeing him who is **i** . . . . Heb 11:27

INWARD
truth in the **i** parts . . . . Ps 51:6

I will put my law in their **i** parts . . . . . Jer 31:33

delight in the law of God after
  the **i** man. . . . . Rom 7:22

the **i** man is renewed . . . . 2 Cor 4:16

IRON
I sharpeneth **i** . . . . Prov 27:17

legs of **i**, his feet part of **i**. . . . . Dan 2:33

conscience seared with a hot **i** . . . . 1 Tim 4:2

ISAAC
By faith Abraham, when he was
  tried, offered up **I** . . . . Heb 11:17

in **I** shall thy seed be called . . . . Heb 11:18

By faith **I** blessed Jacob and Esau . . . . Heb 11:20

ISRAEL
name shall be called no
more Jacob, but **I** . . . . Gen 32:28

they are not all **I**, which are of **I** . . . . . . Rom 9:6

prayer to God, for **I**, that they
might be saved. . . . . Rom 10:1

Did not **I** know? . . . . Rom 10:19

J

JACOB
J have I loved, but Esau have I hated. . Rom 9:13

By faith Isaac blessed **J** and Esau . . . . Heb 11:20

By faith **J** . . . blessed both
the sons of Joseph. . . . . Heb 11:21

JEHOVAH
by my name **J** was I not known . . . . Ex 6:3

whose name alone is **J** . . . . Ps 83:18

for the LORD **J** is my strength . . . . Isa 12:2

in the LORD **J** is everlasting strength . . . . Isa 26:4

JERUSALEM
J, the city which I have chosen . . . . . 1 Kgs 11:36
(See also 2 Kgs 21:7; 23:27; 2 Chr 6:6; 12:13.)

answereth to **J** which now is . . . . Gal 4:25

J which is above is free. . . . . Gal 4:26

new **J**, which cometh down . . . . Rev 3:12
(See also Rev 21:2.)

JESUS
thou shalt call his name **J** . . . . Matt 1:21

I am **J** whom thou persecutest . . . . Acts 9:5

J Christ the same yesterday. . . . . Heb 13:8

JEW
the **J** have no dealings with
Samaritans . . . . John 4:9

salvation is of the **J** . . . . John 4:22

to the **J** first, and also to the Greek . . . Rom 1:16

thou art called a **J**, and restest
in the law. . . . . Rom 2:17

not a **J**, which is one outwardly . . . . . Rom 2:28

he is a **J**, which is one inwardly . . . . . . Rom 2:29

What advantage then hath the **J**? . . . . . Rom 3:1

no difference between the **J** and
the Greek . . . . Rom 10:12

unto the **J** I became as a **J**. . . . . 1 Cor 9:20

being a **J,** livest after the manner
of Gentiles . . . . Gal 2:14

There is neither **J** nor Greek . . . . Gal 3:28
(See also Col 3:11.)

JEZEBEL
sufferest that woman **J** . . . . Rev 2:20

JOIN
What therefore God hath **j** . . . . Matt 19:6;
Mark 10:9

whole body fitly **j** together. . . . . Eph 4:16

JOY
j of the LORD is your strength. . . . . Neh 8:10

j cometh in the morning. . . . . Ps 30:5

Restore unto me the **j** of
thy salvation . . . . Ps 51:12

They that sow in tears shall reap in **j** . . . Ps 126:5

j shall be in heaven over one sinner . . . Luke 15:7

there is **j** in the presence of
the angels . . . . Luke 15:10

Fulfil ye my **j** . . . . Phil 2:2

for the **j** that was set before him . . . . . . Heb 12:2

count it all **j** when ye fall . . . . James 1:2

that our **j** may be full . . . . 2 John 1:12

JUDAEA
let them which be in **J** flee . . . . Matt 24:16;
Mark 13:14; Luke 21:21

unknown by face unto the
churches in **J** . . . . Gal 1:22

both in Jerusalem, and in all **J** . . . . Acts 1:8

JUDGE (n)

the **J** of quick and dead . . . . Acts 10:42

the Lord, the righteous **j** . . . . 2 Tim 4:8

to God the **J** of all . . . . Heb 12:23

the **j** standeth before the door . . . . James 5:9

JUDGE (v)

J not, that ye be not **j** . . . . Matt 7:1

j righteous judgment . . . . John 7:24

who art thou that **j** . . . . Rom 14:4

JUDGMENT

in danger of the **j** . . . . Matt 5:21

Father . . . committed all **j** unto
    the Son . . . . John 5:22

we shall all stand before the **j** seat . . . Rom 14:10

JUST

the **j** shall live by faith . . . . . . Hab 2:4; Rom 1:17;
                            Gal 3:11; Heb 10:38

sendeth rain on the **j** and on
    the unjust . . . . Matt 5:45

JUSTIFY

all that believe are **j** . . . . Acts 13:39

j freely by his grace . . . . Rom 3:24
    (See also Titus 3:7.)

being **j** by faith . . . . Rom 5:1

being now **j** by his blood . . . . Rom 5:9

K

KEEP

Fear God, and **k** his commandments . . Eccl 12:13

If a man love me, he will **k**
    my words . . . . John 14:23

k the unity of the Spirit . . . . Eph 4:3

shall **k** your hearts and minds . . . . Phil 4:7

k yourselves from idols . . . . 1 John 5:21

K yourselves in the love of God . . . . . . Jude 1:21

him that is able to **k** you
    from falling . . . . Jude 1:24

KEY

the **k** of the house of David . . . . Isa 22:22

the **k** of the kingdom of heaven . . . . . Matt 16:19

the **k** of hell and of death . . . . Rev 1:18

hath the **k** of David . . . . Rev 3:7

the **k** of the bottomless pit . . . . Rev 9:1; 20:1

KINDLY

the LORD deal **k** with you . . . . Ruth 1:8

Be **k** affectioned one to another . . . . . Rom 12:10

KING

God is my **K** of old . . . . Ps 74:12

By me **k** reign . . . . Prov 8:15

Curse not the **k** . . . . Eccl 10:20

behold, thy **K** cometh . . . . Zech 9:9
                            Matt 21:5; John 12:15

Blessed be the **K** that cometh . . . . Luke 19:38

The **k** of the Gentiles exercise
    lordship . . . . Luke 22:25

Behold your **K** . . . . John 19:14

unto the **K** eternal, immortal . . . . 1 Tim 1:17

K of kings . . . . 1 Tim 6:15; Rev 17:14; 19:16

thou **K** of saints . . . . Rev 15:3

the way of the **k** of the east might
    be prepared . . . . Rev 16:12

KINGDOM

ye shall be unto me a **k** of priests . . . . . . Ex 19:6

gospel of the **k** . . . . Matt 4:23; 9:35; 24:14

children of the **k** shall be cast out . . . . Matt 8:12

k divided against itself . . . . Matt 12:25;
                            Mark 3:24; Luke 11:17

inherit the **k** . . . . Matt 25:34

Father's good pleasure to give
    you the **k** . . . . Luke 12:32

My **k** is not of this world . . . . John 18:36

into the **k** of his dear Son . . . . Col 1:13

heirs of the **k** which he hath
    promised . . . . James 2:5

into the everlasting **k** . . . . 2 Pet 1:11

KISS

K the Son, lest he be angry . . . . Ps 2:12

Salute one another with an holy **k** . . . Rom 16:16

Greet ye one another with a **k**
of charity . . . . 1 Pet 5:14

KNEW

I never **k** you; depart . . . . Matt 7:23

who **k** no sin . . . . 2 Cor 5:21

KNOW

I **k** that my redeemer liveth . . . . Job 19:25

Be still, and **k** that I am God . . . . Ps 46:10

he **k** our frame . . . . Ps 103:14

let not thy left hand **k** . . . . Matt 6:3

I **k** him not . . . . Luke 22:57

k my sheep, and am **k** of mine . . . . . John 10:14

By this shall all men **k** that ye
are my disciples . . . . John 13:35

we **k** in part . . . . 1 Cor 13:9

and to **k** the love of Christ . . . . Eph 3:19

I **k** whom I have believed . . . . 2 Tim 1:12

thou hast **k** the holy scriptures . . . . . 2 Tim 3:15

I **k** thy works . . . . Rev 2:2, 9, 13, 19; 3:1, 8

KNOWLEDGE

Wise men lay up **k** . . . . Prov 10:14

destroyed for lack of **k** . . . . Hos 4:6

K puffeth up . . . . 1 Cor 8:1

love of Christ, which passeth **k** . . . . Eph 3:19

the excellency of the **k** of Christ . . . . . . Phil 3:8

treasures of wisdom and **k** . . . . Col 2:3

to virtue **k** . . . . 2 Pet 1:5

grow in grace, and in the **k** . . . . 2 Pet 3:18

L

LABOURER

the **l** is worthy of his hire . . . . Luke 10:7

but the **l** are few . . . . Matt 9:37; Luke 10:2

Pray . . . that he will send forth **l** . . . . Matt 9:38;

we are **l** together with God . . . . 1 Cor 3:9

The **l** is worthy of his reward . . . . 1 Tim 5:18

LAMB

God will provide himself a **l** . . . . Gen 22:8

brought as a **l** to the slaughter . . . . Isa 53:7

Behold the **L** of God . . . . John 1:29, 36

He [Jesus] saith unto him,
Feed my **l** . . . . John 21:15

as of a **l** without blemish . . . . 1 Pet 1:19

stood a **L** as it had been slain . . . . Rev 5:6

Worthy is the **L** that was slain . . . . Rev 5:12

hide us . . . from the wrath of the **L**. . . . Rev 6:16

by the blood of the **L** . . . . Rev 12:11

the throne of God and of the **L** . . . . Rev 22:1

LAMP

Thy word is a **l** unto my feet . . . . Ps 119:105

LAW

I delight in thy **l** . . . . Ps 119:70

how love I thy **l** . . . . Ps 119:97

come to destroy the **l** . . . . Matt 5:17

the **l** is holy . . . . Rom 7:12

the **l** is spiritual . . . . Rom 7:14

the **l** was our schoolmaster . . . . Gal 3:24

against such there is no **l** . . . . Gal 5:23

so fulfil the **l** of Christ . . . . Gal 6:2

perfect **l** of liberty . . . . James 1:25

LEAD

he **l** me beside the still waters . . . . Ps 23:2

l me to the rock that is higher than I . . . . Ps 61:2

a little child shall **l** them . . . . Isa 11:6

l us not into temptation . . . Matt 6:13; Luke 11:4

the blind **l** the blind . . . . . Matt 15:14; Luke 6:39

LEAN

l not unto thine own understanding . . . . Prov 3:5

LEARN

l of me; for I am meek . . . . Matt 11:29

Moses was l in all the wisdom . . . . Acts 7:22

But ye have not so l Christ. . . . . Eph 4:20

which ye have both l . . . and seen
   in me, do. . . . . Phil 4:9

I have l in whatsoever state I am,
   therewith to be content . . . . Phil 4:11

Let the woman l in silence . . . . 1 Tim 2:11

LEAST

one of these l commandments . . . . . . Matt 5:19

he that is l in the kingdom . . . . Matt 11:11;
                              Luke 7:28

one of the l of these . . . . Matt 25:40, 45

faithful in that which is l . . . . Luke 16:10

less than the l of all saints. . . . . Eph 3:8

LEAVE

l his father and his mother, and
   shall cleave. . . . . Gen 2:24;
                       Mark 10:7; Eph 5:31

Peace I l with you. . . . . John 14:27

I will never l thee. . . . . Heb 13:5

LEAVEN

kingdom of heaven is like unto l . . . . Matt 13:33

beware of the l of the Pharisees . . . . . Matt 16:11

A little l leaveneth the whole lump . . . 1 Cor 5:6;
                                  Gal 5:9

Purge out therefore the old l . . . . 1 Cor 5:7

LIAR

All men are l . . . . Ps 116:11

he is a l, and the father of it. . . . . John 8:44

all l, shall have their part in the lake . . . Rev 21:8

LIBERTY

he sent me . . . to proclaim l to
   the captives. Isa 61:1

to set at l them that are bruised . . . . . Luke 4:18

where the Spirit of the Lord is,
   there is l . . . . 2 Cor 3:17

Stand fast therefore in the l . . . . Gal 5:1

law of l. . . . . James 1:25; 2:12

LIFE

the tree of l . . . . Gen 2:9; 3:24; Rev 2:7

Take no thought for your l. . . . . Matt 6:25;
                              Luke 12:22

The l is more than meat . . . . Luke 12:23

In him was l. . . . . John 1:4

passed from death unto l . . . . John 5:24;
                             1 John 3:14

that bread of l. . . . . John 6:48

I lay down my l. . . . . John 10:15, 17

the resurrection, and the l . . . . John 11:25

in newness of l . . . . Rom 6:4

the l which I now live. . . . . Gal 2:20

your l is hid. . . . . Col 3:3

the pride of l . . . . 1 John 2:16

LIGHT

The Lord is my l . . . . Ps 27:1

a l unto my path . . . . Ps 119:105

the l of the world . . . . . Matt 5:14; John 8:12; 9:5

Let your l so shine . . . . Matt 5:16

the l of the body is the eye . . . . Matt 6:22

That was the true L . . . . John 1:9

l is come into the world . . . . John 3:19

commanded the l to shine out
   of darkness . . . . 2 Cor 4:6

an angel of l . . . . 2 Cor 11:14

now are ye l in the Lord: walk as
   children of l . . . . Eph 5:8

God is l . . . . 1 John 1:5

walk in the l, as he is in the l . . . . 1 John 1:7

LIGHTNING

as the l . . . so also shall the coming
   of the Son of man . . . . Matt 24:27

Satan as l fall from heaven. . . . . Luke 10:18

LION

a living dog is better than a dead l . . . . . Eccl 9:4

the devil, as a roaring l, walketh . . . . . . 1 Pet 5:8

behold, the **L** of the tribe of Juda. . . . . . . Rev 5:5

LIP
a man of unclean l. . . . . Isa 6:5

honoureth me with their l . . . . Matt 15:8

LITTLE
a l lower than the angels . . . . . . Ps 8:5; Heb 2:7

a l sleep, a l slumber, a l folding
of the hands . . . . Prov 6:10; 24:33

l ones . . . . Matt 10:42; 18:6;
Mark 9:42; Luke 17:2

to whom l is forgiven . . . . Luke 7:47

a l leaven . . . . 1 Cor 5:6; Gal 5:9

bodily exercise profiteth l . . . . 1 Tim 4:8

use a l wine . . . . 1 Tim 5:23

LIVE
not l by bread . . . . Deut 8:3;
Matt 4:4; Luke 4:4

the just shall l by his faith . . . . Hab 2:4

this do, and thou shalt l . . . . Luke 10:28

though he were dead, yet
shall he l . . . . John 11:25

in him we l, and move . . . . Acts 17:28

whether we l, we l unto the Lord . . . . . Rom 14:8

For to me to l is Christ . . . . Phil 1:21

LIVELY
unto a l hope by the resurrection . . . . . . 1 Pet 1:3

as l stones, are built up a
spiritual house . . . . 1 Pet 2:5

LIVING
l waters . . . . Song 4:15; Jer 2:13; 17:13;
Zech 14:8; John 4:10

I am the l bread . . . . John 6:51

LOOK
L unto me, and be ye saved . . . . Isa 45:22

no man . . . l back is fit . . . . Luke 9:62

L not every man on his own things . . . . . Phil 2:4

he l for a city . . . whose builder and
maker is God . . . . Heb 11:10

which things the angels desire
to l into . . . . 1 Pet 1:12

LORD
the **L**, the **L** God, merciful . . . . Ex 34:6

the **L** he is God . . . . Deut 4:35

The **L** our God is one **L**. . . . . Deut 6:4

The **L** be with you. . . . . . . Ruth 2:4; 2 Thess 3:16

It is the **L** . . . . 1 Sam 3:18; John 21:7

the **L**, he is the God . . . . 1 Kgs 18:39

thou, art **L** alone . . . . Neh 9:6

whose God is the **L** . . . . Ps 33:12

Know ye that the **L** he is God . . . . Ps 100:3

This is the **L** doing . . . . Ps 118:23

one **L**, and his name one . . . . Zech 14:9

Not every one that saith
unto me, **L**, **L** . . . . Matt 7:21

L, is it I? . . . . Matt 26:22

L also of the sabbath . . . . . Mark 2:28; Luke 6:5

why call ye me, **L**, **L**? . . . . Luke 6:46

Who is he, **L**? . . . . John 9:36

We have seen the **L** . . . . John 20:25

both **L** and Christ . . . . Acts 2:36

Who art thou, **L**? . . . . Acts 9:5; 26:15

One **L** . . . . Eph 4:5

LOST
the l sheep of the house
of Israel . . . . Matt 10:6; 15:24

to save that which was l . . . . Matt 18:11;
Luke 19:10

LOVE (n)
if ye have l one to another . . . . John 13:35

Greater l hath no man than this . . . . John 15:13

the l of Christ constraineth us . . . . 2 Cor 5:14

the l of Christ, which passeth . . . . Eph 3:19

the l of money is the root
of all evil . . . . 1 Tim 6:10

Let brotherly l continue . . . . Heb 13:1

l is of God . . . . 1 John 4:7

God is l . . . . 1 John 4:8, 16

There is no fear in l . . . . 1 John 4:18

LOVE (v)

l the Lord thy God . . . . Deut 6:5; 11:1;
                                                        19:9; 30:6; Matt 22:37;
                                                        Mark 12:30; Luke 10:27

A friend l at all times . . . . Prov 17:17

A time to l . . . . Eccl 3:8

Hate the evil, and l the good . . . . Amos 5:15

to l mercy, and to walk humbly . . . . Mic 6:8

L your enemies . . . . Matt 5:44; Luke 6:27

That ye l one another . . . . John 15:12, 17

l thou me? . . . . John 21:15, 16, 17

owe no man any thing, but to l . . . . . . Rom 13:8

We l him, because he first l us . . . . . 1 John 4:19

LUST

when he is drawn away of his
   own l . . . . James 1:14

abstain from fleshly l . . . . 1 Pet 2:11

the l of the flesh . . . . 1 John 2:16

M

MADE

This is the day which the Lord
   hath m . . . . Ps 118:24

The Lord hath m all things
   for himself . . . . Prov 16:4

All things were m by him . . . . John 1:3

he hath m him to be sin for us . . . . . 2 Cor 5:21

m nigh by the blood of Christ . . . . Eph 2:13

having m peace . . . . Col 1:20

MAKER

ascribe righteousness to my M . . . . Job 36:3

kneel before the Lord our m . . . . Ps 95:6

the Lord is the m of them all . . . . Prov 22:2

whose builder and m is God . . . . Heb 11:10

MAN

I will not fear; what can m do? . . . . . . Ps 118:6

No m can serve . . . . Matt 6:24

No m hath seen God . . . . John 1:18; 1 John 4:12

Behold the m . . . . John 19:5

though our outward m perish . . . . 2 Cor 4:16

in fashion as a m . . . . Phil 2:8

the m Christ Jesus . . . . 1 Tim 2:5

MANNER

All m of sin and blasphemy shall
   be forgiven . . . . Matt 12:31

holy in all m of conversation . . . . 1 Pet 1:15

MARK (n)

the Lord set a m upon Cain . . . . Gen 4:15

I press toward the m for the prize . . . . . Phil 3:14

MARRIAGE

they that were ready went in with
   him to the m . . . . Matt 25:10

M is honourable in all . . . . Heb 13:4

the m of the Lamb is come . . . . Rev 19:7

Blessed are they which are called
   unto the m supper . . . . Rev 19:9

MASTER

No man can serve two m . . . . Matt 6:24
   (See also Luke 16:13.)

disciple is not above his m . . . . Matt 10:24;
                                                        Luke 6:40

one is your M, even Christ . . . . . . Matt 23:8, 10

Ye call me M and Lord: and ye
   say well . . . . John 13:13

ye also have a M in heaven . . . . Col 4:1

Servants, be subject to your m . . . . . . 1 Pet 2:18

MATTER

conclusion of the whole m . . . . Eccl 12:13

how great a m a little fire kindleth . . . James 3:5

MEASURE (n)

good **m**, pressed down . . . . Luke 6:38

to every man the **m** of faith . . . . Rom 12:3

MEAT

I have **m** to eat . . . . John 4:32

My **m** is to do the will of him that
  sent me . . . . John 4:34

abstain from **m** offered to idols . . . . . Acts 15:29

kingdom of God is not
  m and drink . . . . Rom 14:17

if **m** make my brother to offend . . . . . 1 Cor 8:13

to abstain from **m** . . . . 1 Tim 4:3

MEDIATOR

one **m** between God and men,
  the man Christ Jesus . . . . 1 Tim 2:5

the **m** of a better covenant . . . . Heb 8:6

the **m** of the new testament . . . . Heb 9:15

the **m** of the new covenant . . . . Heb 12:24

MEEK (n)

the **m** shall inherit the earth . . . . Ps 37:11

Blessed are the **m** . . . . Matt 5:5

MERCIFUL

Be ye therefore **m**, as your Father
  also is **m** . . . . Luke 6:36

God be **m** to me a sinner . . . . Luke 18:13

a **m** and faithful high priest . . . . Heb 2:17

MERCY

his **m** endureth for ever . . . . 1 Chr 16:34, 41;
                2 Chr 5:13; 7:3, 6; Ezra 3:11;
                Ps 106:1; 107:1; 118:1;
                136:1; Jer 33:11

Surely goodness and **m** shall follow . . . . . Ps 23:6

I will sing of **m** . . . . Ps 101:1

The earth, O LORD, is full of thy **m** . . . . Ps 119:64

but to do justly, and to love **m** . . . . Mic 6:8

Thou Son of David, have **m** . . . . Matt 9:27;
                Mark 10:47; Luke 18:38, 39

m on whom I will have **m** . . . . Rom 9:15

God, who is rich in **m** . . . . Eph 2:4

obtain **m**, and find grace . . . . Heb 4:16

according to his abundant **m** . . . . 1 Pet 1:3

MERRY

m heart doeth good like
  a medicine . . . . Prov 17:22

than to eat, and to drink,
  and to be **m** . . . . Eccl 8:15

Is any **m**? . . . . James 5:13

MICHAEL

M, one of the chief princes, came to
  help me . . . . Dan 10:13

none that holdeth with me in these
  things, but **M** your prince . . . . Dan 10:21

at that time shall **M** stand up . . . . Dan 12:1

M the archangel, when contending . . . . Jude 1:9

M and his angels fought against . . . . . . Rev 12:7

MIND (n)

the carnal **m** is enmity against God . . . . Rom 8:7

Be of the same **m** . . . . Rom 12:16

of one **m** . . . . 2 Cor 13:11; Phil 2:2

in lowliness of **m** . . . . Phil 2:3

Let this **m** be in you . . . . Phil 2:5

shall keep your hearts and **m** . . . . Phil 4:7

of a sound **m** . . . . 2 Tim 1:7

stir up your pure **m** . . . . 2 Pet 3:1

MOCK

I will **m** when your fear cometh . . . . . . Prov 1:26

God is not **m** . . . . Gal 6:7

MOMENT

his anger endureth but a **m** . . . . Ps 30:5

In a **m** . . . . 1 Cor 15:52

affliction, which is but for a **m** . . . . . 2 Cor 4:17

MONEY

he that hath no **m** . . . . Isa 55:1

Wherefore do ye spend **m** . . . . Isa 55:2

Thy **m** perish with thee . . . . Acts 8:20

the love of **m** . . . . 1 Tim 6:10

MORROW

no thought for the **m** . . . . Matt 6:34

ye know not what shall be
   on the **m** . . . . James 4:14

MOSES

as I was with **M**, so I will
   be with thee . . . . Josh 1:5

Though **M** and Samuel stood
   before me . . . . Jer 15:1

as **M** lifted up the serpent . . . . John 3:14

there appeared **M** and Elias . . . . Matt 17:3
   (See also Luke 9:30.)

there appeared Elias and **M** . . . . Mark 9:4

M truly said . . . A prophet shall the
   Lord your God raise up . . . . Acts 3:22

Michael . . . disputed about the
   body of **M** . . . . Jude 1:9

MOTHER

As is the **m**, so is her daughter . . . . . . Ezek 16:44

Who is my **m?** . . . . Matt 12:48; Mark 3:33

the **m** of Jesus . . . . John 2:1; Acts 1:14

MOUTH

I will keep my **m** with a bridle . . . . Ps 39:1

This people draw near me with
   their **m** . . . . Isa 29:13
   (See also Matt 15:8.)

Out of the **m** of babes . . . . Ps 8:2; Matt 21:16

Out of the same **m** proceedeth . . . . . . James 3:10

MULTITUDE

in the **m** of words there wanteth
   not sin . . . . Prov 10:19

in the **m** of counsellers . . . . Prov 11:14;
                        15:22; 24:6

M, m in the valley of decision . . . . Joel 3:14

m of sins . . . . James 5:20; 1 Pet 4:8

MYSTERY

the wisdom of God in a **m** . . . . 1 Cor 2:7

stewards of the **m** of God . . . . 1 Cor 4:1

though I . . . understand all **m** . . . . . . 1 Cor 13:2

I shew you a **m** . . . . 1 Cor 15:51

This is a great **m** . . . . Eph 5:32

the **m** which hath been hid
   from ages . . . . Col 1:26

the **m** of iniquity doth
   already work . . . . 2 Thess 2:7

N

NAME (n)

The **n** of the Lord is a strong tower . . . Prov 18:10

good **n** . . . . Prov 22:1; Eccl 7:1

I am the Lord: that is my **n** . . . . Isa 42:8

one Lord, and his **n** one . . . . Zech 14:9

Hallowed be thy **n** . . . . Matt 6:9; Luke 11:2

for my **n** sake . . . . Matt 10:22; 19:29;
                Mark 13:13; Luke 21:12;
                 John 15:21; Acts 9:16

little child in my **n** . . . . Matt 18:5

gathered together in my **n** . . . . Matt 18:20

many shall come in my **n** . . . . Matt 24:5;
                Mark 13:6; Luke 21:8

do a miracle in my **n** . . . . Mark 9:39

receive this child in my **n** . . . . Luke 9:48

n are written in heaven . . . . Luke 10:20

if another shall come in
   his own **n** . . . . John 5:43

ye shall ask in my **n** . . . . John 14:13; 16:26

his **n** through faith in his **n** . . . . Acts 3:16

none other **n** under heaven . . . . Acts 4:12

that ye should not teach in this **n** . . . . Acts 5:28

worthy to suffer shame for his **n** . . . . . Acts 5:41

every **n** that is named . . . . Eph 1:21

a **n** which is above every **n** . . . . Phil 2:9

whose **n** are in the book of life . . . . . . Phil 4:3

do all in the **n** of the Lord Jesus . . . . . . Col 3:17

obtained a more excellent **n** . . . . Heb 1:4

a new **n** written, which no man
   knoweth . . . . Rev 2:17

NATION

Blessed is the **n** whose God is
the LORD. . . . . Ps 33:12

Righteousness exalteth a **n** . . . . Prov 14:34

n shall not lift up a sword against **n** . . . . Isa 2:4;
Mic 4:3

n shall rise against **n** . . . . Matt 24:7;
Mark 13:8; Luke 21:10

crooked and perverse **n** . . . . Phil 2:15

tongue, and people, and **n** . . . . Rev 5:9

NEED (n)

God shall supply all your **n** . . . . Phil 4:19

grace to help in time of **n** . . . . Heb 4:16

ye have **n** that one teach you. . . . . Heb 5:12

seeth his brother have **n** . . . . 1 John 3:17

city had no **n** of the sun. . . . . Rev 21:23

NEVER

I **n** knew you . . . . Matt 7:23

shall **n** thirst . . . . John 4:14; 6:35

Charity **n** faileth. . . . . 1 Cor 13:8

I will **n** leave thee . . . . Heb 13:5

NEW

a **n** song . . . . Ps 33:3; 40:3; 96:1; 98:1;
144:9; 149:1; Isa 42:10; Rev 5:9; 14:3

no **n** thing under the sun . . . . Eccl 1:9

n every morning . . . . Lam 3:23

n cloth unto an old garment . . . . Matt 9:16
(See also Luke 5:36.)

A **n** commandment . . . . John 13:34
(See also 1 John 2:7, 8.)

a **n** creature . . . . 2 Cor 5:17; Gal 6:15

n man . . . . Eph 2:15; 4:24; Col 3:10

n and living way . . . . Heb 10:20

n name . . . . Rev 2:17; 3:12

I make all things **n** . . . . Rev 21:5

NOTHING

without me ye can do **n** . . . . John 15:5

brought **n** into this world . . . . 1 Tim 6:7

NOW

n I know in part. . . . . 1 Cor 13:12

the life which I **n** live . . . . Gal 2:20

though **n** ye see him not . . . . 1 Pet 1:8

NUMBER (v)

So teach us to **n** our days . . . . Ps 90:12

he was **n** with the transgressors. . . . . . Isa 53:12;
Mark 15:28

hairs of your head are all **n** . . . . Matt 10:30;
Luke 12:7

multitude, which no man could **n** . . . . . Rev 7:9

O

OBEY

to **o** is better than sacrifice. . . . . 1 Sam 15:22

we ought to **o** God rather
than men . . . . Acts 5:29

o your parents. . . . . Eph 6:1; Col 3:20

O them that have the rule over you. . . Heb 13:17

OBTAIN

So run, that ye may **o** . . . . 1 Cor 9:24

o mercy, and find grace to help . . . . . . Heb 4:16

having **o** eternal redemption . . . . Heb 9:12

OFFEND

brother **o** is harder to be won . . . . Prov 18:19

if thine eye **o** thee. . . . . Matt 5:29; 18:9;
Mark 9:47

OFFER

then come and **o** thy gift . . . . Matt 5:24

o upon the sacrifice and service of
your faith . . . . Phil 2:17

Christ was once **o** to bear the sins
of many. Heb 9:28

OMEGA

I am Alpha and **O** . . . . . . Rev 1:8, 11; 21:6; 22:13

ORDER (n)

the **o** of Melchizedek . . . . Ps 110:4; Heb 5:6;
6:20; 7:11

decently and in **o** . . . . 1 Cor 14:40

OUGHT
We **o** to obey God . . . . Acts 5:29

ye **o** to be teachers . . . . Heb 5:12

what manner of persons **o** ye to be . . . 2 Pet 3:11

OUT
be sure your sin will find you **o** . . . . . Num 32:23

o of it are the issues of life . . . . Prov 4:23

o of the abundance of the heart
the mouth speaketh. . . . . Matt 12:34

instant in season, **o** of season . . . . 2 Tim 4:2

OVERCOME
I have **o** the world . . . . John 16:33

Be not **o** of evil, but **o** evil. . . . . Rom 12:21

victory that **o** the world. . . . . 1 John 5:4

To him that **o** . . . . Rev 2:7, 17; 3:21

P

PAIN
travaileth in **p** . . . . Rom 8:22

neither shall there be any more **p** . . . . . Rev 21:4

PARENTS
children shall rise up
against their **p** . . . . . . Matt 10:21; Mark 13:12

no man that hath left house, or **p** . . . Luke 18:29

ye shall be betrayed both by **p** . . . . . . Luke 21:16

who did sin, this man, or his **p?** . . . . . . John 9:2

disobedient to **p** . . . . Rom 1:30; 2 Tim 3:2

not to lay up for the **p**, but the **p**
for the children. . . . . 2 Cor 12:14

Children, obey your **p** . . . . Eph 6:1; Col 3:20

PARTAKER
p of his hope . . . . 1 Cor 9:10

p with the altar . . . . 1 Cor 9:13

p of that one bread . . . . 1 Cor 10:17

p of the Lord's table. . . . . 1 Cor 10:21

neither be **p** of other men's sins . . . . . 1 Tim 5:22

p of the heavenly calling . . . . Heb 3:1

p of Christ's sufferings . . . . 1 Pet 4:13

a **p** of the glory. . . . . 1 Pet 5:1

p of the divine nature . . . . 2 Pet 1:4

PASS
let this cup **p**. . . . . Matt 26:39

neither can they **p** to us . . . . Luke 16:26

fashion of this world **p** . . . . 1 Cor 7:31

old things are **p** away . . . . 2 Cor 5:17

love of Christ, which **p** knowledge . . . . Eph 3:19

which **p** all understanding. . . . . Phil 4:7

PASTOR
Some, **p** and teachers. . . . . Eph 4:11

PATH
a light unto my **p** . . . . Ps 119:105

make his **p** straight . . . . Matt 3:3;
Mark 1:3; Luke 3:4

PATIENCE
tribulation worketh **p** . . . . Rom 5:3

with **p** wait for it . . . . Rom 8:25

through **p** and comfort . . . . Rom 15:4

the God of **p** . . . . Rom 15:5

as the ministers of God, in much **p** . . . . 2 Cor 6:4

unto all **p** and long suffering . . . . Col 1:11

and **p** of hope. . . . . 1 Thess 1:3

for your **p** . . . . 2 Thess 1:4

faith, love, **p**, meekness. . . . . 1 Tim 6:11

sound in faith, in charity, in **p** . . . . Titus 2:2

ye have need of **p**. . . . . Heb 10:36

run with **p** . . . . Heb 12:1

trying of your faith worketh **p** . . . . James 1:3

let **p** have her perfect work . . . . James 1:4

hath long **p**. James 5:7

of suffering affliction, and of **p** . . . . . James 5:10

Ye have heard of the **p** of Job . . . . James 5:11

and to temperance **p** . . . . 2 Pet 1:6

PEACE
seek **p**, and pursue it . . . . Ps 34:14
   (See also 1 Pet 3:11.)

saying, **P, p**; when there is no **p**. . . Jer 6:14; 8:11

P I leave with you, my **p** I give
   unto you . . . . John 14:27

that in me ye might have **p** . . . . John 16:33

p from God our Father . . . . . Rom 1:7; 1 Cor 1:3;
              2 Cor 1:2; Eph 1:2; Phil 1:2

we have **p** with God . . . . Rom 5:1

the gospel of **p** . . . . Rom 10:15; Eph 6:15

follow after the things which
   make for **p** . . . . Rom 14:19

the God of **p** . . . . Rom 15:33; 16:20;
               Phil 4:9; Heb 13:20

author of confusion, but of **p** . . . . . . 1 Cor 14:33

he is our **p** . . . . Eph 2:14

p to you which were afar off . . . . Eph 2:17

in the bond of **p** . . . . Eph 4:3

p of God, which passeth all
   understanding. . . . . Phil 4:7

and **p,** from God. . . . . Col 1:2; 1 Thess 1:1;
              2 Thess 1:2; Phile 1:3

let the **p** of God rule in your hearts . . . . Col 3:15

PEACEABLE
a quiet and **p** life. . . . . 1 Tim 2:2

pure, then **p**, gentle . . . . James 3:17

PERCEIVE
Jesus **p** their wickedness . . . . Matt 22:18

I **p** that virtue is gone out. . . . . Luke 8:46

I **p** that God is no respecter
   of persons . . . . Acts 10:34

Hereby **p** we the love of God . . . . 1 John 3:16

PERDITION
none of them is lost, but
   the son of **p**. . . . . John 17:12

man of sin be revealed,
   the son of **p** . . . . 2 Thess 2:3

which drown men in destruction
   and **p** . . . . 1 Tim 6:9

who draw back unto **p** . . . . Heb 10:39

beast . . . shall . . . go into **p** . . . . Rev 17:8
   (See also Rev 17:11.)

PERFECT
his way is **p** . . . . 2 Sam 22:31; Ps 18:30

Be ye therefore **p** . . . . Matt 5:48

strength is made **p** in weakness . . . . . 2 Cor 12:9

either were already **p** . . . . Phil 3:12

as many as be **p** . . . . Phil 3:15

present every man **p** . . . . Col 1:28

salvation **p** through sufferings. . . . . . . Heb 2:10

Make you **p** in every good work. . . . . . Heb 13:21

patience have her **p** work. . . . . James 1:4

every good gift and every **p** gift . . . . James 1:17

p law of liberty. . . . . James 1:25

p love casteth out fear. . . . . 1 John 4:18

PERISH
no vision, the people **p** . . . . Prov 29:18

that one of these little ones
   should **p**. Matt 18:14

not willing that any should **p**. . . . . 2 Pet 3:9

PERSECUTE
when men shall revile you, and
   p you . . . . Matt 5:11

why **p** thou me?. . . . . Acts 9:4; 22:7; 26:14

I **p** the church of God . . . . . . 1 Cor 15:9; Gal 1:13

P, but not forsaken . . . . 2 Cor 4:9

Concerning zeal, **p** the church. . . . . Phil 3:6

PERVERSE
a **p** and crooked generation . . . . Deut 32:5

in the midst of a crooked and
   p nation . . . . Phil 2:15

PIERCE
whom they have **p** . . . . . Zech 12:10; John 19:37

p themselves through with many sorrows . . . . 1 Tim 6:10

PIT

they go down quick into the **p** . . . . . Num 16:30

bring them down into the **p** of destruction. . . . . Ps 55:23

shall fall himself into his own **p** . . . . . Prov 28:10

to the hole of the **p** whence ye are digged . . . . Isa 51:1

key of the bottomless **p** . . . . Rev 9:1; 20:1

beast that ascendeth out of the bottomless **p** . . . . Rev 11:7 (See also Rev 17:8.)

cast him into the bottomless **p**. . . . . . . Rev 20:3

PLACE

the **p** whereon thou standest is holy . . . . Ex 3:5; Josh 5:15

The eyes of the LORD are in every **p** . . . . Prov 15:3

see the **p** where the Lord lay . . . . Matt 28:6

with one accord in one **p**. . . . . Acts 2:1

Neither give **p** to the devil . . . . Eph 4:27

PLAGUE

blasphemed God because of the **p** of the hail . . . . Rev 16:21

PLEASE

they that are in the flesh cannot **p** God. . . . . Rom 8:8

not to **p** ourselves . . . . Rom 15:1

it **p** God by the foolishness of preaching . . . . 1 Cor 1:21

as I **p** all men in all things. . . . . 1 Cor 10:33

without faith it is impossible to **p** him . . . . Heb 11:6

PLEASURE

ye ministers of his, that do his **p** . . . . . Ps 103:21

the LORD taketh **p** in his people . . . . Ps 149:4

he hath no **p** in fools . . . . Eccl 5:4

Father's good **p** . . . . Luke 12:32

lovers of **p** . . . . 2 Tim 3:4

the **p** of sin for a season. . . . . Heb 11:25

PLOWSHARE

shall beat their swords into **p** . . . Isa 2:4; Mic 4:3

Beat your **p** into swords. . . . . Joel 3:10

PLUCK

my cheeks to them that **p** . . . . Isa 50:6

offend thee, **p** it out . . . . Matt 5:29; 18:9; Mark 9:47

shall any man p them out of my hand . . . . John 10:28

POOR

Blessed are the **p** in spirit. . . . . Matt 5:3

as **p**, yet making many rich . . . . 2 Cor 6:10

for your sakes he became **p** . . . . 2 Cor 8:9

POSSIBLE

with God all things are **p**. . . . . Matt 19:26; Mark 10:27

if it were **p** . . . . Mark 13:22

if it be **p**, let this cup pass from me. Matt 26:39

all things are **p** to him that believeth . . . . Mark 9:23

all things are **p** unto thee . . . . Mark 14:36

POWER

being girded with **p** . . . . Ps 65:6

Not by might, nor by **p** . . . . Zech 4:6

p on earth to forgive . . . . . . Matt 9:6; Mark 2:10

All **p** is given unto me . . . . Matt 28:18

Jesus returned in the **p** of the Spirit. . . Luke 4:14

his word was with **p** . . . . Luke 4:32

with **p** from on high . . . . Luke 24:49

p to become the sons of God . . . . John 1:12

I have **p** to lay it down . . . . John 10:18

P, after that the Holy Ghost is come . . . . Acts 1:8

Give me also this **p** . . . . Acts 8:19

his eternal **p** and Godhead . . . . Rom 1:20

that I might shew my **p** in thee . . . . . . Rom 9:17

it is raised in **p**. . . . . 1 Cor 15:43

prince of the **p** of the air . . . . Eph 2:2

the effectual working of his **p** . . . . Eph 3:7

the **p** of his resurrection. . . . . Phil 3:10

spirit of fear; but of **p**, and of love . . . . 2 Tim 1:7

form of godliness, but denying
 the **p**. . . . . 2 Tim 3:5

might destroy him that had the **p**
 of death. . . . . Heb 2:14

receive glory and honour and **p** . . . . Rev 4:11

PRAISE (n)

his **p** shall continually be in
 my mouth . . . . Ps 34:1

make his **p** glorious . . . . Ps 66:2

garment of **p** . . . . Isa 61:3

p of the glory of his grace . . . . Eph 1:6

if there be any **p**. . . . . Phil 4:8

offer the sacrifice of **p** . . . . Heb 13:15

PRAISE (v)

All thy works shall **p** thee. . . . . Ps 145:10

Let another man **p** thee. . . . . Prov 27:2

PRAY

they love to **p** standing
 in the synagogues . . . . Matt 6:5

And when ye stand **p**, forgive . . . . . . Mark 11:25

Lord, teach us to **p** . . . . Luke 11:1

men ought always to **p**. . . . . Luke 18:1

I **p** for them: I **p** not for the world. . . . John 17:9

Neither **p** I for these alone . . . . John 17:20

know not what we should **p** for . . . . . . Rom 8:26

P without ceasing. . . . . 1 Thess 5:17

Is any among you afflicted? let
 him **p**. . . . . James 5:13

p one for another . . . . James 5:16

PRAYER

house of **p** . . . . Isa 56:7; Matt 21:13;
 Mark 11:17; Luke 19:46

whatsoever ye shall ask in **p**,
 believing . . . . Matt 21:22

the hour of **p** . . . . Acts 3:1

in every thing by **p** and supplication . . . . Phil 4:6

the **p** of faith shall save the sick . . . . James 5:15

The effectual fervent **p** of a
 righteous man . . . . James 5:16

watch unto **p** . . . . 1 Pet 4:7

PREACH

Jesus began to **p**. . . . . Matt 4:17
 (See also Matt 10:7.)

and **p** every where . . . . Mark 16:20

But we **p** Christ crucified. . . . . 1 Cor 1:23

we **p** not ourselves. . . . . 2 Cor 4:5

Some indeed **p** Christ even of envy
 and strife. . . . . Phil 1:15

P the word; be instant . . . . 2 Tim 4:2

PRECIOUS

p shall their blood be in his sight . . . . . . Ps 72:14

P in the sight of the Lord is the
 death of his saints . . . . Ps 116:15

How **p** also are thy thoughts. . . . . Ps 139:17

more **p** than rubies . . . . Prov 3:15

trial of your faith, being much more
 p than of gold . . . . 1 Pet 1:7

the **p** blood of Christ . . . . 1 Pet 1:19

like **p** faith . . . . 2 Pet 1:1

great and **p** promises . . . . 2 Pet 1:4

PREPARE

P ye the way of the Lord . . . . . Isa 40:3; Matt 3:3

I go to **p** a place for you . . . . John 14:2

PRESENCE

in thy **p** is fulness of joy . . . . Ps 16:11

Cast me not away from thy **p** . . . . Ps 51:11

whither shall I flee from thy **p**? . . . . . . Ps 139:7

PRESENT (adj)

deliver us from this **p** evil world. . . . . . . Gal 1:4

having loved this **p** world . . . . 2 Tim 4:10

in this **p** world . . . . Titus 2:12

PRESENT (n)
to be **p** with the Lord. . . . . 2 Cor 5:8

whether **p** or absent . . . . 2 Cor 5:9

PRESENT (v)
p your bodies a living sacrifice . . . . Rom 12:1

p every man perfect . . . . Col 1:28

p you faultless . . . . Jude 1:24

PRICE
kept back part of the **p** . . . . Acts 5:2

bought with a **p** . . . . 1 Cor 6:20; 7:23

of great **p** . . . . 1 Pet 3:4

PRIDE
P goeth before destruction . . . . Prov 16:18

the lust of the eyes,
    and the **p** of life . . . . 1 John 2:16

PRIEST
Thou art a **p** for ever. . . . . Ps 110:4; Heb 5:6

hath made us kings and **p** unto God . . . . Rev 1:6
    (See also Rev 5:10.)

shall be **p** of God and of Christ, and
    shall reign. Rev 20:6

PRIESTHOOD
an unchangeable **p**. . . . . Heb 7:24

an holy **p** . . . . 1 Pet 2:5

ye are a chosen generation, a royal **p** . . . 1 Pet 2:9

PRINCIPLE
first **p** of the oracles of God . . . . Heb 5:12

leaving the **p** of the doctrine of Christ. . . Heb 6:1

PRISON
thou be cast into **p** . . . . Matt 5:25

in **p**, and ye came unto me. . . . . Matt 25:36

to go with thee, both into **p**, and
    to death . . . . Luke 22:33

spirits in **p** . . . . 1 Pet 3:19

PROCLAIM
to **p** liberty to the captives. . . . . Isa 61:1

To **p** the acceptable year . . . . Isa 61:2

p upon the housetops. . . . . Luke 12:3

PROMISE (n)
p of God in him are yea. . . . . 2 Cor 1:20

the **p** of eternal inheritance . . . . Heb 9:15

died in faith, not having received
    the **p** . . . . Heb 11:13

great and precious **p**. . . . . 2 Pet 1:4

Where is the **p** of his coming? . . . . 2 Pet 3:4

not slack concerning his **p** . . . . 2 Pet 3:9

PROPHESY
your sons and your daughters
    shall **p** . . . . Joel 2:28; Acts 2:17

P unto us, thou Christ . . . . Matt 26:68

P: and the servants did strike . . . . . . Mark 14:65

P, who is it that smote thee? . . . . Luke 22:64

let us **p** according to the proportion . . . Rom 12:6

we **p** in part. . . . . 1 Cor 13:9

covet to **p**. . . . . 1 Cor 14:39

PROPHET
Beware of false **p** . . . . Matt 7:15

A **p** is not without honour. . . . . Matt 13:57;
                                                      Mark 6:4

not a greater **p** than John. . . . . Luke 7:28

I perceive that thou art a **p**. . . . . John 4:19

are all **p**? . . . . 1 Cor 12:29

PROVOKE
How long will this people **p** me? . . . . Num 14:11

is not easily **p**. . . . . 1 Cor 13:5

p one another . . . . Gal 5:26

p not your children to wrath . . . . Eph 6:4

to **p** unto love and to good works . . . . Heb 10:24

PRUNINGHOOKS
shall beat . . . their spears into **p** . . . . . . Isa 2:4;
                                                      Mic 4:3

Beat your . . . **p** into spears . . . . Joel 3:10

PUFF (v)
Knowledge **p** up . . . . 1 Cor 8:1

PURE
Thy word is very **p** . . . . Ps 119:140

whatsoever things are **p**. . . . . Phil 4:8

p conscience. . . . . 1 Tim 3:9; 2 Tim 1:3

keep thyself **p** . . . . 1 Tim 5:22

unto the **p** all things are **p** . . . . Titus 1:15

P religion . . . . James 1:27

first **p**, then peaceable . . . . James 3:17

stir up your **p** minds. . . . . 2 Pet 3:1

even as he is **p**. . . . . 1 John 3:3

PURPOSE (n)
Every **p** is established by counsel . . . . Prov 20:18

the called according to his **p** . . . . Rom 8:28

that the **p** of God according to
    election might stand . . . . Rom 9:11

according to the **p** . . . . Eph 1:11

eternal **p** which he purposed
    in Christ . . . . Eph 3:11

Q

QUENCH
neither shall their fire be **q** . . . . Isa 66:24

fire that never shall be **q** . . . . Mark 9:43

able to **q** all the fiery darts. . . . . Eph 6:16

Q not the Spirit . . . . 1 Thess 5:19

R

RACE
they which run in a **r** run all . . . . 1 Cor 9:24

the **r** that is set before us. . . . . Heb 12:1

RAIMENT
the life more than meat,
    and the body than **r** . . . . Matt 6:25

why take ye thought for **r**? . . . . Matt 6:28

having food and **r** let us be
    therewith content . . . . 1 Tim 6:8

RAIN (n)
r was upon the earth forty days. . . . . . . Gen 7:12

sendeth **r** on the just and on
    the unjust . . . . Matt 5:45

the **r** descended, and the
    floods came . . . . Matt 7:25

RAISE
in the third day he will **r** us up . . . . Hos 6:2

r the dead. . . . . Matt 10:8
    (See also Matt 11:5; Luke 7:22.)

be **r** again the third day . . . . Matt 16:21
    (See also Matt 17:23; Luke 9:22.)

I will **r** him up at the last day. . John 6:40, 44, 54

Whom God hath **r** up . . . . Acts 2:24
    (See also Acts 2:32; 3:15; 4:10; 5:30; 10:40;
    13:30, 33, 34; 17:31; Rom 10:9; 1 Cor 6:14;
    2 Cor 4:14; Gal 1:1; Eph 1:20.)

like as Christ was **r** up from the dead. . . Rom 6:4

Spirit of him that **r** up Jesus. . . . . Rom 8:11

he **r** up Christ: whom he **r** not up . . . 1 Cor 15:15

if Christ be not **r** . . . . 1 Cor 15:17

the Lord Jesus shall **r** up us also . . . . . 2 Cor 4:14

hath **r** us up together. . . . . Eph 2:6

Accounting that God was able to
    r him up . . . . Heb 11:19

and the Lord shall **r** him up . . . . James 5:15

RAM
behind him a ram caught in a thicket
    by his horns . . . . Gen 22:13

there stood before the river a **r** which
    had two horns . . . . Dan 8:3

RANSOM (n)
to give his life a **r** for many . . . . Matt 20:28;
                                                 Mark 10:45

gave himself a **r** for all . . . . 1 Tim 2:6

READY

The spirit truly is **r** . . . . Mark 14:38

I am now **r** to be offered . . . . 2 Tim 4:6

salvation **r** to be revealed in the
    last time . . . . 1 Pet 1:5

be **r** always to give an answer . . . . 1 Pet 3:15

REAP

they sow not, neither do they **r** . . . . . . Matt 6:26
    (See also Luke 12:24.)

He which soweth sparingly shall **r**
    also sparingly . . . . 2 Cor 9:6

whatsoever a man soweth, that shall
    he also **r** . . . . Gal 6:7

REBUKE (v)

He that **r** a man afterwards shall
    find more favour . . . . Prov 28:23

he arose, and **r** the winds . . . . Matt 8:26;
                   Mark 4:39; Luke 8:24

Peter took him, and began to
    r him . . . . Matt 16:22; Mark 8:32

If thy brother trespass against thee,
    r him . . . . Luke 17:3

R not an elder . . . . 1 Tim 5:1

RECEIVE

afterward **r** me to glory . . . . Ps 73:24

ask in prayer, believing, ye
    shall **r** . . . . Matt 21:22

but he **r** it not . . . . Mark 15:23

he was **r** up into heaven . . . . Mark 16:19

R thy sight . . . . Luke 18:42; Acts 22:13

his own **r** him not . . . . John 1:11

as many as **r** him . . . . John 1:12

ask, and ye shall **r** . . . . John 16:24

r my spirit . . . . Acts 7:59

which I have **r** of the Lord Jesus . . . . . Acts 20:24

I have **r** of the Lord that which also
    I delivered . . . . 1 Cor 11:23

every one may **r** the things done in
    his body . . . . 2 Cor 5:10

whatsoever we ask, we **r** of him . . . . 1 John 3:22

RECONCILE

first be **r** to thy brother . . . . Matt 5:24

when we were enemies, we were **r**
    to God . . . . Rom 5:10

that he might **r** both unto God . . . . Eph 2:16

REDEEM

ye were not **r** with corruptible
    things . . . . 1 Pet 1:18

hast **r** us to God by thy blood . . . . Rev 5:9

REDEEMER

I know that my **r** liveth . . . . Job 19:25

As for our **r**, the LORD of hosts is
    his name . . . . Isa 47:4

REDEMPTION

your **r** draweth nigh . . . . Luke 21:28

the **r** of our body . . . . Rom 8:23

sealed unto the day of **r** . . . . Eph 4:30

REIGN

death **r** from Adam to Moses . . . . Rom 5:14

death **r** by one . . . . Rom 5:17

as sin hath **r** unto death, even so
    might grace **r** . . . . Rom 5:21

Let not sin therefore **r** in your
    mortal body . . . . Rom 6:12

If we suffer, we shall also **r**
    with him . . . . 2 Tim 2:12

the Lord God omnipotent **r** . . . . Rev 19:6

REJOICE

in the shadow of thy wings will I **r** . . . . . Ps 63:7

Let the heavens **r** . . . . Ps 96:11

The LORD reigneth; let the earth **r** . . . . . . Ps 97:1

r with the wife of thy youth . . . . Prov 5:18

R not when thine enemy falleth . . . . . Prov 24:17

When the righteous are in authority,
    the people **r** . . . . Prov 29:2

R, O young man, in thy youth . . . . Eccl 11:9

R greatly, O daughter of Zion . . . . Zech 9:9

many shall **r** at his birth . . . . Luke 1:14

R ye in that day, and leap for joy . . . . . Luke 6:23

r, because your names are written
    in heaven . . . . Luke 10:20

In that hour Jesus **r** in spirit . . . . Luke 10:21

Abraham **r** to see my day . . . . John 8:56

If ye loved me, ye would **r** . . . . John 14:28

I will see you again, and your
    heart shall **r** . . . . John 16:22

and **r** in hope of the glory of God . . . . . . Rom 5:2

R with them that do **r** . . . . Rom 12:15

I therein do **r**, yea, and will **r** . . . . Phil 1:18

Finally, my brethren, **r** in the Lord . . . . . Phil 3:1

R in the Lord alway: and again
    I say, **R** . . . . Phil 4:4

R evermore . . . . 1 Thess 5:16

REJOICING
R in hope . . . . Rom 12:12

As sorrowful, yet alway **r** . . . . 2 Cor 6:10

what is our hope, or joy, or
    crown of **r**? . . . . 1 Thess 2:19

REMAIN
we which are alive and **r** unto
    the coming of the Lord . . . . 1 Thess 4:15

There **r** therefore a rest to the
    people of God . . . . Heb 4:9

there **r** no more sacrifice for sins . . . . . Heb 10:26

REMEMBER
R not the sins of my youth . . . . Ps 25:7

Who **r** us in our low estate . . . . Ps 136:23

R now thy Creator . . . . Eccl 12:1

R Lot's wife . . . . Luke 17:32

Lord, **r** me when thou comest into
    thy kingdom . . . . Luke 23:42

R my bonds . . . . Col 4:18

R without ceasing your work
    of faith . . . . 1 Thess 1:3

R them that are in bonds . . . . Heb 13:3

R them which have the rule
    over you . . . . Heb 13:7

R therefore from whence thou
    art fallen . . . . Rev 2:5

R therefore how thou hast received . . . . . Rev 3:3

REMEMBRANCE
in death there is no **r** of thee . . . . Ps 6:5

There is no **r** of former
    things . . . . Eccl 1:11

this do in **r** of me . . . . . . Luke 22:19; 1 Cor 11:24

bring all things to your **r** . . . . John 14:26

REMOVE
r this cup from me . . . . Luke 22:42

will **r** thy candlestick . . . . Rev 2:5

RENDER
R therefore unto Caesar . . . . Matt 22:21;
                  Mark 12:17; Luke 20:25

See that none **r** evil for evil . . . . 1 Thess 5:15

Not **r** evil for evil, or railing
    for railing . . . . 1 Pet 3:9

RENEW
and **r** a right spirit within me . . . . Ps 51:10

thy youth is **r** like the eagle's . . . . Ps 103:5

they that wait upon the LORD shall
    r their strength . . . . Isa 40:31

the inward man is **r** day by day . . . . . . 2 Cor 4:16

be **r** in the spirit of your mind . . . . Eph 4:23

the new man, which is **r** in
    knowledge . . . . Col 3:10

If they shall fall away,
    to **r** them again . . . . Heb 6:6

REPENT
the LORD **r** of the evil . . . . Ex 32:14
    (See also 2 Sam 24:16; 1 Chr 21:15; Jer 18:8;
    26:13, 19; Joel 2:13.)

for he is not a man, that he
    should **r** . . . . 1 Sam 15:29

joy shall be in heaven over
    one sinner that **r** . . . . Luke 15:7

if he **r**, forgive him . . . . Luke 17:3

REPENTANCE

the goodness of God leadeth
thee to **r** . . . . Rom 2:4

not laying again the foundation of **r** . . . . Heb 6:1

to renew them again unto **r** . . . . Heb 6:6

REPORT (n)

Who hath believed our **r**? . . . . Isa 53:1

whatsoever things are of good **r** . . . . . . Phil 4:8

he must have a good **r**. . . . . 1 Tim 3:7

REPUTATION

made himself of no **r** . . . . Phil 2:7

hold such in **r**. Phil 2:29

REQUIRE

what doth the LORD **r** of thee? . . . . . . Deut 10:12;
Mic 6:8

this night thy soul shall be **r**
of thee . . . . Luke 12:20

of him shall be much **r** . . . . Luke 12:48

Jews **r** a sign . . . . 1 Cor 1:22

RESERVE

r in heaven for you. . . . . 1 Pet 1:4

to be **r** unto judgment . . . . 2 Pet 2:4

the **r** unto fire. 2 Pet 3:7

RESIST

who hath **r** his will? . . . . Rom 9:19

God **r** the proud . . . . James 4:6; 1 Pet 5:5

R the devil, and he will flee
from you . . . . James 4:7

RESTORE

He **r** my soul. . . . . Ps 23:3

R unto me the joy of thy salvation . . . . . Ps 51:12

Elias truly shall first come, and **r**
all things . . . . Matt 17:11
(See also Mark 9:12.)

I **r** him fourfold . . . . Luke 19:8

r such a one in the spirit of meekness . . . Gal 6:1

RETURN

unto dust shalt thou **r** . . . . Gen 3:19

naked shall I **r** thither. . . . . Job 1:21

As a dog **r** to his vomit . . . . Prov 26:11

it shall not **r** unto me void. . . . . Isa 55:11

the seventy **r** again with joy . . . . Luke 10:17

now **r** unto the Shepherd and Bishop
of your souls . . . . 1 Pet 2:25

REVEAL

to whom is the arm of the LORD **r**? . . . . . Isa 53:1
(See also John 12:38.)

nothing covered, that shall not
be **r**. . . . . Matt 10:26; Luke 12:2

hast **r** them unto babes . . . . Matt 11:25

flesh and blood hath not **r** it . . . . Matt 16:17

in the day when the
Son of man is **r** . . . . Luke 17:30

wrath of God is **r** from heaven . . . . Rom 1:18

glory which shall be **r** in us . . . . Rom 8:18

it shall be **r** by fire . . . . 1 Cor 3:13

ready to be **r** in the last time . . . . 1 Pet 1:5

when his glory shall be **r** . . . . 1 Pet 4:13

partaker of the glory that shall be **r** . . . . 1 Pet 5:1

REWARD (n)

in keeping of them there is great **r** . . . . . Ps 19:11

great is your **r** in heaven. . . . . Matt 5:12
(See also Luke 6:23.)

They have their **r**. . . . . Matt 6:2, 5, 16

in no wise lose his **r** . . . . Matt 10:42
(See also Mark 9:41.)

your **r** shall be great . . . . Luke 6:35

every man shall receive his own **r** . . . . . 1 Cor 3:8

the labourer is worthy of his **r** . . . . . . 1 Tim 5:18

RICH

give me neither poverty nor **r** . . . . Prov 30:8

with the **r** in his death. . . . . Isa 53:9

let not the **r** man glory in his **r** . . . . Jer 9:23

woe unto you that are **r**! for ye
have received . . . . Luke 6:24

sorrowful: for he was very **r** . . . . Luke 18:23

make known the **r** of his glory . . . . Rom 9:23

the depth of the **r** both of the
    wisdom and knowledge . . . . Rom 11:33

poor, yet making many **r** . . . . 2 Cor 6:10

r, yet for your sakes . . . . 2 Cor 8:9

according to the **r** of his grace . . . . Eph 1:7

God, who is **r** in mercy . . . . Eph 2:4

he might shew the exceeding **r** of
    his grace . . . . Eph 2:7

unsearchable **r** of Christ . . . . Eph 3:8

according to his **r** in glory by Christ. . . . Phil 4:19

r of the glory of this mystery . . . . Col 1:27

be **r** in good works . . . . 1 Tim 6:18

reproach of Christ greater **r** . . . . Heb 11:26

God chosen the poor of this world
    r in faith . . . . James 2:5

the Lamb that was slain to
    receive **r** . . . . Rev 5:12

RIGHT (adj)

The statutes of the LORD are **r** . . . . Ps 19:8

renew a **r** spirit within me . . . . Ps 51:10

The way of a fool is **r** in his
    own eyes. Prov 12:15

There is a way which
    seemeth **r**. . . . . Prov 14:12; 16:25

Every way of man is **r** in his
    own eyes . . . . Prov 21:2

Thou hast answered **r** . . . . Luke 10:28

obey your parents in the Lord: for
    this is **r** . . . . Eph 6:1

RIGHTEOUS

have I not seen the **r** forsaken . . . . Ps 37:25

the LORD loveth the **r** . . . . Ps 146:8

R lips are the delight of kings . . . . Prov 16:13

When the **r** are in authority, the
    people rejoice . . . . Prov 29:2

to call the **r** . . . . Matt 9:13;
                           Mark 2:17; Luke 5:32

the **r** into life eternal . . . . Matt 25:46

they were both **r** before God. . . . . Luke 1:6

Certainly this was a **r** man . . . . Luke 23:47

There is none **r**, no, not one . . . . Rom 3:10

For scarcely for a **r** man will one die . . . Rom 5:7

many be made **r** . . . . Rom 5:19

the Lord, the **r** judge . . . . 2 Tim 4:8

the eyes of the Lord are
    over the **r**. 1 Pet 3:12

Jesus Christ the **r** . . . . 1 John 2:1

RIGHTEOUSNESS

leadeth me in the paths of **r** . . . . Ps 23:3

his **r** endureth for ever . . . . Ps 111:3; 112:3, 9

R exalteth a nation . . . . Prov 14:34

Better is a little with **r** . . . . Prov 16:8

our **r** are as filthy rags . . . . Isa 64:6

THE LORD OUR **R** . . . . Jer 23:6

to fulfil all **r** . . . . Matt 3:15

hunger and thirst after **r** . . . . Matt 5:6

persecuted for **r** sake . . . . Matt 5:10

except your **r** shall exceed the **r** . . . . . . Matt 5:20

John came unto you in the way
    of **r**. . . . . Matt 21:32

the **r** of God. . . . . Rom 1:17; 3:5; 10:3

unto whom God imputeth **r** . . . . Rom 4:6

by the **r** of one . . . . Rom 5:18

so might grace reign through **r** . . . . Rom 5:21

members as instruments of **r** . . . . Rom 6:13

the **r** which is of faith . . . . Rom 9:30

kingdom of God is not meat and
    drink, but **r** . . . . Rom 14:17

Awake to **r** . . . . 1 Cor 15:34

that we might be made the **r**. . . . . 2 Cor 5:21

what fellowship hath **r** with
    unrighteousness? . . . . 2 Cor 6:14

the breastplate of **r**. . . . . Eph 6:14

touching the **r** which is in the law,
    blameless . . . . Phil 3:6

not having mine own **r** . . . . Phil 3:9

follow after **r** . . . . 1 Tim 6:11

laid up for me a crown of **r** . . . . 2 Tim 4:8

Not by works of **r** . . . . Titus 3:5

being dead to sins, should live
   unto **r** . . . . 1 Pet 2:24

RIGHTLY
r dividing the word of truth . . . . 2 Tim 2:15

RISE
the third day he shall **r** again . . . . . . Matt 20:19;
   Mark 10:34; Luke 18:33

The Lord is **r** indeed . . . . Luke 24:34

Thy brother shall **r** again . . . . John 11:23

R, Peter; kill, and eat . . . . Acts 10:13

but now is Christ **r** . . . . 1 Cor 15:20

If ye then be **r** with Christ . . . . Col 3:1

the dead in Christ shall **r** first . . . . . 1 Thess 4:16

RIVER
baptized of him in the **r** of Jordan. . . . . Mark 1:5

on the sabbath we went out of the
   city by a **r** side . . . . Acts 16:13

he shewed me a pure **r** of water. . . . . . . Rev 22:1

on either side of the **r**, was there the
   tree of life . . . . Rev 22:2

ROARING
the devil as a **r** lion. . . . . 1 Pet 5:8

ROCK
must we fetch you water out of
   this **r**? . . . . Num 20:10

lead me to the **r** that is higher than I. . . . Ps 61:2

r of offence . . . . Isa 8:14; Rom 9:33; 1 Pet 2:8

it was founded upon a **r** . . . Matt 7:25; Luke 6:48

upon this **r** I will build my church . . . Matt 16:18

some fell upon a **r**. . . . . Luke 8:6

that **R** was Christ. . . . . 1 Cor 10:4

ROD
thy **r** and thy staff they comfort me . . . . . Ps 23:4

he that spareth his **r** . . . . Prov 13:24

ROOT (n)
there shall be a **r** of Jesse . . . . Isa 11:10;
   Rom 15:12

as a **r** out of a dry ground . . . . Isa 53:2

fig tree dried up from the **r** . . . . Mark 11:20

love of money is the **r** of all evil . . . . . 1 Tim 6:10

ROSE (v)
to this end Christ both died, and **r** . . . . Rom 14:9

buried, and that he **r** again the
   third day . . . . 1 Cor 15:4

which died for them, and **r** again . . . . 2 Cor 5:15

RULE (v)
thy husband, and he
   shall **r** over thee . . . . Gen 3:16

peace of God **r** in your hearts . . . . Col 3:15

One that **r** well his own house . . . . 1 Tim 3:4

elders that **r** well. . . . . 1 Tim 5:17

RUN
my cup **r** over . . . . Ps 23:5

by any means I should **r**,
   or had **r**, in vain . . . . Gal 2:2

let us **r** with patience. . . . . Heb 12:1

S

SABBATH
The **s** was made for man . . . . Mark 2:27

the Son of man is Lord
   also of the **s**. . . . . Mark 2:28; Luke 6:5

SACRIFICE (n)
to obey is better than **s**. . . . . 1 Sam 15:22

The **s** of God are a broken spirit . . . . . . Ps 51:17

than an house full of **s** with strife . . . . Prov 17:1

the **s** of fools . . . . Eccl 5:1

I desired mercy, and not **s** . . . . Hos 6:6

I will have mercy, and not **s**. . . . . Matt 9:13; 12:7

present your bodies a living **s** . . . . Rom 12:1

a **s** to God for a sweetsmelling savour . . . Eph 5:2

the **s** and service of your faith . . . . Phil 2:17

a **s** acceptable, wellpleasing . . . . Phil 4:18

offered one **s** for sins . . . . Heb 10:12

there remaineth no more **s** for sins . . . Heb 10:26

a more excellent **s** . . . . Heb 11:4

let us offer the **s** of praise . . . . Heb 13:15

to offer up spiritual **s** . . . . 1 Pet 2:5

SAINTS
and forsaketh not his **s** . . . . Ps 37:28

he maketh intercession for the **s** . . . . . Rom 8:27

Do ye not know that the **s** shall
    judge the world? . . . . 1 Cor 6:2

concerning the collection for the **s** . . . 1 Cor 16:1

his inheritance in the **s** . . . . Eph 1:18

less than the least of all **s** . . . . Eph 3:8

perfecting of the **s** . . . . Eph 4:12

the **s** in light . . . . Col 1:12

was once delivered unto the **s** . . . . Jude 1:3

SAKE
persecuted for righteousness' **s** . . . . . . Matt 5:10

before rulers and kings for my **s** . . . . . Mark 13:9

before kings and rulers for
    my name's **s**. . . . . Luke 21:12

Wilt thou lay down thy life
    for my **s**? . . . . John 13:38

for his body's **s**, which is the church . . . Col 1:24

for thy stomach's **s** . . . . 1 Tim 5:23

SALVATION
S belongeth unto the LORD . . . . Ps 3:8

Restore unto me the joy of thy **s** . . . . . . Ps 51:12

my rock and my **s** . . . . Ps 62:6

an helmet of **s** upon his head . . . . Isa 59:17

S is of the Lord . . . . Jon 2:9

an horn of **s** for us . . . . Luke 1:69

mine eyes have seen thy **s** . . . . Luke 2:30

Neither is there **s** in any other. . . . . Acts 4:12

the power of God unto **s** . . . . Rom 1:16

sorrow worketh repentance to **s** . . . . . 2 Cor 7:10

the gospel of your **s** . . . . Eph 1:13

the helmet of **s**. Eph 6:17

work out your own **s** . . . . Phil 2:12

for an helmet, the hope of **s** . . . . 1 Thess 5:8

grace of God that bringeth **s**. . . . . Titus 2:11

if we neglect so great **s** . . . . Heb 2:3

the captain of their **s** . . . . Heb 2:10

author of eternal **s** . . . . Heb 5:9

things that accompany **s** . . . . Heb 6:9

your faith, even the **s** of your souls . . . . 1 Pet 1:9

SAME
this **s** Jesus, which is taken up . . . . Acts 1:11

the **s** Lord over all . . . . Rom 10:12

Be of the **s** mind . . . . Rom 12:16

s yesterday, and to day, and for ever . . . Heb 13:8

SANCTIFY
being **s** by the Holy Ghost. . . . . Rom 15:16

husband is **s** by the wife . . . . 1 Cor 7:14

s, and meet for the master's use . . . . . 2 Tim 2:21

perfected for ever them that are **s** . . . . Heb 10:14

s the Lord God in your hearts . . . . 1 Pet 3:15

SATAN
And **S** . . . provoked David to
    number Israel . . . . 1 Chr 21:1

and **S** came also among them. . . . . Job 1:6

Get thee hence, **S** . . . . Matt 4:10

I beheld **S** as lightning fall
    from heaven. . . . . Luke 10:18

Then entered **S** into Judas . . . . Luke 22:3

To deliver such a one unto **S** . . . . 1 Cor 5:5

S himself is transformed into an
    angel of light. . . . . 2 Cor 11:14

the messenger of **S** to buffet me . . . . . 2 Cor 12:7

SAVE
he will **s** . . . . Zeph 3:17

1547

... sins .... Matt 1:21

s his people from .... Matt 18:11;
Luke 19:10

to s that which .... Matt 19:25;
Mark 10:26; Luke 18:26

Who th ... Matt 27:40; Mark 15:30

he cannot s .... Matt 27:42;
Mark 15:31

.... Mark 3:4; Luke 6:9

's lives, but to s .... Luke 9:56

.... Luke 23:35

_hrist, s thyself and us ... Luke 23:39

.e world through him
might be s .... John 3:17

vhat must I do to be s? .... Acts 16:30

:an faith s him? .... James 2:14

he prayer of faith shall s the sick ... James 5:15

f the righteous scarcely be s .... 1 Pet 4:18

SAVIOUR

he is the s of the body .... Eph 5:23

vho is the S of all men .... 1 Tim 4:10

SAW

under the fig tree, I s thee .... John 1:48

Abraham rejoiced to see my day,
and he s it .... John 8:56

SAY

teach thee what thou shalt s .... Ex 4:12

do men s that I the Son of
man am? .... Matt 16:13
(See also Mark 8:27.)

SCATTER

s abroad, as sheep having
no shepherd .... Matt 9:36

he that gathereth not with me s .... Matt 12:30;
Luke 11:23

SCRIBE

exceed the righteousness of the s ..... Matt 5:20

as one having authority, and not
as the s .... Matt 7:29

Beware of the s .... Mark 12:38; Luke 20:46

SCRIPTURE

Search the s .... John 5:39

All s is given by inspiration of God ... 2 Tim 3:16

no prophecy of the s is of any
private interpretation .... 2 Pet 1:20

SEARCH (v)

S me, O God, and know my heart .... Ps 139:23

when ye shall s for me with all
your heart .... Jer 29:13

S the scriptures .... John 5:39; Acts 17:11

he that s the hearts, knoweth
what is the mind .... Rom 8:27

the Spirit s all things .... 1 Cor 2:10

SEASON

To every thing there is a s, and a time. .. Eccl 3:1

be instant in s .... 2 Tim 4:2

pleasures of sin for a s .... Heb 11:25

SEAT

the s of the scornful .... Ps 1:1

chief s in the synagogues .... Matt 23:6;
Mark 12:39

SECRET (n)

when I was made in s .... Ps 139:15

thy Father which seeth in s .... Matt 6:4

pray to thy Father which is in s .... Matt 6:6

in s have I said nothing .... John 18:20

SEE

Having eyes, s ye not? .... Mark 8:18

thou shalt s greater things .... John 1:50

I was blind, now I s .... John 9:25

For now we s through a
glass, darkly .... 1 Cor 13:12

though now ye s him not .... 1 Pet 1:8

we shall s him as he is .... 1 John 3:2

SEEK

s peace, and pursue it ...... Ps 34:14; 1 Pet 3:11

early will I **s** thee . . . . Ps 63:1

those that **s** me early shall find me. . . . Prov 8:17

after all these things
do the Gentiles **s** . . . . Matt 6:32

s ye first the kingdom of God. . . . . . . Matt 6:33

s, and ye shall find . . . . Matt 7:7

adulterous generation **s** after
a sign . . . . Matt 12:39

I know that ye **s** Jesus . . . . Matt 28:5

and **s** diligently till she find it . . . . Luke 15:8

is come to **s** and to save . . . . Luke 19:10

Why **s** ye the living among
the dead? . . . . Luke 24:5

the Father **s** such to worship him . . . . John 4:23

there is none that **s** after God. . . . . . . Rom 3:11

s not her own. 1 Cor 13:5

s those things which are above. . . . . Col 3:1

rewarder of them that diligently
s him. . . . . Heb 11:6

s whom he may devour . . . . 1 Pet 5:8

SEEM
There is a way which **s** right . . . . Prov 14:12

If any among you **s** to be wise. . . . . . . 1 Cor 3:18

SEEN
yet have I not **s** the righteous
forsaken. . . . . Ps 37:25

have **s** a great light . . . . Isa 9:2

neither hath the eye **s** . . . . Isa 64:4
(See also 1 Cor 2:9.)

he that hath **s** me
hath **s** the Father. . . . . John 14:9

whom no man hath **s,** nor can see . . . 1 Tim 6:16

evidence of things not **s**. . . . . Heb 11:1

SEND
Whom shall I **s**, and who
will go for us?. . . . . Isa 6:8

Here am I; **s** me. . . . . Isa 6:8

SENT
work the works of him that **s** me. . . . . John 9:4

and Jesus Christ, whom
thou hast **s** . . . .

how shall they preach, except
they be **s**?. . . . .

God **s** forth his Son. . . . .

SERPENT
be ye therefore wise as **s**. . . . .

as Moses lifted up the **s** . . . .

that old **s**, called the Devil . . . .
(See also Rev 20:2.)

SERVANT
the borrower is **s** to the lender . . . . Prov 22

unprofitable **s** . . . . Luke 17:10

SERVE
No man can **s** two masters. . . . . Matt 6:24

leave the word of God, and **s** tables . . . . Acts 6:2

henceforth we should not **s** sin . . . . Rom 6:6

for ye **s** the Lord Christ . . . . Col 3:24

to **s** the living and true God . . . . 1 Thess 1:9

SERVICE
will think that he doeth God **s** . . . . John 16:2

your reasonable **s** . . . . Rom 12:1

SHADOW
under the **s** of the Almighty . . . . Ps 91:1

neither **s** of turning . . . . James 1:17

SHAKE
I will **s** the heavens . . . . . . Isa 13:13; Hag 2:6, 21
(See also Joel 3:16.)

good measure, pressed down,
s together. Luke 6:38

SHAME
I speak this to your **s** . . . . 1 Cor 6:5; 15:34

put him to an open **s** . . . . Heb 6:6

despising the **s** . . . . Heb 12:2

SHARP
s than any two-edged sword . . . . Heb 4:12

SHEARERS

a sheep before her **s** is dumb . . . . Isa 53:7

SHED

by man shall his blood be **s** . . . . Gen 9:6

is **s** for many for the remission
  of sins . . . . Matt 26:28

without **s** of blood is no remission. . . . . Heb 9:22

SHEEP

the **s** of his hand. . . . . Ps 95:7

the **s** of his pasture . . . . Ps 100:3

All we like **s** have gone astray . . . . Isa 53:6

that entereth in by the door is the
  shepherd of the **s**. . . . . John 10:2

the good shepherd giveth his life
  for the **s**. . . . . John 10:11

Feed my **s** . . . . John 21:16

SHEPHERD

The Lord is my **s** . . . . Ps 23:1

I am the good **s**. . . . . John 10:14

SHILOH

sceptre shall not depart from
  Judah . . . until **S** come. . . . . Gen 49:10

SHINE

upon them hath the light **s** . . . . Isa 9:2

Arise, **s**; for thy light is come. . . . . Isa 60:1

Let your light so **s** . . . . Matt 5:16

God, who commanded the light to **s** . . . 2 Cor 4:6

SHOD

your feet **s** with the preparation
  of the gospel . . . . Eph 6:15

SHORT

come **s** of the glory of God . . . . Rom 3:23

SHOUT

shall descend from heaven
  with a **s** . . . . 1 Thess 4:16

SICK

Is any **s** among you?. . . . . James 5:14

prayer of faith shall save the **s** . . . . . . James 5:15

SIGHT

blind receive their **s** . . . . Matt 11:5
  (See also 20:34; Luke 7:21.)

walk by faith, not by **s**. . . . . 2 Cor 5:7

SIN (n)

my **s** is ever before me . . . . Ps 51:3

Fools make a mock at **s**. . . . . Prov 14:9

s is a reproach to any people. . . . . . . Prov 14:34

not remember thy **s**. . . . . Isa 43:25
  (See also Isa 44:22.)

bare the **s** of many. . . . . Isa 53:12

wash away thy **s** . . . . Acts 22:16

where **s** abounded. . . . . Rom 5:20

Shall we continue in **s**?. . . . . Rom 6:1

made him to be **s** for us. . . . . 2 Cor 5:21

his own self bare our **s** . . . . 1 Pet 2:24

SIN (v)

the soul that **s**, it shall die . . . . Ezek 18:4

s no more. . . . . John 5:14; 8:11

Be ye angry, and **s** not . . . . Eph 4:26

he cannot **s**, because he is born
  of God. . . . . 1 John 3:9

SINGING

come before his presence with **s** . . . . . . Ps 100:2

s and making melody . . . . Eph 5:19

SINNER

eateth your master with publicans
  and **s** . . . . Matt 9:11
  (See also Mark 2:16; Luke 5:30; 15:2.)

over one **s** that repenteth . . . . Luke 15:7, 10

be merciful to me a **s** . . . . Luke 18:13

while we were yet **s** . . . . Rom 5:8

many were made **s** . . . . Rom 5:19

SLAIN

strong men have been **s** by her . . . . Prov 7:26

a Lamb as it had been **s** . . . . Rev 5:6

SLAUGHTER
as sheep for the **s** . . . . Ps 44:22

brought as a lamb to the **s**. . . . . Isa 53:7
   (See also Jer 11:19.)

SLEEP (n)
lest I sleep the **s** of death . . . . Ps 13:3

Yet a little **s**. . . . . Prov 6:10; 24:33

Love not **s**, lest thou come
   to poverty . . . . Prov 20:13

SLEEP (v)
shall neither slumber nor **s**. . . . . Ps 121:4

Why **s** ye? rise and pray . . . . Luke 22:46

We shall not all **s** . . . . 1 Cor 15:51

Awake thou that **s** . . . . Eph 5:14

SLUMBER
that keepeth thee will not **s** . . . . Ps 121:3

Yet a little sleep, a little **s** . . . . . . Prov 6:10; 24:33

SMOKE
the house was filled with **s** . . . . Isa 6:4

SMOOTH
five **s** stones . . . . 1 Sam 17:40
   (See also Isa 57:6.)

SMOTE
with his rod he **s** the rock twice. . . . . Num 20:11

David's heart **s** him . . . . 1 Sam 24:5

SNOW
I shall be whiter than **s**. . . . . Ps 51:7

garment was white as **s**. . . . . Dan 7:9
   (See also Matt 28:3; Mark 9:3.)

SOBER
let us watch and be **s** . . . . 1 Thess 5:6

s, of good behaviour, given to . . . . 1 Tim 3:2

good men, **s**, just, holy . . . . Titus 1:8

SOFT
A **s** answer turneth away wrath . . . . . . Prov 15:1

SOJOURNER
I am a stranger with thee and a **s** . . . . . Gen 23:4
   (See also Ps 39:12.)

SOLDIER
as a good **s** of Jesus Christ . . . . 2 Tim 2:3

SON
unto us a **s** is given . . . . Isa 9:6

no man knoweth the **S**. . . . . Matt 11:27

only begotten **S** . . . . John 1:18; 3:18

the **s** of perdition . . . . . . John 17:12; 2 Thess 2:3

conformed to the image of his **S** . . . . . Rom 8:29

spared not his own **S** . . . . Rom 8:32

bringing many **s** unto glory . . . . Heb 2:10

He that hath the **S** hath life . . . . 1 John 5:12

SONGS
he hath put a new **s** in my mouth . . . . . . Ps 40:3

in psalms and hymns and
   spiritual **s**. . . . . Eph 5:19; Col 3:16

SORROW
a man of **s** . . . . Isa 53:3

godly **s** worketh repentance. . . . . 2 Cor 7:10

SORROWFUL
he went away **s**. . . . . Matt 19:22
   (See also Luke 18:23.)

My soul is exceeding **s**. . . . . Matt 26:38;
                         Mark 14:34

SOUGHT
I **s** the LORD, and he heard me . . . . Ps 34:4

thou shalt be called, **S** out . . . . Isa 62:12

SOUL
man became a living **s**. . . . . Gen 2:7

with all thy **s**. . . . . Deut 30:2; Matt 22:37

Bless the Lord, O my **s** . . . . Ps 103:1; 104:1

to destroy both **s** and body. . . . . Matt 10:28

lose his own **s**. . . . . Matt 16:26; Mark 8:36

SOUND (n)
their **s** went into all the earth . . . . . . Rom 10:18

an uncertain **s** . . . . 1 Cor 14:8

SOW
sower went forth to **s** . . . . Matt 13:3
   (See also Mark 4:3; Luke 8:5.)

whatsoever a man **s**, that shall
   he also reap . . . . Gal 6:7

SPAKE
Never man **s** like this man . . . . John 7:46

holy men of God **s** as they
   were moved . . . . 2 Pet 1:21

SPARE
He that **s** his rod hateth his son . . . . . Prov 13:24

s not his own Son . . . . Rom 8:32

if God **s** not the angels that sinned . . . . 2 Pet 2:4
And **s** not the old world, but
   saved Noah . . . . 2 Pet 2:5

SPEAK
the abundance of the heart
   the mouth **s** . . . . Matt 12:34; Luke 6:45

slow to **s** . . . . James 1:19

SPECIALLY
Saviour of all men, **s** of those
   that believe . . . . 1 Tim 4:10

and **s** for those of his own house . . . . . 1 Tim 5:8

SPEECH
Let your **s** be alway with grace . . . . Col 4:6

SPIRIT
Into thine hand I commit my **s** . . . . Ps 31:5
   (See also Luke 23:46.)

the **s** indeed is willing . . . . Matt 26:41

the **S** like a dove descending
   upon him . . . . Mark 1:10

God is a **S**: and they that
   worship him . . . . John 4:24

S of truth . . . . John 14:17; 15:26;
   16:13; 1 John 4:6

the law of the **S** of life in Christ . . . . . . Rom 8:2

Walk in the **S** . . . . Gal 5:16

the sword of the **S** . . . . Eph 6:17

ministering **s**, sent forth
   to minister . . . . Heb 1:14

believe not every **s**, but try the **s** . . . . . 1 John 4:1

SPIRITUAL
Now concerning **s** gifts . . . . 1 Cor 12:1

against **s** wickedness in high places . . . . Eph 6:12

SPOKEN
a word **s** in due season . . . . Prov 15:23

SPOT
a lamb without blemish and
   without **s** . . . . 1 Pet 1:19

STAND
s ye still, and see the salvation . . . . Ex 14:13;
   2 Chr 20:17

S in awe, and sin not . . . . Ps 4:4

house divided against itself
   shall not **s** . . . . Matt 12:25
   (See also Mark 3:25.)

having done all, to **s** . . . . Eph 6:13

I **s** at the door, and knock. . . . . Rev 3:20

the dead, small and great, **s**
   before God . . . . Rev 20:12

STATURE
Jesus increased in wisdom and **s** . . . . . Luke 2:52

STAY (v)
whose mind is **s** on thee . . . . Isa 26:3

STEAL
thieves break through and **s** . . . . Matt 6:19

thief cometh not, but for to **s** . . . . John 10:10

STEP
The **s** of a good man are ordered . . . . . . Ps 37:23

not in man that walketh to direct
   his **s** . . . . Jer 10:23

that ye should follow his **s** . . . . 1 Pet 2:21

STIFFNECKED
be ye not **s**, as your fathers . . . . 2 Chr 30:8

STILL
beside the **s** waters . . . . Ps 23:2

Be **s**, and know that I am God . . . . Ps 46:10

and said unto the sea, Peace, be **s** . . . . Mark 4:39

STING
O death, where is thy **s**? . . . . 1 Cor 15:55

The **s** of death is sin . . . . 1 Cor 15:56

STOLE
Let him that **s** steal no more . . . . Eph 4:28

STOMACH
a little wine for thy **s** sake . . . . 1 Tim 5:23

STONE
this **s** shall be a witness . . . . Josh 24:27

lest thou dash thy foot against a **s**. . . . . Ps 91:12;
Matt 4:6; Luke 4:11

The **s** which the builders refused. . . . . Ps 118:22;
Matt 21:42; Mark 12:10

the **s** was rolled away. . . . . Mark 16:4; Luke 24:2

let him first cast a **s** at her . . . . John 8:7

STOREHOUSE
Bring ye all the tithes into the **s** . . . . . . Mal 3:10

STRAIGHT
make **s** in the desert a highway. . . . . . . Isa 40:3

make his paths **s** . . Matt 3:3; Mark 1:3; Luke 3:4
(See also John 1:23.)

STRANGER
I am a **s** and a sojourner. . . . . Gen 23:4; Ps 39:12

from the **s** which flattereth. . . . . Prov 7:5

I was a **s**, and ye took me in. . . . . . . Matt 25:35

Be not forgetful to entertain **s** . . . . Heb 13:2

STRENGTH
The Lord is my **s**. . . . . . . Ex 15:2; Ps 28:7; 118:14

God is our refuge and **s** . . . . Ps 46:1
(See also Ps 81:1.)

Wisdom is better than **s**. . . . . Eccl 9:16

he increaseth **s**. . . . . Isa 40:29

STRENGTHEN
to be **s** with might . . . . Eph 3:16

all things through Christ
which **s** me . . . . Phil 4:13

STRONG
Be **s** . . . . 1 Sam 4:9; Isa 35:4; Dan 10:19

The Lord **s** and mighty . . . . Ps 24:8

first bind the **s** man . . . . Matt 12:29

STUDY
S to shew thyself approved
unto God . . . . 2 Tim 2:15

SUBJECT
not **s** to the law of God . . . . Rom 8:7

as the church is **s** unto Christ . . . . Eph 5:24

Servants, be **s** to your masters . . . . 1 Pet 2:18

all of you be **s** one to another. . . . . 1 Pet 5:5

SUBMIT
wives, **s** yourselves. . . . . Eph 5:22

s yourselves therefore to God. . . . . James 4:7

SUBSTANCE
My **s** was not hid from thee . . . . Ps 139:15

Honour the LORD with thy **s** . . . . Prov 3:9

the **s** of things hoped for . . . . Heb 11:1

SUBTIL
the serpent was more **s** than
any beast. . . . . Gen 3:1

SUFFER
s many things . . . . Matt 16:21;
Mark 8:31; Luke 9:22

s little children, and forbid them
not, to come unto me . . . . Matt 19:14
(See also Mark 10:14; Luke 18:16.)

if so be that we **s** with him. . . . . Rom 8:17

If we **s**, we shall also reign . . . . 2 Tim 2:12

Christ also **s** for us, leaving us
an example . . . . 1 Pet 2:21

SUN

S, stand thou still . . . . Josh 10:12

The **s** shall not smite thee by day . . . . . . Ps 121:6

there is no new thing under the **s** . . . . . . Eccl 1:9

he maketh his **s** to rise on the evil . . . . Matt 5:45

let not the **s** go down upon
your wrath . . . . Eph 4:26

SUPPLICATION

with all prayer and **s** in the Spirit . . . . . Eph 6:18

SUPPLY (v)

my God shall **s** all your need . . . . Phil 4:19

SURE

be **s** your sin will find you out . . . . . . Num 32:23

a more **s** word of prophecy. . . . . 2 Pet 1:19

SUSTAIN

he shall **s** thee. Ps 55:22

SWEAT

in the **s** of thy face shalt thou
eat bread. . . . . Gen 3:19

his **s** was as it were great drops
of blood . . . . Luke 22:44

SWIFT

the race is not to the **s** . . . . Eccl 9:11

Their feet are **s** to shed blood . . . . Rom 3:15

SWORD

not to send peace, but a **s** . . . . Matt 10:34

the **s** of the Spirit. . . . . Eph 6:17

sharper than any twoedged **s**. . . . . Heb 4:12

out of his mouth went a sharp **s** . . . . . . Rev 1:16
(See also Rev 19:15.)

T

TABLE

Thou preparest a **t** before me . . . . Ps 23:5

yet the dogs under the **t** . . . . Mark 7:28

TAKE

t not thy holy spirit from me . . . . Ps 51:11

T no thought. . . . . Matt 6:25, 31, 34; 10:19;
Mark 13:11; Luke 12:11

T my yoke upon you. . . . . Matt 11:29

T, eat; this is my body. . . . . Matt 26:26;
Mark 14:22; 1 Cor 11:24

that no man **t** thy crown . . . . Rev 3:11

TALK

while he **t** with us by the way . . . . . . Luke 24:32

it is he that **t** with thee . . . . John 9:37

TAME

the tongue can no man **t** . . . . James 3:8

TASTE (v)

t and see that the Lord is good. . . . . Ps 34:8

t death for every man . . . . Heb 2:9

TEACH

that they may **t** their children . . . . Deut 4:10

t me thy paths . . . . Ps 25:4

T me thy way, O LORD . . . . Ps 27:11; 86:11

the Holy Ghost shall **t** you . . . . Luke 12:12

t every man in all wisdom . . . . Col 1:28

I suffer not a woman to **t** . . . . 1 Tim 2:12

who shall be able to **t** others also . . . . . 2 Tim 2:2

t the young women to be sober . . . . Titus 2:4

TEACHER

I have more understanding than
all my **t** . . . . Ps 119:99

and some, pastors and **t**. . . . . Eph 4:11

TEARS

I have seen thy **t**. . . . . 2 Kgs 20:5; Isa 38:5

They that sow in **t**. . . . . Ps 126:5

the Lord GOD will wipe away **t** . . . . Isa 25:8

God shall wipe away all **t** . . . . . . Rev 7:17; 21:4

TELL

Who can **t** if God will
    turn and repent? .... Jon 3:9

t it unto the church .... Matt 18:17

TEMPLE

he did hear my voice out of his **t** .... 2 Sam 22:7

his train filled the **t** .... Isa 6:1

Destroy this **t** .... John 2:19

ye are the **t** of the living God .... 2 Cor 6:16

TEMPORAL

the things which are seen are **t** ...... 2 Cor 4:18

TEMPT

Ye shall not **t** the LORD your God ..... Deut 6:16
    (See also Matt 4:7; Luke 4:12.)

to be **t** above that ye are able .... 1 Cor 10:13

he himself hath suffered being **t** ...... Heb 2:18

in all points **t** like as we are .... Heb 4:15

God cannot be **t** with evil .... James 1:13

TEMPTATION

lead us not into **t** .... Matt 6:13

There hath no **t** taken you .... 1 Cor 10:13

how to deliver the godly out of **t** ...... 2 Pet 2:9

TESTAMENT

my blood of the new **t** .... Matt 26:28;
    Mark 14:24

This cup is the new **t** in my blood ... Luke 22:20

made us able ministers of the new **t** ... 2 Cor 3:6

the same veil untaken away in the
    reading of the old **t** .... 2 Cor 3:14

was Jesus made a surety of
    a better **t** .... Heb 7:22

he is the mediator of the new **t** .... Heb 9:15

TESTIFY

our sins **t** against us .... Isa 59:12

they which **t** of me .... John 5:39

we have seen and do **t** .... 1 John 4:14

TESTIMONY

I have kept thy **t** .... Ps 119:22

therefore I love thy **t** .... Ps 119:119

for a **t** against them ..... Matt 10:18; Mark 13:9

THANK

God, I **t** thee, that I am not like
    other men .... Luke 18:11

I **t** my God always on your behalf ..... 1 Cor 1:4

I **t** Christ Jesus our Lord .... 1 Tim 1:12

THANKS

he took the cup, and gave **t** .... Matt 26:27;
    Luke 22:17

t be to God, which giveth us
    the victory .... 1 Cor 15:57

Giving **t** always for all things
    unto God .... Eph 5:20

THANKSGIVING

before his presence with **t** .... Ps 95:2

by prayer and supplication with **t** ...... Phil 4:6

THICKET

a ram caught in a **t** .... Gen 22:13

THIEF

and fell among **t** .... Luke 10:30

All that ever came before me are
    t and robbers .... John 10:8

come as a **t** .... 2 Pet 3:10; Rev 16:15

THINK

For as he **t** in his heart, so is he ...... Prov 23:7

What **t** ye? ...... Matt 22:42; 26:66; Mark 14:64

not to **t** of himself more highly
    than he ought to **t** .... Rom 12:3

let him that **t** he standeth .... 1 Cor 10:12

t on these things .... Phil 4:8

THIRST (v)

they which do hunger and thirst
    after righteousness .... Matt 5:6

he that believeth on me shall
    never **t** .... John 6:35

I **t** . . . . John 19:28

THIRSTY
pour water upon him that is **t** . . . . Isa 44:3

THORN
sow not among **t** . . . . Jer 4:3

there was given to me a **t** in
   the flesh . . . . 2 Cor 12:7

THOUGHT (n)
all the imaginations of the **t** . . . . 1 Chr 28:9

my **t** are not your **t** . . . . Isa 55:8

Jesus knowing their **t** . . . . Matt 9:4
   (See also 12:25.)

Take no **t** . . . . Matt 6:25, 31, 34; 10:19;
                  Mark 13:11; Luke 12:11, 22

into captivity every **t** to the
   obedience of Christ . . . . 2 Cor 10:5

and is a discerner of the **t** and
   intents of the heart . . . . Heb 4:12

and are become judges of evil **t** . . . . . . James 2:4

THOUGHT (v)
I will repent of the evil that I **t**
   to do unto them . . . . Jer 18:8

and that **t** upon his name . . . . Mal 3:16

when he **t** thereon, he wept . . . . Mark 14:72

they **t** that he had spoken of
   taking of rest . . . . John 11:13

I **t** as a child . . . . 1 Cor 13:11

t it not robbery to be equal with God . . . Phil 2:6

THOUSAND
a **t** years in thy sight are but
   as yesterday . . . . Ps 90:4

one day is with the Lord as a **t** years . . . 2 Pet 3:8

and a **t** years as one day . . . . 2 Pet 3:8

laid hold on . . . Satan and bound
   him a **t** years . . . . Rev 20:2

lived and reigned with Christ
   a **t** years . . . . Rev 20:4

THREEFOLD
a **t** cord is not quickly broken . . . . Eccl 4:12

THRONE
whether they be **t,** or dominions . . . . . . Col 1:16

come boldly unto the **t** of grace . . . . Heb 4:16

I saw a great white **t** . . . . Rev 20:11

THRUST
God **t** him down, not man . . . . Job 32:13

and **t** my hand into his side . . . . John 20:25

TIDINGS
glad **t** . . . . Luke 1:19; 2:10;
                    Acts 13:32; Rom 10:15

TIME
The LORD will deliver him in **t**
   of trouble . . . . Ps 41:1

What **t** I am afraid . . . . Ps 56:3

and a **t** to every purpose . . . . Eccl 3:1

discern the signs of the **t** . . . . Matt 16:3

Redeeming the **t,** because
   the days are evil . . . . Eph 5:16

grace to help in **t** of need . . . . Heb 4:16

TOGETHER
Can two walk **t**, except they
   be agreed? . . . . Amos 3:3

two or three are gathered **t** in
   my name . . . . Matt 18:20

all things work **t** for good . . . . Rom 8:28

TONGUE
Keep thy **t** from evil . . . . Ps 34:13

A wholesome **t** is a tree of life . . . . Prov 15:4

Whoso keepeth his mouth and his
   t keepeth his soul . . . . Prov 21:23

and bridleth not his **t** . . . . James 1:26

the **t** is a fire . . . . James 3:6

let us not love in word, neither
   in **t** . . . . 1 John 3:18

TOOTH
Eye for eye, **t** for **t** . . . . Ex 21:24; Matt 5:38

TOUCH
neither shall ye **t** it, lest ye die . . . . Gen 3:3

If I may **t** but his clothes . . . . Mark 5:28

Jesus saith unto her, **T** me not . . . . . . John 20:17

TRAIN
his **t** filled the temple . . . . Isa 6:1

TRANSFORM
t by the renewing of your mind . . . . . . Rom 12:2

Satan himself is **t** into an angel
    of light . . . . 2 Cor 11:14

TRANSGRESSION
the sins of my youth, nor my **t** . . . . Ps 25:7

thy tender mercies blot out my **t** . . . . Ps 51:1

he was wounded for our **t** . . . . Isa 53:5

TRAVAIL (v)
the whole creation groaneth and
    t in pain . . . . Rom 8:22

TREASURE
Israel for his peculiar **t** . . . . Ps 135:4

searchest for her as for hid **t** . . . . Prov 2:4

where your **t** is, there will your
    heart be . . . . Matt 6:21; Luke 12:34

out of the good **t** of the heart . . . . Matt 12:35

thou shalt have **t** in heaven. . . . . Matt 19:21;
                    Mark 10:21; Luke 18:22

that layeth up **t** for himself . . . . Luke 12:21

we have this **t** in earthen vessels . . . . . . 2 Cor 4:7

the **t** of wisdom and knowledge . . . . Col 2:3

greater riches than the **t** in Egypt . . . . Heb 11:26

TRESPASS
if ye forgive men their **t** . . . . Matt 6:14

not imputing their **t** unto them . . . . . . 2 Cor 5:19

dead in **t** and sins . . . . Eph 2:1

having forgiven you all **t** . . . . Col 2:13

TRIAL
the **t** of your faith . . . . 1 Pet 1:7

fiery **t** which is to try you . . . . 1 Pet 4:12

TRIBULATION
then shall be great **t** . . . . Matt 24:21

t worketh patience . . . . Rom 5:3

Rejoicing in hope; patient in **t** . . . . . . Rom 12:12

TROUBLE (n)
man is born unto **t** . . . . Job 5:7

a refuge in times of **t** . . . . Ps 9:9

a very present help in **t** . . . . Ps 46:1

even the time of Jacob's **t** . . . . Jer 30:7

TROUBLE (v)
Now is my soul **t** . . . . John 12:27

t on every side . . . . 2 Cor 4:8; 7:5

TRUE
That was the **t** Light . . . . John 1:9

the **t** worshippers shall worship
    the Father . . . . John 4:23

my Father giveth you the **t** bread . . . . . John 6:32

I am the **t** vine . . . . John 15:1

they might know thee the only **t** God. . John 17:3

God is created in righteousness
    and **t** holiness . . . . Eph 4:24

bretheren, whatsoever things are **t** . . . . . Phil 4:8

draw near with a **t** heart . . . . Heb 10:22

This is the **t** God, and eternal life . . . 1 John 5:20

TRUST
Though he slay me, yet will I **t**
    in him . . . . Job 13:15

T in the LORD . . . . Ps 37:3; 40:3; Prov 3:5

T in him at all times . . . . Ps 62:8

he knoweth them that **t** in him . . . . Nah 1:7

He **t** in God; let him deliver
    him now . . . . Matt 27:43

TRUTH
Buy the **t**, and sell it not . . . . Prov 23:23

full of grace and **t** . . . . John 1:14

know the **t**, and the **t** shall make
    you free . . . . John 8:32

I am the way, the **t**, and the life . . . . . . John 14:6

Spirit of **t,** is come, he will guide
you into all **t** . . . . John 16:13

speaking the **t** in love . . . . Eph 4:15

rightly dividing the word of **t** . . . . . . 2 Tim 2:15

TRY
when he hath **t** me, I shall come
forth as gold. . . . . Job 23:10

when he is **t,** he shall receive
the crown . . . . James 1:12

t the spirits whether they are
of God. . . . . 1 John 4:1

TURN
T thou us unto thee, O Lord, and
we shall be **t**. . . . . Lam 5:21

t to him the other also . . . . Matt 5:39

from such **t** away . . . . 2 Tim 3:5

TWINKLING
in the **t** of an eye . . . . 1 Cor 15:52

TWOEDGED
sharp as a **t** sword. . . . . Prov 5:4

any **t** sword, piercing . . . . Heb 4:12

U

UNAWARES
entertained angels **u** . . . . Heb 13:2

crept in **u** . . . . Jude 1:4

UNDEFILED
pure religion and **u**. . . . . James 1:27

an inheritance incorruptible, and **u** . . . . 1 Pet 1:4

UNDERSTAND
Who can **u** his errors?. . . . . Ps 19:12

Hear ye indeed, but **u** not . . . . Isa 6:9

There is none that **u** . . . . Rom 3:11

they that have not heard shall **u**. . . . . . Rom 15:21

u all mysteries . . . . 1 Cor 13:2

I **u** as a child . . . . 1 Cor 13:11

UNDERSTANDING
had **u** of the times . . . . 1 Chr 12:32

I have more **u** than all my teachers . . . Ps 119:99

apply thine heart to **u** . . . . Prov 2:2

lean not unto thine own **u** . . . . Prov 3:5

by **u** hath he established
the heavens . . . . Prov 3:19

He that is slow to wrath
is of great **u** . . . . Prov 14:29

Then opened he their **u** . . . . Luke 24:45

the peace of God, which passeth all **u** . . . Phil 4:7

UNFRUITFUL
the **u** works of darkness . . . . Eph 5:11

u in the knowledge of our Lord
Jesus Christ. . . . . 2 Pet 1:8

UNGODLINESS
revealed from heaven against all **u** . . . . Rom 1:18

they will increase unto more **u** . . . . . . 2 Tim 2:16

UNGODLY
the way of the **u** shall perish . . . . Ps 1:6

Christ died for the **u** . . . . Rom 5:6

UNITY
brethren to dwell together in **u** . . . . Ps 133:1

endeavouring to keep the **u** of
the Spirit. Eph 4:3

UNPUNISHED
the wicked shall not be **u** . . . . Prov 11:21

he that is glad at calamities shall
not be **u** . . . . Prov 17:5

UNRIGHTEOUS
the **u** man his thoughts. . . . . Isa 55:7

Is God **u** who taketh vengeance? . . . . . . Rom 3:5

UNRIGHTEOUSNESS
instruments of **u**. . . . . Rom 6:13

what fellowship hath righteousness
with **u**?. . . . . 2 Cor 6:14

cleanse us from all **u** . . . . 1 John 1:9

All **u** is sin . . . . 1 John 5:17

UNSEARCHABLE

how **u** are his judgments . . . . Rom 11:33

the **u** riches of Christ . . . . Eph 3:8

UNWISE

both to the wise, and to the **u** . . . . Rom 1:14

Wherefore be ye not **u** . . . . Eph 5:17

UPHOLD

U me according unto thy word . . . . . . Ps 119:116

u all things by the word of his power . . . Heb 1:3

UPWARD

as the sparks fly **u** . . . . Job 5:7

the spirit of man that goeth **u** . . . . Eccl 3:21

UTTER

A fool **u** all his mind . . . . Prov 29:11

groanings which cannot be **u** . . . . Rom 8:26

V

VAIN

not take the name of the
 LORD thy God in **v** . . . . Ex 20:7; Deut 5:11

the people imagine a **v** thing . . . . Ps 2:1
 (See also Acts 4:25.)

beauty is **v** . . . . Prov 31:30

use not **v** repetitions . . . . Matt 6:7

receive not the grace of God in **v** . . . . . 2 Cor 6:1

run, or had run, in **v** . . . . Gal 2:2

this man's religion is **v** . . . . James 1:26

VANITY

every man at his best state is
 altogether **v** . . . . Ps 39:5

V of **v**, saith the preacher . . . . . . Eccl 1:2; 12:8

from these **v** unto the living God . . . . . Acts 14:15

VESSEL

the **v** of wrath . . . . Rom 9:22

we have this treasure in earthen **v** . . . . 2 Cor 4:7

to possess his **v** in sanctification . . . . 1 Thess 4:4

giving honour unto the wife, as
 unto the weaker **v** . . . . 1 Pet 3:7

VIAL

pour out the **v** of the wrath of God
 upon the earth . . . . Rev 16:1

VICTORY

Death is swallowed up in **v** . . . . 1 Cor 15:54

v that overcometh the world, even
 our faith . . . . 1 John 5:4

VINE

fruit of the **v** . . . . Matt 26:29;
 Mark 14:25; Luke 22:18

I am the true **v** . . . . John 15:1

VIRGIN

Behold, a **v** shall conceive . . . . Isa 7:14
 (See also Matt 1:23.)

kingdom of heaven be likened
 unto ten **v** . . . . Matt 25:1

I may present you as a chaste
 v to Christ . . . . 2 Cor 11:2

VIRTUOUS

A **v** woman is a crown to
 her husband . . . . Prov 12:4

Who can find a **v** woman? . . . . Prov 31:10

VISION

Where there is no **v**, the
 people perish . . . . Prov 29:18

the valley of **v** . . . . Isa 22:1

young men shall see **v** . . . . . . Joel 2:28; Acts 2:17

VISIT

the son of man, that thou **v** him . . . . Ps 8:4;
 Heb 2:6

I was sick, and ye **v** me . . . . Matt 25:36

To **v** the fatherless and widows . . . . . James 1:27

VOICE

after the fire a still small **v** . . . . 1 Kgs 19:12

v of one crying in the wilderness . . . . . Matt 3:3;
Mark 1:3; Luke 3:4

neither shall any man hear his **v** . . . . Matt 12:19

the **v** of the archangel. . . . . 1 Thess 4:16

if any man hear my **v** . . . . Rev 3:20

VOLUME

in the **v** of the book . . . . Ps 40:7; Heb 10:7

VOW (n)

vowed a **v**. . . . . . . Gen 28:20; 31:13; Judg 11:30

When thou vowest a **v** unto God,
defer not to pay . . . . Eccl 5:4

W

WAGES

changed my **w** ten times . . . . Gen 31:7

the **w** of sin is death . . . . Rom 6:23

the **w** of unrighteousness. . . . . 2 Pet 2:15

WAIL

there shall be **w** and gnashing . . . . . . Matt 13:42

fear of her torment, weeping and **w**. . . Rev 18:15

WAIT

none that **w** on thee be ashamed . . . . . . Ps 25:3

W on the Lord . . . . Ps 27:14; 37:34

w for the consolation of Israel . . . . . . Luke 2:25

w for the adoption . . . . Rom 8:23

to **w** for his Son from heaven. . . . . . 1 Thess 1:10

WALK

Though I **w** in the midst of trouble . . . . Ps 138:7

he **w** on the water . . . . Matt 14:29

Take up thy bed, and **w** . . . . John 5:11, 12

w in newness of life . . . . Rom 6:4

who **w** not after the flesh, but
after the Spirit . . . . Rom 8:1

we **w** by faith. . . . . 2 Cor 5:7

in time past ye **w** according to. . . . . Eph 2:2

w worthy of the vocation. . . . . Eph 4:1

w circumspectly . . . . Eph 5:15

That ye might **w** worthy of the Lord. . . . Col 1:10

ye would **w** worthy of God. . . . . 1 Thess 2:12

how ye ought to **w** . . . . 1 Thess 4:1

w about, seeking whom he
may devour . . . . 1 Pet 5:8

if we **w** in the light . . . . 1 John 1:7

WALL

So built we the **w** . . . . Neh 4:6

broken down, and without **w** . . . . . . Prov 25:28

thou whited **w** . . . . Acts 23:3

the middle **w** of partition. . . . . Eph 2:14

WAR (n)

a time of **w** . . . . Eccl 3:8

neither shall they learn **w**
any more. . . . . Isa 2:4; Mic 4:3

w and rumours of **w** . . . . . Matt 24:6; Mark 13:7

there was **w** in heaven . . . . Rev 12:7

WAR (v)

we do not **w** after the flesh . . . . 2 Cor 10:3

lusts that **w** in your members . . . . James 4:1

from fleshly lusts, which **w** . . . . 1 Pet 2:11

WARM (v)

and **w** himself at the fire . . . . Mark 14:54

stood with them, and **w** himself . . . . John 18:18

be ye **w** and filled. . . . . James 2:16

WASH

w me, and I shall be whiter than snow . . Ps 51:7

began to **w** his feet with tears . . . . . . Luke 7:38

but ye are **w**. . . . . 1 Cor 6:11

our bodies **w** with pure water . . . . Heb 10:22

have **w** their robes . . . . Rev 7:14

WATCH (v)

The Lord **w** between me and thee . . . . Gen 31:49

W therefore, for ye know not . . . . Matt 24:42

W therefore, for ye know neither . . . . Matt 25:13

W and pray . . . . Matt 26:41; Mark 13:33
(See also Mark 14:38.)

W ye therefore . . . . Mark 13:35; Luke 21:36

let us **w** and be sober . . . . 1 Thess 5:6

WATER (n)

beside the still **w** . . . . Ps 23:2

a dry and thirsty land, where no **w** is . . . . Ps 63:1

Stolen **w** are sweet . . . . Prov 9:17

Cast thy bread upon the **w** . . . . Eccl 11:1

Many **w** cannot quench love . . . . Song 8:7

When thou passest through the **w** . . . . . Isa 43:2

baptize you with **w** . . . . Matt 3:11; Mark 1:8;
Luke 3:16; John 1:26

little ones a cup of cold **w** . . . . Matt 10:42

bid me come unto thee on the **w** . . . . Matt 14:28

Except a man be born of **w** . . . . John 3:5

Sir, give me this **w** . . . . John 4:15

flow rivers of living **w** . . . . John 7:38

John truly baptized with **w** . . . . Acts 1:5
(See also Acts 11:16.)

WATER (v)

Apollos **w**; but God gave the increase . . 1 Cor 3:6

WAY

lead me in the **w** everlasting . . . . Ps 139:24

In all thy **w** acknowledge him . . . . Prov 3:6

consider her **w**, and be wise . . . . Prov 6:6

the **w** of life . . . . Prov 6:23; 15:24; Jer 21:8

The **w** of a fool is right in his
own eyes . . . . Prov 12:15

Train up a child in the **w** . . . . Prov 22:6

I am the **w**, the truth, and the life . . . . John 14:6

also make a **w** to escape . . . . 1 Cor 10:13

a more excellent **w** . . . . 1 Cor 12:31

By a new and living **w** . . . . Heb 10:20

unstable in all his **w** . . . . James 1:8

the sinner from the error of his **w** . . . James 5:20

WEAK

let the **w** say, I am strong . . . . Joel 3:10

but the flesh is **w** . . . . . . Matt 26:41; Mark 14:38

w things of the world to confound . . . 1 Cor 1:27

For this cause many are **w** . . . . 1 Cor 11:30

when I am **w**, then am I strong . . . . . 2 Cor 12:10

WEAPON

No **w** that is formed against thee
shall prosper . . . . Isa 54:17

the **w** of our warfare . . . . 2 Cor 10:4

WEARY

fainteth not, neither is **w** . . . . Isa 40:28

they shall run, and not be **w** . . . . Isa 40:31

not be **w** in well doing . . . . Gal 6:9
(See also 2 Thess 3:13.)

WEEP

W not . . . . Luke 7:13; 8:52; Rev 5:5

w not for me, but **w** for
yourselves . . . . Luke 23:28

and **w** with them that **w** . . . . Rom 12:15

WEEPING

w may endure for a night . . . . Ps 30:5

w and gnashing of teeth . . . . Matt 8:12;
Luke 13:28

Mary stood without at the
sepulchre **w** . . . . John 20:11

now tell you even **w** . . . . Phil 3:18

WEIGH

Thou art **w** in the balances . . . . Dan 5:27

WEIGHT

a more exceeding and eternal
w of glory . . . . 2 Cor 4:17

lay aside every **w** . . . . Heb 12:1

WELL (adv)

three things which go **w** . . . . Prov 30:29

Doest thou **w** to be angry? . . . . Jonah 4:4

W done . . . . Matt 25:21
  (See also Luke 19:17.)

when all men speak **w** of you. . . . . . . Luke 6:26

Ye did run **w** . . . . Gal 5:7

WELL (n)
w of living waters. . . . . Song 4:15
  (See also John 4:14.)

w without water. . . . . 2 Pet 2:17

WEPT
beheld the city, and **w** over it . . . . . . Luke 19:41

Jesus **w**. John 11:35

WHETHER
w we live, . . . or die . . . . Rom 14:8

w in the body, I cannot tell; or
  whether out of the body . . . . 2 Cor 12:2

WHITE
they shall be **w** as snow. . . . . Isa 1:18

thou canst not make one hair
  w or black . . . . Matt 5:36

w already to harvest. . . . . John 4:35

WHOLE
not that thy **w** body be cast
  into hell . . . . Matt 5:29

be **w** need not a physician . . . . Matt 9:12

gain the **w** world . . . . Matt 16:26;
                      Mark 8:36; Luke 9:25

if the **w** body were an eye . . . . 1 Cor 12:17

keep the **w** law . . . . James 2:10

for the sins of the **w** world . . . . 1 John 2:2

WHORE
the judgment of the great **w** . . . . Rev 17:1
  (See also Rev 19:2.)

The waters which thou sawest,
  where the **w** sitteth . . . . Rev 17:15

ten horns . . . shall hate the **w** . . . . . . Rev 17:16

WICKED
Let the **w** forsake his way . . . . Isa 55:7

The heart is deceitful above all
  things, and desperately **w** . . . . Jer 17:9

and by **w** hands have crucified
  and slain. . . . . Acts 2:23

put away from among yourselves
  that **w** person . . . . 1 Cor 5:13

the fiery darts of the **w** . . . . Eph 6:16

enemies in your mind by **w** works . . . . Col 1:21

WICKEDNESS
they that plow iniquity, and sow **w**,
  reap the same . . . . Job 4:8

Being filled with all unrighteousness,
  fornication, **w** . . . . Rom 1:29

spiritual **w** in high places. . . . . Eph 6:12

the whole world lieth in **w** . . . . 1 John 5:19

WIFE
the **w** of thy youth . . . . Prov 5:18

Whoso findeth a **w** findeth a
  good thing . . . . Prov 18:22

a prudent **w** is from the LORD . . . . . . Prov 19:14

the **w** whom thou lovest . . . . Eccl 9:9

the unbelieving **w** is sanctified . . . . . . 1 Cor 7:14

the husband is the head of the **w** . . . . . Eph 5:23

the bride, the Lamb's **w** . . . . Rev 21:9

WILL (v)
not as I **w**, but as thou **w** . . . . Matt 26:39

to **w** is present with me . . . . Rom 7:18

both to **w** and to do . . . . Phil 2:13

whosoever **w**, let him take . . . . Rev 22:17

WILLING
not **w** that any should perish . . . . 2 Pet 3:9

WIN
he that **w** souls is wise . . . . Prov 11:30

that I may **w** Christ . . . . Phil 3:8

WINGS
the shadow of thy **w** . . . . Ps 17:8; 36:7; 57:1

under his **w**. . . . . Ps 91:4

the **w** of the morning . . . . Ps 139:9

riches certainly make themselves **w** . . . Prov 23:5

WIPE
wash his feet with tears, and did
w them with the hairs. . . . . Luke 7:38

wash the disciples feet, and to
w them . . . . John 13:5

WISDOM
better is it to get **w** than gold . . . . Prov 16:16

w is justified of her children . . . . Matt 11:19

the **w** of this world is foolishness
with God. . . . . 1 Cor 3:19

If any of you lack **w** . . . . James 1:5

the **w** that is from above
is first pure . . . . James 3:17

to receive power, and riches, and **w** . . . . Rev 5:12

WISE
to make one **w**. . . . . Gen 3:6

Be not **w** in thine own eyes . . . . Prov 3:7

he that winneth souls is **w** . . . . Prov 11:30

w unto salvation . . . . 2 Tim 3:15

WITHER
his leaf also shall not **w** . . . . Ps 1:3

The grass **w**, the flower
fadeth . . . . Isa 40:7; 1 Pet 1:24

the fig tree **w** away. . . . . Matt 21:19
(See also Mark 11:21.)

WITHHOLD
what **w** that he might be
revealed. . . . . 2 Thess 2:6

WITNESS (n)
I have greater **w** than that of John . . . John 5:36

conscience also bearing **w**. . . . . Rom 2:15

the **w** of God is greater . . . . 1 John 5:9

WOMAN
O **w**, great is thy faith. . . . . Matt 15:28

Two **w** shall be grinding . . . . Matt 24:41;
Luke 17:35

blessed art thou among **w** . . . . Luke 1:28

Among those that are born of **w** . . . . . Luke 7:28

a **w** taken in adultery . . . . John 8:3

W, behold thy son . . . . John 19:26

It is good for a man not to
touch a **w** . . . . 1 Cor 7:1

the **w** is the glory of the man . . . . 1 Cor 11:7

God sent forth his Son, made of a **w** . . . . Gal 4:4

w adorn themselves . . . . 1 Tim 2:9

Let the **w** learn in silence . . . . 1 Tim 2:11

WOMB
thou hast covered me in my
mother's **w**. . . . . Ps 139:13

the Lord that made thee, and formed
thee from the **w** . . . . Isa 44:2
(See also Isa 49:5.)

WONDERFUL
Such knowledge is too **w** for me . . . . . . Ps 139:6

his name shall be called **W** . . . . Isa 9:6

WORD
every **w** that proceedeth out
of the mouth of God . . . . Deut 8:3

A **w** fitly spoken . . . . Prov 25:11

every **w** that proceedeth out of
the mouth of God . . . . Matt 4:4

every idle **w** that men shall speak . . . Matt 12:36

my **w** shall not pass away. . . . . Matt 24:35

ashamed of me and of my **w** . . . . Mark 8:38;
Luke 9:26

In the beginning was the **W**. . . . . John 1:1

I have given unto them the **w**
which thou gavest me . . . . John 17:8

not in **w**, but in power. . . . . 1 Cor 4:20

Holding forth the **w** of life. . . . . Phil 2:16

Let the **w** of Christ dwell in you . . . . . . Col 3:16

comfort one another with
these **w** . . . . 1 Thess 4:18

Holding fast the faithful **w**. . . . . Titus 1:9

the **w** of God is quick, and powerful . . . Heb 4:12

And have tasted the good **w** of God .... Heb 6:5

if any be a hearer of the **w** .... James 1:23

take away from the **w** of the book .... Rev 22:19

WORK (n)
Six days shall **w** be done .... Ex 35:2

let her own **w** praise her .... Prov 31:31

This is the **w** of God, that
  ye believe.................... John 6:29

I have finished the **w** .... John 17:4

shew me thy faith without thy **w** ... James 2:18

destroy the **w** of the devil .... 1 John 3:8

WORK (v)
all things **w** together for good .... Rom 8:28

it is the same God which **w** all
  in all .... 1 Cor 12:6

the spirit that now **w**................ Eph 2:2

w out your own salvation .... Phil 2:12

w with your own hands .... 1 Thess 4:11

WORLD
he hath set the **w** in their heart....... Eccl 3:11

gain the whole **w**................ Matt 16:26;
                Mark 8:36; Luke 9:25

He was in the **w** .... John 1:10

which taketh away the sin of the **w**... John 1:29

God so loved the **w**................ John 3:16

the Saviour of the **w** .... John 4:42; 1 John 4:14

not to judge the **w**, but to
  save the **w**.................... John 12:47

the prince of this **w** cometh .... John 14:30

In the **w** ye shall have tribulation ... John 16:33

the **w** itself could not contain
  the books.................... John 21:25

be not conformed to this **w**......... Rom 12:2

the god of this **w** hath blinded .... 2 Cor 4:4

having loved this present **w** .... 2 Tim 4:10

Of whom the **w** was not worthy ..... Heb 11:38

Love not the **w**.................. 1 John 2:15

WORSE
lest a **w** thing come unto thee .... John 5:14

he hath denied the faith, and is
  w than an infidel.............. 1 Tim 5:8

WORSHIP
let us **w** and bow down .... Ps 95:6

Our fathers **w** in this mountain...... John 4:20

must **w**, in spirit and in truth....... John 4:24

w and served the creature more
  than the Creator................. Rom 1:25

WORTHY
not **w** to unloose........ Luke 3:16; John 1:27

the labourer is **w** of his hire........ Luke 10:7

not **w** to be compared with
  the glory...................... Rom 8:18

walk **w** .... Eph 4:1; Col 1:10; 1 Thess 2:12

Of whom the world was not **w** ..... Heb 11:38

WOUND (v)
he was **w** for our transgressions .... Isa 53:5

WRATH
the **w** of man shall praise thee....... Ps 76:10

provoke not your children to **w**....... Eph 6:4

God hath not appointed us to **w** .... 1 Thess 5:9

WRITTEN
What I have **w** I have **w**.......... John 19:22

w for our admonition .... 1 Cor 10:11

w in the Lamb's book of life........ Rev 21:27

Y

YEAR
for all their sins once a **y**............ Lev 16:34

For a thousand **y** in thy sight .... Ps 90:4

To preach the acceptable **y** of
  the Lord...................... Luke 4:19

one day is with the Lord as
  a thousand **y** ... a thousand **y**
  (are) as one day................. 2 Pet 3:8

laid hold on . . . Satan and bound
  him a thousand **y** . . . . Rev 20:2

they lived and reigned with Christ
  a thousand **y**. . . . . Rev 20:4

YIELD
Neither **y** ye your members as
  instruments of unrighteousness
  unto sin . . . but **y** yourselves
  unto God . . . . Rom 6:13

afterward it **y** the peaceable fruit
  of righteousness . . . . Heb 12:11

YOKE
For my **y** is easy . . . . Matt 11:30

and be not entangled again
  with the **y** of bondage . . . . Gal 5:1

YOUTH
thy **y** is renewed like the eagle's . . . . Ps 103:5

Remember now thy Creator in
  the days of thy **y**. . . . . Eccl 12:1

have I kept from my **y** up . . . . Matt 19:20;
                                         Luke 18:21

Let no man despise thy **y** . . . . 1 Tim 4:12

Z

ZEAL
the **z** of thine house . . . . Ps 69:9

My **z** hath consumed me . . . . Ps 119:139

I the LORD have spoken it in my **z** . . . . Ezek 5:13

The **z** of thine house. . . . . John 2:17

your **z** hath provoked very many. . . . . . 2 Cor 9:2

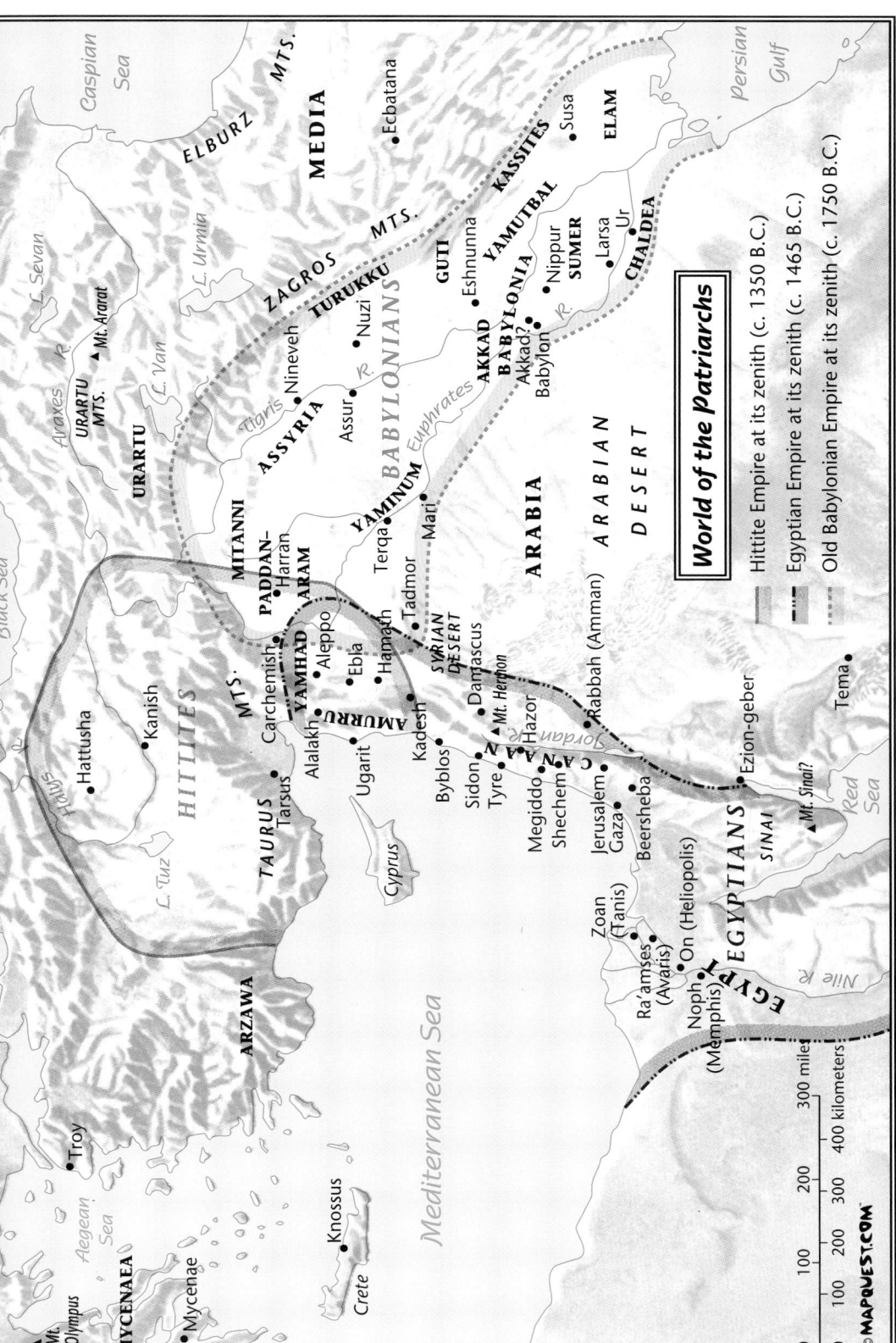

World of the Patriarchs

||| Hittite Empire at its zenith (c. 1350 B.C.)
||| Egyptian Empire at its zenith (c. 1465 B.C.)
||| Old Babylonian Empire at its zenith (c. 1750 B.C.)

© MAPQUEST.COM

| 0 | 100 | 200 | 300 miles |
| 0 | 100 | 200 | 300 | 400 kilometers |

Caspian Sea

ELBURZ MTS.

MEDIA
• Ecbatana

• Susa
ELAM
KASSITES
YAMUTBAL
GUTI
Eshnunna •
• Nuzi
BABYLONIANS
AKKAD
Akkad? •
BABYLONIA
Nippur •
SUMER
Larsa •
Ur •
CHALDEA

Nineveh •
ASSYRIA
Assur •

ZAGROS MTS.
TURUKKU

Tigris R.

Euphrates R.

URARTU
▲ Mt. Ararat
URARTU MTS.
Avaxes R.
L. Van
L. Urmia
L. Sevan

Black Sea

YAMINUM
Mari •
Terqa •
Tadmor •
Hamath •
PADDAN-ARAM
Harran •
MITANNI
• Ebla
Aleppo •
Carchemish •
YAMHAD

AMURRU
Kadesh •
Ugarit •
Byblos •
Sidon •
Tyre •
SYRIAN DESERT
Damascus •
▲ Mt. Hermon
Hazor •
CANAAN
Jordan R.
Rabbah (Amman) •

ARABIA
ARABIAN DESERT

• Tema

Megiddo •
Shechem •
Jerusalem •
Gaza •
Beersheba •
Ezion-geber •
SINAI
▲ Mt. Sinai?
Red Sea

EGYPTIANS
Zoan (Tanis) •
Ra'amses (Avaris) •
On (Heliopolis) •
Noph (Memphis) •
EGYPT
Nile R.

HITTITES
• Kanish
Hattusha •
Halys R.
TAURUS MTS.
Tarsus •
Alalakh •
L. Tuz

Cyprus

ARZAWA

Mediterranean Sea

Troy •
MYCENAEA
Mycenae •
▲ Mt. Olympus
Aegean Sea
Knossus •
Crete

Persian Gulf

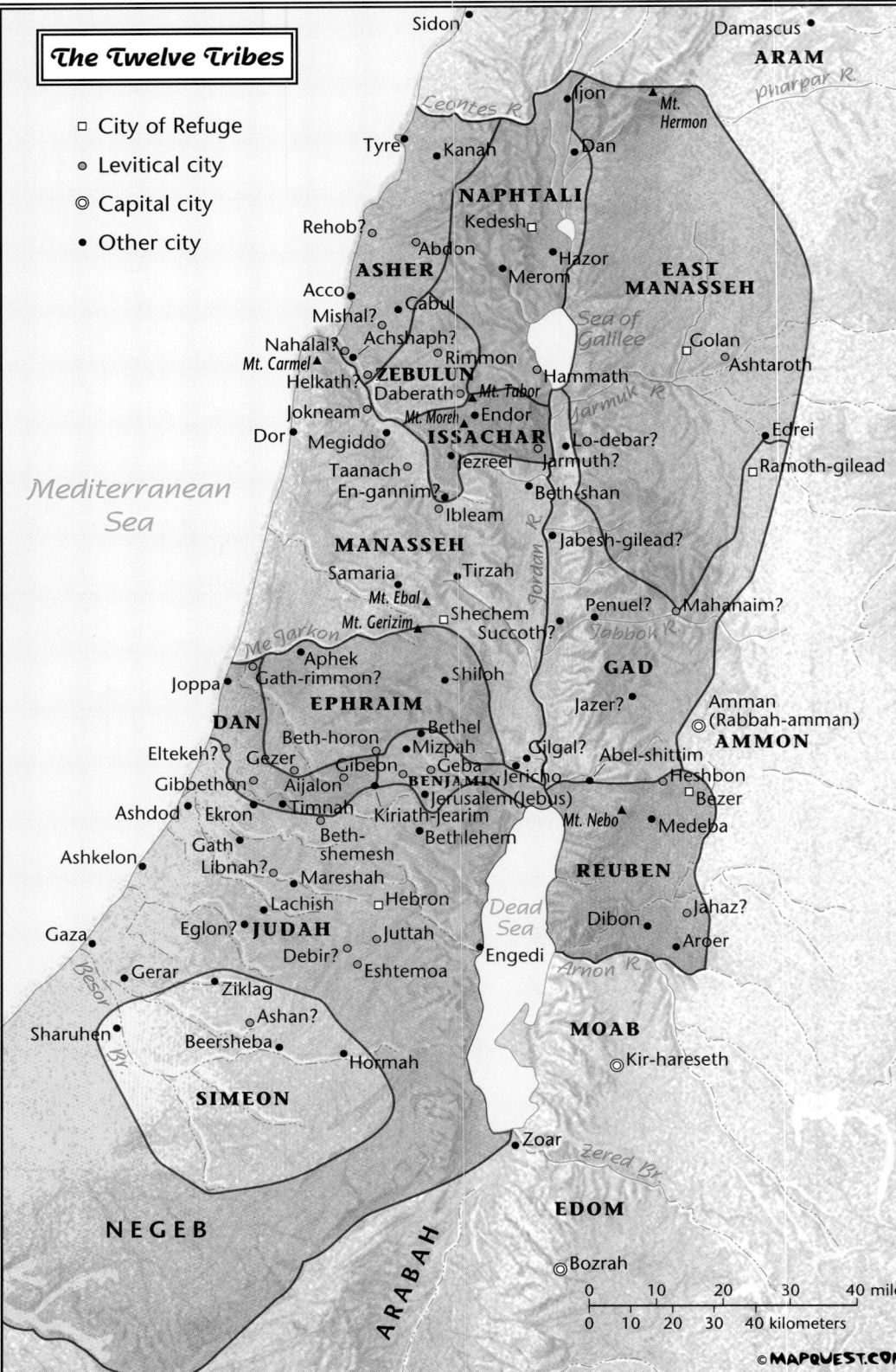

The Twelve Tribes

□ City of Refuge
● Levitical city
◎ Capital city
• Other city

ARAM
Damascus
Sidon
Ijon
Mt. Hermon
Leontes R.
Pharpar R.
Tyre
Kanah
Dan
NAPHTALI
Kedesh
Rehob?
Abdon
Hazor
EAST
MANASSEH
ASHER
Meron
Acco
Cabul
Mishal?
Golan
Nahalal?
Achshaph?
Sea of
Galilee
Ashtaroth
Mt. Carmel
Rimmon
ZEBULUN
Hammath
Helkath?
Daberath
Mt. Tabor
Yarmuk R.
Joknéam
Mt. Moreh
Endor
Edrei
Dor
Megiddo
ISSACHAR
Lo-debar?
Ramoth-gilead
Taanach
Jezreel
Jarmuth?
En-gannim?
Beth-shan
Ibleam
Jabesh-gilead?
MANASSEH
Mediterranean
Sea
Samaria
Tirzah
Mt. Ebal
Penuel?
Mahanaim?
Mt. Gerizim
Shechem
Succoth?
Jabbok R.
Me Jarkon
GAD
Aphek
Shiloh
Joppa
Gath-rimmon?
Jazer?
Amman
(Rabbah-amman)
DAN
EPHRAIM
Bethel
AMMON
Eltekeh?
Beth-horon
Mizpah
Abel-shittim
Gezer
Geba
Gilgal?
Heshbon
Gibeon
Aijalon
Jericho
Bezer
Gibbethon
Timnah
BENJAMIN
Jerusalem (Jebus)
Ashdod
Ekron
Kiriath-jearim
Mt. Nebo
Medeba
Gath
Beth-
shemesh
Bethlehem
Ashkelon
Libnah?
Mareshah
REUBEN
Lachish
Hebron
Dibon
Jahaz?
Gaza
Eglon?
JUDAH
Juttah
Dead
Sea
Aroer
Debir?
Eshtemoa
Engedi
Arnon R.
Gerar
Ziklag
MOAB
Sharuhen
Ashan?
Beersheba
Kir-hareseth
Hormah
SIMEON
Zoar
Zered Br.
Besor Br.
NEGEB
EDOM
ARABAH
Bozrah

0   10   20   30   40 miles
0 10 20 30 40 kilometers

© MAPQUEST.COM

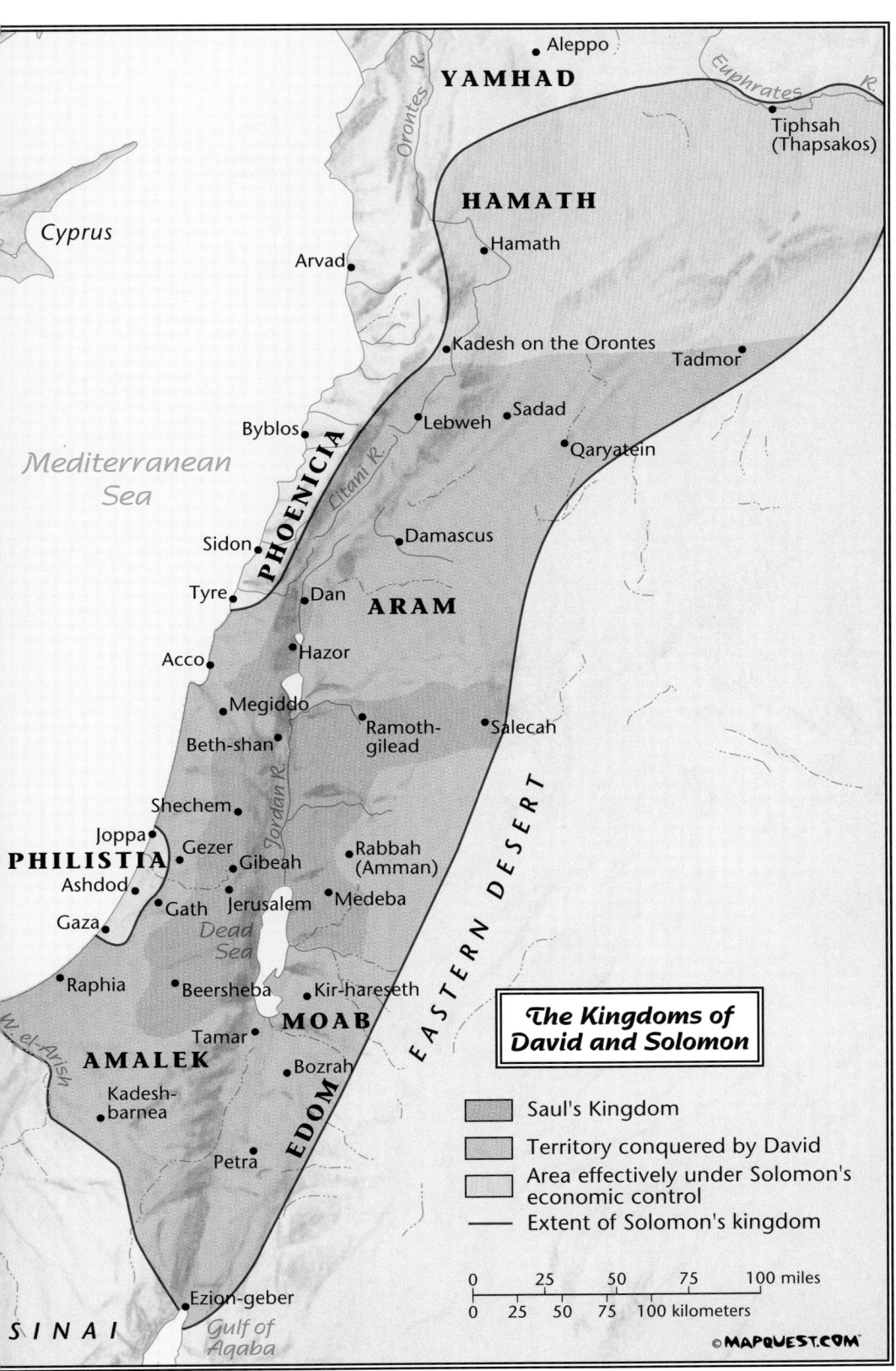

The Kingdoms of David and Solomon

Aleppo

YAMHAD

Euphrates R.

Tiphsah
(Thapsakos)

HAMATH

Hamath

Cyprus

Arvad

Kadesh on the Orontes

Tadmor

Lebweh · Sadad

Byblos

Mediterranean
Sea

Damascus

Qaryatein

Sidon

Tyre · Dan

ARAM

Acco

Hazor

Megiddo

Beth-shan

Ramoth-
gilead

Salecah

Shechem

EASTERN DESERT

Joppa

Gezer

PHILISTIA

Gibeah

Rabbah
(Amman)

Ashdod

Jerusalem

Gath

Medeba

Gaza

Dead
Sea

Raphia

Beersheba

Kir-hareseth

MOAB

Tamar

AMALEK

Bozrah

Kadesh-
barnea

EDOM

Petra

*The Kingdoms of
David and Solomon*

Saul's Kingdom

Territory conquered by David

Area effectively under Solomon's
economic control

Extent of Solomon's kingdom

Ezion-geber

SINAI

Gulf of
Aqaba

0   25   50   75   100 miles

0   25   50   75   100 kilometers

©MAPQUEST.COM

The Kingdoms of Israel and Judah

0 10 20 30 40 miles
0 10 20 30 40 kilometers

Beirut

PHOENICIA

Sidon

Litani R.

Abana R.

Damascus

Mt. Hermon

Pharpar R.

ARAM

Tyre

Dan

Kedesh

Hazor

J. Jarmuk

Acco

Sea of Galilee

Mediterranean Sea

Mt. Carmel

Mt. Tabor

Kishon R.

Yarmuk R.

Ashtaroth

Megiddo

Mt. Moreh

Edrei

Taanach

Beth-shan

Ramoth-gilead

Ibleam

Mt. Gilboa

Jabesh-gilead?

Tirzah

Jordan R.

Samaria

Mt. Ebal

Succoth?

Penuel?

Mahanaim?

Mt. Gerizim

Schechem

Tabbok R.

Yarkon R.

Aphek

Shiloh

ISRAEL

Joppa

Rabbah (Amman)

Bethel

AMMON

Gezer

Jericho

Ashdod

Aijalon

Jerusalem

Mt. Nebo

Heshbon

Gath

Bethlehem

Medeba

Ashkelon

Mareshah

Gaza

Hebron

Dibon

Gerar

Dead Sea

Arnon R.

Raphia

JUDAH

Besor Br.

PHILISTIA

Beersheba

MOAB

Kir-hareseth

Zered Br.

W. el-Arish

Region periodically contested by Judah and Edom

Bozrah

WILDERNESS

Kadesh-barnea

EDOM

WILDERNESS

©MAPQUEST.COM

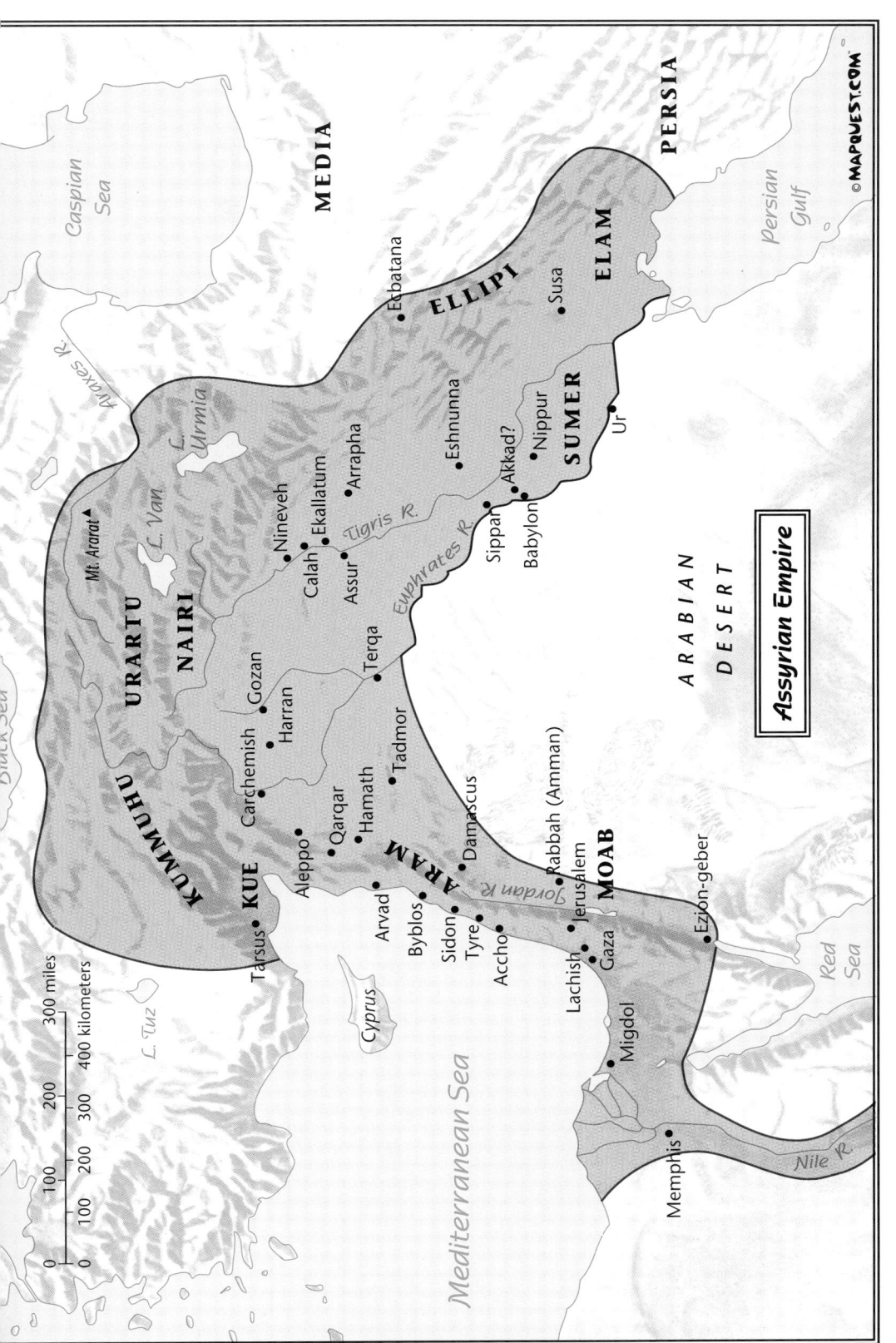

Assyrian Empire

© MAPQUEST.COM

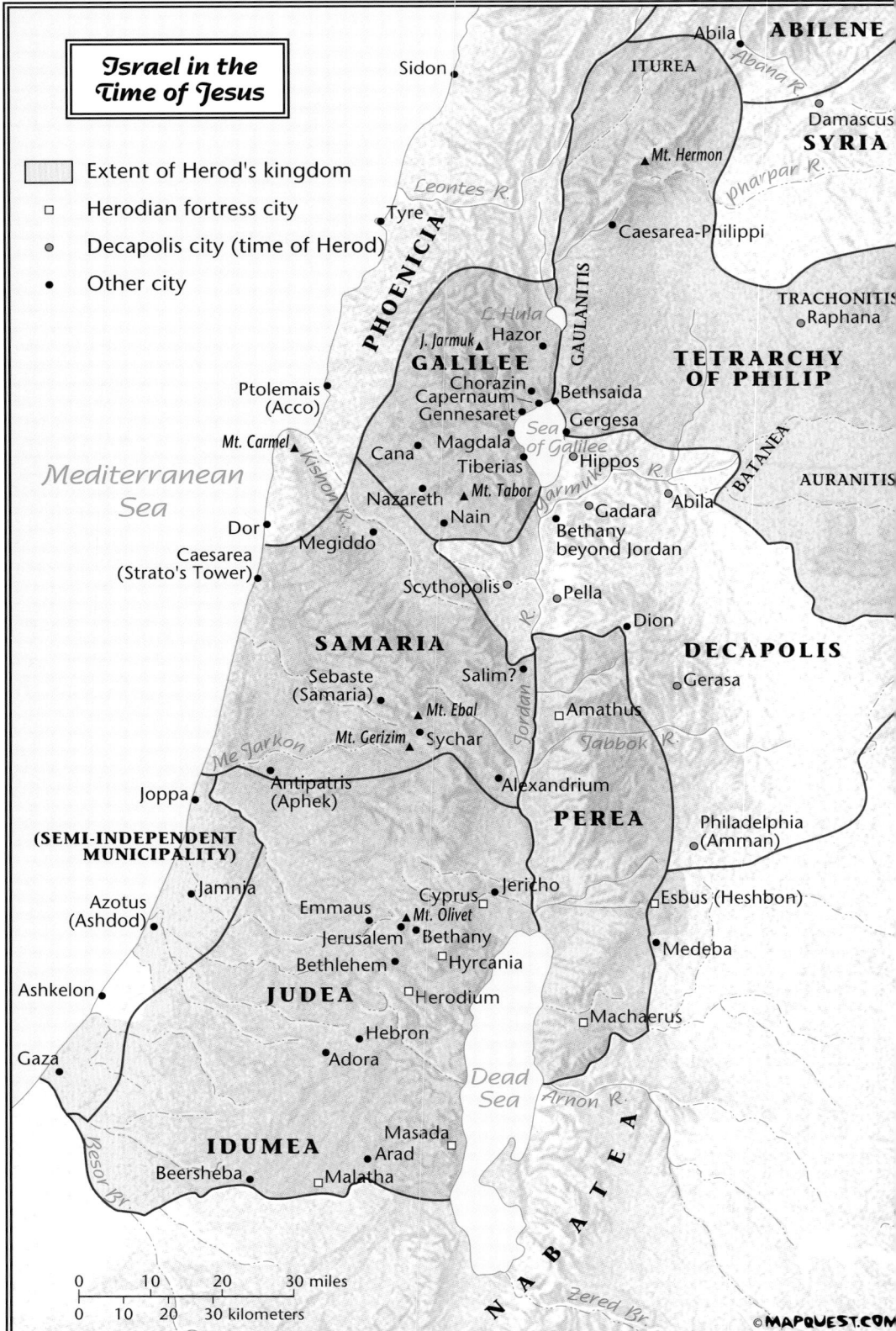

Israel in the Time of Jesus

Legend:
- Extent of Herod's kingdom
- □ Herodian fortress city
- ◦ Decapolis city (time of Herod)
- • Other city

Labels:

Abila — ABILENE
ITUREA
Sidon
Damascus
SYRIA
Mt. Hermon
Leontes R.
Abana R.
Pharpar R.
Tyre
Caesarea-Philippi
PHOENICIA
TRACHONITIS
Raphana
L. Hula
Hazor
J. Jarmuk
GALILEE
GAULANITIS
TETRARCHY OF PHILIP
Chorazin
Capernaum
Bethsaida
Ptolemais (Acco)
Gennesaret
Gergesa
Sea of Galilee
BATANEA
Mt. Carmel
Cana
Magdala
Hippos
AURANITIS
Mediterranean Sea
Kishon R.
Tiberias
Nazareth
Mt. Tabor
Yarmuk R.
Abila
Nain
Gadara
Dor
Megiddo
Bethany beyond Jordan
Caesarea (Strato's Tower)
Scythopolis
Pella
Dion
DECAPOLIS
SAMARIA
Salim?
Gerasa
Sebaste (Samaria)
Mt. Ebal
Amathus
Mt. Gerizim
Sychar
Jabbok R.
Me Jarkon
Antipatris (Aphek)
Alexandrium
PEREA
Joppa
Philadelphia (Amman)
(SEMI-INDEPENDENT MUNICIPALITY)
Jericho
Esbus (Heshbon)
Azotus (Ashdod)
Jamnia
Emmaus
Cyprus
Mt. Olivet
Jerusalem
Bethany
Medeba
Ashkelon
Bethlehem
Hyrcania
JUDEA
Herodium
Gaza
Machaerus
Hebron
Adora
Dead Sea
Arnon R.
IDUMEA
Masada
Arad
NABATEA
Beersheba
Malatha
Resor Br.
Zered Br.

Scale:
0   10   20   30 miles
0   10   20   30 kilometers

©MAPQUEST.COM

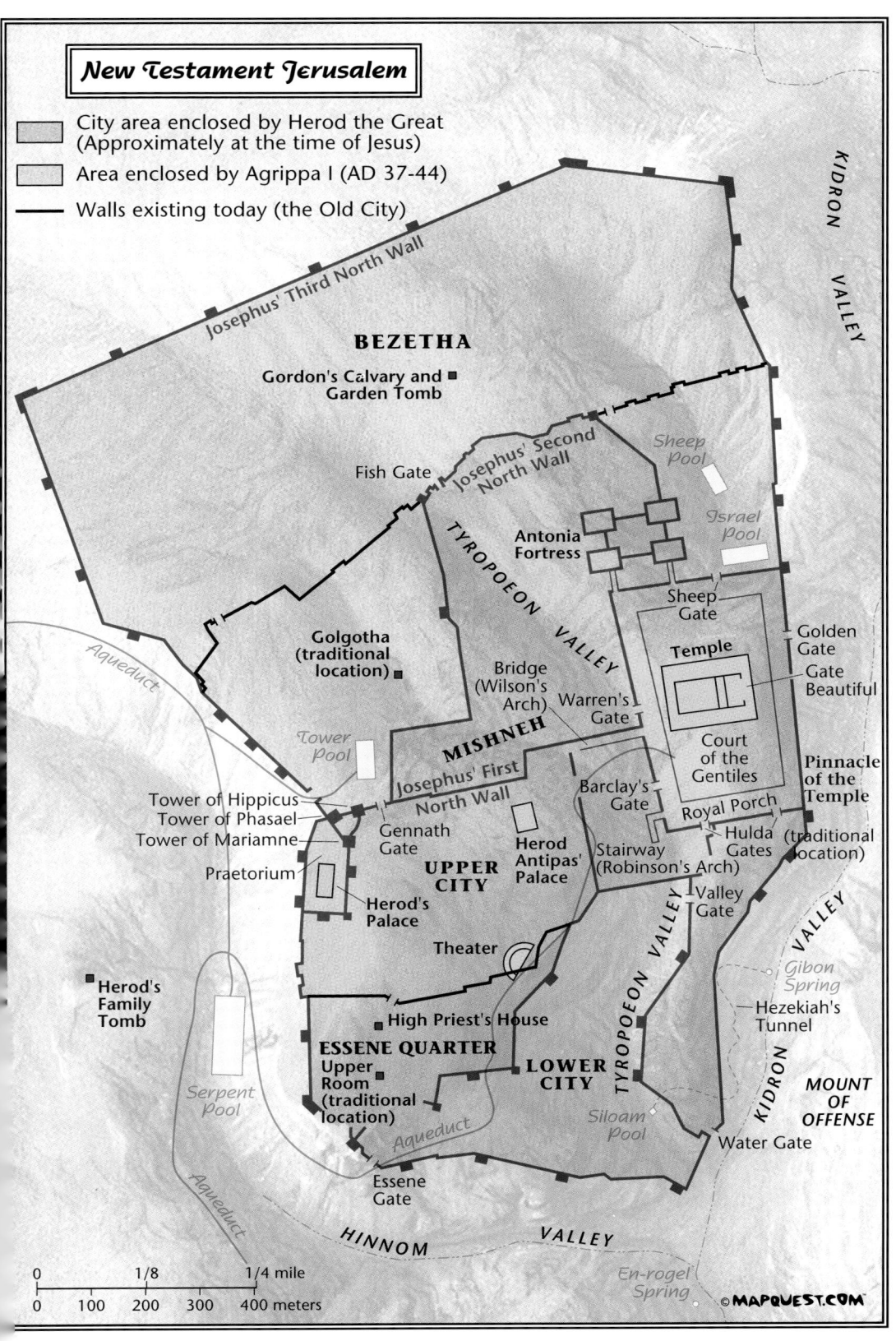

New Testament Jerusalem

- City area enclosed by Herod the Great (Approximately at the time of Jesus)
- Area enclosed by Agrippa I (AD 37-44)
- Walls existing today (the Old City)

KIDRON VALLEY

Josephus' Third North Wall

BEZETHA

Gordon's Calvary and Garden Tomb

Josephus' Second North Wall

Fish Gate

Sheep Pool

Israel Pool

Antonia Fortress

Sheep Gate

TYROPOEON VALLEY

Golgotha (traditional location)

Temple

Golden Gate

Gate Beautiful

Bridge (Wilson's Arch)

Warren's Gate

MISHNEH

Court of the Gentiles

Aqueduct

Tower Pool

Josephus' First North Wall

Barclay's Gate

Royal Porch

Pinnacle of the Temple

Tower of Hippicus
Tower of Phasael
Tower of Mariamne

Gennath Gate

Herod Antipas' Palace

Stairway (Robinson's Arch)

Hulda Gates

Pinnacle of the Temple (traditional location)

Praetorium

UPPER CITY

Valley Gate

Herod's Palace

KIDRON VALLEY

Herod's Family Tomb

Theater

TYROPOEON VALLEY

Gibon Spring

Hezekiah's Tunnel

High Priest's House

ESSENE QUARTER

Upper Room (traditional location)

LOWER CITY

Serpent Pool

Aqueduct

Siloam Pool

Water Gate

KIDRON

MOUNT OF OFFENSE

Essene Gate

Aqueduct

HINNOM VALLEY

En-rogel Spring

© MAPQUEST.COM

| 0 | 1/8 | 1/4 mile |

| 0 | 100 | 200 | 300 | 400 meters |

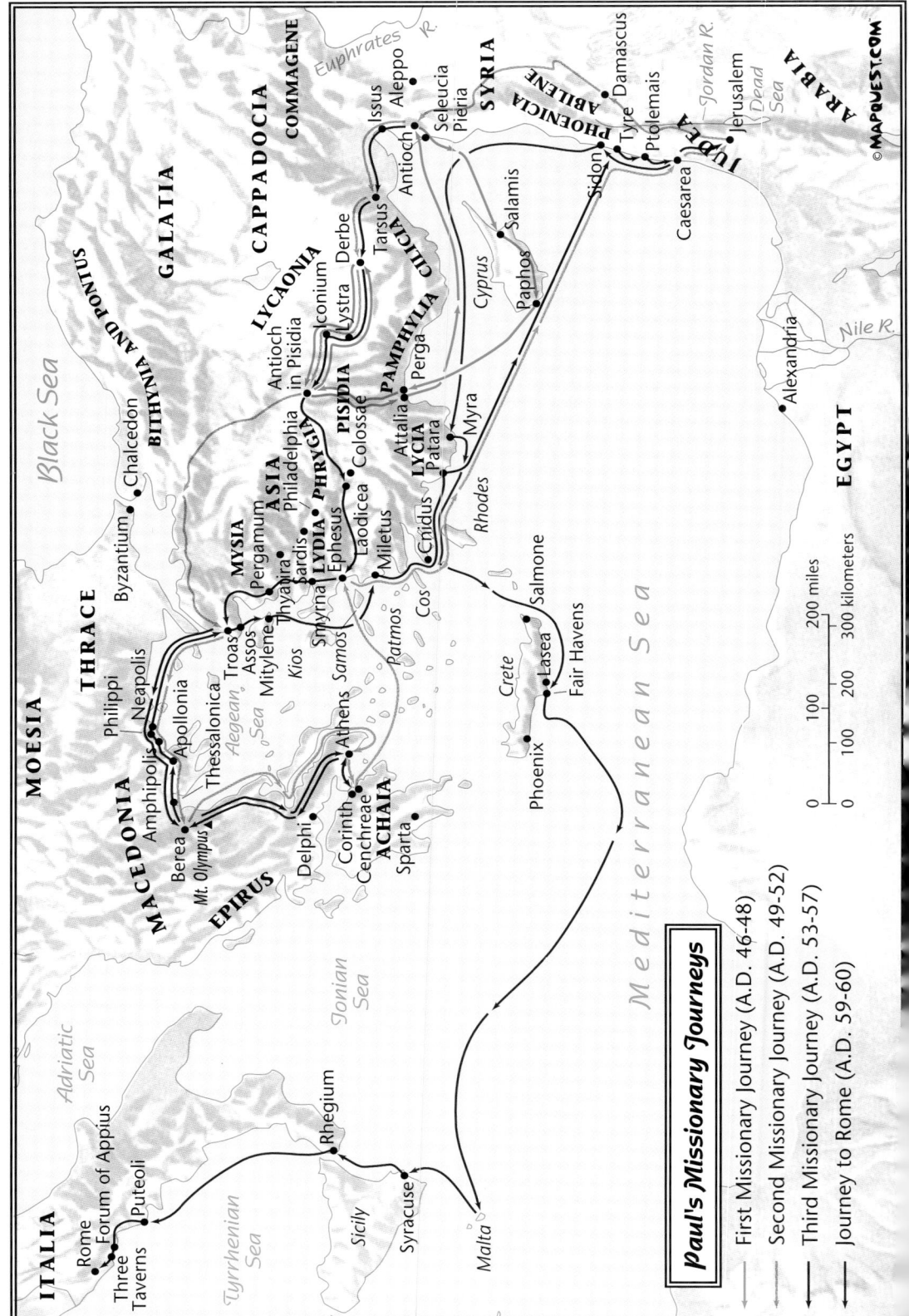

Paul's Missionary Journeys

First Missionary Journey (A.D. 46–48)
Second Missionary Journey (A.D. 49–52)
Third Missionary Journey (A.D. 53–57)
Journey to Rome (A.D. 59–60)

ITALIA
Rome
Forum of Appius
Three Taverns
Puteoli
Rhegium
Sicily
Syracuse
Tyrrhenian Sea
Adriatic Sea
Ionian Sea
Malta

MOESIA
THRACE
Byzantium
Chalcedon
BITHYNIA AND PONTUS
Black Sea

MACEDONIA
Philippi
Neapolis
Amphipolis
Apollonia
Thessalonica
Berea
Mt. Olympus
EPIRUS
Delphi
ACHAIA
Corinth
Cenchreae
Athens
Sparta
Aegean Sea

Troas
Assos
Mitylene
Kios
Samos
Patmos
Cos
Cnidus
Rhodes

GALATIA
CAPPADOCIA
COMMAGENE
Euphrates R.

LYCAONIA
Antioch in Pisidia
Iconium
Lystra
Derbe
Tarsus
CILICIA
Issus
Aleppo
Antioch
Seleucia Pieria
SYRIA
Damascus
ABILENE
PHOENICIA
Tyre
Ptolemais
Sidon
Caesarea
JUDEA
Jerusalem
Dead Sea
Jordan R.
ARABIA

MYSIA
Pergamum
ASIA
Thyatira
Sardis
Smyrna
LYDIA
Ephesus
Philadelphia
PHRYGIA
Colossae
Laodicea
Miletus
PISIDIA
Attalia
Perga
PAMPHYLIA
Patara
LYCIA
Myra

Cyprus
Salamis
Paphos

Crete
Salmone
Lasea
Fair Havens
Phoenix

Mediterranean Sea

EGYPT
Alexandria
Nile R.

0   100   200 miles
0   100   200   300 kilometers

©MAPQUEST.COM